FOUNDATION
GRANTS TO INDIVIDUALS

FOUNDATION
CENTER
Knowledge to build on.

23RD EDITION

FOUNDATION
GRANTS TO
INDIVIDUALS

Edited by
Claire Charles

CONTRIBUTING STAFF

Vice President for Data Acquisition and Architecture _____ Jeffrey A. Falkenstein

Director, Foundation Information Management _____ David G. Jacobs

Coordinator, Foundation Directory and Related Projects _____ Bill Giles

Coordinator, Large Foundations _____ Cindy B. Martinez

Coordinator, Outsourcing _____ Nicole Gardner

Manager, Corporate Philanthropy _____ Andrew Grabois

Liaison, U.S. Public Charities _____ Terrence Aybar

Liaison, New Forms of Philanthropy _____ Linda Calderon

Liaison, Community Foundations _____ David Rosado

Senior Editorial Associates_____ Regina J. Faighes

Elia S. Glenn

Joseph W. Guastella

Marisa Leong

Cynthia Y. Manick

Editorial Associate_____ Lakesha Spiegel-Reneau

Editorial Assistants _____ Carlos Edwin Estremera

Michele Kragalott

Casey Robbins

Publishing Database Administrator _____ Kathye Giesler

System Administrator _____ Emmy So

Director of Communications _____ Vanessa Schnaidt

Production Manager _____ Christine Innamorato

Reference Librarian_____ Robert Bruno

The editor gratefully acknowledges the many other Foundation Center staff who contributed support, encouragement, and information that was indispensable to the preparation of this volume. Special mention should also be made of the staff members of the New York, Washington, DC, Cleveland, San Francisco, and Atlanta libraries who assisted in tracking changes in foundation information. We would like to express our appreciation as well to the many foundations that cooperated fully in updating information prior to the compilation of *Foundation Grants to Individuals.*

CONTENTS

Introduction _____ v

Federal Laws and Grants to Individuals _____ ix

Scholarships and Grants to Individuals: Where to Find Them _____ xi

Glossary _____ xv

Abbreviations _____ xix

Resources for Individual Grantseekers: A Bibliography _____ xxi

Resources of the Foundation Center_____ xxxvii

DESCRIPTIVE DIRECTORY_____ 1

Appendix: Edition 22 Grantmakers Not Included in Edition 23 _____ 1573

Indexes _____ 1577

Geographic Index   1577

International Giving Index   1603

Company Name Index   1607

Specific School Index   1609

Type of Support Index   1623

Subject Index   1649

Grantmaker Name Index   1693

INTRODUCTION

Foundation Grants to Individuals is the most comprehensive directory available of private grantmakers, public charities (also known as public foundations), and corporate giving programs in the United States that provide financial assistance to individuals. The 23rd edition contains 10,126 entries from U.S. grantmakers that the Foundation Center has identified as conducting ongoing grantmaking programs for individuals. It describes giving for a variety of purposes, including scholarships, student loans, fellowships, travel internships, residencies, arts and cultural projects, research, and general welfare. It is intended to be both a grantseeker's guide and a reference tool for those interested in giving to individuals.

The 23rd edition includes the most current information available for eligible entries listed in the previous edition (see the Appendix on p. 1573 to review the list of ineligible entries) as well as 398 entries new to this edition.

To prepare the 23rd edition, Foundation Center staff researched a variety of public records, including 990-PFs and 990s (which all private foundations and public charities are required to file with the IRS), annual reports, newsletters, web sites, and other published information about grantmakers. Entries were then mailed to potential 23rd edition grantmakers for review and correction, and were revised according to the information supplied.

It is important to note that this directory describes only those grantmaker programs providing support to individuals. Most grantmakers also have funding programs for nonprofit organizations and institutions. Often these programs are much more substantial than those for individuals. Information about programs providing funding for nonprofit organizations can be found in other Foundation Center products (see Resources of the Foundation Center on p. xxxvii).

Many of the programs that grantmakers finance through nonprofit organizations are geared toward individual recipients (e.g., funds given by grantmakers to colleges and universities for setting up scholarship programs). Such programs are not included in this volume, as students must apply to their school rather than the grantmaker for assistance. However, information on these types of programs can be obtained through the appropriate financial aid offices. Keep in mind that many alternative sources of funding for individuals are available in the United States. Government grants, scholarships offered directly by colleges and universities, research funds from nonprofit

institutions, and other awards should be fully investigated as you search for financial assistance.

To help individual grantseekers of all kinds learn about alternative funding, a bibliography of reference guides to grants other than those made by grantmakers appears on page xxi. Relevant web addresses are also included here. For many grantseekers, the bibliography may be as useful as the grantmaker entries listed in this volume.

CRITERIA FOR INCLUSION

In order to be included in *Foundation Grants to Individuals*, a grantmaker must meet four criteria:

1. It must initially award grants to individuals totaling $5,000.

2. It must award grants to individuals totaling at least $2,000 annually to maintain eligibility. (The latest financial information for the years 2012 or 2013 were used, however, information from 2010 or 2011 was used in the absence of timely delivery of tax reporting forms from the IRS.) In addition, if a grantmaker gave less than $2,000 in grants to individuals in the latest year available, financial data from previous years was reviewed, and the grantmaker was included if a substantial giving pattern was found to exist.

3. Its grant recipients must be selected by its governing board or an independent selection committee.

4. It must accept applications from individuals directly or through an intermediary. The exception to this is funding by nomination only which includes information on award programs that require nominations from sources other than the individuals themselves (e.g., institutions or organizations affiliated with the grantmaker). These entries have been included for those interested in reviewing the full spectrum of grantmaker support for individuals. **Individuals should not apply directly to grantmakers described as only accepting nominations.**

ARRANGEMENT

Foundation Grants to Individuals is published annually. Entries are listed by state and arranged alphabetically by grantmaker name. Each descriptive entry is assigned a sequence number and references in the indexes are to these entry numbers.

Many grantmakers have more than one type of grantmaking program. For example, a grantmaker might award scholarships and also give support to the needy elderly. Where breakdowns are available and both programs are of substantial size (usually over $2,000 in grant awards per program) both are listed.

Each entry includes, as available, the following:

1. The full legal **name of the grantmaker**.

2. The **former name** of the grantmaker.

3. The **street address, city, and zip code** of the grantmaker's principal office.

4. The **telephone number** of the grantmaker.

5. The name and title of the **contact person** of the grantmaker.

6. The **application address** supplied by the grantmaker, if different from the grantmaker's principal address. Additional telephone or fax numbers as well as e-mail and/or URL addresses may also be listed here.

7. **Grantmaker type:** community, company-sponsored, corporate giving, independent, operating, or public charity.

8. The **purpose** statement describing the restrictions (if any) on giving made by the grantmaker.

9. A list of **publications** of other materials made available by the grantmaker that describes its activities and giving programs. These can include annual or multi-year reports, newsletters, informational brochures, grants lists, etc.

10. The **year-end date** for the grantmaker's accounting period for which financial data is supplied.

11. **Assets:** the total value of the grantmaker's investments at the end of the accounting period. In a few instances, foundations that act as "pass-throughs" for individuals gifts report zero assets.

12. **Asset type:** generally, assets are reported at market value (M) or ledger value (L).

13. **Expenditures:** total disbursements of the foundation, including overhead expenses (salaries; investment, legal, and other professional fees; interest; rent; etc.) and federal excise taxes, as well as the total amount paid for grants, scholarships, and matching gifts.

14. The **total giving** amount and number of grants paid during the year, with the largest grant paid (high) and smallest grant paid (low). The total giving amount represents all the grants awarded by an organization during the fiscal year, and not necessarily funding to individuals.

15. The total amount and number of **grants made directly to or on behalf of individuals**, including scholarships, fellowships, awards, and medical payments. When supplied by the grantmaker, high, low, and average range are also indicated. The grants to individuals amount represents all the grants awarded by an organization.

16. The number of **loans to individuals** and the total amount loaned. When supplied by the grantmaker, high, low, and average are also indicated.

17. The **fields of interest** reflected in the grantmaker's giving program relating to individuals. It is the subjects the grantmaker might support that are relevant to an individual's needs and does not include the giving interests the grantmaker provides to organizations.

18. **Types of support** is generated to denote the types of support a grantmaker might provide to individuals and does not include the types of support the grantmaker provides to organizations.

19. **Application information**, including the preferred form of application, the number of copies of proposals requested, application deadlines, and the general amount of time the grantmaker requires to notify the applicant of the board's decision.

20. **Program description:** the name of the grant or award; its purpose, terms, and conditions; and grantee accountability to the grantmaker.

21. **Company Name:** the specific name of the company supporting employee-related funding.

22. **EIN:** The Employer Identification Number assigned to the grantmaker by the Internal Revenue Service for tax purposes. This number can be useful when ordering or searching for copies of the grantmaker's annual information return, Form 990-PF or 990.

The absence of certain pieces of information in an entry indicates that such information is not pertinent or was not available for that grantmaker. Where full information is not provided and the available data seems to indicate that you might be eligible for assistance, it is advisable to write to the grantmaker. If a contact person is not listed and no specific program is named or described, inquiries should simply be addressed to the grantmaker.

INDEXES

In order to facilitate your research and provide access to the many entries in this volume, seven indexes have been developed. The indexes are the best place to begin when using this directory.

The numbers listed in the indexes correspond to the sequence numbers of individual grantmaker entries in the Descriptive Directory section of the book. In the Grantmaker Name Index, the letter "A" refers to the Appendix, which lists grantmakers from the 22nd edition of *Foundation Grants to Individuals* that have not been included in the 23rd edition. The grantmakers listed in the Appendix have either terminated their operations or no longer meet the criteria for inclusion in this volume. The indexes include the following:

1. **Geographic Index.** This index provides access by state to all grantmaker entries in which a geographic preference or restriction is stated. Grantmakers in boldface type make

grants on a national, regional or international basis; the others generally limit giving to the city, county, or state in which they are located.

2. **International Giving Index.** This index provides access to all grantmaker entries having demonstrated giving interests in specific countries, continents, or regions. The index lists only those grantmakers whose giving goes directly overseas; to further access international interests of grantmakers, see the Subject Index for more information.

3. **Company Name Index.** This index provides access, by company name, to grantmaking programs that are open to a specific company's employees, former employees, and/or their families.

4. **Specific School Index.** This index provides access to grantmakers that make grants to individuals who have attended, are attending, or will attend specific schools.

5. **Type of Support Index.** This index provides access to grantmakers according to the particular kinds of grants they award, such as scholarships, medical expenses, or research grants. Entries are indexed under the applicable terms. Again, related types of support terms should be checked to make certain all potentially relevant entries are reviewed. Grantmakers in boldface type make grants on a national, regional, or international basis; the others generally limit giving to the city, county, or state in which they are located. This index is generated to denote the types of support a grantmaker might provide to individuals and does not include the types of support the grantmaker provides to organizations.

6. **Subject Index.** This index provides access to grantmakers that make grants in specific subject areas. Entries are indexed under the applicable terms. Related subject terms should be checked to make certain all potentially relevant entries are reviewed. Grantmakers in boldface type make grants on a national, regional, or international basis; the others generally limit giving to the city, county, or state in which they are located. This index is generated to denote the fields of interest a grantmaker might support that are relevant to an individual's needs and does not include the giving interests the grantmaker provides to organizations.

7. **Grantmaker Name Index.** This index provides access by grantmaker name to entries in the main section of the book, as well as to those listed in the Appendix (these entries are listed with an "A" next to them).

TO THE GRANTSEEKER: RESEARCHING GRANTMAKER GIVING

Used correctly, *Foundation Grants to Individuals* can be an important tool in the construction of a methodical research strategy designed to uncover those grantmakers that might be able to fulfill your funding needs. It is as much a guide to those programs to which you should not apply as it is a guide to those for which you may qualify. Many grantmakers making grants to individuals are small, have limited assets, and make a limited number of grants each year. Federal laws outline

specific restrictions and requirements for grantmaker giving to individuals and have limited the extent and nature of such programs. An analysis of these laws follows this introduction.

Remember, most of the grantmakers listed in this volume place specific limitations (i.e., by subject area, recipient type, and/or geographic focus) on their giving. Finding out about those limitations before you submit your application will save you time and increase your chances of obtaining assistance. Most grantmakers will automatically reject any applicant who does not qualify under their restrictions.

Do not waste time applying to inappropriate grantmakers. The law of averages does not apply when seeking grants. One hundred applications sent to one hundred grantmakers whose qualifications you do not meet will result in one hundred rejections, or in no responses at all. By demonstrating your knowledge of a grantmaker's programs, you have a better chance of getting your foot in the door. Grantmakers give only a limited amount of money and have a large number of applicants from which to choose. The grantmaker personnel who review your application will be looking for the candidate who best meets the standards and objectives of their programs.

Each entry in this book includes a statement of limitations outlining the specific constraints on that grantmaker's giving program for individuals. In addition, geographic information is indicated in the Subject, Geographic, and International Indexes.

REMEMBER: IF YOU DON'T QUALIFY, DON'T APPLY.

IDENTIFYING FUNDING POSSIBILITIES

As with all grantseeking, the key for individuals to obtain a grant is preparation. Preparation means identifying the grantmakers that make grants in your area and determining whether you qualify. It is important to pay close attention to grantmaker limitation statements, giving patterns, areas of interest, and average grant awards. Applying to a grantmaker that makes grants outside your field of study or to one that only makes grants of a few hundred dollars when you need thousands will prove futile. Instead, learn as much as you can about your funding prospects. Use all the available resources and do your homework.

Identify funding possibilities using the indexes provided in this book. The indexes give you access to the grantmaker entries by subject, type of support, geographic focus, international giving focus, company-related grantmaking, and specific schools. Once you've identified the grantmakers likely to consider your request, try to find out more about their particular programs. Visit the Funding Information Network, which provide a core collection of Center publications as well as a variety of supplementary materials and services in areas useful to grantseekers all free of charge.

If, upon further research, you believe a grantmaker may be receptive to your request, prepare your application or proposal according to the guidelines specified by the grantmaker. Be thorough. Provide all the information requested, give references if required, and be sure to provide carefully planned budgets that show how the money will be spent.

Approach the application process as you would a job application. Explain why you are the best person for that grantmaker to support and emphasize your qualifications.

Take the time to make your case clearly and persuasively.

With all this in mind, you are now ready to begin the process that could lead to the funding you seek.

FEDERAL LAWS AND GRANTS TO INDIVIDUALS

SOME BACKGROUND INFORMATION

Provisions of the Internal Revenue Code establish some special requirements that certain foundation "grants to individuals" (GTIs) programs must meet. Individual grantees should be familiar with these rules, as they affect the grantee as well as the grantmaker grantor.

Charitable organizations in general, and foundations in particular, have traditionally enjoyed favorable treatment in the GTI area more so than individual contributors. If you as an individual know a deserving and needy student, you can give that student the necessary funds for a college education, graduate degree, or research project (assuming you are financially able to do so)—but you won't get the benefit of a charitable contribution for doing so. However, charitable organizations, including foundations, whose funds are already exempt from income taxes and to which tax-deductible contributions can be made, have long been able to make individual grants without adversely affecting their tax status.

LEGISLATIVE HISTORY

The right for foundations to give GTIs came under close scrutiny in 1969, when the current elaborate private foundation rules and restrictions were first under consideration in Congress. The House Ways and Means Committee at one point tentatively decided that, with certain limited exceptions, private foundations should be denied the right to make grants directly to individuals for travel, study, or similar purposes. But the Committee changed its mind and reported a proposed bill allowing private foundations to award GTIs for travel, study, or similar purposes provided selection procedures for these grants were approved in advance by the Treasury Department on a one-time approval basis. This approach was enacted into law and remains in effect.

SOME GROUND RULES AND SOME QUESTIONS

Internal Revenue Code Section 4945 provides the ground rules that private foundations must follow regarding GTIs. A grant to an individual for travel, study, or similar purposes is proscribed, unless the grant is awarded on an objective and nondiscriminatory basis under an approved procedure and the grant:

1. is a scholarship or fellowship as specially defined for study at an educational institution;

2. achieves a specific objective; produces a report or other similar product; or improves or enhances an artistic, scientific, or teaching capacity, skill, or talent of the grantee; or

3. is a prize or award given for the achievement of exempt charitable purposes, where the recipient did not enter into a contest or other proceedings leading to the award and no substantial future services are required of the recipient as a condition to the prize or award.

The IRS requires advanced approval for scholarship and fellowship programs as well as for the specific objective programs. Prize or awards programs are not mandated to follow this rule.

Though few foundations make such grants, the law also permits private foundations to provide direct support to needy individuals. Thus, the regulations to Section 4945 provide that a private foundation may make grants to indigent individuals enabling them to purchase needed goods or services, without regard to whether the criteria cited above are met.

Let's take a closer look at the "objective and nondiscriminatory" and "approved procedure" requirements.

A question that has arisen with increasing frequency in other contexts is whether an educational program can be nondiscriminatory if it benefits particular groups (e.g., women, African Americans, the residents of a particular community or region). In the case of foundation GTIs, it still seems clear that prospective recipients can be limited to a group sufficiently broad to be recognized as a charitable class. The purpose of the individual grant rules was to ensure against arbitrary, whimsical, or personally motivated grants. If a foundation maintains a scholarship program providing aid for residents of a particular county or state, or for a particular group that has been victimized by discrimination, the tax law rules do not require the foundation to change that focus so long as the program is administered in an objective and nondiscriminatory fashion within the group for whom benefits are available. The regulations also recognize that for grants to "achieve a specific objective," as noted in subparagraph two (2) above, selection from a group is not necessary where, taking the grant's purposes into account, one or more persons are selected because they are exceptionally qualified to accomplish these purposes.

Once a grant is made to an individual, the foundation and its individual grantees have additional responsibilities. The foundation must follow up to see to it the funds are being used by the individual grantee for the intended purposes. The foundation must obtain reports at least annually, though reporting and record keeping burdens can be lessened where the grants are paid to the educational institution for the benefit of the grantee rather than to the grantee directly.

A foundation also has a duty to investigate situations where there are indications that the grant is not being used for the purposes intended or is being diverted to improper purposes. A foundation would normally withhold any further funds under the grant until the situation is corrected and, where a diversion occurs, it is obliged to take all reasonable and appropriate steps to recover or to otherwise ensure the restoration of those funds.

Failure to comply with the requirements is sanctioned by a series of penalty excise taxes that can be imposed on the foundation and, in limited circumstances, on its managers. In flagrant cases, the foundation can lose its tax-exempt status.

SIGNIFICANT GUIDELINES FOR PUBLIC CHARITIES

Public charities, known alternately as public foundations (including a sub-class known as community foundations), sometimes administer programs of grants to individuals, but they do not have to meet the rules and regulations that apply to private foundation GTI programs. Regulators do not provide as much oversight for these programs, so that more responsibility for the conduct of the programs is shifted to the charities. The upshot is that these charities must have in-depth legal knowledge and pay close attention to administrative detail.

Community foundations function along the same lines as private foundations. Many public charities also operate this way. While the tax rules and regulations are not binding, charities often use the legal criteria set out in Section 4945 to insure that they are within a safe zone when they file tax returns. Community foundations, however, must comply with the IRS H.R. 4 of 2006, generally referred to as the Pension Protection Act (PPA). For example, with regard to donor-advised funds, community foundations do not allow the donor or the donor-advised fund to take part in the selection of individuals.

One requirement of grantmaking to individuals is that programs must be "objective and non-discriminatory"; public charities and private foundations use the same criteria. As a result of the wider interpretation of the phrase "objective and nondiscriminatory grants," public charities must investigate additional facets of the proposed granting to be sure it meets legal criteria. Another important point to note is that public charities, in contrast to private foundations, are allowed to do some lobbying and are permitted to provide a limited amount of funding for lobbying purposes.

With regard to the approval procedure, contrary to the private foundation requirements, a public charity is not required to seek advanced approval from the IRS, with the exception of company-related GTI programs where funds donated by a corporate foundation for company employee scholarships are to be administered by a community foundation. In addition, the IRS must be notified about amendments to the organization document when the charity undertakes a new GTI program not included in the original articles contained in that document.

Programs for public charity loans to individuals function along the same lines as their GTI programs.

INCOME TAX CONSIDERATIONS

There is a substantial amount of law written on the subject of whether scholarships and similar payments are taxable or tax-exempt income—a subject that is beyond the scope of this section. Please seek legal or accounting advisors to learn more about this area. A few general observations follow:

Under prior law, private foundation scholarship and fellowship grants were generally income tax free to the recipient. However, this rule was substantially curtailed by the Tax Reform Act of 1986. The income-tax exemption is now generally limited to scholarships for degree candidates at educational institutions (also specially defined), and then only for amounts spent for tuition, fees, books, and supplies. Amounts spent for room, board, and other "personal expenses" are subject to tax.

Individuals lucky enough to receive a private foundation grant should not assume that their grant is nontaxable and be aware that tax-exempt treatment is limited to a narrow area.

OTHER PROGRAMS

Bear in mind that many grantmakers provide substantial scholarship dollars but make these funds available to schools and other public charities, thus entrusting the responsibility to the institutions for selecting grant recipients. Students will often find that the source of the money for the scholarship awarded by the school or college of their choice is a grantmaker. The grantmaker community is a major source of support for organizations such as the Eisenhower Exchange Fellowships, the National Merit Scholarship Program, and others. However, such grant programs are generally treated as grants to organizations, and the detailed requirements for GTIs described here do not apply.

CONCLUSION

A relatively small number of grantmakers make grants to individuals because of the restrictions of federal law. However, for the grantmakers that do provide grants to individuals, the general consensus is that the rules are reasonable and provide assurance that grants to individuals made by grantmakers will be rational rather than whimsical, fair rather than arbitrary, and very much in the public interest. For additional information about this area of law visit the IRS at www.irs.gov.

SCHOLARSHIPS AND GRANTS TO INDIVIDUALS: WHERE TO FIND THEM

How can you get a grant to help pay for your education, write a book, make a film, or do research?

There are no easy answers, but there are resources that can help you. *Foundation Grants to Individuals* is an excellent starting point. The purpose of this section, however, is to suggest additional resources on scholarships and grants.

FINANCIAL AID FOR EDUCATION

If you are a student and need financial support to further your education, your first stop should be the financial aid office of the school you plan to attend. Financial aid officers often have information about special scholarships or awards given by government agencies, local corporations, or foundations. Their advice can get you started in the right direction. You might also research the various financial aid directories available to you. A representative list of resources can be found in the bibliography that appears on page xxi. The best approach is to consider your own attributes and the connections you have to associations, corporations, or other organizations. Many scholarships are not based solely on academic merit or financial need. For example, there are scholarships for students from a particular county, for art history majors, for people with disabilities, or for women. Consider your background and the type of support you need, and apply to those programs for which you qualify. Some of the more useful directories include *Peterson's How to Get Money for College and Scholarships, Grants and Prizes* (Peterson's) and *The College Student's Guide to Merit and Other No-Need Funding* (Reference Service Press). These books are well indexed and may suggest additional funding possibilities to you. For answers to frequently-asked questions about individual grantseeking (including information for those seeking financial aid) and links to other web sites with scholarship information, visit the Foundation Center's GrantSpace web site (grantspace.org).

GENERAL RESOURCES FOR GRANTSEEKERS

In addition to the directories of financial aid for education, there are directories covering funding for non-educational purposes. *Annual Register of Grant Support: A Directory of Funding Sources* (Information Today) covers grants for academic and scientific research, project development, travel and exchange programs, publication support, equipment and construction, in-service training, and competitive awards and prizes in a variety of fields. *The Grants Register* (Palgrave Macmillan) is intended for grantseekers at or above the graduate level and for those who require professional or advanced vocational training. It is international in scope and is useful to students from other countries seeking exchange opportunities or international scholarships. *Volume 1 of Awards, Honors, and Prizes* (Gale Cengage Learning) contains details about thousands of prizes and awards for all types of service and special achievement in the United States and Canada. Volume 2 covers awards from countries other than the U.S. and Canada. *The Directory of Research Grants* (Schoolhouse Partners) is a useful source for scholars, grant administrators, faculty members, and others seeking support for research projects. It includes programs supported by private foundations, corporations, professional organizations, and a few state and foreign governments. Also of interest to the researcher is the *Research Centers Directory* (Gale Cengage Learning), which lists university-related and other nonprofit research organizations in the U.S. and Canada.

SPECIALIZED RESOURCES FOR GRANTSEEKERS

In addition to the general directories, there are specialized resources compiled for specific population groups (e.g., women, minorities, etc.) or for specific disciplines and professions (e.g., the arts, medicine, or sciences). Among these specialized resources are the *Directory of Financial Aids for Women* (Reference Service Press), *Financial Aid for African Americans* (Reference Service Press), and the *Directory of Biomedical and Health Care Grants* (Schoolhouse Partners). For information on federal funding, the primary resource is the *Catalog of Federal Domestic Assistance* (Office of Management and Budget, free online at cfda.gov). Use the annual print catalog only as a starting point, since much of the information may be outdated by the time it is published. Follow up by contacting the local or regional office of the appropriate agency. Another useful resource for finding federal grantmaking agencies is the web site Grants.gov (grants.gov).

PROPOSAL WRITING FOR GRANTSEEKERS

Many grantmakers that give grants directly to individuals provide their own application forms and detailed guidelines. If you are applying to one of these grantmakers, be certain to follow their instructions to the letter. However, some funders provide very general application guidelines. The following information will be useful in constructing a proposal for these funders.

Each proposal is a unique document written with a specific funder in mind. The purpose of your proposal is to present you and your ideas in a positive and compelling way and to establish a link between you and the funder. Your proposal should suggest that you are a potential partner in accomplishing their mission, not just a person asking for money.

There are certain characteristics common to most successful proposals:

- They deliver an important idea and address a significant issue.

- They indicate that the applicant has chosen an innovative approach to that issue and has a reasonable plan for implementation.

- They assure the funder that the applicant is capable of success.

- They show how the grant will advance the funder's goals.

- They set forth anticipated results.

The standard elements of a proposal are:

- A **Cover Letter** addressed specifically to the appropriate contact person at the grantmaker.

- A brief **Abstract** (sometimes called an executive summary) that describes very concisely the information that will follow.

- An **Introduction** that helps to establish your credibility as a grant applicant.

- A **Statement of Need** that describes a problem and explains why you require a grant to address the issue.

- **Objectives** that refine your idea and tell exactly what you expect to accomplish in response to the need.

- **Procedures** that describe the methods you will use to accomplish your objectives within a stated time frame.

- An **Evaluation** method for determining how you and the funder will measure your results and effectiveness. This should closely correspond to the objectives you set forth.

- If the project is ongoing, a section about its **Future Funding**, with specific plans for feasible, continuing support.

- A separate **Budget** depicting in dollars precisely how much money will be required and how and when it will be spent in order to accomplish your objectives. Typical components of a budget for an individual's grant project include: wages for personnel (usually your own salary is "donated"), space and equipment costs, travel expenses, telephone, printing, postage, and other direct costs.

In general, proposals from individuals should not exceed five pages in addition to the budget. Begin by writing an outline to help you compose your thoughts and achieve clarity and conciseness. Good grammar and accurate spelling are important. The text should be divided into short paragraphs, with headings and sub-headings used for clarification. It's always good advice to ask someone else to read and critique your proposal before you submit it.

Funders' deadlines are very strict, so allow yourself enough time to do your research and to produce your most polished effort. Creating a checklist will help to ensure that your submission includes all the requested items in the proper order. If you are applying to more than one funder (which is common), you should mention this fact in your cover letter. Remember one important rule of thumb: "If you don't qualify, don't apply." The ultimate success of your effort, like that of nonprofit grantseekers, will rest on the quality of your research aimed at uncovering the best prospective funder. Take your time in using *Foundation Grants to Individuals*— available in both online (gtionline.foundationcenter.org) and print formats— to ensure that you approach only grantmakers that have demonstrated an interest in your field and that give grants in your geographic area.

The Virtual Classroom in GrantSpace (grantspace.org/ Classroom/Online-Classes) offers two courses that may be useful: "Finding Foundation Support for Your Education" and "Grantseeking Basics for Individuals." This page also includes numerous webinars, including one specifically for artists titled "Grantseeking Basics for Individuals in the Arts."

AFFILIATION WITH A TAX-EXEMPT ORGANIZATION

If you are seeking support other than for your own education, you should be aware that few private foundations or corporations make grants directly to individuals. Most, in fact, make grants only to nonprofit tax-exempt organizations (e.g., universities, hospitals, museums, and other organizations with educational, scientific, religious, and/or charitable purposes) to which contributions are tax deductible. Some individual grantseekers become affiliated with tax-exempt organizations that serve as their sponsors in order to obtain the federal tax-exempt status that funders require. To identify organizations to which contributions are tax-deductible, visit the IRS web site to search their online database *Exempt Organizations Select Check* (irs.gov/app/eos). Newsletters, annual reports, and membership lists from state and local arts and humanities councils, Chambers of Commerce, and local United Ways may also help you to locate potential sponsors for your work or project. For a good discussion of the pros and cons of affiliation with a tax-exempt organization and of grantseeking in general, see the *Guide to Fiscal Sponsorship* tutorial on the Foundation Center's web site (foundationcenter.org/getstarted/tutorials/ fiscal). It suggests a number of affiliation possibilities, including forming a consortium with other individuals interested in the same subject; finding a temporary, in name only, tax-exempt sponsor or umbrella group to serve as a fiscal sponsor for your project; making use of your current affiliations with professional societies, trade associations, clubs, alumni groups, etc.; or becoming an employee of a nonprofit institution. There are a number of creative strategies, including teaching in a college or university continuing education program on a part-time basis and developing a "scholar-in-residence" role for yourself. Some organizations may fund your project directly or serve as a fiscal sponsor for you. A fiscal sponsor is an organization that will accept funds on your behalf. It makes the formal application for the grant and retains financial responsibility for the project. If you choose to work with a fiscal sponsor, be sure it has federal tax-exempt status and be aware that there may be strings attached. For example, the organization may insist on retaining administrative controls on your work; it may impose a service fee; it may want to share in subsidiary rights as a co-author; and make further requests. No two fiscal sponsorship relationships are exactly alike. A detailed discussion of alternative arrangements may be found in *Fiscal Sponsorship: 6 Ways to Do It Right* (Study Center Press) by Gregory L. Colvin. GrantSpace also provides Knowledge Base Articles on this topic (grantspace.org/Tools/Knowledge-Base/Individual-Grantseekers/Fiscal-Sponsorship).

FORMING YOUR OWN NONPROFIT ORGANIZATION

Still another option to consider is forming your own nonprofit tax-exempt organization. This will require careful thought and a good deal of administrative work on your part. It also entails legal and financial responsibilities that are likely to require the services of a lawyer. Don't try it alone. To learn more about what's involved in incorporating as a nonprofit or in forming an unincorporated association, there are a number of useful sources, including *Starting and Managing a Nonprofit Organization: A Legal Guide* (John Wiley & Sons) by Bruce R. Hopkins and *How to Form a Nonprofit Corporation* (Nolo Press) by Anthony Mancuso. Books covering incorporation for your particular state can be even more useful. In this category, see *How to Form a Nonprofit Corporation in California* (Nolo Press) and *Procedures for Forming and Changing Not-for-profit Corporations* in New York State (New York State Department of Law, Charities Bureau). Nolo provides basic incorporation steps and advice on its web site (nolo.com/legal-encyclopedia/nonprofit-corporation), and GrantSpace has a Knowledge Base

section on establishing a nonprofit organization (grantspace.org/Tools/Knowledge-Base/Nonprofit-Management/Establishment).

Keep in mind that forming a nonprofit organization and obtaining tax-exempt status are two separate processes. Nonprofit incorporation is a procedure handled on the state level; tax-exempt status is a federal matter. For information on applying for tax-exempt status, see IRS publication 557, *Tax Exempt Status for Your Organization*. You can obtain copies by contacting the Internal Revenue Service at (800) 829-3676, or view it online at irs.gov/pub/irs-pdf/p557.pdf.

Forming a nonprofit organization is not for everyone. In fact, many nonprofit organizations fail in their first few years because the people who established them did not understand what taking such a step would entail. By reviewing the resources mentioned above and discussing your options with a lawyer, you should be better able to decide if this approach is right for you.

Resources for Individual Grantseekers: A Bibliography on page xxi is a list of select resources that may prove valuable as you pursue your research. Scan the general directories first, and then check to see whether there are specific resources related to your status or interests.

Publishers' addresses frequently change, as do edition numbers and the price of publications. Before you order a particular title, check with the publisher to verify that it contains the most current information available. Copies of many of the works mentioned above are also available for reference use at the Foundation Center's New York, Washington, D.C., Cleveland, San Francisco, and Atlanta libraries as well as through the Foundation Center's Funding Information Network. For the nearest location, call the Foundation Center at (212) 620-4230, or check our web site: foundationcenter.org/fin.

GLOSSARY

The following list, arranged alphabetically, includes common terms used by grantmakers and grantseekers.

Accredited Institutions: Entities that meet specific standards for educational programs as determined by regional or national associations.

American College Testing (ACT): A test created by the American College Testing Program, which some colleges require students to take.

Annual Report: A voluntary report issued by a grantmaker that provides financial data and descriptions of grantmaking activities. Annual reports vary in format from simple typewritten documents listing the year's grants to detailed publications that provide substantial information about the grantmaking program. Many organizations post the Annual Report of their web site.

Assets: The total value of the foundation's investments at the end of the accounting period. In a few instances, foundations that act as "pass-throughs" for individual gifts report zero assets.

Award: A gift given in recognition of past achievements usually by nomination only.

Campership: A grant given to enable a child to attend summer camp.

Class Rank: In secondary education, student rank based on GPA or grades relative to the other students in their class.

Community Foundation: A 501(c)(3) organization that makes grants for charitable purposes in a specific community or region. Most community foundations are classified as public charities, which are eligible for maximum income tax-deductibility of contributions.

Community Fund: An organized community program that makes annual appeals to the general public for funds that are usually not retained in an endowment but are used for the ongoing operational support of local social and health service agencies. (*See also* **Federated Giving Program**)

Company-Sponsored Foundation: (also referred to as Corporate Foundation) A private foundation whose grant funds are derived primarily from the contributions of a profit-making business organization.

Conferences/Seminars: Grants that may cover registration, lodging, or transportation for an individual to attend a conference, seminar, or workshop. Often, these grants are awarded in conjunction with a fellowship, internship, or scholarship.

Cooperative Venture: A joint effort between or among two or more grantmakers (including foundations, corporations, and government agencies). Partners might share in funding responsibilities or contribute information and technical resources.

Corporate-Giving Program: A grantmaking program established and administered within a profit-making company. These programs are not subject to the same reporting requirements as private foundations or public charities. Some companies make charitable contributions through both a corporate giving program and a company-sponsored foundation.

Curriculum Vitae: In the academic community, a lengthy document providing a summary of an individual's accomplishments, including employment, education, research, published work, awards, professional memberships, and other biographical information.

Distribution Committee: The board responsible for making grant decisions. For community foundations, it is intended to be broadly representative of the community served by the foundation.

Doctoral Support: Grants to aid dissertation or thesis research.

Donee: The recipient of a grant or scholarship (also known as the grantee or beneficiary).

Emergency Funds: Grants to individuals and families to assist in paying for emergency needs resulting from disaster, natural or otherwise, including expenses for medical and dental care, shelter, repairs, utilities, transportation, and clothing.

Employee-Related Scholarships/Student Loans: Scholarships and student loans to current or former company employees and/or their families.

Employee-Related Welfare: General welfare grants/loans to current or former employees and their families.

Endowment: Funds intended to be kept permanently and invested to provide income for continued support of an organization.

Exchange Program: A program that sends students to study in other countries and allows students from those countries to exchange places with its participants.

Expenditures: Total disbursements of the foundation, including overhead expenses (salaries; investments, legal, and other professional fees; interest; rent; etc.) and federal excise taxes, as well as the total amount paid for grants, scholarships, and matching gifts.

Family Foundation: An independent private foundation whose funds are derived from members of a single family. Family members often serve as officers or board members of the foundation and have a significant role in grantmaking decisions.

Federated Giving Program: A joint fundraising effort usually administered by a nonprofit "umbrella" organization that in turn distributes contributed funds to several nonprofit agencies. The United Way and community chests or funds, the United Jewish Appeal and other religious appeals, the United Negro College Fund, and joint arts councils are examples of federated giving programs. (See also **Community Fund**)

Fellowships: Programs that award stipends to individuals for tuition, travel, books, and other costs of research and study.

Financial Aid Form (FAF): Many private universities require this form, which is more detailed and requires a processing fee, in addition to the FAFSA, (See also **Free Application for Student Aid**).

Fiscal Agent/Sponsor: A nonprofit organization with 501(c)(3) status that has agreed to manage the financial activity of an applicant's grant. The check is sent to the fiscal agent (also known as a fiscal sponsor) who then disburses the funds to the applicant, minus a small administrative fee, usually between 5 percent and 7 percent of the grant.

Foreign Applicants: Applicants from countries other than the U.S. are eligible to apply for certain programs administered by U.S. grantmakers.

Form 990: The annual information return that all public charities must submit to the IRS each year and which is also filed with appropriate state officials. The form requires information on the charity's assets, income, operating expenses, contributions and grants, paid staff and salaries, program funding areas, and grantmaking guidelines.

Form 990-PF: The annual information return that all private foundations must submit to the IRS each year and which is also filed with appropriate state officials. The form requires information on the foundation's assets, income, operating expenses, contributions and grants, paid staff and salaries, program funding areas, grantmaking guidelines and restrictions, and grant application procedures.

Free Application for Student Aid (FAFSA): This is a form commonly used to apply for U.S. Government financial aid. Colleges and many non-institutional programs will use the data on this form to determine entitlement for financial aid (See also **Financial Aid Form**).

501(c)(3): The section of the Internal Revenue Code that defines nonprofit, charitable, tax-exempt organizations; 501(c)(3) organizations are further defined as public charities, private operating foundations, and private non-operating foundations. (See also **Operating foundation; Private foundation; Public Charity**)

General Purpose Foundation: An independent private foundation that awards grants in many different fields of interest.

Graduate Support: Funds awarded to individuals for graduate work through programs administered by the grantmaker.

Grants by Nomination Only: Scholarships, fellowships, research grants, and other awards or grants in which individuals must be nominated by the grantmaker, an allied institution, or a third party in order to be considered.

Grants for Special Needs: Funds given directly to individuals or on their behalf, including grants and/or loans to cover medical expenses and other basic needs for economically disadvantaged individuals.

Independent Foundation: A grantmaking organization classified by the IRS as a private foundation. Independent foundations may also be known as family foundations, general purpose foundations, special purpose foundations, or private non-operating foundations. The Foundation Center classifies independent foundations and company-sponsored foundations separately; however, federal law normally classifies them both as private, non-operating foundations, and both are subject to the same rules and requirements. (See also **Private Foundation**)

In-Kind Gifts: Non-monetary donations to individuals, including donated services or donated products. Examples of donated services include medical services, financial consulting, home weatherization, transportation, job training, and counseling services. Examples of donated products include food, temporary housing, medical equipment, and medication.

Internships: Programs that support individuals in gaining practical experience in their careers. Some internships are paid, and must be undertaken for college credit.

Letter of Recommendation: A letter written by a teacher, school administrator, or professional in a relevant field that indicates the quality of an applicant's abilities or character.

Loans: Funds which usually must be repaid to the lending grantmaker, often with a pre-determined interest percentage added to the loaned amount.

Medical Expenses: Funding which covers medical, dental, or eye care for needy individuals.

Operating Foundation: A 501(c)(3) organization classified by the IRS as a private foundation whose primary purpose is to conduct research, social welfare, or other programs determined by its governing body or establishment charter. Some grants may be made, but the sum is generally small relative to the funds used for the foundation's own programs. (See also **501(c)(3)**)

Payout Requirement: The minimum amount that private foundations are required to expend for charitable purposes (including grants and, within certain limits, the administrative cost of making grants). In general, a private foundation must meet or exceed an annual payout requirement of five percent of the average market value of the foundation's assets.

Pell Grant: Federally-funded educational grants awarded almost exclusively to individuals who have not yet earned a bachelor's degree. Awards are based upon financial need, and the maximum award rarely exceeds $4,000.

Permanent Resident: Non-U.S. citizens who have gained this status from the U.S. immigration and Naturalization Service.

Postdoctoral Study: Funds for the pursuit of advanced research or study after receiving a doctorate degree.

Postgraduate Study: Funds for the pursuit of advanced research or study after receiving a graduate degree.

Precollege Scholarships/Student Loans: Scholarships and loans given for expenses related to elementary or secondary education, such as private school tuition.

Preliminary Student Aptitude Test (PSAT): A standardized test, often taken during the junior year of high school, which prepares the student for the Student Aptitude Test (SAT). (See also **Student Aptitude Test**)

Private Foundation: A nongovernmental, nonprofit organization with funds and programs managed by its own trustees or directors, established to maintain or aid social, educational, religious, or other charitable activities serving the common welfare, primarily through making grants. A private foundation is tax exempt under code section 501(c)(3).

Prizes: Gifts to winners of competitions sponsored by nonprofits or an affiliated organization.

Professorships: Awards to individuals who will serve on the faculty of an institution of higher learning.

Program Development: Grants to support specific projects or programs as opposed to general purpose grants.

Program Officer: A staff member of a grantmaker who reviews grant proposals and processes applications for the board of trustees. Only a small percentage of grantmakers have program officers.

Project Support: Support given to individuals working at the postgraduate level or beyond and/or those seeking support for projects within their professional career.

Proposal: A written application, often with supporting documents, submitted to a foundation or corporate giving program in requesting a contribution. Preferred procedures and formats vary. Consult published guidelines.

Publication: Grants to fund reports or other publications issued by a nonprofit resulting from research or projects of interest to the grantmaker.

Public Charity: In general, an organization that is tax exempt under code section 501(c)(3) and is classified by the IRS as "not a private foundation." Public charities derive their funding or support from the general public in carrying out social, educational, religious or other charitable activities serving the common welfare. Gifts to public charities are eligible for the maximum income tax-deductibility and are not subject to the same rules and restrictions as private foundations. Some are referred to as public foundations. (See also **501(c)(3)**)

Renewable: A scholarship or grant that may be renewed by the recipient, either automatically or through a reapplication process.

Request for Proposal (RFP): When the government issues a new contract or grant program, it sends out RFPs to agencies that might be qualified to participate. The RFP lists project specifications and application procedures. A few grantmakers occasionally use RFPs in specific fields that are initiated by applicants.

Research: Funds to cover the costs of investigations and clinical trials, including demonstration and pilot projects (research grants for individuals are usually referred to as fellowships).

Residencies: A nonmonetary award usually of short duration usually only for artists of all disciplines to further their creative talents. Meals, living quarters, equipment, and studio space may be provided.

Resident: Usually, an individual qualifies for legal residency in a state by living there for a certain length of time. Criteria vary by state.

Resume: A one- to two-page document providing a summary of an individual's accomplishments, including employment, education, research positions, and other biographical information.

Sabbatical: A leave of absence, often with pay, usually granted every seventh year.

Scholarships—General: Funds awarded to individuals through programs administered by the grantmaker that are not specifically categorized elsewhere.

Seed Money: Grants to start, establish, or initiate new projects or organizations; may cover salaries and other operating expenses of a new project. Also called "startup funds."

Seminary: An institution of higher education that offers religious training, usually to prepare the individual for ministry, priesthood, or rabbinate.

Set-Asides: Total funds set aside by the foundation for a specific purpose or project that are counted as qualifying distributions toward the annual payout requirement. Amounts for the project must be paid within five years of the first set-aside.

Special Purpose Foundation: A private foundation that focuses its grantmaking activities in one or a few special areas of interest. For example, a foundation might only award grants in the area of cancer research or child development.

Stipends: Primarily for researchers and artists, fixed allowances to cover salary and expenses during the development of an individual's work.

Student Aid Report (SAR): The SAR is generated when students submit the FAFSA to College Scholarship Services. This report calculates the amount of money the study and/or the student's family should be able to contribute toward educational expenses. Both the student and his/her designated college will receive a copy of this report.

Student Aptitude Test (SAT): Students are often required to take this test for admission to many colleges. It is also administered by the College Board (*See also* **Preliminary Student Aptitude Test**).

Student Loans—General: Loans distributed directly to individuals through programs administered by the grantmaker. Loans for educational expenses which usually must be repaid to the lending grantmaker, often with a pre-paid interest percentage added to the loan amount.

Support for Graduates or Students of Specific Schools: Applicants are restricted to those who attend or have attended a specific school. Some programs may also specify institutions to be attended after graduation. In many cases, an application must be made through the high school or college instead of the grantmaker.

Technical/Vocational School: Postsecondary institution that offers certificates in education directly related to preparation for specific careers, and which require no more than two years of study.

Total Giving: Represents all the grants awarded by an organization during the fiscal year, and not necessarily funded to individuals. Total giving contains grants to organizations, grants to individuals, matching gifts, and sometimes program amount and/or in-kind gifts. When the specific grants to individuals amount is not listed, the total giving will contain a grants to individuals amount.

Transcript: An official record of a student's academic achievement available from the student's school. When a request is made to provide this document, an official copy must be submitted.

Travel Grants: Awards that cover transportation and out-of-town living expenses. Enrollment in a college or university is not usually required.

Undergraduate Support: Funds awarded to individuals for undergraduate work through programs administered by the grantmaker.

Welfare Assistance: Grants or loans to cover basic needs for economically disadvantaged individuals.

Work Study Grants: Grants for educational expenses given to students who engage in a part-time work arrangement. A work commitment of 10-15 hours per week is usually required.

ABBREVIATIONS

The following lists contain standard abbreviations frequently used by the Foundation Center's editorial staff. These abbreviations are used most frequently in the addresses of grantmakers and the titles of corporate and grantmaker officers.

STREET ABBREVIATIONS

1st	First*	N.E.	Northeast
2nd	Second*	N.W.	Northwest
3rd	Third*	No.	Number
Apt.	Apartment	Pkwy.	Parkway
Ave.	Avenue	Pl.	Place
Bldg.	Building	Plz.	Plaza
Blvd.	Boulevard	R.R.	Rural Route
Cir.	Circle	Rd.	Road
Ct.	Court	Rm.	Room
Ctr.	Center	Rte.	Route
Dept.	Department	S.	South
Dr.	Drive	S.E.	Southeast
E.	East	S.W.	Southwest
Expwy.	Expressway	Sq.	Square
Fl.	Floor	St.	Saint
Ft.	Fort	St.	Street
Hwy.	Highway	Sta.	Station
Ln.	Lane	Ste.	Suite
M.C.	Mail Code	Terr.	Terrace
M.S.	Mail Stop	Tpke.	Turnpike
Mt.	Mount	Univ.	University
N.	North	W.	West

*Numerics used always

TWO LETTER STATE AND TERRITORY ABBREVIATIONS

AK	Alaska	NC	North Carolina
AL	Alabama	ND	North Dakota
AR	Arkansas	NE	Nebraska
AZ	Arizona	NH	New Hampshire
CA	California	NJ	New Jersey
CO	Colorado	NM	New Mexico
CT	Connecticut	NV	Nevada
DC	District of Columbia	NY	New York
DE	Delaware	OH	Ohio
FL	Florida	OK	Oklahoma
GA	Georgia	OR	Oregon
HI	Hawaii	PA	Pennsylvania
IA	Iowa	PR	Puerto Rico
ID	Idaho	RI	Rhode Island
IL	Illinois	SC	South Carolina
IN	Indiana	SD	South Dakota
KS	Kansas	TN	Tennessee
KY	Kentucky	TX	Texas
LA	Louisiana	UT	Utah
MA	Massachusetts	VA	Virginia
MD	Maryland	VI	Virgin Islands
ME	Maine	VT	Vermont
MI	Michigan	WA	Washington
MN	Minnesota	WI	Wisconsin
MO	Missouri	WV	West Virginia
MS	Mississippi	WY	Wyoming
MT	Montana		

ABBREVIATIONS USED FOR OFFICER TITLES

Acctg.	Accounting	Govt.	Government
ADM.	Admiral	Hon.	Judge
Admin.	Administration	Inf.	Information
Admin.	Administrative	Int.	Internal
Admin.	Administrator	Intl.	International
Adv.	Advertising	Jr.	Junior
Amb.	Ambassador	Lt.	Lieutenant
Assn.	Association	Ltd.	Limited
Assoc(s).	Associate(s)	Maj.	Major
Asst.	Assistant	Mfg.	Manufacturing
Bro.	Brother	Mgmt.	Management
C.A.O.	Chief Accounting Officer	Mgr.	Manager
C.A.O.	Chief Administration Officer	Mktg.	Marketing
C.E.O.	Chief Executive Officer	Msgr.	Monsignor
C.F.O.	Chief Financial Officer	Mt.	Mount
C.I.O.	Chief Information Officer	Natl.	National
C.I.O.	Chief Investment Officer	Off.	Officer
C.O.O.	Chief Operating Officer	Opers.	Operations
Capt.	Captain	Org.	Organization
Chair.	Chairperson	Plan.	Planning
Col.	Colonel	Pres.	President
Comm.	Committee	Prog(s).	Program(s)
Comms.	Communications	RADM.	Rear Admiral
Commo.	Commodore	Rels.	Relations
Compt.	Comptroller	Rep.	Representative
Cont.	Controller	Rev.	Reverend
Contrib(s).	Contribution(s)	Rt. Rev.	Right Reverend
Coord.	Coordinator	Secy.	Secretary
Corp.	Corporate, Corporation	Secy.-Treas.	Secretary-Treasurer
Co(s).	Company(s)	Sen.	Senator
Dep.	Deputy	Soc.	Society
Devel.	Development	Sr.	Senior
Dir.	Director	Sr.	Sister
Distrib(s).	Distribution(s)	Supt.	Superintendent
Div.	Division	Supvr.	Supervisor
Exec.	Executive	Svc(s).	Service(s)
Ext.	External	Tech.	Technology
Fdn.	Foundation	Tr.	Trustee
Fr.	Father	Treas.	Treasurer
Genl.	General	Univ.	University
Gov.	Governor	V.P.	Vice President
		VADM.	Vice Admiral
		Vice-Chair.	Vice Chairperson

ADDITIONAL ABBREVIATIONS

E-mail	Electronic mail
FAX	Facsimile
LOI	Letter of Inquiry
RFP	Request for Proposals
SASE	Self-Addressed Stamped Envelope
TDD, TTY	Telecommunication Device for the Deaf
Tel.	Telephone
URL	Uniform Resource Locator (web site)

Jan.	January
Feb.	February
Mar.	March
Apr.	April
Aug.	August
Sept.	September
Oct.	October
Nov.	November
Dec.	December

RESOURCES FOR INDIVIDUAL GRANTSEEKERS: A BIBLIOGRAPHY

Compiled by Rob Bruno

The following is a selective bibliography of publications and electronic resources relevant to the individual grantseeker. These items were selected from a variety of sources. Entries with a descriptive abstract were taken from the Foundation Center's bibliographic database, the Catalog of Nonprofit Literature (cnl.foundationcenter.org), or the publisher's web site. The bibliography is divided into the following sections:

- General
- Arts and Humanities
- International Travel and Study
- Media and Communications
- Medicine and Health
- Minorities and Special Populations
- Research
- Scholarships, Fellowships, and Loans
- Writing

GENERAL

Annual Register of Grant Support: A Directory of Funding Sources. 47th ed. Medford, NJ: Information Today, Inc., 2014.
> Includes details on thousands of grant support programs of government agencies, public and private foundations, corporations, community trusts, unions, educational and professional associations, and special-interest organizations. Each program description contains details of the type, purpose, and duration of the grant; amount of funding available for each award and for the entire program; eligibility requirements; geographic restrictions; number of applicants and recipients; and other pertinent information and special stipulations. Published annually. URL: infotoday.com

Atterberry, Tara, ed. Awards, Honors, and Prizes. Volume 1: United States and Canada. 35th ed. Farmington Hills, MI: Gale Cengage Learning, 2014.
> Directory containing information on awards recognizing achievement in advertising, arts and humanities, business and finance, communications, computers, ecology, education, engineering, fashion, film, journalism, law, librarianship, literature, medical research, music, performing arts, photography, public affairs, publishing, radio and television, religion, science, social science, sports, technology, and transportation. Indexed by sponsoring organization, award, and subject area. URL: cengage.com

Atterberry, Tara, ed. Awards, Honors, and Prizes. Volume 2: International. 35th ed. Farmington Hills, MI: Gale Cengage Learning, 2014.
> Contains descriptions for awards offered by organizations in countries outside the U.S. and Canada. The listing is arranged alphabetically by country. Indexed by organization, award name, and award subject. Each entry has the name of the organization administering the award (in English when available, as well as in the original language); contact information; name, purpose, and frequency of the award; year the award was established; sponsor of the award; and the award's former name. URL: cengage.com

Catalog of Federal Domestic Assistance. Washington, DC: Office of Management and Budget, 2013.
> Official directory of federal programs that provide assistance to American organizations, institutions, and individuals. Includes programs open to individual applicants or for individual beneficiaries in the areas of agriculture, commerce, community development, consumer protection, arts and culture, education, employment, energy, environmental quality, nutrition, health, housing, social services, information sciences, law, natural resources, regional development, science and technology, and transportation. Arranged by administering agency, with indexes by applicant eligibility, subject, and authorizing legislation. Published annually. Also available for free online searching or PDF download at cfda.gov. URL: cfda.gov

Internet Sources

Catalog of Federal Domestic Assistance (cfda.gov)
> The online version of the print publication listed above, providing a searchable database of information about federal assistance programs.

Benefits.gov (benefits.gov)
> Includes information on a variety of federal, state, and local benefit and assistance programs for veterans, seniors, students, teachers, children, people with disabilities, disaster victims, caregivers, and others. Allows searching by category, by federal

agency, or by state. Also provides an online questionnaire to help grantseekers determine their eligibility for benefit programs.

Grants for Individuals (staff.lib.msu.edu/harris23/ grants/3subject.htm)
Compiled by staff at the Michigan State University Libraries, this useful list gives information on grants available to individuals covering a wide range of subject areas and population groups.

Grants.gov (grants.gov)
A comprehensive site that calls itself "the central storehouse for information on over 1,000 grant programs" and provides access to approximately $500 billion in annual awards. Managed by the U.S. Department of Health and Human Services, it offers users "full service electronic grant administration" with guidelines and grant applications available online. Search by agency or category, or browse available grant opportunities.

GrantSpace: Resources for Individual Grantseekers (grantspace.org/Tools/Knowledge-Base/Individual-Grantseekers)
Knowledge Base articles compiled by Foundation Center staff answer questions ranging from finding grant funding to obtaining help with personal expenses.

ARTS AND HUMANITIES

American Art Directory. Berkeley Heights, NJ: National Register Publishing Co., 2014.
Includes a section listing art scholarships and fellowships available through various organizations including museums and colleges, as well as a listing of state arts councils. URL: americanartdir.com

Artist's & Graphic Designer's Market. Cincinnati, OH: North Light Books, 2014.
Includes the most current contact and submission information for art markets such as greeting card companies, magazine and book publishers, galleries, art fairs, ad agencies and more. Published annually. URL: writersdigestshop.com

Battenfield, Jackie. *The Artist's Guide: How to Make a Living Doing What You Love*. Philadelphia, PA: Da Capo Press. 2009.
Provides advice and resources for artists in several areas including startup, marketing, exhibitions, networking, financial management, business issues, daily operations, and other topics. Also contains a chapter on residencies, grants, and donations. URL: perseusbooksgroup.com/dacapo

Bhandari, Heather Darcy, and Jonathan Melber. *Art/Work: Everything You Need to Know (and Do) as You Pursue Your Art Career*. New York, NY: Free Press, 2009.
This career guide for visual artists contains a chapter on residencies and grants. The authors discuss key issues to consider before seeking a grant and provide tips on completing applications. URL: books.simonandschuster.com

Cobb, Peter, Susan Ball and Felicity Hogan, eds. *The Profitable Artist: A Handbook for All Artists in the Performing, Literary, and Visual Arts*. New York, NY: Allworth Press, 2011.
Outlines the day-to-day practicalities of running a business in the arts. Includes a section on writing grant proposal applications and soliciting individuals ("the ask"). Copublished by the New York Foundation for the Arts. URL: allworth.com

Cutler, David. *The Savvy Musician*. Pittsburgh, PA: Helius Press, 2009.
This career guide for musicians contains a chapter that discusses grantseeking, donor solicitation, and fundraising activities. Includes a sample business plan. URL: savvymusician.com

Dean, Carole Lee. *The Art of Film Funding: Alternative Financing Concepts*. 2nd ed. Studio City, CA: Michael Wiese Productions, 2012.
Topics covered in this guide include proposals, researching funders, fundraising from individuals and businesses, public funding, branding, partnerships, tax laws, and other areas. The appendix includes a list of possible funders for film projects. URL: shop.mwp.com

Directory of Grants in the Humanities 2012. 22nd ed. Nashville, IN: Schoolhouse Partners, 2011.
This directory highlights over 5,500 current programs from 3,000 sponsors, including U.S. and foreign foundations, corporations, state arts councils and government agencies, and other organizations. URL: schoolhousepartners.net

Dramatists Sourcebook. 26th ed. New York, NY: Theatre Communications Group, 2010.
Contains a "Fellowships and Grants" section listing foundations and organizations that offer funding to playwrights, composers, translators, librettists, and lyricists. Notes guidelines, application procedures, deadlines, remuneration, and frequency of these funding sources. Published biennially. URL: tcg.org

Hytone Leb, Nancy. *Business of Art: An Artist's Guide to Profitable Self-employment*. 2nd ed. Los Angeles, CA: Center for Cultural Innovation, 2012.
This handbook for artists provides guidance in the creation of personal goals, marketing and promotion, legal issues, financial management, and fundraising. URL: cciarts.org

Liberatori, Ellen. *Guide to Getting Arts Grants*. New York, NY: Allworth Press, 2006.
Provides practical advice to help artists obtain grants from foundations and government agencies. Topics covered include developing a plan, creating a portfolio, identifying funders, and completing a grant application. A chapter focuses on proposals submitted by arts organizations, noting that artists may collaborate with arts groups through fiscal sponsorship arrangements. The author also draws upon her prior experience as a program officer to elaborate on how grantmaking decisions are made. URL: allworth.com

Luttrull, Elaine Grogan. *Arts and Numbers: A Financial Guide for Artists, Writers, Non-Profits, and Other Members of the Creative Class*. Chicago, IL: B2 Books, 2013.
The author provides financial management and planning advice for artists. She discusses goal setting, saving, budgeting, writing personal financial statements, raising cash, taxes, and business planning. The appendix outlines common budget costs. URL: agatepublishing.com/B2

Michels, Caroll. *How to Survive and Prosper as an Artist: Selling Yourself Without Selling Your Soul*. 6th ed. New York, NY: Henry Holt & Co., 2009.

> Includes a chapter on grantseeking, and an appendix of useful resources, including art colonies and residencies, publications with internships and apprenticeships, competitions, arts organizations, and an annotated *bibliography on grants and funding*. URL: us.macmillan.com/HenryHolt.aspx

Musical America Worldwide: International Directory of the Performing Arts. 2014 ed. Hightstown, NJ: Musical America, 2013.

> Includes a listing of North American and international contests, foundations and awards in the fields of music and performing arts. URL: musicalamerica.com

Photographer's Market. 36th ed. Cincinnati, OH: North Light Books, 2012.

> Covers markets for photography professionals, including addresses, contacts and terms, specifications, and fees paid. Published annually. URL: writersdigestshop.com

Rosenberg, Gigi. *The Artist's Guide to Grant Writing : How to Find Funds and Write Foolproof Proposals for the Visual, Literary, and Performing Artist*. New York, NY: Watson-Guptill Publications. 2010.

> Targets writers, performers and visual artists who want to learn how to fundraise successfully and write winning proposals. Chapters include tips from successful grant writers, grant officers and fundraising specialists and cover the application process, crafting an artist statement, and budgeting. An annotated appendix lists grants and residencies. URL: randomhouse.com/crown/watsonguptill

Schlachter, Gail A. and R. David Weber. *Money for Graduate Students in the Arts & Humanities 2010–2012*. El Dorado Hills, CA: Reference Service Press, 2010.

> Directory of grants, awards, fellowships, and traineeships for graduate training, study, and research in the humanities. Contains a bibliography of financial aid resources. Indexed by subject, sponsor, location, and deadline. Published biennially. URL: rspfunding.com

Songwriter's Market. 37th ed. Cincinnati, OH: Writer's Digest Books, 2014.

> Includes updated listings for music publishers, record companies, managers and booking agents, record producers, and more. Published annually. URL: writersdigestshop.com

Internet Sources

American Center for Artists (americanartists.org)

> Provides a listing of both public and private organizations that give grants and other forms of support to artists.

American Musicological Society (ams-net.org)

> Maintains a list of ongoing grants and fellowships for the study and teaching of music.

Americans for the Arts (americansforthearts.org/by-topic/funding-resources)

> Information clearinghouse listing funding resources for individuals in all areas of the arts.

American Society of Composers, Authors, and Publishers (ASCAP) Awards Programs (ascap.com/music-career/support)

> Lists prizes and awards to composers in various areas of music.

Art Deadlines List (artdeadlineslist.com)

> Free monthly Internet publication with funding opportunities in the visual arts.

Art List (theartlist.com)

> A monthly online newsletter listing grants, upcoming art contests, competitions, and juried shows across the United States. Sign up for either the free listings or the subscription list with more extensive postings.

Art Support (art-support.com)

> Originally created for fine art photographers, this site has evolved to provide information that is valuable for every artist trying to make it in the field of visual art.

Artist Help Network (artisthelpnetwork.com)

> This site is designed to assist fine artists in locating information, resources, guidance, and advice on a comprehensive range of career-related topics. Includes a list of competitions and juried shows. Based on the appendix of resources in the book How to Survive and Prosper as an Artist: Selling Yourself Without Selling Your Soul.

Arts and Healing Network (artheals.org)

> In the Artist Support section, this site provides information on grants available to artists as well as calls for entry for shows and exhibitions.

BMI Foundation (bmifoundation.org)

> Describes awards, scholarships, internships, and fund programs established to encourage young composers and supports the work of accomplished concert-music composers in areas such as classical music, jazz, and musical theater.

Creative Capital (creative-capital.org)

> A listing of grant opportunities as well as professional development resources for individual artists.

Dance Media (dancemedia.com/who-what-wear?resource=directory)

> From the publisher of Dance Magazine, this directory lists professional dance companies, competitions, and funding resources related to all aspects of dance.

The Field (thefield.org)

> Provides services to performing artists as well as fiscal sponsorship. Offers workshops on fundraising, marketing, and management.

Foundation Center: Requests for Proposals, Arts and Culture (philanthropynewsdigest.org/rfps)

> The Foundation Center's Philanthropy News Digest lists currently open Requests for Proposals (RFPs) in the category of arts, including some aimed at individual artists.

Grammy Foundation (grammy.org/grammy-foundation/grants)

> Provides information on grants that support the archiving and preserving of the music and recorded sound heritage of the Americas, as well as grants that advance research related to the impact of music study on early childhood development, human

development and the medical and occupational well-being of music professionals.

Grants for Individuals: Arts (staff.lib.msu.edu/harris23/grants/3arts.htm)
> Compiled by staff at the Michigan State University Libraries, this comprehensive listing of funding opportunities includes web sites, databases, and books focused on the arts.

Grants for Individuals: Music (staff.lib.msu.edu/harris23/grants/3music.htm)
> Compiled by staff at the Michigan State University Libraries, this comprehensive listing of funding opportunities includes web sites, databases, and books focused on music.

Grants for Individuals: Photography (staff.lib.msu.edu/harris23/grants/3photo.htm)
> Compiled by staff at the Michigan State University Libraries, this comprehensive listing of funding opportunities includes web sites, databases, and books focused on photography.

GrantSpace Resources for Individual Grantseekers: Artists (grantspace.org/Tools/Knowledge-Base/Individual-Grantseekers/Artists)
> Knowledge Base articles compiled by Foundation Center staff provide advice and resources for filmmakers, musicians, performing artists, visual artists, and writers seeking grant funding.

Musical Online (musicalonline.com/foundation_grants.htm)
> A compilation of funding resources including foundations and associations, grants, scholarships, and organizations.

National Arts and Disability Center (www.semel.ucla.edu/nadc/grants)
> The National Arts and Disability Center web site has a listing of funding sources for individual artists and arts organizations of all disciplines.

National Network for Artist Placement (artistplacement.com)
> Profiles over 1,600 internship opportunities (paid and unpaid) that can lead to a permanent career in the arts. Presents a broad range of disciplines, including arts management, dance, theater, music, film, photography, performing arts, and design. Entries give brief program description and eligibility requirements.

National Endowment for the Arts (nea.gov)
> Provides information on funding opportunities for individuals in the areas of music, literature, folk and traditional arts.

New York Foundation for the Arts (NYFA) (nyfa.org)
> The "For Artists" area provides information on fellowships, Strategic Opportunity Stipends (SOS), and fiscal sponsorship for artists.

Savvy Musician (savvymusician.com)
> Affiliated with a book by the same title, the "Resources" section of this web site includes a list of organizations that fund musicians and music related programs.

Sculptor.org (sculptor.org/Jobs/GrantsScholarships.htm)
> Provides information on grants, fellowships, and scholarships open to sculptors.

Theatre Communications Group (tcg.org/grants/individual.cfm)
> The "Grants" section of this web site lists grants to actors, directors, writers, and other theater professionals.

United States Artists (unitedstatesartists.org)
> This organization, funded by foundations and private donors, supports a fellowship program open to artists in all career stages. Fellowships are given across a broad array of disciplines, including architecture and design, craft/traditional art, dance, literature, media arts, music, performance art, theater, and the visual arts.

WomenArts (womenarts.org/funding-resources/index)
> This site offers a listing of resources to help artists find grants and emergency funding, as well as general information on fundraising.

World Wide Arts Resources (wwar.com/categories/Agencies)
> Provides information on arts-related funding opportunities from a variety of organizations, including some international agencies.

INTERNATIONAL TRAVEL AND STUDY

Funding for United States Study 2014: A Guide for International Students and Professionals. New York, NY: Institute of International Education, 2014.
> Provides information on more than 800 grants, fellowships, and scholarships for undergraduate and graduate study, as well as doctoral and postdoctoral research in the United States. In addition, the guide provides informative articles on financial assistance and university funding options. Indexed by field of study and countries of origin. Published annually. URL: iiebooks.org

IIE Passport: The Complete Guide to Study Abroad. New York, NY: Institute of International Education, 2013.
> Includes both short- and long-term programs offered by U.S. and foreign universities and private organizations. With information on application procedures and requirements, academic credit, contact addresses, e-mail, phone, fax, costs, fields of study, language of instruction, housing, travel and orientation. URL: iiebooks.org

International Exchange Locator: A Resource Directory for Educational and Cultural Exchange. Washington, DC: Alliance for International Educational and Cultural Exchange, 2011.
> Lists organizations involved in international exchanges, industry-specific exchanges, research/support organizations, foreign affairs agencies and exchange programs, other federal government exchanges, and key congressional committees and members of congress. Entries contain name and address of the organization, statement of purpose, types of exchange programs, availability of financial assistance, geographic focus, and a list of selected publications. URL: alliance-exchange.org

Schlachter, Gail A. and R. David Weber. *Financial Aid for Research and Creative Activities Abroad 2008–2010.* El Dorado Hills, CA: Reference Service Press, 2008.
> Lists nearly 1,100 scholarships, fellowships, loans, grants, awards, and internships available for research, lectureships, exchange programs, work assignments, conferences attendance, creative activities (like writing or painting), and professional development abroad. Indexed by program title, sponsoring organization, geographic area, subject, and filing deadline. URL: rspfunding.com

Schlachter, Gail A. and R. David Weber. *Financial Aid for Study and Training Abroad 2008–2010*. El Dorado Hills, CA: Reference Service Press, 2008.

> Describes nearly 1,000 financial aid programs sponsored by government agencies, professional organizations, foundations, educational associations, and other public and private agencies. Indexed by program title, sponsoring organization, geographic area, subject, and filing deadline. URL: rspfunding.com

Internet Sources

AllAbroad.us (allabroad.us)

> Offers a free search tool to look for scholarships, fellowships and grants for study abroad. It includes sections focused on funding for underrepresented students and on scholarships for study in "Nontraditional Countries" in Africa, Asia, Latin America, the Middle East and the Caribbean.

Cornell Graduate Fellowship Database (gradschool.cornell.edu/fellowships)

> The Fellowship Database, compiled by the Cornell University Graduate School, offers a large searchable database of graduate fellowships from a wide variety of organizations, including fellowships specifically for international students and study abroad programs.

Diversity Abroad (diversityabroad.com/international-scholarships)

> Allows searching for international scholarships and fellowships using categories including academic status, region, country, subject, and diversity criteria such as disabilities, low-income, and ethnic groups.

EduPASS! The SmartStudent™ Guide to Studying in the USA (edupass.org)

> Provides information for international students who are thinking about pursuing undergraduate, graduate, or professional education in the United States, including a scholarship search engine.

FinAid: Domestic Exchange and Study Abroad Programs (finaid.org/otheraid/exchange.phtml)

> This page on the FinAid site lists a variety of resources on financial aid for study abroad and domestic exchange programs.

Fulbright Foreign Student Program (foreign.fulbrightonline.org)

> The Fulbright Foreign Student Program is administered by bi-national Fulbright Commissions and Foundations or U.S. Embassies and is sponsored by the U.S. Department of State. The program awards grants to international students for Master's degree or Ph.D. study at U.S. universities or other appropriate institutions. This web site provides a list of eligible countries and fields, application procedures, and selection criteria.

Fulbright U.S. Student Program (us.fulbrightonline.org)

> The Fulbright Program is the largest U.S. international exchange program offering opportunities for students, scholars, and professionals to undertake international graduate study, advanced research, university teaching, and teaching in elementary and secondary schools worldwide. This web site lists eligibility requirements, participating countries, types of grants available, and application procedures.

GoAbroad.com (goabroad.com/scholarships-abroad)

> This easy-to-use search engine provides detailed descriptions of scholarship programs for study in the United States and around the world.

GrantSpace Resources for Individual Grantseekers: Students (grantspace.org/Tools/Knowledge-Base/Individual-Grantseekers/Students)

> Knowledge Base articles compiled by Foundation Center staff provide advice and resources for U.S. and international students at all education levels.

Hubert H. Humphrey Fellowship Program (humphreyfellowship.org)

> The Hubert Humphrey Fellowship Program for foreign professionals is administered by the Institute of International Education (IIE) with support from the U.S. Department of State. It provides ten months of non-degree academic study and related professional experiences in the United States.

Institute of International Education Online (iie.org)

> Includes information about international education and training programs, including Fulbright scholarships.

International Education Financial Aid (iefa.org)

> This online directory lists college scholarship and grant information for U.S. and international students wishing to study abroad.

International Scholarships (internationalscholarships.com)

> Has a searchable database of grants, scholarships, and loans for international students wishing to study abroad. It can be searched by field of study, location of study, award type, and keywords.

InternationalStudent.com (internationalstudent.com/scholarships)

> Find college scholarship programs by country, field of study or university name. This site includes information for international students and U.S. study abroad students.

NAFSA: Association of International Educators (nafsa.org/Explore_International_Education/For_Students/)

> Information for American students interested in studying abroad as well as international students who want to study in the United States, including bibliographies and links to other information sites.

Peterson's Scholarship Search (petersons.com/college-search/scholarship-search.aspx)

> This search tool lets international students enter information such as age, gender, ethnicity, residency, and academic record to find suitable scholarship programs. Free registration required.

Social Science Research Council (ssrc.org)

> Supports international fellowships and grant programs in the social sciences.

StudyAbroad.com (studyabroad.com/scholarships.aspx)

> Lists sources and tips on obtaining financial aid, including minority scholarships, Commonwealth Universities scholarships, and study abroad programs in countries such as Germany, England, France, and Turkey.

MEDIA AND COMMUNICATIONS

Davies, Adam P. and Nicol Wistreich. *The Film Finance Handbook: How to Fund Your Film*. London: Netribution, 2007.
> A complete guide to film finance around the world, from web short film through mainstream international multi-million dollar co-production. Provides details on nearly 1,000 funding awards from over 300 international organizations. URL: fundyourfilm.com

Dean, Carole Lee. *The Art of Film Funding: Alternative Financing Concepts*. 2nd ed. Studio City, CA: Michael Wiese Productions, 2012.
> Topics covered in this guide include proposals, researching funders, fundraising from individuals and businesses, public funding, branding, partnerships, tax laws, and other areas. URL: mwp.com

Irving, David K. and Peter W. Rea. *Producing and Directing the Short Film and Video*. 4th ed. Boston: Focal Press, 2010.
> Contains information on funding options for film makers, including foundation grants and corporate sponsorship. URL: focalpress.com

Levison, Louise. *Filmmakers and Financing: Business Plans for Independents*. 7th ed. Waltham, MA: Focal Press, 2012
> Chapters of this step-by-step guide examine the various parts of film business plans: executive summary, the company, the films, the industry, the markets, distribution, risk factors, financing, and the financial plan. Includes a business plan for a fictional company. URL: focalpress.com

Schlachter, Gail A. and R. David Weber. *How to Pay for Your Degree in Journalism & Related Fields 2011–2013*. El Dorado Hills, CA: Reference Service Press, 2011.
> Lists nearly 750 scholarships, fellowships, loans, grants, and awards for both college and graduate study. Entries include contact information, purpose, eligibility, financial data, duration, number awarded, and deadline. URL: rspfunding.com

Trigonis, John T. *Crowdfunding for Filmmakers: the Way to a Successful Film Campaign*. Studio City, CA: Michael Wiese Productions, 2013.
> The author gives a brief history of film financing, explains how to create and personalize a campaign, and offers tips on community engagement. He also discusses the use of online social networks in film fundraising. URL: mwp.com

Warshawski, Morrie. *Shaking the Money Tree: How to Get Grants and Donations for Film and Video Projects*. 3rd ed. Studio City, CA: Michael Wiese Productions, 2010.
> A step-by-step guide that covers planning a project, doing research, writing a proposal, soliciting donations from individuals, and more. The appendices include a bibliography of publications and resources, and sample proposals. URL: mwp.com

Internet Sources

Association of Independent Video and Filmmakers (aivf.org)
> Provides advice on film financing as well as a list of key funding sources for film and video. Its publication The Independent is a leading source of information for independent, grassroots, and activist media-makers.

Corporation for Public Broadcasting (cpb.org/grants)
> CPB is the largest single source of funding for public television and radio programming. This web site lists open grants available to individuals creating radio and television projects as well as for research on public broadcasting.

Dow Jones News Fund (newsfund.org)
> The emphasis for this web site is on education for students and teachers to promote careers in print and online journalism. It includes information on scholarships, internships, and awards, as well as an online publication, "The Journalist's Road to Success," also available in Spanish, which provides guidance on planning a career in journalism.

Foundation Center: Requests for Proposals, Journalism/Media (philanthropynewsdigest.org/rfps)
> The Foundation Center's Philanthropy News Digest lists currently open Requests for Proposals (RFPs) in the category of media and journalism, including some aimed at individuals.

Grantmakers in Film + Electronic Media – Media Database (media.gfem.org)
> This group of media funders maintains a database on current film and media projects. Those seeking grants can post information about their projects in this database, which is available for review by grantmaking organizations.

Grants for Individuals: Communications (staff.lib.msu.edu/harris23/grants/3communi.htm)
> Compiled by staff at the Michigan State University Libraries, this comprehensive listing of funding opportunities in the media and communications field includes web sites, databases, and books.

Grants for Individuals: Film (staff.lib.msu.edu/harris23/grants/3film.htm)
> Compiled by staff at the Michigan State University Libraries, this comprehensive listing of funding opportunities includes web sites, databases, and books for film and video makers.

Grants for Individuals: Journalism (staff.lib.msu.edu/harris23/grants/3jrnlism.htm)
> Compiled by staff at the Michigan State University Libraries, this comprehensive listing of funding opportunities for journalists includes web sites, databases, books, and announcements.

GrantSpace Resources for Individual Grantseekers: Artists (grantspace.org/Tools/Knowledge-Base/Individual-Grantseekers/Artists)
> Knowledge Base articles compiled by Foundation Center staff provide advice and resources for filmmakers and other types of artists seeking grant funding.

Independent Television Service (itvs.org/funding)
> Funds proposals by independent producers and provides production, promotion, marketing and distribution support.

International Documentary Association (documentary.org)
> After a free online registration, this site gives links to production resources such as fiscal sponsorship, grants, and documentary educational materials.

Media Rights (mediarights.org)
> Under "Resources," this site offers a list of funders interested in supporting social-issue documentaries and short films.

Morrie Warshawski (warshawski.com)
This web site, created by a well-known expert on the arts and the nonprofit sector, provides an extensive bibliography on fundraising for independent film projects.

National Alliance for Media Arts and Culture (namac.org)
Provides a directory of organizations (under the "Community" tab) working in the field of media arts, some of which may be potential funders or fiscal sponsors. Also provides useful information on how to research funding, including a fundraising toolkit.

National Endowment for the Humanities (neh.gov)
Supports learning in all areas of the humanities and funds research and education. Includes information on grant guidelines and deadlines.

Newswise (newswise.com)
Includes information on awards and grants for journalists under "Resources."

Radio Television Digital New Association (rtdna.org)
This professional association web site provides an online directory of awards, grants and fellowships focused on journalism and media.

United States Artists (unitedstatesartists.org)
A fellowship program, funded by foundations and private donors, offering support to a broad array of disciplines, including media arts (audio, film, radio, video).

WomenArts (womenarts.org/funding-resources/fundlists)
This site offers a listing of resources to help artists find grants and emergency funding, including a section focused on film and video projects.

MEDICINE AND HEALTH

Directory of Biomedical and Health Care Grants 2012. 23rd ed. Nashville, TN: Schoolhouse Partners, 2012.
Provides listings of thousands of funding opportunities concerned with human health and biomedicine, covering funding for research from laboratory investigations to studies on health care delivery. Indexed by subject, program type, and location. URL: schoolhousepartners.net

Directory of Research Grants 2012. 35th ed. Nashville, TN: Schoolhouse Partners, 2012.
Offering researchers listings of thousands of funding opportunities, this two-volume publication features grants for basic research, equipment acquisition, building construction/renovation, fellowships, and 23 other program types. URL: schoolhousepartners.net

Medical School Admission Requirements 2014. Washington, DC: Association of American Medical Colleges, 2014.
Provides an overview of the complete medical school application process, with application procedures and deadlines, tuition and student fees, financial aid packages, and statistics on acceptance rates from every accredited medical school in the United States and Canada. Published annually. URL: aamc.org

Schlachter, Gail A. and R. David Weber. *Money for Graduate Students in the Biological Sciences 2010–2012.* El Dorado Hills, CA: Reference Service Press, 2010.
Directory of grants, awards, fellowships, and traineeships for graduate training, study, and research in the biological sciences. Indexed by subject, sponsor, location, and deadline. URL: rspfunding.com

Schlachter, Gail A. and R. David Weber. *Money for Graduate Students in the Health Sciences 2010–2012.* El Dorado Hills, CA: Reference Service Press, 2010.
Directory of grants, awards, fellowships, and traineeships for graduate training, study, and research in the health sciences. Indexed by subject, sponsor, location, and deadline. URL: rspfunding.com

Schlachter, Gail A. and R. David Weber. *Money for Graduate Students in the Social and Behavioral Sciences 2010–2012.* El Dorado Hills, CA: Reference Service Press, 2010.
Directory of grants, awards, fellowships, and traineeships for graduate training, study, and research in the social and behavioral sciences. Indexed by subject, sponsor, location, and deadline. URL: rspfunding.com

Schlachter, Gail A. and R. David Weber. *How to Pay for Your Degree in Nursing 2011–2013.* El Dorado Hills, CA: Reference Service Press, 2011.
A list of nearly 800 scholarships, fellowships, grants, awards, loans, traineeships, and other funding programs in support of study, training, research, and creative activities for nursing students and nurses. URL: rspfunding.com

Internet Sources

Association of American Medical Colleges (aamc.org)
The organization aims to improve the nation's health by advancing the quality of education in medicals schools and teaching hospitals. Its web site includes tips on financing one's education as well as information on research grant opportunities.

Fogarty International Center Funding Opportunities (fic.nih.gov/funding)
The Fogarty International Center, part of the National Institutes of Health, publishes this comprehensive compilation of international funding opportunities in biomedical and behavioral research, separated by category.

Grants & Funding (sciencecareers.sciencemag.org/funding)
The staff at the journal Science has compiled a list of sites to search for information on science and health related funding programs.

Grants for Individuals: Medicine (staff.lib.msu.edu/harris23/grants/3med.htm)
Compiled by staff at the Michigan State University Libraries, this comprehensive listing of financial aid and medical research funding opportunities includes web sites, databases, and books.

Grants for Individuals: Medicine – Emergency Medical Assistance (staff.lib.msu.edu/harris23/grants/3medema.htm)
> Compiled by staff at the Michigan State University Libraries, this comprehensive listing of financial aid for those with medical needs includes web sites and databases.

Grants for Individuals: Nursing (staff.lib.msu.edu/harris23/grants/3nursing.htm)
> Compiled by staff at the Michigan State University Libraries, this comprehensive listing of financial aid and scholarship opportunities for nurses includes web sites, databases, books, and announcements.

Grants for Individuals: Psychology and Psychiatry (staff.lib.msu.edu/harris23/grants/3psych.htm)
> Compiled by staff at the Michigan State University Libraries, this comprehensive listing of scholarships and research funding for the fields of psychology and psychiatry includes web sites, databases, and books.

National Institutes of Health (grants.nih.gov)
> This site is the main source for information on NIH's medical and behavioral research grant policies, guidelines and funding opportunities.

Requests for Proposals: Health and Medical Research (philanthropynewsdigest.org/rfps)
> From the Foundation Center's Philanthropy News Digest, these sites provide listings of current requests for proposals (RFPs) from foundations and other grantmaking organizations interested in funding health and medical research related projects and issues. While most of these RFPs are open only to nonprofit organizations, some may be open to individuals for research, education, or direct assistance. Updated weekly.

ScanGrants (scangrants.com)
> ScanGrants is a public service listing of grants and other funding types to support health research, programs and scholarships.

MINORITIES AND SPECIAL POPULATIONS

The Complete Directory for People with Disabilities 2014. 22nd ed. Millerton, NY: Grey House Publishing, Inc., 2013.
> The directory contents include government agencies, foundations and funding resources, independent living centers, camps, veteran services, exchange programs, rehabilitation programs, education, vocational and employment services, along with information on assistive devices. Published annually. URL: greyhouse.com

National Directory of Scholarships, Internships, and Fellowships for Latino Students. 6th ed. Washington, DC: Congressional Hispanic Caucus Institute, 2011.
> Provides a comprehensive list of scholarships, internships, and fellowships targeting Latino students and young professionals. The directory may be downloaded for free at: chci.org

Need a Lift? to Educational Opportunities, Careers, Loans, Scholarships & Employment. 62nd ed. Indianapolis, IN: American Legion, 2013.
> While the focus of this book is to help children of deceased and disabled veterans in their pursuit of higher education, all students can benefit from the information offered. Includes information on federal, state, and private sources of funding, American Legion benefit programs, and annotated bibliography. Published annually. The guide may be downloaded or searched online for free at: needalift.org.

Schlachter, Gail A. and R. David Weber. Directory of Financial Aids for Women 2014–2016. El Dorado Hills, CA: Reference Service Press, 2012.
> Describes nearly 1,500 scholarships, fellowships, loans, grants, awards, internships, and state sources of educational benefits for women. Entries include program title, sponsoring organization, availability, purpose, eligibility, financial data, duration, limitations, number of awards, and application deadline. Includes annotated bibliography of general financial aid directories. Indexed by program title, sponsoring organization, geographic area, subject focus, and calendar deadlines. Published biennially. URL: rspfunding.com

Schlachter, Gail A. and R. David Weber. Financial Aid for African Americans, 2014–2016. El Dorado Hills, CA: Reference Service Press, 2014.
> Lists nearly 1,300 descriptions of scholarships, fellowships, loans, grants, awards, and internships available to African Americans from high school through professional and postdoctoral levels. Published biennially. URL: rspfunding.com

Schlachter, Gail A. and R. David Weber. Financial Aid for Asian Americans, 2014–2016. El Dorado Hills, CA: Reference Service Press, 2014.
> Describes nearly 950 scholarships, fellowships, loans, grants, awards, or internship opportunities for Americans of Asian/Pacific Islander origins. Published biennially. URL: rspfunding.com

Schlachter, Gail A. and R. David Weber. Financial Aid for Hispanic Americans, 2014–2016. El Dorado Hills, CA: Reference Service Press, 2014.
> Provides detailed entries on more than 1,175 scholarships, loans, fellowships, grants, awards, and internships available to Americans of Mexican, Puerto Rican, Cuban, Central American, or other Latin American heritage. Published biennially. URL: rspfunding.com

Schlachter, Gail A. and R. David Weber. Financial Aid for Native Americans, 2014–2016. El Dorado Hills, CA: Reference Service Press, 2014.
> Contains more than 1,400 grants, scholarships, fellowships, internships, and awards open to American Indians, Native Alaskans, Native Hawaiians, Native Samoan, and other Native Pacific Islanders. The funding opportunities cover major subject areas and are sponsored by more than 800 private and public agencies and organizations. Published biennially. URL: rspfunding.com

Schlachter, Gail A. and R. David Weber. Financial Aid for Persons With Disabilities and Their Families, 2012–2014. El Dorado Hills, CA: Reference Service Press, 2012.
> Lists more than 1,400 scholarships, loans, grants-in-aid, and awards from federal, state, and private sources, arranged by disability type, with subject, geographic, sponsor, and filing date indexes. Published biennially. URL: rspfunding.com

Schlachter, Gail A. and R. David Weber. Financial Aid for Veterans, Military Personnel and Their Families, 2012–2014. El Dorado Hills, CA: Reference Service Press, 2012.

> Lists more than 1,400 scholarships, grants-in-aid, loans and other benefit programs for Americans affiliated with the military, from federal, state, and private sources. Indexed by subject, sponsor, geographic area, and filing deadline. Published biennially. URL: rspfunding.com

Schlachter, Gail A. and R. David Weber. *Funding for Persons with Visual Impairments*. Large print ed. El Dorado Hills, CA: Reference Service Press, 2012.

> A large-print listing of scholarships, fellowships, loans, grants-in-aid, awards, and internships that are designated for persons with visual impairments, from high school seniors through professionals and others. More than 300 funding opportunities are described. Published annually. URL: rspfunding.com

Schlachter, Gail A. and R. David Weber. *Money for Christian College Students, 2012–2014*. El Dorado Hills, CA: Reference Service Press, 2012.

> Offers information on 850 scholarships, fellowships, grants, awards, and other funding opportunities available to Christian undergraduate and graduate students. URL: rspfunding.com

Tanabe, Gen S. and Kelly Y. Tanabe. *501 Ways for Adult Students to Pay for College*. 3rd ed. Los Altos, CA: SuperCollege, 2009.

> With information on distance learning and part-time classes and new financial aid, loan and scholarship opportunities, this updated resource shows how to find and win scholarships designed especially for adult students, obtain financial support from employers, negotiate for more financial aid, take advantage of educational tax breaks, and cancel education debts with loan forgiveness programs. URL: supercollege.com

Winds of Change Magazine's Annual College Guide for American Indians. Boulder, CO: Winds of Change.

> Contains information especially for American Indians on tribal colleges, preparing college applications, and financial aid. Published annually as a special issue of Winds of Change Magazine. URL: aises/what/woc

Internet Sources

AbleData (abledata.com)

> A federally funded project whose primary mission is to provide information on assistive   sources to consumers, organizations, professionals, and caregivers within the United States.

African American Scholarships and Internship Opportunities (littleafrica.com/scholarship)

> This site lists hundreds of scholarships, grants, internships, and other financial aid sources for African American students. Provides contact information and deadlines for application submissions.

Alliance for Technology Access (ATA) (ataccess.org)

> Under "ResourceHUB," this organization offers a downloadable publication, "Guide to Low-Cost/No-Cost Online Tools for People with Disabilities," which presents information on funding for assistive technology.

Asian & Pacific Islander American Scholarship Fund (apiasf.org/scholarships.html)

> In addition to its own scholarship programs, the APASF also lists other scholarship programs open to Asian and Pacific Islander American students.

Asian Pacific Fund (asianpacificfund.org/scholarships)

> This organization, supported by Asian American donors, manages a number of scholarship programs focused on students of Asian heritage.

ASPIRA (aspira.org/book/college-information)

> Gives listings of scholarships, fellowships, internships, academic awards, and other financial aid resources aimed at Latino youth.

Black Collegian Online (blackcollegian.com)

> The "Study & Campus" section of this site provides a listing of scholarships, grants, fellowships, and contests for students of color.

Black Excel: The College Help Network (blackexcel.org)

> Provides information on hundreds of scholarship opportunities for minority students, along with general information on applying to colleges and universities.

BlackStudents.com (blackstudents.blacknews.com)

> Gives a listing of scholarships and internships available to African Americans. Also offers a free weekly email newsletter to provide information on new opportunities.

Congressional Hispanic Caucus Institute (chci.org/scholarships)

> In addition to providing information about its own scholarship programs, CHCI also provides free access to a downloadable pdf version of its National Directory of Scholarships, Internships and Fellowships for Latino Students.

Department of Veteran Affairs (va.gov)

> This web site contains information on a wide range of benefits for veterans and their dependents, including health benefits, pension programs, and support for education.

Disability.gov (disability.gov)

> This government web portal presents links to the home pages of federal agencies and programs that provide assistance to people with disabilities, including sections on Medicare, Medicaid, and Social Security benefits.

Disability Resources Monthly (DRM) Guide to Disability Resources on the Internet (disabilityresources.org/GRANTS.html)

> A nonprofit network staffed by volunteers, Disability Resources provides an online guide to disability-related funding opportunities, browsable by funder type.

Federal Benefits for Veterans, Dependents, and Survivors (www.va.gov/opa/publications/benefits_book.asp)

> Information on benefits available to U.S. military veterans and dependents, including pensions, insurance, educational support, and health care. Also available for download in Spanish (www.va.gov/opa/publications/benefits_book/federal_benefits_spanish.pdf).

Financial Aid for Lesbian, Gay, Bisexual, and Transgendered Students (finaid.org/otheraid/lgbt.phtml)
> Lists many different scholarship funds for lesbian, gay, bisexual, and transgendered students, dividing them into general, athletic, regional, and campus specific.

Financial Aid for Native American Students (finaid.org/otheraid/natamind.phtml)
> This site provides information on financial aid and scholarship programs for Native Americans available from a variety of sources.

Financial Aid for Students with Disabilities (finaid.org/otheraid/disabled.phtml)
> Lists a number of information resources about scholarships and fellowships for students with disabilities.

Grants for Individuals: Gays, Lesbians, Bisexual, Transgendered (staff.lib.msu.edu/harris23/grants/3gayles.htm)
> Compiled by staff at the Michigan State University Libraries, this comprehensive listing includes web sites, databases, and books focusing on financial assistance opportunities for GLBT individuals.

Grants for Individuals: Minorities (staff.lib.msu.edu/harris23/grants/3specpop.htm)
> Compiled by staff at the Michigan State University Libraries, this comprehensive listing of funding opportunities for specific ethnic or immigrant groups includes web sites, databases, and books.

Grants for Individuals: Nontraditional, Reentry, or Adult Students (staff.lib.msu.edu/harris23/grants/3nontrad.htm)
> Compiled by staff at the Michigan State University Libraries, this comprehensive listing of funding opportunities for nontraditional or adult students includes web sites, databases, and books.

Grants for Individuals: The Disabled (staff.lib.msu.edu/harris23/grants/3disable.htm)
> Compiled by staff at the Michigan State University Libraries, this comprehensive listing of funding opportunities includes web sites, databases, and books to assist people with disabilities.

Grants for Individuals: Veterans, Military Science Students, or Dependents (staff.lib.msu.edu/harris23/grants/3veteran.htm)
> Compiled by staff at the Michigan State University Libraries, this comprehensive listing of funding opportunities includes web sites, databases, and books to assist veterans and their dependents.

Grants for Individuals: Women (staff.lib.msu.edu/harris23/grants/3women.htm)
> Compiled by staff at the Michigan State University Libraries, this comprehensive listing includes web sites, databases, and books focusing on financial assistance for women.

GrantSpace Resources for Individual Grantseekers: General (grantspace.org/Tools/Knowledge-Base/Individual-Grantseekers/General)
> Knowledge Base articles compiled by Foundation Center staff provide advice and resources for the disabled and other individuals seeking personal financial assistance.

HEATH Resource Center: Online Clearinghouse on Postsecondary Education for Individuals With Disabilities (heath.gwu.edu)
> Sponsored by George Washington University, this online clearinghouse provides information about disability support services, policies, procedures, and adaptations, as well as information about accessing college or university campuses, career-technical schools, and other postsecondary training entities. It also offers guides on financial assistance, scholarships, and materials that help students with disabilities attend colleges, universities, career-technical schools, and other postsecondary programs.

Hispanic Scholarship Fund (hsf.net)
> The Hispanic Scholarship Fund is the nation's largest provider of college financial aid for Latino undergraduate and graduate students.

Human Rights Campaign: LGBT Student Scholarship Database (hrc.org/resources/entry/scholarship-database)
> Includes scholarships, fellowships, and grants for LGBT and allied students at both the undergraduate and graduate level.

Latino College Dollars (latinocollegedollars.org)
> This easy-to-search site provides information on over 300 scholarships aimed at Latino students.

Modest Needs (modestneeds.org)
> Provides short-term emergency grants for those who don't qualify for conventional types of social or charitable assistance.

National Eye Institute - Financial Aid for Eye Care (nei.nih.gov/health/financialaid.asp)
> The National Eye Institute, which supports eye research, does not help individuals pay for eye care. However, this web site does provide a listing of programs and resources that can help search for funding for eye care purposes.

National Organization for Rare Disorders (NORD) (rarediseases.org)
> While NORD does not offer funding itself, it does have a database of patient support organizations under "Rare Diseases Information." Networking with these organizations may provide leads to financial resources for disease sufferers and their families.

National Organization on Disability (NOD): Disability Resources (nod.org/disability_resources)
> NOD offers resources and information for people with disabilities, including resources for legal advocacy, employment, transportation, and emergency services.

Scholarships for Students Regardless of Immigration Status (maldef.org/leadership/scholarships)
> This list, compiled by the Mexican American Legal Defense and Educational Fund, provides information on scholarships that do not require a social security number, legal residency, or citizenship in order to apply.

Supercollege.com (supercollege.com)
> A searchable listing of scholarships, grants, and contests to help pay for higher education, including a section focused on adult students. Also offers guidance on selecting and applying to schools.

United Negro College Fund (scholarships.uncf.org)
> This searchable database provides information on all the scholarship programs administered by UNCF.

RESEARCH

Directory of Biomedical and Health Care Grants 2012. 23rd ed. Nashville, TN: Schoolhouse Partners, 2012.

Provides listings of funding opportunities concerned with human health and biomedicine, covering funding for research from laboratory investigations to studies on health care delivery. Indexed by subject, program type, and location. URL: schoolhousepartners.net

Directory of Research Grants 2012. 35th ed. Nashville, TN: Schoolhouse Partners, 2012.

Offering researchers listings of more than 5,800 funding opportunities, this two-volume publication features grants for basic research, equipment acquisition, building construction/ renovation, fellowships, and 23 other program types. URL: schoolhousepartners.net

The Grants Register, 2014. 32nd ed. New York, NY: Palgrave Macmillan, Ltd., 2013.

Lists scholarships, fellowships, and awards at all levels of graduate study, from regional, national, and international sources; arranged alphabetically by name of organization. Entries provide contact information, subject, eligibility, purpose, type, number of awards offered, frequency, amount of award, length of study, country of study, and application procedure. Includes a subject and eligibility guide to awards. Published annually. URL: us.macmillan.com

International Research Centers Directory. 28th ed. Farmington Hills, MI: Gale Cengage Learning, 2012.

This three-volume set lists government, university, independent, nonprofit, and commercial research and development organizations worldwide, indexed by name, subject, and country. URL: cengage.com

Research Centers Directory. 42nd ed. Farmington Hills, MI: Gale Cengage Learning, 2012.

Guide to over 14,100 university-related and other nonprofit research organizations in a broad range of subject areas, providing information on programs, staffing, publications, and educational efforts. Includes subject, geographic, personal name, and master indexes. Published annually. URL:cengage.com

Schlachter, Gail A. and R. David Weber. *Financial Aid for Research and Creative Activities Abroad 2008–2010.* El Dorado Hills, CA: Reference Service Press, 2009.

Lists nearly 1,100 scholarships, fellowships, loans, grants, awards, and internships available for research, artistic, and professional pursuits abroad. Indexed by program title, sponsoring organization, geographic area, subject, and filing deadline. Published biennially. URL: rspfunding.com

Schlachter, Gail A. and R. David Weber. *Money for Graduate Students in the Physical and Earth Sciences 2010–2012.* El Dorado Hills, CA: Reference Service Press, 2010.

Directory of grants, awards, fellowships, and traineeships for graduate training, study, and research in the earth and physical sciences. Indexed by subject, sponsor, location, and deadline. Published biennially. URL: rspfunding.com

Schlachter, Gail A. and R. David Weber. *Money for Graduate Students in the Social and Behavioral Sciences 2010–2012.* El Dorado Hills, CA: Reference Service Press, 2010.

Directory of grants, awards, fellowships, and traineeships for graduate training, study, and research in the social and behavioral sciences. Indexed by subject, sponsor, location, and deadline. Published biennially. URL: rspfunding.com

Internet Sources

American Historical Association (historians.org)

Describes more than 450 organizations that grant fellowships, awards, and prizes to historians. Some of this information is available online only to members of AHA.

Community of Science (COS) Funding Opportunities (pivot.cos.com)

This site lists thousands of sources of funding for work in all disciplines: physical sciences, social sciences, life sciences, health and medicine, arts and humanities. Covers funding for many purposes, such as research, collaborations, travel, curriculum development, conferences, fellowships, postdoctoral positions, equipment acquisitions, capital or operating expenses.

Fulbright U.S. Student Program (us.fulbrightonline.org)

The Fulbright Program is the largest U.S. international exchange program offering opportunities for students, scholars, and professionals to undertake international graduate study, advanced research, university teaching, and teaching in elementary and secondary schools worldwide. This web site lists eligibility requirements, participating countries, types of grants available, and application procedures.

Grants for Individuals (staff.lib.msu.edu/harris23/ grants/3subject.htm)

Compiled by staff at the Michigan State University Libraries, this useful list gives information on grants available to individuals covering a wide range of subject areas, including some for researchers.

Grants.gov (grants.gov)

A comprehensive site that calls itself "the central storehouse for information on over 1,000 grant programs" and provides access to approximately $500 billion in annual awards. Managed by the U.S. Department of Health and Human Services, it offers users "full service electronic grant administration" with guidelines and grant applications available online. Search by agency or category, or browse available grant opportunities.

Grants & Funding (sciencecareers.sciencemag.org/funding)

The staff at the journal Science has compiled a list of sites to search for information on science and health related funding programs.

National Endowment for the Humanities (neh.gov)

Supports learning in all areas of the humanities and provides funding for research, education, preservation, and public programs.

National Institutes of Health (nih.gov)
Funds grants, cooperative agreements, and contracts that support the advancement of fundamental knowledge about the nature and behavior of living systems to meet the NIH mission of extending healthy life and reducing the burdens of illness and disability.

National Science Foundation (nsf.gov)
Promotes and advances scientific progress in the United States by competitively awarding grants and cooperative agreements for research and education in the sciences, mathematics, and engineering.

Social Science Research Council (ssrc.org)
Offers fellowship and grant programs mostly targeting the social sciences, though many are also open to applicants from the humanities, natural sciences, and relevant professional and practitioner communities.

SCHOLARSHIPS, FELLOWSHIPS, AND LOANS

Asher, Donald. *The Best Scholarships for the Best Students.* Lawrenceville, NJ: Peterson's, 2010.
Offers information on scholarships and fellowships, undergraduate research programs, access and equity programs, internships, and service programs. Also describes how to write a personal statement, prepare your resume, obtain letters of recommendation, and conduct an interview.

College Blue Book. 41st ed. New York, NY: Macmillan Reference USA, 2014.
This six-volume set includes information on nearly 12,000 institutions of higher learning, occupational and technical schools, and distance learning programs. Volume 5 provides an extensive listing of more than 5,000 financial aid sources. Published annually. URL: cengage.com

Scholarship Handbook 2014. New York, NY: College Board Publications, 2014.
Descriptions of more than 2,100 programs that award college funding to 1.7 million students each year. Includes scholarship, internship, and low-cost loan programs. Published annually. URL: store.collegeboard.org

Funding Your Education: The Guide to Federal Student Aid. . Washington, DC: United States Department of Education, 2013.
A comprehensive resource on student financial aid from the U.S. Department of Education, including grants, loans, and work-study programs. Published annually in both English and Spanish. The entire guide may be downloaded online (http://studentaid.ed.gov/sites/default/files/funding-your-education.pdf), or request a copy by calling 1-877-4-ED-PUBS (1-877-433-7827).

Getting Financial Aid 2014. New York, NY: College Board Publications, 2014.
Provides information about scholarships offered by colleges for academics, sports, artistic or musical talent, and ROTC. Also has step-by-step guides to filling out the FAFSA and other forms and the "financial aid picture" for each of more than 3,000 colleges, universities, and technical schools. Published annually. URL: store.collegeboard.org

The Grants Register, 2014. 32nd ed. New York, NY: Palgrave Macmillan, Ltd., 2013.
Lists scholarships, fellowships, and awards at all levels of graduate study, from regional, national, and international sources; arranged alphabetically by name of organization. Entries provide contact information, subject, eligibility, purpose, type, number of awards offered, frequency, amount of award, length of study, country of study, and application procedure. Includes a subject and eligibility guide to awards. Published annually. URL: us.macmillan.com

Leider, Anna. *The A's and B's of Academic Scholarships.* 27th ed. Alexandria, VA: Octameron Associates, 2011.
Describes nearly 100,000 academic merit-based scholarships at over 1,200 colleges and universities. The scholarship amounts range from $200-$35,000. URL: octameron.com

Leider, Anna. *Loans and Grants from Uncle Sam: Am I Eligible and for How Much?* 19th ed. Alexandria, VA: Octameron Associates, 2011.
This book contains simple explanations and useful worksheets to help students understand loans and grants offered by the U.S. government. Published annually. URL: octameron.com

Leider, Anna and Robert Leider. *Don't Miss Out: The Ambitious Student's Guide to Financial Aid.* 35th ed. Alexandria, VA: Octameron Associates, 2011.
Planning guide that discusses procedures and strategies for students seeking financial aid, with tips about public and private funding sources. Special sections on academic and athletic scholarships and on funding for women and minorities. Published annually. URL: octameron.com

Need a Lift? to Educational Opportunities, Careers, Loans, Scholarships & Employment. 62nd ed. Indianapolis, IN: American Legion, 2013.
While the focus of this book is to help children of deceased and disabled veterans in their pursuit of higher education, all students can benefit from the information offered. Includes information on federal, state, and private sources of funding, American Legion benefit programs, and annotated bibliography. Published annually. The guide may be downloaded or searched online for free at: needalift.org.

Peterson's How to Get Money for College: Financing Your Future Beyond Federal Aid 2014. Lawrenceville, NJ: Peterson's, 2013.
Profiles four-year colleges in the United States, and indicates the amount and type of scholarships they offer. Also gives general information about federal and state loan programs. Published annually. URL: petersonsbooks.com

Peterson's Scholarships, Grants and Prizes 2014. Lawrenceville, NJ: Peterson's, 2013.
Contains detailed profiles of awards, based on ethnic heritage, talent, employment experience, military service, and other categories, that are available from private sources, such as foundations, corporations, and religious and civic organizations. URL: petersonsbooks.com

Schlachter, Gail A. and R. David Weber. *The College Student's Guide to Merit and Other No-Need Funding, 2008–2010*. El Dorado Hills, CA: Reference Service Press, 2007.
> More than 1,300 non-need-based funding programs for currently enrolled or returning students, with subject, geographic, and calendar date indexes. Published biennially. URL: rspfunding.com

Schlachter, Gail A. and R. David Weber. *High School Senior's Guide to Merit and Other No-Need Funding 2008–2010*. El Dorado Hills, CA: Reference Service Press, 2008.
> Identifies more than 1,100 no-need funding programs available to high school seniors interested in going to college. URL: rspfunding.com

Schlachter, Gail A. and R. David Weber. *How to Pay for Your Degree in Agriculture & Related Fields, 2012–2014*. El Dorado Hills, CA: Reference Service Press, 2012. URL: rspfunding.com

Schlachter, Gail A. and R. David Weber. *How to Pay for Your Degree in Business & Related Fields, 2012–2014*. El Dorado Hills, CA: Reference Service Press, 2012. URL: rspfunding.com

Schlachter, Gail A. and R. David Weber. *How to Pay for Your Degree in Education & Related Fields, 2011–2013*. El Dorado Hills, CA: Reference Service Press, 2011. URL: rspfunding.com

Schlachter, Gail A. and R. David Weber. *How to Pay for Your Degree in Engineering, 2011–2013*. El Dorado Hills, CA: Reference Service Press, 2011. URL: rspfunding.com

Schlachter, Gail A. and R. David Weber. *How to Pay for Your Degree in Journalism & Related Fields, 2011–2013*. El Dorado Hills, CA: Reference Service Press, 2011. URL: rspfunding.com

Schlachter, Gail A. and R. David Weber. *How to Pay for Your Degree in Library & Information Science, 2010–2012*. El Dorado Hills, CA: Reference Service Press, 2010. URL: rspfunding.com

Schlachter, Gail A. and R. David Weber. *How to Pay for Your Law Degree, 2011–2013*. El Dorado Hills, CA: Reference Service Press, 2011. URL: rspfunding.com

Schlachter, Gail A. and R. David Weber. *Money for Graduate Students in the Arts & Humanities, 2010–2012*. El Dorado Hills, CA: Reference Service Press, 2010.
> Directory of grants, awards, fellowships, and traineeships for graduate training, study, and research in the humanities. Contains a bibliography of financial aid resources. URL: rspfunding.com

Scholarships, Fellowships and Loans: A Guide to Education-Related Financial Aid Programs for Students and Professionals. 31st ed. Farmington Hills, MI: Gale Cengage Learning, 2013.
> Lists a wide range of scholarships, fellowships, loans, grants, and awards not controlled by a college or university. URL: cengage.com

Tanabe, Gen S. and Kelly Y. Tanabe. *The Ultimate Scholarship Book 2013: Billions of Dollars in Scholarships, Grants and Prizes*. Los Altos, CA: SuperCollege, 2012.
> Contains a listing of more than 1.5 million awards which can be used at any college or university. Also lists scholarships that are not based on grades or need. Published annually. URL: supercollege.com

Internet Sources

College Answer (collegeanswer.com)
> Formerly Wired Scholar, this site from Sallie Mae offers guidance on college preparation, evaluation, selection, application, and financing, including a scholarship database.

College Board's Scholarship Search (bigfuture.collegeboard.org/scholarship-search)
> Users can create a personal profile of educational level, talents, and background to search among more than 2,200 sources of undergraduate scholarships, loans, internships, and other financial aid programs from non-college sources.

CollegeData.com (collegedata.com)
> This web site, which has been approved by the National Association for College Admission Counseling, offers the Scholarship Finder, which includes 580,000 awards worth more than $3.4 billion and is searchable by inputting eligibility criteria such as ethnicity/heritage, religion, and area of study.

CollegeNet (collegenet.com/mach25/app)
> Offers a database of over $1.6 billion in scholarships, which can be searched by keyword or by student profile information, such as residence, gender, minority status, and religious affiliation.

College Scholarships (collegescholarships.org)
> This easy-to-browse site, which does not require registration, offers information and advice on financial aid for many different types of students.

Cornell Graduate Fellowship Database (gradschool.cornell.edu/fellowships)
> The Fellowship Database, compiled by the Cornell University Graduate School, offers a large searchable database of graduate fellowships from a wide variety of organizations, including fellowships specifically for international students and study abroad programs.

Fastweb.com (fastweb.com)
> An extensive scholarship search engine that prompts users to enter information about themselves, including area of study, and responds with an appropriate list of available local, national, and college-specific scholarships. Also offers information about internship programs.

Fedmoney.org (fedmoney.org)
> The most comprehensive free full-text online resource on all U.S. federal government student financial aid programs.

FinAid: The SmartStudent™ Guide to Financial Aid (finaid.org)
> Links to funding sources such as scholarships, fellowships, and grants, some of which are focused toward those with particular needs or interests, such as the disabled, minorities, and international students.

FindTuition.com (findtuition.com)
> Includes listings for over $7 billion in scholarships and grants, along with information on student loan programs.

Gradschools.com (gradschools.com)
> In the section titled "Financing" this site provides information on fellowships, scholarships, loans, and assistantships available to graduate students, as well as advice and tips related to financing graduate-level education.

Grants for Individuals (staff.lib.msu.edu/harris23/grants/3subject.htm)

Compiled by staff at the Michigan State University Libraries, this comprehensive listing of funding opportunities includes web sites, databases, books, and announcements. It offers the choice to search by academic level, including Precollege, Undergraduate, Graduate, and Postdoctorate funding.

GrantSpace Resources for Individual Grantseekers: Students (grantspace.org/Tools/Knowledge-Base/Individual-Grantseekers/Students)

Knowledge Base articles compiled by Foundation Center staff provide advice and resources for U.S. and international students at all education levels.

Peterson's Scholarships, Loans, Financial Aid & the FAFSA (petersons.com/college-search/scholarships.aspx)

Gives help, guidance, and answers to frequently asked questions on financial aid, as well as information on organizations that offer private and federal loans. Peterson's Scholarship Search provides information on scholarships, grants, and prizes worth over $8 billion.

Princeton Review (princetonreview.com/scholarships-financial-aid.aspx)

Provides access to a database of scholarships that is searchable by factors such as home state, ethnicity, religion, and disabilities.

Sallie Mae Fund (thesalliemaefund.org)

Search their database for information on over $16 billion in scholarship funding for high school, undergraduate, graduate, and adult students.

Scholarship Experts (scholarshipexperts.com)

Provides a free online scholarship database of 2.4 million scholarships worth over $14 billion.

Scholarships.com (scholarships.com)

A searchable database listing 2.7 million local and national scholarships and grants worth over $19 billion. Also gives a listing of colleges and universities that can be searched by school name, state, or area of study.

Scholarships4Students.com (scholarships4students.com)

This easy-to-use site offers listings of scholarships by major, state, and minority group, as well as by categories such as athletic, artistic, religious and disabilities scholarships.

Student Aid on the Web (studentaid.ed.gov)

The U.S. Department of Education's Federal Student Aid (FSA) programs, described on this web site, are the largest source of student aid in America. The information provided is designed to assist with college planning. The site gives access to and information about the products and services needed throughout the financial aid process, including a link to the FAFSA (Free Application for Federal Student Aid) form.

Supercollege.com (supercollege.com)

A searchable list of scholarships, grants, and contests to help pay for higher education. Also offers guidance on selecting and applying to schools.

Union Plus College Education Resources (unionplus.org/college-education-financing)

Provided by the AFL-CIO, this database offers information on union-sponsored scholarships and aid.

WRITING

Dramatists Sourcebook. 26th ed. New York, NY: Theatre Communications Group, 2010.

Contains a "Fellowships and Grants" section listing foundations and organizations that offer funding to playwrights, composers, translators, librettists, and lyricists. Notes guidelines, application procedures, deadlines, remuneration, and frequency of these funding sources. Published biennially. URL: tcg.org

LMP: Literary Market Place 2014: The Directory of the American Book Publishing Industry. Medford, NJ: Information Today Inc., 2013.

Includes a section listing literary prizes, contests, residencies, fellowships, and grants. Published annually. URL: books.infotoday.com

Poets & Writers Magazine. New York, NY: Poets & Writers, Inc.

Each monthly issue offers a list of grants, awards, conferences, and residencies available to writers, plus a variety of articles related to being a working writer. URL: pw.org

Poet's Market. 27th ed. Cincinnati, OH: Writer's Digest Books, 2013.

Entries include contact information and submission instructions for periodicals, book publishers, and other outlets for poetry. Published annually. URL: writersdigestshop.com

Writer's Market. 93rd ed. Cincinnati, OH: Writer's Digest Books, 2013.

Covers fiction and nonfiction, books, articles, greeting cards, screenplays, and other media. Entries include contact information, how to query the publisher, typical fees paid, and other specifications for aspiring and professional writers. Includes a chapter on contests and awards. Also available as a regularly updated online database via paid subscription. Published annually. URL: writersdigestshop.com

Internet Sources

American Literary Translators Association (utdallas.edu/alta/resources/grants-and-awards)

ALTA's list of grants and awards for the literary translator, including submission dates.

Americans for the Arts (americansforthearts.org/by-topic/funding-resources)

Information clearinghouse that provides material on funding for individuals in all areas of the arts.

Authors League Fund (authorsleaguefund.org)

With funds from professional writers, ALF provides interest-free loans to writers facing financial need.

Dow Jones News Fund (newsfund.org)
The emphasis for this web site is on education for students and teachers to promote careers in print and online journalism. It includes information on scholarships, internships, and awards, as well as an online publication, "The Journalist's Road to Success," also available in Spanish, which provides guidance on planning a career in journalism.

Grants for Individuals: Writing (staff.lib.msu.edu/harris23/grants/3writing.htm)
Compiled by staff at the Michigan State University Libraries, this comprehensive listing of funding opportunities for writers includes web sites, databases, and books.

GrantSpace Resources for Individual Grantseekers: Artists (grantspace.org/Tools/Knowledge-Base/Individual-Grantseekers/Artists)
Knowledge Base articles compiled by Foundation Center staff provide advice and resources for writers and other types of artists seeking grant funding.

National Endowment for the Arts (nea.gov)
Provides information on fellowships in the areas of poetry, prose, music, and the arts.

New York Foundation for the Arts (NYFA) (nyfa.org)
The "For Artists" area provides information on fellowships and fiscal sponsorship for artists.

Newswise (newswise.com)
Includes information on awards and grants for journalists under "Resources."

PEN American Center Grants and Awards Online Database (pen.org/ns-grants-and-awards)
With more than 1,500 listings of domestic and foreign grants, literary awards, fellowships, and residencies, this is the most comprehensive online database available to writers of all income brackets, at work in all genres, and at various levels of achievement. Available online only by subscription or with membership to the PEN American Center. Also available on-site at the five Foundation Center libraries.

Poets & Writers Online (pw.org/grants)
Contains an extensive list of upcoming deadlines for state and national poetry, fiction, and creative nonfiction prizes. Also provides information on conferences and residencies for writers.

Theatre Communications Group (tcg.org/grants/individual.cfm)
The "Grants" section of this web site lists grants to actors, directors, writers, and other theater professionals.

United States Artists (unitedstatesartists.org)
This organization, funded by foundations and private donors, supports a fellowship program open to artists in all career stages. Fellowships will be given across a broad array of disciplines, including literature (fiction, non-fiction, poetry).

FOUNDATION CENTER RESOURCES

Established in 1956 and today supported by close to 550 foundations, Foundation Center is the leading source of information about philanthropy worldwide. Through data, analysis, and training, it connects people who want to change the world to the resources they need to succeed. Foundation Center maintains the most comprehensive database on U.S. and, increasingly, global grantmakers and their grants — a robust, accessible knowledge bank for the sector. It also operates research, education, and training programs designed to advance knowledge of philanthropy at every level. Thousands of people visit Foundation Center's website each day and are served in its five library/learning centers and at more than 470 Funding Information Network locations nationwide and around the world.

ONLINE DATABASES

Foundation Directory Online
Which grantmaker is most likely to fund your organization? *Foundation Directory Online* (FDO) will help you answer this question, making it an essential tool for any grantseeker.

With detailed profiles on 120,000+ grantmakers — including U.S. and international foundations, corporations, and grantmaking public charities — FDO eliminates the guesswork from finding the right funder.

Foundation Directory Online includes:
- **Grantmaker profiles:** Get application information and deadlines, grant limitations, fields of interest, and geographic focus to help narrow your search.
- **Grants information:** Discover grants awarded to organizations similar to yours, with in-depth descriptions.
- **Visualization tools:** Easily map and chart a grantmaker's funding patterns by location and subject area.

Monthly and annual plans are available to fit your research needs.

LEARN MORE: foundationcenter.org/fdo

Foundation Grants to Individuals Online
Need a scholarship, fellowship or award? Visit the new *Foundation Grants to Individuals Online* built specifically for students, artists, researchers, and individuals like you!

$19.95: ONE MONTH
$36.95: THREE MONTHS
$59.95: SIX MONTHS
$99.95: ONE YEAR

TO SUBSCRIBE, VISIT gtionline.foundationcenter.org

TRASI (Tools and Resources for Assessing Social Impact)
Browse or search the TRASI database for proven approaches to social impact assessment, guidelines for creating and conducting an assessment, and ready-to-use tools for measuring social change. TRASI also features a community page where individuals can connect with peers and experts.
FREE

PLEASE VISIT trasi.foundationcenter.org

Foundation Maps
Foundation Maps brings to life data about U.S. and global philanthropy through extensive mapping, charting, and analytic capabilities. This interactive tool for funders is designed to facilitate more transparent, effective, and collaborative philanthropy.

LEARN MORE: maps@foundationcenter.org

Nonprofit Collaboration Database
This database provides hundreds of real-life examples of how nonprofits are working together.

PLEASE VISIT foundationcenter.org/gainknowledge/collaboration

GRANTMAKER DIRECTORIES

The Foundation Directory, 2014 Edition
Key facts include fields of interest, contact information, financials, names of decision makers, and over 51,000 sample grants. Convenient indexes are provided for all *Foundation Directories*.
MARCH 2014 / ISBN 978-1-59542-473-0 / $215 / PUBLISHED ANNUALLY

The Foundation Directory Part 2, 2014 Edition
Thorough coverage for the next 10,000 largest foundations, with nearly 40,000 sample grants.
MARCH 2014 / ISBN 978-1-59542-474-7 / $185 / PUBLISHED ANNUALLY

The Foundation Directory Supplement, 2014 Edition
This single volume provides updates for thousands of foundations in *The Foundation Directory* and the *Directory Part 2*. Changes in foundation status, contact information, and giving interests are highlighted in new entries.
SEPTEMBER 2014 / ISBN 978-1-59542-475-4 / $125 / PUBLISHED ANNUALLY

Guide to Funding for International & Foreign Programs, 11th Edition

Profiles of more than 2,200 grantmakers that provide international relief, disaster assistance, human rights, civil liberties, community development, and education.

MAY 2012 / ISBN 978-1-59542-408-2 / $125

The Celebrity Foundation Directory
5th Digital Edition

This downloadable directory (PDF) includes detailed descriptions of more than 1,880 foundations started by VIPs in the fields of business, entertainment, politics, and sports.

NOVEMBER 2013 / ISBN 978-1-59542-456-3 / $59.95

Foundation Grants to Individuals, 23rd Edition

The only publication devoted entirely to foundation grant opportunities for qualified individual applicants, this directory features more than 10,000 entries with current information including foundation name, address, program description, and application guidelines.

JULY 2014 / ISBN 978-1-59542-489-1 / $75 / PUBLISHED ANNUALLY

The PRI Directory, 3rd Edition
Charitable Loans and Other Program-Related
Investments by Foundations

This *Directory* lists leading funders, recipients, project descriptions, and includes tips on how to secure and manage PRIs. Foundation listings include funder name and state; recipient name, city, and state (or country); and a description of the project funded.

PUBLISHED IN PARTERNSHIP WITH PRI MAKERS NETWORK.

JULY 2010 / ISBN 978-1-59542-214-9 / $95

Grant Guides

Designed for fundraisers who work within specific areas, 15 digital edition *Grant Guides* list actual foundation grants of $10,000 or more. *Guides* include a keyword search tool and indexes to pinpoint grants of interest to you. As a special bonus, each grantmaker entry contains a link to its *Foundation Directory Online Free* profile for even more details, all in a convenient PDF format.

2014 EDITIONS / $39.95 EACH

TO ORDER, VISIT foundationcenter.org/grantguides

FUNDRAISING GUIDES

After the Grant
The Nonprofit's Guide to Good Stewardship

An invaluable and practical resource for anyone seeking funding from foundations, this *Guide* will help you manage your grant to ensure you get the next one.

MARCH 2010 / ISBN 978-1-59542-301-6 / $39.95

Foundation Fundamentals, 8th Edition
Expert advice on fundraising research and proposal development.
A go-to resource in academic programs on the nonprofit sector. *Foundation Fundamentals* describes foundation funding provides advice on research strategies, including how to best use *Foundation Directory Online*.

MARCH 2008 / ISBN 978-1-59542-156-2 / $39.95

Foundation Center's Guide to
Proposal Writing, 6th Edition

Author Jane Geever provides detailed instructions on preparing successful grant proposals, incorporating the results of interviews with 40 U.S. grantmakers.

MAY 2012 / ISBN 978-1-59542-404-4 / $39.95

Guía Para Escribir Propuestas

The Spanish-language translation of *Foundation Center's Guide to Proposal Writing,* 5th edition.

MARCH 2008 / ISBN 978-1-595423-158-6 / $39.95

The Grantseeker's Guide to Winning Proposals

A collection of 35 actual proposals submitted to international, regional, corporate, and local foundations. Each includes remarks by the program officer who approved the grant.

AUGUST 2008 / ISBN 978-1-59542-195-1 / $39.95

Securing Your Organization's Future
A Complete Guide to Fundraising Strategies, Revised Edition

Author Michael Seltzer explains how to strengthen your nonprofit's capacity to raise funds and achieve long-term financial stability.

FEBRUARY 2001 / ISBN 0-87954-900-9 / $39.95

NONPROFIT MANAGEMENT GUIDES

America's Nonprofit Sector
A Primer

The third edition of this publication, by Lester Salamon, is ideal for people who want a thorough, accessible introduction to the nonprofit sector—as well as the nation's social welfare system.

MARCH 2012 / ISBN 978-1-59542-360-3 / $24.95

The 21St Century Nonprofit
Managing in the Age of Governance

This book details the significant improvements in nonprofit management practice that have taken place in recent years.

SEPTEMBER 2009 / ISBN 978-1-59542-249-1 / $39.95

Foundations and Public Policy

This book presents a valuable framework for foundations as they plan or implement their engagement with public policy.

Published in partnership with The Center on Philanthropy & Public Policy.

MARCH 2009 / ISBN 978-1-59542-218-7 / $34.95

Local Mission-Global Vision
Community Foundations in the 21st Century

This book examines the new role of community foundations, exploring the potential impact of transnational evolution on organized philanthropy.

Published in partnership with Transatlantic Community Foundations Network.

AUGUST 2008 / ISBN 978-1-59542-204-0 / $34.95

Wise Decision-Making in Uncertain Times
Using Nonprofit Resources Effectively

This book highlights the critical challenges of fiscal sustainability for nonprofits, and encourages organizations to take a more expansive approach to funding outreach.

AUGUST 2006 / ISBN 1-59542-099-1 / $34.95

Effective Economic Decision-Making by Nonprofit Organizations

Editor Dennis R. Young offers practical guidelines to help nonprofit managers advance their mission while balancing the interests of trustees, funders, government, and staff.
DECEMBER 2003 / ISBN 1-931923-69-8 / $34.95

The Board Member's Book
Making a Difference in Voluntary Organizations, 3rd Edition

Written by former Independent Sector President Brian O'Connell, this is the perfect guide to the issues, challenges, and possibilities facing a nonprofit organization and its board.
MAY 2003 / ISBN 1-931923-17-5 / $29.95

Philanthropy's Challenge
Building Nonprofit Capacity Through Venture Grantmaking

Author Paul Firstenberg explores the roles of grantmaker and grantee within various models of venture grantmaking. He outlines the characteristics that qualify an organization for a venture grant, and outlines the steps a grantmaker can take to build the grantees' organizational capacity.
FEBRUARY 2003 / SOFTBOUND: ISBN 1-931923-15-9 / $29.95
HARDBOUND: ISBN 1-931923-53-1 / $39.95

Investing in Capacity Building
A Guide to High-Impact Approaches

Author Barbara Blumenthal helps grantmakers and consultants design better methods to help nonprofits, while showing nonprofit managers how to get more effective support.
NOVEMBER 2003 / ISBN 1-931923-65-5 / $34.95

ASSOCIATES PROGRAM

For just $995 a year or $695 for six months, the Associates Program experts will answer all of your questions about foundation giving, corporate philanthropy, and individual donors.

You will receive online access to several lists that are updated monthly, including new grantmakers and grantmaker application deadlines. In addition, you will receive most results within the next business day.

JOIN NOW AT foundationcenter.org/associates

ADDITIONAL ONLINE RESOURCES

foundationcenter.org

- *Philanthropy News Digest* is a daily digest of philanthropy-related articles. Read interviews with leaders, look for RFPs, learn from the experts, and share ideas with others in the field.
- Foundation Stats is a web-based tool that provides free and open access to a wealth of data on the U.S. foundation community. The intuitive platform can be used by anyone to generate thousands of custom tables and charts on the size, scope, and giving priorities of the U.S. foundation community.
- Access research studies to track trends in foundation growth and giving in grantmaker policies and practices.
- To stay current on the latest research trends visit foundationcenter.org/gainknowledge.

grantspace.org

GrantSpace, Foundation Center's learning community for the social sector, features resources organized under the 13 most common subject areas of funding research — including health, education, and the arts.

- Dig into the GrantSpace knowledge base for answers to more than 150 questions asked about grantseeking and nonprofits.
- Stay up-to-date on classes and events happening in person and online with the GrantSpace training calendar.
- Add your voice and help build a community-driven knowledge base: share your expertise, rate content, ask questions, and add comments.

glasspockets.org

Glasspockets provides the data, resources, examples, and action steps foundations need to understand the value of transparency, be more open in their own communications, and help shed more light on how private organizations are serving the public good.

- Learn about the online transparency and accountability practices of the largest foundations, and see who has "glass pockets."
- Transparency Talk, the Glasspockets blog and podcast series, highlights strategies, findings, and best practices related to foundation transparency.
- The Giving Pledge is an effort that encourages the world's wealthiest individuals and families to commit the majority of their assets to philanthropic causes. Eye on the Giving Pledge offers an in-depth picture of Giving Pledge participants, their charitable activities, and the potential impact of the Giving Pledge.
- Learn more about the Reporting Commitment, an initiative aimed at developing more timely, accurate, and precise reporting on the flow of philanthropic dollars.

grantcraft.org

GrantCraft combines the practical wisdom of funders worldwide with the expertise of Foundation Center to improve the practice of philanthropy. Since 2001, GrantCraft has delivered the knowledge funders need to be strategic and effective in their work, addressing questions funders face across various strategies and issue areas.

- Search the 13 content types including guides, takeaways, discussions, infographics, and videos to find real-life examples from funders.
- Register for free access to the monthly newsletter, personal dashboard, and to share content and comment.
- All content is free to use and share.

issuelab.org

IssueLab provides free access to resources that analyze the world's most pressing social, economic, and environmental challenges and their potential solutions. The platform contains thousands of case studies, evaluations, white papers, and issue briefs, and represents one the largest collections of social sector knowledge.

- Search and browse the database by social issue area, author, publishing organization, or geography.
- Learn how to add resources to the IssueLab collection.

DESCRIPTIVE DIRECTORY

ALABAMA

1

AAMN Foundation

(also known as American Assembly for Men in Nursing Foundation)
P.O. Box 130220
Birmingham, AL 35213 (205) 956-0146
FAX: (205) 956-0146; E-mail: jimraper@uab.edu;
URL: http://aamn.org/foundation.shtml

Foundation type: Operating foundation
Purpose: Scholarships to deserving Pre-RN and graduate male nursing students.
Financial data: Year ended 12/31/2012. Assets, $41,780 (M); Expenditures, $4,200; Total giving, $3,500; Grants to individuals, 7 grants totaling $3,500 (high: $500, low: $500).
Fields of interest: Nursing school/education; Men.
Type of support: Scholarships—to individuals.
Application information: Applications accepted. Application form required.
Deadline(s): Varies
EIN: 631255992

2

Alabama Forestry Foundation

555 Alabama St.
Montgomery, AL 36104-4395 (334) 265-8733
Contact: Christopher V. Isaacson, Exec. V.P.
FAX: (334) 262-1258;
E-mail: cisaacson@alaforestry.org

Foundation type: Public charity
Purpose: College scholarships to deserving students of AL, pursuing an education in forestry.
Financial data: Year ended 12/31/2011. Assets, $1,049,528 (M); Expenditures, $400,223; Total giving, $1,500; Grants to individuals, totaling $1,500.
Fields of interest: Environment, forests.
Type of support: Scholarships—to individuals.
Application information: Applications accepted. Application form required.
Additional information: Scholarship is based on academic achievement and involvement in extra curricular activities and leadership.
EIN: 630756161

3

Alabama Home Health Care, Inc.

2400 John Hawkins Pkwy.
Birmingham, AL 35244-3500 (205) 981-8000

Foundation type: Public charity
Purpose: Assistance to elderly and terminally ill individuals in AL seeking health care services at home.
Financial data: Year ended 12/31/2011. Assets, $448,680 (M); Expenditures, $146,756; Total giving, $137,681; Grants to individuals, totaling $137,681.
Fields of interest: Human services; Hospices; Aging; Terminal illness, people with.
Type of support: Grants for special needs.
Application information: Contact the organization for further information on application procedures.
EIN: 237207236

4

Alabama Law Foundation, Inc.

P.O. Box 4129
Montgomery, AL 36101-0671 (334) 387-1600
Contact: Tracy Daniel, Exec. Dir.
E-mail: tdaniel@alfinc.org; URL: http://www.alfinc.org

Foundation type: Public charity
Purpose: Scholarships to academically outstanding Alabama students in pursuit of a law education.
Publications: Application guidelines; Grants list; Informational brochure; Newsletter.
Financial data: Year ended 03/31/2013. Assets, $4,800,801 (M); Expenditures, $984,616; Total giving, $524,513; Grants to individuals, totaling $24,250.
Fields of interest: Vocational education, post-secondary; Higher education; Law school/education.
Type of support: Graduate support; Technical education support; Precollege support; Undergraduate support.
Application information: Application form required. Application form available on the grantmaker's web site.
Send request by: Online
Copies of proposal: 1
Deadline(s): 1st Fri. in June for Cabaniss, Johnston, May 1 for Kids' Chance and Apr. 1 for Justice Janie L. Shore
Final notification: Recipients notified in one month
Applicants should submit the following:
1) Transcripts
2) GPA
3) Financial information
4) FAFSA
Additional information: See web site for additional application information.
Program descriptions:
Cabaniss, Johnston Scholarship Fund: This $5,000 scholarship is to recognize and assist academically outstanding second-year law students who are also Alabama residents, and further to help promising law students become lawyers who will make a positive impact on society. A runner-up scholarship of $1,000 may be awarded at the committee's discretion.
Justice Janie L. Shores Scholarship: The organization offers one or more scholarships to female Alabama residents attending an Alabama law school.
William Verbon Black Scholarship: The organization offers scholarships to assist full-time law students at the University of Alabama School of Law. Applicants should be in all respect superior. Alabama residents are given priority. Academic achievement is the key factor, but consideration is also given to consciousness, dependability, civic involvement, financial need and dedication to the highest ethical standards.
EIN: 630951482

5

Alabama Pharmacy Association Scholarship Foundation

(formerly Alabama Pharmaceutical Association Scholarship Foundation)
1211 Carmichael Way
Montgomery, AL 36106-3672 (334) 271-4222

Foundation type: Independent foundation
Purpose: Scholarships only to AL students majoring in pharmaceutical studies.

Financial data: Year ended 12/31/2011. Assets, $16,281 (M); Expenditures, $6,348; Total giving, $5,000.
Fields of interest: Health sciences school/education; Pharmacology.
Type of support: Undergraduate support.
Application information: Applications not accepted.
Additional information: Unsolicited requests for funds not considered or acknowledged.
EIN: 636049895

6

Alsite Scholarships, Inc.

c/o Skipper Consulting
3644 Vann Rd., Ste. 100
Birmingham, AL 35235
Contact: Dr. Robert L. Vecellio, Chair.
Application address: c/o HMR ALSITE Scholarships, Inc., Dept. of Civil Engineering, 238 Harbert Engineering Center, Auburn University, AL 36849-5337
URL: http://www.alsite.org/hmr.shtml

Foundation type: Independent foundation
Purpose: College scholarships to full-time students for attendance at an accredited Civil Engineering school in the state of Alabama pursuing an engineering degree.
Financial data: Year ended 12/31/2012. Assets, $144,032 (M); Expenditures, $6,796; Total giving, $6,250; Grants to individuals, 2 grants totaling $6,250 (high: $3,750, low: $2,500).
Fields of interest: Engineering school/education.
Type of support: Support to graduates or students of specific schools.
Application information: Applications accepted. Application form required.
Deadline(s): Mid-Feb.
Applicants should submit the following:
1) Transcripts
2) Letter(s) of recommendation
3) Financial information
Additional information: Applications can be obtained from faculty members in the Civil Engineering Departments at Auburn University, the University of Alabama, the University of Alabama at Birmingham, the University of Alabama in Huntsville, and the University of South Alabama, January of each year. Payments are made directly to the university on behalf of the student.
EIN: 631115900

7

W. R. Alsobrook Scholarship Trust

c/o Regions Bank, Trust Dept.
P.O. Box 2886
Mobile, AL 36652-2886 (501) 371-6719
Application address: c/o Regions Bank, Attn.: Trust Off., 400 West Capitol Ave., Little Rock, AR 72201-3402, tel.: (501) 371-6719

Foundation type: Independent foundation
Purpose: Scholarships to graduating high school seniors residing in Saline County, AR for higher education.
Financial data: Year ended 12/31/2011. Assets, $113,645 (M); Expenditures, $11,976; Total giving, $6,000; Grants to individuals, 4 grants totaling $6,000 (high: $2,500, low: $875).
Fields of interest: Higher education.
Type of support: Scholarships—to individuals; Support to graduates or students of specific schools.

Application information: Applications accepted. Application form required.

Deadline(s): Vary

Additional information: Application should include transcript.

EIN: 710517178

8

The American Society for Reproductive Medicine

(formerly The American Fertility Society)
1209 Montgomery Hwy.
Birmingham, AL 35216-2809 (205) 978-5000
Contact: Robert W. Rebar M.D., Exec. Dir.
FAX: (205) 978-5005; E-mail: asrm@asrm.org;
URL: http://www.asrm.org

Foundation type: Public charity

Purpose: Grants and awards to support outstanding researchers in the field of reproductive medicine.

Publications: Application guidelines; Annual report; Informational brochure.

Financial data: Year ended 06/30/2012. Assets, $41,082,730 (M); Expenditures, $8,284,329; Total giving, $59,500.

Fields of interest: Reproductive health.

Type of support: Research; Grants to individuals; Awards/prizes; Travel grants.

Application information: Applications accepted. Application form available on the grantmaker's web site.

Initial approach: Application

Deadline(s): May 1 for ASRM Nurse Research Award, June 1 for all others

Additional information: See web site for additional guidelines.

Program descriptions:

ASRM Nurse Research Award: This award recognizes outstanding research conducted by licensed nursing professionals, and allows a group of nurses who are active in research to attend the organization's annual meeting to present the results of their research studies. Eligible applicants include nurses who are presenting oral or poster abstracts.

ASRM/Society for Reproductive Endocrinology and Infertility, National Research Service Institutional Training Award: This program provides selected fellows with one- and two-year National Institutes of Health (NIH) traineeships to conduct cutting-edge research in the laboratories of NIH-funded investigators. In their final year of training, fellows present their research at the society's annual meeting.

Distinguished Researcher Award: This award recognizes a member of the society who has made outstanding contributions to clinical or basic research in reproduction published during the previous ten years. Recipients should have demonstrated sustained long-term commitment to advancing the frontiers of research in reproductive sciences and educating future scholars in the field. Recipients will be awarded with a $1,500 honorarium. Awards are by nomination only.

Ira and Esther Rosenwaks New Investigator Award: This award recognizes a society member who has made outstanding contributions to clinical or basic research in reproductive sciences published within ten years after receiving a doctoral degree or completing residency training. Recipients will have made original research contributions that significantly impact the field independently of his or her mentors; other factors to be considered in making the award include conceptual breakthrough, the significance of the research to allied fields of investigation, and development of new and innovative clinical or research methodologies.

Recipients will be awarded with a $1,000 honorarium, as well as reimbursement for travel, transportation, and food expenses.

Suheil J. Muasher Distinguished Service Award: This award recognizes and honors individuals and organizations that have provided distinguished service to the society. Nominees may either be society members or non-society members; recipients may be selected based on scientific, leadership, organizational, political, or societal service contributions to the society, reproductive medicine, and/or reproductive medicine patients. Recipients will be awarded free registration to the society's annual meeting, as well as travel and room/board reimbursement.

EIN: 042284338

9

American Sports Medicine Institute, Inc.

2660 10th Ave. S., Ste. 505
Birmingham, AL 35205-1626 (205) 918-0000
Contact: Lanier Johnson, Exec. Dir.
FAX: (205) 918-0800; E-mail: info@asmi.org; Tel.: Lanier Johnson : (205) 918-2127; Fax: Lanier Johnson : (205) 918-2177; E-mail For Lanier Johnson: ljohnson@asmi.org; URL: http://www.asmi.org

Foundation type: Public charity

Purpose: Scholarships to students enrolled in athletic training at select Alabama based universities.

Financial data: Year ended 06/30/2012. Assets, $1,165,864 (M); Expenditures, $1,703,403.

Fields of interest: Athletics/sports, training.

Type of support: Scholarships—to individuals.

Application information: Applications accepted.

Additional information: Students are selected by the universities based on need and contribution of that student to their athletic training program. See web site for additional information.

EIN: 630952490

10

Andalusia Health Services Inc.

P.O. Box 56
Andalusia, AL 36420-1200 (334) 222-2030
Contact: Gwen Ryland

Foundation type: Independent foundation

Purpose: Scholarships to residents of Covington County, AL, who are pursuing degrees in nursing, medicine, medical or laboratory technology, occupational therapy, physical therapy, speech therapy or emergency medicine.

Publications: Annual report.

Financial data: Year ended 06/30/2011. Assets, $2,895,722 (M); Expenditures, $198,992; Total giving, $175,700.

Fields of interest: Medical school/education; Nursing school/education; Health sciences school/education; Physical therapy; Speech/hearing centers.

Type of support: Scholarships—to individuals.

Application information: Applications accepted. Application form required.

Deadline(s): Aug. for Emergency Medicine, Mar. for all others

Additional information: Applicant must submit high school and college transcripts.

EIN: 630793474

11

The Baker Foundation

P.O. Box 846
Decatur, AL 35602-0846

Foundation type: Independent foundation

Purpose: Scholarships only to residents of Decatur, AL for higher education.

Financial data: Year ended 12/31/2012. Assets, $2,354,849 (M); Expenditures, $139,462; Total giving, $88,250.

Fields of interest: Higher education.

Type of support: Undergraduate support.

Application information: Applications not accepted.

Additional information: Unsolicited requests for funds not considered or acknowledged.

EIN: 630843636

12

Baptist Health Care Foundation of Montgomery

P.O. Box 244030
Montgomery, AL 36124-4030 (334) 273-4258
Contact: W. Russell Tyner, Pres. and C.E.O.

Foundation type: Public charity

Purpose: Two-year nursing scholarships are available to students in a ASN program or the last two years of a BSN program for tuition and/or school expenses.

Financial data: Year ended 06/30/2012. Assets, $8,642,014 (M); Expenditures, $446,431; Total giving, $394,211.

Fields of interest: Nursing school/education.

Type of support: Scholarships—to individuals.

Application information: Applications accepted. Application form required.

Applicants should submit the following:
1) Transcripts
2) GPA
3) Essay

Additional information: Application must also include two letters of reference and proof of acceptance to a nursing school.

EIN: 237281996

13

Bashinsky Foundation, Inc.

3432 E. Briarcliff Rd.
Birmingham, AL 35223-1309

Foundation type: Company-sponsored foundation

Purpose: Scholarships to students who are currently enrolled in or admitted to a degree-granting program at the University of Alabama.

Financial data: Year ended 12/31/2012. Assets, $10,436,968 (M); Expenditures, $593,583; Total giving, $531,721.

Fields of interest: Higher education.

Type of support: Scholarships—to individuals; Undergraduate support.

Application information: Applications accepted.

Initial approach: Letter

Applicants should submit the following:
1) Letter(s) of recommendation
2) Essay
3) Transcripts

Program description:

Joann F. Bashinsky Scholarship: The foundation awards scholarships to students who are currently enrolled in or admitted to a degree granting program at the University of Alabama. Applicants must

demonstrate solid academic progress and achievement.
EIN: 630968201

14
Lloyd Batre Scholarship Trust Fund
c/o Regions Bank
P.O. Box 2886
Mobile, AL   36652-2886   (251) 380-2255
Contact: Rhonda Shirazi
Application Address: 4000 Dauphin St., Mobile, AL 36608

Foundation type: Independent foundation
Purpose: Scholarships to financially needy students attending Spring Hill College, AL.
Financial data: Year ended 01/31/2013. Assets, $125,458 (M); Expenditures, $8,904; Total giving, $5,100; Grants to individuals, 4 grants totaling $5,100 (high: $1,550, low: $710).
Type of support: Support to graduates or students of specific schools; Undergraduate support.
Application information:
   Initial approach: Letter
   Deadline(s): None
EIN: 636020978

15
The J. L. Bedsole Foundation
P.O. Box 1137
Mobile, AL   36633-1137   (251) 432-3369
Contact: Christopher L. Lee, Exec. Dir.
Contact for scholarships: Scott A. Morton, Dir., e-mail: scott@jlbedsolefoundation.org
FAX: (251) 432-1134;
E-mail: info@jlbedsolefoundation.org; E-mail for Christopher Lee: chrislee@jlbedsolefoundation.org; URL: http://www.jlbedsolefoundation.org

Foundation type: Independent foundation
Purpose: Scholarships to entering college freshmen from southwest AL to attend AL colleges and universities.
Publications: Application guidelines.
Financial data: Year ended 12/31/2012. Assets, $64,134,957 (M); Expenditures, $3,783,502; Total giving, $2,632,710; Grants to individuals, 152 grants totaling $747,500 (high: $6,000, low: $1,500).
Fields of interest: Scholarships/financial aid.
Type of support: Undergraduate support.
Application information: Applications accepted. Application form required.
   Applicants should submit the following:
      1) GPA
      2) ACT
      3) FAFSA
   Additional information: Scholarship information available on foundation web site.
Program description:
   J.L. Bedsole Scholars Program: The scholars program awards college scholarships to future leaders from southwest Alabama. The program offers financial assistance for students with leadership ability, academic achievement and financial need to attend college within Alabama. Candidates for the Bedsole scholarship must express a desire to use their abilities to further the civic, cultural and economic development of southwest Alabama. Leadership is the most important criteria. Scholarship amounts do not exceed $6,000 per academic year. See foundation web site for application information.
EIN: 237225708

16
Blaylock Foundation, Inc.
1020 Indian Hills Dr.
Tuscaloosa, AL   35406-2225   (205) 752-8011
Contact: Elizabeth B. Hollingsworth, Pres.

Foundation type: Operating foundation
Purpose: Grants for assisting religious activities and education in the U.S. and abroad.
Financial data: Year ended 12/31/2011. Assets, $153,501 (M); Expenditures, $24,386; Total giving, $18,152; Grant to an individual, 1 grant totaling $2,300.
Fields of interest: Human services.
Type of support: Grants to individuals.
Application information: Applications accepted.
   Initial approach: Letter
   Deadline(s): None
   Additional information: Contact the foundation for additional information.
EIN: 630967721

17
The Mildred W. Blount Educational & Charitable Foundation
P.O. Box 607
Tallassee, AL   36078-0007   (334) 283-4931
Contact: Arnold B. Dopson, Chair.

Foundation type: Independent foundation
Purpose: Scholarships to students in Elmore County, AL for higher education.
Financial data: Year ended 06/30/2013. Assets, $2,989,256 (M); Expenditures, $181,357; Total giving, $170,000.
Fields of interest: Higher education.
Type of support: Scholarships—to individuals.
Application information: Applications accepted. Application form required.
   Deadline(s): Early May
   Additional information: Students should submit general information to scholarship committee of each high school within Elmore county, AL.
EIN: 630817472

18
John & Billie Boyd Charitable Foundation Trust
c/o Regions Bank, Trust Dept.
P.O. Box 2886
Mobile, AL   36652-2886   (931) 232-5179
Application address: 120 Robertson Hill Rd., Dover TN 37058-5949

Foundation type: Independent foundation
Purpose: Scholarships to financially needy graduates of Stewart County High School, TN for full time postsecondary education at accredited colleges or vocational school.
Financial data: Year ended 09/30/2012. Assets, $305,091 (M); Expenditures, $21,006; Total giving, $15,000.
Fields of interest: Vocational education, post-secondary; Higher education.
Type of support: Support to graduates or students of specific schools.
Application information: Applications accepted. Application form required.
   Deadline(s): None
   Additional information: Application is available at Stewart County High School. Student must maintain a 3.0 GPA.
EIN: 626338983

19
The Greater Brewton Foundation
P.O. Box 87
Brewton, AL   36427-0087
Contact: John D. Finlay, Jr., Pres.

Foundation type: Community foundation
Purpose: Scholarships to graduating students in the Brewton, AL area for tuition, books and other related fees for those seeking a college education.
Publications: Annual report; Informational brochure; Newsletter.
Financial data: Year ended 02/28/2013. Assets, $1,696,077 (M); Expenditures, $43,697; Total giving, $39,694; Grants to individuals, 11 grants totaling $9,100.
Fields of interest: Higher education.
Type of support: Scholarships—to individuals.
Application information: Applications accepted. Application form required. Application form available on the grantmaker's web site.
   Additional information: Applicant must demonstrate financial need, academic merit and other deserving characteristics.
EIN: 631112240

20
Central Alabama Community Foundation, Inc.
(formerly Montgomery Area Community Foundation, Inc.)
35 S. Court St.
Montgomery, AL   36104   (334) 264-6223
Contact: Burton Ward, Pres.; For grants: Caroline Montgomery Clark, V.P., Community Svcs.
FAX: (334) 263-6225;
E-mail: burton.ward@cacfinfo.org; URL: http://www.cacfinfo.org

Foundation type: Community foundation
Purpose: Scholarships to graduating seniors of Montgomery, Pike, Elmore and Lowndes counties, AL for higher education.
Publications: Application guidelines; Annual report; Financial statement; Grants list; Newsletter.
Financial data: Year ended 12/31/2012. Assets, $37,142,203 (M); Expenditures, $5,069,018; Total giving, $3,829,153.
Fields of interest: Higher education.
Type of support: Scholarships—to individuals; Undergraduate support.
Application information: Applications accepted. Application form required. Application form available on the grantmaker's web site.
   Initial approach: Application
   Send request by: Online
   Deadline(s): Apr. 1 for most scholarships
   Applicants should submit the following:
      1) Essay
      2) Financial information
      3) Letter(s) of recommendation
      4) Transcripts
   Additional information: See web site for a complete list of scholarships.
EIN: 630842355

21
Chapman Trust Fund
c/o Regions Bank Trust Dept.
P.O. Box 2886
Mobile, AL   36652-2886   (601) 261-4328
Contact: Lee Gill
Application address: c/o Regions Bank, Attn: Lee Gill, 202 S. 40th Ave., Hattiesburg, MS 39402-1641, tel.: (601) 261-4328

Foundation type: Independent foundation
Purpose: Student loans for males residing in Lawrence County, MS, to attend college.
Financial data: Year ended 12/31/2011. Assets, $256,908 (M); Expenditures, $7,298; Total giving, $0.
Fields of interest: Higher education; Men.
Type of support: Student loans—to individuals.
Application information: Applications accepted.
  Initial approach: Letter or telephone
  Deadline(s): None
  Applicants should submit the following:
    1) Letter(s) of recommendation
    2) Resume
    3) Financial information
EIN: 646023166

22
The Charity League, Inc.
P.O. Box 530233
Birmingham, AL 35253-0233 (205) 934-1598
Application address: c/o Kellie Reece, 115 Hope St., Clanton, AL 35045, tel.: (205) 217-7275, e-mail: kelu@hotmail.com
E-mail: Info@thecharityleague.org; URL: http://www.thecharityleague.org

Foundation type: Public charity
Purpose: Scholarships to speech and hearing impaired college bound students who are residents of Birmingham, AL.
Publications: Application guidelines.
Financial data: Year ended 12/31/2011. Assets, $264,394 (M); Expenditures, $64,625; Total giving, $55,177; Grants to individuals, totaling $4,500.
Fields of interest: Higher education; Deaf/hearing impaired.
Type of support: Scholarships—to individuals.
Application information: Applications accepted. Application form required. Application form available on the grantmaker's web site.
  Initial approach: Letter or e-mail
  Send request by: Mail
  Deadline(s): Apr. 1
  Applicants should submit the following:
    1) Essay
    2) Transcripts
  Additional information: The application should also include two letters of reference.
Program description:
  Virginia Cobb Scholarships: Scholarships range in the amount from $500 to $2,000 to speech and hearing impaired high school seniors entering colleges and universities.
EIN: 630500377

23
Childcare Resources
1904 1st Ave. N.
Birmingham, AL 35203-4006 (205) 252-1991
Contact: Joan Wright, Exec. Dir.
FAX: (205) 251-2076;
E-mail: childcare@ccr-bhm.org; Toll-free tel.: (800) 822-2734; additional fax (HR): (205) 795-2216; E-Mail for Joan Wright: jwright@ccr-bhm.org; URL: http://www.ccr-bhm.org

Foundation type: Public charity
Purpose: Childcare financial assistance to indigent residents of Blount, Jefferson, Shelby, and Walker counties, AL.
Publications: Application guidelines; Annual report; Newsletter.
Financial data: Year ended 09/30/2012. Assets, $214,371 (M); Expenditures, $1,504,739; Total giving, $184,775; Grants to individuals, totaling $184,775.
Fields of interest: Economically disadvantaged.
Type of support: Grants for special needs.
Application information:
  Initial approach: Letter
  Additional information: Contact the organization for eligibility criteria.
EIN: 630882628

24
Civitan International
(formerly Civitan International Foundation)
P.O. Box 130744
Birmingham, AL 35213-0744 (205) 591-8910
Application e-mail: rosemarysmith@civitan.org
FAX: (205) 592-6307; E-mail: civitan@civitan.org; Toll-free tel.: (800)-CIVITAN; URL: http://www.civitan.org

Foundation type: Public charity
Purpose: Undergraduate and graduate scholarships, based on grades, leadership, and community service, to members of Civitan, spouses or children of members, or junior Civitan members.
Publications: Application guidelines.
Financial data: Year ended 09/30/2011. Assets, $2,632,506 (M); Expenditures, $3,130,734; Total giving, $469,782; Grants to individuals, totaling $19,782.
Fields of interest: Higher education.
Type of support: Graduate support; Undergraduate support.
Application information: Applications accepted. Application form required. Application form available on the grantmaker's web site. Interview required.
  Initial approach: Telephone
  Send request by: E-mail
  Deadline(s): Jan. 31
  Final notification: Applicants notified in Apr.
  Additional information: Application must include a scanned copy of your tax forms. Scholarships are paid directly to the educational institution on behalf of the student.
Program description:
  Shropshire Scholarships: Scholarships are awarded to students enrolled in undergraduate or graduate studies. The $1,000 award is to be used only for tuition, room, books, laboratory fees, and academic supplies. Candidates must be a Civitan (or a Civitan's child or grandchild) and must have been a Civitan for at least two years, and/or must be or have been a junior Civitan for no less than two years.
EIN: 636052990

25
Community Action Agency of Baldwin, Escambia, Clarke, Monroe, & Conecuh Counties
26440 N. Pollard Rd.
P.O. Box 250
Daphne, AL 36526-4273 (251) 626-2646
FAX: (251) 626-2613; URL: http://www.caaofbecmcc.org/about.htm

Foundation type: Public charity
Purpose: Services to indigent residents of Baldwin, Clarke, Conecuh, Escambia, and Monroe counties, AL. which includes daycare, food assistance, home weatherization, utility assistance, transportation, and emergency housing.

Financial data: Year ended 09/30/2011. Assets, $1,893,748 (M); Expenditures, $20,011,411; Total giving, $10,730,495; Grants to individuals, totaling $10,730,495.
Fields of interest: Economically disadvantaged.
Type of support: In-kind gifts.
Application information:
  Initial approach: Letter
  Additional information: Applicants must bring all required documentation. Eligibility is determined by the federal poverty guidelines.
EIN: 630510904

26
Community Action Partnership of North Alabama
1909 Central Pkwy., S.W.
Decatur, AL 35601-6822 (256) 355-7843
Contact: Michael Tubbs, C.E.O.
FAX: (256) 260-3200; E-mail: mtubbs@capna.org; URL: http://www.capna.org/

Foundation type: Public charity
Purpose: Utility, weatherization, housing, early childhood development and other assistance to low income individuals residing in Blount, Cherokee, Colbert, Cullman, DeKalb, Franklin, Jackson, Lawrence, Marion, Marshall, Morgan, Walker, and Winston counties, AL.
Publications: Financial statement.
Financial data: Year ended 12/31/2011. Assets, $33,132,982 (M); Expenditures, $30,216,197; Total giving, $2,691,492; Grants to individuals, totaling $2,691,492.
Fields of interest: Economically disadvantaged.
Type of support: Grants for special needs.
Application information:
  Initial approach: Letter
  Additional information: Contact the organization for eligibility criteria.
EIN: 630514875

27
Community Foundation of Greater Birmingham
(formerly The Greater Birmingham Foundation)
2100 First Ave. N., Ste. 700
Birmingham, AL 35203-4223 (205) 327-3800
Contact: Kate Nielsen, Pres.; For grants: James McCrary, V.P., Grants and Evaluation; For scholarships: Sheree Wilkerson, Scholarship Mgr.
FAX: (205) 328-6576;
E-mail: info@foundationbirmingham.org; URL: http://www.foundationbirmingham.org

Foundation type: Community foundation
Purpose: Scholarships to students of Birmingham, AL who might not otherwise have been able to afford college tuition.
Publications: Application guidelines; Annual report; Financial statement; Grants list; Informational brochure; Newsletter; Occasional report.
Financial data: Year ended 12/31/2012. Assets, $169,336,538 (M); Expenditures, $20,058,050; Total giving, $17,706,427; Grants to individuals, 99 grants totaling $317,950.
Fields of interest: Higher education.
Type of support: Scholarships—to individuals; Support to graduates or students of specific schools.
Application information: Applications accepted.
  Initial approach: Varies
  Deadline(s): Varies
  Additional information: The foundation administers a variety of scholarships through

various funds. Some scholarships are limited to students from certain schools or other eligibility requirements, see web site for additional information.
EIN: 631209631

28
Community Foundation of Northeast Alabama
(formerly Calhoun County Community Foundation)
1130 Quintard Ave., Ste. 100
P.O. Box 1826
Anniston, AL 36201 (256) 231-5160
Contact: Jennifer S. Maddox, C.E.O.
FAX: (256) 231-5161;
E-mail: info@yourcommunityfirst.org; Additional e-mail: jmaddox@yourcommunityfirst.org;
URL: http://www.yourcommunityfirst.org/

Foundation type: Community foundation
Purpose: Scholarships to assist students from various public and private schools in Northeast Alabama for postsecondary education.
Publications: Application guidelines; Annual report; Financial statement; Grants list; Informational brochure; Newsletter; Occasional report; Program policy statement.
Financial data: Year ended 09/30/2013. Assets, $34,488,973 (M); Expenditures, $1,789,000; Total giving, $1,118,005. Scholarships—to individuals amount not specified.
Fields of interest: Higher education.
Type of support: Scholarships—to individuals.
Application information: Applications accepted. Application form available on the grantmaker's web site.
Send request by: Online
Deadline(s): Mar. 1
Additional information: See web site for additional application guidelines.
EIN: 630308398

29
Community Service Programs of West Alabama, Inc.
(also known as CSP)
601 Black Bears Way
Tuscaloosa, AL 35401-4807 (205) 752-5429
FAX: (205) 758-7229; Toll-Free Tel.: (855) 211-0950; URL: http://www.cspwal.com

Foundation type: Public charity
Purpose: Grants to low-income and special needs individuals in west-central AL.
Publications: Annual report.
Financial data: Year ended 09/30/2011. Assets, $9,345,704 (M); Expenditures, $16,411,150.
Fields of interest: Disabilities, people with; Economically disadvantaged.
Type of support: Grants for special needs.
Application information:
Initial approach: Telephone or e-mail
Additional information: Applicants must meet financial guidelines.
EIN: 630671915

30
Decatur Policemen & Firemen Death Benefit Fund
c/o Regions Bank
P.O. Box 680
Huntsville, AL 35804 (256) 532-4602
Contact: Kimberly Akins

Foundation type: Independent foundation
Purpose: Financial assistance only to police and fire department employees of Decatur, Alabama.
Financial data: Year ended 12/31/2012. Assets, $169,703 (M); Expenditures, $10,544; Total giving, $7,000.
Type of support: Grants for special needs.
Application information: Applications accepted.
Initial approach: Letter
Deadline(s): None
Additional information: Giving is only for death benefits as instructed in the fund document.
EIN: 636100570

31
The Dixon Foundation
1 Chase Corporate Ctr., Ste 400
Birmingham, AL 35244-7001 (205) 313-6501
Contact: Diane Gentry
FAX: (205) 802-7855

Foundation type: Operating foundation
Purpose: Fellowships in pediatrics research at Children's Hospital, Birmingham, AL, are awarded to residents of AL and GA.
Financial data: Year ended 12/31/2012. Assets, $8,946,151 (M); Expenditures, $1,021,133; Total giving, $397,622.
Fields of interest: Theological school/education; Pediatrics research; Protestant agencies & churches.
Type of support: Fellowships; Research; Postgraduate support.
Application information: Applications accepted.
Initial approach: Letter
Deadline(s): None
Additional information: Applicant must demonstrate financial need.
EIN: 630944809

32
Adrian & Marie Downing Educational Trust
P.O. Box 469
Brewton, AL 36427 (251) 809-2132
Contact: Christy Black

Foundation type: Independent foundation
Purpose: Scholarships to residents of Escambia County, AL, attending post secondary institutions.
Financial data: Year ended 12/31/2012. Assets, $453,291 (M); Expenditures, $24,604; Total giving, $19,000; Grants to individuals, 28 grants totaling $19,000 (high: $1,000, low: $500).
Fields of interest: Higher education.
Type of support: Scholarships—to individuals.
Application information: Applications accepted. Application form required.
Deadline(s): Mar. 1
EIN: 586320669

33
David R. Dunlap, Jr. Memorial Trust
c/o Regions Bank
P.O. Drawer 1628
Mobile, AL 36633-1628 (251) 690-1411
Contact: David R. Dunalp, Jr.

Foundation type: Independent foundation
Purpose: Student loans to residents of Mobile and Baldwin counties, AL, and to employees of Regions Bank and Atlantic Marine, Inc.
Financial data: Year ended 12/31/2012. Assets, $2,378,746 (M); Expenditures, $76,530; Total giving, $0.

Type of support: Employee-related scholarships; Student loans—to individuals.
Application information: Applications accepted. Application form required.
Deadline(s): July
Additional information: Application must include transcripts and educational expenses.
Company names: Regions Bank; Atlantic Marine, Incorporated
EIN: 636020944

34
East Alabama Medical Center Foundation
2000 Pepperell Pkwy.
Opelika, AL 36801-5452 (334) 528-5868
Contact: Julia Pipes, Dir.
URL: http://www.eamcfoundation.org

Foundation type: Public charity
Purpose: Scholarship to a community student of east Alabama pursuing a career in the health care field.
Publications: Application guidelines; Newsletter.
Financial data: Year ended 09/30/2011. Assets, $10,057,590 (M); Expenditures, $697,134; Total giving, $241,149; Grants to individuals, totaling $23,437.
Fields of interest: Higher education; Health care.
Type of support: Scholarships—to individuals.
Application information: Applications accepted.
Additional information: Individuals are nominated by their school and are interviewed by the scholarship committee.
EIN: 630959617

35
Electric Cooperative Foundation Inc.
P.O. Box 244014
Montgomery, AL 36124-4014 (334) 215-2732
URL: http://www.areapower.coop/content.cfm?id=2022

Foundation type: Company-sponsored foundation
Purpose: Scholarships to individuals for postsecondary education who are dependents of members of an Alabama electric cooperative that has contributed principal funds to the foundation.
Publications: Grants list.
Financial data: Year ended 12/31/2011. Assets, $291,527 (M); Expenditures, $80,489; Total giving, $74,600; Grants to individuals, 42 grants totaling $74,600 (high: $10,000, low: $500).
Fields of interest: Higher education.
Type of support: Scholarships—to individuals.
Application information: Applications not accepted.
Additional information: Unsolicited requests for funds not considered or acknowledged.
EIN: 631190086

36
Zelia Stephans Evans Educational Trust
P.O. Box 2450
Montgomery, AL 36102-2450 (334) 230-6105
Application address: c/o Distribution Committee, Attn: Glenda Fr.

Foundation type: Independent foundation
Purpose: Scholarships to full-time students from AL who maintain a B average and a continuous course of study.
Financial data: Year ended 12/31/2012. Assets, $362,963 (M); Expenditures, $30,047; Total giving, $22,000; Grants to individuals, 11 grants totaling $22,000 (high: $2,000, low: $2,000).

Type of support: Scholarships—to individuals.
Application information: Applications accepted.
  Deadline(s): None
  Additional information: Application by essay describing previous experiences, plan of action, desired outcome and outside sources of income.
EIN: 636202940

37

Curtis Finlay Foundation Inc.
P.O. Box 298
Brewton, AL 36427-0298   (251) 867-7706
Contact: Richard D. Finlay, Dir.

Foundation type: Independent foundation
Purpose: Scholarships to residents of Escambia County, AL, and students attending Jefferson Davis Community College, Brewton, AL.
Financial data: Year ended 12/31/2012. Assets, $13,886,982 (M); Expenditures, $700,912; Total giving, $600,000; Grants to individuals, 8 grants totaling $30,000 (high: $4,000, low: $2,000).
Type of support: Support to graduates or students of specific schools; Undergraduate support.
Application information: Applications accepted. Application form not required.
  Deadline(s): None
  Additional information: Contact foundation for additional application guidelines.
EIN: 631080992

38

Blanche N. Fowler Charitable Trust
c/o Regions Bank, Trust Dept.
P.O. Box 2509
Tuscaloosa, AL 35403-2509   (205) 391-5730
Contact: Joann Jackson

Foundation type: Independent foundation
Purpose: Scholarships to students attending four-year colleges in AL.
Financial data: Year ended 12/31/2012. Assets, $347,896 (M); Expenditures, $16,282; Total giving, $8,425.
Type of support: Scholarships—to individuals.
Application information: Application form required.
  Deadline(s): Mar. 31
EIN: 636158965

39

Franklin Foundation
25676 Craft Rd.
Athens, AL 35613-7371   (256) 233-4284
Contact: Olen Britnell, Dir.

Foundation type: Operating foundation
Purpose: Grants and scholarships for religious purposes and human services.
Financial data: Year ended 12/31/2011. Assets, $121,189 (M); Expenditures, $18,645; Total giving, $17,263.
Fields of interest: Human services; Religion.
Type of support: Grants to individuals; Scholarships—to individuals.
Application information:
  Initial approach: Letter
  Deadline(s): None
EIN: 721400061

40

J. C. Freels Scholarship Trust
c/o Regions Bank Trust Department
P.O. Box 2886
Mobile, AL 36652-2886

Foundation type: Independent foundation
Purpose: Scholarships to graduates from Morristown, TN.
Financial data: Year ended 12/31/2012. Assets, $117,131 (M); Expenditures, $12,507; Total giving, $8,703.
Type of support: Support to graduates or students of specific schools; Undergraduate support.
Application information: Applications not accepted.
  Additional information: Unsolicited requests for funds not considered or acknowledged.
EIN: 626049363

41

E. L. Gibson Foundation
482 Oxford Way
Pelham, AL 35124   (205) 664-7885
Contact: Tim Alford, Secy.

Foundation type: Independent foundation
Purpose: Scholarships for health-related study to residents of Coffee County, AL, and bordering counties attending approved universities in AL.
Financial data: Year ended 12/31/2012. Assets, $3,323,693 (M); Expenditures, $155,616; Total giving, $81,198.
Fields of interest: Health sciences school/education.
Type of support: Scholarships—to individuals.
Application information: Applications accepted. Application form required.
  Initial approach: Letter
  Deadline(s): None
EIN: 630383929

42

Carl H. Grisham and Laura Estella Grisham Scholarship Foundation
5184 Caldwell Mill Rd., Ste. 204
P.O. Box 338
Birmingham, AL 35244-1913

Foundation type: Independent foundation
Purpose: Scholarships awarded to graduating Broward County, FL high school seniors with at least a 4.0 cumulative GPA for grade 9 through the first semester of grade 12.
Financial data: Year ended 12/31/2012. Assets, $3,161,044 (M); Expenditures, $224,757; Total giving, $110,000; Grants to individuals, 55 grants totaling $110,000 (high: $2,000, low: $2,000).
Fields of interest: Higher education.
Type of support: Undergraduate support.
Application information:
  Initial approach: Letter
  Deadline(s): Mar. 15
EIN: 203450384

43

Harry E. Griswold Scholarships Fund
(formerly Harry E. Griswold Trust)
c/o Regions Bank, N.A.
P.O. Box 2886
Mobile, AL 36652-2886

Foundation type: Independent foundation
Purpose: Scholarships to graduates of Blue Mound and Taylorville high schools, IL.

Financial data: Year ended 03/31/2013. Assets, $3,812,884 (M); Expenditures, $202,420; Total giving, $162,000.
Type of support: Support to graduates or students of specific schools; Undergraduate support.
Application information: Applications not accepted.
  Additional information: Unsolicited requests for funds not considered or acknowledged.
EIN: 376182916

44

Gulf Regional Childcare Management Agency, Inc.
(also known as GRCMA Early Childhood Directions)
3100 Cottage Hill Rd., Bldg. 4, Ste. 400
Mobile, AL 36606-2913   (251) 473-1060
FAX: (251) 450-3856; E-mail: info@grcma.org;
Additional tel. (from outside Mobile County): (800) 276-2134; URL: http://www.grcma.org

Foundation type: Public charity
Purpose: Financial assistance to daycare providers for special needs kids in the seven county region in the Mobile, AL area. Training for daycare providers and family home providers.
Financial data: Year ended 09/30/2011. Assets, $272,971 (M); Expenditures, $2,562,215; Total giving, $3,324; Grants to individuals, totaling $3,324.
Fields of interest: Day care; Family services, home/homemaker aid.
Type of support: Grants for special needs.
Application information: Funds are paid directly to the daycare providers.
EIN: 631056487

45

Hanna-Spivey Scholarship Fund
11505 US Hwy., Ste. 231
Rockford, AL 35136-5070

Foundation type: Independent foundation
Purpose: Scholarships to residents of Rockford, AL for attendance at accredited colleges or universities.
Financial data: Year ended 12/31/2012. Assets, $363,338 (M); Expenditures, $5,000; Total giving, $4,725; Grants to individuals, 3 grants totaling $4,725 (high: $1,575, low: $1,575).
Type of support: Undergraduate support.
Application information: Applications not accepted.
  Additional information: Unsolicited requests for funds not considered or acknowledged.
EIN: 631225355

46

Harbert Employees Reaching Out Foundation
(formerly Hero Foundation)
P.O. Box 1297
Birmingham, AL 35201-1297   (205) 987-5500
Contact: Liz Deuel, Pres.
FAX: (205) 987-5568; E-mail: skeeton@harbert.net;
URL: http://www.harbert.net/company/community-outreach/

Foundation type: Public charity
Purpose: Grants to needy individuals residing in AL to restore financial independence when there is hardship caused by natural disaster, medical condition or other temporary financial hardship.

Publications: Application guidelines; Financial statement; Newsletter.
Financial data: Year ended 12/31/2011. Assets, $918,759 (M); Expenditures, $750,833; Total giving, $748,400; Grants to individuals, totaling $720,884.
Type of support: Emergency funds.
Application information: Applications accepted. Application form required. Interview required.
  Initial approach: Letter
  Deadline(s): None
  Additional information: Application must include financial information for requests of more than $2,500.
EIN: 631202843

47
Harold L. Harmeson Trust

c/o Regions Bank, Trust Dept.
P.O. Box 2886
Mobile, AL 36652-2886 (765) 659-3305
Contact: Leslie Robison; Karen Rudolph; Allen Remaly; Aaron Hauenstein; Mona Heck
Application address: 2400 S. County Rd., 450 W. , Frankfort, IN 46041-7413, tel.: (765) 659-3305; 50 S. Maish Rd., Frankfort, IN 46041, tel.: (765) 654-5585; 1 Robert Egly Dr., Rossville, IN 46065, tel.: (765) 379-2551; P.O. Box 178, Michigantown, IN 46057, tel.: (765) 249-2255; 2405 Madison Ave., Indianapolis, IN 46225, tel.: (317) 226-2204

Foundation type: Independent foundation
Purpose: Scholarship awards to graduating seniors of Clinton Central Jr./Sr., Clinton Prairie Jr./Sr., Emmerich Manual, Community Schools of Frankfort, and Rossville Jr./Sr. high schools, IN, to attend Purdue University.
Financial data: Year ended 11/30/2012. Assets, $632,816 (M); Expenditures, $36,901; Total giving, $26,005.
Fields of interest: Higher education.
Type of support: Support to graduates or students of specific schools; Undergraduate support.
Application information:
  Initial approach: Letter
  Deadline(s): Vary
EIN: 356221524

48
Clyde W. Harrell Educational Fund

c/o Regions Bank Trust Dept.
P.O. Box 2886
Mobile, AL 36652-2886

Foundation type: Independent foundation
Purpose: Scholarships to graduates of public high schools in the upper end of Hawkins County, TN, to attend colleges and universities in TN.
Financial data: Year ended 02/28/2013. Assets, $62,026 (M); Expenditures, $9,360; Total giving, $4,000.
Fields of interest: Higher education.
Type of support: Support to graduates or students of specific schools; Undergraduate support.
Application information: Applications accepted.
  Deadline(s): Apr. 30
  Additional information: Scholarship recipients are chosen by their high school principal with final approval by the First American Trust Committee. Contact foundation for current application guidelines.
EIN: 626085008

49
Hawkins Educational Foundation

c/o Compass Bank, WMG- Tax Dept.
P. O. Box 10566
Birmingham, AL 35296-0002 (205) 297-6713
Contact: Patsy Alford, Grants Mgr.
E-mail: info@HawkinsScholarship.com;
URL: http://www.hawkinsscholarship.com

Foundation type: Independent foundation
Purpose: Scholarship to residents of Baldwin County, Alabama, with a minimum 2.0 GPA from high school pursuing a higher education.
Financial data: Year ended 07/31/2013. Assets, $4,048,608 (M); Expenditures, $236,334; Total giving, $157,500; Grants to individuals, 46 grants totaling $157,500 (high: $6,000, low: $1,700).
Fields of interest: Higher education.
Type of support: Scholarships—to individuals.
Application information: Applications accepted. Application form required. Interview required.
  Send request by: Mail
  Deadline(s): Jan. 31
  Final notification: Applicants notified Mar. 28
  Applicants should submit the following:
    1) Letter(s) of recommendation
    2) SAT
    3) ACT
    4) Transcripts
  Additional information: See web site for additional application guidelines.
EIN: 616320623

50
Laura Calfee Higdon Charitable Foundation

P.O. Box 469
Brewton, AL 36427-0469 (251) 867-3231

Foundation type: Independent foundation
Purpose: College scholarships to students of Escambia County, AL and Santa Rosa County, FL for higher education.
Financial data: Year ended 12/31/2011. Assets, $1,593,315 (M); Expenditures, $96,203; Total giving, $70,033; Grants to individuals, 109 grants totaling $63,628 (high: $2,000, low: -$260).
Fields of interest: Higher education.
Type of support: Undergraduate support.
Application information:
  Initial approach: Letter
  Additional information: Contact foundation for further application guidelines.
EIN: 636197968

51
C.V. Maybelle & John I Holland Scholarship Foundation for Tullahoma School System Grds.

(formerly C.V. Holland, Maybelle Holland, & John Holland Scholarship Fund)
c/o Regions Bank, N.A., Trust Dept.
P.O. Box 2886
Mobile, AL 36652-2886
Contact: Harry Brittain
Application address: P. O. Box 70, Tullahoma, TN 37388

Foundation type: Independent foundation
Purpose: Scholarships to graduating high school seniors at Tullahoma High School, TN pursuing postsecondary education.
Financial data: Year ended 05/31/2013. Assets, $446,056 (M); Expenditures, $31,260; Total giving, $26,000.
Fields of interest: Higher education.

Type of support: Support to graduates or students of specific schools; Undergraduate support.
Application information: Applications accepted. Application form required.
  Deadline(s): Mar. 31
  Additional information: Students should contact their high school guidance counselor for application information. Payments are made directly to the educational institution on behalf of the students.
EIN: 626141452

52
Infirmary Foundation, Inc.

P.O. Box 2226
Mobile, AL 36652-2226 (251) 435-4447
Contact: D. Mark Nix, Pres.
E-mail scholarship: Robby McClure, robby.mcclure@infirmaryheath.org, tel.: (251) 435-4447
E-mail: foundationevents@infirmaryhealth.org;
URL: http://www.infirmaryhealth.org/foundations/infirmary

Foundation type: Public charity
Purpose: Scholarships for area nursing students and continuing education for health care professionals in southwest AL.
Financial data: Year ended 03/31/2012. Assets, $32,292,148 (M); Expenditures, $3,417,447; Total giving, $3,207,101; Grants to individuals, totaling $265,280.
Fields of interest: Nursing school/education; Health sciences school/education.
Type of support: Scholarships—to individuals.
Application information: Applications accepted.
  Additional information: Contact the foundation for additional information.
EIN: 630870620

53
Internal Medicine Associates Scholarship Fund, Inc.

121 N. 20th St.
Opelika, AL 36801 (334) 749-3385
Contact: W. Park McGehee, Chair.

Foundation type: Independent foundation
Purpose: Scholarships to AL graduating seniors pursuing a health career of any type.
Financial data: Year ended 12/31/2011. Assets, $168,004 (M); Expenditures, $24,677; Total giving, $24,130; Grants to individuals, 14 grants totaling $24,130 (high: $5,969, low: $100).
Fields of interest: Health sciences school/education.
Type of support: Undergraduate support.
Application information: Applications accepted.
  Initial approach: Letter
  Deadline(s): None
  Additional information: Application should include ACT scores. Contact organization for application guidelines.
EIN: 570884128

54
International Retinal Research Foundation, Inc.

1720 University Blvd., Ste. 124
Birmingham, AL 35233-1816 (205) 325-8103
Contact: Sandra Blackwood, Exec. Dir.
FAX: (205) 325-8394;
E-mail: sblackwood@irrfonline.org; URL: http://www.IRRFonline.org

Foundation type: Independent foundation
Purpose: Grants to support research on the diseases of the human eye, especially the macula. Specific consideration will be given to those scientists who are actively working toward discovering the causes, preventions, and cures of macular degeneration and diabetic retinopathy.
Publications: Application guidelines; Grants list; Informational brochure; Newsletter.
Financial data: Year ended 12/31/2012. Assets, $29,225,702 (M); Expenditures, $1,809,687; Total giving, $1,515,656.
Fields of interest: Eye research.
Type of support: Research.
Application information: Application form required. Application form available on the grantmaker's web site.
> Initial approach: Application form on foundation web site
> Copies of proposal: 6
> Deadline(s): Mar. 1
> Applicants should submit the following:
>> 1) Letter(s) of recommendation
>> 2) Proposal
>> 3) Curriculum vitae
>> 4) Budget Information
> Additional information: E-mail applications are not accepted.
EIN: 721342841

55
J. A. & Ophelia Killgore Scholarship Trust Fund
c/o Regions Bank, Trust Dept.
P.O. Box 2886
Mobile, AL 36652-2886

Foundation type: Independent foundation
Purpose: Scholarships to graduating high school seniors from Lee County, AL pursuing postsecondary education at a college or university of their choice.
Financial data: Year ended 09/30/2012. Assets, $2,943,555 (M); Expenditures, $109,157; Total giving, $97,750; Grants to individuals, 79 grants totaling $97,750 (high: $1,500, low: $500).
Fields of interest: Higher education.
Type of support: Support to graduates or students of specific schools; Undergraduate support.
Application information: Applications accepted. Application form required.
> Deadline(s): None
> Additional information: Students are chosen based on their academic achievements. Application should include GPA.
EIN: 636055718

56
John R. Lucash Charitable Private Foundation Trust
(formerly John R. Lucash Scholarship Trust)
c/o Regions Bank, Trust Dept.
P.O. Box 2886
Mobile, AL 36652-2886 (618) 539-5533

Foundation type: Operating foundation
Purpose: Scholarships to graduates of Freeburg High School, IL.
Financial data: Year ended 12/31/2012. Assets, $1,052,968 (M); Expenditures, $67,546; Total giving, $49,000; Grants to individuals, 100 grants totaling $49,000 (high: $490, low: $490).
Fields of interest: Scholarships/financial aid.
Type of support: Scholarships—to individuals; Support to graduates or students of specific schools.

Application information: Applications accepted. Application form required.
> Deadline(s): Dec. 1
EIN: 376342883

57
Macon-Russell Community Action Agency, Inc.
102 Lakeview Rd.
Tuskegee, AL 36083-1964 (334) 727-6100
Contact: James M. Upshaw, Jr., Exec. Dir.

Foundation type: Public charity
Purpose: Services to indigent residents of the Tuskegee, AL area. Examples include home energy assistance, transportation, and emergency food and housing.
Financial data: Year ended 10/31/2011. Assets, $240,306 (M); Expenditures, $2,047,521; Total giving, $1,425,270; Grants to individuals, totaling $1,425,270.
Fields of interest: Economically disadvantaged.
Type of support: In-kind gifts.
Application information:
> Initial approach: Letter
> Additional information: Contact foundation for eligibility criteria.
EIN: 636054092

58
Marshall-Jackson Mental Retardation Authority, Inc.
2024 Gunter Ave.
Guntersville, AL 35976-2113

Foundation type: Public charity
Purpose: Services for individuals in the Guntersville, AL area with mental retardation and their families.
Financial data: Year ended 09/30/2011. Assets, $950,708 (M); Expenditures, $8,513,359; Total giving, $7,619,368; Grants to individuals, totaling $7,619,368.
Fields of interest: Mentally disabled.
Type of support: In-kind gifts.
Application information:
> Initial approach: Letter
> Additional information: Contact foundation for eligibility guidelines.
EIN: 631033473

59
Dewey & Louise Martin Scholarship Fund
c/o Regions Bank Trust Dept.
P.O. Box 2886
Mobile, AL 36652-2886 (615) 748-2008
Contact: Carl Esterhay
Application address: Regions Bank, Attn: Joseph Chickey, 315 Deadrick St., 5th Fl., Nashville, TN 37237

Foundation type: Independent foundation
Purpose: Scholarships to Trousdale county students attending Volunteer State Community College at Gallatin, TN.
Financial data: Year ended 12/31/2012. Assets, $618,161 (M); Expenditures, $49,088; Total giving, $37,025.
Fields of interest: Higher education.
Type of support: Scholarships—to individuals; Support to graduates or students of specific schools.

Application information: Applications accepted. Application form required.
> Deadline(s): None
> Additional information: Application can be obtained at Trousdale county high school.
EIN: 621721707

60
The Charles G. & Alice R. Mayson Scholarship Grant Fund
P.O. Box 27
Atmore, AL 36504 (251) 368-0445

Foundation type: Operating foundation
Purpose: Scholarships by nomination only to students at three local area high schools in Altmore, AL.
Financial data: Year ended 12/31/2011. Assets, $865,972 (M); Expenditures, $50,223; Total giving, $38,424; Grants to individuals, 12 grants totaling $38,424 (high: $3,202, low: $3,202).
Fields of interest: Higher education; Scholarships/ financial aid.
Type of support: Awards/grants by nomination only; Undergraduate support.
Application information: Applications accepted.
> Deadline(s): None
> Applicants should submit the following:
>> 1) Class rank
>> 2) Letter(s) of recommendation
>> 3) GPA
>> 4) ACT
> Additional information: Recipients are nominated by high schools representatives.
EIN: 636161467

61
Lena Y. Meharg Scholarship Trust
c/o Regions Bank Trust Dept.
P.O. Box 2886
Mobile, AL 36652-2886 (205) 326-5713
Contact: Kenny Burns
Application address: P.O. Box 10885, Birmingham, AL 35282

Foundation type: Independent foundation
Purpose: Scholarships for higher education to financially needy young women of the First Presbyterian Church of Anniston, AL, and individuals in the Presbyterian Home for Children at Talladega, AL.
Financial data: Year ended 08/31/2013. Assets, $332,890 (M); Expenditures, $23,502; Total giving, $15,183; Grants to individuals, 19 grants totaling $15,183 (high: $1,299, low: $102).
Fields of interest: Children/youth, services; Christian agencies & churches; Women.
Type of support: Scholarships—to individuals.
Application information: Applications accepted.
> Deadline(s): Mar. 31
EIN: 636017711

62
Kate Kinloch Middleton Fund
c/o Regions Bank
P.O. Box 1628
Mobile, AL 36633-1628 (251) 438-9597
Contact: Betty Thornton
Application address: 1507 Regions Bank Bldg., Mobile, AL 36602

Foundation type: Independent foundation
Purpose: Grants to financially needy residents of Mobile County, AL, to help cover the cost of medical expenses.

Financial data: Year ended 01/31/2013. Assets, $2,719,506 (M); Expenditures, $161,546; Total giving, $100,896; Grants to individuals, 15 grants totaling $100,896 (high: $18,085, low: $540).
Fields of interest: Health care.
Type of support: Grants for special needs.
Application information: Applications accepted. Application form required. Interview required.
  Deadline(s): None
  Additional information: Application should include copies of medical bills and proof of income and expenses.
EIN: 636018539

63
The Miss Alabama Pageant, Inc.
2809 Crescent Ave., Ste. 2
Birmingham, AL 35209-2526 (205) 871-6276
URL: http://www.missalabama.com

Foundation type: Public charity
Purpose: Scholarships to participants in the Miss Alabama pageant.
Financial data: Year ended 11/30/2011. Assets, $557,853 (M); Expenditures, $4,628,120; Total giving, $4,417,662; Grants to individuals, totaling $4,417,662.
Fields of interest: Women.
Type of support: Undergraduate support.
Application information:
  Initial approach: Letter
  Additional information: Contact foundation for complete eligibility requirements.
EIN: 640810076

64
Cecile Moeschle Scholarship Fund
c/o Regions Bank, Bill Newburn, Trust Office
P.O. Box 2886
Mobile, AL 36652-2886
Application addresses: c/o Longview High School, Attn.: Counselor, 201 E. Tomlinson Pkwy., Longview, TX 75604, tel.: (903) 663-1301; c/o Pine Tree High School, Attn.: Counselor, 1005 W. Fairmont St., Longview, TX 75604-3511, tel.: (903) 295-5000

Foundation type: Independent foundation
Purpose: Scholarships to graduates of Longview High School, and Pine Tree High School, both in TX, for attendance at any TX college, university, or community college.
Financial data: Year ended 12/31/2012. Assets, $187,995 (M); Expenditures, $9,102; Total giving, $5,500.
Fields of interest: Higher education.
Type of support: Support to graduates or students of specific schools; Undergraduate support.
Application information: Applications accepted. Application form required.
  Deadline(s): Apr. 1
  Additional information: Applications are available at participating high schools.
EIN: 756349280

65
Montgomery Area Food Bank, Inc.
521 Trade Ctr. St.
Montgomery, AL 36108-2107 (334) 263-3784
FAX: (334) 262-6854;
E-mail: pphinman@earthlink.net; Toll-free tel.: (800) 768-3784; URL: http:// www.montgomeryareafoodbank.org

Foundation type: Public charity

Purpose: Assistance to low-income county residents of south-central AL with food, clothing, shelter, and other services.
Financial data: Year ended 06/30/2012. Assets, $5,142,493 (M); Expenditures, $26,546,091; Total giving, $23,793,714; Grants to individuals, totaling $23,793,714.
Fields of interest: Food banks; Human services.
Type of support: Grants for special needs.
Application information: Applications not accepted.
  Additional information: Contact the organization for assistance.
EIN: 630931846

66
Omega Men of North Alabama, Inc.
P.O. Box 3622
Huntsville, AL 35810-0622 (256) 859-3766
Contact: Houston A. Yarbrough, Treas.
E-mail: themajor@aol.com; Tel./fax: (256) 837-6516; additional tel.: (256) 508-9518

Foundation type: Public charity
Purpose: Scholarships primarily to individuals in AL.
Publications: Annual report; Financial statement.
Financial data: Year ended 12/31/2011. Assets, $420,725 (M); Expenditures, $36,881; Total giving, $4,750; Grants to individuals, totaling $4,000.
Type of support: Scholarships—to individuals; Undergraduate support.
Application information:
  Initial approach: Letter
  Send request by: Mail
  Copies of proposal: 1
  Deadline(s): None
  Final notification: Applicants notified in 30 days
  Applicants should submit the following:
    1) Curriculum vitae
    2) Essay
    3) Financial information
    4) Photograph
    5) Work samples
    6) Transcripts
    7) SAT
    8) Letter(s) of recommendation
    9) GPA
    10) Budget Information
    11) ACT
EIN: 631125716

67
Elizabeth Anne Owens Foundation
P.O. Box 1229
Brewton, AL 36427

Foundation type: Independent foundation
Purpose: Scholarships to residents of Escambia County, AL, students at Jefferson Davis Community College, the University of Alabama, or Auburn University, or women who are attending or are graduates of Westover School, Middlebury, CT, for higher education.
Financial data: Year ended 12/31/2012. Assets, $503,610 (M); Expenditures, $26,805; Total giving, $22,716; Grants to individuals, 10 grants totaling $21,716 (high: $3,000, low: $1,500).
Fields of interest: Higher education; Women.
Type of support: Support to graduates or students of specific schools; Graduate support; Undergraduate support; Postgraduate support.
Application information: Application form required.
  Initial approach: Letter
  Send request by: Mail
  Applicants should submit the following:

1) Letter(s) of recommendation
2) Transcripts
3) SAT
4) ACT
EIN: 631058213

68
Lou & Lillian Padolf Foundation
c/o Regions Bank Trust Dept.
P.O. Box 2886
Mobile, AL 36652-2886 (813) 639-3415
Contact: Jeffrey Cowley
Application address: P.O. Box 2918, Clearwater, FL 33757-2918 tel.: (813) 639-3415

Foundation type: Independent foundation
Purpose: Undergraduate scholarships to graduates of Pinellas County, FL who are residents of mid-Pinellas County, north of Walshingham Rd. and south of Klosterman Rd., to attend college or university within the state of FL.
Financial data: Year ended 12/31/2011. Assets, $762,444 (M); Expenditures, $36,587; Total giving, $25,000; Grants to individuals, 7 grants totaling $25,000 (high: $7,500, low: $1,250).
Fields of interest: Higher education.
Type of support: Scholarships—to individuals; Support to graduates or students of specific schools; Undergraduate support.
Application information: Application form required.
  Initial approach: Letter
  Deadline(s): May 1
  Applicants should submit the following:
    1) Letter(s) of recommendation
    2) Transcripts
    3) Financial information
Program description:
  Lou & Lillian Padolf Scholarship: Scholarships range in the amount of $500 to $1,500 to attend a two or four year accredited college or university within the state of Florida. Applicants must be from a Pinellas County High School in the top 25 percent of their graduating class. Applicants are evaluated based on financial need, academic promise, character and leadership qualities. Awards are for undergraduate work only and are renewable at the discretion of the awarding committee for up to four years.
EIN: 596190737

69
Parker Family Foundation
c/o Regions Bank
P.O. Box 11647
Birmingham, AL 35202-1647 (334) 738-5135
Contact: Jenks C. Parker, Dir.
Application address: 5700 Peachburg Rd., Union Springs, AL 36089

Foundation type: Operating foundation
Purpose: Scholarship to financially needy students who are residents of Bullock County, AL, and will return after postsecondary education to teach in the Bullock County, school system.
Financial data: Year ended 12/31/2012. Assets, $2,321,718 (M); Expenditures, $112,126; Total giving, $103,855; Grants to individuals, totaling $103,855.
Fields of interest: Higher education.
Type of support: Undergraduate support.
Application information: Applications accepted. Application form required.
  Initial approach: Letter
  Deadline(s): Varies
  Applicants should submit the following:
    1) Transcripts

2) Resume
3) Class rank
4) GPA
5) ACT
Additional information: Application should also include two references, extracurricular activities, academic achievements honors and goals.
EIN: 721358823

70
Portraits, Inc. Scholarship Foundation
(formerly Portraits, Inc., Scholarship Foundation)
P.O. Box 131384
Birmingham, AL   35213-6384   (205) 879-1222

Foundation type: Company-sponsored foundation
Purpose: Scholarships to children and grandchildren of artists affiliated with Portrait Brokers of America, Inc., or to children and grandchildren of non-affiliated artists.
Financial data: Year ended 12/31/2012. Assets, $2,141 (M); Expenditures, $7,753; Total giving, $7,000; Grants to individuals, 9 grants totaling $7,000 (high: $1,000, low: $500).
Fields of interest: Higher education.
Type of support: Undergraduate support.
Application information: Application form required.
Initial approach: Letter
Deadline(s): Mar. 15
Applicants should submit the following:
1) Class rank
2) SAT
3) GPA
4) ACT
5) Transcripts
6) Letter(s) of recommendation
EIN: 631241622

71
V. I. Prewett, Jr. Educational Foundation
c/o Julie Morgan
592 Co. Rd., Ste. 284
Fort Payne, AL   35967   (256) 845-5806
Contact: Vicki L. Prewett, Board Member

Foundation type: Independent foundation
Purpose: Scholarships to individuals or dependents of individuals associated with the hosiery industry in DeKalb County, AL, pursuing higher education.
Financial data: Year ended 10/28/2011. Assets, $0 (M); Expenditures, $25,312; Total giving, $24,289; Grants to individuals, 13 grants totaling $24,289 (high: $5,767, low: $510).
Type of support: Undergraduate support.
Application information: Applications accepted. Application form required.
Deadline(s): June 15
EIN: 721350711

72
Protective Life Foundation
P.O. Box 2606
Birmingham, AL   35202-2606   (205) 268-4434
Contact: Kate H. Cotton, Exec. Dir.
FAX: (205) 268-5547;
E-mail: kate.cotton@protective.com; URL: http://www.protective.com/giving-back.aspx

Foundation type: Company-sponsored foundation
Purpose: Scholarships to children of employees of Protective Life Entities.
Publications: Application guidelines; Annual report.
Financial data: Year ended 12/31/2011. Assets, $98,517 (M); Expenditures, $2,605,702; Total

giving, $2,501,148; Grants to individuals, 44 grants totaling $67,579 (high: $2,500).
Type of support: Employee-related scholarships.
Application information: Applications not accepted.
Additional information: Unsolicited requests for funds not considered or acknowledged.
Program description:
Scholarship and Academic Award Program: The foundation awards college scholarships to children of employees of Protective Life who have excelled in academics and/or civic service.
Company name: Protective Life Corporation
EIN: 631129596

73
Joanna F. Reed Medical Scholarship Trust
c/o BankTrust Co.
P.O. Box 469
Brewton, AL   36427-0469   (251) 867-3231

Foundation type: Independent foundation
Purpose: Medical school scholarships to residents of AL or northwest FL, who will attend a private university. Northwest FL is defined as all counties west of the Apalachicola River.
Financial data: Year ended 12/31/2012. Assets, $355,411 (M); Expenditures, $21,000; Total giving, $16,370; Grants to individuals, 3 grants totaling $16,370 (high: $6,500, low: $4,935).
Fields of interest: Medical school/education.
Type of support: Graduate support.
Application information: Application form required.
Deadline(s): May 15
Applicants should submit the following:
1) Transcripts
2) Letter(s) of recommendation
Additional information: Application should also include MCAT scores.
EIN: 630805093

74
Regional Cultural Alliance of Greater Birmingham, Inc.
1731 1st Ave. N., Ste. 190
Birmingham, AL   35203-2055   (205) 458-1393
Contact: Buddy Palmer, Pres. and C.E.O.
FAX: (205) 458-1396;
E-mail: bpalmer@cultural-alliance.com; E-mail for Melissa Schoel: mschoel@cultural-alliance.com; E-mail for grant information: grants@cultural-alliance.com; URL: http://www.cultural-alliance.com

Foundation type: Public charity
Purpose: Grants to individual artists to develop, sustain, promote, and expand arts and cultural activities in Central Alabama.
Publications: Application guidelines.
Financial data: Year ended 12/31/2011. Assets, $305,175 (M); Expenditures, $414,992; Total giving, $72,010. Grants to individuals amount not specified.
Fields of interest: Arts.
Type of support: Grants to individuals.
Application information: Applications accepted.
Initial approach: Telephone or e-mail
Additional information: See web site for additional information.
EIN: 841631034

75
S. M. and Jessie Dell Reynolds Scholarship Trust
2728 Fairmont Rd.
Montgomery, AL   36111-2811   (334) 566-1850
Contact: Myrtle P. Ridolphi, Tr.
tel.: (334) 566-1850

Foundation type: Independent foundation
Purpose: Scholarships to high school graduates in the metropolitan area city of Montgomery, AL.
Financial data: Year ended 12/31/2011. Assets, $55,038 (M); Expenditures, $4,675; Total giving, $3,000; Grants to individuals, 3 grants totaling $3,000 (high: $1,000, low: $1,000).
Fields of interest: Higher education.
Type of support: Scholarships—to individuals.
Application information: Applications accepted.
Initial approach: Letter
Deadline(s): June 15
Additional information: Application should include transcript of grades and list of activities.
EIN: 635841040

76
Riverbend Foundation
635 W. College St.
Florence, AL   35630-5313   (256) 764-3431

Foundation type: Public charity
Purpose: Financial assistance for educational expenses provided to students in the Florence, AL area enrolled in mental health fields of study.
Financial data: Year ended 09/30/2012. Assets, $2,870,926 (M); Expenditures, $73,955; Total giving, $47,300; Grants to individuals, totaling $10,500.
Fields of interest: Mental health/crisis services.
Type of support: Scholarships—to individuals.
Application information: Contact the foundation for additional guidelines.
EIN: 630819544

77
Benjamin & Roberta Russell Foundation, Inc.
(formerly Benjamin and Roberta Russell Educational and Charitable Foundation, Inc.)
P.O. Box 369
Alexander City, AL   35011-0369
Contact: James D. Nabors, Secy.-Treas.

Foundation type: Independent foundation
Purpose: Scholarships to residents of Tallapoosa and Coosa counties in AL for higher education.
Financial data: Year ended 12/31/2012. Assets, $13,188,957 (M); Expenditures, $706,823; Total giving, $586,778; Grants to individuals, totaling $142,778.
Fields of interest: Higher education.
Type of support: Scholarships—to individuals.
Application information: Contact the foundation for additional information.
EIN: 630393126

78
Sheffield Education Foundation
300 W. 6th St.
Sheffield, AL   35660-2802   (256) 383-0400
FAX: (256) 386-5704; URL: http://www.scs.k12.al.us/?DivisionID=4772

Foundation type: Public charity

Purpose: College scholarships to graduating seniors of Sheffield High School, AL for continuing education at institutions of higher learning. Mini grants for teachers of the Sheffield City School District for classroom supplies.
Financial data: Year ended 09/30/2011. Assets, $365,055 (M); Expenditures, $38,303; Total giving, $21,916; Grants to individuals, totaling $21,916.
Fields of interest: Education.
Type of support: Grants to individuals; Support to graduates or students of specific schools.
Application information: Applications accepted.
   Additional information: Selection criteria for scholarship is based on monetary need, access to other scholarship monies, character attributes and potential for success.
EIN: 570899633

79
The Simpson Foundation
P.O. Box 240548
Montgomery, AL   36124-0548   (334) 386-2516
FAX: (334) 386-2521; URL: http://
thesimpsonfoundation.org/

Foundation type: Independent foundation
Purpose: Scholarships to high school students of Wilcox County, AL.
Financial data: Year ended 04/30/2013. Assets, $6,439,713 (M); Expenditures, $356,406; Total giving, $199,200.
Fields of interest: Higher education.
Type of support: Scholarships—to individuals; Support to graduates or students of specific schools.
Application information: Application form required. Interview required.
   Deadline(s): Jan. 1 to Mar. 31.
   Applicants should submit the following:
      1) Transcripts
      2) Letter(s) of recommendation
EIN: 630925496

80
J. Craig and Page T. Smith Scholarship Foundation, Inc.
400 Caldwell Trace Park
Indian Springs, AL   35242   (205) 202-4076
Contact: Ahrian Tyler Dudley, C.E.O.

Foundation type: Operating foundation
Purpose: Scholarships to AL residents who attend college or university in AL, with preference given to students who would be the first in their family to attend college.
Financial data: Year ended 12/31/2012. Assets, $30,545,848 (M); Expenditures, $1,281,428; Total giving, $573,587; Grants to individuals, totaling $573,587.
Fields of interest: Higher education.
Type of support: Undergraduate support.
Application information: Applications accepted. Application form required. Application form available on the grantmaker's web site.
   Initial approach: Letter
   Deadline(s): Jan. 15
   Final notification: Recipients announced late Apr.
   Applicants should submit the following:
      1) Transcripts
      2) Letter(s) of recommendation
EIN: 202224138

81
Southeastern Conference
2201 Richard Arrington Jr., Blvd. N.
Birmingham, AL   35203-1103   (205) 458-3000
URL: http://www.secdigitalnetwork.com/
SECSports/Home.aspx

Foundation type: Public charity
Purpose: Postgraduate scholarships to outstanding student athletes who excel academically and athletically. Grants and fellowships for ethnic minorities and women.
Financial data: Year ended 08/31/2012. Assets, $46,336,049 (M); Expenditures, $270,552,040; Total giving, $4,051,576; Grants to individuals, 197 grants totaling $404,914. Subtotal for scholarships—to individuals: 28 grants totaling $164,000. Subtotal for grants to individuals: 169 grants totaling $240,914.
Fields of interest: Scholarships/financial aid; Recreation; Minorities; Women.
Type of support: Grants to individuals; Scholarships—to individuals; Postgraduate support.
Application information: Applications not accepted.
   Additional information: Unsolicited requests for funds not considered or acknowledged.
EIN: 630377461

82
Southern Phenix Textiles Scholarship Fund Inc.
P.O. Box 1108
Phenix City, AL   36868   (334) 664-3367
Contact: Ronnie Brooks, Secy.-Treas.

Foundation type: Company-sponsored foundation
Purpose: Scholarships to children of Johnston Textiles, Inc., employees residing in Phenix City, AL and surrounding communities for undergraduate education.
Financial data: Year ended 06/30/2012. Assets, $3,671 (M); Expenditures, $4,500; Total giving, $4,000; Grants to individuals, totaling $4,000.
Fields of interest: Higher education.
Type of support: Employee-related scholarships.
Application information: Applications not accepted.
   Additional information: Unsolicited requests for funds not considered or acknowledged.
Company name: Johnston Textiles, Inc.
EIN: 631018039

83
TAV Foundation
P.O. Box 952
Daphne, AL   36526-0952   (251) 990-8872
Contact: Harriet Outlaw, Secy.
Application address: 8872 County Rd. Ste. 34 , Fairhope, AL. 36532 tel.:(251) 990-8872

Foundation type: Independent foundation
Purpose: Scholarships to graduates of public and private high schools in Baldwin County, AL.
Financial data: Year ended 12/31/2012. Assets, $1,501,089 (M); Expenditures, $73,912; Total giving, $55,000; Grants to individuals, 28 grants totaling $55,000 (high: $2,000, low: $1,000).
Type of support: Support to graduates or students of specific schools; Undergraduate support.
Application information: Application form required.
   Initial approach: Letter
   Deadline(s): Mar. 15
   Applicants should submit the following:
      1) Letter(s) of recommendation

      2) GPA
      3) Financial information
      4) ACT
   Additional information: Application must also include a personal statement.
EIN: 630919414

84
Robert H. Todd Scholarship Fund
c/o Regions Bank
P.O. Box 11647
Birmingham, AL   35202-1647

Foundation type: Independent foundation
Purpose: Scholarships to students from Anniston, AL who have no financial means to attend college.
Financial data: Year ended 12/31/2010. Assets, $140,936 (M); Expenditures, $7,655; Total giving, $5,100; Grants to individuals, 4 grants totaling $5,100 (high: $1,275, low: $1,275).
Type of support: Undergraduate support.
Application information: Applications not accepted.
   Additional information: Students are selected by the trustee and a committee. Unsolicited requests for funds not considered or acknowledged.
EIN: 636069304

85
The Tractor and Equipment Company Foundation
5336 Airport Hwy.
Birmingham, AL   35212-1599   (205) 591-2131
Contact: Lloyd Adams, Secy.-Treas.

Foundation type: Company-sponsored foundation
Purpose: Scholarships only to children of Tractor & Equipment Company, Inc. employees residing in AL to attend accredited institutions of higher education.
Financial data: Year ended 12/31/2012. Assets, $18,493 (M); Expenditures, $112,056; Total giving, $111,026.
Fields of interest: Higher education.
Type of support: Employee-related scholarships.
Application information: Application form required.
   Deadline(s): Mar. 1
   Additional information: Applications from individuals who are not within the stated recipient restriction are not accepted. Scholarship application address: c/o James W. Waitzman, Jr., Pres., Tractor & Equipment Co., Inc., P.O. Box 12326, Birmingham, AL 35201.
EIN: 630718825

86
United Way of Central Alabama, Inc.
(formerly The Birmingham Community Chest)
3600 8th Ave. S.
P.O. Box 320189
Birmingham, AL   35232-0189   (205) 251-5131
Contact: Drew Langloh, Pres. and C.E.O.
FAX: (205) 323-8730; E-mail: info@uwca.org;
URL: http://www.uwca.org

Foundation type: Public charity
Purpose: Financial assistance to individuals and families of central AL, with basic needs.
Publications: Annual report.
Financial data: Year ended 12/31/2011. Assets, $90,981,061 (M); Expenditures, $54,634,640; Total giving, $31,378,249; Grants to individuals, 169 grants totaling $152,776.

Fields of interest: Human services; Economically disadvantaged.
Type of support: Grants for special needs.
Application information: Applications accepted.
   Additional information: Payments are made directly to the vendors providing the needed service.
EIN: 630288846

87
Austin L. and Nell S. Venable Educational Trust

c/o Regions Bank
P.O. Box 2450
Montgomery, AL   36102-2450   (334) 230-6171
Contact: Henry E. Moore

Foundation type: Independent foundation
Purpose: Scholarships to individuals who are at least second-generation natives of Elmore County, AL, and who are in the top 25 percent of their high school graduating class.
Financial data: Year ended 06/30/2012. Assets, $587,078 (M); Expenditures, $46,851; Total giving, $33,800; Grants to individuals, totaling $33,800.
Fields of interest: Higher education.
Type of support: Undergraduate support.
Application information: Applications accepted. Application form required.
   Deadline(s): Jan. 1 and Mar. 1
   Additional information: Application forms available from Elmore County, AL, high schools.
EIN: 636158945

88
Vulcan Scholarships, Inc.

P.O. Box 1850
Foley, AL   36536-1850   (251) 943-2645
Contact: Thomas M. Lee, Secy.-Treas.
URL: http://www.vulcaninc.com

Foundation type: Company-sponsored foundation
Purpose: Scholarships to students of Foley High School, Gulf Shores High School and Robertsdale High School, in Baldwin county AL, for study in engineering.
Financial data: Year ended 10/31/2012. Assets, $333,488 (M); Expenditures, $15,702; Total giving, $15,600; Grants to individuals, 12 grants totaling $15,600 (high: $2,100, low: $750).
Fields of interest: Engineering school/education.
Type of support: Support to graduates or students of specific schools; Undergraduate support.
Application information: Application form required.
   Deadline(s): Mid-Feb.
   Applicants should submit the following:
   1) Transcripts
   2) SAT
   3) GPA
   4) ACT
   Additional information: Applicant must demonstrate financial need. Application can be obtained from faculty members at any of the three high schools. Scholarship payments are made directly to the educational institution on behalf of the student.
EIN: 630887786

89
Allyrae Wallace Educational Trust

P.O. Box 433
Camden, AL   36726-0433   (334) 682-4155
Contact: Haas Strother, Tr.

Foundation type: Independent foundation
Purpose: Scholarships for Wilcox County, AL residents to attend college or vocational schools.
Financial data: Year ended 12/31/2012. Assets, $5,973,485 (M); Expenditures, $516,973; Total giving, $390,731; Grants to individuals, totaling $390,731.
Fields of interest: Higher education.
Type of support: Technical education support; Undergraduate support.
Application information: Applications accepted. Application form required.
   Initial approach: Letter
   Deadline(s): Feb. 1
   Additional information: Application should include transcripts.
EIN: 636192432

90
WEDC Foundation, Inc.

(also known as Women's Economic Development Council Foundation)
185 Chateau Dr., Ste. 200-A
Huntsville, AL   35801-7424   (256) 429-4718
E-mail: info@wedcfoundation.org; Mailing address: P.O. Box 4761, Huntsville, AL 35815-4761;
URL: http://wedcfoundation.org/

Foundation type: Public charity
Purpose: Scholarships to economically disadvantaged women residing in Madison, Marshall, Morgan and/or Limestone County, AL.
Publications: Application guidelines.
Financial data: Year ended 09/30/2012. Assets, $430,122 (M); Expenditures, $79,022.
Fields of interest: Women; Economically disadvantaged.
Type of support: Undergraduate support.
Application information: Applications accepted. Application form required. Interview required.
   Initial approach: Letter
   Deadline(s): Varies
   Applicants should submit the following:
   1) Transcripts
   2) Resume
   Additional information: Application should also include two letters of reference.
Program description:
   Scholarships: Scholarships ranging from $500 to $2,500 are available to adult women seeking an academic degree or technical training in order to achieve significant advancement in their current employment. Applicants must have a minimum high school diploma or GED, and must be a resident of Madison County, Alabama, with special consideration going to those with a household income of $32,000 or less and/or who are responsible for dependent care.
EIN: 631207448

91
John M. Will Journalism Scholarship Foundation

c/o Regions Bank Trust Dept.
P.O. Box 2886
Mobile, AL   36652-2886   (251) 432-6751
Contact: Brandon Hughey
Application address: P.O. Box 290, Mobile, AL 36601

Foundation type: Independent foundation
Purpose: Scholarships to students pursuing a career in journalism who attend schools in Mobile, AL and the surrounding areas.
Financial data: Year ended 12/31/2012. Assets, $164,095 (M); Expenditures, $15,732; Total giving, $12,900; Grants to individuals, 8 grants totaling $12,900 (high: $4,500, low: $500).
Fields of interest: Journalism school/education.
Type of support: Scholarships—to individuals.
Application information: Application form required.
   Additional information: Contact the school guidance office for application deadlines.
EIN: 636053159

92
Winston-Marion Counties Association for Retarded Citizens, Inc.

145 County Hwy. 176
Haleyville, AL   35565-3602   (205) 486-2178

Foundation type: Public charity
Purpose: Grants to mentally disabled individuals, primarily in AL.
Financial data: Year ended 09/30/2011. Assets, $367,643 (M); Expenditures, $708,128.
Fields of interest: Mentally disabled.
Type of support: Grants to individuals.
Application information:
   Initial approach: Letter
   Additional information: Contact foundation for current application guidelines.
EIN: 237352161

93
The Woerner Foundation for World Missions, Inc.

(formerly The Woerner Foundation)
P.O. Box 820
Foley, AL   36536-0820

Foundation type: Operating foundation
Purpose: Financial assistance to Christian missionaries, primarily in AL.
Financial data: Year ended 06/30/2012. Assets, $14,103 (M); Expenditures, $5,600; Total giving, $5,600.
Fields of interest: Christian agencies & churches.
Type of support: Grants to individuals.
Application information: Applications not accepted.
   Additional information: Unsolicited requests for funds not considered or acknowledged.
EIN: 650687118

94
The O. G. Wollman, Dorothy Armstrong Wollman and Ella Armstrong Scholarship Fund

c/o Regions Bank Trust Dept.
P.O. Box 2886
Mobile, AL   36652-2886
Contact: Beth Welsh, Committee Member
Application address: 213 Country Club Dr., Tullahoma, TN 37388-0001

Foundation type: Independent foundation
Purpose: Scholarships to students of the senior class of Tullahoma High School, TN, for higher education.
Financial data: Year ended 01/31/2013. Assets, $239,387 (M); Expenditures, $12,178; Total giving, $8,000.
Fields of interest: Higher education.

Type of support: Support to graduates or students of specific schools; Undergraduate support.
Application information: Applications accepted. Application form required.
  Initial approach: Letter
  Deadline(s): None
  Additional information: Contact the bank for additional application information.
EIN: 626266551

95
Marian Gaynor Yanamura Educational Fund, Inc.
P.O. Box 511
Fairhope, AL 36533-0511
Contact: C.O. McCawley, Jr.

Foundation type: Operating foundation
Purpose: Scholarships to graduating seniors from Fairhope High School and Daphne High School, AL.
Financial data: Year ended 09/30/2012. Assets, $2,849,872 (M); Expenditures, $182,131; Total giving, $148,000; Grants to individuals, 37 grants totaling $148,000 (high: $4,000, low: $4,000).
Fields of interest: Higher education.
Type of support: Support to graduates or students of specific schools; Undergraduate support.
Application information: Applications accepted. Application form required.
  Additional information: Application forms are available from the two eligible high schools.
EIN: 721351380

ALASKA

96
Ahtna Heritage Foundation
P.O. Box 213
Glennallen, AK 99588-0213 (907) 822-5778
Contact: Liana Charley-John, Exec. Dir.
FAX: (907) 822-5338; E-Mail For Liana
Charley-John: ahtnaheritage.liana@gmail.com;
URL: http://www.ahtnaheritagefoundation.com

Foundation type: Public charity
Purpose: Scholarships to Ahtna shareholders who are planning to attend an accredited college, university, or vocational school.
Publications: Application guidelines.
Financial data: Year ended 12/31/2011. Assets, $587,251 (M); Expenditures, $981,311; Total giving, $226,200; Grants to individuals, totaling $226,200.
Fields of interest: Vocational education, post-secondary; Higher education.
Type of support: Scholarships—to individuals.
Application information: Applications accepted. Application form required.
   Initial approach: Application
   Send request by: Mail
   Deadline(s): July 15 for fall semester, Dec. 15 for spring semester for Walter Charley Memorial Scholarship
   Applicants should submit the following:
   1) Letter(s) of recommendation
   2) Transcripts
   Additional information: Application should also include official proof of enrollment and registration listing the courses you are registered for, documentation proving you are an Ahtna shareholder and one page letter describing your personal goals. Funds will be paid directly to the educational institution on behalf of the student.
Program descriptions:
   Irene Tansy Memorial Scholarship: A one-time scholarship of $1,500 will be given to a college-bound graduate of Kenny Lake High School. Preference will be given to Alaska Natives, and to applicants seeking a degree in education. Application should include an essay.
   Walter Charley Memorial Scholarship: Renewable scholarships, ranging from $1,000 to $2,000 per semester, are available to college students or recent high school graduates who are Ahtna shareholders. Eligible applicants must be high school graduates (or have a GED), and must be accepted to an accredited college, university, or vocational school.
EIN: 920114292

97
The Alaska Community Foundation
3201 C St., Ste. 110
Anchorage, AK 99503 (907) 334-6700
Contact: Candace Winkler, C.E.O.; For grants: Anne Remick, Prog. Off.; For scholarships: Anna Dalton, Prog. Assoc.
Scholarship inquiry tel.: (907) 274-6710;
Scholarship e-mail: adalton@alaskacf.org
FAX: (907) 334-5780; E-mail: info@alaskacf.org;
URL: http://www.alaskacf.org

Foundation type: Community foundation
Purpose: Scholarships to residents of AK seeking to further their education.

Publications: Annual report; Grants list; Informational brochure; Newsletter.
Financial data: Year ended 12/31/2011. Assets, $55,742,229 (M); Expenditures, $8,223,586; Total giving, $6,038,881; Grants to individuals, 54 grants totaling $71,443.
Fields of interest: Music; Performing arts, education; Higher education; Nursing school/education; Engineering school/education; Athletics/sports, winter sports.
Type of support: Scholarships—to individuals; Support to graduates or students of specific schools; Undergraduate support.
Application information: Applications accepted. Application form required. Application form available on the grantmaker's web site.
   Initial approach: Application
   Send request by: Online
   Deadline(s): Varies
   Additional information: See web site for a complete scholarship listing and application guidelines.
Program description:
   Scholarship Funds: The foundation administers various scholarship funds distributed to individuals for educational purposes based on pre-set criteria. Most scholarships are for students attending two or four year colleges or universities, pursuing degrees in specified subjects, such as music, auto-mechanics or health care. Many are based upon academic success and evidence of financial need. See web site for additional information.
EIN: 920155067

98
Alaska Conservation Foundation
911 W. 8th Ave., Ste. 300
Anchorage, AK 99501 (907) 276-1917
Contact: Ann Rothe, Exec. Dir.
FAX: (907) 274-4145;
E-mail: acfinfo@alaskaconservation.org;
URL: http://www.alaskaconservation.org

Foundation type: Community foundation
Purpose: Awards to individuals advancing solutions to environmental issues in AK.
Publications: Application guidelines; Annual report; Financial statement; Grants list; Informational brochure; Newsletter; Program policy statement.
Financial data: Year ended 06/30/2012. Assets, $9,237,456 (M); Expenditures, $5,396,552; Total giving, $3,160,238. Awards/prizes amount not specified.
Fields of interest: Film/video; Environment.
Type of support: Awards/grants by nomination only; Awards/prizes; Project support.
Application information: Applications accepted. Application form required. Application form available on the grantmaker's web site.
   Initial approach: Letter or telephone
   Send request by: Mail
   Deadline(s): Varies
   Additional information: Awards by nomination, including letter of nomination. Self-nominations are accepted.
Program descriptions:
   ACT Lifetime Achievement Award: Celebrates the accomplishments of remarkable individuals who have made a difference by devoting significant parts of their lives to protecting and enhancing Alaska's natural greatness, and thanks them for their tireless dedication and advocacy. Nominees should be at least 60 years of age or have dedicated 30 or more years of their life to Alaska conservation.
   Alaska Native Fund: In partnership with an Alaska Native Steering Committee, the fund advances Alaska Native priorities for protecting land and

sustaining traditional ways of life. The fund awards annual grants to qualifying Alaska Native nonprofit organizations and individuals. Applicants must perform work that aligns with the priority environmental issues and core strategies supported by the fund. For the 2013 grantmaking cycle, the priority environmental issues are climate change, food security, sustainable economies, energy, and holistic wellness. The fund also will provide up to three grants for qualifying applicants working to implement youth organizing strategies in the priority environmental areas. In 2013, the fund anticipates awarding grants totaling $150,000 - $200,000. Grants to organizations will range from $10,000 to $20,000; grants to individuals will range up to $10,000; and grants for youth organizing will be $5,000.
   Caleb Pungowiyi Award for Outstanding Achievements by an Alaska Native Organization or Individual: This award recognizes an Alaska Native organization, program or individual working to protect their environment and culture through innovative problem solving, collaboration, effective communication, and building conservation support within the Native Community.
   Celia Hunter Award for Outstanding Volunteer Contributions: Honors leaders in the grassroots, volunteer environmental movement in Alaska. These individuals are active on a state or nationwide level, are ardent conservation supporters, and have made a positive, solutions-based difference for Alaska's conservation movement over many years. The award winner has the opportunity to recommend a grant to the organization of their choice.
   Daniel Housebeth Wilderness Image Award for Excellence in Still Photography, Film or Video: Awards film, video, and still photography projects that advance the protection of Alaska's wilderness environment, further discussion of issues relating to habitat and stewardship of Alaska's natural resources, and enhance public education relating to these areas.
   Denny Wilcher Award for Young Environmental Activists: Acknowledges Alaska high school seniors who have made significant contributions to their communities and who seek solutions to environmental problems and issues. These individuals act as leaders among their peers and have demonstrated, through school and extracurricular activities, their care and deep concern for conserving the environment. Cash gift to assist the student in future endeavors. Since this award recognizes service rather than academic achievement, it is not a scholarship, but students are encouraged to use the award to further their education.
   Jerry S. Dixon award for Excellence in Environmental Education: Rewards innovative educators who integrate stewardship of Alaska's natural environment into their instructive efforts. These individuals, who may teach in any discipline and include experiential and outdoor educators, demonstrate a long history of service with students and outstanding, innovative contributions in conservation education.
   Olaus Murie Award for Outstanding Professional Contributions: Recognizes longstanding service to Alaska by individuals working in a non-profit organization or a public agency responsible for the environment. These individuals have demonstrated strong leadership skills and helped build a more influential conservation movement in Alaska. The award winner has the opportunity to recommend a grant to the organization of their choice.
EIN: 920061466

99
Alaska Humanities Forum
161 E. 1st Ave., Door 15
Anchorage, AK 99501-1661 (907) 272-5341
FAX: (907) 272-3979; E-mail: info@akhf.org; E-mail for grants information: grants@akhf.org; E-Mail for Nina Kemppel: nkemppel@akhf.org; URL: http://www.akhf.org

Foundation type: Public charity
Purpose: Grants to AK residents for projects and research in the humanities that will benefit the people of AK.
Publications: Application guidelines; Biennial report; Financial statement; Grants list; Informational brochure; Newsletter.
Financial data: Year ended 09/30/2011. Assets, $2,213,974 (M); Expenditures, $2,417,411; Total giving, $256,527; Grants to individuals, totaling $52,230.
Fields of interest: Humanities; Arts; Community/economic development.
Type of support: Conferences/seminars; Research.
Application information: Applications accepted. Application form required. Application form available on the grantmaker's web site.
Deadline(s): Vary
Applicants should submit the following:
1) Letter(s) of recommendation
2) Resume
EIN: 920042123

100
Alaska Kidney Foundation, Inc.
3201 C St., Ste. 110
Anchorage, AK 99503-3961 (907) 563-8550

Foundation type: Independent foundation
Purpose: Grants to kidney patients who are residents of AK, and have encountered unexpected financial hardship.
Financial data: Year ended 12/31/2012. Assets, $11,232,295 (M); Expenditures, $419,033; Total giving, $269,388; Grants to individuals, totaling $101,866.
Fields of interest: Kidney diseases.
Type of support: Emergency funds; Grants to individuals.
Application information: Application form required.
Deadline(s): None
Additional information: Application must be prepared by a licensed, certified social worker who is associated with a dialysis or transplant facility.
Program description:
Patient Support Grant: The purpose of the grant is to provide direct, immediate assistance to kidney patients who have encountered an unexpected, relatively small expense that their budgets cannot accommodate but which, if unpaid, threatens to undermine the quality of the individual's life.
EIN: 237286827

101
Alaska Youth Bowling Foundation
3717 Minnesota Dr.
Anchorage, AK 99503-5643 (907) 562-2695
Contact: Chris Clapper, Pres.

Foundation type: Independent foundation
Purpose: Scholarships to AK residents who are current members in good standing of a collegiate bowling team.
Financial data: Year ended 12/31/2010. Assets, $51,762 (M); Expenditures, $47,297; Total giving, $5,000; Grants to individuals, 4 grants totaling $5,000 (high: $1,250, low: $1,250).
Fields of interest: Higher education; Athletics/sports, school programs; Recreation.
Type of support: Scholarships—to individuals.
Application information: Applications accepted. Application form required.
Send request by: Mail
Deadline(s): Feb. 1
Additional information: Application should include an essay of at least 100 words about your participation with the collegiate bowling program at the college you are attending.
EIN: 920177971

102
Alaskan International Education Foundation, Inc.
2009 Wildwood Ln.
Anchorage, AK 99517-1332 (907) 279-1380
Contact: Ramona S. Duby

Foundation type: Operating foundation
Purpose: Grants to AK residents for programs to help foster international understanding, and for international students studying in AK.
Financial data: Year ended 12/31/2011. Assets, $1,946,821 (M); Expenditures, $94,018; Total giving, $51,553; Grants to individuals, 2 grants totaling $4,000 (high: $2,500, low: $1,500).
Fields of interest: Higher education.
Type of support: Grants to individuals.
Application information: Applications accepted. Application form required.
Deadline(s): None
Applicants should submit the following:
1) Letter(s) of recommendation
2) Transcripts
EIN: 920154513

103
The Aleut Foundation
703 W. Tudor Rd., Ste. 102
Anchorage, AK 99503-6650 (907) 646-1929
E-mail: taf@thealeutfoundation.org; URL: http://thealeutfoundation.org

Foundation type: Company-sponsored foundation
Purpose: Scholarships to original enrollees of the Aleut Corporation, AK, and their descendants; and to Aleut WWII evacuees and their descendants. Burial assistance for the deaths of original enrollees of the Aleut Corporation, AK, and their descendants.
Financial data: Year ended 03/31/2012. Assets, $215,104 (M); Expenditures, $1,296,804; Total giving, $956,609; Grants to individuals, 2 grants totaling $956,609 (high: $869,025).
Type of support: Grants to individuals; Scholarships—to individuals; Technical education support; Travel grants; Grants for special needs.
Application information: Applications accepted. Application form required. Application form available on the grantmaker's web site.
Deadline(s): June 30 for scholarships; Within six months of the original enrollee's or descendant of an original enrollee's death for Burial Assistance
Applicants should submit the following:
1) Transcripts
2) Letter(s) of recommendation
Additional information: Scholarship application should also include letter of acceptance, letter of intent, birth certificate, and class schedule for the upcoming fall semester/quarter. See web site for further application guidelines.
Program descriptions:
Aleut Foundation Part-Time Scholarships: The foundation awards college scholarships to original enrollees and the descendants of original enrollees of the Aleut Corporation, beneficiaries and the descendants of beneficiaries of the Aleutian Pribilof Islands Restitution Trust, and original enrollees and the descendants of original enrollees of the Isanotski Corporation attending undergraduate, graduate, or master's programs part-time.
Aleut Foundation Scholarships: The foundation awards college scholarships to original enrollees and the descendants of original enrollees of the Aleut Corporation, beneficiaries and the descendants of beneficiaries of the Aleutian Pribilof Islands Restitution Trust, and original enrollees and the descendants of original enrollees of the Isanotski Corporation.
Burial Assistance Grants: The foundation awards $2,000 burial assistance grants to the families of deceased original and the descendents of original enrollees of the Aleut Corporation. Applicant should submit a certified death certificate with the application.
Culture Camp Grants: The foundation awards grants to original and the descendants of original enrollees of the Aleut Corporation to attend culture camp.
Lille Hope McGarvey Scholarship: The foundation awards college scholarships to original enrollees and the descendants of original enrollees of the Aleut Corporation, beneficiaries and the descendants of beneficiaries of the Aleutian Pribilof Islands Restitution Trust, and original enrollees and the descendants of original enrollees of the Isanotski Corporation studying in the medical field.
Company name: Aleut Corporation
EIN: 920124517

104
Arctic Education Foundation
3900 C. St., Ste. 1002
Anchorage, AK 99503 (907) 852-9456
Contact: Carolyn M. Edwards, Mgr.
Tel. and e-mail for Carolyn M. Edwards: (907) 852-8633, cmedwards@asrc@com; Additional tel.: (800) 770-2772; URL: http://www.arcticed.com

Foundation type: Company-sponsored foundation
Purpose: Scholarships to worthy and financially needy Northern Alaska Inupiat Natives residing in the Arctic Slope Region and direct lineal descendants of an original 1971 shareholder of the Arctic Slope Regional Corporation for training and higher education.
Publications: Application guidelines.
Financial data: Year ended 12/31/2012. Assets, $27,716,808 (M); Expenditures, $1,654,701; Total giving, $1,532,335; Grants to individuals, 435 grants totaling $1,532,335 (high: $27,885, low: $1,067).
Fields of interest: Vocational education; Higher education; Native Americans/American Indians.
Type of support: Scholarships—to individuals; Undergraduate support.
Application information: Applications accepted. Application form required. Application form available on the grantmaker's web site.
Send request by: Mail for Award, online for Scholarship
Deadline(s): Mar. 1, May 1, Aug. 1 and Dec. 1 for AEF Scholarships, Apr. 15 for Anagi Leadership Award
Applicants should submit the following:

1) Essay
2) Letter(s) of recommendation
3) Transcripts
4) Financial information
Additional information: For college students pursuing a four-year degree or for graduate students (six to eight year program) the maximum is $6,000 and $10,000 per year respectively, and for training students (two year program or less) the limit is $5,000 per year.

Program description:
Anagi Leadership Award: The foundation awards one scholarship to an original ASRC shareholder or direct lineal descendant of an original ASRC shareholder. The scholarship covers tuition, fees, books, and room and board, and is awarded to acknowledge the leadership of retired Arctic Slope Regional Corporation President, Jacob Anagi Adams.
EIN: 920068447

105
Bering Straits Foundation
110 Front St., Ste. 300
P.O. Box 1008
Nome, AK   99762-1008   (907) 443-4305
Contact: Moriah Sallaffie, Exec. V.P.
FAX: (907) 443-2985;
E-mail: info@beringstraits.com; Toll-free tel.: (800) 478-5079; E-mail for Moriah Sallaffie: msallaffie@beringstraits.com; URL: http://www.beringstraits.com/

Foundation type: Public charity
Purpose: Scholarships to individuals primarily in AK, who are members of Bering Straits Corporation or the children of members, for undergraduate education.
Publications: Application guidelines; Newsletter; Occasional report; Program policy statement; Quarterly report.
Financial data: Year ended 12/31/2012. Assets, $237,050 (M); Expenditures, $381,115; Total giving, $246,224; Grants to individuals, totaling $246,224.
Fields of interest: Vocational education, post-secondary; Higher education; Native Americans/American Indians.
Type of support: Conferences/seminars; Fellowships; Scholarships—to individuals; Graduate support; Technical education support; Undergraduate support.
Application information: Applications accepted. Application form required. Application form available on the grantmaker's web site.
Initial approach: E-mail
Send request by: E-mail
Copies of proposal: 1
Deadline(s): June 30 and Dec. 30 for Higher Education and Vocational Training Scholarship; June 30 for Martin Olson Memorial Scholarship
Applicants should submit the following:
1) Transcripts
2) Letter(s) of recommendation
Additional information: Application should also include a personal statement and copy of birth certificate. See web site for additional application information.
Program descriptions:
Fellowships: The foundation offers cultural and heritage fellowships to individuals who plan to attend non-credit workshops, conferences, or seminars that perpetuate the understanding of Bering Straits Native culture and heritage. Sixteen fellowships of $250 each will be awarded to

individuals who plan to attend the Kawerak Regional Conference; twenty fellowships of $500 each will also be available to individuals who plan to attend national/international events that meet the stated guidelines.
Scholarships: The foundation awards scholarships to full- or part-time students enrolled in an accredited college or vocational school. Eligible applicants must be a shareholder, or lineal descendent of a shareholder of, the Bering Straits Native Corporation, and must have maintained a 3.0 GPA for his/her high school career.
EIN: 920138528

106
Bristol Bay Economic Development Corporation
P.O. Box 1464
Dillingham, AK   99576-1464   (907) 842-4370
Contact: H. Robin Samuelsen, Pres. and C.E.O.
FAX: (907) 842-4336;
E-mail: sockeye1@nushtel.net; URL: http://www.bbedc.com/

Foundation type: Public charity
Purpose: Financial assistance and counseling to eligible Bristol bay, AK residents so that they are able to obtain limited entry permits through a short-term, emergency transfer. Grants of up to 50% of the emergency transfer (lease) fee for Bristol Bay limited entry drift and set permits are available to eligible resident fishers.
Financial data: Year ended 12/31/2011. Assets, $200,690,449 (M); Expenditures, $13,082,535; Total giving, $8,045,201; Grants to individuals, totaling $934,749.
Fields of interest: Animals/wildlife, fisheries; Marine science.
Type of support: Grants to individuals.
Application information: Applications accepted. Application form required. Application form available on the grantmaker's web site.
Initial approach: Letter or e-mail
Additional information: Eligibility is based on residency in one of the 17 BBEDC communities, need for BBEDC assistance, access to a permit and market as well as other criteria.
EIN: 920142567

107
Bristol Bay Native Corp., Education Foundation
111 W. 16th Ave., Ste. 400
Anchorage, AK   99501-6299
Contact: Luanne Pelagio, Exec. Dir.
Additional tel.: (800) 426-3602; URL: http://www.bbnc.net/index.php?option=com_content&view=category&layout=blog&id=19&Itemid=40

Foundation type: Company-sponsored foundation
Purpose: Scholarships to shareholders of Bristol Bay Native Corporation, located in AK.
Publications: Application guidelines; Newsletter (including application guidelines).
Financial data: Year ended 12/31/2012. Assets, $6,747,330 (M); Expenditures, $389,821; Total giving, $313,375; Grants to individuals, 199 grants totaling $313,375 (high: $5,875, low: -$284).
Fields of interest: Higher education.
Type of support: Scholarships—to individuals.

Application information: Applications accepted. Application form required. Application form available on the grantmaker's web site.
Deadline(s): Apr. 1, None for Short-Term Vocational Education Program Scholarships
Applicants should submit the following:
1) Essay
2) Resume
3) GPA
4) Financial information
5) Letter(s) of recommendation
Additional information: Applicants for Short-Term Vocational Education Program Scholarships must also submit a letter of request that includes employment goals, how the training will relate to your employment goals, and employment opportunities after completion of the training.
Program descriptions:
H. Noble Dick Scholarship: Through the H. Noble Dick Scholarship program, the foundation awards one college scholarship of up to $1,000 to a college junior or senior who is an Alaska Native shareholder of Bristol Bay Native Corporation and is majoring in accounting or business management.
Higher Education Scholarships: Through the Higher Education Scholarship program, the foundation awards college scholarships of up to $3,500 to high school seniors who are Alaska Native shareholders of Bristol Bay Native Corporation. The award is based on academic standing, leadership, financial need, and life experiences.
Pedro Bay Scholarship: Through the Pedro Bay Scholarship program, the foundation awards college scholarships of up to $3,000 to high school juniors, seniors, or advanced degree candidates enrolled at a 4 year college who are shareholders of Pedro Bay Corporation.
Short-Term Vocational/Technical Education Program Scholarship: Through the Short-Term Vocational/Technical Education Program, the foundation awards scholarships of up to $600 to Alaska Native shareholders of Bristol Bay Native Corporation to attend short term trainings to enhance their work and career opportunities.
Vocational Education Scholarships: Through the Vocational Education Scholarship program, the foundation awards $500 college scholarships to high school seniors who are Alaska Native shareholders of Bristol Bay Native Corporation. The award is given to encourage educational and career advancement.
Wells Fargo - BBNC Scholarship: Through the Wells Fargo - BBNC Scholarship program, the foundation, in partnership with Wells Fargo, awards one college scholarship of up to $5,000 to a college junior or senior who is an Alaska Native shareholder of Bristol Bay Native Corporation. The scholarship is awarded to further advance the education of Alaska Natives and to encourage interest in the banking profession.
EIN: 920141709

108
Calista Scholarship Fund
(formerly David K. Nicolai Memorial Scholarship Fund)
301 Calista Ct., Ste. A
Anchorage, AK   99518-3028   (907) 279-5516
FAX: (907) 644-6376;
E-mail: scholarships@calistacorp.com; Toll-free tel.: (800) 277-5516; URL: http://www.calistacorp.com/shareholders/scholarshipscalista-heritage-foundation

Foundation type: Public charity

Purpose: Scholarships to AK Natives for continuing educational activities, for the benefit of the region and its people. Giving is limited to shareholders and their descendents of Calista Corporation.
Publications: Application guidelines; Informational brochure.
Financial data: Year ended 12/31/2012. Assets, $2,203,272 (M); Expenditures, $875,250; Total giving, $378,783; Grants to individuals, totaling $378,783.
Fields of interest: Native Americans/American Indians.
Type of support: Scholarships—to individuals.
Application information: Applications accepted. Application form required. Application form available on the grantmaker's web site.
   Initial approach: Letter or telephone
   Deadline(s): June 30
   Applicants should submit the following:
      1) Transcripts
      2) GPA
      3) Financial information
      4) Essay
   Additional information: Application should also include career and educational goals.
Program description:
   Scholarships: Awards scholarships, ranging from $500 to $1,000 per semester for up to two semesters, to Alaska Native shareholders of Calista Corporation or lineal descendants of an Alaska Native shareholder. Applicants must have earned a G.E.D. and be in good academic standing and have at least a 2.0 GPA.
EIN: 920088631

109
Chenega Future, Inc.

3000 C St., Ste. 200 S. Wing
Anchorage, AK   99503-3975   (907) 751-6901
Contact: Patti Andrews, Secy.
Application address: Chenega Future Inc., Shareholder Development Manager, P.O. Box 240988, Anchorage, AK 99524
FAX: (907) 569-6939;
E-mail: pandrews@chenegacorp.com.; URL: http://www.chenegafuture.com/

Foundation type: Operating foundation
Purpose: Scholarships to shareholders of the Chenega Corporation, AK, their spouses and descendants.
Publications: Application guidelines.
Financial data: Year ended 12/31/2012. Assets, $16,673 (M); Expenditures, $1,372,246; Total giving, $328,384; Grants to individuals, 117 grants totaling $328,384 (high: $8,052, low: $15).
Fields of interest: Higher education.
Type of support: Internship funds; Scholarships—to individuals.
Application information: Applications accepted. Application form required. Application form available on the grantmaker's web site.
   Initial approach: Application
   Send request by: Mail
   Deadline(s): May 1 for summer semester, Dec. 1 for spring semester, Aug. 1 for fall semester, 10 days prior to the start of any short-term, vocational or technical training, and Sept. 30 for Chugach School District
   Applicants should submit the following:
      1) FAFSA
      2) Letter(s) of recommendation
      3) Financial information
      4) Transcripts
   Additional information: Application should also include a letter of acceptance from the school you will be attending, program degree or

certificate plan, a goal letter, an educational career plan, a Certificate of Indian Blood (CIB), and a term course schedule.
Company name: Chenega Corporation
EIN: 943111730

110
Choggiung Education Endowment Foundation

P.O. Box 330
Dillingham, AK   99576-0330   (907) 842-5218

Foundation type: Company-sponsored foundation
Purpose: Scholarships to shareholders and children of shareholders of Choggiung Ltd.
Publications: Application guidelines; Program policy statement.
Financial data: Year ended 09/30/2013. Assets, $322,641 (M); Expenditures, $22,569; Total giving, $21,821; Grants to individuals, 18 grants totaling $21,821 (high: $3,000, low: $321).
Type of support: Scholarships—to individuals.
Application information: Applications accepted. Application form required.
   Initial approach: Letter
   Deadline(s): May 31
   Applicants should submit the following:
      1) Letter(s) of recommendation
      2) Transcripts
   Additional information: Applications should also include a letter of interest that includes applicants intentions, expected field of study, goals, and expectations; two letters of reference; and a letter of acceptance from the institution that the applicant plans to attend.
EIN: 920155519

111
Chugach Heritage Foundation

3800 Centerpoint Dr., Ste. 601
Anchorage, AK   99503-4196   (907) 563-8866
URL: http://www.chugachheritagefoundation.org/

Foundation type: Company-sponsored foundation
Purpose: Scholarships to shareholders or legal descendants of original shareholders of the Chugach Alaska Corporation seeking college and university degrees, and vocational certificates.
Publications: Application guidelines.
Financial data: Year ended 12/31/2012. Assets, $243,834 (M); Expenditures, $909,184; Total giving, $821,065.
Fields of interest: Vocational education, post-secondary; Higher education.
Type of support: Undergraduate support.
Application information: Applications accepted. Application form required. Application form available on the grantmaker's web site.
   Send request by: Mail, e-mail, fax, or hand deliver
   Deadline(s): None
   Additional information: The foundation awards associate level scholarships up to $4,800 annually, junior and senior level undergraduate scholarships up to $6,000 annually, and vocational training scholarships up to $4,000 per academic year. Applications should include transcripts, a copy of birth certificates, class schedule, and acceptance letter from the school you are attending. Checks are issued on behalf of the student.
EIN: 920116128

112
Chugiak-Eagle River Foundation

12001 Business Blvd., #108
P. O. Box 770301
Eagle River, AK   99577   (907) 694-4702
Contact: Brad Gamble, Pres.
FAX: (907) 694-1205;
E-mail: info@cerfoundation.org; URL: http://www.cerfoundation.org/

Foundation type: Community foundation
Purpose: Scholarships for higher education to resident of Chugiak-Eagle River who are graduating seniors from an Alaskan secondary school or attending or planning to attend a college or vocational school.
Publications: Grants list.
Financial data: Year ended 01/31/2012. Assets, $567,952 (M); Expenditures, $27,314; Total giving, $19,100; Grants to individuals, 21 grants totaling $10,100.
Fields of interest: Higher education.
Type of support: Scholarships—to individuals.
Application information: Applications accepted. Application form required. Application form available on the grantmaker's web site.
   Initial approach: Application
   Send request by: Mail or hand deliver
   Copies of proposal: 4
   Deadline(s): Apr. 1
   Applicants should submit the following:
      1) Financial information
      2) Letter(s) of recommendation
      3) Resume
      4) Essay
      5) Transcripts
      6) GPA
   Additional information: The maximum amount of a scholarship is $1,500. See web site for additional information.
EIN: 920152780

113
The CIRI Foundation

(also known as The Cook Inlet Region, Inc. Foundation)
3600 San Jeronimo Dr., Ste. 256
Anchorage, AK   99508-2870   (907) 793-3575
FAX: (907) 793-3585;
E-mail: tcf@thecirifoundation.org; Additional tel.: (800) 764-3382; URL: http://www.thecirifoundation.org

Foundation type: Company-sponsored foundation
Purpose: Scholarships, fellowships, internships, and grants to AK Natives enrolled to the Cook Inlet Region under the Alaska Native Settlement Claims Act of 1971. Recipients are original enrollees, their descendants, or their legally adopted descendants.
Publications: Application guidelines; Grants list; Program policy statement.
Financial data: Year ended 12/31/2012. Assets, $50,389,113 (M); Expenditures, $3,895,457; Total giving, $2,616,444; Grants to individuals, 682 grants totaling $2,494,575 (high: $10,000, low: $250).
Fields of interest: Visual arts; Performing arts; Literature; Vocational education; Business school/education; Engineering school/education; Health sciences school/education; Education; Employment, training; Employment; Mathematics; Native Americans/American Indians.
Type of support: Conferences/seminars; Fellowships; Internship funds; Grants to individuals; Scholarships—to individuals; Graduate support; Undergraduate support.

Application information: Applications accepted. Application form required. Application form available on the grantmaker's web site.

Send request by: Mail and Online

Deadline(s): Mar. 31, June 30, Sept. 30, and Dec. 1 for Vocational Training, Career Upgrade, fellowships, and internships, June 1 for Achievement, Excellence Annual, and Special Excellence Annual Scholarships, June 1 and Dec. 1 for General Semester Scholarships

Applicants should submit the following:
1) Transcripts
2) Letter(s) of recommendation

Additional information: Application should also include proof of eligibility, proof of school or program acceptance, and statement of purpose.

Program descriptions:

Achievement Annual Scholarships: The foundation annually awards college and graduate scholarships of up to $8,000 to Alaska Natives maintaining a 3.0 GPA who are original enrollees and the direct lineal descendants of original enrollees of Cook Inlet Region, Inc.

Career Upgrade Grants: The foundation awards grants of up to $4,500 to Alaska Natives who are original enrollees and the direct lineal descendants of original enrollees of Cook Inlet Region, Inc. to enroll in a course of study that contributes to potential employment or employment upgrade.

Excellence Annual Scholarships: The foundation annually awards college and graduate scholarships of up to $10,000 to Alaska Natives maintaining a 3.5 GPA who are original enrollees and the direct lineal descendants of original enrollees of Cook Inlet Region, Inc.

General and Cultural Heritage Fellowships: The foundation awards general fellowships of up to $250 for non-credit workshops or seminars to improve employment skills; and cultural heritage fellowships of up to $250 for the study of visual, literary, and performing arts of Alaska Natives. Fellowships are limited to Alaska Natives maintaining a 2.5 GPA who are original enrollees and the direct lineal descendants of original enrollees of Cook Inlet Region, Inc.

General Semester Scholarships: The foundation awards college and graduate scholarships of up to $2,500 per semester to Alaska Natives maintaining a 2.5 GPA who are original enrollees and the direct lineal descendants of original enrollees of Cook Inlet Region, Inc.

Internship Program: The foundation supports individuals obtaining temporary, supervised, and on-the-job training to develop employment skills and gain practical work experience. The program is limited to Alaska Natives maintaining a 2.5 GPA who are original enrollees and the direct lineal descendants of original enrollees of Cook Inlet Region, Inc.

Special Excellence Annual Scholarships: The foundation awards college and graduate scholarships of up to $20,000 to Alaska Natives maintaining a 3.7 GPA who are original enrollees and the direct lineal descendants of original enrollees of Cook Inlet Region, Inc. Special emphasis is directed toward students studying business, education, math, science, health service, and engineering.

Vocational Training Grants: The foundation awards grants of up to $4,500 to Alaska Natives who are original enrollees and the direct lineal descendants of original enrollees of Cook Inlet Region, Inc. to attend a vocational training program or obtain a technical skills certificate.

EIN: 920087914

114

Copper Mountain Foundation

P.O. Box 650
Cordova, AK 99574 (907) 278-4000

Foundation type: Company-sponsored foundation

Purpose: Scholarships and career enhancement grants to Native Alaskans or Native Alaskan descendants with ancestral ties to the native village of Tatitlek, AK.

Financial data: Year ended 12/31/2012. Assets, $85,420 (M); Expenditures, $98,855; Total giving, $48,566; Grants to individuals, 6 grants totaling $48,566.

Fields of interest: Higher education; Native Americans/American Indians.

Type of support: Scholarships—to individuals.

Application information: Application form required.

Deadline(s): 30 day's prior to your school's payment deadline

Additional information: Application should include transcripts. Scholarships are paid directly to the educational institution on behalf of the students.

EIN: 920137461

115

The Doyon Foundation

615 Bidwell, Ste. 101
Fairbanks, AK 99701-7580 (907) 459-2048
Contact: Doris Miller, Exec. Dir.; for Scholarship: Tonya Garnett, Prog. Mgr.
Tel. for Tonya. Garnett; (907) 459-2049, e-mail: garnett@doyon.com
FAX: (905) 459-2065;
E-mail: foundation@doyon.com; E-mail for Doris Miller: millerd@doyon.com; Additional tel.: (888) 478-4755; URL: http://www.doyonfoundation.com/

Foundation type: Company-sponsored foundation

Purpose: Scholarships to shareholders of Doyon Ltd., and their spouses and lineal descendants attending an accredited college, university, vocational or technical school.

Publications: Application guidelines; Annual report; Informational brochure; Newsletter.

Financial data: Year ended 06/30/2013. Assets, $16,359,338 (M); Expenditures, $1,066,680; Total giving, $426,630; Grants to individuals, 597 grants totaling $426,630 (high: $2,500, low: -$400).

Fields of interest: Vocational education; Higher education; Education.

Type of support: Scholarships—to individuals; Undergraduate support.

Application information: Applications accepted. Application form required. Application form available on the grantmaker's web site.

Initial approach: Complete online application or download application and mail

Deadline(s): Apr. 15 for Competitive Scholarships, Mar. 15, Apr. 15, and Nov. 15 for Basic Scholarships, and Mar. 15, Apr. 15, Sept. 15, and Nov. 15 for Vocational Scholarships

Applicants should submit the following:
1) Letter(s) of recommendation
2) GPA
3) Essay
4) Transcripts

Program description:

Scholarship Program: The foundation awards college scholarships ranging from $400 to $7,000 to shareholders and descendants of shareholders of Doyon, Ltd., enrolled in a part-time or full-time degree program, or enrolled in a vocational program. The foundation awards competitive scholarships of up to $7,000; basic scholarships of up $400 for part-time students and $800 for full-time students; short-term vocational scholarships of up to $400; and advanced college credit scholarships of up $400 for high school students taking college courses.

EIN: 943089624

116

The Eyak Foundation

(formerly Cordova Native Foundation)
360 W. Benson Blvd., Ste. 210A
Anchorage, AK 99503-3953 (907) 334-3940
E-mail: info@eyakfoundation.org; URL: http://www.eyakfoundation.org/

Foundation type: Company-sponsored foundation

Purpose: Scholarships to Alaska Native shareholders and lineal descendants of shareholders of Eyak Corporation.

Publications: Application guidelines; Grants list.

Financial data: Year ended 12/31/2012. Assets, $980,083 (M); Expenditures, $123,903; Total giving, $54,916; Grants to individuals, 33 grants totaling $54,916 (high: $5,000, low: $333).

Fields of interest: Higher education; Native Americans/American Indians.

Type of support: Scholarships—to individuals; Undergraduate support.

Application information: Applications accepted. Application form required. Application form available on the grantmaker's web site.

Initial approach: Application

Send request by: Mail or hand deliver

Deadline(s): Mar. 14 for Spring, Oct. 31 for Fall

Applicants should submit the following:
1) Essay
2) Photograph
3) Transcripts
4) Letter(s) of recommendation

Additional information: Application should also include proof of lineal descent of original Eyak Corporation shareholder, proof of acceptance from college, university, vocational or training program, and course description and requirements of institution for full time students.

EIN: 920161386

117

The Homer Foundation

3733 Ben Walters Ln., Ste. 4
P.O. Box 2600
Homer, AK 99603-2600 (907) 235-0541
Contact: Joy Steward, Exec. Dir.
FAX: (907) 235-2021; E-mail: info@homerfund.org; Additional e-mail: jsteward@homerfund.org; URL: http://www.homerfund.org

Foundation type: Community foundation

Purpose: Scholarships to graduates of Homer High School and/or residents of the southern Kenai Peninsula, AK.

Publications: Application guidelines; Annual report; Financial statement; Grants list; Informational brochure; Newsletter.

Financial data: Year ended 06/30/2012. Assets, $2,445,620 (M); Expenditures, $532,282; Total giving, $418,157; Grants to individuals, 19 grants totaling $19,750 (high: $3,000, low: $500, average grant: $500-$1,000).

Fields of interest: Higher education.

Type of support: Scholarships—to individuals; Support to graduates or students of specific schools; Undergraduate support.

Application information: Applications accepted. Application form required. Application form available on the grantmaker's web site.
- *Initial approach:* Application
- *Send request by:* Mail, hand deliver, or e-mail with signature attached
- *Copies of proposal:* 1
- *Deadline(s):* Varies
- *Additional information:* See web site for application form per scholarship. Faxed application not accepted.

EIN: 920139183

118
Huna Heritage Foundation
9301 Glacier Hwy., Ste. 210
Juneau, AK 99801-9306 (907) 789-3682
FAX: (907) 789-1896;
E-mail: heritage@hunatotem.com; URL: http://www.hunaheritage.org

Foundation type: Company-sponsored foundation
Purpose: Scholarships to AK Huna Totem shareholders and descendants for full-time graduate, undergraduate, cultural education, or vocational study.
Publications: Application guidelines; Annual report; Corporate report; Newsletter.
Financial data: Year ended 12/31/2012. Assets, $240,420 (M); Expenditures, $370,025; Total giving, $175,707; Grants to individuals, 23 grants totaling $70,350 (high: $2,000, low: $300).
Fields of interest: Cultural/ethnic awareness; Vocational education; Higher education; Native Americans/American Indians.
Type of support: Grants to individuals.
Application information: Applications accepted. Application form required. Application form available on the grantmaker's web site.
- *Initial approach:* Application
- *Send request by:* Mail
- *Copies of proposal:* 1
- *Deadline(s):* Jan. 31 and Sept. 30 for Education Assistance, None for Vocational Education Assistance and Cultural Education Assistance
- *Applicants should submit the following:*
  1) Transcripts
  2) Letter(s) of recommendation
  3) Financial information
  4) Budget Information
- *Additional information:* Application should also include GED certificate and letter of acceptance from college, university, vocational school, or administrators of the Apprenticeship Program or Intern Program of On-The-Job-Training (OJT).

Program descriptions:
Cultural Education Assistance: The foundation awards grants of up to $300 to Huna Totem shareholders and descendants for instructional activities associated with traditional practices or art forms. The program is designed to assist in preserving, advocating, and learning the history and culture of the Huna people. Applicants must be accepted into a program to learn an art form which is related to the traditional culture of the Huna people.
Vocational Education Assistance: The foundation awards grants to Vocational Education and Apprenticeship programs for Huna Totem shareholders or descendants to receive training that leads to gainful employment. Vocational Education courses must be approved by a National Accreditation Association or the Alaska Department of Education's Division of Vocational Education. Apprentice programs must be approved by the U.S.

Bureau of Apprenticeship Training. All applicants must be unemployed.
EIN: 943113818

119
Igloo No. 4 Foundation
P.O. Box 70145
Fairbanks, AK 99707-0145 (907) 474-0501

Foundation type: Independent foundation
Purpose: Scholarships to residents of Fairbanks, AK for higher education.
Financial data: Year ended 12/31/2012. Assets, $796,232 (M); Expenditures, $44,329; Total giving, $41,413; Grants to individuals, 2 grants totaling $14,337 (high: $13,000).
Fields of interest: Higher education.
Type of support: Undergraduate support.
Application information:
- *Initial approach:* Letter
- *Deadline(s):* None
- *Additional information:* Contact foundation for additional application guidelines.

EIN: 510186261

120
Juneau Arts & Humanities Council
350 Whittier St., Ste. 101
Juneau, AK 99801-1774 (907) 586-2787
Contact: Nancy DeCherney, Exec. Dir.
FAX: (907) 586-2148; E-mail: info@jahc.org; E-mail For Nancy DeCherney: nancy@jahc.org;
URL: http://www.jahc.org

Foundation type: Public charity
Purpose: Scholarships to qualified applicants who lived in Juneau, AK for at least one year for the purpose of travel to a performing or fine arts camp, tuition or other purposes.
Publications: Application guidelines; Grants list.
Financial data: Year ended 06/30/2012. Assets, $290,158 (M); Expenditures, $623,948; Total giving, $117,652; Grants to individuals, totaling $24,652.
Fields of interest: Performing arts.
Type of support: Scholarships—to individuals.
Application information: Applications accepted. Application form required.
- *Deadline(s):* Apr.
- *Additional information:* See web site for additional application information.

EIN: 237243859

121
Kawerak, Inc.
P.O. Box 948
Nome, AK 99762-0948 (907) 443-5231
Contact: Loretta Bullard, Pres.
URL: http://www.kawerak.org

Foundation type: Public charity
Purpose: Scholarships to tribal members of the Bering Straits, AK, region enrolled at an accredited college or university. Temporary assistance to individuals and families in meeting their basic essential needs.
Financial data: Year ended 12/31/2011. Assets, $22,672,088 (M); Expenditures, $24,640,345; Total giving, $4,350,117; Grants to individuals, totaling $1,027,811.
Fields of interest: Higher education; Safety/disasters; Cemeteries/burial services.
Type of support: Emergency funds; Scholarships—to individuals; Grants for special needs.

Application information: Application form required. Application form available on the grantmaker's web site.
- *Initial approach:* Application
- *Applicants should submit the following:*
  1) Photograph
  2) Letter(s) of recommendation
  3) Transcripts
  4) Budget Information
- *Additional information:* See web site for additional guidelines.

Program descriptions:
Burial Assistance: Eligibility for this program is income-based. Maximum payment for burial assistance is $2,500. If any person or organization pays for a more expensive burial than the minimum provided by this program for the deceased, authorization will not be made. Reasonable transportation costs will be considered in addition to the burial cost.
Emergency Assistance: The maximum amount of assistance awarded is $1,000. This assistance can be made to individuals or families who suffer from a burnout, flood or other destruction of their home and loss or damage to personal possessions. Payments will be made for essential needs and other non-medical necessities.
Scholarship Program: Applicants must be accepted into a two- or four-year degree program and must maintain a minimum GPA of 2.00 or better. Full-time students must complete 12 credits per semester or 10 credits per quarter. Part-time students must complete a minimum of 6 credits. Applicant must be a member of a Native Village in the Bering Straits region (Tribal members of Gambell and Nome Eskimo Community must apply to their local IRA Council)
EIN: 920047009

122
Koniag Education Foundation
4241 B. Street, Suite 303B
Anchorage, AK 99503-5920 (907) 562-9093
Contact: Tyan Hayes, Exec. Dir.
FAX: (907) 562-9023;
E-mail: kef@koniageducation.org; Additional tel.: (888) 562-9093; URL: http://www.koniageducation.org

Foundation type: Company-sponsored foundation
Purpose: Scholarships to Native Alaskan students of the Koniag region, AK, for undergraduate, graduate, vocational or other educational endeavors.
Publications: Application guidelines; Financial statement; Grants list; Informational brochure; Newsletter.
Financial data: Year ended 03/31/2013. Assets, $6,045,140 (M); Expenditures, $589,357; Total giving, $231,415; Grants to individuals, 166 grants totaling $231,415 (high: $11,100, low: $132).
Fields of interest: Vocational education, post-secondary; Higher education; Native Americans/American Indians.
Type of support: Internship funds; Graduate support; Technical education support; Undergraduate support.
Application information: Applications accepted. Application form required. Application form available on the grantmaker's web site.
- *Initial approach:* Application
- *Send request by:* Mail or Online
- *Deadline(s):* Jan. 15 for Angayuk Scholarship & Internship, Mar. 15 for KEF General summer term, June 1 for KEF General fall term, Aug. 10 for Alyeksa, Drabek, ExxonMobil, Godfrey, and Matfay

Applicants should submit the following:
1) Photograph
2) Resume
3) Letter(s) of recommendation
4) GPA
5) Essay
6) Transcripts

Additional information: Application must also include two letters of assessment, applicants letter, achievements, activities and responsibilities.

Program descriptions:

Alyeska: The foundation, in partnership with Alyeska Pipeline Service Company, awards scholarships of up to $2,500 to college students who are Alaska Native shareholders or descendents of shareholders of Koniag, Inc. Applicants must have a GPA of 2.0. and pursue study in select fields: engineering, health, safety, environment, quality, inspection professionals, security, planner/schedulers/project controls, project manager, information technology professionals, business planning, or technical positions.

Career Development Grants: The foundation awards grants of up to $1,000 to Alaska Native shareholders and descendents of Koniag, Inc. who have chosen to further their education through a specific short-term class, seminar, or workshop lasting up to six weeks.

ExxonMobil: The foundation, in partnership with ExxonMobil, awards one $10,000 college scholarship to a student who is an Alaska Native shareholder or a descendent of shareholders of Koniag, Inc. Applicants must have a GPA of 3.0 and must pursue study in a field directly related to the oil and gas industry.

Glenn Godfrey Memorial Scholarship: The foundation awards one $5,000 college scholarship to a college sophomore, junior, or senior who is an Alaska Native shareholder or descendent of a shareholder of Koniag, Inc. Applicants must have a GPA of 2.5 or higher and must demonstrate continued community service or civic duty. The scholarship was created to help Alutiiq people pursue self-improvement and positive leadership roles.

KEF General Scholarship: The foundation awards college scholarships of up to $2,500 to high school seniors with a GPA of 2.0 are higher who are Alaska Native shareholders or descendents of shareholders of Koniag, Inc.

Koniag Angayuk Scholarship & Internship: The foundation awards renewable college scholarships of up to $10,000 to high school seniors who are Alaska Native shareholders or descendents of shareholders of Koniag, Inc. Applicants must have a GPA of 3.0 and agree to intern at any one of Koniag's subsidiaries during the summer months. Students will receive a salary during the internship, travel, and lodging.

Larry Matfay Scholarship: The foundation awards one $1,000 college scholarship to an Alaska Native shareholder or descendent of a shareholder of Koniag, Inc. studying healthcare, anthropology, history, Alaska Native or American Indian studies, or other disciplines involving research and learning about Alutiiq culture.

Magnel Larsen Drabek: The foundation awards one $2,000 college scholarship to a college sophomore, junior, or senior who is an Alaska Native shareholder or descendent of a shareholder of Koniag, Inc. Applicants must have a GPA of 2.0 and must major in education, arts, or cultural studies.

EIN: 920145017

123
Kuskokwim Educational Foundation

4300 B St., Ste. 207
Anchorage, AK   99503-5951   (907) 675-4275
Contact: Sally Hoffman
FAX: (907) 243-2984; E-mail: dg@kuskokwim.com;
Additional tel.: P.O. Box 227, Aniak, AK 99557
(907) 675-4275; URL: http://
www.kuskokwim.com/content/
educational-foundation

Foundation type: Company-sponsored foundation
Purpose: Scholarships to Native Americans and their descendants who are living in the region serviced by Kuskokwim Corporation, AK, for study at colleges, universities, and vocational schools.
Publications: Application guidelines; Corporate report; Informational brochure; Newsletter.
Financial data: Year ended 05/31/2012. Assets, $39,759 (M); Expenditures, $43,090; Total giving, $32,000; Grants to individuals, 48 grants totaling $32,000 (high: $1,250, low: $500).
Fields of interest: Vocational education; Higher education; Business school/education; Medical school/education; Adult/continuing education; Health care; Native Americans/American Indians.
Type of support: Technical education support; Undergraduate support.
Application information: Applications accepted. Application form required. Application form available on the grantmaker's web site.
> *Send request by:* Online
> *Deadline(s):* June 15 for fall semester, Nov. 15 for spring semester
> *Final notification:* Recipients notified July 1 for fall semester, and Dec. 1 for spring semester
> *Applicants should submit the following:*
> 1) Essay
> 2) Photograph
> 3) Letter(s) of recommendation
> 4) Transcripts

Program descriptions:

General Scholarships: The foundation awards scholarships to shareholders and children of shareholders of Kuskokwim Corp. for college and university courses, vocational and continuing education, student exchange programs, and other educational opportunities as determined by the KEF board of directors. Awards range from $100 to $1,500.

Mary Morgan-Wolf Memorial Scholarships: The foundation annually awards a two- or four-year scholarship to a Native student from the middle Kuskokwim region who is entering a health-related field. Applicant must attend a college or vocational institution with a GPA of 2.0 and must be returning to the Kuskokwim area after the degree is received. Award amounts range from $1,500 for the first year to $2,000 or more for the following years.

Nick Mellick Memorial Scholarship Fund: The foundation annually awards scholarships to TKC Region shareholders and descendents to pursue a degree in business or a related field. Applicants must attend a college or vocational institution with a GPA of 3.25 and must be returning to the Kuskokwim area after the degree is received. Award amounts range from $2,500 for the first year to $3,500 or more for the following years.

Suulutaaq Construction Scholarship: The foundation, in partnership with Nugget Construction and TKC, awards scholarships to students interested in heavy equipment, electrical work, carpentry, or a related field.

EIN: 920081529

124
Edna P. McCurdy Scholarship Foundation

P.O. Box 149
Unalaska, AK   99685-0149   (907) 581-1276
Contact: Chris Salts

Foundation type: Company-sponsored foundation
Purpose: Scholarships to shareholders of Ounalashka Corp., and their descendents for educational training.
Publications: Application guidelines.
Financial data: Year ended 12/31/2012. Assets, $625,974 (M); Expenditures, $122,240; Total giving, $119,836; Grants to individuals, 18 grants totaling $119,836 (high: $10,936, low: $2,367).
Fields of interest: Vocational education, post-secondary; Higher education.
Type of support: Graduate support; Undergraduate support.
Application information: Applications accepted. Application form required. Application form available on the grantmaker's web site.
> *Initial approach:* Application
> *Send request by:* Mail
> *Deadline(s):* 30 days prior to your school's deadline
> *Applicants should submit the following:*
> 1) Essay
> 2) Letter(s) of recommendation
> 3) Financial information
> 4) Transcripts
> *Additional information:* Application should also include written evidence of acceptance from a school, and an estimation of school expenses.

Program description:

Scholarships: The foundation awards scholarships of up to $5,000 to shareholders of Ounalashka Corp. and their descendents. Scholarships are available for trade and career schools, Bachelor programs lasting five years, Masters programs lasting two years, and Ph.D. programs lasting one year. Funding for tuition, room, and board are only offered to full-time students living on campus. Students must meet certain criteria including a base GPA.
EIN: 920157058

125
Monroe Foundation, Inc.

215 Betty St.
P.O. Box 71620
Fairbanks, AK   99707-1620   (907) 456-7970

Foundation type: Public charity
Purpose: Scholarships to individuals for attendance at Catholic schools in Fairbanks, AK.
Financial data: Year ended 06/30/2012. Assets, $1,955,680 (M); Expenditures, $1,271,246; Total giving, $1,108,101; Grants to individuals, totaling $8,000.
Fields of interest: Education; Catholic agencies & churches.
Type of support: Precollege support.
Application information: Applications accepted.
> *Additional information:* Contact foundation for current application deadline/guidelines.
EIN: 930747034

126
MTNT Foundation, Inc.

P.O. Box 309
McGrath, AK   99627-0309   (907) 524-3056
Contact: Betty Magnuson, V.P.

Foundation type: Independent foundation

Purpose: Scholarships to family and relatives of shareholders of MTNT, Ltd., for higher education.
Financial data: Year ended 09/30/2011. Assets, $5,090 (M); Expenditures, $25,769; Total giving, $23,284; Grants to individuals, 18 grants totaling $23,284 (high: $2,400, low: $84).
Fields of interest: Vocational education, post-secondary; Higher education.
Type of support: Scholarships—to individuals.
Application information: Applications accepted. Application form required.
> *Deadline(s):* July 30
> *Applicants should submit the following:*
> 1) Transcripts
> 2) Letter(s) of recommendation
> *Additional information:* Application should also include letter of acceptance from college or vocational school. A 2.0 GPA is required to be eligible for further awards. All checks will be sent directly to the educational institution on behalf of the students.
EIN: 920173151

127
Robert "Aqqaluk" Newlin, Sr. Memorial Trust
333 Shore Ave., Ste. 202
P.O. Box 509
Kotzebue, AK 99752-0509 (907) 442-1607
Contact: Erica Nelson, Pres.
FAX: (907) 442-2289;
E-mail: erica.nelson@nana.com; Toll-free tel.: (866) 442-1607; URL: http://aqqaluktrust.com

Foundation type: Public charity
Purpose: Scholarships to Native Alaskans of the Anchorage region who are NANA shareholders or the descendants of NANA shareholders for educational and vocational achievement.
Publications: Application guidelines; Informational brochure (including application guidelines).
Financial data: Year ended 12/31/2011. Assets, $16,788,673 (M); Expenditures, $1,056,868; Total giving, $837,315; Grants to individuals, totaling $837,315.
Fields of interest: Native Americans/American Indians.
Type of support: Technical education support; Undergraduate support.
Application information: Applications accepted. Application form required. Application form available on the grantmaker's web site.
> *Deadline(s):* Contact trust for deadline
> *Applicants should submit the following:*
> 1) Financial information
> 2) Transcripts
> 3) Letter(s) of recommendation
> 4) Essay
> *Additional information:* Application must also include bio and proof of enrollment.
EIN: 943116762

128
Norton Sound Economic Development Corporation
420 L St., Ste. 310
Anchorage, AK 99501-1971 (907) 274-2248
Contact: Janis Ivanoff, Pres. and C.E.O.
FAX: (907) 274-2249; URL: http://www.nsedc.com/

Foundation type: Public charity
Purpose: Scholarships to northwestern AK students, as well as loans of up to $25,000 are available to Norton Sound-area commercial fisherman.

Publications: Application guidelines; Annual report; Newsletter; Quarterly report.
Financial data: Year ended 12/31/2011. Assets, $166,311,143 (M); Expenditures, $14,282,706; Total giving, $3,576,074; Grants to individuals, totaling $840,812.
Type of support: Undergraduate support; Loans—to individuals.
Application information:
> *Initial approach:* Letter
> *Additional information:* Contact foundation for eligibility criteria.
Program descriptions:
> *Employment, Education, and Training (EET) Program Scholarships:* Scholarships of up to $2,000 are available to northwestern Alaska students who are enrolled full-time at an accredited college, university, or vocational school. Eligible applicants must: be residents of the Norton Sound region; be enrolled in an accredited two-year associate program, four-year college or university, master's program, Ph.D. program, or vocational institution; carry a minimum credit load of 12 hours per semester (or ten hours per quarter); and maintain a minimum GPA of 2.0.
> *Revolving Loan Program:* Loans of up to $25,000 are available to Norton Sound-area commercial fisherman who fish commercially for herring, salmon, red king crab, halibut, baitfish, and other species that are authorized for commercial harvest by the Alaska Department of Fish and Game.
EIN: 860710582

129
Old Harbor Scholarship Foundation
2702 Denali St., Ste. 100
Anchorage, AK 99503-0071 (907) 286-2286
Contact: Kim Fraser
Application address: P.O. Box 71, Old Harbor, AK 99643

Foundation type: Company-sponsored foundation
Purpose: Scholarships to Old Harbour Native Corporation shareholders, their dependents, and descendants. Applicants must be either Alaska Natives or descendants thereof.
Financial data: Year ended 12/31/2011. Assets, $146,386 (M); Expenditures, $100,814; Total giving, $25,500; Grants to individuals, 22 grants totaling $25,500 (high: $2,500, low: $1,000).
Type of support: Undergraduate support.
Application information: Applications accepted. Application form required.
> *Additional information:* Application must include proof of college enrollment and letters of recommendation.
EIN: 920154160

130
Pioneer Igloo No. 1
P.O. Box 55
Nome, AK 99762-1101 (907) 443-3565
Contact: Laura Samuelson, Pres.

Foundation type: Public charity
Purpose: Scholarships to residents of Nome, AK.
Financial data: Year ended 12/31/2012. Assets, $33,570 (M); Expenditures, $4,082; Total giving, $1,772; Grants to individuals, totaling $272.
Type of support: Undergraduate support.
Application information:
> *Initial approach:* Letter
EIN: 926003434

131
Providence Alaska Foundation
3400 Health Dr.
P.O. Box 196604
Anchorage, AK 99508 (907) 212-3600
Contact: Susan Ruddy C.F.R.E., Pres.
FAX: (907) 212-3048; URL: http://alaska.providence.org/giving/Pages/about.aspx

Foundation type: Public charity
Purpose: Emergency financial assistance to employees of Providence Health Systems, AK.
Publications: Annual report.
Financial data: Year ended 12/31/2011. Assets, $18,252,090 (M); Expenditures, $3,627,479; Total giving, $2,451,171; Grants to individuals, totaling $37,100.
Type of support: Employee-related welfare.
Application information: Contact foundation for complete application guidelines.
EIN: 920093565

132
Rasmuson Foundation
301 W. Northern Lights Blvd., Ste. 400
Anchorage, AK 99503-2648 (907) 297-2700
Contact: Diane S. Kaplan, C.E.O. and Pres.; Ian Dutton, V.P. and C.O.O.; Sammye Pokryfi, V.P., Prog (s).
FAX: (907) 297-2770;
E-mail: rasmusonfdn@rasmuson.org; Toll free tel. within Alaska: (877) 366-2700; URL: http://www.rasmuson.org

Foundation type: Independent foundation
Purpose: Fellowships and awards to artists residing in AK.
Publications: Application guidelines; Annual report; Grants list; Informational brochure (including application guidelines); Newsletter; Occasional report.
Financial data: Year ended 12/31/2012. Assets, $569,389,107 (M); Expenditures, $29,480,222; Total giving, $16,809,329; Grants to individuals, 37 grants totaling $263,200 (high: $25,000, low: $2,800).
Fields of interest: Folk arts; Media/communications; Visual arts; Performing arts; Choreography; Music composition; Literature; Management/technical assistance; Administration/regulation.
Type of support: Program development; Fellowships; Awards/prizes; Residencies; Stipends.
Application information: Applications accepted. Application form required. Application form available on the grantmaker's web site.
> *Initial approach:* Letter or telephone for fellowships and awards. Online application available.
> *Deadline(s):* Mar. 1 for Project Awards, Distinguished Artist and Artists Fellowships
> *Additional information:* Application for projects, fellowships and awards should include budget information, resume, work samples, project description, artist statement and SASE. See web site for additional application information.
Program descriptions:
> *Artist Fellowship:* The foundation has created three award programs for individual artists living and working in Alaska: 1) Distinguished Artist: one annual $40,000 award for a mature artist of recognized stature with a history of creative excellence and accomplishment in the arts; 2) Project Awards: grants of $7,500 for emerging mid-career, and mature artists for specific, short

term projects that have a clear benefit to the artist and the development of his/her work; and 3) Artist Fellowships: $18,000 awards for mid career or mature artists to focus their energy and attention for a one year period on developing their creative work. The program awards grants in ten artistic disciplines. These awards will provide artists the resources to concentrate and reflect on their work, to immerse themselves in a creative endeavor, and to experiment, explore and develop their artistry more fully. It is the foundation's hope that these investments in individual artists will result in substantial contributions to the culture of Alaska, the vibrancy of its communities, and to the art itself. See the foundation website for more details.

Sabbatical Program: The foundation believes that nonprofit Chief Executive Officers and tribal administrators better serve their organization when they have extended opportunity to reflect on their work, gain insight into what they want to accomplish in their careers, learn better ways to run their agencies, and renew their personal energy. To achieve these objectives and help prevent job related stress and burnout, the foundation endorses the concept of sabbaticals and has committed funds to support time off for outstanding nonprofit and tribal leaders in Alaska. The sabbatical is not only a reward for achievement, it is a motivating factor to keep the best people in the field. This award is for the personal growth or renewal of the applicant - with no bias toward either reason. Activities dedicated to personal renewal as defined by the recipient may include travel, study, time for reflection, or simply rest. Awards will support sabbaticals of a minimum of 60 continuous and a maximum of 180 continuous days. The amount of each grant will be up to $40,000. Although grants will be awarded to the organization, they are to be used specifically for the individual taking the sabbatical to cover salary and expenses during the sabbatical. No distinction will be made between large and small organizations. Applications can be downloaded from the foundation web site.
EIN: 916340739

133

Peter Rooney Wrangell Community Foundation

P.O. Box 775
Wrangell, AK 99929-0775
Contact: Janelle Privett, Pres.
Application address: P.O. Box 1063, Wrangell, AK 99929-1063; URL: http://peterrooneyfund.org

Foundation type: Operating foundation
Purpose: Grants to AK leukemia patients aged 18 or younger who need to travel for treatments.
Financial data: Year ended 12/31/2011. Assets, $206,632 (M); Expenditures, $11,983; Total giving, $7,421; Grant to an individual, 1 grant totaling $7,421.
Fields of interest: Leukemia.
Type of support: Grants for special needs.
Application information: Applications accepted. Application form required. Application form available on the grantmaker's web site.
Initial approach: Letter
EIN: 911834169

134

Harvey Samuelsen Scholarship Trust

P.O. Box 1464
Dillingham, AK 99576-1464 (907) 842-4370
Toll free tel.: (800) 478-4370 for questions regarding scholarship eligibility
FAX: (907) 842-4336; E-mail: kyle@bbedc.com; URL: http://www.bbedc.com/

Foundation type: Independent foundation
Purpose: Scholarships to residents of Aleknagik, Clarks Point, Dillingham, Egegik, Ekuk, Ekwok, King Salmon, Levelock, Manokotak, Naknek, Pilot Point, Port Heiden, Portage Creek, South Naknek, Togiak, Twin Hills, and Ugashik, AK. Undergraduate students must have a 2.0 GPA and graduate students must have a 3.0 GPA.
Financial data: Year ended 12/31/2012. Assets, $9,749,301 (M); Expenditures, $564,989; Total giving, $370,550; Grants to individuals, 88 grants totaling $370,550 (high: $7,480, low: $2,190).
Type of support: Graduate support; Undergraduate support.
Application information: Applications accepted. Application form required.
Send request by: Mail
Deadline(s): June 22
Applicants should submit the following:
  1) Financial information
  2) Transcripts
  3) Photograph
Additional information: Application should also include BBEDC Residency Form, letter of interest, college letter of acceptance, and copy of cost of attendance sheet.
EIN: 300065137

135

Elmer & Ruth Schwantes Scholarship Fund

1029 W. 3rd Ave., Ste. 600
Anchorage, AK 99501-1958 (907) 276-6015

Foundation type: Independent foundation
Purpose: Undergraduate scholarships to graduates of Spencer High School, Spencer, WI and high schools in AK.
Financial data: Year ended 12/31/2011. Assets, $231,265 (M); Expenditures, $32,134; Total giving, $20,000; Grants to individuals, 6 grants totaling $20,000 (high: $4,000, low: $2,000).
Fields of interest: Higher education.
Type of support: Support to graduates or students of specific schools; Undergraduate support.
Application information: Application form required.
Initial approach: Letter
Deadline(s): Vary
Additional information: Contact the fund for current application guidelines.
EIN: 920151161

136

Sealaska Heritage Institute

(formerly Sealaska Heritage Foundation)
1 Sealaska Plz., Ste. 301
Juneau, AK 99801-1245 (907) 463-4844
Contact: Deena LaRue, Mgr., Grants
FAX: (907) 586-9293;
E-mail: scholarship@sealaska.com; URL: http://www.sealaskaheritage.org

Foundation type: Public charity
Purpose: Scholarships and apprenticeships to Alaskan Native Americans who are Sealaska Corporation shareholders for college, university,

and vocational and technical schools. Giving primarily in AK, but giving also in lower 48 states.
Publications: Application guidelines; Informational brochure; Newsletter.
Financial data: Year ended 12/31/2011. Assets, $3,783,744 (M); Expenditures, $2,665,659; Total giving, $360,730; Grants to individuals, totaling $360,730.
Fields of interest: Native Americans/American Indians.
Type of support: Technical education support; Undergraduate support.
Application information: Application form required.
Initial approach: Letter or telephone
Deadline(s): Mar. 1
Final notification: Recipients notified May 1
Applicants should submit the following:
  1) Transcripts
  2) Letter(s) of recommendation
  3) Essay
Additional information: See web site for additional application information.
Program descriptions:
Corporate 7(i) Scholarship: Scholarships are available to applicant's whose major field of study relates to Sealaska Corporation's businesses.
Judson L. Brown Endowment Fund: The program awards one scholarship of $5,000 to an outstanding junior or senior college student.
Sealaska Endowment Scholarship: The institute awards academic scholarships for undergraduate, graduate, and vocational studies at accredited institutions.
EIN: 920081844

137

Jennie J. Seybert Memorial Scholarship Fund

5910 W. Diamond Blvd.
Anchorage, AK 99502-4004 (907) 243-7701
Contact: Orin D. Seybert, Chair.

Foundation type: Independent foundation
Purpose: Scholarships to eligible recipients from communities of Pilot Point or Chignik Lake, AK.
Financial data: Year ended 12/31/2010. Assets, $80,732 (M); Expenditures, $4,078; Total giving, $4,000; Grants to individuals, 4 grants totaling $4,000 (high: $1,000, low: $1,000).
Fields of interest: Education.
Type of support: Scholarships—to individuals.
Application information: Applications accepted.
Initial approach: Letter
Deadline(s): None
Additional information: Applicant must state goals, and what he/she hopes to attain.
EIN: 920162268

138

Sitnasuak Foundation

P.O. Box 905
Nome, AK 99762-0905 (907) 443-4305
Contact: Moriah Sallaffie
Applicationj address: c/o BSF, P.O. Box 1008, Nome, AK 99762 Tel.: (907) 443-4305;
URL: http://www.snc.org/foundation

Foundation type: Company-sponsored foundation
Purpose: Scholarships, stipends, grants, student aid, and other means of support to students of Alaska for educational training at colleges and other institutions.
Financial data: Year ended 12/31/2011. Assets, $1,635 (M); Expenditures, $88,945; Total giving, $88,000.
Fields of interest: Higher education.

Type of support: Scholarships—to individuals.
Application information: Applications accepted.
Initial approach: Letter
Deadline(s): Apr. 30
Applicants should submit the following:
1) Transcripts
2) Letter(s) of recommendation
Additional information: Application should also include letter of acceptance from college, and class enrollment. Scholarship award is based on financial need and applicant's GPA.
EIN: 920148088

139
SNA Foundation
P.O. Drawer L
Seldovia, AK   99663-0250   (907) 234-7625
URL: http://www.snai.com/shareholders/sna-foundation.html

Foundation type: Company-sponsored foundation
Purpose: Scholarships to AK natives, their children and spouses who are native shareholders or descendants of shareholders.
Publications: Application guidelines.
Financial data: Year ended 12/31/2012. Assets, $166,592 (M); Expenditures, $7,168; Total giving, $6,100; Grants to individuals, 6 grants totaling $6,100 (high: $1,500, low: -$400).
Fields of interest: Education; Native Americans/American Indians.
Type of support: Scholarships—to individuals; Graduate support; Undergraduate support.
Application information: Applications accepted. Application form required. Application form available on the grantmaker's web site.
Initial approach: Application
Send request by: Mail or hand delivered
Copies of proposal: 1
Deadline(s): July 1
Applicants should submit the following:
1) Financial information
2) Photograph
3) Transcripts
4) Letter(s) of recommendation
Additional information: Application should also include proof of acceptance letter from college or university.
EIN: 920157596

140
Tanana Chiefs Conference
122 First Ave., Ste. 600
Fairbanks, AK   99701-4871   (907) 452-8251
FAX: (907) 459-3840;
E-mail: info@tananachiefs.org; Toll-free tel. (AK only): (800) 478-6822; toll-free tel. (outside of AK only): (800) 770-8251; URL: http://www.tananachiefs.org

Foundation type: Public charity
Purpose: Funding for vocational education to eligible tribal members residing in the five Interior villages of Birch Creek, Circle, Huslia, Minto, and Tetlin, as well as Fairbanks, AK. Individuals must be degree-seeking and accepted by an accredited vocational training school in Alaska or the United States.
Financial data: Year ended 09/30/2011. Assets, $148,863,210 (M); Expenditures, $99,227,944; Total giving, $9,442,968; Grants to individuals, totaling $9,092,900.
Fields of interest: Adult/continuing education; Education; Native Americans/American Indians.
Type of support: Undergraduate support.

Application information: Applications accepted. Application form required. Application form available on the grantmaker's web site.
Initial approach: E-mail or tel.
Deadline(s): Mar. 15, Apr. 30, Nov. 15
Applicants should submit the following:
1) FAFSA
2) Essay
3) Transcripts
4) Letter(s) of recommendation
Additional information: TCC does not accept faxed applications.
EIN: 920040308

141
Tanaq Foundation
4141 B St., Ste. 301
Anchorage, AK   99503
Contact: Kim Kashevarof

Foundation type: Independent foundation
Purpose: Scholarships to Native St. George Tanaq Corp. shareholders or their children for undergraduate education.
Financial data: Year ended 12/31/2011. Assets, $11,586 (M); Expenditures, $17,999; Total giving, $16,500; Grants to individuals, 10 grants totaling $16,500 (high: $2,500, low: $1,000).
Fields of interest: Native Americans/American Indians.
Type of support: Undergraduate support.
Application information: Application form required.
Deadline(s): June 30 and Nov. 30
Applicants should submit the following:
1) Transcripts
2) Letter(s) of recommendation
3) Essay
Additional information: Application must also include proof of postsecondary enrollment.
EIN: 920150959

142
TDX Foundation
615 E. 82nd Ave., Ste. 200
Anchorage, AK   99518   (907) 278-2312
URL: http://www.tanadgusix.com/

Foundation type: Company-sponsored foundation
Purpose: Educational support to Native Americans residing in AK, and their descendants that are recorded or beneficial owners of TDX common stock.
Financial data: Year ended 09/30/2012. Assets, $101,747 (M); Expenditures, $239,566; Total giving, $51,475; Grants to individuals, 59 grants totaling $51,475 (high: $2,000, low: $500).
Fields of interest: Native Americans/American Indians.
Type of support: Scholarships—to individuals.
Application information: Applications accepted.
Initial approach: Letter
Deadline(s): Aug. 1
Additional information: Application must include transcripts and a letter of acceptance.
EIN: 920144730

143
Territorial Sportsmen Scholarship
P. O. Box 35014
Juneau, AK   99803-5014   (907) 586-1602
Contact: Malin Babcock, Pres.

Foundation type: Public charity
Purpose: Scholarships to graduating seniors from high schools in Juneau, AK, who support

conservation and maintenance of healthy fish and wildlife populations and their habitats, and fair and equitable hunting and fishing rights for sportsmen.
Financial data: Year ended 12/31/2011. Assets, $421,498 (M); Expenditures, $53,070; Total giving, $48,000; Grants to individuals, totaling $48,000.
Fields of interest: Athletics/sports, fishing/hunting.
Type of support: Technical education support; Undergraduate support.
Application information: Applications accepted. Application form required. Interview required.
Applicants should submit the following:
1) Photograph
2) Resume
3) Letter(s) of recommendation
4) ACT
5) SAT
6) Transcripts
Program description:
Scholarships: Scholarships are open to any Juneau Borough graduating senior who supports the goals and objectives of the Territorial Sportsmen, Inc. which are: to actively promote conservation and maintenance of healthy fish and wildlife populations and their habitats; to work for fair and equitable fishing and hunting rights for sportsmen; to promote and maintain friendly and respectful relations between sportsmen and state, federal and private landowners; to educate people in fish and wildlife conservation; and to promote adherence to hunting and fishing regulations and firearms safety. Scholarships are awarded without regard to an applicant's intended field of study. Up to four scholarships of $12,000 each may be awarded each year.
EIN: 920153117

144
Tigara Educational Foundation Inc.
P.O. Box 9
Point Hope, AK   99766-0009   (907) 368-2235

Foundation type: Company-sponsored foundation
Purpose: Scholarships to students who are natives of the Point Hope Region, AK and their dependents for higher education.
Financial data: Year ended 06/30/2013. Assets, $2,829 (M); Expenditures, $57,907; Total giving, $31,700; Grants to individuals, 32 grants totaling $19,200 (high: $600, low: $600).
Fields of interest: Higher education; Native Americans/American Indians.
Type of support: Scholarships—to individuals.
Application information: Applications accepted.
Initial approach: Letter
Deadline(s): Ongoing
Applicants should submit the following:
1) Transcripts
2) GPA
Additional information: Written application must be delivered to the foundation. College students must provide proof of enrollment into college, and applicant must maintain a 2.0 GPA.
EIN: 920158717

145
UIC Foundation, Inc.
3201 C St., Ste. 801
Anchorage, AK   99503   (907) 852-4460
Contact: Rebecca Brower
Application Address: P.O. Box 890, Barrow, AK-99723; URL: http://www.uicalaska.com/

Foundation type: Company-sponsored foundation
Purpose: Scholarships to UIC shareholders and their children to attend any university, college, or training institute.
Publications: Application guidelines; Financial statement.
Financial data: Year ended 12/31/2012. Assets, $60,101 (M); Expenditures, $148,001; Total giving, $147,920; 120 grants totaling $147,920 (high: $3,000, low: $350).
Fields of interest: Vocational education, post-secondary; Higher education.
Type of support: Fellowships; Scholarships—to individuals.
Application information: Application form required. Application form available on the grantmaker's web site.
　Initial approach: Telephone
　Send request by: Mail or fax
　Copies of proposal: 1
　Deadline(s): Mar. 1, May 1, Aug. 1, Dec. 1
　Final notification: Recipients notified in two weeks
　Applicants should submit the following:
　　1) Transcripts
　　2) SAT
　　3) Letter(s) of recommendation
　　4) GPA
　　5) Financial information
　　6) Budget Information
　　7) ACT
　Additional information: Application should also include a letter of acceptance from the school student will attend and a personal statement detailing future career plans after completion of college or training.
EIN: 920157584

146
University of Alaska Foundation
910 Yukon Dr., Ste. 206
P.O. Box 755080
Fairbanks, AK 99775-9702 (907) 450-8030
Contact: Carla Beam, Pres.
FAX: (907) 450-8031;
E-Mail: foundation@alaska.edu; E-Mail for Carla Beam: carla.beam@alaska.edu; Fax for Carla beam: (907) 786-1369; URL: http://www.alaska.edu/foundation/

Foundation type: Public charity
Purpose: Scholarships to students attending any campus of the University of Alaska for higher education. Research grants on migratory bird species, their biology, general ecology and habitat relationships.
Publications: Application guidelines.
Financial data: Year ended 06/30/2012. Assets, $197,524,368 (M); Expenditures, $16,537,519; Total giving, $13,719,810; Grants to individuals, totaling $40,000.
Fields of interest: Higher education; Animals/wildlife, bird preserves; Animals/wildlife.
Type of support: Professorships; Research; Scholarships—to individuals; Awards/prizes.
Application information: Applications accepted.
　Initial approach: Proposal for Research grant
　Send request by: Online for scholarships
　Deadline(s): Feb. 15 for Scholarships, Nov. for Research Grant and Harold T. Caven Professorship, Dec. for Edith R. Bullock Prize
　Final notification: Recipients notified mid-Feb. for Research Grant

Additional information: Application should include FAFSA and an essay approximately 500 words for scholarships. See web site for additional application guidelines for scholarships and grants.
Program descriptions:
　Angus Gavin Migratory Bird Research Grant: This fund provides grants to support research on migratory bird species and their biology, general ecology, and habitat relationships. Grants are used for the support of research on bird species found either permanently or seasonally in Alaska or its coastal waters. Research specific to the management of bird species will be given preference. Proposals for this grant will be accepted from scientists within the University of Alaska system, including graduate students and faculty members employed within the university system.
　Edith R. Bullock Prize for Excellence: The prize is awarded to an individual whose work has demonstrated excellence in support of Alaska's State University. The individual must demonstrate a specific, definable, notable accomplishment which benefits the University and demonstrate general support of the University either through service advocacy or philanthropy. Any individual, regardless of University affiliation, is eligible for nomination for the prize.
　Harold T. Caven Professorship: This award is up to $10,000 each year for up to two years, is given to faculty members in business and finance within the University of Alaska system, and is intended to help carry out activities and projects designed to enhance the field of business and finance beyond those associated with the recipient's normal faculty assignments.
EIN: 237394620

147
The Usibelli Foundation
100 Cushman St., Ste. 210
Fairbanks, AK 99701-4674 (907) 452-2625
Contact: Bill Brophy, Exec. Dir.
E-mail: info@usibelli.com; URL: http://www.usibelli.com/Community_found.php

Foundation type: Company-sponsored foundation
Purpose: Scholarship to students of Alaska for the study of mining and geological engineering, and to individuals for outstanding research, teaching and public service.
Publications: Application guidelines; Program policy statement.
Financial data: Year ended 12/31/2012. Assets, $2,253,027 (M); Expenditures, $118,803; Total giving, $112,210.
Type of support: Scholarships—to individuals; Support to graduates or students of specific schools.
Application information:
　Initial approach: Letter
　Deadline(s): Mar. 1, June 1, Sept. 1, and Dec. 1
　Additional information: Contact foundation for eligibility requirements.
Program descriptions:
　Emil Usibelli Distinguished Teaching, Research, and Service Awards: The foundation annually awards three $10,000 scholarships to individuals who display extraordinary excellence in teaching, research, or public service.
　Tri-Valley High School Scholarships: The foundation annually awards college scholarships to five graduates of Tri-Valley high school based on

academic excellence and class standing. The foundation awards an Emil Usibelli Scholarship for $1,500, a Cecil Lester Memorial Scholarship for $1,250, and three Usibelli Coal Mine Scholarships for $750.
EIN: 943152617

148
Valley Hospital Association, Inc.
950 E. Bogard Rd., Ste. 218
Wasilla, AK 99654-7172 (907) 352-2863
Contact: Elizabeth Ripley, Exec. Dir.
FAX: (907) 352-2865;
E-mail: info@matsuhealthfoundation.org; E-mail For Elizabeth Ripley: eripley@healthymatsu.org;
URL: http://www.matsuhealthfoundation.org

Foundation type: Public charity
Purpose: Scholarships to graduating high school seniors, undergraduate, and graduate students of Mat-Su, AK to complete a degree or certificate program in a health-related major.
Publications: Application guidelines.
Financial data: Year ended 12/31/2011. Assets, $99,227,234 (M); Expenditures, $4,751,777; Total giving, $3,791,159; Grants to individuals, totaling $94,047.
Fields of interest: Health sciences school/education.
Type of support: Scholarships—to individuals; Graduate support; Undergraduate support.
Application information: Applications accepted. Application form available on the grantmaker's web site.
　Send request by: Online
　Deadline(s): Mar. 19
　Additional information: Applicants must submit letter of acceptance from the college or university.
Program description:
　Scholarships: Scholarships, ranging from $1,000 to $10,000, will be available to residents of Matanuska-Susitna Borough who are currently enrolled, or are planning to enroll, in a health-care discipline at an accredited college or university. Each application will be reviewed for clarity of healthcare career goals and the value of those goals to the health care community, demonstrated interest in the healthcare field through job experience, volunteer efforts, internships, or related course offerings, and past academic performance.
EIN: 920019395

149
West High Alumni Association
2525 C St., Ste. 100
Anchorage, AK 99503-2632 (907) 563-6722
Contact: Kivlina Block, Pres.

Foundation type: Public charity
Purpose: Scholarships to graduates of West Anchorage High School, AK.
Financial data: Year ended 12/31/2011. Assets, $372,281 (M); Expenditures, $278,757.
Type of support: Support to graduates or students of specific schools; Undergraduate support.
Application information: Applications accepted. Application form required.
　Initial approach: Letter
EIN: 943079511

ARIZONA

150
The 100 Club of Arizona
5033 N. 19th. Ave., Ste. 123
Phoenix, AZ 85015-3203 (602) 485-0100
Contact: Sharon Knutson-Felix, Exec. Dir.
FAX: (602) 242-1715; E-mail: info@100club.org;
Toll-free tel.: (877) 564-6100, E-Mail For Sharon
Knutson-Felix :sharon@100club.org; URL: http://
www.100club.org

Foundation type: Public charity
Purpose: Scholarships to family members of AZ
public safety officers/firefighters who have suffered
death or injury. Financial assistance to individual
law enforcement officers or their families in time of
need.
Publications: Application guidelines; Newsletter.
Financial data: Year ended 12/31/2011. Assets,
$1,899,141 (M); Expenditures, $1,549,868; Total
giving, $905,111; Grants to individuals, totaling
$685,872.
Fields of interest: Vocational education,
post-secondary; Higher education; Government
agencies.
Type of support: Undergraduate support; Grants for
special needs.
Application information: Applications accepted.
Application form required. Application form
available on the grantmaker's web site. Interview
required.
Initial approach: Letter or telephone
Deadline(s): Varies
Applicants should submit the following:
  1) Essay
  2) Letter(s) of recommendation
  3) Transcripts
Additional information: Application by fax or
  e-mail not accepted.
Program description:
Scholarship Program: This program provides
financial education assistance to family members
of public safety officers and firefighters who have
been killed or injured in the line of duty, as well as
family members of active or retired Arizona public
safety officers and firefighters. Scholarships are
awarded to individuals who wish to pursue a course
of study beyond high school, including accredited
colleges and universities and postsecondary trade
schools. Scholarships are not awarded for
post-graduate study.
EIN: 237172077

151
Adelante Foundation Inc.
P.O. Box 488
Chandler, AZ 85244-0488 (480) 895-9350
Contact: Barbara Jefferson

Foundation type: Independent foundation
Purpose: Scholarships to residents of AZ, for
continuing education at accredited institutions of
higher learning.
Financial data: Year ended 12/31/2012. Assets,
$4,392,077 (M); Expenditures, $272,781; Total
giving, $208,601; Grants to individuals, 13 grants
totaling $20,016 (high: $4,000, low: $303).
Fields of interest: Higher education.
Type of support: Undergraduate support.
Application information: Applications accepted.
Application form required.
Deadline(s): 90 days before needed

Additional information: Application should
  include a 500-word essay outlining the
  applicant's reason for choosing his/her
  course of study.
EIN: 860966575

152
The Agape Foundation
5333 N. 7th St., Ste. C-222
Phoenix, AZ 85014

Foundation type: Independent foundation
Purpose: Awards to families with special needs
children.
Financial data: Year ended 12/31/2012. Assets,
$616,805 (M); Expenditures, $138,656; Total
giving, $135,500.
Fields of interest: Mental health, disorders;
Residential/custodial care; Disabilities, people
with.
Type of support: Grants for special needs.
Application information: Applications not
accepted.
Additional information: Unsolicited requests for
  funds not considered or acknowledged.
EIN: 860840802

153
Alhambra Foundation for the Future
4510 N. 37th Ave.
Phoenix, AZ 85019-3206 (602) 336-2925
FAX: (602) 336-2270;
E-mail: communityrelations@alhambraesd.org;
URL: http://www.alhambraesd.org/

Foundation type: Public charity
Purpose: Scholarships to graduates of any
Alhambra, AZ elementary school attending a junior
college or university in AZ. Scholarships are also
available for post-secondary education such as
trade, craft and technological schools and
health-related programs.
Financial data: Year ended 06/30/2012. Assets,
$1,368,737 (M); Expenditures, $191,429; Total
giving, $189,243; Grants to individuals, totaling
$189,243.
Type of support: Support to graduates or students
of specific schools; Technical education support;
Undergraduate support.
Application information:
Initial approach: Telephone or e-mail
EIN: 860729940

154
Alliance Defense Fund, Inc.
15100 N. 90th St.
Scottsdale, AZ 85260-2901
FAX: (480) 444-0028; URL: http://
www.alliancedefendingfreedom.org/

Foundation type: Public charity
Purpose: Fellowships for law students who have
demonstrated outstanding achievements, aptitude,
leadership, and career potential during their legal
studies.
Financial data: Year ended 06/30/2011. Assets,
$37,374,797 (M); Expenditures, $33,848,974;
Total giving, $2,462,191; Grants to individuals,
118 grants totaling $744,531.
Fields of interest: Law school/education.
Type of support: Fellowships.
Application information: Applications accepted.
Additional information: Contact the fund for
  additional guidelines.
EIN: 541660459

155
Arizona Burn Foundation
(formerly Foundation for Burns and Trauma, Inc.)
333 E. Virginia Ave., Ste. 204
Phoenix, AZ 85004-1210 (602) 230-2041
Contact: Mike Merucci, Exec. Dir.
Application address: Attn: Scholarship Request,
P.O. Box 1329, Phoenix, AZ 85001
FAX: (602) 230-2157;
E-mail: mike.merucci@azburn.org; Mailing Address:
PO Box 1329, Phoenix, AZ, 85001; URL: http://
www.azburn.org

Foundation type: Public charity
Purpose: Scholarships to Arizona residents who
have survived serious burn injury.
Publications: Application guidelines; Financial
statement; Newsletter.
Financial data: Year ended 09/30/2011. Assets,
$1,768,378 (M); Expenditures, $956,931; Total
giving, $100,559; Grants to individuals, totaling
$100,559.
Fields of interest: Higher education.
Type of support: Scholarships—to individuals.
Application information: Applications accepted.
Application form required. Application form
available on the grantmaker's web site.
Initial approach: Application
Send request by: Mail
Deadline(s): One month before the start of the
  semester
Final notification: Applicants notified within two
  weeks after receipt of application
Applicants should submit the following:
  1) Financial information
  2) Letter(s) of recommendation
  3) Transcripts
  4) Essay
Additional information: See web site for
  additional application guidelines.
Program description:
*MacDonald Wood, M.D. Burn Survivor Educational
Scholarship Program:* Scholarships of up to $1,500
per quarter or semester are available to Arizona
residents who survived a serious burn that required
hospitalization. Applicants must be 17 years of age
or older and enrolled in an undergraduate diploma
or certificate program at a state licensed and
accredited institution. Renewal applicants are
required to have passing grades in all courses and
to retain a GPA at or above 2.5 and are required to
have volunteered for at least one Arizona Burn
Foundation sponsored event the previous quarter or
semester. Applicants will be judged on academic
ability, financial need and the recommendation of a
teacher or counselor.
EIN: 860207519

156
Arizona College Scholarship Foundation
4040 E. Camelback Rd., Ste. 220
Phoenix, AZ 85018-8361 (602) 636-1850
Contact: Rich Nickel, Pres. and C.E.O.
FAX: (602) 636-1857; E-mail: info@azcsf.org;
URL: http://www.azcsf.org

Foundation type: Public charity
Purpose: College scholarships to graduates of
Arizona high schools for attendance at colleges or
universities in AZ.
Financial data: Year ended 12/31/2011. Assets,
$17,425,043 (M); Expenditures, $2,506,542;
Total giving, $1,672,150; Grants to individuals,
totaling $1,672,150.
Fields of interest: Higher education.
Type of support: Scholarships—to individuals.

Application information: Applications accepted. Application form required.
  Deadline(s): End of Mar.
  Additional information: Students must be recommended by one of the ACSF partner organizations. Applicant must demonstrate significant financial need.
EIN: 202366755

157
Arizona Community Foundation
2201 E. Camelback Rd., Ste. 405B
Phoenix, AZ 85016-3431   (602) 381-1400
Contact: Paul Velaski, C.F.O.; Peg Reirson, C.P.A.
FAX: (602) 381-1575;
E-mail: pvelaski@azfoundation.org; Grant application e-mail: grants@azfoundation.org;
URL: http://www.azfoundation.org

Foundation type: Community foundation
Purpose: Scholarships to residents of AZ to attend Arizona State University, Northern Arizona University, or University of Arizona.
Publications: Application guidelines; Annual report; Financial statement; Informational brochure; Newsletter; Program policy statement.
Financial data: Year ended 03/31/2013. Assets, $556,710,301 (M); Expenditures, $55,409,581; Total giving, $38,633,992. Scholarships—to individuals amount not specified.
Fields of interest: Higher education; Scholarships/financial aid.
Type of support: Scholarships—to individuals; Support to graduates or students of specific schools; Undergraduate support.
Application information: Applications accepted. Application form required. Application form available on the grantmaker's web site.
  Send request by: Online
  Deadline(s): Varies
  Additional information: See web site for complete listing of scholarships.
Program description:
  Scholarships: Scholarships are paid from more than 80 individual scholarship funds to assist students pursuing higher education. The donor who creates the fund can designate a specific institution, such as a college or vocational school, to receive the funds and select annual award recipients, provide guidance to the foundation on the goals of the scholarship program but leave the selection process to the foundation, or, participate as a member of the selection committee, reviewing individual applications and evaluating award recipients.
EIN: 860348306

158
Arizona Foundation for Legal Services and Education
4201 N. 24th St., Ste. 210
Phoenix, AZ 85016-6288   (602) 340-7366
Contact: Kevin Ruegg Ph.D., Exec. Dir. and C.E.O.
FAX: (602) 773-3105; URL: http://www.azflse.org

Foundation type: Public charity
Purpose: Scholarships to teachers for professional development training and loans to law school graduates to assist them in paying their law school loans.
Publications: Annual report; Newsletter (including application guidelines).
Financial data: Year ended 12/31/2011. Assets, $1,119,431 (M); Expenditures, $3,237,102; Total giving, $1,441,543; Grants to individuals, totaling $24,812.

Fields of interest: Law school/education; Science.
Type of support: Scholarships—to individuals; Loans—to individuals.
Application information: Application form required. Application form available on the grantmaker's web site.
  Initial approach: Letter
  Send request by: Mail, fax or e-mail
  Deadline(s): Oct. 21 for Loan Repayment, none for Scholarship
  Additional information: See web site for complete application information.
Program descriptions:
  Joyce Holsey's Loan Repayment Program: This program provides loan assistance for law school graduates employed in programs dedicated to serving the civil legal needs of the poor, and to supplement low salaries paid to legal aid attorneys by providing forgivable loans to assist in paying law school loans. Eligible applicants must be members of the State Bar of Arizona, be employed by an approved nonprofit legal organization (as listed on the foundation's web site), have an annual income of no more than $65,000, and have outstanding undergraduate or law school loans. Loans of up to $10,000 per year will be awarded, and are forgivable conditional to the applicant's continued employment at an approved nonprofit legal organization.
  Teacher Scholarship Program: Funding is available to attend the foundation's annual Law-Related Education Academy.
EIN: 953351710

159
Arizona Kidney Foundation
360 E. Coronado Rd. Ste. 180
Phoenix, AZ 85018-5341   (602) 840-1644
Contact: Jeffrey D. Neff, C.E.O.
FAX: (602) 840-2360; E-mail: info@azkidney.org;
URL: http://www.azkidney.org

Foundation type: Public charity
Purpose: Scholarships to kidney patients residing in AZ. Financial assistance to kidney patients residing in AZ, for dental needs, food, medications, transportation, nutritional supplements, rent or mortgage payments, and utilities.
Publications: Annual report.
Financial data: Year ended 06/30/2012. Assets, $2,851,188 (M); Expenditures, $1,498,003; Total giving, $196,511; Grants to individuals, totaling $196,511.
Fields of interest: Kidney diseases.
Type of support: Undergraduate support; Grants for special needs.
Application information: Application form required. Application form available on the grantmaker's web site.
  Deadline(s): Contact foundation for current application deadline
  Additional information: Applications are to be reviewed by and submitted by the patient's renal social worker only; See web site for further information.
EIN: 866052343

160
Arizona National Guard Emergency Relief Fund
(formerly Army Reserve Component Emergency Relief Fund)
P.O. Box 64252
Phoenix, AZ 85082-3455   (480) 745-4725
Contact: Danielle Salomon, Fund Admin.
FAX: (602) 267-2954;
E-mail: azng.erfund@gmail.com

Foundation type: Public charity
Purpose: Emergency financial assistance, in the form of loans or grants, to service members of the AZ National Guard and their families.
Publications: Application guidelines.
Financial data: Year ended 12/31/2011. Assets, $94,874 (M); Expenditures, $57,559; Total giving, $57,559. Grants to individuals amount not specified.
Fields of interest: Military/veterans.
Type of support: Grants for special needs; Loans—to individuals.
Application information: Applications accepted. Application form required. Application form available on the grantmaker's web site.
  Initial approach: Mail, fax, telephone or e-mail
  Send request by: Mail, fax or e-mail
  Copies of proposal: 1
  Deadline(s): None
  Final notification: Applicants notified in one to two business days
  Additional information: Applications should include financial information.
EIN: 860837273

161
Arizona Private Education Scholarship Fund, Inc.
6909 E. Greenway Pkwy., Ste. 240
Scottsdale, AZ 85254-8826   (480) 699-8911
FAX: (480) 646-3196; E-mail: helpdesk@apesf.org;
URL: http://www.apesf.org

Foundation type: Public charity
Purpose: Scholarships to qualified students attending private K through 12 schools in Arizona.
Publications: Application guidelines.
Financial data: Year ended 06/30/2012. Assets, $703,193 (M); Expenditures, $1,469,466; Total giving, $1,238,140; Grants to individuals, totaling $1,234,609.
Fields of interest: Education.
Type of support: Scholarships—to individuals.
Application information: Applications accepted. Application form required. Application form available on the grantmaker's web site.
  Deadline(s): Feb. 28
  Additional information: Application should include copies of pages one and two of parents' most recent tax return and copy of each child's most recent report card.
Program description:
  Scholarships: Scholarships are available to students to children in grades K-12 who are enrolled at a qualified Arizona private school.
EIN: 860958161

162
Arizona Scholarship Fund
P.O. Box 2576
Mesa, AZ 85214-2576   (480) 497-4564
FAX: (480) 497-4737;
E-mail: customerservice@azscholarships.org;
URL: http://www.azscholarships.org

Foundation type: Public charity
Purpose: Scholarships to families residing in AZ to send their children to private schools, from K-12th grade.
Publications: Informational brochure; Program policy statement; Program policy statement (including application guidelines).
Financial data: Year ended 06/30/2012. Assets, $2,327,876 (M); Expenditures, $2,936,757; Total giving, $2,527,898.
Fields of interest: Elementary/secondary education.
Type of support: Scholarships—to individuals.
Application information: Applications accepted. Application form required. Application form available on the grantmaker's web site.
  Initial approach: Telephone
  Copies of proposal: 1
  Deadline(s): None
  Applicants should submit the following:
    1) Letter(s) of recommendation
    2) Financial information
    3) FAF
    4) Essay
  Additional information: Tuition is paid directly to the educational institution on behalf of the students.
Program description:
  Scholarship Program: Renewable scholarships of up to $1,000 per child are awarded on a first-come, first-served basis. Students must be Arizona residents, enrolled in grades K-12.
EIN: 860938314

163
Arizona School Choice Trust, Inc.
2875 W. Ray Rd., Ste. 6-314
Chandler, AZ 85224   (623) 414-3429
Contact: Liz Dreckman, Pres. and Exec. Dir.
FAX: (623) 243-6846; E-mail: admin1@asct.org;
E-mail For Liz Dreckman : ldreckman@asct.org;
URL: http://www.asct.org/

Foundation type: Public charity
Purpose: Scholarships to low-income families residing in AZ for tuition at K-12 schools.
Publications: Application guidelines.
Financial data: Year ended 07/31/2012. Assets, $4,449,532 (M); Expenditures, $3,190,133.
Fields of interest: Elementary/secondary education; Economically disadvantaged.
Type of support: Precollege support.
Application information: Applications accepted. Application form required. Application form available on the grantmaker's web site.
  Send request by: Mail
  Deadline(s): May 30
  Final notification: Recipients notified by June 30
  Additional information: Application should include tax returns and the $20 application fee.
Program description:
  ASCT Scholarships: Awards up to $5,400 per child per school year to low-income families and children who are disabled or in foster care who reside in Arizona with children in grades K-12. Awards are on a first-come first-served basis.
EIN: 860712553

164
Arizona Tuition Organization, Inc.
P.O. Box 11900
Prescott, AZ 86304-1900   (602) 295-3033
Contact: Lara Roehr, Exec. Dir.
FAX: (866) 833-5170; E-mail: admin@azto.org;
URL: http://www.azto.org/

Foundation type: Public charity
Purpose: Scholarships and tuition assistance to students from Kindergarten thru 12th grades for attendance at a private schools in Arizona.
Publications: Application guidelines.
Financial data: Year ended 06/30/2012. Assets, $194,943 (M); Expenditures, $1,200,243; Total giving, $1,101,738; Grants to individuals, totaling $1,101,738.
Fields of interest: Scholarships/financial aid; Education; Christian agencies & churches.
Type of support: Scholarships—to individuals.
Application information: Applications accepted. Application form required. Application form available on the grantmaker's web site.
  Send request by: Mail, fax, or e-mail
Program description:
  Scholarships: The organization provides scholarships to children attending Christian secondary schools in Arizona. Scholarships are awarded based on financial need.
EIN: 200575040

165
Arizona Water Association
(formerly Arizona Water and Pollution Control Association, also known as A.W.P.C.A.)
1042 Willow Creek Rd., A101-510
Prescott, AZ 86301-1673   (928) 717-9905
Contact: Deborah Muse, Exec. Dir.
Scholarship application address: c/o Jeanne Jensen, 2355 E. Camelback Rd., Ste. 700, Phoenix, AZ 85016-9044, tel.: (602) 217-1012, e-mail: jjensen@dswa.net
FAX: (928) 717-9910; E-mail: musegroup@aol.com;
Toll-free tel.: (888)-559-8844; E-Mail for Deborah Muse: musegroup@aol.com; URL: http://azwater.org/

Foundation type: Public charity
Purpose: Scholarships to individuals enrolled in an accredited program at colleges or universities pursuing education in water resource issues.
Financial data: Year ended 12/31/2011. Assets, $415,244 (M); Expenditures, $510,998; Total giving, $8,114; Grants to individuals, totaling $8,114.
Fields of interest: Environment, water resources.
Type of support: Graduate support; Undergraduate support.
Application information: Applications accepted.
  Send request by: Mail or on-line
  Deadline(s): Mar.
  Final notification: Apr.
Program description:
  Scholarship: Scholarships are awarded to undergraduate and graduate students at Arizona colleges and universities pursuing studies related to water, wastewater, or environmental resources. Scholarships will be awarded in $1,000 to $500 amounts to students who demonstrate achievement in chosen area of study, understanding of a pertinent water issue in Arizona, applicability of personal history and future plans, and creativity and writing ability. U.S. citizenship is not a requirement.
EIN: 861037705

166
Assistance League of Phoenix, Arizona
9224 N. 5th St.
Phoenix, AZ 85020-2533   (602) 944-7636
Contact: Linda Killmer, Pres.
FAX: (602) 944-7971; E-mail: info@alphx.org;
URL: http://www.phoenix.assistanceleague.org

Foundation type: Public charity
Purpose: Scholarships for tuition to junior and senior students of AZ public universities pursuing a degree from an accredited four year college. Non-cash assistance to various individuals and families who are in need.
Publications: Application guidelines; Annual report.
Financial data: Year ended 05/31/2012. Assets, $3,291,969 (M); Expenditures, $466,203; Total giving, $178,508; Grants to individuals, totaling $178,508.
Fields of interest: Higher education; Economically disadvantaged.
Type of support: Scholarships—to individuals; Grants for special needs.
Application information: Applications accepted. Application form required.
  Additional information: Applicants for scholarship must complete 64 hours of community college to attend a four year college.
EIN: 860193883

167
AZHHA Education Foundation
(also known as Arizona Hospital and Healthcare Association Education Foundation)
2800 N. Central Ave., Ste. 1450
Phoenix, AZ 85004-1054   (602) 445-4300
Contact: John Rivers, Pres. and C.E.O.

Foundation type: Public charity
Purpose: Scholarships to residents of AZ pursuing healthcare-related fields, with an emphasis on field in which a shortage of qualified employees has been identified. Recipients must plan to work in AZ upon graduation.
Financial data: Year ended 12/31/2011. Assets, $255,691 (M); Expenditures, $40,856.
Fields of interest: Nursing school/education.
Type of support: Graduate support.
Application information:
  Initial approach: Letter
  Applicants should submit the following:
    1) GPA
    2) Financial information
  Additional information: Contact foundation for further program information.
EIN: 942851811

168
Baize Gospel Preaching Foundation
707 N. Evelyn Ave.
Tucson, AZ 85710

Foundation type: Independent foundation
Purpose: Grants to Gospel preachers only for religious purposes.
Financial data: Year ended 12/31/2011. Assets, $935,068 (M); Expenditures, $53,600; Total giving, $48,600; Grants to individuals, 7 grants totaling $48,600 (high: $12,000, low: $1,200).
Fields of interest: Religion.
Type of support: Grants to individuals.
Application information: Applications not accepted.
  Additional information: Unsolicited requests for funds not considred or acknowledged.
EIN: 300335419

169
Banner Health
1441 N. 12th St.
Phoenix, AZ 85006-2837 (602) 747-4000
Contact: Peter S. Fine, Pres. and C.E.O.
Scholarship inquiry tel.: (602) 747-6357,
e-mail: nicky.treece@BannerHealth.com
URL: http://www.bannerhealth.com

Foundation type: Public charity
Purpose: Scholarships to Banner Health Registered
Nurses pursuing advanced nursing degrees.
Publications: Application guidelines.
Financial data: Year ended 12/31/2011. Assets,
$6,298,332,280 (M); Expenditures,
$3,925,202,020; Total giving, $1,104,701.
Fields of interest: Nursing school/education.
Type of support: Scholarships—to individuals.
Application information: Applications accepted.
Application form required. Interview required.
　Initial approach: Telephone
　Send request by: Mail
　Deadline(s): Feb. 10 for Anthony J. Jannetti
　　Nursing Scholarship
　Final notification: Recipients notified by Feb. 27
　Applicants should submit the following:
　　1) GPA
　　2) Resume
　　3) Essay
　　4) Letter(s) of recommendation
　　5) Curriculum vitae
Program description:
　Anthony J. Jannetti Nursing Scholarship Award:
One-time scholarships of $1,500 each to registered
nurses associated with one of the organization's
health institutions who are pursuing advanced
degrees in nursing. Applicants must be employed
for at least one year with the organization, be an
R.N. currently employed 32 hours or more at an
Arizona Region Banner Health facility, accepted into
a nursing related degree-granting program in an
accredited institution, and be enrolled part- or
full-time, while maintaining a minimum 3.0 GPA. In
addition to regular scholarships, the organization
will award one recipient with an additional
Excellence Award of $2,500.
EIN: 450233470

170
Banner Health Foundation of Arizona
(formerly The Samaritan Foundation)
2025 N. 3rd St., Ste.250
Phoenix, AZ 85004 (602) 747-4483
Contact: Andy Kramer, Pres. and C.E.O.
FAX: (602) 258-1463; *URL:* http://
www.bannerhealth.com

Foundation type: Public charity
Purpose: Grants and residencies to AZ and CO
medical professionals for research that benefits the
Banner Health System.
Publications: Financial statement; Newsletter.
Financial data: Year ended 12/31/2011. Assets,
$67,042,665 (M); Expenditures, $16,423,861;
Total giving, $12,982,329; Grants to individuals,
totaling $463,468.
Fields of interest: Medical research.
Type of support: Research.
Application information: Applications accepted.
　Additional information: Contact foundation for
　　current application deadlines/guidelines.
EIN: 942545356

171
William A. Barlocker Foundation
849 S. 54th Cir.
Mesa, AZ 85206 (480) 969-0244
Contact: Justin Smith, Chair.

Foundation type: Independent foundation
Purpose: Scholarships primarily to students in AZ
and UT for higher education.
Financial data: Year ended 12/31/2011. Assets,
$219,749 (M); Expenditures, $15,242; Total
giving, $12,250; Grants to individuals, 19 grants
totaling $12,250 (high: $1,050, low: $300).
Fields of interest: Higher education.
Type of support: Scholarships—to individuals.
Application information:
　Initial approach: Letter
　Deadline(s): Aug. 1 and Dec. 1
　Applicants should submit the following:
　　1) Transcripts
　　2) Financial information
　Additional information: Contact foundation for
　　additional application guidelines.
EIN: 742395114

172
The Breast Cancer Society, Inc.
6859 E. Rembrandt Ave., Ste. 128
Mesa, AZ 85212-3630 (480) 284-4014
Contact: James T. Reynolds II, Pres. and Exec. Dir.
FAX: (480) 659-9807;
E-mail: info@breastcancersociety.org; E-Mail for
James T. Reynolds II:
james@breastcancersociety.org; URL: http://
www.breastcancersociety.org/

Foundation type: Public charity
Purpose: Financial assistance to breast cancer
patients in the U.S. and to aid with critical need
such as treatment, recovery, food, shelter,
medicine, education, workshop and other basic
needs.
Financial data: Year ended 12/31/2011. Assets,
$4,501,537 (M); Expenditures, $42,565,914;
Total giving, $29,096,841; Grants to individuals,
totaling $1,583,564.
Fields of interest: Breast cancer.
Type of support: Grants for special needs.
Application information: Contact the society for
additional information.
EIN: 260237089

173
The Breeding Foundation
3157 S. Sycamore Village Dr.
Gold Canyon, AZ 85218 (480) 671-1727
Contact: John G. Breedig, Dir.

Foundation type: Operating foundation
Purpose: Scholarships to graduating students of
Red Rock High School, AZ for continuing their
education at accredited colleges or universities.
Financial data: Year ended 12/31/2012. Assets,
$638,981 (M); Expenditures, $32,636; Total
giving, $29,918.
Fields of interest: Higher education.
Type of support: Support to graduates or students
of specific schools.
Application information: Applications accepted.
Application form required.
　Deadline(s): None
　Applicants should submit the following:
　　1) GPA
　　2) Financial information

Additional information: Application must also
　include applicant's career interests.
EIN: 411808408

174
Dorothea Brinker Scholarship Fund
c/o Wells Fargo Bank, N.A.
P.O. Box 53456, MAC S4035-014
Phoenix, AZ 85072-3456

Foundation type: Independent foundation
Purpose: Scholarships to residents of Clark County,
GA, to attend the University of Las Vegas, NV.
Financial data: Year ended 12/31/2011. Assets,
$263,055 (M); Expenditures, $11,372; Total
giving, $7,251.
Type of support: Support to graduates or students
of specific schools; Undergraduate support.
Application information: Applications not
accepted.
　Additional information: Unsolicited requests for
　　funds not considered or acknowledged.
EIN: 886005302

175
Cancer Aid and Research Fund
20280 N. 59th Ave., Ste. 115-709
P.O. Box 37099
Phoenix, AZ 85069-7099 (623) 561-5893
Contact: Larry Mackay, Pres.
FAX: (602) 674-5254;
E-mail: lmackay106@aol.com; URL: http://
www.canceraidresearch.org

Foundation type: Public charity
Purpose: Grants to cancer patients and their
families for medical assistance.
Financial data: Year ended 09/30/2011. Assets,
$433,875 (M); Expenditures, $2,362,974; Total
giving, $2,054,968.
Fields of interest: Cancer.
Type of support: Grants for special needs.
Application information: Contact the fund for
application guidelines.
EIN: 742520175

176
**Catholic Charities Community Services,
　Inc.**
4747 N. 7th Ave.
Phoenix, AZ 85013-2401 (602) 285-1999
Contact: Robert Brown, Pres. and C.E.O.
FAX: (602) 285-0311; E-mail: info@cc-az.org;
URL: http://www.catholiccharitiesaz.org/

Foundation type: Public charity
Purpose: Emergency assistance to individuals and
families including women, victims, children and the
homeless of northern and central AZ.
Publications: Annual report.
Financial data: Year ended 06/30/2012. Assets,
$14,781,403 (M); Expenditures, $27,311,274;
Total giving, $2,456,323; Grants to individuals,
totaling $2,456,323.
Fields of interest: Human services; Children/youth;
Economically disadvantaged.
Type of support: Emergency funds; Grants for
special needs.
Application information: Funds are paid directly to
vendors on behalf of the clients. Contact the
organization for eligibility determination.
EIN: 860223999

177
Catholic Tuition Organization of the Diocese of Phoenix

2025 N. 3rd St., Ste. 165
Phoenix, AZ 85004-1425 (602) 218-6542
Contact: Paul Mulligan, Pres. and C.E.O.
FAX: (602) 218-6623;
E-mail: info@catholictuition.org; Application address: Financial Aid Independent Review, P.O. Box 484, Rosemount, MN 55068-0484;
URL: http://www.catholictuition.org

Foundation type: Public charity
Purpose: Scholarships and grants to children attending the schools owned and operated by the Roman Catholic Diocese of Phoenix, AZ.
Financial data: Year ended 06/30/2012. Assets, $12,671,148 (M); Expenditures, $11,062,106; Total giving, $10,166,208.
Fields of interest: Catholic agencies & churches.
Type of support: Scholarships—to individuals.
Application information:
    Initial approach: Letter
    Deadline(s): Apr. 16
Program description:
    Scholarships: Parents of students enrolled in a school owned and operated by the Roman Catholic Diocese of Phoenix can apply for tuition assistance. Awards will be given to applicants, primarily based on financial need.
EIN: 860937587

178
The Chapman Fund

(formerly The Chapman Foundation)
14719 W Grand Ave.
Sun City West, AZ 85376 (623) 832-6616

Foundation type: Independent foundation
Purpose: Scholarships to individuals residing in the Sun City, AZ, area, for undergraduate education.
Financial data: Year ended 12/31/2012. Assets, $391,364 (M); Expenditures, $16,572; Total giving, $15,750; Grants to individuals, 23 grants totaling $15,750 (high: $2,000, low: $500).
Type of support: Undergraduate support.
Application information: Application form required.
    Deadline(s): Feb. 28
    Applicants should submit the following:
        1) Letter(s) of recommendation
        2) Transcripts
        3) Financial information
EIN: 860731311

179
Christian Scholarship Foundation

(formerly Prescott Christian School Scholarship Foundation)
2126 W. Charteroak Dr.
Prescott, AZ 86305-7711 (928) 771-2018
Contact: William T. Warren, Chair.
URL: http://www.csf-info.net

Foundation type: Independent foundation
Purpose: Scholarships to graduating seniors of Prescott, AZ local schools.
Financial data: Year ended 12/31/2012. Assets, $303,176 (M); Expenditures, $198,999; Total giving, $181,653; Grants to individuals, 145 grants totaling $181,653 (high: $2,920, low: $38).
Fields of interest: Scholarships/financial aid.
Type of support: Undergraduate support.
Application information: Application form required.
    Deadline(s): None

Additional information: Applications available at local schools.
EIN: 860947958

180
Christian Scholarship Fund of Arizona

P.O. Box 31101
Tucson, AZ 85751-1101 (520) 322-0966
Contact: Thomas R. LaVoie, Pres.
FAX: (520) 881-7392; E-mail: in@csf-az.org;
URL: http://www.csf-az.org

Foundation type: Public charity
Purpose: Scholarships to students of needy families who attend local Christian schools in Arizona.
Financial data: Year ended 06/30/2012. Assets, $524,720 (M); Expenditures, $277,588.
Fields of interest: Education.
Type of support: Scholarships—to individuals.
Application information: Application form required. Application form available on the grantmaker's web site.
    Copies of proposal: 1
    Deadline(s): None
    Additional information: Scholarships are based on independent evaluation and recommendation.
EIN: 860940166

181
Community Food Bank, Inc.

3003 S. Country Club Rd.
Tucson, AZ 85713-4082 (520) 622-0525
Contact: Michael McDonald, C.E.O.
FAX: (520) 624-6349;
E-mail: mmcdonald@communityfoodbank.org;
Mailing address: P.O. Box 26727, Tucson, AZ 85726-6727; toll-free tel. (800) 950-8681;
URL: http://www.communityfoodbank.com

Foundation type: Public charity
Purpose: Emergency assistance to individuals and families in need of food in Tucson and Pima counties, AZ.
Publications: Annual report; Financial statement; Newsletter.
Financial data: Year ended 06/30/2012. Assets, $16,894,593 (M); Expenditures, $51,331,333; Total giving, $40,972,748; Grants to individuals, totaling $40,967,748.
Fields of interest: Food banks; Agriculture/food.
Type of support: Emergency funds; In-kind gifts.
Application information: Applications accepted.
    Additional information: Some assistance require completion of application. Contact the organization for eligibility determination.
EIN: 510192519

182
Community Foundation for Southern Arizona

2250 E. Broadway Blvd.
Tucson, AZ 85719-6014 (520) 770-0800
Contact: J. Clint Mabie, C.E.O.; For scholarship inquiries: Marthena Maley, Prog. Off.
Scholarship and award inquiries: mmaley@cfsaz.org
FAX: (520) 770-1500;
E-mail: philanthropy@cfsoaz.org; URL: http://www.cfsoaz.org

Foundation type: Community foundation
Purpose: Scholarships to students graduating from or attending southern AZ educational institutions.

Awards by nomination only to artists and to those providing services to the disabled in AZ.
Publications: Application guidelines; Annual report; Financial statement; Informational brochure.
Financial data: Year ended 06/30/2012. Assets, $101,388,984 (M); Expenditures, $12,610,631; Total giving, $9,737,507. Awards/prizes amount not specified. Scholarships—to individuals amount not specified.
Fields of interest: Arts education; Visual arts; Opera; Higher education; Scholarships/financial aid; Disabilities, people with.
Type of support: Scholarships—to individuals; Support to graduates or students of specific schools; Awards/grants by nomination only; Awards/prizes; Undergraduate support.
Application information: Applications accepted. Application form required. Application form available on the grantmaker's web site.
    Initial approach: Application
    Send request by: On-line for scholarships
    Deadline(s): Apr. 2 for scholarships
    Final notification: Applicants notified within two months for scholarships
    Applicants should submit the following:
        1) SAR
        2) FAFSA
    Additional information: See web site for a complete listing of scholarships. Also, guidelines for awards.
Program descriptions:
    Buffalo Exchange Arts Award: The award rotates each year between emerging artists in the performing arts and visual arts, and individuals who have made outstanding contributions to the arts through education, organization and advocacy. Individuals may not apply. Recipients are chosen by nomination only.
    Diane Lynn Anderson Memorial Award: The award recognizes individuals who demonstrate patience, respect, compassion, devotion and care to people with disabilities in Pima County, AZ.
    Igor Gorin Memorial Award: Financial assistance for young opera singers who may be eligible for a second year of funding based on the quality of continued singing appearances. Funds may be used for a variety of purposes, including general living expenses or professional development.
    Scholarships: Southern Arizona high school students graduating from public high schools are eligible to apply. Selection criteria includes financial need, academic success, academic potential, interests and activities.
EIN: 942681765

183
Deer Valley Education Foundation, Inc.

20402 N. 15th Ave.
Phoenix, AZ 85027-3636 (623) 445-5012
FAX: (623) 445-5087;
E-mail: Marie.Brennan@dvusd.org; Cell Tel.: (623) 521-2110; URL: http://www.dvef.org

Foundation type: Public charity
Purpose: Scholarships for 7th and 8th grade students of Phoenix, AZ, to attend Space Camp Academy in Huntsville, AL during the summer. Scholarships for high school seniors for higher education.
Financial data: Year ended 06/30/2012. Assets, $382,922 (M); Expenditures, $224,994; Total giving, $118,973; Grants to individuals, totaling $31,898.
Fields of interest: Education.
Type of support: Camperships; Scholarships—to individuals.

Application information: Applications accepted. Application form required. Application form available on the grantmaker's web site.

> *Deadline(s):* Apr. 5 for Space Academy Scholarships, Apr. 18 for McElyea Scholarship
> *Applicants should submit the following:*
> 1) Letter(s) of recommendation
> 2) Essay
> *Additional information:* High School seniors should contact their school counselor. See web site for additional application guidelines.

EIN: 742472475

184

Bill Dickey Scholarship Association

1140 E. Washington St., Ste. 103
Phoenix, AZ 85034-1051 (602) 258-7851
FAX: (602) 258-3412;
E-mail: andrea@bdscholar.org; URL: http://www.nmjgsa.org

Foundation type: Public charity
Purpose: Scholarships to assist college bound minority young men and women in pursuit of a higher education and the development of their golf skills.
Publications: Application guidelines.
Financial data: Year ended 06/30/2012. Assets, $808,919 (M); Expenditures, $330,918.
Fields of interest: Higher education; Athletics/sports, golf; Minorities; Young adults, female; Young adults, male.
Type of support: Scholarships—to individuals; Undergraduate support.
Application information: Application form required. Application form available on the grantmaker's web site.

> *Send request by:* Mail
> *Deadline(s):* Apr. 30
> *Applicants should submit the following:*
> 1) GPA
> 2) Letter(s) of recommendation
> 3) Financial information
> 4) Photograph
> 5) Transcripts
> 6) Essay
> *Additional information:* Application should include two personal references.

Program description:
Scholarships: The association awards scholarship grant and financial aid packages. Awards range from one-time grants of $1,000 to grants for up to four years, at $3,500 annually. Awards are based on academic achievement, entrance exam scores, financial need, references, evidence of community service, and golfing ability. High school seniors as well as undergraduate students that previously received a scholarship as a freshman are eligible to apply.
EIN: 942933804

185

Diocesan Council for the Society of St. Vincent de Paul

420 W. Watkins Rd.
Phoenix, AZ 85003-2830 (602) 266-4673
Contact: Stephen J. Zabilski, Exec. Dir.
E-mail: zap-cr@svdp-phx-az.org; Mailing Address:P.O. Box 13600, Phoenix, AZ 85002;
URL: http://www.stvincentdepaul.net

Foundation type: Public charity
Purpose: Scholarships to high school students from central and northern, AZ who would not be able to attend college without financial help.

Publications: Newsletter.
Financial data: Year ended 09/30/2011. Assets, $32,255,115 (M); Expenditures, $29,189,158; Total giving, $96,253; Grants to individuals, totaling $65,750.
Fields of interest: Higher education; Economically disadvantaged.
Type of support: Scholarships—to individuals.
Application information: Applications not accepted.

> *Additional information:* Students are selected by their high school counselors based on general economic conditions. First generation scholars receive additional consideration in the selection process. Unsolicited requests for funds not considered or acknowledged.

EIN: 860096789

186

Dougherty Foundation, Inc.

3507 N. Central Ave., Ste. 404
Phoenix, AZ 85012-2020 (602) 264-7478
Contact: Linda M. Czarnecki, Secy.-Treas.
URL: http://www.doughertyfoundation.com/

Foundation type: Independent foundation
Purpose: Scholarships and student loans to financially needy AZ students who are U.S. citizens and enrolled in both undergraduate and postgraduate degree programs at accredited colleges in AZ.
Publications: Financial statement; Informational brochure.
Financial data: Year ended 12/31/2012. Assets, $6,146,066 (M); Expenditures, $382,829; Total giving, $141,500; Grants to individuals, totaling $141,500.
Fields of interest: Higher education.
Type of support: Scholarships—to individuals; Student loans—to individuals.
Application information: Applications accepted.

> *Deadline(s):* None
> *Applicants should submit the following:*
> 1) Transcripts
> 2) Financial information
> *Additional information:* Applications are not accepted directly from students. Contact the foundation for eligibility requirement.

EIN: 866051637

187

East Valley Christian School Tuition Organization, Inc.

P.O. Box 6580
Chandler, AZ 85246-6580 (480) 820-0403
Contact: Steve Yarbrough, Exec. Dir.
FAX: (480) 820-2027; E-mail: social@acsto.org;
URL: http://www.acsto.com

Foundation type: Public charity
Purpose: Scholarships to students in grades K-12 for attendance in a Christian private school in Arizona.
Publications: Application guidelines.
Financial data: Year ended 06/30/2012. Assets, $2,636,871 (M); Expenditures, $11,040,911; Total giving, $9,864,238; Grants to individuals, totaling $9,864,238.
Fields of interest: Education.
Type of support: Scholarships—to individuals.
Application information: Applications accepted. Application form required. Application form available on the grantmaker's web site.

> *Send request by:* Mail or fax
> *Deadline(s):* Feb. 28

> *Additional information:* Scholarships are awarded based on financial need, recommendations and other considerations.

Program description:
Scholarships: The organization awards tuition grants to K-12 students attending Christian private schools in Arizona. Eligible applicants must be planning to attend the school by the semester following the award process.
EIN: 860931047

188

Educare Scholarship Fund

4643 E. Thomas Rd.
Phoenix, AZ 85018 (602) 980-2680
Contact: Susan Patterson, V.P.

Foundation type: Public charity
Purpose: Tuition assistance to financially needy students to attend school in Arizona.
Fields of interest: Economically disadvantaged.
Type of support: Undergraduate support.
Application information: Applications accepted. Application form required.

> *Initial approach:* E-mail or letter
> *Additional information:* Application should include transcripts. Assistance is based on scholastic achievement. Contact fund for further program information.

EIN: 860967764

189

Education Endowment of Yavapai County, Inc.

2970 Centerpoint E. Dr.
Prescott, AZ 86301
URL: http://www.education-scholarships-yavapai.org/

Foundation type: Independent foundation
Purpose: Scholarships to Yavapai County school, college, or university graduate who intends to teach in public education.
Financial data: Year ended 12/31/2012. Assets, $307,916 (M); Expenditures, $19,627; Total giving, $18,000; Grants to individuals, 12 grants totaling $18,000 (high: $1,500, low: $1,500).
Fields of interest: Teacher school/education.
Type of support: Scholarships—to individuals.
Application information: Applications accepted. Application form required.

> *Deadline(s):* Mar.

EIN: 861008939

190

Educational Enrichment Foundation

3809 E. 3rd St.
Tucson, AZ 85716-4611 (520) 325-8688
Contact: Pamela Francis, Exec. Dir.
FAX: (520) 325-8579; E-mail: info@eeftucsor.org;
URL: http://eeftucson.org

Foundation type: Public charity
Purpose: Scholarships to TUSD graduating seniors who intend to pursue postsecondary education. Assistance to disadvantaged TUSD students to obtain basic resources necessary to keep needy at-risk children in school.
Publications: Application guidelines; Grants list.
Financial data: Year ended 06/30/2012. Assets, $779,188 (M); Expenditures, $524,357; Total giving, $207,456; Grants to individuals, totaling $207,456.

Fields of interest: Higher education; Science; Mathematics; Engineering.
Type of support: Scholarships—to individuals; Awards/prizes; Grants for special needs.
Application information: Applications accepted. Application form required. Application form available on the grantmaker's web site.
   Initial approach: Telephone
   Send request by: Mail or hand delivered
   Deadline(s): Feb. 3 for proposals for Classroom Grants, Mar. 16 for college scholarships
   Final notification: Students notified in May for scholarships
   Applicants should submit the following:
      1) Transcripts
      2) Letter(s) of recommendation
      3) Essay
   Additional information: See web site for additional guidelines.
Program descriptions:
   Classroom Grants: Grants are awarded once a year for the following school year based on a competitive open call for proposals from TUSD educators who work directly with students.
   College Scholarships for TUSD Seniors: Twenty scholarships ranging from $1,000 to $2,000 are available to TUSD seniors who successfully complete all State and District graduation requirements.
   EEF Interscholastic Scholarships: Academically eligible, financially in-need students in middle school and high school who are unable to pay TUSD's mandatory participation fee for organized co-curricular activities (such as inter-mural team sports, orchestra, band, Academic Decathlon, cheerleading, spirit line, folkloric, mariachi, chess team, and JROTC) may apply for an EEF Interscholastic Scholarship ranging from $20 to $50. Scholarships are granted on a weekly basis.
   Evelyn Jay Excellence in Education Award: The award is given to celebrate Evelyn Jay's dedication to and passion for teaching reading skills to young learners. Each year three outstanding educators are recognized with cash awards for their superlative and innovative work in inspiring a lifelong of reading and books in their young students.
EIN: 742354578

191
Feed My People Childrens Charities, Inc.
3805 E. Huntington Dr.
Flagstaff, AZ   86004-9450   (928) 526-2211
Contact: Kerry D. Ketchum, Exec. Dir.
FAX: (928) 526-9505;
E-mail: info@feedmypeople.org; URL: http://www.feedmypeople.org/

Foundation type: Public charity
Purpose: Emergency assistance to individuals and families in need throughout northern AZ, with food, clothing, medical supplies and other items.
Financial data: Year ended 09/30/2012. Assets, $686,904 (M); Expenditures, $2,065,272; Total giving, $1,610,712; Grants to individuals, totaling $396,756.
Fields of interest: Food services; Food banks; Economically disadvantaged.
Type of support: Emergency funds; In-kind gifts.
Application information: Applications not accepted.
   Additional information: Contact the organization for information on how to receive assistance.
EIN: 731330955

192
The Steven and Lynn Fisher Foundation
1310 W. Island Cir.
Chandler, AZ   85248-3700   (480) 899-2907
Contact: Steven D. Fisher, Pres. and Treas.

Foundation type: Independent foundation
Purpose: Scholarships to individuals for higher education.
Financial data: Year ended 12/31/2012. Assets, $0 (M); Expenditures, $5,453; Total giving, $0.
Type of support: Scholarships—to individuals.
Application information:
   Initial approach: Letter
   Deadline(s): None
EIN: 860686929

193
The Flinn Foundation
1802 N. Central Ave.
Phoenix, AZ   85004-1506   (602) 744-6800
Contact: Jack B. Jewett, C.E.O.
Scholarship tel.: (602) 744-6802,
e-mail: fscholars@flinn.org
FAX: (602) 744-6815; E-mail: info@flinn.org;
URL: http://www.flinn.org

Foundation type: Independent foundation
Purpose: Undergraduate scholarships to Arizona's top high school seniors for study at one of three state universities.
Publications: Annual report; Financial statement; Newsletter; Occasional report.
Financial data: Year ended 12/31/2012. Assets, $194,755,468 (M); Expenditures, $10,138,784; Total giving, $5,250,603. Scholarships—to individuals amount not specified.
Fields of interest: Higher education.
Type of support: Fellowships; Undergraduate support.
Application information: Applications accepted. Application form available on the grantmaker's web site. Interview required.
   Send request by: Online
   Deadline(s): Oct. 19
   Applicants should submit the following:
      1) SAT
      2) ACT
      3) Letter(s) of recommendation
      4) Essay
      5) Transcripts
Program description:
   Flinn Scholars Program: The program, in partnership with Arizona's public universities, annually awards 20 top Arizona high school graduates an educational package that covers the full cost of undergraduate study, plus other benefits including study-related travel abroad. The program aims to strengthen the ability of the universities to compete for Arizona's top students and to provide the students an outstanding academic experience. About 500 students apply every fall for the 20 awards. You may send questions about the application process to application@flinn.org.
EIN: 860421476

194
Food for Children, Inc.
P.O. Box 6759
Chandler, AZ   85246-6759

Foundation type: Public charity
Purpose: Funds to child care providers in Arizona, participating in the federal child care food.
Financial data: Year ended 09/30/2011. Assets, $230,449 (M); Expenditures, $1,221,955.

Fields of interest: Food services; Children, services.
Type of support: Grants to individuals.
Application information: Contact the agency for additional information.
EIN: 953451981

195
Foundation for Montessori Scholarships
9201 N. 7th Ave.
Phoenix, AZ   85021-3518   (602) 870-0004

Foundation type: Public charity
Purpose: Scholarships to students attending Montessori schools in AZ.
Financial data: Year ended 12/31/2010. Assets, $6,500 (M); Expenditures, $80,948; Total giving, $34,350; Grants to individuals, totaling $34,350.
Type of support: Scholarships—to individuals.
Application information:
   Initial approach: Schools request application from the foundation.
   Deadline(s): None
   Final notification: Dec. 1
   Additional information: Application should include financial information.
Program description:
   Grants: Scholarships are available to needy, at-risk students in grades K through 12, who are attending a private school in Arizona. Students will be evaluated based on his/her financial need, academic record, and personal profile.
EIN: 860973909

196
Freeport-McMoRan Copper & Gold Foundation
(formerly Phelps Dodge Foundation)
333 N. Central Ave.
Phoenix, AZ   85004-2189   (602) 366-8116
Contact for Scholarship Program: Brittany Watkins, e-mail: brittany_watkins@fmi.com
FAX: (602) 366-7305; E-mail: foundation@fmi.com;
URL: http://www.freeportinmycommunity.com/

Foundation type: Company-sponsored foundation
Purpose: Scholarships to students pursuing degrees relevant to mining and manufacturing.
Publications: Application guidelines; Corporate report; Grants list; Informational brochure (including application guidelines); Program policy statement.
Financial data: Year ended 12/31/2012. Assets, $7,231,295 (M); Expenditures, $16,101,185; Total giving, $16,100,657.
Fields of interest: Higher education; Scholarships/financial aid; Geology; Engineering.
Type of support: Scholarships—to individuals.
Application information: Applications accepted. Application form required. Application form available on the grantmaker's web site.
   Initial approach: Application
   Send request by: Mail
   Deadline(s): Mar. 30
   Final notification: Applicants notified Apr. 20
   Applicants should submit the following:
      1) Resume
      2) Letter(s) of recommendation
      3) Transcripts
      4) Essay
   Additional information: See web site for participating schools and addresses.
Program description:
   Scholarship Program: The foundation awards scholarships to students pursuing a degree in engineering or mining at select colleges and universities. Special emphasis is directed towards

students entering their junior or senior year studying engineering, sustainability, geology, chemistry, environmental sciences, health and safety, or business. Applicants must apply through participating schools. Scholarship recipients are also encouraged to apply for a 10 to 14 week summer internship following each year in which a scholarship is awarded.
EIN: 136077350

197
Friedman Fund TUW Foundation
(formerly Friedman Scholarship Fund)
c/o Wells Fargo Bank, N.A., Trust Tax Dept.
P.O. Box 53456, MAC S4101-22G
Phoenix, AZ 85072-3456 (208) 393-5486
Applicaion address: 998 W. Main St. Bosie, ID 83702

Foundation type: Independent foundation
Purpose: Scholarships to graduates of Wood River High School, Hailey, ID.
Financial data: Year ended 12/31/2012. Assets, $582,011 (M); Expenditures, $41,685; Total giving, $39,500.
Type of support: Support to graduates or students of specific schools; Undergraduate support.
Application information: Applications accepted. Application form required.
  Initial approach: Letter
  Deadline(s): Mar. 15 and Oct. 1
EIN: 826066650

198
Friendship Village of Tempe Foundation, Inc.
(also known as FVT Foundation, Inc.)
2645 E. Southern Ave.
P.O. Box 381
Tempe, AZ 85282-7649 (480) 831-0880

Foundation type: Public charity
Purpose: Financial assistance to the residents of Friendship Village,Tempe, AZ to cover incidental living expenses for those persons who qualify.
Financial data: Year ended 12/31/2011. Assets, $3,252,013 (M); Expenditures, $161,568; Total giving, $136,409; Grants to individuals, totaling $9,500.
Fields of interest: Economically disadvantaged.
Type of support: Grants for special needs.
Application information: Contact the foundation for eligibility criteria.
EIN: 860564702

199
William M. & Ann K. Grace Foundation
c/o William Matt Grace Development Co.
7575 N. 16th St., Ste. 1
Phoenix, AZ 85020-4625 (602) 956-8254
Contact: Ron Richards, Dir.
FAX: (602) 943-3548;
E-mail: ronrichards@wmgracefoundation.com;
URL: http://www.wmgracefoundation.com

Foundation type: Independent foundation
Purpose: Scholarships to students for all levels of school, including private grade schools, high schools, colleges, and universities, given for merit or need.
Financial data: Year ended 12/31/2012. Assets, $10,727,378 (M); Expenditures, $645,827; Total giving, $642,006. Scholarships—to individuals amount not specified.
Fields of interest: Higher education.

Type of support: Scholarships—to individuals.
Application information: Applications accepted. Application form required. Application form available on the grantmaker's web site.
  Send request by: On-line, mail, fax or e-mail
  Deadline(s): Nov. 15
  Additional information: Application should include GPA. Scholarship application form and specific instructions available on the web site. Students must maintain a 2.0 GPA or greater with 12 or more credit hours/semester.
EIN: 562529760

200
Help From Above
4001 W Indian School Rd.
Phoenix, AZ 85019-3314

Foundation type: Independent foundation
Purpose: Financial assistance to residents of Chandler and Phoenix, AZ, as well as Encinitas, CA, to help pay for living expenses.
Financial data: Year ended 03/31/2011. Assets, $9,011 (M); Expenditures, $3,798; Total giving, $3,798; Grant to an individual, 1 grant totaling $398.
Type of support: Grants for special needs.
Application information: Applications not accepted.
  Additional information: Unsolicited requests for funds not considered or acknowledged.
EIN: 861048274

201
Hopi Foundation Barbara Chester Endowment Fund
c/o Hopi Foundation
P.O. Box 301
Kykotsmovi, AZ 86039 (928) 737-2340
Contact: Heidi Ernst, Grant/Affiliate Admin.
E-mail for nominations:
nominations@barbarachesteraward.org
E-mail: info@hopifoundation.org; URL: http://barbarachesteraward.hopifoundation.org/about/the-hopi-foundation

Foundation type: Public charity
Purpose: Awards by nomination for outstanding clinicians/practitioners who treat victims of torture, their families, and their communities.
Publications: Application guidelines.
Fields of interest: Sexual abuse.
Type of support: Awards/prizes.
Application information:
  Deadline(s): Apr. 6
  Additional information: Nomination forms are available online. See web site for additional guidelines.
Program description:
  Barbara Chester Awards: This award honors outstanding clinicians/practitioners who treat victims of torture, their families, and their communities, and recognizes and honors the worthy persons who undertake the difficult and often dangerous work of providing healing services in circumstances of torture. Recipients are awarded a $10,000 cash prize and a silver sculpture. Eligible candidates must be clinicians or healing practitioners (from the fields of psychology, social work, physical therapy, counseling, psychiatry, Western medicine, or indigenous healing traditions) who provide treatment or healing services directly to survivors of political torture and their communities. Candidates should also exemplify some or all of the following qualities, abilities, and accomplishments undertaken and performed in a

respectful and nonviolent manner: courage; compassion; scholarly contributions; client empowerment; conceptual and intellectual brilliance; tenacity and perseverance; respect for cultural diversity; facilitation of community organization and teamwork; strong, effective client advocacy; the promotion of self-determination for indigenous peoples; and superb therapeutic/ healing skills. Consideration will also be given to candidates whose personal safety may be in jeopardy from working in high-risk situations.

202
The Ingebritson Family Foundation
c/o Arizona Community Foundation
2201 E. Camelback Rd., Ste. 405B
Phoenix, AZ 85016-3431 (602) 381-1400
Contact: Steven G. Seleznow, Pres.

Foundation type: Public charity
Purpose: Scholarships to students of AZ pursuing postsecondary in nursing, education, finance or engineering.
Financial data: Year ended 03/31/2012. Assets, $1,564,638 (M); Expenditures, $184,474; Total giving, $152,600; Grants to individuals, totaling $24,100.
Fields of interest: Higher education.
Type of support: Scholarships—to individuals; Support to graduates or students of specific schools.
Application information: Applications accepted. Application form required.
  Deadline(s): Mar.
  Additional information: Applicants must attend one of the following institutions to qualify for this scholarship: Arizona State University, Northern Arizona University, Maricopa Community Colleges, Yavapai College and Eastern Arizona college. Applicants must be enrolled full time, and demonstrate financial need.
Program description:
  Ingebritson Scholarship: This scholarship is awarded to students selected by the scholarship offices at Arizona universities or colleges. Criteria for scholarships include: having a GPA of 2.5 or better, scoring in the top 15 percent of SAT or ACT scores, and majoring in nursing, engineering, finance, or education.
EIN: 860800012

203
Institute for Better Education
911 S.Craycroft
Tucson, AZ 85711-3777 (520) 512-5438
Contact: Charlotte Beecher, Exec. Dir.
FAX: (520) 203-0184;
E-mail: Services@ibescholarships.org; URL: http://www.ibescholarships.org

Foundation type: Public charity
Purpose: Scholarships primarily to students K through grade 12 residing in the southern AZ area for attendance at private schools.
Publications: Informational brochure; Newsletter.
Financial data: Year ended 06/30/2013. Assets, $7,494,610 (M); Expenditures, $8,609,956; Total giving, $8,046,620.
Type of support: Precollege support.
Application information: Applications accepted. Application form required. Application form available on the grantmaker's web site.
  Deadline(s): Rolling

Additional information: Application should include financial information and a letter of circumstances, if needed.
EIN: 237102832

204
Interfaith Cooperative Ministries
501 S. 9th Ave.
P.O. Box 2225
Phoenix, AZ 85002-2225 (602) 254-7450
FAX: (602) 257-1837; E-mail: info@icmaz.org;
E-Mail for Renea Gentry: renea@icmaz.org;
URL: http://www.icmaz.org

Foundation type: Public charity
Purpose: Emergency assistance to individuals and families in the Phoenix, AZ, area with food, clothing, shelter, rental and utility assistance, and other services.
Publications: Newsletter.
Financial data: Year ended 12/31/2011. Assets, $986,804 (M); Expenditures, $2,067,598; Total giving, $1,656,027; Grants to individuals, totaling $1,656,027.
Fields of interest: Human services, emergency aid; Economically disadvantaged.
Type of support: Grants for special needs.
Application information:
Initial approach: Letter
EIN: 860401223

205
Jewish Family & Children's Service of Southern Arizona, Inc.
4301 E. 5th St.
Tucson, AZ 85711-2005 (520) 795-0300
Contact: Shira M. Ledman, Pres. and C.E.O.
FAX: (520) 795-8206;
E-mail: jcfsinfo@jfctucson.org; URL: http://www.jfcstucson.org

Foundation type: Public charity
Purpose: Emergency financial assistance to individuals and families in need throughout southern AZ.
Publications: Annual report; Newsletter.
Financial data: Year ended 09/30/2011. Assets, $2,812,280 (M); Expenditures, $2,780,033; Total giving, $292,005; Grants to individuals, totaling $292,005.
Fields of interest: Human services.
Type of support: Emergency funds.
Application information:
Initial approach: Telephone, fax, e-mail
Additional information: Funds are paid directly to vendors for the purpose for which it is intended. Contact the foundation for additional information.
Program description:
Emergency Financial Assistance: The organization helps individuals and families throughout southern Arizona with emergency financial assistance to avoid eviction, utility shut-off, and hunger by offering short-term financial assistance with burial arrangements for indigent individuals, food cards, Sun Tran bus passes, rent/mortgage payments, moving expenses, utilities, medical expenses, transportation (including car insurance, if car is needed for work) and work-related expenses.
EIN: 860623896

206
The Janis & Milly Kahvush Trust
10568 E. Laurel Ln.
Scottsdale, AZ 85259-2943

Foundation type: Independent foundation
Purpose: Scholarships to individuals of Latvian origin.
Financial data: Year ended 06/30/2013. Assets, $491,212 (M); Expenditures, $42,252; Total giving, $39,590; Grants to individuals, 3 grants totaling $2,800 (high: $2,150, low: $250).
International interests: Latvia.
Type of support: Scholarships—to individuals.
Application information: Applications accepted.
Additional information: Contact foundation for current application deadline/guidelines.
EIN: 521540658

207
Kingman Regional Hospital Foundation
3269 Stockton Hill Rd.
Kingman, AZ 86401-3619 (928) 757-2101
URL: http://www.azkrmc.com/

Foundation type: Public charity
Purpose: Tuition and scholarships for students of AZ, pursuing education in qualified nursing programs.
Financial data: Year ended 06/30/2011. Assets, $895,211 (M); Expenditures, $234,456; Total giving, $180,105; Grants to individuals, totaling $10,264.
Fields of interest: Nursing school/education.
Type of support: Scholarships—to individuals.
Application information: Applications accepted. Application form required.
Additional information: Applicants for nursing scholarships must have completed all prerequisites and be accepted into an ADN or BSN program at an approved college or university.
EIN: 742388735

208
Russell and Edna Knapp Foundation Trust
(also known as Knapp Foundation)
c/o Wells Fargo Bank, N.A.
P.O. Box 53456, MAC S4101-22G
Phoenix, AZ 85072-3456 (800) 352-3705
Application Address: P.O.Box 40908, Reno, NV 59804-4908

Foundation type: Independent foundation
Purpose: College scholarships to high school graduates from any high school in the Elko County School District, NV, and to residents of Elko County, NV, pursuing higher education at colleges, universities, and technical schools.
Financial data: Year ended 01/31/2013. Assets, $1,261,044 (M); Expenditures, $74,424; Total giving, $50,733; Grants to individuals, 8 grants totaling $50,733 (high: $46,900, low: $333).
Fields of interest: Vocational education, post-secondary; Higher education.
Type of support: Undergraduate support.
Application information: Applications accepted. Application form required.
Deadline(s): None
EIN: 942938337

209
Elizabeth LaForce Scholarship and Grant Fund
c/o Jaqueline Dawson
6320 E. Kings Ave.
Scottsdale, AZ 85254-1338 (480) 443-3311
Contact: for Scholarship: Sherry Pennington, Coord., Financial Aid

Foundation type: Public charity
Purpose: Scholarships for female residents of Arizona for attendance at Cottey College in Nevada, MO for higher education.
Financial data: Year ended 03/31/2012. Assets, $255,045 (M); Expenditures, $43,720; Total giving, $43,575.
Fields of interest: Higher education; Women.
Type of support: Support to graduates or students of specific schools.
Application information: Applications accepted. Application form required.
Deadline(s): Mar.
EIN: 953671820

210
Lapan Memorial Sunshine Foundation, Inc.
(formerly Lapan Educational Loan Foundation, Inc.)
4320 E. Pinnacle Ridge Pl.
Tucson, AZ 85718-3541
Application address: c/o Lapan College Club, Attn: Lucy Kin, 101 W. 44th St., Tucson, AZ 85745, tel.: (520) 360-9881

Foundation type: Operating foundation
Purpose: Scholarships to financially needy individuals residing in CA for higher education, with preference to those from Alameda and Pima counties.
Financial data: Year ended 12/31/2012. Assets, $883,819 (M); Expenditures, $323,917; Total giving, $262,858.
Type of support: Scholarships—to individuals.
Application information:
Initial approach: Letter
Deadline(s): May 1
Applicants should submit the following:
1) Financial information
2) Transcripts
3) Resume
Additional information: Scholarships are paid directly to the institution on behalf of the students.
EIN: 880192311

211
T. W. Lewis Foundation
850 W. Elliot Rd.
Tempe, AZ 85284-1202 (480) 820-0807
FAX: (480) 820-1445;
E-mail: twlfoundation@twlewis.com; URL: http://www.twlewisfoundation.org/

Foundation type: Independent foundation
Purpose: Scholarships to graduates of Maricopa County, AZ, high schools for undergraduate education.
Publications: Grants list.
Financial data: Year ended 12/31/2012. Assets, $16,714,743 (M); Expenditures, $604,006; Total giving, $501,905; Grants to individuals, 38 grants totaling $101,205 (high: $4,683, low: $1,665).
Fields of interest: Higher education.
Type of support: Support to graduates or students of specific schools; Undergraduate support.

Application information: Applications accepted. Application form required. Application form available on the grantmaker's web site. Interview required.

Send request by: Mail or hand deliver
Deadline(s): Feb. 10
Final notification: Recipients notified by May
Applicants should submit the following:
1) Transcripts
2) Financial information
3) Photograph
4) Letter(s) of recommendation
5) Essay
6) Class rank
7) GPA
Additional information: Funds will be paid directly to the educational institution on behalf of the students.

Program description:
Scholarship Program: Scholarships to students in the amount of $20,000 ($5,000 per year) in financial aid for expenses for four years at the college or university of their choice. Applicants must be Maricopa County, AZ, high school students, be enrolled full-time (15 semester hours or more) in a course of study leading to a baccalaureate degree at an accredited college or university located within the U.S., have a minimum SAT score of 1800, have a minimum high school cumulative GPA of 3.0 and rank in the top twenty percent of their graduating class academically.
EIN: 860989236

212
Los Abogados Hispanic Bar Association
P.O. Box 813
Phoenix, AZ 85001-0813
Contact: Gaetano Testini, Pres.
FAX: (855) 999-9329;
E-mail: membership@losabogados.org;
URL: http://losabogados.org

Foundation type: Public charity
Purpose: Scholarships to students of Hispanic descent attending Sandra Day O'Connor College of Law, the James E. Rogers College of Law, and the Phoenix School of Law.
Publications: Newsletter.
Financial data: Year ended 12/31/2011. Assets, $120,239 (M); Expenditures, $30,092; Total giving, $20,000. Scholarships—to individuals amount not specified.
Fields of interest: Law school/education; Hispanics/Latinos.
Type of support: Scholarships—to individuals.
Application information: Applications accepted. Application form required. Application form available on the grantmaker's web site.
Deadline(s): Apr. 13
Additional information: Selection is based on leadership, service and support efforts in the Hispanic community.
EIN: 860601404

213
Lupus Inspiration Foundation for Excellence
P.O. Box 64088
Tucson, AZ 85728-4088 (520) 299-9234
E-mail: life4lupus@hotmail.com; URL: http://www.lifescholarship.org

Foundation type: Public charity
Purpose: Scholarships to deserving college and graduate school students with Lupus, for continuing education.

Publications: Application guidelines.
Fields of interest: Lupus.
Type of support: Scholarships—to individuals.
Application information: Applications accepted. Application form required. Application form available on the grantmaker's web site.
Send request by: Mail
Deadline(s): July 1 for the Aug. award, Dec. 16 for the Jan. award
Applicants should submit the following:
1) Essay
2) Transcripts
3) Letter(s) of recommendation
Additional information: Application should also include a letter from a physician verifying a diagnosis of SLE. The foundation selects students who have demonstrated courage and perseverance in their struggle to overcome the limitations of Lupus. Faxed or e-mailed applications are not accepted.

Program description:
L.I.F.E. Scholarship: The scholarship is awarded to one or more students each year in the month of Aug. and/or Jan., and recipients will receive a minimum award of $500 made payable to the educational institution at which they are enrolled for tuition, fees, and other educational-related expenses. Each applicant must be diagnosed with systemic lupus erythematosus (SLE) and be working towards a degree with a minimum of six credits per semester at an accredited United States college or university. The applicant must have a minimum GPA of 3.0 and be involved in at least one extracurricular activity (e.g., performance group, athletics, clubs/organizations, community service, employment, etc.)
EIN: 861035692

214
Major League Baseball Equipment Managers Association
P. O. Box 2095
Phoenix, AZ 85001 (206) 346-4309
Contact: Lou Cucuzza, Jr., Pres.
FAX: (610) 279-7100; E-mail: info@mlbema.com; URL: http://mlbema.com/

Foundation type: Public charity
Purpose: Scholarships to baseball equipment managers, prospective equipment managers, and their personnel.
Financial data: Year ended 12/31/2011. Assets, $240,436 (M); Expenditures, $68,664; Total giving, $16,125.
Fields of interest: Athletics/sports, baseball.
Type of support: Graduate support; Undergraduate support.
Application information: Application form required.
Deadline(s): Contact foundation for deadline
Additional information: Unsolicited requests for funds not considered or acknowledged.
EIN: 341763294

215
Make-A-Wish Foundation of Arizona, Inc.
711 E. Northern Ave.
Phoenix, AZ 85020-4154 (602) 395-9474
Contact: Elizabeth Reich, Pres. and C.E.O.
Toll-free tel. (Prog. Svcs. Dept.): (800) 324-9474
FAX: (602) 395-0722; E-mail: info@wishaz.org;
E-Mail for Elizabeth Reich: ereich@wishaz.org;
Toll-Free: (800)-324-9474; URL: http://www.wishaz.org

Foundation type: Public charity

Purpose: Grants to fulfill the wishes of central and southern Arizona children who are at least 2 1/2 years of age and less than eighteen years of age who live with life threatening medical conditions.
Publications: Annual report; Newsletter.
Financial data: Year ended 08/31/2011. Assets, $2,306,786 (M); Expenditures, $3,231,528; Total giving, $1,805,473; Grants to individuals, totaling $1,805,473.
Fields of interest: Children/youth; Terminal illness, people with.
Type of support: Grants for special needs.
Application information: Application form available on the grantmaker's web site.
Initial approach: Telephone or e-mail
Additional information: Children may be referred by medical professionals treating the child, a parent or legal guardian or the potential wish child.
EIN: 860409636

216
Roy and Yvonne McNeil Scholarship Fund
9494 Heritage Dr.
Flagsaff, AZ 86004

Foundation type: Operating foundation
Purpose: Scholarships to residents of Traill County, ND for students of May-Port CG Dollars and Hillsboro School.
Financial data: Year ended 12/31/2012. Assets, $1,009,633 (M); Expenditures, $34,758; Total giving, $27,300.
Type of support: Undergraduate support.
Application information: Applications accepted. Application form required.
Initial approach: Letter
Deadline(s): May 15
EIN: 456101161

217
Ed and Patricia McWilliams Trust, Inc.
318 S. Alarest Ave.
Miami, AZ 85539 (925) 473-3303

Foundation type: Independent foundation
Purpose: Scholarships to high school graduates in the Globe-Miami, AZ area for continuing education.
Financial data: Year ended 12/31/2012. Assets, $402,385 (M); Expenditures, $30,151; Total giving, $29,000; Grants to individuals, 22 grants totaling $29,000 (high: $2,000, low: $1,000).
Fields of interest: Higher education.
Type of support: Undergraduate support.
Application information: Application form required.
Deadline(s): Mar. 1
EIN: 800038408

218
Mesa Angels Foundation, Inc.
410 N. 44th St., Ste. 700
Phoenix, AZ 85008-7608 (602) 685-4000
FAX: (602) 685-4352

Foundation type: Public charity
Purpose: Grants and loans to individuals needing short-term emergency assistance due to issues such as medical emergency, natural disasters or other unforeseen, life-changing events.
Publications: Application guidelines.
Financial data: Year ended 09/30/2011. Assets, $153,539 (M); Expenditures, $12,601; Total giving, $12,200. Grants to individuals amount not specified.
Fields of interest: Human services.

Type of support: Emergency funds; Grants for special needs; Loans—to individuals.
Application information: Applications accepted. Application form required. Application form available on the grantmaker's web site.
Initial approach: Letter
Send request by: Mail, fax or e-mail
Deadline(s): First of the month
Additional information): Contact foundation for complete eligibility criteria.
Program description:
Grants: The foundation is available for individuals needing short-term emergency assistance. Potential recipients can apply for grants and loans in times of critical financial need due to issues such as medical emergency, natural disasters, or other unforeseen, life-changing events; individuals can also submit an application on behalf of deserving charitable organizations serving a broad public interest. Applicants will be required to clearly demonstrate a need for grants and loans, and must have exhausted all other methods of funding sources.
EIN: 010720556

219

Miss Arizona Scholarship Foundation
2800 14th Ave.
Douglas, AZ 85607-2627 (520) 364-5308
Contact: Stephen T. Rich, Pres.
FAX: (520) 364-1137;
E-mail: info@miss-arizona.org; E-Mail for Stephen T. Rich: rich@miss-arizona.org; URL: http://www.miss-arizona.org/

Foundation type: Public charity
Purpose: Scholarships to young women of AZ.
Financial data: Year ended 07/31/2012. Assets, $2,674 (M); Expenditures, $76,543; Total giving, $9,153.
Type of support: Undergraduate support.
Application information:
Initial approach: Letter or e-mail
Additional information: Contact foundation for application guidelines and eligibility requirements.
EIN: 942864252

220

Muscular Dystrophy Association, Inc.
3300 E. Sunrise Dr.
Tucson, AZ 85718-3208 (520) 529-2000
Contact: Steven M. Derks, Pres. and C.E.O.
FAX: (520) 529-5454; E-mail: mda@mdausa.org;
Toll-Free Tel.: (800) 572-1717; URL: http://www.mdausa.org/research

Foundation type: Public charity
Purpose: Research grants aimed at developing treatments for the muscular dystrophies and related diseases of the neuromuscular system.
Publications: Application guidelines; Annual report; Financial statement; Grants list; Informational brochure; Newsletter.
Financial data: Year ended 12/31/2011. Assets, $98,307,873 (M); Expenditures, $175,594,205; Total giving, $46,352,169.
Fields of interest: Nerve, muscle & bone diseases; Muscular dystrophy; Nerve, muscle & bone research; Muscular dystrophy research.
Type of support: Research; Postdoctoral support.
Application information: Application form required.
Initial approach: Pre-proposal
Deadline(s): June 15 and Dec. 15
Additional information: See web site for further application information.

Program descriptions:
Development Grant: Grants of up to $45,000 per year for up to three years are available to candidates who may be a member of a research team in the laboratory of an independent investigator (principal investigator), under whose guidance the applicant will be given flexibility to conduct a neuromuscular disease research project. Eligible applicants must: hold a M.D., Ph.D., D.Sc., or equivalent degree; be a member of a research team at an appropriate institution; be qualified to conduct a program of original research under the supervision of a principal investigator; have an acceptable research plan for a specific disease in the association's program; have access to institutional resources necessary to conduct the proposed research project; and have at least eighteen months of post-doctoral research laboratory training at the time of the application.
Research Grant: The association supports research aimed at developing treatments for muscular dystrophies and related diseases of the neuromuscular system. Applicant must be a professional or faculty member at an appropriate educational, medical, or research institution, and be qualified to conduct and supervise a program of original research, have access to institutional resources necessary to conduct the proposed research project, and hold an M.D., Ph.D., or equivalent degree. Funding levels for research grants are unlimited.
EIN: 131665552

221

North American Artist Foundation
c/o .
220 W. Pershing
Phoenix, AZ 85029-1815 (918) 734-8989
Toll-free tel.: (800) 848-3360

Foundation type: Public charity
Purpose: Grants for musical management training to aspiring musicians throughout the U.S.
Fields of interest: Music.
Type of support: Grants to individuals.
Application information: Contact foundation for guidelines.
EIN: 742542564

222

Northern Arizona University Foundation, Inc.
P.O. Box 4094
Bldg. 10, Old Main
Flagstaff, AZ 86011-0001 (928) 523-2012
Contact: Mason Gerety, Pres.
FAX: (928) 523-8877;
E-mail: advancement@nau.edu; Additional E-mail: university.advancement@nau.edu; Toll Free Tel.: (888) 628-2586; URL: http://www.advancement.nau.edu/foundation.shtml

Foundation type: Public charity
Purpose: Scholarships to Northern Arizona University students pursuing higher education.
Financial data: Year ended 06/30/2011. Assets, $116,429,111 (M); Expenditures, $11,397,367; Total giving, $6,899,110; Grants to individuals, totaling $1,771,380.
Fields of interest: Higher education.
Type of support: Scholarships—to individuals; Support to graduates or students of specific schools.
Application information:
Deadline(s): Jan. 31

Additional information: Contributes only to NAU students; unsolicited requests for funds not considered or acknowledged.
EIN: 860193726

223

Old Pueblo Community Services
4501 E. 5th St.
Tucson, AZ 85711-7015 (520) 546-0122
Contact: Nick Jones, C.E.O.
FAX: (520) 777-4512; URL: http://www.helptucson.org/help_tucson/makeadifference.php

Foundation type: Public charity
Purpose: Provides homebuyers assistance, homebuyer education programs, and develops affordable housing for Tucson, AZ low income residents. Assistance to individuals recovering from addiction, substance abuse and veterans returning from service in the U.S. Armed Forces.
Financial data: Year ended 12/31/2011. Assets, $4,587,958 (M); Expenditures, $5,741,484; Total giving, $203,421; Grants to individuals, 30 grants totaling $203,421.
Fields of interest: Substance abuse, services; Housing/shelter, home owners; Housing/shelter; Military/veterans.
Type of support: Grants for special needs.
Application information: Applications accepted. Application form required.
Additional information: Some assistance require an application. See web site for additional guidelines.
EIN: 860836556

224

Father Joseph Patterson Foundation
P.O. Box 25407
Tempe, AZ 85285 (602) 838-8777
Contact: Erin Patterson, Pres.

Foundation type: Independent foundation
Purpose: Scholarships primarily to residents of AZ for attendance at institutions of higher education.
Financial data: Year ended 07/31/2013. Assets, $547,381 (M); Expenditures, $45,783; Total giving, $45,500; Grants to individuals, 30 grants totaling $45,500 (high: $2,000, low: $1,000).
Fields of interest: Higher education.
Type of support: Scholarships—to individuals.
Application information: Applications accepted. Application form required.
Deadline(s): June 15
Applicants should submit the following:
1) Letter(s) of recommendation
2) Transcripts
Additional information: Application should also include a personal cover letter about self, educational, career goals, list of extracurricular activities and honors.
EIN: 953325958

225

Peoria Educational Enrichment Foundation, Inc.
6330 W. Thunderbird Rd.
Glendale, AZ 85306-4002 (623) 486-6040
Contact: Robert Young, Pres.
E-mail: bapperson@peoriaud.k12.az.us

Foundation type: Public charity
Purpose: Scholarships to graduating high school seniors of Peoria, AZ for postsecondary education.
Publications: Application guidelines.

Financial data: Year ended 06/30/2012. Assets, $910,807 (M); Expenditures, $39,500; Total giving, $33,650; Grants to individuals, totaling $33,650.
Fields of interest: Higher education.
Type of support: Support to graduates or students of specific schools.
Application information: Applications accepted. Application form required.
   Initial approach: Application
   Deadline(s): Feb. 18 for Against All Odds Scholarships, Mar. 26 for PEEF Expre$$ Program, Oct. 29 for Annual Grants, Nov. 14 for Community Service Scholarship
   Additional information: See web site for additional application information.
Program descriptions:
   Against All Odds Scholarships: Up to ten $1,000 scholarship each (one for each Peoria district high school) will be awarded to high school seniors who have overcome significant adversity to complete their high school coursework, and who plan to continue on with postsecondary education. Scholarships are intended to honor and support remarkable young men and women who have faced health issues, language barriers, adult responsibilities, family tragedies, and/or financial hardships with courage and fortitude.
   Annual Grants: Grants, ranging from $500 to $2,500, are available to fund innovative projects that demonstrate the potential to significantly improve achievement among Peoria Unified School District students. Grants can be awarded for fine arts, service-learning opportunities, literacy initiatives, special needs, health and wellness initiatives, technology integration, math/science, and principal staff development.
   Community Service Scholarship: Scholarships are available to Peoria Unified School District high school seniors who have demonstrated academic excellence and a strong commitment to the community in which they live.
   PEEF Expre$$ Program: Grants, ranging from $25 to $350, will be available to Peoria Unified School District teachers, administrators, and staff to fund small-scale projects in the classroom and in the school. Grants can be used for instructional supplies, computer supplies, audio-visual supplies, and books and/or periodicals.
EIN: 860607829

226
Phoenix Foundation Trust Fund
c/o Most Worshipful Grand Lodge F&AM of Arizona
345 W. Monroe St.
Phoenix, AZ 85003-1617 (602) 252-1924

Foundation type: Independent foundation
Purpose: Scholarships to individuals attending public colleges and universities in AZ.
Financial data: Year ended 06/30/2012. Assets, $0 (M); Expenditures, $58,936; Total giving, $51,000; Grants to individuals, totaling $51,000.
Type of support: Support to graduates or students of specific schools; Undergraduate support.
Application information: Application form required.
   Initial approach: Letter
   Deadline(s): Feb. 1
EIN: 959013325

227
Phoenix Suns Charities, Inc.
P.O. Box 1369
Phoenix, AZ 85001-1369 (602) 379-7767
Contact: Robin Milne, Exec. Dir.
FAX: (602) 379-7922; E-mail: sburgus@suns.com;
URL: http://www.nba.com/suns/news/charities_index.html

Foundation type: Public charity
Purpose: Scholarships to graduating high school seniors of AZ, for attendance at a college or university of their choice.
Publications: Application guidelines; Grants list.
Financial data: Year ended 06/30/2012. Assets, $1,042,349 (M); Expenditures, $1,275,988; Total giving, $1,133,950; Grants to individuals, totaling $112,335.
Fields of interest: Higher education.
Type of support: Scholarships—to individuals.
Application information:
   Initial approach: Letter or telephone
   Deadline(s): Feb. 1 for SunStudents College Scholarship and Kevin Johnson Scholar Award
   Applicants should submit the following:
      1) Letter(s) of recommendation
      2) Essay
EIN: 860633919

228
Pima Council on Aging, Inc.
8467 E. Broadway Blvd.
Tucson, AZ 85710-4009 (520) 790-7262
Contact: Jim Murphy, Pres. and C.E.O.
FAX: (520) 790-7577; E-mail: help@pcoa.org;
URL: http://www.pcoa.org

Foundation type: Public charity
Purpose: Minor home repairs and adaptations to low-income homeowners age 60 in Pima County, AZ. When funding allows, PCOA accepts applications for major home repairs to provide up to $4,000 in major home repairs such as major electrical/plumbing repairs, new cooling and/or heating units, etc.
Publications: Annual report; Financial statement; Newsletter.
Financial data: Year ended 06/30/2012. Assets, $3,166,825 (M); Expenditures, $8,639,806; Total giving, $4,590,132; Grants to individuals, totaling $111,332.
Fields of interest: Housing/shelter, services; Aging, centers/services; Aging; Economically disadvantaged.
Type of support: In-kind gifts.
Application information: Applications accepted. Application form required.
   Initial approach: Tel. or e-mail
   Applicants should submit the following:
      1) Financial information
   Additional information: Contact foundation for eligibility criteria.
EIN: 860251768

229
The Virginia G. Piper Charitable Trust
1202 E. Missouri Ave.
Phoenix, AZ 85014-2921 (480) 948-5853
Contact: Judy Jolley Mohraz Ph.D., C.E.O. and Pres.
FAX: (480) 348-1316; E-mail: info@pipertrust.org;
URL: http://www.pipertrust.org

Foundation type: Independent foundation
Purpose: Fellowships to Maricopa County, AZ, executives who hold positions of significant responsibility in nonprofit organizations.

Publications: Biennial report; Financial statement; Grants list; Newsletter; Occasional report.
Financial data: Year ended 03/31/2013. Assets, $533,033,849 (M); Expenditures, $23,682,862; Total giving, $15,056,253. Fellowships amount not specified.
Fields of interest: Nonprofit management.
Type of support: Fellowships.
Application information: Applications accepted. Application form available on the grantmaker's web site. Interview required.
   Initial approach: Letter, telephone or e-mail
   Send request by: Mail
   Deadline(s): Sept. 15
   Final notification: Applicants notified in Nov.
   Applicants should submit the following:
      1) Letter(s) of recommendation
      2) Budget Information
      3) Resume
      4) Essay
   Additional information: See web site for additional application guidelines.
Program description:
   Piper Fellows Program: The program acknowledges the never-ceasing demands of nonprofit leadership and offers opportunities for Maricopa County leaders to retool, refresh, and renew. A Piper Fellowship offers the potential for a $90,000 Piper Trust commitment to a Fellow's organization: Piper Trust awards up to $30,000 for study and travel expenses to support the professional development of outstanding senior executives of nonprofit organizations serving Maricopa County. The Trust awards $10,000 for staff and board professional development. And, a Fellowship makes the Fellow's organization eligible for a grant up to $50,000 for a Piper Fellows Organizational Enhancement Award either during the sabbatical or within six months of completion. See web site for application process.
EIN: 866247076

230
Positive Impact, Inc.
P.O. Box 11
Gilbert, AZ 85299-0011 (480) 899-7791
FAX: (480) 545-5137; URL: http://www.positiveimpactinc.org/?page_id=34

Foundation type: Public charity
Purpose: Grants to individuals and families in AZ for medical and temporary living expenses.
Financial data: Year ended 12/31/2011. Assets, $23,240 (M); Expenditures, $114,531; Total giving, $106,808.
Fields of interest: Human services.
Type of support: Grants for special needs.
Application information:
   Initial approach: Letter
EIN: 860920583

231
Prayer Child Foundation
3903 E. Huber St.
Mesa, AZ 85205-3903 (480) 889-6141
E-mail: info@prayerchild.org; URL: http://www.prayerchild.org

Foundation type: Operating foundation
Purpose: Grants to individuals 18 years old and younger in AZ who are in need of physical, emotional and financial assistance.
Publications: IRS Form 990 or 990-PF printed copy available upon request.
Financial data: Year ended 06/30/2013. Assets, $58,804 (M); Expenditures, $226,886; Total

giving, $226,700; Grants to individuals, 333 grants totaling $226,300 (high: $1,000, low: $200).
Fields of interest: Children/youth; Economically disadvantaged.
Type of support: Grants for special needs.
Application information: Applications accepted. Application form required.
> *Additional information:* Contact the foundation for eligibility criteria.
EIN: 030558277

232
Renaissance Performing Arts Co.
12601 E US HIGHWAY 60
Apache Junction, AZ 85118-9791 (520) 463-2600
Contact: Jeff Siegel, Tr.

Foundation type: Company-sponsored foundation
Purpose: Grants to individuals for performance and education relating to the Carolina Renaissance Festival, NC.
Financial data: Year ended 12/31/2012. Assets, $1,373 (M); Expenditures, $32,460; Total giving, $31,885; Grants to individuals, 111 grants totaling $31,885 (high: $2,875, low: $50).
Fields of interest: Performing arts; Performing arts, education.
Type of support: Grants to individuals; Scholarships—to individuals.
Application information: Applications accepted.
> *Additional information:* Contact the company for current application guidelines.
EIN: 411794770

233
Research Corporation for Science Advancement
4703 E. Camp Lowell Dr., Ste. 201
Tucson, AZ 85712-1292 (520) 571-1111
Contact: Daniel Gasch, C.F.O.
FAX: (520) 571-1119; E-mail: awards@rescorp.org;
URL: http://www.rescorp.org

Foundation type: Operating foundation
Purpose: Grants and awards for faculty research in the natural sciences (physics, chemistry, and astronomy) at colleges and universities in the U.S. and Canada. Awards are intended to help strengthen the linkage between research and teaching from high school through the graduate level, and Research Opportunity Awards by nomination only.
Publications: Application guidelines; Annual report; Newsletter; Occasional report.
Financial data: Year ended 12/31/2012. Assets, $146,724,496 (M); Expenditures, $8,752,905; Total giving, $4,169,828.
Fields of interest: University; Education; Research; Science; Physical/earth sciences; Astronomy; Chemistry; Physics.
Type of support: Program development; Research; Awards/grants by nomination only; Awards/prizes.
Application information:
> *Deadline(s):* Sept. 1 for Cottrell Scholars Awards
> *Additional information:* Contact foundation for current application guidelines; See web site for complete program guidelines.
Program description:
> *Cottrell Scholar Awards:* Cottrell Scholar Awards are for beginning faculty members who are committed to excel at both research and teaching. Applications should be tenure-track beginning faculty members whose primary appointment is in a Bachelor's and Ph.D. degree-granting department of astronomy, biochemistry, biophysics, chemistry,

or physics, but not in a school of medicine or engineering. Eligibility is limited to those in the third year after their first tenure-track appointment. The proposal consists of brief proposals for both research and teaching. Originality, feasibility, and the prospect for significant fundamental advances to science are the main criteria for the research plan. Contributions to education, especially at the undergraduate level, aspirations for teaching, and the proposed strategies to achieve educational objectives are factors in assessment of the teaching plan. The ability of applicants to mount a strong research program and their commitment to teaching are weighed in the two-phase review process. The deadline for receipt of proposals is 5 pm (MST) on Aug. 1. Applications must conform to guidelines and directions, and need to be endorsed by the institution. Potential applicants can begin the online submission process by completing the online submission Eligibility Quiz. Consult the complete program guidelines on the website for full details.
EIN: 131963407

234
Rosztoczy Foundation
c/o Wendy Cooper
11111 W. McDowell Rd.
Avondale, AZ 85392-5000
E-mail: ferenc@rosztoczyfoundation.org;
URL: http://www.rosztoczyfoundation.com

Foundation type: Independent foundation
Purpose: Scholarships for Hungarian students to travel to the U.S. to study and research with professors.
Financial data: Year ended 01/31/2013. Assets, $658,477 (M); Expenditures, $367,427; Total giving, $363,100; Grants to individuals, 70 grants totaling $363,100 (high: $30,000, low: $2,000).
Type of support: Research; Scholarships—to individuals; Foreign applicants.
Application information: Applications accepted. Application form required.
> *Send request by:* Mail or e-mail
> *Deadline(s):* None
> *Additional information:* Application must include recommendations.
EIN: 721583507

235
Shirley G. Schmitz Foundation Inc.
11445 E. Via Linda, Ste. 2 442
Scottsdale, AZ 85259-2638 (480) 661-6128
Contact: Shirley G. Schmitz, Chair.
URL: http://www.shirleygschmitz.org

Foundation type: Independent foundation
Purpose: Scholarships for students enrolled full time in accredited universities and community colleges within AZ, that can lead to forming a business.
Financial data: Year ended 12/31/2011. Assets, $442,204 (M); Expenditures, $22,146; Total giving, $14,750; Grants to individuals, 13 grants totaling $14,750 (high: $1,500, low: $1,000).
Fields of interest: College; University; Business school/education.
Type of support: Undergraduate support.
Application information: Applications accepted. Application form required. Application form available on the grantmaker's web site. Interview required.
> *Initial approach:* Letter
> *Send request by:* Mail
> *Deadline(s):* June 1
> *Applicants should submit the following:*

> 1) Letter(s) of recommendation
> 2) Financial information
> *Additional information:* See web site for additional application guidelines.
EIN: 810616358

236
Seed Money for Growth Foundation, Inc.
(also known as SMFG Foundation, Inc.)
4716 N. Dromedary Rd.
Phoenix, AZ 85018-2939

Foundation type: Operating foundation
Purpose: Scholarships to financially needy residents of AZ for attendance at "AMI approved" Montessori schools, Montessori teacher training, development of special talents at the graduate level in the arts and sciences at an AZ institution, and for nurses of free-standing ambulatory surgical centers (FSASC).
Financial data: Year ended 07/31/2013. Assets, $215,516 (M); Expenditures, $16,245; Total giving, $0.
Fields of interest: Arts; Elementary school/education; Education; Health care; Science.
Type of support: Graduate support; Undergraduate support.
Application information: Application form required.
> *Initial approach:* Telephone
> *Copies of proposal:* 1
> *Deadline(s):* None
> *Applicants should submit the following:*
> 1) Financial information
> 2) Budget Information
> *Additional information:* Application should also include W-2 copies and a copy of previous year's IRS filing for income verification.
EIN: 942919372

237
Southern Arizona Foundation for Education-Lutheran
P.O. Box 19139
Tucson, AZ 85731-9139 (520) 349-9873
URL: http://www.safelutheran.org/

Foundation type: Public charity
Purpose: Grants to Lutheran schools in Arizona that provide scholarships to educate needy children in their schools.
Financial data: Year ended 12/31/2011. Assets, $213,623 (M); Expenditures, $270,292; Total giving, $250,029. Scholarships—to individuals amount not specified.
Fields of interest: Scholarships/financial aid; Education.
Type of support: Scholarships—to individuals.
Application information: Applications accepted. Application form required.
> *Additional information:* Selection is based on need. Scholarships are paid directly to the educational institution on behalf of the students.
EIN: 860939957

238
Spencer Scholarship Foundation
42488 N. 108 St.
Scottsdale, AZ 85262 (952) 476-1072
Contact: Dale A. Spencer, Pres.

Foundation type: Independent foundation
Purpose: Scholarships to MN undergraduate students at accredited colleges and universities, or technical and vocational schools.

Financial data: Year ended 12/31/2011. Assets, $45,222 (M); Expenditures, $1,657; Total giving, $0.
Fields of interest: Vocational education.
Type of support: Technical education support.
Application information: Application form required.
   Deadline(s): Feb. 28.
   Additional information: Scholarship amounts are up to $3,000 for college or university, and up to $1,000 for vocational/technical school.
EIN: 411843693

239
The William D. Squires Educational Foundation, Inc.

2338 W. Royal Palm Rd., Rm. J
Phoenix, AZ 85021-9339
E-mail: info@wmdsquiresfoundation.org;
Application address: c/o Cynthia Squires Gross, P.O. 2940, Jupiter, FL 33468-2940, tel.: (561) 741-7751; URL: http://www.wmdsquiresfoundation.org/index.htm

Foundation type: Independent foundation
Purpose: Scholarships to students in OH for higher education who might not otherwise be able to afford tuition.
Financial data: Year ended 12/31/2012. Assets, $2,214,165 (M); Expenditures, $261,973; Total giving, $158,918; Grants to individuals, 26 grants totaling $158,918 (high: $52,000, low: $1,500).
Type of support: Undergraduate support.
Application information: Applications accepted. Application form required.
   Initial approach: Letter
   Deadline(s): Apr. 5
   Applicants should submit the following:
    1) Transcripts
    2) SAR
    3) Letter(s) of recommendation
    4) Essay
EIN: 860946058

240
St. Mary's/Westside Food Bank Alliance

2831 N. 31st Ave.
Phoenix, AZ 85009-1518 (602) 242-3663
Contact: Beverly Damore, Pres. and C.E.O.
FAX: (480) 393-4511;
E-mail: bbdamore@firstfoodbank.org; URL: http://www.firstfoodbank.org

Foundation type: Public charity
Purpose: Grants of food and other necessities to needy residents of AZ.
Financial data: Year ended 06/30/2011. Assets, $33,997,488 (M); Expenditures, $132,038,396; Total giving, $114,322,063; Grants to individuals, totaling $23,281,727.
Fields of interest: Economically disadvantaged.
Type of support: Grants for special needs.
Application information:
   Initial approach: Telephone or in person
EIN: 237353532

241
John Stott Ministries

P.O. Box 189
Cave Creek, AZ 85327 (480) 595-5117
Contact: Benjamin K. Homan, Pres.
FAX: (408) 945-1321;
E-mail: info.jsm@johnstottministries.org;
URL: http://www.johnstottministries.org/

Foundation type: Public charity
Purpose: Financial assistance to Ph.D. candidates from the Majority World in biblical and theological studies.
Publications: Annual report.
Financial data: Year ended 06/30/2012. Assets, $3,199,506 (M); Expenditures, $2,639,222; Total giving, $1,068,672; Grants to individuals, totaling $219,401.
Fields of interest: Theological school/education.
Type of support: Scholarships—to individuals; Postdoctoral support.
Application information: Applications accepted. Application form required.
   Additional information: See web site for additional guidelines.
EIN: 237417198

242
The Stephen H. Sturges & Rose P. Sturges Charitable Trust

P.O. Box 4997
Yuma, AZ 85366-4997
Application address: c/o Amy Gill, 833 Plaza Cir., Yuma, AZ 85364

Foundation type: Independent foundation
Purpose: Scholarships to residents of Yuma, AZ for continuing education at institutions of higher learning.
Financial data: Year ended 11/30/2012. Assets, $4,523,968 (M); Expenditures, $283,728; Total giving, $203,500; Grants to individuals, 67 grants totaling $128,500 (high: $2,500, low: $1,250).
Fields of interest: Scholarships/financial aid.
Type of support: Undergraduate support.
Application information: Application form required.
   Initial approach: Letter
   Additional information: Applications are made to individuals' high schools, which then forward the applications to the foundation, along with their recommendations. Application should include a brief resume.
EIN: 860427923

243
Sulphur Springs Valley Electric Cooperative Foundation, Inc.

(also known as SSVEC Foundation)
350 N. Haskell
Willcox, AZ 85643 (520) 384-5510
Contact: Wayne Crane
URL: http://www.ssvec.org/scholarship-program/

Foundation type: Company-sponsored foundation
Purpose: Scholarships to high school seniors who are children of members of Sulphur Springs Valley Electric Cooperative. Grants to junior high school students to attend an educational tour of Washington, D.C. Awards and prizes to support science and other educational during the Youth Engineering and Science Fair.
Publications: Application guidelines.
Financial data: Year ended 12/31/2012. Assets, $12,153,387 (M); Expenditures, $107,602; Total giving, $26,200; Grants to individuals, 50 grants totaling $18,000 (high: $5,000, low: $500).
Fields of interest: Education; Engineering; Science.
Type of support: Conferences/seminars; Scholarships—to individuals; Awards/prizes; Travel grants.
Application information:
   Initial approach: Complete online application for scholarships, download entry form for YES

Fair, and contact selected high schools for Washington Youth Tour
   Deadline(s): Mar. 4 for scholarships, Feb. 7 for Youth Engineering Science Fair
Program descriptions:
   SSVEC Foundation Scholarship Program: The foundation awards twenty $1,000 college scholarships to high school seniors who are children of members of Sulphur Springs Valley Electric Cooperative. One graduate from Benson, Bowie, Buena, Patagonia, San Simon, St. David, Tombstone, Valley Union, and Willcox high schools will each be awarded a scholarship. One scholarship will also be awarded to 12th grade graduates of home schools, charter schools, and private or public high schools in Cochise, Pima, Graham, or Santa Cruz counties.
   Washington Youth Tour: The foundation sponsors six junior high school students from Benson, Bowie, Buena, Patagonia, St. David, San Simon, Tombstone, Valley Union, or Willcox high schools to attend a one-week educational tour of Washington, D.C.
   YES Fair: The foundation awards grants, equipment, and travel expenses to students and advisors for the Youth Engineering Science Fair (YES Fair), where students in grades 5-12 compete in up to 14 science categories to receive cash awards and prizes. Two grand prize winners in the 9-12 divisions are also selected to compete at the Intel International Science and Engineering Fair.
EIN: 860488826

244
Thunderbird Junior Golf Foundation

9510 S. 7th St.
Phoenix, AZ 85042-7756 (602) 305-7655
E-mail: hsmith@thefirstteephoenix.org;
URL: http://www.thefirstteephoenix.org

Foundation type: Public charity
Purpose: Scholarships to graduating high school seniors of Maricopa county, AZ for higher education.
Financial data: Year ended 05/31/2012. Assets, $2,235,043 (M); Expenditures, $879,123; Total giving, $34,500.
Fields of interest: Higher education; Athletics/sports, golf.
Type of support: Scholarships—to individuals.
Application information: Applications accepted. Application form required.
   Initial approach: Telephone
   Deadline(s): Dec. 4
   Additional information: Applicants must be qualified members of The First Tee of Phoenix.
Program description:
   Cloud 9 Scholarship: The foundation will award scholarships of $250 each to graduating seniors who exemplify the values of honesty, integrity, respect, and sportsmanship on and off the golf course.
EIN: 522103204

245
Rosa Carrillo Torres Memorial Scholarship Fund

c/o Valle del Sol
3807 N. 7th St.
Phoenix, AZ 85014-5005
Application address: Arizona Community Foundation, 2201 East Camelback Rd., Ste. 202, Phoenix, AZ 85016, tel.: (800) 222-8221
FAX: (602) 248-8113; URL: http://www.valledelsol.com/?page_id=267

Foundation type: Public charity
Purpose: Scholarships to high school seniors of Hispanic descent enrolled in the Phoenix Union High School District, AZ who are attending a vocational or postsecondary school in AZ.
Publications: Application guidelines.
Fields of interest: Vocational education, post-secondary; Higher education; Hispanics/Latinos.
Type of support: Scholarships—to individuals.
Application information: Applications accepted. Application form required. Application form available on the grantmaker's web site.
> *Deadline(s):* Mar. 26
> *Final notification:* Applicants notified May 6
> *Applicants should submit the following:*
>   1) Essay
>   2) Letter(s) of recommendation
>   3) Transcripts
> *Additional information:* Application should also include letter of admission to college or university.
Program description:
> *Rosa Carrillo Torres Memorial Scholarship:* The fund provides scholarships of up to $1,000 per year to students of Hispanic heritage who are the first generation in their family pursuing a secondary education. Eligible applicants must be seniors in good standing who will graduate from Phoenix Union High School District, who have a minimum high school GPA of 2.5. in both their junior and senior years of high school, and who are accepted by and plan to enroll as a full-time student at an accredited, postsecondary institution or vocational program in AZ. Preference is given to students who plan to pursue a major in a health-care field or communication, as well as to students who come from low income backgrounds and who are the first generation in their family to attend college. Scholarships are renewable for up to four years.

246
Trico Foundation
c/o Trico Electric Cooperative, Inc.
P.O. Box 930
Marana, AZ   85653-0930   (520) 744-2944
URL: http://www.trico.coop/index.php?option=com_content&view=article&id=107&Itemid=109

Foundation type: Company-sponsored foundation
Purpose: Scholarships to Trico Electric Cooperative consumers, and their dependent children, who reside in Pima, Pinal, and Santa Cruz counties, AZ.
Publications: Application guidelines.
Financial data: Year ended 12/31/2012. Assets, $1,860,262 (M); Expenditures, $68,708; Total giving, $65,320; Grants to individuals, 37 grants totaling $65,320 (high: $4,600, low: $920).
Fields of interest: College; Scholarships/financial aid.
Type of support: Undergraduate support.
Application information: Applications accepted. Application form required. Application form available on the grantmaker's web site.
> *Initial approach:* Application
> *Send request by:* Mail
> *Deadline(s):* Varies
> *Applicants should submit the following:*
>   1) Financial information
>   2) Transcripts
>   3) Letter(s) of recommendation
Program description:
> *Scholarships:* The foundation awards college scholarships to Trcico members and to the immediate family of Trico members. Students attending two-year schools are awarded $1,840

($920 per semester) and students attend four-year schools are awarded $4,600 ($2,300 per semester). Applicants must have a 2.5 GPA or greater.
EIN: 942941045

247
Tucson-Pima Arts Council, Inc.
100 N. Stone Ave., Ste. 303
Tucson, AZ   85701   (520) 624-0595
Contact: Roberto Bedoya, Exec. Dir.
FAX: (520) 624-3001;
E-mail: info@tucsonpimaartscouncil.org; E-mail for Roberto Bedoya:
rbedoya@tucsonpimaartscouncil.org, tel.: (520) 624-0595, ext. 25; URL: http://www.tucsonpimaartscouncil.org

Foundation type: Public charity
Purpose: Grants to individual artists living in Tucson or Pima county AZ.
Publications: Application guidelines.
Financial data: Year ended 06/30/2012. Assets, $641,629 (M); Expenditures, $979,232; Total giving, $354,763; Grants to individuals, totaling $23,300.
Fields of interest: Visual arts; Performing arts; Arts.
Type of support: Grants to individuals.
Application information: Applications accepted. Application form required. Application form available on the grantmaker's web site.
> *Send request by:* Mail or hand deliver
> *Deadline(s):* Mar. 22
> *Final notification:* Recipients notified June 30
> *Applicants should submit the following:*
>   1) Work samples
>   2) Resume
>   3) Budget Information
Program description:
> *New Works Artist Project Grant:* The grants are awarded to working artists living in Tucson or Pima County, AZ for projects to create art that meets the highest standards of excellence across a diverse spectrum of artistic disciplines within Tucson and Pima County. Creation activities may include development and production of new art work, workshops and residencies for artists where the primary purpose is to create new art, opportunities for artists to create or refine their work, projects that employ innovative forms of art-making and design.
EIN: 860465675

248
Turf Paradise Foundation
1501 W. Bell Rd.
Phoenix, AZ   85023-3411
Contact: Vincent Francia, Chair.

Foundation type: Company-sponsored foundation
Purpose: Assistance and/or rehabilitation of individuals associated with horse racing.
Financial data: Year ended 12/31/2012. Assets, $4,366 (M); Expenditures, $49,082; Total giving, $34,000; Grants to individuals, 13 grants totaling $27,000 (high: $6,876, low: $2,100).
Fields of interest: Athletics/sports, equestrianism.
Type of support: Grants to individuals.
Application information: Applications accepted.
> *Deadline(s):* None
EIN: 742442775

249
The Turnbow Foundation
7619 E. Tasman Cir.
Mesa, AZ   85207-1197

Foundation type: Operating foundation
Purpose: Scholarships to economically disadvantaged individuals and families residing in the Mesa, AZ area.
Financial data: Year ended 12/31/2012. Assets, $71,392 (M); Expenditures, $95,037; Total giving, $34,368.
Fields of interest: Family services.
Type of support: Grants for special needs.
Application information: Applications not accepted.
EIN: 860732335

250
United Way of Tucson and Southern Arizona, Inc.
330 N. Commerce Park Loop, Ste. 200
Tucson, AZ   85754-6750   (520) 903-9000
FAX: (520) 903-9002;
E-mail: info@unitedwaytucson.org; URL: http://www.unitedwaytucson.org

Foundation type: Public charity
Purpose: Grants to needy residents of the Tuscon, AZ, area.
Publications: Annual report; Financial statement; Newsletter.
Financial data: Year ended 06/30/2011. Assets, $7,851,746 (M); Expenditures, $16,995,811; Total giving, $11,905,841; Grants to individuals, totaling $67,359.
Fields of interest: Economically disadvantaged.
Type of support: Grants for special needs.
Application information:
> *Initial approach:* Letter
> *Additional information:* Contact foundation for current eligibility requirements.
EIN: 860098932

251
University Medical Center Corporation
1501 N. Campbell Ave.
Tucson, AZ   85724-0001   (520) 694-0111
Contact: Michael Waldrum M.D., Pres. and C.E.O.
E-mail: krollins@umcaz.edu; Toll-Free Tel.: (800) 524-5928; URL: http://www.uahealth.com/

Foundation type: Public charity
Purpose: Assistance to individuals of southern AZ, with prescription drugs from outpatient pharmacy.
Financial data: Year ended 06/30/2012. Assets, $650,129,553 (M); Expenditures, $639,841,274; Total giving, $19,382,429; Grants to individuals, totaling $44,712.
Fields of interest: Health care; Economically disadvantaged.
Type of support: In-kind gifts.
Application information: Applications not accepted.
> *Additional information:* Uninsured patients who cannot pay for prescription are assisted with medication.
EIN: 860492210

252

US Airways Education Foundation, Inc.

(formerly America West Airlines Education
Foundation, Inc.)
c/o Community Rels.
4000 E. Sky Harbor Blvd.
Phoenix, AZ 85034-3802   (480) 693-5748
Contact: Sue Glawe, Pres.
FAX: (480) 693-3715;
E-mail: community.relations@usairways.com;
URL: http://www.usairways.com/en-US/
Resources/_downloads/aboutus/
education_foundation_guidelines.pdf

Foundation type: Public charity
Purpose: Scholarships to dependents of employees
of US Airways, Inc. for undergraduate studies at an
accredited college or university.
Publications: Application guidelines.
Financial data: Year ended 12/31/2011. Assets,
$748,197 (M); Expenditures, $460,023; Total
giving, $460,000; Grants to individuals, totaling
$290,000.
Fields of interest: Higher education.
Type of support: Employee-related scholarships.
Application information: Application form required.
Initial approach: Letter
Applicants should submit the following:
1) Essay
2) GPA
3) Letter(s) of recommendation
4) Transcripts
5) SAT
6) ACT
Company name: US Airways Group, Inc.
EIN: 860670438

253

The Valley Foundation

4729 E. Sunrise Dr., Ste. 307
Tucson, AZ 85718-4534

Foundation type: Independent foundation
Purpose: Scholarships to residents of Pima County,
AZ.
Financial data: Year ended 12/31/2011. Assets,
$785,873 (M); Expenditures, $83,678; Total
giving, $70,500; Grants to individuals, 26 grants
totaling $70,500 (high: $4,000, low: $1,000).
Fields of interest: Higher education.
Type of support: Scholarships—to individuals.
Application information: Application form required.
Deadline(s): Mar. 1
EIN: 931228513

254

Valley of the Sun Hospice Association

1510 E. Flower St.
Phoenix, AZ 85014-5656   (602) 530-6900
Contact: Susan Levine, C.E.O. and Exec.Dir.
FAX: (602) 530-6901; E-mail: info@hov.org;
URL: http://www.hov.org

Foundation type: Public charity
Purpose: Scholarships for nursing degrees to
employees in good standing at Hospice of the
Valley, AZ who agree to work there for at least 24
months following graduation.
Financial data: Year ended 09/30/2011. Assets,
$193,197,842 (M); Expenditures, $151,311,262;
Total giving, $150,425; Grants to individuals,
totaling $5,000.
Fields of interest: Nursing school/education;
Palliative care.
Type of support: Employee-related scholarships.

Application information:
Initial approach: Letter
Additional information: Application should
include letters of recommendation; Contact
foundation for current application guidelines.
EIN: 860338886

255

Valley of the Sun United Way

1515 E. Osborn Rd.
Phoenix, AZ 85014-5386   (602) 631-4800
Contact: Merl Waschler, Pres. and C.E.O.
FAX: (602) 631-4809;
E-mail: information@vsuw.org; URL: http://
www.vsuw.org

Foundation type: Public charity
Purpose: Stipends for child care providers
throughout Maricopa County, AZ.
Financial data: Year ended 06/30/2012. Assets,
$76,865,218 (M); Expenditures, $82,678,656;
Total giving, $71,008,203; Grants to individuals,
1,910 grants totaling $1,537,160.
Fields of interest: Day care; Human services;
Economically disadvantaged.
Type of support: Grants to individuals; Stipends.
Application information: Applications accepted.
Additional information: See web site for other
programs on individual needs.
EIN: 860104419

256

Valley Telephone Cooperative Foundation

P.O. Box 970
Willcox, AZ 85644-0970   (520) 384-2231
FAX: (520) 384-2831; URL: http://www.vtc.net/

Foundation type: Company-sponsored foundation
Purpose: Scholarships to member-patrons and
family members of patrons of Valley Telephone
Cooperative, Inc. in AZ and NM.
Publications: Application guidelines.
Financial data: Year ended 12/31/2012. Assets,
$1,541,536 (M); Expenditures, $73,355; Total
giving, $67,655; Grants to individuals, 39 grants
totaling $62,500 (high: $2,500, low: $1,250).
Type of support: Undergraduate support.
Application information: Applications accepted.
Application form required. Application form
available on the grantmaker's web site.
Send request by: Mail or hand delivered
Deadline(s): Mar. 12
Applicants should submit the following:
1) Letter(s) of recommendation
2) Transcripts
3) Essay
4) Class rank
5) GPA
EIN: 742613547

257

Kurt Warner First Things First Foundation

1 N. 1st St., Ste. 730
Phoenix, AZ 85004-2357   (602) 385-0840
Contact: Marci M. Pritts, Secy.-Treas.
FAX: (602) 385-0841; URL: http://
www.kurtwarner.org

Foundation type: Public charity
Purpose: Scholarships to students of St. Louis, MO
and Iowa for continuing education at accredited
colleges or universities.
Financial data: Year ended 12/31/2011. Assets,
$1,590,954 (M); Expenditures, $649,511; Total

giving, $266,789; Grants to individuals, totaling
$43,932.
Fields of interest: Higher education.
Type of support: Scholarships—to individuals.
Application information: Applications accepted.
Application form required.
Additional information: Scholarship funds are
paid directly to the educational institution on
behalf of the students. Recipients are
selected based on financial need and
community service.
EIN: 431921463

258

**The Washington Education Foundation,
Inc.**

P. O. Box 54356
Phoenix, AZ 85078-4356   (602) 376-6395
Contact: Nancy Putman, Pres.
E-mail: wesdfoundation@cox.net; E-mail for Nancy
Putman: nancy.putman@wesdschools.org;
URL: http://www.wesdfoundation.com

Foundation type: Public charity
Purpose: Grants to teachers in the Washington
School District in Phoenix, AZ, area for the
educational benefit of students in their classrooms.
Publications: Application guidelines.
Financial data: Year ended 06/30/2012. Assets,
$49,997 (M); Expenditures, $48,693; Total giving,
$34,883.
Fields of interest: Elementary/secondary
education.
Type of support: Grants to individuals.
Application information: Applications accepted.
Application form required. Application form
available on the grantmaker's web site.
Deadline(s): Feb. and Oct.
Final notification: Within 30 days after receipt of
application
EIN: 860650710

259

Youth On Their Own

1443 West Prince Rd.
Tucson, AZ 85705-3037   (520) 293-1136
FAX: (520) 888-7233; URL: http://www.yoto.org

Foundation type: Public charity
Purpose: Financial assistance, basic human
necessities and guidance to students in grades 8
through 12 who lack a stable home and parental
involvement in the Tuscon-metro area.
Publications: Newsletter.
Financial data: Year ended 06/30/2011. Assets,
$1,010,074 (M); Expenditures, $629,121; Total
giving, $264,922; Grants to individuals, 516 grants
totaling $264,922. Subtotal for grants to
individuals: 516 grants totaling $264,922.
Fields of interest: Secondary school/education.
Type of support: Emergency funds; Stipends.
Application information: Applications not
accepted.
Program descriptions:
Special Needs Fund: Emergency funds are
available for students in a financial bind who need
assistance with rent, utilities, sports fees and
equipment, summer school, and other fees.
Stipend Program: The program provides a
monthly student stipend of up to $125, dependent
upon grades and school attendance, that assists
students with living expenses such as food, rent,
utilities, and other basic needs.
EIN: 860644388

ARKANSAS

260
The Charlotte D. and Delbert E. Allen, Sr. Charitable and Scholarship Trust
P.O. Box 7200
Siloam Springs, AR 72761-7200 (479) 524-2222

Foundation type: Company-sponsored foundation
Purpose: Scholarships to graduates of Siloam Springs High School, AR for continuing education at accredited colleges or universities.
Financial data: Year ended 12/31/2012. Assets, $506,855 (M); Expenditures, $25,577; Total giving, $25,000.
Type of support: Support to graduates or students of specific schools; Undergraduate support.
Application information: Applications accepted.
  Initial approach: Letter
  Deadline(s): May 31
  Applicants should submit the following:
    1) GPA
    2) Financial information
EIN: 716138517

261
Area Agency on Aging of West Central Arkansas, Inc.
905 W. Grand Ave.
Hot Springs, AR 71913-3438 (501) 321-2811
Contact: TIm Herr, Exec. Dir.
FAX: (501) 321-2650;
E-mail: info@seniorspecialists.org; Toll-free tel.: (800) 467-2170; URL: http://www.seniorspecialists.org

Foundation type: Public charity
Purpose: Assistance to older persons in the west central Arkansas area, to lead independent and dignified lives, with transportation and social services, also in home care services, and other special needs.
Financial data: Year ended 06/30/2012. Assets, $3,206,638 (M); Expenditures, $9,044,424.
Fields of interest: Human services; Aging.
Type of support: Grants for special needs.
Application information: Qualification requirements for specific programs may vary according to income, age, or other factors, the agency endeavors to provide help to all seniors in the coverage area. Contact the agency for eligibility determination.
EIN: 710521904

262
Arkansas Childrens Hospital
1 Children's Way
Little Rock, AR 72202-3591 (501) 364-1100
Contact: Jonathan Bates M.D., Pres. and C.E.O.
Application address: P.O. Box 34114, Little Rock, AR 72203, tel.: (501) 364-1230 or toll free: (800) 280-1230
URL: http://www.archildrens.org/

Foundation type: Public charity
Purpose: Financial assistance to eligible families in Arkansas, who cannot afford to pay for certain services provided by the hospital.
Publications: Annual report; Newsletter; Occasional report.

Financial data: Year ended 06/30/2012. Assets, $720,257,625 (M); Expenditures, $466,892,785; Total giving, $8,115,383; Grants to individuals, totaling $383,437.
Fields of interest: Health care; Children/youth; Economically disadvantaged.
Type of support: Grants for special needs.
Application information: Applications accepted. Application form required. Application form available on the grantmaker's web site.
  Initial approach: Telephone
  Send request by: Mail
  Additional information: See web site for additional information for eligibility determination.
EIN: 710236857

263
Arkansas Eastman Scholarship Trust
c/o Citizens Bank
P.O. Box 2156
Batesville, AR 72503-2156 (870) 698-5524
Application address: c/o Scholarship Comm., P.O. Box 2357, Batesville, AR 72503

Foundation type: Operating foundation
Purpose: Scholarships to full-time students from north-central AR with an interest in math and/or science or other related studies for higher education.
Financial data: Year ended 12/31/2012. Assets, $69,610 (M); Expenditures, $9,750; Total giving, $8,000; Grants to individuals, 8 grants totaling $8,000 (high: $1,000, low: $1,000).
Fields of interest: Higher education.
Type of support: Undergraduate support.
Application information: Applications accepted.
  Deadline(s): None
  Additional information: Contact the foundation for additional application guidelines.
EIN: 582024178

264
Arkansas Farm Bureau - Romeo E. Short Memorial Foundation
(formerly Romeo E. Short Foundation)
P.O. Box 31
Little Rock, AR 72203 (479) 575-4433
Contact: Randy Luttrell Dr.
Applicaton address: 205 Agriculture Bldg., Fayetteville, AR 72701

Foundation type: Independent foundation
Purpose: Scholarships to students enrolled at The University of Arkansas-Fayetteville, Dale Bumper College of Agriculture, Food and Life Sciences.
Financial data: Year ended 10/31/2012. Assets, $429,047 (M); Expenditures, $19,428; Total giving, $19,000.
Fields of interest: Higher education; Formal/general education.
Type of support: Scholarships—to individuals.
Application information: Application form required.
  Deadline(s): Mar. 1
EIN: 716050688

265
Arkansas Farm Bureau Scholarship Foundation
(formerly Farm Bureau-Arkansas Scholarship Foundation, Inc.)
10720 Kanis Rd.
Little Rock, AR 72211-3825 (501) 228-1246
Contact: Chuck Tucker
Application address: P.O. Box 31, Little Rock, AR 72203, tel.: (501) 228-1246

Foundation type: Independent foundation
Purpose: Scholarships to juniors and seniors of AR planning a career in or related to the agricultural industry.
Financial data: Year ended 10/31/2013. Assets, $383,971 (M); Expenditures, $22,697; Total giving, $22,500; Grants to individuals, 20 grants totaling $22,500 (high: $1,125, low: $1,125).
Fields of interest: Higher education; Agriculture.
Type of support: Scholarships—to individuals; Undergraduate support.
Application information: Applications accepted. Application form required.
  Initial approach: Letter
  Deadline(s): June 1
  Applicants should submit the following:
    1) GPA
    2) Financial information
    3) Essay
  Additional information: Selection is based on academic achievement, character, career plans, financial need and leadership potential. Applicants must be children or grandchildren of Farm Bureau Members. Applicants must also have a minimum of two full semesters required for completion of their degree.
EIN: 710888051

266
Arkansas Human Development Corporation
300 S. Spring St., Ste. 800
Little Rock, AR 72201-2424 (501) 374-1103
Contact: Clevon Young, Exec. Dir.
FAX: (501) 374-1413; E-mail: cyoung@arhdc.org; Toll-Free Tel.: (800) 482-7641; URL: http://www.arhdc.org/

Foundation type: Public charity
Purpose: Support to economically disadvantaged individuals in rural AR to improve their standards of living and quality of life.
Publications: Annual report; Informational brochure; Newsletter.
Financial data: Year ended 06/30/2012. Assets, $2,485,079 (M); Expenditures, $3,169,306.
Fields of interest: Economically disadvantaged.
Type of support: Stipends.
Application information: Applications not accepted.
  Additional information: Applications to pre-selected individuals.
EIN: 237248955

267
Arvac, Inc.
613 N. 5th St.
P.O. Box 808
Dardanelle, AR 72834-0808 (479) 229-4861
Contact: Stephanie Ellis, Exec. Dir.
E-mail: arvac@arvacinc.org; URL: http://www.arvacinc.org

Foundation type: Public charity

Purpose: Grants to economically disadvantaged residents of the nine county area in the Arkansas River Valley with food, shelter, energy and other special needs.
Financial data: Year ended 06/30/2012. Assets, $1,373,571 (M); Expenditures, $4,469,405; Total giving, $2,556,228; Grants to individuals, totaling $2,556,228.
Fields of interest: Economically disadvantaged.
Type of support: Grants for special needs.
Application information: Contact the agency for application guidelines.
EIN: 710386402

268
Mabel Brickey Ayres Memorial Foundation, Inc.
709 N. Ermen Ln.
Osceola, AR 72370 (870) 563-2990
Contact: Ann Moore, Secy.

Foundation type: Independent foundation
Purpose: Scholarships to residents of Mississippi County, AR for higher education at accredited institutions.
Financial data: Year ended 12/31/2012. Assets, $205,084 (M); Expenditures, $42,187; Total giving, $29,500.
Fields of interest: Higher education.
Type of support: Scholarships—to individuals.
Application information: Application form required.
Initial approach: Letter or telephone
Additional information: Contact foundation for current application guidelines.
EIN: 237408205

269
Baptist Health Foundation
9601 Interstate 630, Exit 7
Little Rock, AR 72205-7202 (501) 202-1839
URL: http://www.baptist-health.com/give/about/

Foundation type: Public charity
Purpose: Scholarships to nursing students and health care providers at Baptist Health Schools, Little Rock, AR.
Publications: Informational brochure.
Financial data: Year ended 12/31/2011. Assets, $45,152,604 (M); Expenditures, $5,399,439; Total giving, $2,846,332; Grants to individuals, totaling $199,225.
Fields of interest: Nursing school/education.
Type of support: Support to graduates or students of specific schools; Undergraduate support.
Application information: Applications accepted. Application form required.
EIN: 237169407

270
Bearden Lumber Company Scholarship Foundation, Inc.
P.O. Box 137
Bearden, AR 71720-0137 (870) 687-2246

Foundation type: Company-sponsored foundation
Purpose: Scholarships to graduates of Bearden High School, AR, for higher education.
Financial data: Year ended 12/31/2012. Assets, $0 (M); Expenditures, $23,750; Total giving, $23,750; Grants to individuals, 11 grants totaling $23,750 (high: $2,500, low: $1,250).
Type of support: Support to graduates or students of specific schools; Undergraduate support.

Application information: Applications accepted. Application form required.
Deadline(s): Mar. 15
EIN: 710510772

271
George S. & Carrie Lee Boggan Scholarship Fund Trust
P.O. Box 416
Van Buren, AR 72957 (479) 474-3466
Contact: Lori Suggs

Foundation type: Independent foundation
Purpose: Scholarships to students who are residents of Crawford county, AR and one Parish in Natchitoches, LA for higher education.
Financial data: Year ended 12/31/2013. Assets, $9,757 (M); Expenditures, $12,024; Total giving, $12,000; Grants to individuals, 10 grants totaling $12,000 (high: $1,500, low: $750).
Fields of interest: Education.
Type of support: Scholarships—to individuals.
Application information: Application form required.
Deadline(s): None
Additional information: Application forms are furnished upon request.
EIN: 710485290

272
The Buck Foundation
15249 Dutchman's Dr.
Rogers, AR 72756-7868 (479) 925-2597
Contact: Jan Buck, Exec. Dir.
E-mail: info@buckforscholarships.com; Email address for Jan Buck: jan@buckforscholarships.com; URL: http://buckforscholarships.com

Foundation type: Independent foundation
Purpose: Scholarships to graduating seniors from Rogers High School, AR, Bentonville High School, AR or Pea Ridge High School, AR for continuing education at accredited colleges or universities.
Financial data: Year ended 04/30/2013. Assets, $6,160,358 (M); Expenditures, $242,538; Total giving, $228,500; Grants to individuals, totaling $190,500.
Fields of interest: Higher education.
Type of support: Support to graduates or students of specific schools.
Application information: Applications accepted.
Deadline(s): Vary
Additional information: Applications can be obtained from the guidance counselors from the high schools.
EIN: 710824287

273
Cabot Scholarship Foundation, Inc.
200 W. Main St.
Cabot, AR 72023-2945 (501) 843-6515
Contact: Calvin K. Aldridge, Treas.

Foundation type: Public charity
Purpose: Scholarships to graduates of Cabot High School, AR for continuing education at accredited colleges or universities.
Financial data: Year ended 07/31/2011. Assets, $544,429 (M); Expenditures, $59,321; Total giving, $56,691; Grants to individuals, totaling $56,691.
Type of support: Support to graduates or students of specific schools.
Application information: Application form required.

Additional information: Contact guidance counselor for current application guidelines.
EIN: 710713554

274
Communication Arts Institute
(formerly Writers' Colony at Dairy Hollow)
515 Spring St.
Eureka Springs, AR 72632-3032 (479) 253-7444
FAX: (479) 253-9859;
E-mail: director@writerscolony.org; URL: http://www.writerscolony.org

Foundation type: Public charity
Purpose: Residencies to emerging and experienced writers at work on specific projects.
Publications: Application guidelines.
Financial data: Year ended 12/31/2011. Assets, $419,729 (M); Expenditures, $108,442.
Fields of interest: Music composition; Literature.
Type of support: Residencies.
Application information: Application form required.
Send request by: Mail or e-mail
Deadline(s): None
Applicants should submit the following:
  1) Letter(s) of recommendation
  2) Essay
Additional information: Application should also include two work samples that are not returnable and a $35 non-refundable application fee. See web site for complete program information.
Program description:
Residency Fellowships: The organization offers a variety of fellowships, generally ranging from one week to four weeks, for writers on a variety of topics. Fellows receive the time and space needed to work on their project, including a private suite with writing space, private bath, wireless and/or cable hookup, uninterrupted writing time, prepared meals, and the opportunity to discuss works in progress with other professional writers. In turn, recipients will be asked to donate their time for a two-hour in-house event (which can include a lecture, slide show, question-and-answer session, reading, demonstration, gallery showing, etc.)
EIN: 731547467

275
Community Action Program for Central Arkansas
707 Robins St., Ste. 118
Conway, AR 72034-6517 (501) 329-3891
Contact: Archie Musselman, Exec. Dir.
FAX: (501) 329-9247; E-mail: info@capcainc.org; URL: http://www.capcainc.org

Foundation type: Public charity
Purpose: Low-income Home Energy Assistance Program designed to assist eligible persons in central AR with utility bills whose household is at or below the 150% Federal Poverty guidelines.
Publications: Newsletter.
Financial data: Year ended 03/31/2012. Assets, $626,615 (M); Expenditures, $9,373,076; Total giving, $4,288,079; Grants to individuals, totaling $1,788,492.
Fields of interest: Housing/shelter, expense aid; Economically disadvantaged.
Type of support: Grants for special needs.
Application information: Applications accepted. Application form required.
Initial approach: Tel.
Applicants should submit the following:
  1) Financial information

Additional information: Contact 855-267-8341 for further eligibility criteria.
EIN: 710393919

276
Cornerstone Scholarship Charitable Trust
(formerly Mauldin Scholarship Charitable Trust)
c/o Herbert Brooks
12404 Watson Rd.
Sherwood, AR 72120-9719

Foundation type: Independent foundation
Purpose: Scholarships to students of Little Rock, AR.
Financial data: Year ended 12/31/2011. Assets, $0 (M); Expenditures, $4,750; Total giving, $4,000.
Fields of interest: Higher education.
Type of support: Scholarships—to individuals; Technical education support; Undergraduate support.
Application information: Application form required.
   Initial approach: Cover letter
   Deadline(s): Mar. 1
EIN: 710744188

277
El Dorado Promise, Inc.
200 Peach St.
El Dorado, AR 71730-5836 (870) 864-5046
Application address: 2000 Wildcat Dr., El Dorado, AR 71730
URL: http://www.eldoradopromise.com/

Foundation type: Company-sponsored foundation
Purpose: Scholarships to graduates of El Dorado public schools, AR who are admitted to or enrolled at a two or four year accredited college or university pursuing an associate's or bachelor's degree.
Publications: Application guidelines.
Financial data: Year ended 12/31/2011. Assets, $19,600,796 (M); Expenditures, $2,672,501; Total giving, $2,546,316; Grants to individuals, totaling $2,546,316.
Fields of interest: Higher education.
Type of support: Support to graduates or students of specific schools.
Application information: Applications accepted. Application form required. Application form available on the grantmaker's web site.
   Initial approach: Application
   Deadline(s): Student's senior year of high school
   Additional information: Students may submit applications to any El Dorado high school guidance counselor. Funds are paid directly to the educational institution on behalf of the student.
EIN: 208303418

278
Endeavor Foundation
800 Founders Park Dr. E.
Springdale, AR 72762 (479) 361-4624
Contact: Anita Scism, C.E.O.
FAX: (479) 361-5094;
E-mail: anita@endeavorfoundation.net;
URL: http://www.endeavorfoundation.net

Foundation type: Community foundation
Purpose: Scholarships to graduating high school students of AR, pursuing postsecondary education at a two- or four-year college or vocational school.
Publications: Annual report; Biennial report; Informational brochure; Occasional report.

Financial data: Year ended 12/31/2012. Assets, $19,896,547 (M); Expenditures, $2,073,759; Total giving, $1,257,481; Grants to individuals, totaling $3,000.
Fields of interest: Vocational education, post-secondary; College; University.
Type of support: Support to graduates or students of specific schools.
Application information: Applications accepted.
   Deadline(s): Varies
   Applicants should submit the following:
      1) Transcripts
      2) GPA
      3) ACT
   Additional information: See web site for complete listing of scholarship funds and additional area scholarship programs not administered by the foundation.
EIN: 311682365

279
Henry J. and Helen Finkbeiner Memorial Fund for Benton High School Graduates
422 N. Main St.
Benton, AR 72015-3714
Contact: Fred E. Briner, Dir.

Foundation type: Independent foundation
Purpose: Scholarships to Benton High School, AR, seniors for higher education.
Financial data: Year ended 12/31/2012. Assets, $206,574 (M); Expenditures, $8,484; Total giving, $8,000; Grants to individuals, 5 grants totaling $8,000 (high: $2,000, low: $1,000).
Fields of interest: Higher education.
Type of support: Support to graduates or students of specific schools; Undergraduate support.
Application information: Application form required.
   Deadline(s): Vary
   Additional information: Application must include transcript.
EIN: 710557061

280
Gillespie Family Charity Trust
P.O. Box 3010
Russellville, AR 72811 (479) 967-8000

Foundation type: Independent foundation
Purpose: Scholarships to graduates of high schools in Pope County, AR for continuing education at accredited colleges or universities.
Financial data: Year ended 12/31/2012. Assets, $394,839 (M); Expenditures, $22,495; Total giving, $16,948; Grants to individuals, 18 grants totaling $16,948 (high: $2,000, low: $500).
Type of support: Support to graduates or students of specific schools; Undergraduate support.
Application information: Applications accepted.
   Initial approach: Letter
   Deadline(s): None
   Additional information: Application should include academic ability, financial need, disability status and two letters of character reference.
EIN: 716145471

281
Fred & Florence Halstead Charitable Trust
(formerly Fred E. Halstead Scholarship Trust)
2000 Regions Ctr.
400 W. Capitol Ave.
Little Rock, AR 72201-3402 (501) 370-1544
Contact: A. Wyckliff Nisbet, Jr., Tr.

Foundation type: Independent foundation
Purpose: Scholarships to high school graduates of Wynne High School and Arkansas High School, AR for continuing education at higher institutions.
Financial data: Year ended 06/30/2013. Assets, $2,869 (M); Expenditures, $8,795; Total giving, $8,000; Grants to individuals, 6 grants totaling $8,000 (high: $2,000, low: $1,000).
Fields of interest: Higher education.
Type of support: Support to graduates or students of specific schools.
Application information: Applications accepted.
   Initial approach: Letter
   Deadline(s): None
EIN: 716177921

282
Harry O. Hamm Foundation
P.O. Box 469
Van Buren, AR 72957-0469
Application address: Senior Class Counselor, Van Buren High School, 1221 Pointer Trail, Van Buren, AR 72956, tel.: (479) 474-2621

Foundation type: Operating foundation
Purpose: Scholarships to graduates of Van Buren High School, AR, for higher education.
Financial data: Year ended 12/31/2012. Assets, $3,885,343 (M); Expenditures, $195,474; Total giving, $169,806.
Fields of interest: Higher education.
Type of support: Support to graduates or students of specific schools; Undergraduate support.
Application information: Applications accepted. Application form required.
   Deadline(s): Apr. 1
EIN: 710800702

283
Helping Hands of Benton County
(formerly Helping Hands Thrift Shop, Inc.)
320 Airport Rd.
Bentonville, AR 72712-6780 (479) 273-2511
Contact: Bill Crawford, Exec. Dir.
FAX: (479) 273-0838;
E-mail: Bill@HelpingHandsNWA.org; URL: http://www.helpinghandsnwa.org

Foundation type: Public charity
Purpose: Assistance to individuals in northwest Arkansas with food, clothing, rental assistance, utility bills, doctor's visits and limited prescriptions. Assistance also to those affected by fire and other natural disasters.
Financial data: Year ended 12/31/2011. Assets, $1,964,142 (M); Expenditures, $2,800,581; Total giving, $1,795,918; Grants to individuals, totaling $1,795,918.
Fields of interest: Safety/disasters; Economically disadvantaged.
Type of support: Grants for special needs.
Application information: Monetary assistance is provided on a first come first served basis. Contact the agency for eligibility determination.
EIN: 710478243

284
Hornlein Scholarship Trust
P.O. Box 1928
Mountain Home, AR 72654-1928 (870) 425-1801

Foundation type: Independent foundation
Purpose: Scholarships based on financial need, character, and scholastic ability, to graduates of

Mountain Home Arkansas High School, AR, who are enrolled in institutions within the continental U.S. for vocational, undergraduate, and graduate degrees.
Publications: Annual report (including application guidelines); Informational brochure.
Financial data: Year ended 12/31/2012. Assets, $1,521,193 (M); Expenditures, $94,107; Total giving, $63,511; Grants to individuals, 93 grants totaling $63,511 (high: $1,900, low: $161).
Type of support: Support to graduates or students of specific schools; Graduate support; Technical education support; Undergraduate support.
Application information: Applications accepted. Application form required.
  Deadline(s): Dec. 31.
  Applicants should submit the following:
    1) Letter(s) of recommendation
    2) SAT
    3) ACT
    4) Transcripts
    5) Financial information
  Additional information: Application should also include a list of other scholarships received, a current tax return and general information about the applicant.
EIN: 716157456

285
The Harvey and Bernice Jones Charitable Trust No. 2
922 E. Emma Ave.
Springdale, AR   72764

Foundation type: Independent foundation
Purpose: Scholarships to deserving students of Springdale, AR for higher education at colleges or universities.
Financial data: Year ended 11/30/2012. Assets, $1,135,073 (M); Expenditures, $119,618; Total giving, $106,236.
Type of support: Scholarships—to individuals.
Application information: Applications not accepted.
  Additional information: Unsolicited requests for funds not considered or acknowledged.
EIN: 716143264

286
Mickey and Ross Kelder Scholarship Trust
P.O. Box 1928
Mountain Home, AR   72654   (870) 425-2101
Application address: Integrity First Bank

Foundation type: Independent foundation
Purpose: Scholarships to students pursuing studies in foreign languages at the graduate or undergraduate level at a college or university in AR and whose interest is in teaching foreign languages within AR.
Financial data: Year ended 12/31/2012. Assets, $168,256 (M); Expenditures, $8,946; Total giving, $5,124; Grants to individuals, 5 grants totaling $5,124 (high: $2,250, low: $375).
Fields of interest: Language (foreign).
Type of support: Graduate support; Undergraduate support.
Application information: Applications accepted.
  Additional information: Selection is based on academic and extracurricular achievement, and financial need.
EIN: 716182215

287
Phyllis A. Keltner Foundation for Women
(formerly Phyllis A. Widding Foundation for Women)
5320 Country Club Blvd.
Little Rock, AR   72207   (501) 569-3194
Application address: University of AR at LR, 2801 S. University Ave., Little Rock, AR 72204

Foundation type: Independent foundation
Purpose: Scholarships to single women, with dependent children, who are students at the University of Arkansas, Little Rock, AR.
Financial data: Year ended 12/31/2012. Assets, $0 (M); Expenditures, $63,002; Total giving, $60,767; Grants to individuals, 15 grants totaling $60,767 (high: $6,599, low: $387).
Fields of interest: Women.
Type of support: Support to graduates or students of specific schools; Undergraduate support.
Application information: Applications accepted. Application form required.
  Initial approach: Letter
  Deadline(s): Apr. 1
  Additional information: Applicant should demonstrate academic accomplishment and financial need. Application should include a complete written narrative.
EIN: 716168654

288
The Carmen Lehman Charitable Foundation, Inc.
P.O. Box 489
Rogers, AR   72757-0489
URL: http://www.chapleonthecreeks.com

Foundation type: Independent foundation
Purpose: Scholarships to AR individuals for continuning education at institutions of higher learning.
Financial data: Year ended 04/01/2011. Assets, $0 (M); Expenditures, $52,458; Total giving, $3,000.
Fields of interest: Higher education.
Type of support: Undergraduate support.
Application information: Contact foundation for further program deadlines and guidelines.
EIN: 201401671

289
Mashburn Scholarship Foundation
1765 N. College Ave., Ste. 9
Fayetteville, AR   72703-2651   (479) 582-1936
Contact: Jonathan Story, Pres.
E-mail: mashburnfoundation@gmail.com;
URL: http://www.mashburnfoundation.org

Foundation type: Public charity
Purpose: Scholarships to talented and gifted students for full time attendance at the University of Arkansas pursuing a major in vocal performance, music education or musical theater.
Publications: Application guidelines.
Financial data: Year ended 12/31/2011. Assets, $310,382 (M); Expenditures, $78,353; Total giving, $25,050; Grants to individuals, totaling $25,050.
Fields of interest: Theater (musical); Music (choral); Performing arts, education.
Type of support: Scholarships—to individuals.
Application information: Applications accepted. Application form required. Interview required.
  Send request by: Mail
  Applicants should submit the following:
    1) Transcripts
    2) SAT

3) GPA
4) Financial information
5) ACT
  Additional information: Application should also include three letters of reference and a copy of your parents' most recent tax return.
Program description:
  Scholarships: Scholarships of up to $2,000 are available to gifted young people who wish to pursue a career in music education, music history, vocal music, drama, or the performing arts. Applicants will be judged on talent, understanding and ability to meet foundation commitments, dependability, leadership potential, a willingness to serve as a role model and mentor, attitude, maturity, exemplary morals, personal development, poise potential, and financial need. Scholarship recipients will be required to perform at annual fundraisers and other functions, take part in leadership conferences, prepare and meet budgets, learn study skills and time management, and become goodwill ambassadors who promote positive lifestyles and music.
EIN: 710745213

290
John & Lee Ella McDonald Scholarship Fund
c/o Simmons Trust Co.
P.O. Box 3010
Russellville, AR   72811-3010   (479) 965-7150
Application address: c/o Charleston High School, Attn.: Counselor, P.O. Box 188, Charleston, AR 72933

Foundation type: Independent foundation
Purpose: Scholarships to graduates of Charleston Arkansas High School first year students attending a four year college.
Financial data: Year ended 12/31/2012. Assets, $211,584 (M); Expenditures, $12,241; Total giving, $9,000; Grants to individuals, 6 grants totaling $9,000 (high: $3,000, low: $1,000).
Fields of interest: Higher education.
Type of support: Support to graduates or students of specific schools.
Application information: Applications accepted.
  Deadline(s): None
  Additional information: Applicant must show scholastic aptitude and financial need.
EIN: 716182849

291
Vida June Moll Scholarship Trust
c/o Dewitt Bank & Trust Co.
P.O. Box 71
Dewitt, AR   72042-0071   (870) 946-3531
Application address: Dewitt Bank and Trust Company, 215 South Jefferson, Dewitt, AR 72042

Foundation type: Independent foundation
Purpose: Scholarships to residents of DeWitt, AR for higher education.
Financial data: Year ended 12/31/2012. Assets, $207,891 (M); Expenditures, $10,424; Total giving, $8,000; Grants to individuals, 12 grants totaling $8,000 (high: $1,000, low: $500).
Fields of interest: Higher education.
Type of support: Scholarships—to individuals.
Application information: Applications accepted.
  Initial approach: Letter
  Additional information: Contact the trust for additional application guidelines.
EIN: 716124420

292
Julian M. Munyon Scholarship Trust
c/o Simmons First Trust Co., N.A.
P.O. Box 7009
Pine Bluff, AR 71611-7009

Foundation type: Independent foundation
Purpose: Scholarships to graduates of Star City High School, Arkansas, pursuing higher education.
Financial data: Year ended 12/31/2012. Assets, $849,515 (M); Expenditures, $56,961; Total giving, $44,175.
Fields of interest: Higher education.
Type of support: Support to graduates or students of specific schools.
Application information: Applications accepted.
Additional information: Scholarships are paid directly to the educational institution on behalf of the students. Contact the trust for additional application guidelines.
EIN: 716180317

293
Murphy Education Program, Inc.
200 Peach St.
P.O. Box 7000
El Dorado, AR 71730
URL: http://www.murphyoilcorp.com/responsibility/community.aspx

Foundation type: Company-sponsored foundation
Purpose: Scholarships to graduates of El Dorado High School, AR for postsecondary education at any accredited Arkansas public university or community college, or any accredited private or out of state university.
Financial data: Year ended 12/31/2012. Assets, $262,464 (M); Expenditures, $270,693; Total giving, $268,561.
Fields of interest: Education.
Type of support: Scholarships—to individuals; Awards/prizes.
Application information: Applications not accepted.
EIN: 710814094

294
M. W. Murphy Foundation
200 N. Jefferson Ave., Ste. 400
El Dorado, AR 71730-5854   (870) 862-4961
Contact: Martha W. Murphy, Pres. and Treas.

Foundation type: Independent foundation
Purpose: Scholarships to individuals of AR and MS pursuing higher education.
Financial data: Year ended 12/31/2012. Assets, $3,520,011 (M); Expenditures, $193,241; Total giving, $190,500; Grants to individuals, 2 grants totaling $6,600 (high: $3,600, low: $3,000).
Fields of interest: Higher education.
Type of support: Undergraduate support.
Application information: Applications accepted.
Initial approach: Letter
Additional information: Contact the foundation for scholarship guidelines.
EIN: 710802701

295
The Murphy Foundation
200 N. Jefferson Ave., Ste. 400
El Dorado, AR 71730-5854   (870) 862-4961
Contact: Brett Williamson, Secy.-Treas.

Foundation type: Independent foundation

Purpose: Scholarships to students from southern AR, for personal expenses related to students' education as well as tuition.
Financial data: Year ended 04/30/2013. Assets, $62,120,303 (M); Expenditures, $3,262,642; Total giving, $2,908,897; Grants to individuals, 164 grants totaling $677,749 (high: $19,000, low: $786).
Fields of interest: Higher education; Scholarships/financial aid.
Type of support: Scholarships—to individuals.
Application information: Applications accepted.
Initial approach: Letter
Deadline(s): Aug. 1
Additional information: Application should include a copy of applicant's scholastic record.
EIN: 716049826

296
Murphy Oil Corporation Contributions Program
200 Peach St.
P.O. Box 7000
El Dorado, AR 71731-7000   (870) 881-6866
Contact: Katie Sandifer, Community Rels. Mgr.
Application address for El Dorado Promise: 200 W. Oak, El Dorado, AR 71730, tel.: (870) 864-5046
E-mail: sandiks@murphyoilcorp.com; *URL:* http://www.murphyoilcorp.com/responsibility/community.aspx

Foundation type: Corporate giving program
Purpose: Grants to employees of Murphy Oil Corporation for educational assistance and scholarships to children of Murphy Oil Corporation for academic excellence.
Fields of interest: Higher education; Adult/continuing education; Education.
Type of support: Employee-related scholarships.
Application information: Applications not accepted.
Additional information: Unsolicited requests for funds not considered or acknowledged.
Program description:
Employee Educational Assistance Program: Through the Employee Educational Assistance Program, Murphy Oil supports the ongoing needs of its employees. The company reimburses the costs of tuition, textbooks and some required fees that employees incur at accredited colleges, universities, or trade schools. The program is designed to encourage employees to extend their knowledge and capability through outside study.
Company name: Murphy Oil Corporation

297
William H. & Helen L. Nelson Scholarship Fund
P.O. Box 1906
Mountain Home, AR 72653-1906   (870) 508-1000
Application address: c/o Baxter Regional Medical Center, 624 Hospital Dr., Mountain Home, AR 72653, tel.: (870) 508-1000

Foundation type: Independent foundation
Purpose: Scholarships to students of Baxter and Marion counties, AR in pursuit of a nursing career.
Financial data: Year ended 12/31/2011. Assets, $540,496 (M); Expenditures, $21,880; Total giving, $15,267; Grants to individuals, 9 grants totaling $15,267 (high: $3,768, low: $729).
Fields of interest: Nursing school/education.
Type of support: Scholarships—to individuals.

Application information: Applications accepted.
Initial approach: Letter
Deadline(s): None
Additional information: Letter must outline career goals and financial need.
EIN: 201947722

298
Northeast Arkansas Higher Education Charitable Foundation, Inc.
P.O. Box 189
Newport, AR 72112-0189

Foundation type: Public charity
Purpose: Scholarships for graduating seniors from schools in Jackson county, AR or from schools outside Jackson county who will be attending ASU/N. Scholarships to continuing college students attending ASU/N.
Financial data: Year ended 06/30/2012. Assets, $805,358 (M); Expenditures, $182,947; Total giving, $95,824; Grants to individuals, 188 grants totaling $95,824. Subtotal for grants to individuals: 26 grants totaling $5,875. Subtotal for scholarships—to individuals: 162 grants totaling $89,950.
Fields of interest: Higher education.
Type of support: Scholarships—to individuals; Support to graduates or students of specific schools.
Application information: Applications accepted. Application form required. Application form available on the grantmaker's web site.
Send request by: Mail
Deadline(s): Apr. 1
Applicants should submit the following:
1) GPA
2) Class rank
3) SAT
4) ACT
5) Transcripts
6) Financial information
7) Essay
Additional information: Selection is based on need, family income versus number of school-aged children and scholastic achievement. Funds will be paid to the educational institution on behalf of the student.
EIN: 710713937

299
Harold & Bruce Ohlendorf Scholarship Fund
3608 N. Steele, Ste. 202
Fayetteville, AR 72703   (870) 563-2192
Application address: Head Guidance Counselor, Osceola High School, 2800 W. Semmes, Osceola, AR 72370

Foundation type: Independent foundation
Purpose: Scholarships to one or more graduating seniors of Osceola High School, AR who are unable to attend a college or university with financial assistance.
Financial data: Year ended 12/31/2012. Assets, $186,622 (M); Expenditures, $14,202; Total giving, $3,000; Grants to individuals, 3 grants totaling $3,000 (high: $1,000, low: $1,000).
Fields of interest: Higher education.
Type of support: Support to graduates or students of specific schools.
Application information: Applications accepted. Application form required.
Deadline(s): Mar. 31
Applicants should submit the following:

1) Transcripts
2) GPA
3) Financial information
4) ACT
Additional information: Application can be obtained from your high school. Applicant must have a minimum 2.75 GPA.
EIN: 716181584

300
Olds Foundation
P.O. Box 114
Amity, AR   71921-0114   (870) 342-5191
Contact: Millard Aud, Chair. and Genl. Mgr.
E-mail: oldsxaud@windstream.net

Foundation type: Independent foundation
Purpose: Scholarships to graduating seniors of Centerpoint High School and Kirby High School, who are residents of Pike and Clark counties, AR.
Financial data: Year ended 11/30/2013. Assets, $15,573,730 (M); Expenditures, $409,107; Total giving, $260,400; Grants to individuals, totaling $101,000.
Fields of interest: Higher education.
Type of support: Scholarships—to individuals.
Application information: Applications accepted. Application form required. Interview required.
  Initial approach: Letter requesting application form
  Send request by: Mail
  Copies of proposal: 5
  Deadline(s): Varies
  Final notification: Applicants notified within 30 to 90 days
  Applicants should submit the following:
    1) ACT
    2) Budget Information
    3) Curriculum vitae
    4) Essay
    5) Financial information
    6) GPA
    7) Pell Grant
    8) Transcripts
EIN: 710747091

301
Ozark Opportunities, Inc.
P.O. Box 1400
Harrison, AR   72602-1400   (870) 741-9406

Foundation type: Public charity
Purpose: Support to low-income individuals living in Baxter, Boone, Marion, Newton, Searcy, and Van Buren counties, AR. Support includes educational assistance, energy assistance, emergency assistance, home improvement for the elderly, and food.
Financial data: Year ended 02/28/2013. Assets, $1,656,532 (M); Expenditures, $5,208,795; Total giving, $1,034,578; Grants to individuals, totaling $1,034,578.
Fields of interest: Housing/shelter, expense aid; Human services; Family services; Aging, centers/services.
Type of support: Grants for special needs.
Application information: Contact foundation for current application procedures.
EIN: 710407485

302
Mills O. Pierce & Mount Vernon Pierce Charitable Foundation
1923 E. Joyce Blvd., Ste. 138
Fayetteville, AR   72703-5168

Foundation type: Independent foundation
Purpose: Scholarships to graduates of Prairie Grove High School, AR for studies at universities, colleges and vocational/technical institutions.
Financial data: Year ended 12/31/2012. Assets, $160,759 (M); Expenditures, $12,331; Total giving, $12,000; Grants to individuals, 8 grants totaling $12,000 (high: $2,750, low: $750).
Fields of interest: Higher education.
Type of support: Support to graduates or students of specific schools; Undergraduate support.
Application information: Applications accepted. Application form required.
  Deadline(s): June 30
  Additional information: Only graduates of Prairie Grove High School are eligible to apply. Unsolicited requests for funds not considered or acknowledged.
EIN: 710526830

303
Arthur J. & Blanche D. Raef Scholarship Fund Trust
c/o First Security Bank
P.O. Box 1906
Mountain Home, AR   72654   (870) 425-2166

Foundation type: Independent foundation
Purpose: Scholarships to students attending Arkansas State University in Mountain Home, AR.
Financial data: Year ended 12/31/2012. Assets, $631,400 (M); Expenditures, $37,356; Total giving, $29,750; Grants to individuals, 42 grants totaling $29,750 (high: $1,750, low: $500).
Fields of interest: Higher education.
Type of support: Support to graduates or students of specific schools; Undergraduate support.
Application information: Scholarship selection is based on academic achievement, extracurricular activities and financial need. Unsolicited requests for funds not considered or acknowledged.
EIN: 470891370

304
Judge J. P. & Elizabeth Reed Foundation
2305 Spring Lake Rd.
Paragould, AR   72451-1305   (870) 236-3102
Application address: c/o Elizabeth Reed, 1704 Carroll Rd., Paragould, AR 72450, tel.: (870) 236-3102

Foundation type: Operating foundation
Purpose: Scholarships to high school graduates from Greene County, AR planning to pursue Christian ministry or enter the healthcare field.
Financial data: Year ended 12/31/2011. Assets, $24,793 (M); Expenditures, $2,375; Total giving, $2,000; Grant to an individual, 1 grant totaling $2,000.
Fields of interest: Higher education.
Type of support: Scholarships—to individuals.
Application information: Applications accepted. Application form required.
  Applicants should submit the following:
    1) Class rank
    2) GPA
    3) ACT
EIN: 311603716

305
Cle & Dennis Riordan Foundation
23 Diamante Blvd.
Hot Springs Village, AR   71909-7788   (972) 355-8550
Contact: Cledith Ann-Rice Riordan, Pres.
Application address: 1200 Noble Way, Flower Mound, TX 75022

Foundation type: Independent foundation
Purpose: Financial assistance to individuals of TX with housing, food, home repairs, tutoring, dental expense, and other special needs.
Financial data: Year ended 12/31/2012. Assets, $352,667 (M); Expenditures, $148,377; Total giving, $146,285; Grants to individuals, 13 grants totaling $145,285 (high: $50,000, low: $500).
Fields of interest: Economically disadvantaged.
Type of support: Grants for special needs.
Application information: Applications accepted.
  Initial approach: Letter
  Deadline(s): None
  Additional information: Applicant must demonstrate need.
EIN: 452848204

306
RMHC of Arkoma, Inc.
(also known as Ronald McDonald House Charities of Arkoma, Inc.)
518 S. Thompson, Ste. D.
Springdale, AR   72764-1366   (479) 756-5600
Contact: Stephanie Medford, Exec. Dir.
E-mail: stephanie@rmhcofarkoma.org; Tel. for Stephanie Medford: (479) 841-6755; URL: http://www.rmhcofarkoma.org/

Foundation type: Public charity
Purpose: Dental treatments to children in northwest AR who would otherwise go without.
Financial data: Year ended 12/31/2011. Assets, $2,729,429 (M); Expenditures, $477,170; Total giving, $10,000.
Fields of interest: Dental care; Children, services; Children/youth; Economically disadvantaged.
Type of support: In-kind gifts; Grants for special needs.
Application information:
  Initial approach: E-mail
  Additional information: Contact foundation for eligibility criteria.
EIN: 731563945

307
SHARE Foundation
403 W. Oak St., Ste. 100
El Dorado, AR   71730-4573   (870) 881-9015
FAX: (870) 881-9017;
E-mail: dwatts@sharefoundation.com; URL: http://www.sharefoundation.com

Foundation type: Public charity
Purpose: Scholarships for health care education, primarily to residents of Union County, AR.
Publications: Application guidelines; Annual report; Informational brochure; Newsletter.
Financial data: Year ended 12/31/2011. Assets, $63,844,451 (M); Expenditures, $9,272,923; Total giving, $924,315; Grants to individuals, totaling $135,640.
Fields of interest: Elementary/secondary education; Early childhood education; Nursing school/education; Health sciences school/education.
Type of support: Emergency funds; Scholarships—to individuals; Student loans—to individuals;

Support to graduates or students of specific schools; Graduate support; Undergraduate support.
Application information: Applications accepted. Application form required. Application form available on the grantmaker's web site.
  Initial approach: Telephone
  Send request by: Mail
  Copies of proposal: 1
  Deadline(s): Apr. 15 for Smith Family Scholarship Fund; Apr. 1, July 1, and Nov. 1 for all others
  Final notification: Recipients notified in one month
  Applicants should submit the following:
    1) Letter(s) of recommendation
    2) Financial information
    3) GPA
    4) Transcripts
Program descriptions:
  Barton Scholarship Program: Scholarships are exclusively for full-time registered nursing students at Southern Arkansas University. Recipients agree to employment in a nursing career at the Medical Center of South Arkansas immediately following the completion of their course of study for a period of one year for each year funded with a minimum work requirement of one year.
  Curtis W. Kinard Memorial Scholarship: These scholarships are intended to provide tuition and books (in whole or in part) to individuals who live within a 100-mile radius of El Dorado and are pursuing healthcare careers at approved educational institutions. Recipients must agree to employment in a health related career in Union County, Arkansas immediately following the completion of their course of study for a period of one year for each year funded with a minimum work requirement of one year.
  Dr. J.C. Callaway Memorial Scholarship Fund: The scholarship provides tuition and books (in whole or in part) for nontraditional students pursuing medical related careers at South Arkansas Community College, with heavier consideration being given to students accepted into the college's Surgical Technology Program. Recipients must work full-time in their stated career immediately following graduation or completion of their course of study for a period of six consecutive months for each semester funded, with a minimum work requirement of one year (even if only one semester is funded)
  Dr. Warren S. and Wilma "Billie" Riley Scholarship: Scholarships are available to provide and/or reimburse tuition (in whole or in part) to students that are studying, or have studied, to become registered nurses, or for advanced training of registered nurses. Recipients must be willing to work for either the foundation or the Medical Center of South Arkansas immediately following the completion of their course of study for a period of six months for each semester funded, with a minimum work requirement of one year.
  Larkin M. Wilson Memorial Scholarship: These scholarships provide tuition and books (in whole or in part) to Union County, Arkansas residents pursuing healthcare careers at approved educational institutions. Recipients must agree to employment in a health related career at Medical Center of South Arkansas or the foundation immediately following the completion of their course of study for a period of six months for each semester funded, with a minimum work requirement of one year.
  Lucy A. Ring Memorial Scholarship: These scholarships are intended to be used for careers in healthcare or public education in grades K-12. Recipients must be Union County, Arkansas residents, though there are no geographical limits

on the place of study. Recipients must agree to employment in a healthcare career at Medical Center of South Arkansas, the foundation itself, or in Union County, Arkansas public education careers in grades K-12 immediately following the completion of their course of study for a period of one year for each funded (with a minimum work requirement of one year)
  MCSA Auxiliary Helen Wright Memorial Scholarship: The scholarship provides tuition and books (in whole or in part) to individuals who reside within a forty mile radius of El Dorado, limited to the state of Arkansas, who are pursuing health care careers at approved Arkansas educational institutions. Recipients must agree to employment in a health related career at Medical Center of South Arkansas immediately following the completion of their course of study for a period of one year for each year funded, with a minimum work requirement of one year.
  Smith Family Scholarship Fund: One-time scholarships of up to $1,000 for tuition and fees only (room and board not included) are available to graduates of Parkers Chapel High School, after attending a minimum of four years completing grades 9 to 12. Recipients must have maintained a minimum 3.0 GPA while attending the school.
  The John R. Williamson M.D. Memorial Scholarship: These scholarships are intended to provide tuition and books (in full or in part) to individuals who live in Union County, and who are pursuing health-related careers at approved educational institutions. Recipients must agree to employment in a health-related career in Union County immediately following the completion of their course of study for a period of one year for each year funded, with a minimum work requirement of one year.
  UAMS Master of Public Health Scholarship: The scholarship provides tuition in whole or in part for persons pursuing a Master of Public Health Degree from the University of Arkansas for Medical Sciences (UAMS). Applicants must live in Ashley, Bradley, Calhoun, Columbia, Dallas or Union counties in Arkansas. Recipients must agree to become employed in Union County immediately following the completion of their course of study, utilizing their M.P.H. degree ,for a period of six months for each semester funded (with a minimum work requirement of one year)
  Union County Medical Scholarship: The scholarship shall be used for Doctorate of Medicine (D.M.) or Osteopathy (D.O.) candidates who reside within a 75-mile radius of El Dorado, Arkansas. There are no geographical limits on the place of study, as long as they are approved and/or accredited educational institutions. Recipients must agree to become employed in Union County, Arkansas immediately following the completion of their internship and/or residency program for a period of six months for each semester funded, with a minimum work requirement of one year.
EIN: 710236863

308
Shewmaker Family Scholarship Trust
c/o Arvest Trust Co., N.A.
P.O. Box 1229
Bentonville, AR 72712

Foundation type: Independent foundation
Purpose: Scholarships to graduating high school residents of Buffalo, MO.
Financial data: Year ended 10/31/2012. Assets, $232,188 (M); Expenditures, $13,725; Total giving, $8,500; Grants to individuals, 9 grants totaling $8,500 (high: $2,000, low: $500).

Type of support: Undergraduate support.
Application information: Applications not accepted.
  Additional information: Unsolicited requests for funds not considered or acknowledged.
EIN: 716121895

309
Single Parent Scholarship Fund of Northwest Arkansas, Inc.
(formerly Single Parent Scholarship Fund of Washington County, Inc.)
16 W. Colt Square Dr.
Springdale, AR 72764-4400   (479) 935-4888
Contact: Jody Dilday, Exec. Dir.
FAX: (479) 439-1179; E-mail: info@spsfnwa.org;
E-Mail For Jody Dilday: jody@spsfnwa.org;
URL: http://www.spsfnwa.com/

Foundation type: Public charity
Purpose: Scholarships to low-income single parents who are residents of Carroll, Madison or Washington County, AR.
Publications: Application guidelines; Informational brochure; Newsletter.
Financial data: Year ended 12/31/2011. Assets, $1,120,190 (M); Expenditures, $628,284; Total giving, $349,025; Grants to individuals, totaling $349,025.
Fields of interest: Single parents.
Type of support: Technical education support; Undergraduate support.
Application information: Applications accepted. Application form required. Application form available on the grantmaker's web site. Interview required.
  Send request by: Online
  Deadline(s): Oct. 15 for Spring semester, Mar. 15 for Summer semester and June 15 for Fall semester
  Final notification: Recipients notified in sixty days
  Applicants should submit the following:
    1) Transcripts
    2) Letter(s) of recommendation
    3) Financial information
Program description:
  Scholarships for Single Parents: This program provides supplemental financial assistance to those single parents who are pursuing a course of instruction which will improve their income-earning potential. Scholarships may be used for tuition, books, utility bills, car maintenance, childcare, or any other financial need that contributes to the recipient's success in schools. Eligible individuals must be residents of Washington County who: have a high-school diploma or GED; are a single head of household (single, legally separated, divorced, or widowed) with sole custody of one or more children under the age of 18; are pursuing a career-oriented course of study (full- or part-time) to ensure a better standard of living for his/her family; are a low-income person at or near the poverty level; and are the recipient of a Pell Grant, or in the process of obtaining one. Scholarships range from $750 to part-time students to $1,500 for full-time students.
EIN: 680498770

310
Edward Craig Smith Scholarship Foundation
P.O. Box 983
Russellville, AR 72811-0983   (479) 880-8899
Contact: Becky Ellison
Application address: 1020 W. Main St., Russellville, AR 72801

Foundation type: Independent foundation
Purpose: Scholarships to junior and senior nursing students attending University of Arkansas Community College at Morrilton, AR and Arkansas Tech University, AR for college education and to further their nursing career.
Financial data: Year ended 06/30/2012. Assets, $321,506 (M); Expenditures, $18,277; Total giving, $16,800; Grants to individuals, 4 grants totaling $16,800 (high: $5,400, low: $2,000).
Fields of interest: Nursing school/education.
Type of support: Support to graduates or students of specific schools.
Application information: Applications accepted.
  Additional information: Scholarships are awarded for one semester and may be renewed each semester by the board of directors.
EIN: 200926682

311
South Shore Foundation
P.O. Box 209
Flippin, AR   72634-0209   (870) 453-8811
Contact: Deanna Sullivan, Tr.
URL: http://www.southshore.com/south_shore_foundation.php

Foundation type: Company-sponsored foundation
Purpose: Scholarships to high school seniors at schools in the South Shore area or north central Arkansas for attendance at an Arkansas college or university.
Financial data: Year ended 12/31/2011. Assets, $31,356 (M); Expenditures, $40,973; Total giving, $38,949; Grants to individuals, 6 grants totaling $6,000 (high: $1,000, low: $1,000).
Fields of interest: Higher education.
Type of support: Undergraduate support.
Application information:
  Initial approach: Letter
  Additional information: Applicant must demonstrate financial need and academic performance. Contact your guidance counselor for application information.
EIN: 621666363

312
Southern Arkansas University Foundation, Inc.
Slot 26
P.O. Box 9174
Magnolia, AR   71754-9174   (870) 235-4078
Contact: Jeanie Bismark, Exec. Dir.
E-mail: mjbismark@saumag.edu; Tel. for Jeanie Bismark : (870)-235-4991; URL: http://www.saufoundation.org/

Foundation type: Public charity
Purpose: Full and partial scholarships to students for attendance at Southern Arkansas University for higher education.
Publications: Annual report.
Financial data: Year ended 12/31/2011. Assets, $23,572,949 (M); Expenditures, $2,215,152; Total giving, $1,918,936; Grants to individuals, totaling $1,918,936.
Fields of interest: Higher education.
Type of support: Support to graduates or students of specific schools.
Application information: Applications accepted. Application form required. Application form available on the grantmaker's web site.
  Send request by: Mail
  Additional information: Application should include an essay stating your educational goals, and how you expect to benefit from the

scholarship, and why you deserve the award. See web site for scholarships available by the foundation and for additional guidelines.
EIN: 710549140

313
Sparks Employee Good Neighbor Foundation
1001 Towson Ave.
Fort Smith, AR   72901-4921   (479) 441-5452

Foundation type: Public charity
Purpose: Grants for utilities and living assistance to needy individuals in the Fort Smith, AR area.
Financial data: Year ended 06/30/2011. Assets, $292,144 (M); Expenditures, $58,701; Total giving, $58,701.
Fields of interest: Economically disadvantaged.
Type of support: Grants for special needs.
Application information: Applications not accepted.
  Additional information: Unsolicited requests for funds not considered or acknowledged.
EIN: 237025576

314
Roy & Christine Sturgis Foundation
P.O. Box 7
Sparkman, AR   71763-0007   (870) 678-2277
Contact: Donald White, Pres.

Foundation type: Independent foundation
Purpose: Scholarships to students from AR, with preference to those from Sparkman, AR.
Financial data: Year ended 11/30/2011. Assets, $816,725 (M); Expenditures, $10,730; Total giving, $9,500; Grants to individuals, 20 grants totaling $9,500 (high: $800, low: $200).
Type of support: Undergraduate support.
Application information: Applications accepted. Application form required.
  Deadline(s): None
  Additional information: Contact foundation for current application guidelines.
EIN: 716057144

315
W. P. Sturgis Foundation
P.O. Box 394
Arkadelphia, AR   71923-0394
Contact: June Anthony, Secy.-Treas.

Foundation type: Independent foundation
Purpose: Scholarships to AR students with at least a 2.0 GPA. Students who have completed eight or more semesters of undergraduate study will not be considered.
Financial data: Year ended 12/31/2012. Assets, $3,561,564 (M); Expenditures, $261,838; Total giving, $207,391; Grants to individuals, totaling $180,145.
Type of support: Undergraduate support.
Application information: Application form required.
  Deadline(s): May 1 and Dec. 1
  Applicants should submit the following:
    1) Financial information
    2) Photograph
    3) Transcripts
    4) GPA
  Additional information: Application must also include personal statement and most recent federal tax return.
EIN: 716057063

316
Tenenbaum Educational Trust
P.O. Box 15128 G.M.F.
North Little Rock, AR   72231   (501) 945-0881
Contact: Timothy McGrath, Tr.

Foundation type: Independent foundation
Purpose: Scholarships to high school graduates who are residents of AR for medical education expenses.
Financial data: Year ended 12/31/2012. Assets, $52,141 (M); Expenditures, $42,560; Total giving, $42,469; Grants to individuals, 8 grants totaling $42,469 (high: $21,303, low: $708).
Fields of interest: Medical school/education.
Type of support: Undergraduate support.
Application information: Applications accepted. Application form required.
  Initial approach: Letter
  Deadline(s): None
EIN: 710705223

317
Seymour Terry Memorial Scholarship Trust Fund
c/o Iberia Bank
P.O. Box 7299
Little Rock, AR   72217

Foundation type: Independent foundation
Purpose: Scholarships to graduates of Little Rock Central High School, AR, who will attend University of Arkansas.
Financial data: Year ended 06/30/2013. Assets, $709,378 (M); Expenditures, $35,330; Total giving, $24,500; Grants to individuals, 5 grants totaling $24,500 (high: $7,000, low: $3,500).
Type of support: Support to graduates or students of specific schools; Undergraduate support.
Application information: Applications accepted.
  Initial approach: Letter
  Deadline(s): None
  Additional information: Applications must include scholastic record, general records, and financial need.
EIN: 716050556

318
Godfrey Thomas Foundation
c/o Mary Carr
703 S. Tyler St.
DeWitt, AR   72042   (870) 946-1982

Foundation type: Independent foundation
Purpose: Scholarships to residents of DeWitt, AR, for continuing education at institutions of higher learning.
Financial data: Year ended 12/31/2012. Assets, $1,943,245 (M); Expenditures, $107,874; Total giving, $87,700.
Fields of interest: Education.
Type of support: Scholarships—to individuals.
Application information: Application form required.
  Deadline(s): May 1 for fall semester and Nov. 1 for spring semester
  Additional information: Contact foundation for current application guidelines.
EIN: 716065971

319
Trinity Foundation
P.O. Box 7008
Pine Bluff, AR   71611-7008   (870) 534-7120
Contact: Drew Atkinson

Foundation type: Independent foundation
Purpose: Scholarships to graduating high school seniors at specific high schools in Pine Bluff, Little Rock, Benton, and Bauxite, AR.
Financial data: Year ended 09/30/2013. Assets, $16,414,600 (M); Expenditures, $469,997; Total giving, $363,000.
Type of support: Support to graduates or students of specific schools; Undergraduate support.
Application information: Application form required.
   Deadline(s): Apr. 10
   Additional information: Application can be obtained from school's guidance offices.
EIN: 716050288

320
Tyson Family Foundation, Inc.
P.O. Box 2020
Springdale, AR 72765-2020
FAX: (479) 290-7984; Application address: c/o Roberta Gonzales, 2200 Don Tyson Pkwy., Springdale, AR 72762; tel.: (479) 290-5180

Foundation type: Independent foundation
Purpose: Scholarships to Tyson Foods Inc. employees and dependents of employees or growers.
Financial data: Year ended 12/31/2012. Assets, $27,458,868 (M); Expenditures, $1,658,060; Total giving, $1,509,250.
Fields of interest: Higher education.
Type of support: Employee-related scholarships.
Application information: Application form required.
   Initial approach: Letter or telephone
   Additional information: Apply for preprinted application.
Company name: Tyson Foods, Inc.
EIN: 237087948

321
Union County Community Foundation, Inc.
P.O. Box 148
El Dorado, AR 71731-0148 (870) 862-8223
Contact: Rodney Landes, Chair.

Foundation type: Community foundation
Purpose: Scholarships for higher education to students and residents of Union County, AR.
Publications: Financial statement; Grants list; Newsletter.
Financial data: Year ended 09/30/2012. Assets, $13,617,576 (M); Expenditures, $520,001; Total giving, $398,864; Grants to individuals, 53 grants totaling $78,513.
Fields of interest: Nursing school/education; Teacher school/education; Education; Engineering.
Type of support: Support to graduates or students of specific schools; Undergraduate support.
Application information: Contact foundation for application guidelines.
EIN: 311500805

322
Ruth Veasey Educational Foundation Inc.
P.O. Box 326
Dermott, AR 71638 (870) 538-5221
Contact: David Holt, Secy.
Application address: P.O. Box 3, Dermott, AR 71638-0003, tel.: (870) 538-5221

Foundation type: Operating foundation
Purpose: Student loans to graduates of Dermott High School, AR, for education at an accredited college, technical institute or university. If funds

permit, loans are also given to other residents of AR.
Financial data: Year ended 05/31/2012. Assets, $1,360,928 (M); Expenditures, $108,984; Total giving, $96,250; Grants to individuals, 20 grants totaling $96,250 (high: $5,000, low: $1,250).
Type of support: Student loans—to individuals; Support to graduates or students of specific schools; Undergraduate support.
Application information: Application form required.
   Initial approach: Letter or telephone
   Deadline(s): Apr. 30
   Additional information: Application must include three references, one from a local business person if possible.
EIN: 716051103

323
Wallace Trust Foundation
209 W. Oak St.
McGehee, AR 71654
Contact: Gibbs Ferguson, Tr.

Foundation type: Independent foundation
Purpose: Scholarships and grants to residents of McGehee, AR, for educational expenses and assistance for those with hardships.
Financial data: Year ended 12/31/2012. Assets, $500,000 (M); Expenditures, $118,194; Total giving, $117,695; Grants to individuals, 4 grants totaling $18,593 (high: $12,070, low: $600).
Type of support: Undergraduate support; Grants for special needs.
Application information: Applications accepted.
   Initial approach: Letter
   Deadline(s): None
EIN: 710754251

324
Wal-Mart Associates in Critical Need Fund
(also known as Walmart Associates in Critical Need Fund)
702 S.W. 8th St., Dept. 8687
M.S. No. 0555
Bentonville, AR 72716-0555 (800) 530-9925

Foundation type: Public charity
Purpose: Financial assistance to associates or their dependents of Wal-mart when they experience extreme economic hardship due to situations outside of their control, including natural disasters.
Financial data: Year ended 01/31/2013. Assets, $13,573,166 (M); Expenditures, $13,837,747; Total giving, $13,837,747; Grants to individuals, totaling $13,837,747.
Fields of interest: Safety/disasters; Human services.
Type of support: Grants for special needs.
Application information: Applications not accepted.
   Additional information: Contributes only to Wal-mart associates or dependents, unsolicited requests for funds not considered or acknowledged.
EIN: 710858484

325
The Wal-Mart Foundation, Inc.
(formerly Wal-Mart Foundation, also known as The Walmart Foundation)
702 S.W. 8th St., Dept. 8687, No. 0555
Bentonville, AR 72716-0555 (800) 530-9925
Contact: Julie Gehrki, Sr. Dir., Business Integration
FAX: (479) 273-6850; URL: http://walmartfoundation.org

Foundation type: Company-sponsored foundation
Purpose: Scholarships to employees and children of employees of Wal-Mart/Sam's Club, general offices, distribution centers, or other facilities.
Publications: Application guidelines; Program policy statement.
Financial data: Year ended 01/31/2013. Assets, $21,162,257 (M); Expenditures, $182,860,304; Total giving, $182,859,236.
Fields of interest: College; Scholarships/financial aid; Education.
Type of support: Employee-related scholarships; Undergraduate support.
Application information: Applications not accepted.
   Additional information: Unsolicited requests for funds not accepted or acknowledged.
Company name: Wal-Mart Stores, Inc.
EIN: 205639919

326
Grant T. White Foundation
P.O. Box 7
Fort Smith, AR 72902-0007 (479) 788-4343
Contact: Jeannie Wakefield
Application address: 6th Garrison, Fort Smith, AR 72901

Foundation type: Independent foundation
Purpose: Scholarships primarily to high school graduates and college students of Fort Smith, AR.
Financial data: Year ended 05/31/2012. Assets, $1,220,244 (M); Expenditures, $58,291; Total giving, $38,350; Grants to individuals, totaling $38,350.
Fields of interest: Higher education.
Type of support: Undergraduate support.
Application information: Application form required.
   Deadline(s): Apr. 1
   Applicants should submit the following:
    1) SAT
    2) Financial information
    3) Transcripts
    4) Letter(s) of recommendation
    5) ACT
   Additional information: Scholarships are generally for one year, but may be renewed depending on the student's progress and funds available.
EIN: 710561239

327
Ted and Betty Williams Charitable Trust
(formerly Ted Williams Charitable Trust)
c/o Gwynne Hinterthuer
37 Kings River Rd.
North Little Rock, AR 72116
E-mail: eiseman@fridayfirm.com

Foundation type: Independent foundation
Purpose: Scholarships to college bound high school seniors of Arkansas, who demonstrate financial need.
Financial data: Year ended 12/31/2012. Assets, $2,399,241 (M); Expenditures, $156,134; Total giving, $120,000.

Fields of interest: Higher education.
Type of support: Undergraduate support.
Application information: Contact your high school counselors.
EIN: 716172017

328
Robert E and Catherine Woodson Sampley Educational Foundation, Inc.
P.O. Box 1147
Mount Ida, AR 71957-1147
Contact: Robert E. Samply

Foundation type: Independent foundation
Purpose: Renewable scholarships of $2,000 each semester for up to four years to graduates of high schools in Montgomery County, AR, who are in the top third of their class and will attend college or university in AR.
Financial data: Year ended 12/31/2012. Assets, $4,104,814 (M); Expenditures, $232,169; Total giving, $189,000; Grants to individuals, 67 grants totaling $189,000 (high: $18,000, low: $3,000).
Type of support: Scholarships—to individuals.
Application information:
   Deadline(s): Apr.

Applicants should submit the following:
   1) Transcripts
   2) ACT
   3) SAT
   4) Photograph
   5) GPA
Additional information: Application should also include a list of activities and honors.
EIN: 716156225

CALIFORNIA

329
10,000 Degrees
(formerly Marin Education Fund)
1650 Los Gamos Dr., Ste. 110
San Rafael, CA 94903 (415) 459-4240
Contact: Kim Mazzuca, Pres.
FAX: (415) 459-0527;
E-mail: sgoddard@10000degrees.org; E-mail For
Kim Mazzuca: kmazzuca@10000degrees.org;
URL: http://www.10000degrees.org/

Foundation type: Public charity
Purpose: Scholarships to assist low to moderate
income Marin county, CA residents for attendance
at an accredited college or university working
towards their first degree.
Publications: Application guidelines; Annual report;
Newsletter.
Financial data: Year ended 06/30/2012. Assets,
$7,994,769 (M); Expenditures, $4,026,270; Total
giving, $1,740,849; Grants to individuals, totaling
$1,740,849.
Fields of interest: Vocational education,
post-secondary; Higher education.
Type of support: Scholarships—to individuals.
Application information: Applications accepted.
Application form required.
  Deadline(s): Jan. for Child Care Scholarship, Mar.
    for Undergraduate Scholarship
Program descriptions:
  Child Care Scholarships: Provides child care
scholarships ranging from $500 to $9,000 per child
for parents who are enrolled in college. The
scholarship pays for a portion of a child's day care
while the parent is enrolled in college. Children
must be under the age of 11 and attending a
licensed child care facility. The scholarship is
renewable annually provided that the parent
maintains satisfactory progress.
  Undergraduate Scholarships: Scholarships
ranging from $1,000 to $5,000 are available to
residents of Marin County who plan to attend an
accredited college, or university. Applicants must
be planning to enroll in an undergraduate program
leading to an associate's or bachelor's degree or
teaching credential for at least one semester or two
quarters during the academic year for a minimum of
12 units per term.
EIN: 953667812

330
18th Street Arts Complex
1639 18th St.
Santa Monica, CA 90404-3807 (310)
453-3711
FAX: (310) 453-4347;
E-mail: office@18thstreet.org; URL: http://www.
18thstreet.org

Foundation type: Public charity
Purpose: Residencies to emerging and mid-career
contemporary artists. Applicants must be
international or residents of Los Angeles, CA.
Publications: Application guidelines.
Financial data: Year ended 06/30/2011. Assets,
$4,108,265 (M); Expenditures, $1,001,109.
Fields of interest: Visual arts; Arts, artist's
services.
International interests: Australia; Eastern Europe;
Global Programs; Southeastern Asia; Taiwan.
Type of support: Residencies.

Application information: Applications accepted.
Application form required. Application form
available on the grantmaker's web site. Interview
required.
  Send request by: Mail
  Applicants should submit the following:
    1) Work samples
    2) Letter(s) of recommendation
    3) Resume
  Additional information: Application should also
    include personal statement.
Program descriptions:
  International Artists in Residence Program:
Residencies for foreign artists. Citizens of
Australia, Eastern Europe, and Southeast Asia are
eligible. Applicants are selected through
partnerships with foreign governmental agencies
and foundations.
  Residency Program: This program provides
studio space, administrative and fundraising
consultation services, audio/visual equipment, and
opportunities for the artists to display their work.
Residencies last for three years.
EIN: 953825203

331
826 Valencia
826 Valencia St.
San Francisco, CA 94110-1737 (415)
642-5905
FAX: (415) 642-5914;
E-mail: leigh@826valencia.org; URL: http://www.
826valencia.org/

Foundation type: Public charity
Purpose: Scholarships to students in the San
Francisco Bay Area, CA who have a demonstrated
interest and talent in writing. Awards to outstanding
teachers for their dedication, innovation and overall
commitment to challenging students to excel.
Publications: Application guidelines.
Financial data: Year ended 06/30/2011. Assets,
$2,037,479 (M); Expenditures, $1,082,669; Total
giving, $156,500; Grants to individuals, 27 grants
totaling $156,500.
Fields of interest: Vocational education,
post-secondary; Higher education.
Type of support: Scholarships—to individuals.
Application information: Applications accepted.
Application form available on the grantmaker's web
site.
  Deadline(s): 15th of each month for teacher
    awards
  Additional information: Scholarship payments are
    made directly to the educational institution on
    behalf of the student. Teachers must be
    nominated by a previous or current student,
    and one adult past college age.
Program description:
  Scholarships: Each year, the organization awards
four $10,000 scholarships to college-bound
students in the San Francisco Bay Area. Eligible
applicants must be high-school graduates or
graduating seniors who live in the Bay Area,
demonstrate financial need, show an
extracurricular interest in the written word, and
demonstrate intent to enroll in a vocational school,
college, or university. Named scholarships include
the Young Author's Scholarship, the Nathan Jillson
Memorial Scholarship, the Irving Hochman
Memorial Scholarship, and the Taylor Renfrew
Ingham Memorial Scholarship. Preference will be
given to students who attend public high schools in
San Francisco.
EIN: 043694151

332
Mary M. Aaron Memorial Trust
Scholarship Fund
1190 Civic Center Blvd.
Yuba City, CA 95993

Foundation type: Independent foundation
Purpose: Scholarships to residents of Sutter and
Yuba counties, CA, to attend CA institutions of
higher learning. Preference given to students who
begin their education at Yuba College, CA, then
move on to other colleges or universities.
Financial data: Year ended 06/30/2013. Assets,
$1,971,041 (M); Expenditures, $100,225; Total
giving, $65,100; Grants to individuals, 46 grants
totaling $65,100 (high: $3,000, low: $600).
Fields of interest: Scholarships/financial aid.
Type of support: Support to graduates or students
of specific schools; Undergraduate support.
Application information: Application form required.
  Initial approach: Letter
  Deadline(s): Mar. 15
  Applicants should submit the following:
    1) Letter(s) of recommendation
    2) Transcripts
EIN: 941561354

333
Academic Assistance Fund
101 Montgomery St., Ste. 2350
San Francisco, CA 94104-4159 (415)
433-8300
Contact: Patrick A. Cahill, Pres.

Foundation type: Independent foundation
Purpose: Scholarships paid directly to the
independent educational institutions in the San
Francisco area, CA, for continuing education.
Financial data: Year ended 12/31/2012. Assets,
$645,789 (M); Expenditures, $71,671; Total
giving, $63,500.
Type of support: Undergraduate support.
Application information:
  Initial approach: Letter
EIN: 208103824

334
Academy Foundation
8949 Wilshire Blvd.
Beverly Hills, CA 90211-1907 (310) 247-3000
Contact: Bruce Davis, Exec. Dir.
Application address: Academy Film Scholars
Program, Academy of Motion Pictures Arts and
Sciences, 1313 N. Vine St., Los Angeles, CA
90028-8017
FAX: (310) 859-9351; E-mail: ampas@oscars.org;
URL: http://www.oscars.org/education-outreach/
index.html

Foundation type: Public charity
Purpose: Fellowships to screenwriters for
completion of their original works.
Publications: Application guidelines.
Financial data: Year ended 06/30/2011. Assets,
$3,057,523 (M); Expenditures, $5,711,814; Total
giving, $2,304,803; Grants to individuals, 18
grants totaling $102,500. Subtotal for awards/
prizes: 20 grants totaling $109,500.
Fields of interest: Film/video.
Type of support: Fellowships.
Application information: Applications accepted.
Application form available on the grantmaker's web
site.
  Send request by: On-line
  Deadline(s): May 2

Program descriptions:
Academy Film Scholars Program: A $25,000 grant is available to two individuals each year to stimulate and support new and significant works of film scholarship.
Internship Grants: Provides financial support to students and organizations who are financially limited so that they may participate in motion picture production-focused internships.
Nicholl's Fellowships in Screenwriting Program: Awards up to five $30,000 fellowships to screenwriters who have not earned more than $5,000 writing for film or television.
EIN: 952243698

335
Academy of Television Arts and Sciences Foundation
5220 Lankershim Blvd.
North Hollywood, CA 91601-3109   (818) 754-2800
Contact: Norma Provencio Pichardo, Exec. Dir.
FAX: (818) 761-2827;
E-mail: pichardo@emmys.org; URL: http://www.emmysfoundation.org/

Foundation type: Public charity
Purpose: Scholarships and awards to undergraduate and graduate students pursuing careers in television production.
Publications: Application guidelines.
Financial data: Year ended 12/31/2011. Assets, $3,497,666 (M); Expenditures, $2,034,579; Total giving, $91,000; Grants to individuals, totaling $91,000.
Fields of interest: Media/communications; Television; Early childhood education; Child development, education.
Type of support: Internship funds; Scholarships—to individuals; Awards/prizes.
Application information: Applications accepted.
Deadline(s): Jan. 11 for College Awards, Feb. 27 for Rogers Scholarship, and Mar. 15 for Internship Program
Additional information: College awards must be completed on-line; Rogers Scholarship application must include a proposed detailed budget and recommendations from two persons; Internship Program must include a resume, GPA, two letters or recommendation and transcripts. See web site for additional application requirements.
Program descriptions:
College Television Awards: These awards are given to recognize excellence in college student video, digital, and film productions in animation, children's, comedy/comedy series, commercial, documentary, drama/drama series, magazine, music, and newscast categories. Eligible applicants include students (graduate or undergraduate) currently enrolled in a community college, college, or university who wish to enter a video/film/digital production that was created in the year prior to application. Awards range from $500 to $2,000; a $4,000 Seymour Bricker Family Humanitarian Award is also awarded. Winning entries will be honored at a ceremony and broadcast nationally.
Internship Program: These six- to eight-week internships are designed to give qualified full-time students (both undergraduate and graduate) pursuing degrees at colleges at universities in the U.S. in-depth exposure to professional production, techniques, and practices. The foundation will pay a $4,000 stipend to each intern accepted into the program; interns will be responsible for their own housing, transportation (including ownership of a

car and travel to the Los Angeles area), and living expenses.
The Fred Rogers Memorial Scholarships: Three scholarships of $10,000 each are available to support and encourage aspiring upper-division (junior and senior) and graduate (masters or Ph.D.) students to pursue careers in children's media and further the values and principles of the work of Fred "Mister" Rogers. Applicants must demonstrate a commitment (either through coursework or experience) to any combination of at least two of the following fields: early childhood education, child development/child psychology, film/television production, music, and animation. Particular attention will be given to applicants from inner-city or rural communities.
EIN: 952283284

336
Access Foundation
181 Bonetti Dr.
San Luis Obispo, CA 93401-7397
Contact: Felicia Cashin, Pres.

Foundation type: Independent foundation
Purpose: Scholarships for students of CA for attendance at an accredited college or university.
Financial data: Year ended 11/30/2012. Assets, $82,944 (M); Expenditures, $14,653; Total giving, $13,548; Grants to individuals, 6 grants totaling $5,027 (high: $2,003, low: $500).
Fields of interest: Higher education.
Type of support: Scholarships—to individuals.
Application information: Applications accepted.
Initial approach: Letter
Deadline(s): None
Additional information: Student should state purpose, need and expected accomplishment is acceptable.
EIN: 954457341

337
ACEC Califorina Scholarship Foundation
(formerly Consulting Engineers & Land Surveyors Scholarship Foundation)
1303 J St., No. 450
Sacramento, CA 95814-2937   (916) 441-7991
Contact: for Scholarship: Monica Laplander
Scholarship e-mail: mlaplander@acec-ca.org

Foundation type: Public charity
Purpose: Scholarships to deserving college students entering their junior, senior, fifth or graduate year at an accredited college or university in CA and working toward a degree in engineering or land survey.
Publications: Application guidelines.
Financial data: Year ended 06/30/2012. Assets, $307,855 (M); Expenditures, $20,463; Total giving, $19,000.
Fields of interest: Engineering/technology.
Type of support: Scholarships—to individuals; Graduate support; Undergraduate support.
Application information: Applications accepted. Application form required.
Send request by: Mail
Deadline(s): Jan. 6
Applicants should submit the following:
1) Transcripts
2) Letter(s) of recommendation
3) Essay
Program description:
ACEC Scholarships: Each year, the foundation awards scholarships, ranging from $1,000 to $7,500 each, to deserving college students working toward a degree in engineering or land

surveying. Top award recipients are then nominated to apply for the American Council of Engineering Companies (ACEC) national scholarship competition. Applicant must be a U.S. citizen.
EIN: 680124316

338
Adobe Systems Incorporated Corporate Giving Program
c/o Community Rels.
345 Park Ave.
San Jose, CA 95110-2704   (408) 536-6000
FAX: (408) 537-6000; URL: http://www.adobe.com/corporate-responsibility.html

Foundation type: Corporate giving program
Purpose: Adobe sponsors annual nationwide scholarships through the National Society of Black Engineers, the Society of Hispanic Engineers, and the Society of Women Engineers.
Publications: Application guidelines; Corporate giving report.
Financial data: Year ended 12/31/2012. Total giving, $59,579,256.
Fields of interest: Engineering/technology; Engineering; Minorities; African Americans/Blacks; Hispanics/Latinos; Women.
Type of support: Undergraduate support.
Application information:
Initial approach: Letter
Additional information: See each organization's web site for more information about its scholarship program.

339
Advertising Industry Emergency Fund
11700 National Blvd., Ste. L, No. 230
Los Angeles, CA 90064-3669   (310) 397-9267
Contact: Nicole Levitt, Exec. Dir.
FAX: (310) 285-3279; E-mail: nicole@aief.org;
URL: http://www.aief.org

Foundation type: Public charity
Purpose: Emergency aid to individuals and families of the southern CA advertising and promotion industry in times of need.
Publications: Application guidelines.
Financial data: Year ended 12/31/2011. Assets, $434,529 (M); Expenditures, $121,758.
Fields of interest: Human services; Human services, emergency aid.
Type of support: Emergency funds; Grants for special needs.
Application information: Applications accepted. Application form required. Application form available on the grantmaker's web site.
Initial approach: Telephone or e-mail
Send request by: Mail or fax
Additional information: See web site for complete eligibility information.
Program description:
Financial Aid: This fund provides aid in times of need to members of the southern California advertising and promotions industry and their families. Eligible applicants must have been employed for a continuous period of one year by an advertising or promotions entity within southern California, excluding San Diego county, or have worked for an advertising or promotions corporation or organization as a member or an independent contractor. Eligible applicants must not have been absent from the field for more than one year.
EIN: 237236394

340
Advocates for Indigenous California Language Survival
221 Idora Ave.
Vallejo, CA 94591-7318 (707) 486-6806
Contact: Richard Bugbee, Chair.
FAX: (866) 644-7616; URL: http://www.aicls.org/

Foundation type: Public charity
Purpose: Grants to California Natives to work on language revitalization projects.
Financial data: Year ended 06/30/2012. Assets, $136,393 (M); Expenditures, $278,947; Total giving, $5,009; Grants to individuals, totaling $5,009.
Fields of interest: Language/linguistics.
Type of support: Grants to individuals.
Application information: Applications accepted. Application form required.
> *Send request by:* Mail
> *Deadline(s):* Varies
> *Additional information:* Application should include an explanation describing your experience, your activities relating to language preservation and how you would like to further your knowledge through this project.
Program description:
> *Seeds of Language Mini-Grant:* The organization sponsors a mini-grant program to assist California Natives who are working to revitalize their languages through the purchase of recording equipment, attendance at language conferences and workshops, conducting research, or other possible language-related projects. A small number of grants ranging from $100 to $500, depending on need, will be given throughout the year.
EIN: 721584619

341
AEPOCH
c/o Leventhal Kline Mgt.
127 University Ave.
Berkeley, CA 94710-1616 (510) 841-4145
URL: http://www.aepoch.org/arts.html

Foundation type: Public charity
Purpose: Grants to underrepresented individuals, groups and start-up projects that have difficulties in being funded or "valued" in traditional sense with little or no funding history. Fiscal sponsorship is also provided for a few select projects.
Financial data: Year ended 12/31/2011. Assets, $37,676 (M); Expenditures, $522,979; Total giving, $348,831.
Fields of interest: Arts, artist's services.
Type of support: Grants to individuals; Fiscal agent/sponsor.
Application information: Applications not accepted.
> *Additional information:* Grants are by invitation only. Unsolicited requests for funds not considered or acknowledged.
EIN: 204414461

342
Aesthetic Surgery Education and Research Foundation
11262 Monarch St.
Garden Grove, CA 92841-1441 (562) 799-2356
Contact: Joe M. Gryskiewicz M.D., Pres.
FAX: (562) 799-1098; E-mail: aserf@surgery.org; URL: http://www.aserf.org

Foundation type: Public charity

Purpose: Grants and awards for research that directly impacts the clinical practice of plastic surgery.
Publications: Application guidelines; Grants list.
Financial data: Year ended 06/30/2012. Assets, $1,967,696 (M); Expenditures, $166,628; Total giving, $140,400; Grants to individuals, totaling $140,400.
Fields of interest: Surgery research.
Type of support: Research; Awards/prizes.
Application information: Applications accepted. Application form required. Application form available on the grantmaker's web site.
> *Send request by:* E-mail
> *Deadline(s):* Apr. 15
> *Applicants should submit the following:*
> 1) Proposal
> 2) Budget Information
Program descriptions:
> *Best Journal Article Awards:* A $1,000 award will be given to the best aesthetic surgery article published in a scientific journal.
> *Gaspar W. Anastasi Award:* This $250 award is given to the highest-rated resident and/or fellow scientific papers at the society's annual meeting Resident and Fellows Forum.
> *In Chul Song Award for Philanthropic Service:* This $750 award is given to a plastic surgeon whose philanthropic plastic surgery efforts to citizens in less-fortunate countries best exemplifies humanitarian service.
> *Research Grants:* The program funds important research that directly impacts the clinical practice of aesthetic surgery.
EIN: 330613185

343
Aid for Starving Children
(formerly African American Self-Help Foundation)
182 Farmers Lane, Ste. 201
Santa Rosa, CA 95403-3016 (707) 528-3499
Contact: Joseph Spiccia, Vice-Pres.
Application address for Emergency Assistance Fund: AASHF c/o Samaritan Outreach P.O. Box 3842 , Dayton OH 45401
E-mail: info@aidforstarvingchildren.org; Mailing address for information on the African American Single Mothers Program: Attention: Jeff Baugham: P.O. Box 3842, Dayton, OH 454051; URL: http://www.aidforstarvingchildren.org

Foundation type: Public charity
Purpose: Grants to provide relief and self-help to African children and families, through educational assistance, medical immunizations, clothing and food. Also, a limited number of small cash grants to help qualified African American single mothers meet emergency financial needs.
Publications: Annual report.
Financial data: Year ended 04/30/2012. Assets, $272,332 (M); Expenditures, $10,177,047; Total giving, $9,758,534.
Fields of interest: African Americans/Blacks; Women; Adults, women; Single parents; Economically disadvantaged.
Type of support: Foreign applicants; Grants for special needs.
Application information: Applications accepted. Application form required. Application form available on the grantmaker's web site.
> *Initial approach:* Letter explaining need
> *Deadline(s):* None
> *Applicants should submit the following:*
> 1) Essay
> 2) Financial information

Additional information: Contact foundation for further eligibility criteria.
EIN: 521224507

344
AIDS Emergency Fund
12 Grace St., Ste. 300
San Francisco, CA 94103-2954 (415) 558-6999
Contact: Mike Smith, Exec. Dir.
FAX: (415) 558-6990;
E-mail: michael.armentrout@aef-sf.org; E-mail For Mike Smith: kome.muller@aef-sf.org; URL: http://www.aidsemergencyfund.org

Foundation type: Public charity
Purpose: Emergency financial assistance to persons with AIDS or disabling HIV for rent, telephone, medical equipment, and supplies.
Financial data: Year ended 02/28/2012. Assets, $1,270,260 (M); Expenditures, $2,051,262; Total giving, $1,240,618; Grants to individuals, totaling $1,240,618.
Fields of interest: AIDS, people with; Economically disadvantaged.
Type of support: Grants for special needs.
Application information:
> *Initial approach:* Telephone or in person
> *Additional information:* Applicant must be a resident of San Francisco, CA, have a medical diagnosis from a local medical doctor stating you are medically disabled, and provide proof of current income.
Program description:
> *Financial Assistance Program:* Emergency financial assistance of up to $500 per year is available to eligible individuals to cover specific types of expenses. Grants may be used towards rent, utilities, (including gas, electric, and water), past due phone bills, medical insurance premiums, medical expenses not covered by insurance (including optical and dental), and pre-arranged funeral costs. Eligible applicants must have a current monthly income of $1,354 or less.
EIN: 942922039

345
Alalusi Foundation
1975 National Ave.
Hayward, CA 94545-1709 (510) 887-2374
E-mail: info@alalusifoundation.org; URL: http://www.alalusifoundation.org/

Foundation type: Independent foundation
Purpose: Grants to individuals for humanitarian assistance overseas, primarily in China.
Financial data: Year ended 03/31/2013. Assets, $0 (M); Expenditures, $753,871; Total giving, $725,264; Grants to individuals, totaling $65,734.
International interests: China.
Type of support: Emergency funds; Grants for special needs.
Application information:
> *Initial approach:* Letter
> *Deadline(s):* None
> *Additional information:* Application must include a letter of recommendation.
EIN: 912158518

346
Allgemeiner Deutscher Frauen-Hilfsverein
(also known as German Ladies General Benevolent Society)
P.O. Box 27101
San Francisco, CA 94127-0101 (415) 391-9947
Contact: Elke schlosser, Secy. and Treas.

Foundation type: Operating foundation
Purpose: Temporary assistance to financially needy women and children of German descent who reside in the greater San Francisco Bay Area, CA.
Publications: Annual report.
Financial data: Year ended 12/31/2011. Assets, $2,466,650 (M); Expenditures, $114,576; Total giving, $74,721; Grant to an individual, 1 grant totaling $74,721.
Fields of interest: Children/youth, services; Race/intergroup relations; Women.
International interests: Germany.
Type of support: Grants for special needs.
Application information: Applications accepted. Application form required.
  Deadline(s): None
EIN: 941528193

347
Alliance For California Traditional Arts
1243 Van Ness Ave.
Fresno, CA 93721-1711 (559) 237-9812
Contact: Amy Kitchener, Exec. Dir.
Application addresses for Apprenticeship: The Presidio, P.O. Box 29096, San Francisco, CA 94129 (for USPS), or 1007 General Kennedy Ave., Ste. 211, San Francisco, CA 94129 (for UPS, FED EX, or DHL)
FAX: (559) 237-9814; E-mail: info@actaonline.org; URL: http://www.actaonline.org

Foundation type: Public charity
Purpose: Grants to individuals working to preserve and promote traditional arts in CA.
Publications: Application guidelines.
Financial data: Year ended 06/30/2011. Assets, $1,187,077 (M); Expenditures, $1,042,140; Total giving, $499,911; Grants to individuals, totaling $85,620.
Fields of interest: Folk arts; Arts education.
Type of support: Grants to individuals.
Application information: Applications accepted. Application form required. Application form available on the grantmaker's web site.
  Initial approach: Application
  Send request by: Mail
  Deadline(s): July 16 for Apprenticeship Program, none for Traditional Arts Development Program
  Final notification: Recipients notified Dec. 15 for Apprenticeship
  Additional information: See web site for additional guidelines.
Program descriptions:
  Apprenticeship Program: This program encourages the continuation of the state's traditional arts and cultures by contracting master artists to offer intensive, one-on-one training to qualified apprentices. A master artist is someone who is recognized as an exemplary practitioner of a traditional art form by his or her community and peers. Prospective apprentices should demonstrate investment and developed skill in the specific art form they wish to continue learning. The master artist and apprentice must apply together. Each $3,000 contract will support a six- to twelve-month period of concentrated learning.

Traditional Arts Development Program: This program makes contracts of up to $1,500 to support consultancies, mentorships, and travel opportunities that foster a new level of growth for individual folk and traditional artists and organizations engaged in the field in California. Requested services may be focused on organizational, program, and/or artistic development goals. Individual artists and cultural practitioners as well as organizations, whether incorporated or not, may apply.
EIN: 020541202

348
Alliance for Nonprofit Management
731 Market St., Ste. 200
San Francisco, CA 94103-2005 (415) 704-5058
FAX: (415) 541-7708;
E-mail: info@allianceonline.org; URL: http://www.allianceonline.org

Foundation type: Public charity
Purpose: Awards to authors of the most inspirational and useful new book published for the nonprofit sector.
Publications: Application guidelines.
Financial data: Year ended 12/31/2011. Assets, $14,805 (M); Expenditures, $180,653.
Fields of interest: Literature.
Type of support: Awards/grants by nomination only; Awards/prizes.
Application information: Application form available on the grantmaker's web site.
  Deadline(s): Apr. 19 for Terry McAdam Book Award
  Additional information: Awards are by nomination only.
Program description:
  Terry McAdam Book Award: Awarded with support by the New York Community Trust and the Chronicle of Philanthropy, a $1,000 stipend will be made available yearly to recognize the best contribution to nonprofit management literature. Eligible books must specifically address issues of nonprofit management, management consultancy, or advancement of the 501(c)(3) nonprofit sector; books must also be published during the current and preceding year the award will be given out, and must be marketed to the national (or a specific) nonprofit community. Authors of nominated books are not required to be alliance members.
EIN: 522089750

349
Almanor Scholarship Fund
c/o Collins Pine Co.
P.O. Box 796
Chester, CA 96020
Contact: Laura MacGregor, Tr.

Foundation type: Independent foundation
Purpose: Scholarships to residents of the northern half of Plumas County, CA.
Financial data: Year ended 12/31/2012. Assets, $1,532,514 (M); Expenditures, $101,699; Total giving, $78,300; Grants to individuals, 58 grants totaling $78,300 (high: $2,700; low: $600).
Fields of interest: Scholarships/financial aid.
Type of support: Undergraduate support.
Application information: Applications accepted. Application form required.
  Deadline(s): Aug. 1
  Additional information: Contact foundation for complete application guidelines.

Program description:
  Scholarship Program: Scholarships are awarded for undergraduate and graduate study to individuals who will be full-time students and single at the time of registration, and have maintained at least a 3.25 GPA in high school and at least a 3.0 GPA in college. Recipients must have exhibited leadership potential in school, engaged in community activities, and have employment experience.
EIN: 946066722

350
Alta Bates Summit Foundation
(formerly Alta Bates Summit Medical Center Foundation)
2855 Telegraph Ave., Ste. 601
Berkeley, CA 94705-1161 (510) 204-1667
FAX: (510) 883-9303;
E-mail: absfoffice@sutterhealth.org; Mailing address: 2450 Ashby Ave., Berkeley, CA 94705-2067; URL: http://www.absfdn.org

Foundation type: Public charity
Purpose: Career assistance and scholarship support to employees of Alta Bates Summit Medical Center.
Publications: Annual report; Newsletter.
Financial data: Year ended 12/31/2011. Assets, $69,505,697 (M); Expenditures, $6,876,091; Total giving, $2,944,815; Grants to individuals, totaling $29,750.
Fields of interest: Nursing school/education; Health sciences school/education.
Type of support: Scholarships—to individuals.
Application information: Applications not accepted.
  Additional information: Unsolicited requests for funds not considered or acknowledged. Assistance is only for employees of Alta Bates Summit Medical Center.
EIN: 510160184

351
Alta California Regional Center, Inc.
2241 Harvard St., Ste. 100
Sacramento, CA 95815-3305 (916) 978-6400
Contact: Phil Bonnet, Exec. Dir.
FAX: (916) 489-1033; URL: http://www.altaregional.org

Foundation type: Public charity
Purpose: Assistance to individuals with developmental disabilities and their families in Alpine, Colusa, El Dorado, Nevada, Placer, Sacramento, Sierra, Sutter, Yolo, and Yuba counties, CA.
Publications: Application guidelines; Informational brochure.
Financial data: Year ended 06/30/2012. Assets, $27,437,958; Expenditures, $287,959,119; Total giving, $255,699,069; Grants to individuals, totaling $255,699,069.
Fields of interest: Children; Adults; Disabilities, people with.
Type of support: Grants for special needs.
Application information: See web site or contact the organization for eligibility determination.
Program description:
  Center Services: The center provides a wide array of services to children and adults with developmental disabilities and their families for services from the center. A developmental disability is defined in state and federal law as mental retardation, cerebral palsy, epilepsy, and autism. Other substantially disabling conditions closely related to mental retardation or which require

treatment similar to the treatment required by persons with mental retardation may be eligible for services.
EIN: 941720511

352
Amador Community Foundation, Inc.
148 Main St.
P.O. Box 1154
Jackson, CA   95642   (209) 223-2148
Contact: Kathleen Harmon, Exec. Dir.
FAX: (209) 223-4569;
E-mail: acf@amadorcommunityfoundation.org;
URL: http://www.amadorcommunityfoundation.org

Foundation type: Community foundation
Purpose: Provides scholarships to residents of Amador County, CA through various funds.
Publications: Application guidelines; Grants list; Informational brochure.
Financial data: Year ended 12/31/2012. Assets, $1,597,727 (M); Expenditures, $730,667; Total giving, $193,076.
Fields of interest: Higher education.
Type of support: Scholarships—to individuals.
Application information: Applications accepted.
EIN: 680447992

353
American Arabic Educational Foundation
5742 Wish Ave.
Encino, CA   91316-1410

Foundation type: Independent foundation
Purpose: Scholarships for higher education to CA residents of Arab-American heritage with ancestors from Jordan, Libya, Palestine, or Syria.
Financial data: Year ended 12/31/2012. Assets, $374,604 (M); Expenditures, $23,710; Total giving, $22,600; Grants to individuals, 22 grants totaling $22,600 (high: $1,500, low: $1,000).
International interests: Israel; Jordan; Libya; Syria; West Bank/Gaza (Palestinian Territories).
Type of support: Scholarships—to individuals.
Application information: Applications not accepted.
  Additional information: Unsolicited requests for funds not considered or acknowledged.
EIN: 237423734

354
American Association of Critical Care Nurses
101 Columbia
Aliso Viejo, CA   92656-4109
FAX: (949) 362-2020; E-mail: info@aacn.org;
Toll-free tel.: (800) 809-2273; URL: http://www.aacn.org/

Foundation type: Public charity
Purpose: Grants and scholarships to critical care nurses pursuing degrees beyond their basic nursing education.
Financial data: Year ended 06/30/2011. Assets, $83,065,302 (M); Expenditures, $21,168,488; Total giving, $532,313; Grants to individuals, 2 grants totaling $370,231 (high: $10,000, low: $7,150).
Fields of interest: Nursing school/education.
Type of support: Research; Grants to individuals; Scholarships—to individuals.
Application information: Applications accepted. Application form required. Application form available on the grantmaker's web site.

Send request by: On-line
Deadline(s): Nov. 1
Additional information: See web site for additional application guidelines.
Program descriptions:
  AACN Impact Research: The program encourages experienced clinicians and researcher to propose projects that support inquiry and systematic research that generates new knowledge that influence high acuity critical care nursing practice. Research projects lasts for a duration of two years. Up to three grants are awarded annually and amounts to $50,000. Candidates must be AACN members and are expected to present completed studies at the National Teaching Institute& Critical Care Exposition.
  AACN-Philips Healthcare Clinical Outcomes Grant: These grants support experienced nurses in conducting clearly articulated research studies. Qualified proposals should seek to achieve improved outcomes and/or system efficiencies in care of high acuity or critically ill individuals of any age. Up to three awards of $10,000 are available annually. Candidates must be AACN members and is expected to present completed studies at the National Teaching Institute and Critical Care Exposition.
  Continuing Professional Development Scholarships: This scholarship program has expanded to help members enrich their careers and acquire knowledge and skills beyond traditional academic nursing education. A limited number of scholarships for specific academic courses will continue to be awarded. Applicants must assess gaps in their knowledge and skills, identify and evaluate learning opportunities and develop a plan to show how an AACN scholarship will help them achieve their professional learning goals.
EIN: 952706905

355
American Baptist Homes Foundation of the West, Inc.
6120 Stoneridge Mall Rd., 3rd Fl.
Pleasanton, CA   94588-3296
FAX: (925) 227-1032;
E-mail: foundation@abhow.com; Toll-free tel.: (800) 222-2469, ext. 7120; URL: http://www.abhow.com/foundation

Foundation type: Public charity
Purpose: Financial assistance for low income elderly residents in CA with affordable housing and other special needs.
Publications: Annual report.
Financial data: Year ended 09/30/2011. Assets, $38,558,792 (M); Expenditures, $2,506,261; Total giving, $1,962,698; Grants to individuals, totaling $46,763.
Fields of interest: Aging.
Type of support: Grants for special needs.
Application information: Applications accepted.
  Additional information: Residents must be at least age 62 years old to qualify. Contact the foundation for additional information.
EIN: 237039408

356
American Film Institute, Inc.
2021 N. Western Ave.
Los Angeles, CA   90027-1625   (323) 856-7600
FAX: (323) 467-4578; E-mail: information@afi.com;
URL: http://www.afi.com

Foundation type: Public charity

Purpose: Scholarships, grants, and awards to individuals in the film industry who are a part of the AFI Conservatory.
Publications: Annual report.
Financial data: Year ended 06/30/2012. Assets, $42,597,043 (M); Expenditures, $25,720,766; Total giving, $102,112; Grants to individuals, totaling $102,112.
Fields of interest: Film/video; Television.
Type of support: Grants to individuals; Scholarships—to individuals; Awards/prizes.
Application information: Applications accepted.
  Initial approach: Telephone or e-mail
  Deadline(s): Dec.
  Applicants should submit the following:
    1) Transcripts
    2) Resume
    3) Letter(s) of recommendation
  Additional information: See web site for additional guidelines.
EIN: 526072925

357
American Glaucoma Society
P.O. Box 193940
San Francisco, CA   94109-1342   (415) 561-8587
FAX: (415) 561-8531; E-mail: ags@aao.org;
URL: http://www.americanglaucomasociety.net/

Foundation type: Public charity
Purpose: Awards to individuals at the critical stages of their career development as clinician scientists by reducing vision loss from glaucoma through research.
Financial data: Year ended 12/31/2011. Assets, $2,601,701 (M); Expenditures, $1,369,799; Total giving, $425,200.
Fields of interest: Eye research.
Type of support: Awards/prizes.
Application information: Applications accepted.
  Additional information: See web site for additional guidelines.
Program descriptions:
  Mentoring for Advancement of Physician-Scientists (MAPS) Awards: This program provides a mechanism to assist young physician scientists members of the society by providing tools and resources to further their careers as potential leaders in the specialty of glaucoma care. Awards are given to individuals at early stages (within five years of graduation) of their academic careers, and are intended to help awardees overcome barriers and hindrances to their research efforts and in their careers. Awards can include equipment and training necessary to advance their research careers, as well as specific research projects.
  Mid-Career Physician Scientist Awards: These awards are targeted towards individuals between five to twenty years after fellowship. Awards are designed to assist individuals who are starting new avenues of research, including clinicians who have not been actively involved in research but are considering a career shift, as well as more-established clinician scientists embarking on new areas of research where alternate funding is unavailable.
  Young Clinician Scientist Award: These awards are targeted towards clinician scientists in glaucoma in the early stages of their careers, with the goal of encouraging the development of new clinician scientists in glaucoma. Funding is provided for the research projects undertaken within the first five years after graduation.
EIN: 222765077

358
The American Head and Neck Society, Inc.

11300 W. Olympic Blvd., Ste. 600
Los Angeles, CA   90064-1663   (310) 437-0559
Contact: Terry Day, Pres.
FAX: (310) 437-0585; E-mail: admin@ahns.info;
URL: http://www.headandneckcancer.org

Foundation type: Public charity
Purpose: Research grants to individuals for the study of head and neck cancer.
Publications: Application guidelines.
Financial data: Year ended 12/31/2011. Assets, $1,407,904 (M); Expenditures, $425,236; Total giving, $112,376; Grants to individuals, totaling $112,376.
Fields of interest: Cancer research.
Type of support: Research.
Application information: Applications accepted. Application form required. Application form available on the grantmaker's web site.
> *Deadline(s):* Vary
> *Additional information:* The complete listing of programs, as well as application guidelines, are available on the foundation's Web site.
Program descriptions:
AHNS/AAO-HNSF Surgeon-Scientist Career Development Award: Awarded in conjunction with the American Academy of Otolaryngology-Head and Neck Surgery Foundation, this award supports collaborative research projects that foster the development of contemporary basic or clinical research skills focused on neoplastic disease of the head and neck among new full-time academic surgeons. Awards are intended as a preliminary step in clinical investigation career development, and is expected to facilitate the recipient's preparation of a more comprehensive individualized research plan suitable for submission to the National Institutes of Health or comparable funding agency. Eligible applicants must be full-time academic surgeons in faculty positions at the rank of assistant professor or instructor who: are citizens of the U.S., non-citizen nationals, or have been lawfully admitted for permanent residency at the time of application; hold an M.D. degree from an accredited institution; have demonstrated the capacity or potential for a highly-productive independent research career with an emphasis in head and neck surgical oncology; are members or candidate members of the American Academy of Otolaryngology-Head and Neck Surgery or the society; and have completed residency or fellowship training no longer than four years prior to submitting an application. Grants will be awarded for $35,000 per year for two years.
Alando J. Ballantyne Resident Research Grant: This one-year, $10,000 grant is available to support basic, translational, or clinical research projects in head and neck oncology. Clinical or translational research studies are strongly encouraged and should be specifically related to the prevention, diagnosis, treatment, outcomes, or pathophysiology of head and neck neoplastic disease. Eligible applicants must be residents of the U.S. or Canada.
Fellowships: Fellowships, lasting between one and two years, are available to candidates who are eligible to take the examination of the American Board of Surgery, Otolaryngology, or Plastic Surgery. Participating institutions include Johns Hopkins University, MD Anderson Cancer Center, Medical University of South Carolina, Memorial Sloan-Kettering Cancer Center, Ohio State University, Roswell Park Cancer Institute, Stanford University, University of Alabama-Birmingham, University of Alberta, University of California-Davis, University of Cincinnati, University of Iowa, University of Kansas, University of Manitoba, University of Miami, University of Michigan, University of Nebraska, University of Oklahoma, University of Pennsylvania, University of Pittsburgh, University of South Florida, University of Toronto, University of Washington, and Wayne State University.
Pilot Research Grant: This award supports basic, translational, or clinical research projects in head and neck oncology with a one-year, $10,000 award. Clinical or translational research studies are strongly encouraged and should be specifically related to the prevention, diagnosis, treatment, outcomes, or pathophysiology of head and neck neoplastic disease. Eligible applicants must reside in the U.S. or Canada and be medical students, residents, Ph.D.s, or faculty members at the rank of associate professor or below.
Young Investigator Award (with AAOHNS): Awarded in conjunction with the American Academy of Otolaryngology, this award supports a collaborative research project by fostering the development of contemporary basic or clinical research skills focused on neoplastic disease of the head and neck among new full-time academic surgeons. Research supported by this award should be specifically directed toward the pathophysiology, diagnosis, prevention, or treatment of head and neck neoplastic disease, and may be either basic or clinical/translational in approach. Eligible applicants must be physicians with demonstrated potential for excellence in research and teaching, and serious commitment to an academic research career in head and neck surgery; applicants must also be members or candidate members of the American Academy of Otolaryngology-Head and Neck Surgery and/or the society. Priority will be given to fellows or junior faculty who have completed residencies or fellowships within four years of the application receipt date. Awards are for up to two years, at $10,000 per year.
EIN: 237323559

359
American Lung Association of California

424 Pendleton Way
Oakland, CA   94621-2116   (510) 638-5864
Contact: Jill Arnstein, Co-Exec. Dir.
FAX: (510) 638-8984; E-mail: cainfo@lung.org;
URL: http://www.californialung.org

Foundation type: Public charity
Purpose: Research grants, scholarships and fellowships to investigators for the study of lung disease, primarily in CA.
Publications: Application guidelines; Annual report; Informational brochure; Newsletter.
Financial data: Year ended 06/30/2012. Assets, $28,426,401 (M); Expenditures, $12,226,442.
Fields of interest: Nursing school/education; Lung research.
Type of support: Research; Postdoctoral support; Graduate support; Doctoral support.
Application information: Applications accepted. Application form required.
> *Deadline(s):* Sept. 5
> *Additional information:* See Web site for complete program information.
Program descriptions:
Clinical Research Grant: Awards up to $50,000 per year for up to two years, provided that satisfactory progress is demonstrated and funds are available. Applicants must hold a doctoral degree, hold an entry-level rank (e.g. instructor or assistant professor), and have completed two years of postdoctoral research training.
Research Grants: Awards up to $50,000 for two years to applicants who hold an M.D., D.O., Ph.D., ScD., DNSc., or comparable qualifications and who have completed a minimum of two years of research training. The grant supports young investigators during the transition from research training to independent research as junior faculty.
Research Training Fellowships: Awards up to $50,000 for one year to applicants who hold an M.D., Ph.D. (or equivalent) and doctoral nursing candidates seeking further training as scientific investigators.
Scholarships: Awards $6,000 one-year scholarships to fund the second year of study for graduate students enrolled in a master's program in nursing. Applicants must be committed to developing a specialty in pulmonary nursing or acute and/or chronic care.
EIN: 940362650

360
American Society for Enology and Viticulture

P.O. Box 1855
Davis, CA   95617-1855   (530) 753-3142
FAX: (530) 753-3318; E-mail: society@asev.org;
URL: http://www.asev.org

Foundation type: Public charity
Purpose: Scholarships to undergraduate and graduate students pursuing a degree in enology and viticulture at an accredited four year college or university.
Financial data: Year ended 10/31/2011. Assets, $2,886,166 (M); Expenditures, $1,222,432; Total giving, $48,801; Grants to individuals, totaling $48,801.
Fields of interest: Science.
Type of support: Graduate support; Undergraduate support.
Application information: Applications accepted. Application form required.
> *Deadline(s):* Mar. 1
> *Final notification:* Recipients notified in June
> *Applicants should submit the following:*
> 1) Transcripts
> 2) Letter(s) of recommendation
Program description:
Scholarship Program: The society annually awards numerous scholarships to students pursuing a degree in enology, viticulture, or in a curriculum emphasizing a science basic to the wine and grape industry. The awards are not in predetermined amounts and may vary from year to year.
EIN: 946089508

361
Ameritec Foundation

417 W. Foothill Blvd., Ste. 516
Glendora, CA   91741-5301
E-mail: jwatsonameritec@gmail.com

Foundation type: Company-sponsored foundation
Purpose: Awards and prizes to researchers in Los Angeles, CA for medical research targeting spinal cord injury.
Financial data: Year ended 12/31/2012. Assets, $1,484,967 (M); Expenditures, $108,419; Total giving, $105,000.
Fields of interest: Institute; Spine disorders research.
Type of support: Research; Awards/grants by nomination only; Awards/prizes.

Application information:
Initial approach: Letter
Deadline(s): Oct. 15
Additional information: Contact foundation for current nomination guidelines.
EIN: 954147156

362
Amgen Foundation, Inc.
c/o Jewel Smith, Mgr.
1 Amgen Center Dr., M.S. 28-1-B
Thousand Oaks, CA 91320-1799 (805) 447-4056
Contact: Jewel Smith, Mgr., Corp. Contribs.; Eduardo Cetlin, Dir., Corp. Contribs.
FAX: (805) 376-1258;
E-mail: amgenfoundation@amgen.com; Additional e-mail for Eduardo Cetlin: ecetlin@amgen.com; additional e-mail for Jewel Smith: jewels@amgen.com; URL: http://www.amgen.com/citizenship/foundation.html

Foundation type: Company-sponsored foundation
Purpose: Awards to K-12 educators who excel in science teaching.
Publications: Application guidelines; Annual report; Grants list.
Financial data: Year ended 12/31/2012. Assets, $93,229,705 (M); Expenditures, $19,299,061; Total giving, $17,994,001.
Fields of interest: Formal/general education; Science.
Type of support: Grants to individuals; Awards/prizes.
Application information: Applications accepted. Application form required. Application form available on the grantmaker's web site.
Initial approach: Application
Send request by: Online or e-mail
Deadline(s): Feb.
Final notification: Applicants notified in June
Applicants should submit the following:
1) Curriculum vitae
2) Photograph
3) Essay
4) Letter(s) of recommendation
5) Resume
Additional information: Applications should include release forms, a photograph of the applicants classroom, and a lesson plan. Online or PDF via email if in a language other than English (French or Spanish).
Program description:
Amgen Award for Science Teaching Excellence (AASTE): The foundation annually awards grants to K-12 educators who elevate the level of science literacy in the classroom. Recipients are selected based on creativity and effectiveness of teaching methods, the plan for the use of grant money to improve science education resources in their schools, and an innovative science lesson plan showcasing innovative methods in the classroom. The selected winners receive $5,000 and the winner's school receive a restricted grant of $5,000 for expansion or enhancement of a school science program, for science resources, or for the professional development of the school's science teachers. The program is limited to California, Colorado, Kentucky, Massachusetts, Rhode Island, Washington, Puerto Rico, and Canada.
EIN: 770252898

363
Anaheim Arts Council
P. O. Box 1364
Anaheim, CA 92815-1364   (714) 868-6094
Contact: Michael Buss, Pres.
URL: http://www.anaheimartscouncil.com

Foundation type: Public charity
Purpose: Scholarships to graduating high school seniors who are residents of Anaheim, CA or attending school in Anaheim or a school in the Anaheim Union High School District to further their art education.
Financial data: Year ended 06/30/2010. Assets, $182,785 (M); Expenditures, $49,609; Total giving, $45,589.
Fields of interest: Visual arts; Performing arts.
Type of support: Undergraduate support.
Application information:
Deadline(s): May 18
Applicants should submit the following:
1) Letter(s) of recommendation
2) Transcripts
Additional information: See web site for additional guidelines.
Program description:
Violet Wheeler Scholarships: Scholarships are available to high school seniors who are residents of Anaheim, currently enrolled in a visual arts or performing arts class. Awards of $1,000 each will be presented to two talented students to apply toward their tuition for education in the arts. Applicants will audition before a panel of judges and winners must perform for the members of the AAC.
EIN: 912162436

364
Anaheim Community Foundation
200 S. Anaheim Blvd., Ste. 433
Anaheim, CA 92805-3820   (714) 765-4419
Contact: Terry D. Lowe, C.E.O.
FAX: (714) 765-4454;
E-mail: AnaheimCommunityFoundation@gmail.com; URL: http://www.anaheimcommfound.org

Foundation type: Community foundation
Purpose: Scholarships to economically disadvantaged Anaheim youth for participation in the city of Anaheim's Community Services classes and programs.
Publications: Application guidelines; Annual report; Informational brochure.
Financial data: Year ended 06/30/2012. Assets, $722,682 (M); Expenditures, $407,650; Total giving, $392,781; Grants to individuals, totaling $392,781.
Fields of interest: Economically disadvantaged.
Type of support: Scholarships—to individuals.
Application information: Applications accepted. Application form required.
Send request by: Hand delivered
Deadline(s): Feb. 27
Additional information: Applicants must be 17 years old or younger, and show proof of Anaheim residency. See web site for additional application guidelines.
EIN: 330033023

365
Anderson Prize Foundation
c/o Allen Schuh
2727 Vallejo St.
San Francisco, CA 94123   (415) 775-6321

Foundation type: Independent foundation

Purpose: Awards by nomination only to individuals whose efforts have enhanced the quality of life for the gay and lesbian community.
Financial data: Year ended 12/31/2012. Assets, $84,155 (M); Expenditures, $41,722; Total giving, $40,000.
Fields of interest: Civil/human rights, LGBTQ.
Type of support: Awards/grants by nomination only.
Application information: Applications not accepted.
Additional information: Unsolicited requests for funds not considered or acknowledged.
EIN: 363710311

366
Angels Baseball Foundation
2000 E. Gene Autry Way
Anaheim, CA 92806-6100   (714) 940-2000
FAX: (714) 940-2244; URL: http://losangeles.angels.mlb.com/ana/community/baseball_foundation.jsp

Foundation type: Public charity
Purpose: Scholarships to academically talented, financially disadvantaged public middle school students in Orange County, CA pursuing a four-year college degree.
Financial data: Year ended 12/31/2011. Assets, $2,123,241 (M); Expenditures, $671,094; Total giving, $585,800; Grants to individuals, totaling $20,000.
Fields of interest: Higher education.
Type of support: Scholarships—to individuals.
Application information: Applications accepted. Application form required.
Additional information: Students must be a legal resident, of strong character, citizenship, and academic achievement, and enrolled in an avid program all four years of high school. Scholarship is awarded once the student is accepted and enrolled in a four-year college.
EIN: 200713975

367
Angels Gate Cultural Center, Inc.
3601 S. Gaffey St.
San Pedro, CA 90731-6969   (310) 519-0936
Contact: James Cross, Pres.; Residencies: Marshall Astor
FAX: (310) 519-8698;
E-mail: info@angelsgateart.org; URL: http://www.angelsgateart.org/

Foundation type: Public charity
Purpose: Studio space to professional artists of various disciplines.
Publications: Application guidelines.
Financial data: Year ended 12/31/2012. Assets, $155,236 (M); Expenditures, $314,683.
Fields of interest: Visual arts; Literature.
Type of support: Residencies.
Application information: Applications accepted. Application form required. Application form available on the grantmaker's web site.
Initial approach: Letter, telephone, or e-mail
Deadline(s): None
Applicants should submit the following:
1) Curriculum vitae
2) Work samples
Additional information: Application must also include letter of intent, as well as hard copies of work samples, preferably in CD format.
EIN: 953688214

368
The Archeo/ Community Foundation
(formerly Tyche Foundation for Archaeology and Community)
181 2nd Ave., Ste. 400
San Mateo, CA 94401-3838   (650) 344-4348
Contact: John L. Crary, Exec. Dir.
URL: http://archaeocommunity.wikispaces.com/

Foundation type: Independent foundation
Purpose: Grants to academics conducting archaeological research.
Financial data: Year ended 12/31/2011. Assets, $1,930 (M); Expenditures, $12,105; Total giving, $11,715.
Fields of interest: History/archaeology.
Type of support: Grants to individuals.
Application information: Applications accepted.
 Deadline(s): None
 Applicants should submit the following:
  1) Budget Information
  2) Proposal
EIN: 770621337

369
The Ardron Charitable Foundation
940 Sylva Ln.
Sonora, CA 95370-5969

Foundation type: Independent foundation
Purpose: Financial assistance to single mothers residing in Sonora, CA, for medical expenses.
Financial data: Year ended 12/31/2012. Assets, $0 (M); Expenditures, $57,743; Total giving, $57,318.
Fields of interest: Women; Single parents.
Type of support: Grants for special needs.
Application information: Applications not accepted.
 Additional information: Unsolicited requests for funds not considered or acknowledged.
EIN: 311811012

370
Armenian Gospel Mission
2650 E. Foothill Blvd., Ste. 205
Pasadena, CA 91107-3439   (626) 744-3221
FAX: (626) 744-3224;
E-mail: office@armeniangospelmission.org; Mailing address: P.O. Box 5727, Pasadena, CA 91117-0727; URL: http://www.armeniangospelmission.org

Foundation type: Public charity
Purpose: Financial assistance and emergency support to the poor in Armenia with food, clothing, utilities and other special needs.
Financial data: Year ended 12/31/2011. Assets, $1,958,379 (M); Expenditures, $1,754,707; Total giving, $415,496.
Fields of interest: Human services, emergency aid; Christian agencies & churches; Economically disadvantaged.
Type of support: Emergency funds; In-kind gifts.
Application information: Contact the mission for additional information.
EIN: 237089113

371
Armstrong Family Foundation
408 The Strand
Manhattan Beach, CA 90266

Foundation type: Independent foundation

Purpose: Scholarships to graduates of Garfield High School, Los Angeles, CA, for higher education.
Financial data: Year ended 12/31/2011. Assets, $4,038 (M); Expenditures, $3,220; Total giving, $3,000.
Type of support: Support to graduates or students of specific schools; Undergraduate support.
Application information: Applications not accepted.
 Additional information: Unsolicited requests for funds not considered or acknowledged.
EIN: 954251068

372
Arques Charitable Education Trust
30 Liberty Ship Way, Ste. 3380
Sausalito, CA 94965-3322

Foundation type: Independent foundation
Purpose: Scholarships to students majoring in veterinary fields, classical voice, or mechanical arts.
Financial data: Year ended 12/31/2012. Assets, $1,019,526 (M); Expenditures, $183,663; Total giving, $96,090.
Fields of interest: Music; Opera; Veterinary medicine.
Type of support: Scholarships—to individuals; Student loans—to individuals; Graduate support.
Application information: Application form required.
 Initial approach: Letter
 Copies of proposal: 1
 Deadline(s): Mar. 31
 Final notification: Students notified within 30 days
 Applicants should submit the following:
  1) Resume
  2) Proposal
  3) Letter(s) of recommendation
  4) Budget Information
  5) Financial information
EIN: 686044627

373
Art of the Matter Performance Foundation
3288 21st St., Ste. 71
San Francisco, CA 94110-2423   (415) 267-7687
FAX: (415) 332-7171;
E-mail: info@deborahslater.org; URL: http://www.deborahslater.org

Foundation type: Public charity
Purpose: Support to artists through a fiscal sponsorship program.
Publications: Application guidelines.
Financial data: Year ended 12/31/2011. Assets, $25,916 (M); Expenditures, $100,641.
Fields of interest: Arts, artist's services.
Type of support: Fiscal agent/sponsor.
Application information: Applications accepted. Application form required. Application form available on the grantmaker's web site.
 Initial approach: Application
 Send request by: E-mail
 Deadline(s): None
 Additional information: Application should include $30 fee.
Program description:
 Fiscal Sponsorship: The program exists to encourage artists by providing a place where new ideas, diverse art forms, artists and audiences can be encouraged to interact. The foundation offers a low-tech performance space, access to a bulk-mail insignia, the ability to apply for grants requiring 501

(c)(3) sponsorship and a point of view based in experimental dance, theater, music and new media.
EIN: 943085133

374
Art Works Downtown, Inc.
1337 4th St.
San Rafael, CA 94901-2809   (415) 451-8119
E-mail: info@artworksdowntown.org; E-Mail For Elisabeth
Setten:elisabeth@artworksdowntown.org;
URL: http://www.artworksdowntown.org

Foundation type: Public charity
Purpose: Merit scholarships to students in art classes.
Financial data: Year ended 12/31/2011. Assets, $3,716,431 (M); Expenditures, $444,209.
Fields of interest: Cultural/ethnic awareness.
Type of support: Scholarships—to individuals.
Application information: Applications accepted.
 Applicants should submit the following:
  1) Letter(s) of recommendation
  2) Work samples
EIN: 680387761

375
Arthritis Foundation, Inc.
800 W. 6th St., Ste. 1250
Los Angeles, CA 90017-2721   (323) 954-5760
FAX: (323) 954-5790;
E-mail: info.sca@arthritis.org; Toll Free Tel.: (800)-283-7800; URL: http://www.arthritis.org/california/

Foundation type: Public charity
Purpose: Grants to support research in finding a cure for the prevention of arthritis.
Publications: Annual report; Newsletter.
Financial data: Year ended 12/31/2011. Assets, $27,722,142 (M); Expenditures, $11,203,710; Total giving, $417,554.
Fields of interest: Arthritis.
Type of support: Fellowships; Research; Postdoctoral support; Doctoral support.
Application information: Applications accepted. Application form required.
 Additional information: See web site for additional application guidelines.
Program descriptions:
 Innovative Research Grant: This grant is to broaden the base of inquiry in fundamental biomedical science, clinical research or behavioral research with relevance to rheumatic disease by encouraging applications for research proposals that involve an especially high degree of innovation and novelty or represent a special opportunity to address questions. Established investigators with any terminal degree are invited to apply. The award is up to $100,000 per year for two years.
 New Investigators Awards: This award is offered to encourage individuals in health care to carry out innovative research projects in areas related to arthritis and the rheumatic diseases. The award provides salary and research expenses for up to three years. The second year of the award will be based on project progress, and the third year will be issued after competitive renewal. This is for PhD's or equivalent committed to arthritis related questions. Not for Laboratory research. MDs are not eligible. The award is $50,000 per year.
EIN: 951885447

376
Arthritis National Research Foundation
200 Oceangate, Ste. 830
Long Beach, CA 90802-4335
Contact: Helene Belisle, Exec. Dir.
FAX: (562) 983-1410; E-mail: anrf@ix.netcom.com;
Toll-free tel.: (800) 588-2873; URL: http://
www.curearthritis.org

Foundation type: Public charity
Purpose: Research grants to newer postdoctoral investigators for the study of arthritis at nonprofit U.S. institutions.
Publications: Application guidelines; Annual report; Financial statement; Grants list; Informational brochure (including application guidelines); Newsletter.
Financial data: Year ended 03/31/2012. Assets, $7,693,675 (M); Expenditures, $1,334,200; Total giving, $950,000.
Fields of interest: Arthritis research.
Type of support: Conferences/seminars; Fellowships; Research; Grants to individuals; Postdoctoral support; Travel grants.
Application information: Applications accepted. Application form not required.
Initial approach: Letter, telephone, or e-mail
Send request by: Online and mail
Copies of proposal: 3
Deadline(s): Jan. 18
Final notification: Recipient notified Apr. 30
Applicants should submit the following:
1) Resume
2) Proposal
3) Budget Information
Program description:
Grants: Grants between $20,000 and $75,000 to newer investigators holding an M.D. or Ph.D. for study into the causes of arthritis. Salaries, supplies, and equipment directly related to the proposed studies are funded; overhead or indirect costs will not be funded.
EIN: 956043953

377
Arts Council Silicon Valley
4 N. 2nd St., Ste. 500
San Jose, CA 95113-1324 (408) 998-2787
Contact: Connie Martinez, C.E.O.
FAX: (408) 971-9458;
E-mail: admin@svcreates.org; URL: http://
www.artscouncil.org
Additional URL: http://www.artsoplis.com

Foundation type: Public charity
Purpose: Funding to the region's artists and arts organizations for advocacy and technical support services including fellowships to visual and performing artists who are residents of Santa Clara County and adjoining counties in the Silicon Valley, CA, area.
Publications: Application guidelines; Annual report; Grants list; Newsletter; Quarterly report.
Financial data: Year ended 06/30/2011. Assets, $2,093,425 (M); Expenditures, $2,639,439; Total giving, $95,578.
Fields of interest: Visual arts; Performing arts; Humanities.
Type of support: Fellowships; Project support; Fiscal agent/sponsor.
Application information: Applications accepted. Application form required. Application form available on the grantmaker's web site.
Send request by: Mail
Deadline(s): Varies
Applicants should submit the following:
1) Work samples

2) Resume
3) Proposal
4) Curriculum vitae
Program descriptions:
Artist Fellowships: The council annually awards artist fellowships of up to $4,000 in rotating categories to recognize professional working artists and to enable them to continue to pursue their creative work. The artists are selected by a notable panel of experienced judges based upon the following set of criteria: artistic quality (artistic quality and originality of work, based on the examples provided by the applicant); community impact (record of professional activity and achievement, especially during the past three years, with demonstrated impact in Santa Clara County); and professional development (continuity and exploration of the art form by the applicant)
Arts Enrichment Grant Program for Individual Artists: This grant program provides a minimum of $1,500 for artists to be placed in Power of Preschool (POP) classrooms, to teach young children through the arts and to build the skills of early educators to also use the arts as a teaching strategy. Artists will work towards: teaching young children through the arts by providing hands-on arts experiences to young children; increasing awareness of the importance of appropriate artistic engagement through experiential activities as integral to a quality early childhood environment; and assisting children in becoming personally, socially, and physically competent, effective learners, and ready to transition into kindergarten.
EIN: 942825213

378
The Asia Foundation
465 California St., 9th Fl.
San Francisco, CA 94104-1822 (415) 982-4640
Contact: Gordon R. Hein, V.P., Progs.
FAX: (415) 392-8863; E-mail: info@asiafound.org; Additional address (DC office): 1779 Massachusetts Ave., N.W., Ste. 815, Washington, DC 20036-2109, tel.: (202) 588-9420, fax: (202) 588-9409, email: info@asiafound-dc.org; additional mailing address (CA office): P.O. Box 193223, San Francisco, CA 94119-3223; URL: http://www.asiafoundation.org

Foundation type: Public charity
Purpose: Support to junior associates who wish to further their professional development in Asian studies.
Publications: Annual report; Financial statement; Grants list; Occasional report.
Financial data: Year ended 09/30/2011. Assets, $61,636,301 (M); Expenditures, $151,290,491; Total giving, $26,390,978; Grants to individuals, totaling $98,760.
Fields of interest: International affairs.
Type of support: Research; Postgraduate support.
Application information: Applications accepted. Application form available on the grantmaker's web site.
Initial approach: Application
Send request by: Online
Deadline(s): Varies
Applicants should submit the following:
1) Letter(s) of recommendation
2) Transcripts
3) Resume
Additional information: See web site for additional information.
EIN: 941191246

379
Asian Pacific Fund
465 California St., Ste. 809
San Francisco, CA 94104-4224 (415) 395-9985
Contact: Audrey Yamamoto, Pres. and Exec. Dir.
FAX: (415) 433-6866;
E-mail: info@asianpacificfund.org; URL: http://
www.asianpacificfund.org

Foundation type: Public charity
Purpose: Scholarships and awards to Asian-Americans, primarily in the Bay Area, CA, region.
Publications: Annual report.
Financial data: Year ended 06/30/2012. Assets, $10,584,111 (M); Expenditures, $1,118,952; Total giving, $488,580; Grants to individuals, totaling $194,750.
Fields of interest: Asians/Pacific Islanders.
Type of support: Support to graduates or students of specific schools; Awards/prizes; Undergraduate support.
Application information:
Initial approach: E-mail
Additional information: See web site for complete program information.
Program descriptions:
Banatao Filipino American Education Fund College Scholarship: Awards five scholarships of $5,000 each to qualified high school seniors who will be enrolled at four-year colleges or universities. Applicants must be of Filipino heritage with a GPA of at least "B", and who plan to attend a four-year college or university. Awards are based on financial need.
Banatao SAT Prep and College Admissions Counseling Scholarship: High school juniors of at least 50% Filipino heritage with a minimum GPA of 2.7 who have an interest in engineering, math, or science and demonstrate financial need are eligible for a 40-hour Princeton Review or Kaplan SAT preparatory course and/or a private college admissions counseling sessions.
Chang-Lin Tien Educational Leadership Awards: Honors the legacy of Chang-Lin Tien, the first Asian American to head a major U.S. research university as chancellor of UC Berkeley from 1990 to 1997. The program was created to inspire more Asian Americans to aspire to the leadership exemplified by Dr. Tien. Annually, Asian Americans who have significant academic accomplishments and potential to advance to the highest leadership levels in higher education are selected to receive a $10,000 grant. The purpose of the awards is to support the recognition, professional development and advancement of Asian Americans as leaders of colleges and universities.
Frederick and Demi Seguritan Scholarship: A four-year renewable award of $5,000 is available to incoming freshman enrolled full-time at an accredited four year-college or university who has a passion for business. Students must be of Asian heritage, have a minimum GPA of 3.0, demonstrate financial need, and show a commitment to community service.
Growing Up Asian in America: Awards $27,000 in prizes in an annual art & essay contest for K-12 students in the San Francisco Bay area. Winners receive savings bond awards worth $1,000 to $2,000 and are honored at an awards ceremony at the Asian Art Museum. The program provides a unique forum for youth to explore their ideas and to celebrate being both Asian and American and by serving as an important community resource, helping people of all backgrounds better understand the experiences of young Asian Americans and learn more about life in a place as diverse as the San Francisco Bay Area.

Helen and L.S. Wong Memorial Scholarship: One to three awards of $1,000 to $3,000, with $500 to $1,000 renewable for up to four years, are available to incoming freshman at a four-year college who have a minimum GPA of 2.8. Applicants must be of Asian heritage, demonstrate financial need, and be a U.S. citizen or permanent resident.

Hsiao Memorial Economics Scholarship: Students majoring in Economics at a U.S. college who are pursuing a career in academia are eligible for a $1,000 scholarship. Students must be of Asian heritage, preferably of Chinese descent.

Human Capital Scholarship Application: Two awards of $1,500 are available to incoming freshman who are the first generation in their family to attend college. Students must have a minimum GPA of 2.7, demonstrate financial need, and attend any University of California campus. Applicants from any underrepresented minority group are accepted. Preference is given to students in the liberal arts.

Jack and Jeanette Chu Scholarship: Two awards of $2,500 are available to Business Administration majors at UC Berkeley of Asian heritage (preferably Chinese) with a minimum GPA of 3.0. Preference is given to students who have lived in Central America and have a record of community service.

Lapiz Family Scholarship: Two $1,000 scholarships are awarded for students who are farm workers or children of farm or migrant workers, attending the University of California.

Lauren C. Poon, MD Scholarship Application: A $1,000 award is available to a high school graduate of Alameda County who is pursuing a career in medicine, public health, or allied health field, with a minimum GPA of 3.5, who demonstrate financial need and a commitment to community service.

Maria Elena Yuchengco Memorial Journalism Scholarship: Awards one to three scholarships of $1,000 to $3,000 to full-time undergraduate students at San Francisco State University, who are journalism majors of Filipino heritage, and who have a minimum cumulative GPA of 3.0. Awards are based on merit and financial need; applicants must be U.S. citizens or permanent residents.

Philippine International Aid-Wells Fargo Scholarship: Three one-year renewable awards of $1,500 are available to incoming freshman at an accredited four-year college or university in California, who demonstrate financial need, are at least 25% Filipino, and have a minimum GPA of 2.75.

Shui Kuen and Allen Chin Scholarship: Two awards of $1,000 are available to incoming freshman or current, full-time undergraduate students whose parents or themselves are currently or formerly employed at an Asian-owned or Asian cuisine restaurant. Applicants must be U.S. citizens or permanent residents in financial need who have a minimum GPA of 3.0.

Yale Asian Community Service Fellowship: Two $2,500 fellowships are available to Yale undergraduate or recent graduate students who will intern for 10 weeks at a nonprofit organization that serves Asians. Applicants must be of at least 50% Asian heritage and demonstrate financial need.
EIN: 943201522

380
Aspiranet
400 Oyster Point Blvd., Ste. 501
South San Francisco, CA   94080-7600   (650) 866-4080
Contact: Vernon McFarland Brown, C.E.O.
FAX: (650) 866-4081; URL: http://www.aspiranet.org/

Foundation type: Public charity

Purpose: Foster care payments to San Francisco metro area families in the Aspiranet program.
Financial data: Year ended 06/30/2012. Assets, $17,689,345 (M); Expenditures $48,935,098; Total giving, $7,296,958; Grants to individuals, totaling $7,296,958.
Fields of interest: Foster care; Family services.
Type of support: Grants to individuals.
Application information:
   Initial approach: Letter
   Additional information: Contact foundation for eligibility criteria.
EIN: 942442955

381
Aspiration Corporation
P.O. Box 880264
San Francisco, CA   94188-0264
E-mail: info@inspirationtech.org; URL: http://www.aspirationtech.org

Foundation type: Operating foundation
Purpose: Short-term fiscal sponsorship to individuals with software development projects who are in the process of becoming official 501(c)(3) nonprofit organizations.
Financial data: Year ended 12/31/2012. Assets, $130,026 (M); Expenditures, $445,599; Total giving, $0.
Type of support: Fiscal agent/sponsor.
Application information: Applications accepted. Application form required. Application form available on the grantmaker's web site. Interview required.
   Additional information: Applicants must fill out an initial fiscal sponsorship application and submit a non-refundable application fee of $150.
Program description:
   Fiscal Sponsorship: The organization provides short-term fiscal sponsorship to nonprofit software development projects that are in the process of becoming official 501(c)3 nonprofit organizations. Generally, sponsorships last between 1-2 years. The sponsorship model is that of a grantor and grantee relationship, so while the project is being sponsored, the project remains a separate entity with its own Board of Directors who oversees the activities of the project.
EIN: 912106274

382
Assistance League of Newport-Mesa California
2220 Fairview Rd.
Costa Mesa, CA   92627-1624   (949) 645-6929
FAX: (949) 645-3919; E-mail: alnm@sbcglobal.net; URL: http://assistanceleague.publishpath.com/

Foundation type: Public charity
Purpose: Dental and health care services, clothing distribution, financial support for day care, and other services to underprivileged children living in the Newport-Mesa, CA, school district.
Financial data: Year ended 05/31/2012. Assets, $3,958,552 (M); Expenditures, $931,453; Total giving, $110,076; Grants to individuals, totaling $92,752.
Fields of interest: Dental care; Human services; Day care; Children, services.
Type of support: Grants for special needs.
Application information: Contact foundation for current application deadline/guidelines.
EIN: 951942148

383
Assistance League of Orange California, Inc.
124 S. Orange St.
Orange, CA   92866-1424   (714) 532-5800
Contact: Carolyn Seeley, Recording Secy.
Application address: c/o Robin Lyall, 1852 Windes Dr., Orange, CA 92869, tel.: (714) 633-3099
E-mail: AssistanceLeagueOfOrange@Gmail.com;
URL: http://www.aorange.org

Foundation type: Public charity
Purpose: Scholarships to outstanding graduating seniors who reside or attend a school in the Orange Unified School District for continuing their education at accredited colleges or universities.
Financial data: Year ended 05/31/2012. Assets, $1,330,414 (M); Expenditures, $399,227; Total giving, $125,784; Grants to individuals, totaling $125,784.
Fields of interest: Higher education.
Type of support: Scholarships—to individuals.
Application information: Applications accepted.
   Deadline(s): Apr. 14
   Final notification: Applicant notified Apr. 24
   Applicants should submit the following:
      1) Photograph
      2) Transcripts
      3) Letter(s) of recommendation
   Additional information: Applicant must demonstrate financial need, academic achievement, high school activities, extracurricular activities and community service, as well as leadership qualities.
EIN: 956101256

384
Assistance League of Riverside
3707 Sunnyside Dr.
Riverside, CA   92506-2418   (951) 682-3445
Contact: Betty Vaughn, Pres.
FAX: (951) 684-1703; URL: http://riverside.assistanceleague.org

Foundation type: Public charity
Purpose: Scholarships to college bound students of Riverside, CA for postsecondary education.
Financial data: Year ended 05/31/2012. Assets, $1,979,636 (M); Expenditures, $397,916; Total giving, $10,879; Grants to individuals, totaling $10,879.
Fields of interest: Higher education.
Type of support: Scholarships—to individuals.
Application information: Applications accepted. Application form required. Application form available on the grantmaker's web site.
   Send request by: Mail
   Deadline(s): Mar. 31
   Applicants should submit the following:
      1) Transcripts
      2) Letter(s) of recommendation
      3) Essay
   Additional information: Students should contact their guidance counselors for additional application information.
EIN: 952394523

385
Assistance League of Whittier
P.O. Box 386
Whittier, CA   90608-0386   (562) 693-6533
URL: http://whittier.assistanceleague.org/ps.mainpagecenter.cfm?ID=3078

Foundation type: Public charity

Purpose: Assistance to low-income families of the Whittier, CA, area for dental care, clothing, and other services. Scholarships to students at Whittier College, CA, and Rio Hondo College, CA.
Financial data: Year ended 05/31/2012. Assets, $941,278 (M); Expenditures, $178,997; Total giving, $93,087; Grants to individuals, totaling $66,087.
Fields of interest: Dental care; Human services.
Type of support: Support to graduates or students of specific schools; Grants for special needs.
Application information:
Initial approach: Letter
EIN: 952135127

386
Association for the Advancement of Artificial Intelligence
(also known as AAAI)
2275 E. Bayshore Rd. Ste. 160
Palo Alto, CA 94303-3463 (650) 328-3123
Contact: Carol Hamilton, Exec. Dir.
FAX: (650) 321-4457; E-mail: info08@aaai.org;
URL: http://www.aaai.org

Foundation type: Public charity
Purpose: Awards to individuals who have made significant contributions in the area of artificial intelligence.
Financial data: Year ended 12/31/2011. Assets, $7,172,212 (M); Expenditures, $1,632,833; Total giving, $108,959; Grants to individuals, totaling $59,972.
Fields of interest: Science.
Type of support: Awards/prizes.
Application information: Application form available on the grantmaker's web site.
Deadline(s): Feb. 13
Additional information: Application by nomination only. Nomination forms available online.
Program descriptions:
AAAI Classic Paper Award: The award honors the author(s) of paper(s) deemed most influential, chosen from a specific conference year. The award will be presented at the association's annual conference in Chicago. A total of $1,000 in travel support is available to enable the author(s) to travel to the conference to accept the award in person.
AAAI Distinguished Service Award: The award recognizes one individual each year for extraordinary service to the artificial intelligence community. The winner will receive a $1,000 prize.
AAAI Fellows Program: The program recognizes a small group of association members who have made significant, sustained contributions to the field of artificial intelligence, and are recognized as having unusual distinction in the profession.
AAAI INTEL Science and Engineering Awards: The awards are presented at the Intel Science and Engineering Fair for the best projects in the area of computer science with an artificial intelligence component. The current award amount is $5,000 and is split among the winners.
ACM/AAAI Allen Newell Award: The award is presented to an individual selected for career contributions that have breadth within computer science, or that bridge computer science and other disciplines. This endowed award is accompanied by a prize of $10,000.
Robert S. Engelmore Memorial Lecture Award: This award is presented annually to an individual who has shown extraordinary service to AAAI and the AI community. In conjunction with the award, the recipient is invited to present a keynote lecture at the IAAI conference, and to prepare a companion

article for AI Magazine. The award includes a certificate from IAAI and a $1,000 honorarium.
EIN: 942702216

387
Association of American Educators Foundation
27405 Puerta Real, Ste. 230
Mission Viejo, CA 92691-6388 (800) 704-7799
Contact: Gary Beckner, Chair.
FAX: (949) 595-7970;
E-mail: info@aaeteachers.org; Toll-free tel.: (800) 704-7799; URL: http://www.aaeteachers.org/foundation.shtml

Foundation type: Public charity
Purpose: Scholarships and grants to teachers. Funds are provided primarily to student teachers, to mentors of student teachers, and to educators who demonstrate unique expertise in advancing professionalism in their classrooms.
Financial data: Year ended 12/31/2011. Assets, $553,868 (M); Expenditures, $1,138,147; Total giving, $72,768; Grants to individuals, totaling $23,534.
Fields of interest: Secondary school/education.
Type of support: Grants to individuals; Scholarships—to individuals.
Application information: Contact foundation for application guidelines.
EIN: 330623003

388
Association of Black Women Physicians, Inc.
4712 Admiralty Way, Ste. 175
Marina del Rey, CA 90292-6905 (310) 364-1438
E-mail: scholarship@blackwomenphysicians.org

Foundation type: Public charity
Purpose: Scholarships to female medical students of southern CA, or enrolled in southern CA medical schools.
Publications: Application guidelines.
Financial data: Year ended 12/31/2011. Expenditures, $2,944.
Fields of interest: Medical school/education; Women.
Type of support: Scholarships—to individuals.
Application information: Applications accepted. Application form required. Application form available on the grantmaker's web site.
Deadline(s): Sept. 7
Applicants should submit the following:
   1) Transcripts
   2) Letter(s) of recommendation
   3) Curriculum vitae
Additional information: Application should also include a personal statement, and application must be typed. Applications are available through your medical school financial aid office or scholarship contact, or download from web site.
Program description:
Rebecca Lee, M.D. Scholarship Award: The scholarship provides assistance to women medical students who are residents of Southern California or enrolled in Southern California medical schools. The awards range from $1,000 to $5,000 and are based on academic merit, financial need, and commitment to the ABWP mission.
EIN: 953764478

389
Association of Moving Image Archivists
(also known as A.M.I.A.)
1313 N. Vine St.
Los Angeles, CA 90028-8107 (323) 463-1500
FAX: (323) 463-1506; E-mail: amia@amianet.org;
E-mail for Caroline Frick:cfrick@austin.utexas.edu;
URL: http://www.amianet.org

Foundation type: Public charity
Purpose: Scholarships and fellowships to students who wish to pursue careers in moving image archive management.
Publications: Application guidelines; Newsletter.
Financial data: Year ended 12/31/2011. Assets, $664,973 (M); Expenditures, $524,525; Total giving, $29,943; Grants to individuals, totaling $29,943.
Fields of interest: Arts education; Film/video.
Type of support: Fellowships; Internship funds; Scholarships—to individuals; Graduate support.
Application information: Applications accepted. Application form required. Application form available on the grantmaker's web site.
Initial approach: Telephone, fax or e-mail
Deadline(s): May 1 for fellowships; May 15 for scholarships
Applicants should submit the following:
   1) Transcripts
   2) Resume
   3) Letter(s) of recommendation
   4) Essay
   5) Curriculum vitae
Program descriptions:
AMIA Scholarship Program: The program awards five annual scholarships: the Mary Pickford Scholarship; the Sony Pictures Scholarship; the CFI Sid Solow Scholarship; Universal Studios Preservaton Scholarship; and the Rick Chace Scholarship. Financial assistance in the amount of $4,000 is given to students of merit who intend to pursue careers in moving-image archiving.
Kodak Fellowship: Provides students with financial assistance in the amount of a $4,000 scholarship for their formal education, practical experience through an intensive six-week summer internship at Kodak, and an introduction to the film archive community through participation in the AMIA conference.
EIN: 954386715

390
Association of Professors & Scholars of Iranian Heritage Award Fund
P.O. Box 4175
Diamond Bar, CA 91765 (909) 869-2569
FAX: (909) 869-2564; E-mail: nfo@Apsih.org;
URL: http://apsih.org/

Foundation type: Public charity
Purpose: Awards to outstanding high school graduates, outstanding college graduates, advanced degree graduates, and post doctoral associates of Iranain heritage.
Financial data: Year ended 06/30/2012. Assets, $42,310 (M); Expenditures, $15,511; Total giving, $12,150; Grants to individuals, 23 grants totaling $12,150.
Fields of interest: Higher education.
Type of support: Awards/prizes; Postdoctoral support; Graduate support; Precollege support; Undergraduate support.
Application information: Application form available on the grantmaker's web site.
Send request by: On-line
Deadline(s): May 3
Applicants should submit the following:

1) Transcripts
2) Resume
Additional information: Applicants are nominated by anyone including themselves, based on academic performance, scholastic aptitude, class participation, on campus activities, extra-curricular activities, and other qualities that bespeak of one's character and good standing, and positive equities. See web site for additional guidelines.
EIN: 311693573

391
A-T Medical Research Foundation
16224 Elisa Pl.
Encino, CA 91436-3320
Contact: Pamela J. Smith, Pres. and C.F.O.
FAX: (818) 906-2870; E-mail: ATMRF@aol.com

Foundation type: Operating foundation
Purpose: Grants to individuals in Canada, Costa Rica, the Netherlands, Poland, the U.S., Israel, Italy, and Turkey for the foundation's Medical Research Program concerning ataxia-telangiectasia.
Publications: Annual report; Informational brochure; Newsletter.
Financial data: Year ended 09/30/2011. Assets, $1,972 (M); Expenditures, $201,480; Total giving, $200,000.
Fields of interest: Institute.
International interests: Canada; Costa Rica; Israel; Italy; Netherlands; Turkey.
Type of support: Research.
Application information: Applications not accepted.
Additional information: Unsolicited requests for funds not considered or acknowledged.
EIN: 953882022

392
Athena Charitable Trust
5411 Bahia Ln.
La Jolla, CA 92037-7020

Foundation type: Operating foundation
Purpose: Support to individuals for a variety of needs, including educational assistance, general welfare, and medical expenses, primarily in CA.
Financial data: Year ended 06/30/2013. Assets, $104,945 (M); Expenditures, $96,661; Total giving, $33,373; Grants to individuals, 17 grants totaling $21,239 (high: $5,100, low: $100).
Fields of interest: Health care; Economically disadvantaged.
Type of support: Grants for special needs.
Application information: Applications not accepted.
Additional information: Unsolicited requests for funds not considered or acknowledged.
EIN: 336211470

393
Autism Care & Treatment Today
(also known as ACT Today!)
6330 Variel Ave., Ste. 102
Woodland Hills, CA 91367 (818) 340-4010
E-mail: info@act-today.org; URL: http://
www.act-today.org

Foundation type: Public charity
Purpose: Financial support for individuals and families to help their children with autism spectrum disorders, to be used for medications and adaptive treatments.

Publications: Application guidelines.
Financial data: Year ended 06/30/2011. Assets, $154,769 (M); Expenditures, $620,724; Total giving, $385,198; Grants to individuals, totaling $385,198.
Fields of interest: Autism.
Type of support: Grants for special needs.
Application information: Applications accepted. Application form required.
Initial approach: Application
Deadline(s): Jan. 31 for 1st quarter, Apr. 30 for 2nd quarter, July 31 for 3rd quarter, Oct. 30 for 4th quarter
Final notification: Applicants notified Mar. 15, June 15, Sept. 30 and Dec. 15
Additional information: Assistance is provided to families on a quarterly basis. See web site for additional guidelines.
EIN: 201424642

394
The Avant! Foundation
4320 Stevens Creek Blvd., Ste. 168
San Jose, CA 95129-1281 (408) 551-0322
FAX: (408) 551-0324;
E-mail: info@avantifoundation.org; Additional tel.: (408) 737-7168

Foundation type: Company-sponsored foundation
Purpose: Scholarships to high school graduates of the CA Bay Area with tuition and financial support.
Financial data: Year ended 12/31/2012. Assets, $2,000,530 (M); Expenditures, $661,339; Total giving, $445,437; Grants to individuals, 22 grants totaling $102,051 (high: $10,449, low: $532).
Type of support: Undergraduate support.
Application information: Applications not accepted.
Additional information: Unsolicited requests for funds not considered or acknowledged.
EIN: 943290664

395
Avery Dennison Foundation
(formerly Avery International Foundation)
150 N. Orange Grove Blvd.
Pasadena, CA 91103-3534 (626) 304-2000
Contact: Alicia Procello Maddox, Pres. and Exec. Dir.
E-mail: AveryDennison.Foundation@averydennison.
com; URL: http://www.averydennison.com/avy/
en_us/Sustainability/Community

Foundation type: Company-sponsored foundation
Purpose: College scholarships to Chinese students studying engineering, science, and technology.
Publications: Application guidelines; Grants list; Occasional report.
Financial data: Year ended 12/31/2012. Assets, $16,193,506 (M); Expenditures, $1,168,360; Total giving, $848,490.
Fields of interest: Engineering/technology.
International interests: Chile; China.
Type of support: Scholarships—to individuals; Foreign applicants.
Application information:
Initial approach: Letter
EIN: 953251844

396
Avery-Fuller-Welch Children's Foundation
(formerly Avery-Fuller Children's Center)
c/o Pacific Foundation Services, LLC
1660 Bush St., Ste. 300
San Francisco, CA 94109-5308 (415)
561-6540
Contact: Hector Melendez, Exec. Dir.
FAX: (415) 561-6477;
E-mail: hmelendez@pfs-llc.net; URL: http://
www.pfs-llc.net/afw/index.html

Foundation type: Independent foundation
Purpose: Financial assistance to mentally and physically disabled children in San Francisco, Alameda, Contra Costa, San Mateo, and Marin counties, CA, to increase their self-sufficiency. See program description for further limitations.
Publications: Application guidelines; Informational brochure (including application guidelines); Program policy statement.
Financial data: Year ended 06/30/2013. Assets, $5,971,109 (M); Expenditures, $355,704; Total giving, $298,585; Grants to individuals, 8 grants totaling $40,180 (high: $7,200, low: $2,500).
Fields of interest: Physical therapy; Youth development; Children/youth, services; Disabilities, people with.
Type of support: Grants for special needs.
Application information: Application form required.
Initial approach: Letter
Deadline(s): Feb. 15, May 15, Aug. 15, and Nov. 15
Final notification: Applicants notified within four weeks of the deadline
Additional information: Application must be submitted by the professional who has primary care responsibility.
EIN: 941243657

397
Carl & Grace Baker Memorial Scholarship
c/o Bank of Stockton, N.A.
P.O. Box 201014
Stockton, CA 95201-9014 (209) 929-1500
Contact: Robert W. Fay, V.P.

Foundation type: Independent foundation
Purpose: Educational loans to students in the public school system within the territorial jurisdiction of Stockton, CA, Scottish Rite Bodies, for enrollment in a college or university of their choice.
Publications: Informational brochure.
Financial data: Year ended 10/31/2013. Assets, $1,934,892 (M); Expenditures, $29,913; Total giving, $0.
Fields of interest: Higher education.
Type of support: Student loans—to individuals.
Application information: Applications accepted. Application form required.
Send request by: Mail or hand delivered
Deadline(s): May 15 for fall semester and Oct.15 for spring semester
Applicants should submit the following:
1) Transcripts
2) GPA
Additional information: Late applications may be considered if good cause is shown.
EIN: 946618012

398
Bank of Stockton Educational Foundation
P.O. Box 1110
Stockton, CA 95201-1110

Foundation type: Company-sponsored foundation
Purpose: Educational loans to children of full-time employees of the Bank of Stockton, for full-time undergraduate degree programs.
Financial data: Year ended 06/30/2013. Assets, $444,681 (M); Expenditures, $30; Total giving, $0.
Fields of interest: Higher education.
Type of support: Student loans—to individuals.
Application information: Applications not accepted.

> *Additional information:* Unsolicited requests for funds not considered or acknowledged.

Company name: Bank of Stockton
EIN: 311801280

399
The Frank H. Bartholomew Foundation
c/o William W. Godward
101 California St., 5th Fl.
San Francisco, CA   94111-5800   (707) 938-2244
Contact: Scott Clyde, Genl. Mgr.
Application address: P.O. Box 311, Sonoma, CA 95476-0311, tel.: (707) 938-2244

Foundation type: Operating foundation
Purpose: Scholarships to graduating seniors of Sonoma Valley High School, CA, for study at the University of California, Davis, with emphasis on viticulture program.
Financial data: Year ended 12/31/2012. Assets, $15,606,041 (M); Expenditures, $842,847; Total giving, $5,000; Grant to an individual, 1 grant totaling $5,000.
Fields of interest: Higher education.
Type of support: Support to graduates or students of specific schools; Undergraduate support.
Application information: Applications accepted.

> *Initial approach:* Letter
> *Deadline(s):* Spring semester
> *Additional information:* Application must include a recommendation from a Sonoma Valley High School Vice Principal.

EIN: 943129676

400
W. P. Bartlett Trust Fund
27349 Ave., Ste. 138
Porterville, CA   93257-9428   (559) 781-4927
Contact: John C. Richardson, Secy.-Treas.

Foundation type: Independent foundation
Purpose: Scholarships to students of Porterville College, Porterville High School, Monache High School, Granite Hills High School or Strathmore High School, CA for postsecondary education.
Financial data: Year ended 12/31/2012. Assets, $1,620,674 (M); Expenditures, $78,147; Total giving, $76,100; Grants to individuals, 6 grants totaling $8,000 (high: $2,000, low: $1,000).
Type of support: Support to graduates or students of specific schools; Undergraduate support.
Application information: Applications accepted. Application form required. Interview required.

> *Initial approach:* Letter
> *Deadline(s):* End of school year
> *Additional information:* Contact your individual school for application.

Program description:

> *Scholarship Program:* Scholarship recipients are recommended by scholarship committees of Porterville College, Porterville High School, and Monache High School. The aim of the fund is to assist financially needy, qualified students in meeting school expenses for each quarter for two years of schooling. Recipients of the scholarships

must have been attending their high school or college for at least two years prior to application. Applicants are judged on prior academic performance, performance on college aptitude tests, recommendations from instructors, financial need, and an interview with the selection committee.
EIN: 946102005

401
The Basic Fund
268 Bush St., Ste. 2717
San Francisco, CA   94104-3503   (415) 986-5650
Contact: Rachel Elginsmith, Exec. Dir.
FAX: (415) 986-5358;
E-mail: rachel@basicfund.org; URL: http://www.basicfund.org

Foundation type: Public charity
Purpose: Scholarships to children in the Bay Area, CA. The maximum award per student per school year is $1,600.
Publications: Application guidelines.
Financial data: Year ended 06/30/2012. Assets, $14,569,111 (M); Expenditures, $6,831,406; Total giving, $6,191,699; Grants to individuals, totaling $6,191,699.
Fields of interest: Elementary/secondary education; Elementary school/education; Education; Economically disadvantaged.
Type of support: Scholarships—to individuals.
Application information: Applications accepted. Application form required. Application form available on the grantmaker's web site.

> *Initial approach:* Letter
> *Deadline(s):* Mar. 14
> *Applicants should submit the following:*
>   1) Financial information
> *Additional information:* See web site for eligibility criteria.

EIN: 943290699

402
The Peggy and Jack Baskin Foundation
5214F Diamond Heights Blvd., Ste. 808
San Francisco, CA   94131-2175
URL: http://baskinfoundation.org

Foundation type: Independent foundation
Purpose: Scholarships to female students who are CA residents, enrolled for at least one full year at Cabrillo College, Hartnell College, or Monterey Peninsula College.
Financial data: Year ended 12/31/2012. Assets, $3,339,419 (M); Expenditures, $640,410; Total giving, $489,915.
Fields of interest: Scholarships/financial aid; Women.
Type of support: Support to graduates or students of specific schools.
Application information: Applications accepted. Application form required. Application form available on the grantmaker's web site.

> *Initial approach:* Application
> *Additional information:* Scholarship candidates must be nominated by the president of their respective community college. Scholarships are paid directly to the school on behalf of the students. Students must maintain a 3.0 GPA.

EIN: 260677825

403
Battered Women's Assistance
P.O. Box 1119
Santa Cruz, CA   95061-1119

Foundation type: Operating foundation
Purpose: Financial assistance and volunteer guidance to battered women and children in Santa Cruz County, CA.
Financial data: Year ended 12/31/2011. Assets, $6,668 (M); Expenditures, $10,214; Total giving, $10,214; Grants to individuals, totaling $10,214.
Fields of interest: Crime/violence prevention; Domestic violence; Children/youth, services; Domestic violence; Women.
Type of support: Grants for special needs.
Application information: Applications not accepted.

> *Additional information:* Applicants must be referred by another 501(c)(3) agency. Unsolicited requests for funds not considered or acknowledged.

EIN: 770167239

404
K. & F. Baxter Family Foundation Inc.
1563 Solano Ave., No. 404
Berkeley, CA   94707-2116   (510) 524-8145
FAX: (510) 524-4101;
E-mail: staceybell@kfbaxterfoundation.com;
URL: http://www.kfbaxterfoundation.com

Foundation type: Independent foundation
Purpose: Scholarships to multiracial children from Los Angeles, Berkeley, Oakland, and West Contra Costa Unified School Districts, CA.
Financial data: Year ended 12/31/2012. Assets, $158,247 (M); Expenditures, $251,495; Total giving, $214,055.
Type of support: Precollege support; Undergraduate support.
Application information: Applications not accepted.

> *Additional information:* Unsolicited requests for funds not considered or acknowledged.

EIN: 954633505

405
Bay Area Video Coalition
2727 Mariposa St., 2nd Fl.
San Francisco, CA   94110-1401   (415) 861-3282
Contact: for Residency: Carol Varney, Exec.-Dir.
FAX: (415) 861-4316;
E-mail: membership@bavc.org; E-mail Fore Carol Varney: carol@bavc.org; URL: http://www.bavc.org

Foundation type: Public charity
Purpose: Awards and to artists working on media projects.
Publications: Application guidelines; Annual report; Financial statement; Grants list; Newsletter.
Financial data: Year ended 12/31/2011. Assets, $2,137,421 (M); Expenditures, $4,795,961; Total giving, $70,826; Grants to individuals, totaling $70,826.
Fields of interest: Film/video; Arts, artist's services; Arts.
Type of support: Awards/prizes; Residencies; Project support; Fiscal agent/sponsor.
Application information: Applications accepted. Application form required. Application form available on the grantmaker's web site.

> *Copies of proposal:* 1
> *Deadline(s):* Feb. 1 for MediaMaker Award
> *Applicants should submit the following:*

1) Budget Information
2) Proposal
3) Resume
4) SASE
5) Work samples
Additional information: Application must also include list of awards, intended audience, distribution plan, and desired production locations.

Program descriptions:
Innovation Artist-in-Residence: The coalition offers a four-month residency (including technical support, access, and mentorship in the coalition's Community Innovation Lab) with the goal of developing a socially-relevant media project utilizing emerging web or mobile technologies, new software tools, or social networking applications.

James D. Phelan Art Award in Video: Sponsored and administered by the San Francisco Foundation, this biennial award honors California-born artists whose body of work has made significant contributions to the field.

Media Maker Award: The award provides an $8,000 package of services and classes for media projects in the postproduction phase. The award is divided into $6,000 toward postproduction suites and services and $2,000 toward coalition classes. Out-of-pocket expenses (i.e. production insurance, equipment operators, tape stock, etc.) are not covered by the award.

Producers Institute for New Media Technologies: This program is a ten-day residency for eight creative teams (independent producers or public broadcasters) of three people each, all who have a shared goal of developing and prototyping a multi-platform project inspired by, or based on, a significant documentary project. The intention of the project is to develop socially-relevant media projects for emerging one-on-one project development with technical mentors, new media storytelling workshops, and hands-on prototyping of their ideas. The participants adapt and develop film, video, and audio content for delivery using a range of interactive web-based experiences, mobile streaming, multi-user communities, and new educational software. Producers may propose a range of delivery strategies, including cell-phones, other hand-held devices, set-tops, Internet, portable software, and more. The program provides creative mentors, technology consultants, and advisors based on the needs of the project. All projects must be either independently produced (without the support of a commercial or cable broadcaster), or the project of a public broadcast station; project producers, executive producers, or directors should be the lead applicant, and should include two additional creative team members. Other team members should be one visual designer (web, game, etc) and any other appropriate committed program staff who would be relevant for project execution (for example: editors, writers, talent, directors of photography, sound recordists/ editors, or composers)
EIN: 942403876

406
BBCN Bank Scholarship Foundation
(formerly The Nara Bank Scholarship Foundation)
3731 Wilshre Blvd., Ste. 1000
Los Angeles, CA   90010-2830   (213) 639-1700
Contact: Paul Choi, Secy.
URL: http://www.bbcnbank.com/ community_support.asp

Foundation type: Company-sponsored foundation

Purpose: Scholarships to individuals residing in communities served by Nara Bank, N.A. in the states of CA, NY, and NJ.
Publications: Application guidelines; Grants list.
Financial data: Year ended 12/31/2010. Assets, $0; Expenditures, $94,659; Total giving, $92,000; Grants to individuals, 45 grants totaling $90,000 (high: $2,000, low: $2,000).
Fields of interest: Higher education; Asians/Pacific Islanders.
Type of support: Undergraduate support.
Application information: Applications accepted. Application form required.
  Deadline(s): Feb. 28
  Applicants should submit the following:
    1) GPA
    2) Essay
    3) Transcripts
  Additional information: Application must also include a copy of signed family tax return.
Program description:
Scholarships: The foundation awards $2,000 college scholarships to underserved high school graduates located in select counties of California, New Jersey, and New York. Applicants must plan to attend an accredited junior college or four-year college and have an overall GPA of 3.3 or higher. Recipients are selected based on financial need, academic excellence, and leadership in the community.
EIN: 912156704

407
The Dennis and Anne Beaver Foundation
1311 L St.
Bakersfield, CA   93301-4508   (661) 323-7911
Contact: Dennis Beaver, Pres.

Foundation type: Independent foundation
Purpose: Scholarships and travel grants to preselected, gifted students at universities and high schools in Bakersfield, CA, to study abroad in Sweden or France.
Financial data: Year ended 12/31/2011. Assets, $99,082 (M); Expenditures, $39,184; Total giving, $33,169.
Type of support: Undergraduate support; Travel grants.
Application information: Applications not accepted.
EIN: 770557208

408
Arnold and Mabel Beckman Foundation
100 Academy
Irvine, CA   92617-3002   (949) 721-2222
Contact: Jacqueline Dorrance, Exec. Dir.
FAX: (949) 721-2225;
E-mail: administration@beckman-foundation.com;
Mailing address: P.O. Box 13219, Newport Beach, CA 92658; e-mail (for Kathlene Williams, Exec. Asst.): k.williams@beckman-foundation.com;
URL: http://www.beckman-foundation.com

Foundation type: Independent foundation
Purpose: Research support to U.S. citizens and permanent residents with tenure-track appointments in academic and nonprofit organizations to fund research in the chemical and life sciences.
Publications: Application guidelines; Program policy statement.
Financial data: Year ended 08/31/2013. Assets, $548,425,390 (M); Expenditures, $26,561,276; Total giving, $22,625,440.

Fields of interest: Genetic diseases and disorders; Research; Science; Marine science; Chemistry; Biology/life sciences.
Type of support: Research; Awards/prizes.
Application information: Applications accepted. Application form required. Application form available on the grantmaker's web site.
  Initial approach: Application
  Copies of proposal: 2
  Deadline(s): Oct. 1
  Applicants should submit the following:
    1) Curriculum vitae
    2) Proposal
    3) Letter(s) of recommendation
EIN: 953169713

409
Grant Beckstrand Cancer Foundation
20341 Birch St., Ste. 310
Newport Beach, CA   92660-1515   (949) 955-0099
Contact: Lil Spitzer, Pres. and C.E.O.
FAX: (949) 955-0070; URL: http:// www.beckstrand.org

Foundation type: Public charity
Purpose: Financial assistance to cancer patients who reside in Los Angeles or Orange County, LA with living expenses. Scholarships to individuals under age 25 who have been diagnosed with cancer, and plan to attend or attending college and demonstrate financial need.
Financial data: Year ended 12/31/2012. Assets, $1,466,672 (M); Expenditures, $998,607.
Fields of interest: Higher education; Cancer.
Type of support: Scholarships—to individuals; Grants for special needs.
Application information: Applications accepted. Application form required.
  Send request by: Mail
  Deadline(s): Apr. 29 for Scholarship
  Final notification: Scholarship recipients notified July 15
  Additional information: Diagnosis is subject to verification by your doctor.
Program descriptions:
Individual Patient Assistance (IPA): Assistance is given to individuals who reside in Orange or Los Angeles county, CA and have been diagnosed with cancer within the past year or have on-going cancer. Financial assistance is available through medical co-payments and health insurance premiums, prescription reimbursement, rent and mortgage assistance, utilities and auto payments and insurance. Applicant must be a lawful U.S. resident and currently undergoing aggressive treatment, or have just completed treatment within three weeks.
National Scholarship Program: The foundation provides financial support nationwide to individuals under the age of 25 who have been diagnosed with cancer, plan to attend/are attending college, and who demonstrate financial need. Six scholarships of $2,000 are available to U.S. citizens.
EIN: 237416758

410
Bel-Air Film and Arts Foundation, Inc.
5656 W. 5th St.
Los Angeles, CA   90048-4602
E-mail: info@belairfilmarts.org; URL: http:// belairfilmarts.org/

Foundation type: Public charity
Purpose: Provides film school scholarships to students to help with their funding needs.
Publications: Application guidelines.

Financial data: Year ended 12/31/2011. Expenditures, $4,318.
Fields of interest: Film/video.
Type of support: Scholarships—to individuals.
Application information: Applications accepted. Application form required. Application form available on the grantmaker's web site. Interview required.

Initial approach: Application
Final notification: Applicants notified in Oct.

Program description:

Film Scholarship Program: The scholarship program is dedicated to helping students between the ages of eighteen and twenty-four attend film school. Participating schools include Long Beach State University, USC School of Cinematic Arts, and the New York Film Academy. Entries are reviewed by selection committees and board members. Finalists are interviewed in person and winners are announced via email.
EIN: 271459894

411
The Belvedere Cove Foundation

P. O. Box 786
Belvedere, CA 94920-0786 (415) 273-1510
Contact: for Scholarship: Laurel Holm, Scholarship Chair.
E-mail address for scholarship:
laurel.holm@belvederecove.org
URL: http://www.belvederecove.org

Foundation type: Public charity
Purpose: Scholarships to qualified youth of northern CA for participation in sailing programs.
Financial data: Year ended 12/31/2012. Assets, $625,303 (M); Expenditures, $153,699; Total giving, $137,701; Grants to individuals, totaling $8,607.
Fields of interest: Athletics/sports, water sports.
Type of support: Scholarships—to individuals.
Application information: Applications accepted. Application form available on the grantmaker's web site. Interview required.

Initial approach: Letter
Send request by: Online

Program description:

Scholarships: Scholarships are granted to individuals who wish to learn more about sailing, and who wish to pursue coursework related to sailing by providing equipment, facilities, and free or low cost instruction to young individuals by qualified teachers.
EIN: 680010945

412
Bialis Family Foundation

P.O. Box 30590
Santa Barbara, CA 93130-0590
Application address for Nursing Excellence Awards Program: c/o Selection Committee, P.O. Box 30570, Santa Barbara, CA 93130

Foundation type: Independent foundation
Purpose: Grants to individual nurses for excellence in nursing and to individuals who lack resources to meet their basic human needs.
Financial data: Year ended 06/30/2012. Assets, $7,201,317 (M); Expenditures, $395,321; Total giving, $372,160.
Fields of interest: Nursing care; Homeless.
Type of support: Awards/prizes; Grants for special needs.
Application information: Applications accepted. Application form required.

Initial approach: Letter
Deadline(s): Dec. 31 for nursing awards
Additional information: Applicants for the Award for Nursing Excellence must complete the nomination form. Each applicant must be a nurse with at least 5 years continuous experience working as a nurse in Santa Barbara. No faxes, e-mails or telephone calls accepted.
EIN: 953646277

413
Bickerstaff Family Foundation

c/o Gursey Schneider
1888 Century Park, E.
Century City, CA 90067-1702
Contact: Amy White
E-mail: bickfamilyfound@aol.com; Application address: P.O. Box 41100, Long Beach, CA 90853; Tel./Fax: (562) 433-5661

Foundation type: Independent foundation
Purpose: Scholarships to teens and young adults ages 16 to 25 infected with AIDS or HIV to pursue higher education or vocational training. Giving is limited to residents of Los Angeles and Orange counties, CA.
Financial data: Year ended 12/31/2012. Assets, $3,508,532 (M); Expenditures, $1,812,998; Total giving, $1,788,250.
Fields of interest: Higher education; AIDS.
Type of support: Technical education support; Undergraduate support.
Application information: Applications accepted. Application form required.

Initial approach: Letter or e-mail
Send request by: Mail, fax or e-mail
Copies of proposal: 1
Deadline(s): Mar. 15
Final notification: Recipients notified three to four months after deadline
Applicants should submit the following:
1) Transcripts
2) Letter(s) of recommendation
3) GPA
4) Essay
EIN: 954819633

414
Black Rock Arts Foundation

995 Market St., 9th Fl.
San Francisco, CA 94124-1444 (415) 626-1248
Contact: Josie Schimke, Prog. Devel. Asst.
E-mail: info@blackrockarts.org; URL: http://www.blackrockarts.org

Foundation type: Public charity
Purpose: Grants to artists for the creation of community-based interactive art projects.
Publications: Grants list.
Financial data: Year ended 12/31/2011. Assets, $588,129 (M); Expenditures, $577,706; Total giving, $219,080; Grants to individuals, totaling $140,680.
Fields of interest: Visual arts.
Type of support: Seed money.
Application information: Applications accepted. Application form required.

Initial approach: E-mail
Deadline(s): Mar. 13
Final notification: Applicants notified no later than May 15
EIN: 912130056

415
Camron D. Blackburn Athletic & Scholarship Foundation

5 S. Vista De La Luna
South Laguna, CA 92651-6750 (760) 433-5860

Foundation type: Independent foundation
Purpose: Scholarships to high school seniors of Laguna Beach High School, Laguna Beach, CA who exhibit an excellence in athletics while attending school. Scholarships also to students attending the college or university of his or her choice on a full-time basis to cover tuition, room and board and other miscellaneous expenses.
Financial data: Year ended 12/31/2012. Assets, $126,450 (M); Expenditures, $51,260; Total giving, $50,500; Grant to an individual, 1 grant totaling $500.
Fields of interest: Higher education.
Type of support: Support to graduates or students of specific schools.
Application information: Applications accepted. Application form required. Interview required.

Applicants should submit the following:
1) Transcripts
2) Essay
Additional information: High school seniors must maintain at least a 3.5 GPA on a 4.0 scale, and student attending college must maintain at least a 2.0 GPA on a 4.0 scale.
EIN: 953618770

416
Boand Family Foundation

13440 Paramount Blvd., No. G
South Gate, CA 90280-8250

Foundation type: Independent foundation
Purpose: Scholarships to students at Downey High School, CA.
Financial data: Year ended 12/31/2012. Assets, $3,237,299 (M); Expenditures, $175,448; Total giving, $158,000.
Fields of interest: Education.
Type of support: Scholarships—to individuals; Support to graduates or students of specific schools; Awards/prizes.
Application information: Applications not accepted.

Additional information: Unsolicited requests for funds not considered or acknowledged.
EIN: 954262373

417
A. W. Bodine—Sunkist Memorial Foundation

P.O. Box 7888
Van Nuys, CA 91409-7888 (818) 986-4800
Contact: Shannon Gleason, Treas.

Foundation type: Company-sponsored foundation
Purpose: Undergraduate scholarships to financially needy students who have a background or are directly related to someone in the student's immediate family who must have derived the majority of his or her income from CA or AZ agriculture.
Publications: Application guidelines.
Financial data: Year ended 12/31/2012. Assets, $444,243 (M); Expenditures, $40,748; Total giving, $34,000; Grants to individuals, 17 grants totaling $34,000 (high: $2,000, low: $2,000).
Fields of interest: Agriculture.
Type of support: Scholarships—to individuals; Undergraduate support.

Application information: Applications accepted.
Application form required. Application form
available on the grantmaker's web site.
> *Send request by:* Mail
> *Deadline(s):* Apr. 30
> *Applicants should submit the following:*
> 1) GPA
> 2) Letter(s) of recommendation
> 3) SAT
> 4) Transcripts
> 5) Essay
> 6) Financial information

EIN: 953958439

418
Anita Borg Institute for Women and Technology

1501 Page Mill Rd., MS 1105
Palo Alto, CA 94304-1126 (650) 236-4756
Contact: Telle Whitney, Pres. and C.E.O.
FAX: (650) 852-8172; URL: http://anitaborg.org

Foundation type: Public charity
Purpose: Scholarships and awards for students and
faculty to attend the GHC of women in computing
conference.
Publications: Application guidelines; Annual report.
Financial data: Year ended 12/31/2011. Assets,
$1,547,064 (M); Expenditures, $5,135,860; Total
giving, $242,216; Grants to individuals, 206 grants
totaling $172,149.
Fields of interest: Computer science; Women.
Type of support: Scholarships—to individuals;
Awards/prizes.
Application information: Applications accepted.
Application form required.
> *Deadline(s):* Varies
> *Additional information:* See web site for
> additional guidelines.

Program descriptions:
> *Change Agent ABIE Awards:* Three outstanding
> international women (non U.S. residents with an
> emphasis on developing countries) who have
> created opportunities for girls and women in
> technology will be recognized. Nominations are
> encouraged for professional women regardless of
> their age or education level. The award covers the
> winners' expenses to attend the conference.
> *Denice Denton Emerging Leader ABIE Award:* This
> award recognizes a junior faculty member for high
> quality research and significant positive impact on
> diversity. The award includes a prize of $5,000.
> *Social Impact ABIE Award:* This award recognizes
> individuals who have made a positive impact on
> women, technology, and society. Recipients are
> honored by the technical women's community at
> the Grace Hopper Celebration (GHC). The award
> includes a prize of $10,000. Nominees may be an
> individual or a team, and male or female.
> *Technical Leadership ABIE Award:* This award
> recognizes women technologists who demonstrate
> leadership through their contributions to technology
> and achievements in increasing the impact of
> women on technology. Recipients are honored by
> the technical women's community at the Grace
> Hopper Celebration (GHC) and invited to give a
> presentation on their work and accomplishments at
> the conference. The award includes a prize of
> $10,000.

EIN: 770480427

419
The Lawrence Bossola - Colombo Club Scholarship Fund

1343 Locust St., Ste. 201
Walnut Creek, CA 94596-4521 (510) 653-9716

Foundation type: Independent foundation
Purpose: Scholarships to members or children,
grandchildren, or great grandchildren of a member
of the Colombo Club or the Colombo Club Auxiliary,
Oakland, CA.
Financial data: Year ended 12/31/2011. Assets,
$514,847 (M); Expenditures, $22,455; Total
giving, $18,000; Grants to individuals, 12 grants
totaling $18,000 (high: $1,500, low: $1,500).
Type of support: Undergraduate support.
Application information: Applications accepted.
Application form required.
> *Initial approach:* Letter
> *Deadline(s):* Mar. 31

EIN: 721605589

420
Marvin Boyer Scholarship Foundation

(formerly The Marvin Boyer Memorial Scholarship
Fund)
3737 Camino del Rio S., Ste. 109
San Diego, CA 92108-4007
Contact: John C. Mowry, Tr.
Application address: P.O. Box 412, Potosi, MO
63664

Foundation type: Company-sponsored foundation
Purpose: Scholarships to students who
demonstrate financial need to attend a state
university in MO.
Financial data: Year ended 12/31/2013. Assets,
$0 (M); Expenditures, $5,000; Total giving,
$5,000; Grant to an individual, 1 grant totaling
$5,000.
Fields of interest: Higher education.
Type of support: Support to graduates or students
of specific schools; Undergraduate support.
Application information:
> *Initial approach:* Letter
> *Deadline(s):* Dec. 15
> *Additional information:* Application should
> include proof of admission to a state
> university in MO.

EIN: 330245562

421
The Bradley Foundation

1672 Main St., Ste. E-364
Ramona, CA 92065-5257
Contact: Barbara Teets
URL: http://www.bradleyfoundationscholars.org

Foundation type: Independent foundation
Purpose: Scholarships to individuals residing in
San Diego, CA.
Financial data: Year ended 12/31/2012. Assets,
$4,463,001 (M); Expenditures, $458,621; Total
giving, $367,886; Grants to individuals, 4 grants
totaling $72,000 (high: $40,000, low: $5,000).
Type of support: Scholarships—to individuals.
Application information: Applications not
accepted.
> *Additional information:* The application process
> has been suspended until further notice. See
> foundation web site for updates in this area.

EIN: 330771070

422
Breast Cancer Survivors

3843 S. Bristol St., Ste. 152
Santa Ana, CA 92704-7426 (866) 960-9222
Contact: Anna Bell, Exec. Dir.
FAX: (866) 781-6068; E-mail: info@bcsurvivors.org;
URL: http://www.bcsurvivors.org

Foundation type: Public charity
Purpose: Financial assistance only to women
undergoing treatment for breast cancer who are
unable to meet basic living expenses and reside in
Orange, San Diego, Riverside, and San Bernadino
counties, CA.
Publications: Application guidelines.
Financial data: Year ended 12/31/2011. Assets,
$277,810 (M); Expenditures, $722,873; Total
giving, $465,197; Grants to individuals, totaling
$465,197.
Fields of interest: Breast cancer; Women.
Type of support: Grants for special needs.
Application information: Applications accepted.
Application form required. Application form
available on the grantmaker's web site.
> *Additional information:* BCS has a lifetime
> support limit of 9 months, as well as a per
> person monetary limit.

EIN: 330765783

423
Sunshine Brooks Foundation

P.O. Box 34627
San Diego, CA 92163-4627
Contact: Michael Kearney, Dir.
E-mail: mkearney@costco.com; URL: http://
www.sunshinebrooks.com

Foundation type: Independent foundation
Purpose: Scholarships to active employees and
children of employees of Costco Wholesale, or any
of its direct or indirect wholly-owned subsidiaries for
higher education at accredited colleges or
universities.
Financial data: Year ended 06/30/2013. Assets,
$1,576,571 (M); Expenditures, $166,081; Total
giving, $156,000; Grants to individuals, 104 grants
totaling $156,000.
Fields of interest: Higher education.
Type of support: Employee-related scholarships.
Application information: Applications accepted.
Application form required. Application form
available on the grantmaker's web site.
> *Send request by:* Mail
> *Deadline(s):* May 1
> *Final notification:* Applicants notified before Aug.
> 15
> *Applicants should submit the following:*
> 1) Letter(s) of recommendation
> 2) Transcripts
> *Additional information:* Application should also
> include a personal statement. Unsolicited
> requests for funds not considered or
> acknowledged.

EIN: 330190411

424
Sunny Brown Foundation

1760 N. Palm
Upland, CA 91784 (909) 982-1826

Foundation type: Independent foundation
Purpose: Scholarships to graduating seniors at
DeRidder High School, LA and to U.S. citizens
showing skills and a desire to study the visual or
performing arts.

Financial data: Year ended 12/31/2011. Assets, $560,884 (M); Expenditures, $80,163; Total giving, $45,000; Grants to individuals, 9 grants totaling $45,000 (high: $5,000, low: $5,000).
Fields of interest: Arts; Scholarships/financial aid.
Type of support: Support to graduates or students of specific schools; Undergraduate support.
Application information: Applications accepted. Application form required.
   Applicants should submit the following:
      1) ACT
      2) Transcripts
      3) Essay
   Additional information: Application should also include list of activities and college acceptance letter.
Program descriptions:
   Sunny Brown Memorial Scholarships for DeRidder High School: One scholarship per year is awarded to an outstanding senior at DeRidder High School on the basis of merit. Applicants must have an overall GPA of 3.5 and a minimum of 20 on the ACT test, demonstrate outstanding academic talent and exceptional school and/or community service, and plan to attend a four-year college or university. Recipients receive a $12,000 award.
   Sunny Brown Memorial Scholarships for the Arts: Scholarships are awarded to talented graduating high school seniors who are U.S. citizens to pursue study in the creative arts at colleges, universities, and other accredited professional companies or private institutions allowing them to study and train in their artistic fields. Recipients are selected on the basis of talent and achievement in the arts.
EIN: 954190924

425
Helen Ann Buckley Foundation
P.O. Box 2229
Sonoma, CA 95476-2229 (707) 938-2700

Foundation type: Operating foundation
Purpose: Scholarships to residents of Sonoma Valley, CA, for undergraduate and vocational education.
Financial data: Year ended 12/31/2011. Assets, $857,752 (M); Expenditures, $33,090; Total giving, $15,000; Grants to individuals, 5 grants totaling $5,000 (high: $1,500, low: $500).
Fields of interest: Vocational education, post-secondary; Higher education.
Type of support: Technical education support; Undergraduate support.
Application information: Applications accepted.
   Initial approach: Letter
   Deadline(s): Apr. 15
EIN: 686183386

426
Buddhist Film Foundation
2600 10th St., Ste. 409
Zaentz Media Ctr.
Berkeley, CA 94710-3104 (510) 601-5111
Contact: Gaetano Kazuo Maida, Exec. Dir.
E-mail: info@ibff.org; URL: http://www.buddhistfilmfoundation.org

Foundation type: Public charity
Purpose: Fiscal sponsorships to filmmakers concentrating on Buddhist cultures, practices, philosophy, personalities, history, art/aesthetics and interaction with other cultures, religions and philosophies.
Publications: Application guidelines.
Financial data: Year ended 12/31/2011. Assets, $60,530 (M); Expenditures, $126,097; Total

giving, $16,827. No monetary support given for fiscal sponsorships.
Fields of interest: Film/video; Arts, artist's services; Buddhism.
Type of support: Fiscal agent/sponsor.
Application information: Contact the foundation for additional information.
Program description:
   Fiscal Sponsorship: The foundation provides a fiscal sponsorship program to filmmakers seeking grants and donations for appropriate film projects from American funders. The program provides funders with tax-deductibility of their grant or donation; funds raised through the foundation are remitted to the filmmaker within seven business days, less a small administrative fee. In certain cases, for films of merit, the foundation may be able to serve as executive producer if such participation/identification will benefit the film and its potential for completion and distribution.
EIN: 943402911

427
Builder's Exchange of Santa Clara County Scholarship Fund
400 Reed St.
Santa Clara, CA 95050 (408) 727-4000

Foundation type: Independent foundation
Purpose: Scholarships to children and grandchildren of general members of the Builders Exchange of Santa Clara County, CA, and children and grandchildren of employees of member firms that have worked four hundred hours or more for a general member within the previous or current calendar year. Applicants must be pursuing a career in the construction and business industry at a college, university or trade school.
Financial data: Year ended 12/31/2011. Assets, $0 (M); Expenditures, $16,733; Total giving, $15,000; Grants to individuals, 9 grants totaling $15,000 (high: $3,000, low: $1,000).
Fields of interest: Vocational education; Business school/education; Business/industry.
Type of support: Technical education support; Undergraduate support.
Application information: Applications accepted. Application form required. Application form available on the grantmaker's web site. Interview required.
   Send request by: Mail
   Deadline(s): Mar. 30
   Final notification: Applicants notified in May
   Applicants should submit the following:
      1) Essay
      2) Transcripts
      3) Letter(s) of recommendation
   Additional information: Contact foundation for current application guidelines.
EIN: 770304794

428
Burks Charitable Trust
c/o Free & Accepted Masons
3444 E. Shields Ave., Ste. 247
Fresno, CA 93726-6919 (559) 222-8565

Foundation type: Independent foundation
Purpose: Financial assistance, including medical expenses, to needy families who are residents of CA.
Financial data: Year ended 10/31/2013. Assets, $106,649 (M); Expenditures, $4,248; Total giving, $2,986; Grant to an individual, 1 grant totaling $2,986.

Fields of interest: Health care; Family services; Economically disadvantaged.
Type of support: Grants for special needs.
Application information: Applications accepted.
   Initial approach: Letter
   Deadline(s): None
   Additional information: Application should outline financial need and reason for request.
EIN: 946362466

429
Alisa Ann Ruch Burn Foundation
2501 W. Burbank Blvd., Ste. 201
Burbank, CA 91505-2347 (818) 848-0223
Contact: Jennifer Radics, Exec. Dir.
FAX: (818) 848-0296; E-mail: info@aarbf.org; Toll-free tel.: (800)-242-BURN; E-Mail for Jennifer Radics: jradics@aarbf.org; URL: http://www.aarbf.org

Foundation type: Public charity
Purpose: Scholarships to residents of CA who have survived a burn injury.
Publications: Informational brochure; Informational brochure (including application guidelines); Newsletter.
Financial data: Year ended 12/31/2011. Assets, $736,309 (M); Expenditures, $777,179; Total giving, $12,270; Grants to individuals, totaling $12,270.
Fields of interest: Disasters, fire prevention/control.
Type of support: Scholarships—to individuals.
Application information: Applications accepted.
   Additional information: Contact the foundation for additional information.
EIN: 237162017

430
Burwen Education Foundation
1114 Blue Lake Sq.
Mountain View, CA 94040-4561 (650) 967-3403
Contact: Susan Jo Burwen, Secy.-Treas.

Foundation type: Operating foundation
Purpose: Scholarships only to graduating seniors from Mountain View, CA.
Financial data: Year ended 09/30/2012. Assets, $380,370 (M); Expenditures, $121,009; Total giving, $106,613; Grants to individuals, 22 grants totaling $78,783 (high: $15,750, low: $500).
Fields of interest: Higher education.
Type of support: Scholarships—to individuals.
Application information: Applications accepted. Application form required.
   Deadline(s): Sept. 15
   Applicants should submit the following:
      1) Letter(s) of recommendation
      2) FAFSA
      3) Transcripts
   Additional information: Application should also include college acceptance letter and SAT II and AP test scores.
EIN: 770560492

431
Busch Family Foundation
2532 Dupont Dr.
Irvine, CA 92612-1524
Application address: c/o Clinton High School, Attn.: Tim Wilson, Principal, 341 E. Michigan Ave., Clinton, MI 49236-9593

Foundation type: Independent foundation

Purpose: Scholarships to graduates of Clinton High School, MI. Living expense assistance to residence of CA.
Financial data: Year ended 12/31/2012. Assets, $40,425 (M); Expenditures, $38,847; Total giving, $27,525; Grants to individuals, 16 grants totaling $27,525 (high: $4,100, low: $125).
Fields of interest: Vocational education.
Type of support: Support to graduates or students of specific schools; Undergraduate support.
Application information: Application form required.
  Initial approach: Letter or telephone
  Deadline(s): Mid-Apr.
  Applicants should submit the following:
    1) Letter(s) of recommendation
    2) ACT
    3) SAT
    4) Transcripts
    5) Essay
  Additional information: Contact high school guidance office for current application guidelines. Application should include short biographical sketch.
EIN: 382671217

432
Butte Creek Foundation
14916 Eagle Ridge Dr.
Forest Ranch, CA 95942-9707
Contact: John L. Burghardt, Dir.

Foundation type: Independent foundation
Purpose: Scholarships to residents of Butte County, CA.
Financial data: Year ended 12/31/2012. Assets, $3,067,042 (M); Expenditures, $151,979; Total giving, $151,979; Grants to individuals, 3 grants totaling $1,400 (high: $500, low: $400).
Fields of interest: Higher education.
Type of support: Scholarships—to individuals.
Application information: Applications accepted.
  Initial approach: Letter
  Deadline(s): None
EIN: 680111634

433
Cabrillo College Foundation
6500 Soquel Dr.
Aptos, CA 95003-3119 (831) 479-6338
Contact: Melinda Silverstein, Exec. Dir.
FAX: (831) 477-5686;
E-mail: mesilver@cabrillo.edu; URL: http://www.cabrillo.edu/associations/foundation

Foundation type: Public charity
Purpose: Scholarships and financial support for students attending Cabrillo College, CA.
Financial data: Year ended 06/30/2012. Assets, $22,653,833 (M); Expenditures, $3,934,248; Total giving, $2,734,000; Grants to individuals, totaling $590,426.
Fields of interest: Higher education.
Type of support: Support to graduates or students of specific schools.
Application information: Applications accepted.
  Additional information: The foundation administers a large scholarship program to financially needy and academically promising students. Each scholarship has its own criteria to identify qualified recipients as determined by the donors. See web site for additional information.
EIN: 946121953

434
Cacique Foundation
14940 Proctor Ave.
City of Industry, CA 91744 (909) 274-4215

Foundation type: Company-sponsored foundation
Purpose: Scholarships to individuals for study at Mount San Antonio College, CA. The scholarship funds are administered by the Mount San Antonio College Foundation, and are available, in order of priority, to students who are teen mothers sponsored by the Buenanueva Foundation, employees of Cacique, Inc., and other Mount San Antonio College students who are single parents.
Financial data: Year ended 12/31/2012. Assets, $50,033 (M); Expenditures, $103,547; Total giving, $103,427.
Fields of interest: Single parents.
Type of support: Employee-related scholarships; Support to graduates or students of specific schools.
Application information: Applications accepted. Application form required.
  Initial approach: Letter
  Additional information: Scholarship information is available at the office of the Mount San Antonio College Foundation on the campus of Mount San Antonio College.
Company name: Cacique, Inc.
EIN: 954518246

435
Cahp Foundation
2030 V St.
Sacramento, CA 95818-1730 (916) 452-6751
Contact: Jon Hamm, C.E.O.

Foundation type: Public charity
Purpose: Scholarships to dependents of uniformed California Highway Patrol Officers for undergraduate education.
Financial data: Year ended 12/31/2012. Assets, $744,480 (M); Expenditures, $12,034; Total giving, $9,500; Grants to individuals, totaling $9,500.
Fields of interest: Higher education.
Type of support: Employee-related scholarships; Undergraduate support.
Application information: Contact foundation for current application deadline/guidelines.
EIN: 942716339

436
The Cain Family Foundation
195 Oaks Ct.
Tulare, CA 93274

Foundation type: Independent foundation
Purpose: Scholarships to graduates of Tulare, CA high schools. Also, medical grants to needy residents of the Tulare, CA area.
Financial data: Year ended 06/30/2013. Assets, $0 (M); Expenditures, $10; Total giving, $0.
Type of support: Support to graduates or students of specific schools.
Application information: Applications accepted.
  Initial approach: Letter
  Additional information: Contact foundation for current application guidelines.
EIN: 770455208

437
Cal Humanities
(formerly California Council for the Humanities, also known as CCH)
312 Sutter St., Ste. 601
San Francisco, CA 94108-4371 (415) 391-1474
Contact: Jessica Sanchez, Exec. Asst.
FAX: (415) 391-1312; E-mail: info@calhum.org; URL: http://www.calhum.org

Foundation type: Public charity
Purpose: Awards for projects that document aspects of life in CA in film, photography or story form.
Publications: Application guidelines; Biennial report; Financial statement; Grants list; Informational brochure; Newsletter; Occasional report.
Financial data: Year ended 12/31/2011. Assets, $1,310,237 (M); Expenditures, $3,053,895; Total giving, $989,989. Awards/prizes amount not specified.
Fields of interest: Film/video; Radio; Photography; Literature; Historical activities.
Type of support: Program development; Grants to individuals; Project support.
Application information: Applications accepted. Application form required. Application form available on the grantmaker's web site.
  Send request by: Online
  Deadline(s): June 15 for California Story Fund, Apr. 29 for California Documentary Project
  Applicants should submit the following:
    1) Curriculum vitae
    2) Budget Information
    3) Work samples
  Additional information: Application should also include letter of interest from a broadcaster or distributor.
Program description:
  California Documentary Project: This grants program supports documentary film, radio, and new media productions that enhance understanding of California and its cultures, peoples, and histories. Projects must use the humanities to provide context, depth, and perspective and be suitable for California and national audiences through broadcast and/or distribution. CDP grants support projects at the research and development, production, and public engagement stages. Research and Development grant awards range up to $10,000. Production grant awards range up to $50,000.
EIN: 942952469

438
Cal Poly Pomona Foundation, Inc.
3801 W. Temple Ave., Bldg. 55
Pomona, CA 91768-2557 (909) 869-2950
Contact: G. Paul Storey, Exec. Dir.
FAX: (909) 869-4549;
E-mail: gpstorey@csupomona.edu; URL: http://foundation.csupomona.edu/

Foundation type: Public charity
Purpose: Grants and scholarships to students of California State Polytechnic University, Pomona for postsecondary education.
Publications: Annual report; Financial statement; Newsletter.
Financial data: Year ended 06/30/2012. Assets, $168,033,586 (M); Expenditures, $51,878,683; Total giving, $7,054,167; Grants to individuals, totaling $3,123,295.
Fields of interest: Higher education.

Type of support: Support to graduates or students of specific schools.
Application information: Applications not accepted.
  Additional information: Contributes only to students of Cal Poly Pomona; unsolicited requests for funds not considered or acknowledged.
EIN: 952417645

439
Cal State East Bay Educational Foundation
25800 Carlos Bee Blvd., Ste. 908
Hayward, CA 94542-3004 (510) 885-4170

Foundation type: Public charity
Purpose: Scholarship and financial assistance to selected students attending California State University, East Bay, CA for higher education.
Financial data: Year ended 06/30/2012. Assets, $15,108,548 (M); Expenditures, $1,216,891; Total giving, $564,359.
Fields of interest: Higher education.
Type of support: Support to graduates or students of specific schools.
Application information: Unsolicited requests for funds not considered or acknowledged.
EIN: 946128893

440
Calcot-Seitz Foundation
P.O. Box 259
Bakersfield, CA 93302-0259

Foundation type: Independent foundation
Purpose: Scholarships to students from cotton-producing areas in CA and AZ to pursue four-year degrees in agriculture.
Financial data: Year ended 08/31/2013. Assets, $768,068 (M); Expenditures, $14,054; Total giving, $12,150; Grants to individuals, 63 grants totaling $11,150 (high: $1,350, low: -$30,800).
Fields of interest: Agriculture.
Type of support: Scholarships—to individuals.
Application information: Applications accepted. Application form required. Interview required.
  Deadline(s): Mar. 31
  Applicants should submit the following:
    1) Photograph
    2) Letter(s) of recommendation
    3) Essay
    4) Transcripts
    5) GPA
EIN: 953434180

441
California Academy of Family Physicians Foundation
1520 Pacific Ave.
San Francisco, CA 94109-2627 (415) 345-8667
Contact: Callie Langton Ph.D., Exec. Dir.
E-mail for scholarships: dsakharova@familydocs.org
FAX: (415) 345-8668;
E-mail: cafpf@cafpfoundation.org; URL: http://www.cafpfoundation.org/

Foundation type: Public charity
Purpose: Travel grants for CA medical students to attend the AAFP National Conference for Family Medicine Residents and Medical Students. One grant for a medical student to attend the annual Political Leadership Institute (PLI) of the American Medical Student Association. Additionally, full scholarships to two students and two family medicine residents every year.
Publications: Annual report; Newsletter.
Financial data: Year ended 12/31/2011. Assets, $2,991,797 (M); Expenditures, $421,932; Total giving, $4,000.
Fields of interest: Health care.
Type of support: Travel grants; Doctoral support.
Application information: Applications accepted. Application form required. Application form available on the grantmaker's web site.
  Initial approach: Letter or e-mail
  Deadline(s): May 15
  Final notification: Recipients notified May 25
  Applicants should submit the following:
    1) Curriculum vitae
    2) Essay
EIN: 942938597

442
California Association for Bilingual Education
16033 E. San Bernardino Rd.
Covina, CA 91722-3900 (626) 814-4441
FAX: (626) 814-4640;
E-mail: info@bilingualeducation.org; URL: http://www.bilingualeducation.org

Foundation type: Public charity
Purpose: Scholarships only to members of CABE who currently work as teacher assistants/paraprofessionals to pursue a career as a bilingual teacher.
Publications: Application guidelines.
Financial data: Year ended 06/30/2012. Assets, $1,772,056 (M); Expenditures, $2,760,386; Total giving, $22,500; Grants to individuals, totaling $22,500.
Fields of interest: Teacher school/education.
Type of support: Scholarships—to individuals; Awards/prizes.
Application information: Applications accepted. Application form required. Application form available on the grantmaker's web site.
  Deadline(s): Nov. 2
  Additional information: Applications and other documentation should be submitted to your local chapter president or CABE headquarters. Download application from web site.
Program description:
  Teachership Award: The program is a yearly endowment to award teacherships to 10 outstanding paraprofessional CABE members who are pursuing their bilingual teaching credentials. Each awardee will receive $2,000 from CABE Teachership funds. The structure of the teachership is designed to involve CABE chapters directly in the process. Each chapter has the opportunity to nominate one paraprofessional for a teachership award. These nominees applications are then sent to the Region Representatives of each region. Then, the Region Representatives form a committee to review all nominees and then select two to be that region's teachership recipients.
EIN: 953151449

443
California Association of Realtors Scholarship Foundation
525 S. Virgil Ave.
Los Angeles, CA 90020-1403 (213) 739-8200
FAX: (213) 480-7724; E-mail: scholarship@car.org;
URL: http://www.car.org/aboutus/carscholarships/

Foundation type: Public charity
Purpose: Scholarships to students enrolled at a CA college or university for careers related to real estate.
Publications: Application guidelines.
Financial data: Year ended 12/31/2011. Assets, $1,230,728 (M); Expenditures, $61,955; Total giving, $47,000; Grants to individuals, totaling $47,000.
Fields of interest: Higher education.
Type of support: Scholarships—to individuals.
Application information: Applications accepted. Application form required. Application form available on the grantmaker's web site.
  Initial approach: Telephone or e-mail
  Deadline(s): May 2
  Applicants should submit the following:
    1) Transcripts
    2) Letter(s) of recommendation
    3) Financial information
    4) Essay
  Additional information: Faxed or incomplete application not accepted.
Program description:
  Scholarships: The program awards scholarships of $2,000 each to students attending a two-year college, and $4,000 to students attending a four-year college or university.
EIN: 237230340

444
California Bar Foundation
(formerly Foundation of the State Bar of California)
180 Howard St.
San Francisco, CA 94105-1614 (415) 856-0780
Contact: Sonia Gonzales, Exec. Dir.
FAX: (415) 856-0788;
E-mail: info@calbarfoundation.org; E-Mail for Sonia Gonzales: sgonzales@calbarfoundation.org; Tel. for Sonia Gonzales: (415) 856-0780 ext. 303;
URL: http://www.calbarfoundation.org/

Foundation type: Public charity
Purpose: Scholarships to law school students of CA committed to public service meet the financial burden for a legal career serving the community.
Publications: Annual report; Grants list.
Financial data: Year ended 12/31/2011. Assets, $1,721,917 (M); Expenditures, $1,005,142; Total giving, $595,658; Grants to individuals, totaling $297,050.
Fields of interest: Law school/education.
Type of support: Scholarships—to individuals.
Application information: Applications accepted. Application form required. Application form available on the grantmaker's web site.
  Send request by: Mail, e-mail or fax
  Deadline(s): Mar. 16 for Public Interest Scholarship, June 15 for Diversity Scholarship
  Applicants should submit the following:
    1) Transcripts
    2) Letter(s) of recommendation
    3) Resume
  Additional information: See web site for additional information.

Program descriptions:

Diversity Scholarship Awards: Awards of $7,500 recognize incoming first year law students with financial need who demonstrate a desire to make a positive impact as a community leader. The scholarship is designed to pay for tuition, fees, books and other related education expenses.

Public Interest Scholarship: Awards of up to $7,500 recognize law students who demonstrate superior academic achievement, a sustained and extensive commitment to public service, often while overcoming serious personal hardships and obstacles, an intent to pursue a career in public interest law, and financial need. The scholarship helps pay the cost of obtaining a law school education at a California law school, including tuition, fees, books and other related education expenses. Candidates must be nominated by their law school.

Rosenthal Bar Exam Scholarship: Scholarships to 15 aspiring public interest lawyers from California law schools to assist with the costs associated with taking the California Bar Exam. The foundation gives $3,500 each to all 15 scholarship recipients. The top five recipients also receive $2,000 cash awards. Nominated by their law schools, the 15 recipients have demonstrated a commitment to public service, including hundreds of volunteer hours at legal clinics and other nonprofit organizations and past employment in a variety of community service settings and impressive academic records.
EIN: 943104546

445
California Community Foundation
221 S. Figueroa St., Ste. 400
Los Angeles, CA 90012 (213) 413-4130
FAX: (213) 383-2046; E-mail: info@calfund.org;
Grants information e-mail:
grantsmanager@calfund.org; URL: http://www.calfund.org/

Foundation type: Community foundation
Purpose: Scholarships to residents of the greater Los Angeles County, CA, area for higher education. Grants to artists and teachers of the Los Angeles, CA area.
Publications: Application guidelines; Annual report; Financial statement; Informational brochure; Newsletter.
Financial data: Year ended 06/30/2013. Assets, $1,315,930,000 (M); Expenditures, $184,177,000; Total giving, $164,428,000. Scholarships—to individuals amount not specified. Grants to individuals amount not specified.
Fields of interest: Visual arts; Performing arts; Literature; Arts, artist's services; Higher education.
Type of support: Program development; Fellowships; Scholarships—to individuals; Support to graduates or students of specific schools; Undergraduate support.
Application information: Applications accepted. Application form required. Application form available on the grantmaker's web site.
    Deadline(s): Varies
    Additional information: See web site for guidelines for grants and scholarships.
Program descriptions:
    CCF Fellowship for Visual Arts: Grants are awarded annually for L.A.-based emerging and mid-career visual artists. Awardees receive $15,000 to $20,000 grants and professional development support.
    Fedco Teacher Grants: Grants are awarded annually to L.A.-based K-12 teachers in public and private school for experientially-based teaching approaches within their classrooms.
    Scholarships: One of the largest scholarship fund managers in Los Angeles, CCF awards more than $3 million annually to students who seek postsecondary education and workforce training as a means to build a brighter future. CCF has helped to create educational pathways for the most vulnerable student populations for decades. Working with donors, selection committees and partner institutions comprised of high schools, colleges, universities and nonprofit organizations, CCF administers more than 150 high-quality scholarship programs and coordinates student awards for more than 1,200 deserving students in Los Angeles and beyond.
EIN: 953510055

446
California Council on Science and Technology
5005 La Mart Dr., Ste. 105
Riverside, CA 92507-5991 (951) 682-8701
FAX: (951) 682-8702; URL: http://www.ccst.us

Foundation type: Public charity
Purpose: One-year fellowships to CA-based science and technology experts to assist the California state legislature on science and technology-related issues.
Publications: Application guidelines; Annual report; Newsletter; Occasional report.
Financial data: Year ended 12/31/2011. Assets, $5,317,435 (M); Expenditures, $1,757,751.
Fields of interest: Management/technical assistance; Information services; Science.
Type of support: Fellowships.
Application information: Applications accepted. Application form required. Application form available on the grantmaker's web site.
    Send request by: On-line
    Deadline(s): Mar. 31
    Applicants should submit the following:
        1) Essay
        2) Resume
        3) Curriculum vitae
        4) Letter(s) of recommendation
Program description:
    Policy Fellowships: These fellowships place professional scientists and engineers, who are interested in improving the interface between science and legislative decision-making and who want to learn more about the public policy decision-making process, in the California State Legislature for one-year appointments. Fellowships enable participants to work hands-on with policy-makers to develop solutions to complex scientific and technical issues facing California through their interaction with the legislative process.
EIN: 943093624

447
California Dental Association Foundation
(formerly California Dental Association Research Fund, also known as CDA Foundation)
1201 K St., Ste. 1511
Sacramento, CA 95814-3925 (916) 554-4905
Contact: Cathy Mudge, Exec. Dir.
FAX: (916) 498-6182;
E-mail: foundationinfo@cda.org; E-Mail for Cathy Mudge: cathy.mudge@cda.org; Toll Free Tel.: (800) 232-7645; URL: http://www.cdafoundation.org

Foundation type: Public charity

Purpose: Scholarships to students who are interested in becoming dental hygienists, dental assistants, or dental laboratory technicians and are enrolled in state approved programs primarily in CA.
Publications: Application guidelines; Annual report; Grants list; Informational brochure; Newsletter.
Financial data: Year ended 12/31/2011. Assets, $2,559,603 (M); Expenditures, $3,344,832; Total giving, $806,902; Grants to individuals, totaling $274,500.
Fields of interest: Dental school/education; Dental care; Hispanics/Latinos; Economically disadvantaged.
Type of support: Emergency funds; Professorships; Grants to individuals; Scholarships—to individuals; Postgraduate support; Doctoral support.
Application information: Applications accepted. Application form required. Application form available on the grantmaker's web site.
    Initial approach: Application
    Deadline(s): Varies
    Additional information: Application must be submitted on-line only and should include financial information; See web site for additional application information.
Program descriptions:
    Allied Dental Student Scholarship: This scholarship program provides educational grants to students enrolled in dental hygiene, dental assisting, registered dental assisting, or dental lab tech programs; the program also provides dental hygienist, dental assistant, registered dental assistant, and dental lab tech students with scholarships toward completing their education. Awards are up to $1,000.
    Bettie Underwood Dental Assisting Scholarship: Provides scholarships for dental assisting students enrolled in California dental assisting programs. Scholarship awards of $1,000 will be based on financial need, community service and leadership, and achievement.
    CDA Foundation Humanitarian Award: The award recognizes California dentists who have distinguished themselves by a lifetime of outstanding, unselfish leadership, and contributions to fellow human beings in the field of dentistry, through the dedication of extraordinary time and professional skills, to improve the oral health of underserved populations in California, the United States, or abroad. Nominees must hold a California dental license. Winners receive a $2,500 contribution to the nonprofit of the winner's choice.
    CDA Foundation Relief Fund: The fund renders financial aid to dentists, their dependents, or dependents of deceased dentists if an accidental injury, advanced age, physically-debilitating illness, medically-related, natural disaster, or condition prevents them from gainful employment and results in undue financial strain.
    Dental Student Scholarship: Provides educational grants of $5,000 to dental students enrolled full time in a California dental school.
    Dr. Arthur A. Dugoni Faculty Award: The award supports individuals who contribute to the scholarly and creative activities of the school through direct contact with students, and is available to new faculty members, junior faculty members, visiting scientists, and guest lecturers who hold full- or part-time teaching positions affiliated with California's dental schools. Awards are $5,000 per faculty member per year.
    Latinos for Dental Careers Scholarship: Provides ten $1,000 awards to increase the number of Latinos in the dental profession.
    Student Loan Repayment Grant: Provides educational grants and scholarships to dental students (due to graduate in the next six months), recent graduates (within the last three years), and

students enrolled in dental auxiliary programs. This grants provides up to $35,000 per year for three years (for total of up to $105,000), and is directly applied toward the recipient's academic financial account in exchange for providing dental services to the underserved populations for the grant period.
EIN: 680411536

448

California Farm Bureau Scholarship Foundation
2300 River Plaza Dr.
Sacramento, CA 95833-3293 (916) 561-5500
Contact: for Scholarships: Darlene Licciardo
FAX: (916) 561-5695; E-mail: cfbf@cfbf.com;
URL: http://cfbf.com/programs/

Foundation type: Public charity
Purpose: Scholarships to undergraduate students entering or attending a four-year accredited college or university in CA, pursuing a career in the agricultural industry.
Financial data: Year ended 07/31/2012. Assets, $4,319,614 (M); Expenditures, $209,739; Total giving, $203,250; Grants to individuals, totaling $203,250.
Fields of interest: Agriculture.
Type of support: Undergraduate support.
Application information: Applications accepted. Application form required. Interview required.
  Deadline(s): Mar. 1
  Applicants should submit the following:
    1) Transcripts
    2) Letter(s) of recommendation
    3) GPA
    4) Essay
  Additional information: Scholarships are awarded based on academic achievement, career goals, extracurricular activities, determination, leadership skills and a commitment to study agriculture.
EIN: 946070123

449

California Federation of Teachers - AFT 8004
2550 N. Hollywood Way, Ste. 400
Burbank, CA 91505-5008 (818) 843-8226
Application address: Raoul Teilhet Scholarship Program, California Federation of Teachers, 2900 Bristol St., Ste. C107, Costa Mesa, CA 92626, tel.: (714) 754-6638
FAX: (818) 843-4662; URL: http://www.cft.org/

Foundation type: Public charity
Purpose: Scholarships to children and dependents of federation members who are enrolled in two- and four-year courses of study.
Publications: Application guidelines; Informational brochure; Newsletter.
Financial data: Year ended 12/31/2011. Assets, $23,068,207 (M); Expenditures, $24,019,392; Total giving, $590,794; Grants to individuals, totaling $115,000.
Fields of interest: Higher education; Labor unions/organizations.
Type of support: Scholarships—to individuals.
Application information: Applications accepted. Application form required. Application form available on the grantmaker's web site.
  Initial approach: Application

  Send request by: Mail
  Deadline(s): Jan. 10 for high school seniors, July 1 for continuing college students for Raoul Teilhet Scholarship
  Final notification: High school seniors notified by Mar. 31, college students notified by Sept. 20
  Applicants should submit the following:
    1) Financial information
    2) Transcripts
    3) Essay
  Additional information: See web site for additional program description.
EIN: 941271864

450

California HealthCare Foundation
1438 Webster St., Ste. 400
Oakland, CA 94612-3206 (510) 238-1040
Contact: Lisa Kang, Dir., Grants Admin.
FAX: (510) 238-1388; E-mail: info@chcf.org; E-mail for questions regarding Letters of Inquiry: grants@chcf.org; Additional address: 1415 L St., No. 820, Sacramento, CA 95814; tel.: (916) 329-4540; fax: (916) 329-4545; URL: http://www.chcf.org

Foundation type: Public charity
Purpose: A two-year fellowship (CHCF Health Care Leadership Program) to clinically trained health care professionals residing in CA.
Publications: Application guidelines; Informational brochure (including application guidelines); Occasional report; IRS Form 990 or 990-PF printed copy available upon request.
Financial data: Year ended 02/28/2013. Assets, $716,354,350 (M); Expenditures, $52,443,464; Total giving, $31,775,896.
Fields of interest: Health care.
Type of support: Fellowships.
Application information:
  Initial approach: Letter
  Send request by: E-mail
  Deadline(s): None
  Final notification: Applicants notified six to eight weeks after submission of the letter of intent
  Applicants should submit the following:
    1) Budget Information
    2) Proposal
EIN: 954523231

451

The California Highway Patrol 11-99 Foundation
2244 N. State College Blvd.
Fullerton, CA 92831-1361 (714) 529-1199
Contact: Steve Harrington, C.E.O.
Scholarship e-mail: scholarship@chp11-99.org
FAX: (714) 529-1191; E-mail: info@chp11-99.org; URL: http://www.chp11-99.org

Foundation type: Public charity
Purpose: Scholarships to sons, daughters, and spouses of current, retired and Fallen in the Line of Duty California Highway Patrol employees who have graduated from or planning to graduate from high school. Assistance to persons employed with the California Highway Patrol for hardships connected with a death, injury or illness to themselves or a family member.
Publications: Application guidelines; Grants list.
Financial data: Year ended 12/31/2011. Assets, $27,218,802 (M); Expenditures, $2,464,653; Total giving, $1,446,252; Grants to individuals, totaling $1,446,252.
Fields of interest: Higher education; Economically disadvantaged.

Type of support: Scholarships—to individuals; Grants for special needs.
Application information: Applications accepted. Application form required. Application form available on the grantmaker's web site.
  Deadline(s): Mar. 15 for Scholarships
  Final notification: Recipients notified in June for scholarships
  Applicants should submit the following:
    1) GPA
    2) Transcripts
    3) SAR
    4) Letter(s) of recommendation
  Additional information: See web site for further application information.
Program descriptions:
  Broderick Crawford Benefits Program: The foundation provides emergency financial assistance to California Highway Patrol (CHP) employees or their families facing an emergency situation, such as death of a spouse or child, emergency medical expenses, or other unforeseen financial hardship.
  Scholarship Program: The foundation provides scholarships to children of California Highway Patrol employees who seek higher education at a college, university, or trade school.
EIN: 956530738

452

California Human Development Corporation
3315 Airway Dr.
Santa Rosa, CA 95403-2005 (707) 523-1155
Contact: Chris Paige, C.E.O., Opers.
FAX: (707) 523-3776;
E-mail: info@cahumandevelopment.org; E-mail For Chris Paige:
chris.paige@cahumandevelopment.org;
URL: http://www.cahumandevelopment.org/

Foundation type: Public charity
Purpose: Grants to low-income individuals and families of northern CA to help them secure affordable housing, job training and employment, and other services.
Financial data: Year ended 06/30/2012. Assets, $9,023,468 (M); Expenditures, $12,769,181; Total giving, $474,278; Grants to individuals, totaling $474,278.
Fields of interest: Economically disadvantaged.
Type of support: Grants for special needs.
Application information: Contact the corporation or see web site for additional information for assistance.
EIN: 941653023

453

California Japanese American Alumni Association
c/o Emiko Yamada
1060 Tahoe Dr.
Belmont, CA 94002-3011 (510) 559-9277
Contact: Katherine Yoshii, Tr.
E-mail: scholarships@cjaaa.org; Application address: P.O. Box 15235, San Francisco, CA 94115-0235, tel.: (510) 559-9277; URL: http://www.cjaaa.org

Foundation type: Independent foundation
Purpose: Scholarships to Japanese-American students enrolled at one of the nine University of California campuses for undergraduate or graduate education.

Financial data: Year ended 06/30/2013. Assets, $325,857 (M); Expenditures, $1,973; Total giving, $0.
Fields of interest: Asians/Pacific Islanders.
International interests: Japan.
Type of support: Support to graduates or students of specific schools; Graduate support; Undergraduate support.
Application information: Applications accepted. Application form required. Application form available on the grantmaker's web site.
 Initial approach: Letter
 Send request by: Mail
 Deadline(s): May 1
 Applicants should submit the following:
  1) Financial information
  2) Letter(s) of recommendation
  3) Essay
  4) Transcripts
 Additional information: Application should also include two letters of reference, academic achievement, community and college activities. See web site for additional guidelines.
EIN: 941179725

454
California Job's Daughters Foundation, Inc.
303 W. Lincoln Ave., Ste. 210
Anaheim, CA 92805-2928 (714) 491-4994
Scholarship address: Betty Klotz, Schol. Chair., 1228 Moss Rock Ct., Santa Rosa, CA 95404-2532
E-mail: cajdfoundation@hotmail.com; URL: http://www.cajdfoundation.org

Foundation type: Public charity
Purpose: Scholarships to California Job's Daughters graduating from high school or who have graduated and wish to further their education.
Publications: Application guidelines.
Financial data: Year ended 12/31/2011. Assets, $410,885 (M); Expenditures, $43,681; Total giving, $35,092.
Fields of interest: Vocational education, post-secondary; Higher education.
Type of support: Scholarships—to individuals.
Application information: Applications accepted. Application form required.
 Initial approach: Letter or e-mail
 Deadline(s): Mar. 15
 Applicants should submit the following:
  1) Transcripts
  2) Letter(s) of recommendation
EIN: 330692562

455
California Masonic Foundation
1111 California St.
San Francisco, CA 94108-2252 (415) 776-7000
Contact: Arthur H. Weiss, Pres.
FAX: (415) 776-7170;
E-mail: foundation@Freemason.org; URL: http://www.freemason.org

Foundation type: Public charity
Purpose: Undergraduate scholarships to financially needy high school seniors who are U.S. citizens, and current residents of CA for at least one year, for study at accredited two- or four-year college or university.
Publications: Application guidelines.
Financial data: Year ended 10/31/2011. Assets, $21,679,517 (M); Expenditures, $1,458,977;

Total giving, $851,409; Grants to individuals, totaling $412,027.
Fields of interest: Higher education.
Type of support: Undergraduate support.
Application information: Application form required. Interview required.
 Deadline(s): Feb. 15
 Applicants should submit the following:
  1) Letter(s) of recommendation
  2) Essay
  3) SAT
  4) Transcripts
 Additional information: Application should also include name of college where accepted, parents' and students' latest tax returns. Applicant must demonstrate financial need. See web site for additional application information.
Program description:
 Scholarships: In addition to its general scholarship fund, the foundation manages other scholarship programs that grant awards to CA residents. All applications will be evaluated on academic standing, financial need, and student's essay. All scholarships are renewable annually. Applicants should submit only one application for consideration in all scholarship funds. While not required, some preference is given to applicants with Masonic relationships and/or Masonic youth group membership. See web site for a listing of the various scholarships.
EIN: 237013074

456
California New Car Dealers Scholarship Foundation
(formerly California New Car Dealers Association Scholarship Foundation)
1415 L St., Ste. 700
Sacramento, CA 95814 (916) 441-2599
Contact: Bruce Sedlezky, Dir.
FAX: (916) 441-5612; URL: http://www.cncda.org/scholarship/scholarship.html

Foundation type: Independent foundation
Purpose: Scholarships to worthy high school graduates of CA pursuing a degree in automotive technology or automotive management at postsecondary educational institutions.
Financial data: Year ended 12/31/2012. Assets, $880,732 (M); Expenditures, $43,100; Total giving, $34,200; Grants to individuals, 137 grants totaling $34,200 (high: $1,600, low: $125).
Fields of interest: Higher education; Scholarships/financial aid; Business/industry.
Type of support: Undergraduate support.
Application information: Applications accepted. Application form required.
 Initial approach: Letter
 Send request by: Mail
 Deadline(s): July 2
 Applicants should submit the following:
  1) Class rank
  2) Transcripts
  3) GPA
  4) Financial information
 Additional information: Funds are paid directly to the educational institution on behalf of the recipient.
Program description:
 Auto Technician Scholarship: Scholarships to students who are legal residents of the U.S. and reside in California. Students must be high school graduates or the holder of a high school general equivalency diploma and be enrolled in or accepted for enrollment in a postsecondary mechanical automotive technician training program. Applicants

must intend to pursue a career as an auto technician at a California franchised new car dealership. Scholarship recipients must maintain a 2.5 GPA on a 4.0 scale.
EIN: 954454279

457
California Scottish Rite Foundation
2100 N. Broadway, Ste. 350
Santa Ana, CA 92706 (714) 547-7325
Contact: Frank Loui, Pres. and Chair.
FAX: (714) 541-7602; E-mail: info@casrf.org;
URL: http://www.casr-foundation.org

Foundation type: Public charity
Purpose: Scholarships to graduate and undergraduate college students of CA, pursuing higher education.
Publications: Application guidelines.
Financial data: Year ended 06/30/2012. Assets, $41,711,814 (M); Expenditures, $4,001,374; Total giving, $144,000; Grants to individuals, totaling $144,000.
Fields of interest: Higher education.
Type of support: Scholarships—to individuals; Graduate support; Undergraduate support.
Application information: Applications accepted. Application form required.
 Send request by: Mail
 Deadline(s): Feb. 15 for Miller scholarship; Feb. 14 for all others
 Applicants should submit the following:
  1) Letter(s) of recommendation
  2) Transcripts
 Additional information: See web site for additional application guidelines.
Program descriptions:
 Baldwin Scholarships: This scholarship is for students who are California residents pursuing a Masters or Doctorate degree in the field of foreign service, public school administration, or speech language pathology at a fully accredited California graduate school. The total amount of scholarship is $6,000 for one year.
 Lister Scholarship: Scholarship in the amount of $2,000 per year, for a maximum of four years, paid directly to the student, who is a California resident seeking a college degree as an undergraduate student. Grantees must be California young men who are blood relatives of a California Mason and or past or present DeMolay, a citizen of the U.S. and a legal resident of California.
 Ruppert Scholarship: This scholarship is in the amount of $2,000 per year for a maximum of four years, paid directly to the student. Applicant must be a California resident aged 17 to 25 seeking a college degree as an undergraduate at any fully accredited college or university nationwide. This scholarship is only for study in medicine, engineering forestry or public school administration.
 Stovall Scholarship: Grants a total of $6,000 per year, until graduation, and for a maximum of two years to a California resident pursuing a Masters Degree in the field of Public Administration at any accredited college or university located in CA offering the required course of study.
EIN: 946078728

458
California State Summer School Arts Foundation

39 E. Walnut St., No. 8
Pasadena, CA 91103-3832 (626) 584-4055
Contact: Margaret Burt, Exec. Dir.
URL: http://www.cssa.org

Foundation type: Public charity
Purpose: Scholarships for talented and motivated students who attend the CA State Summer School for the Arts pursuing a career in the arts.
Financial data: Year ended 06/30/2012. Assets, $3,603,666 (M); Expenditures, $626,057; Total giving, $441,324; Grants to individuals, totaling $261,324.
Fields of interest: Arts education.
Type of support: Scholarships—to individuals; Support to graduates or students of specific schools.
Application information: Applications accepted. Application form required.
  Deadline(s): Feb. 28
  Additional information: Financial aid is available only to California residents. Unsolicited requests for funds not considered or acknowledged.
EIN: 954111128

459
California State University, Fullerton, Philanthropic Foundation

2600 E. Nutwood Ave., Ste. 850
Fullerton, CA 92831-5455 (657) 278-2786
Contact: Gregory J. Saks, Exec. Dir.
E-mail: foundation@fullerton.edu; *URL:* http://www.fullerton.edu/foundation/about/index.asp

Foundation type: Public charity
Purpose: Scholarships to deserving students for attendance at California State University, Fullerton, CA pursuing and completing a higher education.
Publications: Annual report.
Financial data: Year ended 06/30/2012. Assets, $61,078,982 (M); Expenditures, $8,092,754; Total giving, $3,000,954; Grants to individuals, totaling $1,000.
Fields of interest: Higher education.
Type of support: Support to graduates or students of specific schools.
Application information: Selection is based on need, merit or to a student for a particular academic experience.
EIN: 330567945

460
California Teachers Association Disaster Relief Fund

1705 Murchison Dr.
Burlingame, CA 94010-4504 (650) 697-1400
Additional info.: Regional Resource Center, Santa Fe Springs CTA office, tel.: (562) 942-7970 or the FACT Foundation office, tel.: (818) 729-8105
URL: http://www.cta.org/About-CTA/CTA-Foundation/Disaster-Relief/index.aspx

Foundation type: Public charity
Purpose: Disaster relief assistance for members of the California Teachers Association impacted by natural disaster and other disasters.
Financial data: Year ended 08/31/2011. Assets, $2,384,282 (M); Expenditures, $97,469; Total giving, $47,450; Grants to individuals, totaling $47,450.
Fields of interest: Disasters, preparedness/services.

Type of support: Grants to individuals.
Application information: Applications accepted. Application form required. Application form available on the grantmaker's web site.
Program descriptions:
  Catastrophic Damage Grant: Recipients of the Standard Grant may be eligible for up to another $1,500 if damages exceed $50,000.
  School Site Grant: Members may receive up to $500 for damage to their classroom.
  Standard Grant: CTA members may receive up to $1,500 for significant economic hardship related to damage to their primary residence, displacement or disruption in required utilities.
  Temporary Displacement Grant: Grants of up to $500 may be available for members who are displaced from their primary residence as the result of a disaster, but do not meet the requirements for a Standard Grant.
EIN: 710891612

461
The California Wellness Foundation

6320 Canoga Ave., Ste. 1700
Woodland Hills, CA 91367-2565 (818) 702-1900
Contact: Amy Scop, Dir., Grants Mgmt.
FAX: (818) 702-1999; *E-mail:* tcwf@tcwf.org; Branch Office address: 575 Market St., Ste. 1850, San Francisco, CA 94105, tel.: (415) 908-3000, fax: (415) 908-3001; *URL:* http://www.calwellness.org/

Foundation type: Independent foundation
Purpose: Awards to honorees as an acknowledgement of their commitment to prevent violence and promote peace in their communities, and of their commitment to increasing California's health care workforce and its diversity.
Publications: Application guidelines; Annual report; Annual report (including application guidelines); Grants list; Informational brochure; Informational brochure (including application guidelines); Newsletter (including application guidelines); Occasional report.
Financial data: Year ended 12/31/2012. Assets, $847,982,323 (M); Expenditures, $51,454,654; Total giving, $39,550,105; Grants to individuals, 6 grants totaling $150,000 (high: $25,000, low: $25,000).
Fields of interest: Health care; Crime/violence prevention.
Type of support: Awards/prizes.
Application information: Applications not accepted.
  Additional information: Applications not accepted.
EIN: 954292101

462
Cancer for College

981 Park Ctr. Dr.
Vista, CA 92081-8533 (760) 599-5096
Contact: Greg Flores, Director of Operations
FAX: (760) 599-9208;
E-mail: info@cancerforcollege.org; Additional address: 4508 53rd Ave. N.E., Seattle, WA 98105-3833; E-mail: cancerforcollege@hotmail.com; *URL:* http://www.cancerforcollege.org

Foundation type: Public charity
Purpose: College scholarships to current and former cancer patients who are currently attending either a four year accredited university, junior college and/or graduate school.

Financial data: Year ended 12/31/2011. Assets, $1,515,630 (M); Expenditures, $676,142; Total giving, $258,357; Grants to individuals, totaling $258,357.
Fields of interest: Vocational education, post-secondary; Higher education; College (community/junior); Cancer.
Type of support: Scholarships—to individuals; Graduate support.
Application information: Applications accepted. Application form required. Application form available on the grantmaker's web site.
  Deadline(s): May 1
  Final notification: Recipients notified within three weeks of submission of application
  Additional information: Application must include two letters of recommendation, a copy of acceptance letter, a personal statement and a summary of cancer treatment.
Program description:
  Scholarships: Scholarships are awarded to current and former cancer patients who are currently attending a four year accredited university, junior college, and/or graduate school. Scholarships are also awarded to amputees regardless if they are cancer survivors. Scholarships applicants must already be accepted to a university and/or attending a junior college. Scholarship amounts vary, ranging from $250 one-time scholarships to four-year perpetual scholarships of larger dollar amounts.
EIN: 931144756

463
Iris & B. Gerald Cantor Foundation

(formerly The B. G. Cantor Art Foundation)
1180 South Beverly Dr., Ste. 321
Los Angeles, CA 90035-1154
Contact: Judith Sobol, Exec. Dir.
E-mail: jsobol@ibgcf.org; *URL:* http://www.cantorfoundation.org

Foundation type: Independent foundation
Purpose: Art history research centered on Auguste Rodin.
Financial data: Year ended 04/30/2012. Assets, $41,038,963 (M); Expenditures, $737,173; Total giving, $1,307,202.
Type of support: Publication; Research; Foreign applicants; Travel grants.
Application information: Applications accepted. Application form not required.
  Initial approach: E-mail
  Send request by: Mail
  Copies of proposal: 10
  Deadline(s): None
  Final notification: Applicants are informed of a decision within six months
  Applicants should submit the following:
    1) Budget Information
    2) Curriculum vitae
    3) Proposal
    4) Letter(s) of recommendation
  Additional information: Contact foundation for further program information.
EIN: 136227347

464
Carlston Family Foundation

(formerly Broderbund Foundation)
2933 Quedada
Newport Beach, CA 92660 (415) 388-4763
Contact: Timothy J. Allen, Exec. Dir.
FAX: (949) 640-7841;
E-mail: tima@carlstonfamilyfoundation.com;

Additional telephone: (949) 640-7840;
URL: http://www.carlstonfamilyfoundation.org
Foundation type: Independent foundation
Purpose: Awards by nomination only to teachers in the CA public school system.
Publications: Annual report; Grants list; Program policy statement.
Financial data: Year ended 12/31/2012. Assets, $3,361,903 (M); Expenditures, $313,120; Total giving, $150,730; Grants to individuals, totaling $82,761.
Fields of interest: Education.
Type of support: Awards/grants by nomination only; Awards/prizes.
Application information: Application form available on the grantmaker's web site.
Initial approach: Letter
Deadline(s): None
EIN: 680154752

465
Reynaldo J. Carreon, M.D. Foundation
P.O. Box 1420
Indio, CA   92202-1420
Contact: Gloria Rodirquez
Applicaiton address: 30976 Avenida Ximino, Cathedral City, CA 92234; URL: http://carreonfoundation.org/

Foundation type: Independent foundation
Purpose: Scholarships for undergraduate study to residents of Coachella Valley, Riverside County, CA. Candidates must be of Mexican descent.
Financial data: Year ended 12/31/2012. Assets, $1,379,934 (M); Expenditures, $136,720; Total giving, $41,667; Grants to individuals, totaling $41,667.
Fields of interest: Higher education; Minorities; Hispanics/Latinos.
International interests: Mexico.
Type of support: Undergraduate support.
Application information: Application form required.
Additional information: Contact foundation for current application deadline.
EIN: 330426210

466
Catalyst for Youth
1724 Alberta Ave.
San Jose, CA   95125   (408) 269-3356
Application Address: Catalyst For Youth, Fiscal Sponsorship, 1724 Alberta Ave., San Jose, CA 95125
URL: http://www.catalystforyouth.org

Foundation type: Public charity
Purpose: Fiscal sponsorship to individuals whose projects help at-risk youth through programs that enable them to explore their capabilties and emerge as productive members of society. The foundation focuses on arts-based projects.
Publications: Informational brochure.
Fields of interest: Volunteer services; Crime/violence prevention, youth; Offenders/ex-offenders, services; Youth; Young adults.
Type of support: Project support; Fiscal agent/sponsor.
Application information: Applications accepted. Application form required. Application form available on the grantmaker's web site.
Initial approach: Letter, telephone or e-mail
Send request by: Applications must be submitted by mail.

Copies of proposal: 3
Deadline(s): None
Final notification: 3-4 weeks.
Applicants should submit the following:
1) Essay
2) Financial information
3) Proposal
4) Resume
5) Work samples
6) Budget Information
Program description:
Fiscal Sponsorship Program: A fiscal sponsorship program is available to individuals and organizations whose objectives and projects align with those of Catalyst for Youth. The organization provides access to its 501(c)(3) status and operating budget, a separate fund for grantees' monies, and general guidance on grant proposals and year-end reports. The organization charges a 10 percent fee on all monies received; the organization does not charge for tax-deductible in-kind donations.
EIN: 223863184

467
Catholic Charities CYO of the
Archdiocese of San Francisco
180 Howard St., Ste. 100
San Francisco, CA   94105-6153   (415) 972-1200
Contact: Deborah Dasovich, Pres.
FAX: (415) 972-1201; E-mail: moreinfo@cccyo.org; URL: http://www.cccyo.org

Foundation type: Public charity
Purpose: Giving limited to food, shelter, and clothing assistance for indigents in the San Francisco, CA area.
Financial data: Year ended 06/30/2012. Assets, $27,564,407 (M); Expenditures, $37,001,196; Total giving, $3,231,042; Grants to individuals, totaling $3,231,042.
Fields of interest: Economically disadvantaged.
Type of support: In-kind gifts.
Application information: Applications not accepted.
Additional information: Unsolicited requests for funds not considered.
EIN: 941498472

468
Catholic Charities of San Jose
(also known as Catholic Charities of Santa Clara County)
2625 Zanker Rd.
San Jose, CA   95134-2130   (408) 468-0100
Contact: Gregory R. Kepferle, C.E.O.
FAX: (408) 944-0275; URL: http://www.catholiccharitiesscc.org/

Foundation type: Public charity
Purpose: Financial assistance to low income individuals and families of Santa Clara county, CA with housing, clothing, food, and other general assistance.
Financial data: Year ended 06/30/2012. Assets, $24,505,542 (M); Expenditures, $31,547,702; Total giving, $3,044,012; Grants to individuals, 1,995 grants totaling $3,044,012.
Fields of interest: Human services; Economically disadvantaged.
Type of support: In-kind gifts; Grants for special needs.
Application information: Applications accepted.

Additional information: Some assistance require an application. Contact the organization for eligibility determination.
EIN: 942762269

469
Cavalier Foundation
c/o Carolyn Cavalier Rosenberg
6015 Estate Dr.
Oakland, CA   94611

Foundation type: Independent foundation
Purpose: Scholarships to residents of Oakland, CA for continuing education at institutions of higher learning.
Financial data: Year ended 11/30/2012. Assets, $276,436 (M); Expenditures, $24,776; Total giving, $15,770; Grants to individuals, 12 grants totaling $12,500 (high: $2,000, low: $1,000).
Fields of interest: Education.
Type of support: Scholarships—to individuals.
Application information: Contact the foundation for additional information.
EIN: 205920208

470
Celebrity Fund for Children's Charities
1640 S. Sepulveda Blvd., No. 515
Los Angeles, CA   90025-7538   (818) 885-1575
E-mail: info@cf4cc.org; URL: http://www.cf4cc.org

Foundation type: Public charity
Purpose: Fiscal sponsorship to individuals and companies lacking IRS status who wish to raise money for charitable causes.
Fields of interest: Children, services; Children.
Type of support: Fiscal agent/sponsor.
Application information: Applications accepted.
Additional information: Contact organization for application information and deadlines.
Program description:
Fiscal Sponsorship: The fund acts as a fiscal sponsor for companies involved with charitable donations to children. This allows an agency or person who wishes to raise money for charitable causes to operate under the protection of section 501(c)(3) status of the Internal Revenue Code. Under this umbrella, funds raised can be directed to the charity of interest of the person(s) raising the money.
EIN: 201250075

471
Center for Community and Family
Services
565 N. Rosemead Blvd.
Pasadena, CA   91107-2147

Foundation type: Public charity
Purpose: Financial assistance for child care providers in Los Angeles and Madera counties, CA.
Financial data: Year ended 06/30/2010. Assets, $7,793,578 (M); Expenditures, $59,825,776; Total giving, $33,878,196; Grants to individuals, totaling $33,878,196.
Fields of interest: Day care.
Type of support: Grants for special needs.
Application information: Applications accepted.
Additional information: Child care providers receive financial reimbursement for meals served to children.
EIN: 952627676

472
Center for Cultural Innovation
244 S. San Pedro St., Ste. 401
Los Angeles, CA 90012-3860 (213) 687-8577
Contact: Cora Mirikitani, Pres. and C.E.O.
FAX: (213) 687-8578; E-mail: info@cciarts.org;
Additional address (Bay Area office): 870 Market
St., Ste. 490, San Francisco, CA 94102-3013, tel.:
(415) 288-0530, fax: (415) 288-0529; URL: http://
www.cciarts.org

Foundation type: Public charity
Purpose: Grants to artists In the Bay Area and Los
Angeles, CA, in all stages of their careers with
support in areas where other funding sources may
be limited.
Publications: Application guidelines; Annual report.
Financial data: Year ended 06/30/2012. Assets,
$1,812,516 (M); Expenditures, $1,251,373; Total
giving, $650,368; Grants to individuals, totaling
$440,819.
Fields of interest: Arts, services; Arts, artist's
services; Arts.
Type of support: Grants to individuals.
Application information: Applications accepted.
  Send request by: On-line
  Deadline(s): May 1 for Artists' Resource for
    Completion, July 1 for Investing in Artists,
    Ongoing for Next Gen Arts and Creative
    Capacity Fund
  Additional information: See web site for
    additional guidelines.
Program descriptions:
  Artists' Resource for Completion (ARC) Grants:
These grants provide rapid, short-term assistance
to individual artists in Los Angeles County who wish
to enhance work for a specific, imminent
opportunity that may significantly benefit their
careers. The applicant must already have secured
an invitation from an established arts organization
to present the proposed work. The work must be
scheduled for presentation within six months of the
application deadline. Grants of up to $3,500 may
be requested to support: purchase or rental of
materials, equipment, or space to complete work
already scheduled for a specific event; an
exhibition, performance, publication, reading, etc;
auxiliary travel or shipping associated with the
proposed event, stipends/fees for collaborating
artists (performers, designers, etc.) whose
participation would expand or enhance the
proposed work.
  Creative Capacity Fund Quick Grants:
Administered in conjunction with the San Francisco
Arts Commission, Grants for the Arts/San
Francisco Hotel Tax Fund, the San Francisco
Foundation, San Jose Office of Cultural Affairs, and
the Los Angeles Department of Cultural Affairs, this
initiative works to strengthen the work of artists and
arts administrators in the Los Angeles and San
Francisco Bay Areas by providing them with access
to a wide range of professional development and
peer-learning opportunities. Grants may be used for
tuition or registration fees for classes, workshops,
or conferences focused on building administrative
skill and knowledge; travel and hotel expenses (if
workshop or conference occurs outside a 60-mile
radius of applicant's primary address); and fees to
engage an outside consultant, facilitator, executive
coach, or career counselor in order to build staff
counselor. Priority will be given to organizations that
provide strong rationale on how the proposed
activity will directly enhance the business and
administrative capabilities of an individual or
organization, and have budgets of $250,000 or
under (for San Francisco Bay Area-based
organizations) or $500,000 or under (for Los
Angeles-based organizations). Applicants must also
meet specific requirements of the fund's funding

partners; arts organizations may receive up to
$1,000 per calendar year, while individual artists
are eligible for up to $500.
  Investing in Artists Grants Program: This program
is designed to enhance the working lives and
creative environment for California artists by
funding tools and artistic innovation that will allow
them to create their best work more consistently,
and distribute that work more broadly to new
audiences. Grants are available in two funding
categories: grants for artistic equipment and tools
(one-time implementation grants of up to $10,000
each for individuals to acquire tools, materials, or
equipment that will strengthen their long-term
capacity to create work), and grants for artistic
innovation (grants of up to $10,000 for individual
artists to create new work that pushes the envelope
of an artist's creative process, explores new artistic
collaborations, or supports artistic growth and
experimentation that extends the boundaries of
their art-making). Eligible applicants must: be
individual working artists (defined as adults who
have received training in an artistic discipline or
tradition, spend ten or more hours a week on their
artwork, self-define as professional artists, and
attempt to derive income from work in which they
use their expert artistic practices and skills); show
proof of permanent residency in California for at
least three consecutive years prior to the
application deadline; be 18 years old at the time of
application deadline; and have exhibited,
performed, presented, and/or published artistic
work in a public context within the last three years.
  NextGen Arts Professional Development Grants:
Emerging arts leaders between the ages 18 to 35,
may be eligible to apply for up $1,000 to enroll in
workshops, attend conferences and to work with
consultants or coaches in order to enhance the
skills needed to lead the nonprofit arts sector of
tomorrow.
EIN: 912156812

473
The Center for Land Use Interpretation
9331 Venice Blvd.
Culver City, CA 90232-2621 (310) 839-5722
FAX: (310) 839-5722; E-mail: clui@clui.org;
URL: http://www.clui.org

Foundation type: Public charity
Purpose: Residencies to artists for the production
of work that explores themes related to their stay
in the Great Salt Lake desert region.
Publications: Application guidelines; Informational
brochure; Newsletter.
Financial data: Year ended 12/31/2011. Assets,
$24,098 (M); Expenditures, $172,569.
Fields of interest: Arts.
Type of support: Residencies.
Application information: Applications accepted.
  Initial approach: E-mail
  Deadline(s): None
  Applicants should submit the following:
    1) SASE
    2) Work samples
    3) Resume
    4) Curriculum vitae
    5) Essay
Program description:
  Wendover Residence Program: The center
operates a residence program to support the
development of new interpretive methodologies and
ideas. The program is open to artists, researchers,
theorists, or anyone who works with land and land
use issues in an innovative and engaging manner.
Residents primarily work out of the center's
facilities at Wendover, Utah, and explore and

interpret the landscape of that unique and inspiring
geographic region (including the Great Salt Lake
and its desert and salt-flat environs). Residents
generally stay for a period of three to six weeks,
during which time they will be expected to conduct
work that examines, engages, or reflects the land
uses of the surrounding area; occasionally stipends
and project support are available, but applicants
are encouraged to seek their own funding sources
for project expenses and materials.
EIN: 943198743

474
Central Valley High School Scholarship Fund
P.O. Box 494312
Redding, CA 96049-4312 (530) 229-1652
Contact: Kate Baker, Tr.

Foundation type: Independent foundation
Purpose: Scholarships to graduates of Central
Valley High School, Redding, CA.
Financial data: Year ended 07/31/2013. Assets,
$985 (M); Expenditures, $10,027; Total giving,
$10,000; Grants to individuals, 2 grants totaling
$10,000 (high: $5,000, low: $5,000).
Type of support: Scholarships—to individuals;
Support to graduates or students of specific
schools.
Application information: Application form required.
  Deadline(s): Before end of school year
  Additional information: Application must include
    justification for need.
EIN: 946293818

475
Central Valley Low Income Housing Corporation
2431 W. March Ln., Ste. 350
Stockton, CA 95207-8211 (209) 472-7200
Contact: Bill Mendelson, Exec. Dir.

Foundation type: Public charity
Purpose: Affordable housing and related support
services to low-income households in the Stockton,
CA area.
Financial data: Year ended 06/30/2012. Assets,
$302,997 (M); Expenditures, $5,514,102; Total
giving, $3,993,020; Grants to individuals, totaling
$3,993,020.
Fields of interest: Housing/shelter, services;
Housing/shelter.
Type of support: Grants for special needs.
Application information:
  Initial approach: Letter
  Additional information: Contact foundation for
    eligibility criteria.
EIN: 680256280

476
Challenged Athletes, Inc.
P.O. Box 910769
San Diego, CA 92191-0769 (858) 866-0959
Contact: Virginia Tinley, Exec. Dir.
FAX: (858) 866-0958;
E-mail: caf@challengedathletes.org; URL: http://
www.challengedathletes.org

Foundation type: Public charity
Purpose: Grants to assist physically challenged and
disabled athletes participate in competitive sports
activities.
Financial data: Year ended 03/31/2012. Assets,
$4,192,934 (M); Expenditures, $4,797,491; Total

giving, $1,389,490; Grants to individuals, totaling $1,325,037.

Fields of interest: Athletics/sports, training; Athletics/sports, Special Olympics; Physically disabled.

Type of support: Grants to individuals.

Application information: Contact the organization for additional guidelines.

Program description:

Access for Athletes: This program provides such equipment as adaptive sports wheelchairs, handcycles, and mono skis, so that those with physical challenges can once again, or for the first time, participate in sports.. After being awarded grants for new adaptive sports equipment, prosthetics and/or training and competition expenses, participants in the program can pursue a full and active life that includes sports. To be eligible for a grant, an athlete's disability must be recognized within the International Paralympic Committee (IPC) classifications.

EIN: 330739596

477
Change a Life Foundation

5 Corporate Park, Ste. 210
Irvine, CA 92606-5166   (949) 788-9999
Contact: Lisa C. Fujimoto, Exec. V.P.
FAX: (949) 788-9266; E-mail: info@changealife.org;
URL: http://www.changealife.org

Foundation type: Independent foundation

Purpose: Scholarships to high school seniors in Los Angeles, San Diego, and Orange Counties, CA.

Publications: Annual report; Newsletter; Newsletter (including application guidelines).

Financial data: Year ended 12/31/2012. Assets, $399,732 (M); Expenditures, $2,647,954; Total giving, $1,884,308.

Fields of interest: Higher education.

Type of support: Scholarships—to individuals.

Application information: Applications accepted. Application form required. Application form available on the grantmaker's web site.

Initial approach: Application
Send request by: Application online; mail or fax attachments as needed
Copies of proposal: 2
Deadline(s): Apr. 25
Final notification: Applicants notified within six weeks
Applicants should submit the following:
  1) ACT
  2) Budget Information
  3) FAFSA
  4) Photograph
  5) Transcripts
  6) SAT
  7) Letter(s) of recommendation
  8) GPA
  9) Financial information
  10) Essay
Additional information: Applicants should work directly with their college and/or guidance counselors to apply.

Program description:

Scholarship Program: The foundation currently funds in San Diego, Orange, and Los Angeles counties to provide scholarships to graduating high school seniors from underprivileged families. Most of these at-risk youth are the first in their families to attend a four-year college or university. And many of these youth have already endured challenges beyond most peoples' lifetime, and have had the resilience to overcome those challenges and succeed. The foundation believes that by investing in the education of these young people, a sense of

hope and accomplishment will be instilled in them - propelling them to a bright and promising future. The foundation partners with the Los Angeles County Office of Education, Orange County Office of Education, emancipated youth from foster care throughout California, and the San Diego County Office of Education. Applicants should apply directly online at the foundation's web site.

EIN: 330935713

478
Chaparral Foundation, Inc.

2722 1st Ave.
San Diego, CA 92103

Foundation type: Independent foundation

Purpose: Scholarships primarily to residents of AZ for higher education.

Financial data: Year ended 12/31/2010. Assets, $0 (M); Expenditures, $0; Total giving, $0.

Type of support: Scholarships—to individuals.

Application information: Applications not accepted.

Additional information: Unsolicited requests for funds not considered or acknowledged.

EIN: 861043858

479
Cherith Christian Private Foundation

4260 Newberry Ct.
Palo Alto, CA 94306-4138

Foundation type: Independent foundation

Purpose: Grants to individuals involved with full-time Christian work at churches and parachurch organizations, and scholarships to individuals for tuition at theological seminaries.

Financial data: Year ended 04/30/2013. Assets, $560,919 (M); Expenditures, $114,178; Total giving, $104,442.

Fields of interest: Theological school/education; Christian agencies & churches.

Type of support: Grants to individuals.

Application information: Applications not accepted.

Additional information: Unsolicited requests for funds not considered or acknowledged.

EIN: 954222174

480
The Robert Chesley Foundation, Inc.

c/o Victor Bumbalo
828 N. Laurel Ave.
Los Angeles, CA 90046

Foundation type: Operating foundation

Purpose: Awards to preselected emerging gay or lesbian playwriters to honor their achievements.

Financial data: Year ended 05/31/2012. Assets, $130,225 (M); Expenditures, $9,007; Total giving, $4,500; Grant to an individual, 1 grant totaling $500.

Fields of interest: Theater (playwriting).

Type of support: Awards/prizes.

Application information: Contributes only to preselected individuals, unsolicited requested for funds or manuscripts not considered or acknowledged.

EIN: 133682405

481
William A. Chessall Memorial Scholarship Fund

c/o Scott Yandell
P.O. Box 3600
Ukiah, CA 95482-0419   (707) 463-5253
Contact: Elizabeth Hovland
Application address: 1000 Low Gap Rd., Ukiah CA, 95482

Foundation type: Independent foundation

Purpose: Scholarships to financially needy graduates of Ukiah High School, CA, for study at colleges and universities, including Mendocino Community College.

Financial data: Year ended 03/31/2013. Assets, $784,296 (M); Expenditures, $31,249; Total giving, $28,000; Grants to individuals, 8 grants totaling $28,000 (high: $4,000, low: $1,333).

Fields of interest: College (community/junior); Scholarships/financial aid; Economically disadvantaged.

Type of support: Support to graduates or students of specific schools; Undergraduate support.

Application information: Application form required.

Deadline(s): Early Apr.
Applicants should submit the following:
  1) Essay
  2) Class rank
  3) Transcripts
  4) GPA
Additional information: Application should also include name of college student is planning to attend and complete a two-page activities information worksheet.

EIN: 946515834

482
Chicana Foundation of Northern CA

(also known as Chicana/Latina Foundation)
1419 Burlingame Ave., Ste. W2
Burlingame, CA 94010-4119   (650) 373-1083
Contact: Olga Talamante, Exec. Dir.
FAX: (650) 373-1090;
E-mail: clfinfo@chicanalatina.org; E-mail for Olga Talamante: olga@chicanalatina.org; URL: http://www.chicanalatina.org

Foundation type: Public charity

Purpose: Scholarships to undergraduate and graduate female students of Latina background for higher education.

Publications: Application guidelines.

Financial data: Year ended 06/30/2012. Assets, $403,063 (M); Expenditures, $827,543; Total giving, $61,750; Grants to individuals, totaling $61,750.

Fields of interest: Higher education; Hispanics/Latinos; Women.

Type of support: Scholarships—to individuals.

Application information: Applications accepted. Application form required. Application form available on the grantmaker's web site. Interview required.

Initial approach: Telephone
Send request by: Mail or e-mail
Deadline(s): Mar. 16
Applicants should submit the following:
  1) Transcripts
  2) Letter(s) of recommendation
  3) Essay

Program description:

Scholarship: Scholarships in the amount of $1,500 are awarded to Chicana/Latina women of the Northern CA counties of Alameda, Contra Costa, Marin, Monterey, Napa, Sacramento, San Francisco, San Mateo, Santa Clara, Santa Cruz,

Solano, Sonoma or Yolo. Applicants must have been a resident for at least two years in one of the counties and be enrolled as a full-time college student, have completed a minimum of 15 college semester units after high school graduation, and have at least a 2.5 GPA. Graduate students must provide verification of acceptance to a graduate school. All candidates must have demonstrated leadership and civic/community involvement. Applicants must agree, if awarded a scholarship, to volunteer a minimum of 10 hours in the next year in support of the Chicana/Latina Foundation.
EIN: 942923423

483
Child Development Associates, Inc.
180 Otay Lakes Rd., Ste. 300
Bonita, CA 91902-2442 (619) 427-4411
Contact: Jane McMasters, Co-Exec. Dir.
FAX: (619) 205-6299; Toll Free: (888) 755-2445;
URL: http://www.cdasandiego.com

Foundation type: Public charity
Purpose: Reimbursement for food costs to providers for child care in the San Diego, CA area.
Financial data: Year ended 06/30/2012. Assets, $6,001,317 (M); Expenditures, $51,490,952; Total giving, $42,425,016; Grants to individuals, totaling $42,425,016.
Fields of interest: Day care.
Type of support: Grants for special needs.
Application information: Contact the agency for eligibility determination.
EIN: 330050042

484
Child Nutrition Program of Southern California, Inc.
7777 Alvarado Rd., Ste. 422
La Mesa, CA 91942 (619) 465-4500
Toll-free tel.: (800) 233-8107; URL: http://www.cnpsc.com/

Foundation type: Public charity
Purpose: Assistance for meal reimbursement funds to licensed family child care homes in Riverside and San Diego county, CA.
Publications: Informational brochure; Newsletter.
Financial data: Year ended 09/30/2011. Assets, $1,101,227 (M); Expenditures, $5,994,313; Total giving, $5,166,812; Grants to individuals, totaling $5,166,812.
Fields of interest: Nutrition; Children, services.
Type of support: Grants to individuals.
Application information: Applications not accepted.
   Additional information: Contact the agency for additional guidelines. Unsolicited requests for funds not considered or acknowledged.
EIN: 953579992

485
Children Affected by AIDS Foundation
6033 W. Century Blvd., Ste. 603
Los Angeles, CA 90045-6440 (310) 258-0850
Contact: Angelica M. Valenzuela, V.P., Prog.
FAX: (310) 258-0851; E-mail: caaf@caaf.org;
URL: http://www.caaf4kids.org

Foundation type: Public charity
Purpose: Emergency funds to meet unanticipated needs in the daily lives of children up to the age of 13 and their families whose lives are affected by HIV/AIDS with food, clothing, utility assistance,

transportation, medications and other special needs.
Publications: Application guidelines; Annual report; Grants list; Informational brochure; Newsletter.
Financial data: Year ended 12/31/2012. Assets, $24,323 (M); Expenditures, $269,405.
Fields of interest: AIDS; Children; AIDS, people with.
Type of support: Emergency funds; Grants for special needs.
Application information: Contact the foundation for eligibility determination.
EIN: 954448687

486
Childrens Burn Foundation
5000 Van Nuys Blvd., Ste. 300
Sherman Oaks, CA 91403-1784 (818) 907-2822
FAX: (818) 501-4005; E-mail: info@childburn.org;
Toll-free tel.: (800) 949-8898; URL: http://www.childburn.org

Foundation type: Public charity
Purpose: Assistance to individuals for medical care including surgeries and hospitalization for young burn victims who have been severely burned.
Publications: Annual report; Newsletter.
Financial data: Year ended 06/30/2011. Assets, $4,161,168 (M); Expenditures, $930,386; Total giving, $112,437; Grants to individuals, 49 grants totaling $91,561. Subtotal for in-kind gifts: grants totaling $10,525. Subtotal for emergency funds: 51 grants totaling $101,912.
Fields of interest: Burn centers; Child abuse.
Type of support: In-kind gifts; Grants for special needs.
Application information: Application form required. Application form available on the grantmaker's web site.
   Initial approach: Letter, telephone, fax or e-mail
   Additional information: Reimbursement is based on the bill/invoice submitted by the individuals.
EIN: 953954352

487
Children's Council of San Francisco
445 Church St.
San Francisco, CA 94114-1720 (415) 276-2900
Contact: Elena Schmid, Pres.
FAX: (415) 392-2399;
E-mail: rr@childrenscouncil.org; URL: http://www.childrenscouncil.org

Foundation type: Public charity
Purpose: Financial support to qualified child-care providers for children and families throughout the San Francisco Bay Area, CA.
Publications: Annual report; Newsletter.
Financial data: Year ended 06/30/2012. Assets, $6,062,467 (L); Expenditures, $55,964,715; Total giving, $43,776,865; Grants to individuals, totaling $43,776,865.
Fields of interest: Day care; Children, services.
Type of support: Grants to individuals; Grants for special needs.
Application information: Applications accepted.
   Initial approach: Telephone
   Additional information: Payments to providers are paid in the form of vouchers. Contact the agency for information in participating in the child care program.

Program description:
   Child Care Food Program: The program helps family child care providers serve nutritious meals and snacks to children. Meals are based on U.S. Department of Agriculture (USDA) child nutrition requirements. Providers are reimbursed for costs of serving two main meals and a snack each day. Providers also benefit from workshops on child nutrition and health.
EIN: 942221305

488
Children's Fund, Inc.
348 W. Hospitality Ln., Ste. 110
San Bernardino, CA 92408-1002 (909) 379-0000
Contact: Erin D. Phillips, Pres. and C.E.O.
FAX: (909) 379-0006; URL: http://www.childrensfundsbcounty.org

Foundation type: Public charity
Purpose: Emergency assistance to at-risk children of San Bernardino, CA, who are abused, neglected, impoverished, or abandoned, receive adequate food, clothing, shelter, medical care and education.
Publications: Annual report.
Financial data: Year ended 06/30/2011. Assets, $2,323,380 (M); Expenditures, $2,188,264; Total giving, $1,544,509; Grants to individuals, totaling $1,544,509.
Fields of interest: Child abuse; Foster care; Children, services.
Type of support: Grants for special needs.
Application information: Applications not accepted.
   Additional information: Assistance to children is provided through the Daily Referral program which works with county case workers to provide the necessary assistance.
EIN: 330193286

489
Children's Hunger Fund
13931 Balboa Blvd.
Sylmar, CA 91342
Contact: Dave Phillips, Pres.
FAX: (818) 979-7101;
E-mail: info@childrenshungerfund.org; Toll-free tel.: (800) 708-7589; URL: http://www.childrenshungerfund.org

Foundation type: Public charity
Purpose: The fund provides assistance to individuals, including food distribution, disaster relief and emergency assistance to meet the needs of those most in need.
Publications: Annual report; Financial statement.
Financial data: Year ended 12/31/2011. Assets, $7,532,920 (M); Expenditures, $37,668,400; Total giving, $31,145,625; Grants to individuals, 100,000 grants totaling $12,193,112.
Fields of interest: Safety/disasters; Human services; International relief; Community/economic development; Children/youth.
Type of support: Emergency funds; Grants to individuals.
Application information: Applications not accepted.
   Additional information: See web site for additional information.
EIN: 954335462

490
Children's Medifund Corporation
243 Chenery St.
San Francisco, CA 94131-2764 (415) 641-9176
Contact: Phyllis Kaplan, Pres.

Foundation type: Operating foundation
Purpose: Grants to U.S. residents for college tuition, camp fees, medical needs, food, clothing, transportation, computers, books and other special needs. Grants also to the needy in some Latin American and Asian countries.
Financial data: Year ended 12/31/2012. Assets, $14,804 (M); Expenditures, $37,001; Total giving, $35,198.
Fields of interest: Education; Human services; Economically disadvantaged.
Type of support: Grants for special needs.
Application information: Applications accepted.
  Initial approach: Letter or telephone
  Deadline(s): Vary
EIN: 942370867

491
Children's Network International
5600 Rickenbacker Rd., Bldg. 1B
Bell, CA 90201-6437 (323) 980-9870
Contact: Roger Presgrove, Pres.
FAX: (323) 980-9878;
E-mail: info@helpthechildren.org; Toll-free tel.: (888) 818-4483; mailing address: P.O. Box 911607, Los Angeles, CA 90091-1600; URL: http://www.helpthechildren.org

Foundation type: Public charity
Purpose: Emergency assistance to children and families in need in the U.S. and abroad with housing, food, transportation, and other special needs.
Financial data: Year ended 12/31/2011. Assets, $1,460,958 (M); Expenditures, $75,813,948; Total giving, $74,863,529; Grants to individuals, 4,540,731 grants totaling $45,407,310.
Fields of interest: Human services, emergency aid; Human services; Community/economic development; Children/youth.
Type of support: In-kind gifts.
Application information: Applications accepted.
  Additional information: Contact the organization for eligibility determination.
EIN: 954669871

492
China Times Cultural Foundation
1499 Bayshore Hwy., Ste. 212
Burlingame, CA 94010-1741 (718) 460-4900
Contact: Sophia Hsieh
Application address: P.O. Box 521234, Flushing, NY 11352
E-mail: ctcfmail@yahoo.com

Foundation type: Independent foundation
Purpose: Undergraduate scholarships to individuals of Chinese ancestry. Scholarships for Chinese language school students. Scholarships to Ph.D. candidates in Chinese studies, and project support and travel grants to Chinese scholars to attend conferences relating to the history and development of China.
Financial data: Year ended 12/31/2012. Assets, $1,914,535 (M); Expenditures, $154,206; Total giving, $42,500; Grants to individuals, 15 grants totaling $42,500 (high: $5,000, low: $2,500).
Fields of interest: Humanities; Social sciences; International studies.

International interests: China.
Type of support: Awards/prizes; Graduate support; Undergraduate support; Travel grants.
Application information: Application form required.
  Deadline(s): June 30
  Final notification: Recipients notified in Oct.
  Applicants should submit the following:
    1) Curriculum vitae
    2) Transcripts
  Additional information: Application should also include letter of approval of doctoral candidacy, letter of approved dissertation prospectus, and project description in Chinese and English.
Program description:
  Doctoral Dissertation Research in Chinese Studies: Scholarships in the amount of $5,000 U.S. each are awarded to doctoral candidates in the humanities or social sciences with an approved dissertation prospectus. The scholarships are awarded on the basis of scholastic achievement without regard to academic discipline, race or nationality. A special award will be given to the top winner from the applicants with a cash award of $10,000 U.S. Enrollment in a university in the U.S. or Canada is required.
EIN: 222711422

493
Chinese American Citizens Alliance Foundation
763 Yale St.
Los Angeles, CA 90012-2325 (213) 628-6368

Foundation type: Independent foundation
Purpose: Undergraduate scholarships to students of Chinese ancestry attending colleges or universities in CA.
Financial data: Year ended 12/31/2012. Assets, $252,443 (M); Expenditures, $11,380; Total giving, $9,500; Grants to individuals, 10 grants totaling $9,500 (high: $1,000, low: $500).
Fields of interest: Asians/Pacific Islanders.
International interests: China.
Type of support: Undergraduate support.
Application information: Applications accepted. Application form required.
  Initial approach: Letter
  Deadline(s): June 30
  Additional information: Application should include transcripts.
EIN: 237106480

494
Chopra Center Foundation
2013 Costa Del Mar
Carlsbad, CA 92009-6801 (760) 494-1625
E-mail: foundation@chopra.com; URL: http://deepakchopra.com/chopra-foundation/home/

Foundation type: Public charity
Purpose: Awards to individuals whose devotion and commitment to their passion for finding answers in their field is matched only by their commitment to humanity.
Financial data: Year ended 12/31/2011. Assets, $855,724 (M); Expenditures, $575,209; Total giving, $199,302; Grants to individuals, totaling $150,625.
Fields of interest: Education; Holistic medicine.
Type of support: Awards/prizes.
Application information: Applications not accepted.
  Additional information: Unsolicited requests for funds not considered or acknowledged.
EIN: 421480296

495
Christian Mission to Gaza
2920 Huntington Dr., No. 130
San Marino, CA 91108-2206 (626) 289-8899

Foundation type: Public charity
Purpose: Grants for medical assistance and living expenses to residents of refugee camps and to the local Christian community who have been impoverished by the fighting within Gaza.
Financial data: Year ended 12/31/2011. Assets, $188,081 (M); Expenditures, $79,599; Total giving, $15,725.
Fields of interest: Christian agencies & churches.
Type of support: Foreign applicants; Grants for special needs.
Application information: Applications not accepted.
  Additional information: Unsolicited requests for funds not considered.
EIN: 330873172

496
Chronicle Season of Sharing Fund
P.O. Box 44740
San Francisco, CA 94144-2905 (415) 777-7120
Contact: Jennifer Kirschenbaum, Exec. Dir.
FAX: (415) 546-9291;
E-mail: JKirschenbaum@sfchronicle.com; E-mail for Jennifer Kirschenbaum: JKirschenbaum@sfchronicle.com; URL: http://www.seasonofsharing.org/

Foundation type: Public charity
Purpose: Short-term and one time only grants to low to moderate income families with children who live in one of the following counties: Alameda, Contra Costa, Marin, Napa, San Francisco, San Mateo, Santa Clara, Solano or Sonoma, CA with housing assistance, food and other needs.
Financial data: Year ended 06/30/2012. Assets, $1,922,617 (M); Expenditures, $6,803,461; Total giving, $6,539,004; Grants to individuals, totaling $21,504.
Fields of interest: Economically disadvantaged.
Type of support: Grants for special needs.
Application information: Contact the fund for assistance.
EIN: 943019992

497
Chrysopolae Foundation
P.O. Box 10174
San Rafael, CA 94912-0174

Foundation type: Independent foundation
Purpose: Scholarships to former students of the Tamiscal High School, CA Team Program to attend college or vocational school.
Financial data: Year ended 12/31/2012. Assets, $10,579,526 (M); Expenditures, $542,068; Total giving, $455,529.
Fields of interest: Vocational education, post-secondary; Higher education.
Type of support: Scholarships—to individuals; Support to graduates or students of specific schools.
Application information: Applications accepted. Application form required.
  Send request by: Mail
  Deadline(s): May 15 for undergraduates, Aug. 12 for all others
  Final notification: Undergraduates notified on June 16, all others notified on Sept. 1
  Applicants should submit the following:

1) Financial information
2) Transcripts
3) Essay
Additional information: Application should also include proof of acceptance or enrollment in college. Applicant must demonstrate financial need, academic achievement and community service.
EIN: 943265060

498
The Chung Charitable Foundation Inc.
1000 Dove St., Ste. 300
Newport Beach, CA 92660-2850
URL: http://chungfoundation.org

Foundation type: Independent foundation
Purpose: Scholarships to international graduate students and undergraduate students at a U.S. top ten ranking university with a focus in real estate, architecture, city planning or other related majors. Scholarships to high school students, junior high students and elementary students from Orange county or Los Angeles county, CA.
Financial data: Year ended 12/31/2012. Assets, $1,780,081 (M); Expenditures, $90,139; Total giving, $70,050; Grants to individuals, 7 grants totaling $18,500 (high: $10,000, low: $500).
Fields of interest: Middle schools/education; Elementary school/education; Secondary school/education; Higher education.
Type of support: Scholarships—to individuals; Graduate support; Undergraduate support.
Application information: Applications accepted. Application form required.
Send request by: Mail
Deadline(s): Dec. 1
Applicants should submit the following:
1) Transcripts
2) Resume
Additional information: Application should also include a personal statement. Selection is based on demonstrated academic and/or extracurricular excellence. Individuals will be selected from each candidate group once a year. Awards are in the amount of $100 to $10,000. See web site for additional guidelines.
EIN: 770607988

499
Chung-Ahm-Jeewon & Jong Lee Scholarship Foundation, Inc.
27763 Homestead Rd.
Laguna Niguel, CA 92677 (949) 360-6287
Contact: Jong D. Lee M.D., Secy.-Treas.

Foundation type: Independent foundation
Purpose: Scholarships to individuals for higher education at any educational institution.
Financial data: Year ended 12/31/2012. Assets, $208,068 (M); Expenditures, $14,828; Total giving, $14,500; Grants to individuals, 5 grants totaling $7,000 (high: $3,000, low: $1,000).
Fields of interest: Higher education.
Type of support: Scholarships—to individuals.
Application information: Applications accepted. Application form required.
Deadline(s): None
EIN: 371284091

500
Joseph D. Ciatti Memorial Foundation
1101 5th Ave., No. 170
San Rafael, CA 94901-2916

Foundation type: Independent foundation
Purpose: Scholarships primarily to graduates of high schools in San Rafael, CA.
Financial data: Year ended 10/31/2011. Assets, $264,463 (M); Expenditures, $16,785; Total giving, $14,825; Grants to individuals, 5 grants totaling $13,500 (high: $3,000, low: $1,500).
Fields of interest: Higher education.
Type of support: Support to graduates or students of specific schools; Undergraduate support.
Application information: Applications not accepted.
Additional information: Unsolicited requests for funds not considered or acknowledged.
EIN: 680113940

501
Civic Ventures
114 Sansome St., Ste. 850
San Francisco, CA 94104-3830 (415) 430-0141
FAX: (415) 430-0144;
E-mail: info@civicventures.org; URL: http://www.civicventures.org/contact.cfm

Foundation type: Public charity
Purpose: Awards to outstanding individuals 60 or older who have demonstrated uncommon vision, determination and entrepreneurialism in addressing community and national problems.
Publications: Informational brochure; Newsletter.
Financial data: Year ended 12/31/2011. Assets, $11,653,588 (M); Expenditures, $5,074,809; Total giving, $567,257; Grants to individuals, totaling $75,000.
Fields of interest: Aging.
Type of support: Awards/prizes.
Application information: Applications accepted. Application form required. Application form available on the grantmaker's web site.
Initial approach: Letter or e-mail
Deadline(s): Mar. 22 for Purpose Prize
Program descriptions:
Encore Fellowships: Paid, time-limited fellowships place highly skilled, experienced professionals at the end of their midlife careers in social-purpose organizations. During the fellowship period (typically six to twelve months, half- to full-time), the fellows take on roles that bring significant, sustained impact to their host organizations. While they are working, the fellows earn a stipend, learn about social-purpose work and develop a new network of contacts and resources for the future.
Launch Pad Award: This contest awards $5,000 to help budding social entrepreneurs over 45 in the second half of life get a start on their dream encore careers. Individuals entered the contest, demonstrating a deep interest in helping to solve a serious social problems in their communities or in the world.
Purpose Prize: The award supports outstanding individuals over 60 years of age who are already producing significant social innovation and accomplishing work of great importance. The Prize awards up to $100,000 each to five people in encore careers creating new ways to solve tough social problems. Individuals are nominated for this prize.
EIN: 943274339

502
Donald Clark Scholarship Trust
P.O. Box 60078 SC-MPK-03-M
Los Angeles, CA 90060
Application address: c/o Bridgeport Public Schools, Attn.: Dan Hadden, Principal, P.O. Box 430, Bridgeport, NE 69336, tel.: (308) 262-0346

Foundation type: Independent foundation
Purpose: Scholarships to graduates of Bridgeport High School, NE, who are attending or are planning to attend the University of Nebraska.
Financial data: Year ended 12/31/2012. Assets, $586,820 (M); Expenditures, $34,665; Total giving, $25,000.
Type of support: Support to graduates or students of specific schools; Undergraduate support.
Application information: Applications accepted. Application form required.
Send request by: Mail
Deadline(s): Apr. 1
Applicants should submit the following:
1) Budget Information
2) Transcripts
Additional information: Application must include a letter of no more than 200 words demonstrating need and tax returns.
EIN: 476213232

503
Cloud Forest Institute
P.O. Box 1435
Ukiah, CA 95482-1425 (707) 743-1287
Contact: Freeda Alida Burnstad, Exec. Dir.
E-mail: info@cloudforest.org; URL: http://www.cloudforest.org

Foundation type: Public charity
Purpose: Fiscal sponsorship for projects and organizations whose purposes fall within the Institute's educational mission.
Financial data: Year ended 12/31/2011. Assets, $64,034 (M); Expenditures, $119,725; Total giving, $97,360.
Fields of interest: Education; Environment.
International interests: Ecuador.
Type of support: Fiscal agent/sponsor.
Application information: Contact the institute to set up an interview.
Program description:
Fiscal Sponsorship: The institute acts as 501(c)(3) umbrella for projects and organizations whose purposes fall within its educational mission. The institute organizes educational journeys in Ecuador based on individual and group specifications. It will develop a Service Learning course that will travel to and focus on particular subjects based on your interests and budget.
EIN: 770480093

504
Coastal Community Foundation
162 S. Rancho Santa Fe Rd, Ste. F-50
Encinitas, CA 92024 (760) 942-9245
Contact: Sharon Omahen, Exec. Dir.
E-mail: info@coastalfoundation.org; Mailing address: P.O. Box. 230415, Encinitas, CA 92023-0415; Additional e-mail: sharon@coastalfoundation.org; URL: http://www.coastalfoundation.org

Foundation type: Community foundation
Purpose: Scholarships for higher education to graduating seniors from the Carlsbad, Oceanside and San Diego high schools. Grants also available

to public school teachers in the north coastal San Diego County area, CA.

Publications: Annual report; Financial statement; Grants list; Informational brochure; Newsletter.

Financial data: Year ended 12/31/2011. Assets, $1,602,612 (M); Expenditures, $216,396; Total giving, $139,690; Grants to individuals, 20 grants totaling $13,430.

Fields of interest: Arts education; Music; Elementary school/education; Higher education; Medical school/education; Teacher school/education.

Type of support: Grants to individuals; Scholarships—to individuals; Support to graduates or students of specific schools; Undergraduate support; Camperships.

Application information: Applications accepted. Application form required. Application form available on the grantmaker's web site.

> *Deadline(s):* Varies
> *Applicants should submit the following:*
> 1) FAFSA
> 2) GPA
> 3) Letter(s) of recommendation
> *Additional information:* Most applications should be submitted to your school guidance office/scholarship department. See web site for a complete listing of scholarships and application.

Program descriptions:

College Scholarships: The foundation administers several scholarship funds, open to graduating seniors from the Carlsbad, Oceanside and San Dieguito high schools only. Scholarship awards typically range from $500 to $2,000. Each scholarship has its own unique set of eligibility requirements, including awards for students pursuing a degree in specific subject areas, such as medicine, education, and public administration. See web site for additional information.

Suzuki Music Scholarship: Scholarships are available from the Barbara Schneiderman Fund for Piano Enrichment for San Diego County students to attend a Suzuki camp or convention. Awards are open to students studying Suzuki music (piano only). E-mail or telephone the foundation for additional application information.

EIN: 330216692

505
The David J. and Rosetta Adler Cohen Foundation

3255 Wilshire Blvd., Ste. 1034
Los Angeles, CA   90010-1414   (213) 386-1773
Contact: Jerry Michaels, Pres.

Foundation type: Independent foundation
Purpose: Scholarships primarily to CA residents for higher education.
Financial data: Year ended 12/31/2010. Assets, $0 (M); Expenditures, $4,098; Total giving, $0.
Type of support: Scholarships—to individuals.
Application information: Applications accepted.
> *Initial approach:* Letter
> *Deadline(s):* None
EIN: 954420751

506
Roberta Collister Scholarship Trust

205 W. Alvarado
Fallbrook, CA   92028-2002
Contact: Robert H. James, Tr.

Foundation type: Independent foundation
Purpose: Scholarships to students at Fallbrook Union High School, CA.

Financial data: Year ended 12/31/2012. Assets, $181,825 (M); Expenditures, $18,271; Total giving, $11,868.
Fields of interest: Disabilities, people with.
Type of support: Support to graduates or students of specific schools; Undergraduate support.
Application information: Applications not accepted.
> *Additional information:* Unsolicited requests for funds not considered or acknowledged.
EIN: 336208197

507
Colonnades Theatre Lab Inc.

1880 Century Park E., No. 618
Los Angeles, CA   90067-1622   (310) 552-1808
Contact: Surpin Mayerson Edelstone
URL: http://globalartscorps.org

Foundation type: Independent foundation
Purpose: Grants to individuals primarily in Santa Barbara, CA for project support in film or the theatrical arts.
Financial data: Year ended 06/30/2012. Assets, $319,747 (M); Expenditures, $802,659; Total giving, $0.
Fields of interest: Alliance/advocacy; Performing arts; Arts.
International interests: South Africa.
Type of support: Grants to individuals; Project support.
Application information:
> *Initial approach:* Letter
> *Additional information:* Contact the Lab for application information and guidelines.
EIN: 237293173

508
Columbia Foundation

77 Van Ness Ave., Ste. 200
San Francisco, CA   94102-6042   (415) 861-5657
Contact: Susan Reed Clark, Exec. Dir.
FAX: (415) 861-4937; E-mail: info@columbia.org; Letter of inquiry e-mail: loi@columbia.org; e-mail for confirmation of LOI receipt (if a confirm has not been received within a week following appropriate deadline) Alex Hoskyns-Abrahall: alex@columbia.org; URL: http://www.columbia.org

Foundation type: Independent foundation
Purpose: Grants to filmmakers in the San Francisco Bay area whose projects cover issues related to arts and culture, human rights, and food and farming.
Publications: Application guidelines; Annual report (including application guidelines); Grants list; Program policy statement (including application guidelines).
Financial data: Year ended 05/31/2012. Assets, $69,884,801 (M); Expenditures, $4,475,238; Total giving, $3,495,250.
Fields of interest: Cultural/ethnic awareness; Film/video; Environment; Civil/human rights; Economics.
Type of support: Grants to individuals; Project support.
Application information: Applications accepted. Application form required. Application form available on the grantmaker's web site.
> *Initial approach:* Letter of inquiry
> *Send request by:* E-mail
> *Copies of proposal:* 1
> *Deadline(s):* Mar. 1 for Arts and Culture, Aug. 1 for Human Rights, Dec. 1 for Food and Farming

Additional information: The foundation will only consider proposals from individuals who have obtained a fiscal sponsor for their project.

Program description:
Media: The foundation considers letters of inquiry for media projects in each program area (Arts and Culture, Human Rights, and Food and Farming) if they address the foundation's current program priorities, and relate to the work of organizations already funded by the foundation. If the issue already has received extensive media coverage, the foundation is unlikely to consider the project for funding. The foundation gives priority to San Francisco Bay Area filmmakers; to films or videos that will be used by Columbia Foundation-funded public-interest organizations to further their work on the issue; and to projects for which a grant of $5,000 to $25,000 makes a difference in getting the project started or completed. Applications for media projects should be submitted by the annual deadline for the relevant program area. E-mail address for LOI: loi@columbia.org.
EIN: 941196186

509
Common Counsel Foundation

405 14th St., Ste. 809
Oakland, CA   94612-1238   (510) 834-2995
Contact: Laura Livoti, C.E.O.
E-mail for residency: mesa@commoncounsel.org
FAX: (510) 834-2998;
E-mail: info@commoncounsel.org; URL: http://www.commoncounsel.org

Foundation type: Public charity
Purpose: Residencies to writers working on topics related to economic and environmental sustainability and related social equity issues.
Publications: Application guidelines; Biennial report; Grants list; Informational brochure (including application guidelines).
Financial data: Year ended 12/31/2011. Assets, $3,720,313 (M); Expenditures, $1,437,034; Total giving, $669,100.
Fields of interest: Literature.
Type of support: Residencies.
Application information: Applications accepted. Application form required.
> *Initial approach:* Letter or telephone
> *Deadline(s):* Feb. 1 for spring and early summer, June 1 for late summer and fall
> *Applicants should submit the following:*
> 1) Work samples
> 2) Proposal
> 3) Letter(s) of recommendation
> 4) Resume
Program description:
Mesa Refuge Residency Program: Residency for two or four weeks are available to experienced writers from diverse backgrounds and disciplines, but generally only support projects that address the environment, the economy, and to a more limited extent, social equity issues. Nonfiction projects are generally preferred.
EIN: 943214166

510
Community Foundation for Oak Park

P.O. Box 291
Agoura Hills, CA   91376-0291   (818) 390-0060
Contact: Alon Glickstein, Pres.
E-mail: info@OakParkFoundation.org; URL: http://www.OakParkFoundation.org

Foundation type: Community foundation

Purpose: Scholarships to graduating high school students of Oak Park Unified School District, CA.
Publications: Application guidelines; Financial statement; Grants list; Informational brochure; Occasional report.
Financial data: Year ended 06/30/2013. Assets, $373,748 (M); Expenditures, $249,586; Total giving, $86,915.
Fields of interest: Higher education; Scholarships/financial aid.
Type of support: Scholarships—to individuals; Support to graduates or students of specific schools.
Application information: Applications accepted.
Additional information: Students should contact their guidance counselors for additional information.
EIN: 953416510

511
Community Foundation for San Benito County

829 San Benito St., Ste. 200
Hollister, CA 95023 (831) 630-1924
Contact: Paul Levy, Dir., Opers. and Grants
FAX: (831) 630-1934; E-mail: info@cffsbc.org;
Grant application e-mail: grants@cffsbc.org;
URL: http://www.cffsbc.org/

Foundation type: Community foundation
Purpose: Scholarships to students in the San Benito County, CA area for higher education.
Publications: Application guidelines.
Financial data: Year ended 12/31/2011. Assets, $5,007,728 (M); Expenditures, $2,256,903; Total giving, $1,689,897; Grants to individuals, 16 grants totaling $25,403.
Fields of interest: Higher education.
Type of support: Scholarships—to individuals; Undergraduate support.
Application information: Applications accepted.
Additional information: Students should contact their guidance counselors for application guidelines.
EIN: 770312582

512
The Community Foundation of Santa Cruz County

(formerly Greater Santa Cruz County Community Foundation)
7807 Soquel Dr.
Aptos, CA 95003 (831) 662-2000
Contact: Lance Linares, C.E.O.; For grants: Christina Cuevas, Prog. Dir.; For scholarships: Owen David, Prog. Assoc.
Scholarship inquiry tel.: (832) 662-2072
FAX: (831) 662-2001; E-mail: cfhelp@cfscc.org;
URL: http://www.cfscc.org

Foundation type: Community foundation
Purpose: Scholarships to high school graduates from Santa Cruz County, CA. Fellowships for visual artists.
Publications: Application guidelines; Annual report; Financial statement; Grants list; Informational brochure.
Financial data: Year ended 12/31/2012. Assets, $56,863,547 (M); Expenditures, $5,664,793; Total giving, $3,704,920. Fellowships amount not specified. Scholarships—to individuals amount not specified.
Fields of interest: Visual arts; Vocational education; Higher education; Athletics/sports, training; Recreation; Economically disadvantaged.

Type of support: Fellowships; Scholarships—to individuals; Support to graduates or students of specific schools; Undergraduate support.
Application information: Applications accepted. Application form required. Application form available on the grantmaker's web site.
Initial approach: Application
Send request by: Online
Deadline(s): Feb. 23 for scholarships
Final notification: Applicants notified in May for scholarships
Applicants should submit the following:
1) Class rank
2) Transcripts
3) GPA
Additional information: Application should include transcripts. See web site for application form and a complete listing of scholarships.
Program description:
Scholarships: Donors have established several scholarship funds which the foundation manages, to help students pursue their education beyond the high school level. Each scholarship maintains its own unique eligibility criteria, such as financial need, high academic achievement, attendance at a particular high school or majoring in a particular field of study. See web site for additional information.
EIN: 942808039

513
Community Foundation of the Verdugos

(formerly Glendale Community Foundation)
111 E. Bdwy., Ste. 200
Glendale, CA 91205 (818) 241-8040
Contact: Edna Karinski, C.E.O.
FAX: (818) 241-8045; E-mail: info@cfverdugos.org;
URL: http://www.cfverdugos.org/

Foundation type: Community foundation
Purpose: Scholarships to individuals from La Crescenta, La Canada Flintridge, Glendale, Montrose and Verdugo City, CA, for undergraduate education.
Publications: Application guidelines; Annual report; Financial statement; Grants list; Informational brochure; Newsletter; Program policy statement (including application guidelines).
Financial data: Year ended 12/31/2012. Assets, $9,238,660 (M); Expenditures, $697,756; Total giving, $308,285; Grants to individuals, 62 grants totaling $89,750.
Fields of interest: Education, special; Vocational education, post-secondary; Medical school/education; Teacher school/education; Journalism school/education; Scholarships/financial aid.
Type of support: Exchange programs; Student loans—to individuals; Support to graduates or students of specific schools; Technical education support; Undergraduate support.
Application information: Applications accepted. Application form required. Interview required.
Initial approach: Letter, telephone or e-mail
Copies of proposal: 1
Deadline(s): Mar. 7
Final notification: May 1
Applicants should submit the following:
1) SAR
2) Letter(s) of recommendation
3) ACT
4) SAT
5) Transcripts
6) Essay
Additional information: See web site for complete listing of scholarships and application form.
EIN: 956068137

514
The Community Foundation Serving Riverside and San Bernardino Counties

(formerly Community Foundation of Riverside County)
3700 6th St., Ste. 200
Riverside, CA 92501 (951) 241-7777
Contact: Celia Cudiamat, Exec. V.P.
FAX: (951) 684-1911;
E-mail: info@thecommunityfoundation.net;
URL: http://www.thecommunityfoundation.net

Foundation type: Community foundation
Purpose: Scholarships to deserving college-bound area students of Riverside, CA who otherwise would not be able to attend college.
Publications: Application guidelines; Annual report; Financial statement; Grants list; Informational brochure; Newsletter.
Financial data: Year ended 12/31/2012. Assets, $62,966,618 (M); Expenditures, $9,680,230; Total giving, $8,232,792; Grants to individuals, 158 grants totaling $689,425.
Fields of interest: Higher education.
Type of support: Scholarships—to individuals; Undergraduate support.
Application information: Applications accepted. Application form required. Application form available on the grantmaker's web site.
Send request by: Mail
Deadline(s): Vary
Additional information: Students should contact their guidance counselor or college financial aid office for scholarship information.
Program description:
Scholarships: The foundation averages $1 million a year in scholarships to public two- and four-year colleges and universities in the two-county region, as well as to colleges and universities in other parts of the nation. The awards not only recognize these students' achievements, but also, more significantly, provide hope for those seeking to better themselves through education. Each donor has a different vision for the scholarships they wish to fund. The foundation manages several different scholarships with varied eligibility requirements. See web site for additional information.
EIN: 330748536

515
Community Foundation Sonoma County

(formerly The Sonoma County Community Foundation)
250 D St., Ste. 205
Santa Rosa, CA 95404-4773 (707) 579-4073
Contact: For grants: Robert Judd, V.P., Progs.
FAX: (707) 579-4801; E-mail: info@sonomacf.org;
URL: http://www.sonomacf.org

Foundation type: Community foundation
Purpose: Scholarships to individuals who are Sonoma County, CA, residents for education at an accredited two or four-year college, university or vocational college.
Publications: Application guidelines; Annual report; Financial statement; Informational brochure; Newsletter.
Financial data: Year ended 12/31/2012. Assets, $153,516,532 (M); Expenditures, $13,275,815; Total giving, $9,973,500.
Fields of interest: Arts, artist's services; Higher education; Scholarships/financial aid.
Type of support: Scholarships—to individuals; Undergraduate support.
Application information: Applications accepted. Application form required. Application form

available on the grantmaker's web site. Interview required.

Send request by: Online

Deadline(s): Mar. 2

Applicants should submit the following:
1) FAFSA
2) Financial information
3) Letter(s) of recommendation
4) Essay

Additional information: Most scholarships range from $500 to $5000 per academic year. See web site for complete listing of scholarships and individual eligibility criteria.

Program description:

Connecting a New Generation to a Better Future: A community prospers when it shares and acts on a sense of hope for its future. The foundation believes that the possibility of achieving one's life goals should be accessible to all. Scholarships are available through a new program, Scholarship Sonoma County, which is a partnership of the Community Foundation and 10,000 Degrees.

EIN: 680003212

516
Community Hospital Foundation

P.O. Box HH

Monterey, CA   93942-6032   (831) 624-5311

Contact: Steven Packer M.D., Pres. and C.E.O.

E-mail: information@chomp.org; URL: http://www.chomp.org/

Foundation type: Public charity

Purpose: Financial assistance for qualified patients of Community Hospital of the Monterey Peninsula who need help paying for services that may not be paid for by insurance. The patient's family gross income must not exceed 250% of the current federal poverty level.

Financial data: Year ended 12/31/2011. Assets, $215,486,004 (M); Expenditures, $12,564,267; Total giving, $7,060,991; Grants to individuals, totaling $285,712.

Fields of interest: Health care; Economically disadvantaged.

Type of support: Grants for special needs.

Application information: Applications accepted.

Initial approach: Letter or tel.

Deadline(s): Applications for the Sponsored Care or Discount Payment Program must be submitted to the hospital within 120 days of the date services were provided, or within 90 days of payment made to the hospital by third party coverage.

Applicants should submit the following:
1) Financial information

Additional information: For additional info, call Patient Business Services at (831) 625-4922.

EIN: 942789696

517
Community Initiatives

(formerly Community Initiative Funds of the San Francisco Foundation, also known as CIF of the San Francisco Foundation)

354 Pine St., Ste. 700

San Francisco, CA   94104-4224   (415) 230-7700

Contact: M. Melanie Beene, Pres. and C.E.O.

FAX: (415) 230-7701;

E-mail: melanie@communityin.org; URL: http://www.communityin.org

Foundation type: Public charity

Purpose: Support through a fiscal sponsorship program for collaborative, philanthropic efforts among several foundations; community efforts responding to crises and urgent calls to action; projects of limited duration; and new, incubating organizations.

Publications: Annual report; Informational brochure.

Financial data: Year ended 06/30/2011. Assets, $16,693,217 (M); Expenditures, $17,670,349; Total giving, $3,554,820; Grants to individuals, totaling $58,745.

Type of support: Fiscal agent/sponsor.

Application information: Applications accepted.

Additional information: If the project is approved a $1,000 nonrefundable fee must accompany fiscal sponsorship application.

Program description:

Fiscal Sponsorship: Fiscal sponsorship opportunities are available for organizations not incorporated as independent, nonprofit corporations, that fall into one of the following types: collaborative, philanthropic efforts among several foundations; community efforts responding to crises and urgent calls to action; projects of limited duration; and new, incubating organizations. Services offered include tax and informational returns, payroll tax remittance and filings, monthly financial statements, finance record-keeping, independent audit, insurance (including workers' compensation), human resources administration, payroll processing, personnel policies, technical assistance on personnel issues, benefits administration, permits, and others. The organization charges 10 percent of gross receipts plus 50 percent of interest earned on funds on deposit.

EIN: 943255070

518
Community Projects, Inc.

715 Franklin St.

Napa, CA   94559-2920   (707) 226-7585

Contact: Scholarships: J. Miller

Foundation type: Public charity

Purpose: Four-year scholarships to graduating students attending one of the following Napa Valley, CA, schools: Callistoga High School, St. Helena High School, Justin-Siaena High School, Vintage High School, Napa High School, New Technology High School, Napa Valley College.

Publications: Application guidelines; Annual report; Grants list.

Financial data: Year ended 12/31/2011. Assets, $1,967,941 (M); Expenditures, $650,265; Total giving, $408,251.

Type of support: Support to graduates or students of specific schools; Undergraduate support.

Application information: Applications accepted.

Initial approach: Letter

Send request by: Mail

Copies of proposal: 1

Deadline(s): Contact foundation for current application deadline

Additional information: Application must demonstrate financial need, scholastic excellence and community service. Applications available through guidance counselors at the specified schools.

EIN: 941229581

519
CompassPoint Nonprofit Services

(formerly Support Center for Nonprofit Management)

500 12th St., Ste. 320

Oakland, CA   94607-4087   (415) 541-9000

Contact: Jeanne Bell, C.E.O.

FAX: (415) 541-7708;

E-mail: info@compasspoint.org; Additional address (Silicon Valley Office): 600 Valley Way, Ste. A, Milpitas, CA 95035-4138, tel.: (408) 719-1400, fax: (408) 719-1444; URL: http://www.compasspoint.org

Foundation type: Public charity

Purpose: Support to individuals of color within the San Francisco Bay Area, CA to develop the skills needed to work in high-level nonprofit positions.

Publications: Application guidelines; Annual report; Newsletter.

Financial data: Year ended 12/31/2011. Assets, $2,597,793 (M); Expenditures, $4,149,206.

Fields of interest: Human services.

Type of support: Program development.

Application information: Applications accepted.

Send request by: Online

Deadline(s): Feb. 8

Final notification: Recipients notified by Feb. 15

Program description:

Next Generation Leaders of Color Program: This program provides managers and leaders of color working in Bay Area health and human service organizations with an opportunity to develop the necessary confidence, leadership vision, and practical senior-level management skills needed to thrive in diverse organizations operating in challenging environments. Eligible applicants must be individuals of color who are currently in mid-level management positions within a Bay Area health and human service organization, have at least two years of experience managing people and budgets, have never been an executive director, and have a commitment to social change.

EIN: 931196632

520
Concern Foundation

1026 S. Robertson Blvd., Ste. 300

Los Angeles, CA   90035-1545   (310) 360-6100

Contact: Derek Alpert, Pres.

E-mail address for S. Yu: seunga@concernfoundation.org

FAX: (310) 360-6105;

E-mail: info@concernfoundation.org; URL: http://www.concernfoundation.org

Foundation type: Public charity

Purpose: Grants to researchers in the field of cancer immunology, immunotherapy and the genetics of cancer.

Publications: Application guidelines; Annual report; Grants list.

Financial data: Year ended 12/31/2011. Assets, $3,923,191 (M); Expenditures, $1,529,059; Total giving, $1,166,250.

Fields of interest: Cancer research; Immunology research.

Type of support: Research.

Application information: Applications accepted. Application form required.

Send request by: Online

Deadline(s): Sept. 8 for Letter of Intent, Dec. 8 for application

Additional information: See web site for additional application guidelines.

Program description:
Grants: Grants of $60,000 are available to independent investigators at the level of assistant professor (or equivalent with explanation) for cancer research. The foundation is especially interested in funding young researchers who may initially have difficulty obtaining funding from more traditional sources.
EIN: 237002878

521
The Edward & Elizabeth Conner Foundation
P.O. Box 1318
Venice, CA 90294 (310) 823-5872
Contact: Kathleen Conner, Pres.
E-mail: connerfound@aol.com

Foundation type: Independent foundation
Purpose: Scholarships to graduates of Liberty High School, Brentwood, CA, or Greene High School, Greene, NY, for postsecondary education at two-year institutions.
Financial data: Year ended 12/31/2012. Assets, $1,710,468 (M); Expenditures, $117,872; Total giving, $94,200; Grants to individuals, 38 grants totaling $94,200 (high: $4,800, low: $200).
Fields of interest: Higher education.
Type of support: Support to graduates or students of specific schools; Undergraduate support.
Application information:
Deadline(s): 45 days before scholarship is required
Additional information: Applications must be made through Liberty High School or Greene High School guidance departments.
EIN: 946131053

522
The Conquistador Trust
11436 Corte Playa Laguna
San Diego, CA 92124-1540 (858) 694-0246
Contact: Roy Gilmour, Tr.

Foundation type: Operating foundation
Purpose: Scholarships to female seniors of Serra High School, San Diego, CA for continuing education at a college of their choice.
Financial data: Year ended 12/31/2013. Assets, $4,173 (M); Expenditures, $5,016; Total giving, $5,000; Grant to an individual, 1 grant totaling $5,000.
Fields of interest: Higher education; Women.
Type of support: Support to graduates or students of specific schools.
Application information: Applications accepted. Application form required.
Deadline(s): Mar.
Final notification: Recipients notified in Apr.
Applicants should submit the following:
1) SAT
2) ACT
3) Transcripts
4) Photograph
5) GPA
6) FAFSA
Additional information: Scholarship award is based on achievements in sports, financial need and extracurricular activities.
EIN: 206513443

523
Cops 4 Causes
1776 N. Higland Ave.
Los Angeles, CA 90028-4404
Contact: Christopher T. Landavazo, Pres.
E-mail: office@cops4causes.org; Mailing address: 5482 Wilshire Blvd., Ste. 1562, Los Angeles, CA 90036-4218; toll-free tel.: (888) 964-2677; toll-free fax: (888) 914-2677; E-mail For Christopher T. Landavazo: cl@cops4causes.org; URL: http://www.cops4causes.org

Foundation type: Public charity
Purpose: Emergency funds to families of Los Angeles County, LA police officers who have been killed or disabled in the line of duty. Scholarships to children of peace officers in the Los Angeles, CA area who have been disabled or killed in the line of duty.
Financial data: Year ended 12/31/2012. Assets, $76,625 (M); Expenditures, $78,929; Total giving, $37,511; Grants to individuals, totaling $22,796.
Fields of interest: Higher education.
Type of support: Emergency funds; Scholarships—to individuals.
Application information: Applications not accepted.
Additional information: Contributes only to families of police and peace officers; unsolicited requests for funds not considered or acknowledged.
Program descriptions:
Fallen Heroes Fund: This programs gives funds directly to the families of Los Angeles County officers who have killed or disabled in the line of duty, in order to ensure that families of peace officers who have been rendered disabled or who have paid the ultimate sacrifice while serving and protecting their communities receive assistance.
Rick J. Centanni Fallen Heroes Scholarship Fund: This fund provides scholarships to degree-seeking, full-time college students of peace officers who have been rendered disabled or who have paid the ultimate sacrifice while serving and protecting the community.
EIN: 261452839

524
Randy Couch Memorial Fund
250 Lynd Way
Dixon, CA 95620-3245 (707) 678-2154
Contact: Wayne Couch, Treas.

Foundation type: Independent foundation
Purpose: Scholarships to South Tahoe High School athletic seniors for continuing education at institutions of higher learning.
Financial data: Year ended 12/31/2012. Assets, $0 (M); Expenditures, $6,733; Total giving, $6,250; Grants to individuals, 4 grants totaling $6,250 (high: $2,500, low: $1,250).
Fields of interest: Higher education; Recreation.
Type of support: Scholarships—to individuals.
Application information:
Deadline(s): End of school year
Additional information: Students should contact their guidance department for additional application information.
EIN: 942745884

525
CounterPULSE
1310 Mission St.
San Francisco, CA 94103-2609 (415) 626-2060
E-mail for residency: abby@counterpulse.org
FAX: (415) 626-1643;
E-mail: info@counterpulse.org; URL: http://www.counterpulse.org

Foundation type: Public charity
Purpose: Provides free rehearsal space to low-income emerging and established artists in the San Francisco, CA area and support through a fiscal sponsorship program.
Financial data: Year ended 06/30/2011. Assets, $695,769 (M); Expenditures, $702,613. Grants to individuals amount not specified.
Fields of interest: Performing arts; Arts, artist's services; Economically disadvantaged.
Type of support: Residencies; Stipends; Fiscal agent/sponsor.
Application information: Application form required. Application form available on the grantmaker's web site.
Deadline(s): Feb. 15
Final notification: Applicants notified by Mar. 1
Applicants should submit the following:
1) Work samples
2) SASE
3) Proposal
Additional information: See web site for additional guidelines.
Program descriptions:
Artist in Residence Program: The program provides a nurturing space for low-income and emerging artists committed to innovation and growth. This program offers artists an opportunity to rehearse and perform. Two selected artists or companies will receive up to 100 hours of free rehearsal space and, in exchange, they will present the work developed during the residency in a shared weekend of performances. The organization offers both winter and summer residencies annually.
Fiscal Sponsorship: This program exists to provide managerial support and guidance to dancers and dance organizations so that they may produce temporary projects or begin to develop on-going organization, and assure funding agencies and contributors that funds are well-managed and spent according to their guidelines, and that the artists deliver their proposed services or products. Fiscal sponsorship services are offered to independent artists and companies whose work supports low-income artists.
EIN: 942986114

526
Creative Visions Foundation
18820 Pacific Coast Hwy., Ste. 201
Malibu, CA 90265 (310)-456-1109
Contact: Joey Borgogna, Exec. Dir.
E-mail: info@creativevisions.org; URL: http://www.creativevisions.org

Foundation type: Public charity
Purpose: Support to filmmakers, artists, photographers and other "creative activists" through a fiscal sponsorship program.
Financial data: Year ended 12/31/2011. Assets, $588,383 (M); Expenditures, $476,015.
Fields of interest: Media/communications; Film/video; Photography; Arts, artist's services.
Type of support: Fellowships; Fiscal agent/sponsor.

Application information: Applications accepted. Application form required.
> *Initial approach:* E-mail
> *Additional information:* See web site for additional guidelines.

Program descriptions:
Dan Eldon Fellowship: In association with the Overseas Press Club of America, the foundation awards an annual scholarship to an outstanding young journalist who is pursuing a career in international journalism.

Fiscal Sponsorship: The foundation provides fiscal sponsorship to artists who are committed to creating projects with a social relevance. It acts as ambassador on an artist's behalf, referencing their project to the media; mentors them by providing them with contacts and resources to maximize their opportunities; and acts as a pass-through while artists raise funds for taking inspiration from concept to reality.
EIN: 391902814

527
Croatian National Foundation
555 W. 9th St., Ste. 18
San Pedro, CA   90731

Foundation type: Operating foundation
Purpose: Grants primarily in support of Croatian history and culture.
Financial data: Year ended 12/31/2012. Assets, $38,370 (M); Expenditures, $21,641; Total giving, $0.
International interests: Croatia.
Type of support: Grants to individuals.
Application information: Applications not accepted.
> *Additional information:* Unsolicited requests for funds not considered or acknowledged.

EIN: 954065779

528
Croatian Scholarship Fund
P.O. Box 290
San Ramon, CA   94583-0290
E-mail: vbrekalo@msn.com; Tel./fax: (925) 556-6263; URL: http://www.croatianscholarship.org

Foundation type: Public charity
Purpose: Scholarships to Croatian and Bosnian-Herzegovinan students to attend a university in Croatia.
Publications: Application guidelines; Annual report; Newsletter.
Financial data: Year ended 12/31/2011. Assets, $278,805 (M); Expenditures, $84,384; Total giving, $63,375; Grants to individuals, totaling $63,375.
Fields of interest: Higher education; Scholarships/financial aid.
International interests: Bosnia and Herzegovina; Croatia.
Type of support: Scholarships—to individuals.
Application information: Applications accepted. Application form required. Application form available on the grantmaker's web site.
> *Deadline(s):* May 15
> *Additional information:* Contact the organization for additional application guidelines. Applications must be completed in Croatian.

Program description:
Scholarships: The foundation awards scholarships to Croatian students from Croatia and

Bosnia-Herzegovina to attend universities in Croatia.
EIN: 680231056

529
Croul Family Foundation
18101 Von Karman Ave., Ste. 700
Irvine, CA   92612-0145
Contact: Spencer Behr Croul, Secy.
FAX: (949) 833-9584;
E-mail: grants@croulfoundation.org; Toll free tel.: (877) 968-6328; URL: http://www.croulfoundation.org

Foundation type: Independent foundation
Purpose: Scholarships to the economically disadvantaged in Los Angeles and Orange County, CA.
Publications: Application guidelines; Program policy statement.
Financial data: Year ended 12/31/2012. Assets, $20,794,170 (M); Expenditures, $1,233,791; Total giving, $1,077,850.
Type of support: Scholarships—to individuals.
Application information: Contact foundation for current application deadline/guidelines.
EIN: 201222760

530
Cure Autism Now
(also known as CAN)
5455 Wilshire Blvd., Ste. 2250
Los Angeles, CA   90036-4234   (323) 549-0500
FAX: (323) 549-0547;
E-mail: info@cureautismnow.org; Toll-free tel.: (888) 828-8476; URL: http://www.cureautismnow.org

Foundation type: Public charity
Purpose: Research grants for the investigation of effective biological treatments, prevention and cure of autism and related disorders.
Publications: Application guidelines; Financial statement; Grants list; Informational brochure; Newsletter.
Fields of interest: Autism research.
Type of support: Research; Awards/prizes.
Application information: Applications accepted. Application form required.
> *Initial approach:* Letter of intent
> *Send request by:* Online
> *Copies of proposal:* 1
> *Additional information:* See web site for current application deadline/guidelines.

Program descriptions:
Innovative Technology for Autism (ITA) Bridge Grants: The ITA bridge grants are intended to support projects in areas where traditional funding is not available due to project timeline, area of investigation, or the nature of the need. Examples of possible reasons for applying for funding are: one-time expenses, quick investigation of a new hypotheses, intern expenses, student projects, or investigation of topics that do not fit existing RFPs. To meet the needs of those applying for bridge grants, the application and review procedures are streamlined to provide funding in a timely fashion.

Innovative Technology for Autism Initiative (ITA): The initiative was established to lead in the development of products that provide real world solutions for those with autism, their families, educators, healthcare specialists, and researchers. ITA is intended to create a merger of technology with other fields, such as design, assistive technology, engineering, social science, and neuroscience, yielding an interdisciplinary

approach to the challenge of utilizing technology to improve the lives of people with autism. To enable the efforts of those developing products and technologies related to autism, ITA has established the following programmatic areas: multi-year grants, fast track bridge grants, educational programs, and a workgroup within which investigators can meet, share, and collaborate. The ITA workgroup additionally acts as a conduit for the promotion of relevant technologies, and actively recruits new investigators to the field. In keeping with its mission to innovate, ITA supports projects employing both traditional and emerging research and development methodologies, with the main requirement being a compelling argument as to how the work ultimately will improve the quality of life for those with autism.

Pilot Research Awards: The award supports established investigators from within as well as outside of the field of autism. Research proposals targeting promising hypotheses or using innovative approaches and technologies are a priority. In addition, Cure Autism Now encourage studies focused on generating preliminary data, leading to larger studies and federal funding. These awards are available to investigators at any stage in their career. Funding is available at a maximum of $120,000 for two-year awards ($60,000 per year). Indirect costs are limited to 10 percent and do not include salary for Pilot Investigator.

Treatment-Related Awards: Cure Autism Now recognizes the urgent need to develop effective therapies to treat both core and domain specific features of autism. Research proposals focused on all aspects of transitional research are acceptable for submission. Applications are encouraged both from scientists already focusing on autism and from those new to the field. All proposals must have direct and immediate relevance to autism and its related disorders. Treatment Awards are limited to $60,000 per year for one, two, or three years. Indirect costs may not exceed 10 percent of the total proposed budget and must be included in the $60,000 annual funding limit. We generally do not consider funding of salary costs for the Principal Investigator. In addition, funding equipment purchases over $500 will not be considered. Second year funding is contingent upon a mid-cycle report indicating satisfactory progress and the availability of funds.

Young Investigator Awards: The award is given to promising young scientists to enter the field of autism research. Applicants must be no more than four years out of an M.D. or Ph.D. program and work under the supervision of an established investigator. The mentor need not be directly involved in autism research, but must provide a research environment in which the young investigator can perform research with direct relevance to autism. Funding is available at a maximum of $80,000 for two-year awards ($40,000 per year) in postdoctoral fellowship support ($1,000/year may be used for conferences). Indirect costs are not supported by Young Investigator Awards, nor are equipment purchases over $500.
EIN: 954542637

531
The Curley Foundation
8405 Zeta St.
La Mesa, CA   91942-2842   (619) 589-8151
Contact: Carmen J. Berry, V.P. and Secy.-Treas.

Foundation type: Independent foundation
Purpose: Scholarships to individuals for higher education, with preference given to those who

received their primary and secondary education in San Diego County, CA.

Financial data: Year ended 12/31/2012. Assets, $161,891 (M); Expenditures, $17,499; Total giving, $4,750; Grants to individuals, 6 grants totaling $4,750 (high: $1,000, low: $500).

Fields of interest: Higher education.

Type of support: Support to graduates or students of specific schools; Undergraduate support.

Application information: Applications accepted. Application form required.

> *Deadline(s):* May 31
> *Applicants should submit the following:*
> 1) Transcripts
> 2) Letter(s) of recommendation
> 3) Essay
> *Additional information:* Application forms are available from high schools and colleges in the San Diego area.

EIN: 330640939

532
Cystic Fibrosis Research, Inc.
2672 Bayshore Pkwy., Ste. 520
Mountain View, CA 94043-1016   (650) 904-9975
Contact: David Soohoo, Prog. Dir.; Carroll Jenkins, Exec. Dir.
FAX: (650) 404-9981; E-mail: cfri@cfri.org; Email for Carroll Jenkins: cjenkins@cfri.org; tel. for Carroll Jenkins: (650) 404-9977; email for David Soohoo: dsoohoo@cfri.org; tel. for David Soohoo: (650) 404-9445; URL: http://www.cfri.org

Foundation type: Public charity

Purpose: Grants to individuals performing both clinical and basic research in cystic fibrosis.

Publications: Financial statement; Informational brochure; Newsletter.

Financial data: Year ended 12/31/2011. Assets, $578,266 (M); Expenditures, $771,831; Total giving, $194,600.

Fields of interest: Cystic fibrosis; Cystic fibrosis research.

Type of support: Fellowships; Research.

Application information: Applications not accepted.

> *Additional information:* Unsolicited requests for funds not considered or acknowledged.

EIN: 510169988

533
Cystinosis Foundation, Inc.
58 Miramount Dr.
Moraga, CA 94556-1002   (925) 631-1588
Contact: Valerie Hotz, Exec. Dir.
E-mail: VHotz@cystinosis.com; Toll-free tel.: (888) 631-1588; URL: http://www.cystinosisfoundation.org

Foundation type: Public charity

Purpose: Scholarships to individuals suffering from cystinosis who are planning to attend an accredited college, university, or vocational program.

Publications: Application guidelines; Informational brochure.

Financial data: Year ended 06/30/2012. Assets, $78,103 (M); Expenditures, $163,410; Total giving, $1,000; Grants to individuals, totaling $1,000.

Fields of interest: Scholarships/financial aid; Diseases (rare).

Type of support: Scholarships—to individuals.

Application information: Applications accepted. Application form required. Application form available on the grantmaker's web site.

Initial approach: Application
Deadline(s): Mar. 30
Applicants should submit the following:
1) Budget Information
2) Letter(s) of recommendation
3) Transcripts
4) Essay
Additional information: Applicants must also submit an essay of 500 words, discussing a person who has played a vital role in the student's life.

Program description:
Deanna Lynn Potts Scholarship: This scholarship provides supplemental financial assistance to an undergraduate student diagnosed with cystinosis who is enrolled in an accredited collegiate or vocational program. A $1,000 scholarship is awarded annually.

EIN: 942927892

534
George F. Dales Foundation
3433 Golden Gate Way
Lafayette, CA 94549

Foundation type: Independent foundation

Purpose: Scholarships to U.S. citizens pursuing degree-granting studies and research in ancient civilizations, archaeology, anthropology or professional areas supporting these academic areas.

Financial data: Year ended 12/31/2011. Assets, $0 (M); Expenditures, $5,080; Total giving, $5,000; Grant to an individual, 1 grant totaling $5,000.

Type of support: Graduate support; Doctoral support.

Application information: Application form required.

> *Send request by:* Mail
> *Copies of proposal:* 6
> *Deadline(s):* May 31
> *Final notification:* Recipients are notified by June 30
> *Applicants should submit the following:*
> 1) Letter(s) of recommendation
> 2) Transcripts
> 3) Essay
> *Additional information:* Application must also include official confirmation of enrollment.

EIN: 686083929

535
Dancers' Group, Inc.
44 Gough St, Ste 201
San Francisco, CA 94103-2647   (415) 920-9181
Contact: Wayne Hazzard, Exec. Dir.
FAX: (415) 920-9173;
E-mail: wayne@dancersgroup.org; URL: http://www.dancersgroup.org

Foundation type: Public charity

Purpose: Support to Bay Area, CA choregraphers and dance companies through a fiscal sponsorship program.

Publications: Application guidelines.

Financial data: Year ended 12/31/2011. Assets, $695,121 (M); Expenditures, $1,290,750; Total giving, $580,041.

Fields of interest: Dance; Arts, artist's services.

Type of support: Project support; Fiscal agent/sponsor.

Application information: Applications accepted. Application form required. Application form available on the grantmaker's web site.

> *Deadline(s):* June 30 for Lighting Artists in Dance

Additional information: The fiscal sponsorship review process may take up to one month and submission of an application does not guarantee sponsorship.

Program descriptions:
CA$H Grants: The grants support professionally-oriented theatre and dance artists and small companies with budgets under $100,000. The purpose of these grants is to spark a creative surge throughout northern California's theatre and dance community by providing grants to artists (of up to $1,500) and small-sized organizations (of up to $2,500)

Fiscal Sponsorship: The program provides administrative support and guidance to choreographers and dance organizations, working in a variety of disciplines, so that they may produce community and performance projects; and ensures funding agencies and contributors that donations and grants received on behalf of the artists/projects are well-managed and funds are disbursed according to the grant proposal and their guidelines.

Internships: Provides on-the-job experience to those interested in developing arts administration, journalism, and production management careers.

Lighting Artists in Dance (LAD) Award: This program supports Bay Area lighting designers working in the field of dance and in partnership with a choreographer, dance company, or presenter of dance. Up to $12,000 is available to support public performance projects that encourage an active interaction between designers and choreographer. Projects must be presented in Alameda, Contra Costa, Marin, Napa, San Francisco, San Mateo, Santa Clara, Solano, or Sonoma counties, California.

New Stages for Dance Grants: This program awards theater rental subsidies to San Francisco Bay Area-dance companies and artists presenting work at select theaters in San Francisco (including Dance Mission, ODC Theater, Yerba Buena Center for the Arts, and Z Space at Theater Artaud). Three funding categories are available: shared presentation (performance programs in a participating theater with any combination of two dance companies or dance artists), new theater (for companies or artists performing in a participating theater where they have not previously performed, and which has an increase in seating capacity or technical capacity from prior venues where the artist has presented), and increase performances (for a company or artist presenting work in a participating theater who will propose to significantly increase the number of performances beyond prior years)

Parachute Fund: This program provides grants of up to $500 per request, and $1,500 in a calendar year, to members of the San Francisco Bay Area dance community facing HIV/AIDS or other life-threatening illnesses.

EIN: 942879185

536
Agnes Larsen Darnell Scholarship
3909 Shaker Run Cir.
Fairfield, CA 94533   (707) 422-8212
Contact: Larry Darnell, C.E.O.
Scholarship e-mail: mitchlaurenpeters@gmail.com

Foundation type: Independent foundation

Purpose: Scholarships to Alaska natives for advanced education at accredited colleges and universities and other institutions for postsecondary education.

Financial data: Year ended 12/31/2011. Assets, $96,594 (M); Expenditures, $5,982; Total giving,

$5,000; Grants to individuals, 5 grants totaling $5,000 (high: $1,000, low: $1,000).
Fields of interest: Vocational education, post-secondary; Higher education.
Type of support: Scholarships—to individuals.
Application information: Applications accepted.
Initial approach: E-mail
Deadline(s): Mar. 31
Applicants should submit the following:
1) Transcripts
2) GPA
EIN: 680619368

537
Deaf West Theatre Company, Inc.
5112 Lankershim Blvd.
North Hollywood, CA 91601-3717   (818) 762-2998
FAX: (818) 762-2981; E-mail: info@deafwest.org;
URL: http://www.deafwest.org

Foundation type: Public charity
Purpose: Summer-long training programs for deaf and hard-of-hearing acting students to help them toward the goal of attaining employment in the Los Angeles entertainment industry.
Financial data: Year ended 12/31/2011. Assets, $77,790 (M); Expenditures, $274,516.
Fields of interest: Performing arts; Theater; Deaf/hearing impaired.
Type of support: Residencies.
Application information:
Initial approach: Letter
Program description:
Professional Summer School Program: This program provides training for Deaf and hard-of-hearing acting students every summer, through a three-week program that addresses their specific needs of Deaf and helps them toward the goal of attaining employment in the entertainment industry. Eligible applicants include Deaf and hard-of-hearing high school graduates who are at least 18 years of age. Priority will be given to those with previous professional, community, and/or college performing experience. The program includes three meals per day and housing for individuals who live outside of the Los Angeles area; applicants are responsible for their transportation to and from the school.
EIN: 954315054

538
Desert Valley Charitable Foundation
(formerly Dr. Prem Reddy Charitable Foundation)
16850 Bear Valley Rd., Ste. 200
Victorville, CA 92395-5794
Contact: Jana Bullock
Scholarship address: 16716 Bear Valley Rd., Victorville, CA 92395-5797; tel.: (760) 241-8000

Foundation type: Operating foundation
Purpose: Scholarships to residents of the High Desert, CA communities who are planning to enroll in an accredited program in health care or a medical-related field.
Publications: Application guidelines; Financial statement; Informational brochure.
Financial data: Year ended 12/31/2012. Assets, $6,826,000 (M); Expenditures, $5,171,687; Total giving, $4,371,756; Grants to individuals, 88 grants totaling $104,300 (high: $5,000, low: $500).
Fields of interest: Medical school/education; Health sciences school/education; Health care.
Type of support: Scholarships—to individuals.

Application information: Application form required.
Deadline(s): July 1
Applicants should submit the following:
1) Transcripts
2) Letter(s) of recommendation
Additional information: Application should also include a personal statement of plans and goals, and a copy of individual or parent's tax return.
EIN: 330486173

539
The Discovery Eye Foundation
6222 Wilshire Blvd., Ste. 260
Los Angeles, CA 90048-5123   (310) 623-4466
Contact: Susan Lee DeRemer, V.P., Devel.
FAX: (310) 623-1837;
E-mail: contactus@discoveryeye.org; URL: http://www.discoveryeye.org

Foundation type: Public charity
Purpose: Research and educational grants to physician researchers in finding cures and treatments for corneal and retinal eye disease.
Financial data: Year ended 12/31/2012. Assets, $7,014,683 (M); Expenditures, $2,136,872; Total giving, $846,200.
Fields of interest: Eye diseases.
Type of support: Research.
Application information: Contact the foundation for eligibility determination.
EIN: 954228653

540
The Walt Disney Company Foundation
500 S. Buena Vista St.
Burbank, CA 91521-6444
URL: http://corporate.disney.go.com/responsibility/index.html

Foundation type: Company-sponsored foundation
Purpose: Undergraduate scholarships to children of full-time, regular employees of The Walt Disney Company and its subsidiaries or affiliated companies.
Financial data: Year ended 10/01/2011. Assets, $6,724,245 (M); Expenditures, $2,787,753; Total giving, $2,599,687.
Fields of interest: Higher education; Scholarships/financial aid.
Type of support: Employee-related scholarships.
Application information: Applications not accepted.
Additional information: Unsolicited requests for funds are not considered or acknowledged.
Program description:
Disney Scholars Program: The foundation awards 50 college scholarships of $20,000 to high school seniors who are children of employees of Walt Disney Company and its subsidiaries or affiliated companies. Scholarships are awarded based on academic and extracurricular achievement. The program is administered by the Educational Testing Service.
Company name: The Walt Disney Company
EIN: 956037079

541
Djerassi Resident Artists Program
(formerly The Djerassi Foundation)
2325 Bear Gulch Rd.
Woodside, CA 94062-4405   (650) 747-1250
Contact: Margot Knight, Exec. Dir.
FAX: (650) 747-0105; E-mail: drap@djerassi.org;
E-mail For Margot Knight: margot@djerassi.org;
URL: http://www.djerassi.org

Foundation type: Public charity
Purpose: Residencies for artists working on independent or collaborative projects, with studio and living space, and all meals for a period of approximately one month.
Publications: Application guidelines; Informational brochure (including application guidelines); Newsletter.
Financial data: Year ended 12/31/2012. Assets, $5,204,613 (M); Expenditures, $145,769.
Fields of interest: Media/communications; Film/video; Visual arts; Photography; Sculpture; Design; Painting; Drawing; Ceramic arts; Performing arts; Choreography; Music composition; Literature.
Type of support: Residencies.
Application information: Applications accepted. Application form required. Application form available on the grantmaker's web site.
Initial approach: Letter, telephone, fax or e-mail
Copies of proposal: 1
Deadline(s): Feb. 15
Final notification: Applicants are notified in Aug.
Applicants should submit the following:
1) Work samples
2) SASE
3) Resume
4) Proposal
Additional information: See web site for additional application information.
Program descriptions:
Gerald Oshita Memorial Fellowships: Fellows receive a one-month Djerassi Program residency, during which the recipient is free to compose, study, rehearse, and otherwise advance his or her own creative projects, plus cash stipend.
Residency Program: Residencies are awarded competitively, at no cost, to national and international artists in the disciplines of choreography, literature, music composition, visual arts, and media arts/new genres. The organization seeks applications from emerging and mid-career artists, from whom appointments as resident artists may make a significant difference to their careers, as well as from established artists with national and/or international reputations. Applicants are evaluated by panels of arts professionals in each category. Those selected are offered living and studio space for four- to five-week sessions during the season, which runs from mid-Mar. through mid-Nov.
EIN: 946115995

542
Hans and Margaret Doe Charitable Trust
600 W. Broadway, 8th Fl.
San Diego, CA 92101-3540
Contact: Shirley Woodson
E-mail: swoodson@hechtsolberg.com

Foundation type: Independent foundation
Purpose: Scholarships to students who are children of employees of Vista Irrigation District, CA.
Financial data: Year ended 12/31/2012. Assets, $2,617,681 (M); Expenditures, $155,636; Total giving, $99,062; Grants to individuals, 5 grants totaling $43,062 (high: $8,000, low: $5,000).
Fields of interest: Higher education.

Type of support: Employee-related scholarships.
Application information: Applications accepted.
  Initial approach: Letter or telephone
  Deadline(s): None
EIN: 336080541

543
Doing His Time
1129 State St. 3E
Santa Barbara, CA   93101-8700

Foundation type: Independent foundation
Purpose: Educational grants for offenders and ex-offenders to cover the costs of tuition, books, fees, study materials and other incidental expenses, primarily in CA.
Financial data: Year ended 12/31/2012. Assets, $129,834 (M); Expenditures, $198,036; Total giving, $26,440; Grants to individuals, 2 grants totaling $26,440 (high: $24,055, low: $1,719).
Fields of interest: Correctional facilities; Offenders/ex-offenders, services.
Type of support: Scholarships—to individuals.
Application information: Applications not accepted.
  Additional information: Unsolicited requests for funds not considered or acknowledged.
EIN: 010626360

544
Dorland Mountain Arts Colony
P.O. Box 6
Temecula, CA   92593-0006
E-mail: info@dorlandartscolony.org; URL: http://dorlandartscolony.org/

Foundation type: Public charity
Purpose: Residencies for one to twelve weeks to aspiring, emerging, or professional artists in Temecula, CA.
Publications: Application guidelines; Informational brochure.
Financial data: Year ended 12/31/2011. Assets, $463,572 (M); Expenditures, $68,493. No monetary support given for residencies.
Fields of interest: Visual arts; Design; Dance; Music; Performing arts, education; Literature.
Type of support: Residencies.
Application information: Applications accepted. Application form required.
  Send request by: Mail
  Deadline(s): 45 days prior to requested dates
  Applicants should submit the following:
    1) Curriculum vitae
    2) Work samples
    3) SASE
    4) Resume
  Additional information: Application should also include three letters of reference and a $25 non-refundable application fee. See web site for additional guidelines.
EIN: 953786125

545
The James E. Downey Foundation
23 Brookline
Aliso Viejo, CA   92656-1461   (949) 474-0900
Contact: Karl Jonson, Secy. and C.F.O.

Foundation type: Independent foundation
Purpose: Scholarships to single parents in the Newport Beach, CA area for higher education.
Financial data: Year ended 06/30/2013. Assets, $4,063,334 (M); Expenditures, $559,774; Total

giving, $437,300; Grants to individuals, 275 grants totaling $437,300 (high: $2,000, low: $1,500).
Fields of interest: Education; Single parents.
Type of support: Scholarships—to individuals.
Application information: Applications accepted. Application form required.
  Deadline(s): Apr. 30
  Additional information: Contact the foundation for application forms and additional guidelines.
EIN: 203510627

546
The Dr. Phil Foundation
137 N. Larchmont Blvd., No. 705
Los Angeles, CA   90004-3704   (323) 956-3449
Contact: Steve Davidson, Pres. and C.E.O.
E-mail: info@drphilfoundation.org; URL: http://www.drphilfoundation.org

Foundation type: Public charity
Purpose: Grants to individuals for quality care, tuition, room, board and medical expense.
Financial data: Year ended 07/31/2012. Assets, $665,778 (M); Expenditures, $450,102; Total giving, $277,719; Grants to individuals, 5 grants totaling $106,156.
Fields of interest: Higher education; Human services.
Type of support: Grants to individuals.
Application information: The foundation provides grants to individuals under strict screening guidelines. Contact foundation for further information.
EIN: 200316670

547
The Draper Richards Kaplan Foundation
(formerly The Draper Richards Foundation)
1600 El Camino Real, Ste. 155
Menlo Park, CA   94111-4779   (650) 319-7808
Contact: Jennifer Shilling Stein, Exec. Dir.; Anne Marie Burgoyne, Dir.; Christy Chin, Dir.; Breanna DiGiammarino, Assoc.
FAX: (650) 323-4060;
E-mail: info@draperrichards.org; MA address: 535 Boylston St., 7th Fl., Boston, MA 02116, tel.: (617) 830-7122; Application e-mail: proposals@draperrichards.org; URL: http://www.draperrichards.org/

Foundation type: Operating foundation
Purpose: Fellowships awarding $100,000 annually for three years to individuals starting new non-profit organizations.
Publications: Application guidelines.
Financial data: Year ended 12/31/2012. Assets, $22,225,614 (M); Expenditures, $3,658,984; Total giving, $1,800,000.
Fields of interest: Nonprofit management; Community/economic development; Philanthropy/voluntarism.
Type of support: Seed money; Fellowships.
Application information: Applications accepted.
  Initial approach: Letter
  Send request by: Submit the application online via foundation web site
  Deadline(s): None
  Applicants should submit the following:
    1) Resume
    2) Proposal
  Additional information: See web site for additional information.
Program description:
  Fellowship Program: The Draper Richards Kaplan Foundation provides selected social entrepreneurs with funding of $100,000 annually for three years.

The funds are specifically and solely for entrepreneurs starting new non-profit organizations. The Draper Richards Kaplan Fellowships are highly selective. The foundation only awards six fellowships per year.
EIN: 912172351

548
Dudley-Vehmeyer-Brown Memorial Foundation
325 Channing Ave.
Palo Alto, CA   94301-2763

Foundation type: Independent foundation
Purpose: Scholarships to graduating seniors of Alta Vista High School, Mountain View, CA; Palo Alto High School and Gunn High School, both in Palo Alto, CA; Lowell High School, San Francisco, CA; and Roseville High School, CA.
Financial data: Year ended 12/31/2012. Assets, $1,261,160 (M); Expenditures, $83,101; Total giving, $57,000.
Fields of interest: Higher education.
Type of support: Support to graduates or students of specific schools; Undergraduate support.
Application information: Applications accepted.
  Additional information: Recommendations are made to the foundation by the participating high schools.
EIN: 237355824

549
The Durfee Foundation
1453 3rd St., Ste. 312
Santa Monica, CA   90401-3430
Contact: Claire Peeps, Exec. Dir.
FAX: (310) 899-5121; E-mail: admin@durfee.org; URL: http://www.durfee.org

Foundation type: Independent foundation
Purpose: Grants to artists and musicians residing in Los Angeles, CA. Paid sabbaticals to leaders in the Los Angeles, CA, nonprofit sector.
Publications: Application guidelines; Annual report; Financial statement; Informational brochure; IRS Form 990 or 990-PF printed copy available upon request.
Financial data: Year ended 12/31/2012. Assets, $26,249,676 (M); Expenditures, $2,005,192; Total giving, $1,256,974.
Fields of interest: Music; Arts; Volunteer services.
Type of support: Seed money; Fellowships; Grants to individuals; Sabbaticals.
Application information: Application form required. Application form available on the grantmaker's web site.
  Additional information: See web site for guidelines for specific programs.
Program descriptions:
  Artists' Resource for Completion (ARC): The ARC (Artists' Resource for Completion) grants provide rapid, short-term assistance to individual artists in Los Angeles County, CA, who wish to enhance work for a specific, imminent opportunity that may significantly benefit their careers. Artists in any discipline are eligible to apply. The applicant must already have secured an invitation from an established arts organization to present the proposed work. The work must be scheduled for presentation within six months of the application deadline. The goal of the program is to enhance the careers of Los Angeles artists by enabling them to take the best advantage of imminent opportunities to present their work, thereby fostering a climate of optimism in the Los Angeles arts community. Effective Jan. 2011, Durfee will partner with the

Center for Cultural Innovation to administer the ARC grant program.

Sabbatical Program: In an effort to replenish the stores of energy and inspiration for the community's most gifted leaders, the Durfee Sabbatical Program offers up to six individuals stipends and expenses of up to $35,000 to travel, reflect or otherwise renew themselves in whatever manner they propose. Additional support of up to $5,000 is made available to successful candidates' employing organizations that are willing to establish a permanent, revolving fund for professional staff development. The purpose of the fund is to make it possible for other staff to have access to training programs or short-term leaves that might enhance their professional capacities. In recognition of Durfee's commitment to the professional development of all nonprofit staff, the foundation's contribution starts up the fund. As cash is drawn down, it is expected that the recipient organization will replenish the fund on an annual basis, and maintain it as a permanent line item in its budget. This program is offered biennially.

Student Challenge Awards: In partnership with Earthwatch, the foundation offers students gifted in the arts and humanities an opportunity to spend two intensive weeks during the summer at a scientific research station. The aim is to excite the students' imagination, expand their potential, and stimulate their curiosity about science and technology. Recent research sites include the Los Alamos National Observatory in New Mexico, the Skagit River Basin in Washington, and the Churchill Northern Studies Center in Manitoba, Canada, among others. At present the only national program operated by the foundation, the Challenge Awards are initiated by nominations from high school teachers and guidance counselors throughout the country.

The Springboard Fund: This fund supports dynamic leaders of new social-benefit ventures in Los Angeles, CA, who apply innovative strategies to complex community challenges. The best candidates for the fund will be those who build communities in unexpected ways, by bringing together groups from different sectors with overlapping interests. The fund offers two-year grants of up to $50,000, typically $25,000 each year. Grants are unrestricted, and can be used for general operating support, salaries, technical assistance, equipment purchase or whatever else the organization deems necessary for its development.

The Stanton Fellowship: This program provides up to six fellows with $75,000 each, over a two-year period to think deeply about the intractable problems in their sector, and to tease out solutions that will improve life for the people of Los Angeles, CA.
EIN: 954856207

550
Earth Island Institute, Inc.
2150 Allston Way., Ste. 460
Berkeley, CA 94704-1375 (510) 859-9100
Contact: John A. Knox, Exec. Dir., Opers.
FAX: (510) 859-9091;
E-mail: johnknox@earthisland.org; URL: http://www.earthisland.org

Foundation type: Public charity
Purpose: Awards to young people between the ages of 13 and 22 living in North America who have shown outstanding leadership on a project with positive environmental and social impact in addition to fiscal sponsorship to environmental activists.

Publications: Application guidelines.
Financial data: Year ended 12/31/2011. Assets, $11,049,127 (M); Expenditures, $12,989,684; Total giving, $451,250.
Fields of interest: Environment; Human services.
Type of support: Grants to individuals; Awards/prizes; Fiscal agent/sponsor.
Application information: Applications accepted. Application form required. Application form available on the grantmaker's web site.
   Send request by: Mail or e-mail
   Deadline(s): May 14 for Brower Youth Award
   Additional information: Application should include a photograph.
Program descriptions:
   Brower Youth Award: This annual award recognizes six young people between the ages of 13 and 22 for their outstanding activism and achievements in the fields of environmental and social justice advocacy. Eligible applicants must live in North America and have shown outstanding leadership on a project with positive environmental and social impact. Winners receive a $3,000 cash prize, a professionally produced short film about their work, flight and lodging accommodations for a week long trip to the San Francisco Bay Area.
   Fiscal Sponsorship Program: The institute provides fiscal sponsorship, administrative services, technical assistance, and outreach to more than thirty environmental campaigns and programs. In turn, those projects help to support the institute with a standard nine percent fee on revenue (e.g., grants, donations, licensing). The institute believes this model is a cost-effective and efficient alternative to dozens of nonprofits separately incorporating and duplicating basic administrative functions. Projects function with programmatic autonomy and are responsible for raising their own funds while benefiting from the network's synergetic exchange of experiences, ideas, and energy.
EIN: 942889684

551
Eastcliff Foundation
510 Mission St.
Santa Cruz, CA 95060 (831) 465-8399
Contact: Jeannine Baker, Secy.

Foundation type: Independent foundation
Purpose: Scholarships to high school seniors of Santa Cruz County, CA, public high schools for postsecondary education.
Financial data: Year ended 09/30/2011. Assets, $6,670 (M); Expenditures, $2,000; Total giving, $2,000; Grant to an individual, 1 grant totaling $2,000.
Fields of interest: Higher education; Scholarships/financial aid.
Type of support: Scholarships—to individuals.
Application information: Applications accepted.
   Initial approach: Telephone
   Applicants should submit the following:
      1) FAFSA
      2) Transcripts
      3) Financial information
      4) Essay
   Additional information: Application should also include a copy of the parent's most recent tax form.
EIN: 912150715

552
The Easter Island Foundation
(formerly Inter-American Wildlife Foundation)
P.O. Box 6774
Los Osos, CA 93412 (805) 528-8558

Foundation type: Operating foundation
Purpose: Scholarships to students under the age of 30 with Rapanui ancestry who wish to further their education.
Financial data: Year ended 12/31/2012. Assets, $142,726 (M); Total giving, $25,496; Grants to individuals, 10 grants totaling $25,496 (high: $3,996, low: $2,000).
Fields of interest: Education.
Type of support: Scholarships—to individuals.
Application information: Applications accepted. Application form required. Application form available on the grantmaker's web site.
   Initial approach: Letter
   Deadline(s): None
   Additional information: Application should include past academic performance and a short essay describing the goals of the student and how he/she hopes to apply his/her education.
EIN: 953220730

553
Ebell of Los Angeles Scholarship Endowment Fund
743 S. Lucerne Blvd.
Los Angeles, CA 90005-3707 (323) 931-1277
Contact: Harriette Williams, Chair.
URL: http://www.ebellla.com/

Foundation type: Independent foundation
Purpose: Scholarships to full-time students who are U.S. citizens for attendance at an accredited Los Angeles county, CA educational institution.
Publications: Application guidelines.
Financial data: Year ended 06/30/2012. Assets, $4,063,006 (M); Expenditures, $296,335; Total giving, $227,000; Grants to individuals, 51 grants totaling $227,000 (high: $7,500, low: $1,500).
Fields of interest: Scholarships/financial aid.
Type of support: Undergraduate support.
Application information: Applications accepted. Application form required.
   Deadline(s): Mar. 31
   Applicants should submit the following:
      1) Photograph
      2) Letter(s) of recommendation
      3) Essay
      4) Financial information
      5) Transcripts
      6) GPA
   Additional information: Applications available from the fund or the financial aid office of student's college or university.
EIN: 237049580

554
Anslavs Eglitis & Veronika Janelsins Foundation
5550 Topanga Canyon Blvd., Ste. 210
Woodland Hills, CA 91367-7469 (818) 703-7700
Contact: Laura Conti

Foundation type: Independent foundation
Purpose: Grants to Latvian writers, poets, artists and painters.
Financial data: Year ended 12/31/2011. Assets, $514,264 (M); Expenditures, $75,568; Total

giving, $34,000; Grants to individuals, 3 grants totaling $34,000 (high: $20,000, low: $4,000).
Fields of interest: Arts.
International interests: Latvia.
Type of support: Grants to individuals.
Application information: Applications accepted.
  Deadline(s): None
  Additional information: Application should include a statement of purpose.
EIN: 206280680

555
Stanley W. Ekstrom Family Foundation, Inc.
1329 Potrero Ave.
South El Monte, CA   91733-3012
Contact: Stanley W. Ekstrom, C.E.O.

Foundation type: Independent foundation
Purpose: Scholarships to individuals in pursuit of a higher education in the health, justice, and educational areas with a particular emphasis on programs that support the development and care of children and young adults.
Financial data: Year ended 12/31/2012. Assets, $19,198 (M); Expenditures, $102,544; Total giving, $100,850.
Fields of interest: Higher education.
Type of support: Scholarships—to individuals.
Application information: Applications accepted.
  Deadline(s): None
EIN: 203198081

556
El Dorado Community Foundation
312 Main St., Ste. 201
P.O. Box 1388
Placerville, CA   95667   (530) 622-5621
Contact: William Roby, Dir.; For grants: Marsha Repschlaeger, Acct.
FAX: (888) 404-6855; E-mail: pam@eldoradocf.org; Additional e-mail: megan@eldoradocf.org and bill@eldoradocf.org; For grant inquiries: marsha@eldoradocf.org; URL: http://www.eldoradocf.org

Foundation type: Community foundation
Purpose: Scholarships to residents of El Dorado County, CA.
Publications: Application guidelines; Annual report; Financial statement; Grants list; Informational brochure; Newsletter.
Financial data: Year ended 12/31/2011. Assets, $9,024,270 (M); Expenditures, $767,467; Total giving, $568,458.
Type of support: Undergraduate support.
Application information: Applications not accepted.
  Additional information: Unsolicited requests for funds not considered or acknowledged.
EIN: 680255556

557
El Monte-South El Monte Emergency Resources Association
10900 Mulhall St.
El Monte, CA   91731-1326   (626) 444-7269
Contact: Ricardo Padilla, Pres.

Foundation type: Public charity
Purpose: Emergency assistance to residents in the El Monte, CA, community for basic necessities and living expenses, including food, shelter, transportation, rent, utilities, clothing, furniture, car repair, medical assistance and holiday gift distribution.
Financial data: Year ended 06/30/2012. Assets, $50,700 (M); Expenditures, $321,529; Total giving, $127,640; Grants to individuals, totaling $127,640.
Fields of interest: Health care; Food distribution, groceries on wheels; Housing/shelter, temporary shelter; Housing/shelter, expense aid; Housing/shelter; Human services, transportation; Human services, gift distribution; Human services, emergency aid; Economically disadvantaged.
Type of support: Grants for special needs.
Application information: Applications accepted.
  Initial approach: Telephone
  Additional information: All expenses are paid directly to the vendors on behalf of the individuals. Contact the association for additional guidelines.
EIN: 956097318

558
El Puente Charitable Foundation
4730 Doyle Dr.
San Jose, CA   95129
URL: http://www.elpuentefoundation.com/

Foundation type: Operating foundation
Purpose: Temporary financial assistance to economically disadvantaged individuals for housing, education, medical expenses and living expenses.
Financial data: Year ended 12/31/2012. Assets, $305,492 (M); Expenditures, $13,379; Total giving, $3,491; Grants to individuals, 3 grants totaling $3,491 (high: $1,500, low: $491).
Fields of interest: Economically disadvantaged.
Type of support: Emergency funds; Grants for special needs.
Application information: Applications accepted. Application form required.
  Initial approach: Letter or web site
  Additional information: Benefits are handled on a case-by-case basis. Application should be notarized prior to sending it out. See web site for additional information.
EIN: 770557020

559
Elim Ministry Foundation
4461 S. Santa Fe Ave.
Los Angeles, CA   90058-2101   (323) 277-7930
Contact: Mi Hye Kim, Pres.

Foundation type: Company-sponsored foundation
Purpose: Scholarships to individuals primarily in California for higher education.
Financial data: Year ended 12/31/2012. Assets, $76,945 (M); Expenditures, $10,919; Total giving, $10,180.
Fields of interest: Higher education.
Type of support: Scholarships—to individuals.
Application information: Applications accepted. Application form required.
  Deadline(s): None
  Applicants should submit the following:
    1) Transcripts
    2) Essay
  Additional information: Application should also include reference. Applicant must maintain a minimum 2.5 GPA.
EIN: 030535740

560
Elk Grove Community Foundation
P.O. Box 2021
Elk Grove, CA   95759-2021   (916) 685-7118
FAX: (916) 689-7875;
E-mail: contact@egcommunityfoundation.org; Tel.: 916-685-7118; URL: http://www.egcommunityfoundation.org

Foundation type: Public charity
Purpose: Scholarships to individuals in the Elk Grove, CA, area.
Publications: Application guidelines; Financial statement; Informational brochure; Newsletter (including application guidelines); Occasional report (including application guidelines); Program policy statement.
Financial data: Year ended 12/31/2011. Assets, $2,534,930 (M); Expenditures, $189,179; Total giving, $140,900; Grants to individuals, totaling $140,900.
Type of support: Scholarships—to individuals.
Application information: Applications accepted. Application form required. Application form available on the grantmaker's web site.
  Copies of proposal: 3
  Deadline(s): Jan. 23 if returned in person; Jan. 29 if returned by mail
  Applicants should submit the following:
    1) Photograph
    2) Transcripts
  Additional information: See web site for complete program information.
EIN: 946097642

561
The Lawrence Ellison Foundation
(formerly The Ellison Medical Foundation)
101 Ygnacio Valley Rd., Ste. 310
Walnut Creek, CA   94596-7018   (301) 829-6410
Contact: Kevin Lee Ph.D., Exec. Dir.
E-mail: klee@ellisonfoundation.org; Address for post-award financial reporting: 104 E. Ridgeville Blvd., Mount Airy, MD 21771-5260, tel.: (301) 829-6410, fax: (301) 829-6413; URL: http://www.ellisonfoundation.org

Foundation type: Operating foundation
Purpose: Research grants to U.S. nonprofit institutions and universities on behalf of investigators to study the basic biology of aging.
Publications: Informational brochure.
Financial data: Year ended 12/31/2012. Assets, $0 (M); Expenditures, $48,903,099; Total giving, $46,418,840; Grants to individuals, 209 grants totaling $36,122,869 (high: $291,000, low: $2,000).
Fields of interest: Institute; Geriatrics research.
Type of support: Research; Awards/prizes.
Application information: Applications accepted. Application form required. Application form available on the grantmaker's web site.
  Deadline(s): Mar. 8 for Senior Scholar, Dec. 16 for Julie Martin Mid-Career Award
  Additional information: Applicants for Senior Scholar Awards must complete and submit online letter of intent from foundation's web site.
Program descriptions:
  New Scholar Award in Aging: The objective of the foundation's New Scholars Award is to support new investigators of outstanding promise in the basic biological sciences relevant to understanding aging processes and age-related diseases and disabilities. The award is intended to provide significant support to new investigators to permit them to become established in the field of aging.

The New Scholars Award provides up to $100,000 per year for a four year period for successful candidates. The foundation announced that no new applications will be accepted for New Scholar awards in Aging. All currently funded awards will continue subject to the terms and conditions established in the original award agreement between the foundation and the grantee institution.

Senior Scholar Award in Aging: The program is designed to support established investigators working at institutions in the U.S. to conduct research in the basic biological sciences relevant to understanding lifespan development processes and age-related diseases and disabilities. The award is intended to provide significant support to allow the development of novel, innovative research programs by investigators who are not currently conducting aging research or who wish to develop new research programs in aging. The foundation particularly aims to stimulate new research that has rigorous scientific foundations but is not funded adequately, either because of its perceived novelty, its high risk, or because it is from an area where traditional research interests absorb most funding. Senior Scholar awards provide funding up to $150,000 per year for a four-year period.The foundation announced that no new applications will be accepted for Senior Scholar awards in Aging. All currently funded awards will continue subject to the terms and conditions established in the original award agreement between the foundation and the grantee institution.
EIN: 943269827

562
Emergency Housing Consortium of Santa Clara County
507 Valley Way
Milpitas, CA 95035-4105 (408) 539-2100
Contact: Jenny Niklaus, C.E.O.
FAX: (408) 957-0253;
E-mail: info@ehclifebuilders.org; URL: http://www.ehclifebuilders.org

Foundation type: Public charity
Purpose: Financial assistance for education and related expense for eligible individuals of Santa Clara county, CA. Financial assistance for housing, rental assistance, and utility payments and other living expenses for individuals and families of Santa Clara county, CA.
Publications: Annual report; Financial statement.
Financial data: Year ended 06/30/2012. Assets, $29,373,634 (M); Expenditures, $9,689,943; Total giving, $1,429,639; Grants to individuals, totaling $1,429,639.
Fields of interest: Education; Housing/shelter, homeless; Economically disadvantaged.
Type of support: Grants for special needs.
Application information: The various programs have established guidelines that determine eligibility. Contact the agency for eligibility determination.
EIN: 942684272

563
Emery Education Foundation
1275 61st St.
P.O. Box 8926
Emeryville, CA 94662-8926 (510) 601-4911
Contact: C. Phillip Powell, Exec. Dir.
FAX: (510) 601-4993;
E-mail: phillip.powell@emeryed.org; URL: http://www.emeryed.org
Additional URL: http://www.emeryed.org/wiki

Foundation type: Public charity
Purpose: Scholarships to graduates of the Emery Unified School District, CA.
Publications: Application guidelines; Financial statement; Informational brochure; Occasional report; Program policy statement (including application guidelines).
Financial data: Year ended 06/30/2011. Assets, $629,499 (M); Expenditures, $592,602; Total giving, $307,292; Grants to individuals, totaling $27,750.
Type of support: Support to graduates or students of specific schools; Undergraduate support.
Application information: Applications not accepted.
Additional information: Unsolicited requests for funds not considered or acknowledged.
EIN: 943248242

564
Employees Community Fund of Boeing California, Inc.
(formerly McDonnell Douglas-West Personnel Community Services Inc.)
3855 Lakewood Blvd., MC D802-0011
Long Beach, CA 90846-0001 (562) 593-2612
Contact: Carrie L. Bollwinkle, Exec. Dir.
FAX: (562) 593-0955;
E-mail: carrie.l.bollwinkle@boeing.com;
URL: http://www.ecfboeingca.org

Foundation type: Public charity
Purpose: Scholarships to children (natural, step and adopted) of Boeing employees (active, retired, or deceased) who meet specific eligibility requirements in the CA service area. Assistance to financially distressed Boeing California employees who are temporarily or permanently indigent members of current or former employees of Douglas Aircraft Co., Inc. or a successor company.
Publications: Annual report; Newsletter.
Financial data: Year ended 12/31/2011. Assets, $2,186,145 (M); Expenditures, $3,578,524; Total giving, $3,446,456; Grants to individuals, totaling $43,550.
Fields of interest: Higher education; Economically disadvantaged.
Type of support: Employee-related scholarships; Employee-related welfare.
Application information: Applications not accepted.
Additional information: Unsolicited requests for funds not considered or acknowledged.
EIN: 952311678

565
The Exploratorium
3601 Lyon St.
San Francisco, CA 94123-1019 (415) 561-0360
Contact: Dennis M. Bartels, Exec. Dir.
E-mail: visit@exploratorium.edu; URL: http://www.exploratorium.edu/arts

Foundation type: Public charity
Purpose: Residencies to visual and performing artists for the creation of art for the Exploratorium, a museum of science, art, and human perception located in San Francisco, CA.
Publications: Annual report; Informational brochure; Newsletter.
Financial data: Year ended 06/30/2011. Assets, $157,012,815 (M); Expenditures, $35,171,533; Total giving, $25,000; Grants to individuals, 3 grants totaling $17,000.

Fields of interest: Visual arts; Museums (art); Museums (science/technology); Performing arts.
Type of support: Residencies.
Application information: Applications accepted. Application form not required.
Initial approach: Letter
Deadline(s): Quarterly
Additional information: Application must include background information, slides and other supporting materials. See web site for additional application information.
Program descriptions:
AIR Program: The program has grown to include hundreds of artists and performers. The museum works with individuals and artist groups who are drawn to collaboration, interested in interdisciplinary dialogue, and open to developing new working methods. Projects have taken countless forms, such as multimedia performances, theatrical productions, animated filmmaking, immersive installations, walking tours and online projects. While the room variance, residencies typically unfold over two years and include both an exploratory and project development phase. This program does not accept unsolicited artist materials.
Osher Fellowship: The residence fellowships are generally one to four weeks in duration for artists, scholars, authors and scientists. Osher Fellows work with Exploratorium staff on programs, exhibit projects, and new endeavors, and share their own research and work with staff and the public.
EIN: 941696494

566
Fairmount Tire Charitable Foundation Inc.
2942 Columbia St.
Torrance, CA 90503 (559) 542-2639
Contact: Alvie Kracik
Application address: 56816 Aspen Dr., Springville, CA 93265, tel.: (559) 542-2639

Foundation type: Company-sponsored foundation
Purpose: Scholarships to economically disadvantaged nursing students in the greater Los Angeles, CA, area.
Financial data: Year ended 12/31/2012. Assets, $31,743 (M); Expenditures, $0; Total giving, $0.
Fields of interest: Nursing school/education.
Type of support: Undergraduate support.
Application information: Application form required.
Deadline(s): None
Additional information: Applications are accepted via educational institutions.
EIN: 954424035

567
Faith's Hope Foundation
2271 W. Malvern Ave., Ste. 382
Fullerton, CA 92833-2106 (714) 871-4673
Contact: Deborah Levy, Exec. Dir.
E-mail: fhf@faithshopefoundation.org; Additional address: 444 N. Harbor Blvd. Ste. 200, Fullerton, CA 92832-1968; URL: http://www.faithshopefoundation.org

Foundation type: Public charity
Purpose: Financial assistance to middle and lower-income individuals and families in the California region while tending to loved ones who are hospitalized.
Financial data: Year ended 06/30/2012. Assets, $535,456 (M); Expenditures, $3,523,596; Total giving, $63,556; Grants to individuals, totaling $53,818.
Fields of interest: Economically disadvantaged.

Type of support: Grants for special needs.
Application information: Applications accepted. Application form required. Application form available on the grantmaker's web site.

Send request by: E-mail

Additional information: Those applying for assistance must demonstrate need. Contact the foundation for additional guidelines.
EIN: 300039459

568

Family Care Foundation, Inc.
1373 Marron Valley Rd.
Dulzura, CA   91917-2105   (619) 468-3191
Contact: Lawrence Corley, Exec. Dir.
FAX: (619) 468-6996; E-mail: fcf@familycare.org;
Toll-free tel.: (800) 992-2383; mailing address: P.O. Box 1039, Spring Valley, CA 91979-1039;
URL: http://www.familycare.org

Foundation type: Public charity
Purpose: Emergency assistance and in-kind gifts to families in need throughout the world with medical costs and other assistance for low income families to help meet their needs.
Publications: Annual report; Newsletter.
Financial data: Year ended 12/31/2011. Assets, $2,530,067 (M); Expenditures, $3,389,275; Total giving, $1,243,126; Grants to individuals, totaling $9,798.
Fields of interest: Economically disadvantaged.
Type of support: Emergency funds; Grants for special needs.
Application information: Contact the foundation for eligibility determination.
EIN: 330734917

569

Fansler Foundation
5713 N. West Ave., Ste. 102
Fresno, CA   93711-2366   (559) 432-0544
Contact: Lisa Prudek, Admin. Dir.
FAX: (559) 432-0543; URL: http://www.fanslerfoundation.com

Foundation type: Independent foundation
Purpose: Scholarships to 8th grade students attending public, private, or Diocesan schools in the Fresno county, CA area.
Publications: Application guidelines.
Financial data: Year ended 10/31/2012. Assets, $30,048,646 (M); Expenditures, $2,045,838; Total giving, $1,316,565. Scholarships—to individuals amount not specified.
Fields of interest: Education.
Type of support: Scholarships—to individuals.
Application information: Applications accepted. Application form required.

Send request by: Mail

Deadline(s): Mar. 15

Applicants should submit the following:
1) Financial information
2) Essay
3) Transcripts

Additional information: Applicants must be registered parishioners within The Diocese of Fresno, have a minimum 3.2 GPA for 7th and 8th grade years prior to the application deadline. Parents previous year's tax return must be included. See web site for additional information.
EIN: 770095125

570

Far Northern Coordinating Council on Developmental Disabilities
1900 Churn Creek Rd., Ste. 319
P.O. Box 492418
Redding, CA   96049-2418   (530) 222-4791
Contact: Laura Larson, Exec. Dir.
FAX: (530) 222-8908;
E-mail: mhanson@farnothernnrc.org; URL: http://www.farnothernnrc.org/

Foundation type: Public charity
Purpose: Assistance for individuals with developmental disabilities, in northern California, and their families.
Publications: Newsletter.
Financial data: Year ended 06/30/2012. Assets, $35,893,859 (M); Expenditures, $110,263,590; Total giving, $96,820,367; Grants to individuals, totaling $96,820,367.
Fields of interest: Human services; Disabilities, people with.
Type of support: Grants for special needs.
Application information: Contact the council for eligibility determination.
EIN: 941648724

571

Anne & Jason Farber Foundation
c/o PMB Helin Donovan
1340 Treat Blvd., Ste. 525
Walnut Creek, CA   94597-7984

Foundation type: Independent foundation
Purpose: Research grants for the investigation of brain tumors.
Financial data: Year ended 11/30/2012. Assets, $3,280,184 (M); Expenditures, $356,000; Total giving, $250,000.
Fields of interest: Institute; Cancer research.
Type of support: Research.
Application information: Applications not accepted.
EIN: 942778778

572

Federal Employees Scholarship Foundation Inc.
(formerly Fed-Mart Foundation)
1022 Laguna Seca Loop
Chula Vista, CA   91915-1200
Scholarship application address: P.O. Box 26785, San Diego, CA 92196
E-mail: civilwar49@aol.com

Foundation type: Independent foundation
Purpose: Scholarships to graduating seniors of high schools in San Diego County, CA, with a GPA of 3.0 or higher.
Financial data: Year ended 12/31/2012. Assets, $688,819 (M); Expenditures, $18,998; Total giving, $15,000; Grants to individuals, 5 grants totaling $15,000 (high: $4,000, low: $1,500).
Fields of interest: Scholarships/financial aid.
Type of support: Support to graduates or students of specific schools; Undergraduate support.
Application information: Applications accepted. Application form required.

Deadline(s): Mar.

Applicants should submit the following:
1) Essay
2) Transcripts

Additional information: Applicants must show active participation in school and community activities.
EIN: 330727818

573

The Feminist Majority Foundation
433 S. Beverly Dr.
Beverly Hills, CA   90212-4401   (310) 556-2500
FAX: (310) 556-2509;
E-mail: webmaster@feminist.org; Additional address (east coast): 1600 Wilson Blvd., Ste. 801, Arlington, VA 22209-2511, tel.: (703) 522-2214, fax: (703) 522-2219; URL: http://www.feminist.org

Foundation type: Public charity
Purpose: Scholarships to eligible Afghan women who are eighteen years old and above, and have been admitted in the U.S. as refugees.
Publications: Newsletter.
Financial data: Year ended 12/31/2011. Assets, $3,383,431 (M); Expenditures, $6,196,314; Total giving, $126,686.
Fields of interest: Education; Immigrants/refugees.
Type of support: Scholarships—to individuals.
Application information: Scholarships are provided to those who have a high school certificate or equivalent, documentation of English language skills, and commitment to use higher education to promote women's rights and human rights.
EIN: 541426440

574

Fernando Award Foundation, Inc.
12520 Magnolia Blvd., No. 212
North Hollywood, CA   91607-2350   (818) 980-7867
E-mail: Danialeperry@yahoo.com; URL: http://www.fernandoawards.org

Foundation type: Public charity
Purpose: Scholarships to graduating seniors from public and private high schools in the San Fernando Valley, CA who have excelled in community service.
Financial data: Year ended 12/31/2011. Assets, $41,765 (M); Expenditures, $56,873.
Fields of interest: Higher education.
Type of support: Scholarships—to individuals; Awards/prizes.
Application information: Scholarship candidates are nominated by their schools and winners are selected by the foundation scholarship committee.
EIN: 954576012

575

Film Independent, Inc.
(formerly Independent Feature Project/West)
9911 W. Pico Blvd., 11th Fl.
Los Angeles, CA   90035-2703   (310) 432-1200
Contact: Sean R. McManus, Co-Pres.
FAX: (310) 432-1203;
E-mail: smcmanus@filmindependent.org;
URL: http://www.filmindependent.org

Foundation type: Public charity
Purpose: Fellowships to directors who are prepping feature-length narrative films in Los Angeles, CA.
Publications: Application guidelines.
Financial data: Year ended 09/30/2011. Assets, $2,614,368 (M); Expenditures, $8,697,067; Total giving, $265,500; Grants to individuals, totaling $30,500.
Fields of interest: Film/video.
Type of support: Fellowships.
Application information:

Initial approach: Letter

Deadline(s): Oct. 5

Program descriptions:

Directors Lab: This intensive eight-week program, based each winter in Los Angeles, helps participating directors prepare their feature films and advance their careers through introducing them to film professionals who can advise them on the craft and business of directing. Under the guidance of a lab instructor, directors workshop, work with actors, and construct scenes from their work in the editing process. Fellows receive a one-year membership with the organization, a pass to the Los Angeles Film Festival, and year-round support. Applications must be accompanied by a fee, as dictated on the organization's website.

Producers Lab: A maximum of ten producers will be chosen to complete this intensive seven-week program, designed to help filmmakers develop skills as creative independent producers. During the lab, participants develop a strategy and action plan for bringing their projects to fruition, including a detailed budget, schedule, and business plan. Lab participants have one-on-one meetings with lab advisors (established producers, directors, and other industry professionals) who advise them on both the craft and the business of filmmaking. The labs are open to all filmmakers, regardless of educational background or previous accomplishment in film. Participants with qualifying projects are also eligible for a $25,000 production grant.

Sloan Producers Grant: This new grant program was established as part of the Producers Lab. Grant recipients will receive admission to the Producers Lab, a $25,000 development grant, and year-round support from the organization. The grant is funded by the Alfred P. Sloan Foundation. To be eligible for the grant, the applicant must be attached as producer to the script with which they are applying, and the screenplay should have a scientific, mathematical, and/or technological theme and storyline or have a leading character who is a scientist, engineer, or mathematician.
EIN: 953943485

576
Dorothy K. Fischer Veterans Assistance Foundation
P.O. Box 7166
San Carlos, CA   94070   (650) 595-3896
Contact: Susan O. Robinson, Pres.
URL: http://www.dkfveterans.com

Foundation type: Operating foundation
Purpose: Scholarships to full-time college students who are residents of CA and are military veterans or dependents of deceased military veterans who served in support of Operation Enduring Freedom or Operation Iraqi Freedom within the central command area of responsibility.
Financial data: Year ended 12/31/2012. Assets, $366,033 (M); Expenditures, $35,073; Total giving, $25,000; Grants to individuals, 5 grants totaling $25,000 (high: $5,000, low: $5,000).
Fields of interest: Higher education; Military/veterans.
Type of support: Scholarships—to individuals.
Application information: Applications accepted. Application form required. Application form available on the grantmaker's web site.
> *Additional information:* See web site for additional information.
EIN: 870734862

577
Five Acres-The Boys & Girls Aid Society of Los Angeles County
760 W. Mountain View St.
Altadena, CA   91001-4925   (626) 798-6793
Contact: Chanel Boutakidis, C.E.O.
FAX: (626) 797-7722; E-mail: info@fiveacres.org; TTY: (626) 204-1375; URL: http://www.fiveacres.org

Foundation type: Public charity
Purpose: Specific assistance to children and families in the Los Angeles, Ventura, Orange and San Bernardino counties, CA area with food, clothing, shelter and personal needs.
Publications: Newsletter.
Financial data: Year ended 06/30/2012. Assets, $19,187,917 (M); Expenditures, $31,339,759; Total giving, $1,740,209; Grants to individuals, totaling $1,740,209.
Fields of interest: Foster care; Economically disadvantaged.
Type of support: Grants for special needs.
Application information: Applications accepted.
> *Additional information:* Contact the organization for eligibility determination.
EIN: 951647810

578
Fleishhacker Foundation
P.O. Box 29918
San Francisco, CA   94129-0918   (415) 561-5350
Contact: Christine Elbel, Exec. Dir.
FAX: (415) 561-5345;
E-mail: info@fleishhackerfoundation.org;
URL: http://www.fleishhackerfoundation.org

Foundation type: Independent foundation
Purpose: One-year fellowships by nomination only to assist visual artists, 25 years of age or older, to residents of San Francisco, Marin, Sonoma, Alameda, Contra Costa, San Mateo, and Santa Clara counties, CA.
Publications: Application guidelines; Grants list.
Financial data: Year ended 12/31/2012. Assets, $14,914,940 (M); Expenditures, $833,244; Total giving, $584,500; Grants to individuals, totaling $86,500 (high: $25,000, low: $25,000).
Fields of interest: Visual arts.
Type of support: Fellowships; Awards/grants by nomination only; Awards/prizes.
Application information: Applications not accepted.
> *Additional information:* Artists are nominated by nonprofit art organizations. Unsolicited applications not accepted. Application cycle is every three years.
Program description:
> *Eureka Fellowship Program:* Grant recipients are selected once every three years, based on the nominations received from local nonprofit visual arts organizations. Each artist receives $25,000 for a one-year period.
EIN: 946051048

579
Mr. & Mrs. Charles N. Flint Scholarship Endowment Fund
(formerly The Ebell of Los Angeles/Charles N. Flint Scholarship Endowment Fund)
743 S. Lucerne Blvd.
Los Angeles, CA   90005   (323) 931-1277
Contact: Harnette Williams, Chair.
FAX: (323) 937-0272;
E-mail: scholarship@ebelloflosangeles.com;
URL: http://www.ebellla.com

Foundation type: Independent foundation
Purpose: Undergraduate scholarships to full-time students attending Los Angeles County colleges and universities,.
Financial data: Year ended 06/30/2012. Assets, $1,841,231 (M); Expenditures, $107,205; Total giving, $72,000; Grants to individuals, 16 grants totaling $72,000 (high: $7,000, low: $1,500).
Fields of interest: Higher education.
Type of support: Technical education support; Undergraduate support.
Application information: Applications accepted. Application form required. Application form available on the grantmaker's web site. Interview required.
> *Initial approach:* E-mail
> *Deadline(s):* Apr. 1
> *Applicants should submit the following:*
> 1) Letter(s) of recommendation
> 2) Essay
> 3) Financial information
> 4) Transcripts
> *Additional information:* Applications available from the fund or the financial aid office of student's university or college.
EIN: 956100327

580
Floor Covering Industry Foundation
2211 E. Howell Ave.
Anaheim, CA   92806-6009   (714) 634-0302
FAX: (714) 978-6745; E-mail: info@fcif.org;
URL: http://www.fcif.org

Foundation type: Public charity
Purpose: Financial assistance to individuals who have derived their primary source of income from the floor covering industry and their families who experience catastrophic illness, severe disabilities, or other life-altering hardships.
Publications: Application guidelines.
Financial data: Year ended 12/31/2011. Assets, $1,980,794 (M); Expenditures, $209,036; Total giving, $153,200; Grants to individuals, totaling $153,200.
Fields of interest: Health care; Housing/shelter; Human services.
Type of support: Grants for special needs.
Application information: Applications accepted. Application form required. Application form available on the grantmaker's web site.
> *Additional information:* Application should include financial information and physician's diagnosis.
Program description:
> *Grants:* The foundation provides financial assistance to individuals who have been employed in the floor covering industry. Grants may be provided for emergency medical expenses, continuing healthcare expenses, or for basic necessities such as food, shelter, and utilities.
EIN: 521238188

581
Florsheim Brothers, A California Non-Profit Benefit Corporation
1701 W. March Ln., Ste. D
Stockton, CA 95207-6416 (209) 473-1106
Contact: David Florsheim, Pres.

Foundation type: Public charity
Purpose: Scholarships and education expenses to students of CA. Aid to needy individuals and families of CA.
Financial data: Year ended 12/31/2011. Assets, $721,129 (M); Expenditures, $123,441; Total giving, $118,309; Grants to individuals, totaling $118,309.
Fields of interest: Education; Human services.
Type of support: Scholarships—to individuals; Grants for special needs.
Application information: Applications accepted. Application form required.
Additional information: Contact the foundation for eligibility determination.
EIN: 911775773

582
Marcus A. Foster Educational Institute
8301 Edgewater Dr. St., 203
Oakland, CA 94612-1214 (510) 777-1600
Contact: Alicia Dixon, Exec. Dir.
FAX: (510) 777-1601;
E-mail: info@marcusfoster.org; E-Mail for Alicia Dixon: Adixon@marcusfoster.org

Foundation type: Public charity
Purpose: Scholarships to graduating Oakland, CA seniors pursuing postsecondary education. Grants to children and youth to attend fee-based academic and enrichment activities of their choice. Grants for teachers to improve student academic achievement using innovative instructional methods in the classroom. Fiscal sponsorship is available for projects.
Publications: Application guidelines.
Financial data: Year ended 06/30/2011. Assets, $1,564,703 (M); Expenditures, $967,643; Total giving, $210,045; Grants to individuals, totaling $210,045.
Fields of interest: Vocational education, post-secondary; Higher education.
Type of support: Grants to individuals; Scholarships—to individuals; Fiscal agent/sponsor.
Application information: Applications accepted. Application form required. Application form available on the grantmaker's web site.
Deadline(s): Mar. 31 for Foster Scholarships
Additional information: See web site for additional guidelines.
Program descriptions:
College Scholarships: Scholarship funds are provided to at least 60 graduating high school seniors pursuing a postsecondary degree at a two- or four-year college, or at a vocational training institute. Grants range from $1,000 to $15,000.
Fiscal Sponsorship Program: The institute serves as the fiscal sponsor of several projects that work in tandem with Oakland public schools to provide support and development for students, teachers, and families.
Fund for Teachers: Grants (of up to $5,000 per individual and $10,000 per team) are available for pre-K through grade-12 teachers who have taught for a minimum of three years, spend at least 50 percent of their full time position in the classroom or classroom-like setting, and intend to return to

teaching in school/district in the consecutive school year. Winners may apply every five years.
EIN: 237357906

583
Found Animals Foundation, Inc.
P.O. Box 66370
Los Angeles, CA 90066-0370
Application e-mail:
michelsonprize@foundanimals.org
E-mail: Info@foundanimals.org; URL: http://www.foundanimals.org/

Foundation type: Operating foundation
Purpose: Awards and prizes to graduate students in the U.S. for the development of a permanent, non-surgical sterliant in dogs and cats.
Financial data: Year ended 11/30/2012. Assets, $796,277 (M); Expenditures, $8,971,559; Total giving, $873,447.
Fields of interest: Animal population control; Science; Engineering.
Type of support: Awards/prizes.
Application information: Applications accepted.
Initial approach: Proposal
Send request by: E-mail
Deadline(s): Jan. 12
Applicants should submit the following:
1) Letter(s) of recommendation
2) Curriculum vitae
3) Budget Information
Additional information: Application must be submitted in English. See web site for additional application guidelines.
EIN: 203944602

584
Foundation for California State University San Bernardino
5500 Univ. Pkwy.
San Bernardino, CA 92407-2318 (909) 537-5918
Contact: Deborah Burns, Exec. Dir.
FAX: (909) 537-7036; URL: http://adminfin.csusb.edu/foundation/

Foundation type: Public charity
Purpose: Scholarships to students at California State University, San Bernardino.
Publications: Financial statement.
Financial data: Year ended 06/30/2012. Assets, $18,860,619 (M); Expenditures, $24,869,885.
Fields of interest: Graduate/professional education.
Type of support: Scholarships—to individuals; Support to graduates or students of specific schools.
Application information: Contact foundation for program and application information.
EIN: 956067343

585
The Foundation for College Christian Leaders
(formerly Eckmann Foundation)
2658 Del Mar Heights Rd., Ste. 266
Del Mar, CA 92014-3100 (858) 481-0848
Contact: James K. Eckmann, Dir.
E-mail: LMHays@aol.com; URL: http://www.collegechristianleader.com

Foundation type: Operating foundation
Purpose: Scholarships to financially needy Christian leaders, who are residents of southern CA

or attending schools in southern CA, to obtain a four-year degree in higher education.
Financial data: Year ended 12/31/2012. Assets, $1,030,226 (M); Expenditures, $73,189; Total giving, $53,000; Grants to individuals, 28 grants totaling $53,000 (high: $3,000, low: $1,000).
Fields of interest: Christian agencies & churches.
Type of support: Scholarships—to individuals.
Application information: Applications accepted. Application form required.
Deadline(s): Apr. 22
EIN: 330323974

586
Foundation for Deep Ecology
1062 Fort Cronkhite
Sausalito, CA 94965-2609 (415) 229-9339
Contact: Lizzie Udwin, Prog. Admin.
FAX: (415) 229-9340;
E-mail: info@deepecology.org; URL: http://www.deepecology.org

Foundation type: Independent foundation
Purpose: Awards to individuals in the U.S., Canada, Chile, Argentina and some of Europe for research on biodiversity and wilderness, ecological agriculture, and globalization and megatechnology.
Publications: Multi-year report.
Financial data: Year ended 06/30/2012. Assets, $42,431,433 (M); Expenditures, $2,351,461; Total giving, $1,163,117.
Fields of interest: Natural resources; Environment; Animals/wildlife, preservation/protection; Agriculture.
Type of support: Research; Awards/prizes.
Application information: Applications not accepted.
Additional information: Unsolicited applications not accepted.
EIN: 943106115

587
Foundation for Excellence, Inc.
2620 Augustine Dr., Ste. 185
Santa Clara, CA 95054 (408) 985-2001
Contact: Vijaya Sivamani, Off. Admin.
FAX: (408) 985-2001; E-mail: support@ffe.com; E-Mail for Vijaya Sivamani: VijayaSivamani@ffe.org; URL: http://www.ffe.org

Foundation type: Public charity
Purpose: Scholarships to exceptional students in India pursuing studies in professional courses leading to degrees in engineering, technology or medicine.
Publications: Application guidelines.
Financial data: Year ended 06/30/2012. Assets, $270,881 (M); Expenditures, $759,643; Total giving, $620,400.
Fields of interest: Higher education; Medical school/education; Engineering school/education; Engineering/technology.
Type of support: Scholarships—to individuals; Foreign applicants.
Application information: Applications accepted. Application form required.
Additional information: Scholarships are awarded solely on the basis of academic eligibility and financial need. Renewal of scholarship is dependent on continued academic excellence and financial need.
EIN: 770474749

588
Foundation for Sustainable Development
1000 Brannan St., Ste. 207
San Francisco, CA 94103-1431 (415) 283-4873
Contact: Mireille Cronin Mather, Exec. Dir.
FAX: (415) 621-5476;
E-mail: info@fsdinternational.org; E-mail for Mireille Cronin Mather: mireille@fsdinternational.org;
URL: http://www.fsdinternational.org

Foundation type: Public charity
Purpose: Scholarships to public health graduate students pursuing FSD international internships.
Financial data: Year ended 12/31/2011. Assets, $184,883 (M); Expenditures, $1,429,420; Total giving, $688,698; Grants to individuals, totaling $139,222.
Fields of interest: Public health school/education.
Type of support: Scholarships—to individuals; Graduate support.
Application information: Applications accepted. Application form required.
  Deadline(s): Mar. 15
  Final notification: Recipients notified Apr. 1
  Additional information: Application should include an essay of approximately 500 words. See web site for additional guidelines.
EIN: 561938284

589
Foundation for the Advancement of Mesoamerican Studies Inc.
(also known as FAMSI)
5905 Wilshire Blvd.
Los Angeles, CA 90036
E-mail: famsi@famsi.org; URL: http://www.famsi.org

Foundation type: Independent foundation
Purpose: Research grants to individuals studying the ancient cultures of Mexico, Guatemala, Honduras, Belize and El Salvador (Pre-Columbian Mesoamerica).
Publications: Application guidelines; Grants list; Informational brochure; Informational brochure (including application guidelines); Occasional report; Program policy statement.
Financial data: Year ended 09/30/2012. Assets, $0 (M); Expenditures, $224,306; Total giving, $0.
Fields of interest: Cultural/ethnic awareness; History/archaeology; Language/linguistics; Historical activities; Anthropology/sociology.
International interests: Belize; Central America; El Salvador; Guatemala; Honduras; Mexico.
Type of support: Seed money; Research; Grants to individuals; Foreign applicants; Awards/prizes; Postdoctoral support; Graduate support; Postgraduate support; Travel grants; Doctoral support; Project support.
Application information: Applications accepted. Application form required. Application form available on the grantmaker's web site.
  Initial approach: Letter, fax, or e-mail
  Copies of proposal: 2
  Deadline(s): Sept. 15 for research grants,
  Applicants should submit the following:
    1) Letter(s) of recommendation
    2) Resume
    3) Proposal
    4) Curriculum vitae
    5) Budget Information
  Additional information: Application brochures may be obtained through FAMSI Granting Comm. or Web site.

Program descriptions:
  Awards Program: The foundation supports projects in the disciplines of archaeology, art history, epigraphy, linguistics, ethnohistory, and sociology and encourages interdisciplinary projects. Awards go to the most qualified scholars regardless of degree level, although the foundation favors degree candidates, recent graduates, and professionals whose projects have not had extensive financial support.
  Research Grants: The foundation supports projects in the disciplines of archaeology, art history, epigraphy, linguistics, ethnohistory, and sociology and encourages interdisciplinary projects. Awards go to the most qualified scholars regardless of degree level, although the foundation favors degree candidates, recent graduates, and professionals whose projects have not had extensive financial support.
EIN: 593195520

590
The Foundation for the Elimination of Diseases Attacking the Immune System
(also known as DAISY Foundation)
P.O. Box 788
Glen Ellen, CA 95442-0788
Contact: Bonnie Barnes, Pres.
E-mail: bonniebarnes@daisyfoundation.org;
URL: http://www.daisyfoundation.org

Foundation type: Public charity
Purpose: Grants to registered nurses for research that impact patients or family members of patients with an auto-immune disease or cancer.
Financial data: Year ended 12/31/2012. Assets, $888 (M); Expenditures, $574.
Fields of interest: Cancer research; Leukemia research; Immunology research.
Type of support: Research; Grants to individuals.
Application information: Applications accepted.
  Initial approach: Letter of Intent
  Send request by: Online
  Deadline(s): Apr. 1 and Sept. 16 for LOI, May 27 and Oct. 28 for Application
  Final notification: Recipients notified Apr. 26 and Sept. 30 for LOI, July 15 and Dec. 16 for application
  Additional information: Funds are paid directly to the medical institution on behalf of the individual investigator. See web site for additional guidelines.
Program description:
  J. Patrick Barnes Grants for Nursing Research and Evidence-Based Practice Projects: This program provides support for nurses who continually evaluate their practice, seek answers to clinical questions in an effort to improve their practice, and change their practice based on evidence and evaluation of that change. Applicant must be a registered nurse with a current license. Research must impact patients or family members of patients with an auto-immune disease or cancer. Small grants of up to $2,000 will be made to nurses undertaking clinical inquiry or evidence-based practice projects that directly benefit patients or family members of patients with immune-system related diseases or cancer. Larger grants of up to $5,000 will be made to nurses conducting documented patient-focused research or evidence-based practice projects that develop, implement, and evaluate nursing practice for the care and treatment of patients or family members of patients with immune-system related diseases or cancer.
EIN: 912009739

591
The Foundation Inc.
c/o Chapman Bird & Tessler Inc.
1990 S. Bundy Dr., Ste. 200
Los Angeles, CA 90025-5249 (732) 483-0500
Contact: Jim McDuffie
Application address: 482 Monmouth Rd., West Long Branch, NJ 07764-1260, tel.: (732) 483-0500

Foundation type: Independent foundation
Purpose: Grants for home repairs to low-income homeowners in NJ. Maximum grant is generally $10,000.
Financial data: Year ended 12/31/2012. Assets, $43,257 (M); Expenditures, $61,611; Total giving, $44,701.
Fields of interest: Housing/shelter, repairs; Housing/shelter, expense aid; Housing/shelter; Economically disadvantaged.
Type of support: Grants for special needs.
Application information: Applications accepted.
  Initial approach: Letter
  Additional information: Contact foundation for current application deadline/guidelines.
EIN: 222995739

592
FRAMAX, Inc.
715 G St.
Modesto, CA 95354-3407 (209) 578-4792
FAX: (209) 578-9891; E-mail: jbowers@framax.net;
Toll Free Tel.: (800)-755-4792; URL: http://www.framax.net

Foundation type: Public charity
Purpose: Financial meal reimbursement and nutritional education to family child care home providers in CA.
Financial data: Year ended 09/30/2011. Assets, $113,663 (M); Expenditures, $8,295,677; Total giving, $7,389,806; Grants to individuals, totaling $7,389,806.
Fields of interest: Family services.
Type of support: Grants for special needs.
Application information: Unsolicited requests for funds not considered or acknowledged. Grants are made only to home providers participating in the USDA, CACFP.
EIN: 942767727

593
Frameline
145 9th St., Ste. 300
San Francisco, CA 94103-2640 (415) 703-8650
FAX: (415) 861-1404; E-mail: info@frameline.org;
URL: http://www.frameline.org

Foundation type: Public charity
Purpose: Project support to gay, lesbian, bisexual and transgender media artists in their final stages of film and video production.
Publications: Application guidelines; Newsletter.
Financial data: Year ended 12/31/2012. Assets, $800,204 (M); Expenditures, $1,552,249; Total giving, $30,000; Grants to individuals, totaling $28,000.
Fields of interest: Film/video; Arts, artist's services; Arts; LGBTQ.
Type of support: Grants to individuals; Awards/prizes.
Application information: Applications accepted. Application form required. Application form available on the grantmaker's web site.
  Initial approach: Letter

Send request by: Application should be sent by
mail
Copies of proposal: 7
Deadline(s): Oct. 1
Final notification: Applicants notified three
months after submission
Applicants should submit the following:
1) Budget Information
2) Essay
3) Financial information
4) Proposal
5) Work samples
Program description:
Frameline Film and Video Completion Fund: This
fund assists lesbian and gay media artists with the
final stages of film and video productions by
awarding completion funds ranging from $5,000 to
$10,000. Submissions are accepted for
documentary, educational, narrative, animation or
experimental projects of any length or format.
Women and people of color are encouraged to
apply.
EIN: 942775772

594
The John Douglas French Alzheimer's
Foundation
11620 Wilshire Blvd., Ste. 270
Los Angeles, CA 90025-1767 (310) 445-4650
URL: http://www.jdfaf.org

Foundation type: Public charity
Purpose: Cash grants to scientists to develop a
cure and treatment for Alzheimer's disease.
Publications: Newsletter.
Financial data: Year ended 07/31/2012. Assets,
$9,954,091 (M); Expenditures, $1,151,171; Total
giving, $710,444; Grants to individuals, 11 grants
totaling $710,444.
Fields of interest: Alzheimer's disease research.
Type of support: Research; Grants to individuals.
Application information: Applications not
accepted.
Additional information: Unsolicited requests for
funds not considered or acknowledged.
EIN: 953901768

595
Fresno County Economic Opportunities
Commission
1920 Mariposa Mall, Ste. 300
Fresno, CA 93721-2504 (559) 263-1000
Contact: Brian Angus, C.E.O.
FAX: (559) 263-1286;
E-mail: executiveoffice@fresnoeoc.org;
URL: http://www.fresnoeoc.org/

Foundation type: Public charity
Purpose: Emergency assistance to individuals and
families in need throughout Fresno County, CA.
Publications: Annual report.
Financial data: Year ended 12/31/2011. Assets,
$39,380,638 (M); Expenditures, $121,036,694;
Total giving, $30,525,112; Grants to individuals,
56,453 grants totaling $30,525,112.
Fields of interest: Economically disadvantaged.
Type of support: Emergency funds.
Application information: Applications accepted.
Additional information: Contact the agency for
additional information.
EIN: 941606519

596
Fresno Musical Club
2689 W. San Carlos
Fresno, CA 93711
Contact: Saskia Dyer, C.F.O.

Foundation type: Operating foundation
Purpose: Scholarships to young musicians and
artists in the community of Clovis, CA, to assist in
their music studies.
Financial data: Year ended 06/30/2012. Assets,
$133,856 (M); Expenditures, $17,225; Total
giving, $11,280; Grants to individuals, 14 grants
totaling $11,280 (high: $1,400, low: $200).
Fields of interest: Music; Performing arts,
education.
Type of support: Undergraduate support.
Application information: Applications accepted.
Initial approach: Letter
Deadline(s): None
Additional information: Application must include
resume of musical background and
description of needs, accepted throughout the
year.
EIN: 946075667

597
Fresno Regional Foundation
5250 N. Palm Ave., Ste. 424
Fresno, CA 93704-2210
Contact: For inquiries: Sandra R. Flores, Sr. Prog. Off.
FAX: (559) 230-2078;
E-mail: info@fresnoregfoundation.org; URL: http://
www.fresnoregfoundation.org

Foundation type: Community foundation
Purpose: Scholarships to individuals residing in the
San Joaquin Valley, CA, area, for undergraduate and
graduate education.
Publications: Application guidelines; Annual report;
Financial statement; Informational brochure;
Newsletter; Newsletter (including application
guidelines); Quarterly report.
Financial data: Year ended 12/31/2011. Assets,
$78,348,542 (M); Expenditures, $5,710,161;
Total giving, $3,787,687.
Fields of interest: Higher education; Scholarships/
financial aid.
Type of support: Scholarships—to individuals;
Undergraduate support.
Application information: Applications accepted.
Application form required. Application form
available on the grantmaker's web site.
Additional information: Contact foundation for
additional application guidelines.
Program description:
Scholarships: The foundation manages many
scholarship funds that are awarded to graduating
seniors from area high schools each year. Many of
these scholarships are also renewable for college
students. Some scholarships were started by
families or individuals, others by businesses or
organizations. Each scholarship has its own unique
eligibility criteria. See web site for additional
information.
EIN: 770478025

598
Friedberger Educational Fund
c/o Bank of Stockton
P.O. Box 201014
Stockton, CA 95201-9014 (209) 933-7000

Foundation type: Independent foundation
Purpose: Scholarships by nomination only to
residents of San Joaquin County, CA, who graduate

from preparatory schools and attend colleges and
universities within CA.
Financial data: Year ended 12/31/2012. Assets,
$1,114,366 (M); Expenditures, $60,032; Total
giving, $35,545; Grants to individuals, 57 grants
totaling $35,545 (high: $735, low: $592).
Fields of interest: Scholarships/financial aid.
Type of support: Awards/grants by nomination only;
Undergraduate support.
Application information: Each public and private
high school may nominate two applicants.
Interested students should notify guidance
counselor if interested. Unsolicited requests for
funds not considered or acknowledged.
EIN: 946081078

599
Friends of Civic Arts Education Fund
1666 N. Main St.
Walnut Creek, CA 94596 (925) 939-2787
Contact: Michael S. Weiner, Pres.
FAX: (925) 988-9907;
E-mail: friendsofcae@walnut-creek.org;
URL: http://www.friendsartsed.org/

Foundation type: Public charity
Purpose: Scholarships to Contra Costa county, CA
residents in need of obtaining safe, high quality arts
and preschool programs.
Financial data: Year ended 06/30/2012. Assets,
$128,711 (M); Expenditures, $55,411; Total
giving, $23,034. Scholarships—to individuals
amount not specified.
Fields of interest: Performing arts.
Type of support: Scholarships—to individuals.
Application information: Applications accepted.
Application form required.
Send request by: Mail, hand deliver, fax, or e-mail
Additional information: Scholarships are awarded
on a first-come, first-served basis, and are
based on gross household income and
number of members. See web site for
additional guidelines.
Program description:
Scholarships: A limited number of scholarships
are awarded to assist families needing safe,
high-quality arts and preschool programs for their
children and themselves. The goal is to raise and
allocate funds to families who demonstrate the
greatest need. Scholarships are offered in the form
of reduced payments, and an existing scholarship
fund covers the cost of this program.
EIN: 562522306

600
Friends of Crest
120 N. Park Dr.
El Cajon, CA 92021-4327
Contact: Peggy Meredith

Foundation type: Independent foundation
Purpose: Grants to crest residents affected by the
wildfires (cedar fire) in San Diego county, CA.
Financial data: Year ended 12/31/2010. Assets,
$1,343 (M); Expenditures, $14,026; Total giving,
$6,000.
Fields of interest: Human services, emergency aid.
Type of support: Grants to individuals.
Application information:
Initial approach: Letter
Additional information: Unsolicited requests for
funds not accepted.
EIN: 330660248

601
Friends of the Schindler House
835 N. Kings Rd.
West Hollywood, CA 90069-5409 (323) 651-1510
FAX: (323) 651-2340;
E-mail: office@makcenter.org; URL: http://www.makcenter.org

Foundation type: Public charity
Purpose: Residencies to artists and architects to work in Los Angeles, CA for six months.
Financial data: Year ended 12/31/2012. Assets, $204,396 (M); Expenditures, $86,711.
Fields of interest: Architecture; Arts, artist's services; Arts.
Type of support: Residencies.
Application information: Applications accepted. Application form required. Application form available on the grantmaker's web site.
Initial approach: Letter, telephone or e-mail
Deadline(s): Early Mar.
Additional information: See web site for additional application information.
Program description:
MAK Center Artists and Architects in Residence Program: Residencies for projects in the fields of architecture and the fine arts respectively as part of the MAK Schindler Artists and Architects in Residence Program in Los Angeles, CA. The winners will stay at the Mackey House, one of the two locations of the MAK Center for Art and Architecture, Los Angeles, for six months, realizing the projects they have submitted. This program is open to freelance artists, advanced students of architecture and graduates of architecture immediately after completion of their degree.
EIN: 953161402

602
The James F. and Sarah T. Fries Foundation
(formerly Healthtrac Foundation)
135 Farm Rd.
Woodside, CA 94062 (650) 529-9533
Contact: James F. Fries M.D., Chair.
URL: http://www.friesfoundation.org/

Foundation type: Operating foundation
Purpose: Prizes by nomination only to individuals who have greatly contributed to the health of the public.
Publications: Informational brochure (including application guidelines).
Financial data: Year ended 12/31/2012. Assets, $1,282,792 (M); Expenditures, $153,382; Total giving, $105,000; Grants to individuals, 14 grants totaling $105,000 (high: $60,000; low: $500).
Fields of interest: Formal/general education.
Type of support: Awards/prizes.
Application information:
Initial approach: Telephone, letter, or e-mail
Deadline(s): May 31
Final notification: July 15
Applicants should submit the following:
1) Curriculum vitae
2) Letter(s) of recommendation
Additional information: Self-nominations not accepted.
Program descriptions:
Elizabeth Fries Health Education Award: The Elizabeth Fries Health Education Award is for a health educator who has made a substantial contribution to advancing the field of health education or health promotion through research, program development, or program delivery. The

award amount is $25,000. See foundation web site for additional information.
Fries Prize For Improving Health: The Fries Prize For Improving Health is for major accomplishments in health improvement, unrestricted as to field, with emphasis upon recent contributions to health in the United States. The award amount is $60,000. See foundation web site for additional information.
EIN: 943131228

603
From the Heart Productions, Inc.
1455 Mandalay Beach Rd.
Oxnard, CA 93035-2845 (805) 984-0098
Contact: Carole Dean, Pres.
Application e-mail address: caroleedean@att.net
E-mail: general@fromtheheartproductions.com;
URL: http://www.fromtheheartproductions.com

Foundation type: Public charity
Purpose: Grants to screenwriters and filmmakers to fund films and support documentary filmmakers.
Publications: Application guidelines.
Financial data: Year ended 12/31/2011. Assets, $166,141 (M); Expenditures, $574,424; Total giving, $455,760.
Fields of interest: Film/video.
Type of support: Grants to individuals.
Application information: Applications accepted. Application form required. Application form available on the grantmaker's web site.
Send request by: Online and mail
Copies of proposal: 1
Deadline(s): Apr. 30
Applicants should submit the following:
1) Budget Information
2) Work samples
3) SASE
4) Proposal
Additional information: Application should also include a two- to six-page proposal, and a suggested $38 application fee or $28 for students with a copy of student ID. Faxed applications are not accepted. See web site for additional guidelines.
Program description:
Roy W. Dean Film and Video Grants: This grant is now available for short and low-budget independents as well as documentary filmmakers, and have expanded to further our goals of creating films that are unique and make a contribution to society. Student filmmakers, independent producers or independent production companies are all welcome.
EIN: 954445418

604
Fulfillment Fund
6100 Wilshire Blvd.
Los Angeles, CA 90048-5107 (323) 939-9707
Contact: Kenny Rogers, C.E.O.
FAX: (323) 525-3095; TTY: (323) 525-3098;
URL: http://www.fulfillment.org

Foundation type: Public charity
Purpose: College scholarships are provided to high school students who were enrolled in a Fulfillment Fund program for at least two years.
Publications: Annual report.
Financial data: Year ended 06/30/2012. Assets, $8,817,591 (M); Expenditures, $4,374,542; Total giving, $430,961; Grants to individuals, totaling $430,961.
Type of support: Scholarships—to individuals.
Application information: Applications accepted. Application form required.

Additional information: See web site for additional information.
Program description:
Scholarships: Los Angeles-area high school students who have successfully completed the fund program are eligible to apply for scholarships and internships, and receive one-on-one counseling and assessment, graduate school guidance, resume review and interview skills training, job shadowing and informational interviews with donors and alumni, and workshops and seminars. High-school graduates who had been in the program for at least two years are eligible to apply for up to $1,500 per year for up to five years to assist with tuition, books, supplies, and other expenses.
EIN: 953180934

605
Fundacion La Curacao Para Los Ninos
(also known as Curacao Children's Foundation)
c/o Community Rels. Dept.
1605 W. Olympic Blvd., Ste. 600
Los Angeles, CA 90015-3836
E-mail: Foundationinfo@iCuracao.net; URL: http://www.icuracao.net/Community.aspx?p=1#.UNCPeqyrDTM

Foundation type: Company-sponsored foundation
Purpose: Assistance with free home products to disadvantaged children and families in need in the Los Angeles, CA area. Scholarships to Latino students for higher education.
Publications: Application guidelines.
Financial data: Year ended 12/31/2011. Assets, $0 (M); Expenditures, $222,280; Total giving, $126,427.
Fields of interest: Higher education; Children, services; Family services; Economically disadvantaged.
Type of support: Scholarships—to individuals; Grants for special needs.
Application information: Applications accepted. Application form available on the grantmaker's web site.
Initial approach: Application
Send request by: Online
Deadline(s): None
Additional information: Individuals must be referred by a community organization, church, school, or other entity that works with children. Foundation staff will visit referred families and assess needs.
EIN: 912168952

606
Futuro Infantil Hispano
2227 E. Garvey Ave., N.
West Covina, CA 91791-1500 (626) 339-1824
Contact: Oma Velasco-Rodriguez, Pres. and Exec.Dir.
FAX: (626) 915-4148; Ontario Office Address: 1131 W. 6th St., Ste. 110, Ontario, CA 91762, tel.: (909) 460-1138, fax: (909) 460-0438; URL: http://www.futuroinfantil.org

Foundation type: Public charity
Purpose: Financial assistance to foster families for providing quality care and to improve the life of children that have been abused and abandoned in the Los Angeles, San Bernardino, Riverside and Orange counties, CA area.
Financial data: Year ended 06/30/2012. Assets, $4,185,216 (M); Expenditures, $6,233,304; Total giving, $2,844,123; Grants to individuals, totaling $2,844,123.
Fields of interest: Foster care.

Type of support: Grants for special needs.
Application information:
Initial approach: Telephone
Additional information: Contact the agency for eligibility determination.
EIN: 954494661

607

The Gaines-Jones Education Foundation

P.O. Box 3016
Novato, CA 94948-3016

Foundation type: Operating foundation
Purpose: Scholarship assistance to eligible high school seniors of GA, in meeting their college needs.
Financial data: Year ended 12/31/2012. Assets, $310,012 (M); Expenditures, $25,401; Total giving, $17,148; Grants to individuals, 12 grants totaling $17,148 (high: $2,600).
Fields of interest: Higher education.
Type of support: Scholarships—to individuals.
Application information: Contact the foundation for application guidelines.
EIN: 943326884

608

Gala Foundation

3191 Red Hill Ave., Ste. 100
Costa Mesa, CA 92626 (310) 403-4943
Contact: Dineshchandra Gala, C.E.O.

Foundation type: Independent foundation
Purpose: Scholarships to individuals of Indian descent for higher education.
Financial data: Year ended 09/30/2012. Assets, $423,097 (M); Expenditures, $105,257; Total giving, $104,994.
International interests: India.
Type of support: Scholarships—to individuals.
Application information:
Initial approach: Letter
Deadline(s): Sept. 1
EIN: 330777331

609

Gemological Institute of America, Inc.

5345 Armada Dr.
Carlsbad, CA 92008-4602 (760) 603-4000
Contact: Donna Baker, Pres. and C.E.O.
Additional tel. for scholarship: (800) 421-7250, ext 4175, e-mail: scholarship@gia.edu
FAX: (760) 603-4080; E-mail: marketing@gia.edu;
URL: http://www.gia.edu

Foundation type: Public charity
Purpose: Scholarships to individuals 18 years of age, with a high school diploma or GED equivalent for its Gemology and Jewelry Manufacturing Arts programs, courses and classes.
Publications: Application guidelines.
Financial data: Year ended 12/31/2011. Assets, $324,244,613 (M); Expenditures, $131,101,136; Total giving, $458,965; Grants to individuals, totaling $263,378.
Fields of interest: Higher education.
Type of support: Scholarships—to individuals.
Application information: Applications accepted. Application form required.
Deadline(s): Oct. 31
Final notification: Recipients notified end of Jan.
Applicants should submit the following:
1) Letter(s) of recommendation
Additional information: Application should include a letter of recommendation. See web

site for additional application guidelines and listing of scholarships.
Program descriptions:
Absolute Brilliance Scholarship: This $1,000 scholarship is available for an individual to participate in the institute's On Campus Graduate Diamonds Program, Distance Education Diamonds & Diamond Grading course, or Diamond Grading Lab class.
CJA Peter Hess Scholarship: One $1,000 scholarship is available for an individual to participate in an institute-sponsored On Campus or Distance Education course or program. Recipients must be a member of the California Jewelers Association, or be willing to join the association if awarded this scholarship.
CJA Robert B. Westover Scholarship: One $1,000 scholarship is available for an individual to participate in an institute-sponsored On Campus or Distance Education course or program. Recipients must be a California Jewelers Association member, or be willing to join the association if awarded this scholarship.
Daniel Swarovski & Company Scholarship: Two scholarships of $1,500 each are available for individuals to enroll in the institute's On Campus or Distance Education gemology course or program. Eligible applicants must have a minimum of two years' experience in the jewelry industry; two letters of recommendation are required, one of which must come from within the jewelry industry.
GIA 80th Anniversary Scholarship for On-Campus Students: Six scholarships of $18,000 each are available for individuals to enroll in the institute's On Campus programs and courses, including the Graduate Gemologist or Jewelry Manufacturing Arts program (including Applied Jewelry Arts, Graduate Jeweler, and CAD/CAM/Jewelry Design courses)
Lone Star GIA Associate and Alumni Scholarship: One $500 scholarship will be made available to an individual to participate in an institute-sponsored On Campus or Distance Education course, program, or lab class. Preference will be given to applicants who reside in Texas, Oklahoma, Louisiana, New Mexico, or Arkansas.
North Texas GIA Alumni Association Scholarship: One $1,500 scholarship is available for an individual to participate in an institute-sponsored On Campus or Distance Education course, program, or lab class. Preference will be given to applicants who reside within the following Texas zip codes: 75000-75799, 76000-76999, and 76900-79799.
R. Harder Gallery Scholarship: One On Campus, or two Distance Education, $5,000 scholarships are available to participants of the institute's Graduate Gemologist program. Applicants must reside in the state of Wisconsin, with preference given to applicants who reside in the Fox Valley region (zip codes 54911-54956)
Richard T. Liddicoat Scholarship: Two scholarships of $19,000 each are available (one for an On Campus Graduate Gemologist program, and one for the Distance Education Graduate Gemologist program) to participants of institute-sponsored courses.
Wisconsin Jewelers Association Scholarship: At least five scholarships of $1,000 each are available for an individual to participate in an industry-sponsored On Campus or Distance Education course or program. Eligible applicants must be employees of a Wisconsin Jewelers Association member store.
EIN: 953797687

610

GenCorp Foundation, Incorporated

P.O. Box 15619
Sacramento, CA 95852-0619
Contact: Juanita Garcia, Exec. Dir.
FAX: (916) 355-2515;
E-mail: gencorp.foundation@gencorp.com;
URL: http://www.gencorp.com/pages/gcfound.html

Foundation type: Company-sponsored foundation
Purpose: Scholarships to local high school students who plan to pursue college study in science, technology, engineering or mathematics.
Publications: Application guidelines; Annual report; Informational brochure (including application guidelines); Occasional report.
Financial data: Year ended 11/30/2012. Assets, $16,225,000 (M); Expenditures, $798,985; Total giving, $685,798.
Application information: Applications accepted. Application form required.
Initial approach: Letter
Deadline(s): Apr. 1
Applicants should submit the following:
1) ACT
2) SAT
3) Transcripts
4) Letter(s) of recommendation
5) GPA
6) Essay
Additional information: Applicants must have 3.0 GPA, must be involved in school extra-curricular and community service activities, and have economic need and/or outstanding academic ability and performance.
Program description:
Aerojet Community Scholarships: The foundation awards $1,000 scholarships to local high school seniors who plan to pursue college study in science, technology, engineering, or math. Applicants are selected based on academic ability and economic need.
EIN: 680441559

611

Genentech Access To Care Foundation

1 DNA Way, M.S. #858A
South San Francisco, CA 94080-4918
FAX: (650) 335-1366;
E-mail: info@genentech-access.com; URL: http://www.genentech-access.com/hcp/find-patient-assistance

Foundation type: Operating foundation
Purpose: Pharmaceutical assistance to economically disadvantaged and uninsured individuals.
Publications: Application guidelines.
Financial data: Year ended 12/31/2012. Assets, $62,512,918 (M); Expenditures, $690,746,654; Total giving, $665,582,721; Grants to individuals, totaling $665,582,721.
Fields of interest: Pharmacy/prescriptions; Health care; Economically disadvantaged.
Type of support: Grants to individuals.
Application information: Applications accepted. Application form available on the grantmaker's web site.
Initial approach: Letter, telephone, or online
Deadline(s): None
Additional information: Application should include medical information from the patient's physician and financial information from the patient to determine eligibility. Applicants are

eligible for free medicine for 1 year then they must reapply annually.
EIN: 460500266

612
Wallace Alexander Gerbode Foundation

77 Van Ness Ave., Ste. 200
San Francisco, CA 94102-6042 (415) 391-0911
Contact: Molly Barrons, Admin. Mgr.
FAX: (415) 992-4723; E-mail: info@gerbode.org;
URL: http://www.foundationcenter.org/grantmaker/gerbode/

Foundation type: Independent foundation
Purpose: Awards to California artists by nomination only, through their presenting organization, to support fresh, dynamic collaborations in contemporary dance, theater and music.
Publications: Application guidelines; Annual report; Financial statement; Grants list.
Financial data: Year ended 12/31/2012. Assets, $59,511,941 (M); Expenditures, $3,812,936; Total giving, $2,602,966.
Fields of interest: Performing arts; Dance; Choreography; Theater (musical); Music; Orchestras; Music composition; Performing arts (multimedia).
Type of support: Awards/grants by nomination only; Awards/prizes.
Application information: Application form available on the grantmaker's web site.
   Initial approach: Letter
   Deadline(s): Aug. 24 for composers
   Additional information: Contact foundation for eligibility criteria.
EIN: 946065226

613
The GET Foundation

(formerly Gordon Tam & Elsie K. Tam Charitable Foundation)
46 Eugenia Way
Hillsborough, CA 94010-6263

Foundation type: Independent foundation
Purpose: Scholarships to financially needy graduates from Hong Kong high schools to study at accredited four-year US schools to enhance their future economic prospects. Preference is given to those who wish to pursue a career in science, engineering or teaching.
Financial data: Year ended 12/31/2012. Assets, $38,078 (M); Expenditures, $31,339; Total giving, $10,000; Grants to individuals, 2 grants totaling $10,000 (high: $5,000, low: $5,000).
Type of support: Foreign applicants.
Application information: Applications accepted. Application form required. Application form available on the grantmaker's web site.
   Initial approach: E-mail
   Deadline(s): Apr. 15
   Applicants should submit the following:
     1) Essay
EIN: 946746714

614
J. Paul Getty Trust

1200 Getty Ctr. Dr., Ste. 800
Los Angeles, CA 90049-1679 (310) 440-7320
Contact: The Getty Foundation
FAX: (310) 440-7703;
E-mail: GettyFoundation@getty.edu; URL: http://www.getty.edu

Foundation type: Operating foundation
Purpose: Support to scholars in the art history field, and internships to undergraduate and graduate students interested in exploring career possibilities in the visual arts, museum professions, and art history.
Publications: Application guidelines; Annual report; Grants list.
Financial data: Year ended 06/30/2012. Assets, $10,502,514,302 (M); Expenditures, $282,607,897; Total giving, $14,565,066; Grants to individuals, 155 grants totaling $1,877,485 (high: $67,000, low: $500).
Fields of interest: Research; Visual arts; Art conservation; Museums; Museums (art); Humanities; Art history; Arts; Science; Social sciences; Minorities; African Americans/Blacks; Hispanics/Latinos; Native Americans/American Indians.
International interests: Eastern Europe; Europe.
Type of support: Conferences/seminars; Fellowships; Internship funds; Research; Postdoctoral support; Graduate support; Undergraduate support; Postgraduate support; Residencies; Travel grants; Stipends.
Application information: Applications accepted. Application form required.
   Initial approach: Letter
   Additional information: See web site for further application and program information.
Program descriptions:
   Conservation Guest Scholars: Supports new ideas and perspectives in the field of conservation, this program provides an opportunity for professionals to pursue scholarly research in an interdisciplinary manner across traditional boundaries in areas of wide general interest to the international conservation community. Grants are for established conservators, scientists, and professionals who have attained distinction in conservation and allied fields. Conservation Guest Scholars are in residence at the Getty Center for three to nine consecutive months. A monthly stipend of $3,500 is awarded. For complete application information and guidelines see web site. E-mail:researchgrants@getty.edu.
   Getty Scholar Grants: Recipients are in residence at the Getty Research Institute, where they pursue their own projects free from academic obligations, make use of Getty collections, join their colleagues in a weekly meeting devoted to an annual theme, and participate in the intellectual life of the Getty. These grants are for established scholars, artists, or writers who have attained distinction in their fields. Applications are welcome from researchers of all nationalities who are working in the arts, humanities, or social sciences. A stipend of up to $65,000 per year will be awarded based on length of stay, need, and salary. For complete application information and guidelines see web site. E-mail:researchgrants@getty.edu.
   Graduate Interns: The internships are offered in the four programs of the J. Paul Getty Trust-the J. Paul Getty Museum, the Getty Research Institute, the Getty Conservation Institute, and the Getty Foundation-to students who intend to pursue careers in fields related to the visual arts. Training and work experience are available in areas such as curatorial, education, conservation, research, information management, public programs, and grantmaking. Applicants must be either students currently enrolled in a graduate program leading to an advanced degree in a field relevant to the internship(s) for which they are applying, or individuals who have completed a relevant graduate degree on or after Jan. 1, 2011, with postgraduate activities in their field, paid or unpaid. Internships are located at the Getty Center in Los Angeles or

the Getty Villa in Malibu. All positions are full-time and grant amounts are $17,400 for eight months and $26,000 for twelve months. The grant includes health benefits, but housing and relocation funds are not provided. For complete application information and guidelines see web site. E-mail: gradinterns@getty.edu.
   Leadership and Professional Development: Recognizing that the continued vitality of the fields we serve depends on the quality of their leaders, the Getty Foundation funds professional development opportunities for individuals at various stages of their careers. Current grant programs are Multicultural Graduate Interns, Graduate Internships, Professional Development and Getty Leadership Institute.
   Library Research Grants: Provides partial, short-term support for costs relating to travel and living expenses for scholars whose research requires use of specific collections housed in the Research Library at the Getty Research Institute. Grants are intended for scholars at any level who demonstrate a compelling need to use materials housed in the Research Library, and whose place of residence is more than eighty miles from the Getty Center. Library Research Grants range from $500 to $2,500. The research period may range from several days to a maximum of three months.For complete application information and guidelines see foundation web site. E-mail:researchgrants@getty.edu.
   Multicultural Undergraduate Getty Internships: Internships provide stipends of $3,500 for ten-week summer internships at the Getty Center in Los Angeles and the Getty Villa in Malibu, California. The internships are full time. Health insurance, housing, and transportation are not provided. Students interested in internships at other organizations should refer to the list of available positions throughout Los Angeles County. For more information see web site. E-mail:summerinterns@getty.edu.
   Multicultural Undergraduate Interns: The program has funded substantive, full-time summer work opportunities for students at Los Angeles-area museums and visual arts organizations. The internships are intended specifically for currently enrolled undergraduates and recent graduates residing or attending college in Los Angeles County who are members of groups currently underrepresented in museums and visual arts organizations. Eligible organizations must be a museum or visual arts organization located in Los Angeles County and a nonprofit as defined by section 501(c)(3) of the United States Internal Revenue Service Code. Eligible students must: 1) be of African American, Asian, Latino/Hispanic, Native American, or Pacific Islander descent; 2) currently enrolled undergraduates; 3) reside or attend college in Los Angeles County and be a United States citizen or permanent resident. The internships are full-time (40 hours/week) positions, each with a salary of $3,500. For complete application information and guidelines see web site. E-mail: summerinterns@getty.edu.
   Postdoctoral Fellowship in Conservation Science: The fellowship is a two-year residence program at the Getty Center. Applications are welcome from scientists of all nationalities who are interested in pursuing a career in conservation science and have received a PhD in chemistry/physical science no earlier than 2008. A background in the humanities is helpful, and strong science working practices are essential. For complete application information and guidelines see web site. E-mail:researchgrants@getty.edu.
   Pre- and Postdoctoral Fellowships: The fellowships provide support for emerging scholars to complete work on projects related to the Getty

Research Institute's annual theme. Recipients are in residence at the Getty Research Institute, where they pursue research to complete their dissertations or to expand them for publication. Fellows make use of the Getty collections, join in a weekly meeting devoted to the annual theme, and participate in the intellectual life of the Getty. Applications are welcome from scholars of all nationalities. Predoctoral fellowship applicants must have advanced to candidacy by the time of the fellowship start date and should expect to complete their dissertations during the fellowship period. Postdoctoral fellowship applicants must not have received their degree earlier than 2008. Predoctoral Fellows are in residence from Sept. to June and receive a stipend of $25,000. Postdoctoral Fellows are in residence from September to June and receive a stipend of $30,000. For complete application information and guidelines see web site. E-mail:researchgrants@getty.edu.
EIN: 951790021

615
A. P. Giannini Foundation
(formerly Giannini Family Foundation)
57 Post St., Ste. 510
San Francisco, CA 94104-5020 (415) 981-2966
Contact: John S. Blum, Admin.; Kenneth J. Blum, Admin.
FAX: (415) 981-5218;
E-mail: info@apgianninifoundation.org; URL: http://www.apgianninifoundation.org/
Foundation type: Independent foundation
Purpose: Fellowships to promising young postdoctoral investigators in the early stages of their careers for research who are sponsored by one of the eight medical schools in CA.
Publications: Financial statement; Informational brochure (including application guidelines).
Financial data: Year ended 12/31/2012. Assets, $20,235,738 (M); Expenditures, $1,196,389; Total giving, $821,166.
Fields of interest: Medical research.
Type of support: Fellowships.
Application information: Applications accepted. Application form required. Application form available on the grantmaker's web site. Interview required.
  Initial approach: Telephone, or e-mail
  Send request by: Mail
  Copies of proposal: 1
  Deadline(s): Nov. 4
  Applicants should submit the following:
    1) Proposal
    2) Curriculum vitae
    3) Letter(s) of recommendation
  Additional information: Fellowships are awarded and paid to California medical schools which must sponsor the candidate. No grants or fellowships are paid directly by the foundation to individuals.
EIN: 946089512

616
The Gifford Foundation, Inc.
3130 Alpine Rd., No. 288-250
Portola Valley, CA 94028-7549

Foundation type: Independent foundation
Purpose: Scholarships to individuals residing in CA and HI for undergraduate education. Program development grants to individuals primarily in CA for community baseball programs.

Financial data: Year ended 05/31/2013. Assets, $6,778,052 (M); Expenditures, $1,627,419; Total giving, $1,518,164.
Fields of interest: Athletics/sports, baseball.
Type of support: Program development; Undergraduate support.
Application information: Contact foundation for current application deadlines/guidelines.
EIN: 943303273

617
Girl Scouts Heart of Central California
(formerly Girl Scouts of Tierra Del Oro)
6601 Elvas Ave.
Sacramento, CA 95819-4339 (916) 452-9181
FAX: (916) 452-9182;
E-mail: info@girlscoutshcc.org; Toll-free tel.: (800) 322-4475; Additional address (Stockton office): 7475 Murray Dr., Ste. 3, Stockton, CA 95210-5318, tel.: (209) 473-5914, fax: (209) 473-4446; Additional address (Modesto office): 3621 Forest Glenn Dr., Modesto, CA 95355-1339, tel.: (209) 522-9001, fax: (209) 522-9036;
URL: http://www.girlscoutshcc.org
Foundation type: Public charity
Purpose: Financial assistance support to Girl Scouts throughout central California.
Financial data: Year ended 09/30/2011. Assets, $12,009,985 (M); Expenditures, $7,825,820; Total giving, $166,030; Grants to individuals, totaling $166,030.
Fields of interest: Girl scouts.
Type of support: Grants for special needs.
Application information: Contact the organization for further guidelines.
EIN: 941582429

618
Give A Slice
7755 Center Ave., Ste. 300
Huntington Beach, CA 92647-3084

Foundation type: Independent foundation
Purpose: Financial assistance to employees of BJ's restaurants and to their family members who may have suffered from illness, injury, death, fire or other catastrophic events.
Financial data: Year ended 12/31/2012. Assets, $267,798 (M); Expenditures, $143,500; Total giving, $110,722; Grants to individuals, 41 grants totaling $110,722 (high: $9,500, low: $500).
Fields of interest: Safety/disasters.
Type of support: Grants for special needs.
Application information: Applications not accepted.
  Additional information: Unsolicited requests for funds not considered or acknowledged.
EIN: 020727065

619
Glaucoma Research Foundation
251 Post St., Ste. 600
San Francisco, CA 94108-5017 (415) 986-3162
Contact: Thomas M. Brunner, Pres. and C.E.O.
FAX: (415) 986-3763; E-mail: grf@glaucoma.org; Toll-free tel.: (800) 826-6693; E-Mail for Thomas M. Brunner : tbrunner@glaucoma.org; URL: http://www.glaucoma.org
Foundation type: Public charity
Purpose: Research grants to individuals working on finding a cure for glaucoma. Fellowships by nomination only for study at a U.S. institution to

ophthalmologists from developing countries who have been nominated by their department chairs.
Publications: Application guidelines; Annual report; Financial statement; Grants list; Informational brochure (including application guidelines); Newsletter.
Financial data: Year ended 06/30/2012. Assets, $5,540,004 (M); Expenditures, $3,902,081; Total giving, $2,082,102. Grants to individuals amount not specified.
Fields of interest: Eye diseases; Institute; Eye research.
Type of support: Fellowships; Research; Awards/grants by nomination only.
Application information: Application form required.
  Initial approach: Letter
  Deadline(s): June 1 to July 31 for preliminary proposal; Sept. 30 for formal application
  Additional information: Application should include financial information. For Shaffer International Fellowship contact Jennifer Rulon, Research Specialist.
Program descriptions:
  Shaffer Grant Program: Grant money is provided to initiate new research in important areas of glaucoma research or to stimulate work examining critical issues in glaucoma. The primary focus is in funding collaborative pilot projects across disciplines. Typically, these grants are awarded in the amount of $40,000 for one year. Any papers and abstracts resulting from research funded by the foundation must acknowledge this fact. To be eligible, applicants must possess at least a graduate degree. Interdisciplinary teams and collaborations that may lead to new glaucoma treatments are encouraged.
  Shaffer International Glaucoma Fellowship Program: Ophthalmologists from developing countries are placed in academic institutions in the U.S. for one year, beginning in July, every other year. Upon completion of the fellowship period, the recipient returns to his/her country of origin to apply the research skills and knowledge they've obtained through clinical observation. Fellows each receive a $25,000 stipend and their participating academic institution receives $10,000 for required research materials and supplies for the fellow.
EIN: 942495035

620
The Gleitsman Foundation
c/o Solomon Ross Grey & Co.
16633 Ventura Blvd., Ste. 600
Encino, CA 91436-1835
URL: http://www.gleitsman.org

Foundation type: Independent foundation
Purpose: Awards by nomination only to citizen activist leaders who confront, challenge and correct social injustice, and initiate positive social change.
Financial data: Year ended 03/31/2013. Assets, $218,301 (M); Expenditures, $11,696; Total giving, $10,446.
Fields of interest: Human services; International human rights; Civil/human rights.
Type of support: Awards/grants by nomination only; Awards/prizes.
Application information: Applications not accepted.
  Additional information: Deadline Nov. 2. Self-nominations cannot be considered.
EIN: 954220291

621
Glenn Foundation for Medical Research, Inc.
(formerly Paul F. Glenn Foundation for Medical Research, Inc.)
1270 Coast Village Cir., St. 200
Santa Barbara, CA 93108-3724
Contact: Mark R. Collins, Pres.
E-mail: mrc@glennfoundation.org; URL: http://www.glennfoundation.org

Foundation type: Independent foundation
Purpose: Grants for research on the biology of aging to those engaged in research on mechanisms of the aging process with one or more of the following objectives: delaying or preventing the onset of senility and prolonging the human life span, increasing the stature of the field of gerontology, broadening scientific understanding of the aging process, or advancing the field of biogerontology.
Publications: Grants list; Informational brochure; Program policy statement.
Financial data: Year ended 09/30/2013. Assets, $245,703,267 (M); Expenditures, $10,346,058; Total giving, $6,448,409.
Fields of interest: Biology/life sciences; Gerontology.
Type of support: Fellowships; Research; Awards/grants by nomination only.
Application information: Applications not accepted.
Additional information: Unsolicited requests for funds not considered or acknowledged. Support programs are administered through internal recommendations or by anonymous outside advisors.
EIN: 860710305

622
Glennon Foundation
13091 Pierce Rd.
Saratoga, CA 95070-4211 (408) 867-5440
Contact: William Glennon, Tr.

Foundation type: Independent foundation
Purpose: Scholarships to deserving financially needed students who qualify academically for attendance at schools of higher education within the California State College system.
Financial data: Year ended 12/31/2011. Assets, $63,412 (M); Expenditures, $139,750; Total giving, $138,682; Grants to individuals, totaling $138,682.
Fields of interest: Higher education.
Type of support: Scholarships—to individuals.
Application information: Applications accepted.
EIN: 320037020

623
Global Operations and Development
8332 Commonwealth Ave.
Buena Park, CA 90621-2526 (714) 523-4454
FAX: (714) 523-4474; E-mail: global@godaid.org;
URL: http://godaid.org/index.htm

Foundation type: Public charity
Purpose: Grants to disaster victims with distribution of medicine, medical supplies, food, clothes and other emergency assistance.
Financial data: Year ended 06/30/2012. Assets, $16,717,196 (M); Expenditures, $35,606,793; Total giving, $34,285,276.
Fields of interest: Safety/disasters.
Type of support: Emergency funds.
Application information:
Initial approach: Letter

Additional information: Contact foundation for complete eligibility criteria.
EIN: 953464287

624
The La'Roi Glover Foundation
c/o The Giving Back Fund
6033 W. Century Blvd., Ste. 350
Los Angeles, CA 90045-6444 (310) 649-5222
FAX: (310) 649-5070;
E-mail: laroigloverfoundation@givingback.org

Foundation type: Public charity
Purpose: Scholarships to graduating seniors of Point Loma High School, San Diego, CA for postsecondary education and to college students in San Diego, CA.
Fields of interest: Higher education.
Type of support: Support to graduates or students of specific schools.
Application information:
Applicants should submit the following:
1) Letter(s) of recommendation
2) GPA
3) Essay
Program description:
Scholarships: In an effort to support deserving high school senior students as they endeavor to attend college, the foundation awards two $5,000 scholarship to Point Loma, CA High School graduates. One boy and one girl are selected each year to receive college scholarships, which are awarded based on GPA requirements, extracurricular activities, strong recommendations, and compelling essays about why the student is deserving of the award.

625
Golden Gate Family Foundation
3201 Ash St.
Palo Alto, CA 94306-2240

Foundation type: Independent foundation
Purpose: Scholarships to individuals in pursuit of a higher education. Also, assistance with medical, living and housing expenses.
Financial data: Year ended 12/31/2012. Assets, $122,307 (M); Expenditures, $212,630; Total giving, $194,937; Grants to individuals, 22 grants totaling $194,937 (high: $55,107, low: $1,128).
Type of support: Scholarships—to individuals.
Application information: Applications not accepted.
Additional information: Unsolicited requests for funds not considered or acknowledged.
EIN: 770259505

626
Golden Gate Restaurant Association Scholarship Foundation
(formerly David Rubenstein Memorial Scholarship Foundation)
100 Montgomery St., Ste. 1280
San Francisco, CA 94104-4315 (415) 781-5348
Contact: Rob Black
URL: http://www.ggra.org/education/scholarship-foundation/

Foundation type: Independent foundation
Purpose: Scholarships to students from the greater San Francisco Bay Area pursuing a career in the culinary and hospitality industry.
Financial data: Year ended 12/31/2011. Assets, $299,484 (M); Expenditures, $55,948; Total

giving, $55,728; Grants to individuals, 13 grants totaling $48,000 (high: $6,500, low: $500).
Fields of interest: Business/industry.
Type of support: Graduate support; Undergraduate support.
Application information: Applications accepted. Application form required. Interview required.
Initial approach: Letter or telephone
Send request by: Mail
Deadline(s): Apr. 30
Final notification: Applicants notified two weeks after interview
Applicants should submit the following:
1) Transcripts
2) Letter(s) of recommendation
3) Essay
Program description:
Scholarship Fund: Recipients are selected on the basis of a commitment to pursuing a career in the hospitality industry, personal merit, and evidence of ability to benefit from additional training. In the case of applicants with equal qualifications, preference may be given to students who are immediate family or employees of GGRA members and students attending San Francisco Bay Area foodservice programs.
EIN: 237012819

627
Golden West College Foundation
15744 Goldenwest St.
Huntington Beach, CA 92647-3103 (714) 895-8315
Contact: For Scholarships: Margie Bunten, Dir., Fdn. & Community Relations
M. Bunten e-mail: mbunten@gwc.cccd.edu
URL: http://goldenwestcollege.edu/foundation/

Foundation type: Public charity
Purpose: Scholarships for students attending Golden West College, CA for higher education.
Financial data: Year ended 06/30/2012. Assets, $6,876,300 (M); Expenditures, $1,032,492; Total giving, $484,071; Grants to individuals, totaling $484,071.
Fields of interest: Higher education.
Type of support: Scholarships—to individuals; Support to graduates or students of specific schools.
Application information: Applications accepted. Application form required. Application form available on the grantmaker's web site.
Send request by: Online
Deadline(s): Mar. 8
Final notification: Recipients notified after mid-Apr.
Additional information: Application should include a personal statement. See web site for additional application guidelines.
EIN: 330073702

628
Goldman Environmental Foundation
160 Pacific Ave., Ste. 200
San Francisco, CA 94111-1976 (415) 249-5800
FAX: (415) 772-9137;
E-mail: info@goldmanprize.org; URL: http://www.goldmanprize.org

Foundation type: Independent foundation
Purpose: Awards by nomination only to individuals from six continents in recognition of significant achievement in the field of environmental protection.
Publications: Informational brochure; Newsletter.

Financial data: Year ended 12/31/2012. Assets, $111,517,762 (M); Expenditures, $4,572,681; Total giving, $900,000; Grants to individuals, 6 grants totaling $900,000 (high: $150,000, low: $150,000).
Fields of interest: Natural resources; Environment; Animals/wildlife, preservation/protection.
Type of support: Awards/grants by nomination only; Awards/prizes.
Application information: Applications not accepted.
Additional information: Unsolicited nominations not accepted; 21 organizations and a network of environmentalists are invited to submit nominations to the foundation.
Program description:
Goldman Environmental Prize: The prize is given each year to six environmental heroes - one from each of six continental regions: Africa, Asia, Europe, Island Nations, North America and South/Central America. The award currently stands at $150,000. The prize is the world's largest award for grassroots environmentalists, recognizing courageous individuals working against overwhelming odds to preserve the natural environment. An international environmental network of organizations and individuals submits nominations confidentially. Staff researches each nomination, and the prize jury makes the final selection.
EIN: 943094857

629
Good Friend Ministry
(formerly International Gospel Mission)
15 Santa Rida
Irvine, CA 92606-8874
Contact: Eugene J. Choy, Pres.

Foundation type: Operating foundation
Purpose: Grants to individuals for missions, primarily in CA.
Financial data: Year ended 12/31/2012. Assets, $474,685 (M); Expenditures, $14,262; Total giving, $13,000.
Fields of interest: Media/communications; Human services; Christian agencies & churches.
Type of support: Grants for special needs.
Application information:
Initial approach: Letter
Deadline(s): None
Additional information: Contact the mission for additional guidelines.
EIN: 953842453

630
The Good Shepherd Fund
1641 N. 1st St., Ste. 155
San Jose, CA 95112-4521 (408) 573-9606
FAX: (408) 573-9609;
E-mail: cdenham@goodshepherdfund.org; Toll-free tel.: (888) 422-4904; URL: http://www.goodshepherdfund.org
Foundation type: Public charity
Purpose: Grants to individuals with developmental disabilities and their families living in CA, CO, and OR.
Financial data: Year ended 06/30/2011. Assets, $26,362,545 (M); Expenditures, $1,400,633; Total giving, $268,443; Grants to individuals, totaling $268,443.
Fields of interest: Disabilities, people with; Economically disadvantaged.
Type of support: Grants for special needs.

Application information: Payments on behalf of individuals are based on the needs of the developmentally disabled.
EIN: 237093399

631
Good Tidings Foundation
9 Pier, Ste. 117
San Francisco, CA 94111 (415) 283-1811
FAX: (415) 283-4844;
E-mail: larry@goodtidings.org; Toll-free tel.: (800) 824-7366; URL: http://www.goodtidings.org
Foundation type: Public charity
Purpose: College scholarships to deserving high school seniors of the San Francisco, CA Bay area for serving their community.
Publications: Application guidelines; Annual report.
Financial data: Year ended 12/31/2011. Assets, $3,246,910 (M); Expenditures, $949,326; Total giving, $107,900; Grants to individuals, totaling $107,900.
Fields of interest: Higher education.
Type of support: Scholarships—to individuals.
Application information: Applications accepted. Application form required.
Deadline(s): Nov. 10
Final notification: Recipients notified in two weeks
Applicants should submit the following:
1) Essay
2) Letter(s) of recommendation
3) SAT
4) GPA
5) Financial information
Additional information: Selection is based on those with greatest need.
Program description:
Community Service Scholarships: Twenty $5,000 scholarships are available to high school seniors who have recognized the benefits of serving their community. Eligible applicants must reside in the greater San Francisco Bay area.
EIN: 943219013

632
Jan Gorecki Scholarship Foundation
19306 S. Anza Ave.
Torrance, CA 90503-1405
Contact: Peter Paley, Tr.

Foundation type: Independent foundation
Purpose: Scholarship awards for students of Polish descent living in England, Poland or the U.S.
Financial data: Year ended 09/30/2013. Assets, $221,510 (M); Expenditures, $5,442,217; Total giving, $300,000; Grants to individuals, 6 grants totaling $300,000 (high: $50,000, low: $50,000).
Fields of interest: Higher education.
International interests: England; Poland.
Type of support: Scholarships—to individuals.
Application information: Application form required.
Initial approach: Letter
Deadline(s): None
Additional information: Students must demonstrate high academic achievement.
EIN: 330831210

633
Grace Family Vineyards Foundation
(formerly NAPA Valley Student Enrichment Program)
1210 Rockland Rd.
St. Helena, CA 94574-9704 (707) 963-0808
URL: http://gracefamilyvineyards.com/grace-foundation

Foundation type: Public charity
Purpose: Financial assistance for indigent children's tuition and other education related expenses. Medical assistance for indigent children.
Financial data: Year ended 12/31/2011. Assets, $115,231 (M); Expenditures, $202,788; Total giving, $144,803; Grants to individuals, totaling $17,163.
Fields of interest: Education; Economically disadvantaged.
Type of support: Grants for special needs.
Application information: Applications accepted.
Initial approach: Letter
Additional information: Applicant's request must include nature of need. Contact the foundation for eligibility determination.
EIN: 680331455

634
Florence B. Graham & Clemma B. Fancher Scholarship Fund
115 Atherton Loop
Aptos, CA 95003 (559) 351-5928
Contact: Robert W. Darrow, Tr.

Foundation type: Independent foundation
Purpose: Scholarships to graduating seniors from high schools in northern Santa Cruz County, CA.
Financial data: Year ended 04/30/2013. Assets, $58,434 (M); Expenditures, $8,919; Total giving, $6,400; Grants to individuals, 10 grants totaling $6,400 (high: $1,000, low: $300).
Fields of interest: Higher education.
Type of support: Undergraduate support.
Application information: Applications accepted. Application form required.
Deadline(s): May 1
Additional information: Application should include transcripts. Application forms available through eligible high schools. Scholarships are awarded primarily on the basis of need, but academic standing and high school achievements are also considered.
EIN: 946233118

635
The GRAMMY Foundation
(also known as The NARAS Foundation)
3030 Olympic Blvd.
Santa Monica, CA 90404-5073 (310) 392-3777
Contact: Kristin Murphy, Sr. Coord., Grant Prog.
FAX: (310) 392-2188; E-mail: loi@grammy.com; URL: http://www.grammyfoundation.com/grants

Foundation type: Public charity
Purpose: Scholarships to law students for the research, analyzation, and submission of essays regarding important issues facing the entertainment industry. Research grants to fund projects related to the impact of music on the human condition. Also, grants toward archiving and preservation of the music and recorded sound heritage of the Americas.
Publications: Application guidelines; Annual report; Financial statement; Grants list.

Financial data: Year ended 07/31/2011. Assets, $5,676,998 (M); Expenditures, $4,085,768; Total giving, $609,378; Grants to individuals, totaling $11,000.
Fields of interest: Research.
Type of support: Research; Scholarships—to individuals.
Application information: Applications accepted. Application form required. Application form available on the grantmaker's web site.
   Initial approach: Letter
   Copies of proposal: 1
   Deadline(s): Oct. 1 for letter of inquiry, early Nov. for full application
   Final notification: Recipients notified in Mar.
   Applicants should submit the following:
      1) Proposal
      2) Curriculum vitae
      3) Budget Information
   Additional information: Contact foundation for additional application guidelines.
Program descriptions:
   Archiving and Preservation Projects: Grants are available to organizations and individuals to support music archiving and preservation efforts and for scientific research projects related to the impact of music on the human condition. Two funding categories are available: Preservation Implementation grants award up to $20,000; and Planning, Assessment, and/or Consultation Grants award up to $5,000.
   Scientific Research Projects: Grants of up to $20,000 are available to organizations and individuals to support research on the impact of music on the human condition. Examples might include the study of the effects of music on mood, cognition and healing, as well as the medical and occupational well-being of music professionals and the creative process underlying music. Priority is given to projects with strong methodological design as well those addressing an important research question.
EIN: 953199223

636
Leon L. Granoff Foundation
P.O. Box 2148
Gardena, CA 90247-0148 (323) 321-2810
Contact: Kim Gold, Pres.

Foundation type: Independent foundation
Purpose: Scholarships for California residents to continue their education at CA colleges and universities of their choice, and maintain a 3.25 GPA or better.
Financial data: Year ended 12/31/2012. Assets, $0 (M); Expenditures, $296; Total giving, $0.
Fields of interest: Higher education.
Type of support: Undergraduate support.
Application information: Applications accepted.
EIN: 953184779

637
The Grass Foundation
P.O. Box 241458
Los Angeles, CA 90024-9258 (424) 832-4188
FAX: (310) 986-2252;
E-mail: info@grassfoundation.org; URL: http://www.grassfoundation.org

Foundation type: Independent foundation
Purpose: Fellowships to M.D.s and Ph.D.s, predoctoral and postdoctoral researchers in neurophysiology and allied fields of science and medicine.

Publications: Application guidelines; Informational brochure (including application guidelines); Program policy statement.
Financial data: Year ended 12/31/2012. Assets, $19,834,897 (M); Expenditures, $948,089; Total giving, $181,500.
Fields of interest: Neuroscience; Institute; Neuroscience research; Medical research; Marine science; Biology/life sciences.
Type of support: Fellowships; Research; Postdoctoral support.
Application information:
   Deadline(s): Nov. 1 for Morison Fellowship; Dec. 15 Neuroscience Fellowship
Program descriptions:
   Grass Fellowships in Neuroscience: The fellowship provides support for an outstanding young clinician who wishes to invest two years in basic science research training in preparation for an academic career. Eligible applicants must be M.D.s who will have completed a residency in neurology, neurosurgery, or psychiatry prior to beginning the fellowship. Any concurrent clinical service responsibilities must be limited so as not to interfere with research training. The award provides for a yearly stipend of $40,000 with an additional $4,000 per year available for research expenses and travel to one scientific meeting. An additional letter of recommendation from the residency supervisor should be included, as well as the candidate's and sponsor's CV.
   Robert S. Morison Fellowship: The fellowship provides support for an outstanding young clinician who wishes to invest two years in basic science research training in preparation for an academic career. Eligible applicants must be M.D.s who will have completed a residency in neurology, neurosurgery, or psychiatry prior to beginning the fellowship. Any concurrent clinical service responsibilities must be limited so as not to interfere with research training. The award provides for a yearly stipend of $40,000 with an additional $4,000 per year available for research expenses and travel to one scientific meeting. An additional letter of recommendation from the residency supervisor should be included, as well as the candidate's and sponsor's CV.
EIN: 046049529

638
Lloyd Ellis Griffin Scholarship Foundation Inc.
3535 Linda Vista Dr. 286
San Marcos, CA 92078 (760) 727-9449

Foundation type: Independent foundation
Purpose: Scholarships to residents of San Diego County, CA.
Financial data: Year ended 07/31/2013. Assets, $291,651 (M); Expenditures, $11,173; Total giving, $10,600; Grants to individuals, 5 grants totaling $10,600 (high: $5,000, low: $1,200).
Type of support: Undergraduate support.
Application information:
   Initial approach: Letter
   Deadline(s): Mid-Dec.
EIN: 952418159

639
Mike & Bev Groeniger College Scholarship Fund
331 Guadalupe Terr.
Fremont, CA 94539-5416 (510) 786-3333
Contact: Richard Groeniger, Tr.
Application address: 27750 Insustrail Blvd., Hayward, CA 94540, Tel.: (510) 786-3333

Foundation type: Company-sponsored foundation
Purpose: Scholarships only to children of employees of Groeniger & Company who are high school seniors with a GPA of 2.5 or higher.
Financial data: Year ended 12/31/2012. Assets, $534,441 (M); Expenditures, $921; Total giving, $0.
Fields of interest: Higher education.
Type of support: Employee-related scholarships.
Application information: Applications not accepted.
   Additional information: Unsolicited requests for funds not considered or acknowledged.
Company name: Groeniger & Co.
EIN: 946757910

640
Gunn Senior High School Foundation
780 Arastradero Rd.
Palo Alto, CA 94306-3827 (650) 424-8392
Application address: 3708 Carlson Cir., Palo Alto, CA 94306-4228

Foundation type: Public charity
Purpose: Scholarships to students of Gunn High School, Palo Alto, CA.
Financial data: Year ended 06/30/2012. Assets, $217,840 (M); Expenditures, $43,957; Total giving, $43,500.
Type of support: Support to graduates or students of specific schools; Undergraduate support.
Application information:
   Initial approach: Letter
   Deadline(s): Mar.
EIN: 946182158

641
A. B. Guslander Masonic Lodge Scholarship Fund
P.O. Box 67
Willits, CA 95490-0067
Contact: Charles Raasch, Pres.

Foundation type: Independent foundation
Purpose: Scholarships to graduates of Willits High School, CA.
Financial data: Year ended 12/31/2012. Assets, $0 (M); Expenditures, $706; Total giving, $0.
Type of support: Support to graduates or students of specific schools; Graduate support; Undergraduate support.
Application information: Applications accepted.
   Initial approach: Letter
   Deadline(s): Oct. 31
   Applicants should submit the following:
      1) Transcripts
      2) Essay
EIN: 237323314

642
The Guzik Foundation
2443 Wyandotte St.
Mountain View, CA 94043-2350

Foundation type: Independent foundation

Purpose: Scholarships and cash prizes for music students ages 15 to 20 for performances nationally and internationally.
Financial data: Year ended 12/31/2012. Assets, $38,904,934 (M); Expenditures, $2,188,290; Total giving, $2,008,000.
Fields of interest: Music.
Type of support: Awards/prizes.
Application information: Contact foundation for additional information.
EIN: 770360079

643
Hager Hanger Club Foundation
2163 Harbor Bay Pkwy.
Alameda, CA 94502-3019   (510) 612-5768
Contact: James Hager, Pres.
URL: http://hagerhangerclub.com/

Foundation type: Operating foundation
Purpose: Scholarships for flight training to underprivileged students in CA and Mexico.
Financial data: Year ended 12/31/2012. Assets, $1,154,668 (M); Expenditures, $17,188; Total giving, $9,203; Grants to individuals, 19 grants totaling $9,203 (high: $3,089, low: $35).
Fields of interest: Space/aviation; Economically disadvantaged.
International interests: Mexico.
Type of support: Scholarships—to individuals.
Application information: Applications accepted.
Deadline(s): None
EIN: 943245672

644
Lois Haight Foundation for Foster Children
850 S. Broadway
Walnut Creek, CA 94596   (925) 939-8080
Contact: John Herrington, Tr.
Application Address: 160 Alderwood Ln., Wallnut Creek, CA 945981042

Foundation type: Independent foundation
Purpose: Scholarships to foster children from Contra Costa, CA.
Financial data: Year ended 12/31/2012. Assets, $1,900 (M); Expenditures, $23,500; Total giving, $23,500.
Type of support: Scholarships—to individuals.
Application information: Applications accepted. Application form not required.
Initial approach: Letter
Deadline(s): None
EIN: 680456743

645
Steven L. Hallgrimson Foundation Inc.
10 Almaden Blvd., 11th Fl.
San Jose, CA 95113-2233   (408) 286-5800
Contact: Steven L. Hallgrimson, Pres.

Foundation type: Independent foundation
Purpose: Scholarships primarily to residents of CA.
Financial data: Year ended 12/31/2012. Assets, $404,608 (M); Expenditures, $29,675; Total giving, $27,030.
Type of support: Undergraduate support.
Application information:
Initial approach: Letter
Deadline(s): None
Additional information: Contact foundation for current application guidelines.
EIN: 770140464

646
John Clifford Hamilton Foundation
c/o Thomas McCormack
P.O. Box 849
Rio Vista, CA 94571   (707) 374-5586
Contact: Loretta Abbett
Application Address: 6th St., Rio Vista, CA 94571

Foundation type: Independent foundation
Purpose: Scholarships to graduating seniors of River Delta Unified School District, CA pursuing a career in agriculture.
Financial data: Year ended 12/31/2012. Assets, $127,391 (M); Expenditures, $10; Total giving, $0.
Fields of interest: Agriculture.
Type of support: Support to graduates or students of specific schools; Undergraduate support.
Application information: Applications accepted. Application form required.
Deadline(s): May 1
Applicants should submit the following:
1) Transcripts
2) Class rank
3) GPA
4) Essay
Additional information: Selection is based on scholastic attainment, character, promise and interest in agricultural programs or programs directly relating to agriculture.
EIN: 942439948

647
Harbison Scholarship Trust
P.O. Box 3262
San Bernardino, CA 92413-3262
Contact: Doreen Thornes, Tr.

Foundation type: Operating foundation
Purpose: Four year scholarships to San Bernardino County high school students for college tuition and books.
Financial data: Year ended 10/31/2012. Assets, $4,449,750 (M); Expenditures, $454,472; Total giving, $292,765; Grants to individuals, 14 grants totaling $292,765 (high: $41,941, low: $292).
Fields of interest: Higher education.
Type of support: Support to graduates or students of specific schools.
Application information: Awards are based on previous record of scholarship, character, motivation, interests, skills, extracurricular activities, and financial need.
EIN: 330621341

648
Dan Hartman Arts and Music Foundation
(formerly Dan Hartman Foundation for Music)
6439 Deep Dell Pl.
Los Angeles, CA 90068

Foundation type: Independent foundation
Purpose: Scholarships and teaching to young individuals of CA, showing outstanding artistic ability.
Financial data: Year ended 12/31/2012. Assets, $260,744 (M); Expenditures, $67,907; Total giving, $5,000.
Fields of interest: Music.
Type of support: Scholarships—to individuals.
Application information: Applications accepted. Application form required.
Initial approach: Letter
Deadline(s): None

Additional information: Scholarships are $5,000 per student pursuing arts education. Contact the foundation for additional guidelines.
EIN: 954520564

649
Headlands Center for the Arts
944 Fort Barry
Sausalito, CA 94965-2608   (415) 331-2787
Contact: Sharon Maidenberg, Exec. Dir
FAX: (415) 331-3857; E-mail: info@headlands.org;
URL: http://www.headlands.org

Foundation type: Public charity
Purpose: Residencies to visual, literary, film/video and performing artists. Awards to emerging painters in the San Francisco Bay, CA, area who have graduated from an MFA program in the past five years.
Publications: Application guidelines.
Financial data: Year ended 12/31/2011. Assets, $1,904,380 (M); Expenditures, $1,267,993; Total giving, $70,550; Grants to individuals, totaling $70,550.
Fields of interest: Film/video; Visual arts; Performing arts; Literature.
Type of support: Foreign applicants; Residencies; Travel grants.
Application information: Applications accepted. Application form required.
Initial approach: Telephone
Deadline(s): June 4
Additional information: Contact the center for additional application guidelines.
Program descriptions:
Affiliate Artist Program: The program provides local artists with a place for self-directed investigation and an opportunity to engage with the local, national and international Artists in Residence who live on site each year. Studios range from approximately 100 square feet to 540 square feet.
Artists-In-Residence: The program provides a supportive working environment that allows time for artists to experiment, reflect and grow, both individually and collectively during their stay. The program offers fully sponsored, live-in and live-out residencies to around 30 artists each year from March to November and is distinguished in that there is no fee to participate. Through the support of generous donations, Artists in Residence are provided with a studio, shared housing and five meals a week for live-in artists. A studio and dinner twice weekly are provided for live-out artists. Stipends of up to $500 per month are available pending funding and sponsorships secured each year. Residencies range from one to six months, with an average stay of three months.
Tournesol Award: The award is designed to support a full-year of artistic work and development. The award provides the chosen artist with a $10,000 cash stipend and a studio (live-out) residency for one year at Headlands Center for the Arts. A solo exhibition at a Bay Area venue will show work created at the end of this period.
EIN: 942817843

650
Healdsburg Educational Legacy Partnership Foundation

(also known as The Healdsburg Education Foundation)
P.O. Box 1668
Healdsburg, CA 95448-1668 (707) 433-1223
Contact: Pamela Swan, Exec. Dir.
FAX: (707) 433-8403;
E-mail: info@hefschools.com; E-mail for Pamela Swan: pswan@hefschools.com; URL: http://www.hefschools.com

Foundation type: Public charity
Purpose: Scholarships to graduating seniors of Healdsburg High School, CA pursuing postsecondary education.
Publications: Application guidelines.
Financial data: Year ended 06/30/2012. Assets, $750,804 (L); Expenditures, $345,962; Total giving, $211,066; Grants to individuals, totaling $94,079.
Fields of interest: Vocational education, post-secondary; Higher education.
Type of support: Scholarships—to individuals; Support to graduates or students of specific schools.
Application information: Applications accepted. Application form required.
Additional information: Selection is based on academic excellence and meeting other qualifications. See web site for additional guidelines.
EIN: 680051242

651
Health Professions Education Foundation

(formerly Minority Health Professions Education Foundation)
400 R St., Ste. 460
Sacramento, CA 95811-6513 (916) 326-3640
Contact: Lupe Alonzo-Diaz, Exec. Dir.
FAX: (916) 324-6585;
E-mail: hpef-email@oshpd.ca.gov; Toll-free tel. (in CA): (800) 773-1669; E-Mail for Lupe Alonzo-Diaz: Lupe.Alonzo-Diaz@oshpd.ca.gov; URL: http://www.healthprofessions.ca.gov/

Foundation type: Public charity
Purpose: Scholarships and loan repayment to current health professional students enrolled or accepted into an accredited CA school, college or university, or have graduated with a health professional degree.
Publications: Application guidelines; Annual report; Informational brochure; Newsletter.
Financial data: Year ended 06/30/2011. Assets, $21,521,349 (M); Expenditures, $8,625,818; Total giving, $7,213,125; Grants to individuals, totaling $7,213,125.
Fields of interest: Nursing school/education; Health care.
Type of support: Scholarships—to individuals; Student loans—to individuals.
Application information: Application form required. Application form available on the grantmaker's web site.
Initial approach: Telephone
Deadline(s): Varies
Applicants should submit the following:
1) Transcripts
2) Financial information
Additional information: Application must also include work experience community background and involvement, career goals and prior academic performance.
EIN: 680178150

652
Heart of Compassion Distribution

600 S. Maple Ave.
Montebello, CA 90640-5406 (323) 727-7997
FAX: (323) 727-0170;
E-mail: hocdist@sbcglobal.net; URL: http://hocdistribution.com

Foundation type: Public charity
Purpose: Emergency assistance to individuals and families in need throughout southern CA, with nutritional food, clothing and other needs.
Publications: Newsletter.
Financial data: Year ended 06/30/2011. Assets, $2,604,598 (M); Expenditures, $32,993,600; Total giving, $32,651,462; Grants to individuals, totaling $32,651,462.
Fields of interest: Human services; Economically disadvantaged.
Type of support: Emergency funds.
Application information: Applications not accepted.
Additional information: Contact the agency for additional information.
EIN: 421573926

653
Heart of Los Angeles Youth, Inc.

2701 Wilshire Blvd., Ste. 100
Los Angeles, CA 90057-3231 (213) 389-1148
Contact: Tony M. Brown, Exec. Dir.
FAX: (213) 389-1085;
E-mail: tbrown@heartofla.org; URL: http://www.heartofla.org

Foundation type: Public charity
Purpose: Scholarships, classes and other support are provided to inner city youth in the Los Angeles, CA area.
Publications: Newsletter.
Financial data: Year ended 06/30/2012. Assets, $3,613,775 (M); Expenditures, $2,826,496; Total giving, $200,842; Grants to individuals, totaling $200,842.
Type of support: Scholarships—to individuals.
Application information: Applications accepted. Application form not required.
Additional information: Applicants are judged on academic excellence, civic participation and financial need.
EIN: 954397418

654
Heffernan Group Foundation

1350 Carlback Ave., Ste. 350
Walnut Creek, CA 94596-7328
Contact: Michelle Lonaker, Dir.
FAX: (925) 934-8278;
E-mail: michellel@heffernanfoundation.com; Tel. for Michelle Lonaker: (925) 295-2575; URL: http://www.heffernanfoundation.com/index.php

Foundation type: Company-sponsored foundation
Purpose: Scholarships to Heffernan Group employees or child, grandchild, relative or dependent of a Heffernan Group employee.
Publications: Grants list.
Financial data: Year ended 12/31/2011. Assets, $344,786 (M); Expenditures, $617,773; Total giving, $613,174.
Fields of interest: Education.
Type of support: Employee-related scholarships.
Application information: Applications not accepted.
Additional information: Unsolicited requests for funds not considererd or acknowledged.

Program description:
Garee Lee Smith Scholarship Program: The foundation award five $5,000 scholarships to Heffernan Group employees or to children of Heffernan Group employees. Employees must be in good standing and employed on a full-time permanent basis for at least a year.
Company name: Heffernan Insurance Brokers
EIN: 711010693

655
The Held Foundation

1880 Century Park E.
Los Angeles, CA 90067-1607

Foundation type: Independent foundation
Purpose: Scholarships to individuals who are residents of California.
Financial data: Year ended 12/31/2011. Assets, $2,794,691 (M); Expenditures, $230,272; Total giving, $216,450.
Type of support: Scholarships—to individuals.
Application information: Applications not accepted.
Additional information: Unsolicited requests for funds not considered or acknowledged.
EIN: 954016569

656
The Herbst Foundation, Inc.

30 Van Ness Ave., Ste. 3600
San Francisco, CA 94102-6065
Contact: Dwight L. Merriman, Jr., V.P.

Foundation type: Independent foundation
Purpose: Awards by nomination only to teachers in the San Francisco, CA, area.
Financial data: Year ended 07/31/2012. Assets, $62,218,035 (M); Expenditures, $2,638,649; Total giving, $2,185,622; Grants to individuals, 15 grants totaling $75,000 (high: $5,000, low: $5,000).
Fields of interest: Education.
Type of support: Awards/grants by nomination only; Awards/prizes.
Application information: Applications not accepted.
Additional information: Unsolicited requests for funds not considered or acknowledged.
EIN: 946061680

657
Heritage Club - A Christian Molokan Association

P.O. Box 248
Westminster, CA 92684-0248 (562) 618-9444

Foundation type: Public charity
Purpose: Scholarships to university students who are residents of CA.
Financial data: Year ended 12/31/2011. Assets, $1,288,951 (M); Expenditures, $72,602; Total giving, $44,950; Grants to individuals, totaling $41,400.
Type of support: Undergraduate support.
Application information: Contact foundation for current application deadline/guidelines.
EIN: 953622329

658

Fannie and John Hertz Foundation

(also known as The Hertz Foundation)
2300 1st St., Ste 250
Livermore, CA 94550-3850   (925) 373-1642
Contact: Linda Kubiak, Fellowship Admin.
FAX: (925) 373-6329;
E-mail: askhertz@hertzfoundation.org; URL: http://www.hertzfoundation.org

Foundation type: Public charity
Purpose: Graduate fellowships to students in physical applied sciences at specified nationwide institutions whose education may be of value to the defense of the U.S.
Publications: Informational brochure.
Financial data: Year ended 06/30/2012. Assets, $20,694,567 (M); Expenditures, $3,444,139; Total giving, $1,750,396; Grants to individuals, totaling $1,750,396.
Fields of interest: Engineering school/education; Research; Science; Physical/earth sciences; Astronomy; Chemistry; Mathematics; Physics; Computer science; Biology/life sciences.
Type of support: Fellowships; Support to graduates or students of specific schools; Graduate support.
Application information: Applications accepted. Application form required. Application form available on the grantmaker's web site.
  Deadline(s): Oct. 30
  Applicants should submit the following:
    1) Transcripts
    2) GPA
  Additional information: Application must also include references, and personal statement; Technical interviews covering topics in physics, chemistry, mathematics, and engineering may be required. See web site for a complete listing of selected universities.
EIN: 362411723

659

George E. Hewitt Foundation for Medical Research

1048 Irvine Ave., Ste. 742
Newport Beach, CA 92660-4602
Contact: Lois A. Horness, V.P. and Secy.-Treas.

Foundation type: Operating foundation
Purpose: Grants by nomination only to postdoctorates and M.D.s and Ph.D.s for medical research in CA.
Financial data: Year ended 12/31/2012. Assets, $31,739,082 (M); Expenditures, $1,219,793; Total giving, $748,917; Grants to individuals, 22 grants totaling $748,917 (high: $49,000, low: $3,750).
Fields of interest: Institute.
Type of support: Research; Awards/grants by nomination only; Postdoctoral support.
Application information:
  Deadline(s): None
  Additional information: Application should include resume.
EIN: 953711123

660

Thomas & Jennie Hiebler Memorial Scholarship Fund Trust

P.O. Box 45174
San Francisco, CA 94145-0174

Foundation type: Independent foundation
Purpose: Scholarships to deserving and financially needy students from Montrose High School and

Mancos High School, CO, for attendance at universities in CO.
Financial data: Year ended 06/30/2013. Assets, $316,946 (M); Expenditures, $21,901; Total giving, $15,250.
Fields of interest: Higher education.
Type of support: Scholarships—to individuals; Support to graduates or students of specific schools; Undergraduate support.
Application information: Applications accepted.
  Initial approach: Letter
  Additional information: Scholarships are paid directly to the educational institution on behalf of the students.
EIN: 956111386

661

Colin Higgins Foundation

P.O. Box 29903
San Francisco, CA 94129-0903
Application address: 55 Exchange Pl., Ste. 402, New York, NY 10005; URL: http://www.colinhiggins.org

Foundation type: Independent foundation
Purpose: Grants by nomination only for the foundation's Courage Awards, to individuals of the LGBTQ communities, who have endured overwhelming hostility and hate, yet have handled themselves with the utmost grace.
Financial data: Year ended 12/31/2012. Assets, $438,604 (M); Expenditures, $158,856; Total giving, $75,000; Grants to individuals, 2 grants totaling $20,000.
Fields of interest: Youth development; Children/youth, services; Civil/human rights, LGBTQ; LGBTQ.
Type of support: Grants to individuals; Awards/grants by nomination only; Awards/prizes.
Application information: Application form required. Application form available on the grantmaker's web site.
  Initial approach: Online nomination
  Copies of proposal: 1
  Deadline(s): Mar. 2
  Final notification: Recipients notified within one to two months
  Additional information: Application should include letters of recommendation.
EIN: 954084793

662

High Desert Community Foundation

(formerly Streams in the Desert Foundation)
18838 Hwy. 18, Ste. 5
P.O. Box 2028
Apple Valley, CA 92307-0039   (760) 242-8877
Contact: Lisa Lawrence, Exec. Dir.
FAX: (760) 242-8833; E-mail: hdcf@verizon.net; URL: http://www.hdcfoundation.org

Foundation type: Community foundation
Purpose: Scholarships to graduating high school seniors of San Bernardino county, CA, for continuing education at institutions of higher learning.
Publications: Informational brochure; Occasional report.
Financial data: Year ended 12/31/2012. Assets, $1,742,754 (M); Expenditures, $233,667; Total giving, $90,881.
Fields of interest: Higher education.
Type of support: Scholarships—to individuals; Support to graduates or students of specific schools.

Application information: Applications accepted. Application form required. Application form available on the grantmaker's web site.
  Initial approach: Application
  Send request by: Mail
  Deadline(s): Apr. 2
  Final notification: Applicants notified in May
  Applicants should submit the following:
    1) Transcripts
    2) Letter(s) of recommendation
    3) Essay
  Additional information: Each scholarship has a unique set of eligibility requirements. See web site for a complete listing.
EIN: 841179212

663

William & Alice Hinckley Fund

c/o Mike Clark
611 Veterans Blvd., Ste 100
Redwood City, CA 94063-1802   (415) 776-4580
Contact: Galen Workman
Scholarship application address: c/o First Unitarian Universalist Soc. of S.F., 1187 Franklin St., San Francisco, CA 94109-6813
E-mail: lindaenger@comcast.net

Foundation type: Independent foundation
Purpose: Graduate scholarships limited to northern CA residents of nine Bay Area communities with career plans in humanitarian goals.
Financial data: Year ended 12/31/2011. Assets, $2,280,890 (M); Expenditures, $109,637; Total giving, $91,710; Grants to individuals, 6 grants totaling $30,000 (high: $5,000, low: $5,000).
Fields of interest: Medical school/education; Nursing school/education; Theological school/education; Health care; Mental health, treatment; Leadership development.
Type of support: Graduate support.
Application information: Applications accepted. Application form required.
  Initial approach: Letter
  Deadline(s): Feb. 28
  Applicants should submit the following:
    1) Budget Information
    2) Transcripts
  Additional information: Applications must also include two half-page, single-spaced answers to the following questions: Why do you need a scholarship? What do you see as the humanitarian/social impact of your planned career? Interviews are required. Applications should be sent only by mail. Response to an application is three to four months.
EIN: 946080975

664

Hispanic Scholarship Fund

1411 W. 190th St., Ste. 325
Gardena, CA 90248-4362   (310)-975-3700
FAX: (310)-349-3328; E-mail: info@hsf.net; URL: http://www.hsf.net

Foundation type: Public charity
Purpose: Scholarships to outstanding Latino students throughout the U.S. and Puerto Rico, for higher education.
Publications: Application guidelines; Annual report; Financial statement; Newsletter.
Financial data: Year ended 03/31/2012. Assets, $42,494,710 (M); Expenditures, $42,391,603; Total giving, $33,840,932; Grants to individuals, totaling $33,840,932.
Fields of interest: Higher education; Hispanics/Latinos.

Type of support: Graduate support; Undergraduate support.
Application information: Applications accepted. Application form required. Application form available on the grantmaker's web site.
  Send request by: Online
  Deadline(s): Dec. 15
  Applicants should submit the following:
    1) Transcripts
    2) SAT
    3) SAR
    4) Letter(s) of recommendation
    5) GPA
    6) Financial information
    7) FAFSA
    8) Essay
EIN: 521051044

665
Hoag Hospital Foundation
500 Superior Ave., Ste. 350
Newport Beach, CA 92663-3658 (949) 764-7217
FAX: (949) 764-7201;
E-mail: diana.aston@hoaghospital.org; URL: http://www.hoaghospitalfoundation.org/

Foundation type: Public charity
Purpose: Scholarships to Hoag Registered Nurses of California, pursuing education in nursing at the Bachelor's and Master's degree level.
Publications: Newsletter.
Financial data: Year ended 09/30/2011. Assets, $168,297,521 (M); Expenditures, $30,439,764; Total giving, $18,798,785; Grants to individuals, totaling $20,000.
Fields of interest: Nursing school/education; Health care.
Type of support: Scholarships—to individuals.
Application information: Applications accepted. Application form required. Interview required.
  Applicants should submit the following:
    1) Letter(s) of recommendation
    2) Curriculum vitae
  Additional information: Scholarships are only for Hoag Registered Nurses. Applicant must demonstrate financial need. Unsolicited requests for funds not considered or acknowledged.
EIN: 953222343

666
Hoag Memorial Hospital Presbyterian
1 Hoag Dr.
P.O. Box 6100
Newport Beach, CA 92658-6100 (949) 764-4624
Contact: Richard F. Afable M.D., Pres. and C.E.O.
E-mail: feedback@hoaghospital.org; URL: http://www.hoag.org/Pages/Home.aspx

Foundation type: Public charity
Purpose: Assistance to Hoag Memorial Hospital, CA patients in need with demonstrated financial hardship and eligible low-incomes through a discounted payment and charity care program.
Financial data: Year ended 09/30/2011. Assets, $2,103,471,586 (M); Expenditures, $831,014,882; Total giving, $7,475,467; Grants to individuals, totaling $4,025.
Fields of interest: Health care; Economically disadvantaged.
Type of support: Grants for special needs.

Application information: Applications accepted. Application form required. Application form available on the grantmaker's web site.
  Initial approach: Tel.
  Applicants should submit the following:
    1) Financial information
  Additional information: Patients may request that they be screened for possible financial assistance. If such screening establishes that family income is at or below 200% of the Federal Poverty Level (FPL), the patient is eligible for a 100% write-off of their liability for services.
EIN: 951643327

667
Horizons Foundation
550 Montgomery St., Ste. 700
San Francisco, CA 94111-2900 (415) 398-2333
FAX: (415) 398-4733;
E-mail: info@horizonsfoundation.org; URL: http://www.horizonsfoundation.org

Foundation type: Public charity
Purpose: Scholarships to children with at least one gay or lesbian parent residing in the San Francisco Bay area, CA.
Publications: Application guidelines; Annual report; Financial statement; Grants list; Informational brochure; Newsletter.
Financial data: Year ended 12/31/2012. Assets, $21,454,158 (M); Expenditures, $5,619,172; Total giving, $4,476,734.
Fields of interest: Vocational education; Education; LGBTQ.
Type of support: Scholarships—to individuals; Technical education support; Undergraduate support.
Application information: Applications accepted. Application form required.
  Initial approach: Letter
  Deadline(s): Varies
  Additional information: See web site for additional application guidelines.
Program description:
  Scholarships: These scholarships are focused on supporting and raising the visibility of the LGBT community, including GAPA's George Choy Memorial Scholarship, Bobby Griffith Memorial Scholarship, Markowski-Leach Scholarship, Juan Marquez Scholarship, Pride Law Fund's Thomas H. Steel Fellowship, and Joseph Towner Scholarship for Gay and Lesbian Families.
EIN: 942686530

668
Evelyn Horn Scholarship Trust
c/o Westamerica Bank, N.A.
2893 Sunrise Blvd., Ste. 106
Rancho Cordova, CA 95742-6527 (916) 852-5097
Contact: Kathleen Layton; Ron Chittock

Foundation type: Independent foundation
Purpose: Scholarships to students who have completed two years of education at Folsom Lake College at the El Dorado Center in Placerville, graduates of El Dorado Union High School, Placerville, and graduates of the high school within the Black Oak Mine School, CA pursuing a bachelor's degree.
Financial data: Year ended 09/30/2013. Assets, $311,139 (M); Expenditures, $19,064; Total giving, $14,112; Grants to individuals, 19 grants totaling $14,112 (high: $1,800, low: $262).

Fields of interest: Higher education; Scholarships/financial aid.
Type of support: Support to graduates or students of specific schools; Undergraduate support.
Application information: Application form required.
  Send request by: Mail
  Deadline(s): 2nd Fri. in Jan.
EIN: 686060391

669
Housing Industry Foundation
538-A Valley Way
Milpitas, CA 95035-4106 (408) 935-9201
Contact: Meta S. Ware, Exec. Dir.
FAX: (408) 935-9203; E-mail: meta@HIFinfo.org;
Tel. for Meta S. Ware: (408)-935-9202;
URL: http://www.hifinfo.org

Foundation type: Public charity
Purpose: Grants to low-income families in San Mateo and Santa Clara counties, CA, who are at risk of losing their housing or having to relocate due to an unavoidable crisis.
Publications: Informational brochure; Newsletter.
Financial data: Year ended 06/30/2012. Assets, $515,358 (M); Expenditures, $771,953; Total giving, $506,855.
Fields of interest: Housing/shelter.
Type of support: Grants for special needs.
Application information: Applications not accepted.
  Additional information: Unsolicited requests for funds not considered or acknowledged.
Program description:
  Emergency Housing Grants: The foundation awards one-time grants of up to $1,000 to aid individuals who are unable to pay for rent, mortgages, utilities, or habitability repairs due to unforeseen circumstances. Individuals must be screened and approved by a requesting agency.
EIN: 943100671

670
HP Corporate Giving Program
c/o Office of Global Social Innovation
3000 Hanover St.
Palo Alto, CA 94304-1185 (650) 857-1501
FAX: (650) 857-5518; URL: http://www.hp.com/hpinfo/socialinnovation/index.html

Foundation type: Corporate giving program
Purpose: Scholarships to African American, Latino, and American Indian high school seniors to pursue higher education in a technical field at a HP partner school. Research grants to graduate students to pursue collaborative research on a competitive basis.
Fields of interest: Higher education; Engineering school/education; Engineering/technology; Computer science; Minorities; African Americans/Blacks; Hispanics/Latinos; Native Americans/American Indians.
Type of support: Research; Graduate support; Undergraduate support.
Application information: Applications accepted. Application form required. Application form available on the grantmaker's web site.
  Additional information: See web site for application guidelines.
Program descriptions:
  HP Labs Innovation Research Program (IRP): Through IRP, HP Labs annually awards research grants of up to $75,000 to a graduate student to assist the Principal Investigator conduct a collaborative research project. Research topics include cloud and security, information analytics,

intelligent infrastructure, mobile and immersive experience, networking and communications, printing and content delivery, services, social computing, and sustainable ecosystems. Awards are renewable up to three years based on research outcomes and HP business needs.

HP Scholars: The company awards scholarships to African-American, Latino, and American Indian high school seniors to complete degrees in computer science, computer engineering, or electrical engineering at a HP Scholar partnership university. Scholarship packages include cash, HP internships, HP equipment, and a paid internship at HP during the three summers between their engineering studies.

671
The Humboldt Area Foundation
373 Indianola Rd.
Bayside, CA   95524-9350   (707) 442-2993
Contact: Patrick Cleary, Exec. Dir.; Kathy VanVleet, Admin. Asst.
FAX: (707) 442-9072;
E-mail: kathyv@hafoundation.org; Additional e-mail: patrickc@hafoundation.org; URL: http://www.hafoundation.org

Foundation type: Community foundation
Purpose: Scholarships to students who reside in the Humboldt County, CA, area for undergraduate education.
Publications: Application guidelines; Annual report; Financial statement; Grants list.
Financial data: Year ended 06/30/2013. Assets, $90,470,144 (M); Expenditures, $6,482,013; Total giving, $2,717,169.
Fields of interest: Architecture; Vocational education, post-secondary; Nursing school/education.
Type of support: Support to graduates or students of specific schools; Foreign applicants; Undergraduate support.
Application information: Applications accepted. Application form required. Application form available on the grantmaker's web site.
> *Initial approach:* Application
> *Send request by:* Online
> *Copies of proposal:* 1
> *Deadline(s):* Mar. 15 for scholarships
> *Final notification:* Applicants notified by the second week in July for scholarships
> *Applicants should submit the following:*
> 1) Transcripts
> 2) SAR
> 3) Letter(s) of recommendation
> 4) GPA
> 5) Financial information
> 6) Essay
> *Additional information:* See web site for a complete program listing.
Program descriptions:
Native Cultures Fund: Initiated and led by Native peoples, the mission of this program is to support the renaissance of California Native American arts, culture, sacred sites, and cultural transmission between generations. Funding is provided to individuals as well as nonprofit organizations who are partners with Native artists. See web site for additional information.: www.nativeculturesfund.org.
Scholarships: North Coast residents have created over 200 scholarship funds at the foundation to honor their loved ones, to support higher education and to help foster the improvement of area students as they pursue their diverse ambitions. Scholarships range from $250 to $7,500.
EIN: 237310660

672
Dorothy P. and Howard D. Hunter Foundation
13554 Starbuck St.
Whittier, CA   90605-2254   (562) 693-1105
Contact: Howard D. Hunter, Jr., Pres.

Foundation type: Independent foundation
Purpose: Scholarships to graduating students of Whittier Union High School District attending a vocational or technical college, California.
Financial data: Year ended 12/31/2011. Assets, $554,916 (M); Expenditures, $28,740; Total giving, $23,000; Grants to individuals, 21 grants totaling $23,000 (high: $2,000, low: $1,000).
Fields of interest: Vocational education; Higher education.
Type of support: Scholarships—to individuals.
Application information: Applications accepted. Application form required.
> *Initial approach:* Letter
> *Deadline(s):* Apr. 1
> *Applicants should submit the following:*
> 1) Letter(s) of recommendation
> 2) GPA
> 3) Essay
> *Additional information:* Applicants must have a minimum GPA of 2.0 and submit two letters of recommendation from non-related individuals along with a 100-word essay explaining the reasons behind their choice of career and school.
EIN: 800263956

673
Huntington Beach Police Officers Foundation
20422 Beach Blvd., Ste. 450
P.O. Box 896
Huntington Beach, CA   92648-8301   (714) 842-8851
FAX: (714) 847-0064; URL: http://hbpoa.org/

Foundation type: Public charity
Purpose: Benefit to spouses or children of police officers killed in the line of duty or provide medical assistance to children of police officers in need of help, primarily in Huntington Beach and Orange County, CA.
Financial data: Year ended 12/31/2011. Assets, $13,120 (M); Expenditures, $128,484; Total giving, $73,075.
Fields of interest: Crime/law enforcement, police agencies.
Type of support: Grants for special needs.
Application information:
> *Initial approach:* Letter
> *Additional information:* Contact foundation for eligibility criteria.
EIN: 330932434

674
Henry E. Huntington Library and Art Gallery
1151 Oxford Rd.
San Marino, CA   91108-1218   (626) 405-2194
Contact: Robert C. Ritchie, Dir., Research
FAX: (626) 449-5703;
E-mail: cpowell@huntington.org; URL: http://www.huntington.org

Foundation type: Public charity
Purpose: Fellowships to scholars for research in the arts, humanities and sciences.
Publications: Informational brochure.
Financial data: Year ended 06/30/2011. Assets, $568,715,654 (M); Expenditures, $55,498,627; Total giving, $1,766,474; Grants to individuals, 119 grants totaling $1,606,474. Subtotal for research: 151 grants totaling $1,766,474.
Fields of interest: Humanities; Libraries/library science; Science.
Type of support: Publication; Fellowships; Awards/prizes.
Application information: Applications accepted. Application form not required.
> *Initial approach:* Letter
> *Send request by:* Mail
> *Copies of proposal:* 1
> *Deadline(s):* Dec. 15
> *Applicants should submit the following:*
> 1) Letter(s) of recommendation
> 2) Curriculum vitae
> *Additional information:* See web site for additional application guidelines.
Program description:
Huntington Fellowships: Fellowships are awarded to Ph.D. or equivalents or doctoral candidates at the dissertation stage. Short term fellowship tenures are for one to five months, with an award amount of $2,500 per month. Long term fellowships last nine to twelve months and award up to $50,000.
EIN: 951644589

675
The Hurliman Scholarship Foundation
5150 Fair Oaks Blvd. 101-306
Carmichael, CA   95608-5758
E-mail: hurlimansf@comcast.net; URL: http://www.hurlimanscholarshipfoundation.com/

Foundation type: Operating foundation
Purpose: Scholarships to graduating high school seniors of Fremont, Custer or Pueblo counties, CO for attendance at an accredited college or university.
Financial data: Year ended 12/31/2012. Assets, $6,681,121 (M); Expenditures, $397,343; Total giving, $291,783; Grants to individuals, 18 grants totaling $291,783 (high: $37,416, low: $5,891).
Fields of interest: Higher education.
Type of support: Scholarships—to individuals.
Application information: Applications accepted. Application form required. Application form available on the grantmaker's web site. Interview required.
> *Initial approach:* Application
> *Send request by:* Mail
> *Deadline(s):* Feb. 4
> *Final notification:* Applicants notified Apr. 25
> *Applicants should submit the following:*
> 1) Letter(s) of recommendation
> 2) Essay
> 3) SAT
> 4) ACT
> 5) GPA
EIN: 205993001

676
Hydrocephalus Association
870 Market St., Ste. 705
San Francisco, CA   94102-2902   (415) 732-7040
FAX: (415) 732-7044; E-mail: info@hydroassoc.org; Toll-free tel.: (888) 598-3789; URL: http://www.hydroassoc.org

Foundation type: Public charity
Purpose: Scholarships to young adults with hydrocephalus for attendance at institutions of higher learning.
Financial data: Year ended 12/31/2011. Assets, $1,215,491 (M); Expenditures, $1,805,015; Total giving, $487,827; Grants to individuals, totaling $4,500.
Fields of interest: Education.
Type of support: Scholarships—to individuals.
Application information: Applications accepted. Application form required.
  Initial approach: Telephone
  Deadline(s): Apr. 1
  Final notification: Applicants notified in May
Program description:
  Scholarships: The association provides $500 scholarships to recognize the accomplishments of young adults with hydrocephalus and to assist them with their education beyond high school. The association has six scholarships: Gerard Swartz Fudge Scholarship; Morris L. Ziskind Memorial Scholarship; Anthony Abbene Scholarship Fund; Justin Scot Alston Memorial Scholarship; Mario J. Tocco Hydrocephalus Foundation Scholarship; and Giavanna Marie Melomo Memorial Scholarship. Scholarship applicants must be between the ages of 17 and 30, with hydrocephalus. The scholarship funds must be used for an educational purpose, including, but not limited to: a four-year or junior college; a high school post-graduate four-year, technical, or trade school; an accredited employment training program; or a post-graduate program. Applicants may be in the process of applying to a program or university or be already enrolled. The funds may be used for tuition, books, housing, or an expense directly related to the educational experience.
EIN: 943000301

677

Immunobiology Research Fund
1100 Main St., Ste.200
Woodland, CA 95695-3515 (530) 662-3911
Contact: Stephen C. Bick

Foundation type: Independent foundation
Purpose: Awards and travel grants to international researchers for research in immunology, allergy, and rheumatology.
Financial data: Year ended 12/31/2012. Assets, $300,758 (M); Expenditures, $24,841; Total giving, $20,362; Grants to individuals, 8 grants totaling $20,362 (high: $6,278, low: $669).
Fields of interest: Allergies; Immunology research.
Type of support: Research; Foreign applicants; Awards/prizes; Travel grants.
Application information: Applications accepted. Application form not required.
  Initial approach: Letter
  Deadline(s): None
EIN: 680070880

678

The Impact Fund
125 Univ. Ave., Ste. 102
Berkeley, CA 94710-1616 (510) 845-3473
Contact: Jocelyn Larkin, Exec. Dir.
FAX: (510) 845-3654;
E-mail: impactfund@impactfund.org; E-mail for Jocelyn Larkin: jlarkin@impactfund.org;
URL: http://www.impactfund.org
Foundation type: Public charity

Purpose: Grants for the benefit of public interest in the areas of poverty law, environmental justice and civil and human rights.
Publications: Application guidelines; Annual report; Grants list.
Financial data: Year ended 06/30/2012. Assets, $1,080,549 (M); Expenditures, $1,165,457; Total giving, $214,000; Grants to individuals, totaling $72,500.
Fields of interest: Civil/human rights; Poverty studies.
Type of support: Grants to individuals.
Application information: Applications accepted. Application form required. Application form available on the grantmaker's web site.
  Initial approach: Proposal
  Send request by: Mail, e-mail or fax
  Deadline(s): Vary
  Additional information: See web site for additional guidelines.
Program description:
  Grants: Grants are made in the general areas of social and environmental justice, human and civil rights, and poverty. The fund is particularly interested in receiving applications addressing systemic deprivations of constitutional or statutory rights in the following areas: post-9/11 cases involving denial of rights under the guise of 'homeland security'; criminal justice and immigration; and education access and equity. The average grant size is $5,000 to $15,000, with a maximum of $25,000 available. Grants are made to private attorneys, small legal firms, or nonprofit legal entities that do not have sufficient access to funding sources. Grants are also awarded to cases that could not be effectively prosecuted, and/or in which financial hardship would occur to the applicant, if supplementary funding were not available.
EIN: 943161863

679

INCOSE Foundation
7670 Opportunity Rd., Ste. 220
San Diego, CA 92111-2222 (858) 541-1725
Contact: Dr. William Ewald, C.E.O.
E-mail: foundation@incose.org; Toll-free tel.: (800) 366-1164; E-mail for Dr. William Ewald: wewald@jhu.edu; URL: http://www.incose.org/about/foundation/index.aspx

Foundation type: Public charity
Purpose: Scholarships and grants to outstanding applied systems engineering students.
Publications: Application guidelines; Annual report.
Financial data: Year ended 12/31/2012. Assets, $180,128 (M); Expenditures, $82,805; Total giving, $49,489.
Fields of interest: Higher education; Engineering/technology; Engineering.
Type of support: Research; Scholarships—to individuals; Graduate support; Postgraduate support.
Application information: Applications accepted. Application form required. Application form available on the grantmaker's web site.
  Initial approach: Application
  Deadline(s): May 13 for James E. Long Memorial Post-Doctoral Fellowship and Stevens Doctoral Award for Promising Research in Systems Engineering and Integration, Nov. 1 for JHU/Applied Physics Laboratory Alexander Kossiakoff Scholarship
  Applicants should submit the following:
    1) Letter(s) of recommendation
    2) Proposal
    3) Curriculum vitae

  Additional information: See web site for additional guidelines.
Program descriptions:
  James E. Long Memorial Post-Doctoral Fellowship: This program awards a $5,000 fellowship to post-doctoral researchers who have the potential to produce major improvements in advancing the practice of systems engineering and systems thinking. Eligible applicants must advance the state of the practice of systems thinking or the systems perspective, demonstrate potential for rapid transition from theory to practice (especially in improving systems approaches to solving complex problems), and serve as a catalyst for additional research in the area of systems thinking.
  Johns Hopkins University/Applied Physics Laboratory Alexander Kossiakoff Scholarship: This $5,000 award recognizes and encourages promising applied systems engineering research by students in a master's or doctoral program. Eligible applicants must be U.S. citizens who are admitted students in a master's or doctoral program in systems engineering at an accredited university. Applications will be evaluated on the rigor and creativity of proposed applied research, potential application to applied physics laboratory systems engineering interest, strength of resume and bio sketch, strength of academic recommendations, and additional attributes (noted in the applicant's materials) that go beyond the application requirements.
  Stevens Doctoral Award for Promising Research in Systems Engineering and Integration: This award provides a $5,000 grant to a doctoral student along with a plaque whose research is relevant to the field of systems engineering and integration. Eligible applicants must have qualified Ph.D. status in a degree program, with their research proposal approved.
EIN: 201692992

680

Independent Arts and Media
P.O. Box 420442
San Francisco, CA 94142-0442 (415) 738-4975
Contact: Joshua K. Wilson, Secy.
E-mail: sponsor@artsandmedia.net; URL: http://artsandmedia.net/

Foundation type: Public charity
Purpose: Support to artists, musicians, and media producers for non-commercial projects through a fiscal sponsorship program.
Financial data: Year ended 12/31/2011. Assets, $57,837 (M); Expenditures, $272,060.
Fields of interest: Media/communications; Arts, artist's services.
Type of support: Fiscal agent/sponsor.
Application information: Applications accepted. Application form required. Application form available on the grantmaker's web site.
  Initial approach: E-mail short query letter including a project description.
  Copies of proposal: 1
  Additional information: See web site for application guidelines.
Program description:
  Fiscal Sponsorship: The organization provides fiscal sponsorship to media, arts, and culture programs with an emphasis on important ideas, perspectives, and dialogue that are excluded by existing structures (be they commercial or nonprofit, mainstream or "alternative") and that exemplify First Amendment rights of free expression and democracy's need for open inquiry and the public's right to know. Projects will be evaluated

based on how well the project fits into the organization's mission and values, relevant experience and background of the project's leaders, and the specific needs of the project and its organizational framework. The organization charges a seven-percent administrative fee for all monies received.
EIN: 943355076

681
Independent Television Service
(also known as ITVS)
651 Brannan St., Ste. 410
San Francisco, CA 94107 (415) 356-8383
FAX: (415) 356-8391; E-mail: itvs@itvs.org;
URL: http://www.itvs.org

Foundation type: Public charity
Purpose: Grants to independent film and video artists to produce innovative television programming.
Publications: Application guidelines; Newsletter.
Financial data: Year ended 09/30/2011. Assets, $22,899,529 (M); Expenditures, $18,311,182.
Fields of interest: Film/video; Arts.
Type of support: Grants to individuals.
Application information: Application form required. Application form available on the grantmaker's web site.
> *Initial approach:* Letter or telephone
> *Deadline(s):* Feb. 1 for ITVS International call; Sept. 26 for Diversity Development Fund

Program descriptions:
> *Diversity Development Fund:* This fund seeks talented minority producers to develop projects for public television. Programs can be in any genre, including drama, documentary, docudrama, animation, experimental works, or innovative combinations that will resound in multicultural communities.
> *ITVS International Call:* This initiative is designed to showcase international documentaries with powerful global stores that inform, inspire, and connect Americans to the world at-large by providing production funds for independent producers who are non-U.S. citizens, helping them create documentaries for American television. The initiative will support: programs that bring international perspectives, ideas, events, and people to U.S. television; content that represents diverse communities and advances underrepresented points of view; content that explores globally-significant themes and inspires public dialogue; single, story-driven documentaries with broadcast hour versions; programs that have already begun production and can be realistically completed within one year of contract; and co-production projects with either international broadcast partner(s) or producers from different countries. Eligible applicants must be 'independent' producers (individuals who have artistic, budgetary, and editorial control of the project, and the ability to grant rights to reversion for broadcast) who do not reside in the U.S., and who have previous film or television production experience in a principal role (as producer, co-producer, director, or co-director, as demonstrated by credits on a sample tape of a previously-completed work submitted with the application).
> *Linking Independents and Co-Producing Stations (LINCS):* Matching funds support of up to $100,000 is available to demonstrated partnerships between independent producers and public broadcasting stations for programming of up to one hour in length. Projects must have already begun production; a work-in-progress tape is required with

each application. Programs under consideration should stimulate civic discourse and find innovative ways to explore regional, cultural, political, social, or economic issues.
EIN: 521654276

682
Injured Marine Semper Fi Fund
Wounded Warrior Center
P.O. Box 555193
Camp Pendleton, CA 92055-5193 (760) 725-3680
FAX: (760) 725-3685;
E-mail: info@semperfifund.org; Additional tel.: (703) 640-0181; URL: http://www.semperfifund.org

Foundation type: Public charity
Purpose: Financial assistance to Marines and Sailors, and other service members injured in combat and training.
Publications: Financial statement.
Financial data: Year ended 06/30/2012. Assets, $11,118,270 (M); Expenditures, $15,666,238; Total giving, $12,215,385; Grants to individuals, totaling $12,215,385.
Fields of interest: Family services; Military/veterans' organizations.
Type of support: Emergency funds; Grants for special needs.
Application information: Application form required.
> *Initial approach:* Letter
> *Additional information:* Contact foundation for eligibility criteria.

Program description:
> *Financial Assistance:* The assistance is in the form of a grant with no expectation or repayment. Grants may help with immediate financial needs such as travel, childcare, lodging, or problems resulting from lost family wages. Assistance is also given for long term needs such as modified homes and vans.
EIN: 260086305

683
Inland Counties Regional Center, Inc.
1365 S. Waterman Ave.
San Bernardino, CA 92408-2804 (909) 890-3000
Contact: Carol Fitzgibbons, Exec. Dir.
Tel.: (909) 890-4711 for San Bernardino county residents, (909) 890-4763, for Riverside county residents and Spanish only speaking families
FAX: (909) 890-3001; Mailing Address: P.O. Box 19037; San Bernardino, CA 92423; URL: http://www.inlandrc.org

Foundation type: Public charity
Purpose: Residential care and other assistance to individuals with developmental disabilities residing in San Bernardino and Riverside counties, CA.
Publications: Newsletter.
Financial data: Year ended 06/30/2012. Assets, $60,926,264 (M); Expenditures, $295,352,422; Total giving, $245,837,373; Grants to individuals, totaling $245,837,373.
Fields of interest: Disabilities, people with; Mentally disabled.
Type of support: Grants for special needs.
Application information: Applications accepted.
> *Initial approach:* Telephone
> *Additional information:* Individuals with substantial developmental disability, that originates before age 18 and will likely continue indefinitely are eligible for services.

Contact the agency or see web site for additional information.
EIN: 237121672

684
Inner-City Arts
720 Kohler St.
Los Angeles, CA 90021-1518 (213) 627-9621
Contact: Robert Smiland, Pres. and C.E.O.
FAX: (213) 627-6469;
E-mail: info@inner-cityarts.org; URL: http://www.inner-cityarts.org

Foundation type: Public charity
Purpose: Financial assistance to students in the Los Angeles, CA area seeking post high school education to further their creative or academic endeavors.
Financial data: Year ended 12/31/2011. Assets, $17,529,536 (M); Expenditures, $2,627,147; Total giving, $2,000; Grants to individuals, totaling $2,000.
Fields of interest: Arts; Children; Economically disadvantaged.
Type of support: Grants for special needs.
Application information: Contact the organization for additional guidelines.
EIN: 954239478

685
Institute for Educational Advancement
625 Fair Oaks Ave., Ste. 285
South Pasadena, CA 91030-5836 (626) 403-8900
Contact: Elizabeth D. Jones, Pres.
FAX: (626) 403-8905;
E-mail: ieagifted@educationaladvancement.org;
URL: http://www.educationaladvancement.org/

Foundation type: Public charity
Purpose: Scholarships to exceptionally gifted middle school students for attendance to a high school where they can actualize their intellectual and personal potential.
Publications: Application guidelines.
Financial data: Year ended 12/31/2011. Assets, $2,963,705 (M); Expenditures, $2,313,829; Total giving, $1,216,884; Grants to individuals, totaling $1,216,884.
Fields of interest: Education.
Type of support: Scholarships—to individuals.
Application information: Applications accepted. Application form required. Interview required.
> *Deadline(s):* May 16
> *Final notification:* Applicants notified July 11
> *Applicants should submit the following:*
>   1) Transcripts
>   2) Letter(s) of recommendation
> *Additional information:* See web site for additional application guidelines.

Program description:
> *Caroline D. Bradley Scholarship:* This scholarship identifies exceptionally-gifted middle school students who exhibit advanced intellectual talent and have the ability to demonstrate academic and personal excellence, and provides them with a scholarship to a high school where they can actualize their intellectual and personal potential. Eligible recipients must demonstrate both academic achievement (currently in 7th grade, has achieved a score of at least 97 percent in one or more major academic areas of a school-administered national standardized test in the past two years, has scored 500 or higher in either the verbal or math component of the SAT-1 Reasoning Test) and personal characteristics

(strives for excellence, continually seeks higher challenges, demonstrates leadership abilities, exhibits creative thinking, is extremely curious an has a thirst for knowledge, exhibits a passion for learning, is highly motivated, embraces the ideals of integrity and honesty, demonstrates a high level of maturity and a strong sense of self). Applicants must be a U.S. citizen who resides in Alabama, Arkansas, California, Colorado, Connecticut, Delaware, Florida, Georgia, Idaho, Illinois, Indiana, Iowa, Kansas, Kentucky, Louisiana, Maine, Maryland, Massachusetts, Michigan, Minnesota, Mississippi, Missouri, Montana, Nebraska, Nevada, New Hampshire, New Jersey, New Mexico, New York, North Carolina, North Dakota, Ohio, Oklahoma, Oregon, Pennsylvania, Rhode Island, South Carolina, South Dakota, Tennessee, Texas, Utah, Vermont, Virginia, Washington DC, Washington state, West Virginia, Wisconsin or Wyoming; priority will be given to those who need assistance in finding the optimal high school environment or may experience other challenges that prohibit attending an appropriate school.
EIN: 954695698

686
Intel Corporation Contributions Program
2200 Mission College Blvd.
Santa Clara, CA 95054-1549 (408) 765-8080
URL: http://www.intel.com/community/index.htm

Foundation type: Corporate giving program
Purpose: Assistance for natural disaster relief to residents living in the areas of Intel manufacturing facilities and technology labs.
Publications: Corporate giving report.
Financial data: Year ended 12/31/2010. Total giving, $77,891,526.
Type of support: Emergency funds.
Application information: Applications not accepted.
  Additional information: Unsolicited requests for funds not considered.

687
Interface Children Family Services
4001 Mission Oaks Blvd., Ste. I
Camarillo, CA 93012-5121 (805) 485-6114
Contact: Erik Sternad, Exec. Dir.
E-mail: mdelao@icfs.org; E-Mail For Erik Sternad: esternad@icfs.org; *URL:* http://www.icfs.org

Foundation type: Public charity
Purpose: Emergency shelter for victims of domestic violence; transitional housing for foster, runaway, and homeless youth; mental health services for individuals, couples, and families. All programs are limited to residents of California.
Financial data: Year ended 06/30/2012. Assets, $4,679,623 (M); Expenditures, $6,506,813.
Fields of interest: Housing/shelter, temporary shelter; Youth, services; Family services; Family services, parent education; Domestic violence; Family services, counseling; Human services, emergency aid; Women, centers/services; Human services; Economically disadvantaged.
Type of support: Grants for special needs.
Application information:
  Initial approach: Letter, telephone, or e-mail
  Additional information: Contact the agency for application and program information.
EIN: 952944459

688
International Buddhist Education Foundation
19191 S. Vermont Ave., No. 850
Torrance, CA 90502-1018
Contact: Chang Yu Li, Pres. and C.E.O.

Foundation type: Public charity
Purpose: Scholarships and fellowships to students studying Buddhism at the University of the West, CA.
Publications: Application guidelines.
Financial data: Year ended 12/31/2012. Assets, $3,234,183 (M); Expenditures, $305,560.
Fields of interest: Education; Buddhism.
Type of support: Fellowships; Scholarships—to individuals.
Application information: Applications accepted. Application form required. Application form available on the grantmaker's web site.
  Deadline(s): Nov. 15 and Apr. 1
  Applicants should submit the following:
    1) Essay
    2) Letter(s) of recommendation
    3) Transcripts
  Additional information: See web site for additional guidelines.
Program descriptions:
  Fellowships: Fellowship opportunities are available to encourage Buddhist monastic students who need financial aid to study Buddhism and complete their education. Fellowships of up to $3,000 (per semester) are available to Ph.D.-degree students, while fellowships of $2,000 each (per semester) are available for M.A.- and M.Div.-degree students. Eligible students must be Buddhist monastics who are new or current students in the Department of Religious Studies at the University of the West, and who are not currently receiving any other form of a full scholarship, have a GPA of at least 3.0, and be full-time students.
  Scholarships: Scholarships are available to encourage outstanding students who need financial aid to study Buddhism and complete their education. Ph.D.-degree students receive $4,500 per semester, M.A. and M.Div. degree students receive $3,500 each semester, and B.A.-degree students receive $3,000 each semester. Eligible applicants must be either new or current students in the Department of Religious Studies at the University of the West, at either the undergraduate or graduate level, who have been recommended and sponsored by the head of a Fo Guang Shan or Fo Guang Shan-affiliated organization around the world, or a new or current student in the Department of Religious Studies at the University of the West, at either the undergraduate or graduate level, who are not currently receiving any other form of a full scholarship. Applicant must have a cumulative GPA of 3.5 or higher, and be a full-time student (a minimum of 12 units per semester for undergraduate applicants, or a minimum of 9 units per semester for graduate students).
EIN: 562536373

689
International Documentary Association
(formerly International Documentary, also known as IDA)
1201 W. 5th St., Ste. M270
Los Angeles, CA 90017-1461 (213) 534-3600
Contact: Sandra J. Ruch, Exec. Dir.; Amy Halpin, Prog. Mgr., Fiscal Sponsorship
FAX: (213) 534-3610;
E-mail: info@documentary.org; E-Mail For Sandra J. Ruch: michael@documentary.org; *URL:* http://www.documentary.org

Foundation type: Public charity
Purpose: Support to students and artists to encourage documentary filmmaking through a fiscal sponsorship program.
Publications: Informational brochure.
Financial data: Year ended 12/31/2011. Assets, $1,326,961 (M); Expenditures, $4,714,602; Total giving, $75,000; Grant to an individual, 1 grant totaling $15,000.
Fields of interest: Film/video; Arts, artist's services; Arts.
Type of support: Internship funds; Awards/prizes; Project support; Fiscal agent/sponsor.
Application information: Applications accepted. Application form required. Application form available on the grantmaker's web site.
  Copies of proposal: 3
  Applicants should submit the following:
    1) Letter(s) of recommendation
    2) Proposal
    3) Budget Information
  Additional information: Application must also include a completed Project Summary Sheet; see web site for complete application guidelines.
Program description:
  Fiscal Sponsorship Program: The association acts as a fiscal sponsor for a variety of creative projects. This program has been specifically set up for the documentary filmmaker who qualifies in all other respects for a grant or a donation, but cannot arrange to accept the donation, grant, or gift because the donor insists on the recipient having nonprofit status under 501(c)(3) of the Internal Revenue Code. In such cases, the donation, grant or gift can be made to the association, who will administer and turn the funds over to the documentary filmmaker after deducting a 5 percent administrative fee. Applicants must be members in good standing of the association.
EIN: 953911227

690
International House of Blues Foundation, Inc.
7060 Hollywood Blvd., 2nd Fl.
Hollywood, CA 90028-7419 (323) 769-4901
Contact: Marjorie Gilberg, Exec. Dir.
E-mail: ihobfnational@hob.com; E-mail For Marjorie Gilberg: marjoriegilberg@livenation.com;
URL: http://www.ihobf.org

Foundation type: Public charity
Purpose: Scholarships to college bound high school seniors who have committed to cultural diversity and who wish to pursue studies in the arts.
Publications: Newsletter.
Financial data: Year ended 12/31/2012. Assets, $634,024 (M); Expenditures, $1,112,989; Total giving, $212,569.
Fields of interest: Cultural/ethnic awareness; Arts.
Type of support: Scholarships—to individuals.
Application information: Contact the foundation for further application information.
EIN: 043179950

691
International Myeloma Foundation
12650 Riverside Dr., Ste. 206
North Hollywood, CA 91607-3421 (818) 487-7455
Contact: Susie Novis, Pres.
FAX: (818) 487-7454;
E-mail: TheIMF@myeloma.org; Toll-free tel.: (800) 452-2873; E-mail for Susie Novis:

snovis@myeloma.org; URL: http://
www.myeloma.org
Foundation type: Public charity
Purpose: Research grants to investigators seeking
methods of better treatments, management,
prevention and a cure for myeloma.
Publications: Application guidelines.
Financial data: Year ended 09/30/2011. Assets,
$3,607,952 (M); Expenditures, $8,688,614; Total
giving, $458,661.
Fields of interest: Cancer research.
Type of support: Seed money; Internship funds;
Research; Awards/prizes; Travel grants.
Application information: Applications accepted.
Application form required. Application form
available on the grantmaker's web site.
　Send request by: Mail
　Deadline(s): Sept. 2
　Applicants should submit the following:
　　1) Letter(s) of recommendation
　　2) Proposal
　　3) Curriculum vitae
　Additional information: Application should also
　　include outline of the facilities and equipment
　　to be used, biohazards statement, relevant
　　applicant's publications and a statement
　　detailing any additional funding.
EIN: 954296919

692
International Transactional Analysis
　Association

2843 Hopyard Rd., Ste. 155
Pleasanton, CA 94588-2775 (925) 600-8110
FAX: (925) 600-8112; E-mail: itaa@itaa-net.org;
URL: http://www.itaa-net.org

Foundation type: Public charity
Purpose: Project support for various evaluations
and applications of transactional analysis theory to
help fund program budgets.
Publications: Application guidelines; Informational
brochure; Newsletter.
Financial data: Year ended 12/31/2011. Assets,
$422,572 (M); Expenditures, $198,939.
Fields of interest: Psychology/behavioral science.
Type of support: Program development; Research.
Application information:
　Initial approach: Letter
　Send request by: Mail
　Additional information: See web site for
　　additional guidelines.
Program descriptions:
　Eric Berne Fund for the Future: This fund awards
grants to individuals or organizations, both
nonprofit and for-profit, demonstrating an interest
in the evaluation of effectiveness of various
applications of transactional analysis theory.
Priority is given to those applicants who either are
current members of the association or have
demonstrated a high level of competency in the
theory and practice of TA. There is no formal grant
application.
　Scholarship Grant Fund: This fund awards a
maximum grant of $1,200 per year ($600 per
semester) over a three-year period of $3,600 to
association members in any country who has been
a member for one year prior to making application.
Grants may be considered for training in
transactional analysis, including training fees,
tuition for ongoing training or selected workshops,
room and board, books and supplies, contract filing
fees, and both oral or written exam fees. There will
also be consideration for attending an association
conference in the form of a conference fee waiver

for registration. Application must be completed for
the scholarship grant.
　TALent Program: Dues reductions may be
available for residents of economically
disadvantaged countries. The scholarship is
designed to make the association economically
accessible to everyone, and are supported by the
general membership of the ITAA.
EIN: 946104066

693
Intersection for the Arts

925 Mission St., Ste. 109
San Francisco, CA 94103-3415 (415)
626-2787
Contact: Arthur Combs, Exec. Dir.
FAX: (415) 626-1636;
E-mail: arthur@theintersection.org; URL: http://
www.theintersection.org

Foundation type: Public charity
Purpose: Awards to promising young writers who
are residents of northern California. Support to
emerging artists in the San Francisco Bay Area
through a fiscal sponsorship program.
Publications: Application guidelines.
Financial data: Year ended 06/30/2012. Assets,
$3,147,423 (M); Expenditures, $1,933,088.
Fields of interest: Theater (playwriting); Literature;
Arts, artist's services.
Type of support: Awards/prizes; Fiscal agent/
sponsor.
Application information: Applications accepted.
Application form required.
　Initial approach: Letter
　Deadline(s): Mar. 31 for Awards
　Additional information: Applicants for Jackson,
　　Phelan, and Tanenbaum awards must submit
　　one application form and three copies of a
　　single manuscript.
Program descriptions:
　Awards: Manuscripts from eligible promising
young California writers are invited to apply for three
$2,000 literary awards: the Joseph Henry Jackson
Awards (applicants must be residents of and
currently living anywhere in California north of the
line dividing Monterey County from San Luis Obispo
County, or the state of Nevada, for three
consecutive years immediately prior to the
deadline); the James Duval Phelan Award
(applicants must have been born in the State of
California but need not be current residents, and
unpublished work-in-progress submitted may be
fiction, nonfictional prose, poetry, or drama
submitted in standard script format); and the Mary
Tanenbaum Award for Nonfiction (recognizes
outstanding nonfictional prose; applicants must be
residents of and currently living anywhere in
California north of the line dividing Monterey
County from San Luis Obispo County for three
consecutive years immediately prior to the
deadline)
　Incubator Services: This program provides its
members with assistance in funding, developing,
and promoting their artistic work. A full program of
services and partnerships is available, including
continuing education, networking opportunities,
access to consultants, and resources for
fundraising. Through fiscal sponsorship in
particular, the program encourages funding
agencies and contributors to take risks in funding
new projects and emerging artists, ensuring that
funds are well-managed and spent according to the
funder's guidelines.
EIN: 941593216

694
Invisible Children, Inc.

1600 National Ave.
San Diego, CA 92101-2738 (619) 562-2799
Contact: Ben Keesey, Exec. Dir. and C.E.O.
FAX: (619) 660-0576;
E-mail: info@invisiblechildren.com; Additional fax:
(619) 660-0689; URL: http://
www.invisiblechildren.com

Foundation type: Public charity
Purpose: Scholarships and mentoring to secondary
and university students from Gulu, Amuru, and
Pader districts of northern Uganda.
Publications: Annual report; Financial statement.
Financial data: Year ended 06/30/2012. Assets,
$17,728,929 (M); Expenditures, $15,981,026;
Total giving, $5,262,652.
Fields of interest: Higher education.
Type of support: Scholarships—to individuals;
Undergraduate support.
Application information: Applications accepted.
Interview required.
　Additional information: Applicants are selected
　　based on demonstrated need for school fee
　　support as well as academic drive to succeed.
Program description:
　The Visible Child Scholarship Program: This
initiative focuses on increasing access to
post-primary education, improving learning
environments, and providing mentoring from local
leaders to children in Uganda. Once accepted into
the program, each student is assigned a mentor (an
employed community leader whose purpose is to
build a personal relationship with the student and
provide professional follow-up for each child).
Acceptance into the program is based on a
combination of academic performance and need,
with special consideration given to children who are
total orphans, heads of household, formerly
abducted returnees, those living positively with
HIV/AIDS, and child mothers.
EIN: 542164338

695
The Ioan Foundation

14010 Columbet Ave.
San Martin, CA 95046-9710

Foundation type: Independent foundation
Purpose: Grants to individuals in CA and WA who
demonstrate a need for public or private charitable
support.
Financial data: Year ended 12/31/2011. Assets,
$28,333 (M); Expenditures, $17,904; Total giving,
$17,904.
Type of support: Grants for special needs.
Application information:
　Initial approach: Letter
EIN: 770559484

696
Iranian Scholarship Foundation

P.O. Box 7531
Menlo Park, CA 94026-7531 (650) 331-0508
E-mail: admin@iranianscholarships.com;
URL: http://www.iranianscholarships.com

Foundation type: Public charity
Purpose: Scholarships to Iranian-American
students in need of financial assistance while
encouraging community service.
Financial data: Year ended 08/31/2011. Assets,
$187,189 (M); Expenditures, $132,010; Total
giving, $127,500.
Fields of interest: Higher education.

Type of support: Scholarships—to individuals.
Application information: Applications accepted. Application form required.
Deadline(s): May 31
Final notification: Recipients notified Aug. 31
Applicants should submit the following:
1) SAT
2) Letter(s) of recommendation
3) Essay
4) ACT
Program descriptions:
Dr. Ali Jarrahi Merit Scholarship: Scholarships are awarded to high school students with outstanding academic records, who are entering one of the top 10 universities in the U.S. This scholarship is not need based. Eligible applicants must possess a GPA of 4.0 or higher, have a minimum SAT score of 2300, and be of Iranian descent.
Excellence in Community Service Scholarship: Scholarships are awarded to students with an outstanding record of community service. Student must have a proven record of community service and have maintained a GPA of 3.5 or better.
ISF Undergraduate Scholarships: Scholarships are provided of as high as $10,000 per year, for up to four years, to Iranian-American students. Eligible applicants must be enrolled or accepted at a four-year accredited American university and possess and maintain a GPA of 3.5 or higher.
EIN: 203100594

697
Irwindale Educational Foundation
(formerly Irwindale Educational & Scholarship Foundation)
P.O. Box 2307
Irwindale, CA 91706-2082 (626) 960-6606
Contact: Lisa Bailey, Treas.

Foundation type: Operating foundation
Purpose: Scholarships to individuals who have been residents of Irwindale, CA, for at least three years. A limited number of grants are available to Irwindale Chamber of Commerce members and their children.
Publications: Informational brochure (including application guidelines).
Financial data: Year ended 12/31/2012. Assets, $58,849 (M); Expenditures, $45,628; Total giving, $27,280; Grants to individuals, 23 grants totaling $27,280 (high: $1,240, low: $620).
Type of support: Scholarships—to individuals; Grants for special needs.
Application information: Application form required.
Initial approach: Letter or telephone
Deadline(s): Contact foundation for current application deadline
Applicants should submit the following:
1) Financial information
2) Transcripts
Additional information: Application must also include proof of college acceptance.
EIN: 954274826

698
Italian-American Community Services Agency
(formerly Italian Welfare Agency, Inc.)
678 Green St.
San Francisco, CA 94133-3896
URL: http://www.italiancommunityservices.org/

Foundation type: Operating foundation
Purpose: Assistance to economically disadvantaged Italian-Americans, including senior citizens.

Financial data: Year ended 12/31/2012. Assets, $5,487,580 (M); Expenditures, $537,778; Total giving, $34,036; Grants to individuals, totaling $34,036.
Fields of interest: Aging; Economically disadvantaged.
Type of support: Grants for special needs.
Application information: Applications accepted.
EIN: 941196199

699
Jack in the Box Foundation
9330 Balboa Ave.
San Diego, CA 92123-1516 (858) 571-2544
Contact: Kathy Kovacevich, Secy.
E-mail: kathy.kovacevich@jackinthebox.com;
Additional contact: Brian Luscomb, Pres., tel.: (858) 571-2291, e-mail: brain.luscomb@jackinthebox.com; URL: http://www.jackinthebox.com/corporate/corporate-responsibility/

Foundation type: Company-sponsored foundation
Purpose: Grants to employees of Jack in the Box who are victims of natural or personal disasters.
Financial data: Year ended 09/30/2012. Assets, $580,512 (M); Expenditures, $1,751,035; Total giving, $1,392,061; Grants to individuals, 13 grants totaling $12,345 (high: $1,500, low: $100).
Fields of interest: Safety/disasters.
Type of support: Emergency funds; Employee-related welfare.
Application information: Applications not accepted.
Company name: Jack in the Box, Incorporated
EIN: 330776076

700
William James Association
P.O. Box 1632
Santa Cruz, CA 95061-1632 (831) 607-8952
Contact: Laurie Brooks, Exec. Dir.
E-mail: info@williamjamesassociation.org;
URL: http://www.williamjamesassociation.org

Foundation type: Public charity
Purpose: Support to individuals and organizations to promote work service in the arts, environment, education, and community development.
Publications: Application guidelines.
Financial data: Year ended 06/30/2012. Assets, $77,279 (M); Expenditures, $166,678.
Fields of interest: Arts, services.
Type of support: Fiscal agent/sponsor.
Application information: Applications accepted. Application form required. Application form available on the grantmaker's web site.
Initial approach: Download fiscal sponsorship application form
Deadline(s): None
Additional information: No monetary support given for the Fiscal Sponsor program.
Program descriptions:
Community Youth Arts Project: Through this project the association contracts with professional artists to work with disenfranchised and 'at-risk' youth in alternative schools and detention facilities in and around Santa Cruz, California.
Fiscal Sponsorship Program: Through this program, the association assists individuals and community organizations consistent with its service mission by providing administrative support, tax-exempt status, and fiscal sponsorship. The association charges an eight percent administrative fee for its services.

Prison Arts Project: The project contracts with professional artists to provide in-depth, long-term arts experiences for incarcerated men and women. The program also establishes artist-in-residence programs for the National Endowment for the Arts and the Federal Bureau of Prisons.
EIN: 237320163

701
James Family Foundation
(formerly C.M.J. Private Foundation)
101 Ygnacio Valley Rd., Ste. 310
Walnut Creek, CA 94596-7018
Scholarship address: c/o Laura Alford, Pres., 38 Miller Ave., PMB 114, Mill Valley, CA 94941, tel.: (415) 205-9824

Foundation type: Independent foundation
Purpose: Scholarships for attending an out of state university, Tulane University, New York University, University of California at Berkeley, University of California at Los Angeles, Duke University, Rhode Island School of Design, University of Virginia, MIT, or any ivy league school. In addition, scholarships for fields of study within natural resource conservation and/or environmental studies at Colorado State University, Montana State University, Utah State University, University of Wyoming, Michigan State University, Cornell University, Mississippi State University, Oregon State University, Penn State University, Texas A&M University, University of California at Davis, University of Wisconsin/Stevens Point and Dickinson College.
Publications: Program policy statement.
Financial data: Year ended 11/30/2012. Assets, $10,316,855 (M); Expenditures, $2,180,235; Total giving, $1,994,707; Grants to individuals, totaling $347,416.
Fields of interest: Higher education; Natural resources; Environment.
Type of support: Support to graduates or students of specific schools; Undergraduate support.
Application information: Applications accepted.
Deadline(s): Apr. 1
Applicants should submit the following:
1) Transcripts
2) Letter(s) of recommendation
Additional information: Application should also include a brief personal statement and a signed scholarship agreement form. For scholarship eligibility, students must attend one of the following three high schools for four years: Healdsburg High School, Healdsburg, CA; Harrisburg High School, Harrisburg, IL; Pinedale High School, Pinedale, WY.
EIN: 133864227

702
James Publishing's Kids
3505 Cadillac Ave., Ste. H
Costa Mesa, CA 92626-1461

Foundation type: Independent foundation
Purpose: Scholarships to seniors at Los Angeles and Orange County high schools who have been accepted by a UC or California State University campus.
Financial data: Year ended 12/31/2011. Assets, $0 (M); Expenditures, $31,335; Total giving, $31,150; Grants to individuals, 3 grants totaling $5,750 (high: $3,000, low: $1,000).
Type of support: Scholarships—to individuals; Support to graduates or students of specific schools.

Application information: Applications accepted. Application form required.

> *Deadline(s):* None
> *Additional information:* Application should include transcript.

EIN: 202638616

703
Jedinstvo Athletic Club, Inc.
5038 St Andres Ave.
P.O. Box 292
La Verne, CA   91750-0292   (909) 592-1444
Contact: Desmond Warren, Pres.

Foundation type: Public charity
Purpose: Scholarships to deserving students in the CA area to help with the purchase of text books.
Financial data: Year ended 05/31/2012. Assets, $278,150 (M); Expenditures, $12,298; Total giving, $8,000; Grants to individuals, totaling $8,000.
Fields of interest: Education.
Type of support: Scholarships—to individuals.
Application information: Applications accepted. Application form required.

> *Additional information:* Selection criteria is based on academic achievement, school activities, community service and church participation. Scholarship is not based on financial need.

EIN: 237010837

704
Jefferies Family Scholarship
(formerly Boyd & Stephen Jefferies Educational Grant Program)
11100 Santa Monica Blvd.
Los Angeles, CA   90025-3381
Contact: Regina de Wetter, Progs. Coord.
E-mail: rdewette@jefferies.com; URL: http://jefferiesscholarship.org/

Foundation type: Public charity
Purpose: Scholarships to children of employees of Jefferies Group, Inc., pursuing higher education.
Publications: Application guidelines.
Financial data: Year ended 06/30/2012. Assets, $8,961,655 (M); Expenditures, $413,116; Total giving, $284,629; Grants to individuals, totaling $244,629.
Fields of interest: Higher education.
Type of support: Employee-related scholarships.
Application information: Applications accepted. Application form required. Application form available on the grantmaker's web site.

> *Send request by:* On-line
> *Deadline(s):* Feb. 15
> *Final notification:* Recipients notified May 1
> *Additional information:* Scholarships are awarded for one academic year only. Students must apply each year they are eligible.

EIN: 953594410

705
John Percival and Mary C. Jefferson Endowment Fund
P.O. Box 99
Santa Barbara, CA   93102-0099   (805) 963-8822

Foundation type: Independent foundation
Purpose: Relief assistance to Santa Barbara County, CA, residents of limited means for medical, dental, and living expenses.
Financial data: Year ended 03/31/2013. Assets, $3,651,741 (M); Expenditures, $285,119; Total

giving, $127,841; Grants to individuals, 26 grants totaling $77,841 (high: $7,308, low: $296).
Fields of interest: Dental care; Health care; Economically disadvantaged.
Type of support: Grants for special needs.
Application information: Applications accepted. Application form required. Interview required.

> *Initial approach:* Letter
> *Send request by:* Mail
> *Copies of proposal:* 1
> *Deadline(s):* None
> *Applicants should submit the following:*
>   1) Financial information
>   2) Budget Information

EIN: 956005231

706
Jewish Community Federation of San Francisco, the Peninsula, Marin and Sonoma Counties
121 Steuart St.
San Francisco, CA   94105-1236   (415) 777-0411
Contact: Jennifer Gorovitz, C.E.O.
E-mail: info@sfjcf.org; E-Mail for Jennifer Gorovitz: jenniferg@sfjcf.org; URL: http://www.jewishfed.org/

Foundation type: Public charity
Purpose: Scholarships, awards, and day camp opportunities for individuals throughout San Francisco, the Peninsula, and Marin and Sonoma Counties, CA.
Publications: Application guidelines.
Financial data: Year ended 06/30/2012. Assets, $675,137,451 (M); Expenditures, $134,027,819; Total giving, $97,582,334; Grants to individuals, totaling $111,719.
Fields of interest: Scholarships/financial aid; Education; Jewish agencies & synagogues.
Type of support: Fellowships; Camperships; Travel awards; Scholarships—to individuals; Awards/prizes.
Application information: Applications accepted. Application form available on the grantmaker's web site.

> *Initial approach:* Application
> *Deadline(s):* Varies
> *Additional information:* See web site for additional application guidelines.

Program descriptions:

Alexander M. and June L. Maisin Foundation Scholarship Fund: Scholarships will be made available to Jewish high school seniors who demonstrate a strong academic record, leadership potential, and financial need. The student's parents must be permanent residents of San Francisco, the Peninsula (Sunnyvale and north), or Marin or Sonoma County.

Annual Haas/Koshland Memorial Awards: Each year, the foundation provides up to $20,000 to support college students (from sophomore year through graduate school) who are from, or attend school in, the San Francisco Bay Area, and who wish to broaden their personal and/or academic life with a year of study and personal development in Israel.

Elaine and Barry Gilbert College Scholarship Fund: One to three scholarships, ranging from $3,000 to $5,000, will be available to Jewish high school seniors who will attend a University of California campus. The applicant's parents must be permanent residents of San Francisco, the Peninsula (Sunnyvale and north), or Marin or Sonoma County; applicants must demonstrate financial need, a minimum 3.5 GPA, and demonstrated Jewish involvement. Preference will

be given to graduates of San Francisco's Lowell or Washington High School.

Family Specialty Camp Scholarships: The federation provides need-based scholarships to Jewish children who live in the San Francisco Bay Area to attend a qualified family specialty camp. Both parents and children are eligible to apply; scholarship funds are exclusively for camp tuition for children.

Gail Karp Orgell Scholarship: One to two scholarships, ranging from $2,000 to $4,000 each, are available to Jewish female undergraduate students who are currently attending a four-year university, and who demonstrate a focus on academic excellence, achievements in leadership, and involvement in athletics. The student's parents must be permanent residents of the greater San Francisco Bay Area.

Helen Diller Family Awards for Excellence in Jewish Education: The foundation honors outstanding teachers who encourage youth to explore the rich traditions of the Jewish heritage, to incorporate Jewish values into their own lives, to help build Jewish community, and to take responsibility for the common destiny of the Jewish people. Exceptional educators will be honored who work in early childhood, day school, congregational/community school, and information education settings (outside of a classroom). Nominees must currently be teaching in a program of pre-collegiate Jewish education within the federation's service area, as well as the Jewish Community Foundation of the Greater East Bay (Alameda and Contra Costa counties) or the Jewish Federation of Silicon Valley (San Jose and environs); nominees must also have worked in the field of Jewish education for a minimum of three years, and are encouraged from all religious streams and from all formal and informal institutional frameworks.

Jack and Elisa Klein Scholarship Fund: Eight to ten scholarships, ranging from $3,000 to $5,000, will be available to Jewish undergraduates (and, if funding permits, graduate students) who are accepted to, or currently attending, a four-year accredited college or university. The applicant's students must be permanent residents of San Francisco, the Peninsula (Sunnyvale and north), or Marin or Sonoma counties (on occasion, the foundation will consider requests from applicants whose parents reside outside the above-stated area); applicants must demonstrate financial need, a strong academic record, and Jewish community involvement.

Jewish Day Camp Scholarships: The foundation provides need-based scholarships to Jewish children attending qualified Jewish day camps (both summer and winter) within the federation's service area. Scholarships are only available through specific day camps. Families with children between the ages of 3 and 15 are eligible; scholarship funds may be used for camp tuition and associated before and after care (camp-provided bus transportation is not covered unless included in camp fees).

Jewish Day School Scholarships: The foundation provides need-based scholarships to Jewish children attending qualified Jewish day schools within the federation's service area. Funding is only available to specific schools; scholarships must be 'last resort' funds (supplementing financial assistance provided by the day school, family, and other possible sources), and families must contribute a minimum percentage of total tuition according to their ability to pay.

Jewish Overnight Camp Scholarships: This program provides need-based funds to families with children between the ages of 6 and 18, to attend a qualifying Jewish overnight camp in the U.S., Canada, or Israel. Eligible applicants must live in

San Francisco, Sonoma, or Marin counties, or the Peninsula (from Sunnyvale north); families must contribute a minimum percentage of total tuition according to their ability to pay. Scholarship funds may be used strictly for camp tuition and camp-provided bus transportation to and from camp.

Jewish Preschool Scholarships: This program provides need-based scholarships to Jewish children attending qualified Jewish preschools in the federation's service area. Scholarships are only available to participating preschools.

Marvin Anmuth Scholarship Fund: One scholarship, ranging from $2,500 to $5,000, is available for a Jewish graduate or undergraduate student pursuing a degree program in electrical engineering at an accredited college, university, or graduate school. Applicants must reside within the San Francisco Bay Area and demonstrate financial need, a minimum 3.0 GPA, and leadership in the Jewish or general community.

Nathan Jay Friedman College Scholarship Fund: One to three scholarships, generally ranging from $1,500 to $5,000, are available to Jewish undergraduate students who are accepted to, or who are currently attending, an accredited undergraduate college or university program. The applicant's parents must be permanent residents of San Francisco, the Peninsula (Sunnyvale and north), or Marin, Sonoma, or Alameda Counties; applicants must demonstrate an outstanding academic record and financial need.

One Happy Camper Incentive Grants: Awarded in conjunction with the Foundation for Jewish Camp, these awards provide need-blind grants of up to $1,000 to families with children attending nonprofit, mission-driven Jewish overnight camps for the first time.

Ronald P. Wilmot Scholarship: Four to six scholarships, ranging from $3,000 to $5,000 each, will be available to undergraduate or graduate students who are currently attending accredited institutions of higher learning and/or the arts, and who are children of gay or lesbian parent(s). Both the applicant and his/her parents must be permanent residents of Alameda, Contra Costa, Marin, Solano, or Sonoma counties, San Francisco, or the Peninsula (Sunnyvale and north); applications will be evaluated on academic and/or artistic excellence and financial need.

Sarlo Emigre Youth Fund: At least six scholarships, ranging from $1,000 to $10,000 each, are available to foreign-born first- or second-generation immigrant, undergraduate, or (on occasion) graduate students at accredited institutions of higher learning and/or the arts. Applications will be evaluated on artistic excellence and financial need; applicants must be the first generation in their family to attend a U.S. college or university.

Scholarships for First-Time Teen Trips to Israel: The federation provides need-based scholarships for Jewish teens in grades 8-12 who live in the federation's service area, and who wish to travel on an organized teen trip to Israel for the first time. Funding is only available for specific programs; funds are to be used exclusively for program fees and travels.

Sinton Award for Distinguished Leader of the Year: This award is given in honor of volunteer leadership in the Jewish community, and includes a financial stipend to a Jewish agency or organization chosen by the recipient.

Stephanie G. Hoffman Scholarship Fund: Two to three scholarships, ranging from $2,000 to $5,000, are available to Jewish undergraduate and graduate students accepted to, or attending, an accredited college/university program, and who

wish to major (or are majoring) in library science, English literature, or a related field, with the intention of working with underserved children to excite them through reading to pursue higher education. Both applicants and their parents must be permanent residents of the greater San Francisco Bay Area.
EIN: 941156533

707
Jewish Family and Children's Services of San Francisco, the Peninsula, Marin and Sonoma Counties
(formerly JFCS)
2150 Post St.
San Francisco, CA 94115-3508 (415) 449-1200
Contact: Anita Friedman Ph.D., Exec. Dir.
FAX: (415) 449-3839; E-mail: admin@jfcs.org; TDD: (415) 567-1044; URL: http://www.jfcs.org

Foundation type: Public charity
Purpose: Scholarships and grants to permanent Jewish residents of San Francisco, the Peninsula, Marin, and Sonoma counties, CA. Student loans are also available to permanent Jewish residents of the East Bay, CA area.
Publications: Application guidelines; Annual report; Informational brochure.
Financial data: Year ended 06/30/2012. Assets, $68,195,545 (M); Expenditures, $30,784,540; Total giving, $1,593,607; Grants to individuals, totaling $1,161,597.
Fields of interest: Humanities; Education, special; Vocational education; Higher education; Reading; Children/youth, services; International exchange; Business/industry; Jewish agencies & synagogues.
International interests: Israel.
Type of support: Student loans—to individuals; Technical education support; Undergraduate support.
Application information: Applications accepted. Application form required. Interview required.
Initial approach: Telephone
Program descriptions:
Anna and Charles Stockwitz Children and Youth Fund: Provides loans and grants to assist Jewish children and teens with a valuable educational, social, or psychological experience, including attendance at an undergraduate school. Criteria for grants include financial need and, for loans, ability to repay. Maximum student grant/loan amount is $6,000.
Butrimovitz Family Endowment Fund for Jewish Education: Scholarships of up to $500 are provided to individuals in need who wish to pursue traditional Jewish education in the context of a Jewish day school, undergraduate, or graduate school setting.
Camper Scholarships: Funds are available to assist with the costs of sending San Francisco Bay Area Jewish children to summer camps, study in Israel, and to pursue individualized educational experiences that help to build a strong Jewish community. Primarily, camper scholarships are offered to the children of current organization clients.
David, Nancy, and Liza Cherney Scholarship Fund: The fund provides annual scholarships of up to $100 to enable girls to go to college.
DeHovitz-Senturia Campership Fund: The fund offers grants of up to $600 to provide a Jewish summer camp experience to individuals 26 years old or younger.
Emergency Assistance: The foundation has funds dedicated to providing short-term loans and grants for Jewish residents of the Bay Area who are in crisis and need help to meet basic living expenses

such as food, housing, medical, and other essential expenses.
Esther Shiller Memorial Endowment Loan Fund for College Loans: Provides student loans to worthy college students with limited resources who demonstrate academic promise and the ability to repay. Maximum loan amount is $6,000.
Fogel Loan Fund: Provides loans of up to $6,000 per year to individuals of all ages for college, university, or vocational studies.
Harry and Florence Wornick Endowment Fund: Loan funds of up to $5,800 are provided to Jewish students with higher education or vocational training, with special consideration to students pursuing careers in the use of wood, or careers in music.
Henry and Tilda Shuler Scholarship Fund for Young People: Scholarships of up to $950 are provided to youths for vocational training, college education, or other studies. Applicants must be 26 years of age or younger.
Jacob Rassen Memorial Scholarship: Provides annual scholarships of up to $1,900 to financially and academically deserving Jewish boys or girls under the age of 22 for a study trip to Israel.
Kaminer Family Fund: The fund provides grants of up to $475 to provide a Jewish summer camp experience to individuals 26 years of age or younger. Grants may be made for such general and specific purposes as camperships, counseling, and supportive services.
Lillian Fried Scholarship Fund: The fund provides scholarships of up to $130 for deserving women to pursue collegiate or graduate studies.
Miriam S. Grunfeld Scholarship Fund: The fund provides annual grants of up to $950 to educate young people under 26 years of age who otherwise would not be able to fulfill their educational aspirations.
Rozsi and Jeno Zisovich Jewish Studies Scholarship Fund to Teach the Holocaust: Scholarships are provided to help Jewish or non-Jewish students who hope to pursue careers which will include teaching the Holocaust to future generations, and/or pursue collegiate and/or graduate studies in Holocaust education.
Selig Fund: The fund provides college loans of up to $6,000 for undergraduate studies.
Stanley Olson Youth Scholarship: Provides scholarships of up to $2,500 each to Jewish youths less than 26 years of age for undergraduate or graduate study in the liberal arts.
Vivienne Camp College Scholarship Fund: Provides annual college scholarships of $4,350 per year to two Jewish men and two Jewish women with demonstrated academic achievement, promise, and financial need. Recipients must attend colleges, universities, or other institutions of higher learning in California.
EIN: 941156528

708
Jewish Vocational Service - Los Angeles
6505 Wilshire Blvd., Ste. 200
Los Angeles, CA 90048-4957 (323) 761-8888
Contact: John Goldsmith, Pres.
URL: http://jvsla.org

Foundation type: Public charity
Purpose: Scholarships to Jewish students who are residents of Los Angeles, CA for postsecondary education pursuing studies at community colleges, vocational schools, four year colleges, universities and graduate schools in the U.S.
Financial data: Year ended 12/31/2011. Assets, $11,014,026 (M); Expenditures, $17,054,109;

Total giving, $315,300; Grants to individuals, totaling $315,300.

Fields of interest: Vocational education, post-secondary; Higher education.

Type of support: Scholarships—to individuals; Graduate support; Undergraduate support.

Application information: Applications accepted.

Additional information: Applicant must demonstrate financial need.

Program description:

Scholarship Fund: The JVS Scholarship Fund provides qualified Jewish students whose primary residence is in Los Angeles with need-based financial aid, in the belief that education represents the first step to career success. Applicant must be Jewish, at least 16 years old, and a legal resident of Los Angeles County planning to enroll full-time in an accredited public, private or vocational school in the United States. Applicant must maintain at least a 2.7 GPA and demonstrate verifiable financial need. Scholarship range from $1,000 to $5,000. Complete list of supplemental application materials needed is available on foundation web site.

EIN: 951691012

709

The Ralph and Marguerita Johnson Charitable Trust

P.O. Box 1434
Arroyo Grande, CA   93421-1434   (805) 489-7547
Contact: Arlene Pilkington, Tr.

Foundation type: Independent foundation

Purpose: Scholarships to San Luis Obispo County, CA, residents who are U.S. citizens, for continuing their education at institutions of higher learning.

Financial data: Year ended 12/31/2011. Assets, $1,008,813 (M); Expenditures, $20,329; Total giving, $14,000; Grants to individuals, 14 grants totaling $14,000 (high: $1,000, low: $1,000).

Fields of interest: Higher education.

Type of support: Scholarships—to individuals.

Application information: Application form required.

Deadline(s): Feb. 28

Additional information: Application must include statement of financial need.

EIN: 776180529

710

Magic Johnson Foundation, Inc.

9100 Wilshire Blvd., E. Tower, Ste. 700
Beverly Hills, CA   90212-3401   (310) 246-4400
FAX: (310) 246-1106;
E-mail: mjfprograms@magicjohnsoncharities.com;
URL: http://magicjohnson.org/

Foundation type: Public charity

Purpose: Undergraduate scholarships to graduating high school seniors from Atlanta, Lansing, Detroit, Cleveland, Chicago, Houston, New York, and Los Angeles County, facing socioeconomic challenges.

Publications: Application guidelines; Annual report; Grants list; Informational brochure; Newsletter.

Financial data: Year ended 12/31/2011. Assets, $2,624,716 (M); Expenditures, $2,097,957; Total giving, $463,119; Grants to individuals, 254 grants totaling $401,119.

Fields of interest: Higher education; Minorities.

Type of support: Undergraduate support.

Application information: Applications accepted. Application form required. Application form available on the grantmaker's web site. Interview required.

Initial approach: Letter

Send request by: Mail

Deadline(s): Feb. 12

Final notification: Applicants notified by Apr. 6

Applicants should submit the following:
1) FAFSA
2) Letter(s) of recommendation
3) Transcripts
4) Essay

Additional information: Application should also include a copy of parent/guardian W2 form and college acceptance letter.

Program description:

Taylor Michaels Scholarship Program: The program is designed to provide support for deserving minority high school students who exemplify a strong potential for academic achievement but face social-economic conditions that hinder them from reaching their full potential. Applicant must currently be a senior in high school with plans to attend a four-year college or university in the fall, have at least a 2.5 cumulative GPA, be a current resident of the metropolitan areas of Atlanta, GA, Lansing, MI, Cleveland, OH, Chicago, IL, Detroit, MI, Houston, TX, Los Angeles, CA, or New York City. Applicants must also be involved in extra-curricular activities or community service activities. Scholarships range from $2,000 to $5,000.

EIN: 954349860

711

Richard Myles Johnson Foundation

2855 E. Guasti Rd., Ste. 600
Ontario, CA   91761-1250   (909) 980-8890
Contact: Tena Lozano, Exec. Dir.
Fax and e-mail for scholarship: Fax: (909) 605-6962, e-mail: info@rmjfoundation.org
FAX: (909) 476-5957;
E-mail: tlozano@rmjfoundation.org; Toll-free tel.: (800) 472-1702; URL: http://www.rmjfoundation.org

Foundation type: Public charity

Purpose: Scholarships for credit union staff and volunteers of California and Nevada to attend educational seminars and conferences.

Financial data: Year ended 12/31/2011. Assets, $608,816 (M); Expenditures, $241,964; Total giving, $122,207; Grants to individuals, totaling $39,815.

Fields of interest: Education.

Type of support: Conferences/seminars; Scholarships—to individuals.

Application information: Applications accepted. Application form required.

Send request by: Mail, fax or e-mail

Additional information: Applicant must demonstrate need.

EIN: 956141173

712

John and Dorothy Johnson Missionary Foundation

791 Pordon Ln.
Healdsburg, CA   95448-3728   (707) 433-5075
Contact: J.R. Young, Dir.

Foundation type: Independent foundation

Purpose: Grants to individuals for international missionary support.

Financial data: Year ended 10/31/2012. Assets, $0 (M); Expenditures, $35,874; Total giving, $27,000.

Fields of interest: Christian agencies & churches.

International interests: Italy; Mexico.

Type of support: Travel grants.

Application information:

Deadline(s): Contact foundation for current application deadlines/guidelines

EIN: 481296127

713

Deacon Jones Foundation

751 S. Weir Canyon Rd., No. 601
Anaheim Hills, CA   92808   (714) 281-2842
E-mail: djfoundation@yahoo.com; URL: http://www.deaconjones.com

Foundation type: Public charity

Purpose: Four year scholarships to selected inner-city students for attendance at a university of their choice.

Financial data: Year ended 12/31/2011. Assets, $156,068 (M); Expenditures, $10,227; Total giving, $5,079; Grants to individuals, totaling $5,079.

Fields of interest: Higher education.

Type of support: Scholarships—to individuals.

Application information: Students are selected by the foundation and they are required to participate in the mentoring program and to work as volunteers within their own communities for at least one month each summer. See web site for additional guidelines.

Program description:

Scholarship Program: The foundation has created a seven-year program which begins when youngsters are selected at the end of the ninth grade. The candidates are provided with individual mentors, summer apprenticeships, an investment portfolio, on-the-job training in a corporate and business setting, and a full four-year scholarship to the university of their choice.

EIN: 330737187

714

Joshua Tree National Park Association

74485 National Park Dr.
Twentynine Palms, CA   92277-3533   (760) 367-5525
Contact: Nancy Downer, Exec. Dir.
Application e-mail: josh_hoines@nps.gov
FAX: (760) 367-5583; E-mail: mail@joshuatree.org; URL: http://www.joshuatree.org

Foundation type: Public charity

Purpose: Research grants to support graduate students at accredited institutions for their independent field studies in Joshua Tree National Park.

Financial data: Year ended 09/30/2011. Assets, $1,437,984 (M); Expenditures, $555,227; Total giving, $48,589; Grants to individuals, totaling $48,589.

Fields of interest: Natural resources.

Type of support: Research; Graduate support.

Application information: Application form required. Application form available on the grantmaker's web site.

Send request by: E-mail or submit on disk in PDF format

Deadline(s): May 2

Final notification: Recipients notified by June 7

Additional information: Application should include a curriculum vitae, and a letter of confidence from your faculty advisor on the institution's letterhead and sent directly from the faculty member. See web site for additional guidelines.

Program description:

Graduate Student Research Grant Program: These grants encourage students to conduct

research and provide experience in applying for grants, meeting deadlines, and developing and managing a budget. The student's work should focus on the resources of Joshua Tree National Park. Potential applicants should review the park's research web site to understand existing research and needed areas of research. Applicants need not limit their inquiries to the research preferences identified. Awardees are expected to produce a written report, prepare a webpage detailing their work and conclusions, and publicly present their findings in a suitable forum. Awardees have two years from time of award to complete their fieldwork and meet all award requirements. Grants are up to $4,000.
EIN: 952312513

715
The Herbert W. and Jeanne A. Justin Foundation
2857 Lincoln Ave.
Alameda, CA 94501-3068

Foundation type: Independent foundation
Purpose: Scholarships to students attending the University of Berkeley and San Francisco State University, CA.
Financial data: Year ended 06/30/2013. Assets, $430,037 (M); Expenditures, $23,866; Total giving, $21,574; Grants to individuals, 6 grants totaling $21,574 (high: $4,682, low: $1,553).
Type of support: Support to graduates or students of specific schools.
Application information: Applications not accepted.
    Additional information: Unsolicited requests for funds not considered or acknowledged.
EIN: 943371142

716
The Henry J. Kaiser Family Foundation
2400 Sand Hill Rd.
Menlo Park, CA 94025-6941 (650) 854-9400
Contact: Renee Wells, Contracts Mgr.
FAX: (650) 854-4800; E-mail: rwells@kff.org; Washington, DC Office Address: 1330 G St. N.W., Washington, DC 20005, tel.: (202) 347-5270; fax: (202) 347-5274; URL: http://www.kff.org

Foundation type: Operating foundation
Purpose: Fellowships to media professionals and internship opportunities to young minority journalists in the area of health reporting. Internships for early career journalists interested in specializing in health reporting.
Financial data: Year ended 12/31/2012. Assets, $573,956,985 (M); Expenditures, $59,560,410; Total giving, $757,218.
Fields of interest: Media/communications; Television; Print publishing; Radio; Public health school/education; AIDS; Minorities.
Type of support: Fellowships; Internship funds; Research; Undergraduate support; Travel grants; Stipends.
Application information: Applications accepted. Application form available on the grantmaker's web site.
    Initial approach: Letter
    Deadline(s): Mar. for fellowships, Nov. for mini-fellowships, Dec. for internships
    Additional information: See web site for additional guidelines.
Program description:
    Media Internship: This twelve-week program is for early career journalists who can demonstrate a commitment and ability to report on health issues

affecting diverse and immigrant communities. Priority is given to journalists who are bilingual and/or bicultural, and to journalists who have studied or reported on health issues affecting diverse and immigrant communities. Interns selected are graduating from college and/or journalism school with quite considerable experience, including previous internships at a newspaper, TV or radio station, or at a news organization's website. Applicants must be U.S. citizens or permanent residents.
EIN: 946064808

717
Kaiser Foundation Health Plan of Colorado
One Kaiser Plz., Ste. 1550L
Oakland, CA 94612-3610 (510) 271-6611

Foundation type: Public charity
Purpose: Medical financial assistance to low-income vulnerable patients who are unable to pay for all or part of the cost of urgent or emergent care provided in Kaiser Permanente facilities who are not eligible for other public or privately sponsored coverage.
Financial data: Year ended 12/31/2011. Assets, $1,454,050,830 (M); Expenditures, $2,837,998,618; Total giving, $5,805,600; Grants to individuals, totaling $29,700.
Fields of interest: Hospitals (general); Health care, patient services; Economically disadvantaged.
Type of support: Grants for special needs.
Application information:
    Initial approach: Letter
    Additional information: Contact foundation for eligibility criteria.
EIN: 840591617

718
Kaiser Foundation Hospitals
1 Kaiser Pl., Ste. 15L
Oakland, CA 94612-3610 (510) 271-6611
Contact: George Halvorson, Chair. and C.E.O.

Foundation type: Public charity
Purpose: Scholarships for students enrolled in any California nursing program pursuing advanced nursing degrees or to become registered nurses.
Financial data: Year ended 12/31/2011. Assets, $28,948,439,297 (M); Expenditures, $16,443,912,529; Total giving, $78,199,348; Grants to individuals, 221 grants totaling $407,000.
Fields of interest: Nursing school/education.
Type of support: Scholarships—to individuals.
Application information: Applications accepted.
    Deadline(s): Vary
    Additional information: Scholarships are need and merit based, on academic excellence, offered to students enrolled in approved nursing degree programs in CA.
EIN: 941105628

719
Ralph A. Kerber Memorial Foundation
32 Castellina Dr.
Newport Coast, CA 92657-1616 (949) 715-3474
Contact: Janet C. Kerber, Tr.

Foundation type: Independent foundation
Purpose: Scholarships to individuals or family members that worked in the swimming pool and spa construction and maintenance industries in the

greater Southern California area for attendance at an accredited two or four year educational institution.
Publications: Application guidelines; Newsletter; Newsletter (including application guidelines).
Financial data: Year ended 12/31/2011. Assets, $685,194 (M); Expenditures, $62,627; Total giving, $37,000; Grants to individuals, 25 grants totaling $37,000 (high: $4,000, low: $1,000).
Fields of interest: Vocational education, post-secondary; Business school/education.
Type of support: Scholarships—to individuals; Undergraduate support; Postgraduate support.
Application information: Application form required.
    Initial approach: Letter or telephone
    Send request by: Mail
    Deadline(s): Apr. 1
    Applicants should submit the following:
        1) Letter(s) of recommendation
        2) Financial information
        3) Essay
Program description:
    Ralph A. Kerber Scholarship: Scholarship grants range between $500 and $2,500 to students who demonstrate solid academic performance in high school, and hold a high school diploma, graduate education diploma or equivalent before any grant funds are disbursed. Grants may be requested for any reasonable further education need or career advancement objective, including trade school or any undergraduate or postgraduate institution or higher learning. Applicant must have been a resident of Southern California for at least two years and must be either a U.S. citizen or legal resident of the U.S.
EIN: 336289007

720
Robert W. Kiersted Memorial Scholarship
P.O. Box 755
Fairfax, CA 94978-0755 (408) 867-3411

Foundation type: Independent foundation
Purpose: Scholarships to residents of the Saratoga, CA area.
Financial data: Year ended 12/31/2012. Assets, $76,604 (M); Expenditures, $8,154; Total giving, $8,000; Grants to individuals, 5 grants totaling $8,000 (high: $3,000, low: $1,000).
Type of support: Scholarships—to individuals; Support to graduates or students of specific schools.
Application information: Applications not accepted.
    Additional information: Unsolicited requests for funds not considered or acknowledged.
EIN: 943064364

721
The Kimbo Foundation
72 Santa Ana Ave.
San Francisco, CA 94127-1508
Application addresses: Northern CA: c/o The SF Korea Daily, Attn.: Business Planning Dept., 33288 Central Ave., Union City, CA 94587-2010, tel.: (510) 429-3230, fax: (510) 429-3260, e-mail: kwang@koreadaily.com; Southern CA and other states: c/o The LA Korean Central Daily, Attn.: Business Planning Dept., 690 Wilshire Pl., Los Angeles, CA 90005-3930, tel.: (213) 368-2607, fax: (213) 389-6196, e-mail: info@jkoreadaily.com
E-mail: info@kimbofoundation.org; URL: http://www.kimbofoundation.org

Foundation type: Independent foundation

Purpose: Scholarships to financially needy students of Korean descent for attendance at four-year colleges and universities. High school seniors and current undergraduates may apply.
Financial data: Year ended 12/31/2012. Assets, $0 (M); Expenditures, $339,823; Total giving, $329,200; Grants to individuals, totaling $273,000.
Fields of interest: Higher education.
Type of support: Undergraduate support.
Application information: Applications accepted. Application form required.
> *Deadline(s):* June 30
> *Applicants should submit the following:*
> 1) Essay
> 2) Transcripts
> 3) Letter(s) of recommendation
> *Additional information:* Application must also include parents' or student's tax return. Essay can be written in English or Korean.
EIN: 943047547

722
Jessie Klicka Foundation
c/o Wells Fargo Bank, N.A.
4365 Executive Dr. 18th Fl.
San Diego, CA   92121

Foundation type: Independent foundation
Purpose: Scholarships to graduates of high schools in San Diego City and County, CA.
Financial data: Year ended 12/31/2012. Assets, $1,841,013 (M); Expenditures, $117,115; Total giving, $66,670.
Fields of interest: Higher education; Scholarships/financial aid; Economically disadvantaged.
Type of support: Support to graduates or students of specific schools; Undergraduate support.
Application information: Application form required.
> *Deadline(s):* Apr. 20
> *Additional information:* Application should include financial information.
EIN: 956093455

723
Korean American Volunteer Corps.
690 Wilshire Pl.
Los Angeles, CA   90005-3930   (213) 368-2630
Contact: Kae Hong Ko, C.E.O.

Foundation type: Public charity
Purpose: Financial assistance to low-income individuals and families with clothing and other needs, and scholarships provided to low-income students in the Los Angeles, CA area.
Financial data: Year ended 12/31/2012. Assets, $43,352 (M); Expenditures, $613,528; Total giving, $342,410; Grants to individuals, totaling $142,500.
Fields of interest: Education; Economically disadvantaged.
Type of support: Grants for special needs.
Application information: Applicant must demonstrate financial need.
EIN: 954847500

724
Korean Heritage Scholarship Foundation
P.O. Box 74518
Los Angeles, CA   90004-0518   (213) 738-0908
Contact: Goon Suk Han, Pres.
E-mail: info@koreanheritage.org; URL: http://www.koreanheritage.org

Foundation type: Public charity

Purpose: Scholarships to Korean-Americans of the greater Los Angeles, CA area who are full time college or college bound students in good standing.
Publications: Application guidelines.
Financial data: Year ended 12/31/2012. Assets, $1,386,275 (M); Expenditures, $53,826; Total giving, $45,000; Grants to individuals, totaling $45,000.
Fields of interest: Higher education.
Type of support: Scholarships—to individuals.
Application information: Applications accepted. Application form required. Application form available on the grantmaker's web site.
> *Deadline(s):* Apr. 29
> *Final notification:* Recipients notified May 31
> *Applicants should submit the following:*
> 1) Transcripts
> 2) FAFSA
> 3) Essay
> *Additional information:* Application should also include copy of tax return, Riot Victim Data, if applicable, and Parents' Peace Officer Status, if applicable.
EIN: 954459495

725
Kornberg Family Foundation
50 Glenbrook Ave.
San Francisco, CA   94114-2110
Contact: Thomas Kornberg, Secy.

Foundation type: Operating foundation
Purpose: Fellowships by nomination only to students of Stanford University and University of California at San Francisco for biomedical research.
Financial data: Year ended 12/29/2010. Assets, $0 (M); Expenditures, $90,194; Total giving, $79,368.
Fields of interest: Chemistry; Biology/life sciences.
Type of support: Fellowships; Support to graduates or students of specific schools; Awards/grants by nomination only.
Application information:
> *Deadline(s):* None
> *Additional information:* Contact foundation for current nomination guidelines.
EIN: 943259687

726
Kathryn L. Kurka Children's Health Fund, Inc.
P.O. Box 39531
Los Angeles, CA   90039-0531   (818) 955-6500
Contact: Karen Maiorca, Pres.
FAX: (818) 955-5127;
E-mail: kurkachildrenshealthfund1@yahoo.org;
Additional Tel.: (626)-576-0701; URL: http://www.kurkachildrenshealthfund.org/

Foundation type: Public charity
Purpose: Assistance for underprivileged children in the Los Angeles, CA, area who lack financial resources with vision, dental, medical and mental health care.
Financial data: Year ended 06/30/2012. Assets, $136,175 (M); Expenditures, $123,477; Total giving, $7,850.
Fields of interest: Human services; Children, services; Economically disadvantaged.
Type of support: Grants for special needs.
Application information: Contact the fund for eligibility criteria.
EIN: 954147257

727
La Canada Flintridge Educational Foundation
4490 Cornishon Ave., Rm. 211
La Canada Flintridge, CA   91011-3243   (818) 952-4268
Contact: Deborah Weirick, Exec. Dir.
FAX: (818) 952-4297; E-mail: ed@lcfef.org;
URL: http://www.lcfef.org

Foundation type: Public charity
Purpose: Grants to individual teachers of La Canada Flintridge, CA for outstanding service.
Publications: Informational brochure; Newsletter.
Financial data: Year ended 06/30/2012. Assets, $7,321,141 (M); Expenditures, $2,530,356; Total giving, $2,106,500; Grants to individuals, totaling $6,500.
Fields of interest: Education.
Type of support: Awards/prizes.
Application information: Applications not accepted.
> *Additional information:* Unsolicited requests for funds not considered or acknowledged.
EIN: 953276042

728
La Costa Canyon High School Foundation, Inc.
1 Maverick Way
Carlsbad, CA   92009-8957   (760) 436-6136
Contact: Janice Itterman, Exec. Dir.
FAX: (760) 943-3450;
E-mail: lcfoundation@sduhsd.net; URL: http://www.lcchsfoundation.org

Foundation type: Public charity
Purpose: Scholarships for students attending La Costa Canyon High School, CA.
Financial data: Year ended 06/30/2013. Assets, $497,770 (M); Expenditures, $1,105,563; Total giving, $388,445; Grants to individuals, totaling $6,065.
Fields of interest: Education.
Type of support: Support to graduates or students of specific schools.
Application information: Applications not accepted.
> *Additional information:* Scholarship for students is based on need and scholastic achievement. Unsolicited requests for funds not considered or acknowledged.
EIN: 330708190

729
Ladies of the Grand Army of the Republic
(formerly George A. Thomas Circle No. 32 Dept. of the Grand Army of the Republic, also known as George H. Thomas Circle No. 32, Ladies of the Grand Army of the Republic)
c/o George H. Thomas Cir. 32, Delahunty
1500 Grant Ave., Ste. 200
Novato, CA   94945-3153

Foundation type: Operating foundation
Purpose: Assistance to financially needy individuals, primarily in CA.
Financial data: Year ended 12/31/2011. Assets, $27,871 (M); Expenditures, $28,121; Total giving, $23,270; Grants to individuals, 10 grants totaling $23,270 (high: $4,850, low: $165).
Fields of interest: Economically disadvantaged.
Type of support: Grants for special needs.
Application information: Applications not accepted.
EIN: 946138985

730
Lafayette Arts & Science Foundation
P.O. Box 923
Lafayette, CA   94549-0923   (925) 299-1644
Contact: Myrna Kimmelman, Prog. Mgr.
FAX: (925) 299-1688; E-mail: office@lasf.org;
URL: http://www.lasf.org

Foundation type: Public charity
Purpose: Grants to teachers in the Lafayette School District (LSD) and the Acalanes Union High School District (AUHSD) in CA to improve and enrich the educational experience of their students.
Publications: Annual report; Grants list; Newsletter.
Financial data: Year ended 06/30/2012. Assets, $1,561,663 (M); Expenditures, $1,717,510. Grants to individuals amount not specified.
Fields of interest: Education.
Type of support: Project support.
Application information: Application form required. Application form available on the grantmaker's web site.
> *Deadline(s):* Apr.
> *Additional information:* On-site meeting for mini-grants, and a short presentation for project grants would be required.

Program description:
> *Lafayette Teacher Allocation Grant Program:* The goal of the program is to provide funds to support teachers in the Lafayette School District and Acalanes High School who want to improve and enrich the educational experience of their students. The grants assist both teachers who want to create innovative projects and pilot them at their site or classroom, and teachers who want to adapt successful curriculum projects created within their district or elsewhere and implement them in their own classroom or lab. There are two categories of grants to better address the various needs and objectives of the proposed curriculum projects: mini-grants (grants up to $1,000 which will include a shorter application and on-site interviews with school allocation rep) and project grants (grants over $1,000 that require more detail and a committee review)

EIN: 942699518

731
Lagrant Foundation
600 Wilshire Blvd., Ste. 1520
Los Angeles, CA   90017-2920   (323) 469-8680
Contact: Kim L. Hunter, Chair.
FAX: (323) 469-8683;
E-mail: erickaavila@lagrant.com; URL: http://www.lagrantfoundation.org/

Foundation type: Public charity
Purpose: Scholarships and internships to African American, American Indian/Native American, Asian, Pacific American and Hispanic/Latino undergraduate and graduate students.
Publications: Application guidelines.
Financial data: Year ended 06/30/2013. Assets, $2,099,312 (M); Expenditures, $468,862; Total giving, $214,485; Grants to individuals, 83 grants totaling $214,410.
Fields of interest: Higher education; Asians/Pacific Islanders; African Americans/Blacks; Hispanics/Latinos; Native Americans/American Indians.
Type of support: Scholarships—to individuals; Graduate support; Undergraduate support.
Application information: Applications accepted. Application form required. Application form available on the grantmaker's web site.
> *Initial approach:* Application

> *Send request by:* On-line
> *Deadline(s):* Feb. 28
> *Final notification:* Applicants notified in mid-Mar.
> *Applicants should submit the following:*
> 1) Transcripts
> 2) GPA
> 3) Letter(s) of recommendation
> 4) Resume
> 5) Essay
> *Additional information:* See web site for additional application guidelines.

Program descriptions:
> *Graduate Scholarships:* These scholarships are awarded to graduate students who are U.S. citizens or permanent residents and a member of one of the following ethnic groups: African American, Asian Pacific American, Hispanic/Latino or Native American/Alaska Native. Applicants must be full-time students at an accredited institution. Graduate applicants must have a minimum of 3.2 GPA and must major in a field of study that has an emphasis on public relations, marketing, or advertising. Applicants must have a minimum of two academic semesters left to complete his/her Master's degree.
> *Undergraduate Scholarships:* These scholarships are awarded to current freshmen, sophomores, juniors, and non-graduating seniors who are U.S. citizen's or permanent residents and a member of one of the following ethnic groups: African American, Asian Pacific American, Hispanic/Latino or Native American/Alaska Native. Applicants must be full-time students at a four-year accredited institution, carrying a total of 12 units or more per semester/quarter. Applicants must have a minimum of 2.75 GPA and must major in a field of study that has an emphasis on public relations, marketing, or advertising or must minor in communications with desire to pursue a career in public relations, marketing, or advertising.

EIN: 954657088

732
Lakewood Medical Center Foundation
(formerly Doctors Hospital of Lakewood Foundation)
c/o Lakewood Regional Medical Ctr.
3300 E. South St., Ste. 105
Lakewood, CA   90805-4579

Foundation type: Independent foundation
Purpose: Scholarships to students currently enrolled in accredited schools of medicine, nursing, and pharmacy who have a permanent address within a five-mile radius of Lakewood Regional Medical Center, in Lakewood, CA. Scholarships are limited to residents of record of the following CA cities: Artesia, Bellflower, Cerritos, Compton, Cypress, Downey, Hawaiian Gardens, Lakewood, Long Beach, Norwalk, Paramount, and Signal Hill.
Financial data: Year ended 09/30/2011. Assets, $0 (M); Expenditures, $377,488; Total giving, $367,625; Grants to individuals, 5 grants totaling $24,000 (high: $7,000, low: $4,000).
Fields of interest: Medical school/education; Nursing school/education; Pharmacy/prescriptions.
Type of support: Graduate support; Undergraduate support.
Application information: Applications accepted. Application form required.
> *Initial approach:* Telephone
> *Deadline(s):* May
> *Additional information:* Contact foundation for current application guidelines.

EIN: 510154413

733
Lambda Literary Foundation
5482 Wilshire Blvd., Ste. 1595
Los Angeles, CA   90036-4218   (323) 366-2104
Contact: Tony Valenzuela, Exec. Dir.
FAX: (323) 362-2104;
E-mail: info@lambdaliterary.org; E-mail for Tony Valenzuela: tvalenzuela@lambdaliterary.org;
URL: http://www.lambdaliterary.org

Foundation type: Public charity
Purpose: Awards by nomination only to the lesbian, gay, bisexual, and transgender community to further the creation and dissemination of writings.
Publications: Application guidelines.
Financial data: Year ended 12/31/2012. Assets, $42,309 (M); Expenditures, $296,209; Total giving, $12,750; Grants to individuals, totaling $12,750.
Fields of interest: Literature.
Type of support: Awards/grants by nomination only; Awards/prizes.
Application information: Application form available on the grantmaker's web site.
> *Deadline(s):* Dec. 1
> *Additional information:* Nomination forms can be downloaded from the foundation web site. A $35 administrative fee is required. See web site for additional guidelines.

Program descriptions:
> *Lamba Literary Awards:* The awards are presented in twenty-four categories. The awards are based principally on the quality of the writing and the LGBT content of the work. The sexual orientation of the author is secondary. A book can be nominated only by its author or by its publisher and can be nominated in more than one category. The book must be published and distributed in the U.S. during 2011, and must be published in English. Translations from other languages into English are accepted and encouraged. Self-published books are eligible.
> *Retreat for LGBTQ Writers:* The foundation offers a one-week intensive immersion in fiction, nonfiction, or poetry to LGBT writers, and an opportunity to learn from the very best writers in the LGBT community, to emerging LGBT writers of any age. Scholarships are available for individuals to attend this workshop.

EIN: 521996380

734
Lambda Theta Nu Sorority, Inc.
1220 Rosecrans Ave., Ste. 543
San Diego, CA   92106-2674   (951) 315-8529
E-mail: community@lambdathetanu.org;
URL: http://www.lambdathetanu.org/lambda/about.html

Foundation type: Public charity
Purpose: Scholarships to young high school Latina students in pursuit of a higher education.
Publications: Application guidelines.
Financial data: Year ended 06/30/2012. Assets, $26,012 (M); Expenditures, $109,371; Total giving, $12,801.
Fields of interest: Vocational education, post-secondary; College (community/junior); University.
Type of support: Scholarships—to individuals.
Application information: Applications accepted. Application form required. Application form available on the grantmaker's web site.
> *Deadline(s):* May
> *Applicants should submit the following:*
> 1) Transcripts
> 2) Letter(s) of recommendation

Additional information: Application must also include a personal statement of your scholastic achievement, educational and career goals. Contact the local chapter in your area for additional information.

Program description:

Latina Scholarship Program: Scholarships are available to assist young Latina high school women to pursue their own educational goals. Eligible applicants must: be females of Latino heritage or be able to demonstrate dedication to community service and empowerment of the Latino/a community; be a graduating senior in high school; and plan to attend an accredited community college, university, or technical or vocational school.

EIN: 943292874

735

Lancaster West Rotary Foundation

44288 Lowtree Way
Lancaster, CA 93534-4169
Application addresses: c/o Antelope Valley College, 3041 West Ave. K, Lancaster, CA 93536, tel.: (661) 943-3241

Foundation type: Independent foundation
Purpose: Scholarships to students attending Antelope Valley College, Lancaster, CA for postsecondary education.
Financial data: Year ended 06/30/2012. Assets, $113,770 (M); Expenditures, $32,843; Total giving, $32,168.
Fields of interest: Higher education.
Type of support: Scholarships—to individuals; Support to graduates or students of specific schools.
Application information: Applications accepted.
  Deadline(s): Mar. 2 for Antelope Valley College
  Applicants should submit the following:
    1) Transcripts
    2) Letter(s) of recommendation
EIN: 954430805

736

Lasso Foundation

(formerly LASO Public/Private Partnership Foundation)
3100 Donald Douglas Loop N., Ste. 100
Santa Monica, CA 90405-3089

Foundation type: Independent foundation
Purpose: Scholarships to dependents of sheriffs residing in CA.
Financial data: Year ended 06/30/2013. Assets, $30,008 (M); Expenditures, $54,895; Total giving, $0.
Type of support: Scholarships—to individuals.
Application information: Applications not accepted.
  Additional information: Unsolicited requests for funds not considered or acknowledged.
EIN: 954151708

737

Laurance Family Foundation

(formerly LFT Pacific Trust Foundation)
11100 Santa Monica Blvd., Ste. 600
Los Angeles, CA 90025-3392

Foundation type: Independent foundation
Purpose: Specific assistance to underprivileged CA individuals with special needs and support.

Financial data: Year ended 12/31/2011. Assets, $2,172,140 (M); Expenditures, $239,604; Total giving, $211,424.
Fields of interest: Human services.
Type of support: Grants for special needs.
Application information: Contact foundation for eligibility criteria.
EIN: 266005102

738

League of United Latin American Citizens California Educational Foundation

7731 Laurelton Ave.
Garden Grove, CA 92841 (714) 898-2312
Contact: Angelina Guirindola, V.P.; Scholarships: Vera Marcus, Pres.

Foundation type: Public charity
Purpose: Scholarships of $500 for undergraduate education to students who reside in CA for attendance at U.S. colleges and universities.
Financial data: Year ended 03/31/2010. Assets, $8,446 (M); Expenditures, $14,159; Total giving, $10,176.
Type of support: Graduate support; Undergraduate support.
Application information: Applications accepted. Application form required.
  Initial approach: Letter
  Deadline(s): June 16
  Applicants should submit the following:
    1) GPA
    2) Letter(s) of recommendation
    3) Financial information
  Additional information: Financial need is a determining factor in selection. Application should include extracurricular activities.
EIN: 330297651

739

The L. S. B. Leakey Foundation

(formerly L. S. B. Leakey Foundation for Research Related to Human Origins, Behavior and Survival)
1003B O'Reilly Ave.
San Francisco, CA 94129-1359 (415) 561-4646
Contact: Sharal Camisa, Managing Dir.
FAX: (415) 561-4647;
E-mail: info@leakeyfoundation.org; URL: http://www.leakeyfoundation.org

Foundation type: Public charity
Purpose: Research grants and fellowships to scholars and students for the study of human origins.
Publications: Application guidelines; Financial statement; Grants list; Informational brochure; Newsletter.
Financial data: Year ended 08/31/2011. Assets, $16,945,972 (M); Expenditures, $1,593,058; Total giving, $762,157; Grants to individuals, totaling $492,387.
Fields of interest: Research; Biology/life sciences; Anthropology/sociology.
International interests: Africa.
Type of support: Fellowships; Research; Foreign applicants; Postdoctoral support.
Application information: Application form required.
  Initial approach: Letter
  Send request by: Mail or e-mail
  Copies of proposal: 6
  Deadline(s): Jan. 5 and July 15 for Research Grants, Feb. 15 for new applicants, Mar. 1 for returning applicants for Baldwin Fellowships
  Additional information: See web site for additional guidelines.

Program descriptions:

Franklin Mosher Baldwin Memorial Fellowships: Awards up to $12,000 per year for up to two years to scholars with African citizenship who seek an advanced degree or specialized training in an area of study related to human origins research.

General Research Grants: Research grants are awarded twice annually. Priority for funding is given to the exploratory phases of promising new research projects that meet the stated purpose of the foundation. The majority of the foundation's general research grants to doctoral students are in the $3,000 to $13,500 range. However, larger grants, especially to senior scientist and postdoctoral students, may be funded up to $22,000.
EIN: 952536475

740

Thomas & Dorothy Leavey Foundation

10100 Santa Monica Blvd., Ste. 610
Los Angeles, CA 90067-4110 (310) 551-9936
Contact: Kathleen L. McCarthy, Chair.

Foundation type: Independent foundation
Purpose: Scholarships to children of employees of Farmers Insurance Group, Inc.
Financial data: Year ended 12/31/2012. Assets, $249,171,900 (M); Expenditures, $14,408,495; Total giving, $11,049,188; Grants to individuals, totaling $324,000.
Type of support: Employee-related scholarships.
Application information: Applications accepted.
  Deadline(s): None
Program description:
  Scholarships: Scholarships based on merit and need only to children of employees or agents of Farmers Insurance Group, Inc.
EIN: 956060162

741

LEF Foundation

c/o MLB Assocs.
2422 Debbie Way
Calistoga, CA 94515-1202 (707) 486-6806
Contact: Marina Drummer, Grants Advisor (CA); Lyda Kuth, Dir. (New England)
E-mail: marina@lef-foundation.org; New England and Moving Image Fund address: P.O. Box 382066, Cambridge, MA 02238-2866, tel.: (617) 492-5333, fax: (617) 868-5603; e-mail: lyda@lef-foundation.org; URL: http://www.lef-foundation.org

Foundation type: Independent foundation
Purpose: Grants that foster the creative development of artists including independent film and video, who are living and working in the six New England states.
Publications: Application guidelines; Grants list; Occasional report; Program policy statement.
Financial data: Year ended 06/30/2012. Assets, $6,572,823 (M); Expenditures, $745,763; Total giving, $469,400.
Fields of interest: Film/video; Visual arts.
Type of support: Stipends.
Application information: Applications accepted. Application form required.
  Initial approach: Letter of inquiry
  Deadline(s): Sept. 23
  Applicants should submit the following:
    1) Budget Information
    2) Proposal
    3) Resume
    4) SASE
    5) Work samples

Additional information: Individuals are required to apply through a nonprofit fiscal sponsor.
Program description:
Moving Image Fund: The program supports independent film and video artists living and working in one of the six New England states (CT, MA, ME NH, RI, or VT), and who have a fiscal sponsor. The grantmaking is targeted toward the production of work, with the larger goal of strengthening the voices of media artists and improving the overall environment for the production, exhibition, and distribution of their work. A maximum of seven grants of $5,000 will be awarded to projects in the pre-production phase of development, a maximum of six grants of $15,000 each will be awarded to projects in the production phase, and a maximum of three grants of $25,000 each will be awarded to projects in the post-production. See foundation web site for complete guidelines.
EIN: 680070194

742
Legal Aid Society of San Mateo County
330 Twin Dolphin Dr., Ste. 123
Natalie Lanam Justice Ctr.
Redwood City, CA 94065-1455   (650) 558-0915
Contact: M. Stacey Hawver, Exec. Dir.
FAX: (650) 558-0673;
E-mail: info@legalaidsmc.org; Toll-free tel.: (800) 381-8898; URL: http://www.legalaidsmc.org

Foundation type: Public charity
Purpose: Emergency assistance to low income individuals, families, seniors, persons with disabilities, and domestic violence survivors in San Mateo county, CA with free civil legal services.
Publications: Annual report; Newsletter.
Financial data: Year ended 03/31/2012. Assets, $4,114,910 (M); Expenditures, $2,517,397; Total giving, $7,089; Grants to individuals, totaling $7,089.
Fields of interest: Legal services; Economically disadvantaged.
Type of support: Emergency funds.
Application information:
Initial approach: Telephone
Additional information: Contact the agency for eligibility determination.
EIN: 941451894

743
Level Playing Field Institute
(formerly Institute for Inclusive Work Environments)
2201 Broadway Ste. 101
Oakland, CA 94612-3028   (415) 946-3030
Contact: Jarvis Sulcer Ph.D., Exec. Dir.
FAX: (415) 946-3001; E-mail: info@lpfi.org;
URL: http://www.lpfi.org

Foundation type: Public charity
Purpose: Scholarships to U.C. Berkeley, CA undergraduate low-income students of color who reside in the seven-county Bay area.
Publications: Annual report; Newsletter.
Financial data: Year ended 12/31/2011. Assets, $1,966,441 (M); Expenditures, $3,427,992; Total giving, $330,667; Grants to individuals, totaling $330,667.
Fields of interest: Higher education; Minorities.
Type of support: Support to graduates or students of specific schools.
Application information:
Applicants should submit the following:
1) Transcripts
2) Financial information

3) Essay
Additional information: Unsolicited application not accepted.
EIN: 912088635

744
Liberty Hill Foundation
6420 Wilshire Blvd., Ste. 700
Los Angeles, CA 90048-5547   (323) 556-7200
Contact: Kafi D. Blumenfield, Pres. and C.E.O.
FAX: (323) 556-7240; E-mail: info@libertyhill.org;
URL: http://www.libertyhill.org

Foundation type: Public charity
Purpose: Stipends of $5,000 to young people to help cover basic living costs while they work at a nonprofit organization anywhere in California.
Publications: Application guidelines; Annual report; Financial statement; Grants list; Informational brochure; Newsletter.
Financial data: Year ended 09/30/2011. Assets, $16,384,713 (M); Expenditures, $7,810,070; Total giving, $4,777,192; Grants to individuals, totaling $453,300.
Fields of interest: Young adults.
Type of support: Stipends.
Application information:
Initial approach: Letter
Deadline(s): Mar. 11
Program description:
Bertha Wolf-Rosenthal Foundation for Community Service Stipend: This program will provide up to five young people, ages 18 to 25, with a stipend of $5,000 each to help cover basic living costs (such as rent, food, utilities, transportation, and childcare) while they work at a nonprofit organization anywhere in California during the year. Eligible applicants must show a history of community service work (in and/or out of school), demonstrate financial need, and currently work full-time (at least 30 hours per week) for a nonprofit organization in California.
EIN: 510181191

745
Life Technologies Corporation Contributions Program
(formerly Invitrogen Corporation Contributions Program)
5781 Van Allen Way
Carlsbad, CA 92008-7313   (760) 746-7204
Contact: Heather Virdo, Mgr., Community Rels. & Corp. Comms.
E-mail: Heather.Virdo@lifetech.com; URL: http://www.lifetechnologies.com/us/en/home/communities-social.html

Foundation type: Corporate giving program
Purpose: Grants to outstanding ninth through twelfth grade biotechnology educators who are full-time teachers in U.S. public or private schools.
Publications: Corporate giving report.
Fields of interest: Teacher school/education; Formal/general education; Science.
Type of support: Awards/grants by nomination only; Awards/prizes.
Application information:
Initial approach: Letter, telephone or e-mail
Applicants should submit the following:
1) Transcripts
2) Letter(s) of recommendation
3) Essay
4) Curriculum vitae
Program description:
Biotechnology Institute Genzyme-Life Technologies Biotech Educator Award: Life

Technologies, in partnership with Genzyme Corporation, honors high school educators who are bringing technology into the classroom and encouraging fellow science teachers to do the same. The company awards $10,000 to the first place winner, $5,000 to the second place winner, and $2,500 to the third place winner. Finalists are chosen and nominated among teachers-leaders who participated in the Biotechnology Institute's National Biotechnology Teacher-Leader Program. The award program is administered by the Biotechnology Institute.

746
Robert L. Lippert Foundation
1150 Ballena Blvd., Ste. 250
Alameda, CA 94501-7313
Contact: Edward W. Withrow, Jr., Pres.

Foundation type: Independent foundation
Purpose: Scholarships to graduates of Alameda Unified School District, and St. Joseph Notre Dame High School, CA.
Financial data: Year ended 12/31/2012. Assets, $1,397,132 (M); Expenditures, $30,651; Total giving, $12,000; Grants to individuals, 7 grants totaling $12,000 (high: $2,000, low: $1,000).
Fields of interest: Higher education.
Type of support: Support to graduates or students of specific schools; Undergraduate support.
Application information: Applications not accepted.
Additional information: Unsolicited requests for funds not considered or acknowledged.
EIN: 943108580

747
Little Company of Mary Community Health Foundation
(also known as Providence Little Company of Mary Foundation)
4101 Torrance Blvd.
Torrance, CA 90503-4607   (708) 229-5067
Contact: Dennis Reilly, Pres. and C.E.O.
URL: http://www.lcmhfoundation.org/site/c.apLEJQOyHqE/b.1540419/k.93A5/LCMHbrFoundation.htm

Foundation type: Public charity
Purpose: Financial assistance for registered nurses, licensed vocational nurses, and interested unlicensed employees of Little Company of Mary service area to return to school and pursue a higher degree in nursing.
Publications: Annual report; Newsletter.
Financial data: Year ended 12/31/2011. Assets, $47,869,204 (M); Expenditures, $9,250,636; Total giving, $6,629,875; Grants to individuals, totaling $80,873.
Fields of interest: Nursing school/education.
Type of support: Employee-related scholarships.
Application information:
Initial approach: Letter
Additional information: The scholarship recipients are chosen on a competitive basis, based on their commitment to Little Company of Mary, their commitment to advance their education and their personal financial need.
EIN: 510224944

748
Little People of America, Inc.
(also known as LPA)
250 El Camino Real, Ste. 201
Tustin, CA   92780-3656   (714) 368-3689
Contact: Joanna Campbell, Exec. Dir.
FAX: (714) 368-3367; E-mail: info@lpaonline.org;
Toll-free tel.: (888) 572-2001, E-Mail For Joanna
Campbell: joanna.lpa@earthlink.net; URL: http://
www.lpaonline.org

Foundation type: Public charity
Purpose: Grants and scholarships to short-statured
individuals for education, medical needs and
emergency situations.
Publications: Application guidelines; Annual report.
Financial data: Year ended 09/30/2011. Assets,
$896,560 (M); Expenditures, $197,516; Total
giving, $38,412; Grants to individuals, totaling
$38,412.
Fields of interest: Vocational education,
post-secondary; Higher education.
Type of support: Grants to individuals;
Scholarships—to individuals; Graduate support.
Application information: Applications accepted.
Application form required.
> *Send request by:* Mail
> *Deadline(s):* Apr. 22 for Scholarships, Apr. 30 for
> Kitchen's Travel Fund
> *Applicants should submit the following:*
> 1) Transcripts
> 2) Letter(s) of recommendation
> 3) GPA
> *Additional information:* Application should also
> include a personal statement of at least 500
> words. Scholarship is limited to two
> undergraduate studies and one for graduate
> studies.
Program descriptions:
> *Kitchens First Time Conference Attendees
> Scholarship:* Funding is available to first-time
> attendees of national conferences hosted by the
> organization, to cover partial expenses accrued
> from transportation, lodging, meal expenses, or
> other costs associated with attending the
> conference. Eligible applicants must be members
> of the organization in good standing. Average grants
> range from $100 to $500.
> *Scholarships:* Scholarships are given, in order of
> preference to: organization members who have a
> medically diagnosed form of dwarfism; immediate
> family members of dwarfs who are also paid
> organization members; people with dwarfism who
> are not organization members; disabled students in
> general; and non-disabled students who can
> demonstrate a need for financial educational
> assistance. Awards generally range from $250 to
> $1,000.
EIN: 942965067

749
The Margaret Liu Foundation
44 Montgomery St.
San Francisco, CA   94104

Foundation type: Independent foundation
Purpose: Scholarships to individuals in the CA area
for attendance at accredited colleges or
universities.
Financial data: Year ended 12/31/2011. Assets,
$0 (M); Expenditures, $97,311; Total giving,
$94,634.
Fields of interest: Education.
Type of support: Scholarships—to individuals.
Application information: Applications accepted.

Additional information: Contact the foundation for
application guidelines.
EIN: 943269896

750
Frank Livermore Trust
P.O. Box 7854
Menlo Park, CA   94026-7854
URL: http://www.moah.org/

Foundation type: Independent foundation
Purpose: Four-year Eagle Scout scholarships to
members of the Pacific Skyline Council, Boy Scouts
of America, Palo Alto, California.
Financial data: Year ended 06/30/2012. Assets,
$1,029,907 (M); Expenditures, $113,677; Total
giving, $24,400; Grants to individuals, 11 grants
totaling $24,400 (high: $2,400, low: $1,200).
Fields of interest: Boys clubs; Boy scouts.
Type of support: Scholarships—to individuals.
Application information: Applications not
accepted.
> *Additional information:* Contributes only to
> preselected organizations, unsolicited
> requests for funds not considered or
> acknowledged.
EIN: 770057575

751
Owen Locke Memorial Foundation
3879-B Brockton Ave.
Riverside, CA   92501   (951) 781-7545
Contact: Brenda Johnson, Scholarship Coord.
E-mail: bami_joe@hotmail.com; URL: http://
www.owenlocke.org/

Foundation type: Independent foundation
Purpose: Scholarships to high school graduates of
CA with limited financial resources, for higher
education for attendance at an accredited college,
university, trade school or vocational school.
Financial data: Year ended 02/29/2012. Assets,
$4,987,978 (M); Expenditures, $474,295; Total
giving, $435,866; Grants to individuals, totaling
$385,866.
Fields of interest: Vocational education,
post-secondary; Higher education.
Type of support: Scholarships—to individuals.
Application information: Applications accepted.
Application form required. Application form
available on the grantmaker's web site.
> *Send request by:* Mail
> *Deadline(s):* May 30
> *Applicants should submit the following:*
> 1) Transcripts
> 2) Letter(s) of recommendation
> 3) Essay
> 4) Financial information
> 5) SAR
> 6) SAT
> 7) GPA
> 8) ACT
> *Additional information:* Scholarships are paid
> directly to the educational institution on
> behalf of the students.
Program description:
> *Scholarships:* This program offers funds
> applicable to tuition, school fees and books for
> eligible applicants. Applications for this scholarship
> will be accepted from high school graduates of
> California who will be attending an accredited
> college, university, trade school or vocational
> program (in California or elsewhere). Scholarships
> are distributed on behalf of the applicant to any

accredited college, university or vocational program
in an amount not to exceed $10,000 per year.
EIN: 208561536

752
Lockheed Martin Employees' Foundation
(formerly Lockheed MSC Employees Bucks of the
Month Club)
P.O. Box 3504, Bldg. 153
Sunnyvale, CA   94088-3504   (408) 742-7667
Contact: Patti Voshall, Exec. Dir.

Foundation type: Public charity
Purpose: Financial assistance to employees of
Lockheed Martin who need help due to natural
disasters, illness, or other unforeseen
emergencies.
Financial data: Year ended 10/31/2011. Assets,
$307,687 (M); Expenditures, $569,350; Total
giving, $544,020; Grants to individuals, totaling
$44,239.
Type of support: Emergency funds; Grants for
special needs.
Application information: Applications not
accepted.
EIN: 946165100

753
The G. and R. Loeb Foundation, Inc.
110 Westwood Plz., Rm. F322
Los Angeles, CA   90095-1481   (310) 206-1877
FAX: (310) 825-4479;
E-mail: loeb@anderson.ucla.edu; URL: http://
www.anderson.ucla.edu/x3294.xml

Foundation type: Independent foundation
Purpose: Awards in business journalism,
recognizing writers, editors and producers who have
made significant contributions to the understanding
of business, finance, and the economy for both the
private investor and the general public.
Financial data: Year ended 09/30/2012. Assets,
$411,136 (M); Expenditures, $178,263; Total
giving, $28,250; Grants to individuals, 44 grants
totaling $28,250 (high: $2,000, low: $250).
Fields of interest: Print publishing; Business/
industry; Economics.
Type of support: Awards/grants by nomination only;
Awards/prizes.
Application information:
> *Initial approach:* Telephone or e-mail
> *Send request by:* Online
> *Deadline(s):* Jan. 31
> *Additional information:* Application by nomination
> only.
Program description:
> *Gerald Loeb Awards:* The winning entry in each
> category receives a $2,000 honorarium. If a winning
> entry has more than one contestant, the award will
> be divided equally. If the final judges determine that
> an entry or entries not selected for a prize in a
> particular category merits special recognition, the
> entry may be awarded honorable mention.
> Honorable mentions in each category receive $500.
> Under certain special circumstances, established
> by the final judges, a writer or entry may receive a
> special award. Award finalists are announced in late
> spring, and award winners are announced at the
> banquet and presentation ceremony in early
> summer.
EIN: 136121546

754
Long Beach Rotary Scholarship Foundation
1119 Queens Hwy., Ste. 103
Long Beach, CA 90802-6390   (562) 436-8181
Contact: Craig Dougherty, Chair.
FAX: (562) 436-8811; E-mail: lbrotary@aol.com;
URL: http://www.rotarylongbeach.org/

Foundation type: Public charity
Purpose: Scholarships to Long Beach, CA area students attending Long Beach City College (LBCC) and California State University, Long Beach (CSULB)
Financial data: Year ended 06/30/2012. Assets, $7,278,106 (M); Expenditures, $347,003; Total giving, $281,557; Grants to individuals, totaling $2,500.
Fields of interest: Higher education.
Type of support: Scholarships—to individuals; Support to graduates or students of specific schools.
Application information: Applications accepted. Application form required. Application form available on the grantmaker's web site.
   Deadline(s): Mar.
   Applicants should submit the following:
      1) Essay
      2) Resume
      3) GPA
   Additional information: See web site for additional application guidelines.
EIN: 956070198

755
Los Altos Community Foundation
183 Hillview Ave.
Los Altos, CA 94022-3742   (650) 949-5908
FAX: (650) 949-0807; E-mail: lacf@losaltoscf.org;
Grant inquiry e-mail: CGP@losaltoscf.org;
URL: http://www.losaltoscf.org

Foundation type: Community foundation
Purpose: Scholarships to graduates of Mountain View Los Altos Union School District, CA.
Publications: Application guidelines; Annual report; Financial statement; Grants list; Informational brochure; Newsletter; Occasional report; Program policy statement.
Financial data: Year ended 06/30/2012. Assets, $5,585,801 (M); Expenditures, $1,112,804; Total giving, $540,579.
Fields of interest: Higher education.
Type of support: Support to graduates or students of specific schools.
Application information: Applications accepted. Application form required.
   Initial approach: Letter
   Copies of proposal: 1
   Applicants should submit the following:
      1) Transcripts
      2) Letter(s) of recommendation
      3) GPA
      4) Financial information
      5) FAFSA
      6) Essay
      7) Budget Information
EIN: 770273721

756
Los Angeles Clippers Foundation
6951 S. Centinela Ave.
Playa Vista, CA 90094   (310) 862-6000
Contact: Denise Booth, Dir., Community Rels. and Player Programs
FAX: (310) 862-6039; URL: http://www.nba.com/clippers/community/lacf.html

Foundation type: Public charity
Purpose: Scholarships to Los Angeles, CA area high school seniors who plan to attend a four year college.
Publications: Application guidelines.
Financial data: Year ended 06/30/2013. Assets, $1,408,020 (M); Expenditures, $1,233,895; Total giving, $221,458; Grants to individuals, totaling $37,500.
Fields of interest: Higher education.
Type of support: Scholarships—to individuals.
Application information: Contact the foundation for application guidelines.
EIN: 954493310

757
Los Angeles County Developmental Services Foundation
3303 Wilshire Blvd., Ste. 700
Los Angeles, CA 90010-1710   (213) 383-1300
FAX: (213) 383-6526; E-mail: kyrc@lanterman.org;
URL: http://www.lanterman.org

Foundation type: Public charity
Purpose: Assistance to residents of California who have developmental disabilities, with food, clothing, living/rental help, medical expenses, transportation and other supported living services.
Financial data: Year ended 06/30/2012. Assets, $14,686,651 (M); Expenditures, $119,975,615; Total giving, $104,484,895; Grants to individuals, 13,000 grants totaling $104,483,895.
Fields of interest: Human services; Disabilities, people with.
Type of support: Grants for special needs.
Application information: Contact the organization for eligibility determination.
EIN: 953374648

758
Los Angeles Philharmonic Association
111 S. Grand Ave.
Los Angeles, CA 90012-3034   (323) 850-2000
For fellowship inquiries: education@laphil.org
URL: http://www.laphil.com

Foundation type: Public charity
Purpose: Awards and fellowships to young musicians and composers who reside in the Los Angeles, CA metropolitan area.
Financial data: Year ended 09/30/2011. Assets, $186,511,130 (M); Expenditures, $103,925,230.
Fields of interest: Music; Orchestras; Music composition.
Type of support: Fellowships; Awards/prizes.
Application information:
   Initial approach: Letter
   Additional information: See web site for a complete list of programs.
EIN: 951696734

759
Claude & Ada Low Foundation, Inc.
803 N. Cambridge St.
Orange, CA 92867-6843

Foundation type: Operating foundation
Purpose: Scholarships to graduates of Skyline High School, MO for continued education at accredited colleges or universities.
Financial data: Year ended 12/31/2011. Assets, $174,655 (M); Expenditures, $8,832; Total giving, $8,500; Grants to individuals, 7 grants totaling $8,500 (high: $3,000, low: $500).
Fields of interest: Higher education.
Type of support: Support to graduates or students of specific schools.
Application information: Applications accepted. Application form required.
   Deadline(s): Mar. 1
   Additional information: Applications are available in the principal's office.
EIN: 431628702

760
Oatha & Una Lucky Scholarship Trust
P.O. Box 56
Lakeport, CA 95453-0056   (707) 263-0627
Contact: Lauretta DeWeese, Tr.

Foundation type: Independent foundation
Purpose: Scholarships to financially needy graduating seniors of Clear Lake High School, Lakeport, CA for postsecondary education.
Financial data: Year ended 09/30/2013. Assets, $1,297,868 (M); Expenditures, $59,820; Total giving, $17,800; Grants to individuals, 53 grants totaling $17,800 (high: $500, low: $200).
Fields of interest: Higher education.
Type of support: Support to graduates or students of specific schools; Undergraduate support.
Application information: Application form required.
   Send request by: Mail
   Deadline(s): May 1
   Applicants should submit the following:
      1) Letter(s) of recommendation
      2) Resume
   Additional information: Application forms are available at Clear Lake High School.
EIN: 686121297

761
David Lynch Foundation For Consciousness-Based Education and World Peace
621 S. Highland Ave.
P.O. Box 93158
Los Angeles, CA 90036-3528   (641) 209-6404
Contact: Bob Roth, Exec. Dir.
FAX: (641) 742-1165;
E-mail: info@davidlynchfoundation.org; Toll-free tel.: (866) 962-0108; additional addresses: (New York office): 216 E. 45th St., 12th Fl., New York, NY 10017, tel.: (212) 644-9880; (Fairfield, IA office): 1000 N. 4th St., Fairfield, IA 52557-0001; URL: http://www.davidlynchfoundation.org

Foundation type: Public charity
Purpose: Scholarships for students who are currently enrolled, or have been accepted to Maharishi University of Management in Fairfield, IA to learn Transcendental Meditation (TM). Scholarships are also offered for students in grades 6 through 12.
Publications: Application guidelines.
Financial data: Year ended 06/30/2012. Assets, $2,705,848 (M); Expenditures, $7,011,065; Total giving, $4,335,793.
Type of support: Scholarships—to individuals; Support to graduates or students of specific schools.

Application information: Applications accepted.
Initial approach: Letter
EIN: 830436453

762
Berneice U. Lynn Foundation
1901 Camino Vida Roble, Ste. 110
Carlsbad, CA 92998 (760) 242-3241
Contact: Michael G. Perdue, Mgr.

Foundation type: Operating foundation
Purpose: Scholarships to graduating high school seniors of the high desert area of southern CA, who are studying science, technology or art.
Financial data: Year ended 12/31/2012. Assets, $1,862,873 (M); Expenditures, $180,191; Total giving, $79,158; Grants to individuals, 140 grants totaling $78,820 (high: $1,440, low: $63).
Type of support: Undergraduate support.
Application information: Applications accepted. Application form required.
Additional information: Contact foundation for current application deadline/guidelines.
EIN: 330555611

763
Bertha Russ Lytel Foundation
P.O. Box 893
Ferndale, CA 95536-0893 (707) 786-9236

Foundation type: Independent foundation
Purpose: Scholarships to graduates of Ferndale High School, CA, who are planning to attend a four-year university or college in CA and major in agriculture.
Publications: Application guidelines.
Financial data: Year ended 09/30/2012. Assets, $12,426,731 (M); Expenditures, $2,637,813; Total giving, $2,417,954.
Fields of interest: Formal/general education.
Type of support: Support to graduates or students of specific schools.
Application information: Applications accepted. Application form required.
Initial approach: Letter
Applicants should submit the following:
1) Transcripts
2) Essay
3) Letter(s) of recommendation
4) SAT
5) ACT
6) GPA
Additional information: If there are no eligible Ferndale High School students, students from Fortuna High School, CA, will be invited to participate.
Program description:
Russ Scholarship: Scholarships in the amount of $7,500 per year for four years, for a total of $30,000 to students majoring in agriculture at a four year university or college in California. Applicant must be a full time student (12 units) each term, maintain a minimum cumulative GPA of 2.0, and submit at the conclusion of each term, documentation to verify major, full time status and GPA.
EIN: 942271250

764
Christopher Michael Machado Foundation
c/o Bill Ringer
P.O. Box 676
Linden, CA 95236 (209) 931-6768

Foundation type: Independent foundation

Purpose: Scholarships to students of CA enrolled in a two or four year college or vocational school.
Financial data: Year ended 12/31/2011. Assets, $117,042 (M); Expenditures, $10,042; Total giving, $8,100; Grants to individuals, 4 grants totaling $8,100 (high: $2,600, low: $1,500).
Fields of interest: Vocational education, post-secondary; Higher education.
Type of support: Scholarships—to individuals.
Application information: Applications accepted. Application form required.
Applicants should submit the following:
1) Transcripts
2) GPA
3) Essay
Additional information: Proof of registration is required. Applicant must have an interest in music in school or outside of school and must have participated in two sports.
EIN: 680417725

765
Angus Madden Memorial Trust
6880 Dixon Ave. E.
Dixon, CA 95620-9685 (707) 678-5860
Contact: Dorothy Wallace, Secy.-Treas.

Foundation type: Independent foundation
Purpose: Scholarships to high school graduates of Dixon High School, CA for continuing education at accredited colleges or universities.
Financial data: Year ended 12/31/2011. Assets, $44,507 (M); Expenditures, $2,686; Total giving, $2,200; Grant to an individual, 1 grant totaling $2,200.
Fields of interest: Higher education.
Type of support: Support to graduates or students of specific schools.
Application information: Applications accepted. Application form required.
Deadline(s): Apr.
EIN: 946079999

766
Make-A-Wish Foundation of Sacramento and Northeastern CA
2800 Club Center Dr.
Sacramento, CA 95835 (916) 437-0206
Contact: Melinda Carson, Exec. Dir.
FAX: (916) 515-0649;
E-mail: info@sacnortheast.wish.org; Toll-free tel.: (888) 828-9474; URL: http://www.makeawish-sacto.org

Foundation type: Public charity
Purpose: Grants to fulfill the wishes of children who live with life threatening medical conditions primarily in Sacramento or northeastern CA.
Publications: Annual report; Newsletter.
Financial data: Year ended 08/31/2011. Assets, $10,436,689 (M); Expenditures, $3,035,248; Total giving, $1,417,874; Grants to individuals, totaling $1,417,874.
Fields of interest: Children/youth; Terminal illness, people with.
Type of support: Grants for special needs.
Application information: Applications accepted. Application form required. Application form available on the grantmaker's web site.
Initial approach: Download English or Spanish referral form
Additional information: Children may be referred by medical professionals treating the child such as doctors, nurses, social workers or child-life specialists; a parent or legal

guardian of the child or the potential wish child.
EIN: 680027351

767
Mammoth Lakes Foundation
100 College Pkwy.
P. O. Box 1815
Mammoth Lakes, CA 93546-1815 (760) 934-3781
Contact: Evan Russell, Pres. and C.E.O.
FAX: (760) 934-6019;
E-mail: info@mammothlakesfoundation.org;
URL: http://www.mammothlakesfoundation.org

Foundation type: Public charity
Purpose: Scholarships to high school graduates and residents of Mono County, CA, for higher education.
Financial data: Year ended 06/30/2012. Assets, $9,864,535 (M); Expenditures, $1,255,054; Total giving, $16,393; Grants to individuals, totaling $16,393.
Fields of interest: College (community/junior); Nursing school/education; Journalism school/education; Athletics/sports, winter sports.
Type of support: Scholarships—to individuals; Support to graduates or students of specific schools.
Application information: Applications accepted. Application form required.
Initial approach: Telephone
Additional information: See web site for additional guidelines.
Program description:
Scholarship: College scholarships for residents of the Mono County, CA, area who wish to further their education at the Mammoth Campus of Cerro Coso Community College, and have lived in the county for at least the past two years are eligible to apply. The scholarship covers the cost of enrollment fees and books for each scholarship recipient for up to sixty units or two years. Scholarship ranges from $800 to $1,000 each semester.
EIN: 770245395

768
So Mang Foundation
4538 Briney Point
La Verne, CA 91750

Foundation type: Independent foundation
Purpose: Grants by nomination only to Christian missionaries who need financial assistance in their theology study and pursuit of Christian world missions.
Financial data: Year ended 12/31/2012. Assets, $169,803 (M); Expenditures, $378,742; Total giving, $90,300.
Fields of interest: Theological school/education; Protestant agencies & churches.
Type of support: Grants to individuals.
Application information: Applications not accepted.
Additional information: Unsolicited requests for funds not considered or acknowledged.
EIN: 954658284

769
Marconi Society Inc.
P.O. Box 777
Mountain View, CA 94042-0777 (650) 207-8897
Contact: Hatti L. Hamlin, Exec. Dir.
E-mail: info@marconisociety.org; URL: http://www.marconifoundation.org

Foundation type: Operating foundation
Purpose: Awards by nomination only to individuals who have made an exceptional contribution to communications or information science and technology and thus improving human life.
Financial data: Year ended 06/30/2013. Assets, $0 (M); Expenditures, $419,348; Total giving, $116,681; Grants to individuals, 6 grants totaling $16,681 (high: $5,000, low: $600).
Fields of interest: Science.
Type of support: Research; Awards/grants by nomination only; Awards/prizes.
Application information:
   Send request by: Mail or e-mail
   Deadline(s): May 31 for Young Scholars Program, June 30 for Marconi Fellows Prize
   Applicants should submit the following:
   1) Resume
   2) Letter(s) of recommendation
   3) Curriculum vitae
Program descriptions:
   Marconi Fellows Prize: The Marconi Prize is awarded to individuals who have made a significant contribution to the advancement of communications through scientific or technological discoveries or innovations. Recipients are expected to pursue further creative work that will add to understanding and development of communications technology for the benefit of mankind. Recipients of the Marconi Prize are designated Marconi Fellows.
   Young Scholars Program: Candidates for this program must be actively engaged in research in a field related to information and communications science, and have already made significant contribution to one or more projects. They should have demonstrated entrepreneurial skills via innovation and leadership in application-focused projects. Applicants must be a student or recent graduate at the time the nomination is submitted and be age 27 or younger. Young scholars receive a $4,000 cash prize plus $1,000 in expenses to attend its annual awards gala.
EIN: 133959217

770
The Marguerite Home
(formerly The Marguerite Home, a Charitable Trust)
400 Capital Mall, Ste. 2200
Sacramento, CA 95814

Foundation type: Independent foundation
Purpose: Financial assistance to a group of preselected women who live in the Sacramento, CA, area, and are needy, elderly, and single.
Financial data: Year ended 06/30/2013. Assets, $1,436,908 (M); Expenditures, $69,430; Total giving, $49,410; Grants to individuals, 32 grants totaling $49,410 (high: $5,700, low: $300).
Fields of interest: Aging; Women.
Type of support: Grants for special needs.
Application information: Applications not accepted.
   Additional information: Contributes only to preselected individuals.
EIN: 946065622

771
Mariani Nut Company Foundation, Inc.
709 Dutton St.
P.O. Box 808
Winters, CA 95694-1748
Contact: Martin Mariani, Dir.

Foundation type: Operating foundation
Purpose: Scholarships to residents of Winters, CA in pursuit of a higher education.
Financial data: Year ended 08/31/2012. Assets, $1,256,701 (M); Expenditures, $85,052; Total giving, $67,239.
Type of support: Undergraduate support.
Application information:
   Initial approach: Letter
   Additional information: Contact foundation for eligibility requirements.
EIN: 680143635

772
Marin Community Foundation
5 Hamilton Landing, Ste. 200
Novato, CA 94949-8263 (415) 464-2500
Contact: Vikki Garrod, V.P., Mktg. and Comms.
FAX: (415) 464-2555; E-mail: info@marincf.org; URL: http://www.marincf.org

Foundation type: Community foundation
Purpose: Scholarships to graduating students of Marine County, CA for postsecondary education.
Publications: Application guidelines; Annual report; Informational brochure (including application guidelines); Newsletter.
Financial data: Year ended 06/30/2012. Assets, $1,333,725,159 (M); Expenditures, $59,136,825; Total giving, $59,136,825.
Fields of interest: Higher education.
Type of support: Scholarships—to individuals; Support to graduates or students of specific schools.
Application information: Applications accepted. Application form required.
   Deadline(s): Varies
   Additional information: Application should include letters of recommendation.
EIN: 943007979

773
James J. Marino Memorial Foundation
10671 Civic Center Dr.
Rancho Cucamonga, CA 91730-3804 (909) 476-0343
Contact: Thomas W. Marino, Pres.

Foundation type: Independent foundation
Purpose: Assistance to needy families and individuals in the CA area, who are experiencing financial hardship, and with medical expense.
Financial data: Year ended 12/31/2012. Assets, $16,384 (M); Expenditures, $169,742; Total giving, $168,345; Grants to individuals, 4 grants totaling $166,849 (high: $141,796; low: $450).
Fields of interest: Human services; Family services.
Type of support: Grants for special needs.
Application information:
   Initial approach: Letter
EIN: 710889391

774
Peter and Madeleine Martin Foundation for the Creative Arts
385 Hayes St.
San Francisco, CA 94102-4420

Foundation type: Independent foundation
Purpose: Awards and project support to artists and writers in NM.
Financial data: Year ended 12/31/2011. Assets, $448,513 (M); Expenditures, $34,040; Total giving, $25,475; Grant to an individual, 1 grant totaling $5,000.
Fields of interest: Literature; Arts, artist's services; Arts.
Type of support: Program development; Awards/prizes.
Application information: Applications not accepted.
EIN: 943113049

775
Masonic Homes of California
1111 California St.
San Francisco, CA 94108-2252 (415) 776-7000
E-mail: dismail@californiamasons.org; URL: http://www.masonichome.org

Foundation type: Public charity
Purpose: Scholarships to residents of the Masonic Homes of California or former residents who wish to pursue a defined course of study at an accredited college or university, or technical/vocational school. Assistance to the elderly and children of California with ongoing financial and care support.
Financial data: Year ended 10/31/2011. Assets, $823,335,790 (M); Expenditures, $47,100,257; Total giving, $3,554,999; Grants to individuals, totaling $3,530,549.
Fields of interest: Higher education; Economically disadvantaged.
Type of support: Scholarships—to individuals; Grants for special needs.
Application information: Applications accepted. Application form required.
   Additional information: Applicants must demonstrate need.
EIN: 941156564

776
Mathematical Sciences Research Institute
(also known as MSRI)
17 Gauss Way
Berkeley, CA 94720-5070 (510) 642-0143
Contact: Lisa Jacobs, Exec. Asst.
FAX: (510) 642-8609;
E-mail: msri-inquiries@msri.org; URL: http://www.msri.org

Foundation type: Public charity
Purpose: The institute makes grants and awards to individuals for the advancement and study of mathematics. Support is made to the following levels of study: 1) Postdoctoral; 2) Graduate Student; 3) Undergraduate Student; and 4) K-12 Educators.
Publications: Newsletter.
Financial data: Year ended 07/31/2011. Assets, $24,884,416 (M); Expenditures, $8,652,729; Total giving, $2,259,460; Grants to individuals, totaling $2,220,460.
Fields of interest: Mathematics.
Type of support: Fellowships; Research; Scholarships—to individuals; Awards/prizes.
Application information: Applications accepted.
   Additional information: See institute web site for specific program application guidelines.
Program descriptions:
   Postdoctoral Fellows: These awards provide support for five months for one-semester programs.

MSRI expects Postdoctoral Fellows to be in residence for the entire period of their fellowship while their program is in session. The fellowship stipend is currently $5,000 per month, with a travel subsidy for one round-trip from your current institution, and a research travel budget of $600. Health insurance is also provided. See institute web site for further details and application information.

Research Members: Research memberships may be offered with no support, with a travel allowance and/or with per diem support. Research memberships are normally not offered for stays of less than one month, and preference will be given to those who can attend for longer periods. Research Members who receive support for an extended visit normally are granted a travel allowance for one round-trip from their home institution. The per diem level is currently $100 per day for stays of one month or more; and up to $140 per day for short stays. Members can receive per diem support only during their dates of residency while the program is in session. Members who receive an award of support should hold a Ph.D. at the time of their proposed residency; financial support is not available for graduate students. Some preference is given to U.S. applicants. See institute web site for application information.

Research Professors: Research Professors can receive partial salary compensation at a pay rate of up to $5,000 per month prorated for the duration of residency during the scheduled dates of the program. Members who receive salary support for an extended visit normally are granted a travel allowance for one round-trip from their home institution. Research Professors are automatically eligible for consideration for appointment as Simons Professors or Eisenbud Professors. Nominations for these special professorships are made by the organizing committees of the programs; no separate application is necessary. See institute web site for further information.
EIN: 942650833

777
Matsui Foundation
c/o Teresa Matsui Sanders
1645 Old Stage Rd.
Salinas, CA   93908-9737   (831) 422-6433, Ext. 206
E-mail: teresa@matsuinursery.com; URL: http://andymatsuifoundation.org/

Foundation type: Operating foundation
Purpose: College scholarships to lower income high school graduates who are residents of Monterey county, CA, and to community college sophomores for continuing education.
Financial data: Year ended 12/31/2012. Assets, $1,037,375 (M); Expenditures, $632,765; Total giving, $561,000; Grants to individuals, 64 grants totaling $545,000.
Fields of interest: College (community/junior).
Type of support: Scholarships—to individuals.
Application information: Selection is based on those who demonstrate outstanding potential for success in college but are experiencing economic hardship.
EIN: 200483500

778
McComb Fund
P.O. Box 60078
Los Angeles, CA   90060-0078   (408) 490-2191

Foundation type: Public charity

Purpose: Scholarships to graduating seniors of Thomasville High School, GA for postsecondary education at a public or private institution.
Financial data: Year ended 12/31/2011. Assets, $340,718 (M); Expenditures, $25,754; Total giving, $19,000; Grants to individuals, totaling $19,000.
Fields of interest: Higher education.
Type of support: Support to graduates or students of specific schools.
Application information: Applications accepted. Application form required.
  Send request by: Mail
  Deadline(s): Apr. 20
  Final notification: Applicant notified on or before graduation each year
  Additional information: Applicants must have attended Thomasville High School for at least two years. Scholarships will be awarded on the basis of need, demonstrated ability and desire. Application can be obtained from your high school counselor. Payment will be made directly to the educational institution on behalf of the student.
EIN: 946489554

779
The McConnell Foundation
800 Shasta View Dr.
Redding, CA   96003-8208   (530) 226-6200
Contact: Lee W. Salter, C.E.O. and Pres.
FAX: (530) 226-6230;
E-mail: info@mcconnellfoundation.org; URL: http://www.mcconnellfoundation.org

Foundation type: Independent foundation
Purpose: Scholarships to residents of Modoc, Shasta, Siskiyou, Tehama and Trinity counties, CA, as well as students of Big Valley High School in Lassen County.
Publications: Annual report; Newsletter.
Financial data: Year ended 12/31/2012. Assets, $342,881,858 (M); Expenditures, $19,489,519; Total giving, $6,983,674; Grants to individuals, totaling $706,564.
Fields of interest: Higher education; Scholarships/financial aid.
International interests: Laos; Nepal.
Type of support: Support to graduates or students of specific schools; Undergraduate support.
Application information: Applications not accepted.
  Additional information: Contact foundation for further application guidelines. Unsolicited requests for funds not considered or acknowledged.
Program descriptions:
  The McConnell Scholars Program: This program is for first-time freshman or transfer juniors seeking Bachelor's degrees at qualified four-year colleges and universities. The foundation offers each recipient an award of up to $30K based on need, personal mentoring and professional development opportunities. Any amounts not spent during the Bachelor's degree may be rolled forward towards graduate school.
  The McConnell Vista Program: The program provides financial and non-financial support to students who have the potential to be successful at community college, but who might not otherwise have the opportunity to attend. This program offers up to $30K for students who wish to complete an AA transfer degree, AS degree or Certificate Program at College of the Siskiyous or Shasta College. Recipients are eligible for up to three years of support at a community college. Students who successfully transfer to qualified four-year

institution are eligible for an additional three years, and may carryover any unused amount of the $30K.
EIN: 946102700

780
Margaret L. McQuinn Scholarship Foundation
3263 San Jose Ave.
Alameda, CA   94501-4863   (510) 522-8749
Contact: Linda Larkin, Pres.

Foundation type: Independent foundation
Purpose: Scholarships to deserving and needy high school students in the Alameda/Oakland, CA area for higher education.
Financial data: Year ended 12/31/2012. Assets, $3,954,717 (M); Expenditures, $211,134; Total giving, $195,000; Grants to individuals, 38 grants totaling $195,000 (high: $5,000, low: $1,500).
Fields of interest: Education.
Type of support: Scholarships—to individuals.
Application information: Applications accepted.
  Initial approach: Letter
EIN: 450499860

781
Media Alliance
1904 Franklin St., Ste. 818
Oakland, CA   94612-2926   (510) 684-6853
Contact: Tracy Rosenberg, Exec. Dir.
FAX: (510) 238-8557;
E-mail: information@media-alliance.org; E-mail For Tracy Rosenberg : tracy@media-alliance.org;
URL: http://www.media-alliance.org

Foundation type: Public charity
Purpose: Support to individuals through a fiscal sponsorship program.
Financial data: Year ended 12/31/2011. Assets, $88,856 (M); Expenditures, $56,173.
Fields of interest: Media/communications.
Type of support: Fiscal agent/sponsor.
Application information: Applications accepted.
Program description:
  Fiscal Sponsorship: The alliance provides fiscal sponsorship as a means of support to a small number of outstanding media projects through its arts, organizing and advocacy programs. These projects are able to benefit from 501(c)(3) status and accept tax-deductible contributions, though they are not 501(c)(3) organizations themselves. Both organizations and individuals are eligible to apply.
EIN: 942563400

782
Media Arts Center San Diego
2921 El Cajon Blvd.
San Diego, CA   92102-2705   (619) 230-1938
Contact: Ethan van Thillo, Exec. Dir.
FAX: (619) 230-1937;
E-mail: info@mediaartscenter.org; E-mail for Ethan van Thillo: ethan@mediaartscenter.org;
URL: http://www.mediaartscenter.org

Foundation type: Public charity
Purpose: Fiscal sponsorship support for media artists working in film, video, audio and computer based multi media.
Publications: Newsletter.
Financial data: Year ended 06/30/2011. Assets, $348,086 (M); Expenditures, $1,095,042.
Fields of interest: Film/video; Arts, artist's services.

Type of support: Fiscal agent/sponsor.
Application information: Applications accepted.
  Initial approach: Fiscal sponsorship proposal
  Copies of proposal: 1
  Applicants should submit the following:
    1) Resume
    2) Proposal
    3) Budget Information
  Additional information: Application should also
    include a detailed description of the project.
Program description:
  Fiscal Sponsorship: Under the center's fiscal
  sponsorship program, members can conduct their
  film and video projects under the center's non-profit
  umbrella, allowing them to apply for grants, and to
  accept tax deductible contributions from individuals
  for an administrative charge of five percent.
EIN: 330871577

783
Memorial Scholarship Foundation of the Music Teachers Association of California, Alemada County Branch
2908 Minna Ave.
Oakland, CA   94619-1712
Contact: Grace Yu

Foundation type: Independent foundation
Purpose: Music scholarships and awards to
students of members of the Music Teachers
Association of Alameda County, CA.
Financial data: Year ended 05/31/2013. Assets,
$440,104 (M); Expenditures, $20,950; Total
giving, $13,160.
Fields of interest: Music; Performing arts,
education.
Type of support: Awards/grants by nomination only;
Awards/prizes.
Application information: Applications accepted.
  Additional information: Contact foundation for
    current application deadline/guidelines;
    Auditions required.
EIN: 237165104

784
Menlo Park-Atherton Education Foundation
181 Encinal Ave.
Atherton, CA   94027-3102   (650) 325-0100
Contact: Lynne Van Tilburg, Exec. Dir.
E-mail: mpaef@mpaef.org; E-Mail for Lynne Van
Tilburg : LynneV@mpaef.org; URL: http://
www.mpaef.org

Foundation type: Public charity
Purpose: Grants to teachers who are employed by
the Menlo Park City School District, CA, to fund
classroom instructional programs.
Publications: Annual report; Newsletter.
Financial data: Year ended 06/30/2011. Assets,
$5,230,950 (M); Expenditures, $2,935,183; Total
giving, $2,600,000.
Fields of interest: Elementary/secondary
education; Teacher school/education; Education.
Type of support: Project support.
Application information: Application form required.
Application form available on the grantmaker's web
site.
  Deadline(s): Oct. 15
  Additional information: Application must include
    detailed budget.
EIN: 942871701

785
Merage Foundation for U.S.- Israel Trade
4350 Von Karman Ave., 4th Fl.
Newport Beach, CA   92660-2043
URL: http://www.merage.com/

Foundation type: Operating foundation
Purpose: Stipends by nomination only, to
exceptional immigrant students enrolled at the
Foundation's Partner Universities for participation
in the Merage American Dream Fellows program.
Residencies to youth in Orange county interested in
a career in filmmaking.
Financial data: Year ended 12/31/2011. Assets,
$0 (M); Expenditures, $378,514; Total giving, $0.
Fields of interest: Film/video; Immigrants/
refugees.
Type of support: Fellowships; Awards/grants by
nomination only; Residencies; Stipends.
Application information: Applications accepted.
Application form required. Application form
available on the grantmaker's web site. Interview
required.
  Initial approach: Letter
  Deadline(s): May for Artists in Residence
  Applicants should submit the following:
    1) Letter(s) of recommendation
    2) Transcripts
    3) GPA
  Additional information: See web site for selected
    high schools for Artists in Residence program.
Program descriptions:
  Merage American Dream Fellows: Every year,
  exceptional immigrant students at the Foundation's
  Partner Universities apply to participate in the
  Merage American Dream Fellows program. Each
  Partner University nominates up to three
  candidates for the program. The Foundation selects
  Fellows based on their academic record, their
  leadership, their consistent ethical behavior, the
  clarity of their American Dream, and their potential
  to make an important contribution to America.
  Merage Fellows receive two-year stipends of
  $20,000 ($10,000 each year) to help them pursue
  their American Dream. The Foundation also
  provides Merage Fellows with strategic access to
  mentors and leaders in their chosen careers.
  Candidates must be citizens or permanent
  residents of the United States, be full-time students
  with senior class status, and graduate between the
  December of their year of application and August of
  the following year.
  *Orange County Student Artists in Residence
  Program:* Fourteen talented, low-income high school
  students will work with veteran professors from the
  Dodge College of Film and Media Arts in a two-week,
  educational program. The students will learn the
  language of film, watch and discuss films to explore
  how images create meaning, and learn various
  aspects of the craft of filmmaking, as well as field
  trips in Orange County or Los Angeles. During the
  course of the program, students will work in groups
  thereby improving social and creative
  problem-solving skills, screen their own films, for
  their families and friends at an end-of-the-season
  celebration at the Marion Knott Studios. Interested
  OCHSA students should submit a completed
  application form, a one-page statement about why
  they would like to be part of the Artists in Residence
  program, a five- to ten-minute reel of their work, and
  a statement describing their contribution to the
  material on the reel. Students must be incoming
  juniors or seniors, passed or enrolled in film
  courses and have a 3.0 GPA or above.
EIN: 201836187

786
Mercy Hospital Foundation
3400 Data Dr., 3rd Fl.
Rancho Cordova, CA   95670-7956   (916)
851-2700
FAX: (916) 851-2724;
E-mail: mercyfoundationsac@chw.edu; URL: http://
www.supportmercyfoundation.org/index.htm

Foundation type: Public charity
Purpose: Crespi Scholarships are awarded to
Sacramento City College nursing students based on
financial need and passion for the nursing
profession.
Financial data: Year ended 06/30/2011. Assets,
$35,077,987 (M); Expenditures, $8,727,815;
Total giving, $5,778,229; Grants to individuals,
totaling $12,250.
Fields of interest: Nursing school/education.
Type of support: Support to graduates or students
of specific schools.
Application information: Applications accepted.
Application form required.
  Initial approach: E-mail
  Additional information: Awards are disbursed in
    the summer. For more information about the
    Kimberly Ann Crespi Scholarship, contact
    Trisha Pena at Trisha.Pena@dignityhealth.org.
EIN: 237072762

787
Methodist Foundation of Santa Monica
1008 11th St.
Santa Monica, CA   90403-4107   (310)
393-8258
Contact: John Stutsman, Pres.

Foundation type: Public charity
Purpose: Educational scholarship to college and
trade school students of Santa Monica, CA for
higher education. Assistance in repayment of
educational loans for pastors from related church
pursuing their religious degrees.
Financial data: Year ended 12/31/2012. Assets,
$3,637,899 (M); Expenditures, $139,627; Total
giving, $114,353; Grants to individuals, totaling
$36,518.
Fields of interest: Vocational education,
post-secondary; Higher education; Theological
school/education.
Type of support: Scholarships—to individuals;
Student loans—to individuals.
Application information: Applications accepted.
  Additional information: Scholarship selection is
    based on merit, need and church services.
EIN: 956201324

788
Mexican American Legal Defense and Educational Fund
634 S. Spring St., Ste. 12
Los Angeles, CA   90014-3921   (213) 629-2512
Contact: Thomas A. Saenz, Pres.
FAX: (213) 629-0266; URL: http://
www.maldef.org/

Foundation type: Public charity
Purpose: Scholarships to deserving students
enrolled at an accredited law school in the U.S.
Publications: Application guidelines; Annual report;
Informational brochure; Newsletter.
Financial data: Year ended 04/30/2012. Assets,
$9,269,033 (M); Expenditures, $7,101,262; Total
giving, $359,500; Grants to individuals, totaling
$359,500.

Fields of interest: Law school/education; Hispanics/Latinos.
Type of support: Scholarships—to individuals.
Application information: Applications accepted. Application form required. Application form available on the grantmaker's web site.
Send request by: Mail
Deadline(s): Jan. 2
Applicants should submit the following:
1) Transcripts
2) Resume
3) Financial information
4) Letter(s) of recommendation
Additional information: Application should also include a typed personal statement of 750 words or less detailing academic and extracurricular achievements, background and financial need, record of service to the Latino community, and goals in law. See web site for additional guidelines.
Program descriptions:
DREAM Act Student Activist Scholarship: This scholarship is meant to support college and graduate student leaders who have been outstanding advocates for the DREAM Act and all immigrant rights. Scholarships of up to $5,000 will be awarded to each deserving DREAM Act student activist. All current college and graduate students are eligible to apply. Students seeking to enroll in college or university for the first time (or to re-enroll following a leave of absence) are also eligible to apply if they will be enrolled in a college or university before the end of 2012.
Law School Scholarship: The fund supports matriculated law students during the completion of their degrees through offering five to ten scholarships of up to $5,000 to qualified individuals in pursuit of higher education.
EIN: 741563270

789
Mexico Foundation
(also known as Camellia Foundation)
750 B St., Ste. 3020
San Diego, CA   92101-4275   (619) 814-1400
Contact: Tobias Gorodzinsky, Secy.

Foundation type: Independent foundation
Purpose: Scholarships to Mexican students pursuing higher education.
Financial data: Year ended 01/31/2013. Assets, $469,954 (M); Expenditures, $46,744; Total giving, $35,000; Grants to individuals, 14 grants totaling $35,000 (high: $2,500, low: $2,500).
Fields of interest: Hispanics/Latinos.
Type of support: Scholarships—to individuals; Foreign applicants.
Application information: Applications accepted.
Initial approach: Letter
Deadline(s): None
Applicants should submit the following:
1) Financial information
2) Transcripts
Additional information: Application must also include intended area of study and reason.
EIN: 330099230

790
Madeline Miedema Trust
c/o Wells Fargo Bank, N.A.
P.O. Box 63954, MAC A0348-012
San Francisco, CA   94163-0001

Foundation type: Independent foundation

Purpose: Scholarships to graduates of the Oxnard Unified School District, CA, who are admitted to a four-year college or university in California.
Financial data: Year ended 12/31/2011. Assets, $443,859 (M); Expenditures, $28,212; Total giving, $18,970.
Fields of interest: Higher education.
Type of support: Scholarships—to individuals; Support to graduates or students of specific schools.
Application information: Applications accepted.
Deadline(s): None
Additional information: Recipients of scholarships are selected by a committee.
EIN: 956592661

791
Military Women In Need Foundation
(formerly California Soldiers' Widows Home Association)
10767 National Place, Unit B
Los Angeles, CA   90034   (310) 684-3854
FAX: (310) 380-5277;
E-mail: info@militarywomeninneed.org; Mailing address: c/o Mariana Sosa, Opers. Mgr., 2355 Westwood Blvd., #350, Los Angeles, CA 90064;
URL: http://www.militarywomeninneed.org

Foundation type: Independent foundation
Purpose: Grants to female residents of southern CA who are veterans or widows of U.S. Armed Forces veterans and are in need of housing assistance. Recipients must be at least 55 years of age, have resided in CA for the past five years, have assets of $20,000 or less (excluding one car), be able to live independently, and have an annual income of less than $15,000.
Financial data: Year ended 06/30/2012. Assets, $1,979,650 (M); Expenditures, $327,463; Total giving, $253,800.
Fields of interest: Housing/shelter, expense aid; Women.
Type of support: Grants for special needs.
Application information: Applications accepted.
Initial approach: Letter
Deadline(s): Contact association for current application deadline
Additional information: Application should copy of latest payroll, SSA or other check, income and expense documentation for verification and budget purposes, and documents verifying assets.
EIN: 953533990

792
The Milken Family Foundation
1250 4th St.
Santa Monica, CA   90401-1353
Contact: Richard Sandler, Exec. V.P.
FAX: (310) 570-4801; E-mail: admin@mff.org;
URL: http://www.mff.org

Foundation type: Independent foundation
Purpose: Awards to educators, and scholarships and educational opportunities to high school seniors.
Financial data: Year ended 11/30/2012. Assets, $378,108,280 (M); Expenditures, $11,456,371; Total giving, $7,514,862.
Fields of interest: Higher education; Volunteer services; Leadership development.
Type of support: Research; Scholarships—to individuals; Awards/prizes.
Application information: Applications not accepted.

Additional information: Nominations not accepted for Educator Awards; Unsolicited nominations/applications by individuals are not accepted by the foundation for Jewish Educator Awards, Milken Educator Awards, or Milken Scholars Program.
Program descriptions:
Jewish Educator Awards: The foundation, in cooperation with the Bureau of Jewish Education of Greater Los Angeles (BJE), established the program in 1990. The program annually offers four awards of $15,000 each to educators based upon their demonstrated excellence as teachers, administrators or other education professionals who work directly with students and other teachers in day schools affiliated with BJE. The award recipients are selected by a committee of educators, professional and lay leaders from the Jewish community who have a long-standing concern for and involvement with education in Jewish schools. To be eligible for consideration, educators must teach a minimum of 15 hours per week at the K-12 level and they must have been teaching for a minimum of seven years in a BJE-affiliated school. Applications are not accepted by the Milken Family Foundation.
Milken Educator Awards: Established in 1987, the goals of the program are: 1) to honor and reward outstanding K-12 educators for the quality of their teaching, their professional leadership, their engagement with families and the community, and their potential for even greater contribution to the healthy development of children; 2) to focus public attention on the importance of excellent educators; 3) to encourage able, caring and creative people to choose the challenge, service and adventure of teaching as a career; 4) to create national and state networks of Milken Educators; and 5) to engage corporate and foundation partners in support of Milken Educators and in advocacy of policies that advance education. There is no formal nomination or application process. Every participating state's department of education appoints an independent blue ribbon committee to recommend candidates according to strict criteria, with final selections made by the Milken Family Foundation.
Milken Scholars: The program offers Milken Scholars four years of financial assistance and access to a range of resources. These include career-related counseling and internships, community service activities, shadowing partnerships and a graduate fund to assist Scholars with preparatory courses for either graduate school or the world of work. Scholars are chosen in the spring semester of their senior year of high school through a nomination, review, and interview process that recruits candidates from high schools in Los Angeles, and New York City. Criteria for selection include distinguished academic performance, school and community service, demonstrated leadership, and financial need. Students interested in becoming a Milken Scholar should speak with their college advisor about the nomination process at their school.
EIN: 954073646

793
Casper Mills Scholarship Foundation
1137 2nd. St. Ste. 207
Santa Monica, CA   90403   (310) 449-0143
Contact: Kevin J. Axelrad, Pres. and Dir.
Application Address: 12340 Santa Monica Blvd., Ste. 212, Los Angeles, CA 90025

Foundation type: Independent foundation

Purpose: Graduate and undergraduate scholarships to financially needy orphans and individuals from broken homes, who reside in CA.
Publications: Program policy statement.
Financial data: Year ended 07/31/2013. Assets, $1,899,259 (M); Expenditures, $244,201; Total giving, $52,500; Grants to individuals, 15 grants totaling $52,500 (high: $6,000, low: $2,000).
Fields of interest: Children, services; Residential/custodial care.
Type of support: Graduate support; Undergraduate support.
Application information: Application form required. Interview required.
   Initial approach: Letter
   Deadline(s): Aug. 31
EIN: 510174623

794
William R. Mills Trust B
600 Wilshire Blvd., Ste. 1515
Los Angeles, CA   90017   (562) 423-8777
Contact: Larry Stone
Application address: 300 N. Lake Ave., Ste. 210, Pasadena, CA 91101

Foundation type: Independent foundation
Purpose: Scholarships to financially needy undergraduate students at the University of Southern California and Syracuse University, NY.
Financial data: Year ended 12/31/2011. Assets, $801,540 (M); Expenditures, $31,260; Total giving, $7,500.
Type of support: Support to graduates or students of specific schools; Undergraduate support.
Application information: Applications accepted. Application form required.
   Deadline(s): Apr. 1
EIN: 956487535

795
Mills-Peninsula Hospital Foundation
1501 Trousdale Dr.
Burlingame, CA   94010-4506   (916) 286-6665
URL: http://www.mills-peninsula.org/foundation/

Foundation type: Public charity
Purpose: Scholarships to individuals pursuing a career in the medical or nursing professions, and to employees of Mills Peninsula Hospital, CA.
Financial data: Year ended 12/31/2011. Assets, $41,914,767 (M); Expenditures, $8,860,899; Total giving, $6,140,072; Grants to individuals, totaling $24,000.
Fields of interest: Medical school/education; Nursing school/education.
Type of support: Scholarships—to individuals.
Application information: Applications accepted.
   Initial approach: Letter
   Additional information: Contact foundation for complete eligibility criteria.
EIN: 237288765

796
Missionary Enterprises
P.O. Box 2127
La Habra, CA   90632

Foundation type: Independent foundation
Purpose: Grants to Christian missionaries to support mission projects.
Financial data: Year ended 12/31/2012. Assets, $0 (M); Expenditures, $15,779; Total giving, $9,070.
Fields of interest: Christian agencies & churches.

Type of support: Grants to individuals.
Application information: Applications not accepted.
EIN: 952152466

797
Mitchell-Gantz Educational & Charitable Trust
PO Box 60078 SC-MPK-03-M
Los Angeles, CA   90060

Foundation type: Independent foundation
Purpose: Scholarships to residents of Arthur, Box Butte, Cherry, Dawes, Garden, Grant, Hooker, Morrill, Sheridan, and Sioux counties, NE.
Financial data: Year ended 09/30/2013. Assets, $333,295 (M); Expenditures, $16,968; Total giving, $12,500; Grants to individuals, 14 grants totaling $12,500 (high: $1,000, low: $500).
Fields of interest: Law school/education; Medical school/education.
Type of support: Graduate support.
Application information: Application form required.
   Deadline(s): Mar. 31
   Applicants should submit the following:
      1) Letter(s) of recommendation
      2) Transcripts
      3) Photograph
      4) SAT
      5) ACT
      6) Essay
   Additional information: Application must also include parents' tax returns; Applications available through high school guidance counselors.
EIN: 476080709

798
Modesto Rotary Club Foundation
P.O. Box 672
Modesto, CA   95353-0972   (209) 577-4500

Foundation type: Public charity
Purpose: Scholarships by nomination only to students in the Modesto, CA, area.
Financial data: Year ended 06/30/2012. Assets, $391,322 (M); Expenditures, $96,417; Total giving, $30,357.
Type of support: Awards/grants by nomination only.
Application information: Applications not accepted.
   Additional information: Unsolicited requests for funds not considered or acknowledged.
EIN: 942413021

799
Modesto Union Gospel Mission, Inc.
1400 Yosemite Blvd.
P.O. Box 1203
Modesto, CA   95353-2840   (209) 529-8259
FAX: (209) 529-3450;
E-mail: info@homelessmission.org; *URL:* http://www.homelessmission.org

Foundation type: Public charity
Purpose: Assisstance to men, women and childern with shelter, food, clothing, and other needs in the Modesto, CA, area.
Financial data: Year ended 12/31/2011. Assets, $6,616,358 (M); Expenditures, $5,942,947; Total giving, $3,655,148; Grants to individuals, totaling $3,655,148.
Fields of interest: Human services; Children; Women; Men; Economically disadvantaged.
Type of support: Grants for special needs.

Application information: Applications not accepted.
   Additional information: Contact the mission for assistance See web site or contact the mission for assistance.
EIN: 946102833

800
The Modglin Family Foundation
3100 Airway Ave., Ste. 124
Costa Mesa, CA   92626-4604

Foundation type: Independent foundation
Purpose: Scholarships to students for attendance at southern CA theological seminaries.
Financial data: Year ended 12/31/2012. Assets, $4,517,471 (M); Expenditures, $318,152; Total giving, $278,335.
Fields of interest: Theological school/education; Christian agencies & churches.
Type of support: Graduate support.
Application information: Applications not accepted.
EIN: 330266405

801
Modoc Scholarship Fund, Inc.
510 N. Main St.
Alturas, CA   96101   (530) 233-1999
Contact: Dwight Beesom, Chair.

Foundation type: Operating foundation
Purpose: Scholarships to graduates of Modec High School, Alturas, CA.
Financial data: Year ended 12/31/2012. Assets, $299,216 (M); Expenditures, $5,759; Total giving, $5,000.
Type of support: Support to graduates or students of specific schools.
Application information:
   Initial approach: Letter
EIN: 680143501

802
Montalvo Arts Center
(formerly Montalvo Association)
P.O. Box 158
Saratoga, CA   95071-0158   (408) 961-5800
Contact: Angela McConnell, Exec. Dir.
FAX: (408) 961-5850;
E-mail: nglace@montalvoarts.org; *URL:* http://www.montalvoarts.org

Foundation type: Public charity
Purpose: Residencies to writers, poets, playwrights, filmmakers, musicians, composers, architects, and visual artists to stay at Montalvo, an artists' retreat located in CA.
Financial data: Year ended 09/30/2011. Assets, $13,660,550 (M); Expenditures, $4,687,651. No monetary support given for residencies.
Fields of interest: Film/video; Visual arts; Architecture; Theater; Theater (playwriting); Music; Music composition; Literature.
Type of support: Residencies.
Application information: Applications not accepted.
   Additional information: Applications by invitation only. Applicants are selected by an international pool of recommenders.
Program descriptions:
   Culinary Fellowship: This fellowship is awarded annually to an emerging chef with a strong interest in sustainable agriculture and cuisine. The program is designed to support the chef in gaining the

experience of running their own kitchen and developing their repertoire. The fellow will live on-site for a year, cooking for Artists-in-residence and will be involved in the production of the food as well as workshop events and classes.

The Sally and Don Lucas Artists Program: The residency seeks to support underserved artists who might not find their way into a residency program. Residencies are offered in all contemporary artistic disciplines including the visual arts, design, literary arts, film, choreography, performance art, music and composition, and teaching artists. Nominated artists are invited to apply for a fellowship. All applicants are then juried by professionals in their respective fields. Selected artists are offered a one to three month fellowship.

EIN: 941249283

803
Monterey Bay Marine Sanctuary Foundation

299 Foam St., Ste. D
Monterey, CA 93940-1499 (831) 644-9600
Contact: Scott Hennessy, Pres.
FAX: (831) 647-4244; E-mail: info@mbnmsf.org; URL: http://www.mbnmsf.org

Foundation type: Public charity
Purpose: Support through a fiscal sponsorship program to individuals whose projects are consistent with the goals and mission of the MBSF.
Financial data: Year ended 12/31/2011. Assets, $3,820,561 (M); Expenditures, $1,848,674; Total giving, $270,884.
Fields of interest: Water pollution; Environment, water resources.
Type of support: Fiscal agent/sponsor.
Application information: Applications accepted.
 Initial approach: Submit written grant request
Program description:
 Fiscal Sponsorship: As a fiscal sponsor, the foundation establishes a pre-approved grant relationship with an independent party. The foundation may then, on behalf of the independent party, accept grant funds for projects that are consistent with the goals and mission of the foundation. The foundation funds such projects only to the extent that money is received from donors. An administrative fee is negotiated for services.
EIN: 943225675

804
Monterey County Association of Realtors

201 Calle Del Oaks
Del Rey Oaks, CA 93940

Foundation type: Independent foundation
Purpose: Scholarships to students in CA, for higher education.
Financial data: Year ended 12/31/2013. Assets, $98,939 (M); Expenditures, $24,152; Total giving, $22,500; Grants to individuals, 15 grants totaling $22,500 (high: $1,500, low: $1,500).
Fields of interest: Higher education.
Type of support: Undergraduate support.
Application information: Applications not accepted.
 Additional information: Applications by letter. Unsolicited requests for funds not considered or acknowledged.
EIN: 237165412

805
Morgan Family Foundation, Inc.

6130 Stoneridge Mall Rd., Ste. 185
Pleasanton, CA 94588-3290

Foundation type: Independent foundation
Purpose: Scholarships to students residing in CA for higher education.
Financial data: Year ended 12/31/2012. Assets, $121,276 (M); Expenditures, $736,790; Total giving, $730,781; Grants to individuals, totaling $153,631.
Type of support: Undergraduate support.
Application information: Applications not accepted.
 Additional information: Unsolicited requests for funds not considered or acknowledged.
EIN: 912081052

806
Muriel M. Morris Educational Foundation

6880 Dixon Ave. E.
Dixon, CA 95620-9685 (707) 678-5860
Contact: Dorothy Wallace, Secy.-Treas.

Foundation type: Independent foundation
Purpose: Scholarships to graduates of Dixon High School, CA, for higher education.
Financial data: Year ended 12/31/2011. Assets, $745,643 (M); Expenditures, $39,138; Total giving, $38,250; Grants to individuals, 4 grants totaling $20,000 (high: $5,000, low: $5,000).
Type of support: Support to graduates or students of specific schools; Undergraduate support.
Application information: Application form required.
 Deadline(s): Apr.
EIN: 680311581

807
Motion Picture & Television Fund

23388 Mulholland Dr., No. 220
Woodland Hills, CA 91364-2792 (818) 876-1977
E-mail: info@mptf.com; Toll-free tel.: (855)-760-6783; URL: http://www.mptvfund.org

Foundation type: Public charity
Purpose: Emergency financial assistance to industry members of southern CA, who experience financial hardship due to illness, disability, unemployment or other reasons.
Publications: Financial statement.
Financial data: Year ended 12/31/2011. Assets, $192,929,126 (M); Expenditures, $106,768,494; Total giving, $1,508,093; Grants to individuals, totaling $1,508,093.
Fields of interest: Film/video; Television; Human services.
Type of support: Grants for special needs.
Application information: Applications accepted.
 Additional information: Applicant must show financial need.
Program description:
 Financial Assistance: Temporary emergency financial assistance is available for qualifying industry members who experience financial hardship. Assistance is provided to meet immediate needs including food and shelter, home care and other emergencies.
EIN: 951652916

808
John Muir Health

1400 Treat Blvd., Ste. 300
Walnut Creek, CA 94597-2142 (925) 947-4449
Contact: Calvin Knight, Pres. and C.E.O.
Additional info. for Concord Volunteer Scholarships: John Muir Medical Center, Concord, Volunteer Scholarship Fund, P.O. Box 4110, Concord, CA 94542-4110
E-mail: info@johnmuirhealth.com; URL: http://www.johnmuirhealth.com

Foundation type: Public charity
Purpose: Scholarships for individuals of Concord or Walnut Creek, CA pursuing a career in a medical related or health care field.
Publications: Annual report.
Financial data: Year ended 12/31/2011. Assets, $1,981,626,204 (M); Expenditures, $1,152,899,037; Total giving, $1,551,693; Grants to individuals, 14 grants totaling $49,000.
Fields of interest: Health sciences school/education.
Type of support: Scholarships—to individuals.
Application information: Applications accepted. Application form required.
 Initial approach: Letter
 Deadline(s): May 1 for Concord Volunteer Scholarship
 Additional information: See web site for additional application guidelines.
Program description:
 Walnut Creek Scholarship Program: The Auxiliary offers selective scholarships to high school seniors and college students who have volunteered at John Muir Medical Center, Walnut Creek. Awards are based on academics, leadership, community service, and a desire to pursue a healthcare-related degree.
EIN: 941461843

809
Musicares Foundation, Inc.

3030 Olympic Blvd.
Santa Monica, CA 90404-5073 (310) 392-3777
Contact: Rusty Rueff, Chair.
Additional tel. for Hurricane Sandy Relief Fund: (877) 303-6962, or (877) 626-2748
FAX: (310) 392-2188; Toll-free tel.: (800) 687-4227; URL: http://www.grammy.org/musicares

Foundation type: Public charity
Purpose: Financial assistance to economically disadvantaged individuals in the music recording community. Grants to individuals for projects that advance the archiving and preservation of the music and recorded sound heritage of the Americas, research and research implementation projects related to music, and the medical and occupational well-being of music professionals. Assistance to individuals affected by Hurricane Sandy.
Publications: Annual report.
Financial data: Year ended 07/31/2011. Assets, $13,400,439 (M); Expenditures, $6,317,784; Total giving, $2,953,302; Grants to individuals, totaling $2,852,782.
Fields of interest: Music; Arts, artist's services; Disasters, preparedness/services; Disasters, floods; Economically disadvantaged.
Type of support: Grants to individuals; Grants for special needs.
Application information: Application form required.
 Additional information: See web site for additional application guidelines, and

eligibility requirements and procedures for Hurricane Sandy relief.

Program descriptions:

Emergency Financial Assistance: The program offers funds for music people struggling with financial, medical or personal crises. Assistance includes medical expenses for doctor, dental and hospital bills, as well as basic living expenses such as rent and utilities. The program is available to music people who have experienced an unavoidable emergency. Eligibility includes documented employment in the music industry for at least five years or credited contribution to six commercially released recordings or videos.

MusiCares Hurricane Sandy Relief Fund: This fund has been established to assist music people affected by the devastation of Hurricane Sandy. Initial assistance will provide funds for food and clothing, shelter, utilities, medical expenses, gasoline and transportation, cleanup efforts, relocation costs, instrument and recording equipment replacement, and other critical supplies.

The MusiCares MAP Fund: Awarded in conjunction with the Musicians Assistance Program, this fund works to specifically address addiction and recovery needs for members of the music community, regardless of their financial condition. This program is open to music people who are able to document at least five years of employment in the music industry, or their contribution to air commercially released recordings or videos, and who can demonstrate proof of financial need.
EIN: 954470909

810
The Mutual After Life Foundation
15355 Brookhurst St., Ste. 217
Westminster, CA 92683-6758 (714) 775-1727
Contact: My Tran

Foundation type: Independent foundation
Purpose: Financial assistance to Vietnamese residents of Orange county CA, with funeral costs.
Financial data: Year ended 12/31/2011. Assets, $31,243 (M); Expenditures, $42,593; Total giving, $0.
Fields of interest: Cemeteries/burial services.
Type of support: Grants for special needs.
Application information: Applicants should include a death certificate one month after death.
EIN: 931175018

811
Myers Oceanographic & Marine Biology Trust
2600 Garden Rd., Ste. 320
Monterey, CA 93940 (831) 373-4957
Contact: Stephen B. Ruth, V.P.

Foundation type: Operating foundation
Purpose: Grants to individuals for continuing research in the field of marine biology.
Financial data: Year ended 12/31/2011. Assets, $0 (M); Expenditures, $38,038; Total giving, $36,450; Grants to individuals, 25 grants totaling $34,050 (high: $2,400).
Fields of interest: Marine science.
Type of support: Research.
Application information: Applications accepted. Application form not required.
  Initial approach: Letter
  Deadline(s): None
  Additional information: Contact the trust for additional guidelines.
EIN: 770094228

812
Myotonic Dystrophy Foundation
(also known as MDF)
1259 El Camino Real, Ste. 150
Menlo Park, CA 94025 (650) 267-5562
Contact: Molly K. White, Exec. Dir.
FAX: (650) 267-5564; E-mail: info@myotonic.com; Toll free tel.: (866) 968-6642; Additional Address: 431 Burgess Dr., Ste. 200, Menlo Park, CA, 94025; E-Mail for Molly K. White: molly.white@myotonic.org; URL: http://www.myotonic.com

Foundation type: Public charity
Purpose: Research grants to physicians and scientists in the field of myotonic dystrophy.
Publications: Application guidelines.
Financial data: Year ended 12/31/2011. Assets, $1,890,239 (M); Expenditures, $736,160; Total giving, $208,273.
Fields of interest: Nerve, muscle & bone diseases; Muscular dystrophy; Nerve, muscle & bone research; Muscular dystrophy research.
Type of support: Research.
Application information: Applications not accepted.
  Additional information: Unsolicited requests for funds not considered or acknowledged.
EIN: 205014628

813
NAMM Foundation
(formerly International Foundation for Music Research)
5790 Armada Dr.
Carlsbad, CA 92008-4608 (760) 438-8001
Contact: Mary L. Luehrsen N.A.M.M., Exec. Dir.
FAX: (760) 438-8257; E-mail: lorab@namm.org; URL: http://www.music-research.org

Foundation type: Public charity
Purpose: Grants to support research in the fields of music research, neuroscience, psychology, education, and/or health-related fields to explore the effects of hands-on music making.
Publications: Application guidelines.
Financial data: Year ended 09/30/2011. Assets, $1,621,613 (M); Expenditures, $1,722,750; Total giving, $1,289,740.
Fields of interest: Music; Elementary/secondary education.
Type of support: Research.
Application information:
  Initial approach: Letter
  Deadline(s): Varies by program
  Additional information: See web site for additional eligibility requirements: www.nammfoundation.org.
Program descriptions:
The Sounds of Learning: The Impact of Music Education Initiative: The initiative supports research that examines the role of music education in the lives of school-age children.
The Sounds of Living: The Impact of Music Making Initiative: The initiative will support research that examines the role of active participation in music for children, youth, adults, and seniors. Research funded under the initiative explores the effects of music learning and music making outside of formal educational settings and expands the understanding of the role of music making in health, wellness, socialization, and the inter-connections between mind, body, and spirit that contribute to wellness and overall quality of life.
EIN: 330797657

814
National Alopecia Areata Foundation
(also known as NAAF)
14 Mitchell Blvd.
San Rafael, CA 94903-2050 (415) 472-3780
Contact: Vicki Kalabokes, Pres. and C.E.O.
FAX: (415) 472-5343; E-mail: info@naaf.org; Additional tel.: (415) 456-4644; URL: http://www.naaf.org

Foundation type: Public charity
Purpose: Grants to medical professionals for research on alopecia areata.
Publications: Application guidelines; Annual report; Financial statement; Informational brochure; Newsletter.
Financial data: Year ended 12/31/2012. Assets, $3,678,366 (M); Expenditures, $1,828,119; Total giving, $288,950; Grants to individuals, totaling $37,030.
Fields of interest: Skin disorders; Immunology; Skin disorders research; Medical research.
Type of support: Fellowships; Research; Grants to individuals.
Application information: Applications not accepted.
Program description:
Research Grants: Grants are available to researchers in one of the following five areas dealing with alopecia areata: clinical research; genetics; immunology; use of alopecia areata registry; and use of the alopecia areata mouse model. These five areas are interrelated and reflect the strong desire of patients and clinician/scientists to move from basic biology to applied research to find safe and effective treatments for alopecia areata. Other areas of innovative research will be considered based on scientific merit.
EIN: 942780249

815
National Charity League, Inc.
950 S. Coast Dr., Ste. 200
Costa Mesa, CA 92626-7831 (714) 966-1005
Contact: Iris Swinea, Dir.
FAX: (714) 966-1022; E-mail: info@nclonline.org; E-Mail For Iris Swinea: iris.swinea@nclonline.org; URL: http://www.nationalcharityleague.org/

Foundation type: Public charity
Purpose: Scholarships to high school students who reside in CA for higher education.
Financial data: Year ended 05/31/2012. Assets, $342,843 (M); Expenditures, $233,344; Total giving, $165,604; Grants to individuals, totaling $89,420.
Type of support: Undergraduate support.
Application information: Contact foundation for application guidelines.
EIN: 952136037

816
National Charity League-Newport Chapter
540 W. 19th St.
Costa Mesa, CA 92627-2748 (949) 487-3637

Foundation type: Public charity
Purpose: Scholarships to girls who are members of the National Charity League and have performed many hours of community service through the organization.
Financial data: Year ended 05/31/2012. Assets, $863,979 (M); Expenditures, $506,904; Total giving, $217,854.
Type of support: Undergraduate support.

Application information: Contact foundation for application guidelines.
EIN: 966055016

817

National Council on Crime and Delinquency

1970 Broadway, Ste. 500
Oakland, CA 94612-2217 (510) 208-0500
Contact: Renee Plog, Comm. Mgr.
FAX: (510) 208-0511; E-mail: info@nccdglobal.org; Midwest office address: 426 S. Yellowstone Dr., Ste. 250, Madison, WI, 53719-1063; E-mail for Renee Plog: rplog@sf.nccd-crc.org; Tool-Free Tel.: (800) 306-6223; URL: http://www.nccd-crc.org

Foundation type: Public charity
Purpose: Awards to honor journalists who draw attention to the American justice system.
Publications: Newsletter.
Financial data: Year ended 06/30/2012. Assets, $8,015,446 (M); Expenditures, $12,976,041.
Fields of interest: Media/communications; Journalism; Literature.
Type of support: Awards/prizes.
Application information: Applications accepted. Application form required. Application form available on the grantmaker's web site.
  Copies of proposal: 2
  Deadline(s): Dec. 31 for PASS Awards
  Final notification: Recipients notified Mar. for PASS Awards
  Additional information: See web site for additional guidelines.
Program descriptions:
  Don M. Gottfredson Scholarship Fund: NCCD sponsors this scholarship at California State University, East Bay. Each year Cal State East Bay and Shalom High School in Milwaukee, WI grant a needs-based scholarship of $2,000 to a ward or former ward of the juvenile or family court in memory of Don M. Gottfredson.
  PASS Awards: PASS Awards (Prevention for a Safer Society) recognizes and honors members of the media who try to focus America's attention on criminal justice, juvenile justice, and child welfare systems in a thoughtful and considerate manner.
  Special Recognition Awards: Each year the committee recognizes several deserving individuals. These awards distinguish academics, elected officials, and community advocates whose work aligns with and expands upon NCCD's mission.
EIN: 131624111

818

The National Fragile X Foundation

1615 Bonanza St., No. 202
Walnut Creek, CA 94596-4530 (800) 688-8765
Contact: Robert M. Miller, Exec. Dir.
Application e-mail address: jayne@fragilex.org
FAX: (925) 938-9315; E-mail: natlfx@fragilex.org; URL: http://www.fragilex.org

Foundation type: Public charity
Purpose: Research grants for basic science research, and clinical research, through the support of young researchers and summer student fellowships.
Financial data: Year ended 12/31/2012. Assets, $653,284 (M); Expenditures, $1,732,427; Total giving, $133,065; Grants to individuals, totaling $24,875.
Fields of interest: Genetic diseases and disorders.
Type of support: Fellowships; Research.
Application information: Applications accepted.
  Initial approach: Proposal
  Send request by: E-mail
  Deadline(s): Apr.
  Additional information: See web site for additional application guidelines.
Program description:
  Summer Research Fellowships: Each year, the foundation funds one or more summer student research fellowships at $2,500 each through the Rosen/Weingarden Summer Fellowship Research Fund. The student's work can be in the area of fragile X syndrome (FXS), fragile X-associated tremor/ataxia syndrome (FXTAS) or fragile X-associated primary ovarian insufficiency (FXPOI). Both undergraduate and graduate students are eligible.
EIN: 840960471

819

The National Multiple Sclerosis Society Northern California Chapter

1700 Owens St., Ste. 190
San Francisco, CA 94158-0002 (415) 230-6678
Contact: Janelle Del Carlo, Pres.
FAX: (415) 230-6652;
E-mail: info@msconnection.org; Additional addresses (Central Valley office): 422 McHenry, Modesto, CA 95354-0326, tel.: (209) 214-6022; (Sacramento office): 4221 Northgate Blvd., Ste. 4, Sacramento, CA 95834-1227, tel.: (916) 927-8000; (Silicon Valley office): 2589 Scott Blvd., Santa Clara, CA 95050-2508, tel.: (408) 988-7557; E-mail For Janelle Del Carlo: janelle.delcarlo@nmss.org; URL: http://www.nationalmssociety.org/chapters/CAN/index.aspx

Foundation type: Public charity
Purpose: Limited financial assistance to people in northern California with multiple sclerosis.
Publications: Annual report; Financial statement; Newsletter.
Financial data: Year ended 09/30/2012. Assets, $2,990,284 (M); Expenditures, $4,845,454; Total giving, $112,887; Grants to individuals, totaling $112,887.
Fields of interest: Higher education; Multiple sclerosis.
Type of support: Scholarships—to individuals; Grants for special needs.
Application information:
  Initial approach: Telephone or e-mail
  Deadline(s): None
Program description:
  Financial Assistance Program: The society provides guidance, leverage, and resources to help minimize the financial impact of multiple sclerosis (MS) on individuals and families throughout the northern California area. The program provides support for needed modifications to homes and automobiles, helps with the purchase of wheelchairs and walkers, and provides immediate resources to overcome urgent financial crises.
EIN: 941294935

820

National Multiple Sclerosis Society, Southern California Chapter

2440 S. Sepulveda Blvd., Ste. 115
Los Angeles, CA 90064-1744 (310) 479-4456
FAX: (310) 479-4436; E-mail: ms@cal.nmss.org; URL: http://cal.nationalmssociety.org/

Foundation type: Public charity

Purpose: Research grants for scientists and clinicians to find a cure and treatment for multiple sclerosis.
Publications: Annual report; Newsletter.
Financial data: Year ended 09/30/2011. Assets, $4,316,145 (M); Expenditures, $10,156,379; Total giving, $772,346; Grants to individuals, totaling $239,122.
Fields of interest: Multiple sclerosis research.
Type of support: Research; Grants to individuals.
Application information: Applications accepted. Application form available on the grantmaker's web site.
  Send request by: On-line
  Deadline(s): Vary
  Additional information: See web site for additional application guidelines.
EIN: 951727656

821

National Physical Science Consortium

(also known as NPSC)
3716 S. Hope, Ste. 348
Los Angeles, CA 90007-4344 (213) 743-2409
Contact: Dr. James L. Powell, Exec. Dir.
FAX: (213) 743-2407; E-mail: npschq@npsc.org; Toll-free tel.: (800) 854-6772; URL: http://www.npsc.org

Foundation type: Public charity
Purpose: Fellowships to underrepresented minorities and women pursing PhDs in the physical sciences and related engineering fields.
Publications: Informational brochure.
Financial data: Year ended 06/30/2012. Assets, $672,853 (M); Expenditures, $1,679,799; Total giving, $1,236,500; Grants to individuals, totaling $1,236,500.
Fields of interest: Physical/earth sciences; Engineering; Minorities; Women.
Type of support: Fellowships; Graduate support.
Application information: Applications accepted. Application form required.
  Send request by: Online
  Deadline(s): Nov. 30
  Additional information: See web site for additional guidelines.
Program description:
  Fellowships: The consortium provides graduate degree fellowships. Applications are accepted from any qualified U.S. citizen who has the ability to pursue graduate work at an NPSC member institution. Though the fields supported can vary annually depending on employer needs, in general NPSC covers Astronomy, Chemistry, Computer Science, Geology, Materials Science, Mathematical Sciences, Physics, and their subdisciplines, and related engineering fields such as Chemical, Computer, Electrical, Environmental, Mechanical. Persons who already possess a doctoral degree (Ph.D., M.D., J.D., E.D., etc.) in any field are ineligible.
EIN: 943067172

822

National Urea Cycle Disorders Foundation

75 S. Grand Ave.
Pasadena, CA 91105-1602 (626) 578-0833
Contact: Cindy LeMons, Exec. Dir.
FAX: (626) 578-0823; E-mail: cindy@nucdf.org; URL: http://www.nucdf.org

Foundation type: Public charity
Purpose: Grants to medical doctors and other scientific professionals for research into urea cycle disorders.

Financial data: Year ended 12/31/2011. Assets, $1,102,192 (M); Expenditures, $291,481; Total giving, $50,000. Grants to individuals amount not specified.
Fields of interest: Genetic diseases and disorders research; Diseases (rare) research.
Type of support: Research; Postdoctoral support.
Application information: Contact foundation for application guidelines.
EIN: 411661444

823
Nauheim/Straus Charitable Foundation, Inc.
P.O. Box 843
La Habra, CA 90633-0843 (714) 738-6112
Contact: John J. Barcal, Pres.

Foundation type: Operating foundation
Purpose: Scholarships to graduates of business or law school in the CA, area.
Financial data: Year ended 12/31/2012. Assets, $4,898,623 (M); Expenditures, $297,674; Total giving, $89,500; Grants to individuals, 43 grants totaling $89,500 (high: $2,500, low: $2,000).
Fields of interest: Business school/education; Law school/education.
Type of support: Scholarships—to individuals; Postgraduate support.
Application information: Application form required.
Initial approach: Letter
Deadline(s): Varies
Applicants should submit the following:
1) Letter(s) of recommendation
2) Photograph
3) Transcripts
Additional information: Contact foundation for application guidelines.
EIN: 200661236

824
Nepal Educational Fund, Inc.
700 Front St., No. 2003
San Diego, CA 92101-6012 (619) 232-7788
Contact: Richard D. Della Pena M.D., Pres.

Foundation type: Operating foundation
Purpose: Scholarships to economically disadvantaged students born in Nepal pursuing higher education.
Financial data: Year ended 12/31/2011. Assets, $63,720 (M); Expenditures, $33,038; Total giving, $31,601; Grants to individuals, 4 grants totaling $31,601 (high: $26,101, low: $1,000).
Fields of interest: Higher education.
International interests: Nepal.
Type of support: Scholarships—to individuals; Undergraduate support.
Application information: Applications accepted.
Initial approach: Letter
Deadline(s): None
Additional information: Applicants must demonstrate academic achievement and financial need. Applicant must show proof of Nepal as country of birth.
EIN: 330490545

825
Nestle USA, Inc. Corporate Giving Program
800 N. Brand Ave.
Glendale, CA 91203-1245 (818) 549-6000
Contact: Kenneth Bentley, V.P., Community Affairs
Contact for Nestle Very Best In Youth: Cristina Bastida, Exec. Dir., tel.: (818) 549-6677, e-mail: NestleVeryBestInYouth@us.nestle.com
URL: http://www.nestleusa.com/creating-shared-value/community

Foundation type: Corporate giving program
Purpose: Awards to young people (ages 13 to 18) who have excelled in school and who are making their community and the world a better place.
Publications: Application guidelines.
Fields of interest: Community development, neighborhood development; Youth.
Type of support: Awards/prizes.
Application information: Applications accepted. Application form required. Application form available on the grantmaker's web site.
Initial approach: Application
Send request by: On-line
Applicants should submit the following:
1) Letter(s) of recommendation
2) Transcripts
3) Essay
Additional information: Applications should also include a signed consent form from a parent or legal guardian. E-mail Nestle for more information:
NestleVeryBestinYouth@us.nestle.com.
Program description:
Nestle's Very Best In Youth Program: Nestle USA annually honors young people ages 13 to 18 who have excelled in youth leadership and have contributed to their community. Applicants are selected based on academic records, special contributions to their school, church, or community, good citizenship, and personal obstacles the youth has overcome. Honorees have their story published in the Nestle Very Best in Youth publication and is awarded a trip with his/her parent or legal guardian to Los Angeles for the Nestle Very Best In Youth awards ceremony. The trip includes round-trip air travel, hotel accommodations for three nights, and $500 spending money. Nestle USA also donates $1,000 in the name of each winner to the charity of his or her choice.

826
New Horizons Foundation
700 S. Flower St., Ste. 1222
Los Angeles, CA 90017-4110 (213) 626-4481
Contact: Henry H. Dearing, Pres. and Treas.

Foundation type: Independent foundation
Purpose: Financial assistance to needy members of the First Church of Christ, Scientist, Boston, MA, or an authorized branch.
Financial data: Year ended 05/31/2013. Assets, $627,148 (M); Expenditures, $91,394; Total giving, $84,500; Grants to individuals, 8 grants totaling $84,500 (high: $15,000, low: $6,000).
Fields of interest: Christian agencies & churches; Aging.
Type of support: Grants for special needs.
Application information: Applications accepted. Application form not required. Interview required.
Initial approach: Letter or telephone
Deadline(s): None
Additional information: Applicants must be at least 65 years of age and demonstrate financial need.
EIN: 956031571

827
The Kenny Nickelson Memorial Foundation for Homeless Veterans, Inc.
P.O. Box 3098
Manhattan Beach, CA 90266-1098 (310) 545-2937
FAX: (310) 939-7738; URL: http://www.knmf.org/about/about.html

Foundation type: Public charity
Purpose: Assistance to indigent veterans and families of Los Angeles, CA in the form of food, clothing, medical and dental attention, housing with case management programs, career training, and assistance with entitlement benefits while in recovery programs.
Financial data: Year ended 12/31/2011. Assets, $701,730 (M); Expenditures, $256,122; Total giving, $10,000.
Fields of interest: Human services, emergency aid; Human services; Military/veterans; Homeless.
Type of support: In-kind gifts.
Application information:
Initial approach: Letter
Additional information: Contact foundation for eligibility criteria.
EIN: 954375903

828
NMA Scholarship Foundation
1970 Broadway, Ste. 825
Oakland, CA 94612-2299 (510) 763-1533
Contact: Jen Kempis, Opers. Mgr.
FAX: (510) 763-6186; E-mail: staff@nmaonline.org; Tel. for Jen Kempis: (510) 763-1553; fax for Jen Kempis: (510) 763-6186; e-mail for Jen Kempis: jen@nmaonline.org; URL: http://www.nmascholars.org

Foundation type: Public charity
Purpose: Scholarships to encourage undergraduate students to pursue a degree in the animal, meat, and food sciences.
Publications: Application guidelines.
Financial data: Year ended 06/30/2012. Assets, $395,877 (M); Expenditures, $27,505; Total giving, $27,250.
Fields of interest: Agriculture/food.
Type of support: Undergraduate support.
Application information: Applications accepted. Application form required. Application form available on the grantmaker's web site.
Initial approach: Letter
Deadline(s): May 1
Program description:
Scholarships: Scholarships, ranging from $2,000 to $2,500, are available to sophomores, juniors, and seniors who are pursuing a curriculum that will lead to a B.S. in animal, meat, or food sciences, or a related discipline. Eligible applicants must be attending a four-year college or university, and have a cumulative 2.75 GPA. Named scholarships include the Frank DeBenedetti Memorial Scholarship (one $2,500 award), the Edie Schmidt NMA Memorial Scholarship (one $2,000 award), the Al Piccetti NMA Memorial Scholarship (one $2,000 award), the Lou Gast NMA Memorial Scholarship (one $2,000 award), and NMA Undergraduate Scholarships (one or more scholarships of $2,000 each). In addition, each recipient who attends the National Meat Association Annual Convention will receive a $500 travel stipend and a plaque.
EIN: 943192729

829

North Bay Developmental Disabilities Services, Inc.

10 Executive Ct., No. A
Napa, CA   94558-6267   (707) 256-1100
Contact: Robert Hamilton, Exec. Dir.

Foundation type: Public charity
Purpose: Financial assistance to individuals with developmental disabilities in Napa, Solano, and Sonoma counties, CA with out-of-home care, day programs and transportation.
Financial data: Year ended 06/30/2011. Assets, $34,647,080 (M); Expenditures, $148,233,611; Total giving, $132,613,351; Grants to individuals, 30,000 grants totaling $132,613,351.
Fields of interest: Developmentally disabled, centers & services; Mentally disabled.
Type of support: Grants for special needs.
Application information: Applications accepted.
  Additional information: Contact the agency for eligibility determination.
EIN: 941719894

830

North Los Angeles County Regional Center, Inc.

15400 Sherman Way, Ste. 170
Van Nuys, CA   91406-4271   (818) 778-1900
FAX: (818) 756-6140; URL: http://www.nlacrc.org

Foundation type: Public charity
Purpose: Assistance to residents of California who have developmental disabilities with home services and other special needs.
Publications: Application guidelines.
Financial data: Year ended 06/30/2012. Assets, $121,583,189 (M); Expenditures, $274,399,372; Total giving, $242,968,631; Grants to individuals, totaling $242,968,631.
Fields of interest: Disabilities, people with.
Type of support: Grants for special needs.
Application information: Applications accepted. Application form required.
  Additional information: Applicants receive assistance based on individual need. Contact the organization for eligibility determination.
EIN: 237351340

831

North Valley Community Foundation

(formerly Chico Community Foundation)
3120 Cohasset Rd., Ste. 8
Chico, CA   95973-0978   (530) 891-1150
Contact: Alexa Benson-Valavanis, C.E.O.
FAX: (530) 891-1502; E-mail: nvcf@nvcf.org; Mailing address: P.O. Box 6581, Chico, CA 95927; Additional e-mail: avalavanis@nvcf.org; URL: http://www.nvcf.org

Foundation type: Community foundation
Purpose: Scholarships to individuals for higher education in Butte, Colusa, Glenn, and Tehama counties, CA.
Publications: Annual report; Financial statement; Grants list; Informational brochure; Occasional report.
Financial data: Year ended 06/30/2012. Assets, $9,889,012 (M); Expenditures, $1,946,459; Total giving, $1,277,661; Grants to individuals, 56 grants totaling $51,135.
Fields of interest: Higher education.
Type of support: Scholarships—to individuals.
Application information: Applications accepted.

Additional information: Contact foundation for application guidelines.
EIN: 680161455

832

North Valley Health Education Foundation

(formerly Chico Community Hospital Foundation)
1354 E. Ave., Ste. R
PMB No. 377
Chico, CA   95926-7383   (530) 591-4161
Contact: Sara Beacham, Secy.
E-mail: Board@NVHEF.org; URL: http://www.nvhef.org

Foundation type: Public charity
Purpose: Scholarships to medical students, nursing students, and allied health professionals of Butte College; California State University, Chico; University of California, Davis; and Enloe Medical Center.
Publications: Application guidelines; Informational brochure.
Financial data: Year ended 04/30/2012. Assets, $690,290 (M); Expenditures, $40,068; Total giving, $34,000; Grants to individuals, totaling $33,000.
Fields of interest: Medical school/education; Nursing school/education.
Type of support: Graduate support; Undergraduate support.
Application information: Applications accepted. Application form required. Application form available on the grantmaker's web site. Interview required.
  Deadline(s): Feb. 18 for students at UC Davis and Feb. 25 for all other Scholarship Program
  Applicants should submit the following:
    1) Transcripts
    2) Financial information
  Additional information: See web site for additional application and program information.
Program description:
  Scholarship Program: The foundation awards scholarships, ranging from $500 to $2,5000, to students enrolled in the health professions at Butte College; California State University, Chico; University of California, Davis; and Enloe Medical Center (both employees and volunteers)
EIN: 237280072

833

Northern California Laborers Scholarship Foundation

4780 Chabot Dr., Ste. 200
Pleasanton, CA   94588-3322   (925) 469-6800
URL: http://www.local270.com/scholarships.html

Foundation type: Public charity
Purpose: College scholarships to deserving sons and daughters of Local Union members who might otherwise not be able to afford college.
Publications: Application guidelines.
Financial data: Year ended 12/31/2011. Assets, $141,566 (M); Expenditures, $156,824; Total giving, $150,848; Grants to individuals, totaling $150,848.
Fields of interest: Higher education; Labor unions/organizations.
Type of support: Scholarships—to individuals.
Application information: Applications accepted. Application form required.
  Deadline(s): Apr.
  Applicants should submit the following:
    1) Financial information
    2) Essay

Additional information: Scholarship applications are available at Local 270 and it is only for children of a member of a Local Union affiliated with the Northern California District Council of Laborers. Scholarships are approximately $2,000 each. Unsolicited requests for funds not considered or acknowledged.
EIN: 680319359

834

The Northern California Scholarship Foundation

(formerly The Northern California Scholarship Foundation and the Scaife Scholarship Foundation)
1547 Lakeside Dr.
Oakland, CA   94612-4520
Contact: Clyde Minar, Secy.-Treas.
E-mail: ncsf@pacbell.net; URL: http://www.ncsfscholarships.org

Foundation type: Independent foundation
Purpose: Scholarships to graduating high school seniors attending a Northern or Central CA public school for higher education.
Publications: Application guidelines; Informational brochure; Program policy statement.
Financial data: Year ended 05/31/2013. Assets, $19,166,941 (M); Expenditures, $915,498; Total giving, $776,000; Grants to individuals, totaling $776,000.
Fields of interest: Higher education.
Type of support: Scholarships—to individuals; Undergraduate support.
Application information: Applications accepted. Application form required. Interview required.
  Deadline(s): Mar.
  Final notification: Applicants notified in mid May
  Applicants should submit the following:
    1) Financial information
    2) Transcripts
  Additional information: Applicants are recommended to the foundation by their high school counselor. See web site for additional guidelines.
EIN: 941540333

835

Nuclear Age Peace Foundation

1622 Anacapa St.
Santa Barbara, CA   93101-1910   (805) 965-3443
FAX: (805) 568-0466; Mailing address for Peace Poetry Awards: 1187 Coast Village Rd., Ste. 1, PMB 121, Santa Barbara, CA 93108-2794; URL: http://www.wagingpeace.org

Foundation type: Public charity
Purpose: Awards and prizes to individuals who address and personalize issues of peace and security and to show appreciation to those exhibiting exceptional devotion to promoting peace.
Publications: Informational brochure; Newsletter.
Financial data: Year ended 12/31/2011. Assets, $4,312,308 (M); Expenditures, $853,785; Total giving, $48,215.
Fields of interest: International peace/security; Arms control.
Type of support: Awards/prizes.
Application information:
  Deadline(s): Apr. 1 for Swackhamer Disarmament Video Contest, July 1 for Barbara Mandigo Kelly Peace Poetry Awards
  Final notification: Recipients notified Oct. 1 for Barbara Mandigo Kelly Peace Poetry Awards

Additional information: See web site for additional information.

Program descriptions:

Distinguished Peace Leadership Award: The award is presented annually to individuals who have demonstrated courageous leadership in the cause of peace. Occasionally, the foundation also presented a Lifetime Achievement Award for peace leadership.

Lifetime Achievement Award: The award is presented to individuals who have made a lifetime commitment to pursuing peace.

Swackhamer Disarmament Video Contest: The Contest is an annual contest in which contestants submit short (2-3 minutes) videos on an aspect of nuclear disarmament (the specific topic is announced on Feb. 1 of each year)

World Citizenship Award: This award is presented to individuals who have made outstanding contributions to the human family. This award is generally presented at the Foundation's Annual Evening for Peace.

EIN: 953825265

836
The Oakland Athletics Community Fund

(also known as The Oakland A's Community Fund)
McAfee Coliseum
7000 Coliseum Way
Oakland, CA 94621-1917   (510) 563-2261
Contact: Kendall R. Pries, Dir.; Detra Page, Dir.
E-mail: community@oaklandathletics.com.;
URL: http://oakland.athletics.mlb.com/NASApp/mlb/oak/community/index.jsp

Foundation type: Company-sponsored foundation
Purpose: Scholarships to high school seniors in the Bay Area and to undergraduate students majoring in journalism or broadcasting.
Publications: Application guidelines.
Financial data: Year ended 12/31/2012. Assets, $643,687 (M); Expenditures, $948,567; Total giving, $477,335.
Fields of interest: Media/communications; Radio; Journalism.
Type of support: Undergraduate support.
Application information: Applications accepted. Application form required. Application form available on the grantmaker's web site.
Initial approach: Application
Deadline(s): Feb. for Bay Area All-Star Scholarship Team, May 31 for the Bill King Scholarship
Applicants should submit the following:
1) Letter(s) of recommendation
2) Transcripts
3) Financial information
4) Essay
Additional information: Contact participating high schools for Bay Area All-Star Scholarship Team.

Program descriptions:

Bay Area All-Star Scholarship Team: The foundation awards $3,000 scholarships to successful high seniors residing within the Bay Area's nine counties. Candidates must have a grade point average of 3.0, display leadership qualities and/or inspirational qualities on the athletic field, and demonstrate the value of education, good work ethic, and community outreach.

Bill Kings College Scholarship: The foundation awards one $3,000 scholarship to an undergraduate student majoring in journalism or broadcasting. Applicants must prove financial need, have a grade point average of 3.0, and show a strong interest in pursuing a career in

broadcasting or journalism. The recipient will also receive the opportunity to intern with the A's Broadcasting Department.
EIN: 942826655

837
Oaklandish, LLP Corporate Giving Program

(also known as Oakland Innovators Awards Fund)
3421 Hollis St., Ste. M
Oakland, CA 94608-4109   (510) 652-7490
Contact: Natalie Nadimi, Community Outreach
E-mail: grants@oaklandish.com; URL: http://www.oaklandish.com/community

Foundation type: Corporate giving program
Purpose: Award of $5,000 goes to an Oakland artist for an approved project that is located in public space, or is readily accessible to the public; addresses or reflects the identity, culture, or history of Oakland, CA. Artists must work under a fiscal sponsor in order to be funded.
Publications: Application guidelines.
Financial data: Year ended 12/31/2010. Total giving, $30,000; Grants to individuals, totaling $30,000.
Fields of interest: Visual arts.
Type of support: Awards/prizes; Fiscal agent/sponsor.
Application information: Applications accepted. Application form required.
Initial approach: Letter
Deadline(s): Dec. 1
Final notification: Jan. 31
Additional information: Project description should not exceed 2 pages; history and mission statement of the project or organization should not exceed 2 paragraphs. Work samples can be submitted as a DVD, CD, print, etc. Proposal should include proof of Oakland residency.

838
The Mary Oakley Foundation, Inc.

494 Twin Oaks Ct.
Thousand Oaks, CA 91362-3166   (805) 448-3461
Contact: Deborah Dunn
FAX: (805) 379-4157;
E-mail: MaryOakleyFndtn@aol.com; Application address: 2969 Glen Albyn Dr., Santa Barbara, CA 93105; URL: http://www.maryoakleyfoundation.org

Foundation type: Independent foundation
Purpose: Grants to economically disadvantaged individuals who are residents of the Tri-Counties of Santa Barbara, San Luis Obispo or Ventura, CA, who suffer from Alzheimer's disease or related dementia.
Financial data: Year ended 12/31/2012. Assets, $12,236,473 (M); Expenditures, $1,107,037; Total giving, $989,099; Grants to individuals, totaling $441,929.
Fields of interest: Alzheimer's disease; Aging; Economically disadvantaged.
Type of support: Grants for special needs.
Application information: Application form required. Interview required.
Initial approach: Letter
Additional information: Applicant must be a long time resident of the Tri-counties.
EIN: 770391113

839
Ojai Film Festival

P.O. Box 1029
Ojai, CA 93024-1029   (805) 640-1947
Contact: Jamie Fleming, Exec. Dir.
E-mail: info@ojaifilmfestival.com; URL: http://www.ojaifilmfestival.com

Foundation type: Public charity
Purpose: Trophies, certificates, and cash awards to winners of the Ojai Film Festival in CA.
Financial data: Year ended 12/31/2011. Assets, $6,244 (M); Expenditures, $42,083.
Fields of interest: Film/video.
Type of support: Awards/prizes.
Application information: Applications accepted. Application form required. Application form available on the grantmaker's web site.
Initial approach: E-mail
Additional information: Applications must include SASE, entry fee and film.
EIN: 460471403

840
The Olympic Club Foundation

524 Post St.
San Francisco, CA 94102-1229   (415) 345-5230
Contact: David Hultman, Pres.
E-mail: info@olyclub.com; URL: http://www.olyclubfdn.org

Foundation type: Public charity
Purpose: Scholarships and grants to young athletes in the San Francisco Bay Area, CA.
Publications: Application guidelines.
Financial data: Year ended 12/31/2011. Assets, $1,483,841 (M); Expenditures, $683,679; Total giving, $314,026; Grants to individuals, 2 grants totaling $10,000.
Fields of interest: Athletics/sports, amateur leagues.
Type of support: Grants to individuals; Undergraduate support.
Application information: Applications accepted. Application form required. Application form available on the grantmaker's web site.
Initial approach: Application
Deadline(s): Oct. 15 for Ohleyer Award
Additional information: See web site for complete program information.

Program descriptions:

Athletes Fund: The program provides grants of up to $5,000 each to outstanding amateur athletes between the ages of 10 and 18 from the San Francisco Bay Area who are in need of financial assistance to develop their athletic skills through coaching, training and competition in recognized athletic events associated with their age and skill level. Primary residency and school must be in Alameda, Contra Costa, Marin, Napa, Santa Clara, San Francisco, San Mateo, Solano, or Sonoma counties.

Brian Ohleyer Memorial Award: The award is presented to a student whose athletic and academic interests are matched by personal qualities of leadership, involvement and community service. The foundation will make a $1,000 contribution to the school or organization in the recipient's name and will provide $4,000 in scholarship funds when they graduate from high school and enroll in a 4-year college.
EIN: 943160462

841
Open Circle Foundation
200 Frank H. Ogawa Plz.
Oakland, CA 94612-2005   (510) 836-3223
FAX: (510) 625-8126;
E-mail: opencircle@eastbaycf.org; URL: http://
www.art4environment.org/index.html

Foundation type: Public charity
Purpose: Grants to artists working in communities
in the East Bay, CA area.
Publications: Application guidelines.
Financial data: Year ended 06/30/2012. Assets,
$548,063 (M); Expenditures, $174,617; Total
giving, $161,177.
Fields of interest: Arts, artist's services; Arts.
Type of support: Grants to individuals; Fiscal
agent/sponsor.
Application information: Applications accepted.
Application form available on the grantmaker's web
site.
  Initial approach: Letter of Inquiry
  Deadline(s): July 31
  Additional information: Eligible artists must be
    affiliated with a 501(c)(3) organization, or be
    under the umbrella of a fiscal sponsor.
Program description:
  Grants: The foundation provides up to five grants,
  ranging from $10,000 to $20,000, to artists
  carrying out work in the East Bay area, and whose
  work focuses on a specific community or on an
  issue that cuts across many communities. Eligible
  applicants must have a fiscal sponsor or be working
  with a 501(c)(3) organization that is capable of
  receiving grant monies; priority will be given to
  artists working within Alameda and Contra Costa
  counties.
EIN: 943349692

842
Optimist Boys Home and Ranch, Inc.
(also known as Optimist Youth Homes and Family
Services)
6957 N. Figueroa St.
P.O. Box 41-1076
Los Angeles, CA 90042-1076   (323) 443-3175
Contact: Silvio John Orlando, Exec. Dir.
FAX: (323) 443-3264; E-mail: silorlando@oyhfs.org;
Toll-free tel.: (877) 749-6884; URL: http://
www.oyhfs.org

Foundation type: Public charity
Purpose: Financial assistance to aid Los
Angeles-area foster parents in caring for the
children.
Financial data: Year ended 06/30/2012. Assets,
$15,438,290 (M); Expenditures, $20,168,912;
Total giving, $487,736; Grants to individuals,
totaling $487,736.
Fields of interest: Foster care.
Type of support: Grants to individuals.
Application information: Applications not
accepted.
  Additional information: Unsolicited requests for
    funds not considered.
EIN: 951643340

843
Orange County Community Foundation
4041 MacArthur Blvd., Ste. 510
Newport Beach, CA 92660-0000   (949)
553-4202
Contact: Todd Hanson, V.P., Donor Rels. and Progs.
FAX: (949) 553-4211; E-mail: thanson@oc-cf.org;
URL: http://www.oc-cf.org

Foundation type: Community foundation
Purpose: Scholarships to residents of Orange
County, CA, and to students of Orange County high
schools, community colleges, and universities.
Publications: Application guidelines; Annual report;
Financial statement; Informational brochure;
Newsletter; Occasional report.
Financial data: Year ended 06/30/2012. Assets,
$144,112,000 (M); Expenditures, $32,649,000;
Total giving, $28,664,000.
Fields of interest: Vocational education; Higher
education; College (community/junior); Law
school/education; Teacher school/education;
Hemophilia; Food services; Athletics/sports, water
sports; Business/industry; Hispanics/Latinos;
Economically disadvantaged.
Type of support: Scholarships—to individuals;
Undergraduate support.
Application information: Application form required.
  Initial approach: Application
  Send request by: Online
  Deadline(s): Varies
  Additional information: See web site for eligibility
    criteria and complete listing of scholarships.
EIN: 330378778

844
Orange County Rescue Mission, Inc.
1 Hope Dr.
Tustin, CA 92782-0221   (714) 247-4300
Contact: Jim Palmer, Pres.
FAX: (714) 258-4451; Toll Free Tel. :
(800)-663-3074; URL: http://
www.rescuemission.org

Foundation type: Public charity
Purpose: Assistance in the areas of guidance,
counseling, education, job training, shelter, food,
clothing, health care, and independent living
communities to indigent residents of Orange
County, CA.
Financial data: Year ended 09/30/2011. Assets,
$43,637,620 (M); Expenditures, $13,256,702;
Total giving, $6,325,146; Grants to individuals,
totaling $6,325,146.
Fields of interest: Human services; Economically
disadvantaged.
Type of support: In-kind gifts.
Application information:
  Initial approach: Letter
  Additional information: Contact the mission for
    eligibility criteria.
EIN: 952479552

845
Orangewood Children's Foundation
1575 E. 17th St.
Santa Ana, CA 92705-9506   (714) 619-0200
Contact: Cal Winslow, C.E.O.
FAX: (714) 619-0252;
E-mail: info@orangewoodfoundation.org;
URL: http://www.orangewoodfoundation.org

Foundation type: Public charity
Purpose: Financial assistance and educational
support to current and emancipated foster youth
from Orange County, CA.
Publications: Application guidelines.
Financial data: Year ended 06/30/2012. Assets,
$21,636,321 (M); Expenditures, $7,162,622;
Total giving, $843,619; Grants to individuals,
totaling $843,619.
Fields of interest: Scholarships/financial aid.
Type of support: Scholarships—to individuals.

Application information: Applications accepted.
Application form required.
  Deadline(s): Within 30 days after the first day of
    class (varies by individual)
  Additional information: Application should
    include transcripts.
Program description:
  Children's Trust Fund Program: This program
  provides financial assistance and educational
  support to current and emancipated foster youth in
  Orange County up to their 25th birthday, and
  provides referrals to other financial and educational
  resources as needed. For current foster youth, ages
  0 to 18, up to $250 per year will be made available
  for educational camps, school sports, and other
  extra-curricular activities; driver's education; and
  yearbook and graduation expenses. For
  emancipated foster youth between the ages of 18
  to 21, up to $500 per year will be available to help
  with living expenses (such as rent, groceries, or
  clothing) and medical/dental expenses. For
  emancipated foster youth attending a
  postsecondary school (community college, trade
  school, or university), up to $6,000 per year will be
  available for tuition, books, supplies, and living
  expenses. Eligible applicants must currently be or
  have been an Orange County dependent and must
  maintain a minimum 2.0 GPA.
EIN: 953616628

846
Organic Farming Research Foundation
303 Potrero St., Ste. 29-203
Santa Cruz, CA 95060-2759   (831) 426-6606
Contact: Maureen Wilmot, Exec. Dir.
FAX: (831) 426-6670; E-mail: info@ofrf.org; Mailing
address: P.O. Box 440, Santa Cruz, CA
95061-0440; E-mail for Maureen Wilmot:
maureen@ofrf.org; URL: http://www.ofrf.org

Foundation type: Public charity
Purpose: Grants to individuals for research on
organic farming and food systems. Preference is
given to American researchers, but there is a
limited amount of funding for exceptional
international projects.
Publications: Application guidelines.
Financial data: Year ended 12/31/2011. Assets,
$568,369 (M); Expenditures, $1,387,113; Total
giving, $196,703; Grants to individuals, totaling
$196,703.
Fields of interest: Research; Agriculture;
Agriculture, sustainable programs; Agriculture/
food.
Type of support: Research.
Application information: Applications accepted.
Application form not required.
  Initial approach: Proposal
  Send request by: Mail or online
  Copies of proposal: 7
  Deadline(s): May 16 and Nov. 15
Program description:
  Education and Outreach Grants Program: Grants
  are available to fund research or education/
  outreach projects on any agricultural production,
  social, economic, or policy-related topic of concern
  to organic farmers or ranchers. Specifically, the
  foundation will fund the development of educational
  opportunities and materials that are pertinent to
  organic agricultural production or marketing, and/or
  programs that are aimed at organic producers, or
  those considering making the transition to organic
  certification. Funding is also available for projects
  in the categories of organic seed quality or
  crop-breeding, and projects that promote
  information-sharing among agricultural researchers
  and organic farmers and ranchers. The program is

open to all applicants residing in Canada, Mexico and the U.S. The foundation does not fund projects outside of these countries. Grants of up to $15,000 per year are available.
EIN: 770252545

847
Oro Grande Foundation
17671 Bear Valley Rd.
Hesperia, CA 92345
*Application address:*P.O. box 3523, Apple Valley, CA 92307

Foundation type: Independent foundation
Purpose: Scholarships for residents of CA pursuing a higher education.
Financial data: Year ended 12/31/2012. Assets, $0 (M); Expenditures, $33,314; Total giving, $23,000; Grants to individuals, 14 grants totaling $23,000 (high: $2,000, low: $1,000).
Fields of interest: Higher education.
Type of support: Scholarships—to individuals.
Application information: Application form required.
  Deadline(s): None
  Additional information: Application must include transcripts.
EIN: 952106478

848
Outpost for Contemporary Art
1268 N. Ave. 50
Los Angeles, CA 90042-2732 (323) 982-9461
E-mail: info@outpost-art.org; URL: http://www.outpost-art.org

Foundation type: Public charity
Purpose: Awards residencies to artists from Eastern and Central Europe with a focus on Ukraine, to stay in Los Angeles, CA.
Financial data: Year ended 06/30/2011. Assets, $29,705 (M); Expenditures, $55,570.
Fields of interest: Visual arts.
Type of support: Residencies.
Application information: Applications accepted.
  Initial approach: Contact organization for information
EIN: 260082871

849
OZ Foundation
1804 Garnet Ave., Ste. 389
San Diego, CA 92109-3352

Foundation type: Independent foundation
Purpose: Scholarships primarily to residents of CA in pursuit of a higher education.
Financial data: Year ended 12/31/2011. Assets, $4,151,549 (M); Expenditures, $217,716; Total giving, $189,623; Grants to individuals, 16 grants totaling $149,623 (high: $20,988, low: $1,000).
Fields of interest: Higher education.
Type of support: Scholarships—to individuals.
Application information: Applications not accepted.
EIN: 770556210

850
Pacific Pioneer Fund, Inc.
(formerly Pioneer Fund, Inc.)
P.O. Box 33
Inverness, CA 94937 (650) 996-3122
Contact: Armin Rosencranz, Exec. Dir.
Application address: P.O. Box 5775, Berkeley, CA 94705; URL: http://www.pacificpioneerfund.com

Foundation type: Independent foundation
Purpose: Grants to emerging documentary filmmakers or videographers who live and work in CA, OR, or WA.
Publications: Application guidelines; Grants list; Program policy statement.
Financial data: Year ended 06/30/2013. Assets, $0 (M); Expenditures, $29,464; Total giving, $27,000.
Fields of interest: Film/video.
Type of support: Grants to individuals.
Application information: Applications accepted. Application form required. Application form available on the grantmaker's web site.
  Send request by: Mail
  Deadline(s): Apr. 15, Aug. 15, Dec. 1 and June 1
  Additional information: Application should include a VHS tape or DVD of up to 10 minutes of edited footage from the project for which support is sought.
Program description:
  Media Grants: Grants ranging from $1,000 to $10,000 are made to public charities which undertake to supervise any project from which individuals receive funds. The fund does not support instructional or performance documentaries, or student film projects. Filmmakers are eligible for only one grant from the fund during their careers.
EIN: 942614215

851
Pack Foundation
5005 Texas St., Ste. 305
San Diego, CA 92108-3724

Foundation type: Operating foundation
Purpose: Scholarships to eligible students to attend San Diego State University, CA with tuition, books, fees, and living expenses.
Financial data: Year ended 12/31/2012. Assets, $3,014,905 (M); Expenditures, $116,094; Total giving, $92,400.
Fields of interest: Higher education.
Type of support: Scholarships—to individuals; Support to graduates or students of specific schools.
Application information: Unsolicited requests for funds not accepted.
EIN: 311621613

852
PADI Foundation
(also known as Professional Association of Diving Instructors Foundation)
9150 Wilshire Blvd., Ste. 300
Beverly Hills, CA 90212-3430 (310) 281-3200
Contact: Charles Rettig, Pres.
URL: http://www.padifoundation.org/

Foundation type: Operating foundation
Purpose: Research and project grants to individuals primarily in the fields of aquatic environment and underwater science.
Publications: Application guidelines; Financial statement; Grants list.

Financial data: Year ended 05/31/2013. Assets, $3,994,234 (M); Expenditures, $323,953; Total giving, $273,777.
Fields of interest: Athletics/sports, water sports; Marine science.
Type of support: Research; Grants to individuals.
Application information: Applications accepted. Application form required. Application form available on the grantmaker's web site.
  Send request by: Online
  Deadline(s): Feb. 1
  Final notification: Applicants notified May 3
  Additional information: The foundation utilizes the Common Grant Application, a web-based management program to receive and administer grant proposals.
EIN: 954326850

853
Palos Verdes Peninsula Education Foundation
P.O. Box 2632
Palos Verdes Peninsula, CA 90274-8632 (310) 378-2278
Contact: Andrea Sala, Exec. Dir.
FAX: (310) 378-2078; E-mail: help@pvpef.org; URL: http://www.pvpef.org

Foundation type: Public charity
Purpose: Grants of $500 to $1,000 to K-12 teachers in the Palos Verdes Peninsula School District, CA, for the purpose of enhancing and complementing curriculum already being taught.
Publications: Application guidelines; Financial statement; Newsletter.
Financial data: Year ended 06/30/2011. Assets, $5,746,488 (M); Expenditures, $3,546,070; Total giving, $2,507,093; Grants to individuals, totaling $500.
Fields of interest: Elementary/secondary education.
Type of support: Project support.
Application information: Applications accepted. Application form required. Application form available on the grantmaker's web site.
  Initial approach: Letter
  Deadline(s): Oct. 5
  Applicants should submit the following:
    1) Proposal
    2) Essay
    3) Budget Information
EIN: 953498211

854
Pancreatic Cancer Action Network, Inc.
1500 Rosecrans Ave., Ste. 200
Manhattan Beach, CA 90266-3721 (310) 725-0025
Contact: Julie Fleshman J.D., Pres. and C.E.O.
FAX: (310) 725-0029; E-mail: info@pancan.org; Toll-free tel.: (877) 272-6226; URL: http://www.pancan.org

Foundation type: Public charity
Purpose: Research grants to physicians and academics with a medical or doctoral degree who specialize in pancreatic cancer.
Publications: Application guidelines; Annual report; Grants list; Newsletter.
Financial data: Year ended 06/30/2012. Assets, $12,790,796 (M); Expenditures, $15,153,700; Total giving, $3,445,000.
Fields of interest: Cancer research; Organ research.
Type of support: Fellowships; Research.

Application information: Applications accepted. Application form required.
> *Deadline(s):* Nov. 10
> *Additional information:* See web site for further application and program information.

Program descriptions:

AACR-Pancreatic Cancer Action Network Career Development Awards: These grants, awarded in conjunction with the American Association for Cancer Research, provide two years' worth of support (of $100,000 each year) to early career scientists who are in the first four years of a faculty appointment to conduct pancreatic cancer research and establish successful career paths in their field. Research proposed for funding may be basic, translational, clinical, or epidemiological in nature, and must have direct applicability and relevance to pancreatic cancer. Grants may be used for direct research expenses, which may include salary and benefits of the grant recipient, postdoctoral or clinical research fellows, and/or research assistants, research/laboratory supplies, and equipment. Eligible applicants must have acquired a doctoral degree in a field related to cancer research, may not currently be a candidate for another degree, and must have completed postdoctoral studies or clinical fellowships no more than four years prior to the start of the grant term.

AACR-Pancreatic Cancer Action Network Fellowship: These fellowships, awarded in conjunction with the American Association for Cancer Research, provide a one-year grant of $45,000 to support the salary and benefits of a fellow while working on a mentored pancreatic cancer research project. Proposed research for funding may be basic, translational, clinical, or epidemiological in nature, and must have direct application and relevance to pancreatic cancer. Eligible applicants must have acquired a doctoral degree in a cancer-related field, may not currently be a candidate for another degree, and must be in the first, second, or third year of a postdoctoral or clinical research fellowship at an academic, medical, or research institution within the U.S. Up to 25 percent of the total grant may be designated for direct research support.

AACR-Pancreatic Cancer Action Network Innovative Grants: Awarded in conjunction with the American Association for Cancer Research, these two-year grants, of $200,000 each, are available to junior and senior investigators to develop and study new ideas and approaches that have direct application and relevance to pancreatic cancer. Proposed research may be basic, translational, clinical, or epidemiological in nature; grant funds will support direct research experiences, which may include salary and benefits of postdoctoral/clinical research fellows and/or research assistants, research/laboratory supplies, and equipment. Eligible applicants can be independent investigators at all levels who are affiliated with any academic, medical, or research institution within the U.S. and who are not postdoctoral or clinical research fellows, or the equivalent, who are working under the auspices of a scientific mentor.

AACR-Pancreatic Cancer Action Network Pathway to Leadership Grant: This grant, awarded in conjunction with the American Association for Cancer Research, will provide up to five years of support, for up to $600,000, to mentors at academic, medical, and research institutions across the U.S. The grant consists of two phases. The Mentored Phase, which can last for up to two years, will allow the recipient the time to complete research, publish results, and prepare to bridge to an independent research position. Funds during this phase will support the grantee's salary and research expenses. The Independent Phase of the program allows the recipient to undergo a research project that will be pursued as an independent investigator. Up to $450,000 of support will be allocated to allow the individual to continue to work toward establishing his/her own independent research program in pancreatic cancer research and progress along the path to leadership within this critical field. Eligible applicants must be postdoctoral or clinical research fellows who completed all doctoral degree requirements no more than five years prior to the start of the grant term; individuals currently or previously holding the ranks of instructor, adjunct professor, assistant professor, research assistant professor, the equivalent, or higher are not eligible for this program.
EIN: 330841281

855

Pasadena Methodist Foundation

500 East Colorado Blvd.
Pasadena, CA 91101-2027 (626) 796-0157
Scholarship e-mail: sclairday@charter.net
E-mail: sclairday@pasadenamethodistfoundation.org; URL: http://pasadenamethodistfoundation.org/

Foundation type: Public charity
Purpose: Scholarships to young adults in college and graduate students in the Pasadena, CA area, also scholarships to students earning their Masters of Divinity degree.
Publications: Application guidelines.
Financial data: Year ended 12/31/2011. Assets, $13,697,851 (M); Expenditures, $592,600; Total giving, $458,730; Grants to individuals, totaling $46,597.
Fields of interest: Higher education; Theological school/education.
Type of support: Scholarships—to individuals; Graduate support.
Application information: Applications accepted. Application form required. Application form available on the grantmaker's web site.
> *Initial approach:* Application
> *Send request by:* Mail or e-mail
> *Deadline(s):* May 28
> *Final notification:* Recipients notified after June 30
> *Applicants should submit the following:*
> 1) Transcripts
> 2) Financial information

Program description:
> *Scholarships:* The foundation awards scholarships to seminary students studying to become church ministers, as well as scholarships to other students who wish to pursue full-time undergraduate coursework.
EIN: 956047662

856

Robert J. & Claire Pasarow Foundation

3029 Wilshire Blvd., Ste. 200
Santa Monica, CA 90403-2364 (310) 828-7547
Contact: Susan Pasarow, Secy.

Foundation type: Independent foundation
Purpose: Grants to individuals for medical and scientific research in the fields of cancer, cardiovascular and neuropsychiatric disease.
Financial data: Year ended 10/31/2012. Assets, $2,251,868 (M); Expenditures, $227,877; Total giving, $180,000; Grants to individuals, 9 grants totaling $180,000 (high: $20,000, low: $20,000).
Fields of interest: Institute; Research.
Type of support: Research.

Application information: Applications accepted.
> *Initial approach:* Letter
> *Deadline(s):* Aug. 31
> *Additional information:* Application must include resume and statement of achievements in applicant's field.
EIN: 954079676

857

Pebble Beach Company Foundation

P.O. Box 1767
Pebble Beach, CA 93953-1767 (831) 625-8445
Contact: for Scholarships: Jeanne Sison
FAX: (831) 625-8441

Foundation type: Public charity
Purpose: Scholarships for children of Pebble Beach Company employees for postsecondary education.
Financial data: Year ended 12/31/2011. Assets, $5,559,968 (M); Expenditures, $513,400; Total giving, $339,971; Grants to individuals, totaling $100,600.
Fields of interest: Higher education.
Type of support: Grants to individuals.
Application information: Applications accepted.
> *Initial approach:* Telephone
> *Additional information:* Contact foundation for application guidelines.
EIN: 510189888

858

Mario Pedrozzi Scholarship Foundation

1040 Florence Rd., No. 21
Livermore, CA 94550-5543 (925) 456-3700
FAX: (925) 456-3701;
E-mail: info@pedrozzifoundation.org; URL: http://www.pedrozzifoundation.org

Foundation type: Operating foundation
Purpose: Scholarships to deserving graduates of Livermore high schools in pursuit of higher education, and to graduates of Alameda county high schools who will be attending St. Patrick's Seminary and University in Menlo Park, CA.
Financial data: Year ended 09/30/2013. Assets, $8,578,083 (M); Expenditures, $507,635; Total giving, $286,000.
Fields of interest: Vocational education, post-secondary; Higher education; College (community/junior); Theological school/education.
Type of support: Graduate support; Undergraduate support.
Application information: Applications accepted. Application form required. Application form available on the grantmaker's web site.
> *Send request by:* Mail or hand delivered
> *Deadline(s):* Mar. 16
> *Additional information:* Application should include transcripts.
EIN: 201025764

859

Richard Penjoyan Educational Trust

17321 Rob Roy Cir.
Huntington Beach, CA 92647-5672 (714) 842-8632
Contact: Peggy L. Penjoyan, Tr.

Foundation type: Independent foundation
Purpose: Scholarships to students residing in Orange or Los Angeles county, CA with minimum academic performance who show an aptitude for higher education.

Financial data: Year ended 12/31/2012. Assets, $211,402 (M); Expenditures, $22,841; Total giving, $22,000; Grants to individuals, 6 grants totaling $22,000 (high: $5,000, low: $3,000).
Fields of interest: Education.
Type of support: Scholarships—to individuals.
Application information: Applications accepted. Application form required.
  Deadline(s): Apr. 30
  Additional information: Application should include a short essay. Applicant must show proof of community involvement through volunteer work, employment and participate in sports.
EIN: 336277180

860
Penny Lane Centers
15305 Rayen St.
North Hills, CA 91343-5117 (818) 894-3384
Contact: Ivelise Markovits, C.E.O.
FAX: (818) 892-3574;
E-mail: contact@pennylane.org; URL: http://www.pennylane.org

Foundation type: Public charity
Purpose: Stipends to foster families of southern CA, as well as social services to children and families.
Financial data: Year ended 06/30/2011. Assets, $31,745,155 (M); Expenditures, $37,971,372; Total giving, $3,827,376; Grants to individuals, totaling $3,827,376.
Fields of interest: Children/youth.
Type of support: Grants for special needs.
Application information:
  Initial approach: Letter
EIN: 952633765

861
Performing Arts Center of Los Angeles County
135 N. Grand Ave.
Los Angeles, CA 90012-3013 (213) 972-7211
E-mail: general@musiccenter.org; TTY: (213) 972-7615; URL: http://www.musiccenter.org/

Foundation type: Public charity
Purpose: Scholarships and awards for high school performing and visual artists. Awards for teachers for exemplary education in the arts in the Los Angeles county, CA area.
Publications: Application guidelines.
Financial data: Year ended 06/30/2011. Assets, $89,251,824 (M); Expenditures, $47,145,732; Total giving, $2,061,805; Grants to individuals, totaling $98,750.
Fields of interest: Visual arts; Performing arts; Arts.
Type of support: Scholarships—to individuals; Awards/prizes.
Application information: Applications accepted.
  Deadline(s): Varies
  Additional information: Teachers must be nominated for the BRAVO awards.
Program descriptions:
  BRAVO Awards: This program recognizes teachers and schools for innovation and excellence in arts education, honoring educators who use the arts to revitalize teaching, enhance student achievement, and foster self-esteem, teamwork, and cross-cultural communication and understanding. Four awards are given under this program: the General Education Teacher BRAVO Award (given to classroom teachers whose primarily responsibility is not the arts, but who consistently utilize the arts within the core curriculum in an

exemplary way during the regular instructional school day; nominees must hold a four-year degree and teach regular, continuation, or special education in grades K-12 at least five hours per day and five days per week); Arts Specialists Teacher BRAVE Award (given to classroom teachers who are employed by a school, and whose primary responsibility is teaching an arts discipline during the regular instructional school day; nominees must hold a four-year degree and teach regular, continuation, or special education in grades K-12 at least ten hours per week); Overall School BRAVO Award (awarded to regular, continuation, or special education school in grades K-12); and School Program BRAVO Award (given to schools who do not provide ongoing instruction in all arts disciplines; all students must be able to participate, instruction must be sequential, and more than one teacher must provide the arts instruction). Eligible applicants must be based in Los Angeles County.
  Spotlight Awards: Awards scholarships annually to finalists, semifinalists, and participants who received honorable mention. Sixteen grand prize finalists are chosen, two from each category. First Grand Prizes, $5,000 scholarships. Second Grand Prizes, $4,000. Honorable mentions, $250 scholarships and Semifinalists, $100 scholarships.
EIN: 952217011

862
Performing Arts Scholarship Foundation
2024 Grand Ave.
Santa Barbara, CA 93103 (805) 898-0941
E-mail: info@pasfsb.org; URL: http://www.pasfsb.org

Foundation type: Public charity
Purpose: Scholarships to aid music students in the Santa Barbara, CA area.
Publications: Application guidelines.
Financial data: Year ended 12/31/2011. Assets, $1,530,800 (M); Expenditures, $80,559; Total giving, $62,550; Grants to individuals, totaling $18,600.
Fields of interest: Music.
Type of support: Undergraduate support.
Application information: Applications accepted. Application form required.
  Initial approach: Letter
  Deadline(s): Mar. 6
Program description:
  Scholarships: The foundation provides scholarships to deserving vocal and instrumental students with professional potential who live and/or study in the Santa Barbara area. Funds can be used for many different career development needs, such as tuition at an established institution, study with a master teacher, instrument improvement, or audition expenses. Recipients are based on applications and auditions.
EIN: 953757549

863
The Pergo Foundation
(formerly The Andrew and Denise Goldfarb Family Foundation)
14170 Chandler Blvd.
Sherman Oaks, CA 91401-5714
Contact: Andrew Goldfarb, Pres. and Dir.; Denise Goldfarb, C.F.O., Secy., and Dir.

Foundation type: Independent foundation
Purpose: Scholarships to individuals residing in the Sherman Oaks, CA, area for attendance at institutions of higher learning.

Financial data: Year ended 06/30/2013. Assets, $3,867,283 (M); Expenditures, $253,882; Total giving, $226,059; Grants to individuals, 95 grants totaling $92,349 (high: $1,899, low: $100).
Type of support: Undergraduate support.
Application information: Applications accepted.
  Initial approach: Letter
  Deadline(s): None
EIN: 954610805

864
Pfaffinger Foundation
316 W. 2nd St., Ste. PH-C
Los Angeles, CA 90012-3504
Contact: Roberto F. Valdez, Business Mgr.
FAX: (213) 680-7474;
E-mail: rvaldez@pfoundation.org

Foundation type: Independent foundation
Purpose: Emergency assistance to employees and retirees of the former Times Mirror Co., and employees and retirees of the Los Angeles Times.
Financial data: Year ended 12/31/2012. Assets, $76,271,475 (M); Expenditures, $4,805,774; Total giving, $3,289,201; Grants to individuals, totaling $2,778,995.
Type of support: Grants for special needs.
Application information: Applications accepted. Application form required. Interview required.
  Initial approach: Letter
  Copies of proposal: 1
  Deadline(s): July 15 and Oct. 1
  Final notification: Recipients notified in Sept., and Dec.
  Additional information: Application should include a copy of last two paycheck stubs and income tax statement from the previous year.
EIN: 951661675

865
Philanthropic Ventures Foundation
1222 Preservation Park Way
Oakland, CA 94612-1201 (510) 645-1890
Contact: Bill Somerville, Pres. and Exec. Dir.
FAX: (510) 645-1892;
E-mail: info@venturesfoundation.org; URL: http://www.venturesfoundation.org

Foundation type: Public charity
Purpose: Grants to teachers are available to enhance after school, arts, mathematics, and special education projects.
Publications: Application guidelines; Annual report; Informational brochure; Newsletter.
Financial data: Year ended 12/31/2011. Assets, $16,286,850 (M); Expenditures, $8,517,326; Total giving, $7,992,274.
Fields of interest: Arts education; Elementary/secondary education; Children/youth, services.
Type of support: Grants to individuals.
Application information: Applications accepted. Application form not required.
  Additional information: See web site for additional guidelines.
Program descriptions:
  After School Program Grants: Grants of up to $2,500 are available to Alum Rock, East Side Union High, Franklin-McKinley, Oakland, and Redwood City school district teachers (grades 6-12), to create and maintain after-school programs for their students. Grants are intended to cover costs of equipment, teacher time, and/or refreshments; examples of eligible after-school programs include running clubs, dance clubs, ecology clubs, yearbook clubs, school choirs, skateboarding clubs, drama clubs, chess clubs, school newspaper teams, yoga

clubs, and guitar clubs; school sports teams are ineligible to receive funding.

Arts Resource Grants Program: This program provides grants of up to $500 to public-school teachers (K-8) working in Alum Rock, Belmont, Cabrillo, East Palo Alto, Franklin/McKinley, Menlo Park, Mountain View/Whisman, Pescadero, Redwood City, and San Carlos school districts, to enhance classroom and after-school arts programs. Examples of eligible funding uses include art supplies, costs associated with visiting artists, scripts, instruments, scores, sound equipment, stipends for after-school arts teaching, costumes, props, and professional development.

Geballe Excursion Grants: Grants of up to $1,000 are available to K-5 public school teachers working in Alameda and San Mateo county school districts, to fund classroom excursions. Funds can cover the costs of transportation, admission fees, and food, and can be used to take students to area beaches, museums, ferries, classroom hikes, or picnics.

Mathematics Resource Grants: Grants of up to $500 are available to preschool teachers in programs serving low-income families and public school teachers (grades K-3) who work in San Mateo and Santa Clara counties. Grants can be used to fund books, materials, software, manipulatives, and professional development opportunities related to mathematics.

Social Worker/CASA Resource Grants: Grants of up to $250 will be awarded to social workers or court-appointed special advocates (CASAs) to help meet the critical needs of clients who are children in dependency court. Funding can be used for eye glasses, dental care, medical testing, clothing, school supplies, tutoring, music lessons, and summer camp opportunities. Applicants must be working with foster care youth in Alameda, Contra Costa, San Francisco, San Mateo, and/or Santa Clara counties.

Special Education Resource Grants: Grants of up to $500 are available to public school teachers or therapists serving special-needs children (children with individualized education plans), pre-K through 12th grade, in the Alameda, Contra Costa, and Solano County public school system. Funding can be used for classroom supplies and resources, therapists' pull-out sessions, educational field trips, or professional development opportunities.
EIN: 943136771

866
Philharmonic Society of Orange County
2082 Business Ctr. Dr., Ste. 100
Irvine, CA 92612-1151 (949) 553-2422
Contact: music scholarships: Dean Corey, Pres.
FAX: (949) 553-2421;
E-mail: contactus@philharmonicsociety.org;
URL: http://www.philharmonicsociety.org

Foundation type: Public charity
Purpose: Scholarships to students who display exceptional music talent.
Financial data: Year ended 06/30/2012. Assets, $2,488,146 (M); Expenditures, $3,799,871.
Fields of interest: Music; Performing arts, education.
Type of support: Scholarships—to individuals.
Application information: Recipients are selected by the educational institutions instructors.
EIN: 951805452

867
Physicians Aid Association
(also known as Aleck Sandler and Co.)
c/o Sandler
292 S. La Cienega Blvd., Ste. 212
Beverly Hills, CA 90211-3341

Foundation type: Independent foundation
Purpose: Medical and financial assistance to physicians living or working in Los Angeles County, CA, who are disabled or retired, and to their immediate families.
Financial data: Year ended 12/31/2012. Assets, $4,199,839 (M); Expenditures, $257,090; Total giving, $161,399; Grants to individuals, 12 grants totaling $161,399 (high: $39,200, low: $2,565).
Fields of interest: Disabilities, people with.
Type of support: Grants for special needs.
Application information: Applications accepted. Application form required.
   Initial approach: Letter or telephone
   Deadline(s): None
EIN: 951660852

868
Piedemonte Charitable Trust
555 Laurel Ave., Ste. 614
San Mateo, CA 94401-4154

Foundation type: Operating foundation
Purpose: Scholarships to residents of San Mateo, CA, who wish to attend school in CA.
Financial data: Year ended 12/31/2011. Assets, $34,273 (M); Expenditures, $52,335; Total giving, $51,775; Grants to individuals, 22 grants totaling $47,318 (high: $5,000, low: $1,000).
Type of support: Undergraduate support.
Application information: Applications not accepted.
   Additional information: Unsolicited requests for funds not accepted.
EIN: 946705153

869
Pirkle Jones Foundation
7 Linsdale Ln.
P.O. Box 1048
Point Reyes Station, CA 94956-1048 (415) 663-8533
E-mail: pirkle@earthlink.net; URL: http://www.pirklejones.com/

Foundation type: Public charity
Purpose: Grants to outstanding emerging or mid-level artists residing in Marin County, CA.
Publications: Application guidelines.
Financial data: Year ended 06/30/2012. Assets, $19,842,180 (M); Expenditures, $451,880; Total giving, $102,848; Grants to individuals, totaling $25,000.
Fields of interest: Visual arts; Arts.
Type of support: Grants to individuals.
Application information: Applications accepted. Application form required. Application form available on the grantmaker's web site.
   Deadline(s): Mar. 30
   Final notification: Recipients notified June 15
   Applicants should submit the following:
      1) Resume
      2) Financial information
   Additional information: Application should also include one CD or DVD with five digital images of work (in .jpg format), four copies each of image documentation, and artist statement.

Program description:
   Visual Artists Support Program Grants: The foundation supports promising emerging and mid-career artists living in Marin County with a one-year, $25,000 grant. Eligible applicants must be residents of Marin County who work in one or more of the following mediums, ceramics, collage, drawing, installation, painting, photography, printmaking, sculpture, or static digital art. Applicants must also be 18 years of age or older, and meet maximum annual income guidelines.
EIN: 680664486

870
Placer Community Foundation
219 Maple St.
Auburn, CA 95603 (530) 885-4920
Contact: Veronica Blake, C.E.O.; Jessica Hubbard, Philanthropic Svcs. Mgr.
FAX: (530) 885-4989; E-mail: info@placercf.org; Mailing address: P.O. 9207, Auburn, CA 95604-9207; URL: http://www.placercf.org

Foundation type: Community foundation
Purpose: Scholarships to graduates of Placer Union High School District, CA.
Publications: Application guidelines; Annual report; Financial statement; Grants list; Informational brochure; Newsletter.
Financial data: Year ended 12/31/2011. Assets, $5,183,550 (M); Expenditures, $1,045,736; Total giving, $597,919.
Type of support: Support to graduates or students of specific schools.
Application information: Applications not accepted.
   Additional information: Unsolicited requests for funds not accepted or considered.
EIN: 201485011

871
Peter & Masha Plotkin Foundation
9700 Aviation Blvd., Ste. 1
Los Angeles, CA 90045
URL: http://www.peterplotkinartist.com/

Foundation type: Operating foundation
Purpose: Scholarships to students in CA for higher education and to travel overseas.
Financial data: Year ended 12/31/2012. Assets, $3,426,980 (M); Expenditures, $318,527; Total giving, $21,000; Grant to an individual, 1 grant totaling $3,500.
Type of support: Undergraduate support; Travel grants.
Application information: Applications not accepted.
EIN: 954394293

872
Ploughshares Fund
1808 Wedermeyer St., Ste. 200
San Francisco, CA 94129 (415) 668-2244
E-mail: ploughshares@ploughshares.org; Additional address (DC office): 1430 K St., N.W., Ste. 550, Washington, DC 20005-2504, tel.: (202) 783-4401, fax: (202) 783-4407; URL: http://www.ploughshares.org

Foundation type: Public charity
Purpose: Research grants to individuals who seek to prevent the spread and use of nuclear, chemical, biological and other weapons of war, and to prevent conflicts that could lead to the use of weapons of mass destruction.

Publications: Annual report (including application guidelines); Grants list; Informational brochure (including application guidelines); Newsletter.
Financial data: Year ended 06/30/2012. Assets, $34,271,572 (M); Expenditures, $6,646,219; Total giving, $4,089,957; Grants to individuals, totaling $169,375.
Fields of interest: Arms control.
Type of support: Program development; Seed money; Research.
Application information: Application form not required.
  Initial approach: Letter or e-mail
  Copies of proposal: 1
EIN: 942764520

873
Plumas Community Foundation
P.O. Box 4157
Quincy, CA 95971-4157 (530) 283-2735
Contact: Michele Piller, Secy.
FAX: (530) 283-3647; E-mail: mpiller@ncen.org

Foundation type: Community foundation
Purpose: Educational scholarships to residents of Plumas county, CA.
Publications: Informational brochure.
Financial data: Year ended 12/31/2012. Assets, $71,166 (M); Expenditures, $15,403; Total giving, $0.
Type of support: Undergraduate support.
Application information: Applications not accepted.
  Additional information: Unsolicited requests for funds not considered or acknowledged.
EIN: 943315367

874
The PMC Foundation
12243 Branford St.
Sun Valley, CA 91352-1010

Foundation type: Company-sponsored foundation
Purpose: Scholarships to eligible individuals for higher education at colleges or universities.
Financial data: Year ended 10/31/2012. Assets, $0 (M); Expenditures, $70,946; Total giving, $67,386; Grants to individuals, 20 grants totaling $67,386 (high: $6,600, low: $992).
Type of support: Scholarships—to individuals.
Application information:
  Initial approach: Letter
  Additional information: Contact foundation for current application guidelines.
EIN: 954194948

875
Point Foundation
5757 Wilshire Blvd., Ste. 370
Los Angeles, CA 90036-5810 (323) 933-1234
Contact: Jorge Valencia, Exec. Dir. and C.E.O.
E-mail: info@pointfoundation.org; Toll-free tel.: (866) 337-6468, fax: (866) 397-6468; Additional addresses (New York office): 1357 Broadway, Ste. 401, New York, NY 10018-7101; (Chicago office): 201 W. Lake St., No. 206, Chicago, IL 60606-1803; URL: http://www.pointfoundation.org

Foundation type: Public charity
Purpose: Scholarships to LGBT undergraduate, graduate or postgraduate students attending accredited colleges or universities in the U.S.
Publications: Application guidelines; Annual report.

Financial data: Year ended 06/30/2012. Assets, $7,901,066 (M); Expenditures, $3,144,539; Total giving, $641,009; Grants to individuals, totaling $641,009.
Fields of interest: Higher education; LGBTQ.
Type of support: Undergraduate support.
Application information: Applications accepted. Application form required. Application form available on the grantmaker's web site.
  Initial approach: Letter
  Send request by: Online
  Deadline(s): Feb. 12
  Final notification: Recipients notified May 1
  Applicants should submit the following:
    1) Transcripts
    2) SAT
    3) ACT
Program description:
  Scholarships: The average scholarship award per scholar is $13,600 and the average total program expense that include scholarship funding, mentoring and leadership training is $34,000 per year. It is available to outstanding lesbian, gay, bisexual, and transgender students to cover college or university tuition, books, supplies, room and board, transportation, and living expenses and to set up with the individual college to meet the needs of the Point Scholar. In exchange, all scholars agree to maintain a high level of academic performance and give back to the LGBT community through the completion of an individual community service project.
EIN: 841582086

876
Pomona Valley Community Hospital LTD-Womens Auxiliary
1798 N. Garey Ave.
Pomona, CA 91767-2918
Contact: Marcia Paetau, Pres.

Foundation type: Public charity
Purpose: Scholarships to individuals planning to pursue heath care education.
Financial data: Year ended 12/31/2011. Assets, $459,970 (M); Expenditures, $182,513; Total giving, $117,411; Grants to individuals, totaling $13,750.
Fields of interest: Health sciences school/education; Volunteer services.
Type of support: Undergraduate support.
Application information: Application form required. Interview required.
  Additional information: A committee of auxiliary members evaluates and scores students, those with the highest scores are awarded scholarships.
EIN: 956053224

877
The Leslie Poole Foundation
30 Alhambra Ct.
Portola Valley, CA 94028-7723 (650) 367-9750
E-mail: wgpoole@msn.com

Foundation type: Independent foundation
Purpose: College scholarships to graduating seniors of Woodside High School, CA for continuing education at institutions of higher learning.
Financial data: Year ended 10/31/2012. Assets, $113,837 (M); Expenditures, $12,649; Total giving, $12,500; Grants to individuals, 5 grants totaling $12,500 (high: $2,500, low: $2,500).
Fields of interest: Higher education.
Type of support: Support to graduates or students of specific schools.

Application information: Applications accepted. Application form required.
  Deadline(s): May 1
EIN: 942777559

878
Price Charities
(formerly San Diego Revitalization Corporation)
7979 Ivanhoe Ave., Ste. 520
La Jolla, CA 92037-4513 (858) 551-2321
Contact: Robert Price
Additional address (City Heights office): 4305 University Ave., Ste. 600, San Diego, CA 92105-1695, tel.: (619) 795-2000; URL: http://www.pricecharities.com

Foundation type: Public charity
Purpose: Provides fellowship opportunities for high school students in the San Diego, CA area.
Financial data: Year ended 12/31/2011. Assets, $161,830,774 (M); Expenditures, $9,762,726; Total giving, $1,360,383.
Fields of interest: Education.
Type of support: Fellowships.
Application information: Applications accepted.
  Initial approach: Contact participating school for application
Program description:
  Aaron Price Fellows Program: This program works to enrich the lives of a diverse group of high school students within the City Heights area. Fellows receive a three-year, hands-on look at San Diego's governmental, cultural, and business communities, and participate in trips to state and national capitals. Eligible applicants must be in the 9th grade, attend one of four San Diego Unified School District-area high schools (Lincoln High School, Hoover High School, Point Loma High School, and University City High School), and have good academic standing and attendance.
EIN: 330898712

879
The Price Family Charitable Fund
(formerly The Sol & Helen Price Foundation)
7979 Ivanhoe Ave., Ste. 520
La Jolla, CA 92037-4513 (858) 551-2321
Contact: Terry Malavenda
E-mail: tmalavenda@pricefamilyfund.org; URL: http://www.pricefamilyfund.org

Foundation type: Independent foundation
Purpose: Fellowships and scholarships primarily to residents of San Diego, CA.
Financial data: Year ended 12/31/2012. Assets, $517,568,212 (M); Expenditures, $27,098,099; Total giving, $21,674,976.
Type of support: Fellowships.
Application information: Applications not accepted.
  Additional information: Unsolicited requests for funds not considered or acknowledged.
EIN: 953842468

880
Price Foundation, Inc.
c/o Loren Sanchez
1543 Upland Hills Dr. N.
Upland, CA 91784-9170
Application Address: c/o Price Foundation, P.O. Box 672 Upland, CA 91785

Foundation type: Independent foundation
Purpose: Interest-free student loans to residents of the west end of San Bernardino County, CA.

Financial data: Year ended 12/31/2012. Assets, $1,778,779 (M); Expenditures, $206,682; Total giving, $179,500.
Fields of interest: Vocational education.
Type of support: Student loans—to individuals.
Application information: Applications accepted. Application form required. Interview required.
Initial approach: Letter
Deadline(s): None
Additional information: Application must include GPA, personal statement, and three letters of reference.
EIN: 956069011

881
M. B. Price Foundation, Inc.
P.O. Box 5100
Visalia, CA 93278-5100

Foundation type: Independent foundation
Purpose: Scholarships to residents of Visalia, CA, for higher education.
Financial data: Year ended 10/31/2012. Assets, $1,193,182 (M); Expenditures, $995,207; Total giving, $947,212; Grants to individuals, totaling $443,887.
Type of support: Undergraduate support.
Application information: Applications not accepted.
Additional information: Unsolicited requests for funds not considered or acknowledged.
EIN: 300121911

882
Scott R. Pritchett Trust
c/o Wells Fargo Bank, N.A.
P.O. Box 63954, MAC A0348-012
San Francisco, CA 94163-0001

Foundation type: Independent foundation
Purpose: Scholarships to graduating seniors of Los Molinos High School who are residents of Vina, CA.
Financial data: Year ended 12/31/2011. Assets, $756,339 (M); Expenditures, $46,321; Total giving, $32,456.
Fields of interest: Higher education; Scholarships/financial aid.
Type of support: Undergraduate support.
Application information: Applications not accepted.
Additional information: Contributes only to preselected individuals.
Program description:
S.R. Pritchett Scholarship: The scholarship may be used upon graduation from high schools by students from the Vina area to enable them to pursue their studies, or develop their talents in schools, colleges or universities anywhere in the world. The recipient shall not be determined solely by academic standing but should have at least average grades.
EIN: 946060240

883
Project Tomorrow
15707 Rockfield Blvd., Ste. 330
Irvine, CA 92618-2870 (949) 609-4660
Contact: Kelly Newberry, Grants Mgr.
FAX: (949) 609-4665;
E-mail: knewberry@tomorrow.org; Additional e-mail: jevans@tomorrow.org; URL: http://www.tomorrow.org

Foundation type: Public charity

Purpose: Awards by nomination only to principals and science teachers for exemplary work in the Orange County, CA, area.
Publications: Application guidelines; Annual report; Informational brochure; Newsletter.
Financial data: Year ended 12/31/2011. Assets, $584,076 (M); Expenditures, $622,752.
Fields of interest: Education; Science.
Type of support: Awards/grants by nomination only; Awards/prizes.
Application information:
Send request by: E-mail or fax
Deadline(s): Mar. 15
Final notification: Applicants notified Apr. 12
Additional information: Nominees may be self-nominated or nominated by a district and/or school staff person or other educational organizations.
Program description:
Innovation in Education Awards: This program recognizes educational leaders and students for their innovative uses of science, math, and technology in the classroom and community. Award categories include Innovative School Program, High-Impact Teaching, and Emerging Student Innovator. Eligible applicants include all Orange County public school districts (including ROP districts) and their schools, private schools, and parochial schools, as well as affiliated principals, classroom teachers, and high-school students. Nominations may be self-submitted or may be submitted by a district and/or school staff person, supporting organization (such as a PTA unit), parent advisory committee, or youth-based organization. Winning teachers will receive a $1,000 award to use to expand a science, math, or technology program in their classroom, while students will receive a $2,500 scholarship to put towards tuition at the college of his/her choice.
EIN: 954581958

884
Promises 2 Kids
(formerly Child Abuse Prevention Foundation)
9440 Ruffin Ct., Ste. 2
San Diego, CA 92123-5300 (858) 278-4400
Contact: Tonya Torosian M.S.W., C.E.O.
Additional e-mail: kathie@capfsd.org
FAX: (858) 278-4480; E-mail: info@capfsd.org; Tel. for T. Torosian: (858) 427-1101, e-mail: Tonya@promises2kids.org;; URL: http://www.promises2kids.org

Foundation type: Public charity
Purpose: Scholarships to former foster youth of San Diego, CA, to help ease the financial burden of attending college. Support and assistance for foster youth and former foster youth in the San Diego, CA, area.
Publications: Application guidelines; Informational brochure; Newsletter.
Financial data: Year ended 12/31/2011. Assets, $4,035,498 (M); Expenditures, $2,357,764; Total giving, $831,353. Scholarships—to individuals amount not specified.
Fields of interest: Higher education; Child abuse; Youth, services.
Type of support: Scholarships—to individuals; Grants for special needs.
Application information: Applications accepted. Application form required. Application form available on the grantmaker's web site.
Initial approach: Telephone
Deadline(s): Mar. 7 for scholarships

Additional information: Application should include transcript, class schedule, and a copy of award letter.
EIN: 953655288

885
Prostate Cancer Foundation
(formerly Association for the Cure of Cancer of the Prostate)
1250 4th St.
Santa Monica, CA 90401-1304 (310) 570-4700
Contact: Jonathan W. Simons, Pres. and C.E.O.
FAX: (310) 570-4701;
E-mail: info@prostatecancerfoundation.org; Toll-free tel.: (800) 757-2873; URL: http://www.prostatecancerfoundation.org

Foundation type: Public charity
Purpose: Research grants to scientists studying treatments for prostate cancer.
Publications: Application guidelines; Annual report; Newsletter.
Financial data: Year ended 12/31/2012. Assets, $52,761,398 (M); Expenditures, $42,489,583; Total giving, $29,127,546.
Fields of interest: Prostate cancer; Prostate cancer research.
Type of support: Research.
Application information: Applications accepted. Application form required. Application form available on the grantmaker's web site.
Initial approach: E-mail
Send request by: On-line
Deadline(s): Nov. 6 for Challenge Award, Nov. 13 for Young Investigator Awards
Applicants should submit the following:
1) Budget Information
2) Proposal
3) Essay
Additional information: See web site for additional guidelines.
Program descriptions:
Creativity Awards: This two year award for $300,000 support exceptionally novel projects with great potential to produce breakthroughs for detecting and treating prostrate cancer. They are complementary and integrated with other PCF award programs.
Young Investigator Awards: These awards aim to focus efforts on developing younger and early-career prostate cancer researchers. Applications are encouraged from early-career basic scientists, medical oncologists, pathologists, urologists, radiologists, radiation oncologists, public health experts, or professionals from other medical research disciplines. Investigators with diverse expertise from anywhere in the world are invited to apply. This year, the foundation encourages research molecular pathologists and bioinformaticians to apply. Applicants should be within six years of completing a professional degree or clinical training, such as M.D., Ph.D., M.D.-Ph.D., M.P.H., or equivalent. Awards will be for three years, at $75,000 per year.
EIN: 954418411

886
Public Health Foundation Enterprises, Inc.
12801 Crossroads Pkwy. S., Ste. 200
City of Industry, CA 91746-3505 (562) 699-7320
Contact: Nancy Kindelan, C.E.O.
FAX: (562) 692-6950; E-mail: info@phfe.org;
URL: http://www.phfe.org

Foundation type: Public charity
Purpose: Support to individuals for well established projects through a fiscal sponsorship program.
Financial data: Year ended 06/30/2012. Assets, $21,747,890 (M); Expenditures, $109,533,578.
Fields of interest: Public health.
Type of support: Fiscal agent/sponsor.
Application information: Applications accepted. Application form required. Application form available on the grantmaker's web site.
  Deadline(s): None
  Additional information: Applicants projects must closely align with the foundation's mission. No incubator projects considered.
Program description:
  Fiscal Sponsorship: The foundation provides comprehensive fiscal sponsorship to government, nonprofits and foundations throughout the United States. It seeks to help clients reduce costs, increase efficiency, and build capacity.
EIN: 952557063

887
Public Health Institute
555 12th St., 10th Fl.
Oakland, CA 94607-4046 (510) 285-5500
Contact: Donna Sofaer, V.P., Comms., Devel., and Public Rels.
FAX: (510) 285-5501;
E-mail: communications@phi.org; URL: http://www.phi.org

Foundation type: Public charity
Purpose: Support to investigators and project managers to explore new questions, forge new relationships, and develop new solutions to emerging public health challenges through the institute's various roles of initiator, fiscal sponsor, incubator, partner, and collaborator.
Publications: Application guidelines.
Financial data: Year ended 12/31/2011. Assets, $26,768,101 (M); Expenditures, $96,345,880; Total giving, $7,297,526.
Fields of interest: Public health.
Type of support: Project support; Fiscal agent/sponsor.
Application information: Applications accepted.
  Additional information: Contact the institute for guidelines.
EIN: 941646278

888
Pursuit of Excellence
1795 Hamilton Ave.
Palo Alto, CA 94303-3006 (650) 322-9417
Contact: Carol Mullin, Pres.

Foundation type: Public charity
Purpose: Scholarships to financially needy high school seniors from certain schools in Palo Alto and the Sequoia Union High School District, CA. Family income must be under $20,000.
Financial data: Year ended 05/31/2012. Assets, $1,318,235 (M); Expenditures, $250,151; Total giving, $237,510; Grants to individuals, totaling $237,510.

Type of support: Support to graduates or students of specific schools; Undergraduate support.
Application information: Application form required. Interview required.
  Initial approach: Letter
  Deadline(s): Feb. 15
  Applicants should submit the following:
    1) SAR
    2) FAFSA
    3) Transcripts
    4) Letter(s) of recommendation
    5) Financial information
    6) Essay
  Additional information: Scholarships are renewable.
EIN: 770054289

889
QUALCOMM Incorporated Corporate Giving Program
c/o Community Involvement
5775 Morehouse Dr.
San Diego, CA 92121-1714 (858) 651-3200
Contact: Allison Kelly, Sr. Mgr., Community Involvement
FAX: (858) 651-3255;
E-mail: philanthropy@qualcomm.com; Tel. for Allison Kelly: (858) 651-4027, e-mail: allison@qualcomm.com; URL: http://www.qualcomm.com/about/citizenship/community

Foundation type: Corporate giving program
Purpose: Scholarships to employees of QUALCOMM Incorporated who work at least 40 hours per week. Recipients must be actively employed at both the beginning and end of the educational courses that the scholarship funds.
Publications: Application guidelines; Corporate giving report (including application guidelines); Informational brochure (including application guidelines); Program policy statement.
Fields of interest: Vocational education; Higher education; Adult/continuing education; Education.
Type of support: Employee-related scholarships.
Application information: Applications not accepted.
  Additional information: Unsolicited requests for funds not considered or acknowledged.
Program description:
  Employee Scholarship Program: The company awards reimbursement scholarships of up to $5,250 per calendar year for the cost of tuition, books, and parking for courses toward continuing education, certification programs, and associate's or bachelor's degrees. Reimbursement is based on grade achieved and the program of study must be pre-approved and considered job-related. Employees become eligible on their date of hire.
Company name: QUALCOMM Incorporated

890
Quality Care Health Foundation, Inc.
2201 K St.
Sacramento, CA 95816-4922 (916) 441-6400
Contact: James H. Gomez, Pres. and C.E.O.
FAX: (916) 441-4454; E-mail: info@cahf.org;
URL: http://www.qchf.org

Foundation type: Public charity
Purpose: Scholarships to CA vocational nurse students.
Publications: Application guidelines; Financial statement; Newsletter.
Financial data: Year ended 12/31/2012. Assets, $512,628 (M); Expenditures, $950,092; Total

giving, $42,936; Grants to individuals, totaling $42,936.
Fields of interest: Health care.
Type of support: Undergraduate support.
Application information:
  Initial approach: Letter
  Deadline(s): Sept. 15
Program descriptions:
  Career Climb Scholarships: Scholarships, ranging from $500 to $2,500, are available for applicants with one or more years of work experience in long-term care, who are actively employed in the long-term care industry.
  Vocational Nurse Scholarship and Loan Repayment Program: This program offers up to $8,000 in scholarship and loan repayment for vocational nurse students and graduates accepted or enrolled in an accredited vocational nursing program in California.
EIN: 942878465

891
QueensCare
1300 N. Vermont Ave., Ste. 1002
Los Angeles, CA 90027-6005 (323) 669-4302
Contact: Barbara B. Hines, Pres. and C.E.O.
FAX: (323) 953-6244; URL: http://www.queenscare.org

Foundation type: Public charity
Purpose: Scholarships to assist individuals in the Los Angeles County area in obtaining an education in the health care field who do not have the financial means to pay for an education.
Publications: Annual report; Informational brochure (including application guidelines).
Financial data: Year ended 06/30/2012. Assets, $383,055,000 (M); Expenditures, $20,695,946; Total giving, $9,630,795; Grants to individuals, totaling $4,578,664.
Fields of interest: Nursing school/education; Health sciences school/education; Health care.
Type of support: Scholarships—to individuals.
Application information: Applications accepted. Application form required. Application form available on the grantmaker's web site.
  Initial approach: Letter
  Copies of proposal: 1
  Deadline(s): May 15
  Final notification: Applicants notified in three months
  Applicants should submit the following:
    1) Resume
    2) Letter(s) of recommendation
    3) GPA
    4) Financial information
    5) FAFSA
    6) Essay
    7) Curriculum vitae
  Additional information: Application should also include most recent tax return.
Program description:
  Gene and Marilyn Nuziard Scholarship Fund: Scholarships of up to $9,000 are available towards assisting in alleviating the problem of the years-long shortage of medical healthcare professionals, by providing funds for persons who wish to obtain an education to qualify them as providers of healthcare services and who do not have the financial means to pay for such an education. Scholarships are available primarily for the education of assistants and technicians, nurses, physicians, licensed vocational nurses, registered nurses, nurse practitioners, and primary-care physicians. Eligible applicants must have family incomes at or below 200 percent of the federal poverty level and who

express an interest in working with the underserved in Los Angeles County.
EIN: 951644040

892
Lucille Rader Education Foundation Inc.
5321 Natasha Ct.
Agoura Hills, CA 91301   (818) 889-5410
URL: http://www.raderfoundation.org/

Foundation type: Independent foundation
Purpose: Scholarships to female students attending Catholic schools in the Los Angeles, CA, Archdiocese who excel in academics, team sports, and show moral character.
Financial data: Year ended 12/31/2012. Assets, $509,992 (M); Expenditures, $10,360; Total giving, $8,500; Grants to individuals, 3 grants totaling $8,500 (high: $3,500, low: $1,500).
Fields of interest: Catholic agencies & churches; Women.
Type of support: Scholarships—to individuals.
Application information: Application form required.
 Deadline(s): Mar. 31
 Additional information: Application should include an essay.
EIN: 330949622

893
Raies-Murr Educational Trust
330 N. Brand Blvd., Ste. 200
Glendale, CA 91203-1155

Foundation type: Operating foundation
Purpose: Scholarships to financially needy public high school students residing in the greater Los Angeles, CA, area.
Financial data: Year ended 12/31/2012. Assets, $341,018 (M); Expenditures, $14,000; Total giving, $14,000; Grants to individuals, totaling $14,000 (high: $1,250, low: $750).
Type of support: Undergraduate support.
Application information: Applications not accepted.
EIN: 956932192

894
Micki Rainey Scholarship Fund Inc.
P.O. Box 1088
Danville, CA 94526

Foundation type: Independent foundation
Purpose: Scholarships to individuals for higher education.
Financial data: Year ended 04/30/2013. Assets, $601,954 (M); Expenditures, $29,269; Total giving, $27,000; Grants to individuals, 12 grants totaling $27,000 (high: $2,250, low: $2,250).
Fields of interest: Higher education.
Type of support: Scholarships—to individuals.
Application information: Applications not accepted.
 Additional information: Unsolicited requests for funds not considered or acknowledged.
EIN: 680097366

895
Ramakrishna Foundation
4900 Overland Ave., No. 169
Culver City, CA 90230-4266   (310) 473-4479
Contact: Tapan Chaudhuri, Pres.
E-mail: tapanch@aol.com

Foundation type: Public charity

Purpose: Grants to swamis, monks and brahmacharis to cover expenses for their religious work in India.
Financial data: Year ended 09/30/2011. Assets, $348,813 (M); Expenditures, $556,595.
Fields of interest: Hinduism; Religion.
Type of support: Foreign applicants; Grants for special needs.
Application information: Contact foundation for application guidelines.
EIN: 954587617

896
Ramona's Mexican Food Products Scholarship Foundation
13633 S. Western Ave.
Gardena, CA 90249

Foundation type: Company-sponsored foundation
Purpose: Scholarships to financially needy students of Mexican descent from Garfield, Roosevelt, or Lincoln high schools in east Los Angeles, CA to attend college in CA.
Financial data: Year ended 09/30/2012. Assets, $76,730 (M); Expenditures, $2,443; Total giving, $0.
Fields of interest: Higher education; Hispanics/Latinos.
International interests: Mexico.
Type of support: Support to graduates or students of specific schools; Undergraduate support.
Application information: Applications accepted. Application form required.
 Deadline(s): Apr.
 Additional information: Selection is based on a 3.5 GPA, academic merit and financial need.
EIN: 237425268

897
Rancho Santa Fe Foundation
(formerly Rancho Santa Fe Community Foundation)
162 S. Rancho Santa Fe Rd., Ste. B-30
Encinitas, CA 92024   (858) 756-6557
Contact: Christina Wilson, Exec. Dir.; For grants: Debbie Anderson, Progs. Mgr.
Application e-mail: christy@rsffoundation.org
FAX: (858) 756-6561;
E-mail: info@rsffoundation.org; Mailing address: P.O. Box 811, Rancho Santa Fe, CA 92067;
URL: http://www.rsffoundation.org

Foundation type: Community foundation
Purpose: Financial assistance to residents of North San Diego county, CA pursuing higher education at CA State University San Marcos, Palomar College, Mira Costa College, San Diego State University, University of California at San Diego and the University of San Diego.
Publications: Annual report; Financial statement; Informational brochure; Newsletter.
Financial data: Year ended 12/31/2012. Assets, $59,385,300 (M); Expenditures, $2,670,500; Total giving, $2,143,200. Scholarships—to individuals amount not specified.
Fields of interest: Higher education.
Type of support: Scholarships—to individuals; Support to graduates or students of specific schools.
Application information: Applications accepted. Application form required.
 Send request by: E-mail
 Deadline(s): May 31
 Applicants should submit the following:
 1) Transcripts
 2) GPA

3) Essay
EIN: 953709639

898
Ayn Rand Institute/The Center for the Advancement of Objectivism
2121 Alton Pkwy., Ste. 250
Irvine, CA 92606-4926   (949) 222-6550
Contact: Yaron Brook, Pres. and Exec. Dir.
Application address for individuals: Dept. W, The Ayn Rand Institute, P.O. Box 57044, Irvine, CA 92619-7044, e-mail: essay@aynrand.org (for Anthem and Fountainhead contests)
FAX: (949) 222-6558; E-mail: mail@aynrand.org;
URL: http://www.aynrand.org

Foundation type: Public charity
Purpose: Awards to high school, undergraduate, and graduate students for critical analysis of Ayn Rand's novels.
Publications: Annual report; Financial statement; Informational brochure (including application guidelines).
Financial data: Year ended 09/30/2012. Assets, $7,777,069 (M); Expenditures, $9,962,302; Total giving, $320,720; Grants to individuals, totaling $215,374.
Fields of interest: Literature; Philosophy/ethics.
Type of support: Awards/prizes; Graduate support; Precollege support; Undergraduate support.
Application information:
 Deadline(s): Mar. 20 for 9th and 10th graders; Apr. 25 for 11th and 12th graders; Sept. 17 for undergraduates
 Final notification: Varies
 Additional information: Contact institute for additional application guidelines.
EIN: 222570926

899
The Keaton Raphael Memorial for Neuroblastoma, Inc.
2260 Douglas Blvd., Ste. 150
Roseville, CA 95661-1378   (916) 784-6786
Contact: Teresa Hofhenke, Exec. Dir.
FAX: (916) 784-3384; E-mail: info@childcancer.org;
URL: http://www.childcancer.org

Foundation type: Public charity
Purpose: Grants to childhood cancer patients and their families who reside in and are being treated for childhood cancer at an accredited institution in northern CA. Services are also available that directly impact the quality of life for childhood cancer patients and their families.
Publications: Informational brochure.
Financial data: Year ended 12/31/2012. Assets, $238,469 (M); Expenditures, $646,600; Total giving, $394,220; Grants to individuals, totaling $80,177.
Fields of interest: Cancer; Children.
Type of support: Grants for special needs.
Application information: Applications not accepted.
 Additional information: Unsolicited requests for funds not considered or acknowledged.
EIN: 680406980

900
RCL Foundation
(formerly Richard S. Staley Foundation)
6055 E. Washington Blvd., Ste. 430
Commerce, CA 90040-2431
Contact: Angela Tan, Treas.

Foundation type: Independent foundation
Purpose: Scholarships and student loans primarily to residents of CA who are graduate students in the medical field.
Financial data: Year ended 04/30/2013. Assets, $2,563,150 (M); Expenditures, $101,229; Total giving, $25,650; Grants to individuals, 2 grants totaling $7,500 (high: $5,000, low: $2,500).
Fields of interest: Medical school/education.
Type of support: Graduate support.
Application information: Applications accepted. Application form required.
  Final notification: Recipients notified within two months
  Applicants should submit the following:
    1) Financial information
    2) Letter(s) of recommendation
    3) Transcripts
    4) GPA
EIN: 953387067

901
The Ronald Reagan Presidential Foundation
40 Presidential Dr., Ste. 200
Simi Valley, CA   93065-0600   (805) 522-2977
FAX: (805) 520-9702;
E-mail: info@reaganfoundation.org; URL: http://www.reaganlibrary.com

Foundation type: Public charity
Purpose: Scholarships to high school students in Ventura, CA, for higher education.
Financial data: Year ended 09/30/2011. Assets, $249,376,056 (M); Expenditures, $29,476,656; Total giving, $371,599; Grants to individuals, totaling $269,000.
Fields of interest: Higher education.
Type of support: Scholarships—to individuals.
Application information: Applications accepted.
  Initial approach: Letter
  Additional information: Selection is based on recommendations from school principals, teachers, and an essay written about American government judged by a panel of community leaders.
EIN: 770054631

902
Recruiting Advancement of Instruction & Scholarship for Education in the Graphic Arts, Inc.
(also known as RAISE)
5800 S. Eastern Ave., Ste. 400
Los Angeles, CA   90040-4091   (323) 728-9500
Contact: Robert Lindgren, Pres.

Foundation type: Public charity
Purpose: Scholarships to students of CA for tuition and other expenses at a qualified educational institution pursuing graphic arts.
Financial data: Year ended 12/31/2011. Assets, $581,743 (M); Expenditures, $121,294; Total giving, $94,133; Grants to individuals, totaling $30,580.
Fields of interest: Print publishing; Arts.
Type of support: Scholarships—to individuals.
Application information: Applications accepted. Application form required.
  Additional information: Contact the organization for additional application information.
EIN: 237433575

903
The Red Tab Foundation
1155 Battery St., Levi's Pl.
San Francisco, CA   94111   (415) 501-6554
Contact: Mary Palafox, Exec. Dir.
FAX: (415) 501-1859;
E-mail: RedTabFoundation@levi.com; Toll-free tel. : (800)-544-5498; e-mail for Mary Palafox : mpalafox@levi.com; URL: http://www.redtabfoundation.org/

Foundation type: Public charity
Purpose: Emergency assistance for Levi Strauss & Company employees, retirees and their families with basic needs and unexpected emergencies. Scholarships are also awarded to Levi Strauss & Co. employees' children who plan to continue their education at any college, university or vocational school.
Financial data: Year ended 05/31/2012. Assets, $14,283,874 (M); Expenditures, $2,044,244; Total giving, $1,185,826; Grants to individuals, totaling $879,033.
Fields of interest: Vocational education, post-secondary; Higher education.
Type of support: Employee-related scholarships; Grants for special needs.
Application information: Applications accepted. Application form required.
  Deadline(s): Apr. for Scholarships
Company name: Levi Strauss & Co.
EIN: 942779937

904
Redding Family Foundation
2530 Atlantic Ave., Ste. B
Long Beach, CA   90806-2741   (562) 595-1659

Foundation type: Independent foundation
Purpose: Scholarships to students in Granville County, NC.
Financial data: Year ended 12/31/2011. Assets, $136,473 (M); Expenditures, $10,995; Total giving, $10,350.
Type of support: Undergraduate support.
Application information:
  Initial approach: Telephone
  Additional information: Contact foundation for application guidelines.
EIN: 330210244

905
REDF
221 Main St., Ste. 1550
San Francisco, CA   94105-3935   (415) 561-6677
Contact: Carla Javits, Pres.
Application e-mail: internships@redf.org
FAX: (415) 561-6685; E-mail: info@redf.org; URL: http://www.redf.org

Foundation type: Public charity
Purpose: Fellowships to MBA graduates and individuals with business experience.
Publications: Financial statement; Informational brochure; Newsletter.
Financial data: Year ended 12/31/2011. Assets, $8,088,025 (M); Expenditures, $4,825,130; Total giving, $1,295,284.
Type of support: Fellowships.
Application information:
  Initial approach: E-mail
  Deadline(s): Feb. 5
Program description:
  Farber Fellows Program: Offers one fellowship each year to M.B.A.s and individuals with business experience to work with a portfolio social enterprise on projects to support the business in achieving its goals.
EIN: 542132153

906
Redwood Children's Services, Inc.
780 S. Dora St.
P.O. Box 422
Ukiah, CA   95482-5348   (707) 467-2000
Contact: Camille Schraeder, Exec. Dir.
E-mail: rcs@rcs4kids.org; Toll-free tel.: (800) 219-5800; URL: http://www.rcs4kids.org

Foundation type: Public charity
Purpose: Grants to foster parents in Lake and Mendocino counties, CA.
Publications: Newsletter.
Financial data: Year ended 12/31/2011. Assets, $3,705,630 (M); Expenditures, $10,797,336; Total giving, $1,520,291; Grants to individuals, totaling $1,520,291.
Fields of interest: Foster care.
Type of support: Grants for special needs.
Application information: Contact foundation for eligibility information.
EIN: 680367894

907
Redwood Coast Developmental Services Corporation
1116 Airport Park Blvd.
Ukiah, CA   95482-5997   (707) 462-3832
Contact: Clay Jones, Exec. Dir.

Foundation type: Public charity
Purpose: Grants to individuals with developmental disabilities and their families in Del Norte, Mendocino, Lake, and Humboldt counties, CA.
Publications: Newsletter.
Financial data: Year ended 06/30/2012. Assets, $26,406,834 (M); Expenditures, $75,940,995; Total giving, $68,159,907; Grants to individuals, totaling $68,159,907.
Fields of interest: Disabilities, people with.
Type of support: Grants for special needs.
Application information: Contact foundation for eligibility requirements.
EIN: 942897317

908
Rest Haven Preventorium for Children, Inc.
(also known as Children's Health Fund)
P.O. Box 420369
San Diego, CA   92142-0369   (858) 576-0590
Contact: Peggy McNamara, Exec. Secy.
FAX: (858) 576-0029;
E-mail: resthavenchfund@sbcglobal.net;
URL: http://resthavenchf.org/contact.html

Foundation type: Operating foundation
Purpose: Grants to financially needy children only in San Diego County and Imperial County, CA, for medical, dental, optical, therapy, hearing, childcare, and nutritional expenses.
Financial data: Year ended 12/31/2012. Assets, $10,660,693 (M); Expenditures, $341,912; Total giving, $210,414.
Fields of interest: Dental care; Optometry/vision screening; Pharmacy/prescriptions; Mental health/crisis services; Nutrition; Children/youth, services; Disabilities, people with.
Type of support: Grants for special needs.

Application information: Applications not accepted.
EIN: 952128344

909
Rex Foundation
P.O. Box 29608
San Francisco, CA 94129-0608 (415) 561-3134
Contact: Sandy Sohcot, Exec. Dir.
FAX: (415) 561-3136;
E-mail: info@rexfoundation.org; URL: http://www.rexfoundation.org

Foundation type: Public charity
Purpose: Awards by nomination only to humanitarians and cultural leaders.
Publications: Annual report; Grants list; Newsletter.
Financial data: Year ended 12/31/2011. Assets, $183,434 (M); Expenditures, $249,410; Total giving, $103,000; Grants to individuals, totaling $10,000.
Fields of interest: Music; Arts; Child development, services; Human services; International affairs; Public affairs, political organizations.
Type of support: Awards/grants by nomination only; Awards/prizes.
Application information: Unsolicited requests for funds not considered or acknowledged.
Program descriptions:
Bill Graham Award: This award is designated for organizations and individuals working to assist children who are victims of political oppression and human rights violations.
Jerry Garcia Award: This award is designed to honor and support individuals and groups that work to encourage creativity in young people.
Ralph J. Gleason Award: This award is given to groups and individuals who have made outstanding contributions to culture.
EIN: 680033257

910
The Barbara Keene Richards Education Foundation
P.O. Box 493862
Redding, CA 96049 (530) 524-2788
Contact: Richard Keene, Dir.
Application address: 2914 Henry's Fork Dr., Redding, CA 96002

Foundation type: Independent foundation
Purpose: Scholarships to students from local school districts in Big Valley, CA for higher education.
Financial data: Year ended 12/31/2012. Assets, $653,686 (M); Expenditures, $36,105; Total giving, $31,000; Grants to individuals, 5 grants totaling $31,000 (high: $27,000, low: $750).
Fields of interest: Education.
Type of support: Scholarships—to individuals.
Application information: Applications accepted. Application form required.
Deadline(s): Mar. 31
Additional information: Application should include transcripts.
EIN: 943377678

911
Rio Hondo College Foundation
3600 Workman Mill Rd.
Administration Bldg., Rm. A203
Whittier, CA 90601-1699 (562) 908-3476
Contact: Howard Kummerman, Exec. Dir.
FAX: (562) 463-4648;
E-mail: rhcfoundation@riohondo.edu; E-mail for Howard Kummerman:
howard.kummerman@riohondo.edu; URL: http://www.riohondo.edu/foundation

Foundation type: Public charity
Purpose: Scholarships and grants to students of Rio Hondo College, CA pursuing higher education.
Financial data: Year ended 06/30/2012. Assets, $2,422,060 (M); Expenditures, $289,211; Total giving, $66,807; Grants to individuals, totaling $66,807.
Fields of interest: College.
Type of support: Scholarships—to individuals; Support to graduates or students of specific schools.
Application information: Applications accepted. Application form available on the grantmaker's web site.
Send request by: On-line
Deadline(s): Apr.
Applicants should submit the following:
1) FAFSA
2) Transcripts
3) Letter(s) of recommendation
4) GPA
5) Financial information
6) Essay
Additional information: Scholarships are both need-based and merit awards.
EIN: 954367487

912
Rivendell Stewards' Trust
P.O. Box 6009
Santa Barbara, CA 93160-6009 (805) 964-9999
Contact: Amity Wicks, Admin.
FAX: (805) 823-4594; E-mail: info@rstrust.org; URL: http://www.rstrust.org

Foundation type: Independent foundation
Purpose: Grants to individuals for Christian ministry projects in developing countries.
Financial data: Year ended 12/31/2012. Assets, $21,462,684 (M); Expenditures, $6,934,251; Total giving, $6,670,500.
Fields of interest: Christian agencies & churches.
International interests: Developing Countries.
Type of support: Grants to individuals.
Application information:
Initial approach: Letter
Deadline(s): Sept. 1
EIN: 776016389

913
Riverside Arts Council
3700 6Th St.
Riverside, CA 92501-3304 (951) 680-1345
FAX: (951) 680-1348;
E-mail: info@riversideartscouncil.org; E-mail for Buna Dorr: bdorr@riversideartscouncil.org;
URL: http://riversideartscouncil.org/

Foundation type: Public charity
Purpose: Residencies to performing artists in Riverside County, CA.
Publications: Application guidelines.

Financial data: Year ended 06/30/2011. Assets, $54,447 (M); Expenditures, $597,419; Total giving, $290,000.
Fields of interest: Visual arts; Performing arts; Literature.
Type of support: Residencies.
Application information: Applications accepted. Application form required.
Initial approach: Letter, telephone, or fax
Applicants should submit the following:
1) Work samples
2) Resume
Additional information: Application must also include three work-related references, and sample lesson overview for a 10-week session. Contact the council for additional application guidelines.
EIN: 953265946

914
Riverside County Physicians Memorial Foundation
3993 Jurupa Ave.
Riverside, CA 92506-2229 (951) 686-3342
Contact: Dolores Green, C.E.O.
FAX: (951) 686-1692

Foundation type: Public charity
Purpose: Scholarships to students who are residents of Riverside County, CA pursuing a career in allopathic or osteopathic medicine.
Publications: Application guidelines.
Financial data: Year ended 12/31/2011. Assets, $693,296 (M); Expenditures, $205,688.
Fields of interest: Medical school/education.
Type of support: Scholarships—to individuals.
Application information: Applications accepted. Application form required. Application form available on the grantmaker's web site. Interview required.
Initial approach: Application
Deadline(s): May 15
Applicants should submit the following:
1) Photograph
2) GPA
Additional information: Applications should also include proof of enrollment in an accredited medical program, leading to a degree of medical doctor or doctor of osteopathy, two letters of reference, and a short statement stating reasons for studying medicine.
Program description:
Medical School Scholarship Program: The foundation provides scholarships to medical students, with the goal of encouraging them to practice in Riverside County, CA where there is a demonstrated need of physicians. Eligible applicants must be Riverside County residents for at least a five-year period, be accepted for or enrolled in an accredited allopathic or osteopathic medical school, and be a citizen of the U.S. Preference will be given to applicants who demonstrate a commitment to primary health care (including family practice, general internal medicine, general practice, or obstetrics/gynecology), financial need, and prior experience with populations whose health care needs are underserved.
EIN: 956080778

915
Robert R. Roberts Memorial Foundation
(formerly Memorial Foundation)
2600 Starlight Blvd.
Redding, CA 96001-0920 (530) 243-4750

Foundation type: Public charity
Purpose: Medical and science scholarships for students attending any Shasta County college, CA for higher education.
Financial data: Year ended 06/30/2012. Assets, $617,335 (M); Expenditures, $220,807; Total giving, $42,634; Grants to individuals, totaling $15,300.
Fields of interest: Medical school/education; Health sciences school/education.
Type of support: Scholarships—to individuals.
Application information: Applicant must demonstrate need.
EIN: 946128990

916
Will Rogers Motion Picture Pioneers Foundation
10045 Riverside Dr., 3rd Fl.
Toluca Lake, CA   91602-2543   (818) 755-2300
FAX: (818) 508-9816; E-mail: info@wrinstitute.org;
URL: http://www.wrpioneers.org

Foundation type: Public charity
Purpose: Financial assistance to veterans of the theatrical community who encounter illness, injury or life-changing event, with medical, dental and hospital expenses. Scholarships to employees or a child of an employee in the theatrical entertainment exhibition industry to attend institutions of higher learning in the U.S.
Publications: Annual report; Grants list; Informational brochure; Newsletter.
Financial data: Year ended 03/31/2012. Assets, $22,288,878 (M); Expenditures, $4,509,784; Total giving, $2,272,979; Grants to individuals, totaling $531,861.
Fields of interest: Higher education; Human services.
Type of support: Scholarships—to individuals; Grants for special needs.
Application information: Applications accepted.
  Deadline(s): June 1 for Scholarships
  Additional information: See web site for additional information for scholarship and assistance.
EIN: 150533551

917
Rohr Employees Will-Share Club
(formerly Goodrich-Rohr Will-Share Club)
850 Lagoon Dr., Ste. 29P
Chula Vista, CA   91910-2098   (621) 691-6477

Foundation type: Public charity
Purpose: Financial assistance to employees of Goodrich-Rohr for unforeseen emergencies.
Financial data: Year ended 12/31/2012. Assets, $41,274 (M); Expenditures, $156,004; Total giving, $156,004.
Fields of interest: Human services.
Type of support: Grants for special needs.
Application information:
  Initial approach: Letter
  Additional information: Unsolicited requests for funds not considered or acknowledged.
EIN: 953455271

918
Ronald McDonald House Charities of Southern California, Inc.
765 S. Pasadena Ave.
Pasadena, CA   91105-3019   (626) 744-9449
Contact: Rob Parker, C.E.O.
FAX: (626) 744-9969;
E-mail: mcdonalds@porternovelli.com; URL: http://www.rmhcsc.org

Foundation type: Public charity
Purpose: Scholarships to minorities of southern CA.
Publications: Annual report; Financial statement.
Financial data: Year ended 12/31/2011. Assets, $58,260,599 (M); Expenditures, $10,772,616; Total giving, $751,549; Grants to individuals, totaling $233,000.
Fields of interest: Minorities; Asians/Pacific Islanders; African Americans/Blacks; Hispanics/Latinos; Economically disadvantaged.
Type of support: Undergraduate support.
Application information:
  Initial approach: Letter
  Additional information: Contact foundation for eligibility criteria.
Program descriptions:
  The ASIA Scholarship: Scholarships of $2,000 each are awarded to applicants of Asian descent. Applicants must submit a transcript, personal statement, letter of recommendation, and parental W-2 forms.
  The Future Achievers Scholarship: Scholarships of $2,000 each are awarded to applicants of African-American descent. Applicants must submit a transcript, personal statement, letter of recommendation, and parental W-2 forms.
  The HACER Scholarship: Scholarships of $2,000 each are awarded to applicants of Hispanic descent. Applicants must submit a transcript, personal statement, letter of recommendation, and parental W-2 forms.
  The Scholars of Tomorrow Scholarship: Scholarships of $2,000 each are awarded to applicants of all ethnicities. Applicants must submit a transcript, personal statement, letter of recommendation, and parental W-2 forms.
EIN: 953167869

919
Rose Foundation for Communities and the Environment
1970 Broadway, Ste. 600
Oakland, CA   94612-2218   (510) 658-0702
Contact: Tim Little, Exec. Dir.
FAX: (510) 658-0732; E-mail: rose@rosefdn.org;
URL: http://www.rosefdn.org

Foundation type: Public charity
Purpose: Fiscal sponsorship to individuals for projects located primarily in CA with budgets over $10,000.
Publications: Application guidelines; Financial statement; Grants list; Newsletter; Occasional report.
Financial data: Year ended 12/31/2011. Assets, $4,498,431 (M); Expenditures, $3,511,095; Total giving, $2,809,885; Grants to individuals, totaling $188,520.
Type of support: Fiscal agent/sponsor.
Application information: Applications accepted. Application form available on the grantmaker's web site.
  Additional information: Applicants should consult with the foundation before submitting an application.

Program descriptions:
  Anthony Grassroots Environmental Prize: A $1,000 prize is given to recognize an outstanding example of grassroots environmental activism in California over the previous year.
  Meade Clean Air Scholarship: The foundation annually awards a $1,000 scholarship to a student who is studying air pollution at UCLA's School of Public Health.
EIN: 943179772

920
Rosemary Childrens Services
36 S. Kinneloa Ave., Ste. 200
Pasadena, CA   91107-3853   (626) 844-3033
Contact: Greg Wessels, C.E.O. and Exec. Dir.
FAX: (626) 844-3034;
E-mail: info@rosemarychildren.org; URL: http://www.rosemarychildren.org

Foundation type: Public charity
Purpose: Grants for basic necessities to foster families, primarily in CA.
Publications: Newsletter.
Financial data: Year ended 06/30/2012. Assets, $6,389,757 (M); Expenditures, $9,180,438; Total giving, $1,326,461; Grants to individuals, totaling $1,326,461.
Fields of interest: Foster care; Children/youth.
Type of support: Grants for special needs.
Application information: Contact foundation for eligibility information.
EIN: 951661683

921
Dorothy Sargent Rosenberg Memorial Fund
(formerly Anna Davidson Rosenberg Fund)
P.O. Box 431
The Sea Ranch, CA   95497-0431
Application address: c/o Dorothy Sargent Rosenberg Poetry Prizes, P.O. Box 2306, Orinda, CA 94563
URL: http://www.dorothyprizes.org

Foundation type: Independent foundation
Purpose: Literary awards to promising young poets of exceptional talent to pursue their craft and advance their careers.
Financial data: Year ended 03/31/2013. Assets, $1,471,146 (M); Expenditures, $105,829; Total giving, $96,893; Grants to individuals, 38 grants totaling $96,893 (high: $7,500, low: $250).
Fields of interest: Literature.
Type of support: Awards/prizes.
Application information: Applications accepted. Application form not required.
  Initial approach: Contact Fund for application guidelines
  Additional information: Complete guidelines available on Fund web site.
Program descriptions:
  Anna David Rosenberg Poetry Awards: First prize of $1,000, second prize of $500, and honorable mentions are awarded to original poems in English that in some way address the theme of the Jewish experience. All interested writers are welcome to apply.
  Dorothy Sargent Rosenberg Poetry Prizes: Prizes varying from $1,000 up to as much as $25,000 will be awarded for the finest lyric poems celebrating the spirit of life. The competition is open to any writer under the age of 40. All poets, published or unpublished, are welcome to enter, but only previously unpublished poems are eligible for the competition.

The Dorothy Rosenberg Memorial Prize in Lyric Poetry: Approximately $6,000 will be awarded at the judges' discretion to University of California, Berkeley students for the best original, unpublished lyric poem. At least one prize will be awarded to an undergraduate student and at least one prize will be awarded to a graduate student.
EIN: 300041654

922
Rossmoor Scholarship Foundation
P.O. Box 2056
Walnut Creek, CA 94595-0056 (925) 949-7571

Foundation type: Public charity
Purpose: Scholarships to graduating seniors at Acalanes, Las Lomas, Northgate, Ygnacio, and College Park High Schools, CA, and Diablo Valley College, CA.
Financial data: Year ended 06/30/2012. Assets, $1,445,553 (M); Expenditures, $125,017; Total giving, $113,500; Grants to individuals, totaling $113,500.
Type of support: Support to graduates or students of specific schools; Undergraduate support.
Application information: Contact foundation for current application deadline/guidelines.
EIN: 946126368

923
Rowan Family Foundation
P.O. Box 992335
Redding, CA 96099-2335 (530) 246-9930
Contact: Jane Rowan, Pres.

Foundation type: Independent foundation
Purpose: Scholarships to individuals in pursuit of a higher education.
Financial data: Year ended 12/31/2012. Assets, $441,866 (M); Expenditures, $10,692; Total giving, $8,000; Grants to individuals, 2 grants totaling $2,000 (high: $1,000, low: $1,000).
Type of support: Undergraduate support.
Application information: Applications accepted.
Initial approach: Letter
Deadline(s): None
Additional information: Contact foundation for current application guidelines.
EIN: 943162645

924
S.L. Scholarship Foundation
4435 Santa Cruz Ave.
San Diego, CA 92107-3616 (619) 223-8202
Contact: Lisa Laube, C.F.O.

Foundation type: Independent foundation
Purpose: Scholarships to individuals attending specific schools in San Diego, CA.
Financial data: Year ended 12/31/2012. Assets, $29,084 (M); Expenditures, $16,009; Total giving, $15,370; Grants to individuals, 9 grants totaling $15,370 (high: $3,082, low: $100).
Fields of interest: Higher education.
Type of support: Scholarships—to individuals; Support to graduates or students of specific schools.
Application information: Application form required.
Deadline(s): Varies
Additional information: Application should include financial information.
EIN: 330782054

925
Sacramento Association of REALTORS Scholarship Foundation Trust
(formerly Sacramento Board of Realtors Scholarship Foundation Trust)
2003 Howe Ave.
Sacramento, CA 95825 (916) 922-7711

Foundation type: Independent foundation
Purpose: Scholarships to legal residents of Sacramento County, CA at accredited colleges or universities.
Financial data: Year ended 12/31/2012. Assets, $57,543 (M); Expenditures, $40,699; Total giving, $38,250; Grants to individuals, 30 grants totaling $38,250 (high: $2,500, low: $1,000).
Fields of interest: Higher education.
Type of support: Scholarships—to individuals.
Application information: Applications accepted. Application form required.
Deadline(s): Mar. 31
Applicants should submit the following:
1) Transcripts
2) Essay
Additional information: Application should also include verification of current enrollment. Applicant must be a legal resident for at least one year, or a relative of a SAR or Affiliated Member and have a valid CA Driver's License or CA State ID card.
EIN: 946129111

926
Sacramento Region Community Foundation
(formerly Sacramento Regional Foundation)
955 University Ave., Ste. A
Sacramento, CA 95825 (916) 921-7723
Contact: Linda Beech Cutler, C.E.O.; For scholarships: Tina Bryce, Grants Mgr.
Scholarship contact e-mail: scholarships@sacregcf.org
FAX: (916) 921-7725; E-mail: info@sacregcf.org; URL: http://www.sacregcf.org

Foundation type: Community foundation
Purpose: Scholarships to residents of Sacramento, Yolo, Placer, and El Dorado counties, CA for continuing education at institutions of higher learning.
Publications: Annual report; Financial statement; Informational brochure; Newsletter.
Financial data: Year ended 12/31/2012. Assets, $106,540,710 (M); Expenditures, $6,357,805; Total giving, $4,174,112; Grants to individuals, 259 grants totaling $819,894.
Fields of interest: Vocational education; Higher education; Business school/education; Nursing school/education.
Type of support: Scholarships—to individuals; Support to graduates or students of specific schools; Undergraduate support.
Application information: Applications accepted. Application form required. Application form available on the grantmaker's web site. Interview required.
Initial approach: Application
Send request by: Online
Deadline(s): Varies
Applicants should submit the following:
1) Letter(s) of recommendation
2) Transcripts
3) FAFSA
4) Essay
Additional information: Application should also include list of activities, and additional materials as required by the individual

scholarships. See web site for a complete listing of scholarships and application guidelines.
Program description:
Scholarships: The foundation manages over 40 scholarship funds that provide tuition assistance and recognition to local students as they strive to achieve a wide range of goals through the pursuit of higher education. Each scholarship fund has its own unique eligibility requirements and designates what awards may and may not be used for. Most scholarships are for students attending two or four year colleges and universities pursuing a degree in specified subjects and may only be used for direct educational expenses such as tuition fees, books and supplies and in some cases, room and board. Some scholarships may be used for vocational and technical schools or adult education programs. Annual scholarship awards range from $500 to $5,000. See web site for additional information.
EIN: 942891517

927
The San Carlos Foundation
1065 Creston Rd.
Berkeley, CA 94708-1545 (510) 525-3787
Contact: Davida Coady, Pres.
FAX: (510) 525-3278; E-mail: dcoady@igc.org; URL: http://sancarlosfoundation.org

Foundation type: Public charity
Purpose: Grants for living expenses to professionals (doctors, nurses, lawyers, engineers, teachers, etc.) who volunteer to train residents of the developing world living in extreme poverty.
Financial data: Year ended 04/30/2012. Assets, $23,041 (M); Expenditures, $324,652; Total giving, $323,671. Grants to individuals amount not specified.
Fields of interest: Philanthropy/voluntarism; Immigrants/refugees; Economically disadvantaged.
Type of support: Grants to individuals.
Application information: Applications accepted. Application form required. Application form available on the grantmaker's web site.
Initial approach: E-mail
Applicants should submit the following:
1) Resume
2) Proposal
Additional information: See web site for additional guidelines.
EIN: 680040121

928
San Diego Asian Film Foundation
2508 Historic Decatur Rd., Ste. 140
San Diego, CA 92106-6138 (619) 400-5911
Contact: Lee Ann Kim, Exec. Dir.
FAX: (619) 342-2695; E-mail: info@sdaff.org; E-mail for Lee Ann Kim: leeann.sdaff.org; Tel.: for Lee Ann Kim: (619) 400-5905; URL: http://www.sdaff.org

Foundation type: Public charity
Purpose: Support to individuals for noncommercial projects to educate the community about Asian Pacific culture through a fiscal sponsorship program. Internships are also provided to high school students who attend school in the San Diego County area through the Reel Internship Project.
Publications: Application guidelines.
Financial data: Year ended 12/31/2012. Assets, $488,917 (M); Expenditures, $770,062.
Fields of interest: Film/video; Arts, artist's services; Youth; Asians/Pacific Islanders.

Type of support: Internship funds; Grants to individuals; Fiscal agent/sponsor.
Application information: Application form required. Application form available on the grantmaker's web site.
Initial approach: Download fiscal sponsorship application
Program descriptions:
Fiscal Sponsorship: A fiscal sponsorship program is available as a fundraising tool for filmmakers seeking funds for a current film project. Any filmmaker of Asian Pacific Islander descent, or non-Asian Pacific Islander filmmaker creating an independent, noncommercial project relating to issues affecting the Asian Pacific Islander community, is eligible. Fiscal sponsorship fees vary from 3 percent (for project budgets under $10,000) to 5 percent (for project budgets over $50,000) if the filmmaker has screened at the San Diego Asian Film Festival, and 5 percent if the filmmaker has not.
Reel Voices Project: A one-year internship program is available to offer high-school students in the San Diego area a chance to change their lives through mentorship and access to filmmaking equipment, and cultivate them into more mature, articulate, and accomplished media artists. Services include video production workshops, media literacy classes, reporting assignments, community screenings, film festivals, and advisement from professionals and educators. Interns receive a $500 scholarship. Applicants must be currently enrolled in a San Diego County area high school.
EIN: 331001523

929
San Diego Chargers Charities

(also known as The Chargers Community Foundation)
P.O. Box 609609
San Diego, CA 92160-9609 (858) 874-4500
Contact: Ed Trimble, Pres.

Foundation type: Public charity
Purpose: Awards by nomination only to outstanding volunteers who exemplify leadership, dedication, and a commitment to improving the youth football and cheer experience for children throughout San Diego County, CA.
Financial data: Year ended 12/31/2011. Assets, $49,823 (M); Expenditures, $110,728; Total giving, $89,620; Grants to individuals, totaling $19,120.
Fields of interest: Community/economic development.
Type of support: Awards/grants by nomination only; Awards/prizes.
Application information:
Deadline(s): Nov. 9 for Community Quarterback Award
Program description:
Community Quarterback Award: Winners will receive a $1,000 donation to their youth football or cheer organization; one volunteer will be selected as an overall award winner and receive $2,500 for their organization.
EIN: 330670086

930
San Diego County Citizens Scholarship Foundation

5256 Avenida De Las Vistas
San Diego, CA 92154-5500
Contact: Sammie McCormick, Pres.
Application Address: P.O BOX 7484 San Diego,CA 92167

Foundation type: Independent foundation
Purpose: Scholarships to financially needy students enrolled in high schools in San Diego County, CA, who have been residents of San Diego County for at least one year, and plan to attend San Diego colleges and universities.
Financial data: Year ended 09/30/2012. Assets, $1,361,566 (M); Expenditures, $99,284; Total giving, $94,750; Grants to individuals, 98 grants totaling $94,750 (high: $1,048, low: $966).
Fields of interest: Higher education.
Type of support: Scholarships—to individuals.
Application information: Application form required. Interview required.
Deadline(s): Mar. 1
Applicants should submit the following:
1) Transcripts
2) Financial information
Additional information: Application must also include personal statement, and a copy of the first page of parents' latest 1040 tax form.
EIN: 956111706

931
San Diego County Medical Society Foundation

5575 Ruffin Rd., No. 250
San Diego, CA 92123-1387 (858) 300-2780
Contact: Aron R. Fleck, Exec. Dir.
FAX: (858) 569-1334; E-mail: afleck@sdcms.org; URL: http://sdcmsf.org/

Foundation type: Public charity
Purpose: Low-interest medical student loans, scholarships and grants to qualifying San Diego County residents medical students.
Financial data: Year ended 09/30/2011. Assets, $963,506 (M); Expenditures, $820,693.
Fields of interest: Medical school/education.
Type of support: Scholarships—to individuals; Student loans—to individuals.
Application information: Applications accepted.
EIN: 952568714

932
San Diego County Salute to Education

4001 El Cajon Blvd., Ste. 201
San Diego, CA 92105-1212 (619) 521-2404
FAX: (619) 283-1327; URL: http://www.salutetoeducation.com

Foundation type: Independent foundation
Purpose: Scholarships to high school seniors residing in and attending accredited schools in San Diego County, CA, for undergraduate education.
Financial data: Year ended 12/31/2012. Assets, $130,370 (M); Expenditures, $186,417; Total giving, $115,727; Grants to individuals, 97 grants totaling $115,727 (high: $19,727, low: $1,000).
Fields of interest: Higher education.
Type of support: Undergraduate support.
Application information: Applications accepted. Application form required. Application form available on the grantmaker's web site.
Send request by: Mail
Deadline(s): Feb. 17
Applicants should submit the following:

1) Transcripts
2) Letter(s) of recommendation
3) Essay
Additional information: See web site for additional application guidelines.
EIN: 330773691

933
San Diego Education Fund

c/o Julie Nguyen
4100 Normal St., Ste. 3251
San Diego, CA 92103-2653 (619) 725-7669
Contact: Rebecca Phillpott, Pres.
FAX: (619) 725-7692; E-mail: jnguyen1@sandi.net; Additional email for Sharon LeeMaster: sharon@sharonleemaster.com; additional tel.: (858) 270-3908; additional fax: (858) 273-5742; URL: http://www.sdef.org

Foundation type: Public charity
Purpose: Minority students enrolled in the foundation's program agree to teach for a minimum of three years in the San Diego district after they receive their teaching credential, in exchange for scholarships to be used towards graduate teacher study.
Financial data: Year ended 06/30/2012. Assets, $1,160,049 (M); Expenditures, $310,107; Total giving, $142,250; Grants to individuals, totaling $142,250.
Fields of interest: Elementary/secondary education; Minorities; Economically disadvantaged.
Type of support: Undergraduate support.
Application information: Applications not accepted.
Additional information: Unsolicited requests for funds not considered or acknowledged.
EIN: 956095413

934
The San Diego Foundation

(formerly San Diego Community Foundation)
2508 Historic Decatur Rd., Ste. 200
San Diego, CA 92106-6138 (619) 235-2300
Contact: Robert A. Kelly, C.E.O.
Scholarship inquiry e-mail: arzo@sdfoundation.org
FAX: (619) 239-1710;
E-mail: info@sdfoundation.org; URL: http://www.sdfoundation.org

Foundation type: Community foundation
Purpose: Scholarships to students or adults residing in San Diego County, CA. Project grants to San Diego County, CA, K-6 elementary public school teachers and 9-12 public high school art teachers.
Publications: Annual report; Financial statement; Grants list; Informational brochure; Newsletter.
Financial data: Year ended 06/30/2013. Assets, $612,487,000 (M); Expenditures, $58,670,000; Total giving, $46,906,000. Scholarships—to individuals amount not specified.
Fields of interest: Vocational education; Higher education; Graduate/professional education; Scholarships/financial aid.
Type of support: Scholarships—to individuals; Support to graduates or students of specific schools; Undergraduate support; Project support.
Application information: Applications accepted. Application form required. Application form available on the grantmaker's web site.
Initial approach: Application
Send request by: Mail
Copies of proposal: 1
Deadline(s): Feb. for scholarships
Final notification: Applicants notified late Apr. or early May

Applicants should submit the following:
1) SAT
2) Transcripts
3) SASE
4) Work samples
5) Proposal
6) Letter(s) of recommendation
7) GPA
8) Financial information
9) Essay
10) Budget Information
11) ACT
Additional information: See web site for a complete listing of scholarships.
Program description:
Scholarships: The foundation administers various scholarships for graduating high school seniors, undergraduates, graduate students and adult re-entry students who are attending two-year colleges, four-year universities, trade/vocational schools, graduate, medical and professional schools or teaching credential programs. Scholarships range from $500 to $5,000. See web site for additional information.
EIN: 952942582

935
San Diego Imperial Counties Developmental Services, Inc.
4355 Ruffin Rd., Ste. 200
San Diego, CA   92123-4307   (858) 576-2996
Contact: Carlos Flores, C.E.O.
FAX: (858) 576-2873; E-mail: info@sdrc.org;
URL: http://www.sdrc.org/
Foundation type: Public charity
Purpose: Grants and services to individuals with developmental disorders and their families in the San Diego, CA, area.
Publications: Newsletter.
Financial data: Year ended 06/30/2012. Assets, $41,885,289 (M); Expenditures, $255,835,496; Total giving, $217,219,263; Grants to individuals, totaling $217,219,263.
Fields of interest: Developmentally disabled, centers & services.
Type of support: Grants for special needs.
Application information: Applications accepted.
Additional information: See web site for complete eligibility information.
EIN: 953735517

936
San Diego Martin Luther King Jr. Foundation
2250 4th Ave., Ste. 300
San Diego, CA   92101-2124   (619) 686-5959
Contact: Debra A. Stephens
FAX: (619) 699-4857;
E-mail: smb@carterreese.com; E-mail for Debra A. Stephens: das@carterreese.com; Tel. for Debra A. Stephens : 619-571-5225; URL: http://www.carterreese.com/MLK-Foundation-History.htm
Foundation type: Public charity
Purpose: Scholarships to residents of the San Diego, CA, area who demonstrate qualities reflecting the life and principles of Martin Luther King, Jr.
Financial data: Year ended 12/31/2011. Assets, $111,952 (M); Expenditures, $21,257; Total giving, $17,500; Grants to individuals, totaling $17,500.
Type of support: Undergraduate support.
Application information:
Initial approach: Letter

Additional information: Contact foundation for further information.
EIN: 330736895

937
Greater San Diego Science & Engineering Fair
P.O. Box 15547
San Diego, CA   92175-2658   (619) 957-5046
URL: http://www.gsdsef.orq
Foundation type: Independent foundation
Purpose: Awards to greater San Diego, CA students who are winners of the Science and Engineering fair, and assistance to the students to attend the International Science Fair.
Financial data: Year ended 12/31/2012. Assets, $56,910 (M); Expenditures, $117,787; Total giving, $33,279; Grants to individuals, 38 grants totaling $33,279 (high: $1,500, low: $50).
Fields of interest: Science; Engineering/technology.
Type of support: Awards/prizes.
Application information: Application form not required.
Deadline(s): None
EIN: 237332855

938
San Diego Scottish Rite Community Foundation
1895 Camino del Rio S.
San Diego, CA   92108-3601   (619) 293-4888
Contact: Randy Brill
Foundation type: Independent foundation
Purpose: Scholarships to individuals who are residents of San Diego and Imperial counties, CA for higher education.
Financial data: Year ended 12/31/2012. Assets, $3,720,426 (M); Expenditures, $175,912; Total giving, $163,000; Grants to individuals, 24 grants totaling $67,500 (high: $5,000, low: $1,500).
Fields of interest: Higher education.
Type of support: Scholarships—to individuals.
Application information: Applications accepted. Application form required. Application form available on the grantmaker's web site.
Initial approach: Letter
Deadline(s): May 15
Applicants should submit the following:
1) Letter(s) of recommendation
2) Transcripts
EIN: 330718473

939
San Diego Sports Medicine Foundation
5471 Kearny Villa Rd., Ste. 200A
San Diego, CA   92123-1151   (858) 571-0606
Contact: David J. Chao, Pres.
E-mail for assistance:
lherrmann@oasis-medical.com
FAX: (858) 571-1933; E-mail: info@sdsmf.com;
URL: http://www.sdsmf.com
Foundation type: Public charity
Purpose: Fellowships to physicians of San Diego, CA interested in working in sports medicine. Financial assistance for youth of San Diego, CA with sports-related injuries and limited financial means.
Publications: Application guidelines.
Financial data: Year ended 06/30/2012. Assets, $1,252,018 (M); Expenditures, $212,558; Total giving, $30,427.

Fields of interest: Medical care, rehabilitation; Youth.
Type of support: Fellowships; Grants for special needs.
Application information: Applications accepted.
Send request by: Mail for financial assistance
Additional information: Financial assistance application should include three essays/letters. See web site for additional information and guidelines.
Program descriptions:
Financial Assistance: The foundation provides financial support to young athletes ages 10 to 18 that have a sports-related injury which requires further medical evaluation, and who either do not have medical insurance or have limited financial means to receive costly medical attention.
San Diego Sports Medicine Fellowship: This twelve-month program provides a unique opportunity to provide a high level of training to a new physician, as well as the opportunity for a 'hands-on' experience in an established sports medicine clinic.
EIN: 912143098

940
San Felipe Humanitarian Alliance
(formerly San Felipe del Rio, Inc.)
35441 Paseo Viento
Capistrano Beach, CA   92624
URL: http://sanfelipealliance.org/
Foundation type: Operating foundation
Purpose: Scholarships to dependent, neglected, or abused youths particularly from CA, NM, and OR. Preference is shown to former residents of San Felipe del Rio's Children's Group Home in Taos, NM.
Financial data: Year ended 06/30/2012. Assets, $1,518,264 (M); Expenditures, $239,745; Total giving, $997.
Fields of interest: Children/youth, services.
Type of support: Scholarships—to individuals; Grants for special needs.
Application information: Applications not accepted.
EIN: 237276447

941
San Francisco Children's Art Center
Fort Mason Ctr., Bldg. C
San Francisco, CA   94123-1382   (415) 771-0292
Contact: Carol Berghen, V.P. and Exec. Comm. Chair.
E-mail: sfcac@childrensartcenter.org; URL: http://www.childrensartcenter.org
Foundation type: Public charity
Purpose: Partial to full tuition assistance to children attending the Children's Art Center of San Francisco, CA.
Publications: Application guidelines.
Financial data: Year ended 08/31/2011. Assets, $15,602 (M); Expenditures, $156,161.
Fields of interest: Arts education.
Type of support: Scholarships—to individuals.
Application information: Applications accepted. Application form required. Application form available on the grantmaker's web site.
Initial approach: Telephone or e-mail
Send request by: Mail
EIN: 942448876

942
San Francisco Family Foundation

P.O. Box 6886
San Rafael, CA 94903 (415) 922-4091
Contact: Beryl Kay, Exec. Dir.
Application address: 2269 Chestnut St., No. 255,
San Francisco, CA 94123
URL: http://sffamilyfoundation.org

Foundation type: Independent foundation
Purpose: General welfare assistance, including
food, clothing, medical, dental, and housing
expenses, to individuals who are 62 years of age or
over in the San Francisco Bay Area, who have a
history of helping other people in need.
Financial data: Year ended 12/31/2012. Assets,
$550,112 (M); Expenditures, $107,599; Total
giving, $46,175; Grants to individuals, 46 grants
totaling $46,175 (high: $22,000, low: $187).
Fields of interest: Health care; Human services;
Aging.
Type of support: Grants for special needs.
Application information: Applications accepted.
Application form required.
   Initial approach: Letter or telephone
   Deadline(s): 5th of every month
   Additional information: Applicants must be in
      need of financial assistance which cannot be
      met by other agencies or resources, including
      family resources. Applications on behalf of
      clients must be submitted by case
      management social service agency
      representatives. See web site for additional
      guidelines.
EIN: 680217117

943
San Francisco Film Society

39 Mesa St., The Presidio, No. 110
San Francisco, CA 94129-1025 (415)
561-5000
Contact: Ted Hope, Exec. Dir.
FAX: (415) 440-1760; E-mail: info@sffs.org; E-Mail
for Ted Hope: ed@sffs.org; URL: http://
www.sffs.org

Foundation type: Public charity
Purpose: Grants and support to film artists through
several programs.
Publications: Application guidelines; Newsletter;
Occasional report.
Financial data: Year ended 12/31/2011. Assets,
$4,158,208 (M); Expenditures, $5,633,000; Total
giving, $730,000; Grants to individuals, totaling
$730,000.
Fields of interest: Arts education; Media/
communications; Film/video; Arts, artist's
services.
Type of support: Awards/prizes; Residencies;
Fiscal agent/sponsor.
Application information: Applications accepted.
   Initial approach: Letter
   Deadline(s): Sept. 15 for fiscal sponsorship, Feb.
      23 for Filmmaking Grants
   Additional information: Applicants for fiscal
      sponsorships who are not members of the
      society must submit a $40 fee with their
      application. Contact foundation for full
      eligibility requirements.
Program descriptions:
Filmhouse Residencies: In partnership with the
San Francisco Film Commission, these residencies
will make production office space available
free-of-charge to Bay-area independent filmmakers
actively engaged in various stages of film
production, for periods of one to six months.

Fiscal Sponsorship: Fiscal sponsorships are
available to the society's Filmmaker Pro members
(either individuals or business) that have a U.S.
IRS-issued social security number, tax ID or EIN,
and a valid U.S. mailing address. Eligible projects
must be consistent with the society's mission and
values. There is a seven-percent administrative fee
on all funds managed by the society up to
$100,000; after $100,000, the fee is five percent.
Golden Gate Awards: Each year, the society
awards cash prizes of up to $25,000 to
international and Bay-area filmmakers as part of the
San Francisco International Film Festival.
Kenneth Rainin Foundation Filmmaking Grants:
Grants of up to $50,000 each will be awarded yearly
to films that, through plot, character, theme, or
setting, significantly explore human and civil rights,
antidiscrimination, gender and sexual identity, and
other urgent contemporary social justice issues. In
addition to funding, grant recipients receive free
tuition to one society class or workshop each
trimester session for one year, automatic
consideration for a society residency of up to six
months, waiving of fiscal sponsorship fees, and
invitation to society private events. Eligible
applicants must: be at least 18 years old; be a
society member at the Filmmaker Pro level or
above; be actively engaged in a narrative feature
film project in screenwriting/script development,
preproduction, or post-production; and have a
strong connection to the San Francisco Bay Area
(including Alameda, Contra Costa, Marin, San
Francisco, San Mateo, or Santa Clara counties) and
uplift the Bay Area film community.
EIN: 942663216

944
The San Francisco Foundation

1 Embarcadero Ctr., Ste. 1400
San Francisco, CA 94111 (415) 733-8500
Contact: Dee Dee Brantley, Interim C.E.O.
FAX: (415) 477-2783; E-mail: info@sff.org; Intent to
Apply e-mail: apps@sff.org; URL: http://
www.sff.org

Foundation type: Community foundation
Purpose: Scholarships to residents of CA for upper
level or graduate study at specific institutions.
Awards to artists and community leaders in the San
Francisco, CA, area.
Publications: Annual report; Financial statement;
Grants list; Newsletter; Program policy statement.
Financial data: Year ended 06/30/2013. Assets,
$1,183,262,000 (M); Expenditures,
$99,928,000; Total giving, $86,830,000. Awards/
prizes amount not specified. Scholarships—to
individuals amount not specified.
Fields of interest: Arts education; Media/
communications; Film/video; Print publishing;
Photography; Humanities.
Type of support: Awards/grants by nomination only;
Awards/prizes; Graduate support; Undergraduate
support.
Application information:
   Initial approach: Letter of intent for artist and
      community leader programs
   Deadline(s): Vary
   Additional information: See web site for complete
      program listings and additional application
      information.
Program descriptions:
Art Awards: The foundation bestows artistic
awards in literature, visual arts, and playwriting
each year to artists who exemplify a commitment to
the ever expanding notion of the essential role of
art and artists in the world.

Community Leadership Awards: This award
celebrate visionary leaders doing extraordinary work
to strengthen Bay Area communities. The work may
confront societal or civic issues, address health or
environmental concerns, or promote arts and
humanities.
Koshland Young Leader Awards: This award
recognizes the next generation of leadership in the
community, providing a two-year award of $7,000
to outstanding San Francisco public high school
juniors who balance extraordinary family, economic
and societal pressures with the discipline required
for academic excellence, and the drive to succeed
at community leadership.
Multicultural Fellowship Program: The program
provides young professionals of color with
challenging work experiences and leadership
opportunities in the areas of grantmaking and
community building. It includes an intensive
curriculum and dynamic hands-on professional
experience, and is a full-time two-year salaried
position. Program fellows serve on a program team
where they contribute to the Program Dept. and
engage in the substantive work of the entire team
and cross-team efforts within the planning
foundation. Fellows learn to perform proposal
review and analysis, participate in collaborative and
implementation of joint projects throughout the
organization, and participate in professional
development. Eligible candidates should be college
graduates, graduate level completed preferred;
represent diverse backgrounds and communities;
experienced in the nonprofit sector; and dedicated
to a career in philanthropy, nonprofits, or service.
The fellowship recruitment effort begins each
January. For more information contact the
fellowship coordinator via e-mail:
fellowship@sff.org or tel.: (415) 733-8500.
EIN: 010679337

945
San Francisco Friends of Chamber Music

135 Main St., Ste. 1140
San Francisco, CA 94105-1815 (415)
710-0551
Contact: Dominique Pelletey, Exec. Dir.
E-mail address for Fiscal Sponsorship:
pelletey@sfcm.org
FAX: (415) 820-1530; E-mail: info@sffcm.org;
URL: http://www.sffcm.org

Foundation type: Public charity
Purpose: Grants to musicians, presenters, and
composers who resides and works in one of the 15
counties of the greater San Francisco Bay Area.
Assistance to emerging and existing chamber
ensembles and others who share a commitment to
chamber music through fiscal sponsorship.
Publications: Application guidelines; Newsletter.
Financial data: Year ended 06/30/2012. Assets,
$261,505 (M); Expenditures, $331,091; Total
giving, $163,999; Grants to individuals, totaling
$126,026.
Fields of interest: Music ensembles/groups.
Type of support: Grants to individuals; Fiscal
agent/sponsor.
Application information: Applications accepted.
Application form required.
   Send request by: Mail for Grants, e-mail and mail
      for Fiscal Sponsorship
   Deadline(s): Feb. 15 for Grants, Oct. 1 and Mar.
      1 for Fiscal Sponsorship
   Final notification: Applicants notified in mid-Apr.
      for Grants, within six weeks of deadline for
      Fiscal Sponsorship
   Applicants should submit the following:
      1) Work samples

2) Budget Information
Additional information: See web site for additional guidelines for grants and fiscal sponsorship.

Program descriptions:

Fiscal Sponsorship Program: This program supports chamber music projects that promote artistic excellence, education, commissioning of new works and the awareness of chamber music as an art form. The program also allow ensembles to use the organization's tax-exempt status to facilitate the solicitation of public grants and private donations for a declared project. The organization will take an eight percent fee of all grants and donations awarded to the affiliate's project to see that it is fulfilled, and that proper reporting is completed.

Musical Grants: This program work to support outstanding projects of San Francisco Bay Area professional chamber music ensembles, presenters, and individuals with chamber music projects. The program will award grants of up to $3,000 through a competitive process to creative, well-conceived projects that seek to further the artistic, educational, and administrative goals of this constituency. Funding can be used for artistic purposes (artist fees, concert venues, concert production costs, recording costs, and commissioning), organizational and financial assistance (public relations and marketing, legal counsel, fund raising, web-based technology, and planning), and career development (outreach programming, training, and travel). Applications will be accepted by ensembles, ensembles with a composer, presenters, and individuals with a chamber music project. Applicants must reside and/or work in Alameda, Contra Costa, Marin, Napa, San Francisco, San Mateo, Santa Clara, Solano, or Sonoma counties, have budgets that do not exceed $100,000, and be U.S. citizens or legal permanent residents who are at least 18 years of age.
EIN: 943298643

946
San Francisco Girls Chorus
44 Page St., Ste. 200
San Francisco, CA 94102-5989 (415) 863-1752
FAX: (415) 934-0302;
E-mail: info@sfgirlschorus.org; E-Mail for Melanie Smith: msmith@sfgirlschorus.org; URL: http://www.sfgirlschorus.org

Foundation type: Public charity
Purpose: Scholarships for girls and young women from San Francisco, CA ages five to eighteen for music education and choral training.
Financial data: Year ended 06/30/2012. Assets, $5,336,542 (M); Expenditures, $2,040,432; Total giving, $169,008; Grants to individuals, totaling $169,008.
Fields of interest: Music (choral); Girls; Young adults, female.
Type of support: Scholarships—to individuals.
Application information:
Initial approach: E-mail
EIN: 942711726

947
San Francisco School Alliance
114 Sansome St., Ste. 800
San Francisco, CA 94104-3818 (415) 857-9650
Contact: Terry Bergeson Ed.D., Exec. Dir.
FAX: (415) 857-9699;
E-mail: info@sfschoolalliance.org; E-Mail for Terry Bergeson: execasst@sfschoolalliance.org; URL: http://sfschoolalliance.org/

Foundation type: Public charity
Purpose: Scholarships to high school seniors of the San Francisco Unified School District, CA, for continuing education.
Financial data: Year ended 06/30/2012. Assets, $4,066,363 (M); Expenditures, $4,963,146; Total giving, $588,420; Grants to individuals, totaling $413,020.
Fields of interest: Vocational education, post-secondary; Higher education.
Type of support: Scholarships—to individuals; Support to graduates or students of specific schools.
Application information: Applications accepted. Application form required.
Initial approach: E-mail
Deadline(s): Mar. 2
Applicants should submit the following:
1) Transcripts
2) Essay
3) Letter(s) of recommendation
4) GPA
Additional information: Applicants must demonstrate financial need and commitment to education/career goals.
Program description:
Maisin Scholar Award: This scholarship of up to $2,000 is given to seniors in the San Francisco Unified School District (SFUSD) high schools so they can pursue a higher level of education and open doors to their dreams. Applicants must attend a community college, university, educational institution, an occupational or vocational training program. The scholarship can be renewed for up to four years.
EIN: 943222869

948
San Francisco Study Center, Inc.
944 Market St., Ste. 701
San Francisco, CA 94102-4020 (415) 626-1650
Contact: Geoffrey Link, Exec. Dir.
FAX: (415) 626-7276;
E-mail: leonor@studycenter.org; Toll-free tel.: (888) 281-3757; E-mail for Geoffrey Link : geoff@studycenter.org; URL: http://www.studycenter.org

Foundation type: Public charity
Purpose: Fiscal sponsorship services to Bay Area nonprofits, foundation and public agencies.
Financial data: Year ended 12/31/2011. Assets, $2,137,234 (M); Expenditures, $4,586,522.
Type of support: Fiscal agent/sponsor.
Application information:
Initial approach: E-mail
Additional information: Contact the Center for further information regarding Fiscal Sponsor program.
Program description:
Fiscal Sponsorship: The center provides fiscal sponsorship for several dozen projects, primarily in health, mental health and community arts. The center offers its sponsored projects budget development and tracking; tracking and payment of

vendor invoices; personnel administration including payroll and benefits administration; maintenance of individualized general ledger for each project; contract management, including invoicing and reporting to fenders; individualized monthly statements; and management of organizational insurance requirements.
EIN: 942168838

949
San Gabriel/Pomona Valleys Developmental Services, Inc.
761 Corporate Ctr. Dr.
Pomona, CA 91768-2647 (909) 620-7722
FAX: (909) 622-5123; URL: http://www.sgprc.org/default.html

Foundation type: Public charity
Purpose: Grants and services to individuals with developmental disabilities and their families in the El Monte, Glendora, Monrovia, and Pomona districts of Los Angeles County, CA.
Financial data: Year ended 06/30/2012. Assets, $54,467,166 (M); Expenditures, $164,080,525; Total giving, $142,354,739; Grants to individuals, totaling $142,354,739.
Fields of interest: Disabilities, people with.
Type of support: Grants for special needs.
Application information: Clients living in residential facilities and adults living at home, generally receive day program and transportation services, while children and their families may receive either preventive services or therapeutic, respite, and other support. Contact foundation for eligibility requirements.
EIN: 954059206

950
San Jose State University Foundation
(also known as San Jose State University Research Foundation)
210 N. 4th St., 4th Fl.
San Jose, CA 95112-5569 (408) 924-1400
FAX: (408) 924-1499;
E-mail: cgarcia@foundation.sjsu.edu; URL: http://sjsufoundation.org/

Foundation type: Public charity
Purpose: Research grants for faculty at San Jose State University, CA.
Financial data: Year ended 06/30/2012. Assets, $37,743,523 (M); Expenditures, $71,201,291; Total giving, $4,104,223; Grants to individuals, totaling $4,104,223.
Type of support: Research.
Application information: Applications accepted.
Additional information: Contact foundation for current application deadline/guidelines.
EIN: 946017638

951
San Luis Obispo County Community Foundation
550 Dana St.
San Luis Obispo, CA 93401 (805) 543-2323
Contact: For grants: Janice Fong Wolf, Dir., Grants & Progs.
FAX: (805) 543-2346; E-mail: info@sloccf.org; Additional e-mail: jwolf@sloccf.org; URL: http://www.sloccf.org

Foundation type: Community foundation
Purpose: Scholarships to students of San Luis Obispo county, CA. Awards to individuals of San

Luis Obispo County, CA, who have made a significant contribution in humanitarian efforts, and advocacy for people with disabilities.
Publications: Application guidelines; Annual report; Grants list; Informational brochure; Newsletter; Occasional report.
Financial data: Year ended 12/31/2012. Assets, $36,353,519 (M); Expenditures, $6,731,821; Total giving, $5,744,157. Scholarships—to individuals amount not specified.
Fields of interest: Higher education; Human services; Disabilities, people with.
Type of support: Scholarships—to individuals; Support to graduates or students of specific schools; Awards/prizes; Undergraduate support.
Application information: Applications accepted. Application form required.
  Deadline(s): Varies
  Additional information: See web site for a complete listing of scholarship funds.
Program descriptions:
  Isabel P. Ruiz Humanitarian Award: The award annually recognizes and rewards a local individual for outstanding efforts in advocacy and caring for local people in San Luis Obispo County. This award is also designed to highlight and encourage those who follow in Mrs. Ruiz's footsteps to remain committed to community organizing and advocacy to improve the lives of everyone in San Luis Obispo County. See web site for additional information.
  Paul Wolff Accessibility Advocacy Award: Every year, individuals, organizations, and businesses within San Luis Obispo County make exemplary contributions of time, energy and talents toward the creation of a barrier-free community for people with disabilities. These individuals, organizations, and businesses are nominated and recognized annually through the Paul Wolff Accessibility Advocacy Award (PWAAA), a donor endowment held by the Community Foundation. See web site for additional information.
  Scholarships: The foundation administers several scholarships funds for higher education. For most scholarships, qualifying students must exhibit a strong academic record and financial need. Additional criteria includes specific intended majors and attendance at particular high schools. Each scholarship has its own unique eligibility requirements and application guidelines. See web site for additional information.
EIN: 770496500

952
San Mateo Rotary Foundation
(formerly Rotary Service Foundation of San Mateo)
P.O. Box 95
San Mateo, CA 94401-0095 (510) 781-5138
Contact: Donald Shoecraft, Pres.
URL: http://www.sanmateorotary.com/Foundation.cfm

Foundation type: Public charity
Purpose: Scholarships to residents of the San Mateo, CA, area for higher education.
Financial data: Year ended 06/30/2012. Assets, $1,119,121 (M); Expenditures, $139,444; Total giving, $131,857.
Type of support: Undergraduate support.
Application information: Contact foundation for application guidelines.
EIN: 237101037

953
Sandpipers Philanthropy Trust Fund
P.O. Box 72
Hermosa Beach, CA 90254-0072
Contact: Debbie Felt, Pres.

Foundation type: Public charity
Purpose: Scholarships and grants to needy individuals in the South Bay, Los Angeles, CA.
Financial data: Year ended 06/30/2012. Assets, $2,923,973 (M); Expenditures, $356,737; Total giving, $301,087; Grants to individuals, totaling $251,522.
Type of support: Scholarships—to individuals; Grants for special needs.
Application information: Contact foundation for eligibility information.
EIN: 953501868

954
Santa Barbara Cottage Hospital Foundation
P.O. Box 689
Santa Barbara, CA 93102-0689 (805) 879-8980
Contact: David Dietrich, V.P., Advancement
URL: http://www.cottagehealthsystem.org/GetInvolved/Foundations/SantaBarbaraCottageHospitalFoundation/tabid/552/Default.aspx

Foundation type: Public charity
Purpose: Nursing scholarships and loans to nursing students attending school in Santa Barbara, Ventura, or San Luis Obispo County, CA and currently enrolled in a Licensed Vocational Nurse (LVN), Associate Degree in Nursing (ADN), or Bachelor's Degree in Nursing (BSN) program.
Financial data: Year ended 12/31/2011. Assets, $235,387,874 (M); Expenditures, $5,987,745; Total giving, $148,548; Grants to individuals, totaling $145,848.
Fields of interest: Nursing school/education.
Type of support: Student loans—to individuals.
Application information: Applications accepted. Application form required. Application form available on the grantmaker's web site.
  Initial approach: Telephone
  Deadline(s): Dec. 1 for the Winter/Spring term and July 1 for the Fall term.
EIN: 953802238

955
Santa Barbara Foundation
1111 Chapala St., Ste. 200
Santa Barbara, CA 93101 (805) 963-1873
Contact: Ronald V. Gallo, C.E.O.
FAX: (805) 966-2345;
E-mail: info@sbfoundation.org; Grant application e-mail: grants@sbfoundation.org; URL: http://www.sbfoundation.org

Foundation type: Community foundation
Purpose: Interest-free student loans, and scholarships to residents of Santa Barbara County, CA, who have attended grades 7-12 at Santa Barbara county schools.
Publications: Application guidelines; Annual report; Financial statement; Informational brochure; Newsletter; Occasional report.
Financial data: Year ended 12/31/2012. Assets, $299,473,778 (M); Expenditures, $35,014,687; Total giving, $24,466,934.
Fields of interest: Performing arts, education; Literature; Vocational education; Medical school/education; Women.

Type of support: Student loans—to individuals; Support to graduates or students of specific schools; Undergraduate support.
Application information: Applications accepted. Application form required. Application form available on the grantmaker's web site.
  Initial approach: Application
  Send request by: Online
  Deadline(s): Jan. 31
  Applicants should submit the following:
    1) SASE
  Additional information: See web site for complete scholarship listing.
Program description:
  Scholarships: The foundation offers a variety of scholarships and student aid packages to students from Santa Barbara County in collaboration the Scholarship Foundation of Santa Barbara. In addition to general scholarships, there are several scholarships for high school seniors, and for students studying music and creative writing. Each scholarship has its own unique set of eligibility criteria. See web site for additional information.
EIN: 951866094

956
Santa Cruz County Rotary Endowment
c/o William S. Lynch
545 Pinecone Dr.
Scotts Valley, CA 95066-4422 (831) 438-4490
Contact: Linda Burrpughs, Pres.
Miling Address: P.O. Box 497; Santa Cruz; CA 95061

Foundation type: Public charity
Purpose: Scholarships to graduating seniors of Santa Cruz, CA, high schools for university, college, or vocational education.
Financial data: Year ended 06/30/2012. Assets, $756,795 (M); Expenditures, $59,727; Total giving, $52,250; Grants to individuals, totaling $52,250.
Fields of interest: Vocational education, post-secondary; Higher education.
Type of support: Scholarships—to individuals.
Application information: Applications accepted. Application form required. Interview required.
  Initial approach: In person at local high school
EIN: 942560310

957
Santa Maria Arts Council, Inc.
P.O. Box 5
Santa Maria, CA 93456-0005
Application address: c/o Kate Burridge, SMAC Individual Grants, 1451 Paseo Ladera Ln., Arroyo Grande, CA 93420,
e-mail: grants@smartscouncil.org
E-mail: info@smartscouncil.org; URL: http://www.smartscouncil.org

Foundation type: Public charity
Purpose: Grants for emerging artists 12 years or older from northern Santa Barbara county, CA in music, drama, dance, and visual arts.
Financial data: Year ended 05/31/2012. Assets, $254,804 (M); Expenditures, $15,190; Total giving, $11,750.
Fields of interest: Visual arts; Dance; Theater; Music.
Type of support: Grants to individuals; Awards/prizes.
Application information: Applications accepted. Application form required.
  Send request by: Mail
  Deadline(s): Mar. 23

Applicants should submit the following:
1) SASE
2) Letter(s) of recommendation

Additional information: Application should also include four images of your best current work, either slides or prints. All applicants must attend a Grants Workshop to obtain an application for Individual Grants in the Arts Competition.

Program description:
Individual Grants in the Arts: Grants are awarded to individuals based on artistic excellence and promise to grow in the arts. Applicant must have lived in northern Santa Barbara county for at least two years or have completed as least one Fine Arts class or youth arts program during each of four semesters in the Santa Maria area. A $1,500 first place and $1,000 second place will be presented to the winner in music, drama, dance, and visual arts.
EIN: 237011595

958
Santa Rosa Junior College Foundation
1501 Mendocino Ave.
Santa Rosa, CA 95401-4395 (707) 527-4348
Contact: Kate McClintock, Exec. Dir.
FAX: (707) 524-1806;
E-mail: rcutcher@santarosa.edu; Tel. for Kate McClintock: (707)-527-4797; E-mail for Kate McClintock: kmcclintock@santarosa.edu;
URL: http://www.santarosa.edu/foundation/

Foundation type: Public charity
Purpose: Scholarships to students at Santa Rosa Junior College, CA.
Publications: Newsletter.
Financial data: Year ended 06/30/2012. Assets, $37,054,210 (M); Expenditures, $2,177,722; Total giving, $1,030,511; Grants to individuals, totaling $1,030,511.
Type of support: Support to graduates or students of specific schools.
Application information: Applications accepted.
Additional information: Contact foundation for current application deadline/guidelines.
EIN: 941735861

959
Santa Verena Charity, Inc.
P.O. Box 51206
Irvine, CA 92619-1206 (949) 471-0310
FAX: (949) 471-0311;
E-mail: santaverena@lacopts.org; URL: http://www.santaverena.com/

Foundation type: Public charity
Purpose: Emergency relief and humanitarian aid to the poor and needy families in the U.S. and Egypt by providing food, medicine, housing and other special need.
Financial data: Year ended 12/31/2012. Assets, $1,665,833 (M); Expenditures, $4,457,047; Total giving, $4,270,598; Grants to individuals, totaling $72,443.
Fields of interest: Human services.
Type of support: Emergency funds; Grants for special needs.
Application information: Applications not accepted.
EIN: 954719735

960
The Sarcoma Alliance
775 E. Blithedale Ave., Ste. 334
Mill Valley, CA 94941-1554 (415) 381-7236
Contact: Matthew Anderson M.D. Ph.D.
FAX: (415) 381-7235;
E-mail: info@sarcomaalliance.org; URL: http://www.sarcomaalliance.org

Foundation type: Public charity
Purpose: Financial assistance to sarcoma patients for second opinion consultations by reimbursing expenses related to travel, phone bills, costs of the evaluation, and other directly related charges.
Publications: Application guidelines; Informational brochure (including application guidelines); Newsletter (including application guidelines).
Financial data: Year ended 12/31/2011. Assets, $222,824 (M); Expenditures, $167,964; Total giving, $15,622.
Fields of interest: Health care, support services; Health care, financing; Cancer.
Type of support: Grants for special needs.
Application information: Applications accepted. Application form required. Application form available on the grantmaker's web site.
Initial approach: Letter, telephone or e-mail
Send request by: Mail
Copies of proposal: 1
Deadline(s): Ongoing
Applicants should submit the following:
1) Financial information
Additional information: Application should include insurance, physician, and estimated expense information.
EIN: 680443045

961
Scaife Scholarship Foundation
1547 Lakeside Dr.
Oakland, CA 94612-4520 (510) 451-1906
Contact: Cal Gilbert, Secy.-Treas.

Foundation type: Independent foundation
Purpose: Scholarships to male graduates of public high schools in northern CA whose parents were born in the U.S.
Financial data: Year ended 05/31/2013. Assets, $12,761,843 (M); Expenditures, $601,427; Total giving, $500,500; Grants to individuals, 66 grants totaling $500,500 (high: $8,000, low: -$1,750).
Fields of interest: Men.
Type of support: Scholarships—to individuals.
Application information:
Deadline(s): Mar. 15
Applicants should submit the following:
1) Transcripts
2) Financial information
Additional information: Application must also include College Board scores.
EIN: 943161402

962
Schiffman Memorial Foundation
4719 Quail Lakes Dr., Ste. G-345
Stockton, CA 95219-0345 (209) 944-0740

Foundation type: Independent foundation
Purpose: Scholarships to graduating high school seniors of Stockton, CA pursuing a career in the fields of teaching, counseling, medicine or law enforcement at an accredited college or university.
Financial data: Year ended 12/31/2012. Assets, $959,500 (M); Expenditures, $62,087; Total giving, $38,600.

Fields of interest: Law school/education; Medical school/education; Teacher school/education.
Type of support: Scholarships—to individuals.
Application information: Applications accepted. Application form required.
Additional information: Selection is based on demonstrated merit and academic achievement. Applicant must have a cumulative 2.5 GPA.
EIN: 134220347

963
Damir I. and Virginia A. Schmidek Charitable Foundation
14500 Fruitvale Ave., Ste. 6116
Saratoga, CA 95070

Foundation type: Independent foundation
Purpose: Support to musical interns at San Jose Opera, CA.
Financial data: Year ended 12/31/2013. Assets, $604,757 (M); Expenditures, $50,420; Total giving, $19,142.
Fields of interest: Music.
Type of support: Internship funds.
Application information: Applications accepted.
Initial approach: Letter
Deadline(s): Apr. 1
EIN: 770520075

964
Clara Schmidt Foundation, Inc.
2528 Honolulu Ave.
Montrose, CA 91020-1806 (818) 249-2021
Contact: Richard A. Sill, Pres. and Dir.

Foundation type: Independent foundation
Purpose: Scholarships to outstanding Los Angeles Lutheran High School students and South Bay Lutheran High School students in the Los Angeles, CA area.
Financial data: Year ended 12/31/2012. Assets, $87,995 (M); Expenditures, $13,955; Total giving, $13,000.
Fields of interest: Higher education.
Type of support: Support to graduates or students of specific schools.
Application information: Applications accepted.
Initial approach: Letter
Deadline(s): May 25
Additional information: Selection is based on financial need.
EIN: 954168951

965
Scholarship Foundation of Santa Barbara
P.O. Box 3620
Santa Barbara, CA 93130-3620 (805) 687-6065
Contact: Colette Hadley, Exec. Dir.
FAX: (805) 687-6031;
E-mail: info@sbscholarship.org; Additional address (Santa Maria office): 120 E. Jones St., Ste 100, Santa Maria, CA 93454-5101, E-Mail for Colette Hadley: chadley@sbscholarship.org; URL: http://www.sbscholarship.org

Foundation type: Public charity
Purpose: Scholarships and student loans to Santa Barbara County, CA, high school graduates for undergraduate, graduate, medical, and vocational study.
Publications: Annual report; Financial statement; Informational brochure (including application guidelines).

Financial data: Year ended 06/30/2012. Assets, $42,215,646 (M); Expenditures, $8,435,304; Total giving, $6,755,487; Grants to individuals, totaling $6,706,951.

Fields of interest: Higher education; Education.

Type of support: Scholarships—to individuals; Student loans—to individuals; Support to graduates or students of specific schools; Graduate support; Technical education support; Undergraduate support.

Application information: Applications accepted. Application form required. Application form available on the grantmaker's web site. Interview required.

> *Send request by:* On-line or by Mail
> *Copies of proposal:* 1
> *Deadline(s):* Jan. 31
> *Final notification:* Recipients notified in one month
> *Applicants should submit the following:*
>   1) FAFSA
>   2) Transcripts
>   3) Letter(s) of recommendation
>   4) GPA
>   5) Financial information
>   6) Essay
>   7) Budget Information
> *Additional information:* See web site for additional program guidelines.

Program descriptions:

Art Scholarship Competition: Scholarships are available to graduating high school seniors in southern Santa Barbara County who will major in art at college. A short, special application is required to apply, and an art portfolio must be presented for judging. These awards are made for one academic year only; applicants may reapply to the General Scholarship Program in subsequent years if they wish.

Breitling College Visit Awards Program: Scholarships are available to female high school graduates throughout Santa Barbara County who are planning to attend an approved college outside of the state of California on a full-time basis. Scholarships are intended to help recipients and families visit out-of-state colleges.

Creative Writing Scholarship: Scholarships are awarded to Santa Barbara County students who demonstrate unusual aptitude and potential in the field of creative writing or poetry.

Fleischmann and Floro Awards Program: Scholarships are available to graduating high school students throughout Santa Barbara County who are planning to continue their education. Applicants must have a minimum GPA of 3.5 and a strong record of community service activities.

General Scholarship Program: Awards of $1,000 to $5,000 are available to undergraduates, and graduate, and medical students, based on evaluated financial need, motivation, and potential.

Loan Program: Student loans are available to individuals who have attended at least grades 7 through 12 in Santa Barbara County and have graduated from a Santa Barbara County high school. All applicants must be enrolled full-time (12 units minimum per term) at an approved vocational school or two- or four-year college, and maintain at least a 2.0 GPA to be eligible.

Scholarship Program: Applicants must have attended at least grades 7 through 12 in Santa Barbara County and have graduated from a Santa Barbara County high school. All applicants must be enrolled full-time (12 units minimum per term) at an approved vocational school or two- or four-year college, and maintain at least a 2.0 GPA to be eligible for scholarship funds.

EIN: 237087774

966
Charles Schwab Foundation

211 Main St.
SF211 MN-16-205
San Francisco, CA 94105-1905 (877) 408-5438
Contact: Elinore Robey, Dir. of Progs.; Roger K. Wong, Progs. Mgr.
FAX: (415) 636-3262;
E-mail: charlesschwabfoundation@schwab.com;
URL: http://www.aboutschwab.com/community

Foundation type: Company-sponsored foundation

Purpose: Provides youth ages 13 to18 with basic money management skills and practical ways to save, spend, and invest their money. Successful participants receive a certificate of completion and a Money Matters $2,000 scholarship from the foundation.

Financial data: Year ended 12/31/2011. Assets, $3,071,192 (M); Expenditures, $4,825,919; Total giving, $4,384,981.

Fields of interest: Boys & girls clubs; Human services, financial counseling.

Type of support: Grants to individuals.

Application information:
> *Initial approach:* Letter
> *Additional information:* Contact foundation for further eligibility requirements.

EIN: 943192615

967
SCI Special Fund

27405 Puerta Real, Ste. 120
Mission Viejo, CA 92691-6314
URL: http://www.scispecialfund.org

Foundation type: Independent foundation

Purpose: Supporting apparatuses, free rehabilitative care, and equipment to qualified patients with spinal cord injuries residing in CA.

Financial data: Year ended 12/31/2012. Assets, $423,155 (M); Expenditures, $110,704; Total giving, $81,246; Grants to individuals, 33 grants totaling $81,246 (high: $8,551, low: $158).

Fields of interest: Medical care, rehabilitation; Spine disorders.

Type of support: Grants for special needs.

Application information: Applications not accepted.

> *Additional information:* Unsolicited requests for funds not considered or acknowledged.

EIN: 330310017

968
Science Scholarship Foundation

c/o A.B. Jacobs
P.O. Box 9175
Laguna Beach, CA 92652

Foundation type: Independent foundation

Purpose: Scholarships to students at Saddleback Community College, CA, who are U.S. citizens and have at least a 3.5 GPA in chemistry, mathematics, physics, or allied science courses.

Financial data: Year ended 05/31/2012. Assets, $742,426 (M); Expenditures, $81,388; Total giving, $80,000.

Fields of interest: Science; Chemistry; Mathematics; Physics.

Type of support: Support to graduates or students of specific schools; Undergraduate support.

Application information: Applications not accepted.

> *Additional information:* Unsolicited requests for funds not considered or acknowledged.

EIN: 953646338

969
The Screen Actors Guild Foundation

5757 Wilshire Blvd., 7th Fl.
Los Angeles, CA 90036-3681 (323) 549-6708
Contact: Jill Seltzer, Exec. Dir.
FAX: (323) 549-6710; E-mail: msmith@sag.org;
URL: http://www.sagfoundation.org

Foundation type: Public charity

Purpose: Scholarships to Guild members and their dependents for study at accredited institutions for higher education. Emergency financial assistance to qualified Screen Actors Guild members during times of crisis or personal need.

Publications: Application guidelines.

Financial data: Year ended 09/30/2011. Assets, $23,815,924 (M); Expenditures, $4,345,162; Total giving, $1,194,263; Grants to individuals, totaling $1,129,563.

Fields of interest: Film/video; Higher education; Health care.

Type of support: Undergraduate support; Grants for special needs.

Application information: Applications accepted. Application form required.

> *Initial approach:* Application
> *Deadline(s):* Mar. 15 for John L. Dales Scholarship Fund; none for all others
> *Applicants should submit the following:*
>   1) Financial information
>   2) Transcripts
>   3) SAT
>   4) Letter(s) of recommendation
>   5) Essay
> *Additional information:* Applicant must demonstrate financial need. See web site for additional guidelines.

Program descriptions:

Catastrophic Health Fund: This fund provides grants to eligible Screen Actors Guild (SAG) members and their dependents who suffer from catastrophic illness or injury.

Emergency Assistance Program: This program provides eligible Screen Actors Guild (SAG) members with financial assistance during times of crisis or personal need.

John L. Dales Scholarship Fund: This fund helps qualified Screen Actors Guild (SAG) members and their children reach their educational potential. Two types of scholarships are available under this program. Standard scholarships are awarded to eligible members and children of eligible members for college education, while transitional scholarships are designed to assist experienced SAG members who need further education to change their careers, and who require financial assistance in order to obtain it. Awards will be applied to accredited and licensed universities, colleges, junior colleges, adult specialty schools, and trade/vocational schools.

EIN: 953967876

970
Junior Seau Foundation

5275 Market St., Ste. B
San Diego, CA 92114-2212 (619) 264-5555
Contact: Jamie Ellis, Dir. Business Development
FAX: (619) 264-5035; E-mail: info@juniorseau.org;
Email for Jamie Ellis: Jamie@juniorseau.org;
URL: http://www.juniorseau.org

Foundation type: Public charity

Purpose: Scholarships to San Diego, CA area disadvantaged high school graduates for higher education.
Financial data: Year ended 06/30/2012. Assets, $1,302,797 (M); Expenditures, $480,048; Total giving, $111,280; Grants to individuals, totaling $111,280.
Fields of interest: Higher education.
Type of support: Scholarships—to individuals.
Application information: Applications accepted. Application form required.
  Initial approach: Telephone
  Deadline(s): Apr. 2
  Additional information: Contact the foundation for additional guidelines.
Program description:
  Scholars of Excellence: This program was created to recognize young men and women who are dedicated to both personal and academic excellence. Financial assistance is granted to high school graduates who have the desire, but not the means, to achieve their dreams through higher education.
EIN: 330541799

971
Second Harvest Food Bank of Santa Clara and San Mateo Counties
750 Curtner Ave.
San Jose, CA 95125-2113 (408) 266-8866
Contact: Mr. Norm Taffe, Chair.
FAX: (408) 266-9042; Additional address (San Mateo County): 1051 Bing St., San Carlos, CA 94070-5320, tel.: (650) 610-0800, fax: (650) 610-0808; URL: http://www.shfb.org/

Foundation type: Public charity
Purpose: Emergency assistance to low-income individuals and families living throughout Santa Clara and San Mateo counties.
Publications: Annual report; Newsletter.
Financial data: Year ended 06/30/2012. Assets, $52,131,037 (M); Expenditures, $83,184,796; Total giving, $66,649,526; Grants to individuals, totaling $24,021,095.
Fields of interest: Children; Aging; Economically disadvantaged.
Type of support: In-kind gifts; Grants for special needs.
Application information: Contact the agency for additional information.
EIN: 942614101

972
Theodore H. Sedler Scholarship Fund
P.O. Box 60078, SC-MPK-03-M
Los Angeles, CA 90060

Foundation type: Independent foundation
Purpose: Scholarships to graduating seniors at high schools in Richland County, ND.
Financial data: Year ended 12/31/2012. Assets, $2,028,734 (M); Expenditures, $138,390; Total giving, $61,875.
Fields of interest: Education.
Type of support: Support to graduates or students of specific schools; Graduate support; Undergraduate support.
Application information: Applications accepted. Application form required.
  Deadline(s): Mar. 31
  Additional information: Applicant must include letters of reference and have a 2.0 minimum GPA.
EIN: 456091443

973
SEMA Memorial Scholarship Fund
P.O. Box 4910
Diamond Bar, CA 91765-0910 (909) 396-0289
Contact: Christopher J. Kersting, Pres. and C.E.O.
Scholarship address: Attn: Education Dept., 1575 S. Valley Vista Dr., Diamond Bar, CA 91765
E-mail: education@sema.org; URL: http://www.sema.org/scholarship

Foundation type: Public charity
Purpose: Scholarships to students engaged in studies which will lead to a career in the automotive aftermarket or a related field.
Publications: Application guidelines.
Financial data: Year ended 06/30/2012. Assets, $2,025,463 (M); Expenditures, $114,580; Total giving, $109,856; Grants to individuals, totaling $109,856.
Fields of interest: Higher education; Scholarships/financial aid.
Type of support: Undergraduate support.
Application information: Applications accepted. Application form required. Application form available on the grantmaker's web site.
  Initial approach: E-mail or letter
  Deadline(s): May 15
  Applicants should submit the following:
    1) Photograph
    2) Letter(s) of recommendation
    3) Transcripts
    4) Essay
Program descriptions:
  Memorial Scholarship Fund: The fund awards scholarships of up to $4,000 to graduate and undergraduate students who are pursuing studies leading to a career in the automotive aftermarket or related field. Applicants must have a minimum grade point average of 2.5.
  Ohio Technical College Scholarship: One full-tuition scholarship (of up to $29,400) will be available to a student who plans to attend Ohio Technical College.
EIN: 954131888

974
Sempra Energy Corporate Giving Program
c/o Corp. Community Rels. Dept.
101 Ash St.
San Diego, CA 92101-3017 (619) 696-2000
Contact: Molly Cartmill, Dir., Corp. Community Rels.
E-mail: gifts@sempra.com; URL: http://www.sempra.com/responsibility/index.shtml

Foundation type: Corporate giving program
Purpose: Scholarships to employees of Sempra Energy for use towards the completion of associate's, master's, or bachelor's degrees, or for professional certificates and foreign-language classes.
Publications: Corporate giving report; Program policy statement.
Fields of interest: Vocational education; Higher education; Graduate/professional education; Adult/continuing education.
Type of support: Employee-related scholarships.
Application information: Applications not accepted.
  Additional information: Unsolicited requests for funds not considered or acknowledged.
Program description:
  Employee Tuition Reimbursement Program: Sempra Energy awards reimbursement scholarships of up to $5,250 per year to full-time employees to be used for tuition, registration costs, required books and software, lab fees, or campus parking. Part-time employees become eligible for up to $800 of scholarship money per year after one year of employment.
Company name: Sempra Energy

975
Sequoia Hospital Foundation
170 Alameda De Las Pulgas
Redwood City, CA 94062-2751 (650) 367-5657
Contact: for Scholarship: JoAnn C. Kemist, Pres.
K. Krueger tel.: (650) 367-5854,
e-mail: karen.krueger@chw.edu
E-mail: joann.kemist@dignityhealth.org;
URL: http://www.sequoiahospitalfoundation.org/index.htm

Foundation type: Public charity
Purpose: Nursing scholarships to support student nurses pursuing a major in a health related field at Canada College, CA.
Financial data: Year ended 06/30/2011. Assets, $24,114,421 (M); Expenditures, $1,721,217; Total giving, $1,520,861; Grants to individuals, totaling $81,746.
Fields of interest: Nursing school/education.
Type of support: Scholarships—to individuals.
Application information: Applications accepted. Application form required.
  Additional information: Contact the foundation for additional information and guidelines.
EIN: 942909990

976
Serra Ancillary Care Corporation
825 Colorado Blvd., Ste. 100
Los Angeles, CA 90041-1741 (323) 344-4888
Contact: Terry Goddard II, Exec. Dir.
FAX: (323) 254-2956;
E-mail: info@serraproject.org; URL: http://www.serraproject.org

Foundation type: Public charity
Purpose: Financial assistance to extremely low income persons of Los Angeles, CA living with HIV/AIDS from becoming homeless.
Financial data: Year ended 06/30/2011. Assets, $1,998,598 (M); Expenditures, $7,213,178; Total giving, $3,369,238; Grants to individuals, totaling $3,369,238.
Fields of interest: Housing/shelter, homeless; AIDS, people with; Economically disadvantaged.
Type of support: Grants for special needs.
Application information:
  Initial approach: Telephone
  Additional information: Contact the agency for eligibility determination.
EIN: 954147364

977
Shaklee Cares
4747 Willow Rd.
Pleasanton, CA 94588-2763 (925) 924-2621
Contact: Roger Barbett, Pres.
FAX: (925) 925-3847;
E-mail: shakleecares@shaklee.com; URL: http://www.shakleecares.org/index.html

Foundation type: Public charity
Purpose: Grants to families for natural disaster relief.
Financial data: Year ended 03/31/2012. Assets, $300,053 (M); Expenditures, $162,786; Total giving, $162,746.
Fields of interest: Disasters, floods.
Type of support: Emergency funds.

Application information: Applications accepted.
Application form required.
   Additional information: See web site for disaster
   relief application form.
EIN: 943169989

978
Shasta Regional Community Foundation
1335 Arboretum Dr., Ste. B
Redding, CA   96003-3627   (530) 244-1219
Contact: Kerri Caranci, C.E.O.; For grants: Amanda
Hutchings, Prog. Off.
FAX: (530) 244-0905; E-mail: info@shastarcf.org;
Grant inquiry e-mail: amanda@shastarcf.org;
URL: http://www.shastarcf.org

Foundation type: Community foundation
Purpose: Scholarships to individuals from Shasta
and Sishiyou counties, CA, for undergraduate
education at colleges and universities in the U.S.
Publications: Application guidelines; Annual report;
Grants list; Informational brochure.
Financial data: Year ended 06/30/2013. Assets,
$21,285,013 (M); Expenditures, $3,129,928;
Total giving, $1,385,828; Grants to individuals,
62 grants totaling $135,308 (high: $58,508, low:
$500).
Fields of interest: Music; Business school/
education; Law school/education; Formal/general
education; Athletics/sports, racquet sports;
Science; Women.
Type of support: Scholarships—to individuals;
Support to graduates or students of specific
schools; Undergraduate support.
Application information: Applications accepted.
Application form required. Application form
available on the grantmaker's web site.
   Initial approach: Letter or fax
   Copies of proposal: 1
   Deadline(s): Varies
   Applicants should submit the following:
      1) Transcripts
      2) Letter(s) of recommendation
      3) GPA
      4) Essay
   Additional information: Contact high school
      counselor, see web site or contact the
      foundation for current application guidelines.
EIN: 680242276

979
The Carroll Shelby Foundation
(formerly Carroll Shelby Children's Foundation)
19021 S. Figueroa St.
Gardena, CA   90248-4510   (310) 327-5072
Contact: Jenni Shreeves, Exec. Dir.
FAX: (310) 538-0419; E-mail: jenni@cscf.org;
URL: http://www.cscf.org/

Foundation type: Public charity
Purpose: Financial assistance for children and
medical professionals to help overcome
life-threatening health issues worldwide.
Scholarship money for kids dedicated to enhancing
their lives through continuing educational
opportunities in the automotive field.
Financial data: Year ended 12/31/2011. Assets,
$6,861,900 (M); Expenditures, $655,236; Total
giving, $85,050; Grants to individuals, totaling
$2,400.
Fields of interest: Education; Health care; Heart &
circulatory diseases; Kidney diseases; Youth.
Type of support: Scholarships—to individuals;
Grants for special needs.
Application information: Applications accepted.

Additional information: Contact the foundation for
additional information.
EIN: 954342625

980
Joseph Shinoda Memorial Scholarship Foundation
234 Via La Paz
San Luis Obispo, CA   93401   (805) 544-0717
Contact: Barbara McCaleb
URL: http://www.shinodascholarship.org

Foundation type: Independent foundation
Purpose: Scholarships to students for the study of
floriculture at accredited colleges and universities.
Financial data: Year ended 12/31/2012. Assets,
$597,087 (M); Expenditures, $42,861; Total
giving, $21,700.
Fields of interest: Botanical/horticulture/
landscape services.
Type of support: Undergraduate support.
Application information: Application form required.
Application form available on the grantmaker's web
site.
   Send request by: Mail
   Deadline(s): Mar. 30
   Applicants should submit the following:
      1) Transcripts
      2) Letter(s) of recommendation
EIN: 237213289

981
Side Street Projects
730 N. Fair Oaks Ave.
P. O. Box 90432
Pasadena, CA   91103-3044   (626) 798-7774
Contact: Emily Hopkins, Exec. Dir.
FAX: (626) 798-7747; E-mail: info@sidestreet.org;
E-Mail for Emily Hopkins: emily@sidestreet.org;
URL: http://www.sidestreet.org

Foundation type: Public charity
Purpose: Support to individuals through a Fiscal
sponsorship program.
Financial data: Year ended 06/30/2012. Assets,
$182,701 (M); Expenditures, $291,531.
Fields of interest: Visual arts; Arts, artist's
services.
Type of support: Fiscal agent/sponsor.
Application information: Applications accepted.
   Initial approach: Telephone or e-mail
Program description:
   Fiscal Sponsorship: Fiscal sponsorship
   opportunities are available to organizations and
   individuals that share the mission and goals of the
   organization. Applicants must be dues-paying
   members before being considered for fiscal
   sponsorship.
EIN: 954395168

982
Sierra Pacific Foundation
c/o Jon D. Gartman
P.O. Box 496028
Redding, CA   96049-6028   (530) 378-8000
E-mail: foundation@spi-ind.com; URL: http://
www.spi-ind.com/spf_home.aspx

Foundation type: Company-sponsored foundation
Purpose: Scholarships to dependent children of
Sierra Pacific Industries employees who reside in
CA.
Publications: Grants list.

Financial data: Year ended 06/30/2013. Assets,
$22,599 (M); Expenditures, $801,780; Total
giving, $776,662; Grants to individuals, 311 grants
totaling $342,972 (high: $2,500, low: $375).
Type of support: Employee-related scholarships.
Application information: Applications not
accepted.
   Additional information: Unsolicited requests for
      funds not accepted or acknowledged.
Company name: Sierra Pacific Industries
EIN: 942574178

983
Sierra Vista Child & Family Services
100 Poplar Ave.
Modesto, CA   95354-1018   (209) 523-4573
FAX: (209) 550-5866; URL: http://
www.sierravistacares.org/

Foundation type: Public charity
Purpose: Mental health support services, food, and
clothing for adults, children, and families living in or
around Modesto, CA. Also financial support for
Modesto, CA foster parents.
Financial data: Year ended 06/30/2011. Assets,
$5,824,613 (M); Expenditures, $15,436,838;
Total giving, $978,178; Grants to individuals,
totaling $978,178.
Fields of interest: Health care, patient services;
Mental health/crisis services; Foster care; Family
services.
Type of support: Grants for special needs.
Application information: Applications accepted.
   Initial approach: Letter, telephone or e-mail
   Additional information: See web site for detailed
      application and program information.
EIN: 942158023

984
Philip and Aida Siff Educational Foundation
(formerly Philip Francis Siff Educational Foundation)
1114 State St., Ste. 300
Santa Barbara, CA   93101-6073

Foundation type: Independent foundation
Purpose: Scholarships to graduate students of
University of California, Los Angeles, and to full-time
students of Hunter College of the City University of
New York, University of California, Santa Barbara,
and Santa Barbara City College, CA.
Financial data: Year ended 06/30/2013. Assets,
$2,031,444 (M); Expenditures, $161,472; Total
giving, $105,167.
Fields of interest: Humanities; Science.
Type of support: Scholarships—to individuals;
Support to graduates or students of specific
schools.
Application information: Applications not
accepted.
   Additional information: Unsolicited requests for
      funds not considered or acknowledged.
EIN: 770165960

985
John J. Signer Memorial Trust Fund
P.O. Box 45174
San Francisco, CA   94145-0174
Contact: Douglas G. Moore

Foundation type: Independent foundation
Purpose: Scholarships to graduates of Lick
Wilmerding High School, San Francisco, CA, who
are planning to study electricity, electronics, or
electrical engineering.

Financial data: Year ended 04/30/2013. Assets, $703,924 (M); Expenditures, $40,427; Total giving, $30,384; Grants to individuals, 5 grants totaling $30,384 (high: $10,846, low: $177).
Fields of interest: Business/industry; Engineering.
Type of support: Support to graduates or students of specific schools; Undergraduate support.
Application information: Applications accepted.
  Initial approach: Letter
  Deadline(s): Two months prior to commencement.
EIN: 946288204

986

Silicon Valley Community Foundation

2440 West El Camino Real, Ste. 300
Mountain View, CA 94040-1498 (650) 450-5400
Contact: Vera Bennett, C.O.O. and C.F.O.; Katarina Koster, Exec. Asst. to C.O.O./C.F.O.
Scholarship e-mail: scholarships@siliconvalleycf.org.
FAX: (650) 450-5401;
E-mail: info@siliconvalleycf.org; URL: http://www.siliconvalleycf.org/

Foundation type: Community foundation
Purpose: Scholarships to high school, community college and university students who are current or former residents of San Mateo and Santa Clara counties, CA.
Publications: Application guidelines; Annual report; Financial statement; Grants list; Informational brochure; Newsletter; Occasional report.
Financial data: Year ended 12/31/2012. Assets, $2,903,166,000 (M); Expenditures, $328,238,000; Total giving, $293,996,000; Grants to individuals, 299 grants totaling $918,000 (high: $10,000, low: $160); Loan to an individual, 1 loan totaling $227,986.
Fields of interest: Higher education.
Type of support: Scholarships—to individuals; Support to graduates or students of specific schools; Undergraduate support.
Application information: Applications accepted. Application form required. Application form available on the grantmaker's web site.
  Deadline(s): Varies
  Additional information: See web site for complete listing of scholarships or e-mail foundation for additional information.
Program description:
  Scholarship Programs: The foundation administers a variety of scholarship programs to high school, community college and university students. The majority are designated for current or former residents of San Mateo and Santa Clara counties. All scholarships have been established by generous local individuals, corporations or organizations to assist students with their educational pursuits. Each scholarship has its own unique set of eligibility requirements, such as financial need and minimum cumulative GPA as well as awards for specific areas of study. Scholarship amounts vary between $500 and $15,000. See web site for additional information.
EIN: 205205488

987

Silicon Valley Education Foundation

1400 Parkmoor Ave., Ste. 200
San Jose, CA 95126-3798 (408) 790-9400
FAX: (408) 213-0560;
E-mail: Info@SVEFoundation.org; URL: http://svefoundation.org

Foundation type: Public charity
Purpose: Grants to PreK-12 teachers who work in a school district or charter school in Santa Clara County, CA that have a signed Memorandum of Understanding (MOU) with the foundation. Scholarships to graduating seniors attending Yerba Buena and Andrew Hill High Schools in San Jose, CA.
Publications: Application guidelines.
Financial data: Year ended 06/30/2011. Assets, $5,697,483 (M); Expenditures, $3,682,975; Total giving, $149,480; Grants to individuals, 137 grants totaling $149,480. Subtotal for scholarships—to individuals: 16 grants totaling $16,000. Subtotal for grants to individuals: 121 grants totaling $133,480.
Fields of interest: Elementary/secondary education.
Type of support: Grants to individuals.
Application information: Applications accepted. Application form required.
  Send request by: Online
  Deadline(s): Sept. 30 and Feb. 3 for Grants, Apr. 13 for Scholarships
  Final notification: Recipients notified Oct. 21 and Feb. 24 for Grants
  Additional information: See web site for additional guidelines.
Program description:
  Teacher Innovation Grants: Grants to individual teachers with the extra resources needed to create new and exciting teaching methods and learning experiences for their students. Teachers can apply individually (up to $500) or collaboratively (up to $1,000) to purchase equipment, materials, or other needs that are not part of the regular school budget.
EIN: 205061316

988

Steve Silver Foundation, Inc.

c/o Steven Horowitz
3661 Buchanan St., Ste. 200
San Francisco, CA 94123-1788 (415) 248-1729
Application address: Beach Blanket Babylon Scholarship, c/o Charles Zukow Assoc., 1 Hallidie Plz., Ste. 501, San Francisco, CA 94102-2843
URL: http://www.beachblanketbabylon.com/scholarship/guidelines.shtml

Foundation type: Independent foundation
Purpose: Scholarships to Bay Area high school seniors or home schooled students pursuing an education in the performing arts.
Financial data: Year ended 12/31/2011. Assets, $248,451 (M); Expenditures, $32,890; Total giving, $30,000; Grants to individuals, 3 grants totaling $30,000 (high: $10,000, low: $10,000).
Fields of interest: Performing arts; Dance; Music (choral).
Type of support: Scholarships—to individuals.
Application information:
  Deadline(s): Apr. 30
  Final notification: Applicants notified in May
  Additional information: Application should include VHS, DVD or Digital CD-ROM of a three minute performance. Scholarships are awarded based on talent. Students must show proof of enrollment at an accredited postsecondary institution. See web site for additional guidelines.
EIN: 943215024

989

Silverlake Conservatory of Music

(also known as Bring on the Music, Inc.)
3920 Sunset Blvd.
Los Angeles, CA 90029-2242 (323) 665-3363
FAX: (323) 665-3176; URL: http://www.silverlakeconservatory.com/

Foundation type: Public charity
Purpose: Scholarships to low income children of Los Angeles County, CA who would like to learn a musical instrument, but whose families cannot afford lessons.
Publications: Application guidelines.
Financial data: Year ended 12/31/2011. Assets, $951,422 (M); Expenditures, $1,037,851.
Fields of interest: Music.
Type of support: Scholarships—to individuals.
Application information: Applications accepted. Application form required.
  Additional information: Application should include a copy of the free lunch notice from the student's school, a photocopy of the lunch tickets with the student's name on it or a copy of the W-2 form.
EIN: 270030546

990

Simon Foundation for Education and Housing

(formerly Ronald M. Simon Family Foundation)
620 Newport Center Dr., 12th Fl.
Newport Beach, CA 92660-8012 (949) 270-3644
FAX: (949) 729-8072; E-mail: info@sfeh.org;
URL: http://www.sfeh.org

Foundation type: Independent foundation
Purpose: Scholarships to students facing difficult life and economic circumstances to excell academically and socially so they can successfully complete a four year college degree.
Financial data: Year ended 06/30/2013. Assets, $857,920 (M); Expenditures, $1,429,816; Total giving, $552,836; Grants to individuals, 117 grants totaling $236,336 (high: $6,000, low: $168).
Fields of interest: Higher education; Economically disadvantaged.
Type of support: Undergraduate support.
Application information: Applications accepted. Application form required. Application form available on the grantmaker's web site.
  Applicants should submit the following:
    1) Financial information
    2) Transcripts
    3) Letter(s) of recommendation
    4) Essay
    5) Photograph
    6) GPA
Program description:
  Simon Scholars Program: The program is a unique six year scholarship program that begins during a student's junior year in high school and continues through four years of college. Simon Scholars are required to maintain a minimum 3.0 GPA by the end of their junior year of high school. During high school, students receive a cash stipend, a computer, social skills training, academic support, leadership training and community services activities. Scholars are also provided with college-preparatory assistance through ACT and SAT courses, college tours and assistance in the application process from college coaches. Following the completion of high school, Scholars receive a $16,000 college scholarship. See web site for additional information.
EIN: 680524905

991
SKB Foundation
1247 Elko Dr.
Sunnyvale, CA   94089-2211   (408) 747-1769
Contact: Ho-Tzu Yen, Pres.

Foundation type: Independent foundation
Purpose: Student loans to high school seniors or students in a postsecondary educational institution of Taiwanese or Chinese origin residing in the San Francisco Bay Area, CA for undergraduate education.
Financial data: Year ended 11/30/2012. Assets, $4,628,173 (M); Expenditures, $236,104; Total giving, $223,000.
Fields of interest: Higher education; Asians/Pacific Islanders.
International interests: China; Taiwan.
Type of support: Student loans—to individuals.
Application information: Applications accepted.
  Initial approach: Letter
  Additional information: Selection criteria include academic achievement, involvement in the community or extracurricular activities.
EIN: 943024121

992
Small Angels Foundation and Endowment
326 Old Newport Blvd.
Newport Beach, CA   92663-4121   (949) 631-3300
Contact: Gerald A. Klein, C.E.O. and Pres.

Foundation type: Independent foundation
Purpose: Financial assistance to indigent families residing in Orange County, CA, to help pay for rent and medical bills.
Financial data: Year ended 12/31/2012. Assets, $0 (M); Expenditures, $28,856; Total giving, $27,635.
Type of support: Grants for special needs.
Application information: Applications
  Initial approach: Letter
  Deadline(s): None
  Additional information: Contact foundation for further application guidelines.
EIN: 481268716

993
Smart & Final Scholarship Foundation
600 Citadel Dr.
Commerce, CA   90040-1562   (323) 869-7523

Foundation type: Public charity
Purpose: Scholarships to dependents of employees of Smart & Final.
Financial data: Year ended 12/31/2011. Assets, $1,826,064 (M); Expenditures, $61,456; Total giving, $50,000; Grants to individuals, totaling $50,000.
Type of support: Scholarships—to individuals; Undergraduate support.
Application information: Applications accepted. Application form required.
  Initial approach: Letter
  Send request by: Mail
  Deadline(s): May 4
  Applicants should submit the following:
    1) ACT
    2) SAT
    3) Transcripts
    4) Essay
EIN: 954800664

994
Tavis Smiley Foundation
4434 Crenshaw Blvd.
Los Angeles, CA   90042-1208   (323) 290-1888
Contact: Jacqueline Murray, Pro. Admin.
FAX: (323) 290-1988;
E-mail: jmurray@tavistalks.com; URL: http://www.youthtoleaders.org/2home.asp

Foundation type: Public charity
Purpose: Scholarships to high school and college students who have participated in any of the foundation programs.
Publications: Application guidelines.
Financial data: Year ended 12/31/2011. Assets, $192,930 (M); Expenditures, $398,546; Total giving, $50,000; Grants to individuals, totaling $50,000.
Fields of interest: Higher education.
Type of support: Scholarships—to individuals.
Application information: Applications accepted. Application form required. Application form available on the grantmaker's web site.
  Initial approach: Application
  Deadline(s): Sept. 30
  Final notification: Applicants notified in Nov.
  Applicants should submit the following:
    1) Photograph
    2) Letter(s) of recommendation
    3) Transcripts
    4) Essay
  Additional information: Application should also include a copy of your college acceptance letter. Faxed or e-mail applications are not accepted.
Program description:
  Smiley Scholars Program: The foundation awards scholarships ranging from $1,000 to $5,000, to alumni of its Youth to Leaders program. Two types of scholarships are available in this program: United Health Foundation scholarships (awarded to individuals who are majoring in a field that will lead to a career in the healthcare industry, such as medicine, dentistry, and psychology); and Anheuser-Busch Better World Scholarships (available to individuals in any field of study). Eligible applicants must be U.S. citizens who are attending an accredited college or university in the U.S., have participated in a foundation program (including the Youth to Leaders conference series, the Youth to Leaders National Summit, the Tavis Smiley Foundation Leadership Institute, the Talented Tenth High School Tour, or Youth 2 Leaders Ventures), and have a minimum GPA of 2.5 (on a 4.0 system)
EIN: 954770291

995
Douglas Franklin Smith Memorial Foundation
13100 Filly Ln.
Truckee, CA   96161-1433   (800) 276-6846
Contact: Jill Dobbs, Exec. Dir.
E-mail: jill@charitysmith.org; Toll-free tel.: (800) 276-6546; URL: http://www.charitysmith.org/

Foundation type: Public charity
Purpose: Scholarships and grants to students, artists, and athletes who have achieved excellence through persistence and hard work.
Financial data: Year ended 12/31/2011. Assets, $824,493 (M); Expenditures, $258,080; Total giving, $213,285; Grants to individuals, totaling $41,031.
Type of support: Grants to individuals; Scholarships—to individuals.

Application information: Applications not accepted.
  Additional information: Unsolicited requests for funds not considered or acknowledged.
EIN: 870636433

996
J.A. & Flossie Mae Smith Scholarship Fund
c/o R.D. Taramasco
P.O. Box 1335
Rancho Santa Fe, CA   92067-1335   (858) 756-4884
Contact: R.D. Taramasco, Tr.

Foundation type: Independent foundation
Purpose: Scholarships to graduate and undergraduate students who demonstrate academic ability and financial need and who intend to pursue a full-time academic program, with emphasis on agriculture at an accredited, tax-exempt CA college.
Financial data: Year ended 12/31/2010. Assets, $279,749 (M); Expenditures, $16,309; Total giving, $13,900; Grants to individuals, totaling $13,900.
Fields of interest: Agriculture.
Type of support: Graduate support; Undergraduate support.
Application information: Applications accepted. Application form required. Interview required.
  Deadline(s): None
EIN: 956432440

997
John & Charlene Smylie Foundation
3643 Grand Ave.
San Marcos, CA   92078-2310

Foundation type: Independent foundation
Purpose: Provides supplemental financial aid to enable the student to continue his or her extracurricular and community activities.
Financial data: Year ended 12/31/2011. Assets, $267,838 (M); Expenditures, $14,050; Total giving, $13,800.
Fields of interest: Higher education.
Type of support: Scholarships—to individuals.
Application information: Applications accepted. Application form required.
  Deadline(s): None
  Applicants should submit the following:
    1) Transcripts
    2) Letter(s) of recommendation
  Additional information: Applicant must apply for available federal and state financial aid to be eligible and provide a copy of the award letter or the letter of rejection. The award is renewable on demonstration of continued progress in their educational program and other activities.
EIN: 943252120

998
Social and Environmental Entrepreneurs
23532 Calabasas Rd., Ste. A
Calabasas, CA   91302-5151   (818) 225-9150
Contact: Jennifer Hoffman, Exec. Dir.
FAX: (818) 225-9151;
E-mail: seefinance2@earthlink.net; URL: http://www.saveourplanet.org

Foundation type: Public charity

Purpose: Fiscal sponsorship to individuals for projects that focus on social and ecological innovation that will bring about positive change.
Publications: Application guidelines; Occasional report.
Financial data: Year ended 12/31/2011. Assets, $2,868,424 (M); Expenditures, $4,482,303.
Fields of interest: Environment.
Type of support: Fiscal agent/sponsor.
Application information: Applications accepted. Application form required. Application form available on the grantmaker's web site. Interview required.
  Initial approach: Mail or in person
  Copies of proposal: 1
  Deadline(s): None
  Final notification: 3 - 4 weeks
  Additional information: To be considered for an interview an application must include a budget. Incomplete applications not considered. Proposals sent by fax or e-mail not accepted.
Program description:
  Fiscal Sponsorship: The organization provides fiscal sponsorship to encourage ecological, humanitarian activism, and education for the purpose of creating a more harmonious civilization. The project must be charitable in purpose and must be organized and operated exclusively for purposes set forth; a fiscal fee of 6.5 percent is charged on all monies received.
EIN: 954116679

999
Society for the Preservation & Encouragement of Barbershop Quartet Singing in America

(also known as SPEBSQSA - Far Western District)
10941 Sproul Ave.
Los Angeles, CA 90064-060   (310) 474-0501
Contact: Russell Young, Pres.

Foundation type: Public charity
Purpose: Travel assistance to district quartets and chorus representatives to attend international convention and music schools, primarily in AZ, CA, HI, and NV.
Financial data: Year ended 12/31/2011. Assets, $123,891 (M); Expenditures, $122,592.
Fields of interest: Music (choral); Music ensembles/groups.
Type of support: Conferences/seminars; Scholarships—to individuals; Travel grants.
Application information: Unsolicited requests for funds not considered or acknowledged.
EIN: 956085839

1000
Society of Experimental Test Pilots Scholarship Foundation

P.O. Box 986
Lancaster, CA 93584-0986   (661) 942-9574
Contact: Paula Smith, Exec. Dir.
E-mail: setp@setp.org; URL: http://www.setp.org/scholarship-foundation/scholarship.html

Foundation type: Public charity
Purpose: Scholarships to children of deceased or disabled members of the Society of Experimental Test Pilots.
Financial data: Year ended 12/31/2011. Assets, $4,162,146 (M); Expenditures, $153,702; Total giving, $104,000; Grants to individuals, totaling $104,000.
Type of support: Undergraduate support.

Application information: Applications accepted.
  Initial approach: Letter
  Additional information: Contact foundation for application guidelines.
EIN: 952479396

1001
Society of Singers, Inc.

26500 W. Agoura Rd., Ste. 102-554
Calabasas, CA 91302-1952   (818) 995-7100
Contact: Judy Varley, Exec. Dir.
FAX: (818) 995-7466; E-mail: sos@singers.org;
E-Mail for Judy Varley: judy@singers.org;
URL: http://www.singers.org

Foundation type: Public charity
Purpose: Financial assistance to professional singers due to medical, family, and other crises. Scholarships to deserving students to help them become professional vocalists.
Publications: Application guidelines; Financial statement; Informational brochure (including application guidelines); Newsletter (including application guidelines).
Financial data: Year ended 12/31/2011. Assets, $83,742 (M); Expenditures, $151,112; Total giving, $18,710; Grants to individuals, totaling $18,710.
Fields of interest: Music (choral); Disasters, Hurricane Katrina; Economically disadvantaged.
Type of support: Emergency funds; Undergraduate support; Grants for special needs.
Application information: Application form required. Interview required.
  Initial approach: Telephone
  Deadline(s): Apr. 30 for Vocal Arts Scholarship, none for Financial Aid Services
  Applicants should submit the following:
    1) Resume
    2) Financial information
    3) Budget Information
  Additional information: Applicants must be professional singers for five or more years to be eligible. Checks are paid directly to creditors for utilities, medical bills, etc. Unsolicited requests for funds not considered or acknowledged.
Program descriptions:
  Financial Aid Services: The society aids singers who have dire and/or emergency financial needs that are due to personal, family, and/or medical crises. Grants may be provided for such basic needs as food, shelter, utilities, transportation, and medical/dental expenses (such as substance abuse rehabilitation, psychotherapy, and HIV/AIDS treatment). Grants are paid directly to creditors.
  Vocal Arts Scholarship Program: Scholarships to Masters students to help them meet the expense of their education at nationwide universities and performing arts institutions. $1,500 grants toward tuition are awarded to students who demonstrate the highest level of talent, academic achievement, and financial need.
EIN: 953903182

1002
Society of St. Vincent de Paul, Particular Council of San Mateo, Inc.

50 N. B St.
San Mateo, CA 94401-3917   (650) 373-0623
Contact: Lorraine Moriarty, Exec. Dir.
FAX: (650) 343-9495;
E-mail: svdpinfo@yahoo.com; Tel. for Lorraine Moriarty : (650)-373-0624; URL: http://www.svdp-sanmateoco.org

Foundation type: Public charity
Purpose: Grants to needy residents of San Mateo County, CA.
Financial data: Year ended 09/30/2011. Assets, $5,311,292 (M); Expenditures, $4,546,453; Total giving, $1,209,091; Grants to individuals, totaling $1,209,091.
Fields of interest: Economically disadvantaged.
Type of support: Grants for special needs.
Application information:
  Initial approach: Telephone
  Additional information: Contact foundation for complete eligibility requirements.
EIN: 941375833

1003
Sonora Area Foundation

362 S. Stewart St.
Sonora, CA 95370   (209) 533-2596
Contact: Lin Freer, Prog. Mgr.; Ed Wyllie, Exec. Dir.
FAX: (209) 533-2412;
E-mail: edwyllie@sonora-area.org; Grant application e-mail: leaf@sonora-area.org; URL: http://www.sonora-area.org

Foundation type: Community foundation
Purpose: Scholarships to Tuolumne County, CA, residents for higher education.
Publications: Application guidelines; Annual report; Biennial report; Financial statement; Grants list; Informational brochure; Informational brochure (including application guidelines); Newsletter; Occasional report.
Financial data: Year ended 12/31/2012. Assets, $44,076,675 (M); Expenditures, $2,640,275; Total giving, $2,008,131; Grants to individuals, 162 grants totaling $178,603.
Fields of interest: Higher education.
Type of support: Precollege support; Undergraduate support.
Application information: Application form available on the grantmaker's web site.
  Additional information: Application process is handled through the schools. Unsolicited requests for funds not considered or acknowledged.
EIN: 931023051

1004
South Central Los Angeles Regional Center for Developmentally Disabled Persons, Inc.

650 W. Adams Blvd., Ste. 400
Los Angeles, CA 90007-2545   (213) 744-7000
Contact: Dexter A. Henderson, C.E.O.
URL: http://www.sclarc.org/

Foundation type: Public charity
Purpose: Assistance to individuals with developmental disabilities, of South Central Los Angeles, CA.
Financial data: Year ended 06/30/2012. Assets, $14,779,982 (M); Expenditures, $142,254,557; Total giving, $120,240,163; Grants to individuals, totaling $120,240,163.
Fields of interest: Disabilities, people with; Economically disadvantaged.
Type of support: Grants for special needs.
Application information: Each individual receives different services based on their individual need.
EIN: 953861159

1005
Southern California Asian American Studies Central, Inc.

(also known as Visual Communications)
120 Judge John Aiso St.
Los Angeles, CA   90012-3805   (213) 680-4462
Contact: Shinae Yoon, Exec. Dir.
FAX: (213) 687-4848; E-mail: info@vconline.org;
E-mail for Shinae Yoon: shinae@vconline.org;
URL: http://www.vconline.org/index.html

Foundation type: Public charity
Purpose: Support to media artists through programs focused on and about Asian Pacific Americans.
Publications: Application guidelines.
Financial data: Year ended 12/31/2011. Assets, $534,304 (M); Expenditures, $603,866; Total giving, $5,000; Grants to individuals, totaling $5,000.
Fields of interest: Film/video; Arts, artist's services; Asians/Pacific Islanders.
Type of support: Fellowships; Fiscal agent/sponsor.
Application information: Applications accepted. Application form required.
> *Initial approach:* Download application forms
> *Deadline(s):* Oct. 1 for Armed with a Camera Fellowship for Emerging Artists; Sept. 1 and Nov. 1 for Fiscal Sponsorship

Program descriptions:
Armed with a Camera Fellowship for Emerging Artists: The fellowship allows emerging media artists to capture their world and surroundings as part of a new generation of Asian Pacific Americans. Up to ten fellows will receive $500 to complete, within a four-month span of time, a five-minute digital video. Selected artists will also receive monetary compensation for their artistic work, access to Visual Communication's (VC) post-production facilities, a one-year membership, exhibition of their new work at the VC Filmfest, professional training workshops throughout the year, future use of Visual Communications as a fiscal sponsor, and technical assistance when necessary. Eligible applicants must be of Asian Pacific descent, 30 years old or younger, residents of California, and have had previous work in the VC Filmfest, ChillVisions, any other VC exhibition and/or any film festival (excluding on-campus student festivals)
Fiscal Sponsorship: A fiscal sponsorship arrangement is available through membership with the Visual Communications Filmmaker's Union. Eligible projects for consideration must be imaginative, creative contributions to Asian Pacific media and/or alternative independent media, and must be consistent with the philosophical principles and mission of Visual Communications. Applicants must also join the Friends of Visual Communications, at the rate of $100 per year, to be considered for sponsorship. A fiscal agent fee of 7 percent will be assessed for any monies granted or donated to projects under its fiscal sponsorship.
EIN: 237108393

1006
Southern Exposure

3030 20th St.
San Francisco, CA   94110-2870   (415) 863-2141
Contact: Courtney Fink, Exec. Dir.
Application URL: http://soex.org/alternativeexposure
FAX: (415) 863-1841; E-mail: director@soex.org;
URL: http://soex.org

Foundation type: Public charity
Purpose: Grants to visual artists of the San Francisco Bay, CA area to support projects that provide frameworks of support for artists to create and continue their work.
Publications: Application guidelines.
Financial data: Year ended 12/31/2011. Assets, $586,884 (M); Expenditures, $618,213; Total giving, $65,090; Grants to individuals, totaling $65,090.
Fields of interest: Visual arts.
Type of support: Grants to individuals.
Application information: Applications accepted. Application form available on the grantmaker's web site.
> *Send request by:* On-line
> *Deadline(s):* Sept.
> *Final notification:* Applicants notified in Nov.
> *Additional information:* Application that includes print materials that cannot be submitted digitally should be delivered to Southern Exposure via mail or hand delivery by the deadline. See web site for additional guidelines.
EIN: 931216297

1007
Space Grant Education and Enterprise Institute

(formerly California Space Grant Foundation)
10619 Sunset Ridge Dr.
San Diego, CA   92131
Contact: Claudia Von Wilpert, C.F.O.
URL: http://wwwsgeei.org

Foundation type: Independent foundation
Purpose: Scholarships to individuals to attain high skill technical and professional careers through education and exciting programs.
Financial data: Year ended 12/31/2012. Assets, $5,225 (M); Expenditures, $39,812; Total giving, $18,014; Grant to an individual, 1 grant totaling $314.
Fields of interest: Education; Space/aviation.
Type of support: Scholarships—to individuals.
Application information: Application form not required.
> *Initial approach:* Letter
> *Deadline(s):* None
EIN: 943031747

1008
Spirit Educational Foundation

21070 Centre Pointe Pkwy.
Santa Clarita, CA   91350-2976   (661) 259-5606
Contact: Peggy Rasmussen, Secy.

Foundation type: Independent foundation
Purpose: Scholarships primarily to residents of CA, who will be attending a college or university in CA.
Financial data: Year ended 12/31/2011. Assets, $261 (M); Expenditures, $15,880; Total giving, $15,000.
Type of support: Undergraduate support.
Application information: Applications accepted. Application form required.
> *Initial approach:* Letter
> *Deadline(s):* None
> *Applicants should submit the following:*
> 1) Transcripts
> 2) Essay
> 3) GPA
EIN: 300339604

1009
Sponsors of Musical Enrichment, Inc.

(also known as SOME, Inc.)
P. O. Box 9010
Stockton, CA   95208-5201   (209) 468-2483
Contact: Mike Canote, Pres.
FAX: (209) 952-2442; E-mail: some@someinc.com;
URL: http://www.someinc.com

Foundation type: Public charity
Purpose: Scholarship to a graduating high school senior or a student presently attending an institution of higher learning.
Publications: Application guidelines.
Financial data: Year ended 12/31/2012. Assets, $211,570 (M); Expenditures, $41,022; Total giving, $34,644.
Fields of interest: Music.
Type of support: Scholarships—to individuals.
Application information: Applications accepted. Application form required. Application form available on the grantmaker's web site.
> *Initial approach:* Letter
> *Deadline(s):* July
> *Applicants should submit the following:*
> 1) Transcripts
> 2) Letter(s) of recommendation
> *Additional information:* Applicant must demonstrate financial need, participate in a drum corps, demonstrate leadership qualities, be a music major and be accepted to or in attendance at an institution of continuing education. All drum corps members are encouraged to apply. See web site for additional information.
Program description:
Jim Ott Scholarship: This $3,000 scholarship is presented annually at the Drum Corps International Championships, and is awarded to an outstanding member of the drum and bugle corps activity.
EIN: 942587379

1010
St Joseph Hospital of Orange

1100 W. Stewart Dr.
Orange, CA   92868-3849   (714) 633-9111
URL: http://www.sjo.org/

Foundation type: Public charity
Purpose: Scholarships to employees of St. Joseph Hospital of Orange County, CA who have been accepted into an accredited educational program. Financial assistance to patients for childcare, housing and medication.
Publications: Newsletter.
Financial data: Year ended 06/30/2011. Assets, $922,797,416 (M); Expenditures, $628,595,360; Total giving, $3,205,131; Grants to individuals, totaling $50,605.
Fields of interest: Health sciences school/education.
Type of support: Employee-related scholarships; Grants for special needs.
Application information: Applications accepted.
> *Additional information:* Selection for scholarship is based on financial need, professional and academic achievement, and recommendations from a manager or peer. Assistance for patients, money is disbursed directly to the vendor or to the patient after appropriate supporting documentation is provided.
EIN: 951643359

1011
St. Francis Yacht Club Foundation
c/o Leventhal Kline Mgt.
127 Univ. Ave.
Berkeley, CA 94710-1616 (510) 841-4123
URL: http://www.stfycfoundation.com

Foundation type: Public charity
Purpose: Grants to individuals in northern CA, to promote sailing, racing competition, and maritime education.
Financial data: Year ended 12/31/2011. Assets, $1,497,071 (M); Expenditures, $234,670; Total giving, $150,118; Grants to individuals, totaling $90,798.
Fields of interest: Athletics/sports, water sports; Recreation.
Type of support: Grants to individuals.
Application information: Applications accepted.
  Send request by: On-line
  Deadline(s): Apr. 1, July 1, Oct.1 and Jan. 1
  Applicants should submit the following:
    1) Budget Information
    2) Resume
  Additional information: Applicant must agree to use the funds only for the purposes described in the application, to return any funds not expended, to submit receipts and/or documentation supporting budgeted expenditures, and to submit a brief report at the conclusion of the project, include photos, if available.
EIN: 942956977

1012
St. Helena Family Center
1440 Spring St.
St. Helena, CA 94574 (707) 963-1919
Contact: Sara Cakebread, Exec. Dir.
FAX: (707) 963-2153;
E-mail: info@sthelenafamilycenter.org; E-mail For Sara Cakebread:
scakebread@sthelenafamilycenter.org;
URL: http://sthelenafamilycenter.org/

Foundation type: Public charity
Purpose: Tuition assistance, medical expenses and food, health care, rent and utilities to low income individuals and families of CA.
Financial data: Year ended 12/31/2011. Assets, $236,557 (M); Expenditures, $502,339; Total giving, $112,232; Grants to individuals, totaling $66,590.
Fields of interest: Human services; Economically disadvantaged.
Type of support: Grants for special needs.
Application information: Applications accepted.
  Additional information: Eligibility is based on individual's or family's account of income and expenses. Contact the organization for eligibility determination.
EIN: 680362076

1013
St. Joseph's Family Center
7950 Church St., Ste. A
Gilroy, CA 95020-4401 (408) 842-6662
Contact: David Cox, Exec. Dir.
FAX: (408) 842-5842;
E-mail: davidc@stjosephsgilroy.org; Tel. for David Cox : (408)-842-6662, Ext. 25; URL: http://www.stjosephsgilroy.org

Foundation type: Public charity
Purpose: Emergency assistance to low-income individuals and families of south Santa Clara

county, CA, with food, clothing, transportation, rental, utility assistance and other special needs.
Financial data: Year ended 06/30/2012. Assets, $1,103,128 (M); Expenditures, $5,018,013; Total giving, $4,170,245; Grants to individuals, totaling $4,170,245.
Fields of interest: Human services; Economically disadvantaged.
Type of support: Emergency funds.
Application information: Applicant must be a resident of Gilroy or San Martin to receive assistance.
EIN: 030391775

1014
St. Jude Hospital, Inc.
101 E. Valencia Mesa Dr.
Fullerton, CA 92835-3809 (714) 871-3280
URL: http://www.stjudemedicalcenter.org

Foundation type: Public charity
Purpose: Financial assistance to indigent patients of St. Jude Hospital in Fullerton, CA, who do not qualify for government-sponsored insurance programs, such as Medi-Cal, MSI, Healthy Families, or Medicare.
Publications: Informational brochure; Newsletter.
Financial data: Year ended 06/30/2011. Assets, $826,477,100 (M); Expenditures, $439,973,476; Total giving, $6,548,059; Grants to individuals, totaling $67,660.
Fields of interest: Health care, patient services; Health care; Economically disadvantaged.
Type of support: Grants for special needs.
Application information: Applications accepted. Application form required.
  Initial approach: Tel.
  Applicants should submit the following:
    1) Financial information
  Additional information: For eligibility guidelines, call a Financial Counselor at (714) 446-5141.
EIN: 951643325

1015
St. Shenouda the Archimandrite Coptic Society
1494 SO. Robert Blvd.104 Ste.
Los Angeles, CA 90035-3482
Contact: Hany N. Takla, Pres.
URL: http://stshenouda.com/Society/taxreturns.htm

Foundation type: Independent foundation
Purpose: Educational grants to individuals to attend graduate work in Coptic studies and participate in scholarly conferences.
Financial data: Year ended 09/30/2012. Assets, $104,772 (M); Expenditures, $72,351; Total giving, $38,076; Grants to individuals, 11 grants totaling $4,984 (high: $789, low: $71).
Fields of interest: Museums (sports/hobby); Language (foreign); Theology; Research; Religion.
Type of support: Conferences/seminars; Graduate support.
Application information: Applications accepted.
  Initial approach: Letter
  Deadline(s): June 1
  Additional information: Letter should state course of study, relation to Coptic Studies, University attended/attending, and professional goal or purpose.
EIN: 953797903

1016
Stanford Public Interest Law Foundation
Stanford Law School, Crown Quadrangle
559 Nathan Abbot Way
Stanford, CA 94305-8602 (650) 223-3017
E-mail: opg.spilf@gmail.com; URL: http://spilf.stanford.edu/

Foundation type: Public charity
Purpose: Fellowships to law students of Stanford Law School, CA working for non-profits during the summer.
Publications: Application guidelines; Informational brochure.
Financial data: Year ended 12/31/2011. Assets, $193,450 (M); Expenditures, $44,851; Total giving, $44,751.
Fields of interest: Law school/education; Legal services, public interest law.
Type of support: Fellowships.
Application information: Applications accepted. Application form required.
  Additional information: See web site for additional guidelines.
Program description:
  SPILF-Stanford Law School Public Interest Fellowship: Two fellows will be selected and each fellowship will include a one-year salary of $45,000, benefits that the sponsoring organization would ordinarily provide to an employee at the recipient's level, and a free bar review course in the recipient's state of choice.
EIN: 942536926

1017
Stanislaus Community Foundation
1029 16th St.
Modesto, CA 95354 (209) 576-1608
Contact: Marion Kaanon, C.E.O.; For grants: Amanda Hughes, Prog. Off.
FAX: (209) 576-1609;
E-mail: mkaanon@stanislauscf.org; Grant inquiry e-mail: ahughes@stanislauscf.org; URL: http://www.StanislausCF.org

Foundation type: Community foundation
Purpose: Scholarships to residents of Stanislaus County, CA, or to individuals attending college or university in Stanislaus County, CA.
Publications: Annual report; Informational brochure; Newsletter.
Financial data: Year ended 12/31/2012. Assets, $12,947,136 (M); Expenditures, $1,187,818; Total giving, $912,599; Grants to individuals, 17 grants totaling $12,000.
Fields of interest: Higher education; Health care; Business/industry; Computer science; Physically disabled; Women.
Type of support: Scholarships—to individuals; Support to graduates or students of specific schools; Undergraduate support.
Application information: Applications accepted. Application form required. Application form available on the grantmaker's web site.
  Initial approach: Application
  Deadline(s): Apr. 4
  Applicants should submit the following:
    1) Letter(s) of recommendation
    2) Transcripts
    3) Resume
  Additional information: See web site for application form and complete listing of scholarship funds. Applications are also available from the financial aid officer at local high schools and colleges.

Program description:

Scholarships Funds: Scholarships to be awarded begin at $500 per school year. Each scholarship has its own unique eligibility requirements. General qualifications and guidelines include: 1) students will be residents of Stanislaus County attending any accredited university or college (unless specified otherwise) or any student attending school in Stanislaus County; and 2) students will maintain a B average or above during senior year and the year the scholarship is made available. See the web site for additional information.

EIN: 680483054

1018

Charles E. Stanley Scottish Rite Memorial Fund

c/o Bank of Stockton
P.O. Box 1110
Stockton, CA 95201-1110 (209) 929-1377

Foundation type: Independent foundation
Purpose: Educational loans to students who have graduated from a high school as far north as Galt, as far east as Sonora, as far west as Antioch and as far south as Turlock, CA.
Financial data: Year ended 12/31/2012. Assets, $1,653,059 (M); Expenditures, $22,895; Total giving, $110,000; Loans to individuals, 33 loans totaling $110,000.
Fields of interest: Higher education.
Type of support: Student loans—to individuals.
Application information: Application form required.
  Deadline(s): Mar. 31
  Applicants should submit the following:
    1) Transcripts
    2) Financial information
EIN: 946220263

1019

Mary R. Stauffer Foundation

P.O. Box 4688
Downey, CA 90241-1688 (562) 861-7378
Contact: Mary Stauffer, C.E.O.
E-mail: DRMRS10@aol.com

Foundation type: Operating foundation
Purpose: Grants to students of the Downey High schools, CA pursuing higher education.
Publications: Grants list; Informational brochure; Program policy statement.
Financial data: Year ended 04/30/2013. Assets, $6,571,191 (M); Expenditures, $376,386; Total giving, $365,543.
Fields of interest: Higher education.
Type of support: Support to graduates or students of specific schools.
Application information: Applications accepted.
  Additional information: The foundation does not consider these grants to be scholarships, as this means of giving has evolved in a need program. Students should contact their guidance counselor for additional application information.
Program description:
  Grants: Grants are awarded to students who want to make something of themselves and contribute to society. Selected students are given a check of $500 by the high school bookkeeper after they register at a junior college of their choice. This process can be repeated for four semesters, with the hope that students will either graduate or transfer to a four-year college.
EIN: 954433269

1020

Ella May Stedman Foundation

3607 Sausalito Dr.
Corona del Mar, CA 92625
Contact: Sara Pinkert, Pres.
Application address: 942 Jefferson P.I., Sturgeon Bay, WI 54235

Foundation type: Independent foundation
Purpose: Scholarships to graduating seniors of Sturgeon Bay High School, WI for postsecondary education at institutions of higher learning.
Financial data: Year ended 01/31/2013. Assets, $167,295 (M); Expenditures, $9,802; Total giving, $9,500; Grants to individuals, 4 grants totaling $9,500 (high: $3,500, low: $2,000).
Fields of interest: Higher education.
Type of support: Support to graduates or students of specific schools.
Application information: Applications accepted. Application form required.
  Initial approach: Letter
  Deadline(s): May 15 for high school students, June 15 for college students
EIN: 953545883

1021

The Stensrud Foundation

P.O. Box 501035
San Diego, CA 92150-1035 (858) 513-1245
Contact: Carol A. Stensrud, Pres.

Foundation type: Independent foundation
Purpose: Scholarships to individuals residing in the San Diego, CA, area for undergraduate education.
Financial data: Year ended 12/31/2012. Assets, $754,701 (M); Expenditures, $150,394; Total giving, $138,300.
Fields of interest: Higher education.
Type of support: Scholarships—to individuals.
Application information: Application form required.
  Deadline(s): May 15
  Additional information: Students must be referred by another 501(c)(3) organizations such as the YMCA or Boys and Girls Club.
EIN: 330757049

1022

Cecile Stephens Charitable Foundation

P.O. Box 903
Seal Beach, CA 90740 (714) 422-8541
Contact: Kevin E. Monson, Tr.

Foundation type: Independent foundation
Purpose: Scholarships to graduating seniors at Fountain Valley High School, CA, with a minimum 2.5 GPA and a minimum of three years performing with the Fountain Valley High School Choir.
Financial data: Year ended 12/31/2012. Assets, $586,407 (M); Expenditures, $166,167; Total giving, $73,400; Grants to individuals, 58 grants totaling $46,400 (high: $2,000, low: $500).
Fields of interest: Music (choral).
Type of support: Support to graduates or students of specific schools; Undergraduate support.
Application information: Applications accepted. Application form required.
  Deadline(s): May 1
  Applicants should submit the following:
    1) GPA
    2) Essay
  Additional information: Essay should include future plans, goals and dreams.
EIN: 201106340

1023

Stephenson-Beelard Scholarship Foundation

(formerly Stephenson Scholarship Foundation)
500 Main St.
Vacaville, CA 95688-3989 (707) 448-6894
Contact: Donald P. Stephenson, Pres.

Foundation type: Independent foundation
Purpose: Scholarships to graduating seniors who are residents of Vacaville, CA, at the time that they graduate from a public high school, and/or college undergraduates who resided in Vacaville at the time that they graduated from a public high school.
Financial data: Year ended 06/30/2012. Assets, $177,586 (M); Expenditures, $10,511; Total giving, $10,400; Grants to individuals, 8 grants totaling $10,400 (high: $1,300, low: $1,300).
Fields of interest: Athletics/sports, training.
Type of support: Undergraduate support.
Application information: Application form required. Interview required.
  Initial approach: Letter
  Deadline(s): Early Aug.
  Applicants should submit the following:
    1) Photograph
    2) Class rank
    3) Transcripts
EIN: 237412597

1024

The Marc and Eva Stern Foundation

(formerly The Stern Family Foundation)
865 S. Figueroa St., Ste. 1800
Los Angeles, CA 90017-2593 (213) 244-0744
Contact: Marc I. Stern, Pres.

Foundation type: Independent foundation
Purpose: Scholarships to graduating seniors at Vineland High School, NJ, who plan to study agriculture in college. First preference will be given to students in agricultural sciences or business and agronomy. Students interested in environmental studies or the life sciences may also apply.
Financial data: Year ended 12/31/2012. Assets, $2,512,623 (M); Expenditures, $1,391,229; Total giving, $1,365,755; Grants to individuals, 6 grants totaling $15,000 (high: $2,500, low: $2,500).
Fields of interest: Agriculture.
Type of support: Support to graduates or students of specific schools; Undergraduate support.
Application information: Applications accepted. Application form required.
  Initial approach: Letter
  Applicants should submit the following:
    1) Letter(s) of recommendation
    2) Transcripts
  Additional information: Applicants should also submit a 50-word or less statement concerning their interests and career goals.
EIN: 330220467

1025

Stockton Fire Fighters Gladys Benerd Trust

P.O. Box 692201
Stockton, CA 95269-2201

Foundation type: Operating foundation
Purpose: Scholarships to individuals for higher education who are dependents of firefighters.
Financial data: Year ended 12/31/2011. Assets, $691,223 (M); Expenditures, $44,674; Total giving, $39,905; Grants to individuals, 43 grants totaling $39,905 (high: $1,335, low: $835).
Type of support: Scholarships—to individuals.

Application information:
Initial approach: Letter or telephone
Deadline(s): End of Mar.
Final notification: Applicants will be notified in May
Applicants should submit the following:
1) Essay
2) Transcripts
EIN: 686117555

1026
Max D. Stone Family Foundation, Inc.
1036 W. Robinhood Dr., Ste. 202
Stockton, CA 95207-5627 (209) 478-4048
Contact: R. Jay Allen, C.F.O.

Foundation type: Independent foundation
Purpose: Scholarships to undergraduate or graduate students for attendance at Brigham Young University or other qualified university for tuition, room, board, books, laboratory and other fees associated with the academic endeavor.
Financial data: Year ended 12/31/2012. Assets, $10,132 (M); Expenditures, $25,033; Total giving, $24,331; Grant to an individual, 1 grant totaling $4,711.
Fields of interest: Higher education.
Type of support: Scholarships—to individuals; Support to graduates or students of specific schools.
Application information: Application form required.
Additional information: Applicants are selected from a group of qualified candidates.
EIN: 680345004

1027
Storkan/Hanes McCaslin Research Foundation
(formerly The Richard C. Storkan Foundation)
8770 Hwy. 25
Hollister, CA 95023 (408) 637-0195
Contact: Joanne Vargas, C.E.O.
Application address: 1029 Railroad St., Corona, CA 92882-1948

Foundation type: Independent foundation
Purpose: Scholarships and research grants to graduate students who are residents of the U.S. and who demonstrate interest in soil-borne diseases. Research must be done in the U.S.
Financial data: Year ended 12/31/2012. Assets, $29,752 (M); Expenditures, $27,271; Total giving, $17,500; Grants to individuals, 3 grants totaling $17,500 (high: $7,500, low: $5,000).
Fields of interest: Biology/life sciences.
Type of support: Research; Graduate support.
Application information:
Deadline(s): July 1
Additional information: Application must include proposal and biographical letter.
EIN: 770193922

1028
Donald A. Strauss Scholarship Foundation
4931 Birch St., Ste. 2
Newport Beach, CA 92660-2114 (949) 955-1930
Contact: Barbara Taborek, Admin.
FAX: (949) 833-9053;
E-mail: admin@straussfoundation.org; URL: http://www.straussfoundation.org

Foundation type: Independent foundation

Purpose: Scholarships by nomination only to full-time juniors for senior year of study at four-year colleges or universities in CA.
Financial data: Year ended 06/30/2012. Assets, $3,720,525 (M); Expenditures, $181,040; Total giving, $116,000; Grants to individuals, 22 grants totaling $116,000 (high: $8,000, low: $2,000).
Fields of interest: Education, services.
Type of support: Awards/grants by nomination only; Undergraduate support.
Application information: Application form required.
Deadline(s): 2nd week of Mar.
Applicants should submit the following:
1) Transcripts
2) Resume
3) Proposal
4) Letter(s) of recommendation
Additional information: Applicants must propose a public service project to be carried out between the end of junior year and the spring of senior year.
EIN: 330734363

1029
Studenica Foundation
535 4th St., Ste. 203
San Rafael, CA 94901-3314 (415) 451-6900
Contact: Michael D. Djordjevich, Pres.

Foundation type: Independent foundation
Purpose: Scholarships and publishing support to individuals in the Federal Republic of Yugoslavia.
Financial data: Year ended 12/31/2012. Assets, $4,122,321 (M); Expenditures, $92,089; Total giving, $71,510.
International interests: Yugoslavia.
Type of support: Publication; Scholarships—to individuals; Foreign applicants.
Application information:
Initial approach: Inquiry on official letterhead
EIN: 943186334

1030
The Sukut Family Foundation
4010 W. Chandler Ave.
Santa Ana, CA 92704-5202 (949) 240-6576
Application address: Capistrano Scholarship Fund, 31071 Marbella Vista, San Juan Capistrano, CA 92675

Foundation type: Independent foundation
Purpose: Financial assistance to college students in CA in need, to help them achieve their educational goals so they may better serve society in the future.
Financial data: Year ended 12/31/2012. Assets, $2,797 (M); Expenditures, $14,010; Total giving, $14,000.
Fields of interest: Higher education.
Type of support: Undergraduate support.
Application information:
Deadline(s): None
Additional information: Contact the foundation for additional guidelines.
EIN: 203484622

1031
The Georgia Frasier Sulprizio Scholarship Fund
2730 Peralta St.
Oakland, CA 94607 (510) 893-6476
Contact: Amie Kangeter

Foundation type: Independent foundation

Purpose: Scholarships to high school graduates of the northern California area, for attendance at a CA college or university, also scholarships for students attending trade schools.
Financial data: Year ended 12/31/2012. Assets, $119,219 (M); Expenditures, $3,405; Total giving, $1,739; Grants to individuals, 4 grants totaling $1,739 (high: $700, low: $100).
Fields of interest: Vocational education, post-secondary; Higher education.
Type of support: Scholarships—to individuals.
Application information: Applications accepted. Application form required.
Deadline(s): None
EIN: 911848938

1032
Sunnyvale Community Services
725 Kifer Rd.
Sunnyvale, CA 94086-5123 (408) 738-4321
Contact: Marie Bernard, Exec. Dir.
FAX: (408) 738-1125;
E-mail: info@svcommunityservices.org; E-mail For Marie Bernard: mbernard@svcommunityservices.org; URL: http://www.svcommunityservices.org

Foundation type: Public charity
Purpose: Grants for food, shelter, and other basic necessities to needy residents of Santa Clara County, CA.
Publications: Newsletter.
Financial data: Year ended 06/30/2012. Assets, $3,837,830 (M); Expenditures, $4,248,344.
Fields of interest: Economically disadvantaged.
Type of support: Grants for special needs.
Application information: Contact foundation for complete eligibility requirements.
EIN: 941713897

1033
Sun-Pacific Scholarship Foundation, Inc.
(formerly Allied Exeter Scholarship Foundation, Inc.)
1095 E. Green St.
Pasadena, CA 91106

Foundation type: Independent foundation
Purpose: Scholarships to employees who have worked for any of the Sun Pacific Companies for at least two seasons, or eligible dependents of Sun Pacific employees.
Financial data: Year ended 07/31/2013. Assets, $3,233 (M); Expenditures, $26,136; Total giving, $26,062; Grants to individuals, 8 grants totaling $26,062 (high: $7,500, low: $750).
Fields of interest: Vocational education, post-secondary; Higher education.
Type of support: Employee-related scholarships.
Application information: Application form required.
Deadline(s): Apr.
Applicants should submit the following:
1) Transcripts
2) SAT
3) Letter(s) of recommendation
4) ACT
5) Essay
Additional information: Selection is based on academic performance, financial need, leadership ability and/or community service.
Program description:
Sun Pacific Scholarships: Two scholarships are offered each year, one, a four-year scholarship to any accredited university and another is a one-time scholarship to any accredited trade school or community college. The four year scholarship provides $3,000 per year for four years if studies

continue to be satisfactory. The one-time scholarship provides $3,000 to the selected student. The scholarships are available to high school graduating seniors and are only available to those not currently enrolled in higher education.
EIN: 942863726

1034
Swanson Fund f/b/o Fresno Lodge No. 247, F. & A. M
(also known as Annette Monson Swanson Fund)
3444 E. Shields Ave.
Fresno, CA   93726-6919   (559) 222-8565

Foundation type: Independent foundation
Purpose: Financial assistance to economically disadvantaged residents of CA.
Financial data: Year ended 11/30/2012. Assets, $32,246 (M); Expenditures, $941; Total giving, $0.
Fields of interest: Economically disadvantaged.
Type of support: Grants for special needs.
Application information: Applications accepted.
  Initial approach: Letter
  Deadline(s): None
  Additional information: Applicant should state reason for need.
EIN: 946140827

1035
Sweet Relief Musicians Fund
2601 E. Chapman Ave. Ste. 204
Fullerton, CA   92831   (714) 626-0447
Contact: Rob Max, Exec. Dir.
FAX: (714) 626-0473; E-mail: info@sweetrelief.org;
Toll-free tel.: (888) 955-7880; URL: http://www.sweetrelief.org

Foundation type: Public charity
Purpose: Grants to musicians with financial need who have or recently have had a serious medical condition. Grants also to older retired or semi-retired musicians with financial need for basic necessities.
Financial data: Year ended 12/31/2011. Assets, $66,261 (M); Expenditures, $711,795; Total giving, $433,724; Grants to individuals, totaling $413,393.
Fields of interest: Arts, artist's services; Economically disadvantaged.
Type of support: Grants for special needs.
Application information: Applications accepted. Application form required.
  Initial approach: E-mail
  Additional information: Contact foundation for complete eligibility requirements.
EIN: 954443269

1036
Swift Memorial Health Care Foundation
4001 Mission Oaks Blvd., Ste. A
Camarillo, CA   93012-5121
Application address: c/o Virgina Weber, 1317 Del Norte Rd., Ste. 150, Camarillo, CA 93010;
URL: http://vccf.org

Foundation type: Independent foundation
Purpose: Scholarships for Ventura County, CA residents and/or for students enrolled in schools in Ventura County pursuing a medical career.
Financial data: Year ended 06/30/2012. Assets, $3,662,304 (M); Expenditures, $239,425; Total giving, $185,092.
Fields of interest: Medical school/education.
Type of support: Support to graduates or students of specific schools.

Application information: Applications not accepted.
  Additional information: Unsolicited requests for funds not considered or acknowledged. See web site for eligibility.
EIN: 770132512

1037
The Tatum Foundation
17189 Yuma St.
Victorville, CA   92395

Foundation type: Independent foundation
Purpose: Scholarships only to residents of the Victorville, CA, area. Financial assistance to individuals for special needs.
Financial data: Year ended 12/31/2012. Assets, $41 (M); Expenditures, $2,388; Total giving, $2,250.
Fields of interest: Education; Economically disadvantaged.
Type of support: Scholarships—to individuals; Grants for special needs.
Application information: Applications accepted.
  Deadline(s): None
  Final notification: Applicants notified within 30 days
  Additional information: Contact foundation for application guidelines.
EIN: 470893091

1038
Tawa Charitable Foundation
6281 Regio Ave.
Buena Park, CA   90620-7323

Foundation type: Independent foundation
Purpose: Scholarships to graduating students of southern California for continuing education at institutions of higher learning.
Financial data: Year ended 12/31/2012. Assets, $2,307,165 (M); Expenditures, $67,010; Total giving, $67,000.
Fields of interest: Education.
Type of support: Scholarships—to individuals.
Application information: Contact the foundation for application guidelines.
EIN: 711035371

1039
The Taylor Family Foundation
(formerly Camp Open Arms, Inc.)
5555 Arroyo Rd.
Livermore, CA   94550-9825   (925) 455-5118
Contact: Angie Carmignani, Exec. Dir.
FAX: (925) 455-5008; E-mail: ttff@ttff.org; Tel. for Angie Carmignani: (925) 455-5118; E-Mail For Angie Carmignani: Angie@ttff.org; URL: http://www.ttff.org

Foundation type: Public charity
Purpose: Camperships to indigent northern CA children with life-threatening and chronic illnesses and developmental disabilities.
Financial data: Year ended 12/31/2011. Assets, $9,410,423 (M); Expenditures, $1,105,978; Total giving, $538,926; Grants to individuals, totaling $53,336.
Fields of interest: Camps; Children; Disabilities, people with; Terminal illness, people with; Economically disadvantaged.
Type of support: Camperships.
Application information:
  Initial approach: Letter

Additional information: Contact foundation for eligibility criteria.
EIN: 943262932

1040
Teachers Housing Cooperative
1717 Powell St., Ste. 300
San Francisco, CA   94133-2843

Foundation type: Operating foundation
Purpose: Grants provide financial incentive for teachers who live and work in San Francisco, CA.
Financial data: Year ended 05/31/2013. Assets, $5,773 (M); Expenditures, $147,064; Total giving, $145,900; Grants to individuals, 41 grants totaling $120,900 (high: $3,900, low: $975).
Type of support: Grants to individuals.
Application information: Applications accepted.
  Additional information: Grant recipients are expected to work in the San Francisco Unified School District public schools for a minimum of two years. Contact the cooperative for additional guidelines.
EIN: 943370330

1041
The Tech Museum of Innovation
201 S. Market St.
San Jose, CA   95113-2008   (408) 294-8324
FAX: (408) 279-7167; E-mail: info@thetech.org;
URL: http://www.thetech.org/

Foundation type: Public charity
Purpose: Awards by nomination only to those who are applying technology to solve humanity's most pressing problems.
Publications: Application guidelines.
Financial data: Year ended 06/30/2011. Assets, $46,359,264 (M); Expenditures, $12,115,360; Total giving, $743,790; Grants to individuals, totaling $743,790.
Fields of interest: Museums (science/technology); Science.
Type of support: Awards/grants by nomination only; Awards/prizes.
Application information: Application form required. Application form available on the grantmaker's web site.
  Send request by: Online
  Deadline(s): Apr. 6
  Additional information: See web site for additional guidelines.
Program description:
  Tech Museum Awards: These awards honor innovators from around the world who are applying technology to benefit humanity, and works to inspire global engagement in applying technology to humanity's most pressing problems by recognizing the best of those who are utilizing innovative technology solutions to address the most critical issues facing the planet. Each year, candidates (including individuals, for-profit companies, and nonprofit organizations) are nominated and then asked to submit applications. Self-nominations are also accepted. An international panel of judges reviews applications and chooses five laureates in each of five categories: health, education, economic development, environment, and equality. One laureate per category will receive a $50,000 prize.
EIN: 942864660

1042
Tenderloin Neighborhood Development Corporation
201 Eddy St.
San Francisco, CA 94102-2715 (415) 776-2151
Contact: Don Falk, Exec. Dir.
FAX: (415) 776-3952; E-mail: info@tndc.org; TTY: (415) 776-4819; E-Mail for Don Falk: dfalk@tndc.org; URL: http://www.tndc.org
Foundation type: Public charity
Purpose: Assistance to low-income individuals and families of the Tenderloin neighborhood of San Francisco, CA through rehabilitation and new construction. Some college scholarships for low -income individuals of San Francisco.
Publications: Annual report; Financial statement; IRS Form 990 or 990-PF printed copy available upon request.
Financial data: Year ended 12/31/2011. Assets, $48,109,273 (M); Expenditures, $11,908,136; Total giving, $1,033,314; Grants to individuals, totaling $12,986.
Fields of interest: Higher education; Housing/shelter, rehabilitation; Housing/shelter, temporary shelter; Housing/shelter; Human services; Economically disadvantaged.
Type of support: Scholarships—to individuals; Grants for special needs.
Application information: Scholarship grants are paid directly to the educational institutions of higher learning on behalf of the students. Contact the corporation for additional guidelines.
EIN: 942761808

1043
That Man May See, Inc.
10 Koret Way, Box 0352
San Francisco, CA 94143-0352 (415) 476-4016
Contact: Kathleen Rydar, Pres.; Danielle Pickett, Annual Fund Mgr.; Netta Fedor; Becky Jennings
FAX: (475) 476-5412;
E-mail: tmms@vision.ucsf.edu; E-mail for Kathleen Rydar: rydark@vision.ucsf.edu; URL: http://thatmanmaysee.org
Foundation type: Public charity
Purpose: Fellowships to researchers in the field of eye disease at the University of California, San Francisco, Department of Opthamology.
Publications: Annual report; Newsletter.
Financial data: Year ended 06/30/2012. Assets, $9,037,330 (M); Expenditures, $7,237,698; Total giving, $6,341,523.
Fields of interest: Eye research.
Type of support: Fellowships; Research.
Application information: Applications accepted.
Initial approach: Letter
Additional information: See web site for complete program information.
EIN: 237129943

1044
Theatre Bay Area
1663 Mission St., No. 525
San Francisco, CA 94103-2487 (415) 430-1140
Contact: Brad Erickson, Exec. Dir.
FAX: (415) 430-1145;
E-mail: tba@theatrebayarea.org; URL: http://www.theatrebayarea.org
Foundation type: Public charity

Purpose: Fellowships and grants to theatre and dance artists residing in the San Francisco Bay Area, CA; also, financial assistance also to aforementioned artists with terminal or life-threatening illnesses who are in need of supplemental assistance to improve the quality of their lives as they deal with medical conditions.
Publications: Application guidelines; Grants list.
Financial data: Year ended 06/30/2011. Assets, $822,295 (M); Expenditures, $1,536,480; Total giving, $150,270; Grants to individuals, totaling $66,270.
Fields of interest: Dance; Theater; Human services; Terminal illness, people with.
Type of support: Program development; Seed money; Research; Grants to individuals; Travel grants; Grants for special needs; Project support.
Application information: Applications accepted. Application form required. Application form available on the grantmaker's web site.
Initial approach: Letter or e-mail
Copies of proposal: 6
Deadline(s): Varies
Final notification: Recipients notified in six weeks
Applicants should submit the following:
  1) Work samples
  2) Resume
  3) Letter(s) of recommendation
  4) Essay
Additional information: See web site for additional application information.
Program descriptions:
CA$H Program: This program provides grants to artists and small-sized dance organizations throughout northern California. Grants range from $2,000 (for individual artists) to $4,000 (for small-sized organizations). Eligible artists must be at least 18 years old, working in the art form of the proposed project, and able to document at least one professionally-oriented production that was presented publicly in the last two years. Eligible organizations must have a yearly operational budget of under $100,000, and must be able to document at least two professionally-oriented works that were presented publicly within the last two years.
Eric Landisman Fellowship: This program supports the development of emerging Bay Area designers and technicians by providing two fellowships, ranging from $2,000 to $5,000 per year. Eligible applicants must be training in an internship or mentorship, or must have a commitment with a producer for an upcoming project or series of projects.
Mary Mason Memorial Lemonade Fund: This program provides emergency funding for theater workers with terminal or life-threatening illnesses who are in need of supplemental financial assistance to improve the quality of their lives as they deal with medical conditions. Eligible applicants include any resident of the San Francisco Bay Area who has worked professionally or vocationally in local theater, or has been an active participant in the theater (regardless of income derived from work in the theater, as long as there are two years' experience within the last five years), and who has received a diagnosis of a terminal or life-threatening medical illness or condition. Requests for up to $1,000 may be submitted every six months, though repeated funding is not guaranteed.
New Works Fund: Provides grants to Bay Area Theatre companies working with local playwrights.
EIN: 942476071

1045
The Corinne Rentfrow Therrien Foundation
2925 FallBrook Ln.
San Diego, CA 92117 (619) 685-3159
Contact: Lawrence S. Branton, Dir.

Foundation type: Operating foundation
Purpose: Financial assistance to battered or abused women and chldren and persons in crisis situations resulting from financial or health problems.
Financial data: Year ended 06/30/2012. Assets, $65,220 (M); Expenditures, $7,240; Total giving, $0.
Type of support: Grants to individuals.
Application information: Applications accepted. Application form required.
Additional information: Contact foundation for application form.
EIN: 203337078

1046
The Thiel Foundation
(formerly Shire Philanthropic Foundation)
1 Letterman Dr., Bldg. C, Ste. 400
San Francisco, CA 94129-1495
URL: http://www.thielfoundation.org

Foundation type: Independent foundation
Purpose: Fellowships to budding entrepreneurs between the ages of 14 and 20 to work on developing innovative technology ideas.
Financial data: Year ended 12/31/2012. Assets, $24,783,613 (M); Expenditures, $12,316,484; Total giving, $8,903,410; Grants to individuals, 51 grants totaling $1,890,861 (high: $200,000, low: $4,167).
Fields of interest: Education.
Type of support: Fellowships.
Application information: Applications accepted. Application form available on the grantmaker's web site. Interview required.
Deadline(s): Dec. 31
Final notification: Applicants notified in the Spring
Applicants should submit the following:
  1) Essay
  2) SAT
  3) ACT
Additional information: Application must be submitted in English. See web site for additional guidelines.
EIN: 203846597

1047
Through the Looking Glass
3075 Adeline St., Ste. 120
Berkeley, CA 94703-2204 (510) 848-1112
Contact: Maureen Block, Pres.
E-mail for essay: scholarships@lookingglass.org
FAX: (510) 848-4445; E-mail: tlg@lookingglass.org; Toll-free tel.: (800) 644-2666; toll-free TTY: (510) 848-1005; URL: http://lookingglass.org

Foundation type: Public charity
Purpose: Scholarships to high school seniors or graduates who have grown up with at least one parent with any type of disability.
Publications: Application guidelines.
Financial data: Year ended 06/30/2012. Assets, $2,339,619 (M); Expenditures, $3,383,670; Total giving, $14,479; Grants to individuals, totaling $14,479.
Fields of interest: Higher education; Disabilities, people with.

Type of support: Scholarships—to individuals.
Application information: Applications accepted. Application form required. Application form available on the grantmaker's web site.
  Initial approach: Application
  Send request by: Mail
  Deadline(s): Mar. 17
  Applicants should submit the following:
    1) Letter(s) of recommendation
    2) Transcripts
    3) Essay
  Additional information: Essay should be three pages in length describing the experience of growing up with a parent with a disability. In addition to mailing your application, your essay must be sent via e-mail.
Program description:
  Scholarships: This program provides scholarships specifically for high school seniors or college students who have parents with disabilities. A total of fifteen $1,000 scholarships will be available. High school students should be planning to attend an accredited college, and college students age 21 years or older should be enrolled in an accredited college.
EIN: 942823116

1048
Tides Foundation
P.O. Box 29198
San Francisco, CA 94129-0198 (415) 561-6400
Contact: Christine Coleman, Dir., Comms.
Pizzigati Prize e-mail: pizzigatiprize@tides.org; Jane Bagley Lehman e-mail: jblawards@tides.org
FAX: (415) 561-6401; E-mail: info@tides.org;
URL: http://www.tidesfoundation.org

Foundation type: Public charity
Purpose: A prize to honor a software developer whose work has made an outstanding contribution to the non-profit sector and to ongoing efforts for positive social change.
Publications: Annual report; Informational brochure (including application guidelines).
Financial data: Year ended 12/31/2011. Assets, $156,657,142 (M); Expenditures, $105,964,453; Total giving, $95,948,974; Grants to individuals, totaling $125,500.
Fields of interest: Civil/human rights; Community development, neighborhood development; Computer science.
Type of support: Awards/prizes.
Application information: Application form required.
  Initial approach: Letter
  Deadline(s): Oct. 31 for Pizzigati Prize, Dec. 1 for Jane Bagley Lehman Award, June 30 for Mario Savio Young Activist Award
  Additional information: See web site for additional guidelines.
Program descriptions:
  Antonio Pizzigati Prize for Software in the Public Interest: This annual $10,000 award will honor a software developer whose work has made an outstanding contribution to the nonprofit community and ongoing efforts for social change. In addition to completing an application, each candidate must also be nominated by a peer within the public interest computing world or a leader in the nonprofit community who can speak to the personal qualities that contribute to that individual's leadership, as well as to the product the nominee developed.
  Jane Bagley Lehman Awards for Excellence in Public Advocacy: These awards recognize individuals who have exhibited a deep commitment to the public interest, and whose work

demonstrates innovative approaches to social change. Ideal nominees should share their experiences and findings with as wide an audience as possible, and work to bridge the gap between those at the grassroots level and those who make policy. Recipients will be honored with a $10,000 grant. Self nominations are not accepted.
  Mario Savio Young Activist Award: This award is presented to a young person (or persons) with a deep commitment to human rights and social justice, and a proven ability to transform this commitment into effective action. Applicants must: be between the ages of 16 and 26; be engaged in activism for social change, promoting the values of peace, human rights, economic/social justice, or freedom of express; act within the context of an organization, social movement, or larger community effort; and be considered an inspirational leader or motivating force by others in that context. Preference will be given to candidates who have not yet been widely recognized, and who do not have personal privilege or a strong institutional base of support. The award carries a cash prize of $6,000, to be split between the prize winner and his/her organization.
EIN: 510198509

1049
Robert Toigo Foundation
180 Grand Ave., Ste. 450
Oakland, CA 94612-3762 (510) 763-5771
Contact: Nancy Sims, Pres. and C.E.O.
FAX: (510) 763-5778;
E-mail: info@toigofoundation.org; E-mail for Nancy Sims: nancy.sims@toigofoundation.org, tel.: (510) 763-5771, ext. 10; URL: http://www.toigofoundation.org

Foundation type: Public charity
Purpose: Fellowships to minority MBA students pursuing a career in finance at an accredited U.S. based institution.
Publications: Application guidelines.
Financial data: Year ended 12/31/2011. Assets, $5,124,045 (M); Expenditures, $3,099,525; Total giving, $241,250; Grants to individuals, totaling $241,250.
Fields of interest: Business school/education; Minorities.
Type of support: Fellowships.
Application information: Applications accepted. Application form required. Interview required.
  Send request by: Online
  Deadline(s): Mar. 23
  Additional information: Tuition is paid directly to the educational institution on behalf of the students. A $40 application fee is required.
Program description:
  Fellowship Program: Fellowships are available to first- and second-year minority MBA students who are interested in pursuing a career in finance. Fellowships provide networking opportunities, mentoring, professional development training, finance industry insights, career coaching and employment services, and a merit award of $2,500 per year to be applied to each participant's MBA tuition and costs. Eligible individuals must be U.S. citizens or permanent residents, be a minority, as defined by the U.S. Department of Labor (i.e. African American, Asian American/Pacific Islander, U.S. Latino, Native American/Alaska Native, and/or South Asian American), and be planning a career in financial services after graduation (including, but not limited to, investment management, investment banking, corporate finance, real estate,

private equity, venture capital, sales and trading, research, or financial services consulting)
EIN: 133565420

1050
Torrance Memorial Medical Center Health Care Foundation
3330 Lomita Blvd.
Torrance, CA 90505-5002 (310) 325-9110
E-mail for scholarship: vmulligan@tmmc.org
E-mail: vmulligan@tmmc.com; URL: http://www.torrancememorial.org/Jobs/Healthcare_Career_Scholarships.aspx

Foundation type: Public charity
Purpose: Scholarships to graduating high school seniors from the South Bay, CA, area who are seeking healthcare careers, specifically in nursing, pharmacy, and allied health professions.
Financial data: Year ended 12/31/2011. Assets, $34,929,487 (M); Expenditures, $10,382,424; Total giving, $10,000,000.
Fields of interest: Medical school/education; Nursing school/education.
Type of support: Undergraduate support.
Application information: Applications accepted. Application form required.
  Initial approach: Letter
  Send request by: Mail
  Deadline(s): Apr. 15
  Final notification: Recipients notified by May 15
  Applicants should submit the following:
    1) Letter(s) of recommendation
    2) Transcripts
EIN: 953528452

1051
Eleanora P. Touhey Scholarship Fund
4929 Hildreth Ln.
Stockton, CA 95212-1408

Foundation type: Independent foundation
Purpose: Scholarships to residents of Stockton, CA.
Financial data: Year ended 12/31/2011. Assets, $359,687 (M); Expenditures, $29,104; Total giving, $20,000; Grants to individuals, 4 grants totaling $20,000 (high: $5,000, low: $5,000).
Type of support: Scholarships—to individuals.
Application information: Applications not accepted.
  Additional information: Unsolicited requests for funds not considered or acknowledged.
EIN: 946737480

1052
Tower Hematology Oncology Cancer Research Foundation
9090 Wilshire Blvd., Ste. 350
Beverly Hills, CA 90211-1851 (310) 285-7242
Contact: Pam Blattner, Exec. Dir.
FAX: (310) 205-5733;
E-mail: towercancerresearch@toweroncology.com;
URL: http://www.towercancerfoundation.org/

Foundation type: Public charity
Purpose: Research grants to support southern CA junior faculty members as they begin their careers in academic medicine, focusing on cancer.
Financial data: Year ended 12/31/2010. Assets, $4,659,882 (M); Expenditures, $2,855,584; Total giving, $213,458; Grants to individuals, totaling $3,458.
Fields of interest: Cancer; Cancer research.

Type of support: Fellowships; Research.
Application information: Applications accepted. Application form required. Application form available on the grantmaker's web site.
Initial approach: Letter
Deadline(s): Apr. 15
Additional information: Applicants must have completed a fellowship in hematology and/or oncology.
EIN: 954596354

1053
Perry S. and Stella H. Tracy Scholarship Fund
c/o Wells Fargo Bank NA
P.O. Box 63954 MAC A0348-012
San Francisco, CA 94163
Application address: c/o Bank of America, N.A., 3044 Sacramento St., Placerville, CA 95667-5513, tel.: (530) 622-5919

Foundation type: Independent foundation
Purpose: Scholarships for full-time study to graduating seniors of El Dorado County, CA for postsecondary education.
Financial data: Year ended 05/31/2012. Assets, $1,024,029 (M); Expenditures, $68,639; Total giving, $44,310.
Fields of interest: Scholarships/financial aid.
Type of support: Support to graduates or students of specific schools; Undergraduate support.
Application information: Applications accepted. Application form required.
Send request by: Mail
Deadline(s): Apr. 15 for first time applicants, Apr. 30 for renewal
Applicants should submit the following:
1) Transcripts
2) Letter(s) of recommendation
Additional information: Application can be obtained from the El Dorado County High School.
Program description:
Tracy Scholarship Fund: The scholarship is intended for graduates from El Dorado, Independence, Golden Sierra, Oak Ridge, Ponderosa, or South Lake high schools for continuing education. Students must have been a resident of El Dorado County for at least two years at the time of original application and have a minimum 3.0 GPA. Consideration is given to worthy graduates who would not be able to pursue their education without such aid.
EIN: 946203372

1054
Tri-City Hospital Foundation
4002 Vista Way
Oceanside, CA 92056-4506 (760) 940-3370
FAX: (760) 940-4053;
E-mail: tchfoundation@tcmc.com; E-Mail for Farrah G. Douglas: douglasfg@tcmc.com; URL: http://www.tricityhospitalfoundation.org

Foundation type: Public charity
Purpose: Scholarships to current employees of Tri-City Medical Center who demonstrate need and are working toward nursing and allied health degrees.
Financial data: Year ended 06/30/2011. Assets, $5,490,769 (M); Expenditures, $425,051; Total giving, $189,912; Grants to individuals, totaling $4,350.
Fields of interest: Nursing school/education.
Type of support: Scholarships—to individuals.

Application information: Applications accepted. Interview required.
Additional information: Applicant must demonstrate need. Contact the foundation for additional information.
EIN: 956131483

1055
Tri-Counties Association for the Developmentally Disabled, Inc.
520 E. Montecito St.
Santa Barbara, CA 93103-3278 (805) 962-7881
FAX: (805) 884-7229;
E-mail: tcrcweb@tri-counties.org; URL: http://www.tri-counties.org/

Foundation type: Public charity
Purpose: Support to individuals with developmental disabilities in San Luis Obispo, Santa Barbara, and Ventura counties, CA.
Publications: Annual report.
Financial data: Year ended 06/30/2013. Assets, $28,511,120 (M); Expenditures, $218,636,478; Total giving, $192,287,040; Grants to individuals, totaling $192,287,040.
Fields of interest: Human services; Disabilities, people with.
Type of support: Grants for special needs.
Application information: Applications accepted.
Initial approach: Telephone
Additional information: Contact the association about eligibility for services.
EIN: 952623230

1056
Trinity Christian Center of Santa Ana, Inc.
2442 Michelle Dr.
Tustin, CA 92780-7015

Foundation type: Public charity
Purpose: Financial assistance to individuals and families of Santa Ana, CA in need with food, clothing, shelter, and other special assistance.
Financial data: Year ended 12/31/2011. Assets, $845,832,015 (M); Expenditures, $183,419,695; Total giving, $28,683,752; Grants to individuals, 90 grants totaling $11,085.
Fields of interest: Human services; Economically disadvantaged.
Type of support: Emergency funds.
Application information: Applications accepted.
Additional information: Some assistance require an application process.
EIN: 952844062

1057
Trinity Youth Services
1470 E. Cooley Dr.
P.O. Box 848
Colton, CA 92324-0848 (909) 825-5588
Contact: John Neiuber, C.E.O.
E-mail: info@trinityys.org; URL: http://www.trinityys.org

Foundation type: Public charity
Purpose: Financial assistance to foster care parents. Assistance for children who have been victims of abuse, violence, neglect and abandonment.
Financial data: Year ended 06/30/2011. Assets, $18,145,498 (M); Expenditures, $22,532,686; Total giving, $4,089,975; Grants to individuals, totaling $4,089,975.

Fields of interest: Foster care; Residential/custodial care.
Type of support: In-kind gifts; Grants for special needs.
Application information: Applications accepted. Application form required.
Deadline(s): None
Additional information: Contact the agency for eligibility determination.
EIN: 952480624

1058
Truckee Tahoe Community Foundation
11071 Donner Pass Rd.
Truckee, CA 96161 (530) 587-1776
Contact: Phebe Bell, Prog. Off.
FAX: (530) 550-7985; E-mail: phebe@ttcf.net;
Mailing address: P.O. Box 366, Truckee, CA 96160;
URL: http://www.ttcf.net

Foundation type: Community foundation
Purpose: Scholarships for graduating seniors from Truckee and North Tahoe High Schools in CA, pursuing higher education.
Publications: Application guidelines; Grants list; Newsletter.
Financial data: Year ended 06/30/2012. Assets, $20,393,202 (M); Expenditures, $2,658,235; Total giving, $1,747,830. Scholarships—to individuals amount not specified.
Fields of interest: Higher education.
Type of support: Scholarships—to individuals.
Application information: Applications accepted. Application form required. Application form available on the grantmaker's web site.
Initial approach: Application
Send request by: Mail or hand deliver
Deadline(s): Mid-May
Applicants should submit the following:
1) Transcripts
2) SAT
3) Resume
4) ACT
5) Financial information
6) FAFSA
Additional information: See web site for complete listing of scholarships and application form and guidelines.
EIN: 680416404

1059
True to Life Children's Services
1800 N. Gravenstein Hwy.
Sebastopol, CA 95472-2607 (707) 823-7300
Contact: Jim Galsterer, Exec. Dir.
FAX: (707) 823-3410; E-mail: info@tlc4kids.org;
Mailing address: P.O. Box 2079, Sebastopol, CA. 95473-2079; E-Mail for Jim Galsterer: jim@tlc4kids.org; URL: http://www.tlc4kids.org

Foundation type: Public charity
Purpose: Assistance to individuals and families with emotionally disabled children with food, clothing, school supplies, personal and incidentals in the Sebastopol, CA area.
Publications: Newsletter.
Financial data: Year ended 12/31/2011. Assets, $5,529,738 (M); Expenditures, $7,229,540; Total giving, $897,742; Grants to individuals, totaling $897,742.
Fields of interest: Children, services; Children.
Type of support: In-kind gifts.
Application information: Applications accepted.

Additional information: Assistance to individuals is disbursed based on eligibility and need. Contact the agency for additional guidelines.
EIN: 680008634

1060
Trust for Conservation Innovation
150 Post St., Ste. 342
San Francisco, CA 94108 (415) 421-3774
Contact: Laura Deaton, Exec. Dir.
FAX: (415) 421-3304;
E-mail: carin@trustforconservationinnovation.org;
URL: http://www.trustforconservationinnovation.org

Foundation type: Public charity
Purpose: Grants to individuals for development and support of initiatives that conserve and protect a sustainable environment.
Financial data: Year ended 12/31/2011. Assets, $2,293,806 (M); Expenditures, $5,825,684; Total giving, $1,903,366; Grants to individuals, totaling $10,000.
Fields of interest: Environment.
Type of support: Fellowships; Fiscal agent/sponsor.
Application information: Applications accepted.
   Initial approach: Telephone or e-mail for a preliminary consultation with staff before submitting an application
   Deadline(s): Rolling for fiscal sponsorship
   Additional information: Unsolicited applications not accepted for the Rainer Fellowship.
Program description:
   Fiscal Sponsorship: The trust seeks to offer an alternative in the marketplace for high-value, low-cost fiscal sponsor services to nonprofit projects. Proposed project activities must: be charitable in purpose and offer unique approaches to environmental and social problems; be consistent with and contribute to the mission of the trust; have a need for, and the potential to benefit from, the services provided by the trust; be willing to work in collaboration with and abide by the trust's policies; have a project leadership that is capable of carrying out the project's purpose; and must not already be a 501(c)(3) organization, as determined by the Internal Revenue Service.
EIN: 912166435

1061
Trustees of Ivan V. Koulaieff Educational Fund
c/o Rothstein Kass
101 Montgomery St., Ste. 22
San Francisco, CA 94104-4104

Foundation type: Independent foundation
Purpose: Grants and scholarships to Russians who were political immigrants between 1918 and 1945 throughout the world, and their descendants.
Financial data: Year ended 12/31/2012. Assets, $7,617,283 (M); Expenditures, $520,838; Total giving, $422,100.
Fields of interest: Immigrants/refugees.
International interests: Russia.
Type of support: Scholarships—to individuals; Foreign applicants.
Application information: Applications not accepted.
   Additional information: Unsolicited requests for funds not considered or acknowledged.
EIN: 946088762

1062
The Truth Seeker Foundation
239 S. Juniper St.
Escondido, CA 92025
E-mail: tseditor@aol.com; URL: http://www.truthseekerfoundation.com/

Foundation type: Operating foundation
Purpose: Grants for creative projects that expand freedom, imagination and innovation.
Financial data: Year ended 12/31/2011. Assets, $500 (M); Expenditures, $45,000; Total giving, $45,000.
Type of support: Program development; Project support.
Application information: Applications not accepted.
   Additional information: Unsolicited requests for funds not considered or acknowledged.
EIN: 330763611

1063
Elizabeth Tuckerman Foundation
c/o Wells Fargo Bank, N.A.
P.O. Box 63954 MAC A0348-012
San Francisco, CA 94163

Foundation type: Independent foundation
Purpose: Scholarships to students from Wales and Great Britain who wish to pursue postgraduate studies in the U.S.
Financial data: Year ended 11/30/2012. Assets, $1,662,449 (M); Expenditures, $74,216; Total giving, $60,926.
Type of support: Foreign applicants; Postgraduate support.
Application information: Applications accepted. Application form required.
   Deadline(s): May 12
   Additional information: Applications distributed by universities.
EIN: 956601661

1064
Turn On To America
(also known as T.O.T.A.)
P.O. Box 643
Lafayette, CA 94549-0643 (925) 930-0364
Contact: Janet Raibaldi, Pres.
E-mail: totacharity@hotmail.com; URL: http://www.turnontoamerica.org/

Foundation type: Public charity
Purpose: Food, clothing, and emergency rent assistance to homeless and low-income individuals in the San Francisco Bay Area, CA.
Financial data: Year ended 10/31/2011. Assets, $35,328 (M); Expenditures, $298,086; Total giving, $266,470; Grants to individuals, totaling $264,270.
Fields of interest: Human services, emergency aid; Residential/custodial care; Homeless, human services; Economically disadvantaged.
Type of support: In-kind gifts; Grants for special needs.
Application information: Applications accepted.
   Additional information: Contact foundation for further program and application information.
EIN: 237110313

1065
Twin Towers Orphan Fund
10010 Rosedale Hwy, Ste. 3
Bakersfield, CA 93312-9431 (661) 633-9076
Contact: Michele Ritter, Chair. and C.E.O.
E-mail: info@ttof.org; URL: http://www.ttof.org

Foundation type: Public charity
Purpose: Scholarships and grants for mental and physical healthcare to children who lost parents in the Sept. 11, 2001 terrorist attacks, and to children of victims of future terrorist attacks.
Publications: Annual report.
Financial data: Year ended 12/31/2012. Assets, $4,602,640 (M); Expenditures, $672,032; Total giving, $413,839; Grants to individuals, totaling $413,839.
Fields of interest: Disasters, 9/11/01.
Type of support: Scholarships—to individuals; Grants for special needs.
Application information: Applications accepted. Application form required. Application form available on the grantmaker's web site.
   Initial approach: Application or letter
   Send request by: Online
   Deadline(s): None
EIN: 571197371

1066
Ukiah Educational Foundation
925 N. State St.
Ukiah, CA 95482-3411 (707) 463-5201

Foundation type: Public charity
Purpose: Scholarships to students in the Ukiah, CA, area for higher education.
Financial data: Year ended 07/31/2012. Assets, $1,859,748 (M); Expenditures, $43,058; Total giving, $38,987; Grants to individuals, totaling $24,750.
Fields of interest: Elementary/secondary education.
Type of support: Undergraduate support.
Application information: Application form required.
   Deadline(s): May 1 for fall and Nov. 1 for spring
EIN: 680288281

1067
Union Labor Health Foundation
(formerly Union Labor Hospital Association)
363 Indianola Rd.
Bayside, CA 95524-9350 (707) 442-2417
FAX: (707) 442-2382;
E-mail: ulhf@hafoundation.org; URL: http://www.ulhf.org

Foundation type: Public charity
Purpose: Small grants for health-related expenses and grants for children's dental care who are residents of Humboldt County, CA.
Publications: Application guidelines.
Financial data: Year ended 06/30/2011. Assets, $4,973,813 (M); Expenditures, $295,689; Total giving, $221,056; Grants to individuals, totaling $146,507.
Type of support: Grants for special needs.
Application information: Applications accepted. Application form required. Application form available on the grantmaker's web site.
   Initial approach: Telephone, e-mail or application
   Send request by: Mail, fax or e-mail
   Copies of proposal: 1
   Deadline(s): Thursdays
   Final notification: Applicants notified within two weeks
EIN: 940942427

1068
Union Rescue Mission
545 S. San Pedro St.
Los Angeles, CA 90013-2101 (213) 347-6300
E-mail: thewayhome@urm.org; URL: http://
www.urm.org

Foundation type: Public charity
Purpose: Assistance to homeless individuals in or
around Los Angeles, CA with food, clothing, shelter,
legal aid, health and emergency services.
Financial data: Year ended 06/30/2011. Assets,
$34,224,000 (M); Expenditures, $22,897,000;
Total giving, $4,540,000; Grants to individuals,
totaling $127,000.
Fields of interest: Economically disadvantaged;
Homeless.
Type of support: In-kind gifts.
Application information:
Initial approach: Telephone or in-person
Deadline(s): None
Additional information: Contact the organization
for assistance.
EIN: 951709293

1069
United Animal Nations
3800 J. St., Ste. 100
Sacramento, CA 95816 (916) 429-2457
Contact: Nicole Forsyth, Pres. and C.E.O.
FAX: (916) 378-5098; E-mail: info@uan.org; Mailing
address: P.O. Box 188890, Sacramento, CA
95818-8890; URL: http://www.uan.org

Foundation type: Public charity
Purpose: Grants to animal rescuers and pet owners
to help them care for animals in life-threatening
situations.
Publications: Application guidelines; Annual report;
Informational brochure; Newsletter.
Financial data: Year ended 12/31/2011. Assets,
$2,448,896 (M); Expenditures, $1,414,757; Total
giving, $90,839; Grants to individuals, totaling
$87,339.
Fields of interest: Animal welfare.
Type of support: Grants to individuals.
Application information: Applications accepted.
Application form required. Application form
available on the grantmaker's web site.
Initial approach: Application
Send request by: Online
Copies of proposal: 1
Deadline(s): Rolling
Final notification: Applicants notified in two
business days
EIN: 680124097

1070
United Food and Commercial Workers Union Local 324
(also known as UFCW 324)
8530 Stanton Ave.
P.O. Box 5004
Buena Park, CA 90620-3930 (714) 995-4601
E-mail: wemaster@ufcw324.org; URL: http://
www.ufcw324.org

Foundation type: Public charity
Purpose: Assistance to members of Union Local
324 of Los Angeles county and Orange county, CA,
who demonstrate hardship and financial need.
Scholarships are also awarded.
Financial data: Year ended 12/31/2011. Assets,
$14,269,814 (M); Expenditures, $13,288,546;
Total giving, $142,215; Grants to individuals,
totaling $6,193.

Fields of interest: Labor unions/organizations.
Type of support: Grants for special needs.
Application information: Unsolicited requests for
funds not considered or acknowledged.
EIN: 951144467

1071
United Friends of the Children
1055 Wilshire Blvd., Ste. 1955
Los Angeles, CA 90017-5602 (213) 580-1850
Contact: Polly Wiliams, Pres.
FAX: (213) 580-1820;
E-mail: info@unitedfriends.org; Tel. for Polly
Williams: (213) 580-1840; URL: http://
www.unitedfriends.org

Foundation type: Public charity
Purpose: Scholarships to foster and probation
suitable placement youth from Los Angeles County,
CA.
Publications: Application guidelines.
Financial data: Year ended 06/30/2012. Assets,
$9,285,443 (M); Expenditures, $4,955,486.
Fields of interest: Foster care.
Type of support: Undergraduate support.
Application information: Applications accepted.
Application form required.
Initial approach: Telephone, letter or e-mail
Deadline(s): Jan. 16
Additional information: Contact foundation for
eligibility criteria.
EIN: 953665186

1072
United States Artists
(also known as USA)
5757 Wilshire Blvd., Ste. 580
Los Angeles, CA 90036-3683 (323) 857-5857
Contact: Katharine DeShaw, Exec. Dir.; Debra
Dysart, Dir., Devel. Opers.
FAX: (323) 857-5867;
E-mail: ddysart@unitedstatesartists.org;
URL: http://www.unitedstatesartists.org

Foundation type: Public charity
Purpose: Fellowships by nomination only to
emerging and mid-career artists as well as
individuals who have achieved master arts status.
Publications: Biennial report; Financial statement;
Newsletter.
Financial data: Year ended 06/30/2011. Assets,
$21,060,543 (M); Expenditures, $7,085,595;
Total giving, $3,207,428; Grants to individuals,
totaling $2,929,907. Subtotal for grants to
individuals: 60 grants totaling $2,479,025.
Fields of interest: Media/communications;
Architecture; Design; Performing arts; Music;
Literature.
Type of support: Fellowships; Awards/grants by
nomination only.
Application information: Applications not
accepted.
Additional information: Nominated artists apply
through an online application process.
Unsolicited requests for funds not considered
or acknowledged.
Program description:
USA Fellows Program: The program provides
unrestricted awards of $50,000 to support artists
in all career stages, including emerging and
midcareer artists, as well as individuals who have
achieved master artist status. The fellowships will
be awarded across a broad array of disciplines:
architecture, design, and fashion; crafts and
traditional arts; dance; literature (fiction, nonfiction,
and poetry); media arts (film, media, and radio);

music; performing arts (performance art and
theater); and visual arts. Eligible fellows are
nominated by an anonymous group of arts leaders,
critics, scholars, and artists chosen by
organization; nominators do not know one another.
Nominators are asked to submit names of artists
they believe show an extraordinary commitment to
their craft. Artists at any stage of career
development may be nominated. To be considered
for fellowships, artists must be 21 years of age or
older and U.S. citizens or legal residents in any U.S.
state.
EIN: 223903993

1073
University of California Chinese Alumni Foundation
751-14th Ave.
San Francisco, CA 94118
Application address: University of California,
Berkeley, Attn.: Dean of Studies, Berkeley, CA
94720

Foundation type: Operating foundation
Purpose: Scholarships to students attending the
University of California, Berkeley, CA.
Financial data: Year ended 12/31/2012. Assets,
$1,149,199 (M); Expenditures, $64,910; Total
giving, $60,000.
Type of support: Support to graduates or students
of specific schools; Undergraduate support.
Application information: Applications not
accepted.
Additional information: Unsolicited requests for
funds not considered or acknowledged.
EIN: 237375387

1074
Urbanek-Levy Education Fund
51 University Ave. G
Los Gatos, CA 95030-6037

Foundation type: Independent foundation
Purpose: Scholarships to children of KLA-Tencor
employees, primarily in CA, for undergraduate
education.
Financial data: Year ended 12/31/2012. Assets,
$290,476 (M); Expenditures, $183,160; Total
giving, $171,000; Grants to individuals, totaling
$171,000.
Type of support: Employee-related scholarships;
Undergraduate support.
Application information: Unsolicited requests for
funds not considered or acknowledged.
EIN: 943372793

1075
The Vaccarezza-Murdaca Family Foundation
1266 Winerose Ct.
Lodi, CA 95242-9157 (209) 339-4353

Foundation type: Independent foundation
Purpose: Scholarships to economically challenged
high school students in San Joaquin County, CA, for
higher education.
Financial data: Year ended 12/31/2012. Assets,
$16,531 (M); Expenditures, $113,558; Total
giving, $102,140.
Type of support: Scholarships—to individuals.
Application information: Applications not
accepted.

Additional information: Unsolicited requests for funds not acknowledged or considered.
EIN: 680400296

1076
Valley Mountain Regional Center, Inc.
702 N. Aurora St.
Stockton, CA 95202-2200 (209) 473-0951
Contact: Paul Billodeau, Jr., Exec. Dir.
E-mail: pbillodeau@vmrc.net; Mailing address: P.O. Box 692290, Stockton, CA 95269-2290;
URL: http://www.vmrc.net

Foundation type: Public charity
Purpose: Assistance to children and adults in San Joaquin, Stanislaus, Amador, Calaveras and Tuolumne counties, CA who have developmental disabilities.
Financial data: Year ended 06/30/2011. Assets, $15,350,604 (M); Expenditures, $138,971,754; Total giving, $118,010,350; Grants to individuals, totaling $118,010,350.
Fields of interest: Human services; Disabilities, people with.
Type of support: Grants for special needs.
Application information: Clients assistance is based on individual need. To qualify for ongoing support and services, a person must be found to have a developmental disability which began before the age of 18 and is a substantial handicap. See web site for additional guidelines.
EIN: 942251069

1077
Vanguard Cancer Foundation
750 E. 29th St.
Long Beach, CA 90806-1712 (855) 322-6237
E-mail: info@vanguardcancerfoundation.org;
URL: http://vanguardcancerfoundation.org

Foundation type: Public charity
Purpose: Financial assistance for cancer patients undergoing chemotherapy to receive vital treatment that will enable them to overcome their illness.
Publications: Application guidelines.
Financial data: Year ended 12/31/2011. Assets, $478,490 (M); Expenditures, $215,602; Total giving, $115,812; Grants to individuals, totaling $115,812.
Fields of interest: Cancer.
Type of support: Grants to individuals.
Application information: Contact the foundation for eligibility determination.
Program description:
Financial Assistance: Emergency funding is available to individuals to cover the cost of personalized assay tests, which will help determine the drug(s) that will most likely and most effectively kill cancer cells. Financial aid is determined solely by the individual's ability to pay; individuals are expected, though not required, to cover part of the $3,500 cost of the procedure.
EIN: 954524195

1078
Variety - The Children's Charity of Southern California, Tent 25
4601 Wilshire Blvd., Ste. 260
Los Angeles, CA 90010-3883 (323) 655-1547
Contact: Murray Wood, Exec. Dir.
FAX: (323) 658-8789;
E-mail: murray@varietysocal.org; URL: http://www.varietysocal.org

Foundation type: Public charity
Purpose: Scholarships to at-risk youth from the greater Los Angeles, CA area for attendance at accredited colleges or trade schools.
Financial data: Year ended 09/30/2011. Assets, $2,303,025 (M); Expenditures, $917,390; Total giving, $532,303; Grants to individuals, totaling $123,443.
Fields of interest: Vocational education, post-secondary; Higher education; Youth.
Type of support: Scholarships—to individuals.
Application information: Applications accepted. Application form required. Interview required.
Applicants should submit the following:
1) Transcripts
2) Essay
Additional information: Application should include letter of acceptance to colleges or trade schools.
EIN: 951330495

1079
Variety - The Children's Charity of the U.S.
4601 Wilshire Blvd., Ste. 260
Los Angeles, CA 90010-3883 (323) 655-1547
Contact: Stan E. Reynolds, Pres.
FAX: (323) 658-8789; E-mail: info@usvariety.org;
URL: http://www.usvariety.org/

Foundation type: Public charity
Purpose: Financial assistance and equipment are available for disabled children whose independent mobility is hindered.
Publications: Application guidelines; Newsletter.
Financial data: Year ended 09/30/2011. Assets, $567,622 (M); Expenditures, $887,466; Total giving, $706,903; Grants to individuals, totaling $127,434.
Fields of interest: Disabilities, people with.
Type of support: Grants to individuals; In-kind gifts.
Application information: Applications accepted. Application form required. Application form available on the grantmaker's web site. Interview required.
Initial approach: Application
Send request by: Mail
Applicants should submit the following:
1) Photograph
2) Letter(s) of recommendation
Additional information: Application should also include family financial data, letter(s) of verification from professionals (therapist, doctor, social worker) who are familiar with your child's needs. Funds will be paid directly to the equipment vendor and equipment will be delivered to eligible children.
Program description:
Kids on the Go! Grants: This program aims to help kids and young adults (ages 21 and younger) gain mobility, confidence, freedom, independence, and the chance to join in the life of their community by providing funding for walkers, wheelchairs, specially-designed adaptive bikes, strollers, prosthetic limbs, and other devices to families with the most need. Funding will be given to families whose need for enabling equipment cannot be met by any other source, including school, insurance, and service program resources.
EIN: 251794405

1080
Paul S. Veneklasen Research Foundation
1711 16th St.
Santa Monica, CA 90404 (310) 450-1733
Contact: John Lo Verde, Pres.
URL: http://www.veneklasenresearchfoundation.org

Foundation type: Independent foundation
Purpose: Grants to individuals for scientific research in acoustics.
Financial data: Year ended 11/30/2012. Assets, $2,387,397 (M); Expenditures, $139,248; Total giving, $116,071.
Fields of interest: Research; Visual arts; Performing arts.
Type of support: Research; Grants to individuals.
Application information: Applications accepted.
Initial approach: Letter
Deadline(s): Dec. 1, Apr. 1, Aug. 1
Applicants should submit the following:
1) Proposal
2) Budget Information
3) Resume
Additional information: The application must include a cover letter that summarizes the background and purpose of the applicant requesting funding and how the funds will be used. See web site for additional guidelines.
EIN: 953555062

1081
Ventura County Community Foundation
4001 Mission Oaks Blvd.
Camarillo, CA 93010-8364 (805) 988-0196
Contact: Hugh J. Ralston, C.E.O.; For grants: LaToya Ford, Prog. Assoc. and Grants Mgr.; For scholarships: Virginia Weber, Scholarship Prog. Off.
FAX: (805) 485-2700; E-mail: vccf@vccf.org;
URL: http://www.vccf.org

Foundation type: Community foundation
Purpose: Scholarships for students from Ventura County, CA pursuing a higher education or career training.
Publications: Application guidelines; Annual report (including application guidelines); Financial statement; Informational brochure; Newsletter.
Financial data: Year ended 09/30/2012. Assets, $118,666,128 (M); Expenditures, $6,726,232; Total giving, $4,671,079. Scholarships—to individuals amount not specified.
Fields of interest: Vocational education, post-secondary; Higher education.
Type of support: Scholarships—to individuals; Support to graduates or students of specific schools; Graduate support; Technical education support; Undergraduate support.
Application information: Applications accepted. Application form required. Application form available on the grantmaker's web site.
Initial approach: E-mail
Send request by: Mail
Copies of proposal: 1
Deadline(s): Varies
Applicants should submit the following:
1) Transcripts
2) SAT
3) Proposal
4) Letter(s) of recommendation
5) GPA
6) Financial information
7) Essay
8) ACT
Additional information: See web site for a complete listing of scholarships and application guidelines.

Program description:

Scholarships: The foundation has awarded more than $7 million in scholarships to deserving Ventura County students and is the local leader in granting financial aid to promising scholars. The foundation's Scholarship Program opens doors of educational opportunity for students of all ages. By educating individuals, the entire community is strengthened. The Community Foundation links donors with financial resources to students with potential for future achievement. A scholarship is more than a financial award, it is the key that unlocks the future for our youth by building their confidence.
EIN: 770165029

1082
Visual Aid: Artists for AIDS Relief

57 Post St., Ste. 905
San Francisco, CA 94104-5028   (415) 777-8242
Contact: Julie Blankenship, Exec. Dir.
FAX: (415) 777-8240; E-mail: julie@visualaid.org; URL: http://www.visualaid.org

Foundation type: Public charity
Purpose: Support to seriously ill artists in Alameda, Contra Costa, Marin, Napa, San Francisco, San Mateo, Santa Clara, Solano and Sonomia counties, CA, in the form of vouchers redeemable at participating art supply stores in the San Francisco Bay area. Visual Aid also sponsors public exhibitions of art works by grant recipients.
Publications: Application guidelines; Informational brochure; Newsletter.
Financial data: Year ended 12/31/2012. Assets, $13,529 (M); Expenditures, $220,328.
Fields of interest: Arts, artist's services.
Type of support: Grants for special needs.
Application information: Application form required.
Send request by: Mail
Deadline(s): June 5 and Dec. 5
Final notification: Applicants are notified about one month after submission deadline
Applicants should submit the following:
1) Resume
2) Letter(s) of recommendation
3) Work samples
Additional information: Application must also include artistic statement and proof of diagnosis of a life-threatening illness.
EIN: 943089742

1083
Mary Beth Vogelzang Foundation

(formerly Mary Beth and James C. Vogelzang Foundation)
1129 State St., Ste. 3E
Santa Barbara, CA 93101-6746

Foundation type: Independent foundation
Purpose: Scholarships to individuals from CO pursuing postsecondary education.
Financial data: Year ended 12/31/2011. Assets, $2,255,994 (M); Expenditures, $267,134; Total giving, $205,123; Grants to individuals, totaling $4,600.
Fields of interest: Higher education.
Type of support: Scholarships—to individuals.
Application information: Applications accepted. Application form required.
Additional information: Contact the foundation for application information.
EIN: 841314262

1084
Jeanne Ward Foundation

(formerly Jeanne Ward Faith Foundation)
2425 Mission St., Ste. 1
San Marino, CA 91108-1620   (626) 799-6618
Contact: Timothy J. McKnight, Secy.-Treas.

Foundation type: Independent foundation
Purpose: Scholarships to high school seniors in the Pasadena Community College District, Pasadena City College, Glendale Community College District , CA, and Glendale Community College for study in the visual arts.
Publications: Application guidelines.
Financial data: Year ended 01/31/2012. Assets, $1,531,324 (M); Expenditures, $120,174; Total giving, $60,500; Grants to individuals, 12 grants totaling $21,000 (high: $1,750, low: $1,750).
Fields of interest: Visual arts.
Type of support: Support to graduates or students of specific schools; Awards/grants by nomination only; Undergraduate support.
Application information: Application form required. Interview required.
Initial approach: Letter
Copies of proposal: 1
Deadline(s): Mid-Apr.
Final notification: Applicants notified by Apr. 30
Applicants should submit the following:
1) Work samples
2) Proposal
Additional information: Grants are paid directly to the educational institution on behalf of the students.
EIN: 953761013

1085
Warne Family Charitable Foundation

18101 Von Karman Ave., Ste. 700
Irvine, CA 92612-0145   (877) 968-6328
FAX: (949) 833-9584;
E-mail: grants@warnefoundation.org; URL: http://warnefoundation.org

Foundation type: Independent foundation
Purpose: Scholarships to students whose musical emphasis is a stringed instrument at an accredited college or university in Orange County, CA.
Financial data: Year ended 12/31/2011. Assets, $1,445,214 (M); Expenditures, $285,340; Total giving, $253,656; Grants to individuals, 35 grants totaling $77,181 (high: $5,000, low: $500).
Fields of interest: Music.
Type of support: Undergraduate support.
Application information: Applications accepted. Application form required. Application form available on the grantmaker's web site.
EIN: 330937768

1086
Mary Ellen Warner Educational Trust

P.O. Box 30
Beverly Hills, CA 90213-0030   (310) 275-9389
FAX: (310) 274-0422

Foundation type: Independent foundation
Purpose: Student loans and scholarships in upper division or graduate level students who are permanent residents of CA and attending fully accredited colleges or universities in CA.
Publications: Informational brochure.
Financial data: Year ended 10/31/2012. Assets, $647,192 (M); Expenditures, $35,028; Total giving, $26,250.
Fields of interest: Higher education.

Type of support: Scholarships—to individuals; Student loans—to individuals; Graduate support; Undergraduate support.
Application information: Applications accepted. Application form required. Interview required.
Initial approach: Letter
Deadline(s): None
Additional information: Application should include college or university grade transcripts for the past two years. Applicant must demonstrate financial need.
EIN: 956037882

1087
Washington Township Hospital Service League, Inc.

2000 Mowry Ave.
Fremont, CA 94538-1716   (510) 797-1111
Contact: Sharon Stagg, Pres.

Foundation type: Public charity
Purpose: Scholarships to students enrolled in a health-related course of study at a four-year school.
Financial data: Year ended 02/28/2013. Assets, $121,366 (M); Expenditures, $100,828; Total giving, $75,229; Grants to individuals, totaling $10,000.
Fields of interest: Health care.
Type of support: Undergraduate support.
Application information: Applications not accepted.
Additional information: Unsolicited requests for funds not considered or acknowledged.
EIN: 946086348

1088
Lenore & Richard Wayne Foundation

1641 Gilcrest Dr.
Beverly Hills, CA 90210-2517   (310) 858-8870
Contact: Richard Wayne, Tr.

Foundation type: Independent foundation
Purpose: Encouragement awards to aspiring singers, primarily in CA.
Financial data: Year ended 12/31/2012. Assets, $763,942 (M); Expenditures, $381,035; Total giving, $379,000; Grant to an individual, 1 grant totaling $25,000.
Fields of interest: Music.
Type of support: Awards/prizes.
Application information: Applications accepted.
Initial approach: Letter
Deadline(s): None
EIN: 957066636

1089
Lawrence M. and Susan Werner Educational Opportunity Charitable Trust

336 Buena Vista St.
Balboa Island, CA 92661   (909) 277-3900
Contact: Margaret S. Werner, Tr.

Foundation type: Independent foundation
Purpose: Scholarships to underprivileged high school students who reside in one of the five southern CA counties, who have high academic performance and have an aptitude for higher education.
Financial data: Year ended 12/31/2011. Assets, $91 (M); Expenditures, $3,510; Total giving, $3,500; Grant to an individual, 1 grant totaling $3,500.
Fields of interest: Higher education.

Type of support: Scholarships—to individuals.
Application information: Applications accepted.
Application form required.
Deadline(s): None
Additional information: Applications can be obtained from high school counselor.
EIN: 954696479

1090

West Contra Costa Public Education Fund

(formerly Richmond Unified Education Fund)
217C W. Richmond Ave.
Richmond, CA 94801 (510) 233-1464
Contact: Joel Mackey, Exec. Dir.
FAX: (510) 217-3996; E-mail: info@edfundwest.org;
E-Mail for Joel Mackey: joel@edfundwest.org;
URL: http://www.edfundwest.org

Foundation type: Public charity
Purpose: Grants and scholarships to low-income and at-risk students in the West Contra Costa Unified School district, CA.
Publications: Application guidelines; Financial statement; Grants list; Informational brochure; Newsletter.
Financial data: Year ended 06/30/2011. Assets, $707,241 (M); Expenditures, $700,441; Total giving, $81,539; Grants to individuals, totaling $81,539.
Fields of interest: Vocational education, post-secondary; Higher education.
Type of support: Scholarships—to individuals.
Application information: Applications accepted.
Application form required. Application form available on the grantmaker's web site.
Deadline(s): Feb.
Applicants should submit the following:
1) Letter(s) of recommendation
2) Transcripts
3) SAT
4) GPA
5) Essay
Additional information: See web site for additional application guidelines.
Program descriptions:
Coach Lamb Memorial Scholarships: A $1,000 scholarship is available to a De Anza High School senior who is graduating with at least a 2.5 cumulative GPA, who is involved with athletics, and who is planning to attend a four-year university, two-year college, or trade school.
Irvine Foundation Scholarship: A $2,500 award is given to a student from a West Contra Costa Unified School District high school who will be graduating with a 3.0 cumulative GPA, and who plans to attend a four-year public or private school or two-year community college (with plans to transfer to a four-year college or university)
Living the Dream Scholarship Program by Chevron: A $2,500 scholarship is given to a senior who is graduating from a West Contra Costa Unified School District who has a 3.5 GPA and who plans to attend a four-year public or private college or university, or two-year community college (with plans to transfer to a four-year college or university)
Norma and Arthur Schroeder Scholarship: A $2,500 scholarship is available to a senior who is graduating from El Cerrito High School with at least a 3.0 GPA, and who is planning to attend a four-year public or private college or university, or two-year community college with plans to transfer to a four-year college or university.
EIN: 680005307

1091

The Westphal Family Foundation

60 Berry Dr.
Pacheco, CA 94553-5601

Foundation type: Company-sponsored foundation
Purpose: Scholarships to dependents of Bay Alarm Company employees, primarily in CA.
Financial data: Year ended 12/31/2012. Assets, $20,938 (M); Expenditures, $318,435; Total giving, $318,375.
Type of support: Employee-related scholarships.
Application information: Applications not accepted.
Additional information: Unsolicited requests for funds not considered or acknowledged.
Company name: Bay Alarm Company
EIN: 916491365

1092

Kathryn M. Whitten Trust

302 Pine Ave.
Long Beach, CA 90802

Foundation type: Independent foundation
Purpose: Scholarships to full-time students studying in CA who maintain at least a "B" average.
Financial data: Year ended 12/31/2012. Assets, $598,971 (M); Expenditures, $22,416; Total giving, $15,886; Grants to individuals, 5 grants totaling $15,886 (high: $4,750, low: $2,000).
Type of support: Scholarships—to individuals.
Application information: Applications not accepted.
Additional information: Unsolicited requests for funds not considered or acknowledged.
EIN: 956040517

1093

Whittier Host Lions Club Foundation

P.O. Box 245
Whittier, CA 90608-0245 (562) 907-4745
Contact: Vincent J. Daigneault
Application address: 15141 E. Whittier Blvd., Whittier, CA 90602-2135

Foundation type: Independent foundation
Purpose: Scholarships to eligible high school seniors for attendance at colleges or universities, who are residents of Whittier, CA and have a 3.0 GPA.
Financial data: Year ended 06/30/2012. Assets, $614,942 (M); Expenditures, $93,887; Total giving, $79,285; Grants to individuals, 15 grants totaling $17,000 (high: $1,500, low: $500).
Fields of interest: Higher education.
Type of support: Scholarships—to individuals.
Application information: Applications accepted.
Application form required.
Deadline(s): May 1
Applicants should submit the following:
1) Financial information
2) Class rank
3) Transcripts
4) SAT
5) Letter(s) of recommendation
6) GPA
7) Essay
EIN: 954583564

1094

Ivie Frances Wickam Scholarship Trust

c/o Wells Fargo Bank, N.A.
P.O. Box 63954, MAC A0348-012
San Francisco, CA 94163-0001

Foundation type: Independent foundation
Purpose: Scholarships only to financially needy female graduates of Escondido High School, CA, and Palomar College, CA.
Financial data: Year ended 05/31/2012. Assets, $639,564 (M); Expenditures, $47,065; Total giving, $31,500.
Fields of interest: Higher education; Women.
Type of support: Support to graduates or students of specific schools.
Application information: Application form required.
Interview required.
Additional information: Contact Palomar College or Escondido High School for application information.
EIN: 956530377

1095

The Wilcox Family Foundation

6377 Cardeno Dr.
La Jolla, CA 92037-6955 (734) 455-6222
Contact: Win Schrader, V.P. and Secy.
E-mail: sdodge1@san.rr.com; URL: http://www.wilcoxfoundation.org/

Foundation type: Independent foundation
Purpose: Scholarships to graduating high school seniors in the Plymouth/Canton School District, MI.
Financial data: Year ended 12/31/2011. Assets, $2,969,354 (M); Expenditures, $161,513; Total giving, $91,117.
Type of support: Support to graduates or students of specific schools; Undergraduate support.
Application information: Applications accepted.
Deadline(s): Apr. 1 and Oct. 1
Additional information: Application must include an essay on the history of Plymouth between WWII and Korean Conflict. Essay must be submitted no later than Mar.
EIN: 311804402

1096

Williams Sonoma Foundation

3250 Van Ness Ave.
San Francisco, CA 94109-1012

Foundation type: Company-sponsored foundation
Purpose: Grants to employees of Williams Sonoma who are needy or distressed due to a Presidentially-declared disaster.
Financial data: Year ended 01/31/2013. Assets, $100,750 (M); Expenditures, $224,341; Total giving, $224,250; Grants to individuals, 136 grants totaling $94,500 (high: $3,000, low: $200).
Type of support: Emergency funds; Employee-related scholarships.
Application information: Applications not accepted.
Additional information: Unsolicited requests for funds not considered or acknowledged.
Company name: Williams-Sonoma, Inc.
EIN: 203424952

1097

Winnett Foundation

c/o Macy's West
2850 N. Main St.
Santa Ana, CA 92705 (310) 793-2714
Application address: c/o Macy's West, 21600 Hawthorne Blvd., Torrance, CA 90503, tel.: (310) 793-2714

Foundation type: Independent foundation
Purpose: Aid to financially needy employees and retirees of Macy's stores that were formerly

Bullock's Department Store, CA, for medical, hospital, and other expenses.
Financial data: Year ended 12/31/2011. Assets, $450,480 (M); Expenditures, $26,965; Total giving, $22,000; Grants to individuals, 4 grants totaling $22,000 (high: $7,200, low: $4,800).
Fields of interest: Health care; Economically disadvantaged.
Type of support: Grants for special needs.
Application information: Application form not required.
Initial approach: Letter
Deadline(s): None
EIN: 952036597

1098
Women in Film Foundation
6100 Wilshire Blvd., Ste. 710
Los Angeles, CA 90048-5117   (323) 935-2211
Contact: Gayle Nachlis, Exec. Dir.
FAX: (323) 935-2212; E-mail: info@wif.org; E-Mail for Gayle Nachlis: gnachlis@wif.org; URL: http://www.wif.org/

Foundation type: Public charity
Purpose: Scholarships and grants designed to promote educational and professional opportunities for women working in the entertainment industry.
Publications: Newsletter.
Financial data: Year ended 12/31/2011. Assets, $711,338 (M); Expenditures, $876,336; Total giving, $82,130; Grants to individuals, totaling $10,000.
Fields of interest: Film/video; Arts, artist's services; Women.
Type of support: Grants to individuals.
Application information:
Initial approach: Letter
Additional information: See web site for complete program information. Applications for scholarships are not accepted from the general public.
Program descriptions:
Eleanor Perry Writing Award: This $3,000 award is given to an undergraduate or graduate student at the University of California-Los Angeles for an original screenplay that best depicts women in a present-day historical perspective.
Film Finishing Fund: This fund supports films by, for, or about women by providing cash grants of up to $15,000 and in-kind services to deserving filmmakers needing help to complete their film projects. Eligible applicants must have completed principal photography and a rough cut at the time of application, but need not be Women In Film member to be apply for the FFF. Student projects are not eligible to receive Film Finishing Funds.
Meredith MacRae Memorial Scholarship: This $3,000 scholarship is awarded to a graduate student in the masters of fine arts (MFA) program at Chapman University who have some experience in acting, producing, and directing.
The Bruce Paltrow Endowment: A $1,000 scholarship will be awarded to a film and media student at Tulane University.
Verna Fields Memorial Fellowship: This $1,000 award is given to a woman graduate student at the University of California-Los Angeles's masters of fine arts (MFA) program, to assist with the production of her thesis film.
WIF Crystals Scholarship: Scholarships, ranging from $2,000 to $3,000, are awarded to media students throughout southern California.
Women in Film/Loreen Arbus Endowment: A $2,000 scholarship will be awarded to a student studying cinematography in the masters of fine arts

(MFA) program at the University of California - Los Angeles.
EIN: 237322834

1099
Women's Foundation of California
340 Pine St., Ste. 302
San Francisco, CA 94104-3235   (415) 837-1113
FAX: (415) 837-1144;
E-mail: info@womensfoundca.org; Additional address: 444 S. Flower St., Ste. 4650, Los Angeles, CA 90071-2937, tel. (213) 388-0485, fax: (213) 388-0405; URL: http://www.womensfoundca.org

Foundation type: Public charity
Purpose: Scholarships to children of first-generation immigrants in Fremont, Newark, Menlo Park, East Palo Alto, Redwood City and the North Fair Oaks area, CA.
Publications: Application guidelines; Annual report; Grants list.
Financial data: Year ended 06/30/2011. Assets, $12,671,219 (M); Expenditures, $5,907,653; Total giving, $3,311,587; Grants to individuals, totaling $156,891.
Fields of interest: Immigrants/refugees.
Type of support: Technical education support; Undergraduate support.
Application information: Applications accepted.
Initial approach: Letter
Additional information: Contact foundation for eligibility criteria.
EIN: 942752421

1100
Woodward/Graff Wine Foundation
(formerly Chalone Wine Foundation)
P.O. Box 1753
Sonoma, CA 95476-1753   (707) 935-2102
FAX: (707) 935-2105;
E-mail: info@woodward-graffwinefoundation.org;
URL: http://www.woodward-graffwinefoundation.org

Foundation type: Public charity
Purpose: Scholarships to students interested in the study of wine and food who are residents of CA.
Financial data: Year ended 03/31/2010. Assets, $448,534 (M); Expenditures, $20,873; Total giving, $16,200; Grants to individuals, totaling $16,200.
Fields of interest: Formal/general education.
Type of support: Undergraduate support.
Application information: Contact foundation for current application deadline/guidelines.
EIN: 943297049

1101
World Affairs Council of Northern California
312 Sutter St., Ste. 200
San Francisco, CA 94108-4311   (415) 293-4600
Contact: Jane Wales, Pres. and C.E.O.
FAX: (415) 982-5028; E-mail: info@worldaffairs.org;
URL: http://www.itsyourworld.org

Foundation type: Public charity
Purpose: Scholarships to high school students residing in CA for study abroad, and also to teachers and high school undergraduate, and graduate students for attendance at the Asilomar Conference.

Publications: Application guidelines; Informational brochure; Newsletter (including application guidelines).
Financial data: Year ended 12/31/2011. Assets, $10,559,740 (M); Expenditures, $4,798,335.
Fields of interest: Education; Formal/general education.
Type of support: Program development; Exchange programs; Support to graduates or students of specific schools; Graduate support; Precollege support; Undergraduate support; Travel grants.
Application information: Application form required.
Deadline(s): Vary
Program descriptions:
Asilomar Scholarships: Awards scholarships to at least 10 pre-collegiate teachers and 80 high school, undergraduate, and graduate students annually giving them the opportunity to attend the council's annual conference in early May.
Study Abroad Scholarship: This program awards two to three scholarships of up to $4,000 or more every year to high school students for the Youth for Understanding (YFU) study abroad program. The scholarship covers a portion of the cost of spending a summer, semester, or academic year with a host family in Chile, France, Thailand, or any of the other 35 participating countries worldwide. Sophomores, juniors, or seniors who attend northern California high schools and have a cumulative GPA of 3.0 or above are eligible to apply.
EIN: 943053917

1102
World of Children, Inc.
6200 Stoneridge Mall Rd., 3rd Fl.
Pleasanton, CA 94588-3242   (925) 399-6411
Contact: Lynn Wallace Naylor, Exec. Dir.
FAX: (925) 399-6001;
E-mail: contact@worldofchildren.org; E-mail for Lynn Wallace Naylor: lynn@worldofchildren.org;
URL: http://www.worldofchildren.org

Foundation type: Public charity
Purpose: Awards by nomination only to individuals who have made a difference in the lives of children in the U.S. and across the globe.
Publications: Application guidelines.
Financial data: Year ended 03/31/2012. Assets, $567,518 (M); Expenditures, $883,314; Total giving, $413,025.
Fields of interest: Education; Health care; Youth development; Human services; Children/youth.
Type of support: Awards/grants by nomination only; Awards/prizes.
Application information:
Deadline(s): Apr. 1
Additional information: Completion of formal nomination required.
Program descriptions:
World of Children Health Award: This program awards a maximum grant of $50,000 to an individual who has made a significant contribution to children in the fields of health, medicine, or the sciences. Nominees must have created, managed, or otherwise supported a sustainable program which has significantly contributed to the improved health of children for a minimum of ten years. Nominees must also have an existing nonprofit organization in good standing, which can receive grant funds if awarded.
World of Children Humanitarian Award: This award recognizes an individual who has made a significant lifetime contribution to children in the areas of social services, education, or humanitarian services with a $50,000 award. Nominees must have created, managed, or otherwise supported a sustainable program which has significantly

contributed to children's opportunities to be safe, to learn, and to grow. Nominee must have been involved in this work for a minimum of ten years, and must have an existing nonprofit organization in good standing, which can receive grant funds if awarded.

World of Children Youth Award: A $25,000 award will be made to a youth who is making extraordinary contributions to the lives of other children. Nominees must be under 21 years of age and must have an existing nonprofit organization in good standing, which can receive grant funds if awarded. The nominee must have been doing this work for a minimum of three years by the nomination deadline.
EIN: 311772381

1103
Mabel B. Wright Education Fund
3263 Pinot Blanc Way
San Jose, CA 95135-1143

Foundation type: Independent foundation
Purpose: Scholarships to local high school seniors in the CA, area for higher education.
Financial data: Year ended 08/31/2012. Assets, $590,021 (M); Expenditures, $44,662; Total giving, $42,875; Grants to individuals, 16 grants totaling $19,500 (high: $2,250, low: $750).
Fields of interest: Higher education.
Type of support: Scholarships—to individuals.
Application information: Contact the fund for additional guidelines.
EIN: 061708305

1104
Wu Yee Children's Services
717 California St., Fl. 1
San Francisco, CA 94108-3166 (415) 677-0100
FAX: (415) 393-8070; E-mail: admin@wuyee.org; E-Mail for Monica Walters: monica.walters@wuyee.org; URL: http://www.wuyee.org

Foundation type: Public charity
Purpose: Grants and stipends for childcare professionals in San Francisco, CA, to offset start-up costs and the costs of continuing education and professional development.
Financial data: Year ended 10/30/2011. Assets, $4,051,967 (M); Expenditures, $13,628,857; Total giving, $6,172,659; Grants to individuals, totaling $6,172,659.
Fields of interest: Day care; Children, services.
Type of support: Grants to individuals; Stipends.
Application information: Applications accepted.
Initial approach: Telephone
EIN: 942387002

1105
Yolo Community Foundation
P.O. Box 1264
Woodland, CA 95776-1264 (530) 312-0593
Contact: Cath Posehn, Exec. Dir.; Mary Stephens DeWall, Pres.
E-mail: info@yolocf.org; URL: http://www.yolocf.org

Foundation type: Community foundation
Purpose: Scholarships to Yolo county students in pursuit of post secondary education.
Publications: Application guidelines; Annual report; Informational brochure; Multi-year report; Newsletter; Program policy statement.
Financial data: Year ended 12/31/2011. Assets, $418,086 (M); Expenditures, $48,602; Total

giving, $12,822; Grants to individuals, 4 grants totaling $3,500.
Fields of interest: Higher education.
Type of support: Scholarships—to individuals; Technical education support.
Application information: Applications accepted. Application form required. Application form available on the grantmaker's web site.
Initial approach: Letter
Send request by: Mail or e-mail
Copies of proposal: 1
Deadline(s): Feb.
Applicants should submit the following:
1) SAT
2) GPA
3) ACT
Additional information: Applicant must demonstrate financial need. Student must be involved in school and community activities, show noteworthy achievements, and have a special talent or skill.
EIN: 752971085

1106
Yosemite Lodge No. 99 Scholarship Fund
1810 M St.
Merced, CA 95340-4714 (209) 722-7966
Contact: Mike Krebs
Application address: P.O. Box 756, Merced, CA 95341,

Foundation type: Independent foundation
Purpose: Scholarships to deserving students from Atwater or Merced high schools or the Merced County Regional Occupation Program for continuing education beyond high school level.
Financial data: Year ended 12/31/2012. Assets, $45,795 (M); Expenditures, $16,215; Total giving, $16,000; Grants to individuals, 21 grants totaling $16,000 (high: $1,500, low: $250).
Fields of interest: Vocational education, post-secondary; Higher education.
Type of support: Support to graduates or students of specific schools.
Application information: Applications accepted. Application form required.
Deadline(s): May
Additional information: Application must include two letters of recommendation. Applicants must be sponsored by a member of Yosemite Lodge #99.
EIN: 776082827

1107
Young Musicians Foundation
(also known as YMF)
195 S. Beverly Dr., Ste. 414
Beverly Hills, CA 90212-3044 (310) 859-7668
Contact: Julia Gaskill, Exec. Dir.
FAX: (310) 859-1365; E-mail: info@ymf.org; E-Mail for Julia Gaskill: jgaskill@ymf.org; URL: http://www.ymf.org

Foundation type: Public charity
Purpose: Scholarships to young musicians residing in southern CA, ages 9 to 25, to pay for private music instruction. Prizes also to winners of the annual National Debut Concerto Competition.
Publications: Application guidelines; Newsletter.
Financial data: Year ended 06/30/2012. Assets, $472,400 (M); Expenditures, $770,217; Total giving, $225,301; Grants to individuals, totaling $225,301.
Fields of interest: Music; Orchestras.
Type of support: Scholarships—to individuals; Awards/prizes.

Application information: Applications accepted. Application form required. Application form available on the grantmaker's web site.
Initial approach: E-mail
Deadline(s): May 18
Applicants should submit the following:
1) Letter(s) of recommendation
2) Financial information
Additional information: See web site for additional program information.
Program descriptions:
Chamber Music Program: The program is open to talented elementary through high school piano, string, harp, woodwind, and brass players through the age of 18. Each ensemble receives a grant to pay for coaching sessions with one of Los Angeles' finest master teachers.
Composition Competition: Cash prizes of up to $400 are awarded to high-school composers who submit highly sophisticated and outstanding chamber works.
Debut Orchestra Camp Program: This program strives to provide a healthy balance of intense orchestral experience and recreational activities. Orchestra rehearsals, individual practice time, sectionals, and master classes are combined with organized free-time, recreational activities, including but not limited to basketball, swimming, karaoke, arts/crafts, hiking, and a talent show. Camp participants receive need-based financial aid, ranging from partial to full scholarships for seventy-five of the most talented 10- to 15 year-old musicians from around the country. Participants are also eligible to receive honoraria, ranging from $500 to $2,000.
Scholarship Program: Scholarships are available to instrumentalists through their senior year in high school, and to vocalists through age 25. Scholarships ranging from $250 to $10,000 are granted. All applicants must demonstrate exceptional talent and financial need, and must be residents of southern California. Vocalists must be under 26 years of age at the time of the auditions. Instrumentalists must be under 18 years of age at the time of the auditions and not beyond their junior year in high school at the time of auditions. In addition, applicants' parents must reside in California (if applicant is not a U.S. citizen)
EIN: 952250007

1108
Henry and Carol Zeiter Charitable Foundation
255 E. Weber Ave.
Stockton, CA 95202-2706 (209) 466-5566
Contact: Henry Zeiter, Pres.; Carol Zeiter, Secy.

Foundation type: Independent foundation
Purpose: Scholarships primarily to needy residents of Stockton, CA.
Financial data: Year ended 12/31/2012. Assets, $5,184,880 (M); Expenditures, $208,289; Total giving, $132,475; Grants to individuals, 33 grants totaling $39,975 (high: $1,500, low: $125).
Type of support: Undergraduate support.
Application information:
Initial approach: Letter
Deadline(s): None
EIN: 680369445

1109
The Christopher Zider Scholarship Fund
1900 Embarcadero Rd., Ste. 100
Palo Alto, CA 94303-3310 (650) 233-8700
URL: http://chrisziderscholarship.org/

Foundation type: Company-sponsored foundation
Purpose: Scholarships to residents of Atherton, East Palo Alto, Menlo Park, Palo Alto, Portola Valley, Stanford, Woodside, or Los Altos Hills, CA, high schools, to be used in any of the next six years to attend public or private secondary schools or four-year colleges. Additionally, any sophomore who attends Menlo School, or Woodside High School is eligible.

Publications: Application guidelines.
Financial data: Year ended 12/31/2012. Assets, $154,597 (M); Expenditures, $42,534; Total giving, $36,000; Grants to individuals, 8 grants totaling $36,000 (high: $15,000, low: $1,000).
Fields of interest: Higher education.

Type of support: Support to graduates or students of specific schools; Precollege support; Undergraduate support.
Application information: Applications accepted. Application form required. Interview required.
   Deadline(s): Mar. 26 (preliminary) and May 14 (full applications)
   Additional information: Applicants must participate in competitive athletics throughout high school.
EIN: 946655102

COLORADO

1110
The ACVIM Foundation
(also known as American College of Veterinary
Internal Medicine Foundation)
1997 Wadsworth Blvd., Ste. A
Lakewood, CO 80214-5293 (303) 231-9933
Contact: Angela E. Frimberger D.V.M., Exec. Dir.
E-mail: foundation@acvim.org; Toll-free tel.: (800)
245-9081; URL: http://www.acvimfoundation.org

Foundation type: Public charity
Purpose: Grants to veterinarians for research on
animal health within the specialties of small and
large animal internal medicine, cardiology,
neurology, and oncology, and support through
grants and loans to veterinary residents in training.
Publications: Application guidelines; Annual report.
Financial data: Year ended 09/30/2011. Assets,
$465,711 (M); Expenditures, $479,141; Total
giving, $50,868.
Fields of interest: Veterinary medicine.
Type of support: Research.
Application information: Applications accepted.
Application form required. Application form
available on the grantmaker's web site.
> *Copies of proposal:* 1
> *Deadline(s):* Sept. 7 for Clinical Research
> *Applicants should submit the following:*
> 1) Proposal
> 2) Letter(s) of recommendation
> 3) Curriculum vitae
> 4) Budget Information
> *Additional information:* See Web site for further
> application information.
Program description:
> *Clinical Investigation Grants:* The foundation
improves the health and well-being of animals by
funding humane studies. These grants support
leading veterinary scientists as they take on a range
of critical animal health issues within the
specialties of small and large animal internal
medicine, cardiology, neurology, and oncology. This
work, in turn, holds promise for better preventive
care, better nutrition, and more sensitive screening
and improved treatment for such devastating
diseases as cancer, epilepsy, cardiomyopathy, and
kidney failure. The goal is to support clinical
investigations that lead to new diagnostic,
treatment, and prevention techniques.
EIN: 841541160

1111
Adventure Unlimited
5201 S. Quebec St.
Greenwood Village, CO 80111-1802 (303)
779-3000
Contact: Gina Lindquist, Exec. Dir.
FAX: (303) 773-0291;
E-mail: info@adventureunlimited.org; URL: http://
www.adventureunlimited.org/

Foundation type: Public charity
Purpose: Camperships for young christian
scientists and their friends of CO. Scholarships
adventure unlimited provides year round leadership
and service programs for youth, family and friends
of CO.
Publications: Informational brochure; Newsletter.
Financial data: Year ended 01/31/2012. Assets,
$11,321,768 (M); Expenditures, $4,036,105;
Total giving, $225,218; Grants to individuals,
totaling $225,218.

Fields of interest: Camps; Christian agencies &
churches.
Type of support: Scholarships—to individuals;
Camperships.
Application information: Applications accepted.
Application form available on the grantmaker's web
site.
> *Send request by:* On-line
> *Deadline(s):* Apr. 20
> *Additional information:* Campership grants of up
> tp $1,000 per family (the average tuition cost
> for two weeks at camp) are awarded, as funds
> are available, to qualified applicants. Children
> receiving campership must be regular
> attendees of a Christian Science Sunday
> School. See web site for additional guidelines.
EIN: 430798771

1112
Advocate Safehouse Project
P.O. Box 2036
Glenwood Springs, CO 81602-2036 (970)
945-2632
Contact: Konnie Krahn-Prosence, Pres.
Additional tel.: (970) 285-0209; URL: http://
www.advocatesafehouse.org

Foundation type: Public charity
Purpose: Emergency assistance to survivors of
domestic and sexual violence throughout CO with
medical assistance, transportation, rent, child care
and other special needs.
Publications: Annual report.
Financial data: Year ended 12/31/2011. Assets,
$874,330 (M); Expenditures, $389,729; Total
giving, $13,965; Grants to individuals, totaling
$13,965.
Fields of interest: Domestic violence; Sexual
abuse; Women.
Type of support: Grants for special needs.
Application information: Clients are assessed
individually and resources are provided as needed.
Contact the agency for eligibility determination.
EIN: 841047611

1113
AEG Foundation
(formerly Engineering Geology Foundation)
P.O. Box 460518
Denver, CO 80246 (303) 757-2926
Contact: Becky Roland, Exec. Dir.
FAX: (720) 230-4846;
E-mail: staff@aegfoundation.org; URL: http://
www.aegfoundation.org

Foundation type: Public charity
Purpose: Scholarships and grants to individuals in
the field of geology.
Financial data: Year ended 06/30/2012. Assets,
$864,086 (M); Expenditures, $46,270; Total
giving, $20,062; Grants to individuals, totaling
$20,062.
Fields of interest: Geology.
Type of support: Graduate support; Undergraduate
support.
Application information: Applications accepted.
Application form required. Application form
available on the grantmaker's web site.
> *Send request by:* Mail
> *Deadline(s):* Feb. 1
> *Applicants should submit the following:*
> 1) Letter(s) of recommendation
> 2) Transcripts
> *Additional information:* Application should also
> include copies of pertinent publications and

abstracts and a statement of career goals.
See web site for complete program listing.
EIN: 943168991

1114
AfricAid, Inc.
1031 33rd St., Ste. 174
Denver, CO 80205 (303) 351-4928
Contact: Maria Galter, Exec. Dir.
E-mail: info@africaid.com; E-mail For Maria Galter:
maria@africaid.com; URL: http://www.africaid.com

Foundation type: Public charity
Purpose: Scholarships for needy young girls to
attend Maasai Girls School in Tanzania who would
not have the chance to pursue a secondary
education.
Publications: Informational brochure; Newsletter.
Financial data: Year ended 12/31/2011. Assets,
$236,430 (M); Expenditures, $290,171; Total
giving, $93,618.
Fields of interest: Girls.
Type of support: Scholarships—to individuals.
Application information: See web site for additional
information.
EIN: 841549841

1115
The Alexander Foundation
P. O. Box 1995
Denver, CO 80201-1995 (303) 331-7733
Contact: Joshua Casto, Chair.
FAX: (303) 331-1953;
E-mail: TheAlexanderFoundation@yahoo.com;
URL: http://www.thealexanderfoundation.org

Foundation type: Public charity
Purpose: Grants and scholarships for gay, lesbian,
bisexual, and transgender people in CO.
Publications: Application guidelines; Annual report;
Financial statement.
Financial data: Year ended 12/31/2012. Assets,
$177,788 (M); Expenditures, $61,520; Total
giving, $50,835; Grants to individuals, 150 grants
totaling $42,715.
Fields of interest: LGBTQ.
Type of support: Undergraduate support; Grants for
special needs.
Application information: Applications accepted.
Application form required.
> *Deadline(s):* Vary
Program descriptions:
> *Cancer, Catastrophic Illness and Injury Grant
Program:* This program is intended to provide
support to lesbians, gays, bisexual and
transgendered people who are at risk of losing their
ability to provide basic life needs due to treatment
or complications related to cancer, a catastrophic
illness, or a serious illness. Some examples of
basic life needs are medical care, housing, food,
clothing, phones, utilities, and other special needs.
Unlike the one grant payment provided through the
Emergency Grant Program, this program provides a
fixed monthly grant for up to 12 months. The
amount of the grant is determined by the recipients'
needs but not to exceed $2,400.
> *Holiday Letter Grant Program:* The program
provides grants to gay, lesbian, bisexual or
transgendered people on a onetime basis during
the traditional holiday season. The program is
designed to assist individuals with significant
chronic problems. Applications are received from
potential recipients and from these requests a
random sample is selected, pseudonyms assigned,
and a direct solicitation to the community is made
during Nov. and Dec. The amount of the grant is

based on need and the financial support and response from the community but can range generally from $100 to $500.

Scholarship Grant Program: This program provides scholarships for individuals with financial assistance in pursuit of an undergraduate or graduate degree from a Colorado institution of higher education. Applicants must be gay, lesbian, bisexual or transgender, reside in Colorado and be accepted or enrolled in an accredited Colorado institution of higher education. The applicant must also demonstrate financial need. Annual scholarship award amounts range from $300 to $3,000.
EIN: 742243837

1116
American Indian College Fund
8333 Greenwood Blvd.
Denver, CO 80221-4488   (303) 426-8900
FAX: (303) 426-1200; E-mail: info@collegefund.org;
Toll-free tel.: (800) 776-3863; URL: http://www.collegefund.org

Foundation type: Public charity
Purpose: Scholarship and awards to Native American students at mainstream and tribal colleges and universities.
Financial data: Year ended 06/30/2012. Assets, $69,010,166 (M); Expenditures, $16,137,413; Total giving, $10,319,729; Grants to individuals, totaling $6,218,251.
Fields of interest: Higher education; Education; Native Americans/American Indians.
Type of support: Scholarships—to individuals.
Application information: Applications accepted. Application form required. Application form available on the grantmaker's web site.
  Deadline(s): May 31
  Final notification: Recipients notified in Aug.
  Applicants should submit the following:
    1) Transcripts
    2) GPA
    3) Essay
Program descriptions:
  Scholarship Programs: The fund offers two different scholarship programs, the tribal college scholarship program which determine student eligibility and awards for the tribal college scholarship program, and designated scholarship program which is offered to American Indian students attending both tribal colleges, mainstream four-year colleges and graduate school. See web site for additional information on both programs.
  STEM Leadership Fellowship: This fellowship provides $36,000 in funds for a Tribal College or University faulty member who is ABD in their Ph.D. program in a STEM discipline.
EIN: 521573446

1117
American Society for Theater Research
(also known as ASTR)
P.O. Box 1798
Boulder, CO 80306-1798   (303) 530-1838
Contact: Heather Nathans, Pres.
FAX: (303) 530-1839; E-mail: president@astr.org;
Toll Free Tel.: (888)-530-1838; URL: http://www.astr.org

Foundation type: Public charity
Purpose: Fellowships, scholarships and grants to further instructions in all aspects of theatre and drama.
Publications: Application guidelines.

Financial data: Year ended 05/31/2012. Assets, $697,546 (M); Expenditures, $186,777; Total giving, $19,400; Grants to individuals, totaling $19,400.
Fields of interest: Theater; Theater (playwriting); Theater (musical); Literature.
Type of support: Fellowships; Grants to individuals; Scholarships—to individuals; Awards/prizes.
Application information: Applications accepted.
  Deadline(s): Mar. 15 for Scholar Award and Research Fellowships, Mar. 25 for Kahan Scholar's Prize, Apr. 14 for Hill Award, Apr. 16 for Hewitt Award, Apr. 28 for Chinoy Fellowships, May 15 for Brockett Prize, Aug. 1 for Keller Grants and Marshall Student Awards
  Applicants should submit the following:
    1) Letter(s) of recommendation
    2) Essay
    3) Curriculum vitae
  Additional information: See web site for additional application guidelines.
Program descriptions:
  Bernard Hewitt Award: Awarded each year to the best book in the "theatre history or cognate disciplines" published during the previous calendar year. The books must be written by a scholar or scholars residing in the Americas, or by a scholar or scholars located outside the Americas but writing on an American topic. Plays, edited collections, and anthologies are not eligible for this prize. Authors wishing to be considered for the award should contact their publishers about nominating them. The award carries a cash value of $2,000.
  Distinguished Scholar Award: The award is given each year to a scholar whose body of work has made a significant contribution to the field of theater, dance, opera, and/or performance studies. Nominations will be accepted from society members and previous winners of this award.
  Errol Hill Award: This award is given in recognition of outstanding scholarship in African American theatre, drama, and/or performance studies, as demonstrated in the form of a published book-length project (monograph or essay collection) or scholarly article. The book or article must have been published in the previous calendar year, but all scholars are eligible whether or not they are affiliated with a university or tenured. Author wishing to be nominated are encouraged to contact their publishers or editors, but their direct entries will be accepted as long as the submission guidelines are followed.
  Gerald Kahan Scholar's Prize: An annual award is offered for the best essay written and published in English in a refereed scholarly journal. The essay can be on any subject in theater research, broadly construed. The author must be untenured and within seven years of the doctorate, or must be enrolled in a doctoral program, at the time the essay is published.
  Oscar G. Brockett Essay Prize: This prize is jointly awarded by the American Society for Theatre Research and the Oscar G. Brockett Center for Theatre History and Criticism at the University of Texas-Austin. The prize of $1,500 ($1,000 from the Brockett Center and $500 from ASTR) recognizes the best essay written and published in English in a refereed scholarly journal or volume published by a scholarly press and relating to any subject in theatre research, broadly construed. The author must have been a member of ASTR for at least three years and be at least seven years beyond the Ph.D. Essays must have been published in the calendar year preceding the year in which the award is given. Essays in edited anthologies may not have appeared elsewhere previously.
  Research Fellowships: This fellowship is to underwrite some of the research expenses of

scholars undertaking projects significant to the field of theater and/or performance studies. the total award of up to $3,000 may be divided among multiple winners. The fellowship can be used in conjunction with funding from other sources. Anyone holding a terminal degree and who has been a member of the society for at least three years is eligible to apply.
  Thomas Marshall Graduate Student Awards: Up to three grants of $800 each are awarded to encourage students to become active members of the society by helping them to meet the expenses of attending the society's annual meeting in Nov. Any student majoring in theatre/performance studies in any academic department at any level of higher education is eligible. Students need not be members of ASTR at the time of application.
EIN: 116110103

1118
Anderson Ranch Arts Center
(formerly Anderson Ranch Arts Foundation)
5263 Owl Creek Rd.
P.O. Box 5598
Snowmass Village, CO 81615-5598   (970) 923-3181
Contact: Nancy Wilhelms, Exec. Dir.
FAX: (970) 923-3871;
E-mail: info@andersonranch.org; E-Mail for Nancy Wilhelms: nwilhelms@andersonranch.org;
URL: http://www.andersonranch.org

Foundation type: Public charity
Purpose: Residencies to emerging and established visual artists for a ten week period. Scholarships for graduating high school seniors, currently enrolled undergraduate and graduate students. Scholarship also for adults, children and teens.
Publications: Application guidelines.
Financial data: Year ended 12/31/2012. Assets, $11,726,676 (M); Expenditures, $3,686,470; Total giving, $177,669; Grants to individuals, totaling $177,669.
Fields of interest: Visual arts.
Type of support: Residencies.
Application information: Applications accepted. Application form available on the grantmaker's web site.
  Send request by: On-line
  Deadline(s): Feb. 15 for Residency
  Final notification: Artists are notified by early Apr.
  Additional information: Application should include 10 images of recent work, declaration of professional status, selection of preferred term, statement of purpose, resume or CV, three references, and a $60 application fee for residency. See web site for additional application information for scholarships.
Program description:
  Residencies: This program is designed to encourage the creative, intellectual and personal growth of emerging and established visual artists. There are no specific educational qualifications for entry into the artists residency program. While in residence, artists will be encouraged to pursue their own work amidst a group of artistic peers. The residency is designed to allow artists to take risks and pursue new projects and ideas, free from every day pressures. Resident artists will be provided with housing, studio space, meals and certain other benefits and will be required to submit only a nominal residency fee of $1,500. Studio areas supported by the program include ceramics, digital media/photography, furniture design/wood/sculpture and, painting and drawing, printmaking, and sculpture. Residents are charged a studio

rental fee, and can choose to live on-campus. Limited scholarship funds are available.

EIN: 237267983

1119

Aorn Foundation

2170 S. Parker Rd., Ste. 300
Denver, CO 80231-5711
Contact: Twilla Barlow, Exec. Dir.
FAX: (303) 755-4219; E-mail: ldurgin@aorn.org;
Toll-free tel.: (800) 755-2676; URL: http://www.aorn.org/foundation/

Foundation type: Public charity
Purpose: Scholarships to students who are pursuing bachelor's, master's, and doctoral degrees for a career in perioperative nursing.
Publications: Annual report; Newsletter.
Financial data: Year ended 12/31/2011. Assets, $3,056,950 (M); Expenditures, $1,179,279; Total giving, $305,993; Grants to individuals, totaling $301,643.
Fields of interest: Nursing school/education.
Type of support: Research; Graduate support; Undergraduate support; Postgraduate support; Doctoral support.
Application information: Applications accepted. Application form required.
　Initial approach: Letter
　Send request by: On-line
　Deadline(s): June 15 for Scholarships
　Final notification: Applicants notified by Aug. 15 for scholarships
Program description:
　Academic Scholarship Program: The program provides funding to students who are pursuing a career in perioperative nursing and to registered nurses who are continuing their education in perioperative nursing by pursuing a bachelor's, master's or doctoral degree.
EIN: 841193583

1120

APS Education Foundation

(formerly Aurora Education Foundation)
15701 E. 1st Ave., Ste. 206
Aurora, CO 80011-9060 (303) 365-7807
Contact: Pieter Leenhouts, Exec. Dir.
URL: http://www.auroraedfoundation.org

Foundation type: Public charity
Purpose: Scholarships to current graduating seniors from each of the high schools in the Aurora School District, CO.
Publications: Application guidelines.
Financial data: Year ended 06/30/2012. Assets, $767,414 (M); Expenditures, $608,171; Total giving, $327,641; Grants to individuals, totaling $58,770.
Fields of interest: Higher education.
Type of support: Scholarships—to individuals.
Application information: Applications accepted. Application form required. Application form available on the grantmaker's web site.
　Deadline(s): Mar. 1
　Applicants should submit the following:
　　1) Transcripts
　　2) Letter(s) of recommendation
　　3) Essay
　Additional information: Contact your school guidance office for application information or the foundation web site.
EIN: 742477363

1121

Archuleta County Victims Assistance Program, Inc.

P.O. Box 2913
Pagosa Springs, CO 81147-2913 (970) 264-9075
Contact: Carmen Hubbs, Exec. Dir.
FAX: (970) 264-2186; E-mail: acvap@centurytel.net

Foundation type: Public charity
Purpose: Assistance to residents of Archuleta County, CO, who are victims of domestic violence, sexual assault, and other abusive situations.
Publications: Annual report; Financial statement; Grants list; Informational brochure; Newsletter.
Financial data: Year ended 12/31/2012. Assets, $163,821 (M); Expenditures, $201,489.
Fields of interest: Sexual abuse; Domestic violence.
Type of support: Emergency funds.
Application information:
　Initial approach: Telephone
EIN: 311622803

1122

Arthritis Foundation, Rocky Mountain Chapter

2280 S. Albion St.
Denver, CO 80222-4906 (303) 756-8622
FAX: (303) 759-4349; E-mail: info.rm@arthritis.org;
URL: http://www.arthritis.org/colorado

Foundation type: Public charity
Purpose: Grants to researchers for the prevention, control and cure of arthritis and related diseases.
Publications: Annual report; Newsletter.
Financial data: Year ended 12/31/2010. Assets, $0 (M); Expenditures, $1,333,419. Grants to individuals amount not specified.
Fields of interest: Arthritis; Arthritis research.
Type of support: Research.
Application information: Applications accepted.
　Send request by: Online
　Deadline(s): Aug. 1
　Additional information: See web site for additional program guidelines.
EIN: 840428040

1123

Aspen Valley Medical Foundation, Ltd.

(also known as A.V.M.F.)
P.O. Box 1639
Aspen, CO 81612-1639 (970) 544-1298
Contact: Kristin Hoegh Marsh, Pres. and C.E.O.
FAX: (970) 544-1562; E-mail: info@avmfaspen.org;
URL: http://www.avmfaspen.org

Foundation type: Public charity
Purpose: Scholarships to Roaring Fork Valley-area residents to pursue educational opportunities in the health field. Emergency medical assistance to individuals and families in need who are using Aspen Valley Health (AVH) services.
Publications: Application guidelines; Annual report; Informational brochure; Newsletter.
Financial data: Year ended 12/31/2011. Assets, $10,296,426 (M); Expenditures, $2,751,616; Total giving, $590,378; Grants to individuals, totaling $158,567.
Fields of interest: Nursing school/education; Scholarships/financial aid; Human services.
Type of support: Emergency funds; Scholarships—to individuals.
Application information: Applications accepted. Application form required. Application form available on the grantmaker's web site.

Initial approach: Application
Send request by: Mail
Deadline(s): Jan. 24, Apr. 17, July 10, and Nov. 20 for all scholarships, none for Medical Assistance
Final notification: Applicants notified within four weeks following the deadline for scholarships
Applicants should submit the following:
　1) Photograph
　2) Essay
　3) Transcripts
Additional information: Selection is based on academic achievement, financial need, and commitment to the community for scholarships. See web site for additional guidelines.
Program descriptions:
　Audrey Owings Memorial Scholarship for EMT: Scholarship awards are offered to Roaring Fork Valley residents pursuing emergency medical technician (EMT) and paramedic training.
　AVH Employees Education Scholarships: Scholarships are available to employees of Aspen Valley Health (AVH) who wish to pursue continuing education opportunities, as they relate to employees' professional duties.
　Dr. Rodney E. Kirk Memorial Scholarship: A scholarship award is offered annually to a Roaring Fork Valley resident pursuing education in a health-related field.
　Medical Assistance: The foundation provides medical assistance to individuals and families in need who are currently using Aspen Valley Health (AVH) services. Prescription assistance (of up to $150 per person per year), dental assistance (of up to $150 per person per year, for emergency care only), and medical assistance (of up to $250 per person per year, for extraordinary mental health and/or vision needs) are available.
　Nursing Scholarships: Nursing scholarships are offered for interested locals who are looking to begin or continue their nursing careers. Eligible applicants include Roaring Fork Valley residents currently enrolled in state-accredited schools of nursing or pre-nursing (defined as college or university programs designed as preparation for entrance into a program leading to an associate or baccalaureate degree in nursing) in associate, baccalaureate, or master's degree programs. Scholarships may be used at Colorado Mountain College, University of Northern Colorado or the University of Colorado.
EIN: 840643721

1124

Assistance League of Denver

1400 Josephine St.
Denver, CO 80206-2213 (303) 322-5205
Contact: Rosemarie McDermott, Pres.
FAX: (303) 322-6469;
E-mail: assistanceleaguedenver@yahoo.com;
URL: http://denver.assistanceleague.org

Foundation type: Public charity
Purpose: Scholarships to students of Community College of Denver, Community College of Aurora, and Pickens Technical Center for continuing their education.
Financial data: Year ended 05/31/2012. Assets, $1,563,682 (M); Expenditures, $550,056; Total giving, $291,401; Grants to individuals, totaling $291,401.
Fields of interest: Vocational education, post-secondary; College (community/junior).
Type of support: Scholarships—to individuals.

Application information: Scholarship is based on need and academic performance.
EIN: 840510311

1125
Assistance League of Pueblo, Inc.
515 N. Chester Ave.
Pueblo, CO   81003-3312   (719) 544-1528
Contact: Carol King, Pres.
FAX: (719) 544-1528; E-mail: alpco1@netzero.net;
URL: http://pueblo.assistanceleague.org/
dcontact.cfm

Foundation type: Public charity
Purpose: Provides scholarships to students from low income families in order for them to continue their education. Also, provides new school clothing for elementary school children in need in the Pueblo, CO area.
Financial data: Year ended 05/31/2012. Assets, $1,028,690 (M); Expenditures, $239,929.
Fields of interest: Education; Family services.
Type of support: Scholarships—to individuals; Grants for special needs.
Application information: Contact foundation for guidelines.
EIN: 237127355

1126
Association of Graduates of the United States Air Force Academy
3116 Academy Dr.
USAF Academy, CO   80840-4402   (719) 472-0300
Contact: William Thompson, Pres. and C.E.O.
FAX: (719) 333-4194; E-mail: aog@usafa.org;
URL: http://www.usafa.org

Foundation type: Public charity
Purpose: Scholarships to children of a graduate of the U.S. Air force Academy for postsecondary education.
Publications: Financial statement.
Financial data: Year ended 06/30/2012. Assets, $35,514,919 (M); Expenditures, $6,823,462; Total giving, $3,157,414.
Fields of interest: Higher education; Military/veterans.
Type of support: Scholarships—to individuals.
Application information: Applications accepted. Application form required. Application form available on the grantmaker's web site.
  Initial approach: Telephone
  Send request by: Mail
  Deadline(s): Mar. 6
  Final notification: Applicants notified by the end of May
  Applicants should submit the following:
    1) Letter(s) of recommendation
    2) SAT
    3) ACT
    4) Transcripts
  Additional information: Application should also include list of extracurricular activities, list of employment history with position/duty title. Selection is based on demonstrated merit, however, financial need may be considered. Scholarships are in the amount of $500 to $2,000.
EIN: 840580665

1127
Rudy Balke Trust, Inc.
4955 Sunbird Cliffs Dr.
Colorado Springs, CO   80919   (719) 598-9312
Contact: Jeffrey Williams, Tr.

Foundation type: Independent foundation
Purpose: Grants to economically disadvantaged individuals in the vicinity surrounding Victor, CO for medical care.
Financial data: Year ended 12/31/2011. Assets, $1,188,707 (M); Expenditures, $83,977; Total giving, $65,573.
Fields of interest: Health care.
Type of support: Grants for special needs.
Application information: Applications accepted.
  Deadline(s): None
EIN: 846044826

1128
The Robert M. Barr and Roberta Armstrong Barr Foundation
P.O. Box 1779
Durango, CO   81302-1779   (970) 247-1579
Contact: Rod Humble, Treas.

Foundation type: Independent foundation
Purpose: Scholarships to residents of CO aspiring to get a degree in education.
Financial data: Year ended 06/30/2013. Assets, $304,540 (M); Expenditures, $21,259; Total giving, $20,000; Grants to individuals, 14 grants totaling $20,000 (high: $3,000, low: $750).
Fields of interest: Teacher school/education.
Type of support: Undergraduate support.
Application information:
  Applicants should submit the following:
    1) Essay
    2) Letter(s) of recommendation
    3) Transcripts
  Additional information: Applications should also include information displaying financial need.
EIN: 880493403

1129
Bernard Bianco Foundation
805 Park St.
Trinidad, CO   81082   (719) 846-3871
Contact: Mark Argo, Tr.

Foundation type: Independent foundation
Purpose: Scholarships to graduating seniors in Las Animas County, CO.
Financial data: Year ended 12/31/2012. Assets, $773,501 (M); Expenditures, $24,862; Total giving, $24,500; Grants to individuals, 49 grants totaling $24,500 (high: $500, low: $500).
Type of support: Support to graduates or students of specific schools; Undergraduate support.
Application information: Applications accepted. Application form required.
  Applicants should submit the following:
    1) Transcripts
    2) Financial information
EIN: 841418124

1130
Bonfils-Stanton Foundation
Daniels and Fisher Twr.
1601 Arapahoe St., Ste. 500
Denver, CO   80202-2015   (303) 825-3774
Contact: Gary P. Steuer, C.E.O. and Pres.
FAX: (303) 825-0802;
E-mail: webinfo@bonfils-stanton.org; URL: http://www.bonfils-stantonfoundation.org

Foundation type: Independent foundation
Purpose: Annual awards by nomination only to individuals in CO who have made significant contributions in the fields of arts and humanities, community service, science, and medicine.
Publications: Application guidelines; Annual report (including application guidelines); Grants list.
Financial data: Year ended 06/30/2013. Assets, $77,475,043 (M); Expenditures, $4,382,372; Total giving, $3,328,560; Grant to an individual, 1 grant totaling $35,000.
Fields of interest: Humanities; Arts; Health care; Volunteer services; Science; Science.
Type of support: Awards/grants by nomination only; Awards/prizes.
Application information:
  Initial approach: Letter
  Additional information: Nominations accepted throughout the year.
Program description:
  Johnston R. Livingston Fellowship Program: The purpose of this fellowship is to provide advanced learning and professional development opportunities to promising nonprofit leaders who hold, or aspire to hold, significant leadership roles in Colorado's nonprofit sector. Each year, the foundation's trustees select up to 5 Livingston Fellows who receive awards of up to $25,000, to further their leadership skills and abilities. Recipients use their fellowships to support a program of activities that may include study, research, skill enhancement, professional development, and peer learning. Candidates for Livingston Fellowships are nominated by a panel of CO community leaders, and interviewed by an independent consultant. Fellows are selected on the basis of exceptional leadership ability, promise for significance and unique contributions to the nonprofit sector, and potential for the fellowship experience to enable them to move from success to significance as leaders of people, organizations, and Colorado's nonprofit community.
EIN: 846029014

1131
Boogie's Diner Foundation
(formerly The Weinglass Foundation, Inc.)
P.O. Box 11509
Aspen, CO   81612-9120   (970) 925-3771

Foundation type: Independent foundation
Purpose: Scholarships to individuals, primarily for athletics, in Aspen, CO and MD. Grants to economically disadvantaged residents of Aspen County, CO, primarily for medical treatment and related expenses.
Financial data: Year ended 12/31/2011. Assets, $400,488 (M); Expenditures, $86,012; Total giving, $55,625.
Fields of interest: Athletics/sports, training; Economically disadvantaged.
Type of support: Scholarships—to individuals; Grants for special needs.
Application information: Applications not accepted.

Additional information: Contributes only to preselected individuals, unsolicited requests for funds not considered or acknowledged.
EIN: 521307628

1132
Boulder County Arts Alliance
2590 Walnut St., Ste. 9
Boulder, CO   80302-5700   (303) 447-2422
Contact: Charlotte LaSasso, Exec. Dir.
E-mail: info@bouldercountyarts.org; URL: http://www.bouldercountyarts.org

Foundation type: Public charity
Purpose: Grants and awards for projects and equipment to artists in Boulder County, CO.
Publications: Application guidelines; Annual report; Grants list; Informational brochure; Newsletter.
Financial data: Year ended 12/31/2011. Assets, $1,447,465 (M); Expenditures, $290,880; Total giving, $186,472; Grants to individuals, totaling $186,472.
Fields of interest: Visual arts; Performing arts; Arts, artist's services; Arts.
Type of support: Program development; Fellowships; Grants to individuals; Awards/prizes; Project support; Fiscal agent/sponsor.
Application information: Applications accepted. Application form required. Application form available on the grantmaker's web site.
Initial approach: Letter
Deadline(s): Vary
Program descriptions:
BCAA/Neodata Endowment Grant Program: The endowment supports artistic excellence and promotes stability among individual artists and organizations within Boulder County. The minimum grant award will be $1,000; grants are unlikely to exceed $1,500. Awards are given in the following categories: individual artist projects/equipment, organization projects, organization operation or equipment support, arts education, and individual artist fellowship.
Fiscal Agency: This program entitles individual artists and cultural organizations without 501(c)(3) status to apply to funders under the auspices of the alliance. Applicants must be members of the alliance.
EIN: 840566939

1133
Boys and Girls Clubs of Metro Denver, Inc.
2017 W. 9th Ave.
Denver, CO   80204-3845   (303) 892-9200
Contact: John Arigoni, Pres. and C.E.O.
FAX: (303) 892-9210; E-mail: info@bgcmd.org;
URL: http://www.bgcmd.org

Foundation type: Public charity
Purpose: Scholarships to students of Denver, CO pursuing higher education at accredited colleges and universities.
Publications: Annual report; Newsletter.
Financial data: Year ended 09/30/2011. Assets, $20,540,523 (M); Expenditures, $10,228,003; Total giving, $19,538; Grants to individuals, totaling $19,538.
Fields of interest: Higher education.
Type of support: Scholarships—to individuals.
Application information: Applications accepted.
Additional information: All students granted scholarships are required to send to the organization their grades at the end of the school term. If students fall below a 2.0 GPA, or if they quit their programs, future funds are

disallowed. Scholarships are based on merit and need.
EIN: 840510404

1134
Breckenridge Outdoor Education Center
P.O. Box 697
Breckenridge, CO   80424-0697   (970) 453-6422
Contact: Bruce Fitch, Exec. Dir.
FAX: (970) 453-4676; E-mail: boec@boec.org;
E-Mail for Bruce Fitch: bruce@boec.org;
URL: http://www.boec.org

Foundation type: Public charity
Purpose: Scholarships to qualified individuals with disabilities or serious illnesses to attend therapeutic BOEC programs.
Financial data: Year ended 09/30/2011. Assets, $1,527,002 (M); Expenditures, $1,451,538; Total giving, $153,644; Grants to individuals, totaling $153,644.
Fields of interest: Scholarships/financial aid; Disabilities, people with.
Type of support: Scholarships—to individuals.
Application information: Applications accepted.
Initial approach: Telephone
Additional information: Applicant must demonstrate financial need.
EIN: 840725560

1135
The Broomfield Community Foundation
26 Garden Ctr., Ste. 4D
P.O. Box 2040
Broomfield, CO   80038   (303) 469-7208
Contact: Karen Smith, Exec. Dir.
FAX: (303) 410-1733;
E-mail: info@broomfieldfoundation.org;
URL: http://www.broomfieldfoundation.org

Foundation type: Community foundation
Purpose: Scholarships to qualified applicants from the Broomfield, MI area for higher education.
Publications: Application guidelines; Annual report; Grants list; Informational brochure; Newsletter.
Financial data: Year ended 12/31/2011. Assets, $2,204,833 (M); Expenditures, $301,007; Total giving, $204,530; Grants to individuals, totaling $16,750.
Fields of interest: Higher education; Nursing school/education.
Type of support: Scholarships—to individuals.
Application information: Applications accepted. Application form required. Application form available on the grantmaker's web site.
Initial approach: Application
Send request by: Mail
Deadline(s): Varies
Additional information: Eligibility varies per scholarship fund. See web site for a complete listing.
EIN: 841246756

1136
Lucille Brown Foundation
4949 Bear Paw Dr.
Castle Rock, CO   80109
Contact: Cecilia A. Wells, Secy.

Foundation type: Independent foundation
Purpose: Scholarships only to CO residents doing undergraduate work at CO schools.
Financial data: Year ended 12/31/2012. Assets, $478,203 (M); Expenditures, $23,090; Total

giving, $19,000; Grants to individuals, 8 grants totaling $15,000 (high: $3,000, low: $1,000).
Type of support: Scholarships—to individuals.
Application information: Applications not accepted.
Additional information: Unsolicited requests for funds not considered or acknowledged.
EIN: 846025298

1137
Evelyn Wylie Burton Charitable Trust
c/o Barbara Hoover
8150 Hwy. 7
Allenspark, CO   80510   (217) 379-4715
Application address: Selection Committee, Paxton-Buckley, P.O. Box 192, Paxton, IL 60957

Foundation type: Independent foundation
Purpose: Scholarships and awards to students and teachers of the Paxton, Illinois School District.
Financial data: Year ended 12/31/2012. Assets, $425,412 (M); Expenditures, $23,571; Total giving, $20,000; Grants to individuals, 4 grants totaling $20,000 (high: $5,000, low: $5,000).
Fields of interest: Higher education.
Type of support: Scholarships—to individuals; Awards/prizes.
Application information: Applications accepted. Application form required.
Deadline(s): June 1
Additional information: Application not required for teachers.
EIN: 376152951

1138
CAEYC
(also known as Colorado Association for the Education of Young Children)
P.O. Box 631326
Highlands Ranch, CO   80163-1326   (303) 791-2772
Contact: Linda Adams, Exec. Dir.
FAX: (303) 791-7597;
E-mail: caeyc@coloradoaeyc.org; Toll-free tel.: (888) 892-4453; URL: http://www.coloradoaeyc.org

Foundation type: Public charity
Purpose: Tuition assistance for students of CO, pursuing a degree in early childhood education.
Publications: Application guidelines.
Financial data: Year ended 09/30/2011. Assets, $255,681 (M); Expenditures, $409,170; Total giving, $10,503; Grants to individuals, totaling $10,503.
Fields of interest: Early childhood education; Higher education.
Type of support: Scholarships—to individuals.
Application information: Applications accepted. Application form required. Application form available on the grantmaker's web site.
Send request by: Mail
Deadline(s): Nov. 15 for Marla Bouma Memorial Tuition Award, Mar. 14 for CAEYC Tuition Award
Applicants should submit the following:
1) Transcripts
2) Essay
Additional information: Application should also include references. See web site for additional guidelines.
Program descriptions:
CAEYC Award: Scholarships are available for college juniors or seniors attending college on a full-time basis. Eligible applicants must have U.S. citizenship and Colorado residence, a documented

B cumulative GPA from each college or university attended, acceptance as a full-time junior or senior undergraduate at a Colorado college or university, and a declared academic emphasis on early childhood education. There are no restrictions based on race, creed, color, sex, or marital status, and financial need is not a primary consideration.

Marla Bouma Memorial Tuition Award: This scholarship is available to individuals who are citizens of the U.S., who hold Colorado residency. Applicant must have a documented B cumulative GPA from each college or university attended, a minimum of six semester hours of prior coursework in early childhood-related classes, undergraduate or graduate part-time or full-time at a Colorado college or university, and a demonstrated commitment to early childhood education.

EIN: 840713812

1139
Ernest and Lillian E. Campbell Foundation
P.O. Box 51
Julesburg, CO   80737-0051
Contact: James G. Kontny, V.P.; Terry Hinde, Secy.-Treas.

Foundation type: Independent foundation
Purpose: Scholarships to graduating seniors of high schools in Sedgwick County, CO for higher education.
Financial data: Year ended 12/31/2011. Assets, $1,792,226 (M); Expenditures, $160,619; Total giving, $80,475; Grants to individuals, 21 grants totaling $27,000 (high: $3,750, low: $500).
Fields of interest: Higher education; Scholarships/financial aid.
Type of support: Support to graduates or students of specific schools; Undergraduate support.
Application information: Applications accepted.
  Applicants should submit the following:
    1) Transcripts
    2) Letter(s) of recommendation
  Additional information: Students must maintain a minimum 3.0 GPA on a 4.0 scale to remain eligible for scholarship. Application forms available from the trustees or from the foundation office.
EIN: 841271390

1140
Carbondale Clay Center
135 Main St.
Carbondale, CO   81623-2136   (970) 963-2529
Contact: K. Cesark, Exec. Co-Dir.
FAX: (970) 963-4492;
E-mail: info@carbondaleclay.org; URL: http://www.carbondaleclay.org

Foundation type: Public charity
Purpose: Scholarships for low-income children to attend art classes offered by the Carbondale Clay Center, CO. Residencies at the Carbondale Clay Center, CO, to professional level, emerging clay artists to reach the next stage of development in their careers.
Publications: Newsletter.
Financial data: Year ended 12/31/2011. Assets, $223,970 (M); Expenditures, $163,339.
Fields of interest: Arts education; Ceramic arts.
Type of support: Scholarships—to individuals; Residencies.
Application information: Applications accepted.
  Initial approach: Telephone or e-mail.
  Applicants should submit the following:
    1) Resume
    2) SASE

Additional information: Contact foundation for application guidelines and eligibility. For residencies, application must also include a list of references, and slides or CD.
EIN: 841429155

1141
Care and Share, Inc.
2650 Preamble Pt.
Colorado Springs, CO   80915-1200   (719) 528-1247
URL: http://www.careandshare.org

Foundation type: Public charity
Purpose: Emergency food assistance to low income individuals and families in need throughout southern CO.
Financial data: Year ended 06/30/2012. Assets, $13,670,547 (M); Expenditures, $26,988,480; Total giving, $21,644,108; Grants to individuals, totaling $21,644,108.
Fields of interest: Food services; Food banks.
Type of support: Emergency funds; In-kind gifts.
Application information: Applications not accepted.
  Additional information: Unsolicited requests for funds not considered or acknowledged.
EIN: 840731930

1142
Catholic Health Initiatives - Colorado
c/o Centura Health
188 Inverness Dr. W., Ste. 500
Englewood, CO   80112-5204   (303) 290-6500
URL: http://www.centura.org/

Foundation type: Public charity
Purpose: Hospital bill financial assistance to indigent patients of Centura Health in CO, whose incomes are less than 250 percent of the current year's federal poverty level.
Financial data: Year ended 06/30/2012. Assets, $1,598,067,497 (M); Expenditures, $1,458,348,224; Total giving, $5,498,403.
Fields of interest: Hospitals (general); Health care, patient services; Economically disadvantaged.
Type of support: Grants for special needs.
Application information: Applications accepted. Application form required.
  Initial approach: Tel.
  Additional information: Call 1-888-269-7001 for eligibility criteria.
EIN: 840405257

1143
The Children with Diabetes Foundation
685 E. Wiggins St.
Superior, CO   80027-8009   (303) 475-4312
Contact: Sonia Cooper, Pres.
E-mail: info@cwdfoundation.org; Toll-free fax: (866) 270-4062; URL: http://www.cwdfoundation.org

Foundation type: Public charity
Purpose: Research grants to investigators for the cure and/or prevention of T1DM.
Publications: Application guidelines.
Financial data: Year ended 12/31/2011. Assets, $417,091 (M); Expenditures, $247,684; Total giving, $241,825. Grants to individuals amount not specified.
Fields of interest: Diabetes research.
Type of support: Grants to individuals.
Application information: Applications accepted.

Send request by: E-mail
Deadline(s): None
Final notification: Applicants notified within one month after completion of the review process
Additional information: See web site for additional guidelines.
Program description:
  Investigator Award: Investigators are encouraged to seek multiple sources of funding and specify how funding from the CWDF will supplement any other pending or existing sources of funding. The institution and investigator receiving the award must acknowledge that 100 percent of funding from CWDF will be used for the project. No overhead will be awarded.
EIN: 311585740

1144
Children's Diabetes Foundation at Denver
4380 S. Syracuse St., Ste. 430
Denver, CO   80237-2624   (303) 863-1200
Contact: Bertha Lynn, Exec. Dir.
FAX: (303) 863-1122;
E-mail: cdfcares@childrensdiabetesfdn.org;
URL: http://www.childrensdiabetesfoundation.org

Foundation type: Public charity
Purpose: Scholarships to patients of the Barbara Davis Center for Childhood Diabetes, CO to help young people with diabetes attend college or a trade school.
Financial data: Year ended 12/31/2011. Assets, $11,369,835 (M); Expenditures, $4,308,172; Total giving, $2,533,204; Grants to individuals, totaling $129,620.
Fields of interest: Vocational education, post-secondary; Higher education; Diabetes.
Type of support: Scholarships—to individuals.
Application information: Applications accepted. Application form required.
  Additional information: Recipients are chosen based on an application process.
EIN: 840745008

1145
Christian Chiropractor's Association
2550 Stover St., No. B-102
Fort Collins, CO   80525-4642   (970) 482-1404
FAX: (970) 482-1538; Toll-free tel.: (800) 999-1970; URL: http://www.christianchiropractors.org

Foundation type: Public charity
Purpose: College scholarships to student members of the association for attendence at an accredited chiropractic college.
Publications: Application guidelines.
Financial data: Year ended 06/30/2012. Assets, $461,733 (M); Expenditures, $190,061; Total giving, $67,685; Grants to individuals, totaling $66,285.
Fields of interest: Spine disorders; Chiropractic.
Type of support: Scholarships—to individuals.
Application information: Applications accepted. Application form required.
  Send request by: Mail
  Deadline(s): Apr. 30
  Additional information: Application should include a 500 word essay entitled "What will set me, as a Christian chiropractor, apart from any other ethical chiropractor?" Payments are made directly to the educational institution on behalf of the students.
Program description:
  Auxiliary Scholarships: Three one-time scholarships are awarded to student members of

the Christian Chiropractors Association. The scholarships are in the amount of, 1st place $700, 2nd place $500 and 3rd place $300. Winners are announced at the banquet of the CCA annual convention.
EIN: 846027795

1146
Christian Scholars Foundation
6580 Arequa Ridge Ln.
Colorado Springs, CO 80919 (978) 273-6793

Foundation type: Independent foundation
Purpose: Scholarships to residents of CO attending a Christian college or university.
Financial data: Year ended 12/31/2012. Assets, $239,840 (M); Expenditures, $11,697; Total giving, $10,400; Grant to an individual, 1 grant totaling $10,400.
Fields of interest: Christian agencies & churches.
Type of support: Undergraduate support.
Application information: Applications accepted.
  Deadline(s): May 15
  Applicants should submit the following:
    1) Essay
    2) Letter(s) of recommendation
    3) Curriculum vitae
  Additional information: Application should also include plans for use of the grant.
EIN: 841282938

1147
Cibrowski Family Foundation
6059 S. Quebec St.
Englewood, CO 80111 (303) 740-9497

Foundation type: Independent foundation
Purpose: Scholarships to full-time engineering and/or chemistry students at the University of Denver, CO and Colorado School of Mines, CO.
Financial data: Year ended 12/31/2012. Assets, $357,108 (M); Expenditures, $29,055; Total giving, $16,000; Grants to individuals, 2 grants totaling $4,000 (high: $3,000, low: $1,000).
Fields of interest: Engineering school/education; Chemistry.
Type of support: Support to graduates or students of specific schools; Undergraduate support.
Application information: Application form required. Interview required.
  Initial approach: Letter
  Deadline(s): Apr. 15
  Applicants should submit the following:
    1) SAT
    2) ACT
    3) Letter(s) of recommendation
    4) Essay
    5) GPA
  Additional information: Application should also include list of academic and community achievements.
EIN: 841255065

1148
The Clan MacBean Foundation
7475 W. 5th Ave., Ste. 201A
Lakewood, CO 80226
URL: http://www.clanmacbean.net/

Foundation type: Operating foundation
Purpose: Scholarships to men or women seeking to further skills and knowledge in studies related to Scottish culture.
Financial data: Year ended 12/31/2012. Assets, $43,717 (M); Expenditures, $7,464; Total giving,

$3,000; Grant to an individual, 1 grant totaling $3,000.
Fields of interest: Education.
International interests: Scotland.
Type of support: Graduate support; Undergraduate support.
Application information: Applications accepted. Application form required. Application form available on the grantmaker's web site.
  Initial approach: Letter or telephone
  Send request by: Mail
  Deadline(s): May 1
  Applicants should submit the following:
    1) Letter(s) of recommendation
    2) Transcripts
  Additional information: Application forms can be obtained from the foundation.
Program description:
  MacBean Scholarship: Scholarship in the amount of $5,000 is awarded to high school graduates pursuing a course of study relating directly to Scottish culture, or be in a field that leads directly to the improvement and benefit of the Human Family. The award may be used toward tuition, fees, books, room and board, printing and publishing costs, historical research fees, and initial costs in establishing a project.
EIN: 411445203

1149
James T. Clark Foundation
3033 E. 1st Ave.
Denver, CO 80206-5617
Application Address: c/o ANB Bank Investment Management and Trust

Foundation type: Independent foundation
Purpose: Scholarships to graduates of Fort Morgan High School, CO, to attend Colorado College, Colorado School of Mines, Colorado State University, University of Colorado, or University of Denver.
Financial data: Year ended 09/30/2012. Assets, $1,169,179 (M); Expenditures, $56,983; Total giving, $43,000; Grants to individuals, 14 grants totaling $43,000 (high: $5,000, low: $2,000).
Fields of interest: Higher education.
Type of support: Scholarships—to individuals; Support to graduates or students of specific schools.
Application information: Application form required. Interview required.
  Deadline(s): Mar. 15
  Final notification: Applicants notified by May 1
  Applicants should submit the following:
    1) Transcripts
    2) Letter(s) of recommendation
    3) SAT
    4) ACT
  Additional information: Completed applications should be delivered to the Fort Morgan High School counselor's office. Application should include letter of acceptance from college and a personal statement outlining future plans and goals.
EIN: 841070259

1150
Clark Scholarship Fund
c/o Guaranty Bank and Trust Co.
P.O. Box 1159
Longmont, CO 80502-0001 (303) 776-6014
Application address: c/o Duke Aschenmenner, Principal, Longmont High School, 1040 Sunset, Longmont, CO 80501
URL: http://www.guarantybankco.com/trust/scholarships.php

Foundation type: Independent foundation
Purpose: Scholarships to financially needy graduates of Longmont High School, CO, attending two- or four-year colleges and universities.
Financial data: Year ended 09/30/2013. Assets, $1,877,815 (M); Expenditures, $101,680; Total giving, $85,000; Grants to individuals, 19 grants totaling $85,000 (high: $5,000, low: -$5,000).
Fields of interest: Higher education.
Type of support: Support to graduates or students of specific schools.
Application information: Applications accepted. Application form required.
  Deadline(s): Apr. 1
  Applicants should submit the following:
    1) SAT
    2) Financial information
    3) GPA
    4) Class rank
    5) ACT
  Additional information: Application should also include PSAT score, and counselor recommendation. Applications available at Longmont High School, CO. Awards are based on financial need, and academic and leadership abilities.
EIN: 846270490

1151
Cocker Kids' Foundation, Inc.
P. O. Box 404
Crawford, CO 81415-0404 (970) 921-4855
Contact: Joe Cocker, Dir.
FAX: (970) 921-4857;
E-mail: info@cockerkidsfoundation.com;
URL: http://www.cockerkidsfoundation.com/

Foundation type: Public charity
Purpose: Scholarships to graduating seniors from Paonia High School, CO and Hotchkiss High School, CO for postsecondary education.
Publications: Application guidelines.
Financial data: Year ended 12/31/2011. Assets, $158,171 (M); Expenditures, $129,395; Total giving, $96,884; Grants to individuals, totaling $14,440.
Fields of interest: Higher education.
Type of support: Scholarships—to individuals; Support to graduates or students of specific schools.
Application information: Applications accepted. Application form required.
  Additional information: Application can be obtained from your guidance counselors.
EIN: 954699516

1152
Colfax Community Network, Inc.
1585 Kingston St.
Aurora, CO 80010-2504 (303) 360-9175
Contact: Jennifer Herrera, Exec. Dir.
FAX: (303) 360-0627;
E-mail: jennifer@colfaxcommunitynetwork.org;
Mailing address: P.O. Box 202373, Denver, CO

80220-8373; URL: http://
www.colfaxcommunitynetwork.org

Foundation type: Public charity
Purpose: Assistance to low-income individual and
families of the Denver, CO area with emergency
food, rental assistance, clothing, and medical and
dental assistance.
Publications: Annual report; Newsletter.
Financial data: Year ended 12/31/2011. Assets,
$193,310 (M); Expenditures, $193,861; Total
giving, $12,151; Grants to individuals, totaling
$12,151.
Fields of interest: Economically disadvantaged.
Type of support: Grants for special needs.
Application information: Contact the network for
assistance.
EIN: 841487426

1153
Colorado Academy of Family Physicians Foundation

2224 S. Fraser St., Unit 1
Aurora, CO   80014-4532   (303) 696-6655

Foundation type: Public charity
Purpose: Fellowships to medical students to
practice and pursue family medicine, and to set up
practice in rural CO, also assist new physicians to
set up practice in eastern CO.
Financial data: Year ended 12/31/2011. Assets,
$176,282 (M); Expenditures, $41,850; Total
giving, $41,000.
Fields of interest: Medical school/education.
Type of support: Fellowships.
Application information: Contact foundation for
further information.
EIN: 841150631

1154
The Colorado Health Foundation

(formerly HealthONE Alliance)
501 S. Cherry St., Ste. 1100
Denver, CO   80246-1325   (303) 953-3600
Contact: Sara Guillaume, Dir. of Grants
Management
FAX: (303) 322-4576;
E-mail: grants@coloradohealth.org; Toll-free tel.:
(877) 225-0839; URL: http://
www.coloradohealth.org

Foundation type: Public charity
Purpose: Fellowship to attend the Dorsey Hughes
Symposium for individuals interested in and willing
to work toward improving health and health care in
CO through government, business, consumerism,
media, and established health care channels.
Publications: Application guidelines; Annual report;
Newsletter.
Financial data: Year ended 12/31/2011. Assets,
$2,233,069,046 (M); Expenditures,
$108,853,115; Total giving, $80,679,415; Grants
to individuals, totaling $14,518.
Fields of interest: Reform; Public health.
Type of support: Fellowships.
Application information:
  Initial approach: Letter
  Additional information: Applicants should refer to
    application guidelines at the foundation's web
    site before submitting their proposals.
Program description:
  Colorado Health Foundation Fellows Program:
  Ideal candidates will possess an interest in health
  care reform; demonstrate the ability to work
  collaboratively with others; share a commitment to
  increasing access to high-quality health care and

empowering individuals to take charge of their
health; and commit to attending the full symposium
and additional meetings throughout the year.
Lodging and meals are included with funding.
EIN: 742568941

1155
Colorado Homeless Families, Inc.

P.O. Box 740130
Arvada, CO   80006-0130   (303) 420-6634
Contact: Connie Zimmerman, C.E.O.
FAX: (303) 420-2356; E-mail: chfrb@flashmail.com;
URL: http://www.chfrb.org

Foundation type: Public charity
Purpose: Provides transitional housing and support
services for 18 months to 2 years to homeless
families who are working to make themselves
self-sufficient by the end of the program.
Publications: Annual report.
Financial data: Year ended 12/31/2011. Assets,
$3,775,771 (M); Expenditures, $852,123.
Fields of interest: Housing/shelter, temporary
shelter; Family services; Homeless.
Type of support: Grants for special needs.
Application information: Applications accepted.
Application form not required. Application form
available on the grantmaker's web site. Interview
required.
  Initial approach: Telephone
  Additional information: Applicants must have a
    referral, four character references, good work
    history and a set of goals. See web site for
    additional information.
EIN: 841049318

1156
Colorado Housing Assistance Corporation

670 Santa Fe Dr.
Denver, CO   80204-4427   (303) 572-9445
FAX: (303) 573-9214;
E-mail: chac@chaconline.org; URL: http://
www.chaconline.org

Foundation type: Public charity
Purpose: Loans to help low to moderate income
first time home buyers of Colorado for down
payment and closing cost assistance.
Financial data: Year ended 06/30/2012. Assets,
$11,937,294 (M); Expenditures, $1,186,081;
Total giving, $127,184; Grants to individuals,
totaling $127,184.
Fields of interest: Housing/shelter, home owners.
Type of support: Loans—to individuals.
Application information: Applications accepted.
Application form required.
  Additional information: All borrowers are required
    to have a minimum contribution to the
    transaction, $1,000. All loans require
    repayment. Contact the corporation for
    eligibility determination.
EIN: 742229383

1157
Colorado Institute of Developmental Pediatrics, Inc.

(formerly Adam's C.A.M.P.)
6767 S. Spruce St., Ste. 102
Centennial, CO   80112-1284   (303) 563-8290
Contact: Karel Horney, Exec. Dir.
FAX: (303) 563-8291;
E-mail: Communication@adamscamp.org; E-mail
for Karel Horney : karel@adamscamp.org;
URL: http://www.adamscamp.org/

Foundation type: Public charity
Purpose: Scholarships are awarded for partial
program fees to support physically challenged
children based on financial need, other funding
sources available and commitment to support the
camp through a variety of volunteer activities.
Publications: Application guidelines.
Financial data: Year ended 12/31/2011. Assets,
$1,107,267 (M); Expenditures, $976,243; Total
giving, $54,347; Grants to individuals, totaling
$54,347.
Fields of interest: Children; Disabilities, people
with.
Type of support: Scholarships—to individuals.
Application information: Applications accepted.
  Initial approach: Telephone
  Additional information: Application must include
    copies of first two pages of most recent tax
    return, and volunteer sign-up sheet.
EIN: 742432104

1158
Colorado Insurance and Business Education Foundation

(formerly SLA Foundation)
5529 W. Hoover Dr.
Littleton, CO   80123   (303) 331-9399
Contact: John G. Wethey, Secy.
Application address: PO Box Denver CO
80201-1500

Foundation type: Independent foundation
Purpose: Scholarships to full-time students who are
CO high school graduates, majoring in business
education or a related subject at accredited
colleges and universities.
Financial data: Year ended 12/31/2012. Assets,
$751,486 (M); Expenditures, $48,123; Total
giving, $39,000; Grants to individuals, 15 grants
totaling $39,000 (high: $5,000, low: $1,000).
Fields of interest: Business school/education;
Computer science.
Type of support: Scholarships—to individuals.
Application information:
  Initial approach: Letter
  Send request by: Mail
  Deadline(s): Apr. 21
  Applicants should submit the following:
    1) Class rank
    2) Transcripts
    3) GPA
    4) Resume
    5) Letter(s) of recommendation
  Additional information: Application must also
    include college name and address, major field
    of study, high school information, personal
    information, and work history.
EIN: 841329138

1159
Colorado Legal Services

(formerly Legal Aid Society of Metropolitan Denver)
c/o Billie Hall
1905 Sherman St., Ste. 400
Denver, CO   80203-1181   (303) 837-1321
Contact: Jonathan D. Asher, Exec. Dir.
FAX: (303) 866-9360; URL: http://
www.coloradolegalservices.org

Foundation type: Public charity
Purpose: Civil legal services to the economically
disadvantaged residents of CO, and grants to offset
the costs of court filing fees, process service and
witness fees, and miscellaneous litigation
expenses.
Publications: Annual report.

Financial data: Year ended 12/31/2012. Assets, $4,414,674 (M); Expenditures, $9,986,440.
Fields of interest: Legal services; Economically disadvantaged.
Type of support: Grants for special needs.
Application information:
  Initial approach: Letter
  Additional information: Contact the local branch for further information.
EIN: 840402702

1160
Colorado Masons Benevolent Fund Association

2400 Consistory Ct.
Grand Junction, CO   81501-2009
Scholarship address: c/o Scholarship Admin.: 1130 Panorama Dr., Colorado Springs, CO 80904, tel.: (800) 482-4441
E-mail: tomcox@cmbfa.org; URL: http://www.cmbfa.org/

Foundation type: Operating foundation
Purpose: Scholarships only to graduating seniors in public high schools in Colorado who have been accepted at, and will attend an institution of higher learning in CO.
Financial data: Year ended 10/31/2012. Assets, $9,296,588 (M); Expenditures, $932,535; Total giving, $730,121.
Fields of interest: Higher education.
Type of support: Scholarships—to individuals.
Application information: Applications accepted. Application form required. Application form available on the grantmaker's web site. Interview required.
  Deadline(s): Mar. 7
  Applicants should submit the following:
    1) Letter(s) of recommendation
    2) Transcripts
    3) FAFSA
  Additional information: Scholarships are paid directly to the educational institution on behalf of the students.
EIN: 840406813

1161
Colorado Mountain College Foundation, Inc.

802 Grand Ave.
P.O. Box 1763
Glenwood Springs, CO   81602-1763   (970) 947-8361
Contact: Matthew Spencer, C.E.O.
Email (for scholarships): cefting@coloradomtn.edu
FAX: (970) 947-8385;
E-mail: mspencer@coloradomtn.edu; Toll free Tel. : (800)-621-8559 Ext. 8378; URL: http://www.cmcfoundation.org

Foundation type: Public charity
Purpose: Scholarships to students at Colorado Mountain College.
Publications: Application guidelines; Annual report; Informational brochure.
Financial data: Year ended 06/30/2012. Assets, $13,213,501 (M); Expenditures, $3,095,880; Total giving, $2,188,700; Grants to individuals, totaling $694,007.
Type of support: Support to graduates or students of specific schools.
Application information: Applications accepted. Application form required. Application form available on the grantmaker's web site.
  Send request by: Mail or e-mail

Copies of proposal: 1
Deadline(s): Varies
Final notification: Applicants notified in six weeks
Applicants should submit the following:
  1) Transcripts
  2) Letter(s) of recommendation
  3) GPA
  4) Financial information
  5) FAFSA
  6) Essay
Additional information: See web site for complete program listing.
EIN: 742393418

1162
Colorado Native Plant Society

P.O. Box 200
Fort Collins, CO   80522-0200   (303) 458-4262
Contact: Jan Loechell Turner
E-mail: jlturner@regis.edu; URL: http://www.conps.org

Foundation type: Public charity
Purpose: Grants to individuals to support the study of Colorado plants and plant communities.
Publications: Application guidelines.
Financial data: Year ended 12/31/2012. Assets, $197,435 (M); Expenditures, $26,223; Total giving, $4,500.
Fields of interest: Biology/life sciences; Botany.
Type of support: Research; Grants to individuals.
Application information: Applications accepted. Application form required. Application form available on the grantmaker's web site.
  Initial approach: Proposal
  Deadline(s): Feb. 19
Program descriptions:
  John W. Marr Fund: Grants of up to $1,000 are available to researchers who whish to study the biology of Colorado native plants and plant communities.
  Myrna P. Steinkamp Fund: Grants of up to $1,000 are available to support research on the biology of Colorado rare native plants.
EIN: 840734596

1163
The Colorado Nonprofit Development Center

4130 Tejon St., Ste. A
Denver, CO   80211-1876
FAX: (720) 855-8273; URL: http://www.cndc.org

Foundation type: Public charity
Purpose: Support to individuals to enable them to transform their ideas for community service into operating projects through a fiscal sponsorship program.
Financial data: Year ended 12/31/2011. Assets, $6,094,024 (M); Expenditures, $11,010,275.
Type of support: Project support; Fiscal agent/sponsor.
Application information: Applications accepted. Application form required. Application form available on the grantmaker's web site.
  Initial approach: Proposal
  Send request by: Mail
  Deadline(s): First business day of the month
  Final notification: Recipients notified in four to six weeks
  Applicants should submit the following:
    1) Resume
    2) Budget Information
  Additional information: Application should also include three letters of support, signed Equal Opportunity and Nondiscrimination Policy, and

Brochures or other supporting materials about the project (optional).
Program description:
  Fiscal Sponsorship: The center provides qualified emerging and transitioning nonprofits with comprehensive fiscal sponsorship, which includes operating under its 501(c)(3) umbrella, an existing back-office infrastructure, and the support of a team of nonprofit management professionals for an administrative fee of nine percent of project revenues.
EIN: 841493585

1164
Colorado Professional Fire Fighters Foundation

2342 Broadway
Denver, CO   80205-2178   (303) 308-1992
Contact: Randy Atkinson, Pres.

Foundation type: Public charity
Purpose: Grants to family members of firefighters in CO due to death, injury or illness.
Financial data: Year ended 06/30/2012. Assets, $342,722 (M); Expenditures, $76,229; Total giving, $73,590; Grants to individuals, totaling $73,590.
Fields of interest: Human services.
Type of support: Grants for special needs.
Application information: Applications not accepted.
  Additional information: Unsolicited requests for funds not considered or acknowledged. Grants are only for firefighters family members.
EIN: 752983748

1165
Colorado Rural Health Center

3033 S. Parker Rd., Ste. 606
Aurora, CO   80014-2923   (303) 832-7493
Contact: Michelle Mills, C.E.O.
FAX: (303) 832-7496;
E-mail: info@coruralhealth.org; Toll-free tel.: (800) 851-6782; URL: http://www.coruralhealth.org

Foundation type: Public charity
Purpose: Scholarships to residents of Colorado pursuing a career in medicine, pharmacy or dental school or a nurse seeking advanced training or a medical assistant training to become a lab technician.
Publications: Application guidelines; Newsletter.
Financial data: Year ended 12/31/2011. Assets, $3,886,622 (M); Expenditures, $3,709,817; Total giving, $653,198.
Fields of interest: Dental school/education; Medical school/education; Nursing school/education.
Type of support: Scholarships—to individuals.
Application information: Applications accepted. Application form required.
  Deadline(s): None
  Additional information: See web site for additional application guidelines.
EIN: 841192031

1166
Colorado Springs Camp No. 7226 Modern Woodmen of America Educational Trust

P.O. Box 2343
Colorado Springs, CO   80901-2343
Contact: Jan Michaels, Secy.

Foundation type: Independent foundation
Purpose: Scholarships to graduating seniors from high schools in El Paso or Teller counties, CO, for attendance at a college, university or technical trade school in CO.
Financial data: Year ended 12/31/2011. Assets, $151,393 (M); Expenditures, $6,484; Total giving, $5,000; Grants to individuals, 5 grants totaling $5,000 (high: $1,000, low: $1,000).
Fields of interest: Vocational education, post-secondary; Higher education.
Type of support: Scholarships—to individuals.
Application information: Applications accepted. Application form required.
  Deadline(s): May 15
  Applicants should submit the following:
    1) Letter(s) of recommendation
    2) Transcripts
EIN: 841135674

1167
Colorado State Grange Leadership and Scholarship Foundation

(formerly Colorado State Grange Leadership and Scholarship Foundation)
P.O. Box 521
Akron, CO 80720 (303) 898-5052
Contact: Jim C. Miller, Treas.
URL: http://www.coloradograng.org/

Foundation type: Independent foundation
Purpose: Scholarships to CO residents who are CO Grange members, or the child or grandchild of a Grange member for attendance at institutions of higher learning.
Financial data: Year ended 12/31/2013. Assets, $377,794 (M); Expenditures, $20,556; Total giving, $20,500; Grants to individuals, 18 grants totaling $20,500 (high: $1,500, low: $500).
Fields of interest: Higher education.
Type of support: Scholarships—to individuals.
Application information: Applications accepted. Application form required.
  Initial approach: Letter
  Deadline(s): Apr. 15
EIN: 840776526

1168
Colorado State Patrol Family Foundation

55 Wadsworth Blvd.
Lakewood, CO 80226-1501 (303) 237-7439
Contact: Lonnie J. Westphal, Exec. Dir
FAX: (303) 237-2067; *URL:* http://www.cspff.net

Foundation type: Public charity
Purpose: Grants to CO State Troopers, State Patrol civilian staff and their families in times of traumatic injury, death or personal hardships. Also, scholarships to CO State Patrol members and their families.
Publications: Application guidelines.
Financial data: Year ended 12/31/2011. Assets, $1,495,467 (M); Expenditures, $915,750; Total giving, $62,074; Grants to individuals, totaling $62,074.
Fields of interest: Crime/law enforcement.
Type of support: Undergraduate support; Grants for special needs.
Application information: Applications accepted. Application form required. Application form available on the grantmaker's web site.
  Applicants should submit the following:
    1) Photograph
    2) Transcripts

Program descriptions:
  Fallen Officer's Fund: These scholarships are available to dependent children (ages 17 to 23) of deceased regular members of the Association of Colorado State Patrol Professionals (ACSPP) who have been killed or died in the line of duty. Recipients must obtain a bachelor's degree within 6 years, an associate's degree within 3 years, or complete the trade vocation within the school's prescribed timeframe; there are no specifications on the area of study.
  General Tuition Scholarship: These scholarships are available to full- or part-time students, to be applied against the cost for tuition, books, and fees to a college or trade school of the recipient's choice. Eligible applicants must be a regular member of the Association of Colorado State Patrol Professionals (ACSPP), or the spouse or dependent child (between the ages of 17 and 23) of an ACSPP regular member who has been in good standing for the previous three years. All applicants must provide written documentation of their acceptance by an accredited educational institution prior to receiving any scholarship funds, and must donate 8 hours of community service to an approved nonprofit organization for each year they receive a scholarship.
  Hardship Fund: This fund assist members of the Association of Colorado State Patrol Professionals (ACSPP) who find themselves in a financial situation beyond their control and are in need of assistance.
  Lyle F. Wohlers Scholarship: These scholarships provide up to $3,000 per year to full-time students pursuing a criminal justice- or law enforcement-related degree. Eligible applicants must be the dependent child (between 17 and 23 years old) of a regular member of the Association of Colorado State Patrol Professionals (ACSPP), and provide proof of acceptance by an accredited educational institution and financial need. Recipient must donate 8 hours of community service to a non-profit organization of the recipient's choice.
EIN: 841150452

1169
Colorado State Science Fair, Inc.

Campus Delivery 1802
Colorado State Univ.
Fort Collins, CO 80523-1802 (970) 498-4121
Contact: Carol Morrow, Pres.
Nomination address: c/o Al Bedard, US Dept. of Commerce/NOAA, 325 Broadway, NOAA/ETL, Boulder, CO 80305, tel.: (303) 497-6508, e-mail: alfred.j.bedard@noaa.gov
FAX: (970) 491-2005;
E-mail: csef@lamar.colostate.edu; *URL:* http://www.csef.colostate.edu/

Foundation type: Public charity
Purpose: Scholarships for students, and grants and awards for teachers through competition and participation at the Colorado State Science and Engineering Fair.
Financial data: Year ended 08/31/2012. Assets, $35,791 (M); Expenditures, $84,067; Total giving, $9,750.
Fields of interest: Secondary school/education; Science; Engineering.
Type of support: Scholarships—to individuals; Awards/prizes.
Application information: Applications accepted. Application form required. Application form available on the grantmaker's web site.
  Deadline(s): Mar. 1 for Teacher Awards

Additional information: Teachers must be nominated. E-mailed or faxed nominations are not accepted.
Program description:
  Teacher of the Year Award: The organization awards a $3,000 grant to a science teacher in Colorado, as determined by a vote of its selection committee, through participation in the annual Colorado State Science and Engineering Fair. The teacher must be actively teaching science or mathematics in grades 6 through 12 in CO and support independent research by students and their competition in local, regional, and state science fairs.
EIN: 741884595

1170
Community Foundation of Gunnison Valley

805 W. Tomichi Ave., W. Door
P.O. Box 7057
Gunnison, CO 81230 (970) 641-8837
Contact: Pam Montgomery, Exec. Dir.
FAX: (970) 641-0443; *E-mail:* info@cfgv.org; Grant inquiry e-mail: pam@cfgv.org; Additional Tel.: (970)-349-5966; *URL:* http://www.cfgv.org

Foundation type: Community foundation
Purpose: College scholarships to residents of Crested Butte, Gunnison, and Upper Gunnison Watershed, CO.
Publications: Application guidelines; Annual report; Financial statement; Newsletter.
Financial data: Year ended 12/31/2012. Assets, $6,197,820 (M); Expenditures, $1,145,110; Total giving, $927,085; Grants to individuals, totaling $3,415.
Fields of interest: Higher education.
Type of support: Scholarships—to individuals.
Application information: Applications accepted.
  Send request by: Mail or hand delivered
  Applicants should submit the following:
    1) Photograph
    2) Transcripts
EIN: 311650658

1171
Community Foundation of Northern Colorado

(formerly Fort Collins Area Community Foundation)
4745 Wheaton Dr., Ste. 100
Fort Collins, CO 80525-9403 (970) 224-3462
Contact: Ray Caraway, Pres.
Scholarship inquiry e-mail: scholarships@nocofoundation.org
FAX: (970) 488-1990;
E-mail: info@nocofoundation.org; *URL:* http://www.nocofoundation.org/

Foundation type: Community foundation
Purpose: Scholarships to students from the Larimer County, CO area for higher education.
Publications: Annual report; Newsletter.
Financial data: Year ended 06/30/2012. Assets, $60,784,156 (M); Expenditures, $7,033,464; Total giving, $4,906,671. Scholarships—to individuals amount not specified.
Fields of interest: Higher education.
Type of support: Scholarships—to individuals; Undergraduate support.
Application information: Applications accepted. Application form required. Application form available on the grantmaker's web site.
  Send request by: Online
  Deadline(s): Mar. 29

Additional information: Each scholarship has its own unique set of eligibility criteria. See web site for a complete listing.
EIN: 840699243

1172
Community Foundation Serving Southwest Colorado

1309 E. 3rd Ave.
Smiley Building, St. 20A
Durango, CO 81301 (970) 375-5807
Contact: Briggen Wrinkle, Exec. Dir.
FAX: (970) 375-5806;
E-mail: director@swcommunityfoundation.org;
Mailing address: P.O. Box 1673, Durango, CO
81302-1673; URL: http://
www.swcommunityfoundation.org

Foundation type: Community foundation
Purpose: Scholarships to Southwest Colorado area residents for continuing education at institutions of higher learning.
Publications: Financial statement; Informational brochure; Occasional report.
Financial data: Year ended 12/31/2012. Assets, $3,200,382 (M); Expenditures, $1,117,966; Total giving, $526,350; Grants to individuals, 71 grants totaling $258,497.
Fields of interest: Education.
Type of support: Scholarships—to individuals.
Application information: Applications accepted.
Additional information: Contact the foundation for scholarship information.
EIN: 841474900

1173
Community Partnership for Child Development

2330 Robinson St.
Colorado Springs, CO 80904-3752 (719)
635-1536
Contact: Noreen Landis-Tyson, Pres. and C.E.O.
FAX: (719) 634-8086;
E-mail: cpcdheadstart@cpcd.org; E-Mail for Noreen Landis-Tyson : nlandistyson@cpcd.org; URL: http://
www.cpcdheadstart.org

Foundation type: Public charity
Purpose: Support for young children and families in the Colorado area with classroom lunch, education counseling, and medical and dental services.
Publications: Newsletter.
Financial data: Year ended 10/31/2011. Assets, $5,263,858 (M); Expenditures, $14,757,750; Total giving, $595,321; Grants to individuals, totaling $595,321.
Fields of interest: Children; Youth; Adults; Economically disadvantaged.
Type of support: In-kind gifts; Grants for special needs.
Application information: Applications accepted. Application form required.
Additional information: Contact the organization for eligibility determination.
Program descriptions:
Colorado Preschool Program (CPP): This program is offered to children ages three to five. Children and families receive many of the same services offered for Head Start families, such as health screenings and family support, but the broader eligibility requirements all for families of diverse economic backgrounds to enroll.
Early Head Start Program: This program serves pregnant women and children ages birth to three. The program serves to enhance the development of

very young children while promoting healthy family functioning and school readiness.
Head Start Program: This program provides educational, physical and mental health, and nutritional services to children ages three to five. Families receive education and support to assist them in fulfilling their roles as their child's first and best teacher.
EIN: 841071825

1174
Cheryl D. Conkling Memorial Foundation

2450 Marshfiels Ln.
Fort Collins, CO 80524

Foundation type: Independent foundation
Purpose: Postsecondary scholarships for individuals with preference given to applicants with hearing or other impairments.
Financial data: Year ended 12/31/2012. Assets, $4,155 (M); Expenditures, $10,897; Total giving, $9,000; Grants to individuals, 5 grants totaling $9,000 (high: $3,000, low: $1,500).
Fields of interest: Higher education; Disabilities, people with; Deaf/hearing impaired.
Type of support: Scholarships—to individuals.
Application information: Applications accepted. Application form required.
Deadline(s): Mid-Apr.
EIN: 260045208

1175
Crossroads Ministry of Estes Park, Inc.

851 Dry Gulch Rd.
P.O. Box 3616
Estes Park, CO 80517-3616 (970) 577-0610
Contact: Virgil Good, Exec. Dir.
FAX: (970) 577-9692; URL: http://
crossroadsministryofep.org/

Foundation type: Public charity
Purpose: Assistance in the form of cash vouchers, and non-cash items, food, medical care, housing, transportation, clothing, household items, and other emergency items, to low-income individuals and families of the Estes Park area, CO.
Financial data: Year ended 12/31/2011. Assets, $498,647 (M); Expenditures, $536,472; Total giving, $272,870; Grants to individuals, totaling $272,870.
Type of support: Grants for special needs.
Application information:
Initial approach: Letter
Additional information: Contact foundation for eligibility criteria.
EIN: 742465229

1176
Charles Curtis & Patricia Morse Curtis Foundation

1 Penrose Ln.
Colorado Springs, CO 80906-4218 (719)
635-9470
Contact: Charles Curtis, Pres.

Foundation type: Independent foundation
Purpose: Scholarships to graduating high school seniors of CO, for postsecondary education.
Financial data: Year ended 09/30/2012. Assets, $1,147,458 (M); Expenditures, $60,680; Total giving, $25,076; Grants to individuals, 6 grants totaling $8,667 (high: $3,500, low: $500).
Fields of interest: Higher education.
Type of support: Scholarships—to individuals.

Application information: Applications accepted.
Initial approach: Letter
Additional information: Contact the foundation for application guidelines.
EIN: 841473110

1177
Daniels Fund

101 Monroe St.
Denver, CO 80206-4467 (303) 393-7220
Contact: Peter Droege, V.P., Comms.; Barb Danbom, Sr. V.P., Grants Prog.
FAX: (720) 941-4110; E-mail: info@danielsfund.org; Toll free tel.: (877) 791- 4726; Additional e-mails for general contact: grantsinfo@danielsfund.org; For B. Danbom: bdanbom@danielsfund.org; For P. Droege: pdroege@danielsfund.org; URL: http://
www.danielsfund.org

Foundation type: Independent foundation
Purpose: Scholarships to financially needy individuals in CO, NM, UT, and WY for higher education.
Publications: Annual report; Financial statement; Grants list; Informational brochure; Newsletter; IRS Form 990 or 990-PF printed copy available upon request.
Financial data: Year ended 12/31/2012. Assets, $1,285,511,708 (M); Expenditures, $56,612,619; Total giving, $46,529,706; Grants to individuals, 1,196 grants totaling $13,935,308.
Type of support: Scholarships—to individuals.
Application information: Applications not accepted.
Additional information: Applicants must be referred by a designated Referral Agency. Unsolicited requests for funds not considered or acknowledged.
Program description:
Daniels Scholarships: The scholarships are awarded in the spring to graduating high school seniors and are supplemental after other federal, state, institutional, and private financial aid and scholarships. Students may use their scholarship at any two- or four-year accredited nonprofit college or university in the United States with an intention to complete a bachelor's degree. Applicants must be referred by a designated Referral Agency. Unsolicited requests for funds not considered or acknowledged.
EIN: 841393308

1178
Delta County Memorial Hospital Foundation

1501 E. 3rd St.
Delta, CO 81416-5003 (970) 874-2291
E-mail: ksramek@deltahospital.org; URL: http://
www.dcmhfoundation.org

Foundation type: Public charity
Purpose: Scholarships to high school graduates of Delta, Montrose or Mesa county, CO pursuing an education in the health care field.
Publications: Application guidelines.
Financial data: Year ended 12/31/2011. Assets, $369,803 (M); Expenditures, $37,427; Total giving, $28,177.
Fields of interest: Health sciences school/ education.
Type of support: Scholarships—to individuals.
Application information: Applications accepted. Application form required.
Initial approach: Letter
Send request by: Mail or hand deliver
Applicants should submit the following:

1) Letter(s) of recommendation
2) Transcripts
Additional information: Application should include transcripts, letter of acceptance and tuition bill, and letters of reference. Scholarships are paid directly to the educational institution on behalf of the students.

Program description:
Health Education Scholarship: Scholarships are available to high school graduates residing in Delta, Montrose, and Mesa counties, CO, who are planning to further their education in a health related program. Eligible applicants must show proof of financial need and academic capability, and sustain a 2.5 GPA. Applicants must be U.S. citizens.
EIN: 841609267

1179
Denver Delta, Inc.
P.O. Box 7330
Denver, CO 80207-7330   (720) 468-1690
Contact: Gloria Tanner, Pres.

Foundation type: Public charity
Purpose: Scholarships are awarded to seniors attending Denver, CO metropolitan area high schools pursuing a higher education.
Financial data: Year ended 06/30/2012. Assets, $120,455 (M); Expenditures, $35,208; Total giving, $21,125.
Fields of interest: Higher education.
Type of support: Scholarships—to individuals; Support to graduates or students of specific schools.
Application information: Interview required.
Applicants should submit the following:
1) Letter(s) of recommendation
2) Essay
Additional information: Applicant must demonstrate financial need, must participate in extra curricular activities, and be active in the community.
EIN: 841319279

1180
Denver Fire Fighters Burn Foundation, Inc.
2342 Broadway, Ste. 140
Denver, CO 80205-2178   (303) 297-2989
E-mail: denverff@denverburnfoundation.org; E-mail For Patrick Hynes: Patrick.Hynes@DenverBurnFoundation.org; URL: http://www.denverburnfoundation.org/

Foundation type: Public charity
Purpose: Scholarships to burn and fire victims who are residents of Denver, CO and DC for attendance at colleges or universities.
Publications: Application guidelines.
Financial data: Year ended 12/31/2011. Assets, $71,457 (M); Expenditures, $108,701; Total giving, $73,928.
Fields of interest: Higher education.
Type of support: Undergraduate support.
Application information: Applications accepted. Application form required.
Send request by: Mail
Deadline(s): Aug. 1
Applicants should submit the following:
1) Photograph
2) Letter(s) of recommendation
3) Transcripts

Additional information: Application should also include a list of extracurricular activities (sports, community service, clubs, etc.).
Program description:
Scholarships: Each year, the foundation provides up to $15,000 in scholarships to victims who have received treatment at The Children's Hospital Burn Center, or who has attended any of the Cheley/ Children's Hospital Burn Camp, Winter Camp, or Project challenge. Scholarships can be used for both formal and non-traditional education programs.
EIN: 841098212

1181
The Denver Health and Hospitals Foundation
655 Broadway, Ste. 750
Denver, CO 80203-3462   (303) 602-2970
Contact: Paula Herzmark, Exec. Dir.
FAX: (303) 602-2981;
E-mail: paula.herzmark@dhha.org; URL: http://www.denverhealthfoundation.org/

Foundation type: Public charity
Purpose: The Patient Assistance Fund provides a safety net to indigent Denver patients in difficult situations, covering the many needs that cannot be addressed within the confines of a hospital's operating budget, like co-pays, eyeglasses and hearing aids, and transportation costs.
Financial data: Year ended 12/31/2011. Assets, $17,281,436 (M); Expenditures, $9,389,399; Total giving, $8,539,736; Grants to individuals, 1,850 grants totaling $116,009.
Fields of interest: Economically disadvantaged.
Type of support: In-kind gifts; Grants for special needs.
Application information:
Initial approach: Letter
Additional information: Contact foundation for eligibility criteria.
EIN: 841085196

1182
Denver Rescue Mission
3501 E. 46th Ave.
Denver, CO 80216-4214   (303) 297-1815
Contact: Brad Meuli, Pres. and C.E.O.
FAX: (303) 295-1566; E-mail: info@denrescue.org; E-Mail for Brad Meuli : bmeuli@denrescue.org; URL: http://www.denverrescuemission.org

Foundation type: Public charity
Purpose: Assistance towards shelter, food, clothing, and education to indigent residents of the Denver, CO metropolitan area.
Publications: Financial statement.
Financial data: Year ended 06/30/2012. Assets, $20,613,898 (M); Expenditures, $24,029,096; Total giving, $9,458,418; Grants to individuals, totaling $9,357,985.
Type of support: Grants for special needs.
Application information:
Initial approach: Letter
Additional information: Contact the mission for eligibility criteria.
EIN: 846038762

1183
Denver Young Artists Orchestra
1245 E. Colfax Ave., Ste. 302
Denver, CO 80218-2216   (303) 433-2420
Contact: Peter Hellyer, Exec. Dir.
E-mail: info@dyao.org; E-Mail for Peter Hellyer: Pete@dyao.org; URL: http://www.dyao.org

Foundation type: Public charity
Purpose: Scholarships and educational assistance to orchestra members based on financial need.
Financial data: Year ended 06/30/2012. Assets, $571,347 (M); Expenditures, $473,323; Total giving, $20,514; Grants to individuals, totaling $20,514.
Fields of interest: Orchestras.
Type of support: Scholarships—to individuals.
Application information: Application form required. Application form available on the grantmaker's web site.
Initial approach: E-mail
Deadline(s): Apr. 23 and May 4
Additional information: Contact the orchestra for audition application. See web site for additional information on scholarship awards and competition.
EIN: 840809348

1184
Douglas County Educational Foundation
(also known as DCEF)
620 Wilcox St.
Castle Rock, CO 80104-1739   (303) 387-0505
Contact: Sean B. McGraw, Exec. Dir.; Susan Meek, Dir., Opers.
E-mail for Professional Development Grants: DCEFApps@dcsdk12.org
FAX: (303) 387-0519;
E-mail: sean.mcgraw@dcsdk12.org; URL: http://schools.dcsdk12.org/dcef

Foundation type: Public charity
Purpose: Scholarships to graduates of Eagle Academy, CO, and one student per Douglas County high school, CO. Grants to teachers of Douglas County School District, CO, for attendance at job-related seminars or workshops.
Publications: Application guidelines; Annual report; Financial statement; Grants list; Newsletter.
Financial data: Year ended 06/30/2011. Assets, $2,622,822 (M); Expenditures, $5,999,180; Total giving, $1,317,777; Grants to individuals, totaling $1,317,777.
Fields of interest: Education.
Type of support: Conferences/seminars; Support to graduates or students of specific schools; Undergraduate support.
Application information: Applications accepted. Application form required.
Deadline(s): Nov. for teacher grants
Additional information: Unsolicited requests for funds not considered or acknowledged for scholarships. Budget and essay are required for teacher grants.
Program descriptions:
MFF Matching Grants - 21st Century Classroom/ Reading Plus Grants: Awarded in conjunction with the Morgridge Family Foundation and Mile High United Way, grants will be made available to Colorado educators to increase the reading proficiency of their students. Grants must be matched on a 1:1 basis with funds from other sources.
Professional Development Funds: Grants are available to Douglas County School District employees (excluding administrators) to support staff development through attending job-related

seminars or workshops, bringing in guest speakers/presenters, and providing funding for registration fees, books, travel, lodging, and/or speaker fees. Grants of up to $200 will be awarded to individuals, and grants of up to $500 will be awarded for groups of three or more.

Responsible Citizen Grants: Grants will be awarded to programs that allow Douglas County School District students to acquire the knowledge and abilities needed to become responsible citizens who contribute to society. Grants should address one or more of the following: critical thinking; universal ethical principles; self-motivation; the application of learning; leadership skills; and student ownership/responsibility for well-being.
EIN: 841165175

1185
Durango Foundation for Educational Excellence
201 E. 12th St.
Durango, CO   81301-5206   (970) 385-1491
Contact: Elizabeth Testa, Exec. Dir.
FAX: (970) 375-3999; E-mail: info@dfee.net; E-mail For Elizabeth Testa: 9RFoundation@gmail.com;
URL: http://www.dfee.net/index.html

Foundation type: Public charity
Purpose: Scholarships to graduating seniors of Durango High School, Big Picture High School and DeNier Center pursuing higher education.
Financial data: Year ended 12/31/2012. Assets, $922,805 (M); Expenditures, $128,646; Total giving, $83,703; Grants to individuals, totaling $11,700.
Fields of interest: Higher education.
Type of support: Scholarships—to individuals; Support to graduates or students of specific schools.
Application information: Applications accepted. Application form required.
Send request by: Mail
Deadline(s): Apr. 1
Additional information: The foundation manages several scholarships, each with unique criteria. See web site for a listing of the scholarships and additional application guidelines, or your high school guidance counselors. Payments will be made directly to the educational institution on behalf of the students.
EIN: 742350944

1186
Eagle Foundation
6600 Simms St.
Arvada, CO   80004-2598

Foundation type: Independent foundation
Purpose: Scholarships to high school graduates for attendance at the University of Iowa for postsecondary education.
Financial data: Year ended 12/31/2012. Assets, $0 (M); Expenditures, $8,322; Total giving, $5,500.
Fields of interest: Higher education.
Type of support: Scholarships—to individuals; Support to graduates or students of specific schools.
Application information: Applications accepted. Application form required. Interview required.
Deadline(s): Apr. 1
Applicants should submit the following:
1) Essay
2) Transcripts

3) SAT
4) ACT
5) Letter(s) of recommendation
Additional information: Essay should not exceed 500 words.
EIN: 841480907

1187
Eagle River Scholarship Fund, Inc.
P.O. Box 5850
Avon, CO   81620   (970) 845-8800
Contact: Kerry Donovan, Pres.

Foundation type: Independent foundation
Purpose: Scholarships to graduating seniors of Eagle County high schools, CO pursuing postsecondary education.
Financial data: Year ended 12/31/2011. Assets, $321,730 (M); Expenditures, $11,794; Total giving, $8,000; Grants to individuals, 2 grants totaling $8,000 (high: $6,000, low: $2,000).
Fields of interest: Higher education.
Type of support: Scholarships—to individuals; Support to graduates or students of specific schools.
Application information: Applications accepted. Application form required.
Send request by: On-line
Applicants should submit the following:
1) SAT
2) Essay
3) Transcripts
4) ACT
Additional information: Application should also include student's identification number and proof of enrollment.
EIN: 840745716

1188
East Angel Friends and Alumni Foundation
(formerly East High Angel Foundation)
P.O. Box 201404
Denver, CO   80220-1404   (720) 423-8433
URL: http://www.eastangelfriends.org

Foundation type: Public charity
Purpose: Scholarships for graduating seniors of East High School in Denver, CO pursuing postsecondary education at accredited colleges of universities.
Financial data: Year ended 06/30/2012. Assets, $290,298 (M); Expenditures, $319,177; Total giving, $72,500; Grants to individuals, totaling $72,500.
Fields of interest: Higher education.
Type of support: Scholarships—to individuals; Support to graduates or students of specific schools.
Application information: Applications not accepted.
Additional information: Scholarships are for East High School students only. Unsolicited requests for funds not considered or acknowledged.
EIN: 320069773

1189
EDUCAUSE
282 Century Pl., Ste. 5000
Louisville, CO   80027-1694   (303) 449-4430
FAX: (303) 440-0461; E-mail: info@educause.edu;
URL: http://www.educause.edu

Foundation type: Public charity

Purpose: Awards by nomination only to professionals in higher education information technology management, and to authors of articles in EDUCAUSE Quarterly. Also, fellowships to staff at institutions of higher education, and to information technology professionals to attend EDUCAUSE events.
Publications: Application guidelines.
Financial data: Year ended 12/31/2011. Assets, $29,544,096 (M); Expenditures, $34,925,899; Total giving, $17,753,048.
Fields of interest: Management/technical assistance; Research; Computer science.
Type of support: Fellowships; Awards/grants by nomination only; Awards/prizes.
Application information:
Deadline(s): Oct. 1 for Jane N. Ryland Fellowship Program, varies for all others
Program descriptions:
Diane Balestri Memorial Scholarship: This scholarship helps women who have never attended an organization-sponsored Seminar on Academic Computing to come to the meeting and join larger information technology communities.
EDUCAUSE Leadership Awards: The award acknowledges and celebrates leadership within and of higher education information technology, and recognizes prominent professionals whose work has had significant positive impact on advancing the theory and practice of information technology in higher education. Eligible candidates must be, or have been, contributing members of the information technology professional community, directly associated with managing information technology and resources in higher education, and individuals who have made significant and demonstrable contributions to the field. Award recipients are recognized at the organization's annual conference and receive complimentary registration, travel, and housing for the conference. In addition, contributions are made to a scholarship fund of the recipient's choice in the amount of $3,000.
Paul Evan Peters Award: This award recognizes individual achievements in the creation and use of information resources that advance scholarship and intellectual productivity through communication networks. Recipients of this award will receive a commemorative award and will be asked to present a major address at one of the Coalition for Networked Information (CNI) membership meetings. The winner will receive travel and housing expenses for the meeting.
EIN: 841455437

1190
EI Charitable Foundation
19750 E. Parker Square Dr., Ste. 100
Parker, CO   80134-7302   (720) 851-1717
Contact: Nirav Shah, Pres.
E-mail: info@eitek.com; URL: http://www.eicharity.org/

Foundation type: Company-sponsored foundation
Purpose: Scholarships to economically disadvantaged residents of the Denver, CO metropolitan area.
Financial data: Year ended 09/30/2013. Assets, $169,577 (M); Expenditures, $515; Total giving, $500.
Fields of interest: Education; Economically disadvantaged.
Type of support: Undergraduate support; Grants for special needs.
Application information:
Initial approach: Letter
Deadline(s): None
EIN: 841569279

1191
Maria Elizondo Scholarship Trust
144 South Uncompahgre Ave.
Montrose, CO   81402   (970) 249-4531

Foundation type: Independent foundation
Purpose: Scholarships to individuals in the top 10 percent of the graduating classes of Mesa and Montrose County high schools, CO.
Financial data: Year ended 06/30/2013. Assets, $1,425,130 (M); Expenditures, $52,241; Total giving, $46,500; Grants to individuals, 4 grants totaling $46,500 (high: $12,500, low: $9,000).
Type of support: Support to graduates or students of specific schools; Undergraduate support.
Application information: Applications accepted. Application form required.
> *Deadline(s):* Mar. 21
> *Applicants should submit the following:*
>   1) Class rank
>   2) Transcripts
>   3) SAT
>   4) ACT
EIN: 846328479

1192
The Ethridge Scholarship Foundation
P.O. Box 2087
Centennial, CO   80161-2087

Foundation type: Independent foundation
Purpose: Scholarships to Denver, CO, female high school seniors for teacher education programs.
Financial data: Year ended 06/30/2013. Assets, $463,019 (M); Expenditures, $32,206; Total giving, $28,000; Grants to individuals, 8 grants totaling $28,000 (high: $4,000, low: $2,000).
Fields of interest: Teacher school/education; Women.
Type of support: Support to graduates or students of specific schools.
Application information: Applications accepted. Application form required. Interview required.
> *Initial approach:* Letter
> *Deadline(s):* Mar. 1
> *Applicants should submit the following:*
>   1) Class rank
>   2) Essay
>   3) Transcripts
>   4) SAT
>   5) GPA
>   6) ACT
>   7) Letter(s) of recommendation
> *Additional information:* Applications must also include extracurricular activities, community activities, record of employment and income tax returns for parents/students.
EIN: 841270799

1193
Evergreen Christian Outreach
P.O. Box 1515
Evergreen, CO   80437-1515   (303) 670-1796
Contact: Sharon Smith, Exec. Dir.
FAX: (303) 679-2721;
E-mail: info@echo-evergreen.org; E-mail for Sharon Smith: sharon@echo-evergreen.org; URL: http://www.evergreenchristianoutreach.org/

Foundation type: Public charity
Purpose: Financial assistance to families and individuals in need in Evergreen, Colorado and the surrounding area with food, clothing, utilities and other needs.
Financial data: Year ended 12/31/2012. Assets, $349,256 (M); Expenditures, $1,380,834; Total

giving, $662,094; Grants to individuals, totaling $662,094.
Fields of interest: Human services; Economically disadvantaged.
Type of support: Emergency funds; Grants for special needs.
Application information: Applications accepted. Application form not required.
EIN: 742539728

1194
Federal Employee Education and Assistance Fund
(also known as FEEA)
3333 S. Wadsworth Blvd., Ste. 300
Lakewood, CO   80227-5122   (303) 933-7580
Contact: Steve Bauer, Exec. Dir.
Toll free for emergency assistance: (800) 323-4140
FAX: (303) 933-7587; E-mail: admin@feea.org;
URL: http://www.feea.org

Foundation type: Public charity
Purpose: Merit-based scholarships to federal employees and their dependents and special scholarships to children who lost a federal employee parent in terrorists attacks. Also, grants and no-interest loans to federal employees in need with basic necessities in catastrophic situation and personal emergencies.
Publications: Application guidelines.
Financial data: Year ended 04/30/2012. Assets, $4,111,569 (M); Expenditures, $1,680,643; Total giving, $812,510; Grants to individuals, totaling $812,510.
Fields of interest: Higher education.
Type of support: Employee-related scholarships; Grants for special needs.
Application information: Applications accepted. Application form required.
> *Deadline(s):* Mar. 27 for Scholarships
> *Final notification:* Oct. 31
> *Applicants should submit the following:*
>   1) Transcripts
>   2) SASE
>   3) SAT
>   4) Letter(s) of recommendation
>   5) Essay
>   6) ACT
> *Additional information:* Scholarship applicants are selected based on academic and extracurricular accomplishments. Financial assistance is need-based on a case-by-case basis. See web site for additional application information.
EIN: 521465583

1195
Flatirons Foundation
P.O. Box 4058
Edwards, CO   81632

Foundation type: Operating foundation
Purpose: Scholarships to graduates of Aspen High School, CO for postsecondary education.
Financial data: Year ended 12/31/2012. Assets, $322,214 (M); Expenditures, $16,225; Total giving, $15,500.
Fields of interest: Higher education.
Type of support: Support to graduates or students of specific schools; Undergraduate support.
Application information: Applications accepted. Application form required.
> *Initial approach:* Letter
> *Deadline(s):* May 1

Additional information: Application should include financial information.
EIN: 840563062

1196
Food Bank of the Rockies
10700 E. 45th St.
Denver, CO   80239-2906   (303) 371-9250
Contact: Kevin Seggelke, Pres. and C.E.O.
FAX: (301) 371-9259;
E-mail: kseggelke@foodbankrockies.org; Toll-free tel.: (877) 460-8504; URL: http://www.foodbankrockies.org

Foundation type: Public charity
Purpose: Food and essential non-food items to needy families in northern Colorado and Wyoming.
Publications: Annual report; Informational brochure; Newsletter; IRS Form 990 or 990-PF printed copy available upon request.
Financial data: Year ended 06/30/2012. Assets, $20,375,274 (M); Expenditures, $58,324,146; Total giving, $8,492,780; Grants to individuals, totaling $2,180,518.
Fields of interest: Food banks; Economically disadvantaged.
Type of support: In-kind gifts.
Application information: Application form not required.
> *Initial approach:* Tel.
EIN: 840772672

1197
Fort Lewis College Foundation, Inc.
1000 Rim Dr.
Durango, CO   81301-3999   (970) 247-7121
Contact: Margie Deane Gray, Exec. Dir.
FAX: (970) 247-7175;
E-mail: foundation@fortlewis.edu; E-mail For Margie Deane Gray: gray_m@fortlewis.edu; URL: http://www.fortlewis.edu/foundation/home.aspx

Foundation type: Public charity
Purpose: Provides scholarships for students of Fort Lewis College and funds for the school's academics, cultural programs and facilities. Scholarships offered for a variety of different subjects and interests.
Financial data: Year ended 06/30/2012. Assets, $21,718,274 (M); Expenditures, $3,273,590; Total giving, $851,738; Grants to individuals, totaling $851,738.
Type of support: Scholarships—to individuals.
Application information: Applications accepted. Application form required. Application form available on the grantmaker's web site.
> *Initial approach:* application
> *Deadline(s):* Feb. 15
> *Additional information:* See web site for full list of scholarships.
EIN: 237122114

1198
Foundation for Educational Excellence
4908 Tower Rd., Ste. 108
Denver, CO   80249-6684   (303) 486-8500
Contact: Eric Montoya, Secy.-Treas.
FAX: (303) 843-0745

Foundation type: Independent foundation
Purpose: Scholarships to residents of the northeastern Denver, CO, area.
Publications: Informational brochure; Occasional report.

Financial data: Year ended 12/31/2012. Assets, $533,656 (M); Expenditures, $4,948,689; Total giving, $4,780,512.
Type of support: Technical education support; Undergraduate support.
Application information:
  Deadline(s): Vary
  Additional information: Contact foundation for current application guidelines.
EIN: 841396597

1199
Foundation for Women's Wellness
1000 S. Race St.
Denver, CO 80209-4613   (303) 548-0595
Contact: Sharon Cravitz, Exec. Dir.
FAX: (303) 744-7759; E-mail: info@thefww.org;
URL: http://www.thefww.org

Foundation type: Public charity
Purpose: Research grants for the study of women's health.
Publications: Application guidelines.
Financial data: Year ended 12/31/2012. Assets, $1,085,321; Expenditures, $49,466.
Fields of interest: Health care; Medical research; Women; Adults, women.
Type of support: Research; Grants to individuals.
Application information:
  Initial approach: E-mail
  Deadline(s): Dec. 20
  Additional information: Application must include curriculum vitae. Contact foundation for eligibility requirements.
EIN: 133944997

1200
Front Range Community College Foundation
3645 W. 112th Ave.
Westminster, CO 80031-2105   (303) 404-5463
FAX: (303) 466-1623; URL: http://www.frontrange.edu/About-Us/Foundation/

Foundation type: Public charity
Purpose: Scholarships to students who are currently attending or are planning to attend Front Range Community College.
Publications: Application guidelines; Annual report; Newsletter.
Financial data: Year ended 06/30/2012. Assets, $1,834,517 (M); Expenditures, $699,634; Total giving, $317,813; Grants to individuals, totaling $317,813.
Fields of interest: College (community/junior); Scholarships/financial aid.
Type of support: Support to graduates or students of specific schools; Undergraduate support.
Application information: Applications accepted. Application form required. Application form available on the grantmaker's web site.
  Initial approach: Download application form
EIN: 841311148

1201
Galaway Foundation
2104 CR, Ste. 127
Penrose, CO 81240
Application address: 3337 W. 114th Cir., Unit A, Wesminster, CO 80031-7172, tel.: (303) 438-1454
URL: http://galawayfoundation.org/

Foundation type: Independent foundation

Purpose: Scholarship to students with outstanding leadership potential for attendance at any four year college or university in the U.S. or Canada.
Financial data: Year ended 12/31/2012. Assets, $478,127 (M); Expenditures, $41,510; Total giving, $34,038; Grants to individuals, 3 grants totaling $34,038 (high: $16,388, low: $6,860).
Fields of interest: Higher education.
Type of support: Scholarships—to individuals; Graduate support; Undergraduate support.
Application information: Applications accepted. Application form required. Application form available on the grantmaker's web site.
  Send request by: E-mail or online
  Applicants should submit the following:
    1) Transcripts
    2) Financial information
  Additional information: Funds will be paid directly to the educational institution on behalf of the students. Successful applicants are expected to live in a college dormitory.
Program description:
  Scholarship: The maximum scholarship is $12,755 per academic year for students for tuition, fees including health insurance, and dormitory and meal charges. The scholarship will assist students who have demonstrated leadership and academic potential to secure higher education at an American or Canadian university. The program is intended for students unable to attend or continue college due to lack of economic resources. Applications for graduate study will be considered from students who have previously been awarded a Galaway Foundation scholarship for undergraduate study.
EIN: 841487248

1202
John R. Garone-Nicksich Foundation
37 Calle Del Sol
Pueblo, CO 81008

Foundation type: Independent foundation
Purpose: Scholarships to Pueblo, CO high school seniors for continuing education at institutions of higher learning.
Financial data: Year ended 12/31/2013. Assets, $388,537 (M); Expenditures, $19,764; Total giving, $19,500; Grants to individuals, 3 grants totaling $1,500 (high: $500, low: $500).
Fields of interest: Education.
Type of support: Scholarships—to individuals.
Application information: Applications accepted. Application form required.
  Deadline(s): Oct. 1
  Additional information: Application forms may be obtained from the foundation.
EIN: 841164914

1203
The Gathering Place: A Refuge for Rebuilding Lives
1535 High St.
Denver, CO 80218-1704   (303) 321-4198
Contact: Leslie Foster, Pres. and C.E.O.
FAX: (303) 321-0679;
E-mail: samantha@the-gatheringplace.org;
URL: http://www.the-gatheringplace.org

Foundation type: Public charity
Purpose: Temporary shelter and other emergency services are available for women and children facing homelessness.
Publications: Newsletter.
Financial data: Year ended 09/30/2011. Assets, $7,948,886 (M); Expenditures, $3,084,617; Total

giving, $675,237; Grants to individuals, totaling $675,237.
Fields of interest: Housing/shelter, temporary shelter; Women, centers/services.
Type of support: Grants to individuals.
Application information: Applications not accepted.
EIN: 841021059

1204
Girl Scouts of Colorado
400 S. Broadway
P.O. Box 9407
Denver, CO 80209-1518   (303) 778-8774
Contact: Stephanie Foote, Pres.
FAX: (303) 733-6345;
E-mail: inquiry@gscolorado.org; Toll-free tel.: (866) 827-7033; E-mail For Stephanie Foote: stephanie.foote@gscolorado.org; URL: http://www.girlscoutsofcolorado.org

Foundation type: Public charity
Purpose: Need-based financial assistance is available for girls and adults who do not have the funds needed to participate in the Girl Scout program. Funds are available for summer camps, troop camping, dues, handbooks, uniform, insignia and council-sponsored events.
Publications: Annual report.
Financial data: Year ended 09/30/2012. Assets, $26,741,152 (M); Expenditures, $12,779,307; Total giving, $136,175; Grants to individuals, totaling $136,175.
Fields of interest: Girl scouts; Girls.
Type of support: Grants for special needs.
Application information: Applications accepted. Application form required. Application form available on the grantmaker's web site.
  Additional information: See web site for additional information.
EIN: 840410630

1205
Goodwill Industries of Denver
6850 Federal Blvd.
Denver, CO 80221-2628   (303) 650-7700
Contact: Stuart Davie, C.E.O.
FAX: (303) 650-7783;
E-mail: contactus@goodwilldenver.org; URL: http://www.goodwilldenver.org

Foundation type: Public charity
Purpose: Scholarships for at-risk students in CO.
Publications: Newsletter.
Financial data: Year ended 12/31/2011. Assets, $55,152,730 (M); Expenditures, $50,103,870; Total giving, $43,688; Grants to individuals, totaling $43,688.
Fields of interest: Economically disadvantaged.
Type of support: Scholarships—to individuals.
Application information:
  Initial approach: Letter
  Additional information: Contact foundation for complete eligibility requirements.
EIN: 840405513

1206
The Griffin Foundation, Inc.
303 W. Prospect Rd.
Fort Collins, CO 80526-2003   (970) 482-3030
Contact: David L. Wood, Chair. and Treas.
FAX: (970) 484-6648;
E-mail: carol.wood@thegriffinfoundation.org;
URL: http://www.thegriffinfoundation.org

Foundation type: Independent foundation
Purpose: Scholarships to students who have an associate degree or at least sixty academic hours from a junior or community college and are seeking to complete a baccalaureate degree and are attending Colorado State University (Fort Collins campus), the University of Northern Colorado or the University of Wyoming (Laramie campus)
Publications: Application guidelines.
Financial data: Year ended 12/31/2012. Assets, $3,082,057 (M); Expenditures, $977,585; Total giving, $700,643.
Fields of interest: Higher education.
Type of support: Undergraduate support.
Application information: Applications accepted. Application form required. Application form available on the grantmaker's web site.
  Deadline(s): Mar. 1
  Applicants should submit the following:
    1) Transcripts
    2) Letter(s) of recommendation
  Additional information: See web site for complete information on eligibility.
EIN: 841171483

1207
Gunnison Council for the Arts
102 S. Main St.
P.O. Box 1772
Gunnison, CO   81230-1772   (970) 641-4029
Contact: Jon Schumacher, Pres.
E-mail: gcarts@gunnison.cc; URL: http://www.gunnisonartscenter.org

Foundation type: Public charity
Purpose: Scholarships to residents of Gunnison County, CO for higher education.
Publications: Application guidelines.
Financial data: Year ended 12/31/2011. Assets, $1,055,665 (M); Expenditures, $311,323; Total giving, $2,936; Grants to individuals, totaling $2,936.
Fields of interest: Arts; Scholarships/financial aid.
Type of support: Scholarships—to individuals.
Application information: Applications accepted. Application form required. Application form available on the grantmaker's web site.
  Send request by: Hand deliver
  Deadline(s): None
  Additional information: Application should include a personal letter stating the reason(s) for tuition assistance. Preference will be given to members of Gunnison Arts Center. Recipients are required to submit an evaluation at the end of the class. Failure to do so will disqualify the recipient from future scholarship support.
Program description:
  Scholarships: The council provides scholarships to individuals who live in Gunnison County who wish to attend classes through the council, but who cannot afford class fees. Recipients will be selected based on economic need (generally speaking, an annual income of under $30,000, although there may be other circumstances affecting economic need), personal goals, and a personal interview with a member of the center staff, if determined to be necessary.
EIN: 742325340

1208
H.E.L.P. International
629 SW 14th
Loveland, CO   80534   (303) 678-7788
E-mail: info@helpint.org; Toll-free tel.: (800) 955-9444; additional address: 629 14th St., S.W., Loveland, CO 80537-6329, tel.: (970) 224-2233; URL: http://helpint.org

Foundation type: Public charity
Purpose: Assistance with mission trips, an outreach project, or specific indigent individuals in CO.
Publications: Newsletter.
Financial data: Year ended 12/31/2011. Assets, $44,489 (M); Expenditures, $7,943,723; Total giving, $7,396,185; Grants to individuals, totaling $402,071.
Fields of interest: Religion; Economically disadvantaged.
Type of support: Travel awards; In-kind gifts; Grants for special needs.
Application information:
  Initial approach: Tel.
    Additional information: Call Don Wilson at (303) 523-2720 for eligibility criteria.
EIN: 841531749

1209
Maudean & E. L. Hanson Foundation
P.O. Box 131
Beulah, CO   81023-0131   (719) 485-3172

Foundation type: Independent foundation
Purpose: Scholarships to residents of Pueblo County, CO, attending a university, college, community college or junior college within CO.
Financial data: Year ended 02/28/2013. Assets, $898,781 (M); Expenditures, $42,802; Total giving, $41,550; Grants to individuals, 14 grants totaling $40,800 (high: $3,400, low: $1,700).
Type of support: Support to graduates or students of specific schools; Undergraduate support.
Application information: Application form required.
  Initial approach: Letter
  Deadline(s): June 1 for fall semester, Nov. 15 for spring semester
  Applicants should submit the following:
    1) Transcripts
    2) Letter(s) of recommendation
  Additional information: Application should also include information about academic achievements and school activities.
EIN: 841150453

1210
O. J. & Mary Christine Harvey Educational Foundation
(formerly The Foundation for Educational Advancement)
435 S. 68th St.
Boulder, CO   80303-4308

Foundation type: Independent foundation
Purpose: Scholarships to students in CO or OK, for higher education.
Financial data: Year ended 12/31/2012. Assets, $1,035,282 (M); Expenditures, $68,582; Total giving, $61,000; Grants to individuals, 16 grants totaling $61,000 (high: $5,500, low: $2,500).
Type of support: Undergraduate support.
Application information: Applications not accepted.
  Additional information: Unsolicited requests for funds not considered.
EIN: 841441530

1211
Hasan Family Foundation
1607 N. Elizabeth St.
Pueblo, CO   81003
Contact: Seeme Hasan, Chair.
URL: http://www.hasanfamilyfoundation.com

Foundation type: Independent foundation
Purpose: Fellowships to individuals for environmental research.
Financial data: Year ended 11/30/2012. Assets, $661,544 (M); Expenditures, $205,719; Total giving, $104,550.
Fields of interest: Environment.
Type of support: Fellowships.
Application information: Applications accepted. Application form not required.
  Initial approach: Letter
  Send request by: Mail
  Copies of proposal: 1
  Deadline(s): None
  Additional information: Contact the foundation additional information.
EIN: 841289731

1212
Bettye Heathcock Accordance
25 N. Cascade, Ste. 200
Colorado Springs, CO   80903-1643

Foundation type: Operating foundation
Purpose: Scholarships to students of St. Mary's High School and Immanuel Lutheran School of Colorado Springs, CO for higher education.
Financial data: Year ended 12/31/2012. Assets, $307,018 (M); Expenditures, $34,353; Total giving, $32,625.
Fields of interest: Education.
Type of support: Support to graduates or students of specific schools.
Application information:
  Deadline(s): Spring
EIN: 421578361

1213
Helmar Skating Fund
1228 15th St., Ste. 309
Denver, CO   80202-2122

Foundation type: Independent foundation
Purpose: Grants to U.S. Figure Skating Association recognized amateur ice skaters to help cover the costs of coaching fees and rink rental expenses.
Financial data: Year ended 06/30/2013. Assets, $891,051 (M); Expenditures, $162,692; Total giving, $161,898; Grants to individuals, 11 grants totaling $161,898 (high: $35,954, low: $4,906).
Fields of interest: Athletics/sports, winter sports.
Type of support: Grants to individuals.
Application information: Applications not accepted.
  Additional information: Unsolicited requests for funds not considered or acknowledged.
EIN: 841032757

1214
R. B. Holt Foundation
(formerly R. B. Holt Corporate Foundation)
c/o David Fowler
P.O. Box 370434
Denver, CO   80237-0434   (303) 758-7813
Application Address: c/o R.B. Holt Foundation

Foundation type: Independent foundation

Purpose: Scholarships to graduating seniors of public high schools in Baca County, CO.
Financial data: Year ended 12/31/2012. Assets, $194,779 (M); Expenditures, $7,940; Total giving, $6,000; Grants to individuals, 2 grants totaling $6,000 (high: $3,000, low: $3,000).
Type of support: Support to graduates or students of specific schools; Undergraduate support.
Application information: Application form not required.
> *Initial approach:* Letter
> *Copies of proposal:* 1
> *Deadline(s):* Apr. 1
> *Applicants should submit the following:*
> 1) Transcripts
> 2) SAT
> 3) GPA
> 4) ACT
> *Additional information:* Application should also include work history and community services.
EIN: 846036673

1215
Housing Resources of Western Colorado
524 30 Rd., Ste. 3
Grand Junction, CO   81504-4437   (970) 241-2871
Contact: Peter Robinson, Pres.
FAX: (970) 245-4853;
E-mail: mailbox@housingresourceswc.org;
URL: http://www.housingresourceswc.org

Foundation type: Public charity
Purpose: Affordable housing, home ownership, maintenance and repair for residents with low and moderate incomes in western Colorado.
Publications: Application guidelines.
Financial data: Year ended 06/30/2012. Assets, $10,125,219 (M); Expenditures, $4,010,047; Total giving, $31,660.
Fields of interest: Housing/shelter, development; Housing/shelter, repairs.
Type of support: Grants for special needs.
Application information: Applications accepted. Application form required. Application form available on the grantmaker's web site.
> *Additional information:* See web site for additional information.
Program descriptions:
Housing Rehabilitation Program: Low-interest loans are available for the rehabilitation of owner-occupied homes, for required home repairs (such as roof repair, plumbing, electrical work, and painting) and room additions. Applicants must qualify for loans based on home ownership and income. Loans are unavailable for the repair of outbuildings, fences, or garages.
Self-Help Housing: This 'sweat-equity' home building program provides new construction of single-family homes on subdivision lots for home buyers that earn a low to moderate income; the 'sweat equity' from the owners helps to substantially reduce down payments. Local contractors are used for the site development and construction, such as concrete work, framing, plumbing, heating, electrical wiring, and sheet rock. Eligible individuals must be 18 years of age or older, meet income and credit guidelines, and be willing to work 30 or more hours per week, with a 15-hour-minimum commitment per homeowner, with other hours potentially coming from family and friends (including a few hours each weekday evening, and Saturdays during the day)
Weatherization Program: This program provides funds towards such energy savings measures as furnace turn-ups or replacements, air infiltration reduction, insulation improvements, storm

windows, window replacements, and refrigerator replacements for renters and homeowners in Archuleta, Delta, Delores, Gunnison, Hinsdale, Mesa, Montrose, Ouray, San Juan, and San Miguel counties. Eligible households must have an income at or below 185 percent of federal poverty levels.
EIN: 840879892

1216
Charles J. Hughes Foundation
5890 Drifter St.
Colorado Springs, CO   80918-5250

Foundation type: Independent foundation
Purpose: Scholarships to students with learning disabilities, primarily those who live in CO.
Financial data: Year ended 08/31/2012. Assets, $432,944 (M); Expenditures, $1,368; Total giving, $0.
Fields of interest: Learning disorders.
Type of support: Scholarships—to individuals.
Application information: Applications accepted.
> *Initial approach:* Letter
> *Additional information:* Application must outline financial need.
EIN: 841148636

1217
A. V. Hunter Trust, Inc.
650 S. Cherry St., Ste. 535
Glendale, CO   80246-1897   (303) 399-5450
Contact: Barbara Howie, Exec. Dir
FAX: (303) 399-5499;
E-mail: barbarahowie@avhuntertrust.org;
URL: http://www.avhuntertrust.org

Foundation type: Independent foundation
Purpose: Financial assistance by nomination only from social service workers for economically disadvantaged legal residents of CO.
Publications: Application guidelines; Grants list.
Financial data: Year ended 12/31/2012. Assets, $56,710,136 (M); Expenditures, $3,412,278; Total giving, $2,484,440; Grants to individuals, 503 grants totaling $486,200.
Fields of interest: Human services; Economically disadvantaged.
Type of support: Grants for special needs.
Application information: Applications accepted. Application form required. Application form available on the grantmaker's web site.
> *Initial approach:* Telephone
> *Send request by:* Mail or e-mail
> *Copies of proposal:* 1
> *Final notification:* Applicants notified within one month
> *Additional information:* Application should include financial information. All payments are made directly to the vendor/provider after all conditions are met. See web site for additional application guidelines.
EIN: 840461332

1218
I Have a Dream Foundation of Boulder County
3012 Sterling Cir., Ste. 200
Boulder, CO   80301-2332   (303) 444-3636
FAX: (303) 444-3838;
E-mail: info@ihaveadreamboulder.org; URL: http://www.ihadboulder.org

Foundation type: Public charity

Purpose: Tuition assistance to low-income and at-risk students in the Boulder Valley School District for college or vocational school.
Financial data: Year ended 12/31/2011. Assets, $4,331,789 (M); Expenditures, $1,241,877.
Fields of interest: Vocational education, post-secondary; Higher education.
Type of support: Scholarships—to individuals.
Application information: Contact foundation for additional guidelines.
EIN: 841150542

1219
Impact on Education
(formerly Foundation for Boulder Valley Schools)
728 Front St., Ste. A
Louisville, CO   80027-1801   (303) 524-3865
Contact: Fran Ryan, C.E.O.
FAX: (303) 524-3867;
E-mail: info@impactoneducation.org; URL: http://www.impactoneducation.org

Foundation type: Public charity
Purpose: Scholarships to graduating high school young men and women of CO, pursuing a college degree.
Publications: Application guidelines; Annual report.
Financial data: Year ended 05/31/2012. Assets, $1,300,697 (M); Expenditures, $785,522; Total giving, $412,359; Grants to individuals, totaling $412,359.
Fields of interest: Higher education.
Type of support: Scholarships—to individuals; Support to graduates or students of specific schools.
Application information: Applications accepted. Application form required. Application form available on the grantmaker's web site.
> *Send request by:* Mail
> *Deadline(s):* Varies
> *Applicants should submit the following:*
> 1) Transcripts
> 2) Letter(s) of recommendation
> 3) Essay
> *Additional information:* Students should contact their respective high school counselor for additional application information, or see web site for additional application guidelines.
Program descriptions:
Gould-Foothill Scholarship: This scholarship awards $1,500 per year for four years to one male and one female Boulder high school graduate and must pursue a degree as an elementary school teacher.
Impact Awards: This program recognizes individuals in the Boulder Valley School District who have an extraordinary impact on student learning by valuing education, service to students, and leadership by example. Classroom teachers, specialists, administrators, classified employees, and volunteers are nominated by the community in the early fall.
Sally Smyth Scholarship: This scholarship annually provides a qualifying Boulder High School senior with a four-year scholarship of $5,000 per year to cover educational expenses at a liberal arts college.
EIN: 840943046

1220
Jeffco Action Center, Inc.
8755 W. 14th Ave.
P.O. Box 150609
Lakewood, CO   80215-4863   (303) 237-7704
FAX: (303) 237-6002;
E-mail: office@theactioncenterco.org; E-Mail for
Mag Strittmatter: mags@theactioncenterco.org;
URL: http://theactioncenterco.org/

Foundation type: Public charity
Purpose: Financial assistance to indigent residents
of Jefferson County, CO, for the payment of utilities,
food, clothing, housing, transportation, and medical
bills.
Publications: Newsletter.
Financial data: Year ended 06/30/2012. Assets,
$5,850,726 (M); Expenditures, $9,907,952; Total
giving, $7,156,829; Grants to individuals, totaling
$7,156,829.
Type of support: Grants for special needs.
Application information:
   Initial approach: Letter or e-mail
   Additional information: All applicants must meet
   with the center's Emergency Services
   Counselor. Contact the center for application
   guidelines.
EIN: 237019679

1221
The Jefferson Foundation
809 Quail St., Bldg. No. 1
Lakewood, CO   80215-5587   (303) 982-2210
Contact: Katie Tiernan, Exec. Dir.
FAX: (303) 982-2209;
E-mail: info@jeffersonfoundation.org; E-mail for
Katie Tiernan:
katietiernan@jeffersonfoundation.org; URL: http://
www.jeffersonfoundation.org/

Foundation type: Public charity
Purpose: Scholarships to graduating seniors of
Jeffco public schools, CO for study at an accredited
two or four year college or university pursuing an
associates or bachelors degree.
Publications: Application guidelines; Informational
brochure.
Financial data: Year ended 06/30/2012. Assets,
$826,513 (M); Expenditures, $865,305; Total
giving, $480,007. Scholarships—to individuals
amount not specified.
Fields of interest: Higher education.
Type of support: Scholarships—to individuals;
Support to graduates or students of specific
schools.
Application information: Applications accepted.
Application form required.
   Send request by: Mail or hand deliver
   Deadline(s): Apr. 7
   Applicants should submit the following:
      1) Essay
      2) Transcripts
      3) Letter(s) of recommendation
      4) Financial information
   Additional information: A variety of scholarships
   are available to students from Jeffco public
   schools. Each scholarship has different
   eligibility criteria. See web site for additional
   guidelines.
Program descriptions:
   Christopher Faughnan Memorial Scholarship: The
   scholarship provides one-time scholarships of
   $3,000 to reward Arvada High School graduating
   seniors (no required GPA) and give them an
   opportunity to further their education at accredited
   nonprofit colleges or universities. The scholarship
   is intended to help students further their

aspirations to create a better world. Selection will
be based on the applicant's personal character,
academic achievement and community service.
   Dee Reed Teaching Scholarship: This $1,000
   one-time scholarship rewards well-rounded
   graduating Wheat Ridge High School seniors with a
   2.5 GPA unweighted, who demonstrate community
   service and who have a passion for pursuing higher
   education and teaching as a career. Extra
   consideration is given to students who demonstrate
   financial need.
   Jeffco Schools Community Scholarship: This
   $1,000 one-time scholarship rewards graduating
   seniors from any Jeffco public high school with a 3.0
   GPA unweighted, who demonstrate extraordinary
   leadership and service, and who have changed their
   communities for the better. Extra consideration is
   given to students who demonstrate financial need.
   *Jefferson County Retired School Employees
   Association(JCRSEA) Scholarship:* This one-time
   scholarship of $2,000 recognizes and rewards
   well-rounded graduating seniors from any Jeffco
   public high schools with a 3.0 GPA unweighted.
   Selected students will demonstrate perseverance,
   responsibility, integrity, enthusiasm and
   inquisitiveness. Extra consideration is given to
   students who demonstrate financial need.
   Lillian LaFleur Scholarship: This one-time
   scholarship of $1000 rewards at least one
   outstanding student, who has studied Spanish
   during high school, from any Jeffco public high
   school with a 3.0 GPA unweighted, with an
   opportunity to further his or her education. Selected
   students will have taken Advanced Placement
   Spanish and will have been members of their
   school's Spanish Club or will have demonstrated a
   love of the Spanish language.
   Rebel Character in Athletics Scholarship: The
   scholarship provides one-time awards of $2,500 to
   one male and to one female varsity athlete
   graduating from Columbine High School with a 3.0
   GPA unweighted, who exhibit character and
   leadership in athletics and in the classroom. Extra
   consideration will be given to students who
   overcome adversity.
   *Wheat Ridge High School 50th Anniversary
   Scholarship Fund:* The scholarship provides
   one-time $1,000 scholarships to well-rounded
   graduating Wheat Ridge High School seniors (must
   be in upper 75 percent of graduating class or be
   nominated by a school counselor) who demonstrate
   character, school and community service, work
   experience and who demonstrate financial need.
   *Wheat Ridge Optimists Carl A. Cervany
   Scholarship:* This scholarship awards two one-time
   $1,000 scholarships to recognize well-rounded
   graduating Jefferson High School and Wheat Ridge
   High School seniors (must be in upper 50 percent
   of graduating class by unweighted GPA) who have
   made an outstanding contribution to their school or
   community. Primary consideration will be given to
   students who have demonstrated service and
   leadership in school and community activities and
   who can demonstrate work experience. Selected
   students must be U.S. citizens.
EIN: 840970315

1222
Jewish Family Service of Colorado, Inc.
Joyce and Kal Zeff Bldg.
3201 S. Tamarac Dr.
Denver, CO   80231-4394   (303) 597-5000
FAX: (303) 597-7700;
E-mail: jfc@jewishfamilyservice.org; Additional
address: 3800 Kalmia Ave., Boulder, CO
80301-1827; URL: http://jewishfamilyservice.org/

Foundation type: Public charity
Purpose: Emergency assistance to low income
individuals and families in need throughout the
greater Denver, CO area.
Publications: Annual report; Newsletter.
Financial data: Year ended 06/30/2011. Assets,
$12,869,535 (M); Expenditures, $8,761,959;
Total giving, $1,111,389; Grants to individuals,
5,690 grants totaling $448,690. Subtotal for
in-kind gifts: grants totaling $581,209. Subtotal for
emergency funds: 4,989 grants totaling $98,140.
Subtotal for grants for special needs: 701 grants
totaling $350,550.
Fields of interest: Human services; Aging;
Disabilities, people with; Economically
disadvantaged.
Type of support: Emergency funds; In-kind gifts;
Grants for special needs.
Application information: Contact the organization
for eligibility determination.
EIN: 840402701

1223
Johns Manville Fund, Inc.
(formerly Schuller Fund, Inc.)
717 17th St.
Denver, CO   80217

Foundation type: Company-sponsored foundation
Purpose: Educational grants for dependent children
of full time Johns Manville employees.
Financial data: Year ended 12/31/2012. Assets,
$65,341 (M); Expenditures, $26,574; Total giving,
$25,325.
Type of support: Employee-related scholarships.
Application information: Application form required.
   Initial approach: Application
   Deadline(s): None
Company name: Johns Manville Corporation
EIN: 136034039

1224
Kaiser Foundation, Inc.
6751 Lupine Cir.
Arvada, CO   80007-7075   (307) 587-3075
Contact: Joseph V. Pomajzl
Additional address: 3407 Sandbak Ave., Cody, WY
82414; URL: http://www.kaiserfoundatininc.com

Foundation type: Independent foundation
Purpose: Scholarships to WY high school
graduates.
Financial data: Year ended 12/31/2012. Assets,
$3,810,745 (M); Expenditures, $199,191; Total
giving, $135,000; Grants to individuals, 45 grants
totaling $135,000 (high: $3,000, low: $3,000).
Type of support: Support to graduates or students
of specific schools; Undergraduate support.
Application information: Applications accepted.
Application form required.
   Deadline(s): Mar. 15
EIN: 840278210

1225
Kennedy Foundation
P.O. Box 621609
Littleton, CO   80162   (303) 933-8942
Contact: P. David Kennedy, Pres.
Application address: P.O. Box 27296, Denver, CO
80227

Foundation type: Independent foundation
Purpose: Scholarships to high school students who
are residents of CO.

Financial data: Year ended 06/30/2013. Assets, $601,521 (M); Expenditures, $32,186; Total giving, $24,558.
Type of support: Undergraduate support.
Application information: Applications accepted. Application form required.
  Initial approach: Letter
  Deadline(s): June 30
EIN: 840748729

1226
Keren America
245 S. Benton St., Ste. 100
Lakewood, CO 80226-2459
Contact: David Sebbag, Exec. Dir.

Foundation type: Independent foundation
Purpose: Assistance to economically disadvantaged individuals for living expenses.
Financial data: Year ended 11/30/2012. Assets, $456,874 (M); Expenditures, $67,670; Total giving, $66,702; Grant to an individual, 1 grant totaling $66,702.
Fields of interest: Economically disadvantaged.
Type of support: Grants for special needs.
Application information: Application form not required.
  Deadline(s): None
EIN: 841527140

1227
William C. Kuzell Foundation
(formerly Fund for Arthritis and Infectious Disease Research)
4155 S. University Blvd.
Englewood, CO 80113 (415) 600-1734
Contact: Lowell S. Young, Pres. and Treas.
Application address: 2200 Webster St., R305, San Francisco, CA, 94115, tel.: (415) 600-1734

Foundation type: Independent foundation
Purpose: Research grants for post doctoral fellows at Kuzell Institute, CA.
Financial data: Year ended 10/31/2011. Assets, $792,671 (M); Expenditures, $43,161; Total giving, $30,000.
Fields of interest: Arthritis.
Type of support: Research.
Application information: Applications accepted.
  Deadline(s): July 1 and Jan. 1
  Additional information: Application should include curriculum vitae.
EIN: 942985482

1228
Bonnie Langston Memorial Scholarship Trust
c/o Victor Roushar
144 S. Uncompahgre Ave.
Montrose, CO 81401 (970) 249-4531

Foundation type: Operating foundation
Purpose: Scholarships to graduates of Montrose High School, CO, who are in the top twenty-five percent of their graduating class.
Financial data: Year ended 12/31/2012. Assets, $363,652 (M); Expenditures, $4,126; Total giving, $14,000; Grants to individuals, 2 grants totaling $14,000 (high: $7,000, low: $7,000).
Type of support: Support to graduates or students of specific schools; Undergraduate support.
Application information: Application form required.
  Deadline(s): Prior to end of school year.
  Applicants should submit the following:
    1) SAT

2) Transcripts
3) Letter(s) of recommendation
4) ACT
EIN: 846268159

1229
Lasater Scholarship Foundation
7780 McFerran Rd.
Colorado Springs, CO 80908-4396 (719) 495-3432
Contact: Sally W. Lasater, Pres. and Dir.
Application address: P.O. Box 88122, Colorado Springs, CO 80908-8122 tel.: (719) 495-3432

Foundation type: Independent foundation
Purpose: Scholarships to graduates of Simla High School, Elbert county, CO to continue post secondary education at colleges or universities.
Financial data: Year ended 09/30/2013. Assets, $264,162 (M); Expenditures, $44,794; Total giving, $9,000; Grants to individuals, 5 grants totaling $9,000 (high: $2,000, low: $1,000).
Fields of interest: Higher education.
Type of support: Support to graduates or students of specific schools.
Application information: Applications accepted. Application form required.
  Deadline(s): Apr. 1
  Applicants should submit the following:
    1) SAT
    2) Class rank
    3) Letter(s) of recommendation
    4) GPA
    5) ACT
EIN: 840902070

1230
Edna A. Layton Scholarship Fund
P.O. Box 1159
Longmont, CO 80502-1159 (303) 776-5800

Foundation type: Independent foundation
Purpose: Scholarships to graduates of Saint Vrain district high schools, CO, to pursue a teaching career.
Financial data: Year ended 03/31/2013. Assets, $586,533 (M); Expenditures, $33,106; Total giving, $24,800; Grants to individuals, 16 grants totaling $24,800 (high: $1,600, low: $800).
Fields of interest: Teacher school/education.
Type of support: Support to graduates or students of specific schools; Undergraduate support.
Application information: Applications accepted. Application form required.
  Initial approach: Letter
  Deadline(s): Mar.
  Additional information: Applicants should submit an essay.
EIN: 841494001

1231
Light Ranch at Old Snowmass Charitable Trust, Inc.
c/o Steven H. Lampman
818 Colorado Ave.
P.O. Box 790
Glenwood Springs, CO 81602
Application Address: c/o Basalt High School Scholarship Committee

Foundation type: Independent foundation
Purpose: Scholarships to graduating seniors of Basalt High School, CO for at least two semesters at an accredited college or university with a

minimum 3.0 GPA to be maintained during the first semester of study.
Financial data: Year ended 12/31/2012. Assets, $1,025,872 (M); Expenditures, $62,819; Total giving, $51,000; Grants to individuals, 15 grants totaling $51,000 (high: $6,000, low: $2,000).
Fields of interest: Higher education.
Type of support: Support to graduates or students of specific schools; Undergraduate support.
Application information: Application form required.
  Applicants should submit the following:
    1) Transcripts
    2) Letter(s) of recommendation
    3) Essay
  Additional information: Applicant must be gainfully employed during the summer breaks.
EIN: 841420992

1232
The Lillis Foundation
P.O. Box 1479
Castle Rock, CO 80104
E-mail: glillis@lillisfoundation.org; URL: http://lillysfoundation.org/

Foundation type: Independent foundation
Purpose: Scholarships to underprivileged youth, and grants to economically disadvantaged residents of the Denver, CO, area.
Financial data: Year ended 12/31/2012. Assets, $4,471,307 (M); Expenditures, $111,724; Total giving, $74,551; Grants to individuals, 17 grants totaling $51,510 (high: $5,000, low: $1,000).
Fields of interest: Education; Economically disadvantaged.
Type of support: Scholarships—to individuals; Grants for special needs.
Application information: Unsolicited requests for funds not considered or acknowledged.
EIN: 916520620

1233
Logan County Nurses Scholarship Association
P.O. Box 1306
Sterling, CO 80751-1306 (970) 522-6210
Contact: Mary Sutter, Pres.
Application address: 831 Elwood St., Sterling, CO 80751, tel.: (970) 522-6210

Foundation type: Operating foundation
Purpose: Scholarships to students who reside in Logan, Morgan, Phillips, Sedgwick, Washington, or Yuma counties, CO pursuing a career in nursing.
Financial data: Year ended 06/30/2011. Assets, $113,215 (M); Expenditures, $1,630; Total giving, $1,500; Grants to individuals, 3 grants totaling $1,500 (high: $500, low: $500).
Fields of interest: Nursing school/education.
Type of support: Scholarships—to individuals.
Application information: Applications accepted. Application form required.
  Deadline(s): Apr. 1
  Applicants should submit the following:
    1) Transcripts
    2) Letter(s) of recommendation
    3) Essay
  Additional information: Application should also include three references (only one of which may be from a school administrator), and a letter of acceptance from the nursing/specialized medical department of the college or university (if available). Payments are made directly to the educational institution on behalf of the student.
EIN: 840736731

1234
The Lupus Foundation of Colorado, Inc.
1211 S. Parker Rd., Ste. 103
Denver, CO 80231-2155 (303) 597-4050
Contact: Skip Schlenk, C.E.O.
FAX: (303) 597-4054;
E-mail: info@lupuscolorado.org; Toll-free tel.:
(800)-858-1292; URL: http://
www.lupuscolorado.org

Foundation type: Public charity
Purpose: Emergency assistance to individuals with Lupus who are residents of CO, for payments to landlords, physicians, pharmacy, and utility assistance.
Publications: Informational brochure; Newsletter.
Financial data: Year ended 09/30/2011. Assets, $366,445 (M); Expenditures, $245,963; Total giving, $20,300; Grants to individuals, totaling $20,300.
Fields of interest: Human services.
Type of support: Emergency funds; Grants for special needs.
Application information: Utility assistance is paid directly to the respective vendor/service provider.
EIN: 840763686

1235
Lutheran Social Service of Colorado
363 S. Harlan St., Ste. 200
Denver, CO 80226-3552 (303) 922-3433
Contact: James Barclay, Pres. and C.E.O.
FAX: (303) 922-7335; E-mail: info@lfsco.org;
Toll-free tel.: (800) 579-9496; URL: http://
www.lfsco.org

Foundation type: Public charity
Purpose: Assistance to individuals and families of CO, by providing homes, foster care services, refugee services, support to aging adults and other special needs.
Publications: Annual report; Financial statement; Informational brochure; Newsletter.
Financial data: Year ended 06/30/2012. Assets, $3,190,177 (M); Expenditures, $10,957,335; Total giving, $3,322,369; Grants to individuals, totaling $3,322,369.
Fields of interest: Human services; Adoption; Foster care; Family services, counseling; International migration/refugee issues; Aging.
Type of support: Grants to individuals; Grants for special needs.
Application information: Applications not accepted.
EIN: 840775550

1236
Muriel L. MacGregor Charitable Trust
P.O. Box 4675
Estes Park, CO 80517

Foundation type: Operating foundation
Purpose: Scholarships to graduating seniors of Estes Park High School, CO, who are also residents of Estes Park.
Financial data: Year ended 12/31/2012. Assets, $22,795,006 (M); Expenditures, $325,340; Total giving, $4,500; Grants to individuals, 5 grants totaling $4,500 (high: $1,000, low: $500).
Fields of interest: Higher education.
Type of support: Support to graduates or students of specific schools; Undergraduate support.
Application information: Application form required. Interview required.
> *Initial approach:* Letter

Additional information: Contact the trust for additional guidelines.
EIN: 846154601

1237
Stephen T. Marchello Scholarship Foundation
1170 E. Long Pl.
Centennial, CO 80122-3020 (303) 886-5018
E-mail: fmarchello@earthlink.net; URL: http://
www.stmfoundation.org

Foundation type: Public charity
Purpose: Scholarships to high school seniors of CO and MT who are survivors of childhood cancer.
Publications: Application guidelines; Annual report; Annual report (including application guidelines); Financial statement; Grants list.
Financial data: Year ended 12/31/2012. Assets, $45,201 (M); Expenditures, $15,742; Total giving, $14,175.
Fields of interest: Higher education.
Type of support: Scholarships—to individuals.
Application information: Applications accepted. Application form required. Application form available on the grantmaker's web site.
> *Initial approach:* Application
> *Send request by:* Fax, mail, or e-mail
> *Copies of proposal:* 1
> *Deadline(s):* Mar. 15
> *Final notification:* Recipients notified within four months
> *Applicants should submit the following:*
> 1) Transcripts
> 2) SAT
> 3) Letter(s) of recommendation
> 4) Essay
> 5) ACT

EIN: 841491959

1238
Bryan Merry Basketball Scholarship Fund
2203 Delwood Ave.
Durango, CO 81301-4826 (970) 247-3031
Contact: Duane R. Merry, Pres.

Foundation type: Independent foundation
Purpose: Scholarships to members of the girls and boys basketball and golf teams at Durango High School, CO.
Financial data: Year ended 03/31/2013. Assets, $255,305 (M); Expenditures, $13,353; Total giving, $10,986; Grants to individuals, 5 grants totaling $10,986 (high: $2,500, low: $1,986).
Fields of interest: Higher education; Athletics/sports, basketball; Athletics/sports, golf.
Type of support: Support to graduates or students of specific schools.
Application information:
> *Deadline(s):* Mar. 31
> *Additional information:* Scholarships are awarded on attitude, desire, and academic and athletic excellence.

EIN: 742251706

1239
The Mikkelson Foundation
17665 Minglewood Trail
Monument, CO 80132-8421
Application address: Scholarship Committee, P.O. Box 768, Monument, CO 80132-0768
URL: http://www.mikkelson.com

Foundation type: Independent foundation

Purpose: Scholarships for CO graduating high school seniors pursuing a career in engineering, mathematics, and/or science at an accredited college or university.
Financial data: Year ended 09/30/2013. Assets, $1,742,018 (M); Expenditures, $119,532; Total giving, $110,150; Grants to individuals, 10 grants totaling $30,000 (high: $3,000, low: $3,000).
Fields of interest: Mathematics; Engineering/technology; Science.
Type of support: Scholarships—to individuals; Graduate support; Undergraduate support.
Application information: Applications accepted. Application form required. Application form available on the grantmaker's web site.
> *Send request by:* Mail
> *Deadline(s):* Apr. 27
> *Applicants should submit the following:*
> 1) Transcripts
> 2) Essay
> *Additional information:* Application should also include three references.

EIN: 841519112

1240
Minority Enterprise & Educational Development
(also known as MEED)
6740 E. Hampden Ave., Ste. 106
Denver, CO 80224 (303) 296-2969
FAX: (303) 592-1596;
E-mail: info@meedcolorado.org; URL: http://
www.meedcolorado.org

Foundation type: Public charity
Purpose: Scholarships for disadvantaged youth in the Denver, CO area.
Publications: Annual report.
Financial data: Year ended 12/31/2011. Assets, $263,610 (M); Expenditures, $60,688; Total giving, $18,128.
Fields of interest: Higher education; Youth; Minorities.
Type of support: Scholarships—to individuals.
Application information: Applications not accepted.
> *Additional information:* Unsolicited requests for funds not considered or acknowledged.

EIN: 841347391

1241
Mary Molloy Scholarship Fund
P.O. Box 179
Loveland, CO 80539-0179 (214) 965-2908
Contact: Colleen D. Pritchett
Application address: c/o University of Colorado-Boulder 77 UCB, Boulder, CO 80309

Foundation type: Independent foundation
Purpose: Scholarships to graduates of Loveland and Thompson Valley high schools, CO, for higher education.
Financial data: Year ended 12/31/2012. Assets, $264,003 (M); Expenditures, $7,948; Total giving, $1,000; Grant to an individual, 1 grant totaling $1,000.
Type of support: Support to graduates or students of specific schools; Undergraduate support.
Application information:
> *Initial approach:* Letter
> *Additional information:* Contact fund for current application deadline/guidelines.

EIN: 846214213

1242
Morgan Family Foundation
P.O. Box 1121
Conifer, CO 80433

Foundation type: Independent foundation
Purpose: Scholarships to needy individuals who are residents of CO or Sonora, Mexico, pursuing higher education.
Financial data: Year ended 12/31/2012. Assets, $1,228,933 (M); Expenditures, $118,094; Total giving, $101,260; Grants to individuals, 2 grants totaling $32,260 (high: $17,260, low: $15,000).
Fields of interest: Higher education.
Type of support: Scholarships—to individuals.
Application information: Applications accepted. Application form required. Interview required.
> *Applicants should submit the following:*
> 1) Transcripts
> 2) SAT
> 3) Essay
> 4) Letter(s) of recommendation
> 5) ACT
> *Additional information:* Selection is based on merit and educational and financial need. Awards will be sent directly to the educational institution on behalf of the students upon proof of enrollment.

EIN: 841364137

1243
Morris Animal Foundation
10200 E. Girard Ave., Ste. B430
Denver, CO 80231-5510 (303) 790-2345
Contact: David Haworth, Pres. and C.E.O.
FAX: (303) 790-4066; Toll-free tel.: (800) 243-2345; URL: http://www.morrisanimalfoundation.org

Foundation type: Public charity
Purpose: Veterinary student scholarships, fellowships and awards, by nomination only, to researchers specializing in companion animal or wildlife research, and veterinary student scholarships.
Publications: Application guidelines; Annual report; Informational brochure; Newsletter (including application guidelines).
Financial data: Year ended 06/30/2012. Assets, $78,298,011 (M); Expenditures, $11,738,610; Total giving, $7,440,902; Grants to individuals, totaling $23,693.
Fields of interest: Veterinary medicine.
Type of support: Fellowships; Scholarships—to individuals; Awards/grants by nomination only; Doctoral support.
Application information: Application form required. Application form available on the grantmaker's web site.
> *Initial approach:* Pre-proposal
> *Send request by:* Online
> *Copies of proposal:* 4
> *Deadline(s):* Apr. 5 for Veterinary Student Scholar, mid-July for Large Companion Animal, Mar. for Small Companion Animal and Mid-Nov. for Wildlife
> *Additional information:* See web site for additional information.

Program descriptions:
> *Established Investigator Awards:* These awards are given to seasoned researchers with a published track record in research. Grants will be awarded in the following categories: large companion animals (including horses and llamas/alpacas), wildlife, and small companion animals (including dogs and cats)
> *Fellowship Training Grants:* This grant opportunity provides salary support for training opportunities

that will produce biomedical scientists (veterinarian and/or Ph.D.) committed to a career in companion animal and/or wildlife research. All pre-doctoral students are eligible for funding, though post-DVM, post-residency, or post-Ph.D. applicants will be given preference; all applicants must not have completed more than two years of post-doc training. Funding will be awarded for two years at a maximum of $50,000 per year, with up to an additional 8 percent for indirect costs.
> *First Award:* This program offers veterinary and/or doctoral (Ph.D.) investigators research opportunities early in their career by providing funding for their 'first' projects as principal investigator in companion animal or wildlife research, and pairing them with a 'seasoned' researcher to facilitate launching a successful, long-term scientific career in advancing companion animal and wildlife health. Eligible applicants must be post-DVM, post-Ph.D., and/or post-specialty board; and must have a post-doctoral career appointment (or equivalent faculty position) in a university, accredited zoo, or conservation organization. Funding will be given for two years at up to $50,000 per year, with an additional maximum of 8 percent for indirect costs.
> *Veterinary Student Scholars Program:* This program works to give veterinary students hands-on involvement in research early in their career, so they will consider entering the veterinary field where they are so critically needed. Through this program, veterinary students or non-veterinary graduate students receive stipends of up to $4,000 to participate in clinical or basic animal health and/or welfare research. Applicants devote a minimum of 50 percent of their time to the project for the equivalent of a ten to twelve week period. Eligible applicants must be nominated by their dean of research or equivalent, be in good academic standing, and be paired with a responsible mentor; students enrolled in a combined D.V.M./Ph.D. degree program, or a Ph.D. degree program, are eligible as long as they are not receiving concurrent stipend support at the time of their intended research. Scholars will also be invited to one of three foundation meetings held each year, where they will present their work to foundation-affiliated scientific advisers and trustees and compete for cash awards.

EIN: 846032307

1244
Mountain Protective Association Scholarship Fund
P.O. Box 253
Evergreen, CO 80437-0253 (303) 838-7082
Application address: P.O. Box 1121, Conifer, CO 80433

Foundation type: Independent foundation
Purpose: Scholarships to graduates of Evergreen High School or Conifer High School, CO (mountain area), for postsecondary education.
Financial data: Year ended 06/30/2013. Assets, $143,325 (M); Expenditures, $5,116; Total giving, $3,000.
Fields of interest: Higher education.
Type of support: Scholarships—to individuals; Support to graduates or students of specific schools.
Application information: Applications accepted. Application form required.
> *Send request by:* Mail
> *Deadline(s):* Aug.
> *Additional information:* Contact the association for application guidelines.

EIN: 237457169

1245
The Louis K. Mulford Scholarship Foundation
3 Brassie Way
Littleton, CO 80123 (303) 797-6733
Contact: Joyce Latham, Tr.

Foundation type: Independent foundation
Purpose: Scholarships to graduates of Littleton High School, CO with tuition and fees for higher education.
Financial data: Year ended 12/31/2012. Assets, $348,093 (M); Expenditures, $38,258; Total giving, $24,000; Grants to individuals, 8 grants totaling $24,000 (high: $4,000, low: $2,000).
Fields of interest: Higher education; Scholarships/financial aid.
Type of support: Scholarships—to individuals; Support to graduates or students of specific schools; Undergraduate support.
Application information: Applications accepted. Application form required. Interview required.
> *Initial approach:* Letter
> *Deadline(s):* Apr. 15
> *Additional information:* Application should include letters of recommendation and letter explaining request and outlining qualifications.

EIN: 237398275

1246
Music Associates of Aspen, Inc.
2 Music School Rd.
Aspen, CO 81611-8500 (970) 925-3254
Contact: Mimi Teschner, Dir., Devel.
FAX: (970) 920-3802;
E-mail: mimi@aspenmusic.org; URL: http://www.aspenmusicfestival.com

Foundation type: Public charity
Purpose: Scholarship and fellowship to students of Aspen, CO who exhibit financial need and musical talent.
Financial data: Year ended 09/30/2011. Assets, $66,791,111 (M); Expenditures, $14,035,128; Total giving, $1,986,714; Grants to individuals, totaling $208,124.
Fields of interest: Arts education; Music; Orchestras.
Type of support: Fellowships; Scholarships—to individuals.
Application information: Applications accepted. Application form available on the grantmaker's web site.
> *Initial approach:* Application
> *Additional information:* See web site for additional application guidelines.

Program description:
> *Scholarships and Fellowships:* The organization provides scholarship and fellowship support to student participants in its programs. Scholarships are awarded based on a combination of talent and financial need, and range from partial to full tuition. All students who apply for financial assistance will be considered for scholarship. Fellowships are merit-based and are awarded based either on a live audition or a recorded application and cover full tuition, room, and board in school housing.

EIN: 840445087

1247
National Council on Education for the Ceramic Arts
(also known as N.C.E.C.A.)
77 Erie Village Sq., Ste. 280
Erie, CO   80516-6996   (303) 828-2811
Contact: Josh Green, Exec. Dir.
FAX: (303) 828-0911; E-mail: office@nceca.net;
Toll-free tel.: (866) 266-2322; E-Mail For Josh
Green: josh@nceca.net; URL: http://
www.nceca.net

Foundation type: Public charity
Purpose: Fellowships to full-time graduate and undergraduate students in the field of ceramic arts.
Publications: Application guidelines; Newsletter.
Financial data: Year ended 06/30/2012. Assets, $1,922,651 (M); Expenditures, $1,099,139.
Fields of interest: Ceramic arts.
Type of support: Fellowships; Graduate support; Undergraduate support.
Application information: Applications accepted. Application form required. Application form available on the grantmaker's web site.
  Deadline(s): Nov. 15
  Applicants should submit the following:
    1) Transcripts
    2) Letter(s) of recommendation
  Additional information: Application must also include CD with exactly 10 images of recent work. Nomination form should be submitted online. Self nominations are encouraged, with two letters of support from teachers.
Program descriptions:
  NCECA Graduate Student Fellowships: Annual awards of $2,000 each are available to full-time graduate students who are matriculated in a degree program at an accredited college, university, or art institute in the U.S. Proposals must include a detailed outline of what will be done with the awards; funds cannot be used to pay for tuition. Eligible applicants must be members of the council.
  Regina Brown Undergraduate Student Fellowships: Scholarships of $1,800 each to full-time undergraduate students matriculated at a degree program at an accredited college, university, or art institute in the U.S., and who have attained the classification of at least a junior or its equivalent. Proposals must detail projects to be undertaken with the award; funds cannot be used toward tuition. Eligible applicants must be members of the council.
EIN: 310932682

1248
National Foundation, Inc.
2925 Professional Pl., Ste. 201
Colorado Springs, CO   80904-8136   (719) 447-4620
FAX: (719) 447-4700;
E-mail: nfi@thefoundations.org; URL: http://waterstone.org/

Foundation type: Public charity
Purpose: Scholarship awards for high school students. Financial assistance to American and foreign applicants for ministry support.
Publications: Financial statement; Informational brochure; Newsletter; Program policy statement.
Financial data: Year ended 03/31/2012. Assets, $3,253 (M); Expenditures, $5,541.
Fields of interest: Christian agencies & churches.
Type of support: Scholarships—to individuals; Foreign applicants; Grants for special needs.
Application information: Applications not accepted.
EIN: 541230512

1249
Sadie G. Newland Trust in Memory of Anna L. Frinrock
c/o American National Bank
3033 E. 1st Ave.
Denver, CO   80206-5617   (303) 394-5128

Foundation type: Independent foundation
Purpose: Scholarships to graduating high school seniors from Richmond Senior High School, Richmond, IN pursuing higher education.
Financial data: Year ended 04/30/2013. Assets, $172,451 (M); Expenditures, $10,940; Total giving, $8,000; Grants to individuals, 2 grants totaling $8,000 (high: $4,000, low: $4,000).
Fields of interest: Higher education.
Type of support: Scholarships—to individuals; Support to graduates or students of specific schools.
Application information: Applications accepted. Application form required.
  Additional information: Application should include two letters of reference.
EIN: 846315126

1250
Nine Health Services, Inc.
1139 Delaware St.
Denver, CO   80204-3607   (303) 698-4455
Contact: Rory Donaldson, Dir., Devel.
FAX: (303) 698-4450;
E-mail: rory.donaldson@9healthfair.org; Toll-free tel.: (800) 332-3078; URL: http://www.9healthfair.org

Foundation type: Public charity
Purpose: Scholarships of $1,000 awards for In the Classroom student leaders in CO.
Publications: Application guidelines; Annual report; Financial statement; Newsletter; Occasional report.
Financial data: Year ended 12/31/2011. Assets, $7,792,710 (M); Expenditures, $5,429,280; Total giving, $166,015.
Fields of interest: Higher education.
Type of support: Undergraduate support.
Application information:
  Initial approach: Letter
Program description:
  Alan D. Laff Scholarships: The organization offers scholarships of $1,000 each to outstanding student leaders who help to successfully implement its In the Classroom health program throughout Colorado schools. Eligible applicants must: be attending a middle or high school and are ages 13 to 18; demonstrate involvement in school, community, and extracurricular activities; plan to attend a college upon graduation; and have maintained a minimum GPA of 3.0.
EIN: 742452969

1251
North Colorado Medical Center Foundation, Inc.
1801 16th St.
Greeley, CO   80631-5199   (970) 356-9020
Contact: Chris Kiser, Pres.
FAX: (970) 350-6723;
E-mail: ncmcfoundation@bannerhealth.com; E-mail for Chris Kiser: chris.kiser@bannerhealth.com; URL: http://www.ncmcfoundation.org

Foundation type: Public charity
Purpose: Scholarships to individuals in the community and employees of the North Colorado Medical Center, CO pursuing a career in health care.
Publications: Application guidelines; Annual report; Newsletter; Quarterly report.
Financial data: Year ended 12/31/2011. Assets, $14,910,943 (M); Expenditures, $2,988,975; Total giving, $1,436,535; Grants to individuals, totaling $53,718.
Fields of interest: Nursing school/education.
Type of support: Scholarships—to individuals.
Application information: Applications accepted. Application form required. Application form available on the grantmaker's web site. Interview required.
  Send request by: Mail or hand deliver
  Deadline(s): Mar. 28
  Applicants should submit the following:
    1) Letter(s) of recommendation
    2) Transcripts
    3) Resume
    4) Essay
  Additional information: Selection is based on academic achievement and promise, extra curricular activities and financial need.
Program descriptions:
  Belle M. Loustalet Memorial Nursing Scholarship: This scholarship is for candidates who are accepted into an accredited nursing program with plans to complete a bachelor's or associate's degree in nursing.
  Florence Winograd Educational Scholarship: This scholarship annually recognizes a group of individuals working at North Colorado Medical Center who exemplify excellence in teamwork. A NCMC Team must consist of at least one R.N. and two other employees working together to solve a problem and improve patient care.
  Hansen Nursing Program: This scholarship is awarded annually to a non-traditional student over the age of 25, who is pursuing a bachelor's or master's degree in nursing through courses offered at the University of Northern Colorado. Applicants must have been accepted into the nursing program at UNC. The two year scholarship provides tuition, reimbursement for books and nursing supplies, and a living expense stipend.
  Hansen Nursing Scholarship: This scholarship is open to non-traditional students age 25 or older who is returning to college to pursue a bachelor's or master's degree in nursing through courses offered at the University of Northern Colorado. Applicants must hold a bachelor's degree in a subject other than nursing and have been accepted into the nursing program at UNC. This two year scholarship covers the cost of tuition, books, nursing supplies, and a stipend for living expenses.
  Hansen Nursing Tuition Scholarship: This scholarship is open to any Weld County high school seniors planning to pursue a nursing degree. During the first two years of college, this scholarship covers the cost of in-state tuition and books; during the second two years, it covers these costs in addition to paying student fees and providing a stipend for living expenses. Applicants must be a resident of Weld County, in their senior year of high school, and planning on pursuing a degree in nursing. Applicants must also be a citizen of the U.S.
  Lily E. Widney Memorial Nursing Scholarship: This scholarship is available to assist employees at North Colorado Medical Center in obtaining an associate's or bachelor's of science degree in nursing. Applicants must have been accepted into an approved nursing program.
  NCMC Foundation Surgical Tech: This scholarship is awarded to individuals studying for an Associate's Degree of Applied Science in Surgical Technology through courses at Aims Community College. The scholarship provides assistance with tuition, program fees, and textbooks.

Nurse Education Tuition Assistance: This scholarship provides up to $1,500 to individuals studying to obtain a B.S. degree in nursing, to assist with tuition expenses. Applicants must have been accepted into an approved nursing program and must agree to seek work as a nurse at the North Colorado Medical Center upon completion of their degree.

Unfulfilled Scholastic Achievement (USA) Scholarship: This scholarship is open to employees or family members of current or former employees working in housekeeping or custodial positions for the North Colorado Medical Center, for the purpose of assisting these individuals in furthering or completing their education. Applicants must be an employee or a family member of a current or retired employee working in a custodial position for the North Carolina Medical Center, accumulated a minimum of 24 hours of post-high school course credit, and be furthering or completing education at a college, university, community college, or trade school. Applicants must also be a citizen of the U.S.

Volunteers Scholarship: This scholarship provides individuals the opportunity to become a certified nurse's assistant through courses offered at Aims Community College.
EIN: 840718355

1252
The Norwood Foundation
P.O. Box 792
Manitou Springs, CO 80829-0792
Contact: Christopher S. Jenkins, Secy.-Treas.
Application tel.: (719) 593-2600

Foundation type: Independent foundation
Purpose: Scholarships to worthy Colorado High School graduates pursuing a course of study or instruction at an accredited college or university for undergraduate or graduate degrees.
Financial data: Year ended 02/28/2012. Assets, $7,943 (M); Expenditures, $971,305; Total giving, $971,080.
Fields of interest: Higher education.
Type of support: Support to graduates or students of specific schools.
Application information: Applications accepted. Application form required.
  Applicants should submit the following:
    1) SAT
    2) GPA
    3) ACT
    4) Transcripts
    5) Letter(s) of recommendation
  Additional information: Application must also include two references from high school teachers or counselor, and one reference from high school superintendent or principal.
EIN: 010705471

1253
Operation Game Thief, Inc.
6060 Broadway
Denver, CO 80216-1029 (303) 291-7342
Contact: Bob Thompson
E-mail: robert.thompson@state.co.us

Foundation type: Operating foundation
Purpose: Grants to individuals who provide information that results in citation for violation of CO wildlife regulations.
Financial data: Year ended 12/31/2012. Assets, $152,887 (M); Expenditures, $31,677; Total giving, $9,550.
Fields of interest: Animals/wildlife, preservation/protection.

Type of support: Grants to individuals.
Application information: Applications accepted. Application form not required.
  Deadline(s): None
EIN: 742188212

1254
Outcalt Foundation
815 4th St.
Alamosa, CO 81101-2526 (719) 589-0155
Contact: Angela Lobato, Tr.
Application address: P.O. Box 1925, Alamosa, CO 81101

Foundation type: Independent foundation
Purpose: Scholarships to high school graduates of Colorado enrolled at accredited colleges or universities for higher education.
Financial data: Year ended 12/31/2011. Assets, $962,110 (M); Expenditures, $99,477; Total giving, $49,000.
Fields of interest: Higher education.
Type of support: Scholarships—to individuals.
Application information: Applications accepted. Application form required.
  Deadline(s): Mar. 15
EIN: 207432649

1255
Outreach United Resource Center, Inc.
303 Atwood St.
Longmont, CO 80501-5514 (303) 772-5529
Contact: Edwina Salazar, Exec. Dir.
URL: http://www.ourcenter.org/

Foundation type: Public charity
Purpose: Emergency assistance to low income individuals and families of Longmont, CO with food, shelter, clothing and other basic needs, and low cost child care services for those in need.
Publications: Application guidelines; Annual report; Newsletter.
Financial data: Year ended 06/30/2013. Assets, $3,050,707 (M); Expenditures, $3,542,229; Total giving, $167,125; Grants to individuals, totaling $167,125.
Fields of interest: Economically disadvantaged.
Type of support: Emergency funds; Grants for special needs.
Application information: Contact the center for need of assistance.
EIN: 742448346

1256
Pathways to Spirit
4307 Goldeneye Dr.
Fort Collins, CO 80526-3662 (970) 282-3819
Contact: Carmeen Klausner, Pres.
E-mail: pathwaystospirit@comcast.net;
URL: http://www.pathwaystospirit.org

Foundation type: Public charity
Purpose: Financial assistance to indigent families and individuals in SD, with food, clothing, shelter, utilities and other basic needs. Scholarship to a deserving student who shows interest in pursuing studies in drug and alcohol rehabilitation for youth on the reservations.
Publications: Newsletter.
Financial data: Year ended 12/31/2012. Assets, $27,943; Expenditures, $143,138; Total giving, $136,808.
Fields of interest: Education; Native Americans/American Indians; Economically disadvantaged.

Type of support: Scholarships—to individuals; Grants for special needs.
Application information: Applications accepted.
  Initial approach: Letter for scholarship
  Additional information: Letter should include applicant's educational and future goals.
EIN: 841363370

1257
Pikes Peak Community Action Agency, Inc.
P.O. Box 2468
Colorado Springs, CO 80901 (719) 385-7910
Contact: John Tighe, C.E.O.
E-mail: admin@ppcaa.org; URL: http://www.ppcaa.org

Foundation type: Public charity
Purpose: Assistance to low income individuals and families transition from poverty to permanent self-sufficiency in the El Paso county, CO area.
Publications: Annual report; Informational brochure; Newsletter.
Financial data: Year ended 12/31/2011. Assets, $664,083 (M); Expenditures, $1,115,202; Total giving, $260,489; Grants to individuals, totaling $260,489.
Fields of interest: Human services; Economically disadvantaged.
Type of support: Grants for special needs.
Application information: Contact the agency for eligibility determination.
Program description:
  Transitions to Independence (TIP) Program: This intensive self-sufficiency program offers services to participants motivated to becoming self-sufficient by providing services that primarily focus on education, training, improving skills, and employment. The program offers participants assistance with financial workshops, certification and short-term training fees, licensing fees, book fees for post-secondary education, supportive services while attending school, and transportation. Eligible individuals must meet qualification guidelines.
EIN: 840933888

1258
Pikes Peak Community Foundation
730 N. Nevada Ave.
Colorado Springs, CO 80903-5014 (719) 389-1251
Contact: For grants: Michael R. Hannigan, Exec. Dir.; Jamie Brown, Dir., Community Svcs.
FAX: (719) 389-1252; E-mail: info@ppcf.org; Additional E-mails: jbrown@ppcf.org and mhannigan@ppcf.org; URL: http://www.ppcf.org

Foundation type: Community foundation
Purpose: Scholarships to high school seniors in the Pikes Peak, CO region pursuing higher education.
Publications: Annual report (including application guidelines).
Financial data: Year ended 12/31/2010. Assets, $46,491,626 (M); Expenditures, $6,186,687; Total giving, $3,340,364.
Fields of interest: Higher education.
Type of support: Scholarships—to individuals; Support to graduates or students of specific schools; Undergraduate support.
Application information:
  Initial approach: Telephone or e-mail
  Deadline(s): Varies

Additional information: See web site for complete listing of scholarship funds and application forms.
EIN: 841339670

1259
Population Biology Foundation
1100 N. Ave., Rm. WUB 221C
Grand Junction, CO 81501

Foundation type: Operating foundation
Purpose: Grants to individuals for environmental and conservation research, primarily in Ecuador.
Financial data: Year ended 12/31/2011. Assets, $34,744 (M); Expenditures, $29,339; Total giving, $27,125.
Fields of interest: Physical/earth sciences; Botany.
Type of support: Research.
Application information: Applications not accepted.
Additional information: Unsolicited requests for funds not considered or acknowledged.
EIN: 911836116

1260
Poudre Valley Health System Foundation
(formerly Poudre Valley Hospital Foundation)
2315 E. Harmony Rd., Ste. 200
Fort Collins, CO 80528-8620 (970) 237-7400
Contact: Ruth Lytle-Barnaby, Exec. Dir., Community and Fdn. Devel.
FAX: (970) 237-7490; E-mail: foundation@pvhs.org; URL: http://www.foundation.pvhs.org

Foundation type: Public charity
Purpose: Scholarships to Poudre Valley Health System employees who are furthering their education or obtaining an advanced degree.
Publications: Application guidelines; Annual report; Grants list; Informational brochure; Newsletter; Occasional report.
Financial data: Year ended 12/31/2011. Assets, $8,889,779 (M); Expenditures, $5,522,846; Total giving, $2,143,309; Grants to individuals, totaling $464,781.
Fields of interest: Higher education.
Type of support: Employee-related scholarships.
Application information: Applications accepted.
EIN: 741894581

1261
Project PAVE, Inc.
2051 York St.
Denver, CO 80205-5713 (303) 322-2382
Contact: Mike Johnson, Exec. Dir.
E-mail: info@projectpave.org; URL: http://www.projectpave.org/

Foundation type: Public charity
Purpose: Ten $1,500 scholarships to graduating seniors to pursue post-high school training or education, such as enrollment in a two- to four-year college or university, or vocational or technical training programs, to show how he or she has risen above an emotionally, physically, or sexually violent experience to attain personal achievement.
Publications: Application guidelines.
Financial data: Year ended 06/30/2012. Assets, $458,498 (M); Expenditures, $775,396.
Fields of interest: Crime/abuse victims.
Type of support: Undergraduate support.
Application information:
Initial approach: Letter
Deadline(s): Jan. 30
EIN: 841031533

1262
Public Education & Business Coalition
600 Grant St., Ste. 525
Denver, CO 80203-1846 (303) 861-8661
Contact: Rosann B. Ward, Pres.
FAX: (303) 861-1501; E-mail: info@pebc.org; E-Mail for Rosann B. Ward: rbward@pebc.org; URL: http://www.pebc.org

Foundation type: Public charity
Purpose: Grants for K-12 teachers in the Denver, CO area with an intererst in making a difference in the lives of low-income children.
Financial data: Year ended 06/30/2012. Assets, $2,273,656 (M); Expenditures, $4,084,268; Total giving, $148,628; Grants to individuals, totaling $148,628.
Fields of interest: Elementary/secondary education.
Type of support: Grants to individuals; Residencies.
Application information: Applications accepted. Application form available on the grantmaker's web site. Interview required.
Send request by: On-line
Deadline(s): Sept.
Applicants should submit the following:
1) Essay
2) Transcripts
3) Resume
4) Letter(s) of recommendation
5) Curriculum vitae
Additional information: Application should also include Praxis II/PLACE a copy of your score report (unofficial), copy of CDE statement of eligibility or initial license, Copy of completed Release of Education Records form for Adams State (San Luis Valley), and Adams State University graduate program application. See web site for additional guidelines.
Program description:
Colorado Boettcher Teacher Residency: This program is for individuals who have earned a bachelor's degree from an accredited institution by the end of June, and have maintained a cumulative GPA of 2.75 or higher. Applicant must be a U.S. citizen, permanent resident, or able to work legally in the U.S.
EIN: 742357262

1263
Puddy Educational Foundation
c/o Carol Ann Rothman
1801 Wynkoop St., Ste. 708
Denver, CO 80202-1196 (303) 298-0180
Contact: Carol Ann Rothman, Pres.

Foundation type: Independent foundation
Purpose: Scholarships to residents of CO seeking associate or teaching degrees. Also, scholarships for students in CO public schools for programs outside public education.
Financial data: Year ended 12/31/2012. Assets, $116,692 (M); Expenditures, $9,887; Total giving, $9,805; Grants to individuals, 6 grants totaling $4,251 (high: $1,171, low: $398).
Fields of interest: Public education; Higher education.
Type of support: Scholarships—to individuals.
Application information: Applications accepted. Application form required.
Deadline(s): Apr. 15, Aug. 15 and Nov. 15
EIN: 562406976

1264
Pueblo Hispanic Education Foundation
2200 Bonforte Blvd., Ste. 325
Pueblo, CO 81001-4901 (719) 549-2564
Contact: for Scholarship: Dalton Sprouse, Exec. Dir.
FAX: (719) 549-2546;
E-mail: phef@colostate-pueblo.edu; Tel. for Dalton Sprouse : (719)-549-2564; URL: http://www.phef.net

Foundation type: Public charity
Purpose: Scholarships for low to moderate income students planning to attend college in CO.
Publications: Application guidelines.
Financial data: Year ended 03/31/2012. Assets, $135,090 (M); Expenditures, $159,729; Total giving, $76,975.
Fields of interest: Higher education.
Type of support: Scholarships—to individuals.
Application information: Applications accepted. Application form required. Application form available on the grantmaker's web site.
Deadline(s): Mar. 10 for attendance at the University of Colorado, Apr. 16 for all other colleges or universities
Applicants should submit the following:
1) Transcripts
2) SAR
3) SAT
4) Letter(s) of recommendation
5) GPA
6) Essay
7) ACT
Additional information: Application forms are available in the scholarship offices of Pueblo Community College and Colorado State University-Pueblo. Also, in the counselors offices of local high schools.
EIN: 742498914

1265
Reach Scholars Foundation
3750 Spring Valley Rd.
Boulder, CO 80304 (206) 728-4442
Contact: Deborah Chandler, Pres.
E-mail: info@reachscholars.org; URL: http://www.reachscholars.org

Foundation type: Independent foundation
Purpose: Scholarships to deserving high school seniors currently enrolled at a Seattle, WA area high school pursuing a career in science, engineering, mathematic, computer science, business, economics or finance.
Financial data: Year ended 12/31/2011. Assets, $170,464 (M); Expenditures, $64,908; Total giving, $59,000; Grants to individuals, 23 grants totaling $59,000 (high: $8,000, low: $1,000).
Fields of interest: Business school/education; Science; Mathematics; Computer science; Engineering; Economics.
Type of support: Scholarships—to individuals.
Application information: Applications accepted. Application form available on the grantmaker's web site. Interview required.
Send request by: Online
Deadline(s): May 15
Final notification: Finalists notified by the end of July
Applicants should submit the following:
1) Transcripts
2) Letter(s) of recommendation
Additional information: Application should also include copies of acceptance letters and a copy of parents' tax form. Scholarships are to "first generation" college student who are economically disadvantaged. Letters of

recommendation must be sent via postal service. See web site for additional guidelines.
EIN: 208318195

1266
Red Rocks Community College Foundation
13300 W. 6th Ave.
Campus Box 1
Lakewood, CO   80228-1213   (303) 914-6308
Contact: Ron Slinger, Exec. Dir.
FAX: (303) 914-6318;
E-mail: scholarships@rrcc.edu; E-Mail for Ron Slinger: ron.slinger@rrcc.edu; Tel. for Ron Slinger: (303)-914-6417; URL: http://www.rrcc.edu/foundation/

Foundation type: Public charity
Purpose: Scholarships for students of Colorado attending Red Rocks Community College, CO pursuing higher education.
Publications: Application guidelines.
Financial data: Year ended 06/30/2012. Assets, $4,863,535 (M); Expenditures, $574,180; Total giving, $490,698; Grants to individuals, totaling $490,698.
Fields of interest: Higher education.
Type of support: Support to graduates or students of specific schools.
Application information: Applications accepted. Application form required. Application form available on the grantmaker's web site.
Send request by: Mail, fax or hand deliver
Deadline(s): June 1
Applicants should submit the following:
1) Transcripts
2) SAT
3) Letter(s) of recommendation
4) GPA
5) Financial information
6) ACT
Additional information: The foundation offers a wide variety of scholarships based on need and merit, together with grades, academic and professional goals, financial need, community service, and special circumstances. See web site for additional guidelines and listing of scholarships.
EIN: 841139105

1267
L. & A. Renfrow Foundation
P.O. Box 1089
Delta, CO   81416-1089   (970) 874-7700
Contact: Les Renfrow, Tr.
Application address: 313 Meeker St. Delta CO, 81416

Foundation type: Independent foundation
Purpose: Scholarships worth up to $1,000 to graduating seniors of Delta High School, Delta, CO, and students of Delta-Montrose Area Vocational-Technical Center, Delta, CO.
Financial data: Year ended 12/31/2012. Assets, $46,973 (M); Expenditures, $6,950; Total giving, $6,200; Grants to individuals, 13 grants totaling $6,200 (high: $1,000; low: $300).
Fields of interest: Vocational education, post-secondary; Higher education.
Type of support: Support to graduates or students of specific schools.
Application information: Applications accepted. Application form required.
Deadline(s): Varies
EIN: 841375153

1268
The Harold and Ruth Robinson Foundation
119 Colorado Ave.
Pueblo, CO   81004-4213   (719) 543-2066
Contact: Daniel H. Valentine, Dir.

Foundation type: Independent foundation
Purpose: Scholarships for graduates of any Pueblo County, CO high school for attendance at a college or university in CO.
Financial data: Year ended 03/31/2013. Assets, $55,353 (M); Expenditures, $8,371; Total giving, $7,500; Grants to individuals, 5 grants totaling $7,500 (high: $1,500, low: $1,500).
Fields of interest: Higher education.
Type of support: Scholarships—to individuals.
Application information: Applications accepted. Application form required.
Deadline(s): Mar. 31
Additional information: Applications available at guidance offices in Pueblo County, CO high schools.
EIN: 841166426

1269
Rock Bottom Foundation
248 Centennial Pkwy.
Louisville, CO   80027-1265   (303) 364-4022
Contact: Jessica Newman, Exec. Dir.
FAX: (303) 664-4197; Toll-free tel.: (800) 233-7827; URL: http://craftworksfoundation.org/

Foundation type: Public charity
Purpose: Employee emergency relief grants only to the current corporation employees of Rock Bottom Restaurants, Inc.
Publications: Annual report.
Financial data: Year ended 06/30/2011. Assets, $588,105 (M); Expenditures, $647,361; Total giving, $268,439.
Fields of interest: Food services.
Type of support: Emergency funds; Awards/grants by nomination only; Employee-related welfare; Grants for special needs.
Application information: Application form required.
Initial approach: Telephone
Copies of proposal: 1
Deadline(s): None
Final notification: 2 days after receipt of application
Applicants should submit the following:
1) Letter(s) of recommendation
2) Financial information
3) Essay
4) Budget Information
Additional information: Applications accepted by nomination only.
Company name: Rock Bottom Restaurants, Inc.
EIN: 841560829

1270
Rocky Mountain Cancer Assistance
(formerly Rocky Mountain Cancer Centers Foundation)
P.O. Box 6625
Denver, CO   80206-0625   (720) 229-0303
Contact: Stephanie Shulman, Exec. Dir.
E-mail: steph@rockymountaincancerassistance.org ; Toll-free Fax: (888) 600-4452; URL: http://www.rockymountaincancerassistance.org

Foundation type: Public charity
Purpose: Financial assistance for day-to-day living expenses for cancer patients in Colorado. Assistance includes grants for housing, food, utilities, transportation and medicines.

Publications: Application guidelines; Informational brochure; Newsletter.
Financial data: Year ended 12/31/2011. Assets, $187,579 (M); Expenditures, $526,213; Total giving, $424,114; Grants to individuals, totaling $424,114.
Fields of interest: Health care; Cancer.
Type of support: Grants to individuals.
Application information: Applications accepted. Application form required. Application form available on the grantmaker's web site.
Initial approach: Letter or telephone
Send request by: Mail or fax
Deadline(s): 1st and 15th of each month
Additional information: Application should include financial information and verification of a cancer diagnosis and current treatment from a healthcare professional. See web site for additional information.
Program description:
Emergency Grants: Assistance is for basic needs for cancer patients including: food, rent or mortgage, utilities, telephone, car and car insurance payments, health insurance or CORBRA, and other basic needs. Eligible applicants must have a cancer diagnosis and be receiving active cancer treatment, be CO residents or be receiving treatment in CO, be 18 years old or older, and have a gross income that does not exceed 60 percent of the CO median income base adjusted for household size. Grant applicants may submit one request per 12-month period, up to two times. The maximum award is currently $500 per person.
EIN: 841487121

1271
Rocky Mountain Children's Choir
4340 E. Kentucky Ave., Ste. 352
Denver, CO   80246   (303) 300-0470
FAX: (303) 300-0390;
E-mail: lcameron@rmchildrenschoir.org; URL: http://www.rmchildrenschoir.org

Foundation type: Public charity
Purpose: Membership fee assistance to needy members of the Rocky Mountain Children's Choir, CO.
Financial data: Year ended 06/30/2012. Assets, $80,220 (M); Expenditures, $471,346.
Fields of interest: Music (choral); Children/youth.
Type of support: Grants to individuals.
Application information: Contact foundation for current application deadline/guidelines.
EIN: 841326073

1272
Rocky Mountain Coal Mining Institute
(also known as RMCMI)
3500 S. Wadsworth Blvd.
Lakewood, CO   80235-2019   (303) 948-3300
Contact: Karen L. Inzano, Exec. Dir.; Beth Coen
FAX: (303) 948-1132; E-mail: mail@rmcmi.org; URL: http://www.rmcmi.org

Foundation type: Public charity
Purpose: Scholarships to full time students in their junior or senior year in mining-related industries.
Publications: Application guidelines.
Financial data: Year ended 12/31/2011. Assets, $1,069,816 (M); Expenditures, $550,821; Total giving, $39,750; Grants to individuals, totaling $39,750.
Fields of interest: Geology; Engineering/technology; Engineering.
Type of support: Conferences/seminars; Scholarships—to individuals.

Application information: Applications accepted. Application form required. Application form available on the grantmaker's web site. Interview required.

Initial approach: Telephone
Deadline(s): Feb. 1
Final notification: Recipients notified early Mar.
Applicants should submit the following:
  1) Resume
  2) Letter(s) of recommendation
  3) Essay
Program descriptions:

Engineering/Geology Scholarships: The institute provides scholarships of up to $2,500 per year (for up to two years) to help students further their education as they continue to promote western coal through education. Each year, eight engineering/ geology scholarship (of up to $2,500) are available to students at a four-year university who are entering their junior or senior year, and who are looking for a career in the coal industry. Eligible applicants must be a U.S. citizen and resident of one of the institute's member states (Arizona, Colorado, Montana, New Mexico, North Dakota, Texas, Utah, or Wyoming); applicants must also be, at the time of application, pursuing a degree in a mining-related field or in the engineering disciplines (such as mining, geology, mineral processing, metallurgy, electrical, mechanical, and environmental)

Technical School Scholarships: Eight one-year scholarships of up to $1,000 are awarded to students in technical programs who hope to take their education into the coal industry, where there is great demand for technical applications. Eligible applicants must be: first-year students at a two-year technical trade school who are in good standing at their institution at the time of selection; U.S. citizens who are legal residents of one of the institute's members states (Arizona, Colorado, Montana, New Mexico, North Dakota, Texas, Utah, or Wyoming); and interested in coal as a career path.

EIN: 840516949

1273
Rocky Mountain Lions Eye Bank
P.O. Box 6026
Aurora, CO   80045-0026   (720) 848-3937
Contact: Edmund Jacobs, Exec. Dir.
FAX: (720) 848-3938; E-mail: info@corneas.org;
Toll-free tel.: (800) 444-7479; URL: http://
www.corneas.org/

Foundation type: Public charity
Purpose: Grants to needy individuals to help pay for eye surgery in CO and WY.
Publications: Annual report; Newsletter.
Financial data: Year ended 06/30/2012. Assets, $5,473,171 (M); Expenditures, $4,294,746; Total giving, $308,838; Grants to individuals, 84 grants totaling $182,370.
Fields of interest: Eye diseases; Surgery.
Type of support: Grants for special needs.
Application information: Contact foundation for eligibility requirements.
EIN: 840890204

1274
Ronald McDonald House Charities of Denver, Inc.
1300 E. 21st Ave.
Denver, CO   80205-5218   (303) 832-2667
FAX: (303) 832-3802;
E-mail: ronaldhousepw@earthlink.net; Additional

address (Aurora office): 932 Potomac Cir., Aurora, CO 80011-6714, tel.: (720) 324-2400;
URL: http://www.ronaldhouse.org

Foundation type: Public charity
Purpose: Scholarships to currently enrolled high school seniors of CO, for attendance at two- or four-year colleges, universities, or vocational/ technical schools.
Publications: Application guidelines; Annual report.
Financial data: Year ended 12/31/2011. Assets, $20,076,162 (M); Expenditures, $2,624,619; Total giving, $99,560; Grants to individuals, 42 grants totaling $42,468.
Fields of interest: Vocational education, post-secondary; Higher education; Asians/Pacific Islanders; African Americans/Blacks; Hispanics/ Latinos.
Type of support: Scholarships—to individuals.
Application information: Applications accepted. Application form required. Application form available on the grantmaker's web site.
Initial approach: Application
Send request by: Mail
Deadline(s): Dec. 20
Final notification: Recipients notified by June
Applicants should submit the following:
  1) Transcripts
  2) SAT
  3) Letter(s) of recommendation
  4) GPA
  5) Financial information
  6) FAFSA
  7) ACT
Additional information: Scholarships are paid directly to the educational institution on behalf of the students.
Program descriptions:

HACER Ronald McDonald House Charities Scholarship: Scholarships are available to currently enrolled high school seniors who have at least one parent of Hispanic heritage, and who are eligible to attend a two- or four-year college, university, or vocational/technical school with a complete course of study. Applicants must be legal U.S. residents, be younger than 21 years of age, and reside in the Aurora or Denver metropolitan area.

RMHC African American Future Achievers Scholarship Program: The scholarship is open to currently enrolled high school seniors who have at least one parent of African American or Black Caribbean heritage, and who are eligible to attend a two- or four-year college, university, or vocational/ technical school with a complete course of study. Applicants must be legal U.S. residents, be younger than 21 years of age, and reside in the Aurora or Denver metropolitan area.

RMHC Scholars Program: Scholarships are available to currently enrolled high school seniors who are eligible to attend a two- or four-year college, university, or vocational/technical school with a complete course of study. Applicants must be legal U.S. residents, be younger than 21 years of age, and reside in the Aurora or Denver metropolitan area.

RMHC/Asia Scholarship Program: Scholarships to currently enrolled high school seniors who have at least one parent of Asian-Pacific heritage and who are eligible to attend a two- or four-year college, university, or vocational/technical school. Applicants must be legal U.S. residents, be younger than 21 years of age, and reside in the Aurora or Denver metropolitan area.

EIN: 840728926

1275
Rutherford Foundation
c/o Jan Hall
2720 Woodland Dr.
Lamar, CO   81052-0110   (719) 523-6800
Contact: Carol J. Brown, Tr.
Application address: P.O. Box 81, Springfield, CO 81073

Foundation type: Independent foundation
Purpose: Scholarships to students in the Baca County school district, CO.
Financial data: Year ended 12/31/2011. Assets, $835,177 (M); Expenditures, $43,792; Total giving, $28,250.
Type of support: Scholarships—to individuals; Support to graduates or students of specific schools.
Application information: Applications accepted. Application form required.
Deadline(s): None
Applicants should submit the following:
  1) Transcripts
  2) Letter(s) of recommendation
Additional information: Application should also include the most recent income tax return of the applicant or his/her parent's; a balance sheet of the applicant that includes all assets and liabilities of the applicant or his/her parent's; three letter of recommendation from non-family members.
EIN: 840751642

1276
Saccomanno Higher Education Foundation
P.O. Box 3788
Grand Junction, CO   81502-3788
Address for inquiries or changes: c/o Alpine Trust and Asset Mgmt., Attn: Joanne Cornell or Marsha Harbert, 225 N. 5th St., Grand Junction, CO 81501; Toll free tel.: (877) 808-7878; URL: http:// www.saccomannoed.org

Foundation type: Independent foundation
Purpose: Scholarships to students who are resident of Mesa County, CO, and Carbon County, UT.
Publications: Annual report; Financial statement; Program policy statement.
Financial data: Year ended 06/30/2013. Assets, $17,873,323 (M); Expenditures, $1,123,792; Total giving, $929,260; Grants to individuals, totaling $812,300.
Fields of interest: Higher education.
Type of support: Scholarships—to individuals.
Application information: Applications accepted. Application form required. Application form available on the grantmaker's web site.
Initial approach: Application
Send request by: Mail
Deadline(s): Apr. 2
Applicants should submit the following:
  1) FAFSA
  2) Letter(s) of recommendation
  3) Financial information
Additional information: Applicants 23 years of age or younger, must submit a copy of their federal tax returns and that of their parents', guardians' or stepparents' and, if married, their spouse's federal tax returns. Scholarship are paid directly to the educational institution.
EIN: 841164982

1277
Sachs Foundation

90 S. Cascade Ave., Ste. 1410
Colorado Springs, CO 80903-1680 (719) 633-2353
Contact: Morris A. Esmiol, Jr., Pres.
URL: http://www.sachsfoundation.org

Foundation type: Independent foundation
Purpose: Undergraduate and graduate scholarships to African-American high school seniors who have been residents of CO for at least five years.
Publications: Application guidelines; Financial statement.
Financial data: Year ended 12/31/2012. Assets, $35,910,854 (M); Expenditures, $1,592,703; Total giving, $1,122,789; Grants to individuals, totaling $1,122,789.
Fields of interest: Higher education; African Americans/Blacks.
Type of support: Graduate support; Undergraduate support.
Application information: Applications accepted. Application form required. Application form available on the grantmaker's web site. Interview required.
  Copies of proposal: 2
  Deadline(s): Application accepted from Jan. 1 to Mar. 17 annually
  Applicants should submit the following:
    1) Transcripts
    2) Letter(s) of recommendation
    3) Photograph
    4) SASE
    5) Financial information
  Additional information: Application must also include copy of parents' signed income tax return. Forms available from high school counselors and the foundation. Application information available on foundation web site.
Program description:
  Scholarships: Scholarships are awarded to African-American high school seniors who have been residents of CO for at least five years, and who have a 3.5 GPA, to obtain undergraduate or graduate degrees. Students who receive the scholarship must then maintain a 2.5 GPA average or better without incompletes or failures and be enrolled for a minimum of 12 credit hours. Awards are made for a maximum of four years. The average undergraduate grant is $5,000 per year. Graduate scholarships are considered on a case-by-case basis only to previous recipients of Sachs undergraduate scholarships. The average graduate grant is $6,000 per year. Recipients may attend educational institutions in any state.
EIN: 840500835

1278
Scottish Rite Foundation of Colorado

1370 Grant St.
Denver, CO 80203-2347 (303) 861-2410
Contact: Stephen M. Munsinger, Pres.
FAX: (303) 861-2411;
E-mail: ritecare@scottishritefoundation.org;
Toll-free tel.: (866) 289-6797; *URL:* http://www.scottishritefoundation.org

Foundation type: Public charity
Purpose: Scholarships to graduate students studying speech-language pathology at either the University of Colorado, Boulder or the University of Northern Colorado.
Publications: Annual report; Financial statement; Informational brochure; Newsletter.

Financial data: Year ended 12/31/2011. Assets, $21,035,567 (M); Expenditures, $1,338,355; Total giving, $1,090,993; Grants to individuals, totaling $20,000.
Fields of interest: Education, special; Children.
Type of support: Scholarships—to individuals; Graduate support.
Application information: Applications accepted. Application form required.
  Deadline(s): June 15
  Additional information: Proof of residency is required.
Program description:
  Graduate Scholarship in Speech-Language Pathology: This program awards two $5,000 scholarships to Colorado residents who are graduate students studying speech-language pathology. Applicant must be committed to a career treating children with childhood language disorders and plan to remain in CO after graduation to serve children in the state. Special consideration will be given to applicants who are interested in serving children in rural or underserved areas of CO.
EIN: 846034299

1279
SEAKR Foundation

6221 S. Racine Cir.
Centennial, CO 80111-6427 (303) 790-8499
Contact: Raymond E. Anderson, Chair.
Additional contact: Melissa Coen, Foundation Rep., tel.: (303) 858-4559; *URL:* http://www.seakr.com/about/foundation.html

Foundation type: Company-sponsored foundation
Purpose: Financial assistance to Colorado military families whose spouse/parent was killed in action in Afghanistan or Iraq.
Financial data: Year ended 12/31/2011. Assets, $161,627 (M); Expenditures, $237,140; Total giving, $226,000; Grants to individuals, 11 grants totaling $226,000 (high: $24,000, low: $4,000).
Fields of interest: Military/veterans.
Type of support: Grants for special needs.
Application information: Applications not accepted.
  Additional information: Unsolicited requests for funds not considered or acknowledged.
EIN: 200979291

1280
Seay Foundation

c/o American National Bank & Trust Co., Trust Div.
P.O. Box 9250
Colorado Springs, CO 80932-0250 (719) 381-5623
Application address: c/o American National Bank, 102 N. Cascade Ave., Colorado Springs, CO 80903-1455

Foundation type: Independent foundation
Purpose: Scholarships by nomination only to students for attendance at any college or university for higher education in the U.S.
Financial data: Year ended 12/31/2012. Assets, $18,130,526 (M); Expenditures, $1,610,755; Total giving, $1,364,656; Grants to individuals, totaling $276,056.
Fields of interest: Higher education; Scholarships/financial aid.
Type of support: Awards/grants by nomination only; Undergraduate support.
Application information: Application form required.
  Deadline(s): May 1
  Applicants should submit the following:
    1) Photograph

    2) Transcripts
  Additional information: Completion of formal nomination required, including three reference forms. Applicant must maintain a minimum cumulative 2.5 GPA.
EIN: 436055549

1281
The Servant Leadership Foundation

950 E. Westglow Ln.
Littleton, CO 80121-1375

Foundation type: Independent foundation
Purpose: Scholarships to individuals in full-time ministry who must raise their own financial support to do so, as well as grants to reduce personal debt of individuals with at least ten years experience in the ministry.
Financial data: Year ended 12/31/2012. Assets, $24,698 (M); Expenditures, $231,098; Total giving, $229,300; Grants to individuals, 11 grants totaling $229,000 (high: $26,000, low: $4,000).
Fields of interest: Christian agencies & churches.
Type of support: Scholarships—to individuals; Grants for special needs.
Application information: Applications accepted.
  Initial approach: Letter
EIN: 841400820

1282
The Marie Walsh Sharpe Art Foundation

725 N. Tejon St.
Colorado Springs, CO 80903 (719) 635-3220
E-mail: sharpeartfdn@qwest.net; *URL:* http://www.sharpeartfdn.org

Foundation type: Independent foundation
Purpose: Summer seminar for students gifted in the visual arts who have just completed their junior year of high school. Artist studio spaces in New York, NY, to any nonstudent, U.S. citizen or permanent U.S. resident aged 21 or over.
Financial data: Year ended 02/28/2013. Assets, $4,149,229 (M); Expenditures, $750,071; Total giving, $0.
Fields of interest: Arts education; Visual arts; Arts, artist's services.
Type of support: Precollege support; Residencies.
Application information: Application form required.
  Send request by: Online for Studio Space, Mail for Summer Seminar
  Deadline(s): Jan. 31 for Studio Space, Apr. 4 for Summer Seminar
  Additional information: See web site for additional guidelines.
Program descriptions:
  Studio Spaces: Seventeen free studio spaces in New York, NY are offered to visual artists 21 years and older. Applicants must be U.S. citizens or permanent U.S. residents and not in school at the time of residency. Studios are available for use for periods of up to one year. Studios are nonliving spaces for the making of new works of art. No stipend or equipment is provide.
  Summer Seminar Program: Three, two-week seminars are held in the summer with full tuition, room and board and all seminar related expenses, excluding transportation, available nationally to artistically gifted high school juniors in public and private schools. The two-week program allows each student to gain a stronger foundation of skills and understanding in the visual arts through experiencing college-level drawing and painting classes in a group setting.
EIN: 840956480

1283
Sister Carmen Community Center, Inc.
701 W. Baseline Rd.
Lafayette, CO 80026-1726 (303) 665-4342
Contact: Suzanne Crawford, C.E.O.
FAX: (303) 665-4960;
E-mail: info@sistercarmen.org; URL: http://www.sistercarmen.org

Foundation type: Public charity
Purpose: Grants for basic necessities to financially needy residents of Lafayette, Louisville, Superior, and Erie, CO.
Financial data: Year ended 06/30/2011. Assets, $3,289,081 (M); Expenditures, $3,534,553; Total giving, $2,526,486; Grants to individuals, totaling $2,519,819.
Fields of interest: Economically disadvantaged.
Type of support: Grants for special needs.
Application information: Applications accepted.
  Initial approach: Letter
  Additional information: Application must include valid photo ID and a piece of mail to verify address.
EIN: 840820308

1284
Warren Skrifvars Scholarship Fund
126 Broadway
Pueblo, CO 81004-4203 (719) 544-1056
Contact: Ron Phillips, Chair.

Foundation type: Independent foundation
Purpose: Scholarships to graduating seniors who are residents of Pueblo county, attending Pueblo County high schools, for attendance at a Colorado college or university.
Financial data: Year ended 12/31/2011. Assets, $656,336 (M); Expenditures, $47,063; Total giving, $31,000; Grants to individuals, 14 grants totaling $27,000 (high: $2,000, low: $1,000).
Fields of interest: Higher education.
Type of support: Scholarships—to individuals.
Application information: Applications accepted. Application form required.
  Deadline(s): May 15
EIN: 841605905

1285
Society of Economic Geologists Foundation, Inc.
7811 Shaffer Pkwy.
Littleton, CO 80127-3732 (720) 981-7882
Contact: For Individuals: John A. Thoms
Application e-mail: studentprograms@segweb.org
FAX: (720) 981-7874; E-mail: seg@segweb.org;
URL: http://www.segweb.org/SEG/Foundation/SEG/Foundation.aspx?hkey=18dc5157-3cbd-4cc3-b8bc-7dca63166e04

Foundation type: Operating foundation
Purpose: Grants, awards, lectureships, and travel grants to graduate students and researchers of the science of economic geology.
Publications: Informational brochure; Newsletter.
Financial data: Year ended 12/31/2012. Assets, $4,553,607 (M); Expenditures, $632,506; Total giving, $519,820.
Fields of interest: Research; Physical/earth sciences; Geology.
Type of support: Research; Grants to individuals; Graduate support; Travel grants.
Application information: Applications accepted.

Send request by: On-line
Deadline(s): Feb. 1 for Graduate Student Fellowship Program, Mar. 1 for Student Research Grant
Additional information: Applicant must be a SEG Student Member. See web site for additional guidelines.
Program descriptions:
  Graduate Student Fellowship Program: The program awards one-year fellowships, ranging from $2,500 to $15,000 each year to students who intend to pursue a course of study in economic geology leading to a Professional Master's, Master of Science (M.Sc.) and/or Ph.D. degree. Students from throughout the world with an expressed interest in pursuing graduate studies in economic geology are encouraged to apply.
  Student Research Grants: Grants provide support for graduate student research projects leading to master's or doctoral degrees, and for exceptional BS projects. Grants typically range up to $5,000. Students in mineral resources study programs throughout the world are eligible. Applicants in financial need may also request support for non-research expenses.
EIN: 516020487

1286
Someone Cares Charitable Trust
P.O. Box 669
Kittredge, CO 80457-0669

Foundation type: Independent foundation
Purpose: Grants to economically disadvantaged individuals for education, medical and other support.
Financial data: Year ended 05/31/2013. Assets, $679,664 (M); Expenditures, $178,169; Total giving, $166,750.
Fields of interest: Education; Health care; Economically disadvantaged.
Type of support: Grants for special needs.
Application information: Applications not accepted.
  Additional information: Unsolicited requests for funds not considered or acknowledged.
EIN: 363415880

1287
Sonlight Curriculum Foundation
8024 S. Grant Way
Littleton, CO 80122-2705 (303) 730-8193
Contact: John A. Holzmann, Pres.
FAX: (303) 730-6509;
E-mail: scholarship@sonlight.com

Foundation type: Company-sponsored foundation
Purpose: Scholarships to students who have purchased and used three full Sonlight Curriculum Core programs over four years.
Publications: Application guidelines; Grants list.
Financial data: Year ended 12/31/2012. Assets, $167,048 (M); Expenditures, $78,189; Total giving, $77,931; Grants to individuals, 43 grants totaling $77,931 (high: $5,000, low: $500).
Fields of interest: Higher education; Christian agencies & churches.
Type of support: Undergraduate support.
Application information: Applications accepted. Application form required. Application form available on the grantmaker's web site.
  Send request by: Mail, e-mail or fax
  Deadline(s): Dec. 7
  Final notification: Applicants notified Feb. 15
  Applicants should submit the following:
    1) Letter(s) of recommendation
    2) Photograph
    3) Essay
    4) ACT
    5) SAT
Program description:
  Sonlight Scholarships: The foundation annually awards thirteen four-year scholarships, including one $5,000 ($20,000 total), four $2,500 ($10,000 total, each) and eight $1,000 ($4,000 total, each) to students who will attend college in the fall. Applicants must have purchased and used five Sonlight Curriculum Core programs. Applicants are evaluated on creativity, mission mindedness, or acts of kindness, spiritual mindedness, leadership, academic performance, heart for learning, and activities and interests.
EIN: 841521871

1288
Spanish Peaks Healthcare Foundation
23500 U.S. Hwy. 160
Walsenburg, CO 81089-9524 (719) 738-5176

Foundation type: Public charity
Purpose: Scholarships to area students in Huerfano County, CO pursuing healthcare careers.
Financial data: Year ended 12/31/2012. Assets, $74,387 (M); Expenditures, $28,854; Total giving, $14,400.
Fields of interest: Health sciences school/education.
Type of support: Scholarships—to individuals.
Application information: Applications accepted.
  Additional information: Contact the foundation for application guidelines.
Program description:
  Scholarships: Scholarships are available to Huerfano County residents between the ages of 16 and 22 years old who have a high-school diploma or GED certificate, or who are in their senior year of high school, and who have a desire to work within the health sciences field. Applicants must have applied and/or been accepted to a one- to two-year college, vocational school, or certificate program.
EIN: 841558843

1289
St. Mary's Hospital and Medical Center, Inc.
2635 N. 7th St.
Grand Junction, CO 81502-8209 (970) 244-2273
Toll-free tel.: (800)-458-3888; URL: http://www.stmarygj.org

Foundation type: Public charity
Purpose: Scholarships to individuals who have signed a letter of intent for employment at St. Mary's Hospital, Grand Junction, CO.
Publications: Occasional report.
Financial data: Year ended 12/31/2011. Assets, $511,222,492 (M); Expenditures, $355,606,283; Total giving, $2,177,258; Grants to individuals, totaling $54,632.
Fields of interest: Health care.
Type of support: Scholarships—to individuals.
Application information:
  Initial approach: Letter
  Additional information: Contact foundation for eligibility criteria.
EIN: 840425720

1290
The Richard Seth Staley Educational Foundation

(formerly Richard Seth Staley Foundation for Psychological Development)
P.O. Box 4129
Aspen, CO 81612-4129   (970) 920-9003
Contact: Donald H. Keltner, Pres.

Foundation type: Operating foundation
Purpose: Scholarships to individuals for attendance at U.S. colleges and universities. Some preference is given to individuals attending CA institutions.
Financial data: Year ended 09/30/2012. Assets, $10,871,873 (M); Expenditures, $684,760; Total giving, $364,392.
Fields of interest: Higher education.
Type of support: Scholarships—to individuals.
Application information: Applications accepted. Application form required.
   Deadline(s): None
   Applicants should submit the following:
      1) Budget Information
      2) Transcripts
      3) Letter(s) of recommendation
EIN: 953532336

1291
Stride

5400 W. Cedar Ave.
Lakewood, CO 80226-2429   (303) 238-3580
Contact: Sarah Maxwell, Exec. Dir.
FAX: (303) 238-3586; E-mail: stride@stride-co.org;
Tel.: for Sarah Maxwell : (303) 238-3578; E-mail for Sarah Maxwell : sarahm@stride-co.org;
URL: http://www.stride-co.org

Foundation type: Public charity
Purpose: Grants for down payment assistance to help welfare recipients in the Denver, CO, area become homeowners.
Publications: Annual report; Newsletter.
Financial data: Year ended 06/30/2012. Assets, $422,655 (M); Expenditures, $552,045.
Fields of interest: Economically disadvantaged.
Type of support: Grants for special needs.
Application information: Applications accepted.
   Initial approach: Letter
   Additional information: Contact foundation for complete eligibility requirements.
EIN: 841158946

1292
E. Isabella Stupfel Trust

c/o Michael Polakovic
1777 S. Harrison St., Ste. 450
Denver, CO 80210   (303) 751-5550

Foundation type: Independent foundation
Purpose: Scholarships to financially needy students of CO for continuing education at institutions of higher learning.
Financial data: Year ended 06/30/2012. Assets, $410,342 (M); Expenditures, $24,699; Total giving, $23,000.
Fields of interest: Education.
Type of support: Scholarships—to individuals.
Application information: Applications accepted. Application form required.
   Deadline(s): None
   Additional information: Application must include references, reports, and transcripts.
EIN: 742439595

1293
The Summit Foundation

111 Lincoln Ave.
P.O. Box 4000
Breckenridge, CO 80424-4000   (970) 453-5970
Contact: Lee Zimmerman, Exec. Dir.
FAX: (970) 453-1423;
E-mail: sumfound@summitfoundation.org;
Additional e-mail:
TSFADmin@summitfoundation.org; URL: http://www.summitfoundation.org

Foundation type: Community foundation
Purpose: Scholarships to graduating seniors from Summit High School and neighboring community high schools.
Publications: Application guidelines; Annual report; Grants list; Informational brochure; Newsletter; Program policy statement.
Financial data: Year ended 09/30/2012. Assets, $7,530,121 (M); Expenditures, $2,114,226; Total giving, $1,573,640; Grants to individuals, 109 grants totaling $181,370.
Fields of interest: Higher education; Scholarships/financial aid.
Type of support: Scholarships—to individuals.
Application information: Applications accepted. Application form required. Application form available on the grantmaker's web site.
   Initial approach: Letter
   Send request by: Mail or online
   Copies of proposal: 2
   Deadline(s): Apr. 12 and Aug. 25
   Applicants should submit the following:
      1) ACT
      2) Transcripts
      3) SAT
      4) Letter(s) of recommendation
      5) GPA
      6) Financial information
      7) Essay
      8) Budget Information
   Additional information: Applications for scholarship funds are made available through the counseling offices at the individual high schools. See web site for additional information.
EIN: 742341399

1294
The Salvatore Taddonio Family Foundation

5139 Arbutus St.
Arvada, CO 80002   (303) 420-3845
Contact: Sandra Madsen, Pres. and Treas.

Foundation type: Independent foundation
Purpose: Scholarships to high school graduates who are residents of CO, for undergraduate studies at accredited colleges or universities in CO.
Financial data: Year ended 12/31/2012. Assets, $134,036 (M); Expenditures, $10,998; Total giving, $10,100; Grants to individuals, 7 grants totaling $10,100 (high: $1,900, low: $1,000).
Fields of interest: Higher education.
Type of support: Scholarships—to individuals.
Application information: Application form required.
   Deadline(s): June 30
EIN: 841158317

1295
Telluride Foundation

220 E. Colorado Ave., Ste. 106
P.O. Box 4222
Telluride, CO 81435   (970) 728-8717
Contact: For grants: April Montgomery, Progs. Dir.
FAX: (970) 728-9007;
E-mail: info@telluridefoundation.org; Additional e-mail: april@telluridefoundation.org; URL: http://www.telluridefoundation.org

Foundation type: Community foundation
Purpose: Grants to needy individuals in San Miguel County, CO for emergency assistance in times of financial crisis.
Publications: Application guidelines; Annual report (including application guidelines); Financial statement; Grants list; Newsletter; Program policy statement.
Financial data: Year ended 12/31/2012. Assets, $9,514,293 (M); Expenditures, $3,145,017; Total giving, $2,526,793.
Type of support: Grants for special needs.
Application information: Applications accepted.
EIN: 841530768

1296
The Emma Belle Tolbert Charitable Trust

P.O. Box 337
Springfield, CO 81073-0337   (719) 523-4557
Contact: Larry Porter, Tr.

Foundation type: Independent foundation
Purpose: Scholarships to high school graduates of Baca County, CO for postsecondary education.
Financial data: Year ended 12/31/2011. Assets, $2,357,954 (M); Expenditures, $97,566; Total giving, $33,956; Grants to individuals, 4 grants totaling $10,000 (high: $2,500, low: $2,500).
Type of support: Undergraduate support.
Application information: Applications accepted.
   Initial approach: Letter
   Deadline(s): None
EIN: 846355695

1297
U.S. Bobsled & Skeleton Federation, Inc.

1631 Mesa Ave., Ste. A
Colorado Springs, CO 80906   (719) 636-1513
E-mail: info@usbsf.com; URL: http://www.usbsf.com

Foundation type: Public charity
Purpose: Grants to US bobsled and skeleton athletes for training and participation in national and international competition.
Publications: Newsletter.
Financial data: Year ended 06/30/2012. Assets, $2,126,015 (M); Expenditures, $2,308,739.
Fields of interest: Athletics/sports, winter sports.
Type of support: Grants to individuals.
Application information: Applications not accepted.
   Additional information: Unsolicited requests for funds not considered or acknowledged.
EIN: 161172380

1298
United States Figure Skating Association
20 1st St.
Colorado Springs, CO   80906-3624   (719) 635-5200
FAX: (719) 635-9548;
E-mail: info@usfigureskating.org; URL: http://www.usfsa.org/

Foundation type: Public charity
Purpose: Grants and scholarships to figure skaters to cover skating expenses.
Publications: Financial statement; Newsletter; Program policy statement.
Financial data: Year ended 06/30/2011. Assets, $9,258,201 (M); Expenditures, $13,739,413.
Fields of interest: Athletics/sports, winter sports.
Type of support: Grants to individuals; Scholarships—to individuals.
Application information: Applications accepted. Application form required. Application form available on the grantmaker's web site.
  Initial approach: Letter
  Deadline(s): Vary
  Additional information: Application should include financial information.
Program descriptions:
  Joyce Komperda Athlete Support Fund: This fund provides financial support to up-and-coming skaters at the novice, intermediate, or junior level. Eligible applicants must: be skating at the recognized (and tested) level of novice, intermediate, or junior; have a family income level of $200,000 or below; be under the age of 18, and show exceptional potential.
  Memorial Fund: This fund helps to assist worthy young people who have demonstrated a continuing interest in and devotion to figure skating who are in need of financial assistance in order to obtain a college or university education. Two types of funds are provided under this program. The Competitive Skaters Assistance Program provides funds to help subsidize the training expenses incurred by competitive figure skaters in the singles, pairs, and ice dancing disciplines. Eligible applicants for this program must be a current member of the association, show intent to compete in the applicable season by submitting a qualifying competition entry, and fall in one of four categories: competed in sectional championships and placed sixth or higher at the novice, junior, or senior level; received a competition bye to the U.S. Figure Skating Championships; competed in the U.S. Junior Championships and placed sixth or higher at the juvenile or intermediate level; or been a member of the Team A, B, C, or reserve envelope. The fund also provides academic scholarships to assist figure skaters who are pursuing a college degree. Awards are based on financial need, academic performance, and continued participation in competitive figure skating or current involvement in association activities. Eligible applicants must: be competing or have competed in the past at the novice level or higher at the sectional championships, or be competing or have competed in the past at the collegiate or senior level at the synchronized skating sectional championships; be currently participating in volunteer work in skating if a former skater (i.e., judging, trial judging, officiating, or committee member); be enrolled and pursuing a degree at an accredited four-year college or university, junior college, community college, or graduate school; be carrying at least six credit hours per semester (at the undergraduate level) or three credit hours (at the graduate level); and possess a cumulative GPA of 3.0 or higher on a 4.0 scale, or 3.75 or higher on a 5.0 scale.
EIN: 840768715

1299
United States Olympic Committee
27 S. Tejon St.
Colorado Springs, CO   80903-1538
URL: http://www.teamusa.org/

Foundation type: Public charity
Purpose: Grants to high-performing athletes for training and to athletes and their families for health insurance. Also, scholarships to athletes pursuing a college degree.
Publications: Annual report.
Financial data: Year ended 12/31/2011. Assets, $204,332,217 (M); Expenditures, $185,071,104; Total giving, $64,969,774; Grants to individuals, totaling $20,343,843.
Fields of interest: Athletics/sports, training; Athletics/sports, Olympics.
Type of support: Grants to individuals; Undergraduate support.
Application information:
  Initial approach: Letter
EIN: 131548339

1300
United Way of Larimer County
424 Pine St., Ste. 102
Fort Collins, CO   80524-2421   (970) 407-7000
Contact: Gordon Thibedeau, Pres. and C.E.O.
FAX: (970) 407-7099; E-mail: office@uwaylc.org; URL: http://www.uwaylc.org

Foundation type: Public charity
Purpose: Childcare Scholarships to single mothers who are residents of Larimer County, CO to help with associated costs of attending institutions of higher education.
Publications: Annual report; Informational brochure; Newsletter.
Financial data: Year ended 06/30/2012. Assets, $7,835,726 (M); Expenditures, $7,154,514; Total giving, $3,605,066; Grants to individuals, totaling $120,482.
Fields of interest: Higher education.
Type of support: Scholarships—to individuals.
Application information: Applications accepted. Application form required.
  Additional information: Scholarships are awarded only to single mothers working toward their GED, certificate or degree program. Consideration is given to those taking 12 credits or more.
EIN: 846031503

1301
University of Northern Colorado Foundation, Inc.
1620 Reservoir Rd.
Judy Farr Ctr.
Greeley, CO   80631-8537   (970) 351-2034
Contact: Rod Esch, Pres.
FAX: (970) 351-1835;
E-mail: info@uncfoundation.org; Toll-free tel.: (800) 568-5213; mailing address: Campus Box 20, Greeley, CO 80639; E-mail For Rod Esch: rodney.esch@unco.edu; URL: http://www.uncfoundation.org/

Foundation type: Public charity
Purpose: Scholarship support to students of the University of Northern Colorado.
Publications: Annual report; Financial statement.
Financial data: Year ended 06/30/2012. Assets, $95,406,628 (M); Expenditures, $12,113,211; Total giving, $9,357,324.
Fields of interest: University.

Type of support: Scholarships—to individuals.
Application information: Applications not accepted.
  Additional information: Unsolicited requests for funds not considered or acknowledged.
EIN: 846044833

1302
Vail Valley Foundation, Inc.
90 Benchmark Rd., Ste. 300
Avon, CO   81620   (970) 777-2015
Contact: for Scholarships: Lindsey Myers, Prog. Coord., Youth Foundation
Tel. for scholarships: (970) 949-1999; Karri Casner Scholarship: c/o Cheryl Lindstrom, P.O. Box 2088, Edwards, CO 81632, tel.: (970) 926-5290, fax: (970) 926-5293
FAX: (970) 949-9265; E-mail: info@vvf.org; URL: http://www.vvf.org

Foundation type: Community foundation
Purpose: Scholarships to graduating seniors of Eagle County, CO for postsecondary education.
Publications: Annual report; Grants list; Newsletter.
Financial data: Year ended 09/30/2012. Assets, $24,056,201 (M); Expenditures, $20,125,758; Total giving, $501,871; Grants to individuals, 17 grants totaling $38,101.
Fields of interest: Music; Higher education; Scholarships/financial aid.
Type of support: Scholarships—to individuals; Support to graduates or students of specific schools; Undergraduate support.
Application information: Applications accepted. Application form required. Application form available on the grantmaker's web site. Interview required.
  Deadline(s): Varies
  Additional information: See web site for additional information.
Program description:
  Vail Valley Foundation Scholarships: Scholarships to graduating seniors of Eagle County, CO, high schools who have excelled in academics, leadership, community service, and athletics, and who have financial need. Applicants must have a cumulative GPA of 3.0 or better.
EIN: 742215035

1303
Eldon E. Veirs Scholarship Fund
1812 Ash Mesa Rd.
Delta, CO   81416-8772   (970) 874-5478
Contact: B.J. Brown, Chair.

Foundation type: Operating foundation
Purpose: Scholarships to graduates of Olathe High School, CO, attending institutions of higher learning in CO.
Financial data: Year ended 04/30/2012. Assets, $116,071 (M); Expenditures, $5,837; Total giving, $5,000; Grants to individuals, 4 grants totaling $5,000 (high: $1,500, low: $1,000).
Fields of interest: Higher education.
Type of support: Support to graduates or students of specific schools; Undergraduate support.
Application information: Applications accepted. Application form required.
  Initial approach: Letter
  Deadline(s): Mar. 31
  Applicants should submit the following:
    1) Financial information
    2) Letter(s) of recommendation
EIN: 840935386

1304
VSA arts of Colorado, Inc.
(also known as VSA Colorado/Access Gallery)
909 Santa Fe Dr.
Denver, CO 80204-3936   (303) 777-0797
Contact: Damon McLeese, Exec. Dir.
FAX: (303) 777-1188; TTY: (303) 777-0796;
URL: http://accessgallery.org/

Foundation type: Public charity
Purpose: Scholarships to disabled individuals in CO who wish to study art.
Publications: Newsletter.
Financial data: Year ended 09/30/2011. Assets, $27,887 (M); Expenditures, $189,640.
Fields of interest: Arts education; Arts; Disabilities, people with.
Type of support: Scholarships—to individuals.
Application information: Applications accepted.
EIN: 742131682

1305
WaterStone
(formerly Christian Community Foundation)
10807 New Allegiance Dr., Ste. 240
Colorado Springs, CO 80921-3803   (719) 447-4620
Contact: Steve Leach, C.E.O.
FAX: (719) 447-4700;
E-mail: waterstone@waterstone.org; URL: http://www.waterstone.org

Foundation type: Public charity
Purpose: Professional assistance and travel grants to Christian community leaders and missionaries.
Financial data: Year ended 03/31/2012. Assets, $149,350,333 (M); Expenditures, $40,125,522; Total giving, $34,548,117; Grants to individuals, totaling $278,197.
Fields of interest: Religion.
Type of support: Awards/grants by nomination only; Travel grants.
Application information: Applications not accepted.
  Additional information: Unsolicited requests for funds not considered or acknowledged.
EIN: 751750059

1306
Western Colorado Community Foundation, Inc.
225 North 5th, Ste. 505
P.O. Box 4334
Grand Junction, CO 81502-4334   (970) 243-3767
Contact: Anne Wenzel, Pres.
FAX: (970) 243-9767; E-mail: awenzel@wc-cf.org;
URL: http://www.wc-cf.org

Foundation type: Community foundation
Purpose: Scholarships for graduating high school seniors and college students from Delta, Eagle, Garfield, Gunnison, Mesa, Montrose, Ouray and Rio Blanco counties, CO.
Publications: Application guidelines; Annual report; Informational brochure; Newsletter.
Financial data: Year ended 12/31/2011. Assets, $29,893,642 (M); Expenditures, $3,027,439; Total giving, $1,400,233. Scholarships—to individuals amount not specified.
Fields of interest: Higher education.
Type of support: Scholarships—to individuals; Undergraduate support.
Application information: Applications accepted. Application form required. Application form available on the grantmaker's web site.

Initial approach: Application
Send request by: Mail
Deadline(s): Varies
Applicants should submit the following:
  1) Financial information
  2) Essay
  3) Transcripts
  4) Letter(s) of recommendation
Additional information: See web site for a complete listing of scholarships.
EIN: 841354894

1307
The Mahlon Thatcher White Foundation
(formerly The Thatcher Foundation)
P.O. Box 2097
Pueblo, CO 81004-0097

Foundation type: Independent foundation
Purpose: Scholarships to students who are residents of or have attended school in Pueblo County, CO to further their education.
Publications: Annual report.
Financial data: Year ended 12/31/2012. Assets, $2,004,579 (M); Expenditures, $118,740; Total giving, $61,690.
Fields of interest: Higher education.
Type of support: Scholarships—to individuals.
Application information: Applications accepted. Application form not required.
  Initial approach: Letter
  Deadline(s): Prior to beginning of school term
  Additional information: Application should include transcripts and applicant should show financial need. Unsolicited requests for funds not considered or acknowledged.
EIN: 840581724

1308
The Williams Family Foundation
626 E. Platte Ave.
Fort Morgan, CO 80701-3339
Contact: Edward L. Zorn, Tr.

Foundation type: Independent foundation
Purpose: Scholarships to financially needy students of CO, who intend to pursue a higher education in the medical field.
Financial data: Year ended 12/31/2012. Assets, $13,870,060 (M); Expenditures, $751,542; Total giving, $722,610.
Fields of interest: Higher education; Medical school/education.
Type of support: Scholarships—to individuals.
Application information: Applications accepted. Application form not required.
  Deadline(s): None
  Additional information: Applications can be obtained from the applicant's high school. Applicant must demonstrate financial need.
EIN: 846023379

1309
Yampa Valley Community Foundation
385 Anglers Dr., Ste. B
Sundance Office Plaza
Steamboat Springs, CO 80487   (970) 879-8632
Contact: Mark Andersen, Exec. Dir.
FAX: (970) 871-0431; E-mail: info@yvcf.org; Mailing address: P.O. Box 881869, Steamboat Springs, CO 80488; URL: http://www.yvcf.org

Foundation type: Community foundation
Purpose: Scholarships to local residents in Routt and Moffat counties, CO.

Publications: Application guidelines; Annual report; Financial statement; Grants list; Informational brochure; Newsletter.
Financial data: Year ended 12/31/2012. Assets, $9,052,088 (M); Expenditures, $1,564,236; Total giving, $916,925; Grants to individuals, 98 grants totaling $108,508.
Fields of interest: Education.
Type of support: Scholarships—to individuals; Exchange programs; Graduate support; Technical education support; Undergraduate support.
Application information: Interview required.
  Additional information: Applications are available through the participating schools.
EIN: 840794536

1310
YMCA of the Rockies
2515 Tunnel Rd.
Estes Park, CO 80511-2800   (970) 586-4444
FAX: (970) 586-6088;
E-mail: info@ymcarockies.org; Toll-free tel.: (800) 777-9622; URL: http://www.ymcarockies.org

Foundation type: Public charity
Purpose: Camp and daycare scholarships for children and youth of the YMCA of the Rockies, CO ages 7 to 17.
Financial data: Year ended 12/31/2011. Assets, $112,619,971 (M); Expenditures, $28,846,911; Total giving, $80,490; Grants to individuals, totaling $77,090.
Fields of interest: YM/YWCAs & YM/YWHAs; Children/youth.
Type of support: Scholarships—to individuals.
Application information: Applications accepted. Application form required.
  Deadline(s): None
  Additional information: Scholarships are awarded based on need and on a first come, first served basis.
EIN: 840404913

1311
Young Heroes Project
c/o Barbara A. Richman
545 Pearl St.
Boulder, CO 80302-3612   (303) 440-8075
URL: http://www.barronprize.org

Foundation type: Independent foundation
Purpose: Awards by nomination to outstanding young leaders in the U.S. and Canada who have made a significant positive difference to the people and the planet.
Financial data: Year ended 12/31/2011. Assets, $2,806 (M); Expenditures, $107,489; Total giving, $27,500; Grants to individuals, 13 grants totaling $27,500 (high: $2,500, low: $1,250).
Fields of interest: Environment; Youth; Young adults.
Type of support: Awards/grants by nomination only; Awards/prizes.
Application information:
  Send request by: Mail
  Deadline(s): Apr. 30
  Final notification: Nominees notified by July 1st
  Additional information: Nominations are not accepted by fax or e-mail. See web site for additional guidelines.
Program description:
  Gloria Barron Prize for Young Heroes: Nominees of the Barron Prize may range in age from 8 to 18 years old, and each receive $2,500 to be used for their higher education or to their service project. Nominees must be legal residents of, and currently

residing in the U.S. or Canada at the time of the nomination, and must be nominated as individuals by an adult who is familiar with the young person's service activity (teacher or librarian, school counselor, youth service official, religious leader, or the like). They must have participated in their heroic work within the 12 months prior to the nomination deadline. Winners will also receive a recognition plaque, a certificate of recognition, and other prizes.
EIN: 841566409

1312
Yuma Community Foundation
700 W. 3rd Ave.
Yuma, CO 80759-1834

Foundation type: Public charity
Purpose: Scholarships to residents of Yuma, CO.
Financial data: Year ended 12/31/2012. Assets, $937,800 (M); Expenditures, $37,451; Total giving, $36,506; Grants to individuals, totaling $36,506.
Type of support: Undergraduate support.
Application information:
  Initial approach: Letter
  Additional information: Contact foundation for complete eligibility requirements.
EIN: 841155472

1313
Zac's Legacy Foundation, Inc.
2990 W. 29th St., Ste. 1
Greeley, CO 80631-8539 (970) 330-9000
Contact: John C. Carlson, Exec. Dir.
URL: http://www.zacslegacyfoundation.org

Foundation type: Public charity
Purpose: Grants to parents of dependent children from CO who are in treatment for cancer.
Financial data: Year ended 06/30/2012. Assets, $13,688 (M); Expenditures, $128,134.
Fields of interest: Cancer; Children.
Type of support: Grants for special needs.
Application information: Applications accepted. Application form required.
  Initial approach: Letter
  Additional information: Applications available from CO social workers and medical care providers.
EIN: 841567130

CONNECTICUT

1314
Action for Bridgeport Community Development, Inc.
1070 Park Ave.
Bridgeport, CT 06604-3400   (203) 366-8241
Contact: Charles B. Tisdale, Exec. Dir.
FAX: (203) 394-6175; Toll-Free Tel.: (888)
852-6080; URL: http://www.abcd.org/

Foundation type: Public charity
Purpose: Emergency assistance to low-income
individuals in the greater Bridgeport, CT area with
food, clothing, rent, utilities and other needs.
Financial data: Year ended 09/30/2012. Assets,
$6,783,014 (M); Expenditures, $31,545,240;
Total giving, $6,023,477; Grants to individuals,
totaling $6,023,477.
Fields of interest: Human services; Economically
disadvantaged.
Type of support: Grants for special needs.
Application information:
  Initial approach: Telephone
  Additional information: Contact the agency for
    eligibility determination.
EIN: 060797841

1315
Adams World Foundation for Dyslexic
c/o G.A. Gagliardi
66-7 Ely's Ferry Rd.
Lyme, CT 06371-3447

Foundation type: Independent foundation
Purpose: Grants to dyslexic students for treatment.
Financial data: Year ended 12/31/2012. Assets,
$10,102 (M); Expenditures, $13,100; Total giving,
$12,750.
Fields of interest: Learning disorders.
Type of support: Grants to individuals.
Application information: Applications not
accepted.
  Additional information: Unsolicited requests for
    funds not considered or acknowledged.
EIN: 061531048

1316
The Arnold M. Albero Charitable Trust
60 Wedgewood Dr.
Danbury, CT 06811   (914) 738-8101

Foundation type: Independent foundation
Purpose: Scholarships to graduating high school
seniors of Pelham High School, NY for post high
school college or technical education.
Financial data: Year ended 12/31/2011. Assets,
$29,821 (M); Expenditures, $1,048; Total giving,
$1,000.
Fields of interest: Vocational education,
post-secondary; Higher education.
Type of support: Support to graduates or students
of specific schools.
Application information: Applications accepted.
Application form required.
  Deadline(s): Apr. 30
  Applicants should submit the following:
    1) Transcripts
    2) Letter(s) of recommendation
    3) Essay

Additional information: Application can be
  obtained from high school guidance office.
EIN: 061356530

1317
Alexion Complement Foundation
352 Knotter Dr.
Cheshire, CT 06410-1138   (888) 765-4747

Foundation type: Operating foundation
Purpose: Provides prescription drug Soliris to
uninsured ill patients for treatment of paroxysmal
nocturnal hemoglobinura (PNH) and atypical
hemolytic uremic syndrome (aHUS)
Financial data: Year ended 12/31/2012. Assets,
$491,454 (M); Expenditures, $1,295,710; Total
giving, $1,275,287.
Fields of interest: Pharmacy/prescriptions; Health
care.
Type of support: Grants for special needs.
Application information: Applications accepted.
  Initial approach: Telephone
  Additional information: Contact foundation for
    qualifying application information.
EIN: 208963321

1318
Alliance for Cancer Gene Therapy, Inc.
(also known as ACGT)
96 Cummings Point Rd.
Stamford, CT 06902-7912   (203) 358-8000
Contact: Jill Smith, Fdn. Admin.
FAX: (203) 348-3103;
E-mail: gpedersen@acgtfoundation.org;
URL: http://www.acgtfoundation.org

Foundation type: Public charity
Purpose: Research grants to qualified scientists
working in gene cancer therapy.
Publications: Application guidelines; Annual report;
Financial statement; Grants list; Informational
brochure; Newsletter; Occasional report.
Financial data: Year ended 04/30/2012. Assets,
$4,437,522 (M); Expenditures, $1,053,966; Total
giving, $576,562.
Fields of interest: Genetic diseases and disorders
research; Cancer research; Leukemia research.
Type of support: Research; Awards/prizes;
Postdoctoral support.
Application information: Applications accepted.
Application form required. Application form
available on the grantmaker's web site.
  Initial approach: Pre-application or letter
  Deadline(s): Mar. 26 for Investigator's Award
  Applicants should submit the following:
    1) Proposal
    2) Budget Information
  Additional information: See web site for complete
    program information.
Program descriptions:
  *Fund for Advancement Grants/Investigators
  Award in Clinical Translation of Gene Therapy for
  Cancer:* The award funds the production and
  release-testing of the clinical trial agents under
  cGMP, conduct the necessary pre-clinical
  pharmacological and toxicological studies in
  appropriate animal models, and/or conducting the
  clinical translational trials in patients in support of
  an Investigative New Drug (IND) application to the
  FDA. While the unambiguous demonstration of
  preclinical efficacy in cancer treatment by gene
  therapy is a pre-requisite, entering into the clinical
  trial during the funding period is also a requirement.
  Grants range from $500,000 to $1,000,000
  distributed over three to five years. Candidates

must hold an M.D., Ph.D., or equivalent degree and
be a tenure-track or tenured faculty member.
  *Fund for Discovery Grants/Young Investigator
  Award:* Grants range from $250,000 to $500,000,
  and distributed over three years, to tenure-track
  assistant professors conducting innovative
  exploratory research in cancer gene therapy.
  Specific focus of research include tumor-specific
  replicating viruses and bacteria, anti-angiogenesis,
  immune-mediated gene therapy and cancer
  vaccines, oncogenes/suppressor oncogenes/
  apoptosis directed therapy, tumor targeting and
  vector development, and other cancer cell and gene
  therapy research. Candidates must hold an M.D.,
  M.P.H., Ph.D. or equivalent degree and be a
  tenure-track Assistance Professor within five years
  of their initial appointment to this rank. Research
  supported by the award must be conducted at
  medical schools and research centers only in the
  U.S. and Canada.
  Investigator's Award: The award is designed to
  support production and release-testing of clinical
  trial agents under current good manufacturing
  practices, necessary pre-clinical pharmacological
  and toxicological studies in appropriate animal
  models, and/or clinical translational trials in
  patients in support of an Investigative New Drug
  application to the FDA. The award provides up to
  $500,000 distributed over two to three years,
  inclusive of a maximum of 10 percent indirect
  costs. The funds may be used at the recipient's
  discretion for salary, technical assistance,
  supplies, animals, or capital equipment, but may
  not support staff who are not directly related to the
  project. Purchase of equipment is not allowed in the
  final year of the grant. Continued support is
  contingent upon submission and approval of a
  noncompetitive renewal application each year.
EIN: 061619523

1319
Elizabeth Raymond Ambler Trust
44 Old Ridgefield Rd., Ste. 215
P.O. Box 7266
Wilton, CT 06897-7266   (203) 761-1150
FAX: (203) 555-5555;
E-mail: amblertrust@sbcglobal.net; URL: http://
www.amblertrust.org

Foundation type: Independent foundation
Purpose: Scholarships of 2,500 to 4,000 to
students who are residents of the town of Wilton,
CT, and surrounding areas.
Publications: IRS Form 990 or 990-PF printed copy
available upon request.
Financial data: Year ended 12/31/2011. Assets,
$7,371,477 (M); Expenditures, $478,860; Total
giving, $304,500.
Type of support: Undergraduate support.
Application information: Applications accepted.
Application form required. Application form
available on the grantmaker's web site.
  Send request by: Mail
  Deadline(s): Apr. 30
  Applicants should submit the following:
    1) Financial information
    2) Essay
    3) FAFSA
    4) Letter(s) of recommendation
    5) Transcripts
EIN: 066473263

1320
American Epilepsy Society
(also known as AES)
342 N. Main St.
West Hartford, CT 06117-2507 (860)
586-7505
Contact: Eileen M. Murray, Exec. Dir.
FAX: (860) 586-7550; E-mail: info@aesnet.org;
E-Mail for M. Suzanne C. Berry : sberry@aesnet.org;
URL: http://www.aesnet.org

Foundation type: Public charity
Purpose: Fellowships and research grants to
individuals for epilepsy research.
Publications: Application guidelines; Annual report;
Newsletter.
Financial data: Year ended 06/30/2012. Assets,
$5,406,620 (M); Expenditures, $4,848,035; Total
giving, $1,079,777; Grants to individuals, totaling
$104,250.
Fields of interest: Epilepsy; Epilepsy research.
Type of support: Fellowships; Research.
Application information: Applications accepted.
Application form required. Application form
available on the grantmaker's web site.
  Send request by: E-mail
  Deadline(s): Vary
  Additional information: See web site for
    additional application guidelines.
Program descriptions:
  AES Young Investigator Awards: The award
provides a $1,200 stipend to young investigator
who must be the first author on the abstract, less
than five years out of post doctoral training, and
must have received this award in the last five years.
Applicant must attend the annual meeting if chosen
for the award, or the award will be forfeited if
applicant choose not to attend.
  Grass AES Young Investigator Award: The Grass
Foundation and the American Epilepsy Society have
combined their resources to present Grass
Foundation AES Young Investigator Travel Awards
($1,000, together with waiver of AES meeting
registration fees) to up to eight deserving
candidates to help support travel costs to present
their research at the annual meeting of the AES.
Candidates must be investigators early in their
careers, including graduate students, postdoctoral
fellows, residents, clinical fellows or junior faculty
(M.D., M.D./Ph.D., Ph.D., or the equivalent), who
are conducting basic or clinical research relating to
epilepsy and are less than five years out of
postgraduate training.
  Research Initiative Awards: The awards provide
seed support to encourage innovative, collaborative
basic or clinical research associated with the
epilepsy field. Awards are given to AES members
who are established investigators. The objective of
these awards is to encourage established
investigators to think "outside the box" and involve
other established investigators who may not now be
working in the field of epilepsy. Awards are made
based on the proposed budget, with an anticipated
award of $30,000 to $50,000 per project. Up to
three projects will be funded each year.
EIN: 046112600

1321
American Legion Charles F. Moran Trust
(also known as American Legion Charles F. Moran
Post No. 475, Scholarship Trust and Baseball
Trust)
100 Pearl St., 13 Flr
Hartford, CT 06103
Contact: Downington Area Senior High School

Foundation type: Independent foundation

Purpose: Scholarships to residents of the
Downingtown, PA, area, for higher education.
Financial data: Year ended 12/31/2012. Assets,
$135,161 (M); Expenditures, $7,136; Total giving,
$6,000; Grants to individuals, 2 grants totaling
$6,000 (high: $3,000, low: $3,000).
Type of support: Undergraduate support.
Application information: Applications accepted.
  Deadline(s): Contact foundation for current
    application deadline
  Applicants should submit the following:
    1) Transcripts
EIN: 237718697

1322
American Savings Foundation
(formerly American Savings Foundation of
Connecticut, Inc.)
185 Main St.
New Britain, CT 06051-2296 (860) 827-2556
Contact: David Davison, Pres. and C.E.O.
FAX: (860) 832-4582; E-mail: info@asfdn.org;
URL: http://www.asfdn.org

Foundation type: Independent foundation
Purpose: Scholarships to undergraduate students
who are full-time residents of one of the sixty-four
CT towns served by the foundation, for study at a
two-or four-year college, university or technical/
vocational school. Current college students and
nontraditional adult students working on no higher
than a first bachelor's degree are welcome to apply.
Scholarship awards range from $500 - $3000 for
the academic year, and applicants may reapply for
up to four academic years.
Financial data: Year ended 12/31/2012. Assets,
$79,642,518 (M); Expenditures, $4,331,534;
Total giving, $3,203,884; Grants to individuals,
381 grants totaling $620,571.
Fields of interest: Higher education.
Type of support: Scholarships—to individuals;
Technical education support; Undergraduate
support.
Application information: Applications accepted.
Application form required. Application form
available on the grantmaker's web site.
  Send request by: Online
  Copies of proposal: 1
  Deadline(s): Mar. 31 for scholarships; June 30
    for scholarship renewals
  Final notification: Applicants notified in two
    months
  Applicants should submit the following:
    1) SAR
    2) Transcripts
    3) Letter(s) of recommendation
    4) GPA
    5) Financial information
    6) FAFSA
    7) Essay
  Additional information: See web site for
    additional application guidelines.
Program description:
  The Robert T. Kenney Scholarship: High school
seniors who are residents of New Britain or
Waterbury, CT, and are applying for the ASF
Scholarship may also apply for the Robert T. Kenney
Scholarship. These scholars are selected based on
an exceptional commitment to community service.
Recipients should have made a significant impact
in their communities, going far beyond the
community service requirements for graduation.
Recipients will receive up to $5,000 (depending on
need) for freshman year. Robert T. Kenney Scholars
may continue to apply for the American Savings
Foundation scholarship for the remaining years of
college (up to a total of 4 academic years). See

foundation web site for scholarship nomination
form.
EIN: 300308972

1323
AmeriCares
(also known as AmeriCares Foundation)
88 Hamilton Ave.
Stamford, CT 06902-3111 (203) 658-9500
E-mail: giving@americares.org; Toll-free tel.: (800)
486-4357; URL: http://www.americares.org

Foundation type: Public charity
Purpose: Assistance to people in extreme medical
and financial need in the U.S. who would not
otherwise have access to prescription drugs for
chronic or long-term conditions. Disaster relief and
emergency medical supplies to men, women and
children in sudden crisis around the world.
Publications: Annual report; Financial statement.
Financial data: Year ended 06/30/2012. Assets,
$162,225,980 (M); Expenditures, $520,101,183;
Total giving, $457,549,326; Grants to individuals,
96,064 grants totaling $130,108,572.
Fields of interest: Safety/disasters; Economically
disadvantaged.
Type of support: In-kind gifts; Grants for special
needs.
Application information: Contact the organization
for eligibility determination.
EIN: 061008595

1324
The Anthony Trust Association
c/o Marcum LLP
555 Long Wharf 12th Fl.
North Haven, CT 06511 (203) 865-5429

Foundation type: Operating foundation
Purpose: Grants to members of the Yale community
for wilderness exploration with philosophic, artistic
or scientific intent, or for travel to rural areas or
developing countries for study.
Financial data: Year ended 06/30/2012. Assets,
$7,371,257 (M); Expenditures, $395,712; Total
giving, $7,500; Grants to individuals, 23 grants
totaling $7,500 (high: $2,000, low: $150).
Fields of interest: Natural resources.
Type of support: Grants to individuals; Travel
grants.
Application information: Applications accepted.
Interview required.
  Deadline(s): Mar. 29
  Applicants should submit the following:
    1) Letter(s) of recommendation
    2) Budget Information
  Additional information: Applicants must also
    submit a brief summary of academic
    background, statement of objectives, and
    itinerary.
EIN: 060245162

1325
The Ash Scholarship Trust
P.O. Box 1868
Lakeville, CT 06039-1868 (860) 435-9801
Application address: Diane E.R. Johnstone, c/o
Salisbury Bank & Trust Co., 19 Bissell St.,
Lakeville, CT 06039

Foundation type: Independent foundation
Purpose: Scholarships to individuals residing in
North Canaan or Salisbury, CT who plan to attend
undergraduate, graduate, vocational, college,

university, or art institute in any one state NY, NJ, PA, DE, MD, CT, MA, RI, VT, NH, OR, or ME.
Financial data: Year ended 12/31/2011. Assets, $1,799,554 (M); Expenditures, $162,073; Total giving, $142,729; Grants to individuals, 9 grants totaling $142,729 (high: $18,900, low: $14,829).
Fields of interest: Arts education; Vocational education, post-secondary; Higher education.
Type of support: Scholarships—to individuals; Graduate support; Undergraduate support.
Application information: Applications accepted. Application form required.
  Initial approach: Telephone
  Deadline(s): May 31
  Applicants should submit the following:
    1) Transcripts
    2) Letter(s) of recommendation
    3) Financial information
  Additional information: Application should also include autobiographical letter and form 1040. Applicant must demonstrate financial need.
EIN: 266528097

1326
Eugene Atwood Fund

P.O. Box 270
New London, CT   06320-0270   (860) 443-4357
E-mail: atwood@mcguire-mcguire.com; Application address:The Eugene Atwood Fund, 68 Federal St., New London, CT 06320; URL: http://www.eugeneatwoodfund.org/

Foundation type: Independent foundation
Purpose: Grants and interest free educational loans only to New London County, CT, students enrolled in college at the undergraduate level.
Publications: Annual report.
Financial data: Year ended 03/31/2013. Assets, $1,820,798 (M); Expenditures, $160,531; Total giving, $131,519.
Fields of interest: Higher education.
Type of support: Grants to individuals; Student loans—to individuals.
Application information: Applications accepted. Application form required.
  Initial approach: Letter or telephone
  Send request by: Mail
  Deadline(s): May 1
  Final notification: Recipients notified mid-July
  Applicants should submit the following:
    1) SAR
    2) Transcripts
    3) GPA
    4) Financial information
  Additional information: Application should also include three letters of reference and a copy of parents' or your most recent income tax return.
EIN: 066044477

1327
Avatar Meher Baba Foundation Inc.

P.O. Box 398
Mystic, CT   06355-0398

Foundation type: Independent foundation
Purpose: Grants by nomination only to individuals to participate in the Avatar Meher Baba PPC Trust Spiritual Training Program in India.
Financial data: Year ended 12/31/2012. Assets, $1,376,434 (M); Expenditures, $188,092; Total giving, $168,810; Grants to individuals, 11 grants totaling $19,800 (high: $1,800, low: $1,800).
Fields of interest: Religion.

Type of support: Grants to individuals; Awards/grants by nomination only.
Application information: Applications not accepted.
  Additional information: Unsolicited requests for funds not considered or acknowledged.
EIN: 061516691

1328
Balso Foundation

c/o Frank Leohmann Jr.
433 S., Main St., Ste. 200
West Hartford, CT   06110   (203) 250-2511

Foundation type: Independent foundation
Purpose: Scholarships to high school seniors and college undergraduates in Cheshire, CT, and surrounding towns. Scholarships are only available for undergraduate study and are renewable.
Financial data: Year ended 12/31/2012. Assets, $311,957 (M); Expenditures, $18,333; Total giving, $15,000; Grants to individuals, 15 grants totaling $15,000 (high: $1,000, low: $1,000).
Type of support: Undergraduate support.
Application information: Application form required.
  Deadline(s): Last week of Mar.
EIN: 237159876

1329
The Barden Foundation, Inc.

1146 Barnum Ave.
Bridgeport, CT   06610
Contact: Robin Bergman, Secy.-Treas. and Tr.

Foundation type: Independent foundation
Purpose: Scholarships to children of employees of The Barden Corp. who reside in CT.
Publications: Informational brochure.
Financial data: Year ended 10/31/2012. Assets, $5,372,647 (M); Expenditures, $284,760; Total giving, $260,200.
Type of support: Employee-related scholarships.
Application information: Applications accepted. Application form required.
  Copies of proposal: 1
  Deadline(s): Mar. 31
  Additional information: Application should include a High School Certification completed by the candidate's high school principal and College Board Entrance Exam score.
EIN: 066054855

1330
Barnes Group Foundation Inc.

123 Main St.
Bristol, CT   06010-0489   (603) 627-3870
URL: http://www.barnesgroupinc.com/about_foundation.php

Foundation type: Company-sponsored foundation
Purpose: Scholarships to children of Barnes Group, Inc., active U.S. or Canadian employees who has been employed at least one year by the due date of the scholarship application or a child of a retired Barnes Group, Inc. employee.
Financial data: Year ended 12/31/2012. Assets, $1,615,355 (M); Expenditures, $1,064,942; Total giving, $1,048,966.
Fields of interest: Higher education.
Type of support: Employee-related scholarships.
Application information: Applications not accepted.
  Additional information: Unsolicited requests for funds not considered or acknowledged.

Company name: Barnes Group Inc.
EIN: 237339727

1331
Bartlett Tree Foundation

P.O. Box 3067
Stamford, CT   06905-0067   (434) 971-8086
Contact: Alan H. Jones, Dir.
Application address: 1185 5 Springs Rd., Charlottes Ville, VA 22902

Foundation type: Operating foundation
Purpose: Scholarships to students for attendance at two and four year colleges and vocational programs majoring in forestry, arboriculture, horticulture or related fields to defray tuition.
Financial data: Year ended 09/30/2013. Assets, $1,214,173 (M); Expenditures, $60,883; Total giving, $59,750.
Fields of interest: Environment, forests; Horticulture/garden clubs; Environmental education.
Type of support: Scholarships—to individuals.
Application information: Applications accepted.
  Initial approach: Letter
  Deadline(s): None
EIN: 222770557

1332
Bauer Foundation

c/o Shipman & Goodwin
P.O. Box 1784
Lakeville, CT   06039-1784   (860) 435-2539
Contact: Stuyvesant K. Bearns, Tr.
Application Address: Shipman Goodwin, Porter St., Lakeville, CT 06039

Foundation type: Independent foundation
Purpose: Scholarships to residents of Regional School District No. 1 in Lakeville, CT.
Financial data: Year ended 12/31/2011. Assets, $1,138,225 (M); Expenditures, $60,674; Total giving, $46,470.
Type of support: Scholarships—to individuals.
Application information: Applications accepted. Application form required.
  Deadline(s): May 2
EIN: 066032985

1333
Frederick R. Bauer Fund

c/o Stuyvesant K. Bearns
P.O. Box 1784
Lakeville, CT   06039   (860) 435-2539
Application address: c/o Shipman Goodman, Lakeville, CT 06039

Foundation type: Independent foundation
Purpose: Scholarships to students attending Wellesley College, MA, or Cornell University, NY.
Financial data: Year ended 12/31/2012. Assets, $552,876 (M); Expenditures, $27,781; Total giving, $20,000.
Type of support: Scholarships—to individuals; Support to graduates or students of specific schools.
Application information: Applications accepted. Application form required.
  Deadline(s): July 15
EIN: 066032984

1334
Belgian American Educational Foundation, Inc.
195 Church St.
New Haven, CT 06510-2009
Contact: Emile L. Boulpaep M.D., Chair. and Pres.
E-mail: emile.boulpaep@yale.edu; Tel./Fax: (203) 777-5765; URL: http://www.baef.be

Foundation type: Public charity
Purpose: Fellowships to Belgian graduate students and to American graduate students who are proficient in Dutch, French, or German.
Publications: Application guidelines; Financial statement; Newsletter.
Financial data: Year ended 08/31/2011. Assets, $71,360,206 (M); Expenditures, $3,021,366; Total giving, $2,035,163; Grants to individuals, 52 grants totaling $1,857,835. Subtotal for fellowships: 60 grants totaling $2,027,990. Subtotal for awards/prizes: 1 grant totaling $7,173.
Fields of interest: Graduate/professional education; International exchange, students.
Type of support: Fellowships; Exchange programs; Awards/grants by nomination only; Graduate support.
Application information: Application form required. Application form available on the grantmaker's web site. Interview required.
Initial approach: Letter or e-mail
Copies of proposal: 1
Deadline(s): May 1 for MBA; Oct. 31 for others
Applicants should submit the following:
1) Transcripts
2) Proposal
3) Letter(s) of recommendation
4) Essay
5) Curriculum vitae
Additional information: Candidates must be nominated by the deans of their graduate schools.
Program descriptions:
Fellowships for Belgian Citizens: Non-renewable grants, or interest-free loans, for one academic year of study or for one full year of research in the U.S. are available to Belgian citizens pursuing graduate study, music study, doctoral and post-doctoral research, M.B.A. and management degrees, and civil engineer M.B.A. candidates. Grants range from $20,000 to $100,000 and include health insurance.
Fellowships for U.S. Citizens: The foundation will award one-year fellowships for advanced study or research at a Belgian university or other academic institution of higher learning. The applicant must be a U.S. citizen and either have a Masters or equivalent degree, or be working towards a Ph.D. or equivalent degree. Candidates under 30 years of age and with a speaking and reading knowledge of Dutch, French, or German are preferred. The grant carries a $24,000 stipend and includes health insurance for the fellow. No additional allowance will be granted in payment of tuition or enrollment fees, if any. For periods shorter than 12 months, but not less than six months, the stipend will be reduced proportionally.
EIN: 131606002

1335
Boehringer Ingelheim Cares Foundation, Inc.
900 Ridgebury Rd.
P.O. Box 368
Ridgefield, CT 06877-0358
Contact: Frank A. Pomer Esq., V.P. and Treas.
E-mail: bicaresfoundation.rdg@boehringer-ingelheim.com; Contact for Patient Assistance Prog.: P.O. Box 66745, St. Louis, MO 63166-674555, tel.: (800) 556-8317, fax: (866) 851-2827; URL: http://us.boehringer-ingelheim.com/our_responsibility/grants-and-funding/charitable_donations.html

Foundation type: Operating foundation
Purpose: Assistance to patients who are without pharmaceutical insurance coverage, and who meet certain household income levels with medications to those who need it most, including senior citizens and families living on limited income.
Publications: Application guidelines; Program policy statement.
Financial data: Year ended 12/31/2012. Assets, $35,238,174 (M); Expenditures, $196,635,116; Total giving, $193,329,277; Grants to individuals, totaling $190,059,517.
Fields of interest: Human services; Economically disadvantaged.
Type of support: Grants for special needs.
Application information: Applications accepted. Application form required. Application form available on the grantmaker's web site.
Initial approach: Application
Send request by: Fax or Mail
Deadline(s): None
Additional information: Applications must be filled out by a doctor and should include proof of the applicant's income.
Program descriptions:
Patient Assistance Program: The foundation provides Boehringer Ingelheim pharmaceuticals to patients who are without pharmaceutical insurance and who meet household income levels. Special emphasis is directed toward those who are most in need, including senior citizens and families on limited incomes. Visit https://www.bipatientassistance.com/ for more information.
Product Donation Program: The foundation provides Boehringer Ingelheim pharmaceuticals to qualified nonprofit, health, and government organizations including AmeriCares, Direct Relief International, and MAP International. Patients in need who are served by those organizations may access medications that are critically important to their health and well-being free of charge.
EIN: 311810072

1336
The Bonfire Foundation
26 Hidden Oak Dr.
Farmington, CT 06032-2734 (800) 923-3516
Contact: Heather Diver, Exec. Dir.
URL: http://teambonfire.com

Foundation type: Independent foundation
Purpose: Scholarships to students who show a strong sense of determination, ambition combined with good judgment, to realize their full potential in raising their quality of life as well as the lives of those around them. The foundation highly considers and values those individuals focusing on journalistic/media and/or athletic pursuits.
Financial data: Year ended 12/31/2012. Assets, $1,692,072 (M); Expenditures, $118,793; Total giving, $34,675.
Fields of interest: Scholarships/financial aid.

Type of support: Scholarships—to individuals; Undergraduate support.
Application information: Applications accepted. Application form required. Application form available on the grantmaker's web site.
Initial approach: Letter
Send request by: Mail
Copies of proposal: 1
Deadline(s): Apr. 1
Final notification: Applicants notified in two months
Additional information: Application must include an essay.
EIN: 134039331

1337
Borck Family Foundation, Inc.
1140 Fairfield Ave.
Bridgeport, CT 06605 (310) 373-1975
Contact: Judith L. Borck, Pres. and Treas.
Application address: 2507 Post Rd., Southport, CT 06890; URL: http://www.theborck.org

Foundation type: Independent foundation
Purpose: Scholarships to individuals for continuing education at accredited colleges or universities.
Financial data: Year ended 12/31/2012. Assets, $529,414 (M); Expenditures, $43,197; Total giving, $18,000; Grants to individuals, 7 grants totaling $18,000 (high: $3,000, low: $1,500).
Fields of interest: Higher education.
Type of support: Scholarships—to individuals.
Application information: Applications accepted.
Initial approach: Letter
Deadline(s): June 1
EIN: 222611596

1338
Branford Community Foundation, Inc.
P.O. Box 462
Branford, CT 06405-0462 (203) 488-6063
Contact: Eunice LaSala, Pres.; For grants: John E. Donegan, Secy.
E-mail: info@branfordcommunityfoundation.org; Additional E-mail: eunice.lasala@gmail.com; URL: http://www.branfordcommunityfoundation.org

Foundation type: Community foundation
Purpose: Scholarships to high school seniors and other support to residents of Branford, CT.
Publications: Annual report; Financial statement; Informational brochure; Newsletter.
Financial data: Year ended 12/31/2011. Assets, $1,401,107 (M); Expenditures, $87,437; Total giving, $80,481.
Type of support: Emergency funds; Program development; Conferences/seminars; Publication; Seed money; Fellowships; Research; Grants to individuals; Scholarships—to individuals; Exchange programs; Support to graduates or students of specific schools; Awards/prizes; Graduate support; Technical education support; Workstudy grants; Doctoral support; Grants for special needs; Camperships; Project support.
Application information: Applications accepted. Application form required. Application form available on the grantmaker's web site.
Initial approach: Letter or telephone
Send request by: Mail
Deadline(s): None
Final notification: Recipients notified in one to three months
Applicants should submit the following:
1) Financial information

2) Budget Information
EIN: 061032832

1339
Bridgeport Hospital Foundation, Inc.
267 Grant St.
Bridgeport, CT   06610-2805   (203) 384-3522
FAX: (203) 384-3752; *E-mail:* aschud@bpthosp.org;
URL: http://www.bridgeporthospital.org/
foundation/

Foundation type: Public charity
Purpose: Nursing scholarships and awards are
granted to individuals who are residents of CT, to
assist with tuition and fees.
Financial data: Year ended 09/30/2011. Assets,
$49,577,666 (M); Expenditures, $4,518,798;
Total giving, $2,527,659; Grants to individuals,
totaling $72,700.
Fields of interest: Nursing school/education.
Type of support: Scholarships—to individuals.
Application information:
   Deadline(s): None
   Additional information: Unsolicited requests for
      funds not accepted.
EIN: 222908698

1340
Bristol Yale Scholarship Fund Inc.
c/o Steven G. Mills
44 Cedar Spring Rd.
Burlington, CT   06013-2441

Foundation type: Independent foundation
Purpose: Scholarships to graduates of accredited
secondary schools, public, private, or parochial,
located in Bristol, Plymouth and/or Plainville, CT.
Scholarships to residents who are graduates of
accredited secondary schools, public, private, or
parochial, located outside Bristol, Plymouth, and
Plainville, CT. Scholarships also to graduates of
Lewis S. Mills High School located in Burlington, CT.
Financial data: Year ended 12/31/2012. Assets,
$535,277 (M); Expenditures, $2,471; Total giving,
$0.
Fields of interest: Higher education.
Type of support: Scholarships—to individuals;
Support to graduates or students of specific
schools.
Application information: Applications accepted.
   Deadline(s): May 20
EIN: 066023679

1341
Clayton Brown f/b/o Randolph Uhs
850 Main St., RC 13-505
Bridgeport, CT   06604-4913

Foundation type: Independent foundation
Purpose: Scholarships to graduating students from
Randolph Union High School for continuing
education at accredited colleges or universities.
Financial data: Year ended 12/31/2012. Assets,
$132,002 (M); Expenditures, $10,636; Total
giving, $7,000.
Fields of interest: Higher education.
Type of support: Support to graduates or students
of specific schools.
Application information: Unsolicited requests for
funds not accepted.
EIN: 036020016

1342
Building Hope Foundation, Inc.
(formerly The Vision Fund, Inc.)
c/o Mary Boudreau
433 Meadow St.
Fairfield, CT   06824   (203) 335-7008
Contact: Mary Boudreau

Foundation type: Operating foundation
Purpose: Scholarships to Home Builders &
Remodelers Association members and their
dependants who are pursuing post-secondary
education. Also financial assistance to provide
housing for disabled veterans in Fairfield County,
CT.
Financial data: Year ended 12/31/2012. Assets,
$0 (M); Expenditures, $27,475; Total giving,
$8,000; Grants to individuals, 8 grants totaling
$8,000 (high: $1,000, low: $1,000).
Type of support: Undergraduate support; Grants for
special needs.
Application information:
   Initial approach: Letter
   Deadline(s): Apr. 30
   Applicants should submit the following:
      1) Transcripts
      2) Letter(s) of recommendation
      3) Essay
EIN: 201819560

1343
Trustees of the Bulkeley School
P.O. Box 1426
New London, CT   06320
Contact: William J. Smith, Treas.

Foundation type: Independent foundation
Purpose: Scholarships only to residents of New
London, CT.
Financial data: Year ended 04/30/2013. Assets,
$1,353,687 (M); Expenditures, $87,779; Total
giving, $61,000.
Type of support: Scholarships—to individuals.
Application information: Applications accepted.
Application form required. Interview required.
   Deadline(s): Apr. 1
   Additional information: Application should
      include a copy of financial aid statement.
      Contact foundation for current application
      guidelines.
EIN: 066040926

1344
Byram Rotary Foundation
(formerly Byram-Cos Cob Rotary Foundation)
90 Greenwich Ave.
Greenwich, CT   06830-5504
Contact: L. Pittocco Esq.

Foundation type: Independent foundation
Purpose: Scholarships to individuals from Western
Greenwich and Cos Cob CT, area for higher
education at accredited institutions of higher
learning.
Financial data: Year ended 04/30/2013. Assets,
$58,869 (M); Expenditures, $1,485; Total giving,
$0.
Fields of interest: Higher education.
Type of support: Scholarships—to individuals.
Application information: Applications accepted.
Application form required.
   Deadline(s): May 15
EIN: 066072260

1345
Canaan Exchange Club Charitable Trust
c/o Bob Anderson
P.O. Box 383
East Canaan, CT   06024
Contact: Robert Anderson

Foundation type: Independent foundation
Purpose: Scholarships to local area Canaan, CT,
high school students for higher education.
Financial data: Year ended 12/31/2011. Assets,
$104,886 (M); Expenditures, $27,218; Total
giving, $16,430; Grants to individuals, 33 grants
totaling $13,500 (high: $600, low: $300).
Fields of interest: Education.
Type of support: Undergraduate support.
Application information: Application form required.
   Deadline(s): 30 days prior to award date
   Additional information: Application should
      include transcripts and parents' financial
      information.
EIN: 061030724

1346
Capital Workforce Partners, Inc.
1 Union Pl., 3rd Fl.
Hartford, CT   06103-1490   (860) 522-1111
FAX: (860) 722-2486; *URL:* http://
www.capitalworkforce.org/

Foundation type: Public charity
Purpose: Scholarship to eligible individuals
throughout north-central CT to upgrade their skills,
increase their competitiveness in the workforce,
and increase their skills of their workforce who wish
to improve their job skills.
Publications: Application guidelines.
Financial data: Year ended 06/30/2012. Assets,
$5,399,254 (M); Expenditures, $19,717,569;
Total giving, $14,124,512; Grants to individuals,
2,338 grants totaling $3,632,603.
Fields of interest: Employment, services;
Employment, training; Employment.
Type of support: Scholarships—to individuals.
Application information: Applications accepted.
   Initial approach: Application
   Deadline(s): Oct. 15, Dec. 14, and Feb 15
   Applicants should submit the following:
      1) Financial information
      2) Essay
   Additional information: Contact organization for
      additional guidelines.
Program description:
   Workforce Investment Act Scholarships:
Scholarships are available to individuals throughout
north-central Connecticut who are seeking funding
to improve their job skills. Eligible applicants must
attend organization-sponsored career services
information sessions and workshops, conduct
research into career training programs, and meet
with career agents to determine eligibility for
scholarship support.
EIN: 061013293

1347
Elizabeth Carlson Memorial Scholarship Trust Fund for Performing Arts
90 Kiekwood Road
West Hartford, CT   06117   (860) 666-8038
Contact: Bruce Carlson, Dir.
Application Address: 31 Franklin Cir., Newington CT
06111

Foundation type: Independent foundation
Purpose: Scholarships to high school seniors in CT
to further their studies in performing arts.

Financial data: Year ended 12/31/2010. Assets, $114,505 (M); Expenditures, $16,725; Total giving, $8,000.
Fields of interest: Arts education; Higher education.
Type of support: Scholarships—to individuals.
Application information: Applications accepted. Application form required.
> *Applicants should submit the following:*
> 1) Essay
> 2) Letter(s) of recommendation
> 3) Work samples
> 4) Photograph
> 5) Resume
> *Additional information:* Applications can be picked up at CT high schools and performing arts centers. Applicants should include a VHS or DVD of a two to five minute performance.
EIN: 161622895

1348
The Cawasa Grange Memorial Scholarship Fund, Inc.
23 Thayer Ave.
Canton, CT 06019-3023   (860) 693-7707

Foundation type: Independent foundation
Purpose: Scholarships to high school graduates from Canton High School, CT for postsecondary education.
Financial data: Year ended 06/30/2013. Assets, $819,120 (M); Expenditures, $59,467; Total giving, $52,500; Grants to individuals, 17 grants totaling $52,500 (high: $5,000, low: $2,500).
Fields of interest: Higher education; Scholarships/financial aid.
Type of support: Undergraduate support.
Application information: Applications accepted. Application form required.
> *Send request by:* Mail
> *Deadline(s):* Apr.
> *Applicants should submit the following:*
> 1) Transcripts
> 2) FAFSA
> 3) FAF
> *Additional information:* Application should also include parents' most recent tax return.
Program description:
> *Scholarship:* Selected applicants will be provided with $5,000 per year (in two increments of $2,500 each) for use towards tuition, room and board each year for up to four years of college. Scholarship money will be paid directly to the institution attended by the recipient for four years pending recipient's progress. Applicants must be residents of the town of Canton, CT at the time of graduation.
EIN: 061552895

1349
CCSU Foundation, Inc.
P.O. Box 612
New Britain, CT 06050-0612   (860) 832-1740
Contact: Christopher J. Galligan, Secy.
FAX: (860) 832-2585; Toll-free tel: (888) 733-2279; URL: http://web.ccsu.edu/ccsufoundation/

Foundation type: Public charity
Purpose: Scholarships to students attending Central Connecticut State University, CT.
Financial data: Year ended 06/30/2012. Assets, $43,034,780 (M); Expenditures, $2,137,987; Total giving, $1,217,718; Grants to individuals, totaling $225,956.
Type of support: Support to graduates or students of specific schools.

Application information: Application form required.
> *Deadline(s):* Feb. 1
> *Additional information:* See Web site for complete list of scholarship programs.
EIN: 237354328

1350
Center for Contemporary Printmaking
Mathews Park
299 West Ave.
Norwalk, CT 06850-4002   (203) 899-7999
FAX: (203) 899-7997;
E-mail: info@contemprints.org; URL: http://www.contemprints.org/

Foundation type: Public charity
Purpose: Residencies to mature and emerging artists to preserve and promote the art of printmaking.
Publications: Application guidelines.
Financial data: Year ended 12/31/2011. Assets, $1,923,765 (M); Expenditures, $432,286.
Fields of interest: Print publishing.
Type of support: Awards/prizes; Residencies.
Application information: Applications accepted. Application form required.
> *Initial approach:* Telephone or e-mail
> *Deadline(s):* Oct. 1
> *Applicants should submit the following:*
> 1) SASE
> 2) Letter(s) of recommendation
> 3) Work samples
> 4) Resume
> 5) Proposal
> *Additional information:* Application should also include a $25 application fee.
Program description:
> *Artist in Residence Program:* The center offers fully equipped studios and a compact residence in an historic 19th century artist's cottage adjacent to the center. This space provides mature and emerging artists the time, privacy, and creative atmosphere in which to realize printmaking projects independently, or collaboratively with center printers. Residencies last from a week to a month. The center subsidizes a significant portion of the cost of the program, but there remains a fee to cover on-site housing, orientation, basic technical assistance, and some studio supplies. The fee for subsequent weeks is reduced. A reduction of fees may be available for two artists collaborating in the space. The organization will receive a commission of 50 percent for any of the artist's works sold during the residency.
EIN: 061400371

1351
William H. Chapman Foundation
P.O. Box 1321
New London, CT 06320-1321   (860) 443-2811

Foundation type: Independent foundation
Purpose: Undergraduate scholarships to residents of New London County, CT, for full-time study at an accredited institution or trade school.
Financial data: Year ended 03/31/2013. Assets, $3,361,537 (M); Expenditures, $161,835; Total giving, $119,937.
Fields of interest: Vocational education, post-secondary; Higher education.
Type of support: Undergraduate support.
Application information: Application form required. Interview required.
> *Initial approach:* Letter
> *Deadline(s):* Apr. 1
> *Applicants should submit the following:*

1) Transcripts
2) Letter(s) of recommendation
EIN: 066034290

1352
The Eugene J. Chariott Memorial Scholarship Fund, Inc.
P.O. Box 907
Norwalk, CT 06852-0907

Foundation type: Independent foundation
Purpose: Scholarships to graduating seniors of Norwalk High School, CT in pursuing a degree in journalism.
Financial data: Year ended 12/31/2012. Assets, $15,336 (M); Expenditures, $4,531; Total giving, $6,000; Grants to individuals, 2 grants totaling $6,000 (high: $3,000, low: $3,000).
Fields of interest: Print publishing; Higher education.
Type of support: Support to graduates or students of specific schools.
Application information: Applications accepted.
> *Initial approach:* Letter
> *Deadline(s):* Apr.
EIN: 061030895

1353
Charitable Society in Hartford
c/o Bank of America, N.A.
200 Glastonbury Blvd.
Glastonbury, CT 06033   (860) 561-3728
Contact: Raymond S. Andrews, Jr., Pres. and Treas.
Application address: 1104 Farmington Ave., West Hartford, CT, 06107 tel.: (860) 561-3728

Foundation type: Independent foundation
Purpose: Small grants to needy residents of Hartford, CT, to meet emergency needs such as food, shelter, clothing, and heat.
Financial data: Year ended 08/31/2012. Assets, $842,791 (M); Expenditures, $48,007; Total giving, $32,703; Grants to individuals, 70 grants totaling $18,953 (high: $300, low: $44).
Fields of interest: Human services, emergency aid.
Type of support: Grants for special needs.
Application information: Applications accepted.
> *Deadline(s):* None
> *Additional information:* Applicants must be referred by recognized churches, schools and local service organizations.
EIN: 066026007

1354
The Jane Coffin Childs Memorial Fund for Medical Research
333 Cedar St., SHM L300 MC 0191
P.O. Box 20800
New Haven, CT 06520-8000   (203) 785-4612
Contact: Kim Roberts, Admin. Dir.
FAX: (203) 785-3301; E-mail: jccfund@yale.edu;
E-mail for referees and sponsors with regard to the Fellowship Program: letters@jccfund.org;
URL: http://www.jccfund.org

Foundation type: Independent foundation
Purpose: Postdoctoral fellowships to individuals to pursue research into the causes and origins of cancer.
Publications: Application guidelines; Annual report; Newsletter; Program policy statement.
Financial data: Year ended 06/30/2012. Assets, $48,706,742 (M); Expenditures, $3,893,948;

Total giving, $3,281,036; Grants to individuals, totaling $3,281,036.
Fields of interest: Cancer research.
Type of support: Fellowships; Postdoctoral support.
Application information: Applications accepted.
  Initial approach: Letter or telephone
  Send request by: On-line
  Deadline(s): Feb.
  Additional information: Application should include proposal and previous work experience. Applicants must apply through the host institution, where funds are paid directly to the institution on behalf of the individuals.
Program description:
  Postdoctoral Fellowship Program: Fellowships are awarded for research into the cause, origins, and treatment of cancer. Fellowships are for full-time postdoctoral studies in the medical and related sciences bearing on cancer. Applicants in general should not have more than one year of postdoctoral experience, and must hold either the M.D. degree or the Ph.D. degree in the field in which they propose to study or furnish evidence of equivalent training and experience. The appointment will be for three years. Applicants may be citizens of any country, but for foreign nationals, awards will be made only for study in the United States. American citizens may hold a fellowship either in the United States or in a foreign country. The basic stipend at present is $50,000 the first year, $50,000 the second year and $50,000 the third year, with an additional $1,000 for each dependent child. There is no dependency allowance for a spouse. An allowance of $1,500 a year toward the cost of the research usually will be made available to the laboratory sponsoring the fellow. The research allowance is not to be used for travel. The fellow will have access to $1,800 for travel to science meetings. A travel award will be made to the fellow and family for travel to the sponsoring laboratory.
EIN: 066034840

1355
China Care Foundation, Inc.
P.O. Box 607
Westport, CT 06881-0607 (203) 227-3655
FAX: (203) 227-8084; E-mail: info@chinacare.org;
URL: http://www.chinacare.org

Foundation type: Public charity
Purpose: Help for special-needs Chinese orphans through direct humanitarian service. Services include specialized care for infants who are orphaned, life saving medical treatments and surgeries, and foster care.
Financial data: Year ended 12/31/2011. Assets, $924,293 (M); Expenditures, $2,292,327; Total giving, $1,767,400.
Fields of interest: Adoption.
Type of support: Foreign applicants.
Application information:
  Initial approach: Letter
EIN: 311732062

1356
The Thomas Cholnoky Foundation, Inc.
100 Old Church Rd.
Greenwich, CT 06830 (203) 869-7600
Contact: Thomas Cholnoky, Pres.

Foundation type: Independent foundation
Purpose: Scholarships, research grants, and travel expenses to students and graduates of certain Hungarian universities for study in the U.S.

Financial data: Year ended 12/31/2012. Assets, $396,177 (M); Expenditures, $49,812; Total giving, $47,164.
Type of support: Research; Foreign applicants; Undergraduate support; Travel grants.
Application information: Applications accepted. Application form required.
  Deadline(s): None
  Additional information: Application must also include academic standing, financial need, personal history and cost of program.
EIN: 222610435

1357
CJR Fund, Inc.
P.O. Box 161
Litchfield, CT 06759-0161 (860) 567-9423
Contact: John F. Boyd, Exec. Dir.

Foundation type: Public charity
Purpose: Scholarships to a limited number of alumni from CT, who qualify to pursue higher education.
Financial data: Year ended 06/30/2011. Assets, $13,350,824; Expenditures, $939,169; Total giving, $10,300; Grants to individuals, 10 grants totaling $10,300.
Fields of interest: Higher education; Scholarships/financial aid; Youth.
Type of support: Scholarships—to individuals.
Application information: Applications accepted.
  Additional information: Applicants must provide evidence of enrollment. Scholarship payments are made directly to the educational institution on behalf of the students.
EIN: 061265380

1358
B.M. Clark Foundation
133 W. View Dr.
Meriden, CT 06450

Foundation type: Independent foundation
Purpose: Scholarships to residents of Union, ME for continuing their education at accredited colleges or universities.
Financial data: Year ended 12/31/2012. Assets, $43,372 (M); Expenditures, $5,154; Total giving, $4,500; Grants to individuals, 7 grants totaling $4,500 (high: $700, low: $500).
Fields of interest: Higher education.
Type of support: Scholarships—to individuals.
Application information: Applications accepted.
  Initial approach: Letter
  Deadline(s): None
EIN: 010282855

1359
Coast Guard Foundation, Inc.
394 Taugwonk Rd.
Stonington, CT 06378-1807 (860) 535-0786
Contact: Anne B. Brengle, Pres.
FAX: (860) 535-0944; E-mail: info@cgfdn.org;
E-Mail for Anne B. Brengle: abrengle@cgfdn.org;
URL: http://www.coastguardfoundation.org

Foundation type: Public charity
Purpose: Scholarships to Coast Guard Academy students or enlisted personnel and their dependents.
Publications: Annual report; Informational brochure; Newsletter.
Financial data: Year ended 12/31/2011. Assets, $7,168,110 (M); Expenditures, $4,716,024; Total

giving, $2,078,689; Grants to individuals, totaling $242,111.
Fields of interest: Military/veterans' organizations.
Type of support: Support to graduates or students of specific schools; Undergraduate support.
Application information: Applications accepted. Application form required.
  Initial approach: E-mail
  Deadline(s): Varies
  Applicants should submit the following:
    1) Essay
    2) Transcripts
    3) SAT
    4) ACT
    5) Letter(s) of recommendation
  Additional information: See web site for further program descriptions.
Program descriptions:
  Captain Ernest Fox Perpetual Scholarship: One $1,000 scholarship is awarded each year to employees of ALC.
  Coast Guard Foundation Scholarship: Scholarships of up to $5,000 per year are awarded to dependent children of enlisted members of the U.S. Coast Guard on active duty, retired or deceased, or to reservists who are currently on extended active duty 180 days or more.
  Commander Daniel J. Christovich Scholarship: Scholarships are awarded to dependent children of enlisted members of the U.S. Coast Guard on active duty, retired or deceased, or to reservists who are currently on extended active duty 180 days or more.
  Enlisted Education Grant: The program offers scholarships of up to $350 for active duty enlisted personnel in the pay grades E-3 to E-9 with two or more years of Coast Guard service.
  Keiser University Coast Guard Scholarship: Two full-tuition scholarships, valued at $50,000 each, to Keiser College are awarded to members of the Coast Guard with at least four years of service.
  Lake Superior State University Amy Ignatowski Memorial Scholarship: Scholarship applicants must be an active U.S. Coast Guard member, Coast Guard Reservist or their dependent from USCG Sector Sault Ste. Marie, Michigan, and be accepted as a student in any course of study at Lake Superior State University with a GPA of 2.0 or higher. Active-duty Coast Guard members must have completed a minimum of six months of military service and reservists must be in drilling status.
  RADM Arnold Sobel Scholarship: Four scholarships of up to $5,000 per year are awarded to dependent children of enlisted members of the U.S. Coast Guard on active duty, retired or deceased, or to reservists who are currently on extended active duty 180 days or more.
  U.S.A.A. Family Reserve Enlisted Scholarship: Six scholarships of $1,000 are awarded to U.S. Coast Guard enlisted reservists or their dependents.
  Vander Putten Family Scholarship Fund: Grants of up to $500 a year for text books and miscellaneous educational expenses are available for active duty members E-3 to E-9.
EIN: 042899862

1360
Colburn-Keenan Foundation, Inc.
P.O. Box 811
Enfield, CT 06083-0811 (860) 749-7522
FAX: (860) 763-6494; E-mail: admin@colkeen.org;
Toll free tel.: (800) 966-2431; URL: http://www.colkeen.org

Foundation type: Independent foundation
Purpose: Emergency assistance to individuals and families impacted by chronic inherited bleeding disorders or other chronic illnesses. Scholarships

to undergraduate students with bleeding disorders attending colleges or universities in the U.S.

Publications: Application guidelines.

Financial data: Year ended 12/31/2012. Assets, $10,801,497 (M); Expenditures, $400,872; Total giving, $252,397; Grants to individuals, 105 grants totaling $207,397 (high: $7,745, low: $100).

Fields of interest: Higher education; Health care; Hemophilia.

Type of support: Emergency funds; Scholarships—to individuals; Grants for special needs.

Application information: Applications accepted. Application form required. Application form available on the grantmaker's web site.

  Initial approach: Letter or telephone
  Deadline(s): Apr. 15 for Scholarships, none for Emergency Grants
  Final notification: Applicants notified before the end of June for scholarships
  Applicants should submit the following:
    1) Letter(s) of recommendation
    2) Resume
    3) SAT
    4) Photograph
    5) Transcripts
    6) GPA
    7) ACT
  Additional information: See web site for additional guidelines for emergency grants.

Program description:
  Beth Carew Memorial Scholarship: Under this Program, scholarships are offered to ten undergraduate students with bleeding disorders attending colleges or universities in the United States. Each award is in the amount of $4,000 per student per year. See foundation web site for more information.
EIN: 204634920

1361
Community Foundation of Eastern Connecticut

(formerly The Community Foundation of Southeastern Connecticut, Inc.)
68 Federal St.
P.O. Box 769
New London, CT   06320-6302   (860) 442-3572
Contact: For scholarships: Jennifer O'Brien, Prog. Dir.
Scholarship inquiry e-mail: jennob@cfect.org
FAX: (860) 442-0584; E-mail: bmorgan@cfect.org;
URL: http://www.cfect.org

Foundation type: Community foundation
Purpose: Scholarships to graduating high school students and enrolled college students in the foundation's forty-two town service area in Eastern CT.

Publications: Application guidelines; Annual report; Annual report (including application guidelines); Financial statement; Grants list; Informational brochure; Newsletter; Occasional report; IRS Form 990 or 990-PF printed copy available upon request.

Financial data: Year ended 12/31/2012. Assets, $44,814,192 (M); Expenditures, $4,067,300; Total giving, $3,088,178; Grants to individuals, 202 grants totaling $315,192.

Fields of interest: Higher education; Graduate/professional education.

Type of support: Scholarships—to individuals; Support to graduates or students of specific schools; Graduate support; Undergraduate support.

Application information: Applications accepted. Application form required. Application form available on the grantmaker's web site.

  Initial approach: Application

  Send request by: Mail
  Copies of proposal: 2
  Deadline(s): Apr. 1
  Final notification: Applicants notified early June
  Applicants should submit the following:
    1) ACT
    2) Essay
    3) FAFSA
    4) Letter(s) of recommendation
    5) SAT
    6) Transcripts
  Additional information: Awards generally range from $500 to $20,000 for a single year or over a period of up to four years. See web site for a complete listing of scholarship funds.

Program description:
  Scholarships: The foundation administers scholarship funds with varying eligibility requirements. Most of the scholarships are for high school seniors, college or graduate students but some may also be awarded to non-traditional students who want to further their education. Each scholarship has its own selection criteria which may include town of residence, high school, field of study and other preferences. Recipients must attend or plan to attend accredited educational institutions. See web site for additional information.
EIN: 061080097

1362
The Community Foundation of Northwest Connecticut, Inc.

(formerly Torrington Area Foundation for Public Giving Trust Entity)
32 City Hall Ave.
P.O. Box 1144
Torrington, CT   06790   (860) 626-1245
Contact: Robert Lee August, Recording Secy.
FAX: (860) 489-7517; E-mail: info@cfnwct.org;
URL: http://www.cfnwct.org

Foundation type: Community foundation
Purpose: Scholarships to residents of Litchfield County, CT, for higher education.

Publications: Application guidelines; Annual report; Financial statement; Informational brochure; Informational brochure (including application guidelines); Newsletter; Occasional report.

Financial data: Year ended 12/31/2011. Assets, $4,698,266 (M); Expenditures, $223,698; Total giving, $91,097; Grants to individuals, 41 grants totaling $17,200.

Type of support: Scholarships—to individuals; Graduate support; Undergraduate support.

Application information: Applications accepted. Application form required. Application form available on the grantmaker's web site.

  Initial approach: Application
  Send request by: Mail
  Copies of proposal: 3
  Deadline(s): Apr. 1
  Final notification: Recipients notified in approximately three months
  Applicants should submit the following:
    1) Essay
    2) FAFSA
    3) GPA
    4) SAT
    5) SAR
    6) Transcripts
EIN: 066114199

1363
The Community Renewal Team, Inc.

555 Windsor St.
Hartford, CT   06120-2418   (860) 560-5600
Contact: Lena Rodriguez, Pres. and C.E.O.
E-mail: info@crtct.org; URL: http://www.crtct.org

Foundation type: Public charity
Purpose: Assistance to low income and working poor households in the Connecticut River Valley with help in home heating costs, weatherization, housing and shelter, and other special needs.

Publications: Annual report; Newsletter; Occasional report.

Financial data: Year ended 12/31/2011. Assets, $30,568,313 (M); Expenditures, $82,915,250; Total giving, $29,041,328; Grants to individuals, totaling $26,906,826.

Fields of interest: Economically disadvantaged.
Type of support: Grants for special needs.
Application information: Applications accepted.

  Additional information: Applicants must show proof of income and household size, most recent bank statement and other documentation. Contact the agency for additional guidelines.
EIN: 060795640

1364
The Compass Fund, Inc.

(formerly Navarro Family Foundation, Inc.)
95 Glastonbury Blvd.
P.O. Box 22
Glastonbury, CT   06033

Foundation type: Independent foundation
Purpose: Scholarships to children of low and moderate-income families residing in New London, CT for attendance at public or private schools of their choice.

Financial data: Year ended 12/31/2012. Assets, $246,621 (M); Expenditures, $41,061; Total giving, $36,000; Grants to individuals, 18 grants totaling $36,000 (high: $2,000, low: $2,000).

Fields of interest: Economically disadvantaged.
Type of support: Scholarships—to individuals.
Application information: Applications accepted. Application form required.

  Additional information: Contact the fund for participating schools.
EIN: 061602643

1365
Connecticut Children's Medical Center Foundation, Inc.

282 Washington St.
Hartford, CT   06106-5035   (860) 545-9000
URL: http://connecticutchildrensfoundation.org/Page.aspx?pid=329

Foundation type: Public charity
Purpose: Scholarships to current and former students of Connecticut Children's Medical Center.

Publications: Application guidelines.

Financial data: Year ended 09/30/2011. Assets, $78,280,475 (M); Expenditures, $3,077,945.

Fields of interest: Vocational education, post-secondary; Higher education; Cancer.

Type of support: Scholarships—to individuals.

Application information: Applications accepted. Application form required. Application form available on the grantmaker's web site. Interview required.

  Initial approach: Application

Send request by: Mail
Deadline(s): Mar. 30 for Isidore Wise Scholarship Program, Apr. 20 for Reach for the Stars Survivorship Scholarship
Applicants should submit the following:
1) Photograph
2) Transcripts
3) SAT
4) Letter(s) of recommendation
5) ACT
Additional information: See web site for additional application guidelines.

Program descriptions:
Isidore Wise Scholarship Program: Five scholarships of $4,000 each will be available to individuals attending an accredited postsecondary undergraduate institution in the fall. Applicants must be high school students completing their senior years, and who are either past or present patients of Connecticut Children's Medical Center (CCMC) or Newington Children's Hospital, or current or former students of the CCMC School.

Reach for the Stars Survivorship Program Scholarship: Scholarships of $500 each are available to deserving high school seniors who are past or present oncology patients of the Division of Hematology and Oncology at Connecticut Children's Medical Center. Applicant must be a pediatric cancer survivor seeking an associate's or undergraduate degree, or a trade school educational program certificate, and an individual who demonstrates academic ambition and embraces a way of life that overcomes the obstacles of living with a cancer diagnosis.
EIN: 222619869

1366
The Connecticut Community Foundation
(formerly The Waterbury Foundation)
43 Field St.
Waterbury, CT   06702-1906   (203) 753-1315
Contact: For grants and scholarships: Josh Carey, Dir., Grants Mgmt.
Scholarship inquiry e-mail: scholarships@conncf.org
FAX: (203) 756-3054; E-mail: info@conncf.org;
URL: http://conncf.org

Foundation type: Community foundation
Purpose: Undergraduate scholarships to students residing in the foundation's 21-town service area.
Publications: Application guidelines; Annual report; Informational brochure; Newsletter; Occasional report.
Financial data: Year ended 12/31/2012. Assets, $81,761,965 (M); Expenditures, $4,390,099; Total giving, $3,001,395; Grants to individuals, 341 grants totaling $716,245.
Fields of interest: Arts education; Media/communications; Print publishing; Humanities; Literature; Research; Secondary school/education; Education, special; Higher education; Nursing school/education; Scholarships/financial aid; Reading; Mathematics; Disabilities, people with; African Americans/Blacks; Women.
Type of support: Scholarships—to individuals; Support to graduates or students of specific schools; Awards/prizes; Undergraduate support.
Application information: Applications accepted. Application form required. Application form available on the grantmaker's web site.
Initial approach: Application
Send request by: Online
Deadline(s): Feb. 14 for re-applicants, Mar. 14 for new applicants
Final notification: Recipients notified in eight weeks
Applicants should submit the following:

1) Essay
2) FAFSA
3) Financial information
4) GPA
5) Letter(s) of recommendation
6) Transcripts
Additional information: See web site for a complete listing of scholarships.

Program description:
Scholarship Programs: The foundation administers nearly 120 different scholarship funds, generously established by area donors. Each scholarship has different requirements, such as academic achievement, fields of study, country of residency, and community service. Scholarship awards are primarily in the $2,000 range and are payable to the school the student plans to attend. See web site for additional information.
EIN: 066038074

1367
Connecticut Health Foundation, Inc.
100 Pearl St.
Hartford, CT   06103-4506   (860) 724-1580
Contact: Rochel Lantz, Cont.
FAX: (860) 724-1589; E-mail: info@cthealth.org;
URL: http://www.cthealth.org

Foundation type: Independent foundation
Purpose: Fellowships to residents of CT who demonstrate a basic understanding and potential impact of racial and ethnic health disparities on health status, community stability and the economy of Connecticut.
Publications: Annual report (including application guidelines); Financial statement; Grants list; Informational brochure; Newsletter.
Financial data: Year ended 12/31/2012. Assets, $107,395,324 (M); Expenditures, $6,314,435; Total giving, $2,652,896.
Fields of interest: Mental health, counseling/support groups; Children.
Type of support: Fellowships.
Application information: Applications accepted. Application form required. Application form available on the grantmaker's web site. Interview required.
Send request by: E-mail
Deadline(s): Apr. 2
Final notification: Recipients notified mid-July
Additional information: Application should include a personal statement.

Program description:
Health Leadership Fellows Program: The program focuses specifically on building leadership skills necessary for creating public will and systems change for health equity. Participants hone skills such as understanding and implementing health systems change solutions, developing strategic messaging and communications, and organizing and working in multi-disciplinary teams. Twenty fellows selected through a competitive process must make a ten-month commitment (Sept. to June) to attend two weekend retreats, monthly seminars, and a leadership project at no cost to them. Each applicant must be a resident of Connecticut or his/her primary work must directly impact the people of Connecticut. The ideal class is composed of representation from multiple sectors and groups most affected by racial and ethnic health disparities. For additional information go to www.cthealth.org or contact Nancy Nolan, nancy@cthealth.org or 860-724-1580.
EIN: 061057387

1368
The Connecticut Young Writers Trust
(formerly The Impac Literary Awards for Young Writers Trust)
P.O. Box 8898
New Haven, CT   06532   (203) 843-1423
Contact: Ravi Shankar, Tr.
Application Address: CT Young Writers Awards, Ravi Shanker, 390 Shore Dr., Branford, CT 06405

Foundation type: Operating foundation
Purpose: Awards to young writers between the ages of 13 and 18 who are enrolled in the CT school system.
Financial data: Year ended 04/30/2013. Assets, $17,872 (M); Expenditures, $7,903; Total giving, $5,500; Grants to individuals, 20 grants totaling $5,500 (high: $750, low: $100).
Fields of interest: Literature.
Type of support: Awards/prizes.
Application information: Applications accepted.
Initial approach: Single work poetry or prose submission
Deadline(s): Feb. 1
Additional information: Applicant must be nominated by teacher.
EIN: 311635811

1369
Carle C. Conway Scholarship Foundation, Inc.
c/o Marsha L. Colten
95 Alexandra Dr.
Stamford, CT   06903-1731
Application address: Carle C. Conway Scholarship Program, P.O. Box 6731, Princeton, NJ 08541

Foundation type: Company-sponsored foundation
Purpose: Scholarships to current employee and children of current employee of the successor companies of the former Continental Can, Inc.
Financial data: Year ended 06/30/2013. Assets, $4,191,616 (M); Expenditures, $314,859; Total giving, $266,938; Grants to individuals, 26 grants totaling $216,938 (high: $10,000; low: -$3,938).
Fields of interest: Higher education.
Type of support: Employee-related scholarships.
Application information: Applications accepted.
Initial approach: Letter
Deadline(s): Mar. 1
Additional information: Letter must include student and employee information. Maximum scholarship award is $10,000 for four years.
Company name: Consolidated Container Company LLC
EIN: 136088936

1370
Cornelia de Lange Syndrome Foundation
302 W. Main St., Ste. 100
Avon, CT   06001-3681   (860) 676-8166
Contact: Marie Concklin-Malloy, Exec. Dir.
FAX: (860) 676-8337; E-mail: info@cdlsusa.org;
Toll-free tel: (800)-753-2357 and (800)-223-8355;
E-mail Fot Marie Concklin-Malloy:
outreach@cdlsusa.org; URL: http://
www.cdlsusa.org

Foundation type: Public charity
Purpose: Research grants provided to fund clinical or pilot research relevant to Cornelia de Lange Syndrome (CdLS).
Financial data: Year ended 12/31/2012. Assets, $886,638 (M); Expenditures, $968,563.
Fields of interest: Diseases (rare); Diseases (rare) research; Medical research.

Type of support: Research; Postgraduate support.
Application information: Applications accepted. Application form required. Application form available on the grantmaker's web site.
  Initial approach: Proposal
  Copies of proposal: 3
  Deadline(s): Apr. 15
  Final notification: Recipients announced June 1
  Additional information: Applications must include budget information and IRB approval. See web site for additional information.
Program description:
  Research Grants: Grants are to be used to increase knowledge of the causes and manifestations of CdLS. Up to $15,000 of grant funds are available to basic science and/or clinical research projects on CdLS. Grants are for a twelve-month period and do not support indirect costs.
EIN: 061057497

1371
Criag D. Tifford Foundation
87 Ridgecrest Rd.
Stamford, CT 06903-3120 (203) 321-8426
Contact: Bonnie Brodowski, Dir. of Prog. Devel.
FAX: (203) 321-8426;
E-mail: info@cdtfoundation.org; Contact e-mail: bonnie.brodowski@gmail.com; URL: http://www.cdtfoundation.org

Foundation type: Public charity
Purpose: Financial assistance to individuals with testicular cancer for non-medical expenses.
Financial data: Year ended 12/31/2011. Assets, $57,181 (M); Expenditures, $172,128; Total giving, $141,000; Grants to individuals, totaling $11,000.
Fields of interest: Cancer.
Type of support: Grants to individuals.
Application information: Contact the foundation for additional guidelines.
EIN: 020654363

1372
CTE, Inc.
(also known as The Community Action Agency for the Greater Stamford Area)
34 Woodland Pl.
Stamford, CT 06902-7057 (203) 327-3260
Contact: Phillip McKain, Pres.
FAX: (203) 352-2972; E-mail: info@ctecap.org;
URL: http://ctecap.org

Foundation type: Public charity
Purpose: Assistance to indigent residents of Stamford, Greenwich, and Darien counties, CT.
Publications: Newsletter; Occasional report.
Financial data: Year ended 09/30/2011. Assets, $804,807 (M); Expenditures, $4,824,200; Total giving, $2,038,130; Grants to individuals, totaling $2,038,130.
Fields of interest: Economically disadvantaged.
Type of support: Grants for special needs.
Application information: Applications not accepted.
  Additional information: Unsolicited requests for funds not considered or acknowledged.
EIN: 060797967

1373
Darien Community Association, Inc.
274 Middlesex Rd.
Darien, CT 06820-3314 (203) 655-9050
Contact: Amy Bell, Exec. Dir.
FAX: (203) 655-4009; E-mail: info@dariendca.org;
E-Mail For Amy Bell: amy@dariendca.org;
URL: http://www.dariendca.org

Foundation type: Public charity
Purpose: Scholarships to graduates of Darien High School, CT for postsecondary education at accredited colleges or universities.
Financial data: Year ended 05/31/2012. Assets, $1,953,738 (M); Expenditures, $736,626; Total giving, $52,000; Grants to individuals, 26 grants totaling $52,000.
Fields of interest: Higher education.
Type of support: Undergraduate support.
Application information: Applications accepted. Application form required. Interview required.
  Deadline(s): May
  Additional information: Scholarships are awarded based on financial need, scholastic standing and the potential of the applicant. Application must include parents' tax return.
EIN: 060763897

1374
Deering Foundation, Inc.
c/o The Ashford Company
707 Summer St.
Stamford, CT 06901

Foundation type: Independent foundation
Purpose: Scholarships to Deering, Hillsboro, and Weare, NH, area students. Preference is given to those majoring in medicine, social service, and related fields.
Financial data: Year ended 05/31/2013. Assets, $705,324 (M); Expenditures, $40,556; Total giving, $35,500; Grants to individuals, 15 grants totaling $32,000 (high: $3,000, low: $1,000).
Fields of interest: Medical school/education; Social sciences.
Type of support: Scholarships—to individuals.
Application information: Applications accepted. Application form required.
  Initial approach: Letter
  Deadline(s): May 1
  Additional information: Application must include present and proposed school, field of interest, financial support available from family, and personal income; Scholarships are renewable.
EIN: 026012645

1375
Deloitte Foundation
(formerly Deloitte & Touche Foundation)
10 Westport Rd.
P.O. Box 820
Wilton, CT 06897-0820
Contact for Doctoral Fellowship Program: Peg Levine, tel.: (203) 761-3413,
e-mail: plevine@deloitte.com; URL: http://www.deloitte.com/us/df

Foundation type: Company-sponsored foundation
Purpose: Fellowships to graduate students enrolled in and successfully pursuing a doctoral program in accounting. Scholarships to accountants to pursue a Ph.D. program and transition into academia. Grants to authors who have made a significant contribution to the practice of public accounting and

grants to tax professors to develop new teaching methods.
Publications: Application guidelines; Grants list; Informational brochure.
Financial data: Year ended 06/02/2012. Assets, $14,867,614 (M); Expenditures, $8,303,444; Total giving, $8,196,527.
Fields of interest: Business school/education.
Type of support: Fellowships; Awards/prizes; Doctoral support.
Application information: Applications accepted. Application form required.
  Deadline(s): Oct. 15 for Doctoral Fellowships
  Final notification: Recipients notified in Jan. for Doctoral Fellowships
Program descriptions:
  AAA/Deloitte Wildman Medal: The foundation, in partnership with the American Accounting Association, honors an author or co-authors whose article, book, monograph, or other work published has made a highly significant contribution to the practice of public accounting. The $5,000 honorarium is awarded to support research that advances the theory and practice of accounting. The award is administered by the American Accounting Association. See web site, http://aaahq.org/awards/award1.htm for additional information.
  Accounting Doctoral Scholars: The foundation, in partnership with the AICPA Foundation, awards grants to accountants with public accounting experience in auditing and tax to help them transition into academic roles at the university level. The program includes an annual stipend of $30,000 for a maximum of four years to pursue a Ph.D. and career in academia. The program is administered by the AICPA Foundation. See web site, http://www.adsphd.org/ for additional information.
  Doctoral Fellowship Program: The foundation annually awards up to ten $25,000 fellowships to doctoral accounting students. Fellowships are disbursed in four payments over two years to help cover expenses during the final year of coursework and during the subsequent year of writing a dissertation.
EIN: 136400341

1376
Devon Rotary Foundation Trust Fund
250 Broad St.
Milford, CT 06460-3236
Contact: Paul Lewis Otzel, Secy.-Treas.
URL: http://www.devonrotary.org

Foundation type: Independent foundation
Purpose: Scholarships to graduating high school seniors from Milford, CT for postsecondary education.
Financial data: Year ended 06/30/2012. Assets, $150,711 (M); Expenditures, $28,425; Total giving, $28,010; Grants to individuals, 21 grants totaling $19,000 (high: $1,000, low: $500).
Fields of interest: Higher education; Law school/education; Community development, real estate; Computer science; Anatomy (animal); Science.
Type of support: Support to graduates or students of specific schools.
Application information: Applications accepted. Application form required. Application form available on the grantmaker's web site.
  Deadline(s): Apr.
  Applicants should submit the following:
    1) Class rank
    2) SAT
    3) GPA
    4) Letter(s) of recommendation

5) Transcripts
6) SAR
7) Essay
Additional information: See web site for additional application information.

Program descriptions:
Barbara Burwell Gaynor Memorial Scholarship: This $1,000 scholarship is for any student graduating from a Milford high school or any Milford student graduating from a high school who is continuing his or her education at a four year college. This is designated for a student who will be pursuing a degree in education with the hopes of becoming a teacher. The scholarship is based on service, academics and need.

Devon Rotary City Wide Scholarship: Scholarship in the amount of $1,000 is for any student graduating from a Milford high school or Milford resident graduating from any high school. The award is based on academics, service, need and activities.

Dodie Ireland Memorial Scholarship: This scholarship of $1,000 has been designated for a graduate of Platt RVTS who will be continuing his or education at an accredited postgraduate institution.

Duke Scholarship: A scholarship in the amount of $1,000 is for any student graduating from a Milford high school or Milford resident graduating from any high school who is continuing his or education at an accredited postgraduate institution. It is designated for a student who will be studying animal sciences, pre-veterinary studies or any related major. The scholarship is based on service, need, and academics.

Edward V. Bierne Memorial Scholarship: This one-time $1,000 scholarship is open to students from Jonathan Law High School who are interested in studying Biology or other life sciences at a four year college.

Frederick De Luca Foundation Scholarship: This $1,000 scholarship is made possible through a grant from the DeLuca Foundation. It is designated for a graduating senior from Jonathan Law who will be attending a four-year college in the fall. Preference is given to Subway employees. This scholarship is based on academics, service, need, and high school activities.

John D. Gaynor Memorial Scholarship: A $1,000 scholarship is for any student graduating from a Milford high school or Milford resident graduating from any high school who is continuing his or her education at a four year college. The scholarship is designated for a student who will be pursuing a degree in business, with additional consideration given to students who are interested in entrepreneurship. The scholarship is based on service, academics and need.

Paul Austin Scholarship: A $1,000 scholarship is renewable for four years for a student graduating from Jonathan Law who will be attending a four year college in the Fall. The scholarship is based on academics, service, need and high school activities. It is renewable provided that the student maintains a 3.0 GPA and is enrolled as a full time student.

Steven G. Memorial Scholarship: A scholarship of $1,000 is renewable for four years and is open to any student graduating from a Milford high school or any Milford resident graduating from any high school. This is designated for a student studying marine biology, aquatic sciences, or a related major, or for a student who has shown concern for the environment and an interest in marine life. The scholarship is based on service, academics and need.

The Stanford Family Scholarship: A one-time scholarship of $500 is open to students from

Jonathan Law or Foran High Schools, and is based on need and academics. Special consideration is given for students who have overcome adversity.
EIN: 222959085

1377
Orazio DiMauro Foundation
11 Green Acres Ln.
Trumbull, CT   06611   (203) 261-5967
E-mail: ifidi@aol.com; *URL:* http://www.oraziodimauro.org

Foundation type: Independent foundation
Purpose: Scholarships to Bridgeport, CT, area residents and residents of Siracusa, Italy, for higher education in the fields of engineering and medicine.
Publications: Application guidelines; Informational brochure.
Financial data: Year ended 08/31/2012. Assets, $999,793 (M); Expenditures, $36,751; Total giving, $23,500; Grants to individuals, 9 grants totaling $23,500 (high: $4,700, low: $2,350).
Fields of interest: Medical school/education; Engineering school/education.
International interests: Italy.
Type of support: Graduate support; Undergraduate support.
Application information: Applications accepted. Application form required.
Initial approach: Letter
Deadline(s): Mar. 31
Final notification: Applicants notified in July
Applicants should submit the following:
1) Transcripts
2) Financial information
Additional information: Application should also include a copy of your acceptance letter from the college or medical school where you will enroll.

Program description:
DiMauro Scholarship Awards: Scholarships for engineering students must be a resident of Bridgeport, CT, or surrounding towns, a graduating high school senior or a full-time student with an engineering major at an accredited four-year college, maintain a high school class rank in the top 50 percent of your class or as a college student with a 3.0 GPA, planning to attend an accredited four-year college with an engineering curriculum for a baccalaureate degree, and in financial need of scholarship assistance. Applicants for the medical scholarship must be a resident of Bridgeport, CT, or surrounding towns, a graduating senior in an accredited four-year college planning to attend an accredited medical college that awards the M.D. degree, maintain a 3.2 GPA or greater, and financially in need of scholarship assistance.
EIN: 061044179

1378
Sabina Dolan & Gladys Saulsbury Foundation, Inc.
400 Orange St.
New Haven, CT   06511-6405
Contact: Edward J. Dolan, Pres.

Foundation type: Independent foundation
Purpose: Scholarships and grants to students participating in interscholastic athletics at public high schools in New Haven, CT and grants to needy students in New Haven to enable them to attend summer camps which will teach them athletic skills.
Financial data: Year ended 01/31/2013. Assets, $5,210 (M); Expenditures, $8,400; Total giving, $8,400; Grants to individuals, 2 grants totaling $2,100.

Fields of interest: Athletics/sports, training.
Type of support: Scholarships—to individuals.
Application information: Applications accepted. Application form required.
Deadline(s): None
EIN: 061088838

1379
W. Gordon Dunning Charitable Trust
100 Pearl St., 13th Fl.
Shartford, CT   06103   (215) 412-8544
Contact: Debbie Henninger
Application address: c/o First Niagra Bank, 401 Plymouth Rd., Ste. 600, Plymouth Meeting, PA 19462

Foundation type: Independent foundation
Purpose: Scholarships to graduating high school and college seniors residing in Montgomery or Bucks Counties, PA for attendance at accredited colleges or universities pursuing a career in medicine, education or the ministry.
Financial data: Year ended 12/31/2012. Assets, $2,790,511 (M); Expenditures, $130,666; Total giving, $106,052; Grants to individuals, totaling $106,052.
Fields of interest: Medical school/education; Teacher school/education; Theological school/education.
Type of support: Scholarships—to individuals.
Application information: Applications accepted. Application form required.
Deadline(s): July 10
Additional information: Applicant must demonstrate financial need.
EIN: 237798777

1380
The Eagle Foundation Inc.
11 Henry St.
Greenwich, CT   06830-7039   (203) 532-9486
Contact: Brenda D. Landsman, Dir.

Foundation type: Independent foundation
Purpose: Undergraduate scholarships to high school seniors, who are residents of Fairfield County, CT, and the greater NY area.
Financial data: Year ended 12/31/2012. Assets, $29,291 (M); Expenditures, $86,524; Total giving, $27,500; Grants to individuals, 5 grants totaling $27,500 (high: $10,000, low: $1,750).
Type of support: Undergraduate support.
Application information: Applications accepted. Application form required.
Deadline(s): Apr. 15
Additional information: Contact local high school for application.
EIN: 061442187

1381
Eastern Star Charity Foundation of Connecticut, Inc.
65 Masonic Ave., Ste. 104
Wallingford, CT   06492-3087   (203) 949-1199

Foundation type: Public charity
Purpose: Grants to aid, assist and support aged and dependent female members of the Order of the Eastern Star of CT, with medical and other expenses.
Financial data: Year ended 02/28/2013. Assets, $7,763,439 (M); Expenditures, $377,588; Total giving, $363,525; Grants to individuals, totaling $1,175.
Fields of interest: Human services.

Type of support: Grants for special needs.
Application information: Applications not accepted.
Additional information: Unsolicited requests for funds not considered or acknowledged. Assistance only for female members of the Order of the Eastern Star of CT.
EIN: 066040430

1382
Arthur G. Eastman Memorial Scholarship Fund
850 Main St., RC 13-505
Bridgeport, CT 06604-4913

Foundation type: Independent foundation
Purpose: Scholarships to graduates of Whitingham High School, Jacksonville, VT, who have completed their last two high school years at Whitingham.
Financial data: Year ended 12/31/2012. Assets, $123,881 (M); Expenditures, $7,531; Total giving, $4,525.
Fields of interest: Higher education; Scholarships/ financial aid.
Type of support: Scholarships—to individuals; Support to graduates or students of specific schools.
Application information: Applications accepted. Application form required.
Applicants should submit the following:
    1) Transcripts
    2) Financial information
EIN: 030279845

1383
The Ebony Horsewomen, Inc.
337 Vine St.
Hartford, CT 06112-2028 (860) 293-2914
Contact: Patricia E. Kelly, Pres. and C.E.O.
FAX: (860) 293-0039; E-mail: ehwomen@aol.com; URL: http://www.ebonyhorsewomen.us/

Foundation type: Public charity
Purpose: Financial assistance to graduating seniors for attendance at colleges, and scholarships to youth who cannot afford summer camp for summer recreation in the Hartford, CT area.
Financial data: Year ended 12/31/2011. Assets, $147,570 (M); Expenditures, $298,599; Total giving, $295; Grants to individuals, totaling $225.
Fields of interest: Higher education; Camps; Athletics/sports, equestrianism.
Type of support: Scholarships—to individuals.
Application information: Contact the organization for additional information.
EIN: 061268874

1384
The Elmseed Enterprise Fund
P.O. Box 207148
New Haven, CT 06520-7148 (203) 903-1737
Contact: Jungwon Byun, C.E.O. and Co-Exec. Dir.
E-mail: info@elmseed.org; E-Mail for Jungwon Byun: jungwon.byun@elmseed.org; URL: http://www.elmseed.org

Foundation type: Public charity
Purpose: Small loans to low-income entrepreneurs in the greater New Haven, CT area.
Publications: Informational brochure.
Financial data: Year ended 07/31/2012. Assets, $81,859 (M); Expenditures, $15,007.
Type of support: Seed money; Loans—to individuals.

Application information:
Applicants should submit the following:
    1) Proposal
    2) Letter(s) of recommendation
    3) Financial information
    4) Budget Information
Additional information: Unsolicited application not accepted. Borrowers must form peer groups of three to five small business owners.
EIN: 061624995

1385
Endocrine Fellows Foundation
342 N. Main St., Ste. 301
West Hartford, CT 06117-2507 (877) 877-6515
Contact: Anne Mercer
FAX: (860) 586-7550;
E-mail: info@endocrinefellows.org; URL: http://www.endocrinefellows.org/

Foundation type: Company-sponsored foundation
Purpose: Awards research grants and preceptorships for the study of endocrinology and its related disorders.
Publications: Application guidelines; Grants list; Program policy statement.
Financial data: Year ended 12/31/2011. Assets, $600,374 (M); Expenditures, $832,961; Total giving, $334,000. Grants to individuals amount not specified.
Fields of interest: Public health, obesity; Nerve, muscle & bone diseases; Diabetes; Institute; Diabetes research; Medical specialties research.
Type of support: Research.
Application information: Applications accepted. Application form required. Application form available on the grantmaker's web site.
Initial approach: Application
Send request by: Online or mail
Deadline(s): Sept. 13 for EFF Endocrine Research Grant and the Marilyn Fishman Grant for Diabetes Research, varies for Preceptorships
Final notification: Recipients notified by Nov. 4 for EFF Endocrine Research Grant and the Marilyn Fishman Grant for Diabetes Research
Applicants should submit the following:
    1) Budget Information
    2) Curriculum vitae
Program descriptions:
Marilyn Fishman Grant for Diabetes Research: The foundation, in partnership with Bristol-Myers Squibb and AstraZeneca Pharmaceuticals, awards up to four research grants of $7,500 each. The grant is limited to metabolism, obesity, and Type 2 diabetes clinical and basic research. Successful grantees are expected to present their research at an EFF scientific diabetes forum for fellows.
Preceptorship Program: The foundation sponsors two-week preceptorships in endocrinology at select institutions to enable fellows to increase their skills in specialized areas. The preceptorships include specialty clinics, research, and techniques that are useful in subspecialty areas of endocrinology and metabolism. The program is limited to second and third year fellows.
The EFF Endocrine Research Grant: This grant is awarded twice a year and is for general endocrine topics including but not limited to thyroid, bone, adrenal, pituitary, growth, and reproductive disorders. Up to four grants are awarded at $7,500 each.
EIN: 954511639

1386
Equus Foundation, Inc.
(also known as Horse Charities of America)
168 Long Lots Rd.
Westport, CT 06880-4016 (203) 259-1550
Contact: Lynn Coakley, Pres.
E-mail: equus@equusfoundation.org; URL: http://www.equusfoundation.org

Foundation type: Public charity
Purpose: Awards by nomination to individuals who have devoted personal time to making the quality of life of horses paramount by improving the health and welfare of the horses.
Financial data: Year ended 08/31/2012. Assets, $253,548 (M); Expenditures, $408,845; Total giving, $290,895. Awards/prizes amount not specified.
Fields of interest: Animal welfare; Athletics/sports, equestrianism.
Type of support: Awards/prizes.
Application information:
Send request by: Mail
Deadline(s): Nov. 11
Additional information: Any member of the equestrian community may make a nomination for an individual to be considered for the award. See web site for additional guidelines.
Program description:
Humanitarian Award: The goal of the award is to spotlight and honor the selfless dedication of an individual or a group of individuals to horse welfare, whether on a regional or national scale. The award will be presented to an individual or group of individuals who have devoted considerable personal time to making the quality of life of horses paramount - from improving the health and welfare of the horse to promoting and expanding the general public's appreciation and respect of the diverse role of horses not just in equestrian sports but also as service and therapy animals. The award is limited to individuals. Corporations, organizations, affiliate groups, and businesses are not eligible. Any member of the equestrian community may submit an award nomination. Nominations may be made by individuals or organizations. The awardee will receive a $5,000 grant from the EQUUS Foundation to be presented to the equestrian or horse-related charity of his or her choice.
EIN: 421547242

1387
Fairfield County Community Foundation, Inc.
(also known as FCCF)
383 Main Ave.
Norwalk, CT 06851-1543 (203) 750-3200
Contact: For grants: Sharon Jones, Prog. Admin. Asst.
FAX: (203) 750-3232;
E-mail: info@fccfoundation.org; URL: http://www.fccfoundation.org

Foundation type: Community foundation
Purpose: Scholarships to graduating high school seniors and current undergraduate and graduate students attending an accredited college or university, or enrolled in a specialized or advanced vocational training program.
Publications: Application guidelines; Annual report; Financial statement; Grants list; Informational brochure; Newsletter; Occasional report.
Financial data: Year ended 06/30/2012. Assets, $150,440,396 (M); Expenditures, $20,109,784;

Total giving, $16,628,149; Grants to individuals, 108 grants totaling $443,666.
Fields of interest: Higher education; Graduate/professional education; Law school/education; Nursing school/education; Engineering school/education; Health sciences school/education.
Type of support: Scholarships—to individuals; Support to graduates or students of specific schools; Undergraduate support; Postgraduate support.
Application information: Applications accepted. Application form required.
  Send request by: Online
  Deadline(s): Varies
  Applicants should submit the following:
    1) SAR
    2) Letter(s) of recommendation
    3) SAT
    4) Transcripts
    5) Essay
  Additional information: See web site for complete listing of scholarship funds.
Program description:
  Scholarship Funds: The foundation has nearly 200 scholarship funds established by generous individuals, businesses and organizations that help deserving students pursue college study and strengthen the future of the local communities. These funds each have their own eligibility requirements and cover many different areas of study, such as health care, the arts and engineering. Students from the Greater Bridgeport Area towns of Bridgeport, Easton, Fairfield, Milford, Monroe, Shelton, Stratford, Trumbull or Westport, CT may apply for scholarships. See web site for additional information.
EIN: 061083893

1388
Fidelco Guide Dog Foundation, Inc.
103 Old Iron Ore Rd.
Bloomfield, CT 06002-1424 (860) 243-5200
E-mail: info@fidelco.org; URL: http://www.fidelco.org

Foundation type: Public charity
Purpose: Assistance to men and women who are blind by providing them with the highest quality guide dogs for increased independence and mobility.
Financial data: Year ended 12/31/2011. Assets, $20,530,009 (M); Expenditures, $4,243,586.
Fields of interest: Blind/visually impaired.
Type of support: Grants for special needs.
Application information: Applications accepted. Application form required. Application form available on the grantmaker's web site. Interview required.
  Initial approach: Application
  Send request by: Online
  Deadline(s): Ongoing
Program description:
  Guide Dog Program: Gifts of guide dogs are available to the legally blind. Orientation and mobility training may be required of applicants before they can be considered for a guide dog.
EIN: 066060478

1389
First County Bank Foundation, Inc.
c/o Ron Holbert
117 Prospect St., 4th Fl.
Stamford, CT 06901-1201 (203) 462-4858
Contact: Katherine A. Harris, V.P.
E-mail: foundation@firstcountybank.com;
URL: https://www.firstcountybank.com/first-county-bank-foundation-inc

Foundation type: Company-sponsored foundation
Purpose: Scholarships to graduating high school seniors in the lower Fairfield county, CT area to pursue higher education.
Publications: Application guidelines.
Financial data: Year ended 12/31/2012. Assets, $3,143,765 (M); Expenditures, $636,148; Total giving, $600,371.
Fields of interest: Higher education.
Type of support: Scholarships—to individuals.
Application information: Applications accepted. Application form required. Application form available on the grantmaker's web site.
  Send request by: Online
  Deadline(s): May 31
  Final notification: Applicants notified end of June
  Applicants should submit the following:
    1) Essay
    2) Transcripts
    3) Letter(s) of recommendation
  Additional information: Application should also include three letters of reference.
Program description:
  Richard E. Taber Citizenship Award: The foundation awards $5,000 college scholarships to three high school seniors living in the Fairfield County area. Applicants must demonstrate and excel in citizenship, leadership, academics, service, and sportsmanship. In addition to the scholarships, honorees receive a personalized certificate or plaque honoring the recipient, a congratulatory ad in the local newspaper with a photo, and a mention and photo on the First County Bank Foundation web site.
EIN: 061604469

1390
Maud Glover Folsom Foundation, Inc.
1228 King St., Ste. 5
Greenwich, CT 06830 (860) 729-7498
Contact: For Scholarships: William F. Austin
Application address: 7 Beldenwood Rd., Simsbury, CT 06070-2130
E-mail: sarahdouglas.burdett@snet.net

Foundation type: Independent foundation
Purpose: Scholarships to male U.S. citizens of Anglo-Saxon or German descent between the ages of 14 and 19.
Publications: Informational brochure (including application guidelines).
Financial data: Year ended 07/31/2012. Assets, $9,035,805 (M); Expenditures, $328,397; Total giving, $135,000; Grants to individuals, 26 grants totaling $135,000.
Fields of interest: Genealogy; Children/youth, services; Men.
International interests: England; Germany.
Type of support: Graduate support; Precollege support; Undergraduate support.
Application information: Applications accepted. Application form required. Interview required.
  Initial approach: Letter
  Deadline(s): None
  Additional information: Interviews required in CT at applicant's expense.
EIN: 111965890

1391
Jacob L. and Lewis Fox Foundation
147 Charter Oak Ave.
Hartford, CT 06106-5100
Application address: c/o Arthur Querido, Pres., 45 Lake St., South Windsor, CT 06074, tel.: (860) 644-1995

Foundation type: Independent foundation
Purpose: Scholarships to graduates of Hartford, CT, public high schools.
Financial data: Year ended 12/31/2011. Assets, $4,251,656 (M); Expenditures, $270,631; Total giving, $177,503; Grants to individuals, totaling $177,503.
Type of support: Support to graduates or students of specific schools; Undergraduate support.
Application information: Applications accepted. Application form required.
  Deadline(s): Usually late Jan. or early Feb.
EIN: 066067700

1392
Howard A. Fromson Foundation, Inc.
(formerly Fromson Foundation, Inc.)
c/o Anocoil Corp.
P.O. Box 1318
Rockville, CT 06066 (860) 871-1200

Foundation type: Company-sponsored foundation
Purpose: Scholarships to students of Clark University, MA, for the study of holocaust and genocide studies.
Financial data: Year ended 11/30/2011. Assets, $900,305 (M); Expenditures, $74,124; Total giving, $59,260; Grants to individuals, 30 grants totaling $17,910 (high: $1,410, low: $250).
Type of support: Support to graduates or students of specific schools.
Application information: Applications accepted. Application form not required.
  Initial approach: Letter
  Deadline(s): None
EIN: 061074374

1393
Frank R. Fuller Trust
c/o Bank of America, N.A.
777 Main St.
Hartford, CT 06115-2303
Contact: Carmen Britt
Application address: c/o Fuller Scholarship Committee, 300 Summit St., Hartford, CT 06106, tel.: (203) 527-3157, ext. 365

Foundation type: Independent foundation
Purpose: Scholarships and student loans to seniors of the Protestant faith, attending Hartford County, CT, high schools who are members of the Congregational Church and who plan to attend an accredited degree program at a four-year college or university.
Financial data: Year ended 12/31/2012. Assets, $4,399,496 (M); Expenditures, $327,304; Total giving, $266,841; Grants to individuals, totaling $266,841.
Fields of interest: Christian agencies & churches.
Type of support: Scholarships—to individuals; Support to graduates or students of specific schools; Undergraduate support.
Application information: Application form required.
  Initial approach: Letter
  Deadline(s): Apr. 15 for application, Mar. 1 to request application form
  Applicants should submit the following:
    1) Transcripts

2) Letter(s) of recommendation
Additional information: Application must also include financial aid form.
EIN: 066028136

1394
Mark R. Fusco Foundation
555 Long Wharf Dr.
New Haven, CT   06535   (203) 777-7451
Contact: Dennis Reilly, Secy.-Treas.

Foundation type: Independent foundation
Purpose: Scholarships primarily to residents of CT for higher education at accredited colleges or universities.
Financial data: Year ended 06/30/2012. Assets, $384,610 (M); Expenditures, $50,174; Total giving, $49,924; Grant to an individual, 1 grant totaling $6,500.
Fields of interest: Scholarships/financial aid.
Type of support: Scholarships—to individuals.
Application information: Applications accepted.
Initial approach: Letter
Deadline(s): None
Additional information: Selection of scholarship is based on academic performance, financial need and recommendations from instructors.
EIN: 222566615

1395
The Gilbert Family Foundation
35 Vista Dr.
Greenwich, CT   06830-7128   (203) 629-8757
Contact: G.S. Beckwith Gilbert, Pres.

Foundation type: Independent foundation
Purpose: Scholarships to individuals for college education, primarily in MA.
Financial data: Year ended 12/31/2011. Assets, $7,318 (M); Expenditures, $78,090; Total giving, $77,725; Grants to individuals, 5 grants totaling $77,725 (high: $27,725, low: $10,000).
Type of support: Undergraduate support.
Application information: Applications accepted. Application form required.
Deadline(s): None
Additional information: Contact foundation for current application guidelines.
EIN: 043732752

1396
The Graham Foundation Inc.
P.O. Box 548
Farmington, CT   06034   (860) 677-2621

Foundation type: Independent foundation
Purpose: Scholarships to graduates of Farmington High School, CT, who are or were residents of Farmington at the time of graduation.
Financial data: Year ended 12/31/2012. Assets, $2,455 (M); Expenditures, $18,242; Total giving, $16,500; Grants to individuals, 16 grants totaling $16,500 (high: $1,500, low: $500).
Type of support: Support to graduates or students of specific schools; Undergraduate support.
Application information: Application form required.
Additional information: Application must include an essay regarding career plans.
EIN: 061337821

1397
C. Arthur and Elizabeth Hammers Charitable Trust
100 Pearl St., 13th Fl.
Hartford, CT   06103
Contact: Craig Reichl
Application address: Lehighton Area High School, Lehighton, PA 18235

Foundation type: Independent foundation
Purpose: Scholarships only to graduates of Lehighton Area High School, PA.
Financial data: Year ended 01/31/2013. Assets, $1,086,103 (M); Expenditures, $34,623; Total giving, $22,750; Grants to individuals, 11 grants totaling $22,750 (high: $3,000, low: $1,500).
Fields of interest: Education.
Type of support: Support to graduates or students of specific schools; Undergraduate support.
Application information: Applications accepted.
Additional information: Contact high school guidance office for current application deadline/guidelines.
EIN: 237840919

1398
Greater Hartford Arts Council, Inc.
P.O. Box 231436
Hartford, CT   06123-1436   (860) 525-8629
Contact: Kenneth Kahn, Exec. Dir.
FAX: (860) 278-5461; E-mail: info@letsgoarts.org; URL: http://www.letsgoarts.org

Foundation type: Public charity
Purpose: Fellowships to artists in the greater Hartford, CT, area.
Publications: Application guidelines; Annual report; Financial statement; Grants list; Informational brochure.
Financial data: Year ended 12/31/2011. Assets, $2,893,883 (M); Expenditures, $3,727,091; Total giving, $1,493,514; Grants to individuals, totaling $370,138.
Fields of interest: Arts.
Type of support: Fellowships.
Application information: Applications accepted. Application form required. Application form available on the grantmaker's web site.
EIN: 237111486

1399
Hartford Foundation for Public Giving
10 Columbus Blvd., 8th Fl.
Hartford, CT   06106-1976   (860) 548-1888
Contact: Virgil Blondet, Jr., V.P., Finance and Admin.
Foundation Scholarship URL: http://www.hfpgscholarships.org/Scholarships/Home/tabid/305/Default.aspx
FAX: (860) 524-8346; E-mail: hfpg@hfpg.org; Additional e-mail: vblondet@hfpg.org; URL: http://www.hfpg.org

Foundation type: Community foundation
Purpose: Scholarships to residents of the Greater Hartford, CT area for higher education.
Publications: Application guidelines; Annual report; Financial statement; Grants list; Informational brochure; Newsletter; Occasional report; Program policy statement.
Financial data: Year ended 12/31/2012. Assets, $810,709,993 (M); Expenditures, $39,667,565; Total giving, $29,828,016.
Fields of interest: Higher education; Graduate/professional education.
Type of support: Scholarships—to individuals; Support to graduates or students of specific

schools; Graduate support; Undergraduate support.
Application information: Applications accepted. Application form required. Application form available on the grantmaker's web site.
Send request by: Mail for College Scholarship, varies for others
Deadline(s): Feb. 2 for College Scholarship Program, vary for others
Additional information: Each scholarship maintains unique eligibility requirements and application guidelines, see the foundation's scholarship directory for additional guidelines.
Program descriptions:
Community Scholarships: Recipients for these scholarships are selected by schools, committees or other organizations, and eligibility varies.
Graduate School Scholarships: Various scholarships for students who have completed college and are going to graduate school.
EIN: 060699252

1400
Greater Hartford Jaycees Foundation, Inc.
1 Financial Plz., 2nd Fl.
Hartford, CT   06103-2601   (860) 522-4171
Contact: Shaun Sheridan, Chair.
FAX: (860) 278-5574; E-mail: info@ghjc.org; Email for grant information: ssheridan@whcpa.com; URL: http://www.ghjc.org/index.cfm/foundation/

Foundation type: Public charity
Purpose: Scholarships to college bound students of greater Hartford, CT for postsecondary education.
Publications: Application guidelines; Annual report; Newsletter.
Financial data: Year ended 12/31/2011. Assets, $1,304,536 (M); Expenditures, $94,546; Total giving, $53,500.
Fields of interest: Higher education.
Type of support: Scholarships—to individuals.
Application information: Applications accepted.
Additional information: Selection is based on academic achievement and need. Contact the foundation for additional guidelines.
EIN: 237163426

1401
Hartley Film Foundation
49 Richmondville Ave., Ste. 204
Westport, CT   06880-2052   (203) 226-9500
Contact: Laura Healy, Off. Mgr.
FAX: (203) 227-6938;
E-mail: info@hartleyfoundation.org; Toll-free tel.: (800) 937-1819; URL: http://hartleyfoundation.org

Foundation type: Public charity
Purpose: Seed grants, through fiscal sponsorship, for documentaries in the areas of world religions and spirituality.
Financial data: Year ended 12/31/2013. Assets, $3,464,500 (M); Expenditures, $1,199,725; Total giving, $99,000.
Fields of interest: Film/video; Religion.
Type of support: Seed money.
Application information:
Initial approach: Letter
Additional information: Contact foundation for eligibility criteria.
EIN: 060950982

1402
Doris Banks Henries Scholarship Trust
100 Pearl St., 13th Fl.
Hartford, CT 06103-4506
Application Address: c/o First Niagara Bank, N.A.

Foundation type: Independent foundation
Purpose: Scholarships to individuals from Middlesex County, CT.
Financial data: Year ended 12/31/2011. Assets, $176,844 (M); Expenditures, $9,855; Total giving, $6,000; Grants to individuals, 4 grants totaling $6,000 (high: $2,000, low: $1,000).
Type of support: Undergraduate support.
Application information:
Initial approach: Letter
EIN: 576207750

1403
Hunter's Scholarship Fund in Memory of Bill Lawton & Carol Gillooly
450 W. Main St.
Meriden, CT 06451-2708 (203) 514-5142

Foundation type: Independent foundation
Purpose: Scholarships to residents of Meriden, CT who are pursuing education or training in the fields of emergency medical services, healthcare and related medical services.
Financial data: Year ended 09/30/2012. Assets, $214,869 (M); Expenditures, $43,928; Total giving, $9,045; Grants to individuals, 5 grants totaling $7,725 (high: $3,000, low: $575).
Fields of interest: Health care, EMS.
Type of support: Scholarships—to individuals.
Application information: Applications accepted. Application form required.
Send request by: Mail
Deadline(s): Two months prior to the start of the semester
Applicants should submit the following:
1) Essay
2) Letter(s) of recommendation
EIN: 066429541

1404
Horace C. Hurlbutt Memorial Fund
c/o Peoples United Bank
850 Main St.
Bridgeport, CT 06604

Foundation type: Independent foundation
Purpose: Undergraduate scholarships, and grants to financially needy residents of Westport, CT.
Financial data: Year ended 12/31/2012. Assets, $605,139 (M); Expenditures, $35,987; Total giving, $25,000.
Fields of interest: Higher education.
Type of support: Undergraduate support; Grants for special needs.
Application information: Applications not accepted.
Additional information: Unsolicited requests for funds not considered or acknowledged.
EIN: 066035912

1405
Doc Hurley Scholarship Foundation, Inc.
103 Woodland St.
Hartford, CT 06105-1233 (860) 819-9750
Contact: Muriel Hurley-Carter, Exec. Dir.
E-mail: dhsf@docscholar.org; URL: http://www.docscholar.org

Foundation type: Public charity

Purpose: Scholarships to high school seniors in the greater Hartford, CT, area to pursue higher education.
Fields of interest: Higher education.
Type of support: Undergraduate support.
Application information: Applications accepted. Application form required.
Deadline(s): Third Friday of Mar.
Applicants should submit the following:
1) Transcripts
2) SAR
3) SAT
4) Letter(s) of recommendation
5) Essay
6) ACT
Additional information: Applications can be obtained from the guidance offices of the participating high schools no later than the second week of Jan. See web site for listing of eligible schools.
EIN: 222997358

1406
Leonard & Mildred Igstaedter Foundation
c/o Ellen Shea
72 Whipstick Rd.
Ridgefield, CT 06877-5029

Foundation type: Independent foundation
Purpose: Financial assistance to needy individuals residing in CT.
Financial data: Year ended 12/31/2012. Assets, $303,763 (M); Expenditures, $14,710; Total giving, $9,909.
Type of support: Grants for special needs.
Application information: Applications not accepted.
Additional information: Unsolicited requests for funds not considered or acknowledged.
EIN: 061399555

1407
International Institute of Connecticut, Inc.
670 Clinton Ave.
Bridgeport, CT 06605-1704 (203) 336-0141
Contact: Angela Rossi Zurowski, Exec. Dir.
FAX: (203) 339-4400; E-mail: admin@iiconn.org;
URL: http://www.iiconn.org

Foundation type: Public charity
Purpose: Grants to immigrants, refugees and their families living in CT.
Publications: Annual report; Newsletter.
Financial data: Year ended 12/31/2011. Assets, $272,830 (M); Expenditures, $1,232,694; Total giving, $151,086; Grants to individuals, totaling $151,086.
Fields of interest: Immigrants/refugees.
Type of support: Grants to individuals.
Application information: Applications accepted. Application form not required.
EIN: 060669118

1408
Jewish Community Foundation of Greater Hartford, Inc.
333 Bloomfield Ave., Ste. D
West Hartford, CT 06117-1544 (860) 523-7460
FAX: (860) 231-0576; E-mail: info@jcfhartford.org;
URL: http://www.jcfhartford.org

Foundation type: Public charity

Purpose: Scholarships to residents of greater Hartford, CT enrolled at an accredited institution of higher learning.
Publications: Application guidelines.
Financial data: Year ended 06/30/2011. Assets, $85,462,469 (M); Expenditures, $3,698,211; Total giving, $2,612,742; Grants to individuals, totaling $93,900.
Fields of interest: Higher education; Jewish agencies & synagogues.
Type of support: Scholarships—to individuals.
Application information: Applications accepted. Application form required.
Send request by: Mail
Deadline(s): Mar. 20 and Nov. 20 for Israel Experience Scholarships, Apr. 15 for College Scholarships
Final notification: Applicants notified in June for College Scholarships
Applicants should submit the following:
1) Transcripts
2) Letter(s) of recommendation
3) Financial information
Additional information: See web site for additional application guidelines.
Program descriptions:
College Scholarships: Scholarships of up to $5,000 are available to Jewish students for college and graduate school education. Funding is meant to assist in tuition, fees, and room and board. Eligible applicants must be accepted or currently enrolled at an accredited institution of higher learning, be a current or former resident of the greater Hartford area, or have parents who are current residents, and be a citizen of the U.S.
Israel Experience Scholarships: Scholarships, ranging from $500 to $2,500, are available to encourage Jewish teenagers and young adults residing in the greater Hartford area to participate in qualified educational and internship programs in Israel. Eligible applicants must be of the Jewish faith, be a high school, college, or graduate school student, or a college graduate, demonstrate financial need, and be a U.S. citizen who currently resides, or formerly resided, in the greater Hartford Jewish community.
EIN: 061372107

1409
Jewish Home for Children
341 Fairfield St.
New Haven, CT 06515 (203) 389-6345
Contact: Patricia McKlintick

Foundation type: Independent foundation
Purpose: Scholarships to residents of the greater New Haven, CT, area for higher education.
Financial data: Year ended 12/31/2012. Assets, $911,760 (M); Expenditures, $56,890; Total giving, $44,550; Grants to individuals, 32 grants totaling $43,950 (high: $4,000, low: $150).
Type of support: Scholarships—to individuals.
Application information: Applications accepted. Application form required.
Deadline(s): None
Additional information: Applicant should provide financial information.
EIN: 237059701

1410
Tai Soo Kim Architectural Fellowship Foundation
41 Rear Concord St.
West Hartford, CT 06119 (860) 232-1719
Contact: Tai Soo Kim, Secy.-Treas.
URL: http://www.tskf.org

Foundation type: Operating foundation
Purpose: Fellowships to individuals of Korean descent who are under the age of 35 and hold degrees in architecture.
Financial data: Year ended 12/31/2012. Assets, $646,746 (M); Expenditures, $49,998; Total giving, $48,000; Grant to an individual, 1 grant totaling $10,000.
Fields of interest: Architecture.
Type of support: Fellowships.
Application information: Applications accepted. Application form required.
Deadline(s): Apr. 30
Additional information: Application must include portfolio of work.
EIN: 223136019

1411
Knights of Columbus Charities, Inc.
1 Columbus Plz.
New Haven, CT 06510-3326 (203) 752-4000
Contact: Carl A. Anderson, Pres.
FAX: (203) 752-4118; E-mail: info@kofc.org;
URL: http://www.kofc.org

Foundation type: Public charity
Purpose: Scholarships to children of Knights or Knights pursuing bachelor's degree at Catholic colleges and universities in the U.S., Canada, Mexico, Puerto Rico and the Philippines.
Financial data: Year ended 12/31/2011. Assets, $1,262,376 (M); Expenditures, $10,367,650; Total giving, $10,250,628.
Fields of interest: Higher education; Catholic agencies & churches.
Type of support: Undergraduate support.
Application information: Applications accepted.
Send request by: Mail
Deadline(s): Mar. 1 for U.S. undergraduate students, May 1 for Canadian undergraduate students
Additional information: Scholarship applications are available after Oct. 1. Students attending colleges and universities in Mexico, Philippines and Puerto Rico should contact their local jurisdiction for additional information.
Program description:
Scholarship Program: Knights of Columbus administers various scholarships annually to students for education at universities for four-year programs and at colleges for two- or three-year programs immediately following graduation from high school. Scholarships are awarded on the basis of academic excellence and are renewable each year of study, pending satisfactory academic performance, for a total of four years. Each scholarship has it's own eligibility criteria. See web site for additional information.
EIN: 237227608

1412
Knights of Columbus Charities USA, Inc.
1 Columbus Plz.
New Haven, CT 06510-3325 (203) 752-4323

Foundation type: Public charity

Purpose: Scholarships to members of the Knights of Columbus and their families who are attending a Catholic college or university.
Financial data: Year ended 12/31/2011. Assets, $64,107,045 (M); Expenditures, $5,980,369; Total giving, $3,664,832; Grants to individuals, totaling $944,614.
Fields of interest: Higher education; Catholic agencies & churches.
Type of support: Scholarships—to individuals; Support to graduates or students of specific schools.
Application information: Applications accepted.
Deadline(s): Mar. 1 for U.S. applicants, May 1 for Canadian applicants
Additional information: Unsolicited requests for funds not considered or acknowledged.
Program descriptions:
Arthur F. and Anna Battista Scholarship Fund: This program annually awards scholarships of $2,000 each to students at the Cornwall Collegiate and Vocational School (Cornwall, Ontario); preference will be given to sons, daughters, grandsons, and granddaughters of members of the Knights of Columbus. Scholarships are awarded based on academic excellence, financial need, and extracurricular activities.
Bishop Charles P. Greco Graduate Fellowships: Scholarships of $500 each (per semester, for up to four semesters) are awarded to a son or daughter of a member of the Knights of Columbus who is engaged in or planning a full-time graduate study leading to a master's degree in the field of teaching the educationally-handicapped, with emphasis on persons with mental retardation.
Bishop Thomas V. Daily Vocations Scholarship Fund: This fund provides scholarships of $2,5000 each for seminarians officially enrolled with ecclesiastical approval in major schools of theology.
Estate of Percy J. Johnson Scholarship Fund: Scholarships of $1,500 each are awarded to young men currently attending a Catholic college or university in the U.S.
Father Michael J. McGivney Vocations Scholarship Fund: Scholarships of $2,500 each are available to students who are studying for the priesthood in a diocesan or religious seminary, and of those students who have been formally accepted by a religious order or congregation with a commitment toward a religious profession. Scholarships are intended to be used toward tuition, room, and board.
Fourth-Degree Pro Deo and Pro Patria Scholarship Program: Scholarships of $1,500 each are awarded annually to members of the Knights of Columbus who are attending a Catholic college.
Francis P. Matthews and John E. Swift Educational Trust Fund: This fund provides scholarships to the children of soldiers, firefighters, and law enforcement officers who have been disabled or killed in the line of duty.
John W. McDevitt (Fourth Degree) Scholarship Fund: Scholarships of $1,500 each are available to members of the Knights of Columbus and their wives, widows, and son and daughters, who attend Catholic colleges and universities in the U.S.
Virgil C. and Ann L. DeChant Scholarship Fund: Scholarships of $1,500 each are available to sons or daughters of the Knights of Columbus who are attending a Catholic school. Preference will be given to residents of Rush County, Kansas, and seminarians from the diocese of Dodge City, Kansas.
EIN: 412140273

1413
Larrabee Fund Association
P.O. Box 271724
West Hartford, CT 06127-1724

Foundation type: Independent foundation
Purpose: Relief to elderly, sick, or indigent women in need who live in Hartford, CT or an adjoining town.
Financial data: Year ended 10/31/2011. Assets, $4,993,149 (M); Expenditures, $284,303; Total giving, $250,616.
Fields of interest: Health care; Human services; Aging; Women; Economically disadvantaged.
Type of support: Grants for special needs.
Application information: Applications accepted. Application form required.
Deadline(s): Two deadlines per month, one week before the first and last Thursday of the month.
Additional information: Applications must be submitted through a social worker or case worker. Applications are available upon request. Need must be demonstrated.
EIN: 066038638

1414
Liberty Bank Foundation, Inc.
55 High St.
P.O. Box 1212
Middletown, CT 06457-1212 (860) 638-2961
Contact: Susan Murphy, V.P., Secy., and Exec. Dir.
Application e-mail: Toral Maher, Grants Coord., tmaher@liberty-bank.com
E-mail: smurphy@liberty-bank.com; URL: https://www.liberty-bank.com/your-community/liberty-foundation

Foundation type: Company-sponsored foundation
Purpose: Scholarships to graduating high school seniors from high schools in towns where Liberty Bank has branches for attendance at accredited colleges or universities. Scholarship to a high school graduate with financial need pursuing a major in engineering or a technology-related field in towns where Liberty Bank has branches.
Publications: Application guidelines; Grants list; Program policy statement.
Financial data: Year ended 12/31/2011. Assets, $8,815,570 (M); Expenditures, $950,394; Total giving, $564,464.
Fields of interest: Higher education; Engineering/technology.
Type of support: Scholarships—to individuals.
Application information: Applications accepted. Application form required. Interview required.
Send request by: Mail
Deadline(s): Mar. 29 for Liberty Bank Foundation Scholarships, Early May for Donald B. Wilbur Scholarships
Final notification: June 3 for Liberty Bank Foundation Scholarships
Applicants should submit the following:
1) Transcripts
2) SAR
3) Letter(s) of recommendation
4) Essay
Additional information: Bank locations include Berlin, Cheshire, Clinton, Colchester, Cromwell, Deep River, Durham, East Haddam, East Hampton, East Lyme, Essex, Glastonbury, Groton, Haddam, Madison, Mansfield, Marlborough, Meriden, Middlefield, Middletown, Montville, Mystic, New London, North Haven, Norwich, Old Saybrook, Plainville, Portland, Stonington, Wallingford, Waterford, West Hartford, Wethersfield and Windham. Checks are made

payable to the educational institution on behalf of the student for foundation scholarship.

Program descriptions:

Donald B. Wilbur Scholarships: The foundation awards $1,000 college scholarships to high school seniors living in areas of Liberty operations who plan to pursue a career in engineering or technology-related field. Recipients are selected based on financial need, academic achievement, and extracurricular and community activities.

Liberty Bank Foundation Scholarship Program: The foundation annually awards college scholarships to high school seniors living in areas of Liberty Bank operations. The award consists of $2,000 for the first year, and $1,000 for the three years thereafter at an accredited college or university. Applicants are nominated by their guidance counselor, teacher, or administrator of a participating secondary school. Recipients are selected based on financial need, academic achievement, and extracurricular activities.
EIN: 061479957

1415
Litchfield County University Club
c/o Roger A. Chace
12 Aspetuck Ave.
New Milford, CT 06776-2705 (860) 824-7046
Contact: Marian Browning, Secy.
Application address: P.O. Box 251, Falls Village, CT 06031

Foundation type: Independent foundation
Purpose: Scholarships to graduates of Litchfield County, CT, secondary schools for postsecondary education.
Financial data: Year ended 12/31/2011. Assets, $1,528,345 (M); Expenditures, $86,477; Total giving, $61,500; Grants to individuals, 31 grants totaling $61,500 (high: $3,500, low: $1,500).
Fields of interest: Higher education; Scholarships/financial aid.
Type of support: Support to graduates or students of specific schools; Undergraduate support.
Application information: Application form required. Interview required.
Initial approach: Letter
Deadline(s): None
Additional information: Application should include a copy of you or your parents' most recent tax return. Application forms are available from the guidance counselor.
EIN: 066055891

1416
The MacCurdy Salisbury Educational Foundation, Inc.
(formerly The MacCurdy Salisbury Foundation, Inc.)
P.O. Box 474
Old Lyme, CT 06371-0474 (860) 434-2646
Contact: Edward G. Perkins, Secy.-Treas.
URL: http://maccurdysalisbury.org

Foundation type: Public charity
Purpose: Scholarships only to residents of Lyme and Old Lyme, CT.
Publications: Informational brochure; Newsletter.
Financial data: Year ended 12/31/2011. Assets, $5,528,093 (M); Expenditures, $277,538; Total giving, $233,050; Grants to individuals, totaling $233,050.
Type of support: Scholarships—to individuals.
Application information: Applications accepted. Application form required.
Initial approach: Application

Send request by: Mail
Deadline(s): Apr. 30
Final notification: Applicants are notified in 45 days
Applicants should submit the following:
1) Financial information
2) FAFSA
3) Budget Information
4) Essay
EIN: 066044250

1417
Macricostas Scholarship Trust, Inc.
(formerly Photronics Scholarship Foundation, Inc.)
15 Secor Rd.
Brookfield, CT 06804-3937 (203) 740-5673
Contact: Daniel Lipton

Foundation type: Company-sponsored foundation
Purpose: Scholarships to children of employees of Phototronics, Inc., for higher education.
Financial data: Year ended 10/31/2013. Assets, $156,273 (M); Expenditures, $39,125; Total giving, $36,975; Grants to individuals, 41 grants totaling $36,975 (high: $1,875, low: $375).
Type of support: Employee-related scholarships.
Application information: Applications not accepted.
Additional information: Unsolicited requests for funds not accepted or acknowledged.
Company name: Phototronics, Incorporated
EIN: 061462843

1418
William & Ellen E. Macristy Foundation
259 Wood Pond Rd.
Glastonbury, CT 06033
Contact: J. Bruce Barlow, Pres.

Foundation type: Independent foundation
Purpose: Scholarships to children of employees who have at least two years of continuous service with Connecticut Stamping & Bending, or Tube Bends, or to children of deceased employees who had two years continuous service with the companies immediately prior to death.
Financial data: Year ended 08/31/2013. Assets, $1,756,033 (M); Expenditures, $80,521; Total giving, $79,021; Grants to individuals, 9 grants totaling $27,275 (high: $3,275, low: $3,000).
Fields of interest: Higher education; Engineering.
Type of support: Employee-related scholarships; Scholarships—to individuals.
Application information: Applications accepted. Application form required.
Deadline(s): Jan. 31
Final notification: Applicant notified last week of Mar.
Applicants should submit the following:
1) Transcripts
2) Letter(s) of recommendation
3) Financial information
Additional information: Application should also include academic record in secondary school, extra-curricular activities and community activities. Applicant must demonstrate need.
Program description:
Scholarship: Scholarships are awarded on the basis of character, attitude, academic standing, and financial need. Recipients may study at accredited colleges, universities, or engineering school with a curriculum leading to a bachelor's degree. Scholarships are renewable contingent upon the recipient remaining in good standing and

earning money during the summer vacation. Applicant schools must be located within the U.S.
EIN: 066034030

1419
Main Street Community Foundation
200 Main St.
P.O. Box 2702
Bristol, CT 06011-2702 (860) 583-6363
Contact: Susan Sadecki, Pres. and C.E.O.
FAX: (860) 589-1252;
E-mail: office@mainstreetfoundation.org;
URL: http://www.mainstreetfoundation.org

Foundation type: Community foundation
Purpose: Scholarships to high school students and residents in Bristol, Burlington, Plainville, Plymouth, Southington and Wolcott, CT for higher education, and computers awarded to area students to utilize in college through the Technology for Teens program.
Publications: Application guidelines; Annual report; Financial statement; Informational brochure; Newsletter.
Financial data: Year ended 12/31/2012. Assets, $11,896,235 (M); Expenditures, $648,954; Total giving, $231,062; Grants to individuals, 126 grants totaling $106,581.
Fields of interest: Higher education; Scholarships/financial aid.
Type of support: Computer technology; Scholarships—to individuals; Undergraduate support.
Application information: Applications accepted. Application form required. Application form available on the grantmaker's web site.
Initial approach: Telephone
Send request by: Mail or hand deliver
Deadline(s): Mar. 31
Applicants should submit the following:
1) SAR
2) FAFSA
3) Transcripts
4) Letter(s) of recommendation
5) GPA
6) Financial information
7) Essay
Additional information: Each scholarship has its own unique set of eligibility criteria. See web site for a complete listing of scholarships.
Program descriptions:
Scholarships: The foundation administers over 60 scholarship funds, each with different application criteria requirements. The scholarship program brings together students in need and donors who care about education to enable more students to achieve their educational dreams.
Technology for Teens: The foundation will award several computers to area students to utilize in college. Applicants must be a current member in good standing of the Boys and Girls Club and Family Center of Bristol.
EIN: 061433299

1420
Manchester Scholarship Foundation, Inc.
c/o 3
20 Hartford Rd.
Manchester, CT 06040-5973 (860) 645-1673
E-mail: Lori.msf@gmail.com; URL: http://www.manchesterscholarship.org

Foundation type: Public charity
Purpose: Scholarships to graduating high school seniors, and to eligible adult students of Manchester, CT for postsecondary education at

colleges, universities, community college or vocational school.

Financial data: Year ended 12/31/2011. Assets, $5,794,777 (M); Expenditures, $380,948; Total giving, $319,732; Grants to individuals, totaling $319,732.

Fields of interest: Vocational education, post-secondary; Higher education.

Type of support: Scholarships—to individuals; Support to graduates or students of specific schools.

Application information: Applications accepted. Application form required. Application form available on the grantmaker's web site.

Send request by: Mail

Deadline(s): Apr. 8 for high school seniors, Apr. 25 for adult students

Additional information: High school seniors must demonstrate financial need, scholastic achievement, school or community service and work experience. Adult students must demonstrate financial need, clarity and seriousness of educational objectives and evidence of ability to honor commitments. See web site for additional application guidelines.

Program descriptions:

Adult Learner Scholarship: This is a renewable scholarship awarded to part-time adult students. Eligible students must be at least twenty-one years of age and a Manchester resident for at least six months at the time of application. Scholarships are initially awarded for two academic terms and will pay the school or college up to $600 for those taking one course, and up to $1,000 for those taking two or more courses.

Arthur Goodman Strong Memorial Scholarship: This program awards individuals who have endured a physical disability or mental impairment that substantially limits one or more major life activities as interpreted under the Americans with Disabilities Act and plans on beginning or continuing post-secondary education.

Scholarships: Scholarships are available to Manchester residents (of at least six months' duration) who will be or is a graduate of Manchester High School, East Catholic High School, Howell Cheney Technical School, Cornerstone Christian School, Great Path Academy, or other secondary school, and who is planning to enter an accredited four-year college, university, or other accredited postsecondary school as a full-time student. Scholarships are for one year and are non-renewable.

Traditional Scholarships for Graduating High School Students: This program offers awards to graduating high school residents of (at least six months) Manchester. Applicants must be accepted into a post secondary school, ranked in the top 65% of the graduating class and have financial need.

EIN: 066076924

1421
The Meriden Foundation

c/o Webster Bank, N.A.
123 Bank St.
Waterbury, CT 06702-2205 (860) 692-1751
Contact: Paul M. McAfee

Foundation type: Independent foundation

Purpose: Scholarships primarily to residents of the greater Meriden, CT, area.

Financial data: Year ended 12/31/2012. Assets, $20,927,788 (M); Expenditures, $1,434,124; Total giving, $1,189,779; Grants to individuals, 62 grants totaling $146,185 (high: $5,000, low: $500).

Type of support: Scholarships—to individuals. **Application information:** Applications accepted. Application form required.

Deadline(s): None

Additional information: Application must also include proof of qualifications for scholarships.

EIN: 066037849

1422
The Justin Samela Miceli-Wings of Hope Foundation

992 High Ridge rd., 2nd Fl.
Stamford, CT 06705 (203) 323-6991
Contact: John Miceli, Co.-Pres.
FAX: (203) 355-3686;
E-mail: info@justinswingsofhope.com; URL: http://www.justinswingsofhope.com

Foundation type: Public charity

Purpose: Financial assistance to indigent residents of Stamford, CT. Also, scholarships to students of Holy Name School and Iona Preparatory School, CT.

Financial data: Year ended 12/31/2012. Assets, $67,753 (M); Expenditures, $61,934; Total giving, $31,189; Grants to individuals, totaling $3,500.

Type of support: Support to graduates or students of specific schools; Grants for special needs.

Application information:

Initial approach: Email

EIN: 260848100

1423
Milford Chamber of Commerce Trust Fund

5 N. Broad St.
Milford, CT 06460 (203) 878-0681
Contact: Kathleen Alagno, Exec. V.P.

Foundation type: Independent foundation

Purpose: Scholarships to graduating students of Milford, CT for continuing education at accredited colleges or universities.

Financial data: Year ended 12/31/2012. Assets, $0 (M); Expenditures, $94,923; Total giving, $44,750; Grants to individuals, 26 grants totaling $22,000 (high: $2,500, low: $500).

Type of support: Undergraduate support.

Application information: Application form required.

Initial approach: Letter

Deadline(s): Apr. 8

Applicants should submit the following:

1) Letter(s) of recommendation
2) Essay
3) SAT
4) ACT
5) FAFSA

Additional information: Contact your guidance counselors for application guidelines.

EIN: 061053993

1424
Milford Hospital, Inc.

300 Seaside Ave.
Milford, CT 06460-4603 (203) 876-4000
Contact: Joseph Pelaccia, Pres. and C.E.O.
URL: http://www.milfordhospital.org

Foundation type: Public charity

Purpose: Scholarships to junior volunteers for higher education.

Financial data: Year ended 09/30/2011. Assets, $64,632,155 (M); Expenditures, $192,326,438; Total giving, $89,905; Grants to individuals, totaling $11,318.

Fields of interest: Higher education.

Type of support: Scholarships—to individuals. **Application information:** Applications not accepted.

Additional information: Volunteers must demonstrate a high level of caring and commitment to Milford Hospital and its patients through their volunteer service at the hospital. Unsolicited requests for funds not considered or acknowledged.

EIN: 060646741

1425
Miss Connecticut Scholarship Corporation

72 Cambridge Dr.
Southington, CT 06489

Foundation type: Operating foundation

Purpose: Scholarships to women of Miss Connecticut title selected through the Miss American Beauty Pageant.

Financial data: Year ended 12/31/2012. Assets, $17,162 (M); Expenditures, $134,141; Total giving, $20,200; Grants to individuals, 16 grants totaling $20,200 (high: $5,600, low: $250).

Fields of interest: Higher education; Women.

Type of support: Scholarships—to individuals.

Application information: Applications not accepted.

Additional information: Unsolicited requests for funds not considered or acknowledged. Contact the corporation for eligibility determination.

EIN: 222708060

1426
The Multiple Myeloma Research Foundation, Inc.

383 Main Ave., 5th Fl.
Norwalk, CT 06851-1544 (203) 229-0464
Contact: Scott T. Santarella, Exec. Dir.
FAX: (203) 229-0572; E-mail: info@themmrf.org;
URL: http://www.multiplemyeloma.org

Foundation type: Public charity

Purpose: Grants to individuals for multiple myeloma research.

Publications: Application guidelines; Annual report; Financial statement; Informational brochure; Newsletter.

Financial data: Year ended 12/31/2010. Assets, $25,514,760 (M); Expenditures, $20,141,024; Total giving, $13,614,779.

Fields of interest: Cancer research.

Type of support: Research; Awards/prizes.

Application information: Applications accepted. Application form required.

Initial approach: Letter or telephone

Send request by: Online

Deadline(s): Vary

Additional information: See web site for additional application guidelines.

EIN: 061504413

1427
Henry J. & Marie Munger Scholarship Fund

550 E. Main St., Ste. 32
Branford, CT 06405-2948
Contact: David P. Zuber, Tr.
URL: http://www.munger.org

Foundation type: Independent foundation

Purpose: Scholarships to first- and second-year college students who have resided for at least four years prior to college (excluding military service) in Guilford, Madison, or Clinton, CT for higher education.
Financial data: Year ended 05/31/2010. Assets, $1 (M); Expenditures, $24,975; Total giving, $20,000; Grants to individuals, 5 grants totaling $20,000 (high: $4,000, low: $4,000).
Fields of interest: Higher education.
Type of support: Undergraduate support.
Application information: Application form required.
  Deadline(s): June 6
  Additional information: Applicant should submit transcripts.
EIN: 060968106

1428
My Child's Hand Foundation Trust
47 Hillspoint Rd.
Westport, CT 06880-5108 (203) 221-1288
Contact: William T. Pasqua, Tr.; Lorayne Pasqua, Tr.

Foundation type: Independent foundation
Purpose: Support to families in the NY area dealing with pediatric cancer patients.
Financial data: Year ended 12/31/2011. Assets, $114,368 (M); Expenditures, $15,338; Total giving, $12,208; Grants to individuals, 7 grants totaling $12,208 (high: $3,075, low: $93).
Fields of interest: Cancer; Pediatrics.
Type of support: Grants to individuals.
Application information: Applications accepted.
  Initial approach: Letter
  Deadline(s): None
  Additional information: Contact the trust for additional information.
EIN: 137355037

1429
National Organization for Rare Disorders, Inc.
55 Kenosia Ave.
P.O. Box 1968
Danbury, CT 06813-1968 (203) 744-0100
Contact: Peter L. Saltonstall, Pres. and C.E.O.
FAX: (203) 798-2291;
E-mail: orphan@rarediseases.org; Toll-free tel.: (800) 999-6673 (voicemail only); TDD: (203) 797-9590; URL: http://www.rarediseases.org

Foundation type: Public charity
Purpose: Research grants and fellowships to academic scientists and physicians specializing in rare diseases. Support to individuals diagnosed with specific rare diseases, to obtain medication and treatment.
Publications: Application guidelines; Annual report; Grants list; Informational brochure; Newsletter; Program policy statement.
Financial data: Year ended 12/31/2011. Assets, $14,450,108 (M); Expenditures, $13,006,380; Total giving, $8,784,207; Grants to individuals, totaling $8,514,207.
Fields of interest: Diseases (rare) research; Medical research.
Type of support: Fellowships; Research.
Application information:
  Initial approach: Letter of intent and abstract
  Additional information: Full proposals accepted by invitation only. See web site for additional guidelines for research.
Program description:
  Patient Assistance Program: The organization administers a series of patience assistance programs to help patients obtain life-saving

or -sustaining medication that they could otherwise not afford. Assistance is available to help patients who are without insurance (or who are uninsured) obtain access to medications, to help patients diagnosed with specific diseases with out-of-pocket costs associated with their insurance plans, and to offset travel and lodging costs to patients who are participating in clinical trials. Eligible applicants must be legal U.S. residents who have an applicable diagnosis or physician referral, and who meet specific financial criteria.
EIN: 133223946

1430
New Canaan Community Foundation, Inc.
111 Cherry St.
New Canaan, CT 06840 (203) 966-0231
Contact: Cynthia Gorey, Exec. Dir.
FAX: (203) 966-0831;
E-mail: info@newcanaancf.org; Additional E-mail: cgorey@newcanaancf.org; URL: http://www.newcanaancf.org

Foundation type: Community foundation
Purpose: Scholarships to individuals who are residents of New Canaan, CT.
Publications: Application guidelines; Annual report; Annual report (including application guidelines); Financial statement; Grants list; Informational brochure.
Financial data: Year ended 12/31/2012. Assets, $14,135,638 (M); Expenditures, $1,409,783; Total giving, $903,007; Grants to individuals, 125 grants totaling $181,761.
Fields of interest: Higher education.
Type of support: Scholarships—to individuals; Awards/prizes; Graduate support.
Application information: Applications accepted. Application form required. Application form available on the grantmaker's web site.
  Initial approach: Letter, telephone or e-mail
  Send request by: Mail
  Copies of proposal: 1
  Deadline(s): Apr. 1
  Final notification: Applicant notified in May
  Applicants should submit the following:
    1) SAR
    2) Transcripts
    3) SAT
    4) Letter(s) of recommendation
    5) GPA
    6) Financial information
    7) FAFSA
    8) Essay
EIN: 060970466

1431
Greater New Haven Community Loan Fund, Inc.
171 Orange St., 3rd Fl.
New Haven, CT 06510-3111 (203) 789-8690
Contact: Carla Weil, Exec. Dir.
FAX: (203) 865-6475; E-mail: info@gnhclf.org;
E-Mail for Carla Weil: carla@gnhclf.org; URL: http://www.gnhclf.org

Foundation type: Public charity
Purpose: Financial assistance for first time homebuyers in the New Haven, CT area with down payment and closing costs, and other housing programs.
Publications: Application guidelines; Annual report; Financial statement; Informational brochure (including application guidelines); Newsletter; Quarterly report.

Financial data: Year ended 12/31/2011. Assets, $9,135,140 (M); Expenditures, $2,796,310; Total giving, $1,788,903; Grants to individuals, totaling $117,337.
Fields of interest: Housing/shelter, home owners.
Type of support: Grants for special needs.
Application information: Applications accepted. Application form required.
  Additional information: Contact the fund or see web site for additional application guidelines.
Program description:
  Citizens Bank Home Buyer Down Payment Assistance Program: This program offered in partnership with Citizens Bank, underwrites down payment assistance loans to income-eligible homebuyer. The funds are designed to complement first mortgages from Citizens Bank and are zero percent, deferred loans. The owner may sell or transfer the property at any time and either repay the loan or transfer it to a new income-eligible homebuyer.
EIN: 222889913

1432
New Opportunities, Inc.
232 N. Elm St.
Waterbury, CT 06702-1516 (203) 576-9799
Contact: Dr. James H. Gatling Ph.D., Pres. and C.E.O.
FAX: (203) 755-8254;
E-mail: info@newopportunitiesinc.org; Additional addresses: 74 Cambridge St., Meriden, CT 06450-2211, tel.: (203) 235-0278; 138 Migeon Ave., Torrington, CT 06790-4817, tel.: (860) 482-9749; E-mail For James H. Gatling: DrGatling@NewOpportunitiesInc.org; URL: http://www.newoppinc.org/

Foundation type: Public charity
Purpose: Assistance for economically disadvantaged individuals and families of CT, by providing them with the necessary resources to increase their standard of living.
Publications: Annual report.
Financial data: Year ended 10/31/2012. Assets, $16,663,199 (M); Expenditures, $50,489,092; Total giving, $18,263,540; Grants to individuals, totaling $14,766,346.
Fields of interest: Human services; Economically disadvantaged.
Type of support: In-kind gifts; Grants for special needs.
Application information:
  Initial approach: Letter
  Additional information: Assistance includes daycare, home heating assistance and weatherization, food delivery to the elderly, and emergency shelter services. Contact the foundation for eligibility criteria.
EIN: 066071847

1433
L. Douglas Nolan Foundation, Inc.
P.O. Box 903
New Canaan, CT 06840-0903 (203) 972-2892
Contact: Suzanne M. Wall, Pres. and Treas.
Application address: 11 Meadow Ln., New Canaan, CT 06840-5808

Foundation type: Independent foundation
Purpose: Scholarships to high school graduates who have resided in East Haddam, Lyme and Old Lyme, CT for the past two years to attend an institute of higher education in New England.
Financial data: Year ended 12/31/2011. Assets, $981,094 (M); Expenditures, $104,099; Total

giving, $103,399; Grants to individuals, 36 grants totaling $103,399 (high: $6,000, low: $1,000).
Fields of interest: Higher education.
Type of support: Scholarships—to individuals.
Application information: Applications accepted. Application form required.
> *Initial approach:* Letter or visit to guidance counselor
> *Deadline(s):* Apr. 15
> *Additional information:* Application should include a cover letter, parents' financial information and a confirmation of acceptance into a college or university.

EIN: 223282521

1434
North Haven Rotary Foundation, Inc.
P.O. Box 202
North Haven, CT   06473

Foundation type: Independent foundation
Purpose: Scholarship awards to graduating seniors at North Haven High School who are residents of North Haven, CT, to attend Gateway Technical Community College or Quinnipiac University.
Financial data: Year ended 06/30/2013. Assets, $196,470 (M); Expenditures, $11,000; Total giving, $11,000; Grants to individuals, 11 grants totaling $11,000 (high: $1,000, low: $1,000).
Fields of interest: Higher education.
Type of support: Support to graduates or students of specific schools.
Application information: Contributes only to pre-selected students; unsolicited requests for funds not considered or accepted.
EIN: 237155608

1435
Norwalk Community College Foundation
188 Richards Ave., Ste. E311
Norwalk, CT   06854-1655   (203) 857-7260
Contact: Jane Kiefer, Exec. Dir.
E-mail: nccfoundation@norwalk.edu; E-Mail for Jane Kiefer: jkiefer@norwalk.edu; URL: http://www.ncc.commnet.edu/nccfoundation/contact.asp

Foundation type: Public charity
Purpose: Merit scholarships for students attending Norwalk Community College pursuing higher education.
Financial data: Year ended 12/31/2011. Assets, $26,459,938 (M); Expenditures, $5,737,218; Total giving, $4,879,803; Grants to individuals, totaling $949,295.
Fields of interest: Higher education.
Type of support: Scholarships—to individuals; Support to graduates or students of specific schools.
Application information: Applications accepted. Application form required.
> *Send request by:* Online, mail
> *Deadline(s):* Vary
> *Additional information:* Every NCCF scholarship has different application requirements and deadlines. Selection is based on academic performance. See web site for various scholarship guidelines.

EIN: 066080293

1436
Norwalk Hospital Foundation, Inc.
34 Maple St.
Norwalk, CT   06850-3815   (203) 852-2216
Contact: Mary Franco, Pres.
FAX: (203) 852-2311;
E-mail: foundation@norwalkhealth.org; E-mail for Mary Franco: mary.franco@norwalkhealth.org; URL: http://www.norwalkhospitalfoundation.org

Foundation type: Public charity
Purpose: Undergraduate and graduate scholarships to assist students of Norwalk, CT pursuing careers in nursing and respiratory care.
Financial data: Year ended 09/30/2011. Assets, $37,236,896 (M); Expenditures, $4,167,107; Total giving, $2,171,214; Grants to individuals, totaling $65,500.
Fields of interest: Nursing school/education.
Type of support: Scholarships—to individuals; Support to graduates or students of specific schools; Graduate support; Undergraduate support.
Application information: Applications accepted. Application form required. Application form available on the grantmaker's web site.
> *Send request by:* Mail
> *Deadline(s):* May 1
> *Final notification:* Applicants notified by June 30
> *Applicants should submit the following:*
> 1) Financial information
> 2) Transcripts
> 3) Essay
> *Additional information:* Funds are sent directly to the educational institution on behalf of the students.

Program descriptions:
Carol Bauer Scholarship: This scholarship is for registered nursed employed at Norwalk Hospital pursuing a graduate or post graduate degree in nursing management.
Edward T. Bedford Foundation Scholarship: This scholarship is for Norwalk Hospital employees pursuing a degree in nursing. Three $5,000 scholarships are awarded.
Gertrude Hotchkiss Heyn Scholarship: This scholarship is for undergraduate or graduate students enrolled in nursing programs with financial need.
Grace Cole Jones Scholarship: This scholarship is for high school students with financial need entering nursing programs at Norwalk Community College, Sacred Heart University and Fairfield University.
Lea Ruegg Scholarship: This scholarship is for undergraduate or graduate students enrolled in nursing programs.
Nursing Graduate Education Scholarships: This scholarship is for nurses employed at Norwalk Hospital pursuing graduate level education.
Strassler Nurse Education Scholarship: This scholarship is for students in graduate or undergraduate nursing programs with priority for students in critical care or nursing administration programs.
The Santo and Dorothy Intellisano Scholarship: This scholarship is offered to undergraduate or graduate students enrolled in nursing programs.
The Woman's Board of Norwalk Hospital Nursing Scholarship: This scholarship is for nursing students at Norwalk Community College who has a minimum 2.75 GPA.
The Woman's Board of Norwalk Hospital Respiratory Care Scholarship: This scholarship is for second year students enrolled in the Respiratory Care Program at Norwalk Hospital or Norwalk Community College with a minimum 2.75 GPA and community involvement.
EIN: 222577707

1437
The O'Meara Foundation, Inc.
P.O. Box 290157
Wethersfield, CT   06109-0157   (860) 563-2918
Contact: Claude-Evelyne O'Diata
E-mail: BPINCMAX@aol.com; Application address: 1900 Berlin Tpke., Wethersfield, CT 06109

Foundation type: Independent foundation
Purpose: Scholarships to financially needy residents of Hartford County, CT, for higher education.
Publications: Annual report.
Financial data: Year ended 06/30/2013. Assets, $335,267 (M); Expenditures, $340,158; Total giving, $297,500; Grants to individuals, 125 grants totaling $297,500.
Fields of interest: Higher education.
Type of support: Scholarships—to individuals.
Application information: Applications accepted. Application form required.
> *Initial approach:* Letter
> *Deadline(s):* June 1
> *Applicants should submit the following:*
> 1) Transcripts
> 2) Letter(s) of recommendation
> *Additional information:* Application must include federal tax returns.

EIN: 066034580

1438
Operation Fuel, Inc.
1 Regency Dr., Ste. 200
Bloomfield, CT   06002-2310   (860) 243-2345
Contact: Patricia J. Wrice, Exec. Dir.
FAX: (860) 726-9310; Toll-free tel.: (800) 354-7199; URL: http://www.operationfuel.org

Foundation type: Public charity
Purpose: Emergency energy assistance to low-income and poor families of Connecticut who are experiencing a utility crisis.
Publications: Annual report; Newsletter; Occasional report.
Financial data: Year ended 06/30/2012. Assets, $1,487,936 (M); Expenditures, $3,969,653; Total giving, $3,116,844.
Fields of interest: Economically disadvantaged.
Type of support: Grants for special needs.
Application information: Applications accepted. Application form required.
> *Initial approach:* Contact partner agency for application
> *Additional information:* Contact organization for assistance.

EIN: 061253091

1439
Orange Foundation
P.O. Box 729
Orange, CT   06477-0729   (203) 795-3716
Contact: Robert E. Archambault, Chair.
FAX: (203) 795-3716;
E-mail: thearchambaults@optonline.net; Additional E-Mail: chairman@tofoundation.com; URL: http://www.orangefoundation.org

Foundation type: Community foundation
Purpose: Scholarships and grants to residents of Orange, CT.
Publications: Application guidelines; Annual report; Grants list; Informational brochure; Informational brochure (including application guidelines); Newsletter (including application guidelines); Occasional report.

Financial data: Year ended 12/31/2012. Assets, $1,351,838 (M); Expenditures, $55,141; Total giving, $41,788; Grants to individuals, 9 grants totaling $27,900.
Fields of interest: Higher education; Scholarships/financial aid.
Type of support: Grants to individuals; Scholarships—to individuals; Student loans—to individuals; Support to graduates or students of specific schools; Postgraduate support; Grants for special needs; Project support.
Application information: Applications accepted. Application form required. Application form available on the grantmaker's web site.
Send request by: Mail
Copies of proposal: 1
Deadline(s): Apr. 15
Final notification: Recipients notified by May 30
Applicants should submit the following:
1) Letter(s) of recommendation
2) Transcripts
3) SAT
4) Financial information
Additional information: See web site for complete listing of scholarships.
EIN: 060955006

1440
Elizabeth and John Paul Scholarship Fund
5 Glenwood Rd.
New Milford, CT   06776   (860) 350-6647
Application address: New Milford High School, Danbury Rd., New Milford, CT 06776

Foundation type: Independent foundation
Purpose: Scholarships to graduates of New Milford High School, CT for postsecondary education.
Financial data: Year ended 12/31/2012. Assets, $207,366 (M); Expenditures, $13,457; Total giving, $13,023; Grant to an individual, 1 grant totaling $13,023.
Fields of interest: Higher education.
Type of support: Support to graduates or students of specific schools; Undergraduate support.
Application information:
Initial approach: Letter
Additional information: Application available from high school.
EIN: 216454026

1441
Victoria Glenn Peirce Scholarship Foundation
c/o J. Berger, Jr.
1700 Bedford St., Ste. 101
Stamford, CT   06905   (203) 327-2000
Contact: Judy Ellenthal, Tr.

Foundation type: Independent foundation
Purpose: Scholarships to women who have graduated from a public or private high school or secondary school in Fairfield County, CT.
Financial data: Year ended 03/31/2013. Assets, $260,632 (M); Expenditures, $69,437; Total giving, $62,000; Grants to individuals, 4 grants totaling $62,000 (high: $25,000; low: $7,000).
Fields of interest: Women.
Type of support: Undergraduate support.
Application information: Applications accepted. Interview required.
Initial approach: Letter
Deadline(s): None
Applicants should submit the following:
1) Transcripts

Additional information: Application should also include financial aid application and college acceptance letter.
EIN: 223808034

1442
Person-to-Person, Inc.
1864 Post Rd.
Darien, CT   06820-5802   (203) 655-0048
Contact: Ceci Maher, Exec. Dir.
FAX: (203) 655-8082; E-mail: info@p2pdarien.org;
URL: http://p2pdarien.org/

Foundation type: Public charity
Purpose: Scholarships, camperships, and emergency assistance to indigent residents of the Darien, CT area.
Publications: Annual report.
Financial data: Year ended 12/31/2011. Assets, $5,355,803 (M); Expenditures, $8,676,725; Total giving, $7,465,677; Grants to individuals, totaling $7,465,677.
Fields of interest: Economically disadvantaged.
Type of support: Undergraduate support; Grants for special needs; Camperships.
Application information:
Initial approach: Letter
EIN: 061422248

1443
Phelps Association
P.O. Box 202047
New Haven, CT   06520-2047   (203) 624-1013

Foundation type: Public charity
Purpose: Scholarships to pre-selected students currently attending Yale University, CT.
Financial data: Year ended 06/30/2012. Assets, $5,672,523 (M); Expenditures, $423,890; Total giving, $4,435; Grants to individuals, totaling $4,435.
Type of support: Support to graduates or students of specific schools.
Application information: Applications not accepted.
Additional information: Unsolicited requests for funds not considered.
EIN: 066069051

1444
The Pitney Bowes Relief Fund Charitable Trust
1 Elmcroft Rd., MSC 6101
Stamford, CT   06926-0700   (203) 351-6669
URL: http://www.pb.com/communityinvestments

Foundation type: Public charity
Purpose: Financial assistance to individuals who have experienced natural disasters or catastrophic events. Support include housing assistance, medical expenses, funeral expenses, daycare, house fires, and other needs.
Publications: Annual report.
Financial data: Year ended 08/31/2011. Assets, $430,011 (M); Expenditures, $157,660; Total giving, $82,920.
Type of support: Emergency funds; Grants for special needs.
Application information:
Initial approach: Letter
Additional information: Contact the trust for further application guidelines.
EIN: 223198214

1445
The Prasad Family Foundation, Inc.
268 Grandview Dr.
Glastonbury, CT   06033-3946

Foundation type: Independent foundation
Purpose: Need base merit scholarship to students of CT to further their education at colleges or universities.
Financial data: Year ended 12/31/2011. Assets, $14,018 (M); Expenditures, $45,331; Total giving, $45,281.
Fields of interest: Higher education.
Type of support: Scholarships—to individuals.
Application information: Applications accepted.
Initial approach: Letter
Additional information: Applicant must demonstrate financial need.
EIN: 061564486

1446
Promising Scholars Fund
c/o The Community Foundation for Greater New Haven
70 Audubon St.
New Haven, CT   06510-1248   (203) 777-7068
Contact: Angela Powers, Sr. V.P., Devel., Stewardship, and Donor Svcs., The Community Foundation for Greater New Haven; Scholarships: Marge Johnson, Admin., Scholarship Mgmt. Svcs.
Address for scholarships: 1 Scholarship Way, St. Peter, MN 56082-1693; tel. for Marge Johnson: (507) 931-1682
E-mail: apowers@cfgnh.org; URL: http://www.sms.scholarshipamerica.org/promisingscholars/index.html

Foundation type: Public charity
Purpose: Scholarships to academically talented African American students in CT who wish to attain a college or university education.
Publications: Application guidelines.
Fields of interest: Scholarships/financial aid; Education; African Americans/Blacks.
Type of support: Scholarships—to individuals.
Application information: Applications accepted. Application form required.
Deadline(s): Mar. 20
Applicants should submit the following:
1) GPA
2) Transcripts
3) Financial information
Program description:
Edward A. Bouchet Scholarship: In conjunction with Scholarship Management Services, the fund administers a scholarship program to assist academically talented African-American graduates of selected Connecticut high schools in attending an accredited two- or four-year college or university of the student's choice. Eligible applicants must graduate from a designated Connecticut high school, plan to enroll in full-time undergraduate study at an accredited two- or four-year college or university, be a U.S. and Connecticut resident, and have a minimum GPA of 2.5. Scholarships range from $1,000 to $4,000 per year; scholarships are renewable for each year of post high school study. Preference will be given to male applicants who reside in New Haven County; female applicants are also eligible to apply.

1447
Real Art Ways
56 Arbor St.
Hartford, CT 06106-1201 (860) 232-1006
FAX: (860) 233-6691; E-mail: info@realartways.org;
URL: http://www.realartways.org

Foundation type: Public charity
Purpose: Provides emerging and established artists with resources needed to make and show new, innovative and experimental work in the greater Hartford, CT region.
Financial data: Year ended 09/30/2011. Assets, $1,336,279 (M); Expenditures, $1,185,309.
Fields of interest: Visual arts.
Type of support: Project support.
Application information:
 Initial approach: Proposal
 Deadline(s): Ongoing
 Applicants should submit the following:
  1) Work samples
  2) SASE
  3) Resume
 Additional information: Videos should be submitted on either DVD format, or VHS (NTSC). Audio samples should be submitted on CD only.
EIN: 060958072

1448
Ridgefield Scholarship Group, Inc.
P.O. Box 823
Ridgefield, CT 06877
Contact: Linda Maggs, Treas.
Application address: 118 Ramapoo Rd., Ridgefield, CT 06877.

Foundation type: Independent foundation
Purpose: Scholarships primarily to graduates of Ridgefield High School, CT, who are Ridgefield, CT, residents.
Financial data: Year ended 12/31/2011. Assets, $392,571 (M); Expenditures, $35,504; Total giving, $34,300; Grants to individuals, 18 grants totaling $34,300 (high: $5,000, low: $500).
Type of support: Support to graduates or students of specific schools; Undergraduate support.
Application information: Application form required.
 Deadline(s): Apr. 15
 Additional information: Contact Ridgefield High School Guidance Dept. for application form.
EIN: 061010124

1449
The Riot Relief Fund
c/o Sacks Press & Lacher
600 3rd Ave.
Stonington, CT 06378-1432 (212) 682-6640
URL: http://www.riotrelieffund.org

Foundation type: Public charity
Purpose: Financial assistance for families of the uniform services who have been killed or injured while in faithful discharge of official duty in the city of New York.
Financial data: Year ended 12/31/2012. Assets, $2,137,710 (M); Expenditures, $44,359; Total giving, $17,500; Grant to an individual, 1 grant totaling $17,500.
Fields of interest: Human services.
Type of support: Grants for special needs.
Application information: Applications not accepted.
 Additional information: Unsolicited requests for funds not considered or acknowledged.
EIN: 237036545

1450
Rockville Bank Foundation, Inc.
(formerly Rockville Bank Community Foundation, Inc.)
1645 Ellington Rd.
South Windsor, CT 06074-2764 (860) 291-3652
Contact: Judy Keppner, Secy.
; URL: http://www.rockvillebank.com/category/6522/rockville-bank-foundation.htm

Foundation type: Company-sponsored foundation
Purpose: Scholarships to graduating high school seniors to pursue higher education and vocational awards to high school seniors who have excelled in vocational or agricultural studies and plan to enter the workforce or pursue work-related training.
Publications: Application guidelines.
Financial data: Year ended 12/31/2011. Assets, $10,386,557 (M); Expenditures, $687,500; Total giving, $685,541; Grants to individuals, 42 grants totaling $52,500 (high: $1,250, low: $1,250).
Fields of interest: Vocational education; Education; Agriculture.
Type of support: Scholarships—to individuals.
Application information: Contact foundation for additional application information.
Company name: Rockville Financial, Inc.
EIN: 203000295

1451
The Rogow Greenberg Foundation, Inc.
(formerly The Rogow Birken Foundation, Inc.)
c/o Birken Manufacturing Co.
3 Old Windsor Rd.
Bloomfield, CT 06002-1397 (860) 242-2211
Contact: Gary Greenberg, Pres.

Foundation type: Independent foundation
Purpose: Scholarships to residents of CT, FL, MA, and NY.
Financial data: Year ended 12/31/2012. Assets, $4,535,271 (M); Expenditures, $675,043; Total giving, $519,398; Grants to individuals, 29 grants totaling $77,485 (high: $10,000, low: $500).
Type of support: Scholarships—to individuals.
Application information: Applications accepted.
 Initial approach: Letter
 Deadline(s): None
EIN: 061051591

1452
Roxbury Scholarship Foundation, Inc.
P. O. Box 106
Roxbury, CT 06783-0106 (860) 354-3174
Contact: Hugh Rawson, Pres.

Foundation type: Public charity
Purpose: Scholarships to residents of Roxbury, CT.
Financial data: Year ended 06/30/2012. Assets, $1,873,875 (M); Expenditures, $78,257; Total giving, $58,500; Grants to individuals, totaling $58,500.
Type of support: Undergraduate support.
Application information: Applications accepted.
 Additional information: Contact foundation for current application deadline/guidelines.
EIN: 237073368

1453
Mary B. Rubinow and William Rubinow Scholarship Fund Trust
c/o L. Rubinow
185 Asylum St., 36th Fl.
Hartford, CT 06103 (860) 647-3542
Application address: Manchester High School, Attn.: Guidance Office, Manchester, CT 06040

Foundation type: Independent foundation
Purpose: Interest-free loans only to residents of Manchester, CT, for undergraduate or graduate education.
Financial data: Year ended 12/31/2012. Assets, $184,619 (M); Expenditures, $444; Total giving, $0.
Fields of interest: Higher education.
Type of support: Student loans—to individuals.
Application information: Applications accepted. Application form required.
 Deadline(s): None
 Additional information: Applications available only through the guidance office of Manchester High School.
EIN: 066034723

1454
Save The Children Federation, Inc.
54 Wilton Rd.
Westport, CT 06880-3108 (203) 221-4030
Contact: Carolyn Miles, Pres. and C.E.O.
E-mail: twebster@savethechildren.org; Toll-free tel.: (800) 728-3843; Additional address: 2000 M St., N.W., Ste. 500, Washington, DC 20036-3316, tel.: (202) 293-4170; URL: http://www.savethechildren.org

Foundation type: Public charity
Purpose: Emergency assistance for children in need around the world by achieving immediate and lasting change in their lives by improving their health, education and economic opportunities.
Publications: Annual report; Financial statement.
Financial data: Year ended 12/31/2012. Assets, $292,829,404 (M); Expenditures, $596,049,431; Total giving, $285,047,610.
Fields of interest: International development; Children/youth; Economically disadvantaged.
Type of support: In-kind gifts; Grants for special needs.
Application information: Applications accepted.
 Additional information: Contact the organization for additional information.
EIN: 060726487

1455
Saybrook Charitable Trust
P.O. Box 330265
West Hartford, CT 06133-0265 (860) 232-6853
Contact: Caren Foisie Gaudet, Managing Tr.
E-mail: info@saybrookcharitabletrust.org

Foundation type: Independent foundation
Purpose: Scholarships to high school seniors and undergraduate college students for continuing education at accredited colleges and universities pursuing a career in engineering, technology, sciences or education.
Financial data: Year ended 12/31/2012. Assets, $9,833 (M); Expenditures, $3,792,248; Total giving, $3,650,743; Grants to individuals, 106 grants totaling $311,243 (high: $7,000, low: $333).
Fields of interest: Education; Science; Engineering/technology.

Type of support: Scholarships—to individuals.
Application information: Applications accepted.
Application form required.
> *Deadline(s):* Mar. 31
> *Final notification:* Applicants notified May 15
> *Applicants should submit the following:*
> 1) GPA
> 2) Transcripts
> 3) Letter(s) of recommendation
> 4) Financial information
> 5) FAFSA
> 6) Essay
> *Additional information:* Application should also include copies of applicant and parents' most recent income tax return. Applicants must be residents of or attending school in Hartford and Middlesex counties, CT, Windham County, VT, or Cheshire County, NH.

EIN: 222501925

1456
SBM Charitable Foundation, Inc.
935 Main St., Level C, Unit B-101
Manchester, CT   06040-6050   (860) 533-0355
Contact: Doreen Downham, Exec. Dir.
Scholarship contact/inquiry: Kelley Gunther, Foundation and Scholarship Dir., tel.: (860) 533-1067, e-mail: kgunther@sbmfoundation.org
FAX: (860) 533-0241; URL: http://www.sbmfoundation.org

Foundation type: Independent foundation
Purpose: College scholarships to students who are permanent residents of Hartford, Tolland, and Windham counties CT, who plan to attend an accredited institution of higher learning in CT.
Financial data: Year ended 12/31/2012. Assets, $37,843,533 (M); Expenditures, $2,486,078; Total giving, $2,051,987. Scholarships—to individuals amount not specified.
Fields of interest: Higher education.
Type of support: Scholarships—to individuals; Undergraduate support.
Application information: Applications accepted. Application form required. Application form available on the grantmaker's web site.
> *Deadline(s):* Mar.
> *Applicants should submit the following:*
> 1) Resume
> 2) Financial information
> 3) Transcripts
> 4) Essay
> 5) Letter(s) of recommendation
> 6) SAR
> 7) FAFSA
> *Additional information:* Applicant must have a 2.5 GPA on a 4.0 scale, or be in the top 40 percent of his/her high school class.

EIN: 061574365

1457
Arthur H. Scott Memorial Trust
850 Main St., RC 13-505
Bridgeport, CT   06604-4913

Foundation type: Independent foundation
Purpose: Scholarships to graduating seniors of Champlain Valley Union High School, Hinesburg, VT, Northfield High School, VT, and Chelsea High School, VT, who are majoring in education or the performing arts.
Financial data: Year ended 12/31/2012. Assets, $1,286,854 (M); Expenditures, $81,043; Total giving, $64,404; Grants to individuals, 9 grants totaling $64,404 (high: $7,156, low: $7,156).

Fields of interest: Performing arts, education; Teacher school/education.
Type of support: Support to graduates or students of specific schools; Undergraduate support.
Application information: Applications not accepted.
> *Additional information:* Unsolicited requests for funds not considered or acknowledged.

EIN: 036047004

1458
The Scudder Association Inc.
c/o Richard Williamson
2 Tinywood Rd.
Darien, CT   06820-2429   (215) 548-8642
Contact: Betsy Steel
Application address: 416 W. Springfield Ave., Philadelphia, PA 19118-4105, tel.: 215-548-8642; URL: http://www.scudder.org/philanthropy

Foundation type: Independent foundation
Purpose: Scholarships to financially needy undergraduate and graduate students from the U.S. and India who are studying for the ministry or in the fields of medicine, nursing, or other medically-related careers, teaching, or social services. Preference is shown to renewal applicants and individuals recommended by Scudder Association members or by the financial aid office of Cornell Medical College, NY. Scholarships are renewable for up to a total of four years of undergraduate and/or graduate support.
Financial data: Year ended 12/31/2010. Assets, $1,884,601 (M); Expenditures, $70,514; Total giving, $31,621; Grants to individuals, 9 grants totaling $14,500 (high: $2,000, low: $1,500).
Fields of interest: Medical school/education; Teacher school/education; Theological school/education; Social work school/education.
International interests: India.
Type of support: Graduate support; Undergraduate support.
Application information: Application form required.
> *Deadline(s):* Apr. 15
> *Applicants should submit the following:*
> 1) Financial information
> 2) Transcripts
> 3) Letter(s) of recommendation
> *Additional information:* Application must also include a personal statement of 500 words or less, and verification of financial need from college.

EIN: 135647705

1459
Senior Services of Stamford, Inc.
2009 Summer St., Ste. 301
Stamford, CT   06905-5023   (203) 324-6584
Contact: Michael G. Mezzapelle, Treas.

Foundation type: Independent foundation
Purpose: General welfare assistance and financial aid for medical, dental, living and home care expenses to elderly individuals in Stamford, CT.
Publications: Annual report; Informational brochure.
Financial data: Year ended 02/28/2013. Assets, $13,354,203 (M); Expenditures, $928,284; Total giving, $319,334; Grants to individuals, 545 grants totaling $319,334.
Fields of interest: Dental care; Health care; Housing/shelter, expense aid; Aging.
Type of support: Grants for special needs.
Application information: Applications accepted. Application form required.

Initial approach: Letter or telephone
Deadline(s): None
EIN: 060646916

1460
Harry R. Sheridan Memorial Scholarship
850 Main St., RC 13-505
Bridgeport, CT   06604-4917   (802) 660-2153

Foundation type: Public charity
Purpose: Scholarships to students from the Union 32 School District and the Montpelier, VT area.
Financial data: Year ended 02/28/2013. Assets, $818,838 (M); Expenditures, $52,106; Total giving, $37,650.
Type of support: Support to graduates or students of specific schools; Undergraduate support.
Application information: Applications accepted. Application form required.
EIN: 036048570

1461
The Society for the Increase of the Ministry
924 Farmington Ave., Ste. 100
West Hartford, CT   06107-2224   (860) 233-1732
Contact: Thomas Moore III, Exec. Dir.
FAX: (860) 233-2644; E-mail: info@simministry.org; E-Mail for Thomas Moore III: t.moore@simministry.org; URL: http://www.simministry.org

Foundation type: Public charity
Purpose: Scholarships for theological education to students preparing for ordination in the Episcopal Church.
Publications: Application guidelines; Informational brochure; Newsletter.
Financial data: Year ended 06/30/2011. Assets, $3,996,020 (M); Expenditures, $613,632; Total giving, $247,700; Grants to individuals, totaling $247,700.
Fields of interest: Theological school/education; Protestant agencies & churches.
Type of support: Scholarships—to individuals.
Application information: Applications accepted. Application form required. Application form available on the grantmaker's web site.
> *Deadline(s):* Mar. 1
> *Applicants should submit the following:*
> 1) Resume
> 2) Essay
> 3) Letter(s) of recommendation
> *Additional information:* Contact financial aid officer of seminary or the society for current application guidelines.

EIN: 066053077

1462
Spirol International Charitable Foundation Inc.
30 Rock Ave.
Danielson, CT   06239-1425   (860) 774-8571
Contact: John E. Ferdinandi, Treas.

Foundation type: Company-sponsored foundation
Purpose: Scholarships to graduating seniors or alumni from qualifying high schools and colleges in California, Connecticut, Ohio, and Vermont pursuing a degree in selected disciplines.
Publications: Application guidelines.

Financial data: Year ended 12/31/2012. Assets, $145,638 (M); Expenditures, $74,566; Total giving, $74,500.
Fields of interest: Higher education; Engineering school/education; Science; Engineering/technology.
Type of support: Support to graduates or students of specific schools; Undergraduate support.
Application information: Applications accepted. Application form required. Application form available on the grantmaker's web site.
  Initial approach: Letter
  Send request by: Mail
  Deadline(s): Apr. 16
  Applicants should submit the following:
    1) Letter(s) of recommendation
    2) GPA
    3) Essay
  Additional information: See web site for qualifying high schools, and additional application guidelines.
Program description:
  SPIROL Scholarship Program: The foundation awards four-year college scholarships of up to $20,000 to high school graduates, for full time students at a two-year or four-year accredited college in California, Connecticut, Ohio, and Vermont pursuing a career in Engineering, Basic Sciences, or Manufacturing Technology. Applicants must have a GPA of 3.0 and demonstrate a commitment to community service/involvement.
EIN: 510494974

1463
C. Weaver Squier Trust
100 Pearl St., 13th Fl.
Hartford, CT 06103-4506

Foundation type: Independent foundation
Purpose: Scholarships to high school seniors from East Hampton, CT.
Financial data: Year ended 12/31/2011. Assets, $195,785 (M); Expenditures, $11,858; Total giving, $7,857; Grants to individuals, 3 grants totaling $7,857 (high: $2,619, low: $2,619).
Type of support: Undergraduate support.
Application information: Applications accepted.
  Initial approach: Letter
  Deadline(s): None
EIN: 106004818

1464
Stamford Rotary Trust Fund
P.O. Box 8026
Stamford, CT 06905-8026   (203) 323-1191

Foundation type: Public charity
Purpose: Scholarships to residents of Stamford, CT.
Financial data: Year ended 06/30/2012. Assets, $253,274 (M); Expenditures, $68,230; Total giving, $53,179.
Type of support: Scholarships—to individuals.
Application information: Contact foundation for current application deadline/guidelines.
EIN: 066068805

1465
Stamford Woman's Club Inc.
P.O. Box 16793
Stamford, CT 06905-8793   (203) 972-1475
Contact: Roseanne DeCamillo

Foundation type: Independent foundation

Purpose: Scholarships to residents of the Stamford, CT area for higher education.
Financial data: Year ended 04/30/2012. Assets, $1,011,947 (M); Expenditures, $81,804; Total giving, $86,834; Grants to individuals, 35 grants totaling $35,000 (high: $1,000).
Fields of interest: Education.
Type of support: Scholarships—to individuals.
Application information: Application form required.
  Initial approach: Letter
  Deadline(s): Mar. 1
  Additional information: Contact the woman's club for eligibility criteria.
EIN: 060653184

1466
Staples Free School Trust
P.O. Box 425
Easton, CT 06612-0425   (203) 372-8871
Contact: Sherry Harris

Foundation type: Independent foundation
Purpose: Scholarships to students of Easton, CT, to attend accredited colleges and universities. One-half of the amount must be repaid to the trust within 7 years of disbursement.
Financial data: Year ended 06/30/2011. Assets, $467,250 (M); Expenditures, $41,950; Total giving, $32,520; Grants to individuals, 11 grants totaling $32,220 (high: $4,000, low: $1,470).
Type of support: Scholarships—to individuals.
Application information: Application form required.
  Deadline(s): May 1
EIN: 066038707

1467
John L. Starks Foundation, Inc.
1127 High Ridge Rd., Ste. 331
Stamford, CT 06905-1203   (203) 322-7788
Contact: Jennifer Alpert, Exec. Dir.
E-mail: info@johnstarks.org; URL: http://www.johnstarks.org/index.php

Foundation type: Public charity
Purpose: Scholarships to students from Tulsa, OK; NY; NJ; and CT area high schools based on academic performance, financial need, and community service.
Financial data: Year ended 12/31/2011. Assets, $108,329 (M); Expenditures, $153,451; Total giving, $47,300; Grants to individuals, totaling $40,000.
Type of support: Undergraduate support.
Application information: Applications accepted. Application form required. Application form available on the grantmaker's web site. Interview required.
  Initial approach: Letter
  Deadline(s): Apr. 1
  Final notification: Recipients notified by May 30
  Applicants should submit the following:
    1) Essay
    2) Letter(s) of recommendation
    3) Transcripts
    4) Financial information
  Additional information: Application should also include a list of community service activities.
EIN: 731438056

1468
Steep Rock Arts Association Co.
9 Potash Hill Rd.
Washington, CT 06793-1618   (917) 822-7155
Contact: Erika Klauer, Pres.
Application address: 102 East St., P.O. Box 1463, Washington Depot, CT 06793-1607
E-mail: info@steeprockarts.org; URL: http://www.steeprockarts.org

Foundation type: Operating foundation
Purpose: Grants and residencies for emerging visual artists and curators to stay in CT.
Financial data: Year ended 12/31/2011. Assets, $9,514 (M); Expenditures, $49,455; Total giving, $20,800.
Fields of interest: Visual arts.
Type of support: Grants to individuals; Residencies.
Application information: Applications accepted. Application form required. Application form available on the grantmaker's web site.
  Initial approach: Letter
  Send request by: Online
  Deadline(s): Dec. 31
  Final notification: Applicants notified by mid-Feb.
  Applicants should submit the following:
    1) Letter(s) of recommendation
    2) Work samples
    3) Resume
EIN: 203065933

1469
Ray & Pauline Sullivan Foundation
c/o Bank of America, N.A.
200 Glastonbury Blvd., 2nd Fl.
Glastonbury, CT 06033-4458
Contact: Amy R. Lynch, V.P.

Foundation type: Independent foundation
Purpose: Scholarships and student loans primarily to graduates of St. Bernard High School, CT, and other area schools to acquire educational advantages that might otherwise not be available to them.
Financial data: Year ended 01/31/2013. Assets, $14,556,953 (M); Expenditures, $777,006; Total giving, $611,260.
Fields of interest: Higher education.
Type of support: Student loans—to individuals; Support to graduates or students of specific schools; Undergraduate support.
Application information: Applications not accepted.
  Additional information: Unsolicited requests for funds not considered or acknowledged.
EIN: 066141242

1470
Thames Valley Council for Community Action, Inc.
1 Sylvandale Rd.
Jewett City, CT 06351-2220   (860) 889-1365
Contact: Deborah Monahan, Exec. Dir.
FAX: (860) 376-8782;
E-mail: dmonahan@tvcca.org; URL: http://www.tvcca.org

Foundation type: Public charity
Purpose: Grants for basic necessities to low-income residents of New London County, CT.
Publications: Annual report.
Financial data: Year ended 03/31/2012. Assets, $13,302,501 (M); Expenditures, $26,133,469; Total giving, $6,274,356; Grants to individuals, totaling $6,274,356.
Fields of interest: Economically disadvantaged.

Type of support: Grants for special needs.
Application information:
Initial approach: Letter
Additional information: Contact coouncil for eligibility information.
EIN: 060806128

1471
The J and K Thomas Foundation
74 Boysenberry Ct.
Suffield, CT   06078

Foundation type: Independent foundation
Purpose: Scholarships primarily to residents of Hartford and East Hartford, CT. Also awards smaller grants to economically disadvantaged individuals.
Financial data: Year ended 06/30/2012. Assets, $475,148 (M); Expenditures, $78,762; Total giving, $83,550.
Fields of interest: Economically disadvantaged.
Type of support: Undergraduate support.
Application information: Application form required.
Send request by: Mail
Deadline(s): None
Final notification: Recipients notified in one month
EIN: 061528257

1472
The Tierney Family Foundation, Inc.
17 Butlers Island Rd.
Darien, CT   06820-6203

Foundation type: Independent foundation
Purpose: Scholarships for Native American students. Also, fellowships to support emerging artists in the field of photography.
Financial data: Year ended 12/31/2012. Assets, $6,323,640 (M); Expenditures, $432,376; Total giving, $417,176.
Fields of interest: Photography; Native Americans/American Indians.
Type of support: Fellowships; Undergraduate support.
Application information: Applications not accepted.
Additional information: Unsolicited requests for funds not considered or acknowledged.
EIN: 133541596

1473
The William J. Tomasso Foundation Inc.
(formerly The Tomasso Family Foundation, Inc.)
P.O. Box 488
New Britain, CT   06050

Foundation type: Independent foundation
Purpose: Scholarships to financially needy students graduating from public, private, and parochial schools in New Britain, Plainville, and Berlin, CT, to attend accredited two- or four-year colleges, or technical or vocational schools.
Financial data: Year ended 03/31/2013. Assets, $265,386 (M); Expenditures, $0; Total giving, $0.
Fields of interest: Vocational education.
Type of support: Technical education support; Undergraduate support.
Application information: Application form required.
Deadline(s): Mar. 1
Additional information: Selection is based on financial need, academic performance, and performance on ability and aptitude tests. Application is furnished upon request.
EIN: 060991847

1474
Hertha Traalum Trust
c/o Richard Danen
76 Center St.
Waterbury, CT   06702-2129

Foundation type: Independent foundation
Purpose: Scholarships to CT residents pursuing a degree in music.
Financial data: Year ended 12/31/2011. Assets, $134,961 (M); Expenditures, $2,317; Total giving, $0.
Fields of interest: Music.
Type of support: Scholarships—to individuals.
Application information: Contact the trust for additional information.
EIN: 566609144

1475
Louis D. Traurig Scholarship Trust
c/o Lawrence H. Engelman, Esq.
P.O. Box 369
Middlebury, CT   06762-0369
Contact: Eric Polokoff, Tr.
Application address: 82 Hampton Rd., Southbury, CT 06488-3907

Foundation type: Independent foundation
Purpose: Scholarships to residents of the greater Waterbury, CT, area for higher education.
Financial data: Year ended 12/31/2012. Assets, $551,893 (M); Expenditures, $29,975; Total giving, $27,000; Grants to individuals, 7 grants totaling $27,000 (high: $5,000, low: $2,500).
Type of support: Scholarships—to individuals.
Application information: Application form required.
Initial approach: Letter or telephone
Deadline(s): Feb. 15
Applicants should submit the following:
1) Transcripts
2) Financial information
EIN: 222936329

1476
United Way of Southeastern Connecticut, Inc.
P.O. Box 375
Gales Ferry, CT   06335-0375   (860) 464-7281
FAX: (860) 464-6362; E-mail: info@uwsect.org; URL: http://www.uwsect.org

Foundation type: Public charity
Purpose: Grants for food, utilities, and other basic necessities for needy residents of southeastern CT.
Publications: Annual report; Informational brochure.
Financial data: Year ended 06/30/2011. Assets, $10,003,738 (M); Expenditures, $8,639,835; Total giving, $6,544,658; Grants to individuals, totaling $2,420,447.
Fields of interest: Economically disadvantaged.
Type of support: Grants for special needs.
Application information:
Initial approach: Letter
Additional information: Contact foundation for eligibility requirements.
EIN: 060771393

1477
The Urban League of Greater Hartford, Inc
140 Woodland St.
Hartford, CT   06105-1210   (860) 527-0147
URL: http://www.ulgh.org/

Foundation type: Public charity

Purpose: Grants to low-income African Americans and other residents of the greater Hartford, CT, area.
Financial data: Year ended 06/30/2012. Assets, $3,924,957 (M); Expenditures, $2,349,122; Total giving, $56,923; Grants to individuals, totaling $56,923.
Fields of interest: Economically disadvantaged.
Type of support: Grants for special needs.
Application information:
Initial approach: Letter
Additional information: Contact foundation for complete eligibility requirements.
EIN: 066066491

1478
Voya Financial, Inc. Contributions Program
(formerly ING Life Insurance and Annuity Company Contributions Program)
1 Orange Way, A3S
Windsor, CT   06095-4774
FAX: (860) 580-1665;
E-mail: diana.crecco@us.ing.com; Application address for ING Unsung Heroes Awards: ING Unsung Heroes Awards Prog., c/o Scholarship America, Inc., 1 Scholarship Way, P.O. Box 297, St. Peter, MN 56082, tel.: (800) 537-4180, e-mail: ing@scholarshipamerica.org; URL: http://ing.us/about-ing/responsibility

Foundation type: Corporate giving program
Purpose: Grants for educational programs to full-time K-12 educators who are employed by public or private schools in the U.S.
Publications: Informational brochure; Program policy statement.
Fields of interest: Elementary/secondary education; Teacher school/education; Education.
Type of support: Program development; Awards/prizes; Project support.
Application information: Applications accepted. Application form required. Application form available on the grantmaker's web site.
Initial approach: Letter, telephone or e-mail
Deadline(s): Apr. 30
Applicants should submit the following:
1) Proposal
2) Budget Information
3) Essay
Program description:
ING Unsung Heroes Awards Program: Through the ING Unsung Heroes Awards Program, ING annually awards 100 $2,000 grants to K-12 educators pioneering new methods and techniques that improve student learning. Three top winners are awarded additional grants of $5,000, $10,000, and $25,000, respectively. At least one award will be granted in each of the 50 United States, provided one or more qualified applications are received from each state. Each project is judged by its innovative method, creativity, and ability to positively influence the students. This program is administered by ING and Scholarship America. Questions regarding the program should be directed to Scholarship America at (507) 931-1682.

1479
The Walkabout Foundation
75 Holly Hill Ln.
Greenwich, CT   06830-6098   (203) 629-5290
E-mail: info@walkaboutfoundation.org; URL: http://www.walkaboutfoundation.org/

Foundation type: Public charity

Purpose: Research grants to scientists to find a cure for paralysis and assistance to people with disabilities around the world in need of wheelchairs.
Financial data: Year ended 12/31/2011. Assets, $542,764 (M); Expenditures, $241,678; Total giving, $200,186.
Fields of interest: Spine disorders research; Medical research; Physically disabled; Economically disadvantaged.
Type of support: Grants to individuals; Grants for special needs.
Application information: Applications accepted.
  Additional information: Contact the foundation for additional information.
Program description:
  Research Grants: The foundation provides research grants to scientists and research centers all over the world working to find a cure for paralysis.
EIN: 371582823

1480
Watertown Foundation, Inc.

P.O. Box 117
Watertown, CT   06795-0117   (860) 274-4299
Contact: James Maxwell, Admin.
E-mail: wttnfoundation@sbcglobal.net; *URL:* http://watertownfoundation.com/

Foundation type: Public charity
Purpose: Scholarships to graduating high school seniors of Oakville-Watertown, CT to assist them financially in achieving a postsecondary education.
Publications: Application guidelines; Annual report; Grants list; Informational brochure; Occasional report.
Financial data: Year ended 08/31/2011. Assets, $2,110,335 (M); Expenditures, $160,962; Total giving, $112,174; Grants to individuals, totaling $20,000.
Type of support: Scholarships—to individuals; Undergraduate support.
Application information: Applications accepted. Application form required.
  Copies of proposal: 1
  Deadline(s): Apr. 1
  Applicants should submit the following:
    1) Essay
    2) FAFSA
    3) GPA
    4) Letter(s) of recommendation
    5) SAT
    6) Transcripts
  Additional information: Scholarship is based on financial need, academic merit, and contribution to school or community. Applicant must be a resident of Oakville-Watertown for at least three years.
EIN: 066064660

1481
Weir Farm Trust, Inc.

735 Nod Hill Rd.
Wilton, CT   06897-1309   (203) 761-9945
Contact: Janice Hess, Exec. Dir.
FAX: (203) 761-9116;
E-mail: evanswft@optonline.net; *URL:* http://www.nps.gov/wefa/supportyourpark/artist-in-residence-program.htm

Foundation type: Public charity
Purpose: Residencies to advanced visual artists of all backgrounds.
Publications: Application guidelines.
Financial data: Year ended 06/30/2012. Assets, $5,821,760 (M); Expenditures, $44,601.
Fields of interest: Visual arts; Arts.

Type of support: Residencies; Stipends.
Application information: Applications accepted. Application form required.
  Initial approach: Telephone or e-mail
  Deadline(s): Jan. 15 and July 15
  Final notification: Notification will be sent six to eight weeks following the deadline
  Applicants should submit the following:
    1) SASE
    2) Resume
    3) Letter(s) of recommendation
    4) Work samples
  Additional information: Application must also include a $50 non-refundable application fee.
Program description:
  Artist-In-Residence: Selected artists from all over the country spend two weeks to one month living and working in excellent facilities located within a short walk from the farm with a monthly stipend of $500.
EIN: 223035427

1482
The Weller Foundation, Inc.

P.O. Box 1145
Woodbury, CT   06798-1145   (203) 263-0229
Contact: JoAnn E. Davies, Mgr.

Foundation type: Independent foundation
Purpose: Scholarships and awards to high school students in Newtown, Monroe, Trumbull, Shelton and Redding, CT, as well as grants to outstanding teachers.
Financial data: Year ended 12/31/2012. Assets, $2,628,482 (M); Expenditures, $122,303; Total giving, $63,982; Grants to individuals, 22 grants totaling $46,800 (high: $12,000, low: $800).
Fields of interest: Music; Vocational education; Nursing school/education; Teacher school/education; Health sciences school/education; Scholarships/financial aid; Business/industry; Engineering/technology; Computer science.
Type of support: Support to graduates or students of specific schools; Awards/prizes; Technical education support; Undergraduate support.
Application information: Applications accepted. Interview required.
  Send request by: Mail
  Deadline(s): Varies
Program descriptions:
  Barton L. Weller Scholarship: Scholarships to senior-year students attending one of the following CT high schools: Joel Barlow High School, Masuk High School, Newtown High School, Shelton High School, or Trumbull High School. The award is determined by a regional competition designed to encourage academic excellence in a substantial independent six-month research or study project of the student's choosing. Sample topics include the fine arts, computer projects, economics, science or engineering, mathematics, or political or environmental factors affecting the immediate geographic area. Five proposals will be accepted and each of the finalists will be awarded $200. The winner receives a scholarship of $12,000, payable in four annual increments of $3,000.
  Senior Science Award, Eleanor F. Moore Business Award and Paul W. Broggi Communications Award: These awards are presented annually in each of the five high schools honoring students who have excelled in science, business studies, and communications. The recipients are chosen by the faculties of the individual high schools. No application is required.
  Vincent Voccia Vocational Award: This award provides financial assistance to full time students at Masuk, Newtown, Trumbull, Joel Barlow, or

Shelton high schools to prepare for vocational or technical careers. Correspondence schools and four-year degree programs are not acceptable under this program. One winner is chosen from each school. Financial need is not a factor. Winners receive an award equal to the lesser of $2,500 or 50 percent of the cost of tuition and fees of the vocational-technical program proposed. Payment is made directly to the institution, one half upon enrollment and one half after satisfactory completion of the first half of the program. The program must begin within nine months of the award date. Application forms are available from the schools' guidance offices. Application must include a copy of the student's transcript.
  Weller Collegiate Scholarships: The award is presented annually to incoming freshmen students at local colleges who are from one of the five communities. The recipients are chosen by the local colleges based on financial need. No application form is required.
  Weller Computer Science/Technology Scholarship: This $4,000 scholarship is awarded to full time high school students at Joel Barlow, Masuk, Newtown, Shelton, or Trumbull High Schools and be accepted and enrolled at a four year fully accredited college or university majoring in computer science or computer engineering. Application must include a 500 to 700 word essay and official high school transcript.
  Weller Education Scholarship: The scholarship is presented annually to high school students who have enrolled in conservatories or colleges as music majors with a concentration in instrumental music. Applicants must be full-time seniors at Joel Barlow, Masuk, Newtown, Shelton, or Trumbull high schools and not be related to the foundation's trustees or judges. Financial need is not a consideration. The winner must start a formal education program within six months from the date of receiving the scholarship. The award is payable in four annual installments of $1,000. Proof of enrollment is required for first payment. Recipients must maintain at least a 2.5 GPA to continue receiving payments.
  Weller Eight Grade Scholastic Achievement Award: The achievement award is presented annually to eighth grade students with outstanding scholastic achievement in each of the six middle schools in the foundation's five-town area. Participating schools are Helen Keller Middle School in Easton, Jockey Hollow Middle School in Monroe, Newtown Middle School in Newtown, Intermediate Middle School in Shelton, and Hillcrest and Madison middle schools, both in Trumbull. The recipients are full-time eighth grade students who have achieved the highest final GPA in their classes. The recipients are announced in June, and receive a $200 U.S. Savings Bond and a certificate of honor.
  Weller Excellence in Teaching Award: The award is presented annually in recognition of the teaching quality and innovation exhibited by classroom teachers of grades K-5. Teachers currently teaching in the Monroe, Trumbull, and Newtown public school systems who developed a successful curriculum project that was implemented during the current or previous academic year may apply. The winner receives $500 and a Certificate of Honor. Completion of formal application required.
  Weller Instrumental Music Scholarship: The scholarship is presented annually to high school students who have enrolled in conservatories or colleges as music majors with a concentration in instrumental music. Applicants must be full-time seniors at Joel Barlow, Masuk, Newtown, Shelton, or Trumbull high schools and not be related to the foundation's trustees or judges. Financial need is

not a consideration. The winner must start a formal education program within six months from the date of receiving the scholarship. The award is payable in four annual installments of $1,000. Proof of enrollment is required for first payment. Recipients must maintain at least a 2.5 GPA to continue receiving payments.

Weller Medical/Health Sciences Scholarship: This scholarship is to encourage and financially assist a student upon graduation who has chosen a course of study in the field of Medical/Health Sciences, Healthcare careers acceptable under this Program are Nursing, Therapy, Medical Technology, Paramedics, and other licensed healthcare workers who provide one-on-one healthcare to people. The award is $4,000 or 50 percent of the cost of tuition for the training program, whichever is less. Applicants must be full time seniors at Joel Barlow, Masuk, Newtown, Shelton, or Trumbull High Schools. Application must include a 500 to 700 word essay and official transcript.
EIN: 066068987

1483
Horace Wells Trust Fund
100 Sherman St.
Norwich, CT   06360-4106   (860) 886-1466
Contact: Jeremiah Lowney

Foundation type: Independent foundation
Purpose: Scholarships to dental students from CT, for continuing their education at accredited institutions of higher learning.
Financial data: Year ended 10/31/2012. Assets, $279,875 (M); Expenditures, $13,309; Total giving, $8,000; Grants to individuals, 8 grants totaling $8,000 (high: $1,000, low: $1,000).
Fields of interest: Dental school/education.
Type of support: Scholarships—to individuals.
Application information: Applications accepted.
   Deadline(s): Nov. 15
EIN: 066037032

1484
Westport-Weston Foundation Trust
c/o Peoples United Bank
850 Main St.
Bridgeport, CT   06604-4904

Foundation type: Independent foundation
Purpose: Undergraduate scholarships to financially needy residents of Westport and Weston, CT, only. Grants for assistance with medical and basic living expenses and Christmas presents to financially needy residents of Westport and Weston, CT, only.
Financial data: Year ended 12/31/2012. Assets, $727,520 (M); Expenditures, $47,924; Total giving, $35,500; Grants to individuals, 24 grants totaling $6,000 (high: $1,000, low: $1,000).
Fields of interest: Higher education; Health care; Economically disadvantaged.
Type of support: Scholarships—to individuals; Grants for special needs.
Application information: Applications accepted. Application form required.
   Initial approach: Letter
   Additional information: Interviews may be required for scholarship applicants.
EIN: 066035931

1485
Widows Society
c/o Bank of America
777 Main St.
Hartford, CT   06115   (860) 952-7380
Contact: Pat Staffaroni
Application address: 200 Glastonbury Blvd., 2nd Fl., Glastonbury, CT 06033-4418

Foundation type: Independent foundation
Purpose: Support to financially needy women who reside in the Hartford, CT, area.
Financial data: Year ended 08/31/2012. Assets, $4,768,330 (M); Expenditures, $217,742; Total giving, $186,364; Grants to individuals, 134 grants totaling $174,064 (high: $12,000, low: $16).
Fields of interest: Women.
Type of support: Grants for special needs.
Application information: Applications accepted.
   Initial approach: Letter demonstrating need
   Deadline(s): None
   Additional information: Applicants are generally referred through public or private social service agencies.
EIN: 066026060

1486
Wilkerson Scholarship Fund LLC
7-9 Issac St.
Norwalk, CT   06850-4102

Foundation type: Independent foundation
Purpose: Scholarships to individuals residing in the greater Norwalk, CT, area for undergraduate education.
Financial data: Year ended 12/31/2011. Assets, $415,336 (M); Expenditures, $12,740; Total giving, $9,750; Grants to individuals, 9 grants totaling $9,750 (high: $1,750, low: $250).
Type of support: Undergraduate support.
Application information: Applications accepted. Application form required.
   Deadline(s): May
   Applicants should submit the following:
     1) Essay
     2) Transcripts
     3) GPA
EIN: 061617537

1487
Windsor High School Alumni Scholarship Fund
c/o R.F. Carroll, C.P.A.
43 Poquonock Ave.
Windsor, CT   06095-2548   (860) 687-2020
Application address: c/o Windsor High School, Attn.: Guidance Office, 50 Sage Park Rd., Windsor, CT 06095

Foundation type: Independent foundation
Purpose: Scholarships to students of Windsor High School, CT, for higher education.
Financial data: Year ended 06/30/2012. Assets, $177,924 (M); Expenditures, $1,993; Total giving, $1,500; Grants to individuals, 2 grants totaling $1,500 (high: $1,000, low: $500).
Type of support: Support to graduates or students of specific schools; Undergraduate support.
Application information: Applications accepted.
   Initial approach: Letter
   Additional information: Application must show financial need established by FAFSA. Contact foundation for current application deadline/guidelines.
EIN: 066026061

1488
Woman's Seamen's Friend Society of Connecticut Inc.
c/o Trust Company of Connecticut
P.O. Box 302
New Haven, CT   06502   (203) 777-2165

Foundation type: Independent foundation
Purpose: Scholarships to CT residents majoring in marine sciences, for residents studying at State maritime academies, residents who are merchant seafarers and/or their dependents, or legal residents of other states majoring in marine sciences at a college, university, or other approved institution in CT. Financial assistance to retired seamen or their widows with special needs.
Financial data: Year ended 12/31/2012. Assets, $5,191,758 (M); Expenditures, $187,454; Total giving, $87,590.
Fields of interest: Business/industry; Marine science; Military/veterans' organizations; Women.
Type of support: Undergraduate support; Grants for special needs.
Application information: Application form required.
   Initial approach: Letter
   Deadline(s): Apr. 1 for summer school, May 15 for academic year.
   Applicants should submit the following:
     1) Transcripts
     2) Financial information
   Additional information: Contact the society for application guidelines for financial assistance to widows.
EIN: 060655133

1489
The Workplace, Inc.
350 Fairfield Ave.
Bridgeport, CT   06604-6023   (203) 335-9703
Contact: Joseph Carbone, Pres. and C.E.O.
FAX: (203) 610-8501; E-mail: info2@workplace.org; Fax for Joseph Carbone: (203)-610-8503;
URL: http://www.workplace.org

Foundation type: Public charity
Purpose: Assistance for dislocated and economically disadvantaged individuals in southwestern CT, with tuition, job training, placement and counseling.
Financial data: Year ended 06/30/2011. Assets, $6,444,110 (M); Expenditures, $19,500,090; Total giving, $10,605,772; Grants to individuals, totaling $2,396,492.
Fields of interest: Human services.
Type of support: Grants for special needs.
Application information: Applications not accepted.
EIN: 222484517

1490
Xerox Foundation
45 Glover Ave.
P.O. Box 4505
Norwalk, CT   06856-4505
Contact: Mark J. Conlin, Pres.
E-mail: mark.conlin@xerox.com; URL: http://www.xerox.com/foundation

Foundation type: Company-sponsored foundation
Purpose: Undergraduate scholarships for minority students which is administered by the National Merit Scholarships.
Publications: Application guidelines; Annual report; Corporate report; Corporate giving report (including application guidelines); Informational brochure

(including application guidelines); Program policy statement (including application guidelines).
Financial data: Year ended 12/31/2012. Assets, $344 (M); Expenditures, $558,200; Total giving, $558,200; Grants to individuals, 131 grants totaling $165,500 (high: $10,000; low: $1,000).
Fields of interest: Education; Minorities.
Type of support: Program development; Research; Technical education support; Undergraduate support; Project support.
Application information: Applications accepted.
  Initial approach: Letter of request or proposal
  Copies of proposal: 1
EIN: 060996443

1491
XL America Foundation, Inc.
(formerly NRC Foundation, Inc.)
100 Constitution Plz., 12th Fl.
Hartford, CT 06103 (610) 968-2551
Contact: Eileen Whelley, Dir.

Foundation type: Company-sponsored foundation
Purpose: Scholarships to family members of XL America employees.
Financial data: Year ended 12/31/2012. Assets, $161,962 (M); Expenditures, $25,150; Total giving, $25,000; Grants to individuals, 6 grants totaling $25,000.
Type of support: Employee-related scholarships.
Application information: Application form required.
  Deadline(s): 2nd Mon. in Aug.
  Applicants should submit the following:
    1) ACT
    2) SAT
    3) Letter(s) of recommendation
    4) Transcripts
    5) Essay
Company name: XL America
EIN: 061559574

1492
Zane Foundation, Inc.
182 Cedar St.
Branford, CT 06405-3034

Foundation type: Independent foundation
Purpose: Scholarships to graduating seniors from Branford High School, CT who are residents of Branford, CT for continuing education at institutions of higher learning.
Financial data: Year ended 12/31/2012. Assets, $183 (M); Expenditures, $5,396; Total giving, $5,000; Grants to individuals, 5 grants totaling $5,000 (high: $500; low: $500).
Fields of interest: Higher education.
Type of support: Support to graduates or students of specific schools.
Application information: Applications accepted.
  Additional information: Selection is based on academic achievement, character and citizenship.
EIN: 061378537

DELAWARE

1493
AstraZeneca Patient Assistance Organization
1800 Concord Pike
P.O. Box 15437
Wilmington, DE 19850-5437
Mailing address: AZ&Me Prescription Savings Prog., P.O. Box 898, Somerville, NJ 08876, fax: (800) 961-8323
URL: http://www.astrazeneca-us.com/medicines/help-affording-your-medicines

Foundation type: Public charity
Purpose: Assistance to eligible individuals without insurance with pharmaceutical drugs.
Financial data: Year ended 12/31/2011. Expenditures, $629,187,333; Total giving, $629,187,333; Grants to individuals, 344,206 grants totaling $629,187,333.
Fields of interest: Pharmacy/prescriptions; Economically disadvantaged.
Type of support: In-kind gifts; Grants for special needs.
Application information: Applications accepted.
  Initial approach: Telephone, mail or fax
  Additional information: The organization distributes certain drugs to qualified individuals who demonstrate need.
EIN: 562591004

1494
CenturyLink-Clarke M. Williams Foundation
(formerly Qwest Foundation)
c/o Foundation Source
501 Silverside Road, Ste. 123
Wilmington, DE 19809-1377
URL: http://www.centurylink.com/Pages/AboutUs/Community/Foundation/

Foundation type: Company-sponsored foundation
Purpose: Grants to K-12 teachers in public schools for technology-related classroom projects.
Publications: Application guidelines.
Financial data: Year ended 12/31/2012. Assets, $16,474,473 (M); Expenditures, $4,090,884; Total giving, $3,822,512.
Fields of interest: Elementary/secondary education; Education.
Type of support: Program development; Awards/prizes.
Application information: Applications accepted. Application form required. Application form available on the grantmaker's web site.
  Deadline(s): Oct. 1 to Jan. 10
  Final notification: Apr. 1
  Additional information: See website for local coordinator information.
EIN: 840978668

1495
Chaney Foundation Ltd.
(formerly Eugene Chaney Foundation, Ltd.)
c/o Foundation Source
501 Silverside Rd.
Wilmington, DE 19809-1377
URL: http://www.chaneyenterprises.com/index.cfm/go/WhoWeAre.Chaney-Foundation

Foundation type: Company-sponsored foundation

Purpose: Scholarships to high school seniors in select counties of MD, to pursue higher education at an accredited two- or four-year college.
Financial data: Year ended 12/31/2012. Assets, $427,418 (M); Expenditures, $246,786; Total giving, $235,350.
Fields of interest: Higher education; Business school/education; Environmental education; Engineering.
Type of support: Scholarships—to individuals; Undergraduate support.
Application information: Applications accepted. Application form required. Application form available on the grantmaker's web site.
  Initial approach: Application
  Send request by: Mail
  Deadline(s): Apr. 30
  Applicants should submit the following:
    1) Transcripts
    2) Photograph
    3) Essay
    4) Letter(s) of recommendation
  Additional information: Application should also include letter(s) of acceptance if not currently attending college. The awarded scholarship will be used for tuition and books only and will be paid directly to the college or university.
Program description:
  Chaney Foundation Scholarship: The foundation awards $1,000 college scholarships to high school seniors or graduates residing in Charles, Calvert, St. Mary's, and Caroline Counties, MD. Preference is given to students majoring in building trades, drafting, design, construction or concrete management, environmental science, architecture, or business. The program is currently under restructuring.
EIN: 521525001

1496
Children and Families First Delaware, Inc.
2005 Baynard Blvd.
Wilmington, DE 19802-3917 (302) 658-5177
Contact: Leslie Newman, C.E.O.
URL: http://www.cffde.org/

Foundation type: Public charity
Purpose: Assistance with child and adult day-care cost for working individuals of DE. Assistance with costs of food, rent, utilities, transportation, health care and other necessary items for individuals of DE.
Financial data: Year ended 12/31/2011. Assets, $6,554,625 (M); Expenditures, $14,190,837; Total giving, $3,516,996; Grants to individuals, totaling $3,093,453.
Fields of interest: Human services; Economically disadvantaged.
Type of support: In-kind gifts; Grants for special needs.
Application information: Applications accepted.
  Additional information: Providers for child and adult care receives monthly cash reimbursement, technical assistance, free nutrition and notary services, and monthly feedback. Providers must be licensed by the State of Delaware, have at least one child enrolled, and be willing to serve meals that meet the USDA and child and Adult Care food Program/DelaCare guidelines. See web site for eligibility determination.
EIN: 510065731

1497
Common Wealth Trust
c/o PNC Bank, N.A.-Delaware
222 Delaware Ave.
Wilmington, DE 19899-1621

Foundation type: Independent foundation
Purpose: Distinguished service awards by nomination only to prominent individuals in the dramatic arts, literature, public service, science, invention, government, and mass communications, primarily in OH.
Financial data: Year ended 12/31/2012. Assets, $7,972,510 (M); Expenditures, $541,177; Total giving, $454,000.
Fields of interest: Media/communications; Theater; Science; Government/public administration; Leadership development.
Type of support: Awards/grants by nomination only; Awards/prizes.
Application information: Applications not accepted.
EIN: 510232187

1498
CTW Foundation, Inc.
(formerly Beneficial Foundation, Inc.)
P.O. Box 911
Wilmington, DE 19899-0911 (302) 429-9427
Contact: Robert A. Tucker, Pres. and Dir.
Application address: C/o Hodson Services, LLC, 200 Bellevue Pkwy., Ste. 100, Wilmington, DE 19809

Foundation type: Company-sponsored foundation
Purpose: Scholarships to children of employees of Beneficial Corporation and its affiliated corporations, primarily in DE, NJ and PA.
Financial data: Year ended 12/31/2012. Assets, $12,938,432 (M); Expenditures, $749,870; Total giving, $697,500.
Type of support: Employee-related scholarships.
Application information: Applications accepted. Application form required.
  Deadline(s): Apr. 15
  Additional information: Application should include financial information, biographical and scholastic information.
Company name: Beneficial Corporation
EIN: 516011637

1499
Delaware Center for the Contemporary Arts, Inc.
200 S. Madison St.
Wilmington, DE 19801-5110 (302) 656-6466
Contact: Maxine Gaiber, Exec. Dir.
E-mail: info@thedcca.org; *URL:* http://www.thedcca.org

Foundation type: Public charity
Purpose: Residencies to visual artists.
Publications: Informational brochure.
Financial data: Year ended 07/31/2011. Assets, $4,596,209 (M); Expenditures, $1,091,256.
Fields of interest: Visual arts.
Type of support: Residencies.
Application information: Applications accepted. Application form required.
  Initial approach: E-mail
  Deadline(s): Apr.
  Additional information: Contact foundation or call for submissions and current application information.

Program description:
Art and Community Residency: Under this program, artists make a full-time commitment to collaborate with an under-served community group to create artwork based on issues relevant to the participants' lives. The residency is also geared to offering artists the time, space, and financial assistance to work on their own independent projects. In addition to a stipend, the center provides selected artists with an on-site apartment/studio space for eight weeks. Eligible applicants must be U.S. citizens.
EIN: 510242942

1500

Delaware Community Foundation
100 W. 10th Street, Ste. 115
P.O. Box 1636
Wilmington, DE 19899 (302) 571-8004
Contact: Elizabeth M. Bouchelle, Dir., Grants; For scholarships: Joyce Darling, Acct.
FAX: (302) 571-1553; E-mail: info@delcf.org;
URL: http://www.delcf.org

Foundation type: Community foundation
Purpose: Scholarships to students residing in DE for attendance at U.S. colleges and universities.
Publications: Application guidelines; Annual report; Financial statement; Informational brochure; Newsletter.
Financial data: Year ended 06/30/2013. Assets, $219,684,923 (M); Expenditures, $33,371,595; Total giving, $28,100,711. Scholarships—to individuals amount not specified.
Fields of interest: Formal/general education; Media/communications; Ballet; Theater; Vocational education, post-secondary; Graduate/professional education; Law school/education; Medical school/education; Nursing school/education; Teacher school/education; Engineering school/education; Journalism school/education; Adult/continuing education; Economically disadvantaged.
Type of support: Scholarships—to individuals; Support to graduates or students of specific schools; Awards/prizes; Graduate support; Technical education support; Undergraduate support.
Application information: Applications accepted. Application form required. Application form available on the grantmaker's web site.
Deadline(s): Apr. 1
Applicants should submit the following:
1) SAT
2) ACT
3) SAR
4) GPA
5) Transcripts
6) Letter(s) of recommendation
Additional information: See web site for a complete listing of scholarship funds and application form.
Program description:
Scholarships: The foundation offers a wide range of scholarships established by donors to provide opportunities for individuals with the rising cost of higher education. Each scholarship fund maintains unique eligibility guidelines, including but not limited to particular fields of study, current high school, academic achievement and financial need. Some scholarships are also available for graduate school education. See the web site for additional information.
EIN: 222804785

1501

Delaware Contractors Association Scholarship Trust
P.O. Box 6520
Wilmington, DE 19804-0120 (302) 994-7442

Foundation type: Independent foundation
Purpose: Scholarships to students enrolled in a construction related field for full-time study who are planning to earn a bachelors or associates degree.
Financial data: Year ended 12/31/2012. Assets, $32,515 (M); Expenditures, $4,493; Total giving, $3,500; Grants to individuals, 5 grants totaling $3,500 (high: $1,000, low: $500).
Type of support: Scholarships—to individuals.
Application information: Applications accepted. Application form required.
Initial approach: Letter or telephone
Deadline(s): Varies
EIN: 516172704

1502

Delaware Foundation Reaching Citizens, Inc.
(formerly Delaware Foundation for Retarded Children, Inc., also known as DFRC)
640 Plaza Dr.
4 Seasons Ctr.
Newark, DE 19702-6369 (302) 454-2730
Contact: Anthony T. Glenn Ed.D., Exec. Dir.
FAX: (302) 454-2755;
E-mail: info@dfrcfoundation.org; URL: http://www.dfrcfoundation.org/

Foundation type: Public charity
Purpose: Financial assistance to residents of DE with children who are mentally disabled.
Publications: Application guidelines; Financial statement; Grants list; Newsletter.
Financial data: Year ended 12/31/2011. Assets, $1,149,398 (M); Expenditures, $741,660; Total giving, $124,100.
Fields of interest: Children; Disabilities, people with.
Type of support: Grants for special needs.
Application information:
Initial approach: Letter
Additional information: Contact foundation for further application information.
EIN: 510102390

1503

Delaware HIV Consortium, Inc.
100 W. 10th St., Ste. 415
Wilmington, DE 19801-1647 (302) 654-5471
Contact: Peter Houle M.B.A., Exec. Dir.
FAX: (302) 654-5472;
E-mail: info@delawarehiv.org; URL: http://www.delawarehiv.org

Foundation type: Public charity
Purpose: Financial assistance for rental payments for low income individuals with HIV/AIDS and their families in Delaware.
Publications: Annual report; Newsletter.
Financial data: Year ended 12/31/2011. Assets, $856,656 (M); Expenditures, $2,414,973; Total giving, $1,657,871; Grants to individuals, totaling $1,657,871.
Fields of interest: AIDS, people with; Economically disadvantaged.
Type of support: Grants for special needs.
Application information: Applications accepted.
Additional information: Individuals are referred to the program by local case management

agencies throughout the state. Contact the agency for additional information.
Program description:
Michael Brossette Memorial Fund: The fund seeks to serve people with HIV disease who are experiencing financial hardship and who do not generally qualify for other private, public, or governmental programs. The fund considers types of requests (such as mortgage payments) that are typically denied through other programs. The program may provide up to $500 in assistance per applicant.
EIN: 510348892

1504

Delaware State Golf Association Scholarship Fund, Inc.
(also known as DSGA Junior Golf Scholarship Fund, Inc.)
20 West Buckingham Dr.
Rehoboth Beach, DE 19971-0101
Application Address: P.O. Box 101 Rehoboth Beach, DE 19971

Foundation type: Operating foundation
Purpose: Scholarships to DE high school seniors and graduates who are involved in golf.
Financial data: Year ended 12/31/2012. Assets, $501,292 (M); Expenditures, $34,196; Total giving, $33,850; Grants to individuals, 21 grants totaling $33,850 (high: $3,500, low: $500).
Fields of interest: Athletics/sports, training; Athletics/sports, golf.
Type of support: Scholarships—to individuals.
Application information: Application form required.
Deadline(s): Apr. 1
Applicants should submit the following:
1) Transcripts
2) Letter(s) of recommendation
3) Essay
Additional information: Application should also include a list of other scholarships applied for or received, and a statement outlining financial need, if any.
EIN: 510297378

1505

Eleutherian Mills-Hagley Foundation, Inc.
P. O. Box 3630
Wilmington, DE 19807-0630 (302) 658-2400
Contact: Henry B. Du Pont, Pres.

Foundation type: Public charity
Purpose: Fellowships to individuals researching the business, industrial and technological history of America's Middle Atlantic region.
Publications: Annual report; Informational brochure.
Financial data: Year ended 12/31/2011. Assets, $139,208,199 (M); Expenditures, $9,601,022; Total giving, $29,750; Grants to individuals, totaling $29,750.
Fields of interest: History/archaeology; Historical activities.
Type of support: Fellowships; Internship funds.
Application information: Application form required.
Initial approach: Letter
Additional information: Contact foundation for current application deadline/guidelines.
Program description:
Fellowships: Research fellowships are awarded through an application and evaluation process. The committee, comprised of Hagley experts and outside scholars, assesses applications 4 times per year. Applicants must demonstrate their research will make important scholarly and

academic contributions; potential grant recipients must also make sufficient use of Hagley's research collections. Approximately 30 grants are awarded per year.
EIN: 510070531

1506
Oliver Etnier Charitable Trust
c/o Wilmington Trust Co.
1100 N. Market St., Drop 1050
Wilmington, DE   19801-1243
Contact: Michela Rossi

Foundation type: Independent foundation
Purpose: Scholarships to PA residents with preference for Huntington County, majoring in engineering, physics, applied mathematics, or computer science at one of six qualifying universities.
Financial data: Year ended 04/30/2013. Assets, $15,684,782 (M); Expenditures, $860,674; Total giving, $658,688.
Type of support: Undergraduate support.
Application information: Applications not accepted.
    Additional information: Unsolicited requests for funds not considered.
EIN: 516170516

1507
Farpath Foundation
800 Bay Ave.
Lewes, DE   19958-1005   (302) 645-8328
Contact: Clifford P. Diver, Jr., Pres.

Foundation type: Independent foundation
Purpose: Grants and awards to individuals to promote and enhance artistic endeavors.
Financial data: Year ended 03/31/2012. Assets, $173,750 (M); Expenditures, $28,945; Total giving, $8,313; Grants to individuals, 3 grants totaling $8,313 (high: $4,370, low: $1,000).
Fields of interest: Arts.
Type of support: Grants to individuals.
Application information:
    Deadline(s): None
EIN: 510408833

1508
William P. Frank Scholarship Fund, Inc.
c/o Thomas J. Shopa
270 Presidentia
Wilmington, DE   19807-0566   (302) 656-5500
Contact: Michael Purzycki, Pres.
Mailing Address: P. O. Box 3566; Wilmington, DE 19807

Foundation type: Public charity
Purpose: Scholarships to deserving students of DE, pursuing a career in journalism.
Financial data: Year ended 06/30/2012. Assets, $291,279 (M); Expenditures, $70,854; Total giving, $60,000; Grants to individuals, totaling $60,000.
Fields of interest: Print publishing.
Type of support: Undergraduate support.
Application information: Applications accepted.
    Additional information: Contact the fund for additional application guidelines.
EIN: 510371156

1509
Fresh Start Scholarship Foundation, Inc.
P.O. Box 7784
Wilmington, DE   19803-0784   (302) 892-2299
Contact: Mary E. Maloney, Pres.
E-mail: fsscholar@comcast.net; URL: http://www.wwb.org/

Foundation type: Public charity
Purpose: Financial and mentoring assistance to women returning to school to improve their lives and opportunities.
Financial data: Year ended 06/30/2012. Assets, $197,516 (M); Expenditures, $63,843; Total giving, $61,000.
Fields of interest: Continuing education; Women.
Type of support: Scholarships—to individuals.
Application information: Applications accepted. Application form required. Application form available on the grantmaker's web site.
    Initial approach: Application
    Deadline(s): May 31
    Final notification: July 31
    Additional information: Application should include a personal statement. See web site for additional information.
Program description:
    Scholarships: The program awards scholarships to provide financial incentive and mentoring assistance to a woman returning to school to improve her life and opportunities. Awards are granted without regard to race, color, creed, religion, disability, or national origin.
EIN: 510378642

1510
George E. Gordy Family Educational Fund
c/o Wilmington Trust Co.
1100 N. Market St., Ste. 310780
Wilmington, DE   19890-0900   (302) 855-2814
Contact: Deanne Welsh

Foundation type: Independent foundation
Purpose: Scholarships to financially needy graduates of high schools in Sussex County, DE, for higher education.
Financial data: Year ended 06/30/2013. Assets, $1,117,031 (M); Expenditures, $69,829; Total giving, $53,250; Grants to individuals, 56 grants totaling $53,250 (high: $1,000, low: $375).
Fields of interest: Vocational education.
Type of support: Support to graduates or students of specific schools; Undergraduate support.
Application information: Application form required.
    Send request by: Mail
    Copies of proposal: 5
    Deadline(s): Feb. 15
    Final notification: Recipients notified by May 15
    Applicants should submit the following:
        1) Financial information
        2) Transcripts
        3) Budget Information
Program description:
    The George E. Gordy Scholarship Award: Applicants must be Sussex County high school graduates and must have evidence of acceptance to an accredited institution of postsecondary education. Screening is done by the Scholarship Advisory Committee and a list of qualified applicants is provided to the Selection Committee to determine award recipients. The scholarship must be applied to tuition, room, board, books, transportation, lab fees and student activities. The funds will be sent directly to the college of the student's choice for ultimate disbursement. To remain eligible, the student must maintain a minimum cumulative GPA of 2.5. The maximum

amount of each award is $3,000. In general, participation is limited to four years and to those enrolled in baccalaureate and associate degrees or those working toward completion of the vocational or other educational program in which enrolled.
EIN: 222561832

1511
Gromet Foundation
(formerly The Janice & Ben Gromet Fund for Disadvantaged Children)
40 E. Main St., Ste. 754
Newark, DE   19711-4639   (808) 384-1456
Contact: Sung Stubenberg
E-mail: info@gromet.org; URL: http://www.grometfoundation.org/

Foundation type: Independent foundation
Purpose: Scholarships to financially needy residents of HI, who have graduated from HI high schools.
Financial data: Year ended 12/31/2012. Assets, $10,232,887 (M); Expenditures, $768,857; Total giving, $187,713; Grants to individuals, 50 grants totaling $187,713 (high: $8,495, low: $750).
Fields of interest: Higher education; Scholarships/financial aid; Economically disadvantaged.
Type of support: Scholarships—to individuals.
Application information: Applications accepted. Interview required.
    Initial approach: Letter
    Deadline(s): Nov. 15
    Applicants should submit the following:
        1) Transcripts
        2) Letter(s) of recommendation
        3) SAT
        4) GPA
        5) Financial information
    Additional information: Contact foundation for complete guidelines. Application should include a personal statement, and a copy of the prior year's tax return.
EIN: 990281966

1512
L. Hirsch Scholarship Fund
(also known as The Hirsch Foundation)
c/o Wilmington Trust Co.
1100 N. Market St.
Wilmington, DE   19890-0900   (302) 855-2814
Contact: Deanne M. Welsh

Foundation type: Independent foundation
Purpose: Undergraduate scholarships to students of Milford High School, DE.
Financial data: Year ended 12/31/2012. Assets, $206,101 (M); Expenditures, $10,884; Total giving, $9,525; Grant to an individual, 1 grant totaling $9,525.
Type of support: Support to graduates or students of specific schools; Undergraduate support.
Application information: Applications not accepted.
    Additional information: Unsolicited requests for funds not considered or acknowledged.
EIN: 516013661

1513
Horsemen's Welfare Trust
c/o Delaware SOA
830 Walker Sq.
Dover, DE   19904-2748

Foundation type: Independent foundation

Purpose: Grants for distressed horsemen or their families who are in need of medical care, food, clothing, funeral expenses and other necessities.
Financial data: Year ended 09/30/2013. Assets, $0 (M); Expenditures, $14,396; Total giving, $13,838; Grants to individuals, 3 grants totaling $6,816 (high: $4,420, low: $1,000).
Fields of interest: Economically disadvantaged.
Type of support: Grants for special needs.
Application information:
 Initial approach: Letter
 Deadline(s): None
 Additional information: Contact the trust for additional guidelines.
EIN: 237097419

1514
International Reading Association, Inc.
800 Barksdale Rd.
P.O. Box 8139
Newark, DE 19714-8139 (302) 731-1600
Contact: Marcie Craig Post, Exec. Dir.
FAX: (302) 731-1057;
E-mail: customerservice@reading.org; Toll-free tel. (U.S. and Canada): (800) 336-7323; Washington D.C. Office: 444 North Capitol St., N.W. Ste. 524, Washington, DC 20001-1543, tel.: (202) 624-8800, fax: (202) 624-8826; E-Mail for Marcie Craig Post: mpost@reading.org; URL: http://www.reading.org

Foundation type: Public charity
Purpose: Awards to writers for works aimed at children and young adults; Research awards, grants, professional development awards, and fellowships to those in the fields of reading and reading education.
Publications: Application guidelines.
Financial data: Year ended 06/30/2012. Assets, $23,048,088 (M); Expenditures, $15,282,645; Total giving, $119,098; Grants to individuals, totaling $119,098.
Fields of interest: Language/linguistics; Literature; Elementary/secondary education; Elementary school/education; Adult education—literacy, basic skills & GED; Education.
Type of support: Fellowships; Research; Awards/prizes.
Application information: Applications accepted. Application form required. Application form available on the grantmaker's web site.
 Initial approach: E-mail
 Deadline(s): Varies
 Additional information: See web site for additional guidelines.
Program descriptions:
 Constance M. McCullough Award: Awards $4,000 annually to assist a member of the International Reading Association in the investigation of reading-related problems and to encourage international professional development activities that are carried out in countries outside North America.
 Dina Feitelson Research Award: Awards $500 to recognize an outstanding empirical study published in English in a refereed journal. The work should report on one or more aspects of literacy acquisition, such as phonemic awareness, the alphabetic principle, bilingualism, or cross-cultural studies of beginning reading. Works may be submitted by the author or anyone else.
 Elva Knight Research Grant: Provides up to $8,000 for research in reading and literacy. Projects should be completed within two years and may be carried out using any research method or approach so long as the focus of the project is on research in reading or literacy.

 Grants for Literacy Projects in Countries with Developing Economies: Awards grants up to $2,500 to members of the Association residing in developing countries who seek support for literacy projects in their own countries. The number of grants is determined by the amount of donations made to this fund as of June 30 each year.
 Helen M. Robinson Grant: Awards $1,200 annually to assist doctoral students at the early stages of their dissertation research in the area of reading and literacy. Applicants must be Association members.
 IRA Arbuthnot Award: This $800 award honors an outstanding college or university teacher of children's and young adults' literature. Nominees must be Association members, affiliated with a college or university, and engaged in teacher and/or librarian preparation at the undergraduate and/or graduate level.
 IRA Award for Technology and Reading: The award honors educators in grades K-12 who are making an outstanding and innovative contribution to the use of technology in reading education. All entrants must be educators who work directly with students ages 5 to 18 for all or part of the working day. The grand prize winner is selected as the best application from across all the regions. Nine additional winners, seven U.S. regional winners (Southeast, Plains, Rocky Mountain, Southwest, West, East, and Great Lakes), one Canadian winner, and one outside North America winner will also be chosen.
 IRA Children's and Young Adult's Book Awards: Awards are given for an author's first or second published book written for children or young adults (ages birth to 17 years). Awards are given for fiction and nonfiction in each of three categories: primary, intermediate, and young adult. Books from any country and in any language published for the first time during the current calendar year will be considered. Each award carries a monetary stipend.
 IRA Eleanor M. Johnson Award: Awards a $1,000 prize to recognize a current outstanding elementary classroom teacher of reading/language arts. Candidates must be Association members, have a minimum of 5 years' teaching experience, and be endorsed by four individuals.
 IRA Lee Bennett Hopkins Promising Poet Award: Awards $500 every three years to a promising new poet who writes for children and young adults and who has published no more than two books of children's poetry. A book-length single poem may be submitted. The award is for published works only.
 IRA Paul A. Witty Short Story Award: This award is given to the author of an original short story published for the first time during the current calendar year in a periodical for children. The award carries a $1,000 stipend. The short story should serve as a literary standard that encourages young readers to read periodicals.
 Jeanne S. Chall Research Fellowship: Awards a $6,000 grant established to encourage and support reading research by promising scholars. It supports research efforts in the following areas: beginning reading; reading difficulty; stages of reading development; the relation of vocabulary to reading; readability; and diagnosing and teaching adults with limited reading ability.
 Nila Banton Smith Award: Awards $1,000 to honor a middle or secondary school classroom teacher or reading teacher who has shown leadership in translating theory and current research into practice for developing content area literacy. Applicants must be Association members.
 Outstanding Dissertation of the Year Award: Awards $1,000 for dissertations in reading or related fields. Studies using any research approach (ethnographic, experimental, historical, survey,

etc.) are encouraged. Each study will be assessed in the light of this approach, the scholarly qualification of its report, and its significant contributions to knowledge within the reading field.
 Steven A. Stahl Research Grant: This $1,000 award was established to honor the memory and work of Steven A. Stahl by encouraging and supporting promising graduate students in their research. This grant will be awarded annually to a recipient with at least three years of teaching experience who is conducting classroom research (including action research) focused on improving reading instruction and children's reading achievement.
 Teacher as Researcher Grant: this grant supports classroom teachers in their inquiries about literacy and instruction. Grants will be awarded up to $4,000, although priority will be given to smaller grants (e.g., $1,000 to $2,000) in order to provide support for as many teacher researchers as possible.
 Travel Grants for Educators: Awards grants to provide support to educators from any country for meetings (across continents) sponsored by the Association. Applicants must be members of the Association or one of its affiliated groups.
EIN: 362364659

1515
JBL Scholarship Trust
P.O. Box 4248
Wilmington, DE 19807-0248
Contact: Catherine S. Malone

Foundation type: Independent foundation
Purpose: Undergraduate scholarships for full time students under age 30, for attendance at a college or university in DE.
Publications: Newsletter.
Financial data: Year ended 12/31/2012. Assets, $5,728,842 (M); Expenditures, $301,841; Total giving, $187,150; Grants to individuals, 86 grants totaling $152,150 (high: $3,000, low: $750).
Fields of interest: Higher education; Scholarships/financial aid.
Type of support: Undergraduate support.
Application information: Application form required.
 Deadline(s): Mar. 15 for first time applicants, Mar. 1 for renewal
 Final notification: Applicants notified late June
 Applicants should submit the following:
  1) Letter(s) of recommendation
  2) Photograph
  3) Class rank
  4) Transcripts
  5) Financial information
  6) Essay
 Additional information: Payments are made directly to the educational institution on behalf of named individuals. Applicant must be a permanent resident of the State of Delaware.
EIN: 516016533

1516
Raymond W. & Edith W. Masten Charitable Scholarship Trust
102 Lakelawn Dr.
Milford, DE 19963-1710

Foundation type: Independent foundation
Purpose: Scholarships for students continuing their education at institutions of higher learning.
Financial data: Year ended 12/31/2011. Assets, $99,303 (M); Expenditures, $6,749; Total giving,

$5,500; Grant to an individual, 1 grant totaling $1,000.
Fields of interest: Higher education.
Type of support: Scholarships—to individuals.
Application information: Contact trust for additional application information.
EIN: 516504612

1517
National Multiple Sclerosis Society - Delaware Chapter
2 Mill Rd., Ste. 106
Wilmington, DE 19806-2175 (302) 655-5610
Contact: Kate Cowperthwait, Pres.
FAX: (302) 655-0993; URL: http://www.nationalmssociety.org/ded/index.aspx

Foundation type: Public charity
Purpose: Financial assistance to individuals with demyelinating diseases who live in Delaware.
Financial data: Year ended 09/30/2011. Assets, $900,000 (M); Expenditures, $1,746,868; Total giving, $303,721; Grants to individuals, totaling $303,721.
Fields of interest: Multiple sclerosis.
Type of support: Grants for special needs.
Application information: Applications not accepted.
Additional information: Unsolicited requests for funds not considered or acknowledged.
EIN: 510097777

1518
Orange Home, Inc.
P.O. Box 30617
Wilmington, DE 19805 (302) 998-3549
Contact: Walter C. Wilson, Secy.-Treas.
Application address: 1315 Biggs Rd., Wilmington, DE 19805

Foundation type: Independent foundation
Purpose: Scholarships to full-time college students who are lodge member or are children or grandchildren of lodge members.
Financial data: Year ended 06/30/2013. Assets, $591,197 (M); Expenditures, $41,767; Total giving, $36,000; Grants to individuals, 18 grants totaling $36,000 (high: $2,000, low: $2,000).
Fields of interest: Higher education.
Type of support: Scholarships—to individuals.
Application information: Applications accepted. Application form required.
Deadline(s): June
EIN: 231261147

1519
Ortega Charitable Foundation
c/o Foundation Source
501 Silverside Rd., Ste. 123
Wilmington, DE 19809-1377

Foundation type: Independent foundation
Purpose: Scholarships to employees and children of employees of Latino ancestry in FL and PR who are dependents of brokers of Goya Foods, Inc.
Financial data: Year ended 12/31/2012. Assets, $39,809,973 (M); Expenditures, $1,046,927; Total giving, $725,750.
Fields of interest: Hispanics/Latinos.
Type of support: Employee-related scholarships.
Application information: Applications accepted. Application form required.
Initial approach: Letter
Deadline(s): May 31

Additional information: Applicants must submit their GPA.
EIN: 650014714

1520
The Presto Foundation
1011 Centre Rd., Ste. 310
Wilmington, DE 19805-1267 (715) 839-2119
Contact: Joan Gehler
Application address: 3925 N. Hastings Way, Eau Claire, WI 54703, tel.: (715) 839-2119

Foundation type: Company-sponsored foundation
Purpose: Scholarships to children of employees of National Presto Industries, Inc., with preference given to those in northwestern WI, especially Eau Claire and Chippewa counties.
Financial data: Year ended 05/31/2013. Assets, $20,614,108 (M); Expenditures, $1,363,491; Total giving, $1,622,825.
Type of support: Employee-related scholarships.
Application information: Applications not accepted.
Additional information: Unsolicited requests for funds not considered or acknowledged.
Company name: National Presto Industries, Incorporated
EIN: 396045769

1521
Quarter Century Club Scholarship Fund
c/o JPMorgan Chase, N.A.
P.O. Box 6089
Newark, DE 19714-6089 (507) 931-0426
Scholarship address: c/o Susan Fredrickson, Scholarship America, 1 Scholarship Way, P.O. Box 297, St. Peter, MN 56082

Foundation type: Independent foundation
Purpose: Scholarships to children of current or former employees of Chase Manhattan Bank Corp. and its subsidiaries.
Financial data: Year ended 12/31/2011. Assets, $587,092 (M); Expenditures, $57,206; Total giving, $56,125.
Type of support: Employee-related scholarships.
Application information: Contact foundation for complete application deadline/guidelines.
Company name: JPMorgan Chase & Co.
EIN: 136120404

1522
Charles E. Robinson Memorial Scholarship
(formerly C. E. Robinson Memorial Scholarship Fund)
61 Tenby Chase Dr.
Newark, DE 19711 (302) 740-4634
Contact: Corina M. Montgomery, Tr.

Foundation type: Independent foundation
Purpose: College scholarships to residents of Delaware, Maryland, and Southeast Pennsylvania for continuing education.
Financial data: Year ended 12/31/2011. Assets, $251,198 (M); Expenditures, $11,834; Total giving, $7,200; Grants to individuals, 12 grants totaling $7,200 (high: $800, low: $400).
Fields of interest: Higher education.
Type of support: Scholarships—to individuals.
Application information: Applications accepted. Application form required.
Deadline(s): None

Additional information: Application should include transcript.
EIN: 510270685

1523
W.B. Simpson Educational Fund Inc.
16 N. Main St.
Camden, DE 19934-1228

Foundation type: Independent foundation
Purpose: Scholarships to worthy individuals who are residents of Camden Wyoming, DE.
Financial data: Year ended 12/31/2012. Assets, $134,133 (M); Expenditures, $5,225; Total giving, $5,000; Grant to an individual, 1 grant totaling $5,000.
Fields of interest: Education.
Type of support: Undergraduate support.
Application information: Applications accepted.
Initial approach: Letter
Deadline(s): Apr. 15
EIN: 510351519

1524
Don and Roy Splawn Charitable Foundation West, Inc.
(formerly Roy L. Splawn Charitable Foundation)
c/o Foundation Source
501 Silverside Rd., Ste. 123
Wilmington, DE 19809-1377

Foundation type: Independent foundation
Purpose: Scholarships to financially disadvantaged students who are residents of California, who wish to further pursue their education at an educational or vocational institution of higher learning.
Financial data: Year ended 12/31/2011. Assets, $4,308,232 (M); Expenditures, $262,160; Total giving, $157,500; Grants to individuals, 96 grants totaling $157,500 (high: $15,000, low: $500).
Type of support: Scholarships—to individuals.
Application information: Applications accepted.
Deadline(s): Early Nov.
EIN: 943276752

1525
The John Edgar Thomson Foundation
c/o Wilmington Trust Co.
1100 N. Market St., DE-3-C070
Wilmington, DE 19890-0001

Foundation type: Operating foundation
Purpose: Financial assistance to daughters of deceased railroad employees, until they are 22 years of age. Recipients must attend college, community college, business school, or trade school on a full-time basis.
Financial data: Year ended 12/31/2012. Assets, $15,096,164 (M); Expenditures, $586,997; Total giving, $393,909; Grants to individuals, totaling $393,909.
Fields of interest: Vocational education; Transportation; Women.
Type of support: Technical education support; Undergraduate support.
Application information: Applications not accepted.
Additional information: Unsolicited requests for funds not considered or acknowledged.
EIN: 231382746

1526
University of Delaware Research Foundation
162 The Green
209 Hullihen Hall
Newark, DE   19716-0099   (302) 831-2136
E-mail: udresearch@udel.edu; URL: http://www.udel.edu/research/about/udrf.html

Foundation type: Public charity
Purpose: Research grants to fund faculty research projects of the University of Delaware, DE.
Financial data: Year ended 12/31/2011. Assets, $8,332,632 (M); Expenditures, $418,350; Total giving, $415,000.
Type of support: Research.
Application information: Applications not accepted.
> *Additional information:* Unsolicited requests for funds not considered or acknowledged.

EIN: 516017306

1527
Vocational Technical Educational Foundation of Delaware
1417 Newport Rd.
Wilmington, DE   19804   (302) 995-8020

Foundation type: Public charity
Purpose: Scholarships for vocational and technical education to students attending technical schools in New Castle, Ken County, and Sussex County, DE.

Financial data: Year ended 12/31/2011. Assets, $822,155 (M); Expenditures, $89,726; Total giving, $25,372; Grants to individuals, totaling $25,372.
Fields of interest: Vocational education, post-secondary; Education.
Type of support: Technical education support.
Application information: Applications accepted. Application form required.
> *Initial approach:* Letter
> *Additional information:* Contact the foundation for additional application guidelines.

EIN: 510341061

1528
The Steve and Anita Westly Foundation
c/o Foundation Source
501 Silverside Rd., Ste. 123
Wilmington, DE   19809-1377
E-mail: contact@westly.org; Mailing address: c/o Fidelity Private Foundation Services, P.O. Box 55158, Boston, MA 02205-5158; URL: http://www.westly.org

Foundation type: Independent foundation
Purpose: Awards and prizes to entrepreneurial leaders whose courage and innovation improve the lives of people and the world around us.
Publications: Grants list.
Financial data: Year ended 12/31/2012. Assets, $10,289,575 (M); Expenditures, $1,077,208; Total giving, $792,076; Grants to individuals, 9 grants totaling $92,500 (high: $20,000, low: $2,500).
Fields of interest: Social entrepreneurship; Leadership development.
Type of support: Awards/prizes.
Application information: Applications accepted. Application form required. Application form available on the grantmaker's web site. Interview required.
> *Send request by:* On-line
> *Deadline(s):* Nov.
> *Additional information:* Applicants are required to submit a YouTube video of no more than two minutes in length demonstrating their innovation. See web site for specific guidelines.

Program description:
> *Westly Prize:* Awards to young innovators in CA with creative solutions to community problems. The foundation will award up to four $20,000 prizes. Two of the prizes typically are given to current high school students. Two additional prizes typically are awarded to university students or professionals under the age of 28. See web site for specific guidelines and information.

EIN: 943368338

DISTRICT OF COLUMBIA

1529
AARP Foundation
(formerly American Association of Retired Persons
(AARP) Andrus Foundation)
601 E St., N.W., Tax Dept.
Washington, DC   20049-0001   (202) 434-2018
Contact: Robin Talbert, Exec. Dir.
FAX: (202) 434-6593;
E-mail: plannedgiving@aarp.org; Toll-free tel.: (800)
775-6776; URL: http://www.aarp.org/foundation

Foundation type: Public charity
Purpose: Scholarships to help women 40 or over
overcome financial and employment barriers by
allowing them to participate in education and
training opportunities they could not otherwise
afford.
Publications: Annual report; Financial statement;
Informational brochure; Newsletter.
Financial data: Year ended 12/31/2011. Assets,
$108,083,041 (M); Expenditures, $138,801,516;
Total giving, $78,631,613; Grants to individuals,
totaling $69,372,057.
Fields of interest: Women.
Type of support: Scholarships—to individuals.
Application information: Applications accepted.
Initial approach: Complete online application for
Women's Scholarship Program
Deadline(s): Oct. 31 for Women's Scholarship
Program
Program description:
Women's Scholarship Program: The program
seeks to help women 40 and over overcome
financial and employment barriers by allowing them
to participate in education and training
opportunities they could not otherwise afford. To be
eligible for the scholarships, applicants must be a
female age 40 and over, be able to demonstrate
financial need, and submit a proposal for
enrollment in an accredited post-secondary school
or training program within six months of the
scholarship award date. Scholarship awards will
range from $500 to $5,000, depending on financial
need and the cost of the education or training
program. Priority will be given to applicants in the
following categories: individuals returning to the
workforce after an extended absence; individuals in
jobs with insufficient pay, benefits, or growth
opportunities; or grandmothers with significant
financial responsibility for one or more
grandchildren. Scholarships will be awarded for a
period of one year or less. Recipients may reapply
for the following year's scholarship program if they
continue to meet program eligibility requirements.
EIN: 520794300

1530
The Frederick B. Abramson Memorial
Foundation
P.O. Box 7810
Washington, DC   20044   (202) 470-5425
FAX: (202) 318-2482;
E-mail: info@abramsonfoundation.org; URL: http://
www.abramsonfoundation.org

Foundation type: Public charity
Purpose: Scholarships to economically
disadvantaged DC public high school seniors for
higher education at a four-year college. Fellowships

of $5,000 to graduating law students or judicial law
clerks in DC for one year's employment with either
a public interest law firm or another nonprofit
service organization.
Publications: Application guidelines; Informational
brochure; Newsletter.
Financial data: Year ended 06/30/2012. Assets,
$144,172 (M); Expenditures, $96,229; Total
giving, $27,250.
Fields of interest: Higher education; Legal services,
public interest law.
Type of support: Fellowships; Scholarships—to
individuals.
Application information: Applications accepted.
Application form required. Application form
available on the grantmaker's web site.
Deadline(s): Apr. 13 for scholarships; Aug. 18 for
fellowships
Applicants should submit the following:
1) Resume
2) Letter(s) of recommendation
3) Financial information
Additional information: Applicants for
scholarships should also include test scores,
essay, and transcripts.
EIN: 521800184

1531
Accordia Global Health Foundation
(formerly Academic Alliance Foundation for AIDS
Care and Prevention in Africa)
1825 Connecticut Ave. NW, Ste. 630
Washington, DC   20009   (202) 534-1200
FAX: (202) 534-1220;
E-mail: info@accordiafoundation.org; URL: http://
www.accordiafoundation.org

Foundation type: Public charity
Purpose: Fellowships and scholarships to African
clinicians and researchers to improve healthcare in
Africa. Also, a Leadership Award to an emerging
African leader who has contributed to the field of
infectious disease in Africa and has earned
accomplishments in teaching, research, and/or
clinical science.
Publications: Newsletter.
Financial data: Year ended 12/31/2011. Assets,
$11,344,406 (M); Expenditures, $8,680,931;
Total giving, $5,350,734.
Fields of interest: Research; Research; AIDS; AIDS
research.
International interests: Africa; Sub-Saharan Africa.
Type of support: Fellowships; Foreign applicants;
Postdoctoral support.
Application information: Applications accepted.
Application form required. Application form
available on the grantmaker's web site.
Initial approach: E-mail or tel.
Deadline(s): Jan. 31 for Leadership Award
Additional information: See web site for varying
eligibility requirements for each program.
EIN: 043774897

1532
Afterschool Alliance
1616 H St. N.W., Ste. 820
Washington, DC   20006-4917   (202) 347-2030
Contact: Jodi Grant, Exec. Dir.
FAX: (202) 347-2092;
E-mail: info@afterschoolalliance.org; URL: http://
www.afterschoolalliance.org

Foundation type: Public charity
Purpose: Stipends to ambassadors and fellows of
the alliance identifies afterschool providers and

advocates of special achievement and helps them
raise their voices in support of afterschool.
Publications: Newsletter.
Financial data: Year ended 12/31/2011. Assets,
$5,524,328 (M); Expenditures, $3,000,002; Total
giving, $117,766; Grants to individuals, totaling
$67,766.
Fields of interest: Education.
Type of support: Stipends.
Application information: Applications accepted.
Application form required.
Additional information: Ambassadors are chosen
by application in the spring.
EIN: 522275123

1533
Aga Khan Foundation U.S.A.
1825 K St. N.W., Ste. 901
Washington, DC   20006-1202
Contact: Dr. Mirza Jahani, C.E.O.
URL: http://www.akdn.org/AKF

Foundation type: Public charity
Purpose: Scholarships for postgraduate studies to
outstanding students under 30 years of age from
developing countries who have no other means of
financing their studies.
Publications: Application guidelines; Annual report.
Financial data: Year ended 12/31/2012. Assets,
$153,943,057 (M); Expenditures, $39,968,795;
Total giving, $34,154,296; Grants to individuals,
totaling $82,212.
Fields of interest: Higher education.
International interests: Developing Countries.
Type of support: Postgraduate support.
Application information: Applications accepted.
Application form required. Interview required.
Deadline(s): Mar. 31
Additional information: See web site for detailed
application guidelines.
Program description:
International Scholarship Program: A limited
number of scholarships are provided for
postgraduate studies to outstanding students from
developing countries who have no other means of
financing their studies. Award winners will be
evaluated on excellent academic records, genuine
financial need, admission to a reputable institution
of higher learning, and thoughtful and coherent
educational and career plans. Applicants must be
based in Bangladesh, India, Pakistan, Afghanistan,
Tajikistan, Syria, Egypt, Kenya, Tanzania, Uganda,
Mozambique, Madagascar, France, Portugal, Great
Britain, the U.S., and Canada. Scholarships are
awarded on a 50-percent grant: 50-percent loan
basis; priority is given to master's-level courses
(though consideration will also be given to Ph.D.
programs), and to students under 30 years of age.
EIN: 521231983

1534
Air Force Officers Wives Club of
Washington DC Welfare Fund
P.O. Box 8490
Bolling AFB
Washington, DC   20032-5411   (703) 677-7396

Foundation type: Public charity
Purpose: Scholarships to college bound high school
seniors, spouses of certain USAF members and
learning disabled high school seniors.
Financial data: Year ended 05/31/2012. Assets,
$67,103 (M); Expenditures, $121,098; Total
giving, $93,080. Scholarships—to individuals
amount not specified.

Fields of interest: Higher education; Military/ veterans' organizations; Disabilities, people with.
Type of support: Scholarships—to individuals.
Application information: Application form required.
  Deadline(s): Mar. 3
  Additional information: High school seniors may contact their counseling officer for application. Applicants are judged on academics and citizenship achievements.
EIN: 526057758

1535
Airline Ambassadors International, Inc.

1500 Massachusetts Ave., N.W., Ste. 648
Washington, DC 20005-1830   (415) 359-8006
Contact: Nancy Rivard, Pres.
E-mail: info@airlineamb.org; Toll-free tel.: (866) 153-2486; E-mail for Nancy Rivard: nancy.rivard@airlineamb.org; URL: http:// www.airlineamb.org

Foundation type: Public charity
Purpose: Humanitarian aid to children and families in need in underprivileged communities throughout the world.
Publications: Annual report.
Financial data: Year ended 12/31/2012. Assets, $33,841 (M); Expenditures, $392,966.
Fields of interest: Human services; Children; Adults; Economically disadvantaged.
Type of support: In-kind gifts; Grants for special needs.
Application information: Contact the organization for additional information.
EIN: 752679444

1536
Albert E. and Angela T. Farone Foundation

(formerly A & A Farone Foundation)
620 Michigan Ave., Rm. 260
Cardinal Sta.
Washington, DC 20064-0001   (202) 319-5606

Foundation type: Public charity
Purpose: Scholarships for students attending the Catholic University of America pursuing higher education.
Financial data: Year ended 04/30/2012. Assets, $25,616,958 (M); Expenditures, $577,312; Total giving, $561,700; Grants to individuals, totaling $561,700.
Fields of interest: Higher education; Theological school/education; Catholic agencies & churches.
Type of support: Scholarships—to individuals; Support to graduates or students of specific schools.
Application information: Applications accepted.
  Additional information: Preference will be given to individuals in the order of students from Oswego county, NY, students from Delaware county, NY, and students from any part of the Albany Diocese of the Roman Catholic Church. Consideration is given to applicant's all-around ability, motivation, moral character, and the need for financial assistance to obtain a higher education.
EIN: 160911612

1537
Amazon Conservation Association

1822 R. St. N.W., 4th Fl.
Washington, DC 20009-1604   (202) 234-2356
FAX: (202) 234-2358;
E-mail: info@amazonconservation.org; Additional

tel. (DC office): (202) 234-2357; additional address (La Paz office): Asociacion de Conservacion del Amazonas, Calle Gregorio Reynolds Numero 625, Sopocachi, La Paz, Bolivia, tel.: (519) 2 291-1139, e-mail: jgonzales@amazonconservation.org; URL: http://www.amazonconservation.org

Foundation type: Public charity
Purpose: Grants to researchers who wish to work on conservation projects in Peru.
Publications: Application guidelines; Newsletter.
Financial data: Year ended 12/31/2011. Assets, $2,939,220 (M); Expenditures, $2,880,668; Total giving, $2,129,030.
Fields of interest: Environment.
Type of support: Research; Scholarships—to individuals.
Application information: Applications accepted. Application form required. Application form available on the grantmaker's web site.
  Initial approach: Application
  Deadline(s): Aug. 20 for Research Scholarships
Program description:
  Research Scholarships: This program gives researchers the resources they need to carry pressing field work in tropical forests. The program provides young Peruvian biologists with opportunities for independent research, and brings researchers from around the world to work at the Los Amigos Biological Station (CICRA) and Wayqecha Cloud Forest Biological Station (WCFBS). The majority of the scholarships offered benefit Peruvian researchers who are conducting biological studies at research stations in Cusco and Madre de Dios.
EIN: 522211305

1538
American Academy of Child & Adolescent Psychiatry

3615 Wisconsin Ave., N.W.
Washington, DC 20016-3007   (202) 966-7300
FAX: (202) 966-2891; E-mail: research@aacap.org; URL: http://www.aacap.org

Foundation type: Public charity
Purpose: Scholarship and fellowship opportunities to child and adolescent psychiatrists.
Publications: Application guidelines; Annual report.
Financial data: Year ended 12/31/2011. Assets, $10,867,097 (M); Expenditures, $8,656,512; Total giving, $640,813; Grants to individuals, totaling $120,950.
Fields of interest: Mental health, disorders; Children; Young adults.
Type of support: Fellowships; Awards/prizes.
Application information: Applications accepted. Application form required. Application form available on the grantmaker's web site.
  Initial approach: Application
  Deadline(s): Varies
  Applicants should submit the following:
    1) Essay
    2) Letter(s) of recommendation
Program descriptions:
  AACAP Beatrix A. Hamburg Award for the Best New Research Poster by a Child and Adolescent Psychiatry Residency at the AACAP Annual Meeting: This $1,000 honorarium is present to the author of the best new research poster presented at the academy's annual meeting. Eligible applicants must be a child and adolescent psychiatry resident at an accredited institution, as well as an academy member.
  AACAP Cancro Academic Leadership Award: This award recognizes a currently-serving general psychiatry training director, medical school dean,

chief executive office (CEO) of a training institution, chair of a department of pediatrics, or chair of a department of psychiatry for his or her contributions to the promoting of child and adolescent psychiatry. This award is presented in even-numbered years, and is accompanied by a $2,000 honorarium.
  AACAP Educational Outreach Program for Child and Adolescent Psychiatry Residents: This program provides the opportunity for child and adolescent psychiatry residents to receive a formal overview to the field of child and adolescent psychiatry, establish child and adolescent as mentors, and experience the academy's annual meeting. Participants will be exposed to the breadth and depth of the field of child and adolescent psychiatry, including research opportunities, access to mentors, and various networking opportunities. Participation in this program provides up to $1,000 for travel expenses to the meeting, including airfare, hotel, and meals.
  AACAP Educational Outreach Program for General Psychiatry Residents: This program provides the opportunity for up to twenty general psychiatry residents to receive a formal overview to the field of child and adolescent psychiatry, establish child and adolescent psychiatrists as mentors, and experience the academy's annual meeting. Participants will be exposed to the field of child and adolescent psychiatry, including research opportunities, access to mentors, and various networking opportunities. Participation in this program provides up to $1,500 for travel expenses to the annual meeting. Eligible applicants must be general psychiatry residents at the time of the meeting, be members of the academy, and be currently enrolled in a residency program in the U.S. (including residents in their first, second, or third year of training in their programs, as well as triple-boarders in their first, second, or third year of training)
  AACAP Educational Outreach Program for Residents in Alcohol Research: This program provides the opportunity for up to ten child and adolescent psychiatry and general psychiatry residents to pursue advanced knowledge in adolescent alcohol research; the program also allows residents to expand their knowledge of adolescent alcohol-related issues by attending the academy's annual meeting. Participants will be exposed to the field of child and adolescent psychiatry, including research opportunities, access to mentors, and various networking opportunities. Participation in this program provides up to $1,000 for travel expenses to the annual meeting. Eligible applicants must be child and adolescent psychiatry or general psychiatry residents at the time of the meeting; must be currently enrolled in a child and adolescent psychiatry, general psychiatry, or triple-board residency in the U.S.; and be either members of the academy or have a membership application pending at the time of application.
  AACAP George Tarjan Award for Contributions in Developmental Disabilities: This award recognizes a child and adolescent psychiatrist and academy member who has made significant contributions in a lifetime career, or single seminal work, to the understanding or care of those with mental retardation and developmental disabilities. These contributions must have national and/or international stature and clearly demonstrate lasting effect; contributions may be in areas of teaching, research, program development, direct clinical service, advocacy, or administrate commitment. Awards are accompanied by a $1,000 cash prize.
  AACAP Irving Philips Award for Prevention: This award recognizes a child and adolescent

psychiatrist and academy member who had made significant contributions in a lifetime career or single seminal work to the prevention of mental illness in children and adolescents. These contributions must have national and/or international stature and clearly demonstrate lasting effects. Contributions may be in the areas of teaching, research, program development, direct clinical service, advocacy, or administrative commitment. The award pays $2,500 to the winner, as well as a $2,000 donation to a prevention program or center of the awardee's choice.

AACAP Life Members Mentorship Grants for Medical Students: This program provides the opportunity for seven medical students to attend the academy's annual meeting, and receive an introduction into the field of child and adolescent psychiatry through a mentorship program. The program provides participants with networking opportunities, exposure to varying specialties, and interaction with life members. Eligible applicants must be enrolled in a medical school in the U.S. at the time of the academy's annual meeting, and be in good standing at their medical school.

AACAP Rieger Psychodynamic Psychotherapy Award: This award recognizes the best published or unpublished paper, written by an academy member, that uses a psychodynamic framework and resents clinical material demonstrating the inner life of an infant, child, or adolescent, in order to illustrate the paper's idea or hypothesis. The paper should include consideration of a DSM diagnosis and a focused literature review that includes current psychiatric literature; the material for this paper may be drawn from clinical practice or from clinical research.

AACAP Rieger Service Program Award for Excellence: This award recognizes innovative program that address prevention, diagnosis, or treatment of mental illnesses in children and adolescents, and serve as model programs to the community. Awards are accompanied by a $4,500 cash prize.

AACAP Sidney Berman Award for the School-Based Study and Treatment of Learning Disorders and Mental Illness: This award recognizes an individual or program that has shown outstanding achievement in the school-based study or delivery of intervention for learning disorders and mental illness. This award is accompanied by a $4,500 cash prize.

Catchers in the Rye Awards: Each year, the academy recognizes members that advocate for children. Four awards are given each year at the academy's annual meeting: the Humanitarian Award (honors an individual who has made significant contributions to the field of children's mental health, including advocacy, increasing awareness, entrepreneurship, philanthropy, research, and/or acts of bravery/kindness); the Advocacy Award to an Individual (recognizes an individual for their outstanding advocacy efforts on behalf of children and adolescents); the AACAP Committee Award (recognizes academy committees for their outstanding efforts on behalf of children and adolescents); and the Regional Organization Award (recognizing regional organizations for their outstanding efforts on behalf of children and adolescents)

Jeanne Spurlock Lecture and Award on Diversity and Culture: This award and lecture opportunity supports individuals who have advocated for children, adolescents, and their families from all cultures.

Jeanne Spurlock Research Fellowships in Substance Abuse and Addiction for Minority Medical Students: This fellowship offers a unique opportunity for minority medical students to explore

a research career in substance abuse in relation to child and adolescent psychiatry, gain valuable work experience, and meet leaders in the child and adolescent psychiatry field. This opportunity offers up to $4,000 for twelve weeks of summer research under a child and adolescent psychiatrist researcher/mentor. Eligible applicants will be considered from African-American, Native American, Alaskan Native, Mexican-American, Hispanic, Asian, and Pacific Islander students who are enrolled in accredited U.S. medical schools, and who are U.S. or permanent residents.

Simon Wile Leadership in Consultation Award (supported by the Child Psychiatry Service at Massachusetts General Hospital): This $500 award acknowledges outstanding leadership and continuous contributions in the field of consultation-liaison child and adolescent psychiatry.

Summer Medical Student Fellowships: This fellowship program offers a chance for medical students to explore a career in child and adolescent psychiatry, gain valuable work experience, and meet leaders in the child and adolescent psychiatry field. The opportunity provides up to $3,500 for twelve weeks of clinical or research training under a child and adolescent psychiatrist mentor. Eligible applicants must students enrolled in accredited U.S. medical schools.

Systems of Care Special Program Scholarship: This scholarship is available for child and adolescent psychiatry residents to attend the academy's annual meeting. Awards are for $750, and are intended to cover travel expenses.

The Robinson-Cunningham Award: This $200 award is given for the best manuscript written by a child and adolescent psychiatrist during residency training. The paper must involve children, adolescents, or their families, and be published in a professional, peer-reviewed journal within three to five years of graduation from a residency training program.
EIN: 131958990

1539
American Academy of Nursing
1000 Vermont Ave.,N.W., Ste. 910
Washington, DC   20005-3308   (202) 777-1170
Contact: Cheryl G. Sullivan, C.E.O.
FAX: (202) 777-0107; E-mail: info@aannet.org;
E-Mail for Cheryl G. Sullivan: CEO@AANnet.org;
URL: http://www.aannet.org/

Foundation type: Public charity
Purpose: Awards and fellowships for accomplishments in nursing and health care. Emphasis on research, education and public service. Some awards by nomination from AAN fellows only.
Publications: Application guidelines; Newsletter.
Financial data: Year ended 12/31/2011. Assets, $4,264,442 (M); Expenditures, $10,944,066; Total giving, $2,339,697; Grants to individuals, totaling $2,331,197.
Fields of interest: Business school/education; Health care; Management/technical assistance.
Type of support: Scholarships—to individuals; Awards/prizes; Graduate support.
Application information: Applications accepted. Application form required. Application form available on the grantmaker's web site.
   Deadline(s): July 28 for Media Award, varies for nomination
   Additional information: Application should include nomination form, support letter, examples of work and biographical statement. See web site for additional information.

Program descriptions:
AAN/Hartford Nurse Leader Award in Aging: The winner of this award to recognize service, leadership and research in aging and gerontological nursing will be honored at the AAN Annual Conference Banquet. Nominees should have advanced the field with new insights into care, research or advocacy.

American Academy of Nursing Fellowship Program: Fellowships are available to members in good standing of the academy or one of its international affiliates. Applicants must be sponsored by two fellows in good standing with the academy, and show evidence of outstanding contributions to the improvement of nursing at the national or international level.

Building Academic Geriatric Nursing Capacity Predoctoral Scholarship Program: Awarded in conjunction with the John A. Hartford Foundation, this two-year scholarship of up to $100,000 supports full-time doctoral education for nurses committed to careers in academic geriatric nursing. Eligible applicants must be registered nurses who hold degrees in nursing, be United States citizens or permanent residents, be planning an academic and research career, and demonstrate potential for long-term contributions to geriatric nursing. An additional $5,000 award will be made available to selected candidates whose research focuses on pain in older persons.

Claire M. Fagin Fellowship: Awarded in conjunction with the John A. Hartford Foundation and the Atlantic Philanthropies, a two-year, $120,000 fellowship is available to support full-time advanced research and leadership training for doctorally-prepared faculty committed to careers in academic geriatric nursing. Eligible applicants must be doctorally-prepared registered nurses who hold degrees in nursing, U.S. citizens or permanent U.S. residents, have the potential to develop into independent investigators, and demonstrate potential for long-term contributions to geriatric nursing. An additional $5,000 will be awarded to select candidates whose research focuses on pain in older persons.

Honorary Fellowship: Recognition for individuals ineligible for AAN membership who are making contributions to nursing or general health care, such as putting new approaches or concepts into practice, demonstrating leadership and researching or publishing information with implications in the field.

John A. Hartford Foundation Nurse/MBA Scholarship Award: A $50,000 award will be provided to registered nurses planning to pursue their MBA in anticipation of a career leading or managing institutions designed to serve the elderly. Applicants must be enrolled in or accepted to a highly-ranked business school and must display their commitment to elderly care.

Living Legends Award: Recognition for outstanding fellows who have made sustained and extraordinary contributions to the field over a career. Eligible nominees will have been active or Emeritus fellows for at least fifteen years who are leaders in their specialty and community, and have used their influence to help the profession.

Media Awards: This award is presented to the individual(s) or organization(s) whose use of media has highlighted the unique contribution of nursing and: increased public awareness of the value nursing plays in promoting health and providing health care to the public and/or the need to address the growing nursing shortage; reported the impact of specific public policies on the health status of individuals, communities, or the general population; been responsible for motivating specific actions to improve healthcare for diverse groups of

people; disseminated nursing research findings nationally (and possibly internationally) using both interdisciplinary and public media; and depicted specific examples of health-enhancing interactions, culturally-sensitive health care, health care addressing health disparity issues of underserved and vulnerable populations, health-promoting activities, or healing actions. Examples of items that may be submitted include, but are not limited to, newspaper articles, radio programs, motion pictures, public service announcements, books, feature films, television shows, magazine articles, novels, documentaries, popular literature, creative endeavors, and multimedia projects.
EIN: 522213870

1540

The American Architectural Foundation, Inc.

2101 L St. N.W., Ste. 670
Washington, DC 20037 (202) 787-1001
FAX: (202) 787-1002;
E-mail: info@archfoundation.org; E-mail For Ron Bogle: rbogle@archfoundation.org; URL: http://www.archfoundation.org

Foundation type: Public charity
Purpose: Scholarships by nomination only to high school seniors and college freshmen who plan to study architecture in a program accredited by the National Architectural Accrediting Board (NAAB). Also, fellowships to working architects.
Publications: Application guidelines; Informational brochure (including application guidelines); Newsletter.
Financial data: Year ended 12/31/2011. Assets, $3,175,430 (M); Expenditures, $3,001,621; Total giving, $22,500; Grants to individuals, totaling $22,500.
Fields of interest: Architecture.
Type of support: Awards/grants by nomination only; Undergraduate support.
Application information: Applications accepted. Application form required. Application form available on the grantmaker's web site.
Initial approach: Telephone
Deadline(s): Vary
Applicants should submit the following:
　1) Transcripts
　2) Financial information
　3) Work samples
　4) Letter(s) of recommendation
　5) Essay
Additional information: See web site for detailed application information.
Program descriptions:
Accent on Architecture Community Grant Program: This program assists American Institute of Architects (AIA) components, local architectural foundations, and other local design organizations to organize innovative public education programming. In past years, successful grant recipients have enlisted architects, educators, design professionals, community leaders, government officials, and business leaders to enrich the public's understanding and appreciation of architecture. The grants competition is open to various charitable organizations whose projects result in constructive engagement between the public decision-makers and design professionals around architectural issues. Projects should promote increased awareness, appreciation, and understanding of how the public's involvement in the design process can enhance the quality of life in a community. Only projects that include active public engagement are eligible for funding. Projects must provide meaningful, long-term benefits to a

community. Applications are available annually in November. Grant amounts requested should not exceed $3,000, or 50 percent of total project costs, whichever is less.
AIA/AAF Minority/Disadvantaged Scholarship: This program is open to high school seniors and college freshmen who plan to study architecture in a program that is accredited by the National Architectural Accrediting Board (NAAB). Twenty awards per year are made and may be renewed for two additional years. Scholarship amounts range between $500 and $2,600, and are determined by evaluation of financial need information provided by the student and the school.
Richard Morris Hunt Fellowship: This fellowship provides opportunity for French and American architects to learn and exchange information about their respective country's historic preservation process and techniques. The fellowship includes a stipend of $25,000.
Richard Riley Award: The award, a partnership with KnowledgeWorks Foundation, recognizes design and educational excellence in 'schools as centers of community,' that serve as centers of community provide a rich array of social, civic, recreational, and artistic opportunities to the broader community, often clustering educational and municipal buildings together. These additional services and opportunities often improve student achievement and help maximize local tax dollars. The winning school will receive a $5,000 prize. All public schools, new and old, including charter schools, are eligible to submit entries for the award; individuals are not eligible to receive the award.
EIN: 520847434

1541

American Association for Clinical Chemistry

1850 K. St. N.W., Ste. 625
Washington, DC 20006-2215 (202) 835-8751
Contact: Robert H. Christenson Ph.D., Pres.
FAX: (202) 887-5093; Toll-free tel.: (800) 892-1400; URL: http://www.aacc.org

Foundation type: Public charity
Purpose: Research grants and travel stipends by nomination only to clinical chemists and clinical scientists in the field of clinical laboratory science.
Publications: Application guidelines; Annual report; Grants list.
Financial data: Year ended 12/31/2011. Assets, $22,603,753 (M); Expenditures, $17,174,556; Total giving, $224,713; Grants to individuals, totaling $207,941.
Fields of interest: Medical research.
Type of support: Research; Awards/grants by nomination only; Travel grants.
Application information: Applications accepted.
Initial approach: Nomination letter
Deadline(s): Varies
Additional information: Nominations must include curriculum vitae and letter of evaluation; See web site for complete nomination guidelines and awards listing.
Program descriptions:
Award for Outstanding Contributions in Education: This award recognizes an individual who has devoted a major potion of his/her professional life to enhancing the practice and profession of clinical chemistry through education. Educators selected for this award are recognized for making significant, innovative, and/or cumulatively outstanding contributions to education in clinical laboratory science (including, but not limited to, teaching, directing, mentoring, writing, and speaking abilities that ideally appeal to multiple levels of audiences.

Award for Outstanding Contributions through Service to the Profession of Clinical Chemistry: This award recognizes the individuals who have worked throughout their careers to advance the professional status of clinical chemists and the professional objectives of the association.
Critical Point-of-Care Testing Research Grants Funded by the Van Slyke Foundation: This $5,000 grant will be given to support point-of-care testing outcome studies, undergone by clinical laboratorians who need limited research funds to explore new ideas in areas where funds are not normally available. Applications will be evaluated on the basis of originality, scope, scientific significance, the sounds of the proposed research plan, the degree of achievability, potential for the project to lead to further exploration beyond the grant period, and the transferability of research findings to actual practice.
Edwin F. Ullman Award: This award recognizes an individual (or individuals) for contributions to the field of clinical chemistry through the creation of new technologies or analytical methods, or through significant adaptations for applications to clinical laboratory diagnostics of technologies from other fields. This award is given in odd-numbered years only.
General Research Grant Funded by the Van Slyke Foundation: Small start-up grants will be made available to young investigators who need limited research funds to explore new ideas in areas where funds are not normally available. Applications will be evaluated on the basis of originality, scope, scientific significance, soundness of research plan, degree of achievability, potential for the project to lead to further exploration beyond the grant period, and the transferability of research findings to actual practice. Preference will be given to young investigators.
International Travel Grants: These grants (of up to $2,500) encourage those in underserved areas of the international clinical laboratory to attend the association's annual meeting and foster relationships between scientists of other countries and those in the U.S. Grants are intended to help offset travel expenses (but not to cover of the costs of attending the meeting), and are based on the following criteria: impacting the applicant's future career in clinical laboratory medicine; impacting the state of clinical lab medicine in their country; broadening international participation at the meeting; demonstrating financial need to attend; and impact on the meeting's content. Preference will be given to members of the association.
Outstanding Lifetime Achievement Award in Clinical Chemistry and Laboratory Medicine: This award recognizes individuals who have made significant contributions to the field of clinical chemistry. Individuals selected for this award will have made significant contributions in all aspects of clinical chemistry, particularly service, education, and research; have achieved international stature and reputation by virtue of their efforts; and have demonstrated long-standing service to the association, either at the grassroots, national, and/or international levels.
Outstanding Scientific Achievement by a Young Investigator Awards: This award recognizes and encourages the professional development of a young investigator who has demonstrated exceptional scientific achievements early in his or her career. Awards are given based on the degree of originality exhibited in the individual's creative process and the significance of the research conducted relevant to the field of clinical laboratory medicine, and are designed to be conferred upon an individual who has the potential to be an outstanding investigator of the future.

Wallace H. Coulter Leadership Award: This award recognizes an outstanding individual who has demonstrated a lifetime commitment to, and made important contributions that have had a, significant impact on education, practice, and/or research in laboratory medicine or patient care. Recipients will be given a $10,000 honorarium.
EIN: 390977801

1542

American Association for the Advancement of Science

(also known as AAAS)
1200 New York Ave., N.W.
Washington, DC 20005-3928 (202) 326-6400
Contact: Alan Leshner, C.E.O.
URL: http://www.aaas.org

Foundation type: Public charity
Purpose: Awards to individuals in the scientific, science journalism, and engineering communities, as well as travel grants for research program development to scientists. Also, grants to secondary school students for research projects in the sciences.
Publications: Application guidelines; Annual report; Newsletter.
Financial data: Year ended 12/31/2011. Assets, $160,876,600 (M); Expenditures, $92,855,806; Total giving, $11,867,097; Grants to individuals, totaling $9,859,780.
Fields of interest: Print publishing; Science; Engineering/technology; Government/public administration; Minorities; Women.
Type of support: Research; Awards/prizes; Postdoctoral support.
Application information: Application form available on the grantmaker's web site.
Deadline(s): Vary
Additional information: Nomination guidelines vary by program; See the association's web site for complete guidelines.
Program descriptions:
AAAS Award for Science Diplomacy: This $5,000 award recognizes an individual or number of individuals working together in the scientific or engineering community, for making an outstanding contribution to furthering international cooperation in science and engineering.
AAAS Leadership in Science Education Prize for High School Teachers: Grants of $1,000 will be awarded to high school science teachers who are recognized as having contributed significantly to advancing science education by developing and implementing an innovative and demonstrably effective strategy, activity, or program. Eligible teachers are nominated by a school, district, or state education administrator who is in a position to know the nominee's work and assess its impact on others. Nominated teachers must be employed as a science instructor in a private or public school for grades 9 to 12 in the U.S. or its territories.
AAAS-Kavil Science Journalism Awards: Awarded in conjunction with the Kavil Foundation, these awards recognize outstanding reporting for a general audience and honor individuals for their coverage of the sciences, engineering, and mathematics. Awards will be presented in the following categories: large newspapers (circulation of 100,000 or more), small newspapers (circulation of less than 100,000), magazines, television, radio, and online; an award will also be given to writing in all categories that exemplifies excellence in reporting news on science. Category winners will receive $3,000 each.
L'Oreal USA Fellowship for Women in Science Program: The program provides five annual grants

of up to $60,000 each to postdoctoral researchers engaged in basic research in the life and physical/material sciences, engineering, technology (including computer science), and mathematics. The fellowship is intended to provide career enhancement. Applicants must be women postdoctoral researchers; American born, naturalized citizens, or permanent residents; affiliated with a U.S. based academic or research institution; and conducting their postdoctoral studies and research in the U.S.
Mentor Awards: These $5,000 awards honor individuals who, during their careers, demonstrated extraordinary leadership to increase the participation of underrepresented groups (including women of all racial and ethnic groups, African Americans, Native Americans, Hispanics, and people with disabilities) in science and engineering fields and careers. A Lifetime Mentor Award will be given to an individual who has been identified as a mentor for 25 or more years; a Mentor Award will be given to an individual who has served as a mentor for fewer than 25 years.
Philip Hauge Abelson Prize: This $5,000 prize is awarded annually either to a public servant, in recognition of sustained exceptional contributions to advancing science, or a scientist, whose career has been distinguished both for scientific achievement and for other notable services to the scientific community.
Science and Technology Policy Fellowships: These fellowships help to establish and nurture critical links between federal decision-makers and scientific professionals to support public policy that benefits the well-being of the nation and the planet. The fellowships are designed to: educate scientists and engineers on the intricacies of federal policymaking; provide scientific expertise and analysis to support decision-makers confronting increasingly complex scientific and technical issues; foster positive exchange between scientists and policymakers; empower scientists and engineers to conduct policy-relevant research that addresses challenges facing society; and increase the involvement and visibility of scientists and engineers in the public policy realm.
Scientific Freedom and Responsibility Award: This $5,000 award honors scientists and engineers whose exemplary actions have served to foster scientific freedom and responsibility through acting to protect the public's health, focusing public attention on important potential impacts of science and technology on society by their responsible participation in public policy debates, or establishing important new precedents in carrying out the social responsibilities or in defending the professional freedom of scientists and engineers. Awards carry a $5,000 cash prize.
EIN: 530196568

1543

American Association of Colleges of Nursing

1 Dupont Cir., N.W., Ste. 530
Washington, DC 20036-1135 (202) 463-6930
Contact: Jennifer Butlin, Exec. Dir.
FAX: (202) 785-8320; E-mail: info@aacn.nche.edu;
E-mail For Jennifer Butlin: jbutlin@aacn.nche.edu;
URL: http://www.aacn.nche.edu

Foundation type: Public charity
Purpose: Scholarships to students planning to obtain a bachelor's, master's, or doctoral degree in nursing.
Publications: Application guidelines.
Financial data: Year ended 06/30/2012. Assets, $17,779,464 (M); Expenditures, $9,340,890;

Total giving, $614,980; Grants to individuals, totaling $310,330.
Fields of interest: Nursing school/education; Minorities.
Type of support: Scholarships—to individuals.
Application information: Applications accepted. Application form required.
Initial approach: Application
Send request by: Mail
Deadline(s): May 2 for Johnson & Johnson/AACN Minority Nurse Faculty Scholars, varies for all others
Final notification: Applicants notified by Aug. 3 for AACN Minority Nurse Scholars
Additional information: See web site for additional guidelines.
Program descriptions:
AfterCollege/AACN Scholarship: Awarded in conjunction with AfterCollege, this program provides scholarships of $2,500 each to students who are seeking a baccalaureate, master's, or doctoral degree in nursing. Special consideration will be given to students enrolled in a master's or doctoral program with the goal of pursuing a nursing faculty career, completing an RN-to-baccalaureate program (BSN), or enrolled in an accredited baccalaureate or master's degree nursing program. Eligible applicants must be nursing students enrolled in a baccalaureate, master's, or doctoral degree program in nursing with a G.P.A. of 3.25 or higher.
California Endowment/AACN Nurse Faculty Scholarships: This scholarship supports nursing students from underrepresented groups who are pursuing graduate degrees and who are committed to teaching after graduation.
Hurst Reviews/AACN Nursing Scholarship: Awarded in conjunction with Hurst Review Services, this scholarship program recognizes and rewards entry-level nursing students for outstanding academic performance. Two scholarships of $2,500 each will be awarded twice yearly. Eligible applicants must already be enrolled in an association member institution.
Johnson & Johnson/AACN Minority Nurse Faculty Scholars: This program provides financial support to graduate nursing students from minority backgrounds who agree to teach in a school of nursing after graduation. Eligible students must: be a member of an underrepresented minority group (individuals from American Indian, Alaskan Native, Asian American, Black/African-American, Hispanic/Latino, native Hawaiian, or other Pacific Islanders); be a U.S. citizen, permanent resident, refugee, or qualified immigrant; and be enrolled full-time at (or be accepted into) an accredited doctoral nursing program (i.e., Ph.D., D.N.P.) or clinically-focused nursing master's program (i.e., M.S.N., M.S.). In return, applicants must sign a letter of commitment in which he/she pledges to provide, for each year of scholarship support awarded, a one-year payback at a full-time nursing faculty in an accredited registered nursing program in the U.S. Preference will be given to students in doctoral programs.
EIN: 520971333

1544

American Association of Community Colleges

1 Dupont Cir., N.W., Ste. 410
Washington, DC 20036-1145 (202) 728-0200
FAX: (202) 833-2467; URL: http://www.aacc.nche.edu

Foundation type: Public charity

Purpose: Awards to individuals who have excelled in their fields and have given back to their communities.
Publications: Application guidelines.
Financial data: Year ended 12/31/2011. Assets, $19,529,473 (M); Expenditures, $22,103,253; Total giving, $1,223,459.
Type of support: Awards/grants by nomination only; Awards/prizes.
Application information:
  Deadline(s): Sept. 25
  Additional information: Awards are by nomination only.
EIN: 530196569

1545
American Association of Museums
(also known as AAM)
1575 Eye St., N.W., Ste. 400
Washington, DC 20005-1105 (202) 289-1818
FAX: (202) 289-6578;
E-mail: servicecentral@aam-us.org; URL: http://www.aam-us.org

Foundation type: Public charity
Purpose: Awards by nomination only for professional excellence and for the enhancement of accessibility in the museum field. Also, fellowships for participation in related programs.
Publications: Application guidelines; Annual report.
Financial data: Year ended 12/31/2011. Assets, $4,995,990 (M); Expenditures, $10,633,827; Total giving, $882,792; Grants to individuals, totaling $46,978.
Fields of interest: Museums; Disabilities, people with.
Type of support: Awards/grants by nomination only; Awards/prizes; Stipends.
Application information:
  Initial approach: Telephone or e-mail
  Deadline(s): Jan. 15
  Additional information: See web site for additional information.
Program descriptions:
  AAM Fellowships: Fellowships vary from program to program and generally include complimentary program registration, a travel stipend, recognition on the AAM Professional Development web page and printed program materials, and acknowledgement at the specific program. See web site for additional information.
  Brooking Paper on Creativity in Museums: This writing competition awards a $1,000 (including $500 toward travel expenses to the association's annual meeting) to an author with notable examples of creativity, innovation, and imagination in any aspect of museum operations. The winning paper will be published in Museum Magazine.
  Nancy Hanks Memorial Award for Professional Excellence: Awards a $1,000 stipend to be used in furtherance of the honoree's professional development with less than ten years in the field. Application for the award must be made by the nominee's director. Museums of all types and sizes are encouraged to nominate a candidate. The presentation takes place during the association's annual meeting.
EIN: 530205889

1546
American Association of People with Disabilities
2013 H. St., N.W., 5th Fl.
Washington, DC 20006-3603 (202) 457-0046
FAX: (866) 536-4461; E-mail: aapd@aol.com;
Toll-free tel.: (800) 840-8844; URL: http://www.aapd.com/

Foundation type: Public charity
Purpose: Awards by nomination only to disabled individuals, as well as fellowships to disabled individuals to offset costs associated with completing an internship.
Publications: Application guidelines; Annual report; Newsletter.
Financial data: Year ended 12/31/2011. Assets, $1,794,534 (M); Expenditures, $3,693,595; Total giving, $3,050.
Fields of interest: Disabilities, people with.
Type of support: Fellowships; Internship funds; Awards/prizes.
Application information: Application form required.
  Initial approach: Letter, telephone or e-mail
  Additional information: Nominations must be submitted on official nomination form; See web site for additional information.
Program description:
  Paul G. Hearne/AAPD Leadership Awards: This program awards $10,000 each to three people with disabilities emerging as leaders in their respective fields to help them continue their progress as leaders. Emerging leaders (defined as someone who has demonstrated leadership qualities in his/her personal and professional life, and who has dedicated his/her passion to the pursuit of inclusion, equality, and justice for all people with disabilities) with disabilities of any age are encouraged to apply.
EIN: 521930174

1547
American Association of University Women Educational Foundation
1111 16th St., N.W.
Washington, DC 20036-4809
For application information: AAUW Fellowships and Grants, c/o ACT, Inc., P.O. Box 4030, Iowa City, IA 52243, tel.: (319) 337-1716 ext. 60, e-mail: aauw@act.org
E-mail: connect@aauw.org; URL: http://www.aauw.org/

Foundation type: Public charity
Purpose: Grants and fellowships to support women attending universities throughout the world.
Financial data: Year ended 06/30/2011. Assets, $130,869,060 (M); Expenditures, $15,774,116; Total giving, $3,805,959; Grants to individuals, 201 grants totaling $3,294,571.
Fields of interest: Higher education; Women.
Type of support: Fellowships; Grants to individuals.
Application information: Applications accepted. Application form required. Application form available on the grantmaker's web site.
  Deadline(s): Varies
  Additional information: See web site for additional application guidelines.
EIN: 526037388

1548
American Chemical Society
1155 16th St. N.W.
Washington, DC 20036-4801 (202) 872-4600
Contact: Madeleine Jacobs, Exec. Dir.
E-mail: service@acs.org; Toll-free tel. (within US): (800) 227-5558; URL: http://www.acs.org

Foundation type: Public charity
Purpose: Grants and scholarships to support the advancement of the chemical sciences through research, education, and community projects.
Publications: Application guidelines; Annual report.
Financial data: Year ended 12/31/2011. Assets, $1,121,108,045 (M); Expenditures, $480,399,853; Total giving, $21,413,817; Grants to individuals, totaling $535,219.
Fields of interest: Science; Chemistry; Engineering.
Type of support: Research; Grants to individuals; Scholarships—to individuals.
Application information: Applications accepted.
  Deadline(s): Varies
  Additional information: See web site for additional guidelines.
Program descriptions:
  Ahmed Zewail Award in Ultrafast Science and Technology: This $5,000 award recognizes outstanding and creative contributions to fundamental discoveries or inventions in ultrafast science and technology in the areas of physics, chemistry, biology, or related fields.
  Petroleum Research Fund Undergraduate Faculty Sabbatical Grants: These grants are designed to provide year-long, full-time, research sabbaticals for qualified faculty performing fundamental research in the petroleum field during a sabbatical. Eligible applicants include faculty with tenured appointments in departments that do not offer a doctoral degree, and faculty at two- and four-year institutions. Matching grants of up to $50,000 are available.
  Petroleum Research Fund Undergraduate New Investigator Grants: This program provides funds for scientists and engineers who are beginning their independent careers in academia and have limited or no preliminary results for a research project they wish to pursue. Grants are to be used to illustrate proof of principle, i.e. feasibility, and are accordingly are to be viewed as seed money for generating preliminary results that can be used to apply for continuation funding from the society or from other funding agencies. Eligibility requires that a principal investigator has attained the rank of assistant professor (or the equivalent) within the past three years and is in a department without a doctoral program, and that the students receiving stipends for the work to be done are undergraduates. Awards are for $50,000 for two years.
  Petroleum Research Fund Undergraduate Research Grants: These grants provide $65,000 of funding, payable over three years, for scientists and engineers in the petroleum and energy fields who are affiliated with established programs of research at non-doctoral departments. Eligible principal investigators must hold a primary appointment in a college or university department that does not grant the Ph.D. or any doctoral degree; investigators from Master's degree-granting departments are eligible, and support can be provided for M.S.-level research, but undergraduates must be included in the project.
EIN: 530196572

1549
American College of Cardiology
2400 N St., N.W.
Washington, DC 20037-1153
Contact: Shalom Jacobovitz, C.E.O.
FAX: (202) 375-7000; E-mail: resource@acc.org;
Toll-free tel.: (800) 253-4636, ext. 5603;
URL: http://www.acc.org

Foundation type: Public charity
Purpose: Scholarships, awards, and travel grants to cardiovascular investigators for research and attendance to annual conferences and events.
Publications: Application guidelines.
Financial data: Year ended 12/31/2011. Assets, $16,115,589 (M); Expenditures, $23,517,961; Total giving, $34,067; Grants to individuals, totaling $34,067.
Fields of interest: Health care; Medical research.
Type of support: Fellowships; Scholarships—to individuals; Travel grants.
Application information: Applications accepted. Application form required. Application form available on the grantmaker's web site.
> *Deadline(s):* Varies
Program descriptions:
ACCF Young Investigators Awards Competition: These awards are intended to encourage and recognize young scientific investigators of promise, upon whom progress in the field of cardiology is dependent. Awards will be given in three categories; clinical investigations, congenital heart disease, and cardiac surgery; physiology, pharmacology, and pathology; and molecular and cellular cardiology. First-place winners for each category will receive $2,000, second-place winners will receive $1,000 each, and three honorable mentions in each category will receive $500; travel, hotel, and meal reimbursement expenses of up to $1,500 will be given to all finalists to attend the organization's Annual Scientific Session in Atlanta. Eligible applicants include any physician/scientist presently in a residency or a fellowship training program, who has been in such a program within the past three years; medical students; and Ph.D. candidates.
ACCF/Bristol-Myers Squibb Travel Awards: Twenty awards of $1,250 each will be given to recipients to attend the organization's Annual Scientific Session. Judging will be based on the applicant's major involvement in research activities leading to presentations and publications during cardiovascular-related subspecialty training. Eligible applicants must be from an Accreditation Council for Graduate Medical Education- or American Osteopathic Association-approved training program in cardiology; and must be beyond their first year in a cardiovascular-related subspecialty training program.
ACCF/GE Healthcare Career Development Awards in Cardiovascular Imaging Technologies and Targeted Imaging Agents: Two awards of $65,000 each are available to foster the early research career development of junior cardiovascular faculty in the research area of imaging technologies and targeted imaging agents. Awards are intended to furnish a portion of the faculty member's total salary support. Applicants eligible for the award are those who: will hold the rank of instructor or assistant professor at the time of the initiation of the award and have completed adult, pediatric, or surgical cardiology fellowship training in a program approved by the Accreditation Council for Graduate Medical Education or the American Osteopathic Association; are members of the college; are no more than five years out of training; have the recommendation and agreement of their division chiefs and the chief's assurance that the awards' support will provide protected time for the

applicants to pursue their research programs; and have an agreement with their institutions that the full amount of the award will be designated for the salary support. Awards are intended only to support a portion of the faculty members' total salary support; awards do not cover research supplies, costs, or institutional overhead.
ACCF/Pfizer Career Development Award in Cardiovascular Disease: The organization will award two three-year career development awards of $65,000 each to encourage the development and promotion of talented physician-scientists who wish to pursue research in cardiovascular disease in an academic setting and who demonstrates a strong career interest in academic cardiovascular medicine. All meritorious submissions will be considered, with specials consideration given to submissions that focus on cardiovascular disease and diabetes and cardiovascular disease and thrombosis. Applicants eligible for the award are those who: will hold the rank of instructor or assistant professor at the time of the initiation of the award and have completed adult, pediatric, or surgical cardiology fellowship training in a program approved by the Accreditation Council for Graduate Medical Education or the American Osteopathic Association; are members of the college; are no more than five years out of training; have the recommendation and agreement of their division chiefs and the chief's assurance that the awards' support will provide protected time for the applicants to pursue their research programs; and have an agreement with their institutions that the full amount of the award will be designated for the salary support. Awards are intended only to support a portion of the faculty members' total salary support; awards do not cover research supplies, costs, or institutional overhead.
ACCF/William F. Keating, Esq. Endowment Award for Hypertension and Peripheral Vascular Disease: This $65,000 award recognizes and provides financial support for research efforts by outstanding young cardiovascular scholars. The award is intended to encourage junior faculty in the early phases of their careers in the field of cardiology by providing a year of research support. Applicants eligible for the award are those who: will hold the rank of instructor or assistant professor at the time of the initiation of the award and have completed adult, pediatric, or surgical cardiology fellowship training in a program approved by the Accreditation Council for Graduate Medical Education or the American Osteopathic Association; are members or eligible to become members of the college; are no more than five years out of training; have the recommendation and agreement of their division chiefs and the chief's assurance that the awards' support will provide protected time for the applicants to pursue their research programs; and have an agreement with their institutions that the full amount of the award will be designated for the salary support. Awards are intended only to support a portion of the faculty members' total salary support; awards do not cover research supplies, costs, or institutional overhead.
Douglas P. Zipes Distinguished Young Scientist Award: This $1,000 award recognizes young scientists who have made outstanding contributions to the field of cardiovascular disease and who have amassed an impressive body of scientific research in either the basic or clinical domains. Eligible applicants must be no more than five years out of training from an accredited U.S. institution or comparable international training program.
EIN: 311781555

1550
American College of Cardiology Foundation
2400 N St., N.W.
Washington, DC 20037-1153

Foundation type: Public charity
Purpose: Awards to support the research of young investigators of cardiology and related fields.
Publications: Application guidelines.
Financial data: Year ended 12/31/2011. Assets, $195,946,419 (M); Expenditures, $75,653,867; Total giving, $1,148,254; Grants to individuals, totaling $1,148,254.
Fields of interest: Heart & circulatory research.
Type of support: Scholarships—to individuals; Awards/prizes.
Application information: Applications accepted. Application form required.
> *Initial approach:* Application
> *Deadline(s):* Oct. 15 for Young Investigator Awards, Sept. 24 for all others
Program descriptions:
ACCF/Daiichi Sankyo Career Development Award: This award works to encourage junior faculty in establishing a solid foundation for a continued career in cardiovascular research, and to recognize and provide financial support for research efforts made by these outstanding cardiovascular scholars. The award will provide one junior faculty member with two years of research support, of up to $70,000. Eligible applicants must hold the rank of instructor of assistant professor at the time of the award's initiation, and must have completed adult, pediatric, or surgical cardiology training in a program approved by the Accreditation Council for Graduate Medical Education (ACGME) or the American Osteopathic Association (AOA); are members (or are eligible to become members) of the American College of Cardiology, and are no more than five years out of training.
ACCF/Merck Research Fellowships in Cardiovascular Disease and Cardiometabolic Disorders: Four one-year fellowships will be awarded to support research in adult cardiology. Applications will be accepted that address cardiovascular disease and cardiometabolic disorders, including proposals that address pathophysiology, molecular genetics, metabolic abnormalities leading to cardiovascular disease, hypertension, heart failure, hyperlipidemia, inflammatory mechanisms, and new pathways for drug discovery. Preference will be given to individuals who have had no more than two years of prior full-time experience (either in clinical or basic research), and to projects that disparities of care. Eligible applicants include anyone currently in an adult cardiology fellowship training program recognized by the Accreditation Council for Graduate Medical Education (ACGME) or the American Osteopathic Association (AOA), and who has the recommendation and agreement of his/her training program director and institution.
ACCF/William F. Keating, Esq. Endowment Award for Hypertension and Peripheral Vascular Disease: This award recognizes and provides financial support for research efforts by outstanding young cardiovascular scholars. This award is meant to encourage junior faculty in the early phases of their careers in the field of cardiology, and will offer $70,000 for one year of research. Eligible applicants: must hold the rank of instructor or assistant professor at the time of the initiation of the award, and must have completed adult, pediatric, or surgical cardiology fellowship training in a program approved by the Accreditation Council for Graduate Medical Education (ACGME) or the American Osteopathic Association (AOA); must be members, or eligible to become members, of the

American College of Cardiology; and must be no more than five years out of training.

ISCTR-ACCF Cardiovascular Translational Research Scholarship: This program recognizes and provides financial support for research efforts by outstanding cardiovascular scholars. Scholarships of up to $70,000 awarded by this program are intended for a physician with a strong interest in developing a career in cardiovascular translational research. In this program, fellows will develop the skills and knowledge to take a scientific concept to the bedside, gain substantial knowledge about the steps in cardiovascular translational research, understand product development related to devices or biologics, learn about toxicology study required on small and large animal models that serve for an investigational drug application (IND) or investigational device exemption (IDE) application, understand the statistical design and analysis required for toxicology studies and phase I, II, and III clinical trials, learn about the regulatory pathways for and how to prepare an IND and IDE, and understand fund raising, NIH grant application process, opportunities in the venture capital arena, and developing and maintaining relationships with industry. Eligible applicants must have completed one year of previous interventional cardiology, are members (or are eligible to be members) of the American College of Cardiology, and are willing to relocate to the host institution.

Young Investigator Awards: This program encourages and recognizes young scientific investigators of promise, upon whom progress in the field of cardiology is dependent. Award categories include: clinical investigations, congenital heart disease, and cardiac surgery; physiology, pharmacology, and pathology; molecular and cellular cardiology; and cardiovascular health outcomes and population genetics. Eligible applicants include physicians and other healthcare providers currently in residence or fellowship programs, or within three years of completion of their program; Ph.D., Pharm.D., or D.N.P. candidates within three years of completion of their program; and medical students. The first-place winner for each category receives $2,000, second-place winners receive $1,000, and three honorable mentions in each category receive $500; travel, hotel, and meal reimbursement (of up to $1,500) will be reimbursed for all finalists to attend the college's annual competition.
EIN: 135641985

1551
American College of Obstetricians and Gynecologists

(also known as ACOG)
409 12th St., S.W., Ste. 100
Washington, DC 20024-2188 (202) 638-5577
Contact: Hal C. Lawrence III M.D., Exec. V.P.
FAX: (202) 484-1595; E-mail: history@acog.org;
Additional address: P.O. Box 70620, Washington, DC 20024-9998; URL: http://www.acog.org

Foundation type: Public charity
Purpose: Fellowships to research obstetrics and gynecology.
Publications: Application guidelines; Occasional report.
Financial data: Year ended 12/31/2011. Assets, $132,207,608 (M); Expenditures, $37,059,966; Total giving, $398,000.
Fields of interest: History/archaeology; Health sciences school/education; Reproductive health; Reproductive health, prenatal care; Women.

Type of support: Fellowships; Research; Postdoctoral support; Postgraduate support; Doctoral support.
Application information: Application form required.
  Deadline(s): Oct. 1
Program description:
  ACOG-ORTHO Fellowship in the History of American Obstetrics and Gynecology: One $5,000 fellowship is given each year to a college member, or other qualified individual, who plan to one month in the Washington, DC, area working full-time to complete a specific historical research project that utilizes the college's history library. Although based at the library, fellows are encouraged to use other national, historical, and medical collections in the Washington, DC, area. The results of this research must be disseminated through either publication or presentation at a professional meeting.
EIN: 362217981

1552
American Councils for International Education

1776 Massachusetts Ave., N.W., Ste. 700
Washington, DC 20036-1911 (202) 833-7522
Contact: William J. Brown, V.P., Devel.
FAX: (202) 833-7523;
E-mail: general@americancouncils.org; E-mail for William J. Brown: wbrown@americancouncils.org; URL: http://www.americancouncils.org

Foundation type: Public charity
Purpose: Grants to students for study and training in the U.S., Europe, Eurasia, Asia and the Middle East.
Publications: Annual report.
Financial data: Year ended 06/30/2011. Assets, $22,350,019 (M); Expenditures, $66,135,242; Total giving, $121,751. Grants to individuals amount not specified.
Fields of interest: Humanities; Public education.
Type of support: Fellowships; Exchange programs; Foreign applicants; Awards/prizes; Travel grants.
Application information: Applications accepted. Application form required.
  Deadline(s): Vary
  Additional information: See web site for additional guidelines.
Program descriptions:
  Advanced Russian Language and Area Studies Program: The program provides intensive Russian-language immersion for U.S. undergraduate and graduate students in Russia. The program is open to undergraduate and graduate students with at least two years of college-level Russian.
  Eurasian Regional Language Program: Provides graduate students, advanced undergraduates, scholars, and working professionals with intensive individualized instructions in the languages of Eurasia. Participants may enroll in semester, academic year, or summer programs. Applicants must be 18 years or older to apply.
  FLEX Alumni Grant Program: This program offers previous program participants the opportunity to initiate social, economic, and civic development projects of their own design in Belarus, Russia, Ukraine, Moldova, and the states of Central Asia and the South Caucasus. Individual grants of up to $250 will be provided for community service projects organized by an individual FLEX alumnus or alumna, as well as personal or professional development projects, including attendance at conferences. Group grants of up to $3,000 will be provided for professional development or teaching programs, community service activities, promotion of the English language, and American culture

projects. Not all those participating in the group have to be FLEX alumni, but the grant recipient and the project leader or co-leader must be.
  Tatarstan Higher Education Fellowship Program: Through a partnership with the Republic of Tatarstan, support for 50 undergraduate and graduate students to study for one year at a U.S. university.
  Title VIII Southeastern Europe Language Program: This program provides fellowships for graduate students, faculty, and scholars to study language for a semester, academic year or summer in Albania, Bosnia-Herzegovina, Bulgaria, Croatia, Macedonia, Montenegro, Romania, and Serbia. Graduate students, faculty and scholars who have at least a beginner level of proficiency in the target language are eligible to apply. Fellowship recipients must be U.S. citizens or permanent residents.
EIN: 521067256

1553
American Dental Education Association

1400 K St., N.W., Ste. 1100
Washington, DC 20005-2415 (202) 289-7201
Contact: Richard W. Valachovic D.M.D., M.P.H., Pres. and C.E.O.
FAX: (202) 289-7204;
E-mail: valachovicr@adea.org; Additional tel.: (202) 289-7385; (202) 289-7390; URL: http://www.adea.org

Foundation type: Public charity
Purpose: Scholarships to dental hygiene students who are members of the American Dental Association. Scholarships by nomination only to predoctoral dental hygiene students. Grants to dental hygiene professionals, scholars, and administrators for advanced research.
Publications: Application guidelines.
Financial data: Year ended 06/30/2012. Assets, $19,874,914 (M); Expenditures, $19,876,439; Total giving, $388,765; Grants to individuals, totaling $154,325.
Fields of interest: Dental school/education; Dental care.
Type of support: Awards/grants by nomination only; Awards/prizes; Undergraduate support.
Application information: Application form required. Application form available on the grantmaker's web site.
  Deadline(s): Vary
  Applicants should submit the following:
    1) Transcripts
    2) Letter(s) of recommendation
    3) Budget Information
  Additional information: Application must also include project description, narrative, professional license, and statement of purpose.
Program descriptions:
  ADEA/ADEA Council of Students, Residents, and Fellows/Colgate-Palmolive Co. Junior Faculty Award: A $2,500 award recognizes junior faculty members who demonstrate excellence in teaching, research, and service and a commitment to dental education.
  ADEA/Alpha Omega Foundation/Leonard Abrams Scholar in the ADEA Leadership Institute: An award of $20,000 to participate in the ADEA Leadership Institute is available to promising dental faculty to help them become leaders in dental and higher education.
  ADEA/Colgate Palmolive Allied Dental Educators Fellowship: This fellowship provides the opportunity for an allied dental educator to focus on a broad range of issues affecting allied dental education such as, but not limited to, policy, research, budget and finance, faculty advancement, legislation, and

gender and workforce issues. The recipient can choose to attend the ADEA Leadership Institute through a $4,000 award that is applied directly to the applicant's tuition and fees or the recipient can choose to spend the fellowship at the ADEA office. The fellow receives a stipend of $4,000 to cover travel and expenses for the cumulative three-month experience in Washington, DC.

ADEA/Colgate Palmolive Co. Excellence in Teaching Award: A $2,500 award honors dental educators who demonstrate exemplary standards and promote excellence in dental education through scholarship and innovation.

ADEA/Colgate-Palmolive Co./National Dental Association Jeanne C. Sinkford Scholar in The ADEA Leadership Institute: An award of $15,000 supports a woman dental scholar's participation in the ADEA Leadership Institute.

ADEA/Johnson & Johnson Healthcare Products Preventive Dentistry Scholarships: Twelve scholarships of $2,500 for tuition and fees are available to predoctoral dental students who have demonstrated academic excellence in preventive dentistry.

ADEA/Johnson & Johnson Healthcare Products/ Enid A. Neidle Scholar-in-Residence Program: A $6,000 stipend to pursue a cumulative 3-month fellowship at ADEA in Washington, DC researching issues affecting women faculty.

ADEA/Sigma Phi Alpha Linda DeVore Scholarship: A $1,000 scholarship is awarded to an individual pursuing allied dental education study at the baccalaureate, master's, or doctoral degree level.

ADEA/Sunstar Americas, Inc./Harry W. Bruce, Jr. Legislative Fellowship: Fellows function as a staff member within the ADEA Center for Public Policy and Advocacy in Washington, DC and work on specific ADEA legislative priorities. Fellows receive a stipend of $15,000 to cover travel and expenses for approximately three months.

ADEA/William J. Gies Foundation Education Fellowship: A $10,000 stipend to pursue a cumulative 3-month fellowship at ADEA in Washington, DC researching educational issues facing dental education.

ADEA/Zimmer Dental Implant Education Teaching Award: Awards of $25,000 recognize excellence and innovation in implant dentistry education. Awards are given once every two years and are divided equally between the winning institution and the dental educator team.
EIN: 911993281

1554
American Educational Research Association
1430 K St., N.W.
Washington, DC   20005-2504   (202) 238-3200
FAX: (202) 238-3250; E-mail: flevine@aera.net;
URL: http://www.aera.net

Foundation type: Public charity
Purpose: Scholarship and research support to education researchers.
Publications: Application guidelines; Annual report.
Financial data: Year ended 12/31/2011. Assets, $30,400,145 (M); Expenditures, $9,142,373; Total giving, $1,016,281; Grants to individuals, totaling $507,158.
Fields of interest: Education; Minorities.
Type of support: Fellowships; Research.
Application information: Applications accepted. Application form required.
Additional information: Application should include financial information. Contact the association for eligibility requirements.

Program descriptions:
AERA Minority Fellowships: This program offers doctoral fellowships to enhance the competitiveness of outstanding minority scholars for academic appointments at major research universities by supporting their research and by providing mentoring and guidance toward completion of their doctoral studies. The association will award up to three doctoral fellowships every year. Each fellowship award is for one year, beginning July 1 or later, and is non-renewable. Fellowships are awarded for doctoral thesis research conducted under faculty sponsorship in any accredited university in the United States.

AERA/AIR Fellows Program: This program aims to build the talent pool of highly-skilled education researchers experienced in working on large-scale studies in major research environments. Up to three fellows are selected annually for a two year, rotational position at the American Institutes for Research in Washington, DC, to acquire additional experience that will broaden their training and research skills in selected areas in the scientific study of education. Only U.S. citizens and permanent residents of the United States are eligible to apply for this fellowship program.

AERA/ETS Fellowship Program in Measurement: The fellowship is designed to provide learning opportunities and practical experience to recent doctoral degree recipients and to early career research scientists in areas such as educational measurement, assessment design, psychometrics, statistical analyses, large-scale evaluations, and other studies direct to explaining student progress and achievement. Up to two fellows will be selected for this rotational research position at Educational Testing Service's (ETS) facilities in Princeton, New Jersey. Through the fellowship program, fellows will receive valuable training and methodological experience in the fields of measurement, psychometrics, and assessment, which will prepare them for productive research experiences in a large employment context. Only U.S. citizens and permanent residents of the United States are eligible to apply for this fellowship position. Applicants must have completed their Ph.D./Ed.D. degrees within three years of submitting their application.
EIN: 237003537

1555
American Farm Bureau Foundation for Agriculture
600 Maryland Ave., S.W., Ste. 1000W
Washington, DC   20024-2555   (202) 406-3600
Contact: Bob Stallman, Chair.
FAX: (202) 314-5121; E-mail: foundation@fb.org;
Toll-free tel.: (800) 443-8456; URL: http://www.agfoundation.org

Foundation type: Public charity
Purpose: Stipends to educators for travel expense to attend the foundation's annual conference.
Publications: Application guidelines; Annual report; Newsletter.
Financial data: Year ended 12/31/2012. Assets, $4,212,597 (M); Expenditures, $832,000; Total giving, $24,050; Grants to individuals, totaling $24,050.
Fields of interest: Elementary/secondary education; Agriculture.
Type of support: Travel awards.
Application information: Applications accepted. Application form required.
Initial approach: Application
Deadline(s): Nov. 1

Additional information: See web site for additional application information.
Program description:
White-Reinhardt Teacher Scholarships: Awarded in conjunction with the American Farm Bureau's Women's Leadership Committee, this program provides travel expense funds (of up to $1,500) to educators employed by a school system to attend the foundation's national conference, for the purpose of using the information gained from the conference to expand their outreach to students regarding food, fuel, and fiber. Eligible applicants include educators employed by a school system and working in grades K-12 who have demonstrated involvement in agricultural literacy programs.
EIN: 366169577

1556
American Federation of State, County, and Municipal Employees
1625 L St., N.W.
Washington, DC   20036-5687   (202) 429-1000
Contact: Lee Saunders, Pres.
FAX: (202) 429-1293; TTY: (202) 659-0446;
URL: http://www.afscme.org/

Foundation type: Public charity
Purpose: Scholarships to members of the federation and their children for attendance at an accredited college, or university, community college, technical college or trade school.
Publications: Informational brochure; Newsletter; Occasional report.
Financial data: Year ended 12/31/2011. Assets, $101,599,858 (M); Expenditures, $166,162,040; Total giving, $16,655,489; Grants to individuals, totaling $110,000.
Fields of interest: Scholarships/financial aid; Labor unions/organizations; Employment.
Type of support: Scholarships—to individuals.
Application information: Applications accepted.
Initial approach: Application
Send request by: Mail
Deadline(s): Varies
Additional information: See web site for additional guidelines.
Program descriptions:
AFSCME Family Scholarship: This program annually provides ten $2,000 scholarships to high school seniors. Eligible applicants must be graduating high school seniors who are applying to an accredited college or university and subsequently accepted as a full-time student in a four-year degree program, and who are children or financially-dependent children of active or retired member of the union. Scholarships can be renewed each year for a maximum of four years, provided the student remains enrolled in a full-time course of study; scholarships may be used for any field of study.

AFSCME/UNCF Union Scholars Program: This program identifies and supports skilled, motivated, and passionate activists who are interested in a career in the labor movement. Participating individuals in this program will be given a ten-week summer field placement, during which they will take part in a union-organizing campaign in one of several locations across the U.S. Participants will receive a stipend of up to $4,000, on-site housing, a week-long orientation and training, and an academic scholarship of up to $5,000 for the school year. Eligible applicants must: be a second-semester sophomore or union during the application and interview process; major in ethnic studies, women's studies, labor studies, American studies, sociology, anthropology, history, political science, psychology, social work, economics, or public policy; have at least a 2.5 GPA; be a college student of color (including African American, Hispanic American, Asian/Pacific Islander American, or American Indian/Alaska Native); demonstrate interest in working for social and economic justice through the labor movement; and have a driver's license.

Jerry Clark Memorial Scholarship: A $5,000 scholarship will be awarded annually to two children of union members who are majoring in a social science (including, but not limited to, political science, sociology, ethnic studies, and communication) at an accredited college or university. Recipients will also be given the opportunity to intern at the union's headquarters during the summer between his/her junior and senior year, or for one semester during his/her junior or senior year. Once awarded, the scholarship will be renewed for the senior year of study, provided the students remain enrolled in a full-time course of study as a social science major. Applicants must have a GPA of 2.5 or higher.

Jerry Wurf Memorial Fund: This fund provides three scholarship for recipients to attend the six-week Harvard Trade Union Program, hosted at Harvard University in Cambridge, Massachusetts. The program is designed for full-time union staff at the local or council level who are planning to devote their careers to the trade union movement. Participants will receive course tuition, housing, round-trip transportation, and a $1,500 allowance for meals and books.

Joey Parisi Memorial Scholarship: This $10,000 scholarship is available to full-time union local, council, or international staff, and local union officers with substantial organizing responsibilities.

Nadra Floyd Memorial Scholarship: This $2,000 scholarship is available to union members and staff to enroll in its National Labor College bachelor's degree program.

Union Plus Scholarships: This program, sponsored by the Union Plus Education Foundation, helps members of the federation and their families defray the cost of higher education by providing scholarships to students who are attending, or who are planning to attend, a college or university, a community college, or a technical college or trade school. Eligible applicants include current and retired members of unions participating in any Union Plus program, their spouses, and their dependent children (including foster children, stepchildren, or any other child for whom the individual member provides greater that 50 percent of his or her support). Applicants for scholarships are evaluated according to academic ability, social awareness, financial need, and appreciation of labor; scholarships are one-time cash awards, ranging from $500 to $4,000.
EIN: 530237789

1557
American Friends of the Alexander von Humboldt Foundation
1101 17th St. N.W., Ste. 603
Washington, DC   20036   (202) 783-1907
Contact: Cathleen S. Fisher Ph.D., Pres.
FAX: (202) 783-1908; Email for Cathleen S. Fisher : cathleen.fisher@americanfriends-of-avh.orgTel. For Cathleen S. Fisher : (202) 609-7884; URL: http://www.americanfriends-of-avh.org

Foundation type: Public charity
Purpose: Awards, scholarships and research fellowships designed to encourage international contact and intellectual collaboration between scholars of all nationalities.
Publications: Application guidelines; Newsletter.

Financial data: Year ended 12/31/2011. Assets, $1,231,512 (M); Expenditures, $695,911; Total giving, $600; Grants to individuals, totaling $600.
Fields of interest: Education; International exchange.
Type of support: Fellowships; Research; Scholarships—to individuals; Foreign applicants.
Application information: See web site for a full list of available programs and additional information.
EIN: 522217136

1558
American Historical Association
400 A St. S.E.
Washington, DC   20003-3807   (202) 544-2422
Contact: Jim Grossman, Exec. Dir.
FAX: (202) 544-8307; E-mail: info@historians.org; URL: http://www.historians.org

Foundation type: Public charity
Purpose: Grants and fellowships to individuals with a doctoral degree in history or in a closely related field.
Publications: Application guidelines.
Financial data: Year ended 06/30/2013. Assets, $7,644,372 (M); Expenditures, $3,827,489; Total giving, $136,091; Grants to individuals, totaling $134,091.
Fields of interest: Art history.
Type of support: Fellowships; Postgraduate support.
Application information:
   Deadline(s): Vary
   Additional information: See web site for additional guidelines.
EIN: 530217487

1559
American Hotel and Lodging Educational Foundation
(formerly American Hotel and Lodging Foundation, also known as AH&LEF)
1201 New York Ave. N.W., Ste. 600
Washington, DC   20005-3931   (202) 289-3100
Contact: Joori Jeon C.P.A., Pres. and C.O.O.
FAX: (202) 289-3199; E-mail: ahlef@ahlef.org; URL: http://www.ahlef.org

Foundation type: Public charity
Purpose: Scholarships to college students pursuing an undergraduate degree in hospitality management.
Publications: Application guidelines; Annual report.
Financial data: Year ended 12/31/2011. Assets, $17,417,048 (M); Expenditures, $1,687,020; Total giving, $885,909; Grants to individuals, totaling $389,950.
Fields of interest: Business/industry.
Type of support: Awards/grants by nomination only; Graduate support; Undergraduate support.
Application information: Applications accepted. Application form required. Application form available on the grantmaker's web site.
   Deadline(s): May 1
   Final notification: Applicants notified by July 15
   Applicants should submit the following:
   1) Letter(s) of recommendation
   2) Transcripts
Program descriptions:
   AH & LEF Graduate Scholarship: This $5,000 scholarship is awarded to those with an undergraduate degree in hospitality or four years of employment in the lodging industry after graduation.
   AH & LEF Incoming Freshman Scholarship: These scholarships are awarded to incoming freshman

hotel and lodging students. Preference is given to high school graduates of the Lodging Management Program. $2,000 scholarships are available to full-time students, and $1,000 scholarships are available to part-time students.

American Express Scholarship Program: The program is offered to lodging employees, working a minimum of 20 hours a week at American Hotel & Lodging Association (AH&LA) member properties and to their dependents. The program offers two types of scholarships. Academic Scholarships provide financial support to students enrolled in an accredited undergraduate academic program leading to a degree in hospitality management; scholarship amounts can range between $2,000 and $500 depending on enrollment status. Professional Development scholarships provide financial support to students enrolled in distance-learning courses or professional certifications courses offered through the foundation's Educational Institute (EI). Applicants must be intending to enroll in the Educational Institute program to qualify.

Annual Scholarship Grant Program: The program is co-administered with 84 universities and colleges that are affiliated with the foundation. The schools are required to use a set of minimum eligibility requirements designated by the foundation when selecting the scholarship recipients. Some of the foundation's criteria include full-time enrollment status, a minimum GPA of 3.0, U.S. citizenship or permanent U.S. resident status, and completion of at least one or two years of school. A few scholarships have slightly different criteria, depending on the program; interested students should inquire at their schools in the dean's office. Award amounts range from $500 to $3,000 depending upon enrollment and recommended amount from the school.

Arthur J. Packard Memorial Scholarship: The purpose of the competition is to provide scholarships to the most outstanding student of lodging management and two runner-ups through an annual competition among the foundation-affiliated four-year programs. The first-place winner receives a $5,000 scholarship; the second-place winner receives a $3,000 scholarship, while the third-place winner receives a $2,000 scholarship. Each university nominates the one student most qualified according to the criteria to compete in the national competition. Students should inquire in their dean's office for consideration of the nomination and application.

Ecolab Scholarship Program: This program offers two types of scholarships. Academic scholarships are available to applicants who are enrolled or intend to enroll full-time (at least 12 hours) in a U.S. baccalaureate or associate hospitality degree-granting program for both the upcoming fall and spring semesters. The applicant's school does not have to be affiliated with the foundation. Scholarships are awarded in the amount of $1,000 for enrollment in a two-year program and $2,000 for a four-year program. Certification scholarships are also available to applicants who are hospitality professionals working at an AH&LA member property for a minimum of 35 hours per week, and who qualify for the Educational Institute's certification program. The scholarship includes the cost of the certification study guide, examination fee, and certification fee for the following professional designations: Certified Hotel Administrator, Certified Lodging Manager, Certified Engineering Operations Executive, and Certified Hospitality Housekeeping Executive. Individuals apply directly to the foundation for consideration for both scholarships.

Hyatt Hotels Fund for Minority Lodging Management Students: The fund provides financial aid to minority students pursuing a degree in hotel management. The scholarship is a national competition among the four-year universities that are members of the Council on Hotel, Restaurant, and Institutional Education. Scholarship winners receive a $2,000 award. Each university nominates the one student who is most qualified, according to the criteria to compete in the competition. Students should inquire in their dean's office for consideration of the nomination and application.

Pepsi Scholarship: These scholarships range from $1,000 to $3,000 and are made to graduates of Marriott Hospitality High School who are enrolled in undergraduate hospitality-related degree granting programs at colleges and universities. Marriott Hospitality High School graduates should inquire in their principal's office for consideration of this scholarship.

Rama Scholarship for the American Dream: The purpose of the program is to provide financial aid ranging from $1,000 to $3,000 to students pursuing degrees in hotel management. Scholarships are awarded through a nomination process only.

Steven Hymans Extended Stay Scholarship: The purpose of the scholarship program is to help educate more undergraduate hospitality management students about the needs, interests, and concerns of the extended-stay segment of the lodging industry. Scholarship amounts can range between $1,000 and $3,000, depending on enrollment status. Applicants must have previous work experience at an extended-stay property and a desire to pursue their professional careers in this segment of the industry.

EIN: 136095316

1560
American Institute for Cancer Research
1759 R St., N.W.
Washington, DC 20009-2552 (202) 328-7744
Contact: Susan Higginbotham Ph.D., Dir., Research
FAX: (202) 328-7226; E-mail: aicrweb@aicr.org;
Toll-free tel.: (800) 843-8114; Application address for Marilyn Gentry Fellowship Prog.: June Stevens, Ph.D. c/o Nutrition Human Resources, Univ. of North Carolina at Chapel Hill, Dept. of Nutrition, 2201 McGavran-Greenberg Bldg., CB No. 7461, Chapel Hill, NC 27599-7461, E-mail: nutritionhr@unc.edu; URL: http://www.aicr.org

Foundation type: Public charity
Purpose: Research grants to investigators for the study of diet and nutrition in the prevention and treatment of cancer.
Publications: Application guidelines; Annual report; Financial statement; Grants list; Informational brochure; Newsletter.
Financial data: Year ended 09/30/2011. Assets, $16,703,968 (M); Expenditures, $24,938,251; Total giving, $521,537.
Fields of interest: Cancer research; Nutrition.
Type of support: Research; Postdoctoral support.
Application information: Applications accepted. Application form required.
Initial approach: Letter, telephone, or e-mail
Deadline(s): Feb. 16
Final notification: Applicants notified in Oct.
Additional information: Only one grant application per Principal Investigator per grant cycle is permitted.
Program descriptions:
Investigator-Initiated Grants (IIG): This program provides $75,000 per year for two years, plus 10 percent of indirect costs, to encourage research on

the dietary and nutritional means of preventing and treating cancer. Relevant applications must focus on dietary factors in the treatment and/or prevention of cancer.
Marilyn Gentry Fellowship Program in Nutrition and Cancer: These two-year, $100,000 fellowships are designed to develop leaders in cutting-edge nutritional research as it relates to cancer prevention, treatment, and survivorship. Fellows will be paired with a research mentor who will help the fellow identify a subset of the mentor's research to be set aside for the fellow. Fellows will be appointed at the rank of research Assistant Professor of Nutrition and will receive two years of organized mentoring on the specific skills needed to succeed as academic scientists; fellows will also develop a body of data that will allow them to compete successfully for grant funding and help establish them as independent investigators. Eligible applicants must have completed at least one year of postdoctoral training with intended research focus in nutrition and cancer prevention and treatment.
Matching Grants: These grants, in coordination with industry or individuals, fund research projects in the area of diet, nutrition, and cancer prevention and treatment. Applications should follow the guidelines and application procedures for Investigator-Initiated Grants.
Post-Doctoral Grant Awards (PDA): This program provides $25,000 per year for two years, plus 10 percent of indirect costs, to beginning investigators to support innovative research on the prevention, etiology, and treatment of cancer by dietary or nutritional methods. Applications should propose relevant feasibility studies to obtain data in support of a new hypothesis that then could be expanded to increase understanding of the role of dietary and nutritional factors in the etiology, pathogenesis, prevention, or treatment of cancer. The principal investigator must have a Ph.D. or equivalent degree or M.D. degree that was awarded no more than three years prior to the date of application, and must hold an academic appointment no higher than assistant professor. The applicant must be sponsored by a professor in whose laboratory the applicant is to perform the research.
EIN: 521238026

1561
The American Institute of Architects
(also known as AIA)
1735 New York Ave., N.W.
Washington, DC 20006-5209 (202) 626-7370
FAX: (202) 626-7547; E-mail: infocentral@aia.org;
Toll-free tel.: (800) 242-3837; URL: http://www.aia.org

Foundation type: Public charity
Purpose: Scholarships and awards to individuals in the field of architecture.
Publications: Application guidelines.
Financial data: Year ended 12/31/2011. Assets, $64,649,373 (M); Expenditures, $52,728,546; Total giving, $1,275,957; Grants to individuals, totaling $69,950.
Fields of interest: Architecture.
Type of support: Scholarships—to individuals; Awards/prizes.
Application information: Applications accepted.
Additional information: See web site for complete program listing.
EIN: 530025930

1562
American Legacy Foundation
1724 Massachusetts Ave., N.W.
Washington, DC 20036-1903 (202) 454-5555
Contact: David B. Abrams, Exec. Dir.; Amber Hardy Thornton, Exec. V.P., Prog. Devel.
FAX: (202) 454-5599;
E-mail: info@americanlegacy.org; URL: http://www.americanlegacy.org

Foundation type: Public charity
Purpose: Awards and scholarships to individuals for the study to reduce youth tobacco usage and substance abuse.
Publications: Financial statement.
Financial data: Year ended 06/30/2012. Assets, $1,038,736,480 (M); Expenditures, $51,262,428; Total giving, $4,704,841; Grants to individuals, totaling $15,200.
Fields of interest: Substance abuse, prevention; Smoking; Minorities; Economically disadvantaged; LGBTQ.
Type of support: Grants to individuals; Scholarships—to individuals.
Application information:
Initial approach: Letter
Deadline(s): Apr. 30 for Adams Scholarship
Final notification: Recipients notified June 29 for Adams Scholarship
Additional information: See web site for additional application requirements.
Program descriptions:
Christine O. Gregoire Youth/Young Adult Award for Outstanding Use of Tobacco Industry Documents: The award recognizes a person 24 years of age or younger who has made a contribution to the health of the public in the recent past through use of tobacco documents. The award honors innovation in the use and application of tobacco industry documents to improve the public's health and, where applicable, to further the goals of tobacco prevention and control in order to help build a world where young people reject tobacco and anyone can quit. Those nominated should be individuals who have made a notable impact through innovative use of tobacco industry documents as applied to research, policy, or advocacy. Award amount is $7,500.
Dr. Alma S. Adams Scholarship: This scholarship awards two candidates with $5,000 each to pursue undergraduate or graduate studies at an accredited institution of higher education in the U.S. Applicants must have demonstrated a commitment to community service or used the visual arts or media to convey culturally-appropriate health messages on behalf of a disadvantaged population (including Native Americans/Alaska Natives, Hispanics, African Americans, Asian/Pacific Islanders, lower socioeconomic status, and LGBT communities). Applicants must be full-time students pursuing a course of study in public health, communications, social work, education, liberal arts, or a related field who have a GPA of at least 3.0 and who can provide evidence of service to a community in an economically- or socially-disadvantaged setting. Entries must include creative writing, a musical composition, or a sample from a visual arts medium.
Sybil G. Jacobs Award for Outstanding Use of Tobacco Industry Documents: The award recognizes a person who has made a significant and well-recognized contribution to the health of the public in the recent past through use of tobacco documents. The award honors innovation in the use and application of tobacco industry documents to improve the public's health and, where applicable, to further the goals of tobacco prevention and control in order to help build a world where young people reject tobacco and anyone can quit. Those

nominated should be individuals who have made a notable impact through innovative use of tobacco industry documents as applied to research, policy, or advocacy. Award amount is $7,500.

Travel Scholarship to Increase Diversity in Nicotine and Tobacco Research: These scholarships aim to increase the diversity of qualified individuals interested in nicotine and tobacco research by providing travel support to attend the foundation's annual meeting. Applicants must have an interest in nicotine and tobacco research and be committed to the foundation's mission, hold a junior faculty (assistant professor, instructor, or equivalent), post-doctoral trainee, or graduate student rank at a U.S.-based university, and live at least 50 miles outside of the Portland, OR area. Preference will be given to applicants from minority racial/ethnic groups (American Indian/Alaska Native, Asian American/Pacific Islander, Black/African American, or Latino/Hispanic), the disabled, candidates from lesbian, gay, bisexual, or transgender groups, or candidates from other disadvantaged groups.
EIN: 911956621

1563
American National Red Cross
2025 E. St., N.W.
Washington, DC   20006-5009   (703) 206-6000
Toll-free tels: (800) 733-2767 (English), (800) 257-7575 (Spanish); URL: http://www.redcross.org

Foundation type: Public charity
Purpose: Emergency and financial assistance to individuals affected by disasters worldwide with shelter and food.
Financial data: Year ended 06/30/2012. Assets, $3,777,960,071 (M); Expenditures, $3,329,153,707; Total giving, $212,460,308; Grants to individuals, totaling $65,641,308.
Fields of interest: Safety/disasters; Human services.
Type of support: Emergency funds.
Application information: Eligibility for assistance is based on the needs of the individual.
EIN: 530196605

1564
American Pharmacists Association Foundation
(also known as The APhA Foundation)
2215 Constitution Ave., N.W.
Washington, DC   20037-2907   (202) 429-7565
FAX: (202) 783-2351;
E-mail: info@aphafoundation.org; E-Mail for Mindy D. Smith: msmith@aphanet.org; URL: http://www.aphafoundation.org

Foundation type: Public charity
Purpose: Grants and awards to practitioners in any pharmacy setting. Also, scholarships to full-time pharmacy students who are active in their school's APhA-ASP chapter.
Publications: Annual report; Newsletter.
Financial data: Year ended 12/31/2011. Assets, $8,094,281 (M); Expenditures, $2,548,974; Total giving, $429,994; Grants to individuals, totaling $62,494.
Fields of interest: Pharmacy/prescriptions; Institute.
Type of support: Program development; Research.
Application information: Applications accepted. Application form required.
  Initial approach: Proposal
  Copies of proposal: 1
  Applicants should submit the following:

1) Curriculum vitae
2) Resume
3) Letter(s) of recommendation
4) Essay
5) Transcripts
Program descriptions:
  Incentive Grants: $1,000 grants are awarded each year to practitioners in all practice settings to develop innovative services and share their experiences with other pharmacists. Applicants must be members of the American Pharmacists Association (APA), currently licensed, and actively engaged in ambulatory pharmacy practice.
  Student Scholarships: Nine $1,000, one-year scholarships are available to students who are active members of the APA Academy of Students of Pharmacy and who have demonstrated leadership as a student pharmacist and member of their community.
EIN: 526039142

1565
American Psychological Foundation
(also known as A.P.F.)
750 1st St., N.E.
Washington, DC   20002-4242   (202) 336-5843
Contact: Elizabeth H. Merck, Asst. Dir.
FAX: (202) 336-5812; E-mail: foundation@apa.org;
URL: http://www.apa.org/apf/

Foundation type: Public charity
Purpose: Scholarships, fellowships and grants for the study of psychology.
Publications: Application guidelines; Annual report; Financial statement; Informational brochure (including application guidelines); Newsletter.
Financial data: Year ended 12/31/2011. Assets, $14,889,448 (M); Expenditures, $1,420,947; Total giving, $618,887; Grants to individuals, totaling $151,000.
Fields of interest: Psychology/behavioral science.
Type of support: Fellowships; Travel awards; Research; Grants to individuals; Scholarships—to individuals; Awards/prizes; Postdoctoral support; Graduate support; Precollege support; Doctoral support.
Application information: Applications accepted. Application form required.
  Initial approach: Letter or telephone
  Deadline(s): Varies
  Additional information: See web site for complete program information.
Program descriptions:
  Foundation Grants: Grants ranging from $1,000 to $50,000 are available to individuals and programs that support the foundation's mission of enhancing psychology to elevate the human condition and advance human potential. See web site for more detailed grant information.
  Pearson Early Career Grants: The foundation awards a grant of $12,000 to a clinician working on a scientifically-based project in the area of serious mental illness, serious emotional disturbance, incarcerated or homeless individuals, children with serious emotional disturbance, or adults with serious mental illness.
  Scholarships and Fellowships: The foundation supports a number of programs aimed at helping graduate students further their education in psychology. Scholarships and fellowships range from $300 for travel support to $25,000 for fellowships. See web site for more detailed grant information.
EIN: 526051733

1566
American Public Power Association
(also known as APPA)
1875 Connecticut Ave., Ste. 1200
Washington, DC   20009-5715   (202) 467-2900
FAX: (202) 467-2910; E-mail: deed@appanet.org;
Toll-free tel.: (800) 515-2772; URL: http://www.publicpower.org/

Foundation type: Public charity
Purpose: Grants to students pursuing a career in energy-related disciplines from accredited colleges or univerities in the U.S. or Canada.
Publications: Application guidelines.
Financial data: Year ended 12/31/2011. Assets, $9,987,398 (M); Expenditures, $16,410,440; Total giving, $464,184; Grants to individuals, totaling $16,720.
Fields of interest: Energy.
Type of support: Research; Grants to individuals.
Application information: Applications accepted. Application form required. Application form available on the grantmaker's web site.
  Send request by: Mail
  Deadline(s): Feb. 15 and Oct. 15 for Research Grants and Internships, Oct. 15 for Technical Design Project (TDP)
  Additional information: Application should include transcripts.
Program descriptions:
  Student Research Grants and Internships: These grants and internship opportunities support students studying in energy-related disciplines, increase awareness of career opportunities in public power, and provide assistance to DEED member utility sponsors. Each year up to ten $4,000 student research grants and internships are awarded to students conducting research on an energy-related project. Students must be sponsored by a DEED member utility and are required to write an abstract and final report at the completion of the project.
  Technical Design Project Grants: This program promotes the involvement of students studying in energy-related disciplines in the public power industry by providing a $5,000 award to a student or group of students who are conducting research on an energy-related project. Recipients also receive travel reimbursements of up to $3,000 to present their project during the association's annual Engineering and Operations Technical Conference.
EIN: 530026315

1567
American Road & Transportation Builders Association Foundation
1219 28th St., N.W.
Washington, DC   20007-3389   (202) 289-4434
Contact: Rhonda Britton, Scholarships and Awards Prog. Mgr.
FAX: (202) 289-4435; E-mail: rbritton@artba.org;
URL: http://www.artba.org/about/transportation-development-foundation/

Foundation type: Public charity
Purpose: Scholarships to children of highway workers who died or were permanently disabled at work. Awards also to undergraduate and graduate students for papers on transportation issues.
Publications: Application guidelines; Annual report.
Financial data: Year ended 12/31/2011. Assets, $1,540,201 (M); Expenditures, $1,744,127.
Fields of interest: Higher education.
Type of support: Scholarships—to individuals.

Application information: Applications accepted. Application form required.
Deadline(s): Mar. 31 for Highway Worker Memorial Scholarship
Applicants should submit the following:
1) GPA
2) Letter(s) of recommendation
Additional information: See web site for additional application information.
Program description:
The Lanford Family Highway Worker Memorial Scholarship Program: The program provides up to $5,000 in scholarships to help the sons, daughters, or legally-adopted children of highway workers who die or have become permanently disabled in roadway construction zone accidents.
EIN: 526283894

1568
American Society for Engineering Education
1818 N. St. N.W., Ste. 600
Washington, DC 20036-2476 (202) 331-3500
Contact: Norman Fortenberry, Exec. Dir.
FAX: (202) 265-8504; E-mail: aseeexec@asee.org;
Tel. for Norman Fortenberry : (202)-331-3545;
URL: http://www.asee.org

Foundation type: Public charity
Purpose: Fellowships to further education in engineering and engineering technology.
Publications: Annual report.
Financial data: Year ended 09/30/2011. Assets, $19,309,539 (M); Expenditures, $88,157,146; Total giving, $79,586,523; Grants to individuals, totaling $79,586,523.
Fields of interest: Engineering.
Type of support: Fellowships; Research.
Application information: Applications accepted. Application form required.
Initial approach: Letter
Program descriptions:
Air Force Summer Faculty Fellowship Program: The program offers hands-on exposure to Air Force research challenges through eight- to twelve-week research residencies at participating Air Force research facilities for full-time science and engineering faculty at U.S. colleges and universities. Participants receive a weekly stipend; the weekly stipend amount depends on the faculty status of the participant's application.
Helen T. Carr Fellowship Program: The program seeks to address the lack of engineering faculty role models at historically Black engineering colleges (HBECs) by awarding fellowships to African-American faculty members or students in pursuit of a doctoral degree. Up to $10,000 per year is provided to students who are pursuing a doctoral degree; upon completion of the doctoral degree requirements, a fellow is committed to return to an HBEC institution. Fellowships are available to students who are currently engaged in planning to enter a career in higher education at an HBEC. A candidate must be sponsored by the Dean of Engineering from one of the participating institutions.
NASA Faculty Fellowship Program: The program provides faculty an opportunity to engage in research at one of the participating NASA Centers or the Jet Propulsion Laboratory (JPL). Fellowships are awarded to qualified faculty members at U.S colleges and universities for a ten-week summer research residency with a possible option for extended support during the academic year. Collaborative research projects proposed for this fellowship should be of mutual interest to the fellow and the NASA colleague, and relevant to Center and

Agency missions. The program is jointly administered by the association and the Universities Space Research Association (USRA).
National Defense Science and Engineering Graduate (NDSEG) Fellowship: The fellowship program is sponsored by the Army Research Office, Office of Naval Research, Air Force Office of Scientific Research, and the Department of Defense High Performance Computing Modernization Program. This program is intended for U.S. citizens at or near the beginning of their graduate studies in science and/or engineering programs. The fellowships are for three-year tenures; the stipends begin at $30,500 for first-year fellows, $31,000 for second-year fellows, and $31,500 for third-year fellows. Full tuition and fees and a health insurance allowance are included as part of the program.
Naval Research Laboratory (NRL) Postdoctoral Fellowship Program: This program is open to U.S. citizens and legal permanent residents and offers a competitive stipend as well as insurance, relocation, and travel allowances. This program offers one- to three-year postdoctoral fellowships designed to increase the involvement of scientists and engineers from academia and industry to scientific and technical areas of interest and relevance to the Navy.
Science, Mathematics, and Research for Transformation Defense Scholarship for Service Program (SMART): This scholarship program provides students with a stipend allowance, full tuition, book allowance, room and board, and other normal educational expenses. The purpose of the program is to promote the education, recruitment, and retention of undergraduate and graduate students in science, mathematics, and engineering studies. The program is open only to citizens of the United States, and students must be at least 18 years of age to be eligible.
EIN: 370730118

1569
American Society of Hematology, Inc.
(also known as ASH)
2021 L St. N.W., Ste. 900
Washington, DC 20036-3530 (202) 776-0544
Contact: Martha Liggett Esq., Exec. Dir.
FAX: (202) 776-0545; E-mail: ash@hematology.org;
URL: http://www.hematology.org

Foundation type: Public charity
Purpose: Research grants to hematologists and junior faculty who are interested in hematology aging research.
Publications: Application guidelines; Annual report.
Financial data: Year ended 06/30/2012. Assets, $175,679,169 (M); Expenditures, $35,988,840; Total giving, $4,293,886; Grants to individuals, totaling $4,069,479.
Fields of interest: Hematology; Hematology research.
Type of support: Research.
Application information: Applications accepted.
Initial approach: Letter
Send request by: Mail
Deadline(s): Early May for letter of intent; late Aug. for full proposal
Applicants should submit the following:
1) Curriculum vitae
2) Proposal
Program descriptions:
ASH Alternative Training Pathway Grant: The program is intended to foster the development and implementation of creative new curricula for trainees in clinical and clinical/translational hematology and related fields. Grants of up to

$50,000 will be awarded to support the development and implementation of novel hematology-related training programs as an alternative to traditional training programs. The award may be expended over a one- to two- year period of time. No institutional overhead (i.e., indirect) costs will be supported by this grant. Applicants must be active members of the American Society of Hematology (ASH) at institutions with (an) accredited training program(s) in adult or pediatric hematology or hematology/medical oncology, or in other hematology-related disciplines (e.g., pathology specialties) in the United States, Canada, or Mexico. Awards are limited to only one application per institution.
ASH Research Training Award for Fellows: Designed to encourage junior researchers to choose careers in academic hematology, this award provides funding to fellows in hematology, hematology/oncology, or hematology-related training programs who need protected time to perform research during fellowship training. The award will, on a three-year pilot basis, grant $50,000 for a one-year period to third- and fourth-year trainees (at time of the award) in training who are not yet eligible for scholar awards. The applicant must either be an associate society member or submit a membership application.
EIN: 237080568

1570
American Society of Interior Designers Foundation
608 Massachusetts Ave., N.E.
Washington, DC 20002-6006 (202) 546-3480
Contact: Randy W. Fiser, Exec. V.P. and C.E.O.
FAX: (202) 546-3240; E-mail: foundation@asid.org;
URL: http://www.asidfoundation.org

Foundation type: Public charity
Purpose: Scholarships to individuals who are entering the field of interior design.
Publications: Application guidelines; Grants list.
Financial data: Year ended 09/30/2012. Assets, $3,438,932 (M); Expenditures, $302,832; Total giving, $168,400; Grants to individuals, totaling $35,000.
Fields of interest: Design; Historic preservation/historical societies.
Type of support: Awards/prizes; Graduate support; Undergraduate support.
Application information: Applications accepted. Application form required. Application form available on the grantmaker's web site.
Initial approach: Telephone
Deadline(s): Apr. 30
Program descriptions:
ASID Foundation Grants: The foundation supports endeavors of organizations and individuals that capture and disseminate knowledge, encourage innovation, and benefit the health, safety and welfare of the public through interior design research and education.
Dora Brahms Award: Awards one $1,500 award to educational institutions on behalf of their students in historic preservation and/or restoration studies, to encourage and support the advancement of professional activities in historic preservation and/or restoration.
Irene Winifred Eno Grant: An award of $1,000 for financial assistance to an individual or groups engaged in the creation of an educational program(s) or an interior design research project dedicated to health, safety and welfare.
Joel Polsky Academic Achievement Award: Awards one $1,000 award to recognize an outstanding undergraduate or graduate student's

interior design research or thesis project. Research papers or doctoral and master's theses should address such interior design topics as educational research, behavioral science, business practice, design process, theory, or other technical subjects.

Joel Polsky Prize: Awards one $1,000 prize to recognize outstanding academic contributions to the discipline of interior design through literature or visual communication.

Legacy Scholarships: Scholarships of $4,000 are available to junior, senior, and graduate students enrolled in interior design programs. Scholarships are awarded based on portfolios and academic/creative accomplishment.

Mabelle Wilhelmina Boldt Scholarship: Awards one $2,000 scholarship to students who are enrolled in or have applied for admission to a graduate-level interior design program at a degree-granting institution. Applicants must have been practicing designers for a period of at least five years prior to returning to graduate level.

Yale R. Burge Competition: One $750 award, and up to five certificates of excellence are open to all students in their final year of undergraduate study enrolled in at least a three-year program of interior design. The competition is designed to encourage students to seriously plan their portfolios.
EIN: 132852954

1571
American Society of Nephrology, Inc.
(also known as ASN)
1510 H St., N.W.
Washington, DC   20005-1003   (202) 640-4660
Contact: Bruce A. Molitoris M.D., Pres.
FAX: (202) 637-9793;
E-mail: email@asn-online.org; URL: http://www.asn-online.org/

Foundation type: Public charity
Purpose: Research grants for the advancement of scientific knowledge and the improvement of care in the field of nephrology.
Publications: Application guidelines; Grants list; Newsletter.
Financial data: Year ended 12/31/2011. Assets, $55,907,516 (M); Expenditures, $18,203,401; Total giving, $2,336,777; Grants to individuals, totaling $136,887.
Fields of interest: Kidney diseases; Kidney research.
Type of support: Research.
Application information: Applications accepted. Application form required.
EIN: 526078378

1572
Americans for the Arts
(formerly American Council for the Arts)
1000 Vermont Ave., N.W., 6th Fl.
Washington, DC   20005-4940   (202) 371-2830
Contact: Robert Lynch, Pres. and C.E.O.
FAX: (202) 371-0424; Toll-free tel.: (866) 471-2787; URL: http://www.artsusa.org

Foundation type: Public charity
Purpose: Awards by nomination only to outstanding individual artists for advancement of arts and arts education in their community.
Financial data: Year ended 12/31/2011. Assets, $119,908,128 (M); Expenditures, $11,239,777; Total giving, $505,335; Grants to individuals, totaling $42,398.
Fields of interest: Arts.
Type of support: Awards/grants by nomination only; Awards/prizes.

Application information:
  Send request by: E-mail
  Deadline(s): Mar. 18
  Applicants should submit the following:
    1) Photograph
    2) Resume
    3) Letter(s) of recommendation
  Additional information: Self-nominations are accepted.
Program description:
  Annual Awards: Each year the organization recognizes those who are committed to building communities through the arts, including educators, elected officials, philanthropists, corporate leaders, and legendary artists, through the following awards: Alene Valkanas State Arts Advocacy Award, Arts Education Award, Emerging Leader Award, Michael Newton Award, National Arts Awards, Public Leadership in the Arts Award, Public Art Network Award, and Selina Roberts Ottum Award.
EIN: 521996467

1573
The Amyotrophic Lateral Sclerosis Association
(also known as The ALS Association)
1275 K St., N.W., Ste. 1050
Washington, DC   20005-6822   (202) 407-8580
Contact: Jane H. Gilbert, Pres. and C.E.O.
FAX: (202) 289-6801; Toll-free tel.: (800) 782-4747; additional address (Calabasas Hills office): 27001 Agoura Rd., Ste. 250, Calabasas Hills, CA 91301-5104, tel.: (818) 880-9007, fax: (818) 880-9006; URL: http://www.alsa.org/

Foundation type: Public charity
Purpose: Research grants to investigators to find a cure for ALS and to improve the standard of living for individuals with the disease.
Publications: Annual report; Informational brochure; Newsletter.
Financial data: Year ended 01/31/2012. Assets, $20,256,339 (M); Expenditures, $15,824,207; Total giving, $4,394,391; Grants to individuals, totaling $24,518.
Fields of interest: Nerve, muscle & bone diseases; Nerve, muscle & bone research.
Type of support: Fellowships; Research; Project support.
Application information:
  Initial approach: Proposal
  Additional information: Contact foundation for current application deadline/guidelines.
Program descriptions:
  Clinical Management Research Program: This program awards funds of up to $40,000 per year for up to two years for research into the clinical, psychological, and/or social management aspects of ALS. Research projects that address the content areas described in each year's specific call for abstracts are given preference.
  Clinician Scientist Development Award: In conjunction with the American Academy of Neurology Foundation, a three-year award is available to support research into drug discovery and the development of therapies that will effectively treat amyotrophic lateral sclerosis (ALS), and recognizes the importance of good clinical research in encouraging young investigators in clinical studies. Awards consist of an annual salary of $75,000, plus a $5,000 institutional award. Eligible applicants must be a neurologist interested in an academic career in clinical research; applicants must hold an M.D., D.O., or equivalent clinical degree from an accredited institution and must be licensed to practice medicine in the U.S. Applicants must also have competed residency

training but be less than seven years from completion of their residency when funding begins.
  Milton Safenowitz Post Doctoral Fellowship for ALS Research Award: One to two post-doctoral fellowships, for up to $40,000 per year for up to two years, are available for post-doctoral fellows or those that have been a fellow for no more than one year.
  Multi-Year Grants: Awards grants of up to $80,000 a year to researchers for projects of up to three years. Funding is committed for one year only, with non-competitive renewals conditioned upon receipt of satisfactory interim progress reports.
  Sheila Essay Award for ALS Research: In partnership with the American Academy of Neurology, this $25,000 prize recognizes an individual actively engaged in ALS research who is making significant contributions in research for the cause, treatment, prevention, or cure for amyotrophic lateral sclerosis.
  Starter Grants: These are one-year awards for new investigators entering the field of ALS proposing innovative and novel projects likely to provide important results relevant to ALS research. Alternatively, they can be pilot studies by established ALS investigators. These applications do not require strong preliminary data but must emphasize novelty, feasibility, innovation and relevance to ALS. The maximum amount awarded is $40,000.
EIN: 133271855

1574
Anacostia Community Outreach Center
711 24th St., N.E., Unit 119
Washington, DC   20002-3235   (202) 889-5607
FAX: (202) 889-3219;
E-mail: info@anacostiaoutreach.org; URL: http://www.anacostiaoutreach.org/

Foundation type: Public charity
Purpose: Assistance to individuals and families of the Washiungton, DC area, with emergency food, clothing, rental and utility assistance, job training, youth services and literacy programs.
Financial data: Year ended 12/31/2011. Assets, $122,744 (M); Expenditures, $622,719.
Fields of interest: Human services, emergency aid; Economically disadvantaged.
Type of support: In-kind gifts; Grants for special needs.
Application information: Applications accepted.
  Additional information: Application accepted for certain assistance, contact the agency for eligibility determination.
EIN: 521729564

1575
Animal Welfare Institute
900 Pennsylvania Ave., S.E.
Washington, DC   20003-2140   (202) 337-2332
Contact: Cathy Liss, Pres.
FAX: (202) 466-2131; E-mail: awi@awionline.org; Mailing address: P.O. Box 3650, Washington, DC 20027-0150; toll-free tel.: (888) 260-2271; URL: http://www.awionline.org

Foundation type: Public charity
Purpose: Project grants to farmers for the improvement of animal welfare on farms.
Publications: Application guidelines; Informational brochure; Newsletter; Occasional report.
Financial data: Year ended 06/30/2012. Assets, $13,619,470 (M); Expenditures, $4,794,099; Total giving, $243,374; Grants to individuals, totaling $84,125.

Fields of interest: Animal welfare; Animals/wildlife, preservation/protection; Animals/wildlife.
Type of support: Program development.
Application information: Applications accepted. Application form required. Application form available on the grantmaker's web site.
  Initial approach: Letter
  Deadline(s): Oct. 15
Program description:
  Animal Welfare Approved Good Husbandry Grants for Farmers: Under the organization's Animal Welfare Approved program, grants of up to $5,000 are available to help current farmers associated with the program, and those who have applied to join the program prior to the grant application deadline, to improve animal welfare on their farms. Specifically, grants will be awarded in three focus areas: increased outdoor access, improved genetics, and improved slaughter facilities. Priority will be given to project proposals with the greatest potential impact for improving the welfare of farm animals by affecting the largest number of animals and/or resulting in the most significant increase in welfare benefits; proposals which seek means to revolutionize practices that ultimately can be applied on other farms will receive partiality. Farms may submit a proposal for up to two different projects. See http://www.animalwelfareapproved.org for more information.
EIN: 135655952

1576
Arab American Institute Foundation
1600 K St., N.W., Ste. 601
Washington, DC 20006-2834 (202) 429-9210
Contact: Helen Samhan, Exec. Dir.
FAX: (202) 429-9214; URL: http://www.aaiusa.org/foundation

Foundation type: Public charity
Purpose: Internship funds, scholarships and research grants to students of Arab descent as well as to individuals working on behalf of the Arab-American community.
Publications: Application guidelines.
Financial data: Year ended 12/31/2011. Assets, $456,538 (M); Expenditures, $592,931; Total giving, $62,686; Grants to individuals, totaling $62,686.
Fields of interest: Community/economic development; Immigrants/refugees.
International interests: Algeria; Middle East; Morocco; Northern Africa.
Type of support: Internship funds; Awards/prizes; Graduate support; Undergraduate support.
Application information: Applications accepted. Application form required. Application form available on the grantmaker's web site.
  Deadline(s): Vary
  Additional information: Applications must include a resume.
Program descriptions:
  Helen Abbot Community Service Awards: Honors students and student organizations whose devotion to community service, selfless acts of care, and interest in improving the quality of life for others reflect the life of the Awards' namesake. Three awards are presented annually: two $1,000 prize one $500 grants to high school students with impressive community service records.
  Internships: The Institute offers paid internship positions to part-time students, graduate students and recent college graduates.
  Raymond Jallow Awards for Public Service: Awards are presented to two deserving candidates whose commitment to public service reflects the

life of the Awards' namesake. Two $500 grants are given annually to students and adults who are actively involved in or plan to participate in public service.
EIN: 521959306

1577
The Arc of the United States
1825 K St., Ste. 1200
Washington, DC 20006-1266 (202) 534-3700
Contact: Peter V. Berns, C.E.O.
FAX: (202) 534-3731; E-mail: info@thearc.org;
Toll-free tel.: (800) 433-5255; URL: http://www.thearc.org

Foundation type: Public charity
Purpose: Assistance for people with intellectual and developmental disabilities and their families.
Publications: Annual report; Financial statement.
Financial data: Year ended 12/31/2011. Assets, $9,693,717 (M); Expenditures, $7,266,256; Total giving, $1,510,726.
Fields of interest: Developmentally disabled, centers & services; Disabilities, people with.
Type of support: Grants for special needs.
Application information: Contact the organization for additional information.
EIN: 135642032

1578
Arch Development Corporation
1227 Good Hope Rd. S.E.
Washington, DC 20020-6907 (202) 889-5000
E-mail addresses for The Arch Artist-in-Residency Program: acavanaugh@archdc.org, bevans@archdc.org
FAX: (202) 889-5035; E-mail: info@archdc.org;
E-Mail For Duane Gautier: dgautier@archdc.org;
URL: http://www.archdevelopment.org/

Foundation type: Public charity
Purpose: Residencies in DC for emerging visual artists for a duration of one year.
Publications: Application guidelines.
Financial data: Year ended 09/30/2011. Assets, $1,799,865 (M); Expenditures, $960,336.
Fields of interest: Visual arts.
Type of support: Residencies.
Application information: Applications accepted. Application form required.
  Initial approach: Letter, telephone or e-mail
  Applicants should submit the following:
    1) Letter(s) of recommendation
    2) Work samples
    3) Resume
  Additional information: Application must also include a nonrefundable $25 application fee.
Program description:
  The Arch Artist in Residency Program: Resident artists are chosen by a Selection Panel consisting of Arch staff members, educators and arts organization representatives. The program offers free housing and workspace for eight weeks.
EIN: 521729252

1579
Armed Forces Foundation
16 N. Carolina Ave., S.E.
Washington, DC 20003-2617 (202) 547-4713
Contact: Patricia Driscoll, Pres. and Exec. Dir.
FAX: (202) 547-4712;
E-mail: info@armedforcesfoundation.org;
URL: http://www.armedforcesfoundation.org/

Foundation type: Public charity

Purpose: Financial assistance to Service members and their families facing financial hardship through injury and other service related situations.
Publications: Annual report; Financial statement; Newsletter.
Financial data: Year ended 12/31/2011. Assets, $594,557 (M); Expenditures, $5,844,718; Total giving, $4,485,426; Grants to individuals, totaling $4,470,826.
Fields of interest: Scholarships/financial aid; Family services; Military/veterans.
Type of support: Grants to individuals.
Application information: Applications accepted. Application form available on the grantmaker's web site.
  Initial approach: Application
  Deadline(s): None
  Additional information: Applicant must provide proof of service before assistance is provided.
Program description:
  C.W. Bill and Beverly Young Financial Assistance Fund: This program provides direct financial assistance to cover such expenses as utility bills, rent or mortgage payments (for civilian housing), car payments, childcare during illness or surgery/recovery, and car insurance or registration payments. The foundation also provides bereavement services to the families of service members dealing with a recent loss, of servicemen and servicewomen who have died.
EIN: 753070368

1580
Asian & Pacific Islander American Scholarship Fund
2025 M St. N.W., Ste. 610
Washington, DC 20036-5002 (202) 986-6892
Contact: Neil Horikoshi, Pres. and Exec. Dir.
FAX: (202) 530-0643; E-mail: info@apiasf.org; Toll Free Tel.: (877)-808-7032; Application address: APIASF, c/o Scholarship Program Administrators, Inc., P.O. Box 23737, Nashville, TN 37202-3737; URL: http://www.apiasf.org

Foundation type: Public charity
Purpose: Scholarships to outstanding Asian and Pacific Islander American students entering or enrolled in postsecondary educational programs.
Financial data: Year ended 06/30/2012. Assets, $6,415,678 (M); Expenditures, $13,953,827; Total giving, $12,033,556; Grants to individuals, totaling $12,033,556.
Fields of interest: Higher education; Asians/Pacific Islanders.
Type of support: Scholarships—to individuals.
Application information: Applications accepted. Application form required.
  Applicants should submit the following:
    1) Letter(s) of recommendation
    2) Essay
  Additional information: See web site for a complete listing of scholarship programs.
Program description:
  APIASF Scholarship: Scholarships are provided for students to pursue higher education. Eligible applicants must: be of Asian and/or Pacific Islander ethnicity; be a U.S. citizen, U.S. National, legal permanent resident, or a citizen of the Federated States of Micronesia, Republic of the Marshall Islands, or the Republic of Palau; be a first-time, incoming college student in the fall of the current year; be enrolled full-time in a two or four-year program at a U.S. accredited college or university in the U.S., Guam, American Samoa, and the Commonwealth of the Northern Mariana Islands for the upcoming school year (in the Freely Associated States, this includes the Community Colleges of the

Federated States of Micronesia, the Republic of Marshall Islands and the Republic of Palau); and have a cumulative, unweighted GPA of 2.7 or higher.
EIN: 571192973

1581

Asian Pacific American Bar Association Educational Fund

P.O. Box 2209
Washington, DC 20013-2209 (202) 210-0412
Application address: Phong Nguyen, Baker & Hostetler LLP, 1050 Connecticut Ave., N.W., Ste. 1100, Washington, DC 20036-5318,tel.: (202) 861-1610, e-mail: phong.aef@gmail.com
E-mail: aefboard@yahoo.com; URL: http://www.aefdc.org

Foundation type: Public charity
Purpose: Fellowships to law students engaged in community service internships serving the metropolitan Washington, D.C. community-at-large and/or the Asian Pacific American community.
Financial data: Year ended 12/31/2011. Assets, $187,315 (M); Expenditures, $31,712; Total giving, $29,500.
Fields of interest: Law school/education.
Type of support: Fellowships.
Application information: Applications accepted. Application form required.
Deadline(s): Apr. 30
Applicants should submit the following:
1) Transcripts
2) Essay
3) Resume
4) Letter(s) of recommendation
EIN: 521808563

1582

Asian Pacific American Institute for Congressional Studies, Inc.

1001 Connecticut Ave., N.W., Ste. 320
Washington, DC 20036-5504 (202) 296-9200
Contact: Floyd Mori, Pres. and C.E.O.
FAX: (202) 296-9236; E-mail: apaics@apaics.org;
E-Mail for Floyd Mori: fmori@apaics.org;
URL: http://www.apaics.org

Foundation type: Public charity
Purpose: Summer internships to college and graduate students with a commitment to the Asian Pacific American community and who are interested in the policy-making process in Washington, DC.
Financial data: Year ended 06/30/2012. Assets, $245,901 (M); Expenditures, $909,770; Total giving, $106,518; Grants to individuals, totaling $106,518.
Fields of interest: Public affairs, citizen participation; Asians/Pacific Islanders.
Type of support: Internship funds.
Application information: Applications accepted.
Additional information: Applicants are selected on the basis of their application materials, including answers to an essay question, transcripts, and descriptions of their experience and background.
EIN: 521917903

1583

The Aspen Institute

1 Dupont Cir., N.W., Ste. 700
Washington, DC 20036-1133 (202) 736-5800
Contact: Winnifred Levy, Comms. Mgr.
FAX: (202) 467-0790;
E-mail: info@aspeninstitute.org; Additional address

(Aspen office): 1000 N. Third St., Aspen, CO 81611-1330, tel.: (970) 925-7010, fax: (970) 925-4188; URL: http://www.aspeninstitute.org
Additional URL: http://www.nonprofitresearch.org

Foundation type: Public charity
Purpose: Assistance in the form of tuition, travel, lodging and meals to young leaders in the private, public, and not-for-profit sectors, to attend the foundation's Socrates Society seminars. General and doctoral dissertation research grants for study of nonprofit activities. Also provides limited undergraduate and graduate scholarships.
Publications: Application guidelines; Annual report; Newsletter.
Financial data: Year ended 12/31/2011. Assets, $169,299,444 (M); Expenditures, $73,880,949; Total giving, $3,754,471; Grants to individuals, totaling $75,150.
Fields of interest: Education; Nonprofit management; Management/technical assistance; Philanthropy/voluntarism; Young adults; Minorities.
Type of support: Fellowships; Research; Scholarships—to individuals.
Application information: Applications not accepted.
Additional information: Application should include brief project description, main research questions being addressed, populations being studied, methodology, data collection and analysis, schedule, budget, and additional materials required; See web site for further application and program information. Unsolicited requests for funds not considered or acknowledged.
Program descriptions:
Bezos Scholar Program: This prestigious, seven-day, all-expense-paid scholarship brings together twelve of the U.S.'s top public high school juniors each summer at the Aspen Ideas Festival. Scholars meet visionaries from around the globe, including international leaders, acclaimed thinkers, and creative artists, and engage in seminars, plenary sessions, and informal meetings. An educator from each student's school also will be awarded a full scholarship, thereby offering a unique leadership development opportunity for students and educators. Following their scholarship experience, teams will return home and apply for $1,000 School Award Grants to use in creating local idea festivals in their schools.
Socrates Society Seminar Scholarship: This program invites young leaders from a broad spectrum of organizations in the private, public, and nonprofit sectors to explore contemporary issues through moderated dialogue. By bringing together individuals with very different backgrounds, the program ensures a level of diversity that enriches the experience for all participants. The foundation offers both full and partial scholarship assistance, in the form of tuition, travel, lodging, and meals, to attend weekend-long seminars at the institute. Applicants who are seriously considered will be individuals whose wisdom and professional experience will add a significant dimension to dialogue. To be eligible for financial assistance, the following professional and personal attributes will be taken into account: ethnic and/or geographic diversity; leadership in such fields as academia, medicine, journalism, non-profit management, government office, and social service organizations; and financial need. For more information, contact katie.bartel@aspeninstitute.org.
William Randolph Hearst Endowed Fellowship for Minority Students: As a program under the auspices of the Program on Philanthropy and Social Innovation (PSI), this fellowship provides funding for minority undergraduate or graduate students to

intern for 12 to 15 weeks with the PSI. Through this program, PSI seeks to introduce a diverse group of students to issues relating to philanthropy, volunteerism, and nonprofit organizations. Ideal candidates are highly-motivated continuing graduate or undergraduate students from underrepresented communities of color, who have an excellent academic record, outstanding research skills, a background in the social sciences or humanities, excellent writing and research skills, and American citizenship. Fellowship funds will be approximately $2,000 for fall and spring interns, and approximately $4,000 for summer interns.
EIN: 840399006

1584

Association for Prevention Teaching and Research, Inc.

1001 Connecticut Ave. N.W., Ste. 610
Washington, DC 20036-5507 (202) 463-0550
Contact: Allison L. Lewis, Exec. Dir.
FAX: (202) 463-0555; E-mail: info@aptrweb.org;
Toll-free tel.:(866) 520-APTRE-Mail for Allison L. Lewis : all@aptrweb.org; URL: http://www.atpm.org

Foundation type: Public charity
Purpose: Research grants to APTR members. Also, scholarships to undergraduates and health professionals. Fellowships are also available for recent graduates and leading career professionals with a Master's or Doctoral degree in the fields of prevention and public health.
Publications: Application guidelines.
Financial data: Year ended 12/31/2011. Assets, $1,189,604 (M); Expenditures, $3,835,377; Total giving, $2,300,783; Grants to individuals, totaling $351,868.
Fields of interest: Public health school/education; Public health.
Type of support: Fellowships; Research; Undergraduate support.
Application information: Applications accepted.
Initial approach: Letter of intent
Deadline(s): Varies
Additional information: See web site for current application deadline/guidelines.
EIN: 521314223

1585

Association of American Geographers

(also known as AAG)
1710 16th St., N.W.
Washington, DC 20009-3198 (202) 234-1450
E-mail for application submission:
grantsawards@aag.org
FAX: (202) 234-2744; E-mail: gaia@aag.org;
URL: http://www.aag.org

Foundation type: Public charity
Purpose: Grants and awards for educational and research projects that advance geographic understanding, geographic literacy and geographic learning.
Publications: Application guidelines.
Financial data: Year ended 08/31/2011. Assets, $10,453,826 (M); Expenditures, $4,803,183; Total giving, $470,282; Grants to individuals, 433 grants totaling $344,130.
Fields of interest: Literature; Population studies.
Type of support: Research; Awards/prizes; Travel grants.
Application information: Applications accepted. Application form required. Application form available on the grantmaker's web site.
Deadline(s): Vary
Applicants should submit the following:

1) Proposal
2) Budget Information
3) Transcripts
4) Letter(s) of recommendation
5) Curriculum vitae
Additional information: See web site for additional application guidelines and program information.

Program descriptions:

AAG Dissertation Research Grants: Doctoral dissertation awards in the form of small grants of up to $500 are available to Ph.D. candidates of any geographic specialty. Eligible applicants must have been members for at least one year.

AAG-IGIF Student Paper Award: Grants of up to $200 will be awarded in recognition of outstanding student papers in any area of spatial analysis or geographic information science or systems that was given at a national or international conference or specialized meeting sponsored by a recognized professional organization. Eligible applicants must be full-time students who are currently registered in an undergraduate or graduate degree program at a duly accredited and recognized college, university, or other educational institution located within the U.S. Preference will be given to single-authored papers.

AAG-IGIF Student Travel Grant: This award of $500 is intended to support student travel to national and international symposia or specialized meetings sponsored by recognized professional organizations supporting activities, associated with specific aspects of geographic data analysis and handling and geographic information systems. Student travel expenses to be eligible for this award include reimbursement for the cost of transportation, accommodations, meals, and any other cost or expense reasonably related to travel for attendance at such meetings. Eligible applicants must be full-time students who are currently registered in an undergraduate or graduate degree program providing either a degree or explicit specialization in some area of applied spatial data analysis or GIS study at a duly accredited and recognized college, university, or other educational institution located within the U.S.

Anne U. White Fund: Two grants of $1,500 each are available for individuals to engage in useful field studies. Eligible applicants must be members in good standing of the association for at least two years.

Darrel Hess Community College Geography Scholarship: Two $1,000 scholarships are available to students from community colleges, junior colleges, city colleges, or similar two-year educational institutions who will be transferring as geography major to four-year colleges and universities. Eligible applicants must have completed at least two transfer courses in geography and plan to transfer to a four-year institution as a geography major during the coming academic year.

E. Willard and Ruby S. Miller Award in Geography: This $1,000 award recognizes members of the association who have made truly outstanding contributions to the geographic field due to their special competence in teaching or researching.

Enrichment Funds for the Annual Meeting of the AAG: Awards ranging from $50 to $500 are available to support participation of distinguished non-geographers in the annual meeting of the association. This award is intended to enrich the meeting by allowing individuals who would otherwise not participate to contribute in a meaningful way to the meeting and field of geography. Funds may be used for reimbursement of lodging, meeting registration fees, subsistence, and travel.

George and Viola Hoffman Award: This award, ranging from $350 to $500, will be awarded to student research that leads to a master's thesis or doctoral dissertation on a geographical subject in Eastern Europe (including the countries of east-central and southeast Europe from Poland south to Romania, Bulgaria, and the successor states of the former Yugoslavia). Topics may be historical or contemporary, systematic or original, limited to a small area or comparative.

Globe Book Award for Public Understanding of Geography: A $1,000 award is available to the authors of a book that conveys most powerfully the nature and importance of geography to the non-academic world. Books must be written or co-authored by a geographer.

John Brinckerhoff Jackson Prize: This award of $1,000 is intended to encourage and reward American geographers who write books about the United States which convey the insights of professional geography in language that is interesting and attractive to a lay audience.

Mel Marcus Fund for Physical Geography: This award grants up to $2,000 to faculty applicants to support travel and logistical costs of including students in field research in physical geography, with the intent of fostering personally-formative participation by students in field-based physical geography research in challenging outdoor environments. Research sites may include both national and international locations. Grant funds may be used to cover travel to the research site, as well as expenses related to the logistical support of the student, such as food, fuel, and lodging; the grant does not cover student stipends.

Meridian Book Award for Outstanding Scholarly Work in Geography: This award of $1,000 will be presented to the author(s) of a book that makes an unusually important contribution to advancing the science and art of geography.

Research Grants: Grants of up to $1,000 are available to support research and fieldwork. Eligible applicants must be members of the association for at least two years. Grants are intended to supplement direct expenses of research; grants do not cover salary or overhead costs.

William L. Garrison Award for Best Dissertation in Computational Geography: This bi-annual award gives a $3,500 prize to support innovative research into the computational aspects of geographic science. The award is intended to arouse a more general and deeper understanding of the important role that advanced computation can play in solving the complex problems of space-time analysis that are at the core of geographic science. Proposals should demonstrate high standards of scholarship, and will be accepted from candidates associated with any institution of higher education, anywhere in the world, that is authorized to award the doctorate.
EIN: 530207414

1586
Association of Performing Arts Presenters
1211 Connecticut Ave., N.W., Ste. 200
Washington, DC 20036-2716 (202) 833-2787
Contact: Sandra Gibson, Pres., C.E.O., and Secy.
FAX: (202) 833-1543;
E-mail: info@artspresenters.org; URL: http://www.artspresenters.org/

Foundation type: Public charity
Purpose: Grants to college and university professional performing arts presenters.
Publications: Application guidelines; Annual report; Newsletter.

Financial data: Year ended 06/30/2011. Assets, $4,194,359 (M); Expenditures, $5,104,584; Total giving, $1,542,164. Grants to individuals amount not specified.
Fields of interest: Performing arts.
Type of support: Grants to individuals; Travel grants.
Application information: Applications accepted. Application form available on the grantmaker's web site.
Send request by: Online
Deadline(s): Nov. 16 for Cultural Exchange Fund
Final notification: Recipients notified Dec. for Cultural Exchange Fund
Additional information: See web site for additional guidelines.

Program description:
Cultural Exchange Fund: The organization awards travel subsidies to individual presenting professionals including agents, managers and producers, presenting organizations and to groups of presenting professionals traveling to see the work of artists and companies, or to develop and advance projects with international artists and their collaborators. All applicants must be active members of the Association of Performing Arts Presenters. The maximum amount awarded per individual organization, inclusive of travel costs and per diem, is $2,000. Group travel subsidies will be awarded only to groups of three or more individuals from different member presenting organizations. The maximum award for a group is $10,000, with not more than $2,000 awarded per organization in the group.
EIN: 391131995

1587
Association of Schools of Public Health, Inc.
(also known as ASPH)
1900 M St., N.W., Ste. 710
Washington, DC 20036-3504 (202) 296-1099
FAX: (202) 296-1252; E-mail: info@asph.org;
URL: http://www.asph.org

Foundation type: Public charity
Purpose: Fellowships awarded to early-career public health professionals from accredited graduate schools of public health to further their professional development training.
Financial data: Year ended 09/30/2012. Assets, $5,787,282 (M); Expenditures, $15,621,821; Total giving, $8,911,373; Grants to individuals, totaling $2,727,480.
Fields of interest: Public health.
Type of support: Fellowships.
Application information: Applications accepted. Interview required.
Send request by: Online or mail
Deadline(s): Feb.
Applicants should submit the following:
1) Transcripts
2) Letter(s) of recommendation
3) Essay
EIN: 560734192

1588
Atlas Economic Research Foundation
1201 L St., N.W.
Washington, DC 20005-4027 (202) 449-8449
Contact: Abby Albright, Mktg. and Communications Mgr.
FAX: (202) 280-1259;
E-mail: abby.albright@atlasnetwork.org;
URL: http://atlasnetwork.org/

Foundation type: Public charity
Purpose: Fellowships to support young scholars making contributions to economics, history, and other fields related to the understanding of the workings of a free and prosperous society.
Publications: Application guidelines; Newsletter.
Financial data: Year ended 12/31/2011. Assets, $3,338,042 (M); Expenditures, $8,167,015; Total giving, $3,238,239; Grants to individuals, totaling $217,962.
Fields of interest: Economic development; Business/industry; Economics.
Type of support: Fellowships; Foreign applicants; Awards/prizes.
Application information: Contact foundation for additional guidelines.
Program description:
  Freda Utley Prize for Advancing Liberty: This annual prize will provide a $10,000 award to a single winner who demonstrates excellence in reaching a broad audience or having a substantial impact on opinion-makers, so that concepts relating to freedom become better understood.
EIN: 942763845

1589
Atlas Service Corps
1825 K St., N.W., Ste. 210
Washington, DC 20006 (202) 263-4545
Contact: Scott Beale, C.E.O.
E-mail: info@atlascorps.org; URL: http://www.atlascorps.org

Foundation type: Public charity
Purpose: Fellowships overseas to the best rising nonprofit leaders in Colombia, India, and the US.
Publications: Application guidelines; Annual report; Newsletter.
Financial data: Year ended 12/31/2011. Assets, $208,751 (M); Expenditures, $1,313,194; Total giving, $251,461; Grants to individuals, totaling $247,111.
Fields of interest: International exchange; International affairs; Leadership development.
Type of support: Fellowships; Exchange programs; Foreign applicants.
Application information:
  Initial approach: Letter
  Deadline(s): Jan. 1
Program description:
  Fellows Program: This program selects fellows to spend one year volunteering at a U.S. nonprofit organization. Fellows will receive one month of advanced training (two weeks in their home country and two weeks in the U.S.), a living stipend and health care during their training and fellowship, and a $2,500 stipend after returning home and working in the citizen sector in their home country for one year. Applicants must be citizens of Colombia or India (for fellowships to the United States); or from the United States (for fellowships to Bogota, Colombia). Eligible participants must be emerging leaders with at least four years of experience working in the citizen sector, and must be able to speak, write, and communicate effectively in English.
EIN: 760834735

1590
Ayuda, Inc.
6925 B Willow St., N.W.
Washington, DC 20012 (202) 387-4848
Contact: Jaime Farrant, Exec. Dir.
E-mail: mvivero@ayudainc.org; URL: http://www.ayudainc.org

Foundation type: Public charity
Purpose: Assistance to low-income Spanish speaking and foreign-born individuals in the metropolitan Washington, D.C. area with legal and social services, domestic violence and other special needs.
Publications: Annual report; Financial statement.
Financial data: Year ended 09/30/2011. Assets, $176,174 (M); Expenditures, $1,776,339; Total giving, $120,647; Grants to individuals, totaling $120,647.
Fields of interest: Human services; Civil/human rights, immigrants; Hispanics/Latinos.
Type of support: Grants for special needs.
Application information:
  Initial approach: Telephone
  Additional information: Contact the organization for assistance.
EIN: 520971440

1591
Alexander Graham Bell Association for the Deaf and Hard of Hearing
3417 Volta Pl., N.W.
Washington, DC 20007-2737 (202) 337-5220
FAX: (202) 337-8314; E-mail: info@agbell.org; TTY: (202) 337-5221; URL: http://www.agbell.org

Foundation type: Public charity
Purpose: Financial assistance to parents of infants and pre-school children, school-aged children, arts and sciences students and college-age students who have moderate to profound hearing loss.
Publications: Application guidelines.
Financial data: Year ended 12/31/2011. Assets, $8,125,058 (M); Expenditures, $3,316,658; Total giving, $420,950; Grants to individuals, totaling $408,186.
Fields of interest: Education; Ear, nose & throat diseases; Deaf/hearing impaired.
Type of support: Grants to individuals; Scholarships—to individuals.
Application information: Applications accepted. Application form required. Application form available on the grantmaker's web site.
  Deadline(s): Vary
  Additional information: See web site for additional guidelines.
Program descriptions:
  Arts and Sciences Awards: The program is available to students who are deaf and hard of hearing who are in grades one through twelve to participate in after-school, weekend or summer programs focused on developing skills in the arts or sciences. Programs can be offered through museums, nature centers, art or music centers, zoological parks, space and science camps, dance and theater studios, martial arts studios or any other program with a focus on the arts or sciences. Awards cannot be used for programs that offer academic credit, travel or study abroad, recreational summer camps, sports camps or sports, including figure skating or gymnastics.
  Parent-Infant Financial Aid Program: The program is for families of infants and toddlers ages birth through three who have been diagnosed with a moderately-severe to profound hearing loss who are in pursuit of spoken language outcome for their child. Awards are intended to assist with expenses for services such as auditory support services, speech-language therapy, tuition etc. Families should be committed to a listening and spoken language outcome for their child or children with hearing loss. The program is for individuals only. Awards are made once a year ranging from $500 to

$1,200 and recipients reside in 20 states and Canada.
EIN: 530196644

1592
Best Friends Foundation
5335 Wisconsin Ave., N.W., Ste., 440
Washington, DC 20015-2054 (202) 478-9677
Contact: Elayne G. Bennett, Pres.
FAX: (202) 478-9678;
E-mail: ebennett@bestfriendsfoundation.org;
URL: http://www.bestfriendsfoundation.org

Foundation type: Public charity
Purpose: Undergraduate scholarships to girls who have been members of the foundation's Diamond Girls Program for at least two years of elementary or middle school.
Financial data: Year ended 07/31/2011. Assets, $334,841 (M); Expenditures, $835,100; Total giving, $20,000; Grants to individuals, totaling $20,000.
Fields of interest: Ethics; Girls.
Type of support: Precollege support; Undergraduate support.
Application information: Applications accepted.
  Deadline(s): Varies
  Additional information: Applicants should abstain from pre-marital sex, alcohol, and drugs. Contact local affiliate for complete application information.
EIN: 521844471

1593
The Black Student Fund
3636 16th St., N.W., 4th Fl.
Washington, DC 20010-4116 (202) 387-1414
Contact: Leroy Nesbitt, Exec. Dir.
E-mail: mail@blackstudentfund.org; Additional tel.: (703) 506-3552; URL: http://www.blackstudentfund.org

Foundation type: Public charity
Purpose: Scholarships to African American pre-K-12th grade students residing in the Washington, DC, metropolitan area.
Publications: Annual report; Informational brochure; Newsletter.
Financial data: Year ended 06/30/2012. Assets, $199,347 (M); Expenditures, $603,039; Total giving, $33,062; Grants to individuals, totaling $33,062.
Fields of interest: Elementary/secondary education; Early childhood education; African Americans/Blacks.
Type of support: Scholarships—to individuals.
Application information: Applications accepted.
  Initial approach: Application
  Deadline(s): Jan. 13 for new applicants, Dec. 15 for current applicants for Financial Aid Scholarships
  Additional information: Application should include transcripts. Applicants must also apply for financial aid from their school. Contact fund for current application guidelines.
Program description:
  Financial Aid Scholarships: The fund awards tuition grants, in conjunction with fund member schools, to black children of modest financial means attending academically-challenging institutions, grades pre-kindergarten through 12, throughout the country. Students may apply for aid if they attend, are applying to, or have been accepted into a fund member school (listed on the fund's web site), and must also submit financial aid

applications to applicant schools. Applicants must accurately demonstrate financial need.
EIN: 526053597

1594
Herb Block Foundation
1730 M St. N.W., Ste. 901
Washington, DC   20036-4509   (202) 223-8801
Contact: Sarah Armstrong Alex, C.O.O. and Exec. Dir.
Scholarship address: The Herb Block Scholarship, ISTS, 1321 Murfreesboro Rd., Ste. 800, Nashville, TN 37217, tel.: (855) 670-4787, e-mail: contactus@applyists.com
FAX: (202) 223-8804; E-mail: info@herbblock.org; URL: http://www.herbblockfoundation.org/

Foundation type: Independent foundation
Purpose: Scholarships to high school graduates, first-year college students, and adult learners, who are permanent residents of Washington, DC, Prince George's or Montgomery Counties in MD, Arlington or Fairfax Counties, or the cities of Falls Church or Alexandria in VA who wish to further their education. Prizes to cartoonists for excellence in editorial cartooning.
Publications: Application guidelines; Grants list; Informational brochure; Program policy statement; Program policy statement (including application guidelines).
Financial data: Year ended 09/30/2013. Assets, $53,421,175 (M); Expenditures, $2,875,910; Total giving, $1,554,500.
Fields of interest: Print publishing; Higher education.
Type of support: Scholarships—to individuals; Awards/prizes.
Application information: Applications accepted. Application form required. Application form available on the grantmaker's web site.
  Send request by: Mail
  Deadline(s): July 7 for Fall semester, Nov. 10 for Spring semester for scholarships, Feb. 1 for Herblock Prize
  Applicants should submit the following:
    1) SAR
    2) FAFSA
    3) Letter(s) of recommendation
    4) Transcripts
  Additional information: Applicants must be planning part-time attendance with at least six credits per semester or full-time attendance at one of the foundation's eligible community colleges.
Program descriptions:
  Herblock Prize & Lecture: The foundation awards this prize to honor excellence in editorial cartooning. The prize was created in 2004 to encourage editorial cartooning as an essential tool for preserving the rights of the American people through freedom of speech and the right of expression. The prize is presented each spring at the Library of Congress. The winner receives a tax free $15,000 cash prize as well as a sterling silver Tiffany trophy. The contest is open to any newspaper, magazine, wire service or syndicate cartoonist for editorial or political cartoons published in a daily or weekly newspaper or magazine published in the U.S. or its territories. Cartoons appearing in U.S. editions of foreign publications are also eligible. The foundation will also accept animated cartoons for consideration. See foundation web site for specific entry guidelines and form.
  Scholarship Program: This program is designed to serve high school graduates, first-year college students or those who went to work after high

school, and now wish to resume their studies. The scholarship is last dollar valued at up to $8,000 per academic year, not to exceed $16,000 over the life of the scholarship. The award covers tuition, mandatory fees, books, and supplies, as well as limited transportation and on-campus childcare expenses.
EIN: 260008276

1595
B'nai B'rith
2020 K St., N.W., 7th Fl.
Washington, DC   20006-1828   (202) 857-6600
URL: http://www.bnaibrith.org

Foundation type: Public charity
Purpose: Research grants, awards, and scholarships to individuals in the greater New York, NY, area.
Financial data: Year ended 06/30/2011. Assets, $5,036,031 (M); Expenditures, $13,323,298; Total giving, $2,195,669; Grants to individuals, 35 grants totaling $75,872. Subtotal for scholarships—to individuals: 36 grants totaling $81,872.
Type of support: Research.
Application information: Contact foundation for current application deadline/guidelines.
EIN: 530179971

1596
The Beau Bogan Foundation
P.O. Box 15178
Washington, DC   20003-0178   (202) 543-5545
Contact: Steve A. Wimer

Foundation type: Independent foundation
Purpose: Fellowships to individuals in the arts.
Financial data: Year ended 12/31/2011. Assets, $23,205 (M); Expenditures, $5,614; Total giving, $5,000; Grants to individuals, 2 grants totaling $3,000 (high: $2,000, low: $1,000).
Type of support: Fellowships.
Application information:
  Applicants should submit the following:
    1) Resume
    2) Budget Information
EIN: 650126326

1597
Broadcast Education Association
1771 N St., N.W.
Washington, DC   20036-2891   (202) 429-5355
Contact: Heather Birks, Exec. Dir.
Application address for individuals: 344 Moore Hall, Central Michigan University, Mt. Pleasant, MI, 48859; tel.: (989) 774-7279 on Mon., Wed., Fri.; toll-free tel.: (888) 380-7222; additional URL: http://www.nab.org
FAX: (202) 775-2981; E-mail: hbirks@nab.org; URL: http://www.beaweb.org

Foundation type: Public charity
Purpose: Scholarships to students planning careers in broadcasting.
Publications: Application guidelines; Grants list.
Financial data: Year ended 12/31/2011. Assets, $1,169,309 (M); Expenditures, $633,401; Total giving, $27,000; Grants to individuals, totaling $27,000.
Fields of interest: Media/communications; Television; Radio.
Type of support: Graduate support; Undergraduate support.

Application information: Application form required. Application form available on the grantmaker's web site.
  Send request by: Mail
  Copies of proposal: 4
  Deadline(s): Oct. 12
  Applicants should submit the following:
    1) Transcripts
    2) Letter(s) of recommendation
  Additional information: Application should also include waiver sheet and NAB station or employment internship affidavit.
Program descriptions:
  Abe Voron Scholarships: Awards two scholarships of $5,000 each to individuals interested in pursuing a career in radio.
  Alexander M. Tanger Scholarship: Awards one $5,000 scholarship to a graduate student for study in any area of broadcasting.
  Helen J. Sioussat/Fay Wells Scholarship: Two scholarships of $1,250 each to study any area of broadcasting.
  John Bayliss Scholarship: One scholarship of $1,500 is awarded to students working towards a career in radio.
  Richard Eaton Foundation Award: One scholarship of $1,500 is awarded to students studying any area of broadcasting.
  Two-Year/Community College BEA Award: Awards two $1,500 scholarships for study at a BEA two-year/community college, or a BEA 4-year institution by a graduate of a BEA 2-year campus.
  Vincent T. Wasilewski Scholarship: Awards one $2,500 scholarship to a student interested in a career in radio.
  Walter S. Patterson Scholarship: Awards two $1,750 scholarships for study towards a career in radio.
EIN: 526057288

1598
Capital Partners for Education, Inc.
1413 K St. N.W., 2nd Fl.
Washington, DC   20005-3405   (202) 682-6020
Contact: Khari Brown, Exec. Dir.
FAX: (202) 682-6026; E-mail: info@cpfe.org; E-mail for Khari Brown: khari@cpfe.org; URL: http://www.cpfe.org

Foundation type: Public charity
Purpose: Scholarships to selected high school students in the metropolitan DC, area pursuing higher education.
Publications: Annual report; Newsletter.
Financial data: Year ended 06/30/2012. Assets, $1,410,034 (M); Expenditures, $1,170,850; Total giving, $306,108; Grants to individuals, totaling $306,108.
Fields of interest: Vocational education, post-secondary; Higher education.
Type of support: Scholarships—to individuals.
Application information: Applications accepted. Application form required. Application form available on the grantmaker's web site.
  Send request by: Mail
  Deadline(s): Mar. 8 for Private School Students, Apr. 19 for Charter School Students
  Final notification: Applicants notified in June
  Applicants should submit the following:
    1) Transcripts
    2) Letter(s) of recommendation
    3) Financial information
  Additional information: See web site for additional application guidelines.
Program description:
  Scholarships: Eligible students receive annual scholarships of up to $4,500 per year to help pay

the way at your new private high school or $1,000 per year in college scholarships if you attend one of the charter school partners. CPE provides an on-going array of programs designed to help the students hone their academic skills, prepare for the college application process, and develop other important career proficiencies such as basic financial literacy, resume writing and interviewing skills.

EIN: 521832497

1599
Center for Nonprofit Advancement

1666 K St. N.W., Ste. 440
Washington, DC 20006-1242   (202) 457-0540
Contact: George Jones, Chair.
FAX: (202) 457-0549;
E-mail: info@nonprofitadvancement.org;
URL: http://www.nonprofitadvancement.org

Foundation type: Public charity
Purpose: Awards to individuals working in the nonprofit sector, to continue their professional education development.
Publications: Annual report; Financial statement.
Financial data: Year ended 12/31/2011. Assets, $347,994 (M); Expenditures, $1,262,045; Total giving, $51,760; Grants to individuals, totaling $21,760.
Fields of interest: Philanthropy/voluntarism.
Type of support: Grants to individuals.
Application information: See web site for additional guidelines.
Program description:
Gelman, Rosenberg, and Freedman Excel Award: These awards recognize and spotlight outstanding leadership among Washington-are nonprofit chief executives, especially in the areas of innovation, motivation, community-building, ethical integrity, and strategic leadership. Up to three people will each receive a $5,000 professional development account to be used for the individual's continued professional development; in addition, each recipient's organization will also receive a $2,000 grant to support the professional development of the organization's staff.
EIN: 521139669

1600
Children's Defense Fund

25 E. St., N.W.
Washington, DC 20001-1522   (202) 628-8787
Contact: Marian Wright Edelman, Pres.
FAX: (202) 662-3570;
E-mail: cdfinfo@childrensdefense.org; Toll-free tel.: (800) 233-1200; URL: http://www.childrensdefense.org

Foundation type: Public charity
Purpose: Scholarships to young people residing in VA, MD and Washington DC who are overcoming tremendous obstacles in their lives while displaying academic excellence and giving back to their communities.
Publications: Application guidelines.
Financial data: Year ended 12/31/2011. Assets, $35,079,240 (M); Expenditures, $20,472,958; Total giving, $1,719,675; Grants to individuals, totaling $275,516.
Fields of interest: Children.
Type of support: Technical education support; Undergraduate support.
Application information: Applications accepted. Application form required. Application form available on the grantmaker's web site.
Deadline(s): Vary

Applicants should submit the following:
  1) Essay
  2) Transcripts
  3) Letter(s) of recommendation
Program descriptions:
Beat the Odds Scholarships: This scholarship program works to affirm the success of young people who are overcoming tremendous obstacles in their lives while working hard, demonstrating academic excellence, and giving back to their communities. Recipients continue to be leaders in their schools and mentors to those in need in the community, while developing academic skills necessary to pursue a college education. Nominees for the scholarship must currently be a junior enrolled in the public/alternative school system of Washington, DC; Fairfax, Arlington, or Alexandria counties in Virginia; or Montgomery or Prince George's counties in Maryland who, following graduation, will attend college, technical, or vocational training.
Joshua and Deborah Generation Program: The Joshua & Deborah Program encourages young religious leaders in the movement for children. Scholarships are available to participants of the program who demonstrate both financial need and commitment to the goals of the program.
EIN: 520895622

1601
Christ Child Society, Inc.

5101 Wisconsin Ave., N.W., Ste. 304
Washington, DC 20016-4138   (202) 966-9250
Contact: Kathleen Curtin, Exec. Dir.
FAX: (202) 966-2880;
E-mail: info@christchilddc.org; E-mail For Kathleen Curtin: kcurtin@christchilddc.org; URL: http://www.christchilddc.org

Foundation type: Public charity
Purpose: Scholarships for children with physical and mental disabilities to attend a variety of local day camps in the Washington, DC metropolitan area. School uniform assistance to children in need in the Washington, DC area attending Catholic schools.
Publications: Application guidelines.
Financial data: Year ended 06/30/2012. Assets, $11,990,959 (M); Expenditures, $1,779,793; Total giving, $20,425; Grants to individuals, totaling $20,425.
Fields of interest: Education; Camps; Children; Physically disabled.
Type of support: Scholarships—to individuals; Grants for special needs.
Application information: Applications accepted.
Deadline(s): None
Additional information: Checks are made payable to either the camp the student attends or to the uniform vendors.
Program descriptions:
Mary Virginia Merrick Camp Scholarship: The program provides scholarships only to those with mental or physical disabilities to attend a variety of local day camps.
School Uniform Assistance Program: This program provides assistance of up to $160 per student to children attending Catholic schools in the Washington, DC area (St. Thomas More, Sacred Heart, Washington Middle School for Girls, St. Francis Xavier, Cristo Rey, St. Anthony's, St. Michael the Archangel, and St. Augustine), to be used toward the purchase of uniforms. Assistance is awarded on a first-come, first-serve basis. Priority is given to students served by the society's School Counseling Program.
EIN: 530207408

1602
CIC, Inc.

1049 30th St. N.W.
Washington, DC 20007   (202) 333-9095
Contact: David Yao, Secy.

Foundation type: Independent foundation
Purpose: Scholarships primarily to members of the US military in Washington, DC.
Financial data: Year ended 08/31/2012. Assets, $1,648,975 (M); Expenditures, $188,698; Total giving, $43,700; Grants to individuals, 3 grants totaling $5,000 (high: $2,000, low: $1,500).
Fields of interest: Education.
Type of support: Scholarships—to individuals.
Application information: Applications not accepted.
Additional information: Unsolicited requests for funds not considered or acknowledged.
EIN: 521654193

1603
Citizens Development Corps, Inc.

1030 15th St., N.W.,
Washington, DC 20005-2421   (202) 872-0933
Contact: Michael A. Levett, C.E.O.
FAX: (202) 872-0923; E-mail: info@cdc.org;
Toll-free tel.: (800) 394-1945; URL: http://www.cdc.org

Foundation type: Public charity
Purpose: Stipends to individuals for work in the international area to encourage and assist the development of viable market economics and democratic political systems in emerging and transitioning economies.
Publications: Newsletter.
Financial data: Year ended 09/30/2011. Assets, $1,202,602 (M); Expenditures, $6,558,651.
Fields of interest: Economic development.
Type of support: Stipends.
Application information: Applications not accepted.
Additional information: Unsolicited requests for funding not considered or acknowledged.
EIN: 521706852

1604
Communications Workers of America Disaster Relief Fund

501 3rd St., N.W.
Washington, DC 20001-2797   (202) 797-8700
URL: http://www.cwa-union.org

Foundation type: Public charity
Purpose: Scholarships to CWA members and their spouses, children and grandchildren, including those of retired or deceased members. Emergency grants to Communication Workers of America members and their families who are victims of declared federal, state, or local disasters.
Financial data: Year ended 12/31/2011. Assets, $25,968 (M); Expenditures, $48,786.
Fields of interest: Higher education; Labor unions/organizations; Safety/disasters.
Type of support: Emergency funds; Scholarships—to individuals; Undergraduate support; Grants for special needs.
Application information: Applications accepted. Application form required. Application form available on the grantmaker's web site.
Initial approach: Letter or telephone
Send request by: Online for Scholarship
Deadline(s): Apr. 30 for Scholarship
Additional information: See web site for additional guidelines.

Program description:

CWA Joe Beirne Foundation Scholarship Program: Thirty two-year scholarships, to be paid at the rate of $3,000 annually, are awarded each year to applicants from the U.S.A. and Canada. A second-year award is contingent on academic accomplishment of the first year. Winners are chosen by lottery drawing and only winners will be notified. CWA members, their spouses, children and grandchildren (including dependents of laid-off, retired or deceased CWA members) may apply. Applicants must be high school graduates or at least high school students who will graduate during the year in which they apply. Undergraduate and graduate students returning to schooling may also apply. Prior winners may not reapply.

EIN: 522128973

1605
The Community Foundation for the National Capital Region

(formerly The Foundation for the National Capital Region)
1201 15th St. N.W., Ste. 420
Washington, DC 20005-2842 (202) 955-5890
Contact: Terri Lee Freeman, Pres.
FAX: (202) 955-8084; E-mail: tfreeman@cfncr.org;
URL: http://www.thecommunityfoundation.org

Foundation type: Community foundation
Purpose: Scholarships to residents of the metropolitan Washington, DC, area, and to students from China. Awards to recognize individuals of creativity, vision, and leadership who work in a community in the Washington, D.C., metropolitan area.
Publications: Application guidelines; Annual report; Financial statement; Informational brochure; Newsletter; Program policy statement.
Financial data: Year ended 03/31/2013. Assets, $334,979,789 (M); Expenditures, $101,071,503; Total giving, $95,397,756.
Fields of interest: Arts; Public education; Engineering school/education; Scholarships/financial aid; Education; Government agencies; Minorities; Asians/Pacific Islanders; Women.
Type of support: Internship funds; Employee-related scholarships; Scholarships—to individuals; Support to graduates or students of specific schools; Awards/grants by nomination only; Foreign applicants; Awards/prizes; Employee-related welfare; Graduate support; Undergraduate support; Grants for special needs.
Application information: Applications accepted.

Additional information: Contact foundation staff member identified on web site for each scholarship program.

Program descriptions:

Linowes Leadership Award: This award recognizes individuals of creativity, vision, and leadership to work in a community in the Washington D.C., metropolitan area and who are generally unrecognized. The program seeks nominations of leaders of all ages who are not just exceptional volunteers or employees but who demonstrate initiative and contribute above and beyond their community work. Nominated individuals must live and work in the greater Washington metropolitan area. Three awards recipients will each receive an unrestricted, direct grant of $2,000 and an additional $3,000 to be contributed to the local nonprofit community organization of his/her choice. Self-nominations are not accepted. See web site for additional information.

Scholarships: The foundation administers several scholarships funds to students for higher education. Each scholarship has its own unique application guidelines and eligibility criteria, including attendance at a specific high school, particular fields of study and country of origin. See web site for additional information.

EIN: 237343119

1606
Community Services Agency of the Metropolitan Washington Council

888 16th St., N.W.
Washington, DC 20006-4103 (202) 974-8150
Contact: Joslyn Williams, Pres.
FAX: (202) 974-8152;
E-mail: streetheat@dclabor.org; E-mail for Joslyn Williams: jwilliam@dclabor.org; tel. for Joslyn Williams: (202) 974-8155; URL: http://www.dclabor.org/ht/d/ProgramDetails/i/246/pid/46784

Foundation type: Public charity
Purpose: Emergency funds and lay-off preparation and support to eligible workers and members of the AFL-CIO and their families.
Financial data: Year ended 06/30/2012. Assets, $463,814 (M); Expenditures, $672,484; Total giving, $95,577; Grants to individuals, totaling $95,004.
Fields of interest: Labor unions/organizations.
Type of support: Emergency funds.
Application information: Applications not accepted.
EIN: 521718506

1607
Congressional Hispanic Caucus Institute

300 M St., S.E., 5th Fl., Ste. 510
Washington, DC 20003 (202) 543-1771
Contact: Esther Aguilera, Pres. and C.E.O.
FAX: (202) 546-2143; E-mail: lcrowe@chci.org;
Toll-free tel.: (800) EXCEL-DC; E-Mail for Esther Aguilera: eaguilera@chci.org; URL: http://www.chci.org/

Foundation type: Public charity
Purpose: Internships, including transportation reimbursement, housing, and stipends, to promising Latino undergraduate students. The Caucus also provides scholarships to undergraduate and graduate Latinos as well as fellowships to allow promising Latinos to participate in public service.
Publications: Application guidelines.
Financial data: Year ended 12/31/2011. Assets, $9,035,645 (M); Expenditures, $6,984,214; Total giving, $385,401; Grants to individuals, totaling $385,401.
Fields of interest: Government/public administration; Leadership development; Public affairs; Hispanics/Latinos.
Type of support: Fellowships; Internship funds; Graduate support; Undergraduate support; Travel grants; Stipends.
Application information: Applications accepted. Application form required. Application form available on the grantmaker's web site.

Deadline(s): Jan. 31 for internships; Feb. 28 for fellowship; Apr. 16 for scholarships
Applicants should submit the following:
  1) Transcripts
  2) Letter(s) of recommendation
  3) SAR
  4) Resume
  5) Financial information
  6) Essay

Program descriptions:

CHCI Fellowship Program: The mission of the fellowship is to offer Latino youth the support, training, and resources needed to ultimately become the effective leaders of tomorrow. Every year, the program brings together a pool of educated and civic-minded young individuals in an effort to shape them into the next generation of Latino leaders. The institute provides participants with domestic round-trip transportation to Washington, DC; health insurance; and a gross monthly stipend of $2,200 to help cover housing and local expenses (fellows with a graduate degree receive a $2,600 monthly stipend)

Congressional Internship Program: This program provides college students with Congressional placements on Capitol Hill for a summer period of eight weeks (June to August) and a winter period of twelve weeks (January to April) to learn first-hand about the U.S.'s legislative processes. Housing, travel, and a $2,500 stipend are provided for summer interns, or a $3,750 stipend for spring and fall interns.

Scholarship Awards: This scholarship opportunity is afforded to Latino students who have a history of performing public service-oriented activities in their communities and who plan to continue contributing in the future. There is no GPA or major requirement. Students with excellent leadership potential are encouraged to apply. Recipients will receive a one-time scholarship of: $5,000 to attend a graduate-level academic institution; $2,500 to attend a four-year academic institution; or $1,000 to attend a community college or AA/AS granting institution. The institute will be responsible for managing the disbursement of the scholarship monies to the recipients. In a two-fold effort to monitor the progress of scholarship recipients and promote college retention, total scholarship monies will be equally divided and distributed on a yearly basis as long as recipients maintain good academic standing (i.e., if the scholarship is received as an entering freshman, the $2,500 award will be distributed in four equal installments of $625 per year). Scholarship awards are designed to cover tuition, room and board, textbooks, and other educational expenses associated with college enrollment.
EIN: 521114225

1608
Corcoran Gallery of Art

500 17th St., N.W.
Washington, DC 20006-4804 (202) 639-1700
E-mail: directorsoffice@corcoran.org; URL: http://www.corcoran.org

Foundation type: Public charity
Purpose: Constance Bergfors Travel Research Prize to fund travel and research on an independent creative and/or research project developed by an enrolled graduate student in one of the Corcoran Masters programs. The stipend is $5,000.
Financial data: Year ended 06/30/2012. Assets, $51,683,924 (M); Expenditures, $32,251,291; Total giving, $4,971,310; Grants to individuals, totaling $4,971,310.
Fields of interest: Museums (art).
Type of support: Travel awards.
Application information:
Applicants should submit the following:
  1) Proposal
Additional information: Submit proposal with research area to provostoffice@corcoran.org.
EIN: 530196641

1609
Cornerstone, Inc.

1400 20th St., N.W., Ste. G-3
Washington, DC 20036-5963 (202) 347-7808
Contact: Nancy Liebermann, Pres.; Ellen Ward, Prg. Mgr.
FAX: (202) 347-7803;
E-mail: info@cornerstonedc.org; E-mail for Nancy Liebermann: liebermann@cornerstonedc.org;
E-mail for Ellen Ward: ward@cornerstonedc.org;
URL: http://www.cornerstonedc.org

Foundation type: Public charity
Purpose: Low-interest loans and grants to finance supportive housing for people with mental illness in the District of Columbia area. Grants for low income Veteran homeowners.
Publications: Informational brochure (including application guidelines).
Financial data: Year ended 12/31/2011. Assets, $10,359,064 (M); Expenditures, $1,210,170; Total giving, $775,928; Grants to individuals, totaling $155,464.
Fields of interest: Housing/shelter; Disabilities, people with; Military/veterans.
Type of support: Grants to individuals; Loans—to individuals.
Application information: Applications accepted. Application form required. Application form available on the grantmaker's web site.
Send request by: Mail or e-mail
Additional information: Grants are up to $5,000 for Veteran homewoners to repair and upgrade their homes, and must have served or currently serving in the U.S. military. See web site or contact organization for eligibility determination.
EIN: 521772313

1610
Council for Advancement and Support of Education

1307 New York Ave., N.W., Ste. 1000
Washington, DC 20005-4701 (202) 328-2273
Contact: John Lippincott, Pres.
FAX: (202) 387-4973; E-mail: info@case.org;
URL: http://www.case.org

Foundation type: Public charity
Purpose: Fellowships for journalists to tap into cutting-edge ideas and gain perspectives away from daily pressures of the newsroom. Also, scholarships to staff at a CASE member institution to cover the cost of conference registration.
Publications: Application guidelines; Annual report.
Financial data: Year ended 06/30/2012. Assets, $26,047,095 (M); Expenditures, $15,613,239; Total giving, $512,450; Grants to individuals, totaling $3,806.
Fields of interest: Print publishing.
Type of support: Fellowships; Research.
Application information:
Deadline(s): Vary
Additional information: See Web site for further information.
Program descriptions:
Alice L. Beeman Research Awards in Communications and Marketing for Educational Advancement: This $2,000 award encourages research in communications and marketing for education, including such areas as public relations, government relations, issues management, and institutional image enhancement. Theses, dissertations, and published scholarships must be helpful to educational advancement practitioners in devising strategies and tactics for accomplishing their work in communications and marketing.

Awards are given in two categories: Outstanding Master's Thesis or Doctoral Dissertation, and Outstanding Published Scholarship.
H.S. Warwick Research Awards in Alumni Relations for Educational Advancement: These $2,000 awards encourages research in alumni relations, including such areas as volunteerism, alumni programming, alumni giving, advocacy, student alumni membership, and marketing. Theses, dissertation, and published scholarship must be helpful to educational advancement practitioners in devising strategies and tactics for accomplishing their work in alumni relations. Awards will be given in two categories: Outstanding Master's Thesis or Doctoral Dissertation, and Outstanding Published Scholarship.
John Grezenbach Awards for Outstanding Research in Philanthropy for Educational Advancement: Co-sponsored by the Giving USA Foundation, these awards recognize the work of established researchers and encourage young scholars to continue their work in advancement and educational fundraising. Awards of $2,000 each are given for both outstanding doctoral dissertations and outstanding published scholarship.
Media Fellowships: In recent years, fellowships have covered topics in business, education, the environment, family and social issues, health and medicine, international affairs, science, technology and more. Journalists discover the latest ideas being researched and explored at leading colleges and universities and interact with renowned scholars. They spend several days to a week in one-on-one meetings with senior faculty, engaging in hands-on research on campus and in the field.
U.S. Professors of the Year Program: Co-sponsored by The Carnegie Foundation for the Advancement of Teaching, this program seeks to reward outstanding professors for their dedication to teaching, commitment to students, and innovative instructional methods.
EIN: 521012307

1611
Council of American Overseas Research Centers

(formerly Council of American Research Centers)
P.O. Box 37012
NHB Rm. CE-123, MRC 178
Washington, DC 20013-7012 (202) 633-1599
Contact: Lisa Rogers, Grants Admin.
FAX: (202) 786-2430;
E-mail: fellowships@caorc.org; Additional e-mail: caorc@caorc.org; URL: http://www.caorc.org

Foundation type: Public charity
Purpose: Fellowships to scholars for multi-country research.
Publications: Application guidelines; Newsletter.
Financial data: Year ended 09/30/2011. Assets, $2,328,574 (M); Expenditures, $12,641,300; Total giving, $9,668,205.
Fields of interest: Humanities; International affairs; Social sciences.
Type of support: Fellowships; Research.
Application information: Application form required.
Deadline(s): Dec. 31
Additional information: Application should include a project description, three letters of recommendation, and a transcript (for Ph.D. candidates) or curriculum vitae (for post-doctoral scholarships).
Program descriptions:
Andrew W. Mellon East-Central European Research Fellowships: These fellowships, funded by the Andrew W. Mellon Foundation, enable

Bulgarian, Czech, Estonian, Hungarian, Latvian, Lithuanian, Polish, Romanian, and Slovak scholars in the humanities and allied social sciences to carry out research at institutes of advanced study in other countries. Each cycle will fund short-term residencies for up to three fellows at each of seventeen designated institutes in Austria, England, France, Germany, Greece, India, Israel, Italy, Jordan, the Netherlands, Norway, Scotland, Spain, Turkey, and Yemen. Fellowships are intended to serve younger scholars who have already obtained a Ph.D. or have equivalent experience and who wish to undertake a specific research project at a participating institute; each institute (listed on the council's web site) will issue its own announcement and will handle all matters concerning application and selection.
Critical Language Scholarships for Intensive Summer Institutes: Awarded in conjunction with the United States Department of State and Bureau of Education and Cultural Affairs, this program offers undergraduate, master's, and Ph.D. students and recent graduates who are U.S. citizens the opportunity to study Azerbaijani, Arabic, Bengali, Chinese, Hindi, Korean, Persian, Punjabi, Russian, Turkish, or Urdu at a summer language program at an American Overseas Research Center. Scholarships are intended to cover travel, orientation costs, room, board, travel, and all entrance fees for program activities. Applicants must currently be enrolled in a degree-granting program at the undergraduate or graduate level, or have graduated from an undergraduate or graduate program no more than two years prior to the application date.
Getty Research Exchange Fellowship Program for the Mediterranean Basin and Middle East: This program of research fellowships will serve to build cooperative networks among practitioners and scholars from Afghanistan, Algeria, Cyprus, Egypt, Greece, Italy, Iraq, Israel, Jordan, Morocco, Palestine, Tunisia, Turkey, and Yemen whose research and professional interests focus on studying or preserving cultural heritage. Programs will draw on the resources, facilities, and contacts of American overseas research centers located in Algeria, Cyprus, Egypt, Greece, Italy, Israel, Jordan, Morocco, Tunisia, Turkey, and Yemen to enable the recipients to further their research and to build professional networks in and among the host countries. Up to twelve fellowships will be available to serve scholars who have already obtained a Ph.D. or have professional experience in the study or preservation of cultural heritage and who wish to undertake a specific research project at one of the following research centers: American Academy in Rome, American Center of Oriental Research (Amman), American Institute for Maghrib Studies (Morocco, Tangier, and Algeria), American Institute for Yemeni Studies, American Research Center in Egypt, American Research Institute in Turkey, American School of Classical Studies at Athens, Cyprus American Archaeological Research Institute, and the W.F. Albright Institute of Archaeological Research (Jerusalem).
Multi-County Research Fellowship Program: Ten awards of up to $12,000 each will be given to scholars who wish to carry out research on broad questions of multi-country significance in the field of humanities, social sciences, and related natural sciences. The program is open to U.S. doctoral candidates and scholars who have already earned their Ph.D. in fields in the humanities, social sciences, or allied natural sciences and wish to conduct research of regional or trans-regional significance. Applicants must be U.S. citizens.
EIN: 521395971

1612
Council on Library and Information Resources
1752 N. St. N.W., Ste. 800
Washington, DC 20036-2188 (202) 939-4750
Contact: Charles Henry, Pres.
FAX: (202) 939-4765; URL: http://www.clir.org

Foundation type: Public charity
Purpose: Fellowships for students enrolled in doctoral programs in graduate schools in the U.S.
Publications: Application guidelines; Annual report; Newsletter; Occasional report.
Financial data: Year ended 06/30/2012. Assets, $4,049,841 (M); Expenditures, $3,838,550; Total giving, $634,177; Grants to individuals, totaling $634,177.
Fields of interest: Humanities; Libraries/library science.
Type of support: Fellowships; Doctoral support.
Application information: Applications accepted.
Send request by: On-line
Additional information: See web site for additional guidelines.
Program descriptions:
CLIR Postdoctoral Fellowship Program: Postdoctoral Fellows work on projects that forge and strengthen connections among library collections, educational technologies, and current research. The program offers recent PhD graduates the chance to help develop research tools, resources, and services while exploring new career opportunities. Host institutions benefit from fellows' field-specific expertise by gaining insights into their collections' potential uses and users' scholarly information behaviors, and current teaching and learning practices within particular disciplines.
Peterson Fellowship: This award recognizes an early-career IT professional or librarian who has led a collaborative effort in resolving a significant challenge in IT and digital libraries. Higher education professionals who have worked for five or fewer years in information technology services and/or libraries may be nominated to compete for the fellowship. The selected fellow will demonstrate the acumen necessary for successful collaboration and an understanding of the benefits of reaching out beyond one's professional boundaries. The award covers travel, lodging and registration costs associated with the fellow's participation in NITLE's annual spring symposium and the DLF Forum.
EIN: 521576808

1613
Una Chapman Cox Foundation
1200 18th St., N.W., Ste. 902
Washington, DC 20036-2558 (202) 331-3918
FAX: (202) 833-4555;
E-mail: programs@uccoxfoundation.org;
URL: http://www.uccoxfoundation.org

Foundation type: Public charity
Purpose: Awards to outstanding university students interns at overseas foreign service post and the Department of State by strengthening their professional skills and preparing them as foreign service officer candidates.
Financial data: Year ended 11/30/2011. Assets, $37,615,155 (M); Expenditures, $1,827,138; Total giving, $734,708.
Fields of interest: Government agencies.
Type of support: Grants to individuals; Awards/prizes.
Application information: Contact foundation for current guidelines.

Program description:
Sabbatical Leave Fellowships: The foundation finances mid-career one-year sabbaticals for promising Foreign Service officers. The foundation is also open to requests by individual officers who need assistance in paying for travel to seminars.
EIN: 311680916

1614
Development Fund for Black Students in Science and Technology
2705 Bladensburg Rd., N.E.
Washington, DC 20018-1424 (202) 635-3604
E-mail: Chairperson@dfbsstscholarship.org;
URL: http://www.dfbsstscholarship.org/

Foundation type: Public charity
Purpose: Scholarships to African-American undergraduate students who enroll in scientific or technical fields of study at historically black colleges and universities.
Publications: Application guidelines.
Financial data: Year ended 12/31/2012. Assets, $337,043 (M); Expenditures, $25,314; Total giving, $23,000; Grants to individuals, 18 grants totaling $23,000 (high: $2,000, low: $1,000).
Fields of interest: Science; Mathematics; Engineering/technology; African Americans/Blacks.
Type of support: Support to graduates or students of specific schools; Undergraduate support.
Application information: Applications accepted. Application form required.
Deadline(s): Apr. 15
Applicants should submit the following:
1) Financial information
2) Letter(s) of recommendation
3) Essay
4) SAT
5) Transcripts
Additional information: Applications available from the science or engineering departments at participating schools.
Program description:
Scholarships: The fund provides scholarships of up to $2,000 per year, renewable for up to four years to African-American students who are enrolled in, or who intend to enroll in, a predominately Black college or university. Eligible applicants must be majoring in, or intending to major in, a technical field of study (engineering, math, science), be a U.S. citizen or permanent resident, and be attending (or intend to attend) a historically Black college or university (Bennett College, Clark Atlanta University, Elizabeth City State University, Fisk University, Florida A&M University, Fort Valley State College, Hampton University, Howard University, Langston University, Lincoln University, Morehouse University, Morgan State University, North Carolina A&T State University, Prairie View A&M University, Southern University, Spelman College, Tennessee State University, Tuskegee University, Wilberforce University, and Xavier University of Louisiana). Applicants will be evaluated by academic achievement, strength of personal essays, and recommendations by teachers and guidance counselors; financial need will also be taken into consideration.
EIN: 521342321

1615
William Orr Dingwall Foundation, Inc.
2201 N St. N.W., Ste. 117
Washington, DC 20037-1113
Contact: John D. Ward Esq., Pres.
E-mail: apply@dingwallfoundation.org; URL: http://www.dingwallfoundation.org/

Foundation type: Independent foundation
Purpose: Scholarships to individuals of Korean ancestry for higher education at accredited institutions and to doctoral candidates of any national origin to study the neural basis of language.
Financial data: Year ended 12/31/2012. Assets, $5,719,435 (M); Expenditures, $386,673; Total giving, $355,023; Grants to individuals, 100 grants totaling $355,023 (high: $30,000, low: $500).
Fields of interest: Language/linguistics; Neuroscience; Asians/Pacific Islanders.
Type of support: Fellowships; Undergraduate support.
Application information: Application form required. Application form available on the grantmaker's web site.
Send request by: Online
Deadline(s): Feb. 1
Applicants should submit the following:
1) Curriculum vitae
2) Essay
3) GPA
4) Letter(s) of recommendation
5) Proposal
6) Transcripts
Program description:
Scholarship Program: This program distributes one or more grants of up to $18,000 per year to students who meet its goals. The amount of the stipend will depend on the grantee's justified need. The normal duration of the grant is three years, but may be extended for one additional year. Grantees must be able to maintain at least a 3.0 GPA out of 4.0, and must submit transcripts of their grades each semester as well as annual progress reports.
EIN: 521877552

1616
The District of Columbia Bar Foundation
1420 New York Ave. N.W., Ste. 650
Washington, DC 20036-6964 (202) 467-3750
Contact: Claudia A. Withers, Dir., Progs.
FAX: (302) 467-3753;
E-mail: info@dcbarfoundation.org; E-Mail For Katherine L. Garrett: garrett@dcbarfoundation.org;
URL: http://www.dcbarfoundation.org

Foundation type: Public charity
Purpose: Legal services to indigent residents of Washington DC who are unable to afford legal help.
Publications: Application guidelines; Annual report; Financial statement; Grants list; Informational brochure; Occasional report.
Financial data: Year ended 06/30/2012. Assets, $1,528,641 (M); Expenditures, $4,293,753; Total giving, $3,633,737; Grants to individuals, totaling $96,334.
Fields of interest: Legal services; Economically disadvantaged.
Type of support: Grants for special needs.
Application information:
Initial approach: Letter
Additional information: Contact foundation for eligibility criteria.
EIN: 521109547

1617
District of Columbia College Access Program
(also known as DC-CAP)
1400 L St., N.W., Ste. 400
Washington, DC 20005-6321 (202) 783-7933
Contact: Argelia Rodriguez, Pres. and C.E.O.
FAX: (202) 783-7939; E-mail: dccapcoff@aol.com;
URL: http://www.dccap.org

Foundation type: Public charity
Purpose: Scholarships to District of Columbia students to attend and graduate from college.
Publications: Application guidelines; Multi-year report.
Financial data: Year ended 06/30/2012. Assets, $62,753,987 (M); Expenditures, $7,170,451; Total giving, $2,719,397; Grants to individuals, totaling $2,719,397.
Fields of interest: Higher education.
Type of support: Scholarships—to individuals.
Application information: Application form required.
  Deadline(s): July 31 for Upper Classmen, Aug. 31 for Freshmen and Jan. 31 for first time students entering in the Spring
  Additional information: Application must include copies of SAR, Financial Aid Award Letter, and grades from the previous semesters/years in college.
EIN: 522132835

1618
District of Columbia College Success Foundation
c/o Robert Craves
1220 12th St., S.E., Ste. 110
Washington, DC 20003-3722 (202) 207-1800
Contact: Deborah J. Wilds Ph.D., Pres. and C.O.O.
FAX: (202) 207-1801;
E-mail: rbrown@dccollegesuccessfoundation.org;
Toll-free tel.: (866) 240-3567; URL: http://www.dccollegesuccessfoundation.org

Foundation type: Public charity
Purpose: Scholarships to low-income, high-potential students in the Washington, DC area.
Publications: Application guidelines; Annual report.
Financial data: Year ended 12/31/2011. Assets, $82,537,952 (M); Expenditures, $11,162,877; Total giving, $7,047,562; Grants to individuals, totaling $6,957,534.
Fields of interest: Higher education.
Type of support: Scholarships—to individuals; Support to graduates or students of specific schools.
Application information: Applications accepted. Application form required. Application form available on the grantmaker's web site.
  Deadline(s): ,Apr. 8 for DC Leadership 1000
Program descriptions:
  Chris Cooley Scholarship Program: Administered in conjunction with the Chris Cooley Scholarship Fund, this program provides selected students in the Washington, DC area with up to $5,000 per year, for up to five years, to support their college education.
  CSF/DC Leadership 1000/Washington Redskins Charitable Foundation Scholarship: Awarded in conjunction with the Washington Redskins Charitable Foundation, this program allows donors to provide up to $5,000 per year for up to four years to support the college education of underprivileged Washington, DC students. Eligible applicants must be in their senior year, have a 2.75 GPA or higher, be actively working to prepare for admission to a four-year college, and be Pell Grant-eligible. Application should be submitted online.

DC Achievers Scholarship Program: This scholarship program supports students from six high schools in Washington, DC (Anacostia Senior High School, Ballou Senior High School, HD Woodson Senior High School, Maya Angelou Public Charter High School, Thurgood Marshall Public Charter High School, and Friendship Collegiate Public Charter High School) with high percentages of low-income students.
EIN: 205561911

1619
The Dan Dutko Memorial Foundation
412 1st St. S.E.
Washington, DC 20003-1804 (202) 484-4884
Contact: G. Stephen Perry, Pres.; Fellowships: Mindy Nierenberg
Address for fellowships: c/o Tufts University College of Citizenship and Public Service, Lincoln Filene Hall, Tufts University, Medford, MA 02155
URL: http://activecitizen.tufts.edu/wp-content/uploads/DutkoApplication.pdf

Foundation type: Public charity
Purpose: Fellowships to individuals graduating from Tufts University College of Citizenship and Public Service, MA.
Publications: Informational brochure.
Fields of interest: Higher education.
Type of support: Fellowships; Support to graduates or students of specific schools.
Application information: Applications accepted.
  Deadline(s): Feb. 25
  Applicants should submit the following:
    1) Transcripts
    2) Resume
    3) Letter(s) of recommendation
    4) Essay
EIN: 522248030

1620
The Ellington Fund, Inc.
3500 R St. N.W., Ste. 100
Washington, DC 20007-2326 (202) 333-2555
Contact: Ellen Coppley, Exec. Dir.
E-mail: ecoppley@ellingtonarts.org; URL: http://www.ellingtonschool.org/ellington-fund/

Foundation type: Public charity
Purpose: Scholarships are awarded to seniors of the Duke Ellington School of the Arts for postsecondary education.
Financial data: Year ended 09/30/2011. Assets, $18,804,915 (M); Expenditures, $1,285,731; Total giving, $686,354; Grants to individuals, totaling $33,050.
Fields of interest: Arts education.
Type of support: Scholarships—to individuals; Support to graduates or students of specific schools.
Application information: Applications accepted.
  Additional information: Students must submit a written statement of their achievements, goals, and reason for applying for a scholarship.
EIN: 521152273

1621
Environmental Law Institute
2000 L St., N.W., Ste. 620
Washington, DC 20036-4919 (202) 939-3800
E-mail address for writing competition: connolly@eli.org
FAX: (202) 939-3868; E-mail: law@eli.org;
URL: http://www.eli.org

Foundation type: Public charity
Purpose: Grants to outstanding law student essayists to submit papers exploring current issues of constitutional environmental law.
Publications: Application guidelines; Annual report.
Financial data: Year ended 12/31/2011. Assets, $6,710,303 (M); Expenditures, $5,697,147.
Fields of interest: Law school/education; Environment.
Type of support: Grants to individuals.
Application information:
  Send request by: E-mail
  Deadline(s): Apr. 13
  Additional information: Submissions may be of any length up to a maximum of 50 pages (including footnotes), in a double-spaced, 8.5 x 11-inch page format with 12-point font (10-point for footnotes).
EIN: 520901863

1622
Equal Justice Works
(formerly National Association for Public Interest Law)
1730 M St., N.W., Ste. 1010
Washington, DC 20036-4511 (202) 466-3686
Contact: David Stern, Exec. Dir.
FAX: (202) 429-9766;
E-mail: mail@equaljusticeworks.org; E-Mail for David Stern: dstern@equaljusticeworks.org;
URL: http://www.equaljusticeworks.org

Foundation type: Public charity
Purpose: Fellowship grants and loan repayment assistance to lawyers committed to equal justice and its manifestations, such as domestic violence, unfairly-rationed health care, lack of affordable housing, employment discrimination, consumer fraud, or environmental degradation.
Publications: Application guidelines; Informational brochure; Newsletter.
Financial data: Year ended 06/30/2011. Assets, $11,970,064 (M); Expenditures, $10,417,167; Total giving, $5,718,158; Grants to individuals, totaling $319,437.
Fields of interest: Law school/education; Legal services.
Type of support: Fellowships; Grants to individuals; Postgraduate support; Loans—to individuals.
Application information: Applications accepted. Application form required. Application form available on the grantmaker's web site. Interview required.
  Initial approach: Application
  Send request by: Online
  Deadline(s): Sept. 14 for Equal Justice Works Fellowships
  Additional information: See web site for additional guidelines.
Program descriptions:
  Equal Justice Works Fellowships: Up to $37,500 is available to law students who wish to work in two-year assignments at nonprofit public interest organizations where they implement projects that address pressing community needs. Fellows will receive a salary and benefits comparable to that of a similarly-experienced attorney at the host organization. The organization will provide up to

$37,500 toward the fellow's annual salary, with the host organization providing any funds above that amount. Fellows will also become eligible to apply for a loan repayment assistance program, and will participate in leadership development training programs and networking activities. Eligible applicants must be third-year law students or graduates from a member law school during the academic year in which they apply, who are committed to public interest law and have the relevant skills and initiative to carry out the goals of the fellowship. Funds will be allotted only to projects that target a population located in the U.S. and its territories; funds are not available for projects that propose routine criminal defense work.

Loan Repayment Assistance Program: The LRAP covers both graduate and undergraduate educational debt. It generally covers federally funded and private educational loans, including commercial bar loans. The LRAP does not cover nontraditional, non-commercial loans, such as those made by a relative. A Fellow's eligibility amount will be reduced dollar-for-dollar by any assistance from another program, and Fellows are required to maximize their participation in other LRAPs for which they are eligible. Assistance to incoming Fellows commence at the time the first payment on each loan is due after Sept. 1. New graduates are required to maximize their lenders' grace periods.
EIN: 521469738

1623
Equipment Leasing and Finance Foundation
1825 K. St., N.W. Ste. 900
Washington, DC 20006-4409 (202) 238-3400
FAX: (202) 238-3401;
E-mail: llevine@elfaonline.org; URL: http://www.leasefoundation.org

Foundation type: Public charity
Purpose: Research grants for the study of topics of interest to the equipment leasing and finance industry.
Publications: Application guidelines; Grants list; Informational brochure; Newsletter; Occasional report.
Financial data: Year ended 12/31/2011. Assets, $1,520,835 (M); Expenditures, $689,574; Total giving, $373,980; Grants to individuals, totaling $39,780.
Fields of interest: Business school/education; Mathematics; Economics.
Type of support: Research.
Application information: Applications accepted. Application form required. Application form available on the grantmaker's web site.
Initial approach: E-mail
Send request by: E-mail
Copies of proposal: 1
Deadline(s): 1st of each month
Final notification: Recipients notified in sixty days
Applicants should submit the following:
1) Proposal
2) Curriculum vitae
3) Budget Information
Program description:
Grants: Grants, generally ranging from $10,000 to $15,000, are available to individuals, universities, foundation, associations, and corporation for research studies, booklets, pamphlets, video production, surveys, and statistical gathering. Eligible studies must be future-focused and aligned with the foundation's mission, benefit a major segment of the lease finance industry (e.g. small-ticket, middle-market,

large-ticket, etc.), be broad-based in geographical appeal, contribute to the prosperity and profitability of the industry, and identify emerging issues and/or trends.
EIN: 541527848

1624
Esperantic Studies Foundation, Inc.
1015 15th St., N.W., Ste. 1000
Washington, DC 20005-2621 (208) 863-4952
E-mail: admin@esperantic.com; URL: http://www.esperantic.org

Foundation type: Operating foundation
Purpose: Grants to individuals for research, teaching or publications dealing with interlinguistics.
Financial data: Year ended 12/31/2011. Assets, $2,212,849 (M); Expenditures, $211,791; Total giving, $34,571.
Fields of interest: Language/linguistics.
Type of support: Publication; Research.
Application information: Application form required.
Initial approach: Letter
Deadline(s): None
EIN: 520885287

1625
Families U.S.A. Foundation, Inc.
1201 New York Ave., N.W., Ste. 1100
Washington, DC 20005-6100 (202) 628-3030
Contact: Ronald Pollack, V.P. and Exec. Dir.
Additional e-mails:
wellstonefellowship@familiesusa.org,
villersfellowship@familiesusa.org
FAX: (202) 347-2417; E-mail: info@familiesusa.org;
URL: http://www.familiesusa.org

Foundation type: Public charity
Purpose: Fellowships to foster the advancement of social justice through participation in healthcare advocacy work, and fellowships to inspire and develop the next generation of healthcare justice leaders.
Publications: Application guidelines.
Financial data: Year ended 12/31/2011. Assets, $50,495,441 (M); Expenditures, $7,808,329.
Fields of interest: Public health; Health care; Aging; Minorities.
Type of support: Fellowships.
Application information: Applications accepted. Application form required. Application form available on the grantmaker's web site.
Initial approach: Letter
Send request by: Mail or e-mail
Deadline(s): Jan. 10 for Villers Fellowship, Jan 27 for Wellstone Fellowship
Applicants should submit the following:
1) Transcripts
2) Resume
3) Letter(s) of recommendation
Additional information: Application should also include a personal statement and responses to two short answer questions.
Program descriptions:
Villers Fellowship for Health Care Justice: This fellowship works to inspire and develop the next generation of health care justice leaders by giving fellows the opportunity to work on a variety of health care justice issues during their year-long tenure. Applicants must demonstrate a commitment to social and health care justice advocacy following their fellowship. In addition, fellows must commit to mentoring at least one other person at some point over the course of their careers. Fellows will receive

a one-year stipend of $38,000, along with health benefits.
Wellstone Fellowships for Social Justice: These fellowships are designed to foster the advancement of social justice through participation in health care advocacy work that focuses on the unique challenges facing communities of color (including Black/African American, Latino, Native American, and Asian/Pacific Islander communities). Applicants must demonstrate an interest in health care policy as a tool for reducing racial and ethnic health disparities, and a commitment to contributing to social justice work following their year of hands-on experience as a fellow. Fellows will receive an annual salary of approximately $38,000 for one year, and health benefits.
EIN: 042730934

1626
FINRA Investor Education Foundation
(formerly NASD Investor Education Foundation)
1735 K St., N.W.
Washington, DC 20006-1506 (202) 728-6964
Contact: John M. Gannon, Secy.
FAX: (202) 728-8149; URL: http://www.finrafoundation.org

Foundation type: Public charity
Purpose: Grants to researchers to apply for funding for projects that support and provide Americans with the knowledge, skills, and tools necessary for financial success.
Publications: Grants list; Newsletter.
Financial data: Year ended 12/31/2011. Assets, $51,238,393 (M); Expenditures, $12,512,892; Total giving, $5,105,343.
Fields of interest: Economics; Public affairs, finance; Financial services.
Type of support: Grants to individuals.
Application information:
Initial approach: Letter
Program description:
General Grant Program: Through its grant program, the foundation funds research and/or educational projects that support its mission of providing underserved Americans with the knowledge, skills, and tools necessary for financial success throughout life. The foundation is interested in funding projects that will reach and actively engage at-risk audiences, such as seniors and first-time investors, by offering them access to unbiased information about the markets and fundamental financial issues. There is no set minimum or maximum for the number of grants to be funded or for the amounts of the grants awarded. Each year, the foundation chooses specific targets with which to focus its grantmaking.
EIN: 200863779

1627
Food and Friends, Inc.
219 Riggs Rd., N.E.
Washington, DC 20011-2409 (202) 269-2277
FAX: (202) 635-4261;
E-mail: info@foodandfriends.org; TTY: (202) 855-1234; URL: http://www.foodandfriends.org

Foundation type: Public charity
Purpose: Assistance to men, women and children living with AIDS, cancer and other life-changing illnesses, with life-sustaining nutrition.
Publications: Annual report; Financial statement.
Financial data: Year ended 12/31/2011. Assets, $12,243,518 (M); Expenditures, $8,134,953; Total giving, $1,606,569.

Fields of interest: Health care; Food services; Nutrition.
Type of support: Grants for special needs.
Application information: Application form required.
Additional information: Applicant must have a qualifying primary illness, comprised nutritional status and a limited ability to prepare his/her own meals due to factors such as disability, illness or medical treatment. Contact the organization for additional information.
EIN: 521648941

1628
Thomas B. Fordham Foundation
1016 16th St. N.W., 8th Fl.
Washington, DC 20036-5703 (202) 223-5452
Contact: Chester E. Finn, Jr., Pres.
FAX: (202) 223-9226;
E-mail: letters@edexcellence.net; URL: http://www.edexcellence.net

Foundation type: Independent foundation
Purpose: Fellowships to individuals in the field of education policy. Research grants to advanced doctoral students and junior faculty members working on key issues in American K-12 education.
Publications: Informational brochure.
Financial data: Year ended 12/31/2010. Assets, $47,964,380 (M); Expenditures, $2,604,809; Total giving, $287,706. Fellowships amount not specified.
Fields of interest: Education.
Type of support: Fellowships; Grants to individuals.
Application information: Applications accepted. Application form required. Application form available on the grantmaker's web site.
Send request by: Mail or e-mail
Deadline(s): Apr. 15 for fellowship, Feb. 15 for research grants
Applicants should submit the following:
1) Proposal
2) Curriculum vitae
3) Letter(s) of recommendation
4) Resume
5) Essay
EIN: 316032844

1629
Foundation for Rural Education & Development, Inc.
(formerly Fund for Rural Education & Development)
2020 K St., N.W., 7th Fl.
Washington, DC 20006-1828 (202) 660-2899
Contact: Melissa Korzuch, Exec. Dir.
FAX: (202) 517-9104; E-mail: mak@opastco.org;
URL: http://www.fred.org/

Foundation type: Public charity
Purpose: Scholarships to students living in or attending school in an Organization for Promotion and Advancement of Small Telecommunications Companies (OPASTCO) member service area.
Publications: Annual report; Grants list; Informational brochure (including application guidelines); Newsletter.
Financial data: Year ended 09/30/2011. Assets, $1,962,657 (M); Expenditures, $320,353; Total giving, $144,964; Grants to individuals, totaling $81,813.
Fields of interest: Higher education; Rural development; Telecommunications.
Type of support: Scholarships—to individuals; Undergraduate support.

Application information: Applications accepted. Application form required. Application form available on the grantmaker's web site.
Send request by: Mail
Copies of proposal: 3
Deadline(s): Feb. 13
Applicants should submit the following:
1) Transcripts
2) Letter(s) of recommendation
3) Financial information
4) Essay
Additional information: Application by fax or e-mail not accepted.
Program description:
Scholarship Program: Educational opportunities for those who pursue careers in telecommunications, rural education, or rural development. Scholarships range in size from $1,000 to $5,000 annually.
EIN: 521676879

1630
Franciscan Foundation for the Holy Land
P.O. Box 29086
Washington, DC 20017-9086
Contact: Rev. Peter F. Vasko O.F.M., Pres.
E-mail: info@ffhl.org; Toll-free tel.: (866) 905-3787; Toll-free fax: (866) 905-3788; URL: http://www.ffhl.org

Foundation type: Public charity
Purpose: Scholarships to Christian Palestinian students in Israel and the Occupied Territories. Parents' economic income is a major criteria for deciding whether student will receive a partial or full scholarship.
Publications: Newsletter.
Financial data: Year ended 12/31/2011. Assets, $3,262,359 (M); Expenditures, $2,415,236; Total giving, $1,938,103.
Fields of interest: Christian agencies & churches.
Type of support: Scholarships—to individuals.
Application information: Contact foundation for current application deadline/guidelines. Unsolicited applications not accepted.
EIN: 330628775

1631
The Freedom Forum, Inc.
555 Pennsylvania Ave., NW
Washington, DC 20001-2114 (202) 292-6100
Contact: James Duff, Pres. and C.E.O.
E-mail: news@freedomforum.org; URL: http://www.freedomforum.org

Foundation type: Operating foundation
Purpose: Scholarships to high school juniors pursing a career in journalism. Summer internships for college students to attend a journalism course at the American Indian Journalism Institute. Training, mentoring, paid internships and cash awards to college students or recent graduates who are pursuing careers in the media through the Chips Quinn Scholars. Program.
Publications: Annual report; Occasional report.
Financial data: Year ended 12/31/2012. Assets, $765,567,826 (M); Expenditures, $56,052,317; Total giving, $28,463,754.
Fields of interest: Journalism school/education; Native Americans/American Indians.
Type of support: Internship funds.
Application information: Applications accepted.
Initial approach: Letter or telephone
Send request by: Online
Deadline(s): Feb. 15 for Neuharth Free Spirit Scholarship, Mar. 1 for American Indian

Journalism, Oct. 15 for Chips Quinn Scholars Program
Additional information: See web site for complete program information.
Program descriptions:
American Indian Journalism Institute: The American Indian Journalism Institute began since 2001, in partnership with the University of South Dakota and in cooperation with the Native American Journalist Association (NAJA). AIJI has been a premier journalism training, scholarship and internship program for aspiring journalists from diverse backgrounds. At Institute sessions, students learned basic journalism practices, participated in educational field trips, reported, wrote and produced multimedia projects. The goal of AIJI has been to recruit, train, mentor and retain diverse journalists for media careers. NAJA and the Newseum Institute are working toward a new program beginning in 2014 that will provide training, mentoring and practical experience for those entering the digital, multi-media world of journalism.
Chips Quinn Scholars Program for Diversity: The program offers students hands-on training and mentoring by caring news veterans. The aim is to provide special support and encouragement that will open doors to news careers and bring greater diversity to the newsrooms of the United States. The program provides internships, training, an intense one-week college course in multimedia skills and financial assistance to college students from multicultural backgrounds who are pursuing careers in journalism. Internships are currently offered in spring and summer. The annual application deadline is in Oct. College juniors, seniors or recent graduates with majors in journalism or career goals in journalism are eligible. For program information and applications, contact Karen Catone: e-mail: kcatone@freedomforum.org, tel.: (202) 292-6271.
EIN: 541604427

1632
Freedom House, Inc.
1301 Connecticut Ave. N.W., 6th Fl.
Washington, DC 20036-1802 (202) 296-5101
FAX: (202) 293-2840;
E-mail: info@freedomhouse.org; Additional address (New York office): 120 Wall St., Fl. 26, New York, NY 10005-3904; URL: http://www.freedomhouse.org

Foundation type: Public charity
Purpose: Humanitarian assistance grants to individuals throughout the world.
Publications: Annual report; Occasional report.
Financial data: Year ended 06/30/2012. Assets, $15,144,537 (M); Expenditures, $43,059,213; Total giving, $23,313,874.
Fields of interest: Human services.
Type of support: Grants to individuals.
Application information: Applications accepted.
Additional information: See web site or contact the organization for additional information.
EIN: 131656647

1633
The Alfred Friendly Foundation
1100 Connecticut Ave. N.W., Ste. 440
Washington, DC 20036-4119
E-mail: info@pressfellowships.org; URL: http://www.pressfellowships.org

Foundation type: Operating foundation

Purpose: Fellowships to journalists from countries other than the U.S. to work as reporters for six months on publications so as to further understanding of the press.
Publications: Financial statement.
Financial data: Year ended 12/31/2012. Assets, $1,775,202 (M); Expenditures, $347,988; Total giving, $20,000; Grants to individuals, 4 grants totaling $20,000 (high: $5,000, low: $5,000).
Fields of interest: Print publishing.
Type of support: Fellowships; Foreign applicants.
Application information: Applications accepted. Application form required. Application form available on the grantmaker's web site. Interview required.
  Initial approach: Application
  Send request by: Mail
  Copies of proposal: 1
  Deadline(s): Aug. 1
  Applicants should submit the following:
    1) Work samples
    2) Curriculum vitae
    3) Letter(s) of recommendation
    4) Essay
  Additional information: Application must also include detailed biographical information, and samples of published work, with translations as necessary; English language proficiency exam required.
EIN: 521307387

1634
The Fund for American Studies
1706 New Hampshire Ave., N.W.
Washington, DC 20009-2502 (202) 986-0384
Contact: Roger Ream, Pres.
FAX: (202) 986-0390; E-mail: info@tfas.org;
Toll-free tel.: (800) 741-6964; URL: http://www.tfas.org

Foundation type: Public charity
Purpose: Scholarships to outstanding undergraduate students for attendance at the Institute on Business and Government Affairs (IBGA). Awards to magazine and newspaper reporters.
Publications: Annual report; Financial statement; Informational brochure; Newsletter.
Financial data: Year ended 12/31/2011. Assets, $22,714,493 (M); Expenditures, $10,357,218; Total giving, $2,268,689; Grants to individuals, totaling $1,175,997.
Fields of interest: Print publishing; Public policy; International exchange, students; International affairs; Economics; Political science.
Type of support: Internship funds; Support to graduates or students of specific schools; Awards/prizes; Undergraduate support.
Application information:
  Initial approach: Letter, telephone, or e-mail
  Deadline(s): Mar. 15 for Mollenhoff Award and Award for Excellence in Economic Reporting, Apr. 15 for Novak Journalism Award
  Additional information: See web site for additional guidelines.
Program descriptions:
  Award for Excellence in Economic Reporting: The award is presented to a magazine or newspaper writer, or team of writers whose work best expands the public's understanding of economic theory and reality. The award is open to both reporters and analysts, but the judges seek to award writing that features outstanding original reporting and fact-finding married to superior analysis.
  Clark Mollenhoff Award for Excellence in Investigative Reporting: The award is given annually to the best newspaper or magazine story that

conforms both the definition of investigative reporting as originally defined by Investigative Reporters and Editors (RE) and to the professional standards articulated by Clark Mollenhoff in his critiques of journalism craft. Recipients may be a newspaper reporter, team of reporters or an individual newspaper showing initiative similar to Mollenhoff's.
  Congressional Scholarship Award: This program provides financial support to college students who wish to attend Georgetown University's Institute on Business and Government Affairs. Scholarships are awarded to outstanding students based on leadership skills, academics, and campus and community involvement.
  Robert Novak Collegiate Journalism Award: The award recognizes excellence in collegiate reporting in which the student's work demonstrates an understanding of the basic ideas that support a free society, including freedom of the press, freedom of speech and free-market economic principles.
EIN: 136223604

1635
Fund for Investigative Journalism
529 14th St. N.W., 13th Fl.
Washington, DC 20045-1000 (202) 662-7564
Contact: Sandy Bergo, Exec. Dir.
E-mail: fundfij@gmail.com; URL: http://www.fij.org

Foundation type: Public charity
Purpose: Grants to journalists for investigative stories with a statement of intent to publish from a suitable outlet. No support for journalism education.
Publications: Grants list.
Financial data: Year ended 12/31/2011. Assets, $235,000 (M); Expenditures, $181,665; Total giving, $118,163; Grants to individuals, totaling $68,913.
Fields of interest: Print publishing; Literature.
Type of support: Publication; Grants to individuals; Awards/prizes.
Application information: Applications accepted. Application form required. Application form available on the grantmaker's web site.
  Initial approach: Proposal
  Send request by: Online
  Deadline(s): Nov. 1 for Grants
  Final notification: Recipients notified six weeks after deadline
  Applicants should submit the following:
    1) Work samples
    2) Resume
    3) Budget Information
  Additional information: Application should also include a signed letter or commitment from a news executive for the intended news outlet. Only domestic reporting proposals are considered for this grant cycle. The fund is not currently accepting applications for the Book Award.
Program descriptions:
  Book Award: The fund will award a $25,000 book prize to a work-in-progress that has yet to be published. Consideration will be given to both investigative book projects that have already received fund support as well as projects that have not been previously considered. Applicants should send a letter describing the project and other information that may be helpful, such as a chapter outline or a sample chapter. It is not required that the book be under contract; however, for books under contract, copies of the first and last pages of the contract should be included with the application.

Grants: Grants average $5,000 which covers travel and other reporting expenses for investigative stories that otherwise would not be told. The Fund grants will not cover grantees' writing fees or salaries, the costs of purchasing equipment, or other capital expenses. In exceptional cases, the Fund will consider awarding a small stipend as part of the grant.
EIN: 520895081

1636
Gateway Global Foundation
(also known as Global Gateway Foundation)
1400 16th St., N.W., Ste. 101
Washington, DC 20036-2222
Contact: James S. Turner, Pres.
E-mail: info@globalgatewayfoundation.org; Tel./fax: (202) 462-8800; URL: http://www.globalgatewayfoundation.org

Foundation type: Public charity
Purpose: Funding in small amounts to investigators undertaking research in areas of interest to the foundation through the Competitive Grants Initiative.
Publications: Application guidelines.
Fields of interest: Research; Research.
Type of support: Research.
Application information: Applications accepted.
  Initial approach: Pre-proposal
  Deadline(s): Dec. 10
  Additional information: Contact foundation for current guidelines. Applications from individuals will be considered on a case-by-case basis.
EIN: 205377532

1637
Gay and Lesbian Medical Association
1326 18th St., N.W., Ste. 22
Washington, DC 20036-1876 (202) 600-8037
Contact: Hector Vargas, Exec. Dir.
FAX: (202) 478-1500; E-mail: info@glma.org; E-Mail for Hector Vargas: hvargas@glma.org; URL: http://www.glma.org

Foundation type: Public charity
Purpose: Grants for research projects in the area of lesbian health needs. Also, scholarships to help defray the costs of attending the GLMA conference.
Publications: Application guidelines; Grants list; Informational brochure (including application guidelines); Newsletter.
Financial data: Year ended 12/31/2012. Assets, $131,700 (M); Expenditures, $691,179; Total giving, $47,059.
Fields of interest: Health care; LGBTQ.
Type of support: Conferences/seminars; Grants to individuals.
Application information: Application form required.
  Initial approach: Letter or telephone
  Send request by: E-mail
  Deadline(s): May 15 and Oct. 15 for grants; July 15 for student scholarships
  Applicants should submit the following:
    1) Proposal
    2) Curriculum vitae
    3) Budget Information
Program descriptions:
  Lesbian Health Fund: The fund seeks to define, study, and educate lesbians and their health care providers about lesbian health issues. Grants range from $500 to $10,000.

Symposium Scholarships: The association offers several scholarships to enable medical students to attend the association's annual symposium.
EIN: 942901694

1638
The German Marshall Fund of the United States
1744 R St., N.W.
Washington, DC 20009-2410 (202) 683-2650
Internship/Fellowships Contact: Tisha Spriggs Pugh, Sr. H.R. Coord.
FAX: (202) 265-1662; E-mail: info@gmfus.org;
E-Mail for Craig Kennedy : ckennedy@gmfus.org;
URL: http://www.gmfus.org

Foundation type: Public charity
Purpose: Fellowships and awards to U.S. journalists, and research fellowships to U.S. postdoctoral scholars for the study of transatlantic issues.
Publications: Annual report.
Financial data: Year ended 05/31/2012. Assets, $200,692,260 (M); Expenditures, $37,987,491; Total giving, $6,434,691.
Fields of interest: Print publishing; Language (foreign); Business school/education; Dental school/education; Medical school/education; Nursing school/education; Education; Natural resources; Energy; Environment; Agriculture; Foreign policy; International affairs; Anthropology/sociology; Economics; Political science; Government/public administration; African Americans/Blacks; Economically disadvantaged.
International interests: Eastern Europe; Europe; France; Germany; Hungary; Italy; Poland; Portugal; Spain.
Type of support: Conferences/seminars; Fellowships; Internship funds; Research; Exchange programs; Awards/grants by nomination only; Foreign applicants; Awards/prizes; Postdoctoral support; Undergraduate support; Travel grants.
Application information: See web site for complete description of programs, and application information.
Program descriptions:
APSA Congressional Fellowship: Support is provided annually for two mid-career German professionals to participate in the prestigious ten-month fellowship. Fellows receive a monthly stipend of $3,800 for ten months, plus $2,150 for program-related international travel, $125 for books, and additional travel expenses for the visit to the Canadian Parliament and one trip to the district office of their respective Congress member.
Economics Program: The program supports a wide range of institutions and individuals working to strengthen transatlantic cooperation to solve various economic, trade, agriculture, and development issues.
Internship Program in Berlin: Graduate students and recent recipients of a B.A. are eligible for the program, which offers an academic-year internship in the fund's Berlin office. Strong research and writing skills are important, as is the ability to work independently. Preference is given to applicants who have a demonstrated interest in U.S.-German relations; whose academic work concentrates on political science, public policy or history or whose concentration on the German language is complemented by courses in political science and history; and who are U.S. citizens or permanent residents. Fluency in written and spoken German is required.
Journalism Program: The program works to promote coverage of transatlantic issues by both American and European journalists and to

encourage an open and spirited exchange between media professionals on both sides of the Atlantic.
Marshall Memorial Fellowship: The fellowship provides a unique opportunity for emerging leaders from the U.S. and Europe to explore societies, institutions, and people on the other side of the Atlantic. Fellowships are awarded to leaders in politics, government, business, media, and the nonprofit sector committed to strengthening the transatlantic relationship. American and European Fellows each visit five cities during the 24-day program. They meet formally and informally with a range of policymakers, prominent community members, and local MMF alumni. During the trip, each Fellow has the opportunity to explore his or her individual professional interests beyond the group programs, which focus on a range of domestic and international policy areas. Individuals must be nominated by a recognized leader in their community or professional field.
Peter R. Weitz Award: A prize, worth $10,000, is open to all journalists covering European issues for American newspapers, magazines, and online media, whether they are based in Europe or cover Europe from the U.S.
Transatlantic Academy Fellowships: Four fellows and two junior fellows are supported in residencies at the fund's Washington, D.C. office for up to ten months where they will actively participate in a collaborative environment, sharing and discussing their work with each other and Academy guests. Fellows use research, publications, and ideas to make policy-relevant contributions to policy debates facing the transatlantic community.
Transatlantic Fellows Program: Each year the fund invites a small number of senior policy-practitioners, journalists, businesspeople, and academics to develop a range of programs and initiatives and build important networks of policymakers and analysts in the Euroatlantic community. Fellows work on questions of foreign policy, international security, trade and economic development, immigration, and other topics important to transatlantic cooperation.
Urban and Regional Policy Fellowship: Fellowships provide opportunities for practitioners and policy-makers working on economic and social issues at the urban and regional policy levels to meet with their counterparts across the Atlantic and discuss policies and measures that have been implemented. Fellows can then return from their time overseas equipped with the ideas and insights necessary to effect significant and lasting positive change in their own communities.
EIN: 520954751

1639
Gerontological Society of America
1220 L St. N.W., Ste. 901
Washington, DC 20005-4001 (202) 842-1275
Contact: James Appleby, Exec. Dir.
FAX: (202) 842-1150; E-mail: geron@geron.org; Tel. for James Appleby: (202)-587-2821; Fax for James Appleby: (202)-587-2850; URL: http://www.geron.org

Foundation type: Public charity
Purpose: Grants for the study of gerontological research.
Publications: Application guidelines; Occasional report.
Financial data: Year ended 12/31/2011. Assets, $10,801,170 (M); Expenditures, $6,400,826; Total giving, $1,290,900; Grants to individuals, totaling $1,100,000.
Fields of interest: Health care; Geriatrics; Geriatrics research; Aging.

Type of support: Fellowships; Research; Travel grants.
Application information:
Initial approach: Letter
Deadline(s): Aug. 1
Applicants should submit the following:
1) Proposal
Program descriptions:
Hartford Doctoral Fellows Program: This program provides substantial financial support and professional development enhancement, prepares participants for a tenure track faculty position at a major university, and provides the opportunity to become a leader in an elite network of scholars. The program provides: grants of $25,000 a year for up to two years to students doing dissertations in gerontologic or geriatric social work; supplemental academic career guidance and mentoring; professional development through institutes held at annual society meetings and through the Society for Social Work Research and the Council on Social Work Education; and cohort-building and peer networking among fellows, scholars, leading gerontologists, and social work educators. Applicants must be: enrolled in a full-time doctoral program in the U.S., committed to seeking a full-time faculty position in an MSW program; and be U.S. citizens or have permanent resident status.
Hartford Pre-Dissertation Award Program in Geriatric Social Work: The program offers support and funding to expose more doctoral students to gerontological social work research, expand the number of social work doctoral dissertations that identify and examine a set of research questions that seek to improve the health and well-being of older persons and their families, and enhance the likelihood of writing a successful grant application to the Hartford Doctoral Fellows Program. Support includes: travel expenses and registration to attend the society's annual scientific meetings; attendance at pre-conference institutes to enhance research and grant-writing skills; and opportunities to meet and network with doctoral fellows and faculty scholars.
EIN: 521256181

1640
The Elizabeth Glaser Pediatric AIDS Foundation
1140 Connecticut Ave. N.W., Ste. 200
Washington, DC 20036-4028 (202) 296-9165
Contact: Charles Lyons, Pres. and C.E.O.
FAX: (202) 296-9185; E-mail: info@pedaids.org;
URL: http://www.pedaids.org

Foundation type: Public charity
Purpose: Research grants and awards for the study of pediatric AIDS.
Publications: Annual report (including application guidelines); Financial statement; Informational brochure; Newsletter.
Financial data: Year ended 12/31/2011. Assets, $33,317,641 (M); Expenditures, $164,151,044; Total giving, $56,529,469.
Fields of interest: Pediatrics; AIDS research.
Type of support: Research; Awards/prizes.
Application information: Application form required.
Initial approach: Letter or telephone
Deadline(s): June 13
Program descriptions:
Elizabeth Glaser Scientist Awards: This program provides a five-year grant to top scientists and clinicians in the field of HIV/AIDS research. Notable research activities supported by this award include identifying candidates for an effective and safe pediatric HIV vaccine, understanding the immune response in children living with HIV, and

understanding the dynamics of HIV transmission during the breastfeeding period.

International Leadership Awards: This program provides three-year grants focused on international investigations into preventing mother-to-child transmission of HIV (PMTCT) and HIV care and treatment. Grants can support improving the effectiveness of PMTCT services, strengthening maternal and infant diagnosis of HIV, and examining the impact of antiretroviral drugs on children.
EIN: 954191698

1641
Global Animal Partnership
(formerly Animal Compassion Foundation)
P.O. Box 21484
Washington, DC   20009-0984
URL: http://www.globalanimalpartnership.org/

Foundation type: Operating foundation
Purpose: Research grants to improve livestock rearing and slaughter methods on farms.
Financial data: Year ended 12/31/2012. Assets, $517,394 (M); Expenditures, $259,883; Total giving, $0.
Fields of interest: Animal welfare; Agriculture, livestock issues.
Type of support: Research.
Application information: Applications not accepted.
   Additional information: Unsolicited requests for funds not considered.
EIN: 202234609

1642
Hemophilia Federation of America, Inc.
210 7th St., S.E., Ste. 200B
Washington, DC   20003-4300   (202) 675-6984
Contact: Kimberly Haugstad, Exec. Dir.
FAX: (972) 616-6211;
E-mail: info@hemophiliafed.org; Toll-free tel.: (800)-230-9797; URL: http://www.hemophiliafed.org

Foundation type: Public charity
Purpose: Academic scholarships to members of the bleeding disorder community seeking a postsecondary education.
Financial data: Year ended 12/31/2011. Assets, $690,408 (M); Expenditures, $1,565,097; Total giving, $15,000; Grants to individuals, totaling $15,000.
Fields of interest: Continuing education; Hemophilia.
Type of support: Scholarships—to individuals.
Application information: Applications accepted. Application form required. Application form available on the grantmaker's web site.
   Deadline(s): Apr. 30
   Final notification: Applicants notified June 1
   Applicants should submit the following:
      1) Work samples
      2) Photograph
      3) Transcripts
      4) Letter(s) of recommendation
      5) Essay
   Additional information: Application must also include statement of financial need and proof of enrollment. Interviews may be required. See web site for additional information.
Program descriptions:
   Artistic Encouragement Grant: A grant in the amount of $1,500 for the purpose of funding a creative endeavor will be offered to people with hemophilia or von Willebrand Disease who is

seeking a post-secondary education. This includes mounting an exhibition of one's work, publishing a story or book, writing a play or putting on a recital.

   Educational Scholarships: The federation provides educational scholarships to members of the bleeding disorders community. To qualify, an applicant must have hemophilia or von Willebrand disease (VWD) and must be seeking a postsecondary education from a college, university, or trade school. The applicant must also be able to demonstrate a commitment to improving quality of life by pursuing his/her goals with determination.

   Parent Continuing Education Grant: Scholarships in the amount of $1,500 is offered to a parent of a child with a hemophilia or von Willebrand Disease who is seeking a postsecondary education either from a college, university or trade school. Applicant must be able to demonstrate his/her commitment to improving the quality of their life by pursuing his/her goals with determination.

   Sibling Continuing Education Grant: Scholarships in the amount of $1,500 is offered to the sibling of a person with hemophilia or von Willebrand Disease seeking a postsecondary education from a college, university or trade school. Recipient must be able to demonstrate his/her commitment to improving the quality of their life by pursuing his/her goals with determination.
EIN: 721282316

1643
The Heritage Foundation
214 Massachusetts Ave. N.E.
Washington, DC   20002-4999   (202) 546-4400
Contact: Edwin J. Feulner, Pres.
Application contact for fellowships: Jonathan Butcher, Domestic Policy, tel.: (202) 608-6073, E-mail: familydatabase@heritage.org
FAX: (202) 546-8328; E-mail: info@heritage.org; URL: http://www.heritage.org

Foundation type: Public charity
Purpose: Fellowships to candidates pursuing degrees in the social sciences.
Publications: Annual report; Financial statement; Newsletter.
Financial data: Year ended 12/31/2011. Assets, $174,109,394 (M); Expenditures, $80,033,828; Total giving, $525,384.
Type of support: Fellowships.
Application information:
   Initial approach: E-mail or letter
Program description:
   Family and Society Database Fellowship: Up to ten fellowships are awarded each year to social scientists pursuing a Ph.D. Fellowships are approximately six months long with a stipend of $7,000. In addition, three fellowships are awarded each year (spring, summer, fall). These are approximately three months long with a stipend of $2,000 per month.
EIN: 237327730

1644
Hispanic College Fund, Inc.
1300 L. St., N.W., Ste. 975
Washington, DC   20005-3317   (202) 296-5400
FAX: (202) 296-3774;
E-mail: hcf-info@hispanicfund.org; Toll-free tel.: (800) 644-4223; URL: http://www.hispanicfund.org

Foundation type: Public charity
Purpose: Scholarships to Hispanic high school graduates of the U.S. and Puerto Rico who demonstrate financial need pursuing degrees in

business, science, engineering, technology and math.
Publications: Informational brochure.
Financial data: Year ended 12/31/2011. Assets, $1,549,399 (M); Expenditures, $5,878,745; Total giving, $2,271,175; Grants to individuals, totaling $2,271,175.
Fields of interest: Business school/education; Science; Mathematics; Engineering/technology; Hispanics/Latinos.
Type of support: Scholarships—to individuals.
Application information: Applications accepted. Application form required. Application form available on the grantmaker's web site.
   Deadline(s): Varies
   Final notification: Recipients notified first week of Aug.
   Applicants should submit the following:
      1) GPA
      2) SAR
      3) Transcripts
      4) Resume
      5) Letter(s) of recommendation
      6) Financial information
      7) Essay
   Additional information: Application must be completed online. See web site for a listing of scholarship programs you may be eligible for.
EIN: 521809680

1645
The Hitachi Foundation
1215 17th St., N.W., 3rd Fl.
Washington, DC   20036-3019   (202) 457-0588
Contact: Barbara Dyer, C.E.O. and Pres.; Mark Popovich, Sr. Prog. Off.
FAX: (202) 298-1098;
E-mail: info@hitachifoundation.org; URL: http://www.hitachifoundation.org

Foundation type: Independent foundation
Purpose: Awards for young entrepreneurs in the U.S. for establishing a financially viable business for low-wealth Americans.
Publications: Application guidelines; Annual report; Financial statement; Grants list; Informational brochure; Occasional report.
Financial data: Year ended 12/31/2012. Assets, $23,469,501 (M); Expenditures, $3,334,689; Total giving, $1,535,572.
Fields of interest: Volunteer services; Business/industry; Social entrepreneurship; Community development, small businesses.
Type of support: Awards/prizes.
Application information: Applications accepted. Interview required.
   Deadline(s): Mar. 28
   Additional information: See web site for additional guidelines.
Program description:
   Yoshiyama Young Entrepreneurs Program: This program supports applicants age 18 years old, and applicants must have been 29 years old or younger when their business began generating revenue. The business must be one to five years old and have been generating revenue for a minimum of the past 12 months. The applicant must have established his/her business with the expressed dual purpose of operating a successful business and creating opportunities for low-wealth individuals in the U.S. to enhance their economic security, and the business may be structured as a for-profit or non-profit. If the business is a non-profit, it must depend primarily on an earned-income revenue model and not depend solely on donations and

grants. The award includes a cash prize of $40,000 total for two years.
EIN: 521429292

1646
James R. Hoffa Memorial Scholarship Fund, Inc.
25 Louisiana Ave. N.W.
Washington, DC 20001-2130 (202) 624-7471
Contact: Cheryl L. Johnson, Pres.
E-mail: scholarship@teamster.org; URL: http://www.teamster.org/content/about-james-r-hoffa-memorial-scholarship-fund

Foundation type: Public charity
Purpose: Scholarships for undergraduate education to children, grandchildren, and financial dependents of members of the International Brotherhood of Teamsters.
Financial data: Year ended 12/31/2011. Assets, $10,386,553 (M); Expenditures, $506,486; Total giving, $431,000; Grants to individuals, totaling $360,000.
Fields of interest: Labor unions/organizations.
Type of support: Undergraduate support.
Application information: Application form required.
  Deadline(s): Mar. 31
  Applicants should submit the following:
    1) Transcripts
    2) ACT
    3) SAT
    4) Letter(s) of recommendation
EIN: 522206826

1647
Horticultural Research Institute Endowment Fund, Inc.
1000 Vermont Ave., N.W., Ste. 300
Washington, DC 20005-4914 (202) 789-2900
FAX: (202) 789-1893; URL: http://www.hriresearch.org

Foundation type: Public charity
Purpose: Scholarships to students enrolled in a landscape/horticulture program. Also, research grants for projects that cover the full range of production, environmental and business issues important to the horticulture industry.
Financial data: Year ended 12/31/2011. Assets, $10,112,167 (M); Expenditures, $882,526; Total giving, $229,455; Grants to individuals, totaling $60,000.
Fields of interest: Environment, plant conservation; Botanical/horticulture/landscape services; Horticulture/garden clubs; Environment.
Type of support: Research; Undergraduate support.
Application information: Applications accepted. Application form required. Application form available on the grantmaker's web site.
  Initial approach: Letter
  Deadline(s): Varies
  Applicants should submit the following:
    1) Letter(s) of recommendation
    2) Transcripts
    3) Resume
    4) Essay
  Additional information: Contact fund for further eligibility criteria.
Program descriptions:
  Carville M. Akehurst Memorial Scholarship: Awards scholarships of up to $2,000 to applicants who are residents of one of the three MANTS member states-Maryland, Virginia, or West Virginia. Attendance at an institution within these states is not mandatory. Applicant must be enrolled in an accredited undergraduate or graduate landscape/

horticulture program or related discipline at a two- or four-year institution.
  Muggets Scholarship: Awards scholarships of up to $750 to applicants enrolled in an accredited undergraduate or graduate horticulture, landscape or related discipline at a two- or four-year institution. Students in vocational agriculture programs will also be considered. High school seniors may apply for this scholarship.
  Spring Meadow Nursery Scholarship: Awards scholarships of up to $1,250 to applicants enrolled in an accredited undergraduate or graduate: landscape, horticulture or related discipline at a two- or four-year institution. Students in vocational agriculture programs will also be considered. High school seniors may apply for this scholarship. This fund is dedicated to helping aspiring students from across the country obtain a degree in horticulture.
  The Usrey Family Scholarship: Awards scholarships up to $750 to graduating students in horticulture to be the lifeblood of the green industry. The scholarship is awarded annually to horticulture students enrolled in a California state university or college.
  Timothy S. and Palmer W. Bigelow, Jr. Scholarship: Applicant must be enrolled in an accredited undergraduate or graduate landscape/horticulture program or related discipline at a two- or four-year institution. The student must currently be enrolled in good standing and carry a full-time complement of courses at the time of application and during the semesters that the scholarship is granted. Applicant must be a resident of one of the six New England states (although attendance at an institution within these states in not mandatory): Connecticut, Maine, Massachusetts, New Hampshire, Rhode Island and Vermont. The maximum award is $1,750.
EIN: 521052547

1648
Zora Neale Hurston & Richard Wright Foundation
611 Pennsylvania Ave., S.E. No. 173
Washington, DC 20003
Contact: Marita Golden, Pres. and C.E.O.
E-mail: info@hurstonwright.org; URL: http://www.hurstonwright.org

Foundation type: Public charity
Purpose: Awards and prizes to writers of African descent for the highest quality fiction and nonfiction literature.
Publications: Application guidelines.
Financial data: Year ended 12/31/2012. Assets, $9,906 (M); Expenditures, $36,409.
Fields of interest: Literature; African Americans/Blacks.
Type of support: Awards/prizes.
Application information: Applications accepted. Application form required. Application form available on the grantmaker's web site.
  Initial approach: E-mail
  Deadline(s): Nov. 21 for Legacy Awards, Jan. 13 for College Writers
  Additional information: Application should include a $25 nonrefundable application fee for Legacy award, and $13 nonrefundable submission fee for College writers. Contact foundation for complete program information.
Program descriptions:
  Hurston/Wright Award for College Writers: This award honors excellence in fiction writing by students of African descent enrolled full-time as an undergraduate or graduate student in any college or university in the U.S. Writers who have published a book in any genre are ineligible.

Hurston/Wright LEGACY Award: This award is presented to published writers of African descent by the national community of Black writers. This award consists of prizes of the highest quality writing in the categories of fiction (novel, novella, or short story collection), nonfiction (autobiography, memoir, biography, history, social issues, and literary criticism), and poetry (books in verse, prose poetry, formal verse, and experimental verse)
EIN: 521706969

1649
Independent Sector
1602 L St., N.W., Ste. 900
Washington, DC 20036-5682 (202) 467-6100
Contact: Diana Aviv, Pres. and C.E.O.
FAX: (202) 467-6101;
E-mail: info@independentsector.org; URL: http://www.independentsector.org

Foundation type: Public charity
Purpose: Awards by nomination only to individuals who work in the nonprofit sector and to those who conduct research in that area.
Publications: Annual report.
Financial data: Year ended 12/31/2011. Assets, $49,035,455 (M); Expenditures, $7,910,797. Awards/prizes amount not specified.
Fields of interest: Community/economic development; Philanthropy/voluntarism; Leadership development.
Type of support: Awards/grants by nomination only; Awards/prizes.
Application information: Application form required.
  Deadline(s): Jan. 31
  Additional information: See web site for complete nomination guidelines.
Program description:
  John W. Gardner Leadership Award: The award is presented each year to living Americans working in or with the nonprofit community whose leadership has been transformative and who have mobilized and unified people, institutions, or causes that improve people's lives. The award honors visionaries who have empowered constituencies, strengthened participation and inspired movements. Recipients may be of any age, may be the creators of needed institutions or may concentrate on education and advocacy that changes public opinion. Whatever means they use, their work has transformed their chosen field and has served as a role model to other fields.
EIN: 521081024

1650
Institute of Current World Affairs, Inc.
(also known as The Crane-Rogers Foundation)
4545 42nd St. N.W., Ste. 311
Washington, DC 20016-4623 (202) 364-4068
Contact: Steven Butler, Exec. Dir.
Application e-mail: apply@icwa.org
FAX: (202) 364-0498; E-mail: icwa@icwa.org; URL: http://www.icwa.org

Foundation type: Operating foundation
Purpose: Support for a limited number of long-term fellowships to persons 35 years or younger of exceptional ability to enable them to work in and write about foreign areas of significance to the U.S.
Publications: Application guidelines; Informational brochure.
Financial data: Year ended 12/31/2012. Assets, $6,058,064 (M); Expenditures, $773,735; Total giving, $160,003; Grants to individuals, 2 grants totaling $29,387 (high: $27,632; low: $1,755).

Fields of interest: Research; International exchange, arts; International exchange; International affairs; Social sciences, interdisciplinary studies; International studies.
Type of support: Fellowships; Research.
Application information: Applications accepted. Application form required. Interview required.
  Initial approach: Letter of interest and resume (by email preferred)
  Copies of proposal: 1
  Deadline(s): See Institute web site for deadlines for letter of interest and resume. If appropriate, candidates will be invited to submit a more detailed written application
  Applicants should submit the following:
    1) Curriculum vitae
    2) Proposal
    3) Budget Information
    4) Essay
  Additional information: Complete application information available on Institute web site.
Program description:
  Fellowship Program: The foundation identifies areas or issues of the world in need of in-depth understanding and then selects young persons of outstanding character to study and write about those areas or issues for a minimum period of two years. Fellowships have been given—normally one or two a year—to men and women of varied academic and professional backgrounds. In keeping with its generalist and interdisciplinary approach, the institute's fellowships are not awarded to support work toward academic degrees, nor to underwrite specific studies, the writing of books, or programs of research as such. Full support, including living and travel expenses, is provided. Fellows are required to write periodic reports to the Executive Director, which are circulated to persons in education, business, government, and the professions who are interested in the subject of the Fellow's inquiry. For complete information, see the Institute's web site.
EIN: 131621044

1651
Institute of Turkish Studies
c/o Georgetown Univ., Intercultural Ctr.
P.O. Box 571033
Washington, DC   20057-1033   (202) 687-0295
Contact: Sinan Ciddi, Exec. Dir.
FAX: (202) 687-3780;
E-mail: institute_turkishstudies@yahoo.com;
URL: http://www.turkishstudies.org

Foundation type: Independent foundation
Purpose: Grants to the academic community of U.S. specialists in the field of Turkish studies.
Publications: Application guidelines; Grants list; Informational brochure; Multi-year report.
Financial data: Year ended 09/30/2012. Assets, $596,517 (M); Expenditures, $244,065; Total giving, $58,618; Grants to individuals, 12 grants totaling $38,570 (high: $12,500, low: $1,202).
International interests: Turkey.
Type of support: Research; Postdoctoral support; Travel grants; Doctoral support.
Application information: Applications accepted. Application form required. Application form available on the grantmaker's web site.
  Initial approach: Letter
  Send request by: E-mail or online
  Deadline(s): Mar. 12
  Final notification: Recipients notified mid-May
  Applicants should submit the following:
    1) Letter(s) of recommendation
    2) Proposal
    3) Budget Information

Additional information: See web site for complete program information.
EIN: 521294029

1652
International Association of Fire Fighters
(also known as IAFF)
1750 New York Ave. N.W.
Washington, DC   20006-5301   (202) 737-8484
FAX: (202) 737-8418;
E-mail: membership@iaff.org; URL: http://www.iaff.org

Foundation type: Public charity
Purpose: Scholarships to association members, as well as family members of fire fighters killed in the line of duty for attendance at colleges and universities.
Publications: Application guidelines; Newsletter.
Financial data: Year ended 09/30/2012. Assets, $37,654,634 (M); Expenditures, $53,586,658.
Fields of interest: Disasters, fire prevention/control.
Type of support: Scholarships—to individuals.
Application information: Applications accepted. Application form required.
  Send request by: Mail
  Deadline(s): July 1 for Harvard University Trade Union Program Scholarship, Feb. 1 for McClennan Scholarship
  Applicants should submit the following:
    1) Transcripts
    2) Letter(s) of recommendation
    3) Essay
Program descriptions:
  Harvard University Trade Union Program Scholarship: This scholarship is awarded to two association members in good standing with a local affiliate to attend the Harvard University Trade Union Program. Scholarships are for $1,000 plus cost of tuition.
  W.H. "Howie" McClennan Scholarship: The scholarship provides financial assistance for sons, daughters, or legally-adopted children of fire fighters killed in the line of duty planning to attend a university, accredited college, or other institution of higher learning. Scholarships are for $2,500 per year. Awards are based on financial need, aptitude promise and demonstrated academic achievement.
EIN: 530088290

1653
International Association of Fire Fighters Burn Foundation
(also known as IAFF Burn Foundation)
1750 New York Ave., N.W., Ste. 300
Washington, DC   20006-5395   (202) 737-8484
FAX: (202) 637-0839;
E-mail: burnfoundation@iaff.org; URL: http://burn.iaff.org/

Foundation type: Public charity
Purpose: Grants for burn injury research for the prevention and treatment of the physical and psychological problems that impair the quality of life for a burn patient.
Publications: Annual report; Informational brochure; Program policy statement.
Financial data: Year ended 09/30/2011. Assets, $15,339 (M); Expenditures, $523,163; Total giving, $86,052.
Fields of interest: Burn centers; Institute.
Type of support: Research.
Application information:
  Initial approach: Letter or telephone
  Deadline(s): Jan. 12

Additional information: See web site for additional guidelines.
EIN: 521256006

1654
International Association of Fire Fighters Scholarship Fund
1750 New York Ave., N.W. Ste. 300
Washington, DC   20006-5395   (202) 737-8484

Foundation type: Independent foundation
Purpose: Scholarships to sons, daughters, dependents, and legally adopted children of fire fighters who were members in good standing of the IAFF and were killed in the line of duty.
Financial data: Year ended 09/30/2011. Assets, $465,146 (M); Expenditures, $104,833; Total giving, $93,750; Grants to individuals, 38 grants totaling $93,750 (high: $2,500, low: $1,250).
Fields of interest: Vocational education; Disasters, fire prevention/control.
Type of support: Graduate support; Technical education support; Undergraduate support.
Application information: Applications accepted. Application form required.
  Deadline(s): Feb. 1
  Final notification: Recipients notified Aug. 1
  Applicants should submit the following:
    1) Transcripts
    2) Letter(s) of recommendation
    3) Financial information
    4) Essay
  Additional information: Scholarships are awarded on the basis of financial need, promise, and academic achievement, and are renewable for up to four years. Applicants must have at least a 2.0 GPA. Recipients may attend any postsecondary institution requiring a high school diploma or GED, including vocational/technical schools, training institutions, two- and four-year public or private accredited colleges, universities, and graduate schools. Renewal applications are given preference over new applications. See web site for full application guidelines and requirements.
EIN: 521121279

1655
International Campaign for Tibet
1825 Jefferson Pl., N.W.
Washington, DC   20036-2504   (202) 785-1515
FAX: (202) 785-4343; E-mail: info@savetibet.org;
URL: http://www.savetibet.org

Foundation type: Public charity
Purpose: Awards to Tibetan individuals who make significant contributions to the international community.
Publications: Annual report; Financial statement.
Financial data: Year ended 12/31/2011. Assets, $4,473,640 (M); Expenditures, $3,719,488; Total giving, $176,552; Grants to individuals, totaling $81,584.
Fields of interest: International affairs; Community/economic development.
Type of support: Grants to individuals.
Application information: Applications accepted.
  Deadline(s): Sept. 30
  Applicants should submit the following:
    1) Proposal
    2) Budget Information
Program description:
  Rowell Fund for Tibet: This fund provides grants of up to $7,500 to support Tibetans who can make a significant contribution to their community and/or

an international audience in the fields of visual arts and media, the environment, and women's rights.
EIN: 521570071

1656
The International Center for Journalists, Inc.

1616 H St., N.W., 3rd Fl.
Washington, DC 20006-4903 (202) 737-3700
Contact: Nancy P. Frye, V.P., Finance and Admin.
FAX: (202) 737-0530; E-mail: editor@icfj.org;
Additional URL (for Knight Fellowships): http://www.knight.ifcj.org; E-mail for Nancy Frye: nfrye@icfj.org; URL: http://www.icfj.org
Additional URL: http://www.ijnet.org

Foundation type: Public charity
Purpose: Fellowships and internships to journalists who have exhibited outstanding personal and professional achievement, including technical, managerial and business aspects of a free press and who exhibit a spirit of adventure and willingness to face personal and professional hardships in the field.
Publications: Application guidelines; Newsletter.
Financial data: Year ended 12/31/2011. Assets, $20,542,748 (M); Expenditures, $10,541,973; Total giving, $3,868,970; Grants to individuals, totaling $660,254.
Fields of interest: Print publishing; Environment; International exchange; International affairs; Public affairs; Hispanics/Latinos.
International interests: Africa; Germany; Japan.
Type of support: Fellowships; Internship funds; Research; Exchange programs; Foreign applicants; Undergraduate support; Travel grants.
Application information: Applications accepted. Application form required. Application form available on the grantmaker's web site.
Deadline(s): Varies
Program descriptions:
Arthur F. Burns Fellowship Program: The program offers 10 young print and broadcast journalists from each country the opportunity to share professional expertise with their colleagues across the Atlantic while working as 'foreign correspondents' for their hometown news organizations. This competitive program is open to U.S. and German journalists who are employed by a newspaper, news magazine, broadcast station, or news agency; and to freelancers. Applicants must have demonstrated journalistic talent and a strong interest in U.S.-European affairs. German language proficiency is not required, but encouraged. Each fellow receives a $5,500 stipend to cover basic travel and living expenses during the two-month fellowship; the program also pays living expenses during the orientation in Washington, DC.
Knight International Journalism Fellowships: This program, funded in conjunction with the John S. and James L. Knight Foundation, works to make tangible changes that improve the quality and freeflow of news in the public interest around the world. The year-long program sends international media professionals to countries where there are opportunities to promote reliable, insightful journalists that hold officials accountable.
McGee Journalism Fellowship in Southern Africa: Each year, a fellow is posted to one or more nations in southern Africa for three to four months. The fellow is based at a university, media assistance organization, or journalism association to conduct professional development programs for local journalists in topics that best fit the local journalists' needs and the fellow's expertise. The fellow will also seek out journalists who would benefit from professional development programs in

the U.S. For more information about the fellowship, contact mcgee@icfj.org.
World Affairs Journalism Fellowships: These fellowships are intended for experienced journalists and editors from America's community-based daily newspapers. The goal is to give them an opportunity to establish the connections between local-regional issues and what is happening abroad. Fellows will conduct overseas research and then submit articles to their local papers in an effort to 'internationalize' America's local press. The fellowships are founded on the belief that local news is not limited to one's immediate community and that enterprising reporters and editors can find good international stories in their own backyards. The program is aimed at news managers, editors, commentary writers, and other 'gatekeepers' (those desk editors largely responsible for selecting news agency and correspondent-initiated stories). By supporting overseas research and writing projects for up to three weeks, the fellowships encourage the writing and selection of news articles, analysis, features, and commentary in the local press that will enhance American understanding of the relationship between local and international issues. The program is jointly administered by the center and the Newspaper Association Managers (NAM). Up to eight fellows from the U.S. will be selected and provided support to develop projects that will lead to articles in their home newspapers or in other U.S.-based publications. While overseas, each fellow receives transportation and living expenses, based on the actual cost of traveling to and living in each country while carrying out the approved project.
EIN: 112724905

1657
International City/County Management Association

777 N. Capitol St., N.E., Ste. 500
Washington, DC 20002-4201 (202) 289-4262
Contact: Robert J. O'Neill, Exec.Dir.
FAX: (202) 962-3500; E-mail: roneill@icma.org;
URL: http://www.icma.org

Foundation type: Public charity
Purpose: Scholarships for travel, lodging, and registration of select ICMA conference attendees.
Publications: Application guidelines; Newsletter.
Financial data: Year ended 06/30/2012. Assets, $14,535,932 (M); Expenditures, $33,160,760; Total giving, $660,457; Grants to individuals, totaling $32,006.
Fields of interest: Education.
Type of support: Scholarships—to individuals.
Application information: Applications accepted. Application form required.
Additional information: Applicants must be ICMA members to qualify for assistance. See web site for additional guidelines.
EIN: 362167755

1658
International Leadership Foundation

1300 Pennsylvania Ave., N.W., Ste. 700
Washington, DC 20044-4382 (202) 609-8819
Contact: Paul S. Hsu, Chair.
E-mail: ilf@ileader.org; URL: http://www.ileader.org/

Foundation type: Public charity
Purpose: Scholarships and fellowships for college students from across the U.S. who are placed in

structured internships in government agencies and the private sector.
Publications: Application guidelines; Grants list.
Financial data: Year ended 12/31/2012. Assets, $428,723 (M); Expenditures, $771,756; Total giving, $45,720; Grants to individuals, totaling $45,720.
Type of support: Fellowships.
Application information: Applications accepted. Application form required.
Deadline(s): Feb. 1
Final notification: Applicants notified Mar. 1
Applicants should submit the following:
1) Transcripts
2) Resume
3) Letter(s) of recommendation
Additional information: See web site for additional guidelines.
EIN: 943362322

1659
International Union of Painters and Allied Trades

7234 Parkway Dr.
Washington, DC 21076-1307 (410) 564-5900
Contact: Kenneth E. Rigmaiden, Pres.
E-mail: mail@iupat.org; URL: http://www.iupat.org

Foundation type: Public charity
Purpose: Scholarships to legal dependants of IUPAT members to further their education.
Publications: Application guidelines; Newsletter.
Financial data: Year ended 12/31/2011. Assets, $77,380,764 (M); Expenditures, $38,039,542; Total giving, $190,604; Grants to individuals, totaling $78,540.
Fields of interest: Vocational education, post-secondary; Higher education.
Type of support: Scholarships—to individuals.
Application information: Applications accepted. Application form required.
Deadline(s): Sept. 1 for Monroe/Williams, III Sports Scholarship and Dec. 14 for Raftery Scholarship
Applicants should submit the following:
1) Transcripts
2) Letter(s) of recommendation
3) Financial information
4) Essay
Additional information: Applicants for the sports scholarship must supply a complete history of athletic participation and special recognition in high school.
Program descriptions:
A.L. "Mike" Monroe/Ralph D. Williams, III Sports Scholarship Awards Program: This program offers student athletes the opportunity to pursue their athletic ambitions while earning an advanced educational degree at the academic institution of their choice, by awarding a $5,000 scholarship to each successful candidate for his/her education. Eligible applicants must: be a legal dependent of a union member in good standing; enroll in the school of their choice within one year of the award date; and be registered with the NCAA Clearing House and declare the athletic program in which he/she will be participating.
S. Frank "Bud" Raftery Scholarship: Ten scholarships of $2,000 each are available to sons, daughters, and legal dependents of the International Union of Painters and Allied Trades (IUPAT). Eligible applicants must submit an essay, between 1,000 and 2,000 words, on a chosen topic each year. Scholarship awards are contingent upon the student attending a certified college, university,

vocational technology school, trade school, or another institute of higher learning.
EIN: 350198600

1660

International Women's Media Foundation

1625 K St., N.W., Ste. 1275
Washington, DC 20006-1680 (202) 496-1992
Contact: Elisa Lees Munoz, Exec. Dir.
FAX: (202) 496-1977; E-mail: info@iwmf.org;
URL: http://www.iwmf.org

Foundation type: Public charity
Purpose: Awards by nomination only to women journalists who have shown extraordinary strength of character and courage to report the news under dangerous and difficult circumstances.
Publications: Application guidelines; Annual report; Informational brochure; Newsletter; Occasional report.
Financial data: Year ended 06/30/2012. Assets, $1,663,172 (M); Expenditures, $1,200,565; Total giving, $159,746; Grants to individuals, totaling $60,000.
Fields of interest: Print publishing; Journalism; Women.
Type of support: Fellowships; Awards/grants by nomination only; Foreign applicants; Awards/prizes.
Application information:
Deadline(s): Mar. 2 for Courage in Journalism, Mar. 8 for Women Entrepreneurs in the Global Digital News Frontier Grant, Apr. 30 for Elizabeth Neuffer Fellowship
Final notification: Recipients notified in May for Courage in Journalism, Apr. for Women Entrepreneurs in the Global Digital News Frontier, June 15 for Elizabeth Neuffer Fellowship
Additional information: See web site for additional guidelines.
Program descriptions:
Elizabeth Neuffer Fellowship: This fellowship provides an opportunity for a woman journalist working in the print, broadcast, or Internet media to spend seven months in a tailored program with access to MIT's Center for International Studies as well as media outlets including The Boston Globe and The New York Times. Through these, the fellow will have opportunities to pursue academic research as well as hone her journalistic skills covering topics related to human rights and social justice. Eligible applicants must be dedicated to a career in journalism in the print, broadcast, or Internet media sectors (including freelancers), be committed to coverage of human rights and social justice, describe how the fellowship will be a transformative experience for her career, have three or more years of journalism experience, and have excellent written and verbal English skills. A stipend will be provided, and expenses, including airfare and housing, will be covered. Contact neuffer@iwmf.org for additional information.
Environmental Reporting Fellowship in the Philippines: This program for women in journalism aims to transform news media coverage of environmental issues in the Philippines. Many environmental problems threaten quality of life in the Philippines, yet these issues receive inadequate news media coverage. In addition, much of the reporting being done lacks depth and excludes the voices of those most affected by environmental degradation, especially women. To address this critical gap in coverage, the program will provide advanced training and coaching to10 journalists, preparing them to produce innovative reports about environmental problems and

solutions, incorporating women's roles in and perspectives on environmental issues. By the conclusion of the year-long fellowship, these journalists will become environmental reporting specialists.
HIV/AIDS Reporting in South Africa: This program aims to increase public awareness of the multi-faceted impact the HIV/AIDS epidemic has on South African communities, with fellows telling untold stories through their reporting. Ten accomplished South African journalists are selected to participate in the fellowship program where they will receive advanced training and coaching to produce innovative, high-quality investigative reporting on the complex issues surrounding HIV/AIDS, reflecting women's voices and concerns. Each will produce three to four investigations as part of the IWMF program.
IWMF Leadership Institute for Women Journalists: The institute empower women in the news media to be successful in their careers. The Institute's programs take different forms in different countries, but their goal is to provide the training and the network for women who want to move up the career ladder.
Women Entrepreneurs in the Global Digital News Frontier Grants: Three grants of $20,000 each will be awarded to women journalists who aspire to be digital news media entrepreneurs, with the hopes of diversifying the emerging digital news media landscape by expanding the voice and role of women entrepreneurs. In addition to seed funding, grantees will receive pro-bono coaching, and will participate in a monthly call series featuring leading entrepreneurs and digital news media experts. Eligible applicants must be U.S.-based women journalists who propose a new project that has not yet launched, and which will use digital media in innovative ways to deliver the news. Applicants must also include a business plan that demonstrates sustainability, as well as how the project intend to further the role of women in the news media.
EIN: 521648942

1661

Jack and Jill of America Foundation

1930 17th St., N.W.
Washington, DC 20009-6207 (202) 232-5290
FAX: (202) 232-1747; URL: http://www.jackandjillfoundation.org/

Foundation type: Public charity
Purpose: Scholarships to deserving African American high school seniors pursuing a higher education at an accredited four year institution.
Publications: Application guidelines; Annual report; Newsletter.
Financial data: Year ended 05/31/2012. Assets, $2,880,441 (M); Expenditures, $678,516; Total giving, $303,070.
Fields of interest: Higher education; African Americans/Blacks.
Type of support: Undergraduate support.
Application information: Applications accepted. Application form required. Application form available on the grantmaker's web site.
Initial approach: E-mail or letter
Send request by: Online
Deadline(s): Mar. 14
Applicants should submit the following:
1) Resume
2) GPA
3) Letter(s) of recommendation
4) Transcripts
5) Essay

Program description:
National College Scholarship Awards: Scholarships range from $1,500 to $2,500 for African American high school seniors with a minimum GPA of 3.0 pursuing a bachelor's degree in an accredited postsecondary institution in the U.S. Scholarship will be applied toward tuition, and room and board.
EIN: 510224656

1662

The Jerusalem Fund for Education and Community Development

(formerly The Jerusalem Fund)
2425 Virginia Ave., N.W.
Washington, DC 20037-2637 (202) 338-1958
Contact: Yousef Munayyer, Exec. Dir.
FAX: (202) 333-7742;
E-mail: info@palestinecenter.org; E-Mail for Yousef Munayyer: ymunayyer@thejerusalemfund.org;
URL: http://www.palestinecenter.org

Foundation type: Public charity
Purpose: Scholarships, fellowships, and travel and research grants to residents of Palestinian communities in Israel, the West Bank, and Gaza.
Publications: Annual report; Financial statement; Grants list; Newsletter.
Financial data: Year ended 12/31/2011. Assets, $4,516,469 (M); Expenditures, $835,766; Total giving, $65,300.
Fields of interest: International exchange, students.
Type of support: Research.
Application information: Applications accepted. Application form required. Interview required.
Initial approach: Letter
Deadline(s): Aug. 31 and Dec. 15
Additional information: Application should also include a biographical record, a report on academic and/or professional careers, and a statement of training plans.
Program description:
Internship Program: Internships for graduate and undergraduate students are based in Washington, D.C. Internships provide students with an opportunity to conduct primary-source research, develop writing and organizational skills, build valuable D.C. contacts, gain hands-on experience, and observe the extensive political and policy-related happenings in the D.C. area. Internships are not paid.
EIN: 521238142

1663

Jews United for Justice

2027 Massachusetts Ave., Fl. 3
Washington, DC 20036-1011 (202) 408-1423
E-mail: info@jufj.org; URL: http://www.jufj.org

Foundation type: Public charity
Purpose: Fellowships to educate and train young adults between the ages of 25 and 35 to become the next generation of Jewish social justice change makers.
Publications: Newsletter.
Financial data: Year ended 12/31/2011. Assets, $272,773 (M); Expenditures, $420,868.
Fields of interest: Jewish agencies & synagogues.
Type of support: Fellowships.
Application information:
Initial approach: Letter
Deadline(s): Sept. 8
Program description:
Jeremiah Fellowships: This fellowship opportunity, given in conjunction with the

Progressive Jewish Alliance, works to educate and train a select cohort of young adults (ages 25 to 35) to become the next generation of Jewish social justice change makers. The goals of the fellowship include: empowerment through in-depth training in professional and leadership skills; expanding knowledge of what Jewish text, tradition, and history have to say about putting ethics into action; acquiring tangible organizing and activism skills within a Jewish context; exploring pressing social, political, and economic issues facing the region; and accessing a dynamic network of organizers, advocates, rabbis, artists, and renowned scholars. During the nine-month fellowship, participants will be expected to attend monthly sessions to discuss different models of putting ethics and values into action, develop community organizing and activism skills, and participate in grassroots fundraising activities.
EIN: 522346578

1664
Junior League of Washington, Inc.
3039 M. St., N.W.
Washington, DC 20007-3759 (202) 337-2001
Contact: Shiela Corley, Pres.
FAX: (202) 342-3148; E-mail: office@jlw.org;
URL: http://www.jlw.org/

Foundation type: Public charity
Purpose: Scholarships to graduating seniors of DC public schools for outstanding volunteerism. Also, awards to winners of a poetry contest for DC public school students in grades four through eight.
Publications: Application guidelines.
Financial data: Year ended 05/31/2012. Assets, $3,826,320 (M); Expenditures, $885,916; Total giving, $207,730; Grants to individuals, totaling $10,000.
Fields of interest: Voluntarism promotion; Youth.
Type of support: Awards/prizes; Undergraduate support.
Application information: Applications accepted. Application form required. Application form available on the grantmaker's web site.
Initial approach: Application
Send request by: Mail
Deadline(s): Mar. 15 for Meg Graham Scholarship Endowment Celebrating Service and Leadership
Applicants should submit the following:
1) Essay
2) Letter(s) of recommendation
3) Transcripts
Program description:
Meg Graham Scholarship Endowment Celebrating Service and Leadership: A $10,000 scholarship is available to a Washington, DC high school senior, at a public or charter school, who is matriculating to an accredited four-year, postsecondary institution. Applicant must demonstrate a commitment to volunteerism and have a 3.0 GPA. Recipient must maintain a minimum GPA of 2.75 or higher as a full-time student to be considered for additional scholarship funds.
EIN: 530213317

1665
The Robert F. Kennedy Center for Justice and Human Rights
(formerly Robert F. Kennedy Memorial)
1300 19th St., N.W., Ste. 750
Washington, DC 20036-1859 (202) 463-7575
Contact: Lynn Delaney, Exec. Dir.
FAX: (202) 463-6606; E-mail: info@rfkcenter.org;
URL: http://www.rfkcenter.org

Foundation type: Public charity
Purpose: Awards to individuals for outstanding journalism that reflects that philosophy and personal missions of Robert F. Kennedy.
Publications: Application guidelines.
Financial data: Year ended 12/31/2011. Assets, $6,479,760 (M); Expenditures, $6,198,261; Total giving, $102,064; Grants to individuals, totaling $9,064.
Fields of interest: Print publishing.
Type of support: Awards/prizes.
Application information: Applications accepted. Application form required. Application form available on the grantmaker's web site.
Deadline(s): Jan. 31
Additional information: Submission for the Robert F. Kennedy Book Award must contain four copies of the book being submitted, a press release and descriptive cover letter, and a $75 entry fee. Submission for the Robert F Kennedy Journalism Award must be accompanied by samples of work and a $75 entry fee; see web site for further submission guidelines (including acceptable formats for work).
Program descriptions:
Robert F. Kennedy Book Award: This award is presented to the author of a book that reflects the themes that most interested Robert F. Kennedy during his lifetime: a concern for the poor and the powerless, a struggle for honest and even-handed justice, a conviction that a decent society must assure all young people a fair chance, and a strong faith in a free democracy that can act to remedy disparities of power and opportunity. Both fiction and non-fiction works are eligible for this prize; all entries must have been published in the year prior to application. Awards carry a $2,500 cash prize.
Robert F. Kennedy Journalism Awards: These awards honor outstanding reporting on issues that reflect Robert Kennedy's concerns, including human rights, social justice, the power of individual action in the U.S. and around the world, and reporting on insights into the causes, conditions, and remedies of injustices, as well as the critical analyses of relevant public policies, programs, attitudes, and private endeavors. Eligible entries must have been published or broadcast in the U.S. for the first time between Jan. 1 and Dec. 31 of the year prior to application. Awards will be given in five categories (print, television, radio, photography, and cartoons); recipients will receive a $1,000 cash prize, with a 'grand-prize' winner receiving an additional cash award.
EIN: 132522784

1666
The John F. Kennedy Center for the Performing Arts
2700 F St., N.W.
Washington, DC 20566-0001 (202) 467-4600
Contact: Michael M. Kaiser, Pres.
FAX: (202) 416-8205; Toll-free tel.:
(800)-444-1324; URL: http://www.kennedy-center.org

Foundation type: Public charity

Purpose: Fellowships and residencies to artists.
Publications: Application guidelines; Informational brochure.
Financial data: Year ended 09/30/2011. Assets, $411,406,853 (M); Expenditures, $192,547,577; Total giving, $1,227,707; Grants to individuals, totaling $854,721.
Fields of interest: Management/technical assistance; Performing arts; Performing arts centers; Music; Music composition.
Type of support: Fellowships; Residencies.
Application information: Application form required.
Send request by: Online
Deadline(s): Dec. 1 for Fellowship, Nov. 17 for Jazz Ahead
Applicants should submit the following:
1) Resume
2) Transcripts
3) Letter(s) of recommendation
Program descriptions:
Fellowships: The center offers two fellowship programs for highly-motivated arts managers. The DeVos International Summer Fellowship Program offers international not-for-profit arts managers an immersive program to study arts management strategy. For four weeks each summer, for three consecutive years, international fellows participate in seminars, group projects, individual mentorships and practical rotations supervised by Institute faculty and Center senior staff. The Fellowship program provides comprehensive study to 10 arts managers at the Kennedy Center with coursework in strategic planning, marketing, and development; three practical work rotations in Center departments; and a series of professional development seminars. The paid fellowships are full-time and last nine months from Sept. through May.
Jazz Ahead Residency Program: This residency program identifies emerging jazz artists in their mid-teens and twenties, and brings them together under the tutelage of experienced artist-instructors. Applicants must be under age 30, be proficient in English and be performers as well as composers. The week-long program includes daily workshops and rehearsals with established jazz artists and culminates in three concerts on the Kennedy Center's Millennium Stage. Travel, meal and lodging is provided. This program is currently suspended. Check the web site for future updates on the program.
EIN: 530245017

1667
The Joseph P. Kennedy, Jr. Foundation
1133 19th St. N.W., 10th Fl.
Washington, DC 20036-3604 (202) 393-1250
Contact: Steve Eidelman, Mgr.
Fellowship inquiry: Eidelman@jpkf.org
FAX: (202) 824-0351; E-mail: info@jpkf.org;
URL: http://www.jpkf.org

Foundation type: Independent foundation
Purpose: Grants to individuals in the field of developmental disabilities to learn about public policy through work in government offices.
Financial data: Year ended 12/31/2012. Assets, $14,812,150 (M); Expenditures, $381,310; Total giving, $226,129. Grants to individuals amount not specified.
Fields of interest: Developmentally disabled, centers & services; Research; Disabilities, people with.
Type of support: Fellowships; Research.
Application information: Applications accepted. Interview required.

Initial approach: Letter
Deadline(s): Apr.
Additional information: Policy fellowship applicants should submit a letter of interest and letters of support.
Program description:
Public Policy Fellowship Program: The Foundation awards professionals and family members a stipend to work in Washington for a full year, where they actively participate in public policy development through work on the staff of a congressional committee, or a federal agency. The program offers opportunities to be involved in policy and legislative development in key areas such as special education, health and mental health care for persons with intellectual and developmental disabilities, child care, housing, justice, child welfare and other areas related to improving the quality of life for individuals with intellectual and developmental disabilities.
EIN: 136083407

1668
Landscape Architecture Foundation
1129 20th St. N.W., Ste. 202
Washington, DC 20036 (202) 331-7070
FAX: (202) 331-7079;
E-mail: bdeutsch@lafoundation.org; URL: http://www.lafoundation.org

Foundation type: Public charity
Purpose: Scholarships and grants to students and professionals to further their research or study in the field of landscape architecture.
Publications: Application guidelines.
Financial data: Year ended 12/31/2012. Assets, $4,065,533 (M); Expenditures, $735,097; Total giving, $64,500; Grants to individuals, totaling $64,500.
Fields of interest: Architecture; Landscaping; Minorities.
Type of support: Support to graduates or students of specific schools; Graduate support; Undergraduate support.
Application information: Applications accepted.
Initial approach: Telephone or e-mail
Deadline(s): Feb. 1 for Fellowships, Feb. 15 for Scholarships, Mar. 15 for Olmsted Scholars
Additional information: See web site for additional application guidelines.
Program descriptions:
ASLA Council of Fellows Scholarship: Awards two $4,000 scholarships in the fall to promising students who are third-, fourth-, or fifth-year undergraduates at Landscape Architecture Accreditation Board (LAAB)-accredited programs of landscape architecture. Graduate students are not eligible for this award. Eligible applicants must be permanent U.S. citizens or permanent resident aliens.
Courtland Paul Scholarship: Awards $5,000 to undergraduate students in the final two years of study in Landscape Architecture Accreditation Board-accredited schools. Eligible applicants must be U.S. citizens.
Douglas Dockery Thomas Fellowship in Garden History and Design: This $4,000 fellowship is awarded annually to an exceptional graduate student to assist with study and research at a leading American institution.
EDSA Minority Scholarship: The scholarship was established to help African American, Hispanic, Native American, and minority students of other cultural and ethnic backgrounds entering into their final two years of undergraduate study in landscape architecture continue their education. Each award is $5,000.

Hawaii Chapter/David T. Woolsey Scholarship: The $2,000 award provides funds for a third-, fourth-, or fifth-year undergraduate or graduate student of landscape architecture whose permanent residence is Hawaii.
Landscape Forms Design for People Scholarship: This $3,000 scholarship honors excellence in design for people, addressing how people use spaces and the ways in which the design of spaces and amenities can enhance and enrich the experience of those who use them. Eligible applicants include landscape architecture students who will be starting their final year of full-time undergraduate study in a LAAB-accredited program, and who demonstrate passion, commitment, and competence in creating great spaces for people.
Olmsted Scholarship: This scholarship program aims to identify, recognize, and support students with exceptional leadership potential who are willing to engage current and critical issues through the use of ideas, influence, communication, services, and leadership with a $25,000 scholarship, thus advancing sustainable planning and design and fostering human and societal benefits.
Peridian International, Inc./Rae L. Price, FASLA Scholarship: Awards $5,000 to students in the final two years of study in Landscape Architecture at the University of California at Los Angeles Extension Program, or in the case of UCLA's termination of the program, other California accredited schools of programs in Landscape Architecture.
Rain Bird Scholarship: A $2,500 scholarship will be awarded to a student in his/her final two years of undergraduate study who is in need of financial assistance. Eligible applicants include those who have demonstrated commitment to the profession through participation in extracurricular activities and exemplary scholastic achievements.
Steven G. King Play Environments Scholarship: This $5,000 scholarship recognizes a student who has high potential in the design of play environments. Eligible applicants include landscape architecture students with a demonstrated interest and aptitude in the design of play environments, who are enrolled in graduate or the final two years of undergraduate study in LAAB-accredited schools. Applicants must show an interest in the value of integrating playgrounds into parks, schools, and other play environments, and understand the significant social and educational value of play.
The Dangermond Fellowship: Awards three $10,000 fellowships each year to graduate students in the United States. Recipients are also awarded a computer, ESRI software, technical training access, and travel costs to conferences. The purpose of the fellowship is to promote and facilitate the integration of art, science, method, and technology in the study and profession of landscape architecture, and encourage the use of geographic information systems (GIS) as a framework for exploring integrated approaches to landscape assessment and intervention.
EIN: 526065505

1669
Latino Student Fund
3480 Woodley Rd., N.W., Carriage House- 2ND Floor
P. O. Box 5403
Washington, DC 20016 (202) 244-3438
Contact: Maria Fernanda Borja, Exec. Dir.
Application address: P.O. Box 5403, Washington, DC 20016-1003
FAX: (202) 244-3757;
E-mail: director@latinostudentfund.org; E-mail For Maria Fernanda

Borja:mfborja@latinostudentfund.org; URL: http://www.latinostudentfund.org

Foundation type: Public charity
Purpose: Scholarships to Latino students in grades PreK-12 for enrollment in Washington, DC metropolitan area independent and parochial schools.
Publications: Newsletter.
Financial data: Year ended 08/31/2012. Assets, $385,874 (M); Expenditures, $416,268; Total giving, $88,500; Grants to individuals, totaling $88,500.
Fields of interest: Elementary school/education; Secondary school/education; Hispanics/Latinos.
Type of support: Scholarships—to individuals.
Application information: Applications accepted. Application form required.
Deadline(s): Apr. 15 for returning students, Apr. 21 for new students
Final notification: Applicants notified in early June
Applicants should submit the following:
1) Letter(s) of recommendation
2) Financial information
Program description:
Scholars Program: The program provides financial aid and education-related support to students in grades PreK-12. The program includes mentoring, workshops on higher education, and support for students and their families. Small stipends are provided and are supplemented by a series of workshops designed for family networking and to prepare students and their families for the future. Scholarships are merit-based and fixed depending on the grade level. The scholarship amounts are as follows: Grades K-5, $500; Grades 6-8, $1,000; and Grades 9-12, $1,500. Applicants must be of Latino descent; demonstrate excellent academic achievement; be admitted to a parochial or independent school for the upcoming academic year; and receive financial aid from the school or Archdiocese.
EIN: 521859975

1670
Legal Services Corporation
(also known as LSC)
3333 K St., N.W., 3rd Fl.
Washington, DC 20007-3522 (202) 295-1500
Contact: Jim Sandman, Pres.
FAX: (202) 337-6797; E-mail: info@lsc.gov; E-mail for Jim Sandman: jsandman@lsc.gov; URL: http://www.lsc.gov

Foundation type: Public charity
Purpose: Grants to attorneys throughout the U.S. and its territories, to provide service to low-income individuals.
Publications: Application guidelines; Annual report; Informational brochure; Occasional report.
Financial data: Year ended 09/30/2012. Assets, $74,472,872 (M); Expenditures, $353,151,065; Total giving, $332,753,738; Grants to individuals, 206 grants totaling $575,462.
Fields of interest: Legal services; Economically disadvantaged.
Type of support: Grants to individuals.
Application information: Applications accepted. Application form available on the grantmaker's web site.
Initial approach: Application
Deadline(s): Varies
Additional information: Funding availability varies depending on geographic area served by applicants. See web site for additional information.

Program description:

Legal Aid Grants: The corporation will fund qualified attorneys, organizations, and entities that will most effectively and efficiently provide high-quality legal representation to eligible clients within a comprehensive, statewide integrated delivery system. Grants are intended to allow recipients to provide a full range of legal services throughout each service area, including consumer/finance, family, housing, education, income maintenance, employment, health, and other (including juvenile, individual rights, and wills) services. Grants will be made available in three service areas: Basic Field-General (intended to provide legal services to the general low-income population living in a specific geographical area), Basic Field-Native American (intended to provide legal services to Native Americans living in a specific geographical area, related to their status as Native Americans), and Basic Field-Migrant (intended to provide legal services to migrant farmworkers living in a specific geographical area, related to their status as migrant farmworkers). Eligible applicants include nonprofit organizations that have as a purpose the provision of legal assistance to eligible clients, private attorneys, groups of attorneys or law firms, state and local governments, and sub-state regional planning or coordination agencies that are composed of sub-state areas whose governing boards are controlled by locally-elected officials.
EIN: 521039060

1671
Lupus Foundation of America, Inc.
2000 L St., N.W., Ste. 710
Washington, DC   20036-4916   (202) 349-1155
Contact: Sandra C. Raymond, Pres. and C.E.O.
FAX: (202) 349-1156; E-mail: info@lupus.org;
URL: http://www.lupus.org

Foundation type: Public charity
Purpose: Grants and fellowships to principal investigators who are seeking a cure for lupus.
Publications: Annual report.
Financial data: Year ended 09/30/2011. Assets, $6,701,026 (M); Expenditures, $10,232,403; Total giving, $806,250; Grants to individuals, totaling $5,000.
Fields of interest: Lupus research.
Type of support: Fellowships; Grants to individuals.
Application information: Applications accepted.
  Send request by: Online
  Deadline(s): Mar. 29 for Gina M. Finzi Memorial Student Summer Fellowship Program
  Final notification: Recipients notified May 10 for Gina M. Finzi Fellowship Program
Program description:
  Gina Finzi Memorial Student Summer Fellowships: Awards in the amount of $4,000 is to foster an interest among students in the area of basic, clinical, translational, epidemiological, or behavioral research relevant to lupus under the sponsorship and supervision of an established, tenure-track Principal Investigator who directs a laboratory dedicated at least in part to the investigation of lupus at a U.S. academic, medical or research institution. Although undergraduate students may apply, preference will be given to graduate or medical students who already earned a baccalaureate degree or will have done so prior to their official acceptance of the award.
EIN: 431131436

1672
Marijuana Policy Project
236 Massachusetts Ave., N.E., Ste. 400
P.O. Box 77470
Washington, DC   20002-4980   (202) 462-5747
Contact: Rob Kampia, Exec. Dir.
E-mail: info@mpp.org; URL: http://www.mpp.org

Foundation type: Public charity
Purpose: Grants to individuals to support projects that encourage the legalization of marijuana within the U.S.
Publications: Application guidelines; Annual report.
Financial data: Year ended 12/31/2011. Assets, $1,000,259 (M); Expenditures, $950,584; Total giving, $3,500; Grants to individuals, totaling $500.
Fields of interest: Civil/human rights; Public affairs.
Type of support: Grants to individuals.
Application information: Contact the organization for additional information.
EIN: 521911644

1673
Marijuana Policy Project Foundation
P.O. Box 77492
Capitol Hill
Washington, DC   20013-8492   (202) 462-5747
Contact: Nydia Swaby, Dir., Grants and VIP Outreach; Sara Cannon, Asst. Mgr., Grants and VIP Outreach
FAX: (202) 232-0442; E-mail: scannon@mpp.org;
URL: http://www.mpp.org

Foundation type: Public charity
Purpose: Research support to individuals for projects that seek to increase public understanding of or decriminalize marijuana.
Publications: Application guidelines; Newsletter; Program policy statement.
Financial data: Year ended 12/31/2011. Assets, $165,693 (M); Expenditures, $1,358,686; Total giving, $6,000. Grants to individuals amount not specified.
Fields of interest: Reform; Reform.
Type of support: Research.
Application information: Applications accepted. Application form required. Application form available on the grantmaker's web site.
  Initial approach: Letter
  Deadline(s): Vary
  Additional information: See web site for additional information.
Program descriptions:
  Diagnostic and Statistical Manual Grants: The foundation is interested in providing funding for an individual or organization to influence the American Psychiatric Association's (APA's) definition of marijuana abuse and dependence in the forthcoming "Diagnostic and Statistical Manual V." Currently, the DSM criteria for marijuana abuse and dependence include problems that might be caused or exacerbated by marijuana prohibition, ironically increasing the perceived need for maintaining prohibition. The foundation seeks to make the DSM's definition of marijuana dependence more accurate, so that people who use marijuana responsibly are not mislabeled as having an abuse or dependence problem.
  Grassroots Organizing Projects in Targeted States and Congressional Districts Grants: The foundation seeks to fund organizations and individuals for comprehensive grassroots organizing for marijuana policy reform in targeted states and congressional districts. The areas of grassroots organizing that are eligible for such funding fall into three

categories: organizing to pass medical marijuana legislation in key states, organizing in key states to pass legislation to regulate marijuana similarly to alcohol, and organizing in congressional districts to pressure targeted members of Congress to support the Hinchey-Rohrabacher amendment to de-fund the federal government's war on medical marijuana.
  Marijuana Research Grants Program: The foundation provides funding for projects that will measurably advance marijuana policy reform in the United States. Grants of up to $60,000 are available for objective, publishable, scientifically rigorous research on marijuana and marijuana policy.
  Medical Marijuana Financial Assistance Program: The program seeks to help low-income patients obtain government-issued registry cards that allow patients to legally use marijuana under state law. Low-income patients or caregivers in Colorado, Montana, Nevada, Vermont, and Rhode Island are eligible to apply for financial assistance from the foundation to cover their medical marijuana ID card application fee.
EIN: 521975211

1674
Thurgood Marshall College Fund
(formerly Thurgood Marshall Scholarship Fund, also known as TMCF)
901 F. St. N.W., Ste. 300
Washington, DC   20004   (202) 507-4851
Contact: Johnny C. Taylor, Jr., Pres. and C.E.O.
FAX: (202) 652-2934;
E-mail: johnny.taylor@tmcfund.org; URL: http://www.thurgoodmarshallfund.org

Foundation type: Public charity
Purpose: Scholarships to students pursuing a degree in any discipline at one of the 47 TMCF member schools.
Publications: Annual report; Financial statement; Occasional report.
Financial data: Year ended 12/31/2011. Assets, $7,019,440 (M); Expenditures, $14,907,009; Total giving, $7,068,361; Grants to individuals, totaling $7,068,361.
Fields of interest: Higher education.
Type of support: Scholarships—to individuals; Support to graduates or students of specific schools.
Application information: Applications accepted. Application form required.
  Deadline(s): Apr. and May
  Additional information: Scholarships are paid directly to the educational institution on behalf of the students.
Program description:
  Scholarships: The foundation will award scholarships to students who attend one of the fund's member schools, and who: are U.S. citizens; are full-time students pursuing a degree in any discipline; demonstrate commitment to academic excellence and community service with a high school GPA of at least 3.0; who have a combined verbal/math score of at least 1650 on the Scholastic Aptitude Test (SAT) or a score of 25 on the American College Testing (ACT) examination; are recommended by their high school as academically exceptional or outstanding in the creative or performing arts; and who demonstrate financial need. Scholarships average around $2,200 per student per semester, and can be used for tuition, room and board, books, and fees.
EIN: 411750692

1675

The Masonic Foundation of the District of Columbia

5428 Macarthur Blvd. N.W.
Washington, DC 20016-2524 (202) 686-1811
Contact: Robert Heyat, Pres.

Foundation type: Public charity
Purpose: Scholarships for high school seniors in Washington, DC for postsecondary education.
Financial data: Year ended 03/31/2012. Assets, $6,836,163 (M); Expenditures, $240,025; Total giving, $200,717; Grants to individuals, totaling $147,900.
Fields of interest: Higher education.
Type of support: Scholarships—to individuals.
Application information: Applications accepted.
  Additional information: Students should contact their guidance counselors for application information.
EIN: 526042568

1676

Melanoma Research Alliance Foundation

1101 New York Ave., N.W., Ste. 620
Washington, DC 20005-4269 (202) 336-8935
URL: http://www.melanomaresearchalliance.org

Foundation type: Public charity
Purpose: Young investigator awards, pilot awards, established investigator awards, and development awards for researchers investigating melanoma.
Publications: Application guidelines; Occasional report.
Financial data: Year ended 12/31/2011. Assets, $31,331,243 (M); Expenditures, $6,656,438; Total giving, $5,103,877.
Fields of interest: Cancer; Skin disorders; Cancer research; Skin disorders research.
Type of support: Research.
Application information: Applications accepted. Application form required.
  Initial approach: Letter
  Additional information: Contact foundation for eligibility criteria.
EIN: 261636099

1677

Melanoma Research Foundation

(also known as MRF)
1411 K St., N.W., Ste. 500
Washington, DC 20005-3404 (202) 347-9675
Contact: Steve Silverstein, Chair.
FAX: (202) 347-9678; E-mail: mrf@melanoma.org;
Toll-free tel.: (800) 673-1290; URL: http://
www.melanoma.org

Foundation type: Public charity
Purpose: Research grants to scientists for the study and eventual cure of melanoma.
Publications: Application guidelines; Annual report; Informational brochure; Newsletter.
Financial data: Year ended 12/31/2011. Assets, $2,462,662 (M); Expenditures, $3,263,305; Total giving, $757,000; Grants to individuals, totaling $744,000.
Fields of interest: Skin disorders research.
Type of support: Research; Project support.
Application information: Applications accepted. Application form required. Application form available on the grantmaker's web site.

Initial approach: Application
Deadline(s): May 1 for Career Development and Established Investigator Awards, Nov. 1 for Medical Student Awards
Final notification: Aug. 25 for Career Development and Established Investigator Awards, Jan. 15 for Medical Student Awards
Additional information: See web site for additional application guidelines.
Program descriptions:
  Career Development Awards: Funding of up to $50,000 per year for two years are available to junior investigators working in melanoma research. Eligible researchers include those who are beginning a research career emphasizing melanoma-related projects and have not yet established strong federal funding. Research must be conducted in a nonprofit research organization or medical or educational institution located in the U.S. Eligible applicants must hold a Ph.D. or M.D. degree or equivalent, have a title equivalent to assistant professor, or at least four years of postdoctoral experience, demonstrate evidence of strong departmental or institutional support and commitment and generally be within ten years of their advanced degree or specialty qualifications, and not have previously received any major (e.g., R01) grant support, nor should they hold a tenured position.
  Career Development CURE OM Awards: This award provides funding of up to $50,000 per year for two years to junior investigators in the ocular/ uveal melanoma field.
  Established Investigator Awards: Grants of up to $100,000 per year for two years are available to established melanoma investigators (or senior researchers) who work in closely-related fields who wish to move into melanoma research. Eligible applicants must hold a Ph.D. or M.D. degree (or its equivalent), have a title equivalent to associate professor or higher for no fewer than five years, and show evidence of strong departmental or institutional support and commitment.
  Established Investigator CURE OM Awards: The awards provide funding of up to $100,000 per year for two years to established ocular/uveal melanoma researchers, or senior researchers.
  Medical Student Awards: The award provides funding of up to $3,000 each year for one year to medical students. Applicants must be a medical student in good academic standing at an accredited U.S. medical school or institution.
EIN: 760514428

1678

Mentors, Inc.

1012 14th St. N.W., Ste. 304
Washington, DC 20005-3415 (202) 783-2310
Contact: Deirdre Bagley, Exec. Dir.
FAX: (202) 783-2315;
E-mail: mentors@mentorsinc.org; E-mail For Deirdre Bagley: dbagley@mentorsinc.org; URL: http://
www.mentorsinc.org

Foundation type: Public charity
Purpose: Scholarships to graduating high school seniors of Washington, DC for continuing education at institutions of higher learning.
Publications: Newsletter.
Financial data: Year ended 06/30/2012. Assets, $304,940 (M); Expenditures, $313,206; Total giving, $18,088; Grants to individuals, totaling $18,088.
Fields of interest: Higher education.
Type of support: Scholarships—to individuals.
Application information: Applications accepted. Application form required.

Applicants should submit the following:
  1) Essay
  2) GPA
Additional information: Students receive one half of scholarship for the fall semester. To obtain the second half of the scholarship for the spring semester, applicant must show continuing proof of enrollment, maintain a required GPA and submit an additional essay.
EIN: 521547224

1679

Minbanc Foundation, Inc.

1513 P St., N.W.
Washington, DC 20005-1909 (202) 588-5432
Contact: Laura Friel, Exec. Dir.
FAX: (202) 588-5443; E-mail: lfriel@minbanc.org;
URL: http://www.minbanc.org/

Foundation type: Public charity
Purpose: Scholarships to management and officer-level employees of minority- and women-owned banks.
Financial data: Year ended 12/31/2011. Assets, $1,777,453 (M); Expenditures, $129,966; Total giving, $66,167; Grants to individuals, totaling $66,167.
Fields of interest: Minorities.
Type of support: Scholarships—to individuals.
Application information: Application form required.
  Initial approach: Letter
  Deadline(s): None
Program description:
  Scholarships: Awarded in conjunction with the National Bankers Association, scholarships are available to management and office-level employees of minority- and women-owned banks. Scholarships can be used to attend courses hosted by the American Bankers Association, Bank Marketing Association, State Bankers Associations, Risk Management Association, American Institute of Banking, Independent Community Bankers of America, and Bank Administrators Inc.
EIN: 510386370

1680

Thelonious Monk Institute of Jazz

5225 Wisconsin Ave., N.W., Ste. 605
Washington, DC 20015-2024 (202) 364-7272
Contact: Thomas R. Carter, Pres.
FAX: (202) 364-0176;
E-mail: info@monkinstitute.org; Additional addresses (Los Angeles office): 1801 Ave. of the Stars, Ste. 302, Los Angeles, CA 90067-6001, tel.: (310) 284-8200, fax: (310) 284-8215; (New Orleans office): 6363 St. Charles Ave., Campus Box 8, New Orleans, LA 70118-6143, tel.: (504) 865-2100, fax: (504) 865-2500; URL: http://
www.monkinstitute.org

Foundation type: Public charity
Purpose: Awards to winners of the Thelonious Monk International Jazz Competition.
Publications: Application guidelines.
Financial data: Year ended 12/31/2012. Assets, $2,204,168 (M); Expenditures, $3,514,007; Total giving, $145,433; Grants to individuals, 11 grants totaling $145,433.
Fields of interest: Music.
Type of support: Foreign applicants; Awards/prizes; Graduate support; Undergraduate support.
Application information: Applications accepted. Application form required. Application form available on the grantmaker's web site.
  Initial approach: E-mail

Send request by: Mail

Deadline(s): July 16 for Instrument Competition and for Composers Competition

Additional information: Application should include a one-paragraph biography, photograph, CD or MP3, four copies of the full score, and $50 check or money order. See web site for additional application guidelines.

Program description:

Thelonious Monk International Jazz Competition: This competition aims to discover the next generation of jazz masters. The competition focuses on a different instrument each year and features an all-star judging panel. The prize helps pay tuition for college-level jazz education studies and provides funds for private, specialized instruction. The winner is guaranteed a recording contract with Concord Music Group. The 2012 Composers Competition offers a grand prize to all composers who have not had their jazz compositions recorded on a major label or recorded by a major jazz artist. The 2012 Drums Competition offers prizes of $10,000, $15,000, and $25,000 for the Third, Second, and First place winners, respectively. The Drums Competition is open to all drum set performers who plan to pursue jazz performance as a career. Eligibility is exclusive to drum set performers who are 30 years of age and under as of Sept. 23, 2012 and have never recorded as a leader on a major label or widely distributed independent label.

EIN: 521544030

1681

The National Academy of Education

500 5th St. N.W., No. 307
Washington, DC 20001-2736 (202) 334-2093
Contact: Gregory White, Exec. Dir.; Philip Perrin, Sr. Prog. Off., Professional Devel. Progs.; Jack Busbee
FAX: (202) 334-2350;
E-mail: info@naeducation.org; URL: http://www.naeducation.org/

Foundation type: Operating foundation

Purpose: Fellowships to recent recipients of a Ph.D. or equivalent degree to promote scholarship in the U.S. and abroad on matters relevant to the improvement of education in all its forms.

Publications: Application guidelines; Informational brochure.

Financial data: Year ended 12/31/2012. Assets, $6,769,453 (M); Expenditures, $2,736,370; Total giving, $1,583,750.

Fields of interest: Humanities; Social sciences; Psychology/behavioral science.

Type of support: Research; Postdoctoral support.

Application information: Applications accepted. Application form required. Application form available on the grantmaker's web site.

Initial approach: Proposal

Send request by: Online

Deadline(s): Nov. for Postdoctoral Fellowship, Oct. for Dissertation Fellowship

Final notification: Recipients notified in May

Additional information: See web site for additional application guidelines.

Program descriptions:

National Academy of Education Spencer Postdoctoral Fellowship: National Academy of Education/Spencer Postdoctoral Fellowships supports early career scholars working in critical areas of education research. This nonresidential postdoctoral fellowship funds proposals that make significant scholarly contributions to the field of education. Fellows will receive $55,000 for one academic year of research, or $27,500 for each of

two contiguous years, working half-time. Non-U.S. citizens are welcome to apply.

National Academy of Education/Spencer Dissertation Fellowship: The Dissertation Fellowship Program seeks to encourage a new generation of scholars from a wide range of disciplines and professional fields to undertake research relevant to the improvement of education. These $25,000 fellowships support individuals whose dissertations show potential for bringing fresh and constructive perspectives to the history, theory, or practice of formal or informal education anywhere in the world. This highly competitive program aims to identify the most talented researchers conducting dissertation research related to education.

EIN: 770415802

1682

National Academy of Engineering Fund

2101 Constitution Ave. N.W.
Washington, DC 20418-0007 (202) 334-2281
E-mail: lmersky@nae.edu; URL: http://www.nae.edu

Foundation type: Public charity

Purpose: Awards by nomination only to leaders in engineering.

Financial data: Year ended 12/31/2011. Assets, $60,896,887 (M); Expenditures, $6,787,680; Total giving, $4,841,531; Grants to individuals, totaling $799,512.

Fields of interest: Engineering/technology; Engineering.

Type of support: Awards/grants by nomination only.

Application information:

Initial approach: Tel.

Deadline(s): The Call for Nominations begins January 2 ends April 1

Additional information: To submit a nomination, please go online at www.naeawardsonline.com.

EIN: 237284092

1683

National Academy of Sciences

(also known as NAS)
500 5th St. N.W.
Washington, DC 20418-0007 (202) 334-2000
Contact: Ralph J. Cicerone, Pres.
E-mail: webmailbox@nas.edu; URL: http://www.nasonline.org

Foundation type: Public charity

Purpose: Awards and prizes by nomination only to scholars engaged in scientific and engineering research, who are dedicated to the furtherance of science and technology.

Financial data: Year ended 12/31/2011. Assets, $769,096,742 (M); Expenditures, $345,428,611; Total giving, $39,193,168; Grants to individuals, totaling $34,090,392.

Fields of interest: Science.

Type of support: Awards/grants by nomination only; Awards/prizes.

Application information:

Initial approach: Letter

Deadline(s): Sept. 15

Additional information: Nomination letter should include the candidate's curriculum vitae, including country of citizenship and date of birth, a selected bibliography of the candidate's most significant publications (maximum of 12 publications), and a maximum of three supporting letters. Electronic copies sent by e-mail are preferred. Self-nominations are not accepted.

Program descriptions:

Alexander Hollaender Award in Biophysics: Awarded for outstanding contributions in biophysics.

Arthur L. Day Prize and Lectureship: Awarded to a scientist making new contributions to the physics of the Earth whose four to six lectures would prove a solid, timely, and useful addition to the knowledge and literature in the field.

Award for Behavioral Research Relevant to the Prevention of Nuclear War: Awarded to recognize basic research in any field of cognitive or behavioral science that has employed rigorous formal or empirical methods to advance the understanding of problems or issues relating to the risk of nuclear war.

Award for Chemistry in Service to Society: Awarded for contributions to chemistry, either in fundamental science or its application, that clearly satisfy a societal need.

Award for Scientific Reviewing: Presented to recognize authors whose reviews have synthesized extensive and difficult material, rendering a significant service to science and influencing the course of scientific thought.

Award in Aeronautical Engineering: The award is given for excellence in the field of aeronautical engineering.

Award in Chemical Sciences: Awarded for innovative research in the chemical sciences that in the broadest sense contributes to a better understanding of the natural sciences and to the benefit of humanity.

Award in Mathematics: Awarded for excellence of research in the mathematical sciences published within the past ten years.

Award in Molecular Biology: Awarded for recent notable discovery in molecular biology by a young scientist who is a citizen of the United States.

Award in the Neurosciences: Awarded in recognition of extraordinary contributions to progress in the fields of neuroscience, including neurochemistry, neurophysiology, neuropharmacology, developmental neuroscience, neuroanatomy, and behavioral and clinical neuroscience.

Comstock Prize in Physics: Awarded to a resident of North America for recent innovative discovery or investigation in electricity, magnetism, or radiant energy.

G.K. Warren Prize: Awarded for noteworthy and distinguished accomplishment in fluviatile geology and closely-related aspects of the geological sciences.

John J. Carty Award for the Advancement of Science: Awarded for noteworthy and distinguished accomplishments in any field of science within the charter of the Academy.

Selman A. Waksman Award in Microbiology: Awarded in recognition of excellence in the field of microbiology.

Troland Research Awards: Two awards, each given to young investigators (age 40 or younger), are awarded to recognize unusual achievement and further empirical research in psychology regarding the relationships of consciousness and the physical world. Funds are to be used by the awardee to support his or her research within the broad spectrum of experimental psychology, including, for example, the topics of sensation, perception, motivation, emotion, learning, memory, cognition, language, and action. For both awards, preference will be given to experimental work taking a quantitative or other formal approach, including mathematics and explicit algorithms (e.g., computer modeling) or symbolic logics of various

types, and/or to experimental research seeking physiological explanations.
EIN: 530196932

1684

National Academy of Social Insurance

1776 Massachusetts Ave., N.W., Ste. 400
Washington, DC 20036-1904 (202) 452-8097
Contact: Pamela J. Larson, Exec. Dir.
FAX: (202) 452-8111; E-mail: nasi@nasi.org; E-mail
For Pamela J. Larson: plarson@nasi.org;
URL: http://www.nasi.org

Foundation type: Public charity
Purpose: Internships and research grants to study social insurance policy.
Publications: Application guidelines; Occasional report.
Financial data: Year ended 06/30/2012. Assets, $1,946,590 (M); Expenditures, $2,213,934; Total giving, $58,200.
Fields of interest: Research; Mutual aid societies.
Type of support: Internship funds; Grants to individuals.
Application information:
  Initial approach: Letter
  Deadline(s): Mar. 1 for internship
  Additional information: Contact foundation for further eligibility criteria.
Program descriptions:
  Eileen Sweeney Graduate Internship in Disability Policy: In partnership with the Children's Defense Fund and the Center on Budget and Policy Priorities, a $3,000 honorarium and a 12-week summer internship will be made available to graduate students aspiring to a career in social policy with a focus on disability. Interns will have the opportunity to work with leading disability policy experts, gain valuable work experience, and make professional contacts and attend relevant seminars and symposia.
  John Heinz Dissertation Award: This $1,000 award recognizes and promotes outstanding research by new scholars addressing social insurance policy questions. Any dissertation addressing topics relevant to the planning and implementation of social insurance policy is eligible for nomination, including (but not limited to) analysis of long-term care financing, the labor market effects of Social Security, cross-national comparisons, and family social insurance protections. Nominations are encouraged from many disciplines and professions, including actuarial science, economics, health policy, history, philosophy, political science, social work, and sociology.
  Nathan J. Stark Internship for Non-Profit Development: This $3,000 internship opportunity provides two students with the opportunity to learn about nonprofit organizations, how they work, how they raise funds, and how they make a difference, in a 12-week internship program based in Washington, D.C., at either the academy or the National Health Policy Forum.
  Somers Aging and Long-Term Care Research Internship: A $3,000 honorarium and a 12-week summer semester internship is available to outstanding graduate and upper-division undergraduate students to serve as interns on aging and long-term care policy and research projects in Washington, D.C.
  Washington Internship on Social Insurance: This internship seeks outstanding graduate and upper-division undergraduate students to serve as interns on social insurance policy research and analysis projects for 12 weeks during the summer in Washington, D.C. Students studying economics,

gerontology, journalism, political science, public policy, social work, actuarial science, or related science are urged to apply. Interns will: work with leading experts and officials who are recognized authorities on social insurance policy, Social Security, Medicare, unemployment insurance, Medicaid, the Children's Health Insurance Program, disability long-term care, health care financing, and related public and private programs; gain valuable work experience; make professional contacts and network in their areas of interest; and discuss current policy issues and attend Congressional hearings.
EIN: 521451753

1685

National Association of Hispanic Journalists

(also known as NAHJ)
1050 Connecticut Ave. N.W., 10th Fl.
Washington, DC 20045-2001 (202) 662-7145
Contact: Anna Lopez Buck, Exec. Dir.
FAX: (202) 662-7144; E-mail: nahj@nahj.org; E-Mail
For Anna Lopez Buck: alopez@nahj.org;
URL: http://www.nahj.org

Foundation type: Public charity
Purpose: Scholarships to full time undergraduate and graduate students pursuing a career in journalism.
Publications: Application guidelines.
Financial data: Year ended 12/31/2012. Assets, $522,786; Expenditures, $504,174; Total giving, $54,375.
Fields of interest: Journalism school/education.
Type of support: Scholarships—to individuals; Graduate support; Undergraduate support.
Application information: Applications accepted.
  Send request by: Online
  Applicants should submit the following:
    1) Work samples
    2) Financial information
    3) Transcripts
    4) Resume
    5) Essay
  Additional information: Application should also include two reference letters. Applicants must be current members of NAHJ. See web site for additional guidelines.
Program descriptions:
  Ford Motor Company Scholarships: These scholarships of up to $2,500 are awarded to students pursuing careers in print, broadcast, online and visual journalism. College-bound high school seniors, college undergraduate or graduate students are eligible as long as they have a 2.0 GPA. These scholarships are made possible by Ford Motor Company Fund, an effort to support young aspiring Latino journalists.
  General Scholarships - Ruben Salazar Fund: Scholarships range from $1,000 to $2,000 per student, and are awarded to college-bound high school seniors, college undergraduates and graduate students pursuing careers in English or Spanish-language print, photo, broadcast or online journalism.
  Geraldo Rivera Scholarship: Scholarship of up to $5,000 is awarded to a college senior or a graduate student pursuing a career in English or Spanish-language TV broadcast journalism. This scholarship supports young Latino journalists aspiring to enter the field. The scholarship is for broadcast students only.
  Jane Velez-Mitchell Scholarships: Scholarships up to $5,000 are awarded to undergraduate or graduate students pursuing a career in TV

broadcast journalism. This scholarship for broadcast students only.
  Maria Elena Salinas Scholarships: This scholarship awards up to $5,000 to students who demonstrate a strong desire to pursue a career as a Spanish-language broadcast journalist. The scholarship is awarded to college undergraduate and graduate students. Recipients of the Maria Elena Salinas Scholarship will also have an opportunity to intern with either the news division of the Univision network or with an Univision affiliate. This scholarship is for broadcast students only.
  PepsiCo Scholarships: These scholarships of up to $2,500 is awarded to students pursuing careers in print, broadcast, online and visual journalism. College-bound high school seniors, college undergraduates and graduate students are eligible as long as they have a 2.0 average.
  Soledad O'Brien Scholarships: Scholarships of up to $5,000 are awarded to undergraduate or graduate students pursuing a career in TV broadcast journalism. This scholarship is for broadcast students only.
EIN: 953927141

1686

National Breast Cancer Coalition Fund

(also known as NBCCF)
1101 17th St., N.W., Ste. 1300
Washington, DC 20036-4710 (202) 296-7477
Contact: Ira J. Hillman, C.O.O., Natl. Breast Cancer Coalition; Frances Visco, Pres.
FAX: (202) 265-6854; Toll-free tel.: (800) 622-2838; URL: http://www.breastcancerdeadline2020.org/homepage.html

Foundation type: Public charity
Purpose: Travel grants for lodging for breast cancer advocates to attend science and/or advocacy training programs.
Publications: Application guidelines; Annual report; Financial statement; Informational brochure; Newsletter.
Financial data: Year ended 12/31/2011. Assets, $2,880,523 (M); Expenditures, $6,315,220; Total giving, $687,326; Grants to individuals, totaling $175,672.
Fields of interest: Breast cancer research.
Type of support: Travel grants.
Application information: Applications accepted. Application form required.
  Additional information: Payments are either made as reimbursements or direct payments to the travel or lodging vendor. Contact the fund for additional guidelines.
EIN: 521782065

1687

National Center for Creative Aging

4125 Albemarle St., N.W.
Washington, DC 20016-2105 (202) 895-9456
Contact: Katie Fitzgerald, Dir. Comm.
FAX: (202) 895-9483;
E-mail: info@creativeaging.org; E-mail for Katie Fitzgerald: kfitzgerald@creativeaging.org;
URL: http://www.creativeaging.org

Foundation type: Public charity
Purpose: Awards to researchers in the field of creativity and aging.
Publications: Application guidelines.
Financial data: Year ended 06/30/2012. Assets, $269,426 (M); Expenditures, $691,059.
Fields of interest: Adults; Aging.

Type of support: Research; Awards/grants by nomination only; Awards/prizes.
Application information: Application form not required.

> *Deadline(s):* July 1
> *Applicants should submit the following:*
>   1) Work samples
>   2) Letter(s) of recommendation
>   3) Essay
> *Additional information:* Awards are by nomination only. See web site for additional guidelines.

Program description:

Dr. Gene D. Cohen Research Award in Creativity and Aging: The award is presented annually to a professional whose research in the field of creativity and aging demonstrates these positive attributes. The award includes up to $1,000 to cover travel and lodging expenses, GSA Annual Scientific Meeting registration, a program profile, and recognition on the NCCA web site, at the awards, and through a press release. Nomination is open to any individual who has produced research that demonstrates the benefits of creativity in arts including but not limited to visual arts, music, dance, drama, writing and multi media. Nominees should demonstrate leadership and contributions in the field of creativity and aging through research.
EIN: 870805049

1688
National Credit Union Foundation, Inc.

601 Pennsylvania Ave., N.W., Ste. 600
Washington, DC 20004-2601 (202) 402-8902
Contact: Wendell "Bucky" Sebastian, Exec. Dir.
FAX: (608) 231-4231;
E-mail: bsebastian@ncuf.coop; Additional address: 6710 Mineral Point Rd., Madison, WI 53705; toll-free tel.: (800) 356-9655; URL: http://www.ncuf.coop

Foundation type: Public charity
Purpose: Scholarships to credit union staff and volunteers to attend trainings and workshops. Disaster relief assistance to credit union employees and members to help them recover from major disasters.
Publications: Application guidelines; Annual report; Financial statement; Grants list; Informational brochure; Occasional report.
Financial data: Year ended 12/31/2011. Assets, $6,973,228 (M); Expenditures, $6,048,442; Total giving, $4,122,560; Grants to individuals, totaling $249,360.
Fields of interest: Community development, neighborhood development.
Type of support: Scholarships—to individuals.
Application information: Applications accepted. Application form available on the grantmaker's web site.

> *Initial approach:* Application
> *Additional information:* See web site for additional guidelines.

EIN: 391383650

1689
National Endowment for the Arts

1100 Pennsylvania Ave., N.W.
Washington, DC 20506-0001 (202) 682-5400
Fellowship tel.: (202) 682-5034,
e-mail: LitFellowships@arts.gov
E-mail: webmrg@arts.gov; TTY: (202) 682-5496; URL: http://www.arts.gov

Foundation type: Public charity
Purpose: Fellowships and grants to outstanding individuals working in the arts.

Publications: Application guidelines; Annual report; Occasional report.
Financial data: Year ended 12/31/2012. Total giving, $65,161,200; Grants to individuals, 56 grants totaling $1,200,000.
Fields of interest: Literature.
Type of support: Fellowships.
Application information: Applications accepted. Application form required. Application form available on the grantmaker's web site.

> *Initial approach:* Application
> *Deadline(s):* Jan. 3 for Literature Fellowships: Translation Projects, Feb. 28 for Literature Fellowships
> *Final notification:* Recipients notified in Aug. for Literature Fellowships: Translation Projects, and Dec. for Literature Fellowships
> *Additional information:* See web site for additional guidelines.

Program descriptions:

Literature Fellowships: This program offers grants of $25,000 each to published creative writers that enable recipients to set aside time for writing, research, travel, and general career advancement. Grants will be awarded in both prose (fiction and creative nonfiction) and poetry categories.

Literature Fellowships: Translation Projects: This program supports the translation of specific works of poetry, prose, or drama from other languages into English. Priority will be given to projects that involve work that has not previously been translated into English, as well as the translation of work and writers that are not well represented in English translation. Grants are for $12,500 or $25,000.

1690
National Environmental Education Foundation

(formerly The National Environmental Education & Training Foundation, Inc.)
4301 Connecticut Ave. N.W., Ste. 160
Washington, DC 20008-2326 (202) 833-2933
FAX: (202) 261-6464; E-mail: neetf@neetf.org; URL: http://www.neefusa.org/

Foundation type: Public charity
Purpose: Grants to high school students in the U.S. for projects focused on wildlife conservation.
Publications: Application guidelines; Annual report; Grants list; Informational brochure; Newsletter; Occasional report.
Financial data: Year ended 09/30/2012. Assets, $4,542,666 (M); Expenditures, $3,724,734; Total giving, $592,903; Grants to individuals, totaling $5,000.
Fields of interest: Environment.
Type of support: Grants to individuals.
Application information: Applications accepted.

> *Send request by:* Online
> *Deadline(s):* Feb. 1
> *Additional information:* Applicants must be a member of Planet Connect. See web site for additional application guidelines.

Program description:

Planet Connect Student Grants: This program offers high school students grants of $1,000 to implement their problem-solving projects and participate in a local internship focused on wildlife conservation. Each project's application must include a timeline for implementation, a budget, tools to be used, collaborators, and desired outcomes. If chosen as a winner, the participant will be provided $50 to turn the project idea into reality. After completing the project in June, the participant will attend an 80-hour wildlife conservation or natural resource internship in their community

during the summer with a $500 stipend. Applicant must be 14 to 19 years old.
EIN: 541557043

1691
National Fish and Wildlife Foundation

1133 15th St., N.W., Ste. 1100
Washington, DC 20005-2710 (202) 857-0166
Contact: Jeff Trandahl, C.E.O. and Exec. Dir.
Additional tel.: (503) 417-8700, ext. 21
FAX: (202) 857-0162; URL: http://www.nfwf.org

Foundation type: Public charity
Purpose: Scholarships to graduate and undergraduate students for education in environmental science, natural resource management, biology, public policy, geography, political science, or related fields. Awards by nomination only to outstanding leaders in the field of fish and wildlife preservation and grants to support research, management, conservation and education/outreach activities related to the conservation and recovery of whales.
Publications: Application guidelines; Annual report; Grants list.
Financial data: Year ended 09/30/2012. Assets, $449,917,561 (M); Expenditures, $94,714,673; Total giving, $78,193,306; Grants to individuals, totaling $970,618.
Fields of interest: Higher education; Natural resources; Environmental education; Animals/wildlife, preservation/protection; Public policy; Biology/life sciences; Political science.
Type of support: Research; Scholarships—to individuals; Awards/prizes; Graduate support; Undergraduate support.
Application information: Applications accepted. Application form required.

> *Deadline(s):* Jan. 14 for Scholarships, May 12 for Grants, vary for nominations
> *Applicants should submit the following:*
>   1) Essay
>   2) Letter(s) of recommendation
> *Additional information:* See web site for further application and program guidelines.

Program descriptions:

Budweiser Conservation Scholarship Program: The program supports and promotes innovative research or study that seeks to respond to current pressing conservation issues. The program seeks to support the next generation of leaders by providing scholarships to eligible graduate and undergraduate students who are poised to make a significant contribution to the field of conservation.

Budweiser Conservationist of the Year Award: The award recognizes individuals who have made significant contributions to the outdoors and conservation. A conservation organization is selected to receive a $50,000 grant from Budweiser and the foundation. Three runners-up each direct a $5,000 grant to a conservation organization of their choice. Deadline Oct. 19.

Guy Bradley Award: The award seeks to recognize extraordinary individuals who have made an outstanding lifetime contribution to wildlife law enforcement, wildlife forensics, or investigative techniques that warrant national recognition. This $1,000 will be presented to one state and one federal agency wildlife enforcement officer whose dedication and public service demonstrate outstanding leadership, excellence in implementation and knowledge, and a lifetime commitment to the field of wildlife law enforcement, and whose actions have advanced the cause of wildlife conservation.

Rich Guadagno Memorial Scholarship Fund: The fund is used for a variety of conservation projects, such as scholarships, to support outstanding students with an avid interest in wildlife biology; and funds special conservation projects that support wildlife and habitat protection.

Sea Turtle Conservation Keystone Fund: This program supports sea turtle research and conservation efforts with grants ranging from $25,000 to $150,000 per year. Priority areas include: increasing effective usage of TEDs (both domestic and abroad) and the implementation of other bycatch reduction methods in areas of high bycatch in the Western Hemisphere that will benefit priority sea turtle populations; determining and assessing potential bycatch and/or unsustainably managed legal harvest hotspots for the NWA loggerhead population and the NA and EP leatherback populations; and strategies on priority nesting beaches to reduce adult harvest to zero and nest mortality to less than ten percent of nests laid for beaches of priority sea turtle populations.

EIN: 521384139

1692

National Geographic Society

1145 17th St., N.W.
Washington, DC 20036-4688 (202) 857-7310
FAX: (202) 429-5701; E-mail: foundation@ngs.org;
URL: http://www.nationalgeographic.com/foundation/

Foundation type: Public charity
Purpose: Grants to teachers for projects that will improve student achievement through geography literacy, and cultural understanding.
Publications: Newsletter.
Financial data: Year ended 12/31/2011. Assets, $1,250,753,645 (M); Expenditures, $451,921,544; Total giving, $15,873,203; Grants to individuals, totaling $5,302,059.
Fields of interest: Film/video; Photography; Minorities.
Type of support: Seed money.
Application information: Applications accepted. Application form required.
> Deadline(s): Mar. 15, June 15, Sept., 15 and Dec. 15 for All Roads Film Project

Program description:
All Roads Film Project Seed Grants: The program provides grants ranging from $1,000 to $10,000 for film projects by or about indigenous and underrepresented minority cultures around the globe. The program is open to indigenous and underrepresented minority-culture filmmakers, as well as filmmakers who can demonstrate with documentation that they have been designated by indigenous or minority communities to tell that community's story. Funds are intended to be used toward the development and production of one of the following film categories: short documentary, long documentary, narrative short, narrative feature, music video, or animation.
EIN: 530193519

1693

National Italian American Foundation, Inc.

1860 19th St. N.W.
Washington, DC 20009-5501 (202) 387-0600
Contact: John Viola, Pres. and C.O.O.
FAX: (202) 387-0800; E-mail: info@niaf.org;
URL: http://www.niaf.org

Foundation type: Public charity
Purpose: Undergraduate, graduate, and doctoral scholarships to Italian-American students. Scholarships also to students of any ethnic

background majoring in Italian language, Italian studies, Italian-American studies or a related field. Grants for teaching of Italian language in schools, and for projects related to Italian-American culture or heritage.
Publications: Application guidelines.
Financial data: Year ended 12/31/2011. Assets, $9,806,115 (M); Expenditures, $5,592,585; Total giving, $1,327,810; Grants to individuals, totaling $916,966.
Fields of interest: Cultural/ethnic awareness; Language (foreign); Higher education; Physical/earth sciences; Astronomy.
International interests: Italy.
Type of support: Graduate support; Undergraduate support.
Application information: Application form available on the grantmaker's web site.
> Initial approach: Letter for grants
> Send request by: Online
> Deadline(s): Varies
> Applicants should submit the following:
> 1) FAFSA
> 2) Transcripts
> Additional information: Grant query by letter must be submitted before a full application. See web site for additional guidelines.

Program descriptions:
Grants: The foundation awards grants to U.S.-based nonprofit organizations who seek to enhance the acknowledgement, appreciation, and visibility of Italian and Italian-American culture. Four types of grants are available under this program: Italian Language Grants (grants to organizations, individuals, and schools that foster the development and implementation of programs in schools, communities, and organizations that encourage the teaching and practice of the Italian language); Culture and Heritage Grants (grants to organizations and individuals in the fields of the performing arts, the fine arts, history, archaeology, other humanities, and related heritage and cultural endeavors); Fellowship Grants (grants to organizations, individuals, schools, and communities that provide opportunities to encourage collaboration among students and academics in the U.S. and Italy, and improve the quality of Italian language teaching in the U.S.); and Youth Program Grants (grants to programs that are focused specifically on youth and which ensure that Italian-American heritage and traditions are kept alive, including camps or programs that focus on language, music, sports, or the arts for young people). Grants are awarded in three categories: Category I ($1,000 to $2,500), Category II ($2,501 to $10,000), and Category III ($10,001 and up)
Italian Language and Culture Teacher of the Year Award: This award annually recognizes an outstanding educator in Italian language and culture who has demonstrated dedication and contribution in the field of teaching Italian. Recipients are awarded a continuing education stipend that aims to provide the instruments (content, methodological, and bibliographical) to teachers, so they can continue their professional development. Eligible applicants must be nominated by an accredited American school, must have a minimum of three years' teaching experience, and can be elementary or secondary teachers at public, private, and/or parochial school; candidates should be skilled, dedicated teachers who plan to actively continue classroom teaching, and should demonstrate an ability to inspire a love of learning the Italian language and culture in students of any background.
John R. Mott Foundation Scholarships: Awarded in conjunction with The John R. Mott Scholarship Foundation, this program provides post-secondary

scholarships (of up to $10,000 per year) for Italian citizens. Priority will be given to applicants from the environs of the town of Serra D'Aiello, then to applicants from the city and province of Cosenza, and finally from the region of Calabria.

Scholarship Awards: Scholarships, ranging from $2,000 to $12,000, are available to outstanding students who wish to continue their studies. Two types of scholarships are available: those for Italian-American students who demonstrate outstanding potential and high academic achievements in any academic discipline; and students from any ethnic background majoring or minoring in Italian language, Italian studies, Italian-American studies, or a related field, who demonstrate outstanding potential and high academic achievement. Eligible applicants must: be enrolled in a U.S.-based, accredited institution of higher education; have a GPA of at least 3.5 (on a 4.0 scale); and be a U.S. citizen or a permanent resident alien. Scholarships are intended to cover tuition and university-provided room and board.

The Anthony Campitelli Endowed Fund: This program provides grants to support various humanitarian and community projects in and around Castel Frentano in Abruzzo, Italy, including schools, churches, and eldercare facilities. Applications for scholarships for residents of Castel Frentano and the province of Chieti will also be accepted.
EIN: 521071723

1694

National League for Nursing, Inc.

2600 Virginia Ave., N.W., 8th Fl.
Washington, DC 20037 (212) 363-5555
FAX: (212) 812-0391; E-mail: generalinfo@nln.org;
Toll Free Tel.: (800) 669-1656; URL: http://www.nln.org

Foundation type: Public charity
Purpose: Grants and awards for nursing education research that informs and promotes teaching.
Publications: Application guidelines; Occasional report.
Financial data: Year ended 12/31/2011. Assets, $5,455,975 (M); Expenditures, $9,587,099; Total giving, $175,948.
Fields of interest: Nursing school/education.
Type of support: Grants to individuals.
Application information: Applications accepted. Application form required.
> Send request by: Online
> Deadline(s): June 1 for Sigma Theta Tau International/ NLN Grant, Feb. 23 for NLN Nursing Education Research Grants, Feb. 15 for Doctoral Dissertation Award
> Additional information: See web site for additional guidelines.

Program descriptions:
NLN Nursing Education Research Grants: Each year, the league offers six to eight research grants to NLN individual members and faculty of NLN member schools.

NLN/MNRS Doctoral Dissertation Award: Awarded in conjunction with the Midwest Nursing Research Society (MNRS), this award promotes research conducted by doctoral students that increases the quality and quantity of doctoral dissertation focused on nursing education, advancing the science of nursing education, and increasing awareness of support for nursing education research. Applicants must be members of both the league and the MNRS. Awards are for $2,500 each.

Sigma Theta Tau International/NLN Grant: Awarded in conjunction with Sigma Theta Tau

International, this grant supports research that advances the science of nursing education through the use of technology in the dissemination of knowledge. Eligible candidates must hold a master's or doctoral degree and be a registered nurse. The application process is open to the public, but preference will be given to Sigma Theta Tau International and National League for Nursing members. One grant per year of up to $5,000 is awarded.

EIN: 131896510

1695
National Press Foundation, Inc.
1211 Connecticut Ave., N.W., Ste. 310
Washington, DC 20036-2709 (202) 663-7280
Contact: Linda Topping Streitfeld, Dir., Progs.
E-mail: npf@nationalpress.org; E-mail for Linda Topping Streitfeld: linda@nationalpress.org; URL: http://www.nationalpress.org/index.htm

Foundation type: Public charity
Purpose: Awards by nomination only to accomplished, working journalists in various areas, and support to working professional journalists for professional development.
Publications: Application guidelines; Annual report; Financial statement; Informational brochure; Occasional report.
Financial data: Year ended 12/31/2011. Assets, $2,813,041 (M); Expenditures, $1,007,652.
Fields of interest: Print publishing; Drawing; Literature; Information services; Science; Government/public administration.
Type of support: Fellowships; Awards/grants by nomination only; Awards/prizes; Grants for special needs.
Application information:
Initial approach: Application
Deadline(s): Varies
Additional information: See web site for current application and program information.
Program descriptions:
Benjamin Bradlee Editor of the Year Award: This award recognizes significant achievements that enhance the quality of journalism in the U.S. The award, award, open to an editor at any level, is made in recognition of imagination, professional skill, ethics, and an ability to motivate staff. One top winner will receive $5,000; honorable mentions will receive a cash award of $1,000.
Clifford K. and James T. Berryman Award for Editorial Cartoons: This award confers a $2,500 prize to an editorial cartoonist of newspapers or magazines in the U.S., for work that exhibits power to influence public opinion, plus good drawing and striking effect.
Everett McKinley Dirksen Awards for Distinguished Reporting of Congress: This $5,000 award recognizes individuals whose work shows thoughtful appraisals and insight into the workings of the U.S. Congress. Entries will be judged on how well they cover the workings of the Congress as a whole, helped illuminate the actions of elected officials or congressional staff, or described the workings of congressional policies. One award each will be given to a print and broadcasting journalist.
Evert Clark/Seth Payne Award for Young Science Writers: This award is intended to encourage young science writers by recognizing outstanding reporting in all fields of science. Eligible applicants must be age 30 or younger, and must have had articles published in newspapers, magazines, newsletters, online-only publications, and/or websites. Winners receive a $1,000 award.
Excellence in Online Journalism Award: This $2,500 award recognizes achievement in the

rapidly-changing field of internet journalism, and encourages others through the winner's example. Awards can be made to a site, an individual, or a specific project.
The "Feddie" Award for Reporting on Federal Rules and Local Impact: Each year, the foundation offers two all-expenses-paid fellowships to U.S.-based working print or broadcast journalists for a fellowship experience at the Wharton School at the University of Pennsylvania. Seminars offer participants an opportunity to expand their knowledge of business by attending courses conducted by leading Wharton faculty, hear guest lectures by business leaders, and compete in an intensive, computer-simulated strategic management exercise. Fellowships include full tuition, housing, most meals, and round-trip transportation.
Thomas L. Stokes Award for Best Energy Writing: This award is presented to a journalist for the best writing on the subject of energy. Subjects may be any form of energy (oil, gas, coal, nuclear, water, solar, etc.); writing may be reporting, analysis, or commentary, and can consist of one to three articles on unrelated subjects, or one series of articles on a related subject. Award recipients are given $1,000 and a citation.
EIN: 521069481

1696
National Society Daughters of the American Revolution
(also known as NSDAR)
1776 D St., N.W.
Washington, DC 20006-5303 (202) 628-1776
Contact: Marcy Kimminau, National Chair., Special Project Grants
Application address: National Chairman, DAR Scholarship Committee, P.O. Box 2906, Ridgeland, MS 39158-2906
E-mail: dargrants@dar.org; URL: http://www.dar.org/natsociety/specialprojectsgrants.cfm

Foundation type: Public charity
Purpose: Scholarships to qualified students of the U.S. for attendance at accredited colleges or universities in the U.S.
Publications: Application guidelines.
Financial data: Year ended 02/28/2012. Assets, $90,346,818 (M); Expenditures, $12,779,035; Total giving, $422,466; Grants to individuals, totaling $222,581.
Fields of interest: Higher education; Medical school/education; Nursing school/education.
Type of support: Scholarships—to individuals.
Application information: Applications accepted. Application form required. Application form available on the grantmaker's web site.
Deadline(s): Feb. 15
Applicants should submit the following:
1) Financial information
2) Essay
3) Transcripts
4) Letter(s) of recommendation
Additional information: Application should also include copy of birth certificate, naturalization paper or information page of U.S. passport and self-addressed, stamped postcard. Some scholarships have specific requirements for eligibility. See web site for additional guidelines.
Program descriptions:
Alice W. Rooke Scholarship: This $5,000 award is available to students who have been accepted into or are pursuing an approved course of study to become a medical doctor (no pre-med, osteopathic medicine, veterinarian, or physician assistant) at an

approved, accredited medical school. Award is renewable for up to four years.
Arthur Lockwood Beneventi Law Scholarship: This one-time $2,000 scholarship is awarded to a student who is either enrolled in or attends an accredited law school and has a minimum GPA of 3.25. This scholarship is not automatically renewable, however, recipients must reapply for consideration every year.
Caroline E. Holt Nursing Scholarship: This one-time $1,000 award is given to students who are in financial need and are accepted and enrolled into an accredited school of nursing.
Dr. Aura-Lee A. and James Hobbs Pittenger American History Scholarship: This scholarship is awarded to a graduating high school student who will pursue an undergraduate degree with a concentrated study of a minimum of 24 credit hours in American History and American Government. Renewal is conditional upon maintenance of a 3.25 GPA. This $2,000 award is renewable for up to four years.
Dr. Francis Anthony Beneventi Medical Scholarship: This $5,000 scholarship is renewable annually for up to four consecutive years and is available for students who have been accepted into or who are pursuing an approved course of study to become a medical doctor (no pre-med, osteopathic medicine, veterinarian or physician assistant) at an approved accredited medical school, college, or university. Applicants must have and maintain a minimum 3.25 GPA. Applicants must reapply each year.
Edward G. and Helen A. Borgens Elementary and Secondary Teacher Education Scholarships: Two one-time scholarships of up to $1,500 will be awarded to students 25 years of age or older. One award will be given to students studying to teach at the elementary school level, the other to students studying to teach at the secondary level. Applicants must have at least a 3.5 GPA, be at least a college sophomore, and attend or plan to attend an accredited college or university. The award is based on academic merit and not automatically renewable, however, recipients may reapply for consideration as long as they meet the eligibility requirements.
Enid Hall Griswold Memorial Scholarship: This one-time $1,000 award is given to a deserving junior or senior enrolled in an accredited college or university in the U.S. who is pursuing a major in either political science, history, government, or economics.
Irene and Daisy MacGregor Memorial Scholarship: This $5,000 scholarship is awarded to students of high scholastic standing and character who have been accepted into or are pursuing an approved course of study to become a medical doctor (no pre-med, osteopathic medicine, veterinarian or physician assistant) at an approved, accredited medical school. This scholarship is also available to students who have been accepted into or who are pursuing an approved course of study in the field of psychiatric nursing at the graduate level at accredited medical schools, colleges, or universities. This scholarship is renewable for up to four years.
Lillian and Arthur Dunn Scholarship: This $2,000 scholarship is awarded for up to four years to well qualified, deserving sons and daughters of members of the NSDAR for four years of college. Renewal is conditional upon maintenance of a 3.25 GPA. Outstanding recipients pursuing graduate study may reapply each year for an additional period of up to four years of study. DAR Member Number of mother, who is a current dues paying member, must be on the application.

Madeline Pickett (Halbert) Cogswell Nursing Scholarship: This one-time $1,000 award is given to students who are accepted or enrolled in an accredited school of nursing. Applicants must be members, descendants of members, or be eligible for membership in NSDAR. DAR Member Number must be on the application.

Margaret Howard Hamilton Scholarship: This $1,000 scholarship, renewable for up to four years, is awarded to a graduating high school senior who has been accepted into the Harvey and Bernice Jones Learning Center, housing the Ben Caudle Learning Program at the University of the Ozarks, Clarksville, Arkansas. Applications must be requested directly through the Learning Center upon acceptance into the program for learning disabled students.

Mary Elizabeth Lockwood Beneventi MBA Scholarship: This one-time $2,000 award is given to a student attending graduate school full time in an accredited college or university and majoring in business administration. Applicants must have a minimum GPA of 3.25. The scholarship is not automatically renewable, however, recipients may reapply for consideration each year.

Michael T. and Mary L. Cloyd Scholarship: A one-time only $3,000 award will be given to a student with a minimum 3.0 average at the third year level of undergraduate study or graduate level studying in the field of library science.

Mildred Nutting Nursing Scholarship: This one-time $1,000 scholarship is award to students who have been accepted or are currently enrolled in an accredited school of nursing. Preference will be given to candidates from the greater Lowell, MA area.

Nellie Love Butcher Music Scholarship: This one-time preferred scholarship of $5,000 is awarded annually to a male or female music student who is pursuing an education in piano or voice. Special consideration will be given to students currently attending the Duke Ellington School of the Performing Arts in Washington, DC. The scholarship is for one year, and is not automatically renewable, however, recipients may reapply for consideration each year, for four years based on maintaining a 3.0 GPA.

Occupational/Physical Therapy Scholarship: This one-time $1,000 scholarship is award to students who are in financial needs and have been accepted or are attending an accredited school of occupational therapy (including art, music, or physical therapy).

William Robert Findley Graduate Chemistry Scholarship: This $2,000 scholarship is a one time preferred amount available for a student attending graduate school full-time in an accredited college or university and majoring in chemistry. Applicants must have a minimum GPA of 3.25. Scholarship is not automatically renewable; recipients may reapply for consideration each year.
EIN: 530205923

1697
National Society of Collegiate Scholars
2000 M St., N.W., Ste. 600
Washington, DC 20036-1225 (202) 265-9000
Contact: Stephen Loflin, Exec. Dir.
FAX: (202) 265-9200; E-mail: nscs@nscs.org;
Toll-free tel.: (800) 989-6727; URL: http://www.nscs.org

Foundation type: Public charity
Purpose: Scholarships to NSCS members for their outstanding academic excellence and achievements.
Publications: Annual report.

Financial data: Year ended 08/31/2012. Assets, $2,609,337 (M); Expenditures, $6,061,015; Total giving, $570,602; Grants to individuals, totaling $570,602.
Fields of interest: Higher education.
Type of support: Scholarships—to individuals.
Application information: Applications accepted. Application form required.
Additional information: Application should include an essay. A variety of scholarships are available for students. See web site for additional guidelines.
Program description:
Merit Award: Each year the society awards $1,000 scholarships to thirty outstanding and deserving new members across the country to help defray the cost of tuition expenses.
EIN: 521870777

1698
National Student Achievement Awards
1350 Connecticut Ave. N.W., No.1200
Washington, DC 20036

Foundation type: Operating foundation
Purpose: Scholarships to low-income students from select public high schools in Washington, DC for higher education.
Financial data: Year ended 09/30/2011. Assets, $110 (M); Expenditures, $1,105; Total giving, $0.
Fields of interest: Higher education.
Type of support: Scholarships—to individuals.
Application information: Applications not accepted.
Additional information: Contributes only to preselected individuals. Unsolicited requests for funds not considered or acknowledged.
EIN: 522044109

1699
National Trust for Historic Preservation in the United States
1785 Massachusetts Ave., N.W.
Washington, DC 20036-2117 (202) 588-6192
Contact: Stephanie Meeks, Pres. and C.E.O.
FAX: (202) 588-6038; E-mail: pr@nthp.org; Toll-free tel.: (800) 944-6847; URL: http://www.nthp.org

Foundation type: Public charity
Purpose: Awards by nomination only to individuals for achievement in preservation of historical landmarks.
Publications: Application guidelines; Annual report; Corporate giving report; Grants list; Program policy statement.
Financial data: Year ended 12/31/2012. Assets, $252,611,089 (M); Expenditures, $27,507,033; Total giving, $3,913,448.
Fields of interest: Historic preservation/historical societies.
Type of support: Awards/grants by nomination only; Awards/prizes.
Application information: Application form required.
Send request by: Online
Deadline(s): Mar. 1
Additional information: Application should include a $30 nomination fee, a description (4,000 characters or less including spaces) of the project, up to five supporting brochures or news clippings, and up to three letters of recommendation. See web site for further application information.
Program descriptions:
Great American Main Street Awards: The award recognizes exceptional accomplishments in revitalizing America's historic and traditional

downtowns and neighborhood commercial districts. Five equal awards recognizing overall achievement in historic preservation-based commercial district revitalization are given each year. Each community receives a $2,500 prize to further its revitalization activities, a bronze plaque, two road signs commemorating its achievements, lapel pins, and a certificate marking their achievements.

National Preservation Honor Awards: Awards are given to individuals whose skill and determination have given new meaning to their communities through preservation. These efforts include citizen attempts to save and maintain important landmarks; craftsmen whose work restores the richness of the past; the vision of public officials who support preservation projects and legislation in their communities; and educators and journalists who help Americans understand the value of preservation.
EIN: 530210807

1700
NEA Foundation
(formerly The NEA Foundation for the Improvement of Education)
1201 16th St. N.W., Ste. 417
Washington, DC 20036-3207 (202) 822-7840
Contact: Harriet Sanford, Pres. and C.E.O.; Grants Mgr.: Jesse Graytock, Grants Mgr.
FAX: (202) 822-7779;
E-mail: foundation_info@nea.org; URL: http://www.neafoundation.org

Foundation type: Public charity
Purpose: Classroom project and professional development support to teachers and education professionals.
Publications: Application guidelines; Financial statement; Grants list; Occasional report.
Financial data: Year ended 08/31/2013. Assets, $47,659,109 (M); Expenditures, $7,408,864; Total giving, $3,644,971; Grants to individuals, totaling $650,000.
Fields of interest: Education.
Type of support: Grants to individuals.
Application information: Applications accepted. Application form required. Application form available on the grantmaker's web site.
Send request by: Online
Copies of proposal: 6
Deadline(s): Feb. 1, June 1 and Oct. 15
Final notification: Recipients notified Apr. 15, Sept. 15 and Jan. 15
Applicants should submit the following:
1) Proposal
2) Budget Information
Program descriptions:
Learning and Leadership Grants: These grants provide opportunities for teachers, education support professionals, and higher education faculty and staff to engage in high-quality professional development and lead their colleagues in professional growth. Grant amounts are for $2,000 for individuals and $5,000 for groups engaged in collegial study. Eligible applicants include practicing U.S. public school teachers in grades K-12, public school education support professionals, and faculty and staff at public higher education institutions.

Student Achievement Grants: These grants provide $2,000 to $5,000 to improve the academic achievement of students by engaging in critical thinking and problem-solving that deepen knowledge of standards-based subject matter. The work should also improve students' habits of inquiry, self-directed learning, and critical reflection. Eligible applicants include practicing U.S. public school teachers in grades K-12, public school

education support professionals, and faculty and staff at public higher education institutions.
EIN: 237035089

1701
The Nonprofit Roundtable of Greater Washington

1201 15th St., N.W., Ste. 420
Washington, DC 20005-2842 (202) 955-6187
Contact: Diana Leon-Taylor, Pres. and C.E.O.
FAX: (202) 955-3133;
E-mail: info@nonprofitroundtable.org; URL: http://www.nonprofitroundtable.org

Foundation type: Public charity
Purpose: Fellowships to provide peer coaching, mentoring, skills development, and ongoing support to prepare mid- and senior-level nonprofit professionals to become leaders at small or medium-sized community-based organizations in the Greater Washington, DC area.
Publications: Application guidelines.
Financial data: Year ended 09/30/2012. Assets, $1,382,993 (M); Expenditures, $1,348,256.
Fields of interest: Leadership development.
Type of support: Fellowships.
Application information:
Initial approach: Letter
Deadline(s): May 30
Program descriptions:
Future Executive Directors Fellowships: This nine-month program provides support and training to help develop a pool of motivated, well-trained professionals to take on the challenge of community-based nonprofit executive leadership, and to build a community of strong emerging leaders who are primed to lead, innovate, and make a difference. The program consists of an intensive six-month series conducted over eleven days, followed by three months of ongoing support facilitated by the roundtable, focusing on the following initiatives: visibility and networking, skills development, executive director modeling, advising and peer coaching, mentoring, and personal achievement of learning goals. The fellowship will provide this intensive leadership development and preparation to mid- and senior-level nonprofit professionals who: possess several years of nonprofit work experience; have managerial experience (which may include experience in the private or public sectors that is equivalent and directly transferable); indicate the intention to become a nonprofit executive director or C.E.O. of a small- to medium-sized community-based organization in greater Washington, DC as the next step in their career; and possess the skills and attributes necessary to be a successful executive director, and are aware of areas needing further development.
Roundtable Fellowship Program: The organization provides a nine-month program that helps shape future nonprofit leaders in the greater Washington, DC area into tomorrow's leaders that can not only lead their organizations, but also be a force beyond the walls of their organization, a strong voice for their causes, their communities, and for the sector. The program involves four two-day group seminars, six private executive coaching sessions, four private mentoring sessions, and four 'just lunch' sessions that allow participants to develop personal goals related to their maturation and role as external leaders. Eligible applicants must: be serving in executive director or equivalent positions (with some consideration given to applicants with fewer than five years' experience as an executive director, but who have had significant experience in other senior positions); be a current roundtable

member, or have an application for membership pending; and be available to participate fully in the program, including mid-year, year-end, and follow-up self-assessments and program evaluations.
EIN: 161626729

1702
The Ocean Foundation

1990 M St. N.W., Ste. 250
Washington, DC 20036-3430 (202) 887-8992
FAX: (202) 887-8987; E-mail: info@oceanfdn.org;
E-Mail for Mark J. Spalding :
mspalding@oceanfdn.org; URL: http://www.oceanfdn.org

Foundation type: Public charity
Purpose: Grants to students at the Masters and Ph.D. level for research projects as well as scholarships to undergraduate, Masters and Ph.D study in the U.S. and internationlly.
Publications: Annual report; Informational brochure; Newsletter; Occasional report.
Financial data: Year ended 06/30/2012. Assets, $3,568,985 (M); Expenditures, $5,065,829; Total giving, $1,478,051; Grants to individuals, totaling $31,800.
Fields of interest: Water pollution; Environment, water resources.
Type of support: Grants to individuals; Scholarships—to individuals; Fiscal agent/sponsor.
Application information: Applications accepted. Application form required.
Deadline(s): Mar. 15 for the Boyd N. Lyon program
Additional information: Award announcements for the Boyd N. Lyon program are in May. See web site for further application instructions.
Program descriptions:
Boyd N. Lyon Scholarship: Scholarships are available for Masters and Ph.D. level students that work and/or research in an area consistent with the Boyd Lyon Sea Turtle Fund's mission to support field research projects that further our knowledge of sea turtle behavior and habitat use in the marine environment, as well as those projects that promote their management and conservation in coastal ecosystems. Applications will be considered that address questions from a wide range of fields in sea turtle research and conservation including, but not limited to life history studies, oceanography, marine affairs, environmental sciences, public policy, community planning and natural resources. One merit-based award of $2,500 will be made to a student at the Masters level, or at the Ph.D. level, annually, based upon available funds.
Fiscal Sponsorship Program: The foundation seeks to help reduce the complexity of operating a successful project and enable small organizations and individuals to concentrate on programs and goals by offering fiscal sponsorship. The foundation's projects acquire the organizational infrastructure that frees individuals to conduct work in an effective and results-oriented way. Foundation staff members provide financial, administrative, and counseling support while individuals focus on program, planning, fundraising, and outreach. The foundation prefers to work with projects that serve to advance the field of ocean conservation itself, or ocean philanthropy. Fees for these services are a flat 10 percent of a project budget.
Surfrider Foundation Scholarship Program: The program provides $10,000 to grantees enrolled in an accredited college or university in the U.S. or internationally for the academic year. Awards may be made at the undergraduate, Masters and Ph.D.

levels. Both full and part time students are welcome to apply. The Ocean Foundation administers the program for the Surfrider Foundation.
EIN: 710863908

1703
Jack H. & Lovell R. Olender Foundation

888 - 17th St. N.W., 4th Fl.
Washington, DC 20006-3939 (703) 354-1800
Contact: Lovell Olender; Jack Olender, Pres.
Application address: 4312-J Evergreen Ln., Annandale, VA 22003, tel.: (703) 354-1800

Foundation type: Independent foundation
Purpose: Scholarships to deserving students from low-income families living in Washington, DC.
Financial data: Year ended 12/31/2012. Assets, $340,151 (M); Expenditures, $303,651; Total giving, $296,291; Grants to individuals, 12 grants totaling $12,000 (high: $1,000, low: $1,000).
Fields of interest: Economically disadvantaged.
Type of support: Scholarships—to individuals.
Application information:
Deadline(s): Before start of fall term
Applicants should submit the following:
1) Transcripts
2) Letter(s) of recommendation
3) Essay
Additional information: Application must also include a copy of parents' tax return.
EIN: 521622462

1704
Claire Williams O'Neil Foundation

c/o Michael Flanagan
2720 36th Pl. N.W.
Washington, DC 20007-1415
URL: http://cwofoundation.org/

Foundation type: Independent foundation
Purpose: Scholarships to individuals who are residents of Susquehanna and Thompson, PA, for higher education.
Financial data: Year ended 12/31/2012. Assets, $687,893 (M); Expenditures, $64,916; Total giving, $62,300; Grants to individuals, 5 grants totaling $60,000 (high: $20,000, low: $10,000).
Fields of interest: Higher education.
Type of support: Scholarships—to individuals.
Application information: Applications not accepted.
EIN: 233058554

1705
Optical Society of America

2010 Massachusetts Ave. N.W.
Washington, DC 20036-1012 (202) 223-8130
Contact: Elizabeth A. Rogan, C.E.O.
FAX: (202) 223-1096; E-mail: info@osa.org;
Toll-free tel.: (800) 766-4672; URL: http://www.osa.org

Foundation type: Public charity
Purpose: Travel grants for students presenting papers at conferences, and awards by nomination only to individuals who have made outstanding contributions in the field of optics.
Publications: Application guidelines.
Financial data: Year ended 12/31/2011. Assets, $73,306,376 (M); Expenditures, $30,105,243; Total giving, $769,920; Grants to individuals, 62 grants totaling $35,607.
Fields of interest: Medical school/education; Engineering school/education; Eye research; Science.

Type of support: Awards/grants by nomination only; Awards/prizes; Travel grants.
Application information: Application form required.
Deadline(s): Oct. 1
Additional information: Nominations accepted throughout the year. Completion of formal nomination required.
Program descriptions:
Corning Outstanding Student Paper Competition: This program recognizes innovation, research excellence, and presentation abilities in optical communications by giving awards to outstanding papers given at the Conference on Optical Fiber Communications (OFC) and the National Fiber Optic Engineers Conference (NFOEC). Eligible presenting authors must be undergraduate or graduate students of an educational institution, who is devoting more than half-time to studies within the institution at the time the paper was written. One first-prize winner will receive $1,500, while two honorable-mention winners will receive $1,000.
Emil Wolf Outstanding Student Paper Competition: This competition recognizes the innovation, research, and presentation excellence of students presenting their work during the society's Frontiers in Optics (FiO). Eligible applicants must be undergraduate or graduate students of an educational institution of collegiate grade who is devoting more than half-time to studies within the institution at the time the paper was written; one winner will be selected from each submission category, and will receive a $300 stipend and a complimentary society student membership.
Incubic/Milton Chang Travel Grant: Ten grants of up to $500 each are available to students who wish to present papers at the society's CLEO and Frontiers in Optics meetings, and at other society-sponsored annual meetings. Grants are usually awarded to the presenter and/or first author of the paper.
Jean Bennett Memorial Student Travel Grants: A $1,000 grant will be awarded to a student presenting their work at the society's Frontiers in Optics (FiO). Eligible applicants must be undergraduate or graduate students of an educational institution of collegiate grade who is devoting more than half-time to studies within the institution at the time the paper was written.
Maiman Student Paper Competition: This program recognizes student innovation, research excellence, and presentation skills in the areas of laser technology and electro-optics, by providing awards to outstanding student presentations at CLEO/QELS and CLEO/IQEC. Eligible presenting authors must be undergraduate or graduate students of educational institutions who devote more than half-time to studies within the institution. The top prize winner will receive $3,000 USD, two honorable mention recipients each receive a certificate.
Newport Travel Grants: This program recognizes the research excellence of students presenting their work at the Conference on Lasers and Electro-Optics (CLEO)
OSA Fellow Travel Grants: Individual travel grants of up to $2,000 are available for society fellows to visit and lecture in developing nations, with the goal of fostering optics programs between fellows and optics communities in these areas. Grants are meant to defray travel costs, and are not intended to support international conference attendance.
Robert S. Hilbert Memorial Student Travel Grants: Three grants of $1,100 each are available to recognize the research excellence of students in the areas of optical engineering, lens design, and illumination design. Eligible applicants must be the presenter of an accepted paper at a qualifying

meeting, and must be undergraduate or graduate students of an educational institution of collegiate grade who is devoting more than half-time studies within the institution at the time the paper was written.
Student Travel Grants: Grants of up to $1,000 each are available to students attending Frontiers in Optics, the society's annual meeting, or a society-managed topical meeting. Eligible applicants must: be working or studying in a qualifying developing nation; be enrolled in an accredited undergraduate or graduate program; and demonstrate need for travel support and state the value of attending the conference.
EIN: 530259696

1706
Paralyzed Veterans of America
801 18th St. N.W.
Washington, DC 20006-3517
E-mail: info@pva.org; Toll-free tel.: (800) 424-8200; URL: http://www.pva.org

Foundation type: Public charity
Purpose: Financial assistance to paralyzed veterans, and research grants to find a cure and improve health care for spinal cord injury or disease.
Financial data: Year ended 09/30/2011. Assets, $51,459,785 (M); Expenditures, $114,364,700; Total giving, $8,859,064; Grants to individuals, totaling $197,890.
Fields of interest: Spine disorders research; Military/veterans' organizations.
Type of support: Research; Grants for special needs.
Application information: Applications accepted.
Initial approach: Letter or e-mail
EIN: 131946868

1707
Parents, Families & Friends of Lesbians and Gays, Inc.
1828 L Street., N.W., Ste. 660
Washington, DC 20036-5112 (202) 467-8180
FAX: (202) 349-0788; E-mail: info@pflag.org;
URL: http://www.pflag.org

Foundation type: Public charity
Purpose: Scholarships are available to graduating high school seniors who identify as LGBTQ.
Financial data: Year ended 09/30/2012. Assets, $1,699,468 (M); Expenditures, $3,032,004; Total giving, $138,013; Grants to individuals, totaling $43,000.
Fields of interest: Education; LGBTQ.
Type of support: Scholarships—to individuals.
Application information: Applications accepted. Application form required. Application form available on the grantmaker's web site.
Send request by: Online
Deadline(s): Mar. 16
Final notification: Applicants notified by June 8
Program description:
Scholarships: Graduating seniors entering higher education for the first time who identify as lesbian, gay, bisexual, transgender or as a straight ally are eligible for $5,000, $2,500, and $1,000 scholarships.
EIN: 953750694

1708
Parkinson's Action Network
1025 Vermont Ave. N.W., Ste. 1120
Washington, DC 20005-3516 (202) 638-4101
Contact: Amy Comstock Rick, C.E.O.
FAX: (202) 638-7257;
E-mail: info@parkinsonsaction.org; Toll-free tel.: (800) 850-4726; E-mail For Amy Comstock Rick: arick@parkinsonsaction.org; URL: http://www.parkinsonsaction.org

Foundation type: Public charity
Purpose: Limited financial support to eligible individuals, to be put towards the registration fee, hotel accommodations, travel, and other necessary expenses of attending the Parkinson's Action Network's annual Research & Public Policy Forum.
Publications: Newsletter.
Financial data: Year ended 12/31/2011. Assets, $1,302,187 (M); Expenditures, $1,968,938; Total giving, $49,035; Grants to individuals, totaling $49,035.
Fields of interest: Parkinson's disease; Parkinson's disease research.
Type of support: Travel grants.
Application information: Applications accepted. Application form required.
Initial approach: Letter
Deadline(s): Jan. 3
EIN: 943172675

1709
Patient Access Network Foundation
(also known as PAN Foundation)
1331 F St., N.W., Ste. 975
Washington, DC 20004-1137 (202) 347-9272
Contact: Patrick McKercher, Pres.
FAX: (202) 347-9275;
E-mail: eacland@panfoundation.org; E-Mail for Patrick McKercher: Pmckercher@panfoundation.org; URL: https://www.PANfoundation.org

Foundation type: Public charity
Purpose: Financial assistance to cover out-of-pocket medical expenses for indigent people.
Publications: Annual report; Informational brochure; Newsletter.
Financial data: Year ended 12/31/2011. Assets, $132,290,472 (M); Expenditures, $35,302,824; Total giving, $28,379,485; Grants to individuals, totaling $8,288,625.
Fields of interest: Health care, financing.
Type of support: Grants for special needs.
Application information: Applications accepted. Application form required.
Initial approach: Letter
Additional information: Application template is generated after pre-screening is completed. Contact foundation for eligibility criteria.
EIN: 201184743

1710
Alicia Patterson Foundation
1090 Vermont Ave. NW, Ste. 1000
Washington, DC 20005-4965 (202) 393-5995
Contact: Margaret Engel, Exec. Dir.
FAX: (301) 951-8512;
E-mail: info@aliciapatterson.org; URL: http://aliciapatterson.org/

Foundation type: Operating foundation
Purpose: Grants one-year fellowships for a small number of print journalists and photojournalists to examine and write about areas or problems of special interest; candidates must be U.S. citizens

who have been working professionally as print journalists for five years or longer.

Publications: Application guidelines; Annual report; Grants list; Informational brochure; Newsletter.

Financial data: Year ended 12/31/2013. Assets, $5,537,766 (M); Expenditures, $432,635; Total giving, $274,775; Grants to individuals, 10 grants totaling $234,775 (high: $40,000, low: $3,333).

Fields of interest: Print publishing.

International interests: Global Programs.

Type of support: Fellowships.

Application information: Applications accepted. Application form required. Interview required.

   Initial approach: Letter, telephone, or e-mail
   Send request by: Mail
   Copies of proposal: 3
   Deadline(s): Oct. 1
   Final notification: Recipients notified in early Dec.
   Additional information: Recipients are chosen by an annual competition.

Program description:

Alicia Patterson Journalism Fellowships: The program awards five to seven new fellowships each year to newspaper, magazine, wire service, and freelance journalists, photographers, or editors for a year of travel and inquiry into significant foreign or domestic issues. Fellows write articles on their chosen subject for the APF Reporter, a quarterly magazine published by the foundation. The Reporter is circulated to newspaper and magazine editors and other interested people in business, government, and the professions throughout the U.S. All articles appearing in the magazine may be reprinted freely with proper credit. Fellowships include a $30,000 stipend. Fellows must take a leave of absence from their employer. Past research topics have included organized crime, abortion, immigrants, and issues in Haiti, Mexico, Hungary, and other nations.

EIN: 136092124

1711
Patton Boggs Foundation

2550 M St. NW
Washington, DC   20037-1350   (202) 457-6424
Contact: William J. Ryan, Secy.-Treas.
E-mail: joberdorfer@pattonboggs.com; URL: http://www.pattonboggs.com/about/patton-boggs-foundation

Foundation type: Public charity

Purpose: Fellowships to exceptional first- and second-year law students in the U.S. who demonstrate a steadfast commitment to public service and a developed interest in public policy.

Financial data: Year ended 09/30/2012. Assets, $1,272,860 (M); Expenditures, $72,590; Total giving, $65,000. Fellowships amount not specified.

Fields of interest: Law school/education; Public affairs.

Type of support: Fellowships.

Application information: Applications not accepted.

   Additional information: Students are selected for the fellowships. Unsolicited requests for funds not considered or acknowledged.

EIN: 522284635

1712
PEN/Faulkner Foundation

201 E. Capitol St., S.E.
Washington, DC   20003-1004   (202) 898-9063
Contact: Emma Snyder, Exec. Dir.
FAX: (202) 675-0360;
E-mail: info@penfaulkner.org; E-mail for Emma

Snyder: esnyder@penfaulkner.org; URL: http://www.penfaulkner.org

Foundation type: Public charity

Purpose: Awards only for peer-judged literary awards, and stipends only to authors and teachers who already participate in the Writers in Schools program.

Publications: Informational brochure; Occasional report; Program policy statement.

Financial data: Year ended 06/30/2012. Assets, $295,190 (M); Expenditures, $572,276; Total giving, $50,000; Grants to individuals, totaling $50,000.

Fields of interest: Literature; Arts.

Type of support: Awards/prizes.

Application information: Applications accepted. Application form not required.

   Deadline(s): Oct. 31
   Additional information: Work may be submitted by publishers, agents or authors.

EIN: 521431622

1713
People For the American Way Foundation

1101 15th St., NW, Ste. 600
Washington, DC   20005-5023   (202) 467-4999
E-mail: pfaw@pfaw.org; URL: http://www.pfaw.org

Foundation type: Public charity

Purpose: Grants to outstanding college-age advocates and activists.

Publications: Occasional report.

Financial data: Year ended 12/31/2011. Assets, $8,801,735 (M); Expenditures, $5,451,224; Total giving, $400,000.

Fields of interest: Research.

Type of support: Research; Grants to individuals.

Application information: Contact the foundation for further information.

EIN: 133065716

1714
Pharmaceutical Research and Manufacturers of America Foundation, Inc.

(also known as PhRMA Foundation)
950 F. St. N.W., Ste. 300
Washington, DC   20004-1440   (202) 572-7756
Contact: John Castellani, Pres. and C.E.O.
FAX: (202) 572-7799;
E-mail: foundation@phrma.org; URL: http://www.phrmafoundation.org

Foundation type: Public charity

Purpose: Support to young scientists in disciplines important to the pharmaceutical industry by awarding them competitive research fellowships and grants at a critical decision point at the outset of their careers.

Publications: Annual report; Grants list; Informational brochure (including application guidelines); Newsletter.

Financial data: Year ended 12/31/2011. Assets, $17,505,081 (M); Expenditures, $2,478,702; Total giving, $1,975,485; Grants to individuals, totaling $1,855,791.

Fields of interest: Medical school/education; Pharmacy/prescriptions.

Type of support: Fellowships; Research.

Application information: Applications accepted. Application form required.

   Deadline(s): Feb. 1 for Paul Calabresi Medical Student Fellowship; Sept. 1 for Informatics and Pharmacology/Toxicology, and Oct. 1 for Health Outcomes and Pharmaceutics

Program descriptions:

Clinical Pharmacology: Fellowships are offered to medical or dental students who have substantial interests in research and teaching careers in clinical pharmacology and who are willing to spend full-time in a specific research effort within a pharmacology or clinical pharmacology unit. Fellowships are available for a minimum period of six months or any period of time up to 24 months with a maximum stipend of $18,000.

Health Outcomes: Outcomes research spans a broad spectrum of issues from studies evaluating the effectiveness of a particular pharmaceutical intervention to the impact of reimbursement policies on the outcomes of care. It also ranges from the development and use of tools to perform patient-based assessments to analyses of the best way to disseminate the results of outcomes research to providers or consumers to encourage behavior change.

Informatics: The goal of this area is to promote the use of informatics in an integrative approach to the understanding of biological and disease processes. Informatics awards will support career development of scientists engaged in computational and experimental research to integrate cutting-edge information technology with advanced biological, chemical, and pharmacological sciences.

Pharmaceutics: Awards in this area deal with the design and evaluation of contemporary pharmaceutical dosage forms (or drug delivery systems) so they are safe, effective, and reliable. Pharmaceutics places a strong emphasis on understanding and exploiting the principles underlying drug delivery, whether a drug is a small organic molecule, a higher molecular weight protein, or a peptide derived through the use of biotechnology.

Pharmacology/Toxicology: Pharmacology/ toxicology awards are provided to support career-development activities of scientists prepared to engage in research that integrates information on molecular or cellular mechanisms of action with information on the effects of an agent observed in an intact organism, either in experimental animal or clinical studies or both.

EIN: 526063009

1715
The Phi Beta Kappa Society

1606 New Hampshire Ave. N.W.
Washington, DC   20009-2512   (202) 265-3808
FAX: (202) 986-1601; E-mail: info@pbk.org;
URL: http://www.pbk.org

Foundation type: Public charity

Purpose: Fellowships and awards to those who have excelled in the liberal arts and sciences.

Publications: Informational brochure.

Financial data: Year ended 07/31/2011. Assets, $5,185,124 (M); Expenditures, $7,064,671; Total giving, $2,760,230; Grants to individuals, totaling $161,000.

Fields of interest: Humanities; Arts.

Type of support: Fellowships; Awards/prizes.

Application information: Applications accepted. Application form required.

   Initial approach: Letter
   Deadline(s): Jan. 15 for Mary Isabel Sibley Fellowships; Mar. 31 for Book Awards; Oct. 1 for Walter J. Jensen Fellowship

Program descriptions:

Book Awards: The book awards are given each year in December to outstanding scholarly books published in the United States. Winning works, which are drawn from the fields of the humanities, the social sciences, the natural sciences and mathematics, must be of broad interest and accessible to the general, literate reader. The following awards are available: 1) Christian Gauss Award is offered for books in the field of literary scholarship or criticism; 2) Phi Beta Kappa Award in Science is offered for outstanding contributions by scientists to the literature of science; and 3) Ralph Waldo Emerson Award is offered for scholarly studies that contribute significantly to interpretations of the intellectual and cultural condition of humanity.

Humanities Award: This $25,000 award is given to recognize individuals who have made significant contributions in the field of the humanities.

Mary Isabel Sibley Fellowship: This annual fellowship is awarded alternately in the fields of Greek and French. The award may be used for the study of Greek language, literature, history or archaeology, or the study of French language or literature. The fellowship has a stipend of $20,000. The stipend will be paid in two installments, the first on July 1 of the award year and the second on the next January 1. Candidates must be unmarried women 25 to 35 years of age who have demonstrated their ability to carry on original research. They must hold a doctorate or have fulfilled all the requirements for a doctorate except the dissertation, and they must be planning to devote full-time work to research during the fellowship year. The award is not restricted to members of Phi Beta Kappa or to U.S. citizens.

Romanell-Phi Beta Kappa Professorship: The professorship is awarded annually to scholars in the field of philosophy, without restriction to any one school of philosophical thought. The professorship is intended to recognize not only distinguished achievement but also the recipient's contribution or potential contribution to public understanding of philosophy. The professorship is not renewable. The professorship carries with it a stipend of $7,500, which will be awarded in addition to the recipient's regular salary. Although the awardee need not be a member of Phi Beta Kappa, he or she must be on the faculty of an institution sheltering a chapter of Phi Beta Kappa and must be nominated by that chapter. Phi Beta Kappa chapters are invited to submit nominations for the professorship.

Sidney Hook Memorial Award: This award recognizes national distinction by a single scholar in each of three endeavors - scholarship, undergraduate teaching and leadership in the cause of liberal arts education. The award is in the amount of $7,500.

Walter J. Jensen Fellowship: The fellowship is awarded for at least six months of study in France. The purpose of the award is to help educators and researchers improve education in standard French language, literature and culture and in the study of standard French in the United States. The fellowship is awarded annually and has a stipend of at least $10,000. The society will also cover a single round-trip, economy-class ticket for the recipient to travel to France; some additional support may be available to those with dependents. Candidates must be U.S. citizens under the age of 40 who can demonstrate their career does or will involve active use of the French language. They must have earned a bachelor's degree from an accredited four-year institution with a 3.0 minimum GPA in French language and literature as a major. **EIN:** 530226282

1716
The Phillips Foundation, Inc.
1 Massachusetts Ave., N.W., Ste. 600
Washington, DC 20001-1401 (202) 250-3887
Contact: D. Jeffrey Hollingsworth; John W. Farley, Exec. Dir.
URL: http://www.thephillipsfoundation.org/

Foundation type: Company-sponsored foundation
Purpose: Scholarships to undergraduates attending four-year colleges who demonstrate leadership on behalf of the cause of freedom, American values, and constitutional principles. Fellowships to professional journalists who are U.S. citizens with less than ten years of experience.
Financial data: Year ended 09/30/2012. Assets, $67,491 (M); Expenditures, $961,749; Total giving, $292,000; Grants to individuals, 65 grants totaling $292,000 (high: $30,000, low: $1,000).
Fields of interest: Print publishing; History/archaeology; Higher education; Public policy; Research.
Type of support: Fellowships; Scholarships—to individuals; Undergraduate support.
Application information: Applications accepted. Application form required. Application form available on the grantmaker's web site. Interview required.
Initial approach: Application
Send request by: Mail
Deadline(s): Jan. 17 for scholarships, Feb. 21 for journalism fellowships.
Final notification: Recipients notified late Mar. or early Apr. for scholarships, Mid-May for journalism fellowships
Applicants should submit the following:
1) Budget Information
2) Curriculum vitae
3) Essay
4) GPA
5) Letter(s) of recommendation
6) Proposal
7) Resume
8) Work samples
Additional information: Scholarship applications should include a dean or registrar's certification of full-time enrollment in good standing.
Program descriptions:
Diana Davis Spencer Fellowship: The foundation awards fellowships to working journalists with less than ten years of professional experience in print and online journalism for writing projects focusing on the impact of free enterprise on society.
Environmental Fellowship: The foundation awards fellowships to working journalists with less than ten years of professional experience in print and online journalism for writing projects focusing on the environment from a free market perspective.
Law Enforcement Fellowship: The foundation awards fellowships to working journalists with less than ten years of professional experience in print and online journalism for writing projects focusing on some aspect of law enforcement in the U.S.
Robert Novak Journalism Fellowship Program: The foundation awards $50,000 full-time fellowships and $25,000 part-time fellowships to working journalists with less than ten years of professional experience in print and online journalism. Fellowships are comprised of a one-year writing project on a topic of the applicants choosing, focusing on journalism supportive of American culture and a free society.
Ronald Reagan College Leaders Scholarship Program: The foundation awards four-year renewable scholarships to college undergraduates who demonstrate leadership on behalf of freedom,

American values, and constitutional principles. Scholarships range from $1,000 to $10,000.
EIN: 521707001

1717
Professional Athletes Foundation
1133 20th St. N.W.
Washington, DC 20036-3408

Foundation type: Independent foundation
Purpose: Assistance for former professional and amateur athletes who are faced with unusual financial problems, whether due to medical, educational, or catastrophic events. Grants are available up to $10,000 per recipient.
Financial data: Year ended 12/31/2012. Assets, $23,844,791 (M); Expenditures, $1,525,505; Total giving, $1,245,655; Grants to individuals, 183 grants totaling $986,755 (high: $30,000, low: $62).
Fields of interest: Athletics/sports, amateur leagues; Athletics/sports, professional leagues.
Type of support: Scholarships—to individuals; Grants for special needs.
Application information: Applications not accepted.
Additional information: Unsolicited requests for funds not considered or acknowledged.
EIN: 521205920

1718
Radio and Television News Directors Foundation
529 14th St., N.W., Ste. 425
Washington, DC 20045-1406 (202) 659-6510
Contact: Barbara Cochran, Pres.; For Scholarships: Melanie Lo
FAX: (202) 223-4007; *E-mail:* janen@rtdnf.org;
Toll-free tel.: (800) 807-8332; *URL:* http://www.rtdna.org/pages/about-rtndf.php

Foundation type: Public charity
Purpose: Scholarships and internship opportunities to U.S. residents who are undergraduate or graduate students pursuing radio and television news careers. Fellowships to radio and television journalists.
Publications: Application guidelines; Annual report.
Financial data: Year ended 12/31/2011. Assets, $1,415,571 (M); Expenditures, $591,784; Total giving, $44,025; Grants to individuals, totaling $44,025.
Fields of interest: Media/communications; Print publishing; Journalism school/education; Minorities.
Type of support: Fellowships; Internship funds; Scholarships—to individuals; Exchange programs; Graduate support; Undergraduate support.
Application information: Applications accepted. Application form required. Application form available on the grantmaker's web site.
Initial approach: Letter, telephone, or e-mail
Deadline(s): May 13
Applicants should submit the following:
1) Curriculum vitae
2) Work samples
Additional information: See web site for additional application information.
Program descriptions:
Carole Simpson Scholarship: A $2,000 award will be presented to an aspiring minority journalism student, to help him/her overcome hurdles along their career path.
Ed Bradley Scholarship: A $10,000 scholarship is available to young aspiring minority journalism students.

George Foreman Tribute to Lyndon B. Johnson Scholarship: This $6,000 award will be presented to an outstanding journalism student from the University of Texas at Austin.

German/American Awards Program: This program works to support bi-national exchange between the U.S. and Germany, by awarding cash prizes to journalists whose stories, pieces, reports, and newscasts address an aspect of the relationship between the two nations. Reports can reference politics, economy, society, culture, or current events; winners are invited to the annual award ceremony in Berlin, where all transportation and accommodation expenses are covered.

Lou and Carole Prato Sports Reporting Scholarship: This scholarship presents a $1,000 tuition grant to a deserving student who is planning a career as a sports reporter in television or radio. Applicants should demonstrate strong writing skills.

Michele Clark Fellowship: A $1,000 award will be given to a young, promising minority professional working in television or radio news. Recipients will also be given an expenses-paid trip to the Radio and Television News Directors Association National Conference.

N.S. Bienstock Fellowships: A $2,500 award will be given to a promising minority journalist in radio or television news. Recipients will also be rewarded with an expense-paid trip to the Radio and Television News Directors Association National Conference.

Pete Wilson Journalism Scholarship: This program presents a $2,000 scholarship to a student from the San Francisco Bay area who is pursuing an undergraduate or graduate journalism degree.

The Abe Schechter Graduate Scholarship: A $2,000 scholarship is awarded to an outstanding student pursuing a graduate degree in journalism.

The Mike Reynolds Journalism Scholarship: This $1,000 scholarship will be awarded to an outstanding applicant who is enrolled in journalism school and who demonstrates good writing ability, excellent grades, a dedication to the news business, a strong interest in pursuing a career in electronic journalism, and a demonstrated need for financial assistance.

The Presidents Scholarship: Two $1,000 scholarships are awarded to currently-enrolled sophomores, juniors, and seniors in good standing at their colleges or universities, to be used toward expanding their journalism experience.
EIN: 381860090

1719
Rainy Day Foundation, Inc.
1808 Corcoran St. N.W.
Washington, DC   20009-1608   (202) 234-7515

Foundation type: Public charity
Purpose: Financial assistance and emergency support to eligible homeowners of Washington, DC who experience unforseen short term financial problems with mortgage payments.
Financial data: Year ended 09/30/2012. Assets, $880,442 (M); Expenditures, $473,733; Total giving, $168,804; Grants to individuals, totaling $168,804.
Fields of interest: Housing/shelter, home owners.
Type of support: Emergency funds; Grants for special needs.
Application information: Applications accepted. Application form required.
  Additional information: Contact the foundation for eligibility determination. Assistance to individuals is based on set eligibility criteria by

the organization to ensure the assistance is made to eligible individuals.
EIN: 522346414

1720
The Norman R. Rales and Ruth Rales Foundation
2200 Pennsylvania Ave., Ste. 800W
Washington, DC   20037-1731

Foundation type: Independent foundation
Purpose: Grants to individuals for higher and other education, and for social services.
Financial data: Year ended 11/30/2012. Assets, $13,459,469 (M); Expenditures, $922,438; Total giving, $756,500.
Type of support: Grants to individuals.
Application information: Applications not accepted.
EIN: 596874589

1721
Recycling Research Foundation
1615 L. Street, N.W.
Washington, DC   20036-5610   (202) 662-8500
Contact: Tom Crane

Foundation type: Public charity
Purpose: Developing-level scholarships to anyone whose field of study relates to the scrap processing and recycling industry; and scholarships only to dependents of individuals whose companies are Institute of Scrap Recycling Industries, Inc. (ISRI) members in good standing and whose ISRI chapter has a scholarship program.
Financial data: Year ended 12/31/2011. Assets, $202,337 (M); Expenditures, $140,924; Total giving, $98,181.
Fields of interest: Recycling.
Type of support: Undergraduate support.
Application information:
  Initial approach: Letter
  Additional information: Contact foundation for eligibility criteria.
EIN: 521332690

1722
Red Circle Foundation
600 Pennsylvania Ave. S.E.
P.O. Box 15415
Washington, DC   20003-4316
E-mail: info@RedCircleFoundation.org; URL: http://redcirclefoundation.org/

Foundation type: Public charity
Purpose: Scholarships for children of former and current U.S. Military Special Operational Professionals pursuing higher education. Financial assistance for former or current U.S. Military Special Operations Professional or parent, spouse or child of the community in the event of an unforseen bereavement or other extenuating circumstances.
Fields of interest: Higher education; Military/veterans' organizations.
Type of support: Scholarships—to individuals; Grants for special needs.
Application information: Applications accepted. Application form required.
  Additional information: See web site for eligibility determination for scholarships and financial assistance. Unsolicited requests for funds not considered or acknowledged. Scholarships and assistance only for U.S. Military.

Program descriptions:
  The John M. Zinn Academic Scholarship: The scholarship was developed to support the children of former or current U.S. Military Special Operations professionals in the fulfillment of their educational endeavors. These scholarships are intended to remove economic barriers for students who demonstrate financial need, by providing financial assistance and support for students from elementary through graduate school. Scholarships will be awarded to offset student costs, including, but not limited to tuition, institutional fees, books and other education-related costs, and living expenses. The maximum award for this scholarship is $1,000.
  The John M. Zinn Enrichment Scholarship: The program is designed to send the children of (deployed, former and fallen) Special Operations Professionals to camps, clinics, or enrichment programs which will give their children an opportunity to learn about a "passion" of their father's. The scholarship will fund young children ages 8 to 18 to "follow in their father's footsteps". The maximum award for this scholarship is $500.
EIN: 352450067

1723
Resources for the Future
(also known as RFF)
1616 P St. N.W., Ste. 600
Washington, DC   20036-1434   (202) 328-5000
Contact: Philip Sharp, Pres.
FAX: (202) 939-3460; E-mail: voigt@rff.org; URL: http://www.rff.org

Foundation type: Public charity
Purpose: Grants and fellowships to scholars studying the environmental and natural resource sciences.
Publications: Application guidelines; Annual report; Newsletter.
Financial data: Year ended 09/30/2011. Assets, $41,002,465 (M); Expenditures, $13,547,113; Total giving, $41,500; Grants to individuals, totaling $41,500.
Fields of interest: Research; Natural resources.
Type of support: Fellowships; Research.
Application information: Contact foundation for complete application guidelines.
EIN: 530220900

1724
Angus Robinson, Jr. Memorial Foundation
c/o Reinsurance Association Of America
1445 New York Ave., N.W., 7th Fl.
Washington, DC   20005
Contact: Jackielyn Hayes, Tr.
Application address: 300 1st Stamford Pl., Stamford, CT 06902
Application address: 300 1st Stamford Pl., Stamford, CT 06902

Foundation type: Independent foundation
Purpose: Scholarships to qualified students who are enrolled in an insurance, risk management or actuarial science four-year degree program.
Financial data: Year ended 12/31/2011. Assets, $1,090,808 (M); Expenditures, $143,174; Total giving, $96,000; Grants to individuals, 33 grants totaling $91,000 (high: $5,000, low: $1,000).
Fields of interest: Business school/education.
Type of support: Undergraduate support.
Application information: Application form required.
  Deadline(s): Dec. 16
  Applicants should submit the following:
    1) SAT

2) GPA
3) Letter(s) of recommendation
4) Essay
5) Transcripts
6) Financial information
7) FAF
Additional information: Selection is also based on demonstrated commitment to the pursuit of a career in the insurance industry.
EIN: 061300536

1725
Ronald McDonald House Charities of Greater Washington, DC, Inc.
3727 14th St., N.E.
Washington, DC   20017-8204   (202) 529-8204
FAX: (202) 635-3578; E-mail: info@rmhcdc.org; Tel. for Karen Judson: (202) 529-8204; e-mail for Karen Judson: kjudson@rmhcdc.org; URL: http://www.rmhc.greaterdc.org

Foundation type: Public charity
Purpose: Scholarships to local high school seniors with financial need from DC, MD, VA, and WV to attend college.
Publications: Application guidelines; Annual report; Financial statement; Grants list; Informational brochure (including application guidelines); Newsletter.
Financial data: Year ended 12/31/2012. Assets, $21,685,289 (M); Expenditures, $2,089,619; Total giving, $328,713; Grants to individuals, totaling $40,000.
Type of support: Undergraduate support.
Application information: Applications accepted. Application form required. Application form available on the grantmaker's web site.
   Initial approach: Application
   Copies of proposal: 1
   Deadline(s): Feb. 16
   Applicants should submit the following:
      1) Transcripts
      2) SAT
      3) Letter(s) of recommendation
      4) GPA
      5) Financial information
      6) Essay
      7) ACT
   Additional information: Scholarships are limited to students residing in DC and in specific counties of MD, VA and WV only. Contact foundation for further program guidelines.
EIN: 521132262

1726
The Schimel Lode
2555 Pennsylvania Ave., N.W., No. 514
Washington, DC   20037-1614   (202) 659-1772
Contact: Ruth Schimel, Board Member
E-mail: ruth@theschimellode.net; Additional tel.: (202) 862-5484; URL: http://www.theschimellode.net/

Foundation type: Public charity
Purpose: Grants to individuals for projects that benefit the Washington, DC, area.
Publications: Application guidelines.
Type of support: Program development; Research; Grants to individuals; Project support.
Application information: Applications accepted. Application form not required. Application form available on the grantmaker's web site.
   Initial approach: Letter

Send request by: E-mail
Deadline(s): June 30
Final notification: Applicants notified in two and a half months
Additional information: See web site for complete program information.

1727
Sheet Metal Workers' International Scholarship Foundation, Inc.
1750 New York Ave. N.W., 6th Fl.
Washington, DC   20006-5386   (202) 662-0871
Contact: Rich McClees, Admin.

Foundation type: Public charity
Purpose: Scholarships to members of the Sheet Metal Workers' International Association and their families.
Publications: Application guidelines.
Financial data: Year ended 06/30/2012. Assets, $6,976,694 (M); Expenditures, $123,153; Total giving, $74,500; Grants to individuals, totaling $74,500.
Fields of interest: Education.
Type of support: Undergraduate support.
Application information:
   Initial approach: Letter
   Deadline(s): Mar. 1
   Applicants should submit the following:
      1) Essay
      2) SAT
      3) GPA
   Additional information: Applicants should also include a list of extracurricular activities.
Program description:
   Scholarship Program: The foundation awards scholarships, ranging from $2,000 to $4,000 each, available to applicants who are members of the Sheet Metal Workers' International Association (SMWIA), a covered employee, or a dependent spouse or child of an (SMWIA) member or covered employee.
EIN: 521473935

1728
Sigma Delta Chi Foundation of Washington, DC
P.O. Box 19555
Washington, DC   20036-0555

Foundation type: Independent foundation
Purpose: Scholarships primarily to individuals pursuing journalism degrees in MD and DC.
Financial data: Year ended 06/30/2012. Assets, $63,767 (M); Expenditures, $23,625; Total giving, $23,000; Grants to individuals, 2 grants totaling $2,000 (high: $1,000, low: $1,000).
Fields of interest: Print publishing.
Type of support: Scholarships—to individuals.
Application information: Applications accepted.
   Additional information: Contact foundation for current application deadline/guidelines.
EIN: 526055635

1729
Smithsonian Institution
1000 Jefferson Dr., S.W.
Washington, DC   20560-0008   (202) 633-1000
Contact: For Fellowships: Katherine Harris
Application address: Office of Fellowships: Smithsonian Institution, 470 L'Enfant Plaza SW, Suite 7102, MRC 902, P.O. Box 37012, Washington, D.C. 20012-7012; phone: (202)

633-7070; e-mail: siofg@si.edu; URL: http://www.si.edu/ofg/Applications/cfell/crfellapp.htm
E-mail: info@si.edu; URL: http://www.smithsonian.org

Foundation type: Public charity
Purpose: Fellowships to individuals for study at the Smithsonian.
Publications: Annual report; Informational brochure; Newsletter.
Financial data: Year ended 09/30/2011. Assets, $3,516,523,060 (M); Expenditures, $1,101,404,223; Total giving, $16,118,927; Grants to individuals, totaling $10,048,175.
Type of support: Fellowships.
Application information: Applications accepted. Application form required. Application form available on the grantmaker's web site.
   Initial approach: Letter
   Deadline(s): Jan. 15
   Applicants should submit the following:
      1) Proposal
   Additional information: See web site for a listing of additional programs.
Program descriptions:
   Latino Studies Fellowship Program: The program provides opportunities to U.S. Latino/Latina predoctoral students and postdoctoral and senior scholars to pursue research topics that relate to Latino art, culture, and history. Interdisciplinary subjects are encouraged and can be undertaken at more than one of the institution's museums and/or research units, and advised by one or more research staff members. Stipends for senior and postdoctoral scholars are $40,000 per year; predoctoral studies receive $25,000 per year.
   Minority Internship Program: This program offers internships to increase participation of U.S. minority groups who are underrepresented in scholarly programs, in the disciplines of research conducted at the institution, and in the museum field. This program is designed to provide undergraduate and beginning graduate students the opportunity to learn more about the institution and the student's academic fields through direct experience in research or museum-related internship projects under the supervision of research and professional staff members at the institution's many museums, research institutes, and offices. Internships are full-time (40 hours per week), ten-week appointments during the summer, fall, or spring. Stipend awards are $550 per week, with additional travel allowances offered in some cases.
   Museum Conservation Institute Postdoctoral Fellowship in Mass Spectrometry: Fellowships are available to qualified individuals to work at the mass spectrometry and proteomics laboratory at the Smithsonian Museum Conservation Institute. Fellows will work to develop mass spectrometry and proteomics technologies relevant to museums' specimens, including (but not limited to): species (fungus, etc.) and proteinaceous objects identification using metabolomics and proteomics techniques; biological dating using various MS techniques, such as amino acid racemization; analysis of insoluble proteinaceous or polymeric materials; analysis of paints, inks, etc., using surface ionization techniques; and the development of portable separation-mass spectrometry devices for onsite chemical/biological analysis. Eligible applicants must have a Ph.D. in the area(s) of separation, micro- and nanofabrication, mass spectrometry, and proteomics, and an outstanding academic track record demonstrated by publications in refereed journals. Stipends of up to $40,000 are available, with allowances for health insurance.

National Air and Space Museum (NASM) Charles A. Lindbergh Chair in Aerospace History: This competitive twelve-month fellowship is open to senior scholarship with distinguished records of publication who are working on, or anticipate working on, books in aerospace history. Support of up to $100,000 for one year is available.

National Air and Space Museum (NASM) Guggenheim Fellowship: This fellowship program is a competitive three- to twelve-month in-residence fellowship for pre- or post-doctoral research in aviation and space history. Predoctoral applicants should have completed preliminary coursework and examination and be engaged in dissertation research, while postdoctoral applicants should have received their Ph.D. within the past seven years. A stipend of $30,000 for predoctoral candidates and $45,000 for postdoctoral candidates, with limited additional funds for travel and miscellaneous expenses.

National Air and Space Museum (NASM) Postdoctoral Earth and Planetary Sciences Fellowship: This fellowship opportunity supports scientific research in the areas of earth and planetary sciences. Fellows will concentrate on geologic and geophysical research of the Earth and other terrestrial planets, using remote sensing data obtained from Earth-orbiting and interplanetary spacecraft. Appointments can be made for one or more years; stipends are compatible with other postdoctoral fellowships in the applicant's field.

National Air and Space Museum (NASM) Verville Fellowship: This competitive nine- to twelve-month in-residence fellowship is intended for the analysis of major trends, developments, and accomplishments in the history of aviation or space studies. Fellowships are open to all interested candidates with demonstrated skills in research and writing; an advanced degree in history, engineering, or related fields is not a requirement. A stipend of $55,000 will be awarded for a 12-month fellowship, with limited additional funds set aside for travel and miscellaneous expenses.

National Museum of American History (NMAH) Lemelson Center Fellowships: This fellowship program supports projects that present creative approaches to the study of invention and innovation in American society, including (but not limited to) historical research and documentation projects that result in publications, exhibitions, educational initiatives, and multimedia products. The program provides stipends for up to ten weeks to scholars and professionals who are pre- or post-doctoral candidates, or who have completed advanced professional training; in addition to stipends, fellows also receive access to the Smithsonian's vast artifact and archival collections, as well as the expertise of the institution's research staff.

National Museum of American History (NMAH) Lemelson Center Travel to Collections Award: This program supports research on the history of American invention and innovation, based on the holdings of the Smithsonian's archives centers and curatorial divisions, by offering five short-term (up to ten days) travel awards per year. Awardees receive $150 per day, that are intended to cover transportation and living expenses. Eligible applicants include scholars, graduate students, and independent researchers not resident or attending school within commuting distance of the National Museum of American History.

Smithsonian Postgraduate Fellowships in Conservation of Museum Collections Program: These fellowships are offered to recent graduates of masters programs in art conservation (or the equivalent) who wish to conduct research and gain further training at the institution's conservation laboratories for a period of one year. Additional

facilities may be available to museum or archives fellows for analytical work at the Smithsonian Center for Materials Research and Education (SCMRE). A stipend of $35,000 is offered, plus allowances.
EIN: 530206027

1730
The Society for Cardiovascular Angiography and Interventions
1100 17th St. N.W., Ste. 330
Washington, DC   20036   (202) 741-9854
E-mail address for fellowships: shubka@scai.org
E-mail: info@scai.org; Toll Free Tel.:
(800)-992-7224; Fax: (800)-863-5202;
URL: http://www.scai.org

Foundation type: Public charity
Purpose: Fellowships to physicians in training who have demonstrated medical excellence and whose research promises advancement and contribution to cardiovascular imaging and invasive techniques.
Publications: Application guidelines; Occasional report.
Financial data: Year ended 12/31/2011. Assets, $4,733,323 (M); Expenditures, $8,601,109; Total giving, $1,016,000; Grants to individuals, totaling $3,500.
Fields of interest: Medical school/education; Heart & circulatory research.
Type of support: Fellowships; Research; Graduate support.
Application information: Applications accepted.
  Initial approach: Proposal
  Send request by: E-mail
  Deadline(s): Mar. 16 for Gregory Braden Memorial Fellowship
  Applicants should submit the following:
    1) Curriculum vitae
    2) Letter(s) of recommendation
  Additional information: Selection is based on either cardiologists or radiologists who are currently enrolled as fellows in accredited training programs recognized by the council for graduate medical education.
Program descriptions:
  Greg Braden Memorial Fellow of the Year Award: This award will go to a graduating interventional cardiology fellow who demonstrates excellent interventional skills in multiple cardiovascular (CV) modalities, shows promise for future contribution to CV research through publications or otherwise, strives to contribute to the overall advancement of interventional cardiology, consistently demonstrates dedication to patient care and well-being, and shows potential to become a leader among peers. Recipients will be honored with a $2,500 cash award, a hand-crafted crystal award, and a one year free membership to SCAI post-graduation.
  SCAI/Cordis Fellowship Program for Interventional Cardiology: Awarded in conjunction with the Cordis Cardiac and Vascular Institute, two fellowships will be made available to physicians-in-training whose research promises advances in cardiovascular invasive and/or interventional patient care. Eligible applicants must be serving as a fellow in an accredited invasive/interventional cardiology fellowship training program recognized by the Accreditation Council on Graduate Medical Education, have the approval of the training program director, and are sponsored by a society member or fellow from the applicant's institution (a physician who has a current membership application on file may also act as a sponsor).
EIN: 341266824

1731
Society for Science and the Public, Inc.
(formerly Science Service, Inc.)
1719 N. St., N.W.
Washington, DC   20036-2801   (202) 785-2255
Contact: Larry Sigler, Business Mgr.
FAX: (202) 785-1243; URL: http://www.societyforscience.org/

Foundation type: Public charity
Purpose: Scholarships to graduating high school seniors for original research projects in mathematics, science, or engineering.
Publications: Application guidelines.
Financial data: Year ended 12/31/2011. Assets, $99,153,472 (M); Expenditures, $18,193,353; Total giving, $2,702,481; Grants to individuals, 812 grants totaling $1,829,013. Subtotal for conferences/seminars: 937 grants totaling $1,787,643. Subtotal for grants to individuals: 30 grants totaling $247,961.
Fields of interest: Engineering school/education; Formal/general education; Mathematics; Engineering.
Type of support: Awards/prizes; Undergraduate support.
Application information: Application form required.
  Applicants should submit the following:
    1) ACT
    2) Transcripts
    3) Letter(s) of recommendation
    4) GPA
    5) Essay
  Additional information: Application must also include research plan, and statement from supervising scientist.
Program description:
  Intel Science Talent Search: The program awards high school seniors in the United States and territories, and American students attending school abroad a first-place scholarship prize of $100,000, a second-place scholarship prize of $75,000, and a third-place scholarship prize of $50,000.
EIN: 530196483

1732
Sons of Italy Foundation
219 E St., N.E.
Washington, DC   20002-4922   (202) 547-2900
Contact: Margaret Cirona O'Rourke, Admin. Asst., Scholarships
FAX: (202) 546-8168;
E-mail: scholarships@osia.org; Toll-free tel.: (800) 522-6742; e-mail for Margaret Cirona O'Rourke: morourke@osia.org; URL: http://www.osia.org/sif/index.php

Foundation type: Public charity
Purpose: Scholarships to U.S. citizens of Italian-American descent enrolled full-time in undergraduate or graduate programs at accredited schools, colleges, and universities.
Publications: Application guidelines; Biennial report; Newsletter.
Financial data: Year ended 09/30/2012. Assets, $1,361,131 (M); Expenditures, $966,545; Total giving, $242,181; Grants to individuals, totaling $58,000.
International interests: Italy.
Type of support: Undergraduate support.
Application information: Application form required. Application form available on the grantmaker's web site.
  Initial approach: E-mail
  Send request by: Mail
  Deadline(s): Feb. 28
  Final notification: Recipients notified May 1

Applicants should submit the following:
1) Resume
2) Essay
3) Letter(s) of recommendation
4) Transcripts
5) SAT
6) ACT

Program descriptions:
General Study Scholarships: Scholarships, ranging from $5,000 to $25,000, are available to U.S. citizens of Italian descent (with at least one Italian or Italian-American grandparent) enrolled in an undergraduate or graduate study at a four-year, accredited academic institution.

Henry Salvatori Scholarship: This scholarship is awarded to a college-bound high school senior who demonstrates exceptional leadership, distinguished scholarship, and a deep understanding and respect for the principles of liberty, freedom, and equality. Eligible applicants must be U.S. citizens of Italian descent who are in their senior year of high school, and who are planning to attend an undergraduate program at a four-year accredited academic institution.

Italian Language Scholarship: Scholarships are available to U.S. citizens of Italian descent who are in their junior or senior year of undergraduate study, and who are majoring or minoring in Italian language studies at an accredited academic institution.

Sons of Italy Foundation/George L. Graziadio Scholarship: The foundation provides a scholarship to a U.S. citizen of Italian descent (with at least one Italian or Italian-American grandparent) who is a student at the George L. Graziadio School of Business and Management at Pepperdine University.

Sorrento Lingue Language and Culture Study Abroad Scholarship: A scholarship will be awarded to an outstanding student to study for one semester at the Sorrento Lingue campus in Sorrento, Italy. Eligible applicants must be U.S. citizens of Italian descent who are enrolled in their junior or senior year of undergraduate study, or are enrolled in a graduate program, at a four-year accredited academic institution. Scholarships are intended to cover enrollment and course fees. Travel to and from Italy, accommodations, and other expenses are not included.
EIN: 236276526

1733
Spina Bifida Association of America
4590 MacArthur Blvd. N.W., Ste. 250
Washington, DC   20007-4226   (202) 944-3285
Contact: Cindy Brownstein, Pres. and C.E.O.
FAX: (202) 944-3295; E-mail: sbaa@sbaa.org;
URL: http://www.spinabifidaassociation.org

Foundation type: Public charity
Purpose: Scholarships are provided for students living with spina bifida.
Publications: Application guidelines.
Financial data: Year ended 12/31/2011. Assets, $2,161,421 (M); Expenditures, $3,137,333; Total giving, $219,750; Grants to individuals, totaling $42,150.
Fields of interest: Genetic diseases and disorders; Spine disorders.
Type of support: Scholarships—to individuals.
Application information: Applications accepted. Application form required. Application form available on the grantmaker's web site.
Deadline(s): Mar. 16
Applicants should submit the following:
1) Transcripts
2) Letter(s) of recommendation
3) FAFSA

4) Essay
Additional information: Application should include verification of acceptance by a school or college and a statement of disability from a physician. See web site for additional information.
Program description:
Scholarship Program: The association seeks to enhance opportunities for persons born with spina bifida to achieve their full potential through higher education. Scholarships from the association make it possible for the student to choose educational pursuits that are otherwise outside of financial reach. The association has two scholarship categories. Four-year scholarships are available to high school seniors, and will be granted up to $5,000 every year in tuition and room and board for four years. One-year scholarships are available to high school graduates or individuals who possess a G.E.D., and will be granted for up to $2,000 for one year. Each applicant can select only one scholarship fund for which he or she would like to be considered.
EIN: 581342181

1734
St. John's Mite Association
5428 MacArthur Blvd. N.W.
Washington, DC   20016   (571) 212-4453
Contact: Mark D. Hoffman, Secy.
Application address: 520 E. Alexandria Ave., Alexandria, VA 22301-1611

Foundation type: Independent foundation
Purpose: Grants to Freemasons, their widows, and children under the age of 18 who are residents of the Washington, DC, metropolitan area.
Financial data: Year ended 10/31/2013. Assets, $225,220 (M); Expenditures, $12,909; Total giving, $11,184; Grants to individuals, 5 grants totaling $11,184 (high: $7,934, low: $250).
Type of support: Grants for special needs.
Application information: Applications accepted.
Initial approach: Letter
Deadline(s): None
EIN: 526051971

1735
Teamster Disaster Relief Fund
25 Louisiana Ave. N.W.
Washington, DC   20001-2198   (202) 624-6800
Contact: James P. Hoffa, Pres.

Foundation type: Public charity
Purpose: Grants to individuals in the US and Canada who are victims of disasters such as hurricanes, earthquakes, and terrorist attacks.
Financial data: Year ended 12/31/2011. Assets, $354,605 (M); Expenditures, $49,750; Total giving, $49,750.
Fields of interest: Safety/disasters; Economically disadvantaged.
Type of support: Emergency funds.
Application information: Contact foundation for eligibility requirements.
EIN: 521790540

1736
Travel Industry Association of America Foundation
1100 New York Ave., N.W., Ste. 450W
Washington, DC   20005-3934   (202) 408-8422
FAX: (202) 408-1255

Foundation type: Public charity

Purpose: Scholarships to graduates who have been nominated to participate in travel and tourism programs.
Publications: Grants list.
Financial data: Year ended 12/31/2011. Assets, $27,997 (M); Expenditures, $21,563; Total giving, $21,348.
Type of support: Scholarships—to individuals; Awards/grants by nomination only.
Application information:
Deadline(s): Mar. and Oct.
Additional information: Completion of formal nomination required; Applications are only accepted from students nominated by schools.
EIN: 520231139

1737
Cirtie Mae Turner Memorial Trust
P.O. Box 75333
Washington, DC   20013-0333

Foundation type: Independent foundation
Purpose: Scholarships to individuals in the DC area.
Financial data: Year ended 12/31/2011. Assets, $549,679 (M); Expenditures, $72,018; Total giving, $0.
Type of support: Undergraduate support.
Application information: Applications not accepted.
Additional information: Unsolicited requests for funds not considered or acknowledged.
EIN: 526756358

1738
U.S. Institute of Peace
(formerly Endowment of the U.S. Institute of Peace)
2301 Constitution Ave., N.W.
Washington, DC   20037-2900   (202) 457-1700
Contact: Jim Marshall, Pres.
FAX: (202) 429-6063;
E-mail: grant_program@usip.org; URL: http://www.usip.org

Foundation type: Public charity
Purpose: Fellowships, grants and scholarships for the research and writing of doctoral dissertations concerning international conflict and resolution.
Publications: Application guidelines; Annual report; Newsletter; Occasional report.
Financial data: Year ended 09/30/2011. Assets, $17,338,740 (M); Expenditures, $11,569,734; Total giving, $3,572,880; Grants to individuals, totaling $641,066.
Fields of interest: International peace/security; International conflict resolution; International affairs.
Type of support: Fellowships; Doctoral support.
Application information: Applications accepted. Application form required.
Initial approach: Letter, telephone or e-mail
Deadline(s): Sept. 8 for Jennings Randolph Senior Fellowship Program
Additional information: Interviews are required for Senior Fellowships.
Program descriptions:
Jennings Randolph Peace Scholarship Dissertation Program: These scholarships are awarded to students at U.S. universities who are writing doctoral dissertations on topics related to peace, conflict, and international security; fellowships of up to ten months are also available. Eligible applicants can have backgrounds in any discipline.

Jennings Randolph Senior Fellowship Program: This program provides scholars, policy analysts, policymakers, and other experts with opportunities to spend time in residence at the institute, reflecting and writing on pressing international peace and security challenges. Eight to twelve fellowships will be awarded per year, with up to a maximum of $100,000 available; fellowships generally last for ten months, though shorter-term fellowships are also available. Eligible fellows include citizens of any country, and individuals from a variety of professional backgrounds and from early, middle, and late stages of their career.
EIN: 521503251

1739
UFCW Suffridge/Jimerson Scholarship Fund

(formerly James A. Suffridge UFCW Scholarship Fund)
1775 K St., N.W.
Washington, DC   20006-1521   (202) 223-3111
Contact: Joseph Hansen, Pres.
E-mail: scholarship@ufcw.org; URL: http://www.ufcw.org/scholarship/english/index.cfm

Foundation type: Public charity
Purpose: Scholarships to members of the United Food and Commercial Workers International Union in good standing and their unmarried children.
Publications: Application guidelines.
Financial data: Year ended 04/30/2012. Assets, $62,792 (M); Expenditures, $84,233; Total giving, $84,000; Grants to individuals, totaling $84,000.
Fields of interest: Labor unions/organizations.
Type of support: Scholarships—to individuals.
Application information: Applications accepted. Application form required. Application form available on the grantmaker's web site.
  Send request by: Online
  Copies of proposal: 1
  Deadline(s): Mar. 15
  Final notification: Applicants notified by June 1
  Applicants should submit the following:
    1) Essay
    2) GPA
    3) Transcripts
EIN: 526033919

1740
ULI Foundation

1025 Thomas Jefferson St. N.W., Ste. 500W
Washington, DC   20007-5201   (202) 624-7000
Contact: David Howard, Exec. V.P.
FAX: (202) 624-7140;
E-mail: info@ulifoundation.org; Toll-free tel.: (800) 321-5011; E-Mail for David Howard: dhoward@uli.org; URL: http://foundation.uli.org

Foundation type: Public charity
Purpose: An award for urban development, a prize for industry practice articles that clearly communicate ideas for the benefit of the entire real estate community, and an award for urban design and development proposal for graduate students.
Financial data: Year ended 06/30/2011. Assets, $52,425,831 (M); Expenditures, $7,642,325; Total giving, $5,361,771; Grants to individuals, totaling $65,637.
Fields of interest: Environment, land resources; Urban/community development; Accessibility/universal design.
Type of support: Awards/prizes.
Application information: Applications accepted. Application form required. Application form available on the grantmaker's web site.

Initial approach: E-mail
Deadline(s): Varies by award program
Additional information: See web site for each award's eligibility criteria.
EIN: 237133957

1741
Union Plus Education Foundation

1100 1st St. N.E., Ste. 850
Washington, DC   20002
FAX: (202) 293-5311;
E-mail: shiggins@unionprivilege.org

Foundation type: Independent foundation
Purpose: Scholarships to members of unions participating in any Union Plus program, their spouses, and their dependent children (foster children, step-children, and any other child for whom the individual member provides greater than 50 percent of their support).
Financial data: Year ended 12/31/2011. Assets, $254,130 (M); Expenditures, $145,250; Total giving, $145,250; Grants to individuals, 128 grants totaling $145,250 (high: $4,000, low: $500).
Type of support: Scholarships—to individuals; Graduate support; Technical education support; Undergraduate support.
Application information: Applications accepted. Application form required. Application form available on the grantmaker's web site.
  Initial approach: Letter, telephone, or e-mail
  Send request by: Mail
  Deadline(s): Jan. 31
  Final notification: Recipients notified in approximately four months
  Applicants should submit the following:
    1) Curriculum vitae
    2) FAF
    3) FAFSA
    4) SAT
    5) Letter(s) of recommendation
    6) GPA
    7) Financial information
    8) Essay
    9) ACT
  Additional information: Participating members from Canada, Guam, Puerto Rico and the Virgin Islands are also eligible. The individual must be accepted into an accredited college or university, community college or recognized technical or trade school at the time the award is issued.
EIN: 383647522

1742
Union Privilege Relief Fund Trust

(also known as Union Plus Disaster Relief Fund)
1100 1st St., N.E., Ste. 850
Washington, DC   20002-4894
E-mail: info@unionprivilege.org; URL: http://www.unionplus.org/disaster-relief/sandy-october-2012

Foundation type: Independent foundation
Purpose: Grants to union members harmed by events beyond their control, such as natural disasters, terrorist acts, accidents, and disease.
Financial data: Year ended 12/31/2012. Assets, $220,819 (M); Expenditures, $237,551; Total giving, $237,500; Grants to individuals, totaling $237,500.
Fields of interest: Safety/disasters.
Type of support: Emergency funds.
Application information: Applications not accepted.

Additional information: Unsolicited requests for funds not considered or acknowledged.
EIN: 841678738

1743
United Negro College Fund, Inc.

1805 7th St., N.W.
Washington, DC   20001-3186   (800) 331-2244
Contact: Michael L. Lomax Ph.D., Pres. and C.E.O.
Toll-free tel.: (800) 331-2244; URL: http://www.uncf.org

Foundation type: Public charity
Purpose: Scholarships and fellowships to individuals for undergraduate, graduate and postdoctoral studies at institutions of their choice.
Financial data: Year ended 03/31/2012. Assets, $1,166,608,507 (M); Expenditures, $166,996,857; Total giving, $123,471,713; Grants to individuals, totaling $770,529.
Fields of interest: Science; Asians/Pacific Islanders; African Americans/Blacks; Hispanics/Latinos; Native Americans/American Indians.
Type of support: Fellowships; Graduate support; Undergraduate support.
Application information: Applications accepted. Application form required. Application form available on the grantmaker's web site.
  Initial approach: Download application from web site
  Deadline(s): Dec. 15 for Fellowships, varies for scholarships
  Applicants should submit the following:
    1) Letter(s) of recommendation
    2) GPA
  Additional information: Scholarships are based on need, GPA, community activities and letters of recommendation. UNCF has many scholarship programs and scholarship programs administered by other foundations. The Gates Millenium Scholars Program is an example of an administered program. See web site for a complete list of programs and guidelines.
Program description:
  Gates Millennium Scholars Award: This program, administered in conjunction with the Hispanic Scholarship Fund, the Asian and Pacific Islander American Fund, and the American Indian Graduate Center Scholars, enables thousands of young Americans to attend the undergraduate and graduate institutions of their choice and be prepared to assume important roles as leaders in their professions and communities. These awards give the students an opportunity to reach their fullest potential, and encourage and support them in completing college and in continuing to earn masters and doctoral degrees in disciplines where ethnic and racial groups are currently underrepresented.
EIN: 131624241

1744
The United States Holocaust Memorial Museum

100 Raoul Wallenberg Pl., S.W.
Washington, DC   20024-2126   (202) 488-0400
Contact: Peter J. Fredlake, Coord., Educ. Div.
FAX: (202) 488-0406; URL: http://www.ushmm.org

Foundation type: Public charity
Purpose: Fellowships for the support of siginificant research and writing about the Holocaust.
Publications: Newsletter.
Financial data: Year ended 09/30/2011. Assets, $325,995,357 (M); Expenditures, $95,047,182;

Total giving, $519,750; Grants to individuals, totaling $519,750.

Fields of interest: Museums (history); Museums (specialized).

Type of support: Fellowships; Research.

Application information: Applications accepted. Application form required. Application form available on the grantmaker's web site.

Initial approach: Application

Copies of proposal: 2

Deadline(s): Feb. 10 for Teacher Fellowships, Feb. 17 for Visiting Scholar

Final notification: Recipients notified Mar. 30 for Teacher Fellowships, May for Visiting Scholar

Additional information: See web site for additional guidelines.

Program descriptions:

Museum Teacher Fellowship Program: This program allows up to 20 selected fellows (including educators of grades 7-12 and community college faculty) to participate in a five-day, all-expense-paid summer institute at the museum, and is designed to immerse participants in advanced historical and pedagogical issues. Following the summer institute, fellows are expected to create and implement an outreach project in their schools, colleges, communities, or professional organizations. In July of the following year, fellows will attend a follow-up program at the museum to assess their various efforts and to continue their study of the Holocaust with museum staff and noted speakers. Applicants must show evidence of extensive knowledge of Holocaust history, successful teaching experience, and participation in community and professional organizations.

Visiting Scholars Program: Fellowships are awarded to support significant research and writing about the Holocaust. Awards are granted on a competitive basis. The Center welcomes proposals from scholars in all relevant academic disciplines, including history, political science, literature, Jewish studies, philosophy, religion, sociology, anthropology, comparative genocide studies, law, and others. Fellowships are awarded to candidates working on their dissertations (ABD), postdoctoral researchers, and senior scholars. Applicants must be affiliated with an academic and/or research institution when applying for a fellowship.

EIN: 521309391

1745
VSA arts

2700 F St., N.W.

Washington, DC 20566-0001 (202) 628-2800

Contact: Soula Antoniou, Pres.; Elena Widder, Dir., Performing Arts; GTI: Elena Widder, Dir., Performing Arts

FAX: (202) 429-0868; E-mail: info@vsarts.org; Toll-free tel.: (800) 933-8721; TDD: (202) 737-0645; e-mail for Elena Widder: elenaw@vsarts.org; URL: http://www.kennedy-center.org/education/vsa/

Foundation type: Public charity

Purpose: Awards to outstanding young artists, ages 25 and under, who are disabled. Also awards to teachers and students for plays related to disabilities.

Publications: Application guidelines; Annual report; Financial statement; Grants list.

Financial data: Year ended 09/30/2011. Assets, $422,388 (M); Expenditures, $9,143,194; Total giving, $3,280,087; Grants to individuals, 101 grants totaling $134,623.

Fields of interest: Visual arts; Theater (playwriting); Music; Disabilities, people with.

Type of support: Awards/prizes.

Application information: Applications accepted. Application form required. Application form available on the grantmaker's web site.

Initial approach: Telephone or e-mail

Deadline(s): Varies

Applicants should submit the following:

1) Work samples

Program descriptions:

All Kids Can Create! Competition: In conjunction with CVS Caremark, this art competition is open to all children, ages 5 to 15, who are living in the U.S. and who create artwork that helps them explore new activities, rethink their perceptions, and discover themselves as artists.

Arts Connect All: Presented in conjunction with the MetLife Foundation, this program works to enable more students with disabilities to experience social, cognitive, and cultural development through arts learning alongside their peers without disabilities; create educational access and inclusion in the arts for students with disabilities; and document the contributions that arts organizations make to inclusive education in public schools. A maximum of ten grants of up to $15,000 each will be awarded through the program. Nonprofit performing and exhibiting arts institutions, including museums, theaters, and multidisciplinary arts presenters, who are creating or have established educational programs are encouraged to apply; organizations must have as their primary mission the goal of advancing the arts and/or a specific art form. Arts organizations in the following cities are eligible: Phoenix, Arizona; Los Angeles, San Diego, and San Francisco, California; Denver, Colorado; Hartford, Connecticut; Tampa, Florida; Atlanta, Georgia; Baltimore, Maryland; Boston, Massachusetts; Detroit, Michigan; Minneapolis/St. Paul, Minnesota; Kansas City and St. Louis, Missouri; Charlotte, North Carolina; Tulsa, Oklahoma; Portland, Oregon; Philadelphia and Pittsburgh, Pennsylvania; Providence, Rhode Island; Nashville, Tennessee; Houston, Texas; and Seattle, Washington.

Playwright Discovery Program: The program seeks to challenge middle and high school students of all abilities to take a closer look at the world around them, examine how disability affects their lives and the lives of others, and express their views through the art of writing a one-act play. Young playwrights (either individuals students or collaborations by a group or class of students) with and without disabilities are encouraged to submit a script; playwrights may write from their own experience or about an experience in the life of another person or fictional character. The winning play will be professionally produced at the John F. Kennedy Center for the Performing Arts, and the winning playwright will receive $2,000 and a trip to Washington D.C. to see his/her play performed.

Playwright Discovery Teacher Award: The award was created to recognize teachers in middle and high schools who creatively bring disability awareness to their classrooms through the art of playwriting.

Teaching Fellowship Award: This program works to engage and support teaching artists with disabilities in the visual and performing arts, with hopes of enriching the learning environment and make it more inclusive of disabilities. Fellows are assessed on: their desire to advance teaching, artistic, and professional experience; their artistic accomplishments, as evidenced by formal training and/or years of experience in arts discipline or traditional arts practice; teaching accomplishments; and professional accomplishment (as demonstrated by presentation skills, and by using their voice and body language to captivate audiences). Recipients are awarded a

$1,000 grant to support professional development or career goal objectives.

Universal Design for Learning Award: The award provides financial support to children's museums to support new or existing programs, exhibits, or initiatives that demonstrate best practices and innovation in the implementation of Universal Design Principles. The award is open to nonprofit children's museums in the United States that are voting members in good standing with the Association of Children's Museums (ACM), and that have established partnerships with state affiliates to develop inclusive practices.

VSA Apprenticeship at the AFI-Discovery Channel Silverdocs Documentary Festival and International Documentary Conference: This program provides up to five emerging filmmakers with disabilities (ages 18-30) the opportunity to work with master documentarians in the most current trends in documentary filmmaking. Apprenticeship opportunities include attending sessions, panels, master classes, small group discussions with industry leaders, and networking events that offer the opportunity for participants to hone their skills, increase their knowledge base, and develop their network of professional contacts. Expenses covered by the program include: conference registration, room, and board; round-trip economy class or coach travel to and from Silver Spring, Maryland (including ground transportation); travel, room, and board for a personal care assistant, if required; and reasonable accommodation for the apprentice's disability.

VSA Apprenticeship at the Williamstown Theatre Festival: The organization partners with the Williamstown Theatre Festival in Williamstown, Massachusetts to provide selected students (ages 19-24 and who have a disability) with the opportunity to expand their theater education and knowledge. Up to 70 students will be given the opportunity to work with notable professions in acting, voice, and movement classes, and will learn about the different aspects of running a professional theater company by working in each of the various departments of the festival.

VSA/Volkswagen Group of America, Inc. Exhibition Program: This program, in conjunction with Volkswagen Group of America, Inc. will provide an exhibition opportunity for emerging U.S.-based visual artists with disabilities (ages 16-25) at the Smithsonian Institution's S. Dillon Ripley Center. Fifteen artists will be selected for the exhibition and will share $60,000 in cash awards: a $20,000 grand prize, a $10,000 first award, a $6,000 second award, and twelve awards of excellence at $2,000 each.

Young Soloists Award: This $5,000 award is given annually to four outstanding musicians: two from the United States and two from the international arena. Any individual musician (instrumental or vocal) age 25 and under from the U.S. who has a disability is eligible to apply; any individual musician (instrumental or vocal) age 30 and under from outside the United States who has a disability is eligible to apply. Applications from musical ensembles (two to eight members) will be accepted for the International Young Soloists Award. This includes any type of ensemble from a rock band to a chamber ensemble to a drum corps. In order to be eligible, at least one member of the ensemble must have a disability. All types of music will be accepted, including but not limited to rock/alt rock, pop, indie, classical, country/folk, jazz, R&B/blues, hip hop/rap, Latin, and world.

EIN: 521065313

1746
Washington Performing Arts Society
(also known as WPAS)
2000 L St., N.W., Ste. 510
Washington, DC 20036-4907   (202) 785-9727
Contact: Jenny Bilfield, Pres.
FAX: (202) 331-7678; E-mail: info@wpas.org; E-Mail
for Jenny Bilfield: president@wpas.org; URL: http://
www.wpas.org

Foundation type: Public charity
Purpose: Scholarships to sixth through twelfth
grade string students in the DC area for purchases
of musical instruments, private music lessons or to
attend summer music camp.
Publications: Application guidelines; Informational
brochure.
Financial data: Year ended 08/31/2011. Assets,
$10,993,731 (M); Expenditures, $7,362,860;
Total giving, $22,030; Grants to individuals,
totaling $22,030.
Fields of interest: Music; Performing arts,
education.
Type of support: Awards/prizes; Undergraduate
support.
Application information: Application form required.
Application form available on the grantmaker's web
site. Interview required.
    Initial approach: Telephone
    Copies of proposal: 1
    Additional information: Contact the society for
        application guidelines.
Program description:
    *Joseph and Goldie Feder Memorial String
Competition:* The competition awards cash prizes
for instrument purchases or private lessons, as well
as scholarships to such summer study programs as
Interlochen Arts Camp, to string players in the
Washington, DC area who are in grades 6 through
12.
EIN: 526062439

1747
The Washington Post Company Educational Foundation
1150 15th St. N.W.
Washington, DC 20071-0001
Contact: Carrie Morse
URL: http://www.washingtonpost.com/
community/

Foundation type: Company-sponsored foundation
Purpose: Awards by nomination only for educational
leadership and excellence in teaching.
Publications: Application guidelines.
Financial data: Year ended 12/31/2012. Assets,
$0 (M); Expenditures, $270,513; Total giving,
$237,000.
Fields of interest: Education; Leadership
development.
Type of support: Awards/grants by nomination only;
Awards/prizes; Precollege support; Undergraduate
support.
Application information: Applications not
accepted.
    Additional information: Awards are by nomination
        only. Unsolicited requests for funds not
        considered or acknowledged. See website for
        additional guidelines.
Program descriptions:
    Distinguished Educational Leadership Awards:
The foundation honors one principal from a private
school and 19 principals from local public school
systems in Washington, D.C., Maryland, and
Virginia. The award is designed to recognize
principals who go beyond the day-to-day demands
of their position to create an exceptional

educational environment and to encourage
excellence in school leadership. The award includes
a reception at The Post and participation in an
educational seminar.
    The Agnes Meyer Outstanding Teacher Awards:
The foundation awards $3,000 to an outstanding
teacher selected in each of the 19 local public
systems, and one award to a teacher from a private
school in the metropolitan area. The award is
limited to school systems in Washington, D.C.,
Maryland, and Virginia. The award is designed to
recognize excellence in teaching and to encourage
creative and quality instruction.
EIN: 521545926

1748
Washington Sports & Entertainment Charities, Inc.
c/o WSE Charities Inc
601 F St.
Washington, DC 20004   (202) 661-5099

Foundation type: Public charity
Purpose: Grants to outstanding teachers in DC, MD
and VA.
Financial data: Year ended 12/31/2011. Assets,
$274,517 (M); Expenditures, $33,094; Total
giving, $9,059.
Fields of interest: Youth development;
Economically disadvantaged.
Type of support: Awards/prizes.
Application information:
    Initial approach: Letter
    Additional information: Contact foundation for
        eligibility.
EIN: 521627622

1749
Washington Tennis & Education Foundation
William H.G. FitzGerald Tennis Ctr.
16th & Kennedy Sts., N.W.
Washington, DC 20011   (202) 291-9888
Contact: Eleni A. Rossides, Exec. Dir.
FAX: (202) 291-9887; E-mail: wtef@wtef.org;
URL: http://www.wtef.org/

Foundation type: Public charity
Purpose: Scholarships to graduating seniors of
Washington DC who are enrolled in the
Foundation's Center for Excellence Program for
attendance at colleges or universities.
Publications: Annual report; Newsletter.
Financial data: Year ended 08/31/2011. Assets,
$12,240,614 (M); Expenditures, $1,563,470;
Total giving, $1,500; Grants to individuals, totaling
$1,500.
Fields of interest: Education.
Type of support: Undergraduate support; Grants for
special needs.
Application information: Applications not
accepted.
    Additional information: Unsolicited requests for
        funds not considered or acknowledged.
EIN: 526046504

1750
The Washington Youth Choir
(formerly The Eastern Choral Society, Inc., also
known as Washington Youth Choir)
733 8th St., N.W.
Washington, DC 20001-3721   (202) 293-7508
Contact: Courtney Baker-Oliver, Exec. Dir.
FAX: (202) 347-6078;
E-mail: heather@washingtonyouthchoir.org;
URL: http://www.washingtonyouthchoir.org/

Foundation type: Public charity
Purpose: Scholarships to two, three, and four year
members of the Washington, DC Youth Choir toward
their first year of college for any area of study.
Publications: Annual report; Financial statement.
Financial data: Year ended 06/30/2012. Assets,
$7,420 (M); Expenditures, $98,117; Total giving,
$1,244; Grants to individuals, totaling $1,244.
Fields of interest: Higher education.
Type of support: Scholarships—to individuals.
Application information: Unsolicited requests for
funds not accepted.
EIN: 521833176

1751
The Wilderness Society
1615 M St., N.W.
Washington, DC 20036-3258   (202) 833-2300
Contact: for Scholarships: Anna Wlodarczyk, HR
Associate
A. Wlodarczyk e-mail: anna_wlodarczyk@tws.org
E-mail: member@tws.org; Toll-free tel.: (800)
843-9453; URL: http://www.wilderness.org

Foundation type: Public charity
Purpose: Scholarships to qualified graduate
students who have the potential to make a
difference in the long term protection of wilderness
in the U.S.
Publications: Annual report; Financial statement;
Newsletter.
Financial data: Year ended 09/30/2012. Assets,
$44,865,186 (M); Expenditures, $31,420,103;
Total giving, $259,862; Grants to individuals,
totaling $28,300.
Fields of interest: Natural resources; Environment.
Type of support: Scholarships—to individuals.
Application information: Applications accepted.
    Send request by: Online
    Applicants should submit the following:
        1) Transcripts
        2) Proposal
        3) Letter(s) of recommendation
        4) Curriculum vitae
    Additional information: Graduate students in
        natural resources management, law or policy
        programs are strongly encouraged to apply.
        See web site for additional guidelines.
EIN: 530167933

1752
Woodrow Wilson International Center for Scholars
1 Woodrow Wilson Plz.
1300 Pennsylvania Ave., N.W.
Washington, DC 20004-3027   (202) 691-4000
Contact: Jane Harman, Pres. and C.E.O.
FAX: (202) 691-4001;
E-mail: wwics@wilsoncenter.org; E-mail For Jane
Harman: jane.harman@wilsoncenter.org;
URL: http://www.wilsoncenter.org

Foundation type: Public charity
Purpose: Postdoctoral fellowships to scholars
conducting focused research on the intersection of

civil society, the nonprofit sector, volunteerism, and public policy.
Publications: Application guidelines; Annual report; Informational brochure; Newsletter.
Financial data: Year ended 09/30/2011. Assets, $101,286,661 (M); Expenditures, $20,019,966; Total giving, $1,584,904; Grants to individuals, totaling $685,879.
Type of support: Fellowships.
Application information: Applications accepted. Application form required. Application form available on the grantmaker's web site.
> *Initial approach:* E-mail
> *Copies of proposal:* 10
> *Applicants should submit the following:*
>   1) Proposal
>   2) Letter(s) of recommendation
>   3) Financial information
>   4) Essay
>   5) Curriculum vitae
> *Additional information:* Download applications from web site and mail to foundation. Final notice seven months after deadline.

Program description:
Fellowships: Fellowships are awarded on a competitive basis to individuals engaging research in the social sciences and humanities. Basic criteria for selection include: the significance of the proposed research, including the importance and originality of the project; quality of the proposal in definition, organization, clarity, and scope; capability and achievements of the applicant and the likelihood that the applicant will accomplish the proposed project; and the relevance of the project to contemporary policy issues. Eligible applicants include citizens or permanent residents from any country (foreign nationals must be able to hold a valid passport and obtain a J1 Visa); men and women with outstanding capabilities and experience from a wide variety of backgrounds (including government, the corporate world, professions, and academia); academic candidates holding a Ph.D. (Ph.D. must be received by the application deadline of October); academic candidates demonstrating scholarly achievement by publications beyond their doctoral dissertations; practitioners or policymakers with an equivalent level of professional achievement. English proficiency is required, as the Center is designed to encourage the exchange of ideas among its fellows. Applicants do not need an institutional affiliation to apply. For most academic candidates, a book or monograph is required. Scholars and practitioners who previously held research awards or fellowships at the Wilson Center are not precluded from applying for a fellowship. However, the nature and recency of the prior award may be among the factors considered during the selection process and by the Fellowships Committee of the Board of Trustees. Contact fellowships@wilsoncenter.org for more information.
EIN: 521067541

1753
Women for Women International
2000 M St., N.W., Ste. 200
Washington, DC   20036-3380   (202) 737-7705
FAX: (202) 737-7709;
E-mail: general@womenforwomen.org; Additional address (London office): 35-36 Loman St., London SE1 0EH UK, tel.: 020-7922-7756, fax: 020-7922-7706; URL: http://www.womenforwomen.org

Foundation type: Public charity
Purpose: Financial aid to women in war-torn countries for basic necessities.

Publications: Annual report.
Financial data: Year ended 12/31/2011. Assets, $17,917,610 (M); Expenditures, $30,272,738; Total giving, $5,283,027.
Fields of interest: Civil/human rights, women; Women.
Type of support: Foreign applicants; Grants for special needs.
Application information:
> *Initial approach:* Letter
> *Additional information:* Contact foundation for eligibility criteria.
EIN: 521838756

1754
Women's Research & Education Institute
714 G St., S.E., Ste. 200
Washington, DC   20003-2883   (202) 280-2720
Contact: Susan Scanlan, Pres.
E-mail: wrei@wrei.org; E-mail for Susan Scanlan: scanlan@wrei.org; tel. for Susan Scanlan: (202) 280-2718; URL: http://www.wrei.org

Foundation type: Public charity
Purpose: Fellowships to graduate students in universities around the country for research and study in the offices of congressional members of the causes for women's issues and in selected congressional committees.
Publications: Application guidelines; Informational brochure.
Financial data: Year ended 12/31/2011. Assets, $2,645,199 (M); Expenditures, $1,381,314; Total giving, $52,286; Grants to individuals, totaling $52,286.
Fields of interest: Research; Women.
Type of support: Fellowships; Graduate support.
Application information: Applications accepted. Application form required. Interview required.
> *Send request by:* Mail or e-mail
> *Deadline(s):* June 15
> *Final notification:* Recipients notified by early Sept.
> *Applicants should submit the following:*
>   1) Transcripts
>   2) Essay
> *Additional information:* Application should also include three letters of reference. Selection is made on the basis of academic competence as well as demonstrated interest in the public policy process.

Program description:
Fellowship Program: The institute awards annual fellowships to a select number of graduate students with a proven commitment to equity for women. Fellows gain practical policymaking experience and graduate credit as they work from January to August as Congressional legislative aides in Washington, DC. Fellows receive a stipend of approximately $1,300 per month. An additional sum of up to $500 is provided for the purchase of health insurance with submission of a bill from a provider. The institute will also reimburse fellows up to a maximum of $1,500 ($750 per semester) for the cost of tuition at their home institutions (excluding student fees, books, or non-tuition expenses)
EIN: 521104895

1755
World Wildlife Fund
(formerly The Conservation Foundation)
1250 24th St., N.W., Fl. 6
Washington, DC   20037-1193   (202) 293-4800
Contact: Carter Roberts, Pres.
FAX: (202) 293-2239; Additional address: P.O. Box 97180; URL: http://www.worldwildlife.org

Foundation type: Public charity
Purpose: Scholarships and fellowship grants to individuals in the field of conservation science.
Publications: Application guidelines; Annual report; Informational brochure; Newsletter; Occasional report.
Financial data: Year ended 06/30/2012. Assets, $412,075,560 (M); Expenditures, $191,549,257; Total giving, $59,294,820; Grants to individuals, totaling $128,203.
Fields of interest: Science.
Type of support: Fellowships.
Application information: Applications accepted. Application form required. Application form available on the grantmaker's web site. Interview required.
> *Initial approach:* Letter
> *Deadline(s):* Varies
> *Applicants should submit the following:*
>   1) Letter(s) of recommendation
>   2) Budget Information
>   3) Curriculum vitae
>   4) Proposal

Program descriptions:
Chandra Gurung Memorial Scholarships: These scholarships provide financial assistance to conservationists from Nepal who wish to pursue a master's degree in a conservation-related field.
Jennifer Headley Memorial Scholarship: This scholarship provides financial assistance to a deserving woman candidate who intends to pursue a bachelor's degree in forestry studies at the Institute of Forestry (IOF) - Hetauda Campus.
Jill Bowling Schlaepfer Memorial Scholarships: Each year, the fund offers a scholarship that encourages bright and promising Nepali students from ethnic, indigenous, minority, or Dalit groups to continue or pursue careers in nature conservation.
Kathryn Fuller Doctoral Fellowships: This program supports doctoral research on marine protected areas (MPAs) that will enhance scientific understanding of their ecological and social impacts, and that will strengthen science-based conservation and policy in fund-identified U.S. priority marine regions. Fellows receive either a $15,000 or $20,000 allocation over a period of up to two years to cover research expenses, opportunities to link doctoral research to the fund's global conservation efforts, and networking opportunities with other fellows, scientists, and fund employees. Eligible applicants must: be currently enrolled in an academic program leading to a doctoral degree in a conservation-related field and must have completed at least one year of course work; have at least two years of work experience in conservation; and propose research in the overall topic of evaluating the impacts of marine-protected areas (MPAs) that has direct implications for conservation in a fund-identified marine priority place.
Kathryn Fuller Postdoctoral Fellowships: This fund supports doctoral research on marine-protected areas (MPAs) that will enhance scientific understanding of their ecological and social impacts and that will strengthen science-based conservation and policy in fund-identified U.S. priority marine regions. Fellowships include $140,000 to cover a stipend and research expenses of up to two years, as well as networking opportunities with other fund fellows, scientists,

and employees; in addition, up to $17,500 will be granted to cover indirect costs at the host institution over the two-year fellowship period. Eligible applicants must: have earned their doctoral degree; identified a scientist at an academic or research institution who will serve as co-sponsor; and propose research in the overall topic of evaluating the impact of marine-protected areas (MPAs) that have direct implications for conservation in a fund-identified U.S. priority place.

Mingma Norbu Sherpa Memorial Scholarship: This scholarship supports and encourages bright and promising students from Nepal's rural mountain areas to pursue careers in nature conservation by supporting a student who has completed ten years of compulsory education and would like to pursue a Technical Certificate Level (TCL) in Forestry at the Institute of Forestry, Pokhara Campus.

Nepal Conservation Memorial Scholarship: This scholarship fund will assist students who wish to pursue careers in conservation. Eligible applicants are those who have completed ten years of compulsory education and would like to pursue a Technical Certificate Level (TCL) in Forestry at the Institute of Forestry (IOF), Hetauda Campus.

Russell E. Train Education for Nature Alumni Grants: Grants of up to $3,500 are available to support former Russell E. Train fellows or scholars in their continued professional development. Funds may be used to present a paper at a conference, attend a workshop or short-term training course offered by a university or other institution, or to conduct research within a fund-identified priority place.

Russell E. Train Education for Nature Professional Development Grants: Funding, ranging from $1,500 to $5,000, is available to provide support for mid-career conservationists to pursue short-term, non-degree training to upgrade their knowledge and skills through short courses, workshops, conferences, and study tours, or through practical training such as internships and professional attachments. Funds support all training-related costs, including registration fees and tuition, meals and accomodations, books and materials, international travel, and local transportation. Eligible participants must: be citizens or legal residents of an eligible country (Cambodia, Central African Republic, Democratic Republic of Congo, Ecuador [Galapagos Islands only], Gabon, Guatemala, Guyana, Honduras, Indonesia, Laos, Madagascar, Mozambique, Namibia, Nepal, Papua New Guinea, Philippines, Republic of Congo, Solomon Islands, Surinam, Tanzania, and Vietnam); have at least three years of work experience, paid or unpaid, in conservation or a related field; have his/her current work and proposed training advancing conservation in an eligible country (mentioned above); and be currently working in a conservation-related field and have promise of continued employment at the completion of the proposed training from the employer.

Russell E. Train Education for Nature Training Fellowships: Fellowships are available to support the academic training of conservations in selected countries in Africa, Asia, and Latin America in a wide variety of disciplines, so that they may gain the knowledge and skills necessary to manage natural resources in complex contents. Fellows receive: financial support for education-related costs for a period of up to two years (study can be at the master's or doctoral level and can take place anywhere in the world); financial support for tuition,

books, travel (to and from training institutions), and room and board for their academic programs for up to two years; costs for field research when required by the academic institution; networking opportunities to meet with other grantees, alumni, and fund staff through periodic regional gatherings; and ongoing professional development support. Eligible candidates must be a citizen or legal resident of a participating country (Argentina, Belize, Bolivia, Brazil, Chile, Colombia, Costa Rica, Ecuador, Guatemala, Guyana, Honduras, Mexico, Panama, Paraguay, Peru, Philippines, and Surinam), have a minimum of two years' work experience in conservation, and be enrolled, admitted, or have applied to an institution of higher education. Generally, funding of up to $20,000 is provided, with more funding given in exceptional circumstances.
EIN: 521693387

1756
Young Women's Christian Association of Greater Toledo
(also known as YWCA of Greater Toledo)
2025 M St., N.W., Ste. 550
Washington, DC   20036   (202) 467-0801
Contact: Dara Richardson-Heron M.D, C.E.O.
FAX: (202) 467-0802; E-mail: info@ywca.org; Email for Lisa McDuffie : lmcduffie@ywcatoledo.org;
URL: http://www.ywca.org/site/pp.asp?c=hgLRJONNG&b=91698

Foundation type: Public charity
Purpose: Grants of basic necessities to indigent residents of the greater Toledo, OH, area.
Publications: Annual report; Financial statement.
Financial data: Year ended 06/30/2012. Assets, $8,583,135 (M); Expenditures, $3,499,469; Total giving, $239,854; Grants to individuals, totaling $239,854.
Fields of interest: Economically disadvantaged.
Type of support: Grants for special needs.
Application information:
   Initial approach: Letter
EIN: 344428265

1757
Youth Service America
1101 15th St., Ste. 200
Washington, DC   20005-5002   (202) 296-2992
Contact: Steven A. Culbertson, Pres. and C.E.O.
FAX: (202) 296-4030; E-mail: info@ysa.org;
URL: http://www.ysa.org

Foundation type: Public charity
Purpose: Grants to young people in America, ages 5 to 25, to serve locally, nationally, and globally to increase the quality and quantity of volunteer opportunities.
Publications: Application guidelines; Grants list.
Financial data: Year ended 06/30/2012. Assets, $1,933,076 (M); Expenditures, $3,661,838; Total giving, $916,161.
Fields of interest: Youth development; Human services.
Type of support: Grants to individuals; Awards/prizes.
Application information:
   Initial approach: Letter or e-mail
   Deadline(s): Sept. 30 for Gladys Marinelli Coccia Awards, Oct. 22 for UnitedHealth HEROES Program, varies for all others

Additional information: See web site for additional application guidelines.
Program descriptions:
Gladys Marinelli Coccia Awards: This award recognizes two exceptional young people who are actively engaged in social entrepreneurship and in leading sustainable social change. To be eligible, a nominee must be between 13 and 22 years of age at the time of nomination, be a social entrepreneur who has launched and is leading his or her own program aimed at sustainable social change, have a business plan and a budget for how the award will be used for the social enterprise, and be a located resident of the United States. One of the two honorees will be selected from the Washington, D.C., or West Virginia region. Eligible individuals may be nominated by organizations, peers, or adult mentors. Self-nominations will also be accepted. Each of the honorees will receive $2,000 to support their social enterprise as well as resources and technical assistance from YSA.
Special Olympics Get Into It Grants: Awarded in conjunction with Youth Service America, these grants work to bring together students of all abilities to fight childhood obesity in their schools and communities through helping to develop a service-learning program that gives youth the opportunity to make a change. Grants ranging from $500 to $1,000 will be awarded.
State Farm Keys to the City Grants: Awarded in conjunction with State Farm, these grants support youth-led projects in the Detroit metropolitan area that incorporate service-learning and that address important community needs in Detroit (such as poverty, education, and community movement/desertion). Twenty grants of up to $500 each will be awarded.
STEMester of Service Grants: This program supports middle school educators in STEM subject areas in engaging their students in a Semester of Service. The $5,000 grant supports teachers and afterschool program facilitators as they engage local partners and guide students in addressing local needs through planning and implementing sustainable service projects that launch on Martin Luther King, Jr. Day of Service and culminate on Global Youth Service Day.
EIN: 521500870

1758
YWCA of the USA
2025 M St., N.W., Ste. 550
Washington, DC   20036-5226   (202) 467-0801
Contact: Dr. Dara Richardson-Heron, C.E.O.
FAX: (202) 467-0802; E-mail: info@ywca.org;
URL: http://www.ywca.org

Foundation type: Public charity
Purpose: Scholarships to female high school seniors who exemplify leadership and serve as role models for their contributions to their communities.
Publications: Annual report.
Financial data: Year ended 08/31/2011. Assets, $58,113,051 (M); Expenditures, $4,188,043; Total giving, $115,000.
Fields of interest: YM/YWCAs & YM/YWHAs; Women.
Type of support: Undergraduate support.
Application information: Applications accepted. Application form required.
   Initial approach: Letter
   Additional information: Contact foundation for current application deadline/guidelines.
EIN: 131624103

FLORIDA

1759
2 Life 18 Foundation, Inc.
11111 Biscayne Blvd., Tower III, Ste. 1758
Miami, FL 33181 (858) 345-2518
Contact: David Perez, Pres.
E-mail: information@cohglobal.org; URL: http://www.2life18.com

Foundation type: Public charity
Purpose: Financial assistance, emergency relief with food, water, telephone service, transportation and other ongoing assistance are provided to disaster victims.
Financial data: Year ended 12/31/2012. Assets, $5,163 (M); Expenditures, $143,412; Total giving, $106,616.
Fields of interest: Disasters, preparedness/services; Disasters, domestic resettlement; Human services.
Type of support: Emergency funds.
Application information: Contact the foundation for additional information.
EIN: 203451673

1760
A Gift for Teaching, Inc.
6501 Magic Way Bldg. No. 400C
Orlando, FL 32809-5677 (407) 345-0515
FAX: (407) 345-8454; URL: http://www.agiftforteaching.org/

Foundation type: Public charity
Purpose: School supplies and merchandise to needy teachers and school children in central Florida.
Publications: Annual report.
Financial data: Year ended 06/30/2011. Assets, $3,006,676 (M); Expenditures, $7,996,704; Total giving, $7,006,279; Grants to individuals, totaling $7,006,279.
Fields of interest: Elementary/secondary education; Education; Economically disadvantaged.
Type of support: In-kind gifts.
Application information:
Initial approach: Letter
Deadline(s): None
Additional information: Contact foundation for eligibility criteria.
EIN: 593515162

1761
AAST Scholarship Foundation
(formerly American Association of State Troopers Scholarship Foundation, Inc.)
1949 Raymond Diehl Rd.
Tallahassee, FL 32308-3841 (850) 385-7904
Contact: Ken Howes, Exec. Dir.
E-mail: beverly@statetroopers.orgToll Free : (800) 765-5456; URL: http://www.statetroopers.org/foundation.html

Foundation type: Public charity
Purpose: Scholarships to children of members of the American Association of State Troopers, Inc., for higher education.
Publications: Application guidelines.
Financial data: Year ended 12/31/2011. Assets, $500,824 (M); Expenditures, $312,797; Total giving, $117,000; Grants to individuals, totaling $117,000.

Fields of interest: Crime/law enforcement, police agencies.
Type of support: Scholarships—to individuals.
Application information: Applications accepted. Application form required.
Copies of proposal: 1
Deadline(s): July 31
Applicants should submit the following:
1) Photograph
2) Transcripts
3) Essay
Additional information: Application sent by fax not accepted. Contact foundation for additional guidelines.
Program description:
Scholarships: Scholarships, ranging from $500 to $1,500, are available to children of members of the American Association of State Troopers, either by natural birth or legal adoption, marriage, or legal guardianship. Applicants must have parents who have been association members in good standing for at least one year, and have a minimum GPA of 2.5.
EIN: 593054670

1762
Abernathy Port Charlotte Kiwanis Foundation Inc., Inc.
3440 Conway Blvd., Ste. 1-A
Port Charlotte, FL 33952-7050 (941) 625-4189
Contact: Allen J. Levin, Pres.

Foundation type: Independent foundation
Purpose: Scholarships for deserving Port Charlotte, FL residents.
Financial data: Year ended 06/30/2013. Assets, $398,090 (M); Expenditures, $54,828; Total giving, $49,200; Grants to individuals, 14 grants totaling $38,500 (high: $3,000, low: $600).
Type of support: Undergraduate support.
Application information:
Initial approach: Letter
EIN: 203272490

1763
Abilities Rehabilitation Center Foundation, Inc.
2735 Whitney Rd.
Clearwater, FL 33760-1610 (727) 538-7370
E-mail: fdelucia@abilities.org; URL: http://www.abilitiesfoundation.com

Foundation type: Public charity
Purpose: Emergency assistance to support various low to moderate income individuals from FL and NC, with disabilities with rent, home loans, housing and other special needs. Assistance to those who have suffered catastrophic disasters.
Financial data: Year ended 06/30/2012. Assets, $2,798,251 (M); Expenditures, $442,275; Total giving, $206,528; Grants to individuals, totaling $36,648.
Fields of interest: Housing/shelter; Safety/disasters; Disabilities, people with; Economically disadvantaged.
Type of support: Emergency funds; Grants for special needs.
Application information: Applications accepted.
Additional information: Some assistance require application. Contact the foundation for eligibility determination.
Program descriptions:
Hurricane Hardening Programs: Pinellas county and the State of Florida are offering programs to be used for improvements to lessen storm damage for

residents in Pinellas county. Most grants range from $1,000 to $20,000.
Low-Interest Home Improvement Loans: Up to $20,000 per household is available for qualified homeowners in Pinellas County, FL to renovate and improve their current residence. Funds can be used for major repairs, cosmetic repairs, landscaping, or accessibility modifications. Very low-income homeowners may qualify for loans deferred until sale. This product allows families to stay where they are, modify for aging or disability, or increase in family size.
EIN: 592293228

1764
AIDS Help of Monroe County
1434 Kennedy Dr.
Key West, FL 33040-4008 (305) 296-6196
Contact: Robert G. Walker, Exec. Dir.
FAX: (305) 296-6337; Additional address (Marathon office): 11139 Overseas Hwy., Marathon, FL 33050, tel.: (305) 289-0055, fax: (305) 289-1371; URL: http://www.aidshelp.cc

Foundation type: Public charity
Purpose: Emergency assistance for individuals affected by HIV within Monroe County, FL.
Publications: Application guidelines; Annual report; Financial statement; Newsletter.
Financial data: Year ended 06/30/2011. Assets, $5,838,568 (M); Expenditures, $3,763,965; Total giving, $1,312,746; Grants to individuals, totaling $1,312,746.
Fields of interest: AIDS, people with.
Type of support: Emergency funds.
Application information: Applications accepted.
Deadline(s): None
Program description:
HIV/AIDS Patient Care Assistance: Assistance is available to individuals residing in Monroe County with a documented HIV-positive status. Covered services include doctor visits, case management, dental care, prescription assistance, transportation assistance, housing assistance, health insurance assistance, and housing opportunities. Eligible applicants must be HIV-positive who reside in Florida, are ineligible for other services (such as Medicaid, Project AIDS care, or insurance), and have an income at or below 300 percent of the Federal Poverty Level.
EIN: 592678740

1765
All Sports Community Service, Inc.
P.O. Box 271-506
Tampa, FL 33688-1506 (813) 966-1008
FAX: (813) 348-3999; URL: http://www.allsportscommunity.org/

Foundation type: Public charity
Purpose: Scholarships to "at-risk" college-bound students and student athletes to attend college or successfully pursue other career options with the assistance of mentors.
Financial data: Year ended 12/31/2011. Assets, $22,983 (M); Expenditures, $80,104.
Fields of interest: Higher education; Athletics/sports, training.
Type of support: Scholarships—to individuals.
Application information: Contact organization for additional information.
EIN: 593184150

1766
R. E. & Joan S. Allen Foundation, Inc.
c/o Steve Kurth
2400 S. Federal Hwy.
Stuart, FL 34994 (772) 288-6062
Contact: Karen Allen Ph.D., Secy.
Application address: 2400 S. Federal Hwy., Ste. 200, Stuart, FL 34994-4556

Foundation type: Independent foundation
Purpose: Scholarships to residents of Kenton, OH, and employees of Imperial Bondware and their children.
Financial data: Year ended 12/31/2011. Assets, $1,030,609 (M); Expenditures, $74,884; Total giving, $52,250; Grants to individuals, 81 grants totaling $52,250 (high: $1,000, low: $250).
Type of support: Employee-related scholarships; Scholarships—to individuals.
Application information: Application form required.
  Deadline(s): None
  Additional information: Application must include biographical statement, academic and professional report, statement of educational plans, and letters of reference.
Company name: Imperial Bondware
EIN: 650225533

1767
Alpha-1 Foundation
3300 Ponce de Leon Blvd.
Coral Gables, FL 33134-7211 (305) 567-9888
Contact: John W. Walsh, Pres. and C.E.O.
FAX: (305) 567-1317;
E-mail: info@alpha-1foundation.org; Toll-free tel.: (877) 228-7321; URL: http://www.alpha-1foundation.org/

Foundation type: Public charity
Purpose: Fellowships, research, and travel grants in the area of Alpha-1 Antitrypsin study.
Publications: Application guidelines; Financial statement; Grants list; Informational brochure; Newsletter.
Financial data: Year ended 06/30/2011. Assets, $12,033,241 (M); Expenditures, $4,996,481; Total giving, $2,295,480.
Fields of interest: Ear, nose & throat research; Lung research; Liver research; Medical research.
Type of support: Fellowships; Research; Postdoctoral support; Travel grants.
Application information: Applications accepted.
  Initial approach: Letter of intent
  Additional information: See web site for complete program information.
Program descriptions:
  Ethical, Legal, and Social Issues (ELSI) Related to AAT Deficiency: This grant program provides up to two years of support towards the development of new information that contributes to the understanding of bioethical, legal, economic, and/or social issues associated with AAT deficiency. Proposals may come from a broad spectrum of disciplines, including humanities, social and natural sciences, and health professions; in particular, this grant mechanism seeks to support the development of novel approaches relating to informed consent, conflicts of interest, organ allocations, genetic testing, and/or genetic discrimination.
  Pilot and Feasibility Grant: The objective of this grant is to provide funds to encourage the development and testing of new hypotheses and/or new methods in research areas relevant to AAT deficiency. Proposed work must be hypothesis-generating or hypothesis-testing, reflecting innovative approaches to important questions in AAT research or development of novel methods, and providing sufficient preliminary data to justify the foundation's support. Results should lead to the submission of applications for funding from other agencies, such as, but not limited to, the NIH. At the conclusion of the funding term, applicants are expected to apply for further funding by other mechanisms or from outside agencies. The award is not intended to support continuation of programs begun under other granting mechanisms. Up to $40,000 will be available, for up to one year of support.
  Postdoctoral Research Fellowship: The objective of this grant is to provide support for postdoctoral fellows who are early in their research careers and are working in the laboratories of established researchers or conducting research with the mentorship of established researchers. In addition, this grant category is intended to provide support for postdoctoral research fellows who intend to pursue a career in AAT research. Applications will be accepted from candidates holding an M.D., Ph.D. or equivalent degrees and who are interested in conducting basic science, clinical research, or ethical, legal, or social studies related to alpha-1 antitrypsin deficiency. Applicants must indicate a commitment to AAT-related research by focusing 50 percent of their time to AAT deficiency research or clinical practice. Grant support for up to two years is available, at a maximum of $35,000 per year.
  Research Grant: The objective of this grant is to provide funds to encourage the development of new information that contributes to the understanding of the basic biology of alpha-1 antitrypsin expression, and the pathogenesis/management of alpha-1 antitrypsin deficiency. In addition, consideration will be given to those projects that provide insight into the development of information that may contribute to the development of new therapies for alpha-1 antitrypsin deficiency. All proposals must be hypothesis-generating or hypothesis-testing and provide sufficient preliminary data to justify the foundation's support. Grants of up to $100,000 per year, for up to two years, are available.
  Travel Grant: The objective of this grant is to provide funds (of up to $1,000) for cross training or attendance at scientific meetings. Training must take place at one of the foundation's Clinical Resource Centers and may include training on diagnostic and therapeutic procedures, research-related techniques, or training on specialized equipment or software applicable to alpha-1 antitrypsin-related research. Candidates may also apply for support in order to present alpha-1 antitrypsin-related abstracts or posters at national and international meetings. Candidates must have an M.D., Ph.D., or equivalent degree, and at least one year of recent research experience related to alpha-1 antitrypsin deficiency. The award is primarily intended to be for travel support for a grantee who already holds a foundation award.
EIN: 650585415

1768
Edmond Amateis Irrevocable Trust Foundation
(formerly Edmond Amateis Foundation)
P.O. Box 1908
Orlando, FL 32802-1908
Contact: Melanie Cianciotto
E-mail: fdnsvcs.fl@suntrust.com; Application address: C/o. Suntrust Bank, 200 S. Orange Ave., SOAB-10, Orlando, FL 32801; URL: http://fdnweb.org/amateis

Foundation type: Independent foundation

Purpose: Scholarships to graduates of Lake County high schools and students currently attending Lake/Sumter Community College, FL.
Financial data: Year ended 03/31/2013. Assets, $823,133 (M); Expenditures, $40,722; Total giving, $25,750.
Fields of interest: Scholarships/financial aid.
Type of support: Support to graduates or students of specific schools; Undergraduate support.
Application information: Application form required.
  Deadline(s): June 1
EIN: 596974154

1769
The American Legion Department of Florida
1912A Lee Rd.
Orlando, FL 32810-5714 (407) 295-2631
Contact: for Scholarship: Carol Polk, Prog. Dir.
Application address: P.O. Box 547859, Orlando, FL 32854-7859
FAX: (407) 299-0901; E-mail: hlcs1956@aol.com; Mailing address: P.O. Box 547859, Orlando, FL 32854-7859; URL: http://www.floridalegion.org

Foundation type: Public charity
Purpose: Scholarships to high school seniors who are direct descendants of a veteran who is a member in good standing of the American Legion or a deceased U.S. veteran who would have been eligible for membership in the American Legion.
Financial data: Year ended 06/30/2012. Assets, $3,208,796 (M); Expenditures, $2,887,156.
Fields of interest: Military/veterans' organizations.
Type of support: Scholarships—to individuals.
Application information: Applications accepted. Application form required. Application form available on the grantmaker's web site.
  Deadline(s): Mar. 1
  Applicants should submit the following:
    1) Photograph
    2) Class rank
    3) SAT
    4) GPA
    5) ACT
Program descriptions:
  Eagle Scout of the Year Award: One Eagle Scout will be selected under this title from each department for exemplary citizenship and demonstration of Eagle Scout skills. Recipients will be awarded a $2,500 scholarship, be asked to speak at the Department annual convention in Orlando, and be automatically nominated to compete for the American Legion National Eagle of the Year award. Department first runners-up receive $1,500, second runners-up will receive $1,000, and third runners-up will receive $500. If selected as the American Legion National Eagle Scout of the Year, the awardee will receive a $10,000 scholarship for college expenses; three national runners-up will also be selected and are entitled to $2,500 each for college expenses.
  Florida Outstanding JROTC Cadet of the Year Award: The award recognizes the most outstanding junior ROTC cadet among all the candidates submitted by each high school JROTC program throughout Florida. The first-place winner receives a $2,000 scholarship, the second-place winner receives a $1,000 scholarship, and the third- and fourth-place winners each receive a $500 scholarship.
  General Scholarship: This scholarship is provided to a student who is a direct descendant or a legally adopted child; a member in good standing of the American Legion Department of Florida; or a deceased U.S. veteran who would have been eligible for membership in the American Legion. The

student must also be in their senior year in an accredited Florida high school. The scholarship may be used for undergraduate study only at an accredited U.S. college or university. Disbursement from the scholarship fund will be made jointly to the student and the school at the beginning of each semester or quarter.
EIN: 590142062

1770
American Legion Memorial Scholarship Funds, Inc.
3676 Collin Dr.
West Palm Beach, FL 33406 (561) 963-2812

Foundation type: Independent foundation
Purpose: Scholarships and student loans to financially needy residents of Palm Beach County, FL, who are U.S. citizens. Recipients may study at any accredited U.S. college or university.
Financial data: Year ended 12/31/2012. Assets, $262,684 (M); Expenditures, $52,362; Total giving, $9,000; Grants to individuals, 5 grants totaling $9,000 (high: $2,000, low: $1,000).
Fields of interest: Scholarships/financial aid.
Type of support: Student loans—to individuals; Graduate support; Undergraduate support.
Application information: Application form required. Interview required.
  Deadline(s): May 1
  Applicants should submit the following:
    1) Transcripts
    2) FAFSA
    3) Photograph
  Additional information: Application should also include three letters of recommendation.
EIN: 596151027

1771
American Lung Association of Florida, Inc.
6852 Belfort Oaks Pl.
Jacksonville, FL 32216-6241 (904) 743-2933
Contact: Martha C. Bogdan, Pres. and C.E.O.
FAX: (904) 743-2916; E-mail: alaf@lungfla.org;
Toll-free tel.: (800) 940-2933; E-Mail for Martha C. Bogdan: mbogdan@lungfla.org; URL: http://www.lungfla.org

Foundation type: Public charity
Purpose: Fellowships and research grants for the study of lung disease.
Financial data: Year ended 06/30/2012. Assets, $14,244,924 (M); Expenditures, $8,146,760; Total giving, $765,169; Grants to individuals, totaling $385,701.
Fields of interest: Lung research.
Type of support: Research.
Application information: Applications accepted. Application form required.
  Initial approach: Letter or e-mail
  Deadline(s): Sept. 1
  Additional information: Grants are limited to U.S. citizens and Canadian citizens, or holders of bona fide permanent U.S. visas. Contact foundation for further application guidelines.
Program descriptions:
  Biomedical Research Grant: Grants of $40,000 a year for up to two years provide seed monies for investigators researching the mechanisms of lung disease and general lung biology.
  Clinical Patient Care Research Grant: Grants of $40,000 a year for up to two years provide seed monies for investigators working on traditional clinical studies examining methods of improving patient care and/or treatment for lung disease.

  Lung Health Dissertation Grant: Pre-doctoral support for nurses or students with an academic career focused on the various disciplines of social science. Research areas of particular interest to the American Lung Association are: psychosocial, behavioral, health services, health policy, epidemiological, biostatistical and education matters related to lung disease. Grants are $21,000 for up to two years.
  Senior Research Training Fellowship: Post-doctoral support for MDs and/or PhDs receiving further academic training as scientific investigators. Research areas of particular interest to the American Lung Association are: adult pulmonary medicine, pediatric pulmonary medicine, and lung biology. Grants are $32,500 per year for up to two years.
  Social-Behavioral Research Grant: The grant provides seed monies for investigators working on epidemiological and behavioral studies examining risk factors affecting lung health. Grants of $40,000 a year for up to two years include studies concerning the ethical, legal, and economic aspects of health services and policies.
EIN: 590662271

1772
American Optometric Foundation
2909 Fairgreen St.
Orlando, FL 32803-5043 (321) 710-3936
FAX: (407) 893-9890; E-mail: aof@aaoptom.org;
URL: http://www.aaopt.org/AOF

Foundation type: Public charity
Purpose: Fellowships, scholarships and research grants to outstanding graduate students of optometry and vision science.
Financial data: Year ended 06/30/2012. Assets, $4,202,086 (M); Expenditures, $555,264; Total giving, $335,000; Grants to individuals, 9 grants totaling $139,000.
Fields of interest: Optometry/vision screening; Eye research.
Type of support: Fellowships; Research; Scholarships—to individuals; Graduate support.
Application information: Applications accepted. Application form required.
  Initial approach: Letter, telephone or e-mail
  Send request by: On-line, mail, e-mail
  Deadline(s): Varies
  Additional information: See web site for additional application and program guidelines.
Program descriptions:
  Award of Excellence in Contact Lens Patient Care: This program is designed to recognize outstanding fourth year student clinicians who have demonstrated excellence in contact lens patient care during their optometric education. Sponsored by Vistakon, this award is a $1,000 and a personal plaque.
  Beta Sigma Kappa Research Fellowships: The program's funding is designed to benefit individuals early in their career whose academic curiosity leads them to seek answers to a vast variety of professionally-based questions covering a wide area of vision science, clinical practice, or eye related public health. At least two fellowships will be awarded, each consisting of no less than $1,000 awarded annually. Fellowship requests may exceed $1,000, however, anything in excess of $1,000 will be at the discretion of the BSK Central World Council.
  Douglas W. Hopkins Primary Care Residency Award: This program is intended to promote the practice and development of the field of Primary Care Optometry by providing incentive and support

to talented optometric residents who demonstrate a passion and commitment to practice, research, and education in primary care. The awards amounts to $2,000 plus one $750 travel fellowship to attend the Annual Meeting of the American Academy of Optometry in Seattle, contingent on the individual sitting for their fellowship exam. One award will be granted.
  Ezell Fellowships Program: This program offers support to graduate students, in a full-time program of study and training in vision-related research that leads to a Masters or Ph.D. degree. Fellowships are for one year and the current amount of the award is $8,000. Each student also receives travel grants to the annual meetings of the American Academy of Optometry and the Association for Research in Vision and Ophthalmology, which are $750 each.
  Glenn A. Fry Lecture Award: The award is given annually to a distinguished scientist or clinician scientist in recognition of the quality, significance, impact, and relevance to optometry of his or her current research contributions. Fulfilling these criteria typically requires that the nominee be at the mid-career stage, meaning that current accomplishments are worthy of the award and the nominee is highly likely to continue to make significant contributions to his or her field. The recipient need not be a Fellow of the Academy nor an optometrist.
  Jill and Geoge Mertz Fellowship Program: The Jill and George Mertz Fellowship is a biennial $30,000 award celebrating former American Optometric Foundation President George Mertz and his wife Jill. Mertz Fellowship is available to support travel to another institution to conduct a period of study. Optometrists at any stage of their career are eligible to apply.
  Sheldon Wechsler and George Mertz Contact Lens Residency Awards: This program is intended to promote the practice and development of the field of contact lenses by providing incentive and support to talented optometric residents who demonstrate a passion and commitment to practice, research, and education. The awards amounts to $2,750 each, part of which is in the form of a $750 travel fellowship to attend the Annual Meeting of the American Academy of Optometry in Seattle. Six awards will be granted.
  Terrance N. Ingraham Pediatric Optometry Residency Awards: This award is intended to promote the practice and development of the field of Pediatric Optometry by providing incentive and support to talented optometric residents who demonstrate a passion and commitment to practice, research, and education in the field of children's vision. The award consists of $2,750, part of which is in the form of a $750 travel fellowship to attend the Annual Meeting of the American Academy of Optometry in Oct.
  The Antoinette M. Molinari Scholarship Program: This program was established to assist an exceptional student who has extraordinary financial needs and, as such, would have difficulty meeting the financial requirements of attending optometry school. Financial need is a major criteria for selection, but academic and leadership potential are also important considerations. One scholarship of $6,000 will be awarded for the academic year. The award is made to the institution, who credits the scholarship to the student.
  The Vincent Salierno Scholarship Program: This program provides scholarship for students in the field of optometry. Between two and five scholarships of $2,000 are awarded for each academic year with the award going to the school or college for application to the student's financial aid.
EIN: 430768182

1773
American Orchid Society, Inc.

(also known as AOS)
10901 Old Cutler Rd.
Coral Gables, FL 33156-4233 (305) 740-2010
Contact: Sandra Tillisch-Svoboda, Pres.
FAX: (305) 740-2011; E-mail: theaos@aos.org;
URL: http://www.aos.org/

Foundation type: Public charity
Purpose: Scholarships, fellowships and research grants are provided to support the study of orchids.
Publications: Application guidelines.
Financial data: Year ended 06/30/2013. Assets, $7,657,268 (M); Expenditures, $1,040,148; Total giving, $21,500.
Fields of interest: Horticulture/garden clubs.
Type of support: Fellowships; Research; Grants to individuals.
Application information: Applications accepted. Application form required. Application form available on the grantmaker's web site.
  Deadline(s): Vary
  Additional information: Applications must include a CV and a description of the project. See web site for additional information.
Program descriptions:
  AOS/Norman's Orchids Masters Scholarship: This two-year scholarship provides the recipient with $5,000 per year to support their research. The purpose is to encourage Masters candidates to pursue orchid education, applied and fundamental research in orchids; to attract future generations of educators and scientists to orchidology; to address critical needs in orchid education. Institutional overhead costs will not paid out of these funds, making the entire stipend available to the student. Preference will be given to candidates working in orchid education or applied science, although consideration will not be strictly limited to those fields.
  Conservation Recognition Awards: The awards seek to recognize and reward individuals, groups and affiliated societies for outstanding work in the field of orchid conservation. The society awards up to two first prizes annually of $500 each. At least one of the prizes is designated to recognize efforts benefiting the conservation of orchid species native to Canada, the U.S. or Mexico. One of the prizes need have no geographical limitations. An additional two runner-up awards of $250 each may be given if judged appropriate. Self-nominations are not accepted.
  Graduate Fellowships: $9,000 per year for up to three years will be awarded to encourage doctoral candidates in their pursuit of fundamental and applied research on orchids. Fellows spend up to three years working on orchid-related dissertations that lead to a Ph.D. from an accredited institution. Applications must include college transcripts and a letter of recommendation.
  Philip Keenan Award: This award is intended to recognize the work of an individual in the study or preservation of native orchids of North America north of Mexico. Applicants may be students, amateurs or professionals actively engaged in the study or conservation of native orchids. Prior achievements in these fields will also be considered. Individuals may apply on their own behalf or on that of another they feel is worthy of consideration.
  Research Grants: The society periodically awards grants for non-commercial conservation projects, as well as experimental projects and fundamental and applied research on orchids. The society's goals are to advance the conservation and preservation of orchids in every aspect, and/or advance the scientific study of orchids in every respect, including classification, evolution,

propagation, culture, care and development. Qualified personnel associated with accredited institutions or appropriate institutes or organizations may apply.
EIN: 042161893

1774
American Society for Artificial Internal Organs

7700 Congress Ave., Ste. 3107
Boca Raton, FL 33487-1356 (561) 999-8969
Contact: Mark Slaughter M.D., Pres.
FAX: (561) 999-8972; E-mail: info@asaio.com;
URL: http://www.asaio.com

Foundation type: Public charity
Purpose: Fellowships to young investigators in the field of artificial internal organs to assist with the financial means to participate in the annual conference.
Financial data: Year ended 12/31/2011. Assets, $392,263 (M); Expenditures, $440,527.
Fields of interest: Science.
Type of support: Fellowships; Research.
Application information: Applications accepted. Application form required. Application form available on the grantmaker's web site.
  Send request by: E-mail
  Deadline(s): Mar. 2
  Additional information: Application should include curriculum vitae.
EIN: 236400773

1775
C.M. Amin Foundation Inc.

1802 Nottingham Ln.
Clearwater, FL 33764-6411

Foundation type: Independent foundation
Purpose: Scholarship awards to students in India attending a medical school.
Financial data: Year ended 08/31/2012. Assets, $84,023 (M); Expenditures, $6,871; Total giving, $5,600; Grants to individuals, 20 grants totaling $5,600 (high: $280, low: $280).
Fields of interest: Medical school/education.
Type of support: Foreign applicants.
Application information: Applications not accepted.
  Additional information: Unsolicited requests for funds not accepted.
EIN: 593475679

1776
W. L. Amos, Sr. Foundation, Inc.

c/o William L. Amos, Jr., M.D.
38 Ocean Club Dr.
Amelia Island, FL 32034-6629
Scholarship application address: c/o Cecil Cheves, P.O. Box 1199, Columbus, GA 31902-1199, tel.: (706) 324-0251

Foundation type: Independent foundation
Purpose: Scholarships to individuals who have a parent or grandparent who has worked at AFLAC for at least six months.
Financial data: Year ended 12/31/2012. Assets, $19,851,360 (M); Expenditures, $896,115; Total giving, $870,060.
Type of support: Employee-related scholarships; Undergraduate support.
Application information: Applications accepted. Application form required.
  Initial approach: Letter or telephone
  Deadline(s): May 1

Company name:
EIN: 582399470

1777
Anew Foundation, Inc.

135 E. Morse Blvd.
Winter Park, FL 32789

Foundation type: Operating foundation
Purpose: Financial assistance to qualifying residents of Winter Park, FL, for counseling and medical expenses related to substance abuse.
Financial data: Year ended 12/31/2012. Assets, $529,671 (M); Expenditures, $92,636; Total giving, $9,440.
Fields of interest: Mental health, addictions.
Type of support: Grants for special needs.
Application information: Applications accepted. Application form required.
  Initial approach: Letter
  Applicants should submit the following:
    1) Financial information
    2) Essay
  Additional information: Contact foundation for eligibility criteria.
EIN: 593719013

1778
Aqua Foundation for Women

4500 Biscayne Blvd., Ste. 340
Miami, FL 33137-3227 (305) 576-2782
Scholarship e-mail: scholars@aquafoundation.org
E-mail: robin@aquafoundation.org; URL: http://www.aquafoundation.org

Foundation type: Public charity
Purpose: Scholarships to graduating high school, college or graduate students who are active in South Florida's lesbian, bisexual, and transgender community.
Publications: Application guidelines.
Financial data: Year ended 12/31/2012. Assets, $318,170 (M); Expenditures, $342,719; Total giving, $100,366; Grants to individuals, totaling $50,366.
Fields of interest: Women; LGBTQ.
Type of support: Scholarships—to individuals.
Application information: Applications accepted. Application form available on the grantmaker's web site.
  Send request by: Online
  Applicants should submit the following:
    1) Essay
    2) Photograph
    3) Transcripts
    4) Letter(s) of recommendation
  Additional information: See web site for deadline and additional application information.
Program description:
  Scholarships: The foundation awards scholarships to benefit students who are active in south Florida's lesbian, bisexual, and transgender (LBT) community. Scholarships are given to encourage present and future leadership for the benefit of LBT communities. Applicant must be a resident of south Florida for at least one year, have a history of leadership and service in the community, and identify as an LBT woman. Each scholarship recipient is paired with a mentor for guidance and support.
EIN: 200873622

1779
The Arcadian Foundation
2760 N.E. 55th St.
Fort Lauderdale, FL   33308-3448
Foundation type: Independent foundation
Purpose: Scholarships to Newark Senior High School students in Newark, NY, for higher education.
Financial data: Year ended 12/31/2011. Assets, $3,535 (M); Expenditures, $14,158; Total giving, $14,000; Grants to individuals, 3 grants totaling $14,000 (high: $8,000, low: $2,000).
Fields of interest: Higher education.
Type of support: Support to graduates or students of specific schools; Undergraduate support.
Application information: Applications not accepted.
   Additional information: Contributes to individuals; unsolicited requests for funds not considered or acknowledged.
EIN: 364014560

1780
Area Agency on Aging of Pasco-Pinellas, Inc.
9549 Koger Blvd., Ste. 100
St. Petersburg, FL   33702-2451   (727) 570-9696
Contact: Edward A. Manny, Pres.
URL: http://www.agingcarefl.org
Foundation type: Public charity
Purpose: Support services to elderly individuals and their caregivers who live in Pasco and Pinellas Counties, FL.
Financial data: Year ended 12/31/2011. Assets, $3,043,499 (M); Expenditures, $17,410,605; Total giving, $13,837,002.
Fields of interest: Family services; Personal assistance services (PAS); Senior continuing care; Aging, centers/services; Human services; Aging.
Type of support: Grants for special needs.
Application information:
   Initial approach: Letter, telephone, or e-mail
   Additional information: Contact foundation or see web site for further application and program information.
Program descriptions:
   Information and Assistance: This program provides elders and their caregivers with essential services to help them age with security, dignity, and purpose. Free counseling is offered, and the counselors then direct individuals to the appropriate resources.
   National Family Caregiver Support Program: Support for those who are the primary caregivers for an elderly individual. Families who are economically or socially disadvantaged are preferred, although low income is not an eligibility requirement. The program also serves grandparents aged sixty or over who serve as primary caregivers for their grandchildren. Services provided by this program include screening and assessment, home health aids, adult day care, in-facility care, counseling, chore services, and medical supplies.
   SHINE: Free health insurance counseling services for elderly individuals. Counselors offer expertise on Medicare, Medicaid, Prescription Assistance, and Long-Term Care Planning and Insurance. The counselors focus on beneficiary rights and consumer protection, and also educate and empower elders so they can make informed decisions.
EIN: 311710636

1781
The Areawide Council on Aging of Broward County, Inc.
(also known as Area Agency on Aging of Broward County)
5300 Hiatus Rd.
Sunrise, FL   33351-8701   (954) 745-9567
FAX: (954) 745-9584;
E-mail: webmaster@adrcbroward.org; URL: http://www.adrcbroward.org
Foundation type: Public charity
Purpose: Assistance for home care and other services for elderly individuals in need throughout Broward County, FL.
Financial data: Year ended 12/31/2011. Assets, $16,815,063 (M); Expenditures, $22,138,336; Total giving, $19,223,138; Grants to individuals, 435 grants totaling $884,342.
Fields of interest: Aging, centers/services; Human services; Aging.
Type of support: Grants to individuals.
Application information: Applications accepted.
   Additional information: Some assistance require an application for eligibility determination. Contact the agency for additional guidelines.
EIN: 591529419

1782
Art League of Bonita Springs, Inc.
26100 Old U.S. 41 Rd.
Bonita Springs, FL   34135-6632   (239) 495-8989
Contact: Susan Bridges, Pres.
FAX: (239) 495-3999; E-mail: cfabs@artinusa.com; URL: http://www.artcenterbonita.org
Foundation type: Public charity
Purpose: Scholarships to high school seniors residing in the Bonita Springs, FL, area with financial need who plan to study art on the college level.
Publications: Newsletter.
Financial data: Year ended 05/31/2013. Assets, $3,762,244 (M); Expenditures, $1,785,076.
Fields of interest: Arts education.
Type of support: Scholarships—to individuals.
Application information: Applications accepted. Application form required.
EIN: 650295085

1783
Art League of Marco Island, Inc.
1010 Winterberry Dr.
Marco Island, FL   34145-5427   (239) 394-4221
Contact: Kenneth Stroud, Pres.
E-mail: mail@marcoislandart.com; URL: http://www.marcoislandart.com
Foundation type: Public charity
Purpose: Scholarships to students from Collier County, FL high schools for higher education in the arts.
Publications: Application guidelines.
Financial data: Year ended 09/30/2011. Assets, $1,718,601 (M); Expenditures, $349,805.
Fields of interest: Arts education.
Type of support: Support to graduates or students of specific schools.
Application information: Applications accepted. Application form required. Application form available on the grantmaker's web site.
   Deadline(s): Feb. 15 for Artists Visiting Kids
   Additional information: Contact foundation for current application deadline/guidelines.

Program description:
   Artists Visiting Kids: Funding of up to $4,500 for individual artists or teachers who are acknowledged experts in their fields, so that community youth may become acquainted with professional artists and expose them to a wide variety of media within the visual arts fields.
EIN: 591754367

1784
Ashley Willwerth Memorial Scholarship Foundation
P.O. Box 1685
St. Augustine, FL   32085-1685   (904) 823-9012
E-mail: info@ashleyfoundation.org; URL: http://www.ashleyfoundation.org
Foundation type: Public charity
Purpose: Scholarships to teachers and students of bowed string instruments, such as violin, viola, string bass or cello.
Financial data: Year ended 12/31/2011. Assets, $50,000.
Fields of interest: Music; Orchestras.
Type of support: Scholarships—to individuals.
Application information: Applications accepted. Application form required. Application form available on the grantmaker's web site.
   Send request by: Mail
   Additional information: Application should include two letters of reference.
EIN: 201797704

1785
Astronaut Scholarship Foundation, Inc.
6225 Vectorspace Blvd.
Titusville, FL   32780-8040   (321) 455-7011
Contact: Linn LeBlanc, Exec. Dir.
FAX: (321) 264-9176;
E-mail: linn@astronautscholarship.org; URL: http://www.astronautscholarship.org
Foundation type: Public charity
Purpose: Scholarships by nomination only to deserving college students who exhibit motivation, imagination, and exceptional performance in the science or engineering field of their major.
Financial data: Year ended 12/31/2011. Assets, $7,127,536 (M); Expenditures, $1,230,087; Total giving, $245,000; Grants to individuals, totaling $245,000.
Fields of interest: Space/aviation; Engineering/technology; Science.
Type of support: Awards/grants by nomination only.
Application information: Unsolicited requests for funds not accepted. Scholarship candidates must be nominated by faculty members. Students may not directly apply for the scholarship.
Program description:
   Scholarship Program: Scholarships are provided to engineering, natural or applied science (e.g. astronomy, biology, chemistry, physics, earth science, computer science), or mathematics students with intentions to pursue research or advance their field upon completion of their final degrees. Scholarship candidates must be nominated by faculty members. Students may not apply directly for the scholarship. Scholarship nominees must be U.S. citizens and attend a cooperating education institution.
EIN: 592448775

1786
Ataxia Telangiectasia Children's Project
(also known as A-T Children's Project)
5300 W. Hillsboro Blvd., Ste. 105
Coconut Creek, FL 33073-4395 (954)
481-6611
Contact: Jennifer Thornton, Exec. Dir.
FAX: (954) 725-1153; E-mail: info@atcp.org;
Toll-free tel.: (800) 543-5728; E-mail for Jennifer
Thornton: jennifer@atcp.org; URL: http://
www.communityatcp.org

Foundation type: Public charity
Purpose: Grants for basic and translational
biomedical research projects to elucidate the
genetic neurological defects of Ataxia
Telangiectasia.
Publications: Application guidelines; Grants list;
Informational brochure; Newsletter.
Financial data: Year ended 05/31/2012. Assets,
$295,988 (M); Expenditures, $916,929; Total
giving, $332,087.
Fields of interest: Institute.
Type of support: Research.
Application information: Applications accepted.
Initial approach: By proposal
Copies of proposal: 3
Final notification: 30 days after receipt of
proposal
Additional information: Applicants must submit
hard copies of the proposal as well as an
electronic copy of the proposal in either
MSWord or PDF formats to grants@atcp.org.
See Web site for additional eligibility criteria.
Program description:
Research Grants: Provides competitive grant
awards for basic and translational research grant
related to ataxia-telangiectasa (A-T). One-and
two-year projects are funded up to a maximum total
direct cost of $75,000 per year. Grants range from
$25,000 to $50,000. Priority will be given to
proposals that are relevant to a therapeutic
intervention for A-T and/or proposals that facilitate
translational or clinical research for this disease.
EIN: 650427215

1787
Atlantic Center for the Arts, Inc.
1414 Art Ctr. Ave.
New Smyrna Beach, FL 32168-5560 (386)
427-6975
Contact: Ann Brady, Exec. Dir.
FAX: (386) 427-5669;
E-mail: program@atlanticcenterforthearts.org;
URL: http://www.atlanticcenterforthearts.org

Foundation type: Public charity
Purpose: Residencies to artists of all disciplines for
participation in the Atlantic Center for the Arts
program.
Publications: Application guidelines; Annual report;
Informational brochure; Newsletter.
Financial data: Year ended 12/31/2012. Assets,
$8,385,609 (M); Expenditures, $1,224,531.
Fields of interest: Visual arts; Performing arts;
Literature; International exchange.
International interests: France; Italy; Japan;
Mexico.
Type of support: Exchange programs; Residencies.
Application information: Applications accepted.
Application form required. Application form
available on the grantmaker's web site.
Send request by: Mail
Deadline(s): Varies
Applicants should submit the following:
1) Essay
2) Resume

3) Work samples
Additional information: Applicants must include a
$25 application fee.
Program description:
Residencies: The center provides residencies,
including workspace access and technical support,
to artists working in the visual arts (painting,
sculpture, photography, and film/video),
architecture, music (composition and
performance), literature, modern dance,
performance art, and theater, so that they may
devote complete time and attention to their art in a
community of like-minded artists. Room, board, and
meals will be provided to artists, as well as
collaboration opportunities with other artists.
EIN: 591998321

1788
Aurora Ministries, Inc.
(formerly Bible Alliance, Inc.)
P.O. Box 1848
Bradenton, FL 34206-1848 (941) 748-4100
E-mail: aurora@auroraministries.org; URL: http://
www.auroraministries.org/

Foundation type: Operating foundation
Purpose: Grants of cassette tape recordings of the
Bible made to the blind and print-handicapped.
Financial data: Year ended 12/31/2012. Assets,
$314,452 (M); Expenditures, $150,953; Total
giving, $0.
Fields of interest: Christian agencies & churches;
Religion; Disabilities, people with.
Type of support: Grants for special needs.
Application information: Applications accepted.
Application form required.
EIN: 237178299

1789
AWS Foundation
550 N.W. Lejeune Rd.
Miami, FL 33126-5649 (305) 443-9353
Contact: William A. Rice, Pres.
E-mail: info@aws.org; Toll-free tel.: (800)
443-9353; E-mail for William A. Rice:
brice@oki-bering.com; tel. for William A. Rice: (304)
346-2977; URL: http://www.aws.org/w/a/
foundation/index.html

Foundation type: Public charity
Purpose: Scholarships, fellowships and student
loans to individuals who wish to enter the field of
welding.
Publications: Application guidelines.
Financial data: Year ended 12/31/2011. Assets,
$11,065,753 (M); Expenditures, $591,668; Total
giving, $295,183; Grants to individuals, totaling
$295,183.
Fields of interest: Engineering/technology.
Type of support: Fellowships; Research; Student
loans—to individuals; Foreign applicants;
Postdoctoral support; Graduate support; Technical
education support; Doctoral support.
Application information: Applications accepted.
Application form required. Application form
available on the grantmaker's web site.
Deadline(s): Varies
Additional information: See web site for further
guidelines.
Program descriptions:
District Scholarship Program: The foundation
offers scholarship funds that, once awarded, are
payable directly to the school to which the individual
has been accepted. It will cover the cost of tuition,
books, supplies and related institutional costs.

Applicants must be enrolled in a welding-related
educational or training program.
International Scholarship Program: The
foundation provides financial assistance to
international students wishing to pursue their
education in welding and related joining
technologies who are not assigned to an American
Welding Society (AWS) section. International
scholarships will be awarded to full time
international students pursuing undergraduate or
graduate studies in joining sciences. Applicants can
be matriculating in accredited joining science
programs at institutions anywhere in the world.
Student must be in the top 20 percent of the
institution's grading system.
National Scholarship Program: The foundation
awards a number of individual scholarships, each
worth a minimum of $2,500. Scholarships are for
students pursuing a specific degree at an
accredited four-year college or university.
Research Fellowships: These fellowships, of up
to $25,000 per year, seek to foster university
research in joining and to recognize outstanding
faculty and student talent. A maximum of six
students are funded for a period of up to three years
of research at any one time. Fellowship is awarded
to the student for graduate research toward a
masters or Ph.D. degree under a sponsoring
professor at a North American University.
EIN: 650148545

1790
The Bailey Family Foundation, Inc.
912 W. Platt St., Ste. 200
Tampa, FL 33606-2114 (813) 549-6140
Contact: Ron K. Bailey, Pres.; Kimberly M. Czabaj,
Admin.
Scholarship Admin.: tel.: (813) 549-6139
FAX: (813) 549-6141;
E-mail: contact@bailey-family.org; URL: http://
www.bailey-family.org/

Foundation type: Operating foundation
Purpose: Scholarships to students attending
specific schools in northern VA and FL for higher
education.
Publications: Informational brochure; Newsletter;
Program policy statement.
Financial data: Year ended 12/31/2012. Assets,
$45,284,217 (M); Expenditures, $4,051,494;
Total giving, $2,999,634; Grants to individuals,
totaling $2,350,037.
Type of support: Support to graduates or students
of specific schools; Undergraduate support.
Application information: Applications accepted.
Application form required.
Initial approach: Letter or e-mail
Deadline(s): Mar. 15
Additional information: See web site for full listing
of schools.
Program descriptions:
College Scholarship Program: This program
provides educational scholarships to college
students who have a financial need and have
demonstrated scholastic achievement.
Heritage Scholarship Program: This program
provides educational scholarships to lineal
descendants of George Patton Bailey who
demonstrate scholastic achievement.
High School Scholarship Program: This program
provides educational scholarships to high school
seniors who have a financial need and have
demonstrated scholastic achievement, and a
dedication to community service.

Hope For Tomorrow: This research program is designed to determine how limited scholarship funds are most efficiently utilized.
EIN: 541850780

1791
Baptist Health Care Foundation, Inc.

1717 N. E St., Twr. 1, Ste. 409
Pensacola, FL 32501-6605 (850) 469-7906
Contact: Dion Guest, Exec. Dir.
FAX: (850) 469-7895; E-Mail For Dion Guest:
dion.guest@bhcpns.org; URL: http://
www.baptisthealthcarefoundation.org

Foundation type: Public charity
Purpose: Scholarships to Baptist Hospital, Inc., employees and to Pensacola, FL, area students for health care education.
Financial data: Year ended 09/30/2011. Assets, $6,700,946 (M); Expenditures, $2,051,812; Total giving, $1,816,338; Grants to individuals, totaling $148,329.
Fields of interest: Health sciences school/education.
Type of support: Employee-related scholarships; Undergraduate support.
Application information: Contact foundation for current application deadline/guidelines.
Company name: Baptist Hospital, Incorporated
EIN: 590192265

1792
Baptist Health System Foundation, Inc.

841 Prudential Dr., Ste. 1300
Jacksonville, FL 32207-8202 (904) 202-2919
Contact: Marlene Spalten C.F.R.E., V.P.; John Erstling, Dir., Devel.
FAX: (904) 202-2875;
E-mail: Foundation@bmcjax.com; URL: http://
community.e-baptisthealth.com/foundation/
index.html

Foundation type: Public charity
Purpose: Professional healthcare scholarships based on financial need to students who are residents of northeast FL and southern GA and employed as nurses or other medical professionals with Baptist Health System, Inc. or are studying nursing at a local college or university.
Publications: Informational brochure; Newsletter.
Financial data: Year ended 09/30/2011. Assets, $36,972,858 (M); Expenditures, $15,537,111; Total giving, $12,525,349; Grants to individuals, totaling $515,804.
Type of support: Employee-related scholarships; Scholarships—to individuals.
Application information: Applications accepted. Application form required. Application form available on the grantmaker's web site.
  Initial approach: Application
  Send request by: Mail
  Copies of proposal: 1
  Deadline(s): Contact foundation for current deadline
  Final notification: Recipients notified 7- 10 days after receipt of application
  Applicants should submit the following:
    1) Transcripts
    2) Letter(s) of recommendation
    3) GPA
  Additional information: Application should also include proof of current enrollment and proof of tuition.
EIN: 592487135

1793
The Robert & Aldona Beall Family Foundation

(formerly The Beall Family Foundation)
1806 38th Ave. E.
Bradenton, FL 34208 (941) 747-2355
Contact: Patricia Johnson

Foundation type: Operating foundation
Purpose: Scholarships to members of the Palmetto Youth Center, FL.
Financial data: Year ended 11/30/2012. Assets, $579,473 (M); Expenditures, $14,158; Total giving, $11,563; Grants to individuals, 6 grants totaling $11,563 (high: $2,500, low: $313).
Fields of interest: Neighborhood centers; Children/youth, services.
Type of support: Scholarships—to individuals.
Application information: Applications accepted. Application form required. Interview required.
  Deadline(s): None
  Applicants should submit the following:
    1) Financial information
    2) GPA
  Additional information: Recipients must volunteer for a minimum of ten hours at the Palmetto Youth Center annually.
EIN: 650545213

1794
R. M. Beall, Sr. Charitable Foundation

1806 38th Ave. E.
Bradenton, FL 34208-4708
Contact: Patricia Johnson

Foundation type: Company-sponsored foundation
Purpose: Scholarships to participants in the Palmetto Youth Program for higher education and to children and minor dependents of full-time Beall's, Inc. employees.
Financial data: Year ended 12/31/2012. Assets, $3,898,246 (M); Expenditures, $231,166; Total giving, $183,527.
Fields of interest: Scholarships/financial aid.
Type of support: Employee-related scholarships; Support to graduates or students of specific schools; Undergraduate support.
Application information: Applications accepted. Application form required. Interview required.
  Send request by: Mail
  Deadline(s): Varies
  Final notification: Applicants notified Apr. or May
  Applicants should submit the following:
    1) Letter(s) of recommendation
    2) Transcripts
Program description:
  Palmetto Youth Center Scholarship Program: The foundation awards college scholarships of up to $5,000 to student members of the Palmetto Youth Center in Palmetto, Florida. Recipients are chosen based on the extent of involvement with the Palmetto Youth Center, academic achievement, extracurricular activities, and financial need.
Company name: Beall's, Inc.
EIN: 592851924

1795
R. M. Beall, Sr. Charitable Operating Foundation

1806 38th Ave. E.
Bradenton, FL 34208
Contact: Patricia Johnson, Fdn. Admin.

Foundation type: Operating foundation
Purpose: Scholarship awards to dependents of full-time Beall's employees. Grants to Beall's employees for natural disaster relief. Grants to teachers in FL to promote creative teaching methods.
Financial data: Year ended 11/30/2012. Assets, $1,687,838 (M); Expenditures, $57,591; Total giving, $37,371; Grants to individuals, 44 grants totaling $37,371 (high: $5,000).
Type of support: Employee-related scholarships; Grants to individuals; Employee-related welfare.
Application information: Application form required.
  Additional information: Contact foundation for additional guidelines.
Company name: Beall's, Inc.
EIN: 800025118

1796
The Bennie & Martha Benjamin Foundation, Inc.

55 S.E. 2nd Ave., Ste. 301
Delray Beach, FL 33444-3615 (561) 243-1477
Contact: David A. Beale, Exec. Dir.
URL: http://www.benniebenjaminfoundation.org

Foundation type: Independent foundation
Purpose: Scholarships to individuals who are residents of the U.S. Virgin Islands, for advanced degrees in the allied medical and health fields.
Financial data: Year ended 10/31/2012. Assets, $1,846,834 (M); Expenditures, $258,282; Total giving, $148,582; Grants to individuals, 4 grants totaling $3,128 (high: $1,000, low: $128).
Fields of interest: Medical school/education; Nursing school/education; Public health school/education; Health care.
Type of support: Scholarships—to individuals.
Application information: Applications accepted. Application form required. Application form available on the grantmaker's web site.
  Deadline(s): Apr. 1
  Additional information: Applicants must sign a Contract of Commitment. See web site for specific scholarship programs.
EIN: 133555717

1797
Joe & Mary Helen Bennett Scholarship Fund

2004 Ravinia Cir.
Venice, FL 34292-6118 (317) 745-6431

Foundation type: Operating foundation
Purpose: Scholarships to graduating seniors of Danville Community High School, IN, for attendance at various colleges, universities or trade schools.
Financial data: Year ended 12/31/2012. Assets, $16,470 (M); Expenditures, $3,251; Total giving, $2,200; Grants to individuals, 11 grants totaling $2,200 (high: $200, low: $200).
Fields of interest: Vocational education, post-secondary; Higher education.
Type of support: Support to graduates or students of specific schools; Undergraduate support.
Application information: Applications accepted. Application form required.
  Deadline(s): Apr. 15
  Applicants should submit the following:
    1) Class rank
    2) Transcripts
    3) SAT
  Additional information: Applicants must live in Center or Marion township of Hendricks county, IN.
EIN: 356605585

1798
Biegelsen Foundation, Inc.
740 S. Andrews Ave.
Ft. Lauderdale, FL 33316-1032 (954)
463-6581
Contact: Jeffrey Biegelsen, Pres.
Application address: P.O. Box 210, Hollywood, FL
33022

Foundation type: Independent foundation
Purpose: Grants to doctors for medical research at
the University of Miami School of Medicine, FL.
Financial data: Year ended 09/30/2013. Assets,
$1,069,266 (M); Expenditures, $52,132; Total
giving, $48,250.
Fields of interest: Heart & circulatory research;
Arthritis research; Lupus research.
Type of support: Research; Postdoctoral support.
Application information: Applications accepted.
  Additional information: Contact foundation for
    application guidelines.
EIN: 136103887

1799
Big Bend Hospice, Inc.
1723 Mahan Center Blvd.
Tallahassee, FL 32308-5428 (850) 878-5310
FAX: (850) 309-1638;
E-mail: hospice@bigbendhospice.org; Toll-free tel.:
(800) 772-5862; Additional fax.: (850) 309-1639;
URL: http://www.bigbendhospice.org

Foundation type: Public charity
Purpose: Free drugs and other services to
hospice-bound individuals with terminal illnesses.
Financial data: Year ended 09/30/2011. Assets,
$10,977,867 (M); Expenditures, $19,043,298.
Fields of interest: Medical care, in-patient care; End
of life care; Health care.
Type of support: Grants for special needs.
Application information: Contact the hospice for
further program information.
EIN: 592328806

1800
Blac Hospitality Initiative of Greater
Miami
(formerly Visitor Industry Human Resource
Development Council)
701 Brickell Ave., Ste. 2700
Miami, FL 33131-2847 (305) 539-3097
Contact: Graylyn Swilley, Exec. Dir.
E-mail: gswilley@gmcvb.com; E-mail for Graylyn
Swilley: gswilley@gmcvp.com; URL: http://
www.blackhospitalitymiami.com/about.htm

Foundation type: Public charity
Purpose: Scholarships to minority students in the
hospitality field.
Financial data: Year ended 09/30/2011. Assets,
$162,260 (M); Expenditures, $253,738; Total
giving, $10,088.
Fields of interest: Formal/general education;
Minorities.
Type of support: Scholarships—to individuals.
Application information: Contact foundation for
current application deadline/guidelines.
EIN: 650329273

1801
Blankenship/Justice Scholarship Fund
Trust
P.O. Box 1908
Orlando, FL 32802-1908
E-mail: Cheryl.godwin@suntrust.com

Foundation type: Company-sponsored foundation
Purpose: Scholarships to children or dependents of
a coal miner; disabled coal miners seeking a
degree; individuals seeking a degree in a field
related to coal mine safety and health; and to
individuals who are high school graduates or GED
certified. Scholarships are limited to residents of
Buchanan, Dickenson, Lee, Russell, Scott, Smyth,
Tazewell, Washington, and Wise counties, and
Bristol and Norton, Virginia.
Financial data: Year ended 12/31/2012. Assets,
$1,496,708 (M); Expenditures, $94,162; Total
giving, $69,250; Grants to individuals, 90 grants
totaling $69,250 (high: $2,500, low: $500).
Fields of interest: Education; Geology.
Type of support: Scholarships—to individuals.
Application information: Applications accepted.
Application form required.
  Deadline(s): Mar. 30
  Applicants should submit the following:
    1) Transcripts
    2) FAFSA
  Additional information: Scholarship amount will
    be paid to the institution on behalf of the
    recipient.
EIN: 626398586

1802
David Strouse Blount Educational
Foundation
c/o SunTrust Bank
P.O. Box 1908
Orlando, FL 32802-1908
Application address: c/o SunTrust Bank,
Attn.: Carolyn McCoy, 510 S. Jefferson St.,
Roanoke, VA 24038, tel.: (540) 982-3076

Foundation type: Independent foundation
Purpose: Scholarships to VA residents with
scholastic ability and financial need attending
colleges and universities in VA.
Financial data: Year ended 03/31/2012. Assets,
$2,821,833 (M); Expenditures, $182,358; Total
giving, $136,500; Grants to individuals, 175 grants
totaling $136,500 (high: $750, low: $750).
Type of support: Scholarships—to individuals.
Application information: Application form required.
  Deadline(s): None
  Applicants should submit the following:
    1) Financial information
    2) Transcripts
  Additional information: Apply through financial
    aid office of a VA college or university.
EIN: 546111717

1803
Anquan Boldin Foundation
P.O. Box 412
Pahokee, FL 33476-0412 (561) 755-3560
Contact: Bishop Robert L. Banks, Jr., Pres. and
Exec. Dir.
E-mail: q81foundation@yahoo.com; Additional tel.:
(561) 371-1430; URL: http://www.q81.org/

Foundation type: Public charity
Purpose: Scholarships to graduating students, high
school seniors, underprivileged children, and single
parents to attend college with tuition and fees for

one degree program to create a brighter future for
themselves.
Publications: Application guidelines.
Financial data: Year ended 12/31/2011. Assets,
$11,640 (M); Expenditures, $62,666; Total giving,
$48,426.
Fields of interest: Higher education.
Type of support: Scholarships—to individuals.
Application information: Contact foundation for
additional guidelines.
EIN: 201686580

1804
Kevin L. Boyer M.D. Charitable
Foundation, Inc.
2410 57th St. E.
Bradenton, FL 34208 (941) 920-7196
Contact: Kevin L. Boyer M.D., Pres.

Foundation type: Independent foundation
Purpose: Scholarships to high school seniors of FL,
seeking an education in the health care field.
Financial data: Year ended 12/31/2012. Assets,
$84,104 (M); Expenditures, $11,659; Total giving,
$9,500; Grants to individuals, 11 grants totaling
$9,500 (high: $2,000, low: $500).
Fields of interest: Higher education; Health
sciences school/education.
Type of support: Scholarships—to individuals.
Application information: Applications accepted.
Application form required.
  Initial approach: Letter or telephone
  Deadline(s): Mar. 1
  Additional information: Applicant must
    demonstrate financial need and academic
    achievement.
EIN: 030520299

1805
Bradish Memorial Scholarship Fund
(formerly Norman C. Bradish Trust)
P.O. Box 40200, FL9-100-10-19
Jacksonville, FL 32203-0200

Foundation type: Independent foundation
Purpose: Scholarships to unmarried male
graduates of Decorah High School, IA.
Financial data: Year ended 06/30/2013. Assets,
$1,662,405 (M); Expenditures, $85,840; Total
giving, $58,100; Grants to individuals, 13 grants
totaling $57,400 (high: $7,000, low: $200).
Fields of interest: Men.
Type of support: Support to graduates or students
of specific schools.
Application information: Applications accepted.
Application form not required.
  Initial approach: Letter
  Deadline(s): None
  Additional information: Applicants must have
    excellent academic records and in need of
    financial assistance.
EIN: 596161559

1806
Herbert E. & Marion K. Bragg Foundation
P.O. Box 1908
Orlando, FL 32802-1908
Contact: Carolyn McCoy
Application address: Suntrust Bank, 510 S.
Jefferson St., Roanoke, VA 24011

Foundation type: Independent foundation
Purpose: Scholarships to students at colleges and
universities in ME and VA.

Financial data: Year ended 10/31/2013. Assets, $1,242,290 (M); Expenditures, $93,014; Total giving, $59,684; Grants to individuals, 67 grants totaling $59,684 (high: $2,153, low: $302).
Type of support: Scholarships—to individuals.
Application information:
  Deadline(s): June 15
  Additional information: Applications are received only from colleges and universities through their financial aid departments.
EIN: 546313244

1807
Brevard Heart Foundation, Inc.
P.O. Box 2151
Melbourne, FL   32901-4773   (321) 725-2742

Foundation type: Independent foundation
Purpose: Scholarships to residents of Brevard County, FL, for nursing and medical education.
Financial data: Year ended 12/31/2011. Assets, $371,872 (M); Expenditures, $36,360; Total giving, $25,000; Grants to individuals, totaling $25,000.
Fields of interest: Medical school/education; Nursing school/education.
Type of support: Graduate support; Undergraduate support.
Application information: Application form required.
  Initial approach: By letter in person
  Deadline(s): May 15
  Additional information: Interviews required for first-time applicants and recommended for reapplicants; photo required for file identification. See program description for specific requirements.
EIN: 596150538

1808
R. Carlyle Bronson Scholarship Foundation Inc.
1350 Neptune Rd.
Kissimmee, FL   34744   (407) 847-5987
Contact: Edna T. Prather, V.P.

Foundation type: Independent foundation
Purpose: Scholarships to residents of Osceola County, FL for higher education at accredited institutions.
Financial data: Year ended 12/31/2012. Assets, $418,684 (M); Expenditures, $22,415; Total giving, $21,000; Grants to individuals, 7 grants totaling $21,000 (high: $3,000, low: $3,000).
Type of support: Scholarships—to individuals.
Application information: Applications accepted. Application form required.
  Deadline(s): Prior to beginning of school year
EIN: 593392431

1809
Derrick Brooks Charities
10014 N. Dale Mabry Hwy., Ste. 101
Tampa, FL   33618-4426   (813) 877-8681
Contact: Bonita R. Pulido, Exec. Dir.
FAX: (813) 877-8481;
E-mail: bonita@derrickbrookscharities.org;
URL: http://www.db55.org/

Foundation type: Public charity
Purpose: Scholarships to graduating seniors of FL for attendance at colleges or universities pursuing higher education.
Financial data: Year ended 12/31/2011. Assets, $195,062 (M); Expenditures, $609,537; Total

giving, $185,681; Grants to individuals, totaling $79,227.
Fields of interest: Higher education; Economically disadvantaged.
Type of support: Scholarships—to individuals.
Application information: Applications accepted.
  Additional information: Applicants must have participated in the First and Goal program, maintain a minimum 2.5 GPA, enrolled in at least 12 credit hours per semester, Rites of Passage Program, and a mentoring program for disadvantaged young ladies. All expenses are paid directly to the educational institution on behalf of the students.
EIN: 450496688

1810
Broward Community College Foundation, Inc.
10 E Broward Blvd, Ste. 750
Fort Lauderdale, FL   33301-2208   (954) 201-7414
Contact: Nancy Botero, Exec. Dir.
FAX: (954) 769-9138;
E-mail: foundation@broward.edu; URL: http://www.broward.edu/foundation

Foundation type: Public charity
Purpose: Scholarships to students of Broward College, FL who would not otherwise be able to attend college.
Publications: Annual report.
Financial data: Year ended 12/31/2011. Assets, $65,050,144 (M); Expenditures, $6,054,268; Total giving, $3,582,418.
Fields of interest: Higher education.
Type of support: Support to graduates or students of specific schools.
Application information: Applications accepted. Application form required.
  Additional information: Applicant must demonstrate financial need. See web site for a listing of scholarship programs.
EIN: 237181959

1811
Broward Education Foundation
600 S.E. 3rd Ave., 1st Fl.
Fort Lauderdale, FL   33301-3125   (754) 321-2030
Contact: Claudette Lavoie, Program Coord.
FAX: (754) 321-2706;
E-mail: marie-lee.baxter@browardschools.com;
Additional tel.: (754)321-0000; E-Mail for Claudette Lavoie: claudette.lavoie@browardschools.com;
URL: http://www.browardedfoundation.net/

Foundation type: Public charity
Purpose: Grants to pre-K through 12th grade teachers and school-based administrators in Broward County, FL to help fun original and innovative projects. Also, scholarships to students in Broward County, FL.
Publications: Application guidelines.
Financial data: Year ended 06/30/2011. Assets, $8,985,311 (M); Expenditures, $1,996,352; Total giving, $851,603; Grants to individuals, totaling $851,603.
Type of support: Program development; Grants to individuals; Scholarships—to individuals; Project support.
Application information: Applications accepted.
  Additional information: See web site for complete program listing.
EIN: 592359433

1812
Brown & Brown Disaster Relief Foundation, Inc.
220 S. Ridgewood Ave.
Daytona Beach, FL   32114-4345   (386) 239-7276

Foundation type: Public charity
Purpose: Assistance to employees of Brown & Brown, Inc. and others who have experienced a loss of home or other property and/or physical injury to themselves or members of their families as a result of a natural disaster or other form of emergency hardship.
Financial data: Year ended 12/31/2012. Assets, $185,052 (M); Expenditures, $33,836.
Fields of interest: Safety/disasters.
Type of support: Emergency funds; Employee-related welfare; Grants for special needs.
Application information: Applications not accepted.
  Additional information: Unsolicited requests for funds not considered or acknowledged.
EIN: 203617312

1813
BRRH Foundation, Inc.
(formerly BRCH Foundation, Inc.)
745 Meadows Rd.
Boca Raton, FL   33486-2301   (561) 955-4142
Contact: Randy Scheid, Grantwriter; Susan Vielhauer, Dir., Fdn. Opers.
FAX: (561) 955-4727;
E-mail: foundation@brch.com; Email for Randy Scheid: rscheid@brch.com; email for Susan Vielhauer: svielhauer@brch.com; URL: http://www.brch.com

Foundation type: Public charity
Purpose: Nursing scholarships and support for student nurses at Boca Raton Regional Hospital, FL.
Financial data: Year ended 06/30/2011. Assets, $124,329,552 (M); Expenditures, $9,617,372; Total giving, $6,777,200; Grants to individuals, totaling $123,450.
Fields of interest: Nursing school/education.
Type of support: Undergraduate support.
Application information:
  Initial approach: Letter
  Additional information: Contact foundation for eligibility criteria.
EIN: 592406425

1814
The Trust for Fuller E. Callaway Professorial Chairs
P.O. Box 40200, FL9-100-10-19
Jacksonville, FL   32203-0200

Foundation type: Independent foundation
Purpose: Grants for the benefit of named individuals for professorial chairs, primarily in GA.
Financial data: Year ended 06/30/2013. Assets, $27,309,064 (M); Expenditures, $1,027,735; Total giving, $841,216.
Fields of interest: Higher education.
Type of support: Professorships.
Application information: Applications not accepted.
  Additional information: Unsolicited requests for funds not considered or acknowledged.
EIN: 586075259

1815
Cape Coral Community Foundation
(formerly Philanthropic Foundation of Cape Coral, Inc.)
1405 S.E. 47th St., Unit 2
Cape Coral, FL   33904   (239) 542-5594
Contact: Beth T. Sanger, Exec. Dir.
FAX: (239) 549-8307;
E-mail: cccf@capecoralcf.org; URL: http://www.capecoralcf.planyourlegacy.org/

Foundation type: Community foundation
Purpose: Scholarships to high school students and individuals for higher education in the Cape Coral, FL area.
Publications: Application guidelines; Annual report; Informational brochure; Newsletter.
Financial data: Year ended 06/30/2012. Assets, $7,839,692 (M); Expenditures, $533,419; Total giving, $283,726; Grants to individuals, 35 grants totaling $57,000.
Fields of interest: Higher education; Scholarships/financial aid; Health care; Athletics/sports, training; Recreation; Science.
Type of support: Employee-related scholarships; Scholarships—to individuals.
Application information: Application form required. Application form available on the grantmaker's web site.
  Deadline(s): Varies
  Applicants should submit the following:
    1) GPA
    2) Essay
  Additional information: Scholarship eligibility varies according to the specific criteria of each scholarship fund. See web site for complete scholarship listing and application form.
EIN: 237410312

1816
Katie Caples Scholarship Foundation, Inc.
98 S. Fletcher Ave.
Fernandina Beach, FL   32034-2216   (904) 277-4851

Foundation type: Public charity
Purpose: Scholarships to Bishop Kenny High School students of Jacksonville, FL in pursuit of a higher education at accredited colleges or universities.
Financial data: Year ended 12/31/2011. Assets, $417,214 (M); Expenditures, $208,427; Total giving, $84,656.
Fields of interest: Higher education.
Type of support: Support to graduates or students of specific schools.
Application information: Unsolicited requests for funds not accepted.
EIN: 593580838

1817
Shawn Carter Scholarship Fund
(also known as Shawn Carter Foundation)
c/o MBAF LLP
1001 Brickell Bay Dr., Ste. 9
Miami, FL   33131-4937   (212) 497-2048
E-mail: info@shawncartersf.com; URL: http://www.shawncartersf.com/

Foundation type: Public charity
Purpose: Scholarships to graduating high school seniors, undergraduate college students, and students at vocational or trade school for higher education.
Publications: Application guidelines.

Financial data: Year ended 12/31/2011. Assets, $649,489 (M); Expenditures, $274,176; Total giving, $141,357; Grants to individuals, 30 grants totaling $26,891.
Fields of interest: Vocational education, post-secondary; Higher education; Scholarships/financial aid.
Type of support: Scholarships—to individuals.
Application information: Applications accepted.
  Send request by: On-line
  Applicants should submit the following:
    1) Transcripts
    2) Financial information
  Additional information: Application should also include financial aid award letter. See web site for additional guidelines.
Program description:
  Scholarships: Scholarships range from $1,500 to $2,500 to students who qualify and reapply yearly. The scholarship can be used to cover tuition expenses and related supplemental educational expenses such as books, lab fees, travel and select cost of living. All applicants are required to "give back" by conducting community service and serving as mentors to younger, aspiring scholars. Applicants must be U.S. citizens, 25 years old or younger, and have a minimum 2.0 GPA.
EIN: 113662240

1818
Catalina Marketing Charitable Foundation
200 Carillon Pkwy.
St. Petersburg, FL   33716-1242
Contact: Bill Protz, Pres.

Foundation type: Company-sponsored foundation
Purpose: Scholarships to underprivileged, single parent youths residing in the Tampa Bay, FL community.
Financial data: Year ended 07/31/2013. Assets, $2,824,070 (M); Expenditures, $263,440; Total giving, $231,511.
Type of support: Scholarships—to individuals.
Application information: Applications not accepted.
  Additional information: Unsolicited requests for funds not considered.
EIN: 330489905

1819
Catholic Charities
134 E. Church St.
Jacksonville, FL   32202-3130   (904) 354-4846
Contact: Jennifer Garizio, Exec. Dir.
URL: http://www.ccbjax.org

Foundation type: Public charity
Purpose: Emergency assistance to indigent residents of Jacksonville, FL through services such as making payments for rent, mortgage or utilities and providing food.
Financial data: Year ended 06/30/2012. Assets, $5,926,779 (M); Expenditures, $9,097,951; Total giving, $4,066,979; Grants to individuals, totaling $4,066,979.
Fields of interest: Housing/shelter, expense aid; Economically disadvantaged.
Type of support: In-kind gifts; Grants for special needs.
Application information:
  Initial approach: Tel.
  Applicants should submit the following:
    1) Financial information

Additional information: Contact foundation for eligibility criteria.
EIN: 590862770

1820
Catholic Charities, Diocese of St. Petersburg, Inc.
1213 16th St. N.
St. Petersburg, FL   33705-1032   (727) 893-1313
Contact: Mark Dufva, Exec. Dir.
FAX: (727) 893-9543; E-mail: mdufva@ccdosp.org; URL: http://www.ccdosp.org/

Foundation type: Public charity
Purpose: Services to indigent residents of St. Petersburg, FL who are in danger of becoming homeless or who are in need of emergency utility assistance. A program for refugees also provides microloans for up to a 3 year repayment term for working capital, inventory, machinery, fixtures, tools, supplies, furniture, and building renovation.
Financial data: Year ended 06/30/2012. Assets, $3,367,825 (M); Expenditures, $9,232,517; Total giving, $2,355,586; Grants to individuals, totaling $2,355,586.
Fields of interest: Immigrants/refugees; Economically disadvantaged.
Type of support: Grants for special needs; Loans—to individuals.
Application information: Applications accepted. Application form required.
  Initial approach: Tel.
  Additional information: For eligibility criteria, contact Jeff Currie at (727) 893-1314 Ext# 223.
EIN: 590875805

1821
B. R. Chamberlain Foundation for Public Enrichment
2845 Marquesas Ct.
Windermere, FL   34786-7824   (800) 613-2506
Contact: Edward E. Gamble, Exec. Dir.
FAX: (800) 613-2506;
E-mail: info@brchamberlainfoundation.org; URL: http://www.brchamberlainfoundation.org/

Foundation type: Public charity
Purpose: Scholarships to students pursuing an A.A. or A.S. degree with at least a 2.0 GPA. Also, scholarships to students at Southern Baptist Association of Christian Schools.
Publications: Application guidelines.
Financial data: Year ended 12/31/2011. Assets, $4,706,415 (M); Expenditures, $129,857; Total giving, $26,500; Grants to individuals, totaling $26,500.
Type of support: Scholarships—to individuals.
Application information: Unsolicited requests for funds not considered or acknowledged.
EIN: 593263469

1822
Change, Inc.
P. O. Box 1818
Sanibel, FL   33957   (239) 433-3457

Foundation type: Public charity
Purpose: Emergency assistance to artists in all disciplines with food, utility, rent and medical expense.
Financial data: Year ended 08/31/2011. Assets, $144,818 (M); Expenditures, $76,136; Total

giving, $75,100; Grants to individuals, totaling $75,100.

Fields of interest: Arts, artist's services; Human services.

Type of support: Emergency funds.

Application information: Applications accepted. Application form not required.

Initial approach: Letter
Send request by: Mail
Copies of proposal: 1
Deadline(s): None
Applicants should submit the following:
  1) Work samples
  2) Financial information
Additional information: Applicant must demonstrate financial need.

EIN: 237086878

1823
Child Care of Southwest Florida, Inc.

6831 Palisades Park Ct., Ste. 6
Fort Myers, FL 33912-7132   (239) 278-1002
Contact: Rhea B. Mike, Exec. Dir.
FAX: (239) 278-3031; E-mail: info@ccswfl.org; Toll free tel.: (888) 290-4114; URL: http://www.ccswfl.org

Foundation type: Public charity
Purpose: Reimbursements to providers for nutritious meals and snacks served to children in the southwest FL, area.
Publications: Annual report.
Financial data: Year ended 06/30/2012. Assets, $2,069,793 (M); Expenditures, $7,381,206; Total giving, $3,060,916; Grants to individuals, totaling $1,035,845.
Fields of interest: Day care.
Type of support: Grants for special needs.
Application information: Applications accepted.

Additional information: Providers must be licensed by the State of FL and have at least one unrelated child in their care, serve meals that meet USDA guidelines, keep accurate records, and submit them to the agency. Contact the agency for additional guidelines.

EIN: 596198583

1824
Children's Dream Fund, Inc.

1 Progress Plz., Ste. 820
St. Petersburg, FL 33701-4349   (727) 896-6390
Contact: Cynthia Lake, Exec. Dir.
FAX: (727) 896-6380;
E-mail: info@childrensdreamfund.org; Mailing address: P.O. Box 1881, St. Petersburg, FL 33731-1881; additional address (Tampa area): 314 S. Plant Ave., Tampa, FL 33606, tel.: (813) 490-9970; toll-free tel.: (800) 456-4543, ext. 6736; URL: http://www.childrensdreamfund.org

Foundation type: Public charity
Purpose: Fulfilling dreams for children ages three to eighteen from Florida's west coast who have been diagnosed with a life-threatening illness.
Publications: Financial statement; Newsletter.
Financial data: Year ended 12/31/2011. Assets, $1,016,004 (M); Expenditures, $967,472; Total giving, $540,049; Grants to individuals, totaling $540,049.
Fields of interest: Children/youth; Terminal illness, people with.
Type of support: In-kind gifts; Grants for special needs.

Application information: Referrals are from hospitals on Florida's west coast.
EIN: 592145821

1825
The Children's Forum, Inc.

(formerly Florida Children's Forum)
2807 Remington Green Cir.
Tallahassee, FL 32308-3752   (850) 681-7002
Contact: Phyllis K. Kalifeh, Pres. and C.E.O.
FAX: (850) 681-9816;
E-mail: info@thechildrensforum.com; Toll-free tel.: (888) 352-4453; E-Mail for Phyllis K. Kalifeh: pkalifeh@thechildrensforum.com; URL: http://www.thechildrensforum.com

Foundation type: Public charity
Purpose: Scholarships to early-childhood caregivers and center directors in FL to work toward earning an AS degree in early childhood education, a CDA credential, a FL state credential or a director credential.
Publications: Application guidelines; Annual report; Informational brochure.
Financial data: Year ended 06/30/2012. Assets, $3,608,995 (M); Expenditures, $8,308,378; Total giving, $3,719,023; Grants to individuals, totaling $3,719,023.
Fields of interest: Children, services; Family services.
Type of support: Scholarships—to individuals.
Application information: Applications accepted.

Additional information: Contact foundation for complete application information.

EIN: 650165007

1826
Children's Home Society of Florida

1485 S. Semoran Blvd., Ste. 1448
Winter Park, FL 32792-5508   (321) 397-3000
Contact: David A. Bundy, Pres. and C.E.O.
E-mail: info@chsfl.org; URL: http://www.chsfl.org/

Foundation type: Public charity
Purpose: Provides adoption services, post-adoption family assistance services, and parent/child relationship counseling services to residents of FL.
Financial data: Year ended 06/30/2011. Assets, $89,202,454 (M); Expenditures, $109,655,084; Total giving, $7,044,343; Grants to individuals, totaling $7,044,343.
Fields of interest: Family services; Children.
Type of support: Grants for special needs.
Application information:

Initial approach: Letter
Additional information: Contact the society for eligibility criteria.

EIN: 590192430

1827
The Christian Sharing Center, Inc.

600 N. Hwy. 17-92, Ste. 158
Longwood, FL 32750-3638   (407) 260-9155
Contact: Angie Romagosa, Pres.
FAX: (407) 332-0535;
E-mail: webmaster@thesharingcenter.org;
URL: http://www.thesharingcenter.org

Foundation type: Public charity
Purpose: Assistance to residents of Seminole county, FL with food, clothing, financial assistance with rent/mortgage, utilities, medical prescription and other special needs to individuals.
Publications: Newsletter.

Financial data: Year ended 09/30/2011. Assets, $344,706 (M); Expenditures, $3,471,290; Total giving, $2,314,385; Grants to individuals, totaling $2,314,385.
Fields of interest: Economically disadvantaged.
Type of support: Grants for special needs.
Application information: Applications not accepted.

Additional information: Unsolicited requests for funds not considered or acknowledged.

EIN: 592744535

1828
Cintas Foundation, Inc.

1450 Brickell Ave., Ste. 1800
Miami, FL 33131   (305) 237-8888
URL: http://www.cintasfoundation.org

Foundation type: Independent foundation
Purpose: Fellowships to individuals of Cuban citizenship or lineage for continuing work outside Cuba in architecture, literature, music composition and the visual arts.
Publications: Application guidelines.
Financial data: Year ended 08/31/2013. Assets, $2,344,969 (M); Expenditures, $124,129; Total giving, $32,500; Grants to individuals, 7 grants totaling $32,500 (high: $7,500, low: $2,500).
Fields of interest: Visual arts; Architecture; Music composition; Literature; Arts.
International interests: Cuba.
Type of support: Fellowships; Foreign applicants.
Application information: Application form required. Application form available on the grantmaker's web site.

Initial approach: Telephone or e-mail
Deadline(s): Aug. 29
Additional information: Application should include two letters of recommendation. See web site for additional guidelines.

Program description:

Fellowship Program: Fellowships are awarded annually in the amount of $10,000 each and are paid in quarterly stipends, beginning in Sept., for twelve consecutive months. The award is limited to artists of Cuban citizenship or direct descent (having a Cuban parent or grandparent). The fellowships are not awarded for academic study or research, or to performing artists and are not awarded more than twice to the same person. Second awards are granted only to candidates demonstrating outstanding artistic development.

EIN: 131980389

1829
Cisneros Fontanals Foundation for the Arts

5960 S.W. 57th Ave.
Miami, FL 33143-2345   (305) 455-3333
Contact: Patricia Garcia-Velez
FAX: (305) 860-9401; E-mail: info@cifo.org; Additional address: 1018 N. Miami Ave., Miami, FL 33136, tel.: (305) 455-3335; URL: http://www.cifo.org/index.php

Foundation type: Company-sponsored foundation
Purpose: Grants to emerging and mid-career contemporary multidisciplinary artists from Latin America.
Publications: Grants list.
Financial data: Year ended 12/31/2012. Assets, $40,546 (M); Expenditures, $1,229,403; Total giving, $94,853; Grants to individuals, 8 grants totaling $94,853 (high: $15,000, low: $8,000).
Fields of interest: Visual arts.
Type of support: Grants to individuals.

Application information:
Deadline(s): None
Additional information: An original project not previously exhibited should be sent to the Selection Committee. Artists are nominated by renowned curators and artists from around the world.
EIN: 542081286

1830
Citrus County Circle of Friends, Inc.
(formerly Mike Hampton Pitching in Foundation)
P.O. Box 1168
Lecanto, FL   34460-1168   (352) 302-8177
E-mail: brenthallgroup@gmail.com

Foundation type: Independent foundation
Purpose: Scholarships only to full-time high school students who are residents of Citrus County, FL. The student will receive up to $2,500 per year, providing that the student remains a full-time student and maintains a 2.0 GPA.
Publications: Financial statement; Informational brochure.
Financial data: Year ended 06/30/2012. Assets, $56,219 (M); Expenditures, $457,962; Total giving, $26,629.
Fields of interest: Higher education.
Type of support: Support to graduates or students of specific schools; Undergraduate support.
Application information: Applications must include three teacher references. Only applications from residents of Citrus County, FL are accepted.
EIN: 760660225

1831
Clark Scholarship Trust
(also known as Grace W. Clark, Thomas R. & Elsie T. Clark Scholarship Trust)
P.O. BOX 40200, FL9-100-10-19
Jacksonville, FL   32203-0200   (804) 788-2673
Contact: Sarah Kay
Application address: 1111 E. Main St., VA2-300-12-92, Richmond, VA 23219

Foundation type: Independent foundation
Purpose: Scholarships primarily to graduating high school seniors of Halifax County, VA.
Financial data: Year ended 12/31/2012. Assets, $1,288,886 (M); Expenditures, $51,402; Total giving, $30,948.
Type of support: Scholarships—to individuals.
Application information: Applications accepted. Application form required.
Initial approach: Letter or telephone
Deadline(s): May 1
Applicants should submit the following:
1) GPA
2) Financial information
EIN: 540907369

1832
The Clint Foundation
1015 Atlantic Blvd., PMB 252
Atlantic Beach, FL   32233-3313
URL: http://www.clintfoundation.org

Foundation type: Independent foundation
Purpose: Scholarships to students who will work during the school year to help pay a portion of their own education costs.
Financial data: Year ended 03/31/2013. Assets, $301,777 (M); Expenditures, $54,176; Total giving, $51,000.

Fields of interest: Higher education; Scholarships/ financial aid.
Type of support: Undergraduate support.
Application information: Students who participate in this program must earn some of the money required for their education, maintain passing grades and make a moral commitment to give back to others in the future.
EIN: 593226849

1833
Sarah Cohen Scholarship Fund
c/o Bank of America, N.A.
P.O. Box 40200, FL9-100-10-19
Jacksonville, FL   32203-0200   (804) 625-4595
Application address: c/o Attn.: Ohef Sholom Temple, Rabbi, Stockley Gardens, 530 Raleigh Ave., Norfolk, VA 23507-2116

Foundation type: Independent foundation
Purpose: Scholarships to residents of Norfolk, VA.
Financial data: Year ended 12/31/2012. Assets, $282,719 (M); Expenditures, $9,948; Total giving, $4,500.
Type of support: Scholarships—to individuals.
Application information: Applications accepted. Application form not required.
Initial approach: Letter
Deadline(s): Aug. 1
EIN: 546033744

1834
The Colen Foundation, Inc.
(formerly The On Top of the World Foundation, Inc.)
8447 S.W. 99th St.
Ocala, FL   34481-4547

Foundation type: Independent foundation
Purpose: Grants to support and assist aged individuals maintain a modest standard of living during their declining years.
Financial data: Year ended 11/30/2012. Assets, $8,305,316 (M); Expenditures, $559,703; Total giving, $497,773; Grant to an individual, 1 grant totaling $725.
Fields of interest: Aging.
Type of support: Grants for special needs.
Application information: Applications accepted. Application form required.
Initial approach: Letter
Send request by: Mail
Copies of proposal: 2
Deadline(s): None
Final notification: Applicants notified within six months
EIN: 592474711

1835
The Columbus Phipps Foundation
P.O. Box 40200, FL9-100-10-19
Jacksonville, FL   32203-0200
Application address: c/o Paul D. Buchanan, Tr., P.O. Box 1145, Clintwood, VA 24228-1145

Foundation type: Independent foundation
Purpose: Scholarships to high school graduates of Dickenson County, VA. Scholarships are renewable.
Financial data: Year ended 03/31/2013. Assets, $17,544,856 (M); Expenditures, $856,301; Total giving, $662,572.
Type of support: Support to graduates or students of specific schools; Undergraduate support.
Application information: Applications accepted.

Initial approach: Letter
Deadline(s): May 15 for new applications, June 15 for renewal applications
Applicants should submit the following:
1) Financial information
2) Essay
3) GPA
4) ACT
5) SAT
Additional information: Application should include references and copy of returned Pell Grant Index form.
EIN: 546338751

1836
Common Knowledge Scholarship Foundation, Inc.
P.O. Box 290361
Davie, FL   33329-0361   (561) 750-1040
Contact: Daryl Hulce
E-mail: info@cksf.org; *URL:* http://www.cksf.org

Foundation type: Public charity
Purpose: Scholarships to high school, college, and graduate students competing in on-line exams.
Financial data: Year ended 12/31/2011. Assets, $106,054 (M); Expenditures, $121,048; Total giving, $16,750; Grants to individuals, totaling $16,750.
Fields of interest: Education.
Type of support: Scholarships—to individuals.
Application information:
Deadline(s): None
Additional information: Scholarships are available on a monthly basis and are announced 15 to 30 days in advance of the start date. See web site for scholarship availability.
EIN: 651101565

1837
Community Coordinated Care for Children, Inc.
3500 W. Colonial Dr.
Orlando, FL   32808-7902   (407) 522-2252
Contact: Jeremy Sloane, Chair.
Additional address (Osceola County office): 2220 E. Irlo Bronson Memorial Hwy., Unit 7, Kissimmee, FL 34744-5312; *URL:* http://www.4corlando.org

Foundation type: Public charity
Purpose: Assistance for child-care providers and families throughout Brevard, Orange, Osceola, and Seminole Counties, FL.
Financial data: Year ended 12/31/2011. Assets, $10,868,928 (M); Expenditures, $144,557,144; Total giving, $125,835,419; Grants to individuals, totaling $125,835,419.
Fields of interest: Children/youth, services; Day care; Family services; Human services.
Type of support: Grants to individuals.
Application information: Applications accepted.
Additional information: Contact the agency for eligibility determination.
EIN: 591371754

1838

The Community Foundation, Inc.

(formerly The Community Foundation in Jacksonville, also known as The Community Foundation in Jacksonville)
245 Riverside Ave., Ste. 310
Jacksonville, FL 32202 (904) 356-4483
FAX: (904) 356-7910; E-mail: info@jaxcf.org; Grant application e-mail: applications@jaxcf.org;
URL: http://www.jaxcf.org

Foundation type: Community foundation
Purpose: Grants to emerging artists in the visual, literary, and performing arts who are legal residents of Nassau, Baker, Duval, Clay or St. Johns counties in northeastern FL.
Publications: Application guidelines; Annual report; Informational brochure; Newsletter.
Financial data: Year ended 12/31/2012. Assets, $257,249,260 (M); Expenditures, $33,308,777; Total giving, $30,647,352; Grants to individuals, 47 grants totaling $58,888.
Fields of interest: Visual arts; Performing arts; Literature; Arts, artist's services; Arts.
Type of support: Grants to individuals.
Application information: Application form required. Application form available on the grantmaker's web site.
    Send request by: Mail or hand-delivered
    Copies of proposal: 1
    Deadline(s): June 13
    Final notification: Applicants notified by Nov. 1
    Applicants should submit the following:
        1) Letter(s) of recommendation
        2) Budget Information
        3) Proposal
        4) Resume
        5) Work samples
    Additional information: See web site for application form.
Program description:
    Art Ventures: Individual Artists: Grants of up to $3,500 are available to support individual artists as they advance their work. Applicants must be at least 18 years of age, and have resided in Baker, Clay, Duval, Nassau or St. Johns counties for at least 12 months at the time of application.
EIN: 596150746

1839

Community Foundation for Palm Beach and Martin Counties, Inc.

(formerly Palm Beach County Community Foundation)
700 S. Dixie Hwy., Ste. 200
West Palm Beach, FL 33401-5854 (561) 659-6800
Contact: For grants: Jillian C. Vukusich, V.P., Community Investment
FAX: (561) 832-6542; E-mail: info@cfpbmc.org; Additional tel.: (888) 853-4438; Grant application e-mail: grants@cfpbmc.org; URL: http://www.yourcommunityfoundation.org
Additional URL: http://www.cfpbmc.org

Foundation type: Community foundation
Purpose: Scholarships to graduating high school seniors who are residents of Palm Beach County or Martin County, FL.
Publications: Application guidelines; Annual report (including application guidelines); Grants list; Informational brochure; Newsletter.
Financial data: Year ended 06/30/2012. Assets, $141,319,630 (M); Expenditures, $10,957,640; Total giving, $7,974,419.
Fields of interest: Media/communications; Print publishing; Performing arts, education; Arts;

Vocational education, post-secondary; Higher education; Business school/education; Law school/education; Teacher school/education; Athletics/sports, training; Leadership development.
Type of support: Scholarships—to individuals; Support to graduates or students of specific schools; Technical education support; Undergraduate support.
Application information: Applications accepted. Application form required. Application form available on the grantmaker's web site. Interview required.
    Initial approach: Application
    Send request by: Online
    Deadline(s): Feb. 1
    Applicants should submit the following:
        1) SAR
        2) ACT
    Additional information: See web site for complete program listings and guidelines.
Program description:
    Scholarship Program: All scholarships are for colleges, universities, or vocational schools in the United States. Individual awards vary from a one-time award of $750 to multiple year awards of $2,500 per year. Scholarship awards may be used for tuition, fees, and room and board. Students may apply for more than one scholarship. Most of the scholarships require that applicants be a graduating high school senior in Palm Beach or Martin County, a resident of Palm Beach or Martin County, demonstrate financial need, plan to attend an accredited two or four-year college, university or vocational school, be a full-time student, and demonstrate academic achievement. See web site for additional information.
EIN: 237181875

1840

Community Foundation of Brevard

(formerly Community Foundation of Brevard County, Inc.)
1361 Bedford Dr., Ste. 102
Melbourne, FL 32940 (321) 752-5505
Contact: Sandi Scannelli, C.E.O.; For scholarship inquiries: Robert D. Watts, Grants Mgr.
Scholarship submission e-mail: foundation@cfbrevard.org
E-mail: info@cfbrevard.org; URL: http://www.cfbrevard.org

Foundation type: Community foundation
Purpose: Scholarships to help local students of Brevard county, FL pursue their dreams and goals at accredited colleges and universities.
Publications: Application guidelines; Grants list; Informational brochure.
Financial data: Year ended 12/31/2012. Assets, $12,708,264 (M); Expenditures, $1,934,668; Total giving, $1,580,896.
Fields of interest: Higher education.
Type of support: Scholarships—to individuals; Support to graduates or students of specific schools; Undergraduate support.
Application information: Applications accepted. Application form required. Application form available on the grantmaker's web site.
    Initial approach: Application
    Send request by: E-mail
    Deadline(s): June 25
    Applicants should submit the following:
        1) Essay
        2) Letter(s) of recommendation
        3) FAFSA
        4) Transcripts
        5) SAR

Additional information: Each scholarship has its own specific purpose and eligibility criteria. See web site for a complete listing.
EIN: 592114988

1841

Community Foundation of Broward

(formerly Broward Community Foundation, Inc.)
910 E. Las Olas Blvd., Ste. 200
Fort Lauderdale, FL 33301 (954) 761-9503
Contact: Linda B. Carter, C.E.O.; For grant applications: Sheri Brown, V.P., Grants and Initiatives
FAX: (954) 761-7102;
E-mail: lcarter@cfbroward.org; Tel. for Sheri Brown: (954) 761-9503, ext. 103; Grant application E-mail: sbrown@cfbroward.org; URL: http://www.cfbroward.org

Foundation type: Community foundation
Purpose: Scholarships primarily to graduating high school seniors and adults from Broward County, FL, to pursue a higher education.
Publications: Application guidelines; Annual report; Financial statement; Informational brochure (including application guidelines); Newsletter.
Financial data: Year ended 06/30/2012. Assets, $99,120,940 (M); Expenditures, $6,951,945; Total giving, $4,632,340.
Fields of interest: Education.
Type of support: Scholarships—to individuals; Support to graduates or students of specific schools; Graduate support; Undergraduate support.
Application information: Applications accepted. Application form required. Application form available on the grantmaker's web site.
    Send request by: Mail
    Copies of proposal: 1
    Deadline(s): Apr. 15
    Final notification: Applicants will be notified by Aug. 15
    Applicants should submit the following:
        1) Transcripts
        2) SAT
        3) SAR
        4) Proposal
        5) Letter(s) of recommendation
        6) GPA
        7) Financial information
        8) FAFSA
        9) Essay
        10) ACT
    Additional information: Contact foundation for complete program information.
EIN: 592477112

1842

Community Foundation of Central Florida, Inc.

1411 Edgewater Dr., Ste. 203
Orlando, FL 32804-6361 (407) 872-3050
Contact: Mark Brewer, C.E.O.
FAX: (407) 425-2990; E-mail: info@cfcflorida.org; Additional Address: P.O. Box 2071, Orlando, FL 32802; URL: http://www.cfcflorida.org

Foundation type: Community foundation
Purpose: Educational grants to students of Winter Haven High School, FL, and Lake Region High School, Eagle Lake, FL, who are also residents of Winter Haven, FL.
Publications: Application guidelines; Annual report; Financial statement; Grants list; Informational brochure; Informational brochure (including application guidelines); Newsletter.

Financial data: Year ended 04/30/2013. Assets, $58,085,963 (M); Expenditures, $5,854,187; Total giving, $4,796,146.
Fields of interest: Higher education; Scholarships/financial aid.
Type of support: Scholarships—to individuals; Support to graduates or students of specific schools.
Application information: Contact high school for current application deadline/guidelines.
EIN: 593182886

1843
Community Foundation of Collier County
2400 Tamiami Trail N., Ste. 300
Naples, FL 34103-4435 (239) 649-5000
Contact: For scholarships: Annette Kirk, Grants and Scholarships Coord.
Scholarship inquiry e-mail: akirk@cfcollier.org
FAX: (239) 649-5337;
E-mail: ekeesler@cfcollier.org; URL: http://www.cfcollier.org

Foundation type: Community foundation
Purpose: Scholarships to students from Collier County, FL for higher education.
Publications: Application guidelines; Annual report (including application guidelines); Newsletter.
Financial data: Year ended 06/30/2012. Assets, $63,470,740 (M); Expenditures, $7,449,356; Total giving, $5,719,879; Grants to individuals, 82 grants totaling $171,346.
Fields of interest: Higher education.
Type of support: Scholarships—to individuals.
Application information: Applications accepted. Application form required. Application form available on the grantmaker's web site.
   Initial approach: Application
   Send request by: Mail
   Deadline(s): Mar. 1
   Final notification: Applicants notified by May 12
   Additional information: See web site for a complete listing of scholarships.
Program description:
   Scholarships: Scholarship funds can assist needy students or support a specific education initiative or scholarship fund at a school, college or university. The donor may stay involved as an advisor, name an advisory committee to assist in the selection of recipients, or allow the foundation to select students based upon specific criteria. The foundation has several scholarship funds to assist worthy students in meeting their educational expenses.
EIN: 592396243

1844
The Community Foundation of Sarasota County, Inc.
(formerly The Sarasota County Community Foundation, Inc.)
2635 Fruitville Rd.
Sarasota, FL 34237-5222 (941) 955-3000
Contact: For grants: Patricia Martin, Mgr., Grants and Community Initiatives; For scholarships: Earl Young, Mgr. Scholarships and Special Initiatives
Scholarship inquiries: tel. (941) 556-7114 or e-mail eyoung@cfsarasota.org
FAX: (941) 952-1951; E-mail: info@cfsarasota.org; URL: http://www.cfsarasota.org

Foundation type: Community foundation
Purpose: Scholarships, awards and professional support to financially needy residents of Charlotte, Manatee, and Sarasota counties, FL.

Publications: Application guidelines; Annual report; Grants list; Informational brochure; Newsletter; Occasional report; Program policy statement.
Financial data: Year ended 05/31/2012. Assets, $194,496,143 (M); Expenditures, $16,775,811; Total giving, $12,417,812.
Fields of interest: Vocational education, post-secondary; Higher education; Scholarships/financial aid; Health care.
Type of support: Scholarships—to individuals; Support to graduates or students of specific schools; Awards/prizes; Undergraduate support.
Application information: Applications accepted. Application form required. Application form available on the grantmaker's web site.
   Initial approach: Application
   Send request by: Online
   Copies of proposal: 1
   Deadline(s): Varies
   Additional information: See web site for complete listing of scholarships.
Program description:
   Scholarships: The foundation has a number of scholarship opportunities for traditional students which include high school seniors and those who are 24-years-old, or younger. Selections are based on financial need, leadership potential, academic performance, work experience and commitment to school and community through volunteerism. Some are restricted to students from a specific high school or area of residence. Others are restricted to those pursuing a particular field of study, or a member of a minority. There are also some scholarships available for adult learners to be students who are returning to vocational school or college after having been out of high school for a number of years. See web site for additional information.
EIN: 591956886

1845
Community Foundation of South Lake County, Inc.
(formerly South Lake County Community Foundation, Inc.)
2150 Oakley Seaver Dr.
Clermont, FL 34711-1964 (352) 394-3818
Contact: For grants: Jessica Whitehouse, Prog. Mgr.
FAX: (352) 394-7739;
E-mail: foundationinfo@cfslc.org; Additional e-mail: jessica@cfslc.org; URL: http://www.cfslc.org

Foundation type: Community foundation
Purpose: Scholarships for college-bound residents of South Lake County, FL for continuing education at accredited colleges or universities.
Publications: Application guidelines; Annual report; Financial statement; Grants list; Informational brochure; Newsletter.
Financial data: Year ended 09/30/2012. Assets, $10,758,106 (M); Expenditures, $586,882; Total giving, $239,335; Grants to individuals, 67 grants totaling $51,250.
Fields of interest: Higher education; Scholarships/financial aid.
Type of support: Scholarships—to individuals; Undergraduate support.
Application information: Applications accepted. Application form required. Application form available on the grantmaker's web site.
   Initial approach: Application
   Send request by: Mail
   Deadline(s): Mar. 30
   Applicants should submit the following:
      1) FAFSA
      2) Transcripts
      3) Essay

      4) Letter(s) of recommendation
      5) Resume
   Additional information: Each scholarship has specific requirements as defined by the organization/individual who has established the scholarship. See web site for complete list of scholarships and eligibility criteria.
EIN: 593343026

1846
Community Foundation of Tampa Bay, Inc.
(formerly The Community Foundation of Greater Tampa, Inc.)
550 N. Reo St., Ste. 301
Tampa, FL 33609-1037 (813) 282-1975
FAX: (813) 282-3119;
E-mail: aberg@cftampabay.org; Grant application e-mail: grantapps@cftampabay.org; URL: http://www.cftampabay.org

Foundation type: Community foundation
Purpose: Scholarships to students from Hillsborough, Pasco, and Pinellas counties, FL for higher education.
Publications: Application guidelines; Annual report; Annual report (including application guidelines); Financial statement; Informational brochure; Newsletter.
Financial data: Year ended 06/30/2012. Assets, $146,563,030 (M); Expenditures, $10,740,625; Total giving, $9,258,068; Grants to individuals, 135 grants totaling $277,347.
Fields of interest: Higher education.
Type of support: Scholarships—to individuals.
Application information: Applications accepted.
   Additional information: Scholarships are awarded annually and are available through several means. See web site or contact your school's guidance counselor for available scholarships.
EIN: 593001853

1847
Community Foundation of the Florida Keys, Inc.
300 Southard St., Ste. 201
Key West, FL 33040 (305) 292-1502
Contact: Dianna Sutton, C.E.O.
FAX: (305) 292-1598; E-mail: cffk@cffk.org; URL: http://www.cffk.org

Foundation type: Community foundation
Purpose: Scholarships to residents of Monroe County, FL.
Publications: Financial statement; Grants list; Informational brochure; Newsletter; Occasional report.
Financial data: Year ended 06/30/2012. Assets, $8,050,525 (M); Expenditures, $1,132,491; Total giving, $675,102; Grants to individuals, totaling $149,595.
Type of support: Research; Scholarships—to individuals; Undergraduate support.
Application information: Applications not accepted.
   Additional information: Unsolicited requests for funds not considered or acknowledged.
EIN: 650648968

1848
The Community Foundation Trust of Sarasota County
2635 Fruitville Rd.
Sarasota, FL 34237 (941) 955-3000
Contact: Roxie Jerde, Pres. and C.E.O.
FAX: (941) 952-1951; E-mail: roxie@cfsarasota.org;
URL: http://www.sarasota-foundation.org

Foundation type: Public charity
Purpose: Scholarships to graduating seniors as well as nontraditional students who may be re-entering higher education to attend accredited colleges, or universities or accredited trade or vocational schools.
Financial data: Year ended 05/31/2012. Assets, $39,732,101 (M); Expenditures, $3,058,340; Total giving, $1,723,465; Grants to individuals, totaling $581,250.
Fields of interest: Vocational education, post-secondary; Higher education.
Type of support: Scholarships—to individuals.
Application information: Applications accepted. Application form required.
　Deadline(s): Mar. for Traditional, Sept. for Non-traditional
　Additional information: Application must include you or your parents 1040 tax forms and two letters of reference. Scholarship awards are based on financial need, leadership potential, academic achievement, work experience, school and community activities. See web site for additional application guidelines.
EIN: 650173371

1849
Community Service Foundation, Inc.
925 Lakeview Rd.
Clearwater, FL 33756-3420
Contact: Jerry Spilatro, Exec. Dir.
FAX: (727) 443-6287;
E-mail: jspilatro@csfhome.org; URL: http://www.csfhome.org

Foundation type: Public charity
Purpose: Assistance to Pinellas County, FL families and individuals to give them the opportunity and experience of home ownership.
Publications: Annual report.
Financial data: Year ended 09/30/2011. Assets, $4,402,939 (M); Expenditures, $920,293; Total giving, $19,243; Grants to individuals, totaling $19,243.
Type of support: Grants for special needs.
Application information: Applications not accepted.
　Additional information: Unsolicited requests for funds not considered or acknowledged.
EIN: 590866939

1850
Conn Memorial Foundation
3410 Henderson Blvd., Ste. 200
Tampa, FL 33609-3975
Contact: Beth Doyle, Grant Dir.
tel./fax: (813) 554-1210;
email: Beth@connfoundation.org; URL: http://www.connfoundation.org

Foundation type: Independent foundation
Purpose: Scholarships to residents of Hillsborough County, FL.
Publications: Application guidelines; Informational brochure (including application guidelines); Multi-year report.

Financial data: Year ended 07/31/2013. Assets, $22,982,249 (M); Expenditures, $1,495,902; Total giving, $1,024,000.
Type of support: Scholarships—to individuals.
Application information: Applications accepted. Application form required.
　Initial approach: Letter
　Deadline(s): May 31 and Nov. 30
　Additional information: Application should include financial information.
EIN: 590978713

1851
Corbett Student Loan Program
(formerly Laura R & William Corbett Trust)
P.O. Box 40200, FL9-100-10-19
Jacksonville, FL 32203-0200

Foundation type: Independent foundation
Purpose: Low-interest loans to medical students attending the University of South Carolina School of Medicine.
Financial data: Year ended 12/31/2012. Assets, $3,640,513 (M); Expenditures, $49,710; Total giving, $0.
Fields of interest: Medical school/education.
Type of support: Student loans—to individuals; Support to graduates or students of specific schools; Graduate support.
Application information: Applications accepted. Application form required.
　Initial approach: Letter or telephone
　Deadline(s): Sept. 16
　Applicants should submit the following:
　　1) Financial information
　　2) Budget Information
　Additional information: Applications available at the Office of Student Affairs at the School of Medicine.
Program description:
　Corbett Trust Loan Program: The primary program is for long-term loans to cover costs associated with medical education and provides for extended repayment. The secondary program is for short-term loans designed to meet emergency needs and to be repaid within one calendar year, or upon leaving school, whichever occurs first. A student borrower's indebtedness under the trust's long-term program will not exceed $3,500 per year with a cumulative indebtedness of $14,000 per individual. Under the short-term program, qualified students may borrow up to $1,000 for a period not to exceed one year. This program is to be used as an emergency fund and must be repaid within one year.
EIN: 570685862

1852
Council of St. Petersburg Diocese Society of St. Vincent de Paul, Inc.
4556 S. Manhattan Ave., Ste. A
Tampa, FL 33611-2332 (813) 831-5100
Contact: Marvin Robert, Pres.
FAX: (813) 831-5105; E-mail: ropert@svdpccsp.org;
URL: http://www.svdpccsp.org/

Foundation type: Public charity
Purpose: Grants to the needy and suffering in the Diocese of St. Petersburg, FL.
Financial data: Year ended 09/30/2011. Assets, $62,868 (M); Expenditures, $53,949; Total giving, $17,222.
Fields of interest: Catholic agencies & churches; Economically disadvantaged.
Type of support: Grants for special needs.

Application information: Applications accepted. Application form not required.
　Initial approach: Letter or telephone
EIN: 592617093

1853
The Michael G. Cousin Foundation Inc.
(formerly American Charity Council, Inc.)
9155 94th Ave. N.
Largo, FL 33777-2142 (727) 394-2501
Contact: Michael G. Cousin, Pres.

Foundation type: Operating foundation
Purpose: Financial assistance to an individual who donates services to assist those in distress to prepare for, during and in the aftermath of major disasters.
Financial data: Year ended 12/31/2011. Assets, $50,843 (M); Expenditures, $8,606; Total giving, $6,290.
Fields of interest: Safety/disasters.
Type of support: Grants for special needs.
Application information: Contact the foundation for additional information.
EIN: 593696286

1854
Crealde School of Art
600 St. Andrews Blvd.
Winter Park, FL 32792-2594 (407) 671-1886
Contact: Peter Schreyer, Exec. Dir.
FAX: (407) 671-0311;
E-mail: pschreyer@crealde.org; URL: http://www.crealde.org

Foundation type: Public charity
Purpose: Scholarships to art students who are experiencing economic hardship.
Publications: Newsletter.
Financial data: Year ended 12/31/2011. Assets, $1,133,048 (M); Expenditures, $916,538.
Fields of interest: Arts education; Economically disadvantaged.
Type of support: Scholarships—to individuals.
Application information: Scholarships are determined by income level, economic hardship and talent.
EIN: 591887887

1855
Darden Dimes, Inc.
1000 Darden Ctr. Dr., Corp. Tax Dept.
Orlando, FL 32837-4032 (407) 245-5542
Contact: Daisy Ng., Chair. and C.E.O.

Foundation type: Public charity
Purpose: Financial assistance to indigent residents of the Orlando, FL area for natural disaster relief and unexpected financial catastrophes.
Financial data: Year ended 05/31/2012. Assets, $3,706,413 (M); Expenditures, $1,783,902; Total giving, $1,783,708; Grants to individuals, totaling $1,783,708.
Fields of interest: Economically disadvantaged.
Type of support: Emergency funds.
Application information: Applications not accepted.
　Additional information: Unsolicited requests for funds not considered or acknowledged.
EIN: 593525641

1856
Jesse David & Katie B. Bundy Scholarship Trust

P.O. Box 40200, FL9-100-10-19
Jacksonville, FL 32203-0200 (866) 461-7287

Foundation type: Independent foundation
Purpose: Scholarship to residents of Wilkes County, NC, who are enrolled in educational programs leading to medical careers in technical and supporting fields.
Financial data: Year ended 08/31/2013. Assets, $914,442 (M); Expenditures, $6,519; Total giving, $2,400.
Type of support: Undergraduate support.
Application information: Applications accepted. Application form required.
> *Initial approach:* Letter
> *Applicants should submit the following:*
>   1) Class rank
>   2) SAT
>   3) GPA
>   4) Essay
>   5) Letter(s) of recommendation
>   6) SAR
>   7) Financial information
>   8) Transcripts
> *Additional information:* Contact trust for current application deadline/guidelines.

EIN: 566501861

1857
DeBartolo Family Foundation

15436 N. Florida Ave., Ste. 200
Tampa, FL 33613-1226 (813) 964-8302
Contact: Melissa Johnson, Exec. Dir.
FAX: (813) 964-8321;
E-mail: mjohnson@debartoloholdings.com;
URL: http://www.debartolofamilyfoundation.com

Foundation type: Independent foundation
Purpose: Scholarships to students who reside in FL for college education.
Publications: Grants list; Newsletter.
Financial data: Year ended 01/31/2013. Assets, $3,151,836 (M); Expenditures, $912,291; Total giving, $417,189; Grants to individuals, 32 grants totaling $87,459 (high: $9,959, low: $2,500).
Fields of interest: College.
Type of support: Undergraduate support.
Application information: Applications accepted. Application form required. Application form available on the grantmaker's web site.
> *Initial approach:* Download application from foundation web site
> *Deadline(s):* Apr. 15
> *Additional information:* See web site for application guidelines.

EIN: 311739677

1858
The Thomas and Elsie Deeley Foundation

9580 Sloane St.
Orlando, FL 32827 (407) 851-0252
Contact: Thomas E. Deeley, Jr., Dir.

Foundation type: Independent foundation
Purpose: Scholarships to graduating seniors of Sacred Heart High School, CT for postsecondary education.
Financial data: Year ended 06/30/2013. Assets, $1,163,665 (M); Expenditures, $36,013; Total giving, $28,888.
Fields of interest: Higher education.

Type of support: Scholarships—to individuals; Support to graduates or students of specific schools.
Application information: Application form required. Application form available on the grantmaker's web site. Interview required.
> *Initial approach:* Letter or telephone
> *Send request by:* Online
> *Deadline(s):* Jan. 31
> *Applicants should submit the following:*
>   1) Essay
>   2) Financial information
>   3) Letter(s) of recommendation
> *Additional information:* Selection is based on academic accomplishment, community involvement, work experience, extra-curricular activity, financial need, and college goals.

Program descriptions:
> *Fairfield University Scholarship:* Scholarships of up to $96,000 for four years to students at Fairfield University, CT. The scholarship applies to both tuition and room and board. All applicants must meet the entrance and financial need requirements of Fairfield University. Only candidates who are accepted by Fairfield University and meet the University's financial need requirements are eligible.
> *General Scholarships:* Scholarships of up to $48,000 for four years are awarded to seniors at Sacred Heart High School. These scholarships can be applied toward tuition costs at any college or university. Candidates must meet the financial need requirements of the school they are planning to attend. The foundation at times makes partial awards to deserving students.
> *Quinnipiac University and Southern Connecticut State University Scholarship:* Scholarships of up to $48,000 for four years are awarded to seniors of Sacred Heart High School who have been accepted to Quinnipiac University or Southern Connecticut State University. Only those candidates who are accepted by the schools and meet their financial need requirements are eligible to receive the scholarship.

EIN: 541780341

1859
Delta Sigma Dental Educational Foundation Inc.

(also known as Delta Sigma Dental Educational Foundation, Inc.)
11971 Bramble Cove Dr.
Fort Myers, FL 33905

Foundation type: Operating foundation
Purpose: Educational loans to students attending dental schools with an undergraduate chapter of Delta Sigma Delta.
Financial data: Year ended 06/30/2013. Assets, $668,254 (M); Expenditures, $29,041; Total giving, $14,386; Grants to individuals, 13 grants totaling $10,476 (high: $2,000, low: $125).
Fields of interest: Dental school/education; Students, sororities/fraternities.
Type of support: Student loans—to individuals.
Application information: Applications accepted.
> *Deadline(s):* None
> *Additional information:* Applications available from a Deputy at Delta Sigma Delta.

EIN: 386089377

1860
Wayne M. Densch Charities, Inc.

P.O. Box 536845
Orlando, FL 32853-6845

Foundation type: Operating foundation
Purpose: Grants to economically disadvantaged individuals, primarily in FL, for medical and food assistance.
Financial data: Year ended 12/31/2012. Assets, $16,032,097 (M); Expenditures, $1,262,621; Total giving, $516,900.
Fields of interest: Health care; Food services; Economically disadvantaged.
Type of support: Grants for special needs.
Application information: Applications accepted.
> *Initial approach:* Letter
> *Deadline(s):* None
> *Additional information:* Application should include financial information.

EIN: 582013696

1861
Dick DeVoe Buick Cadillac Scholarship Trust

c/o William Gresh
4035 10th St. N.
Naples, FL 34103-2304 (239) 261-3538

Foundation type: Company-sponsored foundation
Purpose: Scholarships to graduates of Naples High School, FL for college education. Recipients of FL prepaid tuition scholarships must be students of Collier county or Estero high schools.
Financial data: Year ended 12/31/2011. Assets, $20,767 (M); Expenditures, $114,315; Total giving, $113,246; Grants to individuals, 9 grants totaling $113,246 (high: $13,406, low: $6,000).
Fields of interest: Higher education; Scholarships/financial aid.
Type of support: Scholarships—to individuals; Support to graduates or students of specific schools.
Application information: Applications accepted.
> *Initial approach:* Letter
> *Applicants should submit the following:*
>   1) Class rank
>   2) GPA
> *Additional information:* Application should include address, extracurricular activities, honors/awards, state test scores, and demonstration of need.

EIN: 237296264

1862
Diocesan Council of Orlando - Society of St. Vincent de Paul

770 S. Orange Blossom Trail
Apopka, FL 32703-9170 (407) 880-3126
URL: http://www.svdporlando.org

Foundation type: Public charity
Purpose: Provides emergency support to individuals in need in the Orlando, FL area with food, clothing, rent and utilities.
Financial data: Year ended 09/30/2011. Assets, $1,645,443 (M); Expenditures, $2,470,266; Total giving, $1,794,208; Grants to individuals, totaling $1,794,208.
Fields of interest: Human services, emergency aid; Economically disadvantaged.
Type of support: Emergency funds.
Application information: Contact the agency for eligibility determination.

EIN: 592948683

1863
Distilled Spirits Wholesalers of Florida Education Foundation, Inc.
215 S. Monroe St., Ste. 800A
Tallahassee, FL 32301-1858 (850) 681-8700
Contact: Scott Ashley

Foundation type: Public charity
Purpose: Scholarships to students in FL who have completed their sophomore year in a College of Business at any of the nine universities in the Florida University system.
Financial data: Year ended 06/30/2013. Assets, $219,386 (M); Expenditures, $1,362.
Type of support: Support to graduates or students of specific schools.
Application information: Applications accepted. Application form required.
   Initial approach: Letter
   Deadline(s): Mar. 31
   Applicants should submit the following:
     1) Photograph
     2) Transcripts
     3) Financial information
EIN: 237002435

1864
Howard W. Dunbar Scholarship Trust A
P.O. Box 1908
Orlando, FL 32802-1908
Contact: Sally A. Ware
Application address: c/o SunTrust Bank South Fl, 14050 N.W. 14th St., Ste. 100, Sunrise, Fl 33323, Application Address:Attn: Malinda L. Tedrow C/O Sun Trust Bank, P.O. Box 1689, Orlando., FL 32802

Foundation type: Independent foundation
Purpose: Scholarships to students pursuing a career in engineering with demonstrated financial need.
Financial data: Year ended 08/31/2013. Assets, $569,043 (M); Expenditures, $40,785; Total giving, $28,447.
Fields of interest: Engineering school/education.
Type of support: Scholarships—to individuals.
Application information: Applications accepted. Application form required.
   Initial approach: Letter
   Copies of proposal: 1
   Deadline(s): July 31
   Applicants should submit the following:
     1) Photograph
     2) Letter(s) of recommendation
     3) Transcripts
     4) GPA
     5) Financial information
   Additional information: Application should also include a copy of parents' and applicant's most recent tax returns.
EIN: 656000044

1865
Alfred I. duPont Foundation, Inc.
10140 Centurion Pkwy. N.
Jacksonville, FL 32256-0532 (904) 697-4123
Contact: Rosemary C. Wills, Secy.

Foundation type: Independent foundation
Purpose: Giving primarily to elderly persons residing in the souteheastern U.S., who are in distressed situations requiring health, economic, or educational assistance.
Financial data: Year ended 12/31/2012. Assets, $42,372,929 (M); Expenditures, $1,975,333; Total giving, $1,600,615; Grants to individuals,

124 grants totaling $368,700 (high: $6,500, low: $350).
Fields of interest: Aging; Economically disadvantaged.
Type of support: Grants for special needs.
Application information: Applications accepted. Application form required.
   Initial approach: Letter
   Deadline(s): None
EIN: 591297267

1866
The Education Foundation of Palm Beach County
3300 Forest Hill Blvd., Bldg. E, Ste. 50-116
West Palm Beach, FL 33406-5813 (561) 434-7303
Contact: Mary Kay Murray, Exec. Dir.
FAX: (561) 357-5900;
E-mail: murraymk@palmbeach.k12.fl.us;
URL: http://www.palmbeachschools.org/edfoundation/

Foundation type: Public charity
Purpose: Project grants to outstanding teachers in Palm Beach County, FL.
Publications: Application guidelines.
Financial data: Year ended 06/30/2012. Assets, $2,151,815 (M); Expenditures, $1,187,164; Total giving, $370,763; Grants to individuals, totaling $68,250.
Fields of interest: Education.
Type of support: Project support.
Application information: Application form required. Application form available on the grantmaker's web site.
   Deadline(s): June for Citibank, Mar. 31, July 31 and Nov. 30 for Mini-Grants
   Additional information: Contact foundation for current deadlines.
Program descriptions:
   Beginning Teacher of the Year Award: These $1,000 awards are presented annually to an outstanding elementary, middle, and high school first-year school teacher employed by the Palm Beach County School District who has made noteworthy growth in their first year of teaching. Awards may be used for planning lessons and/or supplies for their classrooms.
   License for Learning Mini-Grant Program: The program awards mini-grants for educational programs to support the development of innovative programs that enhance the education opportunities for students in Palm Beach County public schools. Priority will be given to grant proposals that focus on the following: original, creative, and innovative teaching approaches that address student need; projects towards literacy, career education, science, technology, engineering, art, and mathematics; and measurable approaches and clearly-defined processes to evaluate success in academic achievement and bridging barriers to learning. The maximum individual mini-grant award is $1,000; the maximum team mini-grant award is $2,000.
   William Dwyer Awards For Excellence in Education: In recognition of outstanding achievement, support and excellence in teaching, the foundation, in partnership with the Economic Council of Palm Beach County, recognizes exemplary teachers for their vested interest in quality public education.
EIN: 592420369

1867
The Education Fund, Inc.
(formerly Dade Public Education Fund, Inc.)
900 N.E. 125th St., Ste. 110
North Miami, FL 33161-5745 (305) 892-5099
Contact: Linda Lecht, Pres.
FAX: (305) 892-5096;
E-mail: info@educationfund.org; E-mail for Linda Lecht: llecht@educationfund.org; URL: http://www.educationfund.org

Foundation type: Public charity
Purpose: Grants for educators in the public school system to improve the quality of education in Miami/Dade county, FL.
Publications: Application guidelines; Informational brochure.
Financial data: Year ended 06/30/2012. Assets, $1,512,585 (M); Expenditures, $1,464,983; Total giving, $403,829; Grants to individuals, totaling $246,194.
Fields of interest: Elementary/secondary education.
Type of support: Grants to individuals.
Application information: Applications accepted. Application form required.
   Deadline(s): May 1 for IMPACT II Disseminator Grants, Dec. 3 for Teacher Mini Grants, Jan. 7 for IMPACT II Adapter Grants
   Additional information: See web site for additional guidelines.
Program descriptions:
   Citi Team Mentor Grants: The program awards grants ranging from $1,000 to $1,200 to provide an incentive for collaboration between new and veteran teachers. This collaboration centers on classroom-based student learning projects that provide common ground for veteran teachers and new teachers to work together. The aim is to encourage peer-to-peer learning opportunities and ongoing dialogue among teachers. The teacher teams comprise a mentor (a veteran teacher with more than five years of experience) and one or more beginning teachers with less than three years of teaching experience.
   IMPACT II Adapter Grants: Teachers can apply for an Adapter Grant of up to $400 to purchase materials. This grant reaches out to teachers who are looking for a new approach to teaching a specific curriculum. All Miami-Dade County public schools teachers are eligible.
   IMPACT II Disseminator Grants: Awards $750 disseminator grants to educators who are willing to share the successful teaching strategies that they have designed and implemented in their own classrooms. Applications accepted for K-12 projects in all subject areas.
   Teacher Mini-Grants Program: The program awards grants ranging from $300 to $1,000 to teachers to develop and implement instructional projects that motivate and challenge students to learn.
EIN: 592468114

1868
Edwards Family Foundation, Inc.
(formerly William Edwards Foundation, Inc.)
6090 Central Ave.
St. Petersburg, FL 33707-1622

Foundation type: Independent foundation
Purpose: Assistance to individuals of St. Petersburgh, FL, for medical expenses and other needs.
Financial data: Year ended 06/30/2011. Assets, $9,287 (M); Expenditures, $226,944; Total giving,

$160,763; Grants to individuals, totaling $160,763.
Fields of interest: Economically disadvantaged.
Type of support: Grants for special needs.
Application information: Applications not accepted.
  Additional information: Contact the foundation for additional information.
EIN: 200198747

1869
Embassy of Hope Foundation, Inc.
1255 W. International Speedway Blvd.
Daytona Beach, FL 32114-2816 (386) 239-8215
Contact: Michelle V. Carter-Scott, Exec. Dir.
FAX: (386) 254-1718;
E-mail: ann@vincecarter15.com; URL: http://vincecarter15.com/category/embassy-of-hope/

Foundation type: Public charity
Purpose: Scholarships to students in pursuit of a higher education, and special assistance to individuals who are in need.
Publications: Informational brochure.
Financial data: Year ended 08/31/2012. Assets, $65,252 (M); Expenditures, $63,068; Total giving, $24,091; Grants to individuals, totaling $24,091.
Fields of interest: Higher education; Nursing school/education; Athletics/sports, basketball.
Type of support: Scholarships—to individuals.
Application information: Contact the foundation for additional information for scholarship and assistance.
Program descriptions:
  Annie B. Westbrook Memorial Scholarship: A scholarship will be awarded annually to a deserving high school senior in Volusia County who is interested in the field of nursing, and who plans on attending a post secondary college or university.
  Believing in Your Dreams Scholarship: Two $5,000 scholarships are awarded each year to a male and female high school senior in Volusia County who have maintained a 3.0 GPA and have displayed model character and involvement in extra-curricular activities. Scholarships are intended to assist recipients in attending a post secondary college or university.
EIN: 593533429

1870
Englewood Elks Scholarship Trust PC 52-5823900
401 Indiana Ave.
Englewood, FL 34223

Foundation type: Independent foundation
Purpose: Scholarships to students of Lemon Bay High School, FL, or to members of the Englewood Elks Lodge, for higher education.
Financial data: Year ended 03/31/2013. Assets, $432,385 (M); Expenditures, $20,055; Total giving, $17,000; Grants to individuals, 9 grants totaling $17,000 (high: $2,000, low: $1,000).
Type of support: Support to graduates or students of specific schools; Undergraduate support.
Application information: Application form required.
  Initial approach: Letter or telephone
  Additional information: Contact foundation for current application deadline/guidelines.
EIN: 596687568

1871
Episcopal Children's Services, Inc.
8443 Baymeadow Rd., Ste. 1
Jacksonville, FL 32256-7440 (904) 726-1500
Contact: Connie Stophel, C.E.O.
FAX: (904) 726-1520;
E-mail: cstophel@ecs4kids.org; URL: http://ecs4kids.org

Foundation type: Public charity
Purpose: Assistance to child-care providers throughout Baker, Bradford, Clay, Nassau, Putnam, and St. Johns counties, FL.
Financial data: Year ended 06/30/2012. Assets, $10,134,270 (M); Expenditures, $38,072,147; Total giving, $22,683,890; Grants to individuals, 15,335 grants totaling $22,683,890. Subtotal for grants to individuals: grants totaling $21,782,196. Subtotal for in-kind gifts: grants totaling $901,694.
Fields of interest: Early childhood education; Child development, education; Children/youth, services.
Type of support: Grants to individuals.
Application information: Applications accepted.
  Additional information: Contact the agency for additional information.
EIN: 591146765

1872
The Everglades Foundation, Inc.
18001 Old Cutler Rd., Ste. 625
Palmetto Bay, FL 33157-6441 (305) 251-0001
Contact: Stanley Boynton, Exec. V.P.
E-mail: info@evergladesfoundation.org;
URL: http://www.evergladesfoundation.org/

Foundation type: Public charity
Purpose: Fellowships for advanced research to full time graduate students and postdoctoral researchers. Internships to undergraduate juniors or seniors, recent graduates, graduate students and postgraduate associates.
Publications: Annual report; Newsletter.
Financial data: Year ended 12/31/2012. Assets, $2,570,585 (M); Expenditures, $5,932,714; Total giving, $1,237,000.
Fields of interest: Courts/judicial administration; Physical/earth sciences; Engineering; Biology/life sciences; Social sciences; Economics; Population studies.
Type of support: Fellowships; Internship funds.
Application information: Applications accepted. Application form required.
  Send request by: Letter or e-mail
  Deadline(s): Jan. 15 for Fellowships, June 1 for Internships
  Additional information: Early applications are strongly encouraged. See web site for additional application guidelines.
Program descriptions:
  Internships: Internships pay $10 per hour to students or recent graduates in the natural sciences, physico-chemical and biological sciences, engineering, geography, planning, resources management, law, economics, and the social sciences. Students pursuing cross-disciplinary studies are of special interest.
  Research Fellowships: The foundation provides $20,000 a year to Ph.D. student and $10,000 a year to M.Sc. students pursuing degrees in natural sciences, biological sciences, engineering, geography, planning and resources management, and economics. Funding may be used to cover stipends, tuition fees, travel, and other research-related expenses. Research must be to advance the understanding of the Everglades'

physical, chemical, or biological processes, or the economic impacts of environmental changes.
EIN: 593228899

1873
The Exchange Club of Vero Beach Scholarship Foundation Trust
P.O. Box 1982
Vero Beach, FL 32961-1982 (772) 234-8400

Foundation type: Independent foundation
Purpose: Scholarships to graduates of Indian River County, FL, public high schools.
Financial data: Year ended 08/31/2013. Assets, $596,862 (M); Expenditures, $31,185; Total giving, $31,000; Grants to individuals, 13 grants totaling $31,000 (high: $3,500, low: $2,000).
Type of support: Support to graduates or students of specific schools; Undergraduate support.
Application information: Application form required.
  Deadline(s): Apr. 1
  Applicants should submit the following:
    1) Transcripts
    2) SAT
    3) Letter(s) of recommendation
    4) ACT
  Additional information: Application should also include a list of activities.
EIN: 592967807

1874
The Fabela Family Foundation
7401 Bay Colony Dr.
Naples, FL 34108

Foundation type: Independent foundation
Purpose: Assistance to families in IL who demonstrate financial need, and have a child under the age of six.
Financial data: Year ended 12/31/2012. Assets, $1,925,651 (M); Expenditures, $86,151; Total giving, $81,000.
Fields of interest: Children/youth, services; Economically disadvantaged.
Type of support: Grants for special needs.
Application information: Applications accepted. Application form required.
  Deadline(s): None
EIN: 364144423

1875
J. Hugh and Earle W. Fellows Memorial Fund
900 North 12th Ave.
Pensacola, FL 32501 (850) 471-4546
Application address: c/o Virginia Santoni, Assistant, Fellows Memorial Fund, Pensacola State College, 1000 College Blvd., Pensacola, FL 32504-8998, e-mail: vsantoni@pensacolastate.edu
URL: http://www.fellowsfund.org/

Foundation type: Independent foundation
Purpose: Loans to students for studies in nursing, medicine, medical technology, or the ministry who are residents of Escambia, Santa Rosa, Okaloosa, or Walton county, FL pursuing studies at an accredited college in their respective field of study.
Publications: Informational brochure (including application guidelines).
Financial data: Year ended 04/30/2012. Assets, $6,975,649 (M); Expenditures, $121,858; Total giving, $30,000; Loans to individuals, 35 loans totaling $177,260.

Fields of interest: Medical school/education; Nursing school/education; Theological school/education.
Type of support: Student loans—to individuals; Graduate support; Undergraduate support.
Application information: Applications accepted. Application form required. Interview required.
  Initial approach: Letter
  Deadline(s): None
  Applicants should submit the following:
    1) Transcripts
    2) Financial information
  Additional information: Selection is based on financial need, scholastic record and the extent of assistance reasonably required to enable the individual to complete his or her professional training at an accredited institution.
EIN: 596132238

1876
Rose McFarland Finley Foundation
815 Colorado Ave.
Stuart, FL 34994-3053 (772) 528-7654
E-mail: RMFScholarship@aol.com

Foundation type: Operating foundation
Purpose: Scholarships to graduates of schools in Indian River County, FL.
Financial data: Year ended 04/30/2013. Assets, $1,066,390 (M); Expenditures, $100,814; Total giving, $83,000; Grants to individuals, 175 grants totaling $83,000 (high: $500, low: $100).
Type of support: Support to graduates or students of specific schools; Undergraduate support.
Application information: Application form required.
  Deadline(s): Mar. 15
  Applicants should submit the following:
    1) Transcripts
    2) FAFSA
  Additional information: Application must also include parents' tax returns.
EIN: 237414902

1877
Florida Association of Realtors Disaster Relief Fund
7025 Augusta National Dr.
Orlando, FL 32822-5017 (407) 438-1400
Contact: Richard Darling, Pres.
FAX: (407) 438-1411; *E-mail:* drf@far.org; Toll-free tel.: (866) 829-1439; Mailling Address: PO Box 725025;Orlando, FL 32782-5025; URL: http://www.floridarealtors.org/AboutFar/DisasterReliefFund/index.cfm

Foundation type: Public charity
Purpose: Financial assistance to Florida Association of Realtors, including their real estate employees, Realtor board/associations and their staff, in the event of devastation caused by a hurricane, tornado or other natural disaster.
Publications: Application guidelines.
Financial data: Year ended 12/31/2011. Assets, $2,676,150 (M); Expenditures, $115,746; Total giving, $102,500; Grants to individuals, totaling $102,500.
Type of support: Emergency funds; Employee-related welfare.
Application information:
  Initial approach: Letter
  Additional information: Contact the association for eligibility criteria.
EIN: 593138956

1878
The Florida Bar Foundation
875 Concourse Pkwy. S., Ste. 195
Maitland, FL 32751 (407) 960-7000
Contact: Jane E. Curran, Exec. Dir.
FAX: (407) 960-3765;
E-mail: flabarfndn@worldnet.att.net; Mailing address: P.O. Box 1553, Orlando, FL 32802-1553; toll-free tel.: (800) 541-2195; URL: http://www.flabarfndn.org

Foundation type: Public charity
Purpose: Loans and scholarships to law students.
Publications: Annual report; Grants list.
Financial data: Year ended 06/30/2012. Assets, $43,339,886 (M); Expenditures, $26,373,856; Total giving, $22,984,039; Grants to individuals, totaling $1,265,874.
Fields of interest: Law school/education.
Type of support: Scholarships—to individuals; Student loans—to individuals.
Application information: Contact foundation for current application deadline/guidelines.
Program description:
  Legal Services Summer Fellowship Programs: The foundation annually provides summer fellowships (of up to 11 weeks) to first- and second-year law students from Florida law schools. These fellowships aim to involve law students in the provision of civil legal assistance to the poor in critical areas of need, provide an in-depth educational experience in representing the poor and working with individual clients and client groups in civil matters, increase law student interest in and awareness of the legal problems of the poor and the challenges and satisfactions of representing the poor, and promote commitment to pro bono representation of the poor.
EIN: 591004604

1879
Florida Education Fund, Inc.
201 E. Kennedy Blvd., Ste. 1525
Tampa, FL 33602-5828 (813) 272-2772
Contact: Dr. Lawrence Morehouse, Pres. and C.E.O.
Fellowship e-mail: mdf@fefonline.org
FAX: (813) 272-2784; *E-mail:* office@fefonline.org; URL: http://www.fefonline.org

Foundation type: Public charity
Purpose: Fellowships to individuals who intend to seek a Ph.D. in one or more of the disciplines in the Arts and Sciences, Mathematics, Business, Engineering, Health Sciences, Nursing or the Visual and Performing Arts.
Publications: Application guidelines; Newsletter.
Financial data: Year ended 06/30/2012. Assets, $14,225,764 (M); Expenditures, $3,364,696; Total giving, $2,064,399; Grants to individuals, totaling $1,841,399.
Fields of interest: Visual arts; Performing arts; Business school/education; Nursing school/education; Agriculture; Mathematics; Engineering.
Type of support: Fellowships; Doctoral support.
Application information: Applications accepted. Application form available on the grantmaker's web site.
  Send request by: Online
  Deadline(s): Jan. 15 for McKnight Doctoral Fellowship Program, varies for McKnight Junior Faculty Fellowship Program
  Final notification: Applicants notified in Apr.
  Applicants should submit the following:
    1) Letter(s) of recommendation
    2) Transcripts
    3) Resume

  Additional information: See web site for additional guidelines.
Program descriptions:
  McKnight Doctoral Fellowship Program: Up to 50 fellowships are awarded annually to study at one of the nine participating Florida universities: Florida A&M University, Florida Atlantic University, Florida Institute of Technology, Florida International University, Florida State University, University of Central Florida, University of Florida, University of Miami, and University of South Florida. Fellowships are especially encouraged in, but not limited to, the following disciplines: agriculture, biology, business administration, chemistry, computer science, engineering, marine biology, mathematics, physics, or psychology. Each award provides annual tuition of up to $5,000 for each of three academic years, plus an annual stipend of $12,000. Applicants must be African American or Hispanic, U.S. citizens, and hold a minimum of a bachelor's degree from a regionally-accredited college or university. The fellowship is awarded only to persons who intend to seek the Ph.D. degree full-time in a discipline in the arts and sciences, mathematics, business, or engineering. Currently-enrolled doctoral students are not eligible to apply.
  McKnight Junior Faculty Fellowship Program: This program works to promote excellence and teaching and research by underrepresented minorities and women, and to improve their chances of earning tenure and promotion, but awarding one-year sabbaticals with full salary and benefits. During the sabbatical, fellows are required to engage in research and training projects directly related to their efforts to secure tenure and promotion; while the participating university pays the fellow's salary, the fund will pay the university $15,000 to assist with necessary teaching replacements and support costs.
EIN: 592783821

1880
Florida Elks Charities, Inc.
P.O. Box 49
Umatilla, FL 32784-0049 (352) 669-2241
Contact: Victor McClellan, Pres.

Foundation type: Public charity
Purpose: Financial assistance to the family of deceased, disabled and deployed members of the military in the Florida community.
Financial data: Year ended 03/31/2012. Assets, $21,053 (M); Expenditures, $505,516; Total giving, $281,407; Grants to individuals, totaling $52,341.
Fields of interest: Human services; Military/veterans.
Type of support: Emergency funds; Grants for special needs.
Application information: Applications accepted. Application form required.
  Initial approach: Letter
  Deadline(s): None
  Additional information: Assistance only for military personnel in FL. Unsolicited requests for funds not considered or acknowledged.
EIN: 592825884

1881
Florida Endowment Foundation for Vocational Rehabilitation
(also known as The Able Trust)
3320 Thomasville Road, Ste. 200
Tallahassee, FL   32308-7906   (850) 224-4493
Contact: Dr. Susanne F. Homant, Pres. and C.E.O.
FAX: (850) 224-4496; E-mail: info@abletrust.org;
E-mail For Susanne Homant:
Susanne@abletrust.org; URL: http://
www.abletrust.org/

Foundation type: Public charity
Purpose: Grants to disabled FL residents to become independent, productive, and self-supporting members of society.
Publications: Application guidelines; Annual report; Informational brochure; Newsletter.
Financial data: Year ended 06/30/2012. Assets, $27,308,517 (M); Expenditures, $2,755,750; Total giving, $1,284,928; Grants to individuals, totaling $1,284,928.
Fields of interest: Disabilities, people with.
Type of support: Emergency funds; Grants for special needs.
Application information: Applications accepted.
  Send request by: Mail
  Deadline(s): None
  Applicants should submit the following:
    1) Resume
    2) Proposal
    3) Budget Information
  Additional information: Grants are for a one year time frame and recipients must regularly submit progress reports and document the use of grant funds with receipts.
Program description:
  Able Trust Individual Grants: Grants are made in a variety of areas including equipment needed for employment, education where federal or state financial aid is not available, and assistance with small business start-up costs that could not be provided by an agency of the state of Florida or in emergency situations. Grants to individuals for job accommodation average $2,500.
EIN: 593052307

1882
Florida FBLA-PBL Foundation, Inc.
810 Centerbook Dr.
Brandon, FL   33510-3211
URL: http://www.floridafbla-pbl.com/fbla/scholarship.aspx

Foundation type: Independent foundation
Purpose: Scholarships to high school seniors who are residents of FL and member of Florida FBLA for a minimum of two years pursuing a business degree.
Financial data: Year ended 06/30/2012. Assets, $103,030 (M); Expenditures, $17,012; Total giving, $5,012; Grants to individuals, 2 grants totaling $3,112 (high: $1,612, low: $1,500).
Fields of interest: Business school/education.
Type of support: Scholarships—to individuals.
Application information: Applications accepted. Application form required.
  Send request by: Mail
  Applicants should submit the following:
    1) Resume
    2) Transcripts
    3) SAT
    4) Class rank
    5) Letter(s) of recommendation
    6) Essay
    7) ACT

Additional information: Students attend the district conference, state fall leadership conference or the state leadership conference.
EIN: 043691181

1883
Florida Keys Educational Foundation, Inc.
5901 College Rd.
Key West, FL   33040-4315   (305) 296-9081
Contact: Debra Leonard, Recording Secy.
URL: http://www.fkcc.edu/foundation

Foundation type: Public charity
Purpose: Scholarships to graduating high school seniors of FL for attendance at Florida Keys Community College.
Financial data: Year ended 03/31/2012. Assets, $3,975,718 (M); Expenditures, $621,273; Total giving, $138,682; Grants to individuals, totaling $138,682.
Fields of interest: Vocational education, post-secondary; Higher education; Business school/education; Nursing school/education; Marine science.
Type of support: Support to graduates or students of specific schools.
Application information: Applications accepted. Application form required.
  Send request by: On-line
  Deadline(s): July 6 for Management Scholarships, July 13 for Rotary Club of Key West Crime Stoppers Scholarship
  Applicants should submit the following:
    1) Transcripts
    2) GPA
    3) Essay
  Additional information: Selection is based on financial need, GPA, essay, leadership and character. See web site for additional application guidelines.
EIN: 596173174

1884
Florida Prepaid College Foundation, Inc.
(also known as Stanley G. Tate Florida Prepaid College Foundation)
P.O. Box 1117
Tallahassee, FL   32302-1117   (850) 922-6740
Toll-free tel.: (800) 522-4723; TTY: (877) 431-3691; URL: http://
www.myfloridaprepaid.com/foundation/

Foundation type: Public charity
Purpose: Scholarship to graduating seniors of FL for attendance at colleges, universities or select technical schools.
Publications: Application guidelines; Annual report.
Fields of interest: Vocational education, post-secondary; Higher education.
Type of support: Scholarships—to individuals.
Application information: Applications accepted. Application form required. Application form available on the grantmaker's web site.
  Initial approach: E-mail
  Deadline(s): May 3 for Thomas J. Wallace Scholarship, none for STARS Scholarships
  Applicants should submit the following:
    1) Letter(s) of recommendation
    2) Essay
  Additional information: See web site for additional guidelines.
Program descriptions:
  STARS Scholarship: The foundation matches up eligible Florida graduating high school seniors with

scholarship opportunities offered by the foundation.
  Thomas J. Wallace Scholarship: A scholarship is available to a student who writes the most outstanding essay concerning public service. Eligible applicants must be Florida residents who are students in a 9th, 10th, or 11th grade public school located in Gadsden, Jefferson, Leon, Liberty, or Wakulla counties. Applicants must also seek a career in accounting or public service, must possess a valid social security number, and must be part of a family that qualifies to receive free or reduced lunch.
EIN: 593012202

1885
Florida Surveying and Mapping Society Scholarship Fund, Inc.
(formerly Florida Land Surveyors Scholarship Foundation, Inc.)
1689A Mahan Ctr. Blvd.
Tallahassee, FL   32308   (850) 942-1900
Contact: Marilyn C. Evers

Foundation type: Independent foundation
Purpose: Scholarships to students attending the University of Florida, FL.
Financial data: Year ended 10/31/2012. Assets, $12,392 (M); Expenditures, $12,910; Total giving, $12,100; Grants to individuals, 18 grants totaling $12,100 (high: $1,000, low: $400).
Fields of interest: Higher education.
Type of support: Scholarships—to individuals; Support to graduates or students of specific schools.
Application information: Applications accepted. Application form required.
  Initial approach: Letter or telephone
  Deadline(s): Apr. 30
  Additional information: Contact foundation for application forms.
EIN: 596209248

1886
Florida Symphony Youth Orchestra
P.O. Box 2328
Winter Park, FL   32790-2328   (407) 999-7800
Contact: Heide Evans Waldron, Exec. Dir.
FAX: (407) 898-5250; E-mail: info@fsyo.org;
Mailing address: P.O. Box 2328, Winter Park, FL 32790-2328; URL: http://www.fsyo.org

Foundation type: Public charity
Purpose: Scholarships to students who are in good standing, demonstrate musicianship and service.
Financial data: Year ended 06/30/2012. Assets, $856,704 (M); Expenditures, $247,179; Total giving, $8,893; Grants to individuals, totaling $8,893.
Fields of interest: Arts education.
Type of support: Scholarships—to individuals.
Application information: Applications accepted.
EIN: 592225301

1887
Florida Young Artists Orchestra, Inc.
P.O. Box 521947
Longwood, FL   32752-1947   (407) 772-2555
URL: http://fyao.org

Foundation type: Public charity
Purpose: Musical education and orchestra experience for members. Scholarships to members of the FYAO pursuing a major in music.

Financial data: Year ended 05/31/2011. Assets, $98,522 (M); Expenditures, $157,316; Total giving, $2,000; Grants to individuals, totaling $2,000.
Fields of interest: Arts education; Orchestras.
Type of support: Scholarships—to individuals.
Application information: Applications accepted.
  Deadline(s): Mar.
  Final notification: Applicants notified by Apr. 1
  Additional information: Application should include letters of recommendation, and a video recording of the applicant's performance of a major work from the standard repertoire for the instrument, with piano accompaniment. Contact the organization for additional guidelines.
EIN: 593511807

1888
Mary C. Forbes Charitable Foundation
c/o D'Arcy R. Clarie
1101 Pasadena Ave. S., Ste. 3
South Pasadena, FL   33707-2891

Foundation type: Independent foundation
Purpose: Scholarships to students who reside within the Diocese of St. Petersburg, FL and who are in pursuit of a Catholic education at college, graduate, seminary or other schools of religious studies based on the teaching of the Roman Catholic faith.
Financial data: Year ended 06/30/2012. Assets, $3,416,557 (M); Expenditures, $578,420; Total giving, $349,437.
Fields of interest: Higher education; Theological school/education; Catholic agencies & churches.
Type of support: Scholarships—to individuals.
Application information: Applications accepted.
Program description:
  Scholarship: Scholarships are provided to students who are active practitioners of the Roman Catholic faith for the purpose of seeking their Catholic education. The scholarships are available for students residing in the Diocese who are attending or applying to Catholic elementary, middle and high schools. Scholarships are also available for students who pursue their Catholic education at college, graduate, seminary or other schools of religious studies based upon the teaching of the Roman Catholic faith. Awards are based on financial need as well as academic merit, and the recipient must continue to actively practice the Roman Catholic faith. All awards, including awards over $1,000 for college, graduate, seminary and religious studies students are paid directly to the school.
EIN: 597112797

1889
Fort Lauderdale Area Realtors Charitable Foundation Inc.
1765 N.E. 26th St.
Fort Lauderdale, FL   33305-1482   (954) 563-7261
Contact: Richard W. Barkett, Tr.
URL: http://www.r-world.com/

Foundation type: Operating foundation
Purpose: Financial assistance to Broward county, FL residents with medical expense, food, utilities, rent and other special needs.
Financial data: Year ended 12/31/2011. Assets, $96,369 (M); Expenditures, $42,070; Total giving, $32,827; Grants to individuals, 8 grants totaling $23,202 (high: $6,533, low: $1,295).
Fields of interest: Economically disadvantaged.

Type of support: Grants for special needs.
Application information: Applications accepted. Application form required.
  Initial approach: Telephone
  Deadline(s): None
EIN: 650003512

1890
Fort Lauderdale Rotary 1090 Foundation, Inc.
P.O. Box 2399
Fort Lauderdale, FL   33303-2399   (954) 424-0731

Foundation type: Public charity
Purpose: Scholarships to graduating seniors of Fort Lauderdale High School and St. Thomas Aquinas High School for postsecondary education.
Financial data: Year ended 06/30/2012. Assets, $779,345 (M); Expenditures, $181,075; Total giving, $166,435; Grants to individuals, totaling $60,472.
Fields of interest: Vocational education, post-secondary; Higher education.
Type of support: Scholarships—to individuals; Support to graduates or students of specific schools.
Application information: Applications accepted.
  Additional information: Scholarship is based on financial need, leadership ability, GPA, and standing in the senior class. Students should contact their respective high school guidance counselors for application guidelines.
EIN: 237247846

1891
Fort Myers Beach Chamber of Commerce Foundation
17200 San Carlos Blvd.
Fort Myers Beach, FL   33931-5306   (239) 454-7500
FAX: (239) 454-7910; *URL:* http://fortmyersbeachchamber.org/

Foundation type: Public charity
Purpose: Scholarships to students of Fort Meyers Beach, FL for continuing education at institutions of higher learning.
Financial data: Year ended 12/31/2011. Assets, $603,714 (M); Expenditures, $40,157; Total giving, $10,948; Grants to individuals, totaling $5,955.
Fields of interest: Higher education.
Type of support: Scholarships—to individuals.
Application information: Applications accepted. Application form required.
  Initial approach: Telephone, or in person
  Deadline(s): May
  Applicants should submit the following:
    1) Photograph
    2) Essay
  Additional information: Contact the foundation for additional guidelines.
EIN: 592539155

1892
Ft. Myers Beach Kiwanis Club Foundation, Inc.
P.O. Box 2507
Fort Myers Beach, FL   33932-2507   (239) 463-3192
Contact: Trinky Jarrett, Pres.
URL: http://www.fortmyersbeachkiwanis.org/

Foundation type: Public charity
Purpose: Scholarships to students in the Fort Myers Beach, FL area who wish to attend an accredited college, university or skilled training school.
Publications: Application guidelines.
Financial data: Year ended 09/30/2011. Assets, $1,430,992 (M); Expenditures, $474,018; Total giving, $89,941; Grants to individuals, totaling $29,320.
Fields of interest: Vocational education, post-secondary; Higher education; Scholarships/financial aid.
Type of support: Scholarships—to individuals.
Application information: Applications accepted. Application form required. Application form available on the grantmaker's web site. Interview required.
  Send request by: Mail
  Deadline(s): June 15 for Scholarships
  Applicants should submit the following:
    1) Essay
    2) Letter(s) of recommendation
    3) Transcripts
  Additional information: All applications must be accompanied by documentation of at least 20 hours of community service in the past year.
Program description:
  Scholarships: The foundation provides scholarships to students planning to attend an accredited college or university. Eligible applicants must be high school graduates who reside in the 33931 zip code, and who have a GPA of 3.0 or higher. Application is renewable.
EIN: 650469747

1893
C.G. Fuller Foundation
P.O. Box 40200, FL9-100-10-19
Jacksonville, FL   32203-0200   (803) 255-7381

Foundation type: Independent foundation
Purpose: Scholarships to incoming first-year students who are residents of SC to attend SC colleges and universities.
Financial data: Year ended 12/31/2012. Assets, $3,039,764 (M); Expenditures, $180,718; Total giving, $145,225.
Type of support: Undergraduate support.
Application information: Applications accepted. Application form required. Interview required.
  Initial approach: Contact university financial aid office
  Deadline(s): Mar. 31
EIN: 576050492

1894
Gamma Mu Foundation
P.O. Box 23520
Fort Lauderdale, FL   33307-3520   (866) 463-6007
Contact: Jack V. Lewis, Pres.
E-mail: info@gammamufoundation.org; *URL:* http://www.gammamufoundation.org

Foundation type: Public charity
Purpose: Scholarships to gay men under 35 years of age in rural areas for postsecondary education at accredited colleges, universities or vocational and technical training.
Publications: Financial statement; Grants list; Informational brochure; Newsletter.
Financial data: Year ended 06/30/2013. Assets, $2,183,035 (M); Expenditures, $174,947; Total giving, $129,000.
Fields of interest: Higher education; Men; LGBTQ.

Type of support: Undergraduate support; Postgraduate support.
Application information: Applications accepted. Application form required. Application form available on the grantmaker's web site.
  Deadline(s): Mar. 31
  Final notification: Applicants notified May 31
  Additional information: See web site for additional application guidelines.
Program description:
  Scholarships: Scholarships, ranging from $1,000 to $2,500, will be available to gay men who wish to continue their education beyond high school at a college, university, or vocational or professional training program. Eligible applicants must be gay men under 35 years of age who have completed high school (or have received their GED). Preference will be given to students who are from, or plan to attend, school in a rural area; students from all areas who have overcome issues of discrimination and/or marginalization within their community; students from all areas who demonstrate leadership qualities and future goals to benefit the gay community; students from all areas who demonstrate leadership within their community, specifically promoting diversity and tolerance for all citizens; and students from all areas who demonstrate a strong academic performance.
EIN: 330351175

1895
Glades Electric Educational Foundation Inc.
P.O. Box 519
Moore Haven, FL 33471-0519 (863) 946-0061

Foundation type: Company-sponsored foundation
Purpose: Scholarships to graduating seniors whose permanent, legal residence is served directly or indirectly by Glades Electric Cooperative, Inc.
Financial data: Year ended 12/31/2012. Assets, $633,153 (M); Expenditures, $31,624; Total giving, $26,100; Grants to individuals, 33 grants totaling $26,100 (high: $1,000, low: $500).
Fields of interest: Higher education.
Type of support: Undergraduate support.
Application information:
  Initial approach: Letter
  Applicants should submit the following:
    1) ACT
    2) SAT
    3) GPA
    4) Class rank
    5) Transcripts
    6) Financial information
EIN: 651083705

1896
GMAA -Batchelor Aviation Scholarship Fund Inc.
(formerly GMAA Grover Loening Scholarship Fund)
P.O. Box 660834
Miami Springs, FL 33266-0834 (305) 884-4300
Contact: Dan Sullivan
URL: http://www.gmaa.aero/

Foundation type: Operating foundation
Purpose: Scholarships to qualified aviation students pursuing a career in the South Florida Aviation industry.
Financial data: Year ended 12/31/2012. Assets, $754,943 (M); Expenditures, $134,171; Total giving, $51,000; Grants to individuals, 10 grants totaling $51,000 (high: $6,000, low: $5,000).
Fields of interest: Space/aviation.

Type of support: Scholarships—to individuals; Undergraduate support.
Application information: Application form required. Interview required.
  Deadline(s): At least 1 month prior to school enrollment
  Applicants should submit the following:
    1) Financial information
    2) Transcripts
    3) Letter(s) of recommendation
  Additional information: Application forms are available in college financial aid departments or from the scholarship committee. Applicant must be a U.S. citizen, have completed a minimum of 30 college credits, of which 15 must be in Aviation, have a GPA of 3.5 or higher, and must be accepted or pending application by the program for which funding is sought.
EIN: 650270346

1897
Alexander J. Grossman Scholarship Foundation
c/o Regions Bank Trust Dept.
P.O. Box 2918
Clearwater, FL 33757-2918

Foundation type: Independent foundation
Purpose: Undergraduate scholarships in science and engineering to graduates of Dunedin Comprehensive High School, FL, who were in the top ten percent of their class and have been accepted to accredited U.S. colleges and universities.
Financial data: Year ended 03/31/2013. Assets, $2,093,049 (M); Expenditures, $117,136; Total giving, $91,600; Grants to individuals, 16 grants totaling $91,600 (high: $7,000, low: $3,000).
Fields of interest: Engineering school/education; Science.
Type of support: Support to graduates or students of specific schools; Undergraduate support.
Application information: Applications not accepted.
  Additional information: Candidates are sought by the awards committee. Unsolicited requests for funds not considered or acknowledged.
EIN: 596782085

1898
Gulf Coast Community Foundation, Inc.
(formerly Gulf Coast Community Foundation of Venice)
601 Tamiami Trail South
Venice, FL 34285-3237 (941) 486-4600
Contact: Teri A. Hansen, C.E.O./Pres.; Wendy Deming, Chief of Staff and Corp. Secy.
FAX: (941) 486-4699; E-mail: info@gulfcoastcf.org; Additional e-mail: thansen@gulfcoastcf.org;
URL: http://www.gulfcoastcf.org/

Foundation type: Community foundation
Purpose: Scholarships to students of Sarasota and Charlotte counties, or Boca Grande, FL for attendance at a regionally accredited postsecondary institution for full time undergraduate or vocational study.
Publications: Application guidelines; Annual report; Grants list; Informational brochure (including application guidelines); Occasional report.
Financial data: Year ended 06/30/2013. Assets, $232,647,057 (M); Expenditures, $22,670,492; Total giving, $16,432,516. Scholarships—to individuals amount not specified.

Fields of interest: Vocational education, post-secondary; Higher education.
Type of support: Undergraduate support.
Application information: Applications accepted. Application form required. Application form available on the grantmaker's web site.
  Initial approach: Application
  Send request by: Online
  Deadline(s): Mar. 6
  Applicants should submit the following:
    1) Financial information
    2) Transcripts
    3) Letter(s) of recommendation
    4) Essay
    5) SAR
  Additional information: Faxed or mailed applications are not accepted. See web site for complete scholarship listing.
Program description:
  Scholarships: The foundation offers scholarships which are open to students of any age who attend vocational school or college, and who reside in the areas served by Venice, Lemon Bay, and North Port high schools. In addition, the foundation maintains a matching scholarship program which supports several scholarship funds.
EIN: 591052433

1899
Gulf Coast Jewish Family and Community Services, Inc.
(formerly Gulf Coast Jewish Family Services, Inc.)
14041 Icot Blvd.
Clearwater, FL 33760-3702 (727) 479-1800
FAX: (727) 535-4774; E-mail: info@gcjfs.org; Toll-free tel.: (800) 888-5066; URL: http://www.gcjfs.org

Foundation type: Public charity
Purpose: Stipends to individuals and families of FL, in times of need. College student interest-free loans to help Jewish students needed to attend postsecondary education.
Financial data: Year ended 06/30/2012. Assets, $16,916,532 (M); Expenditures, $25,766,533; Total giving, $780,678; Grants to individuals, totaling $780,678.
Fields of interest: Higher education; Jewish agencies & synagogues; Economically disadvantaged.
Type of support: Student loans—to individuals; Grants for special needs.
Application information: Applications accepted. Application form required.
  Send request by: On-line (loans)
  Deadline(s): Apr. 30, Sept. 30 for Loans
  Additional information: Loans are for Jewish students from Florida, Georgia, North Carolina, South Carolina and Virginia. See web site for additional guidelines.
EIN: 591229354

1900
Darrell Gwynn Foundation, Inc.
4850 S.W. 52nd St.
Davie, FL 33314-5526 (954) 792-7223
Contact: Lisa Gwynn, Interim Exec. Dir.
FAX: (954) 581-7223;
E-mail: info@darrellgwynnfoundation.org;
URL: http://www.darrellgwynnfoundation.org

Foundation type: Public charity
Purpose: Funds research designed to prevent, provide for and ultimately cure spinal cord injuries and other debilitating illnesses.

Financial data: Year ended 06/30/2012. Assets, $2,486,162 (M); Expenditures, $1,289,607; Total giving, $341,638; Grants to individuals, 24 grants totaling $308,138.
Fields of interest: Spine disorders.
Type of support: Research.
Application information: Applications not accepted.
EIN: 510430447

1901
The Hand Foundation, Inc.
1499 Forest Hill Blvd., Ste. 116
West Palm Beach, FL   33406-6050   (561) 439-0171
Contact: Ruben Ledesma, Jr., Dir.

Foundation type: Independent foundation
Purpose: Scholarships to residents of FL for higher education.
Financial data: Year ended 12/31/2012. Assets, $26,784 (M); Expenditures, $191,306; Total giving, $191,245; Grants to individuals, 48 grants totaling $191,245 (high: $16,300, low: $1,000).
Fields of interest: Higher education.
Type of support: Undergraduate support.
Application information:
  Applicants should submit the following:
    1) Financial information
    2) Essay
  Additional information: Primary criterion are financial need and personal achievements/goals.
EIN: 650118848

1902
Hard Rock Cafe Foundation, Inc.
6100 Old Park Ln.
Orlando, FL   32835-2466

Foundation type: Company-sponsored foundation
Purpose: Emergency disaster relief grants to employees who suffered hardship and loss of employment due to the effects of a natural disaster.
Financial data: Year ended 12/31/2012. Assets, $962 (M); Expenditures, $2,267,758; Total giving, $2,267,184; Grants to individuals, 91 grants totaling $55,795 (high: $3,000, low: $200).
Fields of interest: Safety/disasters.
Type of support: Grants to individuals.
Application information: Applications not accepted.
  Additional information: Unsolicited requests for funds not considered or acknowledged.
Company name: Hard Rock Cafe International, Inc.
EIN: 593686985

1903
Dwight H. Harrelson Memorial Scholarship Trust
P.O. Box 40200, FL9-100-10-19
Jacksonville, FL   32203-0200
Application address: c/o Bank of America, N.A., 100 Westminister St., Providence, RI 02903

Foundation type: Independent foundation
Purpose: Scholarships to graduating high school seniors of Cherryville High School, NC for postsecondary education.
Financial data: Year ended 04/30/2013. Assets, $298,342 (M); Expenditures, $18,500; Total giving, $13,650.
Fields of interest: Higher education.
Type of support: Support to graduates or students of specific schools; Undergraduate support.

Application information: Applications accepted.
  Send request by: Mail
  Deadline(s): None
EIN: 237159114

1904
Ray M. Harris Educational Fund
P.O. Box 40200, FL9-100-10-19
Jacksonville, FL   32203-0200   (804) 887-8773
Application address: Bank of America, 1111 East Main St., VA2-300-12-92, Richmond, VA 23219-3500

Foundation type: Independent foundation
Purpose: Undergraduate and graduate scholarships to graduates from high schools in Pittsylvania County, VA.
Financial data: Year ended 12/31/2012. Assets, $1,130,054 (M); Expenditures, $77,707; Total giving, $60,000.
Fields of interest: Higher education.
Type of support: Scholarships—to individuals; Graduate support; Undergraduate support.
Application information: Applications accepted. Application form required.
  Deadline(s): Apr. 15
  Applicants should submit the following:
    1) Transcripts
    2) Letter(s) of recommendation
    3) Financial information
  Additional information: Application should also include copies of all financial aid notices.
EIN: 546065353

1905
Harrison & Conrad Memorial Trust
c/o Bank of America, N.A.
P.O. Box 40200, FL9-100-10-19
Jacksonville, FL   32203-0200   (703) 777-3300

Foundation type: Independent foundation
Purpose: Grants only to children from the town of Leesburg and Loudoun County, VA, who are suffering from polio, muscular dystrophy or any other crippling disease, and whose families cannot afford treatment.
Financial data: Year ended 01/31/2013. Assets, $3,273,989 (M); Expenditures, $157,532; Total giving, $116,100; Grants to individuals, 14 grants totaling $116,100 (high: $30,000, low: $216).
Fields of interest: Health care; Muscular dystrophy; Children/youth, services; Disabilities, people with.
Type of support: Grants for special needs.
Application information: Applications accepted. Interview required.
  Initial approach: Letter
  Deadline(s): Apr. 1
  Additional information: Application should include financial information.
EIN: 521300410

1906
Harvest of Hope Foundation, Inc.
P.O. Box 358025
Gainesville, FL   32635-8025   (352) 372-1312
Contact: Philip Kellerman, Pres.
E-mail: info@harvestofhope.net; Toll-free tel.: (888) 922-4673; URL: http://www.harvestofhope.net

Foundation type: Public charity
Purpose: Emergency financial assistance to various migrant farmworkers and their families with transportation assistance, housing, shelter, food, clothing, medical bills and other expenses.

Financial data: Year ended 08/31/2011. Assets, $77,766 (M); Expenditures, $156,049; Total giving, $79,032; Grants to individuals, totaling $79,032.
Fields of interest: Economically disadvantaged.
Type of support: Emergency funds; Grants for special needs.
Application information: Contact the foundation for additional information.
EIN: 161523238

1907
Nina Haven Scholarships, Inc.
(formerly Nina Haven Charitable Foundation)
P.O. Box 1978
Stuart, FL   34995   (772) 287-7645
Contact: Judith Weber, Pres.
FAX: (772) 221-1970; E-mail: info@ninahaven.org; URL: http://www.ninahaven.org

Foundation type: Independent foundation
Purpose: Scholarships to graduates of Martin County, FL, high schools and local community colleges.
Financial data: Year ended 12/31/2012. Assets, $5,156,023 (M); Expenditures, $340,661; Total giving, $277,250.
Type of support: Support to graduates or students of specific schools; Undergraduate support.
Application information: Application form required.
  Deadline(s): Contact school guidance counselor for current application deadline.
  Additional information: Students should demonstrate need, show evidence of scholastic achievement and meet other intangible criteria.
EIN: 136099012

1908
Health First Foundation, Inc.
1350 S. Hickory St.
Melbourne, FL   32901-3224   (321) 434-7353
Contact: Steven Johnson, Pres.
Application address: Health First Foundation, Cape Canaveral Office, 701 W. Cocoa Beach Causeway, Cocoa Beach, FL 32931, tel.: (321) 868-2720, fax: (321) 868-2770
E-mail: Cynthia.Smith@Health-First.org; URL: http://www.health-first.org/ways_to_help/foundation.cfm

Foundation type: Public charity
Purpose: Scholarships to Brevard County area high school students who wish to pursue a career in a medical or healthcare-related field.
Publications: Application guidelines.
Financial data: Year ended 09/30/2011. Assets, $3,706,049 (M); Expenditures, $2,536,995; Total giving, $1,463,585.
Fields of interest: Medical school/education; Scholarships/financial aid.
Type of support: Scholarships—to individuals.
Application information: Applications accepted. Application form required. Application form available on the grantmaker's web site.
  Initial approach: Application
  Send request by: Mail or hand delivered
  Deadline(s): Mar. 25
  Final notification: Applicants notified by end of Apr.
  Applicants should submit the following:
    1) Transcripts
    2) Letter(s) of recommendation
    3) Essay

Additional information: Awards are sent directly to the educational institution on behalf of the student.

Program description:

Scholarship Program: Scholarships of $1,000 each will be awarded to high school seniors graduating from a Brevard County-based high school that plan to pursue a career in a medical or healthcare-related field. Eligible applicants must have a minimum GPA of 3.0, and must be residents of Brevard County.

EIN: 593528774

1909

Hein Family Foundation Corporation

1944 Levine Ln.
Clearwater, FL 33760-1611 (727) 535-9277

Foundation type: Independent foundation
Purpose: Scholarships to graduating seniors of FL for attendance at accredited institutions of higher learning with tuition, fees, and room and board expenses.
Financial data: Year ended 12/31/2011. Assets, $52,899 (M); Expenditures, $53,142; Total giving, $51,573; Grants to individuals, 2 grants totaling $51,573 (high: $26,040, low: $25,533).
Fields of interest: Higher education; Scholarships/financial aid.
Type of support: Undergraduate support.
Application information: Application form required.
Deadline(s): Two months prior to post-high school education
Applicants should submit the following:
1) Transcripts
2) Letter(s) of recommendation
Additional information: Application should also include goals.
EIN: 593708543

1910

Hellenic Foundation

12051 Rosemount Dr.
Fort Myers, FL 33913-8380 (717) 624-7189
Contact: John F. Grove, Jr., Tr.

Foundation type: Company-sponsored foundation
Purpose: Scholarships to financially needy residents of PA, for attendance at colleges and universities. Scholarships cover tuition, books and living expenses.
Financial data: Year ended 06/30/2012. Assets, $283,634 (M); Expenditures, $15,266; Total giving, $2,705.
Fields of interest: Higher education.
Type of support: Scholarships—to individuals.
Application information: Applications accepted.
Deadline(s): None
Additional information: Applications by letter including academic records, recommendations, and statement of financial need.
EIN: 222536161

1911

The John Henry Company—Lou Brand Scholarship Foundation

10620 Gulf Shore Dr., Ste. 301
Naples, FL 34108
Contact: Shahriar Ghoddousi, Chair.

Foundation type: Company-sponsored foundation
Purpose: Scholarships to children of employees of the John Henry Company and its subsidiaries.

Financial data: Year ended 06/30/2013. Assets, $405,740 (M); Expenditures, $20,974; Total giving, $19,500; Grants to individuals, 27 grants totaling $19,500 (high: $1,400, low: $250).
Type of support: Employee-related scholarships.
Application information: Application form required.
Deadline(s): 3rd Monday in May
Applicants should submit the following:
1) Essay
2) Transcripts
3) Letter(s) of recommendation
Additional information: Recipients may be up to 25 years of age as of June 1 of the year of application and must be attending college to obtain an undergraduate degree.
Company name: John Henry Company
EIN: 383243055

1912

The Hermitage Artist Retreat, Inc.

6650 Manasota Key Rd.
Englewood, FL 34223-9213 (941) 475-2098
E-mail: info@hermitage-fl.org; E-Mail for Bruce Rodgers: director@hermitageartistretreat.org;
URL: http://www.hermitage-fl.org

Foundation type: Public charity
Purpose: Competitive grants and fellowships to visual artists, writers and composers who are residents of Sarasota County, FL.
Financial data: Year ended 06/30/2012. Assets, $1,346,420 (M); Expenditures, $410,800; Total giving, $20,000; Grants to individuals, totaling $20,000.
Fields of interest: Literature.
Type of support: Fellowships; Awards/prizes; Residencies.
Application information: Application by nomination.
Program description:
Sarasota County Fellows: Cash awards of $3,000 and $5,000 to artists residing in Sarasota county, Florida. In addition to the cash prize, the panel will award two to three week Hermitage residencies, one to a visual artist and one to a writer or composer.
EIN: 300104608

1913

Howard E. Hill Foundation Inc.

1324 S. Main St.
Belle Glade, FL 33430-4914 (561) 996-4524
Contact: Jennifer Earnest
URL: http://www.hehill.org/

Foundation type: Operating foundation
Purpose: Loans to low income individuals and families of FL, to enable them to purchase, construct, or rehabilitate a principal residence in which a family reside in Hendry and Western Palm Beach counties, FL.
Financial data: Year ended 12/31/2012. Assets, $30,141,217 (M); Expenditures, $3,089,163; Total giving, $716,395.
Fields of interest: Housing/shelter, rehabilitation; Housing/shelter; Economically disadvantaged.
Type of support: Loans—to individuals.
Application information: Applications accepted. Application form required.
Initial approach: Letter
Deadline(s): None
Additional information: See web site or contact the foundation for additional information.
EIN: 311513075

1914

Hillmyer-Tremont Student Athlete Foundation, Inc.

14030 Metropolis Ave., Ste. 200
Fort Myers, FL 33912-6460

Foundation type: Independent foundation
Purpose: Scholarships to deserving Lee County, FL high school athletic seniors for undergraduate study.
Financial data: Year ended 12/31/2012. Assets, $0 (M); Expenditures, $84,316; Total giving, $70,000; Grants to individuals, 16 grants totaling $70,000 (high: $16,000, low: $2,000).
Fields of interest: Recreation.
Type of support: Scholarships—to individuals.
Application information: Awards are based on academic and athletic achievement, as well as financial need.
EIN: 650803239

1915

Hillsborough Educational Partnership Foundation, Inc.

2306 N. Howard Ave.
Tampa, FL 33607-2613 (813) 574-0260
Contact: Phil Jones, Pres.
FAX: (813) 574-0299;
E-mail: hefnews@educationfoundation.com;
Contact Barbara Dick regarding scholarships; tel.: (813) 231-1970;
e-mail:bdick@educationfoundation.com; E-Mail for Phil Jones: pjones@educationfoundation.com;
URL: http://www.educationfoundation.com

Foundation type: Public charity
Purpose: Scholarships to at-risk students and graduating seniors in Hillsborough County Public Schools, FL for postsecondary education.
Publications: Application guidelines; Annual report.
Financial data: Year ended 06/30/2012. Assets, $19,555,977 (M); Expenditures, $5,530,162; Total giving, $697,703.
Type of support: Undergraduate support.
Application information:
Initial approach: Letter
Additional information: Contact foundation for further application information.
EIN: 592883361

1916

Hma Employee Disaster Relief Fund, Inc.

5811 Pelican Bay Blvd., Ste. 500
Naples, FL 34108-2711 (239) 598-3131
Contact: Patrick E. Lombardo, V.P.

Foundation type: Company-sponsored foundation
Purpose: Hurricane disaster relief assistance to employees of Health Management Associates, Inc.
Financial data: Year ended 12/31/2012. Assets, $361 (M); Expenditures, $7,034; Total giving, $6,500; Grants to individuals, 4 grants totaling $6,500 (high: $2,500, low: $1,000).
Fields of interest: Safety/disasters.
Type of support: Emergency funds; Employee-related welfare.
Application information: Applications accepted. Application form required.
Deadline(s): Six months after the President declares the area a disaster
Additional information: Grant amount is based on an individual basis and need.
Company name: Health Management Associates, Inc.
EIN: 201507465

1917
John F. Hoeting Scholarship Trust
P.O. Box 40200, FL9-100-10-19
Jacksonville, FL 32203-0200

Foundation type: Independent foundation
Purpose: Scholarships to graduating seniors of Hudson High School, FL, for higher education.
Financial data: Year ended 06/30/2013. Assets, $405,204 (M); Expenditures, $20,335; Total giving, $17,490.
Type of support: Support to graduates or students of specific schools; Undergraduate support.
Application information: Applications accepted.
Initial approach: Letter
Deadline(s): None
EIN: 597102513

1918
Holland & Knight Charitable Foundation, Inc.
201 N. Franklin St.
P.O. Box 2877
Tampa, FL 33601-2877 (813) 227-8500
Contact: Elias Matsakis, Pres.
Application address for African American Heritage: Holland & Knight LLP, Attn. Lura Battle, 1201 W. Peachtree St., N.E., 1 Atlantic Ctr., Ste. 2000, Atlanta, GA 30309-3453; E-mail and URL for Holocaust Project: holocaust@hklaw.com, www.holocaust.hklaw.com; E-mail for Young Native Writers' Contest: indian@hklaw.com
FAX: (813) 229-0134;
E-mail: foundation@hklaw.com; Toll-free tel.: (866) 452-2737; E-mail for Elias Matsakis: elias.matsakis@hklaw.com; URL: http://foundation.hklaw.com

Foundation type: Public charity
Purpose: Scholarships and awards to graduating high school students in pursuit of a higher education.
Publications: Application guidelines.
Financial data: Year ended 12/13/2011. Assets, $660,730 (M); Expenditures, $1,062,113; Total giving, $857,266; Grants to individuals, totaling $79,000.
Fields of interest: Higher education; African Americans/Blacks; Native Americans/American Indians.
Type of support: Scholarships—to individuals; Awards/prizes.
Application information: Applications accepted. Application form required. Application form available on the grantmaker's web site.
Deadline(s): Apr. 15 for Young Native Writers', Apr. 30 for Holocaust Remembrance , and Dec. for African American Heritage
Additional information: See web site for guidelines on essays and project.
Program descriptions:
Dream Scholarship Program: This program honors the many African Americans who have dreamed for a better America by offering an essay contest and the potential to recieve scholarships to all students age 19 and under who are currently enrolled as juniors or seniors in public high schools in Atlanta and DeKalb counties. The first, second, and third place winners will receive scholarships worth $3,000, $2,000, and $1,000 respectively.
Holocaust Remembrance Project Essay Contest: This program is a national essay contest for high-school students that is designed to encourage and promote the study of the Holocaust. Participation in this project encourages students to think responsibly, be aware of world conditions that undermine human dignity, and make decisions that

promote respect for the value inherent in every person. Eligible applicants include high-school students in the U.S. and Mexico. Scholarships for first place begin at $2,500.
Young Native Writers Essay Contest: This contest allows Native American high school students to write about their experiences, inspiring honest portrayals of the richness of Native American life and history. Five first-place winners will be chosen to receive scholarships ranging from $1,000 to $5,000, and to be flown to Washington D.C. to visit the National Museum of the American Indian and other prominent sites. Eligible applicants include Native American Indian and Alaska Native individuals who are enrolled members of a state- or federally-recognized tribe, and who are also enrolled in high schools or alternative schools, or are homeschooled.
EIN: 311472972

1919
Hollywood Rotary Foundation, Inc.
P.O. Box 1023
Hollywood, FL 33022 (954) 921-4500
Contact: Charles Smith, Pres.

Foundation type: Public charity
Purpose: Scholarships to deserving students throughout the greater Hollywood, FL area for higher education.
Financial data: Year ended 06/30/2012. Assets, $710,765 (M); Expenditures, $50,471; Total giving, $46,195; Grants to individuals, totaling $46,195.
Fields of interest: Education.
Type of support: Scholarships—to individuals.
Application information: Contact the foundation for eligibility requirement.
EIN: 591926198

1920
Lois Holt Foundation of Central Florida
1417 E. Concord St.
Orlando, FL 32803-4602 (407) 849-1569
Contact: Edward A. Hofma, Exec. Dir.

Foundation type: Independent foundation
Purpose: Scholarships to FL residents for higher education.
Financial data: Year ended 06/30/2011. Assets, $1,208,708 (M); Expenditures, $78,355; Total giving, $41,200; Grants to individuals, 37 grants totaling $41,200 (high: $15,000, low: $750).
Type of support: Scholarships—to individuals.
Application information: Applications accepted. Application form required.
Initial approach: Telephone
Deadline(s): Apr. 1
EIN: 593143622

1921
Hope Foundation for the Homeless
149 E. Broadway
Oviedo, FL 32765-4918 (407) 366-3422
Contact: Joan Faulkner, Exec. Dir.
FAX: (407) 542-3959; URL: http://www.helpforthehomeless.net/pages/

Foundation type: Public charity
Purpose: Assistance to individuals and families to become self-sufficient in the central FL area.
Financial data: Year ended 12/31/2011. Assets, $198,519 (M); Expenditures, $1,858,439; Total giving, $1,438,068; Grants to individuals, totaling $1,438,068.

Fields of interest: Housing/shelter, homeless; Human services; Economically disadvantaged.
Type of support: Emergency funds; In-kind gifts.
Application information: Contact the foundation for additional guidelines.
EIN: 208490916

1922
The Horizons Foundation Inc.
1001 Brickell Bay Dr., Ste. 1800
Miami, FL 33131 (404) 876-7725
Contact: Dorothy Rollins, Dir.
Application address: 145 15th St., No. 1229, Atlanta, GA 30309

Foundation type: Operating foundation
Purpose: Grants to Jamaicans for freediving and for undergraduate education in Jamaica and in the U.S.
Financial data: Year ended 12/31/2011. Assets, $1,362,355 (M); Expenditures, $15,167; Total giving, $0.
Fields of interest: Higher education; Athletics/sports, water sports.
International interests: Jamaica.
Type of support: Foreign applicants; Undergraduate support.
Application information:
Initial approach: Letter
Deadline(s): None
Additional information: Letter should describe individual's needs.
EIN: 651121440

1923
Robert Hungerford Chapel Trust
P.O. Box 2822
Winter Park, FL 32790-2822 (321) 277-5973

Foundation type: Independent foundation
Purpose: Scholarships to minority high school and college students based on financial need.
Financial data: Year ended 12/31/2012. Assets, $476,557 (M); Expenditures, $22,459; Total giving, $18,750; Grants to individuals, 18 grants totaling $18,750 (high: $2,000, low: $750).
Fields of interest: Minorities.
Type of support: Scholarships—to individuals.
Application information: Applications accepted. Application form required.
Applicants should submit the following:
1) ACT
2) Financial information
3) SAT
4) Transcripts
EIN: 592350325

1924
The Agnes B. Hunt Trust
c/o SunTrust Bank
P.O. Box 1908
Orlando, FL 32802-1908
Contact: Joseph Walker, Dir.
Application address: c/o P.O. Box 161, Griffin, GA 30224-1610; URL: http://www.agnesbhunttrust.org/

Foundation type: Independent foundation
Purpose: Scholarships to graduating seniors of Griffin High School, GA. The program is administered by the Department of Family and Children Services.
Financial data: Year ended 12/31/2012. Assets, $461,369 (M); Expenditures, $39,005; Total giving, $28,878.

Type of support: Support to graduates or students of specific schools; Undergraduate support.
Application information: Applications accepted.
Additional information: Contact principal for current application deadline/guidelines.
EIN: 586026028

1925
Lonnie Bob Hurst Scholarship Trust
11465 75th Dr.
Live Oak, FL 32060-7118 (386) 364-5210
Contact: Donna C. Long, Tr.

Foundation type: Operating foundation
Purpose: Scholarships to adults wishing to enter the LPN program at Suwannee-Hamilton Area Voc-Tech, FL. Scholarships to Suwannee High School, FL, seniors wishing to enroll in Suwannee-Hamilton Area Voc-Tech, FL, after graduation. Scholarships to Suwannee High School, FL, seniors wishing to enroll in a community or four-year college after graduation.
Financial data: Year ended 06/30/2013. Assets, $87,744 (M); Expenditures, $1,309; Total giving, $600; Grant to an individual, 1 grant totaling $600.
Fields of interest: Vocational education, post-secondary.
Type of support: Support to graduates or students of specific schools; Technical education support; Undergraduate support.
Application information: Applications accepted. Interview required.
Initial approach: Letter
Deadline(s): May 1 for high school seniors; Aug. 1 for LPN students
Applicants should submit the following:
1) GPA
2) Transcripts
3) Letter(s) of recommendation
4) Financial information
EIN: 597011644

1926
Immokalee Foundation, Inc.
3960 Radio Rd., Ste. 207
Naples, FL 34104-3746 (239) 430-9122
Contact: Liz Allbritten, Exec. Dir.
FAX: (239) 262-7701;
E-mail: info@immokaleefoundation.org;
URL: http://www.immokaleefoundation.org

Foundation type: Public charity
Purpose: Scholarships only to graduates of Immokalee High School, FL.
Publications: Application guidelines; Annual report; Grants list; Informational brochure; Newsletter.
Financial data: Year ended 03/31/2012. Assets, $9,151,340 (M); Expenditures, $1,791,301; Total giving, $187,240; Grants to individuals, totaling $125,240.
Type of support: Support to graduates or students of specific schools; Undergraduate support.
Application information: Application form required.
Initial approach: Letter
Copies of proposal: 7
Deadline(s): Jan. 15
Applicants should submit the following:
1) Proposal
2) Financial information
3) Budget Information
EIN: 650315664

1927
Indian River State College Foundation, Inc.
(formerly Indian River Community College Foundation)
3209 Virginia Ave., Bldg. A., Rm. 154
Fort Pierce, FL 34981-5541 (772) 462-4786
E-mail: foundation@ircc.edu

Foundation type: Public charity
Purpose: Scholarships awarded to Fort Pierce, FL students in pursuit of a higher education.
Publications: Application guidelines; Annual report.
Financial data: Year ended 03/31/2012. Assets, $63,878,019 (M); Expenditures, $5,309,133; Total giving, $4,335,872; Grants to individuals, totaling $2,286,288.
Fields of interest: Higher education.
Type of support: Scholarships—to individuals; Support to graduates or students of specific schools.
Application information: Application form required. Application form available on the grantmaker's web site.
Deadline(s): Aug.1 and Oct. 1
Additional information: See web site for a complete listing of scholarship programs.
EIN: 591105591

1928
Myron Jacob Foreman U.S. Scholarship Trust
580 Village Blvd., Ste. 110
West Palm Beach, FL 33409 (561) 585-1938
Contact: Rufus Lee Boozer, Tr.
Application address: 145 Bloomfield Dr., West Palm Beach, FL 33405, tel.: (561) 585-1938

Foundation type: Independent foundation
Purpose: Scholarships for Bahamian medical students.
Financial data: Year ended 06/30/2013. Assets, $1,003,239 (M); Expenditures, $37,247; Total giving, $20,000; Grants to individuals, 2 grants totaling $20,000 (high: $15,000, low: $5,000).
Fields of interest: Medical school/education.
International interests: Bahamas.
Type of support: Foreign applicants; Graduate support.
Application information: Applications accepted. Application form required.
Initial approach: Letter or telephone
Additional information: Application must include transcripts and MedCat scores.
EIN: 656186928

1929
The Robert and Deborah Jacobson Charitable Trust
P.O. Box 3475
West Palm Beach, FL 33402-3475
Scholarship inquiry: admissions@pba.edu, tel.: (561) 803-2992

Foundation type: Independent foundation
Purpose: Scholarships to qualified students of FL, who have been in the top 10 percent of their class upon graduation, pursuing higher education.
Financial data: Year ended 12/31/2011. Assets, $5,569,631 (M); Expenditures, $488,857; Total giving, $345,900; Grants to individuals, 10 grants totaling $66,000 (high: $11,000, low: $2,500).
Fields of interest: Higher education.
Type of support: Scholarships—to individuals.

Application information: Applications accepted. Application form required.
Deadline(s): Mar.13
Additional information: Students must have a minimum SAT of 1400 on the 1600 system or 2100 on the 2400 system. Applicant must exhibit leadership potential and a sense of volunteerism in the activities both inside and outside of the high school experience.
EIN: 656466536

1930
Tom Coughlin Jay Fund Foundation, Inc.
P.O. Box 50798
Jacksonville Beach, FL 32240-0798 (904) 543-2599
Contact: Keli Coughlin, Exec. Dir.
FAX: (904) 285-3616; E-mail: keli@tcjayfund.org; Toll-free tel.: (866) 538-6331; URL: http://www.tcjayfund.org

Foundation type: Public charity
Purpose: Assistance to families with individuals suffering from Leukemia and other cancers. Aid includes travel, special medical procedures, equipment and living expenses while undergoing treatment. College scholarships to survivors of cancer in the Jacksonville, FL, and NY metropolitan area, including Bergen, Essex, Hudson, Passiac, and Union counties, NJ.
Publications: Newsletter; Newsletter (including application guidelines).
Financial data: Year ended 12/31/2011. Assets, $7,784,319 (M); Expenditures, $856,499.
Fields of interest: Cancer; Leukemia.
Type of support: Grants for special needs.
Application information:
Initial approach: Letter
Deadline(s): Apr. 20 for FL scholarships; May 20 for NY/NJ scholarships
EIN: 593426937

1931
F. W. Johnston Scholarship Fund
(formerly F. W. Johnston Foundation)
P.O. Box 1908
Orlando, FL 32802-1908 (804) 273-7448
Application address: c/o Suntrust Bank,P.O Box 26150 Richmond,VA 23261

Foundation type: Independent foundation
Purpose: Scholarships to students from the Roanoke Valley and Gile County areas, VA.
Financial data: Year ended 12/31/2012. Assets, $1,459,890 (M); Expenditures, $86,384; Total giving, $58,831.
Type of support: Support to graduates or students of specific schools; Undergraduate support.
Application information: Applications accepted.
Deadline(s): None
Additional information: Contact fund for application guidelines.
EIN: 546456401

1932
The Joshua Foundation, Inc.
5331 Congo Ct.
Cape Coral, FL 33904-5863

Foundation type: Independent foundation
Purpose: Grants to disadvantaged individuals for charitable assistance.
Financial data: Year ended 12/31/2012. Assets, $934,658 (M); Expenditures, $257,415; Total

giving, $243,000; Grant to an individual, 1 grant totaling $6,000.
International interests: Africa; Estonia; Hungary.
Type of support: Grants for special needs.
Application information: Contact the foundation for assistance.
EIN: 593076339

1933
Bryan W. & Minnie Judge Foundation
P.O. Box 6973
Vero Beach, FL 32961 (772) 778-6903

Foundation type: Independent foundation
Purpose: College scholarships to graduating students of FL who demonstrate financial need, for postsecondary education.
Financial data: Year ended 12/31/2012. Assets, $437,483 (M); Expenditures, $45,414; Total giving, $37,500; Grants to individuals, 75 grants totaling $37,500 (high: $500, low: $500).
Fields of interest: Higher education; Scholarships/financial aid.
Type of support: Scholarships—to individuals.
Application information: Applications accepted. Application form required.
  Deadline(s): Feb. 28
  Applicants should submit the following:
    1) Transcripts
    2) Letter(s) of recommendation
  Additional information: Application should also include a personal statement. Application forms can be obtained from the foundation.
EIN: 592691650

1934
The Julien Collot Foundation
7152 S.W. 66th St.
Miami, FL 33143 (917) 517-1234
Contact: Jaqueline Cannon Collot, Pres.
URL: http://www.thejuliencollotfoundation.org/

Foundation type: Public charity
Purpose: Assistance to families in need whose children are diagnosed with leukemia.
Financial data: Year ended 09/30/2012. Assets, $3,390 (M); Expenditures, $60,958; Total giving, $42,694.
Fields of interest: Leukemia; Girls; Boys; Terminal illness, people with; Economically disadvantaged.
Type of support: Grants to individuals; Grants for special needs.
Application information: Contact the foundation for additional guidelines.
Program description:
  Families in Need: Depending on the circumstances, the foundation donates items or provides financial assistance to families in need.
EIN: 260835004

1935
Kelly Foundation, Inc.
17225 S.W. 77th Ct.
Miami, FL 33157-4859 (800) 232-2282
Contact: Janis Isom, Secy.-Treas.

Foundation type: Company-sponsored foundation
Purpose: Scholarships to undergraduate students in Florida and to children of employees of Kelly Tractor Company and Pantropic Power Products.
Financial data: Year ended 12/31/2012. Assets, $16,776,052 (M); Expenditures, $1,050,726; Total giving, $960,000; Grants to individuals, 246 grants totaling $728,500 (high: $9,000, low: $1,000).

Fields of interest: Scholarships/financial aid; Education.
Type of support: Employee-related scholarships; Scholarships—to individuals.
Application information: Applications accepted. Application form required.
  Initial approach: Contact foundation for application form
  Deadline(s): None
  Applicants should submit the following:
    1) Letter(s) of recommendation
    2) Essay
    3) Transcripts
Company name: Kelly Tractor Company
EIN: 596153269

1936
Ruth Kenney Foundation
c/o Allan R. Kenney
9067 Hilolo Ln.
Venice, FL 34293-7608

Foundation type: Independent foundation
Purpose: Scholarships to individuals for higher education in the Venice, FL area.
Financial data: Year ended 12/31/2012. Assets, $0 (M); Expenditures, $0; Total giving, $0.
Fields of interest: Higher education.
Type of support: Scholarships—to individuals.
Application information: Contact foundation for further guidelines.
EIN: 651055246

1937
The Kerouac Project of Orlando, Inc.
P.O. Box 547477
Orlando, FL 32854-7477 (407) 862-3807
Contact: Bruce Gordy, Pres.
E-mail: webmaster@kerouacproject.org;
URL: http://kerouacproject.org/

Foundation type: Public charity
Purpose: Residencies to writers of any stripe or age living anywhere in the world to stay at Jack Kerouac's FL home.
Publications: Application guidelines.
Financial data: Year ended 06/30/2012. Assets, $264,596 (M); Expenditures, $29,484.
Fields of interest: Literature.
Type of support: Residencies.
Application information: Applications accepted.
  Initial approach: Letter of Intent
  Send request by: Online
  Deadline(s): Apr. 1
  Additional information: An application fee of $25 is required. See web site for additional application information.
Program description:
  Writer in Residence: The project provides four residencies a year to writers in a three month stay at the former residence of Jack Kerouac. Utilities and a food stipend of $800 are included. Upon completion of the program the resident will give a reading at the Kerouac house.
EIN: 593531416

1938
Kids Wish Network, Inc.
4060 Louis Ave.
Holiday, FL 34691-5600 (727) 937-3600
Contact: Anna Lanzatella, Exec. Dir.
E-mail: info@kidswishnetwork.org; Toll-free tel.: (888) 918-9004; URL: http://kidswishnetwork.org

Foundation type: Public charity

Purpose: Funeral assistance to help the families of the Network's "wish kids" in the event of a child's passing.
Financial data: Year ended 05/31/2012. Assets, $5,300,388 (M); Expenditures, $24,938,087; Total giving, $9,165,855; Grants to individuals, totaling $4,044,113.
Fields of interest: Children, services; Children/youth.
Type of support: Grants for special needs.
Application information:
  Initial approach: Telephone or e-mail
  Deadline(s): None
EIN: 311579097

1939
Basil L. King Scholarship Foundation, Inc.
(formerly Fort Pierce Memorial Hospital Scholarship Foundation, Inc.)
c/o Indian River State College Foundation, Inc.
3209 Virginia Ave.
Fort Pierce, FL 34981-5596 (772) 462-7246
E-mail: lthomas@irsc.edu; URL: http://www.blksf.org/

Foundation type: Independent foundation
Purpose: Scholarships to residents of St. Lucie County, FL, who are following a graduate or undergraduate course of study leading to a career in health sciences, medicine, dentistry or pharmacy. Also, funds for health care to needy children under the age of 14 who are residents of St. Lucie County, FL.
Financial data: Year ended 09/30/2013. Assets, $6,032,419 (M); Expenditures, $312,490; Total giving, $247,035.
Fields of interest: Dental school/education; Medical school/education; Health sciences school/education.
Type of support: Graduate support; Undergraduate support; Grants for special needs.
Application information: Application form required.
  Deadline(s): May 17 for scholarships
  Additional information: Application for scholarships should include transcripts and declaration of domicile and citizenship completed by Clerk of the Circuit Court. Applications for indigent medical care should include expenses per the medical provider.
EIN: 590651084

1940
Kiwanis of Little Havana Foundation, Inc.
1400 S.W. 1st St.
Miami, FL 33135-2203
Contact: Enriqueta Fernandez, Exec. Dir.

Foundation type: Independent foundation
Purpose: Scholarships for underserved Hispanic students who are residents of Miami-Dade county FL, pursuing an undergraduate degree from a FL public college or university.
Financial data: Year ended 09/30/2013. Assets, $760,216 (M); Expenditures, $190,719; Total giving, $201,671; Grants to individuals, 48 grants totaling $71,596 (high: $4,363, low: $50).
Fields of interest: Higher education; Hispanics/Latinos.
Type of support: Scholarships—to individuals.
Application information: Applications accepted. Application form required. Application form available on the grantmaker's web site.
  Deadline(s): May 15
  Applicants should submit the following:
    1) Photograph
    2) Transcripts

3) Letter(s) of recommendation
Additional information: Application should also include a copy of you or your parents' latest income tax return. Applicant must demonstrate financial need.
EIN: 650093807

1941
KML Foundation, Inc.
P.O. Box 23943
Tampa, FL 33623-3943 (813) 289-3180
Contact: John E. Kearney, Chair.
E-mail: info@kmlfoundation.org; URL: http://www.kmlfoundation.org

Foundation type: Operating foundation
Purpose: Scholarships and loans to individuals who are residents of Hillsborough, Pasco or Pinellas counties, Florida, facing the economic challenges of obtaining a higher education.
Financial data: Year ended 05/31/2013. Assets, $6,307,479 (M); Expenditures, $332,463; Total giving, $236,826; Grants to individuals, 72 grants totaling $236,826 (high: $8,000, low: $500).
Fields of interest: Vocational education, post-secondary; Higher education.
Type of support: Scholarships—to individuals; Student loans—to individuals.
Application information: Applications accepted. Application form required. Application form available on the grantmaker's web site.
Send request by: Mail or e-mail
Deadline(s): Mar. 31 for Fall semester, and Sept. 30 for Spring semester for traditional institutions, 60 days prior to start of program term for vocational institutions
Applicants should submit the following:
1) Transcripts
2) Essay
3) Letter(s) of recommendation
Additional information: Application should also include proof of residency and a copy of GED certificate/diploma.
EIN: 203344671

1942
Essie W. Krausman Trust
(also known as August P. & Essie W. Krausman Scholarships)
P.O. Box 40200, FL9-100-10-19
Jacksonville, FL 32203-0200 (866) 461-7287
Contact: Brenton Thurston
Application address: 111 Westminster St. Providence, RI 02903Tel:(866) 461-7287

Foundation type: Independent foundation
Purpose: Scholarships to residents of Pinellas County, FL, for undergraduate education based on academic standing, financial need, and lack of other resources.
Financial data: Year ended 08/31/2013. Assets, $605,405 (M); Expenditures, $35,978; Total giving, $19,000; Grants to individuals, 26 grants totaling $19,000 (high: $1,000, low: $500).
Type of support: Undergraduate support.
Application information: Applications accepted. Application form required. Interview required.
Initial approach: Letter of telephone
Deadline(s): Contact foundation for current application deadline
Additional information: Application must include personal statement.
EIN: 596161774

1943
Lake Eustis Institute, Inc.
P.O. Box 1060
Eustis, FL 32727-1060
FAX: (352) 357-3949;
E-mail: LakeEustis135@comcast.net; URL: http://www.lakeeustisinstitute.org/

Foundation type: Operating foundation
Purpose: Awards to a Barto Prize winner for solo piano composition.
Financial data: Year ended 04/30/2013. Assets, $10,405 (M); Expenditures, $2,450; Total giving, $0.
Fields of interest: Music composition.
Type of support: Awards/prizes.
Application information:
Deadline(s): Aug. 30
Additional information: Contact institute for additional contest guidelines.
Program description:
Barto Prize: The Barto Prize is an international competition for the best piano solo composition and is awarded every two years. The competition is open to all original compositions. Compositions must be based on a short poem. There is a trophy and a monetary prize of $5,000.
EIN: 341977626

1944
Lake-Sumter Community College Foundation, Inc.
9501 U.S. Hwy. 441
Leesburg, FL 34788-3950 (352) 323-3688
Contact: Rosanne Brandeburg, Exec. Dir.
E-mail: brandebr@lscc.edu; URL: http://www.lscc.edu/foundation/

Foundation type: Public charity
Purpose: Scholarships to students attending Lake Summer Community College, FL for full time or part time study.
Financial data: Year ended 12/31/2011. Assets, $12,649,359 (M); Expenditures, $887,999; Total giving, $492,556; Grants to individuals, totaling $492,556.
Fields of interest: College (community/junior).
Type of support: Support to graduates or students of specific schools.
Application information: Applications accepted. Application form required. Application form available on the grantmaker's web site.
Deadline(s): Mar. for Summer semester, June for Fall semester, Oct. for Spring semester
Applicants should submit the following:
1) Financial information
2) Essay
EIN: 591990323

1945
Lang Family Foundation Inc.
3836 Aves Island Ct.
Punta Gorda, FL 33950 (507) 931-0430

Foundation type: Company-sponsored foundation
Purpose: Scholarships to children of employees of A & Incorporated.
Financial data: Year ended 12/31/2011. Assets, $329,566 (M); Expenditures, $23,472; Total giving, $18,800.
Fields of interest: Education.
Type of support: Employee-related scholarships.
Application information: Applications accepted.
Deadline(s): Feb. 10
Company name: A & E Incorporated
EIN: 391884671

1946
Kenard Lang Foundation, Inc.
7017 Slate St.
Orlando, FL 32810-6004 (321) 438-6935
E-mail: info@kenardlangfoundation.org;
URL: http://www.kenardlangfoundation.org

Foundation type: Public charity
Purpose: Scholarships to high school seniors of FL for attendance at a two or four year accredited college or university.
Publications: Application guidelines.
Financial data: Year ended 12/31/2012. Assets, $10,052 (M); Expenditures, $34,228; Total giving, $24,026.
Fields of interest: Higher education.
Type of support: Scholarships—to individuals.
Application information: Applications accepted. Application form required. Application form available on the grantmaker's web site.
Deadline(s): Mar. 1
Applicants should submit the following:
1) GPA
2) Photograph
3) Transcripts
4) Essay
Additional information: Application should also include a personal statement about yourself and acceptance letter from an accredited college or university you plan to attend.
Program description:
Tackle Your Talent Scholarship Program: The purpose of the scholarship is to provide financial assistance to individuals seeking to go to college who have a minimum 2.5 GPA. Eligible applicants must currently reside in the state of Florida, currently be a senior in high school, and be accepted to a two- or four-year accredited college or university. Scholarships are distributed in increments of $1,000.
EIN: 364502710

1947
Lauffer Scholarship Fund
(formerly Charles A. Lauffer Trust)
P.O. Box 40200, FL9-100-10-19
Jacksonville, FL 32203-0200 (401) 278-6039
Contact: Maria Botelho
Application address: 111 Westminster St., Providence, RI 02903, tel.: (401) 278-6039

Foundation type: Independent foundation
Purpose: Student loans to students living in the St. Petersburg, FL, area and in the state of PA, pursuing a career, with preference to medical, agriculture and engineering students.
Financial data: Year ended 08/31/2013. Assets, $3,929,644 (M); Expenditures, $340,426; Total giving, $290,026.
Fields of interest: Medical school/education; Engineering school/education; Agriculture.
Type of support: Student loans—to individuals; Graduate support.
Application information: Application form required.
Initial approach: Letter
Deadline(s): None
Applicants should submit the following:
1) GPA
2) Financial information
3) Class rank
Additional information: Application should also include documentation of school attendance and major course of study.
EIN: 596121126

1948
LeGore Scholarship Fund
P.O. Box 40200, MC FL9-100-10-19
Jacksonville, FL 32203-0200

Foundation type: Independent foundation
Purpose: Scholarships to graduates of Sarasota County, FL, high schools who have participated in the annual Sailor Circus performances.
Financial data: Year ended 03/31/2013. Assets, $426,847 (M); Expenditures, $27,208; Total giving, $18,000.
Fields of interest: Higher education; Scholarships/financial aid.
Type of support: Support to graduates or students of specific schools; Undergraduate support.
Application information: Applications accepted. Application form not required.
Deadline(s): Apr. 15
EIN: 656008408

1949
Edith, Samuel and Elizabeth Leinbach Foundation, Inc.
3808 Valentia Way
Naples, FL 34119-7511

Foundation type: Independent foundation
Purpose: Scholarships to individuals attending Grinnell College, IA, or MaCalester College, St. Paul, MN.
Financial data: Year ended 12/31/2011. Assets, $103,529 (M); Expenditures, $6,143; Total giving, $5,000.
Type of support: Support to graduates or students of specific schools; Undergraduate support.
Application information: Applications not accepted.
Additional information: Unsolicited requests for funds not considered.
EIN: 411543086

1950
Lois Pope Life Foundation Inc.
6274 Linton Blvd., Ste. 103
Delray Beach, FL 33484-6508 (561) 865-0955
FAX: (561) 865-0938; E-mail: life@life-edu.org;
URL: http://www.life-edu.org/

Foundation type: Independent foundation
Purpose: Medical scholarships to inner city students for attendance at the City College of New York (CCNY), as well as honors outstanding scientists who have made possible significant medical breakthroughs.
Publications: Newsletter.
Financial data: Year ended 12/31/2012. Assets, $4,032,904 (M); Expenditures, $993,611; Total giving, $650,250.
Fields of interest: Medical school/education; Science.
Type of support: Research; Scholarships—to individuals; Awards/prizes.
Application information: Applications not accepted.
Additional information: Unsolicited requests for funds not considered or acknowledged.
Program descriptions:
Lois Pope LIFE International Achievement Award: Established in 1999, the Lois Pope LIFE International Achievement Award honors outstanding scientists who have made possible significant medical breakthroughs. The honor, which comes with a $100,000 research award, is presented annually by the Lois Pope LIFE

Foundation and has awarded $1,700,000 since its inception.
Unsung Hero Scholarship: $25,000 medical scholarships are awarded each year to four academically deserving, community service oriented and financially needy inner city students who are attending medical school at the City College of New York (CCNY)
EIN: 273158367

1951
Lincoln Foundation
P.O. Box 163
Windermere, FL 34786-0163 (407) 876-1371
Contact: Timothy W. Lincoln, Secy.-Treas.

Foundation type: Operating foundation
Purpose: Scholarships to needy students of the Lexington, VA and Winter Park, FL areas.
Financial data: Year ended 12/31/2012. Assets, $1,620,158 (M); Expenditures, $29,041; Total giving, $12,998; Grants to individuals, 7 grants totaling $12,998 (high: $6,898, low: $400).
Type of support: Undergraduate support.
Application information:
Initial approach: Letter
Deadline(s): Nov. 30
EIN: 383014819

1952
Mollie Parnis Livingston Foundation, Inc.
389 Eagle Dr.
Jupiter, FL 33477-4065

Foundation type: Independent foundation
Purpose: Awards to journalists under 35 years of age who are working for a U.S. publication or broadcast organization.
Financial data: Year ended 12/31/2011. Assets, $2,766,164 (M); Expenditures, $320,738; Total giving, $265,280.
Fields of interest: Media/communications; Print publishing.
Type of support: Awards/grants by nomination only; Awards/prizes.
Application information: Application form required.
Deadline(s): Feb. 1
Additional information: Application form required for journalism awards, along with printed or broadcast entries; No faxed or e-mailed applications will be accepted; Students are ineligible.
Program description:
Livingston Journalism Awards: Awards are given for the best examples of print, on-line or broadcast journalism in three categories: local, national, and international affairs. Features and commentary are eligible; photography is not. One entry per individual. Individuals may apply on their own or be entered by their organization. In addition to the cash award, recipients take part in a prestigious award ceremony. The ceremony is arranged to attract maximum public attention, and is an important part of the award.
EIN: 136265280

1953
Lloyd Family Foundation
688 N. Town and River Dr.
Fort Myers, FL 33919-5931 (239) 481-2153
Contact: Linda R. Lloyd, Treas.
E-mail: welloyd@comcast.net

Foundation type: Independent foundation

Purpose: Scholarships to residents of Page County, IA, majoring in graphic arts or journalism.
Financial data: Year ended 12/31/2012. Assets, $2,799,272 (M); Expenditures, $297,057; Total giving, $293,200; Grants to individuals, 7 grants totaling $30,000 (high: $5,000, low: $2,500).
Fields of interest: Print publishing; Visual arts; Design.
Type of support: Undergraduate support.
Application information: Applications accepted.
Deadline(s): Mar. 10
EIN: 201861923

1954
Lucy B. Long Charitable Trust
P.O. Box 40200, FL9-100-10-19
Jacksonville, FL 32203-0200

Foundation type: Independent foundation
Purpose: Scholarships to residents of GA to attend school in GA.
Financial data: Year ended 08/31/2013. Assets, $151,082 (M); Expenditures, $10,175; Total giving, $6,500.
Type of support: Undergraduate support.
Application information: Applications not accepted.
Additional information: Unsolicited requests for funds not considered or acknowledged.
EIN: 597247101

1955
The LPGA Foundation
100 International Golf Dr.
Daytona Beach, FL 32124-1092 (386) 274-6200
FAX: (386) 274-1099; URL: http://www.lpgafoundation.org/

Foundation type: Public charity
Purpose: Scholarships to female high school seniors who played golf during high school and pursuing a college education. Financial assistance to members of the golf industry who have suffered serious illness, injury, loss of income or other significant hardship.
Publications: Application guidelines.
Financial data: Year ended 12/31/2011. Assets, $3,971,654 (M); Expenditures, $3,384,553; Total giving, $502,389; Grants to individuals, totaling $12,300.
Fields of interest: Higher education; Athletics/sports, golf.
Type of support: Scholarships—to individuals.
Application information: Applications accepted. Application form required.
Deadline(s): May 13 for Scholarship
Final notification: Recipients notified July 29 for scholarship
Applicants should submit the following:
1) Transcripts
2) GPA
3) Letter(s) of recommendation
4) Essay
Program descriptions:
Dinah Shore Scholarship: The scholarship is granted annually to a female high school senior who played golf during high school and is pursuing a college education in the U.S., but will not be playing on a competitive collegiate golf team. One scholarship in the amount of $5,000 is awarded.
Marilynn Smith Scholarship: The objective of the scholarship is to provide scholarship(s) to female high school seniors who have played golf in high school or in organized junior golf programs, and are planning to play competitive golf at an accredited

college or university in the U.S. Seven scholarships are awarded in the amount of $5,000 each.

Phyllis G. Meekins Scholarship: The objective is to provide a need-based scholarship to a female high school senior from a recognized minority background who played golf during high school and is planning to play competitive golf at an accredited college or university in the U.S. One scholarship in the amount of $1,250 is awarded.

EIN: 593085528

1956
Lutheran Services Florida, Inc.
3627A W. Waters Ave.
Tampa, FL 33614-2783 (813) 875-1408
Contact: Samuel M. Sipes, Pres. and C.E.O.
FAX: (813) 875-1302; E-mail: ssipes@lsfnet.org;
URL: http://www.lsfnet.org

Foundation type: Public charity
Purpose: A Matching Grant Program is to help refugees in FL (Amerasians, Cuban and Haitian entrants, asylees and certified victims of trafficking) become self-sufficient within four months without utilizing public assistance. To accomplish this goal, Lutheran Services Florida matches the Office of Refugee Resettlement grant with cash and in-kind contributions of goods and services.
Publications: Annual report; Newsletter.
Financial data: Year ended 06/30/2012. Assets, $10,967,025 (M); Expenditures, $39,980,715; Total giving, $7,890,098; Grants to individuals, totaling $7,890,098.
Fields of interest: Immigrants/refugees.
Type of support: Grants for special needs.
Application information:
Initial approach: Letter
Additional information: To be eligible for assistance from the Matching Grant Program, applicants must provide documentary proof of status as a refugee, asylee, Cuban or Haitian entrant, Amerasian or victim of trafficking, enroll in the Matching Grant Program within 31 days of the date of receiving notice of eligibility, and be employable or at least one member of their refugee family unit must be employable.

EIN: 592198911

1957
The John Lynch Foundation, Inc.
P. O. Box 172247
Tampa, FL 33672-0247
FAX: (813) 831-4441;
E-mail: maggie@johnlynchfoundation.org; Toll-free tel.: (866) 553-4747; URL: http://www.johnlynchfoundation.org

Foundation type: Public charity
Purpose: Scholarships for graduating seniors in the Denver, CO area who were varsity student-athletes in high school.
Publications: Application guidelines.
Financial data: Year ended 12/31/2011. Assets, $832,409 (M); Expenditures, $151,621; Total giving, $69,500; Grants to individuals, totaling $69,500.
Fields of interest: Athletics/sports, school programs.
Type of support: Undergraduate support.
Application information: Applications accepted. Application form required. Application form available on the grantmaker's web site.
Initial approach: Letter
Send request by: Mail or e-mail
Deadline(s): Apr. 4

Applicants should submit the following:
1) GPA
2) Essay
3) Letter(s) of recommendation
EIN: 593665351

1958
Magic Action Team Community Fund, Inc.
(formerly Magic Action Community Fund, Inc.)
8701 Maitland Summit Blvd.
Orlando, FL 32810
Contact: Stephanie Allen

Foundation type: Operating foundation
Purpose: Scholarships to deserving high school seniors of Orange, Osceola, or Seminole counties FL for attendance at accredited colleges or universities in FL.
Financial data: Year ended 06/30/2012. Assets, $0 (M); Expenditures, $45,000; Total giving, $27,500; Grants to individuals, 10 grants totaling $27,500 (high: $5,000, low: $2,500).
Fields of interest: Higher education; Asians/Pacific Islanders; African Americans/Blacks; Hispanics/Latinos; Native Americans/American Indians.
Type of support: Undergraduate support.
Application information: Application form required.
Deadline(s): Feb.
Applicants should submit the following:
1) Essay
2) ACT
3) SAT
4) Transcripts
5) Letter(s) of recommendation
Additional information: Applicants must demonstrate financial need.
Program descriptions:
Magic Achievers Scholarship: A $10,000 scholarship ($2,500 annually) is provided to a high school senior in the specified tri-county area to attend accredited four year college or university in FL. Applicant must have a minimum 1010 SAT or 21 ACT score, and a weighted GPA of 3.0 or above on a 4.0 scale. The scholarship winner will be required to perform 30 hours of community service per semester.
Orlando Magic UCF Minority Scholarship: This scholarship provides two $10,000 scholarships ($2,500 annually) to two minority high school seniors in the specified tri-county area to attend the University of Central Florida. A minority student including but not limited to African-American, Hispanic, Asian, Pacific Islander, American-Indian, or Alaskan Native. The applicant must have a minimum 1010 SAT or 21 ACT score, a weighted cumulative GPA of 3.0 or above on a 4.0 scale, and perform 30 hours of community service per semester. Applicant must be a U.S. citizen or visa-holding permanent resident.
EIN: 593287579

1959
Will Dushek Maine South Scholarship Fund
c/o James F. Dushek
2301 Gulf Shores Blvd. N.
Naples, FL 34103

Foundation type: Independent foundation
Purpose: Scholarships to qualified students of Park Ridge, IL in pursuit of a higher education.
Financial data: Year ended 12/31/2012. Assets, $54,550 (M); Expenditures, $6,500; Total giving, $6,000; Grants to individuals, 3 grants totaling $6,000 (high: $2,000, low: $2,000).
Fields of interest: Higher education.

Type of support: Scholarships—to individuals.
Application information: Applications accepted.
Deadline(s): None
Additional information: Contact the fund for additional application guidelines.
EIN: 391996550

1960
Manatee Community Foundation, Inc.
3103 Manatee Ave. W.
Bradenton, FL 34205-3305 (941) 747-7765
Contact: Marilyn Howard, Exec. Dir.
FAX: (941) 747-7899;
E-mail: marilyn@manateecf.org; URL: http://www.manateecf.org

Foundation type: Public charity
Purpose: Scholarships to graduating seniors and nontraditional students who reside in Manatee county, FL for attendance at any accredited college, university or technical school.
Publications: Informational brochure; Newsletter.
Financial data: Year ended 05/31/2012. Assets, $22,140,571 (M); Expenditures, $2,666,542; Total giving, $2,041,722; Grants to individuals, totaling $112,124.
Fields of interest: Higher education.
Type of support: Scholarships—to individuals.
Application information: Applications accepted.
Deadline(s): Varies
Additional information: See web site for a complete listing of scholarship programs.
EIN: 650833500

1961
Manley Music Scholarship Trust
14025 Riveredge Dr., Ste. 280
Tampa, FL 33637-2015

Foundation type: Independent foundation
Purpose: Scholarships to students at Wabash High School, IN pursuing a career in music or music education.
Financial data: Year ended 12/31/2012. Assets, $396,084 (M); Expenditures, $15,172; Total giving, $8,000.
Fields of interest: Music.
Type of support: Support to graduates or students of specific schools; Undergraduate support.
Application information: Application form required.
Deadline(s): Mar. 1
Applicants should submit the following:
1) Transcripts
2) Letter(s) of recommendation
EIN: 352028289

1962
Marco Island Women's Club Foundation
P.O. Box 40200, FL-100-10-19
Jacksonville, FL 32203-0200
Contact: Lorraine Rodgers, Chair.
Application address: P.O. Box 400, Marco Island, FL 34146-0400

Foundation type: Independent foundation
Purpose: Scholarships only to Marco Island, FL residents.
Financial data: Year ended 04/30/2013. Assets, $568,927 (M); Expenditures, $30,671; Total giving, $26,000.
Type of support: Scholarships—to individuals.
Application information: Application form required. Interview required.
Initial approach: Letter
Deadline(s): Mar. 15

Additional information: Applicants should submit a resume.
EIN: 650144269

1963
G. Roxy & Elizabeth C. Martin Charitable Trust

c/o SunTrust Bank, Charitable Services Group
300 S. Orange Ave., Ste. 1600
Orlando, FL 32801-3382
E-mail: fdnsvcs.fl@suntrust.com; Application address: c/o SunTrust Bank, 200 S. Orange Ave., SOAB-10, Orlando, FL 32801; URL: http://fdnweb.org/martin

Foundation type: Independent foundation
Purpose: Scholarships to individuals in FL for higher education.
Financial data: Year ended 11/30/2013. Assets, $4,071,044 (M); Expenditures, $249,126; Total giving, $202,750; Grants to individuals, 87 grants totaling $112,250 (high: $2,500, low: $750).
Fields of interest: Higher education.
Type of support: Undergraduate support.
Application information: Applications accepted. Application form required.
  Deadline(s): Mar. 31
  Final notification: May
  Applicants should submit the following:
    1) Essay
    2) Letter(s) of recommendation
    3) Transcripts
    4) Photograph
  Additional information: Application must also include honors received, clubs and social activities participated in, talents and interests, three letters of recommendations, a list of job experience, if any, including place of employment dates of employment, job title and duties, Essay should be a brief autobiography including career goals and objectives.
EIN: 596920693

1964
Martin County Community Foundation, Inc.

33 Flagler Ave.
Stuart, FL 34994-2140 (772) 288-3795
Contact: Bridget Dugan Baratta, Exec. Dir.
FAX: (772) 287-8924;
E-mail: bbaratta@yourmccf.org; Additional telephone: (772) 283-2356; URL: http://www.yourmccf.org

Foundation type: Public charity
Purpose: Scholarships to graduating seniors of Martin County high schools, FL pursuing higher education.
Financial data: Year ended 06/30/2012. Assets, $3,824,978 (M); Expenditures, $300,916; Total giving, $172,232; Grants to individuals, totaling $38,267.
Fields of interest: Higher education.
Type of support: Scholarships—to individuals; Support to graduates or students of specific schools.
Application information: Applications accepted. Application form required.
  Additional information: Students should contact their high school guidance counselors for additional application guidelines. Scholarships are paid directly to the educational institution on behalf of the

students. Application should include transcripts.
EIN: 650024030

1965
The Patrick J. Martin Family Foundation

5286 Kensingston High St.
Naples, FL 34105 (303) 931-3723
Contact: Patrick J. Martin, Tr.
FAX: (239) 643-3263;
E-mail: patmartin@qwest.net; Additional tel.: (303) 931-3723; URL: http://thepatrickjmartinfoundation.com/

Foundation type: Independent foundation
Purpose: Scholarships to students for the study of math, science, and engineering at the college or undergraduate level. Preference is given to students who wish to study at Iona College in New Rochelle, NY, or The George Washington University in Washington, DC.
Publications: Application guidelines.
Financial data: Year ended 12/31/2012. Assets, $4,396,087 (M); Expenditures, $300,832; Total giving, $273,844; Grants to individuals, 43 grants totaling $215,000 (high: $5,000, low: $5,000).
Fields of interest: Higher education.
Type of support: Support to graduates or students of specific schools.
Application information: Applications accepted. Application form required. Application form available on the grantmaker's web site.
  Initial approach: Application
  Applicants should submit the following:
    1) Transcripts
    2) Letter(s) of recommendation
    3) Essay
    4) Class rank
    5) SAT
    6) GPA
    7) ACT
  Additional information: See web site for additional application guidelines.
EIN: 206758585

1966
Mayo Clinic Jacksonville

4500 San Pablo Rd.
Jacksonville, FL 32224-1865 (507) 538-1297
Contact: William C. Rupp M.D., Chair. and C.E.O.
URL: http://www.mayoclinic.org/jacksonville/

Foundation type: Public charity
Purpose: Scholarships to U.S. medical students participating in clinical clerkships at any Mayo Clinic locations.
Financial data: Year ended 12/31/2011. Assets, $599,685,540 (M); Expenditures, $614,721,510; Total giving, $42,414,206; Grants to individuals, totaling $1,555.
Fields of interest: Health care.
Type of support: Undergraduate support.
Application information:
  Initial approach: Letter
  Additional information: Contact foundation for eligibility criteria.
EIN: 593337028

1967
E.R. Warner McCabe Testamentary Trust - Georgia

(formerly Society of Cincinnati, Georgia Trust)
P.O. Box 1908
Orlando, FL 32802-1908
Contact: Ward M. LeHardy, Chair.
Application address: c/o 194 Castle Ln., Kilmarnock, VA 22482-3803

Foundation type: Independent foundation
Purpose: Scholarships to commendable children of members of the Society of Cincinnati in GA.
Financial data: Year ended 06/30/2013. Assets, $1,082,155 (M); Expenditures, $53,940; Total giving, $40,292; Grants to individuals, 14 grants totaling $40,292 (high: $2,878, low: $2,878).
Fields of interest: Education.
Type of support: Scholarships—to individuals.
Application information: Application form not required.
  Initial approach: Letter
  Deadline(s): July 15.
  Additional information: Letter should be from parents, including student's transcripts.
EIN: 546131247

1968
E.R. Warner McCabe Testamentary Trust

(formerly Society of Cincinnati - Virginia Trust)
P.O. Box 1908
Orlando, FL 32802-1908
Contact: Robert L. Montague III, Chair.
Application address: c/o McCabe Scholarship Committee, 207 Prince St., Alexandria, VA, 22314

Foundation type: Independent foundation
Purpose: Scholarships to commendable children of members of the Virginia Society of Cincinnati for undergraduate or graduate study at U.S. institutions.
Financial data: Year ended 06/30/2013. Assets, $1,152,863 (M); Expenditures, $57,071; Total giving, $42,930; Grants to individuals, 27 grants totaling $42,930 (high: $1,590, low: $1,590).
Fields of interest: Higher education.
Type of support: Graduate support; Undergraduate support.
Application information:
  Initial approach: Letter
  Deadline(s): June 1
  Additional information: Letter from parents including student's transcripts.
EIN: 546131246

1969
C.N. McCune Scholarship Foundation Trust

P.O. Box 1908
Orlando, FL 32802-1908
Contact: Malinda L. Tedrow; Mark Varca
FAX: (954) 838-4758; Application address: C/o. SunTrust Bank, 200 S. Orange Ave., 5th Fl., Orlando, FL 32802; 14050 N.W. 14th St., Ste. 100, Sunrise, FL 33323

Foundation type: Independent foundation
Purpose: Scholarships to residents of Broward County, FL, and eligible relatives of C.N. McCune toward degrees from community colleges, universities, and graduate schools. Scholarships are renewable.
Financial data: Year ended 08/31/2013. Assets, $258,926 (M); Expenditures, $45,832; Total giving, $36,750; Grants to individuals, 78 grants totaling $36,750 (high: $500, low: $250).

Type of support: Graduate support; Undergraduate support.
Application information: Applications accepted. Application form required.
   Deadline(s): Apr. 15
   Applicants should submit the following:
      1) Financial information
      2) Photograph
      3) Letter(s) of recommendation
      4) Transcripts
   Additional information: Application must also include student's and parents' most recent tax returns.
EIN: 596667689

1970

The McCurry Foundation Inc.

4417 Beach Blvd., Ste. 200
Jacksonville, FL 32207-4783 (904) 398-6063
Contact: Pamela S. Stefansen, Treas.
URL: http://www.mccurryfoundation.org/

Foundation type: Independent foundation
Purpose: Scholarships to students for undergraduate education, with preference to students from Glynn County, GA, and Clay, Duval, Nassau and St. Johns Counties, FL.
Financial data: Year ended 05/31/2013. Assets, $553,628 (M); Expenditures, $18,987; Total giving, $12,750; Grants to individuals, 12 grants totaling $12,750 (high: $1,250, low: $1,000).
Type of support: Undergraduate support.
Application information: Applications accepted.
   Initial approach: Letter
   Send request by: Mail
   Deadline(s): Feb. 15
   Applicants should submit the following:
      1) Letter(s) of recommendation
      2) FAFSA
      3) Transcripts
      4) Resume
      5) Financial information
      6) Essay
EIN: 593287752

1971

The Ellanora McGinty Scholarship Fund Trust

c/o Sanford A. Minkoff
15800 Acorn Cir.
Tavares, FL 32778

Foundation type: Independent foundation
Purpose: Scholarships for graduating seniors of Tavares High School, FL, for continuing education at accredited colleges or universities.
Financial data: Year ended 12/31/2012. Assets, $179,651 (M); Expenditures, $28,644; Total giving, $27,373; Grants to individuals, 15 grants totaling $27,373 (high: $4,387, low: $999).
Fields of interest: Vocational education, post-secondary; Higher education.
Type of support: Scholarships—to individuals; Support to graduates or students of specific schools.
Application information: Applications accepted. Application form required. Interview required.
   Deadline(s): Late Mar. or Apr.
   Applicants should submit the following:
      1) Essay
      2) SAT
      3) GPA
      4) ACT
   Additional information: Selection is based on financial need and academic achievement.
EIN: 596964815

1972

Edgar & Nona McKinney Charitable Trust

(formerly Edgar P. & Nona B. McKinney Foundation)
c/o SunTrust Bank
200 S. Orange Ave., SOAB-10
Orlando, FL 32801 (407) 237-4485
Contact: Melanie Cianciotto
URL: http://fdnweb.org/mckinney

Foundation type: Independent foundation
Purpose: Scholarships only to Lake County, FL students for higher education.
Financial data: Year ended 05/31/2013. Assets, $1,530,572 (M); Expenditures, $104,931; Total giving, $82,000.
Type of support: Scholarships—to individuals.
Application information: Applications accepted. Application form required.
   Deadline(s): Apr. 1
   Additional information: Contact Sun Trust Bank for guidelines and documents required for current application guidelines.
EIN: 597001925

1973

Edwin Budge Mead Scholarship Trust

P.O. Box 40200, MC FL9-100-10-19
Jacksonville, FL 32203-0200
Application address: Principal of Eutis High School, 1300 E Washington Ave. Eustis, FL 32726-4665

Foundation type: Independent foundation
Purpose: Scholarships to graduating seniors who are in the top 25 percent of the class of Eustis High School, FL.
Financial data: Year ended 12/31/2012. Assets, $340,472 (M); Expenditures, $8,026; Total giving, $0.
Fields of interest: Higher education.
Type of support: Support to graduates or students of specific schools; Undergraduate support.
Application information: Contact high school principal for scholarship information.
EIN: 596190681

1974

L. & M. Meador Scholarship Trust

c/o Bank of America, N.A.
P.O. Box 40200, FL9-100-10-19
Jacksonville, FL 32203-0200 (804) 788-2673
Application address: c/o Bank of America, Attn.: Sarah Kay, 1111 E. Main St., VA2-300-12-92, Richmond, VA 23219

Foundation type: Independent foundation
Purpose: Scholarships to residents of Norton and Wise counties, VA, for higher education.
Financial data: Year ended 05/31/2013. Assets, $960,004 (M); Expenditures, $62,187; Total giving, $39,375.
Type of support: Scholarships—to individuals.
Application information: Applications accepted. Application form required.
   Initial approach: Letter or telephone
   Deadline(s): None
   Applicants should submit the following:
      1) Letter(s) of recommendation
      2) Transcripts
EIN: 546385104

1975

The Nicole Megaloudis Foundation

6 Delano Ln.
Sewalls Point, FL 34996-7701 (772) 220-0026
Contact: Gail Rongen, Pres.
E-mail: remembernicole@aol.com; URL: http://www.remembernicole.org

Foundation type: Public charity
Purpose: Scholarships to assist students who hope to attend and graduate from college.
Financial data: Year ended 12/31/2012. Assets, $245,904 (M); Expenditures, $37,502; Total giving, $22,133; Grants to individuals, totaling $22,133.
Fields of interest: Higher education.
Type of support: Scholarships—to individuals.
Application information: Applications accepted. Application form required.
   Additional information: Selection is based on leadership qualities and demonstration of financial need.
EIN: 200857290

1976

Lucy E. Meiller Educational Trust

P.O. Box 1908
Orlando, FL 32802-1908
Contact: Carolyn McCoy

Foundation type: Independent foundation
Purpose: Scholarships to financially needy VA residents with scholastic ability to attend VA colleges and universities.
Financial data: Year ended 08/31/2013. Assets, $484,572 (M); Expenditures, $37,942; Total giving, $22,500; Grants to individuals, 30 grants totaling $22,500 (high: $750, low: $750).
Fields of interest: Higher education.
Type of support: Scholarships—to individuals.
Application information: Application form required.
   Deadline(s): None
   Applicants should submit the following:
      1) Transcripts
      2) Financial information
   Additional information: Application must also include a biographical sketch, scholastic records, and meet other eligibility requirements.
EIN: 546238746

1977

Meninak Charity Foundation Trust

(formerly Meninak Foundation of Jacksonville)
P.O. Box 8626
Jacksonville, FL 32239 (904) 745-3393
Contact: John Roberts, Chair.
E-mail: meninak@comcast.net; URL: http://www.meninak.org/about-meninak/meninak-foundation.html

Foundation type: Public charity
Purpose: Scholarships to residents of Jacksonville, FL who are participants in Youth Leadership Jacksonville.
Publications: Application guidelines; Grants list.
Financial data: Year ended 12/31/2011. Assets, $233,673 (M); Expenditures, $73,310; Total giving, $55,000.
Fields of interest: Higher education.
Type of support: Scholarships—to individuals.
Application information: Application form required.
   Initial approach: Letter.
   Deadline(s): Feb. 15

Program description:

Meninak Leadership Grants: College scholarships in the form of one-time grants are provided to area high school seniors. Winners are chosen from participants in Youth Leadership Jacksonville, a non-profit organization dedicated to developing leadership potential in high school students throughout Northeast FL.

EIN: 596120994

1978
Miami Foundation, The

(formerly Dade Community Foundation)
200 South Biscayne Blvd., Ste. 505
Miami, FL 33131-5330 (305) 371-2711
Contact: Pamelo Olmo, V.P., Finance and C.F.O.; For grants: Charisse L. Grant, Sr. V.P., Progs.; For communications: Matthew Beatty, Comms. Off.; For development: Julie Bindeutel, Devel. Off.
For Miami Fellows: Tamaya Garcia (305) 357-2094
FAX: (305) 371-5342;
E-mail: polmo@miamifoundation.org; URL: http://www.miamifoundation.org

Foundation type: Community foundation
Purpose: Scholarships and fellowships to residents of Dade County, FL.
Publications: Application guidelines; Annual report; Newsletter; Occasional report.
Financial data: Year ended 12/31/2012. Assets, $165,395,575 (M); Expenditures, $24,539,151; Total giving, $13,952,712. Grants to individuals amount not specified.
Fields of interest: Higher education; Business school/education; African Americans/Blacks.
Type of support: Fellowships; Scholarships—to individuals.
Application information: Applications accepted. Application form required. Application form available on the grantmaker's web site.
Initial approach: Application
Send request by: Mail for scholarship, online for fellows
Deadline(s): Feb. 1 for Tuckfield Scholarship, Feb. 28 for Miami Fellows
Final notification: Recipients notified Apr. 12 for Miami Fellows
Additional information: See web site for additional information.
Program descriptions:
Jacki Tuckfield Memorial Graduate Business Scholarship: Business scholarships are awarded to African American students who plan to pursue a professional career in South Florida. This year, the Jacki Tuckfield Memorial Graduate Business Scholarship Fund will award $30,000 in tuition awards.
Miami Fellows Initiative: This leadership development program enables the foundation to actively recruit local community leaders and expose them to leadership, social, and ethical issues, and provide opportunities to enhance their leadership skills. See web site for application guidelines.
EIN: 650350357

1979
Greater Miami Jewish Federation, Inc.

4200 Biscayne Blvd.
Miami, FL 33137-3210 (305) 576-4000
FAX: (305) 573-8115; E-mail: info@gmjf.org;
URL: http://www.jewishmiami.org

Foundation type: Public charity
Purpose: Scholarshps to Jewish students throughout the Miami-Dade metropolitan area, to attend federation-approved programs in Israel and to continue their school work.
Publications: Application guidelines; Annual report; Informational brochure; Newsletter.
Financial data: Year ended 06/30/2013. Assets, $176,876,409 (M); Expenditures, $36,411,049; Total giving, $26,214,224; Grants to individuals, totaling $259,678.
Fields of interest: Education; Jewish agencies & synagogues.
Type of support: Scholarships—to individuals.
Application information:
Initial approach: Application
Deadline(s): Varies
Additional information: See web site for additional guidelines.
Program descriptions:
Israel Programs Scholarship Assistance: Need-based assistance is offered for Miami-Dade county residents, ages 15 to 26, to attend an approved Israel program of at least three weeks in duration. Awards range from $250 to $500 for month-long summer programs, and up to $1,000 for year-long programs.
Jewish Camp Scholarships: Scholarships of $1,000 each are available for children between the ages of 8 and 17 to help make Jewish overnight summer camping affordable to families. Applicants must be living in Miami-Dade County, demonstrate financial need, and have a child who plans on attending a qualified Jewish summer camp (as listed on the federation's web site)
Jewish Education and Communal Service Scholarships: Scholarship assistance is available to college students (junior and senior undergraduate and graduate levels) who are enrolled in professional degree programs, and who are pursuing careers in Jewish education and Jewish communal service.
Supplemental Jewish Day School Scholarships: The federation provides Jewish day schools in Miami with supplemental funds to assist families still struggling after the initial scholarship process.
EIN: 590624404

1980
Miller Family Charitable Foundation, Inc.

6215 E. Sawgrass Rd.
Sarasota, FL 34240

Foundation type: Operating foundation
Purpose: Specific assistance for needy individuals and families with school supplies, transportation and other special needs.
Financial data: Year ended 12/31/2011. Assets, $0 (M); Expenditures, $1,050; Total giving, $500.
Fields of interest: Human services.
Type of support: Grants for special needs.
Application information: Contact foundation for guidelines on assistance.
EIN: 650965684

1981
Momeni Foundation

P.O. Box 322
Clearwater, FL 33757 (727) 433-2133
E-mail: momenifoundation@aol.com; URL: http://www.momenifoundation.org

Foundation type: Operating foundation
Purpose: Scholarships to graduating high school students and full-time college students of Iranian descent.
Financial data: Year ended 12/31/2012. Assets, $250,864 (M); Expenditures, $14,966; Total giving, $9,500; Grants to individuals, 16 grants totaling $9,500 (high: $1,000, low: $500).
Fields of interest: Higher education.
International interests: Iran.
Type of support: Scholarships—to individuals.
Application information: Applications accepted. Application form required. Application form available on the grantmaker's web site.
Send request by: Mail
Deadline(s): June 30
Final notification: Applicants notified by end of Aug.
Applicants should submit the following:
1) Essay
2) Transcripts
3) Resume
4) GPA
5) Financial information
Program descriptions:
Financial Assistance Scholarship: Scholarships ranging from $500 to $1,000 are awarded on the basis of financial need. This scholarship is available to all graduating high school students and current college students of all levels (undergraduate, graduate and PhD) and of Iranian descent regardless of citizenship or country of residency. Students planning to attend or attending universities in Iran are encouraged to apply.
Scholastic Achievement Scholarship: Scholarships in the amount of $1,000 are awarded on the basis of academic achievement. The scholarship is only available to students of Iranian heritage who are graduating from high school and who are citizens or permanent residents of the United States.
EIN: 931317612

1982
The Nat Moore Foundation, Inc.

16911 N.E. 6th Ave.
North Miami Beach, FL 33162-2407 (305) 770-0995
Contact: Bob Pechon, Pres.
FAX: (305) 770-4059;
E-mail: info@natmoorefoundation.org; URL: http://www.natmoorefoundation.net/

Foundation type: Public charity
Purpose: Scholarships to graduating high school seniors from Miami-Dade and Broward County High Schools, FL, pursuing higher education.
Financial data: Year ended 09/30/2011. Assets, $348,229 (M); Expenditures, $581,982; Total giving, $163,115; Grants to individuals, totaling $99,615.
Fields of interest: Vocational education, post-secondary; Higher education.
Type of support: Scholarships—to individuals; Support to graduates or students of specific schools.
Application information: Applications accepted. Application form required.
Send request by: Mail or e-mail
Deadline(s): Jan. 31
Final notification: Applicants notified by Apr. 15
Applicants should submit the following:
1) Transcripts
2) Photograph
3) Letter(s) of recommendation
4) Essay
Additional information: Applicants must demonstrate financial need, and commitment to community service. Payments are made directly to the educational institution on behalf of the students.

Program description:

Urban Scholarship Program: The program provides $10,000 scholarship awards, payable at $2,500 each year over four years. Each year, the recipients must show their good standing by providing proof of continued enrollment in their school of choice and a cumulative 2.0 GPA or above on a 4.0 scale. Applicant must plan to attend a two or four year college, or technical school.
EIN: 650815097

1983

Winifred Morris Family Foundation

10516 NW 57th Ct.
Coral Springs, FL 33065 (954) 341-7408
Contact: James J. Johnston

Foundation type: Operating foundation
Purpose: Scholarships to residents of the Boca Raton, FL metropolitan area, for attendance at a FL school.
Financial data: Year ended 12/31/2011. Assets, $228,574 (M); Expenditures, $20,776; Total giving, $12,000; Grants to individuals, 6 grants totaling $12,000 (high: $2,000, low: $2,000).
Type of support: Undergraduate support.
Application information:
  Initial approach: Letter
  Deadline(s): None
  Additional information: Contact foundation for eligibility criteria.
EIN: 466125063

1984

Glenn W. & Hazelle Paxson Morrison Foundation, Inc.

P.O. Box 7518
Lakeland, FL 33807-7518 (863) 602-2968
Contact: R. Lynn Noris

Foundation type: Independent foundation
Purpose: Scholarships primarily to individuals pursuing higher education for general music and Christian education at Christian schools in Polk County, FL.
Financial data: Year ended 06/30/2013. Assets, $4,074,639 (M); Expenditures, $266,457; Total giving, $209,550; Grants to individuals, 29 grants totaling $83,250 (high: $3,500, low: $1,000).
Fields of interest: Christian agencies & churches.
Type of support: Scholarships—to individuals.
Application information: Applications accepted.
  Additional information: Application should include a copy of the applicant's or parents' tax return.
EIN: 592220612

1985

Mote Marine Laboratory, Inc.

1600 Ken Thompson Pkwy.
Sarasota, FL 34236-1004 (941) 388-4441
College Intern application e-mail: intern@mote.org
URL: http://www.mote.org

Foundation type: Public charity
Purpose: Scholarships to bright and deserving individuals participating in the Mote College Intern Programs.
Publications: Application guidelines; Newsletter.
Financial data: Year ended 12/31/2011. Assets, $48,051,305 (M); Expenditures, $19,670,758; Total giving, $256,317; Grants to individuals, totaling $105,482.
Fields of interest: Marine science.

Type of support: Internship funds; Scholarships—to individuals.
Application information: Applications accepted. Application form required. Application form available on the grantmaker's web site.
  Send request by: E-mail
  Deadline(s): Mar. 1 for summer session, June 1 for fall session, Sept. 1 for winter session, Dec. 1 for spring session
  Final notification: Applicants notified approximately one month after deadline
  Applicants should submit the following:
    1) Resume
    2) Curriculum vitae
    3) Financial information
    4) Transcripts
    5) Letter(s) of recommendation
  Additional information: Applicant must demonstrate financial need. See web site for additional application guidelines and available scholarships.
Program description:

Scholarship: These scholarships are intended to provide partial support for living expenses for a full-time, 10 week or longer internship. Scholarship amount vary according to intern financial need, internship duration and the number of recipients. It is a one-time award of up to $2,500 per recipient. Interns from minority groups under-represented in science are encouraged to apply for scholarships to promote diversity in the marine sciences. Only U.S. citizens and permanent residents candidates having a U.S. social security number are eligible to apply.
EIN: 590756643

1986

Mount Dora Center for the Arts

138 E. 5th Ave.
Mount Dora, FL 32757-5573 (352) 383-0880
Contact: Beth Miller, Exec. Co-Chair.
FAX: (352) 383-7753;
E-mail: nancy@mountdoracenterforthearts.org;
URL: http://www.mountdoracenterforthearts.org

Foundation type: Public charity
Purpose: Scholarships to selected students who have shown a strong interest and ability in the arts.
Publications: Annual report; Informational brochure; Newsletter.
Financial data: Year ended 06/30/2012. Assets, $425,411 (M); Expenditures, $375,965.
Fields of interest: Arts education.
Type of support: Scholarships—to individuals.
Application information: Application form required.
  Additional information: Scholarships available only to MDCA students/participants.
Program description:

Youth Scholarship: Scholarships are available to public, private, and home-schooled students who are residents of Lake County and who are between the ages of 6 and 16, who would like to take part in studio-based arts programs held at the center but are unable to, because of financial restrictions.
EIN: 592470958

1987

Mount Dora Community Trust

714 N. Donnelly St.
P.O. Box 1451
Mount Dora, FL 32756 (352) 267-0957
Contact: Kevin Batliner, Exec. Dir.
FAX: (352) 383-1219;
E-mail: info@mountdoracommunitytrust.com;
URL: http://www.mountdoracommunitytrust.com

Foundation type: Community foundation
Purpose: Scholarships to students at Mount Dora area high schools, FL, for higher education.
Publications: Application guidelines; Annual report; Informational brochure; Newsletter; IRS Form 990 or 990-PF printed copy available upon request.
Financial data: Year ended 08/31/2012. Assets, $9,846,504 (M); Expenditures, $620,715; Total giving, $468,253; Grants to individuals, 56 grants totaling $62,530.
Type of support: Support to graduates or students of specific schools; Undergraduate support.
Application information: Applications accepted. Application form required. Application form available on the grantmaker's web site.
  Initial approach: Letter, telephone or e-mail
  Send request by: Mail
  Copies of proposal: 1 to 8
  Deadline(s): Mar. 20 for new applications, Mar. 31 for continuance applications
  Final notification: Recipients notified one week after application meeting
  Applicants should submit the following:
    1) Essay
    2) Transcripts
    3) SAT
    4) Letter(s) of recommendation
    5) GPA
    6) ACT
EIN: 237227875

1988

Mount Sinai Medical Center Foundation, Inc.

4300 Alton Rd., Ste. 1000
Miami Beach, FL 33140-2800 (305) 674-2777
E-mail: aross@msmc.com; URL: http://www.msmcfoundation.org/

Foundation type: Public charity
Purpose: Financial assistance in the form of scholarship to children of MSMC employees.
Financial data: Year ended 12/31/2011. Assets, $92,799,895 (M); Expenditures, $8,126,660; Total giving, $3,147,343; Grants to individuals, totaling $60,000.
Fields of interest: Education.
Type of support: Employee-related scholarships.
Application information: Applications not accepted.
  Additional information: Unsolicited requests for funds not considered or acknowledged.
EIN: 591711400

1989

Multiple Sclerosis Foundation, Inc.

(also known as MS Foundation)
6520 N. Andrews Ave.
Fort Lauderdale, FL 33309-2130 (954) 776-6805
Contact: Alan Segaloff, Exec. Dir.
FAX: (954) 938-8708; E-mail: admin@msfocus.org; Toll-free tel.: (800)-225-6495; URL: http://www.msfocus.org/

Foundation type: Public charity
Purpose: Grants to individuals with multiple sclerosis to improve the quality of their lives by enhancing safety, self-sufficiency, comfort or well-being.
Publications: Application guidelines; Financial statement; Newsletter.
Financial data: Year ended 12/31/2011. Assets, $2,306,383 (M); Expenditures, $6,787,983; Total giving, $746,783; Grants to individuals, totaling $746,783.

Fields of interest: Multiple sclerosis.
Type of support: Grants for special needs.
Application information: Applications accepted. Application form required. Application form available on the grantmaker's web site.
   Initial approach: Telephone
   Deadline(s): Sept. 1
   Final notification: Recipients notified in Dec.
   Applicants should submit the following:
      1) Financial information
      2) Essay
   Additional information: Applicant must provide personal and financial information, along with a brief essay of 100 words or less, describing their need and how the grant might help them to have A Brighter Tomorrow.
Program description:
   Brighter Tomorrow Grants: Up to $1,000 to individuals with multiple sclerosis 18 years of age or older and diagnosed with MS, or the parent of a minor child diagnosed with MS, and is a permanent U.S. resident. Applications must be accompanied by a brief essay of 100 words or less to describe how the grant would help applicants have 'a brighter tomorrow'.
EIN: 592792934

1990
William H. Murray Memorial Scholarship Trust Fund
P.O. Box 40200, FL9-100-10-19
Jacksonville, FL   32203-0200   (386) 506-3658
Application address: Daytona State College, 1200 W. International Speedway Blvd., Daytona Beach, FL 32120-2811

Foundation type: Independent foundation
Purpose: Scholarships to financially needy students enrolled in the associate nursing degree program at Daytona State College, FL.
Financial data: Year ended 04/30/2013. Assets, $549,472 (M); Expenditures, $31,767; Total giving, $23,400.
Fields of interest: Nursing school/education.
Type of support: Support to graduates or students of specific schools; Undergraduate support.
Application information: Applications accepted. Application form required.
   Deadline(s): None
   Additional information: Application forms available from the Student Financial Aid Office.
EIN: 596722136

1991
The Music Foundation of Southwest Florida
(formerly Jennifer Craig Memorial Fund for the Arts, Inc.)
13300-56 S. Cleveland Ave., PMB 214
Fort Myers, FL   33907-3871   (239) 275-0057
Contact: Ruth Kotush Christman, Exec. Dir.
E-mail: notes@music-foundation.org; URL: http://www.music-foundation.org

Foundation type: Public charity
Purpose: Scholarships to southwest FL high school seniors for study as music majors at the University of Central Florida.
Publications: Newsletter.
Financial data: Year ended 12/31/2011. Assets, $67,473 (M); Expenditures, $48,757; Total giving, $2,500.
Fields of interest: Music; Performing arts, education.

Type of support: Support to graduates or students of specific schools; Undergraduate support.
Application information: Contact foundation for current application deadline/guidelines.
EIN: 650264107

1992
Campbell E. Nall Scholarship Fund, Inc.
P.O. Box 1237
Clewiston, FL   33440-1077   (813) 983-7183
Contact: Earl E. Edwards III, Pres. and Dir.

Foundation type: Independent foundation
Purpose: Scholarships to graduating high school seniors of Clewiston High School, FL pursuing higher education.
Financial data: Year ended 12/31/2012. Assets, $251,290 (M); Expenditures, $12,164; Total giving, $12,000; Grants to individuals, 10 grants totaling $12,000 (high: $1,500, low: $750).
Fields of interest: Higher education.
Type of support: Scholarships—to individuals.
Application information: Applications accepted.
   Initial approach: Letter
   Deadline(s): Apr. 15
   Additional information: Students must be residents of Hendry County, FL.
EIN: 650258071

1993
Naples Woman's Club, Inc.
570 Park St.
Naples, FL   34102-6612   (239) 262-6331
Contact: Ann Cox, Corresponding Secy.
FAX: (239) 262-2302;
E-mail: napleswomansclub@comcast.net; Mailing Address: P.O. Box 7338; Naples, Florida 34101; URL: http://www.napleswomansclub.com/

Foundation type: Public charity
Purpose: Scholarships to qualifying graduating high school seniors of Collier county, FL pursuing higher education.
Financial data: Year ended 04/30/2013. Assets, $2,256,192 (M); Expenditures, $225,973; Total giving, $39,937; Grants to individuals, totaling $39,937.
Fields of interest: Vocational education, post-secondary; Higher education.
Type of support: Scholarships—to individuals.
Application information: Applications accepted. Application form required. Application form available on the grantmaker's web site. Interview required.
   Send request by: Mail or hand deliver
   Deadline(s): Feb. 19
   Final notification: Applicants notified Mar. 14
   Applicants should submit the following:
      1) Transcripts
      2) Financial information
      3) Essay
Program descriptions:
   Beryl B. Paulson Memorial Scholarship: This $1,000 scholarship is given to a young lady who is pursuing advanced education. The scholarship is based on financial need.
   NWC Educational Scholarships: This scholarship recognizes academic excellence and community service and to support and encourage students' quest for higher education by providing financial assistance. The scholarship is for Collier county high school seniors.
EIN: 590907298

1994
Naples Yacht Club Blue Gavel Scholarship Fund
700 14th Ave. S.
Naples, FL   34102-7303   (239) 262-6648
Contact: John E. Flatley, Pres.

Foundation type: Public charity
Purpose: Scholarships to Club employees and staff, as well as graduating high school seniors in Collier County, Florida.
Financial data: Year ended 12/31/2012. Assets, $78,469 (M); Expenditures, $72,571; Total giving, $70,950.
Fields of interest: Higher education.
Type of support: Employee-related scholarships; Scholarships—to individuals.
Application information: Applications not accepted.
   Additional information: Unsolicited requests for funds not considered or acknowledged.
EIN: 593467966

1995
National Kidney Foundation of Florida, Inc.
1040 Woodcock Rd., Ste. 119
Orlando, FL   32803-3510   (407) 894-7325
Contact: Stephanie Hutchinson, C.E.O.
FAX: (407) 895-0051; E-mail: nkf@kidneyfla.org;
Toll-free tel.: (800) 927-9659; URL: http://www.kidney.org/site/index.cfm?ch=204

Foundation type: Public charity
Purpose: Financial assistance to kidney patients in FL for medication, transportation and other related expenses. Also, research grants to nurses, medical technicians, social workers and renal dieticians for the study of kidney disease.
Financial data: Year ended 06/30/2012. Assets, $730,187 (M); Expenditures, $1,301,544; Total giving, $156,494; Grants to individuals, totaling $156,494.
Fields of interest: Kidney diseases.
Type of support: Grants for special needs.
Application information: Applications accepted.
   Additional information: Contact foundation for current application deadline/guidelines.
EIN: 592190073

1996
National Parkinson Foundation, Inc.
1501 N.W. 9th Ave.
Bob Hope Rd.
Miami, FL   33136-1494   (305) 243-6666
Contact: Joyce A. Oberdorf, Pres.; For Research: Pam Olmo C.P.A., Cont.
FAX: (305) 243-6073;
E-mail: contact@parkinson.org; Toll-free tel.: (800) 327-4545; URL: http://www.parkinson.org

Foundation type: Public charity
Purpose: Grants to scientists for Parkinson's disease research.
Publications: Application guidelines.
Financial data: Year ended 06/30/2011. Assets, $21,656,476 (M); Expenditures, $10,427,723; Total giving, $3,614,292.
Fields of interest: Parkinson's disease; Parkinson's disease research.
Type of support: Research.
Application information: Applications accepted. Application form required. Application form available on the grantmaker's web site.
   Initial approach: Letter or e-mail
   Applicants should submit the following:

1) Letter(s) of recommendation
2) Curriculum vitae
3) Budget Information
4) Proposal
Additional information: Contact foundation for current application deadline/guidelines.

Program descriptions:
Investigator-Initiated Research Grants: This program is designed to support projects of the highest scientific caliber from anywhere in the world that: are directly relevant to the study of causes of and a cure for Parkinson's disease; are complementary to, not duplicative of, other research in the field; and are 'high-risk, high yield' projects that are thoughtfully composed and reasonably likely to advance the state of the knowledge about Parkinson's disease. Grants are for up to $50,000; no indirect costs are permitted. Both basic-research and clinical-research proposals are eligible for support. Candidates must be postdoctoral fellows or residents in recognized training programs, or tenure-track and research-track faculty at colleges and universities or research institutes. Preference will be given to scientists who are at an early stage of their professional careers. For more information contact iiresearchgrants@parkinson.org.

The Fight Goes On: Grants up to $1,000,000 are available over a period of up to three years for targeted, time-limited preclinical or clinical studies directly relevant to studying the cause and cure for Parkinson's disease. A premium will be placed on collaborative ventures involving researchers from more than one institution.
EIN: 590968031

1997
National YoungArts Foundation
(formerly National Foundation for Advancement in the Arts)
2100 Biscayne Blvd.
Miami, FL 33137 (305) 377-1140
Contact: Rebecca M. Gentry, V.P., Devel. and Comm.
FAX: (305) 377-1149; E-mail: info@youngarts.org; URL: http://www.youngarts.org

Foundation type: Public charity
Purpose: Grants to promising artists in their senior year of high school.
Publications: Application guidelines; Annual report; Informational brochure; Newsletter.
Financial data: Year ended 06/30/2012. Assets, $52,976,268 (M); Expenditures, $9,099,505.
Fields of interest: Visual arts; Performing arts.
Type of support: Grants to individuals; Scholarships—to individuals; Awards/prizes.
Application information: Applications accepted. Application form required. Application form available on the grantmaker's web site.
Send request by: Online
Copies of proposal: 1
Deadline(s): Oct. 14
Additional information: Application should include work samples.

Program description:
YoungArts Week: This program is available for high school seniors and 17 to 18 year old artists to apply for scholarships up to $10,000 and a week of life-changing experiences including Master Classes with world renowned artists, showcase performances and interdisciplinary workshops with their fellow young artists from across America. In the Studio, New York City, a celebration of the YoungArts Gold and Silver Award Winners, which is a more intensive YoungArts experience with Master teachers and interdisciplinary workshops and

performances. National Recognition Week, Washington, DC, as YoungArts is the sole nominating agency to the Commission on Presidential Scholars for the designation of scholars in the Arts, our students are recognized by the President of the United States and honored in the White House Regional Programs. YoungArts Miami and YoungArts New York, YoungArts regional programs offer workshops and development training to students in the areas of our regional programs.
EIN: 592141837

1998
North Central Florida Health Planning Council, Inc.
1785 N.W. 80th Blvd.
Gainesville, FL 32606-0000 (352) 313-6500
FAX: (352) 313-6515; E-mail: info@wellflorida.org; URL: http://www.wellflorida.org

Foundation type: Public charity
Purpose: Specific assistance to Florida residents with health and dental care, drug assistance, transportation, house related assistance and other outreach and support programs.
Financial data: Year ended 06/30/2011. Assets, $2,617,311 (M); Expenditures, $4,010,656; Total giving, $2,537,642.
Type of support: Grants for special needs.
Application information: Contact council for additional information on assistance.
EIN: 237083163

1999
North Orange Memorial Hospital Trust
P.O. Box 1908
Orlando, FL 32802-1908

Foundation type: Independent foundation
Purpose: Scholarships to individuals who have resided in the North Orange hospital district for at least one year, for study in a medical-related field.
Financial data: Year ended 09/30/2012. Assets, $94,476 (M); Expenditures, $20,215; Total giving, $15,000.
Fields of interest: Medical school/education.
Type of support: Scholarships—to individuals.
Application information: Applications accepted. Application form required.
Deadline(s): Mar. 31
Applicants should submit the following:
1) Transcripts
2) Letter(s) of recommendation
Additional information: Letter of recommendation may come from a school or employer. Application should also include the number of family members and an estimate of financial cost.
EIN: 596730137

2000
Northeast Florida Builders Association Builders Care, Inc.
103 Century 21 Dr., Ste. 108
Jacksonville, FL 32216-9256 (904) 727-3443
Contact: Chris Simons, Exec. Dir.
FAX: (904) 727-3456; Toll-free tel.: (877) 729-3443; e-mail for Chris Simons: csimons@builderscare.org; tel. for Chris Simons: (904) 727-3443; fax for Chris Simons: (904) 727-3456; URL: http://www.builderscare.org

Foundation type: Public charity

Purpose: Critical construction services to indigent elderly and disabled residents of the Jacksonville, FL area, who cannot afford construction services by traditional means.
Financial data: Year ended 06/30/2012. Assets, $308,709 (M); Expenditures, $573,366.
Fields of interest: Housing/shelter, repairs; Aging; Disabilities, people with; Physically disabled; Economically disadvantaged.
Type of support: In-kind gifts.
Application information:
Initial approach: Letter
Additional information: Contact the association for eligibility criteria.
EIN: 593742789

2001
The Northern Palm Beach County Youth Foundation Inc.
11601 Kew Gardens Dr., Ste. 101
Palm Beach Gardens, FL 33410-2852

Foundation type: Independent foundation
Purpose: Scholarships to students in the Riviera Beach, FL, area, for higher education.
Financial data: Year ended 12/31/2011. Assets, $1,429 (M); Expenditures, $11,331; Total giving, $9,600.
Fields of interest: Higher education.
Type of support: Undergraduate support.
Application information: Contact foundation for current application guidelines.
EIN: 311732652

2002
Office Depot Foundation
6600 N. Military Tr.
Boca Raton, FL 33496-2434 (561) 438-8439
Contact: Mary Wong, Pres.
E-mail: communityrelations@officedepot.com; URL: http://www.officedepotfoundation.org/

Foundation type: Public charity
Purpose: Emergency aid to employees of Office Depot who have suffered loss due to a natural disaster such as fire, flood, hurricane or tornado.
Publications: Application guidelines.
Financial data: Year ended 06/30/2012. Assets, $3,742,521 (M); Expenditures, $1,320,536; Total giving, $866,299.
Fields of interest: Safety/disasters.
Type of support: Emergency funds; Employee-related welfare.
Application information: Application form required.
Deadline(s): Contact foundation for current application deadline/guidelines
EIN: 650596803

2003
Okeechobee Educational Foundation, Inc.
700 S.W. 2nd Ave.
Okeechobee, FL 34974-5117 (863) 462-5000
Contact: Linda Syfrett, Pres.
FAX: (863) 462-5017;
E-mail: vinsons@ocsb.okee.k12.fl.us

Foundation type: Public charity
Purpose: Scholarships to graduates of Okeechobee High School, FL for continuing education at accredited colleges or universities.
Publications: Newsletter.
Financial data: Year ended 12/31/2012. Assets, $184,443 (M); Expenditures, $373,025; Total giving, $296,856; Grants to individuals, totaling $296,856.

Fields of interest: Higher education.
Type of support: Support to graduates or students of specific schools.
Application information: Contact the foundation for further guidelines.
EIN: 650219235

2004
Matred Carlton Olliff Foundation
P.O. Box 995
Wauchula, FL 33873-0995
Contact: Doyle E. Carlton III, Tr.
Application address: P.O. Box 144, Wauchula, Florida 33873

Foundation type: Independent foundation
Purpose: Scholarships only to graduates of Hardee High School, Wauchula, FL for higher education at accredited colleges or universities.
Financial data: Year ended 08/31/2013. Assets, $3,387,061 (M); Expenditures, $171,183; Total giving, $145,648; Grants to individuals, 84 grants totaling $54,498 (high: $5,773, low: $250).
Fields of interest: Higher education.
Type of support: Support to graduates or students of specific schools.
Application information:
  Initial approach: Letter
  Deadline(s): July 1
EIN: 592241303

2005
Operafestival di Roma, Inc.
P.O. Box 117900
Gainesville, FL 32611-7900 (352) 273-3189
FAX: (352) 392-0461;
E-mail: operafest@arts.ufl.edu; URL: http://www.operafest.com

Foundation type: Public charity
Purpose: Scholarships to students to further both their musical education and their practical performing experience to study and perform opera in Italy in the summer.
Financial data: Year ended 11/30/2010. Assets, $0 (M); Expenditures, $404,406; Total giving, $52,882.
Fields of interest: Opera; Performing arts, education.
International interests: Italy.
Type of support: Scholarships—to individuals.
Application information: Applications not accepted.
  Additional information: Unsolicited requests for funds not considered or acknowledged.
EIN: 431686401

2006
Operation Hope of Brevard, Inc.
12285 County Rd. 512
Fellsmere, FL 32948-5466 (772) 571-0003
Contact: Jesse Zermeno, Pres.
FAX: (772) 571-0017;
E-mail: hopeo@bellsouth.net; E-mail for Jesse Zermeno: jessez@juno.com; URL: http://operationhopefl.org/

Foundation type: Public charity
Purpose: Assistance to migrant farm workers and needy families in central and southeastern FL by providing food, clothing, and household effects; the organization also provides after-school tutoring in reading, mathematics, English, and computer skills; job placement; and hurricane relief.
Publications: Newsletter.

Financial data: Year ended 12/31/2011. Assets, $5,234,824 (M); Expenditures, $1,263,816; Total giving, $1,038,361; Grants to individuals, totaling $1,038,361.
Fields of interest: Adult education—literacy, basic skills & GED; Employment, services; Food services; Economically disadvantaged; Migrant workers.
Type of support: In-kind gifts.
Application information:
  Initial approach: Letter
  Additional information: Contact foundation for eligibility criteria.
EIN: 593614249

2007
Orange Bowl Committee, Inc.
14360 N.W. 77th Ct.
Miami Lakes, FL 33016-1534 (305) 371-4700
Contact: Eric L. Poms, C.E.O.
FAX: (305) 341-4771; URL: http://www.orangebowl.org

Foundation type: Public charity
Purpose: Scholarships to student athletes, one male and one female from Dade, Broward, and Palm Beach counties, FL for postsecondary education.
Financial data: Year ended 04/30/2012. Assets, $37,406,419 (M); Expenditures, $18,134,779; Total giving, $707,740; Grants to individuals, totaling $22,875.
Fields of interest: Higher education.
Type of support: Scholarships—to individuals; Support to graduates or students of specific schools.
Application information: Each applicant receives $2,500 scholarship. Unsolicited requests for funds not considered or acknowledged.
EIN: 590384382

2008
Orlando Magic Foundation, Inc.
(formerly Orlando Magic Youth Fund, also known as Orlando Magic Youth Foundation)
8701 Maitland Summit Blvd.
Orlando, FL 32810-5915 (407) 916-2641
Contact: Stephanie Allen, Admin.
E-mail: omyf@orlandomagic.com; URL: http://www.nba.com/magic/orlando-magic-youth-foundation

Foundation type: Public charity
Purpose: Scholarships to deserving high school seniors who plan to attend a college or university in Florida.
Publications: Application guidelines; Grants list; Newsletter; Program policy statement (including application guidelines).
Financial data: Year ended 06/30/2012. Assets, $683,319 (M); Expenditures, $858,015; Total giving, $857,400.
Fields of interest: Higher education; Asians/Pacific Islanders; African Americans/Blacks; Hispanics/Latinos; Native Americans/American Indians.
Type of support: Scholarships—to individuals; Support to graduates or students of specific schools.
Application information: Applications accepted. Application form required.
  Initial approach: Email
  Deadline(s): Feb. 4
  Applicants should submit the following:
    1) Financial information
    2) Essay
    3) Transcripts
    4) Letter(s) of recommendation

Additional information: Each recipient will be required to perform 30 hours of community service per semester and attend the annual scholarship retreat in June or July while enrolled.
EIN: 592940230

2009
Richard F. Ott Scholarship Foundation
c/o Anne Golza Folsom & Regions Bank
P.O. Box 291
Clearwater, FL 34617-2918

Foundation type: Independent foundation
Purpose: Scholarships, which are renewable for up to four years of undergraduate study, to financially needy graduates of Clearwater High School, FL, who graduated in the top 25 percent of their classes and display qualities of a high moral character, scholastic achievement, and leadership ability.
Financial data: Year ended 10/31/2013. Assets, $1,286,197 (M); Expenditures, $78,544; Total giving, $44,000; Grants to individuals, 11 grants totaling $44,000 (high: $4,000, low: $4,000).
Type of support: Support to graduates or students of specific schools; Undergraduate support.
Application information: Application form required.
  Deadline(s): May 1
  Applicants should submit the following:
    1) Financial information
    2) Transcripts
EIN: 596833432

2010
The Pagliara Charitable Foundation
P.O. Box 608
Dunedin, FL 34697-0608 (727) 736-2900

Foundation type: Independent foundation
Purpose: Scholarships to individuals for continuing education at accredited colleges or universities. Grants to individuals for medical care.
Financial data: Year ended 12/31/2011. Assets, $102,448 (M); Expenditures, $62,455; Total giving, $39,675.
Fields of interest: Education; Health care.
Type of support: Grants to individuals; Scholarships—to individuals.
Application information: Application form not required.
  Initial approach: Letter
  Deadline(s): None
  Additional information: Contact foundation for application guidelines.
EIN: 596978261

2011
Palm Beach Community College Foundation, Inc.
4200 Congress Ave.
Lake Worth, FL 33461-4796 (561) 868-3572
FAX: (561) 868-3687

Foundation type: Public charity
Purpose: Scholarships to Palm Beach Community College, FL students pursuing higher education.
Financial data: Year ended 12/31/2011. Assets, $26,995,339 (M); Expenditures, $5,921,477; Total giving, $2,569,574; Grants to individuals, totaling $2,569,574.
Fields of interest: College (community/junior).
Type of support: Support to graduates or students of specific schools.
Application information: Applications accepted.

Additional information: Students apply for scholarship through an online process. Contact the foundation for eligibility requirements.
EIN: 591818556

2012
Palm Beach County Cultural Council
601 Lake Ave.
Lake Worth, FL   33460-3810   (561) 471-2901
Contact: Rena Blades, Pres. and C.E.O.
FAX: (561) 687-9484; E-mail: grants@pbccc.org;
Toll-free tel.: (800) 882-2787; E-mail for Rena
Blades: rblades@palmbeachculture.com;
URL: http://www.palmbeachculture.com/

Foundation type: Public charity
Purpose: Residency grants to professional artists in Palm Beach County, FL in exchange for providing discipline-based arts education to children and their families living in neighborhoods in transition and redevelopment. Also, awards for achievement made to individual artists by nomination.
Publications: Application guidelines; Annual report; Financial statement; Grants list; Informational brochure (including application guidelines); Newsletter.
Financial data: Year ended 09/30/2011. Assets, $4,730,218 (M); Expenditures, $1,718,194; Total giving, $98,247.
Fields of interest: Public education; Arts, artist's services; Arts.
Type of support: Residencies.
Application information: Contact foundation for current application deadline/guidelines.
EIN: 591862336

2013
Palm Beach Rotary Foundation
P.O. Box 105
Palm Beach, FL   33480-0105   (561) 799-6154
Application address: Royal Palm Beach Rotary Club, Scholarship Committee, P.O. Box 211015, Royal Palm Beach, FL 33421-1015
URL: http://www.rpbrotary.org/index.php?src=gendocs&ref=RotaryFoundation&category=Main

Foundation type: Public charity
Purpose: Scholarships to graduating seniors of Royal Palm Beach High School, or who reside in the Village of Royal Palm Beach zip code area of 33411.
Publications: Application guidelines.
Financial data: Year ended 06/30/2012. Assets, $700,210 (M); Expenditures, $74,466; Total giving, $62,121; Grants to individuals, totaling $38,500.
Fields of interest: Higher education.
Type of support: Scholarships—to individuals; Undergraduate support.
Application information: Applications accepted. Application form available on the grantmaker's web site. Interview required.
Initial approach: Application
Send request by: Mail
Deadline(s): Mar. 31
Applicants should submit the following:
1) Class rank
2) Photograph
3) Transcripts
Additional information: Application should also include one reference letter.
Program description:
Todd Robiner Scholarship: Scholarships of $1,000 each to individuals who excel in pursuing

their goals in life and providing service to their community.
EIN: 592551031

2014
Drs. Kiran & Pallavi Patel Family Foundation, Inc.
5600 Mariner St., Ste. 227
Tampa, FL   33609-3471
Contact: Kiran C. Patel M.D., Secy.-Treas.

Foundation type: Independent foundation
Purpose: Scholarships to outstanding FL students for higher education.
Financial data: Year ended 06/30/2012. Assets, $3,731,589 (M); Expenditures, $464,669; Total giving, $404,455.
Type of support: Scholarships—to individuals.
Application information: Applications accepted.
Initial approach: Letter
Additional information: Contact foundation for Patel Scholars application and deadline.
EIN: 203916634

2015
Charles A. & Odette W. Patterson Charitable Trust
P.O. Box 40200, FL9-100-10-19
Jacksonville, FL   32203-0200

Foundation type: Independent foundation
Purpose: Scholarships and awards to employees of the St. Petersburg, FL, police and/or fire department(s) enrolled or accepted at an accredited college or university.
Financial data: Year ended 09/30/2013. Assets, $986,257 (M); Expenditures, $58,656; Total giving, $50,297; Grants to individuals, 65 grants totaling $38,311 (high: $1,621, low: $17).
Fields of interest: Higher education; Crime/law enforcement.
Type of support: Employee-related scholarships; Awards/prizes.
Application information: Applications accepted. Application form required.
Applicants should submit the following:
1) GPA
2) Financial information
Additional information: Contact St. Petersburg Chief of Police or Chief of Fire Dept. for application materials. Applicant must pursue a degree deemed appropriate for a fire protection career, but not necessarily limited to fire protection or fire administration degrees.
EIN: 596953716

2016
Perry Memorial Scholarship Trust
(formerly Frank H. & Annie Belle Whilhelm Perry Memorial Scholarships)
P.O. Box 40200, FL9-100-10-19
Jacksonville, FL   32203-0200   (401) 278-6112

Foundation type: Independent foundation
Purpose: Scholarships to students of Lees-McRae College and Montreat College in NC, and Kings College in Kingston, TN.
Financial data: Year ended 01/31/2013. Assets, $443,275 (M); Expenditures, $24,878; Total giving, $18,948.
Fields of interest: Higher education.
Type of support: Support to graduates or students of specific schools.

Application information: Applications accepted.
Initial approach: Letter
Deadline(s): None
EIN: 566290640

2017
Agnes F. Petteys Trust
c/o Regions Bank
P.O. Box 2918
Clearwater, FL   33757-2918

Foundation type: Independent foundation
Purpose: Scholarships to former residents of a facility maintained by Florida Sheriffs Youth Ranches, Inc.
Financial data: Year ended 12/31/2012. Assets, $328,824 (M); Expenditures, $16,445; Total giving, $9,834.
Fields of interest: Higher education.
Type of support: Scholarships—to individuals.
Application information: Applications accepted. Application form required.
Deadline(s): June 30
Additional information: Recipients must be currently enrolled or accepted for enrollment within six months following presentation of the award at a fully accredited university, junior or senior college within the continental U.S. pursuing a degree.
EIN: 597096014

2018
Pinellas County Community Foundation
5200 East Bay Dr., Ste. 202
Clearwater, FL   33764   (727) 531-0058
Contact: Julie Scales, Exec. Dir.
FAX: (727) 531-0053; E-mail: info@pinellasccf.org;
URL: http://www.pinellasccf.org

Foundation type: Community foundation
Purpose: Scholarships to students in Pinellas County, FL through several scholarship funds.
Publications: Application guidelines; Annual report (including application guidelines); Informational brochure; Newsletter; Occasional report.
Financial data: Year ended 12/31/2012. Assets, $78,287,771 (M); Expenditures, $12,494,140; Total giving, $11,727,266.
Fields of interest: Higher education.
Type of support: Scholarships—to individuals.
Application information: Applications accepted.
Initial approach: Telephone
Deadline(s): Varies
EIN: 237113194

2019
Pinellas County Education Foundation, Inc.
12090 Starkey Rd.
Largo, FL   33773-2727   (727) 588-4816
Contact: Terry Boehm, Pres.
E-mail: info@pinellaseducation.org; E-mail For Terry Boehm: boehmt@pinellaseducation.org;
URL: http://pinellaseducation.org

Foundation type: Public charity
Purpose: Scholarships for high school seniors throughout Pinellas County, FL pursuing higher education.
Financial data: Year ended 06/30/2012. Assets, $33,034,312 (M); Expenditures, $5,850,302; Total giving, $3,070,221; Grants to individuals, totaling $2,854,898.
Fields of interest: Higher education.

Type of support: Scholarships—to individuals.
Application information: Applications accepted.
Application form required.

Send request by: On-line
Final notification: Applicants notified in the Spring
Applicants should submit the following:
1) GPA
2) Transcripts
3) Financial information
4) Essay

Additional information: See web site for additional application guidelines and a listing of scholarships. Scholarships eligibility vary. They range in focus from music and drama to science and math, and sports. Some are designed for specific areas of study such as nursing or dentistry while others regard academic performance and community service, and many are base on financial need.
EIN: 592688253

2020
Pinellas County Urban League, Inc.
c/o 0
333 31st St. N.
St. Petersburg, FL 33713-7603 (727) 327-2081
URL: http://www.pcul.org

Foundation type: Public charity
Purpose: Energy assistance to low income individuals and families of Pinellas county, FL who are in financial distress.
Financial data: Year ended 12/31/2011. Assets, $3,484,733 (M); Expenditures, $15,173,376; Total giving, $5,638,933; Grants to individuals, totaling $4,328,104.
Fields of interest: Economically disadvantaged.
Type of support: Emergency funds; Grants for special needs.
Application information: Contact the league for eligibility determination.
EIN: 591665523

2021
Planning & Visual Education Partnership, Inc.
(formerly Planning & Visual Education (P.A.V.E.))
4651 Sheridan St., Ste. 470
Hollywood, FL 33021-3437 (954) 893-7225
FAX: (954) 893-8375; E-mail: pave@paveinfo.org;
URL: http://www.paveinfo.org

Foundation type: Public charity
Purpose: Scholarships and design awards to students interested in the retail industry.
Publications: Application guidelines.
Financial data: Year ended 06/30/2011. Assets, $638,481 (M); Expenditures, $328,450.
Type of support: Scholarships—to individuals; Awards/prizes.
Application information: Applications accepted.
Send request by: Mail
Deadline(s): Nov. 3
Additional information: See web site for complete program information.
EIN: 133689977

2022
The Players Championship Charities
100 PGA Tour Blvd.
Ponte Vedra Beach, FL 32082-3046 (904) 285-3700

Foundation type: Public charity
Purpose: Multiyear need or merit based scholarships to college bound north Florida area students.
Financial data: Year ended 12/31/2011. Assets, $146,355 (M); Expenditures, $375,048; Total giving, $375,000.
Type of support: Undergraduate support.
Application information: Applications accepted.
EIN: 591059920

2023
Police Officer Assistance Trust
1030 N.W. 111 Ave., Ste. 232
Miami, FL 33172-5800 (305) 594-6662
Contact: Angus Butler, Pres.
FAX: (305) 594-0997; E-mail: info@poat.org;
URL: http://www.poat.org

Foundation type: Public charity
Purpose: Financial assistance to police officers and their families residing in FL, for expenses arising as a result of death, disability, illness, injury or some other catastrophic circumstance. Scholarships to graduating sons or daughters of sworn officers working for any law enforcement agency within Miami-Dade county.
Publications: Application guidelines; Informational brochure; Newsletter.
Financial data: Year ended 09/30/2012. Assets, $2,381,191 (M); Expenditures, $330,635; Total giving, $212,448; Grants to individuals, totaling $141,133.
Fields of interest: Visual arts; Crime/law enforcement, police agencies; Chemistry; Biology/life sciences; Science.
Type of support: Scholarships—to individuals; Grants for special needs.
Application information: Applications accepted. Application form required. Application form available on the grantmaker's web site.
Initial approach: Letter or telephone
Send request by: Mail or in person
Deadline(s): May 1 for Scholarships, none for Financial Assistance
Applicants should submit the following:
1) Transcripts
2) Letter(s) of recommendation
Additional information: See web site for additional guidelines.
Program descriptions:
Amanda Haworth Perseverance Scholarship: This $1,000 scholarship is awarded to a Miami-Dade, Broward, or Monroe county high school senior or graduate. Applicant must be the daughter of a sworn officer working for any law enforcement agency within the geographical boundaries of Miami-Dade county. Applicant must maintain a 2.0 minimum GPA.
Financial Assistance: The trust offers financial assistance to police officers on the federal, state, or local level. Funding is available for officers who are injured or disabled in the line of duty, assistance with medical expenses not covered by health insurance, disaster relief, such as needed in the aftermath of a hurricane, house fire, etc., expenses associated with debilitating illnesses that strike officers, their spouses, and/or children, assistance to the families of officers killed in the line of duty, and other catastrophic circumstances where the officer has no means or remedy. Assistance is also available for expenses associated with funeral expense for slain police officers.
Mike Byrd Crime Scene Investigation Scholarship: A $1,000 scholarship is available to a Miami-Dade, Broward, or Monroe County high school senior or

full-time college student who is the son or daughter of a sworn officer working for any law enforcement agency within the geographical boundaries of Miami-Dade County. Eligible applicants must be full-time students who are planning to major in, or are currently majoring in, biology, chemistry, forensics, pathology, or any major affiliated to crime scene investigation. Applicants must also maintain a 2.5 minimum GPA.
Paul Janosky Criminal Justice-Related Majors Scholarship: One scholarship in the amount of $1,000 is awarded to a Miami-Dade, Broward, or Monroe County high school senior or full-time college student majoring in criminal justice, law, or public safety at an accredited college or university. Applicant must be the son or daughter of a sworn officer working for any law enforcement agency within the geographical boundaries of Miami-Dade County. Applicant must also currently maintain a 2.5 minimum GPA.
Roger Castillo Perseverance Scholarship: This $1,000 scholarship is awarded to a Miami-Dade, Broward, or Monroe county high school senior or graduate. Applicant must be the son of a sworn officer working for any law enforcement agency within the geographical boundaries of Miami-Dade county. Applicant must maintain a 2.0 minimum GPA.
EIN: 650164129

2024
Preeclampsia Foundation
6767 N. Wickham Rd., Ste. 400
Melbourne, FL 32940-2025 (321) 421-6957
FAX: (321) 821-0450;
E-mail: info@preeclampsia.org; Application e-mail: visiongrants@preeclampsia.org; Toll Free Tel.: (800)-665-9341; URL: http://www.preeclampsia.org

Foundation type: Public charity
Purpose: Research grants for the pathophysiology, diagnosis, and treatment of hypertensive disorders of pregnancy.
Publications: Application guidelines; Annual report.
Financial data: Year ended 12/31/2011. Assets, $817,626 (M); Expenditures, $307,611; Total giving, $51,439.
Fields of interest: Medical research.
Type of support: Research.
Application information:
Initial approach: Letter
Deadline(s): May 16
Additional information: Contact foundation for further eligibility requirements.
Program description:
Vision Grants: Vision Grants are intended to provide initial funding for innovative ideas focused on the pathophysiology, diagnosis or treatment of preeclampsia, HELLP syndrome and other hypertensive disorders of pregnancy that might otherwise not be pursued due to lack of funding. All novel, well-considered research topics are encouraged. International applicants will be accepted, but applications must be in English. See foundation web site for requests for proposals.
EIN: 912073087

2025
Prime Time Foundation, Inc.
570 Ocean Dr., Ste. 701
Juno Beach, FL 33408-1954
Contact: Judith P. Yanover, Pres. and Treas.

Foundation type: Independent foundation

Purpose: Scholarships to worthy students of Abaco Bahamas and Eleuthera Bahamas, to attend the University of Michigan, Louisiana State University, and the University of Florida.
Financial data: Year ended 12/31/2013. Assets, $1,723,509 (M); Expenditures, $171,412; Total giving, $140,956.
Fields of interest: Higher education.
International interests: Bahamas.
Type of support: Support to graduates or students of specific schools; Foreign applicants.
Application information:
 Initial approach: Letter
 Deadline(s): July 19
Program description:
 Prime Time Scholarship: Scholarship provides room and board as well as tuition to full time residents of Abaco and Eleuthera Bahamas. The scholarship is for one year, and will be extended for up to four years based upon student performance. Applicant must demonstrate financial need and maintain satisfactory academic progress, demonstrate leadership qualities and/or community service. Successful graduates of this program must return home for a minimum of five years to contribute their skills to the improvement of life in the Bahamas.
EIN: 650875903

2026
Progress Village Foundation, Inc.
(formerly Progress Village Foundation)
8306 Fir Dr.
Tampa, FL 33619 (813) 677-1274
Contact: Beverly Webb, Treas.

Foundation type: Operating foundation
Purpose: Grants to high school and college students who are residents of Progress Village, FL for five years and are accepted in college as full time students.
Financial data: Year ended 12/31/2011. Assets, $131,987 (M); Expenditures, $26,317; Total giving, $21,258.
Fields of interest: Higher education.
Type of support: Grants to individuals.
Application information: Applications accepted. Application form required.
 Deadline(s): May 3 of each year
 Applicants should submit the following:
  1) Photograph
  2) Transcripts
  3) Essay
 Additional information: Essay for first time applicants only.
EIN: 592807536

2027
PSS/Gulf South Employee Relief Fund Inc.
4345 Southpoint Blvd.
Jacksonville, FL 32216

Foundation type: Company-sponsored foundation
Purpose: Grants to company employees recover from losses from Hurricane Katrina disaster and winter storms to assist in the process of rebuilding their lives.
Financial data: Year ended 03/30/2012. Assets, $13,920 (M); Expenditures, $1,978; Total giving, $1,219; Grant to an individual, 1 grant totaling $1,219.
Fields of interest: Disasters, Hurricane Katrina; Safety/disasters.
Type of support: Employee-related welfare.

Application information: Applications not accepted.
 Additional information: Unsolicited requests for funds not considered or acknowledged.
EIN: 203423329

2028
The Rawlings Foundation, Inc.
2554 Players Ct.
Wellington, FL 33414-6286

Foundation type: Operating foundation
Purpose: Grants to individuals supporting missionary work, domestic and world wide.
Financial data: Year ended 12/31/2012. Assets, $58,417,915 (M); Expenditures, $12,073,267; Total giving, $1,722,918.
Fields of interest: Christian agencies & churches.
Type of support: Grants to individuals.
Application information: Applications not accepted.
EIN: 651051638

2029
Walter C. & Ella Rawls Educational Trust
P.O. Box 1908
Orlando, FL 32802-1908

Foundation type: Independent foundation
Purpose: Scholarships to graduating high school seniors who reside in Suffolk, Forest Glen, Kennedy, and Sussex, VA, and Gates, NC.
Financial data: Year ended 06/30/2012. Assets, $298,768 (M); Expenditures, $33,778; Total giving, $16,532; Grants to individuals, 7 grants totaling $16,532 (high: $2,362; low: $2,362).
Fields of interest: Vocational education.
Type of support: Undergraduate support.
Application information: Applications not accepted.
 Additional information: Contributes only to preselected individuals.
EIN: 546053305

2030
The Rayni Foundation, Inc.
c/o Raul F. Rodriguez
300 S.W. 124 Ave.
Miami, FL 33184-1418

Foundation type: Operating foundation
Purpose: Scholarships by nomination only to graduates of Archbishop Carroll Catholic High School and the Belen Jesuit School, FL.
Financial data: Year ended 12/31/2012. Assets, $8,337,240 (M); Expenditures, $1,048,423; Total giving, $813,964; Grants to individuals, 3 grants totaling $14,050 (high: $7,000; low: $3,000).
Fields of interest: Catholic agencies & churches.
Type of support: Support to graduates or students of specific schools; Awards/grants by nomination only; Undergraduate support.
Application information: Unsolicited requests for funds not accepted.
EIN: 650838191

2031
The Rayonier Foundation
(formerly The ITT Rayonier Foundation)
1301 Riverplace Blvd., Ste. 2300
Jacksonville, FL 32207-9062 (904) 357-9100
Contact: Charles H. Hood, Pres.
Application address: 50 N. Laura Street, Ste. 1900, Jacksonville, FL 32202, tel.: (904) 357-9120

Foundation type: Company-sponsored foundation
Purpose: Scholarships to students residing in Nassau County, FL, Wayne County, GA, and Clallam, Grays Harbor, and western Jefferson counties, WA, as well as college scholarships to children of employees of Rayonier Inc.
Publications: Application guidelines.
Financial data: Year ended 12/31/2012. Assets, $5,876,782 (M); Expenditures, $542,288; Total giving, $534,826.
Fields of interest: Higher education; Environment, forests; Science; Chemistry; Engineering.
Type of support: Employee-related scholarships; Scholarships—to individuals; Undergraduate support.
Application information: Application form required.
 Initial approach: Contact guidance counselor from participating schools
 Deadline(s): Nov. 13
 Applicants should submit the following:
  1) Financial information
  2) Transcripts
  3) SAT
  4) ACT
  5) Letter(s) of recommendation
Program descriptions:
 Community Scholarship: The foundation annually awards two $1,000 college scholarships to high school seniors to pursue an academic interest in forestry. The program is limited to the Pacific Northwest.
 Engineering Scholarship: The foundation annually awards two $6,000 four-year college scholarships to high school seniors to pursue an academic interest in chemical, mechanical, paper, or science engineering. The program is limited to Nassau County, Florida, Wayne County, Georgia, and the Pacific Northwest.
 Forestry Scholarship: The foundation annually awards a $6,000 four-year college scholarship to a high school senior to pursue an academic interest in forestry. The program is limited to Nassau County, Florida, Wayne County, Georgia, and the Pacific Northwest.
 Rayonier College Scholarship Program: The foundation annually awards $2,500 four year college scholarships to children of employees of Rayonier.
 Technical/Vocational Scholarship: The foundation annually awards three $2,000 two-year college scholarships to high school seniors to pursue an academic interest in manufacturing. The program is limited to Nassau County, Florida and Wayne County, Georgia.
Company name: Rayonier Inc.
EIN: 136064462

2032
Elsie Seller Reed Charitable Trust
P.O. Box 530944
DeBary, FL 32753 (386) 668-4795
Contact: Peter Wilson, Chair.
Application address: 3 Cunningham Ln., DeBary, FL 32713

Foundation type: Independent foundation
Purpose: Scholarships to high school graduates who are residents of DeBary, FL who are enrolled in

an accredited college, university or vocational school.
Financial data: Year ended 12/31/2012. Assets, $262,789 (M); Expenditures, $9,927; Total giving, $2,000; Grants to individuals, 2 grants totaling $2,000 (high: $1,000, low: $1,000).
Fields of interest: Vocational education, post-secondary; Higher education.
Type of support: Scholarships—to individuals.
Application information: Applications accepted. Application form required.
 Deadline(s): None
EIN: 596836787

2033
Rehabilitation Foundation of Northwest Florida, Inc.
2929 Langley Ave., Ste. 202
Pensacola, FL 32504-7355 (850) 478-0297
E-mail: rehabfound@aol.com

Foundation type: Public charity
Purpose: Financial assistance to physically handicapped residents of northwest FL, who, for any reason cannot obtain funds from the usual sources such as insurance, Medicare/Medicaid, and other agencies.
Financial data: Year ended 12/31/2011. Assets, $8,381,177 (M); Expenditures, $280,420; Total giving, $128,686; Grants to individuals, totaling $103,686.
Fields of interest: Physically disabled.
Type of support: Grants for special needs.
Application information: Application form required.
 Initial approach: Letter
 Additional information: Application must accompany a physician's recommendation outlining their prognosis for rehabilitation.
EIN: 592089355

2034
Grace Fleming Reinhold Scholarship Trust
(formerly Grace E. Reinhold Scholarship Trust)
629 Nerita St., Ste. 4H
Sanibel, FL 33957-6808

Foundation type: Independent foundation
Purpose: Scholarships to grade school and high school students for further education who reside in WI.
Financial data: Year ended 12/31/2011. Assets, $68,794 (M); Expenditures, $42,841; Total giving, $42,245.
Fields of interest: Secondary school/education; Higher education.
Type of support: Scholarships—to individuals; Support to graduates or students of specific schools.
Application information: Applications not accepted.
 Additional information: Unsolicited requests for funds not accepted.
EIN: 391682031

2035
Renal Assistance, Inc.
11013 Boston Dr.
Cooper City, FL 33026 (954) 430-9166
Contact: Deborah Kostner, Admin.
Application address: 11011 Sheridan St., Cooper City, FL 33026

Foundation type: Independent foundation
Purpose: Grants to residents of FL who require hemodialysis therapy or have received a renal

transplant, for the purpose of medical assistance, travel assistance, and emergency assistance.
Financial data: Year ended 01/31/2012. Assets, $56,259 (M); Expenditures, $51,413; Total giving, $47,484; Grants to individuals, 2 grants totaling $47,484 (high: $46,979, low: $505).
Fields of interest: Health care; Kidney diseases.
Type of support: Grants for special needs.
Application information: Applications not accepted.
 Additional information: The foundation contributes only to preselected individuals.
EIN: 591429145

2036
Marguerite A. Rhodes Scholarship Fund
c/o Richard J. Hazen
2607 Bayshore Rd.
Nokomis, FL 34275 (941) 468-3683

Foundation type: Independent foundation
Purpose: Scholarships to qualifying high school seniors of WV and WI in pursuit of a higher education at accredited colleges or universities.
Financial data: Year ended 12/31/2012. Assets, $0 (M); Expenditures, $23,045; Total giving, $11,613; Grants to individuals, 2 grants totaling $6,000 (high: $3,000, low: $3,000).
Fields of interest: Higher education.
Type of support: Scholarships—to individuals.
Application information: Applications accepted.
 Initial approach: Letter
 Deadline(s): None
 Additional information: Applications should include scholastic records.
EIN: 026138254

2037
B. Beall & R. Kemp Riechmann Foundation
P.O. Box 25207
Bradenton, FL 34206-5207 (941) 747-2355
Contact: Beverly Beall, Tr.

Foundation type: Operating foundation
Purpose: Scholarships to graduating high school seniors of Manatee High School, FL for higher education at accredited four year colleges or universities.
Financial data: Year ended 11/30/2012. Assets, $1,816,194 (M); Expenditures, $313,867; Total giving, $193,904; Grants to individuals, 75 grants totaling $162,301 (high: $5,000, low: $271).
Fields of interest: Higher education.
Type of support: Scholarships—to individuals.
Application information: Application form required.
 Deadline(s): Apr. 1
 Additional information: Application should include official grade transcripts and copies of acceptance letters.
Program description:
 Scholarship Program: Scholarships are up to $4,000 per year to help fund college education at an accredited four-year college or university. Applicant must show academic achievement, involvement in extracurricular activities, financial need, and sincerity of interest as demonstrated by thorough completion of the scholarship application and accompanying information. Applicant must have a minimum 2.5 GPA on a 4.0 scale.
EIN: 650808807

2038
The John & David Rigsby Memorial Fund, Inc.
9013 Point Cypress Dr.
Orlando, FL 32836-5475 (407) 352-4040
Contact: Mary Jo Camilli
Application address: c/o Dr. Phillips High School, 6500 Turkey Lake Rd., Orlando, FL 32819

Foundation type: Independent foundation
Purpose: Scholarships to graduating seniors of Dr. Phillips High School, Orlando, FL for attendance at an accredited four year college or university.
Financial data: Year ended 07/31/2013. Assets, $28,889 (M); Expenditures, $7,696; Total giving, $7,000; Grants to individuals, 6 grants totaling $7,000 (high: $2,000, low: $1,000).
Fields of interest: Higher education.
Type of support: Support to graduates or students of specific schools.
Application information: Applications accepted.
 Deadline(s): Mar. 28
 Applicants should submit the following:
  1) Essay
  2) Letter(s) of recommendation
  3) Transcripts
 Additional information: Application should include biographical information, education and family background and financial need statement.
Program description:
 Scholarship Program: Scholarships in the amount of $4,000 is awarded to graduating seniors for attendance at an accredited four-year college or university in the U.S. The scholarship is payable at a rate of $1,000 annually and may be used for tuition and fees. Additional one-year non-renewable scholarships of lesser and varying amounts may be offered to other applicants at the discretion of the foundation.
EIN: 593398973

2039
Diana Roberts Memorial Scholarship Fund
c/o Bernard L. Roberts
3600 Oakview Ct.
Delray Beach, FL 33445-3924

Foundation type: Independent foundation
Purpose: Scholarships to graduating high school seniors in Westchester County, NY.
Financial data: Year ended 12/31/2011. Assets, $70,362 (M); Expenditures, $5,311; Total giving, $3,000.
Type of support: Undergraduate support.
Application information: Applications not accepted.
 Additional information: Unsolicited requests for funds not considered or acknowledged.
EIN: 133674048

2040
Buck Rogers Foundation, Inc.
1756 S.W. Barnett Way
Lake City, FL 32025-6953

Foundation type: Operating foundation
Purpose: Grants to financially needy individuals for assistance with medical expense and basic living expenses.
Financial data: Year ended 12/31/2011. Assets, $1,161,861 (M); Expenditures, $26,915; Total giving, $11,177; Grants to individuals, 12 grants totaling $8,677 (high: $2,000, low: $185).
Fields of interest: Human services, emergency aid; Economically disadvantaged.

Type of support: Grants for special needs.
Application information: Applications accepted.
Initial approach: Letter
EIN: 593495484

2041
J. M. Rubin Foundation, Inc.
505 S. Flagler Dr., Ste. 1320
West Palm Beach, FL 33401-5951   (561)
833-3309
FAX: (561) 833-3647; E-mail: info@jmrf.org;
URL: http://www.jmrf.org

Foundation type: Independent foundation
Purpose: Scholarships to residents of Palm Beach
County, FL, for higher education in the U.S.
Publications: Application guidelines.
Financial data: Year ended 11/30/2012. Assets,
$47,183,273 (M); Expenditures, $2,861,976;
Total giving, $1,936,356; Grants to individuals,
237 grants totaling $1,002,556 (high: $7,500,
low: $75).
Fields of interest: Higher education.
Type of support: Scholarships—to individuals.
Application information: Application form required.
Initial approach: Letter
Deadline(s): Mar. 1
Final notification: Applicants notified in May
Applicants should submit the following:
1) Letter(s) of recommendation
2) Financial information
3) Essay
Additional information: Scholarships are paid
directly to the educational institution.
Application must also include test scores, and
intended major. Interviews may be required.
EIN: 591958240

2042
W. R. & A. F. Ruegamer Charitable Trust
P.O. Box 40200, FL9-100-10-19
Jacksonville, FL 32203-0200   (401) 278-6039

Foundation type: Independent foundation
Purpose: Scholarships for undergraduate or
graduate students of high scholastic standing in the
biochemistry or anthropology departments at the
University of Florida.
Financial data: Year ended 07/31/2013. Assets,
$930,250 (M); Expenditures, $101,201; Total
giving, $80,000.
Fields of interest: Higher education; Biology/life
sciences; Anthropology/sociology.
Type of support: Support to graduates or students
of specific schools; Graduate support;
Undergraduate support.
Application information: Applications accepted.
Deadline(s): Mar. 15
EIN: 597213889

2043
Lonza L. Rush Testamentary Trust
(formerly R. Roy Rush Trust)
P.O. Box 1908
Orlando, FL 32802-1908
Contact: Carolyn McCoy
Application address: c/o SunTrust Bank, P.O. Box
13888, Roanoke, VA 24018.

Foundation type: Independent foundation
Purpose: Scholarships to residents of VA for higher
education.
Financial data: Year ended 02/28/2013. Assets,
$1,137,194 (M); Expenditures, $62,108; Total
giving, $48,750.

Type of support: Scholarships—to individuals.
Application information: Applications accepted.
Initial approach: Letter
Deadline(s): None
Additional information: Application should
include a biographical sketch with scholastic
records, financial need analysis report,
parent's confidential statement or a financial
aid form from the college entrance exam
board; Relatives of the trust committee are
not eligible.
EIN: 546138578

2044
Richard B. Russell Foundation
c/o SunTrust Bank
P.O. Box 1908
Orlando, FL 32802-1908

Foundation type: Independent foundation
Purpose: Teaching awards as well as scholarships
to students of University of Georgia, GA.
Financial data: Year ended 12/31/2012. Assets,
$5,163,232 (M); Expenditures, $273,684; Total
giving, $238,319.
Fields of interest: University.
Type of support: Support to graduates or students
of specific schools; Awards/prizes.
Application information:
Initial approach: Letter
Additional information: Contact foundation for
eligibility criteria.
EIN: 237075206

2045
Thomas E. Ryals Scholarship Fund
P.O. Box 40200, FL9-100-10-19
Jacksonville, FL 32203-0200

Foundation type: Independent foundation
Purpose: Scholarships to students who are
residents of Gerogia for attendance at the
University of Virginia, VA or Mercer University, GA
pursuing a law degree.
Financial data: Year ended 12/31/2012. Assets,
$780,620 (M); Expenditures, $52,330; Total
giving, $40,000.
Fields of interest: Law school/education.
Type of support: Support to graduates or students
of specific schools.
Application information: Applications accepted.
Application form required.
Deadline(s): May 1
Additional information: Awards are paid to the
educational institution on behalf of the
students.
EIN: 581958389

2046
The Ryder System Charitable Foundation, Inc.
11690 N.W. 105th St.
Miami, FL 33178-1103   (305) 500-3031
E-mail: foundation@ryder.com; URL: http://
www.ryder.com/aboutus_cinfo_arc.shtml

Foundation type: Company-sponsored foundation
Purpose: Grants to individuals in CA, FL, GA, MI,
MO, OH, and TX for disaster relief.
Publications: Application guidelines; Corporate
giving report.
Financial data: Year ended 12/31/2012. Assets,
$149,989 (M); Expenditures, $1,134,269; Total
giving, $1,134,269.
Fields of interest: Safety/disasters.

Type of support: Emergency funds.
Application information: Applications not
accepted.
Additional information: Unsolicited requests for
funds not considered or acknowledged.
EIN: 592462315

2047
Sailfish Point Foundation, Inc.
c/o Mrs. Merle Ginsburg
P.O. Box 1107
Stuart, FL 34995-1107   (772) 225-1000
Contact: Richard H. Evans, Pres.
Nursing Scholarship: c/o Rachel Perkins, Martin
Memorial Medical Center, 300 S.E. Hospital Ave.,
Stuart, FL 34994-2338
URL: http://
sailfish-point-foundation-inc.idilogic.aidpage.com/
sailfish-point-foundation-inc/

Foundation type: Public charity
Purpose: Scholarships to needy children and adult
residents of Martin County, FL to pursue a career in
nursing.
Financial data: Year ended 12/31/2011. Assets,
$472,429 (M); Expenditures, $230,765; Total
giving, $213,800; Grants to individuals, totaling
$171,000.
Fields of interest: Nursing school/education.
Type of support: Employee-related scholarships;
Graduate support; Undergraduate support.
Application information: Applications accepted.
Application form required.
Initial approach: Letter
Deadline(s): Contact foundation for application
deadline
Applicants should submit the following:
1) Letter(s) of recommendation
2) Financial information
3) Transcripts
4) GPA
5) Essay
EIN: 650978271

2048
Gordon Samstag Fine Arts Trust
c/o Bank of America, N.A.
P.O. Box 40200, FL9-100-10-19
Jacksonville, FL 32203-0200
Application address: c/o Ross Wolfe, Dir., Samstag
Scholarship Program, University of South Australia,
GPO Box 2471, Adelaide, South Australia 5001,
tel.: (08) 8302-0865; fax: (08) 8302-0866;
International Code for Australia is 618
E-mail: samstag@unisa.edu.au

Foundation type: Independent foundation
Purpose: Support for Australian visual art students
to study art abroad at an art institute or university.
Publications: Application guidelines.
Financial data: Year ended 12/31/2012. Assets,
$8,493,486 (M); Expenditures, $511,957; Total
giving, $233,506; Grants to individuals, 8 grants
totaling $233,506 (high: $63,382, low: $206).
Fields of interest: Visual arts.
International interests: Australia.
Type of support: Scholarships—to individuals;
Foreign applicants.
Application information: Application form required.
Application form available on the grantmaker's web
site.
Initial approach: Letter, e-mail, telephone, or see
web site

Send request by: Application forms must be sent by mail. No faxed application forms will be accepted.
Deadline(s): June 30
Final notification: Sept.
Applicants should submit the following:
1) Transcripts
2) Financial information
3) Curriculum vitae
Additional information: Application must also include proof of Australian citizenship, sample works, two references, and an applicant statement. Application guidelines and application form can be downloaded on trust web site for more detailed information.
EIN: 656064217

2049
Santa Fe College Foundation, Inc.
Robertson Admin. Bldg., Rm 207
3000 N.W. 83 St.
Gainesville, FL 32606-6210 (352) 395-5200
Contact: Charles W. Clemons Sr., Exec. Dir.
FAX: (352) 395-5197;
E-mail: chuck.clemons@sfcollege.edu; URL: http://www.sfcollegefoundation.org

Foundation type: Public charity
Purpose: Scholarships to students who are residents of Alachua and Bradford counties, NM for postsecondary education.
Publications: Annual report.
Financial data: Year ended 12/31/2011. Assets, $42,396,111 (M); Expenditures, $2,912,262; Total giving, $2,011,406; Grants to individuals, totaling $20,585.
Fields of interest: Higher education.
Type of support: Scholarships—to individuals.
Application information: Applications accepted. Application form required.
Send request by: Online
Deadline(s): May 31
Applicants should submit the following:
1) Transcripts
2) Essay
Additional information: Students should contact their guidance counselor for application guidelines. Selection is based on financial need, scholastic achievement, or special talent depending on the specific scholarship criteria. See web site for additional information. Online address: http://stars.sfcollege.edu/stars.
EIN: 510240884

2050
C. B. Schmitt Charitable Foundation, Inc.
11050 Overseas Hwy.
Marathon, FL 33050-3459
URL: http://www.gooddeedsinthekeys.org/

Foundation type: Independent foundation
Purpose: Assistance to qualified needy FL residents for living expenses, and medical assistance whose critical needs are not being met through other means.
Financial data: Year ended 09/30/2013. Assets, $335,062 (M); Expenditures, $109,157; Total giving, $79,223; Grants to individuals, 51 grants totaling $72,851 (high: $4,796, low: $156).
Fields of interest: Residential/custodial care; Economically disadvantaged.
Type of support: Grants for special needs.
Application information: Applications accepted.

Additional information: Selection is based on need. Contact foundation for additional guidelines.
EIN: 562286219

2051
Scholarship Assistance Foundation
1700 N. State Rd., Ste. 7
Lauderhill, FL 33313-5006 (954) 735-9600

Foundation type: Public charity
Purpose: Scholarships to public and private high school students of FL, who will attend postsecondary education institutions.
Financial data: Year ended 04/30/2012. Assets, $1,233,841 (M); Expenditures, $711,620; Total giving, $711,560; Grants to individuals, totaling $711,560.
Fields of interest: Higher education.
Type of support: Scholarships—to individuals.
Application information: Applications accepted.
Additional information: Contact the foundation for application guidelines.
EIN: 134233791

2052
Scholarship Fund for Ethiopian Jews
19202 Black Mangrove Ct.
Boca Raton, FL 33498-4835 (561) 852-8498
FAX: (954) 441-6955; URL: http://www.sfej.org

Foundation type: Public charity
Purpose: Scholarships to Jewish individuals of Ethiopian origin who are seeking higher education opportunities in Israel.
Financial data: Year ended 06/30/2012. Assets, $67,395 (M); Expenditures, $13,101; Total giving, $11,340.
Fields of interest: Scholarships/financial aid.
Type of support: Scholarships—to individuals.
Application information: Applications not accepted.
EIN: 650938714

2053
The Matthew Alan Schommer Memorial Scholarship Fund for Nursing
1460 56th Sq. W.
Vero Beach, FL 32966-2396

Foundation type: Independent foundation
Purpose: Nursing scholarships to residents of the Vero Beach, FL metropolitan area.
Financial data: Year ended 12/31/2011. Assets, $87,739 (M); Expenditures, $9,318; Total giving, $7,500; Grants to individuals, 10 grants totaling $7,500 (high: $1,500, low: $500).
Fields of interest: Nursing school/education.
Type of support: Undergraduate support.
Application information: Applications not accepted.
Additional information: Unsolicited requests for funds not considered or acknowledged.
EIN: 204510282

2054
School of the Arts Foundation, Inc.
P.O. Box 552
West Palm Beach, FL 33402-0552 (561) 805-6298
FAX: (561) 805-6299; E-mail: info@soafi.org; URL: http://www.soafi.org

Foundation type: Public charity
Purpose: Scholarships to graduating seniors and students of Dreyfoos School of the Arts in the Palm Beach county area, FL for higher education.
Publications: Informational brochure.
Financial data: Year ended 06/30/2012. Assets, $4,684,322 (M); Expenditures, $1,449,966; Total giving, $992,421.
Fields of interest: Arts education; Visual arts.
Type of support: Support to graduates or students of specific schools.
Application information: Applications accepted. Application form required.
Deadline(s): Varies
Additional information: Contact the foundation for further application information.
EIN: 650395865

2055
Richard L. & F. Annette Scott Foundation
568 9th St. S., Ste. 276
Naples, FL 34102-4971

Foundation type: Independent foundation
Purpose: Scholarships to graduates of North Kansas City High School, MO, for higher education.
Financial data: Year ended 09/30/2013. Assets, $1,850,339 (M); Expenditures, $87,821; Total giving, $80,395.
Type of support: Support to graduates or students of specific schools; Undergraduate support.
Application information: Applications not accepted.
Additional information: Unsolicited requests for funds not considered or acknowledged.
EIN: 621646107

2056
SeaWorld & Busch Gardens Conservation Fund
9205 SouthPark Center Loop, Ste. 400
Orlando, FL 32819-8651
Contact: Brad F. Andrews, Pres. and Exec. Dir.
E-mail: mail@swbgfund.org; Application address for Environmental Excellence Awards: c/o SeaWorld Orlando Education Dept., 7007 SeaWorld Dr., Orlando, FL 32821, tel.: (877) 792-4332 or (407) 363-2389, e-mail: buschgardenseducation@gmail.com; URL: http://www.swbg-conservationfund.org/

Foundation type: Company-sponsored foundation
Purpose: Awards to students and teachers who are working at the grassroots level to protect and preserve the environment.
Publications: Application guidelines; Annual report; Financial statement; Newsletter.
Financial data: Year ended 12/31/2012. Assets, $578,663 (M); Expenditures, $1,240,909; Total giving, $1,214,168.
Fields of interest: Environmental education; Public education; Animals/wildlife, preservation/protection.
Type of support: Awards/grants by nomination only; Awards/prizes.
Application information:
Deadline(s): Mar. 5 for Environmental Excellence Awards for individuals
Additional information: Post a video (less than five minutes) on YouTube and e-mail for Environmental Excellence Awards for individuals. Awards are by nomination only.
Program description:
Environmental Excellence Awards for Individuals: The award of $10,000 recognizes an outstanding youth, adult and environmental educator for

individual personal achievements in helping to
protect wildlife and wild places.
EIN: 113692807

2057
William G. Selby and Marie Selby Foundation
1800 2nd St., Ste. 954
Sarasota, FL 34236-5930 (941) 957-0442
Contact: Evan Jones, Grants Mgr,
FAX: (941) 957-3135; E-mail: ejones@selbyfdn.org;
URL: http://www.selbyfdn.org/

Foundation type: Independent foundation
Purpose: Scholarships to graduating high school
students and graduating students from Manatee
Community College who are residents of Sarasota,
Manatee, Charlotte or DeSoto counties in FL,
pursuing a bachelors degree from a four-year
accredited college or university.
Publications: Application guidelines; Grants list;
Informational brochure (including application
guidelines).
Financial data: Year ended 05/31/2013. Assets,
$69,415,321 (M); Expenditures, $3,593,894;
Total giving, $2,814,007; Grants to individuals,
totaling $811,820.
Fields of interest: Higher education.
Type of support: Undergraduate support.
Application information: Application form required.
Application form available on the grantmaker's web
site. Interview required.
   Send request by: Online
   Copies of proposal: 1
   Deadline(s): Apr. 1
   Final notification: Applicants notified in June
   Applicants should submit the following:
      1) Resume
      2) Pell Grant
      3) GPA
      4) Financial information
      5) Curriculum vitae
      6) Transcripts
      7) SAR
      8) SAT
      9) Letter(s) of recommendation
      10) FAFSA
      11) Essay
      12) ACT
   Additional information: Scholarships will be
      awarded up to $7,000 per year. Students
      must demonstrate financial need and
      maintain a 3.0 (unweighted) GPA.
EIN: 596121242

2058
Selinger Educational Fund
(formerly Sydney & Grace Selinger Educational Trust
Fund)
P.O. Box 1908
Orlando, FL 32802-1908

Foundation type: Independent foundation
Purpose: Scholarships to one male and one female
honor graduating student attending high schools in
South Broward County, FL.
Financial data: Year ended 12/31/2012. Assets,
$215,113 (M); Expenditures, $17,152; Total
giving, $11,000.
Fields of interest: Higher education; Scholarships/
financial aid.
Type of support: Support to graduates or students
of specific schools; Undergraduate support.
Application information: Applications accepted.
Application form required.
   Applicants should submit the following:

      1) Transcripts
      2) Financial information
   Additional information: Applicant must also
      include parents' most recent tax return, and
      must demonstrate financial need.
EIN: 596501141

2059
Senior Volunteer Services, Inc.
(formerly Broward County Grandparents, Inc.)
4701 N.W. 33rd Ave.
Fort Lauderdale, FL 33309-6807 (954)
484-7117
FAX: (954) 484-8292;
E-mail: administration@seniorvolunteerservices.or
g; URL: http://www.seniorvolunteerservices.org

Foundation type: Public charity
Purpose: Grants to elderly persons sixty years of
age and older of Broward county, FL with benefits
such as stipends and travel reimbursement who
render volunteer services to children and other
elderly persons with special needs.
Publications: Newsletter.
Financial data: Year ended 06/30/2011. Assets,
$796,311 (M); Expenditures, $1,659,286.
Fields of interest: Children, services; Aging.
Type of support: Grants for special needs;
Stipends.
Application information: Contact foundation for
information on the volunteer programs.
EIN: 591297932

2060
Charles E. Shepard Trust
P.O. Box 1908
Orlando, FL 32802-1908

Foundation type: Independent foundation
Purpose: Scholarships to graduates of high schools
in Atlanta, GA.
Financial data: Year ended 12/31/2012. Assets,
$5,491,829 (M); Expenditures, $291,923; Total
giving, $224,484.
Type of support: Undergraduate support.
Application information: Applications not
accepted.
   Additional information: Unsolicited requests for
      funds not considered or acknowledged.
EIN: 207039436

2061
The Fred B. Sieber Foundation
119 N. 11th St., Ste. 100
Tampa, FL 33602-4201

Foundation type: Independent foundation
Purpose: Grants to provide temporary financial
assistance to HIV positive individuals residing in FL
who do not qualify for federal or state assistance
because they continue to work, and those who
cannot work and have applied for assistance but
have not yet been approved. Scholarships to
residents of the Tampa, FL metropolitan area.
Financial data: Year ended 03/31/2012. Assets,
$1,487,529 (M); Expenditures, $139,139; Total
giving, $91,400; Grants to individuals, 9 grants
totaling $23,900 (high: $4,500, low: $500).
Fields of interest: AIDS, people with.
Type of support: Grants for special needs.
Application information: Applications not
accepted.
   Additional information: Unsolicited requests for
      funds not considered or acknowledged.
EIN: 593281642

2062
Lin Sing Association, Inc.
c/o Thoas S. Yang
10802 S.W. 83rd Ave.
Ocala, FL 34481-9701 (352) 873-9988
Contact: Yuk-Tsun Wong, Pres.

Foundation type: Public charity
Purpose: Scholarships primarily to residents of
Chinatown in New York, NY.
Financial data: Year ended 12/31/2012. Assets,
$1,309,355 (M); Expenditures, $87,799; Total
giving, $53,150; Grants to individuals, totaling
$15,200.
Type of support: Undergraduate support.
Application information: Letter
   Initial approach: Letter
   Additional information: Contact foundation for
      complete eligibility requirements.
EIN: 131864473

2063
Smigiel Foundation to Benefit Children and Families Inc.
P.O. Box 540669
Lake Worth, FL 33454-0669

Foundation type: Independent foundation
Purpose: Grants to needy individuals and their
families of Palm Beach county, FL.
Financial data: Year ended 11/30/2011. Assets,
$781,935 (M); Expenditures, $144,223; Total
giving, $131,432.
Fields of interest: Economically disadvantaged.
Type of support: Grants for special needs.
Application information:
   Initial approach: Letter
   Deadline(s): None
EIN: 202074054

2064
McGregor Smith Foundation
(formerly The McGregor Smith Foundation)
3 Bulow's Landing
Flagler Beach, FL 32136 (386) 405-5041
Contact: Philip K. Snyder, Treas.

Foundation type: Independent foundation
Purpose: Scholarships and loans to individuals for
higher education in Dade County, FL.
Financial data: Year ended 12/31/2011. Assets,
$885,505 (M); Expenditures, $148,685; Total
giving, $53,000.
Type of support: Scholarships—to individuals;
Student loans—to individuals.
Application information: Applications accepted.
Application form required.
   Initial approach: Letter
   Deadline(s): None
   Applicants should submit the following:
      1) Letter(s) of recommendation
      2) Transcripts
      3) Financial information
EIN: 591038572

2065
Alice F. Smith Scholarship Trust
P.O. Box 1207
Englewood, FL 34295 (941) 474-7768
Contact: R. Earl Warren, Tr.
Application Address: 359 W. Dearborn St.,
Englewood, FL 34223

Foundation type: Independent foundation

Purpose: Scholarships to students educated in the Englewood School System and residing in the Englewood, FL area for postsecondary education at an institution of learning.
Financial data: Year ended 12/31/2012. Assets, $307,199 (M); Expenditures, $7,906; Total giving, $1,500; Grants to individuals, 2 grants totaling $1,500 (high: $1,000, low: $500).
Fields of interest: Higher education.
Type of support: Scholarships—to individuals.
Application information: Applications accepted. Application form required. Interview required.
  Deadline(s): May 15
  Applicants should submit the following:
    1) Photograph
    2) Transcripts
    3) Letter(s) of recommendation
    4) Financial information
    5) Budget Information
  Additional information: Application forms can be obtained from the Trustees' office. Selection of scholarship is based on financial need.
EIN: 656202829

2066
George Snow Scholarship Fund, Inc.
(formerly George Snow Foundation, Inc.)
201 Plaza Real, Ste 260
Boca Raton, FL 33432-6142 (561) 347-6799
Contact: Timothy G. Snow, Pres.
FAX: (561) 347-6380; URL: http://www.scholarship.org/

Foundation type: Public charity
Purpose: Scholarships to students from Palm Beach and Northern Broward Counties, FL. Preference given to those attending college, university, vocational, or technical school in Miami-Dade, Broward, or Palm Beach counties, FL.
Publications: Application guidelines.
Financial data: Year ended 12/31/2011. Assets, $3,283,264 (M); Expenditures, $771,854; Total giving, $317,206; Grants to individuals, totaling $317,206.
Type of support: Technical education support; Undergraduate support.
Application information: Applications accepted. Application form required. Application form available on the grantmaker's web site.
  Initial approach: Letter
  Additional information: See web site for complete program information.
EIN: 592162597

2067
The Southwest Florida Community Foundation, Inc.
8771 College Pkwy., Bldg. 2, Ste. 201
Fort Myers, FL 33919 (239) 274-5900
Contact: For grants: Anne Douglas, Dir., Progs.
FAX: (239) 274-5930;
E-mail: info@floridacommunity.com; URL: http://www.floridacommunity.com

Foundation type: Community foundation
Purpose: Scholarships to students from high schools in Lee, Charlotte, Hendry, Glades and Collier counties, FL.
Publications: Application guidelines; Annual report (including application guidelines); Financial statement; Grants list; Informational brochure; Newsletter; Occasional report; Program policy statement; Program policy statement (including application guidelines); Quarterly report.

Financial data: Year ended 06/30/2012. Assets, $63,957,237 (M); Expenditures, $3,989,627; Total giving, $2,454,892.
Fields of interest: Historic preservation/historical societies; Arts; Environment; Health care; Human services; Physically disabled.
Type of support: Scholarships—to individuals; Support to graduates or students of specific schools; Undergraduate support.
Application information: Applications accepted. Application form required. Application form available on the grantmaker's web site.
  Send request by: Mail
  Copies of proposal: 1
  Deadline(s): Feb.
  Applicants should submit the following:
    1) ACT
    2) Essay
    3) GPA
    4) Letter(s) of recommendation
    5) SAT
    6) Transcripts
  Additional information: The foundation administers a variety of scholarship programs; See web site for program information. Interviews may be required.
EIN: 596580974

2068
The Space Shuttle Children's Trust Fund
c/o Bank of America, N.A.
P.O. Box 40200, FL9-100-10-19
Jacksonville, FL 32203-0200

Foundation type: Independent foundation
Purpose: Scholarships and other financial assistance to children of the victims of the Challenger explosion.
Financial data: Year ended 12/31/2012. Assets, $2,420,794 (M); Expenditures, $142,575; Total giving, $135,791.
Fields of interest: Education; Children.
Type of support: Scholarships—to individuals; Grants for special needs.
Application information: Applications not accepted.
  Additional information: Unsolicited requests for funds not considered or acknowledged.
EIN: 521439509

2069
Special Operations Warrior Foundation
4409 El Prado Blvd.
P.O. Box 89367
Tampa, FL 33629-8301 (813) 805-9400
FAX: (813) 805-0567;
E-mail: warrior@specialops.org; Mailing address: P.O. Box 13483, Tampa, FL 33681-3483; additional tels.: (813) 805-0640, (813) 839-4059; toll-free tel.: (877) 337-7693; URL: http://www.specialops.org

Foundation type: Public charity
Purpose: Scholarships to the children and spouses of Special Operations personnel who were killed in an operational mission or training accident. Financial assistance to the Special Operations men and women who are wounded in combat.
Publications: Annual report; Financial statement; Informational brochure; Newsletter.
Financial data: Year ended 12/31/2012. Assets, $64,329,508 (M); Expenditures, $4,730,783; Total giving, $2,300,785; Grants to individuals, totaling $1,202,069.
Type of support: Undergraduate support; Grants for special needs.

Application information:
  Initial approach: Letter or e-mail
  Additional information: Unsolicited requests for funds not considered or acknowledged.
Program description:
  Scholarships: The foundation provides family assistance to the children and spouses of fallen warriors from the time they enter the foundation family. The foundation begins establishing a relationship with families within 30 days of notification of a fatality; the foundation remains in contact with children and families throughout the years prior to the children reaching college age, continually encouraging students to attend college. When the student is in high school, foundation counselors work with students to develop personalized college education plans. Funding will be provided to up to four years for a college degree.
EIN: 521183585

2070
Kathleen C. Spicer Scholarship Fund
P.O. Box 40200, FL9-100-10-19
Jacksonville, FL 32203-0200 (866) 461-7287
Application address: c/o Bank of America, N.A., Attn.: Michael Pond, 600 Peachtree St., Ste. 1100, Atlanta, GA 30308-2219, tel.: (404) 607-5101

Foundation type: Independent foundation
Purpose: Scholarships to residents of Cobb County, GA, to attend two- and four-year colleges.
Publications: Application guidelines.
Financial data: Year ended 06/30/2012. Assets, $804,381 (M); Expenditures, $46,595; Total giving, $33,000.
Fields of interest: Higher education; Scholarships/financial aid; Volunteer services.
Type of support: Undergraduate support.
Application information: Application form required.
  Deadline(s): Apr. 20
  Applicants should submit the following:
    1) Essay
    2) Letter(s) of recommendation
  Additional information: Selection criteria include a minimum SAT score of 1200, a minimum GPA of 3.65 for high school applicants and 3.5 for college applicants, interscholastic activities, extracurricular activities, community involvement, course of study, and attendance record. No grants are awarded for postgraduate study.
EIN: 581448686

2071
St. Petersburg Times Fund, Inc.
(formerly St. Petersburg Times Scholarship Fund)
P.O. Box 1121
St. Petersburg, FL 33731-1121
Contact: Nancy Waclawek, Tr.
FAX: (727) 892-2257;
E-mail: waclawek@tampabay.com; Application address: Times Fund Inc., 490 1st Ave. S., St. Petersburg, FL 33701-4204; URL: http://www.tampabay.com/company/times-fund/

Foundation type: Independent foundation
Purpose: Undergraduate scholarships to students residing in Hillsborough, Pinellas, Hernando, Citrus, and Pasco counties, FL pursuing a career in journalism or newspaper related.
Publications: Application guidelines; Financial statement; Grants list.
Financial data: Year ended 12/31/2012. Assets, $11,576,695 (M); Expenditures, $695,494; Total giving, $517,071; Grants to individuals, totaling $156,800.

Fields of interest: Print publishing; Higher education.
Type of support: Scholarships—to individuals.
Application information: Applications accepted. Application form required. Application form available on the grantmaker's web site.
Deadline(s): Oct. 15 for Barnes Scholarship, Jan. 5 for Career Journalism Scholarship
Additional information: Applications are available through participating schools.
Program descriptions:
Barnes Scholarships: Scholarships of $2,500 to seniors in a public or private high school from Hillsborough, Pinellas, Pasco, Citrus and Hernando counties of West Central FL, with an interest in a journalism career (print broadcast on-line). This scholarship may be renewed annually over four years of full-time undergraduate study.
Career Journalism Scholarships: Scholarships of $2,500 per year to seniors in a public or private high school from Pinellas, Hillsborough, Pasco, Hernando, and Citrus counties of West Central FL, with an interest in a journalism career (print broadcast on-line). This scholarship may be renewed annually over four years of full-time undergraduate study.
EIN: 596142547

2072
Starks Charitable Foundation
8940 Azalea Cir.
PO Box 170103
Hialeah, FL 33025-2408 (786) 295-2161
Contact: Duane L. Starks, Pres.
FAX: (305) 829-3375; E-mail: scfcares@aol.com; Toll-free tel.: (888) 541-9774; URL: http://www.starksfoundation.org

Foundation type: Public charity
Purpose: Scholarships to economically disadvantaged high school graduates in the FL area, attending an institution of higher learning.
Financial data: Year ended 12/31/2011. Assets, $2,861 (M); Expenditures, $8,424; Total giving, $75.
Fields of interest: Higher education; Economically disadvantaged.
Type of support: Undergraduate support.
Application information: Applications accepted. Application form required. Application form available on the grantmaker's web site.
Initial approach: E-mail
Deadline(s): Apr. 15
Applicants should submit the following:
1) Financial information
2) Letter(s) of recommendation
3) Transcripts
4) GPA
5) Essay
Additional information: Scholarships are awarded on the basis of maintaining a 2.5 GPA or better, and demonstrate financial need.
EIN: 650864604

2073
State College of Florida Foundation, Inc.
(formerly Foundation for Manatee Community College, Inc.)
5840 26th St. W.
Bradenton, FL 34207-3522 (941) 752-5390
Contact: Peg Lowery, Secy. and Exec. Dir.
FAX: (941) 753-0853; E-mail: loweryp@mccfl.edu; Mailing address: P.O. Box 1849, Bradenton, FL 34206-7046; URL: http://scffoundation.net/

Foundation type: Public charity

Purpose: Scholarships for students attending The State College of Florida, Manatee-Sarasota, FL for higher education.
Publications: Application guidelines.
Financial data: Year ended 09/30/2011. Assets, $37,951,998 (M); Expenditures, $3,070,815; Total giving, $2,386,582; Grants to individuals, totaling $1,313,228.
Fields of interest: Higher education.
Type of support: Support to graduates or students of specific schools.
Application information: Application form required. Application form available on the grantmaker's web site.
Deadline(s): Mar. 14
Final notification: Applicants notified by Aug. 13
Applicants should submit the following:
1) Transcripts
2) GPA
3) FAFSA
4) Essay
Additional information: See web site for additional guidelines and a complete listing of scholarship programs.
Program description:
Scholarships: The foundation endows various scholarships funds, each fund with its own purposes and qualifications. While some scholarship programs require additional application procedures, there is a common application for all scholarship funds, and a student can apply to as many funds for which they are eligible. Scholarship amounts vary.
EIN: 591843274

2074
Alexander William Stearn Foundation, Inc.
2448 Indian Trail W.
Palm Harbor, FL 34683-2815 (727) 785-7969
Contact: Peter Gordon Stearn, Pres.

Foundation type: Independent foundation
Purpose: Scholarships by nomination only to financially needy graduating seniors of Lake Clifton Senior High School, Baltimore, MD.
Financial data: Year ended 06/30/2011. Assets, $1,041,171 (M); Expenditures, $67,954; Total giving, $57,000.
Fields of interest: Higher education.
Type of support: Support to graduates or students of specific schools; Awards/grants by nomination only.
Application information: Applications not accepted.
Additional information: Recipients are nominated by the school.
EIN: 521457719

2075
Step Up for Students
(formerly Florida School Choice Fund, Inc.)
P.O. Box 54367
Jacksonville, FL 32245-4367 (813) 402-0186
Contact: Doug Tuthill, Pres.
FAX: (813) 251-2127;
E-mail: info@stepupforstudents.org; E-Mail for Doug Tuthill: dtuthill@stepupforstudents.org; URL: http://www.stepupforstudents.org/

Foundation type: Public charity
Purpose: Scholarships to low-income students currently enrolled in a FL public school to attend a school of their choice that best meets their needs.
Publications: Application guidelines; Annual report; Financial statement; Newsletter.

Financial data: Year ended 06/30/2012. Assets, $217,819,371 (M); Expenditures, $152,642,566; Total giving, $143,774,025; Grants to individuals, totaling $143,674,025.
Fields of interest: Elementary/secondary education; Charter schools; Scholarships/financial aid.
Type of support: Scholarships—to individuals.
Application information: Applications accepted. Application form available on the grantmaker's web site.
Send request by: Online
Deadline(s): None
Program descriptions:
John M. McKay Scholarships for Students with Disabilities: This program provides the opportunity for special-needs children and their parents to experience broader options in education. Parents whose special-needs child has an active individual education plan can choose any public school (if space is available), or may attend an approved private school. Eligible students must have been enrolled and reported for funding by a Florida School District the prior school year, or be a military family transferring from another state. See web site http://www.mckaycoalition.com for more information.
Step Up for Students Scholarships: This program was created to help alleviate the enormous educational challenges faced by children in Florida who live in poverty. The program provides corporate tax credit scholarships to students in grades K-12 who come from low-income families, and allow students to consider a private or out-of-district school that may better suit their individual needs. Eligible applicants must be entering 2nd through 12th grade and attending a Florida public school for the previous school year, or is entering kindergarten or 1st grade, and meets specific income guidelines. The program provides up to $4,106 for private school tuition and books, or up to $500 in transportation costs to an out-of-district public school.
EIN: 593649371

2076
The David L. Strahan Educational Foundation, Inc.
17967 S.E. 87th St., Melrose Ct.
The Villages, FL 32162-4825
Application address for individuals: c/o Wirt County High School, Attn.: Principal, Mulberry St., Elizabeth, WV 26143, tel.: (304) 275-4241

Foundation type: Independent foundation
Purpose: Scholarships to graduates of Wirt County High School, WV.
Financial data: Year ended 06/30/2010. Assets, $257,208 (M); Expenditures, $10,602; Total giving, $7,811; Grants to individuals, 3 grants totaling $7,811 (high: $3,603, low: $2,104).
Type of support: Support to graduates or students of specific schools; Undergraduate support.
Application information: Application form required.
Deadline(s): June 30
Additional information: Application must include transcripts and a 250-word personal statement.
EIN: 550752363

2077
Roberta Leventhal Sudakoff Foundation, Inc.
1800 2nd St., Ste. 954
Sarasota, FL   34236-5930
Contact: Lori A. Andrew, Trust Off.
URL: http://www.selbyfdn.org/
roberta-leventhal-sudakoff-foundation.aspx

Foundation type: Independent foundation
Purpose: Scholarships for students who are residents of Charlotte, DeSoto, Manatee, and Sarasota counties in FL, and who have limited financial means, so that they may pursue a higher education with the goal of not only achieving a meaningful career, but also helping their community. Scholarships will be awarded up to $7,000 per year, not to exceed one-third of the individual's financial need. These awards are renewable, with certain requirements, for the 4 years the student is enrolled full-time at an accredited college or university. A minimum of 3.0 (unweighted) GPA is required.
Publications: Application guidelines.
Financial data: Year ended 12/31/2012. Assets, $17,804,653 (M); Expenditures, $1,143,643; Total giving, $900,000.
Type of support: Scholarships—to individuals.
Application information: Applications accepted. Application form required. Application form available on the grantmaker's web site.
   Initial approach: Application form on foundation web site
   Deadline(s): Apr. 1
   Applicants should submit the following:
      1) Essay
      2) Letter(s) of recommendation
      3) SAT
      4) ACT
      5) Transcripts
   Additional information: Letters of recommendation (from teachers and community members) should include evidence of personal growth potential. Essays should include perspective on personal values and future plans. A personal interview is also required. See foundation website for additional guidelines and information.
EIN: 311483381

2078
Sun Coast Osteopathic Foundation, Inc.
(formerly Sun Coast Hospital Foundation, Inc.)
2101 Indian Rocks Rd., Ste. A
Largo, FL   33774-1096   (727) 483-0661
Contact: Greg Ward, Exec. Dir.
URL: http://www.suncoastosteopathic.org

Foundation type: Public charity
Purpose: Scholarships to osteopathic students who are residents of the state of FL.
Publications: Application guidelines; Informational brochure.
Financial data: Year ended 09/30/2012. Assets, $1,442,507 (M); Expenditures, $126,217; Total giving, $3,000; Grants to individuals, totaling $1,000.
Fields of interest: Scholarships/financial aid; Health care.
Type of support: Scholarships—to individuals.
Application information: Applications accepted. Application form required. Application form available on the grantmaker's web site.
   Initial approach: Application
   Send request by: Online and mail
   Deadline(s): Feb. 18
   Applicants should submit the following:

      1) Photograph
      2) Financial information
      3) Transcripts
      4) Letter(s) of recommendation
Program description:
   Scholarships: The foundation awards scholarships to osteopathic students who have completed one year of training at an accredited school of osteopathic medicine. Preference is given to residents from the west central area of FL. At least five scholarships of $1,000 each will be available.
EIN: 592490651

2079
Sunburst Foundation, Inc.
2285 Potomac Rd.
Boca Raton, FL   33431-5518   (561) 995-7755
Contact: James M. Hankins, Pres.
E-mail: sunfound@bellsouth.net; *URL:* http://www.sunburst-foundation.org/

Foundation type: Independent foundation
Purpose: Scholarship awards to minority seniors graduating from participating Florida high schools who are planning to study the physical sciences at a four year college or university.
Financial data: Year ended 06/30/2013. Assets, $5,488,714 (M); Expenditures, $265,952; Total giving, $227,250; Grants to individuals, 31 grants totaling $102,250 (high: $6,000, low: $1,500).
Fields of interest: Physical/earth sciences.
Type of support: Support to graduates or students of specific schools; Undergraduate support.
Application information: Application form required.
   Additional information: Applications available through high school guidance counselors. Complete guidelines available on foundation web site.
EIN: 592637289

2080
SWS Charitable Foundation, Inc.
1600 N.W. 163rd St.
Miami, FL   33169-5641
Contact: Robert M. Hersh

Foundation type: Company-sponsored foundation
Purpose: Financial aid to employees of Southern Wine and Spirits of America, Inc., who reside in states for emergency assistance resulting from national disasters such as hurricanes and wildfires.
Financial data: Year ended 12/31/2012. Assets, $462,333 (M); Expenditures, $3,547,272; Total giving, $3,546,094.
Type of support: Emergency funds; Employee-related welfare.
Application information: Applications not accepted.
   Additional information: Unsolicited requests for funds not considered or acknowledged.
Company name: Southern Wine & Spirits of America, Inc.
EIN: 651054944

2081
Take Stock in Children, Inc.
8600 N.W. 36th St., Ste. 500
Miami, FL   33166-6688
FAX: (904) 769-2934; Toll-free tel.: (888) 322-4673; *URL:* http://www.takestockinchildren.com

Foundation type: Public charity

Purpose: Scholarships to low-income, at-risk children in FL.
Publications: Annual report.
Financial data: Year ended 12/31/2011. Assets, $9,042,577 (M); Expenditures, $7,192,317; Total giving, $3,624,001; Grants to individuals, totaling $261,186.
Fields of interest: Children/youth, services; Economically disadvantaged.
Type of support: Technical education support; Undergraduate support.
Application information: Contact foundation for eligibility requirements.
EIN: 593331584

2082
Tallahassee Quarterback Club Foundation, Inc.
1713 Mahan Dr.
Tallahassee, FL   32308-1218   (850) 878-8777

Foundation type: Public charity
Purpose: Scholarships to graduating seniors from local public and accredited private high schools in the greater Tallahassee, FL area.
Financial data: Year ended 03/31/2012. Assets, $204,715 (M); Expenditures, $72,861; Total giving, $59,500.
Fields of interest: Higher education.
Type of support: Scholarships—to individuals.
Application information: Applications accepted. Application form required. Interview required.
   Send request by: Mail or hand deliver
   Deadline(s): Jan.
   Final notification: Applicants notified in Feb.
   Applicants should submit the following:
      1) Photograph
      2) Transcripts
      3) Letter(s) of recommendation
EIN: 593237681

2083
Tangelo Park Pilot Program Inc.
9840 International Dr.
Orlando, FL   32819-8111
URL: http://www.tangeloparkprogram.com/

Foundation type: Independent foundation
Purpose: Grants to child-care providers for pre-school students of bona fide residence of Tangelo Park, FL.
Financial data: Year ended 12/31/2012. Assets, $60,125 (M); Expenditures, $475,049; Total giving, $449,370; Grants to individuals, 11 grants totaling $344,400 (high: $37,440, low: $1,320).
Fields of interest: Child development, education; Elementary school/education.
Type of support: Grants to individuals.
Application information: Applications not accepted.
   Additional information: Unsolicited requests for funding not considered or acknowledged.
EIN: 593224659

2084
Taunton Family Children's Home
P.O. Box 870
Wewahitchka, FL   32465
URL: http://www.tauntonhome.org/

Foundation type: Operating foundation
Purpose: Scholarships to students in FL, primarily in Wewahitchka, for undergraduate or technical school education.

Financial data: Year ended 12/31/2012. Assets, $695 (M); Expenditures, $182,179; Total giving, $0.
Fields of interest: Higher education.
Type of support: Technical education support; Undergraduate support.
Application information: Applications not accepted.
> *Additional information:* Unsolicited requests for funds not considered or acknowledged.
EIN: 592335556

2085
Jason Taylor Foundation, Inc.
1575 Northpark Dr., Ste. 99
Weston, FL 33326-3230 (954) 424-0799
Contact: Seth Levit, Exec. Dir.
FAX: (954) 424-7076;
E-mail: info@jasontaylorfoundation.com;
URL: http://www.jasontaylorfoundation.org

Foundation type: Public charity
Purpose: Assistance to low-income, at-risk children of Miami-Dade, Broward and Palm Beach counties, FL.
Financial data: Year ended 12/31/2011. Assets, $193,844 (M); Expenditures, $604,253; Total giving, $379,136; Grants to individuals, totaling $164,793.
Fields of interest: Children; Economically disadvantaged.
Type of support: Grants for special needs.
Application information: Applications accepted. Application form required.
> *Additional information:* See web site for additional guidelines.

Program description:
> *Jason Taylor Scholars:* This program provides scholarship and mentorship for deserving 6th and 7th grade students. Students enter the program by signing a contract along with their parents in support of the program, to commit to meet with a mentor weekly, stay drug/alcohol free, produce grades which are average or above, remain crime free, attend school and display a strong responsibility to their neighborhoods and schools. In return, mentors are recruited to motivate the student to achieve academic success and model social, coping and life skills. Upon graduation from high school, the student is awarded a FL, Prepaid College Program four-year tuition scholarship.

EIN: 201452369

2086
Haywood R. Thornton III Memorial Scholarship Trust
702 Delaware Ave.
Saint Cloud, FL 34769-3477 (407) 892-4095
Contact: Elizabeth Abshier, Tr.

Foundation type: Independent foundation
Purpose: Scholarships to graduates of Saint Cloud High School, FL, for higher education.
Financial data: Year ended 12/31/2012. Assets, $393,732 (M); Expenditures, $21,983; Total giving, $20,000; Grants to individuals, 4 grants totaling $20,000 (high: $5,000, low: $5,000).
Type of support: Support to graduates or students of specific schools; Undergraduate support.
Application information: Application form required.
> *Deadline(s):* Apr. 15
EIN: 596839701

2087
Robert A. Thrush Charitable Trust
2810 E. Oakland Park Blvd., No. 102
Fort Lauderdale, FL 33306-1801 (954) 563-1000
Contact: James L. Case Esq., Tr.

Foundation type: Independent foundation
Purpose: Scholarships to needy and worthy students of Broward county, FL for higher education.
Financial data: Year ended 12/31/2010. Assets, $0 (M); Expenditures, $9,877; Total giving, $7,500; Grants to individuals, 2 grants totaling $7,500 (high: $4,500, low: $3,000).
Fields of interest: Higher education.
Type of support: Scholarships—to individuals.
Application information: Applications accepted.
> *Initial approach:* Letter
> *Additional information:* Application should include transcripts.
EIN: 650136688

2088
Pierre Toussant/Roger Radloff Foundation
13520 S.W. 113 Ct.
Miami, FL 33176 (305) 253-6752
Contact: Frank M. Evans, Tr.

Foundation type: Independent foundation
Purpose: Scholarships and grants to needy students, with preference to talented and artistic Haitians.
Financial data: Year ended 12/31/2012. Assets, $186,801 (M); Expenditures, $47,921; Total giving, $32,910.
International interests: Haiti.
Type of support: Scholarships—to individuals.
Application information: Application form required.
> *Additional information:* Applications must be submitted by the institution which the applicant is attending or plans to attend.
EIN: 656083720

2089
Brigadier General Edward Dorr Tracy, CFSA and 1st Lieutenant William G. Burt, Jr., USAF Fund
c/o 1LT William G. Burt, Jr.
9000 Southside Blvd., FL9-100-10-19
Jacksonville, FL 32256
Contact: Brenton P. Thurston
Application address: 111 Westminster Street. RI1-102-M1-02, Providence RI, 02903

Foundation type: Independent foundation
Purpose: Scholarships to male residents of Monroe County, GA, who attend the University of Georgia.
Financial data: Year ended 12/31/2012. Assets, $1,577,821 (M); Expenditures, $100,106; Total giving, $77,708; Grants to individuals, 20 grants totaling $77,708 (high: $10,136, low: $1,689).
Fields of interest: Men.
Type of support: Support to graduates or students of specific schools.
Application information: Applications accepted. Application form required.
> *Additional information:* Contact foundation for current application guidelines.
EIN: 527077420

2090
The Trolinger Trust
c/o SunTrust Bank
P.O. Box 1908
Orlando, FL 32802-1908
Contact: Henry M. Harvey, Chair.
Application address: 701 Berkley St., Radford, VA 24143

Foundation type: Independent foundation
Purpose: Financial assistance to needy residents of Montgomery County and Radford, VA, and other southwestern VA counties and cities.
Financial data: Year ended 06/30/2013. Assets, $1,693,855 (M); Expenditures, $74,303; Total giving, $43,450.
Type of support: Grants for special needs.
Application information: Applications accepted.
> *Initial approach:* Letter
> *Deadline(s):* None
> *Additional information:* Application must include statement of financial need.
EIN: 546110451

2091
Ethel H. and George W. Tweed Scholarship Endowment Trust
P.O. Box 40200, FL9-100-10-19
Jacksonville, FL 32203-0200

Foundation type: Independent foundation
Purpose: Scholarships by nomination only to graduating seniors of any St. Petersburg, FL high school.
Financial data: Year ended 10/31/2011. Assets, $16,008 (M); Expenditures, $8,100; Total giving, $3,786; Grants to individuals, 3 grants totaling $3,786 (high: $1,262, low: $1,262).
Fields of interest: Higher education; Scholarships/financial aid.
Type of support: Awards/grants by nomination only; Undergraduate support.
Application information:
> *Initial approach:* Letter
> *Deadline(s):* June 1
> *Applicants should submit the following:*
> 1) Essay
> 2) Financial information
> *Additional information:* Applicant should demonstrate financial need and academic achievement.
EIN: 596145533

2092
Two Red Roses the Foundation, Inc.
4190 Corporate Ct.
Palm Harbor, FL 34683 (727) 943-2144
E-mail: email@tworedroses.com

Foundation type: Operating foundation
Purpose: Grants to winners of the Central to the American Arts and Crafts Movement essay contest, which is open to students at college on the west coast of FL.
Financial data: Year ended 12/31/2012. Assets, $57,338,292 (M); Expenditures, $95,670; Total giving, $0.
Fields of interest: Folk arts.
Type of support: Awards/prizes.
Application information:
> *Initial approach:* Letter
> *Additional information:* Contact foundation for current application guidelines.
EIN: 331093993

2093
United Arts of Central Florida, Inc.
2450 Maitland Ctr. Pkwy., Ste. 201
Maitland, FL   32751-4140   (407) 628-0333
Contact: Flora Maria Garcia, Pres. and C.E.O.
FAX: (407) 628-9110; E-mail: uacf@unitedarts.cc;
E-Mail for Flora Maria Garcia :
floramaria@unitedarts.cc; URL: http://
www.unitedarts.cc

Foundation type: Public charity
Purpose: Grants to support emerging or
established artists, and arts administrators who
are residents of Lake, Osceola, Orange or Seminole
counties, FL to further their artistic careers.
Publications: Application guidelines; Annual report;
Financial statement; Grants list; Informational
brochure.
Financial data: Year ended 06/30/2012. Assets,
$4,658,432 (M); Expenditures, $5,463,080; Total
giving, $4,185,569; Grants to individuals, totaling
$32,099.
Fields of interest: Arts.
Type of support: Grants to individuals.
Application information: Application form required.
Application form available on the grantmaker's web
site.
  Deadline(s): Oct. 14
  Applicants should submit the following:
    1) Work samples
    2) Resume
  Additional information: Application should also
    include artist statement. See web site for
    additional guidelines.
EIN: 591166446

2094
United Way of Central Florida, Inc.
5605 U.S. Hwy. 98 S.
P.O. Box 1357
Highland City, FL   33846-1357   (863) 648-1500
E-mail: info@uwcf.org; URL: http://www.uwcf.org

Foundation type: Public charity
Purpose: Emergency assistance to low income
individuals and families in need throughout central
FL, with rent, utilities, food and other special needs.
Publications: Annual report; Informational
brochure; Newsletter.
Financial data: Year ended 06/30/2011. Assets,
$22,191,834 (M); Expenditures, $9,971,555;
Total giving, $6,819,106; Grants to individuals,
71 grants totaling $88,657.
Fields of interest: Human services; Economically
disadvantaged.
Type of support: In-kind gifts; Grants for special
needs.
Application information: Contact the agency for
eligibility determination.
EIN: 592116280

2095
United Way of St. Lucie County, Inc.
4800 S. U.S. 1
Fort Pierce, FL   34982-7078   (772) 464-5300
Contact: Karen Knapp, Pres. and C.E.O.
FAX: (772) 464-7805;
E-mail: karen.knapp@unitedwayslc.org;
URL: http://www.unitedwayslc.org

Foundation type: Public charity
Purpose: Grants for school supplies to needy
children in St. Lucie County, FL.
Publications: Annual report; Newsletter.
Financial data: Year ended 06/30/2011. Assets,
$2,560,516 (M); Expenditures, $1,209,683; Total

giving, $650,536; Grants to individuals, totaling
$41,855.
Fields of interest: Economically disadvantaged.
Type of support: Grants for special needs.
Application information:
  Initial approach: Letter
  Additional information: Contact foundation for
    complete application guidelines.
EIN: 596212157

2096
University Athletic Association, Inc.
P.O. Box 14485
Gainesville, FL   32604-2485   (352) 375-4683
URL: http://www.uaa.ufl.edu

Foundation type: Public charity
Purpose: Athletic scholarships to students at the
University of Florida, FL.
Publications: Financial statement.
Financial data: Year ended 06/30/2012. Assets,
$293,407,800 (M); Expenditures, $106,655,921;
Total giving, $17,307,524; Grants to individuals,
totaling $10,850,186.
Type of support: Support to graduates or students
of specific schools; Undergraduate support.
Application information: Applications not
accepted.
  Additional information: Unsolicited requests for
    funds not considered.
EIN: 596002050

2097
The Volunteer Way, Inc.
7820 Congress St.
New Port Richey, FL   34653-1110   (727)
815-0433
FAX: (727) 848-5494; URL: http://
www.thevolunteerway.org

Foundation type: Public charity
Purpose: Assistance to financially insecure
individuals of Pasco, Hernando, FL and surrounding
counties with food, personal items, resources and
other needs.
Publications: Newsletter.
Financial data: Year ended 12/31/2011. Assets,
$1,180,630 (M); Expenditures, $5,520,995; Total
giving, $5,081,085; Grants to individuals, totaling
$5,081,085.
Fields of interest: Food services; Human services,
emergency aid.
Type of support: Emergency funds; Grants for
special needs.
Application information: Applications not
accepted.
  Additional information: Contact the agency for
    eligibility determination.
EIN: 593555687

2098
Elizabeth C. Wagner Trust
P.O. Box 1908
Orlando, FL   32802-1908

Foundation type: Independent foundation
Purpose: Scholarships to high school graduates of
VA for higher education.
Financial data: Year ended 02/28/2013. Assets,
$1,196,606 (M); Expenditures, $56,830; Total
giving, $51,328.
Fields of interest: Higher education.
Type of support: Scholarships—to individuals.

Application information: Contract the trust for
additional information.
EIN: 546374333

2099
MaliVai Washington Kids Foundation, Inc.
1096 W. 6th St.
Jacksonville, FL   32209-5091   (904) 359-5437
Contact: Terri Florio, Exec. Dir.
FAX: (904) 301-3789;
E-mail: info@malwashington.com; URL: http://
www.malwashington.com

Foundation type: Public charity
Purpose: Scholarship to graduating youth from high
school who are residents of Jacksonville, FL to
further their education.
Financial data: Year ended 06/30/2012. Assets,
$4,501,791 (M); Expenditures, $1,000,155; Total
giving, $23,370; Grants to individuals, totaling
$23,370.
Fields of interest: Higher education; Recreation;
Youth.
Type of support: Scholarships—to individuals.
Application information: Scholarships are awarded
annually, and youth are nominated by program staff
and coaches. Scholarships are awarded for
academic, athletic and community achievements.
EIN: 593559150

2100
Watson Clinic Foundation, Inc.
100 S. Kentucky Ave., Ste. 255
Lakeland, FL   33801-5089   (863) 802-6221
Contact: J. Scott Swygert M.D., Pres.
FAX: (863) 668-3857;
E-mail: cbamberg@watsonclinic.com; URL: http://
www.watsonclinic.com/wcf/default.aspx

Foundation type: Public charity
Purpose: Scholarships to individuals primarily of FL,
in recognition of past scientific and educational
achievements. Support to physicians for research
that is imperative to advance the pool of medical
knowledge related to prevention and treatment of
diseases, as well as improving patient care.
Financial data: Year ended 12/31/2011. Assets,
$1,339,878 (M); Expenditures, $254,339; Total
giving, $17,300; Grants to individuals, totaling
$5,550.
Fields of interest: Health care; Institute.
Type of support: Research; Scholarships—to
individuals.
Application information:
  Initial approach: Letter
  Copies of proposal: 1
  Deadline(s): None
  Additional information: Contact the foundation for
    eligibility criteria.
EIN: 591100876

2101
Frances R. Wertzberger Trust
c/o A.J. Stites
4741 Atlantic Blvd., Ste. B-1
Jacksonville, FL   32207-2168   (904) 399-8011
Application address: c/o Office of Scholarships,
P.O. Box 6688, Raleigh, NC 27628-6688

Foundation type: Independent foundation
Purpose: Scholarships to needy and deserving high
school seniors or students enrolled in college in the
U.S.
Financial data: Year ended 12/31/2011. Assets,
$694,150 (M); Expenditures, $35,587; Total

giving, $17,600; Grants to individuals, 7 grants totaling $17,600 (high: $5,500, low: $500).

Fields of interest: Higher education.

Type of support: Scholarships—to individuals; Graduate support.

Application information: Application form required.

Deadline(s): Dec.1

Final notification: Applicants notified Mar. 15

Applicants should submit the following:
1) Class rank
2) SASE
3) ACT
4) Essay
5) Letter(s) of recommendation
6) SAT
7) Transcripts

Additional information: Application available upon request. Interviews may be required.

Program description:

Scholarship Program: Scholarships are awarded to students enrolled in a college, university, or graduate school within the U.S., for full or partial tuition, room and board, books, fees, and living expenses, depending on need. Applicant must be a U.S. citizen, U.S. national, or U.S. permanent resident. Scholarships are automatically renewed for another year with the student maintaining a 3.0 GPA with no course grade below 2.0, provided the student has not violated the college or university's honor code and remains in good legal standing in the community.

EIN: 597158689

2102

West Palm Beach Rotary Club Charity Fund, Inc.

P.O. Box 353

West Palm Beach, FL   33402-0353   (561) 254-4789

Foundation type: Public charity

Purpose: Scholarships to graduates of an accredited high school or equivalent from West Palm Beach, FL who would otherwise find it difficult, without hardship to acquire a higher education without financial aid and assistance.

Financial data: Year ended 06/30/2012. Assets, $258,061 (M); Expenditures, $84,864; Total giving, $43,711; Grants to individuals, totaling $18,000.

Fields of interest: Higher education.

Type of support: Scholarships—to individuals; Undergraduate support.

Application information: Applications accepted.

Initial approach: Letter

Additional information: Selection is based on good character, intelligence, determination and ability to complete a full course in higher education. Contact the fund for additional guidelines.

EIN: 591002972

2103

Whitehall Foundation, Inc.

P.O. Box 3423

Palm Beach, FL   33480-1623   (561) 655-4474

Contact: George M. Moffett II, Pres.; Catherine M. Thomas, Asst. Treas.

E-mail: email@whitehall.org; Express mail address: 125 Worth Ave., Ste. 220, Palm Beach, FL 33480; URL: http://www.whitehall.org

Foundation type: Independent foundation

Purpose: Support for basic research in vertebrate (excluding clinical) and invertebrate neurobiology.

Publications: Application guidelines; Grants list.

Financial data: Year ended 09/30/2012. Assets, $107,121,135 (M); Expenditures, $5,117,606; Total giving, $4,566,558.

Fields of interest: Research; Science.

Type of support: Research; Postdoctoral support.

Application information: Applications accepted. Application form required.

Initial approach: Letter

Deadline(s): Jan. 15, Apr. 15 and Oct. 1 for letters of intent. June 1, Sept. 1 and Feb. 15 for applications

Additional information: Letters of intent by e-mail not accepted; See foundation web site for further program and application information.

Program descriptions:

Grants-in-Aid: The program is designed for researchers at the assistant professor level who experience difficulty in competing for research funds because they have not yet become firmly established. Grants-in-aid will also be made to senior scientists. All applications will be judged on the scientific merit of the proposal as well as on past performance and evidence of the applicant's continued productivity. Grants-in-aid are awarded for a one-year period and do not exceed $30,000.

Research Grants: Research grants are available to established scientists of all ages working at accredited institutions in the United States. Applications will be judged on the scientific merit and innovative aspects of the proposal as well as on the competence of the applicant. Research grants of up to three years will be provided. A renewal grant with a maximum of two years is possible, but it will be awarded on a competitive basis. Research grants will not be awarded to investigators who have already received, or expect to receive, substantial support from other sources, even if it is for an unrelated purpose. Research grants will normally be in the range of $30,000 to $75,000 per year.

EIN: 135637595

2104

J.J. Wiggins Memorial Trust

P.O. Box 1111

Moore Haven, FL   33471   (863) 946-3400

Contact: Gregory Bond

Foundation type: Operating foundation

Purpose: Scholarships to individuals who have been residents of Glades County, FL, for at least one year, and who are under 21 years old.

Financial data: Year ended 04/30/2013. Assets, $4,363,061 (M); Expenditures, $346,091; Total giving, $68,250.

Fields of interest: Vocational education, post-secondary; Higher education.

Type of support: Technical education support; Undergraduate support.

Application information: Application form required.

Initial approach: Letter

Send request by: Mail

Deadline(s): June 30

Applicants should submit the following:
1) Transcripts
2) SAT
3) GPA
4) ACT

Additional information: Scholarships are paid directly to the educational institution on behalf of the students.

EIN: 592675273

2105

Winged Foot Scholarship Foundation

2390 Tamiami Trail N., Ste. 204

Naples, FL   34103-4484

Foundation type: Independent foundation

Purpose: Scholarships to top athletic students in Collier County's, FL high schools, public and private enrolled at accredited junior college, college or university.

Financial data: Year ended 12/31/2011. Assets, $616,621 (M); Expenditures, $183,197; Total giving, $53,500; Grants to individuals, 13 grants totaling $53,500 (high: $5,000, low: $2,500).

Fields of interest: Athletics/sports, training; Recreation.

Type of support: Scholarships—to individuals.

Application information: Application form required. Interview required.

Initial approach: Letter or telephone

Deadline(s): Apr.

Applicants should submit the following:
1) GPA
2) Transcripts
3) Letter(s) of recommendation

Additional information: Applicant must show academic and leadership achievements as well as athletic accomplishments.

EIN: 650227001

2106

The Frank M. Wolfe Foundation Inc.

P.O. Box 321299

Cocoa Beach, FL   32932-1299   (321) 783-2834

Contact: Frank M. Wolfe, Pres.

Foundation type: Operating foundation

Purpose: Grants to economically disadvantaged residents of FL for tuition, books, lab fees, transportation and other college costs.

Financial data: Year ended 12/31/2012. Assets, $15,049 (M); Expenditures, $2,309; Total giving, $0.

Fields of interest: Economically disadvantaged.

Type of support: Grants for special needs.

Application information: Applications accepted.

Initial approach: Letter

Deadline(s): None

EIN: 593482977

2107

Woman's Exchange, Inc. of Sarasota

539 S. Orange Ave.

Sarasota, FL   34236-0219   (941) 955-7859

Contact: Karen Koblenz, Exec. Dir. and C.E.O.

E-mail: info@sarasotawex.com; E-mail For Karen Koblenz: kkoblenz@sarasotawex.com; URL: http://www.womansexchange.com/

Foundation type: Public charity

Purpose: College scholarships to students of Sarasota and Manatee counties, FL pursuing a career in the arts.

Publications: Application guidelines; Informational brochure.

Financial data: Year ended 06/30/2012. Assets, $1,479,489 (M); Expenditures, $1,068,456; Total giving, $330,120; Grants to individuals, totaling $105,800.

Fields of interest: Performing arts; Theater.

Type of support: Scholarships—to individuals.

Application information: Applications accepted. Application form required. Application form available on the grantmaker's web site.

Initial approach: Letter

Send request by: Mail

Copies of proposal: 12
Deadline(s): Feb. 1
Final notification: Recipients notified in Apr.
EIN: 591109482

2108
Workforce Escarosa, Inc.
9111 Sturdevant St.
Pensacola, FL   32514-3519   (850) 473-0939
Contact: Susan Nelms, Exec. Dir.
TTY: (877) 887-5627; TDD: (800) 955-8771;
URL: http://www.workforceescarosa.com/

Foundation type: Public charity
Purpose: Financial assistance for cars to residents of Escambia and Santa Rosa counties, FL, who are receiving Temporary Assistance for Needy Families and who live in an area not serviced by public transportation.

Financial data: Year ended 06/30/2012. Assets, $540,405 (M); Expenditures, $6,758,554; Total giving, $1,205,368.
Fields of interest: Economically disadvantaged.
Type of support: Grants for special needs.
Application information: Applications accepted. Application form required. Application form available on the grantmaker's web site.
  Initial approach: Letter
  Additional information: Application must include a certified copy of the applicant's driving record for the last three years.
EIN: 593390564

2109
Charm & Goodloe Yancey Foundation
P.O. Box 1908
Orlando, FL   32802-1908
Contact: Blair Curtis, Chair.
Application address: P.O. Box 43326, Atlanta, GA 30378

Foundation type: Independent foundation
Purpose: Scholarships to children of employees of Yancey Brothers, Inc.
Financial data: Year ended 12/31/2011. Assets, $1,373,379 (M); Expenditures, $75,995; Total giving, $65,000; Grants to individuals, 12 grants totaling $24,000 (high: $2,000, low: $2,000).
Type of support: Employee-related scholarships.
Application information: Applications accepted.
  Initial approach: Letter
  Deadline(s): None
Company name: Yancey Brothers, Incorporated
EIN: 581413050

GEORGIA

2110
100 Black Men of America, Inc.
141 Auburn Ave.
Atlanta, GA 30303-2503 (404) 688-5100
Contact: Dr. Mark Alexander, Secy.
FAX: (404) 688-1028; Toll-free tel.: (800)
598-3411; URL: http://www.100blackmen.org

Foundation type: Public charity
Purpose: Scholarships to deserving matriculating
students who will be full-time students at
accredited, postsecondary institutions based on
the foundation's eligibility criteria.
Financial data: Year ended 06/30/2011. Assets,
$2,138,173 (M); Expenditures, $4,203,538; Total
giving, $218,580; Grants to individuals, totaling
$218,580.
Fields of interest: Higher education; Leadership
development.
Type of support: Undergraduate support.
Application information: Applications accepted.
Application form required. Application form
available on the grantmaker's web site.
  Initial approach: Telephone or letter
  Send request by: Mail
  Deadline(s): Feb. 25
  Final notification: Recipients notified by May 27
  Applicants should submit the following:
    1) Essay
    2) Transcripts
    3) Letter(s) of recommendation
    4) GPA
  Additional information: Application should also
    include one non-related family member
    character reference letter.
Program description:
  100 Black Men of America Scholarship:
Scholarship awards must be applied toward tuition,
room and board and range from $1,000 to $3,000.
Eligibility criteria includes:
  · Minimum GPA of 2.5
  · Completed 50 hours of active community
    service within past 12 months with certified
    documentation
  · Leadership involvement
EIN: 581974429

2111
Wesley G. Adair Scholarship Trust
c/o Synovus Trust Co.
P.O. Box 1747
Athens, GA 30603-1747 (706) 357-7115
Contact: Cynthia H. Lester

Foundation type: Operating foundation
Purpose: Scholarships to individuals who are
residents of Barrow County, GA, or lineal
descendents of Wesley G. Adair for undergraduate
and vocational education.
Financial data: Year ended 12/31/2012. Assets,
$569,636 (M); Expenditures, $30,494; Total
giving, $18,250; Grants to individuals, 23 grants
totaling $18,250 (high: $1,000, low: $250).
Fields of interest: Vocational education,
post-secondary; Higher education.
Type of support: Undergraduate support.
Application information: Application form required.
  Send request by: Mail
  Deadline(s): June 1
  Applicants should submit the following:
    1) Letter(s) of recommendation
    2) Transcripts

Additional information: Application should also
  include a copy of the acceptance letter from
  college or vocational school. Applicant must
  be able to establish financial need.
EIN: 586376451

2112
Alpha Delta Pi Foundation, Inc.
1386 Ponce De Leon Ave., N.E.
Atlanta, GA 30306-4604 (404) 378-3164
Contact: Jennifer Polley Webb, Exec. Dir.
FAX: (404) 378-5935;
E-mail: foundation@alphadeltapi.com; E-Mail for
Jennifer Polley Webb: jwebb@alphadeltapi.com;
URL: http://www.alphadeltapi.org

Foundation type: Public charity
Purpose: Scholarships and emergency grants to
members and alumni of the Alpha Delta Pi Sorority.
Publications: Application guidelines; Annual report;
Financial statement; Newsletter.
Financial data: Year ended 07/31/2012. Assets,
$4,414,764 (M); Expenditures, $661,152; Total
giving, $205,587; Grants to individuals, totaling
$113,676.
Fields of interest: Students, sororities/fraternities;
Women.
Type of support: Scholarships—to individuals;
Grants for special needs.
Application information: Applications accepted.
Application form required. Application form
available on the grantmaker's web site.
  Initial approach: Telephone, fax or e-mail
  Deadline(s): Mar. 1 for scholarships
  Applicants should submit the following:
    1) Letter(s) of recommendation
    2) Transcripts
EIN: 581507941

2113
American Cancer Society, Inc.
c/o Extramural Grants Dept.
250 Williams St., N.W., 6th Fl.
Atlanta, GA 30303-1002 (404) 329-7558
FAX: (404) 321-4669; E-mail: grants@cancer.org;
Toll-free tel.: (800) 227-2345; TTY: (866)
228-4327; URL: http://www.cancer.org

Foundation type: Public charity
Purpose: Awards by nomination only to honor
exemplary individuals in the field of tobacco control
and prevention throughout the world.
Publications: Annual report; Financial statement.
Financial data: Year ended 08/31/2011. Assets,
$1,521,867,801 (M); Expenditures,
$373,462,873; Total giving, $113,106,262.
Grants to individuals amount not specified.
Fields of interest: Cancer; Cancer research.
Type of support: Fellowships; Research; Awards/
grants by nomination only; Awards/prizes;
Postdoctoral support; Doctoral support; Stipends.
Application information: Applications accepted.
Application form required. Application form
available on the grantmaker's web site.
  Initial approach: Letter
  Additional information: Contact foundation for
    further eligibility criteria.
Program descriptions:
  *Audrey Meyer Mars International Fellowships in
Clinical Oncology:* This program provides support for
one year of advanced training in clinical oncology at
participating U.S. cancer centers to qualified
physicians and surgeons from other countries,
particularly where advanced training is not readily
available. This program is limited to non-U.S.
citizens and provides up to $45,000 annually.

*Cancer Control Career Development Awards for
Primary Care Physicians:* These awards provide
support for primary care physicians in supervised
programs intended to develop clinical and teaching
expertise and the capacity to perform independent
research or educational innovation in cancer
control. Candidates must have a full-time faculty
appointment and generally be no more than 10
years beyond training at the beginning of the award.
Awards are made for three years with stipends of
$100,000 per year; in addition, salary and benefits
for the mentor may be charged to the grant in the
amount of up to $10,000 per year.
  Clinical Research Professor Grants: The society
offers a limited number of grants to established
investigators in mid-career who have made seminal
contributions that have changed the direction of
clinical, psychosocial, behavioral, health policy, or
epidemiologic cancer research. Furthermore, it is
expected that these investigators will continue to
provide leadership in their research area. Up to two
awards are made annually for a five-year term that
can be renewed once. The award of up to $80,000
per year (direct costs only) may be used for salary
or research project support.
  Doctoral Degree Scholarships in Cancer Nursing:
This program provides awards to doctoral students
in the fields of cancer nursing research, education,
administration, and clinical practice. Initial two-year
grants are available, providing a stipend of $15,000
per year with the possibility of a two-year
competitive renewal.
  Doctoral Training Grants in Oncology Social Work:
This award is made to support the training of
graduate students in doctoral programs focused on
research related to the psychosocial needs of
persons with cancer and their families. An initial
two-year grant with annual funding of $20,000 will
be awarded, with the possibility of a two-year
competitive renewal.
  Graduate Scholarship in Cancer Nursing Practice:
These scholarships provide support for graduate
students pursuing master's degrees in cancer
nursing or doctorates of nursing practice. Awards
may be for two years, with stipends of $10,000 per
year.
  *International Fellowships for Beginning
Investigators (ACSBI):* Funding preference will be
given to candidates who propose to conduct cancer
research projects into preclinical, clinical,
epidemiological, psychosocial, behavioral, or
health services; or health policy, outcomes, or
cancer control. Eligible candidates should hold
assistant professorships or similar positions at
their home institutes and have at least two years of
postdoctoral experience after obtaining their M.D.
or Ph.D. degrees or equivalents. Awards are
conditional on the return of the fellow to the home
institute at the end of the fellowship and on the
availability of appropriate facilities and resources to
apply their newly-acquired skills. Six to eight fellows
are selected each year for awards, with an average
value of $45,000 for travel and stipend support.
  *Mentored Research Scholar Grant in Applied and
Clinical Research:* This program provides support for
mentored research by full-time faculty, typically
within the first four years of their appointment, with
the goal of becoming independent investigators in
clinical, epidemiological, psychosocial, behavioral,
or health services, or health policy research.
Awards are for up to five years and for up to
$135,000 per year (direct costs), plus eight percent
allowable indirect costs. A maximum of $10,000
per year for the mentor(s) (regardless of the number
of mentors) is included in the $135,000.
  Postdoctoral Fellowships: These fellowships
support the training of researchers who have just
received their doctorate to enable them to qualify

for an independent career in cancer research (including basic, preclinical, clinical, psychosocial, behavioral, and epidemiologic research). Awards are made for one to three years with progressive stipends of $44,000, $46,000, and $48,000 per year, plus a $4,000 per year institutional allowance.

Research Professor Grants: The society offers a limited number of grants to investigators in mid-career who have made seminal contributions that have changed the direction of cancer research. Furthermore, it is expected that these investigators will continue to provide leadership in their research area. Up to two awards are made annually for a five-year term that can be renewed once. The award of up to $80,000 per year (direct costs only) may be used for salary or research project support.

Research Scholar Grants: These grants support investigator-initiated research projects across the cancer research continuum. Awards are for up to four years and for up to $200,000 per year, plus 20 percent allowable indirect costs. Eligible applicants include investigators in the first six years of an independent research career or faculty appointment.
EIN: 131788491

2114
American College of Rheumatology
2200 Lake Blvd. N.E.
Atlanta, GA   30319-5310   (404) 633-3777
Contact: Mark Andrejeski, Exec. V.P.
FAX: (404) 633-1870;
E-mail: acr@rheumatology.org; E-mail for Mark Andrejeski: mandrejeski@rheumatology.org;
URL: http://www.rheumatology.org/index.asp

Foundation type: Public charity
Purpose: Travel scholarships for rheumatology researchers and students to attend conferences, and merit award for rheumatology fellows.
Publications: Annual report; Occasional report.
Financial data: Year ended 06/30/2011. Assets, $34,843,483 (M); Expenditures, $25,610,215; Total giving, $6,032,725; Grants to individuals, 567 grants totaling $1,032,725. Subtotal for travel grants: 557 grants totaling $1,017,725. Subtotal for awards/prizes: 10 grants totaling $15,000.
Fields of interest: Medical research.
Type of support: Travel awards; Awards/prizes.
Application information: Applications accepted.
 Send request by: On-line
 Deadline(s): Vary
 Additional information: See web site for additional application guidelines.
Program descriptions:
 Abstract Awards: These awards recognize scholarship in the field of rheumatology and provide medical and graduate students an opportunity to attend the ACR/ARHP Annual Meeting. The awards term is one year and ranges in the amounts of $750 to $1,500.
 Distinguished Fellow Awards Program: The award program recognizes clinical and research fellows who are in a rheumatology fellowship training program and who have performed meritoriously. Ten awards in the amount of $1,500 each is presented by the ACR.
 Education& Training Awards: These awards help to cultivate future generations of rheumatologists and rheumatology health professionals. The awards range from one to three years in the amounts of $1,500 to $180,000.
 Research Awards: These awards are designed to attract early and mid-career investigators to continue vital research into the cause, prevention and treatment of rheumatic diseases. The awards

years range from 1- 3 years in the amounts of $75,000- $400,000.
EIN: 581627547

2115
American College of Rheumatology Research and Education Foundation
2200 Lake Blvd., N.E.
Atlanta, GA   30319-5310   (404) 633-3777
Contact: Steven C. Echard C.A.E., Exec. Dir.
FAX: (404) 633-1870;
E-mail: foundation@rheumatology.org; E-Mail for Steven C. Echard: sechard@rheumatology.org;
URL: http://www.rheumatology.org/ref/

Foundation type: Public charity
Purpose: Research grants and fellowships for individuals researching rheumatoid arthritis.
Publications: Annual report; Newsletter.
Financial data: Year ended 06/30/2012. Assets, $68,122,057 (M); Expenditures, $10,182,051; Total giving, $7,781,289; Grants to individuals, totaling $153,500.
Fields of interest: Arthritis; Arthritis research.
Type of support: Fellowships; Research.
Application information: Applications not accepted.
 Additional information: Unsolicited requests for funds not considered or acknowledged.
EIN: 581654301

2116
American Junior Golf Foundation, Inc.
1980 Sports Club Dr.
Braselton, GA   30517-6000   (770) 868-4200
Contact: Stephen Hamblin, Exec. Dir.
FAX: (770) 868-4211; E-mail: ajga@ajga.org;
URL: http://www.ajga.org

Foundation type: Public charity
Purpose: Financial assistance to talented junior golfers of promise who may not have the opportunity to compete to gain exposure for a college golf scholarship.
Financial data: Year ended 12/31/2011. Assets, $7,429,377 (M); Expenditures, $1,192,795; Total giving, $593,384; Grants to individuals, totaling $312,324.
Fields of interest: Athletics/sports, golf; Young adults, female; Young adults, male.
Type of support: Grants to individuals; Travel grants; Grants for special needs.
Application information: Applications accepted. Application form required. Application form available on the grantmaker's web site.
 Send request by: Online
 Deadline(s): Sept. 1
 Applicants should submit the following:
  1) Financial information
  2) Budget Information
 Additional information: Applicants must become an AJGA member in order to apply for a grant. See web site for additional application guidelines.
Program description:
 Achieving Competitive Excellence Grant Program: The grant provides financial support to seek top-flight golf opportunities for young golfers regardless of financial resources. Applicants must be between 12 and 18 years of age and a U.S. citizen. Grants are used only to reimburse costs associated with either AJGA events or USGA junior amateur events. Grants are not awarded to individuals not planning to attend college, regardless of their financial situation.
EIN: 581447686

2117
Amos-Cheves Foundation, Inc.
(formerly His Trust Foundation, Inc.)
6867 Mountainbrook Dr., Ste. 107
Columbus, GA   31904-3379

Foundation type: Independent foundation
Purpose: Scholarships to students in the Columbus, GA area for attendance at Columbus State University.
Financial data: Year ended 12/31/2012. Assets, $18,313,390 (M); Expenditures, $2,311,082; Total giving, $2,276,202; Grants to individuals, 23 grants totaling $18,500.
Fields of interest: Higher education.
Type of support: Support to graduates or students of specific schools.
Application information: Contact the foundation for additional information.
EIN: 582634947

2118
The Peyton Anderson Foundation, Inc.
577 Mulberry St., Ste. 830
Macon, GA   31201-8223   (478) 743-5359
Contact: Karen J. Lambert, Pres.
Peyton Anderson Scholarship tel. (Scholarship Mgr.): (478) 314-0948,
e-mail: scholarships@pafdn.org
FAX: (478) 742-5201; E-mail: grants@pafdn.org;
URL: http://www.peytonanderson.org/

Foundation type: Independent foundation
Purpose: Scholarships to help fund the college education of highly promising high school students in Bibb County, GA.
Publications: Application guidelines; Grants list; Informational brochure (including application guidelines).
Financial data: Year ended 12/31/2012. Assets, $83,950,135 (M); Expenditures, $5,394,956; Total giving, $3,486,750; Grants to individuals, totaling $267,750.
Fields of interest: Vocational education, post-secondary; Higher education.
Type of support: Scholarships—to individuals; Support to graduates or students of specific schools.
Application information: Applications accepted. Application form required. Application form available on the grantmaker's web site. Interview required.
 Applicants should submit the following:
  1) ACT
  2) Essay
  3) FAFSA
  4) Letter(s) of recommendation
  5) SAT
  6) SAR
  7) Transcripts
 Additional information: Applicants must have been residents of Bibb county for the past two years, must be graduating high school seniors with a 2.0 GPA, graduating from a Bibb County public high school or private high school accredited by the Southern Association of Colleges and Schools (SACS), and demonstrate academic promise, strong character, community involvement, and financial need. Scholarships are paid directly to the school on behalf of the students. See web site for additional guidelines.
EIN: 581803562

2119
Arby's Foundation, Inc.
1155 Perimeter Ctr. W., Ste. 1200
Atlanta, GA 30338-5464 (678) 514-5158
FAX: (678) 514-5334;
E-mail: info@arbysfoundation.org; URL: http://
www.arbysfoundation.org

Foundation type: Public charity
Purpose: Undergraduate scholarships by
nomination only to participants in the Big Brothers
Big Sisters program.
Financial data: Year ended 12/31/2011. Assets,
$13,226,495 (M); Expenditures, $3,959,076;
Total giving, $1,736,643.
Fields of interest: Scholarships/financial aid.
Type of support: Awards/grants by nomination only;
Undergraduate support.
Application information: Applications not
accepted.
EIN: 581692997

2120
Arthritis Foundation, Inc.
1330 W. Peachtree St., Ste. 100
Atlanta, GA 30309-2904 (404) 872-7100
Contact: John A. Hardin M.D., Chief Scientific Off.;
Leigh Hoffner, Grants Specialist
FAX: (404) 872-0457;
E-mail: johnhardin@arthritis.org; URL: http://
www.arthritis.org

Foundation type: Public charity
Purpose: Grants to individuals conducting research
on arthritis.
Publications: Annual report.
Financial data: Year ended 12/31/2011. Assets,
$64,613,117 (M); Expenditures, $54,607,673;
Total giving, $8,475,600.
Fields of interest: Arthritis research.
Type of support: Research.
Application information: Applications not
accepted.
  Additional information: Giving only to preselected
    individuals. Unsolicited requests for funds not
    considered or acknowledged.
Program descriptions:
  *Doctoral Dissertation Award for Arthritis Health
  Professionals:* Awards $30,000 per year to provide
  for one or two years of salary and/or research
  support. The research project must be related to
  arthritis management and/or comprehensive
  patient care in rheumatology practice, research, or
  education; laboratory research is not covered.
  Innovative Research Grant: Awards up to
  $100,000 per year for two years for research
  proposals with an especially high degree of
  innovation and novelty, or that represent a special
  opportunity to address unique and relevant
  research questions.
  Lee C. Howley, Sr. Prize for Arthritis Research:
  Awards a $20,000 prize to recognize an individual
  who has made an outstanding contribution to
  research that represents a major advance in the
  understanding, treatment, or prevention of arthritis
  and rheumatic diseases. Award is by nomination
  only.
  *New Investigator Grant for Arthritis Health
  Professionals:* Awards $50,000 per year for three
  years to encourage individuals in health care to
  carry out innovative research projects in areas
  related to arthritis and rheumatic diseases.
  Laboratory research and M.D.s are not eligible.
  Postdoctoral Fellowship: Provides a salary
  stipend of $50,000 for M.D.s, D.O.s, Ph.D.s, or
  equivalent for a three-year period. Ninety percent of

the awardee's time must be devoted to
arthritis-related research.
EIN: 581341679

2121
Dallas Austin Foundation, Inc.
(also known as Don't Stop the Music Foundation)
582 Trabert Ave.
Atlanta, GA 30309-2260 (678) 686-5676
FAX: (404) 603-8716; E-mail: info@dafme.org;
Additional tel.: (678) 686-5681; Scholarship
e-mail: scholarship@dafme.org; URL: http://
www.dafme.org/

Foundation type: Public charity
Purpose: Scholarships and financial assistance to
deserving college-bound students from the
metropolitan Atlanta, GA area who have chosen
music as their major, and who have demonstrated
superb leadership skills and interest in music.
Publications: Application guidelines.
Financial data: Year ended 12/31/2011. Assets,
$35,802 (M); Expenditures, $53,827; Total giving,
$26,237.
Fields of interest: Media/communications; Film/
video; Children/youth.
Type of support: Scholarships—to individuals.
Application information: Applications accepted.
  Additional information: Contact the foundation for
    additional application guidelines.
EIN: 731677176

2122
The Nathaniel Anthony Ayers Foundation
for the Artistically Gifted Mentally Ill
(also known as 2 Strings Connection, Inc.)
1600 Atlanta Financial Ctr.
3343 Peachtree Rd., N.E., Ste. 1600
Atlanta, GA 30326-1429
E-mail: info@naayers.org; Toll-free tel.: (877)
272-5272; URL: http://www.naayers.org

Foundation type: Public charity
Purpose: Support to artistically gifted individuals
with mental illness who demonstrate exceptional
talent in the arts.
Publications: Application guidelines.
Financial data: Year ended 12/31/2011. Assets,
$16,922 (M); Expenditures, $31,760.
Fields of interest: Performing arts; Mental health,
disorders.
Type of support: Residencies.
Application information: Applications accepted.
  Additional information: Contact the foundation for
    additional guidelines.
Program description:
  Artist-in-Residence Program: The foundation
  partners with nonprofit organizations that share the
  philosophy of utilizing the arts as a mechanism for
  improving the lives and allowing the
  artistically-talented to share their gifts with the
  world. Artists-in-residence will have the opportunity
  to use their talent to encourage mentees to view
  their own abilities constructively, resulting in
  lifestyle changes that enable them to overcome the
  obstacles in their lives. Applicants will be solicited
  from artists who have demonstrated professional
  excellence in the visual arts (oils, pastels,
  watercolor, sculpture, and photography),
  performing arts (dance, music, theater), and literary
  arts (poetry, playwright, fiction/nonfiction)
EIN: 262258760

2123
Clark and Ruby Baker Foundation
c/o US Trust, Bank of America, N.A.
3414 Peachtree Rd. NE GA7-813-14-04
Atlanta, GA 30326-1113 (404) 264-1377
Contact: Quanda Allen, V.P.
E-mail: quanda.allen@ustrust.com; URL: http://
www.bankofamerica.com/grantmaking

Foundation type: Independent foundation
Purpose: Scholarships primarily to residents of GA
who are attending Methodist-affiliated colleges or
universities. Assistance for retired Methodist
ministers.
Financial data: Year ended 12/31/2012. Assets,
$3,252,901 (M); Expenditures, $176,175; Total
giving, $156,000.
Fields of interest: Theology; Higher education;
Theological school/education; Health care;
Protestant agencies & churches; Religion.
Type of support: Scholarships—to individuals;
Grants for special needs.
Application information: Applications accepted.
  Initial approach: Letter
  Additional information: Contact the foundation for
    additional guidelines.
EIN: 581429097

2124
BankSouth Foundation Ltd.
(formerly Citizens Union Bank Foundation, Ltd.)
P.O. Box 89
Greensboro, GA 30642-0089 (706) 453-2236
Contact: Bobby L. Voyles, Chair.
Application address: 200 N. East St., Greensboro,
GA 30642

Foundation type: Company-sponsored foundation
Purpose: Scholarships by nomination only to
residents of Greene County, GA.
Financial data: Year ended 12/31/2012. Assets,
$437,814 (M); Expenditures, $22,736; Total
giving, $22,250; Grants to individuals, 4 grants
totaling $8,000 (high: $2,000, low: $2,000).
Fields of interest: Higher education.
Type of support: Awards/grants by nomination only.
Application information: Applications not
accepted.
  Additional information: Recipients are nominated
    by schools.
Company name: BankSouth
EIN: 581541701

2125
The Bantly Charitable Trust
806 Moss Creek Plantation
Duluth, GA 30097-5958 (770) 736-7534
Contact: Thomas W. Bantly, Tr.

Foundation type: Independent foundation
Purpose: Grants for medical research, religious
study, and missionary support.
Financial data: Year ended 12/31/2012. Assets,
$458,745 (M); Expenditures, $35,772; Total
giving, $30,026.
Fields of interest: Theological school/education;
Institute; Biology/life sciences; Christian agencies
& churches.
Type of support: Research.
Application information: Applications accepted.
Application form required. Application form
available on the grantmaker's web site. Interview
required.
  Initial approach: Letter
  Deadline(s): None

Additional information: Applicants for medical research grants must also submit a memorandum outlining proposed medical research, approximate length of time the research will take, the specific issues the researcher will address or study, how the results will be used, and the applicant's overall assessment of the importance of the research to mental health in general.
EIN: 581637392

2126
James M. Barnett Jr. Foundation, Inc.
c/o Perry & Walters LLP
P.O. Box 71209
Albany, GA 31708-1209
Contact: James E. Reynolds, Jr., Dir.

Foundation type: Independent foundation
Purpose: Scholarships primarily to music students of southwest GA, with preference given to organ students.
Financial data: Year ended 12/31/2011. Assets, $5,101,627 (M); Expenditures, $225,328; Total giving, $133,054; Grants to individuals, 11 grants totaling $49,804 (high: $27,354, low: $500).
Fields of interest: Music.
Type of support: Undergraduate support.
Application information: Applications accepted. Application form required.
Initial approach: Letter
Additional information: Contact foundation for complete application guidelines and eligibility requirements.
EIN: 562360848

2127
Beech Foundation, Inc.
2461 O'Neal Rd.
Conyers, GA 30094-6027
E-mail: jeff@thebeechfoundation.org; Tel./fax: (678) 413-2136; additional e-mail: greta@thebeechfoundation.org; URL: http://www.thebeechfoundation.org

Foundation type: Operating foundation
Purpose: Scholarships to GA students who are striving towards a nonprofit career.
Financial data: Year ended 12/31/2012. Assets, $0 (M); Expenditures, $1,276,993; Total giving, $1,248,523; Grants to individuals, totaling $861,471.
Type of support: Undergraduate support.
Application information: Applications not accepted.
Additional information: Unsolicited requests for funds not considered or acknowledged.
EIN: 611405192

2128
The R. A. Bowen Trust
5300 Zebulon Rd., Cottage 57
Macon, GA 31210
Contact: R.A. Bowen, Jr., Tr.
Application address: P.O. Box 4611, Macon, GA 31208, tel.: (478) 345-0317, fax: (866) 823-9410
E-mail: rabtrust@juno.com; URL: http://www.rabowentrust.org

Foundation type: Independent foundation
Purpose: Scholarships to qualified students of Macon, GA for full time undergraduate study at Wesleyan College, GA or Mercer University, GA.
Publications: Informational brochure (including application guidelines).

Financial data: Year ended 12/31/2012. Assets, $4,210,747 (M); Expenditures, $186,817; Total giving, $181,377. Scholarships—to individuals amount not specified.
Fields of interest: Higher education.
Type of support: Support to graduates or students of specific schools; Undergraduate support.
Application information: Applications accepted. Application form required.
Deadline(s): June 1
Final notification: Recipients notified by July 1
Additional information: Scholarships are granted for a period of one academic year and may be renewed for one or more additional years, up to a maximum of four years. Awards are paid directly to the educational institution on behalf of the students. See web site for additional guidelines.
EIN: 586032145

2129
Boys & Girls Clubs of America
1275 W. Peachtree St. N.E.
Atlanta, GA 30309-3506 (404) 487-5700
Contact: James Clark, Pres. and C.E.O.
E-mail: info@bgca.org; URL: http://www.bgca.org

Foundation type: Public charity
Purpose: Scholarships to active Boys & Girls Club members who exhibit service to the Club and community, academic performance, and spiritual and family dedication.
Publications: Annual report.
Financial data: Year ended 12/31/2012. Assets, $369,127,674 (M); Expenditures, $127,568,134; Total giving, $66,065,361; Grants to individuals, totaling $52,355.
Fields of interest: Boys & girls clubs.
Type of support: Undergraduate support.
Application information: Contact local Boys & Girls Club for current application deadline/guidelines.
Program description:
Youth of the Year Program: Awarded in conjunction with the Reader's Digest Foundation, this award is designed to promote and recognize service to club and community, academic performance, and contributions to family and spiritual life. Competition begins with each club selecting a Youth of the Year, who receives a certificate and medallion and enters state competitions. State winners receive a plaque and a $1,000 scholarship, and then enter one of five regional competitions. Each regional winner receives a $10,000 scholarship and is eligible for the national competition held in Washington, D.C. The winner of the national competition, named as National Youth of the Year, receives an additional $50,000 scholarship and is installed by the President of the U.S.
EIN: 135562976

2130
Braswell Fund
P.O. Box 857
Madison, GA 30650-0857 (706) 343-6500
Contact: Charles Merritt
Application address: 259 North 2nd Ave., Probate Ct., Madison, GA 30650

Foundation type: Independent foundation
Purpose: Scholarships to financially needy, deserving residents of Morgan County, GA, who have been deprived of the care of one or more parent due to death, for postsecondary education.
Financial data: Year ended 06/30/2013. Assets, $334,595 (M); Expenditures, $26,207; Total

giving, $15,600; Grants to individuals, 12 grants totaling $15,600 (high: $1,300, low: $1,300).
Fields of interest: Higher education.
Type of support: Scholarships—to individuals.
Application information: Applications accepted. Application form required.
Initial approach: Letter or telephone
Deadline(s): Mar. 15
Applicants should submit the following:
1) Budget Information
2) Transcripts
3) Financial information
4) Essay
Additional information: Application should also include two references.
Program description:
Scholarship Program: Applicants must have resided in Morgan County, GA, for at least one year prior to application, be deprived of one or both parents due to death, and plan to enroll in an accredited postsecondary institution on a full-time basis for three consecutive quarters or two consecutive semesters within the 13-month period starting June 1st. In addition, applicants must be high school graduates under the age of 26.
EIN: 586033308

2131
A. T. Brightwell School, Inc.
402 W. Cloverhurst Ave.
Lexington, GA 30648-0360
Contact: Hardy Cook, Exec. Secy.

Foundation type: Independent foundation
Purpose: Scholarships to unmarried or divorced (proof of divorce necessary) students under 25 years of age who have lived within the Maxeys, GA, area for at least two years prior to effective date of scholarship. Parents of student must live and remain in Maxeys area for the duration of the scholarship.
Publications: Annual report; Informational brochure.
Financial data: Year ended 06/30/2012. Assets, $68,943 (M); Expenditures, $61,375; Total giving, $53,863; Grants to individuals, 13 grants totaling $53,863 (high: $52,395, low: $970).
Fields of interest: Vocational education; Business school/education.
Type of support: Technical education support; Undergraduate support.
Application information: Applications accepted. Application form required. Interview required.
Initial approach: Letter
Send request by: Mail
Deadline(s): None
Additional information: Application must include a copy of the applicant's birth certificate.
EIN: 586066256

2132
Richard F. Brown & Pearl P. Brown Education Trust
1125 Bob Harmon Rd.
Savannah, GA 31408

Foundation type: Independent foundation
Purpose: Scholarships to students attending Savannah Technical College, Armstrong Atlantic State University and Georgia Southern University for higher education.
Financial data: Year ended 12/31/2011. Assets, $108,675 (M); Expenditures, $40,951; Total giving, $13,898; Grants to individuals, totaling $13,898.
Fields of interest: Higher education.

Type of support: Support to graduates or students of specific schools.
Application information: Unsolicited requests for funds not accepted.
EIN: 586312774

2133
The Thomas C. Burke Foundation
c/o Bank of America, N.A.
3414 Peachtree Rd. NE, Ste. 1475, GA7-813-14-04
Atlanta, GA 30326-1113
E-mail: ga.grantmaking@ustrust.com; URL: http://www.bankofamerica.com/grantmaking

Foundation type: Independent foundation
Purpose: Medical assistance to cancer patients in central GA.
Financial data: Year ended 09/30/2013. Assets, $6,342,378 (M); Expenditures, $315,099; Total giving, $259,748.
Fields of interest: Health care, patient services; Cancer.
Type of support: Grants for special needs.
Application information: Applications accepted.
   Initial approach: Telephone or in person
   Deadline(s): None
   Additional information: Applicants must be referred by their physicians.
EIN: 586047627

2134
Fuller E. Callaway Foundation
209 Broome St.
P.O. Box 790
LaGrange, GA 30241-0014   (706) 884-7348
Contact: H. Speer Burdette III, Genl. Mgr.
Application address for George E. Sims Nursing Scholarship: c/o Gaylene Deason, West Georgia Health, 1514 Vernon Rd., LaGrange, GA 30240-4131, tel.: (706) 845-3722, e-mail: deasong@wghealth.org
FAX: (706) 884-0201; URL: http://www.callawayfoundation.org/fecf_entry.php

Foundation type: Independent foundation
Purpose: Undergraduate scholarships to individuals who have been residents of Troup County or La Grange, GA, for at least two years. Graduate scholarships to children of former employees of Callaway Mills Company, and to applicants who are residents of LaGrange, GA, who were educated in the LaGrange public schools. Nursing scholarships are available each year to nursing students.
Publications: Informational brochure.
Financial data: Year ended 12/31/2012. Assets, $51,648,160 (M); Expenditures, $2,801,126; Total giving, $1,073,217; Grants to individuals, 2 grants totaling $300,481.
Fields of interest: Higher education; Graduate/professional education.
Type of support: Employee-related scholarships; Scholarships—to individuals; Graduate support; Undergraduate support.
Application information: Applications accepted. Application form required. Interview required.
   Send request by: Mail
   Deadline(s): Feb. 15 for undergraduate scholarships and May 15 for graduate scholarships
   Applicants should submit the following:
      1) Photograph
      2) Transcripts
Program descriptions:
   George E. Sims, Jr. Nursing Scholarship: This scholarship is awarded each year to nursing

students based on the applicant's scholastic record, character, leadership qualities, participation in students and community activities, and personal interviews. The scholarships include all costs associated with fulfilling the requirements of a nursing degree. Recipients must work at West Georgia Health for one or two years after graduation, depending upon the duration of the scholarship.
   Hatton Lovejoy Graduate Studies Fund: This scholarship program is to encourage and assist worthy young men and women to advance themselves through postgraduate education to assume roles in community leadership and service. The scholarship grants are open to any person enrolled or accepted in any accredited postgraduate program of study. First preference is given to children of former employees of Callaway Mills Company and second preference is given to those who are residents and graduates of Troup County, GA. Award amounts vary depending on specific circumstances.
   Hatton Lovejoy Scholarship Plan: Scholarships to individuals who have been residents of Troup County, GA, for at least two years at the time of applying. Additionally, applicants must be graduates of, or within six months of graduation from, an accredited high school with a scholastic standing in the upper 25 percent of their class. While in college, recipients must maintain a cumulative scholastic standing in the upper one-half of their college class. The maximum amount of a scholarship award is $1,200 per quarter or $1,800 per semester of college attendance for 12 quarters or 8 semesters, for a total maximum scholarship of $14,400.
EIN: 580566148

2135
Ryan Cameron Foundation
P.O. Box 550469
Atlanta, GA 30355-2969   (404) 784-1171
Contact: Kysha Cameron, C.E.O.
FAX: (404) 393-9283;
E-mail: info@ryancameron.org; URL: http://www.ryancameron.org

Foundation type: Public charity
Purpose: Scholarships to high school seniors of Atlanta, GA pursuing a college degree in communications.
Publications: Application guidelines.
Financial data: Year ended 12/31/2011. Assets, $93,896 (M); Expenditures, $172,307; Total giving, $9,000; Grants to individuals, totaling $6,500.
Fields of interest: Media/communications.
Type of support: Undergraduate support.
Application information: Applications accepted.
   Send request by: Mail
   Deadline(s): May 20
   Final notification: Recipients notified July 8
   Applicants should submit the following:
      1) Transcripts
      2) Essay
   Additional information: Application should also include college acceptance letters.
EIN: 050529934

2136
The Carter Center, Inc.
1 Copenhill
453 Freedom Pkwy.
Atlanta, GA 30307-1400   (404) 420-5100
Contact: Thom Bornemann, Dir., Mental Health Program
FAX: (404) 420-5158;
E-mail: carterweb@emory.edu; Toll-free Tel.: (800) 550-3560; URL: http://www.cartercenter.org

Foundation type: Public charity
Purpose: Fellowships to journalists to study selected topics of mental health or mental illness.
Publications: Annual report; Informational brochure (including application guidelines).
Financial data: Year ended 08/31/2011. Assets, $473,093,418 (M); Expenditures, $73,679,427; Total giving, $9,026,841; Grants to individuals, totaling $71,069.
Fields of interest: Print publishing; Research; Mental health, disorders.
Type of support: Fellowships; Research.
Application information: Applications accepted. Application form not required.
   Deadline(s): Apr. 20
   Applicants should submit the following:
      1) Letter(s) of recommendation
      2) Resume
      3) Work samples
      4) Proposal
   Additional information: Application should also include description of objectives for fellowship. See web site for additional information.
Program description:
   Rosalynn Carter Fellowships for Mental Health Journalism: The goals of the fellowships are to: increase accurate reporting on mental health issues and decrease incorrect, stereotypical information; help journalists produce high-quality work that reflects an understanding of mental health issues through exposure to well-established resources in the field; and develop a cadre of better-informed print and electronic journalists who will more accurately report information through newspapers, magazines, radio, television, film, and the Internet and influence their peers to do the same. Eligible applicants for a fellowship must have at least three years of experience in print or electronic journalism (writing, reporting, editing, producing, and/or filmmaking). Every year, six U.S. fellows are awarded stipends of $10,000 each. International fellows from select countries (South Africa, Romania, and New Zealand) are awarded a comparable stipend. Stipends cover expenses during the fellowship project, including travel, materials, and other incidental expenses.
EIN: 581454716

2137
The Charter Foundation, Inc.
P.O. Box 472
West Point, GA 31833-0472   (706) 645-1391
Contact: Bonnie F. Bonner, Secy.

Foundation type: Independent foundation
Purpose: Scholarships to residents of Troup County, GA; Chambers County, AL; and Lee County, AL.
Financial data: Year ended 12/31/2012. Assets, $6,996,261 (M); Expenditures, $375,757; Total giving, $305,760; Grants to individuals, 16 grants totaling $16,000 (high: $1,000, low: $1,000).
Type of support: Undergraduate support.

Application information: Applications accepted.
  Deadline(s): Aug. 1
EIN: 582144961

2138

The Cherokee Caddy Scholarship Foundation, Inc.
8601 Dunwoody Pl., Bldg. 100, Ste. 100
Atlanta, GA 30350 (770) 993-4401
Contact: Mark Mongell, V.P.
Application address: 665 Hightower Trail, Atlanta, GA 30350

Foundation type: Independent foundation
Purpose: Scholarships to students of GA, for attendance at accredited colleges or universities to deserving youth who had participated in the Cherokee Town & Country Club's caddy program for at least two years.
Financial data: Year ended 12/31/2011. Assets, $187,770 (M); Expenditures, $14,757; Total giving, $8,000; Grants to individuals, 6 grants totaling $8,000 (high: $2,000, low: $1,000).
Fields of interest: Higher education; Athletics/sports, golf; Youth.
Type of support: Scholarships—to individuals.
Application information: Applications accepted. Application form required.
  Deadline(s): None
  Additional information: Recipients are selected on scholarly aptitude, financial need and appropriateness of his/her course of study.
EIN: 582489470

2139

Chick-fil-A, Inc. Corporate Giving Program
5200 Buffington Rd.
Atlanta, GA 30349-2945 (404) 765-8000
URL: http://www.chick-fil-a.com/#ourcommitment

Foundation type: Corporate giving program
Purpose: Scholarships to employees of Chick-fil-A, Inc., for higher education.
Publications: Application guidelines.
Fields of interest: Higher education.
Type of support: Employee-related scholarships; Undergraduate support.
Application information: Application form required.
  Additional information: Applicants must have completed their high school education, be enrolled in a college or university, be active in their community or school, demonstrate a solid work ethic, and possess strong leadership abilities, good teamwork, and a desire to succeed. Contact foundation for further application information.
Program descriptions:
  Chick-fil-A Leadership Scholarship Program: Chick-fil-A offers $1,000 college scholarships to certain qualified franchised Operator Restaurant employees, a Chick-fil-A tradition that has awarded over $30 million in scholarships.
  S. Truett Cathy Scholar Awards: Chick-fil-A awards additional $1,000 college scholarships to high school students who demonstrate excellence in academics, leadership, and community service.
Company name: Chick-fil-A, Inc.

2140

Children of Promise, Inc.
2522 Howell Farms Way
Acworth, GA 30101-6240

Foundation type: Independent foundation

Purpose: Tuition provided for out of school programs for children of diverse background in the Acworth, GA area.
Financial data: Year ended 06/30/2013. Assets, $2,467 (M); Expenditures, $3,705; Total giving, $0.
Type of support: Scholarships—to individuals.
Application information: Applications accepted.
  Initial approach: Letter
  Deadline(s): Mar. 15
  Additional information: Letter should include request for aid.
EIN: 582493269

2141

The Choson Foundation
5903 Peachtree Industrial Blvd.
Norcross, GA 30092-3417
URL: http://www.chosonfoundation.org/

Foundation type: Operating foundation
Purpose: Scholarship assistance to Korean-American students for higher education who are children of a missionary or pastor and legal residents of Georgia.
Financial data: Year ended 12/31/2012. Assets, $0 (M); Expenditures, $190,991; Total giving, $187,768; Grants to individuals, totaling $25,700.
Fields of interest: Scholarships/financial aid.
Type of support: Scholarships—to individuals.
Application information: Application form required. Application form available on the grantmaker's web site.
  Deadline(s): July
  Applicants should submit the following:
    1) Essay
    2) Financial information
    3) Photograph
    4) Letter(s) of recommendation
    5) Transcripts
    6) SASE
  Additional information: Applications must be sent by US first-class mail. See web site for complete guidelines.
EIN: 586456333

2142

Christian Scholarship Foundation, Inc.
668 Clifton Rd. N.E.
Atlanta, GA 30307-1789 (404) 377-6524
Contact: Caral R. Holladay, Pres.
FAX: (404) 377-4234; *URL:* http://csfinc.org

Foundation type: Public charity
Purpose: Fellowships to members of the churches of Christ who are teaching or who plan to teach religion and related subjects in universities, colleges, schools of theology, and Bible chairs.
Fields of interest: Theological school/education.
Type of support: Fellowships.
Application information: Applications accepted. Application form required. Application form available on the grantmaker's web site.
  Initial approach: Letter
Program description:
  Graduate Fellowship Awards: The applicant must have satisfactorily completed at least one full year of study as a candidate for the Ph.D. or equivalent post-graduate degree prior to the year of application. Fellowship awards range from $2,000 to $10,000.
EIN: 581483707

2143

Churches Homes Foundation, Inc.
c/o Buckhead Capital Mgmt.
3330 Cumberland Blvd., Ste. 650
Atlanta, GA 30339-8124
Application address: c/o V. Faye White, 3475 Piedmont Rd. N.E., Atlanta, GA 30305, tel.: (404) 995-3052

Foundation type: Independent foundation
Purpose: Scholarships to individuals where evidence of financial need exists, and a satisfactory prior academic performance.
Financial data: Year ended 03/31/2013. Assets, $5,213,247 (M); Expenditures, $337,214; Total giving, $277,974.
Type of support: Scholarships—to individuals.
Application information: Applications accepted. Interview required.
  Initial approach: Letter
  Additional information: Application should include a resume.
EIN: 580568689

2144

Club of Hearts, Inc.
241 Ralph McGill Blvd., Bin 10230
Atlanta, GA 30308-3374 (404) 506-3030
E-mail: clubhear@southernco.com

Foundation type: Public charity
Purpose: Emergency grants to Georgia Power and Southern Company (Georgia) employees, retirees, and their family dependent members who are experiencing a financial hardship, resulting from a catastrophic event or serious illness.
Financial data: Year ended 12/31/2011. Assets, $292,374 (M); Expenditures, $957,654; Total giving, $957,654; Grants to individuals, totaling $79,791.
Fields of interest: Human services, emergency aid.
Type of support: Emergency funds.
Application information: Applications accepted. Application form required. Application form available on the grantmaker's web site.
  Initial approach: Letter
  Copies of proposal: 1
  Deadline(s): Mar. 31
  Final notification: Applicants notified in 1 month
EIN: 586056698

2145

Coastal EMC Foundation
P. O. Box 109
Midway, GA 31320-0109 (912) 884-3311
Scholarship e-mail: scholarship@coastalemc.com
FAX: (912) 884-2789; *URL:* http://www.coastalemc.com/foundation.aspx?section=c

Foundation type: Public charity
Purpose: Scholarships to individuals in Bryan, Liberty, and McIntosh counties, GA to further their studies. Grants to teachers to support classroom initiatives.
Publications: Application guidelines.
Financial data: Year ended 12/31/2012. Assets, $174,592 (M); Expenditures, $54,065; Total giving, $54,065.
Fields of interest: Higher education.
Type of support: Scholarships—to individuals.
Application information: Applications accepted. Application form required. Application form available on the grantmaker's web site.
  Initial approach: Application

Send request by: Mail, fax, e-mail or hand deliver
Deadline(s): Feb. 13 for Walter Harrison Scholarship, Mar. 30 for Coastal Electric Cooperative Scholarships, Apr. 31 for Bright Ideas
Final notification: Recipients notified in May for Coastal Electric Cooperative
Applicants should submit the following:
1) ACT
2) SAT
3) Letter(s) of recommendation
4) Transcripts
Additional information: See web site for additional application guidelines.
Program descriptions:
Bright Ideas: This program awards grants of up to $2,000 to certified school teachers instructing students in grades K-12 in south Bryan, Liberty, and McIntosh counties, GA. The program encourages teachers to develop creative, innovative programs that might not otherwise be funded through the school system. The competition is open to public and private schools accredited by the Southern Association of Colleges and Schools.
Coastal Electric Cooperative Foundation Scholarships: Scholarships of $1,000 each are available to residents of south Bryan, Liberty, and McIntosh counties who are graduating seniors, college students, or adult students returning to school. Applications are evaluated on the basis of commitment to community, integrity, accountability, innovation, and financial need.
Walter Harrison Scholarship: Each year, the foundation selects three nominees to compete in a state-wide competition for scholarships of $1,000 each. Eligible applicants must be members of the Coastal Electric Cooperative, or dependent children who are graduating seniors or college students. Applications are judged on the basis of academic achievement and financial need.
EIN: 582076664

2146
Coastal Jewish Foundation, Inc.
400 Mall Blvd., Ste. M
Savannah, GA 31406
Contact: Charles Garfunkel

Foundation type: Operating foundation
Purpose: Grants to individuals in southeastern GA, the metropolitan New York, NY, area and as well as in Jerusalem for general welfare.
Financial data: Year ended 08/31/2013. Assets, $5,391 (M); Expenditures, $39,120; Total giving, $39,096; Grants to individuals, 8 grants totaling $25,634 (high: $13,337, low: $500).
Fields of interest: Human services; Jewish agencies & synagogues.
Type of support: Foreign applicants; Grants for special needs.
Application information: Applications accepted. Application form not required.
Deadline(s): June 1
Additional information: Application by letter outlining purpose of grant and other grants received.
EIN: 581053510

2147
Ty Cobb Educational Fund
P.O. Box 937
Sharpsburg, GA 30277-0937
Contact: Cathy Scott, Schol. Coord.
E-mail: tycobb@mindspring.com; URL: http://www.tycobbfoundation.com

Foundation type: Independent foundation
Purpose: Scholarships to undergraduate students who are residents of GA with a "B" average or higher for attendance at an accredited college or university. Graduate scholarships to students who are residents of GA pursuing their dentistry or MD degrees.
Publications: Application guidelines; Informational brochure.
Financial data: Year ended 12/31/2012. Assets, $12,954,021 (M); Expenditures, $641,488; Total giving, $509,000; Grants to individuals, totaling $509,000.
Fields of interest: Higher education; Dental school/education.
Type of support: Graduate support; Undergraduate support.
Application information: Application form required. Application form available on the grantmaker's web site.
Initial approach: Letter or e-mail.
Deadline(s): June 15.
Applicants should submit the following:
1) FAFSA
2) Transcripts
3) Letter(s) of recommendation
Additional information: Application should also include a copy of you or your parents tax return. Scholarships are paid directly to the institution for a full academic year of nine months and are renewable. Students with the greatest financial need will be given priority.
EIN: 586026003

2148
Coca-Cola Scholars Foundation, Inc.
1 Coca-Cola Pl., Ste. 742
Atlanta, GA 30313 (404) 733-5434
Contact: Patricia A. Ross, V.P.
FAX: (404) 733-5439;
E-mail: questions@coca-colascholars.org; Toll-free tel.: (800) 306-2653; address for Coca-Cola Two-Year College Scholarship: P.O. Box 1615, Atlanta, GA 30301-1615, tel.: (800) 306-2653; E-mail For Jane Hale Hopkins: janehopkins@coca-cola.com; E-mail For Patti A. Ross: patross@coca-cola.com; URL: http://www.coca-colascholars.org

Foundation type: Public charity
Purpose: Scholarships to well-rounded, college-bound high school students with highly developed ethics and goals for higher education at accredited two- or four-year institutions in the U.S.
Publications: Application guidelines; Annual report; Informational brochure (including application guidelines).
Financial data: Year ended 12/31/2011. Assets, $39,246,378 (M); Expenditures, $6,293,794; Total giving, $3,823,426; Grants to individuals, totaling $3,383,426.
Fields of interest: Higher education; Scholarships/financial aid.
Type of support: Scholarships—to individuals.
Application information: Applications accepted. Application form required. Application form available on the grantmaker's web site.
Send request by: Online
Deadline(s): Oct. 31 for initial application and Jan. 31 for semi-finalist's candidacy material
Program description:
Coca-Cola Scholars Program: Seniors at secondary schools throughout the United States who meet eligibility requirements may apply for one of 250 four-year merit-based scholarships. Fifty of these are four-year $20,000 scholarships ($5,000 per year for four years), while 200 are designated

as four-year $10,000 scholarships ($2,500 per year for four years). Scholarships can be used at any accredited U.S. college or university. Eligible applicants must: be current high school (or home-schooled) seniors attending schools in the U.S. (or select Department of Defense schools); be U.S. citizens, nationals, permanent residents, temporary residents, refugees, asylees, Cuban-Haitian emigrants, or humanitarian parolees; anticipate completion of a high-school diploma at the time of application; plan to pursue a degree at an accredited U.S. post-secondary institution; and carry a minimum 3.0 GPA at the end of their junior year of high school.
EIN: 581686023

2149
Columbus Regional Medical Foundation, Inc.
707 Center St.
P.O. Box 790
Columbus, GA 31901-1526 (706) 660-6559
Contact: Karen Cook, Dir.
FAX: (706) 660-6219; E-mail: karen.cook@crhs.net; Contact info. for Linda Bush for Bunch McClellan Nursing Scholarships, tel.: (706) 571-1375, e-mail: linda.bush@crhs.net; Nancy Williams for the Mary Ann Pease Scholarship, tel.: (706) 571-1482, e-mail: nancy.williams@crhs.net; Pat Mansell for the Fred Aranas Memorial Scholarship, tel.: (706) 641-5277, e-mail: pmansell@columbusbustech.edu; URL: http://www.columbusregional.com/ColumbusContentPage.aspx?nd=2015

Foundation type: Public charity
Purpose: Student scholarships and fellowships to those working at Columbus Regional Medical Center, GA.
Financial data: Year ended 06/30/2012. Assets, $13,248,755 (M); Expenditures, $3,043,392; Total giving, $2,046,731; Grants to individuals, totaling $19,000.
Fields of interest: Health care, clinics/centers.
Type of support: Fellowships; Doctoral support.
Application information: Applications accepted.
Initial approach: Telephone or e-mail
Additional information: Contact foundation for eligibility criteria.
EIN: 581501642

2150
The Community Foundation for Greater Atlanta
(formerly Metropolitan Atlanta Community Foundation, Inc.)
50 Hurt Plz., Ste. 449
Atlanta, GA 30303-2915 (404) 688-5525
Contact: Alicia Philipp, Pres.
Scholarship information e-mail: scholarships@cfgreateratlanta.org
FAX: (404) 688-3060;
E-mail: info@cfgreateratlanta.org; URL: http://www.cfgreateratlanta.org

Foundation type: Community foundation
Purpose: Scholarships to deserving students of Atlanta, GA, pursuing a higher education.
Publications: Application guidelines; Annual report; Grants list; Informational brochure; Newsletter; Occasional report; Program policy statement.
Financial data: Year ended 12/31/2012. Assets, $793,327,000 (M); Expenditures, $96,133,000; Total giving, $83,044,000.
Fields of interest: Higher education; Medical school/education; Teacher school/education;

Social work school/education; Health sciences school/education.
Type of support: Employee-related scholarships; Scholarships—to individuals; Support to graduates or students of specific schools; Undergraduate support.
Application information: Applications accepted. Application form required. Application form available on the grantmaker's web site.
  Send request by: Mail or online
  Copies of proposal: 1
  Deadline(s): Varies
  Additional information: See web site for application forms and complete program information.
Program description:
  Scholarship Funds: The foundation manages various scholarship funds for the benefit of eligible applicants. Scholarships allow donors to invest in the future by helping deserving students pursue higher education. Students benefit from the financial assistance as well as the academic recognition of being a scholarship recipient. Most scholarships are for graduating seniors to pursue higher education. Each scholarship has its own specific purpose and eligibility criteria and are managed with varying degrees of involvement by the foundation's Education Advisory Committee and staff. See web site for additional information.
EIN: 581344646

2151
Community Foundation of Central Georgia, Inc.
277 Martin Luther King, Jr. Blvd., Ste. 303
Macon, GA 31201-3489 (478) 750-9338
FAX: (478) 738-9214; E-mail: info@cfcga.org;
Additional tel.: (866) 750-9338; Grant inquiry e-mail: grants@cfcga.org; URL: http://www.cfcga.org

Foundation type: Community foundation
Purpose: Scholarships for students from central Georgia, or students who are attending a Central GA academic institution.
Publications: Annual report; Financial statement.
Financial data: Year ended 06/30/2012. Assets, $61,917,824 (M); Expenditures, $5,842,752; Total giving, $4,721,738; Grants to individuals, 64 grants totaling $78,960.
Fields of interest: Higher education.
Type of support: Scholarships—to individuals; Support to graduates or students of specific schools; Graduate support; Undergraduate support.
Application information: Applications accepted. Application form required. Application form available on the grantmaker's web site.
  Send request by: Online
  Deadline(s): Varies
  Additional information: See web site for complete listing of scholarships and application information.
Program description:
  Scholarship Program: The foundation has 20 scholarship funds, which allow donors to invest in the future by helping deserving students pursue higher education. Students benefit from the financial assistance as well as the academic recognition of being a scholarship recipient. Each scholarship has its own unique set of eligibility criteria and application guidelines. See web site for additional information.
EIN: 582053465

2152
Community Foundation of South Georgia, Inc.
(formerly Community Foundation of Southwest Georgia, Inc.)
135 N. Broad St., Ste. 202
Thomasville, GA 31792-8103 (229) 228-5088
Contact: David M. Carlton, Pres.; Randae Davis, Dir., Donor Svcs.
FAX: (229) 228-0848; E-mail: cfsga@rose.net;
Additional tel.: (888) 544-2317; URL: http://www.cfsga.net/

Foundation type: Community foundation
Purpose: Scholarships for deserving students from southwestern GA to pursue their higher education at a post secondary institution or technical school.
Publications: Annual report; Grants list; Informational brochure.
Financial data: Year ended 12/31/2011. Assets, $52,719,564 (M); Expenditures, $5,079,236; Total giving, $4,093,214; Grants to individuals, 112 grants totaling $89,487.
Fields of interest: Higher education.
Type of support: Scholarships—to individuals.
Application information: Applications accepted. Application form required.
  Initial approach: Application
  Send request by: Mail
  Deadline(s): Varies
  Additional information: To check on the availability of a scholarship please call or contact foundation staff. See web site for complete list of scholarships and the varying criteria for each.
EIN: 582210876

2153
Community Welfare Association of Colquitt County, GA
P.O. Box 38
Moultrie, GA 31776-0038 (229) 985-5210
Contact: William J. Vereen, Tr.

Foundation type: Independent foundation
Purpose: Scholarships to graduates of Colquitt County High School, GA.
Financial data: Year ended 12/31/2012. Assets, $3,352,242 (M); Expenditures, $229,110; Total giving, $180,250; Grants to individuals, 8 grants totaling $12,375 (high: $2,250, low: $750).
Type of support: Support to graduates or students of specific schools; Undergraduate support.
Application information: Applications accepted. Application form required.
  Deadline(s): None
  Additional information: Application should include biographical information.
EIN: 586032259

2154
Concerted Services, Inc.
2100 Riverside Ave.
P.O. Box 1965
Waycross, GA 31501-7020 (912) 285-6083
Additional address: 111 Medical Arts Dr., P.O. Box 1550, Reidsville, GA 30453, tel.: (912) 557-6687; URL: http://www.concertedservices.org

Foundation type: Public charity
Purpose: Provides assistance to residents of Southeastern Georgia to help them become self-sufficient.
Financial data: Year ended 10/31/2011. Assets, $4,829,043 (M); Expenditures, $23,744,096;

Total giving, $4,614,267; Grants to individuals, totaling $4,614,267.
Fields of interest: Aging; Economically disadvantaged.
Type of support: Grants for special needs.
Application information: See web site for additional guidelines.
EIN: 581032805

2155
Council of State and Territorial Epidemiologists
2872 Woodcock Blvd., Ste. 303
Atlanta, GA 30341-4015 (770) 458-3811
Contact: for Fellowship: Ashlyn Beavor
Application e-mail: abeavor@cste.org
FAX: (770) 458-8516; URL: http://www.cste.org

Foundation type: Public charity
Purpose: Fellowships to recent master or doctoral level graduates pursuing a career in epidemiology or related field.
Financial data: Year ended 09/30/2011. Assets, $2,036,513 (M); Expenditures, $9,509,538; Total giving, $5,067,403; Grants to individuals, totaling $2,758,588.
Fields of interest: Public health school/education; Public health, epidemiology.
Type of support: Fellowships.
Application information: Applications accepted. Application form available on the grantmaker's web site. Interview required.
  Send request by: On-line
  Deadline(s): Feb. 1
  Applicants should submit the following:
    1) Transcripts
    2) Resume
    3) Letter(s) of recommendation
    4) Curriculum vitae
  Additional information: Application should also include a personal statement, professional experience, program areas of interest, and proof of U.S. citizenship (copy of birth certificate or U.S. passport). See web site for additional guidelines.
Program description:
  Applied Epidemiology Fellowship Program: The fellowship aims to train recent graduates in the expanding field of applied epidemiology. The goal of the fellowship is to provide a high-quality training experience and to secure long-term career placement for fellows at the state or local level. Participating fellows will receive two years of on-the-job training at a state health agency under the guidance of an experienced mentor.
EIN: 237410799

2156
The Coweta Community Foundation, Inc.
(formerly Newnan-Coweta Chamber Foundation)
P.O. Box 236
Newnan, GA 30264-0236 (770) 253-1833
Contact: Mike McGraw, Dir.
E-mail: info@cowetafoundation.org; URL: http://www.cowetafoundation.org/

Foundation type: Community foundation
Purpose: Awards scholarships to Coweta County residents for higher education.
Financial data: Year ended 12/31/2012. Assets, $307,901 (M); Expenditures, $117,380; Total giving, $20,029; Grants to individuals, totaling $430.
Fields of interest: Higher education.
Type of support: Scholarships—to individuals.
Application information: Applications accepted.

Additional information: Contact the foundation for additional information.
EIN: 582348181

2157
Cox Employee Disaster Relief Fund, Inc.
6205 Peachtree Dunwoody Rd.
Atlanta, GA   30328-4524   (202) 776-2728
Contact: Bob Jimenez, Pres.

Foundation type: Public charity
Purpose: Financial assistance to either employees or former employees of Cox Enterprises, Inc. and affiliates, and their family members who are victims of natural disasters, accidents, serious illness or other emergency.
Financial data: Year ended 12/31/2012. Assets, $12,073,904 (M); Expenditures, $206,859; Total giving, $139,008; Grants to individuals, totaling $139,008.
Fields of interest: Safety/disasters.
Type of support: Grants for special needs.
Application information: Funds are distributed directly to eligible individuals who suffered losses as a result of a disaster.
EIN: 203401306

2158
Creative Community Services, Inc.
4487 Park Dr., Ste. A
Norcross, GA   30093-2964   (770) 469-6226
Contact: Sally Buchanan, Exec. Dir.
FAX: (770) 469-6210; E-mail: info@ccsgeorgia.org;
Toll Free Tel. : (866)-618-2823; E-Mail for Sally Buchanan: sbuchanan@ccsgeorgia.org;
URL: http://www.ccsgeorgia.org

Foundation type: Public charity
Purpose: Assistance to children and developmentally disabled adults of GA through a unique foster care program.
Publications: Annual report; Newsletter.
Financial data: Year ended 06/30/2012. Assets, $959,872 (M); Expenditures, $6,724,794; Total giving, $2,504,522; Grants to individuals, totaling $2,504,522.
Fields of interest: Foster care; Children; Adults; Disabilities, people with.
Type of support: Grants for special needs.
Application information: Adults and children are referred to the program by local and other governmental programs.
EIN: 581581610

2159
CURE Childhood Cancer, Inc.
(formerly CURE Childhood Cancer and Leukemia, Inc.)
1117 Perimeter Ctr. W., Ste. N-402
Atlanta, GA   30338-1000   (770) 986-0035
Contact: Kristin Connor, Exec. Dir.
FAX: (770) 986-0038;
E-mail: info@curechildhoodcancer.org; Toll-free tel.: (800) 443-2873; E-mail for Kristin Connor: kristin@curechildhoodcancer.org; URL: http://www.curechildhoodcancer.org

Foundation type: Public charity
Purpose: Emergency financial assistance for families of GA, who have children with cancer.
Publications: Annual report; Informational brochure; Newsletter.
Financial data: Year ended 06/30/2012. Assets, $2,747,049 (M); Expenditures, $2,996,667; Total

giving, $1,697,609; Grants to individuals, totaling $79,127.
Fields of interest: Cancer; Pediatrics.
Type of support: Emergency funds; Grants for special needs.
Application information: Applications accepted. Application form required.
Additional information: Families seeking financial assistance should contact their social worker for eligibility and availability of funds.
EIN: 581244138

2160
Daisy Davies Educational Foundation
(formerly Daisy Davies Educational Foundation of Friendship Class of Peachtree Road Methodist Church)
3750 Peachtree Rd. N.E., Ste. 277
Atlanta, GA   30319   (404) 201-7277
Contact: William C. Lester, Treas.

Foundation type: Operating foundation
Purpose: Scholarships to theology students in GA.
Financial data: Year ended 05/31/2013. Assets, $332,635 (M); Expenditures, $22,108; Total giving, $22,000; Grants to individuals, 3 grants totaling $22,000 (high: $9,000, low: $5,000).
Fields of interest: Theological school/education.
Type of support: Scholarships—to individuals.
Application information: Applications accepted.
Deadline(s): Sept. 1
Additional information: Application by letter, explaining goals and objectives supported by a budget proposal of income and expenses.
EIN: 586030091

2161
The Decatur Education Foundation, Inc.
200 Nelson Ferry Rd., Ste. B
Decatur, GA   30030-2357   (404) 377-0641
Contact: Gail Rothman, Exec. Dir.
E-mail: info@decatureducationfoundation.org;
URL: http://www.decatureducationfoundation.org

Foundation type: Public charity
Purpose: Grants to support innovative teaching and professional development scholarships to teachers of Decatur, GA. College scholarships to students of Decatur High School for continuing education at colleges or universities.
Publications: Application guidelines.
Financial data: Year ended 12/31/2011. Assets, $688,810 (M); Expenditures, $266,088; Total giving, $143,193; Grants to individuals, totaling $40,000.
Fields of interest: Vocational education, post-secondary; Higher education; Teacher school/education.
Type of support: Scholarships—to individuals; Support to graduates or students of specific schools.
Application information: Applications accepted. Application form required.
Send request by: Mail
Deadline(s): Vary
Additional information: See web site for additional guidelines.
Program descriptions:
Bill Mealor, Jr. Memorial Scholarship: The $1,000 scholarship was established in memory of Decatur High School student Bill Mealor, son of Bill and Marie Mealor. The scholarship is presented each year to a graduating senior male who best displays the positive attitude and overall determination and spirit that was characteristic of Bill Mealor.

Blue and Gold Alumni Scholarship: Scholarship to a graduating senior from Decatur High School who is nominated by the high school faculty. Nominees must show an entrepreneurial spirit and strong leadership skills.
Book Fair Bucks: This program supplies funds that help students in kindergarten through second grade to build their own personal libraries.
Carl and Mae Renfroe Memorial Scholarships: The $1,000 scholarship was established in honor of former Superintendent of schools, Dr. Carl Renfroe and his wife Mae. The scholarships are awarded to one male and one female member of each Decatur High School graduating class who demonstrate academic promise and a determination to succeed.
Coye Foundation Scholarship: A $1,000 scholarship is available for postsecondary study to an African-American graduating senior of Decatur High School who has shown commitment to leadership, community service, scholarship and personal growth. The student must be nominated by Decatur High School faculty.
Decatur Youth Fund: The fund provides scholarships to help children and youth participate in after-school programs, summer school, summer camps, and other enrichment opportunities.
Dr. Phyllis Edwards Education Scholarship: The award is given to a graduating senior who has shown interest in pursuing a career in education and who has gained experience through volunteering or interning in an educational setting.
Harry Edwards Class of 1960 Memorial Scholarship: Recipients of the award exemplify citizenship, school spirit, honesty, integrity, and self-discipline. The student must be nominated by Decatur High School faculty.
Mary Elizabeth Brown Wilson Scholarship: The $500 scholarship honors the life and work of Decatur Mayor Emerita Elizabeth Wilson for her dedication and sacrifice to the cause of justice. Ms. Wilson played a key role in the desegregation of Decatur public schools and libraries during the 1960's.
Mary Leila Honiker Student Assistance Fund: This fund provides emergency assistance to students and families in need.
Mini-Grants Program: The program exists to help fund innovative instructional ideas and programs. The grants range from $200 to $1,500 and are available to individual teachers, teaching teams, media specialists, counselors and administrators in the City Schools of Decatur.
Patrick Family Scholarship: The scholarship is available exclusively to Decatur High School students. Recipients of the award are selected based on demonstrated initiative, potential for success in higher education, and financial need. The $5,000 award is renewable for four years of post secondary study.
Student EdVentures: Funds awarded to help Decatur students participate in educational opportunities outside of the regular school day or school year. Funds may be used for travel expenses and/or program costs. All students in grades 6-12 are eligible.
Teacher EdVentures: EdVentures is a program designed to promote professional growth for teachers and administrators in the City Schools of Decatur. Through this program, the foundation provides funds to cover the cost of a substitute while the regular classroom teacher takes a professional field trip. EdVenture participants may go across the hall, across town, or even to another school district to observe educators in action. There are a limited number of scholarships offered each year.

FOUNDATION GRANTS TO INDIVIDUALS, 23RD EDITION   359

The Carriere Family Scholarship for Teachers: This $1,000 scholarship is available to K-5 classroom teachers, 6-12 mathematics or science teachers, or Exceptional Student Services (ESS) teachers. This scholarship is to enhance instruction in mathematics, science, and special education by supporting teachers from City Schools of Decatur who are seeking an advanced degree with an emphasis in one or more of these areas. Teachers must be employed for a minimum of three years with the City Schools of Decatur.

The Westchester Lifeskills Scholarship: A $1,000 scholarship is awarded to a graduating senior from Decatur High School who exemplifies the learning for life and personal life skills that were emphasized at Westchester. The student must be nominated by Decatur High School faculty.

Thomas Hauk Memorial Scholarship: This $1,500 award is given each year to a graduating male from Decatur High School who participated on the wrestling team (or some other competitive sports team) and embodies Thomas's personal qualities of courage, friendship, and peace-making. The student must be nominated by Decatur High School faculty.
EIN: 582601384

2162
DeKalb Medical Center Foundation, Inc.
2701 N. Decatur Rd.
Decatur, GA   30033-5918   (404) 501-5956
Contact: Leigh Minter, Exec. Dir.
Application address: c/o Betty Castellani, D.Min., Dept. of Pastoral Svcs., DeKalb Medical, 2665 N. Decatur Rd., Ste. 130, Decatur, GA 30033
E-mail: foundation@dkmc.org; E-mail For Leigh Minter: leigh.minter@dekalbmedical.org;
URL: http://www.dekalbmedical.org/foundation/

Foundation type: Public charity
Purpose: Scholarships to individuals in GA for attendance at any accredited colleges or universities pursuing a degree in the health care field.
Financial data: Year ended 06/30/2012. Assets, $9,872,225 (M); Expenditures, $2,006,143; Total giving, $1,889,190; Grants to individuals, totaling $38,665.
Fields of interest: Nursing school/education; Health care.
Type of support: Undergraduate support.
Application information: Applications accepted. Application form required. Interview required.
  Deadline(s): Apr. 30 for Audrey and Jack Morgan Scholarship and Dr. Gulshan Harjee Scholarship, Oct. 1 for Dr. Mark Coppage Nursing Scholarship
  Applicants should submit the following:
    1) Letter(s) of recommendation
    2) GPA
    3) Essay
EIN: 581924605

2163
Ray Dellinger Scholarship Fund
P.O. Box 460
Cartersville, GA   30120   (770) 382-4568
Contact: Dot Frasier-Hall

Foundation type: Independent foundation
Purpose: Scholarships to individuals primarily in the Bartow County, GA, area.
Financial data: Year ended 02/28/2013. Assets, $635,540 (M); Expenditures, $17,915; Total giving, $17,000; Grants to individuals, 11 grants totaling $17,000 (high: $3,000, low: $1,000).

Type of support: Scholarships—to individuals.
Application information: Applications accepted. Application form required.
  Deadline(s): Apr. 15
  Additional information: Application should include transcripts.
EIN: 586041060

2164
DeSana Educational Fund, Inc.
320 Dahlonega St.
Cumming, GA   30040   (770) 889-4050
Contact: Roger L. Crow, Dir.

Foundation type: Operating foundation
Purpose: Scholarships to graduating seniors from Forsyth County, Georgia, high schools.
Financial data: Year ended 12/31/2012. Assets, $211,026 (M); Expenditures, $24,438; Total giving, $22,000; Grants to individuals, 16 grants totaling $22,000 (high: $3,000, low: $1,000).
Fields of interest: Vocational education, post-secondary; College.
Type of support: Support to graduates or students of specific schools; Technical education support; Undergraduate support.
Application information: Applications not accepted.
  Additional information: Contributes only to preselected individuals.
EIN: 582353946

2165
Murray DeYoung Educational Foundation, Inc.
740 Latour Dr.
Atlanta, GA   30350-5552   (770) 685-1090
Contact: Thomas Matthews, Pres. and Treas.

Foundation type: Independent foundation
Purpose: Scholarships to individuals based on financial need and recommendations from teachers, counselors, and welfare agencies.
Financial data: Year ended 06/30/2013. Assets, $5,101,092 (M); Expenditures, $313,643; Total giving, $113,613; Grants to individuals, 9 grants totaling $53,613 (high: $8,000, low: $1,613).
Type of support: Scholarships—to individuals.
Application information: Applications not accepted.
  Additional information: Unsolicited requests for funds not considered or acknowledged.
EIN: 592758439

2166
The Dickens Family Foundation
1068 Viscount Ct.
Avondale Estates, GA   30002-1402

Foundation type: Independent foundation
Purpose: Scholarships to students graduating from Gaffney High School, SC, for undergraduate education at a SC institution.
Financial data: Year ended 12/31/2011. Assets, $2,544,983 (M); Expenditures, $171,739; Total giving, $117,012.
Type of support: Scholarships—to individuals; Support to graduates or students of specific schools.
Application information: Application form required.
  Deadline(s): End of each semester
  Additional information: Application should include transcripts. Contact Gaffney High

School Career Services Counseling Center for current application guidelines.
EIN: 582581077

2167
Irving & Natalie Dinnerman Charitable Trust
P.O. Box 249
Adel, GA   31620-0249   (229) 896-4043
Application Address: c/o Trustees of Irving and Natalie, 300 Newton Ave., Adel, GA 31620

Foundation type: Independent foundation
Purpose: Scholarships to residents of Cook County, GA who are currently enrolled or are planning to enroll in an accredited college or university.
Financial data: Year ended 12/31/2011. Assets, $91,846 (M); Expenditures, $1,614; Total giving, $1,500; Grants to individuals, 2 grants totaling $1,500 (high: $1,000, low: $500).
Fields of interest: Higher education.
Type of support: Scholarships—to individuals.
Application information: Applications accepted. Application form required.
  Initial approach: Letter
  Deadline(s): None
  Additional information: Applications can be obtained from the Trust.
EIN: 046548076

2168
Margaret S. Duke Scholarship Fund
5 Summerville Ln.
Augusta, GA   30909-1813
Contact: Jon D. Simowitz, Pres.

Foundation type: Independent foundation
Purpose: Scholarships to students in Augusta, GA, for higher education.
Financial data: Year ended 12/31/2011. Assets, $82,856 (M); Expenditures, $4,339; Total giving, $4,000; Grant to an individual, 1 grant totaling $4,000.
Type of support: Undergraduate support.
Application information:
  Initial approach: Letter
  Deadline(s): None
  Additional information: Contact foundation for current application guidelines.
EIN: 582270126

2169
East Lake Foundation, Inc.
(formerly East Lake Community Foundation, Inc.)
2606 Alston Dr., S.E.
Atlanta, GA   30317-3334   (404) 373-4351
Contact: Rhonda L. Davidson, Dir., Devel.
FAX: (404) 373-4354;
E-mail: rdavidson@eastlakefoundation.org;
URL: http://www.eastlakefoundation.org

Foundation type: Public charity
Purpose: Scholarships to high school and college students employed by the Charlie Yates Golf Course in Atlanta, GA.
Publications: Annual report; Informational brochure; Newsletter.
Financial data: Year ended 12/31/2011. Assets, $30,442,944 (M); Expenditures, $5,582,628; Total giving, $827,882.
Type of support: Employee-related scholarships; Undergraduate support.
Application information:
  Initial approach: E-mail

Additional information: Contact foundation for current application guidelines.
EIN: 582204306

2170
Edmondson-Telford Foundation
P.O. Box 3430
Gainesville, GA 30503-3430

Foundation type: Independent foundation
Purpose: Grants to financially needy residents of the Hall County, GA, area, for medical expenses and general welfare assistance. A small amount is also given for educational expenses.
Financial data: Year ended 03/31/2013. Assets, $141,024 (M); Expenditures, $3,792; Total giving, $2,920; Grants to individuals, 11 grants totaling $2,125 (high: $700, low: $35).
Fields of interest: Education; Health care; Economically disadvantaged.
Type of support: Scholarships—to individuals; Grants for special needs.
Application information: Unsolicited applications not considered or acknowledged.
EIN: 237062020

2171
Empty Stocking Fund
1975 Century Blvd., Ste. 16
Atlanta, GA 30345-3316 (404) 876-8697
E-mail: info@emptystockingfund.org; URL: http://www.emptystockingfund.org/

Foundation type: Public charity
Purpose: Financial assistance to indigents residing in Clayton, Cobb, DeKalb, Douglas, Fayette, Fulton, Gwinnett, Henry and Rockdale counties, GA during the Christmas holiday season.
Financial data: Year ended 12/31/2011. Assets, $713,123 (M); Expenditures, $501,573; Total giving, $499,641; Grants to individuals, totaling $308,591.
Fields of interest: Family services; Economically disadvantaged.
Type of support: Grants for special needs.
Application information: Applications accepted. Application form required.
Initial approach: Letter
Additional information: Application should include financial information.
Program description:
The Stocking Fund: The fund assists children from birth to age 13 living in Clayton, Cobb, DeKalb, Douglas, Fayette, Fulton, Gwinnett and Henry counties who are receiving Temporary Assistance for Needy Families (TANF) or Medicaid insurance benefits through the Department of Family and Children Services. They each receive gift packages around Christmas that include two toys, an educational item, and a clothing item. Total average retail value for these items is approximately $40 to $50.
EIN: 586045083

2172
Dacy Espy Foundation, Inc.
2221 Peachtree Rd. N.E., Ste. D-330
Atlanta, GA 30309-1148 (251) 246-2492
Contact: Ann Petty, Treas. and Dir.
Application address: 6267 Highway 43, Jackson AL

Foundation type: Independent foundation
Purpose: Scholarships primarily to individuals residing in the South, with a focus on GA, for undergraduate education.

Financial data: Year ended 12/31/2011. Assets, $14,259 (M); Expenditures, $25,636; Total giving, $1,353; Grants to individuals, totaling $1,353.
Fields of interest: Higher education.
Type of support: Undergraduate support.
Application information: Applications accepted.
Initial approach: Letter
Deadline(s): Prior to beginning of school year
EIN: 582657354

2173
Eternal Kingdom Enterprises Inc.
801 Old Newman Rd.
Carrollton, GA 30116-9016 (770) 834-9999
Contact: Anthony F. Dermo, Pres.

Foundation type: Operating foundation
Purpose: Grants to individuals to support Christian Evangelism, primarily in GA.
Financial data: Year ended 12/31/2012. Assets, $742,955 (M); Expenditures, $2,686; Total giving, $2,270; Grants to individuals, 7 grants totaling $2,245 (high: $500, low: $100).
Fields of interest: Christian agencies & churches.
Type of support: Grants to individuals.
Application information: Applications accepted. Application form not required.
Deadline(s): None
EIN: 581716080

2174
The Fadel Educational Foundation, Inc.
3503 Lost Tree Ct.
Augusta, GA 30907
Contact: Ayman H. Fadel, Dir.
URL: http://www.fadelfoundation.org

Foundation type: Operating foundation
Purpose: Scholarships to American students of Islamic faith for educational expenses.
Financial data: Year ended 06/30/2013. Assets, $0 (M); Expenditures, $91,811; Total giving, $80,046; Grants to individuals, 44 grants totaling $80,046 (high: $6,664, low: $400).
Fields of interest: Islam.
Type of support: Graduate support; Technical education support; Undergraduate support.
Application information: Application form required. Application form available on the grantmaker's web site.
Initial approach: Letter
Deadline(s): May
Applicants should submit the following:
1) Transcripts
2) Letter(s) of recommendation
EIN: 582330050

2175
Faith in Serving Humanity
(also known as FISH)
700 S. Madison Ave.
P.O. Box 1838
Monroe, GA 30655-6838 (770) 207-4357
Contact: Cindy Little, Exec. Dir.
FAX: (770) 207-9186; E-mail: cindyblittle@aol.com; URL: http://fishofwalton.org/

Foundation type: Public charity
Purpose: Financial assistance to low to moderate income families with rent, utilities, medical expenses, fuel, emergency shelter, education, furniture and clothing only to Walton County residents, GA.
Publications: Informational brochure; Newsletter.

Financial data: Year ended 12/31/2011. Assets, $1,201,070 (M); Expenditures, $1,080,847; Total giving, $282,079; Grants to individuals, totaling $282,079.
Fields of interest: Housing/shelter, expense aid; Human services.
Type of support: Emergency funds.
Application information: Applications accepted. Application form required.
Additional information: Applicants must provide verification of all income and expenses, what caused the emergency, and how applicant will be able to manage in the future on their own, once assistance is given. Requests for assistance only from individuals residing in Walton County, GA all other applications not considered or acknowledged.
EIN: 582113889

2176
Families First, Inc.
1105 W. Peachtree St. N.E.
Atlanta, GA 30309-3608 (404) 853-2800
Contact: Kim Anderson, C.E.O.
FAX: (404) 685-0204; Mailing address: P.O. Box 7948, Station C, Atlanta, GA 30357-0948; addl. fax: (404) 685-0203; URL: http://www.familiesfirst.org

Foundation type: Public charity
Purpose: Assistance to foster children and their families in GA.
Publications: Newsletter; Occasional report.
Financial data: Year ended 06/30/2012. Assets, $8,330,508 (M); Expenditures, $10,737,823; Total giving, $514,307; Grants to individuals, totaling $514,307.
Fields of interest: Human services; Foster care.
Type of support: Grants to individuals.
Application information: Contact the agency for eligibility determination.
EIN: 581054331

2177
The Emile T. Fisher Foundation for Dental Education Foundation, Inc.
(formerly Georgia Dental Education Foundation, Inc.)
P.O. Box 1204
Rome, GA 30162-1204 (706) 235-2158
Contact: Dale Crail, Pres.
Toll-free tel.: (800)-433-4357; URL: http://www.fisherdentaleducation.org/

Foundation type: Public charity
Purpose: Scholarships of $1,000 each to dental students in GA.
Financial data: Year ended 08/31/2011. Assets, $1,079,042 (M); Expenditures, $92,250; Total giving, $62,100.
Fields of interest: Dental school/education.
Type of support: Support to graduates or students of specific schools.
Application information: Contact foundation for current application deadline/guidelines.
EIN: 581623147

2178

Foundation for Improvement of Justice Inc.
1930 Federal Court.
Lawrenceville, GA 30044-6115 (770) 831-9411
Contact: Pam Edinger
FAX: (770) 831-9896;
E-mail: info@justiceawards.com; URL: http://justiceawards.com/

Foundation type: Independent foundation
Purpose: Awards by nomination only to individuals for achievements in the field of justice.
Financial data: Year ended 12/31/2012. Assets, $1,388,358 (M); Expenditures, $118,072; Total giving, $60,000.
Fields of interest: Crime/law enforcement; Law/international law.
Type of support: Awards/grants by nomination only; Awards/prizes.
Application information: Applications accepted. Application form required.
   Initial approach: Letter, telephone, or e-mail
   Deadline(s): June 1
   Additional information: Self-nominations will not be considered. See web site for full program descriptions.
EIN: 581593170

2179

Fragile Kids Foundation
(formerly Foundation for Medically Fragile Children)
3350 Riverwood Pkwy., Ste. 1400
Atlanta, GA 30339-3314 (770) 951-6111
Contact: Carolyn Polakowski, Exec. Dir.; Jill Gossett, Dir., Devel.
FAX: (770) 541-3763;
E-mail: carolyn@fragilekids.org; URL: http://www.fragilekids.org

Foundation type: Public charity
Purpose: Grants to medically fragile children for health care equipment.
Publications: Application guidelines; Annual report.
Financial data: Year ended 12/31/2011. Assets, $641,568 (M); Expenditures, $482,792; Total giving, $140,902; Grants to individuals, totaling $127,149.
Fields of interest: Health care; Children.
Type of support: Grants for special needs.
Application information: Applications accepted.
   Deadline(s): Revolving
   Additional information: Applicants for the Health Care Grants Program must submit proof of residency and a letter of medical necessity. Recipients are notified within two to six weeks.
Program description:
   Healthcare Grants Program: The foundation provides grants to parents and legal guardians of medically-fragile children ages 21 or younger who are legal U.S. citizens and whose primary legal residence is in Georgia.
EIN: 581915583

2180

The Fulton School Employees Charitable Fund, Inc.
786 Cleveland Ave. S.W.
Atlanta, GA 30315-7239 (404) 763-6835
Contact: Christine Estelle, Secy.

Foundation type: Public charity
Purpose: Grants to current Fulton County school employees and children who at the time of the financial emergencies were students in the Fulton County school district.
Publications: Informational brochure.
Financial data: Year ended 12/31/2011. Assets, $93,356 (M); Expenditures, $429,333; Total giving, $427,217; Grants to individuals, 65 grants totaling $35,668.
Fields of interest: Economically disadvantaged.
Type of support: Emergency funds; Grants for special needs.
Application information: Applications not accepted.
   Additional information: Unsolicited requests for funds not considered or acknowledged.
EIN: 581852091

2181

The Fund for Theological Education, Inc.
160 Clairemont Ave., Ste. 300
Decatur, GA 30030 (678) 369-6755
FAX: (678) 369-6757; URL: http://www.thefund.org

Foundation type: Public charity
Purpose: Fellowships and scholarships to young people who are considering vocations in ministry.
Financial data: Year ended 12/31/2011. Assets, $16,704,355 (M); Expenditures, $5,367,909; Total giving, $1,112,898; Grants to individuals, totaling $898,075.
Fields of interest: Theological school/education; African Americans/Blacks.
Type of support: Fellowships; Scholarships—to individuals.
Application information:
   Initial approach: Letter
Program descriptions:
   African American Ph.D./Th.D. Scholars: This fund supports outstanding African-American students pursuing graduate degrees in religion and theology. This work is designed to address the significant shortage of African-American scholars in faculty teaching and research positions. Diversity is crucial to the vitality of the academy and the Christian church. The program offers two kinds of fellowships. Doctoral Fellowships seek to recruit more African-American doctoral degree candidates and support them in the first year of their graduate programs. Dissertation Fellowships help African-American doctoral students successfully complete their dissertations and move toward faculty positions in theological schools and seminaries. Fellows receive a stipend of up to $15,000.
   Ministry Program: The program strives to identify, inspire, and nurture outstanding undergraduates and seminary students from a variety of Christian denominations who are pursuing vocations in ministry and theological scholarship. Together with seminaries, churches, nonprofit organizations, students, ministers, and professors, the program encourages excellence and diversity in the next generation of leaders for the church. The program offers three kinds of fellowships: Undergraduate Fellowships (for rising juniors or seniors nominated by college administrators, faculty, and clergy), Congregational Fellowships (for students entering the first year of a Master of Divinity degree program), and Ministry Fellowships (for students in the second year of a Master of Divinity degree program who have been nominated by their seminary dean or president). Fellows receive a $2,000 stipend.
   North American Doctoral Fellowships: These fellowships are for talented students from racial and ethnic groups traditionally underrepresented in graduate education who are currently enrolled in Ph.D. or Th.D. programs in religion or theology. The fellowship provides financial assistance to outstanding candidates who might not otherwise have the means to complete their studies. Fellows receive a stipend ranging from $5,000 to $10,000.
   Seminary Students: The fund offers financial aid and a network of support for first- and second-year seminarians pursuing vocations in ministry and theological scholarship. These fellowships provide assistance to outstanding candidates who otherwise might not have the means to complete their studies. Three types of fellowships available for seminary students. Congregational Fellowships provide financial aid to first-year seminarians through partnerships between the fund and individual congregations. VEV Fellowships provide financial assistance to first-year seminarians who are recent participants in faith-based volunteer programs through the Volunteers Exploring Vocation initiative. Ministry Fellowships provide financial and mentoring support to second-year seminarians to enrich their formation as ministerial leaders.
EIN: 210725643

2182

Allan C. and Leila J. Garden Foundation
c/o U.S. Trust, Bank of America, N.A.
3414 Peachtree Rd. NE, Ste. 1475, GA7-813-14-04
Atlanta, GA 30326-1113 (404) 264-1377
Contact: Quanda Allen, V.P.
E-mail: quanda.allen@ustrust.com; URL: http://www.bankofamerica.com/grantmaking

Foundation type: Independent foundation
Purpose: Scholarships and student loans to residents of Fitzgerald, GA, and Ben Hill, Irwin, and Wilcox counties, GA.
Financial data: Year ended 05/31/2013. Assets, $5,046,569 (M); Expenditures, $205,589; Total giving, $153,375; Grants to individuals, 43 grants totaling $83,875 (high: $2,250, low: $1,000).
Type of support: Scholarships—to individuals; Student loans—to individuals.
Application information: Applications accepted. Application form required.
   Deadline(s): None
EIN: 586103546

2183

Georgia Association of Realtors Scholarship Foundation, Inc.
3200 Presidential Dr.
Atlanta, GA 30340-3910 (770) 451-1831
Contact: Anne D. Gault, Pres.
FAX: (770) 458-6992; URL: http://www.garealtor.com/professionaldevelopment/scholarships/tabid/157/default.aspx

Foundation type: Public charity
Purpose: Scholarships to individuals for tuition only for the study of real estate related subjects.
Financial data: Year ended 12/31/2011. Assets, $1,287,590 (M); Expenditures, $94,402; Total giving, $66,885; Grants to individuals, totaling $66,885.
Fields of interest: Business school/education.
Type of support: Scholarships—to individuals.
Application information: Applications accepted. Application form required. Application form available on the grantmaker's web site.
   Initial approach: Download application online
   Deadline(s): Apr. 15, July 15, Oct. 15, Jan. 15
   Additional information: Applicant must show proof of course completion.

Program description:

Scholarships: The scholarship program was developed to assist persons in the real estate field who are seeking to obtain a related designation, such as the GRI, CCIM, CPM, CAE, CRS, CRB, and the many other designations in real estate-related fields. Georgia licensees with an active real estate license and/or employees of Georgia real estate trade or professional organizations are all eligible for a scholarship. Scholarships are for tuition only.
EIN: 581627007

2184
Georgia Engineering Foundation
Harris Twr., Ste. 700
233 Peachtree St.
Atlanta, GA 30303-1501 (404) 521-2324
Contact: James R. Wallace P.E., Pres.
FAX: (404) 521-0283; E-mail: info@gefinc.org;
E-mail for James R. Wallace P.E.:
jrwhaw@comcast.net; URL: http://www.gefinc.org

Foundation type: Public charity
Purpose: Scholarships to residents of GA who are pursuing a career in engineering or engineering technology.
Publications: Application guidelines; Annual report.
Financial data: Year ended 09/30/2011. Assets, $618,598 (M); Expenditures, $74,034; Total giving, $61,102; Grants to individuals, totaling $61,102.
Fields of interest: Engineering school/education.
Type of support: Scholarships—to individuals.
Application information: Applications accepted. Application form required. Application form available on the grantmaker's web site.
    Send request by: Online
    Deadline(s): Aug. 31
    Applicants should submit the following:
        1) Photograph
        2) Financial information
        3) Transcripts
        4) GPA
Program description:
Scholarships: The foundation awards scholarships (ranging from $1,000 to $5,000) to worthy Georgia students who are preparing for a career in engineering or engineering technology. Scholarships are competitively awarded based on the student's demonstrated competence in academics, interest in developing a career in engineering, financial need, and school and community involvement. Eligible applicants must be U.S. citizens who are residents of Georgia, and who have enrolled in an Accreditation Board for Engineering and Technology (ABET)-accredited engineering or engineering technology program (at either the undergraduate or graduate level)
EIN: 237193629

2185
Georgia Goal Scholarship Program, Inc.
5 Concourse Pkwy., Ste. 200
Atlanta, GA 30328-6157 (770) 828-4625
Contact: Lisa Kelly, Pres.
FAX: (877) 478-4625;
E-mail: lmkelly@goalscholarship.org; URL: http://www.goalscholarship.org/

Foundation type: Public charity
Purpose: Scholarships for students of Georgia to attend the private K-12 schools of their parents' choice.
Financial data: Year ended 12/31/2011. Assets, $17,522,752 (M); Expenditures, $11,098,136;

Total giving, $10,226,628; Grants to individuals, 2,759 grants totaling $10,226,628.
Fields of interest: Education.
Type of support: Scholarships—to individuals.
Application information: Applications accepted. Application form required.
    Additional information: Application should include financial assistance. Families must provide proof of eligibility. See web site for additional guidelines.
Program description:
Scholarships: This program provides tuition scholarships to children who desire to attend private K-12 schools. Only students who are Georgia residents enrolled in a Georgia secondary or primary public school or who are eligible to enroll in pre-k4, kindergarten or first grade are eligible.
EIN: 651280229

2186
Georgia Health Care Education and Research Foundation, Inc.
160 Country Club Dr.
Stockbridge, GA 30281-7344
Contact: Jon Howell, Member

Foundation type: Independent foundation
Purpose: Scholarships to students who are residents of Georgia in pursuit of a nursing career.
Financial data: Year ended 06/30/2011. Assets, $841,820 (M); Expenditures, $53,413; Total giving, $23,000; Grants to individuals, 19 grants totaling $23,000 (high: $3,000, low: $1,000).
Fields of interest: Nursing school/education.
Type of support: Scholarships—to individuals.
Application information: Applications accepted.
    Deadline(s): None
    Additional information: Application must include transcripts and references.
EIN: 581392531

2187
Georgia Osteopathic Institute
2037 Grayson Hwy.
Grayson, GA 30017-1242 (770) 908-3200
Contact: Whitney Yaksh
FAX: (770) 908-3210; E-mail: info@oisonline.org;
Additional tel.: (800)-934-2495; E-Mail for Whitney Yaksh: whitney@oisonline.org; URL: http://www.goi.org/students/residency-programs.html

Foundation type: Public charity
Purpose: Grants to osteopathic and podiatric physicians for education and residency program within the state of GA.
Financial data: Year ended 08/31/2011. Assets, $1,466,239 (M); Expenditures, $523,378; Total giving, $19,000.
Fields of interest: Medical school/education.
Type of support: Postgraduate support.
Application information:
    Initial approach: Telephone
EIN: 580683826

2188
God's Gift Foundation, Inc.
P.O. Box 5566
Columbus, GA 31906-5605

Foundation type: Independent foundation
Purpose: Grants to economically disadvantaged individuals in the GA area, for housing and medical assistance.

Financial data: Year ended 12/31/2012. Assets, $0 (M); Expenditures, $993,517; Total giving, $985,029.
Fields of interest: Health care; Housing/shelter; Economically disadvantaged.
Type of support: Grants for special needs.
Application information: Applications accepted.
EIN: 582486355

2189
Golden Key International Honour Society, Inc.
1040 Crown Pointe Pkwy., Ste. 900
Atlanta, GA 30308-2842 (678) 689-2200
Contact: Brad Rainey, Exec. Dir.
FAX: (678) 689-2298;
E-mail: memberservices@goldenkey.org; E-mail for Brad Rainey : brainey@goldenkey.org; Tel. for Brad Rainey : (678)-689-2234; URL: http://www.goldenkey.org

Foundation type: Public charity
Purpose: Grants, awards and scholarships are offered for leadership, service and academic excellence. Only memebers of the Golden Key International Honour Society may apply.
Financial data: Year ended 12/31/2011. Assets, $4,499,936 (M); Expenditures, $9,694,134; Total giving, $860,254; Grants to individuals, totaling $730,081.
Fields of interest: Higher education.
Type of support: Grants to individuals; Scholarships—to individuals; Awards/prizes.
Application information: Applications accepted. Application form required. Application form available on the grantmaker's web site.
    Deadline(s): Varies
    Additional information: Some scholarships require a letter of intent to apply. See web site for a full list of scholarships and their individual requirements.
EIN: 581306896

2190
James H. Hall Eye Center
(also known as The James H. Hall Eye Center)
P.O. Box 71288
Albany, GA 31708
Contact: Dinorah Hall

Foundation type: Independent foundation
Purpose: Postdoctoral fellowships in pediatric ophthalmology and pediatric ophthalmology care for the indigent residing in GA.
Financial data: Year ended 09/30/2013. Assets, $247,627 (M); Expenditures, $234,683; Total giving, $11,200; Grant to an individual, 1 grant totaling $10,000.
Fields of interest: Optometry/vision screening; Eye research; Children/youth.
Type of support: Fellowships; Research; Postdoctoral support; Grants for special needs.
Application information: Applications accepted.
    Additional information: Applications should be submitted with a request for funds pertaining to eye care for indigent children in the Atlanta, GA area and rural areas.
EIN: 510174948

2191
John T. Hall Trust
2277 Martha Berry Hwy., N.W.
Mount Berry, GA 30149
Contact: Debbie Emory

Foundation type: Independent foundation
Purpose: Student loans to residents of GA, for undergraduate and graduate education at GA colleges. Preference is given to students attending Berry College, GA.
Financial data: Year ended 12/31/2012. Assets, $2,776,702 (M); Expenditures, $68,661; Total giving, $50,391.
Type of support: Support to graduates or students of specific schools; Graduate support; Undergraduate support.
Application information: Applications accepted. Application form required.
  Deadline(s): None
  Additional information: Applications by letter, including resume; applications should be sent well in advance of school term.
EIN: 586026022

2192
Hambidge Center for Creative Arts and Sciences, Inc.
105 Hambidge Ct.
P.O. Box 339
Rabun Gap, GA 30568-0339 (706) 746-5718
FAX: (706) 746-9933;
E-mail: center@hambidge.org; URL: http://www.hambidge.org

Foundation type: Public charity
Purpose: Residencies to artists working at the professional level in their field.
Publications: Application guidelines; Newsletter.
Financial data: Year ended 12/31/2011. Assets, $853,648 (M); Expenditures, $382,658.
Fields of interest: Visual arts.
Type of support: Residencies.
Application information: Applications accepted. Application form required. Application form available on the grantmaker's web site.
  Initial approach: Letter or telephone
  Copies of proposal: 1
  Deadline(s): Jan. 15, Apr. 15 and Sept. 15
  Applicants should submit the following:
    1) Work samples
    2) SASE
    3) Resume
  Additional information: Application must also include ten 35 mm slides in thin frames, encased in plastic sleeves, and $30 nonrefundable application fee. See web site for additional information.
Program description:
  Artist Residency Program: This program provides a residency program that empowers talented artists to explore, develop, and express their creative voices. The residency provides a sanctuary of time and space in a 600-acre environment in the mountains of northern Georgia, that is intended to inspire artists working in a broad range of disciplines to create works of the highest caliber. Eligible applicants include artists and other creative thinkers from throughout the U.S. and around the world. Resident fellows pay $200 per week (of the $1,250 per week cost); limited scholarships are available, and include the Fulton County Arts Council Fellowship (providing a two-week residency with a $700 stipend) and the Nellie Mae Rowe Fellowship Program (providing a two-week residency to an African-American artist)
EIN: 586001278

2193
Hamilton Holt Kiwanis Scholarship Fund
P.O. Box 27327
Macon, GA 31221

Foundation type: Independent foundation
Purpose: Scholarships to students of Bibb County, GA for higher education at accredited colleges or universities.
Financial data: Year ended 09/30/2013. Assets, $204,217 (M); Expenditures, $6,860; Total giving, $4,337; Grants to individuals, 3 grants totaling $4,337 (high: $1,500, low: $1,337).
Fields of interest: Higher education.
Type of support: Scholarships—to individuals.
Application information: Application form required.
  Initial approach: Letter
EIN: 237363303

2194
Handweavers Guild of America, Inc.
(also known as HGA)
1255 Buford Hwy., Ste. 211
Suwanee, GA 30024-8421 (678) 730-0010
Contact: Sandra Bowles, Exec. Dir.
FAX: (678) 730-0836;
E-mail: hga@weavespindye.org; E-Mail for Sandra Bowles: executivedirector@weavespindye.org; URL: http://www.weavespindye.org

Foundation type: Public charity
Purpose: Grants and scholarships to individuals specializing in fiber arts at accredited institutions.
Publications: Application guidelines.
Financial data: Year ended 03/31/2012. Assets, $752,043 (M); Expenditures, $416,498; Total giving, $6,200; Grants to individuals, totaling $6,200.
Fields of interest: Arts education.
Type of support: Grants to individuals; Scholarships—to individuals.
Application information: Applications accepted. Application form required. Application form available on the grantmaker's web site.
  Send request by: Mail
  Deadline(s): Feb. 1 for Silvio and Eugenia Petrini Grant, Mearl K. Gable II Memorial Grant Fund, and HGA Teach-It-Forward Grant, Mar. 15 for HGA and Dendel Scholarships, Apr. 2 for Convergence Assistantship Grant
  Final notification: Recipients notified Mar. 1 for Petrini, Gable and HGA Teach-it Forward Grants
  Applicants should submit the following:
    1) Transcripts
    2) SASE
  Additional information: Application should also include slides and other visual materials. See web site for additional guidelines.
Program descriptions:
  Convergence Assistantship Grant: The goal of this assistantship program is to provide capable assistants for Convergence Workshop Leaders and Teachers, while providing students enrolled in Fiber Arts programs the chance to assist internationally known instructors and to participate in the convergence experience. Students must be currently enrolled in an accredited academic program.
  HGA and Dendel Scholarships: This program offers scholarships to students enrolled in accredited undergraduate or graduate programs in the U.S., its possessions, and Canada, who wish to pursue further education in the field of fiber arts including training for research, textile history, and conservation. Scholarships of over $4,000 each

are awarded based on artistic and technical merit rather than on financial need.
  HGA Teach-It-Forward Grant: This $500 grant is awarded to guild members, to assist teachers who focus on beginning weavers or spinners. It is available to those who teach weaving or spinning in a private studio, shop, or school who are bringing new people to the craft and who has an innovative plan or proposal.
  Mearl K. Gable II Memorial Grant Fund: The fund provides grants, in amounts over $100 per individual, for study in nonaccredited programs for any skill level. Recipients must be guild members. Grants may be used for research and studies connected with the fiber arts.
  Silvio and Eugenia Petrini Grant: Grants of up to $300 per individual are available to guild members for study in nonaccredited programs for any skill level. Applicants must be HGA members.
EIN: 060866181

2195
Healthcare Georgia Foundation, Inc.
50 Hurt Plz, Ste. 1100
Atlanta, GA 30303-2957 (404) 653-0990
Contact: Racquel Lee-Sin, Grants Mgr.
FAX: (404) 577-8386;
E-mail: info@healthcaregeorgia.org; URL: http://www.healthcaregeorgia.org/

Foundation type: Independent foundation
Purpose: Awards by nomination only to extraordinary GA individuals who are committed to improving the quality of health and healthcare of those they serve.
Publications: Application guidelines; Annual report; Grants list; Informational brochure (including application guidelines); Occasional report; Program policy statement.
Financial data: Year ended 12/31/2012. Assets, $111,633,150 (M); Expenditures, $7,029,474; Total giving, $3,958,525.
Fields of interest: Health care.
Type of support: Awards/grants by nomination only; Awards/prizes.
Application information: Applications accepted. Application form available on the grantmaker's web site.
  Initial approach: Letter
  Send request by: Mail or e-mail
  Copies of proposal: 2
  Deadline(s): Oct. 28
  Final notification: Applicants notified in 90 days
Program description:
  Joseph D. Greene Community Service Award: Five individuals will be selected for the award. Individual nominees must be a volunteer or a previous volunteer for a health-related nonprofit, have made a passionate commitment to improving the quality of health in a Georgia community, be unselfish in contributing their time to community activities, and serve as a role model and inspiration to others. The foundation will also make a donation of $1,000 in the name of the recipient to a Georgia-based nonprofit health organization of the recipient's choice.
EIN: 582418091

2196
Hospice of the Emerald Coast, Inc.
3350 Riverwood Pkwy., Ste. 1400
Atlanta, GA 30339-4627 (770) 951-6450
URL: http://www.gentiva.com

Foundation type: Public charity

Purpose: Assistance to terminally ill patients with in-home care live more independently with a higher quality of life.
Financial data: Year ended 12/31/2011. Assets, $8,904,385 (M); Expenditures, $20,023,886; Total giving, $51,149; Grants to individuals, totaling $51,149.
Fields of interest: Health care.
Type of support: In-kind gifts; Grants for special needs.
Application information:
  Initial approach: Telephone
  Additional information: Contact the provider for eligibility determination.
EIN: 621805874

2197
Idaho Nurses Foundation Inc.
3525 Piedmont Rd., Bldg. 5, Ste. 300
Atlanta, GA   30305-1509   (208) 339-4420
URL: http://www.idahonurses.org/

Foundation type: Operating foundation
Purpose: Scholarships to assist Idaho nursing students or nurses to continue their education in the nursing profession.
Financial data: Year ended 06/30/2013. Assets, $0 (M); Expenditures, $3,986; Total giving, $3,783; Grants to individuals, 3 grants totaling $3,783 (high: $1,261, low: $1,261).
Fields of interest: Nursing school/education.
Type of support: Scholarships—to individuals.
Application information: Applications accepted. Application form required.
  Initial approach: Letter
  Deadline(s): Nov. 1, July 1, and Apr. 1
EIN: 820411280

2198
Jewish Federation of Greater Atlanta
1440 Spring St., N.W.
The Selig Ctr.
Atlanta, GA   30309-2832   (404) 873-1661
Contact: Michael Horowitz, Pres. and C.E.O.
FAX: (404) 874-7043; E-mail: webmaster@jfga.org;
E-mail For Michael Horowitz: mhorowitz@jfga.org;
URL: http://www.shalomatlanta.org

Foundation type: Public charity
Purpose: Scholarships to Jewish teens ages 15 to 19 who are residents of metropolitan Atlanta, GA enrolled in an Israel Experience educational program.
Publications: Annual report.
Financial data: Year ended 06/30/2012. Assets, $112,521,329 (M); Expenditures, $27,934,679; Total giving, $21,703,118; Grants to individuals, totaling $230,029.
Fields of interest: Education; Jewish agencies & synagogues.
Type of support: Scholarships—to individuals.
Application information: Applications accepted. Application form required. Application form available on the grantmaker's web site.
  Initial approach: Application
  Deadline(s): None
  Additional information: Selection is based on need.
Program description:
  Scholarships: This program provides financial assistance (both incentive- and need-based) to local young adults between the ages of 15 and 19 participating on an approved Israel Experience program. The length of the trip should be a minimum of two weeks in Israel or a trip that includes one week in Israel or another country/

region of comparable Jewish experience. Applicants may apply every two years for a need-based scholarship as long as they are in the required age range.
EIN: 581021791

2199
Kajima Foundation, Inc.
3475 Piedmont Rd., Ste. 1600
Atlanta, GA   30305-2993   (404) 564-3900
Contact: Leia J. Wolfe

Foundation type: Company-sponsored foundation
Purpose: Scholarships to students attending the University of Michigan.
Financial data: Year ended 12/31/2012. Assets, $575,844 (M); Expenditures, $41,603; Total giving, $35,240.
Type of support: Support to graduates or students of specific schools; Undergraduate support.
Application information:
  Initial approach: Letter
  Additional information: This program is administered by the National Merit Scholarship Corp. Contact foundation for eligibility requirements.
EIN: 521675796

2200
The Seymour L. Kaplan Scholarship Foundation
c/o Roberts
3435 Kingsboro Rd., Ste. 1603
Atlanta, GA   30326

Foundation type: Independent foundation
Purpose: Scholarships to students of the Columbia Presbyterian Medical Center and the Mount Sinai School of Medicine.
Financial data: Year ended 12/31/2012. Assets, $615,486 (M); Expenditures, $38,755; Total giving, $35,000; Grants to individuals, 7 grants totaling $35,000 (high: $5,000, low: $5,000).
Fields of interest: Medical school/education.
Type of support: Support to graduates or students of specific schools; Graduate support.
Application information: Applications not accepted.
  Additional information: Unsolicited requests for funds not considered or acknowledged.
EIN: 137004964

2201
Abraham J. & Phyllis Katz Foundation
c/o Alexander S. Katz
1579F Monroe Dr., Ste. 933
Atlanta, GA   30324-5016
Contact: Peter A. Katz, Tr.
E-mail: contact@katzfoundation.org; URL: http://katzfoundation.org/

Foundation type: Operating foundation
Purpose: Grants for the support of scientific and medical research, primarily in NY and OH. Support for young musicians both in performance and composition to perform before musically knowledgeable audiences.
Financial data: Year ended 12/31/2012. Assets, $67,944,440 (M); Expenditures, $3,799,545; Total giving, $3,376,647.
Fields of interest: Music composition; Medical research.
Application information: Applications accepted. Application form required.
  Initial approach: Letter

Additional information: Contact foundation for eligibility criteria.
EIN: 116442077

2202
Kids' Chance of Georgia, Inc.
(formerly Kids' Chance)
2024 Powers Ferry Rd., Ste. 225
Atlanta, GA   30339-5011   (770) 933-7767
FAX: (770) 933-6995; E-mail: KidsChance@cox.net;
URL: http://www.kidschancega.org/

Foundation type: Public charity
Purpose: Scholarships to the children of Georgia workers who have been seriously, catastrophically or fatally injured in work-related accidents.
Financial data: Year ended 12/31/2011. Assets, $1,087,911 (M); Expenditures, $225,653; Total giving, $94,950; Grants to individuals, totaling $94,950.
Fields of interest: Disabilities, people with.
Type of support: Undergraduate support.
Application information: Applications accepted. Application form required.
  Initial approach: E-mail
  Additional information: Contact foundation for current application deadline/guidelines.
EIN: 581827365

2203
Swarna Kumar Memorial Scholarship Fund
386 Hurricane Shoals Rd.
Lawrenceville, GA   30046

Foundation type: Independent foundation
Purpose: Scholarships to indigent students to attend the Montessori School of Rome, GA.
Financial data: Year ended 12/31/2012. Assets, $0 (M); Expenditures, $40,000; Total giving, $0.
Type of support: Support to graduates or students of specific schools.
Application information:
  Initial approach: Letter
EIN: 582661515

2204
Ladonna Cares and Shares Inc.
100 Hope Dr.
Rock Spring, GA   30739-2179
Contact: Amy Maynor, Secy.-Treas.

Foundation type: Independent foundation
Purpose: Financial assistance to indigent residents of the Rock Spring, GA area, for help with utilities, food, and medical expenses.
Financial data: Year ended 12/31/2012. Assets, $4,909 (M); Expenditures, $80,782; Total giving, $76,301; Grants to individuals, 13 grants totaling $54,194 (high: $26,313, low: $150).
Fields of interest: Single parents; Aging; Economically disadvantaged.
Type of support: Grants for special needs.
Application information: Applications accepted.
  Initial approach: Letter
  Additional information: Assistance is focused on single parents, the elderly and the less fortunate.
EIN: 205848641

2205
Legislative Black Caucus of the Georgia General Assembly, Inc.
18 Capitol Sq., S.W., Ste. 602
Atlanta, GA 30334-0028 (404) 651-5569
FAX: (404) 651-0040;
E-mail: gablackcaucus@galbc.org; URL: http://www.galbc.org/

Foundation type: Public charity
Purpose: Scholarships to minority students residing in GA for undergraduate education.
Financial data: Year ended 12/31/2011. Assets, $83,572 (M); Expenditures, $206,829; Total giving, $12,928.
Fields of interest: Minorities.
Type of support: Undergraduate support.
Application information: Contact foundation for current application deadline/guidelines.
EIN: 581500919

2206
James D. and Diane S. Magnus Foundation, Inc.
2410 Hilton Way, S.W.
Gainesville, GA 30501-6192

Foundation type: Company-sponsored foundation
Purpose: Scholarships to preselected residents of Gainesville, GA in pursuit of a higher education.
Financial data: Year ended 12/31/2012. Assets, $1,472,970 (M); Expenditures, $351,394; Total giving, $346,000.
Type of support: Undergraduate support.
Application information: Applications not accepted.
Additional information: Unsolicited requests for funds not considered or acknowledged.
EIN: 600000489

2207
Make A Wish Foundation of Georgia and Alabama
1775 The Exchange S.E., Ste. 200
Atlanta, GA 30339-2016 (770) 916-9474
Contact: John Brennan, C.E.O.
FAX: (770) 916-0222;
E-mail: jbrennan@ga-al.wish.org; SW GA regional office address: 2720 Sheraton Dr., Bldg. D, Ste. 235, Macon, GA 31204-6853, tel. (478) 755-8450, fax: (478) 755-8467; SE GA regional office address: 340 Eisenhower Dr., Ste. 1104, Savannah, GA 31406-1608, tel.: (912) 352-3550, fax: (912)352-3549; Birmingham regional office address: 200 Beacon Parkway W., Ste. 203, Birmingham, AL 35209-3149, tel.: (205) 254-9474, fax: (205) 254-9479; URL: http://www.ga-al.wish.org

Foundation type: Public charity
Purpose: Assistance to individuals of Georgia and Alabama to grant wishes to selected individuals that meet specific criteria.
Publications: Annual report; Financial statement; Informational brochure; Newsletter.
Financial data: Year ended 08/31/2011. Assets, $1,294,724 (M); Expenditures, $4,996,255; Total giving, $3,102,979; Grants to individuals, totaling $3,102,979.
Fields of interest: Human services; Children/youth.
Type of support: In-kind gifts; Grants for special needs.
Application information: Applications accepted.
Additional information: Funding is paid directly to vendors for the wish with the exception of travel stipend (i.e. is meals, tips, gas, etc.)

from the budget. Contact the foundation for eligibility determination.
EIN: 582146828

2208
MAP International
4700 Glynco Pkwy.
Brunswick, GA 31525-6800 (912) 265-6010
Contact: Michael J. Nyenhuis, Pres. and C.E.O.
FAX: (912) 265-6170; E-mail: mapus@map.org;
Toll-free tel.: (800) 225-8550; URL: http://www.map.org

Foundation type: Public charity
Purpose: Fellowships to North American senior medical students working with hospitals in developing countries, or working in community health in a Christian context in a poor urban or rural setting.
Publications: Application guidelines; Annual report; Financial statement; Newsletter; Occasional report.
Financial data: Year ended 09/30/2011. Assets, $42,617,418 (M); Expenditures, $163,564,551; Total giving, $422,100; Grants to individuals, totaling $16,156.
Fields of interest: Medical school/education; Association.
Type of support: Fellowships.
Application information: Applications accepted. Application form required. Application form available on the grantmaker's web site. Interview required.
Deadline(s): Mar. 1
Final notification: May 1
Additional information: An application can be obtained from the Student Affairs Office at the medical school.
Program description:
MAP International Medical Fellowship: This fellowship program (formerly known as the MAP-Reader's Digest International Fellowship program) encourages lifelong involvement in global health issues by providing selected medical students firsthand exposure in a Christian context to the health, social, and cultural characteristics of a developing world community. Third- and fourth-year medical students, residents, and interns are eligible. Applications should be submitted during the academic year prior to travel. The fellowship provides 100 percent of the approved round trip airfare to one destination; in most instances, students pay room and board as well as any in-country travel expenses.
EIN: 362586390

2209
The Marena Foundation, Inc.
650 Progress Industrial Blvd.
Lawrenceville, GA 30043-4800 (888) 462-7362

Foundation type: Company-sponsored foundation
Purpose: Financial assistance to indigent residents of the Lawrenceville, GA area.
Financial data: Year ended 12/31/2012. Assets, $6,264 (M); Expenditures, $171,956; Total giving, $170,826.
Fields of interest: Economically disadvantaged.
Type of support: Grants for special needs.
Application information: Applications not accepted.
Additional information: Unsolicited requests for funds not considered or acknowledged.
EIN: 582379368

2210
McDuffie Scholarship & Loan Foundation, Inc.
P.O. Box 1379
Thomson, GA 30824-1379 (706) 738-6641
Contact: Kim Bragg, Exec. Dir.

Foundation type: Public charity
Purpose: Scholarships to various high school graduates of McDuffie county, GA for postsecondary education.
Financial data: Year ended 12/31/2011. Assets, $309,524 (M); Expenditures, $32,325; Total giving, $23,375.
Fields of interest: Higher education.
Type of support: Scholarships—to individuals.
Application information: Awards are based on academic achievement.
EIN: 581794412

2211
Medical Association of Georgia Foundation, Inc.
(also known as MAG Foundation)
1849 The Exchange, Ste. 200
Atlanta, GA 30339-2027 (678) 303-9284
Contact: John D. Watson, Jr. M.D., Pres.
E-mail: fjones@mag.org; Toll-free tel.: (800) 282-0224; URL: http://www.mag.org/organizations/mag-foundation

Foundation type: Public charity
Purpose: Student loans to GA residents attending a GA medical school.
Financial data: Year ended 12/31/2011. Assets, $5,188,048 (M); Expenditures, $258,466; Total giving, $1,000.
Fields of interest: Medical school/education.
Type of support: Student loans—to individuals.
Application information: Applications accepted. Application form required.
EIN: 586066431

2212
Monroe Welfare Foundation
360 Honeymoon Ln.
Waycross, GA 31503

Foundation type: Independent foundation
Purpose: Scholarships and specific assistance to individuals of Ware County, GA.
Financial data: Year ended 05/31/2013. Assets, $2,490,977 (M); Expenditures, $118,317; Total giving, $116,626.
Type of support: Scholarships—to individuals; Grants for special needs.
Application information: Applications accepted.
Initial approach: Letter
Additional information: Application must include financial information.
EIN: 586033825

2213
National Christian Charitable Foundation, Inc.
11625 Rainwater Dr., Ste. 500
Alpharetta, GA 30009-8678 (404) 252-0100
Contact: David Wills J.D., Pres.
FAX: (404) 252-5177;
E-mail: info@nationalchristian.com; Toll-free tel.: (800) 681-6223; URL: http://www.nationalchristian.com

Foundation type: Public charity

Purpose: Scholarships to students in the U.S. for attendance at accredited colleges, universities or trade and technical schools working toward a diploma or degree.
Publications: Annual report; Financial statement.
Financial data: Year ended 12/31/2012. Assets, $1,240,771,328 (M); Expenditures, $625,262,287; Total giving, $601,841,675; Grants to individuals, 88 grants totaling $454,223.
Fields of interest: Higher education.
Type of support: Scholarships—to individuals.
Application information: Applications accepted.
  Additional information: Selection is based on need, academics or other criteria. Contact the foundation for additional guidelines.
EIN: 581493949

2214
Navy Supply Corps Foundation, Inc.
P.O. Box 6228
Athens, GA   30604-6228   (706) 354-4111
FAX: (706) 354-0334; E-mail: cso@usnscf.org;
URL: https://www.usnscf.com

Foundation type: Public charity
Purpose: Provides financial assistance to immediate family members of a qualifying Navy Supply Corps officer or supply enlisted member (active duty, reservist, retired, or prior service)
Financial data: Year ended 12/31/2011. Assets, $5,373,841 (M); Expenditures, $591,817; Total giving, $224,350; Grants to individuals, totaling $224,350.
Fields of interest: Higher education.
Type of support: Student aid/financial aid.
Application information: Applications accepted.
  Additional information: Application form available on foundation webs site.
Program description:
  Scholarship Program: The foundation provides financial assistance to family members (children, grandchildren, or spouses) of a qualifying Navy Supply Corps officer or supply enlisted member (active duty, reservist, retired, or prior service) for undergraduate studies at an accredited two- or four-year post-secondary school institution.
EIN: 237066533

2215
NCR Scholarship Foundation
3095 Satellite Blvd., Bldg. 800, 3rd Fl.
Duluth, GA   30096-5814   (770) 418-4585
E-mail: ncr.scholarship@ncr.com; URL: http://www.hrme_ncr_com/hrx/process/aspx

Foundation type: Company-sponsored foundation
Purpose: Scholarships to children of NCR Corporation employees pursuing higher education.
Financial data: Year ended 12/31/2012. Assets, $287,793 (M); Expenditures, $16,306; Total giving, $12,000; Grants to individuals, 10 grants totaling $12,000 (high: $1,200, low: $1,200).
Fields of interest: Higher education.
Type of support: Employee-related scholarships.
Application information: Applications not accepted.
  Additional information: Unsolicited requests for funds not considered or acknowledged.
Company name: NCR Corporation
EIN: 237431180

2216
Ninth District Opportunity, Inc.
P.O. Drawer L
Gainesville, GA   30503-1912   (770) 532-3191
Contact: Janice Riley, Exec. Dir.
FAX: (770) 534-0548; E-mail: csbg_tech@ndo.org;
URL: http://www.ndo.org

Foundation type: Public charity
Purpose: Employment counseling, utility assistance, home weatherization, medication, food and re-housing programs for indigent residents of north-central GA.
Financial data: Year ended 09/30/2011. Assets, $15,843,114 (M); Expenditures, $39,133,489; Total giving, $8,618,647; Grants to individuals, totaling $8,618,647.
Fields of interest: Economically disadvantaged.
Type of support: In-kind gifts.
Application information: Applications accepted. Application form required. Application form available on the grantmaker's web site.
  Initial approach: Letter
  Additional information: Contact case manager for eligibility criteria.
EIN: 580974656

2217
North Georgia Community Action, Inc.
1344 Talking Rock Rd.
Jasper, GA   30143-0760   (706) 692-5623
Contact: Jonathan Ray, Exec. Dir.
URL: http://www.ngcainc.com/

Foundation type: Public charity
Purpose: Services to improve the quality of life for the low-income, elderly and homebound populations of Catoosa, Chattooga, Cherokee, Dade, Fannin, Gilmer, Pickens, Murray, Walker and Whitfield counties, GA. Services include transportation, home weatherization, home utility assistance, referral services, and prescription help.
Financial data: Year ended 06/30/2011. Assets, $4,677,903 (M); Expenditures, $10,666,401; Total giving, $5,852,016; Grants to individuals, totaling $5,852,016.
Fields of interest: Aging; Economically disadvantaged.
Type of support: In-kind gifts.
Application information:
  Initial approach: Letter
  Additional information: Contact foundation for eligibility criteria.
EIN: 581204839

2218
North Georgia Community Foundation
615F Oak St., Ste. 1300
Gainesville, GA   30501-8562   (770) 535-7880
FAX: (770) 503-0439; E-mail: info@ngcf.org;
Additional tel.: (866) 535-7880; Grant application e-mail: grants@ngcf.org; URL: http://www.ngcf.org

Foundation type: Community foundation
Purpose: Scholarships to help deserving students of the Gainsville, GA area to pursue higher education.
Publications: Application guidelines; Annual report; Financial statement; Informational brochure; Occasional report.
Financial data: Year ended 12/31/2011. Assets, $36,638,115 (M); Expenditures, $3,724,435; Total giving, $2,908,007; Grants to individuals, 145 grants totaling $173,925.
Fields of interest: Higher education.

Type of support: Scholarships—to individuals; Undergraduate support.
Application information: Applications accepted. Application form required.
  Deadline(s): Varies
  Additional information: Each scholarship has its own specific purpose and eligibility criteria, and awards vary in size depending on the amount available in each particular fund. See web site for additional information.
EIN: 581610318

2219
Parents With A Purpose, Inc.
3950 Hicks Rd.
Austell, GA   30106-1524   (770) 432-5459

Foundation type: Public charity
Purpose: Grants and assistance to individuals and families of Austell, GA in need with back to school supplies, utility, rent and other living necessities.
Financial data: Year ended 12/31/2011. Assets, $189,033 (M); Expenditures, $331,844; Total giving, $2,754,510; Grants to individuals, totaling $126,233.
Fields of interest: Human services; Economically disadvantaged.
Type of support: Grants to individuals; Grants for special needs.
Application information: Contact the organization for eligibility determination.
EIN: 582521988

2220
Leanna Bray Park Memorial Scholarship Fund
P.O. Box 909
Zebulon, GA   30295

Foundation type: Operating foundation
Purpose: Scholarships to students of GA, for the purpose of studying environmental science at an accredited college or university.
Financial data: Year ended 12/31/2011. Assets, $383,297 (M); Expenditures, $5,384; Total giving, $5,000; Grants to individuals, 4 grants totaling $5,000 (high: $2,000, low: $1,000).
Fields of interest: Higher education; Environmental education.
Type of support: Scholarships—to individuals.
Application information: Applications accepted. Application form required.
  Deadline(s): Apr. 27
  Additional information: Preference is given to applicants from Pike County, GA.
EIN: 586396579

2221
The Peoples Bank Foundation, Ltd.
P.O. Box 4250
Eatonton, GA   31024-4250

Foundation type: Company-sponsored foundation
Purpose: Scholarships to graduating seniors of Putnam County, GA for continuing education at accredited colleges or universities.
Financial data: Year ended 12/31/2012. Assets, $123,053 (M); Expenditures, $4,995; Total giving, $4,500; Grants to individuals, 7 grants totaling $4,500 (high: $1,000, low: $500).
Fields of interest: Higher education.
Type of support: Undergraduate support.
Application information: Application form required.
  Initial approach: Letter
  Deadline(s): Mar. 1

Additional information: Application forms available upon request.
EIN: 581811866

2222
Phi Mu Foundation
400 Westpark Dr.
Peachtree City, GA 30269-1482 (770) 632-2090
Contact: Julie Cain Burkhard, Exec. Dir.
FAX: (770) 632-2135; E-mail: cflores@phimu.org;
E-mail For Julie Cain Burkhard: jburkhard@phimu.org; URL: http://www.phimufoundation.org

Foundation type: Public charity
Purpose: Scholarships to graduate and undergraduate students who are members of Phi Mu.
Publications: Application guidelines.
Financial data: Year ended 06/30/2012. Assets, $10,843,081 (M); Expenditures, $901,538; Total giving, $273,000. Scholarships—to individuals amount not specified.
Fields of interest: Students, sororities/fraternities; Health care; Women.
Type of support: Support to graduates or students of specific schools; Graduate support; Undergraduate support; Doctoral support.
Application information: Application form required.
Send request by: Online
Deadline(s): Mar. 1
Applicants should submit the following:
1) Transcripts
2) Letter(s) of recommendation
3) GPA
4) Financial information
5) Essay
6) Budget Information
Additional information: See web site for additional application information.
Program description:
Scholarships: Over 100 scholarships totaling more than $100,000 are available to qualified Phi Mu undergraduate and graduate students each academic year. While some scholarships are restricted to field of study, chapter, state, or college, many are unrestricted. Only one application is required to be considered for all scholarships. Eligible recipients must be an initiated member in good standing of Phi Mu Fraternity, have a cumulative GPA of 3.0 or above, and remain in an accredited college or university working toward a degree, credential, or certificate during the academic year. All undergraduate applicants must be enrolled as full-time students as defined by their college or university.
EIN: 626042543

2223
The Nuci Phillips Memorial Foundation
396 Oconee St.
Athens, GA 30601-3606 (706) 227-1515
Contact: Bob Sleppy, Exec. Dir.
FAX: (706) 227-1524; E-mail: space@nuci.org;
E-Mail For Bob Sleppy: bob@nuci.org; URL: http://www.nuci.org

Foundation type: Public charity
Purpose: Provides studio space for Athens, GA musicians to practice, as well as counseling services to these musicians suffering from depression.
Financial data: Year ended 12/31/2011. Assets, $522,819 (M); Expenditures, $591,153; Total

giving, $267,583; Grants to individuals, totaling $267,583.
Fields of interest: Arts, artist's services; Depression.
Type of support: Grants for special needs.
Application information:
Initial approach: Letter
Additional information: Contact foundation for eligibility criteria.
EIN: 582409414

2224
Pickett & Hatcher Educational Fund, Inc.
6001 River Rd., Ste. 408
Columbus, GA 31904-4558 (800) 864-8308, ext. 100
Contact: Scholarships: Kenneth R. Owens, Pres.
FAX: (706) 324-6788; E-mail: info@phef.org;
Mailing address: P.O. Box 8169, Columbus, GA 31908-8169; tel.: (706) 327-6586; e-mail for Scholarships: info@phef.org; URL: http://www.phef.org

Foundation type: Independent foundation
Purpose: Student loans to U.S. residents for attendance at four year colleges and universities. Loans are available to medical health care students studying nursing, and physical therapy.
Publications: Application guidelines; Informational brochure (including application guidelines).
Financial data: Year ended 09/30/2013. Assets, $47,057,882 (M); Expenditures, $4,087,428; Total giving, $3,376,752; Loans to individuals, 520 loans totaling $3,376,752.
Fields of interest: Higher education; Health sciences school/education.
Type of support: Undergraduate support.
Application information: Applications accepted. Application form required. Application form available on the grantmaker's web site.
Send request by: Online
Copies of proposal: 1
Deadline(s): Rolling
Final notification: Applicants notified within two weeks.
Applicants should submit the following:
1) Letter(s) of recommendation
2) Transcripts
3) SAT
4) GPA
5) Budget Information
6) ACT
Additional information: No support for students planning to enter career fields of medicine, law, or the ministry. See web site for latest application guidelines and procedures.
EIN: 580566216

2225
Pilot International Foundation, Inc.
(also known as PIF)
102 Preston Ct.
Macon, GA 31210-5768 (478) 743-7403
Contact: Peggy Davison, Exec.Dir.
FAX: (478) 474-7229; E-mail: pifinfo@pilothq.org;
E-mail for Jennifer Overbay: jennifer@pilotq.org;
URL: http://www.pilotinternational.org/html/foundation/overview.shtml

Foundation type: Public charity
Purpose: Scholarships to undergraduate and graduate students pursuing careers in the health and welfare fields with an emphasis on brain related disorders.
Financial data: Year ended 06/30/2012. Assets, $3,058,060 (M); Expenditures, $530,483; Total

giving, $122,523; Grants to individuals, totaling $122,523.
Fields of interest: Brain disorders; Disabilities, people with.
Type of support: Foreign applicants; Graduate support; Undergraduate support.
Application information: Applications accepted. Application form required. Application form available on the grantmaker's web site.
Initial approach: E-mail
Deadline(s): Feb. 15
Additional information: See web site additional application information.
Program descriptions:
Becky Burrows Memorial Scholarship: This program assists graduate or undergraduate students preparing for a second career, re-entering the job market or obtaining additional training in their current field. The career path must pertain to assisting those with brain-related disorders or brain-related disabilities.
The Marie Newton Sepia Memorial Scholarship Program: This program assists students studying at the master's or doctorate level who are preparing for a career helping children with brain-related disorders or brain-related disabilities.
The Pilot International Foundation Scholarship Program: Provides assistance to undergraduate students preparing for careers working directly with people with disabilities or training those who will. All applicants for a Pilot International Foundation scholarship must be sponsored by a Pilot Club in their home town, or in the city in which their college or university is located.
The Ruby Newhall Memorial Scholarship Program: Provides aid to international students studying in either the U.S. or Canada. Applicants must be full-time students majoring in a field related to human health and welfare and must have spent at least one full academic semester in an accredited college in the U.S. or Canada before applying for a scholarship.
EIN: 237443190

2226
R.A.C.K Foundation
2770 Shumard Oak Dr.
Braselton, GA 30517-6024 (678) 491-4816

Foundation type: Public charity
Purpose: Scholarships to graduating seniors at Apple Valley High School, MN, who are student-athletes.
Financial data: Year ended 12/31/2012. Assets, $906 (M); Expenditures, $24,959; Total giving, $24,250.
Fields of interest: Athletics/sports, school programs.
Type of support: Support to graduates or students of specific schools; Undergraduate support.
Application information: Applications accepted. Application form required.
Deadline(s): Contact foundation for current application deadline
Applicants should submit the following:
1) Letter(s) of recommendation
2) Transcripts
Additional information: Application should also include a list of activities and a personal statement of educational plans.
EIN: 201531172

2227
Ravi Zacharias International Ministries
4725 Peachtree Corners Cir., Ste. 250
Norcross, GA 30092-2586 (770) 449-6766
Internship e-mail: paul.lundblad@rzim.org
FAX: (770) 729-1729; E-mail: rzim@rzim.org;
URL: http://www.rzim.org/

Foundation type: Public charity
Purpose: Scholarships to attend Oxford Center for Christian Apologetics, in the UK. Also, internships in the GA headquarters to provide students and recent graduates with an opportunity to learn more about various aspects of the ministry, i.e., evangelism, apologetics, spiritual disciplines, and training.
Financial data: Year ended 09/30/2011. Assets, $8,735,136 (M); Expenditures, $16,406,896; Total giving, $6,935,526; Grants to individuals, totaling $1,000. Subtotal for grants to individuals: 13 grants totaling $250,608.
Fields of interest: Christian agencies & churches; Religion.
Type of support: Internship funds; Undergraduate support.
Application information:
  Initial approach: E-mail
  Additional information: Contact the ministries for eligibility criteria.
EIN: 133200719

2228
Reynolds Plantation Foundation, Inc.
(formerly Reynolds Foundation, Inc.)
10000 Vista Dr.
Greensboro, GA 30642-3812 (706) 467-3151

Foundation type: Independent foundation
Purpose: College scholarships to high school seniors from Greene, Putnam and Morgan counties, GA in pursuit of a higher education at an accredited two or four year college or university.
Financial data: Year ended 12/31/2012. Assets, $346,270 (M); Expenditures, $14,268; Total giving, $10,500; Grants to individuals, 16 grants totaling $10,500 (high: $1,000, low: $500).
Fields of interest: Higher education.
Type of support: Scholarships—to individuals.
Application information: Applications accepted. Application form required.
  Initial approach: Letter
  Deadline(s): Apr. 15
  Additional information: Application should include an essay.
EIN: 582465812

2229
Murray & Sydell Rosenberg Foundation, Inc.
(formerly Murray M. Rosenberg Foundation)
3330 Cumberland Blvd., Ste. 900
Atlanta, GA 30339-5998

Foundation type: Company-sponsored foundation
Purpose: Financial assistance to needy Jewish families within the U.S. and Israel.
Financial data: Year ended 06/30/2012. Assets, $15,083 (M); Expenditures, $1,671,174; Total giving, $1,667,342; Grant to an individual, 1 grant totaling $85,800.
Fields of interest: Jewish agencies & synagogues.
Type of support: Grants for special needs.
Application information: Applications not accepted.

Additional information: Unsolicited requests for funds not considered or acknowledged.
EIN: 581947342

2230
Saint Vincent De Paul Society, Inc.
2050-C Chamblee Tucker Rd.
Atlanta, GA 30341-3343 (770) 458-9607
E-mail: svdp@svdpatl.org; URL: http://www.svdpatl.org/

Foundation type: Public charity
Purpose: Financial assistance to indigent GA residents, for a range of needs including medical/dental/prescriptions, counseling, rent and housing, utilities, food, legal fees, transportation, and burials.
Publications: Annual report.
Financial data: Year ended 09/30/2011. Assets, $1,632,408 (M); Expenditures, $8,844,801; Total giving, $6,296,574; Grants to individuals, totaling $6,296,574.
Fields of interest: Economically disadvantaged.
Type of support: Grants for special needs.
Application information:
  Initial approach: Tel.
  Additional information: To apply for assistance, call the helpline: 678-892-6163.
EIN: 580967972

2231
The Sapelo Foundation, Inc.
(formerly Sapelo Island Research Foundation, Inc.)
1712 Ellis St., 2nd Fl.
Brunswick, GA 31520-6417 (912) 265-0520
Contact: Phyllis Bowen, Exec. Dir.
FAX: (912) 265-1888;
E-mail: sapelofoundation@mindspring.com;
URL: http://www.sapelofoundation.org

Foundation type: Independent foundation
Purpose: Scholarships to financially needy residents of McIntosh County, GA, who are graduates of McIntosh County Academy for attendance at accredited colleges, universities, or technical colleges.
Publications: Application guidelines; Annual report; Grants list.
Financial data: Year ended 06/30/2012. Assets, $32,492,613 (M); Expenditures, $1,653,655; Total giving, $1,038,044; Grants to individuals, totaling $142,750.
Fields of interest: Vocational education, post-secondary; Higher education; Scholarships/financial aid.
Type of support: Scholarships—to individuals; Support to graduates or students of specific schools.
Application information: Applications accepted. Application form required. Application form available on the grantmaker's web site.
  Initial approach: Application
  Send request by: Online
  Deadline(s): Mar. 1
  Additional information: Funds are paid directly to the educational institution on behalf of the students. Applicants must have a 2.0 GPA or better. See web site for specific application guidelines.
EIN: 580827472

2232
The Savannah Community Foundation
(formerly The Savannah Foundation)
7393 Hodgson Memorial Dr., Ste. 204
Savannah, GA 31406-1507 (912) 921-7700
Contact: K. Russell Simpson, Pres.
E-mail: Russ@SavFoundation.org; Additional e-mails: russ@savfoundation.org and grants@savfoundation.org; URL: http://www.savfoundation.org

Foundation type: Community foundation
Purpose: Scholarships to residents of southeastern GA for postsecondary education.
Publications: Application guidelines; Financial statement; Grants list; Informational brochure (including application guidelines).
Financial data: Year ended 06/30/2012. Assets, $16,415,432 (M); Expenditures, $2,343,992; Total giving, $2,046,211; Grants to individuals, totaling $87,700.
Fields of interest: Higher education.
Type of support: Scholarships—to individuals; Support to graduates or students of specific schools; Undergraduate support.
Application information: Applications accepted. Application form required.
  Deadline(s): Varies
  Additional information: Each scholarship fund has its own set of eligibility requirements. See web site for scholarship application and listing of various scholarships.
EIN: 586033468

2233
Savannah Jewish Council, Inc.
5111 Abercorn St.
P.O. Box 23527
Savannah, GA 31405-5214 (912) 355-8111
Contact: Adam Solender, Exec. Dir.
FAX: (912) 355-8116;
E-mail: jea_federationhotline@savj.org;
URL: http://www.savj.org/

Foundation type: Public charity
Purpose: Emergency financial assistance to Jewish individuals in Savannah, GA, to ensure adequate shelter, nutrition, health and safety.
Financial data: Year ended 09/30/2011. Assets, $4,769,820 (M); Expenditures, $1,286,915; Total giving, $881,545; Grants to individuals, totaling $82,015.
Fields of interest: Human services; Human services, emergency aid; Jewish agencies & synagogues; Minorities; Economically disadvantaged.
Type of support: Grants for special needs.
Application information: Contact the council for further program and application information.
EIN: 580566231

2234
Scheffler Family Foundation
210 Elderberry Cir.
Athens, GA 30605 (706) 534-0416
Contact: Vincent Laviano, Tr.
FAX: (706) 534-0434

Foundation type: Independent foundation
Purpose: Scholarships to the needy students for continuing education at institutions of higher learning.
Financial data: Year ended 12/31/2012. Assets, $891,442 (M); Expenditures, $45,984; Total giving, $22,625; Grants to individuals, 37 grants totaling $22,625 (high: $1,750, low: $315).

Fields of interest: Higher education; Scholarships/financial aid; Disabilities, people with; Economically disadvantaged.
Type of support: Undergraduate support.
Application information: Applications accepted. Application form required.
  Send request by: Mail
  Deadline(s): Sept.
  Applicants should submit the following:
    1) Transcripts
    2) Letter(s) of recommendation
    3) GPA
  Additional information: Application should also include a copy of your parents and your most recent income tax statement.
EIN: 592129811

2235
Service League of Cherokee County
P.O. Box 1132
Canton, GA   30169-1132
E-mail: info@serviceleague.net; URL: http://www.serviceleague.net

Foundation type: Public charity
Purpose: Scholarships to high school seniors attending public high schools in Cherokee County, GA.
Financial data: Year ended 03/31/2012. Assets, $238,276 (M); Expenditures, $108,100; Total giving, $34,195.
Fields of interest: Higher education.
Type of support: Scholarships—to individuals.
Application information: Applications accepted. Application form required.
  Send request by: Mail
  Deadline(s): Apr. 19
  Applicants should submit the following:
    1) ACT
    2) Transcripts
    3) SAT
    4) Letter(s) of recommendation
    5) Essay
  Additional information: Application should also include a copy of college/other educational institution acceptance letter. Students may obtain application from the Counseling Department at their respective schools.
Program description:
  Scholarships: Scholarships of $1,000 each are annually awarded to one deserving student from each of Cherokee County's high schools. The schools included are Cherokee, Creekview, CrossRoads, Etowah, Polaris, Sequoyah, and Woodstock.
EIN: 581685138

2236
Seven Oaks Foundation, Inc.
225 Peachtree St. N.E., Ste. 1200
Atlanta, GA   30303

Foundation type: Independent foundation
Purpose: Scholarships by nomination only to graduating high school seniors who are U.S. citizens, or noncitizens currently working towards citizenship.
Financial data: Year ended 12/31/2012. Assets, $10,993 (M); Expenditures, $15,993; Total giving, $15,000; Grants to individuals, 2 grants totaling $15,000 (high: $10,000, low: $5,000).
Fields of interest: Education.
Type of support: Awards/grants by nomination only.
Application information: Applications not accepted.

Additional information: High school counselors nominate students to compete; Completion of formal application required by nominees only. Scholarship recipients are chosen biannually by competition.
EIN: 581828554

2237
Southeastern Brain Tumor Foundation
5400 Glenridge Dr., N.E., Ste. 44241
P.O. Box 422471
Atlanta, GA   30342-9471   (786) 505-7283
Contact: Costas G. Hadjipanayis M.D. Ph.D., Pres.
E-mail: info@sbtf.org; URL: http://www.sbtf.org

Foundation type: Public charity
Purpose: Research grants to medical personnel in the southeast U.S. in search of a cure for brain tumor.
Publications: Financial statement; Grants list; Program policy statement.
Financial data: Year ended 12/31/2012. Assets, $74,886 (M); Expenditures, $151,599; Total giving, $75,198.
Fields of interest: Brain research.
Type of support: Research.
Application information: Unsolicited requests for funds not considered or acknowledged.
EIN: 582166144

2238
Southern Company Charitable Foundation, Inc.
241 Ralph McGill Blvd., N.E., BIN 10131
Atlanta, GA   30308-3374   (404) 506-6784
Contact: Susan M. Carter, Secy.
FAX: (404) 506-1485; URL: http://www.southerncompany.com/corporate-responsibility/social-responsibility/communityInvolvement.aspx

Foundation type: Company-sponsored foundation
Purpose: Emergency assistance grants to employees of the Southern Company displaced by disaster.
Financial data: Year ended 12/31/2011. Assets, $29,338,399 (M); Expenditures, $1,012,525; Total giving, $861,111.
Fields of interest: Safety/disasters.
Type of support: Emergency funds; Employee-related welfare.
Application information: Applications not accepted.
  Additional information: Unsolicited requests for funds not considered or acknowledged.
Company name: The Southern Company
EIN: 582514027

2239
Southern Tennis Patrons Foundation
5685 Spalding Dr.
Norcross, GA   30092-2504   (770) 368-8200
FAX: (777) 368-9091; E-mail: info@sta.usta.com;
URL: http://www.southern.usta.com/Patrons-Foundation/5712_Patrons_Home/

Foundation type: Public charity
Purpose: Financial assistance to junior tennis players age 12 to 18 years old. Financial assistance for summer camp scholarships for those 13 years old and under.
Financial data: Year ended 12/31/2011. Assets, $4,859,017 (M); Expenditures, $207,707; Total giving, $195,125; Grants to individuals, totaling $189,125.

Fields of interest: Camps; Athletics/sports, racquet sports.
Type of support: Grants for special needs.
Application information: Applications accepted.
  Deadline(s): Ongoing for junior tennis players, Apr. 1 for summer camp scholarship
  Additional information: Selection is based on need. Contact the foundation for additional guidelines.
EIN: 237035657

2240
Southwest Georgia Community Action Council, Inc.
912 1st Ave. S.E.
P.O. Box 3728
Moultrie, GA   31776   (229) 985-3610
Contact: Ann Hires, Exec. Secy.
FAX: (229) 890-1056;
E-mail: ahires@swgacac.com; Toll-free tel.: (800) 642-3384; URL: http://www.swgacac.com/

Foundation type: Public charity
Purpose: Emergency assistance to individuals of southwest GA, who have experienced a loss of income or unexpected expense beyond their control with payment of rent, mortgage, utility bills, deposits, food and other special needs.
Financial data: Year ended 01/31/2012. Assets, $6,348,860 (M); Expenditures, $28,347,710; Total giving, $3,555,390; Grants to individuals, totaling $3,555,390.
Fields of interest: Human services.
Type of support: Emergency funds.
Application information: Applications accepted.
  Additional information: Applicants must verify eligibility by verification of Social Security Numbers (cards) for all household members, verification of all income coming into the household (all members age 18 or older) for the past 30 days, current statements for services requested (utility, rent, and/or mortgage), and additional items as requested. Individuals are required to document all income and expense for the household and demonstrate the ability to pay all future household bills without assistance.
EIN: 580957513

2241
The John and L. A. Spears Foundation, Inc.
706 Holcomb Bridge Rd.
Norcross, GA   30071

Foundation type: Independent foundation
Purpose: Scholarships to individuals in GA for higher education.
Financial data: Year ended 12/31/2011. Assets, $998,040 (M); Expenditures, $34,839; Total giving, $16,384; Grants to individuals, 6 grants totaling $16,384 (high: $3,000, low: $724).
Fields of interest: Higher education.
Type of support: Scholarships—to individuals.
Application information: Application form required.
  Deadline(s): Vary
  Applicants should submit the following:
    1) Transcripts
    2) SAT
    3) ACT
  Additional information: Application forms are mailed up request. Applicant must have a 2.5 GPA or higher. Maximum scholarship is $10,000 not to exceed tuition and fees.
EIN: 582448721

2242
Star Foundation Inc.
218 Highland Dr.
Tallapoosa, GA 30176 (770) 574-2400
Contact: Gail Carnes, Secy.-Treas.
Application address: 895 Hwy. 100, Tallapoosa, GA 30176, Tel:(770) 574-2400

Foundation type: Independent foundation
Purpose: Scholarships to dependents of workers employed at the American Thread Company, Tallapoosa, GA, for study at an accredited four-year institution.
Financial data: Year ended 12/31/2012. Assets, $43,117 (M); Expenditures, $1,880; Total giving, $1,800; Grants to individuals, 3 grants totaling $1,800 (high: $600, low: $600).
Type of support: Employee-related scholarships.
Application information: Applications accepted. Application form required.
  Deadline(s): None
Company name: American Thread Company
EIN: 586043712

2243
Stingrays, Inc.
3023 High Vista Walk
Woodstock, GA 30189-6781
E-mail: iangoss@bellsouth.net

Foundation type: Public charity
Purpose: Full and partial scholarships to financially needy individuals in Cherokee and Cobb counties, GA, for participation on the Stingrays competitive swim team.
Financial data: Year ended 09/30/2011. Assets, $34,142 (M); Expenditures, $1,028,245.
Fields of interest: Athletics/sports, water sports.
Type of support: Scholarships—to individuals.
Application information: Applications accepted.
  Initial approach: Letter
  Applicants should submit the following:
    1) Letter(s) of recommendation
    2) Financial information
  Additional information: Applicants must demonstrate financial hardship, commitment demonstrated by the swimmer at practice, meets and in dealing with other swimmers and coaches, and references, if necessary.
EIN: 581856147

2244
Stovall Hope Foundation, Inc.
P.O. Box 556
Clayton, GA 30525-0014 (770) 831-0835

Foundation type: Public charity
Purpose: Financial assistance for food and temporary housing to individuals with seriously ill children in Atlanta, GA, hospitals.
Financial data: Year ended 12/31/2011. Assets, $4,485 (M); Expenditures, $19,170; Total giving, $18,800.
Fields of interest: Children; Economically disadvantaged.
Type of support: Grants for special needs.
Application information:
  Initial approach: Letter
  Additional information: Contact foundation for complete eligibility requirements.
EIN: 542084612

2245
Student Aid Foundation Inc.
2550 Sandy Plains Rd., Ste. 225
Marietta, GA 30066-7223 (770) 973-7077
Contact: Catherine W. Reynolds, Exec. Secy.
FAX: (770) 973-2220;
E-mail: studentaid@bellsouth.net; URL: http://www.studentaidfoundation.org

Foundation type: Independent foundation
Purpose: Student loans to financially needy full time female students who are residents of GA, or out-of-state residents attending a GA school.
Financial data: Year ended 03/31/2013. Assets, $2,142,427 (M); Expenditures, $76,949; Total giving, $0.
Fields of interest: Vocational education; Higher education; Women.
Type of support: Student loans—to individuals; Graduate support; Undergraduate support.
Application information: Applications accepted. Application form required.
  Send request by: Mail
  Deadline(s): May 1
  Applicants should submit the following:
    1) Photograph
    2) Essay
    3) Transcripts
    4) Financial information
  Additional information: Application should also include two references. See web site for additional guidelines.
Program description:
  Educational Loan: Interest free loans while enrolled in school are $3,500 to $5,000 per year for undergraduate students for freshman and sophomore years. $3,500 to $7,500 for junior and senior years if GPA is 3.0 or better. $7,500 per year for graduate students. Recipients may reapply for loans for each year of study. Applicants must be U.S. citizens.
EIN: 580612611

2246
The Styles Memorial Scholarship Fund Foundation
3589 Bozeman Lake Rd.
Kennesaw, GA 30144-2010 (706) 265-6555
Application address: c/o Dawson County High School, Attn.: Principal, 1665 Perimeter Rd., Dawsonville, GA 30534-4328

Foundation type: Operating foundation
Purpose: Scholarships to students of Dawson County High School, GA for postsecondary education.
Financial data: Year ended 12/31/2012. Assets, $115,474 (M); Expenditures, $8,285; Total giving, $8,000; Grants to individuals, 8 grants totaling $8,000 (high: $1,000, low: $1,000).
Type of support: Undergraduate support.
Application information: Applications accepted. Application form required.
  Deadline(s): May 1
  Additional information: Application can be obtained from the principal's office. Students must be residents of Dawson County, GA.
EIN: 586354416

2247
TAPPI Foundation, Inc.
15 Technology Pkwy. S.
Norcross, GA 30092-2928 (770) 209-7259
FAX: (770) 446-6947;
E-mail: foundation@tappi.org; URL: http://www.tappi.org/

Foundation type: Public charity
Purpose: Scholarships to students pursuing studies in the pulp, paper, and related industries.
Publications: Application guidelines; Annual report; Informational brochure.
Financial data: Year ended 08/31/2012. Assets, $3,153,204 (M); Expenditures, $298,098; Total giving, $164,156; Grants to individuals, totaling $164,156.
Fields of interest: Higher education.
Type of support: Support to graduates or students of specific schools; Awards/grants by nomination only; Awards/prizes; Undergraduate support.
Application information: Application form required.
  Deadline(s): Aug. 1 for William L. Cullison Scholarship; Feb. 15 for all others
  Final notification: Recipients notified July 1 for scholarships
  Applicants should submit the following:
    1) Letter(s) of recommendation
    2) Essay
    3) Transcripts
Program descriptions:
  Coating and Graphic Arts Division Scholarships: This $1,000 scholarship provides financial assistance to selected students in colleges, universities, and other institutions of higher learning. Students should be majoring in scientific or technical disciplines related to the manufacture and/or graphic-arts end-use of coated paper and paperboard. Eligible applicants must: be enrolled as a full-time student in an accredited college or university in a program related to the coated paper and paperboard, or graphic arts, industry; be a student member of the Technical Association of the Paper and Pulp Industry (TAPPI) or member of one of the association's student chapters; have achieved a class level of junior or higher (with graduate students eligible prior to doctoral candidacy); have a minimum cumulative GPA of 3.0 (on a 4.0 scale); and have a demonstrated interest in a career in the coating and graphic arts industry. In addition, this program awards a $1,000 Best Paper Award to a school selected by the winner of the best paper award given at the association's annual conference.
  Corrugated Packing Division Scholarships: Scholarships, ranging from $1,000 to $2,000, are available to students who demonstrate an interest in the corrugated container, pulp, and paper industry. Eligible applicants must be working (full- or part-time) in the box business and attending day/night school for a graduate or undergraduate degree; or be a full-time student in a two- or four-year college, university, or technical school. Applicants must also have a GPA of 3.0 (on a 4.0 scale), be able to demonstrate an interest in the corrugated packaging industry (with preference given to part-time employment or internship in the industry), and be recommended and endorsed by an instructor or faculty member.
  Douglas Barton Memorial Scholarship: This scholarship is intended to support the areas of environmental control as it relates to the pulp, paper, and allied industries. Eligible applicants must: demonstrate attendance at an Accreditation Board for Engineering and Technology, Inc. (ABET) accredited or equivalent college; have full-time student status; be at or above the sophomore level; and have a cumulative GPA of at least 3.0 (on a 4.0 system)

Engineering Division Scholarships: Up to two scholarships of $1,500 each will be awarded to promote interest in the pulp and paper industry among engineering and science students, and to increase the potential in following an engineering career among students with an interest in these industries. One scholarship will be awarded to a student who will be in his or her junior year, will the other will be awarded to a student in his or her senior year. Eligible applicants must be an undergraduate member of a student chapter of the Technical Association of the Paper and Pulp Industry (TAPPI), a student member of the international branch of the association, or submit comparable evidence of professional development and participation related to the paper industry; eligible applicants must also be full-time students (either upcoming juniors or seniors) enrolled in an engineering or science program, and must be maintaining a GPA of 3.0 or higher (on a 4.0 scale)

Gunnar Nicholson Award: This award, usually between $60,000 and $80,000, will be presented to individuals who have made preeminent scientific and engineering achievements of proven applied benefit to the world's pulp, paper, board, and forest production industries (including forestry, derived products, their process technology, and their applications)

Herman L. Joachim Distinguished Service Award: This award gives an cash honorarium equal to five percent of the Herman L. Joachim Distinguished Service Award Fund (generally between $60,000 and $80,000) for exemplary leadership that has significant contributed to the advancement of the association.

Nonwovens Division Scholarship: This $1,000 scholarship supports a students who is currently enrolled in an program prepatory to a career in the nonwovens industry, or who demonstrates an interest in the areas covered by the Technical Association of the Paper and Pulp Industry (TAPPI) Nonwovens Division. Eligible applicants must be enrolled as a full-time student in a state-accredited undergraduate program, have a GPA of 3.0 (on a 4.0 scale), and be recommended and endorsed by an instructor or faculty member.

Paper and Board Division Scholarship: This $1,000 scholarship is intended to encourage talented science and engineering students to pursue careers in the paper industry, and to utilize their talents in advancing the science and technology of papermaking. Eligible applicants must: be a student member of the Technical Association of the Paper and Pulp Industry (TAPPI), or member of a student chapter; be enrolled as a full-time student or participant in a cooperative work-study program recognized and supported by the recipient's educational institution; be a sophomore, junior, or senior at the time of application; and demonstrate a significant interest in the paper industry.

PLACE (Polymers, Laminations, Adhesives, Coatings, and Extrusions) Division Scholarships: This $1,000 scholarship, offered only in even-numbered years, is available to a student who plans to pursue an area of study within the fields of interest in the Technical Association of the Paper and Pulp Industry (TAPPI)'s PLACE (polymers, laminations, adhesives, coatings, and extrusions) division (including packaging, industrial films and laminations, blown and cast films extrusion, extrusion castings and laminations, sheet extrusion, and printing). Eligible applicants must: be a high-school senior, college undergraduate, or graduate student as of the date of application who is attending college full-time on the date of the award (part-time students working full-time and attending night school); exhibit respectable

academic standing; demonstrate responsibility and maturity throughout a history of part-time and summer employment; and demonstrate an interest in the technological areas covered by the PLACE division.

Process and Product Quality Division Scholarship: This $1,000 award is intended to encourage talented science and engineering students to pursue careers in the pulp and paper industry, and to develop awareness of quality management. Eligible applicants must: be a student member of the Technical Association of the Paper and Pulp Industry (TAPPI), or an undergraduate member of an association student chapter; be enrolled as a full-time college or university undergraduate in an engineering or science program related to the manufacture of pulp and paper products; be a sophomore, junior, or senior at the time of application; demonstrate a significant interest in the pulp and paper industry; and describe how pulp and paper production is dependent on quality management techniques.

William L. Cullison Scholarship: Scholarships of up to $4,000 per year are available to students entering their third year of college who wish to work in the pulp and paper, corrugated container, or polymer, lamination, adhesive, coating, and extrusion industries. Eligible applicants must: major in a pulp and paper science course of study at a college or university; maintain a 3.5 GPA (on a 4.0 scale) through the first two years in a four-year program, or first three years in a five-year program; and demonstrate outstanding leadership abilities and significant interest in the pulp and paper industry. Scholarships are intended to support the last two years of a recipient's undergraduate program.
EIN: 581886221

2248
The Tharpe Foundation
(formerly The Robert H. and Kathryne B. Tharpe Foundation)
3796 Apsley Ct. SE
Atlanta, GA 30339

Foundation type: Independent foundation
Purpose: Scholarships to residents of Moultrie, GA.
Financial data: Year ended 12/31/2011. Assets, $522,987 (M); Expenditures, $632,526; Total giving, $625,769.
Type of support: Undergraduate support.
Application information: Applications not accepted.
Additional information: Unsolicited requests for funds not considered or acknowledged.
EIN: 581858404

2249
THDF II, Inc.
(formerly The Homer Fund)
2455 Paces Ferry Rd., Ste. C-17
Atlanta, GA 30339-1834 (770) 384-3889
Contact: Kelly Caffarelli, Pres.
FAX: (770) 384-3908;
E-mail: hd_foundation@homedepot.com; Additional e-mail: small_grants@homedepot.com; contact for The Homer Fund: Erin Cannaday, tel.: (800) 654-0688, ext. 12611, e-mail: Homer_Fund@HomeDepot.com; URL: http://www.homedepotfoundation.org

Foundation type: Public charity
Purpose: Grants and short term emergency financial assistance to qualifying Home Depot associates who have experienced financial

hardship due to catastrophic illness, accident or who are victims of a natural disaster. Scholarships to dependent sons and daughters of full and part-time associates of the Home Depot and its subsidiaries.
Publications: Application guidelines.
Financial data: Year ended 12/31/2011. Assets, $41,119,012 (M); Expenditures, $45,205,678; Total giving, $39,937,075; Grants to individuals, totaling $17,144,260.
Fields of interest: Higher education.
Type of support: Emergency funds; Scholarships— to individuals; Grants for special needs.
Application information: Applications accepted.
Deadline(s): Mar. 1 for Scholarships
Final notification: June
Additional information: Applicant must demonstrate financial need.
Program description:
Scholarship Program: Scholarships, ranging from $1,000 to $2,500 USD ($1,000 USD for Mexico) each, are available to children of Home Depot associates. Eligible applicant must be high school seniors, college freshmen, sophomores, or juniors enrolled as undergraduate students. Parents or legal guardians must be employed by Home Depot for at least one year and still be employed at the time awards are announced. Awards are renewable; recipients and non-recipients are encouraged to reapply each year they are eligible.
EIN: 582491657

2250
Tri-County Protective Agency, Inc.
P.O. Box 1937
Hinesville, GA 31310 (912) 368-8668
Contact: Paula Foerstel, Exec. Dir.

Foundation type: Public charity
Purpose: Provides temporary emergency shelter, food and assistance to victims of domestic/family voilence and their children.
Financial data: Year ended 12/31/2011. Assets, $353,775 (M); Expenditures, $422,048; Total giving, $23,165; Grants to individuals, totaling $23,165.
Fields of interest: Domestic violence; Economically disadvantaged.
Type of support: Emergency funds.
Application information: Applications not accepted.
EIN: 581736408

2251
United Way of Northwest Georgia, Inc.
816 S. Thornton Ave.
P.O. Box 566
Dalton, GA 30722-0566 (706) 226-4357
Contact: Amanda Burt, Pres.
FAX: (706) 226-1029; E-Mail for Amanda Burt : amanda.burt@ourunitedway.orgTel. for Amanda Burt : (706)-876-1588; URL: http://www.ourunitedway.org

Foundation type: Public charity
Purpose: Grants to economically disadvantaged residents of northwest GA.
Publications: Annual report.
Financial data: Year ended 12/31/2011. Assets, $4,949,026 (M); Expenditures, $3,024,188; Total giving, $2,250,000.
Fields of interest: Economically disadvantaged.
Type of support: Grants for special needs.
Application information:
Initial approach: Letter

Additional information: Contact foundation for eligibility requirements.
EIN: 580905881

2252

United Way of the Central Savannah River Area, Inc.

1765 Broad St.
Augusta, GA 30904-3915 (706) 724-5544
FAX: (706) 724-5541; E-mail: uwa@uwcsra.org;
Mailing address: P.O. Box 1724, Augusta, GA
30903-1724; URL: http://www.uwcsra.org

Foundation type: Public charity
Purpose: Grants to needy individuals in Richmond, Columbia, Burke, Lincoln, Wilkes, Taliaferro, Glascock, Warren, Jefferson, Emanuel, Jenkins, and McDuffie counties, GA; and Aiken, Edgefield, and McCormick counties, SC.
Publications: Annual report; Informational brochure.
Financial data: Year ended 12/31/2011. Assets, $4,094,071 (M); Expenditures, $4,626,806; Total giving, $3,271,179.
Fields of interest: Economically disadvantaged.
Type of support: Grants for special needs.
Application information:
   Initial approach: Letter
   Additional information: Contact foundation for current eligibility requirements.
EIN: 580566155

2253

United Way of the Coastal Empire, Inc.

428 Bull St.
P.O. Box 2946
Savannah, GA 31402-4963 (912) 651-7700
FAX: (912) 651-7724; E-mail: rnale@uwce.org;
URL: http://www.uwce.org

Foundation type: Public charity
Purpose: Grants to needy individuals in the Savannah, GA, area.
Publications: Annual report.
Financial data: Year ended 12/31/2011. Assets, $11,167,990 (M); Expenditures, $9,238,595; Total giving, $6,889,856.
Fields of interest: Economically disadvantaged.
Type of support: Grants for special needs.
Application information:
   Initial approach: Letter
   Additional information: Contact foundation for complete eligibility requirements.
EIN: 580623603

2254

University of Georgia Athletic Association, Inc.

456 E. Broad St.
Athens, GA 30602-2504 (706) 542-1197
URL: http://www.sports.uga.edu/

Foundation type: Public charity
Purpose: Scholarships to student athletes at the University of Georgia for higher education.
Financial data: Year ended 06/30/2012. Assets, $347,342,078 (M); Expenditures, $88,173,810; Total giving, $11,388,742; Grants to individuals, totaling $9,388,742.
Fields of interest: Higher education; Athletics/sports, school programs.
Type of support: Support to graduates or students of specific schools.
Application information: Applications accepted.

Additional information: Selection is based on athletic ability and financial need.
EIN: 580652518

2255

Waffle House Foundation, Inc.

(formerly GFF Educational Foundation, Inc.)
5986 Financial Dr.
Norcross, GA 30071-2949 (770) 729-5780
Contact: Tracy Bradshaw, V.P.

Foundation type: Company-sponsored foundation
Purpose: College scholarships to students who are residents of GA, and are in financial need.
Publications: Application guidelines.
Financial data: Year ended 05/31/2012. Assets, $410,978 (M); Expenditures, $199,331; Total giving, $199,331; Grants to individuals, totaling $21,500.
Fields of interest: Higher education.
Type of support: Scholarships—to individuals.
Application information: Application form required.
   Additional information: Contact the foundation for application information.
EIN: 581477023

2256

Charles M. Walker Foundation, Inc.

P.O. Box 1764
Monroe, GA 30655 (770) 867-9002
Contact: Richard D. Hester Sr.

Foundation type: Independent foundation
Purpose: Educational loans to full time students of Walton County, GA for continuing education beyond high school.
Financial data: Year ended 12/31/2012. Assets, $2,057,677 (M); Expenditures, $57,807; Total giving, $33,000; Loans to individuals, 34 loans totaling $105,891.
Fields of interest: Higher education.
Type of support: Student loans—to individuals.
Application information: Applications accepted. Application form required.
   Initial approach: Letter
   Deadline(s): June 30
   Additional information: Application should include a transcript and at least four references.
EIN: 586036759

2257

Harold Warren Charitable Trust

969 Coldwater Creek Rd.
Dewy Rose, GA 30634-2509 (706) 376-9773
Contact: Wade A. Gaines, Tr.

Foundation type: Independent foundation
Purpose: Scholarship to a graduating senior of Hart County High School, GA or Barnes Academy, GA in an approved University, College or Technical school of their choice.
Financial data: Year ended 12/31/2012. Assets, $6,378,187 (M); Expenditures, $345,559; Total giving, $232,000; Grants to individuals, 38 grants totaling $38,000 (high: $1,000, low: $1,000).
Fields of interest: Higher education.
Type of support: Scholarships—to individuals; Support to graduates or students of specific schools.
Application information: Applications accepted. Application form required.
   Deadline(s): Mar. 15
   Applicants should submit the following:
      1) GPA

2) Letter(s) of recommendation
Additional information: Awards will be paid directly to the educational institution on behalf of the student.
EIN: 273033642

2258

Watson-Brown Foundation, Inc.

310 Tom Watson Way
Thomson, GA 30824-0037 (706) 595-8886
Contact: Tad Brown, Pres.
Scholarship contact: Sarah Katherine Drury, Dir., Scholarships & Alumni Rels., tel.: (706) 872-6972, e-mail: skdrury@watson-brown.org
FAX: (706) 595-3948;
E-mail: tbrown@watson-brown.org; URL: http://www.watson-brown.org/

Foundation type: Independent foundation
Purpose: Scholarships of $3,000 and $5,000 to residents in and near the Savannah River valley of GA and SC, for undergraduate education.
Publications: Application guidelines; Newsletter.
Financial data: Year ended 12/31/2012. Assets, $108,975,271 (M); Expenditures, $4,835,605; Total giving, $2,490,198.
Fields of interest: College; Economically disadvantaged.
Type of support: Undergraduate support.
Application information: Applications accepted. Application form required. Application form available on the grantmaker's web site.
   Initial approach: Telephone or e-mail
   Send request by: Mail
   Copies of proposal: 1
   Deadline(s): Feb. 15
   Final notification: Applicants notified after Apr. 15
   Applicants should submit the following:
      1) Transcripts
      2) SAT
      3) Letter(s) of recommendation
      4) Financial information
      5) Essay
      6) ACT
   Additional information: Complete application guidelines available on foundation web site.
EIN: 237097393

2259

Shirley and Billy Weir Scholarship Foundation Trust

7804 Eagles Landing Ct.
Columbus, GA 31909-2028 (706) 573-2255
Contact: Mike McCollum, Tr.
E-mail: mmccollum@weir-foundation.org; Additional e-mail: mcgolf@knology.net; URL: http://www.weir-foundation.org/

Foundation type: Independent foundation
Purpose: Scholarship to employees or children of employees of golf course facilities located within the state of Georgia served by golf professionals who are members of the Georgia section of the PGA America.
Publications: Application guidelines.
Financial data: Year ended 12/31/2012. Assets, $1,553,855 (M); Expenditures, $170,456; Total giving, $145,275; Grants to individuals, 10 grants totaling $145,275 (high: $43,856, low: $268).
Fields of interest: Higher education; Athletics/sports, golf.
Type of support: Employee-related scholarships.
Application information: Applications accepted. Application form required. Application form

available on the grantmaker's web site. Interview required.

Send request by: Mail
Deadline(s): Mar. 6
Applicants should submit the following:
1) Financial information
2) Letter(s) of recommendation
3) Essay

Additional information: Applicant must demonstrate financial need and be accepted to an accredited college or university. See web site for additional application guidelines.
EIN: 597257621

2260
WellStar Foundation, Inc.

(formerly Kennestone Regional Foundation, Inc.)
805 Sandy Plains Rd.
Marietta, GA   30066-6340   (770) 956-7827
Contact: Tracey Atwater, Pres.
FAX: (770) 793-7983;
E-mail: wellstar@wellstar.org; E-Mail for Tracey Atwater: tracey.atwater@wellstar.org; URL: http://www.wellstar.org/foundation/pages/default.aspx

Foundation type: Public charity
Purpose: Scholarships to employees, dependents and residents of the Wellstar service area, primarily in GA, for undergraduate education. Preference is given to applicants pursuing a health care related course of study.
Financial data: Year ended 06/30/2012. Assets, $11,830,069 (M); Expenditures, $7,022,554; Total giving, $10,250; Grants to individuals, totaling $10,250.
Fields of interest: Health sciences school/education.
Type of support: Employee-related scholarships; Scholarships—to individuals; Undergraduate support.
Application information: Applications accepted.
Additional information: Contact foundation for current application deadline/guidelines.
EIN: 581627413

2261
West Georgia Health Foundation, Inc.

1514 Vernon Rd.
Lagrange, GA   30240-4131   (706) 845-3029
URL: http://www.wghealth.org/

Foundation type: Public charity
Purpose: Tuition reimbursement to employees of West Georgia Medical Center. Emergency assistance to employees of West Georgia Medical Center.
Financial data: Year ended 09/30/2011. Assets, $5,721,672 (M); Expenditures, $431,742; Total giving, $351,073; Grants to individuals, 33 grants totaling $17,290.
Fields of interest: Education; Human services.
Type of support: Grants for special needs.
Application information: Applications not accepted.
Additional information: Unsolicited requests for funds not considered or acknowledged.
EIN: 200936376

2262
Harold and Sara Wetherbee Foundation

c/o Regions Bank
P.O. Box 8
Albany, GA   31703   (229) 438-2450
Application Address: 333 W. Broad Ave., Albany, GA 31701

Foundation type: Independent foundation
Purpose: Scholarships to graduating seniors of high schools in Dougherty County and Lee County, GA. Scholarships are made on the basis of grades, financial need, and extracurricular activities.
Financial data: Year ended 11/30/2012. Assets, $1,368,223 (M); Expenditures, $92,699; Total giving, $69,610; Grants to individuals, 52 grants totaling $69,610 (high: $1,500, low: $500).
Fields of interest: Education.
Type of support: Support to graduates or students of specific schools.
Application information: Applications accepted. Application form required.
Deadline(s): Apr. 15
EIN: 586068645

2263
Dr. & Mrs. A. J. Whelchel Student Aid

P.O. Box 729
Cordele, GA   31010-0729   (229) 276-3400

Foundation type: Independent foundation
Purpose: Student loans to residents of Cordele, GA, to study at a college or university in GA.
Financial data: Year ended 12/31/2011. Assets, $69,790 (M); Expenditures, $3,411; Total giving, $14,000; Grants to individuals, 7 grants totaling $14,000 (high: $2,000, low: $2,000).
Fields of interest: Higher education.
Type of support: Student loans—to individuals.
Application information: Applications accepted.
Initial approach: Letter
Deadline(s): None
EIN: 586107960

2264
Whitfield Healthcare Foundation, Inc.

1200 Memorial Dr.
Dalton, GA   30720-2529   (706) 272-6128
E-mail: foundation@hhcs.org; Mailing Address: P.O. Box 1168 Dalton, GA 30722-1168; URL: http://www.hamiltonhealth.com/Foundation

Foundation type: Public charity
Purpose: Financial assistance to indigent individuals seeking care at Hamilton Medical Center, Dalton, GA.
Financial data: Year ended 09/30/2011. Assets, $41,819,210 (M); Expenditures, $925,990; Total giving, $317,983; Grants to individuals, totaling $14,983.
Fields of interest: Health care; Economically disadvantaged.
Type of support: Grants for special needs.
Application information: Applications accepted. Application form required.
Additional information: Applicant must be receiving or have received services from Hamilton Medical center, must be declared indigent and/or medically indigent, not qualify for medicare, medicaid or any other method of financial assistance.
EIN: 510175056

2265
Widows Home

P.O. Box 40007
Augusta, GA   30914   (706) 736-6525
Contact: Meinda M. Murphy, Pres.
Application address: 2822 1/2 Lombardy Ct., Augusta, GA 30909 Tel.: (706) 736-6525

Foundation type: Independent foundation
Purpose: Grants to needy women in Richmond and Columbia counties, GA.
Financial data: Year ended 12/31/2012. Assets, $1,063,686 (M); Expenditures, $46,457; Total giving, $37,582.
Fields of interest: Women.
Type of support: Grants for special needs.
Application information: Applications accepted. Application form required.
Deadline(s): Vary
Additional information: Application must include financial information.
EIN: 580593440

2266
Wine & Spirits Wholesalers of Georgia Foundation, Inc.

3525 Piedmont Rd.
2 Piedmont Ctr., Ste. 320
Atlanta, GA   30305-1536   (404) 656-2202

Foundation type: Independent foundation
Purpose: Undergraduate scholarships to GA residents, enrolled full-time in the University of Georgia or the University of Georgia school system.
Financial data: Year ended 12/31/2011. Assets, $803,311 (M); Expenditures, $48,118; Total giving, $36,665; Grants to individuals, 9 grants totaling $31,115 (high: $6,472, low: $1,388).
Fields of interest: Higher education.
Type of support: Support to graduates or students of specific schools; Undergraduate support.
Application information: Applications accepted. Application form required.
Deadline(s): None
Additional information: Application form can be obtained from the director or student financial aid of the school.
EIN: 586047788

2267
WinShape Foundation, Inc.

(formerly WinShape Centre, Inc.)
5200 Buffington Rd.
Atlanta, GA   30349-2998
Scholarship application address: c/o Berry College, P.O. Box 490159, Mt. Berry, GA 30149-0009, tel.: (706) 236-2215,
e-mail: admissions@berry.edu, collegeprogram@winshape.org
FAX: (706) 238-7742;
E-mail: rskelton@winshape.org; Additional address: P.O. Box 490009, Mt. Berry, GA 30149-0009, tel.: (877) 977-3873, e-mail: info@winshape.org;
URL: http://www.winshape.org

Foundation type: Operating foundation
Purpose: Scholarships to eligible students for attendance at Berry College in Mount Berry, GA.
Publications: Application guidelines; Informational brochure (including application guidelines).
Financial data: Year ended 12/31/2012. Assets, $71,523,969 (M); Expenditures, $26,372,699; Total giving, $569,547. Scholarships—to individuals amount not specified.
Fields of interest: Higher education.

Type of support: Support to graduates or students of specific schools; Undergraduate support.
Application information: Applications accepted. Application form required. Application form available on the grantmaker's web site. Interview required.

Initial approach: Application
Send request by: Online
Deadline(s): Feb. 1
Final notification: Applicants notified Apr. 15
Applicants should submit the following:
1) Resume
2) Essay
3) Letter(s) of recommendation

Additional information: Applicants must apply to the WinShape College Program and to Berry College. See web site for additional guidelines.
EIN: 581595471

2268
Wood Acres Educational Foundation, Inc.
1149 Woodlawn Dr.
Marietta, GA   30068-2757

Foundation type: Independent foundation

Purpose: Scholarships to students at Wood Acres Day School, GA.
Financial data: Year ended 12/31/2011. Assets, $15,577 (M); Expenditures, $10,980; Total giving, $10,900; Grants to individuals, 8 grants totaling $10,900 (high: $2,100, low: $500).
Type of support: Support to graduates or students of specific schools.
Application information: Applications not accepted.

Additional information: Unsolicited requests for funds not considered or acknowledged.
EIN: 593767075

HAWAII

2269
Aiea General Hospital Association Scholarship Fund
P.O. Box 3170, Dept. 715
Honolulu, HI 96802-3170   (808) 566-5570

Foundation type: Independent foundation
Purpose: Scholarships to individuals who reside within one of the following Leeward O'ahu, HI, zip codes: 96701, 96706, 96707, 96782, 96792, or 96797, and pursuing a major in a health-related field.
Financial data: Year ended 03/31/2013. Assets, $387,704 (M); Expenditures, $19,251; Total giving, $7,500; Grants to individuals, totaling $7,500.
Fields of interest: Health sciences school/education.
Type of support: Scholarships—to individuals.
Application information: Application form required.
  Initial approach: Letter or telephone
  Deadline(s): Mar. 1
  Applicants should submit the following:
    1) FAFSA
    2) Letter(s) of recommendation
    3) Essay
    4) Transcripts
    5) SAR
EIN: 990241566

2270
Crown Prince Akihito Scholarship Foundation
P. O. Box 1412
Honolulu, HI 96806-1412   (808) 524-4450
FAX: (808) 524-4451;
E-mail: ehawkins@jashawaii.org; URL: http://www.jashawaii.org/cpas.asp

Foundation type: Public charity
Purpose: Scholarships offered to American students for study in Japan and for Japanese students for study in Hawaii to promote understanding between the U.S. and Japan.
Publications: Application guidelines.
Financial data: Year ended 12/31/2011. Assets, $2,535,430 (M); Expenditures, $275,558; Total giving, $110,664; Grants to individuals, totaling $65,664.
Fields of interest: Higher education.
Type of support: Scholarships—to individuals; Exchange programs.
Application information: Applications accepted. Application form required. Application form available on the grantmaker's web site. Interview required.
  Send request by: Mail
  Deadline(s): Nov.
  Applicants should submit the following:
    1) Letter(s) of recommendation
    2) GPA
Program description:
  Scholarships: This scholarship is awarded to graduates students in Japan for study at the University of Hawaii at Manoa, and American graduate students at the University of Hawaii at Manor for study in Japan who are pursuing a subject area lending to better understanding between Japan and the U.S. American students are eligible for a $30,000 scholarship and $15,000 annual allowance. Japanese students are eligible for a full

tuition scholarship plus $25,000 per year and up to $1,500 for one-time round-trip economy class airfare from Japan to Honolulu. Additional CPASF scholarships provide two $25,000 scholarships and additional $20,000 grants for living expenses from the Shidler School of Business.
EIN: 990261751

2271
Atherton Family Foundation
c/o Hawaii Community Foundation
827 Fort Street Mall
Honolulu, HI 96813-4317   (808) 537-6333
Contact: Amy Luersen, Dir., Philanthropic Svcs., HCF
FAX: (808) 521-6286;
E-mail: foundations@hcf-hawaii.org; Additional tel.: (888) 731-3863 (Hawaii and neighbor islands only); URL: http://www.athertonfamilyfoundation.org

Foundation type: Independent foundation
Purpose: Scholarships to HI residents who are children of Protestant ministers, graduate theological students at a Protestant seminary, or ministers seeking further education.
Publications: Annual report; Financial statement; Grants list.
Financial data: Year ended 12/31/2012. Assets, $92,259,292 (M); Expenditures, $5,061,604; Total giving, $4,069,046; Grants to individuals, 27 grants totaling $129,300 (high: $6,500; low: $500).
Fields of interest: Theological school/education; Christian agencies & churches; Protestant agencies & churches.
Type of support: Graduate support; Postgraduate support.
Application information: Applications accepted. Application form required. Application form available on the grantmaker's web site.
  Send request by: Online only
  Copies of proposal: 1
  Deadline(s): Mar. 1
  Applicants should submit the following:
    1) SAR
    2) Letter(s) of recommendation
    3) Transcripts
    4) Essay
  Additional information: See program description for further information.
Program description:
  Juliette M. Atherton Scholarship Program: The scholarship was named in memory of Mrs. Atherton to ensure the continued association of her name and her special interest in Christianity with the foundation. The scholarship benefits three categories of individuals: 1) active, ordained Protestant ministers residing in Hawaii wishing to continue their education; 2) dependent sons or daughters of ordained, active Protestant ministers in Hawaii pursuing undergraduate studies; and 3) individuals from Hawaii pursuing graduate theological studies at a Protestant seminary with the goal of ordination. Scholarship recipients are selected based on their financial need and academic promise. For sons and daughters of Protestant ministers and seminary students, applications will be available beginning Nov. Application materials, including the application form, transcript of grades, and personal letter must be postmarked on or before Mar. 1. Ordained Protestant ministers wishing to continue their education should contact scholarship staff for application information. Sons or daughters of ministers and ministers applying for continuing education grants must provide the place and date

of ordination, and name of the seminary attended to confirm eligibility.
EIN: 510175971

2272
Bank of Hawaii Foundation
(formerly Bancorp Hawaii Charitable Foundation)
Foundation Admin. No. 758
P.O. Box 3170
Honolulu, HI 96802-3170   (808) 538-4944
Contact: Elaine Moniz, Trust Specialist
FAX: (808) 538-4006; E-mail: emoniz@boh.com; Additional contacts: Flora Williams, Asst. V.P., tel.: (808) 694-4393, e-mail: flora.williams@boh.com; Paula Boyce, Grants Admin., tel.: (808) 538-4945, e-mail: pboyce@boh.com; URL: https://www.boh.com/customer-service/689.asp

Foundation type: Company-sponsored foundation
Purpose: Scholarships to students at Chaminade University, HI.
Publications: Application guidelines; Informational brochure.
Financial data: Year ended 12/31/2012. Assets, $10,102,843 (M); Expenditures, $1,706,485; Total giving, $1,549,259.
Type of support: Undergraduate support.
Application information: Applications not accepted.
  Additional information: Unsolicited requests for funds not considered or acknowledged.
EIN: 990210467

2273
Harriet Bouslog Labor Scholarship Fund
63 Merchant St.
Honolulu, HI 96813   (808) 537-3327
Contact: Mark Bernstein, Pres.

Foundation type: Independent foundation
Purpose: Scholarships to residents of HI. Preference is given to applicants whose parents are members of labor organizations.
Financial data: Year ended 11/30/2012. Assets, $384,920 (M); Expenditures, $147,496; Total giving, $127,500; Grants to individuals, 79 grants totaling $127,500 (high: $2,000; low: $750).
Fields of interest: Labor unions/organizations.
Type of support: Scholarships—to individuals.
Application information: Applications accepted.
  Deadline(s): None
  Final notification: Applicants notified within three months
  Additional information: Applications must include a brief resume of academic qualifications.
EIN: 990268061

2274
Center for Cultural and Technical Interchange Between East and West, Inc.
(also known as East-West Center)
1601 East-West Rd.
Honolulu, HI 96848-1601   (808) 944-7111
FAX: (808) 944-7376; URL: http://www.eastwestcenter.org

Foundation type: Public charity
Purpose: Scholarships and fellowships to individuals in the United States and Asia Pacific.
Publications: Annual report.
Financial data: Year ended 09/30/2011. Assets, $36,282,269 (M); Expenditures, $34,292,447;

Total giving, $5,494,803; Grants to individuals, totaling $5,334,703.
Fields of interest: Education.
Type of support: Fellowships; Scholarships—to individuals; Graduate support.
Application information:
Deadline(s): Varies
Additional information: Benefits to the individual is continued based on satisfactory performance.
EIN: 990161603

2275
Hung Wo & Elizabeth Lau Ching Foundation
841 Bishop St., Ste. 940
Honolulu, HI 96813-3910 (808) 521-4961
Contact: Han Hsin Ching, V.P.; Han P. Ching, V.P.

Foundation type: Independent foundation
Purpose: Academic achievement awards to students attending Molokai High School, HI.
Financial data: Year ended 01/31/2013. Assets, $5,642,679 (M); Expenditures, $462,545; Total giving, $379,900; Grants to individuals, 12 grants totaling $15,000 (high: $2,500, low: $625).
Fields of interest: Education.
Type of support: Support to graduates or students of specific schools.
Application information: Applications accepted.
Initial approach: Letter
Additional information: Contact the foundation for additional guidelines.
EIN: 996008990

2276
Chung Kun Ai Foundation
c/o City Mill Co., Ltd.
P.O. Box 1559
Honolulu, HI 96806-1559 (808) 533-3811

Foundation type: Independent foundation
Purpose: Scholarships to financially needy HI residents who have at least a 2.8 GPA.
Financial data: Year ended 12/31/2011. Assets, $1,796,631 (M); Expenditures, $102,573; Total giving, $85,650.
Type of support: Scholarships—to individuals.
Application information: Applications accepted. Application form required. Interview required.
Deadline(s): None
Applicants should submit the following:
1) Financial information
2) Letter(s) of recommendation
3) Photograph
4) Transcripts
Additional information: Application should also include a personal letter stating reasons for desiring a scholarship, academic interests and vocational plans, and participation in student activities or community services.
EIN: 996003289

2277
Community Assistance Center
(formerly John Howard Association)
200 N. Vineyard Blvd., Ste. 330
Honolulu, HI 96817-3938 (808) 537-2917
Contact: Gerald Reardon, Exec. Dir.
E-mail: jha@hula.net; URL: http://www.cachawaii.org

Foundation type: Public charity
Purpose: Assistance offered in Hawaii to offenders, ex-offenders, crime-prone adults, drug- and

alcohol-abusing youth and their families, with counseling, job placement assistance, housing assistance, education and advocacy within the criminal justice system.
Financial data: Year ended 12/31/2011. Assets, $347,049 (M); Expenditures, $763,112.
Fields of interest: Offenders/ex-offenders, transitional care; Offenders/ex-offenders, rehabilitation.
Application information: Applications not accepted.
EIN: 990093057

2278
Cottington Trust for Gifted Children
P.O. Box 3170, Dept. 715
Honolulu, HI 96802-3170
URL: http://www.boh.com/philanthropy

Foundation type: Independent foundation
Purpose: Scholarships to intellectually gifted children ages 2 to 18 of HI who demonstrate intellectual giftedness by scoring at or above the 98th percentile on a standard IQ test.
Financial data: Year ended 12/31/2012. Assets, $792,216 (M); Expenditures, $46,628; Total giving, $33,500.
Fields of interest: Education, gifted students.
Type of support: Undergraduate support.
Application information: Application form required.
Initial approach: Letter
Additional information: Applicant must demonstrate financial need and be a resident of Hawaii.
EIN: 996044219

2279
Council for Native Hawaiian Advancement
1050 Queen St., Ste. 200
Honolulu, HI 96814-4130 (808) 596-8155
FAX: (808) 596-8156;
E-mail: info@hawaiiancouncil.org; Toll-free tel./fax: (800) 709-2642; URL: http://www.hawaiiancouncil.org

Foundation type: Public charity
Purpose: Financial assistance and down payment assistance to indigent native Hawaiian residents.
Publications: Application guidelines.
Financial data: Year ended 09/30/2011. Assets, $4,843,233 (M); Expenditures, $2,807,365; Total giving, $530,237; Grants to individuals, totaling $530,237.
Fields of interest: Economically disadvantaged.
Type of support: Grants for special needs.
Application information: Contact the council for eligibility requirements.
EIN: 910313383

2280
Diamond Resort Scholarships
2200 Main St., Ste. 400
Wailuku, HI 96793-1691 (808) 242-4535
Contact: B. Martin Luna, Tr.

Foundation type: Company-sponsored foundation
Purpose: Scholarships to graduating seniors of public high schools in Maui County, HI.
Financial data: Year ended 12/31/2012. Assets, $62,439 (M); Expenditures, $9,278; Total giving, $7,000; Grants to individuals, 7 grants totaling $7,000 (high: $1,000, low: $1,000).
Fields of interest: Higher education.
Type of support: Undergraduate support.

Application information: Applications accepted. Application form required.
Initial approach: Letter
Deadline(s): Mar. 1
Final notification: Applicants notified by May 1
Applicants should submit the following:
1) Transcripts
2) SAT
3) Letter(s) of recommendation
Additional information: Application should also include academic achievements, extracurricular, civic and community activities, and honors awards.
EIN: 996055912

2281
Easter Seals Hawaii
710 Green St.
Honolulu, HI 96813-2119 (808) 536-1015
Contact: Christopher E. Blanchard, Pres. and C.E.O.
FAX: (808) 536-3765; Toll-free tel. (neighboring islands only): (888) 241-7450; E-mail For Christopher E. Blanchard: CBlanchard@eastersealshawaii.org; URL: http://hawaii.easterseals.com

Foundation type: Public charity
Purpose: Services provided to children and adults with disabilities and special needs. Support is also available for their families.
Financial data: Year ended 08/31/2012. Assets, $29,052,674 (M); Expenditures, $16,711,009; Total giving, $79,087; Grants to individuals, totaling $79,087.
Fields of interest: Developmentally disabled, centers & services; Disabilities, people with.
Type of support: Grants for special needs.
Application information: Applications not accepted.
EIN: 990075235

2282
Family Programs Hawaii
(formerly Friends of Foster Kids, Inc., also known as Foster Family Programs of Hawaii)
250 Vineyard St.
Honolulu, HI 96813-2445 (808) 521-9531
Contact: Linda Santos LSW, ACSW, Pres. and C.E.O.
FAX: (808) 533-1018; URL: http://familyprogramshawaii.org/

Foundation type: Public charity
Purpose: Provides services to children and families involved in the child welfare system in Hawaii. Children who need funding may be brought to the program's attention by a social worker.
Financial data: Year ended 12/31/2012. Assets, $1,881,022 (M); Expenditures, $3,743,955; Total giving, $453,890; Grants to individuals, totaling $453,890.
Fields of interest: Human services.
Type of support: Emergency funds.
Application information: Applications accepted. Application form not required.
Program descriptions:
Geist Foundation Funds: Funds of up to $500 per child per year are available to foster parents of foster children who have been abused or neglected. Eligible expenses include extracurricular school expenses (athletic uniforms, field trip fees), social activity expenses (prom attire, graduation cap and gown), after-school activities (summer camp), other quality-of-life enhancements (birthday presents, books, toys), and facilitation of transition into adulthood (copy of birth certificate, driver's education). Recipients must be legally-recognized

foster children under the age of 18 who reside in Hawaii and who are not reunited with their birth parents. Applications are completed by the family's social worker.

Hughes Trust Funds: Funds of up to $500 per child per year are available to foster parents of foster children for: emergency clothing, food, and medicine; child's portion of a furniture purchase; portion of rent and/or deposit of one month's utilities; portion of the cost for summer and after-school programs; portion of school fees, tutoring, preschool, or child care; portion of transportation costs; portion of costs related to youth counseling/therapy; or portion of the cost of diapers, toys, dental, hula, car seat, etc. Recipients must be residents of Hawaii under 18 years of age who are in need of financial assistance and must have been abandoned, neglected, or abused, including children in whose households abuse has occurred. Applications are completed by the family's social worker.
EIN: 990280498

2283
Fukunaga Scholarship Foundation
2850 Pukoloa St., Ste. 300
Honolulu, HI 96819-4475   (808) 564-1386
FAX: (808) 523-3937; E-mail: sandyw@servco.com

Foundation type: Independent foundation
Purpose: Scholarships to residents of HI enrolled in a business-related course of study at any accredited four-year college or university who show a desire to return to HI or the Pacific Islands region and contribute to their growth and welfare.
Publications: Application guidelines.
Financial data: Year ended 12/31/2012. Assets, $3,611,035 (M); Expenditures, $193,762; Total giving, $160,499; Grants to individuals, 45 grants totaling $160,499 (high: $5,333, low: $500).
Fields of interest: Business school/education.
Type of support: Undergraduate support.
Application information: Application form required. Interview required.
  Initial approach: Telephone or e-mail
  Send request by: Mail
  Deadline(s): Mar. 1
  Final notification: Scholarship awardees are informed before the end of Apr.
  Applicants should submit the following:
    1) FAFSA
    2) Letter(s) of recommendation
    3) SAT
    4) Transcripts
EIN: 990600370

2284
Gear Up Hawaii Scholarship Trust
P.O. Box 3170, Dept. 715
Honolulu, HI 96802-3170

Foundation type: Independent foundation
Purpose: Scholarships to high school graduates of HI, pursuing a higher education.
Financial data: Year ended 06/30/2012. Assets, $1,344,878 (M); Expenditures, $448,093; Total giving, $371,850; Grants to individuals, 65 grants totaling $371,850 (high: $5,550, low: $2,775).
Fields of interest: Higher education.
Type of support: Scholarships—to individuals.
Application information: Applications accepted.
  Send request by: On-line
  Deadline(s): Feb.
  Applicants should submit the following:
    1) SAR
    2) Transcripts

3) Letter(s) of recommendation
4) Essay
Additional information: Applicant must demonstrate need, academic achievement, and exhibit good moral character.
Program description:
Scholarships: The scholarship program consists of over 160 different scholarship funds established by generous individuals, families, businesses or organizations to assist Hawaii's residents in obtaining a college education. Each scholarship fund has specific eligibility criteria defined by the donor who created the fund. Scholarships are available in many categories, such as area of study, island of residency, high school attended, religious affiliation, and membership in a specific organization.
EIN: 266026352

2285
Victoria S. & Bradley L. Geist Foundation
c/o Hawaii Community Foundation
827 Fort Street Mall
Honolulu, HI 96813-4317   (808) 537-6333
Contact: Amy Luersen, Dir. of Philanthropic Svcs., Hawaii Community Foundation
E-mail: foundations@hcf-hawaii.org; URL: http://www.hawaiicommunityfoundation.org

Foundation type: Independent foundation
Purpose: Scholarships to students of Hawaii who are currently or formerly in the foster care system, pursuing higher education.
Publications: Application guidelines.
Financial data: Year ended 12/31/2012. Assets, $39,611,412 (M); Expenditures, $2,471,557; Total giving, $1,939,363; Grants to individuals, 125 grants totaling $328,000 (high: $8,000, low: $500).
Fields of interest: Vocational education, post-secondary; Higher education; Foster care.
Type of support: Scholarships—to individuals.
Application information: Applications accepted. Application form available on the grantmaker's web site.
  Send request by: On-line
  Copies of proposal: 1
  Deadline(s): Sept.
  Additional information: Applicant must be currently or formerly placed in the foster care system in the State of Hawaii, submit a confirmation letter from DHS or Foster Family Program case worker to verify foster status. See web site for additional guidelines.
EIN: 990163400

2286
Grove Farm Foundation
3-1850 Kaumuali Hwy.
Lihue, HI 96766-7069
URL: http://www.grovefarm.com/giving

Foundation type: Company-sponsored foundation
Purpose: Scholarships to students of Kauai high schools pursuing higher education at a four-year university or college.
Financial data: Year ended 12/31/2012. Assets, $2,273,321 (M); Expenditures, $106,448; Total giving, $105,680.
Fields of interest: Higher education.
Type of support: Scholarships—to individuals; Support to graduates or students of specific schools.
Application information: Applications accepted. Application form required. Application form

available on the grantmaker's web site. Interview required.
  Initial approach: Application
  Deadline(s): Mar. 1
  Applicants should submit the following:
    1) Transcripts
    2) Letter(s) of recommendation
    3) SAT
    4) ACT
    5) GPA
  Additional information: Application should also include a copy of acceptance letter from college or university, brief statement of educational objectives, career goals, past and current extracurricular activities, and how this scholarship will help applicant reach goals. Students should contact their high school guidance counselors for additional information.
Program description:
Grove Farm Scholarship Program: Merit-based scholarships to Kauai high school students to pursue higher education. Recipients are selected based on community service, citizenship, academic accomplishments, and quality of character. Scholarships of up to $20,000 are awarded and is limited to students from Kapaa High School, Kauai High School, and Waimea High School. Applicant must be a Hawaii state resident.
EIN: 990297416

2287
Hana Maui Trust
P.O. Box 646
Hana, HI 96713

Foundation type: Community foundation
Purpose: Scholarship to a graduating student of Hana High School, HI for higher education. Grants to residents of the Hana, HI, community who have special needs.
Financial data: Year ended 12/31/2012. Assets, $797,543 (M); Expenditures, $31,864; Total giving, $19,214; Grants to individuals, totaling $19,214.
Fields of interest: Higher education; Human services.
Type of support: Scholarships—to individuals; Support to graduates or students of specific schools; Grants for special needs.
Application information: Applications accepted.
  Additional information: Scholarships and grants are based on academic achievement and community service and/or need.
EIN: 996011303

2288
Hawaii Children's Cancer Foundation
1814 Liliha St.
Honolulu, HI 96817-2324   (808) 528-5161
Contact: Tara Humphreys, Admin. Mgr.
FAX: (808) 521-4689; E-mail: info@hccf.org;
URL: http://www.hccf.org

Foundation type: Public charity
Purpose: Provides services and programs to children with cancer and their families, including financial assistance, support groups, social events, education, and advocacy.
Publications: Annual report.
Financial data: Year ended 06/30/2012. Assets, $564,098 (M); Expenditures, $370,543; Total giving, $315,611; Grants to individuals, totaling $315,611.
Fields of interest: Cancer; Children, services; Family services.

Type of support: Grants to individuals.
Application information: Applications not accepted.
EIN: 990299937

2289
Hawaii Community Foundation
(formerly The Hawaiian Foundation)
827 Fort St. Mall
Honolulu, HI 96813   (808) 537-6333
Contact: Kelvin H. Taketa, C.E.O.
Scholarship inquiry e-mail:
scholarships@hcf-hawaii.org
FAX: (808) 521-6286; E-mail: info@hcf-hawaii.org;
Additional tel.: (888) 731-3863; URL: http://
www.hawaiicommunityfoundation.org

Foundation type: Community foundation
Purpose: Scholarships to residents of HI who plan to attend an accredited two- or four-year college or university as an undergraduate or graduate student. Grants also to economically disadvantaged senior citizens living in HI.
Publications: Application guidelines; Annual report; Financial statement; Informational brochure; Newsletter; Program policy statement.
Financial data: Year ended 12/31/2011. Assets, $409,290,708 (M); Expenditures, $36,182,273; Total giving, $28,285,200; Grants to individuals, 795 grants totaling $1,377,287.
Fields of interest: Higher education; Aging; Economically disadvantaged.
Type of support: Scholarships—to individuals; Support to graduates or students of specific schools; Undergraduate support; Grants for special needs.
Application information: Applications accepted. Application form required. Application form available on the grantmaker's web site.
Initial approach: Application
Send request by: Online for scholarships
Deadline(s): Feb. 20 for Scholarships
Applicants should submit the following:
1) FAFSA
2) Transcripts
3) SAR
4) Letter(s) of recommendation
5) Essay
Additional information: See web site for complete listing of scholarships and online application form.
Program description:
Scholarship Funds: The foundation's scholarship program consists of more than 85 different funds for higher education. Each fund has specific eligibility criteria defined by the donor. The following criteria apply to the majority of scholarships: 1) be a resident of the state of Hawaii; 2) demonstrate financial need; 3) plan to attend an accredited two or four year institute of higher learning as either undergraduate or graduate student; 4) be a full-time student; 5) demonstrate academic achievement; and 6) demonstrate good moral character. If an applicant does not meet one or some of the criteria above, they may still qualify for one or more of the scholarships. See web site for additional information.
EIN: 990261283

2290
Hawaii Council for the Humanities
(formerly Hawaii Committee for the Humanities)
1st Hawaiian Bank Bldg.
3599 Wai'alae Ave., Rm. 25
Honolulu, HI 96816-2759   (808) 732-5402
FAX: (808) 732-5432;
E-mail: info@hihumanities.org; E-mail for Robert G. Buss: rbuss@hihumanities.org; URL: http://
www.hihumanities.org

Foundation type: Public charity
Purpose: Grants to Hawaiian scholars to conduct research in the humanities, and for publication of humanities research.
Publications: Application guidelines; Annual report; Informational brochure; Newsletter.
Financial data: Year ended 10/31/2011. Assets, $185,787 (M); Expenditures, $766,934; Total giving, $190,275.
Fields of interest: Humanities.
Type of support: Research.
Application information: Application form required. Application form available on the grantmaker's web site.
Initial approach: Letter, telephone or e-mail
Copies of proposal: 10
Deadline(s): Feb. 17, June 15, and Sept. 15
Applicants should submit the following:
1) Resume
2) Proposal
3) Budget Information
Additional information: See web site for additional application information and programs.
EIN: 990153704

2291
Hawaii Hotel Industry Foundation
2270 Kalakaua Ave., Ste. 1506
Honolulu, HI 96815-2519   (808) 923-0407

Foundation type: Public charity
Purpose: Scholarships to graduating high school seniors of Hawaii, pursuing a career in hotel management and hospitality related fields.
Financial data: Year ended 12/31/2011. Assets, $650,627 (M); Expenditures, $993,403; Total giving, $948,431; Grants to individuals, totaling $50,500.
Fields of interest: Business school/education; Asians/Pacific Islanders.
Type of support: Scholarships—to individuals.
Application information: Applications accepted. Application form required.
Additional information: Contact the foundation for application guidelines.
Program description:
Scholarships: Five scholarships in the amount of $1,000 is awarded to each student per year for up to four years. Applicant must be of native Hawaiian ancestry.
EIN: 990194293

2292
Helping Hands Hawaii
2100 N. Nimitz Hwy.
Honolulu, HI 96819-2218   (808) 536-7234
Contact: Jan Harada, Pres. and C.E.O.
FAX: (808) 536-7237;
E-mail: hhh@helpinghandshawaii.org; URL: http://
www.helpinghandshawaii.org

Foundation type: Public charity
Purpose: Limited financial assistance is provided to people in need who experience one-time, short-term

or long-term emergencies or hardships. The program is limited to residents of Hawaii.
Publications: Annual report.
Financial data: Year ended 12/31/2011. Assets, $5,876,148 (M); Expenditures, $3,663,945; Total giving, $190,751; Grants to individuals, totaling $190,751.
Fields of interest: Human services, emergency aid; Human services.
Type of support: Grants for special needs.
Application information: Applications not accepted.
EIN: 237365077

2293
Charles R. Hemenway Scholarship Trust
c/o Bank of Hawaii
P.O. Box 3170, Dept. 715
Honolulu, HI 96802-3170   (808) 694-4393
Application address: c/o Univ. of Hawaii, Financial Aid Office, 2442 Campus Rd., Honolulu, HI 96822, tel.: (808) 956-7251

Foundation type: Public charity
Purpose: Undergraduate scholarships to residents of HI attending the University of Hawaii, or Hawaii community colleges, who are committed to HI and its people.
Financial data: Year ended 06/30/2012. Assets, $4,260,631 (M); Expenditures, $254,177; Total giving, $190,000.
Fields of interest: Higher education.
Type of support: Support to graduates or students of specific schools; Undergraduate support.
Application information: Applications accepted. Application form required. Interview required.
Deadline(s): Apr. 15
Additional information: Applications available from the financial aid offices of the Manoa and Hilo campuses of the University of Hawaii. Applicant must demonstrate financial need.
Program description:
Scholarships: Scholarships are awarded to aid undergraduate students at the University of Hawaii in pursuing their studies as approved by the Charles R. Hemenway Scholarship committee.
EIN: 996003089

2294
Richard and Eleanor Imai Shin Buddhist Scholarship Charitable Foundation
P.O. Box 3170, Dept. 715
Honolulu, HI 96802-3170

Foundation type: Independent foundation
Purpose: Scholarships to deserving high school seniors who are residents of Hawaii in pursuit of higher education at any accredited college, university, or vocational/techincal post-secondary school in the U.S. or its possessions.
Financial data: Year ended 12/31/2012. Assets, $143,281 (M); Expenditures, $8,657; Total giving, $5,000.
Application information: Applications accepted. Application form required.
Deadline(s): Apr. 2
Final notification: May
Applicants should submit the following:
1) Transcripts
2) Photograph
3) Class rank
4) GPA
5) Essay
Additional information: Application must also include involvement in school and community

activities, and awards and distinctions during high school years.
EIN: 996082996

2295
David S. Ishii Foundation
P.O. Box 2927
Aiea, HI   96701-2225   (808) 941-4488
Contact: David Ishii, Pres.
Scholarship contact: Dayton Asato,
d810@yahoo.com
E-mail: info@davidsishiifoundation.org;
URL: http://davidsishiifoundation.org/

Foundation type: Public charity
Purpose: Scholarships for graduating high school students of Hawaii for attendance at an accredited college in the U.S. with the intent to further their golf careers.
Financial data: Year ended 12/31/2012. Assets, $427,857 (M); Expenditures, $32,857; Total giving, $19,000; Grants to individuals, totaling $9,000.
Fields of interest: Higher education; Athletics/ sports, golf.
Type of support: Scholarships—to individuals.
Application information: Applications accepted. Application form required. Application form available on the grantmaker's web site.
> *Send request by:* Mail
> *Deadline(s):* Apr. 30
> *Applicants should submit the following:*
> 1) SAT
> 2) Letter(s) of recommendation
> 3) Transcripts
> 4) Essay
Program description:
> *David S. Ishii Foundation/Yasuko Asada Memorial College Scholarship Fund:* Two grants of $4,000 each awarded to one male student and one female student who are members of high school golf teams throughout Hawaii, and who have demonstrated a high level of academic achievement, and plan on attending college full-time at an accredited U.S. college or university. Applicant must maintain a 2.0 GPA.
EIN: 990345364

2296
Kaiulani Home for Girls Trust
P.O. Box 3170, Dept. 715
Honolulu, HI   96802-3170

Foundation type: Independent foundation
Purpose: Undergraduate and graduate scholarships to financially needy females who are legal residents of HI, with preference given to those of Hawaiian or part Hawaiian ancestry, to attend colleges and universities in the U.S.
Publications: Informational brochure (including application guidelines).
Financial data: Year ended 03/31/2013. Assets, $2,460,395 (M); Expenditures, $173,851; Total giving, $104,250; Grants to individuals, 142 grants totaling $104,250 (high: $1,500, low: $275).
Fields of interest: Higher education; Women.
Type of support: Graduate support; Undergraduate support.
Application information: Application form required. Application form available on the grantmaker's web site.
> *Deadline(s):* Mar. 1
> *Applicants should submit the following:*
> 1) Transcripts
> 2) SAR
> 3) Letter(s) of recommendation

Additional information: Application should also include a personal statement.
EIN: 996003331

2297
Kaneta Foundation
(formerly Kaneta Charitable Foundation)
827 Fort Street Mall
Honolulu, HI   96813-4317   (808) 566-5550
Contact: Lester Kaneta, Pres.; Amy Luersen, Dir. Phil. Svcs.
FAX: (808) 521-6286;
E-mail: info@kanetafoundation.org; *URL:* http:// kanetafoundation.org

Foundation type: Independent foundation
Purpose: Scholarships to graduating Christian high school seniors of HI.
Financial data: Year ended 12/31/2012. Assets, $3,772,109 (M); Expenditures, $387,715; Total giving, $310,127; Grants to individuals, totaling $181,500.
Fields of interest: Higher education.
Type of support: Scholarships—to individuals.
Application information: Applications accepted. Application form required. Application form available on the grantmaker's web site.
> *Initial approach:* Telephone or e-mail
> *Send request by:* On-line
> *Copies of proposal:* 1
> *Deadline(s):* Feb. 22
> *Applicants should submit the following:*
> 1) Financial information
> 2) GPA
> 3) SAT
> 4) ACT
> 5) Letter(s) of recommendation
> *Additional information:* See foundation web site for detailed program information.
Program description:
> *Scholarship Program:* Scholarships to graduating Christian high school seniors throughout HI. Applicants are evaluated according to character, financial need, academic achievement, and past community involvement. Applicants may re-apply each year as long as they maintain a 3.0 GPA. Scholarship amounts vary from $3,000 each year for four year programs, and $1,500 each year for two year programs. Vocational scholarships of $1,000 are also provided.
EIN: 311655882

2298
The Betty C. Kanuha Foundation
(formerly Betty C. Kanuha and Stella Kaipo Fern Foundation)
76-6242 Plumeria Rd.
Kailua-Kona, HI   96740-2253

Foundation type: Independent foundation
Purpose: Scholarships to graduating high school seniors from HI.
Financial data: Year ended 12/31/2012. Assets, $194,627 (M); Expenditures, $29,836; Total giving, $10,361.
Type of support: Undergraduate support.
Application information: Contact foundation for current application deadline/guidelines.
EIN: 990353703

2299
The Kokua Foundation
P.O. Box 4038
Honolulu, HI   96812-4038

Foundation type: Independent foundation
Purpose: Scholarship awards to students of Punahou School, Honolulu, HI.
Financial data: Year ended 12/31/2012. Assets, $121,344 (M); Expenditures, $38,674; Total giving, $36,380; Grants to individuals, 12 grants totaling $36,380 (high: $5,200, low: $600).
Fields of interest: Higher education.
Type of support: Scholarships—to individuals.
Application information: Applications not accepted.
> *Additional information:* Unsolicited requests for funds not accepted.
EIN: 900079969

2300
Learning Disabilities Association of Hawaii
245 N. Kukui St., Ste. 205
Honolulu, HI   96817-3921   (808) 536-9684
Contact: Michael K. Moore, Exec. Dir.
FAX: (808) 537-6780; *E-mail:* ldah@ldahawaii.org;
Toll-free tel. (for HI only): (800)-533-9684; *E-mail* For Michael K. Moore: MMoore@LDAHawaii.org;
URL: http://www.ldahawaii.org

Foundation type: Public charity
Purpose: Financial assistance for children 17 years or younger of HI, with a serious medical condition or special education need.
Publications: Application guidelines.
Financial data: Year ended 12/31/2011. Assets, $557,558 (M); Expenditures, $859,361; Total giving, $8,950; Grants to individuals, totaling $8,950.
Fields of interest: Children; Youth; Disabilities, people with.
Type of support: Grants for special needs.
Application information: Applications accepted. Application form required.
> *Deadline(s):* None
> *Additional information:* Applicants should provide financial information. Payments are made directly to the vendor on behalf of the clients. No payments are made directly to individuals. Preference is given to families with longstanding residence in HI.
EIN: 990119223

2301
Life Foundation
677 Ala Moana Blvd., Ste. 226
Honolulu, HI   96813-5416   (808) 521-2437
FAX: (808) 521-1279;
E-mail: mail@lifefoundation.org; *URL:* http:// www.lifefoundation.org

Foundation type: Public charity
Purpose: Medical assistance and living expenses to clients of HI, living with HIV and AIDS.
Publications: Annual report; Informational brochure; Newsletter.
Financial data: Year ended 06/30/2012. Assets, $656,398 (M); Expenditures, $2,528,564; Total giving, $119,896; Grants to individuals, totaling $119,896.
Fields of interest: AIDS, people with.
Type of support: Grants for special needs.
Application information: Applications accepted.
> *Additional information:* Applications are reviewed for eligibility including medical reports, personal financial statement and income levels and is evaluated by a case by case basis. Majority of direct assistance is paid directly to the vendors (such as utility companies, medical and dental clinics and

bus vouchers), on behalf of the clients, Contact the foundation for eligibiity determination.
EIN: 990230542

2302
Make-A-Wish Hawaii, Inc.
P.O. Box 1877
Honolulu, HI   96805-1877   (808) 537-3118
Contact: Siana Hunt, Pres. and C.E.O.
FAX: (808) 536-5566;
E-mail: info@makeawishhawaii.org; URL: http://www.makeawishhawaii.org

Foundation type: Public charity
Purpose: Fulfilling wishes of terminally-ill children in HI who have reached the age of two and one half and are under the age of 18 who have a life-threatening medical condition.
Publications: Annual report; Financial statement.
Financial data: Year ended 08/31/2011. Assets, $2,526,013 (M); Expenditures, $844,985; Total giving, $361,435; Grants to individuals, totaling $361,435.
Fields of interest: Children; Young adults; Terminal illness, people with.
Type of support: Grants to individuals.
Application information: The physician will make the final determination if the child is medically qualified for the foundation's services.
EIN: 990220777

2303
H. McKee Foundation, Inc.
P.O. Box 6002
Ocean View, HI   96737-6002   (808) 939-9136
Contact: Stephen Sampson, Pres. and Treas.
Application address: P.O. Box 6035, Oceanview, HI 96737-6002

Foundation type: Independent foundation
Purpose: Scholarships to residents of the Big Island of Hawaii for continuous education at institutions of higher learning.
Financial data: Year ended 12/31/2012. Assets, $387,808 (M); Expenditures, $28,815; Total giving, $13,000; Grants to individuals, 13 grants totaling $13,000 (high: $1,000, low: $1,000).
Fields of interest: Education.
Type of support: Scholarships—to individuals.
Application information: Applications accepted.
Initial approach: Letter
Deadline(s): None
EIN: 990216904

2304
Patsy Takemoto Mink Education Foundation for Low Income Women & Children
c/o Jo Ann Kagawa
P.O. Box 479
Honolulu, HI   96809-0479
Contact: Gwendolyn Mink, Tr.
Application address: 230 Justine Ct. N.E., Washington, DC 20002
URL: http://www.patsyminkfoundation.org/

Foundation type: Independent foundation
Purpose: Assistance to low-income women in HI, with children who are pursuing education or training.
Financial data: Year ended 12/31/2012. Assets, $163,503 (M); Expenditures, $21,561; Total

giving, $17,660; Grants to individuals, 2 grants totaling $5,660 (high: $5,000, low: $660).
Fields of interest: Vocational education, post-secondary; Higher education; Women.
Type of support: Graduate support; Technical education support; Undergraduate support; Doctoral support; Grants for special needs.
Application information: Applications accepted. Application form required. Application form available on the grantmaker's web site.
Initial approach: Letter
Send request by: Mail
Copies of proposal: 6
Deadline(s): Aug. 1
Final notification: Recipients notified in Sept.
Applicants should submit the following:
1) Financial information
2) Essay
Additional information: Award may be used for direct school expenses or living expenses while enrolled in an educational program. See web site for additional guidelines.
EIN: 680524691

2305
National Kidney Foundation of Hawaii
1314 S. King St., Ste. 1555
Honolulu, HI   96814-2004   (808) 593-1515
Contact: Glen Hayashida, C.E.O.
FAX: (808) 593-8096; E-mail: info@kidney.org;
Toll-free tel.: (800) 488-2277; URL: http://www.kidneyhi.org/

Foundation type: Public charity
Purpose: Financial assistance to renal patients residing in HI, for medical equipment, medication, transportation, food, rent and utilities.
Financial data: Year ended 06/30/2012. Assets, $3,664,432 (M); Expenditures, $2,328,045; Total giving, $3,777; Grants to individuals, totaling $3,777.
Fields of interest: Kidney diseases; Economically disadvantaged.
Type of support: Grants for special needs.
Application information: Patients submit applications for emergency needs through their social worker and if approved, funds are paid directly to the vendor.
EIN: 990266733

2306
North Kohala Community Resource Center
55-3393 Akoni Pule Hwy.
Hawi, HI   96719-0519   (808) 889-5523
Contact: Christine Richardson, Exec. Dir.
FAX: (808) 889-5527;
E-mail: info@northkohala.org; Mailing address: P.O. Box 519, Hawi, HI 96719-0519; URL: http://northkohala.org

Foundation type: Public charity
Purpose: Fiscal sponsorship to individuals for projects that meet the mission of the center which provides local support, bridges to funding, and education for projects that benefit the North Kohala community.
Publications: Application guidelines; Annual report; Newsletter.
Financial data: Year ended 12/31/2011. Assets, $209,684 (M); Expenditures, $1,200,470; Total giving, $1,059,570.
Type of support: Project support; Fiscal agent/sponsor.

Application information: Applications accepted. Application form required. Application form available on the grantmaker's web site.
Initial approach: Proposal
Send request by: Mail or hand-delivered with signature
Copies of proposal: 1
Deadline(s): None
Final notification: Applicants notified in one to three weeks
Additional information: Application should include budget information.
Program description:
Fiscal Sponsorship: The center supports projects beneficial to the North Kohala community and its residents by supporting project organizers who do not have 501(c)(3) status in planning and managing their projects, in researching funding sources, and writing proposals for grants. Organizations eligible for fiscal sponsorship must be aligned with the mission of the center. An administrative fee based on a percentage of the grants or donations received will be charged, typically between four and eight percent.
EIN: 020553251

2307
Ellison S. Onizuka Scholarship Fund-Kona, Inc.
81-6439 Mamalahoa Hwy.
Kealakekua, HI   96750-8134   (808) 323-3105
Contact: Earl Ogata, Treas.

Foundation type: Independent foundation
Purpose: Scholarships to students of HI who are or will be studying aerospace engineering.
Financial data: Year ended 06/30/2011. Assets, $22,116 (M); Expenditures, $6,756; Total giving, $6,000; Grants to individuals, 4 grants totaling $6,000 (high: $2,000, low: $1,000).
Fields of interest: Engineering school/education.
Type of support: Scholarships—to individuals.
Application information: Applications accepted.
Deadline(s): May 31
Additional information: Application should include school student is currently attending, and reason for scholarship.
EIN: 990246719

2308
Outrigger Duke Kahanamoku Foundation
PMB 202
305 Ward Ave., Ste. 106
Honolulu, HI   96814-4004   (808) 545-4880
E-mail: info@dukefoundation.org; Toll-free fax: (888) 624-0181; URL: http://www.dukefoundation.org

Foundation type: Public charity
Purpose: Scholarships to student athletes of HI, to compete in local and international athletic competitions.
Publications: Application guidelines; Annual report.
Financial data: Year ended 09/30/2012. Assets, $1,710,580 (M); Expenditures, $199,092; Total giving, $117,200; Grants to individuals, 61 grants totaling $111,700.
Fields of interest: Athletics/sports, water sports; Athletics/sports, amateur competition; Recreation.
Type of support: Scholarships—to individuals.

Application information: Applications accepted. Application form required. Application form available on the grantmaker's web site.

Deadline(s): Feb. 15 for Individual and Team Athletic Grants, Aug. 15 for Athletic Event; Apr. 1 for Scholarship Grants

Final notification: Recipients notified end of Apr. for Individual and Team Grants, and end of Nov. for Athletic Event

Applicants should submit the following:
1) Photograph
2) Transcripts
3) Resume
4) Financial information

Additional information: Application should also include a personal statement, two letters of reference, and most recent parents income tax return. Applicant must demonstrate financial need. See web site for additional information.

Program descriptions:

Athletic Grants: These grants sponsor, promote, and encourage individuals and groups in state, national, and international competitions in the sports of canoeing, surfing, kayaking, swimming, water polo, and volleyball. Individual grants are awarded for a specific purpose or competition, while team athletic grants are awarded to local, national, or international teams.

Scholarship Grants: Scholarships are available to Hawai'i residents who have participated in competitive sports during their high school career, and who plan to attend an accredited college as a full-time student.

EIN: 990217299

2309
Pacific and Asian Affairs Council

(also known as PAAC)
1601 E. W. Rd., 4th Fl.
Honolulu, HI 96848-1601 (808) 944-7780
Contact: Ruth Limitiaco, Pres.
Scholarship e-mail: hs@paachawaii.org
FAX: (808) 944-7785;
E-mail: admin@paachawaii.org; URL: http://www.paachawaii.org

Foundation type: Public charity
Purpose: Scholarships to graduating high school seniors of HI, who participate in the council's clubs and/or after school classes pursuing a major in a field related to international affairs.
Publications: Application guidelines.
Financial data: Year ended 06/30/2012. Assets, $608,697 (M); Expenditures, $475,001; Total giving, $10,360; Grants to individuals, totaling $10,360.
Fields of interest: Higher education; International affairs.
Type of support: Scholarships—to individuals.
Application information: Applications accepted. Application form required.

Send request by: Mail
Deadline(s): Apr. 14 for Eddie Tangen Award and Paul S. Honda Scholarships
Applicants should submit the following:
1) SASE
2) Transcripts
3) Letter(s) of recommendation
4) Essay
Additional information: See web site for additional application guidelines.

Program descriptions:

Eddie Tangen Award: A $300 award is given each year to a student council member who is in grades 9 to 11.

Paul S. Honda Scholarship: Three $1,000 and two $500 scholarships are given annually to graduating seniors who have been involved with the council, to promote Asian and International studies in higher education.
EIN: 990073501

2310
Pacific Islanders in Communications

615 Pi'ikoi St., Ste. 1504
Honolulu, HI 96814-3513 (808) 591-0059
Contact: Ruth Bolan, Exec. Dir.
FAX: (808) 591-1114; E-mail: info@piccom.org;
E-Mail for Ruth Bolan: lferrer@piccom.org;
URL: http://piccom.org/

Foundation type: Public charity
Purpose: Scholarships and project grants to Pacific Islanders, Americans, and Americans of Pacific Island heritage to study or create media content that results in a deeper understanding of Pacific Island history, culture, and contemporary challenges.
Publications: Application guidelines; Annual report.
Financial data: Year ended 09/30/2012. Assets, $1,857,289 (M); Expenditures, $1,680,361; Total giving, $663,240; Grants to individuals, totaling $63,740.
Fields of interest: Media/communications; Film/video; Television; Higher education; Asians/Pacific Islanders.
Type of support: Grants to individuals; Scholarships—to individuals.
Application information: Application form required.
Deadline(s): Vary
Additional information: Contact foundation for application information.

Program descriptions:

Open Call For Production and Completion: Grants are available to public television projects at the research and development, production, or completion stages that focus on issues affecting Asian Pacific Islanders. Up to $15,000 is available for research and development; production and completion funds range from $20,000 to $50,000 with preference given to projects in the final stages of post-production. Emphasis will be given to projects in which Pacific Islanders hold key creative production positions and that adhere to public broadcasting standards of objectivity and balance. Eligible applicants must: hold artistic, budgetary, and editorial control and must own the copyright to the proposed project; be at least 18 years of age and a citizen or legal resident of the United States or its territories; provide a video sample of their proposed work that demonstrates their ability to tell a story through the visual medium.

Open Door Completion Fund: This fund supports public television projects in the final stages of post-production. These funds must be the last monies needed to completely finish the program and bring up to broadcast standards. A full-length rough cut must be submitted to be considered for completion funding. Awards range from $20,000 to $50,000.

Scholarships: Scholarship funds of up to $5,000 per year are available to encourage and support Pacific Islanders to pursue excellence in the field of media and/or communications and to cultivate talent that results in a deeper understanding of Pacific Islander history, culture, and contemporary challenges. Eligible applicants must: be 18 years old or older and be a citizen, legal permanent resident, or national of the United States or its territories; be pursuing a degree, certificate, and/or other certification in media and/or communications at the undergraduate, graduate,

and unclassified levels of study; demonstrate academic proficiency and/or have demonstrated experience in media and/or communications or a related field; demonstrate commitment to Pacific Islander community; and demonstrate a need for financial assistance.
EIN: 990293514

2311
Palama Scholarship Foundation Inc.

725 Kapiolani Blvd., Ste. C-110
Honolulu, HI 96813-6012 (808) 847-4427
Contact: Hyo Kyu Lim, Pres.
Application address: 1210 Dillingham Blvd., Honolulu, HI 96817, tel.: (808) 847-4427

Foundation type: Company-sponsored foundation
Purpose: Scholarship awards to residents of HI of at least 25-percent Korean-American ancestry.
Financial data: Year ended 12/31/2012. Assets, $29,151 (M); Expenditures, $47,451; Total giving, $45,000; Grants to individuals, 9 grants totaling $45,000 (high: $5,000, low: $5,000).
Type of support: Undergraduate support.
Application information:
Initial approach: Letter
Deadline(s): Aug. 10
EIN: 990344016

2312
Palama Settlement

810 N. Vineyard Blvd.
Honolulu, HI 96817-3590 (808) 845-3945
Contact: Jackson Nakasone, Pres.
FAX: (808) 847-2873;
E-mail: info@palamasettlement.org; URL: http://www.palamasettlement.org/

Foundation type: Public charity
Purpose: Scholarships to students of Honolulu, HI entering or be enrolled in the ninth grade or higher and have participated in the Palama Settlement program.
Financial data: Year ended 12/31/2011. Assets, $3,718,679 (M); Expenditures, $1,622,094; Total giving, $30,098; Grants to individuals, totaling $30,098.
Fields of interest: Education.
Type of support: Scholarships—to individuals.
Application information: Applications accepted. Application form required. Interview required.
Deadline(s): May
Applicants should submit the following:
1) Transcripts
2) Letter(s) of recommendation
3) GPA
EIN: 990074140

2313
Parents and Children Together

1485 Linapuni St., Ste. 105
Honolulu, HI 96819-3575 (808) 847-3285
FAX: (808) 841-1485;
E-mail: admin@pacthawaii.org; Toll-free tel.: (800) 815-8413

Foundation type: Public charity
Purpose: Provides food and services for children, families and communities in Hawaii who are in financial need.
Publications: Annual report.
Financial data: Year ended 06/30/2011. Assets, $9,647,002 (M); Expenditures, $20,332,165; Total giving, $998,319; Grants to individuals, totaling $998,319.

Fields of interest: Children/youth, services; Family services.
Type of support: Grants for special needs.
Application information: Applications accepted. Application form not required.
EIN: 990119678

2314
People Attentive to Children
(also known as PATCH)
650 Iwilei Rd., Ste. 205
Honolulu, HI 96817-5318 (808) 839-1988
Contact: Katy Chen, Exec. Dir.
FAX: (808) 839-1799;
E-mail: patch@patchhawaii.org; URL: http://www.patchhawaii.org/

Foundation type: Public charity
Purpose: Scholarships and other funds available for people interested in early childhood care and teaching.
Publications: Application guidelines; Annual report; Newsletter.
Financial data: Year ended 06/30/2012. Assets, $1,155,717 (M); Expenditures, $3,069,711; Total giving, $1,203,911; Grants to individuals, totaling $1,203,911.
Fields of interest: Children/youth, services; Day care; Family services.
Type of support: Scholarships—to individuals.
Application information: Applications accepted. Application form required. Application form available on the grantmaker's web site.
> *Initial approach:* Application
> *Deadline(s):* Jan. 15, May 31, and Aug. 31 for PATCH Scholarships
Program description:
> *PATCH Scholarships:* This program allows people to increase their knowledge in current developmentally-appropriate practices and increase the number of people entering into the early care and education profession. Scholarships provide up to $750 to be used toward training reimbursement for early-childhood-specific college courses, workshops, and assessment fees for obtaining a C.D.A. certificate.
EIN: 990167464

2315
Ida M. Pope Memorial Scholarship Fund
c/o Bank of Hawaii, N.A.
P.O. Box 3170, Dept. 715
Honolulu, HI 96802-3170 (808) 566-5570

Foundation type: Independent foundation
Purpose: Scholarships to financially needy female residents of HI who are of Hawaiian or part-Hawaiian ancestry for undergraduate or graduate study. Recipients must attend or have been admitted to an accredited graduate or undergraduate institution and have a 3.0 GPA or better.
Publications: Informational brochure.
Financial data: Year ended 06/30/2013. Assets, $869,226 (M); Expenditures, $47,354; Total giving, $22,000; Grants to individuals, 22 grants totaling $22,000 (high: $1,000, low: $1,000).
Fields of interest: Asians/Pacific Islanders; Native Americans/American Indians; Women.
Type of support: Graduate support; Undergraduate support.
Application information: Applications accepted. Application form required.
> *Send request by:* Mail
> *Deadline(s):* Mar. 1

Additional information: Application should include a copy of applicant's birth certificate to verify Hawaiian ancestry. Contact foundation for complete program information.
EIN: 996003339

2316
Rehabilitation Hospital of the Pacific Foundation
226 N. Kuakini St.
Honolulu, HI 96817-2488 (808) 566-3451
Contact: Jean Nakanishi, Exec. Dir.
FAX: (808) 566-3425;
E-mail: rehabfoundation@rehabhospital.org; E-mail For Jean Nakanishi: jnakanishi@rehabhospital.org;
URL: http://www.rehabhospital.org/foundation

Foundation type: Public charity
Purpose: Assistance to individuals receiving support from the Rehabilitation Hospital of the Pacific.
Financial data: Year ended 09/30/2011. Assets, $14,818,796 (M); Expenditures, $1,652,365; Total giving, $1,020,152; Grants to individuals, totaling $160,007.
Fields of interest: Nursing school/education.
Type of support: Employee-related scholarships; Scholarships—to individuals; Support to graduates or students of specific schools; Awards/grants by nomination only; Awards/prizes.
Application information: See web site for additional guidelines.
EIN: 990241634

2317
John M. Ross Foundation
P.O. Box 3170, Dept. 715
Honolulu, HI 96802-3170 (808) 694-4945
Contact: Paula Boyce
FAX: (808) 694-4006;
E-mail: paula.boyce@boh.com

Foundation type: Independent foundation
Purpose: Scholarships to financially needy residents of the Island of Hawaii, HI, for full-time study at accredited two- and four-year undergraduate or graduate institutions primarily in HI.
Financial data: Year ended 06/30/2013. Assets, $669,145 (M); Expenditures, $36,791; Total giving, $22,725.
Fields of interest: Higher education.
Type of support: Graduate support; Undergraduate support.
Application information: Application form required.
> *Deadline(s):* Mar. 1.
> *Applicants should submit the following:*
> 1) SAR
> 2) Transcripts
> 3) Letter(s) of recommendation
> 4) Essay
EIN: 996007327

2318
Dr. Alvin & Monica Saake Foundation
P.O. Box 894269
Mililani, HI 96789-8269 (808) 537-6333
Application address: c/o Hawaii Community Foundation, 1164 Bishop St., Ste. 800, Honolulu, HI 96813, tel.: (808) 537-6333

Foundation type: Independent foundation
Purpose: Scholarships to HI college juniors, seniors and graduate students who are studying

kinesiology, physical education, sports medicine or physical/occupational therapy.
Financial data: Year ended 12/31/2011. Assets, $3,042,813 (M); Expenditures, $207,041; Total giving, $139,100.
Fields of interest: Medical care, rehabilitation; Physical therapy; Public health, occupational health; Public health, physical fitness.
Type of support: Graduate support; Undergraduate support.
Application information: Applications accepted. Application form required. Interview required.
> *Send request by:* Mail
> *Deadline(s):* Mar. 31
> *Applicants should submit the following:*
> 1) Essay
> 2) Letter(s) of recommendation
> 3) Financial information
> 4) Transcripts
EIN: 731671840

2319
Toyo Sakumoto Charitable Trust
P.O. Box 3170, Dept. 715
Honolulu, HI 96802-3170

Foundation type: Independent foundation
Purpose: Scholarships to college junior, senior, or graduate students born in HI who are of Japanese descent and attend college in HI.
Publications: Informational brochure (including application guidelines).
Financial data: Year ended 03/31/2013. Assets, $722,980 (M); Expenditures, $36,192; Total giving, $25,000; Grants to individuals, 27 grants totaling $25,000 (high: $1,000, low: $500).
International interests: Japan.
Type of support: Undergraduate support.
Application information: Application form required. Application form available on the grantmaker's web site.
> *Deadline(s):* Mar. 1
> *Applicants should submit the following:*
> 1) GPA
> 2) SAR
> 3) Transcripts
> 4) Essay
> *Additional information:* Applicant must also include a personal statement, have a 3.5 minimum GPA.
EIN: 996089401

2320
Servco Foundation
P.O. Box 2788
Honolulu, HI 96803-2788 (800) 564-1386
FAX: (808) 523-3937;
E-mail: donations@servco.com; URL: http://servco.com/philanthropy/servco_foundation.php

Foundation type: Company-sponsored foundation
Purpose: Scholarships to spouses and children of Servco Pacific Inc. employees to pursue studies at any accredited college.
Publications: Application guidelines.
Financial data: Year ended 06/30/2012. Assets, $5,263,375 (M); Expenditures, $290,773; Total giving, $258,759; Grants to individuals, 24 grants totaling $39,333 (high: $2,000, low: $666).
Fields of interest: Higher education; Scholarships/financial aid; Volunteer services; Leadership development.
Type of support: Employee-related scholarships.
Application information: Applications not accepted.

Additional information: Unsolicited requests for funds not considered or acknowledged.

Program description:

Annual Undergraduate Scholarships: The foundation annually awards $4,000 scholarships to spouses and children of Servco Pacific employees to pursue higher education. Applicants must have GPA of 3.0, demonstrated leadership ability through school activities and community service, and financial need.

Company name: Servco Pacific Inc.

EIN: 990248256

2321
Gertrude S. Straub Trust Estate

P.O. Box 3170, Dept. 715
Honolulu, HI 96802-3170

Foundation type: Independent foundation

Purpose: Scholarships to HI public high school graduates to attend mainland U.S. colleges and universities, with a major in a subject relating to better understanding of peace and the promotion of international peace.

Publications: Informational brochure (including application guidelines).

Financial data: Year ended 03/31/2012. Assets, $6,945,094 (M); Expenditures, $370,479; Total giving, $243,150; Grants to individuals, 193 grants totaling $243,150 (high: $2,100, low: $500).

Fields of interest: Higher education.

Type of support: Scholarships—to individuals.

Application information: Application form required.

Initial approach: Letter or telephone

Deadline(s): Mar. 1

Applicants should submit the following:
1) Transcripts
2) SAR
3) Letter(s) of recommendation
4) Essay

Additional information: Application must also include a personal statement.

Program description:

Marion Maccarrell Scott Scholarship Fund: The scholarship is awarded to students who are graduates from a public high school in Hawaii, plan to attend an accredited U.S. mainland college or university, and demonstrate a commitment to world peace.

EIN: 996003243

2322
Mamoru & Aiko Takitani Foundation, Inc.

(formerly Takitani Foundation, Inc.)
81 S. Hotel St., Ste. 308
Honolulu, HI 96813-3145 (808) 228-0209
Mailing address: P.O. Box 10687, Honolulu, HI 96816-0687; Additional tel.: (808) 247-6085;
URL: http://www.takitani.org/

Foundation type: Company-sponsored foundation

Purpose: Scholarships to graduating students of every public high school and major accredited private high school in HI.

Financial data: Year ended 12/31/2012. Assets, $6,137,809 (M); Expenditures, $197,303; Total giving, $142,098; Grants to individuals, 72 grants totaling $114,098 (high: $10,000, low: -$1,000).

Fields of interest: Higher education.

Type of support: Undergraduate support.

Application information: Applications accepted. Application form required.

Additional information: Scholarship applications are submitted directly to the school administrators.

Program description:

Scholarships: The foundation annually awards over 50 $1,000 college scholarships to high school seniors living in Hawaii. In addition, ten state finalists receive an additional $2,000, one student receives a $5,000 Outstanding Award, and two students receive $10,000 Distinguished Awards. Awards are based on financial need, community service, and scholastic achievement.

EIN: 510212114

2323
Mildred Towle Scholarship Trust

c/o First Hawaiian Bank
P.O. Box 3708
Honolulu, HI 96811-3708

Foundation type: Independent foundation

Purpose: Scholarships to HI residents studying overseas or at Boston University, and to African Americans studying in HI. Also, scholarships to international students with student visas (F or J) for study in HI.

Financial data: Year ended 09/30/2013. Assets, $1,225,862 (M); Expenditures, $123,762; Total giving, $95,541.

Fields of interest: African Americans/Blacks.

Type of support: Support to graduates or students of specific schools; Foreign applicants; Undergraduate support.

Application information: Applications not accepted.

Additional information: Giving only to preselected individuals. Unsolicited request for funds not considered or acknowledged.

EIN: 996050638

2324
University of Hawai'i Foundation

2444 Dole St.
Bachman Hall 105
Honolulu, HI 96822-2388 (808) 956-8849
Contact: Donna Vuchinich, Pres. and C.E.O.
E-mail: webinquiry@uhf.hawaii.edu; Toll free Tel. : (866)-846-4262; Mailing Address : P.O. Box 11270 Honolulu, HI 96828-0270; E-Mail for Donna Vuchinich: Donna.Vuchinich@UHFoundation.org; Tel. for Donna Vuchinich: (808)-956-3711; Fax for Donna Vuchinich : (808)-956-5115; URL: http://www.uhf.hawaii.edu

Foundation type: Public charity

Purpose: Scholarships to students for attendance at the University of Hawaii for higher education.

Publications: Annual report; Financial statement; Informational brochure.

Financial data: Year ended 06/30/2011. Assets, $326,628,806 (M); Expenditures, $39,057,436; Total giving, $9,552,613; Grants to individuals, totaling $1,716,620.

Fields of interest: Higher education.

Type of support: Support to graduates or students of specific schools.

Application information: Applications accepted.

Send request by: Online

Deadline(s): Varies

Applicants should submit the following:
1) Transcripts
2) Essay

Additional information: Applicant must be a resident of Hawaii. Scholarship funds are paid directly to the educational institution on behalf of the students. See web site for additional guidelines.

EIN: 990085260

2325
Waimea Educational & Cultural Association

P.O. Box 595
Waimea, HI 96796-0595

Foundation type: Independent foundation

Purpose: Scholarships primarily to students who are residence of Waimea, HI for continuing their education at accredited institutions of higher learning.

Financial data: Year ended 06/30/2012. Assets, $323,570 (M); Expenditures, $20,565; Total giving, $16,000; Grants to individuals, 16 grants totaling $16,000 (high: $1,000, low: $1,000).

Fields of interest: Higher education.

Type of support: Scholarships—to individuals.

Application information: Applications accepted. Application form required.

Initial approach: Letter

Deadline(s): None

EIN: 996005136

2326
J. Watumull Fund

(formerly J. Watumull Estate, Inc.)
P.O. Box 3708
Honolulu, HI 96811
Contact: Galub Watumull, Pres. and Dir.
Application address: Watumull Bldg., 307 Lewers St., 6th Fl., Honolulu, HI 96815

Foundation type: Independent foundation

Purpose: Scholarships to individuals of Indian ancestry.

Financial data: Year ended 12/31/2012. Assets, $11,632,454 (M); Expenditures, $604,043; Total giving, $515,450.

Type of support: Fellowships.

Application information: Applications accepted. Application form not required.

Initial approach: Letter

Send request by: Mail or fax

Copies of proposal: 1

Deadline(s): None

EIN: 510205431

2327
Hans and Clara Davis Zimmerman Foundation

c/o Bank of Hawaii, No. 758
P.O. Box 3170
Honolulu, HI 96802-3170
For scholarship information contact Hawai'i Community Foundation at scholarships@hcf-hawaii.org or tel.: 1-(808) 566-5570 (or toll-free from neighbor islands 1-(888) 731-3863)

Foundation type: Independent foundation

Purpose: Scholarships to financially needy full-time students who are legal residents of HI for studies at accredited two- and four-year colleges and universities that would lead to careers in the fields of medicine, nursing, or other health-related fields (not including sports medicine, psychology or social work)

Financial data: Year ended 12/31/2012. Assets, $13,613,978 (M); Expenditures, $799,948; Total giving, $568,650; Grants to individuals, 199 grants totaling $568,650 (high: $10,000, low: $1,000).

Fields of interest: Medical school/education; Nursing school/education; Health sciences school/education.

Type of support: Undergraduate support.

Application information: Applications accepted. Application form required. Application form available on the grantmaker's web site.

Initial approach: Letter or telephone
Deadline(s): Mar. 1
Applicants should submit the following:
1) Transcripts
2) SAR
3) Letter(s) of recommendation
Additional information: Application must also include a personal statement.

Program description:

Hans & Clara Zimmerman Health and Education Scholarships: The foundation awards these scholarships to students in the last year of a BSN or RN program in HI. To be considered for this scholarship, applicants must respond to the following two questions in their personal statement: Why did you choose nursing as a career? Who or what most influenced your decision to study nursing? All scholarships are based on financial need and are renewable. Applicants to this foundation may automatically be considered for other scholarship programs administered by the Hawaii Community Foundation. Employees or direct relatives of employees of the Hawaii Community Foundation are ineligible.

EIN: 996006669

IDAHO

2328
John & Olive Adams Scholarship Foundation Inc.
445 Gustafson Dr.
Idaho Falls, ID 83402-4635   (208) 282-7893
Contact: Ann Howell, Pres.

Foundation type: Independent foundation
Purpose: Scholarships to qualifying students who plan to further their education at an accredited college, university or technical college located within the state of Idaho pursuing a career in physical science or social science.
Financial data: Year ended 06/30/2013. Assets, $150,909 (M); Expenditures, $14,046; Total giving, $14,000; Grants to individuals, 18 grants totaling $14,000 (high: $1,000, low: $500).
Fields of interest: Higher education; Physical/earth sciences; Social sciences.
Type of support: Scholarships—to individuals.
Application information: Applications accepted. Application form required.
  Deadline(s): Apr. 11
  Applicants should submit the following:
    1) SAT
    2) GPA
    3) ACT
  Additional information: Applicant must demonstrate financial need.
EIN: 943168497

2329
Boise Legacy Constructors Foundation Inc.
(formerly Washington Group Foundation)
102 S. 17th St., Ste. 200
Boise, ID 83702-5172   (208) 424-7622
Contact: Marlene M. Puckett, Secy. and Exec. Dir.
FAX: (208) 424-7627;
E-mail: blcfoundation@qwestoffice.net;
URL: http://
boiselegacyconstructorsfoundation.com/

Foundation type: Operating foundation
Purpose: Welfare assistance to financially needy individuals and families, including employees and former employees, only in specific locations where Washington Group International has operations.
Publications: Application guidelines.
Financial data: Year ended 12/31/2012. Assets, $7,399,546 (M); Expenditures, $338,087; Total giving, $216,978; Grants to individuals, 230 grants totaling $159,944 (high: $9,500).
Fields of interest: Human services.
Type of support: Grants for special needs.
Application information: Applications accepted. Application form required.
  Deadline(s): None
  Additional information: Application should include financial statement and must be referred by an agency.
EIN: 826005410

2330
Chadwick Foundation
P.O. Box 486
Soda Springs, ID 83276-0486   (208) 547-2166
Application address: 89 W. 2nd S., Soda Springs, ID 83276

Foundation type: Independent foundation
Purpose: Scholarships to individuals with preference to applicants from the immediate southeastern ID area.
Financial data: Year ended 12/31/2011. Assets, $884,923 (M); Expenditures, $45,829; Total giving, $20,372; Grants to individuals, 15 grants totaling $20,372 (high: $1,090, low: $500).
Fields of interest: Higher education.
Type of support: Scholarships—to individuals.
Application information: Applications accepted. Application form required.
  Initial approach: Letter or telephone
  Deadline(s): None
  Additional information: Application forms available upon request.
EIN: 820456503

2331
Excel Foundation, Inc.
P.O. Box 2469
Coeur d'Alene, ID 83816   (208) 755-6606
Contact: Jimmy McAndrew, Pres.
Grant application e-mail: excel@cdaschools.org
E-mail: james.t.mcandrew@wellsfargo.com;
URL: http://www.excelfoundation.org

Foundation type: Public charity
Purpose: Grants for teachers of the Coeur d'Alene, ID School District 271 for classroom projects.
Publications: Application guidelines.
Financial data: Year ended 05/31/2012. Assets, $1,036,752 (M); Expenditures, $79,727; Total giving, $67,867; Grants to individuals, totaling $67,867.
Fields of interest: Education.
Type of support: Grants to individuals.
Application information: Applications accepted. Application form available on the grantmaker's web site.
  Send request by: On-line
  Deadline(s): Sept.
  Final notification: Applicants notified in Oct.
  Additional information: Applicant should submit five hard copies of the application. Application must be word processed in a 12 point font.
Program description:
  Grants: The foundation funds grants to teachers in Coeur d'Alene School District 271 who have unique and innovative ideas which will offer students the opportunities to develop higher level thinking skills and depth of knowledge with potential to increase the students' motivation to learn. Grants aim to provide classrooms with equipment and educational materials that support creative and innovative projects designed by the classroom teacher to enhance the curriculum.
EIN: 943034190

2332
Haugse-Cossey Foundation
P.O. Box 828
Boise, ID 83701-0828   (208) 378-7718
Contact: Michael Ballantyne, Tr.

Foundation type: Independent foundation
Purpose: Scholarships to graduates from Ada County high schools, ID.
Financial data: Year ended 06/30/2013. Assets, $1,136,823 (M); Expenditures, $39,680; Total giving, $10,000; Grants to individuals, 7 grants totaling $10,000 (high: $2,000, low: $1,000).
Type of support: Support to graduates or students of specific schools; Undergraduate support.

Application information: Applications not accepted. Unsolicited requests for funds not considered or acknowledged.
EIN: 826055666

2333
The Home Partership Foundation, Inc.
c/o 01
P.O. Box 7899
Boise, ID 83707-1899   (208) 484-7010
E-mail: hpf@ihfa.org; Toll-free tel.: (800) 219-2286;
URL: http://www.ihfa.org/foundation/about-us.aspx

Foundation type: Public charity
Purpose: Financial assistance to individuals and families of ID with financial training to help them towards the down payment on a home. Assistance to homeless needy families and individuals facing foreclosure or eviction.
Financial data: Year ended 12/31/2011. Assets, $1,819,788 (M); Expenditures, $1,169,147; Total giving, $1,026,308; Grants to individuals, totaling $12,000.
Fields of interest: Housing/shelter, homeless; Housing/shelter, home owners.
Type of support: Emergency funds; Grants for special needs.
Application information: Contact the foundation for eligibility requirements.
EIN: 753162969

2334
IDACORP, Inc. Corporate Giving Program
c/o Corp. Contribs.
P.O. Box 70
Boise, ID 83707-0070   (208) 388-2477
Contact: Layne Dodson, Prog. Mgr
Application address for Scholarship for Academic Excellence: Idaho Power Scholarship Program, c/o Scholarship Program Administrator, 301 E. Benton, Pocatello, Idaho 83201; Application address for Larry Wimer Memorial Scholarship: Elly Davis, Idaho Community Foundation, 210 W. State St., Boise, ID 83702; Additional scholarship contact: Claudia Tremelling, tel.: (208) 236-7733, e-mail: ctremelling@idahopower.com
E-mail: ldodson@idahopower.com; URL: http://www.idahopower.com/NewsCommunity/Community/default.cfm

Foundation type: Corporate giving program
Purpose: Scholarships to graduating high school seniors who live within Idaho Power's service area. Scholarships also to students planning full-time undergraduate enrollment in the Department of Natural Resources at the University of Idaho.
Publications: Application guidelines; Corporate giving report.
Fields of interest: Vocational education; Higher education; Engineering.
Type of support: Employee-related scholarships; Support to graduates or students of specific schools; Undergraduate support.
Application information: Applications accepted. Application form required. Application form available on the grantmaker's web site.
  Initial approach: Application
  Send request by: Mail
  Deadline(s): Mar. 1, Apr. 1 for Larry Wimer Memorial Scholarship
  Final notification: Applicants notified Apr. 1 for Scholarship for Academic Excellence, July 1 for Larry Wimer Memorial Scholarship
  Applicants should submit the following:
    1) Transcripts

2) SAT
3) Letter(s) of recommendation
4) GPA
5) Essay
6) ACT
Additional information: Application for the Larry Wimer Memorial Scholarship may include exhibits showing notable achievement in scholarship, leadership, athletics, dramatics, literature, and community service.
Program descriptions:
Douglas E. Sprenger Memorial Scholarship Fund: The company awards scholarships to high school seniors who are children of employees of Idaho Power. Applicants must plan to enroll full-time at an Idaho or Oregon college, university, or vocational technical school. Scholarships are awarded based on academic achievement, leadership potential, and school and community involvement.
Kevin Whittier Memorial Scholarship Fund: The company awards scholarships to high school seniors who are children of employees of Idaho Power and plan to enroll at an Idaho college, university, or vocational-technical school. Applicants must plan to seek a degree in engineering.
Larry Wimer Memorial Scholarship: The company annually awards $500 scholarships to students who plan to enroll in the University of Idaho's Department of Natural Resources.
Scholarships for Academic Excellence: The company annually awards ten $2,000 scholarships to graduating high school students who live within Idaho Power's service area and are planning to enroll at an accredited Idaho or Oregon college, university, or vocational-technical school. The scholarship honors individual achievement, community awareness and involvement, and academic accomplishment.
Company name: IDACORP, Inc.

2335
Idaho Community Foundation
210 W. State St.
Boise, ID   83702-6052   (208) 342-3535
Contact: Holly Motes, Cont.
FAX: (208) 342-3577; E-mail: info@idcomfdn.org; Additional tel.: (800) 657-5357; Additional E-mail: hmotes@idcomfdn.org; Grant inquiry E-mail: grants@idcomfdn.org; URL: http://www.idcomfdn.org

Foundation type: Community foundation
Purpose: Scholarships to high school graduates of Idaho for postsecondary education.
Publications: Application guidelines; Annual report; Financial statement; Grants list; Informational brochure (including application guidelines); Newsletter; Program policy statement.
Financial data: Year ended 12/31/2012. Assets, $94,957,136 (M); Expenditures, $7,628,377; Total giving, $6,669,803; Grants to individuals, 371 grants totaling $1,016,932 (high: $6,895, low: $250).
Fields of interest: Higher education.
Type of support: Scholarships—to individuals.
Application information: Applications accepted. Application form required. Application form available on the grantmaker's web site.
Initial approach: Telephone or e-mail
Send request by: Online, mail, fax or e-mail
Copies of proposal: 1
Deadline(s): Varies
Applicants should submit the following:
1) GPA
2) Essay
3) Transcripts

4) Proposal
5) Letter(s) of recommendation
Additional information: Each scholarship has its own application process and deadline. See web site for a complete listing of all scholarships.
EIN: 820425063

2336
Idaho Humanities Council
217 W. State St.
Boise, ID   83702-6053   (208) 345-5346
Contact: Rick Ardinger, Exec. Dir.
FAX: (208) 345-5347;
E-mail: rick@idahohumanities.org; Toll-free tel.: (888) 345-5346; URL: http://www.idahohumanities.org

Foundation type: Public charity
Purpose: Grants and fellowships to teachers and humanities scholars in ID.
Publications: Application guidelines; Annual report; Informational brochure; Newsletter.
Financial data: Year ended 10/31/2011. Assets, $1,656,572 (M); Expenditures, $843,238.
Fields of interest: Humanities; Elementary/secondary education; Elementary school/education.
Type of support: Fellowships; Project support.
Application information: Application form required. Application form available on the grantmaker's web site.
Initial approach: Proposal
Deadline(s): Dec. 15 and Aug. 15 for draft proposal, Jan. 15 and Sept. 15 for full proposal for Major Grants, Mini-grants, and Teacher Incentive Grants; Aug. 15 for draft proposal and Sept. 15 for full proposal for Research Fellowship Grants; none for Planning Grants
Program description:
Grants: The council awards a variety of grants to Idaho-based organizations and individuals whose programs and projects align with it. Five types of grants are available: major grants (of at least $2,000 each), mini grants (of up to $2,000), teacher incentive grants (of up to $1,000), research fellowship grants, and planning grants. Applications will be accepted in one of the following disciplines: history, philosophy, language (both modern and classical), linguistics, literature, archaeology, jurisprudence, comparative religion, ethics, history/criticism/theory of the arts, those social sciences employing historical or philosophical approaches to their content (including cultural anthropology, sociology, political theory, international relations, and other subjects concerned with questions of human nature), and the study and application of the humanities to the human environment (with particular attention to reflecting humanity's diverse heritage, traditions, and history, and to the relevance of the humanities to the conditions of national life). Eligible applicants include, but are not limited to, social service organizations and clubs, churches, state and local government agencies, business and professional groups, schools, corporations, public radio and television stations, museums, historical societies, public libraries, arts organizations, and colleges and universities; any non-profit organization, institution, individual, or ad hoc group may receive a grant (and nonprofit status is not necessary, so long as applicants are able to demonstrate that they are 'not for profit' and that they can manage all aspects of the project adequately)
EIN: 820315902

2337
Jeker Family Trust
199 N. Capitol Blvd., Ste. 502
Boise, ID   83701-5964

Foundation type: Independent foundation
Purpose: Scholarships to area students of ID, with emphasis on Boise, Eagle, and Moscow.
Financial data: Year ended 12/31/2012. Assets, $15,210,314 (M); Expenditures, $1,057,266; Total giving, $574,805.
Fields of interest: Higher education.
Type of support: Undergraduate support.
Application information: Applications not accepted.
Additional information: Unsolicited requests for funds not considered or acknowledged.
EIN: 204120889

2338
Mr. & Mrs. Henry B. Kingsbury Scholarship Fund
c/o H.F. Magnuson & Co.
P.O. Box 469
Wallace, ID   83873-0469
Contact: Dennis O'Brien, Secy.

Foundation type: Independent foundation
Purpose: Scholarships to high school graduates of Shoshone County, ID.
Financial data: Year ended 12/31/2012. Assets, $132,842 (M); Expenditures, $6,017; Total giving, $4,500.
Type of support: Undergraduate support.
Application information: Applications accepted. Application form required.
Initial approach: Letter
Deadline(s): Apr. 15
EIN: 826005448

2339
Lewis-Clark State College Foundation, Inc.
c/o Lewis-Clark State College
500 8th Ave.
Lewiston, ID   83501-2691   (208) 792-2458
FAX: (208) 792-2201;
E-mail: collegeadvancement@lcsc.edu;
URL: http://www.lcsc.edu/alumni/foundation/index.htm

Foundation type: Public charity
Purpose: Scholarships for graduating high school seniors of Idaho and Asotin county, Washington for attendance at Lewis-Clark State College, ID.
Financial data: Year ended 06/30/2012. Assets, $5,974,253 (M); Expenditures, $502,457; Total giving, $432,113; Grants to individuals, totaling $295,074.
Fields of interest: College.
Type of support: Scholarships—to individuals; Support to graduates or students of specific schools.
Application information: Applications accepted.
Additional information: See web site for additional information.
Program description:
Scholar Program: Scholars are eligible for a scholarship in the amount of $3,000 per year and is renewable for up to four years if criteria are met. Applicants must be enrolled with a minimum of 12 credits per semester and maintain a 3.5 cumulative GPA.
EIN: 820396878

2340
The Lightfoot Foundation
(also known as The E.L. & B.G. Lightfoot Foundation)
c/o U.S. Bank, N.A.
P.O. Box 7928
Boise, ID 83707-1928   (208) 383-7215
Scholarship contact: Mary Frazer, tel.: (208) 383-7215, e-mail: mary.frazer@usbank.com
FAX: (208) 383-7171;
E-mail: info@lightfootfoundation.com; URL: http://www.lightfootfoundation.com

Foundation type: Independent foundation
Purpose: Scholarships to students who reside in any of the 58 towns and cities in the Treasure Valley area for postsecondary education.
Financial data: Year ended 02/28/2013. Assets, $32,417,993 (M); Expenditures, $1,711,329; Total giving, $1,323,470; Grants to individuals, 73 grants totaling $91,300 (high: $2,000, low: $250).
Fields of interest: Higher education.
Type of support: Scholarships—to individuals.
Application information: Applications accepted. Application form required. Application form available on the grantmaker's web site.
  Send request by: Online
  Deadline(s): Apr. 15
  Applicants should submit the following:
    1) Transcripts
    2) Financial information
  Additional information: Applicants may attend any accredited educational institution they choose. See web site for specific application instructions.
EIN: 820454166

2341
Rick and Amy Magnuson Foundation, Inc.
P.O. Box 709
Wallace, ID 83873-0709

Foundation type: Independent foundation
Purpose: Scholarships to graduating students for college tuition and other expenses so they can continue their education at degree granting institutions.
Financial data: Year ended 12/31/2012. Assets, $110,734 (M); Expenditures, $13,393; Total giving, $12,750; Grants to individuals, 2 grants totaling $3,000 (high: $1,500, low: $1,500).
Fields of interest: Higher education.
Type of support: Scholarships—to individuals.
Application information: Applications accepted.
  Initial approach: Letter
  Deadline(s): May 1
  Additional information: Letter must state purpose of scholarship and amount.
EIN: 820524027

2342
Bruce Mitchell Foundation
12038 W. Mesquite Dr.
Boise, ID 83713-0814
Application address: c/o Glenda Leigh, P.O. Box 443, Parma, ID 83660, tel.: (208) 722-5295

Foundation type: Independent foundation
Purpose: Scholarships primarily to graduates of Parma High School, ID.
Financial data: Year ended 06/30/2013. Assets, $5,377,723 (M); Expenditures, $261,293; Total giving, $221,512; Grants to individuals, 92 grants totaling $221,512 (high: $3,000, low: $833).
Fields of interest: Higher education.

Type of support: Support to graduates or students of specific schools; Undergraduate support.
Application information:
  Initial approach: Letter
  Deadline(s): Apr. 15
  Additional information: Contact trust for current application guidelines.
EIN: 943107820

2343
Robert T. Nahas Educational Scholarship Foundation
877 W. Main St.
Boise, ID 83702-6094   (208) 363-7500
Application address: c/o Scholarship Comm., 20630 Patio Dr., Castro Valley, CA 94546

Foundation type: Independent foundation
Purpose: Scholarships to one male and one female graduating senior from high schools in ID, Caldwell, Contennial, Greenleaf, Homedale, Kuna, Marsing, Melba, Meridian, Middleton, Mountain View, Nampa, Nampa Christian, Rimrock, Skyview, and Vallivue for postsecondary education.
Financial data: Year ended 11/30/2011. Assets, $218,968 (M); Expenditures, $24,007; Total giving, $23,475. Scholarships—to individuals amount not specified.
Fields of interest: Higher education.
Type of support: Support to graduates or students of specific schools; Undergraduate support.
Application information: Application form required. Interview required.
  Initial approach: Letter
  Deadline(s): Mar. 1
  Applicants should submit the following:
    1) Transcripts
    2) Letter(s) of recommendation
  Additional information: Application should also include record of community service and a biographical essay.
EIN: 820392827

2344
Charles Hugh & Wilma Marie Perrin Foundation
121 N. 9th St., Ste. 201
Boise, ID 83702   (541) 447-6262

Foundation type: Operating foundation
Purpose: Scholarships to residents of Prineville, OR for higher education.
Financial data: Year ended 12/31/2011. Assets, $376,961 (M); Expenditures, $26,224; Total giving, $21,000; Grants to individuals, totaling $13,000.
Fields of interest: Higher education.
Type of support: Undergraduate support.
Application information: Applications accepted. Application form required.
  Initial approach: Letter
  Additional information: Contact the foundation for additional application guidelines.
EIN: 931283685

2345
Edward Ramsdale Scholarship Fund, Inc.
1150 Alturas Dr., Ste. 104
Moscow, ID 83843-3263
Contact: Brad Malm, Dir.
Application address: c/o Troy High School, Attn: Vickie Bledsoe, Counselor, 101 S. Main St., Troy, ID 83871, tel.: (208) 835-2361
Application address: P.O. Box 280, Troy, ID 83871

Foundation type: Operating foundation
Purpose: Scholarships only to graduating seniors of Troy High School, ID for attendance at schools beyond the high school level.
Financial data: Year ended 12/31/2011. Assets, $578,857 (M); Expenditures, $27,211; Total giving, $26,828.
Type of support: Support to graduates or students of specific schools; Undergraduate support.
Application information: Applications accepted.
  Additional information: Applicant must have attended Troy High School for at least one full year, and must have been a permanent resident within the boundaries of the Troy School district for the preceding five years. Student must submit class schedule to confirm full-time enrollment in a qualified educational program, and a copy of the billing for school tuition.
EIN: 841398428

2346
Rogers Brothers Foundation
c/o The Bank of Commerce
P.O. Box 1887
Idaho Falls, ID 83403-1887   (208) 523-2020
Application address: Rogers Seed Co., Foundation Admin. Committee, 600 N. Armstrong Pl., Boise, ID 41888, tel.: (800) 574-1553

Foundation type: Company-sponsored foundation
Purpose: Scholarships to children of current employees or retirees of Rogers Brothers Company, or Rogers NK Seed Company, or their subsidiaries, who have completed at least 3,000 hours of service.
Financial data: Year ended 06/30/2012. Assets, $1,187 (M); Expenditures, $10,335; Total giving, $9,500; Grants to individuals, totaling $9,500.
Fields of interest: Higher education.
Type of support: Employee-related scholarships.
Application information:
  Deadline(s): None
  Additional information: Application available from the administrative committee. Unsolicited requests for funds not considered or acknowledged.
EIN: 826012018

2347
Rotary Club of Burley, Idaho Scholarship Trust
1329 Albion Ave.
Burley, ID 83318-1817   (208) 878-0466
Contact: Gaylen Smyer, Treas.
Application address: 1137 Six S. Ranch Roa, Declo, ID 833232

Foundation type: Independent foundation
Purpose: Scholarships to residents of the Burley, ID, area for postsecondary education.
Financial data: Year ended 06/30/2013. Assets, $21,092 (M); Expenditures, $8,559; Total giving, $4,100; Grants to individuals, 10 grants totaling $4,100 (high: $500, low: $400).
Fields of interest: Higher education.
Type of support: Scholarships—to individuals.
Application information: Applications accepted.
  Deadline(s): None
EIN: 826009611

2348
Bernard E. Shultz Eagle Scout Foundation
c/o Larry Bledsoe
263 Highland
Hope, ID   83836
Contact: Jill Sanker, Tr.

Foundation type: Independent foundation
Purpose: Scholarships to students from Nampa
High School or Skyview High School, ID.
Financial data: Year ended 12/31/2012. Assets,
$985,120 (M); Expenditures, $51,250; Total
giving, $51,250; Grants to individuals, 40 grants
totaling $51,250 (high: $2,500, low: $100).
Type of support: Support to graduates or students
of specific schools; Undergraduate support.
Application information:
 Deadline(s): Mar. 15
 Additional information: Application available
  through the foundation or at Nampa High
  School or Skyview High School in Nampa, ID.
EIN: 820446208

2349
J. R. Simplot Company Contributions Program
P.O. Box 27
Boise, ID   83707-0027
Contact: Sue Richardson, Dir., Co. Comms.
FAX: (208) 389-7289;
E-mail: sue.richardson@simpson.com; URL: http://
www.simplot.com/community_involvement

Foundation type: Corporate giving program
Purpose: Scholarships to employees of Simplot
Company who have been working full-time for at
least one year.

Fields of interest: Vocational education; Higher
education; Adult/continuing education;
Scholarships/financial aid.
Type of support: Employee-related scholarships.
Application information: Applications not
accepted.
 Additional information: Unsolicited requests for
  funds not considered or acknowledged.
Program description:
 Employee Assistance Program: The company
awards scholarship of up to $5,250 per year to
full-time employees of Simplot to pursue graduate
studies and up to $3,000 to pursue undergraduate
studies. The award supports examinations; GED,
high school, and undergraduate/graduate degrees
from an accredited college/university;
certifications; technical skills training;
correspondence courses; and self study programs.
Applicants are evaluated by managers and human
resource personnel.
Company name: J.R. Simplot Company

2350
Smallwood Scholarship Foundation
812 Main Ave. N.
Twin Falls, ID   83301   (208) 733-6063
Contact: Kendal F. Egbert, Tr.

Foundation type: Independent foundation
Purpose: Scholarships to graduates of Twin Falls
County high schools, ID, for higher education.
Financial data: Year ended 12/31/2011. Assets,
$240,491 (M); Expenditures, $4,100; Total giving,
$4,100.
Fields of interest: Higher education; Scholarships/
financial aid.

Type of support: Support to graduates or students
of specific schools; Undergraduate support.
Application information: Applications accepted.
Application form required.
 Deadline(s): Apr. 1
 Additional information: Applications available at
  Twin Falls County high schools. Scholarship
  for tuition and books only.
EIN: 820504275

2351
Dwain H. and Joyce L. Stufflebeam Educational Foundation, Inc.
P.O. Box 580
Blackfoot, ID   83221-0580

Foundation type: Operating foundation
Purpose: Scholarships to graduates of Blackfoot
High School and other Bingham County, ID, high
schools for higher education.
Financial data: Year ended 12/31/2012. Assets,
$0 (M); Expenditures, $22,507; Total giving,
$21,000.
Fields of interest: Higher education.
Type of support: Scholarships—to individuals.
Application information: Applications not
accepted.
 Additional information: Scholarships only for
  specific high school students. Unsolicited
  requests for funds not considered or
  acknowledged.
EIN: 202076268

ILLINOIS

2352
A & B Family Foundation
601 S. LaSalle St., Ste. 200
Chicago, IL   60605   (212) 388-1698
Contact: Kenneth D. Alpart, Pres.

Foundation type: Independent foundation
Purpose: Financial assistance to indigents residing in the Chicago, IL metropolitan area.
Financial data: Year ended 12/31/2012. Assets, $37,909 (M); Expenditures, $4,059; Total giving, $0.
Fields of interest: Economically disadvantaged.
Type of support: Grants for special needs.
Application information:
  Initial approach: Letter
  Additional information: Contact foundation for eligibility determination.
EIN: 364334606

2353
The Clara Abbott Foundation
1175 Tri-State Pkwy., Ste. 200
Gurnee, IL   60031-9141   (800) 972-3859
Contact: Christy Wistar, V.P. and Exec. Dir.
FAX: (847) 938-6511;
E-mail: claraabbottfoundation@abbott.com;
Additional tel.: (847) 937-1090; URL: http://clara.abbott.com

Foundation type: Independent foundation
Purpose: Scholarships to dependents of employees and retirees of Abbott Laboratories. Special relief grants and loans, and aid for the aged and economically disadvantaged, only to children of employees and retirees who have worked at Abbott Laboratories for at least two years.
Publications: Annual report (including application guidelines); Financial statement; Informational brochure.
Financial data: Year ended 12/31/2012. Assets, $220,498,413 (M); Expenditures, $7,049,286; Total giving, $3,218,096; Grants to individuals, totaling $3,218,096.
Fields of interest: Education; Aging; Economically disadvantaged.
Type of support: Employee-related scholarships; Employee-related welfare.
Application information: Application form required. Application form available on the grantmaker's web site.
  Applicants should submit the following:
    1) Transcripts
    2) Financial information
Program descriptions:
  Financial Assistance Program: The program provides need-based grants to help eligible Abbott employees and retirees in times of financial difficulty if unable to pay for basic living needs. The following criteria must be met in order to receive a grant: current employee with at least two years of service (or two years from date of Abbott acquisition) and eligible for employee benefits; retiree of Abbott (at least 50 years of age, with a minimum of 10 years of Abbott service); spouse of deceased employee/retiree (until remarried); dependent child of deceased employee/retiree until age 23 for full-time students, age 19 otherwise; special-needs children will not lose eligibility based on age; and an employee who is under a disability program (sponsored by Abbott). All applicants must be enrolled in a health plan.

  Scholarship Program: The program offers need-based scholarships to help the dependent children of Abbott employees and retirees attend accredited colleges or universities, community colleges, vocational and trade schools. Awards are offered to students enrolled in full- or part-time studies to obtain their undergraduate degree. The student must meet the following eligibility requirements: be a dependent child of a full-time, part-time or retired Abbott employee (must be financially supported by and/or living with the Abbott employee). The Abbott employee must have at least 24 months of service (or two years from date of Abbott acquisition) for the student to be eligible; be 17 to 24 years of age as of the deadline date; be a high-school senior, high-school graduate, or current undergraduate student; plan to enroll in a full or part-time undergraduate course of study at an accredited school during the upcoming school year; plan to obtain their first undergraduate degree. If the applicant has already obtained their undergraduate degree or is pursuing a graduate degree, they are not eligible to apply. Applicant must reapply each year and maintain a 2.0 GPA on a 4.0 scale (or equivalent.) Abbott employees and their spouses are not eligible.
Company name: Abbott Laboratories
EIN: 366069632

2354
The Abbvie Patient Assistance Foundation
(formerly The Abbott Patient Assistance Foundation)
200 Abbott Park Rd., D-031C AP31-3NW
Abbott Park, IL   60064-6214   (800) 222-6885
URL: http://www.abbviepaf.org/

Foundation type: Operating foundation
Purpose: Assistance with medications, medical nutritionals, and diabetes care products to economically disadvantaged individuals living below the federal poverty line and to individuals lacking prescription drug coverage.
Publications: Application guidelines.
Financial data: Year ended 12/31/2012. Assets, $30,799,815 (M); Expenditures, $651,002,624; Total giving, $646,459,794; Grants to individuals, totaling $646,459,794.
Fields of interest: Economically disadvantaged.
Type of support: Grants to individuals; Grants for special needs.
Application information: Applications accepted. Application form required. Application form available on the grantmaker's web site.
  Initial approach: Application
  Send request by: Mail
  Deadline(s): None
  Additional information: Applications must include copies of all insurance cards (if applicable), proof of income for all household members, including tax returns, W2, or pay stubs, a physician's signature, and the patients signature.
EIN: 261215559

2355
The Academy of Nutrition & Dietetics
(formerly American Dietetic Association Foundation)
120 S. Riverside Plz., Ste. 2000
Chicago, IL   60606-6995   (312) 889-0040
Contact: Mary Beth Whalen, V.P. and Exec. Dir.
E-mail: foundation@eatright.org; Toll-free tel.: (800) 877-1600; Additional address (DC office): 1120

Connecticut Ave., N.W., Ste. 480, Washington, DC 20036-3989, tel.: (202) 775-8277 ext. 4820, toll-free tel.: (800) 877-0877; URL: http://www.eatright.org

Foundation type: Public charity
Purpose: Scholarships for the study of dietetics to members of the American Dietetic Association.
Publications: Application guidelines.
Financial data: Year ended 05/31/2012. Assets, $18,485,308 (M); Expenditures, $3,002,265; Total giving, $759,633; Grants to individuals, totaling $606,655.
Fields of interest: Health sciences school/education; Nutrition.
Type of support: Graduate support; Undergraduate support.
Application information: Application form required.
  Initial approach: Telephone or e-mail
  Send request by: Mail
  Copies of proposal: 6
  Deadline(s): Vary
  Final notification: Applicants notified in June
  Applicants should submit the following:
    1) Letter(s) of recommendation
    2) Transcripts
    3) GPA
  Additional information: Application should also include GRE scores and a statement of race or ethnicity. See web site for a listing of additional programs.
Program descriptions:
  American Overseas Dietetic Association International Project Award: This award gives a $3,000 prize to American Overseas Dietetic Association (AODA) members who wish to foster collaboration and the sharing of knowledge and skills among food and nutrition professionals in the international community. Awards will be given to AODA members who intend to work in partnership with another food or nutrition professional on a project that will benefit the local community of one of the individuals.
  Barbara Ann F. Hughes - NEP DPG Continuing Education Award: This $1,000 award is available to provide educational stipends for nutrition professionals on the subject of policy initiatives, advocacy, and/or private practice. Applicant must be a member of the American Dietetic Association, be a U.S. citizen, and be planning to attend a conference, seminar, or other form of continuing education for policy initiatives, advocacy, private practice, development of curriculum, or presentation on private practice as a business. Preference will be given to individuals seeking training for skill development or curriculum development in areas of education to increase skills that will enable the member to advocate for expanded or new private insurance coverage and payment for nutrition services, education to increase the skills for collecting nutrition services outcomes data (with the intent that the member will share the outcomes data with private insurance company decision makers who can influence coverage decision and payment for nutrition services), education and skill building that allow member direct participation in national policy initiatives (e.g., ADA Public Policy Workshop and/or participation in state legislative lobbying or other efforts), or the development of a student curriculum or presentation for local members to build the student/practitioners' knowledge and skills on business/private practice procedures, including reimbursement for nutrition services.
  CDR Leadership Grant: Grants of up to $5,000 are available to provide support to registered dietitians (RDs) or dietetic technician registered (DTR) to obtain leadership training, that should prepare individuals to move into leadership

positions within their organizations. Applicants must have been RDs or DTRs for a minimum of three years, must be U.S. citizens, and must demonstrate business acumen, strategic ability, and disciplined execution.

Colgate Palmolive Fellowship in Nutrition, Oral Health, and Dental Education: Grants of up to $15,000 are available to support research in nutrition, oral health, and/or dental education by doctoral students seeking a doctorate in nutrition, oral health, and/or dental education.

E. Neigh Todhunter Memorial Doctoral Fellowship: This award provides financial support of up to $5,000 to a masters-prepared dietetics educator or practitioner for doctoral study in nutrition and dietetics, public health nutrition, or food systems management. Applicants must be a registered dietician, be an active members of the American Dietetic Association (ADA), be a U.S. citizen, be admitted to a doctoral program in nutrition and dietetics, public health nutrition, or food systems management, demonstrate potential for leadership in the profession (with preference given to those who have had three or more years' experience as faculty or preceptors for students in dietetic education programs), and have a career goal of teaching in an accredited/approved dietetics education program.

Edna and Robert Langholz International Nutrition Award: This $25,000 award, presented in even-numbered years, will be presented to a person whose contribution to nutrition has had great international significance.

F. Ann Gallagher Award: This $1,000 award is designed to provide financial support to a registered dietitian who is a member of the Dietetics in Health Care Communities DPG. Applicants should have a demonstrated interest in state or federal legislative issues. Grant money may be used to foster participation by dietitians in legislative issues related to dietetics and may include seminar and symposium fees, travel, lodging, and educational materials.

First International Nutritionist/Dietitian (FIND) Fellowship for Study in the USA: A $2,000 award will be provided to assist foreign national who are pursuing postgraduate work in the U.S.A., and who have a clearly-articulated plan to return to their country. Fellowships will be given to deserving, promising nutritionists/dietitians who intend to practice in a developing country with whose culture they are familiar. Preference will be given to those who come from developing country, and those who have a high financial need. Fellowship monies may be used to enable attendance at workshops, and seminars.

Scholarships: Scholarships are available to deserving students of all levels of study who are studying dietetics and nutrition. All eligible applicants must be members of the American Dietetic Association. Scholarships range from $500 to $10,000.

Wimpfheimer-Guggenheim Fund for International Exchange in Nutrition, Dietetics, and Management: This $1,000 award is available to an outstanding essay describing a food nutrition system improvement, coordinated with an allied partner, to work toward raising the nutritional standards of a community. Examples could include (but are not limited to) foodservice, teaching, or public instructions. Essays should describe projects that are easily adaptable to a variety of situations. Essay winners must submit the essay for publication in a dietetics-related newsletter or magazine.
EIN: 366150906

2356
ADA Foundation
211 E. Chicago Ave.
Chicago, IL 60611-2678 (312) 440-2547
Contact: David A. Whiston D.D.S., Pres.
FAX: (312) 440-3526; E-mail: adaf@ada.org;
URL: http://www.ada.org/applyforassistance.aspx

Foundation type: Public charity
Purpose: Scholarships to dental students. Grants for dental research. Financial assistance to dentists and their dependents who, because of accidental injury, a medical condition or advanced age, are not self-supporting. Grants also to members of the dental profession who are victims of disasters.
Publications: Application guidelines; Annual report; Grants list; Informational brochure.
Financial data: Year ended 12/31/2011. Assets, $23,259,667 (M); Expenditures, $7,795,116; Total giving, $1,557,866; Grants to individuals, totaling $523,901.
Fields of interest: Dental school/education; Dental care; Human services, emergency aid; Minorities.
Type of support: Emergency funds; Research; Graduate support; Undergraduate support; Grants for special needs.
Application information: Applications accepted. Application form required.
Initial approach: E-mail
Deadline(s): Oct. 16 for scholarships; Varies for financial assistance
Additional information: Application forms for all ADA Foundation scholarships are available at dental schools and allied dental health programs. Scholarship application should include letters of recommendation, an essay and financial information. Contact foundation for research and financial assistance application guidelines.
Program descriptions:
Awards: The foundation offers multiple awards to individuals that support the foundation's mission. Awards average $5,000. See web site for additional information.
Fellowships: The foundation offers multiple fellowships to individuals pursuing careers in dentistry. Stipends average $4,000. See web site for additional information.
Grants: The foundation offers multiple grants to organizations and individuals that support the foundation's mission. Grants of up to $13,500 are available. See web site for additional information.
Scholarships: The foundation offers multiple scholarships to individuals pursuing careers in dentistry. See web site for additional information.
EIN: 366132046

2357
Dr. E.W. Adamson Scholarship Fund
10 S. Dearborn IL1-0117
Chicago, IL 60603 (520) 364-3462
Application address: The Principal of Douglas H.S., 1500 15th St., Douglas, AZ 85607

Foundation type: Independent foundation
Purpose: Scholarships to male graduates of Douglas High School, AZ.
Financial data: Year ended 03/31/2013. Assets, $373,512 (M); Expenditures, $11,744; Total giving, $4,500; Grants to individuals, 3 grants totaling $4,500 (high: $1,500, low: $1,500).
Fields of interest: Men.
Type of support: Support to graduates or students of specific schools; Undergraduate support.

Application information: Applications accepted. Application form required.
Deadline(s): Apr. 1
Applicants should submit the following:
1) ACT
2) SAT
3) Financial information
4) GPA
EIN: 866042761

2358
After School Matters, Inc.
66 E. Randolph St.
Chicago, IL 60601-7504 (312) 742-4182
Contact: Margaret C Daley, Chair.
FAX: (312) 742-6631; URL: http://www.afterschoolmatters.org/

Foundation type: Public charity
Purpose: Summer internships for teens of of Chicago, IL enrolled in a Chicago Public high school.
Publications: Annual report; Occasional report.
Financial data: Year ended 06/30/2012. Assets, $6,966,328 (M); Expenditures, $16,936,635; Total giving, $3,117,635; Grants to individuals, totaling $3,117,635.
Fields of interest: Elementary/secondary education; Children/youth.
Type of support: Internship funds.
Application information: Applications accepted. Application form available on the grantmaker's web site. Interview required.
Send request by: On-line
Deadline(s): Aug.-Sept. for Fall programs, Nov.-Jan. for Spring programs, Apr.-June for Summer programs
Additional information: Teens are encouraged to apply for up to three programs to increase their chances of being interviewed and accepted into at least one. Teens must be at least 14 years old and must be Chicago residents. Those who participate in the summer program are eligible to earn a monetary award. See web site for additional guidelines.
EIN: 364409182

2359
Aicardi Syndrome Foundation
P. O. Box 3202
St. Charles, IL 60174-7965
Toll-free tel.: (800) 374-8518; URL: http://www.aicardisyndrome.org/site/node/16

Foundation type: Public charity
Purpose: Assistance for the purchase of medical and adaptive equipment for individuals suffering from Aicardi Symdrome.
Financial data: Year ended 06/30/2012. Assets, $203,892 (M); Expenditures, $56,676; Total giving, $53,091.
Fields of interest: Diseases (rare) research; Economically disadvantaged.
Type of support: Grants for special needs.
Application information: Letter must be provided from a doctor or therapist to receive assistance. Contact the foundation for eligibility determination.
EIN: 363781527

2360
AKA Educational Advancement Foundation, Inc.
5656 S. Stony Island Ave., 3rd Fl.
Chicago, IL 60637-1906 (773) 947-0026
Contact: Barbara F. Sutton, Exec. Dir.
FAX: (773) 947-0277; E-mail: akaeaf@akaeaf.org;
Toll Free Tel.: (800)-653-6528; E-Mail for Barbara
F. Sutton: bsutton@akaeaf.net; URL: http://
www.akaeaf.org

Foundation type: Public charity
Purpose: Scholarships and fellowships to
undergraduate and graduate students for
continuing their education at accredited institutions
of higher learning.
Publications: Application guidelines; Annual report;
Informational brochure.
Financial data: Year ended 12/31/2012. Assets,
$7,626,855 (M); Expenditures, $1,306,368; Total
giving, $390,809; Grants to individuals, totaling
$390,809.
Fields of interest: Higher education.
Type of support: Fellowships; Scholarships—to
individuals; Grants for special needs.
Application information: Applications accepted.
Deadline(s): Apr. 15 and Aug. 15
Program descriptions:
Alice S. Marriott Scholarship: Scholarships are
available to minorities who wish to pursue a
professional career in the hospitality industry.
Community Assistance Awards: The program
awards grants to assist individuals and
organizations for a specific civic, educational or
human service program or project.
Fellowships: Fellowships aid the research and
projects that have practical application that will
improve the quality of life of others. Fellowships do
not require enrollment in an academic institution.
Financial Assistance Scholarships: The program
awards scholarships to full-time student,
sophomore or beyond currently enrolled in an
accredited degree granting institution. Applicant
must have a minimum GPA of 2.5 and demonstrate
community service and involvement.
Merit Scholarships: The program awards
scholarships ranging from $1,000 to $2,500 to
undergraduate and graduate students who excel
academically.
Youth Partners Accessing Capital: Scholarship to
college sophomore who are members of Alpha
Kappa Alpha Sorority, Inc. with a minimum 3.0 GPA.
Applicant must demonstrate exceptional academic
achievement or extreme financial need, and
participate in leadership, volunteer, civic or campus
activities.
EIN: 363104692

2361
Max H. Alberts Scholarship Trust
111 W. Monroe St., Tax Div. 10C
Chicago, IL 60603 (920) 699-3481
Application Address: c/o Johnson Creek High
School, 111 S. St., Johnson Creek, WI 53038

Foundation type: Independent foundation
Purpose: Scholarships for undergraduate study to
graduates of Johnson Creek High School, WI.
Financial data: Year ended 04/30/2013. Assets,
$771,733 (M); Expenditures, $46,168; Total
giving, $35,500; Grants to individuals, 5 grants
totaling $35,500 (high: $7,100, low: $7,100).
Type of support: Support to graduates or students
of specific schools; Undergraduate support.
Application information: Applications accepted.

Initial approach: Letter
Deadline(s): Mar. 30
EIN: 396498404

2362
Jessie V. Allhands Education Trust
P.O. Box 100
Albion, IL 62806
Contact: Vicki Litherland
Application address: c/o Edwards County High
School, Attn.: Vicki Litherland, Guidance Counselor,
361 W. Main St., Albion, IL 62806-1011

Foundation type: Independent foundation
Purpose: Scholarships to graduates of Edwards
County High School, IL, who have maintained a "C"
average or better.
Financial data: Year ended 12/31/2012. Assets,
$511,654 (M); Expenditures, $22,608; Total
giving, $19,300; Grants to individuals, 11 grants
totaling $19,300 (high: $3,000, low: $500).
Fields of interest: Higher education.
Type of support: Support to graduates or students
of specific schools.
Application information: Applications accepted.
Application form required.
Deadline(s): Apr. 1
Additional information: See guidance counselor
for application guidelines.
EIN: 376305145

2363
The Allstate Foundation
2775 Sanders Rd., Ste. F4
Northbrook, IL 60062-6127 (847) 402-7849
Contact: Patricia Lara Garza, Dir., Strategic
Philanthropy
E-mail for High School Award:
KeeptheDrive@allstate.com
FAX: (847) 402-7568; E-mail: Grants@Allstate.com;
Additional e-mails: Jan Epstein -
jepstein@allstate.com; Sue Duchak -
sue.duchak@allstate.com; Jennifer McGrath -
jennifermcgrath@allstate.com; Chindaly Griffith -
chindaly.griffith@allstate.com; e-mail for High
School Award: KeeptheDrive@allstate.com;
URL: http://www.allstatefoundation.org/

Foundation type: Company-sponsored foundation
Purpose: Awards to high school teens who address
teen driving through print or broadcast journalism.
Publications: Application guidelines; Program
policy statement.
Financial data: Year ended 12/31/2012. Assets,
$65,952,209 (M); Expenditures, $19,764,214;
Total giving, $17,269,127. Awards/prizes amount
not specified.
Fields of interest: Print publishing; Web-based
media; Journalism; Safety, automotive safety.
Type of support: Grants to individuals; Awards/
prizes.
Application information: Applications accepted.
Application form required. Application form
available on the grantmaker's web site.
Initial approach: Application
Send request by: Online
Deadline(s): Mar. 1
Program description:
Keep the Drive High School Journalism Awards:
The foundation annually awards grants to high
school teens who address through print or
broadcast journalism the importance of stronger
driver laws at the state or national level. Applicants
for the print journalism category and must submit
published newspaper articles and applications for
the broadcast journalism category must upload

broadcast video segments on YouTube. Grand prize
winners receive $2,000, second place winners
receive $1,000, and a third place winner receives
$750. See Web site for additional information,
http://www.keepthedrive.com/.
EIN: 366116535

2364
Ameren Illinois Corporate Giving Program
(formerly Illinois Power Company Contributions
Program)
c/o Corp. Contribs.
300 Liberty St.
Peoria, IL 61602-1404
Scholarship address: Wanda Cruz, Ameren Illinois,
370 South Main St., E-05, Decatur, IL 62523,
e-mail: wcruz@ameren.com
E-mail: communityrelationsil@ameren.com;
URL: http://www.ameren.com/sites/aiu/
Community/Pages/default.aspx

Foundation type: Corporate giving program
Purpose: Scholarships to minority residents of the
Ameren Illinois distribution service area, pursuing a
major in an engineering discipline.
Publications: Application guidelines.
Fields of interest: Economic development;
Engineering; Minorities; Economically
disadvantaged.
Type of support: Scholarships—to individuals;
Undergraduate support.
Application information: Applications accepted.
Application form required. Application form
available on the grantmaker's web site.
Send request by: Mail
Deadline(s): Apr. 8
Applicants should submit the following:
1) GPA
2) Transcripts
3) Financial information
4) Essay
Additional information: The award is paid to the
educational institution on behalf of the
student.
Program description:
Ameren Illinois Minority Scholarship: Through the
Ameren Illinois Minority Scholarship program,
Ameren Illinois awards one, annually renewable,
$2,500 scholarship every year to a minority
graduating, high school senior accepted to an
accredited two year or four year college or university
in the United States. Scholarship recipients must
earn a 2.6 GPA on a 4.0 scale or its equivalent,
major in an engineering discipline, and are invited
to work at Ameren each summer as a summer
intern. Applicant must be a permanent resident with
the Ameren Illinois distribution service area at the
time the scholarship is first awarded.

2365
American Academy of Dermatology, Inc.
930 E. Woodfield Rd.
Schaumburg, IL 60173-4729 (847) 240-1280
Contact: Dirk M. Elston M.D., Pres.
FAX: (847) 240-1859; E-mail: mrc@aad.org; Mailing
address (Schaumburg office): P.O. Box 4014,
Schaumburg, IL 60168-4014; toll-free tel.: (866)
503-7546; additional address: 1350 I St., N.W.,
Ste. 870, Washington, DC 20005-4355, tel.: (202)
842-3555, fax: (202) 842-4355; URL: http://
www.aad.org

Foundation type: Public charity
Purpose: Awards and research grants to individuals
in the field of dermatology. Preference given to
members of the American Academy of Dermatology.

Publications: Application guidelines.
Financial data: Year ended 12/31/2011. Assets, $59,242,222 (M); Expenditures, $26,813,698; Total giving, $1,429,487; Grants to individuals, totaling $574,139.
Fields of interest: Skin disorders research.
Type of support: Research; Awards/grants by nomination only; Awards/prizes.
Application information: Application form available on the grantmaker's web site.
  Deadline(s): Vary
  Applicants should submit the following:
    1) Letter(s) of recommendation
    2) Curriculum vitae
  Additional information: See web site for complete application information.
Program descriptions:
  Awards for Young Investigators in Dermatology: The awards recognize outstanding research by dermatologists-in-training in the United States and Canada, as well as the educational institutions that support their efforts. The purpose of the awards is to acknowledge their contributions to further research for the improvement of diagnosis and therapeutics in the practice and science of dermatology. Two outstanding young investigators are selected as recipients each year and the awards are presented during the foundation's annual meeting. Winners receive an engraved plaque and a $6,000 prize that is shared between the investigator and the nominating institution on a 50:50 basis.
  Diversity Mentorship Program: Medical students who are considered to be underrepresented in medicine may apply to this program, which offers hands-on exposure to students who are interested in learning more about dermatology as a medical specialty. Mentorships encompass 160 hours over the course of one month and include a stipend of $1,500 to help cover the cost of travel, housing, and meals.
  Gold Foundation Humanism in Medicine Award: The award honors practicing dermatologists who exemplify compassionate, patient-centered care. Dermatologists can receive awards of $1,000 and reimbursement of up to $2,000 for travel to the academy's annual meeting.
  Named Lectureships Awards: Cash prizes, ranging from $7,500 to $25,000, are awarded to recognize experts in the field of cancer research, therapy, and dermatology issues.
  Native American Resident Health Service Rotation Program: This program provides funding for four U.S. dermatology residents in their second or third year of residency to participate in a one- to two-week rural health elective in Chinle, Arizona at the Indian Health Service. Residents will have an opportunity to provide dermatologic care to the Navajo Nation population, which doesn't have access to such care. Residents are expected to keep records of consults, prepare lectures, and present a report of activities to the academy.
  Resident International Grant: This grant provides funding for twelve U.S. or Canadian senior dermatology residents to participate in a four-week to six-week elective in Gaborone, Botswana, where participants rotate between the Princess Marina Hospital and the Baylor International Pediatric AIDS Initiative. Residents take part in dermatologic HIV care for both children and adults.
  Scientific Meeting Scholarships and Grants: Scholarships and grants are available to international and U.S. dermatologists and dermatology students to attend the academy's annual meeting or its summer meeting.
  Sulzberger Grants: The program supports technology-based teaching applications to further clinical education in dermatology and dermatologic

surgery. Proposals from dermatologists who are members of the academy will be given preference; however all proposals to develop technology for dermatology education will be considered. Research grants are at present not in excess of $60,000 per year, for a period of one to two years. Grants are preferentially awarded to young dermatologists who have not previously received significant extramural funding. Small grants ($5,000) are earmarked for residents and fellows with little or no research experience but with committed local research mentors. An annual grant ($7,500) is also available for tuition support for education and technology courses accredited by the National Library of Medicine (NLM)
  Volunteer Grant: Grants, ranging from $2,500 to $10,000, are available to physician members of the academy (or potential members who have completed residency training) to volunteer to teach for three to six months or more at the Regional Dermatology Training Center in Moshi, Tanzania, or another approved educational program in a developing country. A minimum three months' commitment is required.
EIN: 410793046

2366
American Academy of Pediatrics
141 Northwest Point Blvd.
Elk Grove Village, IL   60007-1098   (847) 434-4000
Contact: Errol Alden M.D., F.A.A.P., C.E.O. and Exec. Dir.
FAX: (847) 434-8000; URL: http://www.aap.org

Foundation type: Public charity
Purpose: Grants to support pediatricians in the pilot stage of implementing a community-based child health initiative, where children's access to a medical home or specific health services not otherwise available. Research and scholarship grants are also available for the study of pediatrics.
Publications: Application guidelines.
Financial data: Year ended 06/30/2012. Assets, $93,829,702 (M); Expenditures, $100,924,558; Total giving, $2,110,092; Grants to individuals, totaling $2,000.
Fields of interest: Pediatrics; Pediatrics research.
Type of support: Research; Grants to individuals; Scholarships—to individuals; Project support.
Application information:
  Initial approach: Letter
  Deadline(s): Varies
  Additional information: Contact foundation for further eligibility requirements.
Program descriptions:
  Anne E. Dyson Child Advocacy Award: Awards to outstanding pediatricians-in-training as they work in their communities to improve the health of children, and projects designed and implemented by residents, which aim to improve the lives of children. The award includes $300 in funds to advance the winning project's goals, travel and lodging expenses for one resident per project, and press releases and recognition in academy publications.
  CATCH Implementation Funds Grant: Grants from $2,500 to $12,000 are available to support pediatricians in the initial and/or pilot stage of developing and implementing a community-based child health initiative. Priority will be given to projects serving communities with the greatest demonstrated health care access needs and health disparities. Specific initiatives can include promoting medical homes for hard-to-reach populations with disparities, targeting areas with large numbers of uninsured children and poor

health outcomes, demonstrating community collaboration, assessing needs in the community, and collaborating with SCHIP and/or state Medicaid programs. Priority will also be given to programs offered by pediatricians interested in developing projects focused on reducing secondhand tobacco smoke exposure for children and youth.
  Children's Art Contest: The academy annually sponsors an art contest for boys and girls in two groups, grades 3-5, 6-8, and 9-12 that reflects a specific theme chosen by the academy every year. The winner in each group, and their parents and guardians, will be invited to attend the academy's annual national conference and exhibition in Boston. Both winners will receive $500 and up to $1,000 for travel-related expenses; three second-place winners will each receive $250. In addition to individual awards, the four winners' schools will receive matching cash amounts.
  International Elective Award: Each academic year, the academy will provide a minimum of twelve $500 awards to residents who wish to complete a clinical pediatric elective in the developing world during residency. Resident applicants must be enrolled in pediatric residency training programs that are approved for credit toward certification by the American Board of Pediatrics, the American Osteopathic Board of Pediatrics, the Royal College of Physicians and Surgeons of Canada, or La Corporation Professionelle des Medecins du Quebec.
  International Travel Grants: At least ten grants of $500 each are available annually to categorical pediatric or combined-training pediatric residents who wish to complete a clinical pediatric elective in the developing world during residency. Grants are available only to those programs that do not directly provide compensation to its participants.
  NCE Program Delegate Award: Travel grants of $300 will be made available to residents who serve as program delegates to the academy, to attend the academy's annual National Conference and Exhibition. Awards are available to both categorical and combined-training pediatric residents; however, only one award is available per institution.
  Residency Scholarships: Scholarships from $1,000 to $5,000 to help allay financial difficulties for residents in good academic standing. Eligible applicants must: have completed or will have completed an approved internship, or have completed a PL-1 year, by July 1 of the year the scholarship is being applied to; be a pediatric resident (categorical or combined) in a training program and have a definite commitment for another year of residency or chief residency (not fellowship) in a program accredited by the Residency Review Committee for Pediatrics; and have a substantial need for financial assistance.
  Resident Initiative Fund: Twenty grants of up to $1,000 each are available to enable residents to educate fellow residents and/or parents on a specific aspect of one of the academy's national child health priorities: special health care needs; foster care; oral health; mental health; and immunizations.
  Resident Research Grants: Grants of up to $2,000 are available to pediatric residents to initiate and complete research projects related to their professional interest. Applicants will be required to complete their projects during their residency training (within two years)
  Visiting Professorships in Community Pediatrics: This program promotes advocacy for children and works to advance the field of community pediatrics with up to $4,500 to fund a 2- or 3-day educational program focusing on the field of community pediatrics.
EIN: 362275597

2367
American Association of Endodontists Foundation
211 E. Chicago Ave., Ste. 1100
Chicago, IL 60611-2687
E-mail: foundation@aae.org; Tel./Fax: (312) 266-7255; Toll-free tel.: (800) 872-3636;
URL: http://www.aae.org/foundation/

Foundation type: Public charity
Purpose: Research grants and fellowships to educators for clinical research, educational programs and for opportunities in endodontology.
Publications: Application guidelines.
Financial data: Year ended 12/31/2011. Assets, $25,125,946 (M); Expenditures, $2,260,687; Total giving, $1,464,543; Grants to individuals, 213 grants totaling $954,931.
Fields of interest: Dental school/education.
Type of support: Fellowships; Research; Postgraduate support.
Application information: Applications accepted. Application form required.
 Deadline(s): Vary
 Additional information: See web site for additional application guidelines.
EIN: 366143003

2368
American Association of Law Libraries
105 W. Adams St., Ste. 3300
Chicago, IL 60603-6225   (312) 939-4764
Contact: Kate Hagan, Exec. Dir.
E-mail for scholarships: scholarships@aall.org
FAX: (312) 431-1097; E-mail: sfox@aall.org;
URL: http://www.aallnet.org

Foundation type: Public charity
Purpose: Scholarships to students planning to become a law librarian.
Publications: Application guidelines; Occasional report.
Financial data: Year ended 09/30/2012. Assets, $6,387,432 (M); Expenditures, $3,723,739; Total giving, $65,263; Grants to individuals, totaling $62,243.
Fields of interest: Law school/education; Minorities.
Type of support: Scholarships—to individuals; Graduate support.
Application information: Applications accepted. Application form required.
 Initial approach: Telephone or letter
 Deadline(s): Apr. 1
 Applicants should submit the following:
  1) Financial information
  2) Resume
  3) SASE
  4) Letter(s) of recommendation
Program descriptions:
 AALL/George A. Strait Minority Scholarship Endowment Application: These scholarships are awarded annually to college graduates with meaningful law library experience who are members of a minority group as defined by current U.S. government guidelines, are degree candidates in an accredited library or law school, and who intend to have career in law librarianship. Applicants must show evidence of financial need.
 AALL/Marcia J. Koslov Scholarship: The scholarship provides funding for members who serve as librarians in state, court, or county libraries to attend live seminars and conferences presented by the Institute for Court Management, the Center for Legal and Court Technology, the Equal Justice Conference, or other programs that provide continuing education for state, court, or county law libraries.
 Educational Scholarships: Each year, the foundation awards scholarships to applicants who are planning to attend a library or law school, or who are planning to continue their education by taking courses related to law librarianship. Preference will be given to association members, though non-association members are eligible for specific scholarship opportunities.
 LexisNexis John R. Johnson Memorial Scholarship: This program awards a scholarship in the amount of $3,000 to a library school graduate with law library experience who is pursuing a degree in an accredited law school with the intention of having a career in law librarianship. Applicants must have no more that 36 semester credit hours remaining before qualifying for the degree.
EIN: 362536424

2369
American Bar Association
321 N. Clark St.
Chicago, IL 60654-4714   (312) 988-5000
URL: http://www.abanet.org

Foundation type: Public charity
Purpose: Awards and fellowships for law students to attend colleges and universities in the U.S.
Publications: Application guidelines.
Financial data: Year ended 08/31/2011. Assets, $239,942,508 (M); Expenditures, $129,770,486; Total giving, $773,890; Grants to individuals, totaling $82,485.
Fields of interest: Law school/education.
Type of support: Grants to individuals.
Application information: Applications accepted. Application form required.
 Additional information: See web site for additional guidelines.
Program descriptions:
 Diversity Felloeships in Environmental Law: This fellowship encourages disadvantaged or traditionally underrepresented law students to study and pursue careers in environmental law.
 Janed D. Steiger Fellowship Project: The fellowship provides law students the opportunity to work in the consumer protection departments of state and territorial Offices of Attorneys General.
 Law Student Program of the Year Award: This program recognizes the best student-organized educational program or public service project focusing on environmental, energy, or natural resources law.
EIN: 360723150

2370
American Bar Association Fund for Justice and Education
321 N. Clark St., 21st Fl.
Chicago, IL 60610-4714   (312) 988-5927
FAX: (312) 988-6392; E-mail: fje@staff.abanet.org;
Toll-free tel.: (800) 285-2221; URL: http://www.abanet.org/fje

Foundation type: Public charity
Purpose: Scholarships to minority students for attendance at law school.
Publications: Application guidelines; Annual report; Grants list.
Financial data: Year ended 08/31/2011. Assets, $23,735,586 (M); Expenditures, $64,446,639; Total giving, $8,224,385; Grants to individuals, totaling $742,200.
Fields of interest: Law school/education; Minorities.

Type of support: Graduate support.
Application information: Applications accepted. Application form required. Application form available on the grantmaker's web site.
 Send request by: Mail
 Deadline(s): Mar. 1
 Applicants should submit the following:
  1) Transcripts
  2) Letter(s) of recommendation
  3) Essay
  4) Financial information
  5) GPA
Program description:
 Legal Opportunity Scholarship Fund: Scholarships of $5,000 annually awarded to students of racial and ethnic minority to attend an ABA-accredited law school. Awards made to entering first-year students may be renewable for two additional years for a total of $15,000 in financial assistance during student's time in law school. Recipients are chosen based on: whether they are a member of a racial and/or ethnic minority that has been underrepresented in the legal profession; financial need; personal, family and educational background; and participation in community service activities. To be eligible, applicant must: be an entering first-year law student; have a minimum 2.5 GPA (on a 4.0 scale) at his/her undergraduate institution; and be a citizen or permanent resident of the U.S.
EIN: 366110299

2371
American Bar Foundation
750 N. Lake Shore Dr.
Chicago, IL 60611-3152   (312) 988-6500
Contact: Hon. Bernice B. Donald, Pres.
FAX: (312) 988-6579;
E-mail: fellowships@abfn.org; URL: http://www.abf-sociolegal.org

Foundation type: Public charity
Purpose: Fellowships to outstanding students who are postdoctoral scholars, doctoral candidates, graduate and undergraduate students for degrees in social sciences.
Publications: Application guidelines; Annual report; Informational brochure; Newsletter.
Financial data: Year ended 08/31/2011. Assets, $20,348,828 (M); Expenditures, $6,084,527; Total giving, $215,813; Grants to individuals, totaling $215,813.
Fields of interest: Law school/education; Social sciences.
Type of support: Fellowships; Postdoctoral support; Graduate support; Undergraduate support; Doctoral support.
Application information: Applications accepted. Application form required.
 Deadline(s): Dec. 15 for ABF Doctoral Fellowship, Dec. 1 for Law and Social Science Fellowship & Mentoring Program and Feb. 15 for Summer Research Diversity Fellowships
Program descriptions:
 ABF Doctoral Fellowship Program: Applications are invited from outstanding students who are candidates for Ph.D. degrees in the social sciences. Applicants must have completed all doctoral requirements except the dissertation. Fellows receive a stipend of $27,000 for 12 months. Fellows also may request up to $1,500 to reimburse expenses associated with research, travel to meet with advisors, or travel to conferences at which papers are presented. Relocation expenses up to $2,500 may be reimbursed on application.

Law and Social Science Dissertation Fellowship & Mentoring Program: Fellowships are held in residence at the American Bar Foundation in Chicago, IL, where Fellows are expected to participate in the intellectual life of the ABF, including participating in a weekly seminar series. Fellows receive a stipend of $27,000 per year and are eligible for up to two years of support. Fellows also receive up to $1,500 for research and travel expenses each year, and relocation expenses up to $2,500 may be reimbursed one time. Eligible applicants must be third-, fourth-, and fifth-year graduate students specializing in the field of law and social science and whose research interests include law and inequality.

Summer Research Diversity Fellowships in Law and Social Science for Undergraduate Students: Four summer research fellowships will be awarded each year. Each student will be assigned to an American Bar Foundation Research Professor who will involve the student in the professor's research project and who will act as mentor during the student's tenure. The students also will participate in a series of seminars and field visits to acquaint them with the many facets of sociolegal research and the legal system. The students will work at the American Bar Foundation's offices in Chicago, IL for 35 hours a week for a period of 8 weeks. Each student will receive a stipend of $3,600. Applicants must have a 3.0 GPA or higher and be moving toward an academic major in the social sciences or humanities.
EIN: 366110271

2372
American Brain Tumor Association
8550 W. Bryn Mawr Ave., Ste. 550
Chicago, IL 60631-3225 (773) 577-8750
Contact: Elizabeth Wilson, Pres. and C.E.O.
FAX: (773) 577-8738; E-mail: info@abta.org; Toll-free tel.: (800) 886-2282; E-mail For Elizabeth M. Wilson: ewilson@abta.org; URL: http://www.abta.org

Foundation type: Public charity
Purpose: Fellowships and research awards to researchers, to support new and early career scientists entering the field of brain tumor research.
Publications: Annual report; Informational brochure; Informational brochure (including application guidelines); Newsletter.
Financial data: Year ended 06/30/2012. Assets, $3,632,188 (M); Expenditures, $4,445,459; Total giving, $1,969,631; Grants to individuals, totaling $1,656,500.
Fields of interest: Brain disorders; Brain research.
Type of support: Fellowships.
Application information: Applications accepted. Application form available on the grantmaker's web site.
Initial approach: Proposal
Deadline(s): Varies
Additional information: See web site for additional guidelines.
Program descriptions:
Basic Research Fellowships: The intent of the fellowship program is to encourage talented scientists early in their careers to enter, or remain in, the field of brain tumor research. The association hopes that these awards will help ensure a continuum of dedicated, well-trained brain tumor researchers. Fellowships are $100,000 awards payable over a two-year period ($45,000 salary support and $5,000 in discretionary funding per year). Eligible applicants must be M.Ds. who are within two years of resident completion or within five years of post-residency training; or Ph.Ds. who have

their doctorate and no more than five years of postdoctoral laboratory experience. Criteria for selection include the potential of the candidate (including their commitment to neuro-oncology), the training program environment, and the proposed research.

Discovery Research Grant Program: These $50,000 grants are awarded to high-risk, high-impact projects that are deemed to have the potential to change current diagnostic or treatment paradigms for adult and pediatric brain tumor care. Investigators from sciences outside of traditional biology fields are encouraged to apply.

Medical Student Summer Fellowships: These fellowships are intended to motivate talented medical students to pursue a career in neuro-oncology research by providing $3,000 stipend grants to current medical students wishing to spend a summer conducting brain tumor research. The fellowship is to be conducted in a neuro-oncology laboratory with a mentorship setting designed to provide an introductory learning experience.

Neuro-Oncology Nursing Research Award: Awarded in conjunction with the Oncology Nursing Society Foundation, this two-year, $10,000 grant will be made available for research on symptom management, support systems, or quality of life in neuro-oncology patients and their families. Funding preference will be given to projects that involve nurses in the design and conduct of the research activity, and that promote theoretically-based oncology practice.
EIN: 237286648

2373
American College of Allergy, Asthma, and Immunology
85 W. Algonquin Rd., Ste. 550
Arlington Heights, IL 60005-4460 (847) 427-1200
Contact: Bob Q. Lanier M.D., Exec. Dir.
FAX: (847) 427-1294; E-mail: info@acaai.org; URL: http://www.acaai.org

Foundation type: Public charity
Purpose: Awards to researchers in the fields of allergy, asthma, and immunology.
Financial data: Year ended 12/31/2012. Assets, $19,247,403 (M); Expenditures, $6,927,351; Total giving, $229,356; Grants to individuals, totaling $3,000.
Fields of interest: Allergies research; Asthma research.
Type of support: Research.
Application information: Applications accepted. Application form required.
Additional information: Applicant must demonstrate financial need.
EIN: 840457367

2374
American College of Foot and Ankle Surgeons
8725 W. Higgins Rd., Ste. 555
Chicago, IL 60631-2724 (773) 693-9300
Contact: J.C. Mahaffey, Exec. Dir.
FAX: (773) 693-9304; E-mail: info@acfas.org; Toll-free tel.: (800) 421-2237; Toll-free fax: (800) 382-8270; E-mail For J.C. Mahaffey: Mahaffey@acfas.org; URL: http://www.acfas.org

Foundation type: Public charity
Purpose: Scholarships to outstanding students to attend the college's annual scientific conference.

Financial data: Year ended 12/31/2011. Assets, $8,933,275 (M); Expenditures, $4,619,880; Total giving, $44,611; Grants to individuals, totaling $35,598.
Fields of interest: Education.
Type of support: Scholarships—to individuals.
Application information: Applications accepted. Application form available on the grantmaker's web site.
Initial approach: Application
Deadline(s): Varies
Program description:
Scholarships: Scholarships of $1,000 each are available to outstanding students to defray travel expenses to the college's annual scientific conference. Scholarship winners are also granted complimentary conference registration.
EIN: 237171433

2375
American Dental Association
(also known as ADA)
211 E. Chicago Ave.
Chicago, IL 60611-2678 (312) 440-2500
Contact: Dr. Kathleen T. O'Loghlin, Exec. Dir.
URL: http://www.ada.org

Foundation type: Public charity
Purpose: Limited scholarship and student loans for individuals nationwide who are pursuing careers in dentistry.
Publications: Occasional report.
Financial data: Year ended 12/31/2011. Assets, $136,725,969 (M); Expenditures, $113,515,370; Total giving, $6,151,758. Student loans—to individuals amount not specified. Scholarships—to individuals amount not specified.
Fields of interest: Dental school/education.
Type of support: Scholarships—to individuals; Student loans—to individuals.
Application information: Applications accepted.
Additional information: Contact the association for additional guidelines.
EIN: 360724690

2376
American Dental Hygienist Association Institute for Oral Health
444 N. Michigan Ave., Ste. 3400
Chicago, IL 60611-3980 (312) 440-8900
Contact: Pamela L. Quinones, Chair.
E-mail: mail@adha.net; Toll-free tel: (800) 243-2432; URL: http://www.adha.org/ioh/

Foundation type: Public charity
Purpose: Scholarships to undergraduate and graduate dental hygiene students who have completed at least one year in a dental hygiene program. Fellowships and research grants to individuals for excellence in dental hygiene.
Publications: Application guidelines; Annual report.
Financial data: Year ended 06/30/2012. Assets, $867,795 (M); Expenditures, $172,116; Total giving, $100,500; Grants to individuals, totaling $45,500.
Fields of interest: Dental school/education; Dental care.
Type of support: Research; Scholarships—to individuals; Graduate support; Doctoral support.
Application information: Applications accepted. Application form required. Application form available on the grantmaker's web site.
Deadline(s): Feb. 1 for scholarships
Final notification: Applicants notified after July 1 for scholarships
Applicants should submit the following:

1) Curriculum vitae
2) Letter(s) of recommendation
3) Transcripts

Additional information: Applicant must be an active member of the Student American Dental Hygienists' Association (SADHA) or the American Dental Hygienists' Association (ADHA). Application should include financial information. See web site for additional information and scholarship programs.

Program descriptions:

ADHA Institute Scholarship Program: Awards $2,000 each fall to an average of 60 to 80 students. The program exists primarily to help qualified students in their second year or above of dental hygiene school meet their financial needs.

Institute Fellowship Grant Program: Two fellowships of not more than $5,000 will be awarded annually to faculty members pursuing a master of science degree in dental hygiene education or doctoral work.

Rosie Wall Community Spirit Grant Program: Funding for the award is limited to $1,000 to $3,000 to individuals who are involved in specific community health or search projects.

The ADHA Institute Research Grant Program: This grant program is a competition designed to offer funding for student and professional dental hygiene research. Amounts ranging from $1,000 to $10,000 are awarded each spring/summer.

EIN: 363468143

2377
American Hearing Research Foundation

8 S. Michigan Ave., Ste. 1205
Chicago, IL 60603-3385   (312) 726-9670
Contact: Sharon Parmet, Exec. Dir.
FAX: (312) 726-9695;
E-mail: ahrf@american-hearing.org; URL: http://www.american-hearing.org

Foundation type: Public charity
Purpose: Medical research grants relating to the causes, prevention, and cures of deafness, impaired hearing and balance disorders.
Publications: Application guidelines; Newsletter.
Financial data: Year ended 12/31/2011. Assets, $5,360,597 (M); Expenditures, $308,046; Total giving, $125,000. Grants to individuals amount not specified.
Fields of interest: Medical research; Deaf/hearing impaired.
Type of support: Research.
Application information: Applications accepted. Application form required. Application form available on the grantmaker's web site.
Initial approach: Application
Send request by: Mail or e-mail
Copies of proposal: 14
Deadline(s): Aug. 1
Additional information: See web site for details on application guidelines.

Program description:

Georgia Birtman Grant: This grant supports the advancement of research and education in otology and neurotology. The grant is awarded to an exceptional researcher in audiology, otology or neurotology who will work in a lab at Northwestern University. The foundation gives this grant together with the Northwestern Memorial Foundation. The grant is in the amount of $20,000.

EIN: 362612784

2378
American Institute of Indian Studies

1130 E. 59th St.
Chicago, IL 60637-1539   (773) 702-8638
E-mail: aiis@uchicago.edu; URL: http://www.indiastudies.org

Foundation type: Public charity
Purpose: Grants to performing artists for study in India. Fellowships to doctoral candidates and scholars for study of Indian history, culture, and contemporary life in India.
Publications: Application guidelines; Informational brochure; Newsletter.
Financial data: Year ended 06/30/2012. Assets, $8,405,957 (M); Expenditures, $4,541,924; Total giving, $483,640; Grants to individuals, totaling $118,264.
Fields of interest: Performing arts; Arts, artist's services; Graduate/professional education; Education.
International interests: India.
Type of support: Fellowships; Research; Postdoctoral support.
Application information: Applications accepted. Application form required. Application form available on the grantmaker's web site.
Send request by: E-mail
Deadline(s): July 1
Final notification: Applicants notified by Oct.
Applicants should submit the following:
1) Proposal
2) Work samples
3) Transcripts
4) Curriculum vitae
5) Letter(s) of recommendation
Additional information: Application must also include a copy of the applicant's passport and any Indian visa stamps, institutional affiliation form, project information sheet, reviewer worksheet, and a $25 application fee.

Program descriptions:

Junior Research Fellowships: These fellowships are available to doctoral candidates at U.S. colleges and universities in all fields of study. The fellowships are specifically designed to enable doctoral candidates to pursue their dissertation research in India. Fellows establish formal affiliations with Indian universities and Indian research supervisors. Awards are available for up to 11 months. Fellowships for four months or less have significant restrictions. Fellowships for six months or more may include limited coverage for dependents if funds are available.

Senior Performing and Creative Arts Fellowships: These fellowships are available to accomplished practitioners of performing arts of India who demonstrate that study in India would enhance their skills, develop their capabilities to teach or perform in the U.S., enhance American involvement with India's artistic traditions, and strengthen their links with peers in India.

Senior Research Fellowships: These fellowships are available to scholars who hold a Ph.D. or its equivalent and are either U.S. citizens or resident aliens teaching full-time at U.S. colleges and universities. The fellowships are designed to enable scholars specializing in South Asian studies to pursue further research in India. Fellows establish formal affiliations with Indian institutions. Awards are available for up to nine months. Fellowships for four months or less have significant travel restrictions.

Senior Scholarly/Professional Development Fellowships: These fellowships are available to established scholars who have not previously specialized in Indian studies, and to established professionals who have not previously worked or studied in India. Fellows must be formally affiliated

with an Indian institution. Awards may be granted for periods of six to nine months.
EIN: 236297039

2379
American Library Association

50 E. Huron St.
Chicago, IL 60611-2795
Contact: Roberta Stevens, Pres.
FAX: (312) 944-9374; E-mail: ala@ala.org; Toll-free tel.: (800) 545-2433; TDD: (888) 814-7692;
URL: http://www.ala.org

Foundation type: Public charity
Purpose: Graduate scholarships for study in association-accredited master's degree programs. Awards to librarians, authors, and other individuals for contributions to libraries and librarianship. Research grants for the study of library-related topics, and travel grants to attend the organization's annual conference.
Publications: Application guidelines.
Financial data: Year ended 08/31/2011. Assets, $69,724,896 (M); Expenditures, $47,409,564; Total giving, $1,603,527; Grants to individuals, totaling $1,603,527.
Fields of interest: Libraries/library science; Libraries (public).
Type of support: Program development; Research; Scholarships—to individuals; Awards/prizes; Graduate support; Travel grants.
Application information: Applications accepted.
Initial approach: Application
Deadline(s): July 31 for Emerging Leaders, Nov. 4 for Women's National Book Association/ Ann Heidbreder Eastman Grant, Mar. 1 for others. Varies for awards programs
Additional information: Application for graduate scholarship should include an essay, a one-page, typewritten statement of no more than 300 words. See web site for further information and a complete listing of programs.

Program descriptions:

AASL School Librarian's Workshop Scholarship: This program is funded by the Open Society Foundations and administered by the Office of Intellectual Freedom of ALA. This news education program is designed to help students in grades 10-12 learn skills that will help them distinguish fact from opinion, check news and information sources, and distinguish between propaganda and news. Students participating in the program will work with librarians, journalists, and news ethicists to learn to better analyze news coverage and improve their news literacy. Three public libraries will be selected to participate in the second year of the program. The libraries will receive several benefits, including more than $50,000 worth of training and support; the opportunity to provide a chance for young people to work and connect with journalists and become part of a national network; and a stipend for each student who completes the project.

ALA Scholarships for Library Support Staff: Scholarships are available to library support staff currently working in a library and who have applied for admission to a formal program of library and information studies leading to a master's degree. Eligible applicants must be U.S. or Canadian citizens or permanent residents who are attending an association-accredited master's program and have no more than 12 semester hours towards an M.L.S./M.L.I.S./M.I.S. prior to June 1 of the year awarded. Scholarships include the Tom and Robert Drewes Scholarship ($3,000 paid in two installments), the Miriam L. Hornback Scholarship

($3,000 paid in two installments), and the Tony B. Leisner Scholarship ($3,000 paid in two installments). A personal statement must accompany application.

Bechtel Fellowship: A $4,000 stipend is available for qualified children's librarians to conduct research at the Baldwin Library of the George A. Smathers Libraries, University of Florida, Gainesville, a special collection of children's literature. Eligible applicants must have personal membership in the Association for Library Service to Children, currently work and have at least eight years' experience in direct service to children (or be retired members who completed their careers in direct service to children), and have a graduate degree from an association-accredited program.

Bound to Stay Bound Books Scholarship: Four $6,500 awards are available annually towards the education of individuals who intend to pursue an M.L.S. or advanced degree and who plan to work in the area of library service to children. This work may be serving children up to and including the age of 14 in any type library.

Carnegie Corporation of New York/New York Times I Love My Librarian Award: The award encourages library users to recognize the accomplishment of exceptional public, school, college, community college, or university libraries. Up to ten nominated librarians will receive a $5,000 cash award, a plaque, and a $500 travel stipend to attend the awards reception in New York hosted by the New York Times.

Frederic G. Melcher Scholarship: This program provides two $6,000 scholarships for the professional education of men and women who intend to pursue an M.L.S. degree and who plan to work in children's librarianship. This work may be serving children up to and including the age of 14 in any type of library.

Isadore Gilbert Mudge Award: A $5,000 award is available to an individual who has made a distinguished contribution to reference librarianship, including but not limited to an imaginative and constructive program in a particular library, authorship of a specific book or articles in the reference field, creative and inspirational teaching, active participation in professional associations devoted to reference services, or other noteworthy activities which stimulate reference librarians to more distinguished performance.

Schneider Family Book Award: Three awards of $5,000 each are available to honor an author or illustrator for a book that embodies an artistic expression of the disability experience for child and adolescent audiences. Books must portray some aspect of living with a disability or that of a friend or family member, whether that disability is physical, mental, or emotional. One award each will be given to books falling in these categories: birth through grade school (age 0-8), middle school (9-13), and teens (14-18)

Spectrum Doctoral Fellowship: This program provides full tuition support and annual stipends totaling $20,000 to ten new full-time library and information science doctoral students pursuing degrees at participating colleges and universities (University of Pittsburgh, University of Arizona, University of California at Los Angeles, University of Michigan, Rutgers University, Simmons College, Syracuse University, University of Tennessee at Knoxville, University of Texas at Austin, and University of Wisconsin at Madison). Eligible applicants must be citizens or permanent residents of the U.S. and exhibit intellectual curiosity, interest in the library/information science field and its sub-fields, evidence of academic excellence, effectiveness as a communicator, the ability to

excel as a scholar or executive administrator in the library/information science field, and a strong commitment to diversity.

Spectrum Scholarships: A $5,000 scholarship is available to traditionally underrepresented groups (American Indian/Alaska Native, Asian, Black/African American, Hispanic/Latino, or Native Hawaiian/Other Pacific Islander) who are attending an association-accredited graduate program in library and information studies or an association-recognized NCATE School Library Media program, and who have completed no more than a third of the credit requirements toward his/her M.L.I.S. or school library media degree at the time of the award.
EIN: 362166947

2380
American Lung Association
55 W. Wacker Dr., Ste. 1150
Chicago, IL 60601 (202) 785-3355
FAX: (202) 452-1805; E-mail: info@lungusa.org; Toll-free tel.: (800) 586-4872; URL: http://www.lungusa.org

Foundation type: Public charity
Purpose: Grants and awards to researchers to find new and improved treatments and cures for lung disease.
Publications: Application guidelines; Annual report.
Financial data: Year ended 06/30/2012. Assets, $31,049,040 (M); Expenditures, $49,843,529; Total giving, $6,439,114.
Fields of interest: Lung diseases.
Type of support: Fellowships; Research; Awards/prizes.
Application information: Applications accepted. Application form required.

> *Initial approach:* Letter of intent for Lung Cancer Discovery Award
> *Deadline(s):* Oct. 21
> *Additional information:* At time of application, eligible applicants must be U.S. citizens or foreign nationals holding one of the following visa immigration statuses: permanent resident; student; exchange visitor; temporary worker in a specialty occupation; Canadian or Mexican citizens engaging in professional activities; or temporary worker with extraordinary abilities in the sciences. Non-citizens must submit a notarized copy of proof of possession of visa status with their application.

Program descriptions:

ALA/NSF Pickwick Fellowship Award: This fellowship, co-sponsored with the National Sleep Foundation, provides a promising new investigator grant monies to conduct sleep research, specifically as it relates to breathing. Applicants for the fellowship must have a sponsor and plan to conduct research in a recognized U.S. laboratory or program of study with strong mentoring in the appropriate area. Non-U.S. citizens are eligible. Candidates must have received an M.D., D.V.M., Ph.D., or D.O. degree by the time the fellowship begins. No other fellowships maybe held concurrently with this award. The applicant must demonstrate evidence of aptitude for and proficiency in research and interest in pursuing a career in research related to sleep and breathing. Awardees are supported to conduct mentored research for a greater proportion (at least 75 percent) of their time. Fellowships are available for basic, applied, or clinical research.

Biomedical Research Grants: Ten to twelve grants of $40,000 per year are available to provide seed monies for junior investigators researching the

mechanisms of lung disease and general lung biology. Eligible applicants must hold doctoral degrees, be assured of a faculty appointment or equivalent with demonstrated institutional commitment (salary support, research space, etc.) by the start of the award; applicants must also have completed two years of post-doctoral research training by the start of the award.

Clinical Patient Care Research Grant: One to two grants of $40,000 each are available to provide seed monies for junior investigators working on traditional clinical studies that examine methods of improving patient care and/or treatment of lung disease. Eligible applicants must hold doctoral degrees, be assured of a faculty appointment or equivalent with demonstrated institutional commitment (salary support, research space, etc.) by the start of the award; applicants must also have completed two years of post-doctoral research training by the start of the award.

Dalsemer Research Grant: A $40,00 grant is available to provide seed monies for junior investigators researching interstitial lung disease. Eligible applicants must hold doctoral degrees, be assured of a faculty appointment or equivalent with demonstrated institutional commitment (salary support, research space, etc.) by the start of the award; applicants must also have completed two years of post-doctoral research training by the start of the award.

DeSousa Award: A $100,000 grant is available to support investigators, at any level of research experience, who focus on bronchiectasis, infection with atypical mycobacteria (particularly Mycobacterium avium), and/or infection with Nocardia species of bacteria. Eligible applicants must hold a doctoral degree, have a faculty appointment at an academic institution (including research institutions not formally associated with a university), and have completed a training fellowship; applicants must also be self-directed researchers for whom their institutions must provide space and other resources customary for independent investigators.

Lung Cancer Discovery Award: A $100,000 grant is available to support investigators, at any level of research experience, who focus on novel treatments or a cure for lung cancer. Eligible applicants must hold a doctoral degree, have a faculty appointment at an academic institution (including research institutions not formally associated with a university), and have completed a training fellowship; applicants must also be self-directed researchers for whom their institutions must provide space and other resources customary for independent investigators.

Lung Health Dissertation Grant: A one-year grant of $21,000 is available for pre-doctoral support for nurses or students with an academic career focused on the various disciplines of social science. Research areas of particular interest include psychosocial, behavioral, health service, health policy, epidemiological, biostatistical, and educational matters related to lung disease. Eligible applicants must be matriculating students in good standing in a full-time academic program leading to a doctoral degree in one of the above-mentioned fields; individuals with an M.D. degree who wish to acquire a Ph.D. are not eligible, though nurses pursuing a doctoral degree in any field are eligible.

Senior Research Training Fellowships: Eight to ten grants of $32,500 each are available as post-doctoral support for M.Ds. and/or Ph.Ds. receiving further academic training as scientific investigators. Research areas of particular interest include adult pulmonary medicine, pediatric pulmonary medicine, and lung biology. Eligible applicants must hold a doctoral degree and must work in an academic or nonprofit institution. M.D. or D.O. applicants must also have completed their clinical training, have some research training, and be in their 3rd or 4th year of fellowship training; Ph.D applicants and applicants with medical degrees, whose credentials show that they are on a career track which will not include the practice of medicine, must be in their first or second year of full-time postdoctoral research.

Social-Behavioral Research Grant: One to two grants, at $40,000 each, are available to provide seed monies for junior investigators working on epidemiological and behavioral studies examining risk factors affecting lung health. This grant includes studies concerning the ethical, legal, and economic aspects of health services and policies. Eligible applicants must hold doctoral degrees, be assured of a faculty appointment or equivalent with demonstrated institutional commitment (salary support, research space, etc.) by the start of the award; applicants must also have completed two years of post-doctoral research training by the start of the award.
EIN: 131632524

2381
American Marketing Association Foundation
311 S. Wacker Dr., Ste. 5800
Chicago, IL 60606-6629 (312) 542-9000
Contact: Lisa Chernick, Exec. Dir.
FAX: (312) 542-9001; E-mail: foundation@ama.org;
E-mail for Lisa Chernick: lchernick@ama.org;
URL: http://www.themarketingfoundation.org

Foundation type: Public charity
Purpose: Grants and awards to outstanding researchers and scholars in the field of marketing.
Publications: Application guidelines; Annual report.
Financial data: Year ended 06/30/2011. Assets, $2,054,525 (M); Expenditures, $253,140; Total giving, $52,797; Grants to individuals, 79 grants totaling $32,797. Subtotal for grants to individuals: 34 grants totaling $2,040. Subtotal for doctoral support: 3 grants totaling $1,230. Subtotal for scholarships—to individuals: 12 grants totaling $9,457. Subtotal for awards/prizes: 30 grants totaling $20,070.
Fields of interest: Business/industry.
Type of support: Research; Grants to individuals; Scholarships—to individuals.
Application information: Applications accepted. Application form available on the grantmaker's web site.
  Initial approach: Application
  Deadline(s): Varies
  Additional information: See web site for additional application guidelines.
Program descriptions:
  Berry-AMA Book Prize for the Best Book in Marketing: This award recognizes books whose innovative ideas have had significant impact on marketing and related fields. Eligible recipients include authors who have been published within the previous three years, and whose books are published in English and are available for distribution in the U.S. Prizes include a cash award, plaque, and publicity.
  David K. Hardin Memorial Award: This award honors the best article or paper published in the journal Marketing Research in a given year, with a cash award.
  E.G. Chingos Program: This program funds collegiate memberships in American Marketing Association and American Marketing Association-New York chapters for third- and

fourth-year undergraduate students majoring in marketing at Baruch College, College of Staten Island, New York University, and Pace University.
  Erin Anderson Award for an Emerging Female Marketing Scholar and Mentor: This program is given annually to a female marketing professor who has made significant research contributions in both publications (both leading journals and working papers under review) and teaching and service contributions to her department. Recipients will be awarded a cash prize.
  John A. Howard/AMA Doctoral Dissertation Award: This program recognizes excellent dissertations in the field of marketing by students who are completing their degrees in marketing- and buyer behavior-related topics.
  Nonprofit Marketer of the Year Award: Awarded in conjunction with the American Marketing Association (AMA) and the Nonprofit Times, this program honors extraordinary leadership and achievement in the field of nonprofit marketing. Eligible nominees must be currently employed at a nonprofit organization with an active 501(c)(3) tax status, and have current responsibilities that focus on the branding, marketing, and communications aspect of a nonprofit organization. Winners receive a one-year paid membership to the AMA, complimentary registration to the AMA's Nonprofit Marketing Conference, and a travel grant of up to $1,000 (to be used only to cover travel expenses)
  Nonprofit Travel Grant Scholarships: This grants program rewards emerging Ph.D. scholars with an interest in nonprofit marketing by making it possible to attend the foundation's annual Nonprofit Marketing Conference. Eligible applicants include Ph.D. students currently enrolled in a marketing or advertising department of a U.S. or Canadian accredited business school, and who show interest in the study of applying the marketing discipline to the nonprofit sector.
  Richard A. Hammill Scholarship Fund: This fund provides an annual scholarship award for students who are enrolled in the marketing program at Georgia State University.
  Robert J. Lavidge Nonprofit Marketing Research Scholarship: This scholarship provides funds for marketing professionals working in the nonprofit sector to further their marketing research-related education. Scholarships of up to $1,000 are available to use at foundation-approved marketing research-related conferences, classes at a college or university (that are not part of a degree program), or tutorials on specific research methods.
  S. Tamer Cavusgil Award: This award honors the authors of an outstanding articles published in the Journal of International Marketing with a cash award and a plaque.
  Sheth Foundation Research Competition on Nonprofit Marketing: This competition, administered in conjunction with the Jagdish and Madhuri Sheth Foundation and the Marketing Science Institute, provides cash awards to outstanding research designed to improve the marketing competencies of nonprofit organizations.
  Thomas C. Kinnear/Journal of Public Policy and Marketing Award: This award presents a cash prize to the author(s) of an outstanding article published in the Journal of Public Policy and Marketing.
  Valuing Diversity Scholarships: Scholarships of $1,000 each will be awarded to Ph.D. students from underrepresented populations (African-American, Hispanic-American, or Native American) who are currently studying marketing.
  Vijay Mahajan Award: This award works to inspire marking educators through their work in marketing strategies, by awarding an annual cash prize to an educator who has made sustained contributions to

marketing strategy literature over a span of ten or more years.
EIN: 363834880

2382
American Medical Association Foundation
(also known as AMA Foundation)
515 N. State St.
Chicago, IL 60654-5453 (312) 464-4200
Contact: Steven W. Churchill, Exec. Dir.
FAX: (312) 464-4142;
E-mail: steven.churchill@ama-assn.org;
URL: http://www.amafoundation.org

Foundation type: Public charity
Purpose: Scholarships and grants by nomination only to medical students.
Publications: Application guidelines; Informational brochure.
Financial data: Year ended 12/31/2011. Assets, $19,821,875 (M); Expenditures, $2,828,441; Total giving, $681,587; Grants to individuals, totaling $450,534.
Fields of interest: Medical school/education; Medical research; Minorities.
Type of support: Research; Scholarships—to individuals; Awards/prizes.
Application information: Applications accepted. Application form required.
  Copies of proposal: 1
  Deadline(s): Varies
  Applicants should submit the following:
    1) Resume
    2) Proposal
    3) Curriculum vitae
    4) Budget Information
  Additional information: See web site for additional guidelines.
Program descriptions:
  AMA Foundation Health Education Award: This award was established to encourage and to recognize the professional or public health education activities of practicing physicians. Special consideration is given to those physicians working in the areas of drug and alcohol abuse. The award consists of a $3,500 stipend and an appropriate certificate.
  Arthur N. Wilson, M.D. Scholarship: This scholarship provides a $5,000 tuition assistance to a currently enrolled medical student who graduated from a high school in southeast Alaska. This scholarship highlights the importance of supporting future physicians in rural communities.
  Excellence in Medicine Awards: Through these awards, the foundation honors a select group of physicians and medical students who exemplify the medical profession's highest values: commitment to service, community involvement, altruism, leadership and dedication to patient care.
  Healthy Communities/Healthy America Fund: This fund recognizes the efforts of health care professionals and other community volunteers to offer free or low-cost health care to low-income, uninsured, and underinsured populations by offering grants between $10,000 and $25,000 to physician-led free clinics. This year, the program will address diabetes management and education projects. Grant funding may not be used to pay for staff salary or overhead; capital construction or improvements; or prescription drug take-back/ disposal programs.
  Isaac Hays, MD, and John Bell, MD, Award for Leadership in Medical Ethics and Professionalism: This award promotes and underscores the AMA's continuing dedication to the principles of medical ethics and the highest standards of medical

practice. The award consists of a plaque and monetary award of $2,500.

Joan F. Giambalvo Memorial Scholarship: This scholarship is awarded to a male or female medical student or a physician (MD or DO). Applicant must be working alone or collaboratively on the specific research project.

Minority Scholars Awards: In collaboration with the AMA Minority Affairs Consortium and with support from the Pfizer Medical Humanities Initiatives, the foundation awards $10,000 scholarships to approximately seven to twelve minority medical students annually. Nominees must be a current first of second year student and a permanent resident or citizen of the U.S. Eligible students from the traditionally underrepresented groups in the medical profession include African American/Black, American Indian, Native Hawaiian, Alaska Native and Hispanic/Latino.

Physicians of Tomorrow Scholarships: These $10,000 scholarships reward current third-year medical students/individuals who are approaching their final year of medical school. Typically, eight to twelve recipients are selected. Each medical school can nominate one person for each of the different scholarship opportunities (two nominees in total). Each scholarship category takes into consideration academic excellence and financial need.

Seed Grant Research Program: The program was established to encourage medical students, physician residents, and fellows to enter the medical research field. The program provides seed grants to help recipients conduct small basic science, applied, or clinical research projects. The funds are designed to round out new project budgets, rather than sustain current initiatives. Grants of $2,500 each will be awarded to U.S. citizens or permanent residents of the U.S.

The Jordan Fieldman, MD Award: The award will be presented annually to a resident or fellow who has shown an interest in public health advocacy issues. He or she must be a first-time delegate to the AMA-RFS and from a state or district that does not have the funds to support resident/fellow travel to AMA-RFS meetings. The award money will cover resident travel to both the Annual and Interim meetings during the year of the award and necessary expenses while attending these meetings.
EIN: 366080517

2383
American Nuclear Society
(also known as ANS)
555 N. Kensington Ave.
La Grange Park, IL 60526-5535 (708) 352-6611
Contact: Robert C. Fine J.D., CAE., Exec. Dir.
FAX: (708) 352-0499; Toll-free tel.: (800) 323-3044; URL: http://www.ans.org

Foundation type: Public charity
Purpose: Scholarships to post-high school students pursuing a career in nuclear science and technology. Awards by nomination only to professionals for outstanding achievement and meritorious service.
Financial data: Year ended 12/31/2011. Assets, $19,573,857 (M); Expenditures, $12,560,453; Total giving, $449,500; Grants to individuals, totaling $179,100.
Fields of interest: Higher education; Graduate/professional education; Science; Engineering/technology.
Type of support: Scholarships—to individuals; Awards/grants by nomination only; Awards/prizes.

Application information:
Deadline(s): Feb.1, Apr.1 for Scholarships
Additional information: See web site for additional program description for scholarships and awards.
Program descriptions:
ANS Incoming Freshman Scholarship: Up to four scholarships of $1,000 each are awarded to graduating high school seniors who have enrolled full-time in college courses and who are pursuing a degree in nuclear engineering or have the intent to purse a degree in nuclear engineering.
ANS Undergraduate Scholarship: Undergraduate scholarships will be awarded as follows: a maximum of four scholarships for students who have completed one year in a course of study leading to a degree in nuclear science, nuclear engineering, or a nuclear-related field and who will be sophomores in the upcoming academic year; and a maximum of 21 scholarships for students who have completed two or more years and will be entering as juniors or seniors.
Arthur Holly Compton Award in Education: The award is given to an individual who has made an outstanding contribution to education in the field of nuclear science and/or engineering, but does not have to be an ANS member or work primarily in the education field. An engraved plaque and a monetary award of $2,000 is presented to both the recipient and the recipient's academic institution.
Delayed Education Scholarship for Women: One scholarship is awarded to a mature woman whose undergraduate studies in nuclear science, nuclear engineering, or a nuclear-related field have been delayed.
Gerald C. Pomraning Memorial Award: The award provides recognition to individuals who have made outstanding contributions toward the advancement of the fields of mathematics and/or computation in support of advancing the understanding of these topics of interest to members of the society.
Glenn T. Seaborg Congressional Science and Engineering Fellowship: This fellowship provides a stipend to work in a Congressional office (either House or Senate) for a year, providing advice on science and engineering matters to a member of Congress and his or her staff. The purpose of the fellowship is to bring a reasoned and knowledgeable view of nuclear matters to Congress, and to act as a science and engineering resource for Congress. The Fellow will receive a stipend of $55,000, plus a small travel allowance. Eligible applicants are U.S. citizens who have been a national member of ANS for at least two years.
John and Muriel Landis Scholarships: A maximum of eight scholarships are awarded to undergraduate and graduate students who have greater than average financial need. Consideration is given to conditions or experiences that render the student disadvantaged. Applicants should be planning a career in nuclear science, nuclear engineering, or a nuclear-related field; and be enrolled or planning to enroll in a college or university located in the U.S. (but need not be U.S. citizens)
Landis Public Communication and Education Award: The award recognizes a person for outstanding efforts, dedication, and accomplishment in furthering public education and understanding of the peaceful applications of nuclear technology. Both members and non-members are eligible for this award, which consists of a $1,000 monetary award and engraved plaque.
Landis Young Member Engineering Achievement Award: This award was established to recognize outstanding achievement in which engineering knowledge has been effectively applied to yield an engineering concept, design, safety improvement,

method of analysis, or product utilized in nuclear power research and development or commercial application. Recipients receive a $2,000 monetary award and an engraved plaque.
Pittsburgh Local Section Scholarships: Scholarships are given to a graduate student (studying nuclear science and technology) and an undergraduate student (studying nuclear science and technology) who either have some affiliation with western Pennsylvania or who attend school at a nearby university within the region.
EIN: 362386176

2384
American Orthopaedic Foot and Ankle Society
(also known as American Orthopaedic Foot Society)
6300 N. River Rd., Ste. 510
Rosemont, IL 60018-4206 (847) 698-4654
Contact: Steven L. Haddad MD, Pres.
FAX: (847) 235-4855; E-mail: aofasinfo@aofas.org; URL: http://www.aofas.org

Foundation type: Public charity
Purpose: Research grant to investigators on basic science for the advancement in foot and ankle care.
Publications: Application guidelines.
Financial data: Year ended 08/31/2012. Assets, $2,516,838 (M); Expenditures, $2,610,400; Total giving, $81,970; Grants to individuals, totaling $20,000.
Fields of interest: Podiatry.
Type of support: Grants to individuals.
Application information: Applications accepted. Application form required. Application form available on the grantmaker's web site.
Initial approach: Application
Send request by: E-mail or mail
Deadline(s): Dec. 1
Program description:
Research Grants Program: One year research grants of up to $20,000 are awarded to promote the goal of advancing foot and ankle investigation by providing seed funding for promising research projects, and to encourage supplemental submissions to national funding sources.
EIN: 237087029

2385
American Osteopathic Association
142 E. Ontario St.
Chicago, IL 60611-2864 (312) 202-8000
Contact: Adrienne White-Faines, Exec. Dir. and C.E.O.
FAX: (312) 202-8200;
E-mail: research@osteopathic.org; Toll-free tel.: (800) 621-1773; URL: http://www.osteopathic.org/Pages/default.aspx

Foundation type: Public charity
Purpose: Fellowships and grants to U.S. residents for osteopathic medical research.
Publications: Application guidelines.
Financial data: Year ended 05/31/2012. Assets, $58,960,517 (M); Expenditures, $40,003,398; Total giving, $481,878; Grants to individuals, totaling $10,000.
Fields of interest: Medical specialties; Institute.
Type of support: Fellowships; Research.
Application information: Application form required.
Initial approach: Telephone
Deadline(s): Feb. 15 for research fellowships, Dec. 1 for others
Program descriptions:
Research Fellowships: The fellowship program is designed to support research training for the

applicant and will enable the applicant to conduct a basic science or clinical research project that will make a contribution to osteopathic medicine. The fellowship is, in effect, seed funding to encourage an osteopathic physician or physician in training to contribute to research throughout his/her career in osteopathic medicine. The fellowship involves the completion of a project under the direction of a sponsor. Both the sponsor and the applicant accept responsibility for the conduct of the project and the reporting of the scientific results attained. A portion of the fellowship program may be conducted at an institution other than the sponsoring institution under supervision of a consultant approved by the sponsor. The fellowship year starts Aug. 1 and ends July 31; awards are for $5,000 for a one-year project.

Research Grants: Research projects of up to $50,000 are eligible for funding. Research focus may include but is not limited to: mechanisms of action of OMM/OMT; clinical efficacy of AMM/OMT; inter- and intra-rater reliability of palpatory assessment; cost effectiveness of osteopathic health care; osteopathic physician and patient interactions; methods of teaching palpation and OMM/OMT. Investigators should not expect to be funded for more than two years on a single project.
EIN: 362170786

2386
American Osteopathic Foundation

(formerly National Osteopathic Foundation)
142 E. Ontario, Ste. 1450
Chicago, IL 60611-2888 (312) 202-8234
Contact: Vicki L. Heck, Prog. Mgr.
FAX: (312) 202-8216;
E-mail: info@aof-foundation.org; Toll-free tels.: (866) 455-9383; E-mail For Vicki L. Heck: vheck@aof.org; URL: http://www.aof-foundation.org

Foundation type: Public charity
Purpose: Scholarships to students specializing in osteopathic medicine, and some support for doctors practicing osteopathic medicine.
Financial data: Year ended 12/31/2012. Assets, $10,935,099 (M); Expenditures, $1,494,073; Total giving, $305,243; Grants to individuals, totaling $126,911.
Fields of interest: Education.
Type of support: Awards/prizes; Graduate support.
Application information: Application form required.
  Deadline(s): Vary
  Additional information: See web site for further application and program information.
Program descriptions:
  AOA Presidential Memorial Leadership Award: This $5,000 award recognizes an osteopathic medical student entering their second, third or fourth year of studies. Student must have demonstrated leadership potential, noteworthy accomplishments and honors, outstanding academic achievements, drive to be a leader, and is committed to the osteopathic profession.
  AOF Educator of the Year Award: Honors an individual who not only emulates the osteopathic profession's high standards of excellence in teaching, but also exemplifies a significant and low-standing contribution to the academic advancement of osteopathic students and the profession.
  AstraZeneca Spirit of Humanity Award: One $10,000 grant is awarded to an osteopathic physician, center or program that provides urgently needed mental health care services to the indigent, underserved, or those with barriers to quality health care.

Donna Jones Moritsugu Memorial Award: This award recognizes the spouses of graduating students of osteopathic medicine who best exemplify the role of a professional's partner by providing immeasurable support of his or her mate, family and the osteopathic profession while being an individual in their own right. One award recipient will be chosen from each accredited colleges/schools of osteopathic medicine.
  Paul S. McCord, D.O. Memorial Scholarship: Awards $1,500 scholarship annually to one student from the third year class at Chicago College of Osteopathic Medicine at Midwestern University.
  Pfizer Outstanding Resident Award: Four $5,000 awards are presented to osteopathic physicians currently in the second or third year of an AOA-approved residency program in the primary care specialties of family practice, internal medicine, and pediatrics are eligible to apply for this award for exhibiting exemplary characteristics of a good osteopathic primary care physician. In addition, recipients receive a travel grant to attend the Annual Convention and Scientific Seminar of the American Osteopathic Association and the annual scientific session of the recipient's specialty, where recognition will be given.
  Purdue Partners Against Pain Award: Awards $10,000 to an osteopathic physician, center or program that has made great strides in the field of pain research, management, or improving the quality of life for people living with acute and/or chronic pain.
  Welch Scholars Grant: Grants of $2,000 are awarded to students entering their second, third, or fourth year of studies at an accredited college/school of osteopathic medicine.
  William G. Anderson, D.O. Scholarship for Minority Students: Awards one $5,000 scholarship to encourage minority students to pursue careers in osteopathic medicine by helping to overcome financial barriers to attending medical school.
EIN: 366056120

2387
American Pediatric Surgical Association Foundation, Inc.

111 Deer Lake Rd., Ste.100
Deerfield, IL 60015 (317) 274-4681
Contact: Jay L. Grosfeld, Chair.
Application address: 702 Barnhill Dr., Ste. 2500, Indianapolis, IN 46202, tel.: (317) 274-4681; URL: http://www.eapsa.org/

Foundation type: Independent foundation
Purpose: Grants to members of APSA, a current pediatric surgery resident, or those individuals that have completed an ACGME-RRC or Canadian Royal College of surgeons accredited pediatric surgery residency training program.
Financial data: Year ended 12/31/2012. Assets, $521,701 (M); Expenditures, $66,251; Total giving, $50,000.
Fields of interest: Pediatrics; Surgery.
Type of support: Research; Grants to individuals; Postdoctoral support.
Application information:
  Initial approach: Proposal
  Send request by: Online
  Copies of proposal: 1
  Deadline(s): Mar. 1
Program description:
  Grant Program: Two grants of $25,000 to investigators for one year but may under special circumstances be renewable for up to two years. When warranted by the special nature of the project, awards may be approved for a shorter duration in a

set block of time or may be interrupted for periods of variable duration.
EIN: 593243373

2388
American Sleep Medicine Foundation

2510 N. Frontage Rd.
Darien, IL 60561-1511 (630) 737-9700
Contact: Lisa Antignano, Asst. Coord.
Award inquiries: Nick Cekosh, Coord., e-mail: ncekosh@aasmnet.org
FAX: (630) 737-9790;
E-mail: asmfinfo@aasmnet.org; URL: http://www.discoversleep.org/

Foundation type: Public charity
Purpose: Research grants to educate physicians about diagnosis and treatment of sleep disorders.
Publications: Application guidelines.
Financial data: Year ended 12/31/2011. Assets, $5,395,955 (M); Expenditures, $607,116; Total giving, $594,062.
Fields of interest: Medical research.
Type of support: Research.
Application information: Applications accepted. Application form available on the grantmaker's web site.
  Send request by: Online
  Deadline(s): Aug. 15 for Strategic Research Award, Oct. 17 for Physician Scientist Training Awards and Junior Faculty Research Award, Jan. 17 for Educational Projects Award
  Final notification: Recipients notified by Feb. 10 for Physician Scientist Training and Junior Faculty Research Awards, Apr. 16 for Educational Projects Award
  Additional information: See web site for additional application guidelines.
Program descriptions:
  ABSM Junior Faculty Research Award: The foundation aims to assist new faculty in the development of a career in academic sleep medicine by awarding $50,000 to spread over two years to one applicant a year. The host institution must not have received funding for an ABSM Junior Faculty Research Award within two years of the application in order to be considered for this award.
  Educational Projects Awards: This award helps improve awareness about sleep and its disorders to both the public and all levels of the health care provider and physician training/continuing education continum. It has been shown in numerous surveys and studies that education regarding sleep and sleep disorders is suboptimal in both medical school and curricula and residency training programs. Lack of a basic knowledge regarding sleep may diminish a physician's ability to recognize the signs and symptoms of sleep disorders, understand their potential effect on health, quality of life or exacerbation of other co-morbid conditions, order appropriate diagnostic testing, or initiate adequate therapeutic plans. Eligible applicants include physicians (MD or DO) and PhDs actively engaged in the practice of sleep research, clinical Sleep Medicine or Behavioral Sleep Medicine, Advanced Nurse Practitioners, Physician Assistants or other allied health care professional practicing Sleep Medicine on a full time basis.
  Physician Scientist Training Award: The foundation will award up to five one-year grants in the amount of $75,000 each to chosen candidates for research in sleep medicine. Physicians (MD or DO) who are certified in sleep medicine by the American Board of Sleep Medicine or by a member board of the American Board of Medical Specialties, and are within 10 years post sleep medicine

fellowship, or who are currently enrolled in an ACGME-accredited sleep medicine fellowship are eligible to apply for the Best Science Award. Eligible applicants for the Comprehensive Academic Sleep Program of Distinction category include physicians (MD or DO) who have completed or been accepted to an ACGME sleep medicine fellowship at an institution that holds the status of this category. Both awards will include research expenses such as salary support, supplies and overhead for the awardees.

Strategic Research Award: This award provides support to projects that address sleep problems in disadvantaged populations. The foundation is particularly interested in projects that develop or promote novel approaches to address human suffering in under-served populations as it relates to inadequate or non-restorative sleep, or sleep disorders in disadvantaged groups. There is growing awareness that "sleep disparity" is associated with poverty and that sleep problems have a disproportionate impact on those living in poverty. Examples of specific projects that are responsive to this request include, but are not limited to, the following; development of projects that improve sleep conditions or sleep hygiene in children or adults living in suboptimal sleep environments, such as noisy, cold, or unsafe settings; development of programs that incorporate sleep medicine services into clinics that provide care for medically indigent groups and; development of programs to coordinate the distribution of refurbished CPAP machines and supplies to underserved populations. The foundation encourages collaborative projects that integrate the efforts and resources of more than one organization. Although not a formal requirement, the foundation also encourages applicants to collaborate with a physician who is Board certified in sleep medicine and a member of the American Academy of Sleep Medicine (AASM) in each proposal.
EIN: 411920576

2389
American Society for Gastrointestinal Endoscopy Foundation

1520 Kensington Rd., Ste. 202
Oak Brook, IL   60523-2141   (630) 573-0600
FAX: (630) 573-0691; E-mail: info@asge.org;
URL: http://www.asge.org/foundation/

Foundation type: Public charity
Purpose: Grants for research in the area of gastrointestinal endoscopy to members of the ASGE.
Publications: Application guidelines.
Financial data: Year ended 12/31/2011. Assets, $26,887,201 (M); Expenditures, $11,608,943; Total giving, $672,500; Grants to individuals, totaling $28,500.
Fields of interest: Digestive disorders research; Medical research; Medical specialties research.
International interests: Canada; Mexico.
Type of support: Publication; Research; Grants to individuals; Travel grants.
Application information: Application form required.
   Deadline(s): Vary
   Additional information: Contact foundation for further application and program information.
Program descriptions:
ASGE/ConMed Manuscript Award: The award recognizes a fellow or resident in a training program whose manuscript is accepted in the current year for publication in GIE: Gastrointestinal Endoscopy. A $10,000 cash award will be given to the trainee

who is the primary author of the winning manuscript.
Don Wilson Award: The award provides advanced fellows or junior faculty with the opportunity to train outside of their home country with a premier GI endoscopist or group in order to advance their training. The award assists in underwriting reasonable and customary travel and living expenses for a period of one to three months. The award includes a $7,500 cash stipend prior to the recipient's travel.
Endoscopic Research Awards: These research awards are offered to physicians for projects in basic and clinical endoscopic technology research, outcomes, and effectiveness of endoscopy research. Candidate must be an ASGE member, be an M.D. (or have an equivalent degree), and be currently in a gastroenterology-related and endoscopic practice in academic institutions or private practice in North America.
Endoscopic Research Career Development Awards: These awards provide the salary and/or research support necessary for the investigator to enhance his/her career development. The award is $75,000 for two years. Applicants must be ASGE members and hold full-time faculty positions at North American (U.S., Canada, or Mexico) universities or professional institutions at the time of application. The award is not available for fellows, but is intended for faculty who have demonstrated promise and have some record of accomplishment in research.
EIN: 237058604

2390
American Society for Reproductive Immunology

830 W. End Ct., Ste. 400
Vernon Hills, IL   60061-1344   (847) 247-6905
E-mail: stephohr@gmail.com; URL: http://www.theasri.org

Foundation type: Public charity
Purpose: Travel grants and awards to help defray the cost of students to travel to the ASRI annual meeting for the development of reproductive immunology research.
Financial data: Year ended 06/30/2012. Assets, $167,312 (M); Expenditures, $163,578; Total giving, $14,259; Grants to individuals, totaling $14,259.
Fields of interest: Immunology research.
Type of support: Research; Awards/prizes; Postdoctoral support; Graduate support; Travel grants.
Application information: Selection of the award is based on merit of the presentation.
Program descriptions:
American Journal of Reproductive Immunology Award: This award is presented annually to a senior investigator who has made outstanding contributions to the area of reproductive immunology. Contributions can be in the area of clinical or basic research. Awardees do not need to be members of the society.
Distinguished Service Award: The award is given periodically, and not more than annually, to a member of the society who has provided distinguished service to advance the goals and mission of the society.
Dr. John Gusdon Memorial New Investigator Award: The award is given to a new investigator with trainee status (graduate student, postdoctoral scientist, or resident) who has made a significant contribution to the field of reproductive immunology by presenting an outstanding research paper during the society's annual meeting.

J. Christian Herr Award: The award is given annually to a member of the society or International Society for Immunology of Reproduction (ISIR), typically in the first ten to fifteen years beyond accepting a faculty position, who has made outstanding achievements in basic or applied research in reproductive immunology, particularly for investigators involved in technology transfer.
The Michelson Prize and Grants in Reproductive Biology: A $25 million prize will be awarded to the first entity to provide a single dose, non-surgical sterilant that is: safe, effective, and practical for use in male and female, cats and dogs; viable pathway to regulatory approval; feasible manufacturing process and cost; suitable for administration in field setting. Up to $50 million in multiple, multi-year grants are available for research in pursuit of prize goals.
Travel Awards: Awards travel grants to support travel for a clinical scientist in training status, among other travel opportunities.
EIN: 133390665

2391
American Society of Anesthesiologists

520 N. Northwest Hwy.
Park Ridge, IL   60068-2573   (847) 825-5586
Contact: John M. Zerwas M.D., Pres.
FAX: (847) 825-1692;
E-mail: communications@asahq.org; Additional address (DC office): 1501 M St., N.W., Ste. 300, Washington, DC 20005-1736, tel.: (202) 289-2222, fax: (202) 371-0384, e-mail: mail@asawash.org; URL: http://www.asahq.org/

Foundation type: Public charity
Purpose: $1,000 for resident anesthesiologists organizing regional meetings. Five grants are available each year to residents in each of the ASA's caucuses: New England, Southern, Mid-Atlantic, Midwest and Western, to put together seminars with information on practice management, legislative issues, or finance.
Publications: Occasional report.
Financial data: Year ended 12/31/2011. Assets, $73,777,110 (M); Expenditures, $35,785,824; Total giving, $4,566,276; Grants to individuals, totaling $12,000.
Fields of interest: Anesthesiology; Anesthesiology research.
Type of support: Conferences/seminars.
Application information: Applications accepted. Application form required. Application form available on the grantmaker's web site.
   Initial approach: E-mail
   Deadline(s): Feb. 15
   Additional information: Emails with the application information should be sent to the ASARC president.
EIN: 362181944

2392
American Society of Safety Engineers Foundation

1800 E. Oakton St.
Des Plaines, IL   60018-2100   (847) 699-2929
Contact: Fred J. Fortman, Exec. Dir.
FAX: (847) 768-3434;
E-mail: assefoundation@asse.org; E-mail For Fred J. Fortman: ffortman@asse.org; URL: http://www.asse.org/foundation/

Foundation type: Public charity
Purpose: Fellowships to researchers who have doctoral degrees for research on safety issues. Also, scholarships to individuals who are pursuing

a degree in occupational safety and health or a closely-related field.
Publications: Annual report; Newsletter.
Financial data: Year ended 03/31/2012. Assets, $3,299,192 (M); Expenditures, $500,496; Total giving, $288,340; Grants to individuals, totaling $187,720.
Fields of interest: Research.
Type of support: Fellowships; Research.
Application information: Applications accepted. Application form required. Application form available on the grantmaker's web site.
  Deadline(s): Oct. 1 for Research Grants, Dec. 1 for Scholarships, and Apr. 15 for Research Fellowships.
  Additional information: See web site for complete program information.
Program descriptions:
  ASSE Foundation Professional Development Grant Program: Awards ranging from $500 to $5,000 a year are available to safety professionals, ASSE members, and others for conferences, seminars, and other means of professional development.
  Graduate Awards: $1,000 scholarships are available to full-time graduate students.
  Liberty Mutual Research Fellowship Program: Goals of the program are as follows: 1) To encourage research activity in the field of safety; 2) To familiarize graduate students, faculty members and other researchers with current research projects and up-to-date research models and applications to expand the body of knowledge; 3) To expand and stimulate graduate students', faculty members and others in understanding safety research; 4) To provide a forum for linking safety professionals, industry needs, and quality research programs; and 5) To lay the groundwork for graduate students and faculty members to pursue safety/health applied research projects of their choice. Fellows will receive a stipend from the foundation ($2,000 for the first week and $1,500/ week thereafter to cover expenses). Expenses include transportation to and from the Fellow's home to Hopkinton, MA., room and board, rental car as needed and other miscellaneous expenses. Total expenses will not exceed $9,500 per fellow (for a six-week stay). Fellows will also receive reasonable access to current research projects, databases, equipment, researchers, and other resources as necessary.
  PhD Fellowships: Two fellowships are available to two PhD candidates admitted to Oregon State University in the Public Health program, concentrating in Environment, Safety, and Health. Fellows receive free tuition and a stipend of $18,000 for three years. Fellows are required to teach at a university for three years after receiving their degree.
  Research Grant: Awards $20,000 to a safety and health researcher(s) to conduct applied research that would enhance management performance in reducing injuries and illness in the workplace.
  Undergraduate Awards: Scholarships ranging from $1,000 to $6,000 are available to undergraduates.
EIN: 366145045

2393
American Society of Tropical Medicine and Hygiene
111 Deer Lake Rd., Ste. 100
Deerfield, IL 60015-4943   (847) 480-9592
Contact: Karen A. Goraleski, Exec. Dir.
FAX: (847) 480-9282; E-mail: info@astmh.org;
URL: http://www.astmh.org

Foundation type: Public charity
Purpose: Awards and fellowships to support research and education in the field of tropical medicine.
Publications: Grants list.
Financial data: Year ended 12/31/2011. Assets, $10,264,131 (M); Expenditures, $3,546,312; Total giving, $625,957; Grants to individuals, totaling $79,869.
Fields of interest: Tropical diseases research.
Type of support: Fellowships; Awards/prizes.
Application information:
  Deadline(s): Vary
  Additional information: See web side for additional guidelines.
EIN: 570408245

2394
The Christina and John Anagnos Educational Foundation
c/o Helen Theodoropoulos
9217 N. Kenton Ave.
Skokie, IL 60076-1526
Contact: Eleni Andriotaki
Application address: c/o Eleni Andriotaki, Xanthou 5-Athens, Greece 10673, tel.: (011-30) 210-354-5862

Foundation type: Independent foundation
Purpose: Scholarships to medical students residing in Greece to attend a medical school in that country.
Financial data: Year ended 12/31/2011. Assets, $1,585,189 (M); Expenditures, $121,106; Total giving, $82,000; Grants to individuals, 12 grants totaling $82,000 (high: $6,834, low: $6,833).
Fields of interest: Medical school/education.
Type of support: Foreign applicants; Graduate support.
Application information: Applications accepted. Application form required.
  Deadline(s): Dec. 16
  Additional information: Application must include photocopy of identification, proof of medical school enrollment, proof of Greek residence, birth certificate and parents' and student's tax return. Applications in Greek accepted.
EIN: 306022912

2395
Elizabeth M. Anderson Scholarship Trust
c/o The National Bank
1523 8th St.
East Moline, IL 61244-2190   (309) 755-0671
Contact: Kirk Metzger

Foundation type: Independent foundation
Purpose: Scholarships to graduates of United Township High School, East Moline, IL. Preference is shown to students accepted to Augustana College, IL; Iowa State University; University of Michigan; and Washington University, MO.
Financial data: Year ended 02/28/2013. Assets, $834,874 (M); Expenditures, $46,863; Total giving, $37,120; Grants to individuals, 8 grants totaling $37,120 (high: $4,640, low: $4,640).
Fields of interest: Scholarships/financial aid.
Type of support: Support to graduates or students of specific schools; Undergraduate support.
Application information: Applications accepted. Application form required.
  Deadline(s): End of Apr.
  Applicants should submit the following:
    1) Class rank
    2) GPA
    3) SAT
    4) Transcripts

    5) ACT
  Additional information: Application should include a personal statement.
EIN: 366768317

2396
Andrew Family Foundation
14628 John Humphrey Dr.
Orland Park, IL 60462-2642

Foundation type: Independent foundation
Purpose: Scholarships to graduating seniors of Carl Sandburg High School, IL for higher education.
Financial data: Year ended 10/31/2012. Assets, $14,236,556 (M); Expenditures, $793,430; Total giving, $610,025.
Fields of interest: Higher education.
Type of support: Support to graduates or students of specific schools; Undergraduate support.
Application information: Applications accepted. Application form required.
  Initial approach: Letter
EIN: 363926511

2397
Aileen S. Andrew Foundation
10701 Winterset Dr.
Orland Park, IL 60467-1106   (708) 349-4445
Contact: Robert E. Hord, Jr., Pres.

Foundation type: Independent foundation
Purpose: Scholarships to children of Andrew Corporation employees and to graduates of a local high school in Orland Park, IL.
Financial data: Year ended 11/30/2012. Assets, $49,415,782 (M); Expenditures, $2,869,460; Total giving, $2,086,538; Grants to individuals, 9 grants totaling $81,813 (high: $19,164, low: $2,877).
Fields of interest: Scholarships/financial aid.
Type of support: Employee-related scholarships; Undergraduate support.
Application information: Application form required.
  Deadline(s): Generally the beginning of Apr.
  Applicants should submit the following:
    1) ACT
    2) Essay
    3) Letter(s) of recommendation
    4) SAT
    5) Transcripts
EIN: 366049910

2398
Anesthesia Foundation
520 N. Northwest Hwy.
Park Ridge, IL 60068-2573   (847) 825-5586
Contact: John R. Moyers M.D., Pres.
FAX: (847) 825-5658; URL: http://www.anesthesiafoundation.org

Foundation type: Public charity
Purpose: Low interest loans to residents in Anesthesiology in need of financial assistance. Media award for contributions to anesthesia education.
Financial data: Year ended 12/31/2011. Assets, $1,944,807 (M); Expenditures, $38,563.
Fields of interest: Anesthesiology.
Type of support: Student loans—to individuals; Awards/prizes.
Application information: Applications accepted. Application form required. Application form available on the grantmaker's web site.
  Deadline(s): Dec. 15 for Media Award

Additional information: Contact the foundation for the most current loan requirements and application forms. Application should be submitted to the foundation at least 60 days prior to the date of the desired loan, and for further information on Media Award.

Program descriptions:

Anesthesiology Wellness Loan Program (AWLP): The maximum loan amount is $10,000 to an anesthesiologist who has graduated within the recent five years from a residency/fellowship program in anesthesiology and has suffered a loss of income to a recent personal, medical or practice hardship. Applicant must have been in the active practice of the specialty of anesthesiology at least until the current hardship, and is a citizen or permanent resident of the U.S., and is (or their legal representative is) capable of executing legally enforceable instruments such as notes, security pledges, and such other documentation as may be required to create a borrower/lender relationship.

Excellence in Educational Material Award: Awarded for excellence and innovation in books or multimedia with significant impact on the science and practice of anesthesiology, critical care, or pain medicine. No more than two-author submissions are eligible. The award is $5,000 (to be divided if there are two authors).

Resident/Fellow Loan Program: Low interest loans is provided to anesthesiology residents generally in the amount of $500 per month for a total of $6,000 for one year support. The individual must be in an approved training program (anesthesia residency or fellowship) for this 12 month time to receive the entire loan amount.
EIN: 346527631

2399
Angelman Syndrome Foundation

4255 Westbrook Dr., Ste. 219
Aurora, IL   60504-8125   (630) 978-4245
Contact: Eileen Braun, Exec. Dir.
FAX: (630) 978-7408; E-mail: info@angelman.org;
URL: http://www.angelman.org

Foundation type: Public charity
Purpose: Research grants to advance the awareness and treatment of Angelman Syndrome. Grants are given for both general and targeted research.
Financial data: Year ended 09/30/2011. Assets, $1,953,448 (M); Expenditures, $1,656,658; Total giving, $823,720. Grants to individuals amount not specified.
Fields of interest: Diseases (rare); Diseases (rare) research; Medical research.
Type of support: Research.
Application information: Applications accepted. Application form required.
　Initial approach: Proposal
　Deadline(s): Varies
　Applicants should submit the following:
　　1) Proposal
　　2) Curriculum vitae
　　3) Budget Information
　Additional information: Proposal of up to five pages should include hypothesis, background, research plan and significance of the proposed research. Applicants should submit a cover letter, one-page summary abstract and approval by institutional review boards for any proposal involving human or animal research (if applicable). See web site for additional information.

Program description:

Research Grants: The foundation will award one- or two-year grants in amounts ranging from $10,000 to $100,000 per year to research organizations for preclinical, translational, or clinical research projects that investigate any aspect of Angelman syndrome. While all types of AS-related research proposals will be considered, priority will be given to pilot projects designed to test new ideas about the pathogenesis of and therapeutics for AS. Researchers from all countries, all types of organizations, and all types of sciences, including neuroscience, biotechnology, psychology, and all others are encouraged to apply.
EIN: 593092842

2400
Angels for Kids Foundation, Inc.

7020 High Grove Blvd.
Burr Ridge, IL   60527
E-mail: info@angelsforkids.com; Application address: P.O. Box 784, Windermere, FL 34786-0784; URL: http://www.angelsforkids.org

Foundation type: Independent foundation
Purpose: Grants to children under the age of 16 in the central FL area.
Financial data: Year ended 12/31/2012. Assets, $4,661 (M); Expenditures, $11,980; Total giving, $6,620; Grants to individuals, 6 grants totaling $1,237 (high: $300, low: $120).
Fields of interest: Family services; Children.
Type of support: Grants to individuals.
Application information: Applications accepted. Application form required. Application form available on the grantmaker's web site.
　Send request by: Online or mail
　Deadline(s): None
　Final notification: Applicants notified in one or two weeks
EIN: 200707112

2401
Ann and Robert H. Lurie Children's Hospital of Chicago

(formerly Children's Memorial Hospital)
2300 Children's Plz.
Box 268
Chicago, IL   60614-3394   (773) 880-4000
Contact: Fellowships: Ryan Howard, Admin. Fellow
Tel. for Ryan Howard: (773) 880-8390, fax: (773) 975-8667, e-mail: rhoward@childrensmemorial.org
Toll-free tel.: (800) 543-7362; URL: http://www.luriechildrens.org

Foundation type: Public charity
Purpose: Fellowships to recent graduates for pediatric healthcare administration opportunities.
Publications: Application guidelines.
Financial data: Year ended 08/31/2011. Assets, $2,042,087,930 (M); Expenditures, $549,842,853; Total giving, $28,319,947. Fellowships amount not specified.
Fields of interest: Health care; Pediatrics; Children.
Type of support: Fellowships.
Application information: Applications accepted. Interview required.
　Send request by: E-mail
　Deadline(s): Sept. 30
　Applicants should submit the following:
　　1) Transcripts
　　2) Letter(s) of recommendation
　　3) Essay
　　4) Resume
　Additional information: Application should also include a one- to two-page personal statement addressing career goals, why the applicants wants to pursue a fellowship experience, and specific expectations from the hospital. Also, a one-page essay addressing the current challenges facing the pediatric healthcare market.

Program description:

CMH Postgraduate Administrative Fellowship Program: This one-year postgraduate fellowship program is designed to provide individuals interested in pediatric hospital administration to develop leadership training and growth, contribute to the organization through specific assignments and responsibilities, and develop a mentoring relationship for future professional development. Eligible applicants must have an M.H.A., M.P.A., M.P.H., M.B.A., with a concentration in healthcare, or an equivalent from an accredited graduate program, and must have graduated in the year immediately preceding application.
EIN: 362170833

2402
Aon Memorial Education Fund

200 E. Randolph St., 8th Fl.
Chicago, IL   60601-6419   (312) 381-3551
Contact: Beth Gallagher, V.P.
E-mail: beth.gallagher@aon.com; URL: http://www.aon.com/usa/about-aon/aon-memorial-education-fund.jsp

Foundation type: Company-sponsored foundation
Purpose: Scholarships to children of Aon employees who lost their lives in the Sept. 11 World Trade Center disaster for study at educational institutions, as well as funding for education at various levels for individuals with special needs.
Financial data: Year ended 12/31/2012. Assets, $5,989,407 (M); Expenditures, $455,162; Total giving, $411,909.
Fields of interest: Vocational education, post-secondary; Higher education; Disabilities, people with.
Type of support: Employee-related scholarships; Employee-related welfare; Graduate support; Undergraduate support.
Application information: Applications not accepted.
　Additional information: Unsolicited requests for funds not considered or acknowledged.

Program description:

Post-Secondary Education Scholarships: Scholarships in the amount of $20,000 are awarded annually to each individual for tuition and related expenses such as books, supplies and equipment required for courses. Applicant must maintain a "C" GPA or its equivalent for undergraduate studies, and a "B" GPA for graduate studies. An individual will continue to qualify for annual awards as long as he/she is enrolled for study at an approved educational institution and maintains a minimum GPA as stated, and will not qualify for more than six annual awards without making a special application to the Fund. The award does not cover room and board costs.
EIN: 364468038

2403
APICS Educational & Research Foundation, Inc.

8430 W. Bryn Mawr Ave., Ste. 1000
Chicago, IL   60631   (517) 353-8711
Contact: Bob Collins, Exec. Dir.
FAX: (773) 693-3000;
E-mail: foundation@apics.org; Toll-free tel.: (800) 444-2742; URL: http://www.apics.org/about/overview/erfoundation

Foundation type: Public charity

Purpose: Grants for graduate and undergraduate APICS student members to learn more about the supply chain and operations management industry.
Publications: Application guidelines; Informational brochure.
Financial data: Year ended 12/31/2012. Assets, $952,291 (M); Expenditures, $101,744; Total giving, $3,500; Grants to individuals, totaling $3,500.
Fields of interest: Business school/education; Business/industry.
Type of support: Graduate support; Undergraduate support.
Application information: Applications accepted. Application form required.
   Deadline(s): June 14
   Additional information: See web site for additional guidelines.
Program description:
   APICS Scholars Education Program: The program gives APICS student members the opportunity to attend APICS International Conference & Expo build a network of contacts. The students will make valuable contact with operations management professionals, learn real-world applications and solutions, and be more prepared to enter the workforce after graduation. Applicants must be at least 18 years of age and be a current APICS member to apply.
EIN: 366155750

2404
AptarGroup Charitable Foundation
475 W. Terra Cotta Ste. E
Crystal Lake, IL 60014-3407 (815) 477-0424
Contact: Matthew DellamMaria, Secy. and Dir.

Foundation type: Company-sponsored foundation
Purpose: Scholarships to students of Crystal Lake, IL for attendance at accredited colleges or universities.
Publications: Application guidelines.
Financial data: Year ended 12/31/2012. Assets, $112,018 (M); Expenditures, $308,818; Total giving, $308,818.
Fields of interest: Higher education.
Type of support: Undergraduate support.
Application information: Applications not accepted.
   Additional information: Unsolicited requests for funds not considered or acknowledged.
EIN: 363927834

2405
Arbor Falls Foundation
333 W. Wacker Dr., Ste. 1700
Chicago, IL 60606 (847) 317-1280
Contact: Gregory Eaton, Pres. and Dir.
Application address: 2525 Waukegan Rd., Ste. 200, Bannockburn, IL 60015, tel.: (847) 317-1280; URL: http://www.arborfalls.org/af2/

Foundation type: Independent foundation
Purpose: Scholarships to graduating students in the Illinois area for attendance at four year colleges or post high school vocational training.
Financial data: Year ended 12/31/2012. Assets, $7,085 (M); Expenditures, $33,182; Total giving, $30,000.
Fields of interest: Vocational education, post-secondary; Higher education.
Type of support: Scholarships—to individuals.
Application information: Applications accepted. Application form required.
   Deadline(s): July 20

   Additional information: Maximum scholarship is $3,000 per year and is renewable for up to four years. Payments are made to the educational institution on behalf of the students.
EIN: 204962435

2406
ArcelorMittal USA Foundation, Inc.
(formerly Mittal Steel USA Foundation, Inc.)
1 S. Dearborn St., 19th Fl.
Chicago, IL 60603-2307
Contact: William C. Steers, Pres.

Foundation type: Company-sponsored foundation
Purpose: Scholarships to employees and dependents of active employees of ArcelorMittal USA.
Financial data: Year ended 12/31/2012. Assets, $342,400 (M); Expenditures, $1,506,015; Total giving, $1,505,500.
Type of support: Employee-related scholarships.
Application information:
   Initial approach: Letter
EIN: 352121803

2407
William A. Arnold Trust
c/o BB&T
130 N. Water St.
Decatur, IL 62523-1310

Foundation type: Independent foundation
Purpose: Scholarships to deserving students of Decatur, IL to further his or her education in the field of fine arts.
Financial data: Year ended 12/31/2011. Assets, $134,769 (M); Expenditures, $6,075; Total giving, $4,000.
Fields of interest: Arts education; Visual arts.
Type of support: Scholarships—to individuals.
Application information: Applications accepted.
   Additional information: Funds are paid directly to the educational institution on behalf of the students. Contact the trust for additional information.
EIN: 376061351

2408
Association for Surgical Education
Foundation
P.O. Box 19655
Springfield, IL 62794-9655
URL: http://www.surgicaleducation.com

Foundation type: Independent foundation
Purpose: Fellowships and grants to researchers, educators, and clinicians investigating questions, issues and concerns that are integral to surgical education. Applicants must be Association for Surgical Education members.
Financial data: Year ended 06/30/2013. Assets, $168,585 (M); Expenditures, $96,992; Total giving, $90,386.
Fields of interest: Surgery research.
Type of support: Fellowships; Postdoctoral support.
Application information: Application form required.
   Deadline(s): Dec. 15
   Applicants should submit the following:
     1) Proposal
     2) Letter(s) of recommendation
     3) Curriculum vitae
   Additional information: Application must also include outline of prior medical research and published works and description of current

research interests. See Web site for further application information.
Program description:
   Surgical Education Fellowship: Awards up to ten fellowships annually to spend a year studying under an advisor affiliated with the Foundation. Fellowships include $3,000 for tuition, travel to two seminars and costs associated with the Foundation's forum. Fellows are expected to submit the abstract or paper produced to a peer-reviewed forum or journal and to pass a final exam.
EIN: 371305690

2409
Association of University Radiologists
820 Jorie Blvd.
Oak Brook, IL 60523-2284 (630) 368-3730
Contact: Jennifer McBride, Sr. Asst.
FAX: (630) 571-7837; E-mail: aur@rsna.org; E-mail FOr Jennifer McBride: jmcbride@rsna.org;
URL: http://www.aur.org/

Foundation type: Public charity
Purpose: Grants and fellowships to individuals pursuing radiology education.
Financial data: Year ended 06/30/2012. Assets, $2,460,948 (M); Expenditures, $1,604,856; Total giving, $560,000.
Fields of interest: Diagnostic imaging research.
Type of support: Fellowships; Grants to individuals.
Application information: Applications accepted. Application form available on the grantmaker's web site.
   Send request by: On-line
   Deadline(s): Jan.10 for AUR R&E Foundation Grant/Ethics and Professionalism in Radiology Grant, and RSNA/AUR/APDR/ SCARD Radiology Education Research Development Grant, Jan. 16 for AUR GE Radiology Research Academic Fellowship Award (GERRAF)
   Additional information: See web site for additional eligibility guidelines.
Program descriptions:
   AUR GE Radiology Research Academic Fellowship (GERRAF) Award: This program offers qualified candidates interested in a radiology research the opportunity of meeting their needs through an award of up to $70,000 for each of the two years of involvement.
   Ethics and Professionalism in Radiology Project Grant: The purpose of this program is to improve patient care, to improve patient safety, and to promote social responsibility in medical care and practice, by providing funding opportunities for the study and teaching of ethics and professionalism in radiology. Up to $50,000 (USD) in aggregate may be awarded in a single year. This aggregate award may be to one or more individual applications.
   RSNA/AUR/ARDR/SCARD Education Research Development Grant: This program encourages innovation and improvement in health sciences education by providing research opportunities to individuals throughout the world who are in pursuit of advancing the science of radiology education. Awards amounts up $10,000 for a 1-year project to help cover the costs of research materials, research assistant support, and limited primary investigator salary support (no more than half of grant award).
EIN: 237086211

2410
BancTrust Opportunity Foundation
101 S. Central Ave.
P.O. Box 880
Paris, IL 61944-1728 (217) 465-6381
Contact: Sarah Handley

Foundation type: Company-sponsored foundation
Purpose: College scholarships to high school students in Edgar and Clark Counties, IL for postsecondary education.
Publications: Application guidelines.
Financial data: Year ended 12/31/2012. Assets, $54,874 (M); Expenditures, $38,403; Total giving, $37,852; Grants to individuals, 26 grants totaling $37,852 (high: $5,460, low: $1,000).
Fields of interest: Higher education.
Type of support: Scholarships—to individuals.
Application information: Applications accepted. Application form required.
> *Deadline(s):* Mar. 1
> *Additional information:* Application should include academic information, extracurricular activities, community/work/religious involvement, two reference letters, and a statement from the applicant. Application forms are available at all Edgar and Clark county, high schools.

EIN: 300109336

2411
Barber Family Foundation
1800 W. Diversey Pkwy., Ste. F
Chicago, IL 60614-1032
Contact: Ruth Barber, Secy.-Treas.
E-mail: info@barberfamilyfoundation.org;
URL: http://www.barberfamilyfoundation.org

Foundation type: Independent foundation
Purpose: College scholarships to graduating Pittsfield High School seniors under age 25 who are residents of Pike county, IL.
Financial data: Year ended 12/31/2012. Assets, $4,516 (M); Expenditures, $6,650; Total giving, $6,600; Grants to individuals, 6 grants totaling $6,600 (high: $2,000, low: $600).
Fields of interest: Higher education.
Type of support: Support to graduates or students of specific schools.
Application information: Applications accepted. Application form required. Application form available on the grantmaker's web site.
> *Deadline(s):* Apr. 8
> *Applicants should submit the following:*
> 1) Letter(s) of recommendation
> 2) Transcripts
> 3) Financial information
> 4) Essay
> *Additional information:* Application should also include a copy of your parent(s) 1040 tax form. Checks are sent directly to the educational institution on behalf of the students.

EIN: 201619274

2412
Barnard Scholarship Trust
111 W. Monroe St., Tax div. 10C
Chicago, IL 60603

Foundation type: Independent foundation
Purpose: Scholarships to graduates of River Valley High School, Spring Dale, WI, for attendance at a college within the university of WI system, or a state vocational school within WI.

Financial data: Year ended 08/31/2012. Assets, $293,025 (M); Expenditures, $29,465; Total giving, $22,898; Grants to individuals, 7 grants totaling $22,898 (high: $3,666, low: $1,700).
Fields of interest: Vocational education, post-secondary; Higher education.
Type of support: Support to graduates or students of specific schools; Undergraduate support.
Application information: Applications not accepted.
> *Additional information:* Unsolicited requests for funds not considered or acknowledged.

EIN: 396719890

2413
Fay T. Barnes Scholarship Trust
10 S. Dearborn, IL1-0117
Chicago, IL 60603 (214) 965-2914
Application address: JPMorgan, P.O. Box 227237, Dallas, TX 75222-7237

Foundation type: Independent foundation
Purpose: Scholarships to graduating seniors of high schools in Williamson and Travis counties, TX, to attend TX universities and colleges.
Publications: Informational brochure (including application guidelines).
Financial data: Year ended 12/31/2012. Assets, $2,644,543 (M); Expenditures, $105,461; Total giving, $77,000.
Fields of interest: Higher education.
Type of support: Support to graduates or students of specific schools; Undergraduate support.
Application information: Applications accepted. Application form required.
> *Applicants should submit the following:*
> 1) Transcripts
> 2) Letter(s) of recommendation
> 3) Essay

EIN: 742256469

2414
Cary C. Barr Trust
c/o Harris Bank, N.A.
111 West Monroe St., Ste.16W
Chicago, IL 60603
Application address: c/o Streator Township High School, Attn.: Mark Pano, Asst. Supt., 600 N. Jefferson St., Streator, IL 61364-2145

Foundation type: Independent foundation
Purpose: Scholarships to graduates of Streator Township High School, IL for continuing their education at institutions of higher learning. Grants are also made to the deserving poor of the city of Streator, IL and/or the territory within one mile of the Streator city limits.
Financial data: Year ended 12/31/2011. Assets, $329,710 (M); Expenditures, $24,344; Total giving, $17,250.
Fields of interest: Higher education; Economically disadvantaged.
Type of support: Support to graduates or students of specific schools; Grants for special needs.
Application information: Applications accepted. Application form required.
> *Additional information:* Application for scholarship must include recommendations. Applications can be obtained from the director of guidance of Streator Township high school.

EIN: 366029865

2415
BCMW Community Services
909 E. Rexford
P.O. Box 729
Centralia, IL 62801-3033 (618) 532-7388
Contact: Keith O. Brown, Exec. Dir.
FAX: (618) 532-0204; URL: http://www.bcmwcommunityservices.org/

Foundation type: Public charity
Purpose: Scholarships to low-income students residing in Bond, Clinton, Marion, and Washington Counties who are attending college in IL. Emergency assistance to low-income families of Bond, Clinton, Marion, Washington and Franklin counties, IL, with food, shelter, utilities, medication and transportation.
Financial data: Year ended 06/30/2012. Assets, $3,244,781 (M); Expenditures, $14,056,309; Total giving, $8,156,562; Grants to individuals, totaling $8,156,562.
Fields of interest: Higher education; Pharmacy/prescriptions; Food services; Housing/shelter, rehabilitation; Housing/shelter, temporary shelter; Housing/shelter, services; Housing/shelter, repairs; Human services; Transportation; Utilities.
Type of support: Emergency funds; Scholarships—to individuals; Grants for special needs.
Application information: Applications accepted. Application form required. Interview required.
> *Initial approach:* Letter
> *Applicants should submit the following:*
> 1) Financial information
> 2) Letter(s) of recommendation
> 3) GPA

Program descriptions:
> *Emergency Services:* Food, shelter, medication, and transportation services are available to individuals in emergency situations. Eligible applicants must meet 125 percent of federal poverty income guidelines and demonstrate need.
> *Homebuyer Program:* Zero-interest, forgivable loans are available to low-income individuals toward closing costs (up to $1,500) and down payments (up to $7,000). Loans are also available to help rehabilitate property to meet Section 8 Housing Quality standards. Applicants must be at or below the 80 percent area median income level, complete a Homebuyer's Workshop, have satisfactory credit, and be able to provide a mandatory $1,000 down payment.
> *Low-Income Housing Energy Assistance Program (LIHEAP):* Assists low-income households in paying for winter emergency services through a one-time benefit, to be used towards energy bills. Emergency services are also available if household is disconnected from an energy source needed for heating.
> *Weatherization Program:* Designed to help low-income residents save fuel and money while increasing the comfort of their homes. Services include: a whole-house energy audit, weather-stripping/caulking, insulation of attic and walls, repairing windows and doors, replacing windows, and furnace work if needed. Applicants must own their properties, with either an income that does not exceed federal poverty income guidelines or an occupant receiving SSI or TANF grants. Renters who apply must have landlord consent.

EIN: 370899785

2416
Paul Bechtner Education Foundation
(formerly American Colloid Company Foundation)
2870 Forbs Ave.
Hoffman Estates, IL   60192-3702
Contact: Amiel Naiman

Foundation type: Company-sponsored foundation
Purpose: Scholarships for higher education limited to children of AMCOL International Corp. employees.
Financial data: Year ended 12/31/2012. Assets, $30,522 (M); Expenditures, $36,000; Total giving, $36,000; Grants to individuals, 24 grants totaling $36,000 (high: $1,500, low: $1,500).
Type of support: Employee-related scholarships; Undergraduate support.
Application information: Applications accepted. Application form required.
> *Deadline(s):* Apr. 5
> *Applicants should submit the following:*
>   1) Transcripts
>   2) Financial information
>   3) Letter(s) of recommendation
>   4) Essay
> *Additional information:* Application should also include proof of college acceptance.
Company name: AMCOL International Corporation
EIN: 363892273

2417
Davis Becker Scholarship Fund
P.O. Box 803878
Chicago, IL   60680-3878

Foundation type: Independent foundation
Purpose: Scholarships paid directly to the university for students at the University of Miami, FL.
Financial data: Year ended 03/31/2013. Assets, $149,599 (M); Expenditures, $10,766; Total giving, $6,305.
Type of support: Support to graduates or students of specific schools.
Application information: Applications not accepted.
> *Additional information:* Unsolicited requests for funds not accepted.
EIN: 656018838

2418
Charles A. Beebe Scholarship Fund
c/o Soy Capital Bank & Trust Co.
2306 E. Washington St.
Bloomington, IL   61704   (309) 968-6689
Contact: William Heinhorst, Pres.
Application address: Manito Community Bank, 105 S. Adams St., Manito, IL 61546-9518

Foundation type: Independent foundation
Purpose: Scholarships to graduates of Forman Community High School, Manito, IL.
Financial data: Year ended 12/31/2012. Assets, $1,380,110 (M); Expenditures, $121,369; Total giving, $66,480; Grants to individuals, 90 grants totaling $66,480 (high: $870, low: $225).
Type of support: Support to graduates or students of specific schools; Undergraduate support.
Application information: Applications accepted. Application form required.
> *Deadline(s):* May 15
> *Additional information:* Applications available from People's State Bank.
EIN: 376164013

2419
Otto Bender Scholarship Trust
P.O. Box 280
Carlyle, IL   62231-0280   (618) 594-2491

Foundation type: Independent foundation
Purpose: Scholarships to graduates or potential graduates of Community Unit District 1 High School, Carlyle, IL, who plan to attend four years of college.
Financial data: Year ended 05/31/2013. Assets, $325,737 (M); Expenditures, $37,826; Total giving, $16,678; Grants to individuals, 3 grants totaling $16,678 (high: $5,599, low: $5,540).
Fields of interest: Higher education.
Type of support: Support to graduates or students of specific schools; Undergraduate support.
Application information: Applications accepted. Application form required.
> *Deadline(s):* Apr. 1
EIN: 376341841

2420
Phyllis A. Beneke Scholarship Fund
10 S dearborn ILI-0117
Chicago, IL   60603
Application address: Wheeling Park High School, 1976 Park View Rd., Wheeling, Wv 26003

Foundation type: Independent foundation
Purpose: Scholarships to graduates of Ohio County, WV, public high schools.
Publications: Informational brochure (including application guidelines).
Financial data: Year ended 02/28/2013. Assets, $2,903,249 (M); Expenditures, $159,331; Total giving, $124,000; Grants to individuals, 53 grants totaling $124,000 (high: $7,000, low: $1,000).
Type of support: Scholarships—to individuals; Support to graduates or students of specific schools.
Application information: Application form required.
> *Deadline(s):* Third week of May
> *Applicants should submit the following:*
>   1) Transcripts
>   2) SAT
>   3) ACT
>   4) Financial information
>   5) Letter(s) of recommendation
> *Additional information:* Application should also include personal statement of 200 words or less and student information sheet.
EIN: 556106147

2421
Benjamin Trust Fund
620 W. Burlington Ave.
La Grange, IL   60525-2228

Foundation type: Independent foundation
Purpose: Scholarships to graduates of West Chicago Community High School District No. 94, IL.
Financial data: Year ended 02/28/2013. Assets, $250,302 (M); Expenditures, $20,649; Total giving, $14,747; Grants to individuals, 4 grants totaling $14,747 (high: $8,401, low: $2,000).
Type of support: Support to graduates or students of specific schools; Undergraduate support.
Application information: Applications accepted. Application form required.
> *Deadline(s):* Apr. 15
> *Additional information:* Applications available from Superintendent of schools.
EIN: 366552295

2422
M. A. & L. J. Bennett Scholarship Fund
c/o JPMorgan Chase Bank, N.A.
10 S Dearborn IL1-0117
Chicago, IL   60603-2300   (516) 459-0050
Contact: Thomas Cawley
Application Address: c/o NYPD Emerald Society Attn;Thomas Cawley, 1315 Little Neck Ave., Bellmore NY. 11710

Foundation type: Independent foundation
Purpose: Scholarships to children of police officers of the NYPD who are either active, retired, or were killed in the line of duty.
Financial data: Year ended 05/31/2013. Assets, $2,862,685 (M); Expenditures, $151,058; Total giving, $115,550; Grants to individuals, 33 grants totaling $115,550 (high: $7,500, low: $1,250).
Fields of interest: Crime/law enforcement, police agencies.
Type of support: Employee-related scholarships.
Application information: Applications accepted. Application form not required.
> *Deadline(s):* None
> *Additional information:* Contact fund for current application guidelines.
Company name: New York City Police Department
EIN: 133544931

2423
The Berner Charitable and Scholarship Foundation
P.O. Box 06560
Chicago, IL   60606-6560   (312) 782-5885
Contact: Ruben R. Vernof, Tr.

Foundation type: Independent foundation
Purpose: Scholarships/student loans to GA residents who are attending, or who are planning to attend any U.S. college or university.
Financial data: Year ended 12/31/2012. Assets, $8,065,085 (M); Expenditures, $685,931; Total giving, $547,713; Grants to individuals, 43 grants totaling $333,204 (high: $23,299, low: $5,000).
Fields of interest: Veterinary medicine.
Type of support: Scholarships—to individuals; Student loans—to individuals; Graduate support; Postgraduate support.
Application information: Applications accepted.
> *Initial approach:* Letter
> *Deadline(s):* Mar.
> *Additional information:* Contact foundation for current application guidelines.
Program description:
> *Scholarship Program:* Half of the scholarship is given as an interest-free student loan, to be repaid six months after graduation. Recipients generally have five to six years to complete repayment. All applicants must have a "C" average, and be full-time students. Scholarships can be used for undergraduate, master's, or postgraduate degrees.
EIN: 363923844

2424
George V. & Cora Betts Trust No. 113
c/o First State Bank, N.A.
P.O. Box 260
Monticello, IL   61856-0260   (217) 762-9431
Contact: Nikki Mann
Application address: 201 W. Main, Monticello, IL 61856

Foundation type: Independent foundation
Purpose: Scholarships to students who reside in the Atwood-Hammond Community Unit School

District or the Lovington Community School District, IL, and plan to attend a college or university.
Financial data: Year ended 12/31/2012. Assets, $1,194,719 (M); Expenditures, $28,699; Total giving, $10,000; Grants to individuals, 13 grants totaling $10,000 (high: $1,000, low: $500).
Fields of interest: Higher education.
Type of support: Support to graduates or students of specific schools.
Application information: Applications accepted. Application form required.
 Deadline(s): Apr. 1
 Additional information: Applicants must be full time students and have need of financial assistance beyond parental help. Applications are available at Atwood-Hammond high school, Lovington high school, or State Bank of Hammond.
EIN: 376267420

2425
Evelyn E. Biederstedt Scholarship Fund
c/o La Salle State Bank
P.O. Box 462
La Salle, IL   61301-0462

Foundation type: Independent foundation
Purpose: Scholarships to LaSalle-Peru Township High School seniors who plan to attend a two or four year college or university, or pursue studies at a vocational or trade school.
Financial data: Year ended 12/31/2013. Assets, $341,998 (M); Expenditures, $20,552; Total giving, $16,853; Grants to individuals, 6 grants totaling $16,853 (high: $3,813, low: $1,979).
Fields of interest: Music; Music (choral); Vocational education, post-secondary.
Type of support: Support to graduates or students of specific schools.
Application information: Applications accepted. Application form required.
 Deadline(s): Feb. 15
 Applicants should submit the following:
  1) GPA
  2) Essay
 Additional information: Applicant must demonstrate financial need. Applications can be obtained from the guidance counselor.
Program description:
 Biederstest Memorial Scholarship: A one-year scholarship in the amount of $2,000 is granted to an applicant to be used for tuition, books, fees, or other related educational expenses. The applicant must have a cumulative GPA of 3.0 or better, and must have shown interest in music by participating in band or chorus during high school, and must show leadership ability, perseverance, resourcefulness, and personality.
EIN: 611469132

2426
Black Hawk College Foundation
6600 34th Ave.
Moline, IL   61265-5870   (309) 796-5052
Contact: Jim Metz, Chair.

Foundation type: Public charity
Purpose: Scholarships to residents of Community College District No. 503, IL.
Publications: Application guidelines; Annual report; Informational brochure; Newsletter.
Financial data: Year ended 06/30/2012. Assets, $2,454,406 (M); Expenditures, $147,841; Total giving, $100,331; Grants to individuals, totaling $70,578.
Type of support: Undergraduate support.

Application information: Applications accepted.
 Deadline(s): Contact foundation for current application deadline/guidelines.
EIN: 363240562

2427
The Joseph Blazek Foundation
1500 Skokie Blvd., Ste. 301
Northbrook, IL   60062-4114   (847) 849-5551

Foundation type: Independent foundation
Purpose: Scholarships to high school seniors in public or private secondary schools in Cook County, IL, planning to major in engineering, mathematics, chemistry, physics, or related scientific fields.
Publications: Application guidelines.
Financial data: Year ended 06/30/2013. Assets, $68,478 (M); Expenditures, $60,515; Total giving, $52,000.
Fields of interest: Engineering school/education; Science; Chemistry; Mathematics; Physics.
Type of support: Support to graduates or students of specific schools; Undergraduate support.
Application information: Applications accepted. Application form required.
 Send request by: Mail
 Deadline(s): Mar. 15
 Final notification: Applicants notified in late May
 Applicants should submit the following:
  1) Transcripts
  2) Essay
  3) ACT
  4) SAT
  5) Financial information
EIN: 237015800

2428
Katherine Bogardus Trust
c/o State Bank of Lincoln
508 Broadway
Lincoln, IL   62656   (217) 735-5551
Contact: Gail L. Nunnery, V.P.

Foundation type: Independent foundation
Purpose: Educational loans to graduates of high schools in DeWitt County, IL, and to descendants of the first cousins of the creator of this trust.
Financial data: Year ended 12/31/2012. Assets, $1,728,631 (M); Expenditures, $159,798; Total giving, $130,405.
Fields of interest: Education.
Type of support: Student loans—to individuals.
Application information: Application form required. Interview required.
 Deadline(s): None
 Applicants should submit the following:
  1) Transcripts
  2) Budget Information
 Additional information: Applicants must provide evidence of financial need to be considered.
EIN: 376062479

2429
Erik Bohne-Pace Memorial Scholarship Fund
13152 S. Cicero Ave.
P.O. Box 262
Crestwood, IL   60445-1470   (708) 389-0641
FAX: (708) 389-6413;
E-mail: eriksfoundation@comcast.net; URL: http://www.eriksfoundation.org

Foundation type: Public charity
Purpose: Scholarship to an 8th grader of St. Alexander School, St. Christopher School or an

active member of a St. Jude Knight's House League Hockey Team applying to a high school this fall.
Publications: Application guidelines.
Financial data: Year ended 12/31/2010. Assets, $68,141 (M); Expenditures, $16,247; Total giving, $13,000; Grants to individuals, totaling $8,000.
Fields of interest: Education.
Type of support: Scholarships—to individuals; Awards/grants by nomination only.
Application information:
 Initial approach: Online nomination
Program description:
 Scholarships: Scholarships are available to students in the Chicago area, so that they can attend a parochial high school or defer their college expenses. To be eligible for a scholarship, the child needs to be nominated by a faculty member of either St. Alexander School in Palos Heights, IL or St. Christopher School in Midlothian, IL or a coach with the St. Jude Knights Hockey Club of Crestwood, IL. Applicants must also be an 8th-grader applying to a high school in the fall, carry a B or higher school average, and demonstrate respect for and empathy with others.
EIN: 364434098

2430
Bolingbrook Police Benevolent Foundation
375 W. Briarcliff Rd.
Bolingbrook, IL   60440-0951
Contact: Thomas Gallas, Pres.

Foundation type: Public charity
Purpose: Financial assistance to police officers and their families as well as needy families. A scholarship also for the dependent of a Bolingbrook Police Department employee and a scholarship for a Bolingbrook high school senior.
Fields of interest: Education.
Type of support: Scholarships—to individuals; Support to graduates or students of specific schools; Grants for special needs.
Application information: Unsolicited requests for funds not accepted.
EIN: 364313845

2431
Chris and Katherine Boulos Foundation
c/o The National Bank & Trust Co.
230 W. State St., MSC M-300
Sycamore, IL   60178   (815) 895-2125

Foundation type: Independent foundation
Purpose: Scholarships to graduates of DeKalb High School, IL, and Sycamore High School, IL, for study at Kishwaukee College, in Malta, IL.
Financial data: Year ended 12/31/2012. Assets, $1,520,349 (M); Expenditures, $109,771; Total giving, $86,940; Grants to individuals, 80 grants totaling $86,940 (high: $3,400, low: $250).
Type of support: Support to graduates or students of specific schools; Undergraduate support.
Application information: Applications accepted. Application form required.
 Initial approach: Letter or telephone
 Deadline(s): May 1
EIN: 363727751

2432
Bound To Stay Bound Books Foundation
c/o Jacksonville Savings Bank
1211 W. Morton Ave.
Jacksonville, IL   62650-2770

Foundation type: Company-sponsored foundation
Purpose: Scholarships to students pursuing master's or advanced degree in children's librarianship.
Financial data: Year ended 12/31/2012. Assets, $4,131,337 (M); Expenditures, $244,313; Total giving, $216,100.
Fields of interest: Libraries/library science.
Type of support: Scholarships—to individuals; Graduate support.
Application information: Applications accepted. Application form available on the grantmaker's web site.

> *Send request by:* Online
> *Deadline(s):* Mar. 1
> *Final notification:* Recipients notified June 1
> *Applicants should submit the following:*
> 1) Transcripts
> 2) Letter(s) of recommendation
> *Additional information:* All applicants must be accepted at a library school accredited by the American Library Association that offers a full range of courses in children's materials and library services to children.

Program description:

> *ALSC Bound to Stay Bound Books Scholarship:* The foundation annually awards four $7,000 scholarships to individuals pursuing a master's or advanced degree in children's librarianship. Recipients are selected based on academic excellence, leadership qualities, and the desire to work with children up to and including the age of 14 in any type of library. The program is administered by the American Library Association.

EIN: 376227827

2433
Hazel Marie Boyle Scholarship Fund

606 S. Main St.
Princeton, IL 61356

Foundation type: Independent foundation
Purpose: Scholarships to graduates of Putnam County High School, IL.
Financial data: Year ended 12/31/2012. Assets, $200,558 (M); Expenditures, $12,968; Total giving, $10,253; Grants to individuals, 8 grants totaling $10,253 (high: $1,784, low: $700).
Type of support: Support to graduates or students of specific schools; Undergraduate support.
Application information:

> *Deadline(s):* Feb. 1
> *Additional information:* Application must include complete school records.

EIN: 364091370

2434
Boynton-Gillespie Memorial Funds

165 W. Broadway
P.O. Box 245
Sparta, IL 62286-0245

Foundation type: Independent foundation
Purpose: Scholarships to undergraduate students residing within a 30-mile radius of Sparta, IL.
Financial data: Year ended 12/31/2013. Assets, $2,594,175 (M); Expenditures, $131,334; Total giving, $100,500; Grants to individuals, 62 grants totaling $46,500 (high: $750, low: $750).
Fields of interest: Higher education.
Type of support: Scholarships—to individuals.
Application information: Application form required.

> *Initial approach:* Letter
> *Deadline(s):* May 1
> *Applicants should submit the following:*
> 1) Photograph

> 2) Transcripts
> 3) Essay
> *Additional information:* Scholarship is awarded based on merit and need for a one year period, subject for renewal for three additional years.

EIN: 376028930

2435
Elizabeth Breckinridge Scholarship Fund Trust

10 S. Dearborn, IL1-0117
Chicago, IL 60603 (214) 965-2908
Application address: JPMorgan Chase Bank, N.A., 2200 Ross Ave, 5th Fl., Dallas, TX 75201

Foundation type: Independent foundation
Purpose: Scholarships to public high school seniors in Jefferson County, KY, who are interested in teaching.
Financial data: Year ended 05/31/2013. Assets, $295,237 (M); Expenditures, $20,014; Total giving, $19,663.
Fields of interest: Teacher school/education.
Type of support: Support to graduates or students of specific schools; Undergraduate support.
Application information: Applications accepted. Application form not required.
EIN: 616019485

2436
Jonathan D. Brege Memorial Foundation

10 S. Dearborn, IL1-0117
Chicago, IL 60603 (313) 343-8524
Contact: Don N. Sweeny
Application address: JPMorgan Chase Bank, N.A., 685 St. Clair Ave., 2nd Fl., Gross Pointe, MI 48230-1243

Foundation type: Independent foundation
Purpose: Scholarships primarily to graduating students from Onaway High School and New Lothrop High School, MI.
Financial data: Year ended 09/30/2012. Assets, $314,533 (M); Expenditures, $14,388; Total giving, $12,500.
Fields of interest: Higher education.
Type of support: Support to graduates or students of specific schools; Undergraduate support.
Application information: Applications accepted.

> *Initial approach:* Letter
> *Send request by:* Mail
> *Deadline(s):* None

EIN: 386477703

2437
Robert N. Brewer Family Foundation

115 W. Jefferson St., Ste. 200
Bloomington, IL 61702-3986
Application address: 2 North Park Ave., Herrin, IL 62948

Foundation type: Independent foundation
Purpose: Scholarships to graduating seniors of Herrin High School, IL for continuing education at accredited colleges or universities.
Financial data: Year ended 12/31/2012. Assets, $17,142,384 (M); Expenditures, $1,708,894; Total giving, $1,436,200; Grants to individuals, 160 grants totaling $636,000 (high: $6,300, low: $2,125).
Fields of interest: Education.
Type of support: Support to graduates or students of specific schools; Undergraduate support.

Application information: Application form required.
Deadline(s): None
Additional information: Unsolicited requests for funds not accepted.
EIN: 364129119

2438
Verl I. Brooks Scholarship Foundation

P.O. Box 967
Galesburg, IL 61401-0967
Contact: Freda M. Bonnett, Fdn. Mgr.
Application address: 647 Cypress Ln., Galesburg, IL 61401, tel.: (309) 343-1348

Foundation type: Independent foundation
Purpose: Scholarships to high school graduates who were residents of Rivoli Township, Mercer County, IL, for at least two years prior to graduation.
Financial data: Year ended 12/31/2012. Assets, $2,150,153 (M); Expenditures, $104,336; Total giving, $73,589; Grants to individuals, 28 grants totaling $73,589 (high: $7,600, low: $439).
Type of support: Scholarships—to individuals.
Application information: Unsolicited requests for funds not considered or acknowledged.
EIN: 363967580

2439
Fern Brown Memorial Fund

10 S. Dearborn IL1-0117
Chicago, IL 60603 (214) 965-2908

Foundation type: Independent foundation
Purpose: Scholarships to residents of OK.
Financial data: Year ended 06/30/2012. Assets, $162,561 (M); Expenditures, $14,476; Total giving, $8,711.
Type of support: Scholarships—to individuals.
Application information: Applications accepted.

> *Send request by:* Mail
> *Deadline(s):* None

EIN: 736162573

2440
J. Leonard Brown Memorial Scholarship Fund

1515 Charleston Ave.
P.O. Box 529
Mattoon, IL 61938 (217) 728-4040
Contact: John Sohm Rev.
Application address: P.O. Box 464, Sullivan, IL 61951

Foundation type: Independent foundation
Purpose: Scholarships to full time students who are residents of Moultrie county, IL for attendance at colleges, universities, or vocational/technical school.
Financial data: Year ended 12/31/2012. Assets, $123,738 (M); Expenditures, $7,947; Total giving, $5,200; Grant to an individual, 1 grant totaling $5,200.
Fields of interest: Vocational education, post-secondary; Higher education.
Type of support: Scholarships—to individuals.
Application information: Applications accepted. Application form required.

> *Deadline(s):* Apr. 15
> *Applicants should submit the following:*
> 1) GPA
> 2) Financial information
> 3) Essay

Additional information: Application must also include current tax returns and student must demonstrate financial need.
EIN: 376376771

2441
Lorene Brown Scholarship Foundation
c/o National Bank & Trust Co.
230 W. State St., MSC M-300
Sycamore, IL   60178   (815) 895-2125
Contact: Carolyn Swafford

Foundation type: Independent foundation
Purpose: Scholarships to graduates of Genoa-Kingston High School, IL, who are attending the University of Illinois or Northern Illinois University.
Financial data: Year ended 12/31/2012. Assets, $206,401 (M); Expenditures, $12,076; Total giving, $8,000; Grants to individuals, 3 grants totaling $8,000 (high: $3,000, low: $2,500).
Type of support: Support to graduates or students of specific schools; Undergraduate support.
Application information: Application form required.
   Deadline(s): Apr. 15
EIN: 366939275

2442
Raena Brown Trust No. 363
1201 Network Centre Dr.
Effingham, IL   62401

Foundation type: Independent foundation
Purpose: Scholarships to medical students from the Mendota, IL, area.
Financial data: Year ended 12/31/2012. Assets, $287,498 (M); Expenditures, $19,969; Total giving, $14,000.
Fields of interest: Medical school/education.
Type of support: Graduate support.
Application information: Applications accepted. Application form required.
   Initial approach: Letter or telephone
   Deadline(s): None
EIN: 366692001

2443
The Brunswick Foundation, Inc.
1 N. Field Ct.
Lake Forest, IL   60045-4811   (847) 735-4344
Contact: Judith P. Zelisko, Pres. and Dir.
URL: http://www.brunswick.com/company/community/brunswickfoundation.php

Foundation type: Company-sponsored foundation
Purpose: Scholarships to children of full-time Brunswick Corporation employees and Brunswick Corporation dealership employees.
Publications: Application guidelines.
Financial data: Year ended 12/31/2012. Assets, $2,591,161 (M); Expenditures, $272,351; Total giving, $267,113; Grants to individuals, 96 grants totaling $215,538 (high: $2,500, low: $175).
Fields of interest: Vocational education; Higher education; Scholarships/financial aid; Education.
Type of support: Employee-related scholarships.
Application information: Applications not accepted.
   Additional information: Unsolicited requests for funds not considered or acknowledged.
Program descriptions:
   Sons & Daughters Scholarship Program: The foundation awards single-year scholarships of up to $2,500 to high school seniors and college freshman, sophomores, and juniors who are

children of Brunswick employees to attend a college, university, or vocational school. Scholarships are awarded based on academic record, achievement test scores, and leadership abilities as demonstrated by extracurricular activities, and work record.
   The Dealer Sons & Daughters Scholarship Program: The foundation awards single-year college scholarships of up to $2,000 to high school seniors and college freshman, sophomores, and juniors who are children of Brunswick Dealers attend a college, university, or vocational school. Brunswick Deals must have achieved "Gold" or "Platinum" level status as determined by Brunswick Dealer Advantage.
Company name: Brunswick Corporation
EIN: 366033576

2444
Benjamin F. & Ernestine Bruton Foundation
P.O. Box 201328
Chicago, IL   60620-7328
Contact: Alice S. Walker, Secy.
Application address: 4212 Cedarwood Ln., Matteson, IL 60443-1911

Foundation type: Independent foundation
Purpose: Scholarships to individuals in IL pursuing a career in veterinary medicine.
Financial data: Year ended 12/31/2012. Assets, $616,951 (M); Expenditures, $62,079; Total giving, $12,250.
Fields of interest: Veterinary medicine.
Type of support: Scholarships—to individuals.
Application information: Applications accepted.
   Deadline(s): None
EIN: 363385677

2445
Everett S. Bulkley, Jr. Trust
(formerly The Bulkley Foundation Trust)
c/o JPMorgan Chase Bank, N.A.
10 S. Dearborn St., IL1-0117
Chicago, IL   60603-2300
Application address: c/o JPMorgan Chase Bank, N.A., Attn.: Edward Marks, V.P., 122 Main St., New Canaan, CT, 06480-4709, tel.: (203) 972-2205

Foundation type: Independent foundation
Purpose: Scholarships to graduating seniors at Norwalk High School, CT.
Financial data: Year ended 12/31/2012. Assets, $3,660,016 (M); Expenditures, $212,347; Total giving, $171,221; Grant to an individual, 1 grant totaling $13,071.
Type of support: Support to graduates or students of specific schools; Undergraduate support.
Application information: Applications accepted. Application form not required.
   Initial approach: Letter
   Send request by: Mail
   Copies of proposal: 1
   Deadline(s): Nov. 1
   Final notification: Recipients notified Dec. 1
   Applicants should submit the following:
      1) Proposal
      2) Financial information
      3) Budget Information
   Additional information: Contact trust for current application deadline/guidelines.
EIN: 066332021

2446
Henry Bunn Memorial Fund
10 S. Dearborn IL1-017
Chicago, IL   60603   (217) 525-9737
Contact: Heather Stahlberg Smith
Application address: 1 Old State Capitol Plz., 3rd Fl., Springfield, IL 62701

Foundation type: Independent foundation
Purpose: Scholarships to high school seniors who are residents of Sangamon County, IL.
Financial data: Year ended 12/31/2012. Assets, $1,003,337 (M); Expenditures, $53,561; Total giving, $42,155; Grant to an individual, 1 grant totaling $42,155.
Fields of interest: Higher education; Scholarships/financial aid; Economically disadvantaged.
Type of support: Undergraduate support.
Application information: Applications accepted. Application form required.
   Deadline(s): Mar. 1
   Applicants should submit the following:
      1) ACT
      2) SAT
      3) Transcripts
   Additional information: Applications accepted through local high school counselors.
Program description:
   Scholarship Program: Scholarship recipients must exhibit high moral character, industry, and good study habits. Their high school record and qualifications must be superior, indicating the potential for successful college work. They also must demonstrate a need for financial assistance beyond reasonable levels of parent and self-help. The scholarship may be renewed annually for a maximum of three years, provided the student remains in financial need and good academic standing.
EIN: 376041599

2447
William, Agnes & Elizabeth Burgess Memorial Scholarship Fund
c/o First Mid-Illinois Bank & Trust
P.O. Box 529
Mattoon, IL   61938-0529   (217) 258-0633
Contact: Laura Walk

Foundation type: Independent foundation
Purpose: Scholarships to financially needy graduating seniors of Mattoon Community High School, IL.
Financial data: Year ended 03/31/2012. Assets, $3,055,815 (M); Expenditures, $247,897; Total giving, $144,100; Grants to individuals, 137 grants totaling $144,100 (high: $1,100, low: $550).
Type of support: Support to graduates or students of specific schools; Undergraduate support.
Application information:
   Deadline(s): Mar. 15
   Additional information: Application forms available at Mattoon High School.
EIN: 376024599

2448
Dennett L. Burson Memorial Scholarship Fund
11100 Edgebrook Ln.
Indian Head Park, IL   60525-6974

Foundation type: Independent foundation
Purpose: Provides scholarships to students in Indian Head Park, IL.
Financial data: Year ended 06/30/2013. Assets, $7,711 (M); Expenditures, $10,001; Total giving,

$10,000; Grant to an individual, 1 grant totaling $10,000.
Fields of interest: Higher education.
Type of support: Scholarships—to individuals.
Application information: Applications not accepted.
EIN: 363616328

2449
Lila Draper Burton Trust
10 S. Dearborn 1L1-0117
Chicago, IL   60603

Foundation type: Independent foundation
Purpose: Undergraduate scholarships are awarded to residents of Waukesha County, WI, who have graduated from a Waukesha County, WI, high school and who have demonstrated academic achievement, personality and character qualities, school citizenship, and financial need.
Financial data: Year ended 12/31/2012. Assets, $1,607,284 (M); Expenditures, $85,574; Total giving, $65,960; Grants to individuals, 88 grants totaling $65,960 (high: $1,800, low: $480).
Type of support: Support to graduates or students of specific schools; Undergraduate support.
Application information: Application form required.
  Applicants should submit the following:
    1) SAT
    2) ACT
  Additional information: Contact guidance office of any Waukesha County high school for complete application deadline/guidelines.
EIN: 396146782

2450
Busey-Mills Community Foundation
1105 Baytowned Dr. no. 16
Champaign, IL   61822

Foundation type: Independent foundation
Purpose: Scholarships to residents of IL, primarily in Champaign, for higher education.
Financial data: Year ended 12/31/2012. Assets, $227,503 (M); Expenditures, $13,670; Total giving, $13,000.
Type of support: Undergraduate support.
Application information: Applications not accepted.
  Additional information: Unsolicited requests for funds not accepted.
EIN: 371267247

2451
Bushnell Arts Foundation
P.O. Box 149
Bushnell, IL   61422-0149   (309) 772-2171
Contact: Eileen N. Rausehart, Pres.
Application address: 24 Hillcrest Dr., Bushnell, IL 61422-9737

Foundation type: Independent foundation
Purpose: Scholarship to students who reside in the Bushnell-Prairie City School District, Illinois.
Financial data: Year ended 12/31/2012. Assets, $247,351 (M); Expenditures, $11,577; Total giving, $9,400.
Fields of interest: Arts education.
Type of support: Scholarships—to individuals.
Application information: Applications accepted.
  Initial approach: Letter
  Deadline(s): None
EIN: 363151919

2452
Business and Professional People for the Public Interest
25 E. Washington St., No. 1515
Chicago, IL   60602-1852   (312) 641-5570
Contact: E. Hoy McConnell II, Exec. Dir.
FAX: (312) 641-5454; E-mail: info@bpichicago.org;
E-mail For E. Hoy McConnell II:
hmcconnell@bpichicago.org; URL: http://
www.bpichicago.org

Foundation type: Public charity
Purpose: Fellowships to individuals interested in developing the experience, skills, and network critical to a rewarding career in public interest advocacy.
Publications: Application guidelines.
Financial data: Year ended 12/31/2011. Assets, $6,493,790 (M); Expenditures, $1,638,468.
Fields of interest: Education; Legal services, public interest law; Housing/shelter.
Type of support: Fellowships.
Application information: Applications accepted.
  Deadline(s): Oct. 14 for Polikoff-Gautreaux Fellowship
  Applicants should submit the following:
    1) Resume
    2) Essay
    3) Curriculum vitae
  Additional information: Application should also include a cover letter, references and writing sample.
Program description:
  Polikoff-Gautreaux Fellowship: This program offers the opportunity for recent law school and public policy school graduates to develop the experience, skills, and network critical to a rewarding career in public interest advocacy. Fellows receive invaluable learning opportunities through engaging in the organization's day-to-day work, and receive a salary of $46,000 (including medical and dental coverage), as well as debt service on law or graduate school loans for the duration of the fellowship. Eligible applicants must have: either a J.D. or M.A./M.S. in public policy or a related field; demonstrated interest or experience in one of the organization's program areas (affordable housing, public housing, public education, and/or political reform); accomplished oral and writing skills; a strong academic record; initiative, creativity, and flexibility; and a demonstrated ability to work effectively with a variety of organizations, constituent groups, government, and civic leaders.
EIN: 362675852

2453
William Butterworth Memorial Trust
1105 8th St.
Moline, IL   61265   (309) 736-3800
Application Address: c/o Moline Foundation, Attn.: Joy Boruff, Exec. Dir., 817 11th Ave., Moline IL 61265

Foundation type: Operating foundation
Purpose: Scholarships to high school seniors who are residents of Moline District 40, IL pursuing a degree at a two or four year accredited college or university.
Financial data: Year ended 12/31/2012. Assets, $37,134,197 (M); Expenditures, $1,899,321; Total giving, $18,500.
Fields of interest: Higher education.
Type of support: Scholarships—to individuals.
Application information: Applications accepted. Application form required.

Additional information: Applicant must demonstrate financial need, show proof of enrollment, must have achieved high school scholastic performance, participate in community service activities and extracurricular school activities.
EIN: 362255481

2454
C.E.F.S. Economic Opportunity Corporation
1805 S. Banker St.
P.O. Box 928
Effingham, IL   62401-2765   (217) 342-2193
FAX: (217) 342-4701; E-mail: cefs@cefseoc.org;
URL: http://www.cefseoc.org/

Foundation type: Public charity
Purpose: Financial assistance to economically disadvantaged residents of Christian, Clay, Effingham, Fayette, Montgomery, Moultrie and Shelby counties, IL, for payment towards energy bills, home weatherization, homeownership and other needs.
Financial data: Year ended 08/31/2012. Assets, $2,440,075 (M); Expenditures, $18,586,695.
Fields of interest: Aging; Disabilities, people with; Economically disadvantaged.
Type of support: Grants for special needs.
Application information:
  Initial approach: Letter or e-mail
  Additional information: See web site for additional programs and services or contact the corporation for eligibility determination.
Program description:
  Low Income Home Energy Assistance Program: The program offers assistance to low-income households to better afford the rising cost of energy through direct financial assistance, energy counseling, outreach, and education. Particular emphasis is placed on serving the elderly, people with disabilities, and low-income individuals in the corporation's seven-county service area. The program also includes an emergency furnace repair or replacement component for homeowners. Those eligible for assistance have a combined household income at or below 150 percent of federal poverty level guidelines.
EIN: 376053117

2455
Cabot Scholarship Fund
c/o JPMorgan Chase Bank, N.A.
10 S Dearborn IL1-0117
Chicago, IL   60603   (860) 868-6218
Application address: c/o Shepaug Valley Regional High School, 159 South St., Washington, CT 06793

Foundation type: Independent foundation
Purpose: Scholarships to graduates of Shepaug Valley High School, CT, who are residents of Washington, CT.
Financial data: Year ended 02/28/2013. Assets, $227,549 (M); Expenditures, $14,659; Total giving, $9,384; Grants to individuals, 3 grants totaling $9,384 (high: $3,128, low: $3,128).
Fields of interest: Higher education.
Type of support: Support to graduates or students of specific schools; Undergraduate support.
Application information: Application form required.
  Deadline(s): Apr.
  Applicants should submit the following:
    1) SAR
    2) FAFSA
EIN: 066113079

2456
Charles & Marie Caestecker Foundation
20 S. Clark St., Ste. 2310
Chicago, IL 60603-1806 (920) 294-6411

Foundation type: Independent foundation
Purpose: Scholarships to high school seniors who have attended Green Lake Public High School, WI, for full-time study at four-year colleges and universities.
Financial data: Year ended 04/30/2013. Assets, $1,679,183 (M); Expenditures, $53,438; Total giving, $50,000.
Fields of interest: Education.
Type of support: Scholarships—to individuals.
Application information: Application form required.
  Deadline(s): Feb. 1
Program description:
  Educational Program: Recipients are selected on the basis of academic promise as demonstrated by recommendations, test scores, academic record, extracurricular activity, and financial need.
EIN: 363154453

2457
Joan Camp Memorial Scholarship Foundation
11801 N. Princeville-Jubilee Rd.
Princeville, IL 61559-9167 (309) 243-7212
Contact: Jeanne McCoy, Tr.

Foundation type: Independent foundation
Purpose: Scholarships to worthy men and women of the Princeville School District, IL pursuing a college, university, technical and similar advanced education and training in the R.N. and L.P.N. nursing field.
Financial data: Year ended 03/31/2013. Assets, $252,418 (M); Expenditures, $10,049; Total giving, $9,000; Grants to individuals, 3 grants totaling $9,000 (high: $3,000, low: $3,000).
Fields of interest: Nursing school/education.
Type of support: Scholarships—to individuals.
Application information: Applicant must demonstrate financial need and academic achievement.
EIN: 371234288

2458
Lucille Camp Trust R62440004
10 S Dearborn IL1-0117
Chicago, IL 60603 (260) 563-4131
Contact: Steve Eikenberry
Application address: 580 N. Miami St., Wabash, IN 46992

Foundation type: Independent foundation
Purpose: Scholarships to graduating seniors of Wabash High School, IN, or individuals who graduated less than three years before application.
Financial data: Year ended 02/28/2013. Assets, $403,609 (M); Expenditures, $22,146; Total giving, $18,000; Grants to individuals, 12 grants totaling $18,000 (high: $1,500, low: $1,500).
Type of support: Support to graduates or students of specific schools; Undergraduate support.
Application information: Application form required.
  Deadline(s): First Fri. in Mar.
EIN: 356648622

2459
The Cara Program
237 S. Desplaines
Chicago, IL 60661-5515 (312) 798-3300
Contact: Julie Hoffmann, Dir., Devel.
E-mail: info@thecaraprogram.org; Tel. for Julie Hoffmann: (312) 798-3327; URL: http://www.thecaraprogram.org

Foundation type: Public charity
Purpose: Assistance to homeless and at-risk individuals in the Chicago, IL area with job placement, training and education, and support services in an effort to help them achieve a life of self-sufficiency and achievement.
Publications: Annual report.
Financial data: Year ended 12/31/2011. Assets, $11,157,289 (M); Expenditures, $6,462,717; Total giving, $251,003; Grants to individuals, totaling $251,003.
Fields of interest: Economically disadvantaged.
Type of support: Grants for special needs.
Application information: Contact the organization for assistance.
EIN: 364268095

2460
Carpe Diem Foundation of Illinois
c/o Gordon V. Levine
2700 N. Racine
Chicago, IL 60614
Contact: Gordon V. Levine, Exe. Dir.
URL: http://www.carpediemfoundation.org

Foundation type: Operating foundation
Purpose: Merit based scholarships to altruistic U.S. citizens for use at nationally accredited U.S. colleges and universities.
Financial data: Year ended 12/31/2012. Assets, $68,373 (M); Expenditures, $58,013; Total giving, $22,500.
Fields of interest: Performing arts; Literature; Higher education.
Type of support: Undergraduate support.
Application information: Applications accepted. Application form required.
  Send request by: Mail
  Deadline(s): May 9
  Applicants should submit the following:
    1) Essay
    2) Letter(s) of recommendation
    3) Transcripts
  Additional information: Application should also include a $10 payment by check or money order. See web site for additional guidelines.
EIN: 731625173

2461
Evelyn C. Carter Trust
10 S. Dearborn 1L1-0117
Chicago, IL 60603

Foundation type: Independent foundation
Purpose: Scholarships to graduates of Bridgeport High School, WV, who are attending West Virginia University in Morgantown, WV, and who indicate financial need.
Financial data: Year ended 12/31/2012. Assets, $1,442,899 (M); Expenditures, $84,670; Total giving, $66,850.
Type of support: Support to graduates or students of specific schools; Undergraduate support.
Application information: Applications accepted.
  Initial approach: Letter
  Deadline(s): Apr. 30
EIN: 556129783

2462
Caruso-Sperl Irrevocable Charitable Trust
P.O. Box 148
Thayer, IL 62689-0148

Foundation type: Operating foundation
Purpose: Scholarships to students of Catholic elementary and high schools of IL.
Financial data: Year ended 12/31/2012. Assets, $1,042,269 (M); Expenditures, $40,949; Total giving, $39,577.
Fields of interest: Education.
Type of support: Support to graduates or students of specific schools.
Application information: Scholarships are paid directly to the education institution on behalf of the students.
EIN: 376336628

2463
Catholic Charities of the Archdiocese of Chicago
721 N. LaSalle Dr.
Chicago, IL 60654-3503 (312) 655-7291
Contact: Monsignor Michael M. Boland, Pres. and C.E.O.
FAX: (312) 948-6974; Additional addresses : 1717 Rand Rd., Des Plaines, IL 60016-3509, tel.: (847) 376-2121, fax: (847) 390-8214; 1400 S. Austin Blvd., Cicero, IL 60804-1003, tel.: (708) 329-4022, fax: (708) 222-1495; 16100 Seton Dr., South Holland, IL 60473-1863, tel. (708) 333-8379, ext. 222, fax: (708) 333-9519; 7000 W. 111th St., Ste. 101, Worth, IL 60482-1851, tel.: (708) 430-0428, fax: (780) 430-0502; 671 S. Lewis, Waukegan, IL 60085-6101, tel.: (847) 782-4000, fax: (847) 782-1030; URL: http://www.catholiccharities.net/

Foundation type: Public charity
Purpose: Emergency assistance to families and individuals in need throughout Cook and Lake counties, IL with food, clothing, emergency shelter and other special needs.
Financial data: Year ended 06/30/2012. Assets, $134,317,747 (M); Expenditures, $162,508,457; Total giving, $9,829,281; Grants to individuals, totaling $9,829,281.
Fields of interest: Economically disadvantaged.
Type of support: Emergency funds; Grants for special needs.
Application information: Contact the organization for eligibility requirements.
EIN: 362170821

2464
Catholic Charities, Diocese of Joliet
203 N. Ottawa St.
Joliet, IL 60432-4006 (815) 723-3405
FAX: (815) 723-3452; URL: http://www.cc-doj.org

Foundation type: Public charity
Purpose: Limited financial assistance to indigent residents of Will County, IL, for rent, utilities, medical bills, and other miscellaneous needs.
Publications: Annual report.
Financial data: Year ended 06/30/2012. Assets, $6,706,617 (M); Expenditures, $19,048,646; Total giving, $2,878,940; Grants to individuals, totaling $2,878,940.
Type of support: Grants for special needs.
Application information:
  Initial approach: Letter
  Additional information: Contact the organization for application guidelines.
EIN: 362170817

2465
Frank and Edith Catt Educational Fund
1000 South State St.
Jerseyville, IL   62052-2356   (618) 498-6466

Foundation type: Operating foundation
Purpose: Educational loans to graduates of Jersey County, IL, for higher education.
Financial data: Year ended 12/31/2012. Assets, $7,203,852 (M); Expenditures, $117,349; Total giving, $27,000.
Fields of interest: Higher education.
Type of support: Student loans—to individuals; Undergraduate support.
Application information: Application form required. Interview required.
> *Deadline(s):* Dec. 31 for spring semester, Aug. 1 for fall semester
> *Applicants should submit the following:*
> 1) Transcripts
> 2) Letter(s) of recommendation
> *Additional information:* Application should also include proof of admission into a college or university. Applications are available at the Trust Dept., at Jersey State Bank.

EIN: 376352751

2466
Central Illinois Agency on Aging
700 Hamilton Blvd.
Peoria, IL   61603-3617   (309) 674-2071
FAX: (309) 674-3639; E-mail: info@ciaoa.com; Toll Free tel.: (877)-777-2422; URL: http://www.ciaoa.com

Foundation type: Public charity
Purpose: Assistance to seniors and low income seniors with utility allowance, adaptive equipment and other special needs in the Fulton, Marshall, Peoria, Stark, Tazewell and Woodford counties of IL.
Financial data: Year ended 09/30/2012. Assets, $691,479 (M); Expenditures, $3,666,068; Total giving, $2,308,883.
Fields of interest: Aging; Economically disadvantaged.
Type of support: In-kind gifts; Grants for special needs.
Application information:
> *Initial approach:* Telephone
> *Additional information:* Contact the agency for assistance.

EIN: 370983168

2467
Centralia Foundation
115 E. 2nd St.
Centralia, IL   62801-3503   (618) 532-7424
Contact: Verle Besant, Chair.
URL: http://www.centraliafoundation.com/

Foundation type: Public charity
Purpose: Scholarships and interest-free loans primarily to students from Centralia, IL, or one of the surrounding communities for graduate or undergraduate study.
Financial data: Year ended 09/30/2012. Assets, $24,526,875 (M); Expenditures, $1,761,936; Total giving, $130,425; Grants to individuals, totaling $65,520.
Type of support: Support to graduates or students of specific schools; Graduate support; Undergraduate support.
Application information: Application form required.
> *Applicants should submit the following:*
> 1) Letter(s) of recommendation
> 2) Financial information

> 3) Transcripts

EIN: 376029269

2468
Cervical Spine Research Society
6300 N. River Rd., Ste. 727
Rosemont, IL   60018-4226   (847) 698-1628
Contact: K. Daniel Riew M.D., Pres.; For Research Prog.: Peggy Wlezien, Dir.
FAX: (847) 823-0536; E-mail: csrs@aaos.org; E-mail for Peggy Wlezien: wlezien@aaos.org; URL: http://www.csrs.org

Foundation type: Public charity
Purpose: Awards for outstanding unpublished research papers of the cervical spine. In addition to grants for competitive research projects.
Publications: Application guidelines.
Financial data: Year ended 12/31/2011. Assets, $9,574,582 (M); Expenditures, $1,015,850; Total giving, $260,880; Grants to individuals, totaling $10,500.
Fields of interest: Spine disorders research.
Type of support: Research; Awards/prizes.
Application information: Applications accepted. Application form required. Application form available on the grantmaker's web site.
> *Initial approach:* Abstract for Research awards.
> *Deadline(s):* June 15.
> *Additional information:* Research grant applications should include 13 copies of application, budget, proposal, and protocol statement. See web site for further application information.

Program descriptions:
> *Research Awards:* Provides three awards for outstanding, unpublished research papers. Award categories are Outstanding Clinical, Basic Science and Resident/Fellow Papers. Each award is $2,000.
> *Traveling Fellowship:* Awards clinician-scientists who have completed a year or more of spine fellowship training. The program is designed to expose the spine surgeon to other institutions and individuals with expertise in the cervical spine to broaden their experience and help foster his or her academic career.

EIN: 521231718

2469
CF Industries, Inc. Corporate Giving Program
c/o Community Rels.
4 Pkwy. N., Ste. 400
Deerfield, IL   60015-2590
URL: http://www.cfindustries.com/community_relations.html

Foundation type: Corporate giving program
Purpose: Grants to educators who find innovative ways to incorporate agriculture or the environment into a classroom project, with special emphasis on water quality education. CF Industries, Inc., gives primarily in areas of company distribution facilities.
Fields of interest: Environment, water resources; Environmental education.
Type of support: Program development; Project support.
Application information:
> *Initial approach:* Letter
> *Additional information:* Contact foundation for eligibility requirements.

2470
CGH Health Foundation
(formerly Rock River Valley Health Foundation)
100 E. Lefevre Rd.
Sterling, IL   61081-1278   (815) 625-0400
Contact: Joan Hermes, Exec. Dir.
FAX: (815) 622-0473; E-mail: info@cghmc.com; URL: http://www.cghmc.com/index.cfm?pageID=6

Foundation type: Public charity
Purpose: Scholarships to nurses, healthcare workers and employees who are residents of Lee, Ogle, Whiteside, Carroll and Bureau counties, IL.
Publications: Financial statement; Informational brochure; Newsletter.
Financial data: Year ended 04/30/2012. Assets, $2,699,323 (M); Expenditures, $419,380; Total giving, $48,291; Grants to individuals, totaling $18,290.
Fields of interest: Nursing school/education; Health care.
Type of support: Employee-related scholarships; Scholarships—to individuals.
Application information: Applications accepted. Application form required. Application form available on the grantmaker's web site.
> *Applicants should submit the following:*
> 1) Letter(s) of recommendation
> 2) GPA
> 3) Financial information
> *Additional information:* Selection criteria is based on academic standing and financial need. Contact the foundation for additional application information.

EIN: 363576034

2471
CHEST Foundation
3300 Dundee Rd.
Northbrook, IL   60062-2303   (847) 498-8370
Contact: Megan Schagrin, Exec. Dir.
FAX: (847) 498-5460;
E-mail: mschagrin@chestnet.org; Additional tel.: (847) 498-1400; URL: http://www.onebreath.org/

Foundation type: Public charity
Purpose: Research grants to individuals for projects addressing chest diseases and their prevention.
Publications: Application guidelines; Annual report.
Financial data: Year ended 06/30/2012. Assets, $8,716,071 (M); Expenditures, $2,117,550; Total giving, $417,850; Grants to individuals, totaling $16,650.
Fields of interest: Lung research.
Type of support: Research; Awards/prizes; Travel grants.
Application information: Application form required. Application form available on the grantmaker's web site.
> *Initial approach:* Telephone or e-mail
> *Deadline(s):* Apr. 30
> *Additional information:* See web site for additional information.

Program descriptions:
> *Alpha-1 Foundation/CHEST Foundation Clinical Research Award in Alpha-1 Antitrypsin:* Awarded in conjunction with the Alpha-1 Foundation, this $25,000 award will be granted to support research focused on chronic obstructive pulmonary disease (COPD) and Alpha 1-Antitrypsin (AAT) deficiency.
> *Clinical Research Award in Lung Cancer:* The $100,000 award supports a project that is focused on medical and/or surgical detection, treatment, or cure of lung cancer that is based on clinical/translational research. ACCP members who have completed at least two years of pulmonary or critical care fellowship or a thoracic surgery residency and

are within seven years of completing training will be considered for this award. The award is paid off over two years, giving $50,000 each year.

D. Robert McCaffree, MD, Master FCCP Humanitarian Awards: Multiple awards, ranging from $5,000 to $15,000, are given annually for community-based projects supported by the pro-bono work of American College of Chest Physicians (ACCP) members worldwide. Projects must show a clear impact on the community and have the potential for long-term sustainability and replicability. Award funds are paid to the nonprofit or nongovernmental organization where the ACCP member donates time and medical service.

Fourth Eli Lilly and Company Distinguished Scholar in Critical Care: This $150,000 award, given over a three-year period, supports clinical educational projects that improve patient care, and is intended for the investigation of issues that are not easily supported through traditional funding. The award will support an American College of Chest Physicians (ACCP) fellow who proposes a critical care-related project/service that does one or more of the following: establishes an identity for the diagnosis and management of diseases within a critical care environment; promotes alternatives for critical care treatment; educates patients about options for diagnosis and treatment; educates and disseminates new knowledge about diagnosis and treatment within a critical care environment; addresses family issues; and defines new mechanisms leading to innovations and improvements in treatment.

Roger C. Bone Advances in End-of-Life Care Award: This $10,000 award supports leadership in end-of-life care by stressing the importance of communication, compassion, and effective listening. The award is given for leadership in end-of-life care—on the international, national, or local level—and does not fund research or provide seed money for new end-of-life or palliative care programs or projects.

Sheila J. Goodnight, M.D., FCCP Clinical Research Award in Women's Lung Health: This $10,000 award supports a clinical research project related to women's lung health, which can include research on gender difference in various lung diseases (such as chronic obstructive pulmonary disease and tuberculosis)

The CHEST Foundation California Chapter Clinical Research/Medical Education Award: This $5,000 award supports a one-year clinical research or medical education project proposed by an ACCP member who lives in California. Research must be completed July through June.

Young Investigator Awards: A total of $20,000 will be granted to 20 abstract finalists. The top 3 winners will receive $2,275 and the remaining 17 will be awarded $775. Investigators must be enrolled in a training or fellowship program or have completed a fellowship program within 5 years. Finalists are evaluated on the basis of their written abstract and their presentations. Primary authors are considered for all abstract-related awards but may only win one. Award recipients are selected for their outstanding original scientific research by judges from the Scientific Presentations and Awards Committee.
EIN: 363286520

2472
The Chicago Bar Foundation
321 S. Plymouth Ct., Ste. 3B
Chicago, IL 60604-3997   (312) 554-1204
Contact: Ryanne Easley, Dir. of Grants
FAX: (312) 554-1203;
E-mail: proos@chicagobar.org; URL: http://www.chicagobarfoundation.org

Foundation type: Public charity
Purpose: Scholarships and fellowships to dedicated lawyers to pursue careers in legal aid and public interest law.
Publications: Annual report; Newsletter.
Financial data: Year ended 05/31/2012. Assets, $4,997,123 (M); Expenditures, $5,980,637; Total giving, $4,443,798; Grants to individuals, totaling $320,000.
Fields of interest: Law school/education.
Type of support: Fellowships; Scholarships—to individuals; Postgraduate support.
Application information: Applications accepted. Application form required. Application form available on the grantmaker's web site.
>*Initial approach:* Letter of inquiry
>*Send request by:* Mail
>*Deadline(s):* May 11 for Marovitz Scholarship, May for Anderson Fellowship, July for Sun-Times Fellowship
>*Additional information:* See web site for additional guidelines.

Program descriptions:
Abraham Lincoln Marovitz Public Interest Law Scholarship: The scholarship is awarded annually to a student attending one of the nine Illinois law schools (Chicago-Kent College of Law, University of Chicago Law School, DePaul University College of Law, University of Illinois College of Law, John Marshall Law School, Loyola University School of Law, Northern Illinois University Law School, Northwestern University School of Law and Southern Illinois University School of Law). These funds, payable over a three-year period, enable an incoming student who intends to pursue a career in public interest law to have a significant portion of his or her tuition and related expenses covered by scholarship funding. Scholarship winners will receive $10,000 in the first year of law school, $15,000 in the second year, and $15,000 in the third year.

Kimball R. Anderson and Karen Gatsis Anderson Public Interest Law Fellowship: The annual award of $50,000 assists dedicated law school graduates with repayment of their law school debts. Fellowship funds are awarded in ten installments of $5,000 over five years, contingent on continued compliance with the terms of the fellowship.

Moses Scholarship: The award is intended to support an incoming law student who is deeply committed to public interest work so that upon graduation the individual will be best prepared to pursue a public interest legal career. The $50,000 scholarship, payable over three years, provides funds for public interest-minded students so they may complete law school with as little debt burden as possible.

Sun-Times Public Interest Law Fellowship Program: The foundation awards five five-year fellowships every year to outstanding young attorneys who have chosen to pursue careers in legal aid or public interest law at a foundation-funded organization or at a qualifying legal aid organization serving other parts of Illinois. Each fellow will receive a total of up to $50,000 of loan repayment assistance during their five-year fellowship. One fellowship each year may be awarded to legal aid attorneys who serve Illinois residents outside of Cook County. This program is available to recent law graduates who commit to

work full time for minimum of five years at a foundation-funded legal aid organization or, for a limited number of recipients, a qualifying legal aid organization outside of Cook County.
EIN: 366109584

2473
The Chicago Community Trust
225 N. Michigan Ave.
Chicago, IL 60601   (312) 616-8000
Contact: For grants: Ms. Sandy Phelps, Dir., Grants Mgmt.
FAX: (312) 616-7955; E-mail: info@cct.org;
URL: http://www.cct.org

Foundation type: Community foundation
Purpose: Fellowships to leaders of nonprofit or public sector organizations serving residents of the Chicago metropolitan area, IL.
Publications: Application guidelines; Annual report; Financial statement; Grants list.
Financial data: Year ended 09/30/2012. Assets, $1,804,362,755 (M); Expenditures, $196,010,249; Total giving, $169,744,869.
Fields of interest: Volunteer services; Leadership development.
Type of support: Research.
Application information: Applications accepted. Application form required. Application form available on the grantmaker's web site. Interview required.
>*Initial approach:* Application
>*Send request by:* Online
>*Deadline(s):* June
>*Additional information:* The trust holds a Q & A session in May. See web site for additional information and application.

Program description:
Chicago Community Trust Fellowship: The fellowship offers professional development opportunities for both emerging and experienced leaders who are open to new learning, have a track record of accomplishments, have potential for significant community impact and demonstrate commitment to building strong nonprofit and public sectors. Fellowship applicants customize their own professional development plans. Emerging leaders are awarded up to $30,000 and experienced leaders are awarded up to $60,000 to put these plans into practice. The award may fund salary and benefits during a leave of absence from work, costs related to academic courses, coaching or learning from practitioners.
EIN: 362167000

2474
Chicago Foundation for Education
One N. LaSalle St., Ste. 1675
Chicago, IL 60602-3937   (312) 670-2323
Contact: Amy Sheren, Exec. Dir.
FAX: (312) 670-2029; E-mail: cfe@cfegrants.org;
URL: http://www.cfegrants.org/

Foundation type: Public charity
Purpose: Grants to Chicago, IL, elementary public school teachers of grades pre-K through 8 to improve and enhance the educational experience of students.
Publications: Application guidelines; Annual report; Newsletter.
Financial data: Year ended 06/30/2012. Assets, $1,134,506 (M); Expenditures, $805,583; Total giving, $395,051; Grants to individuals, totaling $395,051.

Fields of interest: Alliance/advocacy; Early childhood education; Elementary school/education; Education; Youth development.
Type of support: Program development.
Application information: Applications accepted. Application form required.
Initial approach: Online
Deadline(s): See web site.
Program descriptions:
Action Research Fellowships: The foundation awards $1,250 fellowships to PreK-8th Grade CPS teachers interested in conducting action research for the purpose of improving instruction and enhancing student achievement. Develop recommendations for change within your classroom, school, or across the district.
Fund for Teachers Fellowships: Grants, ranging between $5,000 and $10,000, enable experienced PreK-12th grade CPS teachers to explore the world through intensive professional learning experiences. Self-design a summer odyssey that will profoundly impact your teaching, student, and greater school community.
Small Grants: The foundation awards $500 small grants to Chicago Public School elementary school teachers for the implementation of classroom or school-wide curricular projects for PreK-8th Grade CPS teachers. Individuals and teams of teachers are encouraged to apply. Teachers receive a $100 bonus toward materials when Character Education (SEL) principles are integrated into the teacher's project.
Study Group Coach Grants: $1,000 Coach Grants offer leadership opportunities for exemplary PreK-8th Grade CPS teachers. Share a teaching method that you have successfully implemented to improve classroom learning with other CPS teachers. Guide your teacher colleagues and share a teaching method that you successfully implemented to improve classroom learning.
Study Group Grants: $300 Study Group Grants provide PreK-8th Grade CPS teachers the opportunity to learn new teaching strategies as well as the resources to implement those strategies. Collaborate with colleagues and expand your skills under the guidance of an experienced CFE Study Group Coach.
EIN: 363429023

2475
Chicago Symphony Orchestra
220 S. Michigan Ave.
Chicago, IL 60604-2596 (312) 294-3000
Contact: Deborah F. Rutter, Pres.
FAX: (312) 294-3329; Toll-free tel.: (800) 223-7114; URL: http://www.cso.org

Foundation type: Public charity
Purpose: Scholarships to music students who are members of the Civic Orchestra of Chicago, IL.
Publications: Annual report.
Financial data: Year ended 06/30/2012. Assets, $436,051,982 (M); Expenditures, $80,055,672; Total giving, $604,506; Grants to individuals, totaling $604,506.
Fields of interest: Orchestras; Performing arts, education.
Type of support: Support to graduates or students of specific schools.
Application information: Applications accepted.
Deadline(s): Varies
Program description:
Scholarships: All Regular members of the Civic Orchestra of Chicago receive a $2,800 scholarship intended to further their musical education. Associate members receive scholarship funds if asked to perform in a concert as a substitute or an

extra player. Approximately twenty-five graduate string players, all of whom are Regular members, receive a $3,500 fellowship annually towards the institution they are attending.
EIN: 362167823

2476
Chicago White Metal Charitable Foundation
649 N., Rte. 83
Bensenville, IL 60106 (630) 595-4424

Foundation type: Company-sponsored foundation
Purpose: Scholarships to children of employees of Chicago White Metal Casting, Inc., who have been employed by the corporation for at least three years, and who are not officers or directors of the corporation.
Financial data: Year ended 10/31/2012. Assets, $48,811 (M); Expenditures, $34,823; Total giving, $34,752.
Fields of interest: Education.
Type of support: Employee-related scholarships; Graduate support; Undergraduate support.
Application information:
Deadline(s): None
Additional information: Submit in writing eligibility for scholarship program.
Company name: Chicago White Metal Casting Company, Inc.
EIN: 366069669

2477
Children at the Crossroads Foundation
751 N. State St.
Chicago, IL 60654-3835 (312) 466-0700
FAX: (312) 337-7180; E-mail: pantlej@fxw.org;
URL: http://catc.org/

Foundation type: Public charity
Purpose: Scholarship and educational assistance for students attending Frances Xavier Warde School, IL.
Financial data: Year ended 06/30/2012. Assets, $2,672,987 (M); Expenditures, $963,005; Total giving, $921,260.
Type of support: Support to graduates or students of specific schools; Undergraduate support.
Application information: Applications not accepted.
Additional information: Unsolicited requests for funds not considered or acknoweldged.
EIN: 363654481

2478
The Children's Heart Foundation
620 Margate Dr.
P.O. Box 244
Lincolnshire, IL 60069-0244 (847) 634-6474
FAX: (847) 634-4988;
E-mail: info@childrensheartfoundation.org; E-mail for William Foley:
bfoley@childrensheartfoundation.org; toll-free tel: (888) 248-8140; URL: http://www.childrensheartfoundation.org

Foundation type: Public charity
Purpose: Research grants to individuals for the study of causes of and improvement in the methods of diagnosing, treating and preventing congenital heart defects.
Publications: Application guidelines; Annual report; Newsletter.
Financial data: Year ended 12/31/2011. Assets, $413,259 (M); Expenditures, $1,898,269; Total

giving, $862,755; Grants to individuals, 10 grants totaling $862,755 (high: $150,000; low: $45,590).
Fields of interest: Heart & circulatory research.
Type of support: Research.
Application information: Application form required. Application form available on the grantmaker's web site.
Deadline(s): June
Additional information: Application should include tax forms, biographical information, budget information, research plan and a lay summary.
Program description:
Medical Grants: Through an annual request for proposals, the foundation supports clinical and basic science research in congenital heart disease, including, but not limited to, molecular genetics, biochemistry, pharmacology, devices and procedural research (cardiac catheterization and surgery), and long-term care of adults with congenital heart defects.
EIN: 364077528

2479
Children's Home & Aid Society of Illinois
125 S. Wacker Dr., 14th Fl.
Chicago, IL 60606-4424 (312) 424-0200
E-mail: contact@chasi.org; URL: http://www.childrenshomeandaid.org

Foundation type: Public charity
Purpose: Financial assistance to foster parents of Illinois to help cover costs for child's food, clothing and personal allowance.
Financial data: Year ended 06/30/2011. Assets, $28,876,844 (M); Expenditures, $50,382,295; Total giving, $5,542,577; Grants to individuals, totaling $5,542,577.
Fields of interest: Human services; Foster care.
Type of support: Grants for special needs.
Application information: Contact the society for additional guidelines.
EIN: 362167743

2480
Children's Oncology Services, Inc.
213 W. Institute Pl., Ste. 511
Chicago, IL 60610-3588 (312) 924-4220
Contact: Janie Weisenberg, Exec. Dir.
FAX: (312) 440-8897;
E-mail: jweisenberg@onestepcamp.org;
URL: http://www.onestepcamp.org/

Foundation type: Public charity
Purpose: Grants to children with cancer or leukemia to allow them to lead "normal" lives by providing camping and other experiences. Also, scholarships and textbook reimbursement to support the continuing education of cancer patients and survivors from IL, IN, IA, MI or WI.
Publications: Annual report; Informational brochure; Newsletter.
Financial data: Year ended 09/30/2011. Assets, $3,301,396 (M); Expenditures, $1,470,706; Total giving, $646,322; Grants to individuals, totaling $646,322.
Fields of interest: Cancer; Leukemia; Camps; Children/youth, services.
Type of support: Grants for special needs.
Application information: Applications accepted. Application form available on the grantmaker's web site.
Deadline(s): Vary

Additional information: Contact foundation or see Web site for complete program information.
EIN: 364263831

2481
Albert A. Christ Scholarship Fund
c/o JPMorgan Chase Bank, N.A.
10 S. Dearborn St., 21st Fl
Chicago, IL 60603-2300
Application address: c/o JPMorgan Chase Bank, N.A., Att.: Ed Johnson, 1114 Market St., Wheeling, WV 26003, tel.: (304) 234-4130

Foundation type: Independent foundation
Purpose: Scholarships to deserving young people who reside in the Wheeling, WV, area to attend a college or university or to pursue graduate studies.
Financial data: Year ended 06/30/2012. Assets, $4,375,418 (M); Expenditures, $223,748; Total giving, $180,050; Grants to individuals, 12 grants totaling $180,050 (high: $2,500, low: $250).
Type of support: Graduate support; Undergraduate support.
Application information: Applications accepted.
Initial approach: Letter
Deadline(s): None
EIN: 556129775

2482
Citizens United for Research in Epilepsy
(also known as C.U.R.E.)
430 W. Erie, Ste. 210
Chicago, IL 60654-3920 (312) 255-1801
Contact: Robin Harding, Exec. Dir.
FAX: (312) 255-1809;
E-mail: info@cureepilepsy.org; Toll-free tel.: (800) 765-7118; URL: http://www.cureepilepsy.org

Foundation type: Public charity
Purpose: Medical research grants to investigators to aid in finding a cure for epilepsy.
Publications: Application guidelines; Newsletter.
Financial data: Year ended 12/31/2012. Assets, $11,308,591 (M); Expenditures, $5,008,421; Total giving, $3,405,292.
Fields of interest: Epilepsy research.
Type of support: Research.
Application information: Applications accepted.
Initial approach: Letter
Send request by: Mail
Deadline(s): Sept. for letter of intent; Jan. for application
Applicants should submit the following:
1) Letter(s) of recommendation
2) Curriculum vitae
3) Proposal
4) Budget Information
Additional information: See web site for complete program information.
EIN: 364253176

2483
The Claretknoll Foundation
c/o James Dubina
16737 Richards Dr.
Tinley Park, IL 60477

Foundation type: Independent foundation
Purpose: Funds to support mentally handicapped orphans.
Financial data: Year ended 06/30/2013. Assets, $779,456 (M); Expenditures, $75,865; Total giving, $33,873; Grants to individuals, 19 grants totaling $21,700 (high: $1,500, low: $200).
Fields of interest: Children/youth, services.

Type of support: Grants to individuals.
Application information: Applications accepted.
EIN: 237204918

2484
CNA Foundation
(formerly CNA Insurance Companies Foundation)
333 S. Wabash Ave., 44th Fl.
Chicago, IL 60604-4107 (312) 822-5000
Contact: Rita Wilmes, Prog. Coord.
E-mail: rita.wilmes@cna.com; Tel. for Rita Wilmes: (312) 822-2606; Additional contact: Marlene Rotstein, Dir., tel.: (312) 822-7065, e-mail: marlene.rotstein@cna.com; Additional e-mail: cna_foundation@cna.com; URL: http://www.cna.com/portal/site/cna/about/

Foundation type: Company-sponsored foundation
Purpose: Grants to employees of CNA and its subsidiaries for emergency disaster relief.
Publications: Application guidelines.
Financial data: Year ended 12/31/2011. Assets, $761,689 (M); Expenditures, $2,526,304; Total giving, $2,526,304.
Fields of interest: Safety/disasters.
Type of support: Employee-related welfare.
Application information: Applications not accepted.
Additional information: Unsolicited requests for funds not considered or acknowledged.
Company name: CNA Financial Corporation
EIN: 364029026

2485
William H. Cochrane Educational Trust
c/o The Northern Trust Company
P.O. Box 803878
Chicago, IL 60680

Foundation type: Independent foundation
Purpose: Scholarships to family members of employees of the City of Vero Beach, FL for higher education.
Financial data: Year ended 12/31/2012. Assets, $113,044 (M); Expenditures, $11,370; Total giving, $5,888; Grants to individuals, 12 grants totaling $5,888 (high: $491, low: $490).
Fields of interest: Higher education.
Type of support: Employee-related scholarships.
Application information: Applications accepted. Application form required.
Deadline(s): None
Applicants should submit the following:
1) Financial information
2) GPA
3) SAT
4) ACT
Additional information: Unsolicited requests for funds not considered or acknowledged.
EIN: 596895373

2486
Regina Coeli Foundation Inc.
739 N. Lake St.
Mundelein, IL 60060-1322
Contact: Dawn Rouse

Foundation type: Independent foundation
Purpose: Financial assistance to disadvantaged individuals residing in the Chicago, IL, area.
Financial data: Year ended 05/31/2013. Assets, $34,286 (M); Expenditures, $19,340; Total giving, $19,325; Grants to individuals, 9 grants totaling $15,825 (high: $4,500, low: $765).
Fields of interest: Economically disadvantaged.

Type of support: Grants for special needs.
Application information: Applications accepted.
Initial approach: Letter
Deadline(s): None
Additional information: Applicants must demonstrate financial need.
EIN: 366126117

2487
Coin Op Cares Education & Charitable Foundation
(formerly Amusement and Music Operators Educational Foundation)
600 Spring Hill Ring Rd., Ste. 111
West Dundee, IL 60118-7301 (847) 428-7699
Contact: Gary Brewer, Chair.

Foundation type: Public charity
Purpose: Two scholarship programs designed to assist students further their college education for attendance at accredited colleges or universities for higher learning.
Publications: Application guidelines.
Financial data: Year ended 12/31/2011. Assets, $1,262,412 (M); Expenditures, $90,825; Total giving, $52,000; Grants to individuals, totaling $51,000.
Fields of interest: Music; Arts.
Type of support: Support to graduates or students of specific schools; Undergraduate support.
Application information: Applications accepted. Application form required.
Deadline(s): Jan. 16 for Hesch Scholarship
Additional information: Application for Hesch scholarship must include a transcript.
Program descriptions:
Rich Holley Memorial Music Scholarship: Each year, the program offers up to two scholarships for University of Florida students to pursue music studies.
Wayne E. Hesch Memorial Scholarship: This scholarship program is designed to provide financial support to students who are, or plan or hope to, be engaged in the amusement or music operators profession.
EIN: 364262815

2488
Lillian R. Coleman Scholarship Trust
(formerly William S. and Lillian R. Coleman Scholarship Trust)
10 S. Dearborn IL1-0117
Chicago, IL 60603 (317) 684-3147
Application address: 1 E. Ohio St., 17th Fl., Indianapolis, IN 46204-1912

Foundation type: Independent foundation
Purpose: Scholarships for postsecondary education to graduates of high schools in Rush County, IN.
Financial data: Year ended 01/31/2013. Assets, $2,550,311 (M); Expenditures, $145,059; Total giving, $121,977; Grants to individuals, 140 grants totaling $121,977 (high: $1,335, low: $300).
Type of support: Support to graduates or students of specific schools; Undergraduate support.
Application information: Applications accepted. Application form required.
Deadline(s): Apr. 1 or 60 days prior to beginning of school term
Additional information: Application must include parents' financial information.
EIN: 356279390

2489
College of American Pathologists Foundation
325 Waukegan Rd.
Northfield, IL 60093-2750 (847) 832-7000
Contact: Marion Malone, Exec. Dir.
Application fax: (847) 832-8931
FAX: (847) 832-8000; E-mail: capfdn@cap.org;
URL: http://www.cap.org/apps/cap.portal?
_nfpb=true&_pageLabel=foundation

Foundation type: Public charity
Purpose: Grants and scholarships to medical students, pathology residents and pathologists for education, research and humanitarian projects.
Publications: Application guidelines; Annual report.
Financial data: Year ended 12/31/2012. Assets, $2,912,218 (M); Expenditures, $1,039,884; Total giving, $161,942; Grants to individuals, totaling $82,500.
Fields of interest: Pathology; Pathology research.
Type of support: Research.
Application information:
   Initial approach: Letter
   Send request by: Mail
   Deadline(s): July 1 for Leadership Development, Nov. 1 for Advance Training Elective in Translational Diagnostic, John H. Rippey Grant and Scholars Research Program
Program descriptions:
   Advanced Training Elective in Translational Diagnostics Grants: This program offers awards (of up to $5,000) to young pathologists to support hands-on exposure related to the development of novel antibodies, probes, and companion diagnostics for therapeutic targets. This training rotation will provide the platform to gain working knowledge of the benefits and drawbacks of using immunohistochemistry and in-situ hybridization for target detection. Additionally, participants obtain experience in the use and interpretation of image and analysis as it pertains to diagnostics. Awards are intended to support the recipient's travel and living expenses during the training period. Eligible applicants must be junior members of the College of American Pathologists.
   Gene and Jean Herbek Humanitarian Award: Each year, the foundation will present a monetary award to an outstanding fellow of the College of American Pathologists (CAP) who provides outstanding direct patient services to individuals in underserved communities through a See, Test and Treat program.
   John H. Rippey Grant for Laboratory Quality Assurance: This grant funds up to $10,000 for innovative projects related to quality assurance, quality improvement in pathology, or patient safety, which have resulted in improved patient care. Eligible applicants must be members of the College of American Pathologists.
   Leadership Development Awards: Travel awards of up to $1,000 each to young pathologists, to be used to attend the specialty's institutional, local, state, and national conferences and leadership opportunities. Awards are intended to enhance the education and experience of award recipients by immersing them in the concerns confronting medicine, particularly the specialty of pathology. Eligible applicants must be junior members of the College of American Pathologists.
   Scholars Research Program: Fellowships of up to $12,500 for six months and up to $25,000 for one year, to pathology residents with the opportunity to conduct translational research. Goals of this program include advancing productive investigations, identifying pathology talent, and encouraging careers in academic medicine. Grants are intended for salary support only. The recipient's

institution is expected to contribute benefits, overhead resources, and other supplemental support. Eligible applicants must be at the PGY-2 level up to those in a second-year fellowship, and must be members of the College of American Pathologists.
EIN: 366134600

2490
The Cardiss Collins Scholarship Fund
c/o H. Grannan
601 W. Randolph St., 2nd Fl.
Chicago, IL 60661

Foundation type: Independent foundation
Purpose: Scholarships to African American high school seniors who are residents of the 7th Congressional District of Illinois, pursuing a major in advertising.
Financial data: Year ended 12/31/2012. Assets, $79,961 (M); Expenditures, $822; Total giving, $0.
Fields of interest: Business school/education.
Type of support: Scholarships—to individuals.
Application information:
   Deadline(s): None
   Additional information: Applicant must demonstrate need and have at least a "B" average.
EIN: 363981706

2491
Community Action Partnership of Lake County
1200 Glen Flora Ave.
P.O. Box 9059
Waukegan, IL 60085-1753 (847) 249-4330
Contact: Mary Lockhart White, Exec. Dir. and C.E.O.
E-mail: capservices@caplakecounty.org; Mailing address: P.O. Box 9059, Waukegan, IL 60079-9059; URL: http://caplakecounty.org/

Foundation type: Public charity
Purpose: Assistance to low-income economically disadvantaged individuals and families of Lake County, IL, with utility, housing, emergency food and shelter, youth programs, and head start programs for pre-schoolers.
Financial data: Year ended 12/31/2011. Assets, $11,238,355 (M); Expenditures, $15,064,150; Total giving, $4,189,353; Grants to individuals, totaling $4,189,353.
Fields of interest: Economically disadvantaged.
Type of support: Grants for special needs.
Application information: Applications not accepted.
   Additional information: Unsolicited requests for funds not accepted.
EIN: 362580774

2492
Community Contacts, Inc.
100 S. Hawthorne St.
Elgin, IL 60123-5874 (847) 697-8800
FAX: (847) 697-1698; E-mail: mail@cci-hci.org;
URL: http://cci-hci.org/

Foundation type: Public charity
Purpose: Financial assistance to elderly and handicapped indigent residents of Kane and DeKalb counties, IL, to help pay for energy bills and home weatherization.
Financial data: Year ended 06/30/2012. Assets, $1,324,956 (M); Expenditures, $8,266,015.
Type of support: Grants for special needs.

Application information:
   Initial approach: Letter or e-mail
   Additional information: Contact organization about requirements for assistance.
EIN: 362977001

2493
Community Foundation for the Land of Lincoln
(formerly Sangamon County Foundation)
205 S. 5th St., Ste. 930
Springfield, IL 62701 (217) 789-4431
Contact: John Stremsterfer, C.E.O. and Pres.; Stacy Reed, V.P., Progs.
FAX: (217) 789-4635; E-mail: info@cfll.org;
URL: http://www.cfll.org

Foundation type: Community foundation
Purpose: Scholarships to residents of Sangamon county, IL for higher education.
Financial data: Year ended 12/31/2012. Assets, $16,061,766 (M); Expenditures, $1,542,880; Total giving, $960,033; Grants to individuals, 40 grants totaling $51,700.
Fields of interest: Higher education.
Type of support: Scholarships—to individuals.
Application information: Applications accepted. Application form required. Application form available on the grantmaker's web site.
   Send request by: Online
   Deadline(s): Mar. 1
   Additional information: See web site for complete listing of scholarship programs.
Program description:
   Scholarship Programs: The foundation administers a variety of postsecondary scholarships for students seeking higher education. Each scholarship has its own unique set of application guidelines and eligibility criteria, including awards to students from specific high schools, academic achievement and those pursuing a degree in a particular field of study such as engineering, nursing, and special education. See web site for additional information.
EIN: 204191391

2494
Community Foundation of Central Illinois
(formerly Peoria Area Community Foundation)
331 Fulton St., Ste. 310
Peoria, IL 61602-1449 (309) 674-8730
Contact: Mark Roberts, C.E.O.; For grants: Alison Oaks, Prog. Mgr.
FAX: (309) 674-8754;
E-mail: mark@communityfoundationci.org;
URL: http://www.communityfoundationci.org

Foundation type: Community foundation
Purpose: Scholarships to students in the Peoria, IL, area for continuing education at accredited colleges, univeristies, trade and technical schools. Grants for teachers in Peoria Public Schools District 150 interested in additional projects to enrich the classroom experience.
Publications: Application guidelines; Annual report (including application guidelines); Financial statement; Informational brochure; Newsletter.
Financial data: Year ended 06/30/2012. Assets, $20,486,858 (M); Expenditures, $1,231,427; Total giving, $822,400. Scholarships—to individuals amount not specified.
Fields of interest: Elementary/secondary education; Vocational education; College (community/junior); Nursing school/education; Epilepsy; Military/veterans.

Type of support: Technical education support; Undergraduate support.
Application information: Applications accepted. Application form required.
Initial approach: Telephone or e-mail
Deadline(s): Oct. 1 for Classroom Grants, varies for Scholarships
Additional information: See web site for application guidelines and a list of scholarship funds.
Program description:
District 150 Classroom Grants: Grants are available to District 150 classroom teachers to enhance the students' educational experience. District 150 Classroom Grants are made possible by the Peoria Public Schools Foundation and the Murray and Rena Yeomans Fund of the Community Foundation of Central Illinois.
EIN: 371185713

2495
Community Foundation of Northern Illinois
(formerly Rockford Community Foundation)
946 N. 2nd St.
Rockford, IL   61107-3005   (815) 962-2110
FAX: (815) 962-2116; E-mail: info@cfnil.org; Grant application tel.: (815) 962-2110, ext. 15 and e-mail: bnelson@cfnil.org; URL: http://www.cfnil.org

Foundation type: Community foundation
Purpose: Scholarships to individuals living in or around Winnebago, Boone, Ogle, and Stephenson counties, IL.
Publications: Application guidelines; Annual report; Grants list; Informational brochure (including application guidelines); Newsletter; Program policy statement.
Financial data: Year ended 06/30/2012. Assets, $49,636,480 (M); Expenditures, $2,822,552; Total giving, $1,959,811; Grants to individuals, 129 grants totaling $140,027.
Fields of interest: Higher education.
Type of support: Scholarships—to individuals.
Application information: Applications accepted. Application form required. Application form available on the grantmaker's web site.
Send request by: Online
Copies of proposal: 1
Deadline(s): Mar. 1
Additional information: See web site for complete program listings.
EIN: 364402089

2496
Community Foundation of the Fox River Valley
(formerly The Aurora Foundation)
111 W. Downer Pl., Ste. 312
Aurora, IL   60506-5136   (630) 896-7800
Contact: Sharon Stredde, C.E.O.
E-mail for scholarship: Sch@CommunityFoundationFRV.org
FAX: (630) 896-7811;
E-mail: info@CommunityFoundationFRV.org;
URL: http://www.communityfoundationfrv.org

Foundation type: Community foundation
Purpose: Scholarships to full-time students who reside in the Aurora, IL, area, including Kendall and southern Kane counties, IL.
Publications: Application guidelines; Annual report; Newsletter.
Financial data: Year ended 12/31/2012. Assets, $63,649,777 (M); Expenditures, $6,263,631;

Total giving, $5,491,916; Grants to individuals, 426 grants totaling $823,400.
Fields of interest: Vocational education, post-secondary; Higher education; Graduate/professional education; Scholarships/financial aid.
Type of support: Scholarships—to individuals; Support to graduates or students of specific schools; Graduate support; Undergraduate support.
Application information: Applications accepted. Application form required. Application form available on the grantmaker's web site. Interview required.
Deadline(s): Feb. 3
Final notification: Applicants notified in May
Applicants should submit the following:
1) Transcripts
2) SAT
3) Letter(s) of recommendation
4) GPA
5) Financial information
6) FAFSA
7) Essay
8) ACT
Additional information: See web site for a complete listing of scholarship programs.
EIN: 366086742

2497
Community Foundation of the Quincy Area
(formerly Quincy Area Community Foundation)
4531 Maine, Ste. A.
Quincy, IL   62305   (217) 222-1237
Contact: Jill Arnold Blickhan, Exec. Dir.; For grants: Amy Meyer Lehenbauer, Outreach Coord.
FAX: (217) 222-2260;
E-mail: info@mycommunityfoundation.org; Mailing address: P.O. Box 741, Quincy, IL 62306-0741; Additional e-mail: execdir@mycommunityfoundation.org; Grant inquiry e-mail: grants@mycommunityfoundation.org; URL: http://www.mycommunityfoundation.org

Foundation type: Community foundation
Purpose: Scholarships to graduating high school seniors from the Quincy, IL area for higher education.
Publications: Application guidelines; Annual report; Grants list; Informational brochure; Newsletter.
Financial data: Year ended 12/31/2012. Assets, $14,836,803 (M); Expenditures, $510,497; Total giving, $276,537; Grants to individuals, 9 grants totaling $6,525.
Fields of interest: Higher education.
Type of support: Scholarships—to individuals; Support to graduates or students of specific schools.
Application information: Applications accepted. Application form required.
Deadline(s): Spring
Additional information: See web site for a complete listing of scholarships, including application guidelines and eligibility criteria for each.
EIN: 371366611

2498
Continental Scholarship Fund
233 S. Wacker Dr.
Chicago, IL   60606   (312) 997-8315
Contact: Donna Towle, Chair.

Foundation type: Public charity
Purpose: Scholarships to children and spouses of employees of Continental Airlines and its subsidiaries.

Financial data: Year ended 12/31/2012. Assets, $2,600,756 (M); Expenditures, $919,032; Total giving, $851,000.
Type of support: Employee-related scholarships.
Application information: Application address: c/o Scholarship Mgmt. Svcs., P.O. Box 297, 1 Scholarship Way, St. Peter, MN 56082, tel.: (507) 931-1682.
Company name: Continental Airlines, Inc.
EIN: 760691086

2499
Conway Farms Golf Club Foundation
425 S. Conway Farms Dr.
Lake Forest, IL   60045-2530   (847) 234-6979

Foundation type: Operating foundation
Purpose: Scholarships to employees and caddies completing one year of employment at Conway Farms or to parents who worked at Conway for at least three years.
Financial data: Year ended 12/31/2012. Assets, $108,680 (M); Expenditures, $42,109; Total giving, $40,672; Grants to individuals, 29 grants totaling $40,672 (high: $4,500, low: $500).
Fields of interest: Higher education.
Type of support: Employee-related scholarships.
Application information: Applications accepted. Application form required.
Initial approach: Application
Additional information: Scholarships are awarded every semester. Unsolicited requests for funds not accepted.
EIN: 030523195

2500
Flora Corpening Trust
10 S. Dearborn IL1-0117
Chicago, IL   60603-2300   (304) 842-3693
Application address: c/o Bridgeport High School, attn.: Principal, 515 Johnson Ave., Bridgeport, WV 26330

Foundation type: Independent foundation
Purpose: Scholarships to graduating seniors at Bridgeport High School, WV.
Financial data: Year ended 12/31/2012. Assets, $153,749 (M); Expenditures, $9,333; Total giving, $5,417; Grants to individuals, 5 grants totaling $5,417 (high: $1,084, low: $1,083).
Type of support: Support to graduates or students of specific schools; Undergraduate support.
Application information: Applications accepted. Application form required.
Deadline(s): Apr. 1
Additional information: Application must include a personal letter.
EIN: 556035695

2501
Glenn E. & Bessie R. Costello Trust
(formerly Thomas H. Boyd Memorial Foundation)
220 6th St.
Carrollton, IL   62016   (217) 942-5244
Contact: Richard Gillingham, Treas.

Foundation type: Operating foundation
Purpose: Financial assistance to individuals of Green County, Illinois, for medical expenses.
Financial data: Year ended 12/31/2011. Assets, $0 (M); Expenditures, $7,717; Total giving, $7,602; Grants to individuals, 4 grants totaling $7,602 (high: $3,000, low: $1,000).
Fields of interest: Economically disadvantaged.
Type of support: Grants for special needs.

Application information: Applications accepted. Application form required.

Additional information: Application should include income tax returns for the last two years together with paycheck stubs for the current calendar year.

EIN: 376363926

2502
O.W. Costilow Scholarship Trust
231 S. LaSalle St., IL1-231-10-05
Chicago, IL 60697
Contact: Cathy Geisz
Application address: Ritenour High School, St. Louis, MO 63114-5423

Foundation type: Independent foundation
Purpose: Scholarships to graduates of Ritenour High School, MO.
Financial data: Year ended 09/30/2013. Assets, $201,165 (M); Expenditures, $16,501; Total giving, $11,000; Grants to individuals, 4 grants totaling $11,000 (high: $6,000, low: $1,000).
Type of support: Support to graduates or students of specific schools; Undergraduate support.
Application information: Applications accepted. Application form not required.
Initial approach: Letter
Deadline(s): None
EIN: 436253991

2503
The Cradle Foundation
2049 Ridge Ave.
Evanston, IL 60201-2713 (847) 475-5800
FAX: (847) 475-5871; E-mail: cradle@cradle.org; E-mail for Heidi Bloom: hbloom@cradle.org; URL: http://www.cradle.org/tcf/home.php

Foundation type: Public charity
Purpose: Grants to Cradle families who have adopted a child with special needs.
Publications: Annual report; Informational brochure; Newsletter.
Financial data: Year ended 09/30/2011. Assets, $17,022,325 (M); Expenditures, $3,112,413; Total giving, $1,922,707; Grants to individuals, totaling $28,600.
Type of support: Grants to individuals.
Application information: Applications not accepted.
Additional information: Unsolicited requests for funds not considered or acknowledged.
Program description:
The Siragusa Scholarship for Special Needs Adoptive Families: This program enables The Cradle to award annual scholarships of up to $1,500 to adoptive families raising children with special needs.
EIN: 450506764

2504
Crosswalk Community Action Agency, Inc.
410 W. Main St.
West Frankfort, IL 62896-2259 (618) 937-3581
Contact: Debra Jackanicz, Exec. Dir.
E-mail: reception@crosswalkcaa.com; URL: http://crosswalkcaa.com/

Foundation type: Public charity
Purpose: Financial assistance to low-income and disadvantaged individuals and families of Franklin,

Jackson, Jefferson and Williamson counties, IL, with home repairs, energy assistance, weatherization, homelessness, scholarships and other special needs.
Publications: Application guidelines.
Financial data: Year ended 06/30/2012. Assets, $1,760,793 (M); Expenditures, $7,592,841; Total giving, $6,033,655; Grants to individuals, totaling $6,033,655.
Fields of interest: Education; Housing/shelter; Economically disadvantaged.
Type of support: Scholarships—to individuals; Grants for special needs.
Application information: Applications accepted.
Additional information: Eligibility is based on household income. Contact the agency for eligibility determination.
Program description:
Scholarships: This program is designed to provide financial assistance to low-income and disadvantaged persons of high academic attainment or potential. Scholarships can be used to provide formal education or occupational training at an accredited Illinois institution, with particular consideration given to fields of study in high-technology areas or other growth operations.
EIN: 371193288

2505
Cameron Cunningham Foundation
P.O. Box 1786
Danville, IL 61834-1786 (217) 431-4204
Contact: Leesa A. Cunningham Hubbard, Exec. Dir.

Foundation type: Operating foundation
Purpose: Scholarships primarily to students residing in the Vermilion County, IL, area. Some support also to seriously ill children.
Financial data: Year ended 12/31/2012. Assets, $154,112 (M); Expenditures, $12,416; Total giving, $11,000; Grants to individuals, 22 grants totaling $11,000 (high: $500, low: $500).
Fields of interest: Medical school/education.
Type of support: Scholarships—to individuals; Grants for special needs.
Application information: Application form required.
Deadline(s): Mar. 31
Applicants should submit the following:
1) Transcripts
2) Financial information
3) ACT
Additional information: Scholarship applications available at area high schools; Applications by letter for medical assistance.
EIN: 371346422

2506
Elizabeth B. Damato Scholarship Trust
c/o Ronald Port
8770 W. Bryn Mawr Ave.
Chicago, IL 60631-3515 (773) 304-5050
Contact: Sue Eaglebarger
Appliaction address: Lawson Products, INc., Human Resources Department

Foundation type: Independent foundation
Purpose: Undergraduate scholarships to children of internal employees of Lawson Products who have been working at any Lawson distribution center for at least three years prior to scholarship period.
Financial data: Year ended 12/31/2012. Assets, $198,995 (M); Expenditures, $10,222; Total giving, $10,000; Grants to individuals, 4 grants totaling $10,000 (high: $2,500, low: $2,500).
Fields of interest: Higher education; Scholarships/financial aid.

Type of support: Undergraduate support.
Application information: Application form required.
Initial approach: Letter or telephone
Applicants should submit the following:
1) Class rank
2) Transcripts
3) GPA
EIN: 367034538

2507
Daniels Hamant Foundation
(formerly The Daniels Hamant Patient Assistance Foundation)
1427 William St.
River Forest, IL 60305-1136
URL: http://www.hamantfoundation.org

Foundation type: Independent foundation
Purpose: Financial support for medically needy patients primarily in Chicago, IL and also international giving to Brazil.
Financial data: Year ended 12/31/2012. Assets, $332,165 (M); Expenditures, $285,341; Total giving, $50,353.
Fields of interest: Health care.
Type of support: Grants for special needs.
Application information: Applications accepted. Application form not required.
Initial approach: Letter
Deadline(s): None
EIN: 364022840

2508
Jones S. Davis Foundation
10 S. Dearborn IL1-0117
Chicago, IL 60603 (214) 965-2901

Foundation type: Independent foundation
Purpose: Scholarships to individuals in LA for higher education.
Financial data: Year ended 08/31/2012. Assets, $1,051,470 (M); Expenditures, $62,195; Total giving, $50,250.
Type of support: Undergraduate support.
Application information: Applications accepted.
Send request by: Mail
Applicants should submit the following:
1) Transcripts
2) ACT
Additional information: Applicants should indicate major and college choice.
EIN: 726023237

2509
Walter R. Davis & Marie Foley Davis Memorial Trust
P.O. Box 369
Fairfield, IL 62837-0369
Application address: c/o Peoples National Bank, Trust Dept., 215 S.E. 3rd St., Fairfield, IL 62837-2172

Foundation type: Independent foundation
Purpose: Scholarships to graduating seniors from Fairfield Community High School, IL to attend a college or university in Illinois.
Financial data: Year ended 12/31/2012. Assets, $144,583 (M); Expenditures, $7,850; Total giving, $5,800; Grants to individuals, 4 grants totaling $5,800 (high: $2,800, low: $1,000).
Fields of interest: Higher education.
Type of support: Scholarships—to individuals; Support to graduates or students of specific schools.

Application information: Applications accepted. Application form required.

Deadline(s): May 31

Final notification: Applicants notified in June

Additional information: Applications are available at the guidance office of Fairfield Community High School and at Peoples National Bank Trust Department.

Program description:

Walter R. & Marie F. Davis Memorial Scholarship: The minimum scholarship awarded is $500 and may vary from year to year. These are one time awards, and past recipients may apply for additional scholarship in future years if they continue to meet the minimum criteria. Applicant must maintain an overall GPA of at least 3.5 on a 4.0 scale, need financial assistance and be of good moral character. Applicant must be accepted at a college or university in the State of Illinois for the next school year.

EIN: 376298427

2510
Margaret L. Davis Trust Fund

10 S. Dearborn IL1-0117
Chicago, IL 60603 (317) 684-3069
Application Address: c/o Perry Meridian High School; 410 W. Meridian School Rd. Indianapolis, IN 46217

Foundation type: Independent foundation
Purpose: Scholarships to current graduates of Perry Meridian High School and Southport High School, IN. Scholarships are renewable for up to four years of study provided that the student maintains at least a "B" average.
Financial data: Year ended 10/31/2013. Assets, $499,972 (M); Expenditures, $24,331; Total giving, $20,821.
Type of support: Support to graduates or students of specific schools; Undergraduate support.
Application information: Applications accepted. Application form required.

Initial approach: Letter or telephone
Deadline(s): Apr. 12
Additional information: Application must include an essay and a list of extracurricular activities.

EIN: 351973505

2511
Blanche L. Dawson Nursing Scholarship Fund

6838 E. State St.
Rockford, IL 61108-4610
Contact: Ron Glenn

Foundation type: Independent foundation
Purpose: Scholarships to young women residing in Boone County, IL, pursuing a career in nursing.
Financial data: Year ended 03/31/2013. Assets, $307,201 (M); Expenditures, $19,074; Total giving, $15,100.
Fields of interest: Nursing school/education; Women.
Type of support: Undergraduate support.
Application information: Application form required.

Deadline(s): Apr. 30
Applicants should submit the following:
1) Class rank
2) Transcripts
3) GPA

EIN: 366877151

2512
James L. & Leona B. & Forrest B. & Muriel R. Dawson Scholarship Trust

c/o Edgar County Bank & Trust Co.
P.O. Box 400
Paris, IL 61944 (217) 465-4154
Contact: John Carrington

Foundation type: Independent foundation
Purpose: Scholarships to residents of the Shiloh Unit Two School District in Edgar County, IL, for study at a public university or college in IL.
Financial data: Year ended 12/31/2012. Assets, $219,632 (M); Expenditures, $11,720; Total giving, $8,472; Grants to individuals, 4 grants totaling $8,472 (high: $2,118, low: $2,118).
Type of support: Scholarships—to individuals.
Application information: Application form required.

Deadline(s): May 15

EIN: 376134534

2513
The de Kay Foundation

10 S. Dearborn St., IL1-0117
Chicago, IL 60603
Contact: Yvette Boisnier MSW, Prog. Dir.
Application address: c/o JPMorgan Chase Bank, N.A., Attn.: Daniel Ordan, V.P., 270 Park Ave., New York, NY 10017; tel.: (212) 648-1489

Foundation type: Independent foundation
Purpose: The foundation traditionally awards monthly stipends directly to elderly individuals and couples to help them remain in their home in safety and comfort, to protect their dignity and individuality, and to encourage them to continue contributing to their community. Stipendiary program applicants must be 65 years of age or older and must be referred by social service agencies and have an assigned social worker. Applicants must demonstrate a history of self-sufficiency and minimal dependence on private charitable or government assistance. Individuals should also demonstrate a history of volunteering or engaging in civic or cultural activities. Applicants may have assets up to $25,000, excluding their primary residence.
Publications: Application guidelines.
Financial data: Year ended 02/28/2013. Assets, $32,797,098 (M); Expenditures, $1,307,556; Total giving, $1,051,794; Grants to individuals, totaling $351,794.
Type of support: Grants for special needs.
Application information: Application form required.

Initial approach: Letter
Additional information: Direct applications from individuals not accepted; Applications only accepted from social service agency representatives which must include age, budget, personal history, and needs of client.

EIN: 136203234

2514
DeKalb County Community Foundation (IL)

475 DeKalb Ave.
Sycamore, IL 60178 (815) 748-5383
Contact: Daniel P. Templin, Executive Director; Anita Zurbrugg, Prog. Dir.
FAX: (815) 748-5873; E-mail: dan@dekalbccf.org; URL: http://www.dekalbccf.org

Foundation type: Community foundation
Purpose: Scholarships to high school graduates who are residents of DeKalb County, IL, for higher education.

Publications: Application guidelines; Annual report; Financial statement; Grants list; Informational brochure; Newsletter; Occasional report.
Financial data: Year ended 12/31/2012. Assets, $38,592,381 (M); Expenditures, $1,184,352; Total giving, $793,151.
Fields of interest: Higher education; Scholarships/financial aid.
Type of support: Scholarships—to individuals; Support to graduates or students of specific schools; Graduate support; Undergraduate support.
Application information:

Initial approach: E-mail
Additional information: Application forms can be obtained from your school's guidance counselor.

Program description:

Scholarship Funds: The foundation administers various scholarships established by donors to invest in the future of area students. Each scholarship has its own unique application guidelines and eligibility criteria, including graduation from a specific high school, high academic achievement, involvement in sports, and study in a particular field such as teaching. See web site for additional information.

EIN: 363788167

2515
Depression and Bipolar Support Alliance

730 N. Franklin St., Ste. 501
Chicago, IL 60654-7225 (312) 642-0049
Contact: Allen Doederlein, Pres.
FAX: (312) 642-7243;
E-mail: questions@dbsalliance.org; Toll-free tel.: (800) 826-3632; E-mail for Allen Doederlein: adoederlein@dbsalliance.org; URL: http://www.dbsalliance.org

Foundation type: Public charity
Purpose: Research grants to study depression and bipolar disorders.
Financial data: Year ended 12/31/2012. Assets, $754,930 (M); Expenditures, $1,337,716.
Fields of interest: Mental health, disorders; Depression.
Type of support: Research.
Application information: Applications not accepted.

Additional information: Unsolicited requests for funds not considered or acknowledged.

EIN: 363379124

2516
Dermatology Foundation

1560 Sherman Ave., Ste. 870
Evanston, IL 60201-4808 (847) 328-2256
FAX: (847) 328-0509;
E-mail: dfgen@dermatologyfoundation.org;
URL: http://www.dermatologyfoundation.org

Foundation type: Public charity
Purpose: Research grants that will advance patient care, and help develop and retain tomorrow's teachers and clinical leaders in the specialty of dermatology.
Publications: Application guidelines; Annual report; Newsletter.
Financial data: Year ended 12/31/2011. Assets, $31,709,516 (M); Expenditures, $5,569,040; Total giving, $3,099,500; Grants to individuals, totaling $3,099,500.
Fields of interest: Skin disorders; Skin disorders research.
Type of support: Research.

Application information:
Initial approach: Letter
Deadline(s): Oct. 15
Program descriptions:
Clinical Career Development Award in Dermatologic Surgery: The award supports research projects that will further the practice of dermatologic surgery, and develop the teaching, research and leadership careers of dermatologic surgeons. Priority will be given to new applications from institutions that do not currently have a recipient of this award. The award offers an annual stipend of $55,000.
Clinical Career Development Award in Health Care Policy: The award supports the establishment and development of health policy careers for dermatologists. Health policy research includes outcome studies, information system development, and evaluation of methods for delivery and practice of population-based dermatology. The environment of the candidate, the quality of project, and the ability of the project to clarify the place of dermatologic practice in the changing health care environment will be the primary criteria used to select an award recipient. The award offers an annual stipend of $55,000.
Dermatologist Investigator Research Fellowship: This fellowship supports dermatologists who desire research training and have a commitment to an academic career in medical and surgical dermatology. Consideration will also be given to individuals with substantial training in other areas who are entering into skin research. Fellows receive a $30,000 salary stipend.
Fellowship in Pediatric Dermatology: The fellowship fosters the development of clinical scholars in pediatric dermatology that will advance the field through patient care, research and teaching. This award is co-sponsored by the foundation and the Society for Pediatric Dermatology. The successful candidate must demonstrate a record of academic interest through publication and/or research. The ability to apply for competitive renewal of this award makes a second year of training possible to enable fellows without any previous pediatric training to complete the requirement of two years of fellowship training for accreditation in pediatric dermatology. Fellows receive a $45,000 salary stipend.
Medical Dermatology Career Development Award: This award provides funding for future intellectual leaders, educators, and clinical scholars in that aspect of the specialty that addresses severe dermatologic disease. The award fosters the careers of young dermatologists who will become the future role models and mentors for physicians diagnosing and treating complex skin disease. The award offers an annual stipend of $55,000.
Patient Directed Investigation Grant: The grant exists to support medical and surgical dermatologic studies that have the potential to directly benefit patients. Funding is intended to enhance the career development of clinical investigators in the early stages of career development. Recipients may apply for a second year of funding on a competitive basis. Grant amount is $20,000.
Physician Scientist Career Development Award: The award supports the academic career of a physician-scientist who is devoted to clinical dermatology, and assists in the transition from fellowship to established investigator. This award is intended for the academic investigator demonstrating significant creativity in clinically relevant research. The award offers an annual stipend of $55,000.
Program Development Grant: This grant provides funding to support the development of the scientific infrastructure in a dermatology division which has

not successfully competed for foundation funding during the last five years. The award has a one-year term and offers up to $10,000 in infrastructure support. Funds may be used (but are not limited) to: acquire critical research equipment, stimulate a promising pilot project, facilitate travel of accomplished scientists to the department, or support visits by young potential investigators to established programs at other institutions.
Psoriasis Career Development Award: This award helps to further the career of psoriasis researchers in the early stages of their careers. This award is sponsored by the National Psoriasis Foundation and will be provided to an applicant who demonstrates meritorious work and potential in psoriasis genetics, immunology, or clinical research focused on understanding mechanism of disease. The award offers an annual stipend of $55,000.
Research Career Development Award: This award assists an individual in the transition from fellowship to established investigator. It provides career development support in skin research for a junior investigator. The award offers an annual stipend of $55,000.
Research Grants: These grants provide financial support for research projects in dermatology and cutaneous biology that benefit the dermatology community at large. Special grants are available for research projects relevant to dermatopathology, ichthyosis and epidermolysis bullosa. Grant amount is $20,000.
Science of Human Appearance Career Development Award: This award provides salary support for the career development of individuals who wish to understand the cell and molecular mechanisms of altered human appearance or of therapeutic interventions. This award recognizes the specialty's sizeable increase in focus on human appearance and the paucity of high quality research in the area.
EIN: 046115524

2517
District One Foundation for Quality Education
950 3rd St.
Carrollton, IL 62016-1404 (217) 942-5314
Contact: Kerry Cox
URL: http://www.c-hawks.net

Foundation type: Independent foundation
Purpose: Scholarships to graduates of Carrolton High School, IL, for higher education at a university, college or trade school.
Financial data: Year ended 06/30/2013. Assets, $246,122 (M); Expenditures, $47,622; Total giving, $47,111; Grants to individuals, 33 grants totaling $35,506 (high: $3,200, low: $360).
Type of support: Support to graduates or students of specific schools; Technical education support; Undergraduate support.
Application information: Application form required.
Deadline(s): Apr. 30
Additional information: Application should include transcripts.
EIN: 371314937

2518
W. J. and Amy C. Dodd Educational Trust
c/o Edgar County Bank and Trust Co.
P.O. Box 400
Paris, IL 61944 (217) 465-4154

Foundation type: Independent foundation
Purpose: Scholarships to graduates of Shiloh C.U.S.D. No. 1, IL.

Financial data: Year ended 09/30/2013. Assets, $338,006 (M); Expenditures, $18,096; Total giving, $13,000; Grants to individuals, 6 grants totaling $13,000 (high: $3,000, low: $2,000).
Type of support: Scholarships—to individuals; Support to graduates or students of specific schools.
Application information: Application form required.
Deadline(s): May 15
Additional information: Applications available at Citizens National Bank of Paris.
EIN: 376331158

2519
Verna Lilly Dodd Scholarship Trust
10 S Dearborn St. IL1-0117
Chicago, IL 60603-2300 (318) 647-3944
Application address: c/o Mer Rouge Methodist Church, Attn.: W.T. Blackwell, P.O. Box 400, Mer Rouge, LA 71261

Foundation type: Independent foundation
Purpose: Scholarships to financially needy residents of the Mer Rouge, LA, area who rank in the top half of their class and have at least an 18 on the ACT and a cumulative GPA of 2.75 or greater.
Financial data: Year ended 05/31/2013. Assets, $218,555 (M); Expenditures, $11,512; Total giving, $7,000.
Fields of interest: Higher education; Scholarships/ financial aid; Economically disadvantaged.
Type of support: Undergraduate support.
Application information: Application form required.
Initial approach: Letter
Deadline(s): June 10
EIN: 726118421

2520
Stephen Dexter and Emily Jane Tipton Dole Scholarship Trust
(also known as Emily Oblinger Trust f/b/o Stephen Dexter and Emily Jane Tipton Dole Scholarship)
c/o The First National Bank
P.O. Box 685
Mattoon, IL 61938-5266 (217) 234-6430

Foundation type: Independent foundation
Purpose: Scholarships to high school students from Coles, Cumberland, Moultrie and Douglas counties, IL, for attendance at the University of Illinois.
Financial data: Year ended 12/31/2012. Assets, $3,801,100 (M); Expenditures, $217,546; Total giving, $138,400; Grants to individuals, 34 grants totaling $138,400 (high: $5,600, low: $2,000).
Fields of interest: Higher education.
Type of support: Support to graduates or students of specific schools; Undergraduate support.
Application information: Application form required.
Send request by: Mail
Deadline(s): Apr. 15
Applicants should submit the following:
1) Transcripts
2) GPA
3) Financial information
4) ACT
Additional information: Applications available at The First National Bank and at area high schools.
EIN: 376023196

2521
Mary Barnes Donnelley Family Foundation
30 N. LaSalle St., Ste. 1232
Chicago, IL 60602-3344

Foundation type: Independent foundation
Purpose: Scholarships to individuals for further education.
Financial data: Year ended 12/31/2011. Assets, $2,748,285 (M); Expenditures, $126,209; Total giving, $114,409.
Fields of interest: Higher education.
Type of support: Technical education support; Undergraduate support.
Application information: Applications not accepted.
  Additional information: Contributes only to preselected individuals.
EIN: 363487746

2522
The Donald J. Doody Foundation
15 Salt Creek Ln., Ste. 312
Hinsdale, IL 60521-2964 (630) 904-5357
Contact: James T. Doody, Pres.
Application address: 2351 Fawn Lake Cir., Naperville, IL 60564

Foundation type: Independent foundation
Purpose: Scholarships to students at St. Laurence High School, Marist High School, and Regis High School, IL.
Financial data: Year ended 12/31/2012. Assets, $2,974 (M); Expenditures, $20,730; Total giving, $17,975.
Fields of interest: Education.
Type of support: Support to graduates or students of specific schools; Undergraduate support.
Application information: Applications accepted. Application form required.
  Initial approach: Letter
EIN: 364092822

2523
Drag Racing Association of Women
(also known as DRAW)
4 Hance Dr.
Charleston, IL 61920 (217) 345-6537
Contact: Ashley Yost, Secy.
E-mail: rnoble@consolidated.net; URL: http://www.drawfasthelp.org/

Foundation type: Public charity
Purpose: Grants and services to drag races, including drivers and crew members while participating in the sport of drag racing.
Publications: Financial statement; Informational brochure; Newsletter.
Financial data: Year ended 12/31/2011. Assets, $1,477,489 (M); Expenditures, $388,163; Total giving, $204,000; Grants to individuals, totaling $204,000.
Fields of interest: Athletics/sports, professional leagues; Recreation.
Type of support: Grants for special needs.
Application information: Applications accepted. Application form not required. Application form available on the grantmaker's web site.
EIN: 953950424

2524
Dreams for Kids, Inc.
c/o Thomas Tuohy
155 N. Michigan Ave., Ste. 700
Chicago, IL 60601-7706
Contact: Thomas W. Tuohy, Pres.
FAX: (312) 729-5405;
E-mail: ttuohy@dreamsforkids.org; Toll-free tel.: (888) 729-5454; Additional address (DC office):

926 N. St., N.W., Studio 3, Washington, DC 20001, tel.: (202) 957-4344, e-mail: dc@dreamsforkids.org; URL: http://www.dreamsforkids.org

Foundation type: Public charity
Purpose: Financial assistance, educational and recreational support for disadvantaged children with disabilities in the Chicago, IL area.
Publications: Newsletter.
Financial data: Year ended 12/31/2011. Assets, $90,467 (M); Expenditures, $462,021.
Fields of interest: Children; Disabilities, people with.
Type of support: Grants for special needs.
Application information: Contact the organization for eligibility determination.
Program description:
  Patricia Tuohy Scholarships: This program provides scholarships to struggling single mothers who wish to further their education.
EIN: 363781104

2525
The Richard H. Driehaus Foundation
737 N. Michigan Ave., Ste. 2000
Chicago, IL 60611-6745 (312) 641-5772
FAX: (312) 641-5736; Contact for arts and culture groups with budgets under $500,000: Richard Cahan, Prog. Off., e-mail: RichardCahan@aol.com, tel.: (847) 722-9244; Contact for small theater and dance companies with budgets under $150,000, Peter Handler, Prog. Dir., e-mail: peterhandler@driehausfoundation.org; E-mail for general inquiries, Kim Romero, Admin.: kimromero@driehausfoundation.org; URL: http://www.driehausfoundation.org

Foundation type: Independent foundation
Purpose: Grants to individuals for projects which preserve and enhance built and natural environments through historic preservation, recognition of quality and landscape design, and conservation of open space, primarily in the Chicago, IL area. Also, awards to individual artists.
Publications: Application guidelines; Biennial report; Multi-year report.
Financial data: Year ended 12/31/2012. Assets, $68,459,646 (M); Expenditures, $5,185,749; Total giving, $3,966,529.
Fields of interest: Historic preservation/historical societies; Housing/shelter, development.
Type of support: Grants to individuals.
Application information:
  Initial approach: Letter or telephone
  Additional information: Projects deemed worthy will be asked to sent a full proposal. Unsolicited requests for funds not considered or acknowledged.
EIN: 363261347

2526
Alfred A. & Tia Juana Drummond Foundation
10 S., Dearborn Fl. 21 IL1-0111
Chicago, IL 60603

Foundation type: Independent foundation
Purpose: Scholarships to graduating seniors of public high schools in Marshall County, OK.
Financial data: Year ended 10/31/2012. Assets, $327,707 (M); Expenditures, $21,470; Total giving, $18,000.
Type of support: Support to graduates or students of specific schools; Undergraduate support.

Application information: Applications not accepted.
  Additional information: Recipients are selected by scholarship selection committees at participating Marshall County, OK, high schools. Unsolicited requests for funds not considered or acknowledged.
EIN: 731157648

2527
Grace Norton Dudley Fund
10 S Dearborn IL1-0117
Chicago, IL 60603 (203) 332-7304
Application Address: c/o Guidance Office of the Bridgeport CT High Schools, 45 Lyon Terr., Bridgeport, CT 06604

Foundation type: Independent foundation
Purpose: Scholarships to students graduating from Bridgeport, CT, high schools for studies at an accredited music school.
Financial data: Year ended 12/31/2012. Assets, $30,780 (M); Expenditures, $1,976; Total giving, $0.
Type of support: Support to graduates or students of specific schools; Undergraduate support.
Application information: Application form required.
  Deadline(s): None
  Applicants should submit the following:
    1) Transcripts
    2) FAF
  Additional information: Application should also include letter of acceptance into an accredited music school, and character reference from high school. Applications can be obtained from guidance office at Bridgeport, CT high schools or JPMorgan Chase Bank.
EIN: 066079557

2528
DuPage Medical Society Foundation
1131 Wheaton Oaks Court W.
Wheaton, IL 60187 (630) 681-2870
Contact: Kirk McMurray, Exec. Dir.
E-mail: dcms@dcmsdocs.org; URL: http://www.dcmsdocs.org/foundation.aspx

Foundation type: Public charity
Purpose: Scholarships to DuPage County, IL students enrolled in or accepted for admission to a professional education or training program who exhibit a strong academic background and financial need.
Financial data: Year ended 12/31/2012. Assets, $156,782 (M); Expenditures, $14,495; Total giving, $12,500.
Fields of interest: Public health; Health care.
Type of support: Technical education support; Undergraduate support.
Application information: Applications accepted. Application form required.
  Initial approach: Letter, telephone or e-mail
EIN: 362598874

2529
Dystonia Medical Research Foundation
(also known as DMRF)
1 E. Wacker Dr., Ste. 2810
Chicago, IL 60601-1905 (312) 755-0198
Contact: Janet Hieshetter, Exec. Dir.
FAX: (312) 803-0138;
E-mail: dystonia@dystonia-foundation.org; Toll-free tel.: (800) 377-3978; URL: http://www.dystonia-foundation.org

Foundation type: Public charity
Purpose: Research grants, fellowships, and awards to those studying dystonia and related fields.
Publications: Application guidelines; Annual report; Grants list; Informational brochure; Newsletter.
Financial data: Year ended 12/31/2011. Assets, $3,572,303 (M); Expenditures, $2,743,795; Total giving, $984,912.
Fields of interest: Genetic diseases and disorders; Neuroscience; Institute.
Type of support: Fellowships; Research; Postdoctoral support.
Application information: Applications accepted. Application form required.
  Initial approach: Letter, telephone, or e-mail
  Copies of proposal: 35
  Deadline(s): Dec. 15 for Fellowships and Research Grants
  Applicants should submit the following:
    1) Letter(s) of recommendation
    2) Proposal
    3) Curriculum vitae
    4) Budget Information
  Additional information: See web site for additional guidelines.
Program descriptions:
  Fellowship Program: Awards fellowships of $50,000 per year for two years to assist post-doctoral students to establish careers in dystonia research. Past studies have focused on genetics, new treatments, and the anatomy and physiology of the basal ganglia. In addition to these continuing areas of interest, new areas of study include the development of immunoreagents for TorsinA protein and studies of both normal and mutant TorsinA biology, and the development of model systems for studies of TorsinA biology.
  Research Grants: The foundation encourages and supports research that will lead to effective treatments and ultimately a cure for dystonia. Funding for grants is available in support of research aimed at providing a better understanding of dystonia. Grants are available up to $65,000 per year for one or two years.
  Residency Program: The foundation sponsors a program for second and third year residents interested in movement disorders with a focus on dystonia. The program is offered for residents to be full time "visiting trainee," experiencing broad research and clinical exposure for a four to six week time period with one of several experts in their respective institutions. The foundation reimburses candidates for expenses up to $4,000.
EIN: 953378526

2530
Greater East St. Louis Community Fund
P.O. Box 547
East St. Louis, IL   62202-0547   (618) 271-2200
Contact: Pamela R. Tucker Coaxum, Exec. Dir.
FAX: (618) 271-2247;
E-mail: greaterestlfund@greaterestlfund.org;
URL: http://estlfund.org/

Foundation type: Public charity
Purpose: Scholarships to students who are residents of East St. Louis or Brooklyn, IL.
Publications: Application guidelines; Informational brochure (including application guidelines); Multi-year report.
Financial data: Year ended 12/31/2012. Assets, $2,782,586 (M); Expenditures, $148,177; Total giving, $20,000; Grants to individuals, totaling $20,000.
Fields of interest: Vocational education, post-secondary; Higher education.
Type of support: Scholarships—to individuals.

Application information: Applications accepted.
  Additional information: Contact the fund for additional application information.
Program description:
  Scholarships: Scholarships are available to permanent residents of East St. Louis or Brooklyn, who are citizens of the U.S., and demonstrate financial need. The students receiving this scholarship must have a high school diploma or GED equivalent, must attend either a two-year or four-year accredited college or vocational institution and maintain at least a C+ average.
EIN: 371274971

2531
Elsie C. Eberhardt Trust
200 W. Harrison St.
Sullivan, IL   61951-1954   (217) 728-7369
Contact: Steven K. Wood

Foundation type: Independent foundation
Purpose: Scholarships to high school graduates of Arthur Community School District schools in IL.
Financial data: Year ended 12/31/2012. Assets, $1,333,131 (M); Expenditures, $61,387; Total giving, $52,250; Grants to individuals, 26 grants totaling $13,063 (high: $503, low: $502).
Type of support: Support to graduates or students of specific schools; Undergraduate support.
Application information: Application form required.
  Deadline(s): June 10
  Applicants should submit the following:
    1) Letter(s) of recommendation
    2) Transcripts
    3) Financial information
  Additional information: Application must also include letter of college acceptance and personal statement.
EIN: 376311757

2532
Edgar County Bank & Trust Foundation
P.O. Box 400
Paris, IL   61944-0400
Contact: John D. Carrington, Secy.-Treas.

Foundation type: Company-sponsored foundation
Purpose: Scholarships to students at secondary schools located in Edgar County and contiguous counties of IL and IN, for study at the postsecondary level.
Financial data: Year ended 07/31/2013. Assets, $18,031 (M); Expenditures, $27,826; Total giving, $27,032; Grants to individuals, 30 grants totaling $25,000 (high: $2,000, low: $500).
Fields of interest: Higher education.
Type of support: Scholarships—to individuals.
Application information: Applications accepted. Application form required.
  Deadline(s): None
  Additional information: Application can be obtained from the Edgar County Bank & Trust Co., Paris, IL.
EIN: 371286227

2533
Edgar County Community Foundation
177 W. Wood St.
P.O. Box 400
Paris, IL   61944   (217) 465-4154
E-mail: inquiry@edgarcountyfoundation.org; Grant inquiry e-mail: hfrost@joink.com; URL: http://www.edgarcountyfoundation.org

Foundation type: Community foundation

Purpose: Scholarships to Edgar County high school seniors for higher education.
Financial data: Year ended 12/31/2012. Assets, $1,013,273 (M); Expenditures, $153,884; Total giving, $114,926; Grants to individuals, 71 grants totaling $46,645.
Fields of interest: Higher education.
Type of support: Scholarships—to individuals.
Application information: Applications accepted. Application form required.
  Deadline(s): Varies
  Additional information: See web site for a complete listing of scholarships and application information.
EIN: 371312204

2534
T. Murrell Edmunds Testamentary Trust
c/o JPMorgan Chase Bank, N.A.
10 S Dearborn IL1-0117
Chicago, IL   60603   (434) 239-6139
Contact: John Bower
Application address: 229 Nottingham Cir., Lynchburg, VA 24502-2748; tel.: (434) 239-6139

Foundation type: Independent foundation
Purpose: Scholarships to high school graduates from Lynchburg, VA who are committed to interracial equality and goodwill.
Financial data: Year ended 12/31/2012. Assets, $247,855 (M); Expenditures, $15,341; Total giving, $10,250.
Fields of interest: Education.
Type of support: Undergraduate support.
Application information: Interview required.
  Deadline(s): May 12
  Additional information: Preference given to those who would not be able to attend college without significant financial assistance.
EIN: 756533776

2535
Edward Foundation
801 S. Washington St.
Naperville, IL   60540-7430
E-mail: jhaines@edward.org; URL: http://www.edward.org/foundation

Foundation type: Public charity
Purpose: Scholarships for nurses and student volunteers of Naperville, IL pursuing higher education.
Financial data: Year ended 06/30/2011. Assets, $8,199,733 (M); Expenditures, $1,653,509; Total giving, $1,407,647; Grants to individuals, totaling $24,000.
Fields of interest: Higher education; Nursing school/education.
Type of support: Scholarships—to individuals.
Application information: Applications accepted. Application form required.
  Additional information: Awards are based on GPA and seniority. Payments are made directly to the educational institution on behalf of the students. Contact the foundation for additional guidelines.
EIN: 363723705

2536
Greater Edwardsville Area Community Foundation

(also known as Your Community Foundation)
P.O. Box 102
Edwardsville, IL 62025-1911   (855) 464-3223
Contact: Mary Westerhold, Chair.
E-mail: contact@edwardsvillefoundation.org;
URL: http://www.geacf.org/

Foundation type: Community foundation
Purpose: Scholarships to students in the Edwardsville Community Unit District 7 School district for postsecondary education.
Publications: Informational brochure; Newsletter.
Financial data: Year ended 12/31/2012. Assets, $1,697,395 (M); Expenditures, $547,196; Total giving, $514,265; Grants to individuals, 58 grants totaling $68,950.
Fields of interest: Higher education.
Type of support: Scholarships—to individuals; Support to graduates or students of specific schools; Undergraduate support.
Application information: Applications accepted. Application form required.
   Additional information: See web site for complete listing of scholarship funds; contact your guidance counselor for scholarship application.
EIN: 367146151

2537
Dr. Glenn G. Ehrler Foundation

c/o The Northern Trust Co.
P.O. Box 803878
Chicago, IL 60680-3878

Foundation type: Independent foundation
Purpose: Awards by nomination only to Nobel Prize winners in physiology or medicine.
Financial data: Year ended 03/31/2013. Assets, $309,895 (M); Expenditures, $20,227; Total giving, $13,515.
Fields of interest: Institute; Biology/life sciences.
Type of support: Awards/grants by nomination only; Awards/prizes.
Application information:
   Initial approach: Letter or telephone
EIN: 366907152

2538
Marie and Margaret Ekstrand Educational Trust

c/o Sherry C. Powers
P.O. Box 153
Elmwood, IL 61529-0153   (309) 742-8464
Contact: Roger Alvey, Tr.
Application address: c/o Elmwood Community High School, Attn.: Thomas Kahn, Supt., 301 W. Butternut St., Elmwood, IL 61529-9454, tel.: (309) 742-8464

Foundation type: Operating foundation
Purpose: Scholarships to individuals who graduated from Elmwood Community High School, IL, in School District No. 322, after 1982.
Financial data: Year ended 12/31/2012. Assets, $1,149,446 (M); Expenditures, $32,970; Total giving, $24,150; Grants to individuals, 51 grants totaling $24,150 (high: $1,500, low: $19).
Fields of interest: Higher education.
Type of support: Scholarships—to individuals; Support to graduates or students of specific schools.
Application information: Application form required.

Initial approach: Letter or telephone
Deadline(s): May
Additional information: Application must include personal information, school and academic information and community activities.
EIN: 366773809

2539
The Elburn Scholarship Fund

611 Plamondon Ct.
Wheaton, IL 60187-6305   (630) 665-2776
Contact: Donald G. Westlake Dr., Pres.

Foundation type: Independent foundation
Purpose: Scholarships to graduating seniors of Kaneland High School, Maple Park, IL, for attendance at community colleges or public universities in IL.
Financial data: Year ended 12/31/2012. Assets, $1,050,108 (M); Expenditures, $50,436; Total giving, $46,000; Grants to individuals, 14 grants totaling $39,500 (high: $3,000, low: $2,500).
Type of support: Support to graduates or students of specific schools; Undergraduate support.
Application information: Application form required.
   Deadline(s): Mar. 1
   Additional information: Application forms are available at Kaneland High School, Maple Park, IL.
EIN: 363366640

2540
Elks National Foundation

2750 N. Lakeview Ave.
Chicago, IL 60614-2256   (773) 755-4728
E-mail for scholarship: scholarship@elks.org
FAX: (773) 755-4729; E-mail: enf@elks.org;
URL: http://www.elks.org/enf/

Foundation type: Public charity
Purpose: Scholarships to graduating high school seniors with tuition assistance in pursuit of an undergraduate college education.
Publications: Annual report; Financial statement; Informational brochure; Newsletter.
Fields of interest: Higher education; Scholarships/financial aid.
Type of support: Emergency funds; Scholarships—to individuals; Awards/prizes; Undergraduate support.
Application information:
   Send request by: Online for Legacy Grants
   Deadline(s): Dec. 2 for Most Valuable Student Scholarships, Dec. 31 for New applicants and Oct. 31 for Renewal applicants for Emergency Educational Grants, and Feb. 1 for Legacy Grants
   Additional information: Scholarships are awarded to individuals who were outstanding in scholarship and leadership attainment, character, citizenship, extracurricular activities and in financial need.
Program descriptions:
   Emergency Educational Fund Grants: The program provides financial assistance to children of deceased or totally-disabled Elks, who wish to obtain or further their college education. Grants can range up to $4,000 and are renewable for up to three years. Applicants must demonstrate financial need to qualify for this grant, be unmarried and under the age of 23 as of Dec. 31 in the year of application, and be attending an accredited, degree-granting U.S. college or university as a full-time undergraduate student. Applicants must also have an Elk parent or stepparent that was a member in good standing for at least one year at

the time of his or her death or complete disablement.
   Legacy Awards: Up to 250 $4,000 four-year scholarships are available to children, grandchildren, or legal wards of a living Elk. Applications will be evaluated on how well the applicant exemplifies the core values of the foundation: knowledge, charity, community, and integrity. Applicants must be high-school seniors who are planning to attend a U.S. American school, college, or university; applicants from Guam, Panama, Puerto Rico, and the Philippines may apply Legacy Awards toward schools, colleges, or universities in their respective homes. Great-grandchildren are ineligible.
   Most Valuable Student Scholarships: 500 four-year scholarships, ranging from $1,000 to $15,000 per year, are available to provide tuition assistance for undergraduate college education. Applicants will be judged on financial need, leadership, and scholarship. Graduating seniors, or their related equivalents, who are U.S. citizens within the jurisdiction of the Order of Elks and who are planning to pursue a college degree may apply. Applications must advance through local, district, and state competitions to reach the national judging. Applicants need not be related to a member of the Elks.
EIN: 046038176

2541
Embarras River Basin Agency, Inc.

400 W. Pleasant St.
P.O. Box 307
Greenup, IL 62428-0307   (217) 923-3113
Contact: Marsha Roll, Exec. Dir.
FAX: (217) 923-5155; E-mail: mindyb@erbainc.org;
URL: http://www.erbainc.org/

Foundation type: Public charity
Purpose: Emergency assistance to indigent residents of Clark, Coles, Crawford, Cumberland, Douglas, Edgar, Jasper, Lawrence, and Richland counties, IL who have been or are in danger of being evicted from their home due to nonpayment of rent. These funds can be used to pay one month or current rent (no deposits). Scholarships are available to indigent individuals who will be attending an Illinois college, university, or community college.
Financial data: Year ended 06/30/2012. Assets, $4,282,510 (M); Expenditures, $16,968,279; Total giving, $6,127,788; Grants to individuals, 44,356 grants totaling $6,127,788.
Fields of interest: Education; Economically disadvantaged.
Type of support: Undergraduate support; Grants for special needs.
Application information:
   Initial approach: Letter or tel.
   Deadline(s): Scholarship applications are taken during the spring and summer for fall enrollments.
   Additional information: Contact foundation for eligibility criteria.
EIN: 370890281

2542
Emergency Fund

(formerly Emergency Fund for the Needy People)
651 W. Washington, Ste. 504
Chicago, IL 60661-2125   (312) 379-0301
Contact: Nonie Brennan, C.E.O.
FAX: (312) 379-0304;
E-mail: info@emergencyfund.org; E-mail For Nonie

Brennan: nbrennan@emergencyfund.org;
URL: http://www.emergencyfund.org

Foundation type: Public charity
Purpose: Financial assistance to low-income individuals and families in crisis residing in the Chicago, IL area.
Financial data: Year ended 12/31/2012. Assets, $1,951,651 (M); Expenditures, $4,001,566; Total giving, $3,294,246; Grants to individuals, totaling $3,128,135.
Fields of interest: Economically disadvantaged; Homeless.
Type of support: Grants for special needs.
Application information:
  Initial approach: E-mail or telephone
  Additional information: Contact fund for further application guidelines.
Program description:
  Flexible Financial Fund: The Flexible Financial Fund distributes assistance on behalf of low-income Chicago residents facing emergency situations. The Crisis Solution Grants are designed with the short-term needs faced by the working poor in mind. Families can receive up to $300 in assistance, once per year. Payments are made directly to landlords, utility companies, or other service providers on behalf of the client. The Self-Sufficiency Grants assist families with rent, utilities, and basic necessities while the head of household completes an employment program. Families may receive assistance multiple times within a period of several months, with a limit of $2,500 per year.
EIN: 237359890

2543
Emergency Nurses Association Foundation
(also known as ENAF)
915 Lee St.
Des Plaines, IL 60016-6513 (847) 460-4103
FAX: (847) 460-4004; E-mail: foundation@ena.org;
URL: http://www.ena.org/foundation

Foundation type: Public charity
Purpose: Scholarships to licensed nurses (RN, LPN, LVN) in emergency care for attendance at a NLN, CCNE, or AACN accredited school.
Publications: Application guidelines.
Financial data: Year ended 12/31/2011. Assets, $1,704,569 (M); Expenditures, $311,540; Total giving, $228,895; Grants to individuals, totaling $228,895.
Fields of interest: Nursing school/education.
Type of support: Scholarships—to individuals.
Application information: Applications accepted. Application form required.
  Deadline(s): June 1
  Additional information: Applicants must be current members of the Emergency Nurses Association (ENA), and must provide verification of the schools current accreditation. See web site for additional guidelines and eligibility requirements.
EIN: 363746084

2544
Ende Menzer Walsh & Quinn Retirees' Widows' & Children's Assistance Fund
20 S. Clark St., Rm. 1400
Chicago, IL 60603-1802
URL: http://www.widowsandchildren.org/

Foundation type: Operating foundation

Purpose: The fund provides financial assistance to the neediest widows (whose monthly income is less than $1,200 per month), and children whose parent died while serving as an active member of the Chicago Fire Department.
Publications: Financial statement; IRS Form 990 or 990-PF printed copy available upon request.
Financial data: Year ended 12/31/2012. Assets, $209,589 (M); Expenditures, $839,371; Total giving, $747,750; Grants to individuals, totaling $717,750.
Fields of interest: Children; Women; Economically disadvantaged.
Type of support: Grants to individuals.
Application information: Applications not accepted.
  Additional information: Unsolicited requests for funds not considered or acknowledged.
EIN: 205045585

2545
Energy Assistance Foundation
P.O. Box 1758
Decatur, IL 62525-1758 (217) 424-6424
Contact: Susan Sams, Exec. Dir.
FAX: (217) 424-6515; E-mail: ssams@ameren.com

Foundation type: Public charity
Purpose: Grants to elderly and disabled individuals who reside within Illinois Power's service territory for home weatherization and heating bill payment.
Financial data: Year ended 12/31/2012. Assets, $1,800,269 (M); Expenditures, $1,405,670; Total giving, $1,317,317; Grants to individuals, totaling $1,317,317.
Fields of interest: Housing/shelter, expense aid; Aging; Disabilities, people with.
Type of support: Emergency funds; Grants for special needs.
Application information: Contact foundation for guidelines on assistance.
Program descriptions:
  Warm Neighbors Bill Payment Program: Applicants must be in danger of losing their primary source of heating, and, if eligible, have already applied for federal and/or state fuel assistance. Applicants must also have a household income at or below 200 percent of the poverty level or demonstrate personal or family crisis. This program runs from Dec. 1 through May 31.
  Weatherization Program: Provides home weatherization to the elderly and disabled who do not qualify for other programs. Thirteen volunteer agencies help to approve grantees for this purpose.
EIN: 363216406

2546
The Engine Rebuilders Educational Foundation
500 Coventry Ln., Ste. 180
Crystal Lake, IL 60014-7592 (815) 526-7600
Contact: Paul Hauglie
FAX: (815) 526-7601; E-mail: info@aera.org;
Toll-free tel.: (888) 326-2372; toll-free fax: (888) 329-2372; URL: http://www.eref.org

Foundation type: Public charity
Purpose: Scholarships for higher education to individuals interested in a career in engine rebuilding.
Publications: Application guidelines.
Financial data: Year ended 06/30/2012. Assets, $161,765 (M); Expenditures, $25.
Fields of interest: Vocational education.
Type of support: Scholarships—to individuals.

Application information: Applications accepted. Application form required. Application form available on the grantmaker's web site.
  Initial approach: Letter
  Applicants should submit the following:
    1) Transcripts
    2) Letter(s) of recommendation
Program description:
  Tech & Skills Conference Grants: Grants (of up to $175 per student) are available to students currently enrolled in engine rebuilding classes who register for and wish to attend a foundation-sponsored technology and skills regional conference. Up to five students will be selected for the grant; grant money includes registration fee, and can be used to pay for gas, hotel, and meals.
EIN: 364163715

2547
Engineering Systems Inc., Charitable Foundation
4215 Campus Dr.
Aurora, IL 60504-8106

Foundation type: Independent foundation
Purpose: Scholarships to individuals for higher learning at accredited colleges or universities in the U.S.
Financial data: Year ended 12/31/2012. Assets, $629 (M); Expenditures, $14,562; Total giving, $14,500; Grants to individuals, totaling $14,500.
Fields of interest: Higher education.
Type of support: Scholarships—to individuals.
Application information: Applications accepted.
  Additional information: Contact the foundation for additional guidelines.
EIN: 911987306

2548
Fenton E. English Charitable Trust
10 S. Dearborn, IL1-0117
Chicago, IL 60603

Foundation type: Independent foundation
Purpose: Scholarships to students at Paris High School, IL, and McLean County High School, Calhoun, KY.
Financial data: Year ended 12/31/2012. Assets, $2,325,722 (M); Expenditures, $133,809; Total giving, $101,890.
Fields of interest: Education.
Type of support: Support to graduates or students of specific schools; Undergraduate support.
Application information: Applications not accepted.
  Additional information: Unsolicited requests for funds not considered or acknowledged.
EIN: 376121328

2549
Arnold & Mildred Erickson Charitable Foundation, Inc.
230 W. State St. MSC M-300
Sycamore, IL 60178 (815) 895-2125
Contact: Carolyn Swafford

Foundation type: Independent foundation
Purpose: Scholarships to graduates of Kaneland and Central Community School Districts, IL, who are attending a four-year college or university, and to residents who are attending Waubonsee Community College, IL, and studying the manual or cultural arts.

Financial data: Year ended 12/31/2012. Assets, $1,341,585 (M); Expenditures, $84,509; Total giving, $64,650; Grants to individuals, 62 grants totaling $52,650 (high: $1,200, low: $450).
Fields of interest: Arts education; Arts.
Type of support: Support to graduates or students of specific schools.
Application information: Applications accepted. Application form required.
  Deadline(s): Mar. 1
EIN: 366998667

2550
Alfred Erk Charitable Education Trust
c/o JPMorgan Chase Bank
10 S. Dearborn
Chicago, IL 60603-2300   (214) 965-2950
Application address: 2200 Ross Ave., Dallas, TX 75201-2787

Foundation type: Independent foundation
Purpose: Scholarships to current residents of Middlebury, CT in pursuit of a higher education at accredited institutions.
Financial data: Year ended 09/30/2012. Assets, $169,749 (M); Expenditures, $10,122; Total giving, $7,296.
Fields of interest: Education.
Type of support: Scholarships—to individuals.
Application information: Applications accepted.
  Initial approach: Letter
  Deadline(s): Jan.1 through Apr. 30
  Additional information: Application must include financial aid form, prior year tax return and academic and extracurricular accomplishments.
EIN: 066287322

2551
Alberta Craig Evans Memorial Scholarship Fund
455 N. Main St.
Decatur, IL 62523-1103

Foundation type: Independent foundation
Purpose: Scholarships to graduating seniors at Rochester High School, IL pursuing higher education at accredited colleges or universities.
Financial data: Year ended 12/31/2013. Assets, $32,011 (M); Expenditures, $14,570; Total giving, $12,000; Grants to individuals, 12 grants totaling $12,000 (high: $1,000, low: $1,000).
Fields of interest: Higher education.
Type of support: Scholarships—to individuals; Support to graduates or students of specific schools.
Application information: Applications accepted.
  Deadline(s): Feb. 25
  Additional information: Application should include education and activity information, and autobiographical statement.
EIN: 376370922

2552
Evans Scholars Foundation
1 Briar Rd.
Golf, IL 60029-2000   (847) 724-4600
Contact: John Kaczkowski, Pres. and C.E.O.
FAX: (847) 724-7133;
E-mail: evansscholars@wgaesf.com; URL: http://www.evansscholarsfoundation.com/

Foundation type: Public charity

Purpose: Undergraduate scholarships and other educational opportunities to deserving caddies with full tuition and housing.
Financial data: Year ended 12/31/2011. Assets, $84,566,045 (M); Expenditures, $17,870,904; Total giving, $11,374,045; Grants to individuals, 825 grants totaling $10,084,877.
Fields of interest: Athletics/sports, golf.
Type of support: Scholarships—to individuals; Awards/prizes; Undergraduate support.
Application information: Applications accepted. Application form required. Application form available on the grantmaker's web site.
  Send request by: Online
  Deadline(s): Sept. 30
  Applicants should submit the following:
    1) Essay
    2) Photograph
    3) Financial information
  Additional information: Application should also include your parents' most recent fax return and W-2 forms.
Program description:
  Chick Evans Caddie Scholarship: The scholarship is a one-year grant which covers tuition and housing (when applicable) and may be renewed for up to four years. To qualify, caddies must be nominated by their club and meet four requirements: strong caddie record where candidates must have caddied, successfully and regularly, for a minimum of two years and are also expected to caddie and/or work at their sponsoring club during the summer when they apply for the scholarship, candidates must have completed their junior year of high school with above a B average in college preparatory courses and are required to take the ACT, candidates must clearly establish their need for financial assistance, and must be outstanding in character, integrity, and leadership.
EIN: 362518129

2553
Everett McKinley Dirksen Endowment Fund
2815 Broadway
Pekin, IL 61554-2678   (309) 347-7113
Contact: Frank Mackaman, Exec. Dir.
E-mail: fmackaman@dirksencenter.org;
URL: http://dirksencongressionalcenter.org

Foundation type: Independent foundation
Purpose: Scholarships to study American government at one of the specified IL universities. Grants to fund research on congressional leadership and the U.S. Congress.
Publications: Application guidelines.
Financial data: Year ended 09/30/2012. Assets, $7,833,428 (M); Expenditures, $516,291; Total giving, $42,588.
Fields of interest: Scholarships/financial aid; Political science; Government/public administration.
Type of support: Research; Support to graduates or students of specific schools; Undergraduate support.
Application information: Applications accepted. Application form required. Application form available on the grantmaker's web site.
  Initial approach: Letter, telephone or e-mail
  Deadline(s): June 1 for Ray LaHood Scholarships
  Applicants should submit the following:
    1) Transcripts
    2) Letter(s) of recommendation
    3) Budget Information
  Additional information: See web site for complete program information.

Program descriptions:
  Congressional Research Awards: The program is open to individuals with a serious interest in studying Congress. Political scientists, historians, biographers, scholars of public administration or American studies, and journalists are among those eligible. The Center encourages graduate students who have successfully defended their dissertation prospectus to apply and awards a significant portion of the funds for dissertation research. The awards program does not fund undergraduate or pre-Ph.D. study. Proposals should concentrate on leadership in the Congress, both House and Senate. Topics could include external factors shaping the exercise of congressional leadership, institutional conditions affecting it, resources and techniques used by leaders, or the prospects for change or continuity in the patterns of leadership. In addition, The Center invites proposals about congressional procedures, such as committee operation or mechanisms for institutional change, and Congress and the electoral process. The research for which assistance is sought must be original, culminating in new findings or new interpretation, or both. The awards program was developed to support work intended for publication in some form or for application in a teaching or policy-making setting. Awards range from a few hundred dollars to $3,500.
  Ray and Kathy LaHood Scholarships for the Study of American Government: Awarded through the Dirksen Center, these scholarships promote the study of politics and governance as practiced by the distinguished public servants who have represented Illinois's 18th district in Congress, and provides financial support for tuition, fee, and books to Bradley University juniors who are majoring in a discipline related to the fund's purpose and interest or in a subject related to the study of the federal government. Eligible applicants must: be juniors in good standing who will enter their senior year of study in a field related to the study of the U.S. government (e.g. political science, public administration, American studies, and U.S. history); attend Bradley University; and have a GPA of at least 3.0 overall and 3.75 in their major.
  Robert H. Michel Special Projects Grants: These grants (which generally range from $2,500 to $5,000) are intended to fund work that advances the public understanding of the federal legislature through research and teaching. Examples of eligible projects include conferences that bring together congressional scholars, the collection or publication of resources useful for research, efforts by teachers to develop creative ways to teach about Congress, and publications, especially those with appeal beyond academia.
EIN: 366132816

2554
The James Ewing Foundation
85 W. Algonquin Rd., Ste. 550
Arlington Heights, IL 60005-4422   (847) 427-9600

Foundation type: Public charity
Purpose: Grants to assist individuals to pursue studies in surgical oncology.
Financial data: Year ended 12/31/2011. Assets, $315,038 (M); Expenditures, $116,220; Total giving, $4,500.
Fields of interest: Cancer research.
Type of support: Research; Awards/prizes; Travel grants.
Application information: Applications accepted.
EIN: 112498503

2555
Experimental Sound Studio
5925 N. Ravenswood Ave.
Chicago, IL 60660-3107 (773) 769-1069
Contact: Louis Mallozzi, Exec. Dir.
FAX: (773) 769-1071; E-mail: lmallozzi@artic.edu;
URL: http://www.experimentalsoundstudio.org/

Foundation type: Public charity
Purpose: Residencies to Chicago, IL, area sonic artists, visual artists who wish to incorporate an audio element to their project, and filmmakers for audio postproduction.
Publications: Application guidelines.
Financial data: Year ended 12/31/2012. Assets, $84,943 (M); Expenditures, $125,320.
Fields of interest: Visual arts.
Type of support: Residencies; Fiscal agent/sponsor.
Application information: Application form required.
  Send request by: E-mail
  Applicants should submit the following:
    1) Work samples
    2) SASE
    3) Resume
    4) Proposal
  Additional information: Application should also include preferred dates of residency. See web site for additional application information.
Program descriptions:
  Artists' Residency Program: The studio offers four 40-hour residencies, at least three of which are for Chicago area artists, with one residency open to a non-Chicago U.S. artist. Each residency includes access to the studio's recordings facilities with engineering assistance.
  Fiscal Sponsorship: The studio acts as a fiscal agent to artists or groups who require a 501(c)(3) status in order to receive funds for projects. The studio retains ten percent of the total amount of the donation/grant for administration.
EIN: 363482714

2556
The Elssy Fabela Foundation
161 S. Lincolnway St., Ste. 104
North Aurora, IL 60542 (630) 820-0400
Contact: Elssy Fabela, Chair. and V.P.
FAX: (630) 820-0904

Foundation type: Operating foundation
Purpose: Assistance to families with disadvantaged children and teens in Aurora, IL, to aid them in completing their education and become productive adults in the community.
Publications: Informational brochure.
Financial data: Year ended 12/31/2012. Assets, $2,917,931 (M); Expenditures, $220,676; Total giving, $29,307; Grants to individuals, 41 grants totaling $11,037 (high: $825, low: $29).
Fields of interest: Children/youth, services; Economically disadvantaged.
Type of support: Grants for special needs.
Application information: Applications accepted. Application form required.
  Deadline(s): None
  Additional information: Application must include tax forms, public aid documents, check stubs, information on social security and disability awards, and children's grade reports.
EIN: 364144368

2557
Fairfield Business and Professional Women's Foundation
P.O. Box 429
Fairfield, IL 62837-0429 (618) 842-2107
Contact: Dave Scarlett

Foundation type: Independent foundation
Purpose: Scholarships to female high school graduates of a Community High School of Wayne county, IL for continuing education at an accredited college, university or community college.
Financial data: Year ended 12/31/2012. Assets, $315,749 (M); Expenditures, $13,710; Total giving, $8,000; Grants to individuals, 4 grants totaling $8,000 (high: $2,000, low: $2,000).
Fields of interest: Higher education; College (community/junior).
Type of support: Scholarships—to individuals.
Application information: Applications accepted.
  Initial approach: Letter
  Applicants should submit the following:
    1) Transcripts
    2) SAT
    3) Letter(s) of recommendation
    4) ACT
  Additional information: Applicant must demonstrate financial need, must be active in school and community events, and must maintain a 2.5 cumulative GPA on a 4.0 scale or the equivalent. Students should apply through the school counseling office.
EIN: 204870780

2558
The Fashion Group Foundation of Chicago, Inc.
P. O. Box 7736
Chicago, IL 60680-7736 (312) 527-7750
Contact: Amanda Domaleczny, Pres.
FAX: (312) 726-9520; URL: http://chicagofashionfoundation.com/

Foundation type: Public charity
Purpose: Scholarships to students pursuing careers in fashion at higher educational institutions.
Publications: Application guidelines; Newsletter.
Financial data: Year ended 12/31/2012. Assets, $0 (M); Expenditures, $159,650; Total giving, $156,672.
Fields of interest: Design.
Type of support: Scholarships—to individuals.
Application information: Applications accepted.
  Additional information: Scholarship funds are paid directly to the educational institution on behalf of the students. Contest winners are chosen based on design talent and skills.
Program description:
  Scholarships: Scholarships of up to $5,000 are available to talented students pursuing careers in fashion at a higher education institution.
EIN: 363571476

2559
Feeding America
(formerly America's Second Harvest)
35 E. Wacker Dr., Ste. 2000
Chicago, IL 60601-2200 (312) 263-2303
FAX: (312) 263-5626; Toll-free tel.: (800) 771-2303; Additional address (DC office): 1150 18th St., N.W., Ste. 200, Washington, DC 20036-3815; URL: http://www.feedingamerica.org/

Foundation type: Public charity

Purpose: Awards to outstanding executive directors of food banks throughout the U.S.
Publications: Annual report; Financial statement; Informational brochure; Newsletter.
Financial data: Year ended 06/30/2012. Assets, $62,576,375 (M); Expenditures, $1,559,486,335; Total giving, $1,479,301,687; Grants to individuals, 2 grants totaling $12,500.
Fields of interest: Food banks; Nutrition.
Type of support: Awards/prizes.
Application information: Applications accepted.
  Additional information: Contact the agency for additional information.
EIN: 363673599

2560
Clifford G. & Grace A. Ferris Foundation
111 W. Monroe St., Rm. 10C
Chicago, IL 60603 (715) 845-3121
Contact: David Guilliom
*Application address:*500 3rd St., P.O. Box 209,Wausau,WI 54402

Foundation type: Independent foundation
Purpose: Scholarships to graduating seniors of Wausau, WI, high schools.
Financial data: Year ended 05/31/2013. Assets, $193,441 (M); Expenditures, $11,078; Total giving, $9,000; Grants to individuals, 4 grants totaling $9,000 (high: $3,000, low: $1,000).
Type of support: Support to graduates or students of specific schools; Undergraduate support.
Application information: Applications accepted.
  Send request by: Mail
  Deadline(s): None
EIN: 396716441

2561
The Johnsie Fiock Fildes Foundation, Ltd.
P.O. Box 357
Olney, IL 62450-0357
Application address: c/o Jeffrey E. Fleming, 420 Whittle Ave., Olney, IL 62450, tel.: (618) 395-8491

Foundation type: Independent foundation
Purpose: Scholarships to graduating students of Richland County High School, IL pursuing a career in the medical field.
Financial data: Year ended 12/31/2012. Assets, $5,392,198 (M); Expenditures, $209,392; Total giving, $175,785; Grants to individuals, 26 grants totaling $33,500 (high: $2,500, low: $500).
Fields of interest: Higher education; Medical school/education.
Type of support: Scholarships—to individuals; Support to graduates or students of specific schools.
Application information: Applications accepted. Application form required.
  Deadline(s): Mar. 10, June 30
  Additional information: Contact your school guidance counselor for application information.
EIN: 364542462

2562
First Mid-Illinois Bank & Trust, Trust No. 93-111
P.O. Box 529
Mattoon, IL 61938-0499 (217) 258-0633
Contact: Laura Walk

Foundation type: Company-sponsored foundation
Purpose: Scholarships to students of Coles County, IL, pursuing a career in the field of agriculture.

Financial data: Year ended 07/31/2013. Assets, $2,622,376 (M); Expenditures, $206,945; Total giving, $130,961; Grants to individuals, 18 grants totaling $120,004 (high: $12,167, low: $4,167).
Fields of interest: Agriculture.
Type of support: Undergraduate support.
Application information: Applications accepted. Application form required.
Initial approach: Letter
Deadline(s): Apr. 15
Additional information: Application can be obtained from Coles county high schools.
EIN: 376314454

2563
Lillian L. Fleurot Testamentary Trust
1615 4th St.
Peru, IL   61354-3507   (815) 224-2400
Contact: Louis E. Olivero, Tr.

Foundation type: Independent foundation
Purpose: Scholarships to graduates of Robert E. Lee High School, Staunton, VA, enrolled in a four-year college or university.
Financial data: Year ended 12/31/2012. Assets, $154,550 (M); Expenditures, $15,410; Total giving, $14,000; Grants to individuals, 14 grants totaling $14,000 (high: $1,000, low: $1,000).
Fields of interest: Higher education.
Type of support: Support to graduates or students of specific schools.
Application information: Applications accepted.
Deadline(s): May 20
Applicants should submit the following:
1) Letter(s) of recommendation
2) Transcripts
EIN: 367265450

2564
Flora School District Academic Foundation, Inc.
444 S. Locust St.
Flora, IL   62839-2119   (618) 662-8000
Contact: for Scholarship: Herb Henson, Jr., Treas.
Application address: P.O. Box 98, Flora, IL 62839-0098

Foundation type: Independent foundation
Purpose: Scholarships to students of Flora Community Unit School District #35, Flora, IL.
Financial data: Year ended 06/30/2013. Assets, $966,883 (M); Expenditures, $78,478; Total giving, $39,929; Grants to individuals, 25 grants totaling $16,439 (high: $2,250, low: $183).
Fields of interest: Higher education.
Type of support: Scholarships—to individuals.
Application information:
Deadline(s): Varies
EIN: 371192911

2565
Follett Educational Foundation
2233 West St.
River Grove, IL   60171-1817   (708) 437-2402
URL: http://www.follett.com/CommunityCommitment.cfm

Foundation type: Company-sponsored foundation
Purpose: College scholarships to children of Follett Corporation employees with at least one year of service.
Financial data: Year ended 07/31/2012. Assets, $3,150,523 (M); Expenditures, $338,458; Total giving, $319,505; Grants to individuals, 153 grants totaling $319,505 (high: $4,500, low: $317).

Type of support: Employee-related scholarships.
Application information: Applications not accepted.
Additional information: Unsolicited requests for funds not considered or acknowledged.
Company name: Follett Corporation
EIN: 366104348

2566
The Footprints Foundation
5901 S. Lagrange Rd.
Countryside, IL   60525
Contact: Lisa Weinberger, V.P.

Foundation type: Independent foundation
Purpose: Scholarships to high school seniors of IL for higher education at accredited institution.
Financial data: Year ended 12/31/2012. Assets, $1,090,323 (M); Expenditures, $66,103; Total giving, $48,355.
Fields of interest: Vocational education, post-secondary; Higher education; Business school/education.
Type of support: Scholarships—to individuals.
Application information: Applications accepted. Application form required.
Deadline(s): Vary
Applicants should submit the following:
1) Letter(s) of recommendation
2) Essay
Program descriptions:
Diamond Ward Memorial Scholarship: The scholarship goes toward an applicant who has done community service and/or other humanitarian work to better our global world for fellow human beings. The fund covers 100 percent of one semester's tuition.
John F. Weinberger Continental Motors Challenge Scholarship: The scholarship is for an applicant who has a commitment to reaching their potential through higher education in the automotive and/or business field. The fund covers 100 percent of one semester's tuition.
EIN: 262982850

2567
P&F Foundation
(formerly Flora S. McCourtney Trust)
c/o Bank of America, N.A.
231 S. LaSalle St., IL1-231-10-05
Chicago, IL   60697-0001
Application address: Robert J. (Bob) Glew, 111 Westminster St., Providence, RI 02903; tel.: (401) 278-6035

Foundation type: Independent foundation
Purpose: Scholarships primarily to graduates of high schools in Sangamon County, IL, who are seeking a technical or scientific education.
Financial data: Year ended 09/30/2012. Assets, $7,214,214 (M); Expenditures, $353,185; Total giving, $302,500; Grants to individuals, 51 grants totaling $302,500 (high: $77,500, low: $1,000).
Fields of interest: Vocational education; Science.
Type of support: Support to graduates or students of specific schools; Technical education support; Undergraduate support.
Application information: Applications accepted. Application form required.
Initial approach: Letter
Additional information: Contact foundation for application guidelines.
EIN: 436023586

2568
Foundation for Women's Cancer
(formerly Gynecologic Cancer Foundation, also known as GCF)
230 W. Monroe, Ste. 2528
Chicago, IL   60606-4902   (312) 578-1439
Contact: Karen Carlson, Exec. Dir.
FAX: (312) 578-9769; E-mail: info@f4wc.org;
URL: http://www.thegcf.org

Foundation type: Public charity
Purpose: Medical research grants for the prevention, detection, and treatment of gynecological cancer.
Publications: Application guidelines; Grants list; Informational brochure.
Financial data: Year ended 12/31/2011. Assets, $1,143,506 (M); Expenditures, $1,840,554; Total giving, $228,275; Grants to individuals, totaling $228,275.
Fields of interest: Cancer research.
Type of support: Grants to individuals.
Application information: Applications accepted.
Send request by: Online
Deadline(s): July 18 for research abstract, Oct. 17 for full proposals
Final notification: Recipients notified in Dec.
Program description:
GCF/National Cancer Institute Scholar's Program: The program is jointly sponsored by GCF and the National Cancer Institute (NCI). The purpose of the program is to support the development of outstanding translational scientists. This mechanism provides specialized study for clinically trained professionals who are committed to a career in research and have the potential to develop into independent investigators. The award supports a 1-3 year period of supervised research experience that integrates didactic studies with laboratory or clinically based research. The experience is intended to be of both intrinsic research importance and be a vehicle for learning the methodology, theories, and conceptualizations necessary for a well-trained independent investigator. Applicants must be Full, Associate, Candidate, or applicants for Candidate Membership of the Society of Gynecologic Oncologists (SGO) or a Fellow-In-Training in Gynecologic Oncology. Each of the sponsoring organizations (GCF and NCI) will award salary of $50,000 per year per organization for a total of $100,000 per year per fellow.
EIN: 363797707

2569
Foundation of the American College of Allergy, Asthma, and Immunology
85 W. Algonquin Rd., Ste. 550
Arlington Heights, IL   60005-4460   (847) 427-1200
FAX: (847) 427-1294; E-mail: mail@acaai.org;
URL: http://www.acaai.org/acaai-foundation/Pages/default.aspx

Foundation type: Public charity
Purpose: Clinical fellowship stipends, research grants, young faculty support awards, and scholars return awards to individuals specializing in asthma, immunology or allergies.
Financial data: Year ended 12/31/2012. Assets, $940,101 (M); Expenditures, $190,329; Total giving, $147,790; Grants to individuals, totaling $147,790.
Fields of interest: Allergies research; Asthma research; Immunology research.
Type of support: Research; Awards/prizes.

Application information: See web site for additional guidelines.
EIN: 364305678

2570
The Foundation of the American Society of Neuroradiology
(formerly The Neuroradiology Education and Research Foundation)
800 Enterprise Dr., Ste 205
Oak Brook, IL   60523-4216   (630) 574-0220
Contact: James B. Gantenberg, Exec. Dir. and C.E.O.
FAX: (630) 574-0661;
E-mail: jgantenberg@asnr.org; URL: http://foundation.asnr.org/

Foundation type: Public charity
Purpose: Awards for mid-career women with demonstrated experience and promise for leadership in neuroradiology and/or radiology overall.
Financial data: Year ended 06/30/2012. Assets, $4,496,943 (M); Expenditures, $359,441; Total giving, $215,000. Awards/prizes amount not specified.
Fields of interest: Neuroscience; Diagnostic imaging research; Women.
Type of support: Awards/prizes.
Application information: Applications accepted.
  Send request by: Online
  Deadline(s): Jan. 21
  Final notification: Recipients notified in Mar.
  Additional information: Application should include a personal statement, curriculum vitae and two letters of support. Applications sent by mail or fax are not accepted.
EIN: 364034440

2571
The Foundry Educational Foundation
(also known as FEF)
1695 N. Perry Ln.
Schaumburg, IL   60173   (847) 490-9200
Contact: William W. Sorensen, Exec. Dir.
FAX: (847) 890-6270; E-mail: info@fefoffice.org;
URL: http://www.fefinc.org/

Foundation type: Public charity
Purpose: Scholarships to individuals for education related to careers in metal casting.
Publications: Annual report.
Financial data: Year ended 04/30/2012. Assets, $7,429,468 (M); Expenditures, $922,167; Total giving, $370,991; Grants to individuals, totaling $278,180.
Fields of interest: Engineering school/education; Scholarships/financial aid.
Type of support: Support to graduates or students of specific schools; Graduate support; Undergraduate support.
Application information: Application form required. Application form available on the grantmaker's web site. Interview required.
  Send request by: Online
  Deadline(s): Varies
  Additional information: See web site for further program and application information.
Program descriptions:
  AFS Twin City Memorial Scholarship: Scholarships are awarded to students attending an FEF school and are residents of Minnesota, Western Wisconsin, or Northern Iowa. Preference will be given to students who are in foundry related courses.

AFS WI Past President Scholarship: Scholarships are awarded to students currently in co-op program in Wisconsin involving the cast metal industry. Preference is given to students who are pursuing programs deemed most useful to the cast metal industry and who hold the best scholastic records.
  George J. Barker Memorial Scholarship: Scholarships of up to $5,000 are awarded to individuals pursuing graduate educational programs related to cast metal. Applicant must be a citizen of the U.S., Canada or Mexico. Preference is given to those who are residents of the State of Wisconsin.
  Keith Dwight Millis Scholarship: Scholarships to undergraduate and graduate students who are interested in ductile iron. Students must be registered with FEF. International students are eligible.
  NADCA Indiana Chapter 25 Scholarship: Scholarships are awarded to students currently in a co-op program involving the die casting industry and attending an FEF school in Indiana, a school in Indiana, or an FEF school in a state adjacent to Indiana. Preference is given to candidates pursuing programs deemed most useful to the die casting industry and who have the best scholastic record.
  Ron Ruddle Memorial Scholarship: Scholarships are awarded to graduate students registered with FEF. Applicants must be North American citizen or permanent resident. Applicant must provide a one page or less, biographical sketch of his/her research.
EIN: 340714666

2572
Francies Scholarship Fund
10 S. Dearborn IL1-0117
Chicago, IL   60603   (214) 965-2908
Application Address: c/o JPMorgan Chase Bank, N.A., 2200 Ros Ave. Dallas, TX 75201

Foundation type: Independent foundation
Purpose: Scholarships to students in the fields of political science, government, and social studies, primarily in OH.
Financial data: Year ended 04/30/2013. Assets, $210,087 (M); Expenditures, $9,741; Total giving, $5,031; Grant to an individual, 1 grant totaling $5,031.
Fields of interest: Social sciences; Political science; Government/public administration.
Type of support: Undergraduate support.
Application information: Contact fund for current application deadline/guidelines.
EIN: 316415216

2573
Franciscan Community Benefit Services
1055 W. 175th St., Ste. 202
Homewood, IL   60430-4615
Contact: Judy Amiano, Pres. and C.E.O.
E-mail: fcinfo@francisanservices.com; Toll-free tel.: (800) 524-6126; URL: http://franciscancommunities.com

Foundation type: Public charity
Purpose: Scholarships for girls to attend an all girls Catholic schools.
Publications: Newsletter.
Financial data: Year ended 06/30/2012. Assets, $2,783,028 (M); Expenditures, $212,784; Total giving, $159,350; Grants to individuals, totaling $159,350.
Fields of interest: Education.
Type of support: Scholarships—to individuals.
Application information: Applications accepted.

Initial approach: Application
Send request by: Online
Program description:
  The Madonna Foundation Scholarships: Scholarships are available to female students who wish to attend an all-girls Catholic high school. Students must demonstrate financial need, reside in the north side of Chicago, show academic effort, and a willingness to make positive contributions to their school and community.
EIN: 364454351

2574
Franklin Park Rotary Club Foundation
P.O. Box 2117
Schiller Park, IL   60176   (847) 671-8300

Foundation type: Public charity
Purpose: Scholarships to individuals residing in the area of Franklin Park, IL, for the first year of college.
Financial data: Year ended 12/31/2011. Assets, $137,494 (M); Expenditures, $19,291; Total giving, $7,250.
Type of support: Scholarships—to individuals.
Application information: Contact foundation for current application deadline/guidelines.
EIN: 363273843

2575
Harry S. Fredenburgh Scholarship Fund Trust
10 S. Dearborn IL1-0117
Chicago, IL   60603

Foundation type: Independent foundation
Purpose: Scholarships to graduates of Mynderse Academy, Seneca Falls, NY.
Financial data: Year ended 12/31/2012. Assets, $1,310,424 (M); Expenditures, $80,605; Total giving, $61,300; Grants to individuals, 26 grants totaling $30,500 (high: $2,700, low: -$500).
Type of support: Support to graduates or students of specific schools; Undergraduate support.
Application information:
  Deadline(s): None
  Applicants should submit the following:
    1) Letter(s) of recommendation
    2) Class rank
  Additional information: Application should also include a description of the student's leadership activities and participation in school and community activities.
EIN: 166229781

2576
Friends United for Juvenile Diabetes Research
1700 Ryders Ln.
Highland Park, IL   60035-0585   (847) 831-5558
Contact: Carol Emer, Co-Pres.
E-mail: info@friends-united.org; URL: http://www.friends-united.org

Foundation type: Public charity
Purpose: Research grants to raise the awareness of juvenile diabetes.
Financial data: Year ended 12/31/2011. Assets, $90,739 (M); Expenditures, $131,321; Total giving, $125,000.
Fields of interest: Diabetes research.
Type of support: Research.
Application information: Contact foundation for application guidelines.
EIN: 364256133

2577
Arthur Gabler Scholarship Fund
(formerly Arthur Gabler Scholarship Trust)
c/o JPMorgan Chase Bank, N.A.
P.O. Box 3038
Chicago, IL 60603-2300   (203) 452-4508
Application address: 72 Strobel Rd., Trumbull, CT
06611

Foundation type: Independent foundation
Purpose: Scholarships to graduating seniors of
Trumbull High School who are residents of
Trumbull, CT, for attendance at institutions of
higher learning.
Financial data: Year ended 06/30/2012. Assets,
$303,255 (M); Expenditures, $13,314; Total
giving, $5,000; Grant to an individual, 1 grant
totaling $5,000.
Fields of interest: Higher education.
Type of support: Scholarships—to individuals;
Support to graduates or students of specific
schools.
Application information: Applications accepted.
Application form required.
Send request by: Mail
Deadline(s): Mar. 1
Additional information: Application must include
parents' and student's tax returns and a
financial aid form.
EIN: 066244605

2578
Robert Gaffney Trust
111 W. Monroe St., Tax Div., Ste. 10C
Chicago, IL 60603   (228) 363-0387
Contact: Thomas P. Gaffney, Tr.
Application address: 101 Aguila Ct., Eagle River, WI
54532

Foundation type: Independent foundation
Purpose: Scholarships to graduates of Northern
Pines High School, WI, and Rhinelander High
School, WI, for undergraduate education, with a
focus on those studying education.
Financial data: Year ended 03/31/2013. Assets,
$710,775 (M); Expenditures, $38,123; Total
giving, $27,700.
Fields of interest: Teacher school/education.
Type of support: Support to graduates or students
of specific schools; Undergraduate support.
Application information: Applications accepted.
Initial approach: Letter
Additional information: Application should
include GPA. Selection is based on scholastic
excellence, need and motive toward teaching
field.
EIN: 816106700

2579
Garwin Family Foundation
120 N. Illinois Ave.
Carbondale, IL 62901-1450   (618) 529-5611
Contact: Marsha G. Ryan, Tr.
URL: http://www.garwinfamilyfoundation.org/

Foundation type: Operating foundation
Purpose: Scholarships to law and medical students
at Southern Illinois University.
Financial data: Year ended 12/31/2011. Assets,
$1,291,028 (M); Expenditures, $62,826; Total
giving, $23,000.
Fields of interest: Law school/education; Medical
school/education.
Type of support: Support to graduates or students
of specific schools; Graduate support.

Application information: Applications accepted.
Deadline(s): None
Additional information: Contact foundation for
current application guidelines.
EIN: 731440816

2580
Geneseo Foundation
P.O. Box 89
Geneseo, IL 61254-0089
Application address: c/o Central Bank Illinois,
Attn.: Michael Kelly, Trust Off., 101 N. State St.,
Geneseo, IL 61254, tel.: (309) 944-5601

Foundation type: Independent foundation
Purpose: Scholarships only to graduates of
Geneseo High School, IL, pursuing careers in
agriculture and computer science.
Financial data: Year ended 03/31/2013. Assets,
$7,689,821 (M); Expenditures, $326,373; Total
giving, $290,754; Grants to individuals, 80 grants
totaling $53,542.
Fields of interest: Higher education; Agriculture;
Computer science.
Type of support: Scholarships—to individuals;
Support to graduates or students of specific
schools.
Application information: Application form required.
Deadline(s): 1st week of each month
EIN: 366079604

2581
Geneva All-Sports Boosters, Inc.
P.O. Box 372
Geneva, IL 60134-0372   (630) 208-1118

Foundation type: Public charity
Purpose: College scholarships to senior athletes
who demonstrate combined excellence in athletics,
high moral character and academics.
Financial data: Year ended 06/30/2012. Assets,
$8,521 (M); Expenditures, $122,143; Total giving,
$110,238.
Fields of interest: Higher education; Athletics/
sports, school programs.
Type of support: Support to graduates or students
of specific schools.
Application information: Applications accepted.
Application form required.
Additional information: Application must include
an essay regarding why they wish to receive
the scholarship.
EIN: 363666963

2582
John & Dorothy Geyer Scholarship Fund
10 S. Dearborn IL1-0117
Chicago, IL 60603   (260) 427-8985
Contact: Gary Reiter
Application address: JPMorgan Chase Bank, N.A.,
101 E. Washington Blvd., 4th Fl., Fort Wayne, IN
46802

Foundation type: Independent foundation
Purpose: Scholarships to individuals for higher
education.
Financial data: Year ended 12/31/2012. Assets,
$2,098,557 (M); Expenditures, $122,210; Total
giving, $100,000.
Type of support: Undergraduate support.
Application information: Applications accepted.
Additional information: Contact fund for current
application deadline/guidelines.
EIN: 352113954

2583
Gift of Adoption Fund
(formerly The JSW Adoption Foundation, Inc.)
2001 Waukegan Rd., 5th Fl.
P.O. Box 567
Techny, IL 60082-0567   (847) 205-2784
Contact: Pam Devereux, C.E.O.
FAX: (847) 205-2925;
E-mail: info@giftofadoption.org; Toll-free tel.: (877)
905-2367; Pam Devereux Email:
pdevereux@giftofadoption.org; URL: http://
www.giftofadoption.org/

Foundation type: Public charity
Purpose: Grants to individuals who adopt children
through an agency program, independent adoption
agency, or international adoption agency.
Publications: Application guidelines; Annual report;
Informational brochure (including application
guidelines); Newsletter.
Financial data: Year ended 06/30/2012. Assets,
$569,375 (M); Expenditures, $665,656; Total
giving, $329,547; Grants to individuals, totaling
$329,547.
Fields of interest: Adoption.
Type of support: Grants for special needs.
Application information: Applications accepted.
Application form required. Application form
available on the grantmaker's web site.
Send request by: Mail
Copies of proposal: 1
Deadline(s): Last day of each month
Additional information: Application should
include most recent tax return, check stub,
two letters of reference and a $40 application
fee. Financial need must be demonstrated.
Program description:
Gift of Adoption Grant: Grant amounts are usually
between $1,000 and $7,500 with the average grant
award at $3,500 to any U.S. citizen who has an
approved and current home study from a licensed
and accredited adoption agency is eligible to apply.
The number of biological children or adopted
children in the home does not impact eligibility.
EIN: 391863217

2584
Mary Williams Gillenwater Scholarship Fund R74629008 / 4400378000
10 S. Dearborn IL1-0117
Chicago, IL 60603   (734) 995-8027
Contact: Alan Dowdy
Application address: 1885 Packard Rd., Ypsilanti,
MI 48197, tel.: (734) 995-8027

Foundation type: Independent foundation
Purpose: Scholarships to graduates of Ypsilanti
public schools, Michigan for higher education.
Financial data: Year ended 10/31/2013. Assets,
$823,630 (M); Expenditures, $44,820; Total
giving, $35,908; Grants to individuals, 13 grants
totaling $35,908 (high: $4,000; low: $1,408).
Application information:
Deadline(s): None
EIN: 616335599

2585
The Dorothy and Lillian Gish Prize
c/o JPMorgan Chase Bank, N.A.
10 S. Dearborn St., 21st Fl.
Chicago, IL 60603-2300
Contact: Jonathan G. Horowitz, JPMorgan Chase
Bank, N.A.
E-mail: jonathan.g.horowitz@jpmorgan.com;
URL: http://www.gishprize.com

Foundation type: Independent foundation
Purpose: Annual prize awarded by nomination only to an individual who has made an outstanding contribution to the appreciation of the arts.
Financial data: Year ended 06/30/2013. Assets, $7,169,098 (M); Expenditures, $516,788; Total giving, $300,000; Grant to an individual, 1 grant totaling $300,000.
Fields of interest: Arts.
Type of support: Awards/grants by nomination only; Awards/prizes.
Application information: Application form not required. Application form available on the grantmaker's web site.
  Initial approach: Letter
  Deadline(s): Contact foundation for nomination deadline
  Additional information: Application should include a letter or recommendation.
EIN: 133751413

2586
Golden Apple Foundation for Excellence in Teaching
8 S. Michigan Ave., Ste. 700
Chicago, IL 60603-3463   (312) 407-0006
Contact: Kelli Garcia, Dir., Devel.
FAX: (312) 407-0344;
E-mail: info@goldenapple.org; E-mail For Kelli Garcia: garcia@goldenapple.org; URL: http://www.goldenapple.org

Foundation type: Public charity
Purpose: Awards by nomination only to full-time teachers at schools in Cook, Lake, and DuPage counties, IL, who spend the majority of their assignment time teaching one or more of grades 9 through 12, and student loans to nominated IL high school juniors to pursue teaching careers.
Publications: Annual report; Financial statement; Newsletter.
Financial data: Year ended 12/31/2012. Assets, $6,064,280 (M); Expenditures, $5,278,577; Total giving, $1,174,746; Grants to individuals, totaling $1,174,746.
Fields of interest: Research; Elementary school/education; Higher education; Education.
Type of support: Program development; Awards/grants by nomination only; Awards/prizes; Undergraduate support.
Application information: Applications accepted. Application form required. Application form available on the grantmaker's web site.
  Deadline(s): Dec. 12 for teaching awards; Dec. 1 for student awards
  Additional information: See web site for complete application information.
Program descriptions:
  Golden Apple Awards for Excellence in Teaching: These awards honor ten outstanding teachers who teach grades pre-K to third in Cook, Lake, DuPage, Kane, and Will counties, and who exemplify the highest standards and practices of the teaching profession (including demonstrating distinguished classroom practice, professionalism and collegiality, high standards for themselves and their students, the ability to create a classroom environment conducive to learning, the ability to reflect on practice, creativity, commitment to students an their learning, and contribution to the wider school community). Winners receive a paid semester sabbatical at Northwestern University, a cash award of $3,000, and induction into the Golden Apple Academy of Educators.
  Golden Apple Scholars of Illinois: This is a renewable scholarship loan program for two years which provides $2,500 for freshman and $5,000

for sophomores, with an additional $2,000 stipend provided for each Summer Institute. This program offers advance teacher preparation and financial assistance for college. Scholars must attend one of 54 Illinois colleges and universities that participate in the program. Students must first be nominated for the program by a teacher, counselor, principal, or other non-family adult.
EIN: 363392992

2587
Gary Goodgear Emergency Assistance Foundation, Inc.
4444 W. 147th St.
Midlothian, IL 60445-2644   (708) 389-5922
Contact: Cecilia Moran, Treas.

Foundation type: Independent foundation
Purpose: Grants to economically disadvantaged individuals, primarily for medical expenses.
Financial data: Year ended 06/30/2012. Assets, $431,280 (M); Expenditures, $25,136; Total giving, $24,015.
Fields of interest: Health care; Economically disadvantaged.
Type of support: Grants for special needs.
Application information: Applications accepted.
  Initial approach: Letter
  Deadline(s): None
EIN: 363924161

2588
Gore Family Memorial Foundation
c/o Northern Trust N.A.
P.O. Box 803878
Chicago, IL 60680-3878

Foundation type: Independent foundation
Purpose: Scholarships to Broward County, FL, residents. Severely physically disabled individuals may apply from other parts of the U.S. Relief assistance to financially needy and physically disabled residents of Broward County, FL.
Financial data: Year ended 01/31/2012. Assets, $20,390,283 (M); Expenditures, $730,309; Total giving, $450,770.
Fields of interest: Higher education; Education; Disabilities, people with; Physically disabled; Economically disadvantaged.
Type of support: Scholarships—to individuals; Grants for special needs.
Application information: Applications accepted.
  Initial approach: Letter.
  Deadline(s): None
Program descriptions:
  Assistance Program: Grants are awarded to assist individuals with medical expenses, equipment for the physically disabled, and housing and transportation costs. Most grants are in the form of one-time or short-term assistance.
  Scholarship Program: Grants are awarded to assist individuals with medical expenses, equipment for the physically disabled, and housing and transportation costs. Most grants are in the form of one-time or short-term assistance.
EIN: 596497544

2589
Charles N. Gorham Memorial Fund
10 S Dearborn ILI-0117
chicago, IL 60603

Foundation type: Independent foundation

Purpose: Support to physically disabled children under the age of 15 who are residents of Winnebago County, IL.
Financial data: Year ended 12/31/2012. Assets, $864,929 (M); Expenditures, $41,044; Total giving, $29,353.
Fields of interest: Children/youth, services; Disabilities, people with.
Type of support: Grants for special needs.
Application information: Applications accepted. Application form required.
  Initial approach: Letter or telephone
  Deadline(s): None
EIN: 366032552

2590
Earl J. Gossett Foundation
8200 N. Austin Ave.
Morton Grove, IL 60053-3205   (847) 983-5626
Contact: For loans: Tiffany Mendez

Foundation type: Company-sponsored foundation
Purpose: Student loans to employees of ITT Bell & Gossett and their dependents. All student loans issued are charged two percent per year simple interest.
Financial data: Year ended 04/30/2013. Assets, $261,472 (M); Expenditures, $18,015; Total giving, $18,000; Grants to individuals, 6 grants totaling $18,000 (high: $3,000, low: $3,000).
Type of support: Student loans—to individuals.
Application information: Application form required.
  Deadline(s): Apr. 30
Company name: ITT Corporation
EIN: 366084312

2591
John Graber Scholarship Trust
111 W. Monroe St. Tax Dive 10C
Chicago, IL 60603   (608) 987-2321
Contact: Gary Galle
Application address: 705 Ross St., Mineral Point, WI 53565, tel.: (608) 987-2321

Foundation type: Independent foundation
Purpose: Scholarships to graduates of the Mineral Point Unified School District, WI, for higher education.
Financial data: Year ended 10/31/2013. Assets, $547,032 (M); Expenditures, $45,067; Total giving, $40,000.
Type of support: Support to graduates or students of specific schools; Undergraduate support.
Application information: Applications accepted. Application form required.
  Deadline(s): Apr. 1
EIN: 396603480

2592
Graham Foundation for Advanced Studies in the Fine Arts
4 W. Burton Pl.
Chicago, IL 60610-1416
Contact: Sarah C. Herda, Exec. Dir.
E-mail: grantprograms@grahamfoundation.org;
URL: http://www.grahamfoundation.org

Foundation type: Independent foundation
Purpose: Project and publishing support, and travel grants to U.S. and Canadian residents working within the U.S. in the areas of contemporary architecture, design, and urban planning. Doctoral support by nomination only for Ph.D. candidates in the field of architecture through the Carter Manny Award.

Publications: Application guidelines; Annual report (including application guidelines); Grants list.
Financial data: Year ended 12/31/2012. Assets, $42,354,623 (M); Expenditures, $2,323,204; Total giving, $882,274; Grants to individuals, 51 grants totaling $401,790 (high: $15,000, low: $125).
Fields of interest: Architecture; Design; Urban studies.
Type of support: Program development; Conferences/seminars; Publication; Fellowships; Research; Grants to individuals; Awards/prizes; Postdoctoral support; Travel grants; Doctoral support; Project support.
Application information: Applications accepted. Application form not required.
> *Initial approach:* Proposal
> *Send request by:* E-mail
> *Copies of proposal:* 1
> *Deadline(s):* Sept. 15
> *Applicants should submit the following:*
> 1) Budget Information
> 2) Curriculum vitae
> 3) Letter(s) of recommendation
> 4) Proposal
> 5) Resume
> 6) Work samples
> *Additional information:* See program description for further details.
Program descriptions:
Carter Manny Awards: To support research for academic dissertations by promising scholars who are presently candidates for a doctoral degree, and whose dissertations focus on areas traditionally supported by the Graham Foundation; that is, areas directly concerned with architecture and with other arts that are immediately contributive to architecture. Scholars whose dissertations are directed towards architecture, landscape architecture, interior design, architectural technologies, architectural research, architectural history and theory, urban design and planning, and the fine arts in relation to architectural topics are eligible for support through a Carter Manny Award. Students must be nominated by their department to apply for the Carter Manny Award.
Production and Presentation Grants: Assist individuals and organizations with the production-related expenses that are necessary to take a project from conceptualization to realization and public presentation. These projects may include, but are not limited to, publications, exhibitions, installations, conferences, films, new-media projects, and other public programs. Research and Development Grants: Assist individuals with seed money for research-related expenses such as travel, documentation, materials, supplies, and other development costs.
EIN: 362356089

2593
Jessie E. Griswold Trust
520 N. Main St.
White Hall, IL 62092-1151   (217) 374-2306
Contact: Howard Piper, Tr.

Foundation type: Independent foundation
Purpose: Student loans for students from Green County, IL, for higher education.
Financial data: Year ended 12/31/2012. Assets, $12,102,315 (M); Expenditures, $329,708; Total giving, $179,275; Loans to individuals, totaling $179,275.
Fields of interest: Higher education.
Type of support: Student loans—to individuals.

Application information: Applications accepted. Application form required. Interview required.
> *Deadline(s):* None
> *Additional information:* Application should include transcripts. Renewal of loans will depend on a satisfactory scholastic record.
EIN: 376105072

2594
Sam & Sarah Grossinger Foundation
6900 N. McCormick Ave.
Lincolnwood, IL   60712-2788   (857) 675-8300
Contact: Sharon Grossinger, V.P.

Foundation type: Independent foundation
Purpose: Scholarships primarily to individuals in the Chicago, IL area for postsecondary education.
Financial data: Year ended 09/30/2012. Assets, $3,818,903 (M); Expenditures, $181,412; Total giving, $142,964; Grants to individuals, 16 grants totaling $54,292.
Fields of interest: Higher education.
Type of support: Scholarships—to individuals.
Application information: Applications accepted. Application form required.
> *Additional information:* Contact foundation for application guidelines.
EIN: 366108185

2595
The Eleanor M. Guenther Trust f/b/o West Point Cadet Fund
10S Dearborn IL1-0117
Chicago, IL   60603   (214) 965-2909
Applciation Address: c/o JPMorgan Chase Bank NA., 2200 Ross Ave., 5th fl., Dallas TX 75201

Foundation type: Independent foundation
Purpose: Grants and scholarships for individuals at the US Military Academy at West Point, NY, or the Naval Academy at Annapolis, MD.
Financial data: Year ended 12/31/2012. Assets, $232,477 (M); Expenditures, $13,960; Total giving, $10,992.
Fields of interest: Military/veterans.
Type of support: Support to graduates or students of specific schools.
Application information:
> *Initial approach:* Letter
> *Deadline(s):* None
> *Additional information:* Letter should include amount and detail of needs.
EIN: 136044874

2596
Hairy Cell Leukemia Research Foundation
790 Estate Dr., Ste. 180
Deerfield, IL   60015-4880   (224) 355-7201
Contact: Earl J. Stone, Pres.
E-mail: hairycellpatientservices@hotmail.com;
Toll-free tel.: (866)-376-0046; URL: http://www.hairycellleukemia.org

Foundation type: Public charity
Purpose: Funds research projects dedicated to the study of Hairy Cell Leukemia.
Financial data: Year ended 12/31/2012. Assets, $57,039 (M); Expenditures, $159,868; Total giving, $158,000.
Fields of interest: Leukemia; Leukemia research.
Type of support: Research; Grants to individuals.
Application information: Contact foundation for additional information.
EIN: 363327001

2597
James & Lena Halsey Educational Trust
100 W. Elm St.
Canton, IL   61520
Application address: Canton High School, Attn.: Principal, 1001 N. Main St., Canton, IL 61520

Foundation type: Independent foundation
Purpose: Scholarships to graduates of Canton High School, IL, for higher education.
Financial data: Year ended 12/31/2012. Assets, $554,936 (M); Expenditures, $32,611; Total giving, $27,500; Grants to individuals, 11 grants totaling $27,500 (high: $2,500, low: $2,500).
Type of support: Support to graduates or students of specific schools; Undergraduate support.
Application information: Applications accepted. Application form required.
> *Deadline(s):* Apr. 1
EIN: 367139856

2598
Hansen-Furnas Foundation, Inc.
(formerly Furnas Foundation, Inc.)
28 S. Water St., Ste. 310
Batavia, IL   60510-3103   (630) 761-1390

Foundation type: Independent foundation
Purpose: Undergraduate and graduate scholarships to students who reside within a 12 mile radius of Batavia, IL, for attendance at any accredited college or university.
Publications: Application guidelines; Informational brochure; Program policy statement.
Financial data: Year ended 12/31/2012. Assets, $848,063 (M); Expenditures, $489,605; Total giving, $432,789.
Fields of interest: Higher education; Nursing school/education; Women.
Type of support: Graduate support; Undergraduate support.
Application information: Application form required. Interview required.
> *Initial approach:* Letter
> *Deadline(s):* Mar. 1
> *Final notification:* Recipients notified Apr. 15
> *Applicants should submit the following:*
> 1) Financial information
> 2) Class rank
> 3) Transcripts
> *Additional information:* Students may contact their guidance counselor for application. All applicants must be U.S. citizens.
Program description:
Leto M. Furnas Graduate Scholarship for Women: This scholarship is awarded to a woman planning to enroll, or currently enrolled in, a postgraduate degree. The award offers a maximum of $5,000 per grant.
EIN: 366049894

2599
Hardin Memorial Scholarship Foundation
231 S. LaSalle St., IL1-231-10-05
Chicago, IL   60697-0001   (407) 278-6039
Contact: Maria Botelho
Application address: c/o Bank of America, N.A., 100 Westminster St., Providence, RI 02903, tel.: (401) 278-6039

Foundation type: Independent foundation
Purpose: Scholarships to graduates of high schools in the city of Louisiana, MO, for study at colleges, universities and technical schools.

Financial data: Year ended 06/30/2013. Assets, $1,720,234 (M); Expenditures, $27,177; Total giving, $3,116.
Fields of interest: Vocational education.
Type of support: Support to graduates or students of specific schools; Technical education support; Undergraduate support.
Application information: Applications accepted. Application form required.
   Deadline(s): May 1
   Applicants should submit the following:
     1) Transcripts
     2) GPA
     3) ACT
     4) Letter(s) of recommendation
     5) Essay
EIN: 436395032

2600
Carrie M. Harper Trust
10 S. Dearborn IL1-0117
Chicago, IL 53201-3038

Foundation type: Independent foundation
Purpose: Scholarships to graduates of East Liverpool High School, OH for continuing education at institutions of higher learning.
Financial data: Year ended 12/31/2012. Assets, $1,130,208 (M); Expenditures, $98,252; Total giving, $85,169.
Fields of interest: Higher education.
Type of support: Support to graduates or students of specific schools; Undergraduate support.
Application information: Applications accepted.
   Deadline(s): None
EIN: 346582259

2601
Fred G. Harrison Foundation
101 S. Park Ave.
Herrin, IL 62948-3609 (618) 942-6666

Foundation type: Independent foundation
Purpose: Scholarships primarily to seniors of Herrin High School, IL for higher education.
Financial data: Year ended 12/31/2012. Assets, $15,740,597 (M); Expenditures, $980,002; Total giving, $198,988.
Fields of interest: Higher education.
Type of support: Support to graduates or students of specific schools; Undergraduate support.
Application information: Applications accepted. Application form required.
   Initial approach: Letter or telephone
   Deadline(s): None
   Additional information: Contact the foundation for additional guidelines.
EIN: 376085205

2602
The Selma J. Hartke Community Foundation
c/o U.S. Bank, N.A.
P.O. Box 19264
Springfield, IL 62794-9264

Foundation type: Independent foundation
Purpose: Scholarships to high school graduates in Macoupin and Montgomery counties, IL pursuing postsecondary education.
Financial data: Year ended 03/31/2012. Assets, $8,667,830 (M); Expenditures, $731,127; Total giving, $576,530; Grants to individuals, totaling $525,100.

Fields of interest: Vocational education, post-secondary; Higher education.
Type of support: Scholarships—to individuals; Undergraduate support.
Application information: Applications accepted. Application form required.
   Deadline(s): Feb.
   Applicants should submit the following:
     1) FAFSA
     2) Transcripts
     3) Financial information
     4) Essay
   Additional information: Contact the foundation for additional guidelines.
EIN: 371406237

2603
Hasnia Foundation
1999 N. 15th Ave.
Melrose Park, IL 60160-1402 (708) 325-1322

Foundation type: Company-sponsored foundation
Purpose: Scholarships to students in Pakistan for higher education.
Financial data: Year ended 12/31/2012. Assets, $145,230 (M); Expenditures, $46,036; Total giving, $34,497; Grant to an individual, 1 grant totaling $8,735.
Fields of interest: Higher education.
Type of support: Scholarships—to individuals; Foreign applicants.
Application information: Applications accepted. Application form required.
   Initial approach: Letter
   Deadline(s): May
   Applicants should submit the following:
     1) GPA
     2) Transcripts
     3) Financial information
     4) Letter(s) of recommendation
   Additional information: Application should also include the educational institution student is applying to. Funds are paid directly to the educational institution on behalf of the student. Selection is based on scholastic achievement and financial need.
EIN: 364415277

2604
Milo & Mildred Hayes Educational Foundation
(formerly Mildred & Milo Hayes Educational Foundation)
231 S. LaSalle St., IL1-231-10-05
Chicago, IL 60697
Contact: Eric J. Eide
Application address: 805 Central Ave., Fort Dodge, IA 50501

Foundation type: Independent foundation
Purpose: Scholarships to graduates of Webster County High School, IA, who graduated in the upper 50 percent of the class, for study at IA colleges and universities.
Financial data: Year ended 03/31/2013. Assets, $611,538 (M); Expenditures, $33,057; Total giving, $28,500.
Fields of interest: Higher education.
Type of support: Support to graduates or students of specific schools; Undergraduate support.
Application information: Applications accepted. Application form required.
   Deadline(s): Apr. 1
   Applicants should submit the following:
     1) Transcripts
     2) Resume

     3) Letter(s) of recommendation
   Additional information: Application should also include a letter stating why you deserve this scholarship, and should be returned to your guidance counselor. Payments are made to educational institutions on behalf of the students.
EIN: 426344913

2605
Health Careers Foundation
c/o WCMS
6991 Redansa Dr.
Rockford, IL 61108-1201
Contact: Andrea Homann, V.P.

Foundation type: Independent foundation
Purpose: Scholarships to students who are residents of Winnebago County and have been accepted at specific professional schools in the health care field in Winnebago County, IL.
Financial data: Year ended 09/30/2012. Assets, $396,117 (M); Expenditures, $22,210; Total giving, $17,750; Grants to individuals, 14 grants totaling $17,750 (high: $2,000, low: $750).
Type of support: Support to graduates or students of specific schools.
Application information: Applications accepted. Application form required.
   Initial approach: Letter
   Deadline(s): Varies
EIN: 366115620

2606
Health Education and Relief
141 W. Jackson Blvd., Ste. 1404
Chicago, IL 60604-3103

Foundation type: Independent foundation
Purpose: Scholarships to Chicago-area students who are college-bound and who come from low-income and/or disadvantaged communities.
Publications: Application guidelines; Newsletter.
Financial data: Year ended 12/31/2012. Assets, $1,313,451 (M); Expenditures, $306,775; Total giving, $91,350.
Fields of interest: Higher education.
Type of support: Scholarships—to individuals.
Application information: Applications accepted. Application form required.
   Send request by: Mail
   Deadline(s): Jan. 28
   Applicants should submit the following:
     1) Financial information
     2) Letter(s) of recommendation
     3) Essay
     4) Transcripts
     5) SAT
     6) GPA
     7) ACT
   Additional information: Faxed or e-mail applications are not accepted.
Program description:
   HEAR Foundation Scholarship: Awarded in conjunction with the Daniel Murphy Scholarship Fund, up to $40,000 in scholarships are given annually to college-bound Chicago-area students in need. Emphasis will be given to students who are hardworking, goal-driven, and involved in their communities and/or schools, and whose needs aren't met by other financial packages.
EIN: 204221874

2607
Health Research and Educational Trust
155 N. Wacker, Ste. 400
Chicago, IL 60606-1719 (312) 422-2600
Contact: Dr. Maulik S. Joshi, Pres.
E-mail contact for fellowship: ngoburdhun@aha.org
FAX: (312) 422-4568; URL: http://www.hret.org

Foundation type: Public charity
Purpose: Fellowships to individuals who have demonstrated a consistent pattern of leadership and innovation in healthcare.
Publications: Annual report.
Financial data: Year ended 12/31/2011. Assets, $7,179,517 (M); Expenditures, $14,167,554; Total giving, $1,164,563. Fellowships amount not specified.
Fields of interest: Health care.
Type of support: Fellowships; Awards/prizes.
Application information: Applications accepted.
  Initial approach: Letter or telephone
  Additional information: Application should include a current curriculum vitae and a short bio (less than 200 words). See web site for additional guidelines.
EIN: 362203931

2608
Healthy Smiles, Healthy Children: The Foundation of the AAPD
211 E. Chicago Ave., Ste. 1700
Chicago, IL 60611-2637 (312) 337-2169
Contact: Beverly A. Largent, Pres.
FAX: (312) 337-6329; E-mail: hshc@aapd.org;
URL: http://www.aapd.org/foundation

Foundation type: Public charity
Purpose: Fellowships, grants, and awards to researchers of dental care for underserved children.
Publications: Annual report.
Financial data: Year ended 06/30/2012. Assets, $12,689,429 (M); Expenditures, $1,220,269; Total giving, $121,721; Grants to individuals, totaling $27,421.
Fields of interest: Dental care; Children.
Type of support: Fellowships; Travel awards; Research; Grants to individuals.
Application information: Applications accepted. Application form required. Application form available on the grantmaker's web site.
  Deadline(s): Varies
Program descriptions:
  3M ESPE Preventative Pediatric Dentistry Postdoctoral Research Fellowship: Up to three pediatric dentistry postdoctoral students/residents are selected each year to receive a year-long research fellowship.
  Future Dental Researcher Fellowship: Grants of up to $75,000 per year, for up to three years, are available to investigators in their third year who are focusing their research on the study of dental care programs that target underserved and limited access child populations.
  Jerome B. Miller "For the Kids" Award: A $1,000 cash award and plaque is presented to an up-and-coming clinician, researcher, or academician in pediatric dentistry for his or her outstanding efforts directed to children's oral health and welfare. Applicants must: be 45 years-old or younger; be a current member of the foundation; possess experience in domestic or international community or humanitarian service; serve or have served in a local, state, or national dental association; and have leadership potential.
  Master Clinician Program: Five scholarships are available for selected candidates to attend the Academy for Academic Leadership's Institute for

Teaching and Learning held at the University of North Carolina at Chapel Hill School of Dentistry.
  NuSmile Graduate Student Research Awards: Current and recent pediatric dentistry students and residents who are selected for this program have the opportunity to present their research at the foundation's annual session. Finalists receive complimentary registration for themselves and a guest, travel expense reimbursement, a cash award and plaque presented during the General Assembly at the session, and a matching cash award given to each finalist's training program.
  Oral Health Research Grants: Grants of up to $100,000 per year for three years are available to individuals or organizations affiliated with the American Dental Association's Commission on Dental Accreditation or the Commission on Dental Accreditation of Canada. Research initiatives must be consistent with the American Academy of Pediatric Dentistry's Research Agenda.
  Ralph E. McDonald Award: The award is presented to the Graduate Student Research Award recipient judged to have accomplished the most outstanding research project. The recipient receives an additional cash award.
  Samuel D. Harris Policy and Management Fellowship: Pediatric dental residents and individuals in their first five years post-residency are eligible to apply to participate in governance and advocacy activities, be involved in foundation and related functions, and attend internal organizational and inter-professional meetings. A cash stipend and payment for travel to Chicago and other meeting locations will be provided.
EIN: 363542658

2609
Hebrew Immigrant Aid Society of Chicago
216 W. Jackson, Ste. 700
Chicago, IL 60606-6921 (312) 357-4666
Contact: Jodi Doane, Admin.
E-mail: hiaschicago@jcfs.org; URL: http://hiaschicago.org/

Foundation type: Public charity
Purpose: Scholarship to an immigrant or a son or daughter of a HIAS immigrant for attendance at institutions of higher learning pursuing a career of professional study in counseling, law, or social work.
Financial data: Year ended 06/30/2012. Assets, $4,183,448 (M); Expenditures, $991,971; Total giving, $978,671; Grants to individuals, totaling $24,000.
Fields of interest: Higher education; Civil/human rights, immigrants.
Type of support: Scholarships—to individuals.
Application information: Contact the society for eligibility criteria.
EIN: 362167094

2610
The Heed Ophthalmic Foundation
c/o The Private Bank
120 S. LaSalle St., 7th Fl.
Chicago, IL 60603 (216) 445-8145
Contact: Froncie A. Gutman
FAX: (216) 444-8968; E-mail: admin1@heed.org;
URL: http://www.heed.org/

Foundation type: Independent foundation
Purpose: Fellowships to U.S. citizens pursuing postgraduate fellowship studies and research in the field of ophthalmology and the related visual sciences.

Publications: Application guidelines; Program policy statement.
Financial data: Year ended 12/31/2012. Assets, $4,347,021 (M); Expenditures, $234,780; Total giving, $125,934; Grants to individuals, 25 grants totaling $125,934 (high: $5,838, low: $4,170).
Fields of interest: Eye diseases; Eye research.
Type of support: Fellowships; Research.
Application information: Applications accepted. Application form required. Application form available on the grantmaker's web site.
  Deadline(s): Jan. 15
  Additional information: Application should include a statement of professional objective, letters of recommendation and a letter of acceptance from the institution at which the fellowship will be conducted.
EIN: 366012426

2611
Frances Sawyer Hefti Trust
10 S. Dearborn, IL1-0117
Chicago, IL 60603 (920) 735-1316
Application address: High School Counselor or JPMorgan Chase Bank, N.A., 200 W. College Ave., Appleton, WI 54911

Foundation type: Independent foundation
Purpose: Scholarships to high school seniors at Neenah or Menasha Joint School Districts, WI.
Financial data: Year ended 12/31/2012. Assets, $783,399 (M); Expenditures, $45,226; Total giving, $35,388.
Type of support: Support to graduates or students of specific schools; Undergraduate support.
Application information: Applications accepted. Application form required.
  Deadline(s): Feb. 15
  Additional information: Forms available from guidance counselors.
EIN: 396474920

2612
Father Leo Henkel Scholarship Trust
c/o Heartland Bank
606 S. Main St.
Princeton, IL 61356-2013 (815) 434-0780
Contact: Richard A. Myers
Application address: c/o William Novotney, LaSalle City Regional Supt. of Schools, 119 W. Madison St., Ste. 102, Ottawa, IL 61350-5015, tel.: (815) 434-0780
Application Address: 119 W. Madison St., Ottawa, IL 61350 Tel: (815) 434-0780

Foundation type: Independent foundation
Purpose: Scholarships to students of LaSalle, IL, who have graduated from local, state-accredited high schools for undergraduate study at accredited colleges or universities.
Financial data: Year ended 12/31/2012. Assets, $127,223 (M); Expenditures, $4,906; Total giving, $2,750; Grants to individuals, 5 grants totaling $2,750 (high: $1,000, low: $250).
Fields of interest: Higher education.
Type of support: Undergraduate support.
Application information: Applications accepted. Application form required. Interview required.
  Deadline(s): Apr. 1
  Applicants should submit the following:
    1) Letter(s) of recommendation
    2) Class rank
    3) GPA
    4) ACT
EIN: 363711096

2613
Iva W. & Roy Henry Scholarship Trust
c/o Edgar County Bank & Trust Co.
P.O. Box 400
Paris, IL   61944-0790   (217) 465-4154

Foundation type: Independent foundation
Purpose: Scholarships for residents of Edgar County, IL pursuing postsecondary education at institutions of higher learning.
Financial data: Year ended 12/31/2012. Assets, $224,193 (M); Expenditures, $14,054; Total giving, $10,500; Grants to individuals, 6 grants totaling $10,500 (high: $2,500, low: $500).
Fields of interest: Higher education.
Type of support: Scholarships—to individuals.
Application information: Applications accepted. Application form required.
>   *Deadline(s):* May 15
>   *Additional information:* Application can be obtained from Edgar County Bank and Trust of Paris.

EIN: 376115083

2614
Bernard & Pauline Herbert Scholarship Trust
10 S. Dearborn IL1-0117
Chicago, IL   60603
Application address: c/o JPMorgan Chase Bank, N.A., Scholarship A, 2200 Ross Ave., 5th Fl., Dallas, TX 75201, tel.: (866) 300-6222

Foundation type: Independent foundation
Purpose: Scholarships to students of osteopathic medicine at Des Moines University, Osteopathic Medical Center, Des Moines, IA.
Financial data: Year ended 12/31/2012. Assets, $4,100,560 (M); Expenditures, $243,359; Total giving, $191,913.
Fields of interest: Higher education.
Type of support: Support to graduates or students of specific schools.
Application information: Applications accepted. Application form required.
>   *Deadline(s):* Six weeks before the next tuition bill date
>   *Additional information:* Application should include FAFSA. Applicant must demonstrate financial need and provide written documentation showing that they are either accepted students or matriculated students at the Des Moines University, Osteopathic Medical Center.

EIN: 206945564

2615
Hellmuth Hertz Foundation
c/o The Northern Trust Co.
P.O. Box 803878
Chicago, IL   60680-3878

Foundation type: Independent foundation
Purpose: Postdoctoral fellowships to individuals who have a doctoral degree from a Swedish university in the fields of natural science, medicine, or technology.
Financial data: Year ended 12/31/2012. Assets, $1,426,469 (M); Expenditures, $113,810; Total giving, $106,050; Grants to individuals, 2 grants totaling $106,050 (high: $60,600, low: $45,450).
Fields of interest: Medical school/education; Science; Engineering/technology.
International interests: Sweden.
Type of support: Fellowships; Postdoctoral support.

Application information: Applications accepted.
>   *Initial approach:* Proposal
>   *Additional information:* Contact the foundation for additional guidelines.

Program description:
>   *Fellowships:* Fellowships to individuals who have received their doctoral degrees from a Swedish university in the areas of natural science, medicine, or technology for further study and/or research in these fields. Solicited applicants must submit a detailed proposal of their planned research or course of study a complete biographical record, including academic and professional history, a list of publications, date the Ph.D. exam will be taken, if not already completed, a reference letter from the institution where proposed research or study will occur, and an estimate of financial need. Grants are renewable, contingent upon satisfactory progress. Fellowship recipients are expected to embark upon careers in the stated fields.

EIN: 363741553

2616
William Higgins Trust for Avelena Fund
10 S. Dearborn IL1-0117
Chicago, IL   60603

Foundation type: Independent foundation
Purpose: Financial assistance to aged, indigent residents of IN.
Financial data: Year ended 10/31/2012. Assets, $572,291 (M); Expenditures, $49,466; Total giving, $34,145.
Fields of interest: Aging; Economically disadvantaged.
Type of support: Grants for special needs.
Application information: Applications accepted.
>   *Initial approach:* Letter
>   *Deadline(s):* None
>   *Additional information:* Application should include financial information.

EIN: 356009209

2617
Paul and Julia Mercer Hill Charitable Foundation
101 S. Park Ave.
Herrin, IL   62948-3609   (618) 942-6666

Foundation type: Independent foundation
Purpose: Scholarships to Carterville High School, IL, graduates for attendance at John A. Logan College in Carterville, IL.
Financial data: Year ended 12/31/2012. Assets, $1,172,708 (M); Expenditures, $50,516; Total giving, $42,812.
Fields of interest: Higher education.
Type of support: Scholarships—to individuals; Support to graduates or students of specific schools.
Application information: Applications accepted. Application form not required.
>   *Initial approach:* Telephone or letter
>   *Deadline(s):* None
>   *Additional information:* Contact the foundation for additional guidelines.

EIN: 371394605

2618
Hill-Plath Foundation
4 Clover Leaf Ct.
Savoy, IL   61874-9759   (217) 351-2159
Contact: Jacquetta Hill, Pres.,Secy. and Dir.
URL: http://www.lahudance.org/

Foundation type: Operating foundation
Purpose: Scholarships to children who have one or more parent who are members of the Lahu minority in northern Thailand.
Financial data: Year ended 12/31/2012. Assets, $29,411 (M); Expenditures, $21,208; Total giving, $18,268.
Fields of interest: Minorities.
Type of support: Scholarships—to individuals.
Application information:
>   *Deadline(s):* None

EIN: 371415365

2619
Armin & Esther Hirsch Foundation
4400 S. Kildare Ave.
Chicago, IL   60632-4356

Foundation type: Independent foundation
Purpose: Scholarships to individuals primarily in IL and IN in pursuit of a higher education at accredited colleges or universities.
Financial data: Year ended 12/31/2012. Assets, $7,050,382 (M); Expenditures, $397,656; Total giving, $348,480; Grants to individuals, 9 grants totaling $22,564 (high: $4,000, low: $783).
Fields of interest: Higher education.
Type of support: Undergraduate support.
Application information: Contact the foundation for additional information.
EIN: 363774078

2620
Irma T. Hirschl Trust
c/o JPMorgan Chase Bank, N.A.
10 S. Dearborn St., IL1-0117
Chicago, IL   60603-2300

Foundation type: Independent foundation
Purpose: Awards to biomedical scientists in NY for careers in academic research.
Financial data: Year ended 10/31/2012. Assets, $41,927,704 (M); Expenditures, $2,198,618; Total giving, $1,979,000.
Fields of interest: Biomedicine research; Biology/life sciences.
Type of support: Research; Awards/prizes.
Application information: Applications not accepted.
>   *Additional information:* All applications submitted by designated medical schools. Unsolicited requests for funds not considered or acknowledged.

Program description:
>   *Irma T. Hirschl and Monique Weill-Caulier Research Award Program:* The aim of this program is to support talented biomedical scientists committed to careers in academic research, and in particular those who exhibit an exceptional potential for high quality productive research. Nominees are to be recommended by the Albert Einstein College of Medicine; Columbia University College of Physicians & Surgeons; Cornell Medical College; the Mount Sinai School of Medicine; New York University College of Medicine; and Rockefeller University.

EIN: 136356381

2621
Joseph J. Hohner Scholarship Fund
111 W. Monroe St., Tax Div. 10C
Chicago, IL   60603

Foundation type: Independent foundation

Purpose: Scholarships to students who are legal residents of LaSalle County, IL to pursue further academic or vocational education.
Financial data: Year ended 05/31/2013. Assets, $1,200,218 (M); Expenditures, $67,958; Total giving, $49,188.
Fields of interest: Vocational education, post-secondary; Higher education.
Type of support: Scholarships—to individuals.
Application information: Applications accepted. Application form required.
  Deadline(s): None
  Final notification: Applicants notified in June
  Additional information: Applications can be obtained from any high school or parochial school in LaSalle county.
EIN: 366644741

2622
The Holocaust Educational Foundation
c/o McGladrey, Inc.
1 S. Wacker Dr., Ste. 800
Chicago, IL 60606-4614 (312) 634-3400
FAX: (847) 676-3706; E-mail: hef3@aol.com;
URL: http://www.holocaustef.org

Foundation type: Public charity
Purpose: Research fellowships to faculty members and ABD graduate students at North American colleges or universities.
Publications: Application guidelines.
Financial data: Year ended 12/31/2011. Assets, $4,122,379 (M); Expenditures, $1,290,315; Total giving, $1,063,900; Grants to individuals, totaling $23,400.
Fields of interest: History/archaeology.
Type of support: Fellowships; Research.
Application information: Applications accepted.
  Initial approach: Proposals
  Send request by: Online or mail
  Deadline(s): Feb. 28
  Final notification: Applicants notified in Mar.
  Applicants should submit the following:
    1) Budget Information
    2) Curriculum vitae
  Additional information: Application should also include a project statement and two letters of reference.
Program descriptions:
  Research Fellowships: Four $2,000 fellowships are available to faculty members and graduate students at North American colleges and universities, to be applied towards further research in Holocaust studies. All academic disciplines are eligible. Proposals may request support for any stance of a research project, from initial field work to write-up or publication of results, but must be specific as to purpose (e.g., travel support, the purchase of released time from teaching, and the acquisition of essential source material)
  Summer Institute: The foundation offers a summer institute program at Northwestern University designed to enrich the preparation of current and prospective college and university faculty for teaching courses on the Holocaust. Themes covered include the religious practice and history of the European Jews, problems in Holocaust interpretation, the Holocaust in literature and film, and the pedagogy of the Holocaust. The institute is open to advanced graduate students and faculty at the college or university level. Successful applicants will receive awards covering room, board, and tuition during the program.
EIN: 363197214

2623
HomeStar Education Foundation Inc.
3 Diversatech Dr.
Manteno, IL 60950-9201 (815) 468-2357
Contact: Deborah S. Maw, Treas.

Foundation type: Company-sponsored foundation
Purpose: Scholarships of $2,000 to 2,500 to high school seniors residing in IL whose parent or grandparent is a customer of HomeStar Bank, HomeStar Insurance Services, HomeStar Investment Services or HomeStar Trust Services, to students who are members of the Kankakee County, IL branch of the NAACP and to students with a Hispanic heritage.
Publications: Application guidelines.
Financial data: Year ended 12/31/2012. Assets, $2 (M); Expenditures, $30,500; Total giving, $30,500; Grants to individuals, 31 grants totaling $30,500 (high: $2,000, low: $500).
Fields of interest: Higher education.
Type of support: Undergraduate support.
Application information: Applications accepted. Application form required.
  Deadline(s): Feb. 15
  Applicants should submit the following:
    1) Letter(s) of recommendation
    2) Transcripts
    3) Essay
  Additional information: Application forms are available from area high school guidance counselors and from any Homestar Bank.
EIN: 364452037

2624
Hoover/Hoehn Scholarship Foundation
(formerly O. Robert Hoover Scholarship Foundation, also known as Hoover/Hohen Scholarship Foundation)
230 W. State St., MSC M-300
Sycamore, IL 60178 (815) 895-2125
Contact: Carolyn Swafford

Foundation type: Independent foundation
Purpose: Scholarships to graduates of Genoa-Kingston High School, IL, for undergraduate education.
Financial data: Year ended 12/31/2012. Assets, $242,050 (M); Expenditures, $17,004; Total giving, $12,800; Grants to individuals, 16 grants totaling $12,800 (high: $1,000, low: $400).
Fields of interest: Higher education.
Type of support: Support to graduates or students of specific schools.
Application information: Applications accepted. Application form required.
  Initial approach: Letter
  Deadline(s): Mar. 15
  Additional information: Contact foundation for current application guidelines.
EIN: 363986816

2625
HOPA Research Foundation
8735 W. Higgins Rd., Ste. 300
Chicago, IL 60631-2738
Application address: Susan Floutsakos, e-mail: sfloutsakos@connect2amc.com
E-mail: info@hoparx.org; Toll-free tel.: (877) 467-2791; URL: http://www.hoparx.org/foundation.html

Foundation type: Public charity
Purpose: Research grants for the support of hematology/oncology pharmacy practitioners in optimizing cancer patient care.

Financial data: Year ended 12/31/2011. Assets, $3,323,123 (M); Expenditures, $1,638,383; Total giving, $69,250; Grants to individuals, 44 grants totaling $19,250.
Fields of interest: Cancer research; Hematology research.
Type of support: Grants to individuals.
Application information: Applications accepted.
  Initial approach: Letter of Intent
  Send request by: On-line
  Deadline(s): June for LOI, Sept. for grant proposals
  Final notification: Recipients notified in Nov.
Program description:
  HOPA Research Grants: The program is intended to support projects that are likely to result in facilitating the efforts of hematology/oncology pharmacists to optimize the care of individuals affected by cancer. The HOPA Foundation will fund up to three grants based on the stated scope of work. A total of $50,000 in funding is available to be awarded.
EIN: 201044674

2626
Susan Cook House Educational Trust
c/o JPMorgan Chase Bank, N.A.
10 S. Dearborn St., IL1-0117
Chicago, IL 60603-2300
Application address: 1 East Old State Capitol Plz., 3rd Fl., Springfield, IL 62701, tel.: (217) 525-9737

Foundation type: Independent foundation
Purpose: Scholarships only to residents of Sangamon County, IL for postsecondary education.
Financial data: Year ended 11/30/2012. Assets, $3,266,148 (M); Expenditures, $294,838; Total giving, $221,492.
Fields of interest: Education.
Type of support: Undergraduate support.
Application information: Applications accepted.
  Initial approach: Letter
EIN: 376087675

2627
Laurence E. Hubbard and Ruth J. Hubbard Scholarship & Charitable Trust
1900 W. Iles Ave.
Springfield, IL 62704
Application address: c/o Pike County Illinois High School

Foundation type: Independent foundation
Purpose: Scholarships for students of Pike County High School, IL.
Financial data: Year ended 09/30/2013. Assets, $617,933 (M); Expenditures, $36,619; Total giving, $29,893.
Fields of interest: Higher education.
Type of support: Scholarships—to individuals.
Application information:
  Initial approach: Letter.
EIN: 431910010

2628
Leola W. and Charles H. Hugg Trust
c/o JPMorgan Chase Bank, N.A.
10 S. Dearborn St., IL1-0117
Chicago, IL 60603-2300

Foundation type: Independent foundation
Purpose: Scholarships for students from Williamson County, TX, for higher education.

Financial data: Year ended 12/31/2012. Assets, $7,780,280 (M); Expenditures, $542,045; Total giving, $393,825; Grants to individuals, 218 grants totaling $393,825 (high: $1,450, low: $450).
Fields of interest: Higher education; Scholarships/financial aid.
Type of support: Undergraduate support.
Application information: Applications not accepted.
  Additional information: Unsolicited requests for funds not considered or acknowledged.
EIN: 741907673

2629
Walter M. Hughes Educational Trust
10 S. Dearborn IL1-0117
Chicago, IL 60603 (214) 965-2231
Application address: c/o JPMorgan Chase Bank, Attn: NCAA, 2200 Ross Ave., Dallas, TX 75201

Foundation type: Independent foundation
Purpose: Scholarships to aid and assist worthy young people of Muskingum County, OH for higher education.
Financial data: Year ended 12/31/2012. Assets, $1,023,224 (M); Expenditures, $60,068; Total giving, $47,000; Grants to individuals, 19 grants totaling $47,000 (high: $3,000, low: $1,500).
Fields of interest: Higher education.
Type of support: Scholarships—to individuals.
Application information: Applications accepted. Application form required.
  Initial approach: Letter
  Deadline(s): Mar. 30
  Additional information: Application must include parents and student income tax information.
EIN: 316024847

2630
Hutchison Foundation
P.O. Box 429
Fairfield, IL 62837-0429 (618) 842-2107
Contact: Dave Scarlett

Foundation type: Independent foundation
Purpose: Scholarships to graduating seniors of a Wayne County, IL area high school for postsecondary education at an accredited university, college or community college.
Financial data: Year ended 12/31/2012. Assets, $967,059 (M); Expenditures, $52,097; Total giving, $44,785; Grants to individuals, 13 grants totaling $9,900 (high: $1,250, low: $300).
Fields of interest: College (community/junior); College; University.
Type of support: Scholarships—to individuals; Undergraduate support.
Application information:
  Initial approach: Letter
  Applicants should submit the following:
    1) Letter(s) of recommendation
    2) Transcripts
    3) Financial information
    4) ACT
    5) GPA
  Additional information: Application should also include a list of activities, awards and goals. Students should contact their high school guidance counselor for application guidelines.
EIN: 364126011

2631
Hyatt Foundation
71 S. Wacker Dr., Ste. 4700
Chicago, IL 60606

Foundation type: Independent foundation
Purpose: Awards by nomination only to an individual for significant contribution to architecture.
Financial data: Year ended 12/31/2012. Assets, $17,630,437 (M); Expenditures, $1,635,823; Total giving, $0.
Fields of interest: Architecture.
Type of support: Awards/grants by nomination only; Awards/prizes.
Application information:
  Deadline(s): Nov. 1
  Additional information: Any licensed architect may submit a nomination by e-mail for consideration by the jury for the Prize.
Program description:
  The Pritzker Architecture Prize: The award consists of $100,000 (US) and a bronze medallion to a living architect whose built work demonstrates a combination of those qualities of talent, vision, and commitment, which has produced consistent and significant contributions to humanity and the built environment through the art of architecture. Nominations are accepted internationally from persons from diverse fields who have a knowledge of and interest in advancing great architecture. This prize is granted annually.
EIN: 362981565

2632
James Hynd and Nancy Johnson Trust
c/o Carlen Penfold
10 S. Dearborn
Chicago, IL 60603

Foundation type: Independent foundation
Purpose: Eyeglasses to financially needy residents of Boulder County, CO.
Financial data: Year ended 06/30/2012. Assets, $1,685,724 (M); Expenditures, $102,084; Total giving, $72,620.
Fields of interest: Optometry/vision screening; Disabilities, people with.
Type of support: Grants for special needs.
Application information: Applications not accepted.
  Additional information: Unsolicited requests for funds not considered or acknowledged.
EIN: 846022973

2633
Illinois Bar Foundation
20 S. Clark St., Ste. 910
Chicago, IL 60603-1898 (312) 726-6072
Contact: Lisa Corrao, Exec. Dir.
FAX: (312) 726-6073; URL: http://www.illinoisbar.org/ibf

Foundation type: Public charity
Purpose: Financial assistance to lawyers of the Illinois Bar with limited means who can no longer support themselves due to incapacity. Scholarships to law students for attendance at accredited colleges or universities in the Chicago, IL area.
Publications: Application guidelines; Annual report.
Financial data: Year ended 06/30/2011. Assets, $3,853,647 (M); Expenditures, $829,510; Total giving, $436,960; Grants to individuals, totaling $61,375.
Fields of interest: Law school/education; Economically disadvantaged.

Type of support: Scholarships—to individuals; Grants for special needs.
Application information: Contact the foundation for additional guidelines.
EIN: 370810222

2634
Illinois Broadcasters Association Minority Intern Program, Inc.
200 Missouri Ave.
Carterville, IL 62918

Foundation type: Independent foundation
Purpose: Educational support to students of color studying in colleges of communication at IL institutes of higher education.
Financial data: Year ended 12/31/2012. Assets, $1,680 (M); Expenditures, $18,488; Total giving, $14,263; Grants to individuals, 8 grants totaling $14,263 (high: $1,800, low: $1,663).
Fields of interest: Media/communications; Minorities.
Type of support: Scholarships—to individuals.
Application information:
  Initial approach: Letter or telephone
  Deadline(s): Contact college dean for application deadline
EIN: 371231448

2635
Illinois Conservation Foundation
1 Natural Resources Way
Springfield, IL 62702-1270 (217) 785-2003
Contact: Donna Ferguson, Admin. Asst.
FAX: (217) 785-8405; E-mail: dnr.icf@illinois.gov; URL: http://www.ilcf.org

Foundation type: Public charity
Purpose: Scholarships to outstanding high school seniors of IL, pursuing education in the natural resources field.
Financial data: Year ended 06/30/2012. Assets, $3,006,573 (M); Expenditures, $1,375,372; Total giving, $434,747; Grants to individuals, totaling $10,785.
Fields of interest: Higher education; Natural resources.
Type of support: Scholarships—to individuals.
Application information: Applications accepted. Application form required.
  Additional information: Applicants must demonstrate effective, voluntary, long-term dedication the the preservation, protection, enhancement and/or promotion of IL natural resources. Contact the foundation for additional guidelines.
EIN: 371340071

2636
Illinois Education Foundation
(also known as One Million Degrees)
226 W. Jackson Blvd., Ste. 426
Chicago, IL 60606-6959 (312) 920-9605
Contact: Robin Redmond, Exec. Dir.
FAX: (312) 920-9607;
E-mail: info@onemilliondegrees.org; URL: http://www.onemilliondegrees.org/

Foundation type: Public charity
Purpose: Scholarships to low-income high potential Illinois community college students.
Financial data: Year ended 06/30/2012. Assets, $1,672,577 (M); Expenditures, $1,271,899; Total giving, $549,199; Grants to individuals, totaling $549,199.

Fields of interest: College (community/junior).
Type of support: Scholarships—to individuals.
Application information: Applications accepted.
Application form required.
Additional information: See web site for additional application guidelines.
EIN: 421710230

2637

Illinois High School Activities Foundation

2715 McGraw Dr.
Bloomington, IL 61704-2715
URL: http://www.ihsa.org/

Foundation type: Company-sponsored foundation
Purpose: Scholarships to IL high school students selected to the Illinois High School Association's "All-State Academic Team"
Financial data: Year ended 12/31/2012. Assets, $118,545 (M); Expenditures, $44,264; Total giving, $26,000; Grants to individuals, 26 grants totaling $26,000 (high: $1,000, low: $1,000).
Fields of interest: Higher education.
Type of support: Precollege support; Undergraduate support.
Application information: Application form required.
Initial approach: Letter or telephone
Additional information: Application should include two letters of recommendation. Selection is based on academic achievement, participation in high school athletics and community service. Individuals must be nominated to the All-State Academic Team by their high schools.
EIN: 371322645

2638

Illinois Historic Preservation Agency Trust

Old State Capitol Plz.
Springfield, IL 62701-1507 (217) 785-9045
Contact: Catherine Shannon, Exec. Dir.

Foundation type: Public charity
Purpose: Scholarships to Ph.D. candidates studying historic or library science, primarily in IL.
Financial data: Year ended 06/30/2012. Assets, $2,371,713 (M); Expenditures, $204,550; Total giving, $89,690; Grants to individuals, totaling $2,980.
Fields of interest: Historic preservation/historical societies; Libraries/library science.
Type of support: Doctoral support.
Application information: Applications not accepted.
EIN: 376332661

2639

Illinois Hospital Research and Educational Foundation

1151 E. Warrenville Rd.
P.O. Box 3015
Naperville, IL 60566-9339 (630) 276-5400

Foundation type: Public charity
Purpose: Scholarships to Illinois residents pursuing a degree in health care.
Financial data: Year ended 12/31/2012. Assets, $1,754,876 (M); Expenditures, $1,973,767; Total giving, $1,467,611; Grants to individuals, totaling $27,000.
Fields of interest: Health sciences school/education.
Type of support: Scholarships—to individuals.

Application information: Applications accepted.
Application form required.
Deadline(s): Apr. 15
Additional information: Contact the foundation for additional application guidelines.
Program description:
Scholarship Program: The scholarship is a $1,000 award for tuition, fees, or books to students attending accredited colleges or universities pursuing a hospital-related health care professional curriculum. Scholarships are awarded based on the student's scholastic achievement, financial need and availability of funds. Applicant must have a 3.5 GPA (on a 4.0 scale)
EIN: 237421930

2640

Illinois Lumber and Material Dealers Association Educational Foundation, Inc.

932 S. Spring St.
Springfield, IL 62704-2725 (217) 544-5405

Foundation type: Independent foundation
Purpose: Scholarships to full time building trades students who are residents of Illinois, enrolled in a certificate or degree program in an accredited trade school, two year junior college or four year college or university.
Financial data: Year ended 12/31/2012. Assets, $39,557 (M); Expenditures, $14,187; Total giving, $6,750; Grants to individuals, 8 grants totaling $6,750 (high: $1,000, low: $500).
Fields of interest: Vocational education, post-secondary; College (community/junior); University.
Type of support: Scholarships—to individuals.
Application information: Applications accepted.
Application form required.
Send request by: Mail
Deadline(s): Apr. 1
Applicants should submit the following:
1) Transcripts
2) Letter(s) of recommendation
Additional information: Applications are available from the foundation.
Program description:
Scholarship Program: Scholarships to selected students to pursue industry-related course work at colleges or universities. The scholarship will assist and encourage qualified students further or continue their interest in selecting the lumber and building materials field as a career. Scholarship will be no less than $500 and not more than $2,000. Students may apply each year for up to four years.
EIN: 371293998

2641

Illinois Network of Child Care Resource and Referral Agencies

1226 Towanda Plz.
Bloomington, IL 61701 (309) 829-5327
FAX: (309) 828-1808; E-mail: inccrra@inccrra.org;
Toll-free tel.: (866)-697-8278; URL: http://www.inccrra.org/

Foundation type: Public charity
Purpose: Scholarship for eligible practitioners working in Early Care and Education (ECE) or school-age care programs in IL.
Financial data: Year ended 06/30/2012. Assets, $1,961,680 (M); Expenditures, $13,870,353; Total giving, $8,000,125; Grants to individuals, 5,085 grants totaling $8,000,125.
Fields of interest: Early childhood education.

Type of support: Undergraduate support.
Application information:
Initial approach: Letter or tel.
Deadline(s): The Gateways Scholarship Program accepts applications year round.
Applicants should submit the following:
1) Transcripts
Additional information: The application is available at www.ilgateways.com or call 866-697-8278.
EIN: 364096312

2642

Illinois P.E.O. Home Fund, Inc.

305 W. Thomas St.
Wyoming, IL 61491-1231 (309) 695-3050
Contact: Karen Steward, Pres.

Foundation type: Public charity
Purpose: Direct financial assistance to elderly women in need who reside in IL, particularly for housing expenses.
Financial data: Year ended 03/31/2012. Assets, $1,670,633 (M); Expenditures, $119,999; Total giving, $87,500; Grants to individuals, totaling $87,500.
Fields of interest: Housing/shelter, aging; Human services; Aging; Women; Economically disadvantaged.
Type of support: Grants for special needs.
Application information:
Initial approach: Letter
Additional information: Contact foundation for further eligibility criteria.
EIN: 370697158

2643

Illinois Real Estate Educational Foundation

522 S. 5th St.
Springfield, IL 62701-1822 (866) 854-7333
Contact: Laurie Clayton, Fdn. Mgr.
FAX: (217) 529-5893; E-mail: lclayton@iar.org;
Mailing address: P.O. Box 2607, Springfield, IL 62708; URL: http://www.ilreef.org

Foundation type: Public charity
Purpose: Scholarships to qualified students of Illinois pursuing a degree in the real estate industry.
Publications: Application guidelines; Informational brochure (including application guidelines).
Financial data: Year ended 12/31/2012. Assets, $1,504,407 (M); Expenditures, $218,219; Total giving, $47,745; Grants to individuals, totaling $35,245.
Fields of interest: Business school/education.
Type of support: Scholarships—to individuals.
Application information: Applications accepted.
Application form required.
Deadline(s): Vary
Additional information: See web site for requirements and criteria of various scholarships.
EIN: 237289227

2644
Illinois State Dental Society Foundation
(formerly Paul W. Clopper Memorial Foundation)
206 S. 6th St.
P. O. Box 217
Springfield, IL 62705 (217) 753-1190
Contact: Dr. Keith W. Dickey, Pres.
E-mail: foundation@isds.org; Toll-Free Tel.: (800)
475-4737; URL: http://www.isds.org/
isdsfoundation/

Foundation type: Public charity
Purpose: Financial aid to IL dental students.
Financial data: Year ended 12/31/2012. Assets,
$1,550,289 (M); Expenditures, $1,704,013; Total
giving, $58,573; Grants to individuals, totaling
$58,573.
Fields of interest: Dental school/education.
Type of support: Doctoral support.
Application information:
  Initial approach: Letter
  Additional information: Contact foundation for
    eligibility criteria.
EIN: 237244932

2645
The Illinois State Historical Society
P.O. Box 1800
Springfield, IL 62705-1800 (217) 525-2781
Contact: William Furry, Exec. Dir.
FAX: (217) 525-2783;
E-mail: wfurry@historyillinois.org; URL: http://
www.historyillinois.org

Foundation type: Public charity
Purpose: Awards to Ph.D. students for research in
some part of IL history. Awards to teachers for
contributions to the study and teaching of IL state
and local history. A scholarship to the winner of an
Abraham Lincoln research paper contest open to IL
high school students.
Publications: Application guidelines; Informational
brochure; Newsletter; Occasional report.
Financial data: Year ended 12/31/2012. Assets,
$2,910,303 (M); Expenditures, $377,367; Total
giving, $9,455; Grants to individuals, totaling
$9,455.
Fields of interest: History/archaeology; Historical
activities.
Type of support: Research; Scholarships—to
individuals; Awards/prizes.
Application information: Applications accepted.
Application form required.
  Initial approach: Letter or telephone
  Deadline(s): Varies
  Applicants should submit the following:
    1) Letter(s) of recommendation
    2) Curriculum vitae
Program descriptions:
  King V. Hostick Scholarship: Awarded in
conjunction with the Illinois Historic Preservation
Agency, stipends of up to $3,000 are available to
provide financial assistance to graduate students
of history and library science who are writing
dissertations dealing with Illinois. Eligible
applicants must be enrolled in a recognized
graduate history or library science degree program
at an accredited institution; preference will be given
to research proposals utilizing the Illinois State
Historical Library.
  Olive Foster Outstanding Teacher Award: This
$500 award honors an outstanding Illinois full-time
teacher for his/her contributions to the study and
teaching of state and local history. Three awards
will be given annually, one each to teachers at the
elementary, middle/junior high, and high school
level.

Verna Ross Orndorff Scholarship: This $1,000
scholarship will be made available to an Illinois high
school student who writes an outstanding essay on
Abraham Lincoln or a significant event in the Civil
War period in Illinois. Entries should be between
1,000 and 1,500 words.
EIN: 370767410

2646
Illinois State University Foundation
101 Alumni Ctr., Campus Box 8000
Normal, IL 61790-0001 (309) 438-8901
URL: http://advancement.illinoisstate.edu/
isu-foundation/

Foundation type: Public charity
Purpose: Student scholarships, professorships,
and research for students of Illinois State
University.
Publications: Annual report.
Financial data: Year ended 06/30/2012. Assets,
$108,119,320 (M); Expenditures, $10,003,829;
Total giving, $7,767,521; Grants to individuals,
totaling $2,366,570.
Fields of interest: Education.
Type of support: Support to graduates or students
of specific schools.
Application information:
  Initial approach: Letter
  Additional information: Contact foundation for
    eligibility criteria.
EIN: 376025713

2647
Illinois Telecommunications Access Corporation
3001 Montvale Dr., Ste. D
Springfield, IL 62704-5377 (217) 698-4170
FAX: (217) 698-0942; Toll-free tel./TTY: (800)
841-6167; URL: http://www.itactty.org

Foundation type: Public charity
Purpose: Giving limited to deaf, hard-of-hearing
individuals, and speech-disabled individuals living
in IL and who have a working land-line telephone
service.
Publications: Application guidelines.
Financial data: Year ended 12/31/2012. Assets,
$3,633,592 (M); Expenditures, $4,832,980; Total
giving, $3,651,758; Grants to individuals, totaling
$3,651,758.
Fields of interest: Telecommunications; Blind/
visually impaired; Deaf/hearing impaired.
Type of support: In-kind gifts.
Application information: Applications accepted.
Application form available on the grantmaker's web
site.
  Initial approach: Submit application
  Deadline(s): None
Program descriptions:
  Loan Program: Braille phones, TTYs, and CapTel
services are available to qualified individuals. The
program covers repair and exchange services under
circumstances of normal wear and tear; any
damage to equipment deemed to be "user abuse"
is charged back to the user. Applicants must be a
legal resident of the state of Illinois, have a working
land line in their residence, and be certified by a
physician, audiologist, speech pathologist, or DHS/
DRS counselor. There are no age or income
restrictions.
  Voucher Program: Vouchers are available for
amplified telephones and TTYs, in which the user
owns and is responsible for upkeep of equipment.
Participants in good standing are eligible for a new
voucher every four years. Applicants must be a legal

resident of the state of Illinois, have a working land
line in their residence, and be certified by a
physician, audiologist, speech pathologist, or DHS/
DRS counselor. There are no age or income
restrictions.
EIN: 363591867

2648
Illinois Valley Educational Foundation Inc.
79 W. Monroe St., Ste. 1119
Chicago, IL 60603-4950

Foundation type: Independent foundation
Purpose: Scholarships to financially needy
students attending LaSalle Catholic Schools in
LaSalle, IL for payment of tuition.
Financial data: Year ended 10/31/2012. Assets,
$5,385 (M); Expenditures, $25,107; Total giving,
$25,000.
Fields of interest: Education.
Type of support: Scholarships—to individuals;
Support to graduates or students of specific
schools.
Application information: Applications accepted.
Application form required.
  Additional information: Applications are
    distributed through the school. Contact your
    guidance counselor for application
    information.
EIN: 364120388

2649
The Inner Voice, Inc.
567 W. Lake St., Ste 1150
Chicago, IL 60612-2521 (312) 994-5830
Contact: Jackie Edens, Exec. Dir.
FAX: (312) 994-8351;
E-mail: info@innervoicechicago.org; E-mail For
Jackie Edens: jedens@innervoicechicago.org;
URL: http://www.innervoicechicago.org

Foundation type: Public charity
Purpose: Emergency assistance to low income
individuals and families in the Chicago, IL area with
food, clothing, shelter, transportation and other
special needs.
Financial data: Year ended 06/30/2013. Assets,
$1,436,357 (M); Expenditures, $2,225,568.
Fields of interest: Economically disadvantaged.
Type of support: Grants for special needs.
Application information: Payments are made on
behalf of clients, no money is provided directly to
the clients.
EIN: 363298143

2650
The International Foundation for Ethical Research
53 W. Jackson Blvd., Ste. 1552
Chicago, IL 60604-3782 (312) 427-6025
FAX: (312) 427-6524; E-mail: ifer@navs.org;
URL: http://www.ifer.org

Foundation type: Public charity
Purpose: Fellowships to graduate students that
integrate animal ethics into their research, and/or
promote alternatives to the use of animals in
research, testing, and/or education.
Publications: Application guidelines.
Financial data: Year ended 12/31/2011. Assets,
$106,524 (M); Expenditures, $71,663; Total
giving, $2,500. Grants to individuals amount not
specified.
Fields of interest: Science.
Type of support: Fellowships.

Application information: Applications accepted. Application form available on the grantmaker's web site.

Initial approach: Application

Deadline(s): Mar. 30 for pre-proposal and Aug. 15 for full proposals

Final notification: Recipients notified Oct. 15

Applicants should submit the following:
1) Proposal
2) Curriculum vitae

Additional information: Only applicants with pre-proposals of interest to the foundation will be asked to submit full proposals.

Program description:

Graduate Fellowships for Alternatives to the Use of Animals in Science: This program provides financial incentives of up to $12,500 in stipend support, and up to $2,500 for supplies to graduate students in science that encourage them at the earliest stages of their career to integrate innovation and discovery with ethics and respect for animals. Fellowships are awarded to those candidates whose program of study shows the greatest potential to replace the use of animals and sciences. Proposals should consider how they advance the development of alternatives to the use of animals in research, testing, and/or education, and how they provide training that integrates innovation and discovery with ethics and respect for animals. Fellowships are open to students enrolled in master's and Ph.D. programs in the sciences, and human and veterinary medicine. Fellowships will also be considered for graduate students in other fields, such as education, psychology, humanities, journalism, and the law, for projects that show promise to increase public awareness or to promote changes in the legal system or public policy regarding the use of animals in research, testing, and education.

EIN: 222628153

2651
International Society for Stem Cell Research

(also known as ISSCR)
5215 Old Orchard Rd., Ste. 270
Skokie, IL 60077   (224) 592-5700
Contact: Nancy Witty, Exec. Dir. and C.E.O.
FAX: (224) 365-0004; E-mail: isscr@isscr.org;
E-Mail for Nancy Witty: nwitty@isscr.org;
URL: http://www.isscr.org

Foundation type: Public charity
Purpose: Awards by nomination to investigators for stem cell research.
Publications: Annual report; Newsletter.
Financial data: Year ended 12/31/2011. Assets, $4,125,012 (M); Expenditures, $3,327,536; Total giving, $217,478; Grants to individuals, totaling $18,311.
Fields of interest: Genetic diseases and disorders research; Medical research.
Type of support: Awards/grants by nomination only; Awards/prizes.
Application information: Nomination should include a copy of nominee's CV(s) and listing of up to five of their most relevant publications must also accompany the nomination letter, a statement of up to 100 words highlighting the innovation for which the nominee(s) are being nominated, and an overview of the contributions of the nominee(s) to the field of stem cell research.
EIN: 364491158

2652
The International Society for Traumatic Stress Studies

c/o Sherwood Group
111 Deer Lake Rd., Ste. 100
Deerfield, IL 60015-4943   (847) 480-9028
Contact: Rick Koepke, Exec. Dir.
FAX: (847) 480-9282; E-mail: istss@istss.org;
E-Mail for Rick Koepke : rkoepke@istss.org;
URL: http://www.istss.org

Foundation type: Public charity
Purpose: Grants and awards by nomination to professionals who want to apply knowledge of emotional trauma to improving coverage of violent events.
Publications: Grants list.
Financial data: Year ended 12/31/2012. Assets, $702,419 (M); Expenditures, $1,317,725; Total giving, $5,000; Grants to individuals, totaling $2,000.
Fields of interest: Stress.
Type of support: Travel awards; Awards/prizes.
Application information:

Initial approach: Letter

Deadline(s): June 1

Additional information: See web site for additional guidelines.

Program descriptions:

Chaim Danieli Young Professional Award: This award recognizes excellence in traumatic stress service or research by an individual who has completed his or her training within the last five years.

Frank Ochberg Award for Media and Trauma Study: This award recognizes significant contributions by clinicians and researchers on the relationship of media and trauma.

Lifetime Achievement Award: The award is the highest honor given by ISTSS and is awarded to the individual who has made great lifetime contributions to the field of traumatic stress.

Public Advocacy Award: This award is given for outstanding and fundamental contributions to advancing social understanding of trauma.

Robert S. Laufer Award for Outstanding Scientific Achievement: This award is given to an individual or group who has made an outstanding contribution to research in the field of traumatic stress.

Sarah Haley Memorial Award for Clinical Excellence: This award is given to a clinician or group of clinicians in direct service to traumatized individuals. This written and/or verbal communication to the field must exemplify the work of Sarah Haley.

Student Research Award: This award is presented to Student Members of the society who submit proposals judged to have the greatest potential to contribute to the field of traumatic stress.

Travel Grants: The grant supports conference attendees coming from developing countries and experiencing financial hardship with fees or travel costs. Priority is given to those from developing countries who have not received a travel grant in the past and who will be making a presentation at the ISTSS conference. They are chosen for being in a position to contribute to and influence traumatic stress study and treatment in their own countries.
EIN: 311129675

2653
Rathke, Edward Irrevocable Scholarship Trust

111 W Monroe St. Tax Div. 10C
Chicago, IL 60603   (312) 461-5154
Contact: Hector Ahumada

Foundation type: Independent foundation
Purpose: Scholarships to high school seniors attending schools in Brown and Oconto counties, WI.
Financial data: Year ended 12/31/2012. Assets, $17,714 (M); Expenditures, $12,572; Total giving, $9,000; Grants to individuals, 18 grants totaling $9,000 (high: $500, average grant: $500).
Type of support: Support to graduates or students of specific schools; Undergraduate support.
Application information: Applications accepted. Application form required.

Deadline(s): Apr. 1

Additional information: Application must include name of school and applicant's and parents' financial information.

EIN: 510187617

2654
Tiffany Irwin Scholarship Foundation

522 Waikiki Dr.
Des Plaines, IL 60016-1167

Foundation type: Independent foundation
Purpose: Scholarships to Iowa residents in pursuit of a higher education.
Financial data: Year ended 12/31/2012. Assets, $87,643 (M); Expenditures, $999; Total giving, $0.
Fields of interest: Higher education.
Type of support: Scholarships—to individuals.
Application information: Applications accepted.

Additional information: Contact foundation for application guidelines.

EIN: 364166962

2655
Genelle V. Jackson Education Trust

c/o Citizens National Bank
P.O. Box 100
Albion, IL 62806-0100

Foundation type: Independent foundation
Purpose: Scholarships to residents of Albion, IL for higher education.
Financial data: Year ended 12/31/2011. Assets, $396,817 (M); Expenditures, $20,851; Total giving, $17,300; Grants to individuals, 5 grants totaling $17,300 (high: $4,300, low: $2,500).
Fields of interest: Higher education.
Type of support: Undergraduate support.
Application information: Applications not accepted.

Additional information: Unsolicited requests for funds not considered or acknowledged.

EIN: 376305146

2656
Bruce & Nellie M. Jackson Memorial Fund

100 W. Elm St.
P.O. Box 310
Canton, IL 61520   (309) 647-1820
Application address: Canton High School,1001 N. Main St., Canton,IL 61520

Foundation type: Independent foundation
Purpose: Scholarships to graduates of Canton High School, IL to pursue a four year graduate course of study at accredited colleges or universities.

Financial data: Year ended 12/31/2012. Assets, $333,972 (M); Expenditures, $16,225; Total giving, $13,000; Grants to individuals, 10 grants totaling $13,000 (high: $4,000, low: $1,000).
Fields of interest: Higher education.
Type of support: Support to graduates or students of specific schools.
Application information: Applications accepted. Application form required.
   Additional information: Applications are available at Canton Union School District #66.
EIN: 364529465

2657
Jewish Federation of Metropolitan Chicago

30 S. Wells St.
Chicago, IL   60606-5054   (312) 346-6700
Contact: Steven B. Nasatir P.h.D., Pres.
E-mail: website@juf.org; URL: http://www.juf.org

Foundation type: Public charity
Purpose: Scholarships and low interest educational loans to full time Jewish residents of the metropolitan Chicago, IL area.
Publications: Application guidelines; Annual report.
Financial data: Year ended 06/30/2012. Assets, $763,346,248 (M); Expenditures, $97,443,175; Total giving, $91,215,500; Grants to individuals, totaling $259,154.
Fields of interest: Higher education.
Type of support: Scholarships—to individuals; Student loans—to individuals.
Application information: Applications accepted. Application form required. Application form available on the grantmaker's web site.
   Send request by: Mail
   Deadline(s): Nov. 1 (Winter and Spring) and Mar. 1 (Summer and Fall) for CCIP High School Scholarship; Nov. 1 (Winter and Spring) and Mar. 15 (Summer and Fall) for college Student/Young Adult Scholarship; Mar. 1 for Merit Scholarship
   Final notification: Recipients notified by the end of Dec. for CCIP High School Scholarship and College Student/Young Adult Scholarship (Winter and Spring)
   Applicants should submit the following:
   1) Transcripts
   2) Letter(s) of recommendation
   3) Essay
   Additional information: Applicants must demonstrate financial need and leadership abilities.
Program descriptions:
   CCIP High School Scholarship Program: Awarded in conjunction with the Naftali Steinfeld Memorial Scholarship Fund, this program offers scholarships (based on financial need) for high school students participating in approved Israel Experience programs. Scholarships are intended to help develop Jewish identity and nourish greater understanding and commitment to Israel and the Chicago Jewish community. Eligible applicants must: be enrolled in grades 10, 11, or 12 (and can include graduating seniors who are going on a post-high school program); demonstrate financial need; have applied to, or be in the process of applying to, a federation-approved Israel Experience program; and be committed to participating in communal Jewish activities after returning from Israel.
   College Student/Young Adult Scholarship Program: Awarded in conjunction with the Joseph A. Hochberg Scholarship Fund, this program provides need-based scholarships for college students and young adults (up to 28 years old) who participate in

an approved Israel Experience program. Scholarships are intended to encourage the development of Jewish identity and nourish greater commitment to Israel and the Chicago Jewish community. Eligible applicants must: demonstrate financial need; reside or attend school in metropolitan Chicago; have already graduated from high school at the time of application; be between the ages of 17 and 28; have applied to, or be in the process of applying to, an approved Israel Experience program; and be committed to participating in communal Jewish activities after returning from Israel.
   Ehrlich Student Loan Program: This program works to subsidize loans to Jewish residents of the metropolitan Chicago area, who are full-time students pursuing undergraduate or graduate education at an accredited college or university within the U.S. Eligible recipients can borrow up to $5,000 per year for up to four years, and can qualify for low-interest rates upon repayment.
   Merit Scholarship Program: A limited number of scholarships (of up to $1,000 each) are available annually to high school, college, and graduate students (to age 23) who demonstrate significant leadership skills. Eligible applicants must: be enrolled in either grades 10, 11, or 12, or be no older than 23 years old and enrolled in a college or graduate program; reside in, or attend school in, metropolitan Chicago; have applied to, or be in the process of applying to, an approved Israel Experience program; demonstrate leadership abilities; and be committed to participating in communal Jewish activities after returning from Israel.
EIN: 362167761

2658
Jewish Vocational Service and Employment Center

216 W. Jackson Blvd., Ste. 700
Chicago, IL   60606-6921   (312) 673-3400
Contact: Howard Sitron, Exec. Dir.
FAX: (312) 553-5544; E-mail: info@jvschicago.org; Toll-free tel.: (877) 412-1737; URL: http://www.jvschicago.org

Foundation type: Public charity
Purpose: Scholarships to full-time students who are Jewish, to attend Jewish colleges or universities. Assistance to occupationally disadvantaged residents of metropolitan Chicago, IL, with housing costs, transportation, wages and other needs.
Publications: Application guidelines.
Financial data: Year ended 06/30/2012. Assets, $9,867,971 (M); Expenditures, $14,902,266; Total giving, $4,738,459; Grants to individuals, totaling $4,738,459.
Fields of interest: Higher education; Human services.
Type of support: Scholarships—to individuals; Grants for special needs.
Application information: Applications accepted. Application form required. Application form available on the grantmaker's web site.
   Initial approach: Telephone or email
   Deadline(s): Feb. 15
   Applicants should submit the following:
   1) Transcripts
   2) Budget Information
   Additional information: Application must also include two letters of reference, 1040 income tax form, applicant must demonstrate financial need, and interview required for scholarship.

Program descriptions:
   Illinois SBDC Duman Entrepreneurship Center Loan Program: This program offers entrepreneurial training, business assistance, mentoring, and access to capital to start-ups and pre-existing small business in the Chicago metropolitan area. Under this program, businesses are eligible for zero and low-interest loans (for anywhere from one to three years), and micro-loan amounts of up to $15,000. Eligible applicants include start-ups and small business expansions, entrepreneurs who cannot qualify for traditional bank financing, and residents of the Chicago metropolitan area.
   Jewish Federation Academic Scholarship Program: Scholarships are available to full-time college and graduate students of Jewish descent who live in the metropolitan Chicago area. Eligible applicants will be identified having promise for significant contributions in their chosen careers. Priority will be given to those with demonstrated financial need, as well as those who are pursuing careers in the helping professions. Eligible applicants must: be born and raised in either Cook County, the Chicago metropolitan area (including DuPage, Kane, Make, McHenry, and Will counties), or northwest Indiana (Lake County); intend to remain in the Chicago metropolitan area after completing school; and must be entering their junior or senior year (if an undergraduate) of an accredited professional education program on a full-time basis.
EIN: 362167762

2659
Ethan Allen and Caroline H. Johnson Educational Trust

c/o Soy Capital Bank & Trust Co.
455 N. Main St.
Decatur, IL   62523-1103   (217) 429-8714

Foundation type: Independent foundation
Purpose: Scholarships to residents of Kankakee County, IL, who are under the age of 22.
Financial data: Year ended 12/31/2012. Assets, $983,697 (M); Expenditures, $134,107; Total giving, $99,000.
Type of support: Scholarships—to individuals.
Application information: Applications accepted. Application form required.
   Deadline(s): Contact trust for current application deadline.
   Applicants should submit the following:
   1) SAT
   2) ACT
EIN: 363467018

2660
Joint Civic Committee of Italian Americans

3800 W. Division St.
Stone Park, IL   60165-1115   (708) 450-9050
Contact: Jo Ann Serpico, Exec. Dir.
URL: http://www.jccia.com

Foundation type: Public charity
Purpose: Scholarships to students of Italian heritage in the Chicago, IL metropolitan area.
Publications: Application guidelines.
Financial data: Year ended 12/31/2012. Assets, $267,267 (M); Expenditures, $119,389; Total giving, $44,961; Grants to individuals, totaling $16,743.
Fields of interest: Media/communications; Higher education; Journalism school/education; Women; Men.
Type of support: Scholarships—to individuals.

Application information: Applications accepted. Application form required. Application form available on the grantmaker's web site.

> *Send request by:* Mail
> *Deadline(s):* Apr. 1 for Women's Division Scholarship, Apr. 19 for John Fischetti Scholarship, May 18 for Joseph Cardinal Bernardin Scholarship
> *Applicants should submit the following:*
> 1) ACT
> 2) Photograph
> 3) SAT
> 4) Letter(s) of recommendation
> 5) Essay
> 6) Transcripts

Program descriptions:

John Fischetti Scholarship: Scholarships of $2,000 each are available to male students of Italian ancestry who are majoring in journalism or media communications. Applicants must reside in the Chicago metropolitan area.

Joseph Cardinal Bernardin Scholarship: Scholarships of $2,000 each are available to male students already enrolled in an accredited college or university, or who has been accepted for enrollment by an accredited college or university. Eligible applicants must be 50 percent Italian, is a resident of Chicago's metropolitan area, and must have a GPA of 3.75 or higher.

Women's Division Scholarship: Scholarships of $2,000 each are available to graduating female high school seniors enrolled full-time at a two- or four-year accredited college or university, or at an accredited vocational or technical school. Eligible applicants must be a resident of Illinois, have at least one parent of Italian descent, and have a minimum cumulative GPA of 3.0 on a 4.0 scale.

EIN: 362550020

2661
Thomas B. Jones & Grace Stevenson Jones Charitable Foundation

230 W. State St., MSC M-300
Sycamore, IL 60178-1419 (815) 754-7711

Foundation type: Independent foundation
Purpose: Scholarships to residents of Grant, Iowa, and Lafayette counties in WI, who are attending four-year colleges or universities.
Financial data: Year ended 12/31/2012. Assets, $1,396,896 (M); Expenditures, $94,257; Total giving, $72,050; Grants to individuals, 40 grants totaling $72,050 (high: $2,500, low: $1,250).
Fields of interest: Higher education.
Type of support: Scholarships—to individuals.
Application information: Application form required.

> *Deadline(s):* Mar. 1

EIN: 363470630

2662
Dan and Pat Jorndt Amundsen High School Learning Foundation, Inc.

104 Wilmot Rd., 3rd Fl., Ste. 1434
Deerfield, IL 60015-5121

Foundation type: Independent foundation
Purpose: Scholarships to graduating students and grants to teachers and administrators of Amundsen High School, Chicago, IL.
Financial data: Year ended 12/31/2012. Assets, $139,234 (M); Expenditures, $104,249; Total giving, $103,500; Grants to individuals, 5 grants totaling $103,500 (high: $12,000, low: $2,500).
Fields of interest: Higher education.
Type of support: Grants to individuals; Scholarships—to individuals.

Application information: Applications not accepted.

> *Additional information:* Unsolicited requests for funding not considered or acknowledged.

EIN: 364332401

2663
Journalism Foundation of Metropolitan St. Louis

c/o Bank of America, N.A.
231 S. LaSalle St., IL1-231-10-05
Chicago, IL 60697 (214) 209-0726
Contact: Paige Kendrick
Application address: 411 N. Akard St., Dallas, Tx 75201-3307

Foundation type: Independent foundation
Purpose: Scholarships to students of St. Louis, MO who are majoring in journalism.
Financial data: Year ended 12/31/2012. Assets, $0 (M); Expenditures, $33,522; Total giving, $29,318.
Fields of interest: Print publishing.
Type of support: Scholarships—to individuals.
Application information: Applications accepted.

> *Initial approach:* Letter
> *Deadline(s):* None

EIN: 436121179

2664
F. Ward Just Foundation

(also known as F. Ward Just Scholarship Foundation)
2508 Walnut St.
Waukegan, IL 60087-3123 (847) 623-0411
Contact: Fred Woldt, V.P.

Foundation type: Independent foundation
Purpose: Scholarships to Lake County, IL, high school graduates pursuing an undergraduate degree in journalism or media communications.
Financial data: Year ended 08/31/2013. Assets, $185,692 (M); Expenditures, $28,995; Total giving, $20,000; Grants to individuals, 5 grants totaling $20,000 (high: $5,000, low: $2,500).
Fields of interest: Media/communications; Journalism school/education.
Type of support: Support to graduates or students of specific schools; Undergraduate support.
Application information: Application form required.

> *Deadline(s):* Apr. 15
> *Applicants should submit the following:*
> 1) Transcripts
> 2) Letter(s) of recommendation
> 3) Financial information
> *Additional information:* Application should also include a copy of family income tax return. Applicant must demonstrate financial need.

EIN: 366162896

2665
Juvenile Protective Association

1707 N. Halsted St.
Chicago, IL 60614-5501 (312) 440-1203
FAX: (312) 698-6931; E-mail: sbudde@juvenile.org;
URL: http://www.juvenile.org

Foundation type: Public charity
Purpose: Special assistance to Chicago-based families of children whose social and emotional well-being, or whose physical safety are in jeopardy.
Publications: Newsletter.
Financial data: Year ended 06/30/2012. Assets, $2,245,075 (M); Expenditures, $1,783,059; Total

giving, $8,467; Grants to individuals, 106 grants totaling $8,467.
Fields of interest: Children/youth.
Type of support: Grants for special needs.
Application information: Applications accepted.

> *Initial approach:* Letter
> *Additional information:* Contact the association for eligibility requirements.

EIN: 362167765

2666
Stephen Douglas Kander Scholarship Fund

(formerly Stephen D. Kander Scholarship Fund)
10 S. Dearborn IL1-0117
Chicago, IL 60603 (920) 448-2092

Foundation type: Independent foundation
Purpose: Scholarships to graduates of Luxembourg-Casco High School and Green Bay East High School, WI, who are math, science, or education majors and show academic promise and/or financial need.
Financial data: Year ended 07/31/2012. Assets, $234,934 (M); Expenditures, $13,697; Total giving, $10,690; Grants to individuals, 14 grants totaling $10,690 (high: $1,335, low: $535).
Fields of interest: Teacher school/education; Education; Science; Mathematics.
Type of support: Support to graduates or students of specific schools; Undergraduate support.
Application information: Applications accepted. Application form required.

> *Deadline(s):* Mar. 31

EIN: 396631861

2667
Kankakee County Community Services, Inc.

657 E. Court St., Ste. 207
Kankakee, IL 60901-4055 (815) 933-7883
Contact: Vincent E. Clark, Exec. Dir.
FAX: (815) 933-0635; URL: http://www.kccsi-cap.org

Foundation type: Public charity
Purpose: Assistance to low income individuals and families of Kankakee county, IL to help with utility, housing, emergency food and shelter. Scholarships to low income, at risk individuals of high-academic attainment or potential to attend a college of their choice in IL.
Publications: Annual report.
Financial data: Year ended 12/31/2011. Assets, $1,261,554 (M); Expenditures, $4,373,080; Total giving, $2,881,500; Grants to individuals, totaling $2,881,500.
Fields of interest: Higher education; Minorities; Economically disadvantaged.
Type of support: Scholarships—to individuals; Grants for special needs.
Application information: Applications accepted. Application form required.

> *Additional information:* Students applying for scholarships, preference is given to applicants of racial or ethnic minorities. Contact the agency for guidelines for other programs.

EIN: 363478633

2668
The Karnes Memorial Fund
c/o Bluestem National Bank
606 W. Oak St.
P.O. Box 288
Fairbury, IL 61739 (815) 692-2302

Foundation type: Independent foundation
Purpose: Scholarships to graduates of Prairie Central Community Unit District 8, who are residents of Fairbury, Forrest, and Chatsworth, IL.
Financial data: Year ended 12/31/2012. Assets, $2,212,311 (M); Expenditures, $164,682; Total giving, $86,890; Grants to individuals, 69 grants totaling $86,890 (high: $2,260, low: $400).
Type of support: Support to graduates or students of specific schools; Undergraduate support.
Application information: Application form required.
> *Deadline(s):* Mar. 1
> *Additional information:* Applicants must submit parental financial analysis, general background information, and school and community activities.
EIN: 376243213

2669
Kaufman & Coffman Scholarship Fund
10 S. Dearborn, IL1-0117
Chicago, IL 60603

Foundation type: Independent foundation
Purpose: Scholarships to residents of the Louisville, KY, area who began the first year of higher education after age 30.
Financial data: Year ended 12/31/2012. Assets, $752,445 (M); Expenditures, $38,947; Total giving, $35,500; Grants to individuals, 5 grants totaling $35,500 (high: $7,100, low: $7,100).
Type of support: Undergraduate support.
Application information: Applications accepted.
EIN: 616252774

2670
The Kilts Foundation
(also known as The Kilts Foundation: Alverda & Edwards Kilts)
P.O. Box 339
Somonauk, IL 60552-0339 (815) 498-3429
Contact: Tonya Weakley

Foundation type: Independent foundation
Purpose: Scholarships primarily to residents of Kendall County, IL.
Financial data: Year ended 12/31/2011. Assets, $305,507 (M); Expenditures, $26,571; Total giving, $17,850; Grants to individuals, 27 grants totaling $17,850 (high: $750, low: $250).
Type of support: Scholarships—to individuals.
Application information: Application form required.
> *Additional information:* Contact foundation for application guidelines.
EIN: 363815138

2671
Kiwanis Charities of Rockford, Inc.
P.O. Box 1573
Rockford, IL 61110-0073 (815) 229-5864
Contact: for Scholarships: Phil Davidson
Application address: Kiwanis YES Award Committee, 5486 Ponderosa Dr., Rockford IL 61107-1666, tel.: (815) 654-0844,
e-mail: phdav0802@yahoo.com
URL: http://kiwanisclubofrockford.com/public/pub_page.aspx?PageID=21030

Foundation type: Public charity
Purpose: Scholarships to graduating seniors of Rockford High School, IL for continuing their education at accredited colleges or universities.
Publications: Application guidelines; Newsletter.
Financial data: Year ended 09/30/2012. Assets, $1,413,031 (M); Expenditures, $93,232; Total giving, $82,370; Grants to individuals, totaling $20,000.
Fields of interest: Higher education.
Type of support: Support to graduates or students of specific schools.
Application information: Applications accepted. Application form required.
> *Deadline(s):* Mar. 12
> *Applicants should submit the following:*
> 1) Transcripts
> 2) Letter(s) of recommendation
> 3) Financial information
> *Additional information:* All applications must be typed. No hand written or hand-printed pages will be accepted. Students are recommended for the awards by their high schools.
EIN: 366167609

2672
Arlen Francis Klein Trust Fund
903 N. Dunlap Ave.
Savoy, IL 61874-9611 (217) 359-2497
Contact: Richard Woodworth, Secy.

Foundation type: Operating foundation
Purpose: Grants to a handicapped child or to benefit handicapped children under the age of 21.
Financial data: Year ended 09/30/2013. Assets, $550,903 (M); Expenditures, $20,128; Total giving, $13,631.
Fields of interest: Disabilities, people with.
Type of support: Grants for special needs.
Application information: Applications accepted. Application form required.
> *Deadline(s):* None
> *Additional information:* Contact the trust for application forms.
EIN: 371284503

2673
Beulah Knecht Trust
c/o Shelby County State Bank
130 S. Morgan St.
Shelbyville, IL 62565-2242

Foundation type: Independent foundation
Purpose: Scholarships to graduates of Shelbyville High School, IL, who have been enrolled at accredited four-year colleges, including graduate school.
Financial data: Year ended 02/28/2013. Assets, $218,124 (M); Expenditures, $6,154; Total giving, $4,000; Grants to individuals, 4 grants totaling $4,000 (high: $1,000, low: $1,000).
Fields of interest: Higher education.
Type of support: Support to graduates or students of specific schools; Graduate support; Undergraduate support.
Application information: Applications accepted. Application form required.
> *Deadline(s):* Apr. 15
> *Applicants should submit the following:*
> 1) Class rank
> 2) Transcripts
> 3) Letter(s) of recommendation
> 4) GPA

Additional information: Applicants must re-apply annually to receive the scholarship for a total of four years.
EIN: 376291914

2674
John G. Koehler Fund
c/o Citizens Bank of Chartworth
502 E. Locust St.
P.O. Box 877
Chatsworth, IL 60921 (815) 844-7128
Application address: C/o Tom Herr, 103 N. Main St., Pontiac, IL 61764

Foundation type: Independent foundation
Purpose: College scholarships to graduating high school students of the Chatsworth, IL area for full-time study.
Financial data: Year ended 12/31/2012. Assets, $1,785,913 (M); Expenditures, $69,329; Total giving, $60,038; Grants to individuals, 20 grants totaling $60,038 (high: $3,400, low: $788).
Fields of interest: Higher education.
Type of support: Scholarships—to individuals.
Application information: Applications accepted.
> *Initial approach:* Letter
> *Deadline(s):* June 1
> *Additional information:* Application must include financial information, last three years' tax returns and student's general background.
EIN: 376141953

2675
Elsie Kohen Non-Exempt Charitable Trust
c/o Quad City Bank
3551 7th St., Ste. 100
Moline, IL 61265-6156

Foundation type: Independent foundation
Purpose: Grants to economically disadvantaged residents of the Jewish faith of Rock Island or Moline, IL.
Financial data: Year ended 03/31/2013. Assets, $514,600 (M); Expenditures, $20,807; Total giving, $16,350; Grants to individuals, 4 grants totaling $12,350 (high: $4,650, low: $500).
Fields of interest: Jewish agencies & synagogues; Economically disadvantaged.
Type of support: Grants for special needs.
Application information: Applications accepted. Application form not required.
> *Deadline(s):* None
> *Additional information:* Contact trust for additional information.
EIN: 366616802

2676
Dolores Kohl Education Foundation
1770 1st St., Ste. 500
Highland Park, IL 60035

Foundation type: Operating foundation
Purpose: Awards by nomination only to elementary school teachers in the Chicago, IL, area for exemplary teaching.
Financial data: Year ended 06/30/2013. Assets, $923,618 (M); Expenditures, $395,179; Total giving, $25,000; Grants to individuals, 4 grants totaling $25,000 (high: $10,000, low: $5,000).
Fields of interest: Education.
Type of support: Awards/grants by nomination only; Awards/prizes.
Application information: Applications not accepted.

Additional information: Unsolicited requests for funds not considered or acknowledged.
EIN: 237206116

2677
Leila Kohl Scholarship Trust
111 W. Monroe St., Tax Div. 10C
Chicago, IL 60603 (715) 453-5531
Application address: c/o School District of Tomahawk, Attn.: Dist. Admin. Off., 18 E. Washington Ave., Tomahawk, WI 54487-1370, tel.: (715) 453-5551

Foundation type: Independent foundation
Purpose: Scholarships to qualified graduating students of the Tomahawk School District, WI.
Financial data: Year ended 03/31/2013. Assets, $1,052,890 (M); Expenditures, $62,735; Total giving, $48,200.
Fields of interest: Higher education.
Type of support: Support to graduates or students of specific schools; Undergraduate support.
Application information: Applications accepted. Application form required.
  Deadline(s): None
EIN: 396611696

2678
Kooi Education Fund
(formerly Elmer J. Kooi, Beatrice A. Kooi and Robert J. Kooi Education Fund)
c/o Tax Division
111 W. Monroe St., Apt. 10C
Chicago, IL 60603-4026

Foundation type: Independent foundation
Purpose: Loans to students of Marengo Community High School, IL, for undergraduate and vocational education.
Financial data: Year ended 12/31/2012. Assets, $3,615,973 (M); Expenditures, $34,139; Total giving, $0.
Fields of interest: Vocational education, post-secondary; Higher education.
Type of support: Student loans—to individuals; Support to graduates or students of specific schools; Undergraduate support.
Application information: Applications accepted. Application form required.
  Initial approach: Letter
  Applicants should submit the following:
    1) Transcripts
    2) Financial information
Program description:
  Student Loan Program: Each year two students, one male and one female may apply for an annual $6,000 loan. The students are selected by the high school principal or a committee appointed by the principal. The loan will not exceed $6,000 per year, and a student receiving a loan for the first year in school will be eligible to receive additional loans for each year he or she continues in school until the student graduates or leaves school. A total of no more than four years of aid will be provided to each student over a period of not more than eight years.
EIN: 363899844

2679
Rob Koranda Scholarship Foundation
c/o Kenneth R. Koranda
7 S 541 Donwood Dr.
Naperville, IL 60540
URL: http://www.robkorandascholarship.com

Foundation type: Independent foundation

Purpose: Scholarships to graduating seniors at Naperville North High School, IL, for higher education.
Financial data: Year ended 12/31/2012. Assets, $459,681 (M); Expenditures, $72,433; Total giving, $40,000; Grants to individuals, 8 grants totaling $40,000 (high: $5,000, low: $5,000).
Fields of interest: Higher education; Athletics/sports, school programs.
Type of support: Scholarships—to individuals; Support to graduates or students of specific schools.
Application information: Application form available on the grantmaker's web site.
  Initial approach: E-mail
  Applicants should submit the following:
    1) Letter(s) of recommendation
    2) Resume
  Additional information: See web site for additional application information.
Program description:
  Rob Koranda Scholarship: Scholarship to one senior male and one senior female of NNHS will be selected each year, and will receive a college scholarship grant of $20,000. Students who have participated for four years in a IHSA school sponsored athletic team and have a cumulative high school GPA of 3.5 or higher may be nominated for this award.
EIN: 367417496

2680
Verlin and Laverne Krill Scholarship Fund
10 S. Dearborn IL1-0117
Chicago, IL 60603 (414) 298-2331
Application address: c/o Edgerton High School, Attn.: Principal, 111 E. River, Edgerton, OH 43517

Foundation type: Independent foundation
Purpose: Scholarships to graduating seniors at Edgerton High School, OH, to attend Ohio State University, Columbus, OH.
Financial data: Year ended 07/31/2012. Assets, $458,543 (M); Expenditures, $84,397; Total giving, $75,606; Grants to individuals, 4 grants totaling $75,606 (high: $27,237, low: $11,089).
Fields of interest: Higher education.
Type of support: Scholarships—to individuals.
Application information: Applications accepted. Application form required.
  Initial approach: Application form
  Deadline(s): Apr. 15
  Additional information: Application forms are available at the Edgerton High School Guidance Office.
EIN: 912160510

2681
Ladies Education Society
c/o Millicent R. Deal
1146 W. College Ave.
Jacksonville, IL 62650-2213 (217) 245-6603
Contact: Adah L. Coultas; Suzanne Verticchio
Application address: 1313 Mound, Jacksonville, IL 62650, tel.: (217) 245-660340 Westfair Dr., Jacksonville, IL 62650, tel.: (217) 243-3177

Foundation type: Independent foundation
Purpose: Scholarships to financially needy female students for continuing their education at accredited institutions of higher learning.
Financial data: Year ended 12/31/2012. Assets, $575,054 (M); Expenditures, $31,004; Total giving, $25,600.
Fields of interest: Higher education; Women.
Type of support: Scholarships—to individuals.

Application information: Applications accepted. Application form required.
  Deadline(s): Apr. 15
  Applicants should submit the following:
    1) Financial information
    2) Letter(s) of recommendation
    3) GPA
  Additional information: Application must also include evidence of need.
EIN: 376027579

2682
Lakeview Pantry
3831 N. Broadway
Chicago, IL 60613-3217 (773) 525-1777
Contact: Gary Garland, Exec. Dir.
E-mail: info@lakeviewpantry.org; E-Mail For Gary Garland: Gary@lakeviewpantry.org; URL: http://www.lakeviewpantry.org

Foundation type: Public charity
Purpose: Financial assistance to individuals and families of with food in the Chicago, Il area, also eligible to receive assistance for food stamps.
Publications: Annual report; Financial statement; Newsletter.
Financial data: Year ended 03/31/2012. Assets, $700,877 (M); Expenditures, $4,180,364; Total giving, $3,123,152; Grants to individuals, totaling $3,123,152.
Fields of interest: Economically disadvantaged.
Type of support: In-kind gifts; Grants for special needs.
Application information: Applications accepted. Application form required.
  Send request by: On-line
  Additional information: Eligible applicants can sign up for the Supplemental Nutrition Assistance Program (SNAP). Contact the agency for eligibility determination.
EIN: 362734184

2683
Ruth E. Patterson Lang Benevolent Trust
c/o Hometown National Bank
260 Bucklin St.
LaSalle, IL 61301 (815) 875-3308

Foundation type: Independent foundation
Purpose: Scholarships to students who reside in Princeton and Berlin Townships of Bureau County, IL for postsecondary education.
Financial data: Year ended 05/31/2013. Assets, $567,057 (M); Expenditures, $30,033; Total giving, $22,000; Grants to individuals, 14 grants totaling $22,000 (high: $1,800, low: $1,000).
Fields of interest: Higher education.
Type of support: Scholarships—to individuals.
Application information: Applications accepted. Application form required.
  Deadline(s): June 7
  Final notification: Applicants notified the last week of July or the first week of Aug.
  Applicants should submit the following:
    1) Financial information
    2) Transcripts
  Additional information: Students should contact their guidance counselor for application information. Application should also include a list of activities and awards.
EIN: 366818806

2684
Lucille Flick Larson Scholarship Trust
c/o State Bank of Lincoln
508 Broadway St.
Lincoln, IL 62656-2706   (217) 735-5551
Contact: for Scholarships: Gail L. Nunnery, V.P. & Tr. Officer
Application address: 111 N. Sangamon St., P.O. Box 529, Lincoln, IL 62656-2097

Foundation type: Independent foundation
Purpose: Scholarships to high school graduates from the New Holland, Middletown, and Greenview communities with second preference to high school graduates throughout Logan county, IL.
Financial data: Year ended 12/31/2012. Assets, $452,879 (M); Expenditures, $29,600; Total giving, $23,250.
Fields of interest: Higher education.
Type of support: Scholarships—to individuals.
Application information: Application form required.
　Deadline(s): Apr. 23
　Applicants should submit the following:
　　1) Class rank
　　2) Transcripts
　　3) Letter(s) of recommendation
　　4) ACT
　Additional information: Recommendations must be from two unrelated staff at the applicant's school of attendance.
EIN: 371380182

2685
Michael Lascaris Scholarship Trust
c/o Schiff Hardi
233 S. Wacker Dr.
Chicago, IL 60606-5096
Contact: Sarah K. Severson
E-mail: info@lascaristrust.gr; URL: http://lascaristrust.gr/

Foundation type: Independent foundation
Purpose: Scholarships to Greeks from Greece, Cyprus and Istanbul for the purpose of learning the English language.
Financial data: Year ended 12/31/2011. Assets, $4,761,664 (M); Expenditures, $530,736; Total giving, $206,400; Grants to individuals, 172 grants totaling $206,400 (high: $1,720, low: $860).
Fields of interest: Education.
Type of support: Foreign applicants; Undergraduate support.
Application information: Applications accepted. Application form required. Application form available on the grantmaker's web site.
　Send request by: Hand deliver
　Deadline(s): May 10
　Applicants should submit the following:
　　1) Financial information
　　2) Transcripts
　Additional information: Application should also include a photocopy of Greek Identification Card, Hellenic Descent Card or Birth Certificate, a copy of Baptismal Certificate, copy of report card, diploma or degree, and copy of tax return. Supporting documentation must be submitted in person at the Trust offices in Kolonaki.
Program description:
　Scholarship: The scholarships are only for English language instruction at all levels from Beginner up to and including the Certificate of Proficiency (universities of Cambridge and Michigan) and are applicable to candidates of all ages, provided they have had their 12th birthday. Applicants must also have Greek ancestry and be Greek Orthodox. The scholarship covers all tuition

and educational materials for one year, with the possibility of renewal for further years for those recipients who are conscientious in their study and attendance. Applicant must have physically lived in Greece, Cyprus or Istanbul for at least six months prior to applying, and must be willing to study at one of the two authorized language institutes, i.e. the Estia Neas Smyrnis English Language School or the Dessy Topouzides Institute of Foreign Languages at Voula.
EIN: 367144785

2686
Madalynne F. Laux Memorial Trust
10 S. Dearborn IL1-0117
Chicago, IL 60603-2300   (414) 832-6219

Foundation type: Independent foundation
Purpose: Scholarships to graduating seniors of Appleton High School East and Appleton High School West, both in WI, who rank in the top 15 percent of their classes and whose permanent residence is Appleton, WI.
Financial data: Year ended 05/31/2013. Assets, $1,244,670 (M); Expenditures, $69,342; Total giving, $57,317.
Type of support: Support to graduates or students of specific schools; Undergraduate support.
Application information: Applications accepted. Application form required.
　Deadline(s): Feb. 15.
　Additional information: Application should include an essay.
EIN: 396551972

2687
Lawrence Hall Youth Services
4833 N. Francisco Ave.
Chicago, IL 60625-3698   (773) 769-3500
E-mail: info@lawrencehall.org; URL: http://www.lawrencehall.org

Foundation type: Public charity
Purpose: Assistance to disadvantaged children and youth in the Chicago, IL, area with food, clothing, transportation, medical needs, foster care, educational assistance, and other needs.
Publications: Annual report; Informational brochure; Newsletter.
Financial data: Year ended 06/30/2012. Assets, $44,593,337 (M); Expenditures, $20,839,724.
Fields of interest: Human services; Children/youth; Economically disadvantaged.
Type of support: Grants for special needs.
Application information: Contact the organization for eligibility criteria.
EIN: 362167771

2688
Lemmer-Blazer Scholarship Fund
124 W. Market St.
Havana, IL 62644-1191   (309) 543-2291

Foundation type: Independent foundation
Purpose: Scholarships to graduating seniors of Havana High School, IL pursuing full time postsecondary education.
Financial data: Year ended 12/31/2011. Assets, $665,725 (M); Expenditures, $35,876; Total giving, $30,600; Grants to individuals, 26 grants totaling $30,600 (high: $1,600, low: $600).
Fields of interest: Higher education.
Type of support: Support to graduates or students of specific schools; Undergraduate support.

Application information: Applications accepted. Application form required.
　Deadline(s): July 1
　Final notification: Recipients notified by Aug. 15
　Applicants should submit the following:
　　1) Transcripts
　　2) GPA
　　3) Class rank
　　4) SAT
　　5) ACT
　Additional information: Students should contact their guidance counselor for application information.
EIN: 376233127

2689
Lenore Cletcher-Wessale Trust
c/o Tuscola National Bank
P.O. Box 110
Tuscola, IL 61953-0110   (217) 253-4711

Foundation type: Independent foundation
Purpose: Scholarships to graduates of Tuscola High School, IL, pursuing an education in the area of medicine.
Financial data: Year ended 12/31/2011. Assets, $845,936 (M); Expenditures, $41,505; Total giving, $37,500; Grants to individuals, 8 grants totaling $37,500 (high: $10,000, low: $1,500).
Fields of interest: Higher education.
Type of support: Support to graduates or students of specific schools.
Application information: Applications accepted.
　Initial approach: Letter
　Deadline(s): Aug. 31
　Additional information: Application should include information on background, GPA, schools and why field of study chosen.
EIN: 367191409

2690
Leukemia Research Foundation, Inc.
3520 Lake Ave., Ste. 202
Wilmette, IL 60091-1064   (847) 424-0600
Contact: Cindy Kane, Sr. Dir., Devel.
FAX: (847) 424-0606; E-mail: info@lrfmail.org; E-mail for Cindy Kane: cindy@lrfmail.org; toll-free tel.: (888) 558-5385; URL: http://www.leukemia-research.org

Foundation type: Public charity
Purpose: Grants and fellowships for the study of leukemia, lymphoma, and myelodysplastic diseases for researchers who meet eligibility requirements. Financial assistance to qualified patients and families who reside within 100 mile of Chicago or in the state of IL.
Publications: Application guidelines; Annual report; Informational brochure (including application guidelines); Newsletter.
Financial data: Year ended 06/30/2012. Assets, $1,602,666 (M); Expenditures, $1,915,092; Total giving, $998,714; Grants to individuals, totaling $198,714.
Fields of interest: Cancer research; Leukemia research.
Type of support: Fellowships; Research.
Application information: Application form required.
　Initial approach: Telephone
　Send request by: E-mail
　Deadline(s): Feb. 15 for Hollis Brownstein Research Grants
Program description:
　Hollis Brownstein Research Grants: One-year grants of up to $100,000 each are available to new investigators (individuals beginning to establish

their own laboratories that are no longer under the tutelage of senior scientist mentor) studying leukemia and other related diseases. Grants are intended to allow these innovative scientists to act on their ideas, and to try new procedures and experiments that will hopefully lead to significant breakthroughs. Applicants must be within seven years of their first independent position (years as a resident physician, fellow physician, or post-doctoral fellow are considered to be training years). Preference will be given to proposals that focus on leukemia, lymphoma, and MDS.
EIN: 366102182

2691
Nicole Lynn Levin Foundation
c/o Jewels By Parklane
100 E. Commerce Dr.
Schaumburg, IL 60173-5328 (800) 433-5775
Contact: Shirley Ann Levin, Pres.

Foundation type: Operating foundation
Purpose: Scholarships to qualifying graduating seniors of Barrington High School, IL pursuing postsecondary education.
Financial data: Year ended 11/30/2013. Assets, $8,335 (M); Expenditures, $10,703; Total giving, $10,000; Grants to individuals, 2 grants totaling $10,000 (high: $5,000, low: $5,000).
Fields of interest: Higher education.
Type of support: Scholarships—to individuals; Support to graduates or students of specific schools.
Application information: Applications accepted.
Initial approach: Letter
Deadline(s): None
Applicants should submit the following:
1) Transcripts
2) Essay
3) Financial information
Additional information: Applicants must demonstrate financial needs, extracurricular activities, and future plans for college and beyond.
EIN: 200072130

2692
Roberta Bachmann Lewis Scholarship Fund
1615 S. Christiana Ave.
Chicago, IL 60623 (773) 542-1490
Contact: Irving Lewis, Pres.
FAX: (773) 542-1492;
E-mail: kstonewall@nlcphs.org; URL: http://www.nlcphs.org/RBLScholarshipFund/?p=1

Foundation type: Public charity
Purpose: Scholarships to individuals in financial need for higher education.
Financial data: Year ended 12/31/2012. Assets, $1,323,784 (M); Expenditures, $104,763; Total giving, $100,830; Grants to individuals, totaling $100,830.
Fields of interest: Higher education.
Type of support: Scholarships—to individuals.
Application information: Applications accepted. Application form required. Interview required.
Additional information: Applicants must be recommended by a faculty member.
EIN: 311705330

2693
Lincoln Park Zoological Society
2001 N. Clark St.
Chicago, IL 60614-4712 (312) 742-2000
Contact: Kevin J. Kell, Pres. and C.E.O.
E-mail: czrinsky@lpzoo.org; URL: http://www.lpzoo.org

Foundation type: Public charity
Purpose: Research grants for projects that have a direct impact on wildlife conservation and/or conservation biology. Projects with participation by graduate or undergraduate students are preferred.
Financial data: Year ended 03/31/2012. Assets, $87,271,088 (M); Expenditures, $25,336,565.
Fields of interest: Animals/wildlife, preservation/protection; Animals/wildlife.
Type of support: Program development; Research.
Application information: Applications accepted.
Initial approach: Letter
Additional information: Contact foundation for complete eligibility requirements.
EIN: 362512404

2694
Franklin Lindsay Trust
10 S. Dearborn IL1-0117
Chicago, IL 60603
E-mail: info@franklinlindsay.org; Application address: c/o JPMorgan Chase Bank, N.A.-NCAA, P.O. Box 227237, Dallas, TX 75222

Foundation type: Independent foundation
Purpose: Low interest loans to students who are attending a Texas accredited college or university in pursuit of higher education.
Financial data: Year ended 12/31/2012. Assets, $21,124,564 (M); Expenditures, $205,516; Total giving, $0.
Fields of interest: Higher education.
Type of support: Student loans—to individuals.
Application information: Applications accepted. Application form required. Application form available on the grantmaker's web site. Interview required.
Send request by: Mail or hand deliver
Additional information: Application should include transcripts, a copy of your driver's license or identification card and three personal references. See web site for mailing instructions.
EIN: 746031753

2695
Lithuanian Foundation
14911 127th St.
Lemont, IL 60439-6466 (630) 257-1616
Contact: Arvydas Tamulis, Pres. and C.E.O.
FAX: (630) 257-1647; E-mail: admin@lithfund.org; URL: http://www.lithuanianfoundation.org/

Foundation type: Public charity
Purpose: Scholarships to students worldwide who are of Lithuanian descent. Preference is given to students outside Lithuania.
Publications: Application guidelines; Newsletter.
Financial data: Year ended 12/31/2012. Assets, $14,576,249 (M); Expenditures, $613,317; Total giving, $338,447; Grants to individuals, totaling $39,240.
International interests: Lithuania.
Type of support: Graduate support; Undergraduate support.

Application information: Applications accepted. Application form required. Application form available on the grantmaker's web site.
Deadline(s): Oct. 10
Applicants should submit the following:
1) FAFSA
2) Financial information
3) Letter(s) of recommendation
4) Transcripts
5) Photograph
Additional information: Application should also include copies of birth certificate, passport, Permanent Resident Card, and valid student visa where applicable.
Program description:
Scholarships: Scholarships are available to students of Lithuanian descent (especially Lithuanian emigres) who are pursuing a bachelor's, master's, or doctoral degree in an accredited college or university.
EIN: 366118312

2696
Loaves and Fishes Community Pantry
1871 High Grove Ln.
Naperville, IL 60563-2901 (630) 355-3663
Contact: Charles P. McLimans, Pres. and C.E.O.
FAX: (630) 355-0562;
E-mail: info@loaves-fishes.org; E-mail For Charles P. McLimans: cmclimans@loaves-fishes.org;
URL: http://www.loaves-fishes.org

Foundation type: Public charity
Purpose: Food assistance to indigent residents of Naperville Township and DuPage County, IL.
Publications: Annual report.
Financial data: Year ended 06/30/2012. Assets, $3,739,288 (M); Expenditures, $9,739,526; Total giving, $8,618,114.
Fields of interest: Economically disadvantaged.
Type of support: In-kind gifts.
Application information:
Initial approach: Letter
Deadline(s): None
Additional information: To qualify for food assistance, a household's gross monthly income must be within the guidelines established by the Illinois Department of Human Services income guidelines for their family size.
EIN: 363786777

2697
Jackie Long Foundation
312 Indian Hills Ct.
Rantoul, IL 61866 (217) 893-8884
Contact: Dennis B. Long, Tr.

Foundation type: Independent foundation
Purpose: Grants to needy families in IL.
Financial data: Year ended 12/31/2012. Assets, $193,214 (M); Expenditures, $16,244; Total giving, $15,955; Grants to individuals, 20 grants totaling $15,955 (high: $1,055, low: $400).
Type of support: Grants for special needs.
Application information: Applications accepted. Application form required.
Deadline(s): None
EIN: 371397811

2698
Ora T. & Dessie H. Lower Memorial Scholarship Fund
10 S Dearborn ILI- 0117
Chicago, IL 60603 (214) 965-2908
Application address: c/o JPMorgan Chase Bank, N.A., Attn.: NCAA, 2200 Ross Ave., Dallas, TX 75201-2787

Foundation type: Independent foundation
Purpose: Scholarships to graduates of high schools in Rush County, IN, for college or other postsecondary education.
Financial data: Year ended 01/31/2013. Assets, $816,799 (M); Expenditures, $44,411; Total giving, $35,506.
Fields of interest: Vocational education.
Type of support: Support to graduates or students of specific schools; Undergraduate support.
Application information: Application form required.
Deadline(s): Apr. 1 or 60 days prior to start of the school term
EIN: 237311043

2699
Alois and Twyla Luhr Foundation
416 Covington Dr.
Waterloo, IL 62298 (618) 281-4106
Contact: Bethany Miller, Tr.
Application address: P.O. Box 50, Columbia, IL 62236

Foundation type: Independent foundation
Purpose: Scholarship to graduating seniors of Monroe County, IL, and from communities in which Luhr Bros. Inc. has a presence to enable recipients to obtain a college degree in the construction industry related field.
Financial data: Year ended 06/30/2013. Assets, $135,497 (M); Expenditures, $26,110; Total giving, $26,000; Grants to individuals, 8 grants totaling $26,000 (high: $5,000, low: $1,000).
Fields of interest: Higher education.
Type of support: Scholarships—to individuals.
Application information: Application form required.
Deadline(s): None
Additional information: Applicant must be of good character and demonstrate academic ability.
EIN: 371401178

2700
Founces M. Luley Scholarship & Educational Fund
10 S. Dearborn IL1-0117
Chicago, IL 60603

Foundation type: Independent foundation
Purpose: Scholarships to high school seniors of Warren G. Harding High School, OH and to worthy graduates of other high schools in Trumbull county, OH pursuing an education in music.
Financial data: Year ended 12/31/2012. Assets, $788,401 (M); Expenditures, $43,007; Total giving, $31,500; Grants to individuals, 14 grants totaling $31,500 (high: $3,500, low: $1,000).
Fields of interest: Music; Performing arts, education.
Type of support: Support to graduates or students of specific schools; Undergraduate support.
Application information: Interview required.
Deadline(s): Apr. 21
Additional information: Applicants must rank in the upper 1/3 of their high school graduating class or maintain a 2.8 GPA in college.
EIN: 346672173

2701
LUNGevity Foundation, Inc.
218 S. Wabash Ave., Ste. 540
Chicago, IL 60604 (312) 407-6100
Contact: Andrea Stern Ferris, Pres. and C.E.O.
FAX: (312) 464-0737; E-mail: info@lungevity.org;
URL: http://www.lungevity.org

Foundation type: Public charity
Purpose: Grants to researchers to support lung cancer research.
Publications: Application guidelines; Grants list.
Financial data: Year ended 06/30/2012. Assets, $5,466,087 (M); Expenditures, $5,981,315; Total giving, $3,028,979; Grants to individuals, totaling $3,028,979.
Fields of interest: Cancer; Lung diseases; Cancer research; Lung research.
Type of support: Research; Grants to individuals.
Application information: Applications accepted. Application form available on the grantmaker's web site.
Initial approach: Application
Deadline(s): Dec. 30 for letter of intent, Mar. 19 for full application
Additional information: Only researchers with letters of intent of interest to the foundation will be asked to submit full proposals.
Program description:
Career Development Awards for Translational Research: Grants of up to $100,000 per year, for up to three years, is available to future research leaders who work to keep the field of lung cancer research vibrant with new ideas. Funded projects will be expected to have a direct impact on the early detection of lung cancer, the outcomes of lung cancer, or the providing of clear conceptual or experimental foundations for the future development of methods for early detection and/or individualized treatment. The preference is for studies that are likely to result in patient benefit in the foreseeable future. Applicants may apply as individuals or in teams of up to three investigators. It is strongly encouraged that teams be composed of principal investigators from different institutions. Early Detection Awards may be for a maximum of $600,000 (an annual maximum of $100,000 a year for two years for up to three principal investigators). Applicants must be within the first five years of their faculty award.
EIN: 364433410

2702
Lutheran Child and Family Services of Illinois
7620 Madison St.
P.O. Box 5078
River Forest, IL 60305-2101 (708) 771-7180
Contact: Gene L. Svebakken, Pres. and C.E.O.
FAX: (708) 771-7184; E-mail: lcfs_info@lcfs.org;
URL: http://www.lcfs.org/NETCOMMUNITY/Page.aspx?pid=178&srcid=-2

Foundation type: Public charity
Purpose: Emergency assistance for low income families and individuals throughout Illinois with food, clothing, disaster relief and other needs.
Publications: Annual report; Newsletter.
Financial data: Year ended 06/30/2012. Assets, $16,805,197 (M); Expenditures, $32,070,570; Total giving, $4,596,735; Grants to individuals, totaling $4,596,735.
Fields of interest: Economically disadvantaged.
Type of support: Emergency funds; Grants for special needs.

Application information: Contact the organization eligibility determination.
EIN: 362167778

2703
Lutheran Social Services of Illinois
1001 E. Touhy Ave., Ste. 50
Des Plaines, IL 60018-5817 (847) 635-4600
Contact: David M.A. Jensen, Pres. and C.O.O.
FAX: (847) 635-6764; E-mail: info@lssi.org;
URL: http://www.lssi.org

Foundation type: Public charity
Purpose: Financial assistance to low-income individuals and families throughout Illinois, with food, clothing, shelter, medical, dental, and hospital expense, and other needs.
Publications: Annual report; Financial statement; Newsletter.
Financial data: Year ended 06/30/2012. Assets, $64,309,979 (M); Expenditures, $99,381,345; Total giving, $574,106; Grants to individuals, totaling $574,106.
Fields of interest: Human services; Economically disadvantaged.
Type of support: Grants for special needs.
Application information: Contact the agency for additional information.
EIN: 362584799

2704
The John D. and Catherine T. MacArthur Foundation
140 S. Dearborn St., Ste. 1200
Chicago, IL 60603-5285 (312) 726-8000
Contact: Richard J. Kaplan, Assoc. V.P., Institutional Research and Grants Mgmt.
FAX: (312) 920-6258;
E-mail: 4answers@macfound.org; TDD: (312) 920-6285; URL: http://www.macfound.org

Foundation type: Independent foundation
Purpose: MacArthur fellowships by nomination only to citizens and residents of the U.S.
Publications: Annual report; Newsletter.
Financial data: Year ended 12/31/2012. Assets, $5,987,438,524 (M); Expenditures, $271,209,395; Total giving, $209,859,152; Grants to individuals, 121 grants totaling $12,100,000 (high: $100,000, low: $100,000).
Fields of interest: Literature; Arts; Human services; Social sciences; Leadership development.
Type of support: Fellowships; Awards/grants by nomination only.
Application information: Applications not accepted.
Additional information: Individual applications and informal nominations are not accepted. See program descriptions for detailed application and nomination information.
Program description:
MacArthur Fellows: The program awards unrestricted $625,000 fellowships to talented individuals who have shown extraordinary originality and dedication in their creative pursuits and a marked capacity for self-direction.
EIN: 237093598

2705
Magnus Charitable Trust
600 W. Rand Rd., Ste. A-104
Arlington Heights, IL   60004-2355   (847)
255-1100
Contact: Delores Dorethy
FAX: (847) 632-0616;
E-mail: info@magnuscharitable.org; Toll free tel.:
(888) 259-5044; URL: http://
www.magnuscharitable.org

Foundation type: Independent foundation
Purpose: Scholarships for low-income individuals
who are residents of Cook, DuPage, Lane and Will
counties, IL for attendance at an accredited college
or university.
Financial data: Year ended 12/31/2012. Assets,
$9,865,836 (M); Expenditures, $1,444,082; Total
giving, $479,388.
Fields of interest: Higher education.
Type of support: Undergraduate support.
Application information: Applications accepted.
Application form required.
> *Deadline(s):* Apr. 18
> *Final notification:* Applicants notified in May
> *Applicants should submit the following:*
> 1) Transcripts
> 2) GPA
> 3) Letter(s) of recommendation
> 4) Financial information
> 5) Essay
EIN: 364049284

2706
Majid Family Foundation
1235 S. Prairie Ave., Ste. 1401
Chicago, IL   60605

Foundation type: Independent foundation
Purpose: Grants to individuals for medical
assistance and other needs.
Financial data: Year ended 12/31/2012. Assets,
$29,251 (M); Expenditures, $31,541; Total giving,
$30,250; Grants to individuals, 4 grants totaling
$25,950 (high: $14,000, low: $2,000).
Fields of interest: Economically disadvantaged.
Type of support: Grants for special needs.
Application information: Applications not
accepted.
> *Additional information:* Unsolicited requests for
> funds not considered or acknowledged.
EIN: 364183120

2707
Make-A-Wish Foundation of Illinois, Inc.
640 N. LaSalle Dr., Ste. 280
Chicago, IL   60654-3754   (312) 602-9474
Contact: Stephanie Springs, C.E.O.
FAX: (312) 943-9813; Toll-free tel.: (800)
978-9474; URL: http://www.wishes.org

Foundation type: Public charity
Purpose: Grant wishes to children ages 2 1/2 to 18
living in IL who have been diagnosed with a
life-threatening medical condition.
Publications: Application guidelines; Annual report.
Financial data: Year ended 08/31/2012. Assets,
$9,954,375 (M); Expenditures, $9,537,411; Total
giving, $5,598,951; Grants to individuals, totaling
$5,598,951.
Fields of interest: Children/youth.
Type of support: Grants to individuals.
Application information:
> *Initial approach:* Telephone
> *Deadline(s):* None

Additional information: Referral forms can be
submitted by a child, the child's parent or
legal guardian, or a physician, nurse, social
worker, or child-life specialist.
Program description:
> *Wishes Program:* The foundation works to grant
> wishes to Illinois children with life-threatening
> medical conditions, in the hopes of enriching their
> lives with hope, strength, and joy. Applicants must
> be between the ages of 2 1/2 and 18, live in Illinois,
> and be diagnosed with a life-threatening medical
> condition at the time of referral as determined by
> the child's treating physician.
EIN: 363422138

2708
Marion Memorial Health Foundation
P.O. Box 1815
Marion, IL   62959
Contact: Judy Broemmel

Foundation type: Independent foundation
Purpose: Scholarships to graduating seniors from
Benton, Carrier Mills, Carterville, Christopher, Crab
Orchard, El Dorado, Goreville, Harrisburg, Herrin,
Johnston City, Marion, Thompsonville, Vienna and
West Frankfort high schools, IL, who are seeking
medical careers.
Financial data: Year ended 12/31/2012. Assets,
$0 (M); Expenditures, $60,710; Total giving,
$43,000; Grant to an individual, 1 grant totaling
$16,000.
Fields of interest: Medical school/education;
Public health.
Type of support: Support to graduates or students
of specific schools; Undergraduate support.
Application information: Application form required.
> *Additional information:* Contact foundation for
> current application deadline/guidelines.
Program description:
> *Scholarship Program:* Scholarships are in the
> amount of $1,000 to three seniors at area schools
> (Benton, Carrier Mills, Carterville, Christopher, Crab
> Orchard, Eldorado, Goreville, Harrisburg, Herrin,
> Johnston City, Thompsonville, Vienna or West
> Frankfort) who are planning a career in human
> health care. Two scholarships of $1,000 are
> provided to Marion graduating seniors pursuing a
> career in the human health care field. A $2,000
> "R.D. Morgan, M.D." medical scholarship will be
> awarded to a Marion High School graduating senior
> who is pursuing a career as a medical doctor. If no
> graduating senior meets the necessary
> qualifications, the scholarship will be open to the
> previously-listed schools.
EIN: 371316969

2709
The Marshall Educational Trust Fund
517 Locust St.
P.O. Box 98
Marshall, IL   62441-0098   (217) 826-8051
Contact: Joseph R. Schroeder, Pres.

Foundation type: Independent foundation
Purpose: Student loans to graduates of Marshall
High School, IL to attend accredited two or four year
colleges or universities.
Financial data: Year ended 07/31/2013. Assets,
$468,704 (M); Expenditures, $3,378; Total giving,
$0.
Fields of interest: Higher education.
Type of support: Student loans—to individuals;
Support to graduates or students of specific
schools; Undergraduate support.

Application information: Application form required.
> *Deadline(s):* June 1 and Dec. 1
> *Additional information:* Applicant must
> demonstrate financial need, and must have at
> least a 2.50 GPA for a four year school and
> 2.0 GPA for a two year school.
EIN: 371318513

2710
Martin Education Trust
10 S. Dearborn IL1-0117
Chicago, IL   60603-2003   (214) 965-2908
Application Address: 2200 Ross Ave. Dallas, TX
75201

Foundation type: Independent foundation
Purpose: Scholarships to residents in the city of
Wooster, Wooster Township, Wayne Township or
Wayne County, OH.
Financial data: Year ended 04/30/2013. Assets,
$340,405 (M); Expenditures, $14,186; Total
giving, $10,000; Grants to individuals, 13 grants
totaling $10,000 (high: $1,250, low: $500).
Type of support: Scholarships—to individuals.
Application information:
> *Deadline(s):* Mar. 1
EIN: 346742103

2711
Maryville Academy
1150 N. River Rd.
Des Plaines, IL   60016-1214   (847) 294-1999
E-mail: info@maryvilleacademy.org; URL: http://
www.maryvilleacademy.org

Foundation type: Public charity
Purpose: High school and college scholarships for
Maryville Academy students. Residential care and
shelter for abused, neglected and orphaned
children.
Publications: Annual report.
Financial data: Year ended 06/30/2012. Assets,
$80,303,012 (M); Expenditures, $42,686,435;
Total giving, $487,740; Grants to individuals,
totaling $487,740.
Fields of interest: Education; Human services;
Economically disadvantaged.
Type of support: Scholarships—to individuals;
Grants for special needs.
Application information: Contact the academy for
additional information.
EIN: 362170873

2712
Daisy Mason Scholarship Fund
(formerly Mason Scholarship Fund)
c/o First Mid-Illinois Bank & Trust
P.O. Box 529
Mattoon, IL   61938   (217) 258-0633
Contact: Laura Walk

Foundation type: Independent foundation
Purpose: Scholarships to graduates of Community
Unit District No. 2, Mattoon Senior High School, IL.
Financial data: Year ended 12/31/2012. Assets,
$2,014,703 (M); Expenditures, $191,674; Total
giving, $113,750; Grants to individuals, 99 grants
totaling $113,250 (high: $1,250, low: $1,000).
Type of support: Support to graduates or students
of specific schools; Undergraduate support.
Application information: Application form required.
> *Deadline(s):* Apr.

Additional information: Applications available at First Mid-Illinois Bank & Trust and Mattoon Senior High School.

EIN: 376024616

2713
Massage Therapy Foundation, Inc.
(formerly American Massage Therapy Association Foundation)
500 Davis St., Ste. 900
Evanston, IL 60201-4695   (847) 869-5019
Contact: Gini S. Ohlson, Exec. Dir.
FAX: (847) 864-1178;
E-mail: info@massagetherapyfoundation.org;
E-mail For Gini S. Ohlson:
gohlson@massagetherapyfoundation.org;
URL: http://www.massagetherapyfoundation.org

Foundation type: Public charity
Purpose: Research grants to individuals for the study of massage therapy.
Financial data: Year ended 02/28/2013. Assets, $765,300 (M); Expenditures, $317,682; Total giving, $103,957; Grants to individuals, totaling $29,800.
Fields of interest: Physical therapy; Community/economic development.
Type of support: Program development; Research.
Application information: Applications accepted. Application form required.
  Initial approach: Proposal
  Deadline(s): Mar. 1 for Research Grants
Program descriptions:
  Research Grants: This grant supports high quality, independent research that contributes to the basic science of massage therapy application, including applied research investigating massage therapy as a health/mental health treatment and/or prevention modality. The research grant is available to investigators who have experience in the relevant field of research, and are presently associated with or have secured the cooperation of a university, independent research organization, or other institution qualified and willing to function as a Sponsoring Organization for the purpose of this project. The normal award for 12 months is $1,000 to $30,000 and must be used in the specific time period for which it has been awarded.
  Student Case Report Contest: This contest, with school support, seeks to foster an opportunity for students to develop research skills by conducting their own research case study in which they will summarize the results in the format of a professional research paper. The grand prize winner will receive $2,500, second place winner will receive $2,000, and third place winner will receive $1,500.
EIN: 363735393

2714
Master Educational Assistance Foundation
747 S. Euclid Ave.
Oak Park, IL 60304-1243   (847) 431-5590
Contact: James F. Zangrilli, Exec. Dir.

Foundation type: Independent foundation
Purpose: Scholarships to economically disadvantaged and/or physically or mentally disabled inner-city residents of IL.
Financial data: Year ended 12/31/2012. Assets, $8,168,063 (M); Expenditures, $770,694; Total giving, $668,545; Grants to individuals, totaling $85,710.
Type of support: Scholarships—to individuals.

Application information: Applications accepted. Application form not required.
  Initial approach: Letter
  Deadline(s): None
  Applicants should submit the following:
    1) FAFSA
    2) Essay
EIN: 363542174

2715
Edith L. Masters Trust Fund
P.O. Box 470
Petersburg, IL 62675   (217) 632-2282
Application address: c/o Porta Community Unit School District No. 202, P.O. Box 202, Petersburg, IL 62675

Foundation type: Independent foundation
Purpose: Undergraduate scholarships to graduates of high schools in Menard County, IL.
Financial data: Year ended 12/31/2012. Assets, $322,801 (M); Expenditures, $44,758; Total giving, $24,000; Grants to individuals, 25 grants totaling $24,000 (high: $1,500, low: $500).
Type of support: Scholarships—to individuals; Support to graduates or students of specific schools.
Application information: Applications not accepted.
  Additional information: Application must include previous year's tax return. Unsolicited requests for funds not considered or acknowledged.
EIN: 376141924

2716
Cheryl A. McAllister Scholarship Fund
601 Main St.
P.O. Box 246
Germantown, IL 62245   (618) 523-4202

Foundation type: Independent foundation
Purpose: Scholarships to graduates and graduating seniors of Community Unit District 1 High School, Carlyle, IL, who are planning to attend a junior college, trade school or four-year university.
Financial data: Year ended 05/31/2013. Assets, $45,514 (M); Expenditures, $33,312; Total giving, $32,460; Grants to individuals, 4 grants totaling $32,460 (high: $15,000, low: $4,000).
Type of support: Support to graduates or students of specific schools; Technical education support; Undergraduate support.
Application information: Applications accepted. Application form required.
  Deadline(s): Nov. 30
EIN: 371397902

2717
McClain Scholarship Trust
c/o ECB&T
P.O. Box 400
Paris, IL 61944-0790   (217) 465-4154
Application Address: c/o Edgar County Bank Trust, 177 W. Wood St., P.O. Box 400, Paris, IL. 61944

Foundation type: Independent foundation
Purpose: Student loans to residents of Edgar and Vermilion counties, IL, who are studying agriculture, nursing, teaching, law, medicine, or dentistry.
Financial data: Year ended 12/31/2012. Assets, $2,754,125 (M); Expenditures, $132,672; Total giving, $104,902; Grants to individuals, 28 grants totaling $104,902 (high: $5,000, low: $662).

Fields of interest: Dental school/education; Law school/education; Medical school/education; Nursing school/education; Teacher school/education; Agriculture.
Type of support: Student loans—to individuals.
Application information: Application form required.
  Deadline(s): May 15
  Additional information: Applications available at Citizens National Bank.
EIN: 376185245

2718
Georgine B. McDonald Trust
c/o Tuscola National Bank
P.O. Box 110
Tuscola, IL 61953-0110   (217) 253-4711
Application address: c/o Tuscola National bank, 900 S. Progress Blvd.

Foundation type: Independent foundation
Purpose: Scholarships to students residing in Douglas county, IL and pursuing a career in medicine, agriculture, literature or fine arts.
Financial data: Year ended 12/31/2012. Assets, $414,384 (M); Expenditures, $23,062; Total giving, $22,000.
Fields of interest: Literature; Arts; Medical school/education; Agriculture.
Type of support: Scholarships—to individuals.
Application information: Applications accepted.
  Additional information: Contact the trust for additional application information.
EIN: 726217567

2719
McDonald's Family Charity, Inc.
1 Kroc Dr.
Oak Brook, IL 60523-2275   (630) 623-1584
Contact: Martin J. Coyne, Jr., Pres.

Foundation type: Public charity
Purpose: Assistance to employees of McDonald's, it's subsidiaries' restaurants, offices, as well as employees of McDonald's suppliers who have been impacted by major natural disasters worldwide.
Financial data: Year ended 12/31/2011. Assets, $243,744 (M); Expenditures, $244,090; Total giving, $234,378; Grants to individuals, 224 grants totaling $152,475.
Fields of interest: Safety/disasters.
Type of support: Employee-related welfare.
Application information: Applications not accepted.
  Additional information: Unsolicited requests for funds not considered or acknowledged.
EIN: 364381203

2720
McFarland Charitable Foundation
112 S. Orange St.
P.O. Box 200
Havana, IL 62644-0200   (309) 543-3361
FAX: (309) 543-3441;
E-mail: info@havanabank.com

Foundation type: Independent foundation
Purpose: Scholarships to nursing students residing in the Havana, IL, area attending approved nursing schools in IL.
Publications: Application guidelines.
Financial data: Year ended 12/31/2011. Assets, $2,950,716 (M); Expenditures, $171,222; Total giving, $121,326; Grants to individuals, 8 grants totaling $105,726 (high: $20,490, low: $4,033).
Fields of interest: Nursing school/education.

Type of support: Scholarships—to individuals; Undergraduate support.
Application information: Applications accepted. Application form required. Interview required.
  Initial approach: Letter
  Deadline(s): None
  Additional information: Application is mailed to applicant. Applicants should be high school graduates and accepted into an accredited registered nursing program. Must have a prior employment commitment to return to Havana, IL, to work at an approved facility for a predetermined number of years. Recipients must sign a written contract with co-signers.
EIN: 376022376

2721
McFarland Medical Trust
112 S. Orange St.
P.O. Box 200
Havana, IL 62644   (309) 543-3361
Contact: Larry Thomson, V.P. and Trust Off., Havana National Bank
E-mail: info@havanabank.com; Application address: c/o Havana National Bank 112 South Orange Havana, IL 62644

Foundation type: Independent foundation
Purpose: Scholarships to students pursuing a medical career within the Havana, IL area.
Publications: Informational brochure.
Financial data: Year ended 12/31/2012. Assets, $610,965 (M); Expenditures, $67,641; Total giving, $55,387; Grant to an individual, 1 grant totaling $55,387.
Fields of interest: Medical school/education.
Type of support: Scholarships—to individuals.
Application information:
  Initial approach: Letter
  Deadline(s): None
  Additional information: Application should include a resume.
EIN: 376095841

2722
Eva E. McInnes College Scholarship Fund
c/o First Midwest Bank
3510 W. Elm St.
McHenry, IL 60050

Foundation type: Independent foundation
Purpose: Scholarships to graduating high school students primarily in McHenry, IL.
Financial data: Year ended 12/31/2012. Assets, $1,251,506 (M); Expenditures, $75,239; Total giving, $54,750; Grants to individuals, 34 grants totaling $54,750 (high: $3,000, low: $250).
Type of support: Scholarships—to individuals.
Application information: Applications not accepted.
  Additional information: Unsolicited requests for funds not considered or acknowledged.
EIN: 363756004

2723
Ella G. McKee Foundation
c/o First National Bank Trust Dept.
311 Banker Blvd.
Vandalia, IL 62471

Foundation type: Independent foundation
Purpose: Interest-free student loans to high school seniors who are residents of Fayette County, IL, for at least four years.

Financial data: Year ended 12/31/2012. Assets, $1,704,114; Expenditures, $240,105; Total giving, $201,200; Grants to individuals, 118 grants totaling $201,200 (high: $4,800, low: $400).
Fields of interest: Higher education.
Type of support: Student loans—to individuals.
Application information: Application form required.
  Additional information: Applicant must demonstrate financial need and show academic achievement.
EIN: 376099863

2724
Herbert McLean Memorial Fund
302 E. Jefferson St.
Bloomington, IL 61701   (309) 763-9640
Contact: Barry Weer

Foundation type: Operating foundation
Purpose: Scholarships of $500 to $1,000 is awarded to all students of IL, in pursuing a college degree.
Financial data: Year ended 12/31/2011. Assets, $279,893 (M); Expenditures, $7,715; Total giving, $7,000; Grants to individuals, 8 grants totaling $7,000 (high: $1,000, low: $500).
Fields of interest: Higher education.
Type of support: Scholarships—to individuals.
Application information: Applications accepted.
  Deadline(s): Aug. 1
  Additional information: Contact fund for additional application guidelines.
EIN: 510176145

2725
Reverend John A. McLoraine Educational Trust
1400 E. Central Rd.
Mount Prospect, IL 60056-2650

Foundation type: Independent foundation
Purpose: Scholarships to financially needy, scholastically worthy graduating seniors attending secondary Catholic education facilities in northern IL.
Financial data: Year ended 06/30/2013. Assets, $2,366,446 (M); Expenditures, $130,465; Total giving, $126,900; Grants to individuals, 35 grants totaling $126,900 (high: $5,275, low: $1,950).
Fields of interest: Catholic agencies & churches.
Type of support: Scholarships—to individuals; Precollege support.
Application information: Applicant should submit financial information and also include primary scholastic information.
EIN: 363196087

2726
James and Madeleine McMullan Family Foundation
(formerly James and Milton McMullan Foundation)
800 S. Ridge Rd.
Lake Forest, IL 60045-2756   (601) 635-2718
Contact: Cille Norman
Application Address: c/o Newton Cnty. High School, 16255 Hwy. 503, Decatur, MS 39327

Foundation type: Independent foundation
Purpose: Scholarships to graduates of Newton High School, MS for continuing education at accredited colleges or universities.
Financial data: Year ended 12/31/2011. Assets, $1,953,579 (M); Expenditures, $135,317; Total

giving, $127,000; Grants to individuals, 4 grants totaling $5,000 (high: $1,250, low: $1,250).
Type of support: Support to graduates or students of specific schools; Undergraduate support.
Application information: Applications accepted. Application form required. Interview required.
  Deadline(s): Apr. 1
  Applicants should submit the following:
    1) Transcripts
    2) Letter(s) of recommendation
    3) Essay
  Additional information: Awards based on financial need, scholastic record, personal statements, activity record and faculty recommendation.
EIN: 363506203

2727
Meade Memorial Science Fund
10 S Dearborn ILI -0117
Chicago, IL 60603

Foundation type: Independent foundation
Purpose: Scholarships and interest-free loans to selected graduates of the Hammondsport Central School District, NY, who are continuing their education in engineering or allied fields at accredited universities and colleges, or other education or training institutions.
Financial data: Year ended 12/31/2012. Assets, $257,210 (M); Expenditures, $10,400; Total giving, $7,500; Grant to an individual, 1 grant totaling $7,500.
Fields of interest: Vocational education; Engineering school/education.
Type of support: Scholarships—to individuals; Student loans—to individuals; Support to graduates or students of specific schools.
Application information: Applications not accepted.
  Additional information: Unsolicited requests for funds not considered or acknowledged.
EIN: 166015269

2728
Medical Library Association
65 E. Wacker Pl., Ste. 1900
Chicago, IL 60601-7246   (312) 419-9094
FAX: (312) 419-8950; E-mail: info@mlahq.org;
E-Mail For Carla J. Funk: funk@mlahq.org;
URL: http://www.mlanet.org

Foundation type: Public charity
Purpose: Research grants, scholarships and fellowships to professionals in the health sciences information field.
Publications: Application guidelines; Annual report.
Financial data: Year ended 12/31/2011. Assets, $3,878,974 (M); Expenditures, $2,854,419; Total giving, $40,155; Grants to individuals, totaling $25,233.
Fields of interest: Libraries/library science; Libraries (school); Libraries (medical); Biomedicine research; Minorities; Asians/Pacific Islanders; African Americans/Blacks; Hispanics/Latinos; Native Americans/American Indians.
Type of support: Fellowships; Research; Scholarships—to individuals; Travel grants; Doctoral support.
Application information: Applications accepted. Application form required. Application form available on the grantmaker's web site.
  Initial approach: Telephone
  Deadline(s): Mar. 1 for MLA/NLM Spectrum Scholarship, Apr. 1 for Cunningham Memorial International Fellowships, Nov. 15 for

Lindberg Research Fellowship, Dec. 1 for Hospital Libraries Section/MLA Professional Development Grants

Additional information: See web site for additional guidelines.

Program descriptions:

Continuing Education Awards: Associations members may submit applications for these awards of $100 to $500 to develop their knowledge of the theoretical, administrative, or technical aspects of librarianship. More than one continuing education (CE) award may be offered in a year and may be used either for MLA courses or for other CE activities.

Cunningham Memorial International Fellowship: This fellowship is for health sciences librarians from countries outside the United States and Canada. The award provides for attendance at the association's annual meeting and observation and supervised work in one or more medical libraries in the U.S. and Canada.

David A Kronick Traveling Fellowship: This grant awards each year one $2,000 fellowship to cover the expenses involved in traveling to three or more medical libraries in the United States or Canada, for the purpose of studying a specific aspect of health information management.

Donald A. B. Lindberg Research Fellowship: This $10,000 fellowship is intended to fund research aimed at expanding the research knowledge base of biomedical care, linking the information services provided by librarians to improved health care and advances in biomedical research.

EBSCO/MLA Annual Meeting Grant: This scholarship, sponsored by EBSCO Information Services, enables association members to attend its annual meeting. Each year, awards of up to $1,000 for travel and conference-related expenses will be given to four librarians who would otherwise be unable to attend the meeting. Applicants must be currently employed as health sciences librarians and have between two and five years' experience in a health sciences library.

Hospital Libraries Section/MLA Professional Development Grants: This award, sponsored by the Hospital Libraries Section, provides librarians working in hospital and similar clinical settings with the support needed for educational or research activities. Up to two awards may be granted each year.

Medical Informatics Section/MLA Career Development Grant: This award provides up to two individuals with a $1,500 grant each to support a career development activity that will contribute to advancement in the field of medical informatics.

MLA Research, Development, and Demonstration Project Grant: The purpose of this grant is to provide support for research, development, or demonstration projects that will help to promote excellence in the field of health sciences librarianship and information sciences. Grants range from $100 to $1,000. Grants will not be given to support an activity that is operational in nature or has only local usefulness. More than one award may be granted in a year.

MLA Scholarship: A scholarship for up to $5,000 will be granted to a student who is entering a masters program at an American Library Association (ALA)-accredited library school or who has yet to finish at least one half of the program's requirements in the year following the granting of the scholarship.

MLA Scholarship for Minority Students: A scholarship for up to $5,000 will be granted to a minority student who is entering a Masters program at an American Library Association (ALA)-accredited library school or has yet to finish at least one half of the program's requirements in the year following

the granting of the scholarship. African American, Hispanic, Asian, Native American, or Pacific Islander American individuals who wish to study health sciences librarianship are eligible.

MLA/NLM Spectrum Scholarship: The Medical Library Association (MLA) and the National Library of Medicine (NLM) jointly sponsor two scholarships through the American Library Association (ALA) Spectrum Initiative Scholarship program. The awards are funded by the National Library of Medicine in conjunction with the Houston Academy of Medicine-Texas Medical Center Library. These two organizations make a total annual donation of $6,500 each year to support minority students in their goals to become health sciences information professionals. African American, Hispanic, Asian, Native American, or Pacific Islander individuals attending ALA-accredited library schools are eligible.

Thomson Reuters/MLA Doctoral Fellowship: A $2,000 fellowship is available to foster and encourage superior students to conduct doctoral work in an area of health sciences librarianship or information sciences, and to provide support to individuals who have been admitted to candidacy. The award supports research or travel applicable to the candidates study within a twelve-month period. The award is given every other year in even-numbered years and may not be used for tuition.

EIN: 360540525

2729

The Medline Foundation

1 Medline Pl.
Mundelein, IL   60060-4486   (847) 643-4343

Foundation type: Company-sponsored foundation

Purpose: Disaster relief grants, welfare grants, and college scholarships to employees and children of employees of Medline.

Financial data: Year ended 12/31/2012. Assets, $3,416,018 (M); Expenditures, $714,773; Total giving, $707,477; Grant to an individual, 1 grant totaling $82,900.

Fields of interest: Higher education; Disasters, preparedness/services.

Type of support: Employee-related scholarships; Employee-related welfare.

Application information: Applications not accepted.

Additional information: Unsolicited requests for funds not considered or acknowledged.

Company name: Medline Industries, Inc.

EIN: 421563666

2730

Edward Arthur Mellinger Educational Foundation, Inc.

1025 E. Broadway
Monmouth, IL   61462-1983   (309) 734-2419
FAX: (309) 734-4435; E-mail: info@mellinger.org; URL: http://www.mellinger.org/

Foundation type: Independent foundation

Purpose: Scholarships to undergraduate students from western IL, for attendance at accredited colleges and universities or accredited vocational schools in the U.S. Loans to graduate students who reside in six western IL counties.

Publications: Application guidelines; Program policy statement.

Financial data: Year ended 12/31/2012. Assets, $19,973,976 (M); Expenditures, $1,602,457; Total giving, $1,301,820; Grants to individuals,

730 grants totaling $895,660; Loans to individuals, totaling $7,500.

Fields of interest: Higher education; Scholarships/financial aid.

Type of support: Student loans—to individuals; Graduate support; Undergraduate support.

Application information: Applications accepted. Application form required. Application form available on the grantmaker's web site.

Initial approach: Letter
Deadline(s): May 1
Final notification: Recipients notified in early July
Applicants should submit the following:
1) SAR
2) Financial information
3) Transcripts

Additional information: The western IL counties include Fulton, Henderson, Knox, McDonough, Mercer and Warren. See web site for additional application guidelines.

EIN: 362428421

2731

Gregory Menn Foundation

10 S. Dearbon ILI-0117
Chicago, IL   60603   (920) 832-6212
Application address: c/o Appleton East High School, Attn.: C. Radtke, Guidance Office, 2121 E. Emmers Dr., Appleton, WI 54911

Foundation type: Independent foundation

Purpose: Scholarships to students and graduates of Appleton High School East, WI, who show academic excellence and school participation.

Financial data: Year ended 06/30/2013. Assets, $793,207 (M); Expenditures, $43,705; Total giving, $34,692; Grants to individuals, 8 grants totaling $34,692 (high: $4,673, low: $4,000).

Type of support: Support to graduates or students of specific schools.

Application information: Application form not required.

Deadline(s): May 1
Additional information: Contact foundation for current application guidelines.

EIN: 396143254

2732

Metamora Community Foundation

1200 E. Partridge
P.O. Box 134
Metamora, IL   61548-0134   (309) 696-5322

Foundation type: Community foundation

Purpose: Scholarships to Metamora, IL area high school seniors for higher education at accredited institutions.

Financial data: Year ended 12/31/2012. Assets, $513,329 (M); Expenditures, $9,512; Total giving, $8,000; Grants to individuals, totaling $3,000.

Fields of interest: Higher education.

Type of support: Scholarships—to individuals.

Application information: Applications accepted.

Additional information: Contact the foundation for scholarship information.

EIN: 371194110

2733

Weaver Milburn, Jr. and Lenore Pauline Milburn Trust

1201 Network Ctr. Dr.
Effingham, IL   62401   (217) 342-2141
Application address: 133 W. Jefferson, Effingham, IL 62401

Foundation type: Independent foundation
Purpose: Scholarships to graduating seniors of Ashton High School, IL, ranked in the upper half of their class.
Financial data: Year ended 12/31/2012. Assets, $129,403 (M); Expenditures, $10,924; Total giving, $7,200; Grants to individuals, 21 grants totaling $7,200 (high: $500, low: $150).
Fields of interest: Higher education.
Type of support: Scholarships—to individuals.
Application information: Applications accepted. Application form required.
  Deadline(s): Apr. 1
  Applicants should submit the following:
    1) Letter(s) of recommendation
    2) Essay
  Additional information: Applications can be picked up from the Ashton High School Principal's office.
EIN: 367013908

2734
Miller Scholarship Trust
10 S. Dearborn, IL1-0117
Chicago, IL   60603

Foundation type: Independent foundation
Purpose: Scholarships to graduating seniors of Canton High School, Astoria High School, and Lewistown High School, WI for full time attendance at an accredited college or university.
Financial data: Year ended 12/31/2012. Assets, $471,077 (M); Expenditures, $28,067; Total giving, $23,842.
Fields of interest: Higher education.
Type of support: Support to graduates or students of specific schools; Undergraduate support.
Application information: Application form required.
  Applicants should submit the following:
    1) SAT
    2) Class rank
    3) ACT
    4) Transcripts
    5) Letter(s) of recommendation
  Additional information: Application should also include three personal references and personal letter explaining reason for applying. Application available from the local high school principals. Awards are made directly to the educational institution on behalf of the student.
EIN: 376280528

2735
George W. and Wilma F. Miller Trust
P.O. Box 266
Lewistown, IL   61542   (309) 547-2288
Application address: Lewistown High School, Attn.: Guidance Counselor, 1551 N. Main St., Lewistown, IL 61542

Foundation type: Independent foundation
Purpose: Scholarships, which are renewable, to students of Lewistown School District No. 97, IL, for higher education.
Financial data: Year ended 12/31/2012. Assets, $1,391,225 (M); Expenditures, $106,951; Total giving, $44,109.
Type of support: Support to graduates or students of specific schools; Undergraduate support.
Application information: Applications accepted. Application form required.
  Deadline(s): Apr. 30.
  Applicants should submit the following:
    1) ACT
    2) SAT

    3) Transcripts
    4) Essay
    5) Letter(s) of recommendation
EIN: 371147868

2736
Minner Family Charitable Foundation
c/o Suburban Bank & Trust Co.
9901 S. Western Ave.
Chicago, IL   60643-1800   (815) 476-2594
Application address: c/o Wilmington High School, Attn.: Guidance Office, 715 S. Joliet St., Wilmington, IL 60481-1488

Foundation type: Independent foundation
Purpose: Scholarships to graduating seniors at Wilmington High School, IL in pursuit of a higher education at accredited colleges or universities.
Financial data: Year ended 12/31/2011. Assets, $279,675 (M); Expenditures, $16,534; Total giving, $11,750; Grants to individuals, 12 grants totaling $11,750 (high: $1,500, low: $500).
Fields of interest: Higher education.
Type of support: Scholarships—to individuals.
Application information: Applications accepted. Application form required.
  Deadline(s): May 10
  Applicants should submit the following:
    1) Class rank
    2) SAT
    3) GPA
    4) Essay
    5) ACT
  Additional information: Funds are paid directly to the educational institution on behalf of the student.
EIN: 367057812

2737
The Moline Foundation
817 11th Ave.
Moline, IL   61265-1222   (309) 736-3800
Contact: Joy Boruff, Exec. Dir.; For scholarships: Linda Daily, Asst.
Scholarship e-mail: ldaily@qconline.com
FAX: (309) 736-3721;
E-mail: molinefoundation@qconline.com;
URL: http://www.molinefoundation.org

Foundation type: Community foundation
Purpose: Scholarships to graduating high school seniors or community college students living in Moline School District No. 40., IL.
Publications: Annual report; Grants list; Newsletter.
Financial data: Year ended 09/30/2012. Assets, $16,717,428 (M); Expenditures, $1,425,007; Total giving, $1,078,209; Grants to individuals, totaling $34,614.
Fields of interest: Higher education.
Type of support: Scholarships—to individuals; Support to graduates or students of specific schools.
Application information: Applications accepted. Application form required. Interview required.
  Initial approach: Letter or telephone
  Send request by: Online
  Deadline(s): Mar. 3
  Final notification: Applicants notified by May 1
  Applicants should submit the following:
    1) Transcripts
    2) Letter(s) of recommendation
    3) Essay

Additional information: Transcripts and reference letters should be mailed to the foundation. See web site for additional guidelines.
EIN: 366036867

2738
Morrison Foundation
(formerly Ollege and Minnie Morrison Foundation)
10 S. Dearborn, IL1-0117
Chicago, IL   60603

Foundation type: Independent foundation
Purpose: Scholarships only to graduating seniors of the Livingston Intermediate School District, Livingston, TX, area.
Financial data: Year ended 12/31/2012. Assets, $897,757 (M); Expenditures, $134,269; Total giving, $139,961; Grants to individuals, 88 grants totaling $139,961 (high: $1,500, low: $461).
Type of support: Support to graduates or students of specific schools; Undergraduate support.
Application information: Applications not accepted.
  Additional information: Unsolicited requests for funds not considered or acknowledged.
EIN: 237073336

2739
Mark Morton Memorial Fund
c/o Schiff Hardin LLP
233 S. Wacker Dr., Ste. 6600
Chicago, IL   60606-6360   (312) 258-5588

Foundation type: Independent foundation
Purpose: Grants to needy LA and TX individuals who are verifiable employees of the Morton Salt Company on or before June 30, 1971, to assist with hospital, medical, and surgical expenses, as well as assistance for those who are aged or disabled.
Financial data: Year ended 12/31/2012. Assets, $17,075,845 (M); Expenditures, $1,339,248; Total giving, $1,003,488; Grants to individuals, 72 grants totaling $244,488 (high: $10,656, low: $140).
Fields of interest: Health care; Aging; Disabilities, people with.
Type of support: Grants for special needs.
Application information: Applications not accepted.
  Additional information: Unsolicited requests for funds not considered or acknowledged.
EIN: 237181380

2740
W. B. Munson Foundation
c/o JPMorgan Chase Bank, N.A.
10 S. Dearborn St.
Chicago, IL   60603-2300
Application address: c/o JPMorgan Chase Bank, N.A., 2200 Ross Ave., 7th Fl., Dallas, TX 75201

Foundation type: Independent foundation
Purpose: Scholarships to seniors at Denison High School, TX.
Financial data: Year ended 12/31/2012. Assets, $8,254,174 (M); Expenditures, $468,832; Total giving, $374,240; Grants to individuals, 22 grants totaling $24,000 (high: $2,000, low: $1,000).
Type of support: Support to graduates or students of specific schools; Undergraduate support.
Application information: Applications not accepted.
  Additional information: Unsolicited requests for funds not considered or acknowledged.
EIN: 756015068

2741
Daniel Murphy Scholarship Fund
100 W. Monroe, Ste. 500
Chicago, IL 60603-1921   (312) 455-7800
Contact: Andrew Ditton, Exec. Dir.
FAX: (312) 455-7801; E-mail: andy@dmsf.org;
URL: http://www.dmsf.org

Foundation type: Public charity
Purpose: Scholarships to Chicago-area students to attend college preparatory high schools.
Publications: Application guidelines; Annual report.
Financial data: Year ended 08/31/2011. Assets, $6,825,887 (M); Expenditures, $2,714,288; Total giving, $1,272,627; Grants to individuals, totaling $1,272,627.
Fields of interest: Elementary/secondary education; Secondary school/education; Charter schools; Scholarships/financial aid.
Type of support: Scholarships—to individuals.
Application information: Applications accepted. Application form required. Application form available on the grantmaker's web site. Interview required.
> *Initial approach:* Application
> *Send request by:* Mail or hand deliver
> *Deadline(s):* Oct. 28
> *Applicants should submit the following:*
> 1) SAT
> 2) Letter(s) of recommendation
> 3) Financial information
> 4) Essay
> *Additional information:* Faxed or e-mailed copies are not accepted.

Program description:
> *Scholarships:* Scholarships are intended to make a life-altering difference in the lives of its recipients by providing them with the best opportunity to succeed in high school and college, and by allowing them to attend a high-performing high school, participate in extracurricular activities, benefit from honors and accelerated programs, and take advantage of educational support services and programs. Applicants must live in Chicago, IL or its surrounding communities including Cicero, Berwyn, Maywood, and Bellwood, and demonstrate academic potential, strong character, and financial need.
EIN: 363675466

2742
Mutual Service Foundation
10 S Dearborn IL1-0117
Chicago, IL 60603   (317) 243-8858
Contact: Jeanne Hicks, Secy.
Application address: 2121 N. Fisher Ave., Sppedway, IN 46224

Foundation type: Independent foundation
Purpose: Scholarships and aid to financially needy, self-supporting women residing in Marion County, IN. A limited amount of funds are available for welfare assistance.
Financial data: Year ended 12/31/2012. Assets, $335,888 (M); Expenditures, $18,732; Total giving, $16,950; Grants to individuals, 5 grants totaling $10,950 (high: $3,000, low: $950).
Fields of interest: Higher education; Human services; Women; Economically disadvantaged.
Type of support: Scholarships—to individuals; Grants for special needs.
Application information: Applications accepted.
> *Initial approach:* Proposal
> *Copies of proposal:* 1
> *Deadline(s):* None
EIN: 356047127

2743
National Council of YMCAs of the USA
101 N. Wacker Dr.
Chicago, IL 60606-1784
Contact: Sally McMillan, Sr. Dir. of Devel.
E-mail: fulfillment@ymca.net; Toll-free tel. (domestic): (800) 872-9622; toll-free tel. (international): (312) 977-0031; URL: http://www.ymca.net

Foundation type: Public charity
Purpose: Scholarships for current and prospective YMCA staff members of YMCAs.
Financial data: Year ended 12/31/2011. Assets, $156,207,543 (M); Expenditures, $92,091,146; Total giving, $22,340,165; Grants to individuals, 51 grants totaling $82,718.
Fields of interest: YM/YWCAs & YM/YWHAs; Children/youth.
Type of support: Scholarships—to individuals.
Application information: Applications accepted. Application form required.
> *Additional information:* Contact the organization for additional guidelines.
EIN: 363258696

2744
National Foundation for Ectodermal Dysplasias
6 Executive Dr., Ste. 2
Fairview Heights, IL 62208-1360   (618) 566-2020
Contact: Kelley Atchison, Dir.
FAX: (618) 566-4718; E-mail: info@nfed.org; E-mail For Kelley Atchison : kelley@nfed.org; URL: http://www.nfed.org

Foundation type: Public charity
Purpose: Scholarships and financial assistance for qualified individuals and families affected by ectodermal dysplasias. Also, research grants for those investigating ectodermal dysplasias.
Publications: Application guidelines; Annual report; Financial statement.
Financial data: Year ended 12/31/2012. Assets, $1,505,095 (M); Expenditures, $1,049,405; Total giving, $152,483; Grants to individuals, totaling $77,483.
Fields of interest: Diseases (rare); Diseases (rare) research; Medical research.
Type of support: Research; Scholarships—to individuals; Grants for special needs.
Application information: Applications accepted. Application form required. Application form available on the grantmaker's web site.
> *Initial approach:* Application
> *Deadline(s):* Mar. 7 for Scholarship
> *Final notification:* Recipients notified in May for Scholarship
> *Additional information:* Application should include financial information, letter(s) of recommendation, an essay and a photograph for scholarship. See web site for additional guidelines.

Program descriptions:
> *L. Marie Heard Education Scholarship Program:* Scholarships of up to $10,000 to individuals affected by ectodermal dysplasias, to be used toward postsecondary education (including colleges, universities, trade schools, and junior colleges). Scholarships can only be used for tuition, fees, and/or books.
> *Treatment Assistance Program:* The program provides financial assistance to families for their dental care as well as wigs, air conditioners, cooling vests, or medical care associated with ectodermal

dysplasias. Maximum awards range from $600 to $15,000.
EIN: 371112496

2745
National Headache Foundation
820 N. Orleans St., Ste. 411
Chicago, IL 60610-3498   (312) 274-2650
Contact: Seymour Diamond M.D., Exec. Chair.
FAX: (312) 640-9049; E-mail: info@headaches.org;
Toll-free tel.: (888) 643-5552; URL: http://www.headaches.org

Foundation type: Public charity
Purpose: Grants by nomination only to a worthy candidate for study in a program related to headache research.
Publications: Application guidelines; Grants list; Informational brochure; Newsletter.
Financial data: Year ended 12/31/2012. Assets, $2,949,362 (M); Expenditures, $1,878,463; Total giving, $92,963.
Fields of interest: Medical research.
Type of support: Research; Travel grants.
Application information: Applications accepted. Application form required. Application form available on the grantmaker's web site.
> *Initial approach:* Letter
> *Copies of proposal:* 6
> *Deadline(s):* Feb. 1 for Research Grants, none for Requests for Proposals Headache in Special Populations
> *Final notification:* Recipients notified by Mar. 1 for Research Grants
> *Additional information:* Application must include curriculum vitae.

Program descriptions:
> *Requests for Proposals Headache in Special Populations Program:* Grants of $10,000 each are available to projects and proposals that work to advance the care of the medically-underserved population, and minorities with headache. Eligible applicants must be in health or biomedical sciences, healthcare administration, sociology, social work, health economics, or minority studies, in training or within five years post-completion of their terminal degree. Applicants who are applying prior to completing their terminal degree must be in good academic standing, as evidence in at least two reference letters from people who have worked with them; applicants who have completed their terminal degree must provide at least two reference letters from people who have worked with them.
> *Research Grants:* Grants for research in the field of headache and pain (including offering education and information to headache sufferers and their families). The foundation is interested in research protocols that are objectively sound and whose results can, when published in the medical literature, contribute to a better understanding and treatment of headache and pain. Grants may be used for the purchase of supplies needed for the study (chemical or pharmacological reagents, laboratory animals, tissue culture materials, forms, etc.), and for costs related to the recruitment of patients, data analysis, and interpreting or reading results. Grants of up to $100,000 will be available.
EIN: 237073022

2746

National Kidney Foundation of Illinois, Inc.

215 W. Illinois St., Ste. 1C
Chicago, IL 60654-7163   (312) 321-1500
Contact: Anne Black, C.E.O.
E-mail for Research grant: mlidacis@nkfi.org
FAX: (312) 321-1505; E-mail: kidney@nkfi.org;
URL: http://www.nkfi.org

Foundation type: Public charity
Purpose: Grants to researchers of Illinois for the study of kidney, urologic and related diseases.
Publications: Application guidelines; Annual report; Informational brochure (including application guidelines); Newsletter.
Financial data: Year ended 06/30/2012. Assets, $4,512,983 (M); Expenditures, $1,900,795; Total giving, $494,119; Grants to individuals, 3 grants totaling $90,000.
Fields of interest: Kidney research.
Type of support: Fellowships; Research.
Application information: Applications accepted. Application form required. Application form available on the grantmaker's web site.
   Initial approach: Telephone or e-mail
   Additional information: See web site for additional guidelines.
Program description:
   Research Grants for the Young Investigator Program: This program provides up to $60,000 per year, for up to two years, to young investigators who have research projects that increase the understanding of kidney, urologic, and related diseases and transportation, as well as improve the clinical management and treatment or cure of these diseases. Applicants must be members of a division of nephrology, urology, or renal transportation in Illinois.
EIN: 366009226

2747

National Merit Scholarship Corporation

(also known as NMSC)
1560 Sherman Ave., Ste. 200
Evanston, IL 60201-4897   (847) 866-5100
Contact: Richard L. Sevcik, Corporate Secy.
FAX: (847) 866-5113; URL: http://www.nationalmerit.org

Foundation type: Public charity
Purpose: Scholarships to students who perform exceptionally well on the Preliminary SAT/National Merit Scholarship Qualifying Test.
Publications: Annual report.
Financial data: Year ended 05/31/2012. Assets, $150,045,003 (M); Expenditures, $61,654,400; Total giving, $50,506,839; Grants to individuals, totaling $47,824,351.
Fields of interest: Education.
Type of support: Undergraduate support.
Application information: Applications not accepted.
   Additional information: Unsolicited requests for funds not considered or acknowledged.
Program descriptions:
   National Achievement Scholarship Program: This program provides scholarships to outstanding African-American students throughout the U.S. who have received excellent scores in the Preliminary SAT/National Merit Scholarship Qualifying Test (PSAT/NMSQT) As with the National Merit Scholarship Program, those students with the highest PSAT/NMSQT scores are asked to name two colleges or universities to which they would like to be referred by the corporation; those high scorers will then be notified through their schools that they have qualified as either a Commended Student (to

which no scholarship support is generally given) or Semifinalist. The field of semifinalists is then narrowed down to a field of finalists; from this field of finalists, scholarship support will be awarded to selected outstanding individuals. Each recipient will win a $2,500 scholarship; finalists and semifinalists will also be eligible for corporate-sponsored merit scholarships.
   National Merit Scholarship Program: This program provides scholarships to outstanding students throughout the U.S. who have received excellent scores in the Preliminary SAT/National Merit Scholarship Qualifying Test (PSAT/NMSQT). Those students with the highest PSAT/NMSQT scores are asked to name two colleges or universities to which they would like to be referred by the corporation; those high scorers will then be notified through their schools that they have qualified as either a Commended Student (to which no scholarship support is generally given) or Semifinalist. The field of semifinalists is then narrowed down to a field of finalists; from this field of finalists, scholarship support will be awarded to selected outstanding individuals. Each recipient will win a $2,500 scholarship; finalists and semifinalists will also be eligible for both corporate-sponsored and college-sponsored merit scholarships.
EIN: 362307745

2748

National Multiple Sclerosis Society - Greater Illinois Chapter

525 W. Monroe St., Ste. 900
Chicago, IL 60661-3793   (312) 421-4500
Contact: Sean Gallagher, Chair.
FAX: (312) 421-4544; E-mail: cgic@ild.nmss.org;
Toll-free tel.: (800) 344-4867; URL: http://www.nationalmssociety.org/chapters/ild/index.aspx

Foundation type: Public charity
Purpose: Financial assistance to individuals and families of IL, whose lifes are affected by multiple sclerosis.
Publications: Application guidelines; Informational brochure.
Financial data: Year ended 09/30/2012. Assets, $3,004,877 (M); Expenditures, $6,201,941; Total giving, $170,290; Grants to individuals, totaling $170,290.
Fields of interest: Multiple sclerosis.
Type of support: Grants to individuals.
Application information:
   Initial approach: Letter or telephone
   Deadline(s): None
Program description:
   Financial Assistance: The chapter provides financial assistance to help people living with multiple sclerosis in Illinois maintain independent living and a high quality of life, in order to fund needed services that are not available using other resources such as private insurance, Medicare, Medicaid, or other state, personal, or community resources. Assistance includes counseling, durable medical equipment, home/respite care, home modifications, incontinence supplies, transportation, vehicle modifications, cooling aides, and wellness programs.
EIN: 362249887

2749

National Restaurant Association Educational Foundation

(formerly National Institute for the Food Service Industry)
175 W. Jackson Blvd., Ste. 1500
Chicago, IL 60604-2814   (312) 715-1010
Contact: Ellen Nash
FAX: (312) 715-0807; E-mail: scholars@nraef.org;
Toll-free tel.: (800) 765-2122; URL: http://www.nraef.org

Foundation type: Public charity
Purpose: Scholarships for undergraduate and graduate studies in the restaurant/hospitality area, and industry assistance and work-study grants to teachers and administrators.
Publications: Application guidelines; Annual report; Newsletter.
Financial data: Year ended 12/31/2011. Assets, $21,627,798 (M); Expenditures, $8,405,628; Total giving, $1,872,519; Grants to individuals, totaling $1,102,519.
Fields of interest: Vocational education, post-secondary; Education; Business/industry.
Type of support: Graduate support; Undergraduate support; Workstudy grants.
Application information: Application form required.
   Initial approach: Letter, telephone, or e-mail.
   Deadline(s): Feb. 8 for Professional Development, Feb. 22 for GRI/Giacomo Bologna, Mar. 14 for Al Schuman Ecolab Scholarship and Undergraduate Students/ProStart Alumni/Manage First Students, July 25 for High School/GED Graduate/ProStart Students
   Additional information: See web site for additional guidelines.
Program descriptions:
   Al Schuman Ecolab Undergraduate Entrepreneurial Scholarship: Scholarships, ranging from $3,000 to $5,500, are awarded to current undergraduate students who are committed to their education and careers in the restaurant and foodservice industry while demonstrating a strong entrepreneurial spirit. Applicants must be citizens or permanent residents of the U.S., be enrolled full-time or substantial part-time (minimum of nine credit hours) at a selected U.S.-accredited culinary school, college, or university in a food service-related program (California State Polytechnic University - Pomona, Cornell University, Culinary Institute of America, DePaul University, Johnson and Wales University, Kendall College, Lynn University, Michigan State University, New York University, Pennsylvania State University, Purdue University, University of Denver, University of Houston, University of Nevada - Las Vegas, and University of Massachusetts - Amherst); and have a minimum GPA of at least 3.0 (on a 4.0 scale)
   GRI/Giacomo Bologna Scholarship: Awarded in conjunction with Gruppo Ristoratori Italiani (GRI), this program will award up to six students with an all-expense-paid trip from New York City to Italy, and enable them to participate in various culinary and restaurant industry-related classes and tours. During this program, students will be offered a first-hand experience in Italian winemaking and cooking. Applicants must be citizens or permanent residents of the U.S., be undergraduate students who are currently enrolled full-time in a U.S.-accredited culinary school, college, or university, demonstrate a commitment to Italian viticulture, and have at least two years of culinary experience and/or viticulture training, working directly with a chef in the preparation of food or with a sommelier.

High School/GED Graduate/ProStart Students Scholarships: Awards of $2,500 each are available to students who will be first-time freshmen, including graduating high school seniors, GED graduates, and high school graduates enrolling in college for the first time. Applicant must be a citizen or permanent resident of the U.S., be a first-time freshman (including a graduating high-school senior, a GED graduate enrolling in college for the first time, or a high school graduate enrolling in college for the first time), be accepted and plan to enroll in a U.S.-accredited culinary school, college, or university, and plan to major in culinary arts, restaurant management, or another foodservice-related major.

Professional Development Scholarships for Educators: This program offers scholarships of $1,750 each to restaurant/foodservice educators to attend the foundation's annual Summer Institute, or to participate in its annual 'Hands On' Industry Work Experience Program, with the goal of providing educators the opportunity to enhance their teaching skills by providing practical, industry-related experience that can be brought back to the classroom. Applicant must be a citizen or permanent resident of the U.S., and be an educator in a restaurant/foodservice-related program at a secondary or post-secondary school.

Undergraduate Student/ProStart Alumni/Manage First Students: Scholarships of $2,500 each are available to current undergraduate students enrolled in a foodservice-related program. Applicant must be a citizen or permanent resident of the U.S., be a college student currently enrolled full-time or substantially part-time (with a minimum of nine credit hours) in a foodservice-related program at a U.S.-accredited culinary school, college, or university, and have completed at least one grading term of his/her college or postsecondary program.
EIN: 366103388

2750
National Rosacea Society
196 James St.
Barrington, IL   60010-4681   (847) 382-8971
Contact: Samuel Huff, Exec. Dir.
FAX: (847) 382-5567; E-mail: rosaceas@aol.com;
Toll-free tel.: (888) 662-5874; URL: http://
www.rosacea.org

Foundation type: Public charity
Purpose: Grants to researchers to encourage and support medical research relating to potential causes of Rosacea and other key aspects of the disorder.
Financial data: Year ended 12/31/2011. Assets, $154,889 (M); Expenditures, $618,959; Total giving, $68,550. Grants to individuals amount not specified.
Fields of interest: Skin disorders research.
Type of support: Research.
Application information: Applications accepted. Application form required.
  Initial approach: Proposal
  Deadline(s): May 1
  Additional information: See web site for additional application guidelines.
Program description:
  Research Grants Program: The program was established to encourage and support research into the potential causes and other key aspects of this condition that may lead to improvements in its treatment and potential prevention or cure. High priority is given to research in such areas as the pathogenesis, progression, mechanism of action,

cell biology, and potential genetic factors of rosacea. Grants are typically $10,000 to $25,000.
EIN: 364120334

2751
National Safety Council
1121 Spring Lake Dr.
Itasca, IL   60143-3201   (630) 285-1121
Contact: Janet Froetscher, Pres. and C.E.O.
FAX: (630) 285-1315; E-mail: info@nsc.org;
Toll-free tel.: (800) 621-7615; E-mail For Janet Froetscher: Janet.Froetscher@nsc.org;
URL: http://www.nsc.org/Pages/Home.aspx

Foundation type: Public charity
Purpose: Scholarships to individuals who are pursuing a degree in either safety or industrial hygiene, and plan to go into the safety and/or health fields after graduation.
Publications: Application guidelines; Annual report.
Financial data: Year ended 06/30/2012. Assets, $25,779,264 (M); Expenditures, $37,996,059.
Fields of interest: Safety, education.
Type of support: Scholarships—to individuals.
Application information: Applications accepted. Application form required.
  Initial approach: Application
  Deadline(s): June 1
Program description:
  Billy D. Young Scholarship: This $1,500 scholarship is offered to those who are pursuing a degree in either safety or industrial hygiene. Recipients will be chosen based on safety/health-related work experience, activities and honors related to safety and health, and financial need.
EIN: 362167809

2752
National Society to Prevent Blindness
211 W. Wacker Dr., Ste. 1700
Chicago, IL   60606-1375   (312) 363-6001
Contact: Hugh R. Parry, Pres. and C.E.O.; Jeff Todd, V.P.
E-mail: info@preventblindness.org; Toll-free tel.: (800) 331-2020; URL: http://
www.preventblindness.org/

Foundation type: Public charity
Purpose: Research grants and fellowships to graduate students, postdoctoral fellows and other beginning investigators for clinically-based research related to the burden of illness of eye-related health and safety topics.
Publications: Annual report; Financial statement; Newsletter.
Financial data: Year ended 03/31/2012. Assets, $12,513,873 (M); Expenditures, $4,598,160; Total giving, $586,068; Grants to individuals, totaling $35,000.
Fields of interest: Eye research.
Type of support: Fellowships; Research; Postdoctoral support; Graduate support.
Application information:
  Initial approach: Proposal
  Send request by: Online
  Copies of proposal: 3
  Deadline(s): Mar. 30
  Additional information: Application should include a letter of recommendation. All research grants must focus on preserving sight and preventing blindness.
Program description:
  Prevent Blindness America Investigator Awards: Grants range from $10,000 for a one year period to $30,000 for research investigating public health

related to eye health and safety. Applications will be accepted in the following priority areas in adult vision, children's vision, or eye injury: the burden/economic aspects of eye disease/vision loss on society; best practices to integrate vision screening/follow-up care to system care access; and vision program effectiveness and/or evaluation. All research grants need to promote the core mission of the organization (preventing blindness and preserving sight). This program does not fund basic laboratory science research.
EIN: 363667121

2753
Neal Foundation
P.O. Box 478
Toledo, IL   62468   (217) 849-3331
Application address: c/o Neal Foundation, P.o. Box 158 Toledo, IL 62468

Foundation type: Independent foundation
Purpose: Grants and scholarships to individuals in Toledo, IL or Cumberland County, IL.
Financial data: Year ended 12/31/2012. Assets, $2,554,406 (M); Expenditures, $113,090; Total giving, $98,400; Grants to individuals, 5 grants totaling $5,750 (high: $2,500, low: $250).
Fields of interest: Higher education.
Type of support: Grants to individuals; Scholarships—to individuals.
Application information:
  Deadline(s): None
EIN: 371020959

2754
Nesbitt Medical Student Foundation
c/o National Bank & Trust Co.
230 W. State St., MSC M-300
Sycamore, IL   60178-1419   (815) 895-2125
Contact: Carolyn Swafford, Trust Off.

Foundation type: Independent foundation
Purpose: Scholarships to financially needy students who are residents of IL attending an approved medical school.
Financial data: Year ended 12/31/2012. Assets, $803,081 (M); Expenditures, $54,304; Total giving, $41,000; Grants to individuals, 4 grants totaling $41,000 (high: $15,000, low: $3,000).
Fields of interest: Medical school/education; Women.
Type of support: Graduate support.
Application information: Application form required.
  Initial approach: Letter
  Send request by: Mail
  Deadline(s): June 1
  Final notification: Applicants notified by Aug. 15
  Applicants should submit the following:
    1) Letter(s) of recommendation
    2) Financial information
  Additional information: Application forms are available upon request. Preference is given to women and residents of Dekalb county, IL.
EIN: 510171682

2755
Linda Neville Trust
10 S. Dearborn IL1-0117
Chicago, IL   60603   (214) 965-2914
Contact: Debbie Ottinger
Application address: c/o JPMorgan Chase Bank, N.A., 2200 Ross Ave., Dallas, TX 75201-2914

Foundation type: Independent foundation

Purpose: Assistance to individuals with defective eyesight who are residents of Kentucky.
Financial data: Year ended 12/31/2012. Assets, $2,560,374 (M); Expenditures, $146,425; Total giving, $126,091.
Fields of interest: Eye diseases; Human services.
Type of support: Grants for special needs.
Application information:
Initial approach: Letter
EIN: 616018696

2756
Niccum Educational Trust Foundation
10 S. Dearborn, IL1-0117
Chicago, IL 60603 (214) 965-2231
Application address: JPMorgan Chase Bank, N.A., 121 W. Franklin St., Elkhart, IN 46516

Foundation type: Independent foundation
Purpose: Scholarships to graduates of public high schools in the IN counties of Elkhart, Kosciusko, LaGrange, Marshall, Noble, or St. Joseph pursuing higher education.
Publications: Application guidelines; Program policy statement.
Financial data: Year ended 12/31/2012. Assets, $504,934 (M); Expenditures, $27,202; Total giving, $24,000; Grants to individuals, 12 grants totaling $24,000 (high: $2,000, low: $2,000).
Fields of interest: Higher education; Scholarships/financial aid.
Type of support: Undergraduate support.
Application information: Applications accepted. Application form required.
Initial approach: Letter
Deadline(s): Apr. 15
Applicants should submit the following:
1) Financial information
2) Transcripts
3) Letter(s) of recommendation
Additional information: Application should also include three references. Application can be obtained from JPMorgan Chase Bank.
EIN: 356017515

2757
Robert and Ida Nicoll Educational Trust
10 S Dearborn IL1-0117
Chicago, IL 60603 (312) 732-6411
Application address: 10 S. Dearborn St., Chicago, IL 60603

Foundation type: Independent foundation
Purpose: Scholarships to graduating high school students in Kenosha County, WI, for higher education.
Financial data: Year ended 12/31/2012. Assets, $244,162 (M); Expenditures, $40,491; Total giving, $37,400.
Fields of interest: Higher education.
Type of support: Undergraduate support.
Application information: Applications accepted. Application form required.
Deadline(s): None
Applicants should submit the following:
1) Transcripts
2) FAFSA
Additional information: Application available upon request. Applicants must have received a high school equivalency from Gateway Technical College, WI, or have been a resident of Kenosha county for the two years immediately preceding the scholarship.
EIN: 396576895

2758
North American Spine Society
(also known as NASS)
7075 Veterans Blvd.
Burr Ridge, IL 60527-5614 (630) 230-3600
FAX: (630) 230-3700; E-mail: kjames@spine.org; Additional addresses (Spring Grove office): 8320 St. Moritz Dr., Spring Grove, IL 60081-9256, tel.: (630) 230-3691, fax: (630) 230-3791; additional address (DC office): 777 N. Capitol St., N.E., Ste. 801, Washington, DC 20002-4294; toll-free tel.: (866) 960-6277; URL: http://www.spine.org

Foundation type: Public charity
Purpose: Research funding for evidence-based, and ethical spine care by promoting education, research, and advocacy.
Publications: Application guidelines; Annual report; Grants list.
Financial data: Year ended 12/31/2011. Assets, $26,747,906 (M); Expenditures, $10,893,091; Total giving, $187,425. Grants to individuals amount not specified.
Fields of interest: Spine disorders; Spine disorders research.
Type of support: Fellowships; Research; Travel grants.
Application information: Applications accepted. Application form required. Application form available on the grantmaker's web site.
Initial approach: Letter of Inquiry
Copies of proposal: 1
Deadline(s): Varies
Final notification: Recipients notified four months for notification of awards
Applicants should submit the following:
1) Letter(s) of recommendation
2) Curriculum vitae
3) Budget Information
Additional information: No support for independent manufacturers, industry development, personal business or financial gain.
Program description:
Awards Program: The foundation provides and grants and awards to individual researchers who work in spine research. Special consideration will be given to the following: antibiotic prophylaxis in spine surgery; antithrombotic therapies in spine surgery; degenerative lumbar spondylolisthesis; degenerative lumbar spinal stenosis; and cervical radiculopathy from degenerative disorders.
EIN: 363382069

2759
Northern Illinois University Foundation
Altgeld Hall 135
DeKalb, IL 60115-2882 (815) 753-0782
FAX: (815) 753-0052;
E-mail: niufoundation@niu.edu; URL: http://www.niufoundation.org

Foundation type: Public charity
Purpose: Scholarships to pre-selected students of Northern Illinois University, IL.
Financial data: Year ended 06/30/2011. Assets, $89,183,681 (M); Expenditures, $8,994,015; Total giving, $5,937,563; Grants to individuals, totaling $1,115,319.
Fields of interest: Higher education.
Type of support: Support to graduates or students of specific schools.
Application information: Applications not accepted.
Additional information: Unsolicited requests for funds not considered or acknowledged.
EIN: 366086819

2760
Nuts, Bolts, and Thingamajigs: The Foundation of the Fabricators and Manufacturers Association, Inc.
(formerly Fabricators & Manufacturers Association Foundation)
833 Featherstone Rd.
Rockford, IL 61107-6302 (815) 381-1337
Contact: Bryan Hawkins, Chair.
FAX: (815) 399-8700;
E-mail: foundation@fmanet.org; Toll-free tel.: (888) 394-4362; URL: http://www.nutsandboltsfoundation.org/

Foundation type: Public charity
Purpose: Scholarships to students enrolled in an engineering or manufacturing-related course of study, or a trade or technical program that may lead to a career in manufacturing.
Publications: Application guidelines; Annual report.
Financial data: Year ended 12/31/2012. Assets, $632,123 (M); Expenditures, $82,907; Total giving, $30,400; Grants to individuals, totaling $15,900.
Fields of interest: Vocational education, post-secondary; Engineering school/education.
Type of support: Technical education support; Undergraduate support.
Application information: Applications accepted. Application form required. Application form available on the grantmaker's web site.
Send request by: Online
Deadline(s): Mar. 22
Final notification: Applicants notified in June
Program description:
Scholarships: Scholarships of up to $1,500 are awarded to students in courses of study that may lead to careers in manufacturing. Eligible applicants must be currently enrolled in, or entering, a postsecondary study program at a community college, technical college, or trade school, leading to a career in the manufacturing technology industry, and be a full-time student with a minimum 2.5 GPA. Applicants must be members of FMA, TPA, or OPC, the employee of a member-company, the child of a member, or the child of a member-company's employee.
EIN: 364201897

2761
Oak Park/River Forest Community Foundation
1049 Lake St., No. 204
Oak Park, IL 60301-6708 (708) 848-1560
Contact: Sophia Lloyd, Exec. Dir.
FAX: (708) 848-1531; E-mail: slloyd@oprfcf.org; URL: http://www.oprfcf.org

Foundation type: Community foundation
Purpose: Scholarships to graduating high school seniors in the Oak Park and River Forest, IL, area.
Publications: Application guidelines; Annual report (including application guidelines); Grants list; Informational brochure; Newsletter; Occasional report.
Financial data: Year ended 12/31/2012. Assets, $22,989,653 (M); Expenditures, $2,857,097; Total giving, $2,178,511.
Fields of interest: Music; Higher education; Scholarships/financial aid; Recreation, community; Children/youth, services.
Type of support: Scholarships—to individuals; Support to graduates or students of specific schools; Undergraduate support; Grants for special needs.

Application information: Applications accepted.
Application form required.
   Deadline(s): Varies
   Additional information: See web site for complete
      listing of scholarship funds and application
      information.
Program description:
   Scholarships and Educational Enrichment Grants:
The foundation offers a variety of scholarships and
educational enrichment grants. Each award has its
own set of unique application guidelines and
eligibility criteria, including graduation from specific
high schools, academic achievement, parishioners
of specific churches, involvement in sports, and
particular fields of undergraduate study such as
music and the arts. See web site for additional
information.
EIN: 364150724

2762
Frank L. Oakes Foundation
10 Dearborn IL1-0117
Chicago, IL   60603-2300   (214) 965-2910
Application address: 2200 Ross Ave. Dallas, TX
752012787

Foundation type: Independent foundation
Purpose: Scholarships to graduates of Marion
County, IN, high schools for college or other
postsecondary education.
Financial data: Year ended 05/31/2013. Assets,
$397,850 (M); Expenditures, $24,349; Total
giving, $17,308; Grants to individuals, 4 grants
totaling $17,308 (high: $4,327, low: $4,327).
Fields of interest: College.
Type of support: Support to graduates or students
of specific schools; Awards/grants by nomination
only; Undergraduate support.
Application information: Application form required.
   Deadline(s): Apr. 30
EIN: 356015133

2763
Oberlin Charitable Trust
c/o First Mid-Illinios Bank & Trust
1515 Charleston Ave.
Mattoon, IL   61938-3932   (217) 258-0494

Foundation type: Independent foundation
Purpose: Scholarships to high school graduates
from the Effingham area, IL for full time study at an
accredited college, university, technical school or
community college pursuing careers in business
related majors, computer science or graphic arts.
Financial data: Year ended 12/31/2013. Assets,
$127,139 (M); Expenditures, $30,757; Total
giving, $25,500; Grants to individuals, 39 grants
totaling $25,500 (high: $1,500, low: $500).
Fields of interest: Arts; Higher education; College
(community/junior); Business school/education;
Computer science.
Type of support: Scholarships—to individuals.
Application information: Application form required.
   Deadline(s): Apr.
   Applicants should submit the following:
      1) Transcripts
      2) Letter(s) of recommendation
      3) GPA
      4) ACT
   Additional information: Interviews may be
      required.
EIN: 364323858

2764
Oberweiler Foundation
1250 S. Grove St., Ste. 200
Barrington, IL   60010-5011
FAX: (847) 277-7446;
E-mail: oberw1@ameritech.net

Foundation type: Independent foundation
Purpose: College scholarships to students of Lake
Zurich High School, IL, for higher education.
Financial data: Year ended 12/31/2012. Assets,
$10,115,544 (M); Expenditures, $687,237; Total
giving, $409,771.
Fields of interest: Higher education.
Type of support: Scholarships—to individuals.
Application information: Applications not
accepted.
   Additional information: Unsolicited applications
      not considered or acknowledged.
EIN: 364376705

2765
Jean Paul Ohadi Memorial Foundation
900 Skokie Blvd., Ste. 122
Northbrook, IL   60062-4115   (972) 881-5399
Contact: Cynthia Drey, Secy.
Application address: 4333 Tall Oak Ln., Plano, TX
75074; tel.: (972) 881-5399

Foundation type: Independent foundation
Purpose: Scholarships to gay and lesbian
individuals in IL currently attending or who wish to
attend an institution of higher learning and are at
least 17 years of age.
Financial data: Year ended 06/30/2013. Assets,
$1,785,898 (M); Expenditures, $38,233; Total
giving, $38,092; Grants to individuals, 5 grants
totaling $9,000 (high: $2,000, low: $1,000).
Fields of interest: Higher education; LGBTQ.
Type of support: Scholarships—to individuals.
Application information: Application form required.
   Initial approach: Letter or e-mail
   Deadline(s): May 5
   Applicants should submit the following:
      1) Work samples
      2) Transcripts
      3) Letter(s) of recommendation
      4) Essay
EIN: 364240821

2766
Old Elm Scholarship Foundation
800 Old Elm Rd.
Highland Park, IL   60035-1104   (847) 432-6270
Contact: Jay Tress, Pres.

Foundation type: Public charity
Purpose: Scholarships to Old Elm employees and
their families for continuing education at
institutions of higher learning.
Financial data: Year ended 12/31/2011. Assets,
$1,887,990 (M); Expenditures, $175,925; Total
giving, $174,000; Grants to individuals, totaling
$174,000.
Fields of interest: Higher education.
Type of support: Employee-related scholarships.
Application information: Scholarships are for one
year and are renewable if qualifications are
warranted. Unsolicited requests for funds not
considered or acknowledged.
EIN: 237399476

2767
Olivet Nazarene University Foundation
(formerly Olivet Nazarene College Foundation)
1 Univ. Ave.
Bourbonnais, IL   60914-2345   (815) 939-5080
URL: http://www.olivet.edu/alumniandfriends/
support/onufoundation.aspx

Foundation type: Public charity
Purpose: Scholarships to students of Olivet
Nazarene University, Bourbonnais, IL.
Financial data: Year ended 06/30/2012. Assets,
$34,141,981 (M); Expenditures, $1,382,556;
Total giving, $857,275; Grants to individuals,
totaling $857,275.
Fields of interest: Higher education.
Type of support: Support to graduates or students
of specific schools.
Application information: Applications accepted.
Application form required.
   Additional information: Completed application
      should be submitted to the financial aid office.
EIN: 237063419

2768
The O'Malley Foundation
496 Phillips Ave.
Glen Ellyn, IL   60137-5013
Contact: Christopher T. O'Malley, Treas. and Dir.

Foundation type: Independent foundation
Purpose: Scholarships to seniors of Mound
Westonka High School, MN for full time four year
undergraduate study at an accredited college or
university pursuing a career in art or pyschology.
Financial data: Year ended 06/30/2013. Assets,
$18,174 (M); Expenditures, $23,583; Total giving,
$23,432; Grant to an individual, 1 grant totaling
$2,000.
Fields of interest: Arts; Higher education;
Psychology/behavioral science.
Type of support: Support to graduates or students
of specific schools.
Application information: Applications accepted.
Application form required.
   Deadline(s): None
   Applicants should submit the following:
      1) Letter(s) of recommendation
      2) GPA
   Additional information: Application should also
      include two letters of reference, copies of
      W-2 form and latest income tax return.
EIN: 364264521

2769
The Organization of Black Aerospcae Professionals
(formerly Organization of Black Airline Pilots)
1 Westbrook Corp. Ctr., Ste. 300
Westchester, IL   60154-5709   (708) 449-7755
Scholarship e-mail: obapscholarships@obap.org
E-mail: nationaloffice@obap.org; Toll-free tel.: (800)
538-6227; URL: http://www.obap.org

Foundation type: Public charity
Purpose: Scholarships and fellowships to African
American pilots for advanced training.
Financial data: Year ended 10/31/2011. Assets,
$410,728 (M); Expenditures, $522,126; Total
giving, $7,000; Grants to individuals, totaling
$7,000.
Fields of interest: Higher education; Space/
aviation; African Americans/Blacks.
Type of support: Fellowships; Undergraduate
support.

Application information: Applications accepted. Application form required. Interview required.

Send request by: Online

Deadline(s): May

Applicants should submit the following:

1) Letter(s) of recommendation
2) Photograph
3) Essay

Additional information: See web site for additional application guidelines.

Program descriptions:

Alaska Airlines Maintence and Engineering Scholarships: This $2,500 scholarship provides a deserving individual the opportunity to further their career in the aviation industry as a Mechanic. The training must be OBAP approved and funds will be sent directly to the training facility.

Alaska Airlines Pilot Scholarship: This scholarship is designed for a deserving individual to further their career in the aviation industry as a pilot. The training must be OBAP approved and funds will be sent directly to the training facility.

Duane Moorer Scholarship: A $2,000 scholarship is available to a high school senior who has been accepted into a two- or four-year aerospace degree program. Eligible applicants must have a 2.5 GPA or better. Applicants must also demonstrate verification of organization Flight Academy attendance (ACE, solo, and private) within the past three years.

Edward Horne Scholarship: A $2,500 scholarship is available to a member of the organization who has faced significant life challenges, to be used toward an advanced rating in aviation or occupational development in the aerospace industry. Applicants must possess a current private pilot's license and have participated in at least one organization event.

United Airlines Pilot Scholarships: This scholarships of $4,000 offers funding to an individual seeking to advance their aviation career, and must be enrolled in an accredited collegiate aviation program. Applicant must have a Commercial Certificate & Instrument Rating, multi-engine rating preferred, and a minimum 3.0 GPA.

Wings Financial Scholarship: Two $1,000 scholarships are available to graduating high school seniors attending an accredited college/university or must be enrolled in an aerospace program. Applicant must have a 2.7 GPA or higher.

EIN: 271836543

2770
Orthopaedic Research Education Foundation

(also known as OREF)

6300 N. River Rd., Ste. 700
Rosemont, IL 60018-4261   (847) 698-9980
Contact: James D. Heckman M.D., Vice-Chair., Research Grants
FAX: (847) 698-7806;
E-mail: communications@oref.org; URL: http://www.oref.org

Foundation type: Public charity

Purpose: Grants and awards to individuals for support into the causes and treatment of musculoskeletal diseases.

Publications: Application guidelines; Annual report; Financial statement; Grants list; Newsletter.

Financial data: Year ended 12/31/2011. Assets, $43,586,972 (M); Expenditures, $13,801,410; Total giving, $9,703,802. Grants to individuals amount not specified.

Fields of interest: Nerve, muscle & bone diseases.

Type of support: Grants to individuals.

Application information: Applications accepted. Application form required. Application form available on the grantmaker's web site.

Send request by: Mail

Deadline(s): Vary

Additional information: See web site for additional application guidelines.

Program descriptions:

AAHKS/OREF Research Grant in Adult Reconstruction: This grant provides seed money and start-up funding of up to $40,000 for a new investigator doing clinically-relevant research in the topic area of adult reconstruction. (Co-)Principal investigators must be an orthopaedic surgeon and a member of the American Association of Hip and Knee Surgeons (AAHK); Ph.D.s and D.V.M.s are eligible if they are affiliated with an orthopaedic department and working with an orthopaedic surgeon who is a principal or co-principal investigator.

AAHKS/OREF Resident Clinician Scientist Training Grant in Total Joint Arthroplasty: With support from Zimmer, this grant program provides $20,000 for research expenses (salary excluded), plus a $1,500 travel stipend, to a candidate who is mentored by an active or candidate member of the American Association of Hip and Knee Surgeons (AAHKS) and who can dedicate at least three to six months. Grants are intended to support residents and fellows completing an orthopaedic fellowship in approved orthopaedic programs who intend to make total joint arthroplasty a major career component.

AAOS/OREF Traveling Fellowship Program: Awarded jointly with the American Academy of Orthopaedic Surgeons, this program seeks to expose early career orthopaedic clinician scientists to established peers and fellow scientists, promote professional relationships between early career and established clinician scientists, and provide opportunities for active mentoring of early career clinician scientists. Two applicants are selected annually to receive up to a $10,000 grant to cover the travel expenses of visiting mentors of their choosing.

AFSH/OREF Hand Surgeon-Scientist Award: Awarded in conjunction with the American Foundation for Surgery, this award recognizes a young orthopaedic hand surgeon who has demonstrated success as both a clinician and a researcher, and provides a base of financial support that will ensure sufficient protected time to develop a long and productive career in academic surgery. The award is designed to support young faculty members at teaching institutions with accredited programs in orthopaedic surgery, and provides up to $75,000 per year for up to five years. Preference will be given to fund researchers who are conducting clinical and/or translational research with an emphasis on improving clinical care.

Career Development Awards: These grants encourage a commitment to scientific research in orthopaedic surgery. Candidates must have completed a residency in orthopaedic surgery and demonstrated a sustained interest in research and excellence in clinical training. Awards of up to $75,000 per year for three years will be considered.

Continuing Medical Education Grants: Grants of up to $25,000 are available to support continuing medical education (CME) programs held in the U.S. on the subject of hip and knee arthroplasty, designed to help orthopaedic surgeons learn new procedures and treatment protocols, refine surgical skills, and gain hands-on experience with new implants and other devices. Applicants must be accredited by the Accreditation Council for Continuing Medical Education (ACCME), provide proof of nonprofit status, and demonstrate that no

funds received from this program will be used for entertainment of attendees.

Educational Awards: One-year funding of up to $25,000 is available for educational programs developed in conjunction with a recognized, national organization to evaluate the effectiveness of orthopaedic education at all levels; clinical consensus conferences, workshops, and symposia; research and development of educational electronic media; and innovative approaches to education.

Loan Repayment Program: The program will repay up to $35,000 per year of qualified educational debt. Applicants must be an orthopaedic surgeon who has achieved funding through the National Institutes of Health (NIH) Loan Repayment Program. The foundation will match NIH funds, limited to $70,000 over two years.

NIAMS/OREF National Research Service Award Post-Doctoral Fellowship in Epidemiology, Clinical Trials, and Outcomes Research in Orthopaedic Surgery: In conjunction with the National Institute of Arthritis and Musculoskeletal and Skin Diseases, postdoctoral fellowships are available to support the training of physicians with expertise in orthopaedic surgery, to supplement that knowledge with training in epidemiology, clinical trials, and outcomes research. These fellowships are intended to support up to two years of advanced training in the relevant methodologies, in order to obtain a Masters of Public Health and/or a Ph.D. in epidemiology to qualify the fellow to pursue a career in these areas as they relate to orthopaedic surgery.

OREF Clinical Research Award: This award recognizes outstanding clinical research related to musculoskeletal disease or injury. One award of $20,000 is offered.

OREF Young Investigator Grant in Total Joint and Trauma Surgery: This one-year grant provides up to $50,000 to advance the training of the next generation of orthopaedists who have a clinical or scientific interest in total joint surgery and/or trauma treatment. Eligible applicants must be orthopaedic surgeons in approved orthopaedic residency and fellowship programs, and who have completed formal training within their last four years.

OREF/AAOS Clinical Research Training Fellowship: The goal of this program is to encourage the development of a cadre of orthopaedic surgeons who have the research skills necessary to undertake and manage various types of health services and outcomes research. One two-year fellowship is offered annually at $70,000 per year.

OREF/ASES/Rockwood Clinical Shoulder Research Grant: Members of the American Shoulder and Elbow Surgeon (ASES) department of the foundation are invited to apply for this grant, which provides seed money and start-up funding of up to $50,000 per year for up to two years. (Co-)Principal Investigators must be orthopedic surgeons; Ph.D.s and D.V.M.s are eligible if they are affiliated with an orthopedic department and working with an orthopedic surgeon is a (co-)principal investigator.

OREF/Current Concepts in Joint Replacement Awards: Two awards of $2,000 each are available to recognize excellence in completed investigations focusing on health care policy, clinical outcomes, or translational research that has immediate clinical impact in the diagnosis and treatment of patients. Eligible applicants include all orthopaedic surgeons who have completed residency and/or fellowship training, including those in private practice; clinicians are especially encouraged to apply.

OREF/Goldberg Research Grants in Arthritis: One $50,000 grant is available to new orthopaedic investigators who work in the field of arthritis. (Co-)

Principal investigators must be orthopaedic surgeons; Ph.D.s and D.V.M.s are eligible to apply if affiliated with an orthopaedic department and if working with an orthopaedic who is the principal or co-principal investigator.

OREF/JBJS Journal Club Grants: Supported by The Journal of Bone and Joint Surgeons, these $2,500 grants help resident journal club participants gain experience in evaluating current literature, writing scientific articles, and understanding ethical issues.

OREF/MTF Research Grant: This grant provides up to $100,000 of seed money and start-up funding for a new investigator doing work in the topic areas of stem cells and orthopaedic allograft research. The principal investigator or co-principal investigator must be an orthopaedic surgeon; Ph.D.s and D.V.M.s are eligible if they are affiliated with an orthopaedic department and working with an orthopaedic surgeon who is the principal or co-principal investigator. Funds may not be used for salary support.

OREF/POSNA Research Grant: In conjunction with the Pediatric Orthopaedic Society of North America (POSNA), grants ranging from $30,000 to $40,000 each for two years are available to encourage new investigators by providing seed and start-up funding for promising research projects. Clinical relevance must be clearly noted in the abstract and specific aims and be obvious from the title and study design. Eligible applicants must be members of POSNA; the principal investigator or the co-principal investigator must be an orthopaedic surgeon. Applications must be received by POSNA.

OREF/Zachary B. Friedenberg, M.D. Clinician Scientist Grant: This grant is intended to encourage young surgeons to pursue a career as a clinician scientist, with a special interest on continued research activity. Grants will be made to orthopaedic surgeons to allow the recipient to spend 40 percent or more of his/her time (two workdays each week) in research for a period of up to three years.

ORS/OREF Travel Awards in Orthopaedic Research Translation: These awards recognize clinician scientists and clinical investigators in the early stages of their careers for playing a key or leading role in an ongoing research project in clinical or translational medicine, demonstrating excellence in training and a commitment to orthopaedic research. Five recipients will receive free registration and will present their work at the foundation's annual meeting, and be given a $500 honorarium, up to $1,000 in travel reimbursement, and two additional years of free meeting registration. Eligible applicants must have: obtained an M.D., D.O., D.D.M., D.P.T., D.D.S., or equivalent; have an active independent clinical practice; and be no more than five years past completion of a clinical residency or fellowship program.

Research Grants: These grants encourage new investigators by providing seed money and start-up funding of up to $50,000 per year for up to two years, conditional upon annual review.

RJOS/OREF/DEPUY Career Development Award in Women's Musculoskeletal Health: The goal of this program is to train and develop female orthopaedic surgeons to improve knowledge in the area of women's musculoskeletal health, and to enhance understanding of gender and diversity differences in the outcomes of orthopaedic procedures. The candidate must be a female orthopaedic surgeon who is a member of the Ruth Jackson Orthopaedic Society. The amount of the award is $50,000 for up to one year.

William J. Tipton, Jr., M.D. Leadership Award: This award recognizes and nurtures outstanding orthopaedic leadership by presenting a $5,000 grant to an individual who is recognized as a leader in orthopaedic research among his/her peers, who is committed to the growth and prestige of orthopaedics, understands and demonstrates the values of diversity in the specialty, and shows exemplary mentorship and conflict resolution skills. Eligible individuals must be nominated by an academy fellow in good standing, a candidate member eligible for fellowship, or an orthopaedic resident who has directly and professionally benefited from the activities of the nominee.

Young Investigator Grants: This one-year grant provides up to $50,000 to advance the scientific training of the next generation of orthopaedists. Orthopaedic surgeons in approved residency and fellowship programs, or having completed formal training within the last for years, may apply by submitting a proposal for an individual plan for further research investigation.
EIN: 366009467

2771
Stig P. Orum Memorial Foundation, Inc.
P.O. Box 384
St. Charles, IL   60174   (847) 695-0028
Contact: Irma B. Orum, Pres.

Foundation type: Independent foundation
Purpose: Scholarships to high school students from Fox River Valley area, surrounding St. Charles, IL for higher education.
Financial data: Year ended 12/31/2012. Assets, $609,522 (M); Expenditures, $30,569; Total giving, $28,500; Grants to individuals, 16 grants totaling $27,000 (high: $2,000, low: $1,000).
Fields of interest: Higher education.
Type of support: Undergraduate support.
Application information: Applications accepted. Application form required.
  Deadline(s): Mar. 15
  Applicants should submit the following:
    1) Class rank
    2) SAT
    3) GPA
    4) ACT
EIN: 363727759

2772
OSF Healthcare System
800 N.E. Glen Oak Ave.
Peoria, IL   61603-3200   (309) 655-2850
E-mail: contactus@osfhealthcare.org; URL: http://www.osfhealthcare.org

Foundation type: Public charity
Purpose: Scholarships to those in an OSF Saint Francis Medical Center RN staff position in IL.
Publications: Application guidelines; Annual report; Financial statement; Newsletter.
Financial data: Year ended 09/30/2011. Assets, $2,267,817,172 (M); Expenditures, $1,651,985,387; Total giving, $2,211,639; Grants to individuals, totaling $77,603.
Fields of interest: Nursing school/education.
Type of support: Undergraduate support.
Application information: Applications not accepted.
  Additional information: Unsolicited requests for funds not considered.
EIN: 370813229

2773
Raymond J. Ott Scholarship Fund
1 E. Wacker Dr. Ste. 2610
Chicago, IL   60601-2001   (312) 782-3636
Contact: David B. Pogrund, Tr.

Foundation type: Independent foundation
Purpose: Scholarships to financially needy full-time students with at least a 3.0 GPA to study toward one of the following degrees: bachelor's, master's, Ph.D., M.D., Doctor of Law, or D.V.M.
Financial data: Year ended 12/31/2012. Assets, $219,789 (M); Expenditures, $30,386; Total giving, $20,000; Grants to individuals, 4 grants totaling $20,000 (high: $5,000, low: $5,000).
Fields of interest: Law school/education; Medical school/education; Veterinary medicine.
Type of support: Fellowships; Graduate support; Undergraduate support; Doctoral support.
Application information: Application form required.
  Deadline(s): Varies
  Additional information: Contact respective high schools.
EIN: 366742652

2774
Harlan, Ruby & Phil E. Ott Scholarship Trust
(also known as Phil E. Ott Scholarships)
10 S Dearborn IL1-0117
Chicago, IL   60603

Foundation type: Independent foundation
Purpose: Scholarships to financially needy graduates of Central Noble High School, IN, to attend accredited colleges.
Financial data: Year ended 12/31/2012. Assets, $1,082,008 (M); Expenditures, $85,308; Total giving, $48,299; Grants to individuals, 21 grants totaling $21,150 (high: $1,050, low: $150).
Fields of interest: Higher education.
Type of support: Support to graduates or students of specific schools; Undergraduate support.
Application information: Applications accepted. Application form required.
  Deadline(s): Apr. 28
  Applicants should submit the following:
    1) Transcripts
    2) FAF
  Additional information: Applicant must demonstrate financial need.
EIN: 356455490

2775
Janet Ozinga Memorial Scholarship Foundation
19001 Old LaGrange Rd., Ste. 300
Mokena, IL   60448-8013

Foundation type: Independent foundation
Purpose: Scholarships to high school seniors residing in the Southwest Chicagoland area, IL.
Financial data: Year ended 12/31/2012. Assets, $78,806 (M); Expenditures, $33,844; Total giving, $31,239; Grants to individuals, 7 grants totaling $31,239 (high: $5,000, low: $1,510).
Fields of interest: Higher education.
Type of support: Scholarships—to individuals.
Application information: Application form required.
  Deadline(s): Varies
  Additional information: Application available upon request.
EIN: 363554481

2776
The Paideia Foundation
c/o Klesman & Co.
7110 W. 127th St., Ste. 230
Palos Heights, IL 60463-1580

Foundation type: Independent foundation
Purpose: Grants to teachers employed at the Koraes School in Palos Hills, IL, for work benefiting elementary child education.
Financial data: Year ended 12/31/2011. Assets, $405,015 (M); Expenditures, $31,430; Total giving, $31,000. Grants to individuals amount not specified.
Fields of interest: Elementary school/education; Education.
Type of support: Grants to individuals.
Application information: Applications accepted.
Initial approach: Letter or telephone
Deadline(s): None
Additional information: Contact foundation for application guidelines.
EIN: 363884185

2777
The Walter Curtis Palmer Scholarship Trust
10 S Dearborn IL1-0117
Chicago, IL 60603 (866) 888-5157
Application address: 10 S. Dearborn St., Chicago, IL 60603

Foundation type: Independent foundation
Purpose: Scholarships to residents of Racine, WI, and the surrounding area who are graduating seniors.
Financial data: Year ended 12/31/2012. Assets, $148,974 (M); Expenditures, $11,409; Total giving, $8,010; Grants to individuals, 10 grants totaling $8,010 (high: $810, low: $800).
Type of support: Undergraduate support.
Application information: Contact trust for current application deadline/guidelines.
EIN: 396037713

2778
Palos Bank Foundation, Inc.
c/o Gregory J. Paetow
12600 S. Harlem Ave.
Palos Heights, IL 60463-0927

Foundation type: Operating foundation
Purpose: Scholarships to graduating high school seniors from eight local area high schools, IL for continuing their education beyond high school at a university, college, trade school, or vocational school.
Financial data: Year ended 12/31/2010. Assets, $223 (M); Expenditures, $22,025; Total giving, $22,000; Grants to individuals, 11 grants totaling $22,000 (high: $2,000, low: $2,000).
Fields of interest: Vocational education, post-secondary; Higher education.
Type of support: Support to graduates or students of specific schools; Undergraduate support.
Application information: Application form required.
Deadline(s): Mar. 1
Final notification: Recipients announced by Apr. 16
Additional information: Recipients must maintain a "B" average or better throughout seven terms of high school. Scholarships are annually awarded to one recipient from each of the following schools: Amos Alonzo Stagg High School; Carl Sandburg High School; Alan B. Shepard High School; Marist High School;

Mother McAuley High School; Providence Catholic High School; Chicago Christian High School; Lincoln-Way East High School; Lincoln-Way Central High School; and Lockport High School.
EIN: 364443693

2779
Partners in Charity, Inc.
86 N. Williams St.
Crystal Lake, IL 60014-4444 (800) 705-8350
FAX: (800) 514-9848;
E-mail: info@partnersincharity.org; Toll-free tel.: (800) 705-8350; toll-free fax: (800) 514-9848; URL: http://www.partnersincharity.org

Foundation type: Public charity
Purpose: Down payment assistant to qualified homebuyers in obtaining assistance for home purchases.
Financial data: Year ended 12/31/2011. Assets, $1,953,396 (M); Expenditures, $435,543; Total giving, $4,475.
Fields of interest: Housing/shelter, home owners.
Type of support: Grants to individuals.
Application information: A down payment is provided with no repayment and no second mortgage or lien of any type.
EIN: 364378897

2780
G. F. Patterson Trust
c/o Edgar County Bank & Trust
P.O. Box 400
Paris, IL 61944-0400 (217) 465-4154
Contact: John Carrington

Foundation type: Independent foundation
Purpose: Scholarships to residents of Edgar County, IL for undergraduate or graduate college education.
Financial data: Year ended 12/31/2011. Assets, $907,908 (M); Expenditures, $43,038; Total giving, $31,686; Grants to individuals, 7 grants totaling $31,686 (high: $4,800, low: $3,386).
Fields of interest: Higher education.
Type of support: Graduate support; Undergraduate support.
Application information: Applications accepted. Application form required.
Initial approach: Letter
Deadline(s): May 15
Additional information: Applications are available at Edgar County Bank & Trust of Paris.
EIN: 376343185

2781
Marion A. & Eva S. Peeples Trust
10 S.Dearborn IL1-0117
Chicago, IL 60603-2300 (214) 965-2098
Contact: Anne McCullough
Application address: 2200 Ross Ave., Dallas, TX 75201-2787

Foundation type: Independent foundation
Purpose: Scholarships to IN high school graduates pursuing studies in nursing, or dietetics or seeking training in teaching in the field of industrial arts at accredited colleges or universities in IN.
Financial data: Year ended 06/30/2013. Assets, $1,307,021 (M); Expenditures, $90,378; Total giving, $55,000.
Fields of interest: Nursing school/education; Education; Nutrition; Engineering/technology.

Type of support: Support to graduates or students of specific schools; Undergraduate support.
Application information: Applications accepted. Application form required. Interview required.
Initial approach: Letter
Send request by: Mail
Deadline(s): Mar. 12
Applicants should submit the following:
1) Transcripts
2) Letter(s) of recommendation
3) Financial information
Additional information: Applicant must demonstrate financial need. Scholarship funds are paid directly to the educational institution on behalf of the student.
Program description:
Peeples Scholarship Program: Scholarships are awarded first to graduates of Franklin Community High School, IN, second to graduates of Johnson county high schools, and then to all Indiana high school graduates who plan to attend an IN college or university. Applicants must pursue a course of study leading to a degree in nursing (B.S., R.N., L.P.N. or an approved hospital nursing program), dietetics (B.S.), or teaching in the field of Industrial Arts/Technology Education. Scholarships are generally for one year only but may be extended for up to four years. Scholarship amount is determined by the scholarship committee.
EIN: 356306320

2782
Peoples Resource Center
201 S. Naperville Rd.
Wheaton, IL 60187-5417 (360) 682-5402
Contact: Kim Perez, Exec. Dir.
FAX: (630) 682-5412; URL: http://www.peoplesrc.org/

Foundation type: Public charity
Purpose: Emergency rent and mortgage assistance to qualifying residents of DuPage County, IL, who are unable to pay rent or make a security deposit due to a temporary financial crisis.
Financial data: Year ended 06/30/2012. Assets, $4,689,801 (M); Expenditures, $8,361,138; Total giving, $6,414,269; Grants to individuals, totaling $6,414,269.
Fields of interest: Economically disadvantaged.
Type of support: Grants for special needs.
Application information: Interview required.
Initial approach: Tel.
Applicants should submit the following:
1) Financial information
Additional information: Call 630-682-5402, ext. 323 and leave a message with name, phone number, and a short explanation of the situation.
EIN: 363157600

2783
Mary Perisho-Nina Rall McConkey Scholarship Trust
c/o Edgar County Bank & Trust
P.O. Box 400
Paris, IL 61944-0400 (217) 465-4154
Contact: John D. Carrington

Foundation type: Independent foundation
Purpose: Scholarships to students of Paris High School, IL, to further their education in home economics.
Financial data: Year ended 04/30/2013. Assets, $166,058 (M); Expenditures, $11,726; Total giving, $8,500; Grants to individuals, 6 grants totaling $8,500 (high: $2,550, low: $850).

Fields of interest: Home economics.
Type of support: Scholarships—to individuals;
Support to graduates or students of specific
schools.
Application information: Application form required.
Deadline(s): May 15
Additional information: Application forms
available at Edgar County Bank, Trust Dept.
EIN: 371248386

2784
Alden and Dorothy Perkins Scholarship Fund

6838 E. State St.
Rockford, IL   61108-4610   (815) 547-5200

Foundation type: Independent foundation
Purpose: Scholarships to graduating seniors from
Belvidere High School, IL, pursuing a degree in
pharmacy or education.
Financial data: Year ended 12/31/2012. Assets,
$101,393 (M); Expenditures, $6,254; Total giving,
$4,400.
Fields of interest: Health sciences school/
education; Education.
Type of support: Support to graduates or students
of specific schools; Undergraduate support.
Application information: Applications accepted.
Deadline(s): Apr. 1
Additional information: Application should
include a statement with at least 300 words
detailing why student is pursuing a degree in
pharmacy or education.
EIN: 367381761

2785
The Herman & Katherine Peters Foundation, Corp.

351 W. Glade Rd.
Palatine, IL   60067-6831   (847) 909-3130
Contact: Scot A. Leonard, Pres.

Foundation type: Independent foundation
Purpose: Scholarships to students from AZ, CO, IL,
MI, and WI for higher education in the fields of
forestry/conservation or Christian-based religious
instruction.
Financial data: Year ended 12/31/2012. Assets,
$8,506,252 (M); Expenditures, $449,758; Total
giving, $298,500; Grants to individuals, 21 grants
totaling $97,500 (high: $10,000, low: $2,500).
Fields of interest: Environmental education;
Religion.
Type of support: Undergraduate support.
Application information: Applications accepted.
Application form required. Application form
available on the grantmaker's web site.
Initial approach: E-mail
Send request by: E-mail
Copies of proposal: 1
Deadline(s): Dec. 31
Additional information: Contact school guidance
office for application guidelines.
EIN: 364180010

2786
Alan & Mildred Peterson Charitable Foundation

566 W. Adams St., Ste. 300
Chicago, IL   60661-5790   (312) 544-6540
Contact: Alan E. Peterson, Dir.; Mildred Peterson,
Dir.

Foundation type: Independent foundation

Purpose: Scholarships to individuals for higher
education at accredited colleges or universities.
Financial data: Year ended 12/31/2012. Assets,
$163,577 (M); Expenditures, $243,696; Total
giving, $227,395; Grants to individuals, 15 grants
totaling $58,700 (high: $8,000, low: $1,000).
Fields of interest: Higher education; Graduate/
professional education.
Type of support: Graduate support; Undergraduate
support.
Application information: Applications accepted.
Application form required.
Applicants should submit the following:
1) Essay
2) Transcripts
3) Letter(s) of recommendation
Additional information: Application must include
proof of tuition.
EIN: 363355444

2787
Orlan W. Pflasterer, M.D. Private Foundation

c/o Michael Howell
1115 Birch Ln.
Sparta, IL   62286
Contact: Orlan W. Pflasterer M.D.

Foundation type: Independent foundation
Purpose: Scholarships to graduating seniors from
the IL counties of Randolph, Washington or Perry or
from the IL townships of Marissa, St. Libory,
Fayetteville, New Athens and Lenzberg.
Financial data: Year ended 12/31/2012. Assets,
$132,357 (M); Expenditures, $9,826; Total giving,
$6,000; Grants to individuals, 6 grants totaling
$6,000 (high: $1,000, low: $1,000).
Fields of interest: Higher education.
Type of support: Undergraduate support.
Application information: Applications accepted.
Initial approach: Letter
Deadline(s): None
Additional information: Applications must be
submitted by high school teachers or
administrators.
EIN: 200481826

2788
Phi Chapter Educational Foundation of Phi Gamma Delta Fraternity

c/o R. Marmer
353 N. Clark St., Ste. 4200
Chicago, IL   60654-3456   (312) 923-2688
Contact: Ronald L. Marmer, Pres.

Foundation type: Independent foundation
Purpose: Undergraduate scholarships to students
of Northwestern University and who are members of
the Fraternity of Phi Gamma Delta.
Financial data: Year ended 11/30/2012. Assets,
$119,022 (M); Expenditures, $14,025; Total
giving, $14,000; Grants to individuals, 7 grants
totaling $14,000 (high: $2,000, low: $2,000).
Fields of interest: Higher education; Students,
sororities/fraternities.
Type of support: Undergraduate support.
Application information: Applications accepted.
Application form required.
Deadline(s): None
Additional information: Unsolicited requests for
funds not considered or acknowledged.
EIN: 366118268

2789
Julia Pierson Trust

P.O. Box 29
Carrollton, IL   62016-1015

Foundation type: Operating foundation
Purpose: Scholarships to graduates of Carrollton
Community Unit School District No. 1, IL.
Financial data: Year ended 12/31/2012. Assets,
$2,219,968 (M); Expenditures, $49,416; Total
giving, $45,200.
Fields of interest: Higher education.
Type of support: Support to graduates or students
of specific schools; Undergraduate support.
Application information: Applications accepted.
Initial approach: Letter
Deadline(s): May 1
Additional information: Application must include
academic resume.
EIN: 376321165

2790
A. Franklin Pilchard Foundation

P.O. Box 2690
Palatine, IL   60078-2690   (847) 963-6762
Contact: Robert C. Pacilio, Treas.

Foundation type: Independent foundation
Purpose: Scholarships to students attending
specific educational institutions in IL that are listed
in the foundation's scholarship program. Applicants
must also attend a college or university located in
IL.
Financial data: Year ended 06/30/2013. Assets,
$18,265,194 (M); Expenditures, $752,588; Total
giving, $559,403; Grants to individuals, totaling
$559,403.
Fields of interest: Higher education; Scholarships/
financial aid.
Type of support: Scholarships—to individuals;
Support to graduates or students of specific
schools.
Application information: Application form required.
Deadline(s): Oct. 31
EIN: 363723290

2791
Edward H. & Cora W. Pingel Educational Fund

111 W. Monroe St., Tax Div 10C
Chicago, IL   60603
*Application Addresss:*c/o Board of Education,
Marengo Community High School Marengo, IL
60152

Foundation type: Independent foundation
Purpose: Student loans to graduates of Marengo
Community High School, IL, for certificate,
associate and baccalaureate degree programs.
Financial data: Year ended 12/31/2012. Assets,
$395,774 (M); Expenditures, $15,615; Total
giving, $0.
Fields of interest: Higher education.
Type of support: Student loans—to individuals;
Support to graduates or students of specific
schools.
Application information: Application form required.
Deadline(s): May 15
Applicants should submit the following:
1) Transcripts
2) Financial information
Program description:
Pingel Loan: Students who have graduated from
Marengo Community High School may apply for this
$2,000 loan. Two graduates will be selected each
year. Loans are renewable provided that the

recipient continues as a full-time student leading to termination of education or graduation. No interest will be charged while full-time student status continues. Loans have a four percent per annum charge commencing one month after graduation or termination of schooling.
EIN: 366910594

2792

The Piper Foundation, Inc.
801 Hampton Ct.
Lake Bluff, IL 60044-2425   (847) 858-8943

Foundation type: Independent foundation
Purpose: Scholarships to graduating seniors attending high schools in the Keystone Central School District, PA.
Publications: Annual report.
Financial data: Year ended 12/31/2012. Assets, $1,171,748 (M); Expenditures, $44,997; Total giving, $44,500; Grants to individuals, 11 grants totaling $28,500 (high: $3,000, low: $1,500).
Fields of interest: Higher education.
Type of support: Undergraduate support.
Application information: Applications accepted.
Initial approach: Letter
Additional information: Application must include list of achievements and proof of financial need. Candidates are selected by individual high school administrators.
EIN: 240863140

2793

The Plastic Surgery Foundation
(formerly Plastic Surgery Educational Foundation)
444 E. Algonquin Rd.
Arlington Heights, IL 60005-4654   (847) 228-9900
E-mail: giving@plasticsurgery.org; *Toll-free tel.:* (800) 766-4955; *URL:* http://www.thepsf.org

Foundation type: Public charity
Purpose: Grants to plastic surgeons for research within their field.
Publications: Application guidelines; Grants list.
Financial data: Year ended 06/30/2012. Assets, $14,795,096 (M); Expenditures, $2,013,062; Total giving, $954,311.
Fields of interest: Surgery research.
Type of support: Fellowships; Research.
Application information: Applications accepted. Application form required. Application form available on the grantmaker's web site.
Initial approach: Telephone
Send request by: Online
Deadline(s): Dec. 1
Additional information: See web site for additional application guidelines.
Program descriptions:
AACPS/PSEF Combined Pilot Research Grant: Grants of up to $10,000 are available for a one-year project to support the preliminary or pilot phase or scientific research projects. No salary support will be provided for the Principal Investigator. Applicants must be a M.D., D.O., Ph.D. or in training, and must be an ASPS member or candidate member, or obtain sponsorship from an ASPS or AACPS member or candidate member.
AAHS/PSEF Combined Pilot Research Grant: Awarded in conjunction with the American Association for Hand Surgery, this program will provide funding of up to $10,000 to fund a research project that will advance the scientific knowledge and clinical practice of hand surgery. Eligible applicants must be a M.D., D.O., or Ph.D., or be in training.

AAPS/PSEF Combined Pilot Research Grant: Grants of up to $10,000 are available to support projects designed to explore effective methods of reducing visible scarring, or controlling the scarring process with regeneration over scar formation. Eligible applicants must have an M.D., D.O., or Ph.D., or be in training.
ASPN/PSEF Combined Pilot Research Grant: Grants of up to $10,000 are available for one-year projects that support the preliminary or pilot phase of scientific (basic or clinical) research projects pertaining to peripheral nerve disorders. Applicants must be an ASPN member (active, associate, or candidate), or a trainee (fellow, resident, or student) being supervised by an ASPN member.
ASRM/PSEF Combined Pilot Research Grant: Awarded in conjunction with the American Society for Reconstructive Microsurgery, grants of up to $10,000 are available to support the preliminary or pilot phase of scientific research projects focused on reconstructive microsurgery. Eligible applicants must be an M.D., D.O., or Ph.D., or be in training.
National Endowment for Plastic Surgery Grants: Grants of up to $50,000 are available to support research related to plastic surgery. The principal investigator must be an active or candidate member of ASPS or obtain sponsorship from an active or candidate member of ASPS. Applicants must be an M.D.. D.O., or Ph.D., and hold a full-time position in a Department of Plastic Surgery or equivalent.
Pilot Research Grant: Grants of up to $10,000 are available to provide one year of support for the preliminary or pilot phrase of scientific research projects. Grants are intended to provide seed funding and allows researchers to conduct preliminary studies related to plastic surgery science that set the stage for applications to external funding sources. Eligible applicants must be a M.D., D.O., or Ph.D., and hold a full-time position in a department of plastic surgery at an accredited institution (or its equivalent)
Research Fellowships: The foundation offers two types of fellowships to support plastic surgery professionals: a $50,000 fellowship is available for research training in areas related to breast reconstruction or facial aesthetics, while an additional $50,000 fellowship is available for research training in any area of plastic surgery. Eligible applicants must have an M.D. or D.O., hold a full-time position in a department of plastic surgery (or its equivalent) at an accredited institution, and must be residents or within five years of initial faculty appointment.
EIN: 596144450

2794

The Playboy Foundation
680 N. Lake Shore Dr.
Chicago, IL 60611-4455
Contact: Matthew Pakula, Dir.
FAX: (312) 266-8506;
E-mail: pbfoundation@playboy.com; *E-mail for HMH First Amendment Awards:* hmhfaa@playboy.com; *URL:* http://www.playboyenterprises.com/foundation

Foundation type: Corporate giving program
Purpose: Awards to individuals who have made significant contributions to protect and enhance First Amendment Rights for Americans.
Publications: Application guidelines.
Fields of interest: Media/communications; Film/video; Television; Print publishing; Civil liberties, first amendment.
Type of support: Awards/grants by nomination only; Awards/prizes.

Application information: Application form available on the grantmaker's web site.
Send request by: Mail or e-mail
Deadline(s): None
Additional information: Application should include a resume. Nomination forms should include a description of the candidate's contribution to First Amendment Rights and a list of references.
Program descriptions:
Freedom of Expression Award: Through the Freedom of Expression Award, Playboy awards $25,000 to a nominee who has a project or program dedicated to defending, advocating, or supporting the First Amendment through their personal or professional pursuits. A successful nominee should demonstrate a promising future as a First Amendment advocate based on their history or accomplishment and the potential for the award to facilitate additional work. Preference is given to nominees who would benefit from having financing to relieve inhibitions or burdens of pursuing the First Amendment ideals of their program or project.
Hugh M. Hefner First Amendment Awards: Through the Hugh M. Hefner First Amendment Awards program, Playboy Enterprises honors individuals who have made significant contributions to the ongoing effort to protect and enhance First Amendment rights for all Americans, including high school students, lawyers, journalists and educators have been honored. Nominees traditionally come from the areas of journalism, arts and entertainment, education, publishing, law and government, and winners are selected by a panel of distinguished judges. The winners are given a cash award of $10,000 and a commemorative plaque.

2795

The Poetry Foundation
(formerly The Modern Poetry Association)
61 W. Superior St.
Chicago, IL 60654-5457   (312) 787-7070
Contact: Stephen Young, Prog. Dir.
FAX: (312) 787-6650;
E-mail: mail@poetryfoundation.org; *URL:* http://www.poetryfoundation.org

Foundation type: Operating foundation
Purpose: Fellowships by nomination only to undergraduate and graduate students of creative writing or English.
Publications: Financial statement.
Financial data: Year ended 12/31/2012. Assets, $210,114,297 (M); Expenditures, $8,959,452; Total giving, $834,950; Grants to individuals, 18 grants totaling $201,250 (high: $100,000, low: $500).
Fields of interest: Literature.
Type of support: Fellowships; Awards/grants by nomination only; Awards/prizes.
Application information:
Deadline(s): Apr. 15
Additional information: Completion of formal nomination required, including samples of candidate's work; Recipients must be nominated by program directors or department chairs.
Program descriptions:
Children's Poet Laureate: The award is given to a living American writer in recognition of a career devoted to writing exceptional poetry for the young child. The award aims to raise awareness that children have a natural receptivity to poetry and are its most appreciative audience, especially when poems are written specifically for them. The Children's Poet Laureate will advise the Poetry Foundation on matters relating to children's

literature and may engage in a variety of projects to help instill a love of poetry among the nation's youngest readers. The length of the laureate's tenure is two years and includes a prize of $25,000. The Children's Poet Laureate will also give two major readings for children and their families, teachers, librarians, and friends over the course of the two-year tenure.

Emily Dickinson Award: The award recognizes an American Poet over the age of 50 who has yet to publish a first book. In addition to publication and promotion of the manuscript, the winner receives a prize of $10,000.

Mark Twain Poetry Award: The award of $25,000 recognizes a poet's contributions to humor in American poetry. The award is given in the belief that humorous poetry can also be seriously good poetry, and in the hope that American poetry will in time produce its own Mark Twain. No applications or unsolicited nominations are accepted.

Neglected Masters Award: The Neglected Masters Award of $50,000 brings to the reading public renewed critical attention to the work of an under-recognized, significant American poet. If not previously published or longer in print, the works of Neglected Masters are published in collaboration with the Library of America. No applications or unsolicited nominations are accepted.

Randall Jarrell Award in Criticism: The award recognizes and rewards poetry criticism that is intelligent and learned, as well as lively and enjoyable to read. The prize is intended for criticism aimed at a large general readership rather than an audience of specialists. No applications or unsolicited nominations are accepted.

Ruth Lilly Poetry Prize: Awarded annually, the $100,000 Ruth Lilly Poetry Prize honors a living U.S. poet whose lifetime accomplishments warrant extraordinary recognition.

Verse Drama Award: The prize seeks to bring renewed attention to an underrecognized area of poetry. The prize will honor a living poet who has written a previously unpublished, outstanding original verse drama in English. The award recipient will receive a cash purse of $10,000 and a staged reading of his or her winning manuscript in Chicago. **EIN:** 362490808

2796
Polish American Congress Charitable Foundation

5711 N. Milwaukee Ave.
Chicago, IL 60646-6294 (773) 763-9942
Contact: Virginia Sikora, Pers.
FAX: (773) 763-9943; E-mail: paccf@paccf.org;
URL: http://www.paccf.org/

Foundation type: Public charity
Purpose: Scholarships to undergraduate and graduate students of Polish descent for higher education.
Publications: Application guidelines.
Financial data: Year ended 12/31/2012. Assets, $3,957,927 (M); Expenditures, $307,052; Total giving, $217,802; Grants to individuals, totaling $59,212.
Fields of interest: Higher education.
Type of support: Scholarships—to individuals; Graduate support; Undergraduate support.
Application information: Applications accepted. Application form required. Application form available on the grantmaker's web site.
Initial approach: Letter
Deadline(s): Mar. 15 for The Majer and Lakowski Families Memorial Scholarship, Apr. 15 for Richard Gorecki Scholarship
Applicants should submit the following:

1) Resume
2) Transcripts
3) Essay
Additional information: All payments will be sent directly to the educational institution on behalf of the applicant.
Program descriptions:
Richard Gorecki Scholarship: Scholarships to full-time students enrolled in an accredited undergraduate or graduate program at a college or university. Applicant must become a member of their local PAC Division or if none in their area, then a member thru the National PAC. Scholarship range between $500 and $1,000.
The Majer and Lakowski Families Memorial Scholarship: Scholarships are available to full-time undergraduate and graduate students majoring in engineering or business administration. Applicants must attend a public state university or college. Preference is given to juniors, seniors, or graduate students. The amount of scholarship will be equal to the in state full time student tuition for one year. **EIN:** 362732238

2797
Presence Health Foundation

(formerly Resurrection Development Foundation)
200 S. Wacker, 11th Fl
Chicago, IL 60657-3707 (777) 665-3909
Contact: Amy Day, V.P.
URL: http://www.reshealth.org/sub_rdf/default.cfm

Foundation type: Public charity
Purpose: Hospital bill financial assistance to indigent uninsured and underinsured patients of Presence Health hospitals in IL.
Financial data: Year ended 12/31/2011. Assets, $38,130,060 (M); Expenditures, $8,869,931; Total giving, $5,584,443; Grants to individuals, totaling $90,537.
Fields of interest: Hospitals (general); Health care, patient services; Economically disadvantaged.
Type of support: Grants for special needs.
Application information:
Initial approach: Letter
Applicants should submit the following:
1) Financial information
Additional information: Contact foundation for eligibility criteria.
EIN: 363330929

2798
Joe Prest Educational Trust Fund

c/o Marla Wilkins
13608 Meadow Ln.
Plainfield, IL 60544
Contact: Marla Wilkins, Tr.

Foundation type: Independent foundation
Purpose: Scholarships to individuals from the Steubenville, OH, area with a GPA of at least 2.75 for undergraduate education at U.S. universities and colleges.
Financial data: Year ended 12/31/2011. Assets, $31,351 (M); Expenditures, $6,455; Total giving, $5,500; Grants to individuals, 6 grants totaling $5,500 (high: $1,000, low: $500).
Fields of interest: Higher education.
Type of support: Undergraduate support.
Application information: Applications accepted.
Deadline(s): None
Additional information: Application should include GPA, and applicants must demonstrate participation in athletics,

extracurricular activities, and, when appropriate, financial need.
EIN: 341742248

2799
Dr. Jorge Prieto Community Board

2424 S. Pulaski Rd.
Chicago, IL 60623-3718

Foundation type: Independent foundation
Purpose: Emergency grants for food, housing and utilities to needy Chicago-area individuals and victims of domestic violence.
Financial data: Year ended 12/31/2011. Assets, $279,359 (M); Expenditures, $27,102; Total giving, $24,879. Grants to individuals amount not specified.
Fields of interest: Domestic violence.
Type of support: Emergency funds; Grants for special needs.
Application information:
Initial approach: Letter
Deadline(s): None
Additional information: Contact the organization for eligibility determination.
EIN: 363945780

2800
Ricky Prine Scholarship Award Foundation

25 N. County St.
Waukegan, IL 60085-4342

Foundation type: Operating foundation
Purpose: Scholarship to a graduating senior of McHenry Community High School for attendance at an accredited college or university of his/her choice.
Financial data: Year ended 04/30/2013. Assets, $50,206 (M); Expenditures, $5,261; Total giving, $5,000; Grant to an individual, 1 grant totaling $5,000.
Fields of interest: Higher education.
Type of support: Support to graduates or students of specific schools.
Application information: Applications accepted. Interview required.
Additional information: Contact your high school for application information.
EIN: 363690477

2801
Proctor Health Care Foundation

5409 N. Knoxville Ave., 5th Fl.
Peoria, IL 61614-5069 (309) 693-0414
Contact: Paul E. Macek, Pres. and C.E.O.
FAX: (309) 689-6014;
E-mail: foundation@proctor.org; Additional tel.: (309) 256-4097; URL: http://www.proctorgiving.com/

Foundation type: Public charity
Purpose: Financial assistance to indigents residing in Peoria, IL, to help pay for medical and living expenses.
Publications: Informational brochure; Newsletter.
Financial data: Year ended 12/31/2011. Assets, $18,751,733 (M); Expenditures, $264,851; Total giving, $100,612.
Fields of interest: Economically disadvantaged.
Type of support: Grants for special needs.
Application information:
Initial approach: Letter

Additional information: Contact foundation for further application guidelines.
EIN: 371133429

2802
Puckett Foundation

c/o Fairfield National Bank
P.O. Box 429
Fairfield, IL   62837-0429   (618) 842-2107

Foundation type: Independent foundation
Purpose: Scholarships to graduating seniors at Fairfield Community High School, IL, for continuing education at accredited colleges or universities.
Publications: Application guidelines.
Financial data: Year ended 12/31/2011. Assets, $1,695,040 (M); Expenditures, $85,503; Total giving, $73,000; Grants to individuals, 10 grants totaling $28,500 (high: $3,000, low: $1,500).
Fields of interest: Higher education.
Type of support: Support to graduates or students of specific schools; Undergraduate support.
Application information: Application form required.
  Deadline(s): Mar. 1
  Final notification: Recipients notified by Apr. 15
  Applicants should submit the following:
    1) Class rank
    2) GPA
    3) ACT
  Additional information: The scholarship is awarded on the basis of ability, industry and integrity, and will be terminated if the recipient does not maintain a passing average. Contact your guidance office for application information.
EIN: 136115138

2803
Pugh Foundation Scholarship Fund

(formerly Hazel & Ben Pugh Foundation Scholarship Fund)
c/o JPMorgan Chase Bank, N.A.
10 S Dearborn St.,No.21 FL
Chicago, IL   60603-2300   (262) 363-6200
Contact: Rick Colbo
Application address: 605 W. School Rd., Mukwonago, WI 53149, tel.: (262) 363-6200

Foundation type: Independent foundation
Purpose: Scholarships to graduating seniors of Mukwonago High School, WI, for undergraduate studies at any college or university.
Financial data: Year ended 09/30/2012. Assets, $248,324 (M); Expenditures, $14,785; Total giving, $11,735; Grants to individuals, 5 grants totaling $11,735 (high: $2,347, low: $2,347).
Type of support: Support to graduates or students of specific schools; Undergraduate support.
Application information: Applications accepted. Application form required.
  Deadline(s): May 1
EIN: 396452749

2804
George M. Pullman Educational Foundation

55 W. Monroe St., Ste. 3460
Chicago, IL   60603-5086   (312) 422-0444
Contact: Robin Redman, Exec. Dir.
FAX: (312) 422-0448;
E-mail: info@pullmanfoundation.org; URL: http://www.pullmanfoundation.org

Foundation type: Independent foundation

Purpose: Scholarships by nomination only to high school seniors in Cook County, IL, for children or siblings of alumni of the Pullman Free School of Manual Training, or an immediate family member who has received a Pullman Award.
Publications: Informational brochure.
Financial data: Year ended 07/31/2013. Assets, $27,740,913 (M); Expenditures, $1,539,850; Total giving, $559,683; Grants to individuals, 161 grants totaling $559,683 (high: $6,000, low: $300).
Fields of interest: Vocational education; Higher education.
Type of support: Awards/grants by nomination only; Undergraduate support.
Application information:
  Deadline(s): Jan. 5 for first-year students, May 1 for new upper class students, and June 1 for renewal students
  Additional information: Individual applications not accepted. All candidates must be nominated by their high school guidance counselors. Students must demonstrate academic excellence and financial need.
EIN: 362216171

2805
Pulmonary Fibrosis Foundation

230 E. Ohio St., Ste. 304
Chicago, IL   60611-3201   (312) 587-9272
Contact: Daniel M. Rose, Chiar. and C.E.O.
FAX: (312) 587-9273;
E-mail: info@pulmonaryfibrosis.org; Toll-free tel.: (888) 733-6741; toll-free fax: (866) 587-9158;
E-mail For Daniel M. Rose: dmrose@pulmonaryfibrosis.org; URL: http://www.pulmonaryfibrosis.org

Foundation type: Public charity
Purpose: Grants for researchers to develop new treatment and finding a cure for pulmonary fibrosis.
Publications: Application guidelines; Annual report.
Financial data: Year ended 12/31/2011. Assets, $3,511,296 (M); Expenditures, $2,296,017; Total giving, $259,415; Grants to individuals, totaling $3,000.
Fields of interest: Lung research.
Type of support: Research; Grants to individuals.
Application information:
  Initial approach: Letter of Intent
  Deadline(s): Mid- Nov. for letter of intent, mid-Feb. for full application
  Final notification: Applicants notified Jan. for LOI, May for full application
  Additional information: See web site for additional guidelines.
EIN: 841558631

2806
The Ragdale Foundation

1260 N. Green Bay Rd.
Lake Forest, IL   60045-1106   (847) 234-1063
Contact: Susan Page Tillett, Exec. Dir.
FAX: (847) 234-1063; E-mail: info@ragdale.org;
E-mail for Susan Page Tillett: s.tillett@ragdale.org; URL: http://www.ragdale.org

Foundation type: Public charity
Purpose: Residency to writers, visual artists, composers, and interdisciplinary artists for two to six week stays.
Publications: Application guidelines; Annual report; Financial statement; Informational brochure; Newsletter.

Financial data: Year ended 12/31/2011. Assets, $8,662,242 (M); Expenditures, $831,421. No monetary support given for residencies.
Fields of interest: Visual arts; Literature.
Type of support: Residencies.
Application information: Applications accepted. Application form required. Application form available on the grantmaker's web site.
  Initial approach: Letter, telephone, or e-mail
  Copies of proposal: 1
  Deadline(s): Jan. 15, May 15, Sept. 15
  Final notification: Recipients notified in three months
  Applicants should submit the following:
    1) Resume
    2) Letter(s) of recommendation
    3) Work samples
    4) Proposal
  Additional information: Application should also include artists' statement and work plan, a $40 nonrefundable application fee. There is a residency fee of $35 per day.
Program description:
  Alice Hayes Writing Fellowship: The foundation awards a four-week residency and $500 stipend to a writer who is working on a project designed to bring awareness to a contemporary issue having to do with peace, social justice, or the environment.
EIN: 362937927

2807
Bish Rainey Memorial Trust

231 LaSalle St., IL1-231-10-05
Chicago, IL   60697
Contact: John C. McMullan
Application address: c/o Kennett Public Schools, Attn.: Dr. John C. McMullan, Supt., 1400 W. Washington St., Kennett, MO 63857-1524
Application address: c/o Kennett Public Schools, 1400 W. Washington St., Kennett, MO 63857-1524

Foundation type: Independent foundation
Purpose: Scholarships to graduates of Kennett public schools, MO, for postsecondary education.
Financial data: Year ended 01/31/2013. Assets, $325,271 (M); Expenditures, $16,670; Total giving, $12,250.
Fields of interest: Vocational education, post-secondary; Higher education.
Type of support: Support to graduates or students of specific schools; Undergraduate support.
Application information: Applications accepted. Application form required.
  Deadline(s): Apr.
  Applicants should submit the following:
    1) Class rank
    2) Transcripts
  Additional information: Students should contact their guidance counselor for application information.
EIN: 431223959

2808
Rauch Family Foundation II, Inc.

1800 3rd Ave., No. 302
Rock Island, IL   61201-8019   (309) 788-2300
Contact: Samuel M. Gilman, Pres.
FAX: (309) 788-3298;
E-mail: day.rauch@sbcglobal.net; URL: http://rauchfamilyfoundation.org/index.html

Foundation type: Independent foundation
Purpose: Grants for programs and projects for the enhancement of Judaism, its traditions and people.

Publications: Annual report (including application guidelines).

Financial data: Year ended 12/31/2011. Assets, $1,129,952 (M); Expenditures, $75,197; Total giving, $62,575; Grants to individuals, 2 grants totaling $4,675 (high: $3,500, low: $1,175).

Fields of interest: Camps; Jewish agencies & synagogues.

Type of support: Grants to individuals; Undergraduate support; Travel grants; Camperships.

Application information: Application form not required.

> *Initial approach:* Letter or telephone
> *Deadline(s):* None
> *Additional information:* Applications must include proposal and outline financial need.

EIN: 363570748

2809
Reach for The Moon Foundation

P.O. Box 628
Batavia, IL 60510-0628   (630) 906-6815
FAX: (630) 906-6845;
E-mail: info@reachforthemoonfoundation.com;
URL: http://www.reachforthemoonfoundation.com

Foundation type: Public charity

Purpose: Grants to provide basic necessities to children, primarily in Cook, Kane, and DuPage counties, IL.

Financial data: Year ended 12/31/2011. Assets, $30,286 (M); Expenditures, $73,888. Grants for special needs amount not specified.

Fields of interest: Children/youth, services.

Type of support: Grants for special needs.

Application information: Contact foundation for eligibility requirements.

EIN: 364193196

2810
Realtors Relief Foundation

430 N. Michigan Ave.
Chicago, IL 60611-4011   (312) 329-8200
Additional address (DC office): 500 New Jersey Ave., N.W., Washington, DC 20001-2020; toll-free tel.: (800) 874-6500; URL: https://www.realtor.org/relief

Foundation type: Public charity

Purpose: Grants to needy individuals and their families for housing-related needs arising from natural disasters, with preference to members of the National Association of Realtors.

Publications: Informational brochure; Newsletter.

Financial data: Year ended 12/31/2011. Assets, $455,386 (M); Expenditures, $852,735; Total giving, $852,735; Grants to individuals, totaling $532,735.

Fields of interest: Housing/shelter; Safety/disasters.

Type of support: Emergency funds.

Application information: Contact foundation for eligibility requirements.

Program description:

> *Grants:* Grants are available to individuals and families who have been the victims of a major disaster. Grants can be used toward repair or rebuild efforts, mortgage or rental assistance, and short-term household assistance. Eligible individuals must apply through their state or local Realtor Association, a 501(c)(3) charitable organization working in conjunction with a state or local Realtor Association, or an institute, society, or

council (ISC) of the National Association of Realtors.

EIN: 364468109

2811
Mildred Reinheimer Trust

33 S. 4th St.
Pekin, IL 61554
Application address: c/o Walter Dare, Scholarship Comm., Delavan High School, Delavan, IL 61734, tel.: (309) 244-8285

Foundation type: Independent foundation

Purpose: Scholarships to graduates of Delavan High School, IL for continuing education at accredited colleges or universities.

Financial data: Year ended 05/31/2013. Assets, $251,551 (M); Expenditures, $16,165; Total giving, $12,860.

Fields of interest: Higher education.

Type of support: Support to graduates or students of specific schools.

Application information: Application form required.

> *Deadline(s):* May 1
> *Additional information:* Applications available from Delavan High School.

EIN: 376154891

2812
William M. Reiss Foundation

231 S. LaSalle St., IL1-231-10-05
Chicago, IL 60697-0001   (214) 978-1709
Contact: Annette Walker
Application address: 120 Main St., Dallas, TX 75202-3113, tel: (214) 978-1709

Foundation type: Independent foundation

Purpose: Scholarships to financially needy students at Belleville, IL, area public schools. Students pursuing degrees in medicine are ineligible.

Financial data: Year ended 12/31/2011. Assets, $853,949 (M); Expenditures, $49,743; Total giving, $34,900. Scholarships—to individuals amount not specified.

Fields of interest: Higher education.

Type of support: Support to graduates or students of specific schools; Undergraduate support.

Application information: Applications accepted. Application form required.

> *Deadline(s):* May 1
> *Final notification:* Recipients notified after June 20
> *Applicants should submit the following:*
> 1) SAR
> 2) Transcripts
> 3) Financial information
> 4) FAFSA

EIN: 237056642

2813
Elizabeth Reller Memorial Scholarship Fund

300 Washington St.
Beardstown, IL 62618-1194

Foundation type: Operating foundation

Purpose: Loans to financially needy graduates of Beardstown High School, IL, for higher education.

Financial data: Year ended 12/31/2013. Assets, $2,435,662 (M); Expenditures, $117,350; Total giving, $107,728; Grants to individuals, 28 grants totaling $107,728 (high: $7,500, low: $309).

Fields of interest: Higher education.

Type of support: Student loans—to individuals; Support to graduates or students of specific schools.

Application information: Application form required.

> *Deadline(s):* July 15 and Dec. 15
> *Applicants should submit the following:*
> 1) Essay
> 2) Transcripts
> 3) Letter(s) of recommendation
> 4) Financial information
> *Additional information:* Recipients are required to begin repayment of their loans 30 days after discontinuation of studies or one year after graduation, if they have completed their studies. Repayment of the loan is generally paid in 120 equal monthly installments. No penalty will apply if the loan is paid early. The rate at that time will be two points above the daily prime rate published daily in the Wall Street Journal.

EIN: 371337146

2814
REO Educational Scholarship Fund

(formerly Omer E. Rabideau Education Scholarship Fund)
P.O. Box 38
Clifton, IL 60927-0038
Application address: c/o Clifton Central High School, Attn.: Principal, 1134 E. 3100 N. Rd., Clifton, IL 60927-7084

Foundation type: Independent foundation

Purpose: Scholarships to graduates and graduating seniors of Clifton Central High School, IL.

Financial data: Year ended 12/31/2011. Assets, $442,838 (M); Expenditures, $13,474; Total giving, $13,000; Grants to individuals, 4 grants totaling $13,000 (high: $5,000, low: $1,000).

Fields of interest: Scholarships/financial aid.

Type of support: Support to graduates or students of specific schools; Undergraduate support.

Application information: Applications accepted.

> *Initial approach:* Letter
> *Deadline(s):* Apr. 1
> *Additional information:* Application must outline financial need and list qualifications.

EIN: 363553408

2815
The Republic of Tea Foundation

(formerly Central Wholesale Liquor Foundation)
17577 Mockingbird Rd.
Nashville, IL 62263-3407   (618) 478-5520
Contact: for Scholarships: Steve Lohmann

Foundation type: Operating foundation

Purpose: Scholarships to full or part-time employees children and to full or part-time employees of the Republic of Tea for higher education.

Financial data: Year ended 04/30/2013. Assets, $28,339 (M); Expenditures, $20,214; Total giving, $20,104; Grants to individuals, 15 grants totaling $20,104 (high: $2,000, low: $471).

Fields of interest: Higher education.

Type of support: Employee-related scholarships.

Application information: Applications not accepted.

> *Additional information:* Unsolicited requests for funds not considered or acknowledged.

Company name: The Republic of Tea
EIN: 371264351

2816
Research & Education Foundation of the American Association for the Surgery of Trauma
633 N. Saint Clair, Ste. 2600
Chicago, IL   60611   (312) 202-5252
Contact: Sharon Gautschy, Exec. Dir.
URL: http://www.aast.org/Foundation/Default.aspx

Foundation type: Public charity
Purpose: Scholarships for research and education in the field of trauma.
Publications: Application guidelines; Newsletter.
Financial data: Year ended 12/31/2011. Assets, $3,210,211 (M); Expenditures, $207,485; Total giving, $195,000; Grants to individuals, totaling $195,000.
Fields of interest: Medical school/education; Health sciences school/education.
Type of support: Graduate support; Doctoral support.
Application information: Applications accepted. Interview required.
   Initial approach: Letter
   Additional information: Contact foundation for eligibility guidelines.
Program description:
   AAST/KCI Research Grant: Scholarships of up to $50,000 are available to qualified individuals seeking to research wound care.
EIN: 561918296

2817
Respiratory Health Association of Metropolitan Chicago
(formerly American Lung Association of Metropolitan Chicago)
1440 W. Washington Blvd.
Chicago, IL   60607-1821   (312) 243-2000
FAX: (312) 243-3954;
E-mail: jafrick@lungchicago.org; URL: http://www.lungchicago.org

Foundation type: Public charity
Purpose: Grants to researchers to advance the understanding and treatment of lung disease.
Publications: Application guidelines; Annual report.
Financial data: Year ended 06/30/2012. Assets, $4,495,140 (M); Expenditures, $8,731,158; Total giving, $1,991,900.
Fields of interest: Lung diseases.
Type of support: Research.
Application information: Applications accepted. Application form required.
   Send request by: Mail, e-mail or online
   Additional information: See web site for eligibility criteria and funding guidelines.
Program description:
   Research Grants: On occasion, the association will issue requests for proposals (RFPs) dealing with specific initiatives aimed at improving the respiratory health of individuals and families throughout the metropolitan Chicago region.
EIN: 362222687

2818
Reynolds-Barwick Scholarship Fund
2931 E. 1300 N. Rd.
Sheldon, IL   60966-9775

Foundation type: Independent foundation
Purpose: Scholarships to graduating seniors ranking in the upper 30 percent of the graduating class and who are residents of Iroquois County, IL.

Financial data: Year ended 12/31/2012. Assets, $1,692,192 (M); Expenditures, $237,909; Total giving, $99,000; Grants to individuals, 12 grants totaling $99,000 (high: $9,000, low: $4,500).
Fields of interest: Higher education.
Type of support: Support to graduates or students of specific schools; Undergraduate support.
Application information:
   Deadline(s): Feb. 1
   Additional information: Contributes only to a preselected individuals, unsolicited requests for funds not considered or acknowledged.
EIN: 376245457

2819
Richland Community College Foundation
1 College Pk.
Decatur, IL   62521-8512   (217) 875-7211
Contact: Richard McGowan, Exec. Dir.
FAX: (217) 875-2762;
E-mail: foundation@richland.edu; URL: http://www.richland.edu/foundation/

Foundation type: Public charity
Purpose: Scholarships to students at Richland Community College, IL pursuing higher education.
Publications: Annual report.
Financial data: Year ended 06/30/2012. Assets, $15,978,787 (M); Expenditures, $688,949; Total giving, $554,037; Grants to individuals, totaling $325,096.
Fields of interest: Higher education.
Type of support: Support to graduates or students of specific schools.
Application information: Applications accepted. Application form required. Application form available on the grantmaker's web site.
   Send request by: Mail
   Additional information: See web site for complete list of programs.
EIN: 371210583

2820
Herman Rieger Foundation
c/o Kathy Knayer
P.O. Box 235
Forrest, IL   61741-0169
Contact: Scholarship: Kay Crane, Dir.
Application address: 318 S. Oak St., Forrest, IL 41741

Foundation type: Independent foundation
Purpose: Scholarships to individuals from the Forrest, IL, area for undergraduate education.
Financial data: Year ended 01/31/2012. Assets, $110,695 (M); Expenditures, $3,750; Total giving, $3,750; Grants to individuals, totaling $3,750.
Fields of interest: Higher education.
Type of support: Undergraduate support.
Application information: Applications accepted. Application form required.
   Deadline(s): Mar. 1
   Additional information: Contact foundation for current application guidelines.
EIN: 371206579

2821
Lila Rinker Trust
(also known as Dr. E.B. Rinker Medical Scholarship Fund)
c/o JPMorgan Chase Bank, N.A.
10 S Dearborn St.No.21 Fl.
Chicago, IL   60603-2300

Foundation type: Independent foundation

Purpose: Scholarships to students attending the School of Medicine, Indiana University, IN who show outstanding academic achievement regardless of financial need.
Financial data: Year ended 06/30/2012. Assets, $753,293 (M); Expenditures, $50,487; Total giving, $37,306.
Fields of interest: Medical school/education.
Type of support: Support to graduates or students of specific schools; Graduate support.
Application information: Applications not accepted.
   Additional information: Unsolicited requests for funds not considered or acknowledged.
EIN: 356262657

2822
Lloyd W. & Virginia D. Rittenhouse Charitable Foundation
(formerly Rittenhouse Foundation)
c/o JPMorgan Chase Bank, N.A.
10 S Dearborn
Chicago, IL   60603
Application address: c/o Honeoye Falls-Lima Senior High School, Attn.: Kathleen Walling, Principal, 83 East St., Honeoye Falls, NY 14472-1228, tel.: (585) 624-7050

Foundation type: Independent foundation
Purpose: Scholarships to graduates of Honeoye Falls-Lima Senior High School, Honeoye Falls, NY.
Financial data: Year ended 12/31/2012. Assets, $848,828 (M); Expenditures, $46,125; Total giving, $31,500; Grants to individuals, 4 grants totaling $31,500 (high: $9,000, low: $4,500).
Fields of interest: Higher education.
Type of support: Support to graduates or students of specific schools.
Application information: Applications accepted.
   Deadline(s): Mar.
   Applicants should submit the following:
      1) Financial information
      2) Essay
      3) Letter(s) of recommendation
      4) ACT
      5) SAT
      6) Transcripts
   Additional information: Application should include a record of leadership roles, a record of employment history, and a listing of school activities, honors and awards.
EIN: 311717147

2823
The Riverside Golf Club Memorial Scholarship Fund For Caddies Foundation
2520 S. Des Plaines Ave.
North Riverside, IL   60546-1571   (708) 447-3700
Contact: Randall Womack, Chair.
Application Address: c/o Riverside Golf Club, North Riverside IL 60546

Foundation type: Independent foundation
Purpose: Scholarships to meritorious caddies at the Riverside Golf Club, IL enrolled in an approved college or school.
Financial data: Year ended 09/30/2012. Assets, $278,194 (M); Expenditures, $38,555; Total giving, $33,250; Grants to individuals, 15 grants totaling $33,250 (high: $4,000, low: $1,250).
Fields of interest: Higher education; Athletics/sports, golf.
Type of support: Scholarships—to individuals.

Application information: Applications accepted.
Application form required.
Deadline(s): None
Additional information: Application must include
APP statement. Applicant must maintain
passing grades and be employed as a caddie
for two years.
EIN: 363715404

2824
Riverside HealthCare Foundation

(formerly RMC Foundation, Inc.)
350 N. Wall St.
Kankakee, IL   60901-2901   (815) 933-1671
Contact: Jaymie Simmon, Chair.; Matt McBurnie,
Exec. Dir.
Application address: Riverside HealthCare,
Professional Development Council, Attn: LeAnn
McCormick, RN, Educational Services, 350 North
Wall St., Kankakee, IL 60901, tel.: (815)
935-7256, ext. 4715,
e-mail: leann-mccormick@riversidehealthcare.net
FAX: (815) 933-1681; URL: http://
www.riversidehealthcare.org/giving/
foundation.html

Foundation type: Public charity
Purpose: Scholarships to students pursuing
education and training in health related career
fields from an accredited institution.
Financial data: Year ended 12/31/2011. Assets,
$14,007,471 (M); Expenditures, $867,391; Total
giving, $714,316; Grants to individuals, totaling
$11,059.
Fields of interest: Nursing school/education.
Type of support: Employee-related scholarships.
Application information: Applications accepted.
Application form required. Application form
available on the grantmaker's web site. Interview
required.
Send request by: Mail
Deadline(s): Apr. 30
Applicants should submit the following:
1) Transcripts
2) Letter(s) of recommendation
Additional information: Funds are paid directly to
the educational institution on behalf of the
student. Applicants must present a copy of
their class schedule and previous semester's
grades (spring only) before scholarship funds
are released.
Program descriptions:
Elaine Chesrown Scholarship Fund: Two $2,500
scholarships are available annually to students
employed by, or who intend to be employed by
Riverside, currently working on a degree or
certificate in nursing or allied health.
*Nehmet Sipahi, M.D. Oncology Nursing
Scholarship:* Scholarships totaling $1,500 are
available to assist area students pursuing a career
in oncology nursing. The scholarship may be used
for tuition, books, and room and board expenses for
area students working toward a degree. Fees,
books, coursework and travel expenses for
Riverside employees pursuing oncology nursing
certification. Also, registration and travel expenses
for a Riverside employee pursuing continuing
oncology nursing education.
EIN: 363166033

2825
Mary K. Roberts Scholarship Foundation

c/o The National Bank & Trust Co.
230 W. State St., MSC M-300
Sycamore, IL   60178-1419   (815) 895-2125
Contact: Tom Sullivan

Foundation type: Independent foundation
Purpose: Scholarships to graduates of Sycamore
High School, IL, who are pursuing degrees in social
work, nursing or special education at four-year
colleges and universities.
Financial data: Year ended 12/31/2012. Assets,
$411,845 (M); Expenditures, $31,228; Total
giving, $22,705; Grants to individuals, 11 grants
totaling $22,705 (high: $2,850, low: $1,235).
Fields of interest: Education, special; Nursing
school/education; Reading; Human services;
Anthropology/sociology.
Type of support: Support to graduates or students
of specific schools; Undergraduate support.
Application information: Applications accepted.
Application form required.
Deadline(s): May 1
EIN: 366868922

2826
Mary H. Robinson Trust

c/o Bank of America, N.A.
231 S. LaSalle St., IL1-231-10-05
Chicago, IL   60697-0001
Application address: Bolivar High School, Attn: SR
Scholarships, Michelle Darby, 1401 North Hwy D,
Bolivar, MO 65613

Foundation type: Independent foundation
Purpose: Scholarships to students attending
Bolivar public schools or Bolivar public schools
graduates who are attending a college, university,
trade or vocational school full time.
Financial data: Year ended 12/31/2011. Assets,
$532,817 (M); Expenditures, $19,839; Total
giving, $14,414; Grants to individuals, 22 grants
totaling $8,722 (high: $600, low: $301).
Fields of interest: Vocational education,
post-secondary; Higher education.
Type of support: Support to graduates or students
of specific schools; Technical education support;
Undergraduate support.
Application information: Applications accepted.
Application form required.
Send request by: Mail
Deadline(s): Mar. 11
Additional information: Recipients are
recommended to the trustees of the fund by
the superintendent of schools, the high
school principal, and the president of the
Parent-Teachers Organization.
EIN: 436260501

2827
Rockford Area Arts Council

713 E. State St.
Rockford, IL   61104-1020   (815) 963-6765
E-mail address for grants:
grants@artsforeveryone.org
FAX: (815) 963-8958;
E-mail: info@artsforeveryone.com; URL: http://
www.artsforeveryone.com

Foundation type: Public charity
Purpose: Grants to individuals and organizations of
northern, IL for the underserved and youth, in
accomplishing new art projects.
Publications: Application guidelines; Annual report.

Financial data: Year ended 08/31/2011. Assets,
$400,078 (M); Expenditures, $400,347; Total
giving, $21,663. Grants to individuals amount not
specified.
Fields of interest: Arts education; Visual arts.
Type of support: Grants to individuals.
Application information: Applications accepted.
Application form required. Application form
available on the grantmaker's web site.
Initial approach: Telephone or e-mail
Deadline(s): Nov. 18 for Community Arts Access
Grants
Program description:
Community Arts Access Grants: Grants of up to
$2,500 are available to artists and community
nonprofit organizations for projects that increase
access to the arts for underserved people, and/or
increase the visibility and accessibility of the arts to
youth, in Boone, DeKalb, Ogle, and Winnebago
counties.
EIN: 237039197

2828
The Rockwood Foundation

(also known as Westerhold Family Foundation)
20 N. Wacker Dr., Ste. 960
Chicago, IL   60606-2901   (312) 621-2238
Contact: Richard P. Mrotek, Dir.

Foundation type: Company-sponsored foundation
Purpose: Scholarships to students residing and
attending college in the Chicago metropolitan area,
IL.
Financial data: Year ended 12/31/2012. Assets,
$138,767 (M); Expenditures, $26,387; Total
giving, $15,000; Grants to individuals, 9 grants
totaling $14,000 (high: $2,500, low: $750).
Fields of interest: Higher education.
Type of support: Scholarships—to individuals.
Application information: Applications accepted.
Application form required.
Initial approach: Letter
Deadline(s): May 17
Applicants should submit the following:
1) Letter(s) of recommendation
2) Essay
3) Transcripts
4) SAT
5) ACT
6) SAR
7) FAFSA
Additional information: Application should also
include a copy of parents' most recent tax
return.
EIN: 200248335

2829
Polly W. Roesch Vocal Scholarship Trust

10 S Dearborn IL1-0117
Chicago, IL   60603   (217) 525-9747
Contact: JoAnn Ley
Application address: P.O. Box 3268 - MC IL2-8283,
Springfield, IL 62708-3268

Foundation type: Independent foundation
Purpose: Scholarships to Sangamon County, IL,
residents who are planning to be vocal music
majors.
Financial data: Year ended 12/31/2012. Assets,
$163,094 (M); Expenditures, $9,292; Total giving,
$7,024.
Fields of interest: Music; Performing arts,
education.
Type of support: Scholarships—to individuals.

Application information: Applications accepted. Application form required.

Deadline(s): Mar. 1

Applicants should submit the following:
1) Transcripts
2) SAT
3) ACT

EIN: 376234631

2830

Lon & Jessie Rogers Educational Trust

c/o JPMorgan Chase Bank, N.A.
10 S. Dearborn St., IL1-0117
Chicago, IL 60603-2317
Application address: JPMorgan Chase Bank, N.A., 2200 Ross Ave., Dallas, TX 75201, tel.: (214) 965-2914

Foundation type: Independent foundation
Purpose: Low-interest loans and scholarships to students who are residents of Muhlenberg, Pike, and Ohio Counties, KY.
Financial data: Year ended 09/30/2012. Assets, $11,926,312 (M); Expenditures, $383,739; Total giving, $287,738; Loans to individuals, totaling $142,045.
Fields of interest: Higher education.
Type of support: Scholarships—to individuals; Student loans—to individuals.
Application information: Applications accepted. Application form required.

Initial approach: Letter
Deadline(s): Before tuition due date
Additional information: Preference is given to students who are attending Centre College. Loans and scholarships are limited to students who are attending non-publicly-funded universities and colleges.

EIN: 616019469

2831

Ronald McDonald House Charities

(formerly Ronald McDonald Children's Charities)
1 Kroc Dr.
Oak Brook, IL 60523-2275 (630) 623-7048
Contact: Jennifer Smith, Dir., Comms.
Scholarship address: RMHC U.S. Scholarship Program, International Scholarship and Tuition Services, Inc., P.O. Box 22376, Nashville, TN 37202-2376
FAX: (630) 623-7488; E-mail: info@rmhc.org; URL: http://www.rmhc.org

Foundation type: Public charity
Purpose: Awards to a physician who has made an outstanding contribution in the field of pediatric health care. Also, emergency housing to families who have a child undergoing medical treatment in a hospital, as well as scholarship support to children throughout the U.S.
Publications: Application guidelines; Annual report; Informational brochure.
Financial data: Year ended 12/31/2012. Assets, $131,500,478 (M); Expenditures, $29,752,940; Total giving, $22,440,142; Grants to individuals, totaling $375,000.
Fields of interest: Higher education; Health care; Children; Youth.
Type of support: Scholarships—to individuals; In-kind gifts; Awards/prizes.
Application information: Applications accepted. Application form available on the grantmaker's web site.

Initial approach: Letter

Send request by: Mail or online
Deadline(s): Jan. 28 for Scholarships
Final notification: Applicants notified in May - June
Applicants should submit the following:
1) Transcripts
2) SAT
3) Letter(s) of recommendation
4) GPA
5) Essay
6) Budget Information
7) ACT

Program descriptions:

Awards of Excellence: These awards recognize individual efforts that have improved children's lives. The achievements of a physician who has made an outstanding contribution in the field of health care, and those of an individual who has done the same for the general well-being of children, are honored with a $100,000 grant to be given to the nonprofit children's organization identified by the recipient.

Ronald McDonald Care Mobile Program: The program maintains a fleet of state-of-the-art vehicles that deliver cost-effective medical, dental, and education services directly to underserved children in their own neighborhoods. The vehicles are equipped with telemedicine capabilities that can transmit images and provide remote consultations, video conferencing, and medical/surgical follow-up. The vehicle accommodates two patient examination rooms, a laboratory, and a pharmacy. The mobile provides a number of medical and dental services, including primary care, specialty care, blood collection, diagnosis, treatment, referral, follow-up for serious medical conditions, health education, and federally-assisted health insurance program enrollment.

Ronald McDonald Family Room Program: These rooms provide a haven within the hospital for the families of children undergoing treatment. The family room serves as a place of respite for family members to step away from the stressful hospital environment. Designed to reflect a comfortable environment, many families use the family room to rest and reflect.

Ronald McDonald House Program: This program provides a 'home away from home' for families of seriously ill children receiving treatment at nearby hospitals. The house provides a comfortable, supportive lodging alternative for these families. It serves as a temporary residence near the medical facility where family members can sleep, eat, relax and find support from other families in similar situations. In return, families are asked to make a donation ranging on average from $5 to $20 per day, but if that isn't possible, their stay is free.

Scholarships: Scholarships to high school seniors who have demonstrated academic achievement, leadership, and community involvement. Eligible applicants must: live in an area where there is a participating local organization chapter; be younger than 21 years old; be eligible to attend a two- or four-year college or university with a full course of study; and be a legal U.S. resident. Scholarships are available through one of four channels: RMHC Scholars, RMHC/ASIA (Asian Students Increasing Achievement), RMHC/African-American Future Achievers, and RMHC/HACER.

EIN: 362934689

2832

Charles M. Ross Trust

c/o Weeks and Brucker, LTD
P.O. Box 288
Fairbury, IL 61739-1446 (815) 692-2362
Contact: Thomas Brucker, Exec. Dir.

Foundation type: Independent foundation
Purpose: Graduate scholarships to financially needy gifted students at participating schools studying in the fields of religion, sociology, medicine, and teaching.
Financial data: Year ended 06/30/2013. Assets, $381,403 (M); Expenditures, $26,967; Total giving, $19,000; Grants to individuals, 7 grants totaling $19,000 (high: $4,000, low: $1,000).
Fields of interest: Medical school/education; Teacher school/education; Theological school/education; Anthropology/sociology.
Type of support: Support to graduates or students of specific schools; Graduate support.
Application information: Application form required.

Initial approach: Letter
Deadline(s): Sept. 1
Applicants should submit the following:
1) Class rank
2) Transcripts
3) Financial information
4) Budget Information
Additional information: Students should not apply to the trust, but through their respective school. Application forms may be obtained from one of the named institutions.

Program description:

Scholarship Program: Annual scholarships range from $1,000 to $3,000, and average $11,000 to $15,000 per year to students attending Lexington Theological Seminary, KY, Vanderbilt University, TN, University of Chicago, IL, Marquette University, WI, Brite Divinity School at Texas Christian University, TX and Centenary College of Louisiana, LA. Applicant should be an active member of a local church who can give evidence that he understands the world mission of the church, and applicant should have earned grades in his undergraduate education which are within the first ten percent of his class. This criteria may only be altered or waived in exceptional cases.

EIN: 376075511

2833

Albert J. and Susan E. Rot Foundation

P.O. Box 222
Naperville, IL 60565-0222 (630) 416-2100
Contact: Albert J. Rot, Pres.

Foundation type: Independent foundation
Purpose: Scholarships to individuals for higher education. Students throughout the U.S. may apply, though students from local high schools are given priority.
Financial data: Year ended 12/31/2012. Assets, $977,440 (M); Expenditures, $148,529; Total giving, $142,246; Grants to individuals, 20 grants totaling $71,711 (high: $12,000, low: $100).
Type of support: Scholarships—to individuals.
Application information: Application form required.

Deadline(s): None
Additional information: Application must include a student needs analysis service of ACT.

EIN: 363653679

2834
Rotary Club of Sparta-Henderson Memorial Foundation, Inc.
603 Fox Run Dr.
Sparta, IL 62286-1080 (618) 443-4866
Contact: H. Henderson

Foundation type: Independent foundation
Purpose: Scholarships to deserving high school seniors of Sparta, IL to further their educational goals.
Financial data: Year ended 12/31/2011. Assets, $69,416 (M); Expenditures, $7,510; Total giving, $7,500; Grants to individuals, 2 grants totaling $2,000 (high: $1,000, low: $1,000).
Fields of interest: Higher education.
Type of support: Scholarships—to individuals.
Application information: Applications accepted. Application form required.
  Deadline(s): Feb.
  Additional information: Application should include an essay.
EIN: 300013245

2835
The Rotary Foundation of Rotary International
1 Rotary Ctr.
1560 Sherman Ave.
Evanston, IL 60201-3698 (847) 866-3000
Contact: Edwin H. Futa, Genl. Secy.
FAX: (847) 328-8554; Toll Free No.: (866) 976-8279; URL: http://indyrotary.com/071013wp/

Foundation type: Public charity
Purpose: Scholarships to qualified students who have completed at least two years of college or university work for study in a foreign country, where they serve as unofficial "ambassadors of goodwill".
Publications: Annual report.
Financial data: Year ended 06/30/2013. Assets, $923,705,131 (M); Expenditures, $201,636,118; Total giving, $155,581,144; Grants to individuals, totaling $5,869,212.
Fields of interest: Education; International exchange, students; International exchange; Volunteer services; Volunteer services.
Type of support: Scholarships—to individuals; Exchange programs; Awards/prizes; Graduate support; Undergraduate support; Postgraduate support; Travel grants; Doctoral support; Project support.
Application information: Application form required. Interview required.
  Initial approach: Letter or web site
  Deadline(s): Jan. through July
  Additional information: Applicants should contact their local Rotary club for further information.
Program description:
  Rotary Scholarships: The foundation provides scholarships to Rotary International participants to further their education. Two types of scholarships are available under this program. Global grants fund scholarships of one to four years for graduate-level study, while district grants provide no restriction on the level (secondary, university, or graduate), location (local or international), length, area of study, or cost.
EIN: 363245072

2836
Roy Scholarship Trust
(formerly Roy Scholarship Fund Charitable Trust, also known as Roy Scholarship Fund)
10S. Dearborn IL1-0117
Chicago, IL 60603 (866) 300-6222

Foundation type: Independent foundation
Purpose: Scholarships to graduating seniors from Akins High School, Austin High School, Bowie High School, Crocket High School, Del Valle Independent School District, Eanes Independent School District, Johnson High School, and Travis High School, all of Austin, TX to attend accredited colleges in TX.
Financial data: Year ended 10/31/2013. Assets, $737,521 (M); Expenditures, $44,854; Total giving, $36,683; Grants to individuals, 106 grants totaling $33,529 (high: $3,305, low: $150).
Fields of interest: Higher education.
Type of support: Support to graduates or students of specific schools.
Application information:
  Deadline(s): May 1
EIN: 746086969

2837
Royal Neighbors of America Foundation
230 16th St.
Rock Island, IL 61201-8645
Toll-free tel.: (800) 627-4762; URL: http://www.royalneighborsfoundation.org/Home3.aspx

Foundation type: Public charity
Purpose: Traditional and non-traditional scholarships to members of Royal Neighbors of America pursuing higher education. Disaster relief grants for members who experience extreme financial hardship as a result of illness, accidents or natural disasters.
Financial data: Year ended 12/31/2011. Assets, $1,129,659 (M); Expenditures, $96,414; Total giving, $51,935; Grants to individuals, 29 grants totaling $46,000. Subtotal for emergency funds: 1 grant totaling $5,000. Subtotal for scholarships—to individuals: 28 grants totaling $41,000.
Fields of interest: Vocational education, post-secondary; Higher education; Safety/disasters; Women.
Type of support: Scholarships—to individuals; Grants for special needs.
Application information: Applications accepted. Application form required.
  Send request by: Mail
  Deadline(s): Mar. 1 for scholarships
  Final notification: Applicants notified by May 31 for scholarships
  Additional information: See web site for additional application guidelines.
EIN: 352164486

2838
Russell Scholarship Fund
(formerly Helen B. & Robert H. Russell Scholarship Fund)
10 S Dearborn ILI-0117
Chicago, IL 60603 (304) 234-4130
Application address: JPMorgan chase Bank 1114 Market St., Wheeling, WV 26003

Foundation type: Independent foundation
Purpose: Scholarships to residents of Ohio and Belmont counties, WV, and non-residents attending high schools in those counties who are between the ages of 17 and 25.

Financial data: Year ended 12/31/2012. Assets, $598,139 (M); Expenditures, $43,956; Total giving, $34,100.
Type of support: Scholarships—to individuals.
Application information: Applications accepted. Application form required.
  Applicants should submit the following:
    1) Letter(s) of recommendation
    2) Photograph
    3) Transcripts
    4) FAF
  Additional information: Application must include information about extracurricular activities.
EIN: 556122686

2839
Ryerson Foundation
(formerly Ryerson Tull Foundation)
227 W. Monroe St., 27th Fl.
Chicago, IL 60606
Contact: Suzan Perry
Application address: Ryerson Scholarship Prog., P.O. Box 432, Lansing, IL 60438-0432

Foundation type: Company-sponsored foundation
Purpose: Scholarships to graduating high school seniors who are children or wards of full-time, retired or deceased Ryerson employees with more than one year of continuous service.
Financial data: Year ended 12/31/2012. Assets, $20,188 (M); Expenditures, $87,316; Total giving, $68,000.
Fields of interest: Higher education.
Type of support: Employee-related scholarships.
Application information: Applications not accepted.
  Additional information: Unsolicited requests for funds not considered or acknowledged.
Company name: Ryerson Inc.
EIN: 366046944

2840
The Karla Scherer Foundation
737 N. Michigan Ave., Ste. 2330
Chicago, IL 60611
Contact: Karla Scherer, C.E.O.

Foundation type: Independent foundation
Purpose: Scholarship to women pursuing a degree in the Humanities at the graduate level attending the University of Chicago, IL.
Financial data: Year ended 12/31/2012. Assets, $4,793,892 (M); Expenditures, $236,568; Total giving, $123,141.
Fields of interest: Humanities; Women.
Type of support: Support to graduates or students of specific schools; Graduate support.
Application information: Application form required. Interview required.
  Initial approach: Letter
  Deadline(s): Mar. 1 written request for application form
  Additional information: Contact the foundation for additional guidelines.
EIN: 382877392

2841
Corinne Jeannine Schillings Foundation
10645 Nebraska St.
Frankfort, IL 60423-2223 (815) 534-5598
E-mail: dschillings1@comcast.net; URL: http://www.cjsfoundation.org

Foundation type: Independent foundation

Purpose: Scholarships to deserving young women who have attained the honor of Silver or Gold Girl Scout award, pursuing a major/minor in a foreign language or studying abroad.
Financial data: Year ended 12/31/2013. Assets, $17,227 (M); Expenditures, $26,725; Total giving, $26,000; Grants to individuals, 20 grants totaling $26,000 (high: $1,500, low: $1,000).
Fields of interest: Language (foreign).
Type of support: Scholarships—to individuals.
Application information: Applications accepted. Application form required.
> *Send request by:* Mail
> *Deadline(s):* May 18
> *Applicants should submit the following:*
>   1) Letter(s) of recommendation
>   2) Transcripts
>   3) Essay
> *Additional information:* Applicant must provide proof or receipt of the Silver or Gold award.
Program descriptions:
> *Scholarship to Study a Foreign Language:* The scholarship is to undergraduate women who have attained at least the honor of Silver Award Girl Scout, and who plan to or are currently pursuing a major/minor in foreign language at a four year college/university. The scholarship provides $1,500 per academic year, and may be renewed three times following the initial award, for a total of $6,000 maximum award. Applicants must maintain a "B" or better GPA overall and in a foreign language (3.0 on a 4.0 scale, or 4.0 on a 5.0 scale).
> *Scholarship to Study Abroad:* The scholarship to study abroad provides $1,000 to the awardee upon verification that they have begun their study abroad experience. The foundation will support Silver or Gold Award Girl Scouts who plan to study abroad irrespective of major/minor. Applicant must provide proof that they have been accepted to study in an accredited "study abroad" program and must have attained at least a cumulative "B" average. The Scholarship to Study Abroad is not renewable. The awards are for undergraduate study only.
EIN: 200894400

2842
Scholar Leaders International

(formerly Christian International Scholarship Foundation)
27850 Irma Lee Cir., Ste. 101
Lake Forest, IL   60045-1554   (847) 295-9308
Contact: Larry Smith, Pres.
FAX: (847) 234-1047;
E-mail: info@scholarleaders.org; URL: http://www.scholarleaders.org/

Foundation type: Public charity
Purpose: Scholarships for Christian students from developing countries who are pursuing a graduate degree in theology and have exhausted educational possibilities at home.
Publications: Application guidelines.
Financial data: Year ended 08/31/2012. Assets, $862,640 (M); Expenditures, $908,843; Total giving, $471,148.
Fields of interest: Theological school/education.
Type of support: Scholarships—to individuals.
Application information: Applications accepted. Application form required.
> *Initial approach:* Letter
> *Send request by:* Mail or e-mail
> *Deadline(s):* Jan. 1
> *Final notification:* Recipients notified in May
> *Additional information:* See web site for additional guidelines.

Program description:
> *LeaderStudies Program:* This program encourages and supports strategic Christian leaders in their pursuit of doctoral-level education in theology and related disciplines, and to actively care for these leaders and their families. Grants will be awarded to men and women who have exhausted their educational opportunities in their home country and continent, and have senior leadership positions (such as a presidency or deanship at a recognized Bible college or seminary, a senior faculty appointment at a similar organization, or an executive director position of a relief organization) awaiting for them upon their return home. Applicants are expected to return to their home country to serve, upon completion of their studies.
EIN: 942923639

2843
William Archie Schroeder Scholarship Trust

P.O. Box 470
Petersburg, IL   62675-0470   (217) 632-3241
Contact: Paul Brown
Application address: 321 N. Sixth St., Petersburg IL 62675 tel: (217) 632-3241

Foundation type: Independent foundation
Purpose: Scholarships to financially needy graduates of Menard County, IL, high schools.
Financial data: Year ended 04/30/2013. Assets, $237,815 (M); Expenditures, $6,835; Total giving, $4,750; Grants to individuals, 5 grants totaling $4,750 (high: $1,250, low: $500).
Type of support: Support to graduates or students of specific schools; Undergraduate support.
Application information: Applications accepted. Application form required.
> *Deadline(s):* May 1
> *Applicants should submit the following:*
>   1) Financial information
>   2) Transcripts
>   3) Letter(s) of recommendation
EIN: 376267162

2844
Schuler Family Foundation

28161 N. Keith Dr.
Lake Forest, IL   60045-4528
E-mail: info@schulerprogram.org; URL: http://www.schulerfoundation.org/

Foundation type: Independent foundation
Purpose: Scholarships of $5,000 per year for four years are offered to IL students for college education.
Financial data: Year ended 12/31/2012. Assets, $109,900,452 (M); Expenditures, $4,437,951; Total giving, $1,152,826; Grants to individuals, totaling $1,152,826.
Fields of interest: Higher education.
Type of support: Support to graduates or students of specific schools.
Application information: Applications accepted. Application form required. Interview required.
> *Deadline(s):* Varies
> *Final notification:* Applicants notified within two weeks after final interviews
> *Additional information:* Applications are only accepted for 8th grade students.
EIN: 364154510

2845
The Evalee C. Schwarz Charitable Trust for Education

c/o JPMorgan Chase Bank, N.A.
10 S Dearborn St., 21st Fl.
Chicago, IL   60603-2300   (713) 216-3834
Contact: Karla Dominquez, V.P.
Application address: JPMorgan Chase Bank, N.A., P.O. Box 2558 (TX2-N370), Houston, TX 77252-2558 tel.: (713) 216-3834; URL: http://www.evaleeschwarztrust.org

Foundation type: Independent foundation
Purpose: Interest-free loans to students pursuing undergraduate and graduate degrees at a school in the state where student resides.
Financial data: Year ended 08/31/2013. Assets, $19,654,207 (M); Expenditures, $306,499; Total giving, $0.
Fields of interest: Higher education.
Type of support: Student loans—to individuals; Graduate support; Undergraduate support.
Application information: Applications accepted. Application form required. Application form available on the grantmaker's web site.
> *Send request by:* Mail
> *Deadline(s):* Apr. 9
> *Applicants should submit the following:*
>   1) Transcripts
>   2) Class rank
>   3) SAR
>   4) SAT
>   5) Letter(s) of recommendation
>   6) Essay
>   7) ACT
> *Additional information:* Application should also include a copy of official picture I.D. (driver's license, passport, or state identification card), document stating current school costs and other test scores. Applicant must not be seeking a law degree.
EIN: 766129622

2846
Alice Wilson Schweitzer & William J. Schweitzer Agriculture Education Foundation

57 Public Sq.
Monmouth, IL   61462   (309) 734-3193
Contact: Jane-Hartley Pratt, Secy.

Foundation type: Independent foundation
Purpose: Scholarships to students of IL, for postsecondary education enrolled in agricultural related field.
Financial data: Year ended 12/31/2012. Assets, $1,185,301 (M); Expenditures, $10,856; Total giving, $9,600; Grants to individuals, 6 grants totaling $9,600 (high: $1,600, low: $1,600).
Fields of interest: Higher education; Agriculture.
Type of support: Scholarships—to individuals.
Application information: Application form required.
> *Deadline(s):* None
EIN: 363731364

2847
Ethel Voris Scott Trust

c/o JPMorgan Chase Bank, N.A.
10 S. Darborn St., Ste 21st Fl.
Chicago, IL   60603-2300   (312) 732-4304
Application address: 2200 Ross Ave., 5th Fl., Dallas, TX 75201-2787

Foundation type: Independent foundation
Purpose: Scholarships to dependent orphan children in Montgomery County, IN.

Financial data: Year ended 12/31/2011. Assets, $1,795,581 (M); Expenditures, $107,747; Total giving, $87,910.
Fields of interest: Residential/custodial care.
Type of support: Scholarships—to individuals.
Application information: Applications accepted.
  Initial approach: Letter
  Send request by: Mail
  Deadline(s): None
  Additional information: Application should be submitted in writing with sufficient information to show need.
EIN: 356011994

2848
Serbian Brothers Help, Inc.
19697 W. Grand Ave.
P.O. Box 6008
Lindenhurst, IL   60046-5900   (847) 367-7077
FAX: (847) 265-7079

Foundation type: Public charity
Purpose: Grants to individuals of Serbian origin residing in the U.S. or Canada who are disabled, elderly, or ill.
Financial data: Year ended 03/31/2012. Assets, $731,161 (M); Expenditures, $170,263; Total giving, $13,366; Grants to individuals, totaling $13,366.
Fields of interest: Aging; Disabilities, people with; Economically disadvantaged.
International interests: Serbia.
Type of support: Grants for special needs.
Application information: Contact the organization for application guidelines.
EIN: 366094578

2849
Ida Shapiro Testamentary Scholarship Trust
130 N. Water St.
Decatur, IL   62523

Foundation type: Independent foundation
Purpose: Scholarship awards to four deserving college students: a graduate from Decatur District 61 high schools, a graduate of Clinton Community Unit No. 15 High School, a student attending Illinois Wesleyan University, Bloomington, and a student attending the School of Journalism at Northwestern University.
Financial data: Year ended 12/31/2012. Assets, $324,284 (M); Expenditures, $18,115; Total giving, $11,000; Grants to individuals, 4 grants totaling $11,000 (high: $2,750, low: $2,750).
Type of support: Support to graduates or students of specific schools; Undergraduate support.
Application information:
  Initial approach: Letter
EIN: 367383601

2850
Sharing Connections, Inc.
5111 Chase Ave.
Downers Grove, IL   60515-4012   (630) 971-0565
FAX: (630) 971-9594; URL: http://www.sharingconnections.org

Foundation type: Public charity
Purpose: Assistance to economically disadvantaged individuals and families in need in the Chicago, IL area with clothing, furniture, and other basic necessities.
Publications: Annual report; Financial statement.

Financial data: Year ended 12/31/2011. Assets, $860,386 (M); Expenditures, $2,678,589; Total giving, $2,267,048.
Fields of interest: Human services; Economically disadvantaged.
Type of support: In-kind gifts; Grants for special needs.
Application information:
  Initial approach: Telephone
  Additional information: Clients must be referred to the agency by their current social worker or case manager to obtain household necessities by showing proof of income.
EIN: 364363123

2851
Shawnee Development Council, Inc.
530 W. Washington St.
P.O. Box 298
Karnak, IL   62956-0298   (618) 634-2201
FAX: (618) 634-9551;
E-mail: sdcinc@shawneedevelopment.org;
URL: http://www.shawneedevelopment.org/

Foundation type: Public charity
Purpose: Financial and emergency assistance to low-income families and elderly individuals with utilities, home weatherization, food, clothing, shelter, medical expense and other needs in Alexander, Hardin, Johnson, Massac Pope, Pulaski, and Union counties, IL. Scholarships to low-income individuals from those counties seeking a college education.
Publications: Application guidelines; Informational brochure.
Financial data: Year ended 12/31/2011. Assets, $1,632,377 (M); Expenditures, $5,874,532; Total giving, $2,959,854; Grants to individuals, totaling $2,959,854.
Fields of interest: Higher education; Economically disadvantaged.
Type of support: Undergraduate support; Grants for special needs.
Application information: Application for scholarship is available each spring for the summer or fall semesters.
Program descriptions:
  Emergency Assistance Program: This program provides financial assistance of up to $175 to eligible individuals, to be used to meet such emergency needs as food, clothing, shelter, medical expenses, and fuel.
  Scholarship Program: The council annually awards sixteen scholarships of $500 each to eligible individuals seeking a college education.
EIN: 370888749

2852
Shinaberry Public Scholarship Trust
10 S. Dearborn IL1-0117
Chicago, IL   60603   (304) 799-6565

Foundation type: Independent foundation
Purpose: Scholarships to graduating seniors of either Pocahontas County High School, WV or Tygarts Valley High School, WV for postsecondary education.
Financial data: Year ended 12/31/2012. Assets, $904,220 (M); Expenditures, $53,105; Total giving, $40,629; Grants to individuals, 14 grants totaling $40,629 (high: $3,391, low: $2,535).
Fields of interest: Higher education.
Type of support: Scholarships—to individuals; Support to graduates or students of specific schools.

Application information:
  Deadline(s): Mar. 31
  Additional information: Contact your respective school guidance office for application information. Awards are paid directly to the educational institution on behalf of the student.
EIN: 916528315

2853
J. Leo Short Scholarship Fund
10 S Dearborn IL1-0117
Chicago, IL   60603   (214) 965-2908
Application address: c/o JPMorgan Chase Bank, N.A., 2200 Ross Ave., Dallas TX, 75201-2787

Foundation type: Independent foundation
Purpose: Scholarships to graduating seniors of Denison High School, TX.
Financial data: Year ended 12/31/2012. Assets, $220,697 (M); Expenditures, $14,634; Total giving, $10,804; Grants to individuals, 4 grants totaling $10,804 (high: $2,701, low: $2,701).
Fields of interest: Higher education; Scholarships/financial aid.
Type of support: Support to graduates or students of specific schools; Undergraduate support.
Application information: Application form required.
  Deadline(s): Mar. 31
EIN: 756097737

2854
Paul and Adelyn C. Shumaker Foundation
10 S. Dearborn, IL1-017
Chicago, IL   60603
Application address: Paul & Adelyn C. Shumaker Trust, c/o JPMorgan Chase, 100 E. Broad St., Columbus, OH 43215

Foundation type: Independent foundation
Purpose: Student loans to residents of Richland County, OH, pursuing a career in the field of medicine.
Financial data: Year ended 12/31/2012. Assets, $1,344,387 (M); Expenditures, $99,028; Total giving, $85,627; Loans to individuals, 2 loans totaling $14,915.
Fields of interest: Medical school/education.
Type of support: Student loans—to individuals.
Application information: Applications accepted. Application form required.
  Deadline(s): None
EIN: 346621245

2855
Sigma Chi Foundation
1714 Hinman Ave.
P.O. Box 469
Evanston, IL   60201-4517   (847) 869-3655
Contact: Greg Harbaugh, Pres.
Application e-mail: scholarship@sigmachi.org
FAX: (847) 869-4906;
E-mail: foundation@sigmachi.org; URL: http://foundation.sigmachi.org/

Foundation type: Public charity
Purpose: Scholarships and fellowships to members of the Sigma Chi Fraternity for higher education.
Publications: Application guidelines; Annual report; Grants list; Newsletter.
Financial data: Year ended 06/30/2012. Assets, $21,661,993 (M); Expenditures, $4,906,105; Total giving, $2,434,459; Grants to individuals, 906 grants totaling $440,176.

Fields of interest: Vocational education; Higher education; Business school/education; International economics/trade policy; International affairs; Business/industry; Engineering; Economics; Political science; International studies; Fraternal societies.
Type of support: Fellowships; Graduate support; Technical education support; Undergraduate support.
Application information: Application form required.
   Initial approach: Telephone, fax, or e-mail
   Deadline(s): June 15
   Applicants should submit the following:
      1) Transcripts
      2) Letter(s) of recommendation
Program descriptions:
   Denton Scholarship: This $1,000 award annually provides a grant to a student pursuing a graduate degree in the field of international affairs, with an emphasis in world trade, business, economics, or political science. Eligible applicants must be a member in good standing of Sigma Chi Fraternity, and have a cumulative GPA of at least 3.0 (on a 4.0 scale)
   Herschede Engineering Scholarship: This $1,000 scholarship is available to members of Sigma Chi Fraternity who are pursuing a graduate degree in the field of engineering. Eligible applicants must be members in good standing of the fraternity, and have a cumulative GPA of at least 3.0 (on a 4.0 scale)
   Madison Graduate Scholarship: This scholarship is presented to qualified members of Sigma Chi Fraternity who are pursuing their first year of graduate study in any academic field. Eligible applicants must be members in good standing of the fraternity, and have a cumulative GPA of at least 3.0 on a 4.0 scale.
   Sigma Chi Medical Scholarship: This award is presented annually to at least one graduate student who is pursuing a career in medicine (specifically from a school of osteopathic, allopathic, podiatric, or veterinarian medicine accredited by the American Medical Association). Primary consideration will be given to fraternity members in financial need.
   Undergraduate Scholarships: The foundation provides up to 175 recipients with grants of $1,000 each, to be used toward his qualified educational expenses. Through this, the foundation seeks to recognize undergraduate brothers who have shown outstanding values-based leadership, maintained strong academic performance, and demonstrated financial need. Eligible applicants must be members in good standing of Sigma Chi Fraternity, and must have a cumulative GPA of at least 2.5 (on a 4.0 scale). Named scholarships under this program include the Nebraska - Donald and Lorena Meier Scholarship, the Indiana - Jim and Connie Bash Scholarship, and the Butler - Jim and Connie Bash Scholarship.
EIN: 362208386

2856
Skelton Scholarship Fund
(formerly Ila M. Skelton Trust Fund)
c/o JPMorgan Chase Bank, N.A.
1 E. Old State Capital Plz., Fl. 3
Springfield, IL   62701-1320   (214) 965-2914
FAX: (217) 525-7048;
E-mail: heather.a.smith@jpmorgan.com

Foundation type: Independent foundation
Purpose: Scholarships primarily to IL residents.
Financial data: Year ended 07/31/2012. Assets, $241,867 (M); Expenditures, $15,599; Total giving, $12,500; Grants to individuals, 15 grants totaling $12,500 (high: $1,000, low: $500).

Type of support: Scholarships—to individuals.
Application information: Applications not accepted.
   Additional information: Unsolicited requests for funds not considered or acknowledged.
EIN: 371297171

2857
Skidmore, Owings & Merrill Foundation
224 S. Michigan Ave., Ste. 1000
Chicago, IL   60604-2526   (312) 427-4202
Contact: Mustafa Abadan, Chair.
URL: http://www.somfoundation.som.com

Foundation type: Company-sponsored foundation
Purpose: Fellowships and travel grants for research relating to architecture or architectural engineering.
Publications: Application guidelines; Grants list; Newsletter.
Financial data: Year ended 08/31/2013. Assets, $3,517,592 (M); Expenditures, $129,971; Total giving, $54,038; Grants to individuals, 4 grants totaling $50,000 (high: $25,000, low: $1,000).
Fields of interest: Architecture; Design; Literature; Urban studies.
Type of support: Fellowships; Research; Awards/grants by nomination only; Awards/prizes; Travel grants.
Application information: Application form available on the grantmaker's web site.
   Send request by: Mail
   Deadline(s): Apr. 18 for Intent to Apply form for SOM Prize and Travel Fellowship
   Final notification: Recipients notified Aug. 5 for SOM Prize and Travel Fellowship
   Additional information: Application should include letter(s) of recommendation. Applications for SOM Prize and Travel Fellowship should include a copyright release statement, a 12 page portfolio, and a research abstract and travel itinerary.
Program descriptions:
   China Prize: The foundation annually awards $20,000 traveling fellowships to outstanding Chinese national students of architecture or urban design from an accredited architecture school in China. Applicants must be in the last year of university in the People's Republic of China as an undergraduate or graduate and must be nominated by a faculty member.
   SOM Prize and Travel Fellowship for Architecture, Design, and Urban Design: The foundation annually awards a $50,000 research and travel fellowship to one student to do in-depth research, collaborate with other designers, and pursue independent study outside the realm of established patterns. The winner is expected to disseminate their research and travel experience through a publication, lecture series, exhibits, and other educational means. A $20,000 travel fellowship will also be awarded to the second strongest candidate. Applicant must be an undergraduate or graduate student of accredited U.S. schools of architecture, design, or urban design. Winners are selected based on portfolios, research plans, and travel itineraries.
   Structural Engineering Fellowship: The foundation annually awards a $10,000 independent travel fellowship to a student graduating with a Bachelor's, Master's, or Ph.D. degree in structural engineering to pursue the knowledge and experiences of architecture and engineering first hand.
   UK Award: The foundation annually awards travel fellowships to students of architecture in the United

Kingdom. The award is administered by the Royal Institute of British Architects (RIBA)
EIN: 362969068

2858
Henry J. Smith Charitable Trust
P. O. Box 12
Rantoul, IL   61866-0012   (217) 893-4642
Contact: Carolyn Taylor, Secy. and Treas.

Foundation type: Public charity
Purpose: Grants to teachers of St. Malachy Catholic Grade School, IL based on their level of employment at the school. Scholarships for students with financial need who wish to attend St. Malachy Catholic Grade School, IL.
Financial data: Year ended 12/31/2011. Assets, $1,007,677 (M); Expenditures, $44,087; Total giving, $39,489; Grants to individuals, totaling $6,600.
Fields of interest: Education.
Type of support: Grants to individuals; Scholarships—to individuals.
Application information: Unsolicited requests for funds not considered or acknowledged.
EIN: 376338859

2859
Arline J. Smith Trust
c/o JPMorgan Chase Bank, N.A.
10 S. dearborn St.
Chicago, IL   60605   (212) 977-5000
Application address: c/o Juilliard School of Music, Attn.: Dir. of Financial Aid, 60 Lincoln Ctr. Plz., Rm. 235, New York, NY 10023-6591, tel.: (212) 799-5000, ext. 211

Foundation type: Independent foundation
Purpose: Scholarships to students who are residents of CT attending four years of study and/or graduate students accepted at The Juilliard School, NY.
Financial data: Year ended 08/31/2012. Assets, $490,760 (M); Expenditures, $32,828; Total giving, $24,259.
Fields of interest: Music; Performing arts, education.
Type of support: Support to graduates or students of specific schools; Graduate support; Undergraduate support.
Application information: Application form required.
   Initial approach: Letter
   Deadline(s): Jan., Apr., and June.
EIN: 066246639

2860
Harry L. & John L. Smysor Memorial Fund
c/o First Mid-Illinois Bank & Trust
P.O. Box 529
Mattoon, IL   61938-0529
Contact: Laura Walk
Application address: c/o First Mid-Illinois Bank & Trust, 1515 Charleston Ave., Mattoon, IL 61938-3932, tel.: (217) 258-0633

Foundation type: Independent foundation
Purpose: Scholarships to students of Windsor High School, IL, for higher education.
Financial data: Year ended 05/31/2013. Assets, $13,754,204 (M); Expenditures, $891,945; Total giving, $552,484; Grants to individuals, 160 grants totaling $552,484 (high: $6,364, low: $1,591).
Type of support: Support to graduates or students of specific schools; Undergraduate support.

Application information: Application form required.
  Deadline(s): Apr. 15
  Additional information: Application form available from Windsor, IL, high schools or from trustee bank.
EIN: 371160678

2861
The Rev. John Smyth Standing Tall Charitable Foundation
1100 N. River Rd.
Des Plaines, IL 60016-1214   (847) 294-1801
FAX: (847) 635-1014;
E-mail: info@standingtallfoundation.org;
URL: http://www.standingtallfoundation.org

Foundation type: Public charity
Purpose: Scholarships to underprivileged children of IL pursuing educational and vocational training.
Financial data: Year ended 12/31/2011. Assets, $2,614,112 (M); Expenditures, $706,418; Total giving, $561,848; Grants to individuals, totaling $518,298.
Fields of interest: Education; Children/youth.
Type of support: Scholarships—to individuals.
Application information: Application should include transcripts. Each recipient must maintain a "C" average or better to maintain their funding.
EIN: 320156071

2862
Society for Ambulatory Anesthesia
330 N. Wabash, Ste. 330
Chicago, IL 60611   (312) 321-6872
Contact: Erin Butler, Exec. Dir.
FAX: (312) 673-6620; E-mail: info@sambahq.org;
E-mail For Erin Butler: ebutler@sambahq.org;
URL: http://www.sambahq.org

Foundation type: Public charity
Purpose: Awards and research grants pertaining to ambulatory anesthesiology.
Publications: Grants list; Newsletter.
Financial data: Year ended 12/31/2011. Assets, $2,599,736 (M); Expenditures, $631,921; Total giving, $6,806; Grants to individuals, totaling $5,806.
Fields of interest: Anesthesiology.
Type of support: Research; Awards/prizes.
Application information:
  Initial approach: Letter or telephone
  Deadline(s): Aug. 18 for SAMBA Distinguished Service Awards, Nov. 30 for SAMBA Research Award
  Applicants should submit the following:
    1) Letter(s) of recommendation
    2) Curriculum vitae
Program descriptions:
  Resident Travel Awards: Awards up to $1,000 to anesthesiology residents whose scientific abstracts are accepted for poser presentation at the society's annual meeting. Awards cover expenses to attend the annual meeting.
  SAMBA Distinguished Service Awards: This award is presented to an individual for outstanding achievement in ambulatory anesthesia and is the highest honor which the Society can bestow. Individual must be nominated by a member of the society.
  SAMBA Research Award: This program awards three research grants, totaling $150,000, to further scientific inquiry and clinical knowledge in the field of ambulatory anesthesia. One grant, for $100,000 ($50,000 per year for two years), is intended to address a significant issue in Ambulatory Anesthesia. Two additional grants of $25,000 each

for one year are geared more toward junior faculty who are interested in contributing to scientific knowledge. It is expected that all applicants be members of SAMBA.
EIN: 541355440

2863
The Society for Arts, Ltd.
1112 N. Milwaukee Ave.
Chicago, IL 60642-4017   (773) 466-9612
FAX: (773) 486-9613;
E-mail: societyforarts@societyforarts.com;
URL: http://www.societyforarts.com

Foundation type: Public charity
Purpose: Fellowships for foreign artists, art critics, and art professionals to live for two months at the foundation's Chicago headquarters. The foundation supports projects that represent European art and culture in the form of painting, sculpture, graphics and photography.
Financial data: Year ended 12/31/2011. Assets, $79,140 (M); Expenditures, $391,483.
Fields of interest: Cultural/ethnic awareness; Visual arts; Photography; Sculpture; Painting; Arts.
International interests: Europe.
Type of support: Fellowships.
Application information: Contact foundation for application and program information.
EIN: 521247160

2864
South Holland Business Association Foundation
P.O. Box 334
South Holland, IL 60473-0334

Foundation type: Independent foundation
Purpose: Scholarships to deserving students primarily of South Holland, IL for higher education at accredited colleges or universities.
Financial data: Year ended 05/31/2012. Assets, $0 (M); Expenditures, $5,000; Total giving, $5,000; Grants to individuals, 5 grants totaling $5,000 (high: $1,000, low: $1,000).
Fields of interest: Higher education; Scholarships/financial aid.
Type of support: Undergraduate support.
Application information: Applications accepted.
  Initial approach: Telephone
  Additional information: Recipients of the scholarship must work for a SHBA member or be the spouse, son or daughter or an employee of a SHBA member.
EIN: 363812139

2865
Southern Illinois University Foundation
1235 Douglas Dr.
Coyler Hall, MC 6805
Carbondale, IL 62901-2591   (618) 453-4900
Scholarship contact Tracee Norris tel.: (618) 453-4563, e-mail: tnorris@siu.edu
FAX: (618) 453-2262; URL: http://www.siuf.org

Foundation type: Public charity
Purpose: Scholarships to new and returning students of Southern Illinois University, Carbondale, IL pursuing a music career.
Publications: Annual report; Informational brochure; Newsletter.
Financial data: Year ended 06/30/2012. Assets, $148,503,935 (M); Expenditures, $10,977,306; Total giving, $7,138,590; Grants to individuals, 1,252 grants totaling $1,782,184.

Fields of interest: Music; Education.
Type of support: Scholarships—to individuals; Support to graduates or students of specific schools.
Application information: Preference will be given to graduates of Herrin High School. If no graduates are available from HHS, preference will be given to transfer students from John A. Logan College.
EIN: 376024575

2866
Special People in Need
300 N. LaSalle St., Ste. 4000
Chicago, IL 60654-3422   (312) 715-5235
Contact: Irene S. Peterson, Grant Coord.
FAX: (312) 715-5155;
E-mail: Irene.Peterson@Quarles.com

Foundation type: Independent foundation
Purpose: Limited scholarships to students with disabilities and students who are not disabled but who have had to overcome extremely difficult circumstances, and grants to physically disabled individuals with a strong economic need to engage in productive activity in which he or she otherwise could not engage.
Publications: Annual report.
Financial data: Year ended 12/31/2012. Assets, $4,242,885 (M); Expenditures, $213,190; Total giving, $107,400.
Fields of interest: Arts education; Research; Disabilities, people with; Economically disadvantaged.
Type of support: Undergraduate support; Grants for special needs.
Application information: Applications accepted.
  Initial approach: Letter
  Send request by: Mail
  Copies of proposal: 1
  Deadline(s): Prior to May 1 for Scholarships
  Applicants should submit the following:
    1) Letter(s) of recommendation
    2) Financial information
    3) Essay
    4) Transcripts
  Additional information: Application must also include letter of acceptance from college or university and biographical data. Contact the organization for additional guidelines.
EIN: 581483651

2867
Haley Sperling Memorial Foundation
c/o Harvey J. Barnett
55 W. Monroe St., Ste. 3200
Chicago, IL 60603-5072

Foundation type: Independent foundation
Purpose: Scholarships to residents for higher education who reside in Illinois or Ohio.
Financial data: Year ended 11/30/2012. Assets, $1,297,498 (M); Expenditures, $49,071; Total giving, $42,000.
Fields of interest: Higher education.
Type of support: Scholarships—to individuals.
Application information: Applications not accepted.
EIN: 364132569

2868
St. Clair County Community Action Agency
19 Public Sq., No. 200
Belleville, IL 62220-1695

Foundation type: Public charity
Purpose: Scholarships and financial assistance for low-income residents of St. Clair County, IL.
Financial data: Year ended 12/31/2011. Assets, $428,913 (M); Expenditures, $7,171,624; Total giving, $5,528,233; Grants to individuals, 9,004 grants totaling $3,532,796.
Type of support: Undergraduate support; Grants for special needs.
Application information: Applications accepted.
  Additional information: Contact foundation for current application deadline/guidelines.
EIN: 371119231

2869
St. Clair County Scholarship Trust Fund
1000 S. Illinois St.
Belleville, IL   62220-2537
Contact: Susan Sarfaty

Foundation type: Independent foundation
Purpose: Scholarships to graduates of high schools in St. Clair County, IL.
Financial data: Year ended 12/31/2012. Assets, $0 (M); Expenditures, $21,459; Total giving, $15,800; Grant to an individual, 1 grant totaling $15,800.
Fields of interest: Higher education; Scholarships/financial aid.
Type of support: Support to graduates or students of specific schools; Awards/grants by nomination only; Undergraduate support.
Application information: Application form required. Interview required.
  Deadline(s): Mar. 30.
  Applicants should submit the following:
    1) SAT
    2) ACT
    3) Financial information
    4) Transcripts
    5) Letter(s) of recommendation
    6) GPA
    7) Essay
  Additional information: High school superintendents within the jurisdiction of the St. Claire County Regional Office of Education will be invited to nominate students for the scholarships. A seven-semester transcript should be submitted with the scholarship application.
EIN: 371286750

2870
St. John's Healing Community Board
222 Goethe Ave.
Collinsville, IL   62234-3221   (618) 344-0276
Contact: Nancy J. Berry, Exec. Dir.

Foundation type: Public charity
Purpose: Support and assistance to the elderly and disabled in the form of housework, meals, personal care and community haven adult programs.
Financial data: Year ended 12/31/2011. Assets, $370,682 (M); Expenditures, $953,548; Total giving, $1,831; Grants to individuals, totaling $1,831.
Fields of interest: Human services; Economically disadvantaged.
Type of support: In-kind gifts.
Application information: Applications not accepted.
EIN: 371184962

2871
Steel Founders' Society Foundation
780 McArdle Dr., Unit G
Crystal Lake, IL   60014-8155   (815) 455-8240
Contact: Raymond Monroe, Secy.

Foundation type: Independent foundation
Purpose: Scholarships to engineering students who have completed an internship in the industry.
Financial data: Year ended 06/30/2012. Assets, $200,862 (M); Expenditures, $12,178; Total giving, $7,605; Grant to an individual, 1 grant totaling $5,000.
Fields of interest: Engineering school/education.
Type of support: Undergraduate support.
Application information: Applications not accepted.
  Additional information: Applicants must be recommended by the companies that hire them as interns. Unsolicited requests for funds not considered or acknowledged.
EIN: 364389361

2872
Sterling-Rock Falls Community Trust
302 First Ave.
P.O. Box 1000
Sterling, IL   61081-8000   (815) 622-1302

Foundation type: Independent foundation
Purpose: Scholarships to graduating seniors of an accredited high school in Sterling, or Rock Falls, IL.
Financial data: Year ended 12/31/2010. Assets, $2,545,318 (M); Expenditures, $187,693; Total giving, $161,402.
Fields of interest: Higher education; Scholarships/financial aid.
Type of support: Support to graduates or students of specific schools; Undergraduate support.
Application information: Application form required.
  Deadline(s): Apr. 1
  Applicants should submit the following:
    1) Financial information
    2) Transcripts
  Additional information: Applicants must reside within the boundaries of the Sterling and Rock Falls school district. Application forms and additional information can be obtained from guidance counselors at high schools.
EIN: 366217952

2873
Stevenson Foundation Trust
10 S. Dearborn IL1-0117
Chicago, IL   60603

Foundation type: Independent foundation
Purpose: Scholarships to deserving and financially needy students in the Canandaigua, NY, area who are currently enrolled in a recognized college of medicine.
Financial data: Year ended 12/31/2012. Assets, $92,687 (M); Expenditures, $6,307; Total giving, $5,000.
Fields of interest: Medical school/education.
Type of support: Graduate support.
Application information: Applications not accepted.
  Additional information: Application must include outline of financial need, as well as pertinent information regarding current enrollment in medical school, including name of school and year of study. Unsolicited requests for funds not considered or acknowledged.
EIN: 166102231

2874
Tom Stockert Foundation
c/o JPMorgan Chase Bank, N.A.
10 S. Dearborn St.
Chicago, IL   60603-2300   (214) 965-2874
Application address: JPMorgan Chase Bank, N.A. Attn: NCAA, 2200 Ross Ave., Dallas, TX 75201.
Tel: (214) 965-2874

Foundation type: Independent foundation
Purpose: Scholarships primarily to WV residents for attendance at the University of Virginia College of Law.
Financial data: Year ended 12/31/2011. Assets, $686,529 (M); Expenditures, $41,939; Total giving, $26,650.
Fields of interest: Law school/education.
Type of support: Support to graduates or students of specific schools.
Application information: Applications accepted.
  Initial approach: Letter
  Deadline(s): Last week in Apr.
  Additional information: Application must include academic history and extracurricular activities.
EIN: 546423244

2875
I. F. Doug Stonier and Ella Stonier Educational Trust
328 S. McCoy St.
Granville, IL   61326-0344   (815) 339-2222
Contact: Philip C. Carlson, Pres.

Foundation type: Independent foundation
Purpose: Scholarships to high school graduates in the Putnam County Community Unit School District, IL.
Financial data: Year ended 04/30/2012. Assets, $340,266 (M); Expenditures, $16,280; Total giving, $14,700; Grants to individuals, 7 grants totaling $14,700 (high: $2,100, low: $2,100).
Type of support: Scholarships—to individuals.
Application information: Application form required.
  Deadline(s): June 30
  Applicants should submit the following:
    1) Transcripts
    2) Financial information
EIN: 363204200

2876
Irene Storey Scholarship Fund
c/o First Mid-Illinois Bank & Trust
P.O. Box 529
Mattoon, IL   61938   (217) 234-7454

Foundation type: Independent foundation
Purpose: Scholarships to students who are residents of Mottoon, IL pursuing a degree in the medical field.
Financial data: Year ended 02/28/2013. Assets, $99,762 (M); Expenditures, $6,320; Total giving, $3,400; Grants to individuals, 2 grants totaling $3,400 (high: $1,700, low: $1,700).
Fields of interest: Medical school/education.
Type of support: Scholarships—to individuals.
Application information: Applications accepted. Application form required.
  Deadline(s): Apr. 15
EIN: 371275007

2877
Gladys Stratton Trust
c/o Edgar City Bank & Trust
P.O. Box 400
Paris, IL 61944-0790 (217) 465-4154
Contact: John Carrington

Foundation type: Independent foundation
Purpose: Educational loans to residents of Edgar County, IL, and children of tenants of any land held in the Gladys Stratton Trust.
Financial data: Year ended 12/31/2011. Assets, $1,967,425 (M); Expenditures, $30,908; Total giving, $0.
Type of support: Student loans—to individuals.
Application information: Application form required.
Deadline(s): May 15
Additional information: Contact trust for current application guidelines and forms.
EIN: 376164685

2878
Helaine & Edgar Strauss Opportunity Trust
154 Maple Ave.
Wilmette, IL 60091-3449 (847) 424-1945
Contact: Ronald Strauss, Tr.

Foundation type: Independent foundation
Purpose: Scholarships to minorities and women living in the inner city of Chicago, IL.
Financial data: Year ended 12/31/2012. Assets, $430,799 (M); Expenditures, $14,547; Total giving, $14,000; Grants to individuals, 2 grants totaling $7,000 (high: $2,000, low: $1,000).
Fields of interest: Higher education.
Type of support: Undergraduate support.
Application information: Applications accepted. Application form required.
Deadline(s): Apr. 1
Additional information: Application must include a recommendation of a high school counselor and a statement from the student of their goals and aspirations.
EIN: 363976041

2879
Stump Memorial Scholarship Fund
c/o First National Bank
P.O. Box 685
Mattoon, IL 61938-0685 (217) 234-6430
Contact: Stephanie Dundee

Foundation type: Independent foundation
Purpose: Scholarships to high school graduates from Mattoon, IL, and surrounding communities to attend any IL state-supported college or university.
Financial data: Year ended 07/31/2013. Assets, $1,185,803 (M); Expenditures, $94,067; Total giving, $51,600; Grants to individuals, 43 grants totaling $51,600 (high: $1,350, low: $500).
Type of support: Undergraduate support.
Application information: Application form required.
Deadline(s): Apr. 15
Additional information: Applications available from high schools and The First National Bank.
EIN: 376064295

2880
Seg and Harty Suarez Charitable Foundation
23 Public Sq., Ste. 440
Belleville, IL 62220 (618) 233-0480
Contact: M. Lee Suarez, V.P.
FAX: (618) 233-0601

Foundation type: Independent foundation
Purpose: Scholarships to economically disadvantaged youths in the Fairmont City, IL, area.
Financial data: Year ended 12/31/2012. Assets, $109 (M); Expenditures, $38,226; Total giving, $38,180; Grants to individuals, 23 grants totaling $38,180 (high: $1,660, low: $1,660).
Type of support: Scholarships—to individuals.
Application information: Applications accepted.
Deadline(s): None
Additional information: Contact foundation for application guidelines.
EIN: 431545390

2881
SVI Scholarship Fund
c/o Jack W. Fiene
1000 Adare Dr.
Wheaton, IL 60187 (815) 748-0228
Contact: Sheryl Climenhaga, Pres.
Application address: 155 Harvestore Dr., DeKalb, IL 60115-8675 tel.:(815) 748-0228

Foundation type: Independent foundation
Purpose: Scholarships to graduating high school seniors of Geneva, IL for postsecondary education.
Financial data: Year ended 10/31/2011. Assets, $329,848 (M); Expenditures, $25,858; Total giving, $24,058; Grants to individuals, 8 grants totaling $22,058 (high: $6,000, low: $1,200).
Type of support: Undergraduate support.
Application information: Applications accepted.
Initial approach: Letter
Deadline(s): None
Applicants should submit the following:
1) Letter(s) of recommendation
2) Class rank
3) Transcripts
Additional information: Application must also include verification by principal of enrollment and residence, scores on scholastic aptitude or other tests measuring aptitude for higher education, statement of extracurricular activities, proof of expenses and copy of parents' and student's income tax returns for previous two years.
EIN: 363995732

2882
Swedish American Hospital
1401 E. State St.
Rockford, IL 61104-2315 (815) 966-2087
Contact: William R. Gorski, C.E.O.

Foundation type: Public charity
Purpose: Scholarships to non-managerial employees of Swedish American Hospital, IL.
Financial data: Year ended 05/31/2012. Assets, $454,467,569 (M); Expenditures, $439,788,046; Total giving, $561,606; Grants to individuals, totaling $30,000.
Fields of interest: Education.
Type of support: Scholarships—to individuals.
Application information: Applications not accepted.
Additional information: Unsolicited requests for funds not considered or acknowledged.
EIN: 362222696

2883
Willard Sweitzer American Legion Trust
1004 Westminster Dr.
Washington, IL 61571 (309) 444-3131
Contact: Carol Madden, Tr.
Application address: 130 S. Main St., Washington, IL 61571

Foundation type: Independent foundation
Purpose: Scholarships to graduates of Washington Community High School, IL, who rank in the top ten percent of their class.
Financial data: Year ended 12/31/2012. Assets, $162,134 (M); Expenditures, $3,126; Total giving, $2,500; Grants to individuals, 2 grants totaling $2,500 (high: $1,500, low: $1,000).
Type of support: Support to graduates or students of specific schools; Undergraduate support.
Application information: Applications accepted. Application form required.
Deadline(s): Within 180 days of trust publication notice.
Applicants should submit the following:
1) ACT
2) Class rank
EIN: 376127123

2884
Swiss Benevolent Society of Chicago
P.O. Box 2137
Chicago, IL 60690 (312) 630-5818
E-mail: president@sbschicago.org; URL: http://www.sbschicago.org

Foundation type: Independent foundation
Purpose: Undergraduate scholarships to full-time students of Swiss descent residing in IL or southern WI. Relief assistance to financially needy or elderly Chicago, IL, residents of Swiss descent or nationality.
Financial data: Year ended 12/31/2012. Assets, $1,226,801 (M); Expenditures, $104,034; Total giving, $81,140; Grants to individuals, 8 grants totaling $14,264 (high: $6,950, low: $300).
Fields of interest: Higher education; Aging; Economically disadvantaged.
International interests: Switzerland.
Type of support: Undergraduate support; Grants for special needs.
Application information: Application form required. Application form available on the grantmaker's web site. Interview required.
Initial approach: Letter or e-mail for relief assistance
Deadline(s): Mar. 31 for Two-Week Language Immersion Program, and Apr. 15 for Scholarship Awards for Undergraduate College Students. Applications accepted throughout the year for relief assistance.
Final notification: Scholarship recipients notified after July 31. Recipients for Language Immersion Program notified by Apr. 31
Applicants should submit the following:
1) Transcripts
2) SAT
3) GPA
4) Essay
5) ACT
6) Class rank
Additional information: Application for relief assistance must include proof of Swiss citizenship. See web site for additional guidelines.
EIN: 366076395

2885
Mr. & Mrs. George W. Taylor Foundation
2599 N. Mulford Rd., Ste. 113
Rockford, IL 61114-5643 (815) 637-6363
Contact: James Thiede, Tr.

Foundation type: Independent foundation
Purpose: Scholarships to students in the Rockford, IL, community participating in the engineering program at the University of Minnesota Institute of Technology.
Financial data: Year ended 12/31/2012. Assets, $10,679,811 (M); Expenditures, $215,663; Total giving, $103,820.
Fields of interest: Engineering school/education.
Type of support: Support to graduates or students of specific schools; Technical education support; Undergraduate support.
Application information: Applications accepted.
  Initial approach: Letter
  Deadline(s): None
  Additional information: Scholarship applications are reviewed by a scholarship committee and selection is based on academic and leadership qualifications.
EIN: 363321315

2886
Brent Taylor Perpetual Charitable Trust
c/o Mercantile Trust & Savings Bank
200 N. 33rd St.
P.O. Box 3455
Quincy, IL 62305-3714
Application address: c/o Titan International, Attn.: Courtney Leeser, 2701 Spruce St., Quincy, IL 62301-3473, tel.: (217) 221-4489

Foundation type: Independent foundation
Purpose: Scholarships to residents of Quincy, IL, Ellsworth, MI, and Saltville, VA; and to employees or children of employees of Titan International, Inc.
Financial data: Year ended 12/31/2011. Assets, $178,246 (M); Expenditures, $245,230; Total giving, $241,399; Grants to individuals, 217 grants totaling $241,399 (high: $21,423, low: $1,000).
Type of support: Employee-related scholarships; Undergraduate support.
Application information: Applications accepted. Application form required.
  Initial approach: Letter
  Deadline(s): None
  Additional information: Contact trust for current application guidelines.
EIN: 376353965

2887
Tazwood Community Services, Inc.
2005 S. Main St.
Morton, IL 61550-2915

Foundation type: Public charity
Purpose: Grants primarily for utilities assistance and weatherization to residents of Morton, IL.
Financial data: Year ended 06/30/2011. Assets, $312,630 (M); Expenditures, $5,043,922; Total giving, $4,378,860; Grants to individuals, totaling $4,378,860. Subtotal for in-kind gifts: 213 grants totaling $1,022,170. Subtotal for emergency funds: 10,615 grants totaling $3,680,289.
Fields of interest: Economically disadvantaged.
Type of support: Grants for special needs.
Application information: Contact foundation for complete eligibility requirements.
EIN: 371311590

2888
John B. Templeton Trust Foundation
1105 35th St.
Oak Brook, IL 60523-2764
Application address: c/o Templeton, Kenly & Co., Attn: S. Ruksana, 2525 Gardner Rd., Broadview, IL 60153-3719

Foundation type: Independent foundation
Purpose: Scholarships based on leadership qualities, past and present scholastic achievement, personal character and integrity, and financial need to IL employees and children of employees of Templeton, Kenly & Co., Inc., who are currently enrolled in an accredited collegiate program.
Financial data: Year ended 12/31/2011. Assets, $220,931 (M); Expenditures, $4,551; Total giving, $3,500; Grants to individuals, 2 grants totaling $1,500 (high: $750, low: $750).
Type of support: Scholarships—to individuals.
Application information: Application form required.
  Send request by: Mail
  Deadline(s): June 1
  Applicants should submit the following:
    1) GPA
    2) Transcripts
    3) Resume
    4) Essay
EIN: 366891453

2889
Terra Foundation for American Art
120 E. Erie St., Chicago
Chicago, IL 60611-3154 (312) 664-3939
Contact: Amy Zinck, V.P.
FAX: (312) 664-2052;
E-mail: grants@terraamericanart.org; Additional e-mail: contact@terraamericanart.org and tsr@terraamericanart.org; URL: http://www.terraamericanart.org

Foundation type: Operating foundation
Purpose: Residencies, prizes, grants, professorships, and postdoctoral and teaching fellowships to artists and scholars to study American art in the U.S. or the European Union.
Publications: Application guidelines; Annual report; Grants list.
Financial data: Year ended 06/30/2013. Assets, $331,633,281 (M); Expenditures, $16,978,564; Total giving, $7,256,905; Grants to individuals, 9 grants totaling $66,300 (high: $15,000, low: $5,000).
Fields of interest: Visual arts; Painting; Art history.
International interests: France.
Type of support: Professorships; Fellowships; Awards/prizes; Residencies; Travel grants.
Application information: Applications accepted. Application form required. Application form available on the grantmaker's web site.
  Initial approach: E-mail
  Deadline(s): Jan. 15
  Applicants should submit the following:
    1) Work samples
    2) Essay
    3) Curriculum vitae
    4) Letter(s) of recommendation
    5) Proposal
  Additional information: Application should also include artist statement. Unsolicited applications not accepted.
Program descriptions:
  Fellowships in American Art: These residential foundation Fellowships in American Art at the Smithsonian American Art Museum support full-time independent and dissertation research by scholars from abroad who are researching historical American art (pre-1980) or by U.S. scholars, particularly those who are investigating international contexts for American art. The stipend for a one-year predoctoral fellowship is $30,000, plus research and travel allowances; the stipend for a senior or postdoctoral fellowship is $45,000, plus research and travel allowances.
  International Essay Prize: This prize recognizes excellent scholarship in the field of historical American art (circa 1500-1980) by a non-U.S. scholar. The winning manuscript submission should advance understanding of American art and demonstrate new findings and original perspectives. It will be translated and published in "American Art," the Smithsonian American Art Museum's scholarly journal, which will also cover the cost of image rights and reproductions, and the winner will receive a $500 award. Essays should be submitted by e-mail to terraessayprize@si.edu.
  Postdoctoral Fellowship in American Art 1600-1950: The foundation's Postdoctoral Fellowship in American Art 1600-1950 in the Department of Art History at Northwestern University seeks to aid the development of a scholar embarking on a professional academic career while strengthening the department's established curriculum and scholarly profile. The Terra Fellow in American Art has the opportunity to pursue original research while also instructing and advising undergraduate and graduate students. The fellow teaches three courses per year: one undergraduate-level survey course in American Art prior to 1950; one upper-level undergraduate course; and one graduate seminar. Departmental responsibilities include advising undergraduate senior theses; advising graduate students in American art as a minor field; and serving as a second reader on dissertation committees. Scholars must have received their Ph.D.s in or after 2007 in order to be eligible.
  Postdoctoral Fellowship in Pre-1945 American Art: The foundation's Postdoctoral Fellowship in pre-1945 American Art in the Department of Art History of the University of Chicago seek to aid the development of a young scholar and to strengthen the department's established curriculum, scholarly profile, and working relationships with Chicago museums, curators, and scholars. The Terra Fellow in American Art has the opportunity to pursue and discuss original research in formal and informal settings and to acquire teaching experience. The fellow teaches three courses per year: one undergraduate-level survey course in American Art prior to 1945; one upper-level undergraduate course; and one graduate seminar. Other responsibilities include advising theses for students pursuing a B.A. or a Master of Arts in the Humanities Degree; fostering relationships with local art historians; and sharing his or her work in progress with Chicago colleagues. The fellow is formally affiliated with the Scherer Center, an interdisciplinary institute for the study of American culture. Scholars must have received their Ph.D. after September 2005 in order to be eligible. This fellowship will conclude in the spring of 2013.
  Postdoctoral Teaching Fellowships: These fellowships seek to increase the opportunities in Europe for graduate study of historical American art while providing recipients the opportunity to pursue individual study and research. The fellowships are offered by the Courtauld Institute of Art in London, and the Institut National d'Histoire de l'Art in Paris. The fellowship program that is integrated with the Courtauld Institute of Art is a 2-year program that supports advanced inquiry in the history of art, conservation, and museum studies. The fellow will teach three historical American art courses, participate in scholarly activities organized by the

Courtauld Institute of Art, and organize an international scholarly event. The stipend for the two-year fellowship is $121,550, including health benefits, travel, research, and lodging. Contact for this fellowship: Dr. Caroline Arscott, e-mail: researchforum@courtauld.ac.uk. The fellowship integrated with the Institut National d'Histoire de l'Art is a 2-year program that is focused on the history of American art and transatlantic exchange, and is shared between the departments of art history and American studies at the Ecole Normale Superieure, the Universite Paris Ouest Nanterre La Defense, and the Universite de Tours. The fellow will teach undergraduate and master's-level students, participate in local seminars, and organize an international scholarly event. The stipend for the two-year fellowship is $102,000, including health benefits, travel, research, and lodging. Contact for this fellowship: Dr. Thierry Dufrene, e-mail: thierry.dufrene@inha.fr.

Research Travel Grants to the United States: These grants support travel to the U.S. for research purposes and are available to European scholars, regardless of affiliation, whose research projects concern American art or transatlantic artistic relations prior to 1980. Three predoctoral grants of $5,000 and three postdoctoral grants of $7,500 (for researchers who have been awarded their doctorate within the past ten years) are awarded annually. Applications must be received by one of the partner institutions: 1) Courtauld Institute of Art in London; 2) Institut National d'Histoire de l'Art in Paris; 3) John F. Kennedy Insititute, Freie Universitat in Berlin; and 4) Zentralinstitut fur Kunstgeschichte in Munich.

Terra Summer Residency in Giverny: The foundation annually offers ten summer fellowships to artists and scholars from the U.S. and Europe for the independent study of American art and visual culture within a framework of interdisciplinary exchange and dialogue. During the eight-week stay, senior artists and scholars are in residence to mentor fellows and pursue their own work. Fellowships are awarded to doctoral students researching a subject on American art and visual culture or its role in a context of international artistic exchange, and to artists who have completed their studies at the master's level within the past five years. Fellows are selected on the basis of the quality of the proposed project, the level of excellence and intellectual rigor or artistic creativity achieved in the applicant's previous work or studies, and the applicant's ability to engage in a community environment. Applications are by nomination only. Fellows receive a stipend of $5,000 (artists receive an additional $200 for the purchase of materials) and are provided with lodging and study or studio space, and a program consisting of independent study, meetings, and seminars. E-mail: tsr@terraamericanart.edu.

Visiting Professorships: This program seeks to increase the opportunities in Europe for graduate study of historical American art while providing recipients the opportunity to pursue individual study and research. The professorships are offered by the Courtauld Institute of Art in London, the Freie Universitat Berlin, and the Institut National d'Histoire de l'Art in Paris. For the professorship integrated with the Courtauld Institute of Art in London, two short-term visiting professorships are part of a program designed to expose students to the best of recent scholarship on historical American art. A twelve-week professorship is available in the Spring academic term of either 2011-2012 or 2012-2013: the professor will give one full-term course that is integrated with The Courtauld Institute of Art's curriculum and will participate in other scholarly activities. A one-week intensive study professorship is also available for

either 2011-2012 or 2012-2013, in the alternate year to the twelve-week professorship. Stipends will be determined by the seniority of the scholars. Contact for this professorship: Dr. Caroline Arscott, e-mail: researchforum@courtauld.ac.uk. For the professorship integrated at the John F. Kennedy Institute, Freie Universitat Berlin, three-month visiting professorships are focused on the history of American art and visual culture. Visiting professors will offer specialized courses, seminars, and lectures to students and participate in the larger academic community throughout their stay. Two professorships are available for each academic year: 2011-2012 and 2012-2013. The stipend for a three-month professorship is $36,000, including travel and lodging. Contact for this professorship: Dr. Winfried Fluck, e-mail: kultur@zedar.fu.berlin.de. For the professorship integrated with the Institut National d'Histoire de l'Art in Paris, eight-week visiting professorships at the Institut National d'Histoire de l'Art are focused on the history of American art and transatlantic exchange and are shared between the departments of art history and American studies at the Ecole Normale Superieure, the Universite Paris Ouest Nanterre La Defense, and the Universite de Tours. Visiting professors will give lectures and seminars that build on existing curricula and will participate in workshops, conferences, and other scholarly gatherings organized by the host universities. One visiting professorship is available for each academic year: 2011-2012 and 2012-2013. The stipend for an eight-week professorship is $30,000, including travel and lodging. Contact for this professorship: Dr.Thierry Dufrene, e-mail: thierry.dufrene@inha.fr.
EIN: 362999442

2890
V. M. Slipher Testamentary Trust
(formerly V. M. Slipher Trust)
10 S. Dearborn, IL1-0117
Chicago, IL 60603

Foundation type: Independent foundation
Purpose: Scholarships to third- and fourth-year physics and astronomy undergraduates who are recommended by their department heads and attend Northern Arizona University, Arizona State University, or the University of Arizona.
Financial data: Year ended 12/31/2012. Assets, $522,644 (M); Expenditures, $30,812; Total giving, $23,912; Grants to individuals, 9 grants totaling $11,961 (high: $1,494, low: $538).
Fields of interest: Science; Physics.
Type of support: Support to graduates or students of specific schools; Awards/grants by nomination only; Undergraduate support.
Application information: Applications not accepted.
  Additional information: Unsolicited requests for funds not considered or acknowledged. Contact scholarship office of one of the three participating universities listed above for nomination guidelines.
EIN: 866065266

2891
Muriel Thauer Scholarship Fund
111 W. Monroe St. Tax Div. 10C
Chicago, IL 60603 (920) 262-7500
Application address: c/o Watertown High School, 825 Endeavor Dr., Watertown, WI 53098-1728,

Foundation type: Independent foundation

Purpose: Scholarships to graduates of Watertown High School, WI, to attend an accredited college or university.
Financial data: Year ended 12/31/2012. Assets, $461,877 (M); Expenditures, $37,280; Total giving, $30,375; Grants to individuals, 15 grants totaling $30,375 (high: $3,000, low: $1,125).
Type of support: Support to graduates or students of specific schools; Undergraduate support.
Application information: Applications accepted.
  Initial approach: Letter
  Deadline(s): None
EIN: 396057804

2892
The Thoracic Surgery Foundation for Research and Education
633 N. St. Clair St., 23rd Fl.
Chicago, IL 60611 (312) 202-5868
Contact: Priscilla S. Page, Exec. Dir.
FAX: (773) 289-0871; E-mail: tsfre@prri.com;
E-Mail For Priscilla S. Page: ppage@tsfre.org;
URL: http://www.tsfre.org

Foundation type: Public charity
Purpose: Research grants and fellowships to those studying cardiothoracic surgery.
Publications: Application guidelines; Annual report; Grants list.
Financial data: Year ended 06/30/2011. Assets, $3,934,571 (M); Grants to individuals, totaling $256,568.
Fields of interest: Heart & circulatory research; Surgery research.
Type of support: Fellowships; Research.
Application information: Applications accepted. Application form required. Application form available on the grantmaker's web site.
  Initial approach: Letter
  Deadline(s): Oct. 17
Program descriptions:
  Career Development Award: Provides salary support of up to $50,000 a year for up to 2 years for applicants who have completed their residency training and who wish to pursue investigative careers in cardiothoracic surgery.
  Research Fellowships: Provides support of up to $35,000 a year for up to 2 years for surgical residents who have not yet completed cardiothoracic surgical training.
  Research Grants: Provides operational support of original research efforts by cardiothoracic surgeons who have completed their formal training, and who are seeking initial support and recognition for their research program. Awards of up to $30,000 a year for up to 2 years are made each year to support the work of an early-career cardiothoracic surgeon (within 5 years of first faculty appointment).
  The Nina Starr Braunwald Career Development Award: Provides a biennial award of $120,000 for two years to support the research career development of a woman cardiac surgeon who holds a full-time faculty appointment and is within 10 years of completion of thoracic surgery residency.
EIN: 363635910

2893
Evelyn K. Titus Trust
c/o Midwest Bank of Western Illinois
200 E. Broadway
Monmouth, IL 61462-0440 (309) 734-9401
Application address: c/o Evelyn Titus Memorial Scholarship, 1000 N. Main St., P.O. Box 348, Monmouth, IL 61462-5218

Foundation type: Independent foundation
Purpose: Scholarships to male and female students of Warren county, IL who major in agriculture or home economics at accredited colleges or universities.
Financial data: Year ended 12/31/2012. Assets, $273,275 (M); Expenditures, $21,618; Total giving, $18,000; Grants to individuals, 9 grants totaling $18,000 (high: $2,000, low: $2,000).
Fields of interest: Agriculture; Home economics.
Type of support: Scholarships—to individuals.
Application information: Applications accepted. Application form required.
  Initial approach: Letter
  Deadline(s): May 1
  Additional information: Application must include transcripts.
EIN: 366982233

2894
Tomara Corporation
103 Irene Dr.
Collinsville, IL   62234   (618) 344-0484
Contact: Robert W. Karrer, Tr.

Foundation type: Independent foundation
Purpose: Scholarships to residents of Collinsville, IL, for higher education.
Financial data: Year ended 12/31/2012. Assets, $141,279 (M); Expenditures, $121,552; Total giving, $114,192; Grants to individuals, 41 grants totaling $114,192 (high: $7,000, low: $1,000).
Type of support: Undergraduate support.
Application information: Applications accepted. Application form required.
  Deadline(s): None
  Additional information: Contact corporation for application guidelines.
EIN: 371193115

2895
TPAA Foundation
(also known as Thai Physicians Association of America Foundation)
1507 W. Walnut St.
Marion, IL   62959   (618) 997-9665
FAX: (618) 993-3356;
E-mail: soorntornt@gmail.com; URL: http://www.tpaa.us/content.cfm?smID=33

Foundation type: Public charity
Purpose: Scholarships to students attending medical school in Thailand.
Publications: Annual report; Financial statement; Grants list; Multi-year report.
Financial data: Year ended 12/31/2012. Assets, $447,089 (M); Expenditures, $234,307; Total giving, $229,972.
Fields of interest: Medical school/education.
Type of support: Grants to individuals; Scholarships—to individuals; Support to graduates or students of specific schools; Awards/grants by nomination only.
Application information: Applications not accepted.
  Additional information: Unsolicited requests for funds not considered or acknowledged.
EIN: 371413467

2896
Tree Research and Education Endowment Fund
(also known as TREE Fund)
552 S. Washington St., Ste. 109
Naperville, IL   60540-6669   (630) 369-8300
Contact: M. Janet Bornancin, Pres. and C.E.O.
Tel./fax: (630) 369-8300; URL: http://www.treefund.org/home

Foundation type: Public charity
Purpose: Scholarships to students pursuing a career in aboriculture.
Financial data: Year ended 12/31/2012. Assets, $2,416,423 (M); Expenditures, $650,472; Total giving, $165,290; Grants to individuals, totaling $162,790.
Fields of interest: Environment, plant conservation; Landscaping.
Type of support: Scholarships—to individuals.
Application information: Applications accepted.
  Initial approach: Telephone or letter
  Send request by: Online
  Deadline(s): Apr. 1 for Robert Felix Memorial Scholarship, May 15 for John Wright Memorial Scholarship
Program descriptions:
  John Wright Memorial Scholarship: This $2,000 scholarship is available to high school seniors and returning college students pursuing careers related to arboriculture. This award helps undergraduate students attend college without accumulating burdensome debt.
  TREE Fund Fellowship: This fellowship awards $100,000 over three to five years in support of mentored doctoral research projects in priority areas of arboriculture and urban forestry.
EIN: 371018692

2897
Tri-County Opportunities Council
P.O. Box 610
Rock Falls, IL   61071-0610   (815) 625-7830
Toll-free tel.: (800) 323-5434; URL: http://www.tcochelps.com/

Foundation type: Public charity
Purpose: Grants for financial emergencies and energy costs to residents of Bureau, Carroll, LaSalle, Lee, Marshall, Ogle, Putnam, Stark, and Whiteside counties in IL. Also, scholarships to individuals from those same counties attending a post-secondary educational institution in IL, with preference to students in high tech or other growth fields.
Financial data: Year ended 12/31/2011. Assets, $4,167,935 (M); Expenditures, $21,573,404; Total giving, $9,095,109; Grants to individuals, totaling $9,095,109.
Type of support: Undergraduate support; Grants for special needs.
Application information: Applications accepted.
  Applicants should submit the following:
    1) Class rank
    2) Transcripts
    3) ACT
    4) GPA
    5) Financial information
  Additional information: See web site for income eligibility guidelines.
EIN: 362559180

2898
True Value Foundation
8600 Bryn Mawr Ave.
Chicago, IL   60631-3579   (773) 695-5000
Contact: John Hartmann, Pres. and C.E.O.
URL: http://truevaluecompany.com/about_true_value/true-value-foundation.asp

Foundation type: Public charity
Purpose: Scholarships to children of True Value Company retailers and associates pursuing higher education.
Financial data: Year ended 12/31/2011. Assets, $397,310 (M); Expenditures, $520,243; Total giving, $484,648; Grants to individuals, totaling $84,500.
Fields of interest: Vocational education, post-secondary; Higher education.
Type of support: Employee-related scholarships.
Application information: Applications not accepted.
  Additional information: Scholarships are only for True Value Company children. Unsolicited requests for funds not considered or acknowledged.
EIN: 261897927

2899
Turnaround Management Association
150 N. Wacker Dr., Ste. 900
Chicago, IL   60606-4107   (312) 578-6900
Contact: Gregory J. Fine C.A.E., C.E.O.
FAX: (312) 578-8336; E-mail: info@turnaround.org; E-mail for Gregory J. Fine: gfine@turnaround.org: tel. for Gregory J. Fine: (312) 578-2020; URL: http://www.turnaround.org

Foundation type: Public charity
Purpose: Awards to teachers who have changed the outcome of students' lives and the communities they work in. Prizes also for student essays covering the field of corporate renewal.
Publications: Application guidelines; Annual report.
Financial data: Year ended 12/31/2011. Assets, $5,272,176 (M); Expenditures, $4,707,966; Total giving, $43,509; Grants to individuals, totaling $9,734.
Fields of interest: Elementary/secondary education; Business school/education; Education; Business/industry.
Type of support: Grants to individuals.
Application information: Applications accepted. Application form required. Application form available on the grantmaker's web site.
  Initial approach: Letter
  Deadline(s): May 1 for Butler-Cooley Excellence in Teaching Awards; May 30 for Carl Marks Student Paper Competition
  Additional information: Application should include proposal.
Program descriptions:
  Butler-Cooley Excellence in Teaching Awards: This program honors three to five teachers who have changed the outcome of students' lives and the communities in which they live with a $5,000 stipend. Eligible nominees must be currently licensed or active elementary or secondary school (K-12) teachers at an accredited public or private school, and must have at least five years of teaching experience.
  Carl Marks Student Paper Competition: This competition recognizes outstanding student achievement in the field of corporate renewal, as well as provides research that could offer new insight into the profession and expand the association's university outreach. Papers will be judged in two categories: case analysis (focus on a

company or companies to see how they can be turned around) and theoretical/conceptual (focus on turnaround issues and theories, and understanding the theoretical underpinnings of turnarounds). Eligible authors must have been students enrolled in an MBA program or equivalent business-related master's degree program at an accredited university at the time the paper was written. A $3,000 first-place award and a $1,500 second-place award will be announced for each category.
EIN: 561596880

2900
Uhlich Children's Advantage Network
(also known as UCAN)
3737 N. Mozart St.
Chicago, IL 60618-3615 (773) 588-0180
FAX: (773) 588-7762;
E-mail: info@ucanchicago.org; URL: http://www.ucanchicago.org

Foundation type: Public charity
Purpose: Financial and other emergency assistance to families with children in need throughout the Chicago, IL area.
Financial data: Year ended 06/30/2011. Assets, $38,374,183 (M); Expenditures, $37,073,943; Total giving, $3,385,879; Grants to individuals, totaling $3,385,879.
Fields of interest: Youth; Young adults; Economically disadvantaged.
Type of support: Grants for special needs.
Application information: Contact the agency for eligibility determination.
EIN: 362167937

2901
Jimmie Ullery Charitable Trust
10 S. Dearborn Il1-0117
Chicago, IL 60603 (214) 965-2908
Application address: c/o JPMorgan Chase Bank, N.A. TX 1-2963, 2200 Ross Ave., Dallas, TX 75201

Foundation type: Independent foundation
Purpose: Scholarships to individuals contemplating full-time Christian service, primarily for study at Presbyterian theological seminaries.
Financial data: Year ended 01/31/2013. Assets, $400,549 (M); Expenditures, $24,601; Total giving, $17,102.
Fields of interest: Higher education; Theological school/education; Christian agencies & churches.
Type of support: Scholarships—to individuals.
Application information: Applications accepted.
Deadline(s): None
EIN: 736142334

2902
Union Health Service, Inc.
1634 W. Polk St.
Chicago, IL 60612-4352 (312) 423-4200
URL: http://www.unionhealth.org

Foundation type: Public charity
Purpose: Healthcare services provided to Union Health Service members throughout the Chicago, IL area.
Financial data: Year ended 12/31/2011. Assets, $30,023,285 (M); Expenditures, $56,173,765.
Fields of interest: Pharmacy/prescriptions; Health care.
Type of support: Grants for special needs.
Application information: Applications not accepted.

Additional information: Unsolicited requests for funds not considered or acknowledged.
EIN: 362302593

2903
Union League Boys and Girls Clubs
65 W. Jackson Blvd.
Chicago, IL 60604-3507 (312) 435-5940
Contact: Mary Ann Mahon-Huels, Exec. Dir.
FAX: (312) 583-0320;
E-mail: k.considine@ulbgc.org; URL: http://www.ulbgc.org

Foundation type: Public charity
Purpose: Scholarships to current or former members of any club supported by the foundation, primarily in IL.
Publications: Annual report; Newsletter.
Financial data: Year ended 12/31/2011. Assets, $14,153,211 (M); Expenditures, $3,632,260; Total giving, $61,513; Grants to individuals, totaling $61,513.
Fields of interest: Economically disadvantaged.
Type of support: Scholarships—to individuals.
Application information: Applications accepted. Application form required. Interview required.
Initial approach: Letter
EIN: 362167939

2904
Union League Civic & Arts Foundation
65 W. Jackson Blvd., Ste. 901
Chicago, IL 60604-3598 (312) 427-7800
Contact: Anne Shea, Exec. Dir.
E-mail: caf@civicandarts.org; URL: http://www.civicandarts.org/

Foundation type: Public charity
Purpose: Scholarships to pre-professional musicians and visual arts students in the metropolitan Chicago, IL area; also, awards to poets, writers, and composers in the metropolitan Chicago, IL area.
Publications: Application guidelines; Annual report.
Financial data: Year ended 02/28/2013. Assets, $1,511,534 (M); Expenditures, $609,338; Total giving, $211,292; Grants to individuals, totaling $211,292.
Fields of interest: Arts education; Visual arts; Music; Music composition; Performing arts, education; Literature.
Type of support: Scholarships—to individuals; Awards/prizes; Undergraduate support.
Application information: See web site for complete program information.
Program descriptions:
Classical Music Scholarships: Awards, ranging from $4,000 to $15,000, are awarded to outstanding teenagers and young adults who practice the art of classical music. Three awards are given in this category: two Rose M. Grundman Scholarships ($15,000 each, one for women's voice and one for men's voice), three $6,000 scholarships (in piano, strings, and winds to college and post-graduate students), and three Edward and Ethel Martin Scholarships ($4,000 to high-school students studying piano, strings, and wind). Eligible applicants must be living and studying within a one-hundred-mile radius of the Chicago Loop, be citizens of the U.S.A., and must be between 23 to 30 years of age for voice or 14 to 30 years of age for piano/strings/wind.
Creative Writing Competition: Up to $9,000 in awards are given to support the creative writing efforts of young people. Grants are given in three divisions: high school (three awards, ranging from

$200 to $500), college (three awards, ranging from $600 to $1,200), and young adult (three awards, ranging from $800 to $1,500). Submissions must be original works of creative writing (poems, short stories, novel excepts, or works of creative nonfiction); applicants must be living and or studying within a one-hundred-mile radius of the Chicago Loop, or students registered in an Illinois school within a one-hundred-mile radius of the Chicago Loop.
Jazz Composition Competition: Awards of up to $5,000 are given to outstanding jazz compositions. Eligible applicants must submit an original jazz composition for any number of voices or instruments; eligible applicants must be living and/or studying within a one-hundred-mile radius of the Chicago Loop.
Jazz Improvisation Competition: A total of $16,000 is available to outstanding jazz improvisators. Awards are presented in the following categories: First Division (awards of up to $3,125 to performers, ages 14 to 17) ,Second Division (awards of up to $4,185 to performers, ages 18 to 22), and Third Division (awards of up to $4,690 to performers, ages 23 to 27). In addition, a $3,000 grand prize will be awarded, and two additional awards (a first-place award of $1,000 and a second-place award of $500) will be given via live-audience vote. Instrumentalists and vocalists must improvise, for a maximum of eight minutes, a blues piece and a composition of their choice; vocalists should include words and skat in their performance.
Visual Arts Competition: Up to $30,000 in awards will be given for excellence in visual arts. Awards will be presented in three categories (photography, moving image, and general categories). Within each category, one first-place award of $4,000, one second-place award of $3,000, and one third-place award of $2,000 will be given; in addition, one entrant will be awarded "best in show," and will receive an additional $3,000 prize. Eligible applicants include any student who is 30 years or younger who are enrolled full-time in a visual arts college or university degree program (either on the undergraduate or graduate level), within a one-hundred-mile radius of the Chicago Loop; or any student that is a resident within a one-hundred-mile radius of the Chicago Loop.
EIN: 362446421

2905
United Conveyor Foundation
2100 Norman Dr. W.
Waukegan, IL 60085-6752 (847) 473-5900
Contact: Mary Nelson
E-mail: davidhoyem@unitedconveyor.com

Foundation type: Company-sponsored foundation
Purpose: Scholarships for students whose parents have been employed at United Conveyor Corporation or an affiliated company for at least three years.
Financial data: Year ended 12/31/2012. Assets, $4,568,964 (M); Expenditures, $259,040; Total giving, $256,000; Grants to individuals, 10 grants totaling $35,450 (high: $5,000, low: $150).
Type of support: Employee-related scholarships.
Application information: Applications not accepted.
Additional information: Unsolicited requests for funds not considered or acknowledged.
Company name: United Conveyor Corporation
EIN: 366033638

2906
United Way of McLean County
201 E. Grove St.
Bloomington, IL   61701-5258   (309) 828-7383
FAX: (309) 829-2469; E-mail: scoffer@uwaymc.org;
URL: http://www.uwaymc.org

Foundation type: Public charity
Purpose: Temporary emergency assistance to individuals of McLean county, IL, who did not qualify for assistance from other agency due to unavailable funds.
Publications: Annual report.
Financial data: Year ended 06/30/2012. Assets, $4,458,228 (M); Expenditures, $4,329,577; Total giving, $3,210,738.
Fields of interest: Human services.
Type of support: Emergency funds; In-kind gifts.
Application information: Contact the agency for eligibility criteria.
EIN: 370661505

2907
Urbana-Champaign Independent Media Center
c/o Jason Turner
202 S. Broadway, Ste. 100
Urbana, IL   61801-3319   (217) 344-8820
E-mail: imc@ucimc.org; URL: http://www.ucimc.org

Foundation type: Public charity
Purpose: Fiscal sponsorship for projects focussing on the creation of radical, accurate, and passionate tellings of truth.
Publications: Financial statement; Informational brochure; Program policy statement.
Financial data: Year ended 12/31/2011. Assets, $523,593 (M); Expenditures, $433,087.
Fields of interest: Print publishing; Radio; Arts; Environment.
Type of support: Fiscal agent/sponsor.
Application information:
   Initial approach: E-mail
   Additional information: Contact the center for further information.
Program description:
   Fiscal Sponsorship: Fiscal sponsorship is available for independent media, social justice, and environmental groups whose mission aligns with that of the center and who have a contact who will be in charge. Fiscal sponsor recipients sign a contract and agree to a fee of seven percent of all grant monies received.
EIN: 371403593

2908
Peter Simon Veeder Scholarship Fund Trust
10 S Dearborn IL1-0117
Chicago, IL   60603   (765) 294-2254
Application address: c/o Southeast Fountain High School, 744 E. U.S. 136, Veedersburg, IN 4798

Foundation type: Independent foundation
Purpose: Scholarships to students from Southeast Fountain High School, IN.
Financial data: Year ended 12/31/2012. Assets, $700,474 (M); Expenditures, $45,830; Total giving, $34,713; Grants to individuals, 25 grants totaling $34,713 (high: $2,001, low: $989).
Type of support: Support to graduates or students of specific schools; Undergraduate support.
Application information: Applications accepted.
   Initial approach: Letter or telephone
   Deadline(s): Mar. 31
EIN: 066115230

2909
Otto Villwock Medical Educational Scholarship Fund
c/o JPMorgan Chase Bank, N.A.
10 S. Dearborn St., no 21Fl.
Chicago, IL   60603-2300   (513) 558-5991
Application addresses: c/o Case Western Reserve University, Attn.: Financial Aid Office, 10900 Euclid Ave., Rm. T-303, Cleveland, OH, 44106-4920, c/o University of Wisconsin Medical School, Attn.: Financial Aid Office,1300 University Ave., Madison, WI 53706-1532, Tel.: (608) 263-7135 , and c/o University of Cincinnati Medical School, P.O. Box 670552, Cincinnati, OH 45267-0552, Tel.: (513) 558 5991

Foundation type: Independent foundation
Purpose: Scholarships to financially needy students whose fathers are deceased and who have been admitted to Case Western Reserve University, University of Wisconsin Medical School (Madison) or University of Cincinnati Medical School.
Financial data: Year ended 05/31/2012. Assets, $277,930 (M); Expenditures, $17,096; Total giving, $13,712.
Fields of interest: Medical school/education.
Type of support: Scholarships—to individuals; Support to graduates or students of specific schools.
Application information: Applications accepted. Application form not required.
   Initial approach: Letter
   Deadline(s): Mar. 31
EIN: 510172011

2910
Rich Vogler Scholarship Foundation, Inc.
c/o Dale Vogler
1860 Tower Hill Dr.
Woodridge, IL   60517-7680   (317) 272-4623
E-mail: dale.vogler.corby@gmail.com; URL: http://www.richvoglerscholarship.org

Foundation type: Public charity
Purpose: Scholarships to individuals involved with the racing community.
Financial data: Year ended 12/31/2011. Assets, $144,206 (M); Expenditures, $24,260; Total giving, $17,000.
Fields of interest: Recreation.
Type of support: Scholarships—to individuals.
Application information: Applications accepted. Application form required. Application form available on the grantmaker's web site.
   Initial approach: Letter
   Send request by: Mail or e-mail
   Deadline(s): Feb. 15
   Applicants should submit the following:
      1) Letter(s) of recommendation
      2) Transcripts
EIN: 351863995

2911
Frank C. Wagenknecht Scholarship Trust
c/o Hometown National Bank
260 Bucklin St.
La Salle, IL   61301

Foundation type: Independent foundation
Purpose: Scholarships to the top two (or more if funds permit) GPA students from LaSalle-Peru High School, IL.
Financial data: Year ended 05/31/2013. Assets, $1,704,007 (M); Expenditures, $101,343; Total

giving, $83,606; Grants to individuals, 34 grants totaling $83,606 (high: $2,500, low: $1,106).
Type of support: Support to graduates or students of specific schools; Undergraduate support.
Application information: Applications not accepted.
   Additional information: Applicants are determined by grade-points only; Selections are made by the school.
EIN: 936122496

2912
Leo J. Wahl Foundation
2902 N. Locust
Sterling, IL   61081-9501   (815) 625-6525
Contact: Clipper C. Wahl

Foundation type: Company-sponsored foundation
Purpose: Scholarships to dependents of Wahl Clipper Corporation employees, primarily in IL.
Financial data: Year ended 12/31/2011. Assets, $263,823 (M); Expenditures, $49,288; Total giving, $49,250; Grants to individuals, 45 grants totaling $49,250 (high: $2,600).
Fields of interest: Higher education.
Type of support: Employee-related scholarships.
Application information: Application form required.
   Deadline(s): None
   Applicants should submit the following:
      1) Financial information
      2) Transcripts
      3) GPA
   Additional information: This is an employee-related program. Unsolicited requests for funds not considered or acknowledged.
EIN: 363447061

2913
Walgreen Benefit Fund
104 Wilmot Rd., MS No. 1410
Deerfield, IL   60015-5121   (847) 315-4662
Contact: John Gremer, V.P. and Dir.
URL: http://www.walgreens.com/topic/sr/sr_walgreens_benefit.jsp

Foundation type: Company-sponsored foundation
Purpose: Welfare assistance to financially needy Walgreen employees and retirees and their families.
Publications: Application guidelines; Annual report.
Financial data: Year ended 04/30/2013. Assets, $24,045,833 (M); Expenditures, $1,947,781; Total giving, $1,922,587; Grants to individuals, 1,302 grants totaling $1,922,587.
Type of support: Employee-related welfare.
Application information:
   Initial approach: Letter
   Deadline(s): None
   Additional information: Application address: Ruth D. Crane, Corp. 104, Wilmot Rd., M.S. 1444, Deerfield, IL 60015, tel.: (847) 315-4663, E-mail: ruth.crane@walgreen.com.
Company name: Walgreen Company
EIN: 366051130

2914
Walgreens Assistance, Inc.
104 Wilmot Rd., M.S. 1444
Deerfield, IL   60015-5121
URL: http://www.walgreens.com/topic/sr/sr_giving_back_flu_shot.jsp

Foundation type: Operating foundation

Purpose: Assistance with flu vaccine vouchers to the uninsured or underinsured ill, needy, and infants to prevent influenza and improve health.
Financial data: Year ended 08/31/2012. Assets, $0 (M); Expenditures, $17,197,200; Total giving, $17,197,200; Grants to individuals, totaling $17,197,200.
Fields of interest: Health care; Economically disadvantaged.
Type of support: Grants for special needs.
Application information: The foundation partners with the U.S. Department of Health and Human Services to distribute flu vaccine vouchers to local health agencies and community partners.
EIN: 274521750

2915
Darleen J. and Robert L. Walker Scholarship Fund

27 W. Park Blvd.
Villa Park, IL 60181
Contact: James Reichardt, Pres.
URL: http://www.walkerscholarship.org/

Foundation type: Independent foundation
Purpose: Scholarships to students studying law or about to enter law school in Milwaukee, WI; St. Louis, MO; or IL. Strong preference is given to individuals who are Masons, come from Masonic families or are former residents of the Masonic Children's Home in LaGrange, IL.
Financial data: Year ended 12/31/2012. Assets, $389,828 (M); Expenditures, $44,770; Total giving, $32,000; Grants to individuals, 10 grants totaling $32,000 (high: $4,000, low: $1,500).
Fields of interest: Law school/education.
Type of support: Undergraduate support.
Application information: Applications accepted. Application form required. Application form available on the grantmaker's web site.
Initial approach: Letter
Send request by: Mail, fax or online
Deadline(s): June 30
Additional information: Application must include FAFSA.
EIN: 202263608

2916
Walters Scholarship Fund

111 W. Monroe St., Ste. 10C
Chicago, IL 60603   (715) 847-4606
Contact: Colleen Gostisha
Application address: , 500 3rd St., Wausau, WI 54402

Foundation type: Independent foundation
Purpose: Scholarships to members of the graduating class of Rhinelander High School, Milwaukee, WI, and who are in the top 25 percent of their class and are planning to pursue a full-time engineering course of study in college.
Financial data: Year ended 09/30/2012. Assets, $255,293 (M); Expenditures, $16,180; Total giving, $12,297.
Fields of interest: Engineering school/education.
Type of support: Support to graduates or students of specific schools; Undergraduate support.
Application information: Applications accepted.
Send request by: Mail
EIN: 930834256

2917
Walters Technical Scholarship Fund

111 W. Monroe St., Tax Div. 10C
Chicago, IL 60603   (715) 847-4606
Application Address: c/o BMO Harris Bank N.A., Attn: Colleen Gostisha, 500 3rd St., Wausau WI. 54402

Foundation type: Independent foundation
Purpose: Scholarships to graduating seniors of north-central WI high school enrolled at one of the sixteen WI technical colleges in a program leading to a two-year associate degree in the technical and industrial area.
Financial data: Year ended 09/30/2012. Assets, $254,991 (M); Expenditures, $16,139; Total giving, $12,284.
Fields of interest: Vocational education, post-secondary; College.
Type of support: Technical education support.
Application information: Applications accepted. Application form required.
Deadline(s): Last school day in Mar.
Applicants should submit the following:
1) Transcripts
2) Letter(s) of recommendation
EIN: 396509266

2918
Waubonsee Community College Foundation

Rte. 47 at Waubonsee Dr., 2nd Fl.
Dickson Ctr.
Sugar Grove, IL 60554   (630) 466-7900
E-mail: foundation@waubonsee.edu; *URL:* https://www.waubonsee.edu/about/foundation/

Foundation type: Public charity
Purpose: Scholarships to students at Waubonsee Community College, IL.
Financial data: Year ended 06/30/2012. Assets, $3,163,674 (M); Expenditures, $180,018; Total giving, $146,191; Grants to individuals, totaling $146,191.
Type of support: Support to graduates or students of specific schools; Undergraduate support.
Application information:
Initial approach: Letter
EIN: 362990533

2919
John Wayne Scholarship Trust

127 S. Side Sq.
Macomb, IL 61455-2218   (309) 833-4551

Foundation type: Public charity
Purpose: Financial assistance to graduating seniors from McDonough and Fulton county high schools, IL to pursue bachelor's or advanced degrees.
Financial data: Year ended 12/31/2012. Assets, $335,720 (M); Expenditures, $11,767; Total giving, $9,000; Grants to individuals, 21 grants totaling $9,000 (high: $875, low: $375).
Fields of interest: Higher education.
Type of support: Scholarships—to individuals.
Application information: Applications accepted.
Additional information: Contact the trust for additional application guidelines.
EIN: 376187937

2920
George S. Weeks Trust

10 S. Dearborn IL1-0117
Chicago, IL 60603

Foundation type: Independent foundation
Purpose: Financial assistance to needy, legally blind individuals of Fayette and Bourbon Counties, KY, for equipment, supplies, and training.
Financial data: Year ended 12/31/2012. Assets, $594,326 (M); Expenditures, $30,693; Total giving, $25,857.
Fields of interest: Disabilities, people with; Economically disadvantaged.
Type of support: Grants for special needs.
Application information: Applications not accepted.
Additional information: Unsolicited requests for funds not considered or acknowledged.
EIN: 616208193

2921
Anna B. Welch Memorial Trust

c/o First Mid-Illinois Bank & Trust
P.O. Box 529
Mattoon, IL 61938-0529   (217) 234-7454
Contact: Laura M. Walk

Foundation type: Independent foundation
Purpose: Scholarships to students of Coles and Cumberland counties, IL pursuing careers in the medical fields of study, including nursing and medical technology.
Financial data: Year ended 02/28/2013. Assets, $1,784,846 (M); Expenditures, $122,923; Total giving, $78,200; Grants to individuals, 77 grants totaling $77,000 (high: $1,000, low: $1,000).
Fields of interest: Medical school/education; Nursing school/education.
Type of support: Scholarships—to individuals; Graduate support.
Application information: Application form required.
Deadline(s): Apr. 15
Additional information: Application should include tax returns. Applicant must demonstrate financial need.
EIN: 376284353

2922
Lucile Wells Scholarship Fund

111 W. Monroe St.Tax Div.10C
Chicago, IL 60603   (608) 346-2439
Contact: Martha McHugh
Application address: 2319 Holiday Dr. 1, Janesville, WI 53545, tel.: (608) 346-2439

Foundation type: Independent foundation
Purpose: Scholarships to high school graduates who are members of the Trinity Episcopal Church, Janesville, WI.
Financial data: Year ended 07/31/2012. Assets, $983,509 (M); Expenditures, $64,375; Total giving, $47,468; Grants to individuals, 10 grants totaling $47,468 (high: $8,490, low: $2,000).
Fields of interest: Higher education; Protestant agencies & churches.
Type of support: Scholarships—to individuals; Undergraduate support.
Application information: Applications accepted. Application form required.
Deadline(s): None
EIN: 396694943

2923
Wells Trust Fund

c/o Edgar County Bank and Trust
P.O. Box 400
Paris, IL   61944-1735   (217) 465-7641
Contact: John Carrington, Trust Off., Edgar County
Bank and Trust

Foundation type: Independent foundation
Purpose: Undergraduate scholarships to Protestant residents of Edgar County, IL, attending Depauw University, Eastern Illinois University, Millikin University, and the University of Illinois.
Financial data: Year ended 12/31/2011. Assets, $1,374,549 (M); Expenditures, $82,511; Total giving, $65,000; Grants to individuals, 11 grants totaling $65,000 (high: $10,000, low: $2,000).
Fields of interest: Protestant agencies & churches.
Type of support: Support to graduates or students of specific schools; Undergraduate support.
Application information: Application form required.
   Deadline(s): May 15
   Additional information: Applications are available at Citizens National Bank of Paris.
EIN: 376115126

2924
Western Egyptian Economic Opportunity
   ## Council, Inc.

1 Industrial Park
P.O. Box 7
Steeleville, IL   62288-1246   (618) 965-3458
Contact: Paulette Hamlin, Exec. Dir.
FAX: (618) 965-9421; E-mail: execdir@weeoc.org;
URL: http://www.weeoc.org

Foundation type: Public charity
Purpose: Emergency assistance to low income individuals and families throughout Jackson, Monroe, Perry, and Randolph counties, IL. Scholarships to high-school graduates in Monroe, Perry, and Randolph counties for continuing education at an IL two-year area college, vocational school, or four-year college or university.
Publications: Application guidelines.
Financial data: Year ended 04/30/2012. Assets, $1,236,736 (M); Expenditures, $9,542,341; Total giving, $5,203,620; Grants to individuals, totaling $5,203,620.
Fields of interest: Vocational education, post-secondary; Higher education; Economically disadvantaged.
Type of support: Scholarships—to individuals; Grants for special needs.
Application information: Applications accepted.
   Deadline(s): Mar. 31 for Scholarships
   Additional information: Contact the council for scholarship information.
EIN: 370892145

2925
Western Illinois Regional Council
   ## Community Action Agency

223 South Randolph St.
Macomb, IL   61455-2209   (309) 837-2997
Contact: for Scholarship: Tina Lovejoy, Prog. Coord.
FAX: (309) 836-3640; E-mail: wirc-caa@wirpc.org;
URL: http://www.wirpc.org/communityaction/

Foundation type: Public charity
Purpose: Emergency assistance to individuals and families throughout Hancock, Henderson, McDonough, and Warren counties, IL. Scholarships to individuals desiring to further their educational training through an IL community college, vocational school, college, or university.

Publications: Application guidelines; Newsletter.
Financial data: Year ended 12/31/2011. Assets, $1,503,237 (M); Expenditures, $5,843,061; Total giving, $4,059,501; Grants to individuals, totaling $4,059,501.
Fields of interest: Vocational education, post-secondary; Higher education.
Type of support: Scholarships—to individuals.
Application information: Applications accepted. Application form required. Application form available on the grantmaker's web site. Interview required.
   Initial approach: Application
   Deadline(s): Mar. 23 for Scholarship Program
   Applicants should submit the following:
      1) Financial information
      2) Transcripts
      3) Letter(s) of recommendation
      4) Essay
   Additional information: Scholarship funds will be paid directly to the educational institution on behalf of the students.
Program description:
   Scholarship Program: This program is available for eligible traditional and nontraditional students with a $1,500 scholarship to assist lower income individuals who are residents of Hancock, Henderson, McDonough and Warren counties. Recipients may begin or continue a course of study in a field with high potential for employment at an accredited Illinois two-year community college, technical school, or four-year college or university. Eligible individuals must reside in a household whose total income meets 125 percent of federal poverty levels. An individual may not receive a WIRC-CAA scholarship more than two times.
EIN: 363220629

2926
B. Belle Whitney Scholarship Trust

10 S. Dearborn, IL1-0117
Chicago, IL   60603

Foundation type: Independent foundation
Purpose: Scholarships to financially needy graduates of Danbury, Bethel, Brookfield, New Fairfield, New Milford, Newtown, Redding, Ridgefield or Sherman, CT high schools who are enrolled in an undergraduate program at Vassar College, NY.
Financial data: Year ended 12/31/2012. Assets, $172,449 (M); Expenditures, $10,812; Total giving, $6,721; Grants to individuals, 2 grants totaling $6,721 (high: $3,721, low: $3,000).
Fields of interest: Higher education.
Type of support: Support to graduates or students of specific schools; Undergraduate support.
Application information:
   Deadline(s): None
EIN: 066022861

2927
Don E. & Charlotte J. Williams Charitable
   ## Foundation, Inc.

c/o Frank Nowinski
1000 36th Ave.
Moline, IL   61265-7126

Foundation type: Independent foundation
Purpose: Scholarships to children of Don E. Williams, Co. employees for elementary, secondary, and undergraduate education, primarily in IL and WI.
Financial data: Year ended 12/31/2012. Assets, $2,399,344 (M); Expenditures, $120,890; Total giving, $68,000.

Fields of interest: Elementary school/education; Secondary school/education.
Type of support: Scholarships—to individuals.
Application information: Application form required.
   Deadline(s): Jan. 5
   Applicants should submit the following:
      1) Letter(s) of recommendation
      2) Essay
      3) Transcripts
      4) Financial information
   Additional information: Unsolicited requests for funds not considered or acknowledged.
EIN: 363611702

2928
Veronica Willo Scholarship Fund

10 S. Dearborn IL1-0117
Chicago, IL   60603   (214) 965-2908
Application address: c/o JPmorgan Chase
Bank,N.A ,2200 Ross Ave., Dallas, TX 75201-2787

Foundation type: Independent foundation
Purpose: Undergraduate scholarships by nomination only to graduating seniors of Mahoning County, OH, high schools.
Financial data: Year ended 12/31/2012. Assets, $189,068 (M); Expenditures, $8,319; Total giving, $6,019.
Fields of interest: Higher education; Scholarships/ financial aid.
Type of support: Scholarships—to individuals.
Application information: Applications not accepted.
   Additional information: Nominations are made by Mahoning County, OH, high school principals. Funds are paid directly to the educational institution on behalf of the students. Unsolicited requests for funds not considered or acknowledged.
EIN: 346577619

2929
Dee Wilson Scholarship Fund

c/o Edgar County Bank & Trust
P.O. Box 400
Paris, IL   61944   (217) 465-4154

Foundation type: Independent foundation
Purpose: Scholarships to residents of Community Unit School District #6, Edgar county, IL or to graduates of Scotland and Chrisman High Schools, IL for continuing their education at colleges or universities.
Financial data: Year ended 12/31/2012. Assets, $168,233 (M); Expenditures, $10,351; Total giving, $7,743; Grants to individuals, 20 grants totaling $7,743 (high: $400, low: $198).
Fields of interest: Higher education.
Type of support: Support to graduates or students of specific schools.
Application information: Applications accepted. Application form required.
   Deadline(s): May 15
   Additional information: Applications are available at the bank and at school district #6, P.O. Box 477, Chrisman, IL 61924.
EIN: 376258368

2930
Murray Wise Associates Foundation
(formerly Westchester Foundation)
1605 S. State St., Ste. 110
Champaign, IL 61820 (217) 398-6400
Contact: Richard J. Baker, Exec. Dir.
URL: http://murraywiseassociates.com/
foundation

Foundation type: Independent foundation
Purpose: College scholarships to outstanding students pursuing degrees in agriculture or agriculturally-related subject areas.
Financial data: Year ended 12/31/2012. Assets, $42,796 (M); Expenditures, $20,936; Total giving, $20,500; Grants to individuals, 18 grants totaling $20,500 (high: $1,500, low: $500).
Fields of interest: Public education.
Type of support: Scholarships—to individuals.
Application information: Application form required.
> *Applicants should submit the following:*
> 1) Transcripts
> 2) Letter(s) of recommendation
> *Additional information:* Application available from the foundation upon request.
EIN: 364149509

2931
WKUS Benefits Trust
c/o Tax Dept.
4025 W. Peterson Ave.
Chicago, IL 60646-6085 (773) 866-3879

Foundation type: Public charity
Purpose: Paid time off wages for employees of Wolters Kluwer.
Financial data: Year ended 12/31/2011. Assets, $307 (M); Expenditures, $26,341,900; Total giving, $26,339,400; Grants to individuals, totaling $26,339,400.
Fields of interest: Employment.
Type of support: Employee-related welfare.
Application information: Applications accepted.
> *Additional information:* Wages are only for employees of Wolters Kluwer. Unsolicited requests for funds not considered or acknowledged.
EIN: 363453154

2932
J. Edgar Wolfer Scholarship Fund
33 S. 4th St.
Pekin, IL 61554-4202

Foundation type: Independent foundation
Purpose: Scholarships to graduates of Pekin Community High School, IL for postsecondary education.
Financial data: Year ended 06/30/2012. Assets, $162,709 (M); Expenditures, $4,791; Total giving, $2,400.
Fields of interest: Higher education.
Type of support: Support to graduates or students of specific schools.
Application information: Applications accepted. Application form required.
> *Deadline(s):* May 1
> *Additional information:* Application from available from high school.
EIN: 366863717

2933
Women of the Evangelical Lutheran Church in America
8765 W. Higgins Rd.
Chicago, IL 60631-4101
Contact: Linda Post Bushkofsky, Exec. Dir.
E-mail: women.elca@elca.org; Toll-free tel.: (800) 638-3522; URL: http://www.womenoftheelca.org/

Foundation type: Public charity
Purpose: Scholarships for women to continue their education in ordained ministry, academics and leadership.
Publications: Application guidelines; Grants list.
Financial data: Year ended 12/31/2012. Total giving, $57,525. Scholarships—to individuals amount not specified.
Fields of interest: Theological school/education; Christian agencies & churches; Women.
Type of support: Scholarships—to individuals.
Application information: Applications accepted. Application form required.
> *Deadline(s):* Feb. 15
> *Final notification:* Recipients notified in May
> *Additional information:* See web site for additional guidelines.
Program descriptions:
> *Arne Administrative Scholarship for Women Administrators:* This scholarship provides assistance to women interested in reaching the top of their field as an administrator, either through full-time school attendance, evening/part-time attendance, or summer session attendance. Eligible applicants must be U.S. citizens who hold membership in the Evangelical Lutheran Church in America, and who have at least a bachelor's degree. Grants average $500 each.
> *Herbert W. and Corinne Chistrom Scholarship for Women Preparing for Ordained Ministry:* Scholarships, generally range from $600 to $1,000, are available to provide assistance to Lutheran women who are second-career students entering their final year at a seminary. Eligible applicants must be U.S. citizens, hold membership in the Evangelical Lutheran Church in America, have experienced an interruption in education of at least five years since college graduation, be endorsed by her synodical candidacy committee, and be preparing for ordained ministry.
> *Opportunity Scholarships for Lutheran Laywomen:* These scholarships provide assistance to Lutheran women studying for a career other than ordained ministry. Named scholarships under this program include the Amelia Kemp Scholarship (for women of color in undergraduate, graduate, professional, or vocational courses of study), the Belmer/Flora Prince and Kahler, Vickers/Raup, Wettstein Scholarships (for women studying for service abroad, either in general or in health professions), the Drinkall Franke/Seeley Kndustrup Scholarships (for women in graduate courses of study preparing for occupations in Christian service), and the Cronk Memorial, First Triennium Board, General, Mehring, Paepke, Piero/Wade/Wade, Edwin/Edna Robeck Scholarship (for women in undergraduate, graduate, professional, or vocational courses of study)
> *Schmieder Leadership Scholarship for Women Faculty at ELCA Colleges and Seminaries:* Scholarships, generally range from $2,000 to $4,000, are available to develop and promote women's leadership at colleges and seminaries by assisting women administrators and faculty to participate in a leadership and management training institute. Eligible applicants must be nominated by the president of her institution, may attend the institution of her choice, provided that the program includes work in governance, financial

management, administration, and professional development, must gain admission to the institute of her choice and provide written confirmation of admission to the institute before the scholarship is disbursed, and must show that her institution is sharing the cost of the summer institute by providing financial support in a variety of ways, such as with transportation, staff support as necessary, and so forth.

2934
Women's Bar Foundation
P. O. Box 641068
Chicago, IL 60664-1068 (312) 641-1441
Contact: Bates McIntyre Larson, Pres.
E-mail: illinoiswbf@aol.com; URL: http://www.illinoiswbf.org/

Foundation type: Public charity
Purpose: Scholarships and stipends to female law school graduates pursuing a career in Illinois' not-for-profit or public service sector.
Publications: Application guidelines.
Financial data: Year ended 12/31/2012. Assets, $933,863 (M); Expenditures, $94,778; Total giving, $63,000; Grants to individuals, totaling $63,000.
Fields of interest: Law school/education; Women.
Type of support: Graduate support.
Application information: Applications accepted.
> *Initial approach:* Letter
> *Additional information:* See web site for additional information.
Program description:
> *Public Service Stipend:* The foundation awards a $15,000 stipend annually to a female attorney providing public interest legal service. Applicants must be currently employed with an organization or firm providing legal services in the Illinois nonprofit or pubic sector; possess a strong academic record, demonstrate present and past extracurricular activities reflecting community involvement or participation within and outside of law school that demonstrates a sincere commitment to public service or public interest law, a demonstrated financial need, demonstrate involvement with diversity initiatives within law school or the legal community, and demonstrate personal qualities that suggest a future leadership role in the legal community.
EIN: 366192588

2935
L. S. Wood Charitable Trust
c/o Bank of America, N.A.
231 S. LaSalle St.
Chicago, IL 60697-0001 (312) 828-2055
Application address: c/o Donald H. Parkison, Admin., 1317 Grand Ave., Ste. 228, Glenwood Springs, CO 81601-3841, tel.: (970) 945-4952, fax: (970) 947-9215, e-mail: parkison@sopris.net

Foundation type: Independent foundation
Purpose: Undergraduate scholarships to individuals studying at accredited colleges, universities and technical schools.
Financial data: Year ended 12/31/2012. Assets, $6,887,051 (M); Expenditures, $558,837; Total giving, $392,500; Grants to individuals, totaling $392,500.
Fields of interest: Higher education; Scholarships/financial aid.
Type of support: Undergraduate support.
Application information: Application form required. Interview required.

Initial approach: Letter or telephone
Deadline(s): Feb. 1
Final notification: Applicants notified in July
Applicants should submit the following:
1) Financial information
2) SAT
3) ACT
4) Class rank
5) GPA
6) Transcripts
7) FAFSA

Additional information: Applicant must demonstrate financial need. Funds are paid directly to the educational institution on behalf of the students.

EIN: 366146230

2936
Woodbury Foundation

c/o Christine M. Rhode
222 N. LaSalle St., 24th Fl.
Chicago, IL 60601-1003
Application address: c/o Dean of Admissions, Warren Wilson College, Swannanoa, NC 28778, tel.: (704) 298-3325

Foundation type: Independent foundation
Purpose: Scholarships to individuals for attendance at Warren Wilson College in Asheville, NC.
Financial data: Year ended 05/31/2012. Assets, $16,761,466 (M); Expenditures, $988,321; Total giving, $893,628. Scholarships—to individuals amount not specified.
Fields of interest: Higher education.
Type of support: Scholarships—to individuals; Support to graduates or students of specific schools.
Application information: Applications accepted.
Additional information: The scholarship is based on merit or need. Students requesting the scholarship must submit a biography.
EIN: 363715828

2937
Woodrow W. Woods Educational Trust

c/o JPMorgan Chase Bank, N.A.
10S Dearborn St.
Chicago, IL 60603-2300 (304) 234-4126
Application address: c/o JPMorgan Chase Bank, N.A., 1114 Market St., Wheeling, WV 26003-2906

Foundation type: Independent foundation
Purpose: Loans for higher education to seniors graduating from high schools in Harrison County, WV.
Financial data: Year ended 12/31/2012. Assets, $1,402,318 (M); Expenditures, $14,482; Total giving, $0; Loans to individuals, totaling $118,284.
Fields of interest: Higher education.
Type of support: Student loans—to individuals; Support to graduates or students of specific schools.
Application information: Applications accepted. Application form required.
Deadline(s): May 30
EIN: 546409374

2938
Youth Outreach Services, Inc.

2411 W. Congress Pkwy.
Chicago, IL 60612-3534 (773) 777-7112
Contact: Rick Velasquez, Exec. Dir.
FAX: (773) 777-7611; E-mail for Rick Velasquez: rickv@yos.org; tel. for Rick Velasquez: (773) 777-7112, ext. 7225; URL: http://www.yos.org

Foundation type: Public charity
Purpose: Assistance for low income youth of IL, with safe and caring homes or shelter, and help them develop the skills to become productive adults.
Publications: Annual report; Financial statement; Newsletter.
Financial data: Year ended 06/30/2011. Assets, $3,341,436 (M); Expenditures, $7,607,181; Total giving, $862,616; Grants to individuals, totaling $862,616.
Fields of interest: Young adults; Economically disadvantaged.
Type of support: Grants for special needs.
Application information: Contact the agency for eligibility determination.
EIN: 363297629

2939
The Louise Tumarkin Zazove Foundation, Inc.

6858 N. Kenneth Ave.
Lincolnwood, IL 60712-4705 (847) 674-4468
Contact: Earl Zazove, Pres.
E-mail: earl@ltzfoundation.org; URL: http://www.ltzfoundation.org/

Foundation type: Independent foundation
Purpose: Scholarships and related assistance to people with hearing loss for attendance at accredited non-profit schools within the U.S.
Financial data: Year ended 08/31/2012. Assets, $78,994 (M); Expenditures, $33,941; Total giving, $26,500; Grants to individuals, 9 grants totaling $26,500 (high: $4,500, low: $1,500).
Fields of interest: Deaf/hearing impaired.
Type of support: Scholarships—to individuals.
Application information: Applications accepted. Application form required. Application form available on the grantmaker's web site.
Deadline(s): May 26
Final notification: Applicants notified July 31
Applicants should submit the following:
1) Transcripts
2) Letter(s) of recommendation
Additional information: Application should also include documentation of the severity of the hearing loss (an audiogram or other verification by a qualified professional), first two pages of you and/or your parents' income tax form. See web site for additional guidelines.
EIN: 383658887

2940
Delyte K. Zearing and Robert I. Zearing Trust

606 S. Main St.
Princeton, IL 61356-2080 (815) 875-4444

Foundation type: Independent foundation
Purpose: Scholarships to students at Bureau County, IL, high schools to attend the University of Illinois at Urbana-Champaign for undergraduate or graduate studies.
Financial data: Year ended 12/31/2012. Assets, $1,037,132 (M); Expenditures, $104,972; Total

giving, $36,000; Grants to individuals, 17 grants totaling $36,000 (high: $4,000, low: $1,000).
Fields of interest: Higher education.
Type of support: Support to graduates or students of specific schools; Graduate support; Undergraduate support.
Application information: Application form required. Interview required.
Deadline(s): May 1
Additional information: Application should include three letters of support as well as a letter of acceptance from the University of Illinois at Urbana-Champaign.
Program description:
Delyte K. and Robert I. Zearing Scholarships: A minimum of two $4,000 scholarships are renewable annually for undergraduate or graduate studies provided that the recipient maintains a minimum GPA of 2.75 on the University of Illinois' four-point system during their enrollment and provides evidence of earning a minimum of 15 credit hours per semester. Financial need is not a factor in determining eligibility.
EIN: 366980732

2941
I.P. and Lola Zimmerly Educational Trust

c/o ECB & T
P.O. Box 400
Paris, IL 61944-0790 (217) 465-4154
Contact: John Carrington

Foundation type: Independent foundation
Purpose: Scholarships to individuals who are residents of Edgar county, IL, and are enrolled in institutions of higher learning.
Financial data: Year ended 05/31/2012. Assets, $211,577 (M); Expenditures, $13,064; Total giving, $9,500; Grants to individuals, 7 grants totaling $9,500 (high: $2,000, low: $500).
Fields of interest: College; University.
Type of support: Scholarships—to individuals.
Application information: Applications accepted. Application form required.
Deadline(s): May 15
Additional information: Applications available at Citizens National Bank.
EIN: 376314386

2942
Zonta International Foundation

1211 W. 22nd St., Ste. 900
Oak Brook, IL 60523-3384 (630) 928-1400
Contact: Maureen Powers, Dir., Progs. and Fdn. Admin.
FAX: (630) 928-1559; E-mail: zontafdtn@zonta.org; URL: http://www.zonta.org

Foundation type: Public charity
Purpose: Scholarships and awards to women around the globe overcoming gender barriers to careers in the traditionally male-dominated fields.
Publications: Application guidelines.
Financial data: Year ended 05/31/2012. Assets, $10,779,760 (M); Expenditures, $633,762; Total giving, $588,275; Grants to individuals, totaling $155,050.
Fields of interest: Science; Space/aviation; Engineering/technology; Women.
Type of support: Fellowships; Scholarships—to individuals; Awards/prizes; Doctoral support.

Application information: Applications accepted. Application form required. Application form available on the grantmaker's web site.

> *Deadline(s):* May for Jane M. Klausman Scholarship, Nov. for Amelia Earhart Fellowships
> *Final notification:* Recipients notified in Apr. for Amelia Earhart Fellowships, mid-Oct. for Jane M. Klausman Scholarship
> *Additional information:* Application should include recommendations. See web site for additional guidelines.

Program descriptions:

Amelia Earhart Fellowship Program: Fellowships of $10,000 are awarded to women of any nationality pursuing a Ph.D./doctoral degree who demonstrate a superior academic record in the field of aerospace-related sciences and aerospace-related engineering. The award is for Fellows around the globe, may be used at any university or college offering accredited post-graduate courses and degrees in these fields. Current fellows may apply to renew the Fellowship for a second year and will undergo the same application and evaluation procedures as first-time applicants.

Jane M. Klausman Women in Business Scholarship Program: The scholarship provides awards of $1,000 each for club recipients at the district level and twelve international scholarships in the amount of $5,000 each. The scholarship is awarded annually and may be used for tuition, books or living expenses at any university, college or institution offering accredited business courses and degrees. Applicants must be nominated by a local Zonta club.

Young Women in Public Affairs Award: The award honors young women of any nationality ages 16 to 19, living or studying in a Zonta district/region who demonstrate a commitment to leadership in public policy, government and volunteer organizations. District recipients receive $1,000 and ten international recipients are selected from the district/region recipients to receive awards of $4,000 each.
EIN: 363396932

2943
Harry R. & Gertrude Zweifel Trust
P.O. Box 584
Freeport, IL   61032   (815) 235-1212

Foundation type: Independent foundation
Purpose: Scholarships for postsecondary education to residents of Orangeville, IL, Stephenson County, IL, and Green County, WI.
Financial data: Year ended 12/31/2011. Assets, $324,442 (M); Expenditures, $28,918; Total giving, $14,250; Grants to individuals, 28 grants totaling $14,250 (high: $600, low: $150).
Fields of interest: College; Scholarships/financial aid.
Type of support: Undergraduate support.
Application information: Application form required.

> *Initial approach:* Letter
> *Deadline(s):* Aug. 1

EIN: 366063248

INDIANA

2944
The Joseph and Luella Abell Charitable Trust
P.O. Box 1001
Seymour, IN 47274-1001 (812) 522-3607
Contact: Brandon Hunsley

Foundation type: Independent foundation
Purpose: Scholarships to nursing school students or graduate students of the ministry who are residents of IN.
Financial data: Year ended 12/31/2012. Assets, $1,057,806 (M); Expenditures, $54,265; Total giving, $41,990.
Fields of interest: Nursing school/education; Theological school/education.
Type of support: Scholarships—to individuals; Graduate support.
Application information: Applications accepted. Application form required.
  Deadline(s): Apr. 1
  Applicants should submit the following:
    1) Financial information
    2) Transcripts
EIN: 326009792

2945
Adams County Community Foundation
102 N. 2nd St.
Decatur, IN 46733-1660 (260) 724-3939
Contact: Coni Mayer, Exec. Dir.
FAX: (260) 724-2299;
E-mail: accfoundation@earthlink.net; URL: http://www.adamscountyfoundation.org

Foundation type: Community foundation
Purpose: Scholarships to residents of Adams County, IN, for undergraduate education.
Publications: Annual report.
Financial data: Year ended 12/31/2012. Assets, $13,044,555 (M); Expenditures, $692,664; Total giving, $391,983; Grants to individuals, 319 grants totaling $126,183.
Fields of interest: Higher education.
Type of support: Undergraduate support.
Application information: Application form required.
  Initial approach: Application
  Send request by: Mail
  Copies of proposal: 10
  Deadline(s): 1st Thurs. of June
  Additional information: Each scholarship has its own unique set of eligibility criteria. Application forms available at the foundation web site or each of the high school's web sites.
EIN: 351834664

2946
AIDS Task Force of LaPorte & Porter Counties, Inc.
5490 Broadway, Ste. L3
Merrillville, IN 46410-1663 (219) 985-6170
Contact: Ramone Morton, Pres.
FAX: (219) 985-6097; URL: http://www.thealivenessprojectnwi.org/

Foundation type: Public charity
Purpose: Support and financial assistance to individuals of LaPorte and Porter counties, IN, who are infected and affected by HIV, through education and prevention programs.
Financial data: Year ended 12/31/2011. Assets, $237,355 (M); Expenditures, $1,031,279; Total giving, $275,920; Grants to individuals, totaling $275,920.
Fields of interest: Human services; AIDS, people with.
Type of support: Grants for special needs.
Application information: Applications accepted.
  Additional information: Applicants must produce diagnosis of HIV and income verification. All clients must be verified on an annual basis. Some assistance require an application process.
EIN: 351785024

2947
Allen County Education Partnership, Inc.
(formerly Allen County Local Education Fund, Inc.)
709 Clay St., Ste. 101
Fort Wayne, IN 46802-2019 (260) 423-6447
Contact: Brian White, Exec. Dir.
FAX: (260) 426-8989;
E-mail: abouteducation@abouteducation.org;
E-mail For Brian White:
bwhite@abouteducation.org; URL: http://www.abouteducation.org

Foundation type: Public charity
Purpose: Awards to teachers throughout Allen County, IN to promote, encourage, and reward excellence in schools.
Publications: Application guidelines; Annual report; Financial statement; Grants list; Informational brochure; Newsletter.
Financial data: Year ended 06/30/2013. Assets, $284,560 (M); Expenditures, $396,105.
Type of support: Awards/prizes.
Application information: Applications accepted.
  Initial approach: Telephone
  Additional information: The awards are not offered this year. New awards process will be available in 2013-2014. See web site for updates on the program.
EIN: 351823402

2948
Alpha Chi Omega Foundation, Inc.
5939 Castle Creek Pkwy. N. Dr.
Indianapolis, IN 46250-4343 (317) 579-5050
Contact: Cheri O'Neill, Exec. Dir.
FAX: (317) 579-5051;
E-mail: foundation@alphachiomega.org; E-mail for Cheri O'Neill: coneill@alphachiomega.org;
URL: https://www.alphachiomega.org/axo-foundation/#.UzLf_6hdWSo

Foundation type: Public charity
Purpose: Scholarships and grants to collegiate and alumnae members of Alpha Chi Omega.
Publications: Application guidelines; Annual report; Informational brochure; Newsletter.
Financial data: Year ended 07/31/2012. Assets, $15,758,173 (M); Expenditures, $2,126,059; Total giving, $810,237; Grants to individuals, 202 grants totaling $143,637.
Fields of interest: Students, sororities/fraternities.
Type of support: Fellowships; Scholarships—to individuals; Student loans—to individuals.
Application information: Application form required.
  Deadline(s): Oct. 15 for Educational Assistance Grants; None for other programs
EIN: 310949882

2949
Alpha Epsilon Pi Foundation, Inc.
8815 Wesleyan Rd.
Indianapolis, IN 46268 (240) 235-5087
E-mail: jfeldman@aepi.org; URL: http://www.aepi.org/?page=Foundation

Foundation type: Public charity
Purpose: Educational and scholastic assistance to members of Alpha Epsilon Pi and their families in the U.S. and Canada.
Publications: Informational brochure.
Financial data: Year ended 05/31/2012. Assets, $2,287,904 (M); Expenditures, $847,783; Total giving, $337,507; Grants to individuals, totaling $337,507.
Fields of interest: Students, sororities/fraternities.
Type of support: Fellowships; Internship funds; Grants to individuals; Scholarships—to individuals.
Application information: Applications accepted.
  Deadline(s): Apr. 25 for scholarships
  Final notification: Recipients notified May 1
  Additional information: Eligibility is determined based on educational need. See web site for additional application information and guidelines.
EIN: 136141078

2950
Alpha Gamma Delta Foundation, Inc.
8710 N. Meridian St.
Indianapolis, IN 46260-5389 (317) 663-4242
Contact: Julie Waitman Cretin, Exec. Dir.
FAX: (317) 663-4244;
E-mail: info@alphagammadelta.org; URL: http://www.alphagammadelta.org/agdfoundation

Foundation type: Public charity
Purpose: Scholarships to members of Alpha Gamma Delta who are full-time students and have completed at least one year of college.
Financial data: Year ended 05/31/2012. Assets, $6,511,145 (M); Expenditures, $1,250,911; Total giving, $671,343; Grants to individuals, totaling $108,750.
Type of support: Graduate support; Undergraduate support.
Application information: Applications accepted. Application form required. Application form available on the grantmaker's web site.
  Deadline(s): Mar. 1
  Final notification: Applicants notified by the end of July
  Applicants should submit the following:
    1) Letter(s) of recommendation
    2) Transcripts
    3) Essay
EIN: 352057322

2951
Alpha Kappa Psi Foundation, Inc.
7801 E. 88th St.
Indianapolis, IN 46256-1233 (317) 872-1553
FAX: (317) 872-1567;
E-mail: foundation@akpsi.org; URL: http://www.akpsi.org/?page=foundation

Foundation type: Public charity
Purpose: Scholarships and grants to members of Alpha Kappa Psi fraternity for undergraduate and graduate students, and supports educational programs that develop leadership and professional development skills.
Publications: Application guidelines.
Financial data: Year ended 06/30/2011. Assets, $2,215,604 (M); Expenditures, $269,519; Total

giving, $72,114; Grants to individuals, 119 grants totaling $70,596.

Fields of interest: Higher education; Students, sororities/fraternities.

Type of support: Grants to individuals; Scholarships—to individuals.

Application information: Applications accepted. Application form available on the grantmaker's web site.

Initial approach: Application
Send request by: Online
Deadline(s): Mar. 10 for Academy, varies for Scholarships
Final notification: Applicants notified by Mar. 30 for Academy
Additional information: See web site for additional guidelines for scholarships and academy.

Program descriptions:

Academy: This program provides an all-expense paid trip for fraternity members to a custom-designed, hands-on leadership experienced, intended to make even the best of fraternity members more impactful, value-based leaders. Participants are given opportunities to share ideas, explore issues, and offer insights to others, an integrated curriculum in which diverse teaching techniques will meet the needs and styles of all participants, and an interactive experience in which each participant is not only a learner, but also a teacher. Eligible applicants must have been a member of the fraternity for at least one year prior to membership, and must have at least a 3.0 cumulative GPA.

Scholarships: The foundation provides annual scholarships, of which some are available to all fraternity members, and others specifically targeted to those majoring in specific fields, such as accounting or healthcare management. Scholarships generally range from $500 to $2,500. Applicants should be full-time students in good standing with both their university and their sorority chapter, though specific scholarships may have additional requirements.

EIN: 356016131

2952

Alpha Tau Omega Foundation, Inc.

32 E. Washington St., Ste. 1350
Indianapolis, IN 46204-3516 (317) 472-0935
Contact: Terry Turman, Pres. and C.E.O.
FAX: (317) 472-0945;
E-mail: foundation@atofoundation.org; Toll-free tel.: (800) 508-5131E-Mail for Terry Turman : tturman@atofoundation.orgTel. for Terry Turman : (317)-472-0935 ext. 205; URL: http://www.ato.org/ATOFoundation.aspx

Foundation type: Public charity

Purpose: Graduate and undergraduate scholarships to members of Alpha Tau Omega Fraternity.

Publications: Annual report; Grants list; Informational brochure; Newsletter; Occasional report.

Financial data: Year ended 12/31/2011. Assets, $10,592,767 (M); Expenditures, $1,182,285; Total giving, $648,220; Grants to individuals, totaling $122,122.

Fields of interest: Print publishing; Law school/education; Students, sororities/fraternities.

Type of support: Internship funds; Support to graduates or students of specific schools; Graduate support; Undergraduate support.

Application information: Applications accepted. Application form required. Application form available on the grantmaker's web site.

Send request by: Mail
Deadline(s): Jan. 31 for Richard A. Ports Scholarship, Mar. 4 for National Scholarship and Mar. 26 for Steven Haisley Scholarship
Applicants should submit the following:
  1) Letter(s) of recommendation
  2) Transcripts
Additional information: Applicant must be an initiated member of Alpha Tau Omega. See web site for complete program information.

Program descriptions:

National Scholarships: Scholarships are awarded on the following scale: 40 percent academic achievements, 30 percent demonstrated leadership in ATO, and 30 percent demonstrated leadership on campus and in the community. Applicants must be ATO members in good standing and have a minimum cumulative GPA of 3.5 on a 4.0 scale.

Richard A. Ports Scholarship: This scholarship recognizes an ATO junior with a demonstrated interest in public affairs/political science with an internship in Washington, D.C., when available. The foundation provides a $150 per week stipend, travel to and from Washington, D.C., and housing during the entire internship. Internships last six to eight weeks during the summer or fall semesters.

Stephen Haisley Scholarship: A $1,000 scholarship is available to initiated or pledge members of the Delta Lambda chapter of Alpha Tau Omega. Candidates should excel in academic achievement, extracurricular activities, and individual character.

EIN: 237154214

2953

Amburn Memorial Scholarship Fund

200 E. Jackson St.
Muncie, IN 47305 (317) 844-2399
Contact: Laura Moorman
Application Address: FIRST MERCHANTS TRUST CO.

Foundation type: Independent foundation

Purpose: Scholarships to graduating high school seniors who are residents of Delaware County, IN. Preference is given to elementary education majors.

Financial data: Year ended 12/31/2012. Assets, $426,113 (M); Expenditures, $29,423; Total giving, $22,500; Grants to individuals, 8 grants totaling $22,500 (high: $3,000, low: $1,500).

Fields of interest: Elementary school/education; Teacher school/education.

Type of support: Scholarships—to individuals; Undergraduate support.

Application information: Applications accepted. Application form required.

Deadline(s): Mar. 31
Additional information: Applicants should submit forms to their respective schools.

EIN: 356051256

2954

The American Legion

P.O. Box 1055
700 N. Pennsylvania St.
Indianapolis, IN 46206-1055 (317) 630-1220
FAX: (317) 630-1223; URL: http://www.legion.org/

Foundation type: Public charity

Purpose: Scholarships and awards to children of legion members in pursuit of higher education.

Publications: Application guidelines; Informational brochure; Newsletter; Occasional report.

Financial data: Year ended 12/31/2011. Assets, $119,811,334 (M); Expenditures, $64,384,186; Total giving, $1,486,432; Grants to individuals,

totaling $1,456,705. Subtotal for grants for special needs: 2,744 grants totaling $822,456. Subtotal for scholarships—to individuals: 223 grants totaling $468,269. Subtotal for in-kind gifts: 856 grants totaling $212,626.

Fields of interest: Higher education; Nursing school/education.

Type of support: Scholarships—to individuals.

Application information: Applications accepted. Application form required. Application form available on the grantmaker's web site.

Initial approach: Application
Deadline(s): Varies
Additional information: See web site for additional guidelines.

Program descriptions:

American Legion Baseball Scholarship: This program awards scholarships to players who participate in an American Legion-affiliated baseball team. One outstanding applicant will be awarded a $5,000 scholarship; eight additional players will receive a $2,500 scholarship. Funds can be used toward attendance costs to a university or college.

American Legion Legacy Scholarship: This program works to ensure that children of U.S. servicemembers who died on or around Sept.11, 2001 receive equal opportunities in their pursuit of higher learning. Eligible applicants include biological or legally-adopted children, or a child of a spouse by a prior marriage, of an U.S Armed Service member who died on or after Sept.11, 2001, and who are high school seniors or high school graduates.

Eagle Scout of the Year: Each year, the legion awards the Eagle Scout of the Year (chosen by the Boy Scouts of America) a $10,000 scholarship, while the three runners-up to the award receive a $2,500 scholarship.

National High School Oratorical Contest: The organization provides scholarships each year to outstanding participants in its National High School Oratorical Contest. This program presents participants with an academic speaking challenge that teaches important leadership qualities, the history of U.S. law, the ability to think and speak clearly, and an understanding of the duties, responsibilities, rights, and privileges of American citizenship. The first-place winner receives $18,000, the second-place winner receives $16,000, and the third-place winner receives $14,000. Each individual state winner certified into and participating in the first round of the national contest receives a $1,500 scholarship, while each first-round winner who advances but does not qualify for the finals receives an additional $1,500 scholarship. Eligible participants must be citizens of or lawful permanent residents of the U.S., be 20 years of age or younger, and be presently enrolled in a high school or junior high school (including public, parochial, military, private, or home school).

Samsung American Legion Scholarship: Awarded in conjunction with Samsung, the legion annually awards up to $300,000 in scholarships to nearly one hundred Boys' State and Girls' State participants who are direct descendents of a veteran eligible for legion membership. Eligible applicants include high school juniors who are a direct descent (i.e., child, grandchild, great-grandchild, or legally adopted child) of a U.S. veteran who served during a period of war and is a delegate to a Boys' State or Girls' State program.

The Eight and Forty Lung and Respiratory Disease Nursing Scholarship Fund: This scholarship works to assist registered nurses with advanced preparation for positions in supervision, administration, or teaching. Eligible applicants must have a current registered nurse license and must have employment prospects in specific positions in

hospitals, clinics, or other health departments upon completion of their education, and the position must have a full-time and direct relationship to pediatric lung and respiratory control. Scholarship awards are for $3,000 each.
EIN: 350144250

2955
The American Legion September 11 Memorial Scholarship Trust Fund
P. O. Box 1055
Indianapolis, IN   46206-1055   (317) 630-1200

Foundation type: Public charity
Purpose: College scholarships to assist children of military, national guards, or reserve personnel killed while on active duty on or after Sept. 11.
Financial data: Year ended 12/31/2012. Assets, $7,642,093 (M); Expenditures, $71,286; Total giving, $45,950.
Fields of interest: Higher education; Disasters, 9/11/01; Military/veterans' organizations.
Type of support: Scholarships—to individuals.
Application information: Applications not accepted.
  Additional information: Unsolicited requests for funds not considered or acknowledged.
EIN: 421553035

2956
Anna Needs Neuroblastoma Answers
(also known as Anna Fund)
9651 Bellflower Dr.
Zionsville, IN   46077-8121   (317) 823-9829
Contact: Shannon Conner, Pres.
E-mail: stevehealey@tds.net; URL: http://annafund.com

Foundation type: Public charity
Purpose: Research grants for the study and cure of neuroblastoma, as well as financial assistance to neuroblastoma families for expenses such as rent and utilities.
Financial data: Year ended 12/31/2011. Assets, $64,028 (M); Expenditures, $60,639; Total giving, $59,380.
Fields of interest: Cancer research.
Type of support: Research; Grants for special needs.
Application information:
  Initial approach: Letter
  Additional information: Contact foundation for eligibility criteria.
EIN: 043713218

2957
Area IV Agency on Aging and Community Action Programs, Inc.
660 N. 36th St.
Lafayette, IN   47903-4727   (765) 447-7683
Contact: Elva James, Exec. Dir.
FAX: (765) 447-6862; URL: http://www.areaivagency.org

Foundation type: Public charity
Purpose: Emergency and financial assistance to disabled, elderly, and disadvantaged individuals of mid-northwestern Indiana, IN with housing, food, energy, transportation and other needs.
Financial data: Year ended 12/31/2011. Assets, $1,740,469 (M); Expenditures, $10,482,839; Total giving, $5,669,936; Grants to individuals, totaling $4,856,376.

Fields of interest: Housing/shelter; Aging; Disabilities, people with; Economically disadvantaged.
Type of support: Emergency funds; In-kind gifts; Grants for special needs.
Application information: Program areas include Benton, Carroll, Clinton, Fountain, Montgomery, Tippecanoe and White counties.
EIN: 351329223

2958
Cecil Armstrong Foundation
114 E. Market St.
Warsaw, IN   46581-1387

Foundation type: Independent foundation
Purpose: Scholarships to Kosciusko County, IN, students to improve skills or advance education by attending any properly accredited or certified educational program in IN.
Financial data: Year ended 12/31/2012. Assets, $199,173 (M); Expenditures, $11,867; Total giving, $9,000; Grants to individuals, 18 grants totaling $9,000 (high: $500, low: $500).
Fields of interest: Vocational education; Health sciences school/education.
Type of support: Technical education support; Undergraduate support.
Application information: Application form required.
  Deadline(s): Apr. 1
  Applicants should submit the following:
    1) Letter(s) of recommendation
    2) Transcripts
  Additional information: Applicant should also include list of activities and attendance record. Applications available from local schools and Lake City Bank.
Program description:
  Scholarship Program: Grants for tuition, housing, and school expenses are awarded to students attending colleges, universities, vocational schools, rehabilitation training, or any properly accredited course in IN. For college-bound applicants, SAT, ACT, PSAT, or equivalent test scores will be required. No specific rank in class is required. For vocational, rehabilitation, or any other type of training, sufficient evidence of skills and ability to pursue such a course of study is required. Applicants applying for assistance to continue a course in which they are already enrolled must submit a transcript of grades and present status from the institution or program they are attending. Recipients are chosen by a five-member awards committee, composed of people from the community. Scholarships are renewable.
EIN: 237128298

2959
Arsenal Technical High School Alumni Association, Inc.
1500 E. Michigan St.
P. O. Box 1162
Indianapolis, IN   46201-3079   (317) 693-5459
Contact: Ronald Jackson, Pres.
URL: http://www.athsalumniassociation.org/

Foundation type: Public charity
Purpose: Scholarships and grants to Arsenal Technical High School, IN graduating seniors pursuing higher education.
Financial data: Year ended 12/31/2012. Assets, $603,427 (M); Expenditures, $98,800; Total giving, $73,106; Grants to individuals, totaling $73,106.
Fields of interest: Higher education.

Type of support: Scholarships—to individuals; Support to graduates or students of specific schools.
Application information: Applications accepted. Application form required. Interview required.
  Additional information: Selection is based on student's grades and extracurricular activities.
EIN: 311242602

2960
Arts Council of Indianapolis, Inc.
20 N. Meridian St., Ste. 500
Indianapolis, IN   46204-3040   (317) 631-3301
Contact: Gregory Charleston, Pres.
FAX: (317) 624-2559;
E-mail: indyarts@indyarts.org; URL: http://www.indyarts.org

Foundation type: Public charity
Purpose: Fellowships to individual artists and arts administrators in IN.
Publications: Application guidelines; Annual report; Informational brochure; Newsletter.
Financial data: Year ended 12/31/2011. Assets, $8,909,700 (M); Expenditures, $3,555,592; Total giving, $2,025,699; Grants to individuals, totaling $731,702.
Fields of interest: Arts.
Type of support: Fellowships.
Application information: Application form required.
  Initial approach: Telephone or e-mail
  Deadline(s): July 22 for Beckmann, Jr. Fellowship
  Final notification: Recipients notified late Aug.
Program descriptions:
  Bechmann Emerging Artist Fellowship Program: Awards of two $3,500 fellowships each year to qualified and talented artists in music, dance, theatre, literature, media and/or the visual arts. The program seeks to introduce and provide experiences, connections, and relationships with professional arts institutions and professional artists in central Indiana.
  Creative Renewal Arts Fellowships Program for Professional Individual Artists and Arts Administrators: Awards of $10,000 to each of 40 selected artists and arts administrators. Applicants must reside at three years of consecutive residence in one of the following counties, Marion, Boone, Hamilton, Hendricks, Hancock, Johnson, or Shelby counties. At least ten years of experience in the arts and at least three years in which the applicant's primary source of income was employed in the arts and primary source of income was work in dance, theatre, media arts, music, literature, visual arts or multidisciplinary art forms.
EIN: 311225893

2961
Frank and Margaret Arvin Family Trust
P.O. Box 1008
Jasper, IN   47547-1008

Foundation type: Operating foundation
Purpose: Scholarships to residents of Montgomery, IN for continuing education at institutions of higher learning.
Financial data: Year ended 12/31/2011. Assets, $300,537 (M); Expenditures, $13,289; Total giving, $8,540; Grants to individuals, 9 grants totaling $8,540 (high: $1,000, low: $840).
Type of support: Undergraduate support.
Application information:
  Initial approach: Letter
EIN: 356608360

2962
Association for Research on Non-Profit Organizations & Voluntary Action

(also known as ARNOVA)
550 W. N. St., Ste. 301
Indianapolis, IN   46202-3491   (317) 684-2120
Contact: Shariq Siddiqui, Exec. Dir.
FAX: (317) 684-2128;
E-mail: ssiddiqui@arnova.org; URL: http://
www.arnova.org

Foundation type: Public charity
Purpose: Scholarships and awards to individuals in the U.S. and abroad to participate at the ARNOVA conference.
Publications: Application guidelines.
Financial data: Year ended 06/30/2012. Assets, $1,221,623 (M); Expenditures, $614,517.
Type of support: Fellowships; Travel awards; Scholarships—to individuals; Awards/prizes; Doctoral support.
Application information: Applications accepted. Application form required.
> *Send request by:* E-mail
> *Deadline(s):* Sept. 9 for Emerging Scholar Awards, and Scholarship and Travel Grant, Sept. 19 for Doctoral Student Fellowship and Seminar
> *Additional information:* See web site for additional guidelines.

Program descriptions:
Doctoral Student Fellowship and Seminar: The fellowship award provides recipients with $1,000 as well as free registration to offset the cost of travel and lodging at the seminar and ARNOVA conference. Applicants must have approved dissertation proposals, with preference given to applicants in the early to mid-stages of their research. Fellows may come from any institution and any academic discipline. The research must be focused on a topic related to philanthropy, voluntary action, civil society and nonprofit sector.

Emerging Scholar Awards: The award is designed to help develop the next generation of scholars, foster dissemination of research into practice, and enhance practitioner involvement in the creation of usable knowledge. The program provides funds to enable students and new scholars (those in their first year of appointment in academic or practice positions) to attend the association's annual conference.

Scholarship and Travel Grant: Scholarship support to assist individuals to attend the annual conference for people with limited means to participate in this important event. Scholarships include remission of conference registration fees (from $294 to $145) and a travel stipend of $250. All travel stipends will be paid at the conference. Priority will be given to presenters at the annual conference, first-time attendees, and individuals who have not received a scholarship award since 2009. Applications from under-represented minority students and faculty are encouraged to apply; also U.S. and international doctoral students studying philanthropy, civil society, nonprofit organizations, and related topics; unemployed ARNOVA members; and practitioners in nonprofit organizations.
EIN: 237378021

2963
Weisell Baber Foundation

132 E. Main St.
P.O. Box 162
Peru, IN   46970   (765) 473-7526
Contact: Eric R. Baber, Mgr.

Foundation type: Independent foundation
Purpose: Student loans to graduates of Miami County high schools, IN for postsecondary education.
Financial data: Year ended 12/31/2012. Assets, $2,768,360 (M); Expenditures, $398,780; Total giving, $19,500; Grants to individuals, 10 grants totaling $19,500 (high: $3,000, low: $1,500).
Fields of interest: Higher education.
Type of support: Student loans—to individuals; Support to graduates or students of specific schools; Undergraduate support.
Application information: Applications accepted. Interview required.
> *Deadline(s):* None
> *Additional information:* Loans are granted to individuals for one year. Applicants must reapply for a loan for subsequent years.
EIN: 356024561

2964
Ball State University Foundation

2800 W. Bethel Ave.
Alumni Ctr., Rm 230
Muncie, IN   47304-2619   (765) 285-8312
Contact: Cheri' E. O'Neill, Pres. and C.E.O.
FAX: (765) 285-7060; E-mail: foundation@bsu.edu; Toll-Free Tel.: (888) 235-0058; E-mail for Cheri' E. O'Neill: Ceoneill@bsu.edu; URL: http://www.bsu.edu/bsufoundation/

Foundation type: Public charity
Purpose: Scholarships to students of Ball State University, IN to further their educational goals.
Publications: Annual report; Newsletter.
Financial data: Year ended 06/30/2012. Assets, $197,238,328 (M); Expenditures, $17,524,055; Total giving, $9,644,097.
Fields of interest: Higher education.
Type of support: Support to graduates or students of specific schools.
Application information: Unsolicited requests for funds not considered or acknowledged.
EIN: 356024566

2965
Joseph C. Belden Foundation

2200 U.S. Hwy. 27 S.
Richmond, IN   47374-7279   (765) 983-5232
Contact: Renee Longworth

Foundation type: Independent foundation
Purpose: Undergraduate scholarships to children of employees of Belden, Inc., Richmond, IN, Indianapolis, IN, and Monticello, KY.
Financial data: Year ended 06/30/2012. Assets, $1,310,577 (M); Expenditures, $112,031; Total giving, $83,054; Grants to individuals, 37 grants totaling $83,054.
Fields of interest: Higher education.
Type of support: Employee-related scholarships.
Application information: Applications accepted. Application form required.
> *Deadline(s):* Dec. 31 for applications, Feb. 1 for additional materials
> *Additional information:* Application should include biographical information and transcripts.
EIN: 363781852

2966
Benton Community Foundation

P.O. Box 351
Fowler, IN   47944-0351   (765) 884-8022
Contact: Ashley Bice, Exec. Dir.
FAX: (765) 884-8023; E-mail: info@bentoncf.org; Additional e-mail: ashley@bentoncf.org; URL: http://www.bentoncf.org

Foundation type: Community foundation
Purpose: Scholarships to residents of Benton County, IN for postsecondary education.
Publications: Application guidelines; Annual report; Grants list; Informational brochure; Newsletter.
Financial data: Year ended 12/31/2012. Assets, $4,757,089 (M); Expenditures, $316,604; Total giving, $193,199; Grants to individuals, 30 grants totaling $75,650.
Fields of interest: Vocational education, post-secondary; Higher education.
Type of support: Scholarships—to individuals; Support to graduates or students of specific schools; Undergraduate support.
Application information: Applications accepted. Application form required. Application form available on the grantmaker's web site.
> *Deadline(s):* Late Jan.
> *Applicants should submit the following:*
> 1) Essay
> 2) Financial information
> 3) SAT
> 4) Letter(s) of recommendation
> 5) Transcripts
> *Additional information:* See web site for a complete listing of scholarships.

Program description:
Scholarships: The foundation administers several scholarships. Application procedures and selection criteria vary for each of the scholarships, though many of the funds use one consolidated application. See web site for additional application information and selection procedures.
EIN: 260074023

2967
Blackford County Community Foundation, Inc.

121 N. High St.
P.O. Box 327
Hartford City, IN   47348-0327   (765) 348-3411
Contact: Patricia D. Poulson, Exec. Dir.
FAX: (765) 348-4945;
E-mail: foundation@blackfordcounty.org; Additional e-mail: ppoulson@blackfordcounty.org;
URL: http://www.blackfordcofoundation.org

Foundation type: Community foundation
Purpose: Scholarships to graduating seniors of Blackford High School, Blackford county, IN for continuing their education at accredited institutions of higher learning.
Publications: Application guidelines; Annual report; Financial statement; Grants list; Informational brochure; Newsletter; IRS Form 990 or 990-PF printed copy available upon request.
Financial data: Year ended 12/31/2011. Assets, $5,116,200 (M); Expenditures, $650,387; Total giving, $327,646; Grants to individuals, 157 grants totaling $119,888.
Fields of interest: Higher education.
Type of support: Support to graduates or students of specific schools.
Application information: Applications accepted. Application form required.
> *Deadline(s):* Varies
> *Applicants should submit the following:*
> 1) Financial information

2) Class rank
3) GPA
Additional information: Applications can be obtained from the guidance office. See web site for additional information.
EIN: 351772356

2968
F. Kelsay Blair Scholarship Trust
P.O. Box 8
Fairmount, IN 46928-0008 (765) 948-4330
Contact: David Crouse

Foundation type: Independent foundation
Purpose: Scholarships to high school students in Fairmount Township, IN, for use in obtaining a bachelor's degree at an accredited institution.
Financial data: Year ended 12/31/2011. Assets, $488,102 (M); Expenditures, $25,366; Total giving, $23,742; Grants to individuals, 18 grants totaling $23,742 (high: $1,319, low: $1,319).
Type of support: Undergraduate support.
Application information: Applications accepted.
Deadline(s): None
EIN: 356532077

2969
Lula Mae Blair Scholarship Trust
P.O. Box 8
Fairmount, IN 46928-0008 (765) 948-4330
Contact: David Crouse

Foundation type: Independent foundation
Purpose: Scholarships to high school students residing in Fairmount Township, IN, for use in obtaining a bachelor's degree from an accredited institution.
Financial data: Year ended 12/31/2011. Assets, $327,780 (M); Expenditures, $17,060; Total giving, $15,882; Grants to individuals, 8 grants totaling $15,888 (high: $1,986, low: $1,986).
Type of support: Undergraduate support.
Application information: Applications accepted. Application form not required.
Deadline(s): None
Additional information: Contact trust for current application guidelines.
EIN: 356532078

2970
The Blue River Community Foundation, Inc.
(formerly The Blue River Foundation, Inc.)
54 W. Bdwy. St., Ste. 1
P.O. Box 808
Shelbyville, IN 46176-1267 (317) 392-7955
Contact: For grant applications: Lynne Ensminger, Prog. Admin.
FAX: (317) 392-4545;
E-mail: brf@blueriverfoundation.com; URL: http://www.blueriverfoundation.com

Foundation type: Community foundation
Purpose: Scholarships to financially needy residents of Shelby County, IN.
Publications: Application guidelines; Annual report; Financial statement; Informational brochure.
Financial data: Year ended 12/31/2012. Assets, $25,717,172 (M); Expenditures, $1,266,028; Total giving, $569,635; Grants to individuals, 92 grants totaling $143,612.
Fields of interest: Higher education; Scholarships/financial aid.
Type of support: Scholarships—to individuals; Undergraduate support.

Application information: Applications accepted. Application form required. Application form available on the grantmaker's web site.
Deadline(s): Jan.
Applicants should submit the following:
1) Transcripts
2) SAT
3) Letter(s) of recommendation
4) GPA
5) Financial information
6) Essay
7) ACT
Additional information: Interviews required for some scholarships. See web site for complete program information.
Program description:
Scholarships: The foundation is committed to helping students in the local communities pursue and complete higher education degrees. The foundation's strategy is to grow and create endowment funds that provide renewable scholarships significant enough to help students achieve degree attainment. The scholarship program currently includes over 70 scholarship funds. See web site for additional information.
EIN: 351756331

2971
James S. Boonshot Memorial Scholarship Trust
c/o GAFA
P.O. Box 1008
Jasper, IN 47547-0810 (812) 482-1314
Contact: Janet Esser

Foundation type: Independent foundation
Purpose: Scholarships for graduates of Pike Central High School, IN, for undergraduate and graduate education.
Financial data: Year ended 12/31/2012. Assets, $1,125,070 (M); Expenditures, $41,868; Total giving, $28,675.
Fields of interest: Higher education.
Type of support: Support to graduates or students of specific schools; Graduate support; Undergraduate support.
Application information: Application form required.
Deadline(s): Apr. 15
Applicants should submit the following:
1) Letter(s) of recommendation
2) Transcripts
3) SAT
4) Photograph
5) Class rank
Additional information: Application should also include a brief letter to Pres. of Citizen's State Bank stating your desire for the scholarship, name of university and career choice.
EIN: 356075332

2972
Bowen Foundation, Inc.
8239 Clearwater Pointe
Indianapolis, IN 46240-4916

Foundation type: Independent foundation
Purpose: Scholarships to individuals who reside in Marion county, IN, and attend vocational/technical schools.
Financial data: Year ended 12/31/2011. Assets, $2,140,413 (M); Expenditures, $170,495; Total giving, $148,450.
Type of support: Scholarships—to individuals.
Application information: Applications not accepted.
EIN: 351906672

2973
Brookville Foundation
919 Main St.
Brookville, IN 47012-1429 (765) 647-4031
Contact: Donald M. Jobe, Pres.

Foundation type: Independent foundation
Purpose: Scholarships to residents of Franklin County, IN for continuing education at institutions of higher learning.
Financial data: Year ended 10/31/2013. Assets, $1,084,381 (M); Expenditures, $57,632; Total giving, $50,554; Grants to individuals, 8 grants totaling $4,868 (high: $1,800, low: $302).
Fields of interest: Higher education.
Type of support: Scholarships—to individuals; Support to graduates or students of specific schools.
Application information: Applications accepted. Application form required.
Copies of proposal: 7
Deadline(s): Sept. 1
Applicants should submit the following:
1) Letter(s) of recommendation
2) Transcripts
3) Financial information
Additional information: Applicant must demonstrate financial need.
EIN: 237130825

2974
Brown County Community Foundation, Inc.
91 W. Mound St. Unit 4
P.O. Box 191
Nashville, IN 47448 (812) 988-4882
Contact: Judy Bowling, Office and Financial Mgr.
FAX: (812) 988-0299; E-mail: jenise@bccfin.org;
URL: http://www.bccfin.org/

Foundation type: Community foundation
Purpose: Scholarships to individuals in the Brown County, IN area.
Publications: Application guidelines; Annual report; Financial statement; Informational brochure (including application guidelines); Newsletter.
Financial data: Year ended 12/31/2012. Assets, $8,455,132 (M); Expenditures, $769,143; Total giving, $565,256; Grants to individuals, 250 grants totaling $28,720.
Fields of interest: Higher education.
Type of support: Camperships; Scholarships—to individuals; Support to graduates or students of specific schools; Awards/prizes; Grants for special needs.
Application information: Applications accepted. Application form required. Application form available on the grantmaker's web site.
Initial approach: Letter, telephone or e-mail
Send request by: E-mail preferred
Copies of proposal: 1
Deadline(s): Jan.
Applicants should submit the following:
1) ACT
2) Essay
3) GPA
4) Letter(s) of recommendation
5) SAT
6) Transcripts
Additional information: Individuals must attend a mandatory meeting to receive scholarship application.
EIN: 351960379

2975
Selma McKrill Brown Educational Trust
114 E. Market St.
Warsaw, IN 46580-1387

Foundation type: Independent foundation
Purpose: Scholarships to U.S. citizen residents of Kosciusko County, IN, who are active church members.
Financial data: Year ended 12/31/2012. Assets, $578,273 (M); Expenditures, $31,017; Total giving, $24,000; Grants to individuals, 57 grants totaling $24,000 (high: $500, low: -$1,000).
Fields of interest: Religion.
Type of support: Scholarships—to individuals.
Application information: Applications accepted. Application form required.
> *Deadline(s):* Apr. 1
> *Applicants should submit the following:*
> 1) Photograph
> 2) Transcripts
> *Additional information:* Application should also include a letter from high school principal and pastor of church.
EIN: 356455007

2976
Marion D. Brown Scholarship Trust
c/o Old National Trust Company
P.O. Box 207
Evansville, IN 47702-0207

Foundation type: Independent foundation
Purpose: Scholarships to students of high schools in Vanderburgh County, IN.
Financial data: Year ended 12/31/2012. Assets, $552,449 (M); Expenditures, $30,807; Total giving, $21,500.
Type of support: Support to graduates or students of specific schools; Undergraduate support.
Application information: Students apply for aid at their respective school's financial aid office during the school year, and are then recommended by the institution for the award.
EIN: 356050689

2977
Bobby Buerger Scholarship Fund
c/o Mainsource Bank
P.O. Box 87
Greensburg, IN 47240 (812) 663-4774
Application address: c/o Supt., Greensburg Community Schools, Greensburg, IN 47240

Foundation type: Independent foundation
Purpose: Scholarships to graduating seniors of Greensburg Community High School, IN.
Financial data: Year ended 12/31/2012. Assets, $680,145 (M); Expenditures, $28,099; Total giving, $18,000; Grants to individuals, 12 grants totaling $18,000 (high: $1,500, low: $1,500).
Type of support: Support to graduates or students of specific schools; Undergraduate support.
Application information: Applications accepted. Application form required.
> *Deadline(s):* May 1
> *Applicants should submit the following:*
> 1) FAF
> 2) GPA
> 3) Class rank
> *Additional information:* Application should also include a personal statement and a financial statement.
EIN: 356415393

2978
Carroll-Wyatt Testamentary Education Trust
6576 W. State Rd., Ste. 65
Petersburg, IN 47567 (812) 354-8478
Contact: Michael Malotte
Application address: 1810 E., State Rd., Ste. 56, Petersburg, IN 47567, Tel.: (812) 354-8478

Foundation type: Independent foundation
Purpose: Scholarships to graduates of Pike Central High School, IN.
Financial data: Year ended 12/31/2012. Assets, $142,226 (M); Expenditures, $4,404; Total giving, $3,175; Grants to individuals, 8 grants totaling $3,175 (high: $500, low: -$325).
Fields of interest: Higher education.
Type of support: Support to graduates or students of specific schools.
Application information: Applications accepted. Application form required.
> *Deadline(s):* May 1
> *Applicants should submit the following:*
> 1) Letter(s) of recommendation
> 2) Transcripts
> 3) Photograph
EIN: 356631332

2979
Cass County Community Foundation, Inc.
417 N. St., Ste. 102
P.O. Box 441
Logansport, IN 46947-3172 (574) 722-2200
Contact: Deanna Crispen, Pres.
FAX: (574) 753-7501;
E-mail: cccf@casscountycf.org; Additional e-mail: dcrispen@casscountycf.org; URL: http://www.casscountycf.org

Foundation type: Community foundation
Purpose: Scholarships to high school seniors from Cass County for postsecondary education.
Publications: Application guidelines; Annual report; Informational brochure; Newsletter.
Financial data: Year ended 12/31/2012. Assets, $14,283,051 (M); Expenditures, $823,219; Total giving, $536,980; Grants to individuals, 91 grants totaling $146,673.
Fields of interest: Higher education.
Type of support: Support to graduates or students of specific schools; Undergraduate support.
Application information: Applications accepted. Application form required. Application form available on the grantmaker's web site.
> *Deadline(s):* Feb. 28
> *Additional information:* Attendance at the orientation meeting of each school is mandatory for all students wishing to apply for a scholarship.
EIN: 352125727

2980
Catholic Education Foundation Diocese of Evansville
520 S. Bennighof
Evansville, IN 47714-1528 (812) 402-6700

Foundation type: Public charity
Purpose: Scholarships to financially needy Evansville Deanery students to attend a Catholic high school within the Evansville diocese, IN.
Publications: Application guidelines; Informational brochure.
Financial data: Year ended 12/31/2011. Assets, $644,673 (M); Expenditures, $482,743; Total

giving, $453,892; Grants to individuals, totaling $442,692.
Fields of interest: Secondary school/education; Catholic agencies & churches.
Type of support: Scholarships—to individuals; Support to graduates or students of specific schools.
Application information: Applications accepted. Application form required.
> *Deadline(s):* Mar. 1 for first consideration, July 1 for appeals.
> *Additional information:* Application must include W-2 forms and tax returns.
EIN: 356078141

2981
Donald L. Charlton Educational Trust
P.O. Box 1602
South Bend, IN 46634

Foundation type: Independent foundation
Purpose: Scholarships to students for attendance at accredited colleges or universities in Indiana.
Financial data: Year ended 12/31/2012. Assets, $1,239,982 (M); Expenditures, $66,437; Total giving, $51,900; Grants to individuals, 17 grants totaling $51,900 (high: $3,400, low: $3,000).
Fields of interest: Higher education.
Type of support: Scholarships—to individuals.
Application information: Contact the trust for application guidelines.
EIN: 356759995

2982
Children's Bureau, Inc.
1575 Dr. Martin Luther King Jr. St.
Indianapolis, IN 46202-2250 (317) 264-2700
Contact: Tina Cloer, Pres. and C.E.O.
FAX: (317) 264-2714;
E-mail: info@childrensbureau.org; URL: http://www.childrensbureau.org

Foundation type: Public charity
Purpose: Emergency support for eligible individuals in Indianapolis, IN, including medical supplies and fees, household and personal supplies, food and lunches, children's clothing and school supplies, children's recreation and carfares, foster care, and other material relief to clients.
Publications: Annual report; Newsletter.
Financial data: Year ended 12/31/2011. Assets, $7,175,163 (M); Expenditures, $15,333,226; Total giving, $1,456,467; Grants to individuals, totaling $1,456,467.
Fields of interest: Economically disadvantaged.
Type of support: Grants for special needs.
Application information: Contact the bureau for additional information.
EIN: 351061264

2983
The Children's Museum of Indianapolis, Inc.
3000 N. Meridian St.
Indianapolis, IN 46208-4716 (317) 334-3322
FAX: (317) 921-4019;
E-mail: customerservice@childrensmuseum.org; Toll-free tel..: (800) 820-6214; URL: http://www.childrensmuseum.org

Foundation type: Public charity
Purpose: Scholarships to residents of Marion County who possess artistic or musical talent and have high grades and participation in neighborhood activities. Also, awards by nomination only to

middle and high school students who have made a significant impact on the lives of others, demonstrated selflessness and exhibited a commitment to service and the betterment of society.
Publications: Annual report.
Financial data: Year ended 12/31/2011. Assets, $361,143,462 (M); Expenditures, $33,989,814; Total giving, $36,709; Grants to individuals, totaling $36,709.
Fields of interest: Performing arts.
Type of support: Scholarships—to individuals.
Application information: Applications accepted. Application form required. Application form available on the grantmaker's web site.
  Additional information: Contact foundation for current application guidelines.
EIN: 350867985

2984
Christamore House Guild, Inc.
(formerly Christamore Aid Society, Inc.)
2 W. 64th St.
Indianapolis, IN 46260-4205 (317) 508-8425
URL: http://christamorehouseguild.org/

Foundation type: Public charity
Purpose: Scholarships to high school graduates in IN, and Christamore House staff.
Financial data: Year ended 05/31/2013. Assets, $341,856 (M); Expenditures, $211,514.
Type of support: Scholarships—to individuals.
Application information: Unsolicited requests for funds not considered or acknowledged.
EIN: 311019216

2985
Christian Foundation of Indiana, Inc.
8445 Keystone Crossing, Ste. 200
Indianapolis, IN 46240-4318
URL: http://www.christianfoundation.org

Foundation type: Independent foundation
Purpose: Grants to teachers at the Heritage Christian School, IN who find themselves in unexpected financial needs.
Financial data: Year ended 12/31/2012. Assets, $27,573 (M); Expenditures, $47,736; Total giving, $45,998; Grants to individuals, 23 grants totaling $45,998 (high: $11,472, low: $190).
Fields of interest: Human services.
Type of support: Grants to individuals; Grants for special needs.
Application information: Applications accepted. Application form required.
  Deadline(s): None
  Additional information: See web site for additional information and application form.
EIN: 356048268

2986
CIACO Inc.
4563 W. 200 N.
Anderson, IN 46011-8788 (317) 637-2050
Contact: Nancy M. Arellano, Dir.

Foundation type: Company-sponsored foundation
Purpose: Undergraduate scholarships to residents of the Chicago, IL, metropolitan area. Grants to economically disadvantaged individuals residing in IN for medical expenses, food, shelter, and clothing.
Financial data: Year ended 12/31/2012. Assets, $1,733 (M); Expenditures, $29,654; Total giving,

$28,620; Grants to individuals, 12 grants totaling $22,035 (high: $3,000, low: $200).
Fields of interest: Health care; Housing/shelter; Economically disadvantaged.
Type of support: Undergraduate support; Grants for special needs.
Application information: Application form required.
  Deadline(s): None
  Additional information: Application forms supplied upon request.
EIN: 351756007

2987
Olive B. Cole Foundation, Inc.
6207 Constitution Dr.
Fort Wayne, IN 46804-1517
Contact: Maclyn T. Parker, Pres.
E-mail: gwentip@ligtel.com

Foundation type: Independent foundation
Purpose: Scholarships to graduates of secondary schools in Noble County, IN, and to residents of Noble County, IN.
Publications: Application guidelines; Program policy statement.
Financial data: Year ended 03/31/2013. Assets, $30,527,314 (M); Expenditures, $1,535,774; Total giving, $1,207,099; Grants to individuals, 194 grants totaling $229,706 (high: $1,200, low: $500).
Type of support: Undergraduate support.
Application information: Applications accepted. Application form required. Interview required.
  Initial approach: Letter
  Deadline(s): None
  Additional information: Application forms available from the foundation or any office in the Noble County, IN, secondary school system.
EIN: 356040491

2988
Community Action of Northeast Indiana, Inc.
227 E. Washington Blvd.
P.O. Box 10570
Fort Wayne, IN 46853-0570 (260) 423-3546
FAX: (260) 422-4041;
E-mail: mariannestanley@canihelp.org; Toll-free tel.: (800) 589-2264; URL: http://www.canihelp.org

Foundation type: Public charity
Purpose: Assistance to low income individuals and families of northeast Indiana, in achieving self-sufficiency through transportation, family development, utility, educational opportunities, housing and other special needs.
Financial data: Year ended 10/31/2011. Assets, $5,670,125 (M); Expenditures, $20,115,096; Total giving, $8,430,874; Grants to individuals, totaling $7,818,591.
Fields of interest: Economically disadvantaged.
Type of support: In-kind gifts; Grants for special needs.
Application information: Contact the agency for eligibility determination.
EIN: 351111819

2989
Community Action Program of Evansville and Vanderburgh County, Inc.
27 Pasco Ave.
Evansville, IN 47713-1927 (812) 425-4241
FAX: (812) 425-4255; Additional address (Posey County): 1113 Main St., Mt. Vernon, IN 47620-1563, tel.: (812) 838-4839; additional address (Gibson County): 107 State St., Princeton, IN 47670-1853, tel.: (812) 386-6576; URL: http://capeevansville.org/

Foundation type: Public charity
Purpose: Financial assistance to low-income families of Vanderburgh County, IN.
Publications: Annual report.
Financial data: Year ended 12/31/2011. Assets, $8,129,172 (M); Expenditures, $13,397,359; Total giving, $5,970,425; Grants to individuals, totaling $5,970,425.
Fields of interest: Economically disadvantaged.
Type of support: Grants for special needs.
Application information:
  Initial approach: Letter
  Additional information: Contact foundation for eligibility criteria.
EIN: 351176665

2990
Community Foundation Alliance, Inc.
5000 E. Virginia St., Ste. 4
Evansville, IN 47715 (812) 429-1191
Contact: Jill Tullar, Exec. Dir.
FAX: (812) 429-0840; E-mail: info@alliance9.org; Toll free tel.: (877) 429-1191; URL: http://www.alliance9.org

Foundation type: Community foundation
Purpose: Scholarships to individuals living in Daviess, Gibson, Knox, Perry, Pike, Posey, Spencer, Vanderburgh, and Warrick counties, IN.
Publications: Application guidelines; Annual report; Financial statement; Grants list; Informational brochure; Newsletter.
Financial data: Year ended 06/30/2012. Assets, $63,918,571 (M); Expenditures, $3,877,053; Total giving, $2,289,659; Grants to individuals, 45 grants totaling $196,532.
Fields of interest: History/archaeology; Arts; Higher education; Business school/education; Agriculture.
Type of support: Scholarships—to individuals; Technical education support; Undergraduate support.
Application information: Applications accepted. Application form required. Application form available on the grantmaker's web site.
  Initial approach: Varies
  Deadline(s): Varies
  Applicants should submit the following:
    1) SAT
    2) GPA
    3) Financial information
    4) Essay
    5) ACT
  Additional information: Each scholarship has its own eligibility criteria and guidelines. See web site for complete listing of scholarship funds per Alliance Members.
Program description:
  Scholarships: The Alliance and its members administer more than 100 scholarships to students throughout Southwestern Indiana. These scholarships have been established by individuals, families, businesses, and civic groups wanting to help local students achieve their educational goals. Each scholarship fund has specific eligibility criteria that are defined by donors when funds are

established. Some of these criteria are geographical area, financial need, academic record, recommendations, seriousness of purpose, and school and community involvement. See web site for additional information.
EIN: 351830262

2991
Community Foundation of Bloomington and Monroe County, Inc.
(formerly Bloomington Community Foundation, Inc.)
101 W. Kirkwood Ave., Ste. 321
Bloomington, IN 47404-6129 (812) 333-9016
Contact: Tina Peterson, Pres. and CEO; For grants: Renee Chambers, Prog. Dir.
FAX: (812) 333-1153; E-mail: info@cfbmc.org;
Grant inquiry e-mail: renee@cfbmnc.org;
URL: http://www.cfbmc.org

Foundation type: Community foundation
Purpose: Scholarships and grants to residents of Bloomington and Monroe counties, IN.
Publications: Application guidelines; Annual report; Informational brochure; Newsletter.
Financial data: Year ended 06/30/2012. Assets, $19,817,322 (M); Expenditures, $1,557,125; Total giving, $985,470; Grants to individuals, 15 grants totaling $12,015.
Fields of interest: Higher education.
Type of support: Grants to individuals; Scholarships—to individuals.
Application information: Applications accepted. Application form required. Application form available on the grantmaker's web site.
  Initial approach: Application
  Deadline(s): Varies
  Additional information: See web site for a complete list of programs and additional information.
Program descriptions:
  Indiana Arts Commission Grants: The Indiana Arts Commission grants are administered on behalf of the Region 8 partner, Ivy Tech Community College. The regional partner provides technical assistance to artists through the Gayle and Bill Cook Center for Entrepreneurship and provides communication and resources from the IAC to local artists.
  Scholarships: The foundation administers a number of scholarship funds to support the educational aspirations of community members.
EIN: 351811149

2992
Community Foundation of Boone County, Inc.
60 E. Cedar St.
P.O. Box 92
Zionsville, IN 46077-1501 (317) 873-0210
Contact: For grants: Barbara J. Schroeder, Prog. Dir.; Jen Pendleton, Exec. Dir.
FAX: (317) 873-0219;
E-mail: info@communityfoundationbc.org;
Additional tel.: (765) 482-0024; URL: http://www.communityfoundationbc.org

Foundation type: Community foundation
Purpose: Scholarships to residents of Boone County, IN pursuing higher education.
Publications: Application guidelines; Annual report; Informational brochure; Newsletter.
Financial data: Year ended 12/31/2011. Assets, $18,287,142 (M); Expenditures, $1,426,203; Total giving, $691,060; Grants to individuals, 42 grants totaling $153,383.
Fields of interest: Higher education.

Type of support: Undergraduate support; Grants for special needs.
Application information: Applications accepted. Application form required.
  Initial approach: Letter
  Deadline(s): Vary
  Additional information: See web site for a complete list of programs.
EIN: 351829585

2993
Community Foundation of Grant County
505 W. 3rd St.
Marion, IN 46952-3748 (765) 662-0065
Contact: Dawn Brown, Exec. Dir.; For grants and scholarships: Ashley McKnight, Prog. Mgr.
FAX: (765) 662-1438;
E-mail: foundationoffice@comfdn.org; URL: http://www.comfdn.org

Foundation type: Community foundation
Purpose: Scholarships to graduates of Grant County high schools, IN.
Publications: Application guidelines; Annual report; Financial statement; Newsletter.
Financial data: Year ended 03/31/2013. Assets, $19,465,148 (M); Expenditures, $2,105,587; Total giving, $912,567; Grants to individuals, 266 grants totaling $350,412 (high: $29,941, low: $500).
Fields of interest: Vocational education; Higher education.
Type of support: Scholarships—to individuals; Support to graduates or students of specific schools; Graduate support; Undergraduate support.
Application information: Applications accepted. Application form required. Application form available on the grantmaker's web site.
  Initial approach: Application
  Copies of proposal: 1
  Deadline(s): Mar. 1
  Final notification: Recipients notified in two to three months
  Applicants should submit the following:
    1) Transcripts
    2) SAT
    3) Letter(s) of recommendation
    4) GPA
    5) Financial information
    6) FAFSA
    7) Essay
    8) ACT
  Additional information: See web site for complete listing of scholarships.
Program description:
  Scholarships: The foundation administers various scholarships established by donors to help area students pursue higher education. Scholarships range from $100 to $5,000 each. Each scholarship has its own unique set of eligibility criteria, including graduation from a particular high school, involvement in sports, academic achievement, and to pursue specific fields of study such as social work, nursing, environmental science and hospitality. Visit the foundation's web site for more information.
EIN: 311117791

2994
Community Foundation of Greater Fort Wayne, Inc.
(formerly Fort Wayne Community Foundation)
555 E. Wayne St.
Fort Wayne, IN 46802-2013 (260) 426-4083
Contact: David J. Bennett, Exec. Dir.; For grant application: Christine Meek, Dir., Progs.
FAX: (260) 424-0114; E-mail: info@cfgfw.org;
URL: http://www.cfgfw.org

Foundation type: Community foundation
Purpose: Scholarships to financially needy graduates of high schools in Allen County IN, and to employees of Independent Alliance Banks, Rae Magnet Wire, Agri Stats, Inc. and Mullinix Packaging.
Publications: Application guidelines; Annual report; Financial statement; Grants list; Informational brochure; Informational brochure (including application guidelines); Newsletter; Occasional report; Occasional report (including application guidelines).
Financial data: Year ended 12/31/2012. Assets, $124,160,882 (M); Expenditures, $6,561,439; Total giving, $5,634,310; Grants to individuals, 145 grants totaling $499,952.
Fields of interest: Vocational education, post-secondary; Higher education.
Type of support: Conferences/seminars; Scholarships—to individuals; Support to graduates or students of specific schools; Graduate support; Undergraduate support; Postgraduate support; Camperships.
Application information: Applications accepted. Application form required.
  Initial approach: Application
  Send request by: Mail
  Copies of proposal: 1
  Deadline(s): Varies
  Final notification: Recipients informed in three months
  Applicants should submit the following:
    1) Transcripts
    2) SAT
    3) Letter(s) of recommendation
    4) GPA
    5) Financial information
    6) Essay
    7) Curriculum vitae
  Additional information: Application should also include a personal data sheet and a list of high school activities. See web site for a complete listing of scholarship programs including criteria and contact information.
EIN: 351119450

2995
The Community Foundation of Greater Lafayette
1114 State St.
Lafayette, IN 47905-1219 (765) 742-9078
Contact: Greg Kapp, C.E.O.
FAX: (765) 742-2428; E-mail: info@cfglaf.org;
URL: http://www.cfglaf.org

Foundation type: Community foundation
Purpose: Scholarships to high school seniors at Tippecanoe County high schools for higher education at IN colleges and universities.
Publications: Application guidelines; Annual report; Grants list; Informational brochure; Newsletter.
Financial data: Year ended 12/31/2012. Assets, $36,716,354 (M); Expenditures, $1,606,472; Total giving, $839,269; Grants to individuals, 68 grants totaling $110,361.

Fields of interest: Higher education; Scholarships/
financial aid.
Type of support: Scholarships—to individuals;
Support to graduates or students of specific
schools; Undergraduate support.
Application information: Applications accepted.
Application form required. Interview required.
  Deadline(s): Varies
  Additional information: See web site for a
  complete listing of scholarship funds and
  additional application information.
Program description:
  Scholarship Funds: The foundation administers
various scholarships established by donors for area
students to attend accredited college and
universities. Each scholarship has its own unique
set of application guidelines and eligibility criteria.
See web site for additional information.
EIN: 237147996

2996
The Community Foundation of Howard County, Inc.
215 W. Sycamore
Kokomo, IN 46901 (765) 454-7298
Contact: For grants: Kim Abney, V.P., Progs.
FAX: (765) 868-4123; E-mail: info@cfhoward.org;
URL: http://www.cfhoward.org

Foundation type: Community foundation
Purpose: Scholarships to students in the Howard
County, IN, area, for higher education.
Publications: Application guidelines; Annual report
(including application guidelines); Informational
brochure; Newsletter.
Financial data: Year ended 12/31/2011. Assets,
$41,479,056 (M); Expenditures, $1,751,172;
Total giving, $1,157,566; Grants to individuals,
167 grants totaling $350,280.
Fields of interest: Higher education; Scholarships/
financial aid.
Type of support: Scholarships—to individuals;
Support to graduates or students of specific
schools; Undergraduate support.
Application information: Applications accepted.
Application form required.
  Deadline(s): Varies
  Applicants should submit the following:
    1) Transcripts
    2) Letter(s) of recommendation
    3) Essay
  Additional information: Application should
  include FAFSA. Application can be obtained
  from area high schools or the foundation
  office. See web site for a complete listing of
  scholarships.
Program description:
  Scholarship Funds: The foundation administers
various scholarships established by donors for area
students to further their education. Each
scholarship fund has specific eligibility criteria
defined by the donor when the fund was
established, which includes attendance at a
specific high school, participation in sports,
academic achievement, or particular fields of study
such as science, history, and architecture. The
scholarships are for educational expenses such as
college or university tuition, fees, required books
and equipment. Most funds offer varying award
amounts, which range from $500 to $3,000. See
web site for additional information.
EIN: 351844891

2997
The Community Foundation of Jackson County, Inc.
107 Community Dr.
P.O. Box 1231
Seymour, IN 47274 (812) 523-4483
Contact: Bud Walther, Pres. and C.E.O.
FAX: (812) 523-1433;
E-mail: info@cfjacksoncounty.org; URL: http://
www.cfjacksoncounty.org

Foundation type: Community foundation
Purpose: Scholarships to students at Jackson
County high schools, IN for attendance at four year
colleges or universities and to students attending
schools offering two year associate degrees or
vocational/technical training.
Publications: Application guidelines; Annual report;
Financial statement; Informational brochure
(including application guidelines); Newsletter.
Financial data: Year ended 12/31/2011. Assets,
$10,770,679 (M); Expenditures, $785,138; Total
giving, $328,803; Grants to individuals, totaling
$52,901.
Fields of interest: Vocational education,
post-secondary; Higher education.
Type of support: Seed money; Support to graduates
or students of specific schools; Technical
education support; Undergraduate support.
Application information: Applications accepted.
Application form required. Application form
available on the grantmaker's web site.
  Send request by: Mail
  Copies of proposal: 1
  Deadline(s): Dec. 8
  Applicants should submit the following:
    1) ACT
    2) Curriculum vitae
    3) Essay
    4) Financial information
    5) GPA
    6) Letter(s) of recommendation
    7) Proposal
    8) SAT
    9) Transcripts
  Additional information: Applications are available
  on foundation web site and at high schools in
  Jackson County.
EIN: 311119856

2998
Community Foundation of Jackson County Holding, Inc.
P.O. Box 1231
Seymour, IN 47274-1231 (812) 523-4483
FAX: (812) 523-1433; URL: http://
www.cfjacksoncounty.org

Foundation type: Public charity
Purpose: Scholarships to students of Jackson
County, IN for postsecondary education at
institutions of higher learning. Grants to teachers of
Jackson County schools with creative ideas that will
inspire students.
Publications: Application guidelines; Newsletter.
Financial data: Year ended 12/31/2011. Assets,
$2,276,655 (M); Expenditures, $6,403.
Fields of interest: Vocational education,
post-secondary; Higher education; Adult/continuing
education.
Type of support: Grants to individuals;
Scholarships—to individuals.
Application information: Applications accepted.
Application form required. Application form
available on the grantmaker's web site.
  Initial approach: Application
  Deadline(s): Varies

Additional information: See web site for
  additional application guidelines.
Program descriptions:
  Classroom Education Grants: Grants of $50 to
$250 will be awarded to innovative teachers who
propose projects that are designed to stimulate
learning.
  Lily Endowment Community Scholarship Program:
The program provides full tuition, fees, and a book
stipend for books and required equipment for four
years of undergraduate study on a full-time basis
leading to a baccalaureate degree at any Indiana
public or private college or university accredited by
the North Central Association of Colleges and
Schools.
  Scholarships: The foundation administers 40
different scholarships to students in Jackson
County who are pursuing traditional higher
education or vocational training. Scholarships are
also available to adults pursuing continuing
education.
EIN: 260273005

2999
Community Foundation of Madison and Jefferson County, Inc.
416 W. St., Ste. B
P.O. Box 306
Madison, IN 47250-0306 (812) 265-3327
Contact: Bill Barnes, Pres. and C.E.O.
FAX: (812) 273-0181; E-mail: info@cfmjc.org;
URL: http://www.cfmjc.org

Foundation type: Community foundation
Purpose: Scholarships for post-high school
education to qualified students of Madison
Consolidated Schools, Madison, IN, and
Southwestern Consolidated Schools, Hanover, IN.
Publications: Application guidelines; Annual report;
Financial statement; Grants list; Informational
brochure; Newsletter; Program policy statement.
Financial data: Year ended 12/31/2012. Assets,
$18,126,846 (M); Expenditures, $731,134; Total
giving, $441,429; Grants to individuals, 51 grants
totaling $71,845.
Fields of interest: Higher education.
Type of support: Scholarships—to individuals;
Support to graduates or students of specific
schools; Technical education support;
Undergraduate support.
Application information: Applications accepted.
Application form required. Application form
available on the grantmaker's web site.
  Initial approach: Telephone or e-mail
  Copies of proposal: 1
  Deadline(s): Varies
  Final notification: Recipients notified in two
  months of application deadline
  Applicants should submit the following:
    1) SAT
    2) Transcripts
    3) Resume
    4) Letter(s) of recommendation
    5) GPA
    6) Financial information
    7) FAFSA
    8) Curriculum vitae
  Additional information: Each scholarship has its
  own unique set of eligibility criteria. See web
  site for complete listing of scholarships.
EIN: 351847297

3000

Community Foundation of Morgan County, Inc.

56 N. Main St.
Martinsville, IN 46151-1415   (765) 813-0003
Contact: Tom Zoss, Exec. Dir.
FAX: (765) 813-0017; E-mail: info@cfmconline.org;
URL: http://cfmconline.org

Foundation type: Community foundation
Purpose: Scholarships for residents of Morgan County, IN, or for individuals who graduated from a high school in Morgan County, IN.
Publications: Application guidelines; Annual report; Financial statement; Grants list; Informational brochure; Newsletter.
Financial data: Year ended 12/31/2012. Assets, $5,838,928 (M); Expenditures, $1,800,363; Total giving, $201,481; Grants to individuals, totaling $113,566.
Fields of interest: Higher education; Scholarships/financial aid.
Type of support: Scholarships—to individuals; Support to graduates or students of specific schools; Undergraduate support.
Application information: Applications accepted. Application form required. Application form available on the grantmaker's web site.
> *Initial approach:* Application
> *Send request by:* Online
> *Deadline(s):* Feb. 22
> *Applicants should submit the following:*
>   1) Resume
>   2) Financial information
>   3) SAT
>   4) GPA
>   5) ACT
>   6) Letter(s) of recommendation
>   7) Essay
>   8) Transcripts
> *Additional information:* Application procedures vary depending on specific scholarship. See web site for guidelines.
EIN: 351956929

3001

The Community Foundation of Muncie and Delaware County, Inc.

P.O. Box 807
Muncie, IN 47308-0807   (765) 747-7181
Contact: Roni Johnson, Pres.
FAX: (765) 289-7770;
E-mail: commfound@cfmdin.org; URL: http://www.cfmdin.org

Foundation type: Community foundation
Purpose: Scholarships to individuals from the Muncie and Delaware Counties, IN for undergraduate education at U.S. colleges and universities.
Publications: Application guidelines; Annual report; Financial statement; Grants list; Informational brochure; Newsletter; Occasional report.
Financial data: Year ended 12/31/2012. Assets, $45,648,869 (M); Expenditures, $2,542,788; Total giving, $1,777,631. Scholarships—to individuals amount not specified.
Fields of interest: Higher education; Business school/education; Medical school/education; Engineering school/education.
Type of support: Grants to individuals; Scholarships—to individuals; Support to graduates or students of specific schools; Technical education support; Undergraduate support.

Application information: Applications accepted. Application form required. Application form available on the grantmaker's web site.
> *Deadline(s):* Varies
> *Final notification:* Applicants notified within three weeks
> *Additional information:* Contact your local high school guidance office for further program information. See web site for additional information.
Program descriptions:
> *Robert P. Bell Education Grants:* The grants are awarded to teachers with innovative ideas, programs, or projects that are designed to stimulate learning in their students. Grants range in size from $50 to $450. See web site for additional information.
> *Scholarships:* The foundation offers a variety of scholarships to area students who wish to pursue higher education. Each scholarship the foundation administers has different application guidelines, due dates, and requirements. Many are for students pursuing a particular area of study, such as engineering, medicine, and small business. See web site for additional information.
EIN: 351640051

3002

Community Foundation of Randolph County, Inc.

213 S. Main St.
Winchester, IN 47394-1824   (765) 584-9077
Contact: Ruth B. Mills, Exec. Dir.
FAX: (765) 584-7710;
E-mail: info@cfrandolphcounty.org; Additional e-mail: rmills@cfrandolphcounty.org; URL: http://www.randolphcountyfoundation.org/

Foundation type: Community foundation
Purpose: Scholarships to graduates of Randolph County, IN, high schools for attendance at any accredited college or university in Indiana.
Publications: Application guidelines; Annual report; Newsletter; Occasional report (including application guidelines).
Financial data: Year ended 12/31/2012. Assets, $7,009,628 (M); Expenditures, $521,415; Total giving, $345,126; Grants to individuals, 70 grants totaling $95,331.
Fields of interest: Higher education; Scholarships/financial aid.
Type of support: Scholarships—to individuals; Support to graduates or students of specific schools.
Application information: Applications accepted. Application form required.
> *Deadline(s):* Varies
> *Additional information:* Applications available at Randolph County high school guidance offices.
EIN: 351903148

3003

Community Foundation of Southern Indiana

4104 Charlestown Rd.
New Albany, IN 47150-9538   (812) 948-4662
Contact: For grants: Crystal Gunther, Grants and Prog. Off.
FAX: (812) 948-4678;
E-mail: lspeed@cfsouthernindiana.com;
URL: http://www.cfsouthernindiana.com

Foundation type: Community foundation

Purpose: Scholarships to graduating students in Clark or Floyd, IN for postsecondary education.
Publications: Annual report (including application guidelines); Financial statement; Informational brochure; Newsletter.
Financial data: Year ended 06/30/2012. Assets, $28,263,609 (M); Expenditures, $2,840,592; Total giving, $1,467,039. Scholarships—to individuals amount not specified.
Fields of interest: Higher education.
Type of support: Scholarships—to individuals; Support to graduates or students of specific schools; Undergraduate support.
Application information: Applications accepted. Application form required. Application form available on the grantmaker's web site.
> *Initial approach:* Application
> *Send request by:* Online
> *Deadline(s):* Jan. 17
> *Final notification:* Applicants notified in Apr.
> *Applicants should submit the following:*
>   1) Transcripts
>   2) Essay
>   3) Financial information
> *Additional information:* See web site for common application, complete listing of scholarship funds and basic criteria for each fund.
Program description:
> *Scholarships:* The foundation is committed to assisting students of local community in pursuing and completing higher education degrees. Students who are residents of Clark or Floyd County and who are graduating this current school year from an accredited high school in these counties may apply to the Scholarship Program and, if eligible, can be awarded a scholarship from one or more different funds. Each scholarship has unique eligibility requirements and application guidelines. See web site for additional information.
EIN: 351827813

3004

Community Foundation of St. Joseph County

205 W. Jefferson Blvd., Ste. 610
P.O. Box 837
South Bend, IN 46624-0837   (574) 232-0041
Contact: Angela Butiste, Sr. Prog. Off.
FAX: (574) 233-1906; E-mail: info@cfsjc.org; Additional e-mail: angela@cfsjc.org; Grant application e-mail: grants@cfsjc.org; URL: http://www.cfsjc.org

Foundation type: Community foundation
Purpose: Scholarships to individuals residing in the St. Joseph County, IN, area for undergraduate education.
Publications: Application guidelines; Financial statement; Grants list; Newsletter.
Financial data: Year ended 06/30/2013. Assets, $132,335,082 (M); Expenditures, $5,949,132; Total giving, $4,496,454; Grants to individuals, totaling $250,035.
Fields of interest: Historic preservation/historical societies; Higher education; Teacher school/education; Engineering school/education; Scholarships/financial aid; Labor unions/organizations; Athletics/sports, school programs.
Type of support: Employee-related scholarships; Scholarships—to individuals; Support to graduates or students of specific schools; Graduate support; Undergraduate support.
Application information: Applications accepted. Application form required. Application form available on the grantmaker's web site.
> *Deadline(s):* Varies
> *Applicants should submit the following:*

1) Transcripts
2) SAT
3) Letter(s) of recommendation
4) GPA
5) Financial information
6) Essay
Additional information: See web site for complete program and application information.

Program description:

Scholarship Programs: The foundation has more than 50 scholarship funds which awards over $450,000 to local students each year. The scholarships were established for a variety of reasons-to assist low-income students, encourage children of employees to pursue their dreams, or train medical professionals, teachers, and engineers. Many were established in memory of lost loved ones, turning grief into tribute and helping students achieve their goals in the process. Each scholarship has unique eligibility requirements and application guidelines. See web site for additional information.
EIN: 237365930

3005

Community Foundation of Switzerland County, Inc.

303 Ferry St.
P.O. Box 46
Vevay, IN   47043-1103   (812) 427-9160
Contact: Pam W. Acton, Exec. Dir.
E-mail: info@cfsci.org; URL: http://www.cfsci.org

Foundation type: Community foundation
Purpose: Scholarships to graduating high school seniors and non-traditional applicants residing in the Switzerland County, IN, area for undergraduate education.
Publications: Application guidelines; Annual report; Grants list; Informational brochure; Program policy statement; Program policy statement (including application guidelines).
Financial data: Year ended 12/31/2012. Assets, $10,629,567 (M); Expenditures, $648,810; Total giving, $463,886; Grants to individuals, 59 grants totaling $33,065.
Fields of interest: Higher education; Scholarships/financial aid.
Type of support: Scholarships—to individuals; Support to graduates or students of specific schools; Undergraduate support.
Application information: Applications accepted. Application form required. Application form available on the grantmaker's web site.
Initial approach: Application
Send request by: Online
Deadline(s): Feb. 27
Final notification: Applicants notified in May/June
Applicants should submit the following:
1) SAT
2) GPA
3) Letter(s) of recommendation
4) Transcripts
5) Essay
Additional information: See website for a complete listing of scholarships.
EIN: 352087649

3006

Community Foundation of Wabash County

(formerly North Manchester Community Foundation)
218 E. Main St.
P.O. Box 7
North Manchester, IN   46962   (260) 982-4824
Contact: Patty Grant, Exec. Dir.; For grants: Julie Garber, Prog. Dir.
FAX: (260) 982-8644; E-mail: info@cfwabash.org;
URL: http://www.cfwabash.org

Foundation type: Community foundation
Purpose: Scholarships to Kent county residents and residents of other counties who plan to attend an educational institution.
Publications: Application guidelines; Annual report (including application guidelines); Grants list; Informational brochure; Newsletter; IRS Form 990 or 990-PF printed copy available upon request.
Financial data: Year ended 12/31/2012. Assets, $31,474,782 (M); Expenditures, $1,631,419; Total giving, $1,036,107; Grants to individuals, 94 grants totaling $61,024.
Fields of interest: Higher education.
Type of support: Scholarships—to individuals.
Application information: Applications accepted. Application form required. Application form available on the grantmaker's web site.
Copies of proposal: 1
Deadline(s): Mar. 14
Final notification: Recipients notified in three months
Applicants should submit the following:
1) Transcripts
2) SAT
3) SAR
4) Resume
5) Letter(s) of recommendation
6) GPA
7) Financial information
8) Essay
9) ACT
Additional information: Contact foundation, guidance counselor or see web site for additional guidelines.
EIN: 356019016

3007

The Community Hospital Auxiliary Scholarship Trust

(also known as Munster Medical Foundation, Inc.)
901 Mac Arthur Blvd.
Munster, IN   46321-2901

Foundation type: Independent foundation
Purpose: Scholarships to eligible dependents of qualified employees of Munster Medical Research Foundation, Inc.
Financial data: Year ended 01/31/2013. Assets, $714,704 (M); Expenditures, $54,690; Total giving, $46,500; Grants to individuals, 31 grants totaling $46,500 (high: $1,500, low: $1,500).
Fields of interest: Higher education.
Type of support: Scholarships—to individuals.
Application information:
Initial approach: Letter or telephone
EIN: 356595973

3008

Marvin H. & Gretchen V. Cook Educational Trust

c/o The Fountain Trust Company
P. O. Box 8
Covington, IN   47932   (765) 793-2237

Foundation type: Independent foundation

Purpose: Scholarships to residents of Troy, Wabash, Fulton, Van Buren, and Milcreek townships in Fountain County, IN.
Financial data: Year ended 12/31/2012. Assets, $369,798 (M); Expenditures, $19,807; Total giving, $19,000; Grants to individuals, 38 grants totaling $19,000 (high: $500, low: $500).
Type of support: Undergraduate support.
Application information: Application form required.
Deadline(s): None
Applicants should submit the following:
1) Class rank
2) Transcripts
3) SAT
4) Financial information
Additional information: Application must also include personal statement.
EIN: 356040497

3009

The Mark W. Coy Foundation, Inc.

(formerly The Beverly Aronson Richey Foundation)
7863 N. 700 W.
Fairland, IN   46126-9544   (317) 623-3372
Contact: Beverly Richey, Pres.

Foundation type: Independent foundation
Purpose: Financial assistance to individuals with special needs. Some scholarships to individuals for higher education.
Financial data: Year ended 12/31/2012. Assets, $138,347 (M); Expenditures, $23,624; Total giving, $22,500; Grants to individuals, 10 grants totaling $12,500 (high: $5,000, low: $500).
Fields of interest: Education; Human services.
Type of support: Scholarships—to individuals; Grants for special needs.
Application information:
Deadline(s): None
Additional information: Applicants must demonstrate need.
EIN: 911825285

3010

Crown Point Community Foundation

115 South Court St.
Crown Point, IN   46307   (219) 662-7252
Contact: Patricia Huber, Pres.
FAX: (219) 662-9493; E-mail: info@thepcf.org;
Mailing address: P.O. Box 522, Crown Point, IN 46308-0522; URL: http://www.crownpointcommunityfoundation.org

Foundation type: Community foundation
Purpose: Scholarships to students in northwestern IN, particularly the Crown Point area, who wish to pursue postsecondary education.
Publications: Application guidelines; Annual report; Informational brochure; Newsletter.
Financial data: Year ended 12/31/2012. Assets, $17,668,731 (M); Expenditures, $942,163; Total giving, $644,678; Grants to individuals, 105 grants totaling $242,036.
Fields of interest: Higher education.
Type of support: Scholarships—to individuals.
Application information: Applications accepted. Application form required. Application form available on the grantmaker's web site. Interview required.
Send request by: Mail or in person
Applicants should submit the following:
1) Transcripts
2) Class rank
3) SAT
4) GPA
5) Financial information

6) Essay

7) ACT

Additional information: Application available at foundation office or website. See web site for a complete listing of scholarship programs.

EIN: 310247014

3011

Dead Sea Scrolls Foundation

P.O. Box 1775

Warsaw, IN   46581-1775   (574) 269-5223

Foundation type: Public charity

Purpose: Research grants to individuals for the translation and publication of ancient scrolls as well as the restoration and conservation of original manuscripts.

Financial data: Year ended 12/31/2012. Assets, $3,065 (M); Expenditures, $99,905; Total giving, $31,135.

Fields of interest: History/archaeology.

Type of support: Research.

Application information: Contact foundation for current application deadline/guidelines.

EIN: 351855580

3012

Dearborn Community Foundation

(formerly Dearborn County Community Foundation)

322 Walnut St.

Lawrenceburg, IN   47025   (812) 539-4115

Contact: Fred McCarter, Exec. Dir.; For grants: Denise Sedler, Dir., Progs.

FAX: (812) 539-4119;

E-mail: mccarterf@comcast.net; Grant information e-mail: dsedler@comcast.net; URL: http://www.dearborncf.org

Foundation type: Community foundation

Purpose: Scholarships for residents of Dearborn County, IN for higher education.

Publications: Application guidelines; Annual report; Newsletter.

Financial data: Year ended 12/31/2012. Assets, $14,623,632 (M); Expenditures, $3,886,508; Total giving, $3,372,388; Grants to individuals, 206 grants totaling $318,000.

Fields of interest: Higher education; Engineering school/education.

Type of support: Scholarships—to individuals; Support to graduates or students of specific schools; Technical education support; Undergraduate support.

Application information: Applications accepted. Application form required. Application form available on the grantmaker's web site.

Initial approach: Application

Send request by: Mail or in person

Deadline(s): Jan. 9

Additional information: Application should include an essay. See web site for application forms and complete program listing.

Program description:

Scholarship Programs: The foundation administers several scholarships established through the generosity of donors to help students in the community pursue education opportunities after high school. Each scholarship program has varied eligibility criteria and application procedures. See web site for additional information.

EIN: 352036110

3013

Decatur County Community Foundation, Inc.

101 E. Main St., Ste. 1

P.O. Box 72

Greensburg, IN   47240-2031   (812) 662-6364

Contact: Deb Locke, Exec. Dir.

FAX: (812) 662-8704;

E-mail: contact@dccfound.org; URL: http://www.dccfound.org

Foundation type: Community foundation

Purpose: Scholarships to residents of Decatur County, IN, for undergraduate education at American colleges and universities. Grants to classroom teachers at any school in Decatur County for innovative classroom projects.

Publications: Application guidelines; Annual report (including application guidelines); Financial statement; Informational brochure; Informational brochure (including application guidelines); Newsletter; Occasional report.

Financial data: Year ended 12/31/2011. Assets, $14,873,816 (M); Expenditures, $709,933; Total giving, $465,466; Grants to individuals, 94 grants totaling $186,210.

Fields of interest: Arts education; Music; Management/technical assistance; Higher education; Nursing school/education; Teacher school/education; Engineering school/education; Health sciences school/education; Formal/general education; Athletics/sports, school programs; Formal/general education.

Type of support: Grants to individuals; Scholarships—to individuals; Support to graduates or students of specific schools; Undergraduate support.

Application information: Applications accepted. Application form required.

Initial approach: Application

Send request by: On-line for scholarships, mail for Teacher Grant

Deadline(s): Mar. 1 for scholarships, Oct. 1 and Feb. 1 for Teacher Grants

Applicants should submit the following:

1) GPA

2) Essay

3) Transcripts

Additional information: See web site for a complete listing of scholarships and common application form, and for teacher grants guidelines.

Program descriptions:

Scholarships: Each scholarship has specific requirements, as defined by the donor who established the scholarship. Students should read each description carefully to make sure they qualify, and complete any additional essays or information requested in the requirements.

Thank a Teacher Grants: The foundation recognizes and supports the improvement of educational opportunities throughout our community through scholarships and grants. These grants recognize that there are times when teachers have innovative classroom ideas, but cannot complete them due to budgetary constraints. This grant process will allow teachers to do those different projects. The maximum amount that may be requested is $250. Grants are for projects that enhance or supplement the teacher's curriculum. Grant requests will be awarded on merit and availability of funds. Under most circumstances, the Thank-a-Teacher Grant will not fund equipment and technology, club activities, classroom supplies that are available from the school corporation, or field trips. One grant per teacher per school year.

EIN: 351870979

3014

Dwight & Virginia Deen Schoeff Scholarship Trust

200 E. Jackson St.

Muncie, IN   47305-2835   (317) 844-2399

Foundation type: Independent foundation

Purpose: Scholarships to high school graduates of any high school located in Delaware County, IN with preference to music education majors.

Financial data: Year ended 12/31/2012. Assets, $2,184,018 (M); Expenditures, $130,124; Total giving, $108,650; Grants to individuals, 37 grants totaling $108,650 (high: $3,200, low: $1,450).

Fields of interest: Performing arts, education.

Type of support: Undergraduate support.

Application information: Applications not accepted.

Additional information: Contact local high school guidance office for application. Unsolicited requests for funds are not accepted or considered.

EIN: 206408218

3015

DeKalb County Community Foundation, Inc.

650 W. N. St.

P.O. Box 111

Auburn, IN   46706-0111   (260) 925-0311

Contact: Wendy Oberlin, Exec. Dir.; For grants: Diane Wilson, Grant and Scholarship Mgr.

Scholarship application e-mail: scholarships@dekalbfoundation.org

FAX: (260) 925-0383;

E-mail: woberlin@dekalbfoundation.org; URL: http://www.dekalbfoundation.org

Foundation type: Community foundation

Purpose: Scholarships to full-time DeKalb county, IN, students for undergraduate study in any public or private college or university.

Publications: Application guidelines; Annual report; Financial statement; Grants list; Newsletter.

Financial data: Year ended 12/31/2013. Assets, $14,041,958 (M); Expenditures, $1,112,341; Total giving, $486,546. Scholarships—to individuals amount not specified.

Fields of interest: Higher education.

Type of support: Scholarships—to individuals; Undergraduate support.

Application information: Applications accepted. Application form required. Application form available on the grantmaker's web site. Interview required.

Initial approach: Application

Send request by: E-mail

Deadline(s): Mar.

Applicants should submit the following:

1) Essay

2) ACT

3) GPA

4) SAT

5) Transcripts

Additional information: Each scholarship is awarded based on criteria suggested by the donor or the community organization that sponsors the award. See web site for a complete listing of scholarships and eligibility criteria for each.

EIN: 351992897

3016
Delta Phi Delta
1281 Win Hentschel Blcd.
West Lafayette, IN 47906 (765) 494-3054
Contact: Harry Bulow, Pres.

Foundation type: Independent foundation
Purpose: Scholarships for Fine Arts majors at Purdue University.
Financial data: Year ended 05/31/2013. Assets, $89,116; Expenditures, $3,699; Total giving, $3,600.
Fields of interest: Arts education; Higher education.
Type of support: Scholarships—to individuals.
Application information: Applications accepted. Application form required.
EIN: 356037713

3017
The James & Shirley Dora Foundation
2501 S. High School Rd.
Indianapolis, IN 46241-4919
Contact: Ron Reader
Application address: 3001 Northwestern Ave., West Lafayette, IN 47906-5361

Foundation type: Independent foundation
Purpose: Scholarships to sons, daughters, grandsons, granddaughters, or wards of employees of General Hotels Corporation or one of the hotels it owns and operates.
Financial data: Year ended 12/31/2012. Assets, $8,483 (M); Expenditures, $9,585; Total giving, $6,500; Grants to individuals, 8 grants totaling $6,500 (high: $1,000, low: $700).
Type of support: Employee-related scholarships; Scholarships—to individuals.
Application information: Applications accepted. Application form required.
Deadline(s): First Mon. in Apr.
Applicants should submit the following:
1) Letter(s) of recommendation
2) Transcripts
3) Essay
EIN: 351807219

3018
Dr. Dane & Mary Louise Miller Foundation, Inc.
(formerly The Biomet Foundation, Inc.)
700 Park Ave., Ste. G
Winona Lake, IN 46590-1066
Contact: Cindy Helper, Secy. and Dir.

Foundation type: Company-sponsored foundation
Purpose: Scholarships to financially needy children of full-time Team Members of Biomet, Inc. and its subsidiaries, primarily in IN.
Publications: Informational brochure.
Financial data: Year ended 12/31/2012. Assets, $16,501,537 (M); Expenditures, $855,060; Total giving, $811,803; Grants to individuals, 68 grants totaling $190,500 (high: $3,000, low: -$7,500).
Fields of interest: Education.
Type of support: Employee-related scholarships.
Application information: Applications not accepted.
Additional information: The children of officers and directors of Biomet, subsidiaries, and members of the foundation are ineligible. Unsolicited requests for funds not considered or acknowledged.
Company name: Biomet, Inc.
EIN: 351806314

3019
Dubois County Community Foundation, Inc.
600 McCrillus St.
P.O. Box 269
Jasper, IN 47547-0269 (812) 482-5295
Contact: Brad Ward, C.E.O.
FAX: (812) 482-7461; E-mail: dccf@fullnet.com; URL: http://www.dccommunityfoundation.org/

Foundation type: Community foundation
Purpose: Endowed scholarships to high school graduates of Dubois county, IN for attendance at accredited colleges or universities in Indiana.
Publications: Application guidelines; Annual report; Financial statement; Grants list; Informational brochure; Newsletter.
Financial data: Year ended 12/31/2012. Assets, $21,292,273 (M); Expenditures, $917,937; Total giving, $326,609; Grants to individuals, totaling $33,500.
Fields of interest: Higher education.
Type of support: Scholarships—to individuals.
Application information: Applications accepted. Application form required. Application form available on the grantmaker's web site.
Initial approach: Application
Send request by: Online
Deadline(s): Apr. 1
Applicants should submit the following:
1) Essay
2) Transcripts
3) Class rank
4) SAT
5) ACT
6) GPA
7) Letter(s) of recommendation
Additional information: See web site for a complete listing of scholarships.
EIN: 351990305

3020
Dubois County High School Scholarship Trust, Inc.
1220 Newton St.
Jasper, IN 47546-2811

Foundation type: Independent foundation
Purpose: Scholarships to students of DuBois County high schools, IN who are affiliated with or sponsored by a relative who is a member of American Legion Post 147.
Financial data: Year ended 07/07/2010. Assets, $0 (M); Expenditures, $6,335; Total giving, $5,000; Grants to individuals, 5 grants totaling $5,000 (high: $1,000, low: $1,000).
Fields of interest: Higher education.
Type of support: Support to graduates or students of specific schools.
Application information: Applications accepted. Application form required.
Deadline(s): Mar. 1
Applicants should submit the following:
1) Essay
2) Letter(s) of recommendation
3) Transcripts
Additional information: Applications can be obtained from the schools' guidance offices.
EIN: 352123787

3021
Dr. Ferrell W. Dunn Memorial Fund Trust
200 E. Jackson St.
Muncie, IN 47305-2835

Foundation type: Independent foundation

Purpose: Scholarships to students from Delaware County, IN, schools who have demonstrated an aptitude and desire to study and practice medicine.
Financial data: Year ended 05/31/2013. Assets, $592,558 (M); Expenditures, $39,914; Total giving, $30,000; Grants to individuals, 3 grants totaling $30,000 (high: $10,000, low: $10,000).
Fields of interest: Medical school/education.
Type of support: Support to graduates or students of specific schools; Undergraduate support.
Application information: Application form required.
Initial approach: Letter
Deadline(s): Apr. 1
Additional information: Contact foundation for current application deadline/guidelines.
EIN: 356398629

3022
James W. & Betty Dye Foundation, Inc.
900 Ridge Rd., Ste. M
Munster, IN 46321-1727 (219) 836-1100
Contact: Scholarship Comm.
FAX: (219) 836-6128;
E-mail: info@dyescholarships.org; URL: http://jimandbettydyescholarships.org

Foundation type: Independent foundation
Purpose: Scholarships to graduates of selected high schools in Northwest Indiana to attend Indiana University or Ball State University.
Financial data: Year ended 12/31/2012. Assets, $6,930,057 (M); Expenditures, $220,388; Total giving, $192,458; Grants to individuals, 95 grants totaling $192,458 (high: $6,000, low: $500).
Fields of interest: Scholarships/financial aid.
Type of support: Support to graduates or students of specific schools.
Application information: Applications accepted. Application form required. Application form available on the grantmaker's web site.
Deadline(s): Apr. 1
Applicants should submit the following:
1) SAT
2) GPA
3) Letter(s) of recommendation
4) Essay
Additional information: Application must also include a copy of letter of admission to the university. Applications available in high school guidance offices. See web site for full list of participating schools.
EIN: 351884798

3023
East Allen County Schools Educational Foundation, Inc.
1240 State Rd. 930 E.
New Haven, IN 46774-1732 (260) 446-0100
Contact: Joyce Magner, Pres.

Foundation type: Public charity
Purpose: Scholarships for current students of East Allen County Schools, IN to local colleges and universities through the dual credit program.
Financial data: Year ended 12/31/2012. Assets, $0 (M); Expenditures, $27,217; Total giving, $17,220.
Fields of interest: Higher education.
Type of support: Scholarships—to individuals.
Application information: Contact the foundation for additional information.
EIN: 371487238

3024
Elkhart County Community Foundation, Inc.
101 S. Main St.
P.O. Box 2932
Elkhart, IN 46515 (574) 295-8761
Contact: For grants: Shannon Oakes, Dir., Grants Admin.
FAX: (574) 389-7497;
E-mail: shannon@elkhartccf.org; URL: http://www.elkhartccf.org

Foundation type: Community foundation
Purpose: Scholarships to residents of Elkhart County, IN for higher education.
Publications: Application guidelines; Annual report (including application guidelines); Grants list; Informational brochure; Newsletter; Occasional report.
Financial data: Year ended 06/30/2013. Assets, $197,402,382 (M); Expenditures, $5,900,036; Total giving, $3,638,701.
Fields of interest: Higher education; College.
Type of support: Scholarships—to individuals; Support to graduates or students of specific schools; Graduate support; Precollege support; Undergraduate support.
Application information: Applications accepted. Application form required. Application form available on the grantmaker's web site.
Initial approach: Application
Send request by: Online
Copies of proposal: 1
Deadline(s): Mar. 1
Final notification: Recipients notified by Apr. 1
Applicants should submit the following:
1) Transcripts
2) SAT
3) GPA
4) Essay
5) ACT
Additional information: See web site for a complete listing of scholarship funds.
EIN: 311255886

3025
Harold Ellison Scholarship Fund
200 E. Jackson St.
Muncie, IN 47305-2835

Foundation type: Independent foundation
Purpose: Scholarships to graduates of Delaware County high schools, IN, admitted with distinction to Ball State University, IN, with special skills in fine and performing arts, writing, or athletics.
Financial data: Year ended 10/31/2013. Assets, $1,034,114 (M); Expenditures, $54,895; Total giving, $44,124.
Fields of interest: Performing arts; Literature; Arts; Athletics/sports, training.
Type of support: Support to graduates or students of specific schools; Undergraduate support.
Application information: Applications accepted. Application form required.
Deadline(s): Nov. 2 through Feb. 28.
Additional information: A complete listing of school and community activities, awards or honors achieved, musical or theatrical performances, items written for publication, athletic activities, and a self description.
EIN: 356375836

3026
Mabel S. Epler Scholarship Fund
200 E. Jackson St.
Muncie, IN 47305-2835 (317) 844-2399

Foundation type: Independent foundation
Purpose: Scholarships to graduates of Yorktown High School, IN.
Financial data: Year ended 12/31/2012. Assets, $96,727 (M); Expenditures, $5,404; Total giving, $3,000; Grants to individuals, 3 grants totaling $3,000 (high: $1,000, low: $1,000).
Type of support: Support to graduates or students of specific schools; Undergraduate support.
Application information: Application form required.
Deadline(s): Mar. 31
EIN: 356326717

3027
Eskenazi Health Foundation, Inc.
(formerly Wishard Memorial Foundation, Inc.)
1001 W. 10th St., Rm. W4523
Indianapolis, IN 46202-2859 (317) 630-6451
FAX: (317) 630-8716;
E-mail: info@eskenazihealthfoundation.org; E-mail for Ernie.Vargo:
ernie.vargo@eskenazihealthfoundation.org;
URL: http://eskenazihealthfoundation.org/

Foundation type: Public charity
Purpose: Scholarships and grants to individuals pursuing medical-related degrees at various accredited Indiana colleges.
Publications: Financial statement; Informational brochure; Newsletter.
Financial data: Year ended 12/31/2011. Assets, $66,147,736 (M); Expenditures, $20,100,440; Total giving, $17,252,560; Grants to individuals, totaling $212,182.
Fields of interest: Medical school/education.
Type of support: Scholarships—to individuals.
Application information: Applications accepted.
Additional information: Scholarship payments are paid directly to the educational institution on behalf of the students.
Program descriptions:
Eli Messenger Scholarship Fund: This scholarship is awarded to employees of Wishard Health Services who are pursuing or who plan to pursue, a health-related degree or certification.
George H. Rawls, M.D. Scholarship Fund: The scholarship provides full tuition grants for minority students to study at the IU School of Medicine, and it makes a commitment for four years of study to achieve the degree of medical doctor. Each grant recipient in turn accepts a one-year obligation to provide healthcare to the indigent in Indiana.
EIN: 311132066

3028
Fayette County Foundation
521 N. Central Ave., Ste. A
P.O. Box 844
Connersville, IN 47331 (765) 827-9966
Contact: Anna Dungan, Exec. Dir.; For grants: Katherine Good, Prog. Off.
FAX: (765) 827-5836;
E-mail: info@fayettefoundation.com; Grant application e-mail: kgood@fayettefoundation.com;
URL: http://www.fayettefoundation.com

Foundation type: Community foundation
Purpose: Scholarships to individuals residing in Fayette County, IN, for undergraduate education.
Publications: Annual report; Grants list; Informational brochure; Newsletter.
Financial data: Year ended 12/31/2012. Assets, $9,585,063 (M); Expenditures, $544,052; Total giving, $307,644. Scholarships—to individuals amount not specified.

Fields of interest: Higher education; Nursing school/education.
Type of support: Scholarships—to individuals; Support to graduates or students of specific schools; Undergraduate support.
Application information: Applications accepted. Application form required. Application form available on the grantmaker's web site.
Initial approach: Telephone or e-mail
Copies of proposal: 1
Deadline(s): Varies
Applicants should submit the following:
1) Transcripts
2) SAT
3) Letter(s) of recommendation
4) GPA
5) Financial information
6) Essay
7) ACT
Additional information: See web site for a complete listing of scholarships.
Program description:
Scholarships: The foundation is committed to help students in the local community pursue and complete higher education degrees. The strategy is to grow and create endowments that provide renewable scholarships significant enough to help students achieve degree attainment. Scholarship funds are customized to provide educational opportunities for students for specific fields of studies, such as arts, elementary education, and nursing, at a particular institution, and with certain standards. The foundation administers over 25 scholarship funds.
EIN: 311185980

3029
Ron and Lisa Fenech Foundation
c/o Fenech
P.O. Box 1512
Middlebury, IN 46540-1512 (574) 825-5310

Foundation type: Independent foundation
Purpose: Grants and scholarships to children of Keystone RV Company employees for postsecondary education.
Financial data: Year ended 12/31/2011. Assets, $2,943,863 (M); Expenditures, $199,086; Total giving, $170,600.
Fields of interest: Higher education.
Type of support: Scholarships—to individuals.
Application information: Applications accepted. Application form required.
Deadline(s): June 1
Additional information: Application should include two endorsement sheets and high school or college transcripts.
EIN: 201944647

3030
Joseph C. & Louise Skinner Fitzgerald Foundation, Inc.
P.O. Box 469
Lafayette, IN 47902 (765) 742-9066

Foundation type: Independent foundation
Purpose: Scholarships to students at McCutcheon High School, IN, for higher education.
Financial data: Year ended 12/31/2012. Assets, $139,425 (M); Expenditures, $16,445; Total giving, $8,000; Grants to individuals, 6 grants totaling $8,000 (high: $2,000, low: $1,000).
Fields of interest: Higher education.
Type of support: Scholarships—to individuals.

Application information: Application form not required.
> *Deadline(s):* None
> *Additional information:* Applicant must demonstrate financial need, show academic achievement, cumulative GPA, school activities, citizenship and community service.

EIN: 351903440

3031

Fort Wayne Philharmonic Orchestra, Inc.

4901 Fuller Dr.
Fort Wayne, IN 46835-3277 (260) 481-0770
Contact: J.L. Nave III, Pres. and C.E.O.
FAX: (260) 481-0769; E-mail: jlnave@fwphil.org;
Toll-free tel.: (888)-402-2224; tel. for J.L. Nave, III:
(260) 481-0750; URL: http://www.fwphil.org

Foundation type: Public charity
Purpose: Scholarships to qualified instrumentalists who have not graduated from high school, and are residents of the greater Fort Wayne, IN area.
Publications: Application guidelines; Informational brochure.
Financial data: Year ended 06/30/2012. Assets, $12,855,655 (M); Expenditures, $4,762,725.
Fields of interest: Music; Orchestras.
Type of support: Scholarships—to individuals; Awards/prizes.
Application information: Application form required. Application form available on the grantmaker's web site.
> *Send request by:* Mail
> *Deadline(s):* Oct. 7 for Phil Friends Scholarship; Oct. 16 for Young Artist Competition
> *Additional information:* A $25 non-refundable must accompany applications for Young Artist Competition.

Program descriptions:
Phil Friends Scholarship: This scholarship provides financial aid to promising elementary and/or secondary orchestral instrument/vocal students who need assistance in meeting the cost of private lessons. Scholarships will be awarded in amounts of $100 or more depending on the need, merit, and number of students applying.
Phil Musicians Professional Scholarship Fund: The fund aids students under age 19 who are truly serious about their music and have aspirations for a career in music but need financial assistance in reaching their goals. Selection of recipients will be based on need, talent, and the student's desire to excel as a musician. This program is not intended for beginning-level or collegiate students. Scholarships are awarded specifically for study with Philharmonic musicians. Auditions are held annually in the fall.
Young Artist Competition: This competition is held each November for young students through the age of 18. The winners of each division receive cash prizes and the senior winner the opportunity to play in a concert with the Philharmonic. Entrants must live within a 75-mile driving distance of Fort Wayne.
EIN: 350791163

3032

The Foundation Chapter of Theta Chi Fraternity, Inc.

3330 Founders Rd.
Indianapolis, IN 46268-1333 (317) 824-1881
Contact: James L. Hosterman, Jr.
FAX: (317) 824-1908; E-mail: ihq@thetachi.org;
URL: http://www.thetachi.org/main/foundation/

Foundation type: Public charity
Purpose: Scholarships to full time upper class students and graduate students who are members of Theta Chi Fraternity.
Publications: Application guidelines.
Financial data: Year ended 06/30/2012. Assets, $10,012,784 (M); Expenditures, $705,559; Total giving, $406,216; Grants to individuals, totaling $302,216.
Fields of interest: Students, sororities/fraternities.
Type of support: Scholarships—to individuals.
Application information: Applications accepted. Application form required.
> *Initial approach:* Letter
> *Deadline(s):* Varies
> *Additional information:* See web site for additional application guidelines.

Program descriptions:
Dale A. Slivinske Memorial Scholarship Fund: This fund provides scholarships for members of Theta Chi Fraternity to attend leadership and education events.
Reginald E.F. Colley Award Scholarship Fund: Three scholarships of $1,500 each are available to Theta Chi Fraternity undergraduate members who best demonstrate distinguished service to their alma mater, their fraternity, and their chapter.
Sherwood and Janet Roberts Blue Memorial Scholarship: Scholarships are awarded to graduate and undergraduate students who demonstrate scholastic aptitude and financial need.
Victor Simon Memorial Scholarship: Scholarships are awarded to college and university sophomores, juniors, seniors, and graduate students who are candidates for bachelor, masters, doctoral, or other professional degrees. Applicants must demonstrate financial need and superior scholarship, and be either a member in good standing of Theta Chi Fraternity or an employee of Theta Chi Fraternity.
EIN: 214014559

3033

The Foundations of East Chicago, Inc.

100 West Chicago Ave.
East Chicago, IN 46312-3260 (219) 392-4225
Contact: Russel G. Taylor, Exec. Dir.
FAX: (219) 392-4245; Contact for RFPs: Rosie Pena, rpena@foundationsec.org; URL: http://www.foundationsec.org

Foundation type: Company-sponsored foundation
Purpose: Scholarships to East Chicago Central High School students attending college and to adults pursing continuing education.
Publications: Application guidelines; Financial statement; Grants list; Newsletter (including application guidelines); Program policy statement.
Financial data: Year ended 12/31/2012. Assets, $28,251,619 (M); Expenditures, $7,338,295; Total giving, $5,490,441.
Fields of interest: Education.
Type of support: Scholarships—to individuals; Support to graduates or students of specific schools.
Application information: Applications accepted. Application form required. Application form available on the grantmaker's web site. Interview required.
> *Initial approach:* Application
> *Deadline(s):* Mar. 26 for High School Scholarshiips
> *Applicants should submit the following:*
> 1) Essay
> 2) Transcripts
> 3) Letter(s) of recommendation
> 4) GPA
> 5) FAFSA

Additional information: Requests for High School scholarships should include 3 letters of recommendation that demonstrates evidence of character, leadership, and/or community service, a 300-word essay, and proof of acceptance to a postsecondary educational institution. Inquire in person for Continuing Education Scholarships.

Program descriptions:
Continuing Education Scholarships: The foundation awards college scholarships of up to $1,000 to adults undertaking continuing education.
High School Scholarships: The foundation annually awards 38 college scholarships to East Chicago Central High School students. Scholarships are renewable and range from $1,500 to $6,000.
EIN: 208445003

3034

Elenore Francisco Educational Trust

P.O. Box 207
Evansville, IN 47702 (812) 465-7268
Contact: Carol Hahn, Trust Off., Old National Trust Co.

Foundation type: Operating foundation
Purpose: Student loans to graduates of Union County High School, KY. Maximum loan amount per academic year per student is $2,500.
Financial data: Year ended 12/31/2012. Assets, $480,716 (M); Expenditures, $34,579; Total giving, $27,000.
Type of support: Support to graduates or students of specific schools; Undergraduate support.
Application information: Applications accepted. Application form required.
> *Additional information:* Application must include transcripts.

EIN: 616151610

3035

Jacob, Lillian & Nathan M. Frank Scholarship Fund

c/o Old National Bank, N.A.
P.O. Box 868
Evansville, IN 47708 (812) 464-1200

Foundation type: Independent foundation
Purpose: Scholarships to high school and college students of Vanderburgh County, IN, for higher education at accredited institutions.
Financial data: Year ended 12/31/2011. Assets, $422,414 (M); Expenditures, $29,236; Total giving, $22,000.
Fields of interest: Secondary school/education; Higher education.
Type of support: Scholarships—to individuals; Undergraduate support.
Application information: Applications accepted.
> *Initial approach:* Letter
> *Deadline(s):* None
> *Additional information:* Applicant must demonstrate financial need.

EIN: 356338764

3036
Franklin County Community Foundation, Inc.
527 Main St.
Brookville, IN 47012-1284 (765) 647-6810
Contact: Shelly Lunsford, Exec. Dir.
FAX: (765) 647-0238;
E-mail: fcfoundation@yahoo.com; URL: http://www.franklincountyindiana.info

Foundation type: Community foundation
Purpose: Scholarships to students primarily in Franklin county, IN for undergraduate study on a full time basis at any IN public or private college or university.
Publications: Application guidelines; Annual report; Financial statement; Grants list; Informational brochure; Newsletter.
Financial data: Year ended 08/31/2012. Assets, $3,019,114 (M); Expenditures, $539,938; Total giving, $270,234; Grants to individuals, 49 grants totaling $32,605.
Fields of interest: Higher education.
Type of support: Scholarships—to individuals; Undergraduate support.
Application information: Applications accepted. Application form required. Application form available on the grantmaker's web site.
  Initial approach: Letter
  Send request by: Mail
  Deadline(s): Varies
  Applicants should submit the following:
    1) Photograph
    2) Transcripts
    3) Essay
  Additional information: See web site for a listing of scholarship program.
EIN: 352034336

3037
Franklin Electric Charitable & Educational Foundation
(formerly The Franklin Electric—Edward J. Schaefer and T. W. Kehoe Charitable and Educational Foundation, Inc.)
400 E. Spring St.
Bluffton, IN 46714-3798 (260) 824-2900
Contact: John Haines, Pres.

Foundation type: Company-sponsored foundation
Purpose: Scholarships to children of employees of Franklin Electric Co., Inc. or its wholly-owned subsidiaries to attend accredited institutions.
Financial data: Year ended 12/31/2012. Assets, $37,625 (M); Expenditures, $147,769; Total giving, $145,269; Grants to individuals, 14 grants totaling $22,000 (high: $3,000, low: $1,000).
Fields of interest: Scholarships/financial aid.
Type of support: Employee-related scholarships.
Application information: Applications not accepted.
  Additional information: Unsolicited requests for funds not considered or acknowledged.
Company name: Franklin Electric Company, Inc.
EIN: 237399324

3038
Irene Frees Teaching Scholarship
c/o First National Bank of Monterey, N.A.
P.O. Box 8
Monterey, IN 46960-0008 (574) 542-2121
Contact: Claiborn Wamsley

Foundation type: Operating foundation

Purpose: Scholarships to graduating seniors at North Judson High School, IN, to pursue teaching degrees.
Financial data: Year ended 12/31/2013. Assets, $168,145 (M); Expenditures, $1,035; Total giving, $750; Grant to an individual, 1 grant totaling $750.
Fields of interest: Teacher school/education.
Type of support: Support to graduates or students of specific schools; Undergraduate support.
Application information: Application form required.
  Initial approach: Letter or telephone
  Deadline(s): Spring
EIN: 356530824

3039
Friends of CRAFT, Inc.
1392 W. Dittemore Rd.
Gosport, IN 47433-9531 (812) 876-0080

Foundation type: Public charity
Purpose: Fellowship grants for scientific research in the field of paleoanthropology.
Financial data: Year ended 06/30/2012. Assets, $4,311,821 (M); Expenditures, $555,494; Total giving, $50,700; Grants to individuals, totaling $50,700.
Type of support: Research.
Application information: Contact the organization for eligibility determination.
EIN: 352112461

3040
Future Farmers of America
6060 FFA Dr.
P.O. Box 68960
Indianapolis, IN 46278-0960 (317) 802-4298
Contact: Teri Buchholtz, Prog. Mgr.
FAX: (317) 802-6051; E-mail: scholarships@ffa.org; URL: http://www.ffa.org

Foundation type: Public charity
Purpose: Scholarships are available for agricultural education and support. Some programs are limited to members of FFA.
Publications: Application guidelines; Newsletter.
Financial data: Year ended 12/31/2011. Assets, $27,878,030 (M); Expenditures, $8,247,662; Total giving, $326,780; Grants to individuals, totaling $48,000.
Fields of interest: Public education; Agriculture.
Type of support: Scholarships—to individuals.
Application information: Applications accepted. Application form required. Application form available on the grantmaker's web site.
  Deadline(s): See web site for a full list of programs and additional information
  Applicants should submit the following:
    1) SAT
    2) GPA
    3) Financial information
    4) ACT
EIN: 540524844

3041
Mary K. Garr Scholarship Foundation Trust
200 E. Jackson St.
Muncie, IN 47305 (317) 844-2399

Foundation type: Independent foundation
Purpose: Scholarships to worthy high school graduates who are U.S. citizens and residents of Delaware County, IN, pursuing a career in medicine or nursing.

Financial data: Year ended 12/31/2012. Assets, $1,792,011 (M); Expenditures, $100,764; Total giving, $82,000; Grants to individuals, 15 grants totaling $82,000 (high: $6,000, low: $4,000).
Fields of interest: Medical school/education; Nursing school/education.
Type of support: Scholarships—to individuals.
Application information: Applications accepted. Application form required.
  Deadline(s): Mar.
EIN: 351938040

3042
Robert Gemmill Foundation
1 Indiana Sq., Ste. 801
Indianapolis, IN 46204 (317) 221-6283
Contact: Craig A. Bush

Foundation type: Independent foundation
Purpose: Scholarships to residents of Grant County, IN for attendance at an accredited college or law school.
Financial data: Year ended 12/31/2012. Assets, $637,461 (M); Expenditures, $31,067; Total giving, $19,500; Grants to individuals, totaling $19,500.
Fields of interest: Higher education; Law school/education.
Type of support: Scholarships—to individuals; Undergraduate support.
Application information: Application form required.
  Deadline(s): May 15
  Applicants should submit the following:
    1) Photograph
    2) Transcripts
    3) Letter(s) of recommendation
    4) Essay
  Additional information: Payments are made to the educational institution on behalf of the students.
EIN: 356494321

3043
Gibson Foundation
P.O. Box 146
Plymouth, IN 46563 (574) 936-2122
Contact: Karen Noll

Foundation type: Independent foundation
Purpose: Scholarships primarily to graduates of Marshall County, IN, schools for higher education; some scholarships also to graduates of St. Joseph County Schools, both in IN.
Financial data: Year ended 12/31/2012. Assets, $2,031,141 (M); Expenditures, $95,751; Total giving, $93,103.
Type of support: Support to graduates or students of specific schools; Undergraduate support.
Application information: Application form required.
  Initial approach: Letter
  Deadline(s): Apr. 1
EIN: 351422779

3044
Marian Leota Gilmore Scholarship Trust for Sullivan High School Students
80 E. Jefferson St.
Franklin, IN 46131-2321 (317) 736-7051
Contact: Robert D. Heuchan, Tr.

Foundation type: Independent foundation
Purpose: Scholarships to graduates of Sullivan High School, IN, for higher education.
Financial data: Year ended 12/31/2011. Assets, $488,727 (M); Expenditures, $27,560; Total

giving, $19,000; Grants to individuals, 13 grants totaling $19,000 (high: $4,000, low: $500).
Type of support: Support to graduates or students of specific schools; Undergraduate support.
Application information: Applications accepted. Application form required.

Additional information: Contact trust for current application deadline/guidelines.
EIN: 356700224

3045
Greene County Foundation, Inc.
(formerly Greene County Community Foundation, Inc.)
4513 W St., Hwy. 54
Bloomfield, IN 47424 (812) 659-3142
Contact: Cam Trampke, Exec. Dir.
FAX: (812) 659-3142;
E-mail: gcf@greenecountyfoundation.org; Additional e-mail: ctrampke@greenecountyfoundation.org;
URL: http://www.greenecountyfoundation.org

Foundation type: Community foundation
Purpose: Scholarships to students of Greene County, IN for higher education.
Publications: Annual report; Occasional report.
Financial data: Year ended 12/31/2012. Assets, $5,064,399 (M); Expenditures, $299,206; Total giving, $199,743; Grants to individuals, 29 grants totaling $49,041.
Fields of interest: Vocational education, post-secondary; Higher education.
Type of support: Scholarships—to individuals; Support to graduates or students of specific schools; Undergraduate support.
Application information: Applications accepted. Application form required. Application form available on the grantmaker's web site.

Initial approach: Application
Deadline(s): Mar. 18 for majority of scholarships, varies for others
Applicants should submit the following:
   1) Essay
   2) ACT
   3) SAT
   4) Transcripts
   5) Letter(s) of recommendation
Additional information: Applications are available from local high school guidance counselors. See web site for a complete listing of scholarship funds and application guidelines.
Program description:
Scholarships: The foundation administers over 30 scholarship funds that provide tuition assistance to area students for the continuation of their education. Most scholarships are for graduating high school students from a specified area of Greene County, and some are limited to pursuing a degree in a specific subject area, such as agriculture, nursing and finance. Each scholarship fund has unique eligibility requirements. See web site for additional information.
EIN: 351815060

3046
E. E. & Maud Greenwell Scholarship Trust
1st Financial Plz.
P.O. Box 540
Terre Haute, IN 47808

Foundation type: Independent foundation
Purpose: Scholarships to graduating seniors from high schools in Clay County, IN, for higher education.

Financial data: Year ended 12/31/2012. Assets, $1,938,086 (M); Expenditures, $63,945; Total giving, $48,333; Grants to individuals, 10 grants totaling $48,333 (high: $7,500, low: $833).
Type of support: Support to graduates or students of specific schools; Undergraduate support.
Application information:
Initial approach: Letter
Deadline(s): Mar. 1
Additional information: Application should include school activities and statistics, work experience, and leadership abilities.
EIN: 356613402

3047
Albert Guiliani Scholarship Foundation
c/o First Financial Bank Trust-Danville
P.O. Box 540
Terre Haute, IN 47808-0540 (217) 554-1370

Foundation type: Independent foundation
Purpose: Scholarships primarily to students attending colleges and universities in IL.
Financial data: Year ended 12/31/2012. Assets, $130,633 (M); Expenditures, $7,794; Total giving, $5,000; Grants to individuals, 4 grants totaling $5,000 (high: $3,500, low: $250).
Type of support: Undergraduate support.
Application information: Applications accepted. Application form required.
Additional information: Contact foundation for current application deadline/guidelines.
EIN: 376134954

3048
Greater Hammond Community Services, Inc.
(also known as GHCS)
824 Hoffman St.
Hammond, IN 46327-1830 (219) 932-4800
FAX: (219) 933-3452; Lake Station Office address: 275 E. 29th Ave., Lake Station, IN, 46405-1803, tel.: (219) 936-0261, fax: (219) 962-6276;
URL: http://www.greaterhammond.com/

Foundation type: Public charity
Purpose: Emergency assistance for families with rent, utility, clothing, shelter and food in the Hammond, IN area.
Financial data: Year ended 06/30/2012. Assets, $283,701 (M); Expenditures, $1,199,609; Total giving, $700,192; Grants to individuals, totaling $700,192.
Fields of interest: Human services, emergency aid; Economically disadvantaged.
Type of support: Emergency funds; Grants for special needs.
Application information: Applications accepted.
Initial approach: Telephone
Additional information: Contact the agency for eligibility determination.
Program descriptions:
Congregate Meals: The program is for persons 60 years of age or older at five locations. The meal, which provides 1/3 of the daily nutrition, is part of a four hour program each day. The program is offered at five locations: Hammond, IN; Highland, IN; Lake Station, IN; Hobart, IN; Merrillville, IN.
Emergency Services: Provides assistance for families in emergency situations (such as fire or weather disasters) with rent, utility bills, and clothing.
Energy Assistance Program: Two programs for Winter and Summer provide a one-time credit on utilities for low-income households, credited directly to the utility provider. The winter program

runs yearly from November through May; the summer program runs yearly from June through July 15.
Family Shelter (CAPES House): The program provides shelter assistance for families with children under the age of 18 in emergency situations, including fire or eviction.
Food Pantry Program: The program provides a three- to five-day supply of emergency food to families in need every 30 days or as needed.
Information and Referral Program: The program is operated through the organization to determine a client's needs. Referrals are then made for job training and placement, food stamps, welfare, social security, education, health programs, elderly services, and other programs and services as needed.
Lawn Program: The program offers direct services for the low- and moderate-income elderly, and individuals with physical disabilities, including lawn mowing and raking leaves. These services are available in the City of Hammond.
Weatherization: Services are provided for homes with insulation, storm windows, doors, caulking, etc. to low-income and elderly persons place of residence. Both homeowners and renters are eligible.
EIN: 351398205

3049
Hammond Optimist Youth Foundation
c/o Stanley C. Wolucka
7614 Manor Ave.
Munster, IN 46321-1022

Foundation type: Independent foundation
Purpose: Scholarships to local youth of Lake county, IN for post high school education.
Financial data: Year ended 12/31/2013. Assets, $740,781 (M); Expenditures, $41,162; Total giving, $33,000.
Fields of interest: Higher education; Youth.
Type of support: Scholarships—to individuals.
Application information:
Deadline(s): None
EIN: 364293584

3050
Hannah & Friends
51250 Hollyhock Rd.
South Bend, IN 46637-2411
E-mail: info@hannahandfriends.org; URL: http://www.hannahandfriends.org

Foundation type: Public charity
Purpose: Grants to low- and moderate-income families in FL, IN, KS, NY, and RI, that may be used for families that care for children and adults with special needs.
Publications: Application guidelines.
Financial data: Year ended 12/31/2011. Assets, $4,628,570 (M); Expenditures, $465,642; Total giving, $69,157; Grants to individuals, 31 grants totaling $15,915 (high: $7,000, low: $15).
Fields of interest: Disabilities, people with.
Type of support: Grants for special needs.
Application information: Applications accepted. Application form required.
Send request by: Mail
Deadline(s): June 15
Final notification: Recipients notified Sept. 15
Applicants should submit the following:
   1) Photograph
   2) Letter(s) of recommendation
   3) Financial information

Additional information: Application should also include a signed copy of the most recent tax form. Letters of recommendation must be written by a doctor, teacher or therapist on letterhead. Grants for individuals with developmental disabilities are given priority. See web site for additional guidelines.

Program description:

Hannah's Helping Hands Grant Program: These grants provide low- and moderate-income families with stipends, ranging from $100 to $500, that may be used for a wide variety of supports related to their family member(s) with special needs. Eligible families must have a family member with special needs at home in Florida, Indiana, Kansas, the Kansas City metropolitan area, the greater Michiana area, New York, or Rhode Island. Priority will be given to families with a household income at or under $35,000 (for a family of four)
EIN: 300171137

3051
Anna M. Harber Educational Trust Foundation
P.O. Box 1602
South Bend, IN 46634
Application address: St. Joseph High School

Foundation type: Independent foundation
Purpose: Scholarships to graduates of Roman Catholic high schools in St. Joseph County, IN.
Financial data: Year ended 12/31/2012. Assets, $318,278 (M); Expenditures, $19,837; Total giving, $14,833; Grants to individuals, 17 grants totaling $14,833 (high: $2,000, low: $500).
Fields of interest: Education; Catholic agencies & churches.
Type of support: Support to graduates or students of specific schools; Undergraduate support.
Application information: Applications accepted. Application form required. Interview required.
Applicants should submit the following:
1) SAT
2) Financial information
3) Class rank
4) GPA
5) Transcripts
6) Letter(s) of recommendation
Additional information: Application must also include IQ, attendance record, health records, and record of school activities.
EIN: 356034473

3052
Russell and Betty B. Harcourt Educational Trust
c/o MainSource Bank, N.A.
P.O. Box 87
Greensburg, IN 47240 (812) 663-4711

Foundation type: Independent foundation
Purpose: Scholarship to graduating students of Anderson or Orange townships in Rush County, IN for continuing education.
Financial data: Year ended 12/31/2012. Assets, $315,543 (M); Expenditures, $15,952; Total giving, $8,000; Grants to individuals, 4 grants totaling $8,000 (high: $2,000, low: $2,000).
Fields of interest: Higher education.
Type of support: Scholarships—to individuals.
Application information: Application form required.
Initial approach: Letter or telephone
Deadline(s): May 1
Applicants should submit the following:
1) Class rank
2) GPA

3) Financial information
Additional information: Application must also include a brief statement concerning career goals after completion of education and extracurricular activities.
EIN: 356629083

3053
Phil Harris & Alice Faye Scholarship Foundation, Inc.
P.O. Box 236
Lyons, IN 47443-0236 (812) 659-2288
Application address: c/o Phil Harris Scholarship Comm., 489 N. Main St., Linton, IN 47441-1357, tel.: (812) 847-9263

Foundation type: Public charity
Purpose: Scholarships to graduating seniors of Linton-Stockton high schools, IN, who are attending Vincennes University, IN.
Financial data: Year ended 12/31/2010. Assets, $21,023 (M); Expenditures, $16,505; Total giving, $250.
Type of support: Support to graduates or students of specific schools; Undergraduate support.
Application information: Applications accepted. Application form required.
Applicants should submit the following:
1) Transcripts
2) Letter(s) of recommendation
3) Essay
4) Photograph
5) Resume
6) GPA
EIN: 310992482

3054
Harrison County Community Foundation, Inc.
1523 Foundation Way
P.O. Box 279
Corydon, IN 47112-1552 (812) 738-6668
Contact: Steven A. Gilliland, C.E.O.; For grants: Anna Curts, Grants Mgr.; For scholarships: Heather Stafford, Dir., Progs.
Scholarship inquiry e-mail: heathers@hccfindiana.org
FAX: (812) 738-6864;
E-mail: steveg@hccfindiana.org; URL: http://www.hccfindiana.org

Foundation type: Community foundation
Purpose: Scholarships to graduating high school seniors of Harrison County, IN, pursuing higher education.
Publications: Application guidelines; Annual report; Financial statement; Grants list; Informational brochure; Multi-year report; Newsletter; Program policy statement (including application guidelines).
Financial data: Year ended 12/31/2012. Assets, $122,832,443 (M); Expenditures, $3,181,299; Total giving, $2,658,641. Scholarships—to individuals amount not specified.
Fields of interest: Higher education.
Type of support: Scholarships—to individuals; Undergraduate support.
Application information: Applications accepted. Application form required. Application form available on the grantmaker's web site.
Initial approach: Application
Send request by: On-line
Deadline(s): Jan. 31 for most scholarships, Mar. 31 for adult scholarships

Additional information: See web site for a complete listing of scholarships and eligibility requirements.
EIN: 351986569

3055
Susan Hay Hemminger Scholarship Foundation
P.O. Box 9242
Michigan City, IN 46361-9242

Foundation type: Independent foundation
Purpose: Scholarships to graduates of LaPorte County, IN, high schools, who are residents of LaPorte County, for attendance at two- or four-year colleges and universities.
Financial data: Year ended 08/31/2013. Assets, $758,142 (M); Expenditures, $50,611; Total giving, $42,000; Grants to individuals, 15 grants totaling $42,000 (high: $3,500, low: $1,000).
Fields of interest: Higher education; Scholarships/financial aid.
Type of support: Scholarships—to individuals; Undergraduate support.
Application information: Application form required. Interview required.
Deadline(s): Apr. 15
Applicants should submit the following:
1) Essay
2) Transcripts
3) GPA
4) Financial information
Additional information: Application should also include references and proof of acceptance to, or enrollment at an accredited institution.
EIN: 351900696

3056
Helen L. Henderson Scholarship Fund
P.O. Box 511
Fowler, IN 47944-0511 (765) 884-1200
Contact: Anne Molter, Tr.
Application address: 300 E. 5th St., Fowler, IN 47944-1455

Foundation type: Independent foundation
Purpose: Loans to students who are residents of Benton County, IN or students of Benton Central Junior/Senior High School, IN.
Financial data: Year ended 12/31/2011. Assets, $336,863 (M); Expenditures, $7,342; Total giving, $0; Loans to individuals, totaling $9,500.
Fields of interest: Higher education.
Type of support: Student loans—to individuals; Support to graduates or students of specific schools; Undergraduate support.
Application information: Applications accepted. Application form required.
Deadline(s): None
Additional information: Selection is based on academic standing, financial need, personal history, cost of studies, and recipients ability to finance cost of education.
EIN: 356479328

3057

Hendricks County Community Foundation

(formerly The White Lick Heritage Community Foundation, Inc.)
6319 E. U.S. Hwy. 36, Ste. 211
Avon, IN 46123 (317) 268-6240
Contact: William A. Rhodehamel, Exec. Dir.; For scholarships: Eric Hessel, Prog. Admin.
Scholarship inquiry e-mail:
eric@hendrickscountycf.org
FAX: (317) 268-6164;
E-mail: info@hendrickscountycf.org; URL: http://www.hendrickscountycf.org/
Alternate URL: http://www.HCGives.orgs

Foundation type: Community foundation
Purpose: Scholarships to students in Hendricks County, IN, for higher education.
Publications: Annual report; Financial statement; Informational brochure; Newsletter.
Financial data: Year ended 12/31/2012. Assets, $8,463,511 (M); Expenditures, $1,136,373; Total giving, $650,349; Grants to individuals, 337 grants totaling $149,235.
Fields of interest: Higher education; Scholarships/financial aid.
Type of support: Scholarships—to individuals; Support to graduates or students of specific schools; Undergraduate support.
Application information: Applications accepted. Application form required. Application form available on the grantmaker's web site.
Initial approach: Application
Send request by: Online
Deadline(s): Feb. 18 for most scholarships
Applicants should submit the following:
   1) Transcripts
   2) Letter(s) of recommendation
Additional information: Contact the local guidance counselor or see web site for a complete listing of scholarships.
Program descriptions:
Lilly Endowment Community Scholarship: The scholarship provides full tuition, required fees, and a special allocation of up to $900 per year for required books and required equipment for four years of undergraduate study on a full-time basis, leading to a baccalaureate degree at any Indiana public or private college or university accredited by the Higher Learning Commission of the North Central Association of Colleges and Schools. See web site for additional information.
Scholarship Funds: The foundation administers over 50 scholarship funds for higher education. Each scholarship has its own unique set of eligibility criteria, such as specified major, academic achievement, extra-curricular activities and more. See web site for additional information.
EIN: 351878973

3058

Henry County Community Foundation, Inc.

700 S. Memorial Dr.
P.O. Box 6006
New Castle, IN 47362-6006 (765) 529-2235
Contact: Beverly Matthews, Exec. Dir.
FAX: (765) 529-2284;
E-mail: info@henrycountycf.org; Additional e-mail: beverly@henrycountycf.org; URL: http://www.henrycountycf.org

Foundation type: Community foundation
Purpose: Scholarships to Henry County, IN, residents pursuing higher educational goals.
Publications: Application guidelines; Annual report; Financial statement; Grants list; Informational

brochure (including application guidelines); Newsletter.
Financial data: Year ended 12/31/2011. Assets, $27,197,186 (M); Expenditures, $1,810,210; Total giving, $974,429; Grants to individuals, 193 grants totaling $224,974.
Fields of interest: Higher education.
Type of support: Scholarships—to individuals; Support to graduates or students of specific schools; Undergraduate support.
Application information: Applications accepted. Application form required. Application form available on the grantmaker's web site. Interview required.
Send request by: Mail or hand delivered
Copies of proposal: 1
Deadline(s): Mar. 11 for high school seniors, June 3 for postsecondary students
Final notification: Applicants notified in July
Applicants should submit the following:
   1) Resume
   2) Financial information
   3) GPA
   4) Letter(s) of recommendation
   5) SAT
   6) Transcripts
Additional information: See web site for a complete scholarship listing and application form. Applications are also available at your high school guidance counselor's office.
Program description:
Scholarships: The foundation is committed to assisting students as they pursue their higher educational goals. Through donors who share this vision, the foundation offers over 100 scholarship opportunities, helping students realize their academic dreams. Both traditional and non-traditional student scholarships are available, and each scholarship fund has specific eligibility criteria. Most scholarships offer varying award amounts, which range from $500 to $2,500.
EIN: 311170412

3059

Heritage Fund - The Community Foundation of Bartholomew County

(formerly Heritage Fund of Bartholomew County, Inc.)
538 Franklin St.
P.O. Box 1547
Columbus, IN 47202-1547 (812) 376-7772
Contact: For grants: Kristin Munn, Community Grants and Outreach Mgr.
FAX: (812) 376-0051;
E-mail: info@heritagefundbc.org; URL: http://www.heritagefundbc.com

Foundation type: Community foundation
Purpose: Scholarships primarily to residents of Bartholomew County, IN for higher education.
Publications: Application guidelines; Annual report; Grants list; Informational brochure; Newsletter; Program policy statement.
Financial data: Year ended 12/31/2012. Assets, $53,860,598 (M); Expenditures, $2,463,937; Total giving, $1,675,912; Grants to individuals, 97 grants totaling $173,880.
Fields of interest: Higher education; Scholarships/financial aid.
Type of support: Scholarships—to individuals; Support to graduates or students of specific schools; Undergraduate support.
Application information: Applications accepted. Application form required. Application form available on the grantmaker's web site.
Deadline(s): Varies
Applicants should submit the following:

   1) Letter(s) of recommendation
   2) Transcripts
   3) Essay
Additional information: Applications area available from the foundation or some local area high school guidance offices. See web site for a complete listing of scholarships.
Program description:
Scholarships: The foundation administers various scholarships for residents of the Bartholomew County area to obtain a higher education. Criteria may include certain academic requirements, specific majors, financial need, attendance at specific colleges and/or participation in a particular sport or extracurricular activity. See web site for additional information.
EIN: 351343903

3060

John W. Hillenbrand Memorial Fund

324 Mitchell Ave.
Batesville, IN 47006

Foundation type: Operating foundation
Purpose: Grants for outstanding teachers at schools in the Batesville, IN area.
Financial data: Year ended 12/31/2011. Assets, $63,127 (M); Expenditures, $26,940; Total giving, $26,789.
Type of support: Awards/prizes.
Application information: Contact foundation for current application deadline/guidelines.
EIN: 310934822

3061

J. Herbert Hoch & Martha Hoch Memorial Trust

P.O. Box 188
Francesville, IN 47946-0188
Application address: c/o Winamac Jr.-Sr. High School, Attn.: Guidance Counselor, 715 School Dr., Winamac, IN 46996-1584, tel.: (219) 946 6151

Foundation type: Operating foundation
Purpose: Scholarship to graduating seniors from Eastern Pulaski Community School Corporation of Winamac, IN, who will attend a college or a postsecondary institution in the fall immediately following graduation.
Financial data: Year ended 12/31/2011. Assets, $6,655,710 (M); Expenditures, $216,584; Total giving, $195,598; Grants to individuals, 31 grants totaling $195,598 (high: $12,758; low: $1,630).
Type of support: Scholarships—to individuals.
Application information: Applications accepted.
Deadline(s): Mar. 31
EIN: 776236699

3062

Horseshoe Foundation of Floyd County

(formerly The Caesars Foundation of Floyd County)
33 State St., Ste. 344
New Albany, IN 47150-1800 (812) 945-4332
Contact: Jerry K. Finn, Exec. Dir.
FAX: (812) 945-4334;
E-mail: staff@horseshoefoundation.org;
URL: http://www.horseshoefoundation.org

Foundation type: Public charity
Purpose: Scholarships to deserving high school graduates of Floyd county, IN for attendance at accredited colleges, universities, or vocational institutions.
Publications: Application guidelines; Annual report; Grants list.

Financial data: Year ended 12/31/2011. Assets, $19,967,445 (M); Expenditures, $2,556,900; Total giving, $2,319,275; Grants to individuals, totaling $425,770.
Fields of interest: Higher education.
Type of support: Scholarships—to individuals.
Application information: Applications accepted.
  Additional information: Applicants must contact their school guidance counselor for application information.
EIN: 352086312

3063
Everett R. & Frieda G. Houghton Memorial Trust

c/o First National Bank of Monterey, N.A.
P.O. Box 8
Monterey, IN   46960

Foundation type: Operating foundation
Purpose: Scholarships to graduating seniors of Culver Community School, IN and Eastern Pulaski Community School, IN, who plan to attend college or another post-secondary institution in the fall following graduation.
Financial data: Year ended 12/31/2013. Assets, $833,804 (M); Expenditures, $10,247; Total giving, $9,000; Grants to individuals, 4 grants totaling $9,000 (high: $2,250, low: $2,250).
Type of support: Scholarships—to individuals; Support to graduates or students of specific schools.
Application information: Applications accepted.
  Initial approach: Letter
  Deadline(s): Spring
EIN: 351899190

3064
Housing Assistance Office, Inc.

2410 Grape Rd., No. 2
Mishawaka, IN   46545-3015

Foundation type: Public charity
Purpose: Housing assistance to low and moderate income families of St. Joseph and eight other northern counties of Indiana, with rent, rehabilitation, and new homes.
Financial data: Year ended 09/30/2011. Assets, $5,274,814 (M); Expenditures, $2,108,267; Total giving, $1,085,624; Grants to individuals, totaling $1,085,624.
Fields of interest: Housing/shelter; Economically disadvantaged.
Type of support: Grants for special needs.
Application information: Applications accepted.
  Additional information: Payments are made directly to contractors and not the homeowners. Contact the agency for eligibility determination.
EIN: 351327581

3065
Hughes Owen Memorial Scholarship Trust

(formerly Hughes Owen Memorial Scholarship Fund)
205 E. Navajo St.
West Lafayette, IN   47906-2154

Foundation type: Independent foundation
Purpose: Scholarships to graduating high school seniors of Tell City High School, IN pursuing higher education at accredited colleges in the U.S.
Financial data: Year ended 12/31/2011. Assets, $620,414 (M); Expenditures, $27,188; Total giving, $26,400; Grants to individuals, 8 grants totaling $26,400 (high: $3,300, low: $3,300).

Fields of interest: Higher education; Athletics/sports, school programs.
Type of support: Scholarships—to individuals.
Application information: Applications accepted. Application form required.
  Deadline(s): May 20
  Applicants should submit the following:
    1) Transcripts
    2) Letter(s) of recommendation
    3) Essay
  Additional information: Application should also include extracurricular and community activities. Applicant should demonstrate financial need, and good character.
EIN: 351816502

3066
Bernie H. & Mary L. Humphrey Scholarship Trust

c/o MainSource Wealth Management
P.O. Box 87
Greensburg, IN   47240-0087   (812) 663-0118
Contact: Susan Wildey

Foundation type: Independent foundation
Purpose: Scholarship to graduates of Greensburg Community High School, IN in pursuit of a higher education.
Financial data: Year ended 03/31/2013. Assets, $130,483 (M); Expenditures, $6,044; Total giving, $3,000; Grants to individuals, 2 grants totaling $3,000 (high: $1,500, low: $1,500).
Fields of interest: Higher education.
Type of support: Support to graduates or students of specific schools.
Application information:
  Deadline(s): None
EIN: 356527663

3067
Huntington County Community Foundation, Inc.

(formerly Heritage Fund of Huntington County, Inc.)
356 W. Park Dr.
P.O. Box 5037
Huntington, IN   46750-2636   (260) 356-8878
Contact: Michael Howell, Exec. Dir.
Scholarship e-mail: scholarship@huntingtonccf.org
FAX: (260) 356-0921;
E-mail: info@huntingtonccf.org; URL: http://huntingtonccf.org

Foundation type: Community foundation
Purpose: Scholarships to Huntington County, IN students for higher education at accredited institutions.
Publications: Application guidelines; Annual report; Annual report (including application guidelines); Financial statement; Grants list; Informational brochure; Informational brochure (including application guidelines); Newsletter; Newsletter (including application guidelines); Program policy statement; Program policy statement (including application guidelines).
Financial data: Year ended 12/31/2012. Assets, $11,371,723 (M); Expenditures, $453,831; Total giving, $236,187; Grants to individuals, 79 grants totaling $71,067.
Fields of interest: Higher education.
Type of support: Scholarships—to individuals.
Application information: Applications accepted. Application form required. Application form available on the grantmaker's web site.
  Initial approach: Application
  Send request by: Mail or e-mail
  Deadline(s): Mar. 25

Applicants should submit the following:
    1) Letter(s) of recommendation
    2) GPA
    3) Photograph
Additional information: Each scholarship has its own eligibility requirements. See web site for a complete listing.
EIN: 351838709

3068
Huntington County Help Inc. for Disabled Citizens

P.O. Box 1032
Huntington, IN   46750-1032

Foundation type: Independent foundation
Purpose: Scholarships to residents of Huntington, IN, who are disabled.
Financial data: Year ended 08/31/2013. Assets, $898,450 (M); Expenditures, $95,842; Total giving, $71,750; Grants to individuals, 10 grants totaling $14,250 (high: $1,500, low: $750).
Fields of interest: Physically disabled.
Type of support: Scholarships—to individuals; Undergraduate support.
Application information: Applications not accepted.
  Additional information: Unsolicited requests for funds not considered or acknowledged.
EIN: 351903337

3069
Independent Colleges of Indiana, Inc.

3135 N. Meridian
Indianapolis, IN   46208-4717   (317) 236-6090
Contact: Richard Ludwick, Pres. and C.E.O. and Secy.
FAX: (317) 236-6086;
E-mail: smartchoice@icindiana.org; URL: http://www.icindiana.org

Foundation type: Public charity
Purpose: Scholarships to IN residents attending IN colleges or universities for higher education.
Publications: Application guidelines.
Financial data: Year ended 06/30/2012. Assets, $68,072,029 (M); Expenditures, $21,989,163; Total giving, $18,772,956; Grants to individuals, totaling $18,040,956.
Fields of interest: Higher education; Scholarships/financial aid.
Type of support: Scholarships—to individuals.
Application information: Applications accepted.
  Initial approach: Application
  Deadline(s): Apr. 19 for H. Kent Weldon Scholarship
  Additional information: See web site for additional guidelines.
Program description:
  H. Kent Weldon Scholarship: This program awards two need-based scholarships of $500 each to undergraduate students enrolled in either a four-year private, independent, or state-sponsored public Indiana college or university. Eligible applicants must be residents of Indiana who are juniors or seniors, and who are in good academic standing at his or her college.
EIN: 310901001

3070
Indiana Bar Foundation
230 E. Ohio St., Ste. 400
Indianapolis, IN 46204-2149 (317) 269-2415
Contact: Charles Dunlap, Exec. Dir.
FAX: (317) 269-2420; E-mail: info@inbf.org;
Toll-free tel: (800) 279-8772; E-Mail for Charles
Dunlap: cdunlap@inbf.org; Tel. for Charles Dunlap:
(317)-269-7861; URL: http://www.inbf.org

Foundation type: Public charity
Purpose: Scholarships to young attorneys in
Indiana to participate in the Indiana State Bar
Association's annual meeting. Loan assistance for
law school graduates practicing in IN, and have
incurred siginificant educational debt.
Publications: Application guidelines; Annual report;
Grants list.
Financial data: Year ended 06/30/2012. Assets,
$3,914,792 (M); Expenditures, $1,483,936; Total
giving, $744,955; Grants to individuals, totaling
$1,175.
Fields of interest: Law school/education.
Type of support: Scholarships—to individuals;
Student loans—to individuals; Graduate support;
Undergraduate support.
Application information: Applications accepted.
Application form required.
  Deadline(s): Sept. 1 for Scholarships, Dec. 15 for
    Loans
EIN: 356032377

3071
Indiana University Foundation
1500 N. State Rd., 46 Bypass
Bloomington, IN 47408 (812) 855-8311
Contact: Daniel C. Smith, Pres. and C.E.O.
FAX: (812) 855-6956; E-mail: iuf@indiana.edu;
Toll-free tel.: (800) 558-8311; Additional address
(Indianapolis office): 340 W. Michigan St.,
Indianapolis, IN 46202-3204, tel.: (317)
274-3711, fax: (317) 274-8818; Mailing Address:
P.O. Box 500; Bloomington, IN 47402; URL: http://
iufoundation.iu.edu/

Foundation type: Public charity
Purpose: Scholarships to students attending
Indiana University, IN for higher education.
Publications: Annual report; Financial statement.
Financial data: Year ended 06/30/2012. Assets,
$2,105,534,426 (M); Expenditures,
$151,664,780; Total giving, $107,057,090;
Grants to individuals, totaling $22,500.
Fields of interest: University; Scholarships/
financial aid.
Type of support: Scholarships—to individuals.
Application information: Applications accepted.
  Additional information: Scholarship is based on
    need and special achievements.
EIN: 356018940

3072
Indianapolis Matinee Musicale
53 Timber Ln.
Brownsburg, IN 46112-1048 (317) 852-8119
Contact: Danielle Hurt
Scholarship application address: c/o Roberta
Graham, 53 Timber Ln., Brownsburg, IN 46112,
tel.: (317) 852-8119

Foundation type: Public charity
Purpose: Scholarship awards for residents of IN
studying music.
Fields of interest: Music.
Type of support: Scholarships—to individuals;
Awards/prizes.

Application information:
  Initial approach: Letter
  Additional information: Contact foundation for
    complete eligibility requirements.
EIN: 351096129

3073
Indianapolis Neighborhood Housing Partnership, Inc.
3550 N. Washington Blvd.
Indianapolis, IN 46205-3719 (317) 610-4663
FAX: (317) 925-1408; URL: http://inhp.org

Foundation type: Public charity
Purpose: Assistance to low and moderate income
first time home buyers of Indianapolis, with
rehabilitation expenses, loan closing or down
payment for a new home.
Financial data: Year ended 03/31/2012. Assets,
$35,507,537 (M); Expenditures, $9,576,258;
Total giving, $2,215,324; Grants to individuals,
totaling $156,384.
Fields of interest: Housing/shelter, rehabilitation;
Housing/shelter, home owners.
Type of support: Grants for special needs; Loans—
to individuals.
Application information: Applications accepted.
  Additional information: Contact the organization
    for additional guidelines.
EIN: 351742559

3074
Indianapolis Press Club Foundation, Inc.
P.O. Box 40923
Indianapolis, IN 46240-0923 (317) 701-1130
FAX: (317) 844-5805;
E-mail: jlabalme.indypress@att.net; E-Mail for Jenny
Labalme: jlabalme.indypress@att.net; URL: http://
www.indypressfoundation.org/

Foundation type: Public charity
Purpose: Scholarships to college and high school
students of Indianapolis, IN pursuing a career in
journalism.
Publications: Application guidelines; Annual report;
Grants list.
Financial data: Year ended 12/31/2012. Assets,
$545,143 (M); Expenditures, $39,560; Total
giving, $15,500; Grants to individuals, totaling
$15,500.
Fields of interest: Journalism school/education.
Type of support: Scholarships—to individuals;
Awards/prizes.
Application information: Applications accepted.
Application form required.
  Initial approach: E-mail
  Additional information: Awards are based on a
    writing contest. Contact the foundation for
    additional guidelines.
Program descriptions:
  Lennis Scholarship: This fund of $1,000 is
    geared towards students pursuing a career in
    journalism.
  Maurice and Robert Early Scholarship: The Early
    Scholarship of $2,000 goes to students who are
    pursuing a career in journalism and are enrolled at
    an Indiana college or university.
  Walter E. and Mary E. Hemphill Scholarship: This
    fund grants journalism scholarships based on need
    to talented journalism students.
EIN: 351813985

3075
IPALCO Enterprises, Inc. Corporate Giving Program
c/o Public Affairs
1 Monument Cir.
Indianapolis, IN 46204 (317) 261-8213
Contact: Cindy Leffler
FAX: (317) 261-8324;
E-mail: publicaffairs.ipl@aes.com; URL: http://
www.iplpower.com/Our_Company/Community/
Community_Involvement/

Foundation type: Corporate giving program
Purpose: Awards by nomination only to IN math,
science and technology teachers for excellence in
the classroom.
Publications: Application guidelines.
Fields of interest: Education.
Type of support: Awards/grants by nomination only;
Awards/prizes.
Application information: Applications accepted.
Application form required. Application form
available on the grantmaker's web site.
  Initial approach: Letter
  Deadline(s): Mar. 26
  Applicants should submit the following:
    1) Proposal
    2) Resume
  Additional information: See web site for further
    eligibility criteria.

3076
Jasper Foundation, Inc.
301 N. Van Rensselaer St.
P.O. Box 295
Rensselaer, IN 47978-2630 (219) 866-5899
Contact: Kristen Ziese, Exec. Dir.
FAX: (219) 866-0555; E-mail: jasper@liljasper.com;
Additional e-mail: kziese@jasperfdn.org;
URL: http://www.jasperfdn.org

Foundation type: Community foundation
Purpose: Scholarships to individuals residing in
Jasper and Newton counties, IN for higher
education.
Publications: Application guidelines; Annual report.
Financial data: Year ended 12/31/2012. Assets,
$13,957,576 (M); Expenditures, $449,059; Total
giving, $248,193.
Fields of interest: Higher education; Health
sciences school/education.
Type of support: Scholarships—to individuals;
Undergraduate support.
Application information: Applications accepted.
Application form required.
  Deadline(s): Mar. 14 for General Scholarship
  Applicants should submit the following:
    1) Financial information
    2) GPA
    3) Transcripts
  Additional information: Most applications are
    available from the guidance counselors at the
    local high schools. If a particular application
    is not available contact the foundation office
    for assistance. See web site for additional
    application information.
EIN: 351842404

3077
Jennings County Community Foundation, Inc.

111 N. State St.
North Vernon, IN 47265 (812) 346-5553
Contact: Barbara Shaw, Exec. Dir.
FAX: (812) 352-4061;
E-mail: jccf@jenningsfoundation.net; URL: http://www.jenningsfoundation.net

Foundation type: Community foundation
Purpose: Scholarships to individuals who are graduates from accredited IN, high schools and are residents of Jennings county.
Publications: Application guidelines; Annual report; Financial statement; Informational brochure; Newsletter.
Financial data: Year ended 12/31/2012. Assets, $4,252,446 (M); Expenditures, $373,768; Total giving, $223,967; Grants to individuals, 49 grants totaling $84,157.
Fields of interest: Higher education.
Type of support: Scholarships—to individuals.
Application information: Applications accepted. Application form required.
  Initial approach: Telephone
  Additional information: Application available at the foundation, high school guidance office, and Jennings county public library.
EIN: 351922885

3078
Jewish Federation of Greater Indianapolis, Inc.

6705 Hoover Rd.
Indianapolis, IN 46260-4120 (317) 726-5450
Contact: for Scholarships: Inna Kolesnikova-Shmukler
Tel. for Inna K-Shmukler: (317) 715-9264; Scholarship
e-mail: AcademicsScholarship@jfgi.org;
FAX: (317) 205-0307; E-mail: info@jfgi.org;
URL: http://www.jfgi.org

Foundation type: Public charity
Purpose: Scholarships to Jewish individuals for high school, college and graduate students of the greater Indianapolis, IN area.
Publications: Application guidelines; Newsletter.
Financial data: Year ended 12/31/2011. Assets, $75,000,442 (M); Expenditures, $12,886,638; Total giving, $7,590,194; Grants to individuals, totaling $83,652.
Fields of interest: Higher education; Jewish agencies & synagogues.
Type of support: Scholarships—to individuals; Graduate support.
Application information: Applications accepted. Application form required.
  Deadline(s): Mar. 15
  Applicants should submit the following:
    1) Transcripts
    2) Essay
  Additional information: Application should also include three letters of reference, and a full copy of W-2 and previous year's income tax returns. The scholarship is awarded on the basis of strong academic record, financial need, work ethic, character, and one year of volunteer experience in the Indianapolis Jewish community.
Program descriptions:
  Eugene Friedmann memorial Scholarship: This scholarship is awarded to deserving Jewish individuals seeking to further their education. Preference is given to foreign born applicants and

applicants entering the fields of science, medicine or technology.
  Jules Dorfman Scholarship for Graduate Studies in Jewish Communal Service: This scholarship is granted annually to a qualified graduate student in Jewish communal service, social work or Jewish education.
  Len Perel Memorial Scholarship: The scholarship is awarded to deserving Jewish individuals seeking to further their education. Applicant must demonstrate financial need, academic excellence and volunteer experience in the Indianapolis Jewish community for greater than one year. Preference is given to foreign born applicants.
EIN: 350888017

3079
Johnson County Community Foundation, Inc.

(formerly Greater Johnson County Community Foundation)
398 S. Main St.
P.O. Box 217
Franklin, IN 46131 (317) 738-2213
Contact: Gail Richards, C.E.O.; For grants and scholarships: Stephanie Walls, Prog. Assoc., Grants and Scholarships
FAX: (317) 738-9113; E-mail: frontdesk@jccf.org; Grant and scholarship inquiries e-mail: stephaniew@jccf.org; URL: http://www.jccf.org

Foundation type: Community foundation
Purpose: Scholarships to high school seniors, students already enrolled in college, and non-traditional students from Johnson County, IN.
Publications: Application guidelines; Annual report (including application guidelines); Grants list; Informational brochure (including application guidelines); Newsletter.
Financial data: Year ended 12/31/2012. Assets, $17,410,671 (M); Expenditures, $1,094,601; Total giving, $548,044; Grants to individuals, 130 grants totaling $164,493.
Fields of interest: Higher education.
Type of support: Scholarships—to individuals.
Application information: Applications accepted. Application form required. Application form available on the grantmaker's web site.
  Initial approach: Application
  Send request by: Online
  Deadline(s): Mar. 1 for scholarships
  Additional information: Each scholarship has specific requirements as defined by the donor who established the scholarship. The online application process helps students determine scholarships for which they are qualified. See web site for a complete listing.
EIN: 351797437

3080
The Georgina Joshi Foundation Inc

215 S. Hawthorne Dr.
South Bend, IN 46617-3440
Contact: Yatish J. Joshi, Chair.
URL: http://www.thegeorginajoshifoundation.org/

Foundation type: Independent foundation
Purpose: Awards and scholarships for educational and career development opportunities for young musicians and singers.
Financial data: Year ended 12/31/2012. Assets, $0 (M); Expenditures, $2,358,630; Total giving, $2,249,349.
Fields of interest: Formal/general education; Music; Opera.

Type of support: Scholarships—to individuals; Awards/prizes.
Application information: Contact the foundation for additional guidelines.
Program descriptions:
  Composition Award: This award gives support to an Indiana University's Jacobs School of Music student composer. The award also expands the repertoire for solo voice and instrumental accompaniment. The recipient of the award receives a financial stipend and a commission to compose a musical work for solo voice and instrumental ensemble. The piece is premiered each spring at an Indiana University's New Music Ensemble concert.
  The Georgina Joshi Graduate Fellowship: This scholarship pays for tuition, books, fees, living expenses and other costs associated with living and studying in Bloomington, IN for two years. It also enables the recipient to fully participate in all that The Jacobs School of Music has to offer. As a part of the selection process, each finalist participates in a public recital.
  The Georgina Joshi International Fellowship: This fellowship is awarded to a Jacobs School of Music graduate student to study for two years in the Artist Diploma program at the Benjamin Britten International Opera School at Royal College of Music, London. The scholarship links Indiana University's Jacobs School of Music and Royal College of Music. As part of the selection process, members of the Royal College of Music faculty visit the Jacobs School of Music to meet with and listen to each fellowship candidate. The RCM faculty also conducts a master class open to all Jacobs School of Music students.
  The Georgina Joshi Scholar at the Royal College of Music: The award is given to enable a student to take full advantage of the tremendous opportunities available to them at Royal College of Music (RCM) in London. The scholarship covers full tuition and fees for a student to attend the Benjamin Britten International Opera School at the Royal College of Music, London, and provides a maintenance grant for living expenses and cultural activities while attending the school.
EIN: 208791238

3081
Kaminski Sylvester & Tessie Foundation

(formerly Kaminski Foundation)
P.O. Box 1602
South Bend, IN 46634 (574) 235-2793

Foundation type: Independent foundation
Purpose: Scholarships primarily to residents of South Bend, IN.
Financial data: Year ended 12/31/2012. Assets, $799,413 (M); Expenditures, $65,848; Total giving, $41,506.
Type of support: Scholarships—to individuals.
Application information: Applications not accepted.
  Additional information: Unsolicited requests for funds not considered or acknowledged.
EIN: 237355916

3082
Kappa Alpha Theta Foundation

8740 Founders Rd.
Indianapolis, IN 46268-1337 (317) 876-1870
FAX: (317) 876-1925;
E-mail: kkaiser@kappaalphatheta.org; Toll Free Tel.: (800)-KAO-1870; URL: http://www.kappaalphathetafoundation.org/

Foundation type: Public charity
Purpose: Scholarships and grants to collegiate and alumna members of the Kappa Alpha Theta fraternity.
Financial data: Year ended 06/30/2013. Assets, $30,055,631 (M); Expenditures, $2,282,388; Total giving, $1,224,161; Grants to individuals, totaling $587,988.
Fields of interest: Leadership development; Fraternal societies.
Type of support: Graduate support; Undergraduate support.
Application information: Application form required.
  Deadline(s): Feb. 1 for scholarships
  Final notification: Applicants notified May 5
  Additional information: Application should include letters of recommendation.
Program descriptions:
  Carryl Wischmeyer Khrone Leadership Grant: This $1,500 grant is available to help sorority alumni attend a leadership seminar in her own community, or a workshop or training session offered in her career or volunteer field.
  Eleanor C. and Frederick D. Hunt Grant: An $8,000 grant is available to help sorority chapters fund their Educational Leadership Consultant program.
  Ellen Bowers Hofstead Scholarship: A $9,675 scholarship is available to a sorority member who is in her sophomore or junior year, who exemplifies the spirit of community.
  Founders Memorial Scholarships: Four scholarships of $12,000 each are available to Kappa Alpha Theta members who exemplify the spirit and character of the founding members of the sorority.
  Friendship Fund: This program provides financial assistance to current sorority members and alumni who have experienced severe financial distress, catastrophic illness, natural disaster, or urgent financial crisis. Potential recipients must be nominated by a fellow sorority member or alumnus.
  Gamma Pi Chapter Scholarships: A $1,000 scholarship is available for a Gamma Phi Chapter member who is currently attending Texas Tech.
  Indianapolis Alumnae Chapter Grant: A $2,400 award is available to college and alumni chapters of the society, as well as individual sorority alumni, to support educational or philanthropic endeavors.
  Joyce Ann Vitelli Memorial Scholarship: A $10,000 scholarship is available to an undergraduate or alumnus sorority member; preference will be given to those majoring in music or the fine arts.
  Marjorie Crane Schnacke Memorial Scholarship: A $1,125 scholarship is available to a sorority undergraduate or alumnus member who is a resident of Kansas.
EIN: 366066531

3083
Charles B. & Lenore M. Keitzer Memorial Trust C
c/o First National Bank of Monterey
P.O. Box 8
Monterey, IN 46960 (574) 542-2121

Foundation type: Independent foundation
Purpose: Scholarships to individuals who have resided within a radius of five miles from the central point in the town of Monterey, IN, for at least one year while a high school student, or be a member of the parish of St. Ann's Catholic Church, Monterey, IN. Awards are limited to study for religious or educational purposes.
Financial data: Year ended 09/30/2012. Assets, $1,554,195 (M); Expenditures, $51,131; Total

giving, $47,250; Grants to individuals, 27 grants totaling $47,250 (high: $1,800, low: $450).
Fields of interest: Theological school/education.
Type of support: Scholarships—to individuals.
Application information: Applications accepted. Application form required.
  Deadline(s): None
EIN: 356354152

3084
Lucille L. Keller Foundation
P.O. Box 929
Columbus, IN 47202-0929 (812) 376-1795
Contact: For Student Loans: Melissa Fleetwood

Foundation type: Independent foundation
Purpose: Interest-free student loans for higher education to Bartholomew County, IN, residents, as well awards for a special honors program and awards to Ivy Tech Nursing Students.
Financial data: Year ended 12/31/2012. Assets, $180,438 (M); Expenditures, $17,122; Total giving, $13,500; Grants to individuals, 6 grants totaling $10,500 (high: $2,500).
Type of support: Student loans—to individuals; Awards/prizes; Undergraduate support.
Application information: Application form required.
  Initial approach: Letter or telephone
  Deadline(s): May 31
  Applicants should submit the following:
    1) Transcripts
    2) Financial information
  Additional information: Applicant for interest-free student loan must have at least a 2.0 GPA. Loans are eligible for renewable for four consecutive years, but re-apply each year.
EIN: 356016638

3085
Kendrick Foundation, Inc.
(formerly Kendrick Memorial Hospital, Inc.)
c/o The Academy Bldg.
250 N. Monroe St.
Mooresville, IN 46158-1551 (317) 831-1232
FAX: (317) 831-2854;
E-mail: info@kendrickfoundation.org; Toll free tel.: (855) 280-3095 (tel. is in c/o the Community Foundation of Morgan County, Inc.); URL: http://www.kendrickfoundation.org

Foundation type: Independent foundation
Purpose: Scholarships to Morgan County, IN, residents pursuing a career in the health care field.
Publications: Application guidelines; Annual report; Financial statement.
Financial data: Year ended 06/30/2013. Assets, $29,315,922 (M); Expenditures, $1,852,868; Total giving, $1,590,383; Grants to individuals, 43 grants totaling $378,113 (high: $15,000, low: $1,144).
Fields of interest: Dental school/education; Medical school/education; Nursing school/education.
Type of support: Scholarships—to individuals.
Application information: Applications accepted. Application form required. Application form available on the grantmaker's web site.
  Initial approach: Telephone
  Send request by: Mail
  Copies of proposal: 1
  Deadline(s): Feb.
  Applicants should submit the following:
    1) Transcripts
    2) Letter(s) of recommendation
    3) Essay

Additional information: Application should also include letter of acceptance into college, and letter of acceptance into specific health-related program. Applicant must also show school and community activities, and work experience.
Program description:
  Scholarships: Scholarships are up to a maximum of $15,000 per person per year to Morgan county IN, residents graduated with a diploma from an Indiana high school or an equivalent education. Applicant must be accepted at an accredited college, university or other educational institution to complete a course of study in a health care field (including medicine, dentistry, allied health and nursing). Recipients are free to choose which educational institution they would like to attend, with preference being given to candidates who will attend Indiana schools.
EIN: 351124905

3086
The Kimball International—Habig Foundation Inc.
(formerly The Habig Foundation)
1600 Royal St.
Jasper, IN 47549-1022 (812) 482-8701
E-mail: HabigFoundation@Kimball.com;
URL: http://www.kimball.com/foundation.aspx

Foundation type: Company-sponsored foundation
Purpose: Scholarships limited to children of full-time employees of Kimball International, Inc. and its subsidiaries, for attendance at two- and four-year institutions.
Publications: Application guidelines; Program policy statement.
Financial data: Year ended 06/30/2013. Assets, $575,899 (M); Expenditures, $97,396; Total giving, $93,780; Grants to individuals, 19 grants totaling $43,800 (high: $3,750, low: $1,200).
Fields of interest: Education.
Type of support: Employee-related scholarships; Undergraduate support.
Application information: Applications not accepted.
  Additional information: Unsolicited requests for funds not considered or acknowledged.
Program description:
  Kimball Scholarship Program: The foundation awards college scholarships to high school seniors who are children or dependents of full-time employees. Scholarships of $15,000 are awarded for four-year college programs and scholarships of $3,600 are awarded for two-year college programs. Recipients are chosen based on academic achievement and financial need.
Company name: Kimball International, Inc.
EIN: 356022535

3087
Maurice & Evelyn King Education Trust
P.O. Box 830
Jasper, IN 47547-0830

Foundation type: Independent foundation
Purpose: Scholarships to Springs Valley high school graduates for undergraduate education.
Financial data: Year ended 12/31/2011. Assets, $214,056 (M); Expenditures, $11,041; Total giving, $8,250; Grants to individuals, 10 grants totaling $8,250 (high: $1,250, low: $500).
Type of support: Support to graduates or students of specific schools.

Application information: Applications by letter accepted throughout the year.
EIN: 356678200

3088
Kiwanis Club Foundation, Inc.
621 W. Mill Rd.
Evansville, IN   47710-3963   (812) 423-9368
Contact: Michele Bryant, Pres.

Foundation type: Public charity
Purpose: Scholarships to local high school seniors and college students in the Evansville, IN area for higher education.
Financial data: Year ended 09/30/2011. Assets, $370,828 (M); Expenditures, $18,092; Total giving, $17,885; Grants to individuals, totaling $10,256.
Fields of interest: Higher education.
Type of support: Scholarships—to individuals.
Application information: Applications accepted.
   Additional information: Scholarships are awarded based on scholastic record and qualifying need. Checks are sent directly to the universities on behalf of the students.
EIN: 356039356

3089
Koch Foundation, Inc.
(formerly George Koch Sons Foundation, Inc.)
10 S. 11th Ave.
Evansville, IN   47744-0001
Contact: Jennifer K. Slade, Secy.
URL: http://www.kochenterprises.com/corporate/foundation.htm

Foundation type: Company-sponsored foundation
Purpose: Scholarships to children of employees of Koch Enterprises, Inc., and their subsidiaries.
Publications: Application guidelines.
Financial data: Year ended 12/31/2012. Assets, $24,956,099 (M); Expenditures, $1,078,648; Total giving, $1,005,682.
Fields of interest: Higher education.
Type of support: Employee-related scholarships; Undergraduate support.
Application information: Applications not accepted.
   Additional information: Unsolicited requests for funds not considered or acknowledged.
Program description:
   Mary L. Koch and Robert L. Koch Scholarship Awards: The foundation annually awards two four-year $2,500 college scholarships to children, stepchildren, and adopted children of full-time employees of Koch Enterprises and its subsidiaries.
Company name: Koch Enterprises, Inc.
EIN: 356023372

3090
Kosciusko 21st Century Foundation, Inc.
(also known as K21 Health Foundation)
2170 N. Pointe Dr.
Warsaw, IN   46581-1810   (574) 269-5188
FAX: (574) 269-5193;
E-mail: rhaddad@k21foundation.org; Mailing address: c/o Richard Haddad, C.E.O. and Pres., P.O. Box 1810, Warsaw, IN 46581-1810;
URL: http://www.k21foundation.org

Foundation type: Independent foundation
Purpose: Scholarships to financially needy residents of Kosciusko County, IN, who are pursuing a degree in health-related professions

pertaining to direct patient care, as well as assistance to financially needy individuals who have had a diagnosis of cancer within the last three months, and reside in the Kosciusko County, IN, area.
Publications: Application guidelines; Annual report; Grants list; Newsletter.
Financial data: Year ended 12/31/2012. Assets, $64,068,199 (M); Expenditures, $5,049,765; Total giving, $4,620,004.
Fields of interest: Medical school/education; Cancer; Economically disadvantaged.
Type of support: Scholarships—to individuals; Grants for special needs.
Application information: Applications accepted. Application form required.
   Deadline(s): Apr. 1 for Scholarship
   Applicants should submit the following:
      1) Letter(s) of recommendation
      2) Transcripts
      3) ACT
      4) SAR
      5) FAFSA
      6) Photograph
   Additional information: Medical Scholarship information and requirements maybe found at http://www.kcfoundation.org/seekingfunds/documents/K21FoundationMedicalTraditional.pdf.
Program description:
   Cancer Care Fund Program: This program provides assistance to financially-eligible residents of Kosciusko County, IN, who have been diagnosed with cancer within the last three months. The purpose of the fund is to relieve some of the financial strain that often accompanies the diagnosis. The assistance provided includes, but is not limited to items such as rent or mortgage payments, utilities, insurance, food, car payments, and prescription medications. Contact: Laura Cooper, tel.: (574) 372-3500, e-mail: laura@thebeamanhome.org. See web site for additional information.
EIN: 351187105

3091
Kosciusko County Community Foundation, Inc.
102 E. Market St.
Warsaw, IN   46580-2806   (574) 267-1901
Contact: Suzanne M. Light, Exec. Dir.
FAX: (574) 268-9780;
E-mail: kcf@kcfoundation.org; URL: http://www.kcfoundation.org

Foundation type: Community foundation
Purpose: Scholarships primarily to students and residents of Kosciusko County, IN for attendance at a college, university or trade school.
Publications: Application guidelines; Annual report; Newsletter.
Financial data: Year ended 06/30/2013. Assets, $44,536,243 (M); Expenditures, $3,213,789; Total giving, $1,734,603; Grants to individuals, 2,075 grants totaling $638,137.
Fields of interest: Arts education; Performing arts, education; Historic preservation/historical societies; Higher education; Medical school/education; Nursing school/education; Pharmacy/prescriptions; Athletics/sports, training; Women.
Type of support: Scholarships—to individuals; Support to graduates or students of specific schools; Technical education support; Undergraduate support.
Application information: Applications accepted. Application form required. Application form available on the grantmaker's web site.

Send request by: Online
Copies of proposal: 1
Deadline(s): Apr. 1
Final notification: Applicants notified within two months
Applicants should submit the following:
   1) Financial information
   2) Transcripts
   3) SAT
   4) SAR
   5) Photograph
   6) Letter(s) of recommendation
   7) GPA
   8) Essay
Additional information: See web site for a complete listing of scholarship programs and application.
Program description:
   Scholarships: The foundation has more than 80 scholarship funds available for graduating high school seniors and present college students, as well as for adults returning to school. Each scholarship has its own unique eligibility requirements.
EIN: 356086777

3092
Kuhner Scholarship Foundation
200 E. Jackson St.
Muncie, IN   47305-2835

Foundation type: Independent foundation
Purpose: Scholarships to students from Delaware County, IN, who are studying engineering.
Financial data: Year ended 12/31/2011. Assets, $222,207 (M); Expenditures, $16,777; Total giving, $12,600; Grants to individuals, 7 grants totaling $12,600 (high: $1,800; low: $1,800).
Fields of interest: Theology; Engineering school/education; Science.
Type of support: Scholarships—to individuals; Support to graduates or students of specific schools; Undergraduate support.
Application information: Applications accepted. Application form required.
   Deadline(s): Mar. 31
   Additional information: Applications available from schools in Delaware County, IN.
EIN: 356017351

3093
LaGrange County Community Foundation, Inc.
109 E. Central Ave., Ste. 3
LaGrange, IN   46761-2301   (260) 463-4363
Contact: Laura Lemings, Exec. Dir.; For grants: Laney Kratz, Prog. Off.
FAX: (260) 463-4856; E-mail: lccf@lccf.net;
Additional e-mail: llemings@lccf.net; URL: http://www.lccf.net

Foundation type: Community foundation
Purpose: Scholarships to individuals from the Lagrange county, IN area for undergraduate education in the U.S.
Publications: Annual report; Financial statement; Grants list; Informational brochure; Newsletter; Occasional report.
Financial data: Year ended 12/31/2012. Assets, $10,877,533 (M); Expenditures, $507,725; Total giving, $223,995. Scholarships—to individuals amount not specified.
Fields of interest: Nursing school/education; Teacher school/education; Health sciences school/education; Journalism school/education;

Formal/general education; Athletics/sports, basketball.
Type of support: Camperships; Scholarships—to individuals; Support to graduates or students of specific schools; Technical education support; Precollege support; Undergraduate support; Doctoral support; Fiscal agent/sponsor.
Application information: Applications accepted. Application form required.
Deadline(s): Feb.
Additional information: See web site for additional application information.
EIN: 351834679

3094
Andrew Laird Testamentary Trust
P.O. Box 129
Frankfort, IN 46041-0129 (765) 654-8731

Foundation type: Independent foundation
Purpose: Scholarships to male residents of Clinton County, IN, for higher education.
Financial data: Year ended 12/31/2012. Assets, $287,634 (M); Expenditures, $6,144; Total giving, $1,500.
Fields of interest: Higher education.
Type of support: Scholarships—to individuals.
Application information: Application form required.
Deadline(s): None
Additional information: Application must include parent's and applicant's financial statements, qualification for federal student loan or Farmers Bank educational loan.
EIN: 356016337

3095
Lambda Chi Alpha Educational
Foundation, Inc.
8741 Founders Rd.
Indianapolis, IN 46268-1338 (317) 803-7329
Contact: Mark Bauer, Pres. and C.E.O.
FAX: (317) 875-3828;
E-mail: foundation@lambdachi.org; URL: https://www.lambdachi.org/foundation

Foundation type: Public charity
Purpose: Undergraduate and graduate scholarships to members of the fraternity for continuing education at institutions of higher learning.
Financial data: Year ended 06/30/2012. Assets, $5,927,833 (M); Expenditures, $1,566,336; Total giving, $539,846; Grants to individuals, totaling $49,218.
Fields of interest: Fraternal societies.
Type of support: Graduate support; Undergraduate support.
Application information: Applications accepted. Application form required.
Initial approach: Telephone or e-mail
Deadline(s): Apr. 2
Program descriptions:
Graduate Fellowships: Awards $50,000 to twenty brothers who are in need of funds for graduate studies. Eligible applicants must have a 3.4 cumulative GPA, demonstrate chapter and/or campus participation, community service, and financial need.
Undergraduate Scholarships: Awards $50,000 to eighteen brothers who are in need of funds for undergraduate studies. Eligible applicants must have a 3.0 cumulative GPA, demonstrate chapter participation, community service, and financial need.
EIN: 136266432

3096
Legacy Foundation, Inc.
1000 E. 80th Pl.
Merrillville, IN 46410 (219) 736-1880
Contact: Harry J. Vande Velde III, C.E.O.
FAX: (219) 736-1940;
E-mail: legacy@legacyfdn.org; URL: http://www.legacyfdn.org

Foundation type: Community foundation
Purpose: Scholarships to residents of Lake County, IN.
Publications: Application guidelines; Annual report; Grants list; Informational brochure; Newsletter.
Financial data: Year ended 06/30/2012. Assets, $41,840,679 (M); Expenditures, $2,518,777; Total giving, $1,702,407; Grants to individuals, 243 grants totaling $378,838.
Fields of interest: Athletics/sports, training; Athletics/sports, academies; Recreation, social clubs.
Type of support: Employee-related scholarships; Technical education support; Undergraduate support.
Application information: Application form required.
Deadline(s): Varies
Additional information: See web site for further information about numerous scholarship funds.
EIN: 351872803

3097
Raymond Leo House Scholarship Fund
c/o Wayne Bank & Trust
P.O. Box 210
Cambridge City, IN 47327-0210 (765) 478-5916

Foundation type: Independent foundation
Purpose: Scholarship to graduating seniors at Lincoln High School, Cambridge City, IN, pursuing a career in journalism.
Financial data: Year ended 12/31/2012. Assets, $244,182 (M); Expenditures, $13,423; Total giving, $10,070; Grants to individuals, 7 grants totaling $7,000 (high: $1,000, low: $1,000).
Fields of interest: Higher education; Journalism school/education.
Type of support: Support to graduates or students of specific schools.
Application information: Applications accepted. Application form required.
Deadline(s): Feb. 25
Applicants should submit the following:
1) Transcripts
2) SAT
3) GPA
4) Financial information
5) Essay
6) ACT
Additional information: Applications available at high school.
EIN: 621548055

3098
Mosette Levin Trust
P.O. Box 527
Michigan City, IN 46361 (219) 879-0327

Foundation type: Operating foundation
Purpose: Medical assistance for a child under age 16 or an adult with any type of cancer, and are residents of LaPorte County, IN.
Financial data: Year ended 12/31/2012. Assets, $0 (M); Expenditures, $781,797; Total giving,

$770,737; Grants to individuals, 8 grants totaling $12,913 (high: $3,500, low: $99).
Fields of interest: Cancer; Children; Adults.
Type of support: Grants for special needs.
Application information: Applications accepted. Application form required. Interview required.
Initial approach: Letter
Deadline(s): None
Additional information: Application should outline financial need and medical condition.
EIN: 356031456

3099
Eli Lilly and Company Contributions
Program
Lilly Corporate Ctr.
Indianapolis, IN 46285-0001 (877) 545-5946
Contact for Welcome Back Awards: WBA Committee, P.O. Box 536, New York, NY 10008-0536, tel.: (212) 884-0650, fax: (614) 839-7395; Contact for Journey Awards: Lilly Diabetes Journey Awards Admin., 1427 W. 86th St., No. 218, Indianapolis, IN 46260, tel.: (888) 545-5115; Contact for Lilly Oncology on Canvas: c/o TogoRun, 220 E. 42nd St., 12th Fl., New York, NY 10017, tel.: (866) 991-5662, e-mail: artdirector@mylooc.com; Contact for Reintegration Scholarships: Lilly Secretariat, PMB 327, 310 Busse Hwy., Park Ridge, IL 60068-3251, tel.: (800) 809-8202, e-mail: lillyscholarships@reintegration.com; *E-mail:* grantinfo@lillygrantoffice.com; URL: http://www.lillygrantoffice.com/pages/index.aspx

Foundation type: Corporate giving program
Purpose: Awards by nomination only to members of the mental health community involved with depression. Awards to individuals who have successfully battled diabetes through insulin. Awards to cancer survivor artists for cancer-inspired artwork. Scholarships to individuals diagnosed with schizophrenia or a related disorder to pursue education.
Publications: Application guidelines; Grants list; Informational brochure.
Fields of interest: Mental health, disorders; Depression; Schizophrenia; Mental health/crisis services; Cancer; Diabetes.
Type of support: Scholarships—to individuals; Awards/grants by nomination only; Awards/prizes.
Application information:
Send request by: Mail
Deadline(s): Jan. 1 Welcome Back Awards, none for Journey Awards, varies for scholarships
Final notification: Recipients notified in Spring for Welcome Back Awards
Applicants should submit the following:
1) Financial information
2) Transcripts
3) Essay
4) Letter(s) of recommendation
Additional information: Nominations should include a biography, a one page personal statement, and examples of nominee's accomplishments.
Program descriptions:
Journey Awards: Through the Lilly Diabetes Journey Awards, Eli Lilly honors diabetes patients who have managed their disease with the help of insulin for 25, 50, or 75 years or more. Recipients receive an engraved bronze 25-year medal, silver 50-year medal, or gold 75-year medal.
Lilly Oncology on Canvas: Eli Lilly, in partnership with the National Coalition for Cancer Survivorship, sponsors a biennial art competition for people who have been affected by cancer. The competition is open to artwork that best portrays an inspiring cancer journey and narratives that illustrate the

journey. Prizes consist of monetary awards of up to $10,000 donated directly to the cancer charity of the winners' choice.

Lilly Reintegration Awards: Lilly awards to grants to recognize outstanding achievement in the work of reintegration. Special emphasis is directed toward treatment teams, programs, and services that support people living with severe mental illness; local and national efforts to improve services and decrease the stigma of mental illness; and achievements of people living with severe mental illness who give hope to others facing similar challenges.

Lilly Reintegration Scholarship: Eli Lilly awards scholarships to individuals with bipolar disorder, schizophrenia and/or related schizophrenia-spectrum disorders to help them acquire educational or vocational skills to reintegrate into society. Educational opportunities include high school equivalency programs, trade or vocational schools, or associate, bachelor, or graduate degrees. Applicants must currently receive medical treatment and be actively involved in rehabilitative or reintegrative efforts.

Welcome Back Awards: Eli Lilly annually awards grants in recognition of outstanding achievements in the mental health community. The program is designed to fight the stigma associated with depression and to help the public understand depression is treatable. Winners share a total of $55,000 to be donated to the not-for-profit organizations of their choice. An independent panel of national mental health experts selects honorees in five categories: Lifetime Achievement (award level: $15,000); Destigmatization (award level: $10,000); Community Service (award level: $10,000); Primary Care (award level: $10,000); and Psychiatry (award level: $10,000). Each award recipient and one guest will receive complimentary airfare and accommodations to attend a ceremony in San Francisco in May.

3100
Lilly Cares Foundation, Inc.
c/o Eli Lilly and Co.
Lilly Corp. Ctr.
Indianapolis, IN 46285-0001 (800) 545-6962
Application address: P.O. Box 230999, Centerville, VA 20120, fax: (703) 310-2534; URL: http://www.lilly.com/Responsibility/patients/Pages/PatientAssistance.aspx

Foundation type: Operating foundation
Purpose: Pharmaceutical assistance to ill, infant, and economically disadvantaged people who are below the federal poverty level and who are not eligible for any third-party medication payment assistance.
Publications: Application guidelines.
Financial data: Year ended 12/31/2012. Assets, $0; Expenditures, $609,678,898; Total giving, $609,678,898; Grants to individuals, totaling $609,678,898.
Fields of interest: Economically disadvantaged.
Type of support: Grants for special needs.
Application information: Applications accepted. Application form required. Application form available on the grantmaker's web site.
Initial approach: Application
Send request by: Mail or fax
Deadline(s): None
Final notification: Applicants notified in four weeks
Additional information: Applications must be filled out by a doctor and should include proof of the applicants income.
EIN: 352027985

3101
Lilly Endowment Inc.
2801 N. Meridian St.
P.O. Box 88068
Indianapolis, IN 46208-0068 (317) 924-5471
Contact: Ronni Kloth, Comm. Dir.
FAX: (317) 926-4431; URL: http://www.lillyendowment.org

Foundation type: Independent foundation
Purpose: Fellowships for professional and personal renewal to K-12 public and private school educators who are residents of IN.
Publications: Application guidelines; Annual report (including application guidelines); Occasional report.
Financial data: Year ended 12/31/2012. Assets, $7,281,773,872 (M); Expenditures, $254,711,388; Total giving, $234,410,589; Grants to individuals, 120 grants totaling $960,000 (high: $8,000, low: $8,000).
Fields of interest: Education.
Type of support: Fellowships.
Application information: Application form required. Application form available on the grantmaker's web site.
Send request by: Mail
Copies of proposal: 3
Applicants should submit the following:
1) Budget Information
2) Letter(s) of recommendation
3) Proposal
Additional information: Application must include personal and professional information, and description of project. See www.teachercreativity.org for additional information.
Program description:
Teacher Creativity Fellowship Program: The program supports creative projects that are personally renewing and intellectually revitalizing to individual Indiana teachers and education professionals. Personal renewal and individual intellectual growth continue to be the primary goals of this program. If the proposed projects also will contribute to students' engagement and learning, applicants are encouraged to discuss that aspect in their applications. The endowment will grant up to 100 Teacher Creativity awards of $10,000 each. Proposals will be judged on substance, clarity, originality and feasibility of the project. Proposals simply to develop new course outlines or lesson units typically do not reflect sufficient imagination, creativity, or thought to merit an award. The endowment also encourages teams of eligible individuals to submit collaborative proposals. If a collaborative project is funded, each participant may receive a $10,000 fellowship. Contact: Barbara S. DeHart, Prog. Dir., tel.: (317) 916-7345. See website for eligibility requirements and application procedure.
EIN: 350868122

3102
Alma Verne Line Scholarship Fund Trust II
(formerly Claude & Verne Line Scholarship Fund Trust II)
P.O. Box 207
Evansville, IN 47702
Application address: c/o Jasper High School, Attn.: Robert Johnson, Principal, 1600 St. Charles St., Jasper, IN 47546

Foundation type: Independent foundation
Purpose: Scholarships to graduates of high schools in Dubois County, IN, who attend church in Bubois county, IN pursuing a medical career.

Financial data: Year ended 11/30/2012. Assets, $9,198 (M); Expenditures, $15,000; Total giving, $15,000; Grants to individuals, 15 grants totaling $15,000 (high: $1,000, low: $1,000).
Fields of interest: Medical school/education; Religion.
Type of support: Support to graduates or students of specific schools; Undergraduate support.
Application information: Applications accepted. Application form required.
Deadline(s): Apr. 15
Applicants should submit the following:
1) Class rank
2) GPA
3) Essay
4) Letter(s) of recommendation
5) Transcripts
6) SAR
7) Financial information
Additional information: Application should also include reference letter from clergy that indicate your church membership, list of previous awards and honors received, and reference letter from each of your employers during the past two years.
EIN: 356370018

3103
Little Buns, Inc.
P.O. Box 3427
Carmel, IN 46082-3427 (317) 896-2017
Contact: Vmaxine Jeglum, Exec. Dir.

Foundation type: Public charity
Purpose: Financial assistance to child and adult day care providers throughout IN.
Financial data: Year ended 12/31/2012. Assets, $417,301 (M); Expenditures, $4,905,761; Total giving, $4,408,544; Grants to individuals, totaling $4,408,544.
Fields of interest: Day care; Residential/custodial care, special day care.
Type of support: Grants for special needs.
Application information: Contact the agency for eligibility determination.
EIN: 351851458

3104
Logansport Memorial Hospital Foundation
1101 Michigan Ave.
Logansport, IN 46947-1528 (574) 753-7541
FAX: (574) 753-1410;
E-mail: vbyrd@logansportmemorial.org; Toll-free tel.: (800) 243-4512

Foundation type: Public charity
Purpose: Scholarships to graduating seniors who are Cass County, IN residents enrolled in one of the following schools: Pioneer H.S., Logansport H.S., Caston H.S., or Lewis Cass H.S.
Financial data: Year ended 12/31/2011. Assets, $2,013,204 (M); Expenditures, $192,938; Total giving, $68,093.
Fields of interest: Higher education; Health sciences school/education.
Type of support: Scholarships—to individuals; Support to graduates or students of specific schools.
Application information: Application form required.
Additional information: Applicants for the annual HealthCare Scholarship should contact the foundation or the guidance department at their school.
EIN: 351631001

3105
Loogootee Community School Scholarship

c/o German American Financial Advisors
P.O. Box 1008
Jasper, IN   47547

Foundation type: Independent foundation
Purpose: Scholarships to graduating seniors of the Loogootee Community School District, IN for academic studies at accredited colleges or universities.
Financial data: Year ended 12/31/2012. Assets, $956,341 (M); Expenditures, $57,394; Total giving, $46,950; Grants to individuals, 35 grants totaling $46,950 (high: $2,400, low: $600).
Fields of interest: Higher education.
Type of support: Support to graduates or students of specific schools; Undergraduate support.
Application information: Applications accepted.
 Additional information: Scholarship is based on academic ability and financial need.
EIN: 356399803

3106
Madison County Community Foundation

33 W. 10th St., Ste. 600
P.O. Box 1056
Anderson, IN   46015-1056   (765) 644-0002
Contact: Sally A. DeVoe, Exec. Dir.
FAX: (765) 644-3392; E-mail: info@madisonccf.org;
Additional e-mail: sdevoe@madisonccf.org;
URL: http://www.madisonccf.org

Foundation type: Community foundation
Purpose: Scholarships to high school students of Madison County, IN, in pursuit of a higher education.
Publications: Annual report (including application guidelines); Informational brochure; Newsletter.
Financial data: Year ended 12/31/2011. Assets, $13,874,636 (M); Expenditures, $1,189,387; Total giving, $663,199. Scholarships—to individuals amount not specified.
Fields of interest: Higher education; Business school/education; Medical school/education; Nursing school/education; Teacher school/education; Engineering school/education; Theological school/education; Scholarships/financial aid.
Type of support: Scholarships—to individuals; Support to graduates or students of specific schools; Undergraduate support.
Application information: Applications accepted. Application form required. Application form available on the grantmaker's web site.
 Send request by: Mail
 Copies of proposal: 9
 Deadline(s): Mar. 11
 Applicants should submit the following:
  1) Essay
  2) SAR
  3) Transcripts
  4) Resume
  5) ACT
  6) SAT
  7) Financial information
  8) GPA
 Additional information: See web site for complete listing of scholarships. Applications are also available in the guidance offices of Madison County high schools.
Program description:
 Scholarship Funds: The foundation administers several scholarship funds established by donors for area students to attend college and universities. Selection criteria includes financial need, academic

performance, community service involvement, character and leadership qualities. Scholarships are available for general education as well as study of specific majors including nursing or math, business, engineering, education, medicine and religious studies. See web site for additional information.
EIN: 351859959

3107
The Elizabeth A. Mahnken Foundation, Inc.

12210 N. Mariposa Dr.
Syracuse, IN   46567   (574) 457-5365
Contact: Sally M. Mahnken, Exec. Dir.

Foundation type: Independent foundation
Purpose: Scholarships to graduating students of Kosciusko County High School, IN for attendance at a state-supported university/college or satellite campus.
Financial data: Year ended 12/31/2011. Assets, $553,022 (M); Expenditures, $23,940; Total giving, $18,557; Grants to individuals, 3 grants totaling $18,557 (high: $7,682, low: $4,033).
Fields of interest: Higher education.
Type of support: Support to graduates or students of specific schools.
Application information: Applications accepted. Application form required. Interview required.
 Deadline(s): Mar. 1
 Applicants should submit the following:
  1) Transcripts
  2) Essay
  3) Class rank
  4) SAT
  5) Financial information
  6) GPA
 Additional information: Application should also include copies of parents' income tax forms for the last two years.
EIN: 351873161

3108
The Roderic and Mildred Mann Scholarship Trust

80 E. Jefferson St.
Franklin, IN   46131-2321   (317) 736-7151
Contact: James Bradley, Tr.

Foundation type: Independent foundation
Purpose: Scholarships to selected graduates from Franklin Community High School and Indian Creek High school of Johnson county, IN for higher education.
Financial data: Year ended 12/31/2011. Assets, $220,025 (M); Expenditures, $21,161; Total giving, $15,750; Grants to individuals, 6 grants totaling $15,750 (high: $5,250, low: $1,750).
Fields of interest: Higher education.
Type of support: Support to graduates or students of specific schools.
Application information: Applications accepted. Application form required.
 Additional information: Application forms are distributed to eligible students through the school administration.
EIN: 351992636

3109
Irena Maris Scholarship Foundation

c/o First Financial Bank Trust - Danville
P.O. Box 540
Terre Haute, IN   47808-0540

Foundation type: Independent foundation
Purpose: Scholarships to individuals in the Danville, IL area for higher education.
Financial data: Year ended 12/31/2012. Assets, $166,757 (M); Expenditures, $12,212; Total giving, $9,000; Grants to individuals, 7 grants totaling $9,000 (high: $2,000, low: $1,000).
Type of support: Scholarships—to individuals.
Application information: Unsolicited requests for funds not considered or acknowledged.
EIN: 376261922

3110
Marshall County Community Foundation, Inc.

2701 N. Michigan St.
P.O. Box 716
Plymouth, IN   46563   (574) 935-5159
FAX: (574) 936-8040;
E-mail: info@marshallcountycf.org; URL: http://www.marshallcountycf.org

Foundation type: Community foundation
Purpose: Scholarships to graduates of schools in Marshall County, IN for higher education at accredited colleges or universities.
Publications: Application guidelines; Annual report (including application guidelines); Financial statement; Grants list; Informational brochure (including application guidelines); Newsletter; Program policy statement.
Financial data: Year ended 06/30/2012. Assets, $25,831,909 (M); Expenditures, $1,257,847; Total giving, $840,352. Scholarships—to individuals amount not specified.
Fields of interest: Higher education.
Type of support: Scholarships—to individuals; Support to graduates or students of specific schools; Precollege support; Undergraduate support; Grants for special needs.
Application information: Applications accepted. Application form required.
 Deadline(s): Varies
 Applicants should submit the following:
  1) Essay
  2) Photograph
  3) Transcripts
  4) ACT
  5) SAT
  6) Letter(s) of recommendation
 Additional information: See web site for additional guidelines.
EIN: 351826870

3111
Thomas D. McGrain Cedar Glade Foundation for the Needy of Harrison County

c/o W.M. H. Davis
102 Capitol Ave.
Corydon, IN   47112-1164   (812) 738-3201

Foundation type: Independent foundation
Purpose: Grants to needy residents of Harrison County, IN.
Financial data: Year ended 12/31/2012. Assets, $212,602 (M); Expenditures, $13,574; Total giving, $12,600; Grants to individuals, 15 grants totaling $12,600 (high: $3,000, low: $500).
Fields of interest: Economically disadvantaged.
Type of support: Grants for special needs.
Application information: Applications accepted. Application form not required.

Initial approach: Letter or in person
Deadline(s): None
EIN: 351965505

3112
Ralph E. McKinney Nursing School Loan Trust

P.O. Box 187
Williamsport, IN   47993-0187   (765) 762-6184
Contact: Nancy J. Litzenberger, Tr.
*Application address:*111 E. Second St., P.O. Box 187, Williamsport , IN 47993-0187

Foundation type: Independent foundation
Purpose: Scholarships and loans to graduates of high schools of Warren county, IN who are attending or admitted to attend a school of nursing in Indiana.
Financial data: Year ended 12/31/2012. Assets, $77,350 (M); Expenditures, $3,913; Total giving, $1,500; Grant to an individual, 1 grant totaling $1,500.
Fields of interest: Nursing school/education.
Type of support: Scholarships—to individuals; Student loans—to individuals.
Application information: Applications accepted. Application form required.
  Deadline(s): None
  Applicants should submit the following:
    1) Transcripts
    2) Essay
  Additional information: Nursing school must be affiliated with a hospital or college, and must be at least a three year course of study designed to culminate in eligibility to be licensed as a Registered Nurse. Applicant must be a resident of Warren county, IN.
EIN: 416563228

3113
Memorial Health Foundation, Inc.

615 N. Michigan St.
South Bend, IN   46601-1033   (574) 647-6613
Contact: Kellie Porter, V.P.
FAX: (574) 647-6629;
E-mail: cwilliams@memorialsb.org; E-Mail for Kellie Porter : kporter@memorialsb.org; URL: http://www.qualityoflife.org/foundation

Foundation type: Public charity
Purpose: Scholarships to employees of Memorial Health Systems, Inc. pursuing a career in the health care field.
Publications: Annual report; Newsletter.
Financial data: Year ended 12/31/2011. Assets, $22,210,857 (M); Expenditures, $2,520,492; Total giving, $1,238,765; Grants to individuals, totaling $57,212.
Fields of interest: Health sciences school/education.
Type of support: Employee-related scholarships.
Application information: Applications accepted. Application form available on the grantmaker's web site.
  Send request by: On-line
  Additional information: Applicant should submit recommendations each semester from an immediate supervisor and from the school enrolled in.
EIN: 351536129

3114
Montgomery County Community Foundation

119 E. Main St.
P.O. Box 334
Crawfordsville, IN   47933-1709   (765) 362-1267
Contact: Kelly Taylor, Exec. Dir.; For scholarships: Marty Pool, Scholarship Coord.
Scholarship inquiry e-mail: marty@mccf-in.org
FAX: (765) 361-0562; E-mail: ann@mccf-in.org;
URL: http://www.mccf-in.org

Foundation type: Community foundation
Purpose: Scholarships to individuals from Montgomery County, IN, for higher education.
Publications: Application guidelines; Annual report; Grants list; Informational brochure (including application guidelines); Newsletter.
Financial data: Year ended 12/31/2012. Assets, $34,574,826 (M); Expenditures, $1,534,599; Total giving, $1,126,543; Grants to individuals, 176 grants totaling $212,380.
Fields of interest: Higher education; Scholarships/financial aid.
Type of support: Support to graduates or students of specific schools; Undergraduate support.
Application information: Applications accepted. Application form required.
  Initial approach: Letter or telephone
  Send request by: On-line
  Deadline(s): Mar. 7 for most scholarships
  Applicants should submit the following:
    1) Transcripts
    2) SAT
    3) Essay
    4) Financial information
  Additional information: See web site for additional application guidelines.
EIN: 351836315

3115
James B. Moore Charitable Foundation

989 W. 83 N.
Crawfordsville, IN   47933-1177   (765) 362-7790
Contact: James B. Moore, Tr.

Foundation type: Independent foundation
Purpose: Scholarships to individuals for continuing education in accredited institutions of higher learning.
Financial data: Year ended 12/31/2011. Assets, $0 (M); Expenditures, $68,676; Total giving, $67,696; Grants to individuals, 4 grants totaling $6,500 (high: $3,000, low: $500).
Fields of interest: Higher education.
Type of support: Scholarships—to individuals.
Application information: Application form required.
  Deadline(s): None
EIN: 351966383

3116
Billy J. and Christina R. Moore Scholarship Trust

c/o Citizens State Bank
P.O. Box C
New Castle, IN   47362   (765) 529-5450

Foundation type: Independent foundation
Purpose: Scholarships to graduates of New Castle Chrysler High School, IN for postsecondary education.
Financial data: Year ended 12/31/2011. Assets, $169,358 (M); Expenditures, $11,464; Total giving, $9,125; Grants to individuals, 15 grants totaling $9,125 (high: $1,000, low: $250).
Fields of interest: Higher education.

Type of support: Support to graduates or students of specific schools.
Application information: Applications accepted. Application form required.
  Deadline(s): Feb. 1
  Applicants should submit the following:
    1) Letter(s) of recommendation
    2) Photograph
    3) Essay
    4) Transcripts
  Additional information: Application should also include a copy of last year's federal tax returns for the applicant and his/her parents.
EIN: 356718729

3117
James Moorman Orphans Home

7660 N. U.S. 27
Ridgeville, IN   47380
Contact: Brian Edwards, Secy.-Treas.

Foundation type: Independent foundation
Purpose: Scholarships to graduating seniors of high schools in Randolph County, IN, who have been residents of Randolph County for at least two years.
Financial data: Year ended 09/30/2013. Assets, $227,231 (M); Expenditures, $12,938; Total giving, $12,000; Grants to individuals, 12 grants totaling $12,000 (high: $1,000, low: $1,000).
Fields of interest: Vocational education.
Type of support: Support to graduates or students of specific schools; Undergraduate support.
Application information: Applications accepted. Application form required.
  Deadline(s): Apr. 8
  Applicants should submit the following:
    1) Photograph
    2) Transcripts
    3) Financial information
  Additional information: Application should also include a personal statement. Application forms available through Randolph County, IN, high schools.
Program description:
  James F. Moorman Scholarship: Scholarship awards are considered in relation to the applicant's probability of succeeding in his/her chosen field. Each scholarship is a single grant awarded for a one-year period. Maximum award is $1,500. Special grants may be awarded at the discretion of the governing board. Two applications will be accepted, upon proper recommendation, from each Randolph County high school for each school year.
EIN: 350883508

3118
Maude M. Moran Religious Education Foundation

P.O. Box 1602
South Bend, IN   46634-1602
Application address: c/o First United Methodist Church, Attn.: Minister, 201 East 3rd St., Mishawaka, IN 46544

Foundation type: Independent foundation
Purpose: Scholarships to students of Indiana, pursuing religious training of full time Christian workers.
Financial data: Year ended 12/31/2012. Assets, $111,930 (M); Expenditures, $8,686; Total giving, $6,000; Grants to individuals, 3 grants totaling $6,000 (high: $3,000, low: $1,500).
Fields of interest: Theological school/education.
Type of support: Scholarships—to individuals.

Application information: Applications accepted. Application form required.

Deadline(s): Apr. 1

Additional information: Application available in the Office of Financial Aid.

EIN: 356304819

3119

Harvey H. and Donna M. Morre Research Inc.

1112 Cherry Ln.
West Lafayette, IN   47906-2202   (765) 463-5970
Contact: D. James Morre, Dir.

Foundation type: Independent foundation
Purpose: Grants for cancer research primarily at Purdue University, IN.
Financial data: Year ended 06/30/2013. Assets, $363,029 (M); Expenditures, $169,289; Total giving, $169,289; Grants to individuals, 4 grants totaling $129,125 (high: $117,125, low: $2,000).
Fields of interest: Cancer; Cancer research.
Type of support: Research.
Application information:

Initial approach: Letter or proposal
Deadline(s): None

EIN: 351872727

3120

Muncie Civic & College Symphony Association, Inc.

2000 W. Univ. Ave., Ste. 112
Muncie, IN   47306-0002   (765) 285-5531
Contact: Alena McKenzie, Exec. Dir.
Competition e-mail: jhjohnson@bsu.edu
FAX: (765) 285-9128;
E-mail: munciesymphonyorchestra@gmail.com;
E-mail Fore Alena McKenzie:
alena.mckenzie@gmail.com; URL: http://www.munciesymphony.org

Foundation type: Public charity
Purpose: Awards and scholarships for young musicians, juniors and seniors in the Muncie, IN area.
Financial data: Year ended 06/30/2012. Assets, $939,190 (M); Expenditures, $324,018.
Fields of interest: Music; Orchestras.
Type of support: Scholarships—to individuals; Awards/prizes.
Application information: Application form required. Application form available on the grantmaker's web site.

Deadline(s): Dec.

Additional information: Application must include a biography and performance history or experience (200 words or less). A non-refundable entry fee of $50 for seniors and $40 for juniors ($10 off second applicant from same family). See web site for additional guidelines.

Program description:

Young Artist Competition: The MSO holds a yearly competition for young musicians in the region. Two divisions, the junior and the senior, provide the opportunity to select two winners, a younger player and a more seasoned player. Candidates must reside in Indiana and/or be enrolled in an Indiana school or home school program. Previous winners may not enter a second time in the same division on the same instrument. The competition divisions are: 1) The Ladonna Dingledine Junior Division which provides a $250 award and a performance opportunity. Junior division contestants may select

either a concerto movement (with accompaniment) or a solo movement. 2) The Steve Dingledine Senior Division which provides a $500 award and a performance opportunity. Senior division contestants must play a concerto movement with accompaniment. The concerto must be easily obtained through the Ball State Symphony Orchestra library or a rental company.

EIN: 356041986

3121

National Collegiate Athletic Association

(also known as NCAA)
700 W. Washington St.
P.O. Box 6222
Indianapolis, IN   46204-2710   (317) 917-6222
FAX: (317) 917-6888; URL: http://www.ncaa.org

Foundation type: Public charity
Purpose: Scholarships to outstanding collegiate athlete scholars who participate in association-sanctioned events.
Publications: Application guidelines.
Financial data: Year ended 08/31/2012. Assets, $704,419,990 (M); Expenditures, $791,295,359; Total giving, $522,009,333; Grants to individuals, 240 grants totaling $196,429.
Fields of interest: Higher education; Scholarships/financial aid; Athletics/sports, amateur competition; Recreation.
Type of support: Scholarships—to individuals.
Application information:

Deadline(s): Varies

Program descriptions:

Division I Degree-Completion Award Program: Financial aid is available to assist student-athletes who have exhausted their eligibility for institutional financial aid. Applicants must have completed eligibility for athletics-related aid at a Division I member institution before applying and must be within 30 semester hours of their degree requirements. Full-time students receive grants equal to a full athletics grant at the institution. Part-time students receive tuition and an allowance for books.

Division II Degree-Completion Award Program: Financial aid is available for student-athletes who have exhausted athletics eligibility at an active Division II institution within the past calendar year. Awards are limited to student-athletes during their first 10 semesters or 15 quarters of full-time collegiate attendance. Eligible applicants must have received athletics-related financial aid from the NCAA Division II member institution, be within 32 semesters or 48 quarter hours of completion of his or her first undergraduate degree at the completion of the spring term, and have a 2.50 cumulative GPA.

Ethnic Minority and Women's Enhancement Postgraduate Scholarship for Career in Athletics: Awards 13 scholarships to ethnic minorities and 13 scholarships to female college graduates who will be entering their initial year of postgraduate studies. The applicant must be seeking admission or have been accepted into a sports administration or other program that will help the applicant obtain a career in intercollegiate athletics, such as athletics administrator, coach, athletic trainer or other career that provides a direct service to intercollegiate athletics. The goal of the program is to increase the pool of and opportunities for qualified minority and female candidates in intercollegiate athletics through postgraduate scholarships.

Ethnic Minority and Women's Internship Grant Program: Two grants of $23,100 each are available to Division III member schools to hire women and

individuals identifying as ethnic minorities (American Indian/Alaskan Native, Asian/Pacific Islander, African American/Black, and Hispanic/Latino) for a 10-month, full-time position in administration/coaching, and expose them to opportunities for learning, administrative supervision, and mentorship. Funding is designed to cover the intern's salary and cost of attending professional development activities.

NCAA Postgraduate Scholarship Program: Postgraduate scholarships, awarded equally to men and women, of $7,500 each are available to student-athletes who excel academically and athletically and who are in their final year of intercollegiate athletics competition. Eligibility is restricted to student-athletes at member institutions who, in their final year of eligibility, have performed with distinction as members of varsity teams in the sport for which they were nominated. Nominees must have a minimum GPA of 3.2, be nominated by the faculty athletics representative or designee at their undergraduate institution, and intend to continue academic work beyond the baccalaureate degree as a part-time or full-time graduate student. Scholarships are awarded three times a year, for winter, fall, and spring sports.

The Freedom Forum - NCAA Sports-Journalism Scholarship Program: Eight $3,000 scholarships are available to college juniors who have career goals in sports journalism, and are majoring in journalism or have experience in campus sports journalism. The program is designed to assist deserving full-time students in their final year of study and is designated to foster freedom of speech and press while promoting quality sports journalism education at the collegiate level.

Walter Byers Postgraduate Scholarship Program: Two scholarships of $21,500 each are awarded annually to one male and one female student-athlete in recognition of outstanding academic achievement and potential for success in postgraduate study. Eligible applicants must have an overall undergraduate cumulative GPA of 3.5 or better, have competed in intercollegiate athletics as a member of a varsity team at a member institution, be a graduating senior or be enrolled in graduate study at an member institution while completing the last year of eligibility, and have intentions of applying for admission on a full-time basis into a graduate degree program at a properly-accredited, nonprofit educational institution or into a post-baccalaureate professional degree program at a professionally-accredited law school, medical school, or the equivalent. Eligible applicants must be nominated by the faculty athletics representative or chief academics officer at the institution where the nominee is or was a varsity student.

EIN: 440567264

3122

National FFA Foundation, Inc.

P.O. Box 68960
Indianapolis, IN   46268-0960   (317) 802-6060
FAX: (317) 802-6051; E-mail: foundation@ffa.org;
URL: https://www.ffa.org/donate/foundation/Pages/default.aspx

Foundation type: Public charity
Purpose: Undergraduate and graduate scholarships for students nationwide who are members of the Future Farmers of America (FFA)
Publications: Application guidelines; Annual report; Financial statement.
Financial data: Year ended 12/31/2011. Assets, $15,272,094 (M); Expenditures, $15,552,320;

Total giving, $5,567,586; Grants to individuals, totaling $5,567,586.
Fields of interest: Fund raising/fund distribution; Education; Agriculture/food.
Type of support: Scholarships—to individuals.
Application information: Applications accepted. Application form required. Application form available on the grantmaker's web site.
  Send request by: Online
  Deadline(s): Feb. 15
  Additional information: Scholarships are available for both FFA members and non-members, though the vast majority of funding is reserved for members. Separate applications must be filled out for both members and non-members.
Program description:
  Scholarship Program: Each year, the foundation awards approximately $2 million in scholarship awards to both undergraduate and graduate students in a variety of disciplines. The selection process takes into account the whole student, including Future Farmers of America (FFA) involvement, supervised agricultural experience (SAE), community service, leadership skills, and academics. Scholarships generally range from $1,000 to $2,500; scholarships are available to both FFA members and non-members, though the vast majority of funding is reserved for FFA members.
EIN: 546044662

3123
National Gymnastics Foundation
132 E. Washington St., Ste. 700
Indianapolis, IN 46204-3674 (317) 237-5050
Contact: Robert Wood, Chair.
FAX: (317) 237-5069;
E-mail: rebound@usa-gymnastics.org; URL: http://www.usa-gymnastics.org/pages/aboutus/pages/foundation.html

Foundation type: Public charity
Purpose: Scholarships awarded to participants of the Trampoling and Tumbling Program of USA Gymnastics, to further their educational endeavors.
Publications: Application guidelines.
Financial data: Year ended 12/31/2011. Assets, $5,726,534 (M); Expenditures, $516,029; Total giving, $437,763; Grants to individuals, totaling $52,763.
Fields of interest: Higher education.
Type of support: Scholarships—to individuals.
Application information: Applications accepted. Application form available on the grantmaker's web site.
  Deadline(s): May 20 for Trampoline and Tumbling Program
  Final notification: Applicants notified June 27
Program description:
  Trampoline and Tumbling Program: This program works to provide trampoline and tumbling athletes with funds to continue their education while still training and competing for USA Gymnastics. Eligible applicants must be seventeen years of age or older, be full- or part-time (at least eight hours) students at an accredited college or university, be a currently-registered athlete, training and completing within the Trampoline and Tumbling Program of USA Gymnastics, and have a GPA of at least 2.5.
EIN: 351757753

3124
National Kidney Foundation of Indiana, Inc.
911 E. 86th St., Ste. 100
Indianapolis, IN 46240-1848 (317) 722-5640
Contact: Margie Fort, Exec. Dir.
FAX: (317) 722-5650;
E-mail: nkfi@kidneyindiana.org; Toll-free tel.: (800) 382-9971; URL: http://www.kidney.org/site/index.cfm?ch=303

Foundation type: Public charity
Purpose: Financial assistance to kidney patients residing in IN, for help with expenses, such as utilities, transportation and medication. Research grants to young investigators in IN interested in developing cures and/or treatments for Chronic Kidney Disease.
Publications: Annual report; Informational brochure.
Financial data: Year ended 06/30/2012. Assets, $1,372,860 (M); Expenditures, $777,750; Total giving, $40,411; Grants to individuals, totaling $40,411.
Fields of interest: Higher education; Kidney diseases; Kidney research.
Type of support: Research; Scholarships—to individuals; Grants for special needs.
Application information: Application form required.
  Deadline(s): Nov. for Research Grants
EIN: 351180274

3125
Harold M. Neel and Katharine Klepinger Neel Scholarship Fund
P.O. Box 909
Lafayette, IN 47902-0909
Application address: c/o Charles Max Layden, 201 N. Main St., Ste. 712, Lafayette, IN 47901-1272, tel.: (765) 742-7646

Foundation type: Independent foundation
Purpose: Undergraduate scholarships to graduating students of Frontier High School, IN, who are in the top 25 percent of their classes for attendance at state supported colleges and universities in IN.
Financial data: Year ended 12/31/2012. Assets, $3,880,005 (M); Expenditures, $175,918; Total giving, $123,178; Grants to individuals, 17 grants totaling $123,178 (high: $23,460, low: $100).
Fields of interest: Higher education.
Type of support: Support to graduates or students of specific schools; Undergraduate support.
Application information: Application form required.
  Deadline(s): Apr. 1
EIN: 356529645

3126
Ted & Anna Nesty Charitable Trust
c/o Wabash Valley Community Foundation
2901 Ohio Blvd., Ste. 153
Terre Haute, IN 47803
Contact: Beth Tevlin

Foundation type: Independent foundation
Purpose: Scholarships to graduates of Northview High School of Clay county IN, for higher education.
Financial data: Year ended 12/31/2012. Assets, $117,522 (M); Expenditures, $8,818; Total giving, $6,950; Grant to an individual, 1 grant totaling $1,950.
Fields of interest: Higher education.
Type of support: Support to graduates or students of specific schools; Undergraduate support.
Application information:
  Initial approach: Letter

  Additional information: Application can be obtained from the trustee. Students must be in the upper 15 percent of their class to be considered for a scholarship.
EIN: 311114644

3127
Noble County Community Foundation
1599 Lincolnway S.
Ligonier, IN 46767-9731 (260) 894-3335
Contact: Linda Speakman-Yerick, Exec. Dir.; For grants: Margarita White, Prog. Off.
FAX: (260) 894-9020;
E-mail: info@noblecountycf.org; URL: http://www.noblecountycf.org/

Foundation type: Community foundation
Purpose: Scholarships to eligible residents of Noble County, IN, pursuing higher education.
Publications: Application guidelines; Annual report; Grants list; Informational brochure (including application guidelines); Newsletter.
Financial data: Year ended 12/31/2012. Assets, $20,563,794 (M); Expenditures, $1,248,996; Total giving, $514,080; Grants to individuals, 67 grants totaling $155,547.
Fields of interest: Vocational education, post-secondary; Higher education; Nursing school/education.
Type of support: Scholarships—to individuals; Awards/grants by nomination only; Technical education support; Undergraduate support.
Application information: Application form required. Application form available on the grantmaker's web site.
  Initial approach: Application
  Send request by: Mail or in person
  Copies of proposal: 1
  Deadline(s): Jan. 23
  Applicants should submit the following:
    1) Transcripts
    2) SAT
    3) Letter(s) of recommendation
    4) GPA
    5) Financial information
    6) Essay
    7) ACT
  Additional information: See web site for additional guidelines.
EIN: 351827247

3128
Northwest Indiana Community Action Corporation
5240 Fountain Dr.
Crown Point, IN 46307-1084 (219) 794-1829
FAX: (219) 932-0560; E-mail: director@nwi-ca.org; Toll-free tel.: (800) 826-7871; TTY: (888) 814-7597; URL: http://www.nwi-ca.com/

Foundation type: Public charity
Purpose: Assistance to low-income individuals and families of northwest Indiana with housing, utility bills, weatherization and other needs. Assistance to older adults with physical disabilities.
Publications: Annual report.
Financial data: Year ended 12/31/2011. Assets, $3,424,473 (M); Expenditures, $26,861,218; Total giving, $20,758,404; Grants to individuals, totaling $20,758,404.
Fields of interest: Human services; Aging; Disabilities, people with; Economically disadvantaged.
Type of support: Grants for special needs.
Application information:
  Initial approach: Telephone

Additional information: Areas served are Jasper, Lake, Newton, Porter, Pulaski, and Starke counties in Northwest IN. Contact the agency for eligibility determination.
EIN: 351112290

3129
Julia S. Oberdorfer Scholarship Trust Fund
c/o Citizens State Bank
P.O. Box C
New Castle, IN   47362-1045   (765) 521-7213
Contact: Bill Tucker
Application address: 2602 S. 14th St., New Castle IN 47362

Foundation type: Independent foundation
Purpose: Scholarships to graduating seniors of New Castle Chrysler High School, IN.
Financial data: Year ended 12/31/2012. Assets, $409,944 (M); Expenditures, $17,236; Total giving, $13,000; Grants to individuals, 14 grants totaling $13,000 (high: $3,000, low: $250).
Fields of interest: Higher education.
Type of support: Support to graduates or students of specific schools; Undergraduate support.
Application information: Application form required.
  Deadline(s): Feb. 15
  Applicants should submit the following:
    1) Transcripts
    2) SAT
    3) ACT
  Additional information: Application should also include PSAT test scores, attendance records, and name of college to attend.
EIN: 356238626

3130
Charles D. & Gertrude H. O'Connor Educational Trust
c/o John Demerly
9650 West 400 N.
Wolcott, IN   47995   (765) 427-7509
Contact: John Demerly, Chair.

Foundation type: Operating foundation
Purpose: Scholarships to students residing in White and Benton counties, IN for attendance at institutions of higher learning.
Financial data: Year ended 12/31/2012. Assets, $2,623,096 (M); Expenditures, $130,165; Total giving, $100,000; Grants to individuals, 20 grants totaling $100,000 (high: $5,000, low: $5,000).
Fields of interest: Higher education.
Type of support: Scholarships—to individuals.
Application information: Application form required.
  Deadline(s): Apr. 1
  Additional information: Application must include transcripts and high school activities. Forms are available from the trustees.
EIN: 311012552

3131
Ohio County Community Foundation, Inc.
330 Industrial Access Dr.
P.O. Box 170
Rising Sun, IN   47040   (812) 438-9401
Contact: Peggy Dickson, Exec. Dir.; For grants: Stephanie Scott, Prog. Coord.
FAX: (812) 438-9488;
E-mail: pdickson@occfrisingsun.com; URL: http://www.occfrisingsun.com

Foundation type: Community foundation
Purpose: Scholarships to high school graduates and residents of Ohio County, IN pursuing higher education. Grants to teachers in the Rising Sun-Ohio County School Corporation to fund classroom projects or teaching tools.
Publications: Application guidelines; Annual report; Grants list; Informational brochure; Newsletter.
Financial data: Year ended 12/31/2012. Assets, $24,719,808 (M); Expenditures, $718,822; Total giving, $248,813; Grants to individuals, 138 grants totaling $108,808.
Fields of interest: Higher education.
Type of support: Grants to individuals; Scholarships—to individuals; Support to graduates or students of specific schools.
Application information: Applications accepted. Application form required.
  Deadline(s): Varies
  Additional information: See web site for additional guidelines.
Program descriptions:
  Certification Scholarship Program: This scholarship program financially assists individuals seeking to earn a certification. The scholarship amount is up to $300 per qualified applicant who is a current resident of Ohio County for at least one year and meet all scholarship criteria. Applications will be processed on a first come, first serve basis until funds for the calendar year have been depleted.
  Community/Junior College Scholarship: The goal of this program is to financially assist residents of Ohio County seeking to pursue a two (2) year college degree at a Community or Junior College. Applicant must meet the specific scholarship criteria. While the foundation administers the scholarship, the City of Rising Sun will determine the scholarship award each year. The award amount will be $500.
  Continuing Education Scholarships: The foundation administers a variety of scholarships for residents of Ohio County who may already be enrolled in a college or university, or who have already graduated from high school and pursuing higher education or wishing to start a new career, make a career change, advance in their current job or enhance their job skills.
  High School Scholarships: The foundation administers various scholarships for graduating high school students of the Ohio County area. Each scholarship has its own unique set of eligibility criteria, which may include demonstration of financial need, high academic achievement and concentration in a particular area of study such as medicine, science, and music.
  Teachers' Classroom Tools Grant Program: All teachers employed by the Rising Sun-Ohio County School Corporation are eligible to apply for the foundation's Teachers' Classroom Tools Grants Program to fund classroom projects or teaching tools that enhance classroom learning. Teachers must have submitted all Grant Report Forms for previous grant awards before submitting a new application. Teachers with outstanding Grant Reports will not be considered.
EIN: 352038531

3132
Organization of American Historians
112 N. Bryan Ave.
P.O. Box 5457
Bloomington, IN   47408-4141   (812) 855-7311
Contact: Katherine Finley, Exec. Dir.
FAX: (812) 855-0696; E-mail: oah@oah.org; E-Mail for Katherine Finley: kmfinley@oah.org;
URL: http://www.oah.org

Foundation type: Public charity
Purpose: Awards, fellowships, prizes, and grants to scholars and professionals specializing in American history, and fellowships to students of color in the Ph.D. program in U.S. History at Indiana University, IN.
Publications: Application guidelines; Annual report.
Financial data: Year ended 06/30/2012. Assets, $2,218,760 (M); Expenditures, $2,706,494; Total giving, $21,201; Grants to individuals, totaling $21,201.
Fields of interest: Historical activities; American studies; Minorities.
Type of support: Fellowships; Support to graduates or students of specific schools; Awards/prizes; Graduate support.
Application information: Application form required.
  Deadline(s): Varies
  Additional information: See web site for additional application guidelines.
Program descriptions:
  Avery O. Craven Award: Awards $500 and a certificate for the most original book on the coming of the Civil War, the Civil War years, or the Era of Reconstruction, with the exception of works of purely military history.
  Binkley-Stephenson Award: Awards $500 and a plaque for the best scholarly article published in the Journal of American History during the preceding year.
  Darlene Clark Hine Award: The organization offers a $2,000 award for a book in African-American and gender history.
  David Thelen Award: This award (formerly the Foreign Language Article Prize) is given biennially for the best article on American history published in a foreign language. The winning article will be published in the Journal of American History. Entries must have been published during the preceding two calendar years. To be eligible, an article should be concerned with the past (recent or distant) or with issues of continuity and change. The winning article will be printed in the Journal of American History and its author awarded a $500 subvention for refining the article's English translation.
  Ellis W. Hawley Prize: Awards $500 and a plaque annually for the best book-length historical study of the political economy, politics, or institutions of the United States, in its domestic or international affairs, from the Civil War to the present.
  Erik Barnouw Award: This award is given annually in recognition of outstanding programming on network or cable television, or in documentary film, concerned with American history, the study of American history, and/or the promotion of history. The winning film or video program will be screened and the award will be presented at the organization's annual meeting. The producer(s) of the winning film or video program will receive $1,000 (or $500 should two films be selected)
  Frederick Jackson Turner Award: Awards $1,000 and a plaque to an author for his/her first book on some significant phase of American history, and also to the press that submits and publishes it.
  James A. Rawley Prize: Awards $1,000 and a plaque annually for a book dealing with the history of race relations in the United States.
  Japan Residencies: This program, in conjunction with the Japanese Association for American Studies (JAAS), will send three American scholars to Japanese universities for two-week residencies. There, in English, the American historians give lectures and seminars in their specialty and provide individual consultation to Japanese scholars, graduate students, and sometimes undergraduates studying American history and culture. Visitors also participate in the collegial life of their host institutions and help expand personal scholarly

networks between Japan and the U.S. Round-trip airfare to Japan, housing, and modest daily expenses are covered. Selectees are also encouraged to explore Japan before or after their two-week residency at their own expense. Applicants must be organization members who have a Ph.D. and are scholars of American history. Applicants from previous competitions are welcome to apply again.

John Higham Travel Grants: Travel grants of $500 are awarded to three graduate students each year. Funds are to be used by graduate students toward costs of attending organization annual meetings. The successful candidates will have a preferred area of concentration in American immigration, American ethnic histories, and/or American intellectual history.

Lawrence W. Levine Award: The organization offers an annual award of $2,000 for the best book in American cultural history.

Lerner-Scott Dissertation Prize: Awards $1,000 and a plaque for the best doctoral dissertation in U.S. women's history.

Liberty Legacy Foundation Award: Awards $2,000 and a plaque to an author for the best book on any historical aspect of the struggle for civil rights in the United States from the nation's founding to the present.

Louis Pelzer Memorial Award: Awards $500 and a plaque to graduate degree candidates who submit essays that deal with any period or topic in the history of the United States.

Merle Curti Award: Awards $2,000 (or $1,000 should two books be selected) and a plaque annually for the best book in social and/or intellectual history.

OAH-IEHS Huggins-Quarles Dissertation Award: Named for Benjamin Quarles and Nathan Huggins, two outstanding historians of the African-American past, this award is given annually to one or two graduate students of color at the dissertation research stage of their Ph.D. program. To apply for a $1,000 award ($2,000 if only one is awarded), the student should submit a five-page dissertation proposal (which should include a definition of the project, an explanation of the project's significance and contribution to the field, and a description of the most important primary sources), along with a one-page itemized budget explaining travel and research plans.

OAH/ALBC Abraham Lincoln Higher Education Awards: The organization partners with the Abraham Lincoln Bicentennial Commission to offer two awards to help further graduate study of Abraham Lincoln and Civil War America, 1854-1865. One ABD doctoral fellow will receive an award of $500, and one masters fellow will receive an award of $250. Applicants are required to submit transcripts, a dissertation or thesis proposal/prospectus, and a letter from their current major professors, respectively, that speaks to the current and future potential of the candidate's continued contribution to historical scholarship regarding Abraham Lincoln.

Ray Allen Billington Prize: Awards $1,000 and a plaque biennially for the best book in American frontier history (defined broadly, so as to include the pioneer periods of all geographical areas) and comparisons between American frontiers.

Richard W. Leopold Prize: Awards $1,500 and a plaque every two years for the best book written by a historian connected with federal, state, or municipal government. Areas of study include: foreign policy, military affairs (broadly construed), the activities of the federal government, or biography of one or more outstanding individuals in one of the aforementioned areas.

Tachau Teacher of the Year Award: The organization sponsors an annual $1,000 award to recognize the contributions made by precollegiate or classroom teachers to improve history education. The winner will demonstrate exceptional ability in one or more of the following kinds of activities: initiating or participating in projects which involve students in historical research, writing, or other means of representing their knowledge of history; initiating or participating in school, district, regional, state, or national projects which enhance the professional development of history teachers; initiating or participating in projects to build bridges between precollegiate and collegiate history or social studies teachers; working with museums, historical preservation societies, or other public history associations to enhance the place of public history in precollegiate schools; developing innovative history criteria that foster a spirit of inquiry and emphasize critical skills; or publishing or otherwise publicly presenting scholarship that advances history education or historical knowledge. Applicants must submit the following materials in their application packets: a cover letter of no more than two pages, written by a colleague, indicating why the applicant merits the award; two letters, no more than two pages apiece, written by former or present students; CV (no more than three pages); samples of written work, including article reprints, reports by classroom observers, course outlines, research proposals, and/or other evidence of excellence in some or all of the areas mentioned in the "criteria" section (no more than 15 pages); a narrative describing the goals and effects of applicant's work, both in the classroom and elsewhere, for history education; and names, addresses, and telephone numbers of at least three professional references, including the writer of the cover letter, at least one of whom must be a colleague or supervisor.

Willi Paul Adams Award: This biennial program awards $1,000 and a plaque for the best book on American history published in a foreign language. To be eligible, a book should be concerned with the past (recent or distant), or with issues of continuity and change.
EIN: 470426520

3133
Alfred H. Orth Scholarship Fund
c/o Old National Trust Co.
P.O. Box 207
Evansville, IN 47702-0207

Foundation type: Independent foundation
Purpose: Scholarship to students for attendance at colleges or universities in Alabama or Indiana, with tuition, books and other educational fees.
Financial data: Year ended 12/31/2011. Assets, $161,849 (M); Expenditures, $9,392; Total giving, $7,872; Grant to an individual, 1 grant totaling $3,500.
Fields of interest: Higher education.
Type of support: Scholarships—to individuals.
Application information: Unsolicited requests for funds not considered or acknowledged.
EIN: 356567115

3134
Lawrence L. Osborn Scholarship Trust
126 N. Main St.
Veedersburg, IN 47987-1406 (765) 294-2228

Foundation type: Independent foundation

Purpose: Scholarships to graduates of high schools in the Southeast Fountain School District, Veedersburg, IN.
Financial data: Year ended 09/30/2013. Assets, $325,968 (M); Expenditures, $5,249; Total giving, $4,333; Grants to individuals, 15 grants totaling $4,333 (high: $289, low: $288).
Fields of interest: Higher education.
Type of support: Support to graduates or students of specific schools; Undergraduate support.
Application information: Applications accepted.
Initial approach: Letter
Deadline(s): May 1
Additional information: Written application should be sent to the Southeast Fountain School system.
EIN: 311020161

3135
Osteopathic Medical Foundation, Inc.
c/o Dan Wagner
65723 US 33 E. Ste. 200
Goshen, IN 46526 (574) 271-8646
URL: http://www.omfmichiana.org/

Foundation type: Independent foundation
Purpose: Grants to individuals through a Forgivable Loan Program as well as giving to individuals through a Physician Recruitment Assistance Program to support osteopathic medicine.
Financial data: Year ended 12/31/2011. Assets, $1,283,504 (M); Expenditures, $55,559; Total giving, $34,000; Grants to individuals, 3 grants totaling $30,000.
Fields of interest: Medical research.
Type of support: Grants to individuals.
Application information: Applications not accepted.
Additional information: Contributes only to preselected individuals. Unsolicited requests for funds not considered or acknowledged.
EIN: 351938572

3136
Owen County Community Foundation
201 W. Morgan St., Ste. 202
P.O. Box 503
Spencer, IN 47460-0503 (812) 829-1725
Contact: Mark E. Rogers, Exec. Dir.; For grants: Marilyn Hart, Admin. Dir.
FAX: (812) 829-9958;
E-mail: mark@owencountycf.org; Grant inquiry e-mail: marilyn@owencountycf.org; URL: http://www.owencountycf.org

Foundation type: Community foundation
Purpose: Scholarships to both graduating Owen county, IN high school seniors and to returning or non-traditional college students who are furthering their education.
Publications: Annual report; Grants list; Informational brochure.
Financial data: Year ended 12/31/2012. Assets, $4,391,156 (M); Expenditures, $306,528; Total giving, $120,480; Grants to individuals, 37 grants totaling $19,090.
Fields of interest: Vocational education, post-secondary; Higher education.
Type of support: Scholarships—to individuals.
Application information: Applications accepted. Application form required.
Deadline(s): Feb.
Final notification: Recipients notified in May
Applicants should submit the following:
1) SAT
2) FAFSA

3) ACT
4) Transcripts
5) Letter(s) of recommendation
6) Essay
Additional information: See web site for additional information.
EIN: 351934464

3137
Pace Community Action Agency, Inc.
(formerly Wabash Valley Human Services, Inc.)
525 N. 4th St.
Vincennes, IN 47591-1444   (812) 882-7927
Contact: Bertha Proctor, Exec. Dir.
FAX: (812) 882-7982; E-mail: pace@pacecaa.org;
URL: http://www.pacecaa.org

Foundation type: Public charity
Purpose: Financial assistance to low-income families of southwestern IN, with food, shelter, clothing, energy assistance and other special needs; also, scholarships to graduating seniors of southwestern, IN for continuing education beyond high school.
Publications: Annual report; Financial statement.
Financial data: Year ended 12/31/2011. Assets, $4,835,939 (M); Expenditures, $8,772,446; Total giving, $3,031,490; Grants to individuals, totaling $3,031,490.
Fields of interest: Higher education; Food services; Housing/shelter; Economically disadvantaged.
Type of support: Scholarships—to individuals; Grants for special needs.
Application information: Applications accepted. Application form required.
  Initial approach: Telephone
  Deadline(s): Apr. 1 for Judith K. Bobe Scholarship
  Applicants should submit the following:
  1) Essay
  Additional information: For assistance contact the Client Services office nearest your home in Daviess, Green, Knox, or Sullivan county for an appointment, for scholarship see web site for additional guidelines.
Program description:
  Judith K. Bobe Scholarship: Up to two $500 scholarships will be awarded annually to assist students in the agency's service area who wish to continue their education beyond high school. Eligible applicants must be graduating high school seniors who have been accepted in to an accredited college or university, community college, or recognized technical or trade school, and who have a minimum 2.5 GPA; applicants must also have been enrolled in the Head Start program in Daviess, Greene, Knox, or Sullivan counties.
EIN: 351120537

3138
Pacers Foundation, Inc.
(formerly Pacers Basketball Corporation Foundation, Inc.)
125 S. Pennsylvania St.
Indianapolis, IN 46204-2603   (317) 917-2864
Contact: Dan Gaines
FAX: (317) 917-2599;
E-mail: foundation@pacers.com; URL: http://www.pacersfoundation.org/

Foundation type: Public charity
Purpose: Undergraduate scholarships to students residing in IN who are interested in medicine, sports medicine, physical therapy or a related discipline.
Publications: Application guidelines; Annual report; Grants list; Informational brochure (including application guidelines).

Financial data: Year ended 06/30/2011. Assets, $1,399,309 (M); Expenditures, $798,149; Total giving, $587,450.
Fields of interest: Medical school/education; Health sciences school/education; Physical therapy.
Type of support: Undergraduate support.
Application information: Applications accepted. Application form required.
  Initial approach: E-mail.
  Send request by: Mail
  Deadline(s): July 1 for Linda Craig Memorial Scholarships.
  Applicants should submit the following:
  1) Essay
  2) Letter(s) of recommendation
  3) Transcripts
  Additional information: Application should also include a one-page personal statement. Awards are paid directly to the educational institution on behalf of the student.
Program description:
  Linda Craig Memorial Scholarship Foundation: Two awards of $2,000 are made each year for use at any accredited four-year Indiana college or university or two-year junior or community college to students who are enrolling in, or plan to enroll in, medicine, sports medicine, physical therapy, and/ or related disciplines. Eligible applicants must be enrolled in good standing in an undergraduate college program, must have at least four semesters completed, must have a minimum GPA of 3.0 (on a 4.0 scale), and must be a U.S. citizen.
EIN: 351908365

3139
Parke County Community Foundation, Inc.
115 N. Market St.
P.O. Box 276
Rockville, IN 47872-1719   (765) 569-7223
Contact: Brad C. Bumgardner, Exec. Dir.
FAX: (765) 569-5383;
E-mail: parkeccf@yahoo.com; URL: http://www.parkeccf.org

Foundation type: Community foundation
Purpose: Scholarships to students in the Parke County, IN, area for postsecondary education.
Publications: Financial statement; Newsletter.
Financial data: Year ended 12/31/2012. Assets, $11,249,782 (M); Expenditures, $776,703; Total giving, $488,439; Grants to individuals, 166 grants totaling $202,261.
Fields of interest: Higher education; Scholarships/ financial aid.
Type of support: Scholarships—to individuals.
Application information: Applications accepted. Application form required. Application form available on the grantmaker's web site.
  Initial approach: Application
  Send request by: Mail
  Deadline(s): Apr. 4
  Applicants should submit the following:
  1) Letter(s) of recommendation
  2) Photograph
  3) Transcripts
  4) Essay
  Additional information: Each scholarship has its own set of unique eligibility criteria. See web site for complete listing.
EIN: 351881810

3140
Parkview Hospital Foundation, Inc.
(formerly Parkview Foundation, Inc.)
2120 Carew St.
Fort Wayne, IN 46805-4638   (260) 373-7970
FAX: (260) 373-7976;
E-mail: foundation@parkview.com; URL: http://www.parkview.com/en/Pages/default.aspx

Foundation type: Public charity
Purpose: Emergency assistance and scholarships to employees of Parkview Hospital, IN.
Publications: Application guidelines.
Financial data: Year ended 12/31/2011. Assets, $12,477,890 (M); Expenditures, $1,921,540; Total giving, $772,395; Grants to individuals, totaling $42,411.
Fields of interest: Education; Hospitals (general).
Type of support: Scholarships—to individuals.
Application information: Applications accepted.
  Initial approach: Employees should contact foundation
Program description:
  Florence L.M. Rolland Nursing Scholarship: Scholarships are available to students preparing to enter an R.N. program of study at the University of St. Francis or Indiana University-Purdue University in Fort Wayne. Eligible applicants must reside in Allen, DeKalb, Noble, Whitley, Huntington, Wells, or Adams counties, and must show both academic ability and financial need.
EIN: 237220589

3141
Alene Payton Scholarship Trust
P.O. Box 207
Evansville, IN 47702

Foundation type: Independent foundation
Purpose: Scholarships to graduating seniors of Paoli High School, IN for continuing education at accredited colleges or universities.
Financial data: Year ended 12/31/2012. Assets, $366,274 (M); Expenditures, $20,233; Total giving, $13,950; Grants to individuals, 3 grants totaling $13,950 (high: $4,650; low: $4,650).
Fields of interest: Higher education.
Type of support: Support to graduates or students of specific schools.
Application information: Applications accepted. Application form required.
  Deadline(s): Apr. 1
  Additional information: Selection is based on financial need, academic achievements and extracurricular activities.
EIN: 616304323

3142
Pearson Scholarship Trust
P.O. Box 1602
South Bend, IN 46634

Foundation type: Independent foundation
Purpose: Scholarships to graduates of Argos High School, IN, for full-time study at postsecondary institutions.
Financial data: Year ended 09/30/2013. Assets, $160,204 (M); Expenditures, $11,398; Total giving, $8,000; Grants to individuals, 3 grants totaling $8,000 (high: $3,000; low: $2,000).
Fields of interest: Higher education.
Type of support: Support to graduates or students of specific schools; Undergraduate support.
Application information: Applications accepted. Application form required.
  Applicants should submit the following:

1) Essay
2) FAFSA

Additional information: Application should also include teacher evaluations, test scores, and employment record.
EIN: 356400471

3143
Peoples Charitable Foundation, Inc.
212 W. 7th St.
Auburn, IN 46706-0231

Foundation type: Independent foundation
Purpose: Scholarships to residents of Auburn, IN in pursuit of a higher education.
Financial data: Year ended 12/31/2011. Assets, $1,802,182 (M); Expenditures, $100,047; Total giving, $82,000.
Fields of interest: Higher education.
Type of support: Scholarships—to individuals.
Application information: Applications accepted. Application form required.
Additional information: Contact the foundation for additional guidelines.
EIN: 351897837

3144
Glenn D. Peters Trust
10322 Indianapolis Blvd.
Highland, IN 46322-3508 (219) 853-3531
Contact: Jessica M. Peyton, V.P.

Foundation type: Independent foundation
Purpose: Scholarships to full time law students who are residents of the Northern District of Indiana for attendance at an accredited law school.
Financial data: Year ended 09/30/2013. Assets, $740,396 (M); Expenditures, $37,376; Total giving, $22,500; Grants to individuals, 22 grants totaling $22,500 (high: $1,250, low: $1,000).
Fields of interest: Law school/education.
Type of support: Graduate support.
Application information: Application form required.
Initial approach: Letter requesting application
Deadline(s): June 1
Additional information: Selection is based on academic ability.
EIN: 356218833

3145
PFS Community Foundation
6776 Cross Rd.
Aurora, IN 47001-1777

Foundation type: Company-sponsored foundation
Purpose: Scholarships to students in Dearborn County, Indiana for higher education.
Financial data: Year ended 12/31/2012. Assets, $652,360 (M); Expenditures, $35,151; Total giving, $33,550.
Type of support: Undergraduate support.
Application information:
Initial approach: Letter
Additional information: Contact foundation for eligibility criteria.
EIN: 352152955

3146
The Endowment Fund of Phi Kappa Psi Fraternity, Inc.
5395 Emerson Way
Indianapolis, IN 46226-1415 (317) 275-3400
URL: http://www.pkpfoundation.org

Foundation type: Public charity
Purpose: Scholarships for higher education to members of the Phi Kappa Psi fraternity.
Financial data: Year ended 12/31/2011. Assets, $37,362,673 (M); Expenditures, $6,948,293; Total giving, $3,305,561; Grants to individuals, totaling $431,356.
Fields of interest: Students, sororities/fraternities.
Type of support: Undergraduate support.
Application information: Applications not accepted.
Additional information: Unsolicited requests for funds not considered.
EIN: 366130655

3147
Phi Kappa Theta National Foundation
9640 N. Augusta Dr., Ste. 420
Carmel, IN 46032-9602 (317) 872-9934
Contact: Walter J. Kronzer III, Pres.
FAX: (317) 872-3026; *URL:* http://www.phikaps.org/?page=foundation

Foundation type: Public charity
Purpose: Scholarships to members of Phi Kappa Theta Fraternity, based on leadership, scholarship, moral qualities, and need.
Publications: Application guidelines.
Financial data: Year ended 06/30/2012. Assets, $822,824 (M); Expenditures, $160,320; Total giving, $18,700.
Fields of interest: Higher education; Students, sororities/fraternities.
Type of support: Scholarships—to individuals.
Application information: Applications accepted. Application form required. Application form available on the grantmaker's web site.
Initial approach: Application
Send request by: Mail
Deadline(s): June 1
Applicants should submit the following:
1) GPA
2) Financial information
3) Transcripts
4) Letter(s) of recommendation
5) Essay
Program description:
Scholarships: The foundation awards scholarships to deserving collegiate members of Phi Kappa Theta Fraternity who demonstrate financial need and excel in the areas of academics, chapter leadership, and campus/community involvement. Named scholarships under this program include the Frank Souchak Memorial Scholarship (two awards of up to $875, with applicants required to have a 2.5 minimum GPA), Bernie Zarnick Memorial Scholarship (one award of up to $900, with applicants required to have a 2.5 minimum GPA), Michael T. Welsh Memorial Scholarship (one award of up to $745, with preference given to students attending the University of Detroit - Mercy), Frank Prawdzienski Memorial Scholarship (two awards of up to $565, with applicants required to have a 2.5 minimum GPA), Fairfield/David Caisse and Thomas Brown Memorial Scholarship (one award of up to $445), Paul Hamann Memorial Scholarship (one award of up to $345, with applicants required to have a 2.5 minimum GPA), and Andres Estrada Memorial Scholarship (one award of up to $215, limited to chapter members attending the University of Texas - Pan American)
EIN: 237209653

3148
Plummer Scholarship Fund
c/o KeyBank N.A., Trust Tax Dept.
202 S. Michigan St.
South Bend, IN 46601-2021
Contact: Agnes Marountas
Application address: 127 Public Sq., 16th Fl., Cleveland, OH 44114

Foundation type: Independent foundation
Purpose: Scholarships to financially needy graduates of Howard County, IN, high schools to pursue studies in medicine or nursing at accredited colleges and universities in the U.S.
Financial data: Year ended 10/31/2013. Assets, $309,261 (M); Expenditures, $19,406; Total giving, $13,000; Grants to individuals, 8 grants totaling $13,000 (high: $3,000, low: $1,000).
Fields of interest: Medical school/education; Nursing school/education.
Type of support: Support to graduates or students of specific schools; Undergraduate support.
Application information: Application form required.
Deadline(s): Mar.
EIN: 356510973

3149
Porter Art Foundation Trust
P.O. Box 147
Peru, IN 46970-0370 (765) 473-8336
Contact: Marianne Savage
Application address: 1860 E. Monona Dr., Peru, IN 46970-8381

Foundation type: Independent foundation
Purpose: Scholarships to graduates of high schools in Miami County, IN, for higher education in performing arts.
Financial data: Year ended 12/31/2011. Assets, $9,552 (M); Expenditures, $16,775; Total giving, $13,750; Grants to individuals, 9 grants totaling $13,750 (high: $2,500, low: $937).
Fields of interest: Performing arts, education.
Type of support: Undergraduate support.
Application information: Interview required.
Initial approach: Letter
Deadline(s): None
EIN: 356067146

3150
Porter County Community Foundation, Inc.
57 S. Franklin St., Ste. 207
P.O. Box 302
Valparaiso, IN 46384 (219) 465-0294
Contact: For grants: Brenda Sheetz, V.P.
FAX: (219) 464-2733;
E-mail: info@portercountyfoundation.org; Grant inquiry e-mail:
bsheetz@portercountyfoundation.org; *URL:* http://www.portercountyfoundation.org

Foundation type: Community foundation
Purpose: College scholarships to selected students of Porter County, IN for continuing education at institutions of higher learning.
Publications: Application guidelines; Annual report; Grants list; Newsletter.
Financial data: Year ended 12/31/2012. Assets, $31,456,644 (M); Expenditures, $2,665,117; Total giving, $1,928,407; Grants to individuals, 14 grants totaling $14,000.
Fields of interest: Higher education.
Type of support: Scholarships—to individuals.

Application information: Applications accepted. Application form required.
> *Initial approach:* Telephone or email
> *Additional information:* Contact the foundation for additional application guidelines.

EIN: 352000788

3151
The Portland Foundation
112 E. Main St.
Portland, IN 47371-2105 (260) 726-4260
Contact: Douglas L. Inman, Exec. Dir.; For grant applications: Jessica L. Cook, Prog. Off.
FAX: (260) 726-4273;
E-mail: tpf@portlandfoundation.org; URL: http://www.portlandfoundation.org

Foundation type: Community foundation
Purpose: Scholarships to graduating students of Jay County High School, IN for continuing education at institutions of higher learning.
Publications: Application guidelines; Annual report; Newsletter; IRS Form 990 or 990-PF printed copy available upon request.
Financial data: Year ended 12/31/2012. Assets, $23,726,366 (M); Expenditures, $851,409; Total giving, $500,791; Grants to individuals, totaling $168,327.
Fields of interest: Vocational education; Higher education.
Type of support: Support to graduates or students of specific schools; Undergraduate support.
Application information: Applications accepted. Application form required. Application form available on the grantmaker's web site.
> *Initial approach:* E-mail or telephone
> *Send request by:* E-mail
> *Copies of proposal:* 1
> *Deadline(s):* Feb.
> *Applicants should submit the following:*
> 1) Financial information
> 2) GPA
> 3) FAFSA

EIN: 356028362

3152
Public Education Foundation of Evansville, Inc.
100 N.W. 2nd St., Ste. 120
Evansville, IN 47708-1202 (812) 422-1699
Contact: Amy P. Walker, Exec. Dir.
FAX: (812) 422-2378;
E-mail: info@pefevansville.org; E-mail for Amy Walker: awalker@pefevansville.org; URL: http://www.pefevansville.org

Foundation type: Public charity
Purpose: Grants to public school teachers in Evansville, IN, to take courses to enrich their teaching skills. Scholarships to graduating seniors of Evansville, IN.
Publications: Application guidelines; Annual report.
Financial data: Year ended 08/31/2011. Assets, $772,392 (M); Expenditures, $657,040; Total giving, $73,113; Grants to individuals, totaling $41,735.
Fields of interest: Public education; Higher education; Teacher school/education; Adult/continuing education.
Type of support: Grants to individuals; Scholarships—to individuals.
Application information: Application form required.
> *Deadline(s):* Apr. for Grants
> *Additional information:* Awards are given by the end of each school year.

Program descriptions:
> *PEF 25-Year Anniversary Grant:* Grants, ranging from $2,000 to $5,000, are available to educators working in Evansville public school district, to be used for educational programs. Priority will be given to: education activities that are truly innovative; collaborative efforts among the school faculty, students, community, and/or parents; projects that give back to the community in some way (school, community, or broader); projects that have long-term benefits; and projects that can be accomplished within the school year.
> *TJMaxx Teacher Study Grants:* Grants of up to $500 are available to teachers working within the Evansville public school system, to be used toward professional development opportunities that increase their knowledge base to benefit their classroom teaching skills. Grants can be used to support university or college classes in the teacher's current field, or an enriching area of interest; conferences or workshops to enhance classroom teaching skills and/or opportunities; and seminars that can be offered locally to benefit a large number of interested teachers. A group of teachers may collaborate in applying for a grant to hold a seminar in Evansville that would benefit as many teachers as possible.

EIN: 351660363

3153
Pulaski County Community Foundation, Inc.
127 E. Pearl Street
P.O. Box 407
Winamac, IN 46996 (574) 946-0906
Contact: Wendy Rose, Exec. Dir.
FAX: (574) 946-0971;
E-mail: wrose@emberqmail.com; URL: http://www.pulaskionline.org/content/view/126/460/

Foundation type: Community foundation
Purpose: Scholarships to Pulaski County, IN high school graduates for undergraduate education at accredited Indiana public or private colleges or universities.
Publications: Application guidelines; Annual report; Financial statement; Grants list.
Financial data: Year ended 12/31/2012. Assets, $7,114,288 (M); Expenditures, $417,133; Total giving, $193,922; Grants to individuals, 45 grants totaling $33,402.
Fields of interest: Higher education.
Type of support: Undergraduate support.
Application information: Applications accepted. Application form required.
> *Initial approach:* Application
> *Send request by:* Online
> *Deadline(s):* Mar. 8
> *Additional information:* See web site for a complete list of scholarships or contact your high school guidance counselors for additional information.

EIN: 352127564

3154
The Putnam County Community Foundation
2 S. Jackson St.
P.O. Box 514
Greencastle, IN 46135-0514 (765) 653-4978
Contact: M. Elaine Peck, Exec. Dir.; For scholarships: Dean Gambill, Dir., Community Devel.
Scholarship e-mail: dgambill@pcfoundation.org
FAX: (765) 653-6385;
E-mail: info@pcfoundation.org; URL: http://www.pcfoundation.org

Foundation type: Community foundation
Purpose: Scholarships to residents of Putnam County, IN for postsecondary education.
Publications: Application guidelines; Annual report; Financial statement; Grants list; Informational brochure; Newsletter.
Financial data: Year ended 12/31/2012. Assets, $21,533,458 (M); Expenditures, $950,577; Total giving, $584,015; Grants to individuals, 145 grants totaling $135,413.
Fields of interest: Higher education; Business school/education; Nursing school/education; Scholarships/financial aid; Athletics/sports, school programs.
Type of support: Scholarships—to individuals; Support to graduates or students of specific schools; Undergraduate support.
Application information: Applications accepted. Application form required. Application form available on the grantmaker's web site.
> *Deadline(s):* Varies
> *Final notification:* Recipients notified in three weeks
> *Applicants should submit the following:*
> 1) Letter(s) of recommendation
> 2) SAT
> 3) ACT
> 4) Transcripts
> 5) FAFSA
> 6) Work samples
> 7) Financial information
> 8) Budget Information
> *Additional information:* Eligibility varies per scholarship. See web site for a complete listing and application forms.

EIN: 311159916

3155
Herbert and Gwendolyn Raab Educational Trust
428 E. National Ave.
Brazil, IN 47834-2632

Foundation type: Independent foundation
Purpose: Scholarships to graduates of Clay County School, IN, who will major in elementary education.
Financial data: Year ended 06/30/2013. Assets, $0 (M); Expenditures, $51,142; Total giving, $50,000; Grants to individuals, 9 grants totaling $50,000 (high: $7,000, low: $3,000).
Fields of interest: Elementary school/education.
Type of support: Scholarships—to individuals; Undergraduate support.
Application information:
> *Deadline(s):* Apr. 1
> *Applicants should submit the following:*
> 1) Transcripts
> 2) Financial information
> *Additional information:* Contact trust for current application deadline/guidelines.

EIN: 356645581

3156
Randolph Memorial Scholarship Trust
P.O. Box 207
Evansville, IN 47702-0207

Foundation type: Independent foundation
Purpose: Scholarships to graduates of Henderson County High School, KY, based on character, industry, integrity, and academic achievement.
Financial data: Year ended 12/31/2012. Assets, $99,889 (M); Expenditures, $6,281; Total giving, $4,800; Grants to individuals, 3 grants totaling $4,800 (high: $1,600, low: $1,600).
Type of support: Support to graduates or students of specific schools; Undergraduate support.
Application information: Applications accepted. Application form required.
   Initial approach: Letter
   Deadline(s): Apr. 1
   Additional information: Applications are made through the high school guidance office.
EIN: 616114750

3157
REAL Services, Inc.
1151 S. Michigan St.
P.O. Box 1835
South Bend, IN 46601-3427 (574) 284-2644
FAX: (574) 284-2691;
E-mail: info@realservices.org; Toll-free tel. (IN only): (800) 552-7928; URL: http://www.realservices.org

Foundation type: Public charity
Purpose: Financial assistance to indigent residents of the five-county area of South Bend, IN, for utilities, medical, and living expenses.
Financial data: Year ended 06/30/2012. Assets, $7,537,821 (M); Expenditures, $19,112,859; Total giving, $8,846,881; Grants to individuals, totaling $8,596,999.
Type of support: Grants for special needs.
Application information:
   Initial approach: Letter
   Additional information: Contact foundation for complete eligibility requirements.
EIN: 351157606

3158
Reeves Foundation
c/o Old National Trust Company
P.O. Box 207
Evansville, IN 47702-0207 (812) 479-2149
Application address: c/o University of Evansville, P.O. Box 329, Evansville, IN 47714

Foundation type: Independent foundation
Purpose: Student loans to financially needy residents of Vanderburgh County, IN, who are studying full-time at the University of Evansville and have completed two years of academic work in good standing.
Financial data: Year ended 05/31/2013. Assets, $314,080 (M); Expenditures, $8,248; Total giving, $0.
Fields of interest: Higher education.
Type of support: Support to graduates or students of specific schools.
Application information: Applications accepted. Application form required.
   Initial approach: Letter
   Deadline(s): None
   Additional information: Applicants must submit evidence of financial need and completed two years of academic work. Obtain application form from the University of Evansville.
EIN: 356077653

3159
Reeves Foundation, Inc.
9405 W. U.S. Hwy. 40
Knightstown, IN 46148-9507

Foundation type: Independent foundation
Purpose: Scholarships to students attending Knightstown High School, IN.
Financial data: Year ended 12/31/2012. Assets, $904,954 (M); Expenditures, $33,387; Total giving, $29,700; Grants to individuals, 11 grants totaling $29,700 (high: $3,000, low: $1,350).
Fields of interest: Higher education.
Type of support: Support to graduates or students of specific schools.
Application information: Application form required.
   Deadline(s): May
   Additional information: Application can be obtained from the counselor's office, and application must include autobiographical information.
EIN: 311175067

3160
Charlotte M. Richardt Charitable Trust
P.O. Box 207
Evansville, IN 47702

Foundation type: Independent foundation
Purpose: Scholarships to students of Central High School, IN, for higher education.
Financial data: Year ended 12/31/2011. Assets, $333,366 (M); Expenditures, $22,468; Total giving, $18,000; Grants to individuals, 4 grants totaling $18,000 (high: $5,000, low: $3,000).
Type of support: Support to graduates or students of specific schools; Undergraduate support.
Application information: Applications not accepted.
   Additional information: Contributes only to preselected individuals.
EIN: 616233945

3161
Richmond Art Museum
350 Hub Etchison Pkwy.
Richmond, IN 47374-0816 (765) 966-0256
Contact: Shaun Dingwerth, Exec. Dir.
FAX: (765) 973-3738;
E-mail: shaund@rcs.k12.in.us; URL: http://www.richmondartmuseum.org

Foundation type: Public charity
Purpose: Scholarships to students of Richmond High School, IN to further their interest in the arts.
Financial data: Year ended 05/31/2012. Assets, $1,320,563 (M); Expenditures, $304,816.
Fields of interest: Arts.
Type of support: Scholarships—to individuals.
Application information: Scholarships are determined by the art department of the high school.
EIN: 356005040

3162
Richmond Symphony Orchestra Association
380 Hub Etchison Pkwy.
P.O. Box 982
Richmond, IN 47374-5339 (765) 966-5181
FAX: (765) 962-8447;
E-mail: rso@richmondsymphony.org; URL: http://www.richmondsymphony.org

Foundation type: Public charity

Purpose: Awards to young talented instrumental and vocal musicians of east central, IN and west central, OH.
Financial data: Year ended 06/30/2012. Assets, $1,159,912 (M); Expenditures, $372,900.
Fields of interest: Performing arts; Music; Orchestras.
Type of support: Awards/prizes.
Application information: Application form required. Application form available on the grantmaker's web site.
   Initial approach: Telephone or e-mail
   Deadline(s): Oct. 9
   Additional information: A $15 application fee and audition tapes must accompany each entry form. All music must be memorized.
Program description:
   Young Artist Competition: The competition is open to instrumentalists and singers who reside in Wayne, Randolph, Henry, Fayette, Franklin, or Union counties in Indiana, or in Preble, Darke, or Butler counties in Ohio. The competition is open to students in grades 6 through 12. First-place winners will perform live with the Richmond Symphony Orchestra and receive a $600 cash award, second-place winners will receive a $400 cash award.
EIN: 356042479

3163
Faye Riddleberger Scholarship Trust
2114 North St.
Logansport, IN 46947-3750 (574) 722-3254
Contact: Jan M. Blackburn, Tr.

Foundation type: Independent foundation
Purpose: Scholarships to graduates of high schools in Cass County, IN, or to current students at Ivy Tech, Logansport, or Indiana University, Kokomo, IN.
Financial data: Year ended 12/31/2011. Assets, $459,033 (M); Expenditures, $35,171; Total giving, $26,400; Grants to individuals, 15 grants totaling $26,400 (high: $1,800, low: $1,800).
Fields of interest: Higher education.
Type of support: Scholarships—to individuals; Support to graduates or students of specific schools.
Application information: Application form required.
   Applicants should submit the following:
      1) Letter(s) of recommendation
      2) FAF
   Additional information: The committee solicits applications during the first quarter of each calendar year.
EIN: 356596875

3164
Ripley County Community Foundation, Inc.
4 S. Park, Ste. 210
Batesville, IN 47006 (812) 933-1098
Contact: Sally Morris, Exec. Dir.
FAX: (812) 933-0096;
E-mail: rccfound@etczone.com; Additional tel.: (887) 234-5220; Additional e-mail: smorris@rccfonline.org and office@rccfonline.org; URL: http://rccfonline.org/

Foundation type: Community foundation
Purpose: Scholarships to residents of Ripley County, IN, for higher education.
Publications: Application guidelines.
Financial data: Year ended 12/31/2011. Assets, $7,621,172 (M); Expenditures, $908,457; Total

giving, $363,564; Grants to individuals, 46 grants totaling $40,462.
Type of support: Scholarships—to individuals.
Application information: Applications accepted. Application form required. Application form available on the grantmaker's web site. Interview required.
> *Deadline(s):* Varies
> *Additional information:* Contact foundation for complete list of programs.
EIN: 352048001

3165
Rose Ladies Aid Society
1925 Wabash Ave.
Terre Haute, IN   47807

Foundation type: Independent foundation
Purpose: Financial assistance to low-income families in Vigo County, IN, for medical, dental, educational, and emergency living expenses.
Financial data: Year ended 04/30/2013. Assets, $1,281,611 (M); Expenditures, $72,738; Total giving, $60,271.
Fields of interest: Dental care; Health care; Economically disadvantaged.
Type of support: Grants for special needs.
Application information: Applications not accepted.
EIN: 350911948

3166
RPW Foundation, Inc.
(formerly Wurster Foundation)
8463 Castlewood Dr., 2nd Fl.
Indianapolis, IN   46250   (317) 841-1002
Contact: Russell P. Wurster, Pres.

Foundation type: Operating foundation
Purpose: Scholarships to participants of the Royal Pin Leisure Centers youth league bowling program in IN.
Financial data: Year ended 12/31/2012. Assets, $934,254 (M); Expenditures, $99,205; Total giving, $96,242; Grants to individuals, 47 grants totaling $96,242 (high: $15,994, low: $250).
Fields of interest: Recreation.
Type of support: Scholarships—to individuals.
Application information: Applications accepted. Application form required.
> *Send request by:* Mail
> *Deadline(s):* May 1
> *Applicants should submit the following:*
>   1) Transcripts
>   2) Essay
EIN: 351778480

3167
Rush County Community Foundation, Inc.
c/o Alisa Henderson
117 N. Main St.
Rushville, IN   46173-1927   (765) 938-1177
Contact: Alisa Henderson, Exec. Dir.
FAX: (765) 938-1719;
E-mail: info@rushcountyfoundation.org;
URL: http://www.rushcountyfoundation.org

Foundation type: Community foundation
Purpose: Scholarships to residents of Rush County, IN for postsecondary education.
Publications: Application guidelines; Annual report; Financial statement; Grants list; Informational brochure; Newsletter.
Financial data: Year ended 12/31/2012. Assets, $10,449,544 (M); Expenditures, $391,885; Total

giving, $250,032; Grants to individuals, 115 grants totaling $86,966.
Fields of interest: Vocational education, post-secondary; Higher education; Scholarships/financial aid.
Type of support: Scholarships—to individuals; Support to graduates or students of specific schools; Undergraduate support; Doctoral support.
Application information: Applications accepted. Application form required. Application form available on the grantmaker's web site.
> *Send request by:* Mail or in person
> *Deadline(s):* Feb. 4 for Lilly Endowment Community Scholarship; Mar. 7 for all others
> *Applicants should submit the following:*
>   1) Transcripts
>   2) SAT
>   3) Letter(s) of recommendation
>   4) GPA
>   5) Financial information
>   6) FAFSA
>   7) Curriculum vitae
>   8) ACT
> *Additional information:* See web site for a complete listing of scholarships. Scholarship applications and cover sheets are also available at Rushville Consolidated High School and Knightstown High School counselors' offices beginning on Dec. 1st of each year.
EIN: 351835950

3168
Edmund J. Russell Medical Educational Trust
c/o First National Bank of Monterey
P.O. Box 8
Monterey, IN   46960-0008   (574) 542-2121

Foundation type: Independent foundation
Purpose: Scholarships to high school graduates, one male and one famale of Winamac Community High School, IN pursuing a career in the health care field.
Financial data: Year ended 08/31/2012. Assets, $101,299 (M); Expenditures, $582; Total giving, $489; Grant to an individual, 1 grant totaling $489.
Fields of interest: Higher education.
Type of support: Support to graduates or students of specific schools.
Application information: Applications accepted. Application form required.
> *Deadline(s):* Two weeks before graduation
EIN: 356676512

3169
Saint Joseph's Regional Medical Center, Inc.
5215 Holy Cross Pkwy.
Mishawaka, IN   46545-1469   (574) 335-5000
URL: http://sjmed.com

Foundation type: Public charity
Purpose: Assistance to students enrolled in an accredited institution in IN or MI in their final year of a two-year program or final two years of a four-year program pursuing a healthcare related field.
Publications: Quarterly report.
Financial data: Year ended 06/30/2012. Assets, $68,530,814 (M); Expenditures, $84,313,270; Total giving, $1,193,720.
Fields of interest: Health sciences school/education.
Type of support: Scholarships—to individuals.
Application information: Applications accepted.

Additional information: Applicants should be committed to patient care and community involvement, agree to gain licensure and be eligible for full time employment within 30 days of completing their academic program. Applicants must also agree to repay the scholarship if they do not fulfill the program requirements. Applicants must have a minimum 3.0 GPA.
EIN: 351568821

3170
Salin Foundation, Inc.
10587 Coppergate Dr.
Carmel, IN   46032-9204   (317) 532-2260
Contact: Sherri Fritsch, Secy.-Treas.

Foundation type: Independent foundation
Purpose: Scholarships to high school seniors from select Indiana communities for full time study at an accredited two or four year college, university, or vocational/technical school.
Financial data: Year ended 12/31/2011. Assets, $1,587,126 (M); Expenditures, $26,886; Total giving, $25,270.
Fields of interest: Vocational education, post-secondary; Higher education.
Type of support: Support to graduates or students of specific schools.
Application information: Applications accepted. Application form required.
> *Deadline(s):* Apr. 15
> *Final notification:* Applicants notified late May
> *Additional information:* Contact the foundation for eligibility determination and list of select schools. Selection of scholarship is based on financial need. The scholarship is administered by Scholarship Management Services.
EIN: 352047694

3171
Scering Trust
(formerly Board of Trustees of Scering Trust)
911 Fordice Rd.
Lebanon, IN   46052-1938   (765) 482-1485
Contact: Robert A. Duff, Secy.-Treas.

Foundation type: Independent foundation
Purpose: Scholarships to active members of Sigma Chi Fraternity, Lambda chapter at Indiana University, Bloomington, IN.
Financial data: Year ended 12/31/2012. Assets, $236,435 (M); Expenditures, $15,609; Total giving, $12,000; Grants to individuals, 3 grants totaling $12,000 (high: $5,000, low: $2,000).
Fields of interest: Higher education; Fraternal societies.
Type of support: Scholarships—to individuals.
Application information: Applications accepted. Application form required.
> *Deadline(s):* Second week of Feb.
> *Applicants should submit the following:*
>   1) Transcripts
>   2) Financial information
>   3) Essay
EIN: 316321562

3172
Edgar & Lucile Schergens Foundation, Inc.
727 Main St.
Tell City, IN   47586-1934   (812) 547-5592
Contact: J. David Huber, Secy.-Treas.

Foundation type: Independent foundation
Purpose: Scholarship to a deserving student of Perry, Harrison or Spencer county, IN pursuing a career in the health care profession.
Financial data: Year ended 12/31/2012. Assets, $5,773,259 (M); Expenditures, $294,923; Total giving, $205,345; Grants to individuals, 25 grants totaling $184,801 (high: $12,750; low: $929).
Fields of interest: Health sciences school/education.
Type of support: Undergraduate support.
Application information:
Initial approach: Letter
Deadline(s): None
EIN: 351848445

3173
Walter F. Schmidt Trust
c/o First Financial Bank, N.A.
P.O. Box 540
Terre Haute, IN 47808 (618) 544-8666

Foundation type: Independent foundation
Purpose: Scholarships to graduates of Crawford County, IL, high schools for attendance at Lincoln Trail College, IL.
Financial data: Year ended 06/30/2013. Assets, $1,564,798 (M); Expenditures, $74,934; Total giving, $54,958; Grants to individuals, 92 grants totaling $54,958 (high: $1,279, low: $14).
Type of support: Support to graduates or students of specific schools; Undergraduate support.
Application information: Application form required.
Deadline(s): July 15
Applicants should submit the following:
1) Transcripts
2) Essay
EIN: 376311892

3174
Denglade Scholarship Foundation, Inc.
c/o Janet Davis Hocker
7202 N. Shadeland Ave., Ste. 207
Indianapolis, IN 46250-2031
Contact: Virginia Reeves, Secy.
Application address: 13 Markland Pike, Vevay, IL 47043

Foundation type: Independent foundation
Purpose: Scholarships for students of Switzerland County School, Vevay, IN who have been accepted at a college or university.
Financial data: Year ended 12/31/2012. Assets, $134,093 (M); Expenditures, $6,200; Total giving, $6,200; Grants to individuals, 8 grants totaling $6,200 (high: $1,200, low: $400).
Fields of interest: Higher education.
Type of support: Scholarships—to individuals; Support to graduates or students of specific schools.
Application information: Applications accepted.
Initial approach: Letter
Deadline(s): May 1
EIN: 351767732

3175
Kate W. Schultz Trust
c/o Old National Trust Co.
P.O. Box 746
Mount Vernon, IN 47620-0746 (812) 838-8018

Foundation type: Independent foundation
Purpose: Scholarships to residents of Posey County, IN, for the study of veterinary medicine or engineering.

Financial data: Year ended 12/31/2012. Assets, $193,968 (M); Expenditures, $17,989; Total giving, $13,000.
Fields of interest: Veterinary medicine; Engineering.
Type of support: Undergraduate support.
Application information: Applications accepted. Application form required.
Initial approach: Letter
Deadline(s): None
Applicants should submit the following:
1) Photograph
2) Class rank
3) Transcripts
4) SAT
5) Financial information
Additional information: Application should also include proof of acceptance to college.
EIN: 356024699

3176
Scott County Community Foundation, Inc.
60 N. Main St.
P.O. Box 25
Scottsburg, IN 47170-1129 (812) 752-2057
Contact: Jaime Toppe, Exec. Dir.
FAX: (812) 752-9257;
E-mail: info@scottcountyfoundation.org; E-Mail for Charlotte Boswell
charlotte.boswell@scottcountyfoundation.org;
URL: http://www.scottcountyfoundation.org

Foundation type: Community foundation
Purpose: Scholarships to students graduating from high schools in Scott County, IN. Scholarships for adult and current college students also available.
Publications: Application guidelines; Annual report; Financial statement; Newsletter.
Financial data: Year ended 09/30/2012. Assets, $6,755,112 (M); Expenditures, $337,611; Total giving, $131,559; Grants to individuals, 25 grants totaling $31,025.
Fields of interest: Higher education.
Type of support: Undergraduate support.
Application information: Applications accepted. Application form required. Application form available on the grantmaker's web site.
Initial approach: Application
Send request by: Online
Deadline(s): Mar. 15
Applicants should submit the following:
1) Financial information
2) Essay
3) Letter(s) of recommendation
4) SAT
5) ACT
6) Transcripts
Additional information: See web site for eligibility criteria per scholarship.
EIN: 352014369

3177
Gordon and Ann Scott Trust
P.O. Box 500
Morocco, IN 47963

Foundation type: Independent foundation
Purpose: Scholarships to graduates of North Newton High School, Morocco, IN, or who resides in Washington Township, Newton county, IN for attendance at any accredited college or university.
Financial data: Year ended 12/31/2011. Assets, $87,835 (M); Expenditures, $52,601; Total giving, $4,788; Grants to individuals, 8 grants totaling $3,750 (high: $750, low: $250).
Fields of interest: Higher education.

Type of support: Support to graduates or students of specific schools; Undergraduate support.
Application information: Applications accepted. Application form required.
Applicants should submit the following:
1) Financial information
2) Transcripts
Additional information: Application must also include post-high school plans, and extracurricular activities.
EIN: 356681290

3178
Lloyd & Gene Sellers Scholarship Fund
2 N., Broadway
Peru, IN 46970
Applicaton address: c/o L & G Sellers Scholarship FD - Harris Bank. 111 W., Monroe St., Tax Div 16 W, Chicago IL 60603

Foundation type: Independent foundation
Purpose: Scholarships to graduating seniors of Taylor High School, IN pursuing accredited postsecondary education.
Financial data: Year ended 12/31/2011. Assets, $681,592 (M); Expenditures, $42,983; Total giving, $35,665; Grants to individuals, 60 grants totaling $35,665 (high: $585, low: $581).
Fields of interest: Higher education.
Type of support: Support to graduates or students of specific schools.
Application information:
Initial approach: Letter
Deadline(s): None
EIN: 306130635

3179
Greater Seymour Trust Fund
P.O. Box 1001
Seymour, IN 47274-1001 (812) 522-3607
URL: http://greaterseymourtrustfund.com

Foundation type: Independent foundation
Purpose: Scholarships to students of Seymour High School, IN, and Washington High School in Milwaukee, WI.
Publications: Annual report; Informational brochure.
Financial data: Year ended 06/30/2012. Assets, $7,743,578 (M); Expenditures, $369,437; Total giving, $273,167; Grants to individuals, 134 grants totaling $216,762 (high: $4,816, low: $250).
Fields of interest: Vocational education.
Type of support: Support to graduates or students of specific schools; Graduate support; Undergraduate support.
Application information: Applications not accepted.
Additional information: Unsolicited requests for funds not considered or acknowledged.
EIN: 356208884

3180
John F. and Mary E. Shiel Trust
c/o Jackson County Bank, Trust Dept.
P.O. Box 1001
Seymour, IN 47274-1001 (812) 522-3607
Contact: Brandon Hunsley

Foundation type: Independent foundation
Purpose: Scholarships to graduates of Seymour High School, IN, to attend colleges and universities full-time.
Publications: Application guidelines; Annual report.

Financial data: Year ended 09/30/2012. Assets, $108,063 (M); Expenditures, $5,786; Total giving, $4,000; Grants to individuals, 2 grants totaling $4,000 (high: $2,000, low: $2,000).
Fields of interest: Higher education; Scholarships/financial aid; Volunteer services.
Type of support: Support to graduates or students of specific schools; Undergraduate support.
Application information: Application form required.
  Deadline(s): Apr. 1
  Applicants should submit the following:
    1) Transcripts
    2) SAT
    3) GPA
  Additional information: Applications are available from the Jackson County Bank Trust Dept.
EIN: 316260142

3181
Shoop Sports and Youth Foundation Inc.
(formerly International Palace of Sports, Inc.)
P.O. Box 332
North Webster, IN   46555-0332   (574) 834-4422
Contact: Joan Rhodes, Treas.

Foundation type: Independent foundation
Purpose: Scholarships to high school seniors of Wawasee, Warsaw, and Whitko school districts, IN for continuing education at accredited colleges, universities or trade schools.
Financial data: Year ended 03/31/2013. Assets, $4,225,076 (M); Expenditures, $154,624; Total giving, $118,517; Grants to individuals, 45 grants totaling $97,457 (high: $6,000, low: $500).
Type of support: Support to graduates or students of specific schools; Undergraduate support.
Application information: Application form required.
  Deadline(s): Apr. 1
  Applicants should submit the following:
    1) Class rank
    2) Financial information
EIN: 351331032

3182
Shroyer Scholarship Fund
200 E. Jackson St.
Muncie, IN   47305-2835   (317) 844-2399

Foundation type: Independent foundation
Purpose: Scholarships to children of employees of First Merchants Bank and American National Bank.
Financial data: Year ended 12/31/2011. Assets, $1,017,900 (M); Expenditures, $59,488; Total giving, $46,259; Grants to individuals, 93 grants totaling $46,259 (high: $568, low: $378).
Type of support: Employee-related scholarships.
Application information: Applications accepted. Application form required.
  Deadline(s): Mar. 21
Company names: American National Bank; First Merchants Bank
EIN: 356017466

3183
Sigma Gamma Rho National Education Fund
2801 Hillside Ave.
Indianapolis, IN   46218-2716   (317) 926-1314
Contact: Georgia L. Johnson, Scholarship Chair.
FAX: (919) 678-9721; Scholarship application address: 8020 Maitland Ave., Inglewood, CA 90305; URL: http://www.sgrho1922.org/nef

Foundation type: Public charity

Purpose: Scholarships to needy high school students, undergraduate, and postgraduate students pursuing higher education at an accredited university, college, business college or graduate school.
Publications: Application guidelines.
Financial data: Year ended 12/31/2012. Assets, $518,278; Expenditures, $62,913; Total giving, $34,750; Grants to individuals, 42 grants totaling $34,750 (high: $2,000, low: $500).
Fields of interest: Higher education.
Type of support: Scholarships—to individuals; Undergraduate support; Postgraduate support.
Application information: Applications accepted. Application form required.
  Send request by: Mail
  Deadline(s): Apr. 30
  Applicants should submit the following:
    1) SAT
    2) Photograph
    3) Financial information
    4) Transcripts
  Additional information: Application should also include a copy of current or previous year W-2 form and income tax form, letter of acceptance by institution of higher learning, two letters of reference, and $20.00 money order or cashier's check. Applicant must demonstrate financial need.
EIN: 311144466

3184
Simon Youth Foundation, Inc.
225 W. Washington St.
Indianapolis, IN   46204-3420   (317) 263-2361
Contact: Richard M. Markoff Ph.D., Exec. V.P.
FAX: (317) 263-2371; E-mail: syf@simon.com; Scholarship application address: Scholarship America, Inc., c/o SYF Scholarship Progs., P.O. Box 297, St. Peter, MN 56082; Toll-free tel.: (800) 537-4180; E-mail for Richard M. Markoff, Ph.D.: markoff@simon.com; URL: http://www.syf.org/

Foundation type: Public charity
Purpose: Scholarships to deserving high school seniors in selected communities who plan to enroll in a full-time undergraduate course of study at an accredited two- or four-year college, university or technical school.
Publications: Annual report.
Financial data: Year ended 12/31/2011. Assets, $10,275,320 (M); Expenditures, $2,498,219; Total giving, $906,605; Grants to individuals, totaling $906,605.
Fields of interest: Higher education.
Type of support: Technical education support; Undergraduate support.
Application information: Application form required.
  Deadline(s): Feb. 15
  Additional information: The program is administered by Scholarship America.
EIN: 352035269

3185
Slaughter Scholarship Trust
P.O. Box 1602
South Bend, IN   46634-1602
Application address: c/o 1st Source Bank, 100 N. Michigan St., South Bend, IN 46601-1600

Foundation type: Independent foundation
Purpose: Scholarships to graduates and graduating seniors of South Bend, IN, public and private high schools.
Financial data: Year ended 12/31/2011. Assets, $203,303 (M); Expenditures, $19,465; Total

giving, $15,500; Grants to individuals, 11 grants totaling $15,500 (high: $2,250, low: $750).
Fields of interest: Higher education.
Type of support: Support to graduates or students of specific schools; Undergraduate support.
Application information: Application form required.
  Deadline(s): None
EIN: 356054296

3186
Hazel Dell Neff Smelser Scholarship Fund
P.O. Box 1602
South Bend, IN   46634-1602

Foundation type: Independent foundation
Purpose: Scholarships to high school graduates from public and parochial schools of Marshall or St. Joseph counties, IN, majoring in music.
Financial data: Year ended 12/31/2011. Assets, $500,452 (M); Expenditures, $32,341; Total giving, $24,880; Grants to individuals, 26 grants totaling $24,880 (high: $2,610, low: -$250).
Fields of interest: Music; Performing arts, education; Higher education.
Type of support: Scholarships—to individuals; Undergraduate support.
Application information: Application form required. Interview required.
  Deadline(s): Jan. 15 for regular study, Apr. 11 for summer study
  Applicants should submit the following:
    1) Financial information
    2) Transcripts
    3) Letter(s) of recommendation
    4) Photograph
    5) SAT
  Additional information: Application should also include a brief personal statement and PSAT results. Auditions required.
Program description:
  Scholarship Program: Scholarships are awarded for the study of voice, piano, organ, orchestral string instruments, or other recognized musical instruments. Recipients are determined by academic record, financial need, musical ability, and character. Awards are available to graduating seniors, or students involved in college or university musical training and private study. The scholarship may be renewed by the committee dependent upon available funds, the student's academic record, and evidence of progress in development of student's talent.
EIN: 310884462

3187
Society for Free Radical Biology and Medicine
(formerly The Oxygen Society)
8365 Keystone Crossing, Ste. 107
Indianapolis, IN   46240-2685   (317) 205-9482
Contact: Kent L. Holland-Parlette, Exec. Dir.
FAX: (317) 205-9481; E-mail: info@sfrbm.org; URL: http://www.sfrbm.org

Foundation type: Public charity
Purpose: Grants and awards to students and postdoctoral fellow members engaged in oxygen related research.
Publications: Application guidelines.
Financial data: Year ended 12/31/2011. Assets, $427,078 (M); Expenditures, $541,137; Total giving, $34,000; Grants to individuals, totaling $18,500.
Fields of interest: Science; Chemistry.
Type of support: Grants to individuals; Awards/prizes.

Application information: Applications accepted.
  Deadline(s): Aug. 15 for Travel Awards, Sept. 1 for Young Investigator Awards, Sept. 15 and Mar. 15 for Research Mini-Fellowships, May 7 for Lifetime Achievement Award
  Additional information: See web site for additional program guidelines.
Program descriptions:
  Lifetime Achievement Award: An award of $2,500, to a scientist, with paid travel expenses, and a bronze medal with stand, and a one page bio and picture will be displayed in the SFRBM Abstract/Program book for overall contribution to the field of free radical biology and medicine. The winner will also be invited to publish a review article for Free Radical Biology and Medicine, SFRBM's journal, celebrating their scientific contributions and the presentation of this award. Award is by nomination only.
  Research Mini-Fellowships: This program provides additional research training opportunities for young investigators in the field of free radical biology that are not available at their home institutions. The program allows young investigators to cultivate collaborative relationships with established scientists, develop novel techniques or methodologies and expand their career development and research opportunities. A total of four mini-fellowships of up to $2,500 are funded each in two cycles.
  Travel Awards: Awards to students and postdoctoral fellow members who wish to attend the annual meeting to present their research. Ten awards at $1,000 each will be given to postdoc or student members of SFRBM outside of the United States, those eligible will include members from Canada, Latin and South America as well as all students and postdocs outside SFRR Americas. In addition, ten travel awards at $500 each are presented to postdoc and student members in the U.S.
  Young Investigator Award: This award is presented to students and postdoctoral fellow members based on a submitted research abstract and the presentation of the work at the annual meeting, either in oral or poster symposia. Graduate students must be enrolled in an accredited full time doctoral degree program at the time of abstract submission. Postdoctoral fellows must be engaged in full time postdoctoral research and must have no more than five years of research experience beyond their doctoral degree. Winners receive $500 at the annual meeting awards. Recipients also are given free conference registration to one of the annual meetings as part of the award.
EIN: 721570152

3188
Society for Pediatric Dermatology

8365 Keystone Crossing, Ste. 107
Indianapolis, IN 46240-2685 (317) 202-0224
Contact: Kent Lindeman, Exec. Dir.
FAX: (317) 205-9481; E-mail: spd@hp-assoc.com;
URL: http://www.pedsderm.net/index.php

Foundation type: Public charity
Purpose: Grants are awarded for research in pediatric dermatology for scholarly, clinical or basic research in the field of pediatric dermatology.
Financial data: Year ended 12/31/2011. Assets, $989,484 (M); Expenditures, $577,931; Total giving, $58,897; Grants to individuals, totaling $36,397.
Fields of interest: Pediatrics; Skin disorders research.
Type of support: Research.

Application information: Applications accepted. Application form required. Application form available on the grantmaker's web site.
  Initial approach: Proposal
  Send request by: Mail
  Deadline(s): Apr. 16
Program descriptions:
  Pilot Project Award: Three awards of up to $7,500 supports the initiation of studies important to Pediatric Dermatology. Preference is given to clinical studies and to projects by SPD members. Collaborative clinical studies are encouraged. Recipients of Pilot Project Award are eligible to apply for the William Weston Research Award in subsequent funding cycles.
  William Weston Research Award: One award in the amount of up to $20,000 supports scholarly clinical or basic research. Proposals are evaluated on their importance of pediatric dermatology, their scientific merit and their likelihood of success. Preference is given to young investigators seeking to establish a research program and to members of the Society.
EIN: 510188954

3189
South Madison Community Foundation

233 S. Main St.
Pendleton, IN 46064 (765) 778-8444
Contact: Lisa Floyd, Exec. Dir.; For grants: Tammy Bowman, Devel. Off.
FAX: (765) 778-9144;
E-mail: lisa@southmadisonfoundation.org; Grant inquiry e-mail: tammy@southmadisonfoundation.org; URL: http://www.southmadisonfoundation.org

Foundation type: Community foundation
Purpose: Scholarships to students of South Madison County, IN to assist with college costs.
Publications: Annual report; Financial statement; Grants list; Informational brochure; Newsletter; Occasional report.
Financial data: Year ended 06/30/2012. Assets, $5,699,169 (M); Expenditures, $298,357; Total giving, $0.
Fields of interest: Higher education.
Type of support: Scholarships—to individuals; Support to graduates or students of specific schools; Awards/prizes; Technical education support; Undergraduate support; Postgraduate support.
Application information: Applications accepted. Application form required. Application form available on the grantmaker's web site.
  Initial approach: Application
  Send request by: Mail or hand deliver
  Copies of proposal: 10
  Deadline(s): Apr. 1
  Applicants should submit the following:
    1) Transcripts
    2) GPA
  Additional information: Selection criteria varies per scholarships. See web site for a complete listing.
EIN: 351839759

3190
St. Vincent de Paul Society of St. Joseph County, Inc.

520 Cres. Ave.
South Bend, IN 46617-1920 (574) 234-6000
FAX: (574) 234-6248; E-mail: info@stvinnies.org;
E-mail for Charles Thompson: charlie.thompson@saintvincent-in.org; tel. for

Charles Thompson: (574) 234-6000, ext. 12113;
URL: http://www.saintvincent-in.org/

Foundation type: Public charity
Purpose: Financial assistance to indigent residents of St. Joseph County, IN and surrounding communities.
Financial data: Year ended 09/30/2012. Assets, $1,668,480 (M); Expenditures, $2,252,803; Total giving, $363,219; Grants to individuals, totaling $363,219.
Type of support: Grants for special needs.
Application information:
  Initial approach: Letter or telephone
  Additional information: Contact the society for additional guidelines.
EIN: 350863177

3191
H. Wayne Standerford Trust

P.O. Box 1078
Muncie, IN 47308-1078 (765) 759-0188
Application address: c/o Muncie Elks Lodge, 245 500 SW, Yorktown, IN 47396

Foundation type: Operating foundation
Purpose: Scholarships for tuition and related expenses to individuals in the Muncie, IN area for attendance at accredited four year colleges or universities.
Financial data: Year ended 12/31/2012. Assets, $461,408 (M); Expenditures, $10,007; Total giving, $10,000; Grants to individuals, 2 grants totaling $10,000 (high: $5,000, low: $5,000).
Fields of interest: Higher education.
Type of support: Scholarships—to individuals.
Application information: Applications accepted. Application form required.
  Deadline(s): May 1
EIN: 356705437

3192
Eugene & Florence O. Stanley Scholarship Trust

P.O. Box 1602
South Bend, IN 46634
Application address: c/o First Source Bank, Trust Dept.

Foundation type: Independent foundation
Purpose: Scholarships to graduates of Plymouth Community Schools, IN, who are in the top 30 percent of their classes based on seven semester rankings.
Financial data: Year ended 12/31/2012. Assets, $1,625,558 (M); Expenditures, $102,749; Total giving, $85,983.
Type of support: Support to graduates or students of specific schools; Undergraduate support.
Application information: Application form required.
  Deadline(s): Mar. 25 for first-time applicants, Mar. 1 for renewals
  Applicants should submit the following:
    1) Photograph
    2) Transcripts
    3) Essay
    4) SAT
    5) Letter(s) of recommendation
    6) Financial information
  Additional information: Application must also include PSAT scores (if applicable) and completed confidential sheet.
EIN: 356375193

3193
Steuben County Community Foundation
1701 N. Wayne St.
Angola, IN   46703-2356   (260) 665-6656
Contact: Jennifer Danic, Pres. and C.E.O.; For
grants: Bill Stockberger, Prog. Off.
FAX: (260) 665-8420;
E-mail: sccf@steubenfoundation.org; URL: http://
www.steubenfoundation.org

Foundation type: Community foundation
Purpose: Scholarships to designated Steuben
county, IN high school students.
Publications: Application guidelines; Annual report;
Financial statement; Informational brochure
(including application guidelines); Newsletter;
Occasional report.
Financial data: Year ended 06/30/2012. Assets,
$15,846,903 (M); Expenditures, $1,010,926;
Total giving, $601,341.
Fields of interest: Higher education.
Type of support: Scholarships—to individuals;
Support to graduates or students of specific
schools; Undergraduate support.
Application information: Applications accepted.
Application form required.
  Initial approach: Telephone
  Send request by: Online
  Deadline(s): Feb. 15
  Applicants should submit the following:
    1) Transcripts
    2) Letter(s) of recommendation
    3) GPA
    4) Essay
    5) Budget Information
  Additional information: Contact the foundation for
    application guidelines.
EIN: 351857065

3194
Robert F. Stiens and Glenda M. Stiens Trust
c/o U.S. Bank
P.O. Box 818
Richmond, IN   47374-0818   (765) 965-2293
URL: http://www.usbank.com

Foundation type: Independent foundation
Purpose: Scholarships to graduating students
attending Randolphe Southern High School, Union
High School, and Northeastern High School, IN.
Financial data: Year ended 12/31/2012. Assets,
$352,728 (M); Expenditures, $17,944; Total
giving, $11,003; Grants to individuals, 7 grants
totaling $7,800 (high: $650, low: $650).
Type of support: Support to graduates or students
of specific schools; Undergraduate support.
Application information:
  Deadline(s): None
  Additional information: Application must include
    information on family income, course of study,
    student income, and degree.
EIN: 356332467

3195
Oliver W. Storer Scholarship Foundation
c/o JPMorgan Chase Bank, N.A.
1 E. Ohio St., 16th Fl.
Indianapolis, IN   46204-1912   (317) 684-3113
Contact: Jean Landy, Fiduciary Off.
Application address: c/o Beasley, Gilkison,
Retherford & Buckles, Attn.: Charles E. Retherford,
110 E. Charles St., Muncie, IN 47308, tel.: (765)
289-0661

Foundation type: Independent foundation

Purpose: Scholarships to graduating seniors of
Delaware County, IN, for four years of schooling.
Awards may be capped.
Financial data: Year ended 02/28/2013. Assets,
$5,150,556 (M); Expenditures, $216,644; Total
giving, $144,696; Grants to individuals, totaling
$144,696.
Type of support: Support to graduates or students
of specific schools; Undergraduate support.
Application information: Applications accepted.
  Initial approach: Letter
  Deadline(s): 60 days prior to start of school year
  Additional information: Application must state
    purpose and need.
EIN: 356012044

3196
C. B. Stout Foundation
P.O. Box 207
Evansville, IN   47702-0207

Foundation type: Independent foundation
Purpose: Scholarships to graduates of high schools
in Orange County, IN, with preference shown to
students of Paoli High School.
Financial data: Year ended 12/31/2012. Assets,
$97,010 (M); Expenditures, $3,111; Total giving,
$1,000.
Type of support: Support to graduates or students
of specific schools; Undergraduate support.
Application information: Application form required.
  Deadline(s): May 1
  Applicants should submit the following:
    1) Financial information
    2) Transcripts
    3) SAT
    4) GPA
EIN: 356211379

3197
Jeanette Lyons Surina Scholarship Fund, Inc.
300 N. Meridian St., Ste. 1100
Indianapolis, IN   46204-1736   (317) 633-4700
Contact: Kathleen Surina Grove, Pres.

Foundation type: Operating foundation
Purpose: Scholarships to graduates of public
schools in Greenwood, IN, who have a minimum "B"
average and have contributed services to the
community.
Financial data: Year ended 09/30/2012. Assets,
$89,429 (M); Expenditures, $13,275; Total giving,
$12,000; Grants to individuals, 6 grants totaling
$12,000 (high: $2,000, low: $2,000).
Type of support: Undergraduate support.
Application information: Applications accepted.
Application form required.
  Deadline(s): Apr. 1
  Applicants should submit the following:
    1) Letter(s) of recommendation
    2) Transcripts
EIN: 351905548

3198
The Thomasson Foundation
(formerly Oxford Foundation, Inc.)
P.O. Box 80238
Indianapolis, IN   46280-0238

Foundation type: Independent foundation
Purpose: Undergraduate scholarships to children of
Christian missionaries in the U.S. and foreign
countries in need of financial assistance to attend
institutions of higher learning.

Financial data: Year ended 12/31/2012. Assets,
$26,062 (M); Expenditures, $185,573; Total
giving, $178,500.
Fields of interest: Christian agencies & churches;
Children.
Type of support: Undergraduate support.
Application information: Applications accepted.
  Initial approach: Letter
  Deadline(s): None
  Applicants should submit the following:
    1) SAT
    2) ACT
    3) Letter(s) of recommendation
    4) Essay
    5) Transcripts
    6) Financial information
  Additional information: Application should also
    include extracurricular activities, academic
    honors and achievement awards and
    institutions to which the applicant will apply.
EIN: 351870799

3199
Thorntown Businessmen's Educational Foundation, Inc.
1201 Indianapolis Ave.
Lebanon, IN   46052
Contact: John Randel, Pres.
Application address: 6255 W., Hazelrigg Rd.,
Thorntown, IN 46071

Foundation type: Independent foundation
Purpose: Scholarships to graduates of Western
Boone High School, Thorntown, Indiana, entering an
industrial field.
Financial data: Year ended 12/31/2012. Assets,
$333,038 (M); Expenditures, $12,001; Total
giving, $12,000; Grants to individuals, 3 grants
totaling $12,000 (high: $4,000, low: $4,000).
Type of support: Support to graduates or students
of specific schools; Undergraduate support.
Application information: Applications not
accepted.
  Additional information: Unsolicited requests for
    funds not considered or acknowledged.
EIN: 351939684

3200
Timmy Global Health
(formerly Timmy Foundation, Inc.)
22 E. 22nd St.
Indianapolis, IN   46202-1428   (317) 920-1822
Contact: Matt MacGregor, Exec. Dir.
FAX: (317) 920-1821;
E-mail: info@timmyglobalhealth.org; E-mail For Matt
MacGregor: matt@timmyglobalhealth.org;
URL: http://www.timmyglobalhealth.org/

Foundation type: Public charity
Purpose: Travel scholarships to qualified students
pursuing a career in the medical profession at
accredited institutions in the U.S., and abroad.
Publications: Annual report.
Financial data: Year ended 06/30/2012. Assets,
$931,879 (M); Expenditures, $3,766,338; Total
giving, $66,242.
Fields of interest: Medical school/education.
Type of support: Travel awards; Scholarships—to
individuals.
Application information: Applications accepted.
Application form required.
  Additional information: Selection is based on
    financial need and academic and
    service-oriented merit.

Program description:

Hank Benjamin Memorial Scholarship Fund: The scholarship provides opportunities for aspiring medical professionals to make tangible contributions to the communities and people. The fund will offset the cost of international travel for Timmy Global Health students who want to follow in Hank's footsteps and make a difference in the lives of others during their journey to become medical professionals. Scholarships in various amounts will be provided to students from the more than 20 Timmy academic student chapters at U.S. universities. Applicants will be eligible for travel stipends to participate on Timmy's short term international medical teams, as well as stipends for long-term volunteer placements at Timmy's developing world partner organizations.
EIN: 352012757

3201

Tipton County Foundation, Inc.
1020 W. Jefferson St.
P.O. Box 412
Tipton, IN 46072-0412   (765) 675-8480
Contact: Frank M. Giammarino, Pres. and C.E.O.; For scholarships: Megan Zanto, Educ. Prog. Off.
Scholarship e-mail: megan@tiptoncf.org
FAX: (765) 675-8488; E-mail: tcf@tiptoncf.org; URL: http://www.tiptoncf.org

Foundation type: Community foundation
Purpose: Scholarships to high school seniors of Tipton County, IN pursuing a four year college degree.
Publications: Application guidelines; Annual report; Financial statement; Grants list; Informational brochure; Newsletter; Occasional report; IRS Form 990 or 990-PF printed copy available upon request.
Financial data: Year ended 12/31/2012. Assets, $24,913,580 (M); Expenditures, $1,140,509; Total giving, $782,695; Grants to individuals, 87 grants totaling $142,836.
Fields of interest: Higher education; Scholarships/financial aid.
Type of support: Scholarships—to individuals; Support to graduates or students of specific schools; Undergraduate support.
Application information: Applications accepted. Application form required. Application form available on the grantmaker's web site.
> *Send request by:* Online
> *Deadline(s):* Mar. 28
> *Additional information:* See web site for applications and a complete listing of scholarship funds. Applications are also available at your high school guidance office. Applications are submitted through Dollars for Scholars program.

Program description:
Scholarship Funds: The foundation administers scholarships for high school seniors planning to pursue a four-year degree. Each scholarship has its own unique set of eligibility criteria, such as academic achievement, sense of humor, and intent to study particular fields, including engineering, health care, and visual arts. Certain scholarships require that the recipient be a graduate of a particular school, others are open to some schools, and a few may be awarded to home-schooled graduates. See web site for additional information.
EIN: 311175045

3202

Randall L. Tobias Foundation, Inc.
10330 Laurel Ridge Ln.
Carmel, IN 46032-8818

Foundation type: Independent foundation
Purpose: Grants to enrich learning for children of all ages from infancy through twelfth grade, IN.
Financial data: Year ended 12/31/2011. Assets, $491,941 (M); Expenditures, $275,290; Total giving, $267,000.
Fields of interest: Children/youth, services.
Type of support: Grants for special needs.
Application information: Application form required.
> *Initial approach:* Telephone or e-mail
> *Deadline(s):* Mar. 1 and Sept. 1

Program description:
Assistance Program: Grants generally range between $5,000 and $50,000 although requests for lesser or greater amounts may be considered. Some grants may be paid over a multi-year period.
EIN: 351938355

3203

Edwin C. Tretter Foundation, Inc.
2250 Robin Dr.
Ferdinand, IN 47532-9152   (812) 367-1978
Contact: Matt Tretter, Dir.

Foundation type: Independent foundation
Purpose: Scholarships to students of Indiana for attendance at accredited colleges or universities in IN.
Financial data: Year ended 12/31/2011. Assets, $625,974 (M); Expenditures, $31,428; Total giving, $30,000.
Fields of interest: Higher education.
Type of support: Scholarships—to individuals.
Application information: Applications accepted.
> *Initial approach:* Letter
> *Deadline(s):* None
EIN: 200742747

3204

Union County Foundation, Inc.
404 Eaton St.
Liberty, IN 47353-1407   (765) 458-7664
Contact: Danka Klein, Exec. Dir.
FAX: (765) 458-0522; E-mail: ucf@frontier.com; Additional e-mail: dklein@ucfoundationinc.org; URL: http://www.ucfoundationinc.org

Foundation type: Community foundation
Purpose: Scholarships to residents of Union County, IN for postsecondary education.
Publications: Application guidelines.
Financial data: Year ended 12/31/2012. Assets, $5,378,463 (M); Expenditures, $315,423; Total giving, $157,932; Grants to individuals, 74 grants totaling $73,867.
Fields of interest: Higher education.
Type of support: Undergraduate support.
Application information: Applications accepted. Application form required. Application form available on the grantmaker's web site.
> *Initial approach:* Application
> *Send request by:* Mail
> *Deadline(s):* Apr. 4
> *Additional information:* See web site for a complete listing of scholarships.
EIN: 351769294

3205

United States Diving Foundation, Inc.
P.O. Box 4352
Carmel, IN 46082-4352   (317) 201-7824
Contact: Todd Smith, Pres.
E-mail: info@usadivingfoundation.org; URL: http://www.usadivingfoundation.org/

Foundation type: Public charity
Purpose: Grants to USA diving registered members to enhance diving in American society through the funding of activities that would otherwise not be possible,.
Financial data: Year ended 12/31/2011. Assets, $3,892,288 (M); Expenditures, $334,654; Total giving, $290,286; Grants to individuals, 2 grants totaling $5,000.
Fields of interest: Athletics/sports, water sports.
Type of support: Grants to individuals.
Application information: Applications accepted. Application form required. Application form available on the grantmaker's web site.
> *Send request by:* On-line
> *Deadline(s):* Dec. 1
> *Additional information:* Application should include a detailed budget. Handwritten applications are not accepted. Grant activity must be initiated between Jan. 1 and Dec. 31 of the grant year and completed within 12 months.
EIN: 311153995

3206

United Student Aid Funds, Inc.
P.O. Box 6028
Indianapolis, IN 46206-6028   (317) 849-6510
Contact: Carl Dalstrom, Pres. and C.E.O.
E-mail: contact@usafunds.org; URL: http://www.usafunds.org

Foundation type: Public charity
Purpose: Scholarships and grants to deserving low-income students.
Publications: Annual report; Newsletter.
Financial data: Year ended 09/30/2011. Assets, $1,024,408,298 (M); Expenditures, $355,883,787; Total giving, $12,857,072; Grants to individuals, totaling $1,199,622.
Fields of interest: Higher education.
Type of support: Scholarships—to individuals.
Application information: Applications accepted. Application form required. Application form available on the grantmaker's web site.
> *Deadline(s):* Feb. 15
> *Final notification:* Applicants notified by June 30

Program description:
Scholarships: Four-year scholarships of $6,000 are available for selected undergraduate and graduate students, full- or part-time.
EIN: 946050341

3207

United Way of Allen County, Inc.
334 E. Berry St.
Fort Wayne, IN 46802-2708   (260) 422-4776
FAX: (260) 422-4782; URL: http://www.unitedwayallencounty.org

Foundation type: Public charity
Purpose: Grants to needy residents of Allen County, IN.
Publications: Annual report.
Financial data: Year ended 06/30/2012. Assets, $6,417,657 (M); Expenditures, $5,630,859; Total giving, $3,355,604.
Fields of interest: Economically disadvantaged.

Type of support: Grants for special needs.
Application information:
  Initial approach: Letter
  Additional information: Contact foundation for complete eligibility requirements.
EIN: 350867932

3208
United Way of Central Indiana
3901 N. Meridian St.
P.O. Box 88409
Indianapolis, IN 46208-4042 (317) 923-1466
Contact: Ann D. Murtlow, Pres. and C.E.O.
FAX: (317) 921-1355; E-mail: community@uwci.org;
URL: http://www.uwci.org

Foundation type: Public charity
Purpose: Specific assistance to families in Boone, Hamilton, Hancock, Hendricks, and Morgan counties in central IN, with food, clothing, and utilities.
Publications: Application guidelines; Annual report.
Financial data: Year ended 06/30/2012. Assets, $128,181,539 (M); Expenditures, $61,259,017; Total giving, $47,872,358; Grants to individuals, totaling $1,864,316.
Fields of interest: Human services.
Type of support: In-kind gifts; Grants for special needs.
Application information:
  Initial approach: Telephone
  Additional information: Contact the agency for eligibility criteria.
EIN: 351007590

3209
Unity Foundation of La Porte County, Inc.
115 E. 4th St.
Michigan City, IN 46360 (219) 879-0327
Contact: Margaret A. Spartz, Pres.
FAX: (219) 210-3881; E-mail: info@uflc.net; Mailing address: P.O. Box 527 Michigan City, IN 46361; Additional tel.: (888) 89-UNITY; URL: http://www.uflc.net

Foundation type: Community foundation
Purpose: Scholarships to area students in LaPorte County, IN for educational and vocational opportunities.
Publications: Application guidelines; Annual report; Annual report (including application guidelines); Financial statement; Grants list; Newsletter.
Financial data: Year ended 12/31/2011. Assets, $19,716,807 (M); Expenditures, $1,683,845; Total giving, $885,267; Grants to individuals, 100 grants totaling $179,875 (high: $29,083, low: $250).
Fields of interest: Higher education.
Type of support: Scholarships—to individuals; Precollege support; Undergraduate support.
Application information: Application form required. Application form available on the grantmaker's web site.
  Initial approach: Telephone
  Send request by: Mail
  Copies of proposal: 1
  Deadline(s): Apr. 5
  Final notification: Recipients notified within 90 days
  Applicants should submit the following:
    1) Transcripts
    2) SAT
    3) SAR
    4) GPA
    5) Financial information
    6) Budget Information

    7) ACT
  Additional information: See web site for additional application information.
EIN: 351658674

3210
USA Gymnastics
(formerly United States Gymnastics Federation)
132 E. Washington St., Ste. 700
Indianapolis, IN 46204-3674 (317) 237-5050
FAX: (317) 237-5069;
E-mail: membership@usagym.org; E-Mail for Steve Penny: spenny@usagym.org; URL: http://www.usa-gymnastics.org

Foundation type: Public charity
Purpose: Scholarships and coaching fee payments to members of the National and Olympic gymnastics teams.
Publications: Financial statement; Program policy statement.
Financial data: Year ended 12/31/2011. Assets, $11,082,538 (M); Expenditures, $17,728,778; Total giving, $1,193,783; Grants to individuals, totaling $1,078,256.
Fields of interest: Athletics/sports, training; Athletics/sports, Olympics.
Type of support: Scholarships—to individuals.
Application information: Scholarships by nomination only. Unsolicited requests for funds not considered or acknowledged.
EIN: 751847871

3211
Vermillion County Community Foundation
102 N. Main St.
P.O. Box 532
Clinton, IN 47842-0532 (765) 832-8665
Contact: Vicki Francis, Exec. Dir.
E-mail: director@thevccf.org; URL: http://www.thevccf.org

Foundation type: Community foundation
Purpose: Scholarships to high school seniors of North Vermillion or South Vermillion counties, IN for attendance at IN colleges.
Publications: Application guidelines; Biennial report; Financial statement; Grants list; Informational brochure.
Financial data: Year ended 06/30/2012. Assets, $2,525,488 (M); Expenditures, $262,068; Total giving, $116,367; Grants to individuals, 26 grants totaling $13,000.
Fields of interest: Higher education; Scholarships/financial aid.
Type of support: Scholarships—to individuals; Undergraduate support.
Application information: Applications accepted. Application form required.
  Send request by: Mail
  Copies of proposal: 1
  Deadline(s): Mar. 31
  Applicants should submit the following:
    1) Transcripts
    2) SAT
    3) Resume
    4) Letter(s) of recommendation
    5) GPA
    6) Financial information
    7) FAFSA
    8) Essay
    9) ACT
  Additional information: Contact your guidance counselor for application information.
EIN: 351998550

3212
Visiting Nurse Association Foundation, Inc.
2401 Valley Dr.
Valparaiso, IN 46383-2520
FAX: (219) 462-6020;
E-mail: webmaster@vnaportercounty.org;
URL: http://www.vnaportercounty.org

Foundation type: Public charity
Purpose: Scholarships to assist health care workers enabling them to pursue further education in health care.
Publications: Application guidelines; Annual report.
Financial data: Year ended 09/30/2011. Assets, $6,944,897 (M); Expenditures, $1,014,500; Total giving, $788,544; Grants to individuals, totaling $56,544.
Fields of interest: Nursing school/education; Health care.
Type of support: Scholarships—to individuals; Grants for special needs.
Application information: Application form required. Application form available on the grantmaker's web site.
  Initial approach: Telephone
  Deadline(s): May 31 for Avis Lukach Scholarship, Feb. 1 for Tricia Marie Simpson Russell Scholarship
  Additional information: Application for scholarship should include no more than three recommendations. Contact foundation for further information regarding health care services.
Program descriptions:
  Avis Lukach Memorial Scholarship: This scholarship is awarded locally each year to assist northern Indiana-based healthcare workers who lack access to traditional scholarships, enabling them to pursue further education in health care. Eligible applicants include anyone employed in the healthcare who wish to advance their healthcare-related education through formal courses, certificate courses, or specialized training.
  Tricia Marie Simpson Russell Memorial Scholarship: A $1,500 scholarship will be awarded to a northern Indiana-based nursing student who wishes to advance his/her education. Eligible applicants must be able to provide evidence of application to or current enrollment in a nursing program; preference will be given to single parents with dependent children.
EIN: 351655711

3213
James A. Voland Scholarship Trust
c/o KeyBank N.A.
202 S. Michigan St., Trust Tax Dept.
South Bend, IN 46601-2021 (317) 346-8011
Application addresses: c/o Brown County Community Foundation, Attn.:Marcia Flaherty, P.O. Box 191, Nashville, IN 47448, tel.: (317) 738-2213, c/o Johnson County Community Foundation, Attn.: Cheryl Morphew, P.O. Box 217, Franklin, IN 46131

Foundation type: Independent foundation
Purpose: Scholarships to qualified students from Franklin High School, Johnson county, IN and Nashville High School, Brown county IN, for higher education.
Financial data: Year ended 07/31/2012. Assets, $802,580 (M); Expenditures, $18,581; Total giving, $0.
Fields of interest: Higher education.
Type of support: Scholarships—to individuals.

Application information: Contact your school guidance office for application guidelines.
EIN: 356721104

3214
VSA Arts of Indiana
1505 North Delaware St.
Indianapolis, IN 46202-4466 (317) 974-4123
Contact: Gayle Holtman, Pres. and C.E.O.
FAX: (317) 974-4124; E-mail: info@vsai.org; Email for Gayle Holtman: gholtman@vsai.org;
URL: http://www.vsai.org

Foundation type: Public charity
Purpose: Residencies to professional teaching artists at a school in the Indianapolis, IN area, for a duration of five, ten, or fifteen days to work with students with identified disabilities.
Publications: Application guidelines.
Financial data: Year ended 06/30/2012. Assets, $332,188 (M); Expenditures, $404,563.
Fields of interest: Visual arts; Performing arts; Dance.
Type of support: Residencies.
Application information: Applications accepted. Application form required.
 Additional information: Applications are processed on a first-come, first-served basis. Faxed and e-mailed applications are not accepted.
EIN: 351529183

3215
Wabash Valley Community Foundation, Inc.
2901 Ohio Blvd., Ste. 153
Terre Haute, IN 47803-2239 (812) 232-2234
Contact: Beth A.A. Tevlin, Exec. Dir.; Kate Kollinger, Financial Mgr.
FAX: (812) 234-4853; E-mail: info@wvcf.com; Additional tel.: (877) 232-2230; Additional e-mails: beth@wvcf.com, kate@wvcf.com; URL: http://www.wvcf.com

Foundation type: Community foundation
Purpose: Scholarships to students in Clay, Sullivan and Vigo counties, IN for postsecondary education.
Publications: Application guidelines; Annual report; Financial statement; Grants list; Informational brochure; Newsletter.
Financial data: Year ended 09/30/2012. Assets, $37,761,328 (M); Expenditures, $1,958,665; Total giving, $1,298,876; Grants to individuals, 36 grants totaling $434,475.
Fields of interest: Higher education; Business school/education; Nursing school/education; Science; Mathematics; Engineering/technology.
Type of support: Scholarships—to individuals; Technical education support; Undergraduate support.
Application information: Applications accepted. Application form required. Application form available on the grantmaker's web site.
 Initial approach: Application
 Send request by: Mail
 Deadline(s): Nov. 15
 Final notification: Applicants notified five weeks after receipt of application
 Applicants should submit the following:
  1) Transcripts
  2) SAT
  3) Photograph
  4) GPA
  5) Essay
  6) Letter(s) of recommendation
  7) FAFSA

Additional information: See web site for further program and application information.
EIN: 351848649

3216
Warren County Community Foundation, Inc.
31 N. Monroe St.
Williamsport, IN 47993-1117 (765) 764-1501
Contact: Carol C. Clark, Exec. Dir.
FAX: (765) 764-1501;
E-mail: warrencountyfoundation@yahoo.com;
URL: http://www.warrencountyfoundation.com

Foundation type: Community foundation
Purpose: Scholarships to individuals of Warren county, IN for continuing education at institutions of higher learning.
Publications: Annual report; Grants list; Informational brochure; Informational brochure (including application guidelines); Newsletter.
Financial data: Year ended 12/31/2012. Assets, $2,284,314 (M); Expenditures, $226,197; Total giving, $145,982; Grants to individuals, totaling $18,250.
Fields of interest: Higher education; Scholarships/financial aid; Education.
Type of support: Emergency funds; Program development; Seed money; Scholarships—to individuals.
Application information: Applications accepted. Application form required. Application form available on the grantmaker's web site.
 Initial approach: Application
 Send request by: Mail to foundation or Seeger High School guidance office
 Deadline(s): Mar. 3 for most scholarships, see web site for exceptions
 Applicants should submit the following:
  1) FAFSA
  2) Essay
  3) Letter(s) of recommendation
  4) Transcripts
EIN: 352070789

3217
Wayne County, Indiana Foundation, Inc.
(also known as Wayne County Foundation)
33 S. 7th St., Ste. 1
Richmond, IN 47374-5423 (765) 962-1638
Contact: Steven C. Borchers, Exec. Dir.
E-mail: steve@waynecountyfoundation.org;
URL: http://www.waynecountyfoundation.org

Foundation type: Community foundation
Purpose: Scholarships to graduates of Wayne County, IN high schools for higher education.
Publications: Application guidelines; Annual report; Financial statement; Grants list; Newsletter; Program policy statement (including application guidelines).
Financial data: Year ended 12/31/2012. Assets, $32,419,755 (M); Expenditures, $2,062,214; Total giving, $1,063,876.
Fields of interest: Elementary/secondary education; Higher education; Scholarships/financial aid.
Type of support: Scholarships—to individuals; Support to graduates or students of specific schools; Undergraduate support.
Application information: Applications accepted. Application form required.
 Deadline(s): Varies
 Additional information: Contact your school counselor to review the criteria for each

scholarship and to obtain the appropriate application form.
EIN: 351406033

3218
Weaver Popcorn Foundation, Inc.
14470 Bergen Blvd., Ste. 100
Noblesville, IN 46060-3377 (317) 292-4763
Contact: Brian Hamilton

Foundation type: Company-sponsored foundation
Purpose: Scholarships to residents of Indiana and high school graduates of Huntington North High School to pursue higher education.
Financial data: Year ended 12/31/2012. Assets, $2,959,824 (M); Expenditures, $549,492; Total giving, $535,180.
Fields of interest: Higher education.
Type of support: Scholarships—to individuals.
Application information: Applications accepted. Application form required. Interview required.
 Send request by: Mail
 Deadline(s): Varies
 Applicants should submit the following:
  1) Essay
  2) Letter(s) of recommendation
  3) Financial information
  4) Transcripts
 Additional information: Bob Straight Scholarships are limited to graduating seniors of Huntington North High School in Huntington, IN. Other scholarships are open to Indiana residents to pursue higher education. Contact the foundation or Huntington North High School for application form.
EIN: 352026043

3219
Guyneth B. Webster Scholarship Fund
P.O. Box 929
Columbus, IN 47202-0929 (812) 376-1795
Contact: Melissa Fleetwood

Foundation type: Independent foundation
Purpose: Scholarships by nomination only to graduates of high schools in Bartholomew County, IN.
Financial data: Year ended 12/31/2011. Assets, $170,831 (M); Expenditures, $15,459; Total giving, $12,000.
Type of support: Awards/grants by nomination only; Undergraduate support.
Application information: Applications not accepted.
 Additional information: Unsolicited requests for funds not considered.
EIN: 356714628

3220
The Wells County Foundation, Inc.
360 N. Main St., Ste. C
Bluffton, IN 46714 (260) 824-8620
Contact: Tammy Slater, C.E.O.
FAX: (260) 824-3981;
E-mail: wellscountyfound@wellscountyfound.org;
Additional e-mail: tslater@wellscountyfound.org;
Additional E-mail: light@wellscountyfound.org;
URL: http://www.wellscountyfound.org

Foundation type: Community foundation
Purpose: Scholarships to individuals residing in Wells County, IN pursuing higher education.
Publications: Application guidelines; Annual report; Informational brochure; IRS Form 990 or 990-PF printed copy available upon request.

Financial data: Year ended 12/31/2012. Assets, $15,899,163 (M); Expenditures, $684,174; Total giving, $425,742; Grants to individuals, 97 grants totaling $246,770.
Fields of interest: Higher education; Scholarships/financial aid; Education.
Type of support: Scholarships—to individuals; Support to graduates or students of specific schools.
Application information: Applications accepted. Application form required.
  Deadline(s): Varies
  Additional information: Contact local high school guidance counselor for application. Each scholarships has its own unique set of eligibility criteria. See web site for additional application information and scholarship listings.
EIN: 356042815

3221
Western Indiana Community Action Agency, Inc.
705 S. 5th St.
Terre Haute, IN 47807-4705   (812) 232-1264
Contact: Carole Barr, Exec. Dir.
URL: http://www.wicaa.org

Foundation type: Public charity
Purpose: Assistance to low income families and individuals in Western Indiana with home energy assistance, medical care, weatherization and other special needs.
Publications: Annual report.
Financial data: Year ended 12/31/2011. Assets, $1,729,803 (M); Expenditures, $4,936,810; Total giving, $284,700; Grants to individuals, 7,272 grants totaling $128,201. Subtotal for in-kind gifts: 5,500 grants totaling $156,499. Subtotal for emergency funds: 7,272 grants totaling $128,201.
Fields of interest: Human services; Economically disadvantaged.
Type of support: Grants for special needs.
Application information: Application for energy assistance should include proof of income for all household members over the age of 18, social security cards, copy of lease, current heating and electric bills. See web site for eligibility determination.
EIN: 351115813

3222
Western Indiana Community Foundation, Inc.
(formerly Covington Community Foundation, Inc.)
135 S. Stringtown Rd.
P.O. Box 175
Covington, IN 47932-0175   (765) 793-0702
Contact: Dale A. White, Exec. Dir.; For scholarships: Kim Eaton, Secy.
Scholarship tel.: (765) 793-0702 ext. 3,
e-mail: keaton@wicf-inc.org
FAX: (765) 793-0703; E-mail: info@wicf-inc.org;
URL: http://www.wicf-inc.org

Foundation type: Community foundation
Purpose: Scholarships to high school students residing in Western Indiana for continuing education at institutions of higher learning.
Publications: Application guidelines; Annual report; Financial statement; Informational brochure; Newsletter; Occasional report (including application guidelines).
Financial data: Year ended 12/31/2012. Assets, $10,457,381 (M); Expenditures, $484,766; Total

giving, $275,151; Grants to individuals, totaling $72,053.
Fields of interest: Higher education.
Type of support: Scholarships—to individuals; Support to graduates or students of specific schools.
Application information: Applications accepted. Application form available on the grantmaker's web site.
  Send request by: Online
  Applicants should submit the following:
    1) Financial information
    2) Transcripts
    3) Letter(s) of recommendation
  Additional information: Funds are paid to the student and the educational institution.
EIN: 351814927

3223
Peter V. Westhaysen Medical Education Trust
10322 Indianapolis Blvd.
Highland, IN 46322-5352

Foundation type: Independent foundation
Purpose: Scholarships to individuals, primarily from IN, for medical and nursing education at accredited colleges and universities.
Financial data: Year ended 12/31/2012. Assets, $1,208,368 (M); Expenditures, $73,330; Total giving, $58,050; Grants to individuals, 28 grants totaling $58,050 (high: $3,000; low: $1,450).
Fields of interest: Medical school/education; Nursing school/education.
Type of support: Graduate support; Undergraduate support.
Application information: Application form required.
  Deadline(s): June 1
EIN: 316290396

3224
Lee Whitehall Educational Trust
121 W. Main St.
Attica, IN 47918-1365
Contact: Thomas P. O'Connor, Tr.

Foundation type: Independent foundation
Purpose: Scholarships to graduating students of Fountain and Warren counties, IN for higher education at accredited colleges or universities.
Financial data: Year ended 12/31/2012. Assets, $419,139 (M); Expenditures, $15,750; Total giving, $15,000; Grants to individuals, totaling $15,000.
Fields of interest: Higher education.
Type of support: Scholarships—to individuals.
Application information: Applications accepted. Application form required.
  Deadline(s): Apr. 15
  Additional information: Application can be obtained from the administrator.
EIN: 356560882

3225
Burt Whiteley Charity Fund Trust
c/o Old National Trust
P.O. Box 207
Evansville, IN 47702

Foundation type: Independent foundation
Purpose: Grants for general welfare to individuals in Delaware County, IN, referred by social welfare agencies.

Financial data: Year ended 12/31/2012. Assets, $62,276 (M); Expenditures, $3,949; Total giving, $1,799.
Type of support: Grants for special needs.
Application information: Applications not accepted.
  Additional information: Applicant must be referred by welfare agency. Unsolicited requests for funds not considered or acknowledged.
EIN: 356009797

3226
Whitley County Community Foundation
400 N. Whitley St.
P.O. Box 527
Columbia City, IN 46725   (260) 244-5224
Contact: September McConnell, Exec. Dir.; For grant applications: John Slavich, Prog. Off.
FAX: (260) 244-5724; E-mail: sepwccf@gmail.com;
URL: http://whitleycountycommunityfoundation.org

Foundation type: Community foundation
Purpose: Scholarships to graduates of Whitley County high schools, IN. Financial assistance to economically disadvantaged residents of Whitley County, IN, who are referred by their local church or social service agency. Examples of assistance include prescription medication, travel expenses related to care, and burial costs.
Publications: Application guidelines; Biennial report; Grants list; Informational brochure (including application guidelines); Newsletter.
Financial data: Year ended 12/31/2011. Assets, $16,044,604 (M); Expenditures, $1,819,461; Total giving, $1,281,354; Grants to individuals, 109 grants totaling $124,325.
Fields of interest: Higher education; Scholarships/financial aid.
Type of support: Scholarships—to individuals; Student loans—to individuals; Support to graduates or students of specific schools; Grants for special needs.
Application information: Applications accepted. Application form required. Application form available on the grantmaker's web site.
  Initial approach: Letter or e-mail for economically disadvantaged residents
  Send request by: Mail, fax, e-mail, or online
  Copies of proposal: 1
  Deadline(s): Varies
  Applicants should submit the following:
    1) Financial information
    2) Letter(s) of recommendation
    3) Transcripts
  Additional information: Applications for scholarship are available in high school guidance offices. Unsolicited application not accepted for financial assistance. Contact foundation for additional guidelines.
EIN: 351860518

3227
Charles and Ada Williams Memorial Scholarship Fund, Inc.
c/o A. Wright
P.O. Box 342
Salem, IN 47167-0342

Foundation type: Independent foundation
Purpose: Scholarships to graduates of West Washington High School, IN, for undergraduate education at a state-sponsored college or university in IN.
Financial data: Year ended 08/31/2012. Assets, $0 (M); Expenditures, $4,108; Total giving, $0.

Type of support: Support to graduates or students of specific schools; Undergraduate support.
Application information:
Deadline(s): Spring
Additional information: Applicants must write an essay on soil and water conservation, school administration, or local government.
EIN: 351708866

3228
Williams Scholarship Loan Fund, Inc.
501 Indiana Ave., Ste. 200
Indianapolis, IN 46202-6146 (317) 955-6040
Application address: c/o Marion College, Attn.: John W. Shelton, 3200 Coldspring Rd., Indianapolis, IN 46222

Foundation type: Independent foundation
Purpose: Loans to students at Marian College, IN, who are majoring in dentistry, elementary education, nursing, medicine or veterinary medicine.
Financial data: Year ended 12/31/2012. Assets, $648,581 (M); Expenditures, $42,825; Total giving, $31,860.
Fields of interest: Dental school/education; Medical school/education; Nursing school/education; Teacher school/education; Veterinary medicine.
Type of support: Student loans—to individuals; Support to graduates or students of specific schools; Graduate support; Undergraduate support.
Application information: Application form required.
Deadline(s): None
Additional information: Application should include proof of current enrollment and FAF.
EIN: 352071999

3229
The Winchester Foundation
8335 Allison Pointe Trail., Ste. 300
Indianapolis, IN 46250-1687 (765) 584-2523
Contact: Chris L. Talley, Chair.

Foundation type: Independent foundation
Purpose: Scholarships to residents of Randolph County, IN, and to graduates of Winchester Community High School, IN, who attended the school for the last two years.
Financial data: Year ended 12/31/2012. Assets, $4,395,684 (M); Expenditures, $272,441; Total giving, $229,562; Grants to individuals, 5 grants totaling $59,562 (high: $26,000, low: $2,356).
Fields of interest: Scholarships/financial aid.
Type of support: Scholarships—to individuals; Support to graduates or students of specific schools; Undergraduate support.

Application information: Application form required.
Deadline(s): Spring
Applicants should submit the following:
1) Letter(s) of recommendation
2) Photograph
3) Transcripts
4) Essay
Additional information: Candidates for scholarships other than the Pierre Goodrich Scholarship are pre-selected by a scholarship committee from the Winchester Community High School, IN. Applications accepted only for the Pierre Goodrich Scholarship. Application form required for this scholarship. Application must also include a list of extracurricular activities.
EIN: 237422941

3230
Zeta Tau Alpha Foundation, Inc.
3450 Founders Rd.
Indianapolis, IN 46268-1334 (317) 872-0540
Contact: Deb Ensor, Exec. Dir.
Scholarship e-mail: scholarships@zetataualpha.org
FAX: (317) 876-3948;
E-mail: zetataualpha@zetataualpha.org;
URL: http://www.zetataualpha.org

Foundation type: Public charity
Purpose: Scholarships to members of Zeta Tau Alpha pursuing graduate and undergraduate degrees.
Financial data: Year ended 07/31/2011. Assets, $12,585,367 (M); Expenditures, $2,660,921; Total giving, $853,277; Grants to individuals, totaling $513,700.
Fields of interest: Higher education; Students, sororities/fraternities.
Type of support: Scholarships—to individuals; Graduate support; Undergraduate support.
Application information:
Deadline(s): Mar. 1
Additional information: Selection is based on leadership, academic achievement, active participation in chapter, campus and community activities, and financial need.
EIN: 310987111

3231
C. Thomas Zimmer Memorial Fund
P.O. Box 1602
South Bend, IN 46634
Application address: c/o St. Peter's United Church of Christ Scholarship Fund, 915 N. Ironwood Dr., South Bend, IN 46615

Foundation type: Independent foundation

Purpose: Financial assistance to students who demonstrate financial need as they seek to continue their education. Academic achievement awards to students who have demonstrated academic excellence in their educational pursuit.
Publications: Application guidelines.
Financial data: Year ended 12/31/2012. Assets, $0 (M); Expenditures, $16,329; Total giving, $14,950; Grants to individuals, 8 grants totaling $14,950 (high: $3,500, low: $500).
Fields of interest: Vocational education, post-secondary; Higher education.
Type of support: Scholarships—to individuals; Grants for special needs.
Application information: Applications accepted. Application form required.
Deadline(s): June 1
Applicants should submit the following:
1) Transcripts
2) Financial information
Additional information: Applicants must be members of St. Peter's United Church of Christ, South Bend, IN for two years, or one year if transferring from another church where membership is in good standing.
EIN: 311091804

3232
Geza & Judit Zoltani Foundation, Inc.
242 Linden Ridge Trail
Greenwood, IN 46142 (310) 296-7776
Contact: Csaba K. Zoltani, Pres.
Application address: 8534 Hill Spring Dr., Lutherville, MD 21093-4530

Foundation type: Independent foundation
Purpose: Scholarships to youth whose mother tongue is Hungarian and who demonstrate a need for aid and who desire to further their education while maintaining their cultural identity.
Financial data: Year ended 12/31/2012. Assets, $30,031 (M); Expenditures, $9,007; Total giving, $8,000; Grants to individuals, 19 grants totaling $8,000 (high: $900, low: $200).
Fields of interest: Education; Youth; Minorities.
Type of support: Scholarships—to individuals.
Application information:
Initial approach: Letter
Deadline(s): None
Additional information: Applicant's letter should describe why a grant should be made to them. Consideration is given to applicants from the Hungarian minority in Sub-Carpathia, Transylvania, and Slovakia.
EIN: 352000627

IOWA

3233
Accelerated Learning Foundation
118 N. Ct.
Fairfield, IA 52556 (734) 764-9339
Contact: Layman E. Allen, Pres.
Application address: 5353 Red Fox Run, Ann Arbor, MI 48105; URL: http://www.alf-learning.org/

Foundation type: Operating foundation
Purpose: Scholarships to high school seniors who qualify to go to the National Academic Games Tournament, recommended by their coaches as outstanding.
Financial data: Year ended 12/31/2012. Assets, $1,549,407 (M); Expenditures, $390,502; Total giving, $12,876; Grants to individuals, 3 grants totaling $12,050 (high: $6,000, low: $50).
Fields of interest: Education.
Type of support: Scholarships—to individuals.
Application information:
Deadline(s): Prior to commencement of the Tournament
EIN: 383423350

3234
Affordable Housing Network, Inc.
3000 J St., S.W.
Cedar Rapids, IA 52404-4562 (319) 363-1403
Contact: Joe Lock, Exec. Dir.
FAX: (866) 908-0198; URL: http://www.affordablehousingnetwork.org/

Foundation type: Public charity
Purpose: Assistance to low-income individuals with affordable homes throughout the Cedar Rapids, IA area.
Financial data: Year ended 06/30/2012. Assets, $23,161,509 (M); Expenditures, $7,277,337; Total giving, $3,638,186; Grants to individuals, totaling $264,881.
Fields of interest: Housing/shelter, development; Housing/shelter, home owners; Housing/shelter.
Type of support: Grants for special needs.
Application information: Applications accepted. Application form required. Application form available on the grantmaker's web site.
Send request by: Mail or hand deliver
Additional information: Application should include financial information.
EIN: 208640691

3235
Allen Memorial Hospital Corporation
1825 Logan Ave.
Waterloo, IA 50703-1916 (319) 235-3941
Toll-free tel.: (800) 807-2955; TDD: (319) 235-3180; URL: http://www.allenhospital.com

Foundation type: Public charity
Purpose: Scholarships to individuals who are pursuing a degree in nursing and radiologic technology education.
Financial data: Year ended 12/31/2011. Assets, $240,687,848 (M); Expenditures, $202,127,712; Total giving, $5,783,172; Grants to individuals, 40 grants totaling $12,000.
Fields of interest: Nursing school/education.
Type of support: Scholarships—to individuals.

Application information: Applicant must demonstrate financial need, scholastic achievement and geographic background.
EIN: 420698265

3236
Ames Education Foundation
1921 Ames High Dr.
P.O. Box 1125
Ames, IA 50010-5171 (515) 268-6600
Contact: Ann Arbuckle, Exec. Dir.
FAX: (515) 268-6633;
E-mail: anne.arbuckle@ames.k12.ia.us; E-Mail for Ann Arbuckle : anne.arbuckle@ames.k12.ia.usTel. for Ann Arbuckle : (515)-268-6630; URL: http://www.ameseducationfoundation.org/

Foundation type: Public charity
Purpose: Scholarships to graduating students of Ames, IA for continuing their education at institutions of higher learning.
Publications: Informational brochure; Occasional report.
Financial data: Year ended 06/30/2012. Assets, $1,215,329 (M); Expenditures, $167,834; Total giving, $67,300; Grants to individuals, totaling $46,100.
Fields of interest: Higher education.
Type of support: Support to graduates or students of specific schools.
Application information: Applications accepted.
Deadline(s): Apr.
Additional information: Applications must be returned to the Student Services office at AHS. Electronic applications are not accepted. See web site for a complete listing of scholarships offered.
EIN: 421357966

3237
Kenneth N. Andersen Family Scholarship Trust
2701 Edgewood Pkwy. S.W.
Cedar Rapids, IA 52404 (877) 275-7034

Foundation type: Independent foundation
Purpose: Scholarships to graduates of Center Point-Urbana High School, IA.
Financial data: Year ended 12/31/2012. Assets, $293,982 (M); Expenditures, $17,759; Total giving, $14,000.
Type of support: Support to graduates or students of specific schools.
Application information:
Initial approach: Letter
Deadline(s): None
EIN: 426563588

3238
Kay M. Anderson Foundation
P.O. Box 307
Shenandoah, IA 51601 (712) 246-2029
Contact: Terry Miller

Foundation type: Independent foundation
Purpose: Scholarships to students of Shenandoah High School, IA, for higher education.
Publications: Annual report.
Financial data: Year ended 12/31/2012. Assets, $1,367,929 (M); Expenditures, $97,932; Total giving, $79,750; Grants to individuals, 29 grants totaling $22,000 (high: $1,000, low: $500).
Type of support: Scholarships—to individuals; Support to graduates or students of specific schools.

Application information: Application form required.
Deadline(s): Mar. 1
EIN: 421363292

3239
Ralph W. Anderson Veterans Trust
c/o Janice Billings
27 Mayridge Dr.
Shenandoah, IA 51601-2233
Contact: Janice Billings, Secy.-Treas.

Foundation type: Independent foundation
Purpose: Scholarships, general welfare support, and grants for medical expenses to needy veterans of the U.S. military who reside in the Northboro, Shenandoah, or Farragut, IA, areas, and to their spouses, children, and grandchildren.
Financial data: Year ended 01/31/2013. Assets, $0 (M); Expenditures, $19,371; Total giving, $17,736.
Fields of interest: Vocational education; Health care; Military/veterans' organizations.
Type of support: Scholarships—to individuals; Grants for special needs.
Application information: Applications accepted. Application form required.
Deadline(s): Jan. 30
Additional information: Application should include copy of veteran's active military service release, DD-214 or other similar release from active military service, list of three personal references, and personal statement.
EIN: 426523038

3240
Leah Andrews Scholarship Trust
c/o Fort Madison Bank & Trust Co.
636 Ave. G
Fort Madison, IA 52627
Contact: Linda Schwartz

Foundation type: Independent foundation
Purpose: Scholarships to graduates of high schools in Fort Madison, IA.
Financial data: Year ended 12/31/2012. Assets, $210,237 (M); Expenditures, $8,315; Total giving, $5,750; Grants to individuals, 6 grants totaling $5,750 (high: $1,500, low: $750).
Type of support: Scholarships—to individuals; Support to graduates or students of specific schools.
Application information: Application form required.
Deadline(s): Contact foundation for current application deadline
Additional information: Applications are available at Fort Madison Bank and at area high schools.
EIN: 426529065

3241
Iowa Pharmacy Association Foundation
8515 Douglas Ave., Ste. 16
Urbandale, IA 50322-2900 (515) 270-0713
Contact: Kate Gainer

Foundation type: Operating foundation
Purpose: Scholarships and research grants in pharmacology to residents of IA.
Financial data: Year ended 12/31/2012. Assets, $882,929 (M); Expenditures, $261,422; Total giving, $83,175.
Fields of interest: Pharmacy/prescriptions.
Type of support: Research; Scholarships—to individuals.

Application information: Applications accepted.
Initial approach: Letter
Deadline(s): None
EIN: 426075767

3242
Homer G. Barr Trust
1207 Central Ave.
Fort Dodge, IA   50501   (515) 573-2154

Foundation type: Independent foundation
Purpose: Scholarships and aid to ministerial and medical students and handicapped individuals of Webster City, IA who may otherwise be deprived of an education.
Financial data: Year ended 12/31/2011. Assets, $705,719 (M); Expenditures, $40,737; Total giving, $31,259.
Fields of interest: Medical school/education; Theological school/education; Disabilities, people with.
Type of support: Scholarships—to individuals; Grants for special needs.
Application information: Applications accepted. Application form required.
Deadline(s): None
Additional information: Application forms are available upon request.
EIN: 426299595

3243
Robert T. Bates Foundation
P.O. Box 698
Albia, IA   52531-0698   (641) 932-2144
Contact: Raymond H. Davis, Pres. and Treas.

Foundation type: Independent foundation
Purpose: Grants to individuals for historic preservation projects in Albia, IA.
Financial data: Year ended 12/31/2011. Assets, $2,370,868 (M); Expenditures, $96,315; Total giving, $12,493.
Fields of interest: Historic preservation/historical societies.
Type of support: Grants to individuals.
Application information: Applications accepted.
Initial approach: Letter
Deadline(s): None
EIN: 421392613

3244
Oswald and Sophia Bathalter Scholarship Trust
c/o DeWitt Bank & Trust Co.
P.O. Box 260
DeWitt, IA   52742-0260   (563) 659-3211
Contact: Roger J. Hill, Sr. V.P.

Foundation type: Independent foundation
Purpose: Scholarships to students graduating from a high school in Clinton County, IA.
Financial data: Year ended 03/31/2013. Assets, $304,250 (M); Expenditures, $20,667; Total giving, $10,597; Grants to individuals, 10 grants totaling $10,597 (high: $2,000, low: $347).
Fields of interest: Catholic agencies & churches.
Type of support: Support to graduates or students of specific schools; Undergraduate support.
Application information: Applications accepted. Application form required.
Deadline(s): Apr. 1
Applicants should submit the following:
1) Financial information
2) Letter(s) of recommendation
3) Transcripts

Additional information: Application should also include family information, a list of activities and a personal statement.
EIN: 421368307

3245
Bishop Educational Trust
c/o First National Bank
300 E. 2nd St.
Muscatine, IA   52761-4121
Contact: Scott Snow

Foundation type: Independent foundation
Purpose: Scholarships to deserving students to attend IA colleges, with preference given to students attending Muscatine Community College.
Financial data: Year ended 12/31/2011. Assets, $2,564,296 (M); Expenditures, $165,885; Total giving, $144,284; Grants to individuals, 86 grants totaling $144,284 (high: $5,750, low: $375).
Type of support: Scholarships—to individuals; Support to graduates or students of specific schools.
Application information: Applications accepted. Application form required.
Initial approach: Letter or telephone
Deadline(s): June 1
Additional information: Contact trust for current application guidelines.
EIN: 426531722

3246
Rex & Christine Bishop Perpetual Scholarship Fund for Iowa Valley Community School District
P.O. Box 267
Marengo, IA   52301-0267   (319) 642-5521
Contact: Julie A. Read, Tr.

Foundation type: Independent foundation
Purpose: Scholarships to graduates of the Iowa Valley Community School District, Marengo, IA, for higher education, including college, trade, and technical education within the state of IA.
Financial data: Year ended 12/31/2012. Assets, $958,324 (M); Expenditures, $54,190; Total giving, $52,337; Grants to individuals, 17 grants totaling $52,337 (high: $6,678, low: $1,596).
Fields of interest: Vocational education.
Type of support: Support to graduates or students of specific schools; Technical education support; Undergraduate support.
Application information: Applications accepted. Application form required.
Deadline(s): May 2
EIN: 421187973

3247
Abner & Eliza Black Memorial Fund
c/o Farmers & Merchants State Bank
P.O. Box 230
Winterset, IA   50273-0230   (515) 462-3731
Contact: Jerold B. Oliver

Foundation type: Independent foundation
Purpose: Scholarships to residents of Madison County, IA, who are physically disabled and under the age of 21 at the time of application.
Financial data: Year ended 12/31/2011. Assets, $374,521 (M); Expenditures, $9,646; Total giving, $7,500; Grants to individuals, 6 grants totaling $7,500 (high: $2,500, low: $625).
Fields of interest: Children/youth, services; Disabilities, people with.

Type of support: Scholarships—to individuals.
Application information: Application form required.
Deadline(s): None
Additional information: Application should include two personal references.
EIN: 426062134

3248
James W. & Carolyn Bray Scholarship
109 N. Main St.
P.O. Box 295
Danville, IA   52623-0295   (319) 392-4261

Foundation type: Independent foundation
Purpose: Scholarships to high school graduates who live within a 25 mile radius of Danville, IA.
Financial data: Year ended 12/31/2012. Assets, $21,326 (M); Expenditures, $17,558; Total giving, $17,000; Grants to individuals, 23 grants totaling $17,000 (high: $1,000, low: $500).
Fields of interest: Higher education.
Type of support: Scholarships—to individuals.
Application information: Applications accepted. Application form required.
Deadline(s): Apr. 1
Applicants should submit the following:
1) Class rank
2) Photograph
3) Letter(s) of recommendation
Additional information: Completed applications must be returned to Danville State Savings Bank.
EIN: 352162520

3249
The Brummer-Stiles-Duncan Scholarship Fund
c/o Cherokee State Bank, N.A.
212 W. Willow St.
Cherokee, IA   51012-1857   (712) 225-3000
Contact: Leon Klotz

Foundation type: Independent foundation
Purpose: Scholarships to graduates of high schools in Cherokee County, IA for attendance at a junior college, college, university or similar institution of higher learning.
Financial data: Year ended 09/30/2013. Assets, $164,792 (M); Expenditures, $5,161; Total giving, $3,000; Grants to individuals, 3 grants totaling $3,000.
Type of support: Support to graduates or students of specific schools; Undergraduate support.
Application information: Applications accepted. Application form required.
Deadline(s): None
EIN: 426371803

3250
Daisy L. Burchfield Trust
P.O. Box 477
Panora, IA   50216-0477
Contact: William E. Bump, Tr.

Foundation type: Independent foundation
Purpose: Educational loans to graduates of Panorama Community School District of Panora, IA, for postsecondary educational expenses.
Financial data: Year ended 12/31/2012. Assets, $882,065 (M); Expenditures, $10,535; Total giving, $44,350; Grants to individuals, 15 grants totaling $44,350 (high: $4,000, low: $1,000).
Type of support: Student loans—to individuals; Support to graduates or students of specific schools; Undergraduate support.

Application information: Application form required.
Deadline(s): May 31
Additional information: Application should include parents' tax form.
EIN: 426359761

3251
Camp Hertko Hollow, Inc.
101 Locust St.
Des Moines, IA 50309-1720 (515) 471-8523
Contact: Ann Wolf, Exec. Dir.; Vivian Murray, Camp Dir.
FAX: (515) 288-2531;
E-mail: a.wolf@camphertkohollow.com; Toll-free tel.: (855) 502-8500; URL: http://www.camphertkohollow.com

Foundation type: Public charity
Purpose: Financial assistance for Iowa campers in need, ages 6 through 18 who have diabetes.
Publications: Financial statement; Grants list; Informational brochure; Newsletter; Quarterly report.
Financial data: Year ended 12/31/2011. Assets, $882,882 (M); Expenditures, $748,686.
Fields of interest: Diabetes; Economically disadvantaged.
Type of support: Camperships.
Application information: Applications accepted. Application form required. Application form available on the grantmaker's web site.
Initial approach: Application
Send request by: Mail
Deadline(s): June
Additional information: Application should include a $50 non-refundable check for pre-registration for full campership.
EIN: 760717999

3252
Fred Carlson Company Foundation
202 E. Water St.
Decorah, IA 52101-2341

Foundation type: Independent foundation
Purpose: College scholarships to Iowa students who are dependents of employees of the Fred Carlson Co., IA for furthering their education.
Financial data: Year ended 01/31/2013. Assets, $101,202 (M); Expenditures, $7,120; Total giving, $5,000.
Fields of interest: Higher education.
Type of support: Employee-related scholarships.
Application information: Applications accepted. Application form required.
Deadline(s): Apr. 30
Company name: Fred Carlson Company, Inc.
EIN: 391890567

3253
Carroll High School Memorial Scholarship Fund
721 N. Main St.
Carroll, IA 51401-2327 (712) 792-8001

Foundation type: Operating foundation
Purpose: Scholarships to graduates of Carroll Public High School, IA for higher education.
Financial data: Year ended 12/31/2011. Assets, $74,461 (M); Expenditures, $9,053; Total giving, $8,975; Grants to individuals, 18 grants totaling $8,975 (high: $1,500, low: $150).
Fields of interest: Higher education.
Type of support: Support to graduates or students of specific schools.

Application information: Applications accepted.
Deadline(s): Apr. 1
Additional information: Application should include family data, academic records and a description of future academic plans.
EIN: 421168047

3254
Marie L. & John L. Carter Trust Fund For The Southeast Polk School Dist.
(formerly Marie L. & John L. Carter Trust Fund)
c/o Legacy Bank
215 Center Ave. S.
Mitchellville, IA 50169
Application address: District Superintendent, 8379 N.E. University Ave., Runnells, IA 50237

Foundation type: Independent foundation
Purpose: Scholarships to Southeast Polk High School, Runnells, IA, graduates who will attend four-year IA colleges and universities. Candidates must have excelled in American history, government, and citizenship, and must not plan on becoming trained in social work.
Financial data: Year ended 03/31/2013. Assets, $268,974 (M); Expenditures, $13,631; Total giving, $10,000; Grants to individuals, 10 grants totaling $10,000 (high: $1,000, low: $1,000).
Type of support: Support to graduates or students of specific schools; Undergraduate support.
Application information: Applications accepted. Application form required.
Deadline(s): None
Additional information: Scholarships are for one year and are renewable for a maximum of four years.
EIN: 421179937

3255
The Greater Cedar Rapids Community Foundation
(formerly The Greater Cedar Rapids Foundation)
324 3rd St. SE
Cedar Rapids, IA 52401-1841 (319) 366-2862
Contact: For grants: Karla Twedt-Ball, V.P., Progs.; For scholarship inquiries: Rochelle Naylor, Scholarship Coord.
Scholarship inquiry e-mail: scholarships@gcrcf.org
FAX: (319) 366-2912; E-mail: info@gcrcf.org; URL: http://www.gcrcf.org

Foundation type: Community foundation
Purpose: Scholarships to students of Greater Cedar Rapids, IA area pursuing higher education.
Publications: Application guidelines; Annual report; Informational brochure; Newsletter.
Financial data: Year ended 12/31/2011. Assets, $111,655,824 (M); Expenditures, $7,836,570; Total giving, $5,639,807. Scholarships—to individuals amount not specified.
Fields of interest: Higher education; Scholarships/financial aid.
Type of support: Scholarships—to individuals.
Application information: Applications accepted. Application form required. Application form available on the grantmaker's web site.
Initial approach: Application
Send request by: Mail
Deadline(s): Feb. 28
Applicants should submit the following:
1) Essay
2) Resume
3) Letter(s) of recommendation
4) Transcripts
5) FAFSA

Additional information: See web site for a complete listing of scholarships.
EIN: 426053860

3256
Hal S. Chase Scholarship Fund
c/o Jerrold B. Oliver
P.O. Box 230
Winterset, IA 50273

Foundation type: Independent foundation
Purpose: Scholarships to students graduating from Winterset High School, IA, Interstate 35 High School, IA, and Orient-Macksburg High School, IA.
Financial data: Year ended 12/31/2011. Assets, $0 (M); Expenditures, $5,350; Total giving, $0.
Type of support: Support to graduates or students of specific schools; Undergraduate support.
Application information: Application form required.
Deadline(s): Mar. 1
Additional information: Contact foundation for current application guidelines.
EIN: 421240720

3257
The Clarinda Foundation
114 E. Washington St.
P.O. Box 273
Clarinda, IA 51632 (712) 542-4412
Contact: Pam Herzberg, Exec. Dir.
FAX: (712) 542-4412;
E-mail: clarindafound@iowatelecom.net;
URL: http://www.clarindafoundation.com

Foundation type: Community foundation
Purpose: Scholarships to deserving college bound students in the Clarinda, IA area for postsecondary education.
Publications: Application guidelines; Annual report; Newsletter.
Financial data: Year ended 12/31/2012. Assets, $3,865,321 (M); Expenditures, $589,995; Total giving, $412,119; Grants to individuals, 22 grants totaling $29,328.
Fields of interest: Higher education; Scholarships/financial aid.
Type of support: Scholarships—to individuals; Undergraduate support.
Application information: Applications accepted. Application form required. Application form available on the grantmaker's web site.
Initial approach: Application
Send request by: Mail
Deadline(s): Mar. 15
Applicants should submit the following:
1) Letter(s) of recommendation
Additional information: See web site for complete listing of scholarships.
EIN: 421285187

3258
Code Scholarship Fund
453 7th St.
Des Moines, IA 50309-3702

Foundation type: Independent foundation
Purpose: Scholarships to graduating seniors of IA for postsecondary education at accredited colleges or universities.
Financial data: Year ended 12/31/2012. Assets, $334,270 (M); Expenditures, $46,072; Total giving, $40,000; Grants to individuals, 5 grants totaling $40,000 (high: $10,000, low: $5,000).
Fields of interest: Higher education.
Type of support: Scholarships—to individuals.

Application information: Applications accepted.
Initial approach: Letter or telephone
Additional information: Contact the fund for additional application guidelines.
EIN: 426472809

3259

Community Action Agency of Siouxland
2700 Leech Ave.
Sioux City, IA   51106-1129   (712) 274-1610
FAX: (712) 274-0368;
E-mail: jlogan@cassiouxland.org; Additional address: 2711 S. Helen St., Sioux City, IA 51106-3212; additional tel.: (712) 274-9940Toll Free Tel. : ((800)-352-3725; URL: http://www.caasiouxland.org

Foundation type: Public charity
Purpose: Assistance to low-income Iowa homeowners and renters to pay for a portion of their primary heating costs. Supplemental assistance is based on total household income, household size, type of dwelling, type of heating fuel and other factors.
Publications: Annual report.
Financial data: Year ended 09/30/2011. Assets, $2,625,516 (M); Expenditures, $11,836,534; Total giving, $4,508,371; Grants to individuals, totaling $4,508,371.
Fields of interest: Housing/shelter, expense aid; Economically disadvantaged.
Type of support: Grants for special needs.
Application information:
Deadline(s): Apr. 30
Applicants should submit the following:
1) Financial information
EIN: 420989589

3260

Community Action of Eastern Iowa
(formerly Iowa East Central T.R.A.I.N.)
500 E. 59th St.
Davenport, IA   52807-2623   (563) 324-3236
FAX: (563) 324-7736; Toll-free tel.: (866) 324-3236; URL: http://www.iacommunityaction.org/

Foundation type: Public charity
Purpose: Assistance to indigent residents of eastern IA for home weatherization and utilities.
Financial data: Year ended 10/31/2011. Assets, $4,287,380 (M); Expenditures, $22,059,555; Total giving, $11,171,111; Grants to individuals, totaling $10,321,806.
Fields of interest: Economically disadvantaged.
Type of support: Grants for special needs.
Application information:
Initial approach: Letter
Additional information: Contact foundation for eligibility criteria.
EIN: 420921929

3261

Community Action of Southeast Iowa
2850 Mt. Pleasant St., Ste. 108
Burlington, IA   52601-2002   (319) 753-0193
FAX: (319) 753-0687;
E-mail: community.action@caofseia.org;
URL: http://www.caofseia.org

Foundation type: Public charity
Purpose: Assistance to indigent southeast IA families to help with medical and regional transportation, energy assistance, food, and home weatherization.

Publications: Annual report.
Financial data: Year ended 09/30/2011. Assets, $2,528,218 (M); Expenditures, $14,264,165; Total giving, $6,754,067; Grants to individuals, totaling $6,754,067.
Fields of interest: Human services; Economically disadvantaged.
Type of support: Grants for special needs.
Application information:
Initial approach: Letter
Additional information: Contact the organization for eligibility criteria.
EIN: 420923961

3262

Community Foundation of Johnson County
325 E. Washington St.
Iowa City, IA   52240-3968   (319) 337-0483
Contact: Michael L. Stoffregen, Exec. Dir.
FAX: (319) 338-9958;
E-mail: info@communityfoundationofjohnsoncounty.com; URL: http://www.communityfoundationofjohnsoncounty.org/

Foundation type: Community foundation
Purpose: Scholarships to local Johnson County, IA students for higher education at accredited colleges or universities.
Publications: Annual report; Grants list; Newsletter.
Financial data: Year ended 06/30/2012. Assets, $8,870,600 (M); Expenditures, $1,626,519; Total giving, $1,312,376.
Fields of interest: Higher education.
Type of support: Scholarships—to individuals.
Application information: Applications accepted. Application form required.
Additional information: Contact the foundation for scholarship guidelines.
EIN: 421508117

3263

Community Foundation of Northeast Iowa
(formerly Community Foundation of Waterloo/Cedar Falls and Northeast Iowa)
425 Cedar St., Ste. 310
Waterloo, IA   50701-1351   (319) 287-9106
Contact: For grants: Tom Wickersham, Prog. Dir.; Kaye Englin, C.E.O. and Pres.
FAX: (319) 287-5015; E-mail: kenglin@cfneia.org;
URL: http://www.cfneia.org

Foundation type: Community foundation
Purpose: Scholarships to graduating seniors who plan to enroll as full time students at an accredited public or private university, college, vocational, technical or postsecondary institution in Iowa.
Publications: Application guidelines; Annual report; Financial statement; Grants list; Informational brochure (including application guidelines); Newsletter.
Financial data: Year ended 12/31/2011. Assets, $57,661,682 (M); Expenditures, $4,243,600; Total giving, $3,668,866.
Fields of interest: Vocational education, post-secondary; Higher education; Scholarships/financial aid.
Type of support: Scholarships—to individuals; Support to graduates or students of specific schools; Undergraduate support.
Application information: Applications accepted. Application form required. Application form available on the grantmaker's web site.
Initial approach: Application
Send request by: Online
Deadline(s): Mar. 1

Applicants should submit the following:
1) Letter(s) of recommendation
2) Transcripts
Additional information: See web site for a complete listing of scholarships.
Program description:
Scholarships: The foundation administers various scholarships established by donors for students to obtain higher education. Each scholarship may have its own eligibility requirements, criteria and application deadline. Many scholarships are limited to residents of specific counties, graduates of specific high schools, or students pursuing a degree in a particular area of study such as engineering, nursing and finance. Scholarship awards vary in size from $250 to full tuition. See web site for additional information.
EIN: 426060414

3264

Community Foundation of the Great River Bend
(formerly Davenport Area Foundation)
852 Middle Rd., Ste. 100
Bettendorf, IA   52722-4100   (563) 326-2840
Contact: Susan S. Skora, C.E.O.
Scholarship inquiry e-mail: scholarships@cfgrb.org
FAX: (563) 326-2870; E-mail: info@cfgrb.org;
Additional e-mail: susanskora@cfgrb.org;
URL: http://www.cfgrb.org

Foundation type: Community foundation
Purpose: Scholarships and students loans to individuals in the 12-county area of eastern IA and western IL who attend school in those areas.
Publications: Application guidelines; Annual report; Grants list; Informational brochure; Newsletter.
Financial data: Year ended 12/31/2012. Assets, $93,405,260 (M); Expenditures, $5,410,925; Total giving, $4,109,081.
Fields of interest: Higher education.
Type of support: Scholarships—to individuals; Student loans—to individuals.
Application information: Applications accepted. Application form required. Application form available on the grantmaker's web site.
Initial approach: Application
Send request by: Online
Deadline(s): Feb. 17 for scholarships
Final notification: Recipients notified mid-May for scholarship
Applicants should submit the following:
1) Transcripts
2) SASE
3) Letter(s) of recommendation
4) GPA
5) Financial information
6) FAFSA
7) Essay
8) ACT
Additional information: See web site for a complete listing of scholarship programs and college loan.
Program description:
Scholarships: The foundation administers multiple scholarship funds started by caring donors who are passionate about helping others attain higher education credentials. Each scholarship fund has specific eligibility criteria that were defined by the donor when the fund was established. See specific criteria for each fund on the foundation's web site.
EIN: 426122716

3265
Community Opportunities, Inc.
23751 Hwy. 30 E.
P.O. Box 427
Carroll, IA 51401-2209 (712) 792-9266
Contact: Chad Jensen, C.E.O.
FAX: (712) 792-5723; URL: http://
www.newopp.org/

Foundation type: Public charity
Purpose: Assistance for utilities and home
weatherization for indigent residents of Audubon,
Calhoun, Carroll, Dallas, Greene, Guthrie, and Sac
counties, IA.
Financial data: Year ended 09/30/2011. Assets,
$3,594,647 (M); Expenditures, $10,900,515;
Total giving, $4,873,221; Grants to individuals,
totaling $4,873,221.
Fields of interest: Economically disadvantaged.
Type of support: Grants for special needs.
Application information:
   Initial approach: Letter
   Additional information: Contact the organization
      for eligibility criteria.
EIN: 420923412

3266
Alice Conner Trust
c/o Iowa State Bank & Trust Co.
2301 128th St.
Urbandale, IA 50323-1818 (515) 246-8240
Application address: c/o Scholarship Selection
Comm., P.O. Box 16268, Des Moines, IA
50316-9405

Foundation type: Independent foundation
Purpose: Scholarships to residents of IA to attend
IA colleges and universities.
Financial data: Year ended 12/31/2011. Assets,
$373,263 (M); Expenditures, $27,928; Total
giving, $22,500; Grants to individuals, 28 grants
totaling $20,000 (high: $1,250, low: $400).
Fields of interest: Higher education; Scholarships/
financial aid.
Type of support: Scholarships—to individuals.
Application information: Application form required.
   Initial approach: Letter
   Deadline(s): Apr. 1
   Applicants should submit the following:
      1) Transcripts
      2) Letter(s) of recommendation
EIN: 426430160

3267
Jessie A. Corbin Trust
c/o Farmers & Merchants Bank Trust
P.O. Box 928
Burlington, IA 52601-0928 (319) 754-2250

Foundation type: Independent foundation
Purpose: Scholarships for students enrolled at an
accredited college or university for training areas
related to the care and education of the mentally
handicapped.
Financial data: Year ended 02/28/2013. Assets,
$114,818 (M); Expenditures, $3,830; Total giving,
$2,100; Grants to individuals, 3 grants totaling
$2,100 (high: $700, low: $700).
Fields of interest: Education, special; Mentally
disabled.
Type of support: Scholarships—to individuals.
Application information: Applications accepted.
Application form required.
   Deadline(s): Apr. 1
EIN: 426358491

3268
Credit Bureau of Fort Dodge Trust
P.O. Box 722
Fort Dodge, IA 50501-0722

Foundation type: Operating foundation
Purpose: Scholarships to students of Fort Dodge,
IA for attendance at accredited colleges or
universities.
Financial data: Year ended 12/31/2011. Assets,
$109,714 (M); Expenditures, $4,302; Total giving,
$3,750; Grants to individuals, 5 grants totaling
$3,750 (high: $750, low: $750).
Fields of interest: Higher education.
Type of support: Scholarships—to individuals.
Application information: Applications accepted.
   Additional information: Students of Fort Dodge
      should contact the trust for additional
      application information.
EIN: 421319169

3269
Robert Lloyd and Myrtle Madge Crozier Educational Trust
P.O. Box 268
Knoxville, IA 50138-0268 (641) 828-8000
Application address: c/o Iowa Savings Bank,
attn.: Stuart Job, 222 E. Robinson St., Knoxville, IA
50138-2235

Foundation type: Independent foundation
Purpose: Scholarships to financially needy
Knoxville High School, IA, graduates for higher
education at recognized colleges and universities.
Financial data: Year ended 12/31/2012. Assets,
$502,111 (M); Expenditures, $26,187; Total
giving, $21,281; Grants to individuals, 34 grants
totaling $5,281 (high: $500, low: $450).
Type of support: Support to graduates or students
of specific schools; Undergraduate support.
Application information: Applications accepted.
Application form required.
   Send request by: Mail
   Applicants should submit the following:
      1) Essay
      2) Transcripts
      3) Class rank
      4) Financial information
   Additional information: Application must also
      include name of the accredited state or
      private school applicant will attend.
EIN: 426469990

3270
Margaret E. Dallas Scholarships
400 E. 6th St.
Tipton, IA 52772-1942

Foundation type: Independent foundation
Purpose: Scholarships to residents of Cedar
County, IA, for study at accredited colleges,
universities, nursing schools, technical schools, or
area schools.
Financial data: Year ended 02/28/2013. Assets,
$195,175 (M); Expenditures, $2,231; Total giving,
$1,000; Grants to individuals, 2 grants totaling
$1,000 (high: $500, low: $500).
Fields of interest: Vocational education,
post-secondary; Higher education; Nursing school/
education; Teacher school/education.
Type of support: Technical education support;
Undergraduate support.
Application information: Application form required.
   Initial approach: Letter

Send request by: Mail
Deadline(s): Mar. 1
Final notification: Applicants notified by May 30
Applicants should submit the following:
   1) Financial information
   2) Class rank
   3) GPA
   4) Transcripts
   5) Letter(s) of recommendation
Additional information: Application should also
   include personal biography.
Program description:
   Scholarship Program: Each year at least one
   scholarship of up to $1,500 is available to a
   qualified applicant who has demonstrated a
   commitment to becoming a kindergarten (early
   childhood) teacher. Other scholarships are
   available in allotments of up to $1,500 per year for
   students attending an accredited college,
   university, technical school, or area school.
   Scholarships are granted on a yearly basis.
   Students must reapply annually.
EIN: 421238258

3271
Greater Delaware County Community Foundation
200 E. Main St.
Manchester, IA 52057 (563) 927-4141
E-mail: macc@manchesteriowa.org; URL: http://
www.manchesteriowa.org/GDCCF/index.html

Foundation type: Community foundation
Purpose: Scholarships to graduating seniors of the
Edgewood-Colesburg and West Delaware
community school districts, IA.
Financial data: Year ended 10/31/2012. Assets,
$2,306,147 (M); Expenditures, $233,114; Total
giving, $173,928; Grants to individuals, 172 grants
totaling $67,575.
Fields of interest: Higher education.
Type of support: Support to graduates or students
of specific schools; Undergraduate support.
Application information: Contact foundation for
current application guidelines.
EIN: 421045184

3272
Robert E. & Olive L. Denton Scholarship Trust
c/o Corydon State Bank
P.O. Box 228
Corydon, IA 50060-0228 (641) 872-2343
Contact: Alan Wilson
Application address: 107 W Jackson St., Corydon IA
50060

Foundation type: Independent foundation
Purpose: Scholarships to graduating seniors at
Wayne Community Junior Senior High School in
Corydon, IA.
Financial data: Year ended 12/31/2012. Assets,
$351,828 (M); Expenditures, $8,228; Total giving,
$7,500; Grants to individuals, 4 grants totaling
$7,500 (high: $3,000, low: $500).
Type of support: Support to graduates or students
of specific schools; Undergraduate support.
Application information: Applications accepted.
Application form not required.
   Deadline(s): None
EIN: 426424290

3273
Des Moines Golf and Country Club Educational Foundation
1600 Jordan Creek Pkwy.
West Des Moines, IA 50266-5833 (515) 440-7500
Contact: David Kloock

Foundation type: Independent foundation
Purpose: Scholarships only to employees of the Des Moines Golf and Country Club in IA for undergraduate study.
Financial data: Year ended 12/31/2011. Assets, $175,798 (M); Expenditures, $59,306; Total giving, $51,000; Grants to individuals, 26 grants totaling $51,000 (high: $3,000, low: $750).
Type of support: Employee-related scholarships.
Application information: Applications not accepted.
Additional information: Unsolicited requests for funds not considered or acknowledged.
Company name: Des Moines Golf and Country Club
EIN: 421402068

3274
Des Moines Jewish Foundation
33158 Ute Ave.
Waukee, IA 50263-7538 (515) 987-0899
Contact: Elaine Steinger, Exec. Dir.
URL: http://jewishdesmoines.org/

Foundation type: Public charity
Purpose: Assistance to indigent Jewish families of Des Moines, IA, for living expenses.
Financial data: Year ended 06/30/2012. Assets, $14,276,480 (M); Expenditures, $967,036; Total giving, $779,739.
Fields of interest: Jewish agencies & synagogues; Economically disadvantaged.
Type of support: Grants for special needs.
Application information:
Initial approach: Letter
Additional information: Contact foundation for eligibility criteria.
EIN: 510159835

3275
Harlan O. Diehl Trust
7452 N. 95th Ave. W.
Baxter, IA 50025
Application address: c/o Guidance Office, Baxter Community High School, Baxter, IA 50028

Foundation type: Independent foundation
Purpose: Scholarships to seniors of Baxter Community High School, IA, for higher education at a college in IA.
Financial data: Year ended 05/31/2013. Assets, $0 (M); Expenditures, $20,591; Total giving, $20,000; Grants to individuals, 10 grants totaling $20,000 (high: $2,500, low: $1,250).
Type of support: Support to graduates or students of specific schools; Undergraduate support.
Application information: Application form required.
Deadline(s): Apr. 15
EIN: 426338687

3276
Cornelius Duggan Scholarship Trust
c/o Security National Bank, Trust Dept.
P.O. Box 147
Sioux City, IA 51102-0147

Foundation type: Independent foundation

Purpose: Scholarships to individuals at Iowa private colleges for higher education in Sioux City, IA.
Financial data: Year ended 12/31/2012. Assets, $3,415,773 (M); Expenditures, $265,665; Total giving, $213,750; Grants to individuals, 48 grants totaling $213,750 (high: $4,500, low: $4,500).
Type of support: Undergraduate support.
Application information: Unsolicited requests for funds not accepted.
EIN: 426136907

3277
Louis J. Elbert Trust
200 N. Main St.
P.O. Box 159
Pocahontas, IA 50574 (712) 335-4848
Contact: Diane Stegge

Foundation type: Independent foundation
Purpose: Scholarships to graduates of Pocahontas Area Community School, IA, with a minimum 2.0 GPA.
Financial data: Year ended 12/31/2012. Assets, $337,471 (M); Expenditures, $18,761; Total giving, $15,050.
Type of support: Support to graduates or students of specific schools; Undergraduate support.
Application information: Applications not accepted.
Additional information: Application must include three references and transcripts. Unsolicited requests for funds not considered or acknowledged.
EIN: 421301198

3278
Rich Eychaner Charitable Foundation
P.O. Box 1797
Des Moines, IA 50305 (515) 262-0000
URL: http://www.eychanerfoundation.org/

Foundation type: Independent foundation
Purpose: Scholarships to residents of IA and IL to attend selected colleges in those states.
Financial data: Year ended 11/30/2012. Assets, $38,964 (M); Expenditures, $243,748; Total giving, $137,246; Grants to individuals, 41 grants totaling $137,246 (high: $11,755, low: $500).
Fields of interest: Minorities; LGBTQ.
Type of support: Support to graduates or students of specific schools.
Application information: Applications accepted. Application form required. Interview required.
Deadline(s): Vary
Applicants should submit the following:
1) FAFSA
2) SAR
3) Transcripts
4) Essay
Program descriptions:
Howard and Mildred Eychaner Minority Scholarship: Scholarships are available for minority students (as to sexual orientation, race, national origin and/or physical challenge) who will attend Northern Illinois University. Deadline Mar. 17.
Matthew Shepard Scholarship: Scholarships are available for IA high school students who are openly gay or lesbian and attending Iowa State University, the University of Iowa or the University of Northern Iowa. Deadline Mar. 31.
EIN: 421305042

3279
Juli Ann Farrell Charitable Trust
c/o Wanda Jane Farrell
104 Walnut St.
Hudson, IA 50643-2159

Foundation type: Independent foundation
Purpose: Scholarships primarily to residents of IA for higher education.
Financial data: Year ended 12/31/2011. Assets, $210,560 (M); Expenditures, $10,957; Total giving, $8,000; Grants to individuals, 11 grants totaling $8,000 (high: $1,000, low: $500).
Type of support: Undergraduate support.
Application information: Applications not accepted.
Additional information: Unsolicited requests for funds not considered.
EIN: 426591048

3280
Father Daily Scholarship Foundation
c/o Boerner & Goldsmith Law Firm, P.C.
500 2nd St.
Ida Grove, IA 51445 (712) 364-2421
Contact: Keri Weber

Foundation type: Operating foundation
Purpose: Scholarships to high school seniors who are parishioners of Sacred Heart Parish, IA, to attend college or technical school.
Financial data: Year ended 12/31/2012. Assets, $88,845 (M); Expenditures, $9,760; Total giving, $8,900.
Fields of interest: Vocational education, post-secondary.
Type of support: Technical education support; Undergraduate support.
Application information: Contact foundation for current application deadline/guidelines.
EIN: 421372214

3281
Florence Frisbie Scholarship Fund
212 W. Willow St.
Cherokee, IA 51012-1000

Foundation type: Operating foundation
Purpose: Scholarships to graduating students of Cherokee County high schools, IA for attendance at accredited colleges or universities.
Financial data: Year ended 12/31/2012. Assets, $175,035 (M); Expenditures, $6,122; Total giving, $4,000.
Fields of interest: Higher education.
Type of support: Support to graduates or students of specific schools.
Application information: Contact your school guidance office for application information.
EIN: 426615574

3282
Virgil C. Webb, William Garber, and Flora Webb Garber Foundation
6075 N.E. 78th Ave.
Bondurant, IA 50035-1067
Application address for Music Scholarship, General Scholarship, and Music Education Grants: 5360 N.E. 70th Ave., Altoona, IA 50009-9564

Foundation type: Independent foundation
Purpose: College scholarship and music scholarships to needy students in the Bondurant-Farrar School District, IA.

Financial data: Year ended 09/30/2012. Assets, $2,500,790 (M); Expenditures, $359,508; Total giving, $338,150; Grants to individuals, 52 grants totaling $323,150 (high: $8,500, low: $1,750).
Fields of interest: Music; Performing arts, education; Higher education.
Type of support: Scholarships—to individuals.
Application information: Applications accepted. Application form required.
> *Deadline(s):* Mar. 1 for Music Scholarship and General Scholarship, June 30 and Dec. 31 for Music Education Grant
> *Applicants should submit the following:*
> 1) Essay
> 2) Letter(s) of recommendation
> 3) Transcripts
> *Additional information:* Contact the foundation for additional guidelines.

EIN: 271536903

3283
Genesis Health Services Foundation

1227 E. Rusholme St.
Davenport, IA   52803-2459   (563) 421-6508
Contact: Melinda Gowey, Exec. Dir.
Scholarship e-mail:
scholarships@genesishealth.com, tel.: (563) 421-6869
E-mail: goweym@genesishealth.com; URL: http://www.genesishealth.com

Foundation type: Public charity
Purpose: College scholarships to students attending an accredited IA or IL college or university pursuing a baccalaureate degree in nursing. Scholarships also to employed nurses at Genesis Medical Center, Davenport and Illini Campus, Silvis, IL pursuing BSN or MSN degrees.
Publications: Informational brochure.
Financial data: Year ended 06/30/2012. Assets, $18,122,345 (M); Expenditures, $2,172,405; Total giving, $1,314,558; Grants to individuals, totaling $578,646.
Fields of interest: Nursing school/education.
Type of support: Scholarships—to individuals; Undergraduate support.
Application information: Applications accepted. Application form required. Application form available on the grantmaker's web site.
> *Send request by:* Mail, e-mail or fax
> *Deadline(s):* Mar. 24
> *Final notification:* Recipients notified in May
> *Applicants should submit the following:*
> 1) Transcripts
> 2) Letter(s) of recommendation
> 3) Essay
> *Additional information:* Application should also include a copy of acceptance letter for college/university or acceptance letter into the BSN program. See web site for additional guidelines.

Program description:
> *Gala Nursing Scholarship:* This $10,000 will be awarded as a one-time scholarship to current college students in good academic standing, attending an accredited Iowa or Illinois college or university. Applicants must be residents within the Genesis Health System, bi-state service which includes Clinton, Des Moines, Jackson, Louisa, Muscatine, or Scott Counties in IA or Henry, Mercer, Rock Island, or Whiteside Counties in IL and have a minimum high school cumulative GPA of 3.0 and/or college cumulative GPA of 2.5. The scholarship is awarded as a forgivable loan and recipients are required to sign a Forgivable Loan Agreement and a Promissory Note. Fifty percent of the loan will be forgiven if the nurse works for Genesis Health

System for one year. One hundred percent of the loan will be forgiven if employed full time for two years.
EIN: 421421670

3284
The Roy H. and Joan Huber Gerling Scholarship Trust

c/o Community Bank
229 Main St.
Columbus Junction, IA   52738-1136   (319) 728-2231

Foundation type: Independent foundation
Purpose: Scholarships to graduating high school seniors of Columbus School District, IA, for higher education.
Financial data: Year ended 12/31/2011. Assets, $58,112 (M); Expenditures, $10,808; Total giving, $10,000; Grants to individuals, 9 grants totaling $10,000 (high: $1,250, low: $625).
Fields of interest: Higher education.
Type of support: Scholarships—to individuals; Support to graduates or students of specific schools.
Application information: Applications accepted. Application form not required.
> *Initial approach:* Letter
> *Deadline(s):* Mar. 1
> *Additional information:* One scholarship with be for a girl and one scholarships will be for a boy each year.

EIN: 716213401

3285
Mary Louise Gidley Scholarship Fund

P.O. Box 54
Shenandoah, IA   51601-0054   (712) 246-1581
Contact: Jeff Hiser
Application address: 304 W. Nishna Rd., Shenandoah, IA 51601

Foundation type: Independent foundation
Purpose: Student loans to graduating high school seniors, college students and persons desiring vocational training of Shenandoah, IA who have no reasonable source of financial assistance.
Financial data: Year ended 12/31/2012. Assets, $444,065 (M); Expenditures, $5,973; Total giving, $0; Loans to individuals, 33 loans totaling $37,500.
Fields of interest: Vocational education, post-secondary; Higher education.
Type of support: Student loans—to individuals; Support to graduates or students of specific schools.
Application information: Applications accepted. Application form required. Interview required.
> *Deadline(s):* May 15
> *Applicants should submit the following:*
> 1) Class rank
> 2) GPA
> *Additional information:* Applicants must possess good character, show promise of being worthy, possess scholastic and academic aptitude and have a strong desire for higher education, and vocational or career training. All applications are to be filed at the Shenandoah High School Office.

EIN: 421091743

3286
Grace Foundation

P.O. Box 846
Ames, IA   50010
Contact: Leah Akers Bell, Tr.
Application address: 355 El Dorado Ave., Palo Alto, CA 94306

Foundation type: Operating foundation
Purpose: Scholarships to economically deprived students of China and Southeast Asia only, to work towards improving the welfare of persons in their native countries and promoting the Christian faith.
Publications: Application guidelines; Informational brochure.
Financial data: Year ended 06/30/2013. Assets, $1,034,357 (M); Expenditures, $58,140; Total giving, $46,100; Grants to individuals, totaling $46,100.
Fields of interest: Christian agencies & churches.
Type of support: Grants to individuals; Scholarships—to individuals; Foreign applicants.
Application information: Application form required.
> *Initial approach:* Letter
> *Copies of proposal:* 1
> *Deadline(s):* Feb. 1
> *Final notification:* Recipients notified by May 15
> *Applicants should submit the following:*
> 1) Transcripts
> 2) Letter(s) of recommendation
> *Additional information:* Application must include intended course of study, statement of financial need, brief background, Christian testimony, and name and address of applicant's college or university.

Program description:
> *Grace Foundation Program:* Recipients must meet the following criteria: [BULLET]have satisfactorily completed one or more years at an accredited four-year college or university in or near their native country, or in a developed country where specialized training is offered; special permission may be granted for Bible Schools that offer in-depth postsecondary school training[/BULLET] [BULLET]have excellent character with a strong Christian witness[/BULLET] [BULLET]have strong academic achievement with a minimum GPA of 3.0 or equivalent; for students studying in the U.S., a minimum TOEFL score of 500 is required[/BULLET] [BULLET]be following a course of study in Christian ministry, teaching, health care, or other fields that can be used to assist needy persons in their native country[/BULLET] [BULLET]have financial need. A student must be unable to pursue studies without some form of financial assistance[/BULLET] [BULLET]have the ability to express himself/herself clearly and to personally complete the Grace Foundation Application Form in English[/BULLET] Preference is shown to students who express a strong commitment to return to their native country upon completion of their studies to provide service in Christian ministry, teaching, health care, or welfare assistance to the poor and uneducated. Scholarships are in amounts of up to $3,500 and cover the costs of tuition only. Scholarships are renewable for up to four years of full-time study provided recipient maintains at least a 3.0 GPA. The foundation does not: [BULLET]accept second party referrals[/BULLET] [BULLET]sponsor students for their entire educational cost[/BULLET] [BULLET]provide aid for more than four years, or for additional degrees[/BULLET] [BULLET]provide transportation or living expenses for students and their families.[/BULLET]

EIN: 237294779

3287
Great River Medical Center Staff Foundation
(formerly Burlington Medical Center Staff Foundation)
200 Jefferson St.
Burlington, IA 52601-5211 (319) 754-5000

Foundation type: Independent foundation
Purpose: Loans to children of staff members of the Great River Medical Center of West Burlington, IA.
Financial data: Year ended 12/31/2011. Assets, $86,444 (M); Expenditures, $70,594; Total giving, $0.
Fields of interest: Higher education.
Type of support: Student loans—to individuals.
Application information: Application form required.
  Deadline(s): None
  Additional information: Applicant should include loan amount requested.
EIN: 421153421

3288
Greene County Medical Center Foundation
1000 W. Lincolnway
Jefferson, IA 50129-1645 (515) 386-2114
FAX: (515) 386-3695; URL: http://gcmchealth.com/body.cfm?id=11

Foundation type: Public charity
Purpose: Scholarships to students of Green county, IA pursuing a degree in a health-related field of study. Tuition reimbursement scholarships to employees of Green County Medical Center who have been employed for two years or more and are taking courses directly related to an employee's job or long-term career development.
Financial data: Year ended 06/30/2012. Assets, $2,613,634 (M); Expenditures, $156,193; Total giving, $78,701; Grants to individuals, totaling $9,131.
Fields of interest: Formal/general education.
Type of support: Scholarships—to individuals.
Application information: Scholarship amounts are based on number of applicants and financial need.
EIN: 237163421

3289
Paul and Mary Griffith Scholarship Fund
c/o Farmers & Merchants State Bank
P.O. Box 29
Winterset, IA 50273 (515) 462-3320
Application address: c/o Winterset Community High School, 624 W. Husky Dr., Winterset, IA 50273-2268

Foundation type: Independent foundation
Purpose: Scholarships to graduates of Winterset Community High School, IA for postsecondary education.
Financial data: Year ended 12/31/2011. Assets, $164,153 (M); Expenditures, $7,173; Total giving, $6,000; Grants to individuals, 6 grants totaling $6,000 (high: $1,000, low: $1,000).
Fields of interest: Higher education.
Type of support: Scholarships—to individuals; Support to graduates or students of specific schools.
Application information: Applications accepted. Application form required. Interview required.
  Deadline(s): None
  Additional information: Students should contact their guidance counselor for application information.
EIN: 421172652

3290
Grinnell Mutual Group Foundation
(formerly GMG Foundation)
4215 Hwy., Ste.146
Grinnell, IA 50112-0790 (641) 269-8000
Contact: Barbara Baker, Mgr.
E-mail: jwoods@gmrc.com

Foundation type: Company-sponsored foundation
Purpose: Grants and scholarships for employees of Grinnell Mutual Group.
Publications: Annual report.
Financial data: Year ended 12/31/2012. Assets, $7,001 (M); Expenditures, $90,225; Total giving, $90,225.
Type of support: Employee-related scholarships; Grants to individuals.
Application information: Applications accepted. Application form not required.
  Initial approach: Letter
  Send request by: Mail
  Copies of proposal: 1
  Deadline(s): Varies
  Final notification: Recipients notified quarterly
  Applicants should submit the following:
    1) Proposal
    2) Budget Information
Company name: Grinnell Mutual Reinsurance Company
EIN: 421308146

3291
Stephen R. Grubb Charitable Foundation Inc.
475 S. 50th St., Ste. 100
West Des Moines, IA 50265-6980 (515) 327-1700
Contact: Stephen R. Grubb, Pres.

Foundation type: Company-sponsored foundation
Purpose: Grants to residents of the Des Moines, IA, area for medical and other expenses.
Financial data: Year ended 12/31/2012. Assets, $11,274 (M); Expenditures, $14,829; Total giving, $14,285; Grant to an individual, 1 grant totaling $5,085.
Type of support: Grants for special needs.
Application information: Applications accepted.
  Initial approach: Letter
  Additional information: Contact foundation for complete application deadline/guidelines.
EIN: 391901112

3292
W. H. Guest & E. M. Guest Educational Trust
(formerly William H. Guest & Edith M. Guest Educational Trust)
209 W. Willow St.
Cherokee, IA 51012 (712) 225-3000
Contact: Craig Weise, Tr.
Application address: Cherokee State Bank, 212 W., Willow St. Cherokee, IA 51012

Foundation type: Independent foundation
Purpose: Scholarships to residents of Cherokee, IA, for study at a two-year trade or vocational school.
Financial data: Year ended 12/31/2012. Assets, $447,565 (M); Expenditures, $23,181; Total giving, $21,600; Grants to individuals, 8 grants totaling $21,600 (high: $2,700, low: $2,700).
Fields of interest: Vocational education.
Type of support: Technical education support.
Application information: Applications accepted. Application form required.
  Deadline(s): May 1

  Additional information: Application should include transcript and description of need.
EIN: 426278426

3293
Mary Catherine Hagedorn Trust
P.O. Box 305
Lake View, IA 51450-0305
Contact: William Vonnahme, Tr.
Application address: 1622 N. Main St., Carroll, IA 51401

Foundation type: Operating foundation
Purpose: Scholarships to graduating seniors from the Catholic high schools in the Diocese of Sioux City, IA for higher education.
Financial data: Year ended 10/31/2013. Assets, $483,102 (M); Expenditures, $11,879; Total giving, $9,450; Grants to individuals, 23 grants totaling $9,450 (high: $550, low: $325).
Type of support: Undergraduate support.
Application information: Applications accepted.
  Initial approach: Letter
  Deadline(s): None
  Additional information: Students are recommended for scholarships by their respective high schools.
EIN: 426291418

3294
Harry Hahn, Jr. Educational Trust
c/o First State Bank
P.O. Box 276
Ida Grove, IA 51445-1310 (712) 364-3181
Contact: Wayne Nielsen, Pres.

Foundation type: Operating foundation
Purpose: Limited scholarships to students of Battle Creek School District, IA for continuing education at accredited institutions of higher learning.
Financial data: Year ended 12/31/2012. Assets, $143,881 (M); Expenditures, $7,416; Total giving, $5,000; Grants to individuals, 4 grants totaling $5,000 (high: $1,750, low: $750).
Fields of interest: Higher education.
Type of support: Scholarships—to individuals.
Application information: Application form required.
  Deadline(s): Before graduation each year, May or June
EIN: 426512801

3295
Harper Brush Works Foundation, Inc.
402 N. 2nd St.
Fairfield, IA 52556-0608 (641) 472-7876
Contact: Diana Spates, Pres.

Foundation type: Company-sponsored foundation
Purpose: Scholarships to college students for higher education and grants to teachers primarily in the Fairfield, IA area for outstanding contributions to education.
Financial data: Year ended 08/31/2012. Assets, $4,982 (M); Expenditures, $0; Total giving, $0.
Fields of interest: Education.
Type of support: Scholarships—to individuals; Awards/prizes.
Application information: Applications accepted.
  Deadline(s): None
EIN: 421145331

3296
Hawkeye Area Community Action Program, Inc.
P.O. Box 490
1515 Hawkeye Dr.
Hiawatha, IA   52233-1102   (319) 393-7811
Contact: Jane Drapeaux, C.E.O.
E-mail: info@hacap.org; URL: http://www.hacap.org/

Foundation type: Public charity
Purpose: Financial assistance to low income individuals and families of IA, with food, shelter, utilities and other special needs.
Publications: Annual report.
Financial data: Year ended 09/30/2011. Assets, $11,143,011 (M); Expenditures, $27,837,075; Total giving, $8,527,270; Grants to individuals, totaling $5,717,563.
Fields of interest: Human services; Economically disadvantaged.
Type of support: Grants for special needs.
Application information: Applications accepted. Application form required.
   Additional information: Some assistance require an application, contact the agency for eligibility determination.
EIN: 420898405

3297
Henry County Health Center Foundation
407 S. White St.
Mount Pleasant, IA   52641-2292
URL: http://www.hchc.org/foundation/

Foundation type: Independent foundation
Purpose: Student loans and grants to attract and retain physicians who will provide medical care to citizens of Henry County, IA. Generally, the grants are given to cover the cost of interest on previously given loans.
Financial data: Year ended 06/30/2013. Assets, $1,964,733 (M); Expenditures, $545,726; Total giving, $944,531.
Fields of interest: Health care.
Type of support: Student loans—to individuals.
Application information: Applications not accepted.
EIN: 421354383

3298
Chink and Annie Hermsen Memorial Foundation
c/o Gerald Van Erdewyk
105 Main St.
Breda, IA   51436-8703   (712) 673-2321
Contact: Gerald Van Erdewyk, Dir.

Foundation type: Independent foundation
Purpose: Scholarship to students and graduates of the public and private school systems in Carroll County, IA for tuition, books, and room and board.
Financial data: Year ended 12/31/2010. Assets, $10,408 (M); Expenditures, $22,980; Total giving, $22,500; Grants to individuals, 5 grants totaling $22,500 (high: $5,000, low: $2,500).
Fields of interest: Higher education.
Type of support: Scholarships—to individuals.
Application information: Applications accepted. Application form required.
   Initial approach: Letter
   Deadline(s): None
EIN: 421393722

3299
Elizabeth Hill Trust
1405 S.W. 2nd St.
Eagle Grove, IA   50533-1924
Contact: Opal Gibson, Tr.

Foundation type: Independent foundation
Purpose: Loans for higher education to needy and deserving residents of Eagle Grove, IA. No interest will be charged until six months after completion or termination of training.
Financial data: Year ended 12/31/2011. Assets, $1,246,305 (M); Expenditures, $36,820; Total giving, $31,665; Grants to individuals, 35 grants totaling $31,665 (high: $1,650, low: $100).
Fields of interest: Higher education.
Type of support: Student loans—to individuals.
Application information: Applications accepted. Application form required.
EIN: 426375488

3300
Charles Hockenberry Foundation
c/o City National Bank
116 S. Blossom St.
Shenandoah, IA   51601-1732   (712) 246-2205
Contact: Heather Ritchey

Foundation type: Independent foundation
Purpose: Scholarships to disadvantaged youths residing in Page County, IA, and grants for other needs.
Financial data: Year ended 12/31/2011. Assets, $1,215,797 (M); Expenditures, $84,705; Total giving, $63,138; Grants to individuals, 110 grants totaling $63,138 (high: $5,100, low: $20).
Fields of interest: Music; Education.
Type of support: Grants to individuals; Scholarships—to individuals.
Application information: Applications accepted. Application form required.
   Deadline(s): None
   Additional information: Application must include a copy of parents' most recent tax return.
EIN: 421382905

3301
Phyllis Perry Hulton Educational Trust
c/o Bowman & Miller, PC
P.O. Box 1635
Marshalltown, IA   50158   (641) 753-9337
Contact: James R. Bowman
Application address: 24 E. Main St., Marshalltown, IA 50158-4903

Foundation type: Independent foundation
Purpose: Scholarships to graduates of any Marshall County, IA, high school.
Financial data: Year ended 11/30/2012. Assets, $2,439,136 (M); Expenditures, $104,241; Total giving, $99,600; Grants to individuals, 125 grants totaling $99,600 (high: $800, low: $800).
Type of support: Support to graduates or students of specific schools; Undergraduate support.
Application information: Applications accepted. Application form required.
   Deadline(s): Apr. 20
   Additional information: Application must include academic qualifications, a transcript and financial plans. Applications available in Jan.
EIN: 426526655

3302
Hy-Vee Foundation Inc.
5820 Westown Pkwy.
West Des Moines, IA   50266-8223   (515) 267-2915
Contact: Lynn Hoskins
E-mail: lhoskins@hy-vee.com; URL: http://www.hy-vee.com/company/scholarships/default.aspx

Foundation type: Company-sponsored foundation
Purpose: Scholarships to high school seniors who are children of Hy-Vee or subsidiary employees or full-time college students pursuing any course of study at a four year college.
Financial data: Year ended 09/24/2012. Assets, $0 (M); Expenditures, $85,000; Total giving, $80,000; Grants to individuals, 80 grants totaling $80,000 (high: $1,000, low: $1,000).
Fields of interest: Higher education.
Type of support: Employee-related scholarships.
Application information: Applications accepted. Application form required.
   Send request by: Mail
   Deadline(s): Feb. 10
   Applicants should submit the following:
      1) Letter(s) of recommendation
      2) Transcripts
      3) Resume
   Additional information: Applicant must be a high school senior working for Hy-Vee or subsidiary, or college student employed at a Hy-Vee location or subsidiary location. Unsolicited requests for funds not considered or acknowledged.
EIN: 420942086

3303
Carrie and Oren Igou Scholarship Fund
c/o Krull Law Office
714 Central Ave.
Northwood, IA   50459-0200   (641) 324-2142
Application Address: c/o Guidance Counselor, 704 N. 7th St., Northwood, IA 50459

Foundation type: Operating foundation
Purpose: Scholarships to graduating seniors of Northwood-Kensett high schools, IA for postsecondary education.
Financial data: Year ended 12/31/2012. Assets, $95,964 (M); Expenditures, $6,333; Total giving, $6,000; Grants to individuals, 3 grants totaling $6,000 (high: $2,000, low: $2,000).
Fields of interest: Higher education.
Type of support: Scholarships—to individuals; Support to graduates or students of specific schools.
Application information: Applications accepted. Application form required.
   Initial approach: Letter
   Deadline(s): Apr. 1
   Additional information: Students should contact their guidance counselor for application information.
EIN: 421339046

3304
Iowa City Area Association of Realtors Scholarship Foundation
847 Quarry Rd.
Coralville, IA   52241   (319) 338-6460
E-mail: icaar@icarr.org; URL: http://www.icaar.org

Foundation type: Independent foundation
Purpose: Scholarships are awarded based on community service to junior high and high school

students in the Iowa City Area Association of Realtors service area for attendance at any accredited college, university, community college, technical or trade school.

Financial data: Year ended 06/30/2013. Assets, $193,595 (M); Expenditures, $7,776; Total giving, $6,450; Grants to individuals, 13 grants totaling $6,450 (high: $2,000, low: $100).

Fields of interest: Vocational education, post-secondary; Higher education; College (community/junior).

Type of support: Undergraduate support.

Application information: Applications accepted. Application form required. Application form available on the grantmaker's web site.

  Deadline(s): Apr. 10

  Final notification: Recipients announced by May 1

  Additional information: Application should include a letter of recommendation.

EIN: 412150966

3305
Iowa Farm Bureau Federation

5400 Univ. Ave.
West Des Moines, IA 50266-5950 (515) 225-5400
Contact: Danny J. Presnall, Secy.-Treas. and Exec. Dir.
FAX: (515) 225-5419; URL: http:// www.iowafarmbureau.com

Foundation type: Public charity

Purpose: Scholarships to the sons and/or daughters of Iowa Farm Bureau members pursuing a degree in agriculture at an accredited college, university or community college.

Publications: Informational brochure.

Financial data: Year ended 10/31/2012. Assets, $802,091,986 (M); Expenditures, $28,142,575; Total giving, $1,617,507; Grants to individuals, totaling $211,161.

Fields of interest: Higher education; Agriculture; Agriculture, farm bureaus/granges.

Type of support: Scholarships—to individuals.

Application information: Applications accepted. Application form required.

  Deadline(s): Mar. 1

  Applicants should submit the following:

    1) Transcripts
    2) SAT
    3) GPA
    4) ACT
    5) Financial information
    6) Essay

  Additional information: Application must also include two character references. Completed application must be sent to your county Farm Bureau Office. See web site for additional application information.

EIN: 420331840

3306
Iowa Foundation for Agricultural Advancement

131 240th St.
Durant, IA 52747-9616
Contact: Taci Lilienthal
Application address: c/o Winner's Circle Scholarship, Attn: Dr. Hodson, 30805 595th Ave., Cambridge, IA 50046, tel.: (515) 383-4386

Foundation type: Independent foundation

Purpose: Scholarships to freshman and upper classmen students pursuing educations in

ag-related fields of study at any two-year or four-year IA college or university.

Financial data: Year ended 12/31/2012. Assets, $0 (M); Expenditures, $249,112; Total giving, $144,000; Grants to individuals, 118 grants totaling $144,000 (high: $5,500, low: $100).

Fields of interest: Agriculture.

Type of support: Scholarships—to individuals.

Application information: Application form required.

  Initial approach: Letter or telephone

  Deadline(s): June 1

EIN: 421183067

3307
Iowa Health Foundation

1440 Ingersoll Ave.
Des Moines, IA 50309-3114 (515) 241-6304
FAX: (515) 241-6966; URL: http:// www.iowahealth.org/ contact-iowa-health-foundation.aspx

Foundation type: Public charity

Purpose: Hospital bill financial assistance to indigent patients of Iowa Methodist Medical Center, Iowa Lutheran Hospital, Blank Children's Hospital and Methodist West Hospital. The amount of assistance will depend on household income, number of dependents, and assets.

Publications: Annual report.

Financial data: Year ended 12/31/2011. Assets, $102,522,709 (M); Expenditures, $8,472,785; Total giving, $6,123,452; Grants to individuals, totaling $26,698.

Fields of interest: Hospitals (general); Health care, patient services; Economically disadvantaged.

Type of support: Grants for special needs.

Application information:

  Initial approach: Tel.

  Applicants should submit the following:

    1) Financial information

  Additional information: For eligibility criteria, call 515-362-5111 for a financial advocate.

EIN: 421467682

3308
Iowa Measurement Research Foundation

334 Lindquist Ctr.
Iowa City, IA 52242-1533 (319) 335-5406

Foundation type: Public charity

Purpose: Grants to faculty of the University of Iowa, IA, to support research in measurement of educational goals at elementary, secondary, and college levels.

Financial data: Year ended 09/30/2011. Assets, $19,434,342 (M); Expenditures, $1,128,026; Total giving, $980,000.

Type of support: Research.

Application information:

  Initial approach: E-mail

  Applicants should submit the following:

    1) Proposal
    2) Budget Information

EIN: 420791544

3309
Iowa P.E.O. Project Fund, Inc.

1706 Pikes Peak Ct. NE
Cedar Rapids, IA 52402
Contact: Gaye Roberts, Pres.
E-mail: gaye.roberts@mchsi.com

Foundation type: Independent foundation

Purpose: Scholarships to individuals to attend Cottey College in Nevada, MO. Grants to individuals in IA for medical and other living expenses.

Publications: Annual report; Financial statement; Informational brochure.

Financial data: Year ended 03/31/2013. Assets, $3,779,440 (M); Expenditures, $327,581; Total giving, $311,326; Grants to individuals, 82 grants totaling $242,956 (high: $5,000).

Fields of interest: Higher education; Education; Human services.

Type of support: Scholarships—to individuals; Support to graduates or students of specific schools; Grants for special needs.

Application information:

  Applicants should submit the following:

    1) Financial information

  Additional information: For general welfare grants, applications must be submitted by local IA P.E.O. chapters on behalf of the individual family.

EIN: 420722695

3310
ISED Ventures

1111 9th St., Ste. 380
Des Moines, IA 50314-2527 (515) 283-0940
Contact: Michael Tramontina, Pres. and C.E.O.; Debra Carr, Dir., Economic Devel.
FAX: (515) 283-0348; E-mail: info@isediowa.org; E-mail For Michael Tramontina: mtramontina@isediowa.org; URL: http:// www.isediowa.org/

Foundation type: Public charity

Purpose: Financial incentives to low-income and underserved families of IA to gain and manage assets to achieve economic and family stability.

Publications: Annual report; Financial statement; Informational brochure; Newsletter.

Financial data: Year ended 06/30/2012. Assets, $951,524 (M); Expenditures, $1,350,353.

Fields of interest: Human services; Economically disadvantaged.

Type of support: Grants to individuals.

Application information: Contact foundation for eligibility criteria.

EIN: 201037604

3311
Jasper Community Foundation

c/o Dan Skokan
P.O. Box 924
Newton, IA 50208-0924 (641) 791-2874
Contact: Dan Skokan, Pres.
E-mail: dan.skokan@progressindustries.org; URL: http://www.jaspercommunityfoundation.org

Foundation type: Community foundation

Purpose: Awards to past war veterans by sending them to Washington D.C. for a day to view war memorials and attend a celebratory dinner to thank them for their service.

Financial data: Year ended 12/31/2012. Assets, $2,738,635 (M); Expenditures, $127,748; Total giving, $29,705.

Fields of interest: Military/veterans.

Type of support: Awards/prizes.

Application information: Contact the foundation for additional information.

EIN: 391905948

3312
George S. & Grace A. Jay Memorial Trust
612 1/2 W. Sheridan Ave.
P.O. Box 57
Shenandoah, IA   51601-1708   (712) 246-3399
Contact: Kathrun Martin

Foundation type: Independent foundation
Purpose: Student loans only to worthy graduates of Shenandoah, Essex, and Farragut, IA, high schools for attendance at accredited colleges, universities, or trade schools.
Financial data: Year ended 03/31/2013. Assets, $2,698,069 (M); Expenditures, $61,303; Total giving, $1,500; Grants to individuals, 3 grants totaling $1,500 (high: $500, low: $500).
Fields of interest: Vocational education, post-secondary; Higher education.
Type of support: Support to graduates or students of specific schools; Graduate support; Undergraduate support.
Application information: Applications accepted. Application form required.
  Initial approach: Telephone
  Deadline(s): May 31
  Final notification: Recipients notified by June 30
EIN: 426061515

3313
Jennie Edmundson Memorial Hospital
933 E. Pierce St.
Council Bluffs, IA   51503   (402) 354-4840
Contact: Steven Baumert, Pres.
URL: http://www.bestcare.org/mhsbase/mhs.cfm/SRC=SP/SRCN=hosp_detail/GnavID=28/hospid=5

Foundation type: Public charity
Purpose: Scholarships to nursing and radiology students of IA pursuing their medical education. Specific assistance to individuals for medical expenses, care and other special needs.
Financial data: Year ended 12/31/2011. Assets, $64,622,876 (M); Expenditures, $91,469,512; Total giving, $5,065,862; Grants to individuals, totaling $4,995,000.
Fields of interest: Nursing school/education.
Type of support: Scholarships—to individuals; Grants for special needs.
Application information:
  Initial approach: Letter
  Additional information: Scholarship selection is based on family income, number of children and special circumstances, by admissions examinations, participation in extracurricular activities and rank in graduating class.
EIN: 420680355

3314
Jepsen Educational Trust
c/o Citizens First National Bank
P.O. Box 1227
Storm Lake, IA   50588-1227   (712) 732-5440
Contact: Citizens First National Bank, Tr.

Foundation type: Independent foundation
Purpose: Scholarships to students graduating from Galva-Holstein Community School District, IA.
Financial data: Year ended 06/30/2013. Assets, $128,961 (M); Expenditures, $5,564; Total giving, $4,000; Grants to individuals, 4 grants totaling $4,000 (high: $1,000, low: $1,000).
Type of support: Support to graduates or students of specific schools; Undergraduate support.
Application information: Applications accepted.

Additional information: Contact foundation for current application deadline/guidelines.
EIN: 426507732

3315
Donald K. Johnson Charitable Scholarship Foundation
2701 Edgewood Pkwy., S.W.
Cedar Rapids, IA   52404
Application address: c/o St. Paul's Lutheran Church, 419 S. 12th St., Fort Dodge, IA 50501

Foundation type: Independent foundation
Purpose: Scholarships to graduates of St. Paul's Lutheran School, IA.
Financial data: Year ended 12/31/2012. Assets, $243,916 (M); Expenditures, $14,968; Total giving, $9,025.
Type of support: Support to graduates or students of specific schools; Precollege support.
Application information: Applications not accepted.
  Additional information: Unsolicited requests for funds not considered or acknowledged.
EIN: 426401180

3316
Kansas State Alpha Tau Omega Students' Aid Endowment Fund
14400 Briarwood Ln.
Urbandale, IA   50323-2038
Contact: William L. Muir, Pres.
Application address: 2040 Shirley Ln., Manhattan, KS 66502-2059

Foundation type: Independent foundation
Purpose: Scholarships to one male and one female student who are Blue Key members attending Kansas State University.
Financial data: Year ended 06/30/2013. Assets, $355,853 (M); Expenditures, $133,828; Total giving, $130,290; Grants to individuals, 56 grants totaling $29,290 (high: $2,000, low: $55).
Fields of interest: Higher education; Students, sororities/fraternities.
Type of support: Support to graduates or students of specific schools; Undergraduate support.
Application information: Applications accepted. Application form required.
  Applicants should submit the following:
    1) Transcripts
    2) GPA
    3) Financial information
  Additional information: Selection is based on good character and sound academic standing, and who have substantially contributed to the quality of student life and outstanding leadership at Kansas State University.
EIN: 486111125

3317
E. R. Keig and Alice Keig Scholarship Fund
P.O. Box 1567
Mason City, IA   50402-1567

Foundation type: Independent foundation
Purpose: Scholarships to graduates of North Fayette Senior High School, West Union, IA. Also, awards to outstanding teachers.
Financial data: Year ended 12/31/2011. Assets, $709,014 (M); Expenditures, $52,944; Total giving, $42,000; Grants to individuals, 9 grants totaling $42,000 (high: $5,000, low: $2,000).

Type of support: Support to graduates or students of specific schools; Undergraduate support.
Application information: Applications not accepted.
  Additional information: Unsolicited requests for funds not considered or acknowledged.
EIN: 596952608

3318
Wilbert J. & Carol A. Keppy Charitable Foundation
2532 E., Locust St.
Davenport, IA   52803

Foundation type: Independent foundation
Purpose: Scholarships to young IL and MN individuals interested in pursuing a career as farmers. Giving to assist interested and qualified individuals in training to become medical doctors at world renowned hospitals.
Financial data: Year ended 12/31/2012. Assets, $2,971,684 (M); Expenditures, $121,112; Total giving, $105,400.
Type of support: Grants to individuals; Scholarships—to individuals.
Application information: Applications not accepted.
  Additional information: Unsolicited requests for funds not considered or acknowledged.
EIN: 421497252

3319
Jane R. King Charity Fund Trust
P.O. Box 453
Jewell, IA   50130

Foundation type: Independent foundation
Purpose: Student loans only to graduates of South Hamilton School District, IA.
Financial data: Year ended 12/31/2013. Assets, $395,175 (M); Expenditures, $11,166; Total giving, $7,500; Grant to an individual, 1 grant totaling $500.
Type of support: Student loans—to individuals; Support to graduates or students of specific schools.
Application information: Applications accepted. Application form required.
  Deadline(s): None
  Additional information: Loan limit is $750 per semester.
EIN: 426081131

3320
Marcella Kingfield Memorial Scholarship Trust
326 4th St.
Lake View, IA   51450

Foundation type: Independent foundation
Purpose: Scholarships to members of St. Mary's Catholic Church, Sac City, IA.
Financial data: Year ended 12/31/2011. Assets, $0 (M); Expenditures, $5,268; Total giving, $4,000; Grants to individuals, 4 grants totaling $4,000 (high: $1,000, low: $1,000).
Type of support: Undergraduate support.
Application information: Applications accepted. Application form required.
  Initial approach: Letter
  Deadline(s): May 1
EIN: 426558164

3321
H. Carl & William Lage Loan & Scholarship Trust Fund
2309B Chatburn Ave.
P.O. Box 551
Harlan, IA 51537-0551 (712) 755-2152
Contact: Justin Wegner
Application address: c/o Harlan Community Schools, Attn.: Supt., 2102 Durant St., Harlan, IA 51537-1221, tel.: (712) 755-2152

Foundation type: Operating foundation
Purpose: Student loans to graduates of Harlan Community High School, IA, who are in the top half of their classes for attendance at four-year colleges and universities.
Financial data: Year ended 10/31/2011. Assets, $1,045,034 (M); Expenditures, $61,822; Total giving, $46,546.
Fields of interest: Higher education.
Type of support: Student loans—to individuals; Support to graduates or students of specific schools; Undergraduate support.
Application information: Applications accepted. Application form required.
Additional information: Applicants must be residents of Harlan, IA.
EIN: 420369519

3322
Lake-Matthews Educational Fund
P.O. Box 307
Shenandoah, IA 51601
Contact: Heather Weiss, Pres.
Application address: 1000 Mustang Dr., Shenandoah, IA 51601-

Foundation type: Independent foundation
Purpose: Scholarships to students of the Shenandoah Community High School, IA, for higher education.
Financial data: Year ended 12/31/2012. Assets, $506,657 (M); Expenditures, $17,255; Total giving, $16,000; Grants to individuals, 17 grants totaling $16,000 (high: $1,000; low: $500).
Type of support: Support to graduates or students of specific schools; Undergraduate support.
Application information: Applications accepted. Application form required.
Deadline(s): Jan. 31
Additional information: Application should include three or four letters of recommendation.
EIN: 421491841

3323
Lucile Latta Charitable Trust
P.O. Box 147
Sioux City, IA 51102-0147

Foundation type: Independent foundation
Purpose: Scholarships to high school graduates who are residents of Harrison County, IA.
Financial data: Year ended 12/31/2012. Assets, $4,520,001 (M); Expenditures, $269,261; Total giving, $207,488; Grants to individuals, 44 grants totaling $207,488 (high: $6,000, low: $1,181).
Type of support: Scholarships—to individuals.
Application information: Applications not accepted.
Additional information: Unsolicited requests for funds not considered or acknowledged.
EIN: 426554228

3324
Lee Endowment Foundation
c/o First Citizens Trust Co., N.A.
2601 4th St., S.W.
P.O. Box 1708
Mason City, IA 50402-1708 (641) 423-1600
Scholarship application address: Muse Scholarship Program, 500 College Dr., Mason City, IA 50401, tel.: (641) 422-4168

Foundation type: Independent foundation
Purpose: Scholarships primarily to residents of Mason City and Cerro Gordo County, IA.
Financial data: Year ended 12/31/2011. Assets, $290,912 (M); Expenditures, $137,634; Total giving, $130,217; Grants to individuals, 5 grants totaling $5,200 (high: $650; low: $650).
Fields of interest: Vocational education.
Type of support: Graduate support; Technical education support; Undergraduate support; Postgraduate support.
Application information: Applications accepted. Application form required.
Deadline(s): Feb. 1
Applicants should submit the following:
1) Transcripts
2) Financial information
Program description:
Muse Scholarship Program: Selection is made on the basis of scholarship, financial need, and good moral character. Scholarships may be used for any course of study or education beyond the high school level. This includes, but is not limited to, trade schools, craft schools, college courses leading to degrees, and college postgraduate courses of every kind and nature. Scholarships are renewable.
EIN: 421074052

3325
The Leeper Scholarship Foundation
308 Central Ave.
Clio, IA 50052 (641) 876-6312
Contact: Janet A. Mortimore, Secy.

Foundation type: Operating foundation
Purpose: Scholarships to residents of Wayne county IA, Clinton, Grand River, Jefferson and Warren; Decatur county IA, Eden, Hamilton, Morgan and Woodland.
Financial data: Year ended 12/31/2012. Assets, $470,911 (M); Expenditures, $23,291; Total giving, $22,700; Grants to individuals, 18 grants totaling $22,200.
Fields of interest: Higher education.
Type of support: Scholarships—to individuals.
Application information: Application form required.
Deadline(s): Mar. 20
Additional information: Application forms available from high school counselors or from the foundation.
EIN: 470818991

3326
Life Investors Fortunaires Club
5123 Middle Rd.
Bettendorf, IA 52722-6059 (563) 449-9181

Foundation type: Public charity
Purpose: Scholarships to children, grandchildren of current Fortunaries. Scholarships to children of Home Office employees, of Transamerica Life & Protection (L&P) Cedar Rapids enrolled in an accredited school.
Financial data: Year ended 12/31/2011. Assets, $691,894 (M); Expenditures, $46,791; Total

giving, $40,770; Grants to individuals, totaling $21,500.
Fields of interest: Higher education.
Type of support: Employee-related scholarships.
Application information: Applications accepted. Application form required. Application form available on the grantmaker's web site.
Send request by: Mail
Deadline(s): Mar. 15
Applicants should submit the following:
1) Letter(s) of recommendation
2) Essay
3) Transcripts
4) SAT
5) ACT
EIN: 420929419

3327
Lindhart Educational Trust
c/o Humboldt Rotary Club
P.O. Box 97
Dakota City, IA 50529-0097 (515) 332-1681
Contact: Jana Bratland, Treas.

Foundation type: Independent foundation
Purpose: Student loans to graduates of high schools in Humboldt County, IA for attendance at an accredited college or community college or accredited vocational trade school.
Publications: Application guidelines.
Financial data: Year ended 12/31/2012. Assets, $117,167 (M); Expenditures, $604; Total giving, $0; Loans to individuals, totaling $18,500.
Fields of interest: Vocational education, post-secondary; Higher education.
Type of support: Student loans—to individuals.
Application information: Applications accepted. Application form required.
Deadline(s): July 1
Final notification: Applicants notified by July 15
Additional information: Application should include transcripts.
EIN: 426051376

3328
LSB Foundation
c/o JAMES E. THIELEN
242 Tower Park Dr.
Waterloo, IA 50701-9002 (319) 233-1900
Contact: James E. Thielen, Tr.

Foundation type: Company-sponsored foundation
Purpose: Relief assistance to individuals for man-made and natural distasters, including floods and tornadoes.
Publications: Application guidelines.
Financial data: Year ended 07/31/2013. Assets, $130,728 (M); Expenditures, $129,367; Total giving, $125,198.
Fields of interest: Safety/disasters.
Type of support: Emergency funds; Grants to individuals.
Application information: Applications accepted. Application form available on the grantmaker's web site.
Additional information: Disaster grant application forms available at the offices of Lincoln Savings Bank or on foundation web site.
EIN: 201653464

3329
A. J. Magnus Home
500 Cedar St.
Muscatine, IA   52761-4208   (563) 264-2727
Contact: Mike Haggerty, Pres.

Foundation type: Independent foundation
Purpose: Assistance with room and board for elderly men in the city and County of Muscatine, IA.
Financial data: Year ended 10/31/2011. Assets, $1,253,576 (M); Expenditures, $136,652; Total giving, $73,051.
Fields of interest: Aging; Men.
Type of support: Grants for special needs.
Application information: Applications accepted. Application form required.
  Deadline(s): None
  Additional information: Application should include a physician's signed assessment of applicant's physical and mental condition. Applicant must be of good moral character and reasonably good health. The minimum age is 70, but men who are 65 are required to pay an additional fee.
EIN: 420950682

3330
Dora Mahanay Educational Trust
P.O. Box 27
Jefferson, IA   50129   (515) 386-5428
Application address: 101 N., Grimmell Rd., Jefferson, IA 50129

Foundation type: Independent foundation
Purpose: Low-interest educational loans to students attending post high school colleges, universities or vocational/trade schools of IA and NE for study at accredited schools.
Financial data: Year ended 12/31/2012. Assets, $0 (M); Expenditures, $100,392; Total giving, $0.
Type of support: Student loans—to individuals.
Application information: Applications accepted. Application form required.
  Deadline(s): None
EIN: 426091712

3331
Marek Trust Fund
c/o Central State Bank
301 Iowa Ave.
Muscatine, IA   52761   (319) 653-6543
Application addresses: Scholarship Committee, Washington Community School District, 404 W. Main St., Washington, IA 52353

Foundation type: Independent foundation
Purpose: Scholarships to financially needy individuals from Washington, Wellman, and Kalona, IA, who are pursuing degrees in medically-related, agriculturally-related, and other socially-related fields that benefit humanity.
Financial data: Year ended 12/31/2012. Assets, $215,526 (M); Expenditures, $9,829; Total giving, $6,000; Grants to individuals, 4 grants totaling $6,000 (high: $2,000, low: $1,000).
Fields of interest: Medical school/education; Agriculture; Human services.
Type of support: Scholarships—to individuals; Support to graduates or students of specific schools.
Application information: Applications accepted. Interview required.
  Initial approach: Letter
  Additional information: Application must also include past academic performance, college

aptitude test scores, recommendations from instructors and statement of financial need.
EIN: 426397123

3332
James Matheson & Marian Matheson Scholarship Trust Fund
508 Main St.
Reinbeck, IA   50669-1052   (319) 788-6441

Foundation type: Independent foundation
Purpose: Scholarships to economically disadvantaged graduates of Reinbeck, IA, public schools for study at accredited colleges and comparable technical or vocational schools.
Financial data: Year ended 12/31/2011. Assets, $48,616 (M); Expenditures, $4,155; Total giving, $3,600; Grants to individuals, 6 grants totaling $3,600 (high: $600, low: $600).
Fields of interest: Vocational education.
Type of support: Support to graduates or students of specific schools; Technical education support; Undergraduate support.
Application information: Application form required.
  Deadline(s): May 1
  Applicants should submit the following:
    1) Transcripts
    2) Financial information
  Additional information: Application must also include standardized test scores, and references.
EIN: 421172985

3333
R. J. McElroy Trust
425 Cedar St., Ste. 312
Waterloo, IA   50701-1351   (319) 287-9102
Contact: Stacy Van Gorp, Exec. Dir.
FAX: (319) 287-9105;
E-mail: vangorp@mcelroytrust.org; Additional e-mail: office@mcelroytrust.org; URL: http://www.mcelroytrust.org

Foundation type: Independent foundation
Purpose: Fellowships by nomination only to graduates of select colleges located within 15 counties in northeast IA, pursuing a Ph.D. degree. The trust also awards Gold Star Awards to teachers in Black Hawk County, IA.
Publications: Application guidelines; Grants list; Informational brochure; Informational brochure (including application guidelines); Program policy statement; Program policy statement (including application guidelines).
Financial data: Year ended 12/31/2012. Assets, $39,977,113 (M); Expenditures, $2,190,439; Total giving, $1,412,591; Grants to individuals, 24 grants totaling $74,300 (high: $10,000, low: $100).
Fields of interest: Education.
Type of support: Fellowships; Awards/grants by nomination only; Awards/prizes; Graduate support.
Application information: Applications not accepted.
  Additional information: Unsolicited requests for funds not considered or acknowledged. See web site for nomination guidelines.
Program descriptions:
  Fellowship Program: The foundation awards fellowships to graduates of liberal arts colleges located within the KWWL viewing area in northeast Iowa. Candidates must be pursuing a Ph.D. degree and be nominated by their college.
  Gold Star Awards for Outstanding Teaching: Each year ten teachers are nominated by students, parents and teachers themselves, and each Gold

Star Award recipient receive $1,000 in cash. The selection committee will look for teachers who rise above everyday standards and expectations to help students achieve their fullest potential.
EIN: 426173496

3334
Milburn A. McKay Trust
c/o Washington State Bank
P.O. Box 311
Washington, IA   52353-0311

Foundation type: Independent foundation
Purpose: Scholarships to graduates of Washington High School, IA, pursuing a major in music.
Financial data: Year ended 12/31/2012. Assets, $100,948 (M); Expenditures, $2,965; Total giving, $2,200; Grant to an individual, 1 grant totaling $2,200.
Fields of interest: Music.
Type of support: Support to graduates or students of specific schools; Undergraduate support.
Application information:
  Deadline(s): Spring
  Additional information: Preference is given to students studying instrumental music.
EIN: 426593433

3335
Leona Thiele McKenney Trust
c/o Cambridge Law Firm, P.L.C.
P.O. Box 496
Atlantic, IA   50022

Foundation type: Independent foundation
Purpose: Scholarships to students of Cass County, IA for continuing education at institutions of higher learning.
Financial data: Year ended 12/31/2012. Assets, $0 (M); Expenditures, $2,324; Total giving, $1,950; Grants to individuals, 12 grants totaling $1,950.
Type of support: Undergraduate support.
Application information:
  Initial approach: Letter
  Deadline(s): Aug. 15 and Jan. 15
EIN: 426449326

3336
J. Ralph and Gladys Meier Scholarship Trust
2701 Edgewood Pkwy SW
Cedar Rapids, IA   52404   (877) 275-7034
Contact: Wesley Hilleshiem

Foundation type: Independent foundation
Purpose: Scholarships for graduates of high schools in the counties of Wapello, Keokuk, and Mahaska, IA, to attend postsecondary schools.
Financial data: Year ended 12/31/2012. Assets, $152,634 (M); Expenditures, $13,947; Total giving, $8,700.
Fields of interest: Higher education.
Type of support: Scholarships—to individuals.
Application information: Applications accepted. Application form required.
  Deadline(s): Feb. 15
  Additional information: Application must include transcript and one-page letter stating educational and career goals, personal interests, and any extraordinary factors.
EIN: 426387434

3337
Michels Family Educational Trust
300 E. 2nd St.
Muscatine, IA   52761   (563) 263-4221
Contact: Scott Snow
Application addres: c/o First National Bank.

Foundation type: Independent foundation
Purpose: Scholarships to financially needy
students to attend Muscatine Community College,
IA, or Drake University, IA, of Des Moines, with
preference given to students from Muscatine and
Louisa counties, IA.
Financial data: Year ended 12/31/2011. Assets,
$259,114 (M); Expenditures, $22,250; Total
giving, $19,500.
Fields of interest: Higher education.
Type of support: Support to graduates or students
of specific schools; Undergraduate support.
Application information: Applications accepted.
   Initial approach: Letter or telephone
   Deadline(s): None
   Additional information: Applicant must
      demonstrate financial need.
EIN: 426570941

3338
Carroll C. Mongan Trust
231 W. Maple
Cherokee, IA   51012-0398   (712) 225-6117

Foundation type: Independent foundation
Purpose: Scholarships and student loans to
residents of Cherokee County, IA.
Financial data: Year ended 12/31/2011. Assets,
$405,747 (M); Expenditures, $23,987; Total
giving, $18,250; Grants to individuals, 7 grants
totaling $18,250.
Type of support: Scholarships—to individuals;
Student loans—to individuals.
Application information: Applications accepted.
   Additional information: Contact trust for
      application deadline/guidelines.
EIN: 426550538

3339
Elsie H. Munson Trust
208 Main St.
Albert City, IA   50510-0128   (712) 843-2211

Foundation type: Independent foundation
Purpose: Scholarships to students of Garfield or
Herdland townships in Clay county, IA pursuing a
career in nursing, medicine or other careers in
medicine.
Financial data: Year ended 12/31/2011. Assets,
$156,609 (M); Expenditures, $1,778; Total giving,
$8,250; Grants to individuals, 5 grants totaling
$8,250 (high: $1,850, low: $1,000).
Fields of interest: Higher education; Medical
school/education; Nursing school/education.
Type of support: Scholarships—to individuals.
Application information: Applications accepted.
Application form required.
   Deadline(s): Mar. 1
   Additional information: Application should
      include grades and course of study.
      Application forms are available through the
      local high school guidance counselors.
EIN: 206263812

3340
Duane & Evelyn Munter Charitable Trust
c/o Citizens State Bank
P.O. Box 4
Strawberry Point, IA   52076-0004

Foundation type: Operating foundation
Purpose: Scholarships to graduating seniors of
Strawberry Point high schools, IA pursuing higher
education.
Financial data: Year ended 07/31/2013. Assets,
$288,620 (M); Expenditures, $8,563; Total giving,
$6,317; Grants to individuals, 8 grants totaling
$5,369 (high: $845, low: $544).
Fields of interest: Higher education.
Type of support: Support to graduates or students
of specific schools; Undergraduate support.
Application information: Applications accepted.
   Additional information: Contact the trust for
      additional guidelines.
EIN: 421286829

3341
Dennis L. & Hildreth M. Murphy
Scholarship Trust
c/o Corydon State Bank
201 W. Jackson St.
Corydon, IA   50060-0228   (641) 872-2343
Contact: Alan Wilson
Application address: 107 W. Jackson St., Corydon,
IA 50060-1416

Foundation type: Independent foundation
Purpose: Scholarships to graduating seniors at
Wayne Community High School, IA for
postsecondary education.
Financial data: Year ended 12/31/2011. Assets,
$883,092 (M); Expenditures, $24,545; Total
giving, $23,500; Grants to individuals, 29 grants
totaling $23,500 (high: $2,500, low: $200).
Fields of interest: Higher education.
Type of support: Support to graduates or students
of specific schools; Undergraduate support.
Application information: Applications accepted.
Application form not required.
   Deadline(s): None
   Additional information: Application should
      include grades, activities and qualifications.
EIN: 421486268

3342
Murray Trust
(also known as Murray XII Trust)
110 N. Marshall St.
Rock Rapids, IA   51246-1516   (712) 472-4051
Contact: Jessica Harman
Application address: c/o Central Lyon Community
School, 1010 S. Greene St., Rock Rapids, IA 51246

Foundation type: Independent foundation
Purpose: Scholarships to graduates of Central Lyon
High School of Rock Rapids, IA for postsecondary
education.
Financial data: Year ended 12/31/2012. Assets,
$1,769,797 (M); Expenditures, $169,392; Total
giving, $78,005; Grant to an individual, 1 grant
totaling $78,005.
Fields of interest: Vocational education,
post-secondary; Higher education.
Type of support: Support to graduates or students
of specific schools; Technical education support;
Undergraduate support.
Application information: Applications accepted.
Application form required.
   Deadline(s): Apr. 30
   Applicants should submit the following:

1) Transcripts
2) Financial information
   Additional information: Application should also
      include an affidavit of nonsupport if applicant
      is self-supporting. Graduates need to apply
      each year they continue to be enrolled in a
      college or technical school.
EIN: 237181382

3343
Nishnabotna Valley Foundation
P.O. Box 714
Harlan, IA   51537-0714
Contact: Janell Cheek
URL: http://www.nvrec.com/aspx/general/
clientpage.aspx?
pageid=794&n=1363&n1=1465&n2=1496

Foundation type: Company-sponsored foundation
Purpose: Scholarships to residents of counties
served by Nishnabotna Valley Rural Electric
Cooperative in IA.
Publications: Application guidelines.
Financial data: Year ended 12/31/2012. Assets,
$15,546 (M); Expenditures, $2,009; Total giving,
$2,000.
Type of support: Undergraduate support.
Application information: Applications accepted.
Application form required.
   Initial approach: Letter
   Deadline(s): Mar. 1
   Additional information: Contact foundation for
      application guidelines.
EIN: 421467824

3344
Nick Norris Memorial Foundation
c/o United Bank Trust
2101 S. Center St.
Marshalltown, IA   50158   (641) 753-5900
Contact: Mike Bloom

Foundation type: Independent foundation
Purpose: Scholarships primarily to graduating high
school seniors of the Marshalltown, IA area
pursuing higher education.
Financial data: Year ended 12/31/2012. Assets,
$72,559 (M); Expenditures, $4,067; Total giving,
$2,900; Grants to individuals, 3 grants totaling
$2,900 (high: $1,500, low: $400).
Fields of interest: Higher education.
Type of support: Scholarships—to individuals.
Application information: Applications accepted.
   Initial approach: Letter
   Additional information: Contact the foundation for
      additional application information.
EIN: 426083955

3345
North Iowa Area Community College
Foundation
500 College Dr.
Mason City, IA   50401-7213   (641) 422-4382
Contact: Katherine Grove, Secy.-Treas.
URL: http://www.niacc.edu/foundation/

Foundation type: Public charity
Purpose: Scholarships to students of the North
Iowa Area Community College pursuing higher
education.
Financial data: Year ended 06/30/2011. Assets,
$17,662,322 (M); Expenditures, $974,844; Total
giving, $827,660; Grants to individuals, totaling
$21,650.
Fields of interest: Medical school/education.

Type of support: Scholarships—to individuals; Support to graduates or students of specific schools.
Application information: Applications accepted. Application form required.
> *Send request by:* Online, mail
> *Deadline(s):* Mar. 1 for Christopherson Medical Scholarship
> *Additional information:* Application should include a transcript and verification of acceptance to medical school for Christopherson Medical Scholarship.

Program descriptions:
> *Charles City Scholarship:* This $500 scholarship is awarded to part-time adult students who are from Floyd County and/or within 20 miles of Charles City. Preference will be given to students who are not previous recipients of the Charles City scholarship. Applicant must be at least 18 years of age.
> *Christopherson Medical Scholarship:* This scholarship is for pre-medical and medical students for full-time study at any accredited public or private postsecondary educational institution. Awards are based on academic achievement, financial need, moral character, and such additional criteria as may be deemed appropriate. Awards are for one year only and must be fully expended by the completion of the academic year. Applicant must have satisfactorily completed a course of study from a recognized high school or possess a General Education Development (GED) diploma.

EIN: 237023677

3346
Northeast Iowa Charitable Foundation
P.O. Box 203
Oelwein, IA 50662-0203   (319) 283-1056

Foundation type: Independent foundation
Purpose: Scholarships to graduates of Oelwein Community Schools, Oelwein, IA.
Financial data: Year ended 12/31/2012. Assets, $8,984,415 (M); Expenditures, $521,216; Total giving, $469,736.
Type of support: Support to graduates or students of specific schools.
Application information:
> *Initial approach:* Letter or telephone
> *Deadline(s):* None

EIN: 421341188

3347
Northwest Iowa Hospital Corporation
2720 Stone Park Blvd.
Sioux City, IA 51104-3734   (712) 279-3500
Contact: Peter Thoreen, Pres. and C.E.O.
URL: http://www.stlukes.org/

Foundation type: Public charity
Purpose: Scholarships to individuals affiliated with St. Lukes Health System pursuing a career in nursing.
Financial data: Year ended 12/31/2011. Assets, $182,750,126 (M); Expenditures, $119,992,718; Total giving, $1,498,715; Grants to individuals, totaling $10,631.
Fields of interest: Nursing school/education.
Type of support: Scholarships—to individuals.
Application information: Applications accepted.
> *Additional information:* Selection is based on financial need and academic achievement.

EIN: 421019872

3348
Operation Threshold, Inc.
1535 Lafayette St.
P.O. Box 4120
Waterloo, IA 50704-4120   (319) 291-2065
Contact: Barbara Grant, Exec. Dir.
E-mail: bgrant@operationthreshold.org; Additional address (Buchanan County office): 1707 1st St., E-3, Independence, IA 50644-9300, tel.: (319) 334-6081; additional address (Grundy County): 1606 G. Ave, Grundy Center, IA 50638-1056, tel. (319) 824-3460; URL: http://www.operationthreshold.org

Foundation type: Public charity
Purpose: Assistance to low to moderate-income families and individuals residing in Black Hawk, Buchanan, and Grundy Counties, IA, to help meet their basic needs and create opportunities for self-sufficiency.
Publications: Annual report; Newsletter.
Financial data: Year ended 09/30/2011. Assets, $6,750,178 (M); Expenditures, $13,418,333; Total giving, $8,501,462; Grants to individuals, totaling $3,388,499.
Fields of interest: Education; Housing/shelter; Human services; Family services; Economically disadvantaged.
Type of support: Emergency funds; Grants to individuals; Grants for special needs.
Application information: Applications accepted.
> *Initial approach:* Submit application

EIN: 420982549

3349
P.E.O. Foundation
3700 Grand Ave.
Des Moines, IA 50312-2899   (515) 255-3153
Contact: Anne Pettygrove, C.E.O.
FAX: (515) 255-3820; URL: http://www.peointernational.org/peo-foundation

Foundation type: Public charity
Purpose: Scholarships and loans to qualified women in the U.S. and Canada seeking higher education.
Financial data: Year ended 06/30/2012. Assets, $81,881,808 (M); Expenditures, $3,924,681; Total giving, $3,438,512; Grants to individuals, totaling $1,003,619.
Fields of interest: Higher education; Women.
Type of support: Scholarships—to individuals.
Application information: Applications accepted. Application form required.
> *Additional information:* Applicants must provide proof of enrollment from the applicable college or university prior to receiving any funding. See web site for additional application guidelines.

Program descriptions:
> *P.E.O. Educational Loan:* Loans are available to qualified women who desire higher education and are in need of financial assistance. An applicant must be recommended by a local chapter of the P.E.O. Sisterhood and be within two years of completing her course of study. The current maximum loan is $12,000 ($20.000 for doctoral degree) at 3 percent interest and due six years from the date of issue.
> *P.E.O. International Peace Scholarship:* The program provides scholarships for international women students to pursue graduate study in the United States and Canada.
> *P.E.O. Program for Continuing Education:* This program provides need based grants to women in the United States and Canada whose education has been interrupted and who find it necessary to return

to school to support themselves and/or their families.
> *P.E.O. Scholars Award:* The scholars awards was established to provide substantial merit-based awards for women of the United States and Canada who are either pursuing a doctoral level degree or engaged in postgraduate study or research at an accredited college or university.
> *P.E.O. Star Scholarship:* This scholarship provides a $2,500 award to high school senior women who wish to pursue postsecondary education.

EIN: 426094564

3350
P.E.O. International Peace Scholarship Fund
3700 Grand Ave.
Des Moines, IA 50312-2806   (515) 255-3153
Contact: Project Supvr.
FAX: (515) 255-3820; URL: http://www.peointernational.org/sites/www.peointernational.org/files/IPS_Info_Card_8-3-10_WEB.pdf

Foundation type: Public charity
Purpose: Scholarships for foreign women to study in the U.S. and Canada.
Publications: Application guidelines; Informational brochure.
Financial data: Year ended 06/30/2012. Assets, $5,838,785 (M); Expenditures, $1,465,419; Total giving, $1,346,500; Grants to individuals, totaling $1,295,500.
Fields of interest: Higher education; Women.
Type of support: Scholarships—to individuals; Graduate support.
Application information: Applications accepted. Application form required. Application form available on the grantmaker's web site.
> *Deadline(s):* Dec. 15 and Jan. 31
> *Final notification:* Recipients notified in four to six weeks
> *Applicants should submit the following:*
>   1) Transcripts
>   2) Resume
>   3) Letter(s) of recommendation
>   4) Financial information
>   5) Curriculum vitae
>   6) Budget Information
> *Additional information:* Individuals receiving scholarships must be women outside the U.S. and Canada for graduate study.

EIN: 426078058

3351
P.E.O. Program for Continuing Education
3700 Grand Ave.
Des Moines, IA 50312-2899   (515) 255-3153
FAX: (515) 255-3820; URL: http://www.peointernational.org

Foundation type: Public charity
Purpose: Financial assistance to women whose education has been interrupted and who find it necessary to resume studies due to changing demands in their lives.
Publications: Informational brochure.
Financial data: Year ended 06/30/2012. Assets, $6,476,893 (M); Expenditures, $2,465,096; Total giving, $2,365,650; Grants to individuals, totaling $2,298,750.
Fields of interest: Adult/continuing education; Women.
Type of support: Scholarships—to individuals.

Application information: Applications accepted. Application form required.
Send request by: Mail
Additional information: Applications for grants must be made through a P.E.O. chapter.
Program description:
Program for Continuing Education: Grants of up to $3,000 are available to women seeking to continue their education. Grants are intended to be used for such expenses as tuition, books, transportation, or childcare, necessary to reach the applicant's education goals. Applicants must be citizens of the U.S. or Canada, be studying in the U.S. or Canada, have had at least 24 consecutive months as a non-student sometime in her adult life, be within 24 consecutive months of completing her education goal, and not be enrolled in a doctoral degree program (e.g., educational, law, medical, or clinical). Applicants need not be members of P.E.O. International, but must be sponsored by their local chapter.
EIN: 237405311

3352

P.E.O. Sisterhood International, California Chapter

3700 Grand Ave.
Des Moines, IA   50312-2806   (515) 255-3153
FAX: (515) 255-3820; URL: http://www.peointernational.org

Foundation type: Public charity
Purpose: Scholarships and loans to qualified women for higher education.
Publications: Application guidelines.
Financial data: Year ended 03/31/2012. Assets, $1,616,651 (M); Expenditures, $1,796,788; Total giving, $911,914; Grants to individuals, totaling $111,000.
Fields of interest: Higher education; Women.
Type of support: Student loans—to individuals; Undergraduate support.
Application information: Applications accepted. Application form required.
Deadline(s): Jan 31 for International Peace Scholarship and Star Scholarship; Nominations for Scholar Awards are accepted between Sept. 1 and Dec. 1
Additional information: Contact foundation for full eligibility criteria.
Program descriptions:
Education Loan Fund: The program makes loans available to qualified women who desire higher education and are in need of financial assistance. An applicant must be recommended by a local chapter of the P.E.O. Sisterhood and be within two years of completing her course of study. The current maximum loan is $9,000 at 4 percent interest and due six years from the date of issue. Following the graduation date originally stated on the application, interest will begin accruing and will be billed on an annual basis. Interest accruals and payments will not be deferred if the student continues with further study.
International Peace Scholarship: The program provides scholarships for international women students to pursue graduate study in the United States and Canada. The scholarships are need-based and the current maximum award is $10,000. Upon completion of degree, student must immediately return to her country to pursue her professional career.
Program for Continuing Education: The program provides need based grants to women in the United States and Canada whose education has been interrupted and who find it necessary to return to school to support themselves and/or their families.

Current maximum award is $2,000. Candidates must have at least 24 consecutive months as a non-student sometime in her adult life, and must be within 24 months of completing educational goal. Applicants must be recommended by a PEO Chapter.
Scholar Awards: Awards merit-based scholarships to U.S. or Canadian citizens women who are pursuing a doctoral level degree or are engaged in post graduate study or research. Candidates must be within 2 years of completing doctoral work and must be nominated by local PEO Chapter. Amount contingent on funds available.
Star Scholarship: Awards scholarships of up to $2,500 to high school seniors under the age of 20 with a minimum 3.0 GPA. Applicants must be nominated by local PEO Chapter.
EIN: 946183854

3353

Elise Miller Palmer & Ben A. Miller Scholarship Trust

P.O. Box E
Reinbeck, IA   50669   (319) 788-6441
Application address: c/o Scholarship Trust, 508 Main St., Reinbeck, IA 50669

Foundation type: Independent foundation
Purpose: Scholarships to graduates of Gladbrook-Reinbeck Community High School, IA for postsecondary education.
Financial data: Year ended 12/31/2012. Assets, $0 (M); Expenditures, $3,897; Total giving, $3,600; Grants to individuals, 6 grants totaling $3,600 (high: $600, low: $600).
Fields of interest: Higher education.
Type of support: Support to graduates or students of specific schools; Undergraduate support.
Application information: Applications accepted. Application form required.
Deadline(s): May 1
Applicants should submit the following:
1) SAR
2) Budget Information
3) FAFSA
4) Financial information
5) Letter(s) of recommendation
6) Transcripts
7) FAF
8) ACT
Additional information: Application should also include written references, FFS, and parents' and student's tax returns. Applicant must be an outstanding student in the use of the English language or outstanding in mathematics.
EIN: 421189787

3354

Ruth Parks Trust for the Education of Nurses

c/o United Bank of Iowa
500 2nd St.
Ida Grove, IA   51445-1305   (712) 364-3393
Contact: Sandy Sykes

Foundation type: Operating foundation
Purpose: Scholarships to individuals pursuing an education in nursing. Preference is given to individuals living within 20 miles of Ida Grove, IA, and/or those who are seeking an R.N. degree.
Financial data: Year ended 12/31/2012. Assets, $146,157 (M); Expenditures, $3,300; Total giving, $2,000.
Fields of interest: Nursing school/education.
Type of support: Scholarships—to individuals.

Application information: Applications accepted. Application form required.
Deadline(s): May 1
Applicants should submit the following:
1) Class rank
2) Financial information
3) GPA
Additional information: Application must also include a statement of career plans.
EIN: 426378004

3355

Pella Rolscreen Foundation

102 Main St.
Pella, IA   50219-2147
Contact: Mary A. Van Zante, Secy. and Exec. Dir.
FAX: (641) 621-6950;
E-mail: mavzante@pella.com; URL: http://www.pellarolscreen.com/

Foundation type: Company-sponsored foundation
Purpose: Scholarships to children of employees of Pella Corporation, IA.
Publications: Application guidelines; Annual report; Program policy statement.
Financial data: Year ended 12/31/2012. Assets, $10,895,336 (M); Expenditures, $1,270,382; Total giving, $1,148,608.
Fields of interest: Education.
Type of support: Employee-related scholarships.
Application information: Applications accepted. Application form required. Application form available on the grantmaker's web site.
Initial approach: Letter
Copies of proposal: 1
Deadline(s): None
Final notification: Applicants notified in one to four months
Applicants should submit the following:
1) Financial information
2) Budget Information
Company name: Pella Corporation
EIN: 237043881

3356

Siegfried Petersen Educational Trust

P.O. Box 151
Tipton, IA   52772

Foundation type: Independent foundation
Purpose: Scholarships to needy individuals of Bennett Community School District, IA and Cedar county, IA pursuing any course of study at the undergraduate or graduate level at any educational institution.
Financial data: Year ended 12/31/2011. Assets, $0 (M); Expenditures, $15,850; Total giving, $15,500; Grants to individuals, 9 grants totaling $15,500 (high: $2,500, low: $1,000).
Fields of interest: Higher education.
Type of support: Scholarships—to individuals; Graduate support; Undergraduate support.
Application information: Applications accepted. Application form required.
Deadline(s): Mar.
Final notification: Recipients notified by May
Applicants should submit the following:
1) Financial information
2) Transcripts
3) Letter(s) of recommendation
Additional information: Applicant must be of good moral character.
EIN: 201021305

3357
Frank Pierce Trust
102 E. Church St.
Marshalltown, IA   50158-2942

Foundation type: Independent foundation
Purpose: Low-interest loans to students at or a graduate of Marshalltown Community High School. Loans also to students attending an IA college or university who have been residents of the Marshalltown Community School District for the last six years for undergraduate or professional study.
Financial data: Year ended 12/31/2011. Assets, $2,770,150 (M); Expenditures, $39,759; Total giving, $0.
Fields of interest: Higher education.
Type of support: Student loans—to individuals; Support to graduates or students of specific schools.
Application information: Application form required.
   Deadline(s): May 1
   Applicants should submit the following:
      1) Photograph
      2) Transcripts
   Additional information: Application must also include test scores, college grades to date, and the consent of co-signer. Loans are not granted for graduate study.
EIN: 420737535

3358
Pioneer Hi-Bred International, Inc. Foundation
P.O. Box 1000
Johnston, IA   50131-1000   (515) 535-6677
Contact: Michelle Gowdy, Pres.
URL: http://www.pioneer.com/home/site/about/business/pioneer-giving/

Foundation type: Company-sponsored foundation
Purpose: Scholarships to students working toward graduate level degrees in plant breeding at non-U.S. institutions.
Publications: Application guidelines.
Financial data: Year ended 12/31/2012. Assets, $671,895 (M); Expenditures, $2,538,877; Total giving, $2,538,877.
Fields of interest: Agriculture.
Type of support: Scholarships—to individuals; Graduate support.
Application information: Applications accepted. Application form required. Application form available on the grantmaker's web site.
   Initial approach: Application
   Send request by: Online
   Deadline(s): None
   Additional information: See web site for additional information.
Program description:
   International Scholarships: The foundation awards international scholarships to outstanding students working toward graduate level degrees in plant breeding. Scholarships are limited to the University of Buenos Aries, Federal University of Vicos, Federal University of Santa Maria, China Agricultural University, Henan Agricultural University, University of Qingdao Agriculture, Maharana Pratap University of Agriculture and Technology, Tamil Nadu Agricultural University, Gandhi Krishi Vignana Kendra, University of Ag Sciences, Punjab Agricultural University, Universidad Autonoma Agraria, and the University of Los Banos. Recipients are selected based on academic excellence, proposed study program/area, future professional plans, leadership, and other experiences.
EIN: 421388269

3359
Greater Poweshiek Community Foundation
1510 Penrose St.
P.O. Box 344
Grinnell, IA   50112-1203   (641) 236-5518
Contact: Tom Marshall, Pres.
FAX: (641) 236-5590; E-mail: gpcf@greaterpcf.org;
URL: http://www.greaterpcf.org

Foundation type: Community foundation
Purpose: Scholarships to residents of Poweshiek County, IA, for postsecondary education.
Financial data: Year ended 12/31/2011. Assets, $4,789,200 (M); Expenditures, $1,174,916; Total giving, $843,203; Grants to individuals, totaling $37,865.
Type of support: Undergraduate support.
Application information: Application form required.
   Deadline(s): Contact foundation for current application deadline
EIN: 421298055

3360
Elmer O. & Ida Preston Educational Trust
801 Grand Ave., Ste. 3700
Des Moines, IA   50309-2727   (515) 243-4191
Contact: Monica Morgan

Foundation type: Independent foundation
Purpose: Scholarships and student loans limited to worthy and financially needy young Protestants residing in IA to pursue collegiate or professional studies in IA in preparation for a career in Christian service.
Publications: Annual report.
Financial data: Year ended 12/31/2012. Assets, $2,368,170 (L); Expenditures, $121,215; Total giving, $61,300; Grants to individuals, 33 grants totaling $61,300 (high: $6,250, low: $250).
Fields of interest: Protestant agencies & churches.
Type of support: Scholarships—to individuals; Student loans—to individuals.
Application information: Applications accepted. Application form required. Interview required.
   Initial approach: Letter or telephone
   Additional information: Awards are given in the form of half grant and half loan.
EIN: 426053621

3361
Pritchard Educational Trust
c/o Cherokee State Bank
212 W. Willow St.
Cherokee, IA   51012-1857   (712) 225-3000
Contact: James Mohn

Foundation type: Independent foundation
Purpose: Free interest loans to students of the Cherokee Community School District, IA, for undergraduate or graduate education.
Publications: Annual report.
Financial data: Year ended 12/31/2012. Assets, $11,461,999 (M); Expenditures, $89,900; Total giving, $0; Loans to individuals, totaling $494,360.
Fields of interest: Higher education.
Type of support: Student loans—to individuals; Support to graduates or students of specific schools; Graduate support; Undergraduate support.
Application information: Applications accepted. Application form required. Interview required.
   Deadline(s): May 1
   Applicants should submit the following:
      1) Financial information

2) GPA
EIN: 426051872

3362
Helen Raider Memorial Trust
c/o Two Rivers Bank & Trust
P.O. Box 728
Burlington, IA   52601-5214

Foundation type: Independent foundation
Purpose: Scholarships to graduates of Des Moines County, IA, high schools for undergraduate education at U.S. universities and colleges.
Financial data: Year ended 12/31/2011. Assets, $401,520 (M); Expenditures, $19,127; Total giving, $14,994; Grants to individuals, 19 grants totaling $14,994 (high: $1,738, low: $188).
Type of support: Support to graduates or students of specific schools; Undergraduate support.
Application information: Applications accepted. Application form required.
   Deadline(s): Mar. 15
EIN: 426372386

3363
Red Rock Area Community Action Program, Inc.
1009 S. Jefferson Way, Ste. 2
Indianola, IA   50125-3221   (515) 961-6271
Contact: Bill Peppmeier, Exec. Dir.
E-mail: bpeppmeier@rracap.org

Foundation type: Public charity
Purpose: Grants for basic necessities to individuals who are needy, elderly, victims of domestic violence, victims of sexual assault, or mentally or physically challenged in Boone, Jasper, Marion, Rural Polk, and Warren counties, IA.
Financial data: Year ended 09/30/2011. Assets, $1,018,181 (M); Expenditures, $6,960,250; Total giving, $5,241,526; Grants to individuals, totaling $5,225,070.
Fields of interest: Economically disadvantaged.
Type of support: Grants for special needs.
Application information:
   Initial approach: Letter, telephone, or e-mail
   Additional information: Contact foundation for eligibility requirements.
EIN: 421078280

3364
The Donna Reed Foundation for the Performing Arts
1305 Broadway
Denison, IA   51442-1923   (712) 263-3334
Contact: Gwen Ecklund, Exec. Dir.
FAX: (712) 263-8026; E-mail: info@donnareed.org;
URL: http://www.donnareed.org

Foundation type: Public charity
Purpose: Scholarships to graduating high school seniors who are residents and attended high school in Crawford County, IA pursuing a career in performing arts.
Publications: Application guidelines; Informational brochure (including application guidelines); Newsletter.
Financial data: Year ended 09/30/2012. Assets, $570,988 (M); Expenditures, $69,671.
Fields of interest: Performing arts; Theater; Theater (musical).
Type of support: Undergraduate support.

Application information: Applications accepted. Application form required.

Deadline(s): May 6

Additional information: Application forms are available at the guidance offices at the Denison-Schleswig, Charter Oak-Ute, Ar-We-Va, and IKM-Manning high schools.

EIN: 421285098

3365
Reifel-Elwood Educational Trust

(also known as Kenneth Rech)
1023 Corning St.
Red Oak, IA   51566-2001   (712) 623-3218
Contact: Kenneth Rech, Tr.

Foundation type: Independent foundation
Purpose: Scholarships to high school seniors who are residents of Montgomery County, IA.
Financial data: Year ended 01/31/2013. Assets, $117,057 (M); Expenditures, $3,946; Total giving, $2,800.
Type of support: Technical education support; Undergraduate support.
Application information: Application form required.
Send request by: Mail
Deadline(s): Apr. 30
EIN: 426149714

3366
Leo B. Riley Family Scholarship Fund

c/o Security National Bank
P.O. Box 147
Sioux City, IA   51102-0147

Foundation type: Independent foundation
Purpose: Scholarships to students who are registered members of St. Michaels Church, South Sioux City, NE.
Financial data: Year ended 07/31/2013. Assets, $157,498 (M); Expenditures, $10,133; Total giving, $6,184; Grants to individuals, 8 grants totaling $6,184 (high: $1,000, low: $184).
Fields of interest: Higher education.
Type of support: Scholarships—to individuals.
Application information: Applications accepted.
Deadline(s): Feb. 28
Additional information: Contributes only to members of St. Michaels Church of S. Sioux City, NE; unsolicited requests for funds not considered or acknowledged.
EIN: 426620636

3367
Michelle Rima Memorial Scholarship, Inc.

P.O. Box 223
Strawberry Point, IA   52076
Contact: Mark Rima, Pres.

Foundation type: Independent foundation
Purpose: Scholarships to graduating seniors of Starmond School District, IA pursuing a higher education.
Financial data: Year ended 12/31/2012. Assets, $0 (M); Expenditures, $7,849; Total giving, $3,000; Grant to an individual, 1 grant totaling $3,000 (high: $1,000, low: $1,000).
Fields of interest: Higher education.
Type of support: Scholarships—to individuals.
Application information: Applications accepted.
Initial approach: Letter
Deadline(s): Mar. 1
Additional information: Application should include GPA, name of institution applicant

plans to attend, planned field of study, and extracurricular activities.
EIN: 260164317

3368
Rotary Club of North Scott Educational Foundation

P.O. Box 79
Eldridge, IA   52748-0079   (563) 285-9965
Contact: Caroline Scheibe
Application Address: 220 W. Davenport St., Eldridge, IA 52748.

Foundation type: Operating foundation
Purpose: Scholarships primarily to residents of IA in pursuit of a higher education.
Financial data: Year ended 06/30/2013. Assets, $167,196 (M); Expenditures, $11,439; Total giving, $10,000; Grants to individuals, 5 grants totaling $10,000 (high: $2,000, low: $2,000).
Fields of interest: Higher education.
Type of support: Scholarships—to individuals.
Application information: Applications accepted.
Initial approach: Letter
Deadline(s): None
EIN: 421395093

3369
Merlin & Ethyl Rufer Scholarship Trust

501 2nd St.
Ida Grove, IA   51445-1304   (712) 364-3393
Contact: Sandy Sikes
Application address: Sandy Sikes, United bank of Iowa, 501 2nd St., Ida Grove, IA 51445 tel: (712) 364-3393; URL: http://www.unitedbk.com/

Foundation type: Independent foundation
Purpose: Scholarships to children of members of Yorkrite Masons of the Masonic Temple Association or the First Presbyterian Church, Fort Dodge, IA.
Financial data: Year ended 12/31/2011. Assets, $249,392 (M); Expenditures, $9,505; Total giving, $7,930; Grants to individuals, 36 grants totaling $7,930 (high: $275, low: $100).
Type of support: Undergraduate support.
Application information: Application form required.
Deadline(s): None
EIN: 421350542

3370
Scanlan Foundation

1403 Main St.
Rock Valley, IA   51247-1223   (712) 476-5411

Foundation type: Independent foundation
Purpose: Student loans to members of St. Mary's Catholic Church in Rock Valley, IA.
Financial data: Year ended 12/31/2012. Assets, $487,990 (M); Expenditures, $1,285; Total giving, $6,000; Grants to individuals, 2 grants totaling $6,000 (high: $4,000, low: $2,000).
Fields of interest: Catholic agencies & churches.
Type of support: Student loans—to individuals.
Application information: Application form required.
Initial approach: Letter or telephone
Deadline(s): Semi-annual
EIN: 421373828

3371
Scanlan Memorial Scholarship Fund

1403 Main St.
Rock Valley, IA   51247-1223   (712) 476-5411

Foundation type: Independent foundation
Purpose: Loans to financially needy high school seniors or graduates of Rock Valley Community School, IA, for postsecondary education.
Financial data: Year ended 12/31/2012. Assets, $102,027 (M); Expenditures, $1,441; Total giving, $3,150; Loans to individuals, 7 loans totaling $3,150.
Fields of interest: Higher education.
Type of support: Student loans—to individuals; Support to graduates or students of specific schools.
Application information: Application form required.
Deadline(s): May
Additional information: Selection is based on merit and financial necessity.
EIN: 421453663

3372
Marjorie Schlagenbusch Scholarship Trust

c/o Fort Madison Bank & Trust Co.
636 Ave. G
Fort Madison, IA   52627
Contact: Linda Schwartz
URL: https://www.fortmadisonbank.com

Foundation type: Independent foundation
Purpose: Scholarships to graduates of Ft. Madison High School, IA, who wish to pursue a teaching career.
Financial data: Year ended 12/31/2012. Assets, $119,551 (M); Expenditures, $22,967; Total giving, $21,077; Grants to individuals, 3 grants totaling $21,077 (high: $12,474, low: $3,249).
Fields of interest: Teacher school/education.
Type of support: Support to graduates or students of specific schools.
Application information: Applications accepted. Application form required.
Deadline(s): Apr. 15
EIN: 426608574

3373
Karl Schooler Scholarship Trust Fund

P.O. Box K
Carlisle, IA   50047-0710   (515) 988-4335
Contact: William R. Schooler Sr., Tr.

Foundation type: Independent foundation
Purpose: Scholarships to financially needy students who are residents of Warren county, IA.
Financial data: Year ended 10/31/2011. Assets, $646,454 (M); Expenditures, $28,136; Total giving, $24,460; Grants to individuals, 6 grants totaling $24,460 (high: $4,910, low: $2,410).
Fields of interest: Education.
Type of support: Scholarships—to individuals.
Application information: Application form required.
Deadline(s): None
Additional information: Application forms available upon request.
EIN: 421494825

3374
Florence M. Schrader Trust

P.O. Box 260
Dewitt, IA   52742   (563) 659-3211
Contact: Roger Hill, Tr.
Application address: Dewitt Bank and Trust, 815 6th Ave., Dewitt, IA 52742

Foundation type: Independent foundation

Purpose: Scholarships to graduating seniors of Central Community High School, IA in pursuit of a higher education.
Financial data: Year ended 12/31/2012. Assets, $197,919 (M); Expenditures, $11,262; Total giving, $8,000; Grants to individuals, 13 grants totaling $8,000 (high: $1,000, low: $500).
Fields of interest: Higher education.
Type of support: Support to graduates or students of specific schools.
Application information: Applications accepted. Application form required.
> *Deadline(s):* Apr. 1
> *Additional information:* First priority will be given to students of Central Community High School, second priority will be given to other graduating students of other high schools in Clinton county, IA.
EIN: 421331033

3375
Dale D. Schroeder Trust
12086 120th St.
Rippey, IA 50235-4703 (866) 228-8142
E-mail: daleschroeder@act.org; URL: http://www.act.org/daleschroeder/

Foundation type: Independent foundation
Purpose: Scholarships to high school graduates of Iowa for attendance at Iowa State University, University of Iowa or University of Northern Iowa pursuing a bachelor's degree.
Financial data: Year ended 12/31/2012. Assets, $1,285,525 (M); Expenditures, $276,665; Total giving, $209,105; Grants to individuals, 21 grants totaling $209,105 (high: $22,749, low: $2,916).
Fields of interest: Higher education.
Type of support: Support to graduates or students of specific schools.
Application information: Applications accepted. Application form required. Application form available on the grantmaker's web site.
> *Deadline(s):* Apr. 5
> *Additional information:* If selected as a semifinalist, applicants should provide a copy of SAR and income tax returns.
EIN: 206519954

3376
Ernie P. Schwartz Foundation
2701 Edgewood Pkwy., S.W.
Cedar Rapids, IA 52404 (515) 284-8579
URL: https://bankiowa.com/

Foundation type: Independent foundation
Purpose: Scholarships primarily to residents of Des Moines, IA for continuing education at institutions of higher learning.
Financial data: Year ended 09/30/2013. Assets, $252,567 (M); Expenditures, $12,353; Total giving, $6,350; Grants to individuals, 4 grants totaling $6,350 (high: $2,200, low: $500).
Type of support: Scholarships—to individuals.
Application information: Contact foundation for additional information.
EIN: 426277194

3377
The Seidler Foundation
c/o Harvey Kadlec
P.O. Box 1297
Des Moines, IA 50305-1297
Contact: Stanley B. Seidler, Pres.

Foundation type: Company-sponsored foundation

Purpose: Scholarships primarily to residents of the Cedar Rapids and Iowa City, IA metropolitan area.
Financial data: Year ended 12/31/2012. Assets, $9,123,190 (M); Expenditures, $466,720; Total giving, $446,020.
Type of support: Undergraduate support.
Application information: Applications not accepted.
> *Additional information:* Unsolicited requests for funds not considered or acknowledged.
EIN: 421209825

3378
Charles E. Shellabarger Educational Trust
c/o Community Bank, N.A.
229 Main St.
Columbus Junction, IA 52738-1136 (319) 728-2231

Foundation type: Independent foundation
Purpose: Scholarships to high school graduates of the Columbus Community School District, IA.
Financial data: Year ended 12/31/2011. Assets, $261,219 (M); Expenditures, $12,727; Total giving, $8,500.
Type of support: Support to graduates or students of specific schools; Undergraduate support.
Application information: Applications accepted.
> *Initial approach:* Letter
> *Deadline(s):* Mar. 1
EIN: 426574321

3379
Mabel E. Sherman Educational Fund
c/o Citizens First National Bank
P.O. Box 1227
Storm Lake, IA 50588 (712) 732-5440

Foundation type: Independent foundation
Purpose: Student loans to students of Buena Vista University, Cornell College, or Morningside College, all in IA. Preference goes to residents of Ida and Cherokee counties, IA, but residents of other parts of IA may be considered.
Financial data: Year ended 06/30/2012. Assets, $5,542,848 (M); Expenditures, $199,143; Total giving, $150,108.
Fields of interest: Higher education.
Type of support: Support to graduates or students of specific schools; Undergraduate support.
Application information:
> *Deadline(s):* None
> *Additional information:* Contact the financial aid offices of fund-supported colleges for current application guidelines.
EIN: 426278859

3380
Nellie R. Sherwood Trust
1026 A Ave. N.E.
Cedar Rapids, IA 52402-5036 (319) 369-7020
Contact: Marcia Schmidt
E-mail: Schmidma@crstlukes.com

Foundation type: Public charity
Purpose: Grants to retired teachers of the Cedar Rapids Community School District, IA, to pay medical, dental, and hospital bills.
Financial data: Year ended 12/31/2011. Assets, $129,668 (M); Expenditures, $23,256; Total giving, $22,765.
Type of support: Grants for special needs.
Application information: Unsolicited requests for funds not considered or acknowledged.
EIN: 426061621

3381
Joseph J. Sinek Scholarship Trust
200 N. Main St.
P.O. Box 50574
Pocahontas, IA 50574 (712) 335-4848
Application address: c/o Pocahontas Area Community School, Attn.: Diane Stegge, Guidance Counselor, Pocahontas Area Comm School, Pocahontas, IA 50574

Foundation type: Independent foundation
Purpose: Undergraduate scholarships only to graduates of Pocahontas Area Community School, Pocahontas, IA.
Financial data: Year ended 12/31/2012. Assets, $1,290,138 (M); Expenditures, $86,558; Total giving, $72,150.
Type of support: Support to graduates or students of specific schools; Undergraduate support.
Application information: Application form required.
> *Deadline(s):* Apr. 1
> *Applicants should submit the following:*
> 1) Class rank
> 2) Transcripts
> 3) Essay
> 4) ACT
> 5) Financial information
EIN: 426336481

3382
Siouxland Community Foundation
(formerly Siouxland Foundation)
505 5th St., Ste. 412
Sioux City, IA 51101-1507
Contact: Debbie Hubbard, Exec. Dir.
FAX: (712) 293-3303;
E-mail: office@siouxlandcommunityfoundation.org;
URL: http://www.siouxlandcommunityfoundation.org

Foundation type: Community foundation
Purpose: Scholarships to graduating seniors who attend high school within a 50-mile tri-state radius of Sioux City, IA.
Publications: Application guidelines; Annual report; Annual report (including application guidelines); Grants list; Informational brochure; Newsletter.
Financial data: Year ended 12/31/2012. Assets, $16,086,227 (M); Expenditures, $2,062,415; Total giving, $2,062,415; Grants to individuals, totaling $222,755.
Fields of interest: Higher education; Medical school/education; Nursing school/education; Teacher school/education; Health sciences school/education; Journalism school/education; Scholarships/financial aid.
Type of support: Scholarships—to individuals; Support to graduates or students of specific schools; Undergraduate support.
Application information: Applications accepted. Application form required. Application form available on the grantmaker's web site.
> *Initial approach:* Mail application(s) and required documents to the foundation
> *Copies of proposal:* 1
> *Deadline(s):* Feb. 15
> *Final notification:* Recipients notified in approximately six weeks
> *Applicants should submit the following:*
> 1) SAT
> 2) Financial information
> 3) Transcripts
> 4) Resume
> 5) Letter(s) of recommendation
> 6) GPA
> 7) Essay
> 8) ACT

Additional information: See web site for complete listing of scholarships.

Program description:

Scholarships: Each year scholarships are awarded to deserving students from funds established by generous donors who want to make an investment in the future of Siouxland's youth. Every scholarship has its own unique criteria reflecting the personal interests of the donor. Selection of recipients is based on such factors as scholastic performance, community service activities, work history and recommendations. Some scholarships are awarded to students pursuing a degree in a particular area of study such as nursing, education, and journalism. Visit the foundation's web site for more information.

EIN: 421323904

3383
Freda B. & William H. Smith Trust

c/o Dennis J. Evans
P.O. Box 10
Conrad, IA 50621-0010 (641) 366-2165

Foundation type: Operating foundation
Purpose: Scholarships to graduates of Beaman-Conrad-Liscomb High School, IA.
Financial data: Year ended 12/31/2012. Assets, $1,140,838 (M); Expenditures, $42,467; Total giving, $30,100; Grants to individuals, 29 grants totaling $30,100 (high: $1,200, low: $900).
Type of support: Undergraduate support.
Application information: Application form required.
Deadline(s): Dec. 1
EIN: 426478959

3384
Goodwin Sonstegard Scholarship Foundation

105 N. 4th St.
Estherville, IA 51334-2144

Foundation type: Operating foundation
Purpose: Scholarships for children of employees of Sonstegard Foods, Inc. for higher education.
Financial data: Year ended 12/31/2011. Assets, $56,474 (M); Expenditures, $15,000; Total giving, $15,000; Grants to individuals, 20 grants totaling $15,000 (high: $1,000, low: $500).
Fields of interest: Education.
Type of support: Scholarships—to individuals.
Application information:
Deadline(s): None
Additional information: Application must include biographical and academic records, academic and career plans, letters of reference, and statement of need.
EIN: 421335347

3385
Southern Iowa Economic Development Association

226 W. Main St.
P.O. Box 658
Ottumwa, IA 52501-0658 (641) 682-8741
Toll-free tel.: (800) 622-8340; URL: http://www.sieda.org/

Foundation type: Public charity
Purpose: Services to indigent residents of Appanoose, Davis, Jefferson, Keokuk, Mahaska, Van Buren & Wapello counties, IA such as home energy assistance and home weatherization.
Publications: Annual report; Newsletter.

Financial data: Year ended 06/30/2011. Assets, $1,942,632 (M); Expenditures, $10,664,504; Total giving, $5,080,819; Grants to individuals, 8,181 grants totaling $4,976,401.
Fields of interest: Economically disadvantaged.
Type of support: In-kind gifts.
Application information:
Initial approach: Letter
Applicants should submit the following:
1) Financial information
Additional information: Contact foundation for eligibility criteria.
EIN: 420923813

3386
Spencer Community School Foundation

23 E. 7th St.
P. O. Box 200
Spencer, IA 51301-0237 (712) 262-8950
Contact: Dick Montgomery, Pres.
FAX: (712) 262-1116;
E-mail: foundation@spencer.k12.ia.us;
URL: http://www.spencerschoolfoundation.com

Foundation type: Public charity
Purpose: Scholarships to graduating seniors at Spencer High School, IA for continuing education at institutions of higher learning.
Financial data: Year ended 12/31/2012. Assets, $1,490,928 (M); Expenditures, $122,100; Total giving, $76,228; Grants to individuals, totaling $53,150.
Fields of interest: Higher education.
Type of support: Support to graduates or students of specific schools; Undergraduate support.
Application information: Applications accepted. Application form required.
Deadline(s): Feb. 17 for scholarships
Applicants should submit the following:
1) FAFSA
2) SAR
3) SAT
4) Letter(s) of recommendation
5) GPA
6) Financial information
7) Essay
8) ACT
Additional information: See web site for additional application information.
EIN: 421306327

3387
St. Luke's Health Care Foundation

1026 A Ave. N.E., Ste. 105
Cedar Rapids, IA 52402-5036 (319) 369-7211
Contact: Susan Rigo, Pres.
FAX: (319) 369-8822;
E-mail: foundation@crstlukes.com/; URL: http://www.stlukesfoundation.com

Foundation type: Public charity
Purpose: Nursing scholarship to a St. Luke's associate, volunteer, or auxilian or their family members, residing in IA.
Publications: Application guidelines.
Financial data: Year ended 12/31/2011. Assets, $32,030,568 (M); Expenditures, $2,876,292; Total giving, $1,105,245; Grants to individuals, totaling $21,500.
Fields of interest: Nursing school/education.
Type of support: Undergraduate support.
Application information:
Deadline(s): Varies
Applicants should submit the following:
1) Letter(s) of recommendation
2) Transcripts

3) Essay
Program descriptions:
Awards: The foundation provides awards to St. Luke's Hospital associates to continue their educations by attending an appropriate educational seminar or conference. Named awards include the Outstanding New Graduate Award, Nancy Lamb Skogsbergh & Edna Lamb Nursing Leadership Award, Excellence in Behavioral Health Awards, 100 Great Iowa Nurses Award, C.A.R.E. Service Award, LaMorgese Award for Excellence in Neurological Nursing, Carroll H. and Lena Nelson Critical Care Award, Dr. Stephen and Peg Vanourny Award for Excellence in Obstetrical and Gynecological Nursing, Social Work Award, Elaine Young Leadership Award, Anna Purna Ghosh Oncology Nursing Award, Darrell Dennis Pulmonary Medicine Award, Smulekoff Family Award for Nursing Excellence, and Dale and Ruby Morgan and Mable Ray Endowment Award.
Scholarships: The foundation awards scholarships to employees of St. Luke's Hospital, to be used toward furthering their education. Named scholarships include St. Luke's Auxiliary Scholarships, Greta N. Schuchmann Scholarship, Nursing Scholarship, Beatha Kuntz Scholarship, May G. Gortner Scholarship, Natalie and Joe Cohn Scholarship, Dr. J. Stuart McQuiston Scholarship, and Dr. Charles Schwartz Scholarship.
EIN: 421106819

3388
St. Luke's Methodist Hospital

1026 A Ave. N.E.
Cedar Rapids, IA 52402-5036 (319) 369-7211
URL: http://www.stlukescr.org

Foundation type: Public charity
Purpose: Assistance to individuals affected by flooding and tornadoes in eastern IA.
Publications: Annual report.
Financial data: Year ended 12/31/2011. Assets, $396,324,331 (M); Expenditures, $332,929,413; Total giving, $5,287,667; Grants to individuals, totaling $4,000.
Fields of interest: Health care.
Type of support: Emergency funds.
Application information: Contact hospital for assistance.
EIN: 420504780

3389
Teresa Treat Stearns Trust

1207 Central Ave.
Fort Dodge, IA 50501-0798 (515) 955-0681
Contact: Dianne Dennis

Foundation type: Independent foundation
Purpose: Scholarships to graduates of Webster City High School, IA for continuing education at an accredited college, university, or vocational school.
Financial data: Year ended 06/30/2013. Assets, $739,963 (M); Expenditures, $44,634; Total giving, $33,655.
Fields of interest: Higher education.
Type of support: Scholarships—to individuals; Support to graduates or students of specific schools.
Application information: Application form required.
Initial approach: Letter or telephone
Deadline(s): May 21
Additional information: Students who are in their junior or senior year of college, or second year of a two year vocational program will be given priority. Application should include two

references and a brief summary of activities in high school, college and the community.

EIN: 426099826

3390

Helen T. & Mildred Stewart Trust

920 Main St.
P.O. Box 713
Grinnell, IA 50112-0713   (641) 236-6128

Foundation type: Independent foundation
Purpose: Scholarships to graduates of Grinnell-Newburg High School, IA, pursuing a career in library science.
Financial data: Year ended 12/31/2012. Assets, $331,952 (M); Expenditures, $21,700; Total giving, $14,112.
Fields of interest: Libraries/library science.
Type of support: Support to graduates or students of specific schools; Undergraduate support.
Application information: Applications accepted. Application form required.
   Initial approach: Letter
   Send request by: Mail
   Deadline(s): Apr. 15
   Applicants should submit the following:
      1) Financial information
      2) Essay
   Additional information: Secondary consideration goes to graduates enrolled in any liberal arts program. Application should also include a list of scholastic and extracurricular activities.
EIN: 426242034

3391

Straub Family Foundation

(formerly Straub Foundation)
7306 Oliver Smith Dr.
Urbandale, IA 50322   (515) 276-9143
Contact: Tim Lockner, Pres.

Foundation type: Independent foundation
Purpose: Scholarships to individuals who are residents of Iowa for continuing their education at accredited colleges or universities.
Financial data: Year ended 12/31/2012. Assets, $155,440 (M); Expenditures, $4,652; Total giving, $2,750; Grants to individuals, 5 grants totaling $2,000 (high: $750, low: $750).
Fields of interest: Higher education.
Type of support: Scholarships—to individuals.
Application information: Applications accepted. Application form required.
   Deadline(s): None
EIN: 426059605

3392

R. L. and Ethel Stubbs Scholarship Trust

c/o Security National Bank
P.O. Box 147
Sioux City, IA 51102

Foundation type: Independent foundation
Purpose: Scholarships to students for higher education in the Galva-Holstein Community School District, IA.
Financial data: Year ended 12/31/2012. Assets, $887,480 (M); Expenditures, $56,167; Total giving, $41,310.
Fields of interest: Higher education.
Type of support: Support to graduates or students of specific schools.
Application information: Application form required.
   Initial approach: Letter

Additional information: Applications can be obtained at the Galva Holstein Community School.
EIN: 421386035

3393

Sidney A. Swensrud Scholarship Fund

P.O. Box 167
Northwood, IA 50459-0167

Foundation type: Independent foundation
Purpose: Scholarships to graduating seniors of Northwood-Kensett High School in Northwood, IA.
Financial data: Year ended 12/31/2012. Assets, $3,499,968 (M); Expenditures, $109,379; Total giving, $105,500.
Type of support: Support to graduates or students of specific schools; Undergraduate support.
Application information: Application form required.
   Deadline(s): May 1
EIN: 426061933

3394

Wesley and Barbara Swiler Memorial Scholarship Trust Fund

c/o Two Rivers Bank & Trust
P.O. Box 728
Burlington, IA 52601-0728   (319) 753-9136
Contact: John Walz

Foundation type: Independent foundation
Purpose: Scholarships to students at Burlington Community High School, IA, and Notre Dame High School, Burlington, IA.
Financial data: Year ended 02/28/2013. Assets, $261,414 (M); Expenditures, $18,821; Total giving, $16,000; Grants to individuals, 8 grants totaling $16,000 (high: $3,000, low: $1,000).
Type of support: Support to graduates or students of specific schools; Undergraduate support.
Application information: Application form required.
   Deadline(s): Mar. 15
   Applicants should submit the following:
      1) Letter(s) of recommendation
      2) Photograph
      3) Class rank
      4) GPA
      5) Essay
      6) ACT
EIN: 426485815

3395

C. H. "Buck" Taylor Scholarship

P.O. Box 8
Guthrie Center, IA 50115

Foundation type: Independent foundation
Purpose: Scholarships to graduates of Guthrie Center High School or Adair-Casey High School, IA for continuing education.
Financial data: Year ended 12/31/2012. Assets, $0 (M); Expenditures, $7,573; Total giving, $7,250; Grants to individuals, 2 grants totaling $6,000 (high: $3,000, low: $3,000).
Fields of interest: Higher education.
Type of support: Support to graduates or students of specific schools.
Application information: Applications accepted. Application form required.
   Deadline(s): May 15
   Additional information: Unsolicited requests for funds not considered or acknowledged.
EIN: 421354075

3396

Traer Community Foundation

611 2nd St.
P.O. Box 435
Traer, IA 50675-1230   (319) 478-2148
FAX: (319) 478-2023; E-mail: info@traer.com

Foundation type: Community foundation
Purpose: Scholarships to residents of the Traer, IA, area.
Financial data: Year ended 12/31/2011. Assets, $1,176,667 (M); Expenditures, $68,180; Total giving, $44,451; Grants to individuals, 9 grants totaling $5,150.
Type of support: Undergraduate support.
Application information: Applications accepted.
   Initial approach: Letter
   Additional information: Contact foundation for eligibility criteria.
EIN: 421366419

3397

Trinity Health Foundation

(formerly T.R.H. Development Foundation)
802 Kenyon Rd.
Fort Dodge, IA 50501-5740   (515) 574-6506
E-mail: Jonesmv@ihs.org; URL: http://www.trinityqc.com/Ways-to-Give/Trinity-Foundation.aspx

Foundation type: Public charity
Purpose: Scholarships to individuals residing in IA for studies that relate to future occupations in the healthcare professions.
Publications: Application guidelines.
Financial data: Year ended 12/31/2011. Assets, $16,888,355 (M); Expenditures, $1,218,558; Total giving, $708,838; Grants to individuals, totaling $14,359.
Fields of interest: Health sciences school/education.
Type of support: Employee-related scholarships; Scholarships—to individuals.
Application information: Applications accepted.
   Deadline(s): None
   Additional information: Each scholarship fund has specific criteria and recipients are selected by a committee based upon academic merit, leadership, citizenship, career objectives and financial need. Scholarships are issued each semester.
Program descriptions:
   Andrea Reed Scholarship: Preference will be given to a healthcare worker pursing an associate degree in nursing, with a career goal to become a registered nurse. Preference will also be given to single parent families. Scholarships are available to both part-time and full-time students.
   Arthur Moeller Scholarship: Provides a scholarship to a deserving Iowa Central Community College (ICCC) nursing student or one seeking an advanced nursing degree in an accredited program. This scholarship is available to both part- and full-time students.
   Dr. Clyde A. Lindquist Scholarship: Awarded to a student in an accredited higher education program, majoring in a health science field. Both undergraduate and graduate students are eligible.
   Lores Coulson Scholarship: Awarded to an outstanding Trinity Regional Medical Center employee who is continuing their education for the purpose of enhancing knowledge and skills.
   McMillen Scholarship: This scholarship is given to individuals who have completed the nursing program at Iowa Central Community College (ICCC) and are seeking an advanced nursing degree at an accredited educational institution. Nursing

students enrolled in the ICCC nursing program also may submit applications. This scholarship is available to both part-time and full-time students.

The Roselpha Lovrien Nursing Scholarship: Preference in awarding this scholarship is given to individuals who have completed the nursing program at Iowa Central Community College (ICCC) and are seeking an advanced nursing degree at an accredited educational institution. Nursing students enrolled in the ICCC nursing program also may submit applications.

Tom and Margaret Welch Scholarship: The scholarship is awarded to students who are certified nurse aides or other health workers who aspire to obtain an associate or baccalaureate degree in nursing. The scholarship is available to both part-time and full-time students.
EIN: 421222381

3398
U.S. Navy Warner Trust
262 S. Chestnut St.
Fremont, IA 52561-7702
Contact: Susan Sieran, Tr.

Foundation type: Independent foundation
Purpose: Scholarships to high school graduates residing in the Fremont School District of IA, who meet minimum GPA requirements and maintain at least three-quarter credit hour schedules each semester.
Financial data: Year ended 12/31/2012. Assets, $240,000 (M); Expenditures, $17,818; Total giving, $14,850; Grants to individuals, 27 grants totaling $14,850 (high: $550, low: $550).
Type of support: Scholarships—to individuals.
Application information: Applications accepted. Application form not required.
Initial approach: Letter
Additional information: Application must include college choice.
EIN: 426348143

3399
United Fire Group Foundation
118 2nd Ave. S.E.
Cedar Rapids, IA 52401-1212

Foundation type: Company-sponsored foundation
Purpose: Grants to individuals for higher education and disaster relief.
Financial data: Year ended 12/31/2011. Assets, $9,049 (M); Expenditures, $747,985; Total giving, $747,985.
Fields of interest: Higher education; Education; Disasters, preparedness/services.
Type of support: Emergency funds; Grants to individuals.
Application information: Applications not accepted.
EIN: 421492320

3400
United Way of Central Iowa
1111 9th St., Ste. 100
Des Moines, IA 50314-2527 (515) 246-6500
E-mail: contactus@unitedwaydm.org; URL: http://www.unitedwaydm.org

Foundation type: Public charity
Purpose: Grants to needy residents of central IA.
Publications: Annual report; Financial statement; Informational brochure; Newsletter.
Financial data: Year ended 06/30/2011. Assets, $29,663,332 (M); Expenditures, $23,738,229;

Total giving, $18,982,729; Grants to individuals, 213 grants totaling $17,314.
Fields of interest: Economically disadvantaged.
Type of support: Grants for special needs.
Application information:
Initial approach: Letter
Additional information: Contact foundation for complete eligibility requirements.
EIN: 420680425

3401
Upper Des Moines Opportunity, Inc.
101 Robins St.
P.O. Box 519
Graettinger, IA 51342-0519 (712) 859-3885
Contact: Jamey Whitney, Exec. Dir.
Toll Free Tel.: (800)-245-6151; URL: http://www.udmo.com/

Foundation type: Public charity
Purpose: Assistance to indigent residents of IA, such as home energy assistance to help homeowners and renters pay for a portion of their primary heating costs for the winter heating season.
Financial data: Year ended 09/30/2011. Assets, $3,348,671 (M); Expenditures, $17,370,079; Total giving, $7,212,133; Grants to individuals, 32,084 grants totaling $7,212,133.
Fields of interest: Economically disadvantaged.
Type of support: Grants for special needs.
Application information:
Initial approach: Letter
Additional information: The assistance is based on household income, household size, type of fuel and type of housing.
EIN: 420923424

3402
Mabel Vacek Scholarship Trust
c/o Remley, Willems, McQuillen, & Voss
301 E. Main
P.O. Box 228
Anamosa, IA 52205-0228 (563) 488-2292
Application address: Midland HS, 109 W. Green, Wyoming, IA 52632,

Foundation type: Operating foundation
Purpose: Scholarships to individuals, primarily in Oxford Junction, IA.
Financial data: Year ended 12/31/2012. Assets, $247,695 (M); Expenditures, $8,855; Total giving, $5,604; Grants to individuals, 5 grants totaling $5,604 (high: $1,000, low: $901).
Type of support: Scholarships—to individuals.
Application information: Applications accepted.
Additional information: Contact foundation for current application deadline/guidelines.
EIN: 426580517

3403
The Van Buren Foundation, Inc.
c/o Community First Bank
714 First St.
Keosauqua, IA 52565-0130 (319) 293-3794
Contact: George Manning

Foundation type: Independent foundation
Purpose: Scholarships and student loans limited to graduating seniors of Van Buren Community High School, IA, and Harmony High School, IA. Educational loans to individuals studying in medical- and healthcare-related fields who are residents of Van Buren County, IA.
Financial data: Year ended 12/31/2012. Assets, $6,547,557 (M); Expenditures, $325,075; Total

giving, $228,766; Grants to individuals, 19 grants totaling $36,831 (high: $3,000, low: $500); Loans to individuals, 3 loans totaling $13,666.
Fields of interest: Medical school/education; Nursing school/education; Health care.
Type of support: Scholarships—to individuals; Student loans—to individuals.
Application information: Applications accepted. Application form required.
Deadline(s): None
Additional information: Application forms available from the foundation or high school counselors in Van Buren County, IA.
EIN: 426062589

3404
VDTA Bernie Epstein Scholarship Fund
2724 2nd Ave.
Des Moines, IA 50313-4933 (515) 282-9101
Toll-free tel.: (800) 367-5651; URL: http://www.vdta.com/besf.html

Foundation type: Public charity
Purpose: Scholarships for children of the manufacturers, distributors, suppliers and dealers of the sewing machine industry. Grandchildren of members and their employees are also eligible.
Publications: Application guidelines.
Financial data: Year ended 12/31/2011. Assets, $167,699 (M); Expenditures, $20,157; Total giving, $15,000.
Fields of interest: College; University.
Type of support: Employee-related scholarships.
Application information: Application form required.
Initial approach: Telephone
Deadline(s): Nov. 1
Applicants should submit the following:
1) GPA
2) Essay
3) Transcripts
4) Letter(s) of recommendation
Program description:
The VDTA/Bernie Epstein Scholarship: Awards up to $10,000, over a four-year period to a student who demonstrates involvement in his/her community, who is actively involved in humanitarian organizations and activities, and who shows great leadership abilities, sportsmanship, and/or participation in recreational sports activities. Eligible applicants must be a dependent of a Vacuum Dealers Trade Association (VDTA) or Sewing Dealers Trade Association (SDTA) member or the dealer member's employees, and must have a 2.5 GPA.
EIN: 421416381

3405
Adolph and Esther Vestergaard Memorial Scholarship Fund
P.O. Box 908
Spencer, IA 51301-0908 (712) 262-1500

Foundation type: Independent foundation
Purpose: Scholarships to residents of Clay and Dickinson counties, IA, for higher education.
Financial data: Year ended 12/31/2011. Assets, $758,669 (M); Expenditures, $44,939; Total giving, $37,000.
Type of support: Scholarships—to individuals.
Application information: Applications not accepted.
Additional information: Application must include college student will attend, extracurricular activities, and other scholarships. Unsolicited

requests for funds not considered or acknowledged.
EIN: 421369816

3406
Waverly Community Foundation
c/o State Bank & Trust Co., N.A.
P.O. Box 58
Waverly, IA   50677-0058   (319) 352-6000
Contact: Alan M. Charlson
FAX: (319) 352-5718;
E-mail: acharlson@sbtcompany.com

Foundation type: Independent foundation
Purpose: Scholarships to graduating seniors of Bremer county high schools, IA for higher education. Grants to Bremer county senior citizens.
Publications: Application guidelines.
Financial data: Year ended 12/31/2011. Assets, $1,856,939 (M); Expenditures, $111,272; Total giving, $90,198.
Fields of interest: Higher education; Aging.
Type of support: Support to graduates or students of specific schools; Undergraduate support; Grants for special needs.
Application information: Applications accepted.
  Initial approach: Letter
  Send request by: Mail or fax
  Copies of proposal: 1
  Deadline(s): Jan. 1 and Apr. 1
  Final notification: Recipients notified in 60 days
  Applicants should submit the following:
    1) Resume
    2) FAFSA
  Additional information: Applicant should demonstrate need. Contact the foundation for eligibility criteria.
EIN: 426058774

3407
West Central Community Action
(formerly West Central Development Corporation)
P.O. Box 709
Harlan, IA   51537-0709   (712) 755-5135
FAX: (712) 755-3235;
E-mail: info@westcentralca.org; Toll-free tel.: (800) 945-9778; URL: http://westcentralca.org/

Foundation type: Public charity
Purpose: Grants to low-income residents of west-central IA.
Financial data: Year ended 09/30/2011. Assets, $7,076,708 (M); Expenditures, $20,250,113; Total giving, $7,561,067; Grants to individuals, totaling $7,561,067.
Fields of interest: Economically disadvantaged.
Type of support: Grants for special needs.
Application information:
  Initial approach: Letter
  Additional information: Contact foundation for complete eligibility requirements.
EIN: 420919214

3408
Winkel Family Foundation
c/o Long Lines - Jon Winkel
P.O. Box 67
Sergeant Bluff, IA   51054

Foundation type: Independent foundation
Purpose: Scholarships to residents of Sergeant Bluff, IA for postsecondary education.
Financial data: Year ended 12/31/2012. Assets, $52,450 (M); Expenditures, $6,062; Total giving, $5,000.
Fields of interest: Higher education.
Type of support: Undergraduate support.
Application information: Applications not accepted.
  Additional information: Unsolicited requests for funds not considered or asknowledged.
EIN: 421464738

3409
The Jim and Marie Wood Foundation
c/o Alan Anderson
110 N. 2nd Ave.
Logan, IA   51546-1332

Foundation type: Independent foundation
Purpose: Scholarships to residents of the Logan, IA, area for higher education.
Financial data: Year ended 12/31/2011. Assets, $3,721,376 (M); Expenditures, $213,249; Total

giving, $179,457; Grants to individuals, 21 grants totaling $122,000 (high: $7,500, low: $2,500).
Type of support: Scholarships—to individuals.
Application information: Contact the foundation for additional application guidelines.
EIN: 931044500

3410
World Food Prize Foundation
666 Grand Ave., Ste. 1700
Des Moines, IA   50309-2500   (515) 245-3783
Contact: Judith Pim, Dir., Secretariat Operations
E-mail for Judith Pim: jpim@worldfoodprize.org
FAX: (515) 245-3785;
E-mail: wfp@worldfoodprize.org; URL: http://www.worldfoodprize.org

Foundation type: Independent foundation
Purpose: Awards prizes to individuals for achievement in improving the world food supply.
Publications: Informational brochure; Informational brochure (including application guidelines).
Financial data: Year ended 12/31/2012. Assets, $48,839,505 (M); Expenditures, $4,107,841; Total giving, $250,000; Grant to an individual, 1 grant totaling $250,000.
Fields of interest: Agriculture.
Type of support: Research; Awards/prizes.
Application information: Applications accepted. Application form not required.
  Deadline(s): Apr. 1
  Additional information: See foundation web site for application and nomination information.
EIN: 421356715

KANSAS

3411
Jennie G. and Pearl Abell Education Trust
717 Main St.
P.O. Box 487
Ashland, KS 67831 (620) 635-2228
Contact: Jane S. Rankin, Tr.

Foundation type: Independent foundation
Purpose: Scholarships to financially needy graduates of Clark County, KS, high schools and current Clark County, KS, residents.
Financial data: Year ended 05/31/2013. Assets, $2,143,114 (M); Expenditures, $124,044; Total giving, $89,500; Grants to individuals, 34 grants totaling $89,500 (high: $5,500, low: $500).
Fields of interest: Education.
Type of support: Support to graduates or students of specific schools; Undergraduate support.
Application information: Applications accepted. Application form required.
> *Send request by:* Mail, fax or e-mail
> *Deadline(s):* June 15
> *Applicants should submit the following:*
> 1) Financial information
> 2) SAR
> 3) Transcripts
> *Additional information:* Applications should be obtained from the trust.

EIN: 237454791

3412
Alpha Nu Educational Foundation
6017 W. 89th Tr.
Overland Park, KS 66207-2011 (913) 642-2916

Foundation type: Public charity
Purpose: Scholarships in the form of small cash awards to students at the University of Kansas.
Financial data: Year ended 04/30/2012. Assets, $19,773 (M); Expenditures, $20,153; Total giving, $500.
Fields of interest: Higher education.
Type of support: Scholarships—to individuals.
Application information: Applications accepted.
> *Additional information:* Applicants are selected based upon need, academic performance, and participation in campus activities. Contact foundation for further application information.

EIN: 486115179

3413
American Academy of Family Physicians Foundation
(also known as AAFP Foundation)
11400 Tomahawk Creek Pkwy., Ste. 440
Leawood, KS 66211-2627
Contact: Craig M. Doane, Secy. and Exec. Dir.
FAX: (913) 906-6095; E-mail: found@aafp.org;
Toll-free tel.: (800) 274-2237; URL: http://www.aafpfoundation.org

Foundation type: Public charity
Purpose: Grants and scholarships to family physicians to support research projects on topics relevant to family medicine.
Publications: Application guidelines; Annual report; Informational brochure; Newsletter.

Financial data: Year ended 12/31/2011. Assets, $21,347,994 (M); Expenditures, $5,894,490; Total giving, $2,857,622; Grants to individuals, totaling $36,934.
Fields of interest: Health care.
Type of support: Research.
Application information: Applications accepted. Application form required. Application form available on the grantmaker's web site.
> *Initial approach:* Telephone or letter
> *Copies of proposal:* 1
> *Deadline(s):* June 1 and Dec. 1 for Joint Grant Awards; Mar. 1 and Sept. 1 for Research Stimulation Grant and Practiced Based Research Network (PBRN) Stimulation Grants
> *Additional information:* Application must include proposal.

Program descriptions:
> *AAFP Foundation Physicians With Heart Resident Scholarship:* The scholarship allows a Family Medicine resident to accompany the delegation in the fall on the Physicians With Heart airlift to Kyrgyzstan. The scholarship will cover all expenses from the departure city to Kyrgyzstan and in-country expenses including housing, transportation, and food. Candidates must be resident members of the AAFP and have an interest and experience in International Family Medicine or humanitarian efforts.
> *James G. Jones, M,D Student Scholarship:* The scholarship sends one medical student to the Family Medicine Congressional Conference held in Washington, DC.
> *Joint Grant Awards Program:* Awards a maximum of $50,000 to support research projects that pose questions of high relevance to family medicine using rigorous design and appropriate statistical analysis.
> *Pfizer Teacher Development Awards:* Sixteen community-based family physicians and part-time teachers are selected to receive a $2,000 scholarship based on their scholastic achievement, leadership qualities, and dedication to Family Medicine. A $500 stipend is provided for their teaching center to host a recognition ceremony.
> *Practiced Based Research Network (PBRN) Stimulation Grants:* $7,500 is provided to projects to support research conducted by family physicians affiliated or associated with a PBRN in Family Medicine.
> *Research Stimulation Grant:* Awards grants of up to $7,500 that address clinical research questions of importance to family physicians and their patients and can be implemented within a typical family medicine setting.
> *Resident and Student Initiatives Fund for National Conference Scholarships:* More than 125 scholarships are provided for students and residents to attend the National Conference annually. This enables residents and students the opportunity to explore Family Medicine through clinical sessions, procedural workshops and interaction with family physicians from across the country. Many scholarship recipients solidify their commitment to the specialty and develop their leadership skills through participation in the National Conference of Family Medicine Residents and Medical Students.
> *Resident Research Grants:* Grants of up to $2,000 are given to support five short-term projects conducted by Family Medicine residents. Each grantee will give a 15 minute presentation on his or her research project at the National Conference.

EIN: 446013671

3414
Heather Lynn Arnold Memorial Scholarship
161 Emmer Rd. S.W.
Gridley, KS 66852-9244 (620) 836-4315
Contact: Greg Arnold, Tr.

Foundation type: Independent foundation
Purpose: Scholarships to graduating seniors at Gridley High School, KS, for higher education.
Financial data: Year ended 12/31/2012. Assets, $208,119 (M); Expenditures, $13,630; Total giving, $11,200; Grants to individuals, 10 grants totaling $11,200 (high: $1,400, low: $700).
Fields of interest: Scholarships/financial aid.
Type of support: Support to graduates or students of specific schools; Undergraduate support.
Application information: Applications accepted. Application form required.
> *Deadline(s):* Contact foundation for current application deadline

EIN: 481170140

3415
Atchison Community Educational Foundation
(formerly Atchison Community Foundation)
625 Commercial
Atchison, KS 66002

Foundation type: Community foundation
Purpose: Scholarships to minorities and at-risk students to attend colleges or universities for higher education.
Financial data: Year ended 06/30/2013. Assets, $353,918 (M); Expenditures, $37,278; Total giving, $36,337.
Fields of interest: Higher education; Minorities.
Type of support: Scholarships—to individuals.
Application information: Applications accepted. Application form required. Interview required.
> *Applicants should submit the following:*
> 1) Transcripts
> 2) Essay
> *Additional information:* Application must also include four written references and acceptance letter from the college applicant plan to attend.

EIN: 481186798

3416
Babson's Midwest Memorial Foundation, Inc.
408 E. 3rd St.
Eureka, KS 67045-2031 (620) 583-8630
Contact: Debbie Burtin
Application address: P.O. Box 430, Eureka, KS 67045

Foundation type: Independent foundation
Purpose: Scholarships to graduates of high schools in Greenwood County, KS.
Publications: Newsletter.
Financial data: Year ended 12/31/2011. Assets, $1,434,640 (M); Expenditures, $112,450; Total giving, $96,500; Grants to individuals, 45 grants totaling $96,500 (high: $6,000, low: $500).
Type of support: Support to graduates or students of specific schools; Undergraduate support.
Application information: Applications accepted. Application form required.
> *Deadline(s):* Apr. 15
> *Applicants should submit the following:*
> 1) Essay
> 2) Financial information
> 3) Transcripts

Additional information: Application can be obtained from high school.
EIN: 237086922

3417
J. H. Baker Trust
802 Main Box 280
La Crosse, KS   67548-0280   (785) 222-2537
Contact: Thomas V. Dechant, Tr.
Apllication address: P.O. Box 280 La Crosse KS 67548

Foundation type: Independent foundation
Purpose: Low-interest undergraduate student loans to graduates of high schools in Rush, Barton, Ellis, Ness, and Pawnee counties, KS, who are under 25 years of age.
Financial data: Year ended 12/31/2011. Assets, $1,253,329 (M); Expenditures, $77,271; Total giving, $46,000.
Fields of interest: Vocational education; College; University.
Type of support: Student loans—to individuals; Support to graduates or students of specific schools; Undergraduate support.
Application information: Applications accepted. Application form required.
Deadline(s): Jan. 15 for spring, July 15 for fall
Final notification: Recipients notified by Aug. 15
Applicants should submit the following:
 1) Letter(s) of recommendation
 2) GPA
 3) Class rank
 4) Transcripts
EIN: 510210925

3418
Earl Bane Foundation
P.O. Box 201
Salina, KS   67402-0201
Application address: c/o Robert Buster, 315 N. 9th St., Salina, KS 67401, tel.: (785) 827-1492

Foundation type: Independent foundation
Purpose: Scholarships to individuals from schools in Salina, KS, for attendance at KS universities and colleges.
Financial data: Year ended 04/30/2013. Assets, $15,203,786 (M); Expenditures, $482,399; Total giving, $383,600.
Type of support: Undergraduate support.
Application information:
Initial approach: Letter
Deadline(s): None
Additional information: Contact foundation for current application guidelines.
EIN: 481152429

3419
Jon C. Beal, Jr. Memorial Trust
310 N. Wabash
Norton, KS   67654-1814   (785) 874-4699
Contact: Kim Fiscus, Tr.

Foundation type: Independent foundation
Purpose: Scholarships to graduates of Fredonia High School, KS for continuing education at accredited colleges or universities.
Financial data: Year ended 12/31/2012. Assets, $185,048 (M); Expenditures, $6,258; Total giving, $6,133; Grants to individuals, 4 grants totaling $6,133 (high: $2,000, low: $1,133).
Fields of interest: Higher education.
Type of support: Support to graduates or students of specific schools.

Application information: Applications accepted.
Initial approach: Letter
Deadline(s): None
Additional information: Application should include social security number, parents' names, school activities, college plans, and a 200-word essay on why he/she wants to attend college.
EIN: 480959834

3420
Lois & Max Beren Foundation
100 N. Main St., Ste. 700
Wichita, KS   67202-1384   (303) 761-1572
Contact: Carla Beren Garrity, Tr.
Application address: 3360 S. Columbine Cir., Englewood, CO 80113-7605

Foundation type: Independent foundation
Purpose: Scholarships to individuals for higher education. Preference is given to students at specific high schools.
Financial data: Year ended 12/31/2012. Assets, $2,416,923 (M); Expenditures, $131,182; Total giving, $110,236.
Type of support: Scholarships—to individuals.
Application information: Application form required.
Initial approach: Letter
Deadline(s): Dec. 31
EIN: 486107224

3421
M C Hess and Margaret Hess Boyle Educational Fund of the Margaret Hess Boyle Trust
(formerly Margaret Hess Boyle Trust)
1903 N St.
P.O. Box 541
Belleville, KS   66935   (913) 874-2000
Contact: Rodney R. Peake, Tr.
Application Address: 21569 N 58th Ave. Glendale, AZ 853086232

Foundation type: Independent foundation
Purpose: Scholarships to students who are residents of KS.
Financial data: Year ended 06/30/2013. Assets, $776,115 (M); Expenditures, $41,024; Total giving, $17,500; Grants to individuals, 11 grants totaling $17,500 (high: $3,000, low: $500).
Type of support: Scholarships—to individuals.
Application information: Applications accepted. Application form required.
Deadline(s): Apr. 1
Applicants should submit the following:
 1) Transcripts
 2) Letter(s) of recommendation
 3) Financial information
 4) Essay
EIN: 481216273

3422
Brown Memorial Foundation
409 N.W. 3rd St., Ste. A
P.O. Box 187
Abilene, KS   67410-0187

Foundation type: Operating foundation
Purpose: Scholarships to graduating seniors of Abilene High School, KS, to attend accredited colleges, universities, and technical schools in KS. Scholarships are awarded on the basis of financial need, grades, class rank, test scores, moral character, citizenship, and motivation.

Financial data: Year ended 12/31/2012. Assets, $25,582,016 (M); Expenditures, $908,634; Total giving, $25,285; Grants to individuals, 8 grants totaling $16,500 (high: $2,800, low: $100).
Application information: Applications not accepted.
Additional information: Unsolicited requests for funds are not considered or acknowledged.
EIN: 480573809

3423
Child Care Links Association
(formerly Reno County Child Care Association, Inc.)
21 W. 2nd
Hutchinson, KS   67501-5207   (620) 669-0291
Contact: Doris Vanek, Exec. Dir.

Foundation type: Public charity
Purpose: Provides nutrition education and other training to child care providers in Reno County, KS, and reimburses providers for food costs of serving nutritious meals.
Financial data: Year ended 09/30/2011. Assets, $54,706 (M); Expenditures, $1,504,024.
Fields of interest: Day care; Children, services.
Type of support: Grants to individuals.
Application information: Applications not accepted.
Additional information: Unsolicited requests for funds not considered.
EIN: 480840803

3424
Christian Foundation for Children & Aging
1 Elmwood Ave.
Kansas City, KS   66103-3719
Contact: Martin Kraus, Dir., Finance
FAX: (913) 384-6500; E-mail: mail@cfcausa.org; Toll-free tel.: (800) 875-6564; URL: http://www.cfcausa.org

Foundation type: Public charity
Purpose: Scholarships to students located at the foundation's project sites throughout the developing world. Sponsored grants to individuals throughout the developing world.
Publications: Annual report; Occasional report.
Financial data: Year ended 12/31/2011. Assets, $39,884,294 (M); Expenditures, $109,349,454; Total giving, $94,977,446. Subtotal for emergency funds: 0 grants totaling $91,440,332.
Type of support: Scholarships—to individuals.
Application information: Applications not accepted.
Additional information: Unsolicited requests for funds not considered or acknowledged.
EIN: 431243999

3425
Clay County Educational Endowment Association, Inc.
P.O. Box 205
Clay Center, KS   67432-0205

Foundation type: Independent foundation
Purpose: Scholarships to graduates of Unified School District 379, KS and to qualifying students participating in specific programs in Kansas.
Financial data: Year ended 12/31/2012. Assets, $912,583 (M); Expenditures, $35,858; Total giving, $31,772; Grants to individuals, 36 grants totaling $30,772 (high: $5,000, low: $150).
Fields of interest: Education.
Type of support: Scholarships—to individuals.

Application information: Applications accepted. Application form required.
EIN: 481202509

3426
Cloud County Children's Trust

c/o Citizens National Bank
115 W. 6th St.
Concordia, KS   66901   (785) 243-3211
Contact: Amy DeGraff
Application address: P.O. Box 409, Concordia, KS 66901

Foundation type: Independent foundation
Purpose: Grants to Cloud County, KS, children age 12 and under with special needs, and their families.
Financial data: Year ended 06/30/2013. Assets, $498,192 (M); Expenditures, $32,676; Total giving, $24,908; Grants to individuals, 18 grants totaling $7,894 (high: $2,500, low: $50).
Fields of interest: Education, special; Reading; Physical therapy; Mental health, counseling/support groups; Disabilities, people with.
Type of support: Grants for special needs.
Application information: Applications accepted. Application form required.
   Deadline(s): None
   Additional information: Application should include first page (front and back) of last year's federal income tax return, including W-2 forms, and current financial statement.
EIN: 510196634

3427
The Otto R. Coffman Charitable Education Trust

P.O. Box 328
Yates Center, KS   66783-0328
Contact: John Danler, Tr.

Foundation type: Independent foundation
Purpose: Scholarships to graduates of Woodson County, Kansas high schools who have demonstrated the desire to attend a college or university or who seek vocational training in an accredited vocational training institution.
Financial data: Year ended 12/31/2012. Assets, $461,840 (M); Expenditures, $4,456; Total giving, $3,500; Grants to individuals, 5 grants totaling $3,500 (high: $1,000, low: $500).
Fields of interest: Vocational education, post-secondary; Higher education.
Type of support: Support to graduates or students of specific schools; Graduate support; Technical education support; Undergraduate support.
Application information: Applications accepted. Application form required.
   Send request by: Mail
   Applicants should submit the following:
      1) Essay
      2) SAT
      3) Photograph
      4) Transcripts
      5) ACT
   Additional information: Application should also include three references.
EIN: 486377667

3428
Columbus Community Foundation

P.O. Box 323
Columbus, KS   66725   (620) 429-3107
Contact: Jim Dahmen, Dir.
E-mail: chairperson@columbuscommunityfoundation.com; URL: http://columbuscommunityfoundation.com

Foundation type: Community foundation
Purpose: Scholarships to high school seniors residing in Columbus, KS for higher education at accredited institutions.
Publications: Application guidelines; Informational brochure; Occasional report.
Financial data: Year ended 12/31/2012. Assets, $1,161,636 (M); Expenditures, $53,451; Total giving, $34,812; Grants to individuals, totaling $7,210.
Fields of interest: Higher education.
Type of support: Scholarships—to individuals.
Application information: Applications accepted.
   Deadline(s): Varies
   Additional information: Counselors at the high school determine scholarship awardees by making recommendations to the foundation based on applications.
EIN: 481101272

3429
Community Foundation of Southwest Kansas

(formerly Dodge City Area Foundation)
114 Gunsmoke
P.O. Box 1313
Dodge City, KS   67801-1313   (620) 225-0959
Contact: Pat Hamit, Exec. Dir.
FAX: (620) 225-4946;
E-mail: pat.cfsk@sbcglobal.net; URL: http://www.communityfoundationswks.com

Foundation type: Community foundation
Purpose: Scholarships to students of southwest KS for full time enrollment for postsecondary education.
Publications: Application guidelines; Annual report; Grants list; Informational brochure; Newsletter; Occasional report.
Financial data: Year ended 12/31/2012. Assets, $19,859,183 (M); Expenditures, $597,779; Total giving, $404,903; Grants to individuals, 149 grants totaling $126,255.
Fields of interest: College; University.
Type of support: Scholarships—to individuals; Undergraduate support.
Application information: Applications accepted. Application form required. Application form available on the grantmaker's web site.
   Initial approach: Application
   Send request by: Mail
   Deadline(s): Feb. 1
   Final notification: Applicants notified by May 1
   Applicants should submit the following:
      1) SAT
      2) ACT
      3) Photograph
      4) Transcripts
      5) Letter(s) of recommendation
      6) GPA
      7) Financial information
      8) Essay
      9) Budget Information
   Additional information: See web site for additional application guidelines.
   Program description:
   Scholarship Program: The foundation's scholarship program reflects a direct effort to

recognize and reward those students who have demonstrated consistent and outstanding academic achievement in high school and college and tend to be a worthy student of good character. Numerous scholarship funds are available to assist qualified applicants to offset some of the costs of higher education at an accredited institution. The program lists various scholarships which students, with proven academic records, financial need or demonstrated leadership potential in any area, should not hesitate to apply under one or more of the available funds. See web site for additional information.
EIN: 481117413

3430
Esther Davis Foundation

P.O. Box 10
Norton, KS   67654-0010   (785) 877-5143
Contact: Karen L. Griffiths, Tr.

Foundation type: Independent foundation
Purpose: Interest-free loans to graduates of Norton Community High School, Norton, KS in pursuit of a college education.
Financial data: Year ended 12/31/2012. Assets, $45,063 (M); Expenditures, $290; Total giving, $1,500; Grant to an individual, 1 grant totaling $1,500.
Fields of interest: Higher education.
Type of support: Support to graduates or students of specific schools.
Application information: Applications accepted.
   Initial approach: Letter
   Deadline(s): June 1
   Additional information: Letter of application must include transcript.
EIN: 481040541

3431
James A. and Juliet L. Davis Foundation Inc.

1 Compound Dr.
Hutchinson, KS   67502-4349   (620) 662-8331
Contact: Merl F. Sellers, Pres.

Foundation type: Independent foundation
Purpose: Scholarships to students graduating from Hutchinson High School, KS. The foundation also gives Educator of the Year Awards.
Financial data: Year ended 12/31/2012. Assets, $4,329,044 (M); Expenditures, $216,954; Total giving, $171,450; Grants to individuals, 33 grants totaling $119,000 (high: $6,000, low: $2,000).
Fields of interest: Education.
International interests: Global Programs.
Type of support: Support to graduates or students of specific schools; Awards/prizes; Undergraduate support.
Application information: Applications accepted.
   Deadline(s): Mar. 15
EIN: 486105748

3432
Christine Dolechek Trust

P.O. Box 128
Ellsworth, KS   67439-0128   (785) 472-3141
Contact: John Thaemert
Application address: 203 N. Douglas, Ellsworth, KS 67439 Tel.: (785)472-3141

Foundation type: Independent foundation
Purpose: Medical scholarships to residents of Ellsworth County, KS.

Financial data: Year ended 01/31/2013. Assets, $218,600 (M); Expenditures, $14,158; Total giving, $10,785.
Fields of interest: Medical school/education.
Type of support: Graduate support.
Application information: Applications not accepted.
> *Additional information:* Unsolicited requests for funds not considered or acknowledged.
EIN: 481042904

3433
Douglas County Community Foundation
900 Massachusetts St., Ste. 406
Lawrence, KS 66044-2868 (785) 843-8727
Contact: Chip Blaser, Exec. Dir.; For grants: Marilyn Hull, Prog. Off.
FAX: (785) 843-8735;
E-mail: dccfoundation@sbcglobal.net; Additional tel.: (785) 843-8735; Grant proposal e-mail: marilynhull@dccfoundation.org; URL: http://www.dccfoundation.org

Foundation type: Community foundation
Purpose: Scholarships for Baldwin High School seniors seeking higher education at a community college, technical school, college or university, and students interested in the practice of professional pharmacy in the Douglas County, KS area.
Publications: Application guidelines; Annual report; Annual report (including application guidelines); Grants list.
Financial data: Year ended 12/31/2012. Assets, $21,132,010 (M); Expenditures, $2,060,787; Total giving, $1,748,165; Grants to individuals, 8 grants totaling $5,500.
Fields of interest: Higher education; Health sciences school/education; Scholarships/financial aid.
Type of support: Scholarships—to individuals.
Application information:
> *Initial approach:* Contact foundation
EIN: 481209687

3434
Leva & Frank Duclos Foundation
c/o Citizens National Bank
115 W. 6th St.
Concordia, KS 66901-0409 (785) 243-3211
FAX: (785) 243-1833; Application address: Citizen National Bank Trust Dept., 115 W 6th St., Concordia, KS 66901 (785)243-3211

Foundation type: Independent foundation
Purpose: Emergency assistance to indigent individuals and families in Cloud, Republic, and adjacent KS counties for medical hardship and loss due to a natural disaster. Net worth of applicants must not exceed $5,000 for individuals and $10,000 for families.
Financial data: Year ended 12/31/2011. Assets, $2,146,950 (M); Expenditures, $104,361; Total giving, $84,690.
Fields of interest: Health care; Safety/disasters; Economically disadvantaged.
Type of support: Emergency funds; Grants for special needs.
Application information: Applications accepted. Application form required.
> *Deadline(s):* Apr. 30 and Nov. 30.
> *Additional information:* Individuals applying for medical hardship needs and disaster requests should contact the Trust Dept. at the bank for current income and net worth guidelines.
EIN: 237222272

3435
D. C. Duer Foundation
P.O. Box 10
Norton, KS 67654-0010

Foundation type: Operating foundation
Purpose: Scholarships to residents of Smith County, KS.
Financial data: Year ended 09/30/2013. Assets, $170,809 (M); Expenditures, $5,032; Total giving, $4,330.
Type of support: Scholarships—to individuals.
Application information: Applications accepted.
> *Additional information:* Contact foundation for current application deadline/guidelines.
EIN: 480947751

3436
Eggleston Educational Trust
P.O. Box 188
Medicine Lodge, KS 67104-0188 (620) 886-3439
Contact: Nola Fowler, Tr.

Foundation type: Independent foundation
Purpose: Scholarships to financially needy graduates of high schools in Barber County, KS.
Financial data: Year ended 08/31/2013. Assets, $342,698 (M); Expenditures, $18,839; Total giving, $16,000; Grants to individuals, 15 grants totaling $15,000 (high: $1,000, low: $1,000).
Fields of interest: Higher education.
Type of support: Support to graduates or students of specific schools; Undergraduate support.
Application information: Application form required.
> *Deadline(s):* Apr. 1
> *Additional information:* Application should be returned to the guidance counselor's office.
EIN: 486320356

3437
Virginia Ehlers Leavenworth High School Scholarship Charitable Educational Fund Trust
P.O. Box 100
McLouth, KS 66054 (913) 796-6133
Contact: Fern H. Braksick, Tr.

Foundation type: Independent foundation
Purpose: Scholarships to deserving high school graduates from Leavenworth High School, KS, Oskaloosa High School, KS, and Jefferson County North High School, KS for continuing education at accredited colleges or universities.
Financial data: Year ended 12/31/2011. Assets, $81,034 (M); Expenditures, $4,293; Total giving, $4,000; Grants to individuals, 4 grants totaling $4,000 (high: $1,000, low: $1,000).
Fields of interest: Higher education.
Type of support: Support to graduates or students of specific schools.
Application information: Applicant must have attended the mentioned high schools for at least one full school term. Recipient must show verification of enrollment in the school of his/her choice prior to receiving payment.
EIN: 486265669

3438
Marlin & Virginia Ehlers Oskaloosa High Scholarship Charitable Educational Trust
P.O. Box 100
McLouth, KS 66054 (913) 796-6133
Contact: Fern H. Braksick, Tr.

Foundation type: Independent foundation
Purpose: Scholarships to students who have attended Oskaloosa High School, KS, for at least one full school term.
Financial data: Year ended 12/31/2011. Assets, $79,324 (M); Expenditures, $4,276; Total giving, $4,000; Grants to individuals, 4 grants totaling $4,000 (high: $1,000, low: $1,000).
Fields of interest: Higher education.
Type of support: Support to graduates or students of specific schools.
Application information: Applications accepted. Application form required.
EIN: 486265672

3439
The Ellis Foundation
(formerly Danny and Willa Ellis Foundation)
P.O. Box 54
Fort Scott, KS 66701-0054 (620) 223-2232
Contact: Danny Ellis, Pres.; Willa Ellis, Secy.-Treas.
FAX: (620) 223-2236;
E-mail: dan@theellisfoundation.org; Additional e-mails:chris@theellisfoundation.org; julie@theellisfoundation.org; URL: http://www.theellisfoundation.org

Foundation type: Public charity
Purpose: Scholarships to high school graduates who have limited resources for postsecondary education.
Financial data: Year ended 06/30/2012. Assets, $11,425,091 (M); Expenditures, $1,658,997; Total giving, $1,149,237; Grants to individuals, totaling $1,108,237.
Fields of interest: Higher education.
Type of support: Scholarships—to individuals; Undergraduate support.
Application information: Applications accepted. Application form required. Application form available on the grantmaker's web site. Interview required.
> *Additional information:* The foundation does not accept scholarship applications from individuals or high schools that are not participating in the foundation's program. See web site for participating schools.
Program description:
> *Scholarship Program:* The foundation awards scholarships of $1,000 each per semester, for up to eight semesters, to students attending a participating college. Scholarships can be used for tuition, books, computer fees, and on-campus dormitory fees. Eligible applicants must have a minimum GPA of 2.5 and present proof of full-time employment (at least 12 credit hours per semester)
EIN: 481093604

3440
John G. Ellis Scholarship Fund
1551 N Waterfront Pkwy.
P.O. Box 637
Wichita, KS 67201-0637 (316) 261-3682
Contact: Brian N. Adams

Foundation type: Independent foundation
Purpose: Scholarships to graduates of El Dorado High School, KS, or any Butler County, KS, high

school to attend Kansas State University, California Maritime Academy, or the University of Southern California.
Financial data: Year ended 12/31/2012. Assets, $432,503 (M); Expenditures, $25,976; Total giving, $21,000; Grants to individuals, 10 grants totaling $21,000 (high: $3,100, low: $500).
Fields of interest: Engineering.
Type of support: Support to graduates or students of specific schools; Undergraduate support.
Application information:
 Initial approach: Letter
 Deadline(s): None
 Additional information: Contact fund for current application guidelines.
EIN: 486250894

3441
Cliff & Nina Fell Foundation
c/o First State Bank
116 W. 6th St.
Larned, KS   67550-3044

Foundation type: Independent foundation
Purpose: Scholarships to residents of Pawnee County, KS attending colleges and universities in KS.
Financial data: Year ended 12/31/2012. Assets, $115,833 (M); Expenditures, $11,995; Total giving, $8,000; Grants to individuals, 4 grants totaling $8,000 (high: $2,000, low: $2,000).
Fields of interest: Higher education.
Type of support: Scholarships—to individuals.
Application information: Applications accepted. Application form required.
 Deadline(s): May 1
EIN: 486332829

3442
Morris Fingersh Scholarship Fund
c/o Valley View Financial Group Trust Co.
5901 College Blvd., Ste. 100
Overland Park, KS   66211-1503   (913) 327-8153
Contact: Gary Hedberg
Application address: 5801 W. 115 St., Overland Park, KS 66211, tel.: (913) 327-8153

Foundation type: Independent foundation
Purpose: Scholarships to financially needy students attending the Hyman Brand Hebrew Academy in Overland Park, KS.
Financial data: Year ended 12/31/2012. Assets, $148,279 (M); Expenditures, $8,105; Total giving, $6,000.
Fields of interest: Elementary school/education; Secondary school/education; Jewish agencies & synagogues.
Type of support: Scholarships—to individuals; Student loans—to individuals.
Application information:
 Initial approach: Letter
 Deadline(s): May 31
EIN: 486235742

3443
Marie G. & Greta M. Fink Scholarship Trust
c/o The Peoples Bank
P.O. Box 307
Smith Center, KS   66967-0307   (785) 454-3332
Application Address: c/o Downs Public Schools, Attn: School Principal, 1306 N. Morgan, Downs, KS 67437

Foundation type: Independent foundation
Purpose: Scholarships to graduates of Downs High School, KS in pursuit of a higher education.
Financial data: Year ended 03/31/2013. Assets, $71,875 (M); Expenditures, $7,952; Total giving, $7,000.
Fields of interest: Higher education.
Type of support: Support to graduates or students of specific schools.
Application information: Applications accepted.
 Initial approach: Letter
 Deadline(s): Apr. 1
EIN: 481163243

3444
Fort Hays State University Foundation
(formerly Fort Hays State University Endowment Association)
P.O. Box 1060
Hays, KS   67601-4010   (785) 628-5620
Contact: Tim Chapman, Pres. and C.E.O.
FAX: (785) 628-5625;
E-mail: foundation@fhsu.edu; Toll Free Tel.: (888)-628-1060; E-Mail for Tim Chapman: tdchapman@fhsu.edu; URL: http://foundation.fhsu.edu/

Foundation type: Public charity
Purpose: Scholarships to students attending Fort Hays State University, and to promote the continuing education of former students of the university.
Financial data: Year ended 06/30/2012. Assets, $51,010,648 (M); Expenditures, $4,486,035.
Fields of interest: Higher education.
Type of support: Support to graduates or students of specific schools.
Application information:
 Initial approach: Telephone or e-mail
EIN: 486108086

3445
R. E. French Family Educational Foundation
P.O. Box 203
Gridley, KS   66852-0203

Foundation type: Independent foundation
Purpose: Scholarships to graduates of Kansas high schools, who have demonstrated the desire to attend a college or university, or who seek vocational training in an accredited vocational training institution.
Financial data: Year ended 06/30/2012. Assets, $11,530,543 (M); Expenditures, $664,188; Total giving, $474,022; Grants to individuals, 284 grants totaling $395,750 (high: $1,500, low: $750).
Fields of interest: Higher education.
Type of support: Undergraduate support.
Application information: Applications accepted. Application form required.
 Initial approach: Letter
 Send request by: Mail
 Applicants should submit the following:
  1) SAT
  2) Photograph
  3) Letter(s) of recommendation
  4) Transcripts
  5) ACT
  6) Essay
 Additional information: Application should also include attendance records.
EIN: 480926521

3446
Blanche E. French Scholarship Foundation
16 W. Jackson
Iola, KS   66749
Contact: Charlotte Young, Tr.
Application address: 605 S.W. Fairland Rd., Topeka, KS 66611

Foundation type: Independent foundation
Purpose: Scholarships to graduating seniors of high schools in Coffey, Woodson and Greenwood counties, KS.
Financial data: Year ended 09/30/2012. Assets, $250,937 (M); Expenditures, $1,628; Total giving, $0.
Type of support: Support to graduates or students of specific schools; Awards/grants by nomination only; Undergraduate support.
Application information: Application form required.
 Applicants should submit the following:
  1) Essay
  2) Transcripts
  3) Photograph
EIN: 480868018

3447
Golden Belt Community Foundation
1307 Williams St.
P.O. Box 1911
Great Bend, KS   67530
Contact: Christy L. Tustin, Exec. Dir.
E-mail: gbcf@goldenbeltcf.org; URL: http://www.goldenbeltcf.org/

Foundation type: Community foundation
Purpose: Scholarships to graduating high school seniors from the Golden Belt, KC area for higher education. One scholarship available to college sophomores from specified area colleges to further their education.
Publications: Application guidelines; Annual report.
Financial data: Year ended 12/31/2012. Assets, $10,629,065 (M); Expenditures, $472,850; Total giving, $234,843; Grants to individuals, 23 grants totaling $15,850.
Fields of interest: Higher education.
Type of support: Scholarships—to individuals; Undergraduate support.
Application information: Applications accepted. Application form required.
 Send request by: On-line
 Deadline(s): Varies
 Additional information: See web site for scholarship descriptions and eligibility criteria.
EIN: 742804940

3448
Grasshopper Trust
c/o Lynn Chance
P.O. Box 50
Fowler, KS   67844   (620) 646-5253
Contact: Vicki McDowell

Foundation type: Independent foundation
Purpose: Scholarships to students who reside, or whose parents reside, in Clark, Ford, Grant, Gray, Meade, Morton, or Stevens counties, KS.
Financial data: Year ended 07/31/2013. Assets, $270,134 (M); Expenditures, $33,565; Total giving, $53,800; Grants to individuals, 140 grants totaling $53,800 (high: $900, low: $100).
Type of support: Scholarships—to individuals.
Application information: Applications accepted. Application form required.

Initial approach: Letter
Deadline(s): Apr. 15
Applicants should submit the following:
1) Essay
2) Financial information
3) SAR
4) Transcripts
Additional information: Essay should be a personal statement handwritten and in ink relevant to your application for a scholarship.
EIN: 486213027

3449
Garnette E. Greene and Ethlyne R. Greene Memorial Scholarship Fund

(formerly G. E. & E. R. Greene Memorial Scholarship Fund)
P. O. Box 570
Goodland, KS   67735-0570   (785) 899-2000
Contact: Darlene R. Lauer, Mgr.

Foundation type: Public charity
Purpose: Scholarships to college-bound graduates of high schools in Cheyenne County, KS.
Financial data: Year ended 12/31/2012. Assets, $719,559 (M); Expenditures, $19,582; Total giving, $9,500; Grants to individuals, totaling $9,500.
Fields of interest: College.
Type of support: Scholarships—to individuals.
Application information: Applications accepted. Application form required.
EIN: 481064924

3450
The Philip D. Griffith Family Charitable Foundation

P.O. Box 313
Neodesha, KS   66757-0313   (620) 325-2626
Contact: Dennis D. Depew, Secy.-Treas.
Application address: 620 Main, Neodesha, KS 66757

Foundation type: Independent foundation
Purpose: Scholarships to graduates of Neodesha High School, KS, and students in Las Vegas, NV.
Publications: Application guidelines.
Financial data: Year ended 12/31/2013. Assets, $25,983 (M); Expenditures, $78,458; Total giving, $68,782; Grants to individuals, 101 grants totaling $68,782 (high: $4,091, low: $250).
Type of support: Support to graduates or students of specific schools; Undergraduate support.
Application information: Application form required.
Send request by: Mail
Deadline(s): Mar. 1
Additional information: Application must include transcript. Incomplete or unsigned applications will not be accepted.
EIN: 481076347

3451
Dane G. Hansen Foundation

P.O. Box 187
Logan, KS   67646-0187   (785) 689-4832
Contact: Don Stahr, Tr.
FAX: (785) 689-4833; URL: http://www.danehansenfoundation.org

Foundation type: Independent foundation
Purpose: Scholarships to graduating high school seniors of the 26 counties in northwest KS to attend KS colleges and universities.

Financial data: Year ended 09/30/2013. Assets, $161,755,823 (M); Expenditures, $7,067,413; Total giving, $5,527,436.
Fields of interest: Vocational education; Higher education; Scholarships/financial aid.
Type of support: Awards/prizes; Technical education support; Undergraduate support.
Application information: Applications accepted. Application form required. Interview required.
Initial approach: Letter or telephone
Deadline(s): Oct. 9 for Vocational Education Scholarships and Community College Scholarships
Applicants should submit the following:
1) Photograph
2) Transcripts
3) Letter(s) of recommendation
4) GPA
5) Essay
Additional information: Scholarship seekers should call or write the foundation for additional eligibility requirements, application forms, and interviews. See web site for eligible counties.
Program descriptions:
Community College Scholarships: Twenty scholarships of $3,000 are available for Kansas Community and Technical College students transferring to an accredited four-year public, private or church related Kansas college or university. For renewal applicants must have completed college work with a 3.0 GPA or better and possess good character and leadership qualities. Scholarship can be renewed for one additional year.
Hansen Leaders of Tomorrow Scholarships: Scholarships of $5,000 each are awarded annually to 10 students planning to attend four-year KS colleges and universities of their choice. Recipients must be graduating high school seniors with at least a 3.5 high school GPA and a record of service and extracurricular activities. Scholarships are awarded on the basis of their "moral and leadership qualities as shown through past participation in community, church, scout, school, and other youth activities, with special emphasis on diligence towards chosen tasks, the recognition accorded them by their peers and a final evaluation by the screening board." Recipients must be proficient in written and verbal skills. Scholarships are renewable for up to three additional years contingent upon recipient maintaining a 3.0 GPA in college.
Hansen Scholar Awards: The same general conditions as set forth in the Leaders of Tomorrow scholarships are observed in the Scholar competition. Up to fifty Hansen Scholar Scholarship Awards are offered annually. They have a stipend of $3,000 and are renewable for one additional year provided the student has attained a 3.0 GPA at the college level. Recipients must attend an accredited four-year public, private or church related Kansas college or university.
Hansen Student Scholarships: One hundred Hansen Student Scholarships may be awarded to qualified high school seniors. The scholarships carry a stipend of $2,000 and are renewable for one additional year, providing the recipient has achieved at least a 3.00 GPA at the college level. With one renewal, the scholarship will be $4,000 over the two-year period. Recipients of the scholarships must attend an accredited community, public, private or church related college or university in Kansas.
EIN: 486121156

3452
Chester and Sylvia Hartley Scholarship Trust

1003 S Pearl
Pratt, KS   67124   (620) 388-1483
Contact: Megan Klausmeyer, Tr.

Foundation type: Independent foundation
Purpose: Scholarships for children and grandchildren of members of Penalosa United Methodist Church. Scholarships for area Kansas students who are not members of the church.
Financial data: Year ended 12/31/2012. Assets, $236,398 (M); Expenditures, $12,754; Total giving, $12,300; Grants to individuals, 4 grants totaling $12,300 (high: $4,100, low: $500).
Fields of interest: Higher education.
Type of support: Undergraduate support.
Application information:
Deadline(s): Dec. 31
Additional information: Unsolicited requests for funds not considered or acknowledged.
EIN: 486353578

3453
Helping Hand Foundation

5370 W. 95th St.
Prairie Village, KS   66207-3204   (913) 383-9248
E-mail: info@helpingfoundation.org; Application address: c/o Rachel Craig, P.O. Box 6861, Leawood, KS 66206-0861, tel.: (913) 385-0604; URL: http://www.helpingfoundation.org

Foundation type: Independent foundation
Purpose: One-time grants to individuals and families of Kansas City, KC who are confronted with crisis situations such as medical expense, housing, and other special needs.
Financial data: Year ended 12/31/2011. Assets, $4,550 (M); Expenditures, $10,000; Total giving, $10,000.
Fields of interest: Economically disadvantaged.
Type of support: Grants for special needs.
Application information: Applications accepted.
Additional information: Cash is not sent to individuals, funding is paid directly to outside parties on behalf of the individuals.
EIN: 421537494

3454
Herbert & Gertrude Henderson Scholarship Foundation

P.O. Box B
Paola, KS   66071-0702   (620) 365-5116

Foundation type: Independent foundation
Purpose: Scholarships for high school seniors for attendance at Allen County Community College, KS.
Financial data: Year ended 12/31/2012. Assets, $337,359 (M); Expenditures, $14,585; Total giving, $10,966; Grants to individuals, 8 grants totaling $10,966 (high: $2,285, low: $1,000).
Fields of interest: College (community/junior).
Type of support: Support to graduates or students of specific schools; Undergraduate support.
Application information: Application form required.
Initial approach: Letter or telephone
Deadline(s): Apr. 1st for fall semester, Dec. 1 for spring semester
Additional information: Application should include transcripts.
EIN: 486322955

3455
Jud W. Hines Honorary Scholarship
P.O. Box 532
Chapman, KS 67431-0532 (785) 922-6515
Contact: Sarah Will, Tr.

Foundation type: Independent foundation
Purpose: Scholarships to graduates of Chapman High School, KS.
Financial data: Year ended 12/31/2012. Assets, $227,813 (M); Expenditures, $4,868; Total giving, $4,200; Grants to individuals, 9 grants totaling $4,200 (high: $750, low: $200).
Type of support: Support to graduates or students of specific schools; Undergraduate support.
Application information: Applications accepted.
  Initial approach: Letter
  Deadline(s): Apr. 1
EIN: 480930179

3456
Jimmy V. & Lucile A. Hoar Memorial Scholarship Fund
P.O. Box 103
Lewis, KS 67552-0103 (620) 324-5650
Contact: Floyd Crockett, Chair.
Application address: 2375 S. Rd., Lewis, KS 67552

Foundation type: Independent foundation
Purpose: Scholarships to graduates of Lewis High School, KS.
Financial data: Year ended 12/31/2012. Assets, $817,993 (M); Expenditures, $49,794; Total giving, $42,000; Grants to individuals, 14 grants totaling $42,000 (high: $3,250, low: $1,500).
Type of support: Support to graduates or students of specific schools.
Application information: Application form required.
  Deadline(s): May 25
EIN: 431917366

3457
Hoover-Koken Foundation, Inc.
811 N. Washington St.
Junction City, KS 66441-2446

Foundation type: Independent foundation
Purpose: Scholarships to residents of Geary County, KS; Jasper County, MO; and Fort Riley, KS.
Financial data: Year ended 12/31/2012. Assets, $1,744,639 (M); Expenditures, $43,985; Total giving, $30,360.
Type of support: Scholarships—to individuals.
Application information:
  Initial approach: Letter or telephone
  Deadline(s): May 1
EIN: 481026087

3458
George Hoy Family Scholarship Fund
P.O. Box 607
Beloit, KS 67420-0607 (785) 738-2942
Application addresses: Office of Principal, Beloit Jr.-Sr. High School, 1711 N. Walnut, Beloit, KS 67420; Office of Principal, St. John's High School, 209 Cherry St., Beloit, KS 67420

Foundation type: Independent foundation
Purpose: Scholarships to graduating seniors at Beloit High School, KS and St. John's High School, Beloit, KS for continuing education at institutions of higher learning.
Financial data: Year ended 12/31/2011. Assets, $59,217 (M); Expenditures, $3,358; Total giving,

$3,000; Grants to individuals, 6 grants totaling $3,000 (high: $500, low: $500).
Fields of interest: Higher education; Scholarships/financial aid.
Type of support: Support to graduates or students of specific schools; Undergraduate support.
Application information: Applications accepted.
  Initial approach: Letter
  Deadline(s): One month before each school term ends
  Additional information: Application should state college and career objectives, and why financial aid is needed.
EIN: 486203636

3459
Ralph & Lucile Hunter Scholarship Trust
c/o Emprise Bank
P.O. Box 2970
Wichita, KS 67201 (785) 628-4408

Foundation type: Independent foundation
Purpose: Scholarships to graduating female students from western Kansas for full time attendance at Fort Hays State University.
Financial data: Year ended 12/31/2012. Assets, $1,381,247 (M); Expenditures, $84,499; Total giving, $69,000.
Fields of interest: Higher education; Young adults, female.
Type of support: Support to graduates or students of specific schools; Undergraduate support.
Application information: Applications accepted. Application form required.
  Deadline(s): Mar. 15
  Additional information: Applicant must have graduated from a Kansas high school, display outstanding citizenship and maintain a 3.0 GPA.
EIN: 486297085

3460
Hutchinson Community Foundation
1 N. Main St., Ste. 501
P.O. Box 298
Hutchinson, KS 67504-0298 (620) 663-5293
Contact: Aubrey Abbott Patterson, Pres.; For grants: Eileen Yamauchi, Donor Svcs. Assoc.
FAX: (620) 663-9277; E-mail: info@hutchcf.org;
Grant inquiry e-mail: eileen@hutchcf.org;
URL: http://www.hutchcf.org

Foundation type: Community foundation
Purpose: Scholarships for postsecondary education to individuals in Hutchison and Reno County, KS.
Publications: Application guidelines; Annual report; Financial statement; Grants list; Informational brochure; Newsletter; Occasional report; Program policy statement.
Financial data: Year ended 12/31/2011. Assets, $32,148,448 (M); Expenditures, $4,686,070; Total giving, $3,498,887.
Type of support: Undergraduate support.
Application information: Applications accepted. Application form required.
  Initial approach: Letter
  Copies of proposal: 15
  Deadline(s): June 1
  Additional information: Applications should include financial information and be sent to the foundation from the schools; Recipients notified within 90 days.
EIN: 481076910

3461
Independence Community College Foundation
P. O. Box 82
Independence, KS 67301-0218 (620) 331-2480
FAX: (620) 331-2480; E-mail: lshaw@indycc.edu;
URL: http://www.indycc.edu/alumni/

Foundation type: Public charity
Purpose: Financial assistance to students in need attending Independence Community College, KC.
Financial data: Year ended 06/30/2012. Assets, $3,424,848 (M); Expenditures, $241,345; Total giving, $62,774; Grants to individuals, totaling $62,774.
Fields of interest: College (community/junior).
Type of support: Support to graduates or students of specific schools.
Application information: Applications not accepted.
  Additional information: Selection is based on academic achievement and financial need. Unsolicited requests for funds not considered or acknowledged.
EIN: 480759236

3462
Jellison Benevolent Society Inc.
P.O. Box 145
Junction City, KS 66441-0145 (785) 762-5566
Contact: Susan E. Williams
FAX: (785) 762-4242;
E-mail: s_williams1948@yahoo.com

Foundation type: Independent foundation
Purpose: Scholarships to residents of KS, with preference shown toward residents of Geary County, KS, to attend undergraduate colleges and technical schools.
Publications: Application guidelines.
Financial data: Year ended 12/31/2011. Assets, $3,601,491 (M); Expenditures, $215,729; Total giving, $153,750.
Fields of interest: Vocational education; Higher education.
Type of support: Undergraduate support.
Application information: Applications accepted. Application form required.
  Initial approach: Letter, telephone, or e-mail
  Send request by: Mail, fax, or e-mail
  Copies of proposal: 1
  Deadline(s): June 20 for fall scholarships, Nov. 20 for spring scholarships and charitable organizations
  Final notification: Recipient notified ten days after meeting
  Applicants should submit the following:
    1) ACT
    2) Budget Information
    3) Financial information
    4) GPA
    5) Letter(s) of recommendation
    6) SAT
    7) Transcripts
  Additional information: Funds paid directly to the educational institution for the benefit of the student only.
EIN: 486106092

3463
Jewish Federation of Greater Kansas City
5801 W. 115th St., Ste. 201
Overland Park, KS 66211-1800 (913) 327-8100
FAX: (913) 327-8110; URL: http://www.jewishkansascity.org

Foundation type: Public charity
Purpose: Camp scholarships are provided to indigent Kansas City Jewish children in 1st-8th grade. The camp program provides activities for 8 weeks in the summer.
Publications: Annual report; Newsletter.
Financial data: Year ended 09/30/2011. Assets, $19,782,197 (M); Expenditures, $7,159,036; Total giving, $3,743,046; Grants to individuals, totaling $9,000.
Fields of interest: Camps; Jewish agencies & synagogues; Children/youth; Economically disadvantaged.
Type of support: Camperships.
Application information:
Initial approach: Letter or tel.
Additional information: Contact foundation for eligibility criteria.
EIN: 440545913

3464
Walter S. and Evan C. Jones Foundation
(also known as Jones Foundation, Inc.)
2501 W. 18th Ave., Ste. D
Emporia, KS 66801-6195 (620) 342-1714
Contact: Sharon L. Tidwell, Exec. Dir.
FAX: (620) 342-4701; E-mail: dir@jonesfdn.org;
URL: http://www.jonesfdn.org

Foundation type: Independent foundation
Purpose: Scholarships to financially needy individuals, and assistance with medical expenses to individuals under the age of 21 who have been continuous residents of Lyon, Coffey, or Osage counties, KS, for a minimum of one year.
Publications: Informational brochure; Program policy statement.
Financial data: Year ended 06/30/2013. Assets, $30,191 (M); Expenditures, $2,253,951; Total giving, $2,076,361.
Fields of interest: Vocational education; Higher education; Hospitals (general); Dental care; Optometry/vision screening; Health care.
Type of support: Technical education support; Undergraduate support; Grants for special needs.
Application information: Applications accepted. Application form required.
Initial approach: Telephone or in person
Send request by: Mail or in person
Deadline(s): July 15 and Dec. 15 for scholarships; None for medical assistance
Applicants should submit the following:
1) Pell Grant
2) FAFSA
3) Financial information
4) SAR
5) Transcripts
Additional information: Scholarship applications and supporting documents including applicant's Institution Financial Award Letter, should be mailed or personally returned to the foundation's office.
EIN: 237384087

3465
Jordaan Foundation, Inc.
P.O. Box 360
Larned, KS 67550-0360 (620) 285-6931

Foundation type: Independent foundation
Purpose: Scholarships to graduates of Pawnee County, KS, high schools to attend KS colleges and universities.
Publications: Application guidelines.
Financial data: Year ended 12/31/2012. Assets, $843,905 (M); Expenditures, $55,939; Total giving, $36,000; Grants to individuals, 24 grants totaling $36,000 (high: $2,000, low: $1,000).
Type of support: Support to graduates or students of specific schools; Undergraduate support.
Application information: Application form required.
Initial approach: In person
Deadline(s): Apr. 5
Additional information: Applications available from Pawnee County high school principals, foundation, or trustee bank; Applications not accepted by mail.
EIN: 480950585

3466
Journalism Education Association
c/o Kansas State Univ.
103 Kedzie Hall
Manhattan, KS 66506-1505 (785) 532-5532
Contact: Kelly Furnas, Exec. Dir.
Additional info.: Candace Perkins Bowen, e-mail: cbowen@kent.edu, tel.: (303) 672-8297
FAX: (785) 532-5563; E-mail: jea@spub.ksu.edu;
URL: http://www.jea.org

Foundation type: Public charity
Purpose: Scholarships to individuals pursuing studies in scholastic journalism.
Financial data: Year ended 06/30/2012. Assets, $1,233,216 (M); Expenditures, $813,140; Total giving, $31,037; Grants to individuals, totaling $31,037.
Fields of interest: Journalism school/education.
Type of support: Scholarships—to individuals.
Application information: Applications accepted. Application form required. Application form available on the grantmaker's web site.
Send request by: Mail
Deadline(s): July 1
Applicants should submit the following:
1) Letter(s) of recommendation
2) Essay
3) Transcripts
Additional information: See web site for additional application guidelines.
Program description:
Future Teacher Scholarships: The association sponsors up to three $1,000 scholarships for education majors who intend to teach scholastic journalism. Each recipient must be an upper-division or master's degree student in a college program designed to prepare him/her for teaching at the secondary-school level. Current secondary-school journalism teachers who are in a degree program to improve their journalism teaching skills are also eligible.
EIN: 410947788

3467
Kansas Association of Child Care Resource and Referral Agencies
1508 A E. Iron
P.O. Box 2294
Salina, KS 67402-2294 (785) 823-3343
Contact: Leadell Ediger, Exec. Dir.
FAX: (785) 823-3385;
E-mail: info@ks.childcareaware.org; Toll-free tel.:
(855)-750-3343; E-mail for Leadell Ediger:

leadell@ks.childcareaware.org; URL: http://www.kaccrra.org

Foundation type: Public charity
Purpose: Scholarships for child care providers in KS to further their education and training.
Financial data: Year ended 12/31/2011. Assets, $2,675,603 (M); Expenditures, $11,621,361; Total giving, $6,035,382; Grants to individuals, totaling $1,188,254.
Fields of interest: Early childhood education.
Type of support: Undergraduate support.
Application information:
Initial approach: Letter
Additional information: Contact foundation for eligibility criteria.
EIN: 481102008

3468
Kansas Athletics Inc.
(formerly University of Kansas Athletic Corp.)
1651 Naismith Dr.
Lawrence, KS 66045-7800 (785) 864-7970
E-mail: kuathletics@ku.edu; URL: http://kuathletics.cstv.com

Foundation type: Public charity
Purpose: Athletic scholarships to full time students enrolled at the University of Kansas.
Financial data: Year ended 06/30/2012. Assets, $78,409,729 (M); Expenditures, $79,336,623; Total giving, $9,950,673; Grants to individuals, totaling $9,134,971.
Fields of interest: Higher education.
Type of support: Scholarships—to individuals; Support to graduates or students of specific schools.
Application information: Applications not accepted.
Additional information: Student athletes must meet certain academic standards and eligibility standards to receive financial aid. Unsolicited requests for funds not considered or acknowledged, as scholarships are only for the University of Kansas students.
EIN: 486033929

3469
Kansas Bar Association
(formerly Kansas Bar Foundation)
1200 S.W. Harrison St.
P.O. Box 1037
Topeka, KS 66612-1806 (785) 234-5696
Contact: Jordan E. Yochim, Exec. Dir.
FAX: (785) 234-3813; E-mail: info@ksbar.org;
E-mail for Jordan E. Yochim: jeyochim@ksbar.org;
URL: http://www.ksbar.org/

Foundation type: Public charity
Purpose: Scholarships to law students and recent law school graduates of KS, to further their law education.
Financial data: Year ended 12/31/2011. Assets, $2,894,232 (M); Expenditures, $357,788; Total giving, $93,184; Grants to individuals, totaling $8,684.
Fields of interest: Law school/education.
Type of support: Scholarships—to individuals.
Application information: Applications accepted. Application form required.
Applicants should submit the following:
1) Transcripts
2) Letter(s) of recommendation
Additional information: Application should also include letter of interest and other supporting documents. Awards vary from $1,000 to

$2,000. See web site for specific requirements for the various scholarships.
EIN: 486116429

3470
Kansas Children's Service League
1365 N. Custer St.
Wichita, KS 67203-6634 (316) 942-4261
Contact: Dona Booe, Pres. and C.E.O.
Toll-free tel.: (877) 530-5275; E-Mail for Dona Booe: dbooe@kcsl.org; URL: https://www.kcsl.org

Foundation type: Public charity
Purpose:
Financial data: Year ended 12/31/2011. Assets, $9,842,605 (M); Expenditures, $16,525,207; Total giving, $83,346; Grants to individuals, totaling $83,346.
Fields of interest: Human services; Adoption; Foster care.
Type of support: Grants for special needs.
Application information: Applications accepted.
Initial approach: Telephone
Additional information: Contact the agency for additional information or eligibility determination.
EIN: 480543749

3471
Kansas Masonic Foundation, Inc.
2909 S.W. Maupin Ln.
Topeka, KS 66614-5335 (785) 357-7646
FAX: (785) 357-7406; E-mail: info@kmfonline.org; URL: http://www.kmfonline.org

Foundation type: Public charity
Purpose: Low interest loans to Kansas residents for attendance at Kansas institutions of higher learning.
Publications: Newsletter.
Financial data: Year ended 03/31/2012. Assets, $26,754,831 (M); Expenditures, $1,027,077; Total giving, $52,510; Grants to individuals, totaling $52,510.
Fields of interest: Higher education.
Type of support: Student loans—to individuals.
Application information: Applications accepted. Application form required. Application form available on the grantmaker's web site. Interview required.
Initial approach: Telephone
Deadline(s): Apr. 15
Applicants should submit the following:
1) Photograph
2) Transcripts
3) Letter(s) of recommendation
4) GPA
5) Financial information
6) Essay
Additional information: Application should also include a copy of you and/or your parents' income tax forms for the last three years. See web site for additional application guidelines.
EIN: 486127355

3472
Kansas State University Foundation
2323 Anderson Ave., Ste. 500
Manhattan, KS 66502-2911 (785) 532-6266
Contact: Fred Cholick, Pres. and C.E.O.
FAX: (785) 532-7545;
E-mail: foundation@found.ksu.edu; Toll-free tel.: (800) 432-1578; E-mail for Fred Cholick:

fcholick@found.ksu.edu; URL: http://www.found.k-state.edu

Foundation type: Public charity
Purpose: Scholarships, awards and prizes for undergraduate and graduate students attending Kansas State University, KS.
Publications: Annual report; Newsletter.
Financial data: Year ended 06/30/2012. Assets, $491,303,240 (M); Expenditures, $74,307,808; Total giving, $44,471,436; Grants to individuals, totaling $9,647,796.
Fields of interest: University; Scholarships/financial aid.
Type of support: Fellowships; Scholarships—to individuals; Awards/prizes.
Application information: Applications not accepted.
Additional information: Scholarships are for Kansas State University students only. Unsolicited requests for funds not considered or acknowledged.
EIN: 480667209

3473
Key Charitable Trust
P.O. Box 389
Fort Scott, KS 66701-0389 (620) 223-2000
Contact: Penny Pollock-Barnes, Tr.

Foundation type: Independent foundation
Purpose: Scholarships to individuals in KS for higher education.
Financial data: Year ended 12/31/2012. Assets, $3,553,334 (M); Expenditures, $150,257; Total giving, $128,860.
Type of support: Undergraduate support.
Application information: Applications accepted.
Initial approach: Letter
Deadline(s): None
EIN: 486107304

3474
Cecil H. Kleppe Scholarship Fund
c/o Michael K. Schmitt
P.O. Box 240
Hiawatha, KS 66434-2306 (785) 742-2181
Contact: Michael K. Schmitt, Tr.
Application address: 117 S. 6th St., Hiawatha, KS 66434

Foundation type: Independent foundation
Purpose: Scholarships only to graduating resident students of high schools in Brown County, KS, who are enrolled in a college, university or vocational school.
Financial data: Year ended 06/30/2010. Assets, $18,750 (M); Expenditures, $162,707; Total giving, $101,000; Grants to individuals, totaling $101,000.
Fields of interest: Vocational education.
Type of support: Support to graduates or students of specific schools; Technical education support; Undergraduate support.
Application information: Applications not accepted.
Additional information: Deadline Apr. 2. Unsolicited requests for funds not considered or acknowledged.
EIN: 486364390

3475
Knights of Columbus Charities Aid Foundation
P.O. Box 280
La Crosse, KS 67548-0280 (785) 222-2537
Contact: Donald L. Wagner, Pres.
URL: http://www.kansas-kofc.org/

Foundation type: Public charity
Purpose: Assistance to people in Kansas with food, clothing, and temporary shelter who have incurred losses due to floods, fire, tornadoes, hurricane and other natural disasters.
Financial data: Year ended 04/30/2012. Assets, $1,218,529 (M); Expenditures, $589,338; Total giving, $504,056; Grants to individuals, totaling $43,742.
Fields of interest: Safety/disasters; Economically disadvantaged.
Type of support: Grants for special needs.
Application information:
Initial approach: Telephone
Additional information: Contact the foundation for eligibility criteria.
EIN: 480698358

3476
Koch Cultural Trust
(formerly Kansas Cultural Trust)
c/o Howard Ellington
255 N. Roosevelt St.
Wichita, KS 67208-3720 (800) 666-9040
URL: http://www.kochculturaltrust.org

Foundation type: Independent foundation
Purpose: Awards to promising visual and performing artists whose study has advanced beyond degree-granting programs and who are or were KS residents or graduates of KS universities and colleges.
Publications: Application guidelines.
Financial data: Year ended 12/31/2012. Assets, $23,869 (M); Expenditures, $142,360; Total giving, $101,600; Grants to individuals, 34 grants totaling $101,600 (high: $5,000, low: $1,000).
Fields of interest: Visual arts; Sculpture; Design; Painting; Performing arts; Dance; Music.
Type of support: Awards/prizes.
Application information: Application form required. Application form available on the grantmaker's web site.
EIN: 480989992

3477
The Fred C. and Mary R. Koch Foundation, Inc.
(formerly The Fred C. Koch Foundation)
4111 E. 37th St. N.
Wichita, KS 67220-3203
Contact: Grant Admin.
Scholarship e-mail: scholarships@fmkfoundation.org
E-mail: email@fmkfoundation.org; URL: http://www.fmkfoundation.org/

Foundation type: Independent foundation
Purpose: Scholarships only to dependents of employees of Koch Industries, Inc., and its subsidiaries.
Publications: Application guidelines.
Financial data: Year ended 12/31/2012. Assets, $31,775,151 (M); Expenditures, $2,127,153; Total giving, $2,043,000; Grants to individuals, 204 grants totaling $405,000 (high: $2,000, low: $2,000).

Fields of interest: Higher education; Scholarships/financial aid.
Type of support: Employee-related scholarships.
Application information: Applications not accepted.
Additional information: Refer to foundation web site for scholarship guidelines.
Company name: Koch Industries, Inc.
EIN: 486113560

3478
Laham Family Foundation
150 N. Market St.
Wichita, KS 67202   (316) 292-3950
Contact: George E. Laham II, Secy.-Treas.

Foundation type: Independent foundation
Purpose: Scholarships and grants to individuals residing in KS.
Financial data: Year ended 07/31/2013. Assets, $7,216 (M); Expenditures, $88,264; Total giving, $78,424.
Fields of interest: Higher education; General charitable giving; Economically disadvantaged.
Type of support: Grants to individuals; Scholarships—to individuals.
Application information: Applications accepted.
Initial approach: Letter
Deadline(s): None
EIN: 810582512

3479
Legacy, A Regional Community Foundation
1216 Main St.
P.O. Box 713
Winfield, KS 67156   (620) 221-7224
Contact: Pamela Moore, Exec. Dir.
FAX: (620) 221-0532;
E-mail: admin@legacyregionalfoundation.org;
Additional tel.: (855) 470-7224; URL: http://www.legacyregionalfoundation.org

Foundation type: Community foundation
Purpose: College scholarships to students of Cowley county, KS and the surrounding area for higher education.
Publications: Application guidelines; Annual report; Financial statement; Grants list; Informational brochure; Newsletter.
Financial data: Year ended 12/31/2012. Assets, $4,235,407 (M); Expenditures, $381,151; Total giving, $172,940; Grants to individuals, totaling $25,716.
Fields of interest: Higher education.
Type of support: Scholarships—to individuals.
Application information: Applications accepted.
Additional information: Students are selected based on leadership potential. Contact the foundation for additional guidelines.
EIN: 481187957

3480
Loofbourrow Educational Trust
c/o D. Pfalzgraf
522 N. Washington Ave.
Wellington, KS 67152-4061

Foundation type: Independent foundation
Purpose: Scholarships to graduates of accredited high schools of Sumner County, KS, for higher education.
Financial data: Year ended 12/31/2012. Assets, $1,465,600 (M); Expenditures, $78,776; Total

giving, $58,750; Grants to individuals, 20 grants totaling $58,750 (high: $3,500, low: $1,500).
Fields of interest: Higher education; Scholarships/financial aid.
Type of support: Support to graduates or students of specific schools; Undergraduate support.
Application information: Application form required.
Deadline(s): Feb. 1
Additional information: Application forms are available from the guidance counselors at the various high schools in Sumner county.
EIN: 486329154

3481
Mansfield Family Foundation
109 E. 3rd St.
Washington, KS 66968   (785) 325-2149
Application address: c/o Mansfield Family Foundation, P.O Box 104 Washington, KS 66968

Foundation type: Independent foundation
Purpose: Scholarships to graduates from Washington County, KS, pursuing postsecondary education.
Financial data: Year ended 12/31/2012. Assets, $562,574 (M); Expenditures, $38,998; Total giving, $31,135; Grants to individuals, 6 grants totaling $15,000 (high: $3,000, low: $1,000).
Fields of interest: Higher education.
Type of support: Support to graduates or students of specific schools; Undergraduate support.
Application information: Applications accepted. Application form required.
Deadline(s): June 15
Applicants should submit the following:
1) SAR
2) Letter(s) of recommendation
3) Essay
4) Transcripts
5) GPA
6) ACT
EIN: 486256918

3482
The Ira and Dena McKinnis Educational Trust
P.O. Box H
Pratt, KS 67124-1108   (620) 672-5533
Contact: Mike Lewis, Tr.

Foundation type: Independent foundation
Purpose: Student loans and scholarships to graduates of high schools in Pratt County, KS.
Financial data: Year ended 12/31/2011. Assets, $598,966 (M); Expenditures, $49,577; Total giving, $31,250; Grants to individuals, 21 grants totaling $31,250 (high: $6,000, low: $750).
Type of support: Scholarships—to individuals; Student loans—to individuals; Support to graduates or students of specific schools.
Application information: Applications accepted.
Initial approach: Letter
Additional information: Application must include personal and academic information.
EIN: 486247592

3483
McPherson Church of Christ Scholarship and Charitable Trust
609 E. Wickersham Dr.
McPherson, KS 67460-2202
Contact: James L. Ketcherside, Tr.

Foundation type: Independent foundation

Purpose: Scholarships to students who participate in McPherson Church of Christ, KS, to attend a college affiliated with the church.
Financial data: Year ended 12/31/2011. Assets, $153,951 (M); Expenditures, $13,485; Total giving, $11,500.
Fields of interest: Higher education; Christian agencies & churches.
Type of support: Scholarships—to individuals.
Application information: Applications accepted. Application form required.
EIN: 746451417

3484
McPherson County Community Foundation
206 S. Main
P.O. Box 616
McPherson, KS 67460   (620) 245-9070
Contact: Becky Goss, C.E.O.
FAX: (620) 245-0238;
E-mail: info@mcphersonfoundation.org; Toll Free Tel.: (866) 245-9070; Grant deadlines and information e-mail:
sharon@mcphersonfoundation.org; URL: http://www.mcphersonfoundation.org/

Foundation type: Community foundation
Purpose: Scholarships to residents of McPherson, KS for higher education.
Publications: Application guidelines; Annual report; Financial statement; Grants list; Informational brochure; Newsletter.
Financial data: Year ended 08/31/2012. Assets, $11,091,012 (M); Expenditures, $899,536; Total giving, $505,520; Grants to individuals, 222 grants totaling $138,009.
Fields of interest: Higher education.
Type of support: Scholarships—to individuals.
Application information: Applications accepted. Application form required. Application form available on the grantmaker's web site.
Send request by: Mail or fax
Copies of proposal: 1
Deadline(s): Mar. 1
Final notification: 60 days after receipt of application
Applicants should submit the following:
1) Transcripts
2) Essay
3) ACT
EIN: 481238797

3485
The Amy E. Mehaffy Foundation, Inc.
P.O. Box 437
Baxter Springs, KS 66713-0437

Foundation type: Independent foundation
Purpose: Scholarships to graduating seniors from Baxter Springs, Kansas High School, KS for continuing education at accredited institutions of higher learning.
Financial data: Year ended 06/30/2013. Assets, $414,875 (M); Expenditures, $11,257; Total giving, $7,500; Grants to individuals, 3 grants totaling $7,500 (high: $3,000, low: $1,500).
Fields of interest: Higher education.
Type of support: Support to graduates or students of specific schools.
Application information: Applications accepted.
EIN: 486284765

3486
The Mitchelson Foundation, Inc.
P.O. Box 610
Pittsburg, KS 66762-0610

Foundation type: Independent foundation
Purpose: Scholarships to high school graduates from Pittsburg, KS for postsecondary education.
Financial data: Year ended 12/31/2012. Assets, $1,436,060 (M); Expenditures, $122,729; Total giving, $109,500; Grants to individuals, 5 grants totaling $8,000 (high: $2,000, low: $1,000).
Fields of interest: Higher education.
Type of support: Scholarships—to individuals.
Application information: Applications accepted.
  Additional information: Contact the foundation for application guidelines.
EIN: 481158378

3487
Moberley F H Scholarship Trust
c/o Trust Tax Dept.
P.O. Box 1
Wichita, KS 67201-5001 (620) 582-2181
Contact: Linda Basnett
Application address: P. O. Box 721, Coldwater, KS 670290721, tel.: (620) 582-2181

Foundation type: Independent foundation
Purpose: Scholarships to graduates of Comanche County, KS, high schools.
Financial data: Year ended 04/30/2013. Assets, $226,141 (M); Expenditures, $14,984; Total giving, $10,000; Grants to individuals, 10 grants totaling $10,000 (high: $1,000, low: $1,000).
Type of support: Support to graduates or students of specific schools; Undergraduate support.
Application information: Application form required.
  Deadline(s): May 10
  Additional information: Application must also include Family Financial Statement (FFS), Financial Aid Package, personal statement, transcripts, and three references.
EIN: 481002542

3488
The Monarch Cement Company Academic Achievement Award
(formerly Monarch Cement Co. Academic Achievement Award)
P.O. Box 1000
Humboldt, KS 66748-0900 (620) 473-2251

Foundation type: Company-sponsored foundation
Purpose: Scholarships to graduating seniors of Humboldt High School, Humboldt, KS for higher education.
Financial data: Year ended 12/31/2012. Assets, $115,448 (M); Expenditures, $4,390; Total giving, $3,174; Grants to individuals, 4 grants totaling $3,174 (high: $1,595, low: $427).
Fields of interest: Higher education.
Type of support: Support to graduates or students of specific schools; Undergraduate support.
Application information:
  Initial approach: Letter
  Send request by: Mail
  Deadline(s): Prior to graduation
  Applicants should submit the following:
    1) Financial information
    2) Essay
  Additional information: Applicants must have a GPA in the top 10 percent of the graduating class.
EIN: 481055534

3489
Roy L. & Aleata M. Moore Scholarship Fund
117 S. 6th St.
P.O. Box 240
Hiawatha, KS 66434-2306 (785) 742-2181
Contact: Michael K. Schmitt, Tr.
E-mail: mschmitt@rainbowtel.net

Foundation type: Independent foundation
Purpose: Scholarships to graduating seniors of Hiawatha High School, KS, who will enroll in a university, college, community college, graduate school, or vocational or proprietary school.
Financial data: Year ended 05/31/2013. Assets, $2,111,110 (M); Expenditures, $123,340; Total giving, $98,275; Grants to individuals, 100 grants totaling $98,275.
Fields of interest: Vocational education; Higher education; Scholarships/financial aid.
Type of support: Scholarships—to individuals; Support to graduates or students of specific schools.
Application information: Applications accepted. Application form required.
  Additional information: Application must include financial information and three reference questionnaires.
EIN: 486348470

3490
Thomas D. Morgan Irrevocable Trust No. 1
120 S. State St.
Norton, KS 67654-2142 (785) 877-3985
Contact: Warren A. White, Chair.
Application address: 302 N.W. St., Norton, KS 67654 Tel.: (785) 877-3985

Foundation type: Independent foundation
Purpose: Scholarships to graduating high school seniors of Norton Community High School, KS for postsecondary education.
Financial data: Year ended 06/30/2013. Assets, $306,860 (M); Expenditures, $59,332; Total giving, $41,500; Grants to individuals, 14 grants totaling $41,500 (high: $4,000, low: $2,000).
Fields of interest: Vocational education, post-secondary; Higher education.
Type of support: Support to graduates or students of specific schools; Undergraduate support.
Application information: Applications accepted. Application form required.
  Deadline(s): May 15 for fall semester and two and one half months prior to start of semester for spring and summer
  Additional information: Application forms are distributed at school.
EIN: 481038549

3491
Moyer Brothers Educational Trust
P.O. Box 413
Abilene, KS 67410-0413 (785) 263-1370
Contact: Robert H. Royer, Jr., Tr.

Foundation type: Independent foundation
Purpose: Scholarships to graduating high school seniors from Abilene High School or Chapman High School, KS for postsecondary education.
Financial data: Year ended 12/31/2012. Assets, $54,069 (M); Expenditures, $14,041; Total giving, $14,000; Grants to individuals, 7 grants totaling $14,000 (high: $2,000, low: $2,000).
Fields of interest: Higher education.

Type of support: Support to graduates or students of specific schools; Undergraduate support.
Application information: Applications accepted. Application form required.
  Deadline(s): Apr. 15
  Additional information: Application can be obtained from the trustee.
EIN: 481010595

3492
Irene Murdock Educational Trust
P.O. Box 1120
Dodge City, KS 67801 (620) 227-8586
Application address: The Respective School Board, Local, Ness Country, KS 67560

Foundation type: Independent foundation
Purpose: Scholarships to former graduates of Ness County, KS high schools to attend college in Kansas.
Financial data: Year ended 12/31/2012. Assets, $170,431 (M); Expenditures, $3,134; Total giving, $738; Grants to individuals, 8 grants totaling $738 (high: $300, low: $62).
Fields of interest: Higher education.
Type of support: Scholarships—to individuals.
Application information: Applications accepted. Application form required.
  Initial approach: Letter
  Deadline(s): None
  Additional information: Applications should be mailed to the applicant's school board.
EIN: 746456632

3493
Naftzger Fund for Fine Arts
c/o Southwest National Bank
P.O. Box 1401
Wichita, KS 67201 (316) 267-5259
Application Address: c/o Naftzger Auditions, 225 W. Douglas Ste. 207 Century II Concert Hall

Foundation type: Independent foundation
Purpose: Awards to young KS, MO, or OK pianists, vocalists, and instrumentalists who are winners of the Naftzger Young Artist Competition.
Financial data: Year ended 12/31/2012. Assets, $873,041 (M); Expenditures, $61,519; Total giving, $55,649.
Fields of interest: Performing arts; Music.
Type of support: Awards/prizes.
Application information: Applications accepted. Application form required.
  Deadline(s): Mar.
  Additional information: Application must include tape recording. Auditions may be required for finalists.
EIN: 486106125

3494
Lawrence R. Nell Trust
c/o Commerce Bank, N.A.
P.O. Box 637
Wichita, KS 67201-0637 (800) 627-6808
Contact: Brian Adams

Foundation type: Independent foundation
Purpose: Scholarships to graduates of Sedgwick County, KS, high schools who are pursuing graduate study in medicine or some other healthcare field and will return to KS to practice.
Financial data: Year ended 09/30/2013. Assets, $582,560 (M); Expenditures, $36,435; Total giving, $26,500; Grants to individuals, 19 grants totaling $26,500 (high: $2,000, low: $500).

Fields of interest: Medical school/education; Health care.
Type of support: Support to graduates or students of specific schools; Graduate support; Undergraduate support.
Application information: Applications not accepted.
Additional information: Unsolicited requests for funds not considered or acknowledged.
EIN: 486274160

3495
Hazel T. Nelson Scholarship Fund
c/o Citizens Bank & Trust Co.
P.O. Box 360
Hiawatha, KS   66434-0360   (785) 742-2101
Contact: James Bush, Tr.

Foundation type: Independent foundation
Purpose: Scholarships to graduates of Brown County, KS, high schools for postsecondary education.
Financial data: Year ended 04/30/2013. Assets, $269,694 (M); Expenditures, $16,822; Total giving, $14,400; Grants to individuals, 14 grants totaling $14,400 (high: $1,200, low: $900).
Fields of interest: Higher education.
Type of support: Support to graduates or students of specific schools; Undergraduate support.
Application information: Applications accepted. Application form required.
Initial approach: Letter or telephone
Deadline(s): Vary
Additional information: Applications available from Citizens State Bank, KS.
EIN: 481046006

3496
Noah's Ark Christian Day Care Center, Inc.
208 N. Lincoln Ave.
Chanute, KS   66720-1822   (620) 431-1832
Contact: Mary Kay Barclay, Exec. Dir.

Foundation type: Public charity
Purpose: Funds to KS home care providers, and provides instructional material, workshops, and in-service training for teachers and day-care workers.
Financial data: Year ended 09/30/2011. Assets, $291,123 (M); Expenditures, $3,314,453; Total giving, $2,832,748; Grants to individuals, totaling $2,832,748.
Fields of interest: Children/youth, services; Day care.
Type of support: Grants to individuals; In-kind gifts.
Application information:
Initial approach: Letter
Additional information: Contact foundation for eligibility criteria.
EIN: 480960961

3497
S. T. & Mabel I. Nuttycomb Charitable Trust
(formerly S. T. & Mabel I. Nuttycomb Charitable Trust No. 2)
P.O. Box 266
Phillipsburg, KS   67661   (785) 543-6561

Foundation type: Independent foundation
Purpose: Scholarships to students from Phillips and Norton Counties, KS planning to attend a post secondary institution.

Financial data: Year ended 09/30/2013. Assets, $989,250 (M); Expenditures, $68,757; Total giving, $47,000.
Fields of interest: Higher education.
Type of support: Scholarships—to individuals.
Application information: Applications accepted. Application form required.
Deadline(s): Dec. 31
Additional information: Application form may be obtained from any Phillips or Norton County, Kansas high school principal or counselor.
EIN: 481027799

3498
Arthur F. Pape Educational Fund Trust
1017 Ctr. P.O. 150
Marysville, KS   66508

Foundation type: Independent foundation
Purpose: Student loans to graduates of high schools in Marshall County, KS, to attend trade schools, and two- and four-year colleges.
Financial data: Year ended 07/31/2013. Assets, $828,628 (M); Expenditures, $25,131; Total giving, $0.
Fields of interest: Vocational education; Higher education.
Type of support: Student loans—to individuals; Support to graduates or students of specific schools.
Application information: Application form required.
Deadline(s): July 1
Applicants should submit the following:
1) GPA
2) Financial information
Additional information: Application must also include information on the college or university the student is planning to attend. Loans are limited to $1,500 per semester, or $3,000 per year. The maximum loan is $12,000 over a period of six years. The interest on the loan must be repaid semi-annually while the student is in school. The principal must be repaid on an amortized basis after graduation, termination of schooling, or six years from the time of the initial loan. The minimum monthly payment is $75. The maximum repayment term for a loan of $9,001 to $12,000 is ten years; for a loan of $6,001 to $9,000 is eight years; and for a loan of less than $6,000, up to six years. The current interest rate is 6.5 percent. The parents of the recipients must co-sign the loan.
EIN: 480941171

3499
W.N. Parsons Scholarship Foundation
P.O. Box C
Pratt, KS   67124-1103   (800) 889-9887
Contact: Wyan Alexander
Application address: c/o Peoples Bank, 101 E. Main St., Coldwater, KS 67029-9757

Foundation type: Independent foundation
Purpose: Scholarships to residents of Commanche, Kiowa, and Clark counties, KS, for attendance at vocational and trade schools, and community colleges.
Financial data: Year ended 12/31/2011. Assets, $560,278 (M); Expenditures, $39,249; Total giving, $34,500.
Fields of interest: Vocational education.
Type of support: Technical education support; Undergraduate support.

Application information: Applications accepted. Application form required.
Deadline(s): None
Additional information: Application must include GPA and a personal statement.
EIN: 481086241

3500
Frances Patterson Trust
P.O. Box 332
Fredonia, KS   66736   (620) 378-2172

Foundation type: Independent foundation
Purpose: Scholarships to graduates of Fredonia High School, KS pursuing higher education.
Financial data: Year ended 12/31/2011. Assets, $124,249 (M); Expenditures, $4,680; Total giving, $4,500; Grants to individuals, 5 grants totaling $4,500 (high: $1,125, low: $500).
Fields of interest: Higher education.
Type of support: Support to graduates or students of specific schools; Undergraduate support.
Application information: Applications accepted.
Initial approach: Letter
Deadline(s): Varies
Additional information: Application should be a letter of no more than three pages with appropriate attachments.
EIN: 446008159

3501
George & Belle Pearce Trust
P.O. Box 913
Hutchinson, KS   67504-0913   (620) 694-2258
Contact: Timothy G. Givan
Application address: 1 North Main, Hutchinson, KS 67501, tel.: (620) 694-2258

Foundation type: Independent foundation
Purpose: Scholarships only to residents of Hutchinson and Reno County, KS, who are attending Hutchinson Community College, KS.
Financial data: Year ended 12/31/2012. Assets, $507,789 (M); Expenditures, $35,136; Total giving, $28,000.
Type of support: Support to graduates or students of specific schools; Undergraduate support.
Application information: Applications accepted.
Initial approach: Letter
Additional information: Contact Hutchinson Community College for application guidelines.
EIN: 486186188

3502
Evelyn Perdue Education Trust
(formerly Evelyn Perdue Education Fund)
c/o Midwest Trust Company
5901 College Blvd.
Overland Park, KS   66211   (913) 837-2941
Contact: Amy Wright
Application address: c/o Louisburg High School, 505 E. Amity St., Louisburg, KS 66053, tel.:(913) 837-2941

Foundation type: Independent foundation
Purpose: Scholarships to students or graduates of Unified School District No. 416, Louisburg, KS, for attendance at colleges, universities, or vocational schools.
Financial data: Year ended 09/30/2013. Assets, $560,775 (M); Expenditures, $31,274; Total giving, $22,500; Grants to individuals, 9 grants totaling $22,500 (high: $2,500, low: $2,500).
Fields of interest: Vocational education; Higher education.

Type of support: Support to graduates or students of specific schools; Technical education support; Undergraduate support.
Application information: Applications accepted. Application form required.
　Deadline(s): May 1
　Applicants should submit the following:
　　1) Financial information
　　2) Letter(s) of recommendation
　　3) Transcripts
EIN: 486297052

3503
Peterson Industries Foundation
136 S. Main
P.O. Box 307
Smith Center, KS　66967-0307　(785) 282-6825
Application address: Peterson Industries, Inc., 617 E. Hwy. 36 Smith Center, KS 66967, tel.: (785) 282-6825

Foundation type: Company-sponsored foundation
Purpose: Scholarships to children or spouses of employees of Peterson Industries pursuing a college or vocational educational training program.
Financial data: Year ended 03/31/2013. Assets, $60,589 (M); Expenditures, $3,126; Total giving, $2,300.
Fields of interest: Vocational education, post-secondary; Higher education.
Type of support: Employee-related scholarships.
Application information: Applications accepted.
　Initial approach: Letter
　Deadline(s): June 1
　Additional information: Applicants must have GED or be a graduate of an accredited high school.
Company name: Peterson Industries, Inc.
EIN: 481158653

3504
Pi Beta Phi Educational Foundation
c/o Douglas C. Miller
5735 High Dr.
Shawnee Mission, KS　66208-1126
Contact: Joanna Glaze, V.P.
Application address: 1023 Westover Rd., Kansas City, MO 64113-1123

Foundation type: Independent foundation
Purpose: Scholarships to female students at the University of Kansas who have had a 2.21 GPA for the previous two years.
Financial data: Year ended 09/30/2013. Assets, $1,363,032 (M); Expenditures, $57,558; Total giving, $48,862; Grants to individuals, 2 grants totaling $8,000 (high: $4,000, low: $4,000).
Fields of interest: Women.
Type of support: Support to graduates or students of specific schools; Undergraduate support.
Application information:
　Send request by: Mail
　Deadline(s): Mar. 1
　Applicants should submit the following:
　　1) Letter(s) of recommendation
　　2) GPA
　　3) Financial information
　Additional information: Applicant must demonstrate financial need. Applicant do not have to be a member of a sorority.
EIN: 486111427

3505
Donald R. Pitts & Zelma C. Pitts Scholarship Fund
c/o The Peoples Bank
P.O. Box 307
Smith Center, KS　66967-0307

Foundation type: Independent foundation
Purpose: Scholarships to graduates of Smith Center High School, KS planning to attend an accredited university, college, junior college, or vocational/technical school.
Financial data: Year ended 03/31/2013. Assets, $104,341 (M); Expenditures, $5,317; Total giving, $4,164.
Fields of interest: Vocational education, post-secondary; Higher education; College (community/junior).
Type of support: Support to graduates or students of specific schools; Technical education support.
Application information: Applications accepted. Application form required.
　Deadline(s): Apr. 1
　Applicants should submit the following:
　　1) Transcripts
　　2) GPA
　　3) Essay
　Additional information: Application should also include scholastic, extracurricular activities, work history, achievements and accomplishments.
EIN: 486364411

3506
Laura E. Porter Trust
P.O. Box H
Pratt, KS　67124-1108　(620) 672-5533
Contact: James Van Blaricum, Tr.

Foundation type: Independent foundation
Purpose: Student loans and scholarships to male graduates from Pratt County Community College, KS, to further their education at universities approved by the trustees.
Financial data: Year ended 12/31/2011. Assets, $1,406,500 (M); Expenditures, $71,470; Total giving, $32,750; Grants to individuals, 17 grants totaling $32,750 (high: $5,000, low: $750); Loans to individuals, 9 loans totaling $49,000.
Fields of interest: Higher education; Men.
Type of support: Student loans—to individuals; Support to graduates or students of specific schools; Undergraduate support.
Application information: Applications accepted.
　Deadline(s): None
　Additional information: Application should include general, personal and academic information.
EIN: 486105318

3507
William Preston & Belvah McFadden Scholarship Fund
P.O. Box B
Paola, KS　66071　(913) 294-3811

Foundation type: Independent foundation
Purpose: Two-year scholarships to financially needy graduates of high schools in Allen County, KS, and to children of residents of Allen County, KS, for full-time study at a four-year Kansas State Board of Regents' college or university.
Publications: Application guidelines; Informational brochure.
Financial data: Year ended 06/30/2013. Assets, $1,269,341 (M); Expenditures, $46,999; Total

giving, $35,000; Grants to individuals, 7 grants totaling $35,000 (high: $5,000, low: $5,000).
Type of support: Undergraduate support.
Application information: Application form required.
　Deadline(s): Nov. 1
　Applicants should submit the following:
　　1) Essay
　　2) Photograph
　　3) Financial information
　　4) Transcripts
　　5) ACT
　Additional information: Application should also include attendance record. Forms may be obtained from high school guidance counselors and Team Bank, N.A. No scholarship shall be given to any applicant who has been a student at a community college that is supported by taxes levied upon the taxpayers of that county.
EIN: 481070866

3508
Florence M. Robinson Scholarship Trust
c/o Midwest Trust Co.
5901 College
Overland Park, KS　66211-1834　(785) 229-8020
Contact: Ryan Cobbs, Principal
Applicatio address: c/o Ottawa High School, 11th ASH, Ottawa, KS 66067

Foundation type: Independent foundation
Purpose: Scholarships to students of Unified School District No. 290, Ottawa, KS.
Financial data: Year ended 08/31/2013. Assets, $343,122 (M); Expenditures, $19,189; Total giving, $12,940; Grants to individuals, 22 grants totaling $12,940 (high: $720, low: $350).
Fields of interest: Vocational education; Teacher school/education.
Type of support: Support to graduates or students of specific schools; Undergraduate support.
Application information: Application form required.
　Deadline(s): May 1
　Applicants should submit the following:
　　1) Transcripts
　　2) GPA
　　3) Letter(s) of recommendation
　Additional information: One letter of recommendation must be from someone in the community.
EIN: 486295973

3509
David and Mary P. Rush Educational Trust
c/o Dennis Bieker
P.O. Box 579
Hays, KS　67601-0579　(785) 625-3537

Foundation type: Independent foundation
Purpose: Scholarships to financially needy graduates of Graham County, KS, high schools who are full-time students and have at least a 2.0 GPA.
Financial data: Year ended 01/31/2012. Assets, $5,404,716 (M); Expenditures, $322,876; Total giving, $219,000.
Fields of interest: Higher education.
Type of support: Scholarships—to individuals; Support to graduates or students of specific schools.
Application information: Application form required.
　Deadline(s): May 1
　Additional information: Student must demonstrate financial need. Awards are paid

to the educational institution on behalf of the students.
EIN: 486243254

3510
Greater Salina Community Foundation
113 N. 7th St., Ste. 201
P.O. Box 2876
Salina, KS   67402-2876   (785) 823-1800
Contact: Betsy Wearing, Pres.
FAX: (785) 823-9370;
E-mail: communityfoundation@gscf.org;
URL: http://www.gscf.org

Foundation type: Community foundation
Purpose: Scholarships for students residing in or around Saline County, KS for higher education.
Publications: Annual report; Financial statement; Newsletter.
Financial data: Year ended 06/30/2012. Assets, $77,404,131 (M); Expenditures, $3,732,513; Total giving, $3,252,409; Grants to individuals, 306 grants totaling $122,263 (high: $2,500, low: $15).
Fields of interest: Higher education; Business school/education; Law school/education; Engineering school/education; Athletics/sports, baseball.
Type of support: Grants to individuals; Scholarships—to individuals; Support to graduates or students of specific schools; Awards/prizes; Undergraduate support.
Application information: Applications accepted. Application form required. Application form available on the grantmaker's web site.
> *Send request by:* Mail application and attachments to foundation
> *Copies of proposal:* 14
> *Deadline(s):* Varies
> *Additional information:* See web site for all scholarship forms and guidelines.
Program descriptions:
> *Scholarship Funds:* The foundation administers 25 scholarship funds. These scholarships are funded by donors who believe in the youth of the local area and beyond, and want to support their pursuit of higher education. Each scholarship fund has specific eligibility criteria which were defined by the donor when the fund was established. See web site for additional information.
> *Youth Baseball Grants:* Grants are reserved for individual players or teams who play in a local league (traveling teams are not eligible), and who might otherwise not be able to participate in baseball due to limited financial resources.
EIN: 481215503

3511
Sarver Charitable Trust
c/o The Peoples Bank
P.O. Box 307
Smith Center, KS   66967-0307   (785) 346-5445
Application address: c/o Paul Gregory, P.O. Box 12, Osborne, KS 67473

Foundation type: Independent foundation
Purpose: Scholarships to graduating high school students and current college students from Osborne County, KS.
Financial data: Year ended 12/31/2012. Assets, $11,540,941 (M); Expenditures, $383,440; Total giving, $281,436; Grants to individuals, 136 grants totaling $117,950 (high: $1,800, low: $300).
Type of support: Undergraduate support.

Application information: Applications accepted. Application form required.
> *Deadline(s):* Apr. 1
> *Applicants should submit the following:*
> 1) Transcripts
> 2) GPA
EIN: 486298990

3512
Elma Schmidt Scholarship Fund
(formerly Dodge City Business & Professional Women's Club-Elma Schmidt Fund)
P.O. Box 1803
Dodge City, KS   67801-1803   (620) 227-8803
Contact: Patty Huckaby, Pres.

Foundation type: Independent foundation
Purpose: Scholarships to financially needy women from southwestern KS who are U.S. citizens, have a high school degree or GED, and are enrolled in six or more credits per semester or in a qualified vocational program.
Financial data: Year ended 03/31/2013. Assets, $191,392 (M); Expenditures, $12,547; Total giving, $9,000; Grants to individuals, 9 grants totaling $9,000 (high: $2,646, low: $300).
Fields of interest: Vocational education; Women.
Type of support: Technical education support; Undergraduate support.
Application information: Applications accepted. Application form required.
> *Deadline(s):* Apr. 1 for fall semester and Nov. 1 for spring semester.
> *Additional information:* Application must include a transcript, GED certificate and a personal statement of 300 words or less.
EIN: 237430868

3513
Paul A. & Daisy E. Schuneman Scholarship Trust
P.O. Box 360
Hiawatha, KS   66434-2231   (785) 742-2101
Contact: James Bush

Foundation type: Independent foundation
Purpose: Scholarships to graduates of Hiawatha High School, KS for postsecondary education.
Financial data: Year ended 12/31/2011. Assets, $337,086 (M); Expenditures, $31,457; Total giving, $28,775; Grants to individuals, 46 grants totaling $11,250 (high: $250, low: $250).
Fields of interest: Higher education.
Type of support: Support to graduates or students of specific schools.
Application information: Application form required.
> *Deadline(s):* Varies
EIN: 336324829

3514
Sidwell Charitable Trust
P.O. Box 757
Winfield, KS   67156-0754   (620) 221-4600
Contact: Gretchen Herlocker
Application address: P.O. Box 754, Winfield, KS 67156

Foundation type: Operating foundation
Purpose: Grants to financially needy individuals over the age of 60 who reside in Winfield, KS.
Financial data: Year ended 12/31/2011. Assets, $167,143 (M); Expenditures, $46,906; Total giving, $40,836; Grants to individuals, 47 grants totaling $40,836 (high: $3,000, low: $150).

Fields of interest: Aging; Economically disadvantaged.
Type of support: Grants for special needs.
Application information: Applications accepted. Application form required.
> *Deadline(s):* None
> *Additional information:* Application should include a personal statement.
EIN: 486290978

3515
Smick Memorial Loan Fund
(formerly Citizens Scholarship Foundation)
P.O. Box 362
Oberlin, KS   67749
Contact: Ken Shobe, Secy.-Treas.
Application address: P.O. Box 263, Oberlin, KS 67749

Foundation type: Independent foundation
Purpose: Interest-free loans to students graduating from high schools in Decatur County, KS, to attend colleges or other approved postsecondary schools.
Financial data: Year ended 12/31/2012. Assets, $172,175 (M); Expenditures, $302; Total giving, $14,625; Grants to individuals, 15 grants totaling $14,625 (high: $1,125, low: $500).
Type of support: Support to graduates or students of specific schools; Undergraduate support.
Application information: Applications accepted. Application form required.
> *Initial approach:* Letter
> *Deadline(s):* July 1
EIN: 237121059

3516
H. L. Snyder Medical Foundation
(formerly H.L. Snyder Medical Research Institute)
1407 Wheat Rd.
Winfield, KS   67156-4705   (620) 221-4080
Contact: C. John Snyder, Exec. Dir.
E-mail: tsmith@snydermri.org; URL: http://www.snydermf.org

Foundation type: Public charity
Purpose: Scholarships to residents of Winfield, KS, who are seeking education in the medical and biomedical fields. Grants to residents of Winfield, KS, who are healthcare professionals including hospital or nursing home employees, lab and x-ray techs, aides, nurses, and LPNs who wish to advance their knowledge and skills in caring for their patients.
Publications: Application guidelines; Annual report; Informational brochure.
Financial data: Year ended 06/30/2012. Assets, $8,771,461 (M); Expenditures, $423,295; Total giving, $352,107; Grants to individuals, totaling $67,812.
Fields of interest: Medical school/education; Formal/general education; Biomedicine.
Type of support: Research; Undergraduate support.
Application information: Applications accepted. Application form required. Application form available on the grantmaker's web site.
> *Initial approach:* Download application form
> *Deadline(s):* May 1 for scholarships, Rolling basis for Healthcare grants
> *Additional information:* Application for scholarship should include letters of recommendation, financial information and an essay. Application for healthcare professional should include an essay and budget information. See web site for complete program information.

Program descriptions:

Healthcare Grants: Grants are available to residents of Winfield who are going into or already are in the healthcare and bioscience field, and who would like to advance their knowledge and skill. Applicants must be a resident of Winfield for the last three years, or a graduate of Winfield High School (USD 465), and must be enrolled in a healthcare or bioscience program. Requests focusing on veterinary medicine, acupuncture, chiropractics, Chinese herbal medicine, homeopathy, or similar related fields will not be accepted.

Scholarships: Scholarships are available to assist Winfield students who are going into the healthcare and bioscience field. Eligible applicants must be a resident of Winfield for the last three years or a graduate of Winfield High School (USD 465), who have a 3.0 GPA or higher, and who are enrolled full-time (12 hours or more) in an accredited university or college program in the healthcare field. Scholarships are unavailable to students who are studying veterinary medicine, acupuncture, chiropractics, Chinese herbal medicine, homeopathy, or similar related fields.
EIN: 480622380

3517

South Central Community Foundation
114 W. 5th St.
P.O. Box 8624
Pratt, KS   67124   (620) 672-7929
Contact: Bekki Pribil, Exec. Dir.
FAX: (620) 672-7669;
E-mail: sccf@southcentralcommunityfoundation.com; Additional e-mail: ed@sccfks.org; URL: http://sccfks.org/

Foundation type: Community foundation
Purpose: Scholarships to graduating high school seniors of Barber, Comanche, Kiowa, Kingman, Pratt, Reno or Stafford counties, KS for postsecondary education.
Publications: Application guidelines; Annual report; Informational brochure; Newsletter.
Financial data: Year ended 12/31/2012. Assets, $11,705,721 (M); Expenditures, $395,368; Total giving, $213,948.
Fields of interest: Higher education.
Type of support: Scholarships—to individuals; Support to graduates or students of specific schools; Undergraduate support.
Application information: Applications accepted. Application form required.
   Initial approach: Application
   Send request by: Mail or hand-deliver
   Deadline(s): Apr. 1
   Additional information: See web site for complete listing of scholarships, including application forms and guidelines.
EIN: 481156704

3518

Southwest Kansas Area Agency On Aging, Inc.
P.O. Box 1636
Dodge City, KS   67801-1636   (620) 225-8230
FAX: (620) 225-8240;
E-mail: swkaaa@hotmail.com; Toll-free tel.: (800) 742-9531; URL: http://www.swkaaa.org/

Foundation type: Public charity
Purpose: Financial assistance to elderly Kansans age 60 or older, and disabled and handicapped individuals living in southwest, KS with rental

assistance, food, in home care, legal services and other needs.
Publications: Informational brochure.
Financial data: Year ended 09/30/2011. Assets, $1,534,721 (M); Expenditures, $5,275,239; Total giving, $2,224,385; Grants to individuals, totaling $2,224,385.
Fields of interest: Aging; Disabilities, people with; Economically disadvantaged.
Type of support: Grants for special needs.
Application information:
   Initial approach: E-mail
   Additional information: Applicants should contact the agency for eligibility determination.
EIN: 480854950

3519

Melvin Spitcaufsky Memorial Foundation
c/o Diane Peters Accounting Svcs.
10435 Bond St.
Overland Park, KS   66214-2717
Contact: Larry S. Spitcaufsky, Pres. and Treas.

Foundation type: Independent foundation
Purpose: Scholarships to Arrow Truck Sales employees and their families.
Financial data: Year ended 12/31/2012. Assets, $1,880,533 (M); Expenditures, $100,850; Total giving, $94,615; Grants to individuals, 4 grants totaling $4,000 (high: $1,000, low: $1,000).
Type of support: Employee-related scholarships; Undergraduate support.
Application information: Applications accepted. Application form required.
   Initial approach: Letter
   Deadline(s): Apr. 30
   Additional information: Contact foundation for current application guidelines.
EIN: 431186049

3520

Rose Spurrier Scholarship Fund
P.O. Box 473
Kingman, KS   67068-0473   (620) 532-3108
Contact: Robert S. Wunsch, Tr.
Application address: 401 N. Main, Kingman, KS 67068 Tel.: (620) 532-3108

Foundation type: Independent foundation
Purpose: Scholarships to qualified graduates of Kingman City High School, KS for attendance at colleges, universities or other institutions of higher education.
Financial data: Year ended 12/31/2012. Assets, $1,703,626 (M); Expenditures, $102,371; Total giving, $66,800.
Type of support: Support to graduates or students of specific schools; Undergraduate support.
Application information: Interview required.
   Applicants should submit the following:
      1) Financial information
      2) Letter(s) of recommendation
   Additional information: Selection is based on scholastic performance, character, extent and quality of extracurricular activities, educational goals and financial need.
EIN: 480978238

3521

Fred T. & John H. Steffens Scholarship Trust
P.O. Box 627
Phillipsburg, KS   67661

Foundation type: Independent foundation

Purpose: Scholarships to graduates of Phillipsburg High School, KS, for postsecondary education at KS institutions.
Financial data: Year ended 12/31/2012. Assets, $373,819 (M); Expenditures, $13,853; Total giving, $10,500; Grants to individuals, 7 grants totaling $10,500 (high: $3,250, low: $500).
Type of support: Support to graduates or students of specific schools; Technical education support; Undergraduate support.
Application information: Application form required.
   Deadline(s): Apr. 1.
   Additional information: Application should include transcripts.
EIN: 486346084

3522

Ross W. Stice Trust
103 N. Union St.
P.O. Box 212
Council Grove, KS   66846-1228   (620) 767-6825
Contact: D. Randall Heilman, Tr.

Foundation type: Independent foundation
Purpose: Scholarships to students of Council Grove High School, KS, who have resided within the Alta Vista, KS, school district or have had significant contact with the Alta Vista community, to attend Kansas State University, University of Kansas, or Emporia State University, KS.
Financial data: Year ended 06/30/2012. Assets, $279,759 (M); Expenditures, $11,963; Total giving, $9,150.
Type of support: Support to graduates or students of specific schools; Undergraduate support.
Application information: Applications not accepted.
   Additional information: Deadline is July 15 for fall semester and Dec. 31 for spring semester. Unsolicited requests for funds not considered or acknowledged.
EIN: 480874854

3523

Stockard Charitable Trust
1017 Broadway
P.O. Box 150
Marysville, KS   66508-1815   (785) 562-2344

Foundation type: Independent foundation
Purpose: Scholarships to one male graduate in the top 25 percent and one female graduate in the top 20 percent of each graduating class of Marysville High School, KS, for undergraduate education at any accredited college, university, vocational or trade school.
Financial data: Year ended 12/31/2012. Assets, $923,312 (M); Expenditures, $51,378; Total giving, $40,602; Grants to individuals, 10 grants totaling $28,429 (high: $2,000, low: $1,000).
Fields of interest: Vocational education, post-secondary; Higher education; Scholarships/financial aid.
Type of support: Scholarships—to individuals; Support to graduates or students of specific schools.
Application information: Application form required.
   Deadline(s): July 1
   Applicants should submit the following:
      1) Class rank
      2) GPA
      3) Financial information
EIN: 746452154

3524
Richard J. & Florence J. Tenholder Trust
(also known as The Griffis Memorial Scholarship in Art and Theatre)
801 S. 8th St.
Atchison, KS 66002-2724
Contact: Ann Marie Shepard, Tr.

Foundation type: Operating foundation
Purpose: Scholarships and achievement awards to women seeking a degree in art or theatre at Benedictine College, KS.
Financial data: Year ended 12/31/2012. Assets, $380,936 (M); Expenditures, $21,400; Total giving, $18,574.
Fields of interest: Arts education; Theater; Women.
Type of support: Support to graduates or students of specific schools; Undergraduate support.
Application information: Applications accepted. Application form required.
> *Deadline(s):* June 15
> *Final notification:* Applicants notified in two months
> *Applicants should submit the following:*
> 1) Transcripts
> 2) Letter(s) of recommendation
> 3) Financial information
> *Additional information:* Art applicants must submit a portfolio. Theatre applicants must have an audition or interview.

EIN: 481061565

3525
C. D. Terry Scholarship Foundation
756 Minnesota Ave.
Kansas City, KS 66101-2704 (913) 667-8022
Contact: Susan Martley
Application address: P.O. Box 335, 2649 S. 142nd St., Bonner Springs, KS 66012, Tel.: (913) 667-8022

Foundation type: Company-sponsored foundation
Purpose: Scholarships to full-time employees or the spouses, children and grandchildren of full-time employeees of Berkel and Co. Contractors, Inc., for college or vocational schools.
Financial data: Year ended 12/31/2012. Assets, $9,983 (M); Expenditures, $32,086; Total giving, $32,086; Grants to individuals, 41 grants totaling $32,086 (high: $1,000, low: -$235).
Fields of interest: Vocational education, post-secondary.
Type of support: Employee-related scholarships.
Application information:
> *Final notification:* Applicants normally notified of a decision within two weeks
> *Additional information:* Application must include transcripts, current class schedule and itemized statement of college costs. Application address: c/o Berkel & Co. Contractors, Inc., P.O. Box 335, Bonner Springs, KS 66012.

Company name: Berkel & Co. Contractors, Inc.
EIN: 486316064

3526
Throckmorton-Riser Foundation, Inc.
P.O. Box 610
Pittsburg, KS 66762-0610

Foundation type: Independent foundation
Purpose: College scholarships to high school graduates who are residents of Anderson county, Kansas to further their postsecondary education.
Financial data: Year ended 12/31/2012. Assets, $1,829,645 (M); Expenditures, $65,945; Total giving, $43,500; Grants to individuals, 18 grants totaling $43,500 (high: $3,000, low: $1,500).
Fields of interest: Higher education.
Type of support: Scholarships—to individuals.
Application information: Applications accepted.
EIN: 481103316

3527
Willis & Imogene Toothaker Trust
P.O. Box 235
Hoxie, KS 67740-0235

Foundation type: Independent foundation
Purpose: Scholarships to individuals of Hoxie, KS, for undergraduate or vocational education.
Financial data: Year ended 12/31/2011. Assets, $1,246,323 (M); Expenditures, $67,686; Total giving, $55,000; Grants to individuals, 12 grants totaling $25,200 (high: $2,100, low: $2,100).
Fields of interest: Vocational education, post-secondary; Higher education.
Type of support: Technical education support; Undergraduate support.
Application information: Applications accepted. Application form required.
> *Additional information:* Contact your high school guidance office for additional application information.

EIN: 486363592

3528
Topeka Community Foundation
5431 S.W. 29th St., Ste. 300
Topeka, KS 66614-4483 (785) 272-4804
Contact: Roger K. Viola, Pres.; For grants: Marsha Pope, V.P.
FAX: (785) 273-4644;
E-mail: info@topekacommunityfoundation.org;
URL: http://www.topekacommunityfoundation.org

Foundation type: Community foundation
Purpose: Scholarships to graduating high school students in Topeka and Shawnee County, KS.
Publications: Application guidelines; Annual report; Financial statement; Informational brochure; Informational brochure (including application guidelines); Newsletter; Quarterly report.
Financial data: Year ended 12/31/2012. Assets, $43,295,040 (M); Expenditures, $3,622,108; Total giving, $2,631,362; Grants to individuals, 150 grants totaling $147,052.
Fields of interest: Higher education; Scholarships/ financial aid.
Type of support: Scholarships—to individuals; Support to graduates or students of specific schools.
Application information: Applications accepted. Application form required. Application form available on the grantmaker's web site.
> *Initial approach:* Application
> *Send request by:* Mail or hand deliver
> *Deadline(s):* Early Feb.
> *Final notification:* Applicants notified by Apr. 1
> *Additional information:* See web site for a complete listing of scholarships.

Program description:
> *Scholarships:* The foundation administers various scholarships established by donors for residents of the Topeka area to obtain a higher education. Each scholarship has its own set of application guidelines and eligibility criteria, including graduating from a particular high school and/or study in a specific field, such as nursing and law enforcement. See web site for additional information.

EIN: 480972106

3529
John E. Trembly Foundation
P.O. Box 274
Council Grove, KS 66846-0274 (620) 767-5192

Foundation type: Independent foundation
Purpose: Scholarships to graduating seniors of Council Grove High School, KS for post-graduate education at accredited colleges or universities in KS.
Financial data: Year ended 12/31/2011. Assets, $1,201,071 (M); Expenditures, $61,937; Total giving, $47,000.
Fields of interest: Higher education; Scholarships/ financial aid.
Type of support: Scholarships—to individuals.
Application information: Application form required.
> *Deadline(s):* Apr. 15
> *Applicants should submit the following:*
> 1) Essay
> 2) Transcripts
> *Additional information:* Application can be obtained from Council Grove High School.

EIN: 486106606

3530
Paul and Ida Trump Scholarship Fund
c/o Valley View Fin. Group Trust Co.
5901 College Blvd., Ste. 100
Overland, KS 66211-1503 (913) 319-0350

Foundation type: Independent foundation
Purpose: Scholarships to graduates of Osawatomie High School, KS.
Financial data: Year ended 04/30/2012. Assets, $185,260 (M); Expenditures, $21,237; Total giving, $18,000; Grants to individuals, 9 grants totaling $18,000 (high: $2,000, low: $2,000).
Type of support: Support to graduates or students of specific schools; Undergraduate support.
Application information: Applications accepted.
> *Initial approach:* Letter
> *Deadline(s):* Contact fund for current application deadline

EIN: 481240121

3531
H. T. Ungles Educational Trust
641 Rd.220
Satanta, KS 67870 (620) 649-2337
Contact: Clinton L. Stalker, Jr., Tr.

Foundation type: Independent foundation
Purpose: Scholarships to graduates of Satanta High School, KS, and to lineal descendants of Dr. J.B. Ungles or Elizabeth Smith.
Financial data: Year ended 12/31/2012. Assets, $681,911 (M); Expenditures, $28,387; Total giving, $26,700; Grants to individuals, 15 grants totaling $26,700 (high: $3,200, low: $500).
Type of support: Support to graduates or students of specific schools; Undergraduate support.
Application information: Applications accepted.
> *Initial approach:* Letter
> *Deadline(s):* Mar. 1

EIN: 481243580

3532
Unified School District No. 380 Endowment Association
209 School St.
Vermillion, KS 66544 (785) 382-6216

Foundation type: Independent foundation

Purpose: Scholarships to students in KS for higher education.
Financial data: Year ended 12/31/2012. Assets, $1,161,825 (M); Expenditures, $56,603; Total giving, $5,469; Grants to individuals, 11 grants totaling $5,469 (high: $910, low: $100).
Fields of interest: Higher education.
Type of support: Undergraduate support.
Application information: Application form required.
> *Deadline(s):* May 1
> *Applicants should submit the following:*
> 1) Transcripts
> 2) Letter(s) of recommendation
> 3) Essay
> *Additional information:* Application must also include list of other scholarships received.
EIN: 481122532

3533
Vernon A. & Ada L. Vesper Educational Trust
c/o First State Bank
P.O. Box 369
Hill City, KS   67642-0369   (785) 421-2168
Contact: Dexter Potter, Tr.
Application address: First State Bank, Attn; Dexter Potter, 101 E. Cherry, Hill City, Kansas 67642

Foundation type: Independent foundation
Purpose: Student loans to graduates of high schools in Graham County, KS. Preference is given to students of medicine, dentistry, nursing, medical technology, and related courses of study. Students attending schools of osteopathic, chiropractic, and naturopathic study are ineligible.
Financial data: Year ended 10/31/2012. Assets, $235,592 (M); Expenditures, $53,970; Total giving, $52,000; Loans to individuals, 35 loans totaling $52,000.
Fields of interest: Dental school/education; Medical school/education; Nursing school/education; Health sciences school/education.
Type of support: Support to graduates or students of specific schools; Undergraduate support.
Application information: Applications accepted.
> *Initial approach:* Letter
> *Deadline(s):* None
EIN: 486121219

3534
The J.L. Weigand, Jr. Notre Dame Legal Education Trust
P.O. Box 9632
Wichita, KS   67277
Contact: Claudette Glenn, Dir.
URL: http://www.jlweigand.org

Foundation type: Operating foundation
Purpose: Scholarships to students who are legal residents of Kansas for a minimum of ten cumulative years for attendance at the University of Notre Dame Law School, Washburn University School of Law, or University of Kansas School of Law in pursuit of a law degree.
Financial data: Year ended 12/31/2012. Assets, $4,533,120 (M); Expenditures, $281,964; Total giving, $66,878; Grants to individuals, 9 grants totaling $66,878 (high: $18,353, low: $3,600).
Fields of interest: Law school/education.
Type of support: Support to graduates or students of specific schools.
Application information: Applications accepted. Application form required. Application form available on the grantmaker's web site.
> *Deadline(s):* Feb. 15
> *Applicants should submit the following:*

1) Photograph
2) Class rank
3) Transcripts
4) SAT
5) Resume
6) Letter(s) of recommendation
7) ACT
> *Additional information:* A personal statement must be submitted with each application.
EIN: 166542975

3535
Western Industrial Training Foundation
U.S.D., No. 281
P.O. Box 309
Hill City, KS   67642   (785) 421-2135
Contact: Jim Hickel, Pres.

Foundation type: Independent foundation
Purpose: Scholarships to students who are residents of Graham county, KS for postsecondary vocational/ technical education.
Financial data: Year ended 12/31/2012. Assets, $96,554 (M); Expenditures, $9,400; Total giving, $8,600.
Fields of interest: Vocational education, post-secondary.
Type of support: Scholarships—to individuals.
Application information: Applications accepted. Application form required.
> *Deadline(s):* Vary
> *Applicants should submit the following:*
> 1) Transcripts
> 2) Financial information
> *Additional information:* Scholarships are made payable to the school on behalf of the student.
EIN: 486117520

3536
Marvin White Foundation, Inc.
27 East 30th Ave., Suite B
Hutchinson, KS   67502   (620) 585-2145
Contact: Jeffrey W. Smith, Secy.
Application address: 717 4th Ave., Inman, KS 67546. Tel: (620) 585-2145

Foundation type: Independent foundation
Purpose: Scholarships to graduating seniors of McPherson County, KS, and to individuals for attendance at colleges in McPherson County pursuing a career in math, or science.
Financial data: Year ended 12/31/2012. Assets, $120,113 (M); Expenditures, $8,219; Total giving, $6,000.
Fields of interest: Higher education; Science; Mathematics.
Type of support: Undergraduate support.
Application information: Applications accepted. Application form required. Interview required.
> *Send request by:* Mail
> *Deadline(s):* Mar.
> *Applicants should submit the following:*
> 1) Transcripts
> 2) Letter(s) of recommendation
> *Additional information:* Application forms are available from high school guidance offices and, the science and math departments of McPherson County colleges.
EIN: 486244419

3537
Wichita Community Foundation
(formerly Greater Wichita Community Foundation)
301 N. Main, Ste. 100
Wichita, KS   67202   (316) 264-4880
FAX: (316) 264-7592; E-mail: wcf@wichitacf.org;
URL: http://www.wichitacf.org

Foundation type: Community foundation
Purpose: Scholarships to graduating seniors from the greater Wichita, KS area pursuing higher education.
Publications: Application guidelines; Annual report; Financial statement; Informational brochure; Newsletter.
Financial data: Year ended 06/30/2012. Assets, $51,512,223 (M); Expenditures, $3,973,233; Total giving, $3,337,375; Grants to individuals, 914 grants totaling $234,484.
Fields of interest: Higher education; Scholarships/ financial aid.
Type of support: Scholarships—to individuals; Support to graduates or students of specific schools.
Application information: Applications accepted. Application form required. Application form available on the grantmaker's web site.
> *Initial approach:* Application
> *Send request by:* On-line
> *Deadline(s):* Mar. 15
> *Final notification:* Applicants notified by May 15
> *Applicants should submit the following:*
> 1) Transcripts
> 2) Letter(s) of recommendation
> *Additional information:* See web site for additional application guidelines. Scholarship awards are paid directly to the educational institution on behalf of the students.
EIN: 481022361

3538
Wichita Consistory Midian Temple Crippled Children's Fund
332 E. 1st St. N.
Wichita, KS   67202-2402   (316) 263-4218
Contact: Jim Davenport, Tr.

Foundation type: Independent foundation
Purpose: Grants to economically disadvantaged children 18 or younger in KS.
Financial data: Year ended 12/31/2012. Assets, $0 (M); Expenditures, $6,412; Total giving, $6,186; Grants to individuals, 18 grants totaling $6,186 (high: $1,500; low: $105).
Fields of interest: Economically disadvantaged.
Type of support: Grants for special needs.
Application information: Applications accepted.
> *Initial approach:* Letter
> *Deadline(s):* None
> *Additional information:* Applicant must demonstrate need.
EIN: 481117049

3539
Wichita State University Foundation
1845 Fairmount St.
Wichita, KS   67260-0002   (316) 978-3040
Contact: Elizabeth King Ph.D., Pres. and C.E.O.
FAX: (316) 978-3277;
E-mail: foundation@wichita.edu; E-mail for Elizabeth King: elizabeth.king@wichita.edu; Tel. for Elizabeth King: (316)-978-3510; URL: http:// foundation.wichita.edu

Foundation type: Public charity

Purpose: Scholarships to undergraduate students and fellowships to graduate students at Wichita State University, KS.
Publications: Annual report; Newsletter.
Financial data: Year ended 06/30/2011. Assets, $234,553,930 (M); Expenditures, $17,278,027; Total giving, $3,865,689; Grants to individuals, 1,792 grants totaling $3,865,689.
Type of support: Fellowships; Support to graduates or students of specific schools; Undergraduate support.
Application information: Applications accepted. Application form required.
 Initial approach: Letter
 Additional information: See web site for complete program information.
EIN: 486121167

3540
Wildlife Disease Association, Inc.
(also known as WDA)
c/o Allen Press, Inc.
P.O. Box 7065
Lawrence, KS   66044   (800) 627-0326
FAX: (785) 843-6153;
E-mail: wda@allenpress.com; E-mail for Dave Jessup: wda.manager@gmail.com; URL: http://www.wildlifedisease.org

Foundation type: Public charity
Purpose: Scholarships and awards to students for outstanding academic and research accomplishment, leadership, and service to wildlife disease and health.
Financial data: Year ended 12/31/2011. Assets, $1,432,671 (M); Expenditures, $508,489; Total giving, $15,032; Grants to individuals, totaling $5,263.

Fields of interest: Environmental education; Animals/wildlife.
Type of support: Scholarships—to individuals; Awards/prizes; Graduate support; Doctoral support.
Application information: Applications accepted.
 Additional information: See web site for additional guidelines.
Program descriptions:
 WDA Student Poster Competition: This annual award acknowledges the most outstanding poster presentation of research findings at the WDA annual international conference.
 Wildlife Disease Association Scholarship: The scholarship is awarded annually to a student who is pursuing a master's or doctoral degree specializing in research on wildlife disease.
 Wildlife Disease Graduate Student Research Recognition Award: This award is offered annually to the student judged to have the best research project in the field of wildlife disease.
EIN: 366098737

3541
The Lloyd E. & Katherine S. Winslow Education Trust
P.O. Box 327
Iola, KS   66749-0327   (620) 237-4250
Contact: David Hardage Supt.
Application address: P.O. Box 35, Moran, KS 66755

Foundation type: Independent foundation
Purpose: Scholarships to high school graduates from Allen County, KS, with preference to graduates of Marmaton Valley High School, KS.
Financial data: Year ended 12/31/2011. Assets, $854,853 (M); Expenditures, $117,674; Total

giving, $88,900; Grants to individuals, 114 grants totaling $88,900 (high: $1,600, low: $200).
Type of support: Scholarships—to individuals.
Application information: Application form required.
 Deadline(s): May 15, July 15 or Dec. 15
 Applicants should submit the following:
  1) Transcripts
  2) SAT
  3) Financial information
  4) ACT
EIN: 481060065

3542
Woolsey Scholarship Fund
c/o Linda M. Burket
P.O. Box 375
Kingman, KS   67068

Foundation type: Independent foundation
Purpose: Scholarships to current year valedictorian(s) of Kingman High School, KS.
Financial data: Year ended 11/30/2012. Assets, $289,920 (M); Expenditures, $11,225; Total giving, $3,700; Grant to an individual, 1 grant totaling $3,700.
Fields of interest: Higher education.
Type of support: Support to graduates or students of specific schools.
Application information:
 Deadline(s): None
 Additional information: No applications are submitted, the awardees are determined by class standing.
EIN: 486107561

KENTUCKY

3543
AAEP Foundation, Inc.
(also known as American Association of Equine Practitioners)
4075 Iron Works Pkwy.
Lexington, KY 40511-8462 (859) 233-0147
Contact: Pam Shook
FAX: (859) 233-1968;
E-mail: aaepoffice@aaep.org; Toll free tel.: (800) 443-0177; E-Mail for Pam Shook: pshook@aaep.org; URL: http://foundation.aaep.org/

Foundation type: Public charity
Purpose: Research grants and scholarships to individuals for equine medicine.
Publications: Application guidelines; Annual report.
Financial data: Year ended 12/31/2011. Assets, $2,072,720 (M); Expenditures, $449,153; Total giving, $234,678; Grants to individuals, 12 grants totaling $36,500.
Fields of interest: Veterinary medicine.
Type of support: Graduate support.
Application information: Applications accepted. Application form required. Application form available on the grantmaker's web site.
> *Deadline(s):* Apr. 1 for The AAEP Foundation and Zoetis Scholarship, Aug. 1 for all others
> *Additional information:* Application should include an essay. See web site for additional guidelines.

Program descriptions:
AAEP Foundation Past Presidents' Research Fellow Scholarship: A $5,000 scholarship is available to American Association of Equine Practitioners member graduates and residents completing their respective residencies or graduate programs while participating in equine research.

EQUUS Foundation Research Fellowship: This $5,000 scholarship is awarded annually to two American Association of Equine Professional member graduates or residents who are completing their residency or a graduate program while participating in equine research.

Markel Insurance Company Inc./AAEP Foundation Scholarship: Eight outstanding veterinary students who have committed their careers to equine practice annually are selected to receive $2,500 scholarships from Market Insurance Company and the foundation. These scholarships are available to fourth-year veterinary students who are proven leaders in their veterinary school, advocates for equine welfare and academic achievers.

Winner's Circle Scholarship: A $1,500 scholarship is awarded annually to fourth-year veterinary students at each University that has a National AAEP Student Chapter in North America and the West Indies. An additional $3,000 is available to qualified applicants.
EIN: 611259683

3544
American Federation of Riders
(also known as A.F.R., Inc.)
2863 Presidential Dr.
Hebron, KY 41048-8629 (859) 322-2537
URL: http://www.afr-1982.org/

Foundation type: Public charity
Purpose: Medical assistance, trust funds, and scholarships to economically disadvantaged,

orphaned, handicapped, abused and neglected children, primarily in OH.
Financial data: Year ended 10/31/2011. Assets, $28,089 (M); Expenditures, $5,562; Total giving, $1,715.
Fields of interest: Disabilities, people with; Economically disadvantaged.
Type of support: Undergraduate support; Grants for special needs.
Application information: Application form not required.
EIN: 311041172

3545
Appalachian College Association
210 Center St.
Berea, KY 40403-1733 (859) 986-4584
Contact: Dr. Irene Burgess, V.P., Academic Progs.
FAX: (859) 986-9549; E-mail: paulc@acaweb.org; URL: http://www.acaweb.org

Foundation type: Public charity
Purpose: Fellowships to qualified candidates who hold full-time faculty or student status at an ACA institution for improving education in the Appalachian region.
Publications: Application guidelines; Annual report; Financial statement.
Financial data: Year ended 06/30/2012. Assets, $26,554,471 (M); Expenditures, $4,613,112; Total giving, $491,778; Grants to individuals, totaling $491,778.
Fields of interest: Scholarships/financial aid; Education; Legal services; Crime/law enforcement; Science.
Type of support: Fellowships.
Application information: Applications accepted. Application form required. Application form available on the grantmaker's web site.
> *Send request by:* Fax, online, or mail
> *Deadline(s):* Varies
> *Additional information:* Electronic submissions are preferred. Funds are paid directly to the educational institution on behalf of the student. See web site for additional application.

Program descriptions:
Barbara Paul Robinson Scholarships: A $2,500 scholarship is available to a current student who shows great interest in and potential to be an attorney, and who is dedicated to making a positive change in Appalachia. Eligible applicants must be students of an association member institution who will be full-time seniors, and who have a GPA of 3.0 or higher (on a four-point scale). Preference will be given to students who have been accepted to, or can show documentation of applying to, an accredited law school.

Colonel Lee B. Ledford Awards: Awards of a maximum of $5,120 will be available to support research experiences for students enrolled at association-member institutions. Various forms of research will be supported, including laboratory and field work, interviews, analyzing special collection, and participant observation. Eligible applicants must be: a full-time student, returning to an association-member institution for at least one semester following the research term; have graduated from high school or been home-schooled in a designated Appalachian or contiguous county, as defined by the Appalachian Regional Commission; have a 2.0 GPA or better (on a four-point scale); and have the support of a faculty member who will agree to serve as mentor throughout the research project. Students from a variety of disciplines (including English, sociology, history, biology, computer science, and religious

studies) are welcome to apply; in addition to the maximum amount, a $1,000 stipend will be awarded for equipment and travel expenses.

NSF Scholarships for STEM Majors: Awarded in conjunction with the National Science Foundation, scholarships of $6,000 per year (with the possibility of a one-year renewal) will be made available to students studying the natural sciences, technology, engineering, or mathematics. Eligible applicants must be U.S. citizens (or have documented refugee or permanent resident status), and be a full-time sophomore, junior, or senior at the beginning of the year in which he/she is applying for aid; eligible applicants must also qualify for financial aid and have a grade point average of 3.0 or higher (on a four-point scale)
EIN: 561758784

3546
Appalachian Foothills Housing Agency, Inc.
1214 Riverside Dr.
Wurtland, KY 41144-2107 (606) 836-0911
Contact: Diane Blankenship, Exec. Dir.
URL: http://www.afha.net/index.html

Foundation type: Public charity
Purpose: Assistance to low income families in the Wurtland, KY area with decent, safe, and sanitary housing and to promote self-sufficiency and economic independence for Section 8 participants.
Financial data: Year ended 06/30/2012. Assets, $961,335 (M); Expenditures, $3,930,177; Total giving, $3,485,677; Grants to individuals, totaling $3,485,677.
Fields of interest: Housing/shelter; Economically disadvantaged.
Type of support: Grants for special needs.
Application information: Applications accepted. Application form required.
> *Additional information:* Application should include financial information. Contact the agency for eligibility criteria.
EIN: 610934381

3547
Baker/Geary Memorial Fund, Inc.
P.O. Box 24292
Louisville, KY 40224 (502) 426-6665
Contact: Michael Conliffe, Dir.

Foundation type: Independent foundation
Purpose: Scholarships to financially needy KY individuals pursuing higher education.
Financial data: Year ended 12/31/2011. Assets, $245,223 (M); Expenditures, $116,544; Total giving, $102,500; Grant to an individual, 1 grant totaling $1,000.
Fields of interest: Higher education; Athletics/sports, golf; Recreation.
Type of support: Scholarships—to individuals.
Application information: Applications accepted. Application form required.
> *Initial approach:* Letter
> *Deadline(s):* Dec. 1
> *Additional information:* Applicants must demonstrate financial need, have passing grades, active in extracurricular activities and have an interest in golf.
EIN: 611234349

3548
Raymond & Mary D. Barnett Foundation, Inc.
P.O. Box 39
Milton, KY 40045-0039   (502) 532-7350
Contact: Zane Peyton, Dir.
Application address: 61 Chilton Ct., Campbellsburg, KY 40011-1439, tel.: (502) 532-7350

Foundation type: Independent foundation
Purpose: Scholarships of $5,000 for a two-year period to individuals who are residents of Kentucky for attendance at accredited colleges or universities.
Financial data: Year ended 12/31/2011. Assets, $890,864 (M); Expenditures, $45,990; Total giving, $42,000.
Fields of interest: Higher education.
Type of support: Scholarships—to individuals.
Application information: Applications accepted.
Initial approach: Letter
Deadline(s): None
Additional information: Applicant must include the name of institution of higher learning, verification of student full-time enrollment, and verification of a 2.5 GPA on a 4.0 scale.
EIN: 611371025

3549
Fred (B. A.) Batterton Fund Trust
c/o Kentucky Bank
P.O. Box 157
Paris, KY 40362-0157   (859) 988-1316

Foundation type: Independent foundation
Purpose: Scholarships to residents of Bourbon County, KY, for medical education.
Financial data: Year ended 12/31/2011. Assets, $908,543 (M); Expenditures, $46,179; Total giving, $34,978; Grants to individuals, 12 grants totaling $25,317 (high: $4,000, low: $1,000).
Fields of interest: Medical school/education.
Type of support: Graduate support.
Application information: Applications accepted.
Initial approach: Letter
Deadline(s): None
EIN: 616128598

3550
Bible Students Aid Foundation
c/o Stock Yards Bank & Trust Co.
P.O. Box 34290
Louisville, KY 40232-4290

Foundation type: Independent foundation
Purpose: Emergency aid for Bible students for utilities, groceries, prescriptions, rent or mortgage payments, etc.
Financial data: Year ended 12/31/2011. Assets, $3,105,717 (M); Expenditures, $134,080; Total giving, $105,945; Grants to individuals, 16 grants totaling $105,945 (high: $15,000, low: $2,000).
Fields of interest: Theological school/education.
Type of support: Grants for special needs.
Application information: Applications accepted.
Initial approach: Letter
Deadline(s): None
Additional information: Application should include a supporting letter from a Bible student elder.
EIN: 616176491

3551
Big Sandy Area Community Action Program, Inc.
2nd Fl., 230 Court St.
Paintsville, KY 41240-1607   (606) 789-3641
Information on services and programs: Larry Dotson, Coord., tel.: (606) 432-2775
FAX: (606) 789-8344; URL: http://bsacap.org/

Foundation type: Public charity
Purpose: Scholarships to KY high school graduates or college/vocational school students entering/returning to college/vocational school. Assistance to low-income families and individuals of Pike, Martin, Magoffin, Floyd, and Johnson counties, KY, with rent, home heating and utility assistance, food, shelter and repairs to home.
Financial data: Year ended 10/31/2011. Assets, $3,017,817 (M); Expenditures, $20,836,412.
Fields of interest: Vocational education; Higher education; Housing/shelter, services; Human services.
Type of support: Scholarships—to individuals; Grants for special needs.
Application information: Application form required.
Initial approach: Letter, telephone or fax
Additional information: Applicant must provide household size, income, social security numbers and birth dates. See web site for complete program information.
Program description:
Community Services Block Grant Scholarship Program: One-time scholarship funds are available on a competitive basis to eligible clients in each county served, who have graduated from high school and plan on entering or returning to college or vocational school. All eligible applicants must meet 100 percent of federal income guidelines.
EIN: 610653946

3552
Blue Grass Community Foundation, Inc.
(formerly Blue Grass Foundation, Inc.)
499 E. High St., Ste. 112
Lexington, KY 40507   (859) 225-3343
Contact: For grants: Kassie L. Branham, Dir., Grants and Scholarships
FAX: (859) 243-0770; E-mail: info@bgcf.org; URL: http://www.bgcf.org

Foundation type: Community foundation
Purpose: Scholarships to students of central and eastern, KY seeking educational opportunities beyond high school.
Publications: Application guidelines; Annual report; Financial statement; Grants list; Quarterly report.
Financial data: Year ended 06/30/2012. Assets, $54,169,892 (M); Expenditures, $5,528,516; Total giving, $3,521,198; Grants to individuals, 151 grants totaling $276,901.
Fields of interest: Higher education; Graduate/professional education; Nursing school/education.
Type of support: Employee-related scholarships; Scholarships—to individuals; Support to graduates or students of specific schools; Graduate support; Undergraduate support.
Application information: Applications accepted. Application form required. Application form available on the grantmaker's web site.
Copies of proposal: 1
Deadline(s): Varies
Additional information: See web site for complete listing of scholarship funds and application guidelines.
Program description:
Scholarships: The foundation administers over 30 different scholarship funds established by

donors, each striving to benefit students who have a passion for learning. Awards are mostly for high school students pursuing higher education degrees in specific subjects, including business, engineering, veterinary medicine and various others. Some scholarships are available for graduate study. Eligibility requirements and application guidelines vary per fund. See web site for additional information.
EIN: 616053466

3553
Boneal Charitable Foundation Inc.
611 Winchester Rd.
P.O. Box 640
Mount Sterling, KY 40353

Foundation type: Company-sponsored foundation
Purpose: Scholarships to residents of Menifee County, KY.
Financial data: Year ended 12/31/2011. Assets, $127,085 (M); Expenditures, $4,381; Total giving, $4,000.
Type of support: Undergraduate support.
Application information: Applications not accepted.
Additional information: Unsolicited requests for funds not considered.
EIN: 611358724

3554
Jeff Caudill Optimist Scholarship Fund, Inc.
P.O. Box 906
London, KY 40743-0906   (606) 864-2486

Foundation type: Public charity
Purpose: Two college scholarships to graduating seniors of London, KY one each of the two high schools in the county for higher education at accredited colleges or universities.
Financial data: Year ended 12/31/2010. Assets, $156,421 (M); Expenditures, $12,000; Total giving, $12,000.
Fields of interest: Higher education.
Type of support: Scholarships—to individuals.
Application information: Applications accepted.
Applicants should submit the following:
1) GPA
2) Financial information
3) Essay
Additional information: Students essay should include why they should receive one of the scholarships.
EIN: 311498863

3555
The Children's Hospital Foundation
234 E. Broadway 5th Fl.
Louisville, KY 40202-2025   (502) 629-3409
URL: http://www.nortonhealthcare.com/body.cfm?id=142

Foundation type: Public charity
Purpose: Financial support to patients who cannot afford medical care in KY and southern IN, as well as nursing scholarships.
Publications: Annual report; Newsletter.
Financial data: Year ended 12/31/2011. Assets, $75,044,697 (M); Expenditures, $6,898,609; Total giving, $4,653,051; Grants to individuals, totaling $260,514.
Fields of interest: Health care.
Type of support: Grants for special needs.

Application information:
Initial approach: Letter
Additional information: Contact foundation for eligibility criteria.
EIN: 616027530

3556
Christian Appalachian Project, Inc.
P.O. Box 59911
Lexington, KY 40555-5911
E-mail: capinfo@chrisapp.org; Toll-free tel.: (866) 270-4227; URL: http://www.christianapp.org

Foundation type: Public charity
Purpose: Assistance to individuals and families in need throughout the Appalachian region. Scholarship support to select individuals.
Publications: Annual report; Financial statement.
Financial data: Year ended 08/31/2012. Assets, $26,060,451 (M); Expenditures, $131,318,061; Total giving, $105,259,480; Grants to individuals, 12,621 grants totaling $557,951.
Fields of interest: Education; Human services.
Type of support: Scholarships—to individuals; In-kind gifts; Grants for special needs.
Application information: Applications accepted.
Additional information: Applicants must demonstrate need.
EIN: 610661137

3557
Commercial Bank Foundation
208 E. Main St.
Grayson, KY 41143-1304 (606) 474-7811
Contact: Jack W. Strother, Jr., Tr.; Mark Strother, Tr.

Foundation type: Company-sponsored foundation
Purpose: Scholarships to graduating seniors from high schools in Carter County, KY.
Financial data: Year ended 12/31/2012. Assets, $570,370 (M); Expenditures, $36,109; Total giving, $35,700; Grants to individuals, 14 grants totaling $14,000 (high: $1,000, low: $1,000).
Fields of interest: Higher education.
Type of support: Support to graduates or students of specific schools; Undergraduate support.
Application information: Application form required.
Deadline(s): Apr. 15
Applicants should submit the following:
1) GPA
2) Essay
3) ACT
Additional information: Applicant must have participated in at least one extracurricular activity for each year of high school.
EIN: 611087988

3558
Community Action Council for Lexington-Fayette Bourbon, Harrison, and Nicholas Counties
710 W. High St.
Lexington, KY 40508-2451 (800) 244-2275
Contact: Jack Burch, Exec. Dir.
FAX: (859) 244-2219; URL: http://www.commaction.org/

Foundation type: Public charity
Purpose: Help to indigent residents of Lexington-Fayette, Bourbon, Harrison and Nicholas counties in KY in the form of food, clothing, elderly transport, emergency rent/mortgage assistance, home weatherization, utility/energy assistance and home repairs.

Financial data: Year ended 06/30/2012. Assets, $9,996,643 (M); Expenditures, $23,311,624; Total giving, $4,361,033; Grants to individuals, totaling $2,808,393.
Fields of interest: Housing/shelter, repairs; Economically disadvantaged.
Type of support: In-kind gifts; Grants for special needs.
Application information:
Initial approach: Tel.
Applicants should submit the following:
1) Financial information
Additional information: Call 859-233-4600 for eligibility criteria.
EIN: 610650121

3559
The Community Foundation of Louisville, Inc.
(formerly Louisville Community Foundation, Inc.)
Waterfront Plz. Bldg.
325 W. Main St., Ste. 1110
Louisville, KY 40202-4251 (502) 585-4649
Contact: For scholarships: Meredith Zahirovic, Community Leadership Assoc.
Scholarship URL: http://scholarship.cflouisville.org; Scholarship inquiry e-mail: meredithz@cflouisville.org
FAX: (502) 587-7484; E-mail: info@cflouisville.org; URL: http://www.cflouisville.org

Foundation type: Community foundation
Purpose: Scholarships to individuals in the greater Louisville, KY, area for postsecondary education.
Publications: Annual report; Informational brochure; Newsletter; Program policy statement.
Financial data: Year ended 06/30/2012. Assets, $354,979,910 (M); Expenditures, $43,260,225; Total giving, $36,612,890. Scholarships—to individuals amount not specified.
Fields of interest: Vocational education; Business school/education; Nursing school/education; Adult/continuing education; Environmental education; Agriculture; Jewish agencies & synagogues; Women.
Type of support: Program development; Employee-related scholarships; Graduate support; Technical education support; Precollege support; Undergraduate support.
Application information: Applications accepted. Application form required. Application form available on the grantmaker's web site.
Initial approach: Application
Send request by: On-line
Deadline(s): Mar. 14
Additional information: See web site for additional application guidelines.
EIN: 310997017

3560
Community Foundation of West Kentucky
(formerly Paducah Area Community Foundation)
333 Broadway, Ste. 615
P.O. Box 7
Paducah, KY 42002-0007 (270) 442-8622
Contact: Tony Watkins, C.E.O.
FAX: (270) 442-8623; E-mail: info@cfwestky.org; URL: http://www.cfwestky.org

Foundation type: Community foundation
Purpose: Scholarships to graduating seniors of West Kentucky pursuing higher education.
Publications: Annual report; Informational brochure; Newsletter.
Financial data: Year ended 12/31/2012. Assets, $16,972,502 (M); Expenditures, $1,249,485;

Total giving, $712,350; Grants to individuals, 35 grants totaling $42,000 (high: $2,000, low: $500).
Fields of interest: Higher education.
Type of support: Scholarships—to individuals.
Application information: Applications accepted. Application form required.
Additional information: Contact the foundation for additional guidelines, or your guidance counselor.
EIN: 611304905

3561
Alvah Cox Memorial Scholarship
c/o Fowler Durham CPA's
P.O. Box 338
Munfordville, KY 42765-0338 (270) 524-1375

Foundation type: Independent foundation
Purpose: Scholarships to residents of Munfordville, Cub Run and Bonneville areas of Hart County, KY.
Financial data: Year ended 05/31/2013. Assets, $180,328 (M); Expenditures, $2,917; Total giving, $2,500; Grants to individuals, 5 grants totaling $2,500 (high: $500, low: $500).
Fields of interest: Higher education.
Type of support: Scholarships—to individuals.
Application information: Applications accepted.
Deadline(s): Prior to May award date
EIN: 611191892

3562
Disabled American Veterans
3725 Alexandria Pike
Cold Spring, KY 41076-1712 (859) 441-7300
Nomination address: National Headquarters, P.O. Box 14301, Cincinnati, OH 45250-0301
Mailing Address: P.O. Box 14301; Cincinnati, OH 45250-0301; URL: http://www.dav.org

Foundation type: Public charity
Purpose: Assistance to disabled veterans and their families in obtaining benefits and services. Scholarships to young volunteers for continued education who play active roles in the Department of Veterans Affairs Voluntary Service (VAVS)
Financial data: Year ended 12/31/2011. Assets, $388,911,658 (M); Expenditures, $116,591,022; Total giving, $5,038,982; Grants to individuals, totaling $154,850.
Fields of interest: Vocational education, post-secondary; Higher education; College (community/junior); College; University.
Type of support: Scholarships—to individuals; Awards/grants by nomination only.
Application information: Application form available on the grantmaker's web site.
Deadline(s): Feb. 25 for Scholarship
Additional information: Applicants must be nominated for the scholarship award. Self nomination is encouraged, and must include an essay. See web site for additional guidelines.
Program description:
Jesse Brown Memorial Youth Scholarship Program: Scholarships are awarded to any volunteer who is age 21 or younger and has volunteered for a minimum of 100 hours at a VA medical center during the previous calendar year. All hours must be credited to the Disabled American Veterans. Scholarships can be used at any accredited institution of higher learning which includes universities, colleges, community colleges, vocational schools, etc., and must be utilized in full prior to the recipient attaining the age of 25, or within six years of receiving the scholarship, whichever is later. Immediate family

members of DAV national organization are eligible to receive a scholarship.
EIN: 310263158

3563
Disabled American Veterans (DAV) Charitable Service Trust, Inc.

3725 Alexandria Pike
Cold Spring, KY   41076-1712   (859) 441-7300
Contact: Nancy L. O'Brien, Admin.
FAX: (859) 442-2088; E-mail: cst@dav.org;
URL: http://www.dav.org/cst

Foundation type: Public charity
Purpose: Relief grants to disabled veterans for the purpose of providing food, clothing, temporary shelter or to obtain relief from injury, illness or personal loss not covered by insurance or other disaster relief agencies.
Publications: Application guidelines; Annual report; Financial statement; Informational brochure.
Financial data: Year ended 12/31/2011. Assets, $19,574,604 (M); Expenditures, $4,415,503; Total giving, $4,012,359.
Fields of interest: Disabilities, people with; Military/veterans; Economically disadvantaged.
Type of support: Emergency funds; In-kind gifts.
Application information:
Initial approach: E-mail or tel.
Additional information: Contact foundation for eligibility guidelines and application information.
EIN: 521521276

3564
The Dream Factory, Inc.

120 W. Broadway, Ste. 300
Louisville, KY   40202-2110   (502) 561-3001
FAX: (502) 561-3004;
E-mail: dfinfo@dreamfactoryinc.com; Toll-free tel.: (800) 456-7556; URL: http://www.dreamfactoryinc.com

Foundation type: Public charity
Purpose: Grants for dreams to critically and/or chronically ill children ages 3 through 18.
Publications: Annual report.
Financial data: Year ended 08/31/2012. Assets, $3,347,508 (M); Expenditures, $1,781,449; Total giving, $1,423,378; Grants to individuals, totaling $1,423,378.
Fields of interest: Diseases (rare); Children/youth.
Type of support: Grants to individuals.
Application information: Applications accepted.
Additional information: The illness must be documented and affirmed by a treating physician, and the child must be able to communicate his or her dream to a volunteer screening representative of The Dream Factory. Referrals will only be considered for children who reside in communities where chapters exist. See web site for additional information or to find local chapters.
EIN: 611220742

3565
Eastern Kentucky Concentrated Employment Program, Inc.

941 N. Main St.
Hazard, KY   41701-1377   (606) 436-5751
Contact: Jeff Whitehead, Exec. Dir.
FAX: (606) 436-5755; E-mail: ekcep@ekcep.org;
E-Mail For Jeff Whitehead: jwhitehead@ekcep.org;
Fax: (606) 436-5755; URL: http://www.ekcep.org

Foundation type: Public charity
Purpose: Assistance for the unemployed and underemployed of eastern KY, with services and training that enable them to enter the workforce, raise their workforce skills, or return to the workforce after losing their jobs.
Financial data: Year ended 06/30/2012. Assets, $811,626 (M); Expenditures, $11,780,141; Total giving, $10,899,409; Grants to individuals, totaling $10,899,409.
Fields of interest: Economically disadvantaged.
Type of support: Grants to individuals.
Application information: See web site for additional information.
EIN: 610674045

3566
Eastern Kentucky PRIDE, Inc.

2292 S. Hwy. 27
Somerset, KY   42501-2905   (606) 677-6150
Contact: Karen Kelly, Pres. and C.E.O.
FAX: (606) 677-6055; Toll-free tel.: (888) 577-4339; URL: http://www.kypride.org

Foundation type: Public charity
Purpose: Grants for low-income homeowners in established homes in the 42 counties served by eastern, KY PRIDE.
Publications: Application guidelines.
Financial data: Year ended 06/30/2012. Assets, $617,424 (M); Expenditures, $962,285; Total giving, $357,396; Grants to individuals, totaling $357,396.
Fields of interest: Water pollution; Environment.
Type of support: Grants for special needs.
Application information: Applications accepted.
Send request by: Mail
Additional information: Application for low income homeowners should include proof of income, copy of deed showing ownership, recent copy of utility bill. Application is reviewed on a first-come, first serve basis.
Program description:
Homeowner Septic System Grant Program: These grants to low-income homeowners allow them the opportunity to replace their straight pipes, outhouses or failing septic systems with sanitary wastewater treatment systems, which are required by state and federal laws.
EIN: 611321358

3567
Energy & Mineral Law Foundation

340 S. Broadway, Ste. 101
Lexington, KY   40508-2553   (859) 231-0271
FAX: (859) 226-0485; E-mail: info@emlf.org;
URL: http://www.emlf.org

Foundation type: Public charity
Purpose: Scholarships to law students studying energy, environmental, natural resource, and mineral law at schools holding membership in the Energy & Mineral Law Foundation.
Publications: Application guidelines.
Financial data: Year ended 06/30/2012. Assets, $1,502,738 (M); Expenditures, $651,205; Total giving, $50,000; Grants to individuals, totaling $50,000.
Fields of interest: Law school/education; Public policy; Natural resources; Energy; Environment.
Type of support: Scholarships—to individuals.
Application information: Applications accepted. Application form required. Application form available on the grantmaker's web site.
Send request by: Mail, fax or e-mail
Deadline(s): Apr. 18

Applicants should submit the following:
1) Financial information
2) Transcripts
3) Class rank
4) Letter(s) of recommendation
5) GPA
Additional information: Two letters of recommendation are required, with at least one from a law school dean, faculty member, or member of the legal profession. Application should also include a personal statement.
Program description:
EMLF Law Student Scholarships: The foundation provides educational assistance to encourage the study of energy, environmental, natural resources, and mineral law. Scholarship awards include: the ELMF Presidents' Scholarship ($5,000), the Paul N. Bowles Scholarship ($1,000), the James H. Davis Scholarship ($1,000), and the Mary Sue Schulberg Scholarship ($1,000). Schools must hold membership with the foundation. See web site for a list of eligible schools.
EIN: 251385547

3568
Farm Income Improvement Foundation, Inc.

9201 Bunsen Pkwy.
P.O. Box 20700
Louisville, KY   40250-0700
Contact: David S. Beck, Secy.-Treas.

Foundation type: Operating foundation
Purpose: Grants to farmers in KY for various types of equipment and services.
Financial data: Year ended 12/31/2012. Assets, $162,001 (M); Expenditures, $8,927; Total giving, $0.
Fields of interest: Agriculture, farm bureaus/granges.
Type of support: Grants for special needs.
Application information: Application form required.
Initial approach: Letter
Deadline(s): Apr. 1 and May 1
Additional information: Applications postmarked prior to Feb. 1 not accepted; Application must be mailed individually and not hand-delivered or sent by fax.
EIN: 311525389

3569
Foundation for Affordable Housing

169 Deweese St.
Lexington, KY   40507-1937   (859) 252-6642

Foundation type: Public charity
Purpose: Assistance to low- and moderate-income families and veterans for establishment and maintenance of affordable housing.
Financial data: Year ended 12/31/2011. Assets, $2,067,439 (M); Expenditures, $479,506; Total giving, $207,639; Grants to individuals, totaling $207,639.
Fields of interest: Economically disadvantaged.
Type of support: Grants for special needs.
Application information: Contact the foundation for eligibility determination.
EIN: 611192747

3570
Foundation for United Methodists, Inc.

204 N. Lexington Ave.
Wilmore, KY   40390-1129   (859) 858-2283
Contact: Dexter W. Porter, Treas.

Foundation type: Public charity
Purpose: Scholarships to United Methodist students at Asbury Theological Seminary, KY on the basis of academic achievement, conference and financial need.
Financial data: Year ended 04/30/2012. Assets, $1,012,921 (M); Expenditures, $118,877; Total giving, $102,260; Grants to individuals, totaling $102,260.
Type of support: Support to graduates or students of specific schools.
Application information: Applications accepted. Application form required.
  Initial approach: Letter or telephone
  Deadline(s): May
  Additional information: Contact the foundation for application guidelines.
EIN: 237015220

3571
Annie Gardner Foundation
620 S. 6th St.
Mayfield, KY 42066-2316
Contact: Nancy H. Sparks, Dir.

Foundation type: Operating foundation
Purpose: Student loans to residents of Graves County, KY, who are graduates of Graves County High School or Mayfield High School. Financial assistance to indigent residents of Graves County, KY, to help pay for rent, utilities, medical bills, and clothing.
Financial data: Year ended 05/31/2013. Assets, $10,202,510 (M); Expenditures, $1,129,699; Total giving, $784,253; Grants to individuals, totaling $784,253.
Fields of interest: Scholarships/financial aid.
Type of support: Support to graduates or students of specific schools; Undergraduate support; Grants for special needs.
Application information: Application form required.
  Deadline(s): July 1
  Additional information: Contact foundation for further application guidelines.
Program description:
  Student Loan Program: Maximum loan amounts are $2,000 and $3,000 per year for undergraduate and graduate students respectively. If student attends summer school, he or she may receive an additional $500.
EIN: 610564889

3572
Gateway Community Services Organization, Inc.
151 University Dr.
P.O. Box 367
West Liberty, KY 41472-0367 (606) 743-3133
FAX: (606) 743-1130; E-mail: info@gcscap.org;
E-mail for Dennis Gulley: dennis.gulley@gcscap.org;
URL: http://www.gcscap.org

Foundation type: Public charity
Purpose: Emergency assistance to low-income individuals and families with affordable housing, weatherization, transportation, food and other needs in the Bath, Menifee, Montgomery, Morgan and Rowan counties, KY.
Publications: Financial statement.
Financial data: Year ended 06/30/2012. Assets, $756,395 (M); Expenditures, $7,024,560.
Fields of interest: Economically disadvantaged.
Type of support: Grants for special needs.
Application information: Households must meet eligibility criteria to receive assistance.
EIN: 610865874

3573
God's Pantry Food Bank, Inc.
1685 Jaggie Fox Way
Lexington, KY 40511-1084 (859) 255-6592
Contact: Marian F. Guinn, C.E.O.
FAX: (859) 254-6330;
E-mail: godspantryinfo@godspantry.org; E-Mail for Marian F. Guinn: marian@godspantry.org;
URL: http://godspantry.org

Foundation type: Public charity
Purpose: Emergency assistance to low income families and individuals in need throughout central and eastern KY with food, clothing, and shelter.
Publications: Annual report; Newsletter.
Financial data: Year ended 06/30/2012. Assets, $12,039,978 (M); Expenditures, $28,547,054; Total giving, $24,311,922; Grants to individuals, totaling $24,311,922.
Fields of interest: Nutrition; Economically disadvantaged.
Type of support: Emergency funds.
Application information:
  Initial approach: Telephone
  Additional information: Clients are referred by a social worker or a social service agency. Contact the agency for eligibility determination.
EIN: 310979404

3574
The Governors Scholars Program Foundation, Inc.
1024 Capital Center Dr., Ste. 210
Frankfort, KY 40601-7514 (502) 573-1630
Contact: Laban Jackson, Jr., Dir.

Foundation type: Public charity
Purpose: Scholarships awarded to agri-business students.
Financial data: Year ended 12/31/2011. Assets, $2,476,043 (M); Expenditures, $228,800; Total giving, $32,500; Grants to individuals, totaling $32,500.
Fields of interest: Education.
Type of support: Scholarships—to individuals.
Application information: Applications accepted.
  Additional information: Contact foundation for further information.
EIN: 611393028

3575
Habitat for Humanity of Metro Louisville, Inc.
1620 Bank St.
Louisville, KY 40203-1314 (502) 637-6265
Contact: Rob Locke, Exec.Dir.
FAX: (502) 637-6266; Tel. for Rob Locke: (502) 805-1412; URL: http://www.hfhlouisville.org

Foundation type: Public charity
Purpose: Assistance to families of Louisville, KY with new homes or rehabilitated existing homes who are in need and who have invested necessary time and education into the responsibilities of homeownership and the construction of the home itself.
Publications: Newsletter.
Financial data: Year ended 12/31/2011. Assets, $14,103,503 (M); Expenditures, $5,167,715; Total giving, $2,088,777; Grants to individuals, totaling $2,018,630.
Fields of interest: Housing/shelter, home owners.
Type of support: In-kind gifts.
Application information: Applications accepted. Application form required. Application form

available on the grantmaker's web site. Interview required.
  Send request by: Mail
  Additional information: See web site for additional guidelines.
EIN: 581735528

3576
The Jim Hedrick & Janice O. Lantz Charitable Foundation
120 Woodhill Rd.
Bardstown, KY 40004-9166 (502) 350-0009

Foundation type: Independent foundation
Purpose: Scholarships to residents of Nelson county, KY pursuing a career in the teaching or medical profession, as well as to individuals of minority or handicapped status.
Financial data: Year ended 12/31/2011. Assets, $23,814 (M); Expenditures, $41,775; Total giving, $41,755.
Fields of interest: Higher education; Medical school/education; Teacher school/education; Disabilities, people with; Minorities.
Type of support: Scholarships—to individuals.
Application information: Applications accepted.
  Deadline(s): None
  Additional information: Applicants must demonstrate academic strength, individual talent, or economic need.
EIN: 200238894

3577
Michael E. Horn Family Foundation Inc.
P.O. Box 1944
Owensboro, KY 42302-1944 (270) 313-0245
Contact: Kathryn Crowe, Dir.
URL: http://www.hornfamilyfoundation.org

Foundation type: Independent foundation
Purpose: Scholarships to students for higher education in the Owensboro and Daviess county and surrounding areas in KY.
Financial data: Year ended 12/31/2012. Assets, $8,457,282 (M); Expenditures, $620,615; Total giving, $410,425; Grants to individuals, 26 grants totaling $35,500 (high: $1,000, low: $500).
Fields of interest: Higher education.
Type of support: Scholarships—to individuals.
Application information: Applications accepted. Application form required.
  Deadline(s): Mar. 1
  Additional information: Applicants should be active members in a school organization, community or church, and demonstrate financial need. Students should see their guidance counselor for application information.
EIN: 261375584

3578
Independence Foundation, Inc.
2425 Frederica St.
P.O. Box 988
Owensboro, KY 42302 (270) 686-1776

Foundation type: Company-sponsored foundation
Purpose: Financial assistance to indigent employees of Independence Bank for utilities and medical bills and college scholarships to high school seniors in a seven county area.
Financial data: Year ended 12/31/2012. Assets, $115,167 (M); Expenditures, $435,919; Total giving, $435,919.
Fields of interest: Education; Human services.

Type of support: Scholarships—to individuals; Employee-related welfare.
Application information: Applications accepted. Application form required. Interview required.
Initial approach: Letter
Deadline(s): Feb. 15 for scholarships
Applicants should submit the following:
1) Transcripts
2) SAT
3) Financial information
4) ACT
5) Essay
Additional information: A personal interview may be requested for scholarship finalists.
Company name: Independence Bank
EIN: 261568393

3579
Beatrice Jackson Scholarship
c/o Ballard County Board of Education
3465 Paducah Rd.
Barlow, KY 42024-9704 (270) 665-8400

Foundation type: Independent foundation
Purpose: Scholarships by nomination only to African-American students and graduates of Ballard Memorial High School, KY, for higher education, including vocational training.
Financial data: Year ended 08/31/2013. Assets, $153,767 (M); Expenditures, $1,194; Total giving, $830; Grants to individuals, 5 grants totaling $830 (high: $350, low: $120).
Fields of interest: Minorities.
Type of support: Awards/grants by nomination only; Technical education support; Undergraduate support.
Application information:
Deadline(s): None
Additional information: Candidates are nominated by Ballard Memorial High School counselors and administration.
EIN: 611225206

3580
The Jones Educational Foundation Inc.
P.O. Box 289
Somerset, KY 42502 (606) 678-0880
Contact: Sonya Jones, Pres. and C.E.O.
E-mail: drjones@jonesfoundation.net; URL: http://www.jonesfoundation.net/

Foundation type: Independent foundation
Purpose: Scholarships to KY students planning to attend four year institutions of higher learning in KY.
Financial data: Year ended 07/31/2013. Assets, $38,028 (M); Expenditures, $12,783; Total giving, $2,000; Grants to individuals, 2 grants totaling $1,000 (high: $500, low: $500).
Type of support: Undergraduate support.
Application information: Applications accepted.
Initial approach: Letter
Deadline(s): One month before the scholarships are presented at the end of the school year.
EIN: 616312867

3581
KD-FC, Inc.
419 Washington St.
Shelbyville, KY 40065-1127 (502) 633-1220
Application address: Rusty Newton Deputy Judge-Executive

Foundation type: Independent foundation

Purpose: Scholarships to residents of Shelbyville, KY, who are pursuing an education in the health-related field.
Financial data: Year ended 12/31/2012. Assets, $570,901 (M); Expenditures, $2,626; Total giving, $2,000; Grants to individuals, 2 grants totaling $2,000 (high: $1,000, low: $1,000).
Fields of interest: Health sciences school/education.
Type of support: Scholarships—to individuals.
Application information: Applications accepted.
Initial approach: Letter
Additional information: Application must outline course of study and school applicant will attend. The scholarship is limited to $2,000 per academic year.
EIN: 611147608

3582
Kentucky Foundation for Women, Inc.
1215 Heyburn Bldg.
332 W. Broadway
Louisville, KY 40202-2184 (502) 562-0045
FAX: (502) 561-0420; E-mail: team@kfw.org; Toll free tel.: (866) 654-7564; URL: http://www.kfw.org

Foundation type: Independent foundation
Purpose: Grants to feminist artists living in KY to promote social change through varied feminist expressions in the arts.
Publications: Application guidelines; Annual report; Grants list; Newsletter.
Financial data: Year ended 06/30/2013. Assets, $12,934,418 (M); Expenditures, $637,884; Total giving, $205,000; Grants to individuals, 54 grants totaling $144,775 (high: $7,444, low: $1,000).
Fields of interest: Arts; Civil/human rights, women.
Type of support: Program development.
Application information: Application form required. Application form available on the grantmaker's web site.
Initial approach: Letter or telephone
Deadline(s): First week of Sept. for Artist Enrichment and first week for Mar. for Art Meets Activism
Final notification: Recipients notified early June for Arts Meets Activism and early Dec. for Artist Enrichment
Applicants should submit the following:
1) Letter(s) of recommendation
2) Budget Information
3) Work samples
Additional information: See web site for further information.
Program descriptions:
Art Meets Activism Program: The Art Meets Activism Program supports feminist artists and organizations in the development and implementation of art activities that are directly focused on progressive social change in Kentucky. Applicants should be able to demonstrate their commitment to feminism and their understanding of the relationship between art and social change.
Artist Enrichment Program: The Artist Enrichment Program provides opportunities for feminist artists and arts organizations to enhance their abilities and skills to create art for progressive social change. Applicants should be able to demonstrate their commitment to feminism and their understanding of the relationship between art and social change.
EIN: 611070429

3583
Kentucky Fried Chicken Foundation, Inc.
(formerly Colonel's Kids, Inc.)
1900 Colonel Sanders Ln.
Louisville, KY 40213-5910 (502) 874-2075
Contact: John Cywinski, Pres.
E-mail: kfcscholars@act.org; URL: http://www.kfcscholars.org

Foundation type: Public charity
Purpose: Scholarships to high school seniors pursuing a college education at accredited public institution within their states of residence.
Publications: Application guidelines; Grants list.
Financial data: Year ended 12/31/2011. Assets, $7,749,824 (M); Expenditures, $1,950,572; Total giving, $1,255,975; Grants to individuals, totaling $1,235,617.
Fields of interest: Higher education.
Type of support: Scholarships—to individuals.
Application information: Applications accepted. Application form required. Application form available on the grantmaker's web site.
Deadline(s): Feb. 10
Final notification: Recipients notified in May
Additional information: Selection is based on financial need, perseverance and entrepreneurial spirit.
Program description:
Scholarships: The program provides scholarship awards of up to $5,000 annually for up to four years.
EIN: 611337601

3584
Kentucky Law Enforcement Memorial Foundation
521 Lancaster Ave.
Funderburk Bldg., EKU
Richmond, KY 40475-3102 (859) 622-8081
Contact: Pam Smallwood
FAX: (859) 622-8256;
E-mail: pam.smallwood@ky.gov; URL: http://www.klemf.org

Foundation type: Public charity
Purpose: Scholarships to law enforcement officers, telecommunicators, their survivors, and immediate family members for attendance at accredited colleges or universities or a recognized vocational or trade school.
Publications: Application guidelines.
Financial data: Year ended 12/31/2012. Assets, $864,936 (M); Expenditures, $125,841; Total giving, $55,750; Grants to individuals, totaling $55,750.
Fields of interest: Vocational education, post-secondary; Higher education; Government agencies.
Type of support: Scholarships—to individuals.
Application information: Applications accepted. Application form required.
Deadline(s): June 30
Additional information: Selection criteria is based on financial need.
Program description:
Gerald F. Healy Kentucky Law Enforcement Memorial Foundation Scholarship: Up to twenty-five scholarships, ranging from $1,000 to $2,000, will be available to provide financial education assistance to law enforcement officers, telecommunicators, their survivors, and immediate family members who demonstrate financial need. Scholarships may be used at any accredited school or university (including two-year and community colleges), or at a recognized or certified vocational or trade school. Eligible applicants must be current,

retired, or disabled Kentucky sworn police officers or telecommunicators, or a survivor or dependent of the same; priority will be given to survivors and dependents.
EIN: 611356926

3585
Kentucky Lions Eye Foundation, Inc.
301 E. Muhammed Ali Blvd.
Louisville, KY 40202-1511 (502) 583-0564
Contact: Wenda Owen, Exec. Dir.
FAX: (502) 852-6596;
E-mail: kylionseye@hotmail.com; URL: http://www.kylionseye.org/

Foundation type: Public charity
Purpose: Financial assistance to KY indigents who are in need of eye care.
Publications: Annual report; Newsletter.
Financial data: Year ended 06/30/2012. Assets, $2,914,960 (M); Expenditures, $1,543,088; Total giving, $77,782; Grants to individuals, totaling $77,782.
Fields of interest: Health care, support services; Eye diseases; Economically disadvantaged.
Type of support: Grants for special needs.
Application information: Contact foundation for eligibility criteria.
EIN: 610516171

3586
Kentucky Racing Health and Welfare Fund, Inc.
422 Heywood Ave.
Louisville, KY 40208-1324 (502) 636-2900
Contact: Richard P. Riedel, Exec. Dir.
FAX: (502) 636-2955;
E-mail: krhwf@kyracinghealth.org; Toll-free tel.: (800) 548-3662; e-mail for Richard P. Riedel: rriedel@kyracinghealth.org; URL: http://www.kyracinghealth.com

Foundation type: Public charity
Purpose: Aid, relief and assistance to eligible individuals in the Kentucky thoroughbred racing industry.
Financial data: Year ended 12/31/2011. Assets, $6,407,811 (M); Expenditures, $2,404,814; Total giving, $1,688,939; Grants to individuals, totaling $1,432,616.
Type of support: Grants for special needs.
Application information: Funding includes payment of medical, hospital, vision and funeral expenses. Individual must demonstrate need. See web site for additional information.
EIN: 610958300

3587
Kincaid Foundation
P.O. Box 1360
Lexington, KY 40590 (859) 253-6251
Contact: Marcia Wave
Application address: c/o Central Bank & Trust Co., 300 W. Vine St., Ste. 3, Lexington, KY 40507-1666,

Foundation type: Independent foundation
Purpose: Scholarships to graduates of Fayette County, KY, high schools for enrollment in four-year college degree programs.
Financial data: Year ended 12/31/2012. Assets, $556,022 (M); Expenditures, $42,787; Total giving, $40,500; Grants to individuals, 14 grants totaling $40,500 (high: $4,000, low: $1,500).

Fields of interest: Higher education; Scholarships/financial aid.
Type of support: Support to graduates or students of specific schools; Undergraduate support.
Application information: Application form required.
Deadline(s): Apr. 1
Applicants should submit the following:
1) Essay
2) Financial information
3) GPA
EIN: 616033698

3588
Kings Daughters Health Foundation, Inc.
2201 Lexington Ave.
Ashland, KY 41101-2843 (606) 408-9330
FAX: (606) 408-6995; URL: http://www.kdhealthfoundation.com/

Foundation type: Public charity
Purpose: Scholarships to students who are residents of KY, OH, or WV pursuing a career in the healthcare-related fields.
Financial data: Year ended 09/30/2011. Assets, $663,252 (M); Expenditures, $32,780; Total giving, $17,319; Grants to individuals, totaling $17,319.
Fields of interest: Medical school/education; Nursing school/education; Health sciences school/education; Health care.
Type of support: Scholarships—to individuals; Grants for special needs.
Application information: Applications accepted. Application form required. Application form available on the grantmaker's web site. Interview required.
Send request by: Mail
Deadline(s): Apr. 25
Applicants should submit the following:
1) Financial information
2) Transcripts
3) Letter(s) of recommendation
4) SAT
5) ACT
Additional information: Applicant must demonstrate financial need. See web site for additional application guidelines.
Program descriptions:
Boyd County Medical Society Scholarship: This non-renewable scholarship of $1,500 is for the first school year's tuition, room and board, books and lab fees for any field of study. The foundation will disburse $750 directly to the recipients school of choice at the start of each semester. Applicants are required to maintain a 2.50 GPA with a minimum of 12 hours of classes per semester. In order to receive their next payment applicants must provide the foundation with a copy of their transcript at the end of the fall semester. Applicants must be a senior at one of these schools, Boyd County High School, Fairview High School, Paul G. Blazer High School or Russell High School.
Edna and Mildred Monk Memorial Nursing Scholarship: This $1,000 scholarship is for the dependents of King's Daughters Team Members and is for the first school year's tuition, room and board, books and lab fees for students pursuing the field of nursing and is non-renewable. Three scholarships will be awarded. The foundation will mail $500 directly to the recipients school of choice at the beginning of each semester. Applicants are required to maintain a 2.50 GPA with a minimum of 12 hours of classes per semester, and must provide the foundation with a copy of their transcript at the end of the fall semester, in order to receive the second payment of the scholarship.

King's Daughter Scholarship: A scholarship in the amount of $2,500 is awarded for the first school year, and the use is limited to tuition, room and board, books and lab fees for a student pursuing a career in healthcare. The scholarship of $1,250 will be mailed directly to the recipient's school at the beginning of each semester and is non-renewable. In order to receive the second payment winners are required to maintain a 2.50 GPA with a minimum of 12 hours of classes per semester, and must provide the foundation with a copy of their transcript at the end of each semester. Applicants must be residents of one of the states and counties: KY - Boyd, Carter, Greenup, Lawrence; OH - Lawrence; WV - Wayne.
EIN: 611035701

3589
Lexmark International, Inc. Corporate Giving Program
(formerly Lexmark International Group, Inc. Corporate Giving Program)
740 W. New Circle Rd.
Lexington, KY 40550-0001
Contact: Juli Gaworski, Community Rels. Specialist
Scholarship contact: recruiting@lexmark.com
E-mail: citizenship@lexmark.com; URL: http://www1.lexmark.com/en_US/about-us/corporate-responsibility/index.shtml

Foundation type: Corporate giving program
Purpose: Scholarships to Lexmark International employees and to dependents of Lexmark International employees for undergraduate and graduate study.
Publications: Corporate giving report; Informational brochure (including application guidelines); Program policy statement.
Financial data: Year ended 12/31/2011. Total giving, $1,750,000.
Fields of interest: Higher education.
Type of support: Employee-related scholarships.
Application information: Applications not accepted.
Additional information: Unsolicited requests for funds not considered or acknowledged.
Company name: Lexmark International, Inc.

3590
Licking Valley Community Action Program
203 High St.
Flemingsburg, KY 41041-1236 (606) 845-0081
Contact: Judy L. Planck, Exec. Dir.
FAX: (606) 854-0418; Toll-free tel.: (800) 327-4321; Additional tel.: (606) 849-4321;
URL: http://www.lvcap.com/

Foundation type: Public charity
Purpose: Assistance to KY low-income families, the handicapped, and elderly with food, shelter and clothing.
Financial data: Year ended 06/30/2012. Assets, $4,655,477 (M); Expenditures, $9,221,805.
Fields of interest: Human services.
Type of support: Grants for special needs.
Application information: Contact organization for guidelines to obtain assistance.
EIN: 610660543

3591
Lincoln Foundation
200 W. Broadway, Ste. 500
Louisville, KY 40202-2125 (502) 585-4733
Contact: Larry M. McDonald, Pres.
FAX: (502) 585-9648; E-mail: info@lincolnfdn.org;
Toll-free tel.:(877) 336-1910; e-mail for Larry M.
McDonald: lmcdonald@lincolnfdn.org; URL: http://
www.lincolnfdn.org

Foundation type: Public charity
Purpose: Educational enrichment programs for
economically disadvantaged seventh grade
students in the Louisville, KY metro area.
Publications: Annual report; Newsletter.
Financial data: Year ended 12/31/2012. Assets,
$7,619,798 (M); Expenditures, $1,126,254; Total
giving, $66,868; Grants to individuals, totaling
$66,868.
Fields of interest: Economically disadvantaged.
Type of support: Program development.
Application information: Applications accepted.
Application form required.
> *Deadline(s):* Mar. 31
> *Final notification:* Applicants notified by Apr. 30
> *Applicants should submit the following:*
> 1) Transcripts
> 2) GPA
Program description:
> *Whitney M. Young Scholars Program:* The program
> recruits academically talented,
> economically-disadvantaged seventh-grade
> students in the greater Louisville area, and over a
> six-year period, prepares them for high school
> graduation and successful matriculation into
> postsecondary educational institutions. This
> preparation includes: introducing more structure
> into the scholar's personal environment;
> maintaining and improving the scholar's academic
> performance; enhancing the scholar's self-esteem;
> developing the scholar's values, character, and
> ethics; facilitating parental/guardian advocacy for
> each scholar; providing positive peer and mentor
> interaction for the scholar in a stimulating
> environment that is conducive to learning; and
> enhancing cultural awareness.
EIN: 610449631

3592
Louisville Male High School Foundation, Inc.
2907 Iris Way
Louisville, KY 40220-1234
Contact: George E. Mercker, Pres.

Foundation type: Independent foundation
Purpose: Scholarships to seniors at Louisville Male
Traditional High School, KY.
Financial data: Year ended 12/31/2012. Assets,
$444,164 (M); Expenditures, $10,057; Total
giving, $8,600.
Fields of interest: Men.
Type of support: Support to graduates or students
of specific schools; Undergraduate support.
Application information: Applications accepted.
> *Initial approach:* Letter
> *Deadline(s):* None
EIN: 616033780

3593
Mackin Foundation, Inc.
545 S. Third St., Ste. 310
Louisville, KY 40202-1838

Foundation type: Company-sponsored foundation

Purpose: Scholarships to children of employees of
Interlock Industries, and its subsidiaries.
Publications: Application guidelines.
Financial data: Year ended 12/31/2012. Assets,
$6,025,718 (M); Expenditures, $340,979; Total
giving, $263,500.
Fields of interest: Education.
Type of support: Employee-related scholarships.
Application information: Applications not
accepted.
> *Additional information:* Unsolicited requests for
> funds not considered or acknowledged.
Company name: Interlock Industries, Inc.
EIN: 352069109

3594
Mallory-Taylor Foundation, Inc.
P.O. Box 53
La Grange, KY 40031-0053
Contact: Barry D. Moore, Chair.

Foundation type: Independent foundation
Purpose: Health care assistance to residents of
Oldham County, KY, who do not have any other form
of medical coverage.
Financial data: Year ended 12/31/2012. Assets,
$661,242 (M); Expenditures, $21,076; Total
giving, $8,311.
Fields of interest: Health care, financing; Health
care.
Type of support: Grants for special needs.
Application information: Application form required.
> *Send request by:* Mail
> *Deadline(s):* None
> *Additional information:* Applicants must have
> been residents of Oldham County, KY, for at
> least six months prior to submission of
> application.
EIN: 611187509

3595
Ephraim McDowell Foundation
P.O. Box 636
Belfry, KY 41514-0636

Foundation type: Independent foundation
Purpose: Scholarships to residents of the Tug
Valley area (Pike and Martin counties, KY, and
Mingo County, WV), with priority given to financially
needy individuals pursuing health-related studies.
Financial data: Year ended 06/30/2013. Assets,
$557,180 (M); Expenditures, $52,007; Total
giving, $41,625; Grants to individuals, 26 grants
totaling $41,625 (high: $4,000, low: $725).
Fields of interest: Health sciences school/
education.
Type of support: Undergraduate support.
Application information: Applications accepted.
> *Initial approach:* Letter
> *Deadline(s):* June 10 and Nov. 10.
> *Additional information:* Application should
> include proof of enrollment in a health-related
> field of study. Scholarships are awarded on
> the basis of financial need and GPA.
EIN: 610647946

3596
Metro United Way, Inc.
334 E. Broadway
P.O. Box 4488
Louisville, KY 40204-0488 (502) 583-2821
Contact: Joseph Tolan, Pres. and C.E.O. and Secy.
FAX: (502) 583-0330; Additional addresses
(southern IN office): 405 E. Court Ave., No. 3,

Jeffersonville, IN 47130-3474, tel.: (812)
206-7515; (Shelby County office): 179 Alpine Dr.,
Shelbyville, KY 40065-8878, tel.: (502) 633-4484;
URL: http://www.metrounitedway.org

Foundation type: Public charity
Purpose: Scholarships to high school graduates
residing in Clark, Floyd, or Harrison Counties, IN, or
Bullitt, Jefferson, Oldham, or Shelby Counties, KY,
who have demonstrated a strong commitment to
community service during high school. Grants to
economically disadvantaged individuals to assist
with rent, housing, utilities, medical, and
bereavement assistance.
Publications: Application guidelines.
Financial data: Year ended 04/30/2012. Assets,
$27,345,879 (M); Expenditures, $26,820,319;
Total giving, $18,812,641.
Fields of interest: Higher education; Economically
disadvantaged.
Type of support: Scholarships—to individuals;
Grants for special needs.
Application information: Application form required.
> *Deadline(s):* Mar. 25 for Scholarships
> *Final notification:* Recipients notified by end of
> May for Scholarships
> *Applicants should submit the following:*
> 1) Letter(s) of recommendation
> 2) Transcripts
EIN: 610444680

3597
MGM Charitable/Scholarship Foundation
2116 Broadway
Paducah, KY 42001-7110 (270) 443-4500

Foundation type: Independent foundation
Purpose: Scholarships to students residing in
McCracken County, KY, for undergraduate
education, with preference to those planning to
study outside of KY.
Financial data: Year ended 11/30/2012. Assets,
$179,378 (M); Expenditures, $274,213; Total
giving, $246,500.
Fields of interest: Higher education.
Type of support: Undergraduate support.
Application information: Applications accepted.
Application form required.
> *Deadline(s):* Apr. 1
> *Final notification:* Applicants notified in May
> *Applicants should submit the following:*
> 1) Transcripts
> 2) SAT
> 3) Essay
> 4) Financial information
EIN: 616264013

3598
Perry W. & Lucy Compton Miller Scholarship Fund
6223 Gamaliel Rd.
Gamaliel, KY 42140-9205

Foundation type: Independent foundation
Purpose: Scholarships to graduates of Monroe
County, KY, schools for higher education.
Financial data: Year ended 05/30/2013. Assets,
$559,733 (M); Expenditures, $46,591; Total
giving, $45,409; Grants to individuals, 14 grants
totaling $40,409 (high: $4,000, low: $1,000).
Fields of interest: Higher education.
Type of support: Scholarships—to individuals.
Application information: Applications not
accepted.

Additional information: Unsolicited requests for funds not considered or acknowledged.
EIN: 311600526

3599
J. L. Morrill Fund
Berea College
Berea, KY 40404-0001

Foundation type: Independent foundation
Purpose: Scholarships to residents of the Southern Mountain District to pursue an education in medicine or nursing and who plan to make their home in the area.
Financial data: Year ended 12/31/2012. Assets, $127,128 (M); Expenditures, $15,447; Total giving, $15,000; Grant to an individual, 1 grant totaling $15,000.
Fields of interest: Medical school/education; Nursing school/education.
Type of support: Undergraduate support.
Application information: Applications accepted. Application form required.
  Applicants should submit the following:
    1) Essay
    2) Financial information
    3) Transcripts
  Additional information: Applicant must explain immediate and future plans, including the name of the institution where professional study is being or will be undertaken.
EIN: 616035200

3600
Louisa S. Morrill Fund
c/o Berea College
C.P.O. 2172
Berea, KY 40404-0001

Foundation type: Independent foundation
Purpose: Interest-free student loans to women who are studying medicine or nursing (preference for graduate study), and who are residents of the Southern Mountain District of the U.S., meaning the mountainous regions of VA, WV, TN, KY, GA, NC, and SC.
Financial data: Year ended 12/31/2012. Assets, $155,128 (M); Expenditures, $20,120; Total giving, $19,600; Grants to individuals, 7 grants totaling $19,600 (high: $2,800, low: $2,800).
Fields of interest: Medical school/education; Nursing school/education; Women.
Type of support: Graduate support.
Application information: Application form required.
  Deadline(s): Three months prior to term for which funds are requested.
  Additional information: Application should include an essay explaining financial need, future plans including the name of the educational institution where professional study is being or will be undertaken and where the medical or nursing profession will be practiced.
EIN: 616035227

3601
Sam Murphy Jr. Trust
c/o Kentucky Trust Company
218 W. Main St.
Danville, KY 40422 (606) 787-6941
Application address: Casey County High School, Attn.: Guidance Office, 1922 N. US RT 127, Liberty, KY 42539

Foundation type: Independent foundation

Purpose: Scholarships to residents of Casey County, KY, with a 2.5 GPA or higher, for postsecondary education.
Financial data: Year ended 12/31/2012. Assets, $127,201 (M); Expenditures, $10,607; Total giving, $9,000; Grants to individuals, 10 grants totaling $9,000 (high: $1,500, low: $500).
Fields of interest: Higher education.
Type of support: Undergraduate support.
Application information: Applications accepted. Application form required.
  Deadline(s): None
  Applicants should submit the following:
    1) Essay
    2) GPA
EIN: 616201556

3602
The Mustard Seed Foundation
200 Big Run Rd.
Lexington, KY 40503-2903

Foundation type: Independent foundation
Purpose: Grants to individuals promoting ministry to college students abroad.
Financial data: Year ended 12/31/2011. Assets, $72,007 (M); Expenditures, $627,093; Total giving, $494,316. Grants to individuals amount not specified.
Fields of interest: Theological school/education; Religion.
Type of support: Grants to individuals.
Application information: Applications accepted.
  Additional information: Contact the foundation for additional guidelines.
EIN: 611390910

3603
Shelley R. and Alice S. Norris Scholarship
P.O. Box 415
Burkesville, KY 42717-0415

Foundation type: Independent foundation
Purpose: Scholarships to individuals for medical or nursing education who wish to practice in KY.
Financial data: Year ended 12/31/2012. Assets, $260,539 (M); Expenditures, $0; Total giving, $0.
Fields of interest: Medical school/education; Nursing school/education.
Type of support: Graduate support.
Application information: Applications accepted.
  Initial approach: Letter
  Deadline(s): Aug.
EIN: 311497834

3604
Northern Kentucky Community Action Commisson, Inc.
717 Madison Ave.
Covington, KY 41011-2479 (859) 581-6607
Contact: Florence W. Tandy, Exec. Dir.
E-mail: ftandy@nkcac.org; Toll-free tel.: (800) 784-6607; URL: http://www.nkcac.org

Foundation type: Public charity
Purpose: Financial assistance to KY individuals for basic and special needs.
Publications: Annual report.
Financial data: Year ended 06/30/2011. Assets, $4,904,391 (M); Expenditures, $12,392,109; Total giving, $4,227,370; Grants to individuals, totaling $4,227,370.
Fields of interest: Pharmacy/prescriptions; Food services; Housing/shelter.
Type of support: Grants for special needs.

Application information: Applications not accepted.
  Additional information: Unsolicited requests for funds not considered or acknowledged.
EIN: 610667805

3605
Norton Healthcare, Inc.
224 E. Broadway - 5th Fl.
Louisville, KY 40202-2025 (502) 629-8249
Norton Scholars tel.: (502) 629-7411; Toll-free tel.: (866) 662-0003
URL: http://www.nortonhealthcare.com/

Foundation type: Public charity
Purpose: Undergraduate scholarships for students in the Louisville, KY area pursuing a career in the health care field. Assistance to current Norton health care clinical personnel.
Financial data: Year ended 12/31/2011. Assets, $935,991,735 (M); Expenditures, $194,117,660; Total giving, $3,527,307; Grants to individuals, totaling $95,000.
Fields of interest: Health sciences school/education; Health care.
Type of support: Scholarships—to individuals.
Application information: Applications accepted. Application form required.
  Send request by: Online for Norton Scholars
  Deadline(s): Sept. 1 for Spring semester, May 1 for Fall semester for Norton Healthcare Scholars
  Applicants should submit the following:
    1) Transcripts
    2) Letter(s) of recommendation
  Additional information: High school seniors should contact their guidance office. See web site for additional guidelines.
EIN: 611028725

3606
Norton Healthcare Foundation, Inc.
234 E. Gray St., Ste. 450
Louisville, KY 40202-1900 (502) 629-8060
Contact: Lynnie Meyer, Exec. Dir.
FAX: (502) 629-8059;
E-mail: foundations@nortonhealthcare.org; Toll-free tel.: (800) 444-2523E-Mail for Lynnie Meyer : lynnie.meyer@nortonhealthcare.org; URL: http://www.nortonhealthcare.com/body.cfm?id=224

Foundation type: Public charity
Purpose: Financial assistance to students of KY and southern IN who are interested in pursuing certain types of health care careers. Nurse externships are also available.
Publications: Annual report; Newsletter.
Financial data: Year ended 12/31/2011. Assets, $39,385,501 (M); Expenditures, $2,586,653; Total giving, $1,865,415; Grants to individuals, totaling $17,000.
Fields of interest: Hospitals (general).
Type of support: Undergraduate support.
Application information: Applications accepted. Application form required. Application form available on the grantmaker's web site.
  Initial approach: Letter
  Applicants should submit the following:
    1) Transcripts
    2) Resume
    3) Letter(s) of recommendation
    4) ACT
    5) GPA
EIN: 310914919

3607
Ogden College Foundation
c/o Daryl Greattinger Regent
1894 N. Main St.
Monticello, KY   42633-2048
Application address: Leigh Jones, P.O. Box 3350, Bowling Green, KY 42102-3350, tel.: (606) 348-9329

Foundation type: Independent foundation
Purpose: Scholarships to graduates of KY public and private high schools who have a grade average of "B" or better and who intend to pursue a major or minor at the Ogden College of Science, Technology and Health at Western Kentucky University. Professorships, fellowships, and science awards are also granted.
Publications: Informational brochure (including application guidelines).
Financial data: Year ended 06/30/2012. Assets, $2,188,767 (M); Expenditures, $209,695; Total giving, $168,500.
Fields of interest: Health sciences school/education; Science; Engineering/technology.
Type of support: Undergraduate support.
Application information: Applications accepted. Application form required. Interview required.
> *Deadline(s):* None, however, scholarships are awarded on a first-come, first-served basis, so submission by at least Jan. 1 is encouraged
EIN: 237078715

3608
Operation Open Arms, Inc.
1400 Envoy Cir., Ste. 1416
Louisville, KY   40299   (502) 493-5007

Foundation type: Operating foundation
Purpose: Financial assistance to needy foster parents, and related expense to the children's care which is provided by the foster parents.
Financial data: Year ended 12/31/2012. Assets, $66,824 (M); Expenditures, $316,084; Total giving, $79,303; Grants to individuals, 7 grants totaling $79,303 (high: $13,437, low: $3,300).
Fields of interest: Adoption; Foster care.
Type of support: Grants for special needs.
Application information: Applications not accepted.
> *Additional information:* Unsolicited requests for funds not considered or acknowledged.
EIN: 311787756

3609
Owensboro Medical Health System, Inc.
811 E. Parrish Ave.
Owensboro, KY   42303-3258   (270) 688-2000
Contact: Jeff Barber, Pres. and C.E.O.
URL: http://www.omhs.org

Foundation type: Public charity
Purpose: Assistance with tuition, fees and books for Owensboro Medical Health System employees pursuing a career in nursing.
Financial data: Year ended 05/31/2012. Assets, $1,044,932,854 (M); Expenditures, $368,831,686; Total giving, $1,573,213; Grants to individuals, totaling $283,757.
Fields of interest: Nursing school/education; Health care.
Type of support: Scholarships—to individuals.
Application information: Applications accepted. Application form required. Interview required.
> *Initial approach:* Telephone
> *Deadline(s):* July
> *Applicants should submit the following:*

1) Letter(s) of recommendation
2) Transcripts
3) Essay
> *Additional information:* Application should also include official acceptance letter from an accredited nursing program. See web site for additional application guidelines.
EIN: 611286361

3610
Owenton Rotary Student Loan Fund
285 Green Acres Rd.
Owenton, KY   40359-8200
Contact: Ronnie Roberts, Pres.
Application address: 7050 Cull Rd., Worthville, KY

Foundation type: Operating foundation
Purpose: Student loans to individuals in Owen County, KY.
Financial data: Year ended 12/31/2012. Assets, $96,092 (M); Expenditures, $10,034; Total giving, $10,000; Grants to individuals, 7 grants totaling $10,000 (high: $3,000, low: $1,000).
Type of support: Student loans—to individuals.
Application information: Applications accepted.
> *Initial approach:* Letter
> *Deadline(s):* None
> *Additional information:* Application should include transcript.
EIN: 311533803

3611
Papa John's International, Inc. Corporate Giving Program
2002 Papa Johns Blvd.
Louisville, KY   40299-2334
Address for Papa John's Scholars: Scholarly Pursuits, c/o Scholarship Admin., 4005 Briar Ridge Rd., LaGrange, KY 40031; E-mail for "The Works" Scholarship: pjtws@aol.com; URL: http://www.papajohns.com/about/community.shtm

Foundation type: Corporate giving program
Purpose: Scholarships to graduating high school seniors in areas of Papa John's restaurants to attend an accredited college or university of their choice, and college scholarships to employees of Papa John's.
Fields of interest: Higher education; Education.
Type of support: Employee-related scholarships; Undergraduate support.
Application information: Applications accepted. Application form required.
> *Initial approach:* Letter
> *Deadline(s):* Vary
> *Additional information:* High school seniors should contact their guidance counselor.
Program description:
> *Papa John's Pizza Scholars Program:* Papa John's awards college scholarships of up to $1,000 to high school seniors located in immediate delivery areas of participating Papa John's restaurants. Recipients are selected based on academic achievement, demonstrated leadership, community involvement, athletic achievement, and obstacles overcome.
Company name: Papa John's International, Inc.

3612
Papa John's Team Member Emergency Relief Fund, Inc.
P.O. Box 99900
Louisville, KY   40269-0900   (502) 261-4227

Foundation type: Public charity

Purpose: Financial assistance is provided to Papa John's employees who are in need.
Financial data: Year ended 12/31/2011. Assets, $96,664 (M); Expenditures, $65,951; Total giving, $64,700.
Fields of interest: Human services.
Type of support: Employee-related welfare.
Application information: Unsolicited requests for funds not considered or acknowledged.
EIN: 201892180

3613
Jack Paxton Memorial Scholarship Fund, Inc.
555 Jefferson St.
Paducah, KY   42001

Foundation type: Independent foundation
Purpose: Scholarships to residents of western KY for continuing education at accredited colleges or universities.
Financial data: Year ended 12/31/2011. Assets, $494,648 (M); Expenditures, $27,342; Total giving, $25,000.
Fields of interest: Higher education.
Type of support: Scholarships—to individuals.
Application information: Application form required.
> *Deadline(s):* Apr. 15
EIN: 611093502

3614
Charles G. Pearl Scholarship Fund
P.O. Box 709
London, KY   40743   (606) 878-7010
Application address: Charles G. Pearson Scholarship Committee, 160 Reed Valley Rd., London, KY 40744

Foundation type: Independent foundation
Purpose: Scholarships to members of First Baptist Church, in London, KY.
Financial data: Year ended 12/31/2012. Assets, $379,168 (M); Expenditures, $10,804; Total giving, $8,533.
Type of support: Undergraduate support.
Application information: Applications not accepted.
> *Additional information:* Unsolicited requests for funds not considered or acknowledged.
EIN: 263196987

3615
Pflughaupt Charitable Foundation
(formerly Eugene B. and Margery Ames Pflughaupt Charitable Foundation, Inc.)
6336 Finchville Rd.
Shelbyville, KY   40065   (502) 633-2344
Contact: Ernestine Jennings, Secy.-Treas.

Foundation type: Independent foundation
Purpose: Scholarships to graduating seniors at Shelby County High School, Shelby County, KY for postsecondary education.
Financial data: Year ended 12/31/2011. Assets, $0 (M); Expenditures, $21,062; Total giving, $20,000; Grants to individuals, 4 grants totaling $20,000 (high: $5,000, low: $5,000).
Fields of interest: Higher education.
Type of support: Support to graduates or students of specific schools.
Application information: Applications not accepted.
EIN: 611274891

3616
PHP, Inc.
c/o William P. Mundy
P.O. Box 319
Hopkinsville, KY 42240-0319 (270) 886-0267
Contact: William P. Munday, Pres.
Application address: 1003 S. Virginia St.
Hopkinsville KY 42240

Foundation type: Independent foundation
Purpose: Scholarships to financially needy residents of Christian County, KY. Medical expenses and household utility payments to financially needy residents of Christian County, KY.
Financial data: Year ended 12/31/2012. Assets, $674,878 (M); Expenditures, $1,081,479; Total giving, $87,583; Grants to individuals, 3 grants totaling $3,000 (high: $1,000, low: $1,000).
Fields of interest: Education; Economically disadvantaged.
Type of support: Scholarships—to individuals; Grants for special needs.
Application information: Applications accepted.
Deadline(s): None
Additional information: Contact foundation for additional application guidelines.
EIN: 311041193

3617
Process Machinery Charitable Foundation, Inc.
1636 Isaac Shelby Dr.
Shelbyville, KY 40065-9173

Foundation type: Independent foundation
Purpose: Grants primarily to residents of KY for financial hardship assistance.
Financial data: Year ended 10/31/2011. Assets, $12,912 (M); Expenditures, $9,595; Total giving, $8,100.
Fields of interest: Human services; Economically disadvantaged.
Type of support: Grants for special needs.
Application information: Applications accepted. Application form not required.
Deadline(s): None
Additional information: Contact foundation for current application guidelines.
EIN: 611315964

3618
Shayne Quinkert Memorial Foundation
7711 Jonquil Dr.
Louisville, KY 40258
Contact: Lin D. Quinkert Ashcraft, Pres.
Application address: 4629 Payne Koehler Rd., New Albany, IN 47150-9554

Foundation type: Operating foundation
Purpose: Scholarships to residents of Floyd and Clark Counties, IN, and Jefferson and Oldham Counties, KY.
Financial data: Year ended 12/31/2011. Assets, $7,905 (M); Expenditures, $4,838; Total giving, $4,800; Grant to an individual, 1 grant totaling $4,800.
Fields of interest: Higher education.
Type of support: Scholarships—to individuals.
Application information:
Deadline(s): None
EIN: 311516337

3619
Rhoads Scholarship Trust
c/o PBI Bank
751 Campbell Ln.
Bowling Green, KY 42104

Foundation type: Independent foundation
Purpose: Scholarships to financially needy female graduating seniors with at least a 3.0 GPA.
Financial data: Year ended 12/31/2011. Assets, $271,910 (M); Expenditures, $16,141; Total giving, $13,125; Grants to individuals, 12 grants totaling $13,125 (high: $1,250, low: $625).
Fields of interest: Higher education; Women.
Type of support: Scholarships—to individuals.
Application information: Applications accepted.
Initial approach: Letter or telephone
Deadline(s): Mar. 15
Applicants should submit the following:
1) Transcripts
2) ACT
Additional information: Application must also include biographical sketch.
EIN: 611089770

3620
The River Foundation, Inc.
P.O. Box 328
Stanford, KY 40484-0328 (606) 365-6956
Contact: Dan Lewis, Exec. Dir.

Foundation type: Public charity
Purpose: Grants to low-income and needy individuals who are experiencing hardship.
Financial data: Year ended 12/31/2011. Assets, $98,461 (M); Expenditures, $1,591,900; Total giving, $1,568,011.
Fields of interest: Economically disadvantaged.
Type of support: Loans—to individuals.
Application information: Applications not accepted.
EIN: 611190262

3621
Scott Rose Foundation, Inc.
P.O. Box 5001
London, KY 40745-5001 (606) 864-6235
Contact: Lawrence Kuhl, Treas.

Foundation type: Independent foundation
Purpose: Support for medical and general welfare needs of disabled and disadvantaged children and young adults living in southeastern KY.
Financial data: Year ended 06/30/2012. Assets, $239,905 (M); Expenditures, $15,966; Total giving, $14,999; Grants to individuals, 8 grants totaling $11,999 (high: $1,500, low: $499).
Fields of interest: Children/youth, services; Disabilities, people with.
Type of support: Grants for special needs.
Application information: Applications accepted.
Initial approach: Letter or telephone
Deadline(s): None
EIN: 611048189

3622
Rural Kentucky Medical Scholarship Fund
c/o Katie Rafferty
4965 U.S. Hwy. 42, Ste. 2000
Louisville, KY 40222-6372 (502) 426-6200
FAX: (502) 426-6877; URL: http://www.kyma.org/content.asp?q_areaprimaryid=5&q_areasecondaryid=4

Foundation type: Public charity

Purpose: Grants and loans to promote an increase in the number of primary care physicians to practice medicine in critically underserved Kentucky counties.
Publications: Application guidelines.
Financial data: Year ended 12/31/2011. Assets, $2,306,006 (M); Expenditures, $105,390; Total giving, $78,593; Grants to individuals, totaling $78,593.
Fields of interest: Medical school/education; Health care.
Type of support: Grants to individuals; Loans—to individuals.
Application information: Applications accepted. Application form required. Application form available on the grantmaker's web site.
Send request by: Mail
Deadline(s): Mar. 1
Program description:
Establish Practice Grant Program: The fund awards grants for practice startup assistance to students currently in medical school who agree to the full-time practice of primary care medication in critically-underserved counties of Kentucky (including the areas of family practice, general practice, internal medicine, pediatrics, medical pediatrics, obstetrics/gynecology, and psychiatry). Recipients will be awarded four disbursements over a seven-year period (after the physician's first, third, fifth, and seventh year of practice): $20,000 after the first year, and $30,000 after subsequent years. Eligible applicants must be members of the Kentucky Medical Association.
EIN: 610967967

3623
School CHOICE Scholarships, Inc.
1228 E. Breckinridge St.
Louisville, KY 40204 (502) 254-7274
Contact: Heather Huddleston, Exec. Dir.
FAX: (502) 253-6555;
E-mail: info@schoolchoiceky.org; E-mail For Heather Huddleston: Heather@SchoolChoiceKy.org;
URL: http://www.schoolchoiceky.org

Foundation type: Public charity
Purpose: Scholarships to students entering grades K-6 who are living and attending school in Jefferson County, KY and qualify as low-income as defined by the Federal School Lunch Guidelines to attend a private school.
Publications: Application guidelines.
Financial data: Year ended 06/30/2012. Assets, $751,080 (M); Expenditures, $631,805; Total giving, $425,470; Grants to individuals, totaling $425,470.
Type of support: Precollege support.
Application information: Applications accepted. Application form required. Application form available on the grantmaker's web site.
Initial approach: Telephone, letter or e-mail
Send request by: Mail
Final notification: Applicants notified in the third week of Apr.
Applicants should submit the following:
1) Financial information
2) Budget Information
EIN: 311589289

3624
Scottish Rite Foundation in Kentucky
200 E. Gray St.
Louisville, KY 40202-2012

Foundation type: Independent foundation

Purpose: Fellowships to individuals who are pursuing a doctorate in Public Education Administration at the University of Louisville, University of Kentucky or Eastern Kentucky University.

Financial data: Year ended 06/30/2013. Assets, $1,096,185 (M); Expenditures, $117,174; Total giving, $107,950.

Fields of interest: Administration/regulation; Public education.

Type of support: Fellowships; Doctoral support.

Application information: Applications not accepted.

Additional information: Unsolicited requests for funds not considered or acknowledged.

EIN: 616036090

3625
Hugh Bell Smith Scholarship Fund

401 Fredena St., Ste. 204D
Owensboro, KY 42301
Contact: Melissa Rensi, Chair.
Application address: 817,Wahington,Brington,MI 48116

Foundation type: Independent foundation

Purpose: Scholarships to financially needy female graduates of McLean County High School, KY, who attend a public university in KY and intend to pursue careers in science or education.

Financial data: Year ended 12/31/2011. Assets, $25,104 (M); Expenditures, $578; Total giving, $0.

Fields of interest: Women.

Type of support: Support to graduates or students of specific schools; Undergraduate support.

Application information: Applications accepted. Application form required.

Deadline(s): Mar. 30

Additional information: Application should include an essay.

EIN: 611346025

3626
Bessie Sparks Scholarship Fund

101 N. Main St.
P.O. Box 8
Owenton, KY 40359-0008 (502) 484-2296
Contact: Jennifer Powers
Application address: Jennifer Powers, c/o Owen County High School, 2340 Hwy. 22 E., Owenton, KY 40359-9115, tel.: (502) 484-2715

Foundation type: Independent foundation

Purpose: Scholarships to students of Owen County High School, KY for postsecondary education.

Financial data: Year ended 12/31/2012. Assets, $205,278 (M); Expenditures, $3,211; Total giving, $1,000; Grants to individuals, 2 grants totaling $1,000 (high: $500, low: $500).

Fields of interest: Higher education.

Type of support: Support to graduates or students of specific schools; Precollege support.

Application information: Application form required.

Deadline(s): Third week in May

Additional information: Application can be obtained at the high school. Individuals are selected by a committee.

EIN: 616143459

3627
Hugh and Della Spear Scholarship, Inc.

P.O. Box 415
Burkesville, KY 42717
Contact: Harlan E. Judd, Jr., Pres.

Foundation type: Independent foundation

Purpose: Scholarships to residents of Cumberland County, KY.

Financial data: Year ended 12/31/2012. Assets, $0 (M); Expenditures, $6,750; Total giving, $6,750; Grants to individuals, 4 grants totaling $6,750 (high: $2,500, low: $1,250).

Type of support: Undergraduate support.

Application information: Applications accepted.

Deadline(s): May 15

Applicants should submit the following:
1) Essay
2) Financial information
3) Transcripts

EIN: 320130945

3628
St. Joseph Hospital Foundation, Inc.

1 St. Joseph Dr.
Lexington, KY 40504-3742 (859) 313-1705
Contact: Barry A. Stumbo, Pres. and C.E.O. and V.P., Devel.
FAX: (859) 313-2016; *URL:* http://www.sjhlex.org/hospital-foundation

Foundation type: Public charity

Purpose: Scholarships to students enrolled in a nursing program at a local college or university. In exchange, recipients agree to become full-time employees of St. Joseph Healthcare after graduating and passing state certification.

Financial data: Year ended 06/30/2011. Assets, $7,806,251 (M); Expenditures, $588,023; Total giving, $282,840; Grants to individuals, 10,622 grants totaling $18,731. Subtotal for grants for special needs: 10,622 grants totaling $18,731.

Fields of interest: Nursing school/education.

Type of support: Undergraduate support.

Application information: Applications accepted. Interview required.

Initial approach: Letter

Additional information: Contact foundation for current application guidelines.

EIN: 611159649

3629
Trover Clinic Foundation, Inc.

900 Hospital Dr.
Madisonville, KY 42431-1644 (270) 825-5201
Contact: E. Berton Whitaker, Pres. and C.E.O. and Secy.
Application address: 200 Clinic Dr., Third Center East, Madison, KY 42431, tel.: (270) 824-3440, e-mail: pslrp@trover.org
E-mail: info@trover.org; *Toll-free tel.:* (800) 998-5100

Foundation type: Public charity

Purpose: Loans to qualified physicians for medical school expenses who agree to practice in at least one of the non-metropolitan Kentucky Delta Region counties.

Financial data: Year ended 12/31/2011. Assets, $179,705,649 (M); Expenditures, $181,303,656; Total giving, $57,840.

Fields of interest: Medical school/education.

Type of support: Student loans—to individuals.

Application information: Applications accepted. Application form required.

Send request by: Mail
Deadline(s): Apr. 1
Final notification: Recipients notified May 1
Additional information: See web site for additional application guidelines.

EIN: 610654587

3630
Marie R. & Ervine Turner Educational Foundation, Inc.

P.O. Box 620
Jackson, KY 41339-0620 (606) 666-9366
Contact: Lesley Warrix-Allen, Exec. Dir.

Foundation type: Operating foundation

Purpose: Scholarships to residents of KY, primarily in Breathitt County, for higher education.

Financial data: Year ended 12/31/2012. Assets, $12,618,774 (M); Expenditures, $322,444; Total giving, $224,750; Grants to individuals, 45 grants totaling $224,750 (high: $118,000, low: $500).

Type of support: Scholarships—to individuals.

Application information: Application form required.

Additional information: Applications available at foundation office or schools in Breathitt County, KY. Contact foundation for current application deadline/guidelines.

EIN: 611333558

3631
United States Achievement Academy Scholarship Foundation, Inc.

2528 Palumbo Dr.
Lexington, KY 40509-1203 (859) 269-5671
URL: http://www.usaa-academy.com/schfacts.html

Foundation type: Operating foundation

Purpose: Scholarships by nomination only to members of the U.S. Achievement Academy, KY.

Financial data: Year ended 12/31/2012. Assets, $2,385 (M); Expenditures, $192,754; Total giving, $80,200; Grants to individuals, 410 grants totaling $80,200 (high: $10,000, low: $100).

Type of support: Awards/grants by nomination only.

Application information: See web site for nomination eligibility.

EIN: 200145934

3632
United States Equestrian Federation, Inc.

(also known as USEF)
4047 Iron Works Pkwy.
Lexington, KY 40511-8483 (859) 258-2472
Contact: Chrystine Tauber, Pres.
FAX: (859) 231-6662; *E-Mail for Chrystine Tauber:* cjtauber@usef.org; *URL:* http://www.usef.org

Foundation type: Public charity

Purpose: Scholarships to junior equestrian athletes who wish to further their education. The scholarship may be used to pursue academic or equestrian education.

Financial data: Year ended 11/30/2011. Assets, $16,905,353 (M); Expenditures, $24,619,470; Total giving, $1,520,866; Grants to individuals, totaling $1,518,478.

Fields of interest: Athletics/sports, equestrianism.

Type of support: Scholarships—to individuals.

Application information:

Initial approach: Letter

Additional information: Applicants are judged based on written exam or essay scores displaying the greatest understanding of equestrian knowledge.

EIN: 562350714

3633
University of Louisville Foundation, Inc.
Controller's Office
Univ. of Louisville
Louisville, KY 40292-2001 (502) 852-7072
Contact: Dr. James Ramsey, Pres.
URL: http://www.louisvillefoundation.org/

Foundation type: Public charity
Purpose: Scholarships and awards to qualified students of the University of Louisville, IL for higher education.
Financial data: Year ended 06/30/2011. Assets, $961,073,320 (M); Expenditures, $83,386,680; Total giving, $9,284,361; Grants to individuals, totaling $8,844,846.
Fields of interest: Higher education.
Type of support: Support to graduates or students of specific schools.
Application information: Applications accepted.
  Additional information: Scholarships are awarded based on availability of funds.
EIN: 237078461

3634
University of Louisville Research Foundation, Inc.
Controller's Office - Service Complex
Louisville, KY 40292-1802 (502) 852-7072

Foundation type: Public charity
Purpose: Scholarships and fellowships to qualified students of KY for higher education.
Financial data: Year ended 06/30/2012. Assets, $143,021,535 (M); Expenditures, $371,929,340; Total giving, $41,778,897; Grants to individuals, totaling $41,424,063.
Fields of interest: Higher education.
Type of support: Fellowships; Scholarships—to individuals.
Application information: Applications accepted.
  Additional information: Students are selected by the Dean's offices based on requirements of each individual scholarship.
EIN: 611029626

3635
USA Cares, Inc.
562 N. Dixie Blvd., Ste. 3
Radcliff, KY 40159-0759 (270) 352-5481
Contact: Peter L. Giusti, Pres.
E-mail: info@usacares.us; Toll-free tel.: (800)-773-0387; URL: http://www.usacares.org

Foundation type: Public charity
Purpose: Financial support to military families in times of need.
Financial data: Year ended 06/30/2012. Assets, $1,153,614 (M); Expenditures, $2,698,015; Total giving, $1,001,571; Grants to individuals, totaling $896,571.
Fields of interest: Military/veterans.
Type of support: Grants for special needs.
Application information: Applications accepted. Application form required. Application form available on the grantmaker's web site.
  Initial approach: Letter
  Send request by: Online
  Deadline(s): None
  Applicants should submit the following:
    1) Financial information
  Additional information: Application should include bills and proof of military status.
EIN: 050588761

3636
Glen, Frieda and John Wells Education Fund
P.O. Box 70
Hartford, KY 42347-0070 (270) 298-3249
Application Address: c/o Ohio County Board of Education, Ohio County High School, 315 E. Union St., Hartford, KY 42347
URL: http://www.ohio.kyschools.us/

Foundation type: Independent foundation
Purpose: Scholarships to graduates of Ohio County High School, KY, for higher education at any college, university or technology center in KY.

Financial data: Year ended 12/31/2012. Assets, $1,181,262 (M); Expenditures, $61,190; Total giving, $61,190; Grants to individuals, 91 grants totaling $61,190 (high: $1,118, low: $267).
Fields of interest: Vocational education, post-secondary; Higher education.
Type of support: Support to graduates or students of specific schools; Undergraduate support.
Application information: Application form required.
  Applicants should submit the following:
    1) Essay
    2) SAT
    3) GPA
    4) ACT
  Additional information: Contact your guidance counselor for application information.
EIN: 611362784

3637
Pauline C. Young Scholarship Foundation, Inc.
115 W. Short St.
Lexington, KY 40507-1301
URL: http://www.classesandcareers.com/schooldegrees/fusion.php?leadcat=pgmms2&v=24&sid=29151bf2f71f4d8b9feda238089c2f85

Foundation type: Operating foundation
Purpose: Scholarships to KY residents who will be attending college in KY.
Financial data: Year ended 12/31/2011. Assets, $8,539 (M); Expenditures, $1,712; Total giving, $0.
Type of support: Undergraduate support.
Application information: Applications not accepted.
  Additional information: Unsolicited requests for funds not considered or acknowledged.
EIN: 010693937

LOUISIANA

3638
100 Black Men of Metropolitan Baton Rouge, Ltd.
2050 N. Foster Dr.
Baton Rouge, LA 70806-1009 (225) 356-9444
Contact: Adell Brown, Jr., Pres. and Chair.
FAX: (225) 356-9453;
E-mail: info@100bmbr.brcoxmail.com; E-Mail for Adell Brown Jr.:
president@100bmbr.brcoxmail.com; URL: http://www.100blackmenbr.org/

Foundation type: Public charity
Purpose: Scholarships to high school graduates of Baton Rouge, LA pursuing postsecondary education at colleges, universities, vocational school or job training.
Financial data: Year ended 06/30/2012. Assets, $281,882 (M); Expenditures, $164,291; Total giving, $5,000; Grants to individuals, 7 grants totaling $5,000 (high: $1,500, low: $500).
Fields of interest: Vocational education, post-secondary; Higher education.
Type of support: Scholarships—to individuals.
Application information: Applications accepted. Application form required. Interview required.
  Deadline(s): May
  Applicants should submit the following:
    1) Letter(s) of recommendation
    2) Transcripts
    3) SAT
    4) Essay
    5) ACT
  Additional information: Applicant must provide proof or enrollment in a college/university, vocational school or other training program, have participated in 100 Black Men of Metropolitan Baton Rouge's activities for at least three years, and display good character traots.
EIN: 721235682

3639
Academic Distinction Fund
8550 United Plaza Blvd., Ste. 301
Baton Rouge, LA 70809-2256 (225) 922-4560
Contact: Martis Jones Ph.D., Exec. Dir.
FAX: (225) 922-4562; E-mail: info@adfbr.org; E-Mail for Martis Jones: martis.jones@adfbr.org;
URL: http://www.adfbr.org

Foundation type: Public charity
Purpose: Grants and fellowships to public school employees in the East Baton Rouge Parish, LA, public school system who work directly with students in an academic setting, including classroom teachers, reading recovery teachers, math specialists, librarians, technology directors, deans of students and counselors.
Publications: Application guidelines.
Financial data: Year ended 07/31/2011. Assets, $195,926 (M); Expenditures, $233,856.
Fields of interest: Education.
Type of support: Fellowships; Grants to individuals; Awards/prizes; Travel grants; Project support.
Application information: Application form required.
  Send request by: Online
  Deadline(s): Apr. 14
Program descriptions:
  ADF Fellows: Fellowships of $2,500 plus an additional $1,000 for individual activities and/or

travel to public school teachers to recognize their outstanding leadership. Deadline Sept. 10.
  Grants for Teachers: Grants up to $1,000 each to teachers who want to implement new learning strategies in the classroom. These grants enable teachers to purchase materials that will enhance instruction. Through a competitive proposal process, teachers are challenged to improve student performance.
  Student Achievement Grant: $500 to $2,500 grants available to meet very different needs from school to school. This grant is a result of combination of the Grants for Teachers and Teachers Learning Together.
EIN: 721300995

3640
Albemarle Foundation
451 Florida St.
Baton Rouge, LA 70801-1700 (225) 388-7552
Contact: Sandra M. Holub, Mgr.
E-mail: AlbemarleFoundation@albemarle.com;
E-mail for Sandra Holub:
sandra_holub@albemarle.com; URL: http://www.albemarle.com/Sustainability/Albemarle-Foundation-42.html

Foundation type: Company-sponsored foundation
Purpose: Scholarships to graduating high school seniors who are dependent children of any regular U.S. employee of Albemarle for attendance at accredited four year colleges or universities.
Publications: Application guidelines; Grants list; Informational brochure.
Financial data: Year ended 12/31/2012. Assets, $10,121,573 (M); Expenditures, $3,883,642; Total giving, $3,591,091.
Fields of interest: Higher education.
Type of support: Employee-related scholarships.
Application information: Applications not accepted.
  Additional information: Unsolicited requests for funds not considered or acknowledged.
Company name: Albemarle Corporation
EIN: 204798471

3641
American Counsel Scholarship Foundation, Inc.
c/o Stanley J. Cohn
Pan-American Life Ctr., 601 Poydras St., 27th Fl.
New Orleans, LA 70130-6029

Foundation type: Operating foundation
Purpose: Scholarship to a deserving law student in the Seventh U.S. Judicial Circuit.
Financial data: Year ended 12/31/2013. Assets, $46,896 (M); Expenditures, $701; Total giving, $0.
Fields of interest: Law school/education.
Type of support: Scholarships—to individuals.
Application information:
  Applicants should submit the following:
    1) Transcripts
    2) Financial information
  Additional information: Student must demonstrate financial need.
EIN: 521720223

3642
Arts Council of Greater Baton Rouge, Inc.
(formerly Arts and Humanities Council of Greater Baton Rouge)
427 Laurel St.
Baton Rouge, LA 70801-1810 (225) 344-8558
Contact: Eric Holowacz, Pres. and C.E.O.
FAX: (225) 344-7777; E-mail: acgbr@aol.com;
E-mail For Eric Holowacz: eric@acgbr.com;
URL: http://www.acgbr.com

Foundation type: Public charity
Purpose: Grants to artists in the Baton Rouge, LA, area.
Publications: Application guidelines.
Financial data: Year ended 06/30/2012. Assets, $2,085,384 (M); Expenditures, $2,237,790; Total giving, $577,737.
Fields of interest: Arts; Minorities.
Type of support: Grants to individuals; Awards/prizes.
Application information: Applications accepted. Application form required. Application form available on the grantmaker's web site.
  Deadline(s): Feb. 1
  Applicants should submit the following:
    1) Work samples
    2) SASE
    3) Resume
  Additional information: See web site for additional guidelines.
Program description:
  Arts Ambassador Award: Awards of $1,000 for Emerging Artist, and $2,000 for Established Artist who are residents of East Baton Rouge Parish for two or more years. Applicants in the Emerging Artist category must be practicing professional artists for at least two but no more than nine years. Applicants in the Established Artist category must be practicing professional artists for ten or more years. Applicants must be of ethnic minority, including but not limited to African-American, American Indian, Asian, Latino, and Pacific Islander.
EIN: 720735814

3643
The Ascension Fund, Inc.
P. O. Box 670
Gonzales, LA 70707-0670 (225) 647-0606

Foundation type: Public charity
Purpose: Grants to teachers in Ascension Parish, LA, schools to enhance education.
Financial data: Year ended 03/31/2010. Assets, $1,129,093 (M); Expenditures, $48,652; Total giving, $38,697.
Fields of interest: Education.
Type of support: Grants to individuals.
Application information:
  Initial approach: Proposal
  Additional information: Contact the fund for additional information.
EIN: 721186479

3644
Baton Rouge Area Foundation
402 N. 4th St.
Baton Rouge, LA 70802-5506 (225) 387-6126
Contact: John G. Davies, C.E.O.
FAX: (225) 387-6153; E-mail: jdavies@braf.org;
Additional tel.: (877) 387-6126; Grant information e-mail: lsmyth@braf.org; URL: http://www.braf.org

Foundation type: Community foundation
Purpose: Scholarships to graduating seniors and college students from the Baton Rouge, LA, area.

Publications: Application guidelines; Annual report (including application guidelines); Informational brochure; Newsletter.
Financial data: Year ended 12/31/2011. Assets, $556,584,976 (M); Expenditures, $42,756,547; Total giving, $26,826,403.
Fields of interest: Higher education.
Type of support: Scholarships—to individuals; Undergraduate support.
Application information: Applications accepted. Application form required. Application form available on the grantmaker's web site.
 Initial approach: E-mail
 Deadline(s): Vary
 Additional information: See web site for a complete list of programs.
EIN: 726030391

3645
Baton Rouge State Fair Foundation
(formerly Baton Rouge Jaycee Foundation)
P.O. Box 15010
Baton Rouge, LA 70895-5010 (225) 755-3247
E-mail: gbrsf@eatel.net; URL: http://www.gbrsf.com/

Foundation type: Independent foundation
Purpose: Scholarships to residents of Baton Rouge, LA, in pursuit of a higher education.
Financial data: Year ended 12/31/2012. Assets, $1,776,025 (M); Expenditures, $988,045; Total giving, $184,563; Grants to individuals, 27 grants totaling $13,500 (high: $500, low: $500).
Fields of interest: Higher education.
Type of support: Scholarships—to individuals.
Application information: Applications accepted.
 Deadline(s): None
 Additional information: Contact foundation for application guidelines.
EIN: 721036440

3646
Nathan Bernstein Scholarship Fund
c/o Regions Bank
333 Texas St., SH2069
Shreveport, LA 71101-3666

Foundation type: Independent foundation
Purpose: Scholarships to medical students for attendance at Louisiana State University School of Medicine.
Financial data: Year ended 09/30/2013. Assets, $2,343,144 (M); Expenditures, $132,074; Total giving, $107,693.
Fields of interest: Medical school/education.
Type of support: Scholarships—to individuals; Support to graduates or students of specific schools; Graduate support.
Application information: Application form required.
 Deadline(s): June 15
 Applicants should submit the following:
  1) Financial information
  2) Letter(s) of recommendation
  3) FAFSA
 Additional information: Awards are based on merit and financial need.
EIN: 726103061

3647
Dr. and Mrs. C. R. Brownell Charitable Fund
1316 Federal Ave.
Morgan City, LA 70380-3120

Foundation type: Independent foundation

Purpose: Scholarships to full-time students who maintain a 3.0 GPA, and attend a LA university or college.
Financial data: Year ended 12/31/2011. Assets, $232,392 (M); Expenditures, $11,434; Total giving, $8,000; Grants to individuals, 4 grants totaling $8,000 (high: $2,500, low: $1,500).
Fields of interest: Higher education.
Type of support: Scholarships—to individuals.
Application information: Applications accepted. Application form required.
 Deadline(s): None
 Applicants should submit the following:
  1) Transcripts
  2) ACT
 Additional information: Application must also include a thesis.
EIN: 721228886

3648
The William T. and Ethel Lewis Burton Foundation
641 W. Prien Lake Rd.
Lake Charles, LA 70601-8315
Contact: William T. Drost, Dir.

Foundation type: Independent foundation
Purpose: Scholarships available to Southwest Louisiana High School seniors and members of the McNeese State University, Lousiana football team.
Financial data: Year ended 05/31/2013. Assets, $5,096,508 (M); Expenditures, $1,082,817; Total giving, $1,069,033; Grants to individuals, 8 grants totaling $10,000 (high: $1,250, low: $1,250).
Fields of interest: Athletics/sports, school programs; Athletics/sports, football.
Type of support: Support to graduates or students of specific schools; Undergraduate support.
Application information: Applications accepted. Application form not required.
 Initial approach: Letter
 Deadline(s): None
 Additional information: Recipients are selected by their institutions.
EIN: 726027957

3649
CS Foundation Inc.
10965 Cornerstone Pl.
Keithville, LA 71047-8587 (318) 524-1880
Contact: Michael E. Jones, Pres.
Application address: 9203 Stonebriar Cir., Shreveport, LA 71115

Foundation type: Independent foundation
Purpose: Assistance to low income individuals primarily of LA who have limited income, with medical and household bills.
Financial data: Year ended 12/31/2012. Assets, $1,113 (M); Expenditures, $155,485; Total giving, $155,350; Grant to an individual, 1 grant totaling $4,400.
Fields of interest: Economically disadvantaged.
Type of support: Grants for special needs.
Application information: Applications accepted.
 Deadline(s): None
 Additional information: Assistance is on a case by case basis. Contact foundation for eligibility determination.
EIN: 721486456

3650
ECD Global Alliance, Inc.
P.O. Box 775
DeRidder, LA 70634-0775 (337) 515-6987
E-mail: support@erdheim-chester.org; URL: http://www.erdheim-chester.org/

Foundation type: Public charity
Purpose: Grants to investigators who seek to conduct research to find the cause, treatment or cure for Erdheim Chester Disease (ECD)
Financial data: Year ended 12/31/2011. Assets, $189,277 (M); Expenditures, $46,569; Total giving, $37,309.
Fields of interest: Diseases (rare).
Type of support: Research.
Application information: Applications accepted.
 Initial approach: Letter of Intent
 Send request by: On-line, mail
 Deadline(s): Apr. 1
 Additional information: See web site for detailed additional application guidelines.
Program description:
 ECD Global Alliance Grants: Grant are provided in amounts up to $50,000 per year to principal investigators who hold post-doctoral positions or beyond. Projects will ordinarily be funded for one year, where appropriate, funding requests for follow on study is encouraged. Proposed projects must have specific relevance to ECD, and show promise for contributing to the scientific advancement in this field of study.
EIN: 270759192

3651
Entergy Corporation Contributions Program
639 Loyola Ave.
New Orleans, LA 70161-1000 (504) 576-6980
Contact: Patty Riddlebarger, Dir., Corp. Social Responsibility
URL: http://www.entergy.com/our_community

Foundation type: Corporate giving program
Purpose: Scholarships to children of employees of Entergy Corporation for college or vocational programs.
Publications: Application guidelines; Corporate report.
Fields of interest: Vocational education; Higher education; Education.
Type of support: Employee-related scholarships.
Application information: Applications accepted.
 Initial approach: Contact the Entergy Contributions Coordinator before submittng an application
Program description:
 Community Power Scholarship: The company awards scholarships to children and dependents of its employees to pursue college or vocational school programming.
Company name: Entergy Corporation

3652
The Food Bank of Central Louisiana, Inc.
3223 Baldwin Ave.
Alexandria, LA 71301-3506 (318) 445-2773
Contact: Jayne Wright-Velez, Exec. Dir.
E-mail: jwrightvelez@fbcenla.org; URL: http://www.fbcenla.org/

Foundation type: Public charity
Purpose: Food assistance and emergency supplies to indigent residents of central LA who fall within the poverty levels set by the federal government.

Financial data: Year ended 06/30/2012. Assets, $1,876,800 (M); Expenditures, $7,360,507; Total giving, $6,099,141; Grants to individuals, totaling $176,141.
Fields of interest: Food banks; Economically disadvantaged.
Type of support: In-kind gifts.
Application information:
Initial approach: In person
Deadline(s): None
Additional information: An applicant must provide the following information to The Food Bank: government issued picture ID, proof of income of everyone in the household, proof of address, verification of the members of the household.
EIN: 721154072

3653
Friends of a Studio in the Woods
13401 Patterson Rd.
New Orleans, LA   70131-3204   (504) 392-4460
FAX: (504) 394-5977;
E-mail: info@astudiointhewoods.org; URL: http://astudiointhewoods.org/index.php

Foundation type: Public charity
Purpose: Four six-week residencies to New Orleans established and emerging artists.
Publications: Application guidelines.
Financial data: Year ended 06/30/2012. Assets, $253,884 (M); Expenditures, $112,517.
Fields of interest: Environment.
Type of support: Residencies.
Application information: Applications accepted.
Deadline(s): June 18
Final notification: Recipients notified July 30
Applicants should submit the following:
1) Resume
2) Work samples
3) SASE
Additional information: Application should also include artist statement, and references, and an application fee of $30. See web site for additional guidelines.
Program description:
Environmental Residencies: The call is open to artists of all disciplines who have demonstrated an established dialogue with environmental issues and a commitment to seeking and plowing new ground. Artists are invited to design their own interface with the public and are encouraged to propose ways to engage the larger community of New Orleans and beyond. Four six-week residencies which include a stipend and supply budget are to be offered between September 2010 and April 2011.
EIN: 721502728

3654
Goldring Family Foundation
524 Metairie Rd.
Metairie, LA   70005-4308   (504) 849-6078
Contact: Trudi Briede, Dir.
FAX: (504) 849-6511; E-mail: trudi@gff1.com

Foundation type: Independent foundation
Purpose: Scholarships to children of employees of Goldring Affiliates and Sazerac Company, for higher education at accredited colleges and universities.
Financial data: Year ended 11/30/2012. Assets, $70,970,952 (M); Expenditures, $4,113,623; Total giving, $3,450,644. Scholarships—to individuals amount not specified.
Fields of interest: Higher education.
Type of support: Employee-related scholarships; Scholarships—to individuals.

Application information: Applications not accepted.
Additional information: Unsolicited requests for funds not considered or acknowledged.
EIN: 726022666

3655
House of Ruth, Inc.
1111 Newton St., Ste. 203
New Orleans, LA   70114-2500   (504) 366-3921
Contact: Brigitte Karmona, Exec. Dir.
E-mail: info@houseofruthnola.org; E-mail For Brigitte Karmona: swilliams@houseofruthnola.org; URL: http://www.houseofruthnola.org/

Foundation type: Public charity
Purpose: Short-term assistance for homeless LA families (with children) who have experienced a sudden loss of income. Assistance with rent, utility, food, clothing, furnishing, personal and household needs is provided.
Financial data: Year ended 06/30/2012. Assets, $70,460 (M); Expenditures, $566,770.
Fields of interest: Human services.
Type of support: Grants for special needs.
Application information:
Initial approach: Letter
Additional information: Contact the organization for eligibility criteria.
EIN: 581766752

3656
Larry & Gladys Hunter Scholarship Fund, Inc.
412 Pine St.
Minden, LA   71055-3120   (318) 377-6846
Contact: Don Hunter, Pres.

Foundation type: Independent foundation
Purpose: Scholarships to graduates of the Minden Public School System, LA, for undergraduate education. Scholarships are renewable, for a maximum of $6,000 over four years.
Financial data: Year ended 12/31/2012. Assets, $130,400 (M); Expenditures, $7,629; Total giving, $6,750; Grants to individuals, 5 grants totaling $3,750 (high: $1,500, low: $750).
Type of support: Support to graduates or students of specific schools; Undergraduate support.
Application information: Applications accepted. Application form required.
Deadline(s): Mar. 10
EIN: 720942291

3657
The JL Foundation
21223 Waterfront E. Dr.
Maurepas, LA   70449-5303   (225) 698-1010
Contact: Robert P. Leslie, Pres.
FAX: (225) 698-1313;
E-mail: jlfoundation@jlfoundation.org; URL: http://www.jlfoundation.org/

Foundation type: Public charity
Purpose: Financial assistance to families of leukemia patients of Louisiana. Scholarships to leukemia patients who are residents of LA.
Publications: Financial statement; Informational brochure.
Financial data: Year ended 02/28/2013. Assets, $160,980 (M); Expenditures, $153,026; Total giving, $152,676.
Fields of interest: Leukemia; Economically disadvantaged.

Type of support: Scholarships—to individuals; Grants for special needs.
Application information:
Initial approach: Letter
Additional information: Contact the foundation for eligibility criteria. Grants are only for leukemia patients of LA.
EIN: 752976320

3658
Lafayette Education Foundation
315 S. College Rd., Ste. 180
Lafayette, LA   70503-3277   (337) 234-3229
Contact: Becky Credeur, Exec. Dir.
FAX: (337) 234-9146;
E-mail: becky@lefoundation.org; Mailing address: P.O. Box 53649, Lafayette, LA 70505-3649; E-Mail for Becky Credeur: becky@lefoundation.org; URL: http://www.lefoundation.org

Foundation type: Public charity
Purpose: Grants to any Lafayette Parish, LA, public school classroom or special education teacher, librarian, or guidance counselor, social worker, or other education professional directly involved in classroom instruction. Awards by nomination only to active academic educators.
Publications: Application guidelines; Grants list; Informational brochure; Newsletter.
Financial data: Year ended 12/31/2011. Assets, $1,855,311 (M); Expenditures, $380,178; Total giving, $180,443; Grants to individuals, totaling $180,443.
Fields of interest: Education.
Type of support: Program development; Awards/grants by nomination only; Awards/prizes.
Application information: Application form required. Application form available on the grantmaker's web site.
Initial approach: Telephone or e-mail
Deadline(s): Mar. 1 for Mini grants, Nov. 1 for grants by nomination only
Program descriptions:
Mini-Grants: Grants of up to $1,000 are awarded to any Lafayette Parish public school classroom or special education teacher, librarian, or guidance counselor, social worker, or other education professional directly involved in classroom instruction. There is a limit of two applications per teacher per year.
Teacher Awards: Nominees must be active academic educators. Eligible educators are teachers, counselors, librarians, or speech therapists, in Lafayette Parish public, private, or parochial school systems in grades K-12.
EIN: 581849198

3659
Lafourche Education Foundation, Inc
P.O. Box 529
Thibodaux, LA   70302-0529   (985) 448-4315
Contact: Judy Theriot
URL: http://www.seeds4success.org

Foundation type: Independent foundation
Purpose: Grants to full-time public school teachers Pre-K- 12 from Lafourche Parish School System, LA.
Financial data: Year ended 06/30/2013. Assets, $33,620 (M); Expenditures, $68,183; Total giving, $27,367; Grants to individuals, 18 grants totaling $12,440 (high: $5,000, low: $500).
Type of support: Project support.

Application information: Applications accepted. Application form required. Application form available on the grantmaker's web site.

> *Deadline(s):* Feb. 15
> *Final notification:* Recipients notified in May
> *Additional information:* A maximum of two Paul Ruth Teacher grant applications may be submitted from each school within the parish.

EIN: 311574723

3660
The Fritz Lang Foundation

P.O. Box 6300
Lake Charles, LA 70606-6300   (337) 474-2840
Contact: Wanda N. Borel, Admin.
FAX: (337) 474-2838;
E-mail: wanda@fritzlangfoundation.org;
URL: http://fritzlangfoundation.org

Foundation type: Independent foundation
Purpose: Scholarships to graduating students from Vermilion and Jefferson Davis parishes, LA, who are pursuing undergraduate and graduate degrees in agriculture and related fields. Scholarships are currently $1,200 per fall and spring semesters. Late applications may be considered and placed on a waiting list for unclaimed funds. Selection will be based on academic achievement and financial need. Students must have and maintain a 2.5 GPA or better.
Publications: Application guidelines.
Financial data: Year ended 06/30/2012. Assets, $1,139,642 (M); Expenditures, $362,899; Total giving, $303,100; Grants to individuals, 139 grants totaling $303,100 (high: $3,000, low: $1,000).
Fields of interest: Agriculture.
Type of support: Professorships; Support to graduates or students of specific schools; Graduate support; Undergraduate support.
Application information: Applications accepted. Application form required.

> *Deadline(s):* Apr. 1
> *Applicants should submit the following:*
> 1) GPA
> 2) Financial information
> 3) Curriculum vitae
> 4) ACT
> 5) Transcripts
> 6) Letter(s) of recommendation
> *Additional information:* Late applications may be considered and placed on a waiting list for unclaimed funds. Application must also include a copy of parents' or personal tax return, as well as evidence of acceptance in college (high school students) or college registration for upcoming semester (already attending college) and a current college transcript, if applicable. Two letters of recommendation are required. Application guidelines and form are available on foundation web site.

EIN: 581854369

3661
The Jerry Ledet Foundation

3404 Wakefield Ave.
Houma, LA 70363-5414   (985) 879-1360
Contact: Gerald C. Ledet, Pres.

Foundation type: Independent foundation
Purpose: Scholarships to residents of Houma and Terrebone Parish, LA, and TX.
Publications: Application guidelines.
Financial data: Year ended 12/31/2011. Assets, $118,224 (M); Expenditures, $20,055; Total giving, $19,500.

Type of support: Undergraduate support.
Application information:

> *Initial approach:* Letter
> *Additional information:* Contact foundation for eligibility requirements.

EIN: 721141584

3662
The Louisiana Association of Community Action Partnerships, Inc.

11637 Industriplex Blvd.
Baton Rouge, LA 70809-5139   (225) 298-3323
Contact: Jane Killen, Exec. Dir.

Foundation type: Public charity
Purpose: Financial assistance to low-income individuals and families in Louisiana, reduce their expenditure and improve their health and safety, and improve energy efficiency of their home.
Financial data: Year ended 10/31/2011. Assets, $7,754,195 (M); Expenditures, $73,117,632; Total giving, $67,461,879; Grants to individuals, totaling $104,062.
Fields of interest: Economically disadvantaged.
Type of support: Grants for special needs.
Application information: Applications accepted.

> *Additional information:* Contact the agency for eligibility determination.

EIN: 581717009

3663
Louisiana Bar Foundation

1615 Poydras St., Ste. 1000
New Orleans, LA 70112-4063   (504) 561-1046
Contact: Donna C. Cuneo, Exec. Dir.
FAX: (504) 566-1926;
E-mail: donna@raisingthebar.org; URL: http://www.raisingthebar.org

Foundation type: Public charity
Purpose: Financial assistance for attorneys of Louisiana who have incurred law school debt.
Publications: Application guidelines; Annual report.
Financial data: Year ended 06/30/2012. Assets, $8,018,757 (M); Expenditures, $7,196,667; Total giving, $6,083,410.
Fields of interest: Law school/education.
Type of support: Loans—to individuals.
Application information: Applications accepted. Application form required.

> *Deadline(s):* Dec. 1

Program description:

> *Public Interest Attorney Loan Repayment Assistance Program (LRAP):* The foundation provides one-year loans up to $5,000 to new or current public interest attorneys with law school debt employed by foundation grantees. The loan amount is disbursed to the recipients on a quarterly basis and is forgiven after completion of 12 months of employment with the grantee. Recipients of this funding are eligible to re-apply annually for loans until receiving five years' of funding.

EIN: 237100704

3664
Louisiana Cultural Economy Foundation

1540 Canal St.
New Orleans, LA 70115-4237   (504) 895-2800
Contact: Aimee Smallwood, C.E.O.
FAX: (504) 910-3001;
E-mail: info@culturaleconomy.org; E-Mail for Aimee Smallwood : aimee@culturaleconomy.org;
URL: http://www.culturaleconomy.org

Foundation type: Public charity
Purpose: Grants, ranging from $250 to $2,500, are available to individual economy cultural workers who are professionally active in their discipline (artistic or cultural), earn income through their talents, and reside in LA.
Publications: Application guidelines.
Financial data: Year ended 12/31/2011. Assets, $181,363 (M); Expenditures, $642,423; Total giving, $122,231; Grants to individuals, totaling $122,231.
Fields of interest: Arts; Community/economic development.
Type of support: Grants to individuals.
Application information: Applications accepted. Application form required.

> *Initial approach:* Letter
> *Deadline(s):* July 6
> *Additional information:* Contact foundation for eligibility criteria.

EIN: 203598297

3665
Louisiana Endowment for the Humanities

938 Lafayette St., Ste. 300
New Orleans, LA 70113-1782   (504) 523-4352
Contact: Michael Sartisky Ph.D., Pres. and Exec. Dir.
FAX: (504) 529-2358; E-mail: lahum@leh.org; Toll-free tel.(in LA): (800) 909-7990; E-Mail for Brian Boyles: sartisky@leh.org; URL: http://www.leh.org/

Foundation type: Public charity
Purpose: Grants for assistance with publication projects to scholars and photodocumentarians applying the humanities to LA history/culture and/or issues impacting life in LA.
Publications: Application guidelines; Annual report; Grants list; Informational brochure.
Financial data: Year ended 10/31/2011. Assets, $6,593,067 (M); Expenditures, $2,699,999; Total giving, $137,326.
Fields of interest: Cultural/ethnic awareness; Photography; Humanities.
Type of support: Publication.
Application information: Applications accepted. Application form required. Application form available on the grantmaker's web site.

> *Initial approach:* Telephone or letter
> *Send request by:* Mail
> *Copies of proposal:* 8
> *Deadline(s):* Feb. 15
> *Final notification:* Applicants notified in 45 days

EIN: 720795568

3666
Louisiana Poultry Industries Educational Foundation, Inc.

P.O. Box 931
Natchitoches, LA 71458-0931
Application address: c/o LSU, Attn.: Poultry Science Dept., 120 Ingram Hall, Baton Rouge, LA 70803-0001

Foundation type: Independent foundation
Purpose: Scholarships to students in Louisiana institutes of higher learning who demonstrate a sincere interest in the poultry area.
Financial data: Year ended 12/31/2012. Assets, $214,927 (M); Expenditures, $4,255; Total giving, $4,250; Grants to individuals, 10 grants totaling $4,250 (high: $500, low: $250).
Fields of interest: Agriculture.
Type of support: Scholarships—to individuals.

Application information: Applications accepted. Application form required.
> *Initial approach:* Letter
> *Send request by:* Mail
> *Deadline(s):* May
> *Applicants should submit the following:*
> 1) Essay
> 2) Transcripts
> 3) Letter(s) of recommendation
EIN: 721148406

3667
Masonic Educational Foundation Inc.
5746 Masonic Dr.
Alexandria, LA   71301   (318) 443-5610

Foundation type: Independent foundation
Purpose: Scholarships only to residents of the Masonic Home for Children, LA, for higher education.
Financial data: Year ended 09/30/2013. Assets, $0 (M); Expenditures, $10,895; Total giving, $8,000; Grants to individuals, 6 grants totaling $8,000 (high: $2,000, low: $750).
Type of support: Undergraduate support.
Application information: Applications accepted. Application form required.
> *Initial approach:* Letter and proof of college admission
> *Deadline(s):* None
EIN: 237423947

3668
Garnie W. & Zoe McGinty Trust
500 E. Reynolds Dr.
Ruston, LA   71270-2821

Foundation type: Public charity
Purpose: Undergraduate scholarships and graduate fellowships to students attending Louisiana Tech University.
Financial data: Year ended 08/31/2012. Assets, $1,291,607 (M); Expenditures, $79,080.
Fields of interest: Higher education; Engineering school/education.
Type of support: Support to graduates or students of specific schools.
Application information: Application form not required.
> *Additional information:* Unsolicited requests for funds not accepted.
EIN: 726081740

3669
Arlene & Joseph Meraux Charitable Foundation, Inc.
417 Friscoville Ave.
Arabi, LA   70032   (504) 439-8191
Contact: Rita O. Gue, Pres.
URL: http://merauxfoundation.org/

Foundation type: Independent foundation
Purpose: Scholarships to high school graduates of St. Bernard Parish, LA for postsecondary education.
Financial data: Year ended 12/31/2012. Assets, $58,996,797 (M); Expenditures, $2,129,643; Total giving, $161,213.
Fields of interest: Higher education.
Type of support: Undergraduate support.
Application information: Applications accepted. Application form required.
> *Initial approach:* Letter
> *Additional information:* Contact the foundation for additional application guidelines.
EIN: 721400981

3670
National Kidney Foundation of Louisiana, Inc.
8200 Hampson St., Ste. 425
New Orleans, LA   70118-1063   (504) 861-4500
Contact: Torie Kranze, C.E.O.
FAX: (504) 861-1976; E-mail: info@kidneyla.org; Toll-free tel.: (800) 462-3694; E-mail For Torie Kranze: torie@kidneyla.org; URL: http://www.kidneyla.org

Foundation type: Public charity
Purpose: Financial assistance to kidney patients residing in LA, for dialysis treatment and transportation. Research grants to support postdoctoral work on kidney disease.
Publications: Newsletter.
Financial data: Year ended 06/30/2012. Assets, $661,024 (M); Expenditures, $529,328; Total giving, $16,656; Grants to individuals, totaling $6,656.
Fields of interest: Kidney diseases; Kidney research.
Type of support: Research; Postdoctoral support; Grants for special needs.
Application information: Contact foundation for application guidelines.
EIN: 720649707

3671
The Humphrey T. Olinde, Jr. Family Foundation
4970 Bluebonnet Blvd., Ste. B
Baton Rouge, LA   70809-3089
Application address for individuals: c/o Henry D.H. Olinde, Sr., 7225 Barford Ave., Baton Rouge, LA 70808

Foundation type: Independent foundation
Purpose: Scholarships to graduate and undergraduate students who demonstrate academic ability and financial need.
Financial data: Year ended 12/31/2012. Assets, $13,089 (M); Expenditures, $127,950; Total giving, $125,506; Grant to an individual, 1 grant totaling $5,000.
Fields of interest: Higher education.
Type of support: Scholarships—to individuals.
Application information: Applications accepted. Application form required.
> *Initial approach:* Application
> *Send request by:* Mail
> *Applicants should submit the following:*
> 1) Essay
> 2) Financial information
> 3) Letter(s) of recommendation
> 4) Transcripts
> *Additional information:* Application forms available at college guidance offices.
EIN: 203098668

3672
Our Lady of the Lake Regional Medical Center
7777 Hennessy Blvd.
Baton Rouge, LA   70808-4375   (225) 765-6565
Contact: K. Scott Wester, C.E.O.
URL: http://www.ololrmc.com/

Foundation type: Public charity
Purpose: Emergency assistance with medical care for needy individuals of Baton Rouge, LA.
Financial data: Year ended 06/30/2012. Assets, $1,250,161,461 (M); Expenditures, $724,998,648; Total giving, $5,152,314; Grants to individuals, totaling $25,500.

Fields of interest: Health care; Economically disadvantaged.
Type of support: Emergency funds.
Application information: Applications accepted.
> *Additional information:* Some assistance require completing an application.
EIN: 720423651

3673
Park West Children's Fund, Inc.
(also known as Friend Ships Unlimited)
1019 N. 1st Ave.
Lake Charles, LA   70601-1705   (337) 433-5022
Contact: Sandra G. Tipton, Pres.
FAX: (337) 433-3433; E-mail: info@friendships.org; URL: http://www.friendships.org/

Foundation type: Public charity
Purpose: Relief assistance to victims of natural disaster with food, clothing, home repairs and other emergency assistance in the U.S. and abroad.
Financial data: Year ended 02/28/2013. Assets, $7,492,431 (M); Expenditures, $1,408,512; Total giving, $804,808.
Fields of interest: Safety/disasters; Human services.
Type of support: In-kind gifts; Grants for special needs.
Application information: Contact the organization for additional guidelines.
EIN: 953917951

3674
Willis & Mildred Pellerin Foundation
P.O. Box 400
Kenner, LA   70063-0400   (504) 467-9591
Contact: Lynne Hotfelter

Foundation type: Independent foundation
Purpose: Scholarships to highly qualified and financially needy residents of LA who are enrolled in a LA college or university for full-time undergraduate study.
Financial data: Year ended 05/31/2013. Assets, $1,563,075 (M); Expenditures, $72,150; Total giving, $57,350; Grants to individuals, 78 grants totaling $57,350.
Type of support: Undergraduate support.
Application information: Application form required.
> *Initial approach:* Letter
> *Deadline(s):* 180 days prior to the beginning of the school term
> *Applicants should submit the following:*
> 1) Photograph
> 2) Transcripts
> 3) Letter(s) of recommendation
> *Additional information:* Application must also include a handwritten explanation of need, and certification of acceptance for enrollment. Applicants are required to repay one-half of the grant in equal weekly installments. The grants will be repaid without interest except for an 8 percent per annum charge on late payments.
EIN: 510166877

3675
Brad Pitt's Make It Right Foundation
(also known as Make It Right)
912 Magazine St.
New Orleans, LA   70130-3814
Contact: Anna Leighman
Toll-free tel.: (888) 647-6652; URL: http://www.makeitrightnola.org

Foundation type: Public charity
Purpose: Financial assistance to qualified homeowners in the Lower 9th Ward, New Orleans, LA with closing costs and affordable mortgage.
Publications: Financial statement.
Financial data: Year ended 12/31/2011. Assets, $44,362,172 (M); Expenditures, $13,398,142; Total giving, $444,490; Grants to individuals, totaling $413,294.
Fields of interest: Housing/shelter, rehabilitation; Housing/shelter, home owners; Community development, neighborhood associations.
Type of support: Grants to individuals.
Application information: See web site for additional guidelines.
EIN: 260723027

3676
Oscar Lee Putnam Cultural Endowment
701 Poydras St., Ste. 3640
New Orleans, LA   70139-7700   (504) 865-5720
Contact: James M. MacLaren, Tr.
Application address: c/o Rbert C. Cudd Hall, Newcomb-Tulane College, New Orleans, LA 70118

Foundation type: Independent foundation
Purpose: Scholarships to students who are residents of LA for higher education.
Financial data: Year ended 12/31/2012. Assets, $319,784 (M); Expenditures, $15,849; Total giving, $10,950.
Fields of interest: Higher education.
Type of support: Scholarships—to individuals.
Application information: Applications accepted.
  Initial approach: Letter
  Deadline(s): June 15
  Additional information: Application must outline financial need and high school academic record.
EIN: 726022138

3677
Southeastern Louisiana University Development Foundation
10293 Southeastern Lousiana Univ.
Hammond, LA   70402-0001   (985) 549-2239
FAX: (985) 549-2257; E-mail: sdf@selu.edu;
Toll-free tel.: (866) 474-4438; URL: http://www.selu.edu/alumni_donors/dev_foundation/

Foundation type: Public charity
Purpose: Scholarships to students of Southeastern Louisiana University, LA pursuing undergraduate and graduate studies.
Financial data: Year ended 06/30/2012. Assets, $30,448,843 (M); Expenditures, $2,056,955; Total giving, $362,328; Grants to individuals, totaling $362,328.
Fields of interest: Higher education.
Type of support: Support to graduates or students of specific schools.
Application information: Applications accepted.
  Additional information: Contact the financial aid office for additional scholarship information.
EIN: 726028821

3678
St. Vincent de Paul Store of Houma
107 Point St.
Houma, LA   70360-4348   (985) 872-0113
Contact: James E. Lagarde, Mgr.
FAX: (985) 223-1931

Foundation type: Public charity

Purpose: Grants of basic necessities to needy individuals in the Houma, LA, area.
Financial data: Year ended 09/30/2012. Assets, $608,417 (M); Expenditures, $1,304,552; Total giving, $909,759; Grants to individuals, totaling $909,759.
Fields of interest: Economically disadvantaged.
Type of support: Grants for special needs.
Application information:
  Initial approach: Letter
  Additional information: Contact foundation for eligibility requirements.
EIN: 720573879

3679
Patrick F. Taylor Foundation
1 Lee Cir.
New Orleans, LA   70130-3931
Contact: Phyllis M. Taylor, Pres.
FAX: (504) 589-0408; URL: http://www.pftaylorfoundation.org

Foundation type: Independent foundation
Purpose: Scholarships to graduating Louisiana high school students attending a four-year LA undergraduate institution, based on financial need and academic performance.
Publications: Application guidelines.
Financial data: Year ended 12/31/2012. Assets, $18,198,077 (M); Expenditures, $3,179,051; Total giving, $3,134,144; Grants to individuals, totaling $171,700.
Fields of interest: Higher education; Scholarships/financial aid.
Type of support: Scholarships—to individuals; Support to graduates or students of specific schools.
Application information: Applications accepted. Application form required.
  Initial approach: Telephone
  Deadline(s): July 15
  Applicants should submit the following:
    1) Transcripts
    2) GPA
    3) ACT
    4) SAR
  Additional information: Application should also include a letter of acceptance to a LA college or university, and must be able to provide information regarding amounts of financial assistance (college, federal and state grant awards). Students are required to submit one character-reference letter. High school students who meet the foundation's criteria may apply in June. See web site for scholarship programs.
Program description:
  The Taylor/Audubon Students and Scholars Program: Eligible students earn a one-year membership to the Audubon Aquarium of the Americas and the Audubon Butterfly Garden and Insectarium for achieving a 2.5 grade point average or higher. Students who earn a 3.0 GPA or above also qualify for a one-year membership to the Audubon Zoo. The program is open to all Louisiana students in grades 7th through 12th, whether attending public, private, or parochial schools. One parent or guardian may accompany students free of charge to these sites. See web site for additional information.
EIN: 581686754

3680
Total Community Action, Inc.
1420 S. Jefferson Davis Pkwy.
New Orleans, LA   70125-1744   (504) 872-0334
Contact: Thelma Harris French, Pres. and C.E.O.
FAX: (504) 872-0339; E-mail: tca@tca-nola.org;
URL: http://www.tca-nola.org

Foundation type: Public charity
Purpose: Grants for residents of the New Orleans, LA, area to help pay energy bills. Special emphasis is given to households with elderly, the disabled, and children age 5 and under.
Financial data: Year ended 12/31/2011. Assets, $11,485,808 (M); Expenditures, $39,202,777; Total giving, $14,968,768; Grants to individuals, totaling $4,933,719.
Fields of interest: Housing/shelter, services; Economically disadvantaged.
Type of support: Grants for special needs.
Application information:
  Initial approach: Telephone or letter
  Additional information: Contact foundation for complete eligibility criteria.
EIN: 720599165

3681
Olive Tupper Foundation
P.O. Box 6300
Lake Charles, LA   70606-6300   (337) 474-2840
Contact: Wanda N. Borel, Admin.
URL: http://www.tupperfoundation.org

Foundation type: Independent foundation
Purpose: Scholarships to financially needy full-time undergraduate and graduate nursing students who have graduated from an accredited high school and plan to attend McNeese State University, LA, or other qualified schools.
Publications: Application guidelines.
Financial data: Year ended 08/30/2012. Assets, $2,831,924 (M); Expenditures, $91,977; Total giving, $80,000; Grants to individuals, 52 grants totaling $80,000 (high: $1,900, low: $900).
Fields of interest: Nursing school/education.
Type of support: Support to graduates or students of specific schools; Graduate support; Undergraduate support.
Application information: Application form required.
  Deadline(s): 60 days prior to start of the semester
  Applicants should submit the following:
    1) Essay
    2) ACT
    3) GPA
    4) Letter(s) of recommendation
    5) Transcripts
  Additional information: High school students should provide evidence of college acceptance and most recent tax return.
Program description:
  Nursing School Scholarship Program: Applicants must possess good character, ambitious purpose, and positive qualities, and should be capable of using educational opportunities to enhance personal excellence and to contribute to his/her community. Residents of Allen and Jefferson Davis parishes, LA, will be given priority. Applicants must also be nursing students accepted to or currently attending McNeese State University, LA, except in the case where enrollment precludes the applicant's admission to McNeese. In addition, applicants must have a maximum adjusted gross income, (as determined by the federal tax return) of $20,000 plus $3,000 for each child under the age of 23 residing at home or in school.
EIN: 721277047

3682
Roy A. Waters Scholarship Fund
c/o John F. Schneider
23473 Hwy. 22 E.
Ponchatoula, LA   70454-5903   (985) 386-2694
Contact: Bruce Bishop

Foundation type: Public charity
Purpose: Scholarships to deserving young individuals to foster support for the sport of canoeing.
Financial data: Year ended 12/31/2012. Assets, $140,321 (M); Expenditures, $4,811; Total giving, $4,661. Scholarships—to individuals amount not specified.
Fields of interest: Camps; Athletics/sports, water sports.
Type of support: Scholarships—to individuals.
Application information: Applications accepted.
Additional information: Scholarships are paid directly to the camp on behalf of the individuals.
EIN: 640616282

3683
The Woldenberg Foundation
(formerly Dorothy & Malcolm Woldenberg Foundation)
524 Metairie Rd.
Metairie, LA   70005-4308   (504) 849-6078
Contact: Trudi Briede, Dir.
FAX: (504) 849-6511; E-mail: trudi@gff1.com

Foundation type: Independent foundation
Purpose: Scholarships to dependent children of employees of Goldring Affiliates & Republic National Distributing Co.
Financial data: Year ended 12/31/2012. Assets, $31,140,801 (M); Expenditures, $2,593,580; Total giving, $2,284,067.
Fields of interest: Higher education.
Type of support: Employee-related scholarships.
Application information: Applications not accepted.
Additional information: Unsolicited requests for funds not considered or acknowledged.
EIN: 726022665

3684
Fred B. and Ruth B. Zigler Foundation
P.O. Box 986
Jennings, LA   70546-0986   (337) 824-2413
FAX: (337) 824-2414;
E-mail: frzigler@bellsouth.net; URL: http://www.ziglerfoundation.org/

Foundation type: Independent foundation
Purpose: Scholarships to graduating seniors from accredited Jefferson Davis Parish, LA, high schools.
Publications: Annual report; IRS Form 990 or 990-PF printed copy available upon request.
Financial data: Year ended 12/31/2012. Assets, $11,144,258 (M); Expenditures, $768,808; Total giving, $480,200.

Fields of interest: College; Scholarships/financial aid.
Type of support: Scholarships—to individuals.
Application information: Application form required.
Initial approach: Letter
Applicants should submit the following:
   1) SAT
   2) ACT
   3) Financial information
   4) GPA
   5) Letter(s) of recommendation
   6) Transcripts
Additional information: Scholarships are awarded on the basis of financial need and the ability to perform college-level work.
EIN: 726019403

MAINE

3685
Acadia Foundation
30 Peabody Dr.
Northeast Harbor, ME 04662   (207) 276-5266
Contact: Richard Estes, Pres.

Foundation type: Independent foundation
Purpose: Cash grants and housing for artists (painters) aiding them in the creative process.
Financial data: Year ended 12/31/2012. Assets, $12,915 (M); Expenditures, $9,029; Total giving, $2,500; Grant to an individual, 1 grant totaling $2,500.
Fields of interest: Painting.
Type of support: Grants to individuals.
Application information: Applications accepted.
  Initial approach: Letter
  Deadline(s): None
EIN: 208046397

3686
Anson Academy Association
P.O. Box 416
North Anson, ME 04958-0073   (207) 635-3399
Application address: c/o Carrabec High School, Attn.: Guidance Counselor, Solon Rd., N. Anson, ME 04958, tel.: (207) 635-2296

Foundation type: Public charity
Purpose: Scholarships to graduates of MSAD No. 74 who have completed one semester of higher education, to be applied to second semester tuition.
Financial data: Year ended 12/31/2011. Assets, $350,382 (M); Expenditures, $12,428; Total giving, $7,600.
Fields of interest: Higher education.
Type of support: Scholarships—to individuals.
Application information: Applications accepted.
  Initial approach: Letter
  Deadline(s): May 15
EIN: 016048483

3687
Associated General Contractors of Maine Education Foundation
P.O. Box 5519
Augusta, ME 04332-5519   (207) 622-4741
Contact: Matt Marks, Secy.
Application address: 181 Whitten Rd., P.O. Box N. Augusta, ME 04332 tel: (207) 622-4741; URL: http://agcmaine.org/

Foundation type: Independent foundation
Purpose: Scholarships to ME students interested in a career in the construction industry.
Financial data: Year ended 12/31/2011. Assets, $488,283 (M); Expenditures, $30,865; Total giving, $25,750; Grants to individuals, 12 grants totaling $25,750 (high: $4,000, low: $1,250).
Fields of interest: Business/industry.
Type of support: Scholarships—to individuals.
Application information: Applications accepted. Application form required.
  Deadline(s): None
  Additional information: Application should include written goals summary.
EIN: 010445998

3688
Augusta Kiwanis Scholarship Foundation
c/o Clayton Rollins
P.O. Box 966
Augusta, ME 04332-0966

Foundation type: Independent foundation
Purpose: Scholarships by nomination only to high school students in ME.
Financial data: Year ended 12/31/2012. Assets, $363,651 (M); Expenditures, $18,245; Total giving, $14,400; Grants to individuals, 14 grants totaling $14,400 (high: $1,200, low: $600).
Type of support: Awards/grants by nomination only.
Application information: Applications not accepted.
  Additional information: Unsolicited requests for funds not considered or acknowledged.
EIN: 237089761

3689
Bangor Fuel Society
c/o Eaton Peabody
P.O. Box 1210
Bangor, ME 04402-1210
Contact: Calvin E. True, Pres.
Application address: 80 Exchange St., Bangor, ME 04401

Foundation type: Operating foundation
Purpose: Deliveries of home heating fuel to low-income residents of Bangor, ME and adjoining communities.
Financial data: Year ended 10/31/2013. Assets, $938,669 (M); Expenditures, $46,921; Total giving, $45,463; Grants to individuals, totaling $45,463.
Fields of interest: Housing/shelter, services; Economically disadvantaged.
Type of support: Grants for special needs.
Application information:
  Deadline(s): None
  Additional information: Applications available through local services agencies.
EIN: 016010608

3690
Robert W. Belknap, M.D. Free Bed Fund
P.O. Box 7
Damariscotta, ME 04543-0007   (207) 563-5864
Contact: David J. Belknap, Pres.

Foundation type: Independent foundation
Purpose: Financial assistance to needy individuals of ME, for hospital expenses.
Financial data: Year ended 12/31/2012. Assets, $239,406 (M); Expenditures, $14,227; Total giving, $12,000; Grants to individuals, 29 grants totaling $12,000 (high: $1,200, low: $50).
Fields of interest: Hospitals (general); Health care.
Type of support: Grants for special needs.
Application information:
  Deadline(s): None
  Additional information: Applicant must show evidence of need. Payments are made directly to hospital on behalf of the individual.
EIN: 016011506

3691
Camden Home for Senior Citizens
8 Harrison Ave.
Camden, ME 04843   (207) 236-9467
Contact: Jean Payne

Foundation type: Independent foundation
Purpose: Financial assistance with a maximum amount of $400 per month is granted to elderly residents of Camden, Rockport, Hope, and Lincolnville, ME, for heating, food, rent, real estate taxes, medication, and other medical needs.
Financial data: Year ended 05/31/2013. Assets, $3,507,379 (M); Expenditures, $180,176; Total giving, $155,200; Grants to individuals, totaling $155,200.
Fields of interest: Aging, centers/services; Aging; Economically disadvantaged.
Type of support: Grants to individuals.
Application information: Applications accepted. Application form required.
  Deadline(s): None
EIN: 010248064

3692
Corporal Works of Mercy Society of St. Mary's Church
87 Whiskeag Rd.
Bath, ME 04530

Foundation type: Independent foundation
Purpose: Grants to economically disadvantaged individuals residing in Bath, ME.
Financial data: Year ended 12/31/2012. Assets, $82,160 (M); Expenditures, $22,751; Total giving, $22,251; Grants to individuals, totaling $22,251.
Fields of interest: Economically disadvantaged.
Type of support: Grants for special needs.
Application information: Applications accepted. Application form not required.
  Deadline(s): None
EIN: 237218514

3693
George P. Davenport Trust Fund
65 Front St.
Bath, ME 04530-2508   (207) 443-3431
Contact: Barry M. Sturgeon, Tr.
E-mail: davenporttrust@myfairpoint.net

Foundation type: Independent foundation
Purpose: Scholarships to graduates of Morse High School who reside in Bath, ME area.
Financial data: Year ended 12/31/2012. Assets, $6,576,416 (M); Expenditures, $375,008; Total giving, $288,425; Grants to individuals, 106 grants totaling $92,750 (high: $1,500, low: $250).
Fields of interest: Higher education.
Type of support: Scholarships—to individuals; Student loans—to individuals; Support to graduates or students of specific schools.
Application information: Applications accepted. Application form required.
  Initial approach: Telephone
  Deadline(s): None
  Additional information: Applicants must submit a copy of their financial aid package as established by the college or university they plan to attend.
EIN: 016009246

3694
Down East AIDS Network, Inc.
(also known as DEAN)
25A Pine St.
Ellsworth, ME 04605-2023   (207) 667-3506
FAX: (207) 664-0574;
E-mail: machiashelp@downeastaidsnetwork.org;
URL: http://www.downeastaidsnetwork.org

Foundation type: Public charity

Purpose: Financial support to people living with HIV and AIDS for medical and nonmedical assistance.
Financial data: Year ended 12/31/2011. Assets, $69,183 (M); Expenditures, $340,192.
Fields of interest: AIDS.
Type of support: Grants to individuals; Grants for special needs.
Application information: Contact the organization for further guidelines.
EIN: 010441229

3695
Eastern Frontier Educational Foundation Inc.

P.O. Box 472
Jonesport, ME   04649   (845) 278-1211
Contact: Stephen T. Dunn, Pres.
Application address: 2022 Rte. 22, Brewster, NY 10509 Tel.: (845) 278-1211; URL: http://www.easternfrontier.com

Foundation type: Operating foundation
Purpose: Residencies for visual artists, writers, and composers to develop and share their work at Norton Island, ME.
Financial data: Year ended 05/31/2013. Assets, $574,147 (M); Expenditures, $63,584; Total giving, $0.
Fields of interest: Visual arts; Music composition; Literature.
Type of support: Residencies.
Application information: Applications accepted. Application form required.
Initial approach: Letter or e-mail
Send request by: Mail
Deadline(s): Mar. 1
Final notification: Applicants notified by Apr. 15
Additional information: Application should include $25 application fee, and work samples.
Program description:
Residency Program: The residency provides room and board, food, and working space. The program takes place in the remote wilderness with limited, basic facilities. The general residency lasts for three weeks. Eight writers of fiction, poetry, and drama, and nonfiction and three visual artists are selected by a jury that judges applicants on talent alone.
EIN: 010535353

3696
Franklin Savings Bank Community Development Foundation

198 Front St.
P.O. Box 825
Farmington, ME   04938-0825   (207) 778-3339
Contact: Peter Judkins, Pres.

Foundation type: Company-sponsored foundation
Purpose: Scholarships to graduating students from Mt. Blue High School, Mountain Valley High School, Mt. Abram High School, Dirigo High School, Jay High School, Livermore Falls High School, Madison High School, Skowhegan Area High School and Rangeley Lakes Regional School pursuing a career in a business related field.
Publications: Application guidelines.
Financial data: Year ended 12/31/2012. Assets, $2,348,203 (M); Expenditures, $165,443; Total giving, $164,630.
Fields of interest: Higher education.
Type of support: Support to graduates or students of specific schools.

Application information: Applications accepted. Application form required. Application form available on the grantmaker's web site.
Additional information: Application must be submitted at your guidance offices. Scholarship is awarded based on academic achievement, community involvement, extracurricular activities and financial need.
EIN: 311719226

3697
Friends of Acadia

43 Cottage St.
P.O. Box 45
Bar Harbor, ME   04609-0045   (207) 288-3340
Contact: Marla O'Byrne, Pres.
FAX: (207) 288-8938;
E-mail: info@friendsofacadia.org; Toll-free tel.: (800) 625-0321; URL: http://www.friendsofacadia.org

Foundation type: Public charity
Purpose: Cash prizes and awards to poets to promote and recognize distinctive nature poetry.
Publications: Newsletter.
Financial data: Year ended 12/31/2011. Assets, $19,703,339 (M); Expenditures, $2,639,750; Total giving, $1,108,806.
Fields of interest: Literature.
Type of support: Awards/prizes.
Application information:
Deadline(s): Apr. 30
Additional information: Nature-based poems must be 30 lines or fewer. There is no application fee. Entries must be original, unpublished and not submitted elsewhere.
EIN: 010425071

3698
Alice G. Gadd and F. Frederick Romanow, Jr. Charitable Foundation

(formerly Alice G. Gadd Charitable Foundation)
P.O. Box 211
Belfast, ME   04915-1712

Foundation type: Operating foundation
Purpose: Grants to individuals with diabetes residing in Waldo County, ME.
Financial data: Year ended 12/31/2012. Assets, $324,257 (M); Expenditures, $14,500; Total giving, $5,193; Grants to individuals, totaling $4,193.
Fields of interest: Diabetes.
Type of support: Grants for special needs.
Application information: Applications accepted.
Initial approach: Letter
Deadline(s): None
Additional information: Contact foundation for current application guidelines.
EIN: 223177652

3699
Girl Scouts of Maine

138 Gannett Dr.
P.O. Box 9421
South Portland, ME   04116-9421   (207) 772-1177
Contact: Joanne Crepeau, C.E.O. and C.F.O.
FAX: (207) 874-2646;
E-mail: jcrepeau@gsmaine.org; Toll-free tel. (ME only): (888) 922-GSME; additional address (Bangor office): 359 Perry Rd., Ste. B, Bangor, ME 04401-6723, tel.: (207) 989-7474, fax: (207) 989-7478; URL: http://www.girlscoutsofmaine.org

Foundation type: Public charity
Purpose: Financial assistance to attend girl scouts program and tuition reduction for camperships in the ten counties of southern and central ME.
Financial data: Year ended 09/30/2012. Assets, $3,906,505 (M); Expenditures, $3,720,294; Total giving, $190,818; Grants to individuals, totaling $190,818.
Fields of interest: Girl scouts.
Type of support: Grants for special needs.
Application information: Applications accepted. Application form required.
Send request by: Mail
Additional information: Applicant must demonstrate financial need. See web site for additional guidelines.
EIN: 010269802

3700
Arthur George Goodrich Scholarship Trust

135 High St.
P.O. Box 1100
Ellsworth, ME   04605-1100

Foundation type: Independent foundation
Purpose: Scholarships to graduates of Mount Desert Island High School, ME, who were in the top 75 percent of their class.
Financial data: Year ended 12/31/2012. Assets, $85,749 (M); Expenditures, $4,843; Total giving, $3,615.
Type of support: Support to graduates or students of specific schools; Undergraduate support.
Application information: Applications accepted. Application form required.
Deadline(s): May 1
Applicants should submit the following:
1) Financial information
2) Transcripts
3) Essay
Additional information: Applications should also include a personal statement of 500 words or less telling of aspirations, recommendation from high school guidance counselor. Recipient selected by high school staff. Student must maintain a "C" average or better to renew.
EIN: 656430473

3701
Theodore and Wanda Gray Scholarship Trust

P.O. Box 1401
Bangor, ME   04402-1401

Foundation type: Independent foundation
Purpose: Scholarships to individuals who have attended George Stevens Academy, ME for four years and have been residents of Blue Hill ME for at least seven years, to attend post-secondary school.
Financial data: Year ended 12/31/2011. Assets, $0 (M); Expenditures, $20,372; Total giving, $18,300; Grants to individuals, 4 grants totaling $18,300 (high: $15,000, low: $1,100).
Type of support: Support to graduates or students of specific schools; Undergraduate support.
Application information: Applications accepted. Application form required.
Deadline(s): Apr. 30
EIN: 016160331

3702

Sumner O. Hancock Scholarship Fund

P.O. Box 295
Casco, ME 04015
Contact: Matt Hancock

Foundation type: Independent foundation
Purpose: Scholarships to residents of the Casco, ME, area, including graduates of Lake Region High School, Naples, ME.
Financial data: Year ended 12/31/2012. Assets, $104,579 (M); Expenditures, $13,297; Total giving, $10,900; Grants to individuals, 24 grants totaling $10,900.
Type of support: Support to graduates or students of specific schools; Undergraduate support.
Application information: Applications accepted. Application form required.
  Deadline(s): May 15
EIN: 016028898

3703

Holocaust and Human Rights Center of Maine

46 University Dr.
Augusta, ME 04330-1644 (207) 621-3530
Contact: Robert Bernheim Ph.D., Exec. Dir.
FAX: (207) 621-3534; E-mail: infohhrc@maine.edu;
URL: http://hhrc.uma.edu/

Foundation type: Public charity
Purpose: Scholarships to high school seniors who are residents of ME. Also, awards to ME students who have written a piece of literature, or who have created a piece of visual or performance art relating to the Holocaust and/or issues of human rights.
Publications: Application guidelines; Newsletter.
Financial data: Year ended 03/31/2012. Assets, $2,956,482 (M); Expenditures, $297,522.
Fields of interest: Visual arts; Performing arts; Literature; Civil/human rights.
Type of support: Undergraduate support.
Application information: Applications accepted. Application form required. Application form available on the grantmaker's web site.
  Initial approach: Letter
  Send request by: Mail
  Deadline(s): Mar. 31
  Applicants should submit the following:
    1) Essay
    2) SASE
Program descriptions:
  Lawrence Alan Speigel Remembrance Scholarship: This $1,000 scholarship is available to any high school senior or home-schooler who is a resident of Maine and who has been accepted to an accredited college, university, or technical school that is Title IV eligible.
  Take a Stand Award: This award, ranging from $250 to $500, recognizes a Maine citizen of any age who, at considerable personal risk, takes a public stand against a situation, person, or action in which another person's rights or personal integrity were being denied. Such action need not have been grandiose; it need only have demonstrated a courageous determination to speak out against the denial of fair and unprejudiced treatment of a fellow human being, lest such abuse feed and grow strong on the silence of bystanders. Eligible recipients must be nominated by another individual.
EIN: 010406624

3704

Hungarian-American Enterprise Scholarship Fund

c/o CIEE
300 Fore St.
Portland, ME 04101-4110 (207) 553-4194
FAX: (207) 553-5194; E-mail: mivanova@ciee.org;
Contact for application, acceptance and pre-departure information and questions: Kati Szalay c/o HAESF, CIEE Exchanges, Inc., Kereskedelmi Kepviselete, Andrassy ut 61., I/5, Budapest 1062, Hungary, tel.: (36-1) 413-0018, fax: (36-1) 413-0019, e-mail: info@haesf.org; Contact for Fellowship placement questions and support-related issues: Maggie Ivanova at Portland, ME, address, tel., fax or e-mail; URL: http://www.haesf.org

Foundation type: Independent foundation
Purpose: Scholarships, fellowships, awards and exchange programs between the U.S. and Hungary to outstanding individuals for the senior leaders and scholarship fellowship and for the professional internship programs.
Financial data: Year ended 09/30/2012. Assets, $7,306,941 (M); Expenditures, $1,097,625; Total giving, $804,780; Grants to individuals, 72 grants totaling $804,780 (high: $36,112; low: $180).
Fields of interest: Education; International exchange, students.
Type of support: Fellowships; Scholarships—to individuals; Exchange programs.
Application information: Applications accepted. Application form required. Application form available on the grantmaker's web site. Interview required.
  Deadline(s): Oct. 15 and Apr. 1 for Professional Internship Program, and Senior Leaders & Scholars Fellowship, Sept. 15 and Feb. 15 for Entrepreneurship Development Program
  Final notification: Recipients notified Dec. 15 and June 15 for Professional Internship Program, and Senior Leaders & Scholars Fellowship. Nov. 15 and Apr. 30 for Entrepreneurship Development Program
  Applicants should submit the following:
    1) Photograph
    2) Transcripts
    3) Resume
    4) Letter(s) of recommendation
    5) Curriculum vitae
  Additional information: See web site for application guidelines for each program.
Program descriptions:
  Entrepreneurship Development Program: Endowed by U.S. Treasury funds, this program grants fully funded four to six month traineeships at prominent American companies to the most accomplished young talent from Hungary. The goal of the program is to provide promising future entrepreneurs of Hungary an opportunity to have a meaningful international training experience, with the intention of enhancing their contribution to their home country and its development upon their return. Selected participants will be placed in traineeships that further their professional and personal development, provide them with leadership and entrepreneurial acumen, improve their English language acquisition, and help them grow their businesses as they return to their home country. See web site for additional information.
  Professional Internship Program: Endowed by U.S. Treasury funds, this program grants fully funded six to twelve month internships at prominent American companies to the most accomplished young talent from Hungary. The goal of the program is to provide promising future leaders of Hungarian society an opportunity to have a meaningful international training experience, with the intention of enhancing their contribution to their home country and its development upon their return. Selected Fellows will be placed in career-related internships that further their professional and personal development, provide them with leadership and cross-cultural communication skills, improve their English language acquisition and help them advance as they attend graduate school and enter the work force at home. See web site for additional information.
  Senior Leaders & Scholars Fellowship: Endowed by U.S. Treasury funds, this program provides fully funded three to twelve month long Fellowships to accomplished professionals and leaders from Hungary. The program provides significant funding to distinguished mid-level and senior-level Hungarian professionals in business, public administration, research, non-profit organizations and academia enabling them to pursue independently organized projects in the United States. At the heart of the program, it is meant to foster the exchange of ideas between Hungarians and Americans and to stimulate international collaboration and research efforts. It promotes interchange, mutual enrichment, and experiential sharing, further strengthening ties between the nations and providing invaluable career and personal development opportunities for participants to leverage in their leadership roles upon their return to Hungary. See web site for additional information.
EIN: 200490204

3705

Information Technology Exchange

156 Searsport Ave.
Belfast, ME 04915-7223 (207) 338-4233
FAX: (207) 338-4033; E-mail: info@itec3.org;
Mailing address: P.O. Box 589, Searsport, ME 04974-0589; URL: http://www.itec3.org/

Foundation type: Public charity
Purpose: Free computers and technical support to low-income individuals and families throughout ME.
Publications: Application guidelines.
Financial data: Year ended 12/31/2011. Assets, $194,324 (M); Expenditures, $501,759.
Fields of interest: Employment; Family services; Engineering/technology.
Type of support: In-kind gifts.
Application information: Applications accepted. Application form required. Application form available on the grantmaker's web site.
  Initial approach: Application
  Deadline(s): None
Program description:
  PCs for Maine: This program is a computer access and literary project that provides low-cost personal computer ownership for individuals, families, schools, and nonprofits who are engaged in job skills development and education. Eligible individuals and organizations include: individuals or representatives of a family engaged in education (pre-K-12, GED, adult education, or college); individuals engaged in career skills development or starting a small business; individuals representing a nonprofit that provides community support, advocates for the disabled, or offers literary instruction; or public pre-K-12 schools. Individual participants must be legal citizens of the U.S. Nonprofit groups must be recognized as 501(c)(3) exempt organizations by the IRS, and must show an IRS determination letter or official educational charter with application.
EIN: 550788650

3706
Island Institute
386 Main St.
P.O. Box 648
Rockland, ME   04841-3345   (207) 594-9209
Contact: Rob Snyder, Pres.
FAX: (207) 594-9314;
E-mail: inquiry@islandinstitute.org; E-Mail for Rob
Snyder: rsnyder@islandinstitute.org; E-Mail for
Kathy Lane: klane@islandinstitute.org; URL: http://
www.islandinstitute.org

Foundation type: Public charity
Purpose: Scholarships to individuals who reside in
the islands and communities of the Gulf of Maine.
Financial data: Year ended 06/30/2012. Assets,
$21,122,221 (M); Expenditures, $4,766,834;
Total giving, $212,554; Grants to individuals,
totaling $119,054.
Type of support: Scholarships—to individuals.
Application information: Applications accepted.
Application form required.
  Deadline(s): Mar. 15, June 15, Sept. 15, and
    Dec. 15 for Fund for Maine Island Education;
    Apr. 1 for all other scholarships
Program descriptions:
*Academic and Community Leadership
Scholarship:* The scholarship provides the top
graduating senior from Maine's fourteen year-round
unbridged island communities with a $5,000
scholarship toward his or her first year of college.
This scholarship seeks to find the individual who
partners civic leadership with academic
achievement. The recipient will not only be an
outstanding scholar but also an outstanding
member of the community who serves as a leader
for his or her peers.
Fund for Maine Island Education: The fund
provides scholarships to broaden educational
opportunities in Maine's unbridged island
communities.
Maine Island Higher Education Scholarship: The
scholarship supports Maine's unbridged island
students in their pursuit of academic excellence at
high schools, colleges, and universities across the
U.S.
Otter Island Scholarship: This scholarship
provides assistance to year-round island students
who attend one of a select group of secondary
schools or post-secondary institutions. Secondary
schools are: Pomfret School, Groton School, St.
Georges School, and Northfield-Mt. Hermon School.
Eligible colleges and universities are: Connecticut
College, Vanderbilt University, Texas Christian
University, Duke University, Colorado College,
University of Utah, and Harvard Business School.
The $5,000 awards are renewable every year during
the recipient's enrollment at one of the eligible
schools.
EIN: 222786731

3707
Kieve-Wavus Education, Inc.
(formerly Kieve Affective Education)
42 Kieve Rd.
P.O. Box 169
Nobleboro, ME   04555-8444   (207) 563-5172
Contact: Henry R. Kennedy, Exec. Dir.
FAX: (207) 563-5215; URL: http://www.kieve.org

Foundation type: Public charity
Purpose: Grants to ME individuals to attend Kieve
Camp for Boys or Wavus Camp for Girls for the
summer.
Financial data: Year ended 12/31/2011. Assets,
$26,049,260 (M); Expenditures, $6,625,028;

Total giving, $802,193; Grants to individuals,
totaling $802,193.
Fields of interest: Elementary/secondary
education; Camps.
Type of support: Camperships.
Application information: Contact organization for
eligibility criteria.
EIN: 237352599

3708
Hattie A. and Fred C. Lynam Trust
P.O. Box 1100
Ellsworth, ME   04605-1100   (877) 475-5399
Scholarship application address: c/o Maine
Community Foundation, 245 Main St., Ellsworth,
ME 04605-1613, tel.: (207) 667-9735, toll
free: (877) 700-6800, fax: (207) 667-0447
Grant application address: c/o Julie Zimmerman,
Trust Officer, Bar Harbor Trust Services, P.O. Box
1100, Ellsworth, ME 04605; email for Julie
Zimmerman: jzimmerman@bhbt.com; URL: http://
www.lynamtrust.com

Foundation type: Independent foundation
Purpose: Scholarships to high school graduates of
Mount Desert Island High School, ME who are
residents of Mount Desert Island for continuing
education at institutions of higher learning.
Financial data: Year ended 12/31/2012. Assets,
$5,109,317 (M); Expenditures, $321,853; Total
giving, $273,738.
Fields of interest: Higher education.
Type of support: Support to graduates or students
of specific schools.
Application information: Applications accepted.
Application form required.
  Deadline(s): May 1
  Applicants should submit the following:
    1) Transcripts
    2) Letter(s) of recommendation
    3) Financial information
    4) Essay
  Additional information: Students must reapply
    each year for consideration, ranked in the top
    75 percent of their class, must be in good
    academic standing and maintain a "C"
    average or better. Students should contact
    their school's guidance office for further
    application information.
EIN: 010222218

3709
Maine Alliance for Arts Education
P.O. Box 872
Augusta, ME   04332-0872   (207) 615-8233
Contact: Peter Alexander, Exec. Dir.
Additional e-mail:
maaemidcoast@suscom-maine.net
FAX: (207) 743-6234;
E-mail: info@maineartsed.org; E-Mail for Peter
Alexander: peter@maineartsed.org; URL: http://
www.maineartsed.org

Foundation type: Public charity
Purpose: Fellowships to permanently assigned arts
teachers in K-12 public schools in ME.
Publications: Application guidelines.
Financial data: Year ended 09/30/2011. Assets,
$36,789 (M); Expenditures, $167,477.
Fields of interest: Arts education.
Type of support: Fellowships.
Application information: Applications accepted.
Application form required.
  Initial approach: Telephone or e-mail
  Additional information: See web site for
    additional guidelines.

Program description:
Maine Arts Teachers Fellowship Program: The
program is a fellowship opportunity for Maine's
K-12 arts teachers (music, theater, creative writing,
visual or performing arts) to design a program that
provides them with the opportunity to interact with
professional artists and to enhance their
understanding or current techniques, activity, and
thinking in their primary artistic medium. Selected
fellows will receive up to $4,000 each, with a
complementary grant of $1,000 to support
post-fellowship activities. The fellowship award may
be used to defray the costs of tuition and other
fees, room and board, travel, purchase of materials
and/or equipment for personal art-making,
childcare and other relevant expenses.
EIN: 222710493

3710
Maine Bar Foundation
40 Water St., 1st Fl.
Hallowell, ME   04347-1437   (207) 622-3477
Contact: Diana Scully, Exec. Dir.
FAX: (207) 623-4140; E-mail: info@mbf.org; E-mail
for Diana Scully: dscully@mbf.org; URL: http://
www.mbf.org

Foundation type: Public charity
Purpose: Loans to assist attorneys interested in
public service with repayment of their law school
debts.
Publications: Application guidelines.
Financial data: Year ended 09/30/2012. Assets,
$3,966,516 (M); Expenditures, $1,599,144; Total
giving, $1,216,567; Grants to individuals, totaling
$23,950.
Fields of interest: Law school/education.
Type of support: Loans—to individuals.
Application information: Applications accepted.
Application form required. Application form
available on the grantmaker's web site.
  Initial approach: Letter
  Deadline(s): Mar. 31
  Final notification: Recipients notified one month
    from deadline
Program description:
Loan Repayment Assistance Program: The loan
program assists attorneys employed by the
Participating Providers, whether full time or part
time, who have outstanding law school loans, are
eligible to participate for a ten-year period. The
maximum amount of loans to any recipient during a
program year will be $5,000.
EIN: 222559133

3711
Maine Cancer Foundation
170 US Route 1, Ste. 250
Falmouth, ME   04105-0553   (207) 773-2533
Contact: Tara Hill, Exec. Dir.
Application e-mail: grants@mainecancer.org
FAX: (207) 773-2386;
E-mail: joyce@maincancer.org; URL: http://
www.mainecancer.org

Foundation type: Public charity
Purpose: Scholarships for oncology nurses and
other professionals of ME, for cancer research,
education and patient support programs.
Publications: Application guidelines; Annual report;
Financial statement; Grants list; Informational
brochure; Newsletter.
Financial data: Year ended 06/30/2012. Assets,
$3,656,296 (M); Expenditures, $1,730,198; Total
giving, $987,344. Scholarships—to individuals
amount not specified.

Fields of interest: Medical research.
Type of support: Research; Scholarships—to individuals.
Application information: Applications accepted. Application form required.
  Send request by: Letter or e-mail
  Additional information: See web site for additional application guidelines.
EIN: 010351077

3712
The Maine Community Foundation, Inc.
245 Main St.
Ellsworth, ME 04605-1613   (207) 667-9735
FAX: (207) 667-0447; E-mail: info@mainecf.org;
URL: http://www.mainecf.org

Foundation type: Community foundation
Purpose: Scholarships for students, camperships, and professional development grants for teachers and residents of ME.
Publications: Application guidelines; Annual report; Financial statement; Grants list; Informational brochure; Newsletter.
Financial data: Year ended 12/31/2012. Assets, $318,658,874 (M); Expenditures, $19,795,722; Total giving, $17,832,771. Camperships amount not specified. Grants to individuals amount not specified. Scholarships—to individuals amount not specified.
Fields of interest: Arts education; Film/video; Literature; Historic preservation/historical societies; Management/technical assistance; Secondary school/education; Higher education; Graduate/professional education; Adult/continuing education; Camps; Youth development, agriculture; Science.
Type of support: Grants to individuals; Scholarships—to individuals; Camperships.
Application information: Applications accepted. Application form required. Application form available on the grantmaker's web site.
  Deadline(s): Varies
  Additional information: Each scholarship has its own eligibility requirements. See web site for a complete list of programs.
Program descriptions:
  John and Ellen Emery Science Grants: The program encourages all AOS #91 teachers to promote the study of science in their classrooms. These grants should increase opportunities for students to understand science and its relevance to their daily lives and, perhaps, inspire some of them to pursue careers in science and related fields. Proposals are invited from full-time teachers working in any AOS #91 school. Grant size ranges from $100 to $2,000.
  Leonard and Renee Minsky Fund for Arts Education: The program helps elementary school teachers in Washington and Penobscot Counties to bring art into the classroom.
EIN: 010391479

3713
Maine Higher Education Assistance Foundation
c/o Marc Owen
489 Congress St., 3rd. Fl.
Portland, ME 04101-3415

Foundation type: Independent foundation
Purpose: Scholarships to Maine high school graduates for continuing education at institutions of higher learning pursuing a business program.
Financial data: Year ended 09/30/2012. Assets, $247,702 (M); Expenditures, $11,695; Total giving, $11,000; Grants to individuals, 11 grants totaling $11,000 (high: $1,000, low: $1,000).
Fields of interest: Higher education; Business school/education.
Type of support: Scholarships—to individuals.
Application information: Selection criteria includes academics and financial need.
EIN: 010265587

3714
Maine Humanities Council
674 Brighton Ave.
Portland, ME 04102-1012   (207) 773-5051
Contact: Hayden Anderson, Exec. Dir.
FAX: (207) 773-2416;
E-mail: info@mainehumanities.org; Toll-free tel.: (866) 637-3233; E-mail for Hayden Anderson: hayden@mainehumanities.org; URL: http://www.mainehumanities.org

Foundation type: Public charity
Purpose: Stipends for teachers of ME, to attend the Teaching American History program for professional development and enable them to teach more effectively.
Publications: Application guidelines; Annual report; Grants list; Informational brochure; Newsletter.
Financial data: Year ended 10/31/2011. Assets, $3,276,463 (M); Expenditures, $1,620,123; Total giving, $183,321; Grants to individuals, totaling $54,100.
Fields of interest: Humanities; Education.
Type of support: Stipends.
Application information: Applications accepted.
  Additional information: Contact the council for additional guidelines. See web site for additional teacher programs.
EIN: 010339295

3715
Maine Technology Institute
(also known as MTI)
8 Venture Ave.
Brunswick Landing
Brunswick, ME 04011-5037   (207) 582-4790
FAX: (207) 582-4772;
E-mail: info@mainetechnology.org; URL: http://www.mainetechnology.org

Foundation type: Public charity
Purpose: Seed grant money to individuals and companies across Maine who are looking to develop new ideas and new products.
Publications: Annual report; Financial statement; Grants list; Newsletter.
Financial data: Year ended 06/30/2012. Assets, $31,878,922 (M); Expenditures, $20,393,176; Total giving, $18,831,762; Grants to individuals, totaling $49,687.
Fields of interest: Research; Engineering/technology.
Type of support: Seed money.
Application information: Applications accepted. Application form required. Application form available on the grantmaker's web site.
  Initial approach: Application
  Deadline(s): Oct. 14 for Seed Grant Program
  Additional information: Application should include budget information.
Program description:
  Seed Grant Program: Grants of up to $12,500 are offered six times a year to support very early-stage research and development activities for new products and services that lead to the market. All projects must fall under one of seven targeted technology sectors: advanced technologies for forestry and agriculture, aquaculture and marine technology, biotechnology, composite materials technology, environmental technology, information technology, and precision manufacturing technology. Eligible projects include business planning, market research, patent filing, and technical assistance.
EIN: 010529871

3716
Maine Veterinary Education Foundation
97A Exchange St., Ste. 305
Portland, ME 04101   (207) 752-1392
Contact: William Bell, Exec. Dir.
URL: http://www.mainevetmed.org

Foundation type: Independent foundation
Purpose: Scholarships to students enrolled in approved colleges of veterinary medicine or veterinary technicians from the state of ME.
Financial data: Year ended 12/31/2012. Assets, $553,279 (M); Expenditures, $29,850; Total giving, $27,600; Grants to individuals, 8 grants totaling $27,600 (high: $8,000, low: $100).
Fields of interest: Veterinary medicine.
Type of support: Scholarships—to individuals.
Application information:
  Initial approach: Letter
  Deadline(s): Prior to beginning of college year
  Additional information: Application can be obtained from the foundation.
EIN: 311599553

3717
Maine Writers and Publishers Alliance
314 Forest Ave., Rm. 318
Portland, ME 04101-2010   (207) 228-8263
FAX: (207) 228-8150;
E-mail: info@mainewriters.org; URL: http://www.mainewriters.org

Foundation type: Public charity
Purpose: Awards by nomination only to writers and publishers who are residents of Maine.
Financial data: Year ended 06/30/2012. Assets, $34,181 (M); Expenditures, $97,150; Total giving, $17,934.
Fields of interest: Literature.
Type of support: Awards/prizes.
Application information: Applications accepted. Application form required.
  Deadline(s): Dec. 15
  Additional information: Application must include two copies of each book or manuscript, along with a registration form and entry fee.
EIN: 010375832

3718
MELMAC Education Foundation
188 Whitten Rd.
Augusta, ME 04330-6021   (207) 622-3066
FAX: (207) 622-3053;
E-mail: info@melmacfoundation.org; Toll free tel.: (866) 622-3066; URL: http://www.melmacfoundation.org

Foundation type: Independent foundation
Purpose: Scholarships to high school seniors in ME for postsecondary education.
Financial data: Year ended 12/31/2012. Assets, $36,809,252 (M); Expenditures, $1,340,091; Total giving, $1,020,106; Grants to individuals, totaling $210,000.
Fields of interest: Higher education.
Type of support: Undergraduate support.

Application information: Applications not accepted.

Additional information: Unsolicited requests for funds not considered or acknowledged.

EIN: 010390854

3719
Anita Card Montgomery Foundation

c/o Fran Moore
P.O. Box 815
Camden, ME   04843-0815   (207) 763-4220

Foundation type: Independent foundation

Purpose: Assistance to financially needy individuals of Camden, Rockport, Lincolnville, and Hope, ME, including medical, dental, and eyecare expenses.

Financial data: Year ended 12/31/2011. Assets, $57,764 (M); Expenditures, $24,455; Total giving, $23,611; Grants to individuals, 15 grants totaling $23,611 (high: $6,000, low: $161).

Fields of interest: Dental care; Optometry/vision screening; Health care; Economically disadvantaged.

Type of support: Grants for special needs.

Application information: Applications accepted. Application form required.

Deadline(s): None

Additional information: Application should include copies of bills and estimated costs from medical professionals.

EIN: 237091570

3720
North Haven Foundation

P.O. Box 664
Rockland, ME   04841   (207) 594-4421

Foundation type: Community foundation

Purpose: Awards scholarships and other educational assistance to residents of North Haven, ME for higher education.

Publications: Annual report.

Financial data: Year ended 06/30/2013. Assets, $2,602,490 (M); Expenditures, $149,812; Total giving, $141,714; Grants to individuals, 18 grants totaling $132,714.

Fields of interest: Higher education; Scholarships/financial aid.

Type of support: Scholarships—to individuals; Undergraduate support.

Application information: Applications accepted. Application form required.

Initial approach: Contact foundation

Deadline(s): None

EIN: 016022839

3721
David Marshall Ohmart Memorial Fund

c/o Bangor Savings Bank
P.O. Box 930
Bangor, ME   04402-0930
Application address: c/o Brewer High School, Attn.: Guidance Counselor, 79 Pkwy. S., Brewer, ME 04412-1699

Foundation type: Independent foundation

Purpose: Scholarships to graduates of Brewer High School, ME for postsecondary education.

Financial data: Year ended 12/31/2011. Assets, $60,614 (M); Expenditures, $5,135; Total giving, $3,200.

Fields of interest: Higher education.

Type of support: Support to graduates or students of specific schools; Undergraduate support.

Application information: Applications accepted.

Deadline(s): Mar. 28

Additional information: Contact foundation for additional application guidelines.

EIN: 237424856

3722
The Opportunity Alliance

(formerly People's Regional Opportunity Program)
50 Monument Sq.
Portland, ME   04101-4039   (207) 553-5800
Contact: Catherine Fellenz, Pres. and C.E.O.
FAX: (207) 553-5888;
E-mail: admin@propeople.org; TTY: (207) 874-1013; toll-free tel.: (800) 698-4959; additional address : 510 Cumberland Ave., Portland, ME 04101-2220; URL: http://www.wherepeoplecomefirst.org/

Foundation type: Public charity

Purpose: Assistance to families of Cumberland County, ME which include housing, substance abuse support, heat assistance, and health care programs.

Financial data: Year ended 06/30/2011. Assets, $5,803,596 (M); Expenditures, $17,467,005; Total giving, $6,402,182; Grants to individuals, totaling $6,402,182.

Type of support: Grants for special needs.

Application information:

Initial approach: Letter

EIN: 010274725

3723
Oxford Hills Scholarship Foundation

1570 Main St.
Oxford, ME   04270-3390

Foundation type: Independent foundation

Purpose: Scholarships primarily to residents of ME School Admin. District 17 who have been accepted in accredited colleges or postsecondary program or course.

Financial data: Year ended 06/30/2012. Assets, $5,140,988 (M); Expenditures, $287,060; Total giving, $218,177; Grants to individuals, totaling $218,177.

Fields of interest: Vocational education, post-secondary; Higher education.

Type of support: Support to graduates or students of specific schools.

Application information:

Deadline(s): None

EIN: 010523143

3724
A. Nina Paganelli Trust

P.O. Box 31
Portland, ME   04112-0031
Application address: c/o Sanford High School, Attn.: Principal, 52 Sanford High Blvd., Sanford, ME 04073-3427

Foundation type: Independent foundation

Purpose: Scholarships to graduating seniors of Sanford High School, ME who are residents of Sanford, ME, to attend the University of Maine at Orone, ME.

Financial data: Year ended 04/30/2013. Assets, $584,757 (M); Expenditures, $26,938; Total giving, $22,906.

Fields of interest: Higher education.

Type of support: Support to graduates or students of specific schools.

Application information: Applications accepted. Application form not required.

Deadline(s): None

EIN: 223180798

3725
Penquis Community Action Program

262 Harlow St.
P.O. Box 1162
Bangor, ME   04402-1162   (207) 973-3500
FAX: (207) 973-3699; Toll-free tel.: (800) 215-4942; URL: http://www.penquis.org

Foundation type: Public charity

Purpose: Assistance to indigent residents of ME, for help with utilities, transportation, and medication.

Publications: Annual report; Financial statement; Newsletter.

Financial data: Year ended 09/30/2011. Assets, $13,553,806 (M); Expenditures, $32,970,562; Total giving, $9,165,875; Grants to individuals, totaling $8,700,760.

Fields of interest: Economically disadvantaged.

Type of support: Grants for special needs.

Application information:

Initial approach: Letter

Additional information: Contact foundation for eligibility criteria.

EIN: 016023748

3726
Portland Female Charitable Society

82 2 Lights Rd.
Cape Elizabeth, ME   04107   (207) 838-6240
Contact: Lee Wilson, Treas.

Foundation type: Independent foundation

Purpose: Aid limited to financially needy residents of the City of Portland, ME, for dental care, prescriptions, hearing aids, glasses, or other needs having to do with health, food, or shelter, with emphasis on the needs of children, the elderly, and the ill.

Financial data: Year ended 09/30/2013. Assets, $241,590 (M); Expenditures, $9,312; Total giving, $8,205.

Fields of interest: Dental care; Optometry/vision screening; Health care; Housing/shelter; Children/youth, services; Aging; Disabilities, people with.

Type of support: Grants for special needs.

Application information: Applications accepted. Interview required.

Deadline(s): None

Additional information: Applications from individuals residing outside of stated geographic restriction not accepted; Requests usually presented by social workers, public health nurses, counselors, etc.

EIN: 010370961

3727
Portland Seamen's Friend Society

14 Lewis St.
Westbrook, ME   04092-2614

Foundation type: Operating foundation

Purpose: Financial assistance to indigent seamen who reside in the state of ME.

Financial data: Year ended 12/31/2011. Assets, $262,630 (M); Expenditures, $77,689; Total giving, $67,160.

Fields of interest: Military/veterans' organizations.

Type of support: Grants for special needs.

Application information: Applications accepted.
Initial approach: Letter or telephone
Deadline(s): None
Additional information: Applications by letter
outlining financial need and including
references; Interviews required.
EIN: 010211545

3728
Ross Powers Foundation
P.O. Box 7532
Portland, ME   04112-7532
E-mail: info@rosspowersfoundation.org

Foundation type: Public charity
Purpose: Financial assistance to VT athletes who
have resided or who have attended school in VT for
at least the past two years.
Publications: Application guidelines.
Financial data: Year ended 06/30/2012. Assets,
$196,653 (M); Expenditures, $147,199; Total
giving, $126,674.
Fields of interest: Athletics/sports, training;
Athletics/sports, winter sports.
Type of support: Grants for special needs.
Application information: Applications accepted.
Application form required. Application form
available on the grantmaker's web site.
Initial approach: Letter
Send request by: Mail
Deadline(s): Feb. 15, May 15, Aug. 15 and Nov.
15
Additional information: Application should
include most recent tax return.
Program description:
Grants: Grants are available to promising
athletes whose opportunity to pursue excellence in
sport would otherwise be limited by their financial
situation. Evaluation criteria include level of athletic
potential, financial need, proposed use of funds,
availability of alternative sources of funding, and
NCAA amateur eligibility. Grants may be
awarded to cover costs related to training,
coaching, equipment, and/or event participation,
including related travel expenses.
EIN: 010541580

3729
The W. Scott Reid Scholarship Fund
c/o U/W W Scott Reid
80 Caron Ln.
Auburn, ME   04210   (207) 786-3638

Foundation type: Independent foundation
Purpose: Scholarships to residents of ME who are
pursuing a nursing degree from an institution of
higher learning in ME.
Financial data: Year ended 12/31/2012. Assets,
$438,390 (M); Expenditures, $27,181; Total
giving, $23,000; Grants to individuals, 22 grants
totaling $23,000 (high: $1,200, low: $1,000).
Fields of interest: Nursing school/education.
Type of support: Scholarships—to individuals.
Application information: Applications accepted.
Application form required.
Deadline(s): Mar. 1
Additional information: Application must include
family information, statement of preparation,
employment while in school, transcript, and
agreement to advise of academic progress at
end of each semester.
EIN: 016141002

3730
Ricker College Endowment Fund
P.O. Box 1016
Houlton, ME   04730-1016
URL: http://rickerscholarship.com/

Foundation type: Independent foundation
Purpose: Scholarships to graduates of high schools
in Aroostook and Washington counties, ME, who are
in the top 25 percent of their classes. Preference is
shown to descendants of graduates of Ricker
Classical Institute, Ricker Junior College, Ricker
College, and to descendants of longtime Ricker
teachers and staff. Scholarships are generally in
the amount of $1,500 per year and are renewable
for up to four years.
Publications: Application guidelines; Informational
brochure (including application guidelines).
Financial data: Year ended 12/31/2012. Assets,
$2,602,375 (M); Expenditures, $167,516; Total
giving, $117,100; Grants to individuals, 74 grants
totaling $117,100.
Type of support: Support to graduates or students
of specific schools; Undergraduate support.
Application information: Application form required.
Deadline(s): 4th Fri. of Apr.
Applicants should submit the following:
1) Letter(s) of recommendation
2) Transcripts
3) Financial information
Additional information: Application must also
include proof of acceptance in a
baccalaureate program.
EIN: 222709285

3731
John W. Robinson Welfare Trust
P.O. Box 101
Gardiner, ME   04345-0026

Foundation type: Independent foundation
Purpose: Scholarships to financially needy
graduating seniors of Gardiner Area High School,
ME, for attendance at accredited universities,
colleges, junior colleges, vocational/technical
schools, or professional schools.
Financial data: Year ended 12/31/2011. Assets,
$1,273,695 (M); Expenditures, $87,058; Total
giving, $68,700.
Fields of interest: Vocational education,
post-secondary; Higher education.
Type of support: Support to graduates or students
of specific schools.
Application information: Applications accepted.
Application form required. Interview required.
Deadline(s): Apr.
Applicants should submit the following:
1) Essay
2) Letter(s) of recommendation
3) Transcripts
Additional information: Payments are made
directly to the educational institution on
behalf of the students.
EIN: 016009329

3732
Ross Scholarship Loan
P.O. Box 31
Portland, ME   04112-0031

Foundation type: Independent foundation
Purpose: Student loans to worthy graduates of any
Sanford, ME high schools.
Financial data: Year ended 01/31/2013. Assets,
$410,401 (M); Expenditures, $1,158; Total giving,
$0.

Fields of interest: Higher education.
Type of support: Student loans—to individuals;
Support to graduates or students of specific
schools.
Application information:
Deadline(s): None
Additional information: Contact your school's
guidance counselor for application guidelines.
EIN: 016075602

3733
Clyde Russell Scholarship Fund
P.O. Box 2457
Augusta, ME   04338-8005   (207) 622-5865
Contact: Lois Kilby-Chesley
URL: http://www.clyderussellscholarshipfund.org

Foundation type: Public charity
Purpose: Scholarships to students residing in ME
for the study of teaching.
Financial data: Year ended 08/31/2012. Assets,
$838,048 (M); Expenditures, $50,414; Total
giving, $12,500; Grants to individuals, totaling
$12,500.
Fields of interest: Teacher school/education.
Type of support: Undergraduate support.
Application information: Applications not
accepted.
Additional information: Contributes only to
preselected individuals.
EIN: 222535972

3734
Savings Bank of Maine Scholarship Foundation
(formerly Gardiner Savings Institution FSB
Scholarship Foundation Savings Bank of Maine
Scholarship Foundation)
P.O. Box 190
Gardiner, ME   04345   (207) 582-5550
Contact: Dennis Carolin, Treas.

Foundation type: Company-sponsored foundation
Purpose: Scholarships to graduating high school
seniors of ME upon recommendation of school.
Financial data: Year ended 03/31/2012. Assets,
$348,146 (M); Expenditures, $28,690; Total
giving, $26,000; Grants to individuals, totaling
$26,000.
Fields of interest: Higher education.
Type of support: Undergraduate support.
Application information: Applications accepted.
Initial approach: Letter
Additional information: Selection is based on
need, leadership, scholarship, and other
criteria.
EIN: 222853667

3735
William Searls Scholarship Fund
c/o The First, N.A.
P.O. Box 940
Damariscotta, ME   04543
Contact: Margo Stanley
Application address: P.O. Box 461, Southwest
Harbor, ME 04679

Foundation type: Independent foundation
Purpose: Scholarships to graduates of Pemetic
High School in Southwest Harbor, ME.
Financial data: Year ended 12/31/2012. Assets,
$364,470 (M); Expenditures, $26,648; Total
giving, $21,300.
Fields of interest: Higher education; Scholarships/
financial aid.

Type of support: Support to graduates or students of specific schools; Undergraduate support.
Application information: Applications accepted. Application form required.
Deadline(s): Apr. 15 for June graduates and May 1 for all others.
Additional information: Application must include elementary school record, birth certificate, parents' confidential financial statement and income tax return for the current year.
EIN: 016009698

3736
Spruce Run Association
P.O. Box 653
Bangor, ME   04402-0653   (207) 945-5102
FAX: (207) 990-4425;
E-mail: sprucerun@sprucerun.net; Toll-free tel.: (800) 863-9909; URL: http://www.sprucerun.net

Foundation type: Public charity
Purpose: Grants for basic necessities to individuals affected by domestic abuse, primarily in ME.
Financial data: Year ended 09/30/2012. Assets, $1,388,609 (M); Expenditures, $1,276,558.
Fields of interest: Abuse prevention; Domestic violence.
Type of support: Grants for special needs.
Application information:
Initial approach: Letter
Additional information: Contact foundation for complete eligibility requirements.
EIN: 010358090

3737
Eleanor F. Stich Scholarship Fund
c/o Acadia Trust, N.A.
511 Congress St., 9th Fl.
Portland, ME   04101   (207) 667-2504
Application Address: c/o Camden National Bank, P.O. Box 807, Ellsworth, ME. 04605

Foundation type: Independent foundation
Purpose: Scholarships to students for attendance at accredited colleges or universities in the Ellsworth, ME area.
Financial data: Year ended 12/31/2012. Assets, $93,685 (M); Expenditures, $4,135; Total giving, $2,500; Grants to individuals, 3 grants totaling $2,500 (high: $1,000, low: $500).
Fields of interest: Higher education.
Type of support: Scholarships—to individuals.
Application information:
Deadline(s): None
EIN: 016154953

3738
Robert and Patricia Switzer Foundation
(formerly Switzer Foundation)
P.O. Box 293
Belfast, ME   04915-0293   (207) 338-5654
Contact: Erin Lloyd, Prog. Off.
E-mail: info@switzernetwork.org; Application e-mail: erin@switzernetwork.org; URL: http://www.switzernetwork.org/

Foundation type: Independent foundation
Purpose: Fellowships by application only to individuals from New England and CA whose studies are directed toward improving the quality of the natural environment.
Publications: Application guidelines; Annual report.
Financial data: Year ended 06/30/2013. Assets, $18,088,083 (M); Expenditures, $969,600; Total giving, $502,097.

Fields of interest: Higher education; Graduate/professional education; Research; Formal/general education; Natural resources.
Type of support: Fellowships.
Application information: Applications accepted. Application form required. Application form available on the grantmaker's web site.
Initial approach: Application
Send request by: Online
Deadline(s): Feb. 1
Final notification: Recipients notified in six months
Applicants should submit the following:
  1) Resume
  2) Transcripts
  3) Letter(s) of recommendation
  4) Financial information
Additional information: See web site for additional information.
Program descriptions:
Professional Development Fund: A program designed to provide support for professional development for Switzer Fellowship Alumni only. Funds may be requested for training in nonprofit management, communications, leadership, or other relevant professional skills, or for attendance at a conference, or other professional activity that will clearly advance the Fellow's career goals. Awards are made on a rolling basis. See foundation Web site for application guidelines.
Switzer Environmental Fellowship Program: The goal of the Switzer Environmental Fellowship Program is to support highly talented graduate students in New England and California whose studies are directed toward improving environmental quality and who demonstrate leadership in their field. Awards have been made to students pursuing environmental policy studies, economics, engineering, public health, and law as well as the more traditional sciences: biology, chemistry and physics. Technical knowledge, analytical skills and environmental experience are important components of a successful application, regardless of field of study. Please see foundation web site for contact and application information.
Switzer Leadership Grant Program: Funds are available for non-profit organizations and public agencies to hire a Switzer Fellow in a leadership staff or consulting position to work on a critical environmental issue. See web site for guidelines and requirements.
EIN: 341504501

3739
Douglas A. Thom Memorial Corporation
P.O. Box 332
Camden, ME   04843   (207) 230-2152
Contact: Aline Taylor, Treas.
Application address: Camdem National Bank, 2 Elm St., Camdem, ME 04843

Foundation type: Independent foundation
Purpose: Loans for scholarships to graduating seniors from the Camden-Rockport High School in Rockport, ME.
Financial data: Year ended 12/31/2012. Assets, $450,291 (M); Expenditures, $4,394; Total giving, $0.
Fields of interest: Higher education.
Type of support: Student loans—to individuals; Support to graduates or students of specific schools.
Application information: Application form required.
Deadline(s): June 1
Applicants should submit the following:
  1) Financial information
  2) Transcripts

Additional information: Application should also include a reference from guidance counselor or College Advisor. Letter from a teacher giving general character and achievement of applicant in school.
EIN: 016019126

3740
Donato J. Tramuto Foundation
P.O. Box 1728
Ogunquit, ME   03907-1728
E-mail: dtramuto@maine.rr.com; URL: http://www.djtfoundation.com

Foundation type: Independent foundation
Purpose: Scholarships to graduating high school seniors from Wells-Ogunquit High School, ME and Fredonia High School, NY for postsecondary education.
Financial data: Year ended 12/31/2011. Assets, $10,855 (M); Expenditures, $164,393; Total giving, $110,052; Grants to individuals, 16 grants totaling $11,845 (high: $1,500, low: $100).
Fields of interest: Higher education.
Type of support: Support to graduates or students of specific schools; Undergraduate support.
Application information: Applications accepted. Application form required.
Deadline(s): Mar. 15
Applicants should submit the following:
  1) Class rank
  2) Transcripts
  3) SAT
  4) Letter(s) of recommendation
  5) ACT
Additional information: Selection is based on overall academic excellence, leadership qualities and financial need. Application available from the guidance department.
EIN: 030373845

3741
Camden Student Trust Fund
(formerly Camden Trust Fund for Student Loans, also known as Camden Student Trust Fund)
c/o Canden National Bank
2 Elm St.
Camden, ME   04843   (207) 236-8821
Contact: Susan Westfall, Tr.
Application address: c/o P.O. Box 310, Camden, ME 04843

Foundation type: Independent foundation
Purpose: Grants to citizens of Camden, Maine for relief, education or recreation.
Financial data: Year ended 12/31/2012. Assets, $49,051 (M); Expenditures, $2,643; Total giving, $1,800; Grants to individuals, 9 grants totaling $1,800 (high: $200, low: $200).
Fields of interest: Education; Recreation.
Type of support: Grants to individuals; Grants for special needs.
Application information: Applications accepted.
Initial approach: Letter
Deadline(s): None
EIN: 016015938

3742
Mark E. and Emily Turner Foundation
P.O. Box 365
Presque Isle, ME   04769-2524
Contact: Marcus J. Barresi, Chair.
Application address: P.O. Box 807, Presque Isle, ME 04769, tel.: (207) 764-5639

Foundation type: Independent foundation
Purpose: Scholarships to Presque Isle, ME, area residents, primarily for the first year of college.
Financial data: Year ended 12/31/2012. Assets, $4,983 (M); Expenditures, $39,837; Total giving, $39,650.
Type of support: Undergraduate support.
Application information: Applications accepted.
  Initial approach: Letter
  Deadline(s): None
  Additional information: Application must include course of study and qualifications of applicant.
EIN: 016019456

3743
United Way, Inc.

1 Canal Plz., Ste. 300
P.O. Box 15200
Portland, ME   04112-5200   (207) 874-1000
FAX: (207) 874-1007;
E-mail: info@unitedwaygp.org; URL: http://www.unitedwaygp.org

Foundation type: Public charity
Purpose: Scholarships awarded to children in the Portland, OR area to attend summer camp; scholarships also awarded to high-school students who wish to further their education.
Publications: Annual report; Financial statement.
Financial data: Year ended 06/30/2011. Assets, $17,446,571 (M); Expenditures, $9,305,526; Total giving, $6,337,697; Grants to individuals, totaling $499,414.
Fields of interest: Education.
Type of support: Grants to individuals; Camperships.
Application information: Interview required.
  Additional information: Selection is based on financial need, academic standing and recommendations.
EIN: 010241767

3744
Waldo Community Action Partners

9 Field St.
P.O. Box 130
Belfast, ME   04915-0130   (207) 338-6809
Contact: Keith E. Small, Exec. Dir.
FAX: (207) 338-6812; E-mail: tlowe@waldocap.org; URL: http://www.waldocap.org

Foundation type: Public charity
Purpose: Emergency assistance to low-income individuals and families throughout Waldo County, ME with housing, utilities, food, transportation and other special needs.
Financial data: Year ended 12/31/2011. Assets, $1,406,190 (M); Expenditures, $6,195,071; Total giving, $1,863,955; Grants to individuals, totaling $1,863,955.
Fields of interest: Human services; Economically disadvantaged.
Type of support: Emergency funds; Grants for special needs.
Application information: Some assistance require application, contact the organization for eligibility criteria.
EIN: 016020566

3745
Watershed Center for Ceramic Arts

19 Brick Hill Rd.
Newcastle, ME   04553-3901   (207) 882-6075
Contact: Fran Rudoff, Exec. Dir.
FAX: (207) 882-6045;
E-mail: info@watershedceramics.org; E-mail For Fran Rudoff: director@watershedceramics.org;
URL: http://www.watershedceramics.org

Foundation type: Public charity
Purpose: Residencies for ceramic artists from across the country and abroad.
Financial data: Year ended 12/31/2011. Assets, $1,127,504 (M); Expenditures, $266,366.
Fields of interest: Ceramic arts.
Type of support: Residencies.
Application information: Applications accepted. Application form required. Application form available on the grantmaker's web site.
  Initial approach: E-mail
  Deadline(s): Apr. 1
  Applicants should submit the following:
    1) Work samples
    2) Letter(s) of recommendation
    3) SASE
    4) Resume
  Additional information: Application must also include application fee cover letter.
EIN: 010427824

3746
The Horace Williams Memorial Fund

c/o Kennebec Savings Bank
150 State St.
Augusta, ME   04332   (207) 622-5801
Contact: Andrew E. Silsby, Tr.
Application address: P.O. Box 50, Augusta, ME 04332, tel.: (207) 622-5801

Foundation type: Independent foundation
Purpose: Scholarships to residents of ME for continuing education at institutions of higher learning.
Financial data: Year ended 08/31/2011. Assets, $241,379 (M); Expenditures, $13,216; Total giving, $11,000; Grants to individuals, 22 grants totaling $11,000 (high: $500, low: $500).
Fields of interest: Higher education.
Type of support: Scholarships—to individuals.
Application information: Applications accepted. Application form not required.
  Initial approach: Letter or telephone
  Deadline(s): None
EIN: 016008547

3747
The Woman's Literary Union

202 Woodford St.
Portland, ME   04103-2733   (207) 797-6333

Foundation type: Independent foundation
Purpose: Scholarships to students of greater Portland, ME, high schools.
Financial data: Year ended 03/31/2013. Assets, $717,987 (M); Expenditures, $107,118; Total giving, $20,000; Grants to individuals, 4 grants totaling $20,000 (high: $5,000, low: $5,000).
Type of support: Support to graduates or students of specific schools; Undergraduate support.
Application information:
  Deadline(s): End of academic year
  Additional information: Seniors are recommended by high school guidance counselors.
EIN: 010220139

3748
Worcester Institute for Student Exchange

52 Park St.
Orono, ME   04473-4406   (201) 947-0111
Contact: Charles D. Hanson, Dir.

Foundation type: Operating foundation
Purpose: Scholarships and grants to students from Eastern Europe studying at U.S. college and medical schools.
Financial data: Year ended 09/30/2011. Assets, $499,923 (M); Expenditures, $61,960; Total giving, $17,825; Grants to individuals, 18 grants totaling $17,825 (high: $4,760, low: $100).
Fields of interest: Medical school/education.
Type of support: Scholarships—to individuals.
Application information: Applications accepted.
  Initial approach: Letter
  Additional information: Application should include letters of recommendation.
EIN: 043139523

3749
York County Community Action Corporation

6 Spruce St.
P.O. Box 72
Sanford, ME   04073-2917   (207) 324-5762
FAX: (207) 490-5026; Toll-free tel.: (800) 965-5762; URL: http://www.yccac.org

Foundation type: Public charity
Purpose: Financial assistance to the poor and elderly persons in York County, ME for advocacy, transportation, housing, fuel assistance, hunger prevention, preschool education, nutrition, daycare, emergency housing assistance and other social services.
Publications: Annual report.
Financial data: Year ended 10/31/2011. Assets, $6,738,417 (M); Expenditures, $15,503,607; Total giving, $5,039,782; Grants to individuals, totaling $5,039,782.
Fields of interest: Housing/shelter, home owners; Housing/shelter, repairs; Housing/shelter; Utilities; Infants/toddlers; Children/youth; Economically disadvantaged.
Type of support: Emergency funds; Grants to individuals; Grants for special needs; Loans—to individuals.
Application information: Applications accepted.
  Initial approach: Download application for the Women Infants Children program
  Additional information: Contact organization for eligibility criteria.
Program descriptions:
  Affordable Housing Program: The program provides financial assistance to help qualified home buyers pay some of the out-of-pocket costs involved in purchasing a home. These expenses may include down payment, closing costs, and home repairs. Income eligible clients may receive "forgivable" loans, a portion of which may be forgiven over time. The program assists any potential homebuyers with the preparation and submission of Rural Development mortgage applications. The program also assists any potential homebuyers with the preparation and submission of applications for a twenty-year, one-percent subsidized loan to repair an existing home. Grants (that do not have to be repaid) are also available only to income-eligible people age 62 or over.
  Energy Crisis Intervention Program: The program provides emergency financial assistance for home heating fuel bills or heating system repairs. Consumers must be pre-approved, Low-Income

Housing Energy Assistance Program (LIHEAP)-eligible within the past year, and have less than 1/8 tank full at time of application.

Low Income Assistance Program: The program provides financial assistance for apartment/home electric bills. Eligibility determined by annual income and cost/usage for Central Maine Power customers. All Kennebunk Power and Light customers are eligible.

Low Income Home Energy Assistance Program: The program provides financial assistance for apartment or home heating fuel bills to income eligible households. Payments are made directly to dealers of oil, kerosene, LP gas, coal, electricity, or wood. Consumers may choose their dealer.

Refrigerator Replacement Program: The program replaces 10-year or older refrigerators with energy efficient models.

Telephone Assistance Program: The program provides financial assistance for installation and monthly payment of telephone bills.

Women, Infants, Children: The program offers health information, nutritious foods, assistance with access to health care and much more. These services are provided to eligible women, infants, and children at no cost.

EIN: 016020406

MARYLAND

3750
The William L. and Victorine Q. Adams Foundation, Inc.

1040 Park Ave., Ste. 300
Baltimore, MD   21201-5635   (410) 783-3203
Contact: Blanche Rodgers, Prog. Off.
E-mail: scholarship@adamsfound.org

Foundation type: Operating foundation
Purpose: Undergraduate scholarships to financially needy African American residents of the City of Baltimore, MD, who are U.S. citizens, for the study of business.
Financial data: Year ended 09/30/2013. Assets, $3,140,514 (M); Expenditures, $426,373; Total giving, $323,487; Grants to individuals, 8 grants totaling $42,777 (high: $12,519, low: $814).
Fields of interest: Business school/education; Business/industry; Economics; African Americans/Blacks.
Type of support: Undergraduate support.
Application information: Application form required. Interview required.
> *Deadline(s):* May 1
> *Applicants should submit the following:*
>   1) Photograph
>   2) Transcripts
>   3) SAR
>   4) Letter(s) of recommendation
>   5) GPA
>   6) Financial information
EIN: 521369556

3751
AICE, Inc.

(also known as American-Israeli Cooperative Enterprise)
2810 Blaine Dr.
Chevy Chase, MD   20815-3040   (301) 565-3918
E-mail: aiceresearch@gmail.com; URL: http://www.jewishvirtuallibrary.org/about/index.shtml

Foundation type: Public charity
Purpose: Grants to U.S. and Israel scholars for acceptance into a graduate program.
Financial data: Year ended 12/31/2011. Assets, $580,489 (M); Expenditures, $2,196,050; Total giving, $1,394,525; Grants to individuals, totaling $195,000.
Fields of interest: Education.
Type of support: Grants to individuals; Graduate support.
Application information: Students must demonstrate an interest in Israel studies. Emphasis is placed on academic achievement and in interest and competence in Israel studies.
EIN: 521865861

3752
Airmen Memorial Foundation, Inc.

5211 Auth Rd.
Suitland, MD   20746-4339   (301) 899-3500
Contact: John R. Mccauslin, C.E.O. and Chair.
URL: http://www.hqafsa.org/Content/NavigationMenu/About/AirmenMemorialFoundation/default.htm

Foundation type: Public charity

Purpose: Scholarship to dependent children of Air Force enlisted personnel, Air National Guard or Air Force Reserve for post high school undergraduate education at accredited colleges and accredited vocational schools.
Financial data: Year ended 12/31/2011. Assets, $1,189,802 (M); Expenditures, $112,383; Total giving, $71,000; Grants to individuals, totaling $66,000.
Fields of interest: Vocational education, post-secondary; Higher education; Military/veterans.
Type of support: Technical education support; Undergraduate support.
Application information: Recipients are selected by the board of directors. Awards are paid directly to the institution on behalf of the student.
EIN: 521323592

3753
Allegany Arts Council, Inc.

9 N. Centre St.
Cumberland, MD   21502-2364   (301) 777-2787
Contact: Andy Vick, Exec. Dir.
FAX: (301) 777-7719; E-mail: arts@allconet.org;
URL: http://www.alleganyartscouncil.org

Foundation type: Public charity
Purpose: Small monetary grants to individuals residing in Allegany County, MD, who are in need of financial assistance to pursue an interest or experience in the arts.
Publications: Application guidelines.
Financial data: Year ended 06/30/2011. Assets, $303,634 (M); Expenditures, $435,656; Total giving, $86,573; Grants to individuals, 48 grants totaling $13,832.
Fields of interest: Arts.
Type of support: Grants to individuals.
Application information: Applications accepted. Application form required. Application form available on the grantmaker's web site.
> *Initial approach:* Application
> *Deadline(s):* July 2 for Hadra Scholarship Fund
> *Additional information:* Preference will be given to first-time applicants.
Program description:
> *Hadra Scholarship Fund:* The fund provides small monetary grants to individuals residing in Allegany County who are in need of financial assistance to pursue an interest or an experience in the arts. Fundable requests include, but are not limited to, class/workshop fees, tickets for art performances or events, travel expenses to art performances or events, art-related supplies or materials, etc. Funds may not be used to help pay for credited classes at local educational institutions. The maximum amount awarded to any individual will be $100.
EIN: 521062379

3754
The Allemall Foundation, Inc.

P.O. Box 25
Libertytown, MD   21762-0025

Foundation type: Independent foundation
Purpose: Scholarships to needy children primarily in MD, who have an interest in education related to wildlife and nature conservation, and to provide health assistance to indigent children.
Financial data: Year ended 06/30/2012. Assets, $2,974,143 (M); Expenditures, $619,267; Total giving, $104,000; Grants to individuals, 17 grants totaling $38,000 (high: $3,000, low: $1,000).
Fields of interest: Environment; Animals/wildlife; Children.

Type of support: Scholarships—to individuals; Grants for special needs.
Application information: Applications accepted. Application form required.
> *Additional information:* Contact foundation for additional guidelines.
EIN: 200514500

3755
Alpha Phi Alpha Education Foundation

2313 St. Paul St.
Baltimore, MD   21218-5211   (410) 554-0040
Contact: Jodie A. James, Dir., Educational Activities
FAX: (401) 554-0054;
E-mail: edfoundation@apa1906.net; URL: http://www.alpha-phi-alpha.com/page.php?id=102

Foundation type: Public charity
Purpose: Scholarships to full time Alpha men pursuing undergraduate degrees or newly admitted to a graduate/professional program.
Publications: Application guidelines.
Financial data: Year ended 12/31/2012. Assets, $204,270 (M); Expenditures, $12,496.
Fields of interest: Higher education; Graduate/professional education; Students, sororities/fraternities.
Type of support: Scholarships—to individuals; Graduate support.
Application information: Applications accepted. Application form required. Application form available on the grantmaker's web site.
> *Send request by:* Mail
> *Deadline(s):* May 1
> *Applicants should submit the following:*
>   1) Transcripts
>   2) Resume
>   3) Letter(s) of recommendation
>   4) Essay
EIN: 386107756

3756
American Association of Anatomists

(also known as AAA)
9650 Rockville Pike
Bethesda, MD   20814-3998   (301) 634-7910
Contact: Shawn Boynes C.A.E., Exec. Dir.
FAX: (301) 634-7965; E-mail: exec@anatomy.org;
E-mail for Shawn Boynes: sboynes@anatomy.org;
URL: http://www.anatomy.org

Foundation type: Public charity
Purpose: Grants and awards to postdoctoral students to further the cause of anatomical science through research and education.
Financial data: Year ended 12/31/2011. Assets, $6,939,325 (M); Expenditures, $1,582,758; Total giving, $103,500; Grants to individuals, totaling $103,500.
Fields of interest: Anatomy (human); Science.
Type of support: Research; Grants to individuals; Postdoctoral support.
Application information: Application form required.
> *Send request by:* On-line
> *Deadline(s):* Varies
> *Applicants should submit the following:*
>   1) Curriculum vitae
>   2) Letter(s) of recommendation
> *Additional information:* Each award has its own criteria regarding who may make a nomination, who may be nominated, and what materials must be submitted. See web site for additional guidelines for the nomination process and on-line address.

Program descriptions:

AAA Postdoctoral Fellowship Program: The fellowships offers salary support to association members who are postdoctoral fellows working in any aspect of biology relevant to the anatomical sciences. Applicants must have been association members for one year preceding the application deadline and are expected to remain members for the duration of the fellowship. Candidates should be working on a research project encompassing any aspect of biology that is relevant to the anatomical sciences. Approaches can include (but are not limited to) cellular, molecular, genetic or histological techniques, and/or emphasize development, evolution, morphology or human health. The association will provide $20,000, plus travel support and registration fee (at early registration rate) to the next appropriate meeting.

AAA/Wiley A.J. Ladman Exemplary Service Medal: The award is presented to an association member distinguished in the field of anatomical sciences who has provided exceptional service to the society and/or mentorship in the discipline. The recipient will receive a plaque, a $1,000 honorarium and travel reimbursement (two nights) to receive the medal at the AAA Banquet.

Basmajian Award: This award recognizes health science faculty who are in the formative stages of their career (within ten years of their highest earned degree at time of nomination), teach human or veterinary gross anatomy, can document excellence in their contribution to the teaching of gross anatomy, and have outstanding accomplishments in biomedical research or scholarship in education. The recipient receives a plaque and a $1,000 honorarium. The recipient will also receive two years free membership and registration (at early registration rate) at the EB meeting will be waived for two years, including the year of the award. Only association members may submit a nomination. However, the proposed award recipient need not be a member.

C.J. Herrick Award in Neuroanatomy: This award recognizes investigators who have made important contributions to the field of comparative neuroanatomy, and who have demonstrated remarkable promise of future accomplishments. Applicants will receive a plaque, a $1,000 honorarium, travel reimbursement (coach airfare plus three nights) two years free membership and two years free registration.

H.W. Mossman Development Biologist Award: This award recognizes investigators in the early stages of their careers who have made important contributions to the field of developmental biology, and who have demonstrated remarkable promise of future accomplishments. Each applicant receives a plaque, a $1,000 honorarium, travel reimbursement, two years free membership and two years free registration.

Henry Gray/Elsevier Distinguished Educator Medal: This award is for human anatomy education in the anatomical sciences as broadly-defined (including gross anatomy, embryology, histology, and neuroanatomy) at the medical/dental, graduate, or undergraduate level of teaching. Only association members may submit a nomination. Nominees must be full-time or emeritus faculty members of accredited colleges or universities and members of the association. The recipient receives a plaque and a $4,000 honorarium, receives travel support for two nights, and organizes an education symposium or present a lecture at the annual meeting.

Henry Gray/Lippincott Williams & Wilkins Scientific Achievement Medal: This award recognizes unique and meritorious contributions to and achievements in anatomical sciences by a distinguished association member. The recipient receives a plaque, a $1,500 honorarium, and travel reimbursement (two nights) to receive the medal at the association banquet.

Keith & Marion Moore Young Anatomists Publication Award: The award recognizes the best publication by a young anatomist published in The Anatomical Record, Anatomical Sciences Education or Developmental Dynamics. Students, postdocs, and assistant professors without tenure who are first or last author (assuming the last author is laboratory director) or a paper published in the calendar year preceding the presentation of the award. The applicant will receive a $500 honorarium and $500 in travel support to attend the annual meeting, together with a ticket to the banquet.

Lippincott Williams Wilkins/AAA Education Research Scholarship: The scholarship supports an association member who is a graduate student in a mentored project, or a postdoctoral fellow or junior faculty member (ranked no higher than assistant professor) who wishes to develop a project that shows promise as a model for improving the quality of teaching and learning in anatomical education. It is anticipated that the proposed project will help foster a learning environment for students that is characterized by creativity, originality, and rigor. The scholarship consists of $5,000, plus travel support and registration fee to the next appropriate association annual meeting. Applicants must be association members for the year in which they apply and through the completion of their scholarship project.

R.R. Bensley Award in Cell Biology: This award recognizes a cell biologist who has made a distinguished contribution to the advancement of anatomy through discovery, ingenuity, and publications in the field of cell biology. The successful candidate will be an independent cell biologist whose publication have had substantial impact on his/her field. The candidate will receive a plaque, a $1,000 honorarium, travel reimbursement, two years free membership, and two years free registration.
EIN: 236239047

3757
American Association of Physics Teachers

1 Physics Ellipse
College Park, MD   20740-3845   (301) 209-3300
Contact: Beth A. Cunningham, Exec. Off.
E-mail address for Awards and Recognition Prog.: awards@aapt.org
FAX: (301) 209-0845; E-mail: aapt-prog@aapt.org;
E-mail For Beth A. Cunningham:
bcunningham@aapt.org; URL: http://www.aapt.org

Foundation type: Public charity
Purpose: Scholarships and awards to physics teachers and students who wish to become high school physics teachers.
Publications: Application guidelines.
Financial data: Year ended 12/31/2011. Assets, $4,521,333 (M); Expenditures, $4,974,033; Total giving, $55,179.
Fields of interest: Education; Physics.
Type of support: Scholarships—to individuals; Awards/prizes; Precollege support; Undergraduate support.
Application information: Applications accepted. Application form required. Application form available on the grantmaker's web site.
Initial approach: Telephone
Deadline(s): Jan. 1 for Barbara Lotze Scholarships for Future Teachers, July 1 for

Hashim A. Yamani Fund, July 1 and Dec. 1 for Frederick and Florence Bauder Endowment for the Support of Physics Teaching, Dec. 1 for High School Physics Teacher Grant
Additional information: See web site for additional scholarship and awards information.
Program descriptions:

AAPT Venture Fund: The fund provides support of up to $25,000 for projects that promote the development and marketing of innovative teaching products and services for physics and other sciences. Applicant must be a member of the American Association of Physics Teachers.

Awards and Recognition Programs: The program was established to recognize and honor those who have made contributions to the association, to physics education, and to physics research. The AAPT recognizes several types of accomplishment with awards, medals or citations, some of which are presented every year and a few of which are presented only occasionally. Nominations remain active for a period of five years from the date of submission. Self nomination is not appropriate for any award.

Barbara Lotze Scholarships for Future Teachers: The association offers two scholarships for future high school physics teachers. These scholarships are available only to U.S. citizens attending a U.S. school. Undergraduate students enrolled, or planning to enroll, in physics teacher preparation curricula and high school seniors entering such programs are eligible. The two successful applicants will each receive a stipend of up to $2,000.

E. Leonard Joseem International Education Fund: This program provides grants to individuals in support of international programs dealing with teaching and learning of physics. Funds are available for two different categories: collaborations between U.S. and developing countries (where funding should facilitate interactions and exchanges of ideas between U.S. physics educators and/or students and those in developing countries), and international meetings and conferences focused on physics education (which should involve direct contact between physics educators and furnish the interactions that stimulate new ideas and lasting collaborations). Funds are available to any association member actively engaged in the teaching and learning of physics: graduate students, post-doctoral fellows, and high school, college, and university faculty.

Frederick and Florence Bauder Endowment for the Support of Physics Teaching: The endowment was established to support special activities in the area of physics teaching. Activities that the grant can support include, but are not limited to provide grants for the development and distribution of innovative apparatus for physics teaching, provide funds of up to $500 to fund local workshops for teachers who spread the use of demonstration and laboratory equipment, to obtain and or build and support traveling exhibits of apparatus. Only AAPT members may apply.

Harold Q. and Charlotte Mae Fuller Fund: The fund provides free memberships to physics teachers in developing countries with nonconvertible currencies. Application by nomination only.

Hashim A. Yamani Fund: This award provides recipients with regular electronic memberships to the American Journal of Physics, The Physics Teacher, and Physics Today. Eligible applicants must be either undergraduate seniors who are planning careers teaching physics to start upon completion of their undergraduate degree, or graduate students who are in their last two years before receiving their final post-baccalaureate degree and who are planning a career teaching physics. Priority will be given to students from the Middle East, Africa, and Southeast Asia.

High School Physics Teacher Grant: Grants of $100 to $500 are awarded to teachers with the best proposal to promote better teaching practice, student understanding and interest, and/or increased enrollment.

EIN: 520749775

3758
American Composers Forum of Washington, DC, Inc.

3309 Bunker Hill Rd.
Mount Rainier, MD 20712-1922 (301) 715-3779
Contact: Jonathan Morris, Chair., C.E.O., and Exec. Dir.

Foundation type: Public charity
Purpose: Grants and support to artists such as fiscal agency, professional development support, referrals for other regional services, networking opportunities, and member meetings.
Financial data: Year ended 06/30/2011. Assets, $3,019 (M); Expenditures, $402.
Fields of interest: Performing arts; Arts, artist's services.
Type of support: Grants to individuals; Residencies; Fiscal agent/sponsor.
Application information: Applications accepted.
Additional information: Artist-in-Residence program not funded in 2007; See web site for further guidelines.
EIN: 200485641

3759
American Gastroenterological Association

4930 Del Ray Ave.
Bethesda, MD 20814-2512 (301) 654-2055
FAX: (301) 654-5920; E-mail: member@gastro.org;
URL: http://www.gastro.org

Foundation type: Public charity
Purpose: Awards to outstanding researchers in the field of gastroenterology.
Financial data: Year ended 03/31/2012. Assets, $54,658,605 (M); Expenditures, $18,102,529; Total giving, $1,167,025; Grants to individuals, totaling $42,025.
Fields of interest: Digestive diseases; Digestive disorders research.
Type of support: Research.
Application information: Applications accepted. Application form required.
Deadline(s): July 27
Applicants should submit the following:
    1) Letter(s) of recommendation
    2) Curriculum vitae
Additional information: Application should also include a $150 non-refundable fee. See web site for additional guidelines.
EIN: 366066325

3760
American Horse Trials Foundation, Inc.

221 Grove Cove Rd.
Centreville, MD 21617-2686 (443) 262-9555
FAX: (443) 262-9666; E-mail: ahtf@att.net;
URL: http://www.ahtf3day.org

Foundation type: Public charity

Purpose: Financial support for qualified riders pay for their training and competition expenses national and internationally.
Publications: Application guidelines.
Financial data: Year ended 12/31/2011. Assets, $1,213,742 (M); Expenditures, $1,979,125; Total giving, $1,804,309; Grants to individuals, totaling $1,804,309.
Fields of interest: Athletics/sports, equestrianism; Athletics/sports, amateur competition.
Type of support: Grants to individuals.
Application information: Applications accepted. Application form required. Application form available on the grantmaker's web site.
Initial approach: Application
Applicants should submit the following:
    1) Letter(s) of recommendation
    2) Budget Information
Additional information: See web site for eligibility criteria.
Program description:
Grants: The foundation provides competition grants to qualified active riders (as defined by the United States Equestrian Federation). Eligible applicants include amateur athletes who have finished in the upper half of a national Three-Day-Event competition within three years of the application date.
EIN: 521495923

3761
American Institute of Physics, Inc.

1 Physics Ellipse
College Park, MD 20740-3843 (301) 209-3100
Contact: H. Frederick Dylla, C.E.O. and Exec. Dir.
FAX: (301) 209-0882; E-mail: aipinfo@aip.org;
URL: http://www.aip.org/aip/writing

Foundation type: Public charity
Purpose: Science writing awards to scientists, journalists and broadcast media professionals for published works on physics, astronomy, and allied science fields.
Publications: Application guidelines; Annual report; Informational brochure.
Financial data: Year ended 12/31/2011. Assets, $168,262,314 (M); Expenditures, $73,163,421; Total giving, $347,402; Grants to individuals, totaling $222,106.
Fields of interest: Print publishing; Astronomy; Physics.
Type of support: Fellowships; Research; Scholarships—to individuals; Awards/prizes; Stipends.
Application information: Applications accepted.
Send request by: Mail
Deadline(s): Varies
Program descriptions:
Abraham Pais Prize for the History of Physics: This annual prize of $10,000 is awarded to an individual for his/her outstanding scholarly achievement in the history of physics.
AIP State Department and Congressional Science Fellowships Program: These fellowships are designed to enhance the science and/or technical capacity of the U.S. Department of State and Congress by enabling at least three scientists annually to work in Washington, D.C. headquarters for a one-year term. The fellowship offers a unique opportunity for a scientist to contribute scientific and technical expertise to the Department and raise awareness of the value of scientific input; in turn, scientists broaden their experience by interacting with policymakers in the federal government and learning about the foreign policy process. Eligible applicants must: be a member of one or more of the ten institute member societies at the time f

application; be a U.S. citizen; have a Ph.D. in physics or a closely-related field; have eligibility for security clearance; and have an interest and/or experience in science and/or technical aspects of foreign policy, excellent science credentials, outstanding interpersonal and communication skills, and sound judgment and maturity in decision-making. Fellows are for one year, usually running from September to August, and are awarded a stipend of $70,000 per year, a relocation allowance, an allowance for in-service travel for professional development, and reimbursement for health insurance premiums.

Andrew W. Gemant Award: This annual award recognizes the accomplishments of a person who has made significant contributions to the cultural, artistic, or humanistic dimension of physics. The awardee is invited to deliver a public lecture in a suitable forum; the awardee receives a cash award of $5,000 and is asked to designate an academic institution to receive a grant of $3,000 to further the public communication of physics. Award is by nomination only.

Dannie Heineman Prizes for Astrophysics and Mathematical Physics: These prizes award $10,000 to recognize outstanding work in the field of astrophysics and mathematical physics.

Fluid Dynamics Prize: This $10,000 award is designed to recognize and encourage outstanding achievement in fluid dynamics research.

Karl Taylor Compton Medal for Leadership in Physics: Awards a quadrennial award of $10,000, a bronze medal, and a certificate to a distinguished physicist who has made an outstanding contribution to physics.

Meggers Project Award: This biennial award of $25,000 is designed to fund projects for the improvement of high-school physics teaching in the U.S., that work to raise the level of interest in physics and boost the quality of physics education. Preference will be given to proposals that directly involve pre-college teachers and/or students.

Prize for Industrial Applications of Physics: Co-sponsored with the American Physics Society (APS) and General Motors, this award recognizes outstanding contributions by an individual or individuals to the industrial application of physics. The award is accompanied with a $10,000 cash prize.

Science Writing Award in Physics and Astronomy for Broadcast Media: Awards are given for works written for radio or television broadcast in English, published in the previous calendar year. Winning authors receive a $3,000 prize, a Windsor Chair, and a testimonial. The publisher of the winning work receives a certificate.

Tate Medal for International Leadership in Physics: Awards a biennial award of $10,000, a bronze medal, and a certificate to a foreign national in recognition for their leadership and service to the physics community on an international level.
EIN: 131667053

3762
American Kidney Fund, Inc.

11921 Rockville Pike, Ste. 300
Rockville, MD 20852-3914 (301) 881-3052
Contact: LaVarne A. Burton, Pres. and C.E.O.
Email for scholarships: scholarship@kidneyfund.org
E-mail: helpline@kidneyfund.org; Toll-free tel.: (800) 638-8299; URL: http://www.kidneyfund.org

Foundation type: Public charity
Purpose: Financial assistance to individuals living with chronic kidney disease. Scholarships for clinical research fellowships in the field of Nephrology.

Publications: Application guidelines.
Financial data: Year ended 12/31/2012. Assets, $24,435,902 (M); Expenditures, $196,544,287; Total giving, $180,444,780; Grants to individuals, 83,806 grants totaling $180,444,780.
Fields of interest: Kidney diseases; Economically disadvantaged.
Type of support: Fellowships; Research; Grants for special needs.
Application information: Applications accepted.
Deadline(s): Dec. 1 for Research
Final notification: Applicant notified Feb. for Research Program
Additional information: See web site for additional guidelines for financial assistance and scholarships.
EIN: 237124261

3763
American Music Therapy Association

8455 Colesville Rd., Ste. 1000
Silver Spring, MD 20910-3392 (301) 589-3300
Contact: Andrea Farbman, Exec. Dir.
FAX: (301) 589-5175;
E-mail: info@musictherapy.org; URL: http://www.musictherapy.org

Foundation type: Public charity
Purpose: Scholarships and awards to individuals who are current members of AMTA for music therapy education and professional development.
Publications: Application guidelines; Annual report; Informational brochure; Newsletter.
Financial data: Year ended 06/30/2011. Assets, $1,178,100 (M); Expenditures, $1,567,029; Total giving, $23,875; Grants to individuals, totaling $23,875.
Fields of interest: Music; Substance abuse, treatment; Mental health, treatment.
Type of support: Research; Scholarships—to individuals; Awards/prizes; Undergraduate support.
Application information: Unsolicited requests for funds not considered or acknowledged.
Program descriptions:
AMTA Conference Scholar: Awards two cash prizes of $500 for conference expenses, free conference registration and free participation in continuing music education courses and institutes. Applicants must be current, professional AMTA members.
Anne Emery Kyllo Professional Scholarship: Awards $500 for continuing music therapy education activities, and for continuing education courses that meet the Educational Activity guidelines as established by the Certification Board of Music Therapists.
Arthur Flagler Fultz Research Fund: Awards up to $10,000 for up to 18 months to support music therapy research in the following areas: Clinical Research: to assess the efficacy of music therapy interventions and help define best practice and Health Services Research: to assess the role of music therapy practices in the context of emerging health care delivery models. Research projects that are a collaboration between a practicing music therapy technician and an experienced researcher are preferred.
Brian Smith Memorial Scholarship: Awards $500 to music therapy interns pursuing training in chemical dependency or in adolescent programs.
E. Thayer Gaston Writing Competition: Awards $500 to undergraduate and undergraduate equivalency students enrolled in a college or university approved by the American Music Therapy Association.

Edwina Eustis Dick Scholarship for Music Therapy Interns: Awards two scholarships of $500 to current student members of AMTA.
Florence Tyson Grant to Study Music Psychotherapy: Provides registration to attend annual AMTA conference to a musical therapist with a current credential of MT-BC or current professional designation of ACMT, CMT, or RMT. Applicants must be AMTA members.
EIN: 486107868

3764
American Nurses Foundation, Inc.

(formerly American Nurses Association Foundation)
8515 Georgia Ave., Ste. 400
Silver Spring, MD 20910-3403 (301) 628-5227
Contact: Kate Judge, Exec. Dir.
FAX: (301) 628-5354; E-mail: anf@ana.org; E-Mail for Kate Judge: kate.judge@ana.org; URL: http://www.anfonline.org

Foundation type: Public charity
Purpose: Grants to beginning and experienced registered nurse researchers with a bachelor's or higher degree to conduct studies that contribute toward the advancement of nursing science and the enhancement of patient care.
Publications: Application guidelines; Annual report; Informational brochure; Newsletter.
Financial data: Year ended 12/31/2011. Assets, $4,274,513 (M); Expenditures, $1,070,163; Total giving, $378,215.
Fields of interest: Research; Nursing care.
Type of support: Research.
Application information: Application form required.
Deadline(s): 1st Mon. in May
EIN: 131893924

3765
American Occupational Therapy Foundation

4720 Montgomery Ln.
P.O. Box 31220
Bethesda, MD 20814-5320 (240) 292-1079
Contact: Charles Christiansen, Exec. Dir.; for Scholarships: Jeanne Y. Cooper
FAX: (240) 396-6188; E-mail: aotf@aotf.org; URL: http://www.aotf.org/

Foundation type: Public charity
Purpose: Scholarships to members of the American Occupational Therapy Association who are enrolled full time in either a professional occupational therapy educational program or an occupational therapy assistant program and must meet all eligibility requirements.
Publications: Annual report; Financial statement; Informational brochure; Newsletter.
Financial data: Year ended 09/30/2011. Assets, $20,273,894 (M); Expenditures, $1,122,990; Total giving, $51,500; Grants to individuals, totaling $51,500.
Fields of interest: Physical therapy.
Type of support: Graduate support; Undergraduate support; Postgraduate support.
Application information: Applications accepted. Application form required. Application form available on the grantmaker's web site.
Send request by: Online
Deadline(s): Nov. 11
Final notification: Applicants notified by Mar.
Applicants should submit the following:
1) Essay
2) Letter(s) of recommendation
3) Transcripts

Additional information: Application should also include Program Directors Statement.
Program description:
Scholarships: Awards range from $150 to $5,000 to occupational therapy students who are currently enrolled and have completed at least one year of occupational therapy specific coursework in an AOTA accredited or developing post-professional level program or enrolled in an occupational therapy assistant program.
EIN: 136189382

3766
American Society of Health-System Pharmacists Research and Education Foundation

(also known as ASHP Research and Education Foundation)
7272 Wisconsin Ave.
Bethesda, MD 20814-4836 (301) 644-8612
Contact: Stephen J. Allen, C.E.O. and Exec. V.P.
FAX: (301) 634-5712;
E-mail: foundation@ashp.org; URL: http://www.ashpfoundation.org

Foundation type: Public charity
Purpose: Research grants for licensed pharmacists.
Publications: Application guidelines; Annual report; Newsletter.
Financial data: Year ended 05/31/2012. Assets, $10,865,231 (M); Expenditures, $3,763,481; Total giving, $1,369,149; Grants to individuals, totaling $106,324.
Fields of interest: Pharmacy/prescriptions; Diabetes.
Type of support: Fellowships; Research; Travel grants.
Application information: Applications accepted. Application form required. Application form available on the grantmaker's web site.
Initial approach: E-mail
Deadline(s): Vary
Additional information: See web site for additional application information.
Program descriptions:
ASHP Foundation-AFPE Undergraduate Gateway to Research Scholarship: A $5,000 grant is offered to outstanding pharmacy students enrolled at U.S. schools and college of pharmacy and outstanding undergraduate science students at any U.S. college or university. The grant is to be used for a faculty-supervised pharmaceutical sciences research project.
Award for Excellence in Medication-Use Safety: This $50,000 award honors a pharmacist-led multidisciplinary team and its significant institution-wide system improvements relating to medication use, and recognizes on a national level pharmacy professionals who have assumed a leadership role in promoting safety in the medication-use process. Nominations will be evaluated on medication-use system initiative and scope, planning and implementation, measurable outcomes and impact, and innovation and applicability. Eligible applicants include practitioners from all hospitals and health systems within the U.S. Two finalists also receive $10,000 each.
Awards: A variety of awards are given. Each of the following awards a $4,000 honorarium, a $1,000 expense allowance to attend the ASHP Mid-year Clinical meeting for the award presentation, and a plaque: (1) Award for Sustained Contributions to the Literature of Pharmacy Practice; (2) Drug Therapy Research Award; (3) Award for Innovation in Pharmacy Practice; (4) Pharmacy Practice Research

Award. The Student Research Award consists of a $1,500 honorarium, a $1,000 expense allowance to attend the ASHP Mid-year Clinical meeting for the award presentation, and a plaque. Please Web site for criteria.

Federal Services Junior Investigator Grant Program: Awards two grants of $25,000 to junior investigators whose research focuses on optimizing drug therapy in patients older than 60 years of age who receive care in a federal services health care facility.

Junior Investigator Research Grant: Awards two $20,000 grants to support health services research in medication use that is conducted by pharmacist junior investigators.

Pharmacy Resident Practice-Based Research Grant: Awards six $5,000 grants to support worthy research projects devoted to improving medical safety, demonstrates the role of the pharmacist in safe medication use, and fosters mentorship of pharmacy residents by an experienced practitioner.

Promoting Influenza Prevention: Pharmacists as Immunization Advocates: A $25,000 grant will be awarded to pharmacist investigators to provide funding for specific practice-based research related to the pharmacist's role in promoting vaccination against seasonal influenza and are not intended for long-term support of research programs.

Student Leadership Awards: The $2,500 award recognizes students with an interest in pharmacy practice in health-systems who have demonstrated leadership ability.

Traineeships: Traineeships are short-term and planned for postgraduates as self-study and experiential programs in specific areas of pharmacy practice. Self-study requirements vary from 10 to 15 hours of work, while the experiential portion requires the participant to attend training sessions at a predetermined site for five to ten days. Programs are offered in antithrombotic pharmacotherapy, oncology patient care, and pain and palliative care.

EIN: 237033369

3767
The American Society of Human Genetics
9650 Rockville Pike
Bethesda, MD   20814-3998   (301) 634-7300
Contact: Joann Boughman, Exec. V.P.
FAX: (301) 634-7079; E-mail: society@ashg.org;
E-Mail for Joann Boughman : jboughman@ashg.org;
URL: http://www.ashg.org

Foundation type: Public charity
Purpose: Awards and prizes by nomination to investigators pursuing human genetics.
Publications: Newsletter.
Financial data: Year ended 12/31/2011. Assets, $9,755,052 (M); Expenditures, $5,403,071; Total giving, $153,750; Grants to individuals, totaling $120,250.
Fields of interest: Science; Mathematics.
Type of support: Research; Awards/prizes.
Application information:
Deadline(s): Apr. 16
Additional information: Nominations must be submitted on-line. Posthumous nominations are not accepted.
EIN: 521419397

3768
American Speech-Language-Hearing Foundation
2200 Research Blvd.
Rockville, MD   20850-3289   (301) 296-8700
Contact: Nancy Minghetti, Exec. Dir.
FAX: (301) 296-8567;
E-mail: foundation@asha.org; E-Mail for Nancy Minghetti : nminghetti@asha.orgTel. for Nancy Minghetti : (301)-296-8701; URL: http://www.ashfoundation.org/grants/default.htm

Foundation type: Public charity
Purpose: Scholarships and research grants to graduate and postgraduate students in the areas of communication sciences and disorders.
Publications: Application guidelines.
Financial data: Year ended 12/31/2011. Assets, $8,539,774 (M); Expenditures, $789,849; Total giving, $271,519; Grants to individuals, totaling $171,519.
Fields of interest: Language/linguistics; Scholarships/financial aid; Speech/hearing centers; Ear, nose & throat research; Psychology/behavioral science; Disabilities, people with; Minorities.
Type of support: Research; Graduate support; Postgraduate support.
Application information: Applications accepted. Application form required. Application form available on the grantmaker's web site.
Deadline(s): Vary
Program descriptions:
Graduate Student Scholarships: The program awards scholarships of $5,000 to full-time master's or doctoral students in communication sciences and disorders programs demonstrating outstanding academic achievement.
Minority Student Scholarship: The program awards a $5,000 scholarship to racial/ethnic minority students who are U.S. citizens and who are accepted for graduate study in audiology or speech-language pathology.
New Investigators Research Grant: The program awards grants of $5,000 to new scientists earning their latest degree in communication sciences within the last five years to pursue research in audiology or speech-language pathology.
Research Grant in Speech Science: The program awards a grant of $5,000 every other year to individuals who have received a doctoral degree within the last five years, and who wish to further research activities in the areas of speech communication.
Student Research Grant in Audiology: The program awards a $2,000 grant for a proposed one-year study to master's and doctoral students in communication sciences and disorders desiring to conduct research in audiology.
Student Research Grant in Early Childhood Language Development: The program awards a $2,000 grant to master's and doctoral students in communication sciences and disorders desiring to conduct research in early childhood language development.
Student with a Disability Scholarship: The program awards scholarships of $4,000 to full-time graduate students with a disability who are enrolled in a communication sciences and disorders program, and who demonstrate outstanding academic achievement.
EIN: 526055761

3769
American Urological Association, Inc.
1000 Corporate Blvd.
Linthicum, MD   21090-2260   (410) 689-3700
FAX: (410) 689-3800; E-mail: aua@auanet.org;
Toll-free tel.: (866) 746-4282; URL: http://www.auanet.org

Foundation type: Public charity
Purpose: Awards honors the contribution of physician researchers and educators to the field of medicine, the specialty of urology, and the AUA. Scholarships and programs provide young urology faculty with an international perspective on urologic medicine.
Publications: Newsletter.
Financial data: Year ended 12/31/2011. Assets, $9,120,910 (M); Expenditures, $11,485,436; Total giving, $2,066,400; Grants to individuals, totaling $26,000.
Fields of interest: Health care; Medical specialties research.
Type of support: Grants to individuals.
Application information:
Deadline(s): Jan. 27 for Pfizer Visiting Professorships Program
Additional information: See web site for additional guidelines.
Program descriptions:
AUA Eugene Fuller Triennial Prostate Award: This award is given once every three years to an individual who has made an outstanding contribution to the study of the prostate gland and its associated diseases; the recipient receives an honorarium.
AUA Gold Cystoscope Award: This award is given annually to a urologist distinguished by outstanding contributions to the profession within ten years of completing residency training; the recipient receives an engraved gold cystoscope and an honorarium.
AUA Hugh Hampton Young Award: This award is presented annually to an individual whose contributions to the study of genitourinary tract disease are considered to be outstanding; the recipient receives an honorarium.
AUA Ramon Guiteras Award: This is awarded annually to an individual who is deemed to have made outstanding contributions to the art and science of urology; the recipient of this award receives an honorarium.
AUA Retrospectroscope Award: This $1,000 prize is awarded to the best presentation on the history of urology given at the annual History of Urology Forum.
AUA-EAU Academic Fellowship Exchange: In association with the European Association of Urology, this program allows young urology faculty to share information and research with one another, and provides an international perspective on urologic medicine. The program provides funding for all lodging, travel, and expenses. Eligible applicants must be younger than 42 years of age, possess an M.D. degree and full-time academic appointment at rank of assistant professor or higher, be an active member of the AUA, and have a strong interest and availability to travel for approximately three weeks. Applicants are nominated by their academic institutions.
Pfizer Visiting Professorships Program: In cooperation with Pfizer, up to ten grants of $7,500 each are available to select host institutions to provide for in-depth, educationally-focused visits by prominent medical experts to U.S. medical schools and/or teaching hospitals. Grants are intended to cover the visiting professor's honorarium, travel, and other direct expenses. U.S. medical schools and/or affiliated teaching with divisions or

departments of urology are strongly encouraged to apply.

Visiting Scholar Program: In cooperation with the Confederacion Americana de Urologia (CAU), this program allows one CAU scholar to visit one U.S. host institution for a three-month period, which is then followed by a partner site in a South American country. The scholar observes urologic surgeries and procedures, and attends clinics and staff activities; the scholar does not perform hands-on surgery. Monthly stipends, travel expenses, and accommodations are provided.

EIN: 522205122

3770
American Urological Association Foundation

(formerly American Foundation for Urologic Disease, Inc., also known as AUA Foundation)
1000 Corporate Blvd.
Linthicum, MD   21090-2260   (410) 689-3700
Application information: Rodney Cotten, Research Mgr., tel.: (410) 689-3750, fax: (410) 689-3998, e-mail: grants@auafoundation.org
FAX: (410) 689-3998;
E-mail: auafoundation@auafoundation.org; Toll-free tel. (U.S. only): (800) 828-7866; URL: http://www.urologyhealth.org/

Foundation type: Public charity
Purpose: Research grants for the prevention and cure of urologic disease.
Publications: Application guidelines; Newsletter.
Financial data: Year ended 12/31/2011. Assets, $17,749,105 (M); Expenditures, $3,043,391; Total giving, $777,748; Grants to individuals, totaling $12,250.
Fields of interest: Medical research.
Type of support: Research.
Application information: Applications accepted. Application form required. Application form available on the grantmaker's web site.
  Initial approach: Telephone or e-mail
  Deadline(s): Sept. 1
  Final notification: Applicants notified in four months
  Additional information: See web site for additional information.
Program descriptions:
  Arkansas Urologic Society Residency Research Award: The fund supports a urology resident in Arkansas for one year while they fulfill their obligation for research training.
  AUA Foundation Bridge Awards: This program works to expand and support research in urologic diseases by provide awards of up to $15,000 to assist AUA member investigators in continuing vital research efforts while awaiting new funding. Applicants must be current AUA members in good standing.
  AUA Foundation/Astellas Rising Star in Urology Research Award: These grants, awarded in conjunction with Astellas Pharma US, Inc., provide supplemental salary support to career development awardees to ensure that their research salary compensation is competitive with other academic urology faculty. Salary supplements are awarded for a period of up to five years, with an escalating payment each year. Eligible applicants must be board-certified or board-eligible urologists who have successfully competed for a new externally-funded, peer-reviewed career development award.
  AUA Foundation/NIDDK/NCI Surgeon-Scientist Award: Awarded in conjunction with the National Institute of Diabetes & Digestive & Kidney Diseases (NIDDK) and the National Cancer Institute (NCI), these grants support urology faculty with the

potential and desire to become independent investigators with up to five years of funding, on an escalating basis, solely for salary supplementation. Eligible applicants must be board-certified or board-eligible urologists, or participating in a training program to obtain board certification in urology; and have successfully competed for KIDD or NIC career development funding within the previous fiscal year.

  AUA Foundation/Robert J. Krane, M.D. Urology Research Success Award: Awards up to $10,000 to assist urology researchers in continuing vital urology research efforts while awaiting new funding.

  Herbert Brendler, M.D. Summer Medical Student Fellowship Program: The program encourages medical students to join the field of urology through a summer fellowship program.

  LUTS and Bladder Dysfunction Research Exploration Awards: This award encourages research by M.D. and Ph.D. researchers to advance the understanding of the basic mechanisms underlying the function of the lower urinary tract and the pathobiology underlying LUTS and bladder dysfunction. Investigators at the doctoral level are eligible to apply for up to $75,000 to support their research for an 18 month performance period. Funds may be used to cover salary, research supplies, technical support, animal costs and other research-related costs. Up to three awards are granted.

  Pfizer/AUA Foundation Female Urology and Voiding Dysfunction Research Training Awards: Provides up to three grants, each up to $37,500 per year for a period of two consecutive years for the establishment of research programs in female urology and voiding dysfunction.

  Research Scholars Program: The program provides an opportunity for young scientists to begin a career in urologic research at a time when many urology departments across the country are faced with budget challenges that limit research opportunities. M.D. Post-resident Fellowships of $60,000 per year are available to trained urologists who are within five years of completing their residency, who aspire to learn scientific techniques, are committed to a career in research, and who are able to provide evidence of current and/or prior interest/accomplishments in research. Ph.D. Post-doctoral Fellowships of $30,000 per year are available to basic scientists who are within five years of earning a Ph.D. with a related interest in urologic diseases and conditions, and/or related diseases and dysfunctions. M.D./Ph.D. One-Year Fellowships of $30,000 each are available to trained urologists or basic scientists who are within five years of completing their residency or doctorate, and who aspire to learn scientific techniques, are committed to a career in urologic research, and who are able to provide evidence of current and/or prior interest/accomplishments in research.

  Russell Scott, Jr., M.D. Urology Residency Research Award: This award funds an outstanding urology resident for a period of one year while the resident fulfills his or her obligation for research training.

EIN: 203210212

3771
AMVETS National Service Foundation

4647 Forbes Blvd.
Lanham, MD   20706-4356   (301) 459-6181
Contact: Joseph T. Piening, Exec. Dir.
FAX: (301) 459-5578; E-mail: vwortz@amvets.org; URL: http://www.amvetsnsf.org

Foundation type: Public charity

Purpose: Scholarships to veterans/active military, their sons, daughters or grandchildren. Scholarships to deserving high school seniors, high school JROTC students and veterans pursuing a higher education.
Publications: Financial statement.
Financial data: Year ended 08/31/2012. Assets, $8,587,034 (M); Expenditures, $15,868,381; Total giving, $2,122,062; Grants to individuals, totaling $316,602.
Fields of interest: Higher education; Military/veterans.
Type of support: Scholarships—to individuals; Undergraduate support.
Application information: Applications accepted. Application form required. Application form available on the grantmaker's web site.
  Send request by: Mail
  Deadline(s): Apr. 15
  Applicants should submit the following:
    1) FAFSA
    2) Transcripts
    3) SAT
    4) Resume
    5) Essay
    6) ACT
  Additional information: Application should include a copy of parents income tax form, acceptance letter from the accredited school, and proof of college expenses.
Program descriptions:
  Dr. Aurelio M. Caccomo Scholarship: One $3,000 scholarship for veterans/guardsman/reservists is awarded nationwide per year, for the duration of the grant, without regard for district boundaries. The scholarship is for veterans, including members of the National Guard and Reserves, seeking new skills in order to be more competitive in the job market. This one-time scholarship may be used for undergraduate courses, accredited degree or certificate programs, including on-line schools.
  Scholarships: The foundation annually awards scholarships to the sons, daughters or grandchildren of American Veterans (AMVETS) members or of a deceased veteran who would have been eligible for AMVETS membership. Opportunities include six $4,000 scholarships for high school seniors ($1,000 per year of a four-year undergraduate program or at an accredited technical/trade leading to certification or a degree, with one selected from each district), three $4,000 scholarships for veterans ($1,000 per year of a four-year undergraduate program or certification/degree from an accredited technical/trade school, with no regard for district boundaries), and one $1,000 scholarship for a JROTC high school senior entering any undergraduate program.
EIN: 520970963

3772
Annapolis Area Ministries, Inc.

10 Hudson St.
P.O. Box 6149
Annapolis, MD   21401-3111   (410) 349-5056
Contact: Elizabeth Kinney, Exec. Dir.
E-mail: info@annapolislighthouse.org; E-mail For Elizabeth Kinney:
ekinney@annapolislighthouse.org; URL: http://annapolislighthouse.org/

Foundation type: Public charity
Purpose: Provides shelter, food, resources and services to homeless and disadvantaged individuals and families in the Annapolis, MD area to promote self-sufficiency.
Financial data: Year ended 06/30/2013. Assets, $9,493,704 (M); Expenditures, $2,511,950; Total

giving, $688,876; Grants to individuals, totaling $688,876.

Fields of interest: Human services; Homeless.
Type of support: Emergency funds.
Application information: Applications not accepted.

Additional information: Unsolicited requests for funds not considered or acknowledged.

EIN: 521671388

3773
Anxiety Disorders Association of America

(also known as ADAA)
8730 Georgia Ave., Ste. 600
Silver Spring, MD   20910-3643   (240) 485-1001
FAX: (240) 485-1035;
E-mail: information@adaa.org; URL: http://www.adaa.org

Foundation type: Public charity
Purpose: Awards and research grants to professionals in the field of anxiety disorders.
Publications: Application guidelines; Newsletter.
Financial data: Year ended 12/31/2011. Assets, $476,990 (M); Expenditures, $838,733; Total giving, $10,700; Grants to individuals, totaling $9,200.
Fields of interest: Mental health, disorders.
Type of support: Research; Awards/prizes; Postdoctoral support; Graduate support; Travel grants.
Application information: Application form required. Application form available on the grantmaker's web site.

Deadline(s): Vary
Applicants should submit the following:
1) Curriculum vitae
2) Letter(s) of recommendation
3) Proposal
Additional information: See Web site for complete program information.

Program descriptions:
Career Development Travel Awards: The awards aim to help young professionals with a career interest in fields related to anxiety disorders, such as basic and clinical neuropsychopharmacology, clinical psychology, genetics, neuroimaging, and epidemiology. Recipients receive a $500 travel stipend and free registration to the ADAA Annual Conference.

Donald F. Klein Early Career Investigator Award: The foundation awards $1,000, plus up to $1,000 to cover travel expenses, and complimentary registration to the Annual Conference to investigators who have completed their terminal degree and are currently at a rank of assistant professor or below. Applicants must be the first or senior author on the submitted paper, which must be original research on anxiety and anxiety-related disorders focusing on neurobiology, psychosocial treatments, or experimental psychopathology. The paper may not be published or in press.

EIN: 521248820

3774
Aplastic Anemia & MDS International Foundation, Inc.

(formerly Aplastic Anemia Foundation of America, Inc.)
100 Park Ave., Ste. 108
Rockville, MD   20850-2621   (301) 279-7202
Contact: John M. Huber, Exec. Dir.
FAX: (301) 279-7205; E-mail: help@aamds.org; Toll free tel.: (800) 747-2820; URL: http://www.aamds.org

Foundation type: Public charity
Purpose: Support for research into prevention and treatment of aplastic anemia, myelodysplastic syndromes, and other bone marrow failure.
Publications: Application guidelines; Annual report; Newsletter.
Financial data: Year ended 12/31/2012. Assets, $4,027,621 (M); Expenditures, $3,512,900; Total giving, $262,506; Grants to individuals, totaling $22,506.
Fields of interest: Health care; Heart & circulatory diseases; Nerve, muscle & bone diseases.
International interests: Global Programs.
Type of support: Research; Scholarships—to individuals.
Application information: Application form required. Application form available on the grantmaker's web site.

Initial approach: Letter or telephone
Send request by: Mail or e-mail
Copies of proposal: 5
Deadline(s): Feb 27
Final notification: Recipients notified in three to four months

Program description:
Research Grants: The foundation invites researchers to apply for two-year grants of $30,000 per year to test new ideas and to explore other research leads for aplastic anemia and myelodysplastic syndromes. Applications are ranked according to merit by a distinguished panel of research scientists and funded by the generosity of families and patients. Established investigators and new investigators (including applicants who hold a doctor of medicine, doctor of philosophy, or other doctoral-level degree, [e.g. PharmD]) in bone marrow disease can apply for awards; second-year funding is contingent upon progress in the first year.

EIN: 521336903

3775
The Arc of Prince George's County, Inc.

1401 McCormick Dr.
Largo, MD   20774-5507   (301) 925-7050
FAX: (301) 925-4387;
E-mail: info@thearcofpgc.org; E-Mail for Mac Ramsey : mramsey@thearcofpgc.orgTel. for Mac Ramsey : (301)-925-7050, Ext. 234; URL: http://www.thearcofpgc.org

Foundation type: Public charity
Purpose: Grants to residents of Prince George's County, MD, with disabilities and their families through the Developmental Disabilities Administration process.
Publications: Annual report; Financial statement; Informational brochure; Newsletter.
Financial data: Year ended 06/30/2012. Assets, $13,431,657 (M); Expenditures, $26,008,297; Total giving, $2,609,546; Grants to individuals, totaling $2,609,546.
Fields of interest: Mentally disabled.
Type of support: Grants for special needs.
Application information:

Initial approach: Letter
Additional information: Contact foundation for eligibility requirements.

EIN: 520715246

3776
Arts and Humanities Council of Montgomery County

801 Ellsworth Dr.
Silver Spring, MD   20910-4438   (301) 565-3805
FAX: (301) 565-3809;
E-mail: info@creativemoco.com; E-Mail for Suzan E. Jenkins: suzan.jenkins@creativemoco.com;
URL: http://www.creativemoco.com/

Foundation type: Public charity
Purpose: Grants to artists or scholars in Montgomery County, MD, for their artistic or scholarly development.
Publications: Application guidelines; Annual report; Financial statement; Grants list; Informational brochure.
Financial data: Year ended 06/30/2013. Assets, $547,303 (M); Expenditures, $3,721,035; Total giving, $3,041,367; Grants to individuals, totaling $72,870.
Fields of interest: Media/communications; Visual arts; Performing arts; Humanities.
Type of support: Grants to individuals; Awards/prizes.
Application information: Applications accepted. Application form required. Application form available on the grantmaker's web site.

Initial approach: Telephone
Deadline(s): Vary
Applicants should submit the following:
1) Work samples
2) Resume
3) Essay
4) Curriculum vitae
5) Budget Information
Additional information: See web site for additional application information.

Program descriptions:
Artists and Scholars in the Community Grants: These grants are intended to support a variety of arts and humanities programs that bring high-quality artists and scholars to community-based audiences in Montgomery County; it is also intended that these grants will bring the arts and/or humanities to underserved populations that have fewer opportunities to participate in programs available to the general community. Eligible artists and scholars chosen to present must be registered with the council; organizations will be given between $250 and $1,500 to compensate presenting artists and scholars.

Artists and Scholars Roster for Community Programs: This initiative of the council provides the public with access to a list of pre-screened, high-quality artists and scholars who are available to present programs and workshops for any organization that wishes to arrange for an artist or scholar to present at its facility. Acceptance onto the roster will also qualify participating artists and scholars for future grants from the council. Eligible community-based organizations must provide programs in Montgomery County to underserved populations (individuals who, by virtue of their age, economic status, locale, physical ability, or other characteristics, have fewer opportunities to participate in programs available to the general community)

Arts Integration Residency Grants: These grants support artists who collaboratively develop an arts-integrated program with classroom teachers in a public, private, or parochial elementary, middle, or high school in Montgomery County. Artists must be chosen from the council's Teaching Artists Roster.

Grants to Individual Artists and Scholars: Grants, ranging from $1,000 to $5,000, are available to

support the work of Montgomery County-based individual artists and scholars, collaborations of artists and scholars, and small arts and humanities groups that may not be formally incorporated as nonprofit organizations. Three types of grants are available under this program: Grants for Creation of New Work (such as producing a new film; creating new paintings, photographs, sculpture, or prints; conducting research in preparation for writing a book; creating work products based on variations or new arrangements of traditional or historical works; and writing poetry), Professional Development Grants (working with a mentor, artists, or teacher in the applicant's field; creating a business or marketing plan; supporting travel and/or registration expenses for workshops or training programs; or developing promotional materials not related to a specific product or program), and Community Connections Grants (funding for: performance, presentation, or exhibition of a visual, performing, or media art form; festivals and events, such as folk, literary, or visual arts; history presentations, archeological programs, or historical reenactments; community mural projects or family arts days; or debates, public forums, seminars, or town meetings)
EIN: 521086825

3777
The Associated: Jewish Community Federation of Baltimore, Inc.
101 W. Mount Royal Ave.
Baltimore, MD   21201-5708   (410) 727-4828
Contact: Mark B. Terrill, Pres.
FAX: (410) 837-1327;
E-mail: information@associated.org; URL: http://www.associated.org

Foundation type: Public charity
Purpose: Fellowship and outstanding service awards to individuals of the Jewish community of Baltimore, MD.
Financial data: Year ended 06/30/2011. Assets, $30,247,791 (M); Expenditures, $44,060,457; Total giving, $27,255,338; Grants to individuals, 23 grants totaling $27,586. Subtotal for awards/prizes: 8 grants totaling $338. Subtotal for fellowships: 15 grants totaling $27,248.
Fields of interest: Jewish agencies & synagogues.
Type of support: Fellowships.
Application information: Applications accepted.
  Additional information: Contact the federation for additional guidelines.
EIN: 520607957

3778
Association of Public Health Laboratories, Inc.
8515 Georgia Ave., Ste. 700
Silver Spring, MD   20910-3477   (240) 485-2745
Contact: Scott J. Becker M.S., Exec. Dir.
Tel. and e-mail for fellowships: (240) 485-2778, fellowships@aphl.org
FAX: (240) 485-2700; E-mail: info@aphl.org; URL: http://www.aphl.org

Foundation type: Public charity
Purpose: Fellowships to students for careers in public health laboratories. Support for specialized training for practicing scientists.
Publications: Annual report.
Financial data: Year ended 06/30/2012. Assets, $8,297,579 (M); Expenditures, $30,596,397; Total giving, $1,771,383; Grants to individuals, totaling $1,410,880.

Fields of interest: Public health school/education; Health sciences school/education; Environment.
Type of support: Fellowships; Research.
Application information: Applications accepted. Interview required.
  Send request by: On-line
  Deadline(s): Vary
  Additional information: See web site for additional application guidelines.
Program descriptions:
  Bioinformatics in Public Health (BPH) Fellowship: This program aims to train and prepare bioinformaticians to apply their expertise within public health and design tools to aid existing public health and design tools to aid existing public health personnel in the use of bioinformatics. The fellowship program was developed to meet the need for expertise in the analysis of the vast amounts of genetic data that are generated through molecular sequencing techniques and to harness that data to solve public health problems. The fellowship types are post-doctoral fellows and practical fellows.
  Emerging Infectious Diseases Laboratory Fellowships: The EID Advanced Laboratory Training Fellowship is a one-year program designed for bachelor's or master's level scientists, with emphasis on the practical application technologies, methodologies and practices related to emerging infectious diseases. The EID Laboratory Research Fellowship is a two-year program designed for doctoral-level scientists to conduct high-priority research in infectious diseases.
  Environmental Health Traineeships and Fellowships: This program offers short term (two to six weeks) specialized training in environmental health to public health laboratory scientists for traineeships and long term (one to two years) hostings for fellowships.
EIN: 521800436

3779
Association of Schools and Colleges of Optometry, Inc.
6110 Executive Blvd., Ste. 420
Rockville, MD   20852-3942   (301) 231-5944
Contact: Marty Wall, Exec. Dir.
FAX: (301) 770-1828; E-mail: mwall@opted.org; URL: http://www.opted.org/

Foundation type: Public charity
Purpose: Stipends and awards for faculty to visit other schools and colleges of optometry sharing their expertise in contact lenses.
Publications: Application guidelines.
Financial data: Year ended 06/30/2012. Assets, $3,586,107 (M); Expenditures, $1,447,228; Total giving, $42,000; Grants to individuals, totaling $9,500.
Fields of interest: Eye diseases; Eye research.
Type of support: Travel awards.
Application information: Applications accepted. Application form available on the grantmaker's web site.
  Deadline(s): 60 days before anticipated date of lecture
  Final notification: Recipients are notified within 30 days of receipt
Program description:
  Alcon Guest Lecture Program: This program, coordinated in conjunction with Alcon, encourages the sharing of faculty expertise in contact lenses, lens care, and ocular surface conditions among association member schools and colleges by developing opportunities for new faculty to visit

other schools. Awardees receive funding to travel cover expenses and a $1,000 honorarium.
EIN: 521005768

3780
Autism Society of America, Inc.
4340 E.W. Hwy., Ste. 350
Bethesda, MD   20814-4411   (301) 657-0881
Contact: Scott Badesch, Pres. and C.E.O. and C.O.O.
Toll-free tel.: (800) 328-8476; E-mail For Scott Badesch: sbadesch@autism-society.org;
URL: http://www.autism-society.org

Foundation type: Public charity
Purpose: Awards to professionals who have made a significant contribution in the autism field. Scholarships to qualified individuals with autism.
Financial data: Year ended 12/31/2011. Assets, $1,735,876 (M); Expenditures, $3,443,468; Total giving, $144,859.
Fields of interest: Autism.
Type of support: Awards/prizes; Undergraduate support.
Application information:
  Initial approach: Letter
  Deadline(s): Mar. 31
  Final notification: Apr. 30
Program descriptions:
  Autism Professional of the Year Award: This award is for professionals (educators, speech language therapists, social workers, occupational therapists, psychologists, psychiatrist medical doctors, or researchers) who have made a significant contribution in the autism field. This list is not exhaustive; nominations for all types of professionals are welcome. Conference registration and an award of $750 are given to the winner.
  CVS/All Kids Can Scholars Program: The program provides a scholarship in the amount of $1,000 to a qualified individual with autism to be applied toward the completion of an accredited, postsecondary educational or vocational program of study (e.g., college, trade school, etc.). The scholarship is available to an individual with autism who has successfully met all the requirements for admission into an accredited post-secondary program of study.
  Outstanding Individual With Autism of the Year Award: The award is given to an individual with autism who has excelled in one or more areas of life experiences or contributions. Conference registration and a cash award of $1,000 is given to the winner.
  Parent/Parents of the Year Award: This award is given for demonstration of unusual dedication or effort on the part of a parent (or parents) of an individual with autism toward furthering the cause of autism, such as community awareness, advocacy, or another significant accomplishment. Conference registration and a cash award of $1,000 are given to the winner.
EIN: 521020149

3781
Autism Society of America Foundation
4340 E.W. Hwy, Ste. 350
Bethesda, MD   20814-3015   (301) 657-0881
Contact: Scott Badesch, Pres. and C.O.O.
E-mail: asaf@autism-society.org; Toll-free tel.: (800) 328-8476E-Mail for Scott Badesch : sbadesch@autism-society.org; URL: http://www.autism-society.org

Foundation type: Public charity

Purpose: Research grants for the study of autism and the causes, cure and treatment thereof.
Financial data: Year ended 12/31/2011. Assets, $449,194 (M); Expenditures, $487,740; Total giving, $370,792.
Fields of interest: Autism; Autism research.
Type of support: Research; Graduate support; Technical education support; Undergraduate support.
Application information:
  Initial approach: E-mail
  Additional information: Contact foundation for application guidelines.
Program description:
  The CVS/All Kids Can Scholars Program: The program awards a scholarship of $1,000 to a qualified individuals with autism to be applied toward the completion of an accredited, postsecondary educational, or vocational program of study (e.g. college, trade school, etc.)
EIN: 522007155

3782
Baltimore Clayworks, Inc.
5707 Smith Ave.
Baltimore, MD   21209-3609
Contact: Paul Derstine, Interim Exec. Dir.
FAX: (410) 578-0058;
E-mail: paul.derstine@baltimoreclayworks.org;
URL: http://www.baltimoreclayworks.org

Foundation type: Public charity
Purpose: Residencies and fellowships to emerging clay artists with studio space in the Baltimore, MD area.
Publications: Annual report.
Financial data: Year ended 12/31/2011. Assets, $3,010,457 (M); Expenditures, $1,193,945.
Fields of interest: Sculpture.
Type of support: Residencies; Stipends.
Application information: Applications accepted. Application form required. Application form available on the grantmaker's web site.
  Initial approach: Letter of intent
  Send request by: Mail
  Deadline(s): Mid-Apr.
  Applicants should submit the following:
    1) Work samples
    2) Resume
Program description:
  Lormina Salter Fellowship: The residency includes a year of studio space, a $100/month stipend, a solo exhibition, and access to facilities. It requires at least 24 hours weekly on the premises doing working, up to 10 hours annually in community outreach, participation in the collective life of the studio, a solo exhibition, and a residence established in Baltimore.
EIN: 521409133

3783
The Baltimore Community Foundation
2 E. Read St., 9th Fl.
Baltimore, MD   21202-6903   (410) 332-4171
Contact: Gigi Wirtz, Dir., Comms.; For grants: Maya Smith, Prog. Asst.
FAX: (410) 837-4701; E-mail: questions@bcf.org;
URL: http://www.bcf.org

Foundation type: Community foundation
Purpose: Scholarships primarily to students in the Baltimore, MD area for higher education.
Publications: Application guidelines; Annual report; Financial statement; Grants list; Informational brochure; Newsletter.

Financial data: Year ended 12/31/2012. Assets, $148,500,109 (M); Expenditures, $44,271,737; Total giving, $20,855,776.
Fields of interest: Higher education; Scholarships/financial aid.
Type of support: Scholarships—to individuals; Undergraduate support.
Application information: Applications accepted. Application form required. Application form available on the grantmaker's web site.
  Send request by: Online
  Deadline(s): Apr. 1
  Applicants should submit the following:
    1) Transcripts
    2) Letter(s) of recommendation
    3) Financial information
    4) Essay
  Additional information: See web site for details of eligibility criteria and application process per scholarship.
EIN: 237180620

3784
Baltimore Washington Medical Center Foundation, Inc.
301 Hospital Dr.
Glen Burnie, MD   21061-5803   (410) 328-6984
Contact: Beth A. Peters, Exec. Dir.
TTY : (410)-787-4498; URL: http://www.bwmc.umms.org/giving_opportunities/index.html

Foundation type: Public charity
Purpose: Scholarships to active associates of BWMC with financial support to pursue a career in nursing/allied health.
Financial data: Year ended 06/30/2012. Assets, $6,790,769 (M); Expenditures, $135,254; Total giving, $93,957; Grants to individuals, totaling $25,000.
Fields of interest: Nursing school/education; Health sciences school/education.
Type of support: Scholarships—to individuals.
Application information: Applications accepted.
  Applicants should submit the following:
    1) Transcripts
    2) Letter(s) of recommendation
  Additional information: Applicants must be assigned to a work schedule of 20 hours a week, must have completed a minimum of twelve months of employment, letter of acceptance or be enrolled in a degree or certification program in nursing and allied health, have satisfactory work and attendance records with no disciplinary action in the past twelve months. Contact the foundation for additional guidelines.
EIN: 521813656

3785
Beth Davis in Good Company, Inc.
5715 Ridgway Ave.
Rockville, MD   20851-1927   (301) 881-1537
E-mail: bdingdco@mindspring.com; URL: http://bethdavisingoodcompany.org

Foundation type: Public charity
Purpose: Fiscal sponsorship for area choreographers and dance companies.
Fields of interest: Dance; Arts, artist's services.
Type of support: Fiscal agent/sponsor.
Application information: Contact the organization for application information.
EIN: 521804843

3786
Bowie Interfaith Pantry and Emergency Aid Fund
3120 Belair Dr.
Bowie, MD   20715-3101   (301) 262-6765
FAX: (301) 262-5177;
E-mail: info@bowiefoodpantry.org; URL: http://www.bowiefoodpantry.org

Foundation type: Public charity
Purpose: Financial assistance and emergency food to residents of Bowie and Prince George's county, MD who are experiencing a crisis.
Financial data: Year ended 09/30/2011. Assets, $131,070 (M); Expenditures, $445,722; Total giving, $408,257; Grants to individuals, totaling $408,257.
Fields of interest: Economically disadvantaged.
Type of support: Emergency funds; Grants for special needs.
Application information: Applicant must demonstrate need.
EIN: 202314965

3787
Tim Brierley Memorial Charitable Foundation, Inc.
10228 Clubhouse Ct.
Ellicott City, MD   21042-2119

Foundation type: Independent foundation
Purpose: Scholarships to graduates of Centennial High School, MD. The program is administered by Centennial High School.
Financial data: Year ended 12/31/2013. Assets, $10,095 (M); Expenditures, $2,000; Total giving, $2,000.
Type of support: Support to graduates or students of specific schools.
Application information: Applications not accepted.
  Additional information: Unsolicited requests for funds not considered.
EIN: 522288009

3788
Bright Star Foundation, Inc.
c/o Shale D. Stiller
6225 Smith Ave.
Baltimore, MD   21209-3600   (410) 235-2287
Contact: Kenneth L. Greif, Pres.
Application address: 3707 Greenway, Baltimore, MD 21218-2402, tel.: (410) 235-2287

Foundation type: Independent foundation
Purpose: Scholarships to residents of Baltimore, MD, for secondary and postsecondary education.
Financial data: Year ended 12/31/2012. Assets, $5,003 (M); Expenditures, $46,836; Total giving, $46,800; Grants to individuals, 4 grants totaling $20,800 (high: $10,000, low: $800).
Type of support: Precollege support; Undergraduate support.
Application information: Applications not accepted.
  Additional information: Unsolicited applications not considered or acknowledged.
EIN: 237083731

3789
Brightfocus Foundation
(formerly American Health Assistance Foundation)
22512 Gateway Center Dr.
Clarksburg, MD 20871-2005
FAX: (301) 258-9454; E-mail: info@brightfocus.org;
Toll-free tel.: (800) 437-2423; URL: http://
www.ahaf.org

Foundation type: Public charity
Purpose: Research grants for study of Alzheimer's disease, glaucoma, macular degeneration, heart disease and stroke. Grants to Alzheimer's patients and caregivers to help ease financial burdens.
Publications: Application guidelines; Annual report; Financial statement; Informational brochure.
Financial data: Year ended 03/31/2013. Assets, $42,238,889 (M); Expenditures, $23,574,306; Total giving, $7,527,500.
Fields of interest: Eye research; Alzheimer's disease research; Medical research.
Type of support: Research; Grants for special needs.
Application information: Applications accepted. Application form available on the grantmaker's web site.
  Initial approach: E-mail or telephone
  Send request by: Online
  Deadline(s): Oct. 19 for Alzheimer's Disease Research, Oct. 26 for National Glaucoma Research, and Nov. 9 for Macular Degeneration Research (by invitation only)
  Additional information: See web site for additional application guidelines.
Program descriptions:
  Alzheimer's Disease Research Program: The program supports promising research in fields ranging from molecular biology to epidemiology. Grants are awarded on the basis of the scientific merit of the proposed research and the relevance of the research to understanding aspects of the disease that lead to improved treatments, prevention strategies, and diagnoses. Applications will be accepted for the following awards: Standard Awards, which are $400,000 for three years; Pilot Project Awards, which are $150,000 for two years; and Research Fellowships which are $100,000 for two years. For the Standard and Pilot awards, the principal investigator must be an independent researcher and hold the academic rank of assistant professor (or equivalent, such as assistant research professor) or higher. Research fellowships are available to junior and senior postdoctoral fellows. Grants are available to U.S. and international researchers working at nonprofit organizations, including universities, medical centers, and independent research institutions. Grants are made to the organization, not to individual researchers.
  Macular Degeneration Research Program: Awards research grants into the cause(s) of and treatment(s) for macular degeneration. Grants of up to $50,000 per year for up to two years are available. Any area of research is eligible for support, but potential relevance to macular degeneration should be an important component of the funding evaluation. The program is particularly interested in funding new investigators and established investigators seeking to explore new directions in macular degeneration research. Collaborative projects are also encouraged.
  National Glaucoma Research Program: The program supports basic research into the causes and potential treatments of glaucoma. In order to be eligible for grant funding from the program, the principal investigator must be an independent researcher and hold the academic rank of assistant professor or higher. Grants are available to U.S. and international researchers working at nonprofit organizations, including universities, medical centers, and independent research institutions. Grants are made to the organization, not to individual researchers. The maximum grant request that will be considered is $100,000 ($50,000 per year for two years)
EIN: 237337229

3790
Vernon W. Brown, Fulton Maryland Scholarship Trust Fund
8386 Ct. Dr.
Ellicott City, MD 21043 (410) 465-5366

Foundation type: Independent foundation
Purpose: Scholarships to students from the Fulton, MD area who desire to work in the field of medicine.
Financial data: Year ended 12/31/2012. Assets, $106,524 (M); Expenditures, $6,816; Total giving, $6,000; Grants to individuals, 2 grants totaling $6,000 (high: $3,000, low: $3,000).
Fields of interest: Medical school/education.
Type of support: Postgraduate support.
Application information: Applications accepted. Application form required.
  Deadline(s): Spring
  Applicants should submit the following:
    1) Resume
    2) Financial information
  Additional information: Application should also include community activities and a list of awards and honors.
EIN: 526945939

3791
Jack Burbage Foundation Inc.
9428 Stephen Decatur Hwy.
Berlin, MD 21811-2674 (410) 213-1900
Contact: John H. Burbage, Jr., Dir.

Foundation type: Independent foundation
Purpose: Financial assistance to needy individuals in Worcester, Wicomico, Somerset and Sussex counties, MD, for necessities such as food, housing, medical care and education.
Financial data: Year ended 06/30/2013. Assets, $11,476 (M); Expenditures, $52,213; Total giving, $52,193.
Fields of interest: Human services; Economically disadvantaged.
Type of support: Grants for special needs.
Application information:
  Initial approach: Letter
  Deadline(s): None
EIN: 522207846

3792
Carroll County Arts Council
91 W. Main St.
Westminster, MD 21157-4800 (410) 848-7272
Contact: Sandy Oxx, Exec. Dir.
FAX: (410) 848-8962;
E-mail: info@CarrollCountyArtsCouncil.org; E-Mail for Sandy Oxx: sandy@carrollcountyartscouncil.org;
URL: http://www.carr.org/arts/

Foundation type: Public charity
Purpose: Scholarships to high school seniors in Carroll County, MD who are pursuing a degree in arts at the college level.
Publications: Annual report; Informational brochure; Newsletter.
Financial data: Year ended 06/30/2012. Assets, $532,441 (M); Expenditures, $521,424; Total giving, $60,660; Grants to individuals, totaling $125.
Fields of interest: Arts.
Type of support: Undergraduate support.
Application information: Applications accepted. Application form required.
  Send request by: Mail
  Deadline(s): Apr. 18
  Final notification: Applicants notified within 45 days
EIN: 521072680

3793
Carson Scholars Fund, Inc.
305 W. Chesapeake Ave., Ste. L-020
Towson, MD 21204-4417 (410) 828-1005
Contact: Amy Warner, Exec. Dir.
FAX: (410) 828-1007;
E-mail: awarner@carsonscholars.org; E-Mail for Amy Warner: awarner@carsonscholars.org;
URL: http://www.carsonscholars.org

Foundation type: Public charity
Purpose: Scholarships in all 50 states with concentration in MD, DE, DC, Pittsburgh, PA, Battle Creek, MI, Atlanta, GA, and Indianapolis, IN.
Publications: Annual report; Financial statement; Informational brochure; Newsletter.
Financial data: Year ended 06/30/2012. Assets, $6,546,445 (M); Expenditures, $1,479,784; Total giving, $402,000; Grants to individuals, totaling $402,000.
Fields of interest: Education, gifted students.
Type of support: Scholarships—to individuals; Awards/prizes.
Application information: Applications are sent to qualifying students. Unsolicited applications not accepted.
Program description:
  Scholarships: This program recognizes and rewards students in grades 4-11 who earn the highest level of academic achievement and who display strong humanitarian qualities. Recipients are designated as "Carson Scholars" and receive a $1,000 scholarship award to be invested in college. Eligible applicants must be nominated by an educator, demonstrate humanitarian qualities in school and community through school programs and/or community service above and beyond what is required, and have a GPA of 3.75 in the following academic subjects: English, reading, language arts, math, science, social studies, and foreign languages.
EIN: 521851346

3794
The Annie E. Casey Foundation
701 St. Paul St.
Baltimore, MD 21202-2311 (410) 547-6600
Contact: Satonya C. Fair, Dir., Grants Mgmt.
FAX: (410) 547-6624; E-mail: webmail@aecf.org;
URL: http://www.aecf.org

Foundation type: Independent foundation
Purpose: Fellowships to individuals to work and study at youth and family organizations and agencies.
Publications: Financial statement; Informational brochure; Newsletter; Occasional report.
Financial data: Year ended 12/31/2012. Assets, $2,666,068,266 (M); Expenditures, $225,437,214; Total giving, $98,681,016.
Fields of interest: Youth development; Human services; Family services; Research.
Type of support: Fellowships; Awards/grants by nomination only.

Application information: Applications accepted. Application form required.
- *Initial approach:* Letter
- *Deadline(s):* None
- *Additional information:* Candidates who are nominated for a Children and Family Fellowship will be invited to submit a full application.

Program description:
Children and Family Fellowship: The fellowship is a 20-month leadership development program for accomplished professionals. It explicitly strives to increase the pool of leaders with the vision and ability to frame and sustain major system reforms and community capacity-building initiatives that benefit large numbers of children and families. The foundation solicits nominations for the fellowship program from a prestigious, national network of organizations and individuals who lead many of the most dynamic systems, institutions, and programs in America today. Once nominated, candidates are invited to complete a fellowship application. The Fellowship Selection Committee, comprised of a diverse team of Casey staff, Fellowship alumni, and partners in the Foundation's work, reviews all applications and recommends candidates for further consideration. For more information see web site or contact Barbara Squires, Dir. of Leadership Development, tel.: (800) 222-1099, extension 2938.
EIN: 521951681

3795
Caves Valley Golf Club Foundation, Inc.
(formerly Caves Valley Scholars Foundation, Inc.)
2910 Blendon Rd.
Owings Mills, MD   21117-2360

Foundation type: Independent foundation
Purpose: Scholarships to students who caddie at golf courses in the greater Baltimore, MD, area, for higher education.
Financial data: Year ended 12/31/2012. Assets, $1,179,753 (M); Expenditures, $41,304; Total giving, $18,848; Grants to individuals, 7 grants totaling $16,000 (high: $3,000, low: $1,500).
Type of support: Undergraduate support.
Application information: Applications not accepted.
- *Additional information:* Unsolicited requests for funds not considered or acknowledged.
EIN: 521900251

3796
Cecil County Bar Foundation, Inc.
157 E. Main St.
Elkton, MD   21921   (410) 398-1918
Contact: Robert Jones, Dir.

Foundation type: Independent foundation
Purpose: Scholarships to students who reside in the Elkton, MD, area.
Financial data: Year ended 02/28/2013. Assets, $21,622 (M); Expenditures, $27,711; Total giving, $27,600; Grants to individuals, 16 grants totaling $7,600 (high: $500, low: $100).
Fields of interest: Higher education.
Type of support: Scholarships—to individuals.
Application information:
- *Initial approach:* Letter
- *Send request by:* Mail
- *Deadline(s):* None
- *Additional information:* Applications should include transcripts.
EIN: 522058962

3797
The Central Scholarship Bureau, Inc.
(also known as CSB)
6 Park Center Ct. 211
Owings Mills, MD   21117   (410) 415-5558
Contact: Jan Wagner, Pres.
FAX: (410) 415-5501;
E-mail: contact@central-scholarship.org;
URL: http://www.centralsb.org

Foundation type: Public charity
Purpose: Interest-free loans and grants to students to attend accredited institutions within the U.S.
Financial data: Year ended 06/30/2012. Assets, $9,887,837 (M); Expenditures, $1,624,206; Total giving, $859,907; Grants to individuals, totaling $859,907.
Fields of interest: Higher education; Education.
Type of support: Scholarships—to individuals; Student loans—to individuals.
Application information: Applications accepted. Application form required. Application form available on the grantmaker's web site.
- *Initial approach:* Complete online application
- *Deadline(s):* May 31
- *Additional information:* Applicants need only submit one application to be considered for all programs.
EIN: 526012589

3798
Charlotte Hall School Board of Trustees Inc.
24665 Hollywood Rd.
Charlotte Hall, MD   20626

Foundation type: Independent foundation
Purpose: Scholarships only to high school students of Charles and St. Mary's counties, MD, for higher education.
Financial data: Year ended 12/31/2012. Assets, $718,438 (M); Expenditures, $36,380; Total giving, $30,500; Grants to individuals, 20 grants totaling $30,500 (high: $2,000, low: $1,250).
Type of support: Scholarships—to individuals.
Application information: Applications not accepted.
- *Additional information:* Unsolicited requests for funds not considered or acknowledged.
EIN: 521609924

3799
Chesapeake Bay Trust
60 W. St., Ste. 405
Annapolis, MD   21401-2400   (410) 974-2941
Contact: Jana Davis Ph.D., Exec. Dir.
FAX: (410) 269-0387; E-mail: hadams@cbtrust.org;
E-mail For Jana Davis: jdavis@cbtrust.org;
URL: http://www.cbtrust.org

Foundation type: Public charity
Purpose: Scholarships and awards to outstanding students, teachers, and community volunteers who take action to restore and protect the Chesapeake Bay and its rivers.
Publications: Application guidelines; Annual report; Informational brochure (including application guidelines); Newsletter.
Financial data: Year ended 06/30/2012. Assets, $10,340,888 (M); Expenditures, $6,293,054; Total giving, $4,244,691.
Fields of interest: Natural resources.
Type of support: Scholarships—to individuals; Awards/prizes.

Application information: Applications accepted. Application form required.
- *Initial approach:* Telephone
- *Additional information:* See web site for additional information.

Program description:
Chesapeake Bay Trust Awards: Each year, the Trust sponsors five annual award programs: the Melanie Teems Awards for an outstanding project of the year, the Ellen Fraites Wagner Award for steward of the year, the Honorable Arthur Dorman Scholarship of $5,000 to a high school or college student, the Teacher of the Year Award of $2,500, and the Student of the Year Scholarship of $5,000 to a high school or college student.
EIN: 521454182

3800
Chesapeake Research Consortium, Inc.
(also known as CRC)
645 Contees Wharf Rd.
Edgewater, MD   21037-3702   (410) 798-1283
Contact: Kevin G. Sellner, Exec. Dir.
FAX: (410) 798-0816; E-mail For Kevin Sellner: sellnerk@si.edu; URL: http://www.chesapeake.org

Foundation type: Public charity
Purpose: Scholarships to graduating seniors accepted to four year colleges or universities seeking higher education in watershed-related fields.
Financial data: Year ended 06/30/2012. Assets, $648,731 (M); Expenditures, $1,781,110; Total giving, $318,517; Grants to individuals, totaling $90,205.
Fields of interest: Science.
Type of support: Scholarships—to individuals.
Application information: Applications accepted. Application form required.
- *Deadline(s):* May 15
- *Final notification:* Applicants notified late June
- Applicants should submit the following:
  1) Transcripts
  2) Resume
  3) GPA
  4) FAFSA
  5) Essay
- *Additional information:* Application should also include acceptance letter from a four year college or university.

Program description:
Scholarship in Natural or Social Sciences: The consortium offers a $500 renewable annual scholarship to deserving high school seniors seeking higher education in watershed-related fields. Graduating seniors from the watershed's public and private high schools who have been accepted to four-year colleges or universities and plan to enroll in natural or social science programs are eligible. Students interested in air, land, or water-related disciplines are encouraged to apply.
EIN: 237245037

3801
The Childhood Brain Tumor Foundation, Inc.
20312 Watkins Meadow Dr.
Germantown, MD   20876-4259   (301) 515-2900
Contact: Jeanne P. Young, Pres.
E-mail: cbtf@childhoodbraintumor.org; Toll-free tel.: (877) 217-4166; URL: http://www.childhoodbraintumor.org

Foundation type: Public charity

Purpose: Medical research and programs to benefit and improve the treatment of children with brain tumors.
Publications: Application guidelines; Newsletter.
Financial data: Year ended 09/30/2012. Assets, $513,524 (M); Expenditures, $236,376; Total giving, $166,220. Grants to individuals amount not specified.
Fields of interest: Brain research; Children.
Type of support: Research.
Application information: Applications accepted. Application form available on the grantmaker's web site.
Initial approach: Proposal
Send request by: On-line
Deadline(s): Mar. 14
Final notification: Recipients notified by July 25
Additional information: See web site for additional guidelines.
Program description:
Research Grants: Two grants are available to research that helps to improve the treatment and understanding of childhood brain tumors. The Pediatric Brain Tumor Grant anticipates funding up to three (3) research proposals that are a maximum of two years in duration. Funding requests cannot exceed $30,000 per year or a maximum of $60,000 over the course of the award. While, the Astrocytoma Research Award has specific funds for one, one-year research proposal related to all grades of astrocytoma. The funding request for this award can be up to a maximum of $50,000.
EIN: 522122976

3802
Choice Hotels International Foundation
10750 Columbia Pike
Silver Spring, MD   20901-4427   (301) 592-5000
Contact: Kelly Kane, Exec. Dir.
Scholarship application address: 4225 E. Windrose Dr., Phoenix, AZ 85032; Tel. for Women's Business Alliance Scholarship Program: (602) 953-4478
FAX: (301) 592-6274;
E-mail: choice_foundation@choicehotels.com;
URL: http://www.choicehotels.com/en/responsibility/roomtogive?sid=xBzpH.WEwNOgSY3.10

Foundation type: Company-sponsored foundation
Purpose: Scholarships to the dependents of associates of Choice Hotels, and a college scholarship to a deserving female with an interest in or link to the hospitality industry.
Publications: Application guidelines; Annual report.
Financial data: Year ended 12/31/2012. Assets, $122,904 (M); Expenditures, $525,376; Total giving, $492,866.
Fields of interest: Adults, women.
Type of support: Employee-related scholarships; Scholarships—to individuals.
Application information: Applications accepted. Application form required. Application form available on the grantmaker's web site.
Initial approach: Download application form and mail to foundation
Deadline(s): Feb. 1
Final notification: May 14
Applicants should submit the following:
1) Transcripts
2) Letter(s) of recommendation
3) Essay
Program descriptions:
Scholarship Program for Dependent Children: The foundation awards $2,000 college scholarships to the dependents of associates of Choice Hotels.
Women's Business Alliance Scholarship Program: The foundation annually awards a $2,000 college

scholarship to a deserving female with an interest in or link to the hospitality industry. This award is open to undergraduate and post-graduate students. Visit URL: http://www.choicehotels.com/en/about-choice/wba for more information.
Company name: Choice Hotels International, Inc.
EIN: 522184905

3803
Collegebound Foundation, Inc.
300 Water St., Ste 300
Baltimore, MD   21202-3237   (410) 783-2905
Contact: Jimmy Tadlock, Exec. Dir.
FAX: (410) 727-5786;
E-mail: info@collegeboundfoundation.org; E-mail For Jimmy Tadlock: jtadlock@collegeboundfoundation.org; URL: http://www.collegeboundfoundation.org

Foundation type: Public charity
Purpose: Grants are provided to Baltimore-area high school students whose expected contributions and financial aid are less than the cost of attending college.
Publications: Application guidelines.
Financial data: Year ended 06/30/2012. Assets, $22,905,634 (M); Expenditures, $3,098,418; Total giving, $544,778; Grants to individuals, totaling $544,778.
Type of support: Scholarships—to individuals.
Application information: Applications accepted. Application form required. Application form available on the grantmaker's web site.
Initial approach: Application
Deadline(s): Mar. 1
Additional information: See web site for a list of eligible schools and additional information.
Program descriptions:
Competitive Scholarships: The foundation provides college scholarships to Baltimore City Public High School students. Some awards recognize and reward community service efforts; others are directed to support efforts of students pursuing specific career goals.
Last Dollar Grant: The grant is a need-based award for Baltimore City public high school graduates whose expected family contribution and financial aid package total less than the cost to attend college. Recipients are eligible to receive a grant of up to $3,000 per year, renewable for up to five years of college or the maximum amount of $15,000. This money is gift money which does not have to be repaid. Eligible applicants must be accepted to and attend one of the following Maryland colleges: Bowie State University, Coppin State University, Frostburg State University, Morgan State University, St. Mary's College of Maryland, Towson University, University of Maryland College Park, University of Maryland Eastern Shore, or Villa Julie College.
EIN: 521598921

3804
Community Assistance Network, Inc.
7900 E. Baltimore St.
Baltimore, MD   21224-2010   (410) 285-4674
FAX: (410) 285-6707;
E-mail: info@canconnects.org; URL: http://www.canconnects.org

Foundation type: Public charity
Purpose: Advocacy, emergency funds, food, employment assistance, eviction prevention and other services are provided for low-income residents, including the elderly and disabled of Baltimore County, MD.

Publications: Annual report; Newsletter.
Financial data: Year ended 08/31/2011. Assets, $1,202,796 (M); Expenditures, $4,494,396; Total giving, $674,862; Grants to individuals, totaling $674,862.
Fields of interest: Aging; Disabilities, people with; Economically disadvantaged.
Type of support: Emergency funds; Grants for special needs.
Application information: Applications accepted. Application form not required.
Additional information: Contact the agency for additional information for assistance.
EIN: 520823186

3805
Community Foundation of Carroll County, Inc.
255 Clifton Blvd. St. 313
Westminster, MD   21157-4690   (410) 876-5505
Contact: Audrey S. Cimino, Exec. Dir.
FAX: (410) 871-9031;
E-mail: cfccinfo@carrollcommunityfoundation.org;
URL: http://www.carrollcommunityfoundation.org

Foundation type: Community foundation
Purpose: Scholarships to graduating seniors of Carroll county, MD for attendance at accredited four-year institutions of higher learning.
Financial data: Year ended 12/31/2011. Assets, $4,659,369 (M); Expenditures, $1,054,694; Total giving, $581,799; Grants to individuals, 206 grants totaling $320,212.
Fields of interest: Higher education.
Type of support: Scholarships—to individuals.
Application information: Applications accepted. Application form required.
Deadline(s): Varies
Additional information: Applications are available at all Carroll county high schools. Home-schooled and privately schooled students may call the foundation for additional information. Application must include transcripts.
EIN: 521865244

3806
The Community Foundation of Frederick County, MD, Inc.
312 E. Church St.
Frederick, MD   21701-5611   (301) 695-7660
Contact: Elizabeth Y. Day, Pres.
FAX: (301) 695-7775;
E-mail: info@frederickcountygives.org; URL: http://www.frederickcountygives.org/

Foundation type: Community foundation
Purpose: Scholarships to residents of Frederick County, MD, for higher education.
Publications: Application guidelines; Annual report; Grants list; Informational brochure; Newsletter.
Financial data: Year ended 06/30/2012. Assets, $81,977,151 (M); Expenditures, $4,042,725; Total giving, $2,741,633; Grants to individuals, 209 grants totaling $369,390 (high: $39,799, low: $120).
Fields of interest: Higher education.
Type of support: Scholarships—to individuals.
Application information: Applications accepted. Application form required. Application form available on the grantmaker's web site.
Initial approach: Application
Deadline(s): Feb. 15
Applicants should submit the following:
1) Transcripts
2) Letter(s) of recommendation

3) FAFSA
Additional information: See web site for additional guidelines.
EIN: 521488711

3807
Community Foundation of Howard County
(formerly The Columbia Foundation)
10630 Little Patuxent Pkwy.
Century Plaza Ste. 315
Columbia, MD   21044   (410) 730-7840
Contact: Beverley White-Seals, C.E.O.; For grants: Tracy Locke-Kitt, Prog. Off.
FAX: (410) 997-6021; E-mail: info@cfhoco.org; Additional e-mail: bwhiteseals@columbiafoundation.org; Grant inquiry e-mail: tlockekitt@cfhoco.org; URL: http://www.cfhoco.org/

Foundation type: Community foundation
Purpose: Scholarships for Howard County, MD students who wish to attend a two-or four-year college/university or trade school.
Publications: Application guidelines; Annual report; Grants list; Informational brochure; Newsletter; Program policy statement.
Financial data: Year ended 12/31/2012. Assets, $15,316,463 (M); Expenditures, $1,350,165; Total giving, $691,761; Grants to individuals, 28 grants totaling $42,950.
Fields of interest: Vocational education, post-secondary; Higher education.
Type of support: Scholarships—to individuals.
Application information: Applications accepted. Application form required. Application form available on the grantmaker's web site.
  Initial approach: Application
  Deadline(s): Varies
  Applicants should submit the following:
    1) Essay
    2) Transcripts
    3) Letter(s) of recommendation
  Additional information: See web site for additional application information. Guidelines and requirements vary per scholarship.
EIN: 520937644

3808
Community Foundation of the Eastern Shore, Inc.
1324 Belmont Ave., Ste. 401
Salisbury, MD   21804   (410) 742-9911
FAX: (410) 742-6638; E-mail: cfes@cfes.org; URL: http://www.cfes.org

Foundation type: Community foundation
Purpose: Scholarships to graduating seniors and residents of lower Eastern Shore of the MD, area, encompassing Somerset, Wicomico, and Worcester counties.
Publications: Application guidelines; Annual report; Financial statement; Informational brochure; Newsletter.
Financial data: Year ended 06/30/2012. Assets, $78,742,845 (M); Expenditures, $5,344,395; Total giving, $4,559,601.
Fields of interest: Higher education; Scholarships/financial aid.
Type of support: Scholarships—to individuals; Support to graduates or students of specific schools; Undergraduate support.
Application information: Applications accepted. Application form required. Application form available on the grantmaker's web site.
  Deadline(s): Varies

Additional information: Eligibility criteria varies per scholarship. See web site for a complete listing.
Program description:
  Scholarships: The foundation administers over 80 local scholarship funds. Each scholarship fund has its own application, guidelines and eligibility criteria, which may include specific geographic area, high school, academic achievement, financial need and field of study. See web site for additional information.
EIN: 521326014

3809
Community Support Systems, Inc.
P.O. Box 206
Aquasco, MD   20608-0206   (301) 372-1491
Contact: Claudia Raskin M. Ed
E-mail: CSS1995@aol.com; URL: http://www.communitysupportsystems.org/

Foundation type: Public charity
Purpose: Assistance for low- and moderate-income individuals, families and senior citizens of southern Prince George's and northern Charles counties, MD with access to services and supplies, which include food pantries and a senior living home.
Financial data: Year ended 06/30/2012. Assets, $88,861 (M); Expenditures, $198,323; Total giving, $81,970; Grants to individuals, totaling $81,970.
Fields of interest: Human services; Aging; Economically disadvantaged.
Type of support: Emergency funds; Grants for special needs.
Application information: Applications not accepted.
Program description:
  Advocacy Program: The program gives low- to moderate-income families access to essential resources and information. Services include applying for energy assistance and food stamps, a temporary cash assistance fund, help with care repairs, job search and families facing homelessness.
EIN: 521949052

3810
The Credit Union Foundation of Maryland and the District of Columbia, Inc.
(formerly The Maryland Credit Union Foundation, Inc.)
8975 Guilford Rd., Ste. 190
Columbia, MD   21046-2386   (443) 325-0771
Contact: Kyle Y. Swisher, Exec. Dir.
FAX: (253) 663-9557; E-mail: info@cufound.org; URL: http://www.cufound.org

Foundation type: Operating foundation
Purpose: Scholarships to members of credit unions in Maryland and Washington DC for higher education and for staff and volunteer training.
Publications: Application guidelines; Newsletter.
Financial data: Year ended 12/31/2012. Assets, $3,324,593 (M); Expenditures, $273,157; Total giving, $80,849; Grants to individuals, 14 grants totaling $21,621 (high: $2,326, low: $1,000).
Fields of interest: Education; Financial services, credit unions.
Type of support: Conferences/seminars; Scholarships—to individuals.

Application information: Applications accepted. Application form required. Application form available on the grantmaker's web site.
  Deadline(s): None for Staff and Volunteer Training Scholarships, Mar. 31 for College Scholarship Awards Program
Program descriptions:
  College Scholarship Awards Program: The foundation awards ten $1,000 college scholarships to members of Maryland and District of Columbia credit union whose winning essay best describes a credit union that is strictly run by people under the age of 30. The foundation also award one $1,000 college scholarship to a member of Maryland and District of Columbia credit union whose video best describes the difference between credit unions and banks.
  Staff and Volunteer Training Scholarships: The foundation awards tuition reimbursement scholarships to Maryland and D.C. based credit unions to attend training courses designed to improve services to their members and communities. Total annual tuition reimbursements are limited to $750 per credit union.
EIN: 521749045

3811
Crossway Community, Inc.
3015 Upton Dr.
Kensington, MD   20895-1937   (301) 929-2505
Contact: Kathleen Guinan, C.E.O.
FAX: (301) 949-4741;
E-mail: reception@crossway-community.org; URL: http://www.crossway-community.org

Foundation type: Public charity
Purpose: Assistance to families of all ethnic and economic backgrounds with a focus on outreach to low-income and at-risk families.
Financial data: Year ended 06/30/2012. Assets, $1,002,268 (M); Expenditures, $3,003,637; Total giving, $637,405; Grants to individuals, totaling $637,405.
Fields of interest: Education; Women; Economically disadvantaged.
Type of support: Grants for special needs.
Application information: Applications accepted. Application form required. Interview required.
  Initial approach: Telephone
  Additional information: See web site for additional information.
Program description:
  Family Leadership Academy: The program is for single mothers 18 years of age or older who have completed high school or have a G.E.D. (work experience in lieu of a high school diploma will be considered). Those who enter the program must be willing to live onsite for a minimum of three years, commit to education, maintain employment, improve career opportunities, and/or pursue further education, and manage living independently, including housekeeping, meal planning, family hygiene and health.
EIN: 521253460

3812
Cystic Fibrosis Foundation
6931 Arlington Rd., 2nd Fl.
Bethesda, MD   20814-5200   (301) 951-4422
Contact: Robert J. Beall Ph.D., Pres. and C.E.O.
FAX: (301) 951-6378; E-mail: info@cff.org; Toll-free tel.: (800) 344-4823; Additional e-mail: grants@cff.org; URL: http://www.cff.org

Foundation type: Public charity

Purpose: Research grants and fellowships for the study of cystic fibrosis and related areas.
Publications: Application guidelines; Annual report; Informational brochure; Newsletter.
Financial data: Year ended 12/31/2011. Assets, $216,321,364 (M); Expenditures, $125,721,614; Total giving, $74,501,565; Grants to individuals, totaling $1,212,242.
Fields of interest: Cystic fibrosis research; Pediatrics research; Medical research.
Type of support: Fellowships; Research; Awards/prizes; Postdoctoral support.
Application information: Applications accepted. Application form required. Application form available on the grantmaker's web site.
  Deadline(s): Varies
  Additional information: Application should be sent online at Proposal Central, https://proposalcentral.altum.com.
Program descriptions:
  CF Foundation/National Institute of Health (NIH) Funding Award: This award supports excellent cystic fibrosis (CF)-related research projects that have been submitted to and approved by the NIH, but cannot be supported by available NIH funds. Applications must fall within the upper 40th percentile with a priority score of 200 or better. Foundation support ranges from $75,000 to $125,000 per year for up to two years.
  Clinical Fellowships: These awards encourage specialized training early in a physician's career, and prepare candidates for careers in academic medicine. Training must take place in one of the foundation's care centers, and must encompass diagnostic and therapeutic procedures, comprehensive care, and CF-related research. Applicants must be eligible for board certification in pediatrics or internal medicine by the time the fellowship begins. Awards provide a $47,600 (first year) and $49,250 (second year) stipend; third-year fellowships of up to $68,250 ($58,250 for stipend and $10,000 for research costs) is also available for additional basic and/or clinical research training. Recipients are expected to be subspecialty board-eligible at the completion of the program. Applicants and sponsors must submit a proposal of the research studies to be undertaken and other specialized training that will be offered during this third year. U.S. citizenship or permanent resident status is required.
  Clinical Research Grants: These awards offer support to clinical research projects directly related to CF treatment and care. Projects may address diagnostic or therapeutic methods related to CF or the pathophysiology of CF. Applicants must demonstrate access to a sufficient number of CF patients from accredited foundation care centers and appropriate controls. A letter of intent to apply must be submitted by potential applicants. Up to $100,000 per year for up to three years (plus 8 percent of indirect costs) may be requested for single-center clinical research grants. For multi-center clinical research, the potential award is up to $225,000 per year for up to three years (plus 8 percent of indirect costs)
  Harry Shwachman Clinical Investigator Award: This three-year award provides the opportunity for clinically-trained physicians to develop into independent biomedical research investigators who are actively involved in CF-related areas. It is also intended to facilitate the transition from post-doctoral training to a career in academic medicine. Support is available for up to $76,000 per year plus $15,000 for supplies. U.S. citizenship or permanent resident status is required.
  Leroy Matthews Physician/Scientist Award: This award will provide up to six years of support for outstanding, newly trained pediatricians and

internists (M.D.'s and M.D./Ph.D.'s) to complete subspecialty training, develop into independent investigators, and initiate a research program. Institutional and individual grants are available. Support ranges from $48,000 (stipend) plus $10,000 (research and development) for the first year, to $76,000 (stipend) plus $15,000 (research and development) for the sixth year. Furthermore, the foundation will underwrite the interest payments for educational loans for up to $7,000 per year. U.S. citizenship or permanent resident status is required.
  Pilot and Feasibility Awards: These grants support the development and testing of new hypotheses and/or new methods of CF research, and to support promising new investigators as they establish themselves in research areas relevant to CF. Proposed work must be hypothesis-driven and must reflect innovative approaches to critical questions in CF research. The award is not meant to support the continuation of programs begun under other granting mechanisms. Up to $40,000 per year, plus up to 8% of indirect costs, for two years may be requested.
  Post-Doctoral Research Fellowships: These awards are offered to M.D.'s, Ph.D.'s, and M.D./Ph.D.'s interested in conducting basic or clinical research related to CF. Awards are offered through the foundation's network of research centers or through individual applications submitted to the foundation. Stipends are $39,000 (first year), $40,100 (second year), and $42,300 (optional third year). Research expenses of $3,500 per year are available, as well. U.S. citizenship or permanent resident status is required.
  Research Grants: This grant mechanism is intended to encourage the development of new information that contributes to the understanding of the basic etiology and pathogenesis of CF. In addition, consideration will be given to those projects that provide insight into the development of information that may contribute to the development of new therapies of CF. All proposals must be hypothesis-driven, and sufficient preliminary data must be provided to justify support. Support is available for $90,000 per year for a period of two years, at which time a grant may be competitively renewed for an additional two years of funding.
  Student Traineeships: Traineeships are offered to introduce students to research related to CF. Applicants must be students in or about to enter a doctoral program (M.D., Ph.D., or M.D./Ph.D.); senior-level undergraduates planning to pursue graduate training may also apply. Each applicant must work with a faculty sponsor on a research project related to CF. The award is $1,500.
  Summer Scholarships in Epidemiology: Awards of up to $2,000 are available to cover tuition and expenses for selected summer epidemiology programs to M.D.s currently working in cystic fibrosis, to increase their skills in epidemiology. Course work should include biostatistics and epidemiology, particularly clinical epidemiology and/or clinical trials.
EIN: 131930701

3813
Joe Davies Scholarship Foundation
c/o Lawrence R. Beebe
4600 East West Hwy., Ste. 900
Bethesda, MD 20814-3423

Foundation type: Independent foundation
Purpose: Scholarships to financially needy graduating high school seniors who are residents of Dodge, Jefferson, and Dane counties, WI.

Financial data: Year ended 12/31/2012. Assets, $704,468 (M); Expenditures, $52,613; Total giving, $45,000.
Type of support: Support to graduates or students of specific schools; Undergraduate support.
Application information: Application form required.
  Deadline(s): Contact foundation for current application deadline.
  Additional information: Application form available from the Board of Education in each community.
EIN: 530218110

3814
Dellon Foundation
1122 Kenilworth Dr., Ste. 18
Towson, MD 21204 (410) 366-9825
Contact: A. Lee Dellon, Dir.

Foundation type: Independent foundation
Purpose: Grants provided to individuals to conduct neuroscience research.
Financial data: Year ended 12/31/2012. Assets, $6,902 (M); Expenditures, $87; Total giving, $0.
Fields of interest: Neuroscience research.
Type of support: Research; Grants to individuals.
Application information:
  Initial approach: Proposal
  Deadline(s): None
  Additional information: Applications should include a description of neuroscience research papers.
EIN: 521317729

3815
Discovery Communications, Inc.
Corporate Giving Program
1 Discovery Pl.
Silver Spring, MD 20910-3354 (240) 662-2000
URL: http://impact.discovery.com/

Foundation type: Corporate giving program
Purpose: Cash awards and prizes to middle school students grades 5 through 8 who compete in a nationwide science competition.
Fields of interest: Elementary/secondary education; Education; Youth development; Formal/general education; Science.
Type of support: Awards/prizes; Undergraduate support.
Application information: Applications accepted. Application form available on the grantmaker's web site.
  Initial approach: Complete online registration and submit video entry
  Deadline(s): Apr. 15
  Additional information: Parents or guardians must complete online parental consent form.
Program description:
  Discovery Education 3M Young Scientist Challenge: Through the Discovery Education 3M Young Scientist Challenge, the company annually awards cash prizes and trips to middle school students in grades 5-8 competing in a nationwide science competition. The program is designed to encourage exploration of science and innovation among youth and promote the importance of science communication. Ten finalists are awarded an all-expense paid trip to competition finals, $1,000, a contest medal or trophy, a chance to win a trip from Discovery Student Adventures, and participation in a summer mentorship program. The first place winner is awarded $25,000, a trip from Discovery Student Adventures, a contest trophy, and the title of "America's Top Young Scientist"

3816

Harry F. Duncan Foundation, Inc.

409 Washington Ave., Ste. 900
Towson, MD 21204-4905

Foundation type: Independent foundation
Purpose: Scholarships to individuals in FL and MO for higher education.
Financial data: Year ended 12/31/2012. Assets, $3,453,893 (M); Expenditures, $181,882; Total giving, $160,210; Grants to individuals, 10 grants totaling $32,000 (high: $5,000, low: $2,000).
Type of support: Undergraduate support.
Application information: Applications not accepted.
  Additional information: Unsolicited requests for funds not considered or acknowledged.
EIN: 526054187

3817

ELECTRI International

(formerly The Electrical Contracting Foundation, Inc.)
3 Bethesda Metro Ct., Ste. 1100
Bethesda, MD 20814-5372 (301) 215-4538
Contact: Russell J. Alessi, Pres.
FAX: (301) 215-4536; E-mail: rja@necanet.org;
URL: http://www.electri21.org

Foundation type: Public charity
Purpose: Grants to researchers whose projects and proposals support the growth and development of the electrical industry. Career awards which focus on an issue of significance to the electrical construction industry.
Publications: Application guidelines; Annual report; Informational brochure; Newsletter.
Financial data: Year ended 12/31/2011. Assets, $18,552,200 (M); Expenditures, $1,454,392; Total giving, $38,760; Grants to individuals, totaling $28,760.
Fields of interest: Engineering/technology.
Type of support: Research; Awards/prizes.
Application information: Applications accepted. Application form required. Application form available on the grantmaker's web site.
  Initial approach: Proposals
  Deadline(s): Nov. 13 (one-page summary of project) and Jan. 5 (full proposals) for research, Apr. 23 for Early Career Awards
  Additional information: See web site for additional guidelines.
Program description:
  Early Career Awards: Two Early Career Awards in the amount of $7,000 are awarded annually to engineering and construction management faculty at U.S. colleges and universities with the rank of assistant professor are eligible to submit proposals. Only one proposal per investigator can be submitted. Recipients of the award will become ineligible for future Early Career Awards, however these individuals will be strongly encouraged to submit proposals to other ELECTRI research programs. An Early Career Awards pilot study might be used as the basis for a subsequent larger scale EI research project.
EIN: 521643734

3818

Endocrine Society

8401 Connecticut Ave., Ste. 900
Chevy Chase, MD 20815-5817 (301) 941-0200
Contact: Scott Hunt, C.E.O. and Exec. Dir.
FAX: (301) 941-0259;
E-mail: societyservices@endo-society.org; Toll Free

Tel.: (888)-363-6274; URL: http://www.endo-society.org

Foundation type: Public charity
Purpose: Grants and awards to promising undergraduate, graduate, and medical students who intend to pursue careers in endocrinology.
Publications: Application guidelines.
Financial data: Year ended 12/31/2011. Assets, $44,296,181 (M); Expenditures, $25,476,431; Total giving, $531,298; Grants to individuals, totaling $311,400.
Fields of interest: Medical school/education; Medical specialties research.
Type of support: Fellowships; Travel awards; Awards/prizes; Graduate support; Undergraduate support.
Application information: Applications accepted.
  Deadline(s): Vary
  Additional information: See web site for additional guidelines.
EIN: 730531256

3819

Enterprise Community Partners, Inc.

(formerly The Enterprise Foundation)
10227 Wincopin Cir., Ste. 500
Columbia, MD 21044-3400
FAX: (410) 964-1918;
E-mail: mail@enterprisefoundation.org; Toll-free tel.: (800) 624-4298; URL: http://www.enterprisefoundation.org

Foundation type: Public charity
Purpose: Fellowships to architects to encourage them to become lifelong leaders in public service and community development.
Publications: Application guidelines; Annual report; Financial statement; Informational brochure; Newsletter.
Financial data: Year ended 12/31/2011. Assets, $185,651,350 (M); Expenditures, $62,600,035; Total giving, $19,914,851.
Fields of interest: Architecture; Housing/shelter, development; Urban/community development; Urban studies.
Type of support: Fellowships.
Application information: Applications accepted. Application form required. Application form available on the grantmaker's web site.
  Initial approach: Letter
  Additional information: See web site for additional guidelines.
Program descriptions:
  Enterprise Bart Harvey Fellowship: Fellows provide substantial and creative support to Enterprise's senior management on projects selected for their strategic importance to the partners' mission. One applicant is selected every other year for the two-year fellowship. Key selection criteria are an evidenced commitment to public service and demonstration of exceptional skills in technical analysis, teamwork, leadership, and communications.
  Enterprise Rose Architectural Fellowship: The fellowship creates partnerships between new architects and community-based organizations to direct the skills and passions of the architects in the service of low- and moderate-income communities. The fellowship is designed to promote architectural and community design in low-income communities and encourages architects to become life-long leaders in public service and community development.
EIN: 521231931

3820

Environmental Leadership Program, Inc.

P.O. Box 907
Greenbelt, MD 20768-0907 (202) 332-3320
Contact: Errol Mazursky, Exec. Dir.
FAX: (202) 332-3327; E-mail: info@elpnet.org;
E-Mail for Errol Mazursky: errol@elpnet.org;
URL: http://www.elpnet.org

Foundation type: Public charity
Purpose: Fellowships to individuals with three to ten years of work experience or post-undergraduate academic studies related to environmental issues who are engaged in environmental and social change work.
Publications: Application guidelines.
Financial data: Year ended 12/31/2011. Assets, $195,901 (M); Expenditures, $242,306.
Fields of interest: Environment.
Type of support: Fellowships.
Application information: Applications accepted. Application form required. Application form available on the grantmaker's web site.
  Initial approach: Letter or e-mail
  Deadline(s): Apr. 1
  Applicants should submit the following:
    1) Resume
    2) Letter(s) of recommendation
    3) Essay
Program description:
  Fellowship Program: The fellowship provides training, project support, and a vibrant peer network to individuals each year from all sectors of the environmental field (including nonprofits, business, government, and higher education) in three key areas: community and diversity; media and communications; and collaborations, coalitions, and strength-based leadership. Eligible applicants must: work or reside in one of the program's regional networks (CT, DE, MA, ME, NH, NJ, NY, eastern PA, RI, and VT); have at least three years of work experience or post-undergraduate academic studies related to environmental or social change issues, broadly defined; have demonstrated leadership capacity; and articulate how his/her work fits into social and environmental issues. Tuition for training programs is $750 and includes room and board for the three overnight retreats, participation in ten days of training and community building, and access to a large network of senior fellows.
EIN: 043521791

3821

Epilepsy Foundation of America

8301 Professional Pl.
Landover, MD 20785-2353 (866) 330-2718
Contact: Jeanette Montgomery RN, Ph.D., CNS, Dir., Clinical Svcs.
FAX: (301) 577-2684; E-mail: info@efa.org; Toll-free tel.: (800) 332-7223; toll-free tel. (en espanol): (866) 748-8008; URL: http://www.epilepsyfoundation.org

Foundation type: Public charity
Purpose: Fellowships and research grants to scientists for the study of epilepsy.
Publications: Application guidelines; Annual report; Financial statement; Informational brochure (including application guidelines).
Financial data: Year ended 06/30/2012. Assets, $18,225,598 (M); Expenditures, $13,034,662; Total giving, $2,614,557.
Fields of interest: Epilepsy research; Social sciences.
Type of support: Program development; Seed money; Fellowships; Research; Exchange

programs; Postdoctoral support; Graduate support; Postgraduate support; Doctoral support.
Application information: Applications accepted. Application form required. Application form available on the grantmaker's web site.

Initial approach: Proposal
Send request by: Online
Deadline(s): Varies
Additional information: See web site for complete program information.

Program descriptions:
Behavioral Sciences Post-Doctoral Fellowship: The fellowship of up to $40,000 seeks to develop excellent behavioral scientists to teach appropriate psychosocial intervention techniques used in working with people with epilepsy, and contribute to the body of behavioral research in epilepsy. Individuals who will have received their doctoral degrees in a field of the social sciences by the time the fellowship commences, and desire additional postdoctoral research experience, may apply.

Behavioral Sciences Student Fellowship: The fellowship seeks to stimulate individuals to pursue careers in epilepsy in either research or practice settings. Appropriate fields include sociology, social work, psychology, anthropology, nursing, economics, vocational rehabilitation, counseling, political science, and others relevant to epilepsy research or practice. Both graduate and undergraduate students are eligible. A $3,000 stipend is available.

Health Sciences Student Fellowship: The fellowship seeks to stimulate individuals to pursue careers in epilepsy in either research or practice settings. Predoctoral training students in the health sciences may be accepted at any point in their schooling, following acceptance but before beginning the first year, or in the period immediately following their final year. A $3,000 stipend is available.

New Therapy Grants Program: Awarded in conjunction with the Epilepsy Therapy Project, this program seeks to advance the development of specific new therapies (including new medicines and therapeutic devices) for epilepsy, accelerating the advancement of research from the laboratory to the patient. Funding will be provided for grants supporting the research and development of new therapies in both academic and commercial settings worldwide. All grant proposals must demonstrate a clear path from the lab to the patient; other areas of consideration include, but are not limited to, seed funding for preliminary and targeted work deemed necessary to explore novel therapeutic approaches, projects which if successful offer a clear path to downstream development, proposals that support the commercialization of exceptional academic research projects, and research to bring new approaches and therapy to children. Preference will be given to proposals that already have a commercial partner engaged to assist with development, as well as to proposals that have committed or matched funding from their sponsoring institution, commercial partner, or other third-party source.

Postdoctoral Research Fellowship: The fellowship of up to $45,000 seeks to develop academic physicians and scientists committed to research related to epilepsy. Applications are considered equally from individuals interested in acquiring experience either in basic laboratory research or in the conduct of human clinical studies. Physicians or Ph.D. neuroscientists who desire postdoctoral research experience are eligible to apply.

Predoctoral Research Training Fellowship: The fellowship of up to $20,000 supports pre-doctoral students with dissertation research related to

epilepsy, thus strengthening their interest in establishing epilepsy research as a career direction. Graduate students pursuing a Ph.D. degree in neuroscience, physiology, pharmacology, psychology, biochemistry, genetics, nursing, or pharmacy may apply.

Research and Training Fellowships for Clinicians: This fellowship program of up to $50,000 is for clinically trained professionals. This fellowship is one-year of supervised study and research. Individuals with an M.D. or D.O. who will have completed residency training in neurology, neurosurgery, pediatrics, internal medicine, or psychiatry by the time the fellowship commences may apply. Other clinically-trained professionals (i.e. PharmD, Doctor of Nursing) are also eligible to apply.

Research Grants Program: The program stimulates epilepsy research by providing funding for investigators in the early stages of their careers. Seed grants of up to $50,000 are awarded to clinical investigators or basic scientists for support of biological or behavioral research which will advance the understanding, treatment, and prevention of epilepsy. Applications from established investigators (associate professor level or above) are ineligible.

Targeted Research Initiatives: Targeted research initiatives award up to $50,000 to investigators researching in a specific area. Areas are subject to change, but currently include: cognitive and psychiatric aspects of epilepsy; morbidity and mortality rate of epilepsy, severe symptomatic epilepsies, epilepsy in youth, women with epilepsy, and health care systems and their affect on epilepsy.
EIN: 520856660

3822
Epilepsy Research Foundation

8301 Professional Pl.
Landover, MD 20785-2237 (301) 459-3700
Contact: Phil Gattone, Pres. and C.E.O.
Application address: (Via Courier) Epilepsy Therapy Project, 10 N. Pendleton St., 2nd Fl., Middleburg, VA 20177, tel.: (540) 687-8077; (Via Mail) Epilepsy Therapy Project, P.O. Box 742, Middleburg, VA 20118
FAX: (301) 577-2684; E-mail: ContactUs@efa.org; Toll-Free Tel.: (800) 332-1000; URL: http://www.epilepsyfoundation.org/research/new-therapy-grant-program.cfm

Foundation type: Public charity
Purpose: Research grants to investigators to discover new treatment options and ultimately find a cure for epilepsy.
Financial data: Year ended 06/30/2012. Assets, $3,813,486 (M); Expenditures, $951,710; Total giving, $951,710.
Fields of interest: Epilepsy research.
Type of support: Grants to individuals.
Application information:

Initial approach: Letter of Intent
Send request by: Mail
Copies of proposal: 1
Deadline(s): Sept. 2 for LOI, Oct. 21 for full proposal
Applicants should submit the following:
1) Proposal
2) Budget Information
Additional information: See web site for detailed information for proposal.

Program description:
New Therapy Grants Program: The program seeks to advance the development of specific new therapies including new medicines and therapeutic

devices. Consistent with the theme of translational research, all grant proposals must demonstrate a clear path from the lab to the patient. Preference will be given to proposals that already have a commercial partner engaged to assist with development and to proposals that have committed or matched funding from the sponsoring institution, commercial partner or other third party source. Proposals for research originating from outside the U.S. are welcome.
EIN: 562369930

3823
Estonian-Revelia Academic Fund, Inc.

12901 Clearfield Dr.
Bowie, MD 20715 (301) 464-0552
Contact: Juri Taht, Dir.

Foundation type: Independent foundation
Purpose: Scholarships to students of Estonian nationality for higher education.
Financial data: Year ended 12/31/2012. Assets, $611,846 (M); Expenditures, $58,675; Total giving, $31,500; Grants to individuals, 21 grants totaling $31,500 (high: $1,500, low: $1,500).
Type of support: Foreign applicants; Undergraduate support.
Application information: Applications accepted.
Deadline(s): Mid-Oct.
Applicants should submit the following:
1) Transcripts
2) Resume
Additional information: Application should also include certificate of enrollment.
EIN: 521901554

3824
The Evergreen House Foundation, Inc.

4545 N. Charles St.
Baltimore, MD 21210-2693 (410) 516-0341
E-mail: joregan@jhu.edu; URL: http://www.jhu.edu/evrgreen

Foundation type: Public charity
Purpose: Residency to a visual artist residing outside of MD.
Publications: Application guidelines.
Financial data: Year ended 06/30/2012. Assets, $6,292,823 (M); Expenditures, $297,302; Total giving, $20,000; Grants to individuals, totaling $20,000.
Fields of interest: Visual arts.
Type of support: Residencies; Stipends.
Application information: Applications accepted.
Initial approach: Letter, telephone, or e-mail
Deadline(s): Jan. 15
Applicants should submit the following:
1) Resume
2) SASE
Additional information: Application must also include 20 slides of recent work, slide script, statement, and reviews.

Program description:
Artist-in-Residence Program: The foundation offers a two-month summer residency for visual artists living outside of Maryland. The program provides housing, individual studio space, and a stipend, allowing an artist the time and space to produce new work. The art produced during the residency will form the basis of a solo exhibition scheduled at Evergreen House for the following year. While in residence, the artist will have access to the extraordinary and diverse collections of the historic house and to the 25 acres of gardens and meadows of the estate. Evergreen's unique setting may inspire the artist to respond by producing work

that may not have been made otherwise. One residency is offered per year.
EIN: 520627782

3825
Ethel & Emery Fast Scholarship Foundation, Inc.

12620 Rolling Rd.
Potomac, MD 20854-1963 (301) 762-1102
Contact: Carol A. Minami, Secy.-Treas.

Foundation type: Operating foundation
Purpose: Graduate and undergraduate scholarships to financially needy Native Americans who have successfully completed one year of postsecondary studies and are full-time students.
Financial data: Year ended 12/31/2012. Assets, $878,226 (M); Expenditures, $194,551; Total giving, $73,100; Grants to individuals, 67 grants totaling $73,100 (high: $2,500, low: $250).
Fields of interest: Native Americans/American Indians.
Type of support: Graduate support; Undergraduate support.
Application information: Application form required.
Initial approach: Letter or telephone
Deadline(s): Jan. 15 for spring semester and Aug. 15 for fall semester.
Applicants should submit the following:
1) Transcripts
2) Financial information
Additional information: Application must also include signed copy of parents income tax form, letter confirming enrollment, course verification form and personal statement no more than two typed pages.
EIN: 521817707

3826
Fisher House Foundation, Inc.

111 Rockville Pike, Ste. 420
Rockville, MD 20850-5168 (888) 294-8560
Contact: Cindy Campbell, V.P., Community Rels.
FAX: (301) 294-8562;
E-mail: info@fisherhouse.org; E-mail for Cindy Campbell: ccampbell@fisherhouse.org;
URL: http://www.fisherhouse.org

Foundation type: Public charity
Purpose: Scholarships to children of active duty military personnel, reserve/guard members, and retired commissary customers.
Publications: Annual report; Informational brochure; Newsletter.
Financial data: Year ended 12/31/2011. Assets, $33,776,988 (M); Expenditures, $52,837,485; Total giving, $48,510,319; Grants to individuals, 6,575 grants totaling $1,268,208.
Fields of interest: Higher education; Military/veterans' organizations.
Type of support: Scholarships—to individuals.
Application information: Applications accepted. Application form required. Application form available on the grantmaker's web site.
Send request by: Mail or hand deliver
Deadline(s): Jan. 31 for Military Spouse Scholarships, Feb. 28 Scholarships for Military Children, Mar. 15 for Heroes' Legacy Scholarship
Applicants should submit the following:
1) Transcripts
2) Letter(s) of recommendation
3) Essay
Additional information: See web site for additional application guidelines.

Program descriptions:
Heroes' Legacy Scholarship: The program is open to dependent unmarried children under age 23 of all who have died or have become disabled through their active military service since Sept. 11, 2001. Applicants must be enrolled or planning to enroll in a full time undergraduate degree program in the fall in an accredited U.S. college or university or junior/community college. This is a $5,000 non-renewable scholarship.
Joanne Holbrook Patton Military Spouse Scholarships: Scholarships are available to military spouses only (active duty, retiree, Reserve, National Guard and/or survivor) to help them prepare for meaningful employment and to better contribute to their family's financial security and to obtain professional certification or attend postsecondary or graduate school. Scholarship funds may be used for tuition, fees, and school room and board. Application accepted online only.
Scholarships for Military Children: A minimum of one $2,000 scholarship will be awarded at every commissary location where qualified applications are received. The scholarship provides for payment of tuition, books, lab fees, and other related expenses. Applicant must have a cumulative 3.0 GPA or above on a 4.0 basis.
EIN: 113158401

3827
Sid & Mary Foulger Foundation, Inc.

9600 Blackwell Rd., Ste. 200
Rockville, MD 20850-4315

Foundation type: Independent foundation
Purpose: Scholarships primarily but not solely to residents of UT for higher education.
Financial data: Year ended 12/31/2012. Assets, $708,764 (M); Expenditures, $662,763; Total giving, $623,670; Grants to individuals, 37 grants totaling $183,670 (high: $32,016, low: $458).
Type of support: Undergraduate support.
Application information: Applications not accepted.
Additional information: Unsolicited requests for funds not considered or acknowledged.
EIN: 522062781

3828
Foundation Fighting Blindness, Inc.

(also known as FFB)
7168 Columbia Gateway Dr., Ste. 100
Columbia, MD 21046-3256 (410) 423-0600
Contact: William T. Schmidt, C.E.O.
E-mail: info@fightblindness.org; Toll-free tel.: (800) 683-5555; TDD: (800) 683-5551; URL: http://www.blindness.org

Foundation type: Public charity
Purpose: Research grants to Ph.D.s, M.D.s, D.O.s, and D.V.M.s at institutions to discover the causes, treatments, preventions and cures for retinal degenerative diseases.
Publications: Application guidelines; Annual report; Financial statement; Informational brochure; Newsletter.
Financial data: Year ended 06/30/2012. Assets, $60,105,388 (M); Expenditures, $29,725,362; Total giving, $15,859,736.
Fields of interest: Pharmacy/prescriptions; Genetic diseases and disorders; Eye research.
Type of support: Research; Awards/prizes.
Application information: Applications not accepted.
Additional information: Contributes only to preselected individuals.

Program descriptions:
Career Development Award: This program emphasizes specialized and rigorous training both in research and in clinical ophthalmology to be arranged at select locations. Ph.D.s, M.D.s, D.O.s, D.V.M.s, or equivalent foreign degrees are eligible. The foundation will undertake salary and research support and, to the degree necessary, other special needs as indicated by the individual circumstances. Awards may be made for up to three years.
Clinical/Research Fellowship Awards: Grants of $65,000 to support post-residency clinical fellowships in inherited orphan retinal degenerations are available to clinicians who possess an M.D., D.O., or recognized equivalent foreign degree, and are eligible to apply for a CRFA.
Individual Investigator Grant Awards: At the present time, individual research awards are available in the areas of genetics, gene therapy, transplantation, pharmaceutical therapy, cell biology, visual prosthesis, clinical studies, and medical therapy assessment (annual models). Ph.D.s, M.D.s, D.O.s, D.V.M.s, or equivalent foreign degrees are eligible. Funding is provided based upon the needs of the proposal and may range from $20,000 to $100,000 per year. Grants are normally funded for a three-year period.
Research Center Awards: The foundation's centers were designed as mechanisms to foster collaboration and cooperation among multiple clinical and/or basic researchers to conduct high quality research into the etiology of retinal degenerations. The proposed research areas or modules should adhere to the mission of the foundation, which is to ultimately discover preventions, treatments, and cures for retinal degenerative diseases. Prior to beginning the application process, the applicant must speak with the organization's Special Science Programs Director or the Chief Scientific Officer. Clinical and/or basic researchers possessing a M.D., Ph.D., D.O., D.V.M., or equivalent foreign degree from accredited academic institutions are eligible. Members of a proposed center may be located at the same institution or, if the interactions between the proposed participants of a center are strong, they may be located at different universities or institutions. Funding is provided based upon the needs of the proposal and may range from $50,000 to $100,000 per year. They are normally awarded for a five-year period.
Young Investigator Award: An average award of $50,000 per year for a three-year period is offered to junior basic and clinical scientists, to encourage the pursuit of studies in the field of retinal degeneration. Ph.D.s, M.D.s, D.O.s, D.V.M.s, or equivalent foreign degrees with a minimum of two and maximum of five years postdoctoral training and experience are eligible.
EIN: 237135845

3829
Foundation for Digestive Health and Nutrition

(also known as American Digestive Health Foundation)
4930 Del Ray Ave.
Bethesda, MD 20814-3015 (301) 222-4002
Contact: Stacey Hinton, Dir., Devel.
FAX: (301) 222-4010; E-mail: info@fdhn.org;
URL: http://www.fdhn.org

Foundation type: Public charity
Purpose: Research grants and fellowships to students and faculty specializing in digestive diseases.

Publications: Application guidelines; Annual report; Grants list; Informational brochure; Newsletter.
Fields of interest: Cancer research; Ear, nose & throat research; Liver research; Digestive disorders research; Medical research; Science.
Type of support: Fellowships; Research; Grants to individuals; Awards/prizes; Graduate support; Doctoral support; Stipends.
Application information: Applications accepted. Application form required. Application form available on the grantmaker's web site.
Send request by: E-mail
Deadline(s): Vary
Additional information: Application must include letter of recommendation. For most programs, membership in American Gastroenterological Association is required. See web site for further application information.
Program descriptions:
AGA Horizon Pharma Fellow Abstract Prizes: Awards of $1,000 are available to M.D. gastroenterology fellows or Ph.D. postdoctoral fellows to stimulate interest in GI research careers through competition and recognition.
AGA Horizon Pharma Student Abstract Prizes: Awards of $500 for travel and $1,000 for abstracts are available to high school, college, graduate, and medical students.
Elsevier Pilot Research Awards: A research initiative grant of $25,000 for one year is offered to investigators to support pilot research projects in gastroenterology- or hepatology-related areas.
Fellowship to Faculty Transition Awards: Four awards at $40,000 per year for two years are made to advanced fellows/trainees, to provide salary support for additional full-time research training in basic science.
Funderburg Research Scholar Award in Gastric Biology Related to Cancer: One award of $50,000 per year for two years is made to support the research of an established investigator working on novel approaches to gastric cancer.
Moti L. and Kamla Rustigi International Travel Awards: Two awards of $500 are given to young basic, translational and clinical investigators residing outside North America to provide travel expenses to attend DDW.
Research Scholar Awards: Six awards of $60,000 per year for two years, potentially three years, are made to support promising junior faculty protecting research time. All applicants with a focus on gastroenterology, hepatology, or related areas will be considered for this award. Eligible applicants must hold an M.D., Ph.D., or equivalent degree; and must hold full-time faculty positions at North American universities or professional institutes at the time the award begins.
Student Research Fellowship Awards: Awards of $2,500 are given each year to support high school and undergraduate students performing digestive disease or nutrition research for a minimum of ten weeks.
EIN: 521764955

3830
Foundation for the National Institutes of Health, Inc.
9650 Rockville Pike
Bethesda, MD   20814-3999   (301) 402-5311
Contact: Maria Freire Ph.D., Pres. and Exec. Dir.
FAX: (301) 480-2752; E-mail: foundation@fnih.org;
E-mail For Maria Freire: mfreire@fnih.org;
URL: http://www.fnih.org

Foundation type: Public charity
Purpose: Fellowships, internships and awards to improve health through scientific research.

Publications: Annual report.
Financial data: Year ended 12/31/2011. Assets, $98,055,767 (M); Expenditures, $50,503,879; Total giving, $25,483,921; Grants to individuals, totaling $288,050.
Fields of interest: Medical research.
Type of support: Fellowships; Internship funds; Research; Grants to individuals; Awards/prizes.
Application information: Applications accepted.
Additional information: See foundation web site for program guidelines.
Program descriptions:
Clinical Research Training Program (CRTP): This year-long program is designed to attract medical and dental students to the intramural campus of the National Institutes of Health (NIH) in Bethesda, Maryland. As many as 30 students a year come to the NIH campus for an intensive 12-month clinical or translational research project. The participants, known as fellows, are paired with senior physician-scientist mentors on projects matched to their interests. Fellows attend clinics, see patients in wards, and participate in interactive group forums with leading NIH researchers and one another. They work with a principal investigator in both the laboratory and at the bedside to learn about translational research, the transformation of basic research into patient therapies.
Sallie Rosen Kaplan Fellowship for Women Scientists in Cancer Research: This program honors the memory of Sallie Kaplan, who held an abiding interest in education and in expanding opportunities for women. These post-doctoral fellowships are given annually to one or more outstanding women scientists at the National Cancer Institute. Funds provided are used to design a Women's Health Postdoctoral Fellowship Program to address the health disparity in sex and gender biomedical research.
EIN: 521986675

3831
Full Citizenship of Maryland, Inc.
4910 Decatur St.
Hyattsville, MD   20781-2300   (301) 209-0696
Contact: Pansy Stancil -Diaz, Exec. Dir.
FAX: (301) 209-0699; E-mail: fullcit@comcast.net

Foundation type: Public charity
Purpose: Provides residential, employment and behavioral support services to residents of Montgomery and Prince George's counties, MD who live with mental or neurological impairments and disabilities.
Financial data: Year ended 06/30/2012. Assets, $5,635,071 (M); Expenditures, $5,135,650.
Fields of interest: Developmentally disabled, centers & services; Disabilities, people with.
Type of support: Grants for special needs.
Application information: Applications accepted. Application form required. Interview required.
EIN: 521542816

3832
GEICO Philanthropic Foundation
c/o GEICO Corp.
5260 Western Ave.
Chevy Chase, MD   20815-3701   (301) 986-2750
Contact: Donald R. Lyons, Chair.
Contact for Military Service Awards: Mike Baker, Military Dept., Dir., GEICO, One GEICO Plaza,

Washington, DC 20076; tel.: (800) 824-5404, ext. 3906, e-mail: mbaker@geico.com
URL: http://www.geico.com/information/military/service-awards/

Foundation type: Company-sponsored foundation
Purpose: Grants to military personnel to recognize outstanding personal achievement.
Financial data: Year ended 12/31/2012. Assets, $58,293,306 (M); Expenditures, $8,963,658; Total giving, $8,960,704; Grants to individuals, 6 grants totaling $15,000 (high: $2,500, low: $2,500).
Fields of interest: Scholarships/financial aid; Military/veterans' organizations.
Type of support: Grants to individuals.
Application information: Applications accepted. Application form required.
Send request by: Mail
Deadline(s): Oct. 31 for Military Awards
Additional information: Contact selected military service channels for Military Service Awards.
Program description:
Military Service Awards: The foundation annually awards six $2,500 grants, one to an enlisted member from each Military service branch, and one to a member of the reserve/national guard component. The award is given to recognize outstanding achievement in the following categories: drug and alcohol abuse prevention; fire safety and fire prevention; and traffic safety and accident prevention.
EIN: 521202740

3833
The German Society of Maryland, Inc.
1819 Leadburn Rd.
Towson, MD   21204-1830   (410) 685-0450
Application address: P.O. Box 22585, Baltimore, MD 2120

Foundation type: Independent foundation
Purpose: Scholarships to individuals of German descent attending colleges in MD.
Financial data: Year ended 12/31/2011. Assets, $546,295 (M); Expenditures, $53,140; Total giving, $11,300; Grants to individuals, 7 grants totaling $5,300 (high: $3,200, low: $100).
International interests: Germany.
Type of support: Undergraduate support.
Application information: Applications accepted.
Initial approach: Letter
Applicants should submit the following:
1) Transcripts
2) FAF
EIN: 520326115

3834
Ginger Cove Foundation, Inc.
4000 River Crescent Dr.
Annapolis, MD   21401-7721   (410) 266-7300
Contact: Nicholas Goldsborough, Pres.
E-mail: foundation@gingercove.com; URL: http://www.gingercove.com/about-us/charitable-giving/

Foundation type: Public charity
Purpose: Scholarships to employees of Annapolis Life Care, Inc. to further their education.
Financial data: Year ended 06/30/2012. Assets, $1,380,567 (M); Expenditures, $479,895; Total giving, $342,005; Grants to individuals, totaling $40,300.
Fields of interest: Education.
Type of support: Employee-related scholarships.
Application information: Applications accepted. Application form required. Interview required.

Additional information: Applicants must submit registration forms from their school and obtain a recommendation from their supervisor. The educational opportunities sought must be related in some way to the activities and/or exempt purpose of the organization. Scholarship payments are made directly to the educational institution on behalf of the student.

EIN: 113656031

3835
Girl Scouts of Central Maryland, Inc.

4806 Seton Dr.
Baltimore, MD   21215-3247   (410) 358-9711
Contact: Traci A. Barnett, C.E.O.
FAX: (410) 358-9918;
E-mail: generalinfo@gscm.org; Toll-Free Tel.: (800)-492-2521; E-mail For Traci A. Barnett: tbarnett@gscm.org; URL: http://www.gscm.org

Foundation type: Public charity
Purpose: A variety of awards, grants and scholarships are available to members of Girl Scout troops in central Maryland.
Publications: Annual report.
Financial data: Year ended 08/31/2012. Assets, $15,402,770 (M); Expenditures, $5,583,068; Total giving, $72,913; Grants to individuals, totaling $72,913.
Fields of interest: Girl scouts; Girls.
Type of support: Grants to individuals; Scholarships—to individuals; Awards/prizes.
Application information: Applications accepted. Application form required. Application form available on the grantmaker's web site.
Additional information: See web site for a full list of awards and additional information.
EIN: 520780207

3836
Global Health Council

1111 19th St. N.W., Ste. 1120
P.O. Box 13469
Baltimore, MD   21203   (202) 833-5900
Contact: Jeffrey Sturchio, Pres. and C.E.O.
FAX: (202) 833-0075;
E-mail: ghc@globalhealth.org; Additional address: 1111 19th St. N.W., Ste. 1120, Washington, DC 20036-3636, tel.: (202) 833-5900, fax: (202) 833-0075

Foundation type: Public charity
Purpose: Awards by nomination only to a leading practitioner in health and human rights.
Financial data: Year ended 09/30/2011. Assets, $2,118,381 (M); Expenditures, $6,392,204; Total giving, $1,005,000.
Fields of interest: Public health; International human rights.
Type of support: Awards/grants by nomination only; Awards/prizes.
Application information: Applications not accepted.
Additional information: Online nomination must be submitted in English. Nomination deadline Jan. 15.
Program descriptions:
Best Practices in Global Health Award: The award is given annually to celebrate and highlight the efforts of a public health practitioner or organization dedicated to improving the health of disadvantaged and disenfranchised populations, and to recognize programs that effectively demonstrate the links among health, poverty, and development. The person or organization selected for this award must

be able to demonstrate the success of their program(s) and measurable results in the field, as well as possess the ability and expertise to share, inspire, and extend best practices for improving health.
Excellence in Media Award for Global Health: The award is given each year to a journalist (print, electronic, and/or visual) who has in the prior year most effectively captured the essence of a major issue in global health and conveyed it to a broad audience. Selection of the awardee is based on the quality of the reporting as well as its wide reach among readers and viewers.
Jonathan Mann Award for Global Health and Human Rights: Co-sponsored by Association Francois-Xavier Bagnoud, Doctors of the World, and John Snow, Inc., the award is bestowed annually to a leading practitioner in health and human rights and comes with a substantial financial reward to allow its recipients a measure of freedom to pursue their work in the important area of global health and human rights.
EIN: 521048393

3837
Govans Ecumenical Development Corporation

1010 E. 33rd St.
Baltimore, MD   21218   (410) 433-2442
Contact: Nichole Doye Battle, C.E.O.
FAX: (410) 433-4834; E-mail: info@gedco.org; E-mail for Nichole Doye Battle: nbattle@gedco.org; URL: http://www.gedco.org

Foundation type: Public charity
Purpose: Provides housing for people with special needs and food, advocacy and financial assistance to low-income individuals in the Baltimore, MD area.
Financial data: Year ended 03/31/2012. Assets, $3,961,882 (M); Expenditures, $7,002,446; Total giving, $6,369,685; Grants to individuals, totaling $1,044,943.
Fields of interest: Human services.
Type of support: Grants for special needs.
Application information: Applications not accepted.
EIN: 521767577

3838
Government Employees Benefit Association Scholarship Foundation

P.O. Box 206
Annapolis Junction, MD   20701-0206   (301) 688-7912
URL: http://www.geba.com/

Foundation type: Company-sponsored foundation
Purpose: Scholarships for GEBA members or their spouses, children and grandchildren for full time study at an accredited postsecondary educational institution, trade and vocational schools.
Financial data: Year ended 12/31/2012. Assets, $10,400 (M); Expenditures, $57,718; Total giving, $50,000; Grants to individuals, 25 grants totaling $50,000 (high: $2,000, low: $2,000).
Fields of interest: Vocational education, post-secondary; Higher education.
Type of support: Undergraduate support.
Application information: Applications accepted. Application form required. Application form available on the grantmaker's web site.
Deadline(s): Apr. 14
Additional information: Application should include educational history, future plans, extracurricular activities and commitment to community service. Applicant or sponsor must

have been a current member who has an active GEBA or GEMBA plan in effect since for the last three years.
EIN: 320143828

3839
Hariri Foundation

7501 Wisconsin Ave., Ste. 715
Bethesda, MD   20814-3602
URL: http://www.haririfoundationusa.org/

Foundation type: Independent foundation
Purpose: Student loans to deserving Lebanese high school students for study at Lebanese institutions of higher learning in order to build up the human resources of Lebanon through educational programs.
Financial data: Year ended 12/31/2012. Assets, $1,591,778 (M); Expenditures, $447,091; Total giving, $87,317.
Type of support: Student loans—to individuals; Undergraduate support.
Application information: Application form required. Interview required.
Additional information: Contact foundation for current application deadline. Initial application must be made in Beirut, Lebanon.
EIN: 521386338

3840
The HealthWell Foundation

c/o Covance Market Access Svcs.
P.O. Box 4133
Gaithersburg, MD   20885-4133   (800) 675-8416
Contact: Mary P. Sundeen, Pres.
FAX: (800) 282-7692;
E-mail: info@healthwellfoundation.org; URL: http://www.healthwellfoundation.org

Foundation type: Public charity
Purpose: Financial assistance for patients living with chronic and life-altering illnesses for prescription drug copayments, deductibles and health insurance premiums.
Publications: Informational brochure.
Financial data: Year ended 12/31/2011. Assets, $66,318,603 (M); Expenditures, $65,518,601; Total giving, $49,521,777; Grants to individuals, totaling $49,521,777.
Fields of interest: Pharmacy/prescriptions; Health care, insurance; Economically disadvantaged.
Type of support: Grants for special needs.
Application information: Applications accepted. Application form available on the grantmaker's web site.
Initial approach: Telephone
Send request by: Online
Additional information: Contact the foundation for eligibility determination.
Program description:
Financial Assistance: The foundation provides financial assistance to eligible patients, and takes into account an individual's financial, medical, and insurance status when determining who is eligible for assistance. Financial criteria are based upon multiples of the federal poverty level, which takes into account a family's size. Families with incomes of up to four times the federal poverty level may qualify. The foundation also considers the cost of living in a particular city or state.
EIN: 200413676

3841
Hispanic National Bar Foundation, Inc.
(also known as HNBF)
8401 Connecticut Ave., Ste. 1202
Chevy Chase, MD   20815-5804   (240)
395-4500
Contact: Christie Lewis, Interim Exec. Dir.
E-mail: clewis@hnbf.org; URL: http://www.hnbf.org

Foundation type: Public charity
Purpose: Scholarships to Hispanic college students and high school graduates who demonstrate leadership and an interest in pursuing a law degree.
Financial data: Year ended 10/31/2011. Assets, $182,021 (M); Expenditures, $163,494; Total giving, $15,000.
Fields of interest: Law school/education; Hispanics/Latinos.
Type of support: Scholarships—to individuals.
Application information: Applications accepted. Application form required.
  Additional information: See web site for a listing of scholarship programs and additional guidelines.
EIN: 592681611

3842
George Cragg Hopkins, Jr., Arts Endowment, Inc.
P.O. Box 194
Great Mills, MD   20634   (301) 475-5511
Contact: Lynne Morgan Smoot, V.P.
Application address: 23160 Moakley St., Ste. 101, Leonardtown, MD 20650 Tel.: (301) 475-5511

Foundation type: Independent foundation
Purpose: Awards to art students of St. Mary's County, Maryland.
Financial data: Year ended 12/31/2012. Assets, $0 (M); Expenditures, $25,298; Total giving, $20,000.
Type of support: Awards/prizes.
Application information: Application form required.
  Initial approach: Letter with samples
  Deadline(s): None
  Additional information: Application must include work samples.
EIN: 300139108

3843
Housing Opportunities Community Partners
10400 Detrick Ave.
Kensington, MD   20895-2440   (240) 773-9327
FAX: (301) 949-1229; URL: http://www.hocommunitypartners.org

Foundation type: Public charity
Purpose: Assistance to low-income families in Mongomery county, MD to become self-sufficient and to improve the quality of their lives.
Financial data: Year ended 12/31/2011. Assets, $94,788 (M); Expenditures, $462,625; Total giving, $453,079.
Fields of interest: Economically disadvantaged.
Type of support: Grants for special needs.
Application information: Contact the agency for eligibility criteria.
EIN: 522149054

3844
Howard County Arts Council
8510 High Ridge Rd.
Ellicott City, MD   21043-3308   (410) 313-2787
FAX: (410) 313-2790; E-mail: info@hocoarts.org;
URL: http://www.hocoarts.org

Foundation type: Public charity
Purpose: Scholarships to students of Howard county, MD pursuing a career in the arts with tuition costs and fees. Choreography awards to individuals from Howard, Ann Arundel, Baltimore and Carroll counties, and Baltimore city, MD.
Publications: Application guidelines; Annual report; Grants list; Informational brochure; Newsletter.
Financial data: Year ended 06/30/2011. Assets, $685,464 (M); Expenditures, $887,972; Total giving, $380,089; Grants to individuals, totaling $8,750.
Fields of interest: Arts.
Type of support: Grants to individuals; Scholarships—to individuals; Awards/prizes.
Application information: Applications accepted. Application form required. Application form available on the grantmaker's web site.
  Send request by: Mail
  Copies of proposal: 9 for scholarships, 6 for choreography
  Deadline(s): Jan. 9 for Scholarships, May for Choreography
  Final notification: Apr. 3
  Applicants should submit the following:
    1) Proposal
    2) Curriculum vitae
    3) Budget Information
    4) Work samples
    5) Transcripts
    6) Letter(s) of recommendation
    7) GPA
    8) Essay
Program descriptions:
  Arts Scholarships: The program provides funding to college-bound seniors committed to pursuing a career in the arts.
  Mark Ryder Original Choreography Grant Program: The program recognizes individual creative expression and provides financial assistance to choreographers to create new original work.
  Rising Star Emerging Performing Artist Award: The award recognizes individual creative expression and provides financial assistance for emerging performers to further their career.
EIN: 521219079

3845
The Huether/McClelland Foundation, Inc.
(formerly The Huether Foundation, Inc.)
P.O. Box 370
1300 Brass Mill Rd.
Belcamp, MD   21017-0370
Contact: H. Douglas Huether, Chair.

Foundation type: Independent foundation
Purpose: Scholarships to seniors at Harford County, MD, high schools to pursue postsecondary education in engineering.
Financial data: Year ended 12/31/2012. Assets, $5,536,831 (M); Expenditures, $279,229; Total giving, $274,473.
Fields of interest: Engineering school/education.
Type of support: Support to graduates or students of specific schools; Undergraduate support.
Application information: Applications accepted.
EIN: 521435090

3846
Howard Hughes Medical Institute
c/o Office of Grants and Special Progs.
4000 Jones Bridge Rd.
Chevy Chase, MD   20815-6789   (301)
215-8500
Contact: For general inquiries: Dr. Peter J. Bruns, V.P., Grants and Special Progs.; Dr. William R. Galey, Prog. Dir, Grad. Prog.; Stephen A. Barkanic, Prog. Dir., Undergrad Prog.; Dr. Jill G. Conley, Prog. Dir., International Prog., Precollege Prog., Research Resources Prog.; Dr. Dennis Liu, Prog. Dir., Educational Products
Toll-free tel.: (800) 448-4882
FAX: (301) 215-8888;
E-mail: grantswww@hhmi.org; URL: http://www.hhmi.org

Foundation type: Public charity
Purpose: Fellowships and research grants to medical students, graduate students, and non-U.S. scientists for the study of biology and related sciences. Grants by nomination only to university science professors to create undergraduate science education initiatives.
Publications: Application guidelines; Annual report; Informational brochure (including application guidelines); Newsletter; Occasional report; Program policy statement.
Financial data: Year ended 08/31/2012. Assets, $18,717,543,067 (M); Expenditures, $1,084,168,259; Total giving, $88,120,850. Grants to individuals amount not specified.
Fields of interest: Dental school/education; Medical school/education; Biomedicine research; Formal/general education; Biology/life sciences.
Type of support: Research; Grants to individuals; Awards/grants by nomination only; Foreign applicants.
Application information: Application form required.
  Deadline(s): Varies
  Additional information: Academic institutions receive and administer these fellowships and grants on behalf of the individual recipients.
Program descriptions:
  Exceptional Research Opportunities Program (EXROP): This program links the resources of HHMI's Science and Grant programs to provide selected undergraduate students with outstanding summer research experiences that encourage them to pursue careers in academic science. EXROP students also attend meetings at HHMI headquarters where they present their research in a poster session, network with their peers and HHMI scientists, and hear from scientists from various backgrounds and stages in their careers. EXROP students are also eligible for continued support in their doctoral education via HHMI's Gilliam Fellowships for Advanced Study. Complete information available on program web page: http://www.hhmi.org/grants/individuals/exrop.html.
  Gilliam Fellowships for Advanced Study: For students who have participated in the Exceptional Research opportunities Program (EXROP) of the Howard Hughes Medical Institute, HHMI offers an opportunity to pursue graduate studies in the life sciences. The Gilliam Fellowships provide full support for up to four years of study toward a Ph.D. for outstanding students who are from groups underrepresented in the sciences or from disadvantaged backgrounds. Gilliam fellows attend the university of their choice and work alongside distinguished scientists. Chosen for their academic excellence and scientific potential, they will become the leaders of a new generation of biomedical researchers.
  HHMI Professors: Grants through this initiative support research-active undergraduate faculty. The grants are intended to empower leading scientists

at doctoral and research universities to work more closely with undergraduates at their home institutions, and provide other institutions with innovative models for transmitting the excitement and values of scientific research to undergraduate education.

HHMI-NIH Research Scholars (Cloister Program): This program was established to give outstanding students at U.S. medical schools the opportunity to receive research training at the National Institutes of Health in Bethesda, MD. Students in good standing at medical, dental, and veterinary schools in the United States are eligible to apply to the program. Research Scholars spend nine months to a year on the NIH campus, conducting basic, translational or applied biomedical research under the direct mentorship of senior NIH research scientists. The Howard Hughes Medical Institute provides the administration and funding for the program, including the salaries and benefits for the Research Scholars. The NIH provides advisors, mentors, laboratory space, and equipment and supplies for laboratory work.

International Student Research Fellowships: This program supports outstanding international predoctoral students studying in the U.S., who are ineligible for fellowships or training grants through U.S. federal agencies. The Institute will award three-year fellowships to international students to support years three, four, and five of a Ph.D. program. Eligible biomedical-related fields include biology, chemistry, physics, math, computer science, engineering, and plant biology, as well as interdisciplinary research. Each fellow will receive an annual stipend of $30,000, plus an educational allowance. Participation in this program is by invitation only. Refer to program web page for complete information: http://www.hhmi.org/grants/individuals/intl_fellows.html.

Medical Research Fellows Program ("Med Fellows Program"): This program supports a year of full-time biomedical research training for medical, dental, and veterinary students. This includes joint initiatives with: the Foundation Fighting Blindness for students conducting research in ophthalmology, particularly inherited retinal degenerative diseases; with the GM Trust for a student researcher in a field related to Duchenne Muscular Dystrophy; and the Burroughs Wellcome Fund for veterinary students. A new initiative, the Medical Research Fellows Program at Janelia Farm, offers students with an interest in neuronal networking and/or imaging an intense year-long research training experience, living and working at the HHMI Janelia Farm Research Campus in Ashburn, VA in the Washington, DC, area. Refer to program web page for further information: http://www.hhmi.org/grants/individuals/medfellows.html.
EIN: 590735717

3847
Humanity First U.S.A.
300 E. Lombard Str., Ste. 840
Baltimore, MD 21202
Contact: Munum Naeem, Exec. Dir.
E-mail: info@humanityfirst.org; Tel./Fax: (877) 994-3872; URL: http://usa.humanityfirst.org/

Foundation type: Public charity
Purpose: Disaster relief assistance to individuals and families in poorer communities in the U.S. and other countries around the world.
Financial data: Year ended 12/31/2011. Assets, $877,720 (M); Expenditures, $935,696; Total giving, $703,100.
Fields of interest: Safety/disasters.

Type of support: In-kind gifts; Grants for special needs.
Application information: See web site for additional information.
EIN: 200464012

3848
Immune Deficiency Foundation, Inc.
40 W. Chesapeake Ave., Ste. 308
Towson, MD 21204-4843
Contact: Marcia Boyle, Pres.
FAX: (410) 321-9165;
E-mail: info@primaryimmune.org; Toll-free tel.: (800) 296-4433; URL: http://www.primaryimmune.org/

Foundation type: Public charity
Purpose: Scholarships of $500 to $1,000 for one or two years of undergraduate or technical training to students with primary immune deficiencies requiring financial assistance for their studies.
Publications: Application guidelines; Newsletter.
Financial data: Year ended 12/31/2011. Assets, $5,687,750 (M); Expenditures, $5,735,821; Total giving, $119,500; Grants to individuals, totaling $43,000.
Fields of interest: Vocational education.
Type of support: Undergraduate support.
Application information: Application form required. Application form available on the grantmaker's web site.
   Initial approach: Letter or telephone.
   Deadline(s): Mar. 31.
   Additional information: Applicant's doctor must provide documentation of the student's primary immune deficiency disease; selection is based on financial need and academic participation.
EIN: 521214782

3849
International Youth Foundation
(also known as IYF)
32 South St., Ste. 500
Baltimore, MD 21202-7503 (410) 951-1500
FAX: (410) 347-1188; E-mail: youth@iyfnet.org;
URL: http://www.iyfnet.org

Foundation type: Public charity
Purpose: Awards to individuals between 18 and 29 years of age who are working to bring a positive change in their communities.
Publications: Application guidelines; Annual report.
Financial data: Year ended 12/31/2011. Assets, $39,138,828 (M); Expenditures, $24,950,559; Total giving, $8,483,965; Grants to individuals, 42 grants totaling $173,370.
Fields of interest: Youth development; Community/economic development.
Type of support: Awards/prizes.
Application information: Applications accepted. Application form required. Application form available on the grantmaker's web site.
   Initial approach: Letter
   Deadline(s): Mar. 16
   Final notification: Applicants notified by May 26
   Additional information: See web site for additional guidelines.
EIN: 382935397

3850
The Ivy Community Charities of Prince George's County, Inc.
6118 Walton Ave.
Suitland, MD 20746 (301) 702-7312
Contact: Cheryl Petty Garnette, Exec. Dir.
Application address: Scholarship Committee, The Ivy Community Charities of Prince George's County, Inc., c/o 14440 Cherry Lane Ct., Ste., 102, Laurel, MD 20707
FAX: (301) 390-3868; E-mail: info@iccpgc.org; URL: http://iccpgc.org/

Foundation type: Public charity
Purpose: Scholarships to high school seniors residing and attending school in Prince George's county, MD for attendance at a two or four year college or university.
Financial data: Year ended 12/31/2012. Assets, $646,141 (M); Expenditures, $132,610; Total giving, $53,805; Grants to individuals, totaling $51,105.
Fields of interest: Higher education.
Type of support: Scholarships—to individuals.
Application information: Applications accepted. Application form required. Application form available on the grantmaker's web site. Interview required.
   Send request by: Mail
   Deadline(s): Feb.
   Applicants should submit the following:
      1) Transcripts
      2) Essay
   Additional information: Scholarships are awarded on the basis of merit and need.
EIN: 521515992

3851
Ivy Vine Charities, Inc.
(formerly Theta Omega Omega Charities, Inc.)
43 Randolph Rd. PMB 102
Silver Spring, MD 20904-5476 (301) 368-2105
Contact: Cynthia D. Jiles R.Ph., Pres.
FAX: (301) 774-2910;
E-mail: ivyvinecharities@gmail.com; URL: http://ivyvinecharities.org

Foundation type: Public charity
Purpose: Scholarships to high school seniors attending a Montgomery County School, District of Columbia or Prince George's County school or be a past or current participant in a Ivy Vine Charities, Inc. debutante cotillion.
Financial data: Year ended 12/31/2011. Assets, $36,955 (M); Expenditures, $42,481.
Fields of interest: Higher education; Students, sororities/fraternities.
Type of support: Scholarships—to individuals.
Application information: Applications accepted. Application form required.
   Deadline(s): Apr.
   Applicants should submit the following:
      1) SAT
      2) GPA
      3) Transcripts
      4) Letter(s) of recommendation
      5) Essay
EIN: 521903943

3852
Jeremy Foundation, Inc.
11610 Primrose Ct.
Ijamsville, MD   21754-8914   (301) 363-8184
Contact: Dianne Ryan, Pres.
FAX: (301) 363-8184;
E-mail: jeremyfoundationinc@comcast.net;
URL: http://www.jeremyfoundation.com

Foundation type: Public charity
Purpose: Grants to families of children in outpatient or in patient treatment for cancer.
Financial data: Year ended 12/31/2012. Assets, $7,337 (M); Expenditures, $31,807.
Fields of interest: Cancer; Children/youth.
Type of support: Grants for special needs.
Application information:
   Initial approach: E-mail
EIN: 550830656

3853
Jewish Social Service Agency
200 Wood Hill Rd.
Rockville, MD   20850-8724   (301) 838-4200
Contact: Jeffrey F. Abramson, Pres.; For scholarships: Donna Becker
FAX: (301) 309-2596; E-mail: contactus@jssa.org;
Additional address (Fairfax office): 3018 Javier Rd., Fairfax, VA 22031-4609, tel.: (703) 204-9100;
URL: http://www.jssa.org

Foundation type: Public charity
Purpose: Scholarships and interest-free educational loans to Jewish residents of the Washington DC metropolitan area. Financial assistance to individuals and families with special needs.
Financial data: Year ended 06/30/2012. Assets, $56,562,619 (M); Expenditures, $16,292,964; Total giving, $725,046; Grants to individuals, totaling $687,546.
Fields of interest: Jewish agencies & synagogues.
Type of support: Scholarships—to individuals; Student loans—to individuals; Grants for special needs.
Application information: Applications accepted. Application form required. Application form available on the grantmaker's web site.
   Initial approach: E-mail
   Deadline(s): Apr. 1 for Scholarships
   Applicants should submit the following:
      1) Essay
      2) Letter(s) of recommendation
      3) Transcripts
      4) FAFSA
   Additional information: Applications must also include financial aid award letter and letter of admission. See web site for complete listing of scholarship programs.
EIN: 530196598

3854
Job Opportunities Task Force, Inc.
231 E. Baltimore St., Ste. 1500
Baltimore, MD   21202-3457   (410) 234-8040
Contact: Jason Perkins-Cohen, Exec. Dir.
FAX: (410) 234-8929; E-mail: info@jotf.org; E-mail for Jason Perkins-Cohen: jason@jotf.org;
URL: http://www.jotf.org/

Foundation type: Public charity
Purpose: Assistance to students of Baltimore, MD to become licensed carpenter, plumber or electrician.
Publications: Newsletter.

Financial data: Year ended 06/30/2011. Assets, $1,693,487 (M); Expenditures, $2,019,220; Total giving, $533,986; Grants to individuals, totaling $349,662.
Fields of interest: Vocational education, post-secondary; Employment.
Type of support: Grants to individuals.
Application information: Applications accepted.
   Additional information: Applicants must be Baltimore City residents, have a high school diploma or GED, and have reading and math ability at the 9th grade level or higher. See web site for additional information.
EIN: 522278450

3855
The Roy Jorgensen Foundation Inc.
P.O. Box 70
Buckeystown, MD   21717-0070
E-mail: john_jorgenson@royjorgensen.com

Foundation type: Company-sponsored foundation
Purpose: Scholarships to students pursuing college degrees in civil engineering with an aim of promoting design excellence in highway maintenance management.
Financial data: Year ended 12/31/2012. Assets, $349,841 (M); Expenditures, $18,835; Total giving, $18,000; Grant to an individual, 1 grant totaling $15,000.
Fields of interest: Engineering.
Type of support: Scholarships—to individuals.
Application information: Applications accepted. Application form required. Application form available on the grantmaker's web site. Interview required.
   Initial approach: E-mail
   Send request by: Mail
   Deadline(s): July 31
   Final notification: Recipients notified by Aug. 15
   Applicants should submit the following:
      1) Transcripts
      2) Letter(s) of recommendation
   Additional information: Application should also include graduate school letters of appplication receipt or of acceptance, and a written statement of career objectives and life goals.
Program description:
   Roy E. Jorgensen Memorial Scholarship: The foundation annually awards a $15,000 scholarship to an undergraduate college senior or graduate student enrolled at an accredited school of engineering in the U.S. Recipients are selected based on academic record, career objectives and life goals, extracurricular activities, and community activities. Preference is given to qualified residents of Maryland. Applicant must be a citizen of the U.S.
EIN: 202052767

3856
Kerri Ann Kattar Memorial Fund, Inc.
414 E. Diamond Ave.
Gaithersburg, MD   20877-3018   (301) 963-5900
Contact: Candace Kattar, Pres.

Foundation type: Independent foundation
Purpose: Scholarships to students pursuing careers in academic, athletic or sports-related fields, and in the arts.
Financial data: Year ended 12/31/2011. Assets, $35,890 (M); Expenditures, $20,201; Total giving, $17,074.
Fields of interest: Arts; Recreation.
Type of support: Scholarships—to individuals.

Application information: Application form required.
   Initial approach: Letter
   Applicants should submit the following:
      1) Letter(s) of recommendation
      2) Financial information
      3) Essay
   Additional information: Application must also include federal or state tax return.
EIN: 042725274

3857
Keswick Foundation, Inc.
700 W. 40th St.
Baltimore, MD   21211-2104   (410) 662-4201

Foundation type: Public charity
Purpose: Scholarships to Baltimore, MD area high school students to obtain degrees in nursing, geriatric nursing assistant's certification and licensed nursing degrees.
Financial data: Year ended 06/30/2012. Assets, $152,389,510 (M); Expenditures, $5,468,088; Total giving, $4,743,223.
Fields of interest: Nursing school/education.
Type of support: Undergraduate support.
Application information:
   Initial approach: Letter
EIN: 521066144

3858
Kids Campaign, Inc.
3800 Hooper Ave.
Baltimore, MD   21211-1313   (410) 467-3000
Contact: Edward Kiernan, Pres.

Foundation type: Public charity
Purpose: General welfare grants to residents of Baltimore, MD.
Financial data: Year ended 12/31/2011. Assets, $397,535 (M); Expenditures, $310,974; Total giving, $310,974; Grants to individuals, totaling $48,712.
Type of support: Grants for special needs.
Application information:
   Initial approach: Letter
   Additional information: Recipients receive gift certificates to enable their families to celebrate the holiday season.
EIN: 521304326

3859
The Larry King Cardiac Foundation
15720 Crabbs Branch Way, Ste. D
Rockville, MD   20855-2678
Contact: Holly Lee, Dir., Devel.
Toll-free tel.: (866) 302-5523; URL: http://www.lkcf.org

Foundation type: Public charity
Purpose: Assistance with medical and hospital expenses for economically disadvantaged individuals requiring cardiac surgery.
Publications: Annual report; Financial statement.
Financial data: Year ended 12/31/2011. Assets, $594,594 (M); Expenditures, $1,293,010; Total giving, $430,270; Grants to individuals, totaling $33,003.
Fields of interest: Heart & circulatory diseases.
Type of support: Grants for special needs.
Application information: Applications accepted.
   Deadline(s): Contact foundation for application deadline
   Additional information: Application by biographical letter including physician's letter,

financial statement, and health insurance documentation.

Program description:

Financial Assistance: The foundation provides funds solely for life saving cardiac procedures for individuals who, due to limited means and inadequate insurance, would be otherwise unable to receive life saving treatment. Eligible patients must be U.S. citizens or have a legal right to be in the U.S. (proof of passport, visa, green card, etc. required); must not have financial resources to pay for the procedures themselves; must not have any insurance; must not qualify for any state or federal support (i.e., Medicare, Medicaid); and must be free of any criminal conviction.

EIN: 521563547

3860
The Kirchner Family Foundation, Inc.
P.O. Box 404
Queenstown, MD   21658-0404   (410) 827-4264
Contact: Suzanne B. Kirchner, Pres.

Foundation type: Independent foundation
Purpose: Scholarship awards to residents of Queenstown, MD, with financial need.
Financial data: Year ended 12/31/2012. Assets, $191 (M); Expenditures, $33,951; Total giving, $0.
Fields of interest: Higher education.
Application information: Applications accepted. Application form required.
  Initial approach: Letter
  Deadline(s): Apr. 1 and Oct. 1
  Applicants should submit the following:
    1) Letter(s) of recommendation
    2) SAT
    3) GPA
EIN: 134222352

3861
Rabbi Chaim Nachman Kowalsky Memorial Ahavas Yisroel Fund, Inc.
6400 Cross Country Blvd.
Baltimore, MD   21215-3111   (410) 358-7975
Contact: Rabbi Baruch Brull, V.P.
E-mail: eli@ahavasyisrael.org; URL: http://www.ahavasyisrael.org

Foundation type: Public charity
Purpose: Specific assistance to the needy with food, clothing, shelter and other assistance to the poor in the metropolitan Baltimore, MD, area.
Financial data: Year ended 12/31/2011. Assets, $1,455,955 (M); Expenditures, $1,421,800; Total giving, $1,338,135; Grants to individuals, totaling $1,338,135.
Fields of interest: Economically disadvantaged.
Type of support: Grants for special needs.
Application information: Contact the fund for eligibility criteria.
EIN: 521219478

3862
Dr. Henry P. and Marion Page Durkee Laughlin Foundation, Inc.
(formerly National Psychiatric Endowment Fund, Inc.)
307 Upper College Terr.
Frederick, MD   21701-4818

Foundation type: Independent foundation
Purpose: Awards by nomination only to MD graduating psychiatric residency students in honor of their scholarship and academic leadership.

Financial data: Year ended 12/31/2012. Assets, $3,727,098 (M); Expenditures, $444,590; Total giving, $177,000; Grants to individuals, 26 grants totaling $22,800 (high: $1,200, low: $400).
Fields of interest: Health sciences school/education; Mental health, treatment.
Type of support: Awards/grants by nomination only; Graduate support; Doctoral support.
Application information: Applications not accepted.
  Additional information: Unsolicited requests for funds not considered or acknowledged.
EIN: 526080760

3863
Leadership Maryland, Inc.
134 Holiday Ct., Ste. 318
Annapolis, MD   21401-7008   (410) 841-2101
Contact: Nancy Minieri, Pres. and C.E.O.
FAX: (410) 841-2104;
E-mail: info@leadershipmd.org; E-mail for Nancy Minieri: nancy@leadershipmd.org; URL: http://www.leadershipmd.org

Foundation type: Public charity
Purpose: Scholarships to qualified participants form non-profit organizations, small businesses, education and the public sector.
Publications: Application guidelines.
Financial data: Year ended 12/31/2011. Assets, $1,479,059 (M); Expenditures, $516,835; Total giving, $22,000; Grants to individuals, totaling $22,000.
Fields of interest: Leadership development.
Type of support: Scholarships—to individuals.
Application information: Applications accepted. Application form required. Interview required.
  Send request by: Mail or hand deliver
  Deadline(s): Oct.
  Additional information: Application should include 13 copies of completed application, 13 copies of one letter of recommendation, an application feel of $250, and tuition assistance form. See web site for detailed application guidelines.

Program description:

Leadership Maryland Program: Each year, fifty diverse and accomplished leaders from around Maryland are selected to participate in a series of classes and hands-on experience that highlight local, regional, and statewide issues. Applicants must be senior-level leaders with significant achievements in career and community, expressed concern about the future of Maryland and a personal commitment to help shape the future, willingness to commit the time and energy necessary to complete the program, and full support of the organization or business that applicant represents, and a willingness to continue supporting the efforts of the organization after graduation. Applicant must work or live in MD.

EIN: 521804780

3864
Klein G. & Mary Lee Leister Foundation Inc
409 Washington Ave., Ste. 900
Towson, MD   21204

Foundation type: Independent foundation
Purpose: Scholarships to residents of Pocomoke City, MD for continuing education at institutions of higher learning.
Financial data: Year ended 11/30/2011. Assets, $170,502 (M); Expenditures, $11,524; Total

giving, $9,650; Grants to individuals, 7 grants totaling $9,600 (high: $2,500, low: $700).
Type of support: Scholarships—to individuals.
Application information: Applications not accepted.
  Additional information: Unsolicited requests for funds not considered or acknowledged.
EIN: 521402453

3865
Life Sciences Research Foundation
3520 San Martin Dr.
Baltimore, MD   21218-2440   (410) 467-2597
Contact: Christine Pratt, Treas.
Application address: Susan DiRenzo, Life Sciences Research Foundation, c/o Lewis Thomas Laboratory, Princeton University, Washington Rd., Princeton, NJ 08544, tel.: (609) 258-3551, e-mail: sdirenzo@molbio.princeton.edu
E-mail: lsrf@ciwemb.edu; URL: http://www.lsrf.org

Foundation type: Independent foundation
Purpose: Three-year fellowships will be awarded on a competitive basis to graduates of medical and graduate schools in the biological sciences holding M.D., Ph.D., D.V.M. or D.D.S. degrees. Awards will be based solely on the quality of the individual applicant's previous accomplishments, and on the merit of the proposal for postdoctoral research. Persons doing a second postdoc are eligible only if they are transferring to a different supervisor's laboratory and embarking on a new project not connected to their previous research. All U.S. citizens are eligible to apply with no geographic restriction on the laboratory of their choice. Foreign applicants will be eligible for study in U.S. laboratories. LSRF fellows must carry out their research at nonprofit institutions. LSRF fellows can change projects, laboratories, and/or institutions during the fellowship as long as the eligibility rules listed here are not violated. A person holding a faculty appointment is not eligible to apply for an LSRF fellowship.
Publications: Application guidelines; Annual report; Financial statement; Grants list; Informational brochure.
Financial data: Year ended 05/31/2012. Assets, $2,224,234 (M); Expenditures, $2,685,280; Total giving, $2,601,556; Grants to individuals, 52 grants totaling $2,601,556 (high: $56,000, low: $1,201).
Fields of interest: Research; Biology/life sciences.
Type of support: Fellowships; Research.
Application information: Applications accepted.
  Deadline(s): Oct. 1
  Additional information: See web site for additional application information.
EIN: 521231801

3866
Brandon James Malstrom Memorial Foundation, Inc.
c/o William Malstrom
15 Edgarwood Ct.
Phoenix, MD   21131
Application address: 13815 Jarretsville Pike,Phoenix,MD 21131

Foundation type: Independent foundation
Purpose: Scholarships to graduates of Dulaney High School, MD, who have a GPA of 3.0.
Financial data: Year ended 12/31/2012. Assets, $140,469 (M); Expenditures, $25,244; Total giving, $19,534; Grants to individuals, 7 grants totaling $19,534 (high: $5,000, low: $1,034).

Type of support: Support to graduates or students of specific schools.
Application information: Applications accepted. Application form required.
>*Deadline(s):* June 1
>*Applicants should submit the following:*
>1) SAT
>2) ACT
>3) Transcripts
>4) Letter(s) of recommendation
>5) Essay
>*Additional information:* Contact foundation for current application guidelines.

EIN: 431988527

3867
Manna Food Center, Inc.
9311 Gaither Rd.
Gaithersburg, MD 20877-1417 (301) 424-1130
Contact: Amy G. Gabala, Exec. Dir.
E-mail: info@mannafood.org; URL: http://www.mannafood.org

Foundation type: Public charity
Purpose: Assistance to needy individuals and families of Montgomery county, MD, with food, clothing, shelter and other assistance.
Publications: Newsletter.
Financial data: Year ended 06/30/2012. Assets, $2,213,462 (M); Expenditures, $7,170,290; Total giving, $5,642,686; Grants to individuals, totaling $5,642,686.
Fields of interest: Human services.
Type of support: Grants for special needs.
Application information:
>*Initial approach:* Phone
>*Additional information:* Contact foundation for eligibility criteria.

EIN: 521289203

3868
The Thelma March Scholarship Foundation
5719 York Rd.
Baltimore, MD 21212

Foundation type: Operating foundation
Purpose: Scholarships to graduating seniors from Dunbar High School, MD and Douglas High School, MD for postsecondary education.
Financial data: Year ended 12/31/2012. Assets, $162,721 (M); Expenditures, $7,245; Total giving, $4,500; Grants to individuals, 5 grants totaling $4,500 (high: $1,500, low: $750).
Fields of interest: Higher education.
Type of support: Support to graduates or students of specific schools.
Application information:
>*Deadline(s):* None
>*Additional information:* Contact your school's guidance office for application information.

EIN: 521208748

3869
Maryland 4-H Foundation, Inc.
8020 Greenmead Dr.
College Park, MD 20740-4000 (301) 314-7835
Contact: Amanda Brown Clougherty, Exec. Dir.
FAX: (301) 314-7146;
E-mail: info@mymaryland4hfoundation.com;
URL: http://www.mymaryland4hfoundation.com/

Foundation type: Public charity

Purpose: Scholarships to current 4-H members or alumni(ae) for attendance at an accredited college, university or vocational institution.
Publications: Application guidelines; Annual report; Financial statement.
Financial data: Year ended 06/30/2012. Assets, $3,265,588 (M); Expenditures, $675,279; Total giving, $101,255; Grants to individuals, totaling $22,500.
Fields of interest: Vocational education, post-secondary; Higher education.
Type of support: Scholarships—to individuals.
Application information: Applications accepted. Application form required. Application form available on the grantmaker's web site.
>*Send request by:* Mail
>*Deadline(s):* June
>*Final notification:* Applicants notified by Oct. 1
>*Applicants should submit the following:*
>1) Letter(s) of recommendation
>2) Transcripts
>3) Financial information
>*Additional information:* Application should also include leadership abilities and resourcefulness, and 4-H background. See web site for additional guidelines.

Program description:
>*Scholarships:* Each year, the foundation awards a variety of scholarships to current 4-H members or alumni who will be enrolled at an accredited college, university, or post high school vocational program in the fall of the year in which they apply. See web site for special criteria for selected scholarships.

EIN: 526056016

3870
Maryland Association of Elementary School Principals, Inc.
(formerly Found Advancement Maryland Education, Inc.)
9752 Gudel Dr.
Ellicott City, MD 21042-1797 (410) 961-2360
Contact: Debbie Drown, Exec. Dir.
FAX: (410) 465-4230;
E-mail: debbiedrown@verizon.net; URL: http://www.maesp.org/

Foundation type: Public charity
Purpose: Grants and awards to educators of MD to advance the quality of education.
Publications: Application guidelines.
Financial data: Year ended 06/30/2012. Assets, $34,491 (M); Expenditures, $97,615; Total giving, $5,000; Grants to individuals, totaling $5,000.
Fields of interest: Education.
Type of support: Awards/prizes.
Application information:
>*Deadline(s):* Feb. for National Distinguished Principal, Apr. 4 for Dr. Kenneth E. Mann Scholarship Award, Dec. for Family Involvement Grants
>*Additional information:* See web site for additional application guidelines.

Program descriptions:
>*Dr. Kenneth E. Mann Scholarship Awards:* A $1,000 scholarship is annually available to recognize a successful elementary teacher education applicant who must graduate from a Maryland public high school and plan to pursue their elementary teaching degree at a college, trade school, or university in the state of MD.
>*Family Involvement Grants:* Six grants of $500 each are available to members of the association who wish to create and implement programs and activities in their schools that encourage families to become more involved in school and their children's education.

National Distinguished Principals (NDP) Program: This program recognizes elementary and middle-level principals who set high standards for instruction, student achievement, character, and climate for the students, families, and staff in their learning communities. Eligible nominees must be practicing principals with at least five years experience in the principalship, who plans to continue as a practicing principal, be a member of the association, and demonstrate evidence of outstanding contributions to the community and to the education profession, and should lead a school that is clearly committed to excellence, has programs designed to meet the academic and social needs of all students, and has firm ties to parents and the community.

EIN: 200623308

3871
Maryland Congress of Parents and Teachers, Inc.
5 Central Ave.
Glen Burnie, MD 21061-3441 (410) 760-6621
Contact: Ray Leone, Pres.
FAX: (410) 760-6344; E-mail: office@mdpta.org;
Toll-free tel.: (800) 707-7972; URL: http://www.mdpta.org

Foundation type: Public charity
Purpose: Scholarships to high school graduates who plan to pursue a career in education in the public schools of MD.
Publications: Application guidelines.
Financial data: Year ended 12/31/2012. Assets, $705,770 (M); Expenditures, $371,151; Total giving, $4,000; Grants to individuals, totaling $4,000.
Fields of interest: Teacher school/education.
Type of support: Undergraduate support.
Application information: Applications accepted. Application form required. Application form available on the grantmaker's web site.
>*Initial approach:* Letter
>*Deadline(s):* Mar. 15
>*Applicants should submit the following:*
>1) Essay
>2) Resume
>3) Transcripts
>4) Financial information
>*Additional information:* Applicant must obtain sponsorship of a Maryland PTA local unit in good standing.

EIN: 520667483

3872
Maryland Hall for the Creative Arts, Inc.
801 Chase St.
Annapolis, MD 21401-3530 (410) 263-5544
Contact: Linnell Bowen, Pres. and C.E.O.
FAX: (410) 263-5114; E-mail: info@mdhallarts.org;
Toll-free tel: (866) 438-3808; URL: http://www.mdhallarts.org

Foundation type: Public charity
Purpose: Residencies to MD, NJ, NY and PA artists who specialize in the performing, visual, and language arts.
Financial data: Year ended 06/30/2012. Assets, $5,030,112 (M); Expenditures, $2,272,205.
Fields of interest: Visual arts; Performing arts; Language/linguistics.
Type of support: Residencies; Stipends.
Application information: Applications accepted. Application form required.
>*Deadline(s):* May 17 for Local AIR Program, June 1 for Visiting AIR Program

Applicants should submit the following:
1) Resume
2) Letter(s) of recommendation
3) Work samples
4) SASE

Program descriptions:
Local Artist-in-Residence Program: Provides support to Maryland artists who wish to share their vision with the community in a specific manner. Accepted artists are reviewed on an annual basis for up to three years at which time artists may apply to the program.
Visiting Artist-in-Residence Program: This program consists of a residency taking place in a one to three month time period. Artists creating original work in any media, including visual, performing, and the language arts, who live in New Jersey, New York, and Pennsylvania are eligible to apply.
EIN: 521164469

3873
Maryland Media, Inc.
P.O. Box U
College Park, MD   20741-3019   (301) 314-8000
Contact: Steve Lamphier, Pres.

Foundation type: Public charity
Purpose: Scholarships to talented graduating high school seniors in the MD, area pursuing a career in journalism.
Financial data: Year ended 08/31/2012. Assets, $4,067,179 (M); Expenditures, $1,027,548; Total giving, $6,966; Grants to individuals, totaling $6,966.
Fields of interest: Print publishing; Higher education.
Type of support: Scholarships—to individuals.
Application information: Applications accepted. Application form required. Interview required.
Applicants should submit the following:
1) Transcripts
2) Letter(s) of recommendation
3) Class rank
4) SAT
5) GPA
EIN: 520942033

3874
Maryland Ornithological Society, Inc.
(also known as MOS)
P.O. Box 105
Monrovia, MD   21770-0105   (301) 490-0444
Toll-Free Tel.: (800) 823-0050; URL: http://www.mdbirds.org

Foundation type: Public charity
Purpose: Scholarships to Maryland teachers, youth leaders, park rangers, camp counselors, community volunteers and others who intend to make nature education a career. Research grants to individuals for the study of birds in Maryland.
Publications: Application guidelines.
Financial data: Year ended 04/30/2012. Assets, $2,915,457 (M); Expenditures, $132,988; Total giving, $9,588; Grants to individuals, totaling $9,588.
Fields of interest: Natural resources; Environmental education.
Type of support: Research; Scholarships—to individuals.
Application information:
Deadline(s): Jan. 31 for Scholarships, June 1 and Dec. 1 for Research
Final notification: Recipients notified mid-Mar. for scholarships

Additional information: Scholarship recipients should include a written statement in the form of a letter, a resume, and two letters of recommendation. Proposals are accepted for research grants.

Program descriptions:
Ecology and Ornithology Scholarships: The society awards ecology and ornithology scholarships to Maryland teachers, youth leaders, park rangers, and nature center staff to attend weeklong summer ecology and ornithology workshops at Audubon camps in Maine. Each award covers the cost of tuition, room, and board for an intensive six-day course of study and instruction in ornithology, ecology, conservation, or natural history. All together, about ten to fifteen scholarships are awarded each year, and applicant must be eighteen years or older. Applicants need not be members of MOS, but must be endorsed by a chapter or a member of MOS. Each scholarship is approximately $1,000.
Research Grants: The society's research grants encourage ecological and conservation research on birds in Maryland. Graduate school projects, projects which involve volunteers, and proposals which are not normally funded through traditional academic, governmental or professional sources are of most interest. Applications for projects which are funded from a variety of sources are strongly encouraged, but grants are open to all levels of researchers from amateurs to graduate students to professionals. The number of grants awarded varies each year depending upon the number of entries and the amount of the available grants. The combined value of all grants seldom exceeds $3,000, but individual grants may range from a few hundred, up to one or two thousand dollars.
EIN: 526046316

3875
Maryland Society for Educational Technology
(formerly Maryland Instructional Computers Coordinators Association, also known as MSET)
103 Little Neck Rd.
Stevensville, MD   21666-2801
Address for grant application:
theajones4@gmail.com
URL: http://www.msetonline.org/

Foundation type: Public charity
Purpose: Grants and awards to MD educators who wish to bring technology into their classrooms.
Publications: Application guidelines; Informational brochure.
Financial data: Year ended 08/30/2011. Assets, $112,630 (M); Expenditures, $382,619; Total giving, $12,317; Grants to individuals, 17 grants totaling $12,317.
Fields of interest: Education.
Type of support: Grants to individuals; Awards/prizes.
Application information: Applications accepted. Application form required.
Send request by: On-line for Grants
Deadline(s): Dec.
Additional information: See web site for additional guidelines.

Program descriptions:
Grants: Grants are offered to educators who are MSET members who are focusing on personalized learning in their innovative work with technology. Grants are in the amount of up to $2,000.
Outstanding Educator Award: This award recognizes one educator for his or her use of educational technology in the teaching and learning process in Maryland schools. Applicants include

any teacher in a Maryland public or private school whose primary job responsibility is the direct instruction of students in an early childhood through grade 12 classroom may be nominated. Educators must be currently responsible for the day-to-day instruction of PreK-12 students. A nominee for this award may include a library media specialist and/or technology integration specialist, if at least 75 percent of his/her responsibilities include the direct instruction of PreK-12 students. Application by nomination only.
Outstanding Leader Award: This award recognizes an educator outside the classroom who has made exemplary contributions to the implementation of technology in Maryland schools. Applicants include any full-time educator or administrator employed by an educational entity in the state of Maryland, whose primary job responsibility is not teaching in an Early Childhood through Grade12 classroom. Application by nomination only.
EIN: 521635549

3876
Maryland-Delaware-D.C. Press Foundation, Inc.
Capital Gazette Bldg.
2000 Capital Dr.
Annapolis, MD   21401-3151
FAX: (410) 721-4557;
E-mail: foundation@mddcpress.com; Contact Jen Thornberry: (855) 721-6332 x2, e-mail: jthornberry@mddcpress.com; URL: http://www.mddcpress.com/mc/page.do?sitePageId=72868&orgId=mdp

Foundation type: Operating foundation
Purpose: Scholarships to senior staff members of high school newspapers and awards journalism internships at local newspapers.
Publications: Application guidelines.
Financial data: Year ended 12/31/2011. Assets, $77,949 (M); Expenditures, $21,955; Total giving, $20,700.
Fields of interest: Print publishing.
Type of support: Internship funds; Scholarships—to individuals; Awards/prizes.
Application information: Applications accepted. Application form required. Application form available on the grantmaker's web site. Interview required.
Initial approach: Application
Send request by: Mail
Deadline(s): Jan. 31 for Michael S. Powell High School Journalist of the Year, Nov. 12 for the Reese Cleghorn MDDC Internship Program
Applicants should submit the following:
1) Letter(s) of recommendation
2) Essay
Additional information: Applications for the Michael S. Powell High School Journalist of the year must submit five articles mounted on unlined paper and an autobiographical review of the applicant's journalism background and experience.

Program descriptions:
Michael S. Powell High School Journalist of the Year: The foundation awards a $1,500 scholarship to an outstanding senior staff member of a Delaware, District of Columbia, or Maryland high school newspaper. The winner is also honored at the MDDC Editorial Conference in the spring.
The Reese Cleghorn MDDC Internship Program: The foundation supports an eight week internship program at participating newspapers. The program is open to student journalists attending any four-year college in Delaware, District of Columbia,

or Maryland or residents in the MDDC region who attend four-year colleges out of state. Each intern is provided a $2,400 stipend and internships are available in news reporting, copy editing, and photojournalism.
EIN: 522135767

3877
The McGeehin Educational Foundation Inc.
1375 Piccard Dr., Ste. 375
Rockville, MD   20850   (301) 840-4600

Foundation type: Independent foundation
Purpose: Scholarships to students of Magruder High School, MD, pursuing a degree in education at a four-year college or university. Applicants from additional high schools in MD, PA and other states may be considered depending on the availability of funds.
Financial data: Year ended 04/30/2013. Assets, $62,333 (M); Expenditures, $5,101; Total giving, $5,000; Grants to individuals, 2 grants totaling $5,000 (high: $2,500, low: $2,500).
Fields of interest: Teacher school/education.
Type of support: Support to graduates or students of specific schools.
Application information: Application form required.
  Deadline(s): Apr. 30
  Additional information: Application should include work history and copy of the past two years' 1040 tax forms.
EIN: 521977515

3878
Medical Education Foundation in Gynecology & Obstetrics
2130 Priest Bridge Dr., Ste. 7
Crofton, MD   21114-2457

Foundation type: Public charity
Purpose: Awards to outstanding teachers in ob-gyn medical education. Research grants for the study of reproductive medicine and female health care.
Fields of interest: Obstetrics/gynecology; Obstetrics/gynecology research.
Type of support: Research; Awards/prizes.
Application information:
  Initial approach: Letter
  Deadline(s): Oct. 1
  Additional information: Application should include a proposal.
EIN: 521435273

3879
Memorial Hospital Foundation, Inc.
219 S. Washington St.
Easton, MD   21601-2678
E-mail: jmarlowe@shorehealth.org; URL: http://www.shorehealth.org/giving/

Foundation type: Public charity
Purpose: Financial assistance to patients of memorial Hospital, MD with medical expenses. Financial assistance to employees of Memorial Hospital, MD for tuition espenses.
Financial data: Year ended 06/30/2011. Assets, $57,504,712 (M); Expenditures, $1,434,451; Total giving, $769,717; Grants to individuals, totaling $42,791.
Fields of interest: Health care; Human services.
Type of support: Employee-related welfare; Grants for special needs.
Application information: Applications accepted.

Additional information: Employees and patients must demonstrate financial need. contact the foundation for eligibillity determination.
EIN: 521282080

3880
Memorial Scholarship Foundation of the Rotary Club of Westminster, Maryland in Memory of Colonel Sherman E. Flanagan, Jr.
939 Winchester Dr.
Westminster, MD   21157-5736   (410) 751-3630
Application address: c/o Westminster High School, 1225 Washington Rd., Westminster, MD 21157

Foundation type: Independent foundation
Purpose: Scholarships to graduating seniors of Westminster High School, MD pursuing higher education.
Financial data: Year ended 06/30/2012. Assets, $135,881 (M); Expenditures, $4,198; Total giving, $4,000; Grants to individuals, 4 grants totaling $4,000 (high: $1,000, low: $1,000).
Fields of interest: Higher education; Scholarships/financial aid.
Type of support: Support to graduates or students of specific schools; Undergraduate support.
Application information: Applications accepted. Application form required.
  Initial approach: Letter
  Deadline(s): Apr. 1
  Additional information: Application should include college of choice, and accomplishments warranting selection. Applications available from high school guidance office.
EIN: 237037815

3881
Mental Health Association of Montgomery County, MD, Inc.
1000 Twinbrook Pkwy.
Rockville, MD   20851-1201   (301) 424-0656
Contact: Scot Marken, C.E.O.
FAX: (301) 738-1030; E-mail: info@mhamc.org;
URL: http://www.mhamc.org

Foundation type: Public charity
Purpose: Financial assistance to residents of Montgomery County, MD with long-term mental illness.
Publications: Informational brochure.
Financial data: Year ended 06/30/2012. Assets, $3,278,779 (M); Expenditures, $4,474,789; Total giving, $97,917; Grants to individuals, totaling $97,917.
Fields of interest: Mentally disabled.
Type of support: Grants for special needs.
Application information: Assistance to clients is provided based on financial need. Contact the association for eligibility requirement.
EIN: 520681147

3882
Metropolitan Center for the Visual Arts
(also known as VisArts at Rockville)
155 Gibbs St., Ste. 300
Rockville, MD   20850-0353   (301) 315-8200
Additional e-mail for Residencies:
education@visartscenter.org
FAX: (301) 315-8296;
E-mail: info@visartscenter.org; E-Mail for Alice

Nappy: anappy@visartscenter.org; URL: http://www.visartscenter.org

Foundation type: Public charity
Purpose: Residencies for visual artists with studio space.
Publications: Financial statement; Grants list; Newsletter; Occasional report.
Financial data: Year ended 06/30/2011. Assets, $2,738,843 (M); Expenditures, $946,620.
Fields of interest: Photography; Sculpture; Design; Painting; Ceramic arts.
Type of support: Residencies.
Application information: Applications accepted. Application form required.
  Initial approach: Telephone or e-mail
  Send request by: Mail
  Applicants should submit the following:
    1) Work samples
    2) SASE
    3) Resume
  Additional information: Contact the center for additional guidelines.
Program description:
  Residencies: The center offers residency opportunities at its Rockville, MD facility. Artists can rent studios and work with the disciplines of painting, ceramics, photography, sculpture, jewelry, glass, mixed media, fiber, and media arts. The center offers all residents paid teaching opportunities at the center.
EIN: 521549839

3883
Ronald G. Michels Fellowship Foundation, Inc.
P.O. Box 122
Riderwood, MD   21139-0122   (914) 722-0664
Contact: Karen Baranick, Exec. Secy.
FAX: (914) 722-0465;
E-mail: karen.baranick@michelsfoundation.org;
URL: http://www.michelsfoundation.org

Foundation type: Public charity
Purpose: Grants to outstanding second year vitreoretinal fellows training in the U.S.
Financial data: Year ended 12/31/2011. Assets, $500,384 (M); Expenditures, $39,170; Total giving, $20,000; Grants to individuals, totaling $20,000.
Fields of interest: Eye diseases.
Type of support: Fellowships; Grants to individuals.
Application information: Applications accepted. Application form required.
  Deadline(s): Sept.
  Applicants should submit the following:
    1) Photograph
    2) Curriculum vitae
    3) Letter(s) of recommendation
EIN: 521715328

3884
Mid Atlantic Arts Foundation
201 N. Charles St., Ste. 401
Baltimore, MD   21201-4199   (410) 539-6656
Contact: Alan W. Cooper, Exec. Dir.
FAX: (410) 837-5517;
E-mail: maaf@midatlanticarts.org; TDD: (410) 539-4241; URL: http://www.midatlanticarts.org

Foundation type: Public charity
Purpose: Residencies and fellowships to visiting artists for the creation of new work for a duration of one and six months.

Publications: Application guidelines; Biennial report; Financial statement; Grants list; Informational brochure; Newsletter.
Financial data: Year ended 06/30/2012. Assets, $6,130,500 (M); Expenditures, $4,346,130; Total giving, $2,172,895; Grants to individuals, totaling $354,167.
Fields of interest: Arts.
Type of support: Residencies.
Application information: Applications accepted. Application form required.
> *Initial approach:* Letter or telephone
> *Deadline(s):* Dec. 7 and Apr. 19 for USArtists International, Feb. 8 for Southern Exposure
> *Applicants should submit the following:*
> 1) Work samples
> 2) Resume
> 3) Budget Information
Program descriptions:
Mid Atlantic Creative Fellowships: These fellowships support one artist from each member state in a month-long residency at either the Millay Colony for the Arts in Austerlitz, NY or the Virginia Center for the Creative Arts in Sweet Briar, VA. These centers cater primarily to writers, composers and visual artists, allowing them undisturbed time to pursue artistic projects in a supportive environment.

Southern Exposure: Performing Arts of Latin America: Performing Arts of Latin America is a national initiative that brings exemplary performing artists in dance, music, or theater, to communities across the United States. Projects will include public performances, community activities, and robust contextualization that enhance appreciation for the artists and provide greater understanding of the cultures from which they derive. Only rant requests between $5,000 and $25,000 will be considered.

State Fellowship Administration: The Foundation provides administrative services for individual artist fellowship programs for the states of Delaware, Maryland, and New Jersey. The states participating in this partnership annually award over $500,000 to the fellowship winners. Each state has a formalized application procedure and eligibility requirements. See web site for additional information.

USArtists International: This program ensures that the impressive range of expression of the performing arts in the United States is represented abroad, and American artists are presented with opportunities for creative and professional development through international cultural exchange and access to the global marketplace. The program provides support for American dance, music and theater ensembles and solo artists who have been invited to perform at significant international arts festivals or engagements that present extraordinary career opportunities anywhere in the world outside of the United States and its territories. Grants, which will seldom cover the applicant's total expenses, generally range from $1,000 to $10,000, and will not exceed $15,000.
EIN: 521169382

3885
The Mid-Atlantic Securities Traders Foundation, Inc.

(formerly The Securities Association of Virginia Foundation, Inc.)
c/o McGladrey, LLP
100 International Dr., Ste. 1400
Baltimore, MD 21202 (800) 552-7757
Contact: Linda W. Ludeke, Pres.
Application address: 4474 Flaherty Dr., Mechanicsville, VA 23111, tel: (800) 552-7757; URL: http://www.midatlanticsecuritytraders.org/foundation.html

Foundation type: Independent foundation
Purpose: Scholarships to undergraduates who are currently sophomore or junior business majors with a concentration in finance or economics and who are enrolled at a four-year state-sponsored college or university.
Financial data: Year ended 12/31/2012. Assets, $241,278 (M); Expenditures, $26,956; Total giving, $24,000.
Fields of interest: Business school/education; Economics.
Type of support: Scholarships—to individuals; Undergraduate support.
Application information: Applications accepted. Application form required.
> *Send request by:* Mail
> *Deadline(s):* May 1
> *Applicants should submit the following:*
> 1) Letter(s) of recommendation
> 2) GPA
> 3) Transcripts
EIN: 541932369

3886
Middle East Fellowship

(formerly Holy Land Trust)
510 Pinefield Dr.
P.O. Box 1252
Severna Park, MD 21146 (562) 653-4252
E-mail: info@middleeastfellowship.org; URL: http://www.middleeastfellowship.org

Foundation type: Public charity
Purpose: Fellowship opportunities to travel to Syria and Palestine.
Publications: Application guidelines.
Financial data: Year ended 12/31/2011. Assets, $82,767 (M); Expenditures, $455,542; Total giving, $376,368.
Fields of interest: Christian agencies & churches; Children/youth.
Type of support: Fellowships.
Application information: Applications accepted. Application form required. Application form available on the grantmaker's web site.
> *Initial approach:* Application
> *Deadline(s):* Apr. 28 and May 30 for Palestine Summer Encounter, June 3 for Damascus Summer Encounter
> *Additional information:* Applicants must pay fellowship costs in full. Limited financial aid is available under the Lucius Battle Peace Fellows Program.
Program descriptions:
Damascus Summer Encounters: Administered in conjunction with the Greek Orthodox Patriarchate of Antioch and All the East, this program provides individuals with an extraordinary opportunity to experience life in Damascus, Syria. Participants will have the opportunity to experience life in Damascus for one to two months, meet with local community and business leaders in Syrian society, learn about the evolving Iraqi refugee crisis, participate in

intensive Arabic language classes, volunteer at local organizations, and explore sights of extreme historical and religious significance. Limited financial aid is available under the Lucius Battle Peace Fellows Program.

Palestine Summer Encounters: Administered in conjunction with the Holy Land Trust, this program provides an opportunity for interested individuals to experience life in the Palestinian territories not as a tourist, but as a guest and participant in the community. Participants can spend one to three months in the summer living with a Palestinian Christian or Muslim host family, participating in Arabic classes, and serve as a volunteer assigned to a local organization; participants will also have the opportunity to meet with Palestinian and Israeli peacemakers to learn more about the roots of, and solutions to, the present conflict. Limited financial aid is available under the Lucius Battle Peace Fellows Program.
EIN: 953910004

3887
Mid-Shore Community Foundation, Inc.

102 E. Dover St.
Easton, MD 21601-3002 (410) 820-8175
Contact: W. W. "Buck" Duncan, Pres.
FAX: (410) 820-8729; E-mail: info@mscf.org; Additional e-mail: wduncan@mscf.org; URL: http://www.mscf.org

Foundation type: Community foundation
Purpose: Scholarships to residents of the mid-shore and eastern-shore areas, MD (Caroline, Dorchester, Kent, Queen Anne's and Talbot counties).
Publications: Application guidelines; Annual report; Financial statement; Informational brochure; Newsletter.
Financial data: Year ended 06/30/2012. Assets, $41,109,757 (M); Expenditures, $2,141,791; Total giving, $1,089,144; Grants to individuals, 17 grants totaling $9,164.
Fields of interest: Higher education; Scholarships/financial aid.
Type of support: Scholarships—to individuals; Undergraduate support.
Application information: Applications accepted. Application form required. Application form available on the grantmaker's web site.
> *Initial approach:* Letter or telephone.
> *Deadline(s):* Feb. 1
> *Final notification:* Applicants notified in Apr.
> *Additional information:* Scholarships are also available through local high school guidance offices. See web site for additional guidelines.
EIN: 521782373

3888
Montgomery Child Care Association, Inc.

(also known as MCCA)
3204 Tower Oaks Blvd., Ste. 330
Rockville, MD 20852-4250 (301) 984-7680
Contact: Michelle Martineau Green, Exec. Dir.
FAX: (301) 984-7686; E-mail: info@mccaedu.org; URL: http://www.mccaedu.org

Foundation type: Public charity
Purpose: Grants to economically disadvantaged families residing in Montgomery County, MD, for assistance with caring for children.
Publications: Financial statement; Newsletter.
Financial data: Year ended 08/31/2012. Assets, $4,032,961 (M); Expenditures, $9,519,964.
Fields of interest: Children/youth, services; Family services; Economically disadvantaged.

Type of support: Grants for special needs.
Application information: Applications not accepted.

> *Additional information:* Unsolicited requests for funds not considered or acknowledged.

EIN: 520880656

3889
M. Eddie Moore Scholarship Trust
8700 Ashwood Dr., 2nd Fl.
Capitol Heights, MD   20743   (301) 333-2356
Contact: Joe Savia, Tr.

Foundation type: Independent foundation
Purpose: Scholarships only to unmarried natural or adopted children and financial dependents of a member of the Steamfitters Local Union 602 of the United Association of Journeymen and apprentice of the plumbing and pipefitting industry of the U.S. and Canada.
Financial data: Year ended 12/31/2011. Assets, $57,192 (M); Expenditures, $10,321; Total giving, $10,000; Grants to individuals, 2 grants totaling $10,000 (high: $5,000, low: $5,000).
Type of support: Scholarships—to individuals.
Application information: Application form required.

> *Deadline(s):* July
> *Applicants should submit the following:*
> 1) Transcripts
> 2) Letter(s) of recommendation
> *Additional information:* Application must also include evidence of enrollment/acceptance to an accredited university, and a written statement of achievement.

EIN: 526489401

3890
The Aaron R. Moore, Jr. Charitable Trust
P.O. Box 198
Kensington, MD   20895   (301) 804-3385
URL: http://www.armeducationgrants.org

Foundation type: Independent foundation
Purpose: Scholarships to academically qualified but financially disadvantaged students from the Washington, D.C., metropolitan area in pursuit of a higher education or degree.
Financial data: Year ended 12/31/2012. Assets, $119,228 (M); Expenditures, $12,570; Total giving, $10,000; Grants to individuals, 2 grants totaling $10,000 (high: $5,000, low: $5,000).
Fields of interest: Higher education.
Type of support: Scholarships—to individuals.
Application information: Applications accepted. Application form required.

> *Deadline(s):* Oct. 15
> *Final notification:* Recipients notified within 60 days
> *Applicants should submit the following:*
> 1) Class rank
> 2) Transcripts
> 3) SAT
> 4) GPA
> 5) Financial information
> 6) Essay
> 7) ACT
> *Additional information:* Activities designed to assist recipients, primarily but not limited to, the Washington, D.C., metropolitan area.

EIN: 200524688

3891
Edward & Sarah Moran Scholarship Trust
P.O. Box 557
Oakland, MD   21550-4557

Foundation type: Independent foundation
Purpose: Scholarships to graduating high school seniors of Mt. Ridge High School, MD pursuing higher education.
Financial data: Year ended 07/31/2013. Assets, $547,883 (M); Expenditures, $48,836; Total giving, $43,400; Grants to individuals, 12 grants totaling $43,400 (high: $4,800, low: $2,300).
Fields of interest: Higher education.
Type of support: Support to graduates or students of specific schools; Undergraduate support.
Application information: Applications accepted. Application form not required.

> *Deadline(s):* Prior to graduation
> *Additional information:* Contact trust for additional application guidelines.

EIN: 556069479

3892
NASDAQ OMX Group Educational Foundation, Inc.
(formerly The Nasdaq Stock Marked Educational Foundation, Inc.)
805 King Farm Blvd.
Rockville, MD   20850   (800) 842-0356
E-mail: foundation@nasdaqomx.com; *URL:* http://www.nasdaqomx.com/services/initiatives/educationalfoundation

Foundation type: Company-sponsored foundation
Purpose: Fellowships to specifically qualified individuals for the purpose of conducting independent academic study or research on financial markets.
Publications: Application guidelines; Grants list.
Financial data: Year ended 12/31/2012. Assets, $27,463,287 (M); Expenditures, $4,679,411; Total giving, $4,309,768.
Fields of interest: Economics.
Type of support: Fellowships.
Application information: Applications accepted. Application form not required.

> *Initial approach:* Letter of inquiry
> *Send request by:* E-mail or mail
> *Copies of proposal:* 1
> *Deadline(s):* Feb. 1 and Aug. 1
> *Final notification:* Recipients notified Mar. 1 and Sept. 1
> *Additional information:* Ph.D. dissertation fellowships are granted in a set amount of $15,000. Applicants may be invited to submit a full proposal at a later date.

EIN: 521864429

3893
National Blood Foundation Research and Education Trust Fund
c/o AABB
8101 Glenbrook Rd.
Bethesda, MD   20814-2749   (301) 907-6977
Contact: Karen L. Shoos Jd., Exec. Dir.
FAX: (301) 907-6895; *E-mail:* nbf@aabb.org;
URL: http://www.aabb.org

Foundation type: Public charity
Purpose: Grants awarded to principal investigators and researchers pertaining to transfusion medicine and cellular therapies.
Publications: Application guidelines; Financial statement; Grants list; Newsletter.

Financial data: Year ended 09/30/2011. Assets, $7,918,535 (M); Expenditures, $659,580; Total giving, $440,500; Grants to individuals, totaling $365,500.
Fields of interest: Medical specialties research.
Type of support: Postdoctoral support.
Application information: Applications accepted. Application form required.

> *Deadline(s):* Dec.
> *Additional information:* See web site for additional application guidelines.

Program description:

> *Scientific Research Grant Program:* Grants are available for research into the scientific, aspects of blood banking and transfusion medicine. Grant terms may be for one or two years, with a maximum total award per grant of $50,000. Applicants must be doctors (M.D. or Ph.D.), medical technologists, or transfusion medicine professionals and be conducting his/her research in the United States.

EIN: 522059102

3894
National Electronic Museum, Inc.
P.O. Box 1693, MS 4015
Baltimore, MD   21203-1693
URL: http://www.nationalelectronicsmuseum.org/

Foundation type: Operating foundation
Purpose: Scholarships to individuals attending University of Maryland at College Park and the University of Maryland Baltimore County pursuing a career in engineering.
Financial data: Year ended 12/31/2012. Assets, $598,770 (M); Expenditures, $130,971; Total giving, $10,500.
Fields of interest: Engineering school/education.
Type of support: Undergraduate support.
Application information: Scholarships are awarded to students in their sophomore, junior or senior year.
EIN: 521226197

3895
National Fallen Firefighters Foundation
P.O. Drawer 498
Emmitsburg, MD   21727-0498   (301) 447-1365
Contact: Ronald Jon Siarnicki, Exec. Dir.
FAX: (301) 447-1645; *E-mail:* firehero@firehero.org;
URL: http://www.firehero.org

Foundation type: Public charity
Purpose: Scholarships to dependents of fallen firefighters honored at the National Fallen Firefighters Memorial in Emmitsburg, MD.
Publications: Application guidelines; Annual report; Financial statement; Informational brochure; Newsletter.
Financial data: Year ended 12/31/2011. Assets, $7,350,513 (M); Expenditures, $5,656,126; Total giving, $409,168; Grants to individuals, totaling $202,802.
Type of support: Scholarships—to individuals; Graduate support; Technical education support; Undergraduate support.
Application information: Applications accepted. Application form required. Application form available on the grantmaker's web site.

> *Initial approach:* Download application form
> *Send request by:* Mail
> *Deadline(s):* Apr. 1
> *Applicants should submit the following:*
> 1) GPA
> 2) Letter(s) of recommendation

Program description:

Sarbanes Scholarship Program: Scholarships are awarded for undergraduate and graduate studies, vocational-technical training, and certification and job training programs. Spouses, life partners, children, and stepchildren of firefighters honored at the National Fallen Firefighters Memorial are eligible to apply for educational assistance. They may be used for study at in-state or out-of-state public and private schools. Children must currently be under the age of 30 and have been under the age of 22 at the time of their firefighter's death.
EIN: 521832634

3896
National Foundation for Cancer Research
4600 East-West Hwy., Ste. 525
Bethesda, MD   20814-6900   (301) 654-1250
Contact: Franklin C. Salisbury, Jr., Pres.
FAX: (301) 654-5824; E-mail: info@nfcr.org;
Toll-free tel.: (800) 321-2873; URL: http://
www.nfcr.org

Foundation type: Public charity
Purpose: Award by nomination only to a distinguished individual who has demonstrated significant advancement in the field of cancer research.
Publications: Application guidelines; Annual report; Financial statement.
Financial data: Year ended 12/31/2011. Assets, $10,554,856 (M); Expenditures, $14,529,686; Total giving, $2,502,564; Grants to individuals, totaling $25,000.
Fields of interest: Cancer; Cancer research.
Type of support: Awards/grants by nomination only; Awards/prizes.
Application information: Application form available on the grantmaker's web site.
Initial approach: Letter
Send request by: Mail or e-mail
Deadline(s): Sept. 30
Applicants should submit the following:
 1) Letter(s) of recommendation
 2) Curriculum vitae
Additional information: Application should also include a listing of fifteen of the nominee's most important published papers, in the view of the nominator. Press clippings are not accepted. See web site for additional guidelines.
Program description:

Albert Szent-Gyorgyi Cancer Research Prize for Progress in Cancer Research: This award honors an outstanding researcher whose scientific achievements have expanded the understanding of cancer and cancer causation, whose vision has moved cancer research in new directions, and whose discoveries have resulted in notable advances in cancer prevention, diagnosis, and treatment. The prize also promotes public awareness of the importance of basic cancer research, and encourages the sustained investment needed to accelerate the translation of these research discoveries into new cancer treatments. The award carries with it a $25,000 cash prize.
EIN: 042531031

3897
The National Foundation for Infectious Diseases
(also known as NFID)
4733 Bethesda Ave., Ste. 750
Bethesda, MD   20814-5278   (301) 656-0003
Contact: Leonard Novick, Exec. Dir.
FAX: (301) 907-0878; E-mail: info@nfid.org;
URL: http://www.nfid.org

Foundation type: Public charity
Purpose: Fellowships and grants for education and research in the field of infestious diseases.
Publications: Annual report; Informational brochure (including application guidelines); Newsletter.
Financial data: Year ended 06/30/2012. Assets, $13,372,124 (M); Expenditures, $4,622,544.
Fields of interest: Public health, epidemiology; Biomedicine; Institute; Medical research; Minorities.
Type of support: Fellowships; Research; Postdoctoral support.
Application information:
Initial approach: Letter
Deadline(s): Jan. 15 and Feb. 15
Additional information: See web site for additional application and program information.
Program descriptions:

New Investigator Matching Grants: New scientists are provided with $2,000 each to be matched by their institution for pilot monies to help pay for supplies and equipment during the first year of independent research. Applicants must be legal residents or citizens of the U.S., with full-time junior faculty status at a recognized, accredited institution of higher education in the U.S. or Canada.

NFID Fellowships in Infectious Disease: Fellowships encourage and assist young, qualified U.S. physicians who have completed at least three years of postgraduate medical training to become specialists and researchers in infectious diseases. A $24,000 award is provided, plus $1,000 for travel and supplies.

NFID John P. Utz Postdoctoral Fellowship in Medical Mycology: The grant encourages and assists qualified U.S. physicians in becoming specialists and researchers in the field of medical mycology (fungi). A $29,000 award is given, plus $1,000 for travel and supplies. Applicants must be sponsored by a university-affiliated medical center.

Postdoctoral Fellowship: A $50,000 stipend is provided to encourage and assist a qualified U.S. physician in becoming a recognized authority on emerging infectious diseases and epidemiology. The fellowship is awarded for a one-year period. Recipients will be assigned to the National Center for Infectious Diseases, CDC, in Atlanta, GA.

Postdoctoral Fellowship in Nosocomial Infection Research and Training: Fellowships provide a $24,000 stipend and $1,000 for travel and supplies to encourage and assist a qualified U.S. physician researcher in becoming a specialist and investigator in the field of nosocomial infections. The fellowship is awarded for a one-year period.
EIN: 237198530

3898
National Gaucher Care Foundation, Inc.
5410 Edson Ln., Ste. 220
Rockville, MD   20852-3106   (301) 963-4489
Contact: Brian Berman, Pres.

Foundation type: Public charity
Purpose: Financial assistance to individuals suffering from Gaucher disease, primarily for medical and medication needs.

Financial data: Year ended 05/31/2012. Assets, $1,204,356 (M); Expenditures, $2,509,351; Total giving, $2,358,047; Grants to individuals, totaling $2,358,047.
Fields of interest: Health care.
Type of support: Grants for special needs.
Application information:
Initial approach: Telephone
Additional information: Applicant must demonstrate financial hardship. Contact the foundation for additional guidelines.
EIN: 521815708

3899
National Kidney Foundation of Maryland, Inc.
c/o Heaver Plaza
1301 York Rd., Ste. 404
Lutherville, MD   21093-6007   (410) 494-8545
Contact: Cassie Schafer, Pres. and C.E.O.
FAX: (410) 494-8549;
E-mail: cshafer@kidneymd.org; URL: http://
www.kidneymd.org

Foundation type: Public charity
Purpose: Research grants to support advancement of research related to all aspects for kidney and urinary tract disease.
Publications: Application guidelines.
Financial data: Year ended 06/30/2012. Assets, $4,349,721 (M); Expenditures, $1,578,574; Total giving, $179,815; Grants to individuals, totaling $179,815.
Fields of interest: Kidney research.
Type of support: Research.
Application information: Applications accepted. Application form available on the grantmaker's web site.
Send request by: E-mail
Deadline(s): Mar. 20
Additional information: Faxed or mailed applications are not accepted.
EIN: 526069952

3900
National Medical Association, Inc.
8403 Colesville Rd., Ste. 920
Silver Spring, MD   20910-2852   (202) 347-1895
Contact: Darryl R. Matthews, Exec. Dir.
Application address for individuals: Special Awards Programs, National Medical Fellowships, Inc., 110 W. 32nd St., New York, NY 10001-3205, tel.: (212) 483-8880
FAX: (202) 898-2510;
E-mail: programs@nmanet.org; URL: http://
www.nmanet.org

Foundation type: Public charity
Purpose: Scholarships to deserving medical students pursuing a health-related career.
Financial data: Year ended 12/31/2011. Assets, $5,671,244 (M); Expenditures, $7,363,235; Total giving, $103,100; Grants to individuals, totaling $12,000.
Fields of interest: Medical school/education; Health care.
Type of support: Scholarships—to individuals.
Application information: Applications accepted. Application form required.
Additional information: Selection is based on academic merit and financial need.
Program descriptions:

NMA Award for Medical Journalism: This program awards $2,500 to third- and fourth-year medical students who have written, produced, or directed health-related films, commercials, or videos.

NMA Emerging Scholars Award: Awards $2,250 to current first-, second-, and third-year medical students for academic achievement, leadership, and potential for distinguished contributions to medicine, who have a need component.

NMA Health Care Recovery Fund Grant: To assist members who where affected in disaster areas, the association will be awarding small practice restoration grants to those who apply and meet established criteria. Grants will be made up to $2,500 to association member physicians who are planning to restore and/or rebuild their damaged practices within affected disaster areas.

Pattie LaBelle Medical Student Scholarship: This scholarship awards up to $5,000 to deserving African-American students selected by the association.
EIN: 536010805

3901

Neighborhood Service Center, Inc.
126 Port St.
Easton, MD   21601-2600   (410) 822-5015
Contact: Sandra B. Reed, Exec. Dir.
E-mail: info@neighborhoodservicecenter.org;
URL: http://www.neighborhoodservicecenter.org/

Foundation type: Public charity
Purpose: Financial assistance to needy, low-income, and elderly residents of Talbot county, MD with temporary shelter, rent or mortgage assistance, monetary assistance for those faced with evictions and foreclosures, and other special needs.
Financial data: Year ended 06/30/2011. Assets, $1,233,280 (M); Expenditures, $1,282,605; Total giving, $459,972; Grants to individuals, totaling $459,972.
Fields of interest: Aging; Economically disadvantaged.
Type of support: Grants for special needs.
Application information: Contact the center for assistance.
EIN: 520982396

3902

Nexion Health Foundation
6937 Warfield Ave.
Sykesville, MD   21784-7454   (410) 552-4800
URL: http://www.nexion-health.com/about-us/

Foundation type: Company-sponsored foundation
Purpose: Scholarships to Nexion Associates or the children of associates who attend an accredited college or vocational school to pursue careers related to health and/or elder care. Financial assistance to Nexion Associates and their dependents who suffer loss due to unforeseen circumstances.
Financial data: Year ended 12/31/2012. Assets, $119,402 (M); Expenditures, $27,906; Total giving, $27,449; Grants to individuals, 22 grants totaling $25,949 (high: $2,931, low: $250).
Fields of interest: Vocational education, post-secondary; Higher education; Safety/disasters.
Type of support: Employee-related scholarships; Grants for special needs.
Application information: Applications not accepted.
Additional information: Unsolicited requests for funds not considered or acknowledged.
Program descriptions:
Emergency Relief: The foundation provides financial assistance to Nexion Associates and their dependents who suffer loss as a result of widespread natural disasters or other major, unforeseeable life circumstances. The Emergency Relief Program provides funds for shelter, medical attention, clothing, food and other basic needs.

Excellence Through Education Scholarship: The foundation awards $1,000 scholarships to eligible Associates, or the children of Associates, who attend an accredited college or vocational school. Primary consideration will be given to applicants pursuing careers related to health and/or elder care.
Company name: Nexion Health, Inc.
EIN: 412129020

3903

Joanna M. Nicolay Melanoma Foundation
255 Clifton Blvd., Ste. 203
Westminster, MD   21157-4786   (410) 857-4890
Contact: Denise L. Safko, Secy.-Treas.
E-mail: contact@melanomaresource.org;
URL: http://www.melanomaresource.org

Foundation type: Public charity
Purpose: Research grants for the prevention, detection, care and cure of melanoma, primarily in MD.
Publications: Application guidelines; Informational brochure; Newsletter.
Financial data: Year ended 12/31/2012. Assets, $225,816 (M); Expenditures, $249,827; Total giving, $70,000; Grants to individuals, totaling $70,000.
Fields of interest: Skin disorders research.
Type of support: Research.
Application information: Applications accepted. Application form not required.
Initial approach: Letter
Copies of proposal: 2
Deadline(s): Dec. 31
Final notification: Recipients notified by Mar. 1
Applicants should submit the following:
   1) Resume
   2) Proposal
   3) Letter(s) of recommendation
   4) Financial information
   5) Essay
   6) Curriculum vitae
   7) Budget Information
Program description:
Research Scholar Awards: Awards of $10,000 each are available to graduate students conducting melanoma research at National Cancer Institute (NCI)-designated cancer center, NCI-designated comprehensive cancer centers, and/or research institutional members of the Association of American Cancer Institutes (AACI)
EIN: 550855653

3904

The Obesity Society
(formerly NAASO, The Obesity Society)
8757 Georgia Ave., Ste. 1320
Silver Spring, MD   20910-3818   (301) 563-6526
Contact: Francesca M. Dea C.A.E., Exec. Dir.
FAX: (301) 563-6595; E-mail: fdea@obesity.org;
URL: http://www.naaso.org

Foundation type: Public charity
Purpose: Grants and awards to individuals for research for the treatment and prevention of obesity.
Publications: Application guidelines.
Financial data: Year ended 03/31/2012. Assets, $1,661,391 (M); Expenditures, $2,587,131; Total giving, $84,500; Grants to individuals, totaling $84,500.
Fields of interest: Eating disorders.
Type of support: Grants to individuals; Awards/prizes.
Application information: Applications accepted.
Additional information: See web site for additional guidelines.
Program descriptions:
Atkinson-Stern Public Service Award: This award recognizes an individual or organization whose work has significantly improved the lives of those affected by obesity, whether through research, public policy, patient care, or other means. Recipients receive a plaque and a $1,000 award.

Ethan Sims Young Investigator Awards: This award recognizes excellence in research by young investigators based on their submitted abstracts and presentation during the society's annual scientific meeting. Five finalists are selected during the call for abstracts and each will receive up to $1,000 to cover meeting expenses. The award is presented during a plenary session at which the five finalists are invited to present their oral abstracts. The recipient will be announced at the conclusion of the session and will receive an additional $1,000 cash prize.

Lilly Scientific Achievement Award: This award recognizes excellence in an established research career and is made possible through an annual grant from the Eli Lilly Pharmaceutical Company. Recipients receive a plaque and $5,000 cash prize plus a travel grant to the society's annual scientific meeting. The award is presented during a plenary session at which the recipient is invited to present the Lilly Scientific Achievement Award Lecture. To be eligible for this award, the recipient must be within 15 years of receiving his or her terminal degree.

Mickey Stunkard Lifetime Achievement Award: The program is designed to recognize people who have made a lifetime of outstanding contributions to the field of obesity in terms of scholarship, mentorship, and education. Recipients receive a plaque and $1,000 cash prize. The award is presented during a plenary session at which the recipient is invited to present the Friends of Mickey Stunkard Award Lecture. This award is by nomination.

The George Bray Founders Award: This program recognizes an individual for significant contributions that advance the scientific or clinical basis for understanding or treating obesity and for extensive involvement with the society. Recipients receive a plaque and a $1,000 cash prize. The award is presented during a plenary session at which the recipient is invited to present the George Bray Founders Award Lecture.

The Obesity Awards for Outstanding Journal Research: This award recognizes exemplary research in basic, clinical, or population manuscripts published in the journal Obesity. The awards are presented during the opening session and the first author of each award (two are given annually) receive a $500 cash prize and a plaque.
EIN: 541438429

3905

Order of the Alhambra Charity Fund, Inc.
4200 Leeds Ave.
Baltimore, MD   21229-5496   (410) 242-0660
Contact: Roger Reid, Exec. Dir.
FAX: (410) 536-5729;
E-mail: info@orderalhambra.org; URL: http://www.OrderAlhambra.org

Foundation type: Public charity

Purpose: Financial assistance, education and residences for persons developmentally disabled by mental retardation.
Financial data: Year ended 06/30/2012. Assets, $3,186,897 (M); Expenditures, $248,348; Total giving, $124,491; Grants to individuals, totaling $38,000.
Fields of interest: Mentally disabled.
Type of support: Grants for special needs.
Application information: Contact the fund for additional guidelines.
EIN: 521571850

3906
Osteogenesis Imperfecta Foundation, Inc.
804 W. Diamond Ave., Ste. 210
Gaithersburg, MD 20878-1414 (301) 947-0083
FAX: (301) 947-0456; E-mail: bonelink@oif.org; Toll-free tel.: (800) 981-2663; Mailing Address: P.O. Box 824061; Philadelphia, PA 19182-4061; URL: http://www.oif.org

Foundation type: Public charity
Purpose: Fellowships to qualified individuals for research on osteogenesis imperfecta (OI).
Publications: Application guidelines; Annual report; Grants list; Newsletter; Occasional report.
Financial data: Year ended 06/30/2012. Assets, $2,762,282 (M); Expenditures, $1,464,888; Total giving, $311,321; Grants to individuals, totaling $146,321.
Fields of interest: Nerve, muscle & bone research.
Type of support: Seed money; Fellowships; Research.
Application information: Applications accepted. Application form required. Application form available on the grantmaker's web site.
   Copies of proposal: 11
   Deadline(s): Varies
   Additional information: Application should include letter and curriculum vitae from applicant's mentor.
Program descriptions:
   Michael Geisman Fellowships: Awards are available to post-doctoral trainees (those with an M.D., D.D.S., D.O., or Ph.D.) who are currently working on projects with clear relevance to osteogenesis imperfect (OI), or who have projects that will enable them to develop expertise in OI research. Fellowship awards provide up to $50,000 per year, which can be used for salary, fringe benefits, and supplies. Eligible applicants must be appointed at the level of a post-doctoral trainee (or equivalent) within the past five years; research must be done under the supervision of a mentor with training and experience in OI research, or research in a related field.
   Seed Grants: Grants are available for new or established principal investigators who seek to initiate basic or clinical research studies with clear relevance to osteogenesis imperfecta (OI). Two types of seed grants are available under this program. Seed grants for basic research provide up to $60,000 for one year, while seed grants for clinical research provide up to $120,000 for up to two years. Seed grants cannot be used for Principal Investigator salaries or indirect costs. Qualified applicants must hold an M.D., D.D.S., D.O., or Ph.D., and have a faculty-level appointment within an academic institution or an affiliated health care system.
EIN: 237076021

3907
Parent Encouragement Program
10100 Connecticut Ave.
Kensington, MD 20895-3809 (301) 929-8824
Contact: Cheryl Wieker, Exec. Dir.
FAX: (301) 929-8834;
E-mail: office@PEPparent.org; URL: http://www.pepparent.org/

Foundation type: Public charity
Purpose: Scholarships to low income parents in the DC, MD, VA area for parenting classes and workshops.
Financial data: Year ended 06/30/2012. Assets, $441,621 (M); Expenditures, $438,200; Total giving, $4,119; Grants to individuals, totaling $4,119.
Fields of interest: Education; Family services, parent education.
Type of support: Scholarships—to individuals.
Application information: Contact the organization for eligibility determination.
EIN: 521379642

3908
The Passano Foundation, Inc.
c/o Waverly Management, LLC
1122 Kenilworth Dr., Ste. 115
Baltimore, MD 21204
FAX: (410) 825-0997;
E-mail: passanofoundation@verizon.net; URL: http://www.passanofoundation.org

Foundation type: Independent foundation
Purpose: Awards by nomination only to distinguished scientists and medical researchers in the U.S.
Publications: Informational brochure.
Financial data: Year ended 12/31/2012. Assets, $1,211,180 (M); Expenditures, $164,969; Total giving, $125,000.
Fields of interest: Institute; Research.
Type of support: Awards/grants by nomination only; Awards/prizes.
Application information:
   Deadline(s): Nov. 2
   Additional information: Completion of formal nomination. Nominations accepted via e-mail only.
EIN: 526036968

3909
Penn-Mar Organization, Inc.
310 Old Freeland Rd.
Freeland, MD 21053-9676 (410) 343-1069
Contact: Gregory T. Miller, Pres. and C.E.O.
FAX: (410) 343-1770;
E-mail: gmiller@penn-mar.org; Toll-free tel.: (888)-273-4507; URL: http://www.penn-mar.org

Foundation type: Public charity
Purpose: Support to families and individuals with disabilities in the MD community in improving their earning potential or human service needs.
Publications: Annual report.
Financial data: Year ended 06/30/2011. Assets, $10,701,685 (M); Expenditures, $10,222,689; Total giving, $57,027; Grants to individuals, totaling $57,027.
Fields of interest: Disabilities, people with.
Type of support: Grants to individuals.
Application information: Contact the organization for eligibility requirements.
EIN: 521590195

3910
The Pet Care Trust
2105 Laurel Bush Rd., Ste. 200
Bel Air, MD 21015-5200
FAX: (443) 640-1086;
E-mail: info@petsintheclassroom.org; URL: http://www.petcaretrust.org

Foundation type: Public charity
Purpose: Awards to graduating veterinary medical students with an interest in companion animals.
Publications: Application guidelines; Grants list; Informational brochure.
Financial data: Year ended 12/31/2011. Assets, $1,603,626 (M); Expenditures, $327,687; Total giving, $27,500.
Fields of interest: Scholarships/financial aid; Veterinary medicine.
Type of support: Scholarships—to individuals.
Application information: Applications accepted.
   Additional information: Contact the trust for additional guidelines.
Program description:
   Sue Busch Memorial Award: Scholarships are awarded each year to graduating veterinary medical students who have displayed leadership with companion animals in the community. The trust sends applications for this award to participating veterinary schools each year.
EIN: 521684353

3911
Phi Sigma Sigma Foundation, Inc.
8178 Lark Brown Rd., Ste. 202
Elkridge, MD 21075-6424 (410) 799-1224
FAX: (410) 779-9186;
E-mail: foundation@phisigmasigma.org; E-Mail for Michelle Soucy: msoucy@phisigmasigma.org; URL: http://www.phisigmasigmafoundation.org

Foundation type: Public charity
Purpose: Grants and scholarships to both collegiate and graduate members of Phi Sigma Sigma to further their education.
Publications: Application guidelines.
Financial data: Year ended 06/30/2012. Assets, $2,026,323 (M); Expenditures, $391,840; Total giving, $114,500; Grants to individuals, totaling $72,500.
Fields of interest: Higher education; Students, sororities/fraternities.
Type of support: Grants to individuals; Scholarships—to individuals.
Application information: Applications accepted. Application form available on the grantmaker's web site.
   Send request by: Online
   Deadline(s): Apr. 10
   Final notification: Applicants notified in Aug.
   Additional information: Unsolicited requests for funds not considered or acknowledged.
Program description:
   Educational Grants: Grants are awarded annually to Phi Sigma Sigma collegiate and alumnae sisters based on the criteria of financial need, scholarship, and service to Phi Sigma Sigma and the community. Grants generally range from $250 to $4,250. In addition, numerous named scholarships are made available each year, given to students and sorority alumni who meet established criteria.
EIN: 205942561

3912
Phoenix Scholarship Foundation Inc.
3200 Crain Hwy., Ste. 100
Waldorf, MD   20603-4964   (301) 638-2001
Contact: Parran Foster, Dir.

Foundation type: Operating foundation
Purpose: Scholarships to individuals for higher
education.
Financial data: Year ended 12/31/2012. Assets,
$75,644 (M); Expenditures, $15,920; Total giving,
$10,000.
Type of support: Scholarships—to individuals;
Undergraduate support.
Application information: Contact foundation for
current application deadlines/guidelines.
EIN: 311490141

3913
The PNH Research & Support Foundation
P.O. Box 10983
Rockville, MD   20849-0983
E-mail: info@pnhfoundation.org; Toll-free tel./fax:
(888) 582-9993; URL: http://
www.pnhfoundation.org

Foundation type: Public charity
Purpose: Grants for medical research into finding
new treatments, and ultimately a cure for PNH
disease. Financial assistance for eligible U.S.
patients with PNH disease.
Financial data: Year ended 12/31/2012. Assets,
$65,041 (M); Expenditures, $70,636; Total giving,
$60,000.
Fields of interest: Diseases (rare) research.
Type of support: Research; Grants for special
needs.
Application information: Applicant must
demonstrate financial need for patient assistance.
Program description:
   Patient Support: The foundation will provide up to
   $3,000 per eligible U.S.-based PNH patient for
   funds to see a PNH specialist for the first time that
   are not covered by insurance, and related travel
   costs, travel and housing for PNH patients
   undergoing a bone marrow transplant, unrelated
   donor searches for those in need of a bone marrow
   transplant, and costs for human leukocyte antigen
   (HLA) testing to determine sibling compatibility for
   a bone marrow transplant.
EIN: 200577614

3914
The Martin Pollak Project, Inc.
3701 Eastern Ave.
Baltimore, MD   21224-4208   (410) 685-2525
Contact: Tom Pollak Esq., Pres.
FAX: (410) 685-0575; Additional address (DC
office): 4406 Georgia Ave., N.W., Washington, DC
20011-7124, tel.: (800) 590-1145; toll-free tel.:
(800) 590-1145; URL: http://www.mppi.org

Foundation type: Public charity
Purpose: Grants for food, shelter, and clothing,
particularly to at-risk children in the foster care
system in Baltimore, MD.
Publications: Newsletter.
Financial data: Year ended 06/30/2012. Assets,
$3,016,461 (M); Expenditures, $7,753,956; Total
giving, $2,317,305; Grants to individuals, totaling
$2,317,305.
Fields of interest: Foster care; Economically
disadvantaged.
Type of support: Grants for special needs.

Application information: Contact foundation for
eligibility requirements.
EIN: 521171384

3915
Prince George's Arts Council, Inc.
(also known as Prince George's Arts and
Humanities Council)
6525 Belcrest Rd., Ste.132
Hyattsville, MD   20782-2003   (301) 277-1402
Contact: Rhonda Dallas, Exec. Dir.
FAX: (301) 277-7215;
E-mail: info@princegeorgesartscouncil.org;
URL: http://www.pgahc.org

Foundation type: Public charity
Purpose: Fellowships, awards, internships,
residencies, and general grants to artists who are
residents of Prince George's County, MD for two
years or more.
Publications: Application guidelines; Annual report
(including application guidelines); Grants list;
Informational brochure (including application
guidelines); Newsletter.
Financial data: Year ended 06/30/2012. Assets,
$74,254 (M); Expenditures, $289,308; Total
giving, $49,992; Grants to individuals, totaling
$12,000.
Fields of interest: Arts, artist's services.
Type of support: Fellowships; Internship funds;
Awards/prizes; Residencies.
Application information: Applications accepted.
Application form required. Application form
available on the grantmaker's web site.
   Initial approach: Letter or telephone
   Additional information: Applicant must show
      proof of residency.
Program description:
   Grants: The council provides financial support to
   programs that demonstrate innovative artistic and
   creative expression, organizational capacity
   building, arts and learning, and artistic and creative
   growth and development. Funding is available to
   both individuals and organizations. Eligible
   individuals must show evidence of at least two
   years of work in their respective discipline, as well
   as at least two years of residency in Prince George's
   County. Eligible organizations must be incorporated
   in Maryland as nonprofit, 501(c)(3) organizations,
   with preference given to organizations based in
   Prince George's County; organizational grants
   require a 1:1 cash match.
EIN: 521295007

3916
Pulmonary Hypertension Association
801 Roeder Rd., Ste. 1000
Silver Spring, MD   20910-4496   (301) 565-3004
Contact: Rino Aldrighetti, Pres. and C.E.O.
FAX: (301) 565-3994;
E-mail: giving@phassociation.org; Toll-free tel.:
(800) 748-7274; URL: http://
www.phassociation.org

Foundation type: Public charity
Purpose: Research grants and scholarships are
provided for work and study to seek a cure for
pulmonary hypertension; grants are provided for
advanced research, while scholarships are
need-based.
Publications: Application guidelines; Newsletter.
Financial data: Year ended 12/31/2011. Assets,
$14,366,401 (M); Expenditures, $7,762,277;
Total giving, $464,449.
Fields of interest: Heart & circulatory diseases;
Heart & circulatory research.

Type of support: Research; Scholarships—to
individuals.
Application information: Applications accepted.
Application form required. Application form
available on the grantmaker's web site.
   Initial approach: Application
   Deadline(s): Varies
   Additional information: See web site for
      additional information.
Program descriptions:
   Mentored Clinical Scientist Award (K08): In
   conjunction with the National Heart, Lung, and
   Blood Institute, funding is available to support the
   development of outstanding clinician research
   scientists in the area of pulmonary hypertension.
   The award of $137,500 is intended to support a
   five-year period of supervised research experience
   that integrates didactic studies with laboratory- or
   clinically-based research. The proposed research
   should have both intrinsic research importance and
   be a vehicle for learning the methodology, theories,
   and conceptualizations necessary for a well-trained
   independent researcher.
   *Mentored Patient-Oriented Research Career
   Development Award (K23):* In conjunction with the
   National Heart, Lung, and Blood Institute, this
   award of $137,500 is intended to support the
   career development of investigators who have
   made a commitment to focus their research
   endeavors on patient-oriented research, through
   providing support for three to five years of
   supervised study and research for clinically-trained
   professionals who have the potential to develop
   into productive, clinical investigators focusing on
   patient-oriented research in pulmonary
   hypertension. Areas of research include
   mechanisms of human disease, therapeutic
   interventions, clinical trials, and development of
   new technologies. Candidates must demonstrate
   that they have received training in, or will participate
   in courses such as, data management,
   epidemiology, study design, hypothesis
   development, drug development, and legal and
   ethical issues associated with research on human
   subjects.
   PHA/AHA Post Doctoral Fellowship Award:
   Fellowship opportunities are available in
   conjunction with the American Heart Association.
   The objective of the fellowship is to help a trainee
   embark upon a career dedicated to the study of
   pulmonary hypertension through basic or clinical
   research. This represents a training award, which
   supports an individual before he/she is ready for
   some stage of independent research.
   *PHA/ATS/Pfizer Research Fellowship in
   Pulmonary Arterial Hypertension:* In conjunction with
   the American Thoracic Society and Pfizer, two
   research grants of up to $50,000 a year for two
   years will be awarded to support novel studies of
   the diagnosis, pathogenesis, treatment, or
   outcomes of pulmonary hypertension. Eligible
   applicants must have completed their primary
   research training and have a firm commitment from
   their home institution for a faculty position.
   Partnerships between junior and senior
   investigators are strongly encouraged, particularly
   for new investigators who are within one to five
   years of the completion of their training.
   PHA/Pfizer Proof of Concept Research Grants:
   This program supports new research projects that
   are in the early exploratory and developmental
   stages and have the potential to lead to advances
   in the scientific understanding of PH. Proposed
   projects should result in preliminary data that will
   enable the investigator to apply for support for a
   larger, hypotheses-driven research project.
   Applicants may request up to $25,000 in direct
   costs for one year to be used for salaries and/or

supplies to conduct this research. Grants cover ten percent of indirect costs. Investigators based in the U.S. and abroad are encouraged to apply.

The American Thoracic Society/Pulmonary Hypertension Association Partnership Grant for Pulmonary Hypertension: In conjunction with the American Thoracic Society, two research grants (up to $50,000/year for two years) will be awarded to support novel studies of the diagnosis, pathogenesis, treatment, or outcomes of pulmonary hypertension. Eligible applicants must have completed their primary research training (Ph.D. or sub-specialty fellowship training) and have a firm commitment from their home institution for a faculty position. Partnerships between junior and senior investigators are strongly encouraged, particularly for new investigators who are within one to five years of the completion of their training.
EIN: 650880021

3917
Pyramid Atlantic, Inc.
8230 Georgia Ave.
Silver Spring, MD 20910-4511 (301) 608-9101
Contact: Jose Dominguez, Exec. Dir.
FAX: (301) 608-9102;
E-mail: hello@pyramid-atlantic.org; E-Mail for Jose Dominguez: jdominguez@pyramid-atlantic.org;
URL: http://www.pyramidatlanticartcenter.org

Foundation type: Public charity
Purpose: Residencies to emerging and established artists who practice the disciplines of bookmaking, papermaking, printmaking and digital media.
Publications: Application guidelines.
Financial data: Year ended 06/30/2012. Assets, $3,248,407 (M); Expenditures, $548,361.
Fields of interest: Multipurpose centers/programs; Visual arts.
Type of support: Residencies.
Application information:
  Initial approach: Letter or e-mail
  Deadline(s): June 20 for Summer residencies, July 15 for Fall residencies, Dec. 1 for Spring residencies
  Additional information: See web site for additional guidelines.
Program description:
  Residency: Residencies last for two weeks to one month. The facility supplies housing, meals, travel, and studio space.
EIN: 521233802

3918
Queen Anne's County Art Council, Inc.
206 S. Commerce St.
P.O. Box 218
Centreville, MD 21617-1118 (410) 758-2520
Contact: Darcey Schoeninger, Exec. Dir.; Andrea Hearn, Prog. Coord.
FAX: (410) 758-1222;
E-mail: questions@arts4u.info; URL: http://www.arts4u.info

Foundation type: Public charity
Purpose: Scholarships to students enrolled in a high school located in Queen Anne's county, MD who have been accepted into a college which supports an art program.
Publications: Application guidelines; Annual report; Grants list; Informational brochure; Newsletter.
Financial data: Year ended 06/30/2012. Assets, $657,368 (M); Expenditures, $187,284; Total giving, $11,637; Grants to individuals, totaling $11,637.
Fields of interest: Arts education.

Type of support: Support to graduates or students of specific schools.
Application information: Applications accepted. Application form required.
  Additional information: Two $1,000 scholarships are awarded annually.
EIN: 521160383

3919
The Bill Raskob Foundation, Inc.
P.O. Box 507
Crownsville, MD 21032-0507 (410) 923-9123
Contact: Edward H. Robinson, Corp. Secy.
FAX: (410) 923-9124; E-mail: ed@billraskob.org;
URL: http://www.billraskob.org

Foundation type: Independent foundation
Purpose: Undergraduate and graduate interest-free student loans to American citizens enrolled at accredited institutions within the U.S.
Publications: Application guidelines; Program policy statement.
Financial data: Year ended 12/31/2012. Assets, $4,517,714 (M); Expenditures, $280,195; Total giving, $96,500; Loans to individuals, totaling $96,500.
Fields of interest: Higher education.
Type of support: Student loans—to individuals.
Application information: Applications accepted. Application form required.
  Initial approach: Letter
  Send request by: Mail
  Deadline(s): May 15
  Applicants should submit the following:
    1) Transcripts
    2) Letter(s) of recommendation
    3) Essay
    4) Financial information
  Additional information: Application should also include a copy of applicant's or parents' most recent tax return, school acceptance letter and a copy of financial aid award letter from school. A personal interview may be required. See web site for additional guidelines.
EIN: 510110185

3920
Ravens All-Community Team Foundation, Inc.
(formerly Ravens Foundation for Families, Inc.)
1 Winning Dr.
Owings Mills, MD 21117-4776 (410) 701-4166

Foundation type: Public charity
Purpose: Scholarships to high school seniors who attend Baltimore City, Baltimore County or Carroll County, MD public high schools pursuing higher education at a four year institution in the Mid-Atlantic region.
Financial data: Year ended 12/31/2011. Assets, $1,056,702 (M); Expenditures, $1,107,399; Total giving, $938,928; Grants to individuals, totaling $50,000.
Fields of interest: Higher education.
Type of support: Scholarships—to individuals; Support to graduates or students of specific schools.
Application information: Applications accepted. Application form required.
  Additional information: Contact the foundation for additional application guidelines.
Program description:
  Baltimore Ravens Scholarship Program: Five $5,000 scholarship enable local youth to continue their education on a collegiate level. This renewable scholarship is based on financial need and

academic achievement. Applicants must be U.S. citizens or permanent residents.
EIN: 521987065

3921
Resource Connections of Prince George's County, Inc.
4550 Forbes Blvd., Ste. 120
Lanham, MD 20706-6305 (301) 429-9300
Contact: Joyce Sims, Exec. Dir.
FAX: (301) 429-9257; E-mail: brodgers@rcpgc.org;
E-mail for Joyce Sims : jsims@resconnect.org, Tel. No.: (240)-898-9303; URL: http://www.rcpgc.org

Foundation type: Public charity
Purpose: Assistance to residents of Prince George County, MD with intellectual and developmental disabilities.
Financial data: Year ended 06/30/2012. Assets, $1,282,909 (M); Expenditures, $3,473,460; Total giving, $31,526; Grants to individuals, totaling $31,526.
Fields of interest: Disabilities, people with.
Type of support: Awards/prizes.
Application information: Applications accepted. Interview required.
  Additional information: Applicants must be referred by the Southern Maryland Regional Office (SMRO) of DDA.
EIN: 043758711

3922
Ellen Marie Roche Memorial Fund, Inc.
11620 Reisterstown Rd., Ste 930
Reisterstown, MD 21136-3301 (410) 833-2323
Contact: Bernard J. Roche, Jr., Pres.

Foundation type: Independent foundation
Purpose: Scholarships to individuals pursuing degrees in biology, animal sciences, medicine or veterinary medicine.
Financial data: Year ended 06/30/2013. Assets, $0 (M); Expenditures, $51,240; Total giving, $49,000.
Fields of interest: Medical school/education; Animals/wildlife; Biology/life sciences.
Type of support: Scholarships—to individuals.
Application information: Applications accepted.
  Additional information: Application should include college and curriculum information.
EIN: 522337355

3923
Joseph Sacco Scholarship Fund
(formerly SIU Scholarship Foundation and Trust)
5201 Auth Way
Camp Springs, MD 20746-4211
Contact: David Heindel, Tr.

Foundation type: Operating foundation
Purpose: Scholarships to children of SIU employees for attendance at an accredited college or university and at a school that offers academic degrees.
Financial data: Year ended 12/31/2012. Assets, $133,339 (M); Expenditures, $10,263; Total giving, $10,250.
Fields of interest: Higher education.
Type of support: Scholarships—to individuals.
Application information: Application form required.
  Deadline(s): Apr. 15
  Applicants should submit the following:
    1) Photograph
    2) Transcripts
    3) SAT

4) ACT
Additional information: Application should also include reference letters, autobiographical statement, and birth certificate.
EIN: 521642751

3924
Salisbury Neighborhood Housing Service, Inc.
(also known as S.N.H.S.)
540 Riverside Dr, Ste. 18
Salisbury, MD 21801-5624 (410) 543-4626
Contact: Cheryl Meadows, Exec. Dir.
FAX: (410) 543-9204;
E-mail: cherylm@salisburynhs.org; URL: http://www.salisburynhs.org

Foundation type: Public charity
Purpose: Grants for home repairs generally related to health and safety factors to Salisbury, MD, residents with a total household income below 80% of the Area Median Income.
Financial data: Year ended 06/30/2012. Assets, $3,894,048 (M); Expenditures, $491,686.
Fields of interest: Housing/shelter, repairs.
Type of support: Grants for special needs.
Application information: Applications accepted.
Additional information: Contact foundation for eligibility requirements.
EIN: 521859345

3925
Salisbury Wicomico Arts Council
104-A Poplar Hill Ave.
P.O. Box 884
Salisbury, MD 21803-0884 (410) 543-2787
Contact: Therese Hamilton, Exec. Dir.
E-mail: arts4shore@yahoo.com; URL: http://www.543arts.org/

Foundation type: Public charity
Purpose: Scholarships to young artists form Wicomico county, MD, who are pursuing academic careers in the arts.
Financial data: Year ended 06/30/2013. Assets, $364,560 (M); Expenditures, $154,833; Total giving, $20,794. Scholarships—to individuals amount not specified.
Fields of interest: Media/communications; Visual arts; Theater (playwriting); Theater (musical).
Type of support: Scholarships—to individuals.
Application information: Applications accepted. Application form required. Application form available on the grantmaker's web site. Interview required.
Send request by: Mail or hand deliver
Deadline(s): Mar. 10
Final notification: Applicants notified late Apr.
Applicants should submit the following:
1) Transcripts
2) Letter(s) of recommendation
Additional information: Scholarships are awarded on the basis of artistic merit and artistic potential. See web site for additional guidelines.
Program descriptions:
Herbert D. Brent Arts Scholarship: Scholarships are for high school seniors or full time college students who reside in Wicomico county or attend college in Wicomico county or be a legal resident of Wicomico county who is attending college elsewhere. Applicant must be or will be a full-time college student enrolled in formal academic study leading to a certificate or degree in the visual, performing, playwright, media or communication arts (minor or major)

Paul S. Hyde Arts Scholarship: This scholarship is for high school seniors or full time college students, who reside in Wicomico county or attend college in Wicomico county or be a legal resident of Wicomico county who is attending college elsewhere. Applicant must be or will be a full time college student enrolled in a formal academic study leading to a certificate or degree in the playwright or performing arts, and be will be a graduate of a Wicomico County Public School.
EIN: 237006845

3926
Jerold J. & Margaret M. Samet Foundation
1000 Parrs Ridge Dr.
Spencerville, MD 20868-9743 (301) 989-1511
Contact: Jerold J. Samet, Pres.

Foundation type: Independent foundation
Purpose: Scholarships to individuals who demonstrate commitment to freemasonry and DeMolay & Youth Leaders International.
Financial data: Year ended 12/31/2011. Assets, $847,016 (M); Expenditures, $611,943; Total giving, $125,167.
Fields of interest: Higher education; Spirituality; Fraternal societies.
Type of support: Scholarships—to individuals.
Application information: Applications accepted.
Deadline(s): None
Additional information: Application by letter accepted throughout the year.
EIN: 522128751

3927
Lillie Murray Sawyer Teacher Scholarship Trust Fund
8601 Manchester Rd., Ste. 312
Silver Spring, MD 20901 (301) 587-8175
Contact: Plugenia Smith Robinson, Pres.

Foundation type: Independent foundation
Purpose: Scholarships to high school seniors residing in DC, who intend to become teachers.
Financial data: Year ended 12/31/2012. Assets, $457,792 (M); Expenditures, $14,714; Total giving, $10,646; Grants to individuals, 3 grants totaling $10,646 (high: $4,323, low: $2,000).
Fields of interest: Teacher school/education.
Type of support: Scholarships—to individuals.
Application information: Applications accepted. Application form required.
Deadline(s): July 1
EIN: 521794412

3928
School Nutrition Foundation
(formerly Child Nutrition Foundation)
120 Waterfront St., Ste. 300
Oxon Hill, MD 20745-1142 (301) 686-3100
E-mail: snf@schoolnutrition.org; E-Mail for Julie Abrera: jabrera@schoolnutrition.org; URL: http://www.schoolnutrition.org/foundation.aspx?id=252

Foundation type: Public charity
Purpose: Scholarships to School Nutrition Association (SNA) members or their dependents for education related to food services.
Publications: Application guidelines; Annual report; Informational brochure.
Financial data: Year ended 07/31/2011. Assets, $5,437,726 (M); Expenditures, $1,568,791; Total giving, $103,888; Grants to individuals, totaling $103,888.
Fields of interest: Nutrition.

Type of support: Program development; Conferences/seminars; Research; Scholarships—to individuals; Foreign applicants; Awards/prizes; Precollege support; Undergraduate support; Travel grants.
Application information: Applications accepted. Application form required.
Initial approach: Telephone
Copies of proposal: 5
Deadline(s): Apr. 15
Applicants should submit the following:
1) Essay
2) Transcripts
3) Letter(s) of recommendation
Program descriptions:
GED Jump Start Scholarship: Awards $200 to eligible individuals with funds to pay for GED classes, GED study materials, and the GED test fee. To qualify for the scholarship the applicant must be a School Nutrition Association member, not currently have a high school diploma or a GED diploma, and plan on earning a GED within one year of receiving the scholarship.
Kathleen Stitt Award: Awards $500 to selected graduate students enrolled full-time in a M.S. or Ph.D. program at an accredited college or university, or to faculty members employed at an accredited college or university.
Nancy Curry Scholarship: One $500 scholarship is available to American School Food Service Association (ASFSA) members employed in school foodservice who undertake undergraduate or graduate study at a vocational/technical institution, community college or university. Children of active ASFSA members who pursue a school foodservice related field of study are also eligible.
Schwan's Food Service Scholarship: Awards scholarships of up to $2,500 to American School Food Service Association (ASFSA) members who pursue formal education in a school foodservice-related field and express a desire to make foodservice a career. Children of active ASFSA members who pursue a school foodservice-related field of study are also eligible.
SNF Professional Growth Scholarship: Awards scholarships of up to $2,500 to qualified American School Food Service Association (ASFSA) members who meet the criteria for the Schwan's Food Service Scholarship and who have also successfully completed at least one course toward a master's degree.
Winston Industries Build Your Future Scholarship: Winston Industries contributes funds to the foundation to provide scholarships of up to $2,500 for school nutrition professionals and their children.
Winston/ANC Scholarship: Awards 50 $500 scholarships to employee-level and manager-level School Nutrition Association (SNA) members who are nominated by a district director for them to attend the foundation's annual national conference in Los Angeles.
EIN: 846039412

3929
Seabee Memorial Scholarship Association
P.O. Box 6574
Silver Spring, MD 20916-6574 (301) 570-2850
Contact: Joseph Leahy, Exec. Dir.
FAX: (301) 570-2873; E-mail: smsa@erols.com; URL: http://www.seabee.org

Foundation type: Public charity
Purpose: Scholarships to deserving children and grandchildren of the men and women who have served or are now serving the Naval Construction Force, also known as Seabees, or the Naval Civil

Engineer Corps. Scholarships are for four-year bachelor's degree programs only.

Publications: Grants list; Informational brochure; Newsletter.

Financial data: Year ended 12/31/2011. Assets, $3,800,616 (M); Expenditures, $627,819; Total giving, $151,051; Grants to individuals, totaling $151,051.

Type of support: Undergraduate support.

Application information: Application form required. Application form available on the grantmaker's web site.

> *Deadline(s):* Apr. 15
> *Applicants should submit the following:*
> 1) Essay
> 2) Transcripts
> 3) SAR
> *Additional information:* Application must also include proof of service, list of extracurricular activities and work experience.

EIN: 520910325

3930
Shepherd's Staff, Inc.

30 Carroll St.
P.O. Box 127
Westminster, MD 21157-4831 (410) 857-5944
Contact: Brenda Meadows, Exec. Dir.
FAX: (410) 857-6122;
E-mail: shepstaff@comcast.net; URL: http://www.shepstaff.org

Foundation type: Public charity

Purpose: Assistance to low income individuals of Carroll county, MD with housing, food, clothing, medical expenses, utilities and transportation.

Publications: Newsletter.

Financial data: Year ended 12/31/2011. Assets, $148,490 (M); Expenditures, $275,945; Total giving, $140,202; Grants to individuals, totaling $140,202.

Fields of interest: Human services; Economically disadvantaged.

Type of support: Grants for special needs.

Application information: Applications accepted.

> *Additional information:* Contact the foundation for eligibility determination.

EIN: 521710096

3931
Shore Up!, Inc.

520 Snow Hill Rd.
Salisbury, MD 21804-6031 (410) 749-1142
Contact: Freddy L. Mitchell, Exec. Dir.
FAX: (410) 742-9191; E-mail: agency@shoreup.org;
TDD: (410) 860-8800; URL: http://www.shoreup.org

Foundation type: Public charity

Purpose: Grants to individuals and families in Somerset, Wicomico, and Worcester counties, MD, who require assistance because of age, disability, or economic conditions.

Publications: Annual report.

Financial data: Year ended 06/30/2011. Assets, $7,299,929 (M); Expenditures, $21,890,005; Total giving, $4,253,226; Grants to individuals, totaling $4,253,226.

Fields of interest: Economically disadvantaged.

Type of support: Grants for special needs.

Application information: Contact foundation for complete eligibility requirements.

EIN: 520886996

3932
The Sioda Family Foundation Inc

7330 Apple Dr.
Boonsboro, MD 21713-2200 (301) 790-2800
Contact: Leon Brumback

Foundation type: Operating foundation

Purpose: Scholarships primarily to residents of Washington County, MD; Franklin County, PA; and Berkeley and Jefferson counties, WV.

Financial data: Year ended 12/31/2012. Assets, $40,008 (M); Expenditures, $37,671; Total giving, $36,190; Grants to individuals, 5 grants totaling $36,190 (high: $14,737, low: $250).

Type of support: Undergraduate support.

Application information: Applications not accepted.

> *Additional information:* Unsolicited requests for funds not considered or acknowledged.

EIN: 204004369

3933
Sisters Together and Reaching, Inc.

1505 Eutaw Pl.
Baltimore, MD 21217-3641 (410) 383-1903
FAX: (123) 456-5679;
E-mail: info@sisterstogetherandreaching.org;
URL: http://www.sisterstogetherandreaching.org

Foundation type: Public charity

Purpose: Financial assistance for rent, utilities, food, transportation, and pharmacy bills to needy HIV-positive individuals.

Financial data: Year ended 03/31/2012. Assets, $53,330 (M); Expenditures, $589,501.

Fields of interest: AIDS; Terminal illness, people with.

Type of support: Grants for special needs.

Application information: Applications accepted.

> *Initial approach:* Letter
> *Additional information:* Application must include picture ID and proof of HIV status. Contact foundation for complete eligibility requirements.

EIN: 521772563

3934
The Skaters Education & Training Fund, Inc.

8504 Southfields Cir.
Lutherville, MD 21093-3979
URL: http://skaterseducationandtrainintfund.org/

Foundation type: Independent foundation

Purpose: Scholarships to competitive skaters residing in the Baltimore-Towson, MD metropolitan area.

Financial data: Year ended 12/31/2011. Assets, $232,094 (M); Expenditures, $1,000; Total giving, $1,000; Grant to an individual, 1 grant totaling $1,000.

Fields of interest: Athletics/sports, training.

Type of support: Undergraduate support.

Application information: Applications not accepted.

> *Additional information:* Unsolicited requests for funds not considered.

EIN: 521750624

3935
Sodexo Foundation, Inc.

(formerly Sodexho Foundation, Inc.)
9801 Washingtonian Blvd.
Gaithersburg, MD 20878-5355 (301) 987-4902
Application email: info@applyists.com, tel.: (615) 320-3149
E-mail: stophunger@sodexofoundation.org;
URL: http://www.stop-hunger.org

Foundation type: Public charity

Purpose: Scholarships to students in kindergarten through graduate school who have made a significant impact in the fight against hunger and its root causes in the U.S.

Publications: Application guidelines.

Financial data: Year ended 12/31/2011. Assets, $882,784 (M); Expenditures, $2,241,796; Total giving, $2,214,302. Scholarships—to individuals amount not specified.

Fields of interest: Higher education; Education.

Type of support: Undergraduate support.

Application information: Applications accepted. Application form required.

> *Initial approach:* Letter
> *Deadline(s):* Dec. 5
> *Additional information:* See web site for additional application guidelines.

Program description:

> *Stephen J. Brady STOP Hunger Scholarship:* The program honors students working to build awareness and mobilize youth as catalysts for innovative solutions to ending hunger in U.S. communities in their lifetime. To be eligible, students must be enrolled in an accredited education institution in the United States and be able to demonstrate an ongoing commitment to hunger-alleviation activities in their community. Up to five students will be selected as national winners, with each receiving a $5,000 scholarship and a $5,000 grant for their anti-hunger charity of choice. The Foundation also will recognize twenty regional honorees with a $1,000 donation for their preferred hunger charity.

EIN: 311652380

3936
Southern Prince George's County Community Charities

P.O. Box 44762
Fort Washington, MD 20749 (202) 497-9465
Contact: Cherise Cole, Exec. Dir.

Foundation type: Public charity

Purpose: Scholarships primarily to residents of Prince George's County, MD, with financial need.

Financial data: Year ended 12/31/2011. Assets, $39,321 (M); Expenditures, $17,291; Total giving, $13,106.

Type of support: Undergraduate support.

Application information:

> *Initial approach:* Letter
> *Additional information:* Contact foundation for current application deadline/guidelines.

EIN: 522228330

3937
The Steeplechase Fund

400 Fair Hill Dr.
Elkton, MD 21921
Contact: Peter McGivney, Exec. Dir.
URL: http://www.nationalsteeplechase.com/fund.html

Foundation type: Independent foundation

Purpose: Financial assistance and medical expenses to former steeplechase jockeys and their widows and families.
Financial data: Year ended 12/31/2012. Assets, $602,957 (M); Expenditures, $39,012; Total giving, $14,634; Grants to individuals, 10 grants totaling $14,634 (high: $4,200, low: $50).
Fields of interest: Athletics/sports, equestrianism; Women.
Type of support: Grants for special needs.
Application information:
  Initial approach: Letter
  Additional information: Application must include medical bills and information about the applicant's disability.
EIN: 136067724

3938
Stepping Stones Shelter, Inc.
P.O. Box 712
Rockville, MD   20848-0712   (301) 251-0567
Contact: Denise Fredericks, Exec. Dir.
FAX: (301) 762-0040;
E-mail: info@steppingstonesshelter.org; E-mail For Denise Fredericks:
Denise@SteppingStonesShelter.org; URL: http://www.steppingstonesshelter.org

Foundation type: Public charity
Purpose: Grants for basic necessities to homeless individuals and families in the Montgomery County, MD, area.
Financial data: Year ended 06/30/2012. Assets, $709,511 (M); Expenditures, $667,747.
Fields of interest: Economically disadvantaged.
Type of support: Grants for special needs.
Application information: Contact foundation for complete eligibility information.
EIN: 521281647

3939
Sudden Infant Death Syndrome Alliance, Inc.
1314 Bedford Ave., Ste. 210
Baltimore, MD   21208-6605   (410) 653-8226
E-mail: info@firstcandle.org; Toll-free tel.: (800) 221-7437; URL: http://www.firstcandle.org

Foundation type: Public charity
Purpose: Research funds to individuals conducting studies related to Sudden Infant Death Syndrome.
Publications: Annual report; Financial statement; Newsletter.
Financial data: Year ended 06/30/2011. Assets, $2,064,801 (M); Expenditures, $2,712,772; Total giving, $362,690.
Fields of interest: SIDS (Sudden Infant Death Syndrome); SIDS (Sudden Infant Death Syndrome) research.
Type of support: Research.
Application information: Contact foundation for eligibility requirements.
EIN: 521591162

3940
Louis C. Talarico Scholarship Fund
c/o Evelyn T. Bolduc
8820 Columbia 100 Pkwy., Ste. 400
Columbia, MD   21045-2163

Foundation type: Independent foundation
Purpose: Scholarships to current employees or dependent children of current employees of the Lewiston, ME fire department accepted or currently enrolled in an accredited postsecondary institution.

Financial data: Year ended 12/31/2012. Assets, $2,519 (M); Expenditures, $9,524; Total giving, $9,500.
Fields of interest: Higher education.
Type of support: Scholarships—to individuals.
Application information: Applications accepted. Application form required.
  Deadline(s): Apr. 30
  Additional information: Employee must be employed for at least one year.
EIN: 010472527

3941
Columbus W. Thorn, Jr. Foundation
109 E. Main St.
Elkton, MD   21921   (410) 398-0611
Contact: Doris P. Scott, Tr.; Charles L. Scott, Tr.

Foundation type: Independent foundation
Purpose: Educational loans to worthy and needy high school graduates of Cecil County, MD.
Publications: Application guidelines.
Financial data: Year ended 12/31/2012. Assets, $18,739,153 (M); Expenditures, $927,151; Total giving, $774,950; Loans to individuals, 138 loans totaling $774,950.
Fields of interest: Higher education; Scholarships/financial aid.
Type of support: Student loans—to individuals; Undergraduate support; Postgraduate support.
Application information: Applications accepted. Application form required.
  Initial approach: Telephone
  Send request by: Mail or hand deliver
  Deadline(s): None
Program description:
  Loan Program: Repayment of the loan is required within four years after completion or discontinuation of student's advanced education. Repayment is guaranteed by student's parents. Interest rate on the loan is five percent from graduation or discontinuation of study.
EIN: 237153983

3942
Robert E. Torray and Anne P. Torray Family Foundation
7501 Wisconsin Ave., Ste. 1100
Bethesda, MD   20814-6523   (301) 493-4600
Contact: William Lane

Foundation type: Independent foundation
Purpose: Need-based scholarships to individuals for educational advancement.
Financial data: Year ended 05/31/2012. Assets, $19,305 (M); Expenditures, $49,550; Total giving, $47,064; Grants to individuals, 4 grants totaling $47,064 (high: $21,664, low: $2,000).
Fields of interest: Higher education.
Type of support: Scholarships—to individuals.
Application information: Applications accepted.
  Deadline(s): None
EIN: 526930570

3943
Florence B. Trueman Educational Trust
401 Fairleigh Ct.
Tracys Landing, MD   20779-2405   (410) 741-5602
Contact: J. Scott Whitney, Tr.
E-mail: JScottWhitney@aol.com

Foundation type: Independent foundation

Purpose: College scholarships to students who attended public high schools in Calvert County, MD.
Financial data: Year ended 06/30/2012. Assets, $720,435 (M); Expenditures, $62,191; Total giving, $33,850; Grants to individuals, 30 grants totaling $33,850 (high: $1,500, low: $1,000).
Fields of interest: Higher education.
Type of support: Scholarships—to individuals.
Application information: Applications accepted. Application form required.
  Initial approach: Letter
  Deadline(s): None
  Applicants should submit the following:
    1) Class rank
    2) Transcripts
    3) SAR
    4) SAT
    5) Letter(s) of recommendation
    6) GPA
    7) Financial information
    8) Essay
EIN: 521649301

3944
Theresa F. Truschel Charitable Foundation Inc.
P.O. Box 19142
Baltimore, MD   21284-9142   (410) 494-4490
FAX: (410) 494-4492;
E-mail: theresaftruschel@gmail.com; URL: http://theresaftruschel.googlepages.com

Foundation type: Independent foundation
Purpose: Academic grants to students of all levels attending Catholic schools in MD and DC.
Financial data: Year ended 12/31/2011. Assets, $878,371 (M); Expenditures, $126,784; Total giving, $74,778.
Fields of interest: Catholic agencies & churches.
Type of support: Scholarships—to individuals.
Application information: Applications accepted. Application form required.
  Initial approach: Letter
  Deadline(s): Apr. 30
  Final notification: Recipients notified in June
EIN: 207279912

3945
The Trustees of McDonough Charity School
P.O. Box 607
La Plata, MD   20646-0607   (301) 753-1510

Foundation type: Independent foundation
Purpose: Scholarships to residents of the McDonough Charity School District in Charles County, MD.
Financial data: Year ended 01/31/2013. Assets, $1,061,255 (M); Expenditures, $57,526; Total giving, $46,000; Grants to individuals, 20 grants totaling $46,000 (high: $4,000, low: $1,000).
Type of support: Support to graduates or students of specific schools; Undergraduate support.
Application information: Applications accepted. Application form required.
  Deadline(s): None
  Additional information: Applications should include letters of recommendation; applications available from district schools.
EIN: 526048878

3946
The U.S. Silica Company Education Foundation
8490 Progress Dr., Ste. 300
Frederick, MD 21701 (800) 243-7500
Contact: Richard A. Johnson, V.P. and Treas.

Foundation type: Company-sponsored foundation
Purpose: Scholarships of $4,000 each to individuals for course of study which leads to either a four year degree or two year vocational program.
Financial data: Year ended 12/31/2012. Assets, $42,002 (M); Expenditures, $26,000; Total giving, $26,000; Grants to individuals, 5 grants totaling $26,000 (high: $6,000, low: $4,000).
Fields of interest: Higher education.
Type of support: Undergraduate support.
Application information: Applications accepted. Application form required.
Deadline(s): Beginning of year
Applicants should submit the following:
1) SAT
2) ACT
EIN: 550760222

3947
The Ulman Cancer Fund for Young Adults
6310 Stevens Forest Rd., Ste. 210
Columbia, MD 21046-1036 (410) 964-0202
Contact: Brock Yesto, Pres. and C.E.O.
Application address: Ulman Cancer Fund for Young Adults, Attn: Scholarship, 921 East Fort Ave., Ste. 325, Baltimore, MD 21230-5149
E-mail: info@ulmanfund.org; Additional address (Baltimore address): 921 E. Fort Ave., Ste. 325, Baltimore, MD 21230-5149; toll-free tel.: (888) 393-3863; E-mail for Brock Yesto: brock@ulmanfund.org; URL: http://www.ulmanfund.org

Foundation type: Public charity
Purpose: Scholarships for college students in the Mid-Atlantic region whose life has been impacted by cancer.
Publications: Application guidelines.
Financial data: Year ended 12/31/2011. Assets, $488,796 (M); Expenditures, $1,054,046; Total giving, $49,750; Grants to individuals, totaling $49,750.
Fields of interest: Higher education; Cancer; Young adults.
Type of support: Scholarships—to individuals.
Application information: Applications accepted. Application form required.
Initial approach: Application
Send request by: Mail
Deadline(s): Mar. 30
Program descriptions:
Marilyn Yetso Memorial Scholarship Award: This award was established to support the financial needs of young adults who have lost a parent or guardian to cancer, or currently have a parent or guardian with cancer, and who are seeking higher education. Eligible applicants must: be either a permanent resident of Maryland, Virginia, or Washington DC, or be attending (or plan to attend) an educational institution as a degree-seeking student in Maryland, Virginia, or Washington DC; be no older than 35 at the time of application; have had (or currently have) a parent who has been diagnosed with cancer when the applicant was between the ages of 15 and 35; exhibit financial need; and demonstrate leadership abilities and commitment to their community.
Satola Family Scholarship Award at the University of Virginia: This scholarship is available to current students of the University of Virginia whose life has

been affected by cancer. Eligible applicants must be a young adult cancer survivor or patient diagnosed between the ages of 15 and 39, or a young adult who has either lost a parent, guardian, or sibling to cancer or who has a parent, guardian, or sibling who has been diagnosed with cancer. Applicants must also be U.S. citizens, be 39 years of age or younger at the time of application, exhibit financial need, and demonstrate leadership abilities and commitment to their community.
Sean Silver Memorial Scholarship: This award supports the financial needs of young adults currently undergoing active treatment for cancer and seeking to obtain a degree in higher education. Eligible applicants must be 30 years of age or young at the time of application, be a U.S. citizen or permanent resident, be currently attending (or be accepted to) a four-year college or university in the U.S., and exhibit financial need.
Vera Yip Memorial Scholarship Award: This award is available to individuals who have been diagnosed with cancer, or who have had a parent or guardian diagnosed with cancer, and who seek higher education. Eligible applicants must: be a permanent resident of Maryland, Virginia, or Washington D.C., or attending (or plan to attend) an educational institution in Maryland, Virginia, or Washington D.C.; be no older than 35 years old at the time of application; demonstrate financial need; and be actively involved in their community with demonstrated leadership abilities.
EIN: 522057636

3948
United Communities Against Poverty, Inc.
1400 Doewood Ln.
P.O. Box 31356
Capitol Heights, MD 20731-0356 (301) 322-5700
Contact: Gwendolyn Ferguson, Pres. and C.E.O.
FAX: (301) 322-3381; E-mail: mail@ucappgc.org; E-mail for Gwendolyn Ferguson: gferguson@ucappgc.org; URL: http://www.ucappgc.org

Foundation type: Public charity
Purpose: Emergency and financial assistance to low-income residents of Prince George's county, MD, with housing, food, utilities and other special needs.
Publications: Annual report.
Financial data: Year ended 06/30/2011. Assets, $713,237 (M); Expenditures, $3,848,470; Total giving, $494,190; Grants to individuals, totaling $494,190.
Fields of interest: Economically disadvantaged.
Type of support: Grants for special needs.
Application information: Contact the agency for eligibility determination.
EIN: 520822919

3949
United Way of Frederick County, Inc.
22 S. Market St., Ste. 5
Frederick, MD 21701-5572 (301) 663-4231
Contact: Joshua B. Pedersen, C.E.O.
Mailing address: P.O. Box 307, Frederick, MD 21705-0307
FAX: (301) 663-1855;
E-mail: info@unitedwayfrederick.org; Mailing Address : P.O. Box 307, Frederick, MD 21705-0307E-Mail for Joshua B. Pedersen : joshpedersen@unitedwayfrederick.org;
URL: http://www.unitedwayfrederick.org

Foundation type: Public charity

Purpose: Grants for basic necessities to needy residents of Frederick County, MD.
Publications: Annual report; Financial statement; Informational brochure; Newsletter.
Financial data: Year ended 06/30/2011. Assets, $1,653,287 (M); Expenditures, $1,012,125; Total giving, $563,118.
Fields of interest: Economically disadvantaged.
Type of support: Grants for special needs.
Application information:
Initial approach: Letter
Deadline(s): None
Additional information: Contact foundation for complete eligibility requirements.
EIN: 520607973

3950
Izaak Walton League of America - Rockville Chapter
18301 Waring Sta. Rd.
P.O. Box 2255
Germantown, MD 20875-2255 (301) 972-1645
Contact: Lee Hays, Pres.
Application address: c/o A.L. Hays, 18 Morning Light Ct., Gaithersburg, MD 20878-2093, tel.: (301) 977-3951
FAX: (301) 972-1645; URL: http://www.iwla-rockville.com/

Foundation type: Public charity
Purpose: College scholarships to graduating seniors of Montgomery county, MD majoring in areas of conservation or environmental sciences.
Publications: Newsletter.
Financial data: Year ended 12/31/2011. Assets, $430,590 (M); Expenditures, $114,873; Total giving, $7,500; Grants to individuals, totaling $7,500.
Fields of interest: Higher education; Natural resources; Environment, forests.
Type of support: Scholarships—to individuals.
Application information: Applications accepted. Application form required.
Deadline(s): Apr. 15
Applicants should submit the following:
1) Class rank
2) Transcripts
3) GPA
4) Letter(s) of recommendation
5) Essay
Additional information: Application should also include four personal references.
EIN: 521481039

3951
Anna Emory Warfield Memorial Fund, Inc.
P.O. Box 674
Riderwood, MD 21139-0674 (410) 453-0345
Contact: Louis Hargrave, Pres.

Foundation type: Independent foundation
Purpose: Relief assistance to aged and dependent women in the Baltimore, MD, area.
Publications: Application guidelines.
Financial data: Year ended 12/31/2012. Assets, $5,130,794 (M); Expenditures, $319,806; Total giving, $237,000; Grants to individuals, 30 grants totaling $237,000 (high: $194,400, low: $17,400).
Fields of interest: Aging; Women; Economically disadvantaged.
Type of support: Grants for special needs.
Application information: Applications accepted.
Initial approach: Letter
Deadline(s): None

Additional information: Application should include personal and financial information.
EIN: 520785672

3952
Womens Board of Montgomery General Hospital
18101 Prince Philip Dr.
Olney, MD   20832-1514   (301) 774-8840
Contact: for Scholarship: Casey Poole
Scholarship tel.: (301) 570-7210,
e-mail: womensboard@montgomerygeneral.com
E-mail: womensboard@medstarmontgomery.org;
URL: http://www.montgomerygeneral.org/
body.cfm?id=126

Foundation type: Public charity
Purpose: Scholarships to individuals from MD pursuing an education in a nursing or allied health field.
Publications: Application guidelines.
Financial data: Year ended 06/30/2011. Assets, $175,185 (M); Expenditures, $128,491; Total giving, $70,009; Grants to individuals, totaling $70,009.
Fields of interest: Nursing school/education; Health sciences school/education.
Type of support: Scholarships—to individuals.
Application information: Applications accepted. Application form required. Application form available on the grantmaker's web site.
   Send request by: Mail or on-line
   Deadline(s): Mar. 15
   Final notification: Applicants notified by May 13
   Applicants should submit the following:

1) ACT
2) SAT
3) Transcripts
4) Letter(s) of recommendation
Additional information: Selection is based on financial need, and academic achievement. Payment of scholarship is made to the educational institution on behalf of the student.
EIN: 526039600

3953
Worcester County Arts Council
6 Jefferson St.
Berlin, MD   21811-1425   (410) 641-0809
Contact: Anna Mullis, Exec. Dir.
FAX: (410) 641-3947;
E-mail: curator@worcestercountyartscouncil.org;
URL: http://www.worcestercountyartscouncil.org

Foundation type: Public charity
Purpose: Scholarships to graduating high school seniors who are residents of Worcester County, MD, and who will major in the visual, performing, music or media arts.
Publications: Application guidelines.
Financial data: Year ended 06/30/2012. Assets, $160,153 (M); Expenditures, $125,884; Total giving, $38,850; Grants to individuals, totaling $8,000.
Fields of interest: Arts.
Type of support: Undergraduate support.
Application information: Applications accepted. Application form required. Application form available on the grantmaker's web site.

Initial approach: Letter
Send request by: Mail
Deadline(s): Apr. 1
Final notification: Applicants notified in early May
Applicants should submit the following:
   1) Letter(s) of recommendation
   2) Work samples
Additional information: Contact foundation for eligibility criteria.
EIN: 521083071

3954
Yvorra Leadership Development, Inc.
P.O. Box 408
Port Republic, MD   20676-0408   (410)586-3047
Contact: Michael Hildebrand
Application address: 2446 Azalea Ln., Port Republic, MD 20676-2605

Foundation type: Operating foundation
Purpose: Scholarships for leadership development to individuals with professional or volunteer backgrounds in fire and emergency services.
Financial data: Year ended 06/30/2012. Assets, $132,097 (M); Expenditures, $13,029; Total giving, $7,500; Grants to individuals, 3 grants totaling $7,500 (high: $2,500, low: $2,500).
Fields of interest: Leadership development.
Type of support: Scholarships—to individuals.
Application information: Applications accepted.
   Initial approach: Letter
   Deadline(s): Aug. 15
   Additional information: Application should include letters of recommendation.
EIN: 521560287

MASSACHUSETTS

3955
47 Palmer, Inc.
26 Church St., Ste. 300
Cambridge, MA 02138-3708 (617) 492-5300
Contact: Dan Hogan, Exec. Dir.
Scholarship e-mail: jon@passim.org
E-mail: info@passim.org; URL: http://
www.clubpassim.org

Foundation type: Public charity
Purpose: Music school scholarships to deserving
individuals in the Cambridge, MA area, who
demonstrate a dedication to the class and music
and who are unable to afford the financial burden
of the class.
Publications: Informational brochure; Newsletter.
Financial data: Year ended 12/31/2012. Assets,
$232,364 (M); Expenditures, $1,228,622; Total
giving, $41,574; Grants to individuals, totaling
$41,574.
Fields of interest: Music; Economically
disadvantaged.
Type of support: Scholarships—to individuals.
Application information: Applications accepted.
Application form required.
  Initial approach: E-mail
  Additional information: Students may take more
  than one course per term and no more than
  two courses per calendar year,and must
  reapply for the scholarship each term that
  they require financial assistance. See web
  site for additional information.
Program description:
  Bob and Rae Ann Donlin Scholarship Fund: This
fund provides scholarship opportunities for
members of the public who would like to enroll in
the Passim School of Music, but are unable to
afford class fees. Scholarships offer financial
assistance for instruments and voice classes and
music education workshops.
EIN: 043255365

3956
James N. Abbott, Jr. Trust
c/o Michael Sanborn
P.O. Box 330
Gloucester, MA 01930 (978) 283-7079
Contact: Rosa Keenan
Application address: c/o Casb Trust Dept., 109
Main St., Gloucester, MA 01930, tel.:(978)
283-7079

Foundation type: Independent foundation
Purpose: Scholarships to residents of Gloucester,
Essex, and Rockport, MA, who have graduated from
Gloucester High School, MA, or Rockport High
School, MA, and plan to return to the area to
practice their professions after college. Applicants
must have consistent strong academic records, and
possess high moral standards.
Financial data: Year ended 12/31/2011. Assets,
$663,518 (M); Expenditures, $40,022; Total
giving, $35,000; Grants to individuals, 10 grants
totaling $35,000 (high: $3,500, low: $3,500).
Type of support: Support to graduates or students
of specific schools; Undergraduate support.
Application information: Applications accepted.
Application form required.
  Initial approach: Letter
  Deadline(s): Apr.
  Applicants should submit the following:
    1) Letter(s) of recommendation

2) Essay
3) Transcripts
Additional information: Application must also
  include letter indicating qualifications and
  proof of acceptance to an accredited school
  of higher education.
EIN: 046707573

3957
Action, Inc.
180 Main St.
Gloucester, MA 01930-6002 (978) 282-1000
FAX: (978) 283-0523;
E-mail: actioninc@actioninc.org; Additional tel.
(Spanish-language): (978) 282-1007; additional
tel. (Portuguese-language): (978) 282-1008;
URL: http://actioninc.org/

Foundation type: Public charity
Purpose: Emergency assistance to low-income
individuals and families of Gloucester, Ipswich,
Rockport, Essex, Manchester-by-the-Sea and
Hamilton/Wenham, MA.
Publications: Annual report.
Financial data: Year ended 09/30/2012. Assets,
$8,937,719 (M); Expenditures, $34,310,172.
Fields of interest: Housing/shelter; Economically
disadvantaged.
Type of support: Emergency funds; Grants for
special needs.
Application information: Contact the organization
for information on additional services.
EIN: 042389332

3958
Affordable Housing Management Training Foundation
c/o Maloney Properties, Inc.
27 Mica Ln.
Wellesley, MA 02481 (781) 237-4893
Contact: Diana J. Kelly, Pres.
E-mail: info@ahmtf.org

Foundation type: Independent foundation
Purpose: Grants to individuals who work in the
affordable housing property management industry
for tuition, seminars, conferences, classes and
other types of training in housing management and
maintenance.
Financial data: Year ended 04/30/2013. Assets,
$0 (M); Expenditures, $0; Total giving, $0.
Fields of interest: Management/technical
assistance; Housing/shelter, repairs.
Type of support: Conferences/seminars;
Scholarships—to individuals; Graduate support;
Technical education support; Precollege support;
Undergraduate support.
Application information: Applications accepted.
Application form required. Application form
available on the grantmaker's web site.
  Initial approach: Telephone
  Send request by: Mail or fax
  Additional information: Application should
    include documentation showing the cost of
    the training and a resume.
EIN: 043528460

3959
John J. Ahern Scholarship Inc.
P.O. Box 393
Foxborough, MA 02035 (508) 543-0100
Contact: Francis J. Spillane, Pres. and Dir.

Foundation type: Independent foundation

Purpose: College scholarships to graduating high
school seniors of Foxborough, MA pursuing higher
education.
Financial data: Year ended 12/31/2012. Assets,
$299,857 (M); Expenditures, $16,054; Total
giving, $16,000; Grants to individuals, 4 grants
totaling $16,000 (high: $4,000, low: $4,000).
Fields of interest: Higher education.
Type of support: Scholarships—to individuals.
Application information: Applications accepted.
Application form required.
  Deadline(s): Apr. 1
  Applicants should submit the following:
    1) Class rank
    2) Financial information
    3) Essay
  Additional information: Selection is based on
    academic achievement, financial need,
    extracurricular activities and community
    service.
EIN: 870790992

3960
Aid for Cancer Research
P.O. Box 376
Newton Centre, MA 02459-0004 (617)
782-0500
Contact: Susan Kohen, Recording Secy.
E-mail: info@aidforcancerresearch.org; URL: http://
www.aidforcancerresearch.org

Foundation type: Public charity
Purpose: Fellowships to qualified individuals in the
field of cancer research in the greater Boston, MA
area.
Publications: Application guidelines.
Financial data: Year ended 07/31/2012. Assets,
$383,494 (M); Expenditures, $158,868; Total
giving, $63,000.
Fields of interest: Cancer research.
Type of support: Fellowships.
Application information: Applications accepted.
  Deadline(s): Oct. 15
  Final notification: Applicants notified Jan. 31
Program description:
  Fellowships: Fellowship opportunities support
qualified individuals in the field of cancer research.
Fellowships are for two years, with stipends of
$37,500 for the first year and $40,000 for the
second. Eligible applicants must be U.S. citizens or
legal residents of the U.S., and have an M.D. and/
or Ph.D. degree. Research must be done in
Massachusetts.
EIN: 046049863

3961
The AIDS Action Committee of Massachusetts, Inc.
75 Amory St.
Boston, MA 02119-1051 (617) 437-6200
Contact: Rebecca Haag, Pres. and C.E.O.
FAX: (617) 437-6445; E-mail: info@aac.org;
URL: http://www.aac.org

Foundation type: Public charity
Purpose: Emergency financial assistance to people
affected with AIDS and HIV in the Boston, MA area.
Financial data: Year ended 04/30/2012. Assets,
$4,398,275 (M); Expenditures, $13,594,735;
Total giving, $771,257; Grants to individuals,
totaling $759,824.
Fields of interest: AIDS, people with.
Type of support: Emergency funds; Grants for
special needs.
Application information: Applications accepted.
Interview required.

Additional information: Eligibility of recipients are determined through documents, referrals and applications.
EIN: 222707246

3962
ALS Therapy Alliance, Inc.
16 Oakland Ave.
Needham, MA 02492-3150 (603) 664-5005
Contact: Traci Bisson, Project Research Mgr.
E-mail: info@alstherapyalliance.org; E-mail for Traci Bisson: traci@alstherapyalliance.org; URL: http://alstherapyalliance.org/

Foundation type: Public charity
Purpose: Grants to researchers who are working to find a cure for amyotrophic lateral sclerosis (ALS)
Publications: Application guidelines.
Financial data: Year ended 12/31/2011. Assets, $9,613,171 (M); Expenditures, $2,078,955; Total giving, $1,495,563. Grants to individuals amount not specified.
Fields of interest: ALS research.
Type of support: Grants to individuals.
Application information: Applications accepted. Application form available on the grantmaker's web site.
> *Send request by:* E-mail
> *Deadline(s):* Feb. 15 and Sept. 15
> *Applicants should submit the following:*
> 1) Curriculum vitae
> 2) Budget Information
> *Additional information:* Applications must be limited to no more than ten pages (including application outline, abstract, background and significance, preliminary data, and experimental design). In addition, applications must include a list of references.

Program description:
Research Grants: This program provides grants to ALS researchers, and whose goals and missions align with those of the alliance. Grants ranging from $100,000 to $1 million over one to three years are awarded to projects, including but not limited to basic, clinical, and translational research and clinical trials, working toward a better understanding of and/or treatments for ALS. National and international nonprofit organizations and for-profit companies are eligible to apply.
EIN: 010621493

3963
American Antiquarian Society
185 Salisbury St.
Worcester, MA 01609-1634 (508) 755-5221
Contact: For Scholarships: Ellen S. Dunlap, Pres.
E-mail for Paul Erickson: perickson@mwa.org
FAX: (508) 753-3311;
E-mail: library@americanantiquarian.org; E-Mail for Ellen S. Dunlap: edunlap@mwa.org; URL: http://www.americanantiquarian.org

Foundation type: Public charity
Purpose: Residency fellowships of one to twelve months at the American Antiquarian Society for research and writing in American history and culture through the year 1876.
Publications: Application guidelines; Annual report; Informational brochure (including application guidelines); Newsletter.
Financial data: Year ended 08/31/2011. Assets, $63,631,455 (M); Expenditures, $5,794,328; Total giving, $321,563; Grants to individuals, totaling $319,713.
Fields of interest: Media/communications; Visual arts; Performing arts; Humanities; Literature;

Historical activities; Historic preservation/historical societies; Libraries (academic/research).
Type of support: Fellowships; Postdoctoral support; Residencies; Travel grants; Stipends.
Application information: Applications accepted. Application form required. Application form available on the grantmaker's web site.
> *Initial approach:* Letter, telephone, or e-mail
> *Send request by:* Mail
> *Copies of proposal:* 9
> *Deadline(s):* Varies
> *Final notification:* Recipients notified in three months
> *Applicants should submit the following:*
> 1) Letter(s) of recommendation
> 2) Resume

Program descriptions:
AAS Visiting Fellowships for Creative and Performing Artist & Writers: The fellowship provides a stipend of $1,200 for one month's residencies and use of the Society's library. An allowance for travel expenses is also provided. Recipients of these grants may be creative and performing artists, designers, illustrators, sculptors, painters, filmmakers, and journalists. Deadline in Oct.

AAS-American Society for Eighteenth-Century Studies Fellowships: Awarded in conjunction with the American Society of Eighteenth-Century Studies (ASECS), this fellowship supports one month of research at the society for projects related to the American eighteenth century. Fellowship holders must be an ABD graduate student or post-doctoral, holding a Ph.D. or equivalent degree at the time of application. ASECS membership is not required of applicants; awardees who are not already members must join. Stipends are for $1,850, or for $1,350 plus housing in the society's Goddard-Daniels House.

AAS-National Endowment for the Humanities Fellowships: Fellowships for four to twelve months each are awarded to both senior scholars working on sweeping subjects and younger scholars at work on more narrowly focused monographs. Maximum stipend is $50,400. These fellowships are not open to degree candidates or non-U.S. citizens, except those who have been U.S. residents for at least three years preceding their award.

AAS-Northeast Modern Language Association Fellowship: Awarded in conjunction with the Northeast Modern Language Association (NEMLA), this fellowship supports research for one month at the society into the literary history of America and the Atlantic world in the eighteenth and nineteenth centuries that can be supported by the society's collections. Membership in NEMLA is not required of applicants; awardees who are not already members must join. Stipends are for $1,850, or $1,350 plus housing in the society's Goddard-Daniels House.

ACLS Frederick Burkhardt Fellowships: The American Council of Learned Societies awards one-year fellowships to recently tenured humanists.

American Historical Print Collectors Society Fellowship: Jointly awarded with the American Historical Print Collectors Society, this one-month fellowship supports research at the society on American prints of the eighteenth and nineteenth centuries, or for projects using these prints as primary documentation. Stipends are for $1,850, or for $1,350 including housing in the society's Goddard-Daniels House.

Fellowships for Creative and Performing Artists and Writers: Fellowships in historical research are available to creative and performing artists, writers, filmmakers, journalists, and other persons whose goals are to produce imaginative, non-formulaic works dealing with pre-twentieth century American history. Fellowships will provide recipients with the

opportunity for a period of uninterrupted research, reading, and collegial discussion at the society for four weeks, as well as a $1,350 stipend for fellows residing on campus, and $1,850 for fellows residing off campus. Successful applicants are those whose work is for the general public rather than for academic or educational audiences.

Hench Post-Dissertation Fellowship: Scholars who are no more than three years beyond receipt of their doctorate are eligible to apply for a special year-long residential fellowship at the American Antiquarian Society to revise their dissertation for publication. The purpose of the program is to provide the recipient with time and resources to extend research and/or to revise the dissertation for publication. Any topic relevant to the society's library collections and programmatic scope—that is, American history and culture through 1876—is eligible. Applicants may come from such fields as history, literature, American studies, political science, art history, music history and others relating to America in the period of the society's coverage. The twelve-month stipend for this fellowship is $35,000.

Jay and Deborah Last Fellowships: This fellowship supports one month of research at the society that focuses on American art, visual culture, and other projects that will make substantial use of graphic materials as primary sources. Fellowship can be from one to three months, with a provision of $1,850 per month, or $1,350 per month including housing in the society's Goddard-Daniels House.

Joyce Tracy Fellowship: One-month fellowships are available for research on newspapers and magazines or for projects that use these resources as primary documentation and that fit within the scope of the society. Stipends are for $1,850, or for $1,350 plus housing in the society's Goddard-Daniels House.

Kate B. and Hall J. Peterson Fellowships: Fellowships are available to individuals engaged in scholarly research and writing (including doctoral dissertations) in any field of American history and culture through 1876. Fellowships can last between one and three months; stipends are $1,850 per month, or $1,350 per month including housing in the society's Goddard-Daniels House.

Reese Fellowship: This fellowship supports one month of research at the society in American bibliography and projects in the history of the book in America. Stipends are for $1,850, or $1,350 plus housing in the society's Goddard-Daniels House.

Stephen Botein Fellowships: One-month fellowships are available for research in the history of the book in American culture. Stipends are for $1,850, or for $1,350 plus housing in the society's Goddard-Daniels House.

The "Drawn to Art" Fellowship: This fellowship supports research on American art, visual culture, or others projects that will make substantial uses of graphic materials as primary sources. Fellowships are for one month, with a stipend of $1,850, or $1,350 and housing in the society's Goddard-Daniels House.

The Christoph Daniel Ebeling Fellowship: Jointly administered by the German Association for American Studies and the foundation, the fellowship is open to German citizens or permanent residents at the post-graduate of postdoctoral stages of their careers. Fellows are selected on the basis of scholarly qualifications and the appropriateness of their proposed studies. The fellowship includes up to 1,800 Euros and lodging in the Goddard-Daniels House.

The Legacy Fellowship: This fellowship is awarded to individuals engaged in scholarly research and writing (including doctoral

dissertations) for research on any topic supported by the society's collections. Stipends are for $1,850, or for $1,350 plus housing in the society's Goddard-Daniels House.
EIN: 042103652

3964
American Association of Plastic Surgeons
500 Cummings Ctr., Ste. 4550
Beverly, MA   01915-6183   (978) 927-8330
Contact: John A. Persing, Pres.
FAX: (978) 524-8890; URL: http://www.aaps1921.org

Foundation type: Public charity
Purpose: Fellowships to individuals conducting research in plastic surgery.
Publications: Application guidelines; Newsletter.
Financial data: Year ended 12/31/2012. Assets, $3,802,229 (L); Expenditures, $873,111; Total giving, $134,487; Grants to individuals, totaling $124,645.
Fields of interest: Surgery research.
Type of support: Fellowships; Research.
Application information: Applications accepted. Application form required. Application form available on the grantmaker's web site.
   Send request by: Mail or e-mail
   Deadline(s): Nov. 1 for Academic Scholar Program; Jan. 30 for John D. Constable Traveling Fellowship
   Applicants should submit the following:
      1) Curriculum vitae
      2) Budget Information
      3) Proposal
      4) Letter(s) of recommendation
Program descriptions:
   Academic Scholarships: The program offers two-year faculty research scholarships to surgeons entering academic careers in plastic and reconstructive surgery. Awards are for $30,000 per year, and provide salary and/or direct costs for research. Applicants must demonstrate their potential to work as independent investigators. The scholarship may be renewed once.
   John D. Constable Traveling Fellowship Award: A fellowship of $7,500 per year to provide an opportunity for international plastic surgeons to come to America. Candidates must be fully trained in their respective country in plastic surgery, a member in good standing of their national society, and have been in practice in their country for a minimum of five years.
EIN: 946118700

3965
American Federation for Medical Research
500 Cummings Ctr., Ste. 4550
Beverly, MA   01915-6183   (978) 927-8330
Contact: Abraham Thomas, Pres.
FAX: (978) 524-8890; URL: http://www.afmr.org

Foundation type: Public charity
Purpose: Awards are given to foster medical research and support the development of the careers of physician scientists.
Financial data: Year ended 12/31/2012. Assets, $458,657 (M); Expenditures, $648,090; Total giving, $72,715; Grants to individuals, totaling $72,715.
Fields of interest: Medical research.
Type of support: Research; Grants to individuals.

Application information: Applications accepted. Application form required. Application form available on the grantmaker's web site.
   Deadline(s): Jan. for Henry Christian Awards, and Junior Physician-Investigator Awards, Feb. for Outstanding Investigator Awards
   Additional information: Applicants must be AFMR members in good standing to qualify. Non-members must submit a membership application with their award application. See web site for additional information.
Program descriptions:
   Henry Christian Awards: The awards are given to the presenters and first authors of outstanding abstracts submitted in each abstract category for the AFMR Regional Meetings. Award winners will be required to present their work via poster at the annual meeting in Washington, DC. Candidates must be physicians who are post-M.D. trainees, including residents. clinical fellows, physicians pursuing graduate degrees, PhDs and other post-doctoral fellows. Awardees will receive a Certificate of Excellence and a $1,250 honorarium.
   Junior Physician-Investigator Awards: These awards were created to honor young investigators whose research projects complement an overall program of research, teaching and clinical medicine. To be considered, a candidate must be a physician who has held a full-time medical school faculty appointment for five years or less and must have submitted an abstract for the AFMR Regional Meetings. Winners will be required to present their work in person via poster at the annual meeting in Washington, DC. A certificate and $2,500 will be presented to two winners.
   Outstanding Investigator Awards: This award is presented annually to an investigator age 45 or younger in recognition of excellence in biomedical research. The recipient of this award will receive $5,000 and compensation for travel expenses. The recipient will be required to present his/her research at the awards and dinner.
EIN: 526056060

3966
American Foundation for Bulgaria, Inc.
167 Newbury St.
Boston, MA   02116-2834   (212) 842-1228
Contact: Theodore Vassilev, Exec. Dir.
E-mail: contact@afbulgaria.org

Foundation type: Public charity
Purpose: Provides grants and scholarships to promote education and artistic achievement in Bulgaria.
Financial data: Year ended 12/31/2011. Assets, $3,179,686 (M); Expenditures, $697,334; Total giving, $387,836.
Fields of interest: Arts; Higher education.
International interests: Bulgaria.
Type of support: Scholarships—to individuals.
Application information: Applications not accepted.
   Additional information: Unsolicited requests for funds not considered or acknowledged.
Program description:
   Secondary Education Scholarship Program: The program provides scholarships to outstanding students in the fields of mathematics, informatics, physics, biology, chemistry, and foreign languages from the secondary schools in humanities, arts, and culture.
EIN: 200361839

3967
American Meteorological Society
45 Beacon St.
Boston, MA   02108-3693   (617) 227-2425
Contact: Keith L. Seitter, Exec. Dir.
Application info.: Donna Fernandez, tel.: (617) 226-3907, e-mail: dfernandez@ametsoc.org; Stephanie Armstrong, tel.: (617) 226-3906, e-mail: armstrong@ametsoc.org
FAX: (617) 742-8718;
E-mail: amsinfo@ametsoc.org; URL: http://www.ametsoc.org/

Foundation type: Public charity
Purpose: Scholarships and fellowships to outstanding graduate and undergraduate students pursuing a career in the atmospheric and related oceanic or hydrologic sciences.
Publications: Application guidelines; Annual report; Financial statement; Grants list; Informational brochure; Newsletter; Program policy statement.
Financial data: Year ended 12/31/2011. Assets, $22,964,730 (M); Expenditures, $16,058,737; Total giving, $295,839; Grants to individuals, totaling $295,839.
Fields of interest: Science; Physical/earth sciences; Mathematics; Engineering/technology; Minorities.
Type of support: Fellowships; Graduate support; Undergraduate support.
Application information: Applications accepted. Application form required. Application form available on the grantmaker's web site.
   Initial approach: Letter or e-mail
   Send request by: Mail
   Deadline(s): Jan. 17 for AMS Graduate Fellowships, Feb. 7 for AMS Minority Scholarships, AMS Freshman Undergraduate Scholarship, AMS Named Scholarship, AMS Graduate Fellowship in the History of Science, June 13 for Macelwane Award in Meteorology
   Applicants should submit the following:
      1) SAT
      2) Essay
      3) ACT
      4) Budget Information
      5) Letter(s) of recommendation
      6) Transcripts
   Additional information: See web site for additional guidelines.
Program descriptions:
   AMS Freshman Undergraduate Scholarships: This scholarship is open to all high school students and designed to encourage study in the atmospheric, or related oceanic or hydrologic sciences. Applicants must be entering their freshman year of college in the fall as a full-time student. The program provides scholarship stipends of $5,000, awarding $2,500 each year (for the freshman and sophomore years). The second year funding is dependent on successful completion of the first year.
   AMS Graduate Fellowships in the History of Science: The fellowship is to be awarded to a student in the process of completing a dissertation on the history of the atmospheric, or related oceanic or hydrologic sciences. The award carries a $15,000 stipend and will support one year of dissertation research. The goal of the graduate fellowship is to support dissertation topics in the history of the atmospheric, or related oceanic and hydrologic sciences, and to foster close working relations between historians and scientists. An effort will be made to place the student into a mentoring relationship with an AMS member at an appropriate institution.
   The Father James B. Macelwane Award in Meteorology: The recipient for this award will receive a stipend of $1,000 to stimulate interest in meteorology among college students through the

submission of original student papers concerned with some phase of the atmospheric sciences. The student must be enrolled as an undergraduate at the time the paper is written, and no more than two students from any one institution may enter papers in any one contest.
EIN: 042103657

3968
American Optical Foundation
100 Mechanic St., Bldg. 80
Southbridge, MA   01550-2570   (508) 765-7085

Foundation type: Company-sponsored foundation
Purpose: Scholarships and student loans to children of employees of American Optical Corporation who reside in MA.
Financial data: Year ended 12/31/2012. Assets, $1,190,287 (M); Expenditures, $89,673; Total giving, $76,555; Grants to individuals, 21 grants totaling $62,750 (high: $10,000, low: $50).
Type of support: Employee-related scholarships.
Application information: Applications accepted. Application form required.
  Deadline(s): Apr. 25
  Applicants should submit the following:
    1) SAT
    2) Essay
    3) Transcripts
    4) Letter(s) of recommendation
Company name: American Optical Corporation
EIN: 046028058

3969
American Physicians Fellowship for Medicine in Israel
(also known as APF)
2001 Beacon St., Ste. 210
Boston, MA   02135-7787   (617) 232-5382
FAX: (617) 739-2616; E-mail: info@apfmed.org; URL: http://www.apfmed.org

Foundation type: Public charity
Purpose: Fellowships to young Israeli physicians and nurses undertaking specialty training in North America who are committed to returning to Israel. Grants are also awarded to young Israelis for medical research.
Publications: Application guidelines; Informational brochure; Newsletter.
Financial data: Year ended 12/31/2011. Assets, $615,464 (M); Expenditures, $504,533; Total giving, $153,659; Grants to individuals, totaling $126,170.
Fields of interest: Medical school/education; Association; Nursing care; Institute.
Type of support: Fellowships; Research; Foreign applicants.
Application information: Applications accepted. Application form required. Application form available on the grantmaker's web site.
  Deadline(s): None
  Applicants should submit the following:
    1) Proposal
    2) Budget Information
    3) Letter(s) of recommendation
    4) Photograph
    5) Curriculum vitae
Program descriptions:
  Fellowships: Awards $5,000 annual grants to gifted Israeli physicians, nurses, and key medical administrators in the advancement of their education and careers by providing specialty training currently unavailable in Israel, at prestigious medical centers in the United States and Canada. With this training, they return to Israel

better equipped to treat the diverse population of new immigrants, veteran, Israelis, and indigenous peoples.
  Kitzberg Fellowship for Oncology Study and Research: This fellowship enables Israeli physicians to spend time at leading medical centers in North America performing oncology related clinical work or engaging in oncology research of the highest caliber.
  Research Grants: Research grants are comprised of two awards, Edward H. Kass Medical Research Award and Isaac Knoll Research Award. Awards of $10,000 are made to an outstanding young Israeli physician conducting research in Israel at a medical institution, hospital or university. No overhead or administrative fees may be deducted.
  Rosenblatt Foundation Grants: Grants of up to $25,000 a year for post-residency training in oncology at a leading U.S. or Canadian medical center.
EIN: 042207701

3970
Andona Society
P.O. Box 256
Andover, MA   01810-0005   (978) 686-6434
Contact: Paula Colby-Clements, Pres.
E-mail: inquiry@andonasociety.org; URL: http://www.andona.org

Foundation type: Public charity
Purpose: Scholarships to permanent residents of Andover, MA, graduating from Andover High School, Greater Lawrence Regional Technical High School, or a private school.
Publications: Application guidelines.
Financial data: Year ended 07/31/2011. Assets, $114,954 (M); Expenditures, $54,000; Total giving, $52,750.
Fields of interest: Vocational education, post-secondary; Higher education.
Type of support: Scholarships—to individuals; Support to graduates or students of specific schools.
Application information: Applications accepted. Application form required. Application form available on the grantmaker's web site.
  Deadline(s): Apr. 14
  Applicants should submit the following:
    1) Transcripts
    2) Letter(s) of recommendation
    3) Essay
  Additional information: Applications are available from the Andover high school guidance office. Applications should be addressed to Jennifer Priest Insero, Chair., Andona Scholarship Committee. See web site for additional information.
Program description:
  Scholarships: Each year, the society makes available five $2,000 scholarships to high school seniors whose principal residence is Andover, who are ranked in the upper 50 percent of their high school class, and who have plans to continue their education after graduation from high school.
EIN: 046192700

3971
Animal Umbrella, Inc.
320B Charger St.
Revere, MA   02151   (508) 877-1194
Contact: Annamarie Taylor, Pres.
E-mail: annamarie.taylor@worldnet.att.net; URL: http://www.animalumbrella.org/

Foundation type: Public charity

Purpose: Assistance to individuals for providing humane services to animals.
Publications: Newsletter.
Financial data: Year ended 12/31/2011. Assets, $19,881 (M); Expenditures, $107,373.
Fields of interest: Animal welfare.
Type of support: Grants for special needs.
Application information: Financial need must be determined. Payments made on behalf of individuals are verified by bills from medical or shelter providers.
EIN: 222662445

3972
Armenian Relief Society, Inc.
80 Bigelow Ave.
Watertown, MA   02472-2012
URL: http://www.ars1910.org/

Foundation type: Public charity
Purpose: Scholarships for students interested in pursuing educational studies at full-time undergraduate or graduate accredited college or university. Summer camps for Armenian children in the U.S. or abroad.
Financial data: Year ended 05/31/2012. Assets, $3,391,922 (M); Expenditures, $1,005,218; Total giving, $493,596; Grants to individuals, totaling $8,500.
Fields of interest: Recreation.
Type of support: Camperships.
Application information: Applications accepted. Application form required.
  Deadline(s): May 31
  Additional information: Scholarship selection is based on merit, need and Armenian community involvement. Camp selection is based on financial need and to those who have not attended an Armenian summer camp. See web site for additional guidelines.
EIN: 042219512

3973
Associates of the Boston Public Library
700 Boylston St.
Boston, MA   02116-2813   (617) 536-3886
Contact: Louisa Stephens, Exec. Dir.
FAX: (6170 536-3813; E-mail: ask@bpl.org; URL: http://www.bpl.org/general/associates/

Foundation type: Public charity
Purpose: Financial assistance to an emerging children's writer of Boston, MA with office space needed to complete one literary work for children or yong adults.
Publications: Application guidelines.
Financial data: Year ended 06/30/2012. Assets, $2,726,742 (M); Expenditures, $409,729; Total giving, $127,337; Grants to individuals, totaling $21,000.
Fields of interest: Literature.
Type of support: Residencies; Grants for special needs.
Application information: Applications accepted. Application form required. Application form available on the grantmaker's web site.
  Initial approach: Application
  Send request by: Mail
  Deadline(s): Apr. 1
  Final notification: Applicant notified in June
  Applicants should submit the following:
    1) SASE
    2) Work samples
    3) Proposal
  Additional information: See web site for additional application guidelines.

Program description:

Children's Writer-in-Residence Program: This program is intended to provide an emerging children's writer with the financial and administrative support needed to complete a literary work. The Children's Writer-in-Residence receives a $20,000 stipend and office space at the BPL's Central Library. He or she must work a minimum of 19 hours per week at the BPL during the nine-month residency. Projects eligible for this program are fiction, non-fiction, a script, or poetry, intended for children or young adults. Eligible individuals must be U.S. citizens and cannot have published more than three books to date.

EIN: 042900822

3974
Association for the Relief of Aged Women of New Bedford

432 County St.
New Bedford, MA   02740-5018

Foundation type: Operating foundation

Purpose: Financial assistance and relief to needy, aged women in New Bedford, Dartmouth, Fairhaven, and Acushnet, MA.

Financial data: Year ended 03/31/2013. Assets, $17,699,049 (M); Expenditures, $1,014,387; Total giving, $771,509; Grants to individuals, totaling $349,693.

Fields of interest: Aging; Women.

Type of support: Grants for special needs.

Application information: Applications not accepted.

Additional information: Recipients are nominated by nonprofit agencies.

EIN: 046056367

3975
William Harold Francis Austin Trust

c/o Eastern Bank
605 Broadway, LF 42
Saugus, MA   01906   (781) 581-4274
Contact: Robert M. Wallask, V.P., Eastern Bank

Foundation type: Independent foundation

Purpose: Non-interest bearing student loans for residents of MA whose natural fathers are deceased and who are in pursuit of a college education.

Financial data: Year ended 07/31/2013. Assets, $981,630 (M); Expenditures, $59,781; Total giving, $48,000.

Fields of interest: Residential/custodial care.

Type of support: Student loans—to individuals.

Application information: Applications accepted. Application form required.

Deadline(s): June 1

Additional information: Application should include transcripts and copy of father's death certificate.

EIN: 042714929

3976
Lloyd G. Balfour Foundation

c/o US Trust, Bank of America, N.A.
225 Franklin St., 4th Fl.
Boston, MA   02110-2801   (866) 778-6859
Contact: Miki C. Akimoto, Market Dir.
Scholarship contact: Wendy Holt, Exec. Dir., Attleboro Scholarship Foundation, tel.: 1 (508) 226-4414
E-mail: ma.grantmaking@ustrust.com; URL: http://www.bankofamerica.com/grantmaking

Foundation type: Independent foundation

Purpose: Scholarship aid to former employees of The Balfour Co. The program is administered by the Attleboro Scholarship Foundation.

Publications: Application guidelines.

Financial data: Year ended 03/31/2013. Assets, $106,987,027 (M); Expenditures, $5,215,669; Total giving, $4,239,030.

Type of support: Scholarships—to individuals.

Application information:

Initial approach: Letter

Program description:

Balfour Employee-Related Scholarships: The foundation provides scholarship aid, via the Attleboro Scholarship Foundation, to former company employees. On an on-going basis, the foundation provides scholarship support to former employees, their children and grandchildren. Grants awarded in this category are administered by the Attleboro Scholarship Foundation. Please contact Wendy Holt, Exec. Dir., Attleboro Scholarship Foundation at tel.: (508) 226-4414.

EIN: 222751372

3977
Balfour Gold Dusters

P.O. Box 733
Raynham Center, MA   02768

Foundation type: Independent foundation

Purpose: Financial assistance to retirees of the Balfour Gold Dusters for utilities and medical assistance only in RI and MA.

Financial data: Year ended 08/31/2013. Assets, $80,080 (M); Expenditures, $90,618; Total giving, $77,574.

Fields of interest: Supported living.

Type of support: Grants for special needs.

Application information: Applications not accepted.

Additional information: Unsolicited requests for funds not considered or acknowledged.

EIN: 042828143

3978
Lillian M. Bassett Private Foundation

c/o Eastern Bank
605 Broadway LF 41
Saugus, MA   01906-3200   (617) 295-0632
Contact: David Olaksen
Application address: 265 Franklin St., Boston, MA 02110

Foundation type: Independent foundation

Purpose: Scholarships to seniors of Swampscott High School, MA.

Financial data: Year ended 12/31/2012. Assets, $223,408 (M); Expenditures, $11,234; Total giving, $8,000.

Type of support: Support to graduates or students of specific schools; Undergraduate support.

Application information: Applications accepted. Application form required.

Deadline(s): None

EIN: 046606391

3979
Baystate Health Foundation, Inc.

280 Chestnut St.
Springfield, MA   01104-3563   (413) 794-5444
Additional e-mail: michelle.graci@bhs.org,
tel.: (413) 794-7654
FAX: (413) 794-7616; URL: http://baystatehealth.com/Baystate/Main+Nav/About+Us/Foundation

Foundation type: Public charity

Purpose: Stipends for a 10-week summer mentored research program at Baystate Medical Center, MA for rising college seniors and medical students who are exploring the potential of a career in medical, biomedical, public health, or behavioral health research.

Publications: Newsletter.

Financial data: Year ended 09/30/2011. Assets, $111,656,645 (M); Expenditures, $12,240,993; Total giving, $186,500.

Fields of interest: Hospitals (general); Medical research.

Type of support: Stipends.

Application information: Applications accepted. Application form required. Application form available on the grantmaker's web site.

Initial approach: Letter

Applicants should submit the following:

1) Transcripts
2) Letter(s) of recommendation

Additional information: See http://www.baystatehealth.com/cbr/SummerScholar.html for further program information.

EIN: 043549011

3980
Frank Huntington Beebe Fund for Musicians

45 School St., 5th Fl.
Boston, MA   02108-3204   (617) 523-1635
Contact: Peter P. Brown, Tr.

Foundation type: Independent foundation

Purpose: Travel grants to talented, advanced-level musicians at the New England Conservatory of Music, MA, to pursue music study abroad, primarily in Europe.

Financial data: Year ended 06/30/2013. Assets, $1,373,583 (M); Expenditures, $52,456; Total giving, $22,410; Grants to individuals, 2 grants totaling $22,410 (high: $16,910, low: $5,500).

Fields of interest: Music.

International interests: Europe.

Type of support: Travel grants.

Application information: Application form required. Application form available on the grantmaker's web site.

Initial approach: Letter

Applicants should submit the following:

1) Financial information
2) Letter(s) of recommendation
3) Transcripts
4) Proposal

Program description:

Fellowship Fund: Provides fellowships for gifted young musicians, generally performers and composers in classical disciplines, who wish to pursue advanced music study and performance abroad, usually in Europe. Fellowships are awarded to musicians at the outset of their professional lives, for whom this would be the first extended period of study abroad. Applicants must demonstrate a solid base of accomplishment in order to be considered and are generally not older than their mid-twenties. A strong, well-planned

project of study will enhance the applicant's life in music must be proposed. Enrollment in a school or university is not required unless such study is an essential part of the project. The fund provides financial support and transportation, living and other expenses, approximately $16,000. Fellowships are for one year and are generally not renewable.
EIN: 046112830

3981
The Belmont Golf Scholarship Fund, Inc.
151 Tremont St.
Boston, MA   02111-1125   (617) 542-2122

Foundation type: Public charity
Purpose: Scholarships are awarded to residents of Belmont, who work in MA as caddies.
Financial data: Year ended 12/31/2011. Assets, $140,429 (M); Expenditures, $60,266; Total giving, $58,300.
Fields of interest: Athletics/sports, golf.
Type of support: Scholarships—to individuals.
Application information: Applications accepted.
Program description:
 Scholarship Program: Scholarship to individuals who reside in Belmont, who work in MA as caddies or other employees for golf courses or individuals who work in Belmont as caddies or other employees of golf courses. Children whose parents fall in to these categories are also eligible to receive scholarships.
EIN: 201723275

3982
Doris L. Benz Trust
c/o Wendell P. Weyland, Trustee
309 Ipswich Rd.
Boxford, MA   01921-1505   (603) 225-6641

Foundation type: Independent foundation
Purpose: Scholarships to graduates of Interlakes Regional High School, NH, or any students residing in Carroll County, NH. Scholarships are administered by the New Hampshire Charitable Foundation.
Financial data: Year ended 06/30/2013. Assets, $9,151,176 (M); Expenditures, $450,778; Total giving, $357,302.
Type of support: Support to graduates or students of specific schools.
Application information: Applications accepted. Application form required.
 Initial approach: Letter
 Deadline(s): Apr. 26
EIN: 046504871

3983
Berkshire Bank Foundation, Inc.
(formerly Greater Berkshire Charitable Foundation)
P.O. Box 1308
Pittsfield, MA   01202-1308   (413) 447-1724
Contact: Peter J. Lafayette, Exec. Dir.
E-mail for scholarships:
scholarshipinfo@berkshirebank.com
E-mail: foundation@berkshirebank.com;
URL: http://www.berkshirebank.com/about-us/in_the_community/berkshire-bank-foundation

Foundation type: Company-sponsored foundation
Purpose: Scholarships to high school seniors in a town or city in Massachusetts, New York, and Vermont served by Berkshire Bank.
Publications: Application guidelines.

Financial data: Year ended 12/31/2012. Assets, $16,139,742 (M); Expenditures, $1,390,248; Total giving, $907,415.
Fields of interest: Vocational education, post-secondary; Higher education.
Type of support: Scholarships—to individuals.
Application information: Applications accepted. Application form required. Application form available on the grantmaker's web site.
 Initial approach: Application
 Send request by: Mail
 Deadline(s): Mar. 28
 Final notification: Applicants notified in May
 Applicants should submit the following:
  1) Resume
  2) Essay
  3) Transcripts
 Additional information: Contact the foundation for additional information.
Program description:
 Berkshire Bank Foundation Scholarship Awards Program: The foundation awards $2,000 college scholarships to high school seniors in a town or city in MA, NY, and VT served by Berkshire Bank. Applicants must have a record of volunteerism in the community in non-school sponsored activities and participation in extracurricular activities, a minimum 3.0 GPA, a family income under $75,000, and a plan to attend a two or four year college or technical school.
EIN: 043365869

3984
Berkshire Community Action Council, Inc.
1531 East St.
Pittsfield, MA   01201-5314   (413) 445-4503
FAX: (413) 447-7871; URL: http://www.bcacinc.org

Foundation type: Public charity
Purpose: Emergency financial assistance to low income individuals and families of Berkshire county, MA with food, shelter, fuel and other needs.
Financial data: Year ended 09/30/2011. Assets, $1,937,352 (M); Expenditures, $12,739,391; Total giving, $6,206,044; Grants to individuals, totaling $6,206,044.
Fields of interest: Human services.
Type of support: Emergency funds; Grants for special needs.
Application information: Applications accepted. Application form required. Application form available on the grantmaker's web site.
 Send request by: E-mail
 Additional information: Funds are based on income eligibility.
Program description:
 Neighbor-to-Neighbor Grant: The foundation makes small grants up to $500 (possibly up to $1,000 in special circumstances) to help pay overdue utilities, medical bills, short-term housing costs, car insurance/repair or other expenses that will alleviate the immediate crisis and leverage other support to assist the family or individual in distress. The grant provides immediate assistance to residents of Berkshire county, MA in difficult financial circumstance and need an emergency financial boost in a particular area of their lives that will help stabilize their situation and help avert a deeper crisis. Payment is made directly to the vendor on behalf of the individual in need.
EIN: 042422074

3985
Berkshire Community College Foundation, Inc.
1350 W. St.
Pittsfield, MA   01201-5720   (413) 499-4660
Contact: John Jeffrey Doscher, Exec. Dir.
URL: http://www.berkshirecc.edu/BCC%20Foundation

Foundation type: Public charity
Purpose: Scholarships to students at Berkshire Community College, MA.
Financial data: Year ended 06/30/2012. Assets, $8,193,229 (M); Expenditures, $822,312; Total giving, $707,549.
Type of support: Support to graduates or students of specific schools.
Application information: Applications accepted.
EIN: 042736585

3986
Berkshire Taconic Community Foundation
800 N. Main St.
P.O. Box 400
Sheffield, MA   01257-0400   (413) 229-0370
Contact: Jennifer Dowley, Pres.; Jill S. Gellert, V.P., Finance and Admin.; For grants: Maeve M. O'Dea, Prog. Dir.
FAX: (413) 229-0329;
E-mail: info@berkshiretaconic.org; Additional tel.: (413) 528-8039; Grant inquiry e-mail: maeve@berkshiretaconic.org; URL: http://www.berkshiretaconic.org

Foundation type: Community foundation
Purpose: Scholarships and grants to residents of the Berkshire Taconic region in New England. Grants to mid-career artists residing in New England.
Publications: Application guidelines; Annual report; Financial statement; Informational brochure (including application guidelines); Occasional report.
Financial data: Year ended 12/31/2012. Assets, $103,766,733 (M); Expenditures, $8,737,625; Total giving, $7,395,552. Scholarships—to individuals amount not specified.
Fields of interest: Visual arts; Literature; Arts; Higher education; Environment.
Type of support: Grants to individuals; Undergraduate support; Residencies; Stipends.
Application information: Applications accepted. Application form required. Application form available on the grantmaker's web site.
 Initial approach: Application
 Deadline(s): Varies
 Final notification: Applicants notified within eight to twelve weeks of the deadline for scholarships
 Applicants should submit the following:
  1) Resume
  2) Work samples
  3) Transcripts
  4) Letter(s) of recommendation
  5) Essay
  6) SAR
  7) FAFSA
  8) FAF
 Additional information: Applicant should create online account on the foundation's application portal. See web site for additional guidelines and a complete listing of programs.
EIN: 061254469

3987
Beta Kappa Phi Alpha Gamma Rho Scholarship Foundation

(formerly The Beta Kappa Phi Alpha Gamma Rho Scholarship Foundation)
P.O. Box 154
Westborough, MA 01581   (508) 366-5659
Contact: Mike Cormacchia

Foundation type: Independent foundation
Purpose: Scholarships to lineal descendants of Beta Kappa Phi-Alpha Gamma Rho fraternity members. Scholarships also to disadvantaged students of University of Massachusetts, Amherst.
Financial data: Year ended 12/31/2012. Assets, $346,994 (M); Expenditures, $28,877; Total giving, $21,292; Grants to individuals, 11 grants totaling $21,292 (high: $8,792, low: $500).
Fields of interest: Higher education; Students, sororities/fraternities.
Type of support: Scholarships—to individuals; Support to graduates or students of specific schools.
Application information: Applications accepted. Application form required.
  Deadline(s): June 30
  Applicants should submit the following:
    1) ACT
    2) SAT
    3) Letter(s) of recommendation
    4) Transcripts
    5) Financial information
    6) GPA
EIN: 043124308

3988
Grace T. Blanchard Trust

c/o Eastern Bank
605 Broadway, LF41
Saugus, MA 01906-3200   (781) 581-4292
Contact: Christine Drew
Application address: c/o Eastern Bank & Trust Co., 605 Braodway Saugus, MA 01906

Foundation type: Independent foundation
Purpose: Scholarships limited to MA residents for attendance either at Harvard University, MA, or Radcliffe College, MA.
Financial data: Year ended 12/31/2012. Assets, $220,690 (M); Expenditures, $13,888; Total giving, $10,500.
Type of support: Support to graduates or students of specific schools; Undergraduate support.
Application information: Applications accepted. Application form required.
  Deadline(s): None
  Additional information: Contact trust for current application guidelines.
EIN: 046015965

3989
Blue Cross Blue Shield of Massachusetts Foundation, Inc. for Expanding Healthcare Access

(formerly Wellchild, the Foundation of Health for Life)
Landmark Ctr.
401 Park Dr.
Boston, MA 02215-3325   (617) 246-3744
Contact: Celeste Reid Lee, Interim Pres.
Contacts for fellowships: Larry Tye, 26 Grant St., Lexington, MA 02420, e-mail: larrytye@aol.com; Anna Gosline, e-mail: Anna.Gosline@bcbsma.com
FAX: (617) 246-3992;
E-mail: info@bluecrossmafoundation.org;
URL: http://www.bcbsmafoundation.org

Foundation type: Company-sponsored foundation
Purpose: Fellowships to New England reporters and editors from newspapers, radio stations, and television outlets for healthcare training.
Publications: Application guidelines; Grants list; IRS Form 990 or 990-PF printed copy available upon request; Program policy statement.
Financial data: Year ended 12/31/2012. Assets, $103,240,974 (M); Expenditures, $7,991,487; Total giving, $3,512,006.
Fields of interest: Health care.
Type of support: Fellowships.
Application information: Applications accepted. Application form required. Application form available on the grantmaker's web site.
  Initial approach: Application
  Send request by: Mail
  Deadline(s): Varies
  Applicants should submit the following:
    1) Work samples
    2) Resume
  Additional information: Application should include a half-page summary of the applicants journalism career to date and 10 year professional plan and a page outlining the health issues central to the applicant and how the fellowship will help cover them.
Program description:
  Health Coverage Fellowship: Through the Health Coverage Fellowship, the foundation trains members of the media to cover critical healthcare issues. The program focuses on issues ranging from insuring the uninsured to mental illness, backups in emergency rooms, ethnic and economic disparities in the delivery of care, and environmental health. The fellowship is housed at Babson College's Center for Executive Education in Wellesley, and brings journalists together with leading health officials, policy makers, and researchers. The fellows also learn first-hand how the system works, from joining mental health case workers patrolling the streets at night to riding a Medflight helicopter. The foundation selects ten journalists each year from across the country for an intensive nine days and nights of training.
EIN: 043148824

3990
The Boch Family Foundation

95 Morse St.
Norwood, MA 02062-4623
Contact: Carla Tardif
E-mail: carla@musicdrivesus.org; Mailing address: 7 Seneca Rd., Winchester, MA 01890-3443;
URL: http://www.musicdrivesus.org

Foundation type: Independent foundation
Purpose: Scholarships to worthy individuals in the New England area to attend music camps, programs and instruction.

Publications: Application guidelines.
Financial data: Year ended 12/31/2012. Assets, $1,391,372 (M); Expenditures, $205,236; Total giving, $88,201.
Fields of interest: Music.
Type of support: Scholarships—to individuals.
Application information: Applications accepted.
  Deadline(s): May 4
  Final notification: Applicants notified July 15
  Additional information: Application must be completed online.
EIN: 203429592

3991
Boston Art Dealers Association Trust

c/o Joanna Fink
67 Newbury St.
Boston, MA 02116-3010   (617) 267-9060

Foundation type: Public charity
Purpose: Scholarhips to students who are entering their final year in studio art programs at colleges in Boston, MA.
Financial data: Year ended 12/31/2011. Assets, $131,393 (M); Expenditures, $106,438; Total giving, $97,000. Scholarships—to individuals amount not specified.
Fields of interest: Visual arts.
Type of support: Scholarships—to individuals; Awards/prizes.
Application information: Applications accepted.
  Deadline(s): June 1
  Final notification: Recipients notified in Sept.
EIN: 046866932

3992
Boston Chapter CPCU Trust

c/o Insurance Library Assn.
156 State St.
Boston, MA 02109-2505   (508) 760-1490
Contact: Thomas C. Radziewicz
Application address: 24 School St., P.O. Box 483, West Dennis, MA 02670-0483

Foundation type: Operating foundation
Purpose: Scholarship only to spouses or dependent of a member in good standing in the Boston Chapter of CPCU.
Financial data: Year ended 12/31/2011. Assets, $52,121 (M); Expenditures, $6,445; Total giving, $4,000; Grants to individuals, 2 grants totaling $4,000 (high: $2,000, low: $2,000).
Fields of interest: Education.
Type of support: Scholarships—to individuals.
Application information: Applications accepted. Application form required.
  Deadline(s): None
  Additional information: Contact the trust for additional information.
EIN: 046392433

3993
Boston Fatherless & Widows Society

Exchange Pl., Ste. 2200
Boston, MA 02109-2881   (617) 570-1987
Contact: Susan L. Abbott, Treas.
FAX: (617) 227-8591;
E-mail: sabbott@goodwinprocter.com

Foundation type: Independent foundation
Purpose: Grants to economically disadvantaged widows who are residents of the greater Boston, MA, area, to cover expenses for food, housing, clothing, and medical treatment.

Financial data: Year ended 11/30/2012. Assets, $6,485,752 (M); Expenditures, $341,882; Total giving, $264,550.
Fields of interest: Housing/shelter; Residential/custodial care; Women.
Type of support: Grants for special needs.
Application information: Applications accepted. Application form not required.
Initial approach: Letter
Send request by: Mail
Deadline(s): None
Final notification: Applicants are informed of decision within two months
Additional information: Potential applicants are referred from agencies and other nonprofits. Application must demonstrate financial need.
EIN: 046006506

3994
Boston Leather Trade Benevolent Society
532 E. Broadway
South Boston, MA   02127-4407
Contact: Daniel D. Gallagher, Secy.

Foundation type: Independent foundation
Purpose: Grants to financially needy individuals who have been affiliated with the leather trade in New England.
Financial data: Year ended 12/31/2012. Assets, $33,203 (M); Expenditures, $40,300; Total giving, $29,900; Grants to individuals, 6 grants totaling $29,900 (high: $7,300, low: $1,900).
Fields of interest: Business/industry.
Type of support: Grants for special needs.
Application information: Applications accepted.
Initial approach: Letter
Deadline(s): None
Additional information: Application must demonstrate financial need and background in the leather trade.
EIN: 237219487

3995
Boston Local Development Corporation
43 Hawkins St.
Boston, MA   02114-2907   (617) 918-5404

Foundation type: Public charity
Purpose: Financial assistance to eligible homebuyers purchasing a residential home in Boston, MA.
Financial data: Year ended 06/30/2011. Assets, $7,270,663 (M); Expenditures, $2,056,294; Total giving, $1,674,223; Grants to individuals, totaling $630,421.
Fields of interest: Housing/shelter.
Type of support: Grants to individuals.
Application information: Grants are provided under the Boston Home Certificate Initiative. Contact organization for application guidelines.
EIN: 042681311

3996
Boston Scientific Foundation, Inc.
1 Boston Scientific Pl., MS B2
Natick, MA   01760-1537   (508) 650-8554
Contact: Jacqueline Boas, Fdn Admin.
FAX: (508) 650-8579;
E-mail: bscifoundation@bsci.com; URL: http://www.bostonscientific.com/corporate-citizenship/giving/foundation.html

Foundation type: Company-sponsored foundation
Purpose: Scholarships to children of employees of Boston Scientific and post-graduate medical

fellowships at academic and training institutions in select fields of study.
Publications: Application guidelines; Annual report.
Financial data: Year ended 12/31/2012. Assets, $18,355,968 (M); Expenditures, $3,515,251; Total giving, $3,168,440; Grants to individuals, 90 grants totaling $178,600 (high: $2,000, low: $1,000).
Fields of interest: Health care; Medical research.
Type of support: Fellowships; Employee-related scholarships.
Application information: Applications accepted. Application form required. Application form available on the grantmaker's web site.
Initial approach: Application
Send request by: Mail
Deadline(s): Mar. 1-30 for Fellowships
Final notification: Applicants notified in three to six months
Additional information: Fellowship applications should include a copy of the institutions W9, a comprehensive fellowship description, and a letter of request on the institution's letterhead signed by the director of the fellowship program.
Program description:
Fellowship Grants: The foundation awards post-graduate medical fellowships in fields of study that are of interest to Boston Scientific. Fields of study include Cardiac Rhythm Management & Electrophysiology, Interventional Cardiology and Peripheral Interventions, and Urology and Women's Health. The program is designed to inspire the next generation of leaders, innovators, and caregivers. The program is administered by Boston Scientific's CRM Grant Committee.
Company name: Boston Scientific Corporation
EIN: 043556844

3997
Bridgewater State College Foundation
25 Park Terrace
P.O. Box 42
Bridgewater, MA   02324-0042
Contact: Molly Fannon Williams, Exec. Dir.
URL: http://www.bridgew.edu/theuniversity/president-leadership/bridgewater-state-university-foundation

Foundation type: Public charity
Purpose: Scholarship for financially qualified students of Bridgewater State College, MA.
Publications: Annual report; Financial statement; Informational brochure.
Financial data: Year ended 06/30/2012. Assets, $23,325,133 (M); Expenditures, $925,508; Total giving, $558,632; Grants to individuals, totaling $337,222.
Fields of interest: Higher education.
Type of support: Support to graduates or students of specific schools.
Application information: Student are nominated for the scholarship.
EIN: 222678005

3998
Lou and Lucienne Brightman Scholarship Foundation
c/o Eastern Bank
605 Broadway, Ste. LF41
Saugus, MA   01906-3200   (781) 581-4241
Contact: Robert M. Wallask, V.P., Eastern Bank & Trust Co.

Foundation type: Independent foundation

Purpose: Scholarships to graduating high school seniors who are residents of MA and will attend an accredited college or university.
Financial data: Year ended 07/31/2013. Assets, $412,963 (M); Expenditures, $22,326; Total giving, $17,000; Grants to individuals, 17 grants totaling $17,000 (high: $1,000, low: $1,000).
Type of support: Undergraduate support.
Application information: Applications accepted. Application form required.
Deadline(s): June 1
Additional information: Application should include transcripts.
EIN: 046500798

3999
Bristol Elder Services, Inc.
1 Father Devalles Blvd., Ste. 101
Fall River, MA   02723-1511   (508) 675-2101
Contact: Nancy Munson, Exec. Dir.
FAX: (508) 679-0320; E-mail: info@bristolelder.org; Additional tel.: (508) 324-4619, TTY: (508) 646-9704; URL: http://www.bristolelder.org

Foundation type: Public charity
Purpose: Financial assistance and other benefits to elders and their families throughout southeastern MA.
Financial data: Year ended 06/30/2012. Assets, $8,543,255 (M); Expenditures, $21,677,431; Total giving, $12,205,249; Grants to individuals, totaling $11,900,418.
Fields of interest: Aging; Economically disadvantaged.
Type of support: Grants for special needs.
Application information: Applications accepted.
Initial approach: Telephone or e-mail
Additional information: Contact the agency for additional information and guidelines.
EIN: 042545767

4000
British Society, Inc.
(formerly British Charitable Society)
3 Channing Rd.
Mattapoisett, MA   02739   (508) 758-2713
Contact: Charles Platt, Pres.
Application address: 5 Channing Rd., Mattapoisett, MA 02739; URL: http://www.britcharity.org/

Foundation type: Independent foundation
Purpose: Awards made to individuals of British birth or descent located within the New England area.
Financial data: Year ended 12/31/2012. Assets, $847,666 (M); Expenditures, $69,533; Total giving, $33,439; Grant to an individual, 1 grant totaling $33,439.
International interests: United Kingdom.
Type of support: Emergency funds; Grants for special needs.
Application information: Applications accepted. Interview required.
Initial approach: Letter
Deadline(s): None
Additional information: The society prefers to receive applications generally through social service agencies. Application should include financial information.
EIN: 046054689

4001
Brockton Rotary Charitable & Educational Fund, Inc.
195 Westgate Dr.
P. O. Box 537
Brockton, MA   02303-0537   (508) 583-6524
Contact: Robert Tufts, Pres.

Foundation type: Public charity
Purpose: Scholarships to needy individuals in the Brockton, MA, area.
Financial data: Year ended 06/30/2012. Assets, $335,445 (M); Expenditures, $6,103; Total giving, $6,000.
Type of support: Scholarships—to individuals.
Application information:
Deadline(s): Apr. 1
Additional information: Contact foundation for current application guidelines.
EIN: 046071645

4002
Florence Evans Bushee Foundation, Inc.
c/o Hemenway & Barnes, LLP
P.O. Box 961209
Boston, MA   02196-1209
Application address: c/o R. Robert Woodburn, 60 State St., Boston, MA 02109-1899

Foundation type: Independent foundation
Purpose: Undergraduate scholarships to residents of the Newbury, MA, area. Applicants must be graduates of Triton, Pentucket, Newburyport, Governor, or Dummer high schools.
Publications: Application guidelines; Informational brochure.
Financial data: Year ended 12/31/2012. Assets, $4,601,232 (M); Expenditures, $330,752; Total giving, $255,900; Grants to individuals, 112 grants totaling $249,900 (high: $5,600, low: $500).
Type of support: Support to graduates or students of specific schools; Undergraduate support.
Application information: Application form required. Interview required.
Initial approach: Letter
Deadline(s): May 1
Additional information: Application must include transcripts.
EIN: 046035327

4003
Ella Lyman Cabot Trust Inc.
c/o GMA Foundations
77 Summer St., 8th Fl.
Boston, MA   02110   (617) 391-3087
Contact: Michelle Jenney, Clerk
FAX: (617) 426-7087;
E-mail: mjenney@gmafoundations.com;
URL: http://www.cabottrust.org

Foundation type: Independent foundation
Purpose: Grants primarily to individuals for projects (sometimes involving a departure from one's usual vocation or a creative extension of it) with a promise of good to others.
Publications: Application guidelines.
Financial data: Year ended 12/31/2011. Assets, $3,154,541 (M); Expenditures, $165,503; Total giving, $136,201; Grants to individuals, 5 grants totaling $98,448 (high: $25,000, low: $1,000).
Fields of interest: Arts; Education; Environment; Health care; Civil/human rights; Community/ economic development; Science; Social sciences; Religion.
Type of support: Grants to individuals.

Application information: Applications accepted. Application form required.
Initial approach: Proposal
Deadline(s): Mar. 1 and Oct. 1
Additional information: If the project outlined in the proposal letter falls within the scope of the Trust, an application form will be supplied. Awards are usually made on a one-year basis and are not renewed.
EIN: 042111393

4004
Cambridge Savings Charitable Foundation Inc.
1374 Massachusetts Ave.
Cambridge, MA   02138-3822

Foundation type: Company-sponsored foundation
Purpose: Scholarships to graduating high school seniors from Cambridge, Acton-Boxborough, Arlington, Bedford, Belmont, Burlington, Concord-Carlisle, Lexington, Newton, Somerville, and Watertown for higher education.
Financial data: Year ended 12/31/2012. Assets, $1,180,698 (M); Expenditures, $445,468; Total giving, $438,018; Grants to individuals, 16 grants totaling $40,000 (high: $2,500, low: $2,500).
Fields of interest: College.
Type of support: Scholarships—to individuals.
Application information: Applications accepted. Application form required.
Additional information: Contact participating school's guidance office for scholarship application form.
Program description:
Kevin J. Fitzgerald Scholarship Program: The foundation awards college scholarships to graduating high school seniors attending schools in Acton-Boxborough, Arlington, Bedford, Belmont, Burlington, Cambridge, Concord-Carlisle, Lexington, Newton, Somerville, and Watertown. Two scholarships will be awarded to seniors from each high school, one $2,500 scholarship to a senior attending a four-year college, and the second to a senior attending a vocational school, community college, or other two-year college program.
EIN: 481307731

4005
Alfred Campanelli Charitable Foundation
P.O. Box 850985
Braintree, MA   02185-0985
Contact: Robert DeMarco, Tr.
Application address: 1 Campanelli Dr., Braintree, MA 02184-5215

Foundation type: Independent foundation
Purpose: Scholarships to local MA high school students for higher education.
Financial data: Year ended 12/31/2012. Assets, $44,686 (M); Expenditures, $24,066; Total giving, $24,025; Grants to individuals, 4 grants totaling $8,000 (high: $2,000, low: $2,000).
Type of support: Undergraduate support.
Application information:
Initial approach: Letter or telephone
Deadline(s): None
Additional information: Contact foundation for application guidelines.
EIN: 042991588

4006
The Cape Cod Community College Educational Foundation, Inc.
2240 Iyannough Rd.
West Barnstable, MA   02668-1599   (508) 362-2131
Contact: Kathy McNamara, Exec. Dir.
E-mail: kmcnamara@capecod.edu; *URL:* http://www.ccccfoundation.org

Foundation type: Public charity
Purpose: Scholarships to graduating high school students for attendance at Cape Cod Community College, MA.
Publications: Annual report.
Financial data: Year ended 06/30/2013. Assets, $8,184,464 (M); Expenditures, $2,620,512; Total giving, $2,307,124; Grants to individuals, totaling $325,307.
Fields of interest: Higher education.
Type of support: Support to graduates or students of specific schools.
Application information: Selection is based on academic excellence, accomplishments and financial need.
Program description:
Scholarships: Scholarships range from $500 to $10,000, for endowed scholarships, to current, incoming, and graduating students. Recipients ranged from students directly out of high school starting college in the fall, to high school students who participated in Dual Enrollment and already have college credit, to many returning students studying toward their degree, to students graduating with a perfect 4.0 GPA.
EIN: 222475111

4007
The Cape Cod Foundation
(formerly The Community Foundation of Cape Cod)
259 Willow St.
P.O. Box 406
Yarmouthport, MA   02675-1762   (508) 790-3040
Contact: For grants: Kristin O'Malley, Exec. Dir.; For scholarships: Dara Bryan, Prog. Off.
Scholarship e-mail: dbryan@capecodfoundation.org
FAX: (508) 790-4069;
E-mail: info@capecodfoundation.org; *URL:* http://www.capecodfoundation.org

Foundation type: Community foundation
Purpose: Scholarships to graduating high school seniors and continuing college students from Barnstable, Duke and Nantucket counties, MA, for higher education.
Publications: Application guidelines; Annual report; Informational brochure; Newsletter.
Financial data: Year ended 12/31/2012. Assets, $40,793,851 (M); Expenditures, $3,268,739; Total giving, $2,489,912. Scholarships—to individuals amount not specified.
Fields of interest: Music; Medical school/ education.
Type of support: Undergraduate support.
Application information: Application form required.
Initial approach: Telephone
Send request by: On-line
Deadline(s): Apr. 1 for most scholarships
Final notification: Recipients notified late May early June
Applicants should submit the following:
1) Financial information
2) FAFSA
3) Letter(s) of recommendation
Additional information: See web site for scholarship descriptions for specific criteria.

Program description:

Scholarships: The foundation currently administers more than 60 active scholarship funds totaling approximately $18 million in principal. The Foundation's scholarship office coordinates all scholarship activity and provides students, parents and school officials with an available resource for scholarship information. Unless otherwise noted, the Cape Cod Foundation's scholarships serve graduating high school seniors and continuing college students from Barnstable, Dukes, and Nantucket counties. Most of the awards are based on academic merit and financial need. See web site for additional information.
EIN: 510140462

4008
Cape Cod Times Needy Fund, Inc.
P.O. Box 36
Hyannis, MA   02601-0036   (508) 778-5661
Contact: Betsey Sethares, Exec. Dir.
E-mail: fund-drive@needyfund.org; URL: http://www.needyfund.org

Foundation type: Public charity
Purpose: Grants to economically disadvantaged individuals in the Cape Cod, MA, area.
Financial data: Year ended 11/30/2011. Assets, $434,978 (M); Expenditures, $725,561.
Fields of interest: Economically disadvantaged.
Type of support: Grants for special needs.
Application information: Applications accepted.
Initial approach: Telephone, e-mail or letter
Additional information: Contact fund for current application deadline/guidelines.
EIN: 222480332

4009
Robert C. Carco 31 Charitable Foundation
7 Wainwright Rd., Ste. 109
Winchester, MA   01890-2394   (781) 729-4424
Contact: Mario P. Carco, Tr.

Foundation type: Independent foundation
Purpose: Scholarships to graduates of Belmont High School, MA for continuing education at accredited colleges or universities.
Financial data: Year ended 12/31/2011. Assets, $210,088 (M); Expenditures, $11,461; Total giving, $11,150.
Fields of interest: Higher education.
Type of support: Support to graduates or students of specific schools.
Application information: Applications accepted.
Applicants should submit the following:
1) Transcripts
2) Letter(s) of recommendation
3) Financial information
Additional information: Application must be submitted to the scholarship committee of Belmont High School.
Program description:
Scholarship Program: Scholarships are awarded on the basis of financial need, community and civic involvement, industry, and scholastic ability as measured by grades, performance, and recommendations.
EIN: 043060962

4010
Caring for Carcinoid Foundation, Inc.
198 Tremont St.
Box 456
Boston, MA   02116-4705   (617) 948-2514
Contact: Lauren Erb, Dir., Research
E-mail: info@caringforcarcinoid.org; URL: http://www.caringforcarcinoid.org

Foundation type: Public charity
Purpose: Research grants to leading scientists who undertake cutting-edge, genetically-based carcinoid research.
Publications: Application guidelines; Annual report; Financial statement; Informational brochure; Newsletter.
Financial data: Year ended 12/31/2011. Assets, $1,732,133 (M); Expenditures, $1,190,634; Total giving, $853,500; Grants to individuals, totaling $853,500.
Fields of interest: Cancer research.
Type of support: Research.
Application information: Applications accepted.
Initial approach: Proposal
Deadline(s): Sept. 15
Additional information: Letter of intent, no more than 2 pages, should be sent via e-mail to research@caringforcarcinoid.org. The foundation will e-mail the applicant to confirm receipt of the letter of intent within five business days, and will contact individuals with successful letters of intent to continue the application process.
Program description:
Research Grants: The organization awards two-year grants of $250,000 over the grant term ($125,000 per year), to investigators pursuing innovative ideas and approaches that have a direct application and relevance to carcinoid cancer or pancreatic neuroendocrine cancer. Applications are invited from researchers currently in the field, as well as from investigators with experience in other areas of cancer research. Research areas may be basic, translational, clinical or epidemiological in nature.
EIN: 201945347

4011
The Carman Family Charitable Foundation
P.O. Box 61223
Longmeadow, MA   01116-6223
Contact: Tracy E. Carman, Tr.

Foundation type: Independent foundation
Purpose: Scholarships to individuals for higher education who reside in Palm Beach County, FL, Hampden County, MA, and New York, NY.
Financial data: Year ended 12/31/2012. Assets, $5,112 (M); Expenditures, $4,675; Total giving, $4,242.
Fields of interest: Higher education.
Type of support: Scholarships—to individuals.
Application information: Application form required.
Initial approach: Letter
Additional information: Letter should include personal information, reason for request, applicable transcripts and other pertinent information which applicant would like considered.
EIN: 046115611

4012
Carroll Charitable Foundation
(formerly Small Business Service Bureau, Inc. Charitable Foundation)
554 Main St.
P.O. Box 15014
Worcester, MA   01615-0014   (508) 756-3513
Contact: Francis Carroll, Tr.

Foundation type: Company-sponsored foundation
Purpose: Scholarships to children of employees of Small Business Service Bureau and college students conducting research on small businesses.
Financial data: Year ended 06/30/2011. Assets, $508,295 (M); Expenditures, $43,811; Total giving, $41,455.
Type of support: Employee-related scholarships; Undergraduate support.
Application information:
Initial approach: Letter
Additional information: Contact foundation for eligibility requirements.
Company name: Small Business Service Bureau, Inc.
EIN: 222546670

4013
The Anne Carroll Foundation Inc.
c/o John J. Carol, Jr.
10 Brooks Hill Rd.
Lincoln, MA   01773-1406

Foundation type: Independent foundation
Purpose: Grants to graduating seniors from Eastern MA high schools for undergraduate education.
Financial data: Year ended 11/30/2013. Assets, $95,474 (M); Expenditures, $3,323; Total giving, $0.
Type of support: Undergraduate support.
Application information: Applications accepted. Application form required.
Deadline(s): None
Additional information: Scholarship awards are based on academic achievement, acceptance in an accredited degree program, teacher recommendations, creative abilities in arts, cost of the program pursued and ability to overcome hardships.
EIN: 043493735

4014
Isaac Harris Cary Educational Fund
c/o Christine Mitchell
25 Fletcher Ave.
Lexington, MA   02420   (781) 862-0422
Contact: Steven T. Balthaser, Pres.
Application Address: 41 Woodland Rd., Lexington, MA 02420

Foundation type: Independent foundation
Purpose: Scholarships to young men of New England parentage for continuing education at accredited colleges or universities.
Financial data: Year ended 04/30/2013. Assets, $1,334,575 (M); Expenditures, $73,257; Total giving, $51,000; Grants to individuals, 38 grants totaling $51,000 (high: $2,830, low: $162).
Fields of interest: Higher education; Men.
Type of support: Undergraduate support.
Application information: Application form required.
Applicants should submit the following:
1) Transcripts
2) Financial information
Additional information: Application must also include a copy of parent's tax form.
EIN: 046023807

4015
The Center for Independent Documentary, Inc.
(formerly The Newton Television Foundation)
680 S. Main St.
Sharon, MA 02067-2868 (781) 784-3627
Contact: Susi Walsh, Exec. Dir.
FAX: (781) 784-8254;
E-mail: Susi@documentaries.org; URL: http://documentaries.org/

Foundation type: Public charity
Purpose: Support to filmmakers working on documentaries on issues from perspectives that are not usually addressed in mainstream media.
Publications: Occasional report.
Financial data: Year ended 12/31/2011. Assets, $1,660,263 (M); Expenditures, $2,382,351.
Fields of interest: Film/video; Arts, artist's services.
Type of support: Fiscal agent/sponsor.
Application information:
Initial approach: Proposal for fiscal sponsorship
Copies of proposal: 1
Deadline(s): None
Final notification: Recipients notified in two to four weeks
Program description:
Fiscal Sponsorship: The center acts a fiscal sponsor for documentary projects in order to manage funds, provide creative or technical support, and also offer advice on fundraising and distribution. The center charges an administrative fee of 5 percent from any funds that the project receives in grants and donations.
EIN: 042738458

4016
Center for Retirement Research
c/o Boston College
140 Commonwealth Ave.
Chestnut Hill, MA 02467-3800 (617) 552-1677
Contact: Alicia H. Munnell, Dir.
Application inquiry: Marina Tsiknis, (617) 552-1092, e-mail: tsiknis@bc.edu
E-mail: amy.grzybowski@bc.edu; URL: http://crr.bc.edu/

Foundation type: Public charity
Purpose: Grants and fellowships for scholars and doctoral candidates in areas of retirement income and disability insurance research.
Fields of interest: Pensions.
Type of support: Fellowships; Grants to individuals.
Application information: Applications accepted.
Send request by: On-line
Deadline(s): Feb. 14 for Grants, and Fellowships
Final notification: Recipients notified in Apr.
Applicants should submit the following:
1) Budget Information
2) Proposal
3) Transcripts
4) Letter(s) of recommendation
5) Curriculum vitae
Additional information: See web site for additional guidelines.
Program descriptions:
Dissertation Fellowship Program: This program supports dissertation research in Retirement Income and Disability Insurance Research. The program is funded by the U.S. Social Security Administration and provides funding opportunities for doctoral candidates to pursue cutting-edge research on retirement issues. Up to two fellowships of $28,000 will be awarded to doctoral candidates enrolled in an accredited program at a U.S. university.

Steven H. Sandell Grant Program: This program supports scholars in the field of retirement income and disability insurance research. The program is funded by the U.S. Social Security Administration to provide opportunities for scholars from all academic disciplines and senior scholars working in a new area to pursue cutting-edge projects on retirement income and disability insurance issues. Up to two grants of $45,000 are awarded based upon the proposal and the proposed budget.

4017
Central Boston Elder Services, Inc.
2315 Washington St.
Boston, MA 02119-3214 (617) 277-7416
Contact: Catherine Hardaway, Exec. Dir.
FAX: (617) 516-0296;
E-mail: hhardaway@centralboston.org; URL: http://www.centralboston.org

Foundation type: Public charity
Purpose: Extensive in-home services to elderly Boston, MA residents, including personal care, transportation, home delivered meals and health services.
Financial data: Year ended 06/30/2012. Assets, $27,991,409 (M); Expenditures, $42,736,766; Total giving, $30,364,617; Grants to individuals, totaling $30,364,617.
Fields of interest: Aging.
Type of support: Grants for special needs.
Application information:
Initial approach: Letter
Additional information: Contact the organization for eligibility criteria.
EIN: 042546441

4018
Charles River Laboratories Foundation, Inc.
(formerly Charles River Foundation)
251 Ballardvale St.
Wilmington, MA 01887-1096
FAX: (802) 785-2900

Foundation type: Company-sponsored foundation
Purpose: Scholarships to residents of MA, who wish to study biomedical research and the humane care of laboratory animals.
Financial data: Year ended 10/31/2012. Assets, $4,654 (M); Expenditures, $138; Total giving, $0.
Fields of interest: Animal welfare; Biomedicine research.
Type of support: Scholarships—to individuals.
Application information:
Initial approach: Letter
Additional information: Contact foundation for eligibility requirements.
EIN: 510188208

4019
The Chatham Citizens Scholarship Trust Fund
P.O. Box 244
North Chatham, MA 02650-1334 (508) 945-0990
Contact: John P. Farrell, Tr.
Application address: 90 Old Harbor Rd., Chatham, MA 02633 tel.: (508) 945-0990

Foundation type: Independent foundation
Purpose: Scholarships to graduates of Chatham High School and Cape Cod Regional High School, MA.

Financial data: Year ended 09/30/2012. Assets, $135,280 (M); Expenditures, $7,147; Total giving, $6,802.
Type of support: Support to graduates or students of specific schools.
Application information: Applications not accepted.
Additional information: The program is administered by Scholarship America. Unsolicited requests for funds not considered or acknowledged.
EIN: 222589632

4020
Chelonian Research Foundation
168 Goodrich St.
Lunenburg, MA 01462-1612 (978) 582-9668
Contact: Anders G.J. Rhodin, Dir.

Foundation type: Operating foundation
Purpose: Research grants to individuals for the dissemination of information on turtles and tortoises.
Financial data: Year ended 12/31/2010. Assets, $257,062 (M); Expenditures, $243,530; Total giving, $209,364.
Fields of interest: Research.
Type of support: Research; Awards/prizes.
Application information: Applications accepted. Application form required.
Copies of proposal: 1
Deadline(s): Nov. 15 for Linnaeus Fund Awards, none for general program fund
Additional information: Application must include proposal.
EIN: 046705444

4021
Chester High School Alumni Association
100 Skyline Trail
Middlefield, MA 01243-9800 (413) 623-5519
Contact: Maurice H. Pease, Scholarship Committee Treas.

Foundation type: Operating foundation
Purpose: Scholarships to financially needy residents of Chester, MA, for study at graduate and undergraduate colleges and universities, and technical schools.
Financial data: Year ended 06/30/2010. Assets, $168,089 (M); Expenditures, $6,834; Total giving, $4,275; Grants to individuals, totaling $4,275.
Type of support: Technical education support; Undergraduate support.
Application information: Applications accepted. Application form required.
Deadline(s): None
EIN: 046058373

4022
Children's Hospital Corporation
300 Longwood Ave.
Boston, MA 02115-5724 (617) 355-6000
URL: http://www.childrenshospital.org

Foundation type: Public charity
Purpose: Scholarships to Children's Hospital Boston employees and their family members for health-related education and training.
Financial data: Year ended 09/30/2011. Assets, $3,369,546,205 (M); Expenditures, $1,316,184,583; Total giving, $10,009,615; Grants to individuals, totaling $1,572,658.
Fields of interest: Nursing school/education; Health care.

Type of support: Scholarships—to individuals.
Application information: Contact foundation for complete application guidelines.
Program description:
Sylvia Orth Young Scholarship: Scholarships to Children's Hospital Boston employees and their family members for college courses leading to a healthcare-related certificate or degree.
EIN: 042774441

4023
Citizens for Citizens, Inc.
(also known as CFC)
264 Griffin St.
Fall River, MA 02724-2702 (508) 679-0041
FAX: (508) 324-7503; E-mail: editor@cfcinc.org;
URL: http://www.cfcinc.org

Foundation type: Public charity
Purpose: Financial assistance to indigent residents of the greater Fall River/Taunton area, MA, to help pay for utilities and other living expenses.
Financial data: Year ended 06/30/2011. Assets, $9,665,196 (M); Expenditures, $33,468,264.
Type of support: Grants for special needs.
Application information:
Initial approach: Letter or e-mail
Additional information: Contact the agency for further guidelines.
EIN: 046134724

4024
City Year, Inc.
287 Columbus Ave.
Boston, MA 02116-5114 (617) 927-2500
FAX: (617) 927-2510; URL: http://www.cityyear.org

Foundation type: Public charity
Purpose: Stipends to corps program participants, to cover the costs of living expenses.
Publications: Application guidelines; Annual report.
Financial data: Year ended 06/30/2011. Assets, $62,350,450 (M); Expenditures, $73,877,630; Total giving, $18,215,450; Grants to individuals, 1,767 grants totaling $18,127,950.
Fields of interest: Education.
Type of support: Stipends.
Application information: Applications accepted.
Initial approach: Application
Send request by: Online
Deadline(s): Feb. 15, Apr. 30, Sept. 30, and Nov. 15
Additional information: See web site for select locations in the U.S. Application must be submitted to the site of your choice.
Program description:
Service Corps Program: Each year, a select group of individuals are chosen to serve full-time in underperforming schools in select locations for ten months as tutors, mentors, and role models. Corps members work to help students stay on track and get back on track to graduate by improving their attendance, behavior, and course performance. Participants receive a modest stipend (varying by location) to help meet living expenses while participating in the program, and will also receive a $5,500 education award at the end of the City Year service, which can be used toward a college degree, a graduate school program, or existing or future qualified student loans. Eligible applicants must have a college degree, have attended some college, or have a high school diploma or GED, be able to dedicate ten months to full-time service, be between the ages of 17 and 24, be a U.S. citizen or legal permanent resident alien, and have served

no more than three terms in another AmeriCorps, NCCC, or VISTA program.
EIN: 222882549

4025
Admiral Sir Isaac Coffin's Lancasterian School
P.O. Box 1225
Nantucket, MA 02554 (508) 228-2505
Contact: Jean Hughes, Pres.; Linda Davis, Treas.

Foundation type: Independent foundation
Purpose: Scholarships to students of Nantucket, MA for postsecondary education.
Financial data: Year ended 12/31/2012. Assets, $3,522,912 (M); Expenditures, $106,233; Total giving, $41,000; Grants to individuals, 16 grants totaling $28,500 (high: $4,000, low: $500).
Fields of interest: Higher education.
Type of support: Scholarships—to individuals.
Application information: Applications accepted. Application form required.
Initial approach: Letter
Additional information: Letter should include amount and purpose of scholarship.
EIN: 042167469

4026
Saul B. and Naomi R. Cohen Foundation Inc.
87 Hammond St.
Chestnut Hill, MA 02467-1132

Foundation type: Independent foundation
Purpose: Grants for gifted students and performing artists, primarily in MA.
Financial data: Year ended 12/31/2012. Assets, $1,201 (M); Expenditures, $6,440; Total giving, $3,000; Grants to individuals, 2 grants totaling $2,000 (high: $1,000, low: $1,000).
Fields of interest: Performing arts.
Type of support: Grants to individuals.
Application information: Applications not accepted.
Additional information: Unsolicited requests for funds not considered or acknowledged.
EIN: 043419905

4027
College Club of Greater Lawrence
202 Pleasant St.
Methuen, MA 01844-7137 (978) 807-5359
Contact: Colleen Carney, Pres.
E-mail: collegeclubofgreaterlawrence@yahoo.com;
URL: http://
www.collegeclubofgreaterlawrence.com/index.html

Foundation type: Public charity
Purpose: Scholarships to residents of Andover, Lawrence , Methuen or North Andover, MA.
Financial data: Year ended 03/31/2013. Assets, $266,578 (M); Expenditures, $16,711; Total giving, $7,000.
Fields of interest: Higher education.
Type of support: Scholarships—to individuals.
Application information: Applications accepted. Application form required.
Deadline(s): 1st week of Apr.
Applicants should submit the following:
1) Resume
2) SAT
3) Essay
4) Letter(s) of recommendation

5) Transcripts
EIN: 222524154

4028
Community Action, Inc.
145 Essex St.
Haverhill, MA 01832-5528 (978) 373-1971
FAX: (978) 373-8966;
E-mail: info@communityinaction.org; URL: http://
www.communityactioninc.org/

Foundation type: Public charity
Purpose: Scholarship support to postsecondary, high school, and GED graduates, also administers emergency funding for low-income individuals in MA.
Publications: Application guidelines; Financial statement.
Financial data: Year ended 12/31/2011. Assets, $4,980,532 (M); Expenditures, $15,905,059; Total giving, $6,537,255; Grants to individuals, totaling $6,537,255.
Fields of interest: Single organization support; Education; Human services.
Type of support: Emergency funds; Scholarships—to individuals.
Application information: Applications accepted. Application form required. Application form available on the grantmaker's web site.
Initial approach: Download application
Deadline(s): Feb. 26 for postsecondary applicants and May 7 for high school graduate/graduating senior and GED applicants for Gerald Goldman Memorial Scholarships
Applicants should submit the following:
1) Essay
2) Letter(s) of recommendation
Program description:
Gerald Goldman Memorial Scholarships: Three $1,000 scholarships are available to residents of Haverhill, Amesbury, Newbury, Salisbury, Groveland, Georgetown, Boxford, Rowley, West Newbury, and Merrimac. Eligible applicants must supply proof of their enrollment in a full-time college program and/or demonstrate in writing their acceptance in a college program; GED applicants must have received a GED and show acceptance into a college program. There are no income eligibility requirements for this scholarship.
EIN: 042383153

4029
Community Foundation of Western Massachusetts
1500 Main St., Ste. 2300
P.O. Box 15769
Springfield, MA 01115-1000 (413) 732-2858
Contact: Ronald E. Ancrum, Pres.; For grants: Sheila Toto, Prog. Off.
Scholarship e-mail:
scholar@communityfoundation.org
FAX: (413) 733-8565;
E-mail: wmass@communityfoundation.org;
URL: http://www.communityfoundation.org

Foundation type: Community foundation
Purpose: Scholarships to residents of western Massachusetts, and Hartford County, CT for higher education.
Publications: Application guidelines; Grants list; Informational brochure; Newsletter.
Financial data: Year ended 03/31/2013. Assets, $103,619,620 (M); Expenditures, $11,428,328; Total giving, $9,474,217.
Fields of interest: Higher education.

Type of support: Scholarships—to individuals; Student loans—to individuals; Support to graduates or students of specific schools; Undergraduate support.
Application information: Applications accepted. Application form required. Application form available on the grantmaker's web site.
  Initial approach: Application
  Send request by: Online
  Deadline(s): Mar. 31
  Final notification: Applicants notified by the end of June
  Applicants should submit the following:
    1) SAR
    2) Transcripts
    3) SAT
    4) GPA
    5) FAFSA
  Additional information: See web site for a complete listing of scholarships and loans. Scholarships are paid directly to the educational institution on behalf of the student.
Program description:
  Scholarship and Loan Program: The foundation administers, through one centralized application process, over 100 scholarship and loan funds. These scholarship and interest-free student loan funds support students seeking access to the opportunities offered by higher education and play a substantial role in providing an educated citizenry. Some of the funds help students from a particular school or area. Others provide financial assistance to those pursuing a specific field of study. Others assist students that are most in need. See web site for additional information.
EIN: 223089640

4030
The Jennie & Samuel J. Costa Educational Trust

c/o John E. McDonald,Jr.
55 Oregon Ave.
Braintree, MA   02184
Contact: John E. McDonald, Jr., Tr.

Foundation type: Independent foundation
Purpose: Scholarships to current seniors or recent graduates of Waltham High School, MA, who are of Italian descent.
Financial data: Year ended 12/31/2012. Assets, $287,750 (M); Expenditures, $11,988; Total giving, $4,500.
Fields of interest: Higher education.
Type of support: Support to graduates or students of specific schools; Undergraduate support.
Application information: Applications accepted. Application form required.
  Deadline(s): None
  Additional information: Applications available at Waltham High School.
EIN: 043031308

4031
Bobby Costello Scholarship Fund

2 S. Kimball St.
P.O. Box 5248
Bradford, MA   01835-7418   (978) 374-6352
Contact: William J. Costello, Tr.

Foundation type: Independent foundation
Purpose: Merit-based scholarships for graduates of Haverhill High School, MA attending Saint Anslem College, NH.

Financial data: Year ended 12/31/2011. Assets, $131,905 (M); Expenditures, $3,601; Total giving, $3,546.
Fields of interest: Higher education.
Type of support: Scholarships—to individuals; Support to graduates or students of specific schools.
Application information:
  Deadline(s): June 1
  Additional information: Unsolicited requests for funds not accepted.
EIN: 043575889

4032
Luther E. Crist and Phyllis C. Crist Trust

150 Second Rd.
Marlborough, MA   01752-4222

Foundation type: Independent foundation
Purpose: Grants to residents of Marlsborough, MA, for medical expenses.
Financial data: Year ended 12/31/2012. Assets, $324,224 (M); Expenditures, $14,050; Total giving, $8,000; Grants to individuals, 4 grants totaling $8,000 (high: $2,500, low: $1,500).
Fields of interest: Health care; Economically disadvantaged.
Type of support: Grants for special needs.
Application information: Applications not accepted.
  Additional information: Unsolicited requests for funding not considered or acknowledged.
EIN: 046802292

4033
The Paul H. D'Amour Fellowship Foundation

2145 Roosevelt Ave.
Springfield, MA   01104-1650   (413) 504-4218

Foundation type: Company-sponsored foundation
Purpose: Scholarships to Big Y customers or their dependents in the Big Y marketing areas of CT and MA.
Financial data: Year ended 06/30/2013. Assets, $163,239 (M); Expenditures, $10,113; Total giving, $10,000; Grants to individuals, 5 grants totaling $10,000 (high: $2,000, low: $2,000).
Type of support: Scholarships—to individuals.
Application information: Applications accepted.
  Initial approach: Letter
  Deadline(s): Feb. 1
  Applicants should submit the following:
    1) SAT
    2) Transcripts
    3) Letter(s) of recommendation
  Additional information: Scholarships are awarded to academically outstanding students in the Big Y market area.
EIN: 222626366

4034
The Gerald & Paul D'Amour Founders Scholarship for Academic Excellence

2145 Roosevelt Ave.
Springfield, MA   01104   (413) 504-4218

Foundation type: Company-sponsored foundation
Purpose: Scholarships to students residing in the Big Y Foods, Inc. marketing area (parts of MA and CT) to attend any two year college, or four year college, community college or junior college.
Publications: Application guidelines; Grants list.

Financial data: Year ended 06/30/2013. Assets, $1,829,854 (M); Expenditures, $220,037; Total giving, $219,078; Grants to individuals, 296 grants totaling $219,078 (high: $1,026, low: $500).
Fields of interest: Higher education.
Type of support: Scholarships—to individuals.
Application information: Applications accepted. Application form required. Application form available on the grantmaker's web site.
  Initial approach: Application
  Send request by: Mail
  Deadline(s): Feb. 1
  Applicants should submit the following:
    1) SAT
    2) Transcripts
    3) Letter(s) of recommendation
  Additional information: Scholarships are based on academic achievement.
EIN: 223305742

4035
The Danny Foundation for Autism

166 Mill St.
Stoughton, MA   02072   (781) 436-8421
Contact: Janet Abrahamson, Tr.

Foundation type: Operating foundation
Purpose: Scholarships for individuals with autism and some support for their families.
Financial data: Year ended 12/31/2012. Assets, $70,270 (M); Expenditures, $7,880; Total giving, $7,380; Grants to individuals, 22 grants totaling $5,180 (high: $400, low: $100).
Fields of interest: Higher education; Autism.
Type of support: Grants to individuals; Grants for special needs.
Application information: Applications accepted. Application form not required.
  Initial approach: Letter
  Deadline(s): None
EIN: 043426612

4036
Amelia Davis Fund for INCAP Alumni

42 Adams Rd.
Framingham, MA   01701-2456   (508) 872-9770
URL: http://www.alumnihouse.org

Foundation type: Independent foundation
Purpose: Need-based financial assistance to alumni of Framingham State College.
Financial data: Year ended 04/30/2013. Assets, $127,508 (M); Expenditures, $11,425; Total giving, $6,900; Grants to individuals, 6 grants totaling $6,900 (high: $1,500, low: $600).
Type of support: Grants to individuals; Support to graduates or students of specific schools.
Application information: Applications not accepted.
  Additional information: Unsolicited requests for funds not considered or acknowledged.
EIN: 046133792

4037
Faye H. Deane Scholarship Fund

P.O. Box 382
Woods Hole, MA   02543-0382
Contact: Thomas A. Maddigan, Tr.
*Application Address:*c/o Prinicipal Middleboro H.S., 71 E. Grove St., Middleborough, MA, 02346

Foundation type: Independent foundation
Purpose: Scholarships to financially needy students who have graduated or are graduating

from Middleborough High School, MA, for higher education.

Financial data: Year ended 12/31/2012. Assets, $461,533 (M); Expenditures, $12,710; Total giving, $6,276; Grants to individuals, 7 grants totaling $6,276 (high: $1,000, low: $500).

Type of support: Scholarships—to individuals; Support to graduates or students of specific schools.

Application information: Application form required.

Deadline(s): End of Apr.

Additional information: Application should include needs and grades; Application form available from the high school principal.

EIN: 042900642

4038
Dedham Women's Exchange, Inc.
445 Washington St.
Dedham, MA 02026-4418   (781) 326-0627
Contact: Ginna Parker, Pres.

Foundation type: Public charity
Purpose: College scholarships to one male and one female graduating senior of Dedham High School, MA for continuing education at accredited colleges or universities.
Financial data: Year ended 01/31/2013. Assets, $253,395 (M); Expenditures, $91,951; Total giving, $5,910; Grants to individuals, totaling $1,600.
Fields of interest: Higher education.
Type of support: Support to graduates or students of specific schools.
Application information: Applications accepted. Application form required.

Additional information: Unsolicited requests for funds not considered or acknowledged.

EIN: 042258361

4039
Sarah A. W. Devens Trust
c/o RH&B, Inc.
50 Congress St., Ste. 900
Boston, MA 02109   (617) 227-1782

Foundation type: Independent foundation
Purpose: Financial assistance to elderly, economically disadvantaged women over the age of 65 residing in MA.
Financial data: Year ended 11/30/2012. Assets, $1,609,298 (M); Expenditures, $71,878; Total giving, $44,170; Grants to individuals, 5 grants totaling $12,575 (high: $4,000, low: $225).
Fields of interest: Aging; Women; Economically disadvantaged.
Type of support: Grants for special needs.
Application information: Applications accepted. Application form not required.

Deadline(s): None

Additional information: Applicants must be recommended by a social service center.

EIN: 046291053

4040
Emilio A. & Mary A. Difelice Scholarship Trust
c/o Eastern Bank
605 Broadway, LF 42
Saugus, MA 01906   (781) 581-4271
Contact: Doreen Dibari

Foundation type: Independent foundation
Purpose: Scholarships to graduating students who reside in Beverly, Salem, Danvers, Peabody,

Hamilton or Manchester, MA for postsecondary education.

Financial data: Year ended 12/31/2012. Assets, $852,338 (M); Expenditures, $51,706; Total giving, $41,061.

Fields of interest: Higher education.

Type of support: Scholarships—to individuals.

Application information: Applications accepted. Application form required.

Deadline(s): None

Additional information: Application forms are available upon request. Students must have a "B" average or better in the year prior at high school, prep school or prior year of college.

EIN: 046941137

4041
Documentary Educational Resources, Inc.
101 Morse St.
Watertown, MA 02472-2554   (617) 926-0491
Contact: Alice Apley, Pres. and Treas. and Exec. Dir.
FAX: (617) 926-9519; *E-mail:* docued@der.org;
Toll-free tel.: (800) 569-6621; E-Mail for Alice Apley:
alice@der.org; URL: http://www.der.org

Foundation type: Public charity
Purpose: Grants to individual artists for the production and distribution of documentary films.
Publications: Application guidelines; Financial statement; Grants list; Informational brochure; Newsletter; Program policy statement.
Financial data: Year ended 04/30/2012. Assets, $416,287 (M); Expenditures, $2,107,889; Total giving, $1,518,527; Grants to individuals, totaling $1,518,527.
Fields of interest: Film/video; Arts, artist's services.
Type of support: Internship funds; Research; Grants to individuals; Fiscal agent/sponsor.
Application information: Applications accepted. Application form not required.

Initial approach: Letter, Telephone, or e-mail (preferred)
Send request by: E-mail (two) and one by mail.
Copies of proposal: 3
Deadline(s): Rolling
Final notification: Applicants notified in three to four weeks
Applicants should submit the following:
1) Work samples
2) Resume
3) Proposal
4) Financial information
Program description:
Fiscal Sponsorship: The organization provides fiscal sponsorship to independent documentary filmmakers who are interested in world cultures, anthropology, film studies, international communication, documentary film, the arts, immigration issues, and human rights. Eligible applicants must be a U.S. citizen residing in the U.S. A small percentage of grant money raised by funding efforts is given to the organization in exchange for the sponsorship.
EIN: 042498206

4042
Kenneth S. Donnell Trust
P.O. Box 354
Nantucket, MA 02554

Foundation type: Independent foundation
Purpose: Scholarships and camperships to people under age 17 who are residents of Nantucket, MA.

Financial data: Year ended 12/31/2012. Assets, $549,322 (M); Expenditures, $28,378; Total giving, $22,057; Grants to individuals, 45 grants totaling $22,057 (high: $900, low: $150).

Type of support: Scholarships—to individuals; Precollege support; Camperships.

Application information: Application form required.

Additional information: Contact trust for current application deadline/guidelines.

EIN: 046635207

4043
Dover and Sherborn Education Fund, Inc.
P. O. Box 421
Dover, MA 02030-0421   (508) 785-2433
Contact: Amy Davis, Exec. Admin.
E-mail: dsef@dsef.com; URL: http://dsef.com/

Foundation type: Public charity
Purpose: Grants to teachers and staff working with limited resources in the public schools in Dover and Sherborn, MA.
Publications: Application guidelines.
Financial data: Year ended 06/30/2012. Assets, $166,561 (M); Expenditures, $148,221; Total giving, $120,428; Grants to individuals, totaling $120,428.
Fields of interest: Education.
Type of support: Grants to individuals.
Application information: Applications accepted. Application form required. Application form available on the grantmaker's web site.

Deadline(s): Fri. before Feb. vacation
Applicants should submit the following:
1) Proposal
2) Budget Information
EIN: 222549842

4044
Cora Du Bois Charitable Trust
c/o Nixon Peabody
100 Summer St.
Boston, MA 02110   (617) 345-1000

Foundation type: Independent foundation
Purpose: Scholarships to graduate students in anthropology and other fields.
Financial data: Year ended 12/31/2012. Assets, $1,153,551 (M); Expenditures, $44,336; Total giving, $23,000; Grants to individuals, 7 grants totaling $23,000 (high: $5,000, low: $3,000).
Fields of interest: Anthropology/sociology.
Type of support: Graduate support.
Application information: Application form required.

Deadline(s): Feb. 15
Applicants should submit the following:
1) Transcripts
2) Letter(s) of recommendation
Additional information: Applicants should demonstrate financial need.
EIN: 046689812

4045
Martin W. Dugan Foundation
(also known as Martin W. Dugan Trust)
c/o Eastern Bank, N.A.
605 Broadway, LF 41
Saugus, MA 01906-3200   (781) 581-4220
Contact: Shawn McCarthy

Foundation type: Independent foundation
Purpose: Scholarships to financially needy residents of Newbury, Newburyport, or West Newbury, MA, for studies in science, technology, law, medicine, or Catholic priesthood.

Financial data: Year ended 12/31/2012. Assets, $489,749 (M); Expenditures, $26,857; Total giving, $20,700.
Fields of interest: Law school/education; Medical school/education; Theological school/education; Science; Engineering/technology; Catholic agencies & churches.
Type of support: Scholarships—to individuals.
Application information: Applications accepted. Application form required.
  Deadline(s): None
EIN: 046193022

4046
Arleen and Arthur H. Dunham Educational Trust

c/o Thomas A. Maddigan, Trustee
P.O. Box 382
Woods Hole, MA 02543-0382 (508) 946-2010
Application address: c/o Middleborough High School, Attn.: Principal, 71 E. Grove St., Middleborough, MA 02346-1847, tel.: (508) 946-2010

Foundation type: Independent foundation
Purpose: Scholarships to students who have graduated or is graduating from Middleborough High School, MA, with sufficient grades and needs to attend college.
Financial data: Year ended 12/31/2012. Assets, $187,443 (M); Expenditures, $16,390; Total giving, $13,693; Grants to individuals, 5 grants totaling $13,693 (high: $3,766, low: $1,450).
Fields of interest: Higher education.
Type of support: Scholarships—to individuals; Support to graduates or students of specific schools.
Application information: Application form required.
  Deadline(s): Apr. 30
  Additional information: Applications available from the principal of Middleborough high school, and must include letter of need and grades.
EIN: 046252943

4047
Dunkin Brands Disaster Relief Fund, Inc.

130 Royall St.
Canton, MA 02021 (781) 737-3000
Contact: Mary Ann Dimascio

Foundation type: Independent foundation
Purpose: Emergency funds to employees of Dunkin Brands, Inc., and its affiliates and their families and to franchises of Dunkin Brands, their employees and families who have become victims of natural, terrorist or other similar disasters or catastrophic events.
Financial data: Year ended 12/31/2012. Assets, $43,804 (M); Expenditures, $59,574; Total giving, $59,300; Grants to individuals, 45 grants totaling $59,300 (high: $2,500, low: $500).
Fields of interest: Disasters, preparedness/services; Safety/disasters.
Type of support: Employee-related welfare.
Application information: Applications not accepted.
  Additional information: Unsolicited request for funds not considered or acknowledged.
EIN: 203493525

4048
J. Franklin Dyer Trust

109 Main St.
Gloucester, MA 01930-5701 (978) 283-9233
Contact: J. Michael Faherty, Tr.
Application address: 111 Main St., Gloucester, MA 01930

Foundation type: Independent foundation
Purpose: Scholarships to graduating students attending Gloucester High School, MA.
Financial data: Year ended 03/31/2013. Assets, $152,228 (M); Expenditures, $2,579; Total giving, $0.
Fields of interest: Higher education.
Type of support: Support to graduates or students of specific schools; Undergraduate support.
Application information: Application information can be obtained through the Gloucester school system.
EIN: 046545848

4049
Earthwatch Institute, Inc.

(formerly Earthwatch Expeditions, Inc.)
114 Western Ave.
Boston, MA 02134-1037 (978) 461-0081
FAX: (978) 461-2332; E-mail: info@earthwatch.org; Toll-free tel.: (800) 776-0188; URL: http://www.earthwatch.org

Foundation type: Public charity
Purpose: Fellowships and research grants to individuals for projects in the biological, physical, social, and cultural sciences. Grants also to individual field researchers specializing in archaeology, marine ecology, and zoology.
Publications: Application guidelines; Grants list; Informational brochure; Newsletter.
Financial data: Year ended 09/30/2011. Assets, $6,664,235 (M); Expenditures, $10,015,430; Total giving, $2,208,812; Grants to individuals, totaling $560,393.
Fields of interest: History/archaeology; Research; Natural resources; Animals/wildlife, preservation/protection; Marine science; Anthropology/sociology.
Type of support: Fellowships; Research; Awards/grants by nomination only; Awards/prizes; Travel grants.
Application information: Application form required.
  Initial approach: Telephone
  Deadline(s): Varies
  Additional information: See web site for additional guidelines.
Program descriptions:
  Research Program: The organization supports doctoral and post-doctoral researchers, or researchers with equivalent scholarship or commensurate life experience. The program welcomes proposals from advanced scholars and professionals of any nationality, covering any geographic region. Applicants intending to conduct research in foreign countries are strongly encouraged to include host country nationals as part of their research staff. The organization awards research grants on a per capita basis; the total grant amount is determined by multiplying the per capita grant by the number of volunteers participating on a project. Per capita grants average $800, and the average project grant range is between $16,000 and $48,000 for one full field season. Each grant may be renewed annually, contingent on staff evaluations of the project's scientific, logistical, and budgetary success in the field. The program encourages long-term research projects and requests that Principal Investigators indicate their projected research term.
  Student Challenge Awards Program: The program offers students aged 16 to 18 gifted in the arts and humanities an opportunity to spend two to three intensive weeks during the summer at a scientific research station. The aim is to excite the students' imagination, expand their potential, and stimulate their curiosity about science and technology.
EIN: 237168440

4050
East Cambridge Savings Charitable Foundation, Inc.

292 Cambridge St.
East Cambridge, MA 02141-1203 (617) 354-7700

Foundation type: Company-sponsored foundation
Purpose: Scholarships to children of East Cambridge Savings Bank employees for undergraduate education.
Financial data: Year ended 12/31/2012. Assets, $115,654 (M); Expenditures, $121,320; Total giving, $120,700; Grants to individuals, 16 grants totaling $22,750 (high: $15,000, low: $750).
Type of support: Employee-related scholarships; Undergraduate support.
Application information: Applications accepted. Application form required.
  Deadline(s): Contact foundation for application form
Company name: East Cambridge Savings Bank
EIN: 043399319

4051
East Longmeadow Rotary Memorial Scholarship Foundation, Inc.

537 Prospect St.
East Longmeadow, MA 01028-3118

Foundation type: Independent foundation
Purpose: Scholarships to residents of East Longmeadow, MA, or to a child of a member of the East Longmeadow Rotary Club.
Publications: Application guidelines.
Financial data: Year ended 06/30/2013. Assets, $290,181 (M); Expenditures, $16,314; Total giving, $14,000; Grants to individuals, 8 grants totaling $14,000 (high: $3,500, low: $1,000).
Fields of interest: Higher education; Scholarships/financial aid.
Type of support: Undergraduate support.
Application information: Applications accepted.
  Initial approach: Letter
  Deadline(s): Mar. 31
  Additional information: Application should include three letters of recommendation.
EIN: 042961763

4052
Easter Chapter Order of the Eastern Star Charitable Trust

2 Wagon Wheel Rd.
North Attleboro, MA 02760 (508) 699-3966

Foundation type: Independent foundation
Purpose: Scholarships to deserving Foxborough High School seniors who are residents of Foxborough, MA and have been accepted at an accredited postsecondary institution.
Financial data: Year ended 12/31/2012. Assets, $47,877 (M); Expenditures, $4,756; Total giving,

$4,000; Grants to individuals, 2 grants totaling $4,000 (high: $2,000, low: $2,000).

Fields of interest: Higher education.

Type of support: Support to graduates or students of specific schools.

Application information: Applications accepted. Application form required. Interview required.

Deadline(s): Apr. 10

Applicants should submit the following:
1) Class rank
2) Transcripts
3) Letter(s) of recommendation
4) Financial information

Additional information: Application must also include a personal statement describing career goals and life interest. Applicant must demonstrate high moral standards and character, extracurricular and community activities. Application can be obtained from guidance counselor's office.

EIN: 202044479

4053

Georgiana Goddard Eaton Memorial Fund

c/o Welch & Forbes LLC
45 School St.
Boston, MA   02108-3204   (617) 523-1635
Contact: Oliver A. Spadling, Tr.

Foundation type: Independent foundation

Purpose: Pensions to former employees of Community Workshops, Inc.

Financial data: Year ended 06/30/2012. Assets, $9,743,787 (M); Expenditures, $580,782; Total giving, $397,412.

Type of support: Grants to individuals.

Application information: Applications accepted.

Deadline(s): None

EIN: 046112820

4054

Educational Foundation of the Massachusetts Society of Certified Public Accountants

105 Chauncy St., 10th Fl.
Boston, MA   02111-1726   (617) 556-4000
Contact: Kenneth W. Kirkland, Pres.
FAX: (617) 556-4126;
E-mail: biannoni@mscpaonline.org; URL: https://www.mscpaonline.org/about/educational_foundation

Foundation type: Public charity

Purpose: Scholarships and awards to undergraduate and graduate students who are residents of Massachusetts, pursuing studies in the accounting field.

Publications: Application guidelines.

Financial data: Year ended 04/30/2012. Assets, $357,320 (M); Expenditures, $1,942,806; Total giving, $71,000; Grants to individuals, totaling $66,000.

Fields of interest: Business school/education.

Type of support: Graduate support; Undergraduate support.

Application information: Applicants must demonstrate financial need and academic excellence.

EIN: 046139571

4055

Edwards Scholarship Fund

89 South St., Ste. 603
Boston, MA   02111-2651   (617) 737-3400

Foundation type: Independent foundation

Purpose: Scholarships to students under the age of 25 whose families have resided in Boston, MA, since the start of the student's junior year in high school.

Publications: Application guidelines.

Financial data: Year ended 07/31/2012. Assets, $7,905,831 (M); Expenditures, $353,373; Total giving, $196,991; Grants to individuals, 108 grants totaling $196,991 (high: $5,000, low: $1,000).

Fields of interest: Scholarships/financial aid.

Type of support: Graduate support; Undergraduate support.

Application information: Application form required. Application form available on the grantmaker's web site. Interview required.

Initial approach: Letter, telephone or e-mail
Send request by: Mail or e-mail
Copies of proposal: Varies
Deadline(s): Mar. 1
Final notification: Applicants notified in five months
Applicants should submit the following:
1) Letter(s) of recommendation
2) Transcripts
3) SAT
4) SAR
5) Financial information

Additional information: Application should also include copies of parents' W-2 forms. Unsolicited applications not accepted.

Program description:

Scholarship Program: The purpose of the fund is to further the development of good citizenship through education. The fund offers scholarships to men and women of good character and ability who are in need of financial aid for higher education. Students must have their family home in Boston and be enrolled in a program that leads to an associate's, bachelor's, or higher degree. Undergraduates receive preference. Applicants must be under 25 years of age, and may receive scholarship aid for six years. Recipients have a moral obligation to repay any amount granted when they are able to do so.

EIN: 046002496

4056

Dorothy Harrison Egan Foundation

c/o Gilmore, Rees & Carlson, P.C.
70 Walnut St.
Wellesley, MA   02481-2102
Application address: c/o Claire D. Graves, P.O. Box 3366, Nantucket, MA 02584-3366, tel.: (508) 228-9868

Foundation type: Independent foundation

Purpose: Scholarship to qualified candidates pursuing health care or any other related subjects in college, medical school or other institutions offering courses of study in these fields.

Financial data: Year ended 09/30/2013. Assets, $4,198,759 (M); Expenditures, $333,223; Total giving, $268,727; Grants to individuals, 25 grants totaling $123,727 (high: $10,000, low: $855).

Fields of interest: Higher education; Medical school/education.

Type of support: Scholarships—to individuals.

Application information: Applications accepted.

Initial approach: Letter
Send request by: Mail
Deadline(s): Late winter, early spring
Applicants should submit the following:
1) Letter(s) of recommendation
2) Transcripts

EIN: 571191002

4057

Elder Services of Cape Cod

68 Rte. 134
South Dennis, MA   02660-3710   (508) 394-4630
Contact: Leslie Scheer, Exec. Dir.
FAX: (508) 394-3712; E-mail: info@escci.org; Toll Free Tel.: (800)-244-4630; URL: http://www.escci.org/

Foundation type: Public charity

Purpose: Provides eligible elders of the Cape Cod, MA area with supportive services at home, such as meals, shopping, homemaking, personal care, emergency response systems, or adult day care.

Financial data: Year ended 06/30/2012. Assets, $4,425,988 (M); Expenditures, $15,619,343; Total giving, $7,897,583; Grants to individuals, totaling $7,752,812.

Fields of interest: Aging; Economically disadvantaged.

Type of support: In-kind gifts.

Application information: Application form not required.

Initial approach: Letter
Deadline(s): None
Additional information: A professional care manager from Elder Services will make a home visit to verify eligibility for services. While there, the care manager will assess health and social needs. Must be a resident of Massachusetts, be sixty years of age or older, have a "critical need" for services, and must meet certain income guidelines.

EIN: 042523904

4058

Elderhostel, Inc.

11 Ave. de Lafayette
Boston, MA   02111-1746   (617) 426-7788
Contact: James Moses, Pres. and C.E.O.
FAX: (617) 426-0701;
E-mail: Registration@elderhostel.org; Toll-free tel.: (800) 454-5768; Toll-free Fax : (877) 426-2166; URL: http://www.elderhostel.org

Foundation type: Public charity

Purpose: Grants to help senior citizens travel.

Publications: Annual report; Financial statement; Informational brochure; Newsletter.

Financial data: Year ended 09/30/2012. Assets, $88,866,900 (M); Expenditures, $182,150,503; Total giving, $209,685; Grants to individuals, totaling $209,685.

Fields of interest: Education; Aging.

Type of support: Grants to individuals.

Application information: Applications accepted. Application form required. Application form available on the grantmaker's web site.

Initial approach: E-mail
Send request by: Mail
Final notification: Applicants notified in four to six weeks

EIN: 042632526

4059

Essex County Community Foundation, Inc.

175 Andover St., Ste. 101
Danvers, MA   01923-2833   (978) 777-8876
Contact: David Welbourn, C.E.O. and Pres.; For grants: Julie Bishop, V.P., Grants and Svcs.
FAX: (978) 777-9454; E-mail: info@eccf.org; Grant inquiry e-mail: j.bishop@eccf.org; Grant application

e-mail: grantsubmit@eccf.org; URL: http://www.eccf.org

Foundation type: Community foundation
Purpose: Scholarships to assist students of Essex county, MA for secondary or postsecondary education.
Publications: Application guidelines; Annual report; Financial statement; Grants list; Informational brochure; Newsletter.
Financial data: Year ended 06/30/2012. Assets, $18,764,384 (M); Expenditures, $3,260,512; Total giving, $2,269,654. Scholarships—to individuals amount not specified.
Fields of interest: Education.
Type of support: Undergraduate support.
Application information: Applications not accepted.
Additional information: Unsolicited requests for funds not considered or acknowledged.
EIN: 043407816

4060
Essex Veterans of World War II
c/o Eastern Bank & Trust Co.
605 Broadway, LF 41
Saugus, MA   01906-3200

Foundation type: Independent foundation
Purpose: Scholarships to graduating seniors of Essex, MA, public schools who are children of U.S. veterans.
Financial data: Year ended 12/31/2012. Assets, $210,389 (M); Expenditures, $11,311; Total giving, $8,750.
Fields of interest: Military/veterans' organizations.
Type of support: Scholarships—to individuals.
Application information: Applications accepted.
Deadline(s): None
Additional information: Applications by essay.
EIN: 046697373

4061
Fallon Clinic Foundation
(formerly Fallon Foundation)
Worcester Off. Twr.
100 Front St., 14th Fl.
Worcester, MA   01608-1425   (508) 368-5498
Contact: Kelsa Zereski CFRE, Exec. Dir. and Clark
FAX: (508) 890-9942;
E-mail: kelsa.zereski@fallonclinic.org; URL: http://www.fallonfoundation.org

Foundation type: Public charity
Purpose: Scholarships to employees and dependants of employees of Fallon Clinic and Fallon Community Health Plan, MA.
Publications: Application guidelines; Financial statement; Grants list; Informational brochure.
Financial data: Year ended 09/30/2011. Assets, $4,764,817 (M); Expenditures, $397,006; Total giving, $163,721.
Type of support: Scholarships—to individuals.
Application information:
Applicants should submit the following:
1) GPA
2) Financial information
3) SAT
4) Transcripts
Additional information: Unsolicited requests for funds not considered or acknowledged.
EIN: 222912515

4062
Farm Aid
501 Cambridge St., 3rd Fl.
Cambridge, MA   02141-1104   (617) 354-2922
Contact: Hilde Steffey, Prog. Dir.
FAX: (617) 354-6992; E-mail: info@farmaid.org;
Toll-free tel.: (800) FARM-AID; URL: http://www.farmaid.org

Foundation type: Public charity
Purpose: Scholarships to undergraduate students pursuing agriculture and agriculture-related studies at colleges and universities in the region in which Younkers, Inc. does business.
Publications: Application guidelines; Annual report; Informational brochure; Newsletter.
Financial data: Year ended 12/31/2012. Assets, $1,953,615 (M); Expenditures, $1,798,375; Total giving, $538,543; Grants to individuals, 3 grants totaling $23,643.
Fields of interest: University.
Type of support: Scholarships—to individuals.
Application information:
Deadline(s): Vary
Additional information: Students must rank in the top 50 percent of the graduating class, demonstrate financial need and leadership.
EIN: 363383233

4063
Edwin S. Farmer Trust
c/o Simonds, Winslow, Willis & Abbott
50 Congress St., Ste. 925
Boston, MA   02109-4075   (617) 227-8662
Contact: John L. Worden III Esq., Tr.

Foundation type: Independent foundation
Purpose: Grants to aged, economically disadvantaged women and married couples with preference to residents of Arlington, MA.
Financial data: Year ended 12/31/2012. Assets, $722,748 (M); Expenditures, $31,708; Total giving, $20,793; Grants to individuals, 12 grants totaling $20,793 (high: $4,500, low: $100).
Fields of interest: Health care; Aging; Women; Economically disadvantaged.
Type of support: Grants for special needs.
Application information: Applications accepted.
Initial approach: Letter
Deadline(s): None
Additional information: Applicant must state marital status, gender, age, and financial circumstances.
EIN: 046257543

4064
Henry Farnam Trust
c/o Day Pitney LLP
1 International Pl.
Boston, MA   02110-2602   (860) 823-3778
Contact: Beverly J. Goulet, Tr.
Application address: c/o City of Norwich, Dept. of Social Services, City Hall, 80 Broadway, Norwich, CT 06360, tel.: (860) 823-3778

Foundation type: Independent foundation
Purpose: Assistance to poor and meritorious widows who reside in the city of Norwich, CT.
Financial data: Year ended 06/30/2012. Assets, $363,641 (M); Expenditures, $22,103; Total giving, $15,000; Grants to individuals, 30 grants totaling $15,000 (high: $500, low: $500).
Fields of interest: Women.
Type of support: Grants for special needs.

Application information: Applications accepted. Application form not required.
Deadline(s): None
EIN: 046057931

4065
The Fassino Foundation, Inc.
42 Eliot Hill Rd.
Natick, MA   01760-5534   (508) 653-4554
Contact: Edward G. Fassino, Pres.

Foundation type: Independent foundation
Purpose: Scholarships primarily to MA residents for higher education.
Financial data: Year ended 12/31/2011. Assets, $2,742,308 (M); Expenditures, $222,988; Total giving, $197,000.
Type of support: Scholarships—to individuals.
Application information: Application form not required.
EIN: 043177633

4066
Harriet M. Faunce Trust
c/o Cape Cod Five Cents Savings Bank
P.O. Box 20
Orleans, MA   02653-0020   (877) 409-5600
Contact: Deborah M. Burgess, Secy.
Application address: P.O. Box 3067, Bourne, MA 02532-0767

Foundation type: Independent foundation
Purpose: Scholarships to eligible students from the towns of Bourne and Sandwich, MA.
Financial data: Year ended 12/31/2011. Assets, $500,295 (M); Expenditures, $32,171; Total giving, $21,500.
Type of support: Scholarships—to individuals.
Application information: Applications accepted. Application form required.
Deadline(s): None
Additional information: Forms are obtained from the guidance department of eligible schools.
EIN: 046035572

4067
Major & Mrs. Frank H. Ferdian Education Foundation
P.O. Box 4256
Springfield, MA   01101-4256   (413) 783-6240
Contact: Michael Cross, Tr.

Foundation type: Independent foundation
Purpose: Scholarships and awards to high school and college students for continuing education at accredited colleges or universities.
Financial data: Year ended 12/31/2010. Assets, $228,057 (M); Expenditures, $24,445; Total giving, $18,872; Grants to individuals, 21 grants totaling $18,872 (high: $1,800, low: $200).
Fields of interest: Higher education.
Type of support: Scholarships—to individuals.
Application information: Applications accepted. Application form required.
Deadline(s): None
EIN: 043448574

4068
Fine Arts Work Center in Provincetown, Inc.
24 Pearl St.
Provincetown, MA   02657-1504   (508) 487-9960
Contact: Hunter O'Hanian, Exec. Dir.
FAX: (508) 487-8873; E-mail: general@fawc.org;
URL: http://www.fawc.org

Foundation type: Public charity
Purpose: Fellowships to visual artists and writers who are in the early phase of their careers.
Publications: Application guidelines; Financial statement; Informational brochure (including application guidelines); Newsletter.
Financial data: Year ended 09/30/2011. Assets, $4,948,947 (M); Expenditures, $1,329,698.
Fields of interest: Visual arts; Literature; Arts.
Type of support: Fellowships; Awards/prizes; Residencies.
Application information: Application form required. Application form available on the grantmaker's web site.
  Initial approach: Letter, telephone, fax, or e-mail
  Deadline(s): Dec. 1 for Writing Fellowship, February 1 for Visual Arts Fellowship
  Applicants should submit the following:
    1) SASE
    2) Work samples
  Additional information: The application fee for writing fellowship is $45. The application fee for the visual arts online submission is $57.
Program description:
  Fellowships: Visual artists and emerging writers are required to be residents in Provincetown, MA during the seven-month fellowship. Fellows are provided living accommodations and a monthly stipend of $750. Visual fellows are also provided separate studio space.
EIN: 042487373

4069
First Literacy, Inc.
(also known as Boston Adult Literacy Fund)
160 Boylston St.
Boston, MA   02116-4620   (617) 482-3336
Contact: Skye Morrison Kramer, C.E.O.
FAX: (617) 482-2554; E-mail: info@firstliteracy.org;
E-Mail for Skye Morrison Kramer:
skramer@firstliteracy.org; URL: http://www.firstliteracy.org/

Foundation type: Public charity
Purpose: Scholarships to individuals residing in the greater Boston, MA, area who have completed Adult Basic Education or English for Speakers of Other Languages. Some support also to individuals who mentor such students.
Publications: Application guidelines; Annual report; Grants list; Newsletter.
Financial data: Year ended 06/30/2011. Assets, $1,288,249 (M); Expenditures, $669,246; Total giving, $276,000; Grants to individuals, totaling $15,000.
Fields of interest: Adult education—literacy, basic skills & GED; Education, ESL programs.
Type of support: Scholarships—to individuals; Support to graduates or students of specific schools.
Application information: Applications accepted. Application form required. Application form available on the grantmaker's web site.
  Initial approach: Application
  Send request by: Mail or e-mail

Copies of proposal: 1
Deadline(s): May 30
Final notification: Recipients notified June 30
Applicants should submit the following:
  1) Letter(s) of recommendation
  2) Essay
Additional information: Applicant must be enrolled in a community based literacy program during the last calendar or last school year.
Program description:
  First Literacy Scholarships: The fund awards scholarships to adults who have completed their Adult Basic Education (ABE) or English for Speakers of Other Languages (ESOL) studies at a greater Boston community-based literacy program and are continuing on to higher education or vocational training. Scholarships will be awarded for up to $1,000.
EIN: 042997446

4070
First Priority Credit Union Charitable Foundation
(formerly Boston Post Office Employees Credit Union Charitable Foundation)
100 Swift St.
East Boston, MA   02128-1102

Foundation type: Independent foundation
Purpose: Scholarships to residents of MA for higher education.
Financial data: Year ended 12/31/2011. Assets, $35 (M); Expenditures, $5,035; Total giving, $5,000; Grants to individuals, 5 grants totaling $5,000.
Type of support: Scholarships—to individuals.
Application information:
  Initial approach: Letter
  Deadline(s): Varies
EIN: 043553922

4071
Fisher and Fuel Society of Beverly
150 Pine St.
Danvers, MA   01923-2630   (351) 201-9583
Contact: Avis A. Beaulieu, Secy.-Treas.

Foundation type: Independent foundation
Purpose: Grants to residents of Beverly, MA, for special assistance in times of illness or misfortune.
Financial data: Year ended 09/30/2013. Assets, $1,754,059 (M); Expenditures, $88,053; Total giving, $71,414; Grants to individuals, 44 grants totaling $35,239 (high: $1,400, low: $31).
Type of support: Grants for special needs.
Application information: Applications accepted.
  Deadline(s): None
  Additional information: Individual applications not accepted; Applications by written appeal from clergy, social welfare agency, or other recognized agency attesting to the need of the person(s) requesting aid.
EIN: 046039361

4072
Albert W. Fleming Insurance Trust
c/o Choate LLP
P.O. Box 961019
Boston, MA   02196   (617) 248-5000
Contact: A. Silvana Giner, Tr.
Application address: c/o Choate LLP, 2 International Pl., Boston, MA 02110

Foundation type: Independent foundation

Purpose: Scholarships to individuals attending college in MA for any education purpose, or those who are enrolled or have been accepted for enrollment at any college or university in the U.S. and display financial need.
Financial data: Year ended 10/31/2013. Assets, $401,015 (M); Expenditures, $25,040; Total giving, $19,000; Grants to individuals, 5 grants totaling $19,000 (high: $4,000, low: $3,000).
Type of support: Undergraduate support.
Application information: Application form required.
  Initial approach: Letter
  Deadline(s): Apr. 30
  Applicants should submit the following:
    1) Transcripts
    2) Letter(s) of recommendation
  Additional information: Application must also include a personal statement.
EIN: 046646727

4073
The Forbes Kirkside Foundation Inc.
(formerly The Kirkside, Inc.)
P.O. Box 855
Westborough, MA   01581-3346   (508) 366-4195
Contact: Bruce Lopatin, Treas.

Foundation type: Independent foundation
Purpose: Personal aid grants to residents and former residents of Westboro, MA.
Financial data: Year ended 12/31/2011. Assets, $716,467 (M); Expenditures, $28,061; Total giving, $19,261; Grants to individuals, 22 grants totaling $19,261 (high: $3,109, low: $100).
Type of support: Grants for special needs.
Application information: Applications accepted.
  Deadline(s): None
  Additional information: Applications by proposal.
EIN: 042311010

4074
Ernest Fortin Memorial Foundation, Inc.
c/o Martha Rice Martini Esq.
15 Front St.
Salem, MA   01970

Foundation type: Independent foundation
Purpose: Scholarships to individuals residing in the Brighton, MA, area for graduate education.
Financial data: Year ended 12/31/2012. Assets, $322,289 (M); Expenditures, $43,453; Total giving, $36,750; Grants to individuals, 20 grants totaling $24,750 (high: $2,000, low: $750).
Type of support: Graduate support.
Application information: Applications not accepted.
  Additional information: Unsolicited requests for funds not considered or acknowledged.
EIN: 043544279

4075
George B. Foster Memorial Trust
2036 Washington St.
Hanover, MA   02339-1617   (207) 336-2891
Contact: Jerald Wiley, Tr.
Application address: P.O. Box 35, Buckfield, ME 04220 tel.: (207) 336-2891

Foundation type: Independent foundation
Purpose: Scholarships to sons of members of Evening Star Lodge, Buckfield, ME for undergraduate education.
Financial data: Year ended 12/31/2012. Assets, $245,777 (M); Expenditures, $14,654; Total

giving, $12,000; Grant to an individual, 1 grant totaling $12,000.
Type of support: Undergraduate support.
Application information: Applications accepted. Application form required.
Deadline(s): May 1
EIN: 046725453

4076
Fraxa Research Foundation, Inc.
45 Pleasant St., 2nd Fl.
Newburyport, MA   01950-2605   (978) 462-1866
Contact: Katherine Clapp M.S., Pres.
FAX: (978) 463-9985; E-mail: info@fraxa.org;
URL: http://www.fraxa.org

Foundation type: Public charity
Purpose: Fellowships and research grants at finding a specific treatment for Fragile X syndrome.
Publications: Application guidelines; Annual report; Financial statement; Grants list; Informational brochure; Newsletter.
Financial data: Year ended 12/31/2011. Assets, $2,843,593 (M); Expenditures, $1,776,588; Total giving, $1,388,464.
Fields of interest: Genetic diseases and disorders research.
Type of support: Fellowships; Research; Postdoctoral support.
Application information: Applications accepted. Application form not required.
Send request by: Mail and e-mail
Deadline(s): Feb. 1
Final notification: Recipients notified in two months
Applicants should submit the following:
1) Letter(s) of recommendation
2) Curriculum vitae
3) Budget Information
Additional information: See web site for additional application guidelines.
Program description:
Postdoctoral Fellowships: Fellowships of $45,000 per year for two years (for salary, fringe benefits and consumable costs) is offered to support postdoctoral fellows who want to pursue research in Fragile X. Applicants must be full time and have MD, PhD or MD/PhD. Successful applicants will likely work in established labs with secure overall funding, which have funding for supplies and any required animal handling costs.
EIN: 043222167

4077
Matthew B. Friary Scholarship Trust
790 Norton Ave.
Taunton, MA   02780   (508) 823-0050

Foundation type: Operating foundation
Purpose: Scholarships to seniors at Taunton High School, MA.
Financial data: Year ended 12/31/2011. Assets, $66,502 (M); Expenditures, $10,000; Total giving, $10,000; Grants to individuals, 3 grants totaling $10,000.
Type of support: Support to graduates or students of specific schools.
Application information: Applications accepted. Application form required.
Deadline(s): May 1
Additional information: Application must include transcript.
EIN: 043199847

4078
General Charitable Fund, Inc.
c/o First Financial
100 Erdman Way
Leominster, MA   01453-1804
Contact: Peter Armbruster, Treas., First Financial Trust, N.A.

Foundation type: Independent foundation
Purpose: Scholarships to qualified individuals for higher education.
Financial data: Year ended 12/31/2012. Assets, $343,628 (M); Expenditures, $23,691; Total giving, $20,000; Grants to individuals, 11 grants totaling $20,000 (high: $2,500, low: $1,500).
Fields of interest: Higher education.
Type of support: Scholarships—to individuals.
Application information: Application form required.
EIN: 046048360

4079
General Charitable Society of
Newburyport
P.O. Box 365
Newburyport, MA   01950-0465

Foundation type: Operating foundation
Purpose: Scholarships to residents of Newburyport, MA. Financial assistance only to residents of Newburyport, MA.
Financial data: Year ended 10/31/2013. Assets, $1,134,789 (M); Expenditures, $53,766; Total giving, $29,392; Grant to an individual, 1 grant totaling $17,300 (high: $17,300).
Fields of interest: Higher education; Human services.
Type of support: Scholarships—to individuals; Grants for special needs.
Application information: Application form required.
Deadline(s): May 1.
EIN: 042589680

4080
Genzyme Charitable Foundation, Inc.
500 Kendall St.
Cambridge, MA   02142-1108
E-mail: CharitableAccessProgram@genzyme.com;
Additional tel.: (617) 768-9009; URL: http://www.genzyme.com/commitment/patients/free_programs.asp

Foundation type: Operating foundation
Purpose: Grants to individuals for prescription medication based on financial and medical need.
Financial data: Year ended 12/31/2012. Assets, $11,036 (M); Expenditures, $54,453,742; Total giving, $54,452,742; Grants to individuals, totaling $54,452,742.
Fields of interest: Health care, patient services.
Type of support: Grants for special needs.
Application information: Applications accepted. Application form required.
Initial approach: Telephone
Additional information: Applications should include financial information, a letter of intent to treat from a physician, and a statement of medical necessity from a physician.
Program description:
Charitable Access Program (CAP): The foundation provides prescription medication to people who are uninsured and lack the financial means to purchase treatment. The program currently provides Cerezyme for Gaucher disease, Myozyme for Pompe disease, Aldurazyme for MPS I disease, Leukine to help increase white blood cells, Clolar for Leukemia; Fabrazyme for Fabry disease, Campath

to patients suffering from B-CLL, Fludara for B-Cell chronic lymphocytic leukemia (CLL), Thyrogen for Hypothyroidism, and Mozobil for non-Hodgkin's Lymphoma or multiple myeloma. This program is designed to be a temporary measure and patients are expected to explore alternative resources for funding in the future.
EIN: 043236375

4081
German Aid Society of Boston Inc.
8 County St.
P.O. Box 207
Walpole, MA   02081-2313   (508) 668-8827
Contact: Norbert Zimmermann
Application address: 65 Norton Dr., Norwood, MA 02090

Foundation type: Independent foundation
Purpose: Financial assistance to needy individuals and families in the Boston, MA, area.
Financial data: Year ended 04/30/2013. Assets, $755,957 (M); Expenditures, $68,965; Total giving, $47,900; Grant to an individual, 1 grant totaling $35,550.
Fields of interest: Economically disadvantaged.
Type of support: Grants for special needs.
Application information: Applications accepted. Application form required. Interview required.
Deadline(s): None
EIN: 046038293

4082
Gerondelis Foundation Inc.
56 Central Ave., Ste. 201
Lynn, MA   01901-1112   (781) 595-3311
Contact: Gregory C. Demakis, Dir.

Foundation type: Independent foundation
Purpose: Scholarships to Essex County, MA, high school graduates who are of at least one half Greek descent and rank in the top 15 percent of their classes.
Financial data: Year ended 12/31/2012. Assets, $5,197,420 (M); Expenditures, $531,129; Total giving, $434,100.
International interests: Greece.
Type of support: Undergraduate support.
Application information: Applications accepted. Application form required.
Initial approach: Letter
Additional information: Applicant must demonstrate financial need.
EIN: 046130871

4083
Giovanni Armenise-Harvard Foundation for
Scientific Research
401 Park Dr., Ste. 22 W.
Boston, MA   02215-3325   (617) 998 8858
Contact: Lisa Mayer, Exec. Dir.
FAX: (617) 384 8487;
E-mail: amanda_pullen@hms.harvard.edu; E-mail For Lisa Mayer: lisa_mayer@hms.harvard.edu;
URL: http://www.armeniseharvard.org/

Foundation type: Public charity
Purpose: Grants to physicians, scientists, and other professionals to support research in the fields of medicine and agriculture.
Publications: Application guidelines.
Financial data: Year ended 06/30/2012. Assets, $70,363,620 (M); Expenditures, $5,762,257; Total giving, $5,052,998; Grants to individuals, totaling $60.

Fields of interest: Science.
Type of support: Research; Postdoctoral support; Graduate support.
Application information:
Initial approach: Proposal
Additional information: See web site for additional application guidelines.
Program descriptions:
Career Development Program: This program provides up to three years of support for newly-independent scientists at an agreed host institute in Italy, and is intended to foster the development of outstanding scientists and enable them to expand their potential to make significant contributions to their field of research. The award also provides an incentive for Italian research institutes to strengthen their departments by providing a sufficiently attractive package to invite applications from the best possible candidates. Awards will be given at a rate of $200,000 per year per scholar.
HMS Junior Faculty Armenise-Harvard Grant: Three successful candidates will receive an award of $75,000 for two years to support basic scientific research at Harvard Medical School. Applications are limited to assistant and associate professors conducting basic science research at the school.
Science Writer Fellowship: Two Italian science writers working in Italy who are at the beginning or mid-career stage are selected to spend a week in June or July at Harvard Medical School. Writers will have the opportunity to interview top HMS researchers from diverse fields, tour laboratories, attend Armenise-Harvard and/or HMS symposia and conferences, meet science writers from the HMS community, and work with editors at HMS. Roundtrip economy airfare, hotel accommodation, and meal and transport expenses of up to $50 a day are provided.
The Armenise-Harvard Ph.D. Award: The award will be available through the Harvard University Division of Medical Sciences and will cover, for the first two years, a twelve-month stipend of $20,000, $24,000 for tuition and fees (including UHS/BCBS), a $200 book allowance, a healthcare allowance of $140, and a travel allowance of $600. In the final two years, the host laboratory will provide the stipend and research costs. One year of postdoctoral funding at a level of $50,000 is also available for work carried out when the candidate returns to work in Italy. This funding will be available for up to 10 years after receiving a Harvard Ph.D. Candidates must be a young science graduate who has been accepted into one of the four Ph.D programs within the Harvard University Division of Medical Sciences (biological and biomedical sciences, immunology, neuroscience, or virology), be an Italian citizen living in Italy, and have some previous research experience.
EIN: 043293162

4084
The Giving Circle
(formerly Berry Fund Charitable Foundation)
99 Conifer Hill Dr.
Danvers, MA   01923-1151   (978) 774-1057

Foundation type: Public charity
Purpose: Financial assistance to low income individuals and families of Danvers, MA with relocation, utilities, and other special needs.
Financial data: Year ended 12/31/2011. Assets, $104,403 (M); Expenditures, $219,953; Total giving, $139,063; Grants to individuals, 15 grants totaling $59,998.
Fields of interest: Human services; Economically disadvantaged.

Type of support: Emergency funds; Grants for special needs.
Application information: Applications accepted.
Additional information: Contact the foundation for eligibility determination.
EIN: 043484211

4085
Global Routes, Inc.
1 Short St.
Northampton, MA   01060-2567   (413) 585-8895
FAX: (413) 585-8810;
E-mail: mail@globalroutes.org; URL: http://www.globalroutes.org

Foundation type: Public charity
Purpose: Financial assistance to students who wish to participate in a volunteer overseas program, but who are unable to due to financial constraints.
Publications: Application guidelines.
Financial data: Year ended 09/30/2010. Assets, $1,920 (M); Expenditures, $238,980; Total giving, $82,570. Grants to individuals amount not specified.
Fields of interest: Scholarships/financial aid.
Type of support: Travel grants.
Application information: Applications accepted. Application form available on the grantmaker's web site.
Initial approach: Application
Deadline(s): Apr. 1
Additional information: Application should include financial information. See web site for addtional guidelines.
Program description:
Global Routes Diversity Fund: This fund allows students who wish to volunteer for overseas work, and who otherwise (due to financial reasons) would not have the opportunity, to be able to contribute their energy and special gifts to international service. Financial aid is given based on student merit, student need, and space availability.
EIN: 043078212

4086
Goddard Health Services Inc.
43 Belmont St., No. C
South Easton, MA   02375-1902

Foundation type: Independent foundation
Purpose: Scholarships to residents of Brockton and Bridgewater, MA.
Financial data: Year ended 09/30/2012. Assets, $5,293,027 (M); Expenditures, $144,578; Total giving, $115,000.
Type of support: Scholarships—to individuals.
Application information: Applications not accepted.
Additional information: Unsolicited requests for funds not considered or acknowledged.
EIN: 042852328

4087
Goldin Foundation for Excellence in Education
85 Grove St.
Wellesley, MA   02482   (781) 444-7660
Contact: Harriet K. Goldin, Exec. Dir.

Foundation type: Operating foundation
Purpose: Awards to outstanding educators in MA, CA and TX.

Financial data: Year ended 12/31/2011. Assets, $0 (M); Expenditures, $18,264; Total giving, $9,500.
Type of support: Awards/prizes.
Application information: Applications not accepted.
Additional information: Unsolicited requests for funds not considered or acknowledged.
EIN: 043090548

4088
Noble Symond Golub and Leila J. Golub Educational Trust
99 Fordham Rd.
Wilmington, MA   01887   (781) 665-6466
Application address: Trustees S/F Aleppo Temple A.A.O.N.M.S.
URL: http://www.alepposhriners.com

Foundation type: Independent foundation
Purpose: Scholarships to students for higher education, with emphasis on residents of MA.
Financial data: Year ended 12/31/2011. Assets, $259,236 (M); Expenditures, $15,947; Total giving, $14,000; Grants to individuals, 14 grants totaling $14,000 (high: $1,000, low: $1,000).
Type of support: Undergraduate support.
Application information: Applications accepted. Application form required.
Initial approach: Letter
Deadline(s): May 1
Additional information: Application must include transcript, personal background, list of activities in school or community and course of study in college and what plans applicant has after college. Contact foundation for current application guidelines.
EIN: 046796825

4089
Gravity Research Foundation
41 Kirkland Cir.
Wellesley Hills, MA   02481-4812
Contact: Louis Witten, V.P.
E-mail: grideoutjr@aol.com; Application address: c/o University of Cincinnati, 2600 Clifton Ave., Cincinnati, OH 45221-0001; URL: http://www.gravityresearchfoundation.org/

Foundation type: Operating foundation
Purpose: Awards to writers for the best essays on the subject of gravitation.
Publications: Application guidelines.
Financial data: Year ended 06/30/2012. Assets, $972,881 (M); Expenditures, $113,417; Total giving, $7,500.
Fields of interest: Physical/earth sciences.
Type of support: Awards/prizes.
Application information:
Send request by: E-mail
Deadline(s): Apr. 1
Final notification: Recipients notified after May 15
Additional information: Essay must be in English. See web site for additional guidelines.
Program description:
Awards for Essays on Gravitation: Five awards, ranging from $500 to $4,000 each, for short essays of 1,500 words or less (excluding abstracts, diagrams, references and minimal equations), on the subject of gravitation, its theory, applications or effects. The organization holds an annual essay contest on the scientific study of gravity for the purpose of stimulating thought and encouraging work on gravitation. The award-winning essays will be published in a special issue of the International

Journal of Modern Physics D (IMPD). Authors of essays designated Honorable Mention will be invited to submit their essays to the IMPD where these may undergo additional refereeing at editorial discretion for possible publication.
EIN: 046002754

4090
The Harold Grinspoon Charitable Foundation
67 Hunt St., Ste. 100
Agawam, MA 01001-1913 (413) 276-0700
Contact: Joanna S. Ballantine, Exec. Dir.
FAX: (413) 276-0804; E-mail: info@hgf.org;
URL: http://www.hgf.org

Foundation type: Independent foundation
Purpose: Grant funding is available for professional development for Jewish educators to attend conferences and workshops, and travel to Israel for study.
Publications: Financial statement; Multi-year report.
Financial data: Year ended 08/31/2012. Assets, $7,676,501 (M); Expenditures, $945,923; Total giving, $636,421.
Fields of interest: Education.
Type of support: Conferences/seminars; Grants to individuals; Travel grants.
Application information: Applications accepted. Application form required. Application form available on the grantmaker's web site.
> *Additional information:* The maximum grant is 600 per teacher per experience. Conferences that cost less than 50 will not be funded. See web site for guidelines and information.

EIN: 222738277

4091
The Harold Grinspoon Foundation
380 Union St.
West Springfield, MA 01089-4132 (413) 736-2552
Contact: Joanne S. Ballantine, Exec. Dir.
FAX: (413) 732-2632; E-mail: info@hgf.org;
URL: http://www.hgf.org

Foundation type: Public charity
Purpose: Assistance to Jewish students attending local Jewish day schools in western Massachusetts and southern Vermont.
Publications: Application guidelines; Annual report.
Financial data: Year ended 08/31/2011. Assets, $233,209,287 (M); Expenditures, $17,264,243; Total giving, $8,062,976; Grants to individuals, totaling $810,671.
Fields of interest: Education; Jewish agencies & synagogues.
Type of support: Grants to individuals.
Application information: Grants to individuals are non-needs based.
EIN: 046685725

4092
Thomas S. Gunning Scholarship Foundation, Inc.
100 Grossman Dr., Ste. 300
Braintree, MA 02184-4965 (781) 849-3220
Contact: Thomas J. Gunning, Pres.

Foundation type: Independent foundation
Purpose: Scholarship awards for contractor members of the Building Trade Employers'

Association, their employees, and immediate family members.
Financial data: Year ended 12/31/2011. Assets, $173,332 (M); Expenditures, $76,318; Total giving, $74,500; Grants to individuals, 30 grants totaling $74,500 (high: $2,500, low: $2,000).
Type of support: Employee-related scholarships.
Application information:
> *Initial approach:* Letter
> *Deadline(s):* Aug. 1

EIN: 043464855

4093
Hampden Savings Foundation, Inc.
P.O. Box 2048
Springfield, MA 01102-2048 (413) 452-5150
Contact: Robert A. Massey, Pres. and Treas.
E-mail: rmassey@hampdenbank.com; Application address: 19 Harrison Ave., Springfield, MA 01103, tel.: (413) 452-5181; URL: https://www.hampdenbank.com/about

Foundation type: Company-sponsored foundation
Purpose: Scholarships to indigent residents of Springfield, MA.
Financial data: Year ended 10/31/2012. Assets, $654,646 (M); Expenditures, $193,953; Total giving, $193,500.
Type of support: Undergraduate support.
Application information: Applications not accepted.
> *Additional information:* Unsolicited requests for funds not considered.

EIN: 043583365

4094
HAP, Inc.
322 Main St.
Springfield, MA 01105-2473 (413) 233-1500
FAX: (413) 731-8723;
E-mail: admin@haphousing.org; Toll-free tel.: (800) 332-9667; TDD: (413) 233-1699; URL: http://www.haphousing.org

Foundation type: Public charity
Purpose: Provides housing assistance and technical assistance for low-income and disabled individuals in western MA.
Financial data: Year ended 06/30/2012. Assets, $22,799,674 (M); Expenditures, $54,029,177; Total giving, $41,425,975; Grants to individuals, totaling $40,964,658.
Fields of interest: Housing/shelter, homeless; Housing/shelter, repairs; Housing/shelter, expense aid; Housing/shelter; Domestic violence; Human services, emergency aid; Aging; Disabilities, people with; Economically disadvantaged.
Type of support: Grants for special needs.
Application information: Applications accepted. Application form required.
> *Additional information:* Contact foundation for application information.

Program descriptions:
> *Home Modification Loans:* Loans (some with deferred payments) of up to $30,000 are available to make access modifications for individuals with disabilities. Homeowners can apply for funds to construct ramps or make modifications to their bathrooms, kitchens or other rooms to allow people to safely remain in their homes. These funds are available to homeowners in Springfield, Agawam, W. Springfield, Chicopee, Holyoke, Northampton, and Westfield.
> *Rental Assistance Program:* The program allows families with very low incomes to be able to rent

decent, safe housing at an affordable rent. Eligibility is primarily based on household income.
> *Residential Assistance to Families in Transition (RAFT) Program:* The program is designed to help families who are homeless or at risk of homelessness. Eligibility criteria include: total household income at or below 50 percent of area median income; homeless; at risk of homelessness (such as overcrowding, domestic violence, health or safety violations in the unit, utility shutoff, eviction notice); or cannot pay more than 50 percent of income for housing expenses but can demonstrate the ability to sustain housing expenses after receiving assistance. Single individuals are not eligible. Assistance can be used for security deposits, first and last month's rent, rent and/or utility arrears, and mortgage arrears.

EIN: 042518368

4095
Harvard Center for Neurodegeneration and Repair, Inc.
c/o Harvard Medical School
220 LOngwood Ave.
Goldenson Bldg., Rm. 524
Boston, MA 02115-6092 (617) 432-3370
FAX: (617) 432-3364;
E-mail: hcnr@hms.harvard.edu; URL: http://www.neurodiscovery.harvard.edu

Foundation type: Public charity
Purpose: Research fellowships to individuals working in the field of neurology and neurobiology.
Financial data: Year ended 06/30/2012. Assets, $11,545,773 (M); Expenditures, $4,404,112; Total giving, $2,281,328; Grants to individuals, totaling $2,599.
Fields of interest: Neuroscience research.
Type of support: Fellowships; Research.
Application information:
> *Deadline(s):* Varies

Program descriptions:
> *Camille and Henry Dreyfus New Faculty Awards Program:* This award aims to provide funding for new center faculty members to help initiate their independent research programs. A key feature of this award is an unrestricted research grant of $50,000 that is awarded before the new faculty member formally begins their first year appointment. Eligible applicants must have no more than three years of postdoctoral experience in the fields of chemistry, biochemistry, and chemical engineering.
> *Damon Runyan Cancer Research Foundation Clinical Investigator Award:* This program supports early-career physician-scientists conducting patient-oriented research (research conducted with human subjects, epidemiologic and behavioral studies, and/or outcomes and health services research), with the goal of increasing the number of physicians capable of moving seamlessly between the laboratory and the patient's bedside in the search for breakthrough treatments. Eligible applicants must be assistant professors or instructors in the Harvard University system whose research is oriented toward the cancer field. Grants are for $100,000 per year, plus research allowance and a debt repayment program.
> *David and Lucile Packard Foundation Fellowships for Science and Engineering:* This program provides funding of up to $125,000 per year for up to five years to help encourage the nation's most promising young professors to pursue science and engineering research with few funding restrictions and limited paperwork requirements, and to provide support for unusually creative researchers early in their careers. Applicants must be within the first

three years of their 'faculty career' (their initial faculty appointment, whether at Harvard or another institution before Harvard), and be engaged in research in the natural sciences or engineering (including physics, chemistry, mathematics, biology, astronomy, computer science, earth science, ocean science, and all branches of engineering)

Ellison Medical Foundation New Scholars Program in Aging: This program aims to support new investigators of outstanding promise in the basic biological and clinical sciences relevant to understanding aging processes and age-related diseases and disabilities. The award is intended to provide new faculty with support during the especially critical first three years of their independent research careers. Applicants must be holding a full-time faculty appointment in the Harvard University system.

Henry Dreyfus Teacher-Scholar Awards Program: This program works to strengthen the teaching and research careers of talented young faculty in the chemical sciences and to provide discretionary funding to faculty at early stages in their careers. It is intended to encourage young scholars who embrace and demonstrate excellence in the academic research and teaching missions, and is based on accomplishments in teaching and scholarly research with respect to primary undergraduates and undergraduate institutions. Eligible applicants must be holding a full-time tenure track academic appointment in the chemical sciences field, be between the fourth and twelfth year of their independent academic careers, and engage in teaching and research primarily with undergraduates.

Norman E. Zinberg Fellowship in Addiction Psychiatry Research: This award provides $44,000 to support training in research on alcohol and/or drug use disorders. Theoretical or applied research projects that include a social-psychological, public policy, or psychotherapeutic dimension or component will be given priority. The fellowship is available through the Research Committee of the Department of Psychiatry at Harvard Medical School. Applicants must have an M.D. degree (at PGY-4 level or higher) and/or Ph.D. degree at time of application, with no more than three years passing since the end of training; applicants cannot hold a faculty appointment of assistant professor or higher during the fellowship period.

Predoctoral Fellowships: Provides qualified young students with an interest in neuroscience support for four years (tuition, fees and stipend for the first two years, and tuition for the final two). The program aims to support the training and development of new investigators.

Rita Allen Foundation Scholars Awards: This award targets individuals who show promise of becoming leaders in research in the cure and treatment of cancer, cerebral palsy, multiple sclerosis, and euphorics and analgesics for the terminally ill, with a stipend of $50,000 per year for each eligible year of funding. Preference will be given to candidates who are in the early stages of their careers of appointment at a faculty level. Applicants must have completed training and provided persuasive evidence of distinguished achievement or extraordinary promise in research in one of the relevant fields, and have been on a tenure track for no more than three years (support will be reconsidered if a chosen applicant is awarded tenure)

The Dana Clinical Hypothesis Research Program in Brain in Immuno-Imaging: Using Brain and Immune Imaging Innovations to Improve Human Health: This program seeks to advance the application of imaging research to improve

understanding of the brain, the immune system, and their interactions in health and disease by supporting pilot-testing of high-risk innovative hypotheses to understand brain function and immune system function, and how these are altered in human conditions and diseases. Applicants must be at the Assistant Professor level within the Harvard University system, or early in their Associate Professor career; senior investigators will only be considered if they can convincingly demonstrate a new research direction. Funding is for up to $100,000 to support conventional brain systems imaging of brain tissues, and up to $200,000 to support the use of emerging cellular/molecular imaging technologies, either alone or in combination with conventional systems imaging techniques, of brain cells or immune cells (or their interactions)

William T. Grant Foundation Scholars Program: This program supports promising post-doctoral researchers from diverse disciplines whose research deepens and broadens the knowledge base in areas that contribute to creating a society that values young people and helps them live up to their potential. Priority research areas include youth development and improving programs, policies, and institutions affecting young people. Applicants must be within seven years of receiving a terminal degree (M.D., M.D./Ph.D., or Ph.D.) at the time of application, and must spend at least have of paid time conducting research.

EIN: 311745145

4096
Harvard Musical Association
57A Chestnut St.
Boston, MA 02108-3506 (617) 523-2897
URL: http://www.hmaboston.org

Foundation type: Independent foundation
Purpose: Awards to secondary school students and conservatory students in MA, for recognition of artistic achievement.
Financial data: Year ended 06/30/2013. Assets, $4,130,814 (M); Expenditures, $326,990; Total giving, $28,000; Grants to individuals, 2 grants totaling $3,000 (high: $2,000, low: $1,000).
Fields of interest: Performing arts; Music; Secondary school/education.
Type of support: Awards/prizes.
Application information: Applications accepted. Application form required.
  Initial approach: Letter
  Deadline(s): Apr. 1
  Additional information: See web site for current application guidelines.
EIN: 042104284

4097
Harvard-Yenching Institute
2 Divinity Ave.
25 Francis Ave., Ste. 20, Vanserg Hall
Cambridge, MA 02138-2020 (617) 495-4050
Contact: Elizabeth J. Perry, Dir.
FAX: (617) 496-7206;
E-mail: yenching@fas.harvard.edu; Additional address: c/o Harvard Management Co., 600 Atlantic Ave., Boston, MA 02210-2211; Additional tel.: (617) 523-4400; URL: http://www.harvard-yenching.org

Foundation type: Public charity
Purpose: Fellowships for scholars from Asia to conduct research at Harvard University, to participate in special training programs, or to attend

graduate school through a Joint Scholarship Program.
Publications: Application guidelines; Program policy statement.
Financial data: Year ended 06/30/2012. Assets, $194,316,014 (M); Expenditures, $7,007,563; Total giving, $5,966,697; Grants to individuals, totaling $2,583,753.
Fields of interest: Education.
Type of support: Fellowships; Research; Awards/grants by nomination only; Graduate support.
Application information:
  Deadline(s): Vary
  Additional information: Selection is by nomination only. The Institute does not accept individual applications. Scholars are chosen through a competitive selection process. See web site for additional guidelines.
Program descriptions:
  Coordinate Research Program: The program provides Harvard faculty with a chance to invite faculty members (no graduate students) to join them in collaborative research projects in established Asian Studies. Priority is given to invitees based on universities and research institutions in Asia. While joint research is the primary focus, collaboration may also include co-teaching and/or co-organizing conferences and workshops. This grant is not intended to extend the stay of a scholar currently at Harvard.
  Grants: The Institute offers grants for Asia-based scholars to travel to Harvard for conferences, and for Asia-based senior scholars to conduct humanities and/or social science research in one or more of the specialized collections of Asian-language materials available only at the Harvard-Yenching Library.
  NUS-HYI Joint Scholarship: This joint scholarship program is for young faculty at HYI partner institutions in Vietnam, Thailand, and Cambodia to complete a Ph.D. at the national University of Singapore, with 12 to 18 months of dissertation research at Harvard University. Applicants are required to have a Master's degree in a relevant discipline or an Honors degree or equivalent in a relevant discipline. They must hold a teaching position at one of HYI's partner institutions in Southeast Asia, or have teaching experience at one of these partner institutions, with assurance that the candidate will be strongly considered for reemployment after graduation from the program.
  Visiting Fellows Program: This program provides advanced Ph.D. candidates at the partner institutions an opportunity to conduct dissertation research at Harvard University for three semesters. Preference is given to those in East Asian Studies whose research would benefit from the resources of the Harvard-Yenching Library. Successful applicants join researchers at the Institute, and have access to all Harvard University libraries.
  Visiting Scholars Program: This program offers younger faculty members in the humanities and social sciences the opportunity to undertake ten months of post-doctoral research at Harvard University. The proposed research project should be related to the humanities and social sciences with an emphasis on culture. Asian and comparative studies are especially welcome. Successful applicants join researchers at the Harvard-Yenching Institute, and gave access to the Harvard University libraries.
EIN: 042062394

4098
Haverhill Female Benevolent Society
58 Marshland St.
Haverhill, MA 01830-3317 (978) 373-0817
Contact: Nadine Bradley
Application address: 45 Lackey St., Haverhill, MA 01830-6708

Foundation type: Independent foundation
Purpose: Grants to economically disadvantaged individuals in the Haverhill, MA, area for food, clothing and utility assistance.
Financial data: Year ended 09/30/2013. Assets, $677,570 (M); Expenditures, $20,511; Total giving, $15,275; Grants to individuals, totaling $15,275.
Fields of interest: Economically disadvantaged.
Type of support: Grants for special needs.
Application information: Applications accepted. Application form not required.
  Initial approach: Letter
  Deadline(s): None
  Additional information: Application should outline financial need.
EIN: 046047957

4099
Esther H. Hawks Trust
c/o Nutter, McClennen & Fish, LLP
P.O. Box 51400
Boston, MA 02205-8982
Contact: John B. Newhall, Tr.
Application addresses: P.O. Box 765, Manchester, MA 01944-1448

Foundation type: Independent foundation
Purpose: Scholarships to graduating high school students of Lynn, MA, for full time study at U.S. colleges.
Financial data: Year ended 12/31/2012. Assets, $1,825,544 (M); Expenditures, $95,711; Total giving, $70,000; Grants to individuals, 35 grants totaling $70,000 (high: $2,000, low: $2,000).
Fields of interest: Higher education; Scholarships/financial aid.
Type of support: Scholarships—to individuals; Undergraduate support.
Application information: Application form required.
  Deadline(s): May 1 for first time applicants, May 15 for renewal applicants
  Final notification: Recipients notified in early June
  Applicants should submit the following:
    1) SAT
    2) GPA
    3) ACT
    4) Financial information
    5) SAR
    6) Transcripts
  Additional information: Application should also include two references. Application available from guidance counselors at Lynn high schools and, for renewal applicants, from trustees.
EIN: 046035212

4100
Josiah Willard Hayden Recreation Centre, Inc.
24 Lincoln St.
Lexington, MA 02421-6830 (781) 862-8480
URL: http://www.jwhayden.org

Foundation type: Operating foundation
Purpose: Four-year scholarships to students pursuing postsecondary education who are residents of Lexington, MA.

Financial data: Year ended 08/31/2013. Assets, $23,092,175 (M); Expenditures, $3,029,878; Total giving, $36,800; Grants to individuals, 61 grants totaling $36,800 (high: $2,000, low: -$300).
Type of support: Undergraduate support.
Application information: Application form required.
  Deadline(s): Apr.
  Additional information: Application must include tuition cost and family financial information.
EIN: 042203700

4101
Health Resources in Action, Inc.
(formerly The Medical Foundation)
95 Berkeley St.
Boston, MA 02116-6230 (617) 451-0049
Contact: Ray Considine M.S.W., Pres.
FAX: (617) 451-0062; E-mail: rconsidine@hria.org;
TTY: (617)-451-0007; URL: http://www.hria.org/

Foundation type: Public charity
Purpose: Medical research grants to postdoctoral fellows for biomedical research.
Publications: Application guidelines.
Financial data: Year ended 06/30/2012. Assets, $11,376,992 (M); Expenditures, $14,684,965; Total giving, $6,052,659; Grants to individuals, totaling $4,456,901.
Fields of interest: Medical research.
Type of support: Fellowships.
Application information: Candidates are chosen based on their qualifications and topic of research.
Program descriptions:
  Charles A. King Trust Postdoctoral Fellowship Program: The program was created to support the investigation of diseases of human beings, and the alleviation of human suffering through the improved treatment of human diseases. In keeping with these principles, the program supports postdoctoral fellows in the basic sciences, as well as clinical and health services research. The program awards two-year grants ranging from $43,000 to $50,000 per year, which includes a $2,000 expense allowance.
  Charles H. Hood Foundation Child Health Research Awards: Two-year grants of $150,000 ($75,000 per year and inclusive of 10 percent indirect costs) are awarded to junior faculty who are within five years of their first independent faculty appointment. Researchers must be working in non-profit academic or medical research institutions within the six New England states. Grants support hypothesis-driven clinical, basic science, public health, health services research, and epidemiology proposals with direct relevance to pediatric diseases. Projects in the field of pediatric behavioral science or genetics of behavior will also be considered.
  Deborah Munroe Noonan Memorial Fund: One-year grants of up to $80,000 (inclusive of 10 percent indirect costs) support innovative projects aimed at improving the quality of life for children and adolescents with physical and developmental disabilities. Research proposals are accepted from both non-profit organizations and academic institutions that serves children with physical or developmental disabilities and associated health-related complications in the greater Boston area.
  Lymphatic Research Foundation (LRF) Postdoctoral Fellowship Awards Program: This program works to expand and strengthen the pool of outstanding junior investigators in the field of lymphatic research. Awards will support investigators who have recently received their doctorates, a critical point in career development when young scientists choose their lifelong

research focus. Two-year fellowships ranging from $82,000 to $95,000 will be awarded to fellows who have completed no more than three years of postdoctoral training by July 1 of the LRF funding cycle.
  Smith Family New Investigator Awards Program: Supports the careers of newly independent biomedical researchers with the ultimate goal of achieving medical break-throughs. Applicants may focus on all fields of basic biomedical science and may also be submitted by investigators in physics, chiemisty and engineering. Three-year grants of $300,000 ($100,000 per year inclusive of five percent indirect costs) target new faculty who are within two years of their first independent appointment as of July 1 of the application year.
EIN: 042229839

4102
Katharine A. Heberton Scholarship Trust
(formerly K. A. Heberton Scholarship Trust)
P.O. Box 1330
Hyannis, MA 02601 (508) 945-5130

Foundation type: Independent foundation
Purpose: Scholarships to graduates of Chatham High School, MA, Worcester High School, MA and Cape Cod Regional Tech School, MA for higher education.
Financial data: Year ended 12/31/2012. Assets, $2,045,400 (M); Expenditures, $122,225; Total giving, $89,700; Grants to individuals, 13 grants totaling $89,700 (high: $11,600, low: $2,500).
Fields of interest: Higher education.
Type of support: Support to graduates or students of specific schools.
Application information: Applications accepted. Application form required.
  Deadline(s): May 1
  Additional information: Application can be obtained from each guidance department.
EIN: 566623518

4103
Evan Henry Foundation for Autism, Inc.
145 Norwell Ave.
Norwell, MA 02061-1211 (617) 347-2068
E-mail: evansway1@gmail.com; URL: http://www.evanhenry.org/foundation.htm

Foundation type: Public charity
Purpose: Scholarships to graduating seniors of Norwell High School, MA who have either helped individuals with autism or are interested in special education.
Financial data: Year ended 12/31/2011. Assets, $29,262 (M); Expenditures, $43,918; Total giving, $41,452.
Fields of interest: Education, special; Higher education.
Type of support: Support to graduates or students of specific schools.
Application information: Applications accepted. Application form required.
  Additional information: Applications are available from guidance department.
EIN: 043545439

4104
High Meadow Foundation, Inc.
30 Main St.
Stockbridge, MA 01262 (413) 298-1605
Contact: Tamara T. Stevens, Secy.
Application address: 312 Monument Valley Rd., Gt.
Barrington, MA 01230

Foundation type: Independent foundation
Purpose: Support primarily for the performing arts, especially theater and music. Giving also for health, social services, and education in Berkshire County, MA.
Financial data: Year ended 09/30/2013. Assets, $884,292 (M); Expenditures, $125,004; Total giving, $108,750; Grants to individuals, 15 grants totaling $15,750 (high: $1,500, low: $750).
Fields of interest: Performing arts; Theater; Music; Education; Health care; Human services.
Type of support: Grants for special needs.
Application information: Applications accepted.
  Initial approach: Letter
  Additional information: Contact foundation for additional application guidelines.
EIN: 222527419

4105
Hill House, Inc.
127 Mt. Vernon St.
Boston, MA 02108-1127 (617) 227-5838
Contact: for Scholarships: Lauren Hoops-Schmieg, Exec. Dir.
Fax and e-mail for J. Bracken: (617) 227-9251, jbracken@hillhouseboston.org
E-mail: lschmieg@hillhouseboston.org; URL: http://www.hillhouseboston.org

Foundation type: Public charity
Purpose: Need-based scholarships to students of Boston, MA for higher education.
Publications: Application guidelines.
Financial data: Year ended 06/30/2012. Assets, $4,732,652 (M); Expenditures, $1,113,702; Total giving, $25,060.
Application information: Applications accepted. Application form required.
  Initial approach: Application
  Send request by: Online
  Additional information: Application should include a current W2 form. Selection is based on need and availability.
Program description:
  Hill House Scholarships: The organization provides financial support to individuals and families who wish to attend activities and classes held at the organization, but who cannot afford to do so.
EIN: 046141765

4106
Hitchcock Free Academy
P.O. Box 155
Brimfield, MA 01010 (508) 347-9301
Application address: c/o Guidance Office Tantasqua Regional High School Sturbridge, MA 01566

Foundation type: Operating foundation
Purpose: Scholarships to high school seniors from Brimfield, Fiskdale, Holland, Sturbridge and Wales, MA for postsecondary education.
Financial data: Year ended 12/31/2012. Assets, $3,550,258 (M); Expenditures, $200,686; Total giving, $6,000; Grants to individuals, 12 grants totaling $6,000.
Fields of interest: Higher education; Scholarships/financial aid.

Type of support: Undergraduate support.
Application information: Application form required. Interview required.
  Deadline(s): Apr. 3
  Applicants should submit the following:
    1) Photograph
    2) Transcripts
    3) Letter(s) of recommendation
EIN: 042277210

4107
Ruth H. Holmes Trust
(formerly Ruth H. Holmes Trust f/b/o Elizabeth V. Cushman Scholarship Fund)
2036 Washington St.
Hanover, MA 02339 (508) 947-2662
Application address: c/o Apponequet Regional High School, 100 Howland Rd., Lakeville, MA 02347

Foundation type: Independent foundation
Purpose: Scholarships to graduates of high schools in Middleboro, Lakeville, and Carver, MA.
Financial data: Year ended 12/31/2012. Assets, $624,458 (M); Expenditures, $29,104; Total giving, $20,500.
Type of support: Support to graduates or students of specific schools; Undergraduate support.
Application information: Applications accepted. Application form required.
  Deadline(s): May 1
  Additional information: Applications should include financial information and are available from guidance counselors.
EIN: 046044854

4108
Holt & Bugbee Foundation, Inc.
1600 Shawsheen Ave.
Tewksbury, MA 01876-0037

Foundation type: Company-sponsored foundation
Purpose: Scholarships to residents of Tewksbury, MA for higher education.
Financial data: Year ended 12/31/2012. Assets, $335,081 (M); Expenditures, $22,926; Total giving, $18,000.
Fields of interest: Higher education.
Type of support: Undergraduate support.
Application information: Applications not accepted.
  Additional information: Unsolicited requests for funds not considered or acknowledged.
EIN: 200446975

4109
Holyoke Community College Foundation, Inc.
303 Homestead Ave.
Holyoke, MA 01040-1099 (413) 538-7000
Contact: Erica Broman, Exec. Dir.
E-mail: ebroman@hcc.mass.edu; URL: http://www.hcc.edu/the-hcc-foundation

Foundation type: Public charity
Purpose: Scholarships to students attending or transferring from Holyoke Community College, MA.
Publications: Annual report; Informational brochure.
Financial data: Year ended 06/30/2012. Assets, $9,093,923 (M); Expenditures, $730,424; Total giving, $507,436; Grants to individuals, totaling $140,186.
Type of support: Support to graduates or students of specific schools.

Application information:
  Initial approach: Letter
EIN: 237181691

4110
Home Builders Foundation of Western Massachusetts, Inc.
240 Cadwell Dr.
Springfield, MA 01104-1743

Foundation type: Operating foundation
Purpose: Scholarships to students who attend a secondary educational vocational institution, an accredited college or university on a full-time basis or a graduate program relating to the construction industry.
Financial data: Year ended 12/31/2012. Assets, $11,495 (M); Expenditures, $16,975; Total giving, $15,000.
Fields of interest: Vocational school, secondary; Business/industry.
Type of support: Graduate support; Technical education support; Precollege support; Undergraduate support.
Application information: Applications accepted.
EIN: 043212851

4111
Charles H. Hood Fund
6 Kimball Ln.
Lynnfield, MA 01940-2682 (617) 887-8475
Contact: Linda R. Thompson, Exec. Dir.

Foundation type: Independent foundation
Purpose: Scholarships to children of employees of H.P. Hood, Inc., for higher education.
Publications: Application guidelines.
Financial data: Year ended 12/31/2011. Assets, $1,708,945 (M); Expenditures, $159,762; Total giving, $144,659.
Fields of interest: Higher education; Scholarships/financial aid.
Type of support: Scholarships—to individuals.
Application information: Application form required.
  Initial approach: Letter or telephone
Company name: HP Hood LLC
EIN: 046036788

4112
The Hopedale Foundation
43 Hope St.
Hopedale, MA 01747-0123 (508) 473-2871
Contact: Vincent J. Arone, Treas.
Application address: P.O. Box 123, Hopedale, MA 01747

Foundation type: Independent foundation
Purpose: Student loans and scholarships only to graduates of Hopedale High School in MA.
Financial data: Year ended 10/31/2012. Assets, $9,526,076 (M); Expenditures, $481,418; Total giving, $416,787; Grants to individuals, 5 grants totaling $17,500 (high: $5,000, low: $2,500).
Fields of interest: Education.
Type of support: Student loans—to individuals; Support to graduates or students of specific schools; Undergraduate support.
Application information: Applications accepted.
  Initial approach: Letter
  Deadline(s): June 1, for student loans
EIN: 046044779

4113
Dorothy K. Hopkins Scholarship Fund
P.O. Box 1330
Hyannis, MA   02601   (617) 737-3637
Contact: Jason Arceley
Application address: TD Bank, N.A., 200 State St.,
Boston, MA 02109 Tel.: (617) 737-3637

Foundation type: Independent foundation
Purpose: Scholarships to high school students of
Gardner, MA seeking postsecondary education for
undergraduate and graduate studies.
Financial data: Year ended 12/31/2012. Assets,
$710,609 (M); Expenditures, $46,501; Total
giving, $35,000; Grants to individuals, 10 grants
totaling $35,000 (high: $3,500, low: $3,500).
Type of support: Graduate support; Undergraduate
support.
Application information:
   Deadline(s): None
EIN: 046661947

4114
Ednah Horner Charitable Foundation
c/o Eastern Bank
605 Broadway, LF41
Saugus, MA   01906-3200   (781) 581-4277
Contact: Scholarships: Bridget Spencer

Foundation type: Independent foundation
Purpose: Scholarships to students in the Peabody,
MA, area.
Financial data: Year ended 12/31/2012. Assets,
$646,955 (M); Expenditures, $38,740; Total
giving, $31,240; Grants to individuals, 21 grants
totaling $31,240 (high: $16,000, low: $690).
Type of support: Scholarships—to individuals.
Application information: Contact foundation for
current application deadline/guidelines.
EIN: 043468419

4115
Houghton Mifflin Harcourt Publishing
   Company Contributions Program
222 Berkeley St.
Boston, MA   02116-3748
URL: http://www.hmhco.com/content/
corporate-social-responsibility

Foundation type: Corporate giving program
Purpose: Houghton Mifflin annually awards two
four-year $2,500 college scholarships to the
children of its employees. The program is
administered by the National Merit Scholarship
Corporation.
Fields of interest: Education.
Type of support: Employee-related scholarships.
Application information: Applications accepted.
Application form required.
   Additional information: Contact the organization
      for further application and program
      information.
Company name: Houghton Mifflin Harcourt
Publishing Company

4116
Howard Benevolent Society
14 Beacon St., Rm. 804
Boston, MA   02108-3727   (617) 742-2952
Contact: Marcia T. Burley

Foundation type: Operating foundation
Purpose: Welfare assistance to sick and destitute
residents of the Boston, MA, area.

Financial data: Year ended 09/30/2013. Assets,
$4,909,880 (M); Expenditures, $413,823; Total
giving, $123,389.
Fields of interest: Human services.
Type of support: Grants for special needs.
Application information: Applications accepted.
Application form not required.
   Initial approach: Letter or telephone
   Deadline(s): None
EIN: 042129132

4117
Trustees of the Howard Funds 1993
756 Orchard St.
Raynham, MA   02767-1028   (508) 583-9055
Application Address: W. Bridgewater High, MA
02379

Foundation type: Independent foundation
Purpose: Scholarships to residents of West
Bridgewater, MA for postsecondary education.
Financial data: Year ended 06/30/2013. Assets,
$990,949 (M); Expenditures, $36,383; Total
giving, $29,857.
Fields of interest: Higher education.
Type of support: Scholarships—to individuals.
Application information: Application form required.
   Deadline(s): Apr. 11
EIN: 042105774

4118
Samuel C. Howes Trust
c/o Nutter, McClennen & Fish, LLP
P.O. Box 51400
Boston, MA   02205-8982
Contact: Thomas P. Jalkut, Tr.

Foundation type: Independent foundation
Purpose: Scholarships to financially needy and
deserving college students, primarily at seminary
and religious schools.
Financial data: Year ended 09/30/2013. Assets,
$2,445,950 (M); Expenditures, $127,931; Total
giving, $101,005.
Type of support: Scholarships—to individuals;
Support to graduates or students of specific
schools.
Application information:
   Initial approach: Letter
   Deadline(s): None
   Additional information: Contact foundation for
      current application guidelines.
EIN: 046077889

4119
Ernest G. Howes Trust f/b/o Sick &
   Needy Persons
c/o Nutter, McClennen & Fish, LLP
P.O. Box 1400
Boston, MA   02205   (617) 439-2372
Contact: Thomas P. Jalkut, Tr.
Application Address: 155 Seaport Boulevard,
Boston, MA 02110-2604

Foundation type: Independent foundation
Purpose: Financial assistance to needy residents of
PA for medical care.
Financial data: Year ended 09/30/2013. Assets,
$160,854 (M); Expenditures, $6,087; Total giving,
$4,200; Grants to individuals, 2 grants totaling
$4,200 (high: $2,100, low: $2,100).
Fields of interest: Economically disadvantaged.
Type of support: Grants for special needs.
Application information: Applications accepted.
Application form not required.

Initial approach: Letter
Deadline(s): None
Additional information: Letter must describe
   individual and purpose for funds.
EIN: 046022100

4120
Howland Fund for Aged Women
63 Union St.
New Bedford, MA   02740-6728

Foundation type: Independent foundation
Purpose: Relief assistance by referral only to
financially needy, aged women residing in the New
Bedford, MA, area.
Financial data: Year ended 02/29/2012. Assets,
$357,916 (M); Expenditures, $43,707; Total
giving, $34,900; Grants to individuals, 18 grants
totaling $34,900 (high: $2,200, low: $500).
Fields of interest: Aging; Women.
Type of support: Grants for special needs.
Application information: Applications not
accepted.
   Additional information: Unsolicited requests for
      funds not considered or acknowledged.
EIN: 046050865

4121
Humane Society of the Commonwealth of
   Massachusetts
51 Grove St., Ste. A
Chestnut Hill, MA   02467   (617) 232-6242
Contact: Beth Nilsson
URL: http://www.masslifesavingawards.com

Foundation type: Independent foundation
Purpose: Grants, medals, and certificates, by
nomination only, to individuals residing in MA who
have heroically saved or attempted to save
someone's life.
Financial data: Year ended 02/28/2013. Assets,
$4,882,332 (M); Expenditures, $226,890; Total
giving, $134,100; Grants to individuals, 33 grants
totaling $133,000 (high: $5,000, low: $1,000).
Fields of interest: Ethics; Disasters, search/
rescue.
Type of support: Awards/grants by nomination only;
Awards/prizes.
Application information: Recipients may be entitled
to receive a reward not exceeding forty dollars in
money, or either of the medals or the certificate of
the Society. Unsolicited requests for funds not
considered or acknowledged.
EIN: 042104291

4122
Helena W. Hunt Trust
2036 Washington St.
Hanover, MA   02339-1617   (781) 871-0541

Foundation type: Independent foundation
Purpose: Scholarships to graduates of Rockland
High School, MA.
Financial data: Year ended 06/30/2013. Assets,
$378,640 (M); Expenditures, $20,818; Total
giving, $17,000; Grant to an individual, 1 grant
totaling $17,000.
Type of support: Support to graduates or students
of specific schools; Undergraduate support.
Application information: Applications accepted.
Application form required.
   Deadline(s): None
   Additional information: Application forms
      available at Rockland High School.
EIN: 046384141

4123
The Samuel Huntington Fund, Inc.
40 Sylvan Rd.
Waltham, MA 01748 (781) 907-3358
Contact: Amy Stacy
E-mail: amy.stacy@us.ngrid.com

Foundation type: Independent foundation
Purpose: Awards to graduating college seniors to pursue a one year public service project anywhere in the world immediately following graduation.
Financial data: Year ended 06/30/2013. Assets, $188,167 (M); Expenditures, $44,165; Total giving, $37,500; Grants to individuals, 6 grants totaling $37,500 (high: $10,000, low: $5,000).
Type of support: Awards/prizes; Graduate support.
Application information: Application form required. Application form available on the grantmaker's web site. Interview required.
> *Initial approach:* Proposal
> *Send request by:* Mail
> *Copies of proposal:* 1
> *Deadline(s):* Jan. 18
> *Applicants should submit the following:*
> 1) Budget Information
> 2) Transcripts
> 3) Proposal
> 4) Resume
> 5) Letter(s) of recommendation
> *Additional information:* Awards are based on quality of proposal, academic record and other personal achievements.

Program description:
Samuel Huntington Public Service Award: The award provides a $10,000 stipend for a one-year public service project. $5,000 is awarded at the beginning of the project and the remaining $5,000 is awarded upon receipt of a six-month progress report. The award allows recipients to engage in a meaningful public service activity for one year before proceeding on to graduate school or a career.
EIN: 043021374

4124
Marjorie and Doris Hutchinson Scholarship Fund
P.O. Box 1330
Hyannis, MA 02601 (617) 737-3637

Foundation type: Independent foundation
Purpose: Scholarships to girls who graduate from Gardner High School, MA, to attend school at Mt. Holyoke College, MA.
Financial data: Year ended 12/31/2012. Assets, $258,196 (M); Expenditures, $17,452; Total giving, $13,000; Grants to individuals, 10 grants totaling $13,000 (high: $1,300, low: $1,300).
Type of support: Support to graduates or students of specific schools; Undergraduate support.
Application information: Applications accepted. Application form required.
> *Deadline(s):* May 1
> *Applicants should submit the following:*
> 1) Essay
> 2) Transcripts
EIN: 316655884

4125
Institution for Savings Charitable Foundation, Inc.
(formerly Institution for Savings in Newburyport & Its Vicinity Charitable Foundation, Inc.)
93 State St.
P.O. Box 510
Newburyport, MA 01950-6618 (978) 462-3106
Contact: Michael J. Jones, Pres. and Tr.
Application address: 2 Depot Sq., Ipswich, MA 01938

Foundation type: Company-sponsored foundation
Purpose: Scholarship to a graduating senior from Newburyport High School or Triton Regional High School to pursue higher education.
Publications: Application guidelines; Grants list.
Financial data: Year ended 06/30/2013. Assets, $8,488,235 (M); Expenditures, $901,076; Total giving, $891,998.
Fields of interest: Higher education; Education.
Type of support: Scholarships—to individuals; Support to graduates or students of specific schools.
Application information: Applications accepted. Application form required. Application form available on the grantmaker's web site.
> *Initial approach:* Application
> *Send request by:* Mail
> *Deadline(s):* Apr. 1
> *Applicants should submit the following:*
> 1) Financial information
> 2) Transcripts
> 3) Essay
EIN: 043353621

4126
International Foundation for Gender Education, Inc.
(also known as IFGE)
84 Keyes Rd.
Gardner, MA 01440-1800 (781) 899-2212
E-mail: info@ifge.org; *URL:* http://ifge.org/

Foundation type: Public charity
Purpose: Scholarships to transgender identified students enrolled in postsecondary institutions.
Financial data: Year ended 12/31/2011. Assets, $54,839 (M); Expenditures, $65,680.
Fields of interest: LGBTQ.
Type of support: Undergraduate support.
Application information: Applications accepted. Application form required.
> *Deadline(s):* Feb. 1
> *Additional information:* Application materials sent by e-mail or fax are not accepted. See web site for additional application guidelines.

Program description:
Scholarships: Scholarships are made to outstanding transgender undergraduate and graduate full-time students at accredited college, university or institution in the U.S. Applicant must be "out" as transgender to their academic communities, and demonstrate a commitment or contribution to the transgender communities. Consideration will include academic performance, honors, personal/financial hardship, and especially service to the transgender communities.
EIN: 042790259

4127
International Society for Infectious Diseases, Inc.
(also known as ISID)
9 Babcock Str., 3rd Fl.
Brookline, MA 02446-3202 (617) 277-0551
Contact: Norman Stein, Exec. Dir.
FAX: (617) 278-9113; *E-mail:* info@isid.org;
URL: http://www.isid.org

Foundation type: Public charity
Purpose: Research grants to investigators for the prevention, and treatment of infectious diseases in low resource countries.
Publications: Application guidelines.
Financial data: Year ended 12/31/2011. Assets, $4,643,453 (M); Expenditures, $2,134,372; Total giving, $106,000.
Fields of interest: Medical research.
International interests: Developing Countries; Eastern Europe.
Type of support: Fellowships; Research.
Application information: Applications accepted. Application form required.
> *Deadline(s):* Mar. 1 for ISID Scientific Fellowship and ISID/ESCMID Fellowship, Apr. 1 for SSI/ISID Fellowship, and Apr. 1 and Oct. 1 for ISID Small Grants
> *Final notification:* Applicants notified after June 1 for ISID/ESCMID Fellowship and ISID Scientific Fellowship, by July 1 for SSI/ISID Fellowships, after June 1 and after Dec. 1 for ISID Small Grants

Program descriptions:
ISID/ESCMID Fellowship Program: With the European Society of Clinical Microbiology and Infections Diseases (ESCMID), the foundation offers up to two fellowships a year to researchers of infection diseases to continue their research in Europe. Fellowships are funded for up to three-month cycles for up to $7,500.

Scientific Exchange Fellowship Program: This program seeks to promote collaboration among researchers in different countries by enabling infectious disease researchers in the formative stages of their careers to extend their research experience in institutions outside of their region. These awards are not restricted to physicians and are intended to support young scientists from developing countries in updating their knowledge of new, relevant laboratory techniques or in learning specific skills and techniques. Applicants are to be investigators (younger than 40 years) already working in a research area, but who have not had the opportunity to work or to study outside their countries or region. Funding will be provided for up to three months for up to $7,500.

Small Grants Program: The program is designed to fund pilot research projects by young investigators in developing countries. The goal is to support and foster the professional development of young individuals in the field of infectious diseases research by helping them to acquire additional skills and data to apply for other grants. Up to five grants of up to $6,000 each will be awarded annually.

SSI/ISID Fellowship Program: The purpose of this program, jointly sponsored by the Swiss Society for Infectious Diseases (SSI), is to support infectious disease physicians and scientists from developing and middle-income countries through multidisciplinary clinical and laboratory training at select biomedical institutions in Switzerland. Opportunities for training and research in a variety of areas ranging from basic studies of the mechanism of disease to studies in public health, epidemiology, diagnostics, therapeutics, and vaccine development, are available through this program. A financial stipend of up to 36,000 SF per

year (approximately $35,500 U.S.) will be given to fellows to cover travel costs and living expenses.
EIN: 222473000

4128

Wilhelmina W. Jackson Trust

c/o Bank of America, N.A.
P.O. Box 55850
Boston, MA 02205-8271
Scholarship application address: c/o Marcia Hostetter (for art scholarships), P.O. Box 47, Marblehead, MA 01945; c/o Rev. Dean Pederson (for medical scholarships), 40 Monument Ave., Swampscott, MA 01907

Foundation type: Independent foundation
Purpose: Scholarships to residents of Swampscott and Marblehead, MA, for the study of medicine, and for the study of any form of the creative arts at a college, university or art school.
Financial data: Year ended 12/31/2012. Assets, $8,155,894 (M); Expenditures, $452,865; Total giving, $347,000; Grants to individuals, 67 grants totaling $346,500 (high: $21,808, low: $500).
Fields of interest: Photography; Sculpture; Design; Painting; Ceramic arts; Art history.
Type of support: Undergraduate support.
Application information: Application form required. Interview required.
   Deadline(s): June 1
   Final notification: July 30
   Applicants should submit the following:
      1) Letter(s) of recommendation
      2) Transcripts
      3) Photograph
Program description:
   William Denning Jackson Art Scholarships: Selection is based on financial need, artistic ability, character and work habits, and GPA. The scholarship is awarded for up to four years. Forms of the creative arts included are painting, sculpture, graphics, printmaking, industrial design, illustration, photography, ceramics, and art history.
EIN: 046024405

4129

Jacob's Pillow Dance Festival, Inc.

358 George Carter Rd.
Becket, MA 01223-4001 (413) 243-0745
Contact: Ella Baff, Exec. Dir.
FAX: (413) 243-0749;
E-mail: info@jacobspillow.org; URL: http://www.jacobspillow.org

Foundation type: Public charity
Purpose: Scholarships to dancers in MA to attend the School at Jacob's Pillow.
Publications: Application guidelines.
Financial data: Year ended 11/30/2011. Assets, $17,828,203 (M); Expenditures, $4,829,792; Total giving, $74,900; Grants to individuals, totaling $74,900.
Fields of interest: Dance; Performing arts, education.
Type of support: Scholarships—to individuals.
Application information: Applications accepted. Application form required. Application form available on the grantmaker's web site.
   Deadline(s): Mar. 16
   Additional information: Application must include financial information.
Program description:
   Scholarships: Scholarships are provided for participants of Jacob's Pillow School. Partial scholarships assist as many dancers as possible, while full scholarships are reserved for

exceptionally-talented dancers. Named scholarships include the Lorna Strassler Award for Student Excellence (providing a full scholarship and $2,500 cash to a young artist demonstrating excellence in performance and/or choreography, combined with exemplary dedication to the field), the Marcia Simon Kaplan Award (providing one full scholarship for a New World School of the Arts student to pursue coursework in contemporary arts), and American Dance Guild Erna Lindner-Gilbert Scholarship (providing one full scholarship to an applicant for the school's Choreographers Lab)
EIN: 046002993

4130

The John J.and Nora Jennings Foundation, Inc.

46 Gaston St.
Medford, MA 02155 (781) 391-5016
Contact: David C. Johnson, Treas.

Foundation type: Independent foundation
Purpose: Scholarships to residents of MA for undergraduate education.
Financial data: Year ended 12/31/2012. Assets, $81,851 (M); Expenditures, $28,553; Total giving, $25,000; Grants to individuals, 10 grants totaling $25,000 (high: $2,500, low: $2,500).
Type of support: Undergraduate support.
Application information: Contact foundation for current application deadline/guidelines.
EIN: 550797079

4131

Marlene F. Johnson Memorial Fund for Scholarly Research on Christian Science

22 Concord Ave.
Cambridge, MA 02138 (617) 497-3322
Contact: David B. Sand, Pres.
URL: http://www.johnsonfund.org

Foundation type: Independent foundation
Purpose: Grants and awards to individuals for research on Christian Science. Awards are for up to $40,000 per year, and are renewable.
Financial data: Year ended 04/30/2013. Assets, $397,668 (M); Expenditures, $25,593; Total giving, $0.
Fields of interest: Protestant agencies & churches.
Type of support: Research; Awards/prizes.
Application information: Applications accepted. Application form not required.
   Initial approach: Proposal
   Send request by: Mail
   Deadline(s): Mar. 31
   Applicants should submit the following:
      1) Letter(s) of recommendation
      2) Work samples
      3) Curriculum vitae
EIN: 043453095

4132

Clinton O. & Lura Curtis Jones Memorial Trust

4 2nd St., Ste. 2
Pittsfield, MA 01201-6204 (413) 443-1183
Contact: Joseph H. Skutnik, Tr.

Foundation type: Independent foundation
Purpose: Scholarships to Berkshire County, MA, residents for higher education at accredited colleges or universities.

Financial data: Year ended 12/31/2012. Assets, $967,194 (M); Expenditures, $45,875; Total giving, $37,000; Grants to individuals, 42 grants totaling $37,000 (high: $5,000, low: $250).
Type of support: Scholarships—to individuals.
Application information: Application form required.
   Initial approach: Letter
   Deadline(s): Apr. 15
   Applicants should submit the following:
      1) Transcripts
      2) Financial information
      3) Essay
   Additional information: Application must also include parents' federal income tax return.
EIN: 046173271

4133

Grace B. Jones Trust

(formerly Grace Jones Trust)
c/o TD Bank, Tax Dept.
P.O. Box 1330
Hyannis, MA 02601 (508) 255-1505
Contact: Nauset Regio
Application address: 100 Cable Rd., Eastham, MA 02642

Foundation type: Independent foundation
Purpose: Scholarships to graduates of Nauset Regional High School, North Eastham, MA.
Financial data: Year ended 12/31/2012. Assets, $463,417 (M); Expenditures, $42,052; Total giving, $35,000; Grants to individuals, 12 grants totaling $35,000 (high: $3,000, low: $2,500).
Type of support: Support to graduates or students of specific schools; Undergraduate support.
Application information: Applications accepted.
   Initial approach: Letter
   Deadline(s): None
   Additional information: Applicants must submit a formal letter stating their background and why they feel they should be chosen.
EIN: 046466327

4134

The Jurassic Foundation Inc.

c/o Braver P.C.
117 Kendrick St., Ste. 800
Needham, MA 02494
URL: http://jurassicfoundation.org/

Foundation type: Company-sponsored foundation
Purpose: Research grants to students, postdoctoral researchers, and other researchers with limited funding opportunities for the study of dinosaur paleobiology.
Financial data: Year ended 12/31/2012. Assets, $102,670 (M); Expenditures, $32,505; Total giving, $29,900.
Fields of interest: Biology/life sciences; Anatomy (animal); Science.
Type of support: Research.
Application information: Applications accepted. Application form required. Application form available on the grantmaker's web site.
   Send request by: Mail or e-mail
   Deadline(s): Mar. 15 and Oct. 15
   Final notification: Recipients notified June 15 and Jan. 15 respectively
   Additional information: Grantees are required to submit a brief, one-page summary of work completed under their grant.
EIN: 043448123

4135
Edward Bangs and Elza Kelley Foundation, Inc.

20 N. Main St.
South Yarmouth, MA 02664
Contact: DeWitt Davenport, V.P.
URL: http://www.kelleyfoundation.org

Foundation type: Independent foundation
Purpose: Scholarships to individuals of Barnstable county, MA who intend to pursue their education in health, human services and related fields.
Publications: Application guidelines; Annual report (including application guidelines); Informational brochure.
Financial data: Year ended 12/31/2012. Assets, $5,802,871 (M); Expenditures, $396,529; Total giving, $128,611.
Fields of interest: Health sciences school/education.
Type of support: Scholarships—to individuals.
Application information: Applications accepted. Application form required. Application form available on the grantmaker's web site.
  Initial approach: Letter or telephone
  Send request by: Mail
  Deadline(s): Apr. 30
  Additional information: Application must include three letters of reference and most recent transcript for new applicants, for re-applicants, transcript and letter of recommendation from a faculty member.
EIN: 046039660

4136
Mary A. Kelly Scholarship Fund

P.O. Box 464
Newburyport, MA 01950-7364

Foundation type: Independent foundation
Purpose: Scholarships to students pursuing studies in science at a four-year college or university, whose parents are members of the Congregation of Immaculate Conception Roman Catholic Church, Newburyport, MA.
Financial data: Year ended 12/31/2011. Assets, $709,481 (M); Expenditures, $19,500; Total giving, $11,825; Grants to individuals, 6 grants totaling $11,825 (high: $2,465, low: $1,000).
Fields of interest: Science; Catholic agencies & churches.
Type of support: Undergraduate support.
Application information: Applications accepted. Application form required.
  Initial approach: Letter
  Deadline(s): Apr. 15
EIN: 046042274

4137
John F. Kennedy Library Foundation, Inc.

c/o Doris Drummond
Columbia Point
Boston, MA 02125-3313 (617) 514-1550
FAX: (617) 436-3395;
E-mail: foundation@jfklfoundation.org; Toll-free tel.: (866) 535-1960; URL: http://www.jfklibrary.org/JFK+Library+and+Museum/Kennedy+Library+Foundation/

Foundation type: Public charity
Purpose: Grants to scholars doing significant research using the holdings of the Library, and awards by nomination only to individuals in government to recognize political courage. Awards to secondary school students for essays on government.
Publications: Application guidelines; Grants list; Informational brochure; Newsletter.
Financial data: Year ended 12/31/2011. Assets, $42,482,312 (M); Expenditures, $6,630,292; Total giving, $35,550; Grants to individuals, totaling $35,550.
Fields of interest: Literature; Research; Government/public administration; Leadership development.
Type of support: Fellowships; Internship funds; Research; Awards/grants by nomination only; Awards/prizes; Precollege support; Undergraduate support.
Application information: Application form required.
  Initial approach: Telephone or e-mail
  Deadline(s): Mar. 15 and Aug. 15
  Applicants should submit the following:
    1) Curriculum vitae
    2) Budget Information
    3) Proposal
  Additional information: See program description for more information.
Program descriptions:
  Abba P. Schwartz Fellowships: The fellowship carries a stipend of up to $3,100, and is intended to support a scholar in the production of a substantial work in the areas of immigration, naturalization, or refugee policy. The successful candidate will develop at least a portion of her or his work from original research in archival materials from the collections of the Kennedy Library.
  Arthur M. Schlesinger, Jr. Fellowship: The fellowship carries a stipend of up to $5,000, which may be awarded to a single individual or divided between two recipients, and is intended to support scholars in the production of substantial works on the foreign policy of the Kennedy years (especially with regard to the western hemisphere), or on Kennedy domestic policy (especially with regard to racial justice and to the conservation of natural resources). Successful candidates will develop at least a portion of their work from original research in archival materials from the collections of the Kennedy Library and related materials. Proposals are invited from all sources, but preference will be given to those from applicants specializing in the areas indicated above. Preference is also given to projects not supported by large grants from other institutions.
  Ernest Hemingway Research Grants: The foundation provides funds for the award of a number of research grants for scholars and students in the range of $200 to $1,000 to help defray living, travel, and related costs incurred while doing research in the Ernest Hemingway Collection. Grant applications are evaluated on the basis of expected utilization of the Hemingway Collection, the degree to which they address research needs in Hemingway and related studies, and the qualifications of applicants. Preference is given to dissertation research by Ph.D. candidates working in newly opened or relatively unused portions of the collection.
  Essay Contest for High School Students: This program invites students from across the nation to write an essay about a political issue at the local, state, or national level, and an elected official in the U.S. who has acted courageously to address that issue. Winners receive between $500 and $3,000, with the nominating teacher of the winning student receiving an additional $500 to be applied towards school projects involving student leadership and civic engagement.
  Kennedy Research Grants: Each year in the spring and fall, the foundation awards a number of research grants in the range of $500 to $2,500 to help defray living, travel, and related costs incurred while doing research in the textual and non-textual holdings of the library. Preference is given to dissertation research by Ph.D. candidates working in newly opened or relatively unused collections, and to the work of recent Ph.D. recipients who are expanding or revising their dissertations for publication.
  Marjorie Kovler Fellowship: The fellowship carries a stipend of up to $2,500 and is intended to support a scholar in the production of a substantial work in the area of foreign intelligence and the presidency or a related topic. The successful candidate will develop at least a portion of her or his work from original research in archival materials from the collections of the Kennedy Library.
  Profile in Courage Award: This award was created to recognize and promote the quality of political courage and leadership that President Kennedy valued. The award is presented annually on or near May 29, the anniversary of Kennedy's birthday, to a current or former elected official whose actions best demonstrate the kind of political courage that Pres. Kennedy described in his Pulitzer Prize-winning book, "Profiles in Courage." The award can be made to municipal, state, or federal officials who have demonstrated an act of political courage. The award consists of $25,000 and a silver lantern. With the establishment of the Profile in Courage Award Essay Contest and Scholarship, the foundation has further enhanced the scope of the award and its impact as an important educational tool for young people. The main purpose of this contest is to encourage students in grades 9-12 to work with elected officials to gain a greater understanding of the process of political decision-making and its integral role in the American democratic system. Judges by the same committee that selects the winner of the Profile in Courage Award, the winning essay is published in the John F. Kennedy Library Foundation Newsletter. The winner receives a $2,000 scholarship and is honored at the Profile in Courage Award Ceremony.
  Theodore C. Sorensen Fellowships: The fellowship carries a stipend of up to $3,600, and is intended to support a scholar in the production of a substantial work in the areas of domestic policy, political journalism, polling, press relations or a related topic. The successful candidate will develop at least a portion of her or his work from original research in archival materials from the collections of the Kennedy Library.
EIN: 046113130

4138
Kernwood Scholarship Foundation

c/o Goldman
990 Paradise Rd.
Swampscott, MA 01907
Application address: c/o Kernwood Country Club, 1 Kernwood Ave., Salem, MA 01970

Foundation type: Operating foundation
Purpose: Scholarships to local high school graduates including Danvers, Beverly, Salem Peabody and Bishop Fenwisk High Schools of Salem, MA.
Financial data: Year ended 12/31/2011. Assets, $63,455 (M); Expenditures, $13,710; Total giving, $12,500; Grants to individuals, totaling $12,500.
Type of support: Undergraduate support.
Application information: Applications accepted.
  Initial approach: Letter
  Deadline(s): June 30
EIN: 223215746

4139
The D. Kim Foundation for The History of Science and Technology In East Asia, Inc.

663 Lowell St.
Lexington, MA   02420-1961
E-mail: info@dkimfoundation.org; URL: http://www.dkimfoundation.org

Foundation type: Independent foundation
Purpose: Fellowships and grants to support graduate students and young scholars in the field of history of science and technology in East Asia.
Financial data: Year ended 06/30/2013. Assets, $3,843,156 (M); Expenditures, $219,839; Total giving, $136,500; Grants to individuals, 8 grants totaling $136,500 (high: $55,000, low: $2,500).
Fields of interest: Science.
Type of support: Fellowships; Grants to individuals; Graduate support.
Application information: Applications accepted. Application form required. Application form available on the grantmaker's web site.
  Send request by: Mail
  Deadline(s): Dec. 15
  Final notification: Recipients notified in late Jan.
  Applicants should submit the following:
    1) Letter(s) of recommendation
    2) Proposal
    3) Curriculum vitae
  Additional information: See web site for additional guidelines.
Program descriptions:
  Dissertation Fellowship: One or two fellowships up to $25,000 each will be awarded annually to Ph.D. candidates who are writing their dissertations. Applicants should include at least two draft chapters with their application.
  Group Grants: Several grants up to $5,000 each will be available to groups that organize workshops or international meetings. These meetings should be conducted in English.
  Post-doctoral Fellowship: One fellowship up to $55,000 will be awarded annually to a distinguished young scholar who has received his/her doctoral degree within the previous five years. Applicants should include an invitation letter from their host institution. The institution cannot be changed without permission from the foundation.
  Traveling/Research Grant: Several grants up to $2,500 each will be awarded annually to scholars who are traveling either to present papers at international conferences, workshops or annual meetings, or for short-term research projects (less than a month). Applicants who do not reside in the U.S. should contact the foundation for eligibility.
EIN: 800297127

4140
Charles A. King Trust

c/o Bank of America, N.A.
225 Franklin St.
Boston, MA   02110-2801
E-mail: miki.akimoko@ustrust.com; Application address: Miki Akimoko, Market Dir., Charles A. King Trust, c/o U.S. Trust, Bank of America, N.A., 225 Franklin St., MA1-225-04-02, Boston, MA 02110-2801; URL: https://www.bankofamerica.com/philanthropic/grantmaking.go

Foundation type: Independent foundation
Purpose: Postdoctoral fellowships for research in medicine and surgery at institutions within MA. Grants are paid to institutions on behalf of individuals.
Publications: Application guidelines.

Financial data: Year ended 12/31/2012. Assets, $21,302,933 (M); Expenditures, $1,166,420; Total giving, $859,083.
Fields of interest: Association; Surgery; Institute; Medical research; Biomedicine research.
Type of support: Fellowships; Research; Postdoctoral support.
Application information: Application form required.
  Deadline(s): Oct. 15 for projects to start on or after Feb. 1 of the following year
Program description:
  Medical Research Program: Grants are made for research in medicine or surgery as they are connected with the investigation of diseases of human beings and the alleviation of human suffering through improved methods of treatment. Support is for a postdoctoral research fellowship program in the biomedical sciences, including clinical investigation and problems of health in the community. Candidates are sought who have already completed a minimum of two or three years of postdoctoral research during which they have demonstrated competency and potential for a career in research. A primary goal of the fellowship program is to help assure future leadership of research in Boston area hospitals and other biomedical institutions. Reflecting this long-term objective, particular interest is taken in applicants whose sponsoring institutions indicate that a future career appointment is contemplate.
EIN: 046012742

4141
Knights of Columbus Massachusetts State Council Charity Fund

470 Washington St.
Norwood, MA   02062-2337   (781) 884-1928

Foundation type: Public charity
Purpose: Grants for the intellectually challenged children and adults of Norwood, MA, with medical equipment.
Financial data: Year ended 04/30/2012. Assets, $2,459,684 (M); Expenditures, $463,033; Total giving, $382,717.
Fields of interest: Children; Adults; Disabilities, people with.
Type of support: Grants to individuals.
Application information: Applications accepted.
  Additional information: Application should include a letter of need from a medical doctor, and a request from the parents or guardian of the individual.
EIN: 040616108

4142
Koster Insurance Scholarship Fund Inc.

500 Victory Rd.
Quincy, MA   02171-3139   (617) 770-9889
URL: http://www.kosterweb.com/

Foundation type: Operating foundation
Purpose: Scholarships to students studying for a career in the healthcare field.
Publications: Application guidelines.
Financial data: Year ended 12/31/2011. Assets, $46,285 (M); Expenditures, $44,520; Total giving, $37,500; Grants to individuals, 10 grants totaling $37,500 (high: $5,000, low: $2,500).
Fields of interest: Health care.
Type of support: Undergraduate support.
Application information: Applications accepted. Application form required. Application form available on the grantmaker's web site.

Send request by: Online
Deadline(s): May 18
Final notification: Applicants notified in Aug.
Applicants should submit the following:
  1) GPA
  2) Financial information
Program description:
  Health Careers Scholarship Program: The foundation annually awards college scholarships to students in their junior or senior year of undergraduate study at an accredited institution that prepares them for a career in healthcare. Qualifying degree programs include pre-medicine, nursing, public/community health, physical therapy, occupational therapy, pharmacy, biology, chemistry, psychology, social work, dentistry, and optometry. Recipients are selected based on academic excellence, motivation to pursue a healthcare career, dedication to community service, and financial need.
EIN: 043542547

4143
Kurzweil Foundation, Inc.

15 Walnut St.
Wellesley Hills, MA   02481-2101

Foundation type: Independent foundation
Purpose: Scholarships to visually impaired students of Cambridge, MA, who are also provided with scanners for computer usage.
Financial data: Year ended 04/30/2012. Assets, $2,460 (M); Expenditures, $35,240; Total giving, $30,000.
Fields of interest: Eye diseases; Disabilities, people with.
Type of support: Undergraduate support.
Application information: Applications not accepted.
  Additional information: Unsolicited requests for funds not considered or acknowledged.
EIN: 042921512

4144
Lake View Pavilion Charitable Foundation

45 Lakeview Rd.
Foxborough, MA   02035-1739   (508) 543-9099
Contact: Anastasia Tsoumbanos, Dir.

Foundation type: Company-sponsored foundation
Purpose: Scholarships to residents of Foxborough, MA for attendance at a four-year college.
Financial data: Year ended 12/31/2012. Assets, $6,607 (M); Expenditures, $6,010; Total giving, $5,475; Grants to individuals, 3 grants totaling $1,500 (high: $500, low: $500).
Type of support: Scholarships—to individuals.
Application information: Applications accepted. Application form required.
  Initial approach: Letter
  Deadline(s): Apr. 1
  Additional information: Contact local high school for application form. Student must submit an essay and provide background information on their schooling.
EIN: 043116285

4145
The Lalor Foundation, Inc.
c/o GMA Foundations
77 Summer St., 8th Fl.
Boston, MA   02110-1006   (617) 391-3088
Contact: Hannah Blaisdell
FAX: (617) 426-7087;
E-mail: hblaisdell@gmafoundations.com;
URL: http://www.lalorfound.org

Foundation type: Independent foundation
Purpose: Postdoctoral research fellowship awards
by nomination only in mammalian reproductive
biology as related to the regulation of fertility.
Publications: Application guidelines; Grants list.
Financial data: Year ended 09/30/2012. Assets,
$12,786,442 (M); Expenditures, $608,368; Total
giving, $438,136.
Fields of interest: Research; Biology/life sciences.
Type of support: Fellowships; Research; Awards/
grants by nomination only; Postdoctoral support.
Application information: Application form required.
Application form available on the grantmaker's web
site.
> *Send request by:* Online
> *Copies of proposal:* 5
> *Deadline(s):* Jan. 15 for Postdoctoral
> Fellowships, May 1 and Nov. 1 for Anna Lalor
> Burdick concept papers
> *Additional information:* See web site for
> additional guidelines.

Program descriptions:
Anna Lalor Burdick Program: This program
focuses particularly on young women who have
inadequate access to information regarding
reproductive health, including the subjects of
contraception and pregnancy termination, and as
such may be particularly lacking options in their
lives.
Postdoctoral Fellowship Program: One of the
foundation's major objectives has been to give
assistance and encouragement to capable
investigators embarking on teaching and research
careers in universities and colleges. This program's
mission is to support these researchers early in
their work so that they can become independently
funded in the field of mammalian reproductive
biology as related to the regulation of fertility. See
foundation web site for additional information.
E-mail: fellowshipmanager@gmafoundations.com.
EIN: 516000153

4146
Lend A Hand Society
89 South St., Ste. 203
Boston, MA   02111-2750   (617) 338-5301
Contact: Nancy Cooper

Foundation type: Independent foundation
Purpose: Relief assistance to financially needy
individuals for food, rent, clothing, medicine,
utilities, and camperships in the Boston, MA, area.
Financial data: Year ended 12/31/2011. Assets,
$2,016,042 (M); Expenditures, $191,492; Total
giving, $128,169; Grants to individuals, totaling
$128,169.
Type of support: Grants for special needs.
Application information: Applications accepted.
> *Initial approach:* Letter
> *Deadline(s):* Mar. 31 for camperships
> *Additional information:* Application should be
> submitted by a licensed social worker from a
> recognized agency.
EIN: 042104384

4147
Elizabeth Levin Trust f/b/o Lynn English
348 Park St., Ste. 108 E.
North Reading, MA   01864-2153

Foundation type: Independent foundation
Purpose: Scholarships to graduating students of
Lynn English High School, MA for continuing their
education at institutions of higher learning.
Financial data: Year ended 12/31/2012. Assets,
$339,536 (M); Expenditures, $23,078; Total
giving, $16,000; Grants to individuals, 4 grants
totaling $16,000 (high: $4,000, low: $4,000).
Fields of interest: Higher education.
Type of support: Support to graduates or students
of specific schools.
Application information: Applications accepted.
Application form required.
> *Additional information:* Application forms
> available upon request. Scholarships are
> awarded based on scholastic ability and
> financial needs.
EIN: 367405684

4148
Liberty Mutual Group Corporate Giving Program
175 Berkeley St.
Boston, MA   02116-5066   (617) 357-9500
URL: http://www.libertymutualgroup.com/
omapps/ContentServer?pagename=LMGroup/
Views/LMG&ft=3&fid=1138356728819&ln=en

Foundation type: Corporate giving program
Purpose: Scholarships to undergraduate students
who start a service or volunteer program at the
college or university where they are enrolled.
Fields of interest: College; University.
Type of support: Scholarships—to individuals;
Undergraduate support.
Application information: Applications accepted.
Application form available on the grantmaker's web
site.
> *Initial approach:* Application
> *Send request by:* Online

Program description:
Liberty Mutual Responsible Scholars: The
company awards scholarships to five
undergraduate students who initiate a service or
volunteer program that impacts or engages their
campus community. Students must be current
freshmen, sophomore, or juniors attending a full
time, undergraduate four-year degree program at an
accredited college or university in the U.S. Applicant
must have a cumulative GPA of 3.0 or better on a
4.0 scale. In addition to awarding scholarships,
Liberty Mutual hosts a trip to Boston where the
students meet with Liberty Mutual executives, learn
about career opportunities, and tour the city.

4149
Lift Up Africa
P.O. Box 3112
Woburn, MA   01888-1912   (503) 408-6838
Contact: Richard M. Levy, C.E.O.
FAX: (503) 408-5766; E-mail: info@liftupafrica.org;
Toll-free tel.: (888) 854-3887; URL: http://
www.liftupafrica.org

Foundation type: Public charity
Purpose: Support to individual projects through a
fiscal sponsorship program.
Publications: Financial statement; Informational
brochure; Newsletter; Occasional report; Program
policy statement.

Financial data: Year ended 12/31/2012. Assets,
$453,858 (M); Expenditures, $564,299; Total
giving, $339,019.
Fields of interest: International development.
Type of support: Fiscal agent/sponsor.
Application information: Applications accepted.
Application form not required. Application form
available on the grantmaker's web site.
> *Initial approach:* Application
> *Deadline(s):* None
> *Additional information:* See web site for
> additional guidelines.

Program description:
Fiscal Sponsorship Program: The organization
offers fiscal sponsorship and project management
services to individuals and projects that do not have
501(c)(3) status and whose programs and
initiatives fit with its mission statement of helping
African people in meaningful ways. Eligible projects
will be evaluated on their relevance and significance
to public interest projects, their legal status or
recognition as a bona fide project in the nation(s) in
which it plans on doing its work, sound financial
management, likelihood of the project or
organization being successful, budget and
planning, fundraising ability, and the demonstrated
ability of key project personnel.
EIN: 743116756

4150
Michael J. Lorden II Memorial Scholarship Corp.
69 Endmoor Rd.
Westford, MA   01886   (978) 692-4711
Application Address: c/o Nashoba Technical High
School, 110 Littleton Rd., Westford, MA 01886; c/
o Westford Academy, 30 Patten Rd., Westford MA
01886, tel.: (978) 692-5570; URL: http://
www.michaellorden.com

Foundation type: Independent foundation
Purpose: Scholarships to student athletes of
Westford Academy and Nashoba Technical High
School with a work history, community service and
financial need.
Financial data: Year ended 12/31/2012. Assets,
$84,723 (M); Expenditures, $6,385; Total giving,
$3,900; Grants to individuals, 2 grants totaling
$3,000 (high: $1,500, low: $1,500).
Fields of interest: Recreation.
Type of support: Support to graduates or students
of specific schools.
Application information: Applications accepted.
Application form required.
> *Deadline(s):* Mar. and Apr.
> *Additional information:* Students must have a
> GPA greater than 2.5. Nashoba Tech students
> must be advancing their career in Plumbing/
> Heating.
EIN: 202897564

4151
Mary Friese Lowe Memorial Educational Fund
c/o Latanzi, Spaulding & Landreth
P.O. Box 2300
Orleans, MA   02653-6300   (508) 255-2133
Contact: Brooks S. Thayer; Richard J. Barber, Jr., Tr.

Foundation type: Independent foundation
Purpose: Scholarships to graduating high school
seniors who are residents of Orleans, MA, and Rye,
NY for postsecondary education.
Financial data: Year ended 06/30/2013. Assets,
$2,047,468 (M); Expenditures, $98,994; Total

giving, $78,000; Grants to individuals, 42 grants totaling $78,000 (high: $2,000, low: $1,000).
Fields of interest: Higher education; Scholarships/financial aid.
Type of support: Undergraduate support.
Application information: Application form required.
  Deadline(s): Apr. 15
  Applicants should submit the following:
    1) Transcripts
    2) SAT
    3) Letter(s) of recommendation
  Additional information: Application should also include parents' tax return. Interviews may be required.
EIN: 133040569

4152
Amy Lowell 10th Clause Trust
c/o Choate, Hall & Stewart, LLP
2 International Pl.
Boston, MA 02110-4101   (617) 248-5253
Contact: Laura Reidy, Admin.
E-mail: amylowell@choate.com; URL: http://www.amylowell.org/

Foundation type: Public charity
Purpose: Scholarships to individuals for higher education who are MA residents, and U.S. citizens by birth.
Publications: Application guidelines.
Financial data: Year ended 11/30/2011. Assets, $17,850,993 (M); Expenditures, $948,207; Total giving, $749,746; Grants to individuals, totaling $105,000.
Fields of interest: Higher education.
Type of support: Undergraduate support.
Application information: Unsolicited requests for funds not considered or acknowledged.
EIN: 046016148

4153
Greater Lowell Community Foundation
100 Merrimack St., Ste. 202
Lowell, MA 01852-1723   (978) 970-1600
Contact: Raymond E. Riddick, Jr., Exec. Dir.
FAX: (978) 970-2444;
E-mail: ray@glcfoundation.org; URL: http://www.glcfoundation.org

Foundation type: Community foundation
Purpose: Scholarships to local students of Lowell, MA for higher education at accredited college or universities.
Publications: Application guidelines; Annual report; Financial statement; Grants list.
Financial data: Year ended 12/31/2012. Assets, $23,739,426 (M); Expenditures, $1,755,450; Total giving, $982,729; Grants to individuals, 150 grants totaling $203,818.
Fields of interest: Higher education.
Type of support: Scholarships—to individuals.
Application information: Applications accepted. Application form required.
  Additional information: Application should include proof of enrollment before funds are released. See web site for additional guidelines.
EIN: 043401997

4154
The Lyceum Fellowship, Inc.
c/o Mark Spaulding
1000 Massachusetts Ave., 4th Fl.
Cambridge, MA 02138
URL: http://www.lyceum-fellowship.org

Foundation type: Independent foundation
Purpose: Travel fellowships to students of invited selected schools of architecture.
Financial data: Year ended 12/31/2011. Assets, $5,349 (M); Expenditures, $39,893; Total giving, $13,000; Grants to individuals, 2 grants totaling $13,000 (high: $11,500, low: $1,500).
Fields of interest: Architecture.
Type of support: Fellowships; Awards/prizes; Travel grants.
Application information: Applications accepted.
  Send request by: Mail
  Deadline(s): Mar.
  Additional information: Application should include a $10 fee. See web site for selected schools and additional guidelines.
Program description:
  Lyceum Competition: The competition welcomes students attending selected schools, where travel awards are intended to enrich the academic experience with all competitors required to have at least one year of study remaining so that a travel award may be fulfilled prior to the completion of the current or an immediately subsequent architectural degree program. Students should work individually, submissions resulting from individual work completed in a design studio are encouraged. Travel prizes are, first prize $12,000 for six months travel abroad, second prize $7,500 for three months travel abroad, and a third prize of $1,500 grant.
EIN: 043655746

4155
William A. Lynch Trust
c/o Eastern Bank
605 Broadway, LF42
Saugus, MA 01906-3200   (978) 921-6132
Application address: c/o Beverly High School, Attn.: Principal, 100 Sohier Rd., Beverly, MA 01915-2654

Foundation type: Independent foundation
Purpose: Scholarships to deserving Catholic graduates of public high schools in Beverly, MA, and nearby Catholic schools.
Financial data: Year ended 12/31/2012. Assets, $46,943 (M); Expenditures, $3,575; Total giving, $2,300; Grants to individuals, 3 grants totaling $2,300 (high: $1,000, low: $300).
Fields of interest: Catholic agencies & churches.
Type of support: Undergraduate support.
Application information: Applications accepted. Application form required.
  Initial approach: Letter
  Deadline(s): June 1
EIN: 046016042

4156
Mack Industrial School
c/o Cabot Money Mgmt.
216 Essex St.
Salem, MA 01970-3705   (978) 745-9233
Contact: Diana Cummings, Chair.
Application address: 11 Valiant Way, Salem, MA 01970

Foundation type: Independent foundation

Purpose: Scholarships to female residents of Salem, MA, who are graduating high school seniors and have been accepted to a vocational school or college for the fall semester following graduation. Recipients are chosen on academic record and need.
Financial data: Year ended 08/31/2013. Assets, $447,603 (M); Expenditures, $20,094; Total giving, $20,000; Grants to individuals, 20 grants totaling $20,000.
Fields of interest: Vocational education, post-secondary; Women.
Type of support: Scholarships—to individuals.
Application information: Applications accepted. Application form required.
  Copies of proposal: 1
  Deadline(s): May 1
  Additional information: Application forms available only at the guidance offices of eligible area high schools.
EIN: 046032773

4157
Make-A-Wish Foundation of Massachusetts, Inc.
1 Bulfinch Pl., 2nd Fl.
Boston, MA 02114-2903   (617) 367-9474
Contact: Charlotte A. Beattie, C.E.O.
FAX: (617) 367-1059;
E-mail: boston@mass.wish.org; URL: http://www.mass.wish.org

Foundation type: Public charity
Purpose: Cash and non-cash assistance for children between the ages of 2 1/2 and 18 years in MA and RI with life-threatening medical conditions.
Financial data: Year ended 08/31/2011. Assets, $8,042,655 (M); Expenditures, $5,627,087; Total giving, $3,416,754; Grants to individuals, totaling $3,316,754.
Fields of interest: Children; Economically disadvantaged.
Type of support: Grants for special needs.
Application information: Applications not accepted.
  Additional information: Unsolicited requests for funds not considered or acknowledged. Contact the foundation for eligibility determination.
EIN: 222867371

4158
William E. Maloney Foundation
275 Massachusetts Ave.
Lexington, MA 02420-4088   (781) 862-3400
Contact: John W. Maloney, Tr.
Application address: P.O. Box 515, Lexington, MA 02173

Foundation type: Independent foundation
Purpose: Scholarships to individuals in MA for undergraduate education at accredited institutions of higher learning.
Financial data: Year ended 12/31/2012. Assets, $835,680 (M); Expenditures, $24,888; Total giving, $22,003.
Fields of interest: Higher education.
Type of support: Undergraduate support.
Application information: Applications accepted.
  Initial approach: Letter
  Deadline(s): None
EIN: 046131998

4159
Marblehead Female Humane Society, Inc.
P.O. Box 425
Marblehead, MA   01945-0425   (978) 762-3848
Contact: Lee Weed, Pres.

Foundation type: Operating foundation
Purpose: Financial assistance to residents of Marblehead, MA.
Financial data: Year ended 09/30/2012. Assets, $2,471,104 (M); Expenditures, $217,254; Total giving, $170,644; Grants to individuals, totaling $97,981.
Fields of interest: Economically disadvantaged.
Type of support: Grants for special needs.
Application information: Applications accepted.
  Initial approach: Letter
  Deadline(s): None
  Final notification: Applicants notified within 60 days
  Additional information: Application must include financial information.
EIN: 042104694

4160
Marine Biological Laboratory
(also known as MBL)
7 MBL St.
Woods Hole, MA   02543-1015   (508) 548-3705
Contact: Gary G. Borisy Ph.D., Pres.
Tel. for Ann Woolford: (508) 289-7173,
e-mail: awoolford@mbl.edu
FAX: (508) 289-7934; E-mail: helpdesk@mbl.edu;
URL: http://www.mbl.edu

Foundation type: Public charity
Purpose: Research grants and fellowships for the study of biology, biomedicine, and ecology.
Publications: Application guidelines; Annual report.
Financial data: Year ended 12/31/2011. Assets, $152,250,850 (M); Expenditures, $48,266,642; Total giving, $4,389,675; Grants to individuals, totaling $1,342,811.
Fields of interest: Biomedicine; Neuroscience; Brain research; Medical research; Science.
Type of support: Fellowships; Research.
Application information: Applications accepted. Application form required. Application form available on the grantmaker's web site.
  Initial approach: Application
  Send request by: Mail or e-mail
  Copies of proposal: 1
  Deadline(s): Jan. 15
  Final notification: Recipients notified within six weeks
Program descriptions:
  Albert and Ellen Grass Faculty Grant: This program works to promote innovative research collaborations, ideally between investigators from different institutions. Preference will be given to junior investigators; junior investigators are a required member of any team seeking this fellowship support.
  The Laura and Arthur Colwin Endowed Summer Research Fellowship Fund: This endowed fund provides support for independent investigators conducting research in the fields of cell and developmental biology during the summer months at the laboratory.
EIN: 042104690

4161
Maria Marino Scholarship Fund
c/o Avon Town Treasurer
Avon Town Hall
Avon, MA   02322   (508) 583-4822
Contact: Marilyn Malcomson
Application address: Avon High School, Avon, MA 02322

Foundation type: Independent foundation
Purpose: Scholarships to graduating students at Avon High School, MA, for college education.
Financial data: Year ended 12/31/2012. Assets, $91,147 (M); Expenditures, $5,806; Total giving, $5,000; Grants to individuals, 7 grants totaling $5,000 (high: $1,000, low: $500).
Type of support: Support to graduates or students of specific schools; Undergraduate support.
Application information: Application form required.
  Deadline(s): Apr. 1
  Applicants should submit the following:
    1) Financial information
    2) Transcripts
    3) Essay
    4) FAFSA
EIN: 510181012

4162
Henry B. Martin Fund, Inc.
10 Post Office Sq., 6th Flr.
Boston, MA   02109-4603   (617) 227-7940
Contact: David H. Morse, Clerk., Treas.
Application address: 60 state St., Boston MA 02109 tel.:(617) 227-7940

Foundation type: Independent foundation
Purpose: Relief assistance to financially needy elderly citizens who currently or previously have had a connection to the town of Milton, MA.
Financial data: Year ended 12/31/2012. Assets, $1,408,060 (M); Expenditures, $137,243; Total giving, $80,000; Grants to individuals, 50 grants totaling $80,000 (high: $2,000, low: $500).
Fields of interest: Aging; Economically disadvantaged.
Type of support: Grants for special needs.
Application information: Grants are most often used to pay for current expenses related to rent, gas, electricity, telephone, food, fuel, medical, dental, counseling, taxes, home repair and childcare.
EIN: 046031995

4163
Massachusetts Bar Foundation, Inc.
20 West St.
Boston, MA   02111-1204   (617) 338-0500
Contact: Elizabeth Lynch, Exec. Dir.
FAX: (617) 338-0550;
E-mail: foundation@massbar.org; URL: http://www.massbarfoundation.org

Foundation type: Public charity
Purpose: Stipends to law students who intern during the summer at nonprofit organizations providing civil legal services to low-income individuals in MA.
Publications: Application guidelines; Annual report; Grants list; Newsletter.
Financial data: Year ended 12/31/2011. Assets, $7,128,282 (M); Expenditures, $3,742,844; Total giving, $3,397,671.
Fields of interest: Law school/education.
Type of support: Internship funds; Graduate support.
Application information: Application form required.

Initial approach: Telephone or e-mail
Send request by: Mail
Deadline(s): Mar. 16
Final notification: Applicants notified in Apr.
Applicants should submit the following:
  1) Transcripts
  2) Essay
  3) Resume
Additional information: Application should also include a letter of reference from a supervisor, professor or similar professional contact. Application by e-mail or fax not accepted.
Program description:
Legal Intern Fellowship Program: The program awards up to six stipends of $6,000 each to law students who intern during the summer months at nonprofit organizations providing civil legal services to low-income clients in Massachusetts. Stipends are paid directly to the intern's organization. Applicants must be currently enrolled in a U.S. law school. Preference will be given to permanent/future residents of MA.
EIN: 046130261

4164
Massachusetts Charitable Fire Society
c/o J.M. Forbes & Co., LLP
121 Mt. Vernon St.
Boston, MA   02108   (617) 423-5705
Contact: G. West Saltonstall, Treas.

Foundation type: Independent foundation
Purpose: Giving limited to individuals in the Boston, MA, area, who have suffered loss due to fire and require assistance in replacing necessities.
Financial data: Year ended 07/31/2013. Assets, $1,954,117 (M); Expenditures, $95,677; Total giving, $82,000.
Fields of interest: Housing/shelter, expense aid; Safety/disasters.
Type of support: Emergency funds.
Application information: Applications accepted.
  Initial approach: Letter
  Deadline(s): None
  Additional information: Applications must include a description of the event giving rise to the need and the specific items for which relief is requested.
EIN: 042305919

4165
Massachusetts College of Liberal Arts Foundation, Inc.
375 Church St.
North Adams, MA   01247-4124   (413) 662-5000
URL: http://www.mcla.edu/

Foundation type: Public charity
Purpose: Scholarships to students at Massachusetts College of Liberal Arts for higher education.
Financial data: Year ended 06/30/2012. Assets, $12,755,754 (M); Expenditures, $2,747,165; Total giving, $2,217,817; Grants to individuals, totaling $220,403.
Fields of interest: Arts education.
Type of support: Scholarships—to individuals.
Application information: Contact foundation for additional guidelines.
EIN: 042613803

4166
Massachusetts Library Aid Association
2 Memorial Dr.
Ashburnham, MA   01430-1299   (800) 952-7403
Contact: Shelly Quezada, Dir.
Application address: 648 Beacon St., Boston, MA
02215, tel.: (800) 952-7403

Foundation type: Independent foundation
Purpose: Grants to librarians or library assistants
who are presently employed in MA public library.
Financial data: Year ended 12/31/2012. Assets,
$292,425 (M); Expenditures, $12,177; Total
giving, $11,158; Grants to individuals, 8 grants
totaling $3,570 (high: $500, low: $250).
Fields of interest: Libraries/library science.
Type of support: Grants to individuals; Travel
grants.
Application information: Applications accepted.
Application form required.
  Deadline(s): None
  Additional information: Maximum education
    award is $500 and maximum travel award is
    $100 for a combined limit of $600. Award
    must be used towards special training in
    library science techniques.
EIN: 046038185

4167
Massachusetts Medical Society
860 Winter St.
Waltham, MA   02451-1411   (781) 891-4610
FAX: (781) 893-8009; E-mail: info@massmed.org;
URL: http://www.massmed.org

Foundation type: Public charity
Purpose: Grants for students and resident
physician members of the Massachusetts Medical
Society to study abroad. Preference is given to
applicants planning careers serving underprivileged
populations in the world.
Publications: Annual report; Newsletter.
Financial data: Year ended 05/31/2012. Assets,
$248,779,761 (M); Expenditures, $106,943,460;
Total giving, $1,181,978; Grants to individuals,
totaling $85,000.
Fields of interest: Health care.
Type of support: Grants to individuals; Travel
grants.
Application information: Applications accepted.
Application form required. Application form
available on the grantmaker's web site.
  Initial approach: Letter
  Send request by: E-mail
  Deadline(s): Sept. 15
  Final notification: Decisions generally made
    within 45 days of deadline
  Applicants should submit the following:
    1) Budget Information
    2) Letter(s) of recommendation
  Additional information: Application should
    include a description of career plans.
EIN: 042050773

4168
Massachusetts Society of Mayflower Descendants
175 Derby St., Ste. 13
Hingham, MA   02043-4036   (781) 875-3194
E-mail: msmd@massmayflower.org; URL: http://
www.massmayflower.org

Foundation type: Public charity
Purpose: Scholarships to members of the
Wampanoag tribe in MA who can prove their

ancestry and who are currently registered at a
college or university.
Publications: Application guidelines; Informational
brochure; Newsletter.
Financial data: Year ended 12/31/2012. Assets,
$2,095,012 (M); Expenditures, $209,159; Total
giving, $2,000; Grants to individuals, totaling
$2,000.
Fields of interest: Native Americans/American
Indians.
Type of support: Undergraduate support.
Application information: Applications accepted.
Application form required.
  Initial approach: Letter
Program descriptions:
  Sears Scholarship: A $1,000 award will be given
to a student who is currently attending a New
England college or university.
  Thanksgiving Day Scholarship: Each year, two
scholarships are presented to college students who
are of the Wampanoag Indian tribe and who can
prove their ancestry. Scholarships are for $1,500
and can be used for undergraduate or graduate
study.
EIN: 042104712

4169
Dennis and Marion Mavrogenis Trust Fund
c/o Eastern Bank & Trust Dept.
605 Broadway, RT1 LF41
Saugus, MA   01906   (781) 581-4219
Contact: Shawn McCarthy

Foundation type: Independent foundation
Purpose: Scholarships to financially needy
residents of Salem, MA, for higher education.
Financial data: Year ended 12/31/2011. Assets,
$2,128,086 (M); Expenditures, $78,672; Total
giving, $51,450; Grants to individuals, 11 grants
totaling $51,450 (high: $5,250, low: $2,100).
Fields of interest: Higher education.
Type of support: Undergraduate support.
Application information: Applications accepted.
  Initial approach: Letter
  Deadline(s): May 1
EIN: 043179137

4170
Maya Educational Foundation
P.O. Box 1483
Wellfleet, MA   02667-1483
Contact: Elisabeth S. Nicholson, Secy. and Exec.
Dir.
E-mail: mef@mayaedufound.org; URL: http://
www.mayaedufound.org

Foundation type: Public charity
Purpose: Scholarships to individuals of Mayan
descent in Central America and Mexico.
Publications: Annual report; Informational
brochure; Newsletter.
Financial data: Year ended 06/30/2012. Assets,
$1,783,147 (M); Expenditures, $607,844; Total
giving, $565,377.
Fields of interest: Native Americans/American
Indians.
International interests: Central America;
Guatemala; Mexico.
Type of support: Program development; Graduate
support; Technical education support; Precollege
support; Undergraduate support; Doctoral support.
Application information: Applications accepted.
  Initial approach: Letter
  Deadline(s): None

Additional information: Contact foundation for
  additional information.
EIN: 030335159

4171
John McElaney Trust f/b/o Town of Avon
c/o Heald Hoffmeister & Co.
105 Chestnut St., No. 10
Needham, MA   02492   (508) 583-4822
Application address: c/o Avon High School,
Attn.: Guidance Counselor, 285 W. Main St., Avon,
MA 02322

Foundation type: Independent foundation
Purpose: Scholarships to graduates of Avon High
School, MA, who plan to pursue studies at higher
education institutions.
Financial data: Year ended 12/31/2012. Assets,
$261,791 (M); Expenditures, $32,668; Total
giving, $13,510; Grants to individuals, 10 grants
totaling $13,510 (high: $3,510, low: $500).
Type of support: Support to graduates or students
of specific schools; Undergraduate support.
Application information: Application form required.
  Deadline(s): Apr. 10
EIN: 046060702

4172
The McLaughlin Foundation
546 Fishers St.
Walpole, MA   02081   (508) 660-1142
Contact: James McGrath, Pres. and Dir.

Foundation type: Independent foundation
Purpose: Scholarships to MT residents attending
Harvard University, MA, and other colleges.
Financial data: Year ended 12/31/2012. Assets,
$507,594 (M); Expenditures, $26,765; Total
giving, $25,000.
Type of support: Scholarships—to individuals;
Support to graduates or students of specific
schools.
Application information: Applications accepted.
  Deadline(s): None
  Additional information: Applicants should submit
    a brief resume of academic qualifications.
EIN: 237416882

4173
MetroWest Health Foundation
(formerly MetroWest Community Health Care
Foundation, Inc.)
c/o The Meadows Bldg.
161 Worcester Rd., Ste. 202
Framingham, MA   01701-5232   (508) 879-7625
Contact: Martin Cohen, Pres.
FAX: (508) 879-7628; E-mail: info@mwhealth.org;
URL: http://www.mwhealth.org

Foundation type: Independent foundation
Purpose: Scholarships to residents of the 25-town
MetroWest region of MA, for the study of medicine,
nursing, dentistry and the allied health fields.
Publications: Application guidelines; Annual report;
Financial statement; Grants list; Newsletter;
Occasional report.
Financial data: Year ended 09/30/2013. Assets,
$99,955,446 (M); Expenditures, $4,690,784;
Total giving, $2,418,094.
Type of support: Undergraduate support.
Application information: Application form required.
Application form available on the grantmaker's web
site.
  Initial approach: Telephone
  Applicants should submit the following:

1) Transcripts
2) Letter(s) of recommendation
3) GPA
4) FAFSA
Additional information: Contact foundation for further eligibility requirements.

Program description:
Health Professions Scholarship Program: Scholarships of $2,000 per academic year are available to students who live or work in the MetroWest area and are accepted in a nursing, medical, or clinical program at an accredited institution.
EIN: 042121342

4174
Middlesex Savings Charitable Foundation, Inc.

c/o Middlesex Savings Bank
6 Main St.
Natick, MA 01760-4506 (508) 315-5360
Contact: Dana M. Neshe, Pres.
E-mail: dneshe@middlesexbank.com; URL: http://www.middlesexbank.com/community/charitablefoundation/

Foundation type: Company-sponsored foundation
Purpose: Scholarship to a high school senior who demonstrates leadership through an essay submission. Scholarships to area graduates of public and vocational high schools for higher edcuation.
Publications: Application guidelines; Grants list; Program policy statement.
Financial data: Year ended 12/31/2012. Assets, $8,158,727 (M); Expenditures, $471,079; Total giving, $424,800.
Fields of interest: Vocational education, post-secondary; Higher education.
Type of support: Scholarships—to individuals; Support to graduates or students of specific schools; Awards/grants by nomination only.
Application information: Application form required. Application form available on the grantmaker's web site.
  Initial approach: Application
  Send request by: Mail
  Deadline(s): Mar. for A. James Lavoie Essay Contest Scholarship
  Final notification: Applicants notified in May for A. James Lavoie Essay Contest Scholarship
  Applicants should submit the following:
    1) FAFSA
    2) Essay
    3) Transcripts
  Additional information: Recipients must be nominated by individual schools.

Program description:
A. James Lavoie Essay Contest Scholarship: The foundation awards a $5,000 scholarship to a graduating senior from one of 24 area public or vocational schools with plans to attend a four-year college program. Applicants must submit a 2-3 page essay describing a developed skill through hard work and perseverance and plans to use that skill to improve the community. Essay topics may change yearly. Applicants must also present evidence of good academic standing, exhibit active involvement in the community, and demonstrate financial need.
EIN: 043521246

4175
Christina M. Mihos Youth Foundation

c/o OLDE Northeast Realty
22 Christys Dr., Ste. 4
Brockton, MA 02301 (508) 427-6111
Contact: Linda Ann Mihos, Tr.
Application address: 29 Harlow St., N. Easton, MA 02356; URL: http://www.cmmyfoundation.org

Foundation type: Independent foundation
Purpose: Scholarships to graduating seniors of Oliver Ames High School, MA, whose immediate family are members of the Greek Orthodox Church in Brockton, MA, and to students who have completed at least one year of full-time study at Stonehill College, MA.
Financial data: Year ended 06/30/2013. Assets, $34,756 (M); Expenditures, $4,803; Total giving, $3,018.
Fields of interest: Higher education; Scholarships/financial aid.
Type of support: Support to graduates or students of specific schools; Undergraduate support.
Application information: Applications accepted.
  Initial approach: Letter
  Deadline(s): None
  Applicants should submit the following:
    1) Transcripts
    2) Financial information
  Additional information: Application should also include letter outlining academic performance and course of study.
EIN: 043164157

4176
Dr. Max & Ida L. Millman Foundation

c/o Hampden District Medical Society
1111 Elm St., Ste. 22
West Springfield, MA 01089-1540

Foundation type: Independent foundation
Purpose: Loans and scholarships to medical students who reside in Hampden County, MA.
Financial data: Year ended 12/31/2012. Assets, $0 (M); Expenditures, $6,725; Total giving, $6,000; Grants to individuals, 3 grants totaling $6,000 (high: $2,000, low: $2,000).
Fields of interest: Medical school/education.
Type of support: Scholarships—to individuals; Student loans—to individuals.
Application information: Applications accepted. Application form required.
  Deadline(s): Sept. 1
EIN: 046397476

4177
John Milton Society for the Blind

c/o Perkins School for the Blind
175 N. Beacon St.
Watertown, MA 02472-2751 (617) 924-3434
Contact: Steven Rothstein, Pres. ans Treas.
FAX: (617) 926-2027

Foundation type: Public charity
Purpose: Scholarships to students who are either from or planning to attend school in NY, who are enrolled at Overbrook School for the Blind, Philadelphia, PA, or Perkins School for the Blind, Watertown, MA, for future work with the blind.
Financial data: Year ended 06/30/2012. Assets, $773,793 (M); Expenditures, $33,967; Total giving, $21,000; Grants to individuals, totaling $21,000.
Fields of interest: Eye diseases; Blind/visually impaired.
Type of support: Scholarships—to individuals.

Application information: Application form required.
  Additional information: Applicants must contact their schools for application forms, or be recommended by the New York State Commission for the Blind.
Program description:
  Scholarship Program: Scholarships are distributed among students enrolled in the International Program at Overbrook School for the Blind (Philadelphia, PA), the Educational Leadership Program at Perkins School for the Blind (Watertown, MA), and one or two students who are from or planning to attend school in New York State (chosen by the New York State Commission for the Blind)
EIN: 135562284

4178
Miss Massachusetts Scholarship Foundation

170 N. Washington St.
North Attleboro, MA 02760-1733 (508) 695-5831
URL: http://www.missmass.org/

Foundation type: Independent foundation
Purpose: Scholarships to young women in MA who are involved in the Miss America organization.
Financial data: Year ended 09/30/2013. Assets, $29,048 (M); Expenditures, $53,601; Total giving, $0.
Fields of interest: Higher education; Women.
Type of support: Undergraduate support.
Application information:
  Deadline(s): None
  Additional information: Contact foundation for current application guidelines.
EIN: 222586251

4179
Everett W. & Marion E. Mitchell Foundation

c/o Nixon Peabody LLP
100 Summer St.
Boston, MA 02110-2131 (617) 345-1000
Contact: Ronald Garmey, Tr.

Foundation type: Independent foundation
Purpose: Scholarships to students residing in the town of Middleton, PA on the basis of citizenship, academic proficiency, and financial need.
Financial data: Year ended 08/31/2013. Assets, $7,595,936 (M); Expenditures, $382,600; Total giving, $302,885; Grants to individuals, 18 grants totaling $150,679 (high: $14,012, low: $4,950).
Type of support: Undergraduate support.
Application information:
  Initial approach: Letter
EIN: 207088204

4180
John Joseph Moakley Charitable Foundation, Inc.

c/o Shaevel Krems
141 Tremont St.
Boston, MA 02111-1209 (617) 556-0244
Contact: William Shaevel, Treas.
URL: http://www.moakleyfoundation.com

Foundation type: Independent foundation
Purpose: Scholarships for a post high school vocational education program or to an institution of higher education for undergraduate or graduate support to residents of MA.

Publications: Application guidelines.
Financial data: Year ended 12/31/2012. Assets, $877,901 (M); Expenditures, $144,809; Total giving, $120,300; Grants to individuals, 30 grants totaling $115,300 (high: $5,000, low: $300).
Fields of interest: Higher education.
Type of support: Scholarships—to individuals.
Application information: Applications accepted. Application form required. Application form available on the grantmaker's web site.
 Initial approach: Letter
 Deadline(s): Apr. 1
 Applicants should submit the following:
  1) Financial information
  2) Essay
 Additional information: Application should also include proof of acceptance in a vocational or higher education program.
Program description:
 Scholarships: Scholarships of up to $5,000 each are awarded on a competitive basis each spring to successful applicants who demonstrate: a desire to contribute to one's community through public or charitable services as a vocation or in extracurricular activities; acceptance to a post-high-school vocational education program or institute of higher education for undergraduate or graduate study; financial need; and residency in Massachusetts, with special consideration given to Boston, Braintree, Brockton, Canton, Dedham, Easton, Medfield, Milton, Needham, Norwood, Randolph, Stoughton, Taunton, Walpole, and Westwood.
EIN: 043551974

4181
Michael A. Molloy Scholarship Trust Fund

85 Exchange St.
Lynn, MA 01901-1417
Contact: T. Richard Cuffe, Jr., Tr.

Foundation type: Independent foundation
Purpose: Scholarships to graduates of St. Mary's Regional Junior/Senior High School, Lynn, MA.
Financial data: Year ended 12/31/2011. Assets, $218,896 (M); Expenditures, $56,527; Total giving, $48,000; Grants to individuals, 23 grants totaling $48,000 (high: $4,000, low: $2,000).
Type of support: Support to graduates or students of specific schools; Undergraduate support.
Application information: Application form required.
 Deadline(s): May 1
 Applicants should submit the following:
  1) Class rank
  2) SAT
  3) Transcripts
 Additional information: Applications should also include school activities and financial data of parent or custodian.
EIN: 043484055

4182
The Mary E. Murphy and John F. Murphy Jr., Charitable Trust

P.O. Box 68
Winchester, MA 01890 (781) 729-2542
Contact: Peter J. Segerstrom, Tr.; James R. Willing, Tr.

Foundation type: Independent foundation
Purpose: College scholarships to eligible students residing in Precinct 8 who are graduates of or graduating seniors at Winchester High School, MA, or to residents of Winchester, MA, who graduated from a regional or vocational high school offering other education of a specialized nature.

Financial data: Year ended 12/31/2012. Assets, $616,676 (M); Expenditures, $30,371; Total giving, $22,245; Grants to individuals, 22 grants totaling $22,245 (high: $2,500, low: $81).
Fields of interest: Vocational education, post-secondary; Higher education.
Type of support: Support to graduates or students of specific schools; Undergraduate support.
Application information: Applications accepted. Application form required.
 Send request by: Mail
 Deadline(s): Apr. 15
 Final notification: Applicants notified by May 15
 Applicants should submit the following:
  1) Financial information
  2) Transcripts
  3) Letter(s) of recommendation
 Additional information: Applicants evaluated by need and character.
EIN: 046772198

4183
F. Leo Murray & Irene D. Murray Scholarship Fund

P.O. Box 127
Winchendon, MA 01475-0250 (978) 297-2042
Contact: Robert LaFortune

Foundation type: Operating foundation
Purpose: Scholarships to qualified young men and women of Winchendon, MA pursuing higher education.
Financial data: Year ended 12/31/2011. Assets, $343,021 (M); Expenditures, $22,555; Total giving, $16,000; Grants to individuals, 8 grants totaling $16,000 (high: $2,000, low: $2,000).
Fields of interest: Higher education.
Type of support: Scholarships—to individuals.
Application information: Applications accepted. Application form required.
 Additional information: Contact the fund for application guidelines.
EIN: 046635075

4184
Museum of Fine Arts

465 Huntington Ave.
Boston, MA 02115-5597 (617) 267-9300
E-mail: webmaster@mfa.org; URL: http://www.mfa.org

Foundation type: Public charity
Purpose: The Maud Morgan Prize is given every other year to a female MA artist who has demonstrated creativity and vision, and who has made significant contributions to the contemporary arts landscape. The prize includes $10,000 and a one-person show at the museum.
Financial data: Year ended 06/30/2012. Assets, $1,135,859,886 (M); Expenditures, $149,185,619; Total giving, $5,336,096; Grants to individuals, totaling $5,336,096.
Fields of interest: Visual arts; Arts; Women.
Type of support: Awards/prizes.
Application information:
 Initial approach: Letter
 Additional information: Contact foundation for eligibility criteria.
EIN: 042103607

4185
Museum of Science

1 Science Park
Boston, MA 02114-0000 (617) 723-2500
Contact: Ioannis N. Miaoulis, Pres.
FAX: (617) 589-0187;
E-mail: information@mos.org; TTY: (617)-589-0417; URL: http://www.mos.org/

Foundation type: Public charity
Purpose: Summer residencies for teachers at Boston's Museum of Science to collaborate on a relevant Museum project, participate in a weekly seminar, and work on an independent project. Stipends of $3,000.
Financial data: Year ended 06/30/2012. Assets, $200,089,508 (M); Expenditures, $52,471,315; Total giving, $5,110,138; Grants to individuals, totaling $441,429.
Fields of interest: Museums (children's); Museums (science/technology).
Type of support: Residencies.
Application information: Applications accepted. Application form required. Application form available on the grantmaker's web site.
 Initial approach: E-mail
 Deadline(s): Feb. 25 until Apr. 7
 Final notification: May 6
EIN: 042103916

4186
Nantucket Community Music Center

11 Ctr. St.
P.O. Box 1352
Nantucket, MA 02554-3638 (508) 228-3352
E-mail: ncmc@verizon.net; URL: http://nantucketcommunitymusiccenter.org/

Foundation type: Public charity
Purpose: Scholarships to adults and children in the Nantucket community for music instruction in theory, voice and instruments.
Financial data: Year ended 06/30/2012. Assets, $203,030 (M); Expenditures, $272,240; Total giving, $11,222; Grants to individuals, totaling $11,222.
Fields of interest: Music.
Type of support: Scholarships—to individuals.
Application information: Applications accepted.
 Additional information: Scholarship applicants are reviewed by a committee.
EIN: 510194502

4187
Nantucket Island School of Design and the Arts, Inc.

23 Wauwinet Rd.
P.O. Box 958
Nantucket, MA 02554-4210 (508) 228-9248
FAX: (508) 228-3648;
E-mail: nisdaartsnantucket@nisda.org;
URL: http://www.nisda.org

Foundation type: Public charity
Purpose: Residencies to emerging and professional artists and educators in all fields.
Publications: Application guidelines.
Financial data: Year ended 06/30/2012. Assets, $1,551,143 (M); Expenditures, $254,647.
Fields of interest: Photography; Painting; Ceramic arts; Music.
Type of support: Residencies.
Application information: Application form required.
 Initial approach: Telephone, e-mail or fax
 Applicants should submit the following:
  1) Proposal

2) Work samples
3) Resume
Additional information: Application should also include a $30 application processing fee.

Program description:

Artist-In-Residency Program: Emerging and professional artists including, but not limited to, the studio arts in photography, painting, ceramics, textiles, writing, music, performance, and any alternative projects committed to the creative process may apply to the program. The residency is a self-structured experience that provides time and climate for personal renewal. Residents live at the school's Harbor Cottages in Nantucket Town.
EIN: 042642384

4188
National Fire Protection Association

1 Batterymarch Pk.
Quincy, MA 02169-7471 (617) 770-3000
Contact: James M. Shannon, Pres. and C.E.O.
FAX: (617) 770-0700; E-mail: custserv@nfpa.org;
URL: http://www.nfpa.org

Foundation type: Public charity
Purpose: Grants and other assistance to invividuals in the U.S. Scholarships for outstanding achievements to individuals in the U.S.
Publications: Application guidelines; Newsletter; Occasional report.
Financial data: Year ended 12/31/2011. Assets, $239,473,110 (M); Expenditures, $65,588,141; Total giving, $395,725; Grants to individuals, totaling $62,400.
Fields of interest: Education.
Type of support: Scholarships—to individuals.
Application information: Applications accepted. Application form required.
Additional information: Contact the association or see web site for additional guidelines.

Program descriptions:

Arthur E. Cote Scholarship: A $5,000 scholarship will be given to one or more undergraduate students enrolled in fire protection engineering programs in either the U.S. or Canada. Eligible applicants must demonstrate scholarship achievement, leadership qualities, concern for others/volunteerism, and intention to pursue a career in fire safety engineering.
Charles S. Morgan Scholarship: A $5,000 scholarship will be awarded to a student enrolled in the four-year fire protection and safety engineering technology program at Oklahoma State University's Center for Academic Services.
David B. Gratz Scholarship: At least one $5,000 scholarship with be awarded to one or more graduate students enrolled in a fire science or fire engineering program at an institution outside the U.S. or Canada. Recipients will be chosen based on scholarship achievement, leadership qualities, concern for others/volunteerism, and contributions to international/national fire safety activities.
Frank J. Fee Scholarship: A $5,000 scholarship is awarded to students enrolled in fire protection engineering programs at the University of Maryland's Department of Fire Protection Engineering.
George D. Miller Scholarship: Scholarships of $5,000 each will be awarded to one or more undergraduate or graduate students enrolled in a fire service or public administration program in either the U.S. or Canada. Applicants will be evaluated on the completion of at least one academic year of post-high school credits, scholastic achievement, leadership qualities, and concern for others/volunteerism.

John L. Jablonsky Scholarship: At least one $5,000 scholarship will be awarded to one or more graduate students enrolled in fire protection engineering programs in either the U.S. or Canada. Applicants will be evaluated on scholastic achievement, leadership qualities, concern for others/volunteerism, and intention to pursue a career in fire safety engineering.
Percy Bugbee Scholarship: A $5,000 scholarship will be awarded to a fire protection engineering student who is enrolled at Worcester Polytechnic Institute, demonstrates excellence in academic achievement, and intends to perform a thesis or graduate project actively aimed at improving fire protection engineering methods.
Warren E. Isman Educational Grant: At least one $5,000 grant will be made to a hazardous materials response team (with a maximum of five members) to register for specialized training at a national hazardous materials conference each year. Any established hazardous materials incident response team from a fire department, police department, or other public-funded program may apply; preference will be given to teams which demonstrate leadership qualities and communications abilities.
EIN: 041653090

4189
National Multiple Sclerosis Society, Central New England Chapter

101-A 1st Ave., Ste. 6
Waltham, MA 02451-1115 (781) 890-4990
FAX: (781) 890-2089; Toll-free tel.: (800) 344-4867; URL: http://mam.nationalmssociety.org/site/PageServer?pagename=MAM_homepage

Foundation type: Public charity
Purpose: Scholarships to high school seniors who have MS or who has a parent with MS, for attendance at an accredited postsecondary school for the first time pursuing a degree, license, or certificate.
Publications: Annual report; Financial statement; Newsletter.
Financial data: Year ended 09/30/2011. Assets, $3,170,226 (M); Expenditures, $9,551,145; Total giving, $602,454; Grants to individuals, totaling $302,860.
Fields of interest: Vocational education, post-secondary; Higher education; Multiple sclerosis.
Type of support: Scholarships—to individuals.
Application information: Applications accepted.
Send request by: Online
Deadline(s): Jan. 15
Applicants should submit the following:
1) Transcripts
2) Financial information
3) Essay
Additional information: Applicants are selected based on demonstrated financial need, academic record, leadership and participation in school or community activities, work experience, outside appraisal, goals and aspirations, and special circumstances regarding the impact of MS on their life. See web site for additional guidelines.
EIN: 042178884

4190
National Patient Safety Foundation

268 Summer St., 6th Fl.
Boston, MA 02210-1108 (617) 391-9900
Contact: Tejal K. Gandhi, Pres.
E-mail: info@npsf.org; E-mail For Tejal K. Gandhi: tgandhi@npsf.org; URL: http://www.npsf.org

Foundation type: Public charity
Purpose: Research grants to study human and organizational error and prevention of accidents in health care.
Publications: Application guidelines; Annual report.
Financial data: Year ended 12/31/2011. Assets, $4,530,005 (M); Expenditures, $3,913,345; Total giving, $199,989.
Fields of interest: Safety, education.
Type of support: Research; Awards/prizes.
Application information:
Initial approach: Letter
Deadline(s): Sept. 6 for LOI, Jan. 27 for full proposal
Applicants should submit the following:
1) Curriculum vitae
Additional information: See web site for additional application information.

Program description:

Research Grant Program: This program provides grants of up to $100,000 to stimulate new, innovative projects directed toward enhancing patient safety in the U.S. Grants are intended to promote studies leading to the prevention of human errors, system errors, patient injuries, and the consequences of such adverse events in the healthcare setting. Eligible applicants must be official members of a nonprofit institution in the U.S.
EIN: 367166993

4191
Needymeds, Inc.

P.O. Box 219
Gloucester, MA 01931-0219 (978) 281-6666
Contact: Rich Sagall M.D., Pres.
FAX: (206) 260-8850; E-mail: info@needymeds.org;
Toll-Free Tel.: (800) 503-6897; E-mail For Rich Sagall: richsagall@needymeds.org; URL: http://www.needymeds.org

Foundation type: Public charity
Purpose: Assistance for low-to-moderate-income, uninsured and under-insured individuals with free or discounted medicines.
Financial data: Year ended 12/31/2011. Assets, $504,587 (M); Expenditures, $31,729,932; Total giving, $30,650,180; Grants to individuals, totaling $30,650,180.
Fields of interest: Health care.
Type of support: Grants for special needs.
Application information: Applications accepted. Application form required.
Additional information: Individuals must complete comprehensive applications to qualify for assistance. See web site for additional information.
EIN: 752982439

4192
Ladies Branch of the New Bedford Port Society

15 Johnny Cake Hill
New Bedford, MA 02740
Contact: Betsy Pye

Foundation type: Operating foundation

Purpose: Scholarships only to needy students from the greater New Bedford, MA, area, whose families or descendants had some connection with the sea or who are engaged in maritime studies.
Publications: Application guidelines.
Financial data: Year ended 12/31/2010. Assets, $1,298 (M); Expenditures, $2,062; Total giving, $1,075.
Fields of interest: Military/veterans' organizations.
Type of support: Undergraduate support.
Application information: Application form required.
> *Initial approach:* Letter
> *Deadline(s):* Apr. 1
> *Applicants should submit the following:*
> 1) GPA
> 2) Financial information
> 3) Essay
> 4) Curriculum vitae
> 5) Budget Information
> 6) ACT
> 7) SASE
> *Additional information:* Applications from individuals residing outside of stated geographic restriction not accepted. Application mailed to all area high schools and to Massachusetts Maritime Academy.
EIN: 046079892

4193
New England Biolabs Foundation
240 County Rd.
Ipswich, MA 01938-2723 (978) 998-7990
Contact: Susan Foster, Asst. Dir.; Jessica Brown, Exec. Dir.
FAX: (978) 356-3250; E-mail: fosters@nebf.org; URL: http://www.nebf.org

Foundation type: Company-sponsored foundation
Purpose: Limited support to individuals, in the Boston, MA, area and outside of the U.S. for small environmental research projects.
Publications: Application guidelines; Grants list; Informational brochure (including application guidelines).
Financial data: Year ended 12/31/2012. Assets, $7,367,626 (M); Expenditures, $636,022; Total giving, $384,325.
Fields of interest: Natural resources.
Type of support: Research; Grants to individuals.
Application information: Application form not required.
> *Initial approach:* Letter
> *Send request by:* E-mail
> *Copies of proposal:* 1
> *Deadline(s):* Mar. 1 and Aug. 29 for proposals
> *Final notification:* Two months after submission of application
> *Applicants should submit the following:*
> 1) Financial information
> 2) Letter(s) of recommendation
> 3) Curriculum vitae
> *Additional information:* Application should also include specific project details, bank references, list of the other grants applied for over past two years, and personal materials relevant to the project.
EIN: 042776213

4194
New England Education Society
c/o Day Pitney, LLP
1 International Pl.
Boston, MA 02110
Contact: E.B. Kidd
Application address: Boston University School of Theology

Foundation type: Independent foundation
Purpose: Loans to graduate students for theological education in Christian ministry at seminaries located in New England.
Financial data: Year ended 04/30/2013. Assets, $2,044,573 (M); Expenditures, $103,411; Total giving, $79,070; Grants to individuals, 29 grants totaling $79,070 (high: $3,000, low: $1,000).
Fields of interest: Theological school/education.
Type of support: Student loans—to individuals.
Application information: Applications accepted.
> *Initial approach:* Letter
EIN: 046067431

4195
New England Farm Workers Council, Inc.
11-13 Hampden St.
Springfield, MA 01103-1293 (413) 272-2200
FAX: (413) 731-5399; URL: http://www.partnersforcommunity.org/default/index.cfm/about-pfc/affiliates-programs/nefwc/

Foundation type: Public charity
Purpose: Emergency assistance for migrant workers and their families throughout CT, MA and RI with home energy assistance, day care, emergency sheltering, employment and job training, and youth programs.
Financial data: Year ended 06/30/2012. Assets, $18,193,731 (M); Expenditures, $58,491,167; Total giving, $52,652,124; Grants to individuals, totaling $52,635,124.
Fields of interest: Education, ESL programs; Agriculture/food; Housing/shelter, homeless; Human services, emergency aid; Developmentally disabled, centers & services; Human services; Hispanics/Latinos; Economically disadvantaged; Migrant workers.
Type of support: Grants for special needs.
Application information: Applications accepted.
> *Additional information:* Some assistance require application forms. Contact the council or see web site for additional guidelines.
EIN: 060872959

4196
New England Foundation for the Arts
(also known as NEFA)
145 Tremont St., 7th Fl.
Boston, MA 02111-1214 (617) 951-0010
Contact: Abigail Maulion, Comms. Coord.
FAX: (617) 951-0016; E-mail: info@nefa.org; E-mail for Abigail Maulion: amaulion@nefa.org;
URL: http://www.nefa.org

Foundation type: Public charity
Purpose: Residencies and stipends to artists, primarily within New England, who seek to make vital connections between artists and audiences, and to build strength, knowledge and leadership of the region's creative sector.
Publications: Application guidelines; Annual report; Newsletter.
Financial data: Year ended 05/31/2013. Assets, $18,812,857 (M); Expenditures, $7,622,534; Total giving, $3,522,630.
Fields of interest: Arts.

Type of support: Grants to individuals.
Application information: Applications accepted.
> *Send request by:* Online or mail
> *Deadline(s):* Rolling for National Native Artist Exchange, Feb. 15 and Sept. 14 for Native Arts New England
> *Applicants should submit the following:*
> 1) Work samples
> 2) Resume
> *Additional information:* Individual choreographers and artists may apply for grant support if fiscally sponsored by an arts organization with 501(c)(3) status. See web site for complete program list and guidelines.
Program description:
> *Native Arts New England:* Grants in amounts up to $3,000 each are available to support Native artists residing in New England. The program supports projects that focus on artmaking, and the involvement of and benefit to New England communities. Projects may address preservation of arts and cultural traditions, contemporary native arts and/or training and technical assistance that will support and/or enhance the artists current work.
EIN: 042593591

4197
Mary Nichols Trust
c/o Eastern Bank
605 Broadway, LF 41
Saugus, MA 01906-3200 (781) 581-4292
Contact: Christine Drew

Foundation type: Independent foundation
Purpose: Scholarships to graduating high school seniors of the Salem, MA, area for postsecondary education.
Financial data: Year ended 12/31/2012. Assets, $169,119 (M); Expenditures, $10,763; Total giving, $8,000; Grants to individuals, 6 grants totaling $8,000 (high: $1,400, low: $1,000).
Fields of interest: Higher education.
Type of support: Scholarships—to individuals.
Application information: Applications accepted. Application form required.
> *Deadline(s):* June 30
> *Additional information:* Application forms available upon request.
EIN: 046342221

4198
Anna Niconchuk Scholarship Trust
c/o Eastern Bank
605 Broadway, LF42
Saugus, MA 01906-3200
Application address: c/o Peabody Veterans Memorial High School, Attn.: School Comm. of the Principal, 485 Lowell St., Peabody, MA 01960-1329

Foundation type: Independent foundation
Purpose: Scholarships to graduates of Peabody Veterans Memorial High School, MA, for attendance at accredited colleges and universities.
Financial data: Year ended 12/31/2011. Assets, $82,794 (M); Expenditures, $6,602; Total giving, $5,000; Grants to individuals, totaling $5,000.
Fields of interest: Higher education.
Type of support: Support to graduates or students of specific schools; Undergraduate support.
Application information: Applications accepted. Application form required.
> *Deadline(s):* None

Additional information: Students should contact their guidance counselor for application information.
EIN: 042775813

4199
North Attleboro Scholarship Foundation
P.O. Box 926
North Attleboro, MA   02760

Foundation type: Company-sponsored foundation
Purpose: Scholarships to graduating seniors of North Attleboro High School MA, for postsecondary education.
Financial data: Year ended 06/30/2012. Assets, $2,294,321 (M); Expenditures, $78,824; Total giving, $62,970; Grants to individuals, 45 grants totaling $62,970 (high: $10,400, low: $250).
Fields of interest: Higher education.
Type of support: Support to graduates or students of specific schools; Undergraduate support.
Application information: Applications not accepted.
Additional information: Unsolicited requests for funds not considered or acknowledged.
EIN: 046056778

4200
North Central Massachusetts Community Foundation, Inc.
649 John Fitch Hwy.
Fitchburg, MA   01420-5998   (978) 345-8383
Contact: Philip M. Grzewinski, Pres.; For grants: Kathy Heintz, Grant Mgr.
FAX: (978) 345-1459; E-mail: info@cfncm.org; Additional e-mail: philg@cfncm.org; Grant inquiry e-mail: kathy@cfncm.org; Grant inquiry tel.: 978-345-8383; URL: http://www.cfncm.org

Foundation type: Community foundation
Purpose: Scholarships to deserving students from area high schools in Massachusetts for higher education.
Publications: Application guidelines; Annual report; Informational brochure; Newsletter.
Financial data: Year ended 06/30/2013. Assets, $33,716,967 (M); Expenditures, $7,183,027; Total giving, $6,886,623; Grants to individuals, 172 grants totaling $417,069.
Fields of interest: Education.
Type of support: Scholarships—to individuals.
Application information: See web site for additional application information.
EIN: 043537449

4201
North East Roofing Educational Foundation, Inc.
100 Grossman Dr., Ste. 300
Braintree, MA   02184-4965   (781) 849-0555
Contact: Patricia Sweeney, Clerk.

Foundation type: Operating foundation
Purpose: Scholarships to family members or associates of NERCA members.
Financial data: Year ended 06/30/2012. Assets, $576,976 (M); Expenditures, $60,067; Total giving, $32,500; Grants to individuals, 13 grants totaling $32,500 (high: $2,500, low: $2,500).
Fields of interest: Higher education.
Type of support: Scholarships—to individuals.
Application information: Applications accepted. Application form required.
Deadline(s): May 1

Additional information: Application should include transcript, work experience, awards and description of other activities.
EIN: 043466803

4202
North Shore Community Action Programs, Inc.
98 Main St.
Peabody, MA   01960-5553   (978) 531-0767
Contact: Laura M. MacNeil, Exec. Dir.
FAX: (978) 531-1012; URL: http://www.nscap.org

Foundation type: Public charity
Purpose: Temporary emergency housing, home fuel/energy assistance, financial advice, referral services, and job training for indigent residents of Salem, Peabody, Beverly and Danvers, MA.
Financial data: Year ended 09/30/2011. Assets, $1,353,763 (M); Expenditures, $9,802,402.
Fields of interest: Human services; Economically disadvantaged.
Type of support: In-kind gifts.
Application information:
Initial approach: Letter or e-mail
Additional information: Contact foundation for eligibility criteria.
EIN: 042385280

4203
The Northern California DX Foundation
27 Pill Hill Ln.
Duxbury, MA   02332   (707) 255-5424
Contact: Bruce Butler
FAX: (707) 255-7355; E-mail: president@ncdxf.org; Application Address: c/o Bruce Buttler, 4220 Chardonnay Court, Napa, CA 94558; URL: http://www.ncdxf.org

Foundation type: Operating foundation
Purpose: Grants to individuals who use amateur radio communications to advance and promote education, science and international goodwill. Scholarships for qualified college-level radio amateurs.
Financial data: Year ended 12/31/2011. Assets, $566,901 (M); Expenditures, $147,865; Total giving, $130,985; Grants to individuals, 10 grants totaling $52,019 (high: $26,850, low: $500).
Fields of interest: Media/communications; Radio.
Type of support: Grants to individuals.
Application information: Applications accepted. Application form required. Application form available on the grantmaker's web site.
Send request by: Online
Deadline(s): Mar. 21 for Grants
Additional information: See web site for additional application information.
Program description:
Grants: Cash grants for projects that will benefit amateur radio in general and DXing in particular. Major support is normally restricted to expeditions that generate world-wide interest by going to locations high on the most-wanted lists published by various organizations around the world. A smaller amount of support is sometimes awarded to other expeditions and projects which in the judgment of the NCDXF directors are unusually strong in supporting the goals of the NCDXF. Expeditions to unusual locations as defined by the Islands on the Air (IOTA) program, Grid Square awards and various radio contests are not supported unless the support can be justified without reference to these activities.
EIN: 942853576

4204
Grace Swift Nye & Alfred Gibbs Nye Scholarship Trust
P.O. Box 55806
Boston, MA   02205-5806
Application address: P.O. Box 271369, West Hartford, CT 06127-1369, tel.: (806) 521-5694
FAX: (860) 521-7247

Foundation type: Independent foundation
Purpose: Scholarships to graduating high school seniors in Bourne, Plymouth, Sandwich, and Wareham, MA.
Publications: Application guidelines.
Financial data: Year ended 12/31/2012. Assets, $3,506,186 (M); Expenditures, $308,631; Total giving, $227,113; Grants to individuals, 143 grants totaling $227,113 (high: $5,000, low: $1,250).
Type of support: Undergraduate support.
Application information: Applications accepted.
Deadline(s): None
Additional information: Scholarships are restricted to permanent residents of the towns listed. Unsolicited applications not considered or acknowledged.
EIN: 066421534

4205
Ocean State Power Scholarship Foundation, Ltd.
59 Elmdale Rd.
Uxbridge, MA   01569

Foundation type: Operating foundation
Purpose: Scholarships to students of Uxbridge, MA, to attend a four-year college or university.
Financial data: Year ended 12/31/2011. Assets, $612,272 (M); Expenditures, $47,629; Total giving, $37,686; Grants to individuals, 22 grants totaling $37,686 (high: $4,000, low: $500).
Fields of interest: Higher education.
Type of support: Graduate support; Undergraduate support.
Application information: Applications accepted. Application form required.
Initial approach: Letter
Deadline(s): Varies
EIN: 222908697

4206
One Family, Inc.
240 Newbury St., 2nd Fl.
Boston, MA   02116   (617) 423-0504
Contact: Valerie Paric, Exec. Dir.
FAX: (617) 423-5615;
E-mail: vparic@onefamilyinc.org; URL: http://www.onefamilyinc.org/

Foundation type: Public charity
Purpose: College scholarship program that breaks the cycle of poverty and family homelessness for low income single parents in MA.
Financial data: Year ended 06/30/2012. Assets, $1,919,183 (M); Expenditures, $1,534,974; Total giving, $412,940; Grants to individuals, totaling $412,940.
Fields of interest: Higher education; Economically disadvantaged; Homeless.
Type of support: Scholarships—to individuals.
Application information: Applicant must be a permanent residents of MA, and a U.S. citizen or Resident Alien. See web site for eligibility criteria.
Program description:
One Family Scholars Program: This program is committed to ending family homelessness, one family at a time, by providing financial support for

higher education, interwoven in a system of support services that parents need in order to clear the barriers that often prevent them from preparing for, and achieving, financial security. Its mission is based on the premise that education, linked with essential support services and mentoring, is the most reliable and direct route to economic independence and self-esteem. Once accepted into the program, Scholars are eligible for a grant of up to $12,000 per year, based on his/her individual need.
EIN: 542076936

4207
Orange Scholarship Foundation
P.O. Box 298
Orange, MA   01364-0298   (978) 544-6304

Foundation type: Independent foundation
Purpose: Scholarships to graduates of Ralph C. Mahar Regional High School, Orange, MA. Graduates of Franklin County Technical School, who are residents of Orange, New Salem, and Wendell, are eligible to apply for Orange High School Alumni Scholarships. Home school students who otherwise would have graduated from Ralph C. Mahar Regional High School are eligible to apply when they have completed one semester of college.
Financial data: Year ended 12/31/2012. Assets, $636,645 (M); Expenditures, $33,767; Total giving, $32,300; Grants to individuals, 54 grants totaling $32,300 (high: $1,000, low: $25).
Type of support: Support to graduates or students of specific schools; Undergraduate support.
Application information: Application form required.
  Send request by: Mail
  Deadline(s): May 27
  Applicants should submit the following:
    1) Transcripts
    2) Financial information
EIN: 046138742

4208
The Francis Ouimet Scholarship Fund, Inc.
300 Arnold Palmer Blvd.
Norton, MA   02766-1365   (774) 430-9090
FAX: (774) 430-9091; URL: http://www.ouimet.org

Foundation type: Public charity
Purpose: Renewable need- and merit-based scholarships for students who have at least two years of service in golf as a caddy, pro shop employee or course superintendent in Massachusetts.
Publications: Application guidelines.
Financial data: Year ended 03/31/2012. Assets, $8,391,181 (M); Expenditures, $2,260,007; Total giving, $1,501,840; Grants to individuals, 276 grants totaling $1,501,840.
Fields of interest: Higher education; Athletics/ sports, golf.
Type of support: Scholarships—to individuals.
Application information: Applications accepted. Application form required. Application form available on the grantmaker's web site. Interview required.
  Initial approach: Telephone
  Deadline(s): Dec. 1
  Applicants should submit the following:
    1) FAFSA
    2) Transcripts
    3) Letter(s) of recommendation
    4) Essay
  Additional information: Complete online application-request form to receive application packet.

Program description:
  Ouimet Scholarship: This competitive undergraduate scholarship ranges from $1,500 to $7,500 per year depending on the applicant's financial need. Eligible applicants must have completed at least two years' service to golf as caddies, helpers in a pro shop, or a course superintendent of operations at a club in Massachusetts.
EIN: 042234126

4209
Charles J. Paine Scholarship Fund Trust
c/o Taylor, Ganson & Perrin, LLP
160 Federal St.
Boston, MA   02110-1723

Foundation type: Independent foundation
Purpose: Scholarships to residents of Weston, MA, attending Harvard University or Massachusetts Institute of Technology.
Financial data: Year ended 12/31/2011. Assets, $264,585 (M); Expenditures, $16,758; Total giving, $11,500.
Type of support: Support to graduates or students of specific schools; Undergraduate support.
Application information: Applications accepted. Application form required.
  Initial approach: Letter
  Deadline(s): None
  Additional information: Letter should state need and personal background.
EIN: 046028710

4210
Marc & Ernest Pallotta Foundation, Inc.
579 Millbury St.
Worcester, MA   01610   (508) 753-2115
Contact: Laura Pallotta, Dir.
Application address: 61 Fox Run Rd., Bolton, MA 01740

Foundation type: Operating foundation
Purpose: Scholarships to residents of central MA, for higher education.
Financial data: Year ended 12/31/2011. Assets, $615 (M); Expenditures, $10,356; Total giving, $9,940; Grants to individuals, 8 grants totaling $7,500 (high: $1,000, low: $500).
Fields of interest: Higher education.
Type of support: Scholarships—to individuals.
Application information:
  Deadline(s): None
  Additional information: Applicants must be recommended by secondary school principals and teachers.
EIN: 223351769

4211
Clyde Park Charitable Foundation
(formerly Clyde Park Trust)
c/o Eaton Vance Trust Company
2 International Pl.
Boston, MA   02110   (617) 672-8771

Foundation type: Independent foundation
Purpose: Grants to worthy employees of the Brookline Country Club, MA who are in need of financial assistance.
Financial data: Year ended 05/31/2013. Assets, $507,422 (M); Expenditures, $54,930; Total giving, $52,850; Grants to individuals, 30 grants totaling $52,850 (high: $7,500, low: $350).
Type of support: Employee-related welfare; Grants for special needs.

Application information: Applications accepted.
  Initial approach: Letter
  Deadline(s): Mar. 31
EIN: 046051719

4212
Grace And Bill Peabody Foundation Inc.
69 E. Housatonic St.
Pittsfield, MA   01201   (603) 362-4003
Contact: William S. Peabody, Pres. and Dir.
Application address: 53 Walker Rd., Atkinson, NH 03811, tel.: (603) 362-4003

Foundation type: Independent foundation
Purpose: Scholarships to children of staff and employees of Wilmington, MA schools.
Financial data: Year ended 12/31/2011. Assets, $402 (M); Expenditures, $17,637; Total giving, $17,500; Grants to individuals, 4 grants totaling $17,500 (high: $5,000, low: $3,750).
Type of support: Scholarships—to individuals.
Application information:
  Initial approach: Letter
  Additional information: Contact foundation for further information.
EIN: 043571773

4213
Henry O. Peabody School for Girls
c/o William T. Simonds
34 Chestnut St.
Concord, MA   01742-2609
Application address: Henry O. Peabody Scholarship Program, Scholarship America, One Scholarship Way, P.O. Box 297, St. Peter, MN 56082

Foundation type: Independent foundation
Purpose: Scholarships to women in Norfolk County, MA, for the purpose of obtaining post-high school instruction to enable them to be self-supporting and to acquire an independent livelihood. The program is administered by Scholarship America.
Financial data: Year ended 03/31/2012. Assets, $3,298,796 (M); Expenditures, $192,251; Total giving, $135,000.
Fields of interest: Adults, women; Young adults, female.
Type of support: Undergraduate support.
Application information: Applications accepted. Application form required.
  Initial approach: Letter
EIN: 046003671

4214
Donald H. and Helen D. Peach Scholarship Fund
c/o Allan J. Martin
6 Cliffside Rd.
Marblehead, MA   01945
Contact: James Keating
Application Address: P.O. Box 605, Marblehead, MA, 01945

Foundation type: Operating foundation
Purpose: Scholarships to worthy graduates of Marblehead High School, MA for attendance at Salem State College, MA for undergraduate or graduate studies.
Financial data: Year ended 12/31/2012. Assets, $254,440 (M); Expenditures, $20,007; Total giving, $14,250; Grants to individuals, 10 grants totaling $14,250 (high: $2,250, low: $750).
Fields of interest: Higher education.
Type of support: Support to graduates or students of specific schools.

Application information: Application form required.
Initial approach: Telephone
Deadline(s): May 15
Additional information: Applications can be obtained from student's guidance office or from the web site marbleheadmasons.org.
EIN: 046721931

4215

The Perfect Storm Foundation, Inc.

248 E. Main St.
P.O. Box 1941
Gloucester, MA 01930-1941 (978) 283-2903
FAX: (978) 282-9550

Foundation type: Public charity
Purpose: Scholarships to children of people employed by the commercial fishing industry in working maritime communities.
Financial data: Year ended 12/31/2012. Assets, $0 (M); Expenditures, $4,088; Total giving, $1,500.
Fields of interest: Marine science.
Type of support: Scholarships—to individuals.
Application information: Applications accepted. Application form required.
Send request by: Mail
Deadline(s): Rolling
Additional information: Grants normally range from $250 to $1,000. Applications are not accepted by fax or e-mail.
EIN: 043418631

4216

Permanent Endowment Fund for Martha's Vineyard

P.O. Box 1182
Oak Bluffs, MA 02557-0000 (508) 338-4665
FAX: (508) 338-4665; *E-mail:* info@endowmv.org;
URL: http://www.permanentendowmv.org

Foundation type: Community foundation
Purpose: Scholarships primarily to graduates of Martha's Vineyard Regional High School, MA, Martha's Vineyard Charter School, MA, and residents of Martha's Vineyard.
Publications: Application guidelines; Annual report.
Financial data: Year ended 12/31/2012. Assets, $7,740,935 (M); Expenditures, $380,349; Total giving, $252,151; Grants to individuals, 78 grants totaling $140,370.
Fields of interest: Higher education; Nursing school/education; Scholarships/financial aid; Natural resources; Dental care.
Type of support: Scholarships—to individuals; Support to graduates or students of specific schools; Awards/prizes; Graduate support; Undergraduate support.
Application information: Applications accepted. Application form required. Application form available on the grantmaker's web site. Interview required.
Initial approach: Application
Deadline(s): Mar. 15
Final notification: Recipients notified early June
Additional information: Scholarships are awarded annually and range in size from approximately $500 to $5,000 with the criteria for applicants established by each scholarship fund. See web site for complete listing of scholarships.
EIN: 042774790

4217

Charles & Olivina Perron Memorial Trust

(also known as Charles A. Perron Memorial Trust f/b/o Graduates of High School Serving the City of North Adams)
P.O. Box 1330
Hyannis, MA 02601

Foundation type: Independent foundation
Purpose: Scholarships to graduates or former graduates of high schools in North Adams, MA.
Financial data: Year ended 12/31/2011. Assets, $128,466 (M); Expenditures, $10,091; Total giving, $6,000; Grants to individuals, 12 grants totaling $6,000 (high: $500, low: $500).
Type of support: Support to graduates or students of specific schools; Undergraduate support.
Application information: Applications accepted.
Initial approach: Letter
Additional information: Applicant must demonstrate financial need, achievement of high scholastic standing in high school and must be of high moral and ethical principles.
EIN: 222672860

4218

Pettee-Chace Memorial Scholarship Fund

P.O. Box 694
Sandwich, MA 02563-0694 (508) 297-1140
Contact: Thomas N. Sampson, Pres.
Application address: 130 Liberty St., Ste. 10, Brockton, MA 02301

Foundation type: Operating foundation
Purpose: Scholarships to students of Abington High School, MA, and Brockton High School, MA, for higher education.
Financial data: Year ended 12/31/2011. Assets, $191,296 (M); Expenditures, $14,801; Total giving, $12,300; Grants to individuals, 4 grants totaling $12,300 (high: $4,500, low: $1,650).
Type of support: Support to graduates or students of specific schools; Undergraduate support.
Application information: Application form required.
Deadline(s): Apr. 1
Applicants should submit the following:
  1) Transcripts
  2) SAT
  3) Financial information
  4) Essay
Additional information: Application available from guidance department of Abington and Brockton High Schools.
EIN: 223051579

4219

The Catherine E. Philbin Memorial Fund

c/o Josephine Veglia
275 Main St.
Oxford, MA 01540-2358 (508) 987-3981

Foundation type: Independent foundation
Purpose: Scholarships to individuals enrolled at local colleges in Massachusetts, pursuing a nursing career.
Financial data: Year ended 12/31/2011. Assets, $283,402 (M); Expenditures, $25,782; Total giving, $14,000; Grants to individuals, 7 grants totaling $14,000 (high: $3,000, low: $1,000).
Fields of interest: Nursing school/education.
Type of support: Scholarships—to individuals.
Application information: Applicants must provide letters describing achievements, education and career goals, financial needs, activities, commitments, and community leadership.
EIN: 043406706

4220

Philips Electronics North American Foundation

(formerly North American Philips Foundation)
c/o Philips Tax Dept.
3000 Minuteman Rd.
Andover, MA 01810-1032

Foundation type: Company-sponsored foundation
Purpose: Scholarships to the children of current, retired, or deceased employees of Philips Electronics North America.
Financial data: Year ended 12/31/2012. Assets, $1,886 (M); Expenditures, $319,614; Total giving, $321,500; Grants to individuals, 120 grants totaling $321,500 (high: $10,000, low: $1,000).
Fields of interest: Higher education; Scholarships/financial aid; Athletics/sports, school programs; Leadership development.
Type of support: Employee-related scholarships.
Application information: Applications not accepted.
Additional information: Unsolicited requests for funds not considered or acknowledged.
Company name: Philips Electronics North America Corporation
EIN: 132961300

4221

Edwin Phillips Foundation

P.O. Box 610075
Newton Highlands, MA 02461-0075
E-mail: grants@epfgrants.org; *URL:* http://www.edwinphillipsfoundation.org

Foundation type: Independent foundation
Purpose: Grants to physically and mentally handicapped children under the age of 22 residing in Marshfield and Plymouth counties, MA.
Publications: Application guidelines.
Financial data: Year ended 12/31/2012. Assets, $11,942,728 (M); Expenditures, $679,755; Total giving, $459,787.
Fields of interest: Health care, patient services; Children/youth, services; Disabilities, people with.
Type of support: Grants for special needs.
Application information: Applications accepted. Application form required. Application form available on the grantmaker's web site.
Initial approach: Letter or telephone
Send request by: Mail
Copies of proposal: 1
Deadline(s): Apr. 1 and Oct. 1
Final notification: Applicants notified within two to three months
Additional information: Evidence of financial and medical need must be documented. The tax returns for the last two years and the doctor's letter are required. Sources of other funding, either received or sought, should also be listed.
Program description:
Assistance Program: Grants to help individuals live in their own homes. Grants are used to provide prosthetic appliances, wheelchairs, beds, or other forms of assistance.
EIN: 046025549

4222
Stephen Phillips Memorial Charitable Trust
P.O. Box 870
Salem, MA 01970-0970   (978) 744-2111
Contact: Karen Emery, Scholarship Coord.
FAX: (978) 744-0456;
E-mail: staff@spscholars.org; URL: http://
www.phillips-scholarship.org/

Foundation type: Independent foundation
Purpose: Scholarships for permanent residents of New England states to attend any college or university in the U.S.
Publications: Application guidelines; Informational brochure (including application guidelines); Newsletter.
Financial data: Year ended 12/31/2012. Assets, $6,956,969 (M); Expenditures, $4,094,662; Total giving, $2,924,200; Grants to individuals, totaling $2,924,200.
Fields of interest: Higher education; Economically disadvantaged.
Type of support: Undergraduate support.
Application information: Applications accepted. Application form required. Application form available on the grantmaker's web site.
   Send request by: On-line
   Deadline(s): Mar. 21 for renewal application, Apr. 15 and May 1 for new applicants
   Applicants should submit the following:
      1) Transcripts
      2) Letter(s) of recommendation
   Additional information: Applicant must demonstrate academic excellence, seriousness of purpose, good citizenship and character, a strong work ethic, and meet the foundation's financial-need requirements. See web site for additional guidelines.
EIN: 237235347

4223
Katharine C. Pierce Trust
c/o U.S. Trust, Philanthropic Solutions
225 Franklin St., 4th Fl.
Boston, MA 02110-2801   (866) 778-6859
Contact: Miki Akimoto, Market Director
E-mail: miki.akimoto@ustrust.com

Foundation type: Independent foundation
Purpose: Financial assistance to needy and deserving gentlewomen residing in MA. Preference is shown to the elderly.
Publications: Application guidelines; Grants list.
Financial data: Year ended 12/31/2012. Assets, $4,921,405 (M); Expenditures, $306,009; Total giving, $245,760.
Fields of interest: Aging; Women.
Type of support: Grants to individuals; Grants for special needs.
Application information: Applications accepted. Application form required.
   Initial approach: Letter
   Send request by: Mail
   Copies of proposal: 1
   Deadline(s): Mar. 1, June 1, Sept. 1 and Dec. 1
   Final notification: Recipients notified three months after receipt of application
   Applicants should submit the following:
      1) Letter(s) of recommendation
      2) Financial information
EIN: 046095694

4224
Pilgrim Foundation
P.O. Box 3400
Brockton, MA 02303-3400   (508) 586-6100
Contact: Jane Southworth

Foundation type: Independent foundation
Purpose: Scholarships to residents of Brockton, MA. Welfare assistance to economically disadvantaged families and children who are residents of Brockton, MA.
Publications: Informational brochure.
Financial data: Year ended 12/31/2012. Assets, $4,590,189 (M); Expenditures, $221,739; Total giving, $175,851.
Fields of interest: Higher education; Family services; Economically disadvantaged.
Type of support: Scholarships—to individuals; Grants for special needs.
Application information:
   Initial approach: Telephone for scholarships; Letter for welfare assistance
   Send request by: Mail
   Deadline(s): Apr. 1 for graduating high school seniors and May 1 for returning college students
   Additional information: Application form required for scholarships and must include a proposal, name of college or university, courses of study, educational history, parents' history, financial information, and a copy of applicant's federal aid forms or parents' federal income tax return. Application by letter for welfare assistance including eight copies of proposal.
EIN: 042104834

4225
Pittsfield Rotary Club Foundation Inc.
P.O. Box 78
Pittsfield, MA 01202-0078

Foundation type: Independent foundation
Purpose: Scholarships to residents of Pittsfield, MA for higher education at colleges or universities.
Financial data: Year ended 06/30/2013. Assets, $416,534 (M); Expenditures, $62,842; Total giving, $47,838; Grants to individuals, 6 grants totaling $8,500 (high: $1,500, low: $1,250).
Fields of interest: Higher education.
Type of support: Scholarships—to individuals; Undergraduate support.
Application information: Applications accepted.
   Additional information: Contact the foundation for guidelines for scholarships.
EIN: 043349204

4226
Plymouth Fragment Society
P.O. Box 6386
Plymouth, MA 02360   (508) 746-9452
Contact: Claire Jesse, Treas.
Application address: 6 Grandview Dr., Plymouth, MA 02360

Foundation type: Independent foundation
Purpose: Financial assistance to senior citizens and economically disadvantaged individuals residing in MA for rent, fuel, medical, food and other needs.
Financial data: Year ended 09/30/2013. Assets, $470,598 (M); Expenditures, $18,160; Total giving, $16,820; Grants to individuals, 31 grants totaling $16,194 (high: $1,250, low: $89).
Fields of interest: Aging; Economically disadvantaged.

Type of support: Grants for special needs.
Application information: Applications accepted.
   Deadline(s): None
   Additional information: Applicants must be Plymouth residents.
EIN: 046043957

4227
Thomas H. Pope Scholarship Fund
c/o Jeffrey Pope
5 Curtis Pt.
Beverly, MA 01915

Foundation type: Independent foundation
Purpose: College scholarships to graduating high school seniors of Danvers, MA, pursuing higher education.
Financial data: Year ended 06/30/2013. Assets, $36,175 (M); Expenditures, $30,438; Total giving, $30,000; Grants to individuals, 6 grants totaling $30,000 (high: $5,000; low: $5,000).
Fields of interest: Higher education.
Type of support: Scholarships—to individuals; Undergraduate support.
Application information: Applications accepted.
   Additional information: Contact the fund for additional application guidelines.
EIN: 046850495

4228
Trustees of the Pratt Free School
c/o Diane Smith
2 Murdock St.
Middleboro, MA 02346

Foundation type: Operating foundation
Purpose: Scholarships to college bound high school students of Middleboro, MA pursuing higher education.
Financial data: Year ended 12/31/2012. Assets, $1,054,939 (M); Expenditures, $39,779; Total giving, $18,400; Grants to individuals, 3 grants totaling $13,000 (high: $5,000, low: $3,000).
Fields of interest: Higher education.
Type of support: Undergraduate support.
Application information: Applications accepted. Application form required.
   Additional information: Contact the trustees for additional guidelines.
EIN: 042121370

4229
Fannie B. Pratt Trust Clause No. 31
c/o Dane & Howe
45 School St.
Boston, MA 02108-3204
Contact: Marion K. Daley, Tr.
Application address: 49 Paul Revere Rd., Needham, MA 02494, tel.: (781) 449-2766

Foundation type: Operating foundation
Purpose: Financial assistance to economically disadvantaged widows of Boston, MA.
Financial data: Year ended 12/31/2011. Assets, $885,617 (M); Expenditures, $60,822; Total giving, $49,534; Grants to individuals, 25 grants totaling $49,534 (high: $9,842, low: $300).
Fields of interest: Women; Economically disadvantaged.
Type of support: Grants for special needs.
Application information: Applications not accepted.
   Additional information: Recipients are chosen by referral and evaluation only.
EIN: 046027727

4230
President and Fellows of Harvard Corporation

(formerly President and Fellows of Harvard College)
1033 Massachusetts Ave., 3rd Fl.
Cambridge, MA 02138-3846 (617) 495-7792
URL: http://www.harvard.edu/harvard-corporation

Foundation type: Public charity
Purpose: Scholarships, grants, and awards to students (both undergraduate and graduate) and faculty of Harvard University, MA.
Financial data: Year ended 06/30/2012. Assets, $56,370,683,000 (M); Expenditures, $4,361,276,872; Total giving, $640,715,440; Grants to individuals, totaling $483,357,819.
Fields of interest: University; Scholarships/financial aid; Education.
Type of support: Fellowships; Research; Grants to individuals; Scholarships—to individuals; Student loans—to individuals; Support to graduates or students of specific schools; Awards/prizes; Postdoctoral support; Stipends.
Application information: Contact the organization for additional information.
EIN: 042103580

4231
The George K. Progin Scholarship Fund

c/o Darmondy, Merlino & Co., LLP
75 Federal St.
Boston, MA 02110-1913 (978) 790-0996

Foundation type: Independent foundation
Purpose: Scholarships to graduates of Fitchburg High School, MA for continuing education at institutions of higher learning.
Financial data: Year ended 12/31/2011. Assets, $794,078 (M); Expenditures, $75,056; Total giving, $65,000; Grants to individuals, 8 grants totaling $65,000 (high: $10,000, low: $5,000).
Fields of interest: Higher education.
Type of support: Support to graduates or students of specific schools.
Application information: Applications accepted.
 Initial approach: Letter
 Additional information: Contact your guidance counselor for application information.
EIN: 200913756

4232
William Lowell Putnam Prize Fund for the Promotion of Scholarship

c/o Boston Family Office
88 Broad St., 2nd Fl.
Boston, MA 02110-3407

Foundation type: Independent foundation
Purpose: Awards to regularly enrolled undergraduates, in colleges and universities of the U.S. and Canada who have not yet received a college degree, and to eligible high school students in a mathematics competition.
Financial data: Year ended 12/31/2012. Assets, $9,557,956 (M); Expenditures, $639,258; Total giving, $407,750.
Fields of interest: Mathematics.
Type of support: Awards/prizes.
Application information: Applicants may apply only through their respective schools.
EIN: 043414102

4233
Quabaug Corporation Charitable Foundation

c/o Eric Rosen
18 School St.
North Brookfield, MA 01535-1937 (508) 867-7731
Contact: Eric Rosen, Tr.

Foundation type: Company-sponsored foundation
Purpose: Scholarships to students attending North Brookfield High School, MA for continuing education at accredited colleges or universities.
Financial data: Year ended 12/31/2011. Assets, $363,379 (M); Expenditures, $59,144; Total giving, $52,600. Scholarships—to individuals amount not specified.
Fields of interest: Higher education.
Type of support: Support to graduates or students of specific schools; Undergraduate support.
Application information: Applications accepted.
 Initial approach: Letter
 Deadline(s): None
 Additional information: Students must maintain a GPA in the top 10 percent of their class each year.
EIN: 510179366

4234
Quincy Community Action Programs, Inc.

1509 Hancock St.
Quincy, MA 02169-5241 (617) 479-8181
Contact: Beth Ann Strollo, Exec. Dir.
FAX: (617) 479-7228;
E-mail: malexander@qcap.org; URL: http://www.qcap.org

Foundation type: Public charity
Purpose: Grants to low-income individuals and families for energy assistance, rent assistance, and child care payments. Giving limited to residents of Quincy, Weymouth, Braintree, Milton, Hull and surrounding South Shore and Norfolk County, MA.
Financial data: Year ended 09/30/2011. Assets, $15,823,123 (M); Expenditures, $21,565,160; Total giving, $10,650,992; Grants to individuals, totaling $10,650,992.
Fields of interest: Housing/shelter; Children, services; Economically disadvantaged.
Type of support: Grants for special needs.
Application information:
 Initial approach: Letter or telephone
 Additional information: Contact the agency for further application guidelines.
EIN: 042391348

4235
The Francis J. Quirico Educational Foundation

c/o John C. Donna, Esq.
P.O. Box 1158
Pittsfield, MA 01202-1158 (413) 443-3440
Contact: John C. Donna Esq., Tr.

Foundation type: Independent foundation
Purpose: Scholarships to graduates of Pittsfield High School, MA for postsecondary education.
Financial data: Year ended 12/31/2012. Assets, $4,200,775 (M); Expenditures, $147,516; Total giving, $132,467; Grants to individuals, 52 grants totaling $132,467 (high: $7,000, low: $318).
Fields of interest: Higher education.
Type of support: Support to graduates or students of specific schools.

Application information: Applications accepted. Application form required.
 Deadline(s): Feb. 28
 Applicants should submit the following:
  1) Transcripts
  2) SAT
  3) Letter(s) of recommendation
  4) Essay
 Additional information: Applicant must demonstrate financial need.
EIN: 207145260

4236
The R.O.S.E. Fund, Inc.

(formerly Ryka Rose Foundation)
200 Harvard Mill Sq., Ste. 310
Wakefield, MA 01880-3209 (617) 482-5400
Contact: Dan Walsh, Chair. and Exec.Dir.
FAX: (617) 482-3443; E-mail: info@rosefund.org; Toll-free tel.: (800) 253-6425; E-mail for Dan Walsh: dwalsh@rosefund.org; URL: http://www.rosefund.org

Foundation type: Public charity
Purpose: Scholarships and awards to women who have survived violent crimes and are now serving as role models for others.
Publications: Application guidelines; Financial statement; Grants list; Informational brochure; Newsletter.
Financial data: Year ended 12/31/2011. Assets, $21,007 (M); Expenditures, $37,409; Total giving, $1,325; Grants to individuals, totaling $1,325.
Fields of interest: Higher education; Domestic violence; Civil/human rights, women; Women.
Type of support: Scholarships—to individuals; Support to graduates or students of specific schools; Undergraduate support; Grants for special needs.
Application information: Applications accepted. Application form required. Application form available on the grantmaker's web site.
 Initial approach: Download application form
 Deadline(s): June 22 for scholarships; Oct. 31 for grants
Program descriptions:
 R.O.S.E. Scholarship: The program provides scholarships of up to $10,000 to women survivors of domestic violence who attend colleges or universities. The scholarships are primarily awarded to women who have successfully completed one full year of undergraduate studies, and will be applied to tuition and expenses at any accredited college or university in New England.
 R.O.S.E. Scholarship at UMASS Boston: The fund annually awards scholarships to accepted University of Massachusetts - Boston students who are women survivors of domestic violence, have a proven record of college success, and who are or will be enrolled in a minimum of nine credits per semester.
 Reconstructive Surgery: The program seeks to help women heal the physical and emotional scars of abuse by funding facial cosmetic and functional surgery in order to improve their lives.
EIN: 043154445

4237
Michael G. Ratte Charitable Foundation

c/o Roger Dubuque
228 Park Ave.
Worcester, MA 01609 (508) 757-5675
Contact: Roger Dubuque, Tr.

Foundation type: Independent foundation

Purpose: Scholarships to graduates of Doherty High School who live in the Tatnuck Square area of Worcester, MA.
Financial data: Year ended 12/31/2012. Assets, $155,019 (M); Expenditures, $10,499; Total giving, $10,000.
Fields of interest: Higher education.
Type of support: Support to graduates or students of specific schools.
Application information: Applications accepted.
  Initial approach: Letter
  Deadline(s): June 30
  Additional information: Applicants must be exemplary citizens who are involved in similar charitable and educational organizations as Michael G. Ratte, such as Christ the King Church, Boy Scouts of America and the Tatnuck Little League Association.
EIN: 043396856

4238
Raytheon Company Contributions Program
Waltham Woods
870 Winter St.
Waltham, MA 02451-1449 (781) 522-5119
Contact: Michael Greenberg, Community Rels. Opers. Mgr.
E-mail: corporatecontributions@raytheon.com;
URL: http://www.raytheon.com/responsibility/community/local/giving/

Foundation type: Corporate giving program
Purpose: Grants to Raytheon Company employees for disaster relief assistance.
Publications: Application guidelines.
Fields of interest: Safety/disasters.
Type of support: Awards/grants by nomination only; Employee-related welfare.
Application information: Applications not accepted.
  Additional information: Unsolicited requests for funds not considered or acknowledged.
Program description:
  Raytheon Employee Disaster Relief Fund: The company awards disaster relief grants of up to $2,500 to employees of Raytheon who have faced catastrophic events. Recipients must be working in a full or part-time capacity at the time of the disaster and must be nominated by a Raytheon Company Human Resources Manager.
Company name: Raytheon Company

4239
Real Colegio Complutense, Inc.
26 Trowbridge St.
Cambridge, MA 02138-5326 (617) 495-3536
FAX: (617) 496-3401;
E-mail: rcc-info@camail.harvard.edu; URL: http://www.realcolegiocomplutense.harvard.edu

Foundation type: Independent foundation
Purpose: Scholarships and fellowships to students, scholars, and researchers from Spanish universities for study and research in any discipline at Harvard University, MA.
Financial data: Year ended 12/31/2012. Assets, $1,143,462 (L); Expenditures, $1,044,012; Total giving, $255,345; Grants to individuals, totaling $160,475.
International interests: Spain.
Type of support: Fellowships; Research; Scholarships—to individuals; Foreign applicants.
Application information: Applications accepted. Application form required. Application form available on the grantmaker's web site.

Initial approach: Letter or telephone
Send request by: Mail or e-mail
Copies of proposal: 1
Applicants should submit the following:
  1) Budget Information
  2) Financial information
  3) Letter(s) of recommendation
  4) Proposal
  5) Resume
EIN: 043134531

4240
The Red Sox Foundation, Inc.
4 Yawkey Way
Boston, MA 02215-3409 (617) 226-6614
Contact: Meg Vaillancourt, Exec. Dir.
E-mail: redsoxfoundation@redsox.com;
URL: http://www.redsoxfoundation.org

Foundation type: Public charity
Purpose: Scholarships to at risk and low income Boston Public School students in MA, in preparation for high school graduation, for attendance at accredited colleges or universities.
Financial data: Year ended 12/31/2011. Assets, $11,120,237 (M); Expenditures, $6,329,704; Total giving, $4,472,844; Grants to individuals, totaling $158,648.
Fields of interest: Education.
Type of support: Scholarships—to individuals; Support to graduates or students of specific schools.
Application information: Applications accepted. Application form required. Application form available on the grantmaker's web site. Interview required.
  Send request by: Mail
  Deadline(s): Feb.
  Applicants should submit the following:
    1) Transcripts
    2) Essay
  Additional information: The scholarship is paid directly to the educational institution of choice on behalf of the students.
Program description:
  Red Sox Scholars: Each year, the foundation provides tutoring, mentoring, enrichment opportunities to ten academically gifted, economically disadvantaged 7th grader students in the Boston Public School District or Boston Public Charter Schools with college scholarships of $10,000 each pending graduation from high school. The scholarships, which are held in their name and will be paid directly to the college of their choice, are conditional upon the students maintaining their academic standing and good citizenship.
EIN: 331007984

4241
Relief Association, Inc.
(formerly Relief Association Trust)
c/o Joan Fisher
P.O. Box 585
Nantucket, MA 02554-0585

Foundation type: Independent foundation
Purpose: Welfare assistance to the aged and indigent of Nantucket, MA, who are recommended by the Center of Elderly Affairs.
Financial data: Year ended 12/31/2011. Assets, $739,582 (M); Expenditures, $43,696; Total giving, $33,530; Grants to individuals, 15 grants totaling $16,350 (high: $1,800; low: $300).
Fields of interest: Aging; Economically disadvantaged.

Type of support: Grants for special needs.
Application information: Applications not accepted.
  Additional information: Recipients are recommended by the Center of Elderly Affairs.
EIN: 046066321

4242
William B. Rice Aid Fund Inc.
P.O. Box 868
Hudson, MA 01749-0868 (978) 562-7994
Contact: George Sousa, Treas.

Foundation type: Operating foundation
Purpose: Scholarships to graduating high school seniors who are residents of Hudson, MA for continuing education at accredited colleges or universities.
Financial data: Year ended 12/31/2011. Assets, $1,019,182 (M); Expenditures, $67,180; Total giving, $48,000; Grants to individuals, 21 grants totaling $42,000 (high: $2,000; low: $2,000).
Fields of interest: Higher education.
Type of support: Scholarships—to individuals.
Application information: Applications accepted. Application form required.
  Initial approach: Letter
  Deadline(s): Apr. 1
  Additional information: Application should include transcripts.
EIN: 046058104

4243
Mary T. & William A. Richardson Fund Corporation
605 Broadway, LF 41
Saugus, MA 01906-3200 (781) 581-4241
Contact: Maureen Trefry, Tr.

Foundation type: Independent foundation
Purpose: Scholarships to residents of MA who are pursuing an undergraduate degree, with preference to those who are graduating high school seniors.
Financial data: Year ended 12/31/2012. Assets, $32,796 (M); Expenditures, $17,826; Total giving, $15,000.
Type of support: Scholarships—to individuals.
Application information: Application form required.
  Deadline(s): Apr. 15
  Applicants should submit the following:
    1) Essay
    2) Transcripts
    3) Letter(s) of recommendation
    4) Financial information
EIN: 510152650

4244
Raymond E. Riddick Memorial Scholarship Fund
22 Blake's Hill Rd.
Westford, MA 01886

Foundation type: Independent foundation
Purpose: Scholarships to graduates of Lowell High School, Lowell, MA.
Financial data: Year ended 06/30/2013. Assets, $194,547 (M); Expenditures, $12,436; Total giving, $10,000; Grants to individuals, 5 grants totaling $10,000 (high: $2,000; low: $2,000).
Fields of interest: Higher education.
Type of support: Support to graduates or students of specific schools.

Application information: Applications accepted. Application form required.

> *Deadline(s):* Apr. 1
> *Additional information:* Applications available from Lowell High School guidance department.

EIN: 042636854

4245
Rockland Trust Charitable Foundation

(formerly Benjamin Franklin Bank Charitable Foundation)
288 Union St.
Rockland, MA 02370 (781) 982-6637
Contact: Jeanne Travers, Clerk
E-mail: Jeanne.Travers@RocklandTrust.com;
URL: http://www.rocklandtrust.com/community-focus/rockland-trust-charitable-foundation.aspx

Foundation type: Company-sponsored foundation
Purpose: Scholarships to graduating seniors from selected high schools in Massachusetts and to a student attending Dean College.
Financial data: Year ended 12/31/2011. Assets, $4,999,842 (M); Expenditures, $184,093; Total giving, $168,238.
Fields of interest: Scholarships/financial aid.
Type of support: Support to graduates or students of specific schools.
Application information: Applications accepted. Application form required.

> *Additional information:* Contact guidance department at participating high schools for application information.

Program description:

> *Rockland Trust Charitable Foundation Scholarship Program:* The foundation awards a $2,500 scholarship to a graduating senior from Franklin High School, Tri-Country Regional Vocational High School, Bellingham High School, Foxborough High School, Milford High School, Medfield High School, Waltham High School, Newton North High School, Learning Prep School, Blackstone Valley Vocational Regional High School, and a student attending Dean College. The award is based on strong character, community involvement, academic achievement, and financial need.

EIN: 202668833

4246
ROFEH, Inc.

1710 Beacon St.
Brookline, MA 02445-2124 (617) 734-5101
Contact: Rabbi Naftali Horowitz, Treas.
E-mail: info@rofeh.org; Additional tel.: (617) 566-9182; URL: http://www.rofeh.org

Foundation type: Public charity
Purpose: Assistance with housing, social services, and medical referrals to Hebrew patients and families who visit the Boston, MA metro area for medical help.
Financial data: Year ended 12/31/2011. Assets, $1,232,043 (M); Expenditures, $563,539; Total giving, $78,670; Grants to individuals, totaling $78,670.
Fields of interest: Health care; Housing/shelter; Human services; Jewish agencies & synagogues.
Type of support: In-kind gifts.
Application information: Contact the organization for eligibility criteria.
EIN: 042661329

4247
Rosenberg Fund for Children, Inc.

116 Pleasant St., Ste. 348
Easthampton, MA 01027-2752 (413) 529-0063
Contact: Jenn Meeropol, Asso. Dir.
FAX: (413) 529-0802; E-mail: rfc@rfc.org; E-Mail for Jenn Meeropol: jenn@rfc.org; URL: http://www.rfc.org/

Foundation type: Public charity
Purpose: Grants to the children of targeted progressive activists, and youth who are targeted activists themselves.
Publications: Application guidelines; Financial statement; Grants list; Informational brochure; Multi-year report; Newsletter; Program policy statement.
Financial data: Year ended 12/31/2011. Assets, $3,483,258 (M); Expenditures, $713,276; Total giving, $307,477; Grants to individuals, totaling $307,477.
Fields of interest: Scholarships/financial aid; Offenders/ex-offenders, services; Youth development; Human services; Children/youth, services; Family services; Human services, transportation; Human services, mind/body enrichment; Human services, travelers' aid; Human services, victim aid; Civil/human rights; Philanthropy/voluntarism.
Type of support: Grants to individuals; Travel grants.
Application information: Application form required.

> *Initial approach:* Telephone or e-mail
> *Deadline(s):* Mar. 21 and Oct. 13
> *Additional information:* Contact foundation for further application information.

Program descriptions:

> *Attica Fund Prison Visit Program:* This program provides funding for children and youth, up to age 24, to visit activist parents from whom they have been separated because of the parents' imprisonment.
> *Carry It Forward Awards:* This program provides up to $600 per year to beneficiaries, ages 19 to 24, to help with the cost of books and supplies associated with post-high-school education and training.
> *Regular Granting Program:* The fund provides grants of up to $3,000 to eligible children and dependents (18 years old or younger) of individuals who have been targeted for their progressive activities. Funding can be used for school tuition, camp tuition, counseling, cultural lessons, recreational programs, or after-school programs.
> *Special Development Grants for Targeted Activist Youth:* This program provides targeted progressive activist youth, ages 18 to 24, with special development grants of up to $1,000 per year to further their education, support their emotional needs, or develop their organizing skills. Applicants are eligible for a maximum of four of these grants (one per year), which are intended to support their development as activists and their transition to adulthood.

EIN: 043095890

4248
Rotary Club Education Fund of Framingham

c/o Tim Sullivan
1 Carriage Hill Cir.
Southborough, MA 01772 (508) 877-4317

Foundation type: Public charity

Purpose: Scholarships to graduating seniors of Ashland, Framingham, Holliston or Hopkinton high schools, MA.
Financial data: Year ended 06/30/2012. Assets, $982,640 (M); Expenditures, $40,821; Total giving, $39,340; Grants to individuals, totaling $39,340.
Type of support: Support to graduates or students of specific schools; Undergraduate support.
Application information: Applications not accepted.

> *Additional information:* Unsolicited requests for funds not considered or acknowledged.

EIN: 046136783

4249
Rotch Travelling Scholarship, Inc.

P.O. Box 55806
Boston, MA 02205-5806
Application address: c/o Boston Society of Architects, 52 Broad St., Boston, MA 02109, fax: (617) 951-0845
URL: http://www.rotchscholarship.org

Foundation type: Operating foundation
Purpose: Grants to practicing architects under 35 years of age for foreign travel and study in architecture. Also, grants to faculty members in all NAAB accredited schools of architecture in the U.S. for travel anywhere in the world.
Publications: Informational brochure (including application guidelines).
Financial data: Year ended 12/31/2011. Assets, $1,228,507 (M); Expenditures, $87,725; Total giving, $66,500; Grants to individuals, 4 grants totaling $46,500 (high: $25,500, low: $1,500).
Fields of interest: Architecture.
Type of support: Travel grants.
Application information: Application form required.

> *Initial approach:* Letter
> *Send request by:* E-mail
> *Deadline(s):* Oct. 21 for Proposals for Studio Scholarship, Jan. 13 for Travelling Scholarship
> *Additional information:* See web site for additional guidelines.

Program descriptions:

> *Rotch Travelling Scholarship:* Awarded annually to provide for eight months of foreign travel and study in the field of architecture. First place award is in the amount of $35,000 for 8 to 12 months of foreign travel. Applicants must be U.S. citizens who have either received a professional degree from an accredited U.S. school of architecture and have one year of full-time professional experience in a MA architecture firm as of Jan. 1 of the competition year or received a professional degree from an accredited MA school of architecture and have one year of full-time professional experience in any architecture firm as of Jan. 1 of the competition year.
> *Rotch Travelling Studio:* Grants to faculty members in schools of architecture for study by their students in a foreign country. Grants are provided to enable faculty member to lead a "studio" for a group of students from the faculty member's school of architecture. The annual foreign-travel grant that provides up to $20,000 toward enhancing students' architectural education.

EIN: 046062249

4250
Travis Roy Foundation
c/o Hemenway and Barnes LLP
60 State St., 8th Fl.
Boston, MA 02109-1892 (617) 619-8257
Contact: Brenda Taylor, Fdn. Coord.
FAX: (617) 227-0781;
E-mail: administrator@travisroyfoundation.org;
URL: http://www.travisroyfoundation.org

Foundation type: Public charity
Purpose: Grants for equipment and home maintenance to paraplegics and quadriplegics paralyzed due to spinal cord injury.
Financial data: Year ended 09/30/2011. Assets, $746,687 (M); Expenditures, $691,025; Total giving, $606,599; Grants to individuals, totaling $329,192.
Fields of interest: Disabilities, people with.
Type of support: Grants for special needs.
Application information: Applications accepted. Application form required.
  Send request by: Mail
  Deadline(s): None
  Additional information: Application must include three estimates of the cost of equipment or home modifications.
EIN: 043327883

4251
Royal Arcanum Scholarship Fund, Inc.
61 Batterymarch St.
Boston, MA 02110 (617) 426-4135
Contact: Dotti Pagnani
URL: http://www.royalarcanum.com

Foundation type: Independent foundation
Purpose: Competitive and non-competitive scholarships and grants to Royal Arcanum members who are in good standing.
Financial data: Year ended 12/31/2012. Assets, $212,098 (M); Expenditures, $51,415; Total giving, $50,750; Grants to individuals, 62 grants totaling $50,750 (high: $2,250, low: $250).
Fields of interest: Higher education.
Type of support: Scholarships—to individuals.
Application information: Applications accepted. Application form required.
  Deadline(s): Oct. 31
EIN: 201236826

4252
Ruffini Charitable Foundation
2036 Washington St.
Hanover, MA 02339 (508) 830-4400
Scholarship address: Plymouth North High School, Attn.: Scholarship Committee, Plymouth, MA 02360

Foundation type: Independent foundation
Purpose: Scholarships to graduating seniors at North Plymouth High School, MA for postsecondary education.
Financial data: Year ended 06/30/2013. Assets, $2,031,016 (M); Expenditures, $111,070; Total giving, $64,900.
Fields of interest: Higher education.
Type of support: Support to graduates or students of specific schools; Undergraduate support.
Application information: Applications accepted.
  Initial approach: Letter or telephone
  Deadline(s): None
  Additional information: Application can be obtained from North Plymouth High School.
EIN: 043030385

4253
Salem Female Charitable Society
c/o Fiduciary Trust Co.
P.O. Box 55806
Boston, MA 02205-5806
Contact: Rosamond Dennis
Application address: 140 Bay View Ave., Salem, MA 01970

Foundation type: Independent foundation
Purpose: Assistance to aged and indigent women of Salem, MA.
Financial data: Year ended 04/30/2013. Assets, $891,921 (M); Expenditures, $58,296; Total giving, $44,850; Grants to individuals, 41 grants totaling $44,850 (high: $2,800, low: $75).
Fields of interest: Aging; Women; Economically disadvantaged.
Type of support: Grants for special needs.
Application information: Applications accepted. Application form not required.
  Initial approach: Letter
  Copies of proposal: 1
  Deadline(s): None
  Additional information: Application should outline financial need.
EIN: 046014190

4254
Samaritan Society
17 Orne Sq.
Salem, MA 01970-2421 (646) 806-4649

Foundation type: Independent foundation
Purpose: Grants to economically disadvantaged residents of Salem, MA, for rent, medications, fuel, and emergencies.
Financial data: Year ended 12/31/2011. Assets, $210,109 (M); Expenditures, $11,696; Total giving, $10,329.
Fields of interest: Economically disadvantaged.
Type of support: Grants for special needs.
Application information: Application form not required.
  Additional information: Maximum grant is $100 per month.
EIN: 046062897

4255
The SAMFund
89 S. St., Ste. LL02
Boston, MA 02111-3611 (617) 938-3484
Contact: Samantha Eisenstein Watson, Exec. Dir.
FAX: (484) 842-2643;
E-mail: info@thesamfund.org; Toll-free tel.: (866) 439-9365; E-Mail for Samantha Eisenstein Watson: sam@thesamfund.org; URL: http://www.thesamfund.org

Foundation type: Public charity
Purpose: Grants and scholarships for individuals between the ages of 17 and 35 who have had cancer and are finished with active treatment.
Publications: Application guidelines.
Financial data: Year ended 06/30/2012. Assets, $283,306 (M); Expenditures, $313,906; Total giving, $130,767; Grants to individuals, totaling $130,767.
Fields of interest: Cancer.
Type of support: Scholarships—to individuals; Grants for special needs.
Application information:
  Initial approach: Letter of intent
  Deadline(s): July 12
EIN: 206018710

4256
Elizabeth and George L. Sanborn Foundation for the Treatment and Cure of Cancer, Inc.
P.O. Box 417
Arlington, MA 02476-0052 (781) 643-7775
Contact: Evelyn Smith-Demille
URL: http://www.sanbornfoundation.org/

Foundation type: Independent foundation
Purpose: Financial assistance to economically disadvantaged residents of Arlington, MA for medical supplies, prescription drugs, hospice care, medical treatments and health insurance premiums.
Financial data: Year ended 12/31/2011. Assets, $5,307,743 (M); Expenditures, $268,978; Total giving, $148,824.
Fields of interest: Hospitals (general); Health care, emergency transport services; Cancer.
Type of support: Grants for special needs.
Application information: Applications accepted.
  Deadline(s): Before the second Tues. of Mar.
  Additional information: Applicant must be residents of Arlington, MA.
EIN: 043452444

4257
Sanders Fund, Inc.
50 Congress St., Ste. 800
Boston, MA 02109-4034

Foundation type: Independent foundation
Purpose: Grants to economically disadvantaged individuals in Boston, Cambridge, and Salem, MA.
Financial data: Year ended 12/31/2010. Assets, $0 (M); Expenditures, $41,957; Total giving, $39,563; Grant to an individual, 1 grant totaling $225.
Fields of interest: Economically disadvantaged.
Type of support: Grants for special needs.
Application information:
  Deadline(s): Nov. 15
  Additional information: Unsolicited requests for funds not considered or acknowledged.
EIN: 042265212

4258
The Sandwich Women's Club
P.O. Box 757
Sandwich, MA 02563-0757
E-mail: info@sandwichwomensclub.org;
URL: http://www.sandwichwomensclub.org

Foundation type: Public charity
Purpose: Scholarships to graduating high school seniors of Sandwich, MA for postsecondary education.
Publications: Application guidelines; Newsletter.
Fields of interest: Higher education.
Type of support: Scholarships—to individuals.
Application information: Applications accepted. Application form required.
  Send request by: Mail
  Deadline(s): Apr. 30
  Applicants should submit the following:
    1) Transcripts
    2) Essay
  Additional information: Application should also include a brief history of your community service during high school, and two letters of reference.

4259
Saugus High School Scholarship Fund, Inc.
c/o Michael Carlson, Sentinel Financial
55 Walkers Brook Dr., Ste. 100
Reading, MA 01867 (781) 231-5027
Contact: Joseph Diorio
Application address: 1 Pearce Memorial Dr., Saugus, MA 01906
Application Address: 1 Pearce Memorial Dr., Saugus, MA 01906

Foundation type: Independent foundation
Purpose: Scholarship awards to graduating seniors of Saugus High School, MA.
Financial data: Year ended 06/30/2013. Assets, $741,898 (M); Expenditures, $36,990; Total giving, $35,200; Grants to individuals, 33 grants totaling $35,200 (high: $5,000, low: -$1,000).
Type of support: Support to graduates or students of specific schools; Undergraduate support.
Application information:
   Initial approach: Letter
   Additional information: Application should include a resume.
EIN: 200698608

4260
Lewis G. Schaeneman, Jr. Memorial Scholarship Foundation, Inc.
1385 Hancock St.
Quincy, MA 02169-5100

Foundation type: Independent foundation
Purpose: Scholarships to qualified Stop & Shop employees for undergraduate education.
Financial data: Year ended 12/31/2011. Assets, $460,119 (M); Expenditures, $28,087; Total giving, $25,048; Grants to individuals, 11 grants totaling $25,048 (high: $7,548, low: $500).
Type of support: Employee-related scholarships; Undergraduate support.
Application information: Applications not accepted.
   Additional information: Unsolicited requests for funds not considered or acknowledged.
Company name: The Stop & Shop Supermarket Company LLC
EIN: 043476066

4261
Scholarship Fund of Kappa Sigma Fraternity Inc.
c/o John K. Stanchfield
P.O. Box 3592
Peabody, MA 01960-3592 (781) 576-9247
Application address: Kappa Sigma Fraternity Scholarship Committee, P.O. Box 218, Wrentham, MA 02093

Foundation type: Independent foundation
Purpose: Undergraduate scholarships to individuals whose relatives are Kappa Sigma Fraternity alumni in MA, for higher education at the University of Massachusetts-Amherst.
Financial data: Year ended 12/31/2011. Assets, $159,278 (M); Expenditures, $25,362; Total giving, $12,000; Grants to individuals, 6 grants totaling $12,000 (high: $2,000, low: $200).
Fields of interest: Students, sororities/fraternities.
Type of support: Undergraduate support.
Application information: Application form required.
   Deadline(s): June 1
   Applicants should submit the following:
      1) Letter(s) of recommendation
      2) Essay

Additional information: Application must also include proof of admission to college, and an additional reference from a Kappa Sigma Fraternity alumnus.
EIN: 042986731

4262
Scholarship Fund of Tau Beta Beta, Inc.
c/o Nancy Saunders
35 Mayo Rd.
Wellesley, MA 02482-1037 (781) 237-1786
Contact: Joyce Austen, Chair.

Foundation type: Public charity
Purpose: Scholarships to young women residing in the communities of Brookline, Newton and Wellesley, MA for furthering their education through college or vocational training as designated by Tau Beta Beta.
Financial data: Year ended 12/31/2011. Assets, $1,197,194 (M); Expenditures, $60,746; Total giving, $57,500; Grants to individuals, totaling $57,500.
Type of support: Undergraduate support.
Application information: Unsolicited requests for funds not considered or acknowledged.
EIN: 042705767

4263
Scleroderma Foundation, Inc.
300 Rosewood Dr., Ste. 105
Danvers, MA 01923-1389 (978) 463-5843
FAX: (978) 463-5809;
E-mail: sfinfo@scleroderma.org; Toll-free tel.: (800) 722-4673; URL: http://www.scleroderma.org

Foundation type: Public charity
Purpose: Research grants to improve treatment and find a cure for scleroderma.
Publications: Application guidelines; Annual report; Grants list; Informational brochure; Newsletter.
Financial data: Year ended 06/30/2012. Assets, $10,615,606 (M); Expenditures, $4,446,158; Total giving, $1,727,178; Grants to individuals, totaling $21,137.
Fields of interest: Diseases (rare) research.
Type of support: Research.
Application information: Application form required. Application form available on the grantmaker's web site.
   Initial approach: Telephone or e-mail
   Send request by: Mail
   Copies of proposal: 5
   Deadline(s): Sept. 15
   Final notification: Recipients notified in Jan.
   Applicants should submit the following:
      1) Proposal
      2) Budget Information
EIN: 521375827

4264
Woman's Auxiliary Board of the Scots Charitable Society of Boston, Massachussetts
c/o Beverly Rawson
39 Charles St.
Georgetown, MA 01833 (617) 543-9243
Contact: Barbara O'Sullivan, Treas.

Foundation type: Independent foundation
Purpose: Scholarships to individuals of Scottish descent in MA and NH.
Financial data: Year ended 12/31/2012. Assets, $292,735 (M); Expenditures, $15,586; Total

giving, $13,200; Grants to individuals, 10 grants totaling $12,600 (high: $1,900, low: $1,000).
Type of support: Undergraduate support.
Application information: Applications accepted. Application form required.
   Deadline(s): May 30
EIN: 046054237

4265
Ronald G. Segel Memorial Scholarship Fund Inc.
2 Newton Pl., Ste. 350
Newton, MA 02458-1637 (615) 320-3151

Foundation type: Company-sponsored foundation
Purpose: Scholarships to children of active employees of Reed Elsevier, Inc. enrolled in undergraduate and graduate degree programs at accredited U.S. institutions.
Financial data: Year ended 05/31/2012. Assets, $0 (M); Expenditures, $2,000; Total giving, $2,000; Grants to individuals, 2 grants totaling $2,000 (high: $1,000, low: $1,000).
Fields of interest: Higher education.
Type of support: Employee-related scholarships.
Application information: Applications accepted. Application form required. Application form available on the grantmaker's web site.
   Send request by: Mail or on-line
   Deadline(s): Apr.
   Applicants should submit the following:
      1) Class rank
      2) GPA
      3) Transcripts
      4) ACT
      5) SAT
      6) Letter(s) of recommendation
Company name: Reed Elsevier Inc.
EIN: 223187139

4266
Self-Help, Inc.
780 W. Main St.
Avon, MA 02322-1744 (508) 588-0447
FAX: (508) 588-1266;
E-mail: carolm@selfhelpinc.org; URL: http://www.selfhelpinc.org

Foundation type: Public charity
Purpose: Financial assistance such as fuel, weatherization, and childcare services to eligible low income residents of the greater Brockton, MA, area.
Financial data: Year ended 09/30/2011. Assets, $7,925,955 (M); Expenditures, $27,372,216.
Type of support: Grants for special needs.
Application information: Applications accepted. Application form required.
   Initial approach: Letter or e-mail
   Additional information: Applicants must be referred. Contact the agency for additional application guidelines.
EIN: 042376180

4267
SEVEN Fund
(also known as Social Equity Venture Fund)
c/o Andreas Widmer
152 Summer St.
Somerville, MA 02143-2611 (617) 331-3071
E-mail: info@sevenfund.org

Foundation type: Public charity

Purpose: Scholarships, prizes, and research opportunities to individuals who seek solutions to ending enduring poverty throughout the world.
Publications: Application guidelines.
Financial data: Year ended 03/31/2012. Assets, $0 (M); Expenditures, $2,319,862; Total giving, $676,098.
Fields of interest: Media/communications; International affairs; Research; Economic development; Community/economic development; Economics; Poverty studies; Social sciences; Economically disadvantaged.
Type of support: Fellowships; Research; Scholarships—to individuals.
Application information: Applications accepted. Application form required.
   Deadline(s): Varies
Program descriptions:
   Cinema Prosperite Film Competition: This film competition strives to create images of poverty that move beyond the stark, evocative, powerful, and persistent, to imagery that focuses on fostering solutions to ending poverty and reshaping how people view other parts of the world, and even their own backyard. This competition will provide an opportunity for amateur and professional filmmakers around the globe to help tell the stores of real people who understand that ending global poverty is serious business. The competition is open to all individuals. A grand prize of $20,000 will be awarded to the top-ranked video (with $10,000 going to the filmmaker and $10,000 to the profiled entrepreneur); a second prize of $10,000 and a third prize of $5,000, to be divided equally among both the filmmaker and the profiled entrepreneur, will also be made available.
   Enterprise-Based Solutions to Poverty RFP: Two research grants of up to $100,000 each are available to researchers whose projects focus on one or more of the following goals: to expand scientific inquiry to include disciplines fundamental to deep understanding of entrepreneurship and economic development that are currently unsupported by conventional grant sources (including those that introduce fresh thinking and new directions into the discourse of poverty reduction and sustainable economic development); to forge and maintain useful collaborations between researchers and on-the-ground actors; to provide the public with a deeper understanding in this area, and its potential implications; and to find, research, and analyze role-model entrepreneurs and companies whose lessons may inspire others. Applicants may include, but are not limited to, think tanks, economics, professors, researchers, business experts, strategy experts, graduate and post-graduate student researchers, economic development experts, business strategists, and nongovernmental organizations.
   SEVEN-CIFA Essay Competition: Awarded in conjunction with the Center for Interfaith Action on Global Poverty, this program seeks essays on enterprise solutions to poverty from around the globe that are faith-based, faith-inspired, or interfaith efforts. Illustrations may come from any domain, including healthcare, education, consumer products, human rights, and others; examples must represent innovative private solutions to public problems. Two prizes of $5,000 each will be awarded to the two best essays.
   Student Essay Competition: This competition will award a graduate student $20,000, and an undergraduate student $10,000, for the best essay that addresses a topic on poverty and international human rights chosen by the fund every year. Any full-time student who studies at an accredited educational institution worldwide, or a student who has been confirmed acceptance and matriculation

for the following academic year, may submit an essay in English, as long as the essay reflects the scope and guidelines stated in the call for essays. Essays must not exceed 2,000 words.
   Teaching Fellowship Competition: This program provides an opportunity for four K-12 teachers (three from a public school setting, one from a faith-based school) to spend two weeks in Rwanda to study enterprise solutions to poverty. Fellows will spend two weeks in Rwanda, meeting with leaders in the private, government, and education sectors, as well as individual meetings and trips that will coincide with the individual interests of the participants. Fellows will also receive a $1,000 prize.
   The WHY Prize: This $50,000 prize will be awarded to two or more individuals from different disciplines that have collaborated together to make a major contribution to the field of enterprise-based solutions to poverty. Currently, the prize is focusing on successful collaborations between macroeconomists and anthropologists. Works must have been published in a major venue or a peer-reviewed journal, and must add to the dialogue around enterprise solutions to poverty by proposing solutions that represent the best integration of actionable insights and thought leadership. Priority will be given to teams that consist of experienced authors and/or Ph.D., experts in their own domains, teams that consist of different ethnicities, and teams whose members reside on different continents and are affiliated with different institutions; however, any act of collaboration that fulfills eligibility guidelines is acceptable.
EIN: 208981997

4268
Ruth A. Shultz Trust
25 Main St.
Lenox, MA   01240   (855) 843-4716
Contact: Elizabeth Gore

Foundation type: Independent foundation
Purpose: Scholarships to high school graduates of the Caanan, CT, area for continuing education in college.
Financial data: Year ended 12/31/2012. Assets, $173,683 (M); Expenditures, $8,424; Total giving, $4,500; Grants to individuals, 4 grants totaling $4,500 (high: $1,500, low: $1,000).
Type of support: Undergraduate support.
Application information: Applications accepted. Application form required.
   Deadline(s): Thirty days prior to award
   Applicants should submit the following:
      1) Transcripts
      2) Financial information
EIN: 066205123

4269
The Smalley Foundation, Inc.
c/o Ellin Smalley
P.O. Box 1385
Brookline, MA   02446

Foundation type: Independent foundation
Purpose: Scholarships to public high school graduates from Worcester, MA, and Yonkers, NY, who have been accepted to institutions where the foundation has established scholarships.
Financial data: Year ended 12/31/2011. Assets, $1,550,112 (M); Expenditures, $176,054; Total giving, $92,283.
Type of support: Support to graduates or students of specific schools; Undergraduate support.

Application information: Applications accepted. Application form required.
   Deadline(s): Contact schools for application deadline.
EIN: 136225947

4270
The Horace Smith Fund
1441 Main St.
Springfield, MA   01103   (413) 739-4222
FAX: (413) 739-1108; URL: http://www.horacesmithfund.org

Foundation type: Independent foundation
Purpose: Scholarships and fellowships to financially needy residents and secondary school graduates of Hampden County, MA.
Financial data: Year ended 03/31/2012. Assets, $6,568,392 (M); Expenditures, $437,375; Total giving, $251,329; Grants to individuals, totaling $251,329.
Fields of interest: Education.
Type of support: Fellowships; Undergraduate support.
Application information: Application form required.
   Deadline(s): Jan. 10 for scholarships; Feb. 1 for fellowships
   Final notification: Recipients notified Apr. 15
   Additional information: Applications available after Sept. 1 for fellowships. See program description for further information.
Program descriptions:
   Walter S. Barr Fellowships: Awarded to Hampden County residents for full-time graduate study; determined on the basis of scholastic record and financial need. See Fund web site for complete guidelines.
   Walter S. Barr Scholarships: Awarded to seniors in secondary schools in Hampden County, MA, for undergraduate education. Application forms are available in the guidance offices of these schools. Recipients are selected on the basis of school records, college entrance exams, general attainment, and financial need. Scholarships are renewable for up to four years. See Fund web site for complete guidelines.
EIN: 042235130

4271
Society of St. Vincent De Paul
18 Canton St.
Stoughton, MA   02072-5500   (781) 344-3100
Contact: Edward J. Resnick, Exec. Dir.
FAX: (781) 341-4560;
E-mail: svdpinfo@svdpboston.org; Toll-free tel.: (800) 675-2882; E-Mail for Edward J. Resnick: ejresnick@svdpboston.com; URL: http://www.svdpboston.com

Foundation type: Public charity
Purpose: Specific assistance to the poor and needy in the Boston, MA area with food, clothing, housing assistance, utilities and other special needs.
Publications: Newsletter.
Financial data: Year ended 09/30/2011. Assets, $10,756,885 (M); Expenditures, $4,040,509; Total giving, $533,513; Grants to individuals, totaling $461,513.
Fields of interest: Economically disadvantaged.
Type of support: Grants for special needs.
Application information: Contact society for eligibility requirements.
EIN: 042104826

4272
South Mountain Association

P.O. Box 23
Pittsfield, MA 01202 (413) 442-2106
Contact: Lou R. Steigler, Exec. Dir.

Foundation type: Operating foundation
Purpose: Scholarships to residents or students in Berkshire County, MA, who are pursuing careers in music (violin, viola, and cello players only). Preference is given to high school seniors, but candidates may apply up to their 25th birthday.
Financial data: Year ended 12/31/2011. Assets, $3,307,629 (M); Expenditures, $236,738; Total giving, $11,500; Grants to individuals, 2 grants totaling $11,500 (high: $6,500, low: $5,000).
Fields of interest: Music; Performing arts, education.
Type of support: Undergraduate support.
Application information: Application form required.
  Initial approach: Letter
  Deadline(s): May 1
  Final notification: Recipients notified by June 1.
  Applicants should submit the following:
    1) Letter(s) of recommendation
    2) Essay
  Additional information: Application must include a recorded sample of the applicant's recent playing.
EIN: 046049419

4273
South Shore Antique Auto Foundation, Inc.

c/o Eric Johnson
199 Grove St.
Kingston, MA 02364
Contact: Eileen Diggle
Application address: 21 Summer St., Fairhaven, MA 02719-4021

Foundation type: Independent foundation
Purpose: Scholarships to high school graduates only (or equivalent) accepted by two years or more accredited degree or certificate-granting educational institutions.
Financial data: Year ended 12/31/2012. Assets, $34,362 (M); Expenditures, $15,553; Total giving, $13,500; Grants to individuals, 9 grants totaling $12,500 (high: $1,500, low: $1,500).
Fields of interest: Higher education.
Type of support: Scholarships—to individuals.
Application information: Applications accepted. Application form required.
  Deadline(s): July 15
  Additional information: Application must include transcripts, educational goals, and academic performance.
EIN: 043133703

4274
South Shore Community Action Council, Inc.

265 S. Meadow Rd.
Plymouth, MA 02360-4782 (508) 747-7575
Contact: Patricia Daly, Exec. Dir.
FAX: (508) 747-1250; URL: http://sscac.org/

Foundation type: Public charity
Purpose: Grants to economically disadvantaged residents of the South Shore, MA, area, for fuel and weatherization assistance as well as food, shelter and clothing.
Financial data: Year ended 09/30/2011. Assets, $5,118,834 (M); Expenditures, $18,794,070;

Total giving, $10,117,395; Grants to individuals, totaling $10,117,395.
Fields of interest: Food services; Housing/shelter; Human services; Economically disadvantaged.
Type of support: Grants for special needs.
Application information: Contact the council for current application deadline/guidelines.
EIN: 046125732

4275
South Shore Elder Services, Inc.

(also known as SSES)
1515 Washington St.
Braintree, MA 02184-5203 (781) 848-3910
FAX: (781) 843-8279; Additional tel.: (781) 383-9790; TDD: (781) 356-1992; URL: http://www.sselder.org

Foundation type: Public charity
Purpose: Grants to elderly individuals in Braintree, Cohasset, Hingham, Holbrook, Hull, Milton, Norwell, Quincy, Randolph, Scituate, and Weymouth, MA, for care to help remain independent in their homes.
Publications: Application guidelines; Grants list.
Financial data: Year ended 06/30/2012. Assets, $3,564,267 (M); Expenditures, $16,076,476; Total giving, $9,745,823; Grants to individuals, totaling $9,570,442.
Fields of interest: Aging.
Type of support: Grants for special needs.
Application information: Applications accepted.
  Initial approach: Telephone or letter
  Additional information: Contact foundation for complete eligibility requirements.
EIN: 042596213

4276
Albert H. & Ruben S. Stone Fund

P.O. Box 1008
Gardner, MA 01440 (978) 630-2800
Contact: Carlton E. Nichols, Jr., Tr.

Foundation type: Independent foundation
Purpose: Scholarships only to residents of Gardner, MA, who are full-time students.
Financial data: Year ended 12/31/2012. Assets, $3,055,359 (M); Expenditures, $110,273; Total giving, $76,973; Grants to individuals, totaling $76,973.
Type of support: Scholarships—to individuals.
Application information: Application form required. Interview required.
  Initial approach: Letter
  Deadline(s): Early in second semester
  Additional information: Applications may be obtained personally through group appointments set with guidance department of high school or by mail; Past recipients of grants receive applications automatically each spring.
EIN: 046050419

4277
Sudbury Foundation

326 Concord Rd.
Sudbury, MA 01776-1819 (978) 443-0849
Contact: Marilyn Martino, Exec. Dir.
FAX: (978) 579-9536;
E-mail: contact@sudburyfoundation.org;
URL: http://www.sudburyfoundation.org

Foundation type: Independent foundation
Purpose: Scholarships to graduating seniors who are residents of Sudbury, MA, or the descendents

of residents, students of Lincoln-Sudbury Regional High School, and dependents of full-time employees of the Town of Sudbury, MA, or Lincoln-Sudbury Regional High School.
Publications: Application guidelines; Financial statement; Informational brochure; Program policy statement.
Financial data: Year ended 12/31/2012. Assets, $30,420,278 (M); Expenditures, $1,599,436; Total giving, $1,196,757; Grants to individuals, 64 grants totaling $309,447 (high: $7,500, low: $1,200).
Type of support: Undergraduate support.
Application information: Application form required. Application form available on the grantmaker's web site. Interview required.
  Send request by: Mail
  Copies of proposal: 1
  Deadline(s): Feb. 1
  Final notification: Recipients notified Mid-Mar.
  Applicants should submit the following:
    1) Transcripts
    2) Letter(s) of recommendation
  Additional information: Application must also include standardized test scores and personal statement.
Program description:
  The Atkinson Scholarship Program: The program was established in 1995 to recognize local students with financial need, academic promise, and the capacity to make a meaningful contribution to society.
EIN: 046037026

4278
Bob Sullivan Memorial Foundation

c/o Sullivan Tire Co., Inc.
41 Accord Park Dr.
Norwell, MA 02061-1614 (781) 871-2260
Contact: Paul Sullivan, Pres.

Foundation type: Public charity
Purpose: Scholarships and grants to residents of Norwell, MA.
Financial data: Year ended 12/31/2011. Assets, $272,882 (M); Expenditures, $19,298; Total giving, $19,000.
Fields of interest: Higher education.
Type of support: Scholarships—to individuals; Undergraduate support.
Application information:
  Initial approach: Letter
EIN: 043214451

4279
Supreme Council Education and Charity Fund

33 Marrett Rd.
Lexington, MA 02421-5703 (781) 862-4410
FAX: (781) 863-1833; URL: http://www.scottishritenmj.org/

Foundation type: Public charity
Purpose: Scholarships to residents of the 15 states which comprise the Scottish Rite Northern Masonic Jurisdiction.
Financial data: Year ended 07/31/2011. Assets, $8,068,154 (M); Expenditures, $501,714; Total giving, $500,500; Grants to individuals, 327 grants totaling $500,500. Subtotal for scholarships—to individuals: 327 grants totaling $500,500.
Fields of interest: Fraternal societies.
Type of support: Scholarships—to individuals.

Application information: Applications not accepted. Unsolicited requests for funds not considered or acknowledged.
EIN: 046116087

4280
Swan Society in Boston
(formerly Widows Society in Boston)
581 Boylston St., Ste. 705
Boston, MA   02116-3626   (617) 536-7951
Contact: Jackie Husid, Exec. Dir.
FAX: (617) 536-0725

Foundation type: Operating foundation
Purpose: Financial assistance to widowed, divorced, and single women who are over 65 years old and who live within 25 miles of the Massachusetts State House in Boston, MA, so that they may continue to live independently.
Publications: Application guidelines; Annual report; Informational brochure.
Financial data: Year ended 10/31/2013. Assets, $5,055,202 (M); Expenditures, $289,609; Total giving, $229,232.
Fields of interest: Aging; Women; Economically disadvantaged.
Type of support: Emergency funds; Grants for special needs.
Application information: Applications accepted. Application form required.
   Initial approach: Letter or telephone
   Copies of proposal: 1
   Deadline(s): None
   Additional information: Application should include budget information. The society's licensed social worker screens recommended applicants, who are informed of the funding decision within two weeks.
EIN: 042306840

4281
Take a Swing at Cancer, Inc.
P. O. Box 5245
Framingham, MA   01701-0445   (781) 690-0350
Contact: Kristen Dion, Pres.
E-mail: info@takeaswing.org; E-mail For Kristen Dion: KristenDion@takeaswing.org; URL: http://www.takeaswing.org

Foundation type: Public charity
Purpose: Grants to individuals and families in New England who have been adversely affected by cancer for expenses not traditionally covered by insurance.
Financial data: Year ended 12/31/2011. Assets, $22,748 (M); Expenditures, $30,505; Total giving, $29,000.
Fields of interest: Cancer.
Type of support: Grants for special needs.
Application information: Applications accepted. Application form required. Application form available on the grantmaker's web site.
   Send request by: Mail
   Deadline(s): None
   Additional information: Application should include an adult oncology release form.
EIN: 043427280

4282
Tanne Foundation
c/o Loring Wolcott & Coolidge
230 Congress St.
Boston, MA   02110
URL: http://www.tannefoundation.org

Foundation type: Independent foundation
Purpose: Fellowships to MA and NY artists who have demonstrated exceptional talent and creativity, for recognition of prior achievement, and to enrich their artistic lives.
Financial data: Year ended 06/30/2013. Assets, $1,141,518 (M); Expenditures, $60,473; Total giving, $36,000; Grants to individuals, 4 grants totaling $26,500 (high: $7,500, low: $4,000).
Fields of interest: Arts.
Type of support: Fellowships.
Application information: Applications not accepted.
EIN: 020500550

4283
Frank C. Taylor & Helen M. Taylor Educational Fund
13 Ventura Dr.
North Dartmouth, MA   02747-1244   (508) 998-6152

Foundation type: Operating foundation
Purpose: Scholarships to graduating seniors of New Bedford High School, Dartmouth High School, Bishop Stang High School, Greater New Bedford Vocational Technical High School, and Fairhaven High School, MA.
Financial data: Year ended 12/31/2011. Assets, $0 (M); Expenditures, $11,550; Total giving, $8,500; Grants to individuals, 17 grants totaling $8,500 (high: $500, low: $500).
Fields of interest: Vocational education; Higher education.
Type of support: Support to graduates or students of specific schools; Undergraduate support.
Application information: Application form required.
   Deadline(s): Apr. 15
   Applicants should submit the following:
   1) Transcripts
   2) Essay
EIN: 046071778

4284
Nathaniel Taylor Fund, Inc.
2036 Washington St.
Hanover, MA   02339-1617
Contact: Carolyn Hubbard, Treas.
Application address: P.O. Box 693, Marshfield, MA 02050-0693

Foundation type: Independent foundation
Purpose: Financial assistance to residents of Marshfield, MA, who are in need due to sickness or other unfortunate circumstances. A small amount for scholarships is also given to local high school graduates to study nursing or a related subject.
Financial data: Year ended 09/30/2012. Assets, $422,940 (M); Expenditures, $23,993; Total giving, $20,000.
Fields of interest: Higher education.
Type of support: Undergraduate support; Grants for special needs.
Application information: Applications accepted.
   Initial approach: Letter
   Deadline(s): None
EIN: 046065495

4285
Tenney Educational Fund, Inc.
89 Main St.
Andover, MA   01810   (978) 474-4447
Contact: John C. Oakley, Treas.

Foundation type: Operating foundation

Purpose: Scholarships to graduates of Methuen High School, MA for higher education.
Financial data: Year ended 04/30/2011. Assets, $859,745 (M); Expenditures, $26,639; Total giving, $23,000. Scholarships—to individuals amount not specified.
Fields of interest: Higher education.
Type of support: Support to graduates or students of specific schools; Undergraduate support.
Application information: Applications accepted. Application form required.
   Deadline(s): May 15
   Additional information: Students should contact their guidance couselor for additional application guidelines.
EIN: 046038700

4286
The Robert F. Terry, Jr. Foundation
993 Massachusetts Ave., Ste. 127
Arlington, MA   02476-4518   (617) 248-6690

Foundation type: Public charity
Purpose: Financial assistance for non-medical expenses to families with children suffering from pediatric brain tumors, particularly in MA.
Financial data: Year ended 12/31/2011. Assets, $8,143 (M); Expenditures, $9,989; Total giving, $7,500; Grants to individuals, totaling $7,500.
Fields of interest: Brain disorders.
Type of support: Grants for special needs.
Application information: Non-medical expenses include mortgage, rent, utilities and other needs. Contact the foundation for eligibility requirements.
EIN: 201310278

4287
Theta Delta Chi Educational Foundation, Inc.
214 Lewis Wharf
Boston, MA   02110-3927   (617) 742-8886
Contact: William A. McClung, Exe. Dir.

Foundation type: Public charity
Purpose: Scholarships to MA members of Theta Delta Chi to attend accredited institutions.
Financial data: Year ended 06/30/2012. Assets, $3,890,483 (M); Expenditures, $421,321; Total giving, $54,099; Grants to individuals, totaling $30,941.
Fields of interest: Fraternal societies.
Type of support: Undergraduate support.
Application information:
   Initial approach: Letter
   Additional information: Apr. 30.
EIN: 043026850

4288
Albert A. and Ruth W. Thomas Scholarship Fund
(also known as Ruth W. Thomas Trust)
P.O. Box 382
Woods Hole, MA   02543-0382
Contact: Thomas A. Maddigan, Tr.
Application address: c/o Middleboro High School, 71 E. Grove St., Middleboro, MA 02346-1847

Foundation type: Independent foundation
Purpose: Scholarships to students who have graduated or is graduating from Middleborough High School, MA with sufficient grades to attend college.
Financial data: Year ended 12/31/2012. Assets, $124,316 (M); Expenditures, $12,897; Total

giving, $10,290; Grants to individuals, 4 grants totaling $10,290 (high: $3,425, low: $1,720).
Fields of interest: Vocational education, post-secondary; Higher education.
Type of support: Support to graduates or students of specific schools.
Application information: Applications accepted. Application form required.
 Deadline(s): End of Apr. (prior to awards night)
 Additional information: Application can be obtained from principal of Middleborough High School.
EIN: 046392636

4289
Henry David Thoreau Foundation, Inc.
(formerly Northeast Educational Services, Inc.)
265 Medford St., Ste. 102
Somerville, MA 02143-1963 (617) 666-6900
Contact: John R. Galvin, Pres.
FAX: (617) 666-0345; URL: http://www.thoreauscholar.org

Foundation type: Independent foundation
Purpose: Scholarships to individuals who are residents of Massachusetts and graduated from a high school in Massachusetts for attendance at an accredited college or university pursuing a career in the environmental field.
Financial data: Year ended 12/31/2012. Assets, $9,668,508 (M); Expenditures, $449,980; Total giving, $178,250; Grants to individuals, 3 grants totaling $1,500 (high: $500, low: $500).
Fields of interest: Higher education; Environment.
Type of support: Scholarships—to individuals.
Application information: Applications accepted. Application form required.
 Initial approach: Telephone or web site
 Deadline(s): Feb. 1
 Final notification: Applicants notified Apr. 30
 Applicants should submit the following:
  1) Transcripts
  2) SAT
  3) Resume
  4) Letter(s) of recommendation
  5) Financial information
  6) Essay
  7) ACT
 Additional information: Interview may be required.
EIN: 042077934

4290
John M. & Ethel C. Thorne Foundation Inc.
3 Sea Meadow Dr.
Sandwich, MA 02563 (508) 759-3320
Contact: Edward Linhares, Treas.
Application address: 32 Beach Rd., Monument Beach, MA 02553

Foundation type: Independent foundation
Purpose: Scholarships to residents of Bourne, Falmouth, Sandwich, and Wareham, MA for higher education.
Financial data: Year ended 04/30/2012. Assets, $490,416 (M); Expenditures, $28,568; Total giving, $20,100; Grants to individuals, 9 grants totaling $9,000 (high: $1,000, low: $1,000).
Fields of interest: Higher education.
Type of support: Scholarships—to individuals.
Application information: Applications accepted.
 Deadline(s): None
 Additional information: Contact the foundation for additional information.
EIN: 046047689

4291
Ernest & Anna Torbet Scholarship Trust
64 Gothic St., Ste. 6
Northampton, MA 01060 (413) 587-1344

Foundation type: Independent foundation
Purpose: Scholarships to deserving graduating seniors of Northampton High School, MA for attendance at educational institutions beyond high school.
Financial data: Year ended 12/31/2012. Assets, $47,620 (M); Expenditures, $9,373; Total giving, $4,000; Grants to individuals, 4 grants totaling $4,000 (high: $1,000, low: $1,000).
Fields of interest: Higher education.
Type of support: Support to graduates or students of specific schools.
Application information: Applications accepted. Application form required.
 Deadline(s): Mar. 1
 Additional information: Application can be obtained from Northampton High School guidance office, or from the trustee.
EIN: 046539428

4292
Tourism Cares, Inc.
(formerly Tourism Cares for Tomorrow, Inc.)
275 Turnpike St., Ste. 307
Canton, MA 02021-3013 (781) 821-5990
Contact: Carolyn Viles, Dir., Grants and Scholarship Progs.
FAX: (781) 821-8949;
E-mail: info@tourismcares.org; URL: http://www.tourismcares.org

Foundation type: Public charity
Purpose: Scholarships primarily to juniors or seniors at undergraduate level or graduate students pursuing degrees in hospitality or travel and tourism-related fields at an accredited university in the United States or Canada.
Publications: Application guidelines; Grants list; Informational brochure; Newsletter; Program policy statement (including application guidelines).
Financial data: Year ended 12/31/2011. Assets, $2,338,193 (M); Expenditures, $1,335,596; Total giving, $277,520; Grants to individuals, totaling $97,620.
Fields of interest: Higher education.
Type of support: Research; Scholarships—to individuals; Support to graduates or students of specific schools; Graduate support; Undergraduate support; Postgraduate support.
Application information: Applications accepted. Application form required. Application form available on the grantmaker's web site.
 Initial approach: Application
 Send request by: Mail
 Copies of proposal: 1
 Deadline(s): Mar. 1 and July 2 for Worldwide Grant Program, Apr. 1 for Academic Scholarships, June 1 for Professional Development Scholarships
 Final notification: Recipients notified in six to eight weeks
 Applicants should submit the following:
  1) Essay
  2) Letter(s) of recommendation
  3) Transcripts
  4) Resume
  5) GPA
Program descriptions:
 Academic Scholarships: Merit-based scholarships, ranging from $1,000 to $5,000, are awarded annually to both undergraduate and graduate level students, in travel and

tourism-related, or hospitality-related, programs of study. Scholarships for undergraduates may be used to cover expenses for tuition, books, and educational fees. Scholarships for graduate level students may be used to cover expenses for tuition, books, educational fees, and research-related expenses. All applicants must be enrolled in school for the upcoming fall semester to be eligible to receive the scholarship award. Applicants must be citizens or permanent residents of the U.S. or Canada.
 Professional Development Scholarships: Merit-based scholarships are awarded annually to applicants, who are entering or continuing the travel-and-tourism or hospitality industry, and who have completed and fully paid for a travel-and-tourism or hospitality certificate program at an accredited or state-licensed educational institution in the U.S., Guam, Puerto Rico, or Canada, or attended the applicable conference or symposium held by a accredited or state-licensed educational institution in the U.S.
EIN: 202013457

4293
Transgender Scholarship and Education Legacy Fund
c/o TSELF Awards Committee
P.O. Box 540229
Waltham, MA 02454-0229 (781) 899-2212
Contact: Julie Johnson
FAX: (781) 899-5703; E-mail: julie@tself.org

Foundation type: Public charity
Purpose: Scholarships to transgender identified students who will be enrolled in a postsecondary program in the helping and caring professions including social services, health care, religious instruction, teaching and the law.
Publications: Application guidelines.
Fields of interest: Education; LGBTQ.
Type of support: Scholarships—to individuals.
Application information: Applications accepted.
 Send request by: Mail
 Deadline(s): Jan. 10
Program descriptions:
 Chicago Gender Society Leadership Award: This award is sponsored by the Chicago Gender Society, and is given with special consideration to students who have been involved in community building activities.
 General Achievement Awards: Several, non-specific awards are available for students in the helping and caring professions. These include, but are not limited to, Social Services, Health Care, Religious Instruction, Teaching and the Law. The awards seek to reflect a broad range of interests, including social services, HIV/AIDS education, law, teaching and education, religious instruction (all denominations), medical and health care as well as the sciences.
 Lee Frances Heller Memorial Award: The award, sponsored by Julie Ann Johnson is limited to a Christian student, who is or will be attending a college, university or other institutions for religious studies. Applicants must indicate how transgender identity and involvement in the Christian church have related to one another. Applicants should include the name of their home congregation and any leadership experience they have had in the Christian church and/or transgender organizations.
 Schools Education Award: Awards are limited to students seeking degrees in education and teaching. Special consideration will be given to students who have been involved in teaching primary and secondary school students and who can articulate how these experiences have

motivated them to provide leadership in the transgender communities.

The HIV/AIDS Prevention and Treatment Award: Students will be given special consideration with this award for the involvement in HIV/AIDS prevention, care, and treatment activities.

Youth Award: The award is limited to youth under the age of 22 attending their first or second year of postsecondary education during the next academic year.

4294
Travelers Aid Family Services, Inc.
727 Atlantic Ave.
Boston, MA 02111-2907 (617) 542-7286
Contact: Bruce Liddell, Exec. Dir.
FAX: (617) 542-9545; E-mail: info@tafsboston.org; E-Mail for Bruce Liddell : bliddell@tafsboston.orgTel. for Bruce Liddell : (617)-542-7286 Ext. 264; URL: http://www.taboston.org

Foundation type: Public charity
Purpose: Emergency assistance to low-income homeless families in the Boston, MA, area who are in need of shelter or transportation assistance.
Publications: Annual report; Financial statement.
Financial data: Year ended 06/30/2012. Assets, $3,241,837 (M); Expenditures, $5,156,826; Total giving, $2,509,018; Grants to individuals, totaling $2,509,018.
Fields of interest: Human services; Human services, transportation; Economically disadvantaged.
Type of support: Emergency funds.
Application information:
  Initial approach: Telephone
  Additional information: Contact the agency for additional information.
EIN: 042105756

4295
The Charles Irwin Travelli Fund
c/o Tyler & Reynolds
77 Summer St.
Boston, MA 02110-1006
Application address: c/o Geoffrey Andrews, 58 Bowen St., Newton, MA 02159, tel.: (617) 332-0548

Foundation type: Independent foundation
Purpose: Scholarships to individuals residing in the New England area for higher education.
Financial data: Year ended 11/30/2012. Assets, $1,834,422 (M); Expenditures, $1,154,321; Total giving, $1,084,300; Grants to individuals, totaling $1,028,800.
Fields of interest: Higher education.
Type of support: Scholarships—to individuals; Undergraduate support.
Application information: Application form required.
  Deadline(s): Varies
  Additional information: Application forms are available in the financial aid offices of the participating institutions. Applicant must demonstrate financial need, and participate in academic and extracurricular activities.
EIN: 042260155

4296
Tri-City Community Action Program, Inc.
110 Pleasant St.
Malden, MA 02148-4901 (781) 332-4125
Contact: Philip Bronder-Giroux, Exec. Dir.
FAX: (781) 324-7717; URL: http://www.tri-cap.org

Foundation type: Public charity
Purpose: Financial assistance to low-income residents of Everett, Malden, Melrose, Stoneham, Winchester, and Woburn, MA, to pay a portion of their utility bills.
Publications: Newsletter.
Financial data: Year ended 06/30/2011. Assets, $4,547,261 (M); Expenditures, $10,209,791; Total giving, $4,744,663; Grants to individuals, totaling $4,744,663.
Fields of interest: Housing/shelter, expense aid.
Type of support: Grants for special needs.
Application information:
  Initial approach: Telephone
  Deadline(s): Nov.- Apr.
  Additional information: Contact foundation for income guidelines.
EIN: 042658101

4297
Richard J. Trifiro Foundation
c/o Atlantic Mgmt. Corp.
205 Newbury St.
Framingham, MA 01701

Foundation type: Independent foundation
Purpose: Scholarships to graduating high school students of Boston English High School, MA, for postsecondary education.
Financial data: Year ended 12/31/2012. Assets, $759,172 (M); Expenditures, $35,308; Total giving, $33,100; Grants to individuals, 14 grants totaling $33,100 (high: $5,000; low: $100).
Fields of interest: Higher education.
Type of support: Undergraduate support.
Application information: Applications not accepted.
  Additional information: Unsolicited requests for funds not considered or acknowledged. Scholarships are only for Boston English High school students.
EIN: 046912472

4298
Trustees of Partridge Academy in Duxbury
P.O. Box 2552
Duxbury, MA 02331 (781) 934-7600

Foundation type: Independent foundation
Purpose: Scholarships to graduates of Duxbury Junior and Senior High School, MA.
Financial data: Year ended 12/31/2012. Assets, $2,373,256 (M); Expenditures, $114,408; Total giving, $110,100; Grants to individuals, 42 grants totaling $110,100 (high: $9,000; low: $300).
Type of support: Support to graduates or students of specific schools; Undergraduate support.
Application information: Applications accepted.
  Deadline(s): Spring of senior year
  Additional information: Applicants should contact guidance counselors for specific application guidelines.
EIN: 222838857

4299
Trustees of the Perley Free School
17 Larch Rd.
Georgetown, MA 01833-1525 (978) 352-7067
Contact: Steven A. Desisto, V.P.
Application address: 15 School St., George town, MA 01833, tel.: (978) 352-7067

Foundation type: Independent foundation
Purpose: Scholarships to residents of Georgetown, MA. Grants to the poor of Georgetown, MA are also available.
Financial data: Year ended 04/30/2013. Assets, $1,223,078 (M); Expenditures, $64,671; Total giving, $34,600; Grant to an individual, 1 grant totaling $33,900.
Fields of interest: Higher education; Economically disadvantaged.
Type of support: Scholarships—to individuals; Grants for special needs.
Application information: Applications accepted.
  Deadline(s): May 15
  Additional information: Scholarship application must include secondary school record, estimated college expenses, and work experience.
EIN: 046032270

4300
Trustees of the Putnam Free School
P.O. Box 562
Newburyport, MA 01950-0762 (978) 462-2197
Contact: Donald Mitchell, Pres.
Application tel.:(978) 356-3600

Foundation type: Independent foundation
Purpose: Scholarships to residents of one of the eleven towns in the Newburyport, MA area.
Financial data: Year ended 10/31/2013. Assets, $1,823,785 (M); Expenditures, $81,227; Total giving, $65,044; Grants to individuals, totaling $65,044.
Fields of interest: Higher education.
Type of support: Undergraduate support.
Application information: Applications accepted. Application form required.
  Deadline(s): July 1
  Additional information: Application should include age, residence, school last attended, college or institution to be attended, proof of acceptance, and proof of financial need. Applicant must take courses in English and Mathematics during the first year.
EIN: 046040535

4301
Trustees of Warren Academy
c/o Glenn Johnson
13 Hilltop Cir.
Woburn, MA 01801

Foundation type: Independent foundation
Purpose: Scholarships to graduating high school seniors of Woburn High School, MA, for attendance at colleges and universities.
Financial data: Year ended 02/28/2012. Assets, $206,276 (M); Expenditures, $6,157; Total giving, $5,900; Grants to individuals, 4 grants totaling $5,900 (high: $1,475, low: $1,475).
Fields of interest: Higher education.
Type of support: Support to graduates or students of specific schools; Undergraduate support.
Application information: Applications not accepted.
  Additional information: Unsolicited requests for funds not considered or acknowledged.

Recipients are chosen on the basis of class rank.
EIN: 046032875

4302
Turning Leaf Foundation Inc.
c/o Kahn Litwin Renza & Co., Ltd.
800 South St., No. 300
Waltham, MA 02453

Foundation type: Independent foundation
Purpose: Scholarships to individuals for post-secondary education for whom such education would not otherwise be available.
Financial data: Year ended 12/31/2011. Assets, $789,214 (M); Expenditures, $141,247; Total giving, $136,492.
Fields of interest: Higher education; Economically disadvantaged.
Type of support: Scholarships—to individuals.
Application information: Applications not accepted.
EIN: 043397818

4303
Two Ten Footwear Foundation, Inc.
1466 Main St.
Waltham, MA 02451-1623 (781) 736-1500
Contact: Peggy K. Meill, Pres.
FAX: (781) 736-1555;
E-mail: scholarship@twoten.org; Toll-free tel.: (800) 346-3210; URL: http://www.twoten.org

Foundation type: Public charity
Purpose: Assistance and resources to needy individuals in the shoe industry, leather trade, and allied trades.
Publications: Application guidelines; Annual report; Informational brochure; Newsletter.
Financial data: Year ended 06/30/2011. Assets, $32,508,024 (M); Expenditures, $4,079,502; Total giving, $1,983,069; Grants to individuals, totaling $1,892,069.
Fields of interest: Business/industry; Economically disadvantaged.
Type of support: Scholarships—to individuals; Grants for special needs.
Application information: Applications accepted. Application form required.
Initial approach: Telephone
Deadline(s): Feb. 15
Additional information: See web site for further information.
EIN: 222579809

4304
Ray Tye Medical Aid Foundation
175 Campanelli Dr.
P.O. Box 850376
Braintree, MA 02184-0376
Contact: Terri Carlson, Dir.
FAX: (781) 356-4551;
E-mail: rtmaf@unitedliquors.com; Additional e-mail: info@rtmaf.org; URL: http://www.rtmaf.org

Foundation type: Independent foundation
Purpose: Grants for the medical care of individuals who are not otherwise eligible.
Publications: Newsletter.
Financial data: Year ended 12/31/2012. Assets, $3,998,269 (M); Expenditures, $813,531; Total giving, $780,347.
Type of support: Grants for special needs.
Application information: Applications accepted. Application form not required.

Initial approach: Letter
Send request by: E-mail
Copies of proposal: 1
Final notification: Recipients notified in 30 days
EIN: 046958143

4305
University Club Scholarship Fund
426 Stuart St.
Boston, MA 02116-5007 (617) 266-5600
FAX: (617) 266-5554; E-mail: bholk@uclub.org;
URL: http://www.uclub.org/club/scripts/library/view_document.asp?
GRP=14110&NS=PUBLIC&APP=80&DN=SCHOLARSHIP

Foundation type: Public charity
Purpose: Scholarships to graduates of the Boston, MA, public school system for undergraduate education.
Financial data: Year ended 12/31/2011. Assets, $395,558 (M); Expenditures, $45,185; Total giving, $45,000; Grants to individuals, totaling $45,000.
Type of support: Undergraduate support.
Application information: Applications not accepted.
EIN: 042618671

4306
University of Massachusetts Dartmouth Foundation, Inc.
285 Old Westport Rd.
North Dartmouth, MA 02747-2300 (508) 999-8000
Contact: Michael Eatough, Exec. Dir.
FAX: (508) 999-8773; Tel. for Michael Eatough: (508)-999-8802; URL: http://www.umassd.edu/institutional_advancement/foundation/

Foundation type: Public charity
Purpose: Scholarships to needy students attending the University of Massachusetts Dartmouth, MA.
Publications: Annual report; Informational brochure.
Financial data: Year ended 06/30/2011. Assets, $44,289,268 (M); Expenditures, $2,262,969; Total giving, $2,194,720; Grants to individuals, 201 grants totaling $512,180.
Type of support: Support to graduates or students of specific schools; Undergraduate support.
Application information:
Initial approach: Letter
EIN: 237336988

4307
USO Council of New England, Inc.
427 Commercial St.
Boston, MA 02109-1027 (617) 720-4949
Contact: Steven Wujciak, Exec. Dir.
FAX: (617) 720-0982;
E-mail: generalmail@uso-newengland.org;
URL: http://www.uso-newengland.org/

Foundation type: Public charity
Purpose: Financial assistance to military families, specifically active duty service personnel, reserve forces, and the national guard.
Financial data: Year ended 06/30/2011. Assets, $0 (M); Expenditures, $517,114; Total giving, $283,643; Grants to individuals, totaling $283,643.
Fields of interest: Military/veterans' organizations.
Type of support: Grants for special needs.

Application information:
Initial approach: Letter or e-mail
Additional information: Unsolicited requests for funds not considered or acknowledged.
EIN: 042318250

4308
Mary G. Voght Trust
(formerly Voght Scholarship Fund)
P.O. Box 1330
Hyannis, MA 02601
Application address: c/o TD Bank, N.A., attn.: Holly Lawson, 99 West St., Pittsfield, MA 01201

Foundation type: Independent foundation
Purpose: Scholarships to individuals for higher education.
Financial data: Year ended 12/31/2011. Assets, $163,765 (M); Expenditures, $10,210; Total giving, $6,000; Grants to individuals, 11 grants totaling $6,000 (high: $600, low: $600).
Type of support: Scholarships—to individuals.
Application information: Applications accepted.
Additional information: Contact trust for current application guidelines.
EIN: 046555019

4309
Gygi Von Wyss Foundation
(formerly Hans Gygi Foundation)
201 Jones Rd.
Waltham, MA 02451-1600
Contact: Stacy Compora, Secy.
Application address: 6211 Ann Arbor Rd., Dundee, MI 48131

Foundation type: Company-sponsored foundation
Purpose: Scholarships to high school seniors who are children or stepchildren of employees of Holcim (U.S.), Inc. and its wholly-owned subsidiaries.
Financial data: Year ended 12/31/2012. Assets, $14,330 (M); Expenditures, $153,120; Total giving, $143,349; Grants to individuals, 25 grants totaling $143,200 (high: $10,666).
Fields of interest: Scholarships/financial aid.
Type of support: Employee-related scholarships; Undergraduate support.
Application information: Applications not accepted.
Additional information: Unsolicited requests for funds not considered or acknowledged.
Company name: Holcim (US), Inc.
EIN: 382472472

4310
Arno & Roberta E. Wagner Scholarship Fund
370 Main St., Ste. 800
Worcester, MA 01608-1741 (508) 756-2423
Contact: Ann K. Molloy, Tr.

Foundation type: Independent foundation
Purpose: Scholarships to residents of the town of Douglas, MA seeking to continue their education beyond high school.
Financial data: Year ended 12/31/2012. Assets, $285,680 (M); Expenditures, $26,279; Total giving, $20,300.
Fields of interest: Higher education.
Type of support: Scholarships—to individuals.
Application information: Applications accepted. Application form required.
Deadline(s): May 15
Applicants should submit the following:
1) Letter(s) of recommendation

2) Essay

Additional information: Applications are available at the Douglas town hall, Douglas High School and Simon Fairfield Library.

EIN: 562319340

4311
Warren Benevolent Fund, Inc.
120 Prospect St.
Ashland, MA   01721-0114   (508) 881-3293
Contact: Anne Gentile, Treas.
Application address: P.O. Box 114, Ashland, MA 01721-0114, tel.: (508) 881-3293

Foundation type: Independent foundation
Purpose: Scholarships and student loans to graduates of Ashland High School, MA.
Financial data: Year ended 12/31/2011. Assets, $525,583 (M); Expenditures, $14,167; Total giving, $10,075; Grants to individuals, 2 grants totaling $10,075 (high: $5,000, low: $5,000).
Fields of interest: Higher education.
Type of support: Support to graduates or students of specific schools; Undergraduate support.
Application information: Applications accepted.
Initial approach: Letter
Additional information: Letter should include information about college attending.
EIN: 042309470

4312
Ann White Washburn Scholarship Fund
2036 Washington St.
Hanover, MA   02339-1617   (508) 946-2014

Foundation type: Independent foundation
Purpose: Scholarships to graduates of Middleboro High School, Kingston High School, and Rochester High School, MA seeking to continue their education.
Financial data: Year ended 12/31/2012. Assets, $136,006 (M); Expenditures, $8,522; Total giving, $6,600; Grants to individuals, 11 grants totaling $6,600 (high: $900, low: $400).
Fields of interest: Higher education.
Type of support: Support to graduates or students of specific schools.
Application information: Applications accepted. Application form required.
Deadline(s): May 1
Additional information: Applications can be obtained from the guidance counselors of the respective high schools.
EIN: 046059111

4313
Marion Huxley West Scholarship Fund
2036 Washington St.
Hanover, MA   02339-1617   (508) 946-2010
Application address: c/o Middleboro High School, Attn.: Principal, 71 E. Grove St., Middleboro, MA 02346-1847

Foundation type: Independent foundation
Purpose: Scholarships only to graduates of Middleboro High School, MA, for attendance at a four-year college or university.
Financial data: Year ended 06/30/2012. Assets, $148,370 (M); Expenditures, $7,669; Total giving, $6,000; Grants to individuals, totaling $6,000.
Fields of interest: Higher education.
Type of support: Support to graduates or students of specific schools.

Application information: Applications accepted. Application form required.
Deadline(s): None
Additional information: Application available at Middleboro High School.
EIN: 043397114

4314
Wesley Weyman Trust
45 School St., 5th Fl.
Boston, MA   02108-3204   (617) 496-3253
Contact: Christoph Wolff Prof., Tr.
Application address: c/o Harvard University, Cambridge, MA 02138

Foundation type: Independent foundation
Purpose: Scholarships to students enrolled in qualified institutions for study in the field of music.
Financial data: Year ended 01/31/2013. Assets, $226,579 (M); Expenditures, $13,549; Total giving, $9,000; Grants to individuals, 21 grants totaling $9,000 (high: $600, low: $100).
Fields of interest: Music; Performing arts, education.
Type of support: Scholarships—to individuals.
Application information:
Deadline(s): None
EIN: 046118681

4315
Wheelwright Scientific School
81 State St.
P.O. Box 510
Newburyport, MA   01950-6617   (978) 462-8749
Contact: John C. Elwell, Tr.
Application address: 266 High St., Newburyport, MA 09150, tel.: (978) 462-8749

Foundation type: Independent foundation
Purpose: Scholarships to residents of Newburyport, MA, pursuing a field of study in engineering or basic science.
Financial data: Year ended 06/30/2012. Assets, $3,342,125 (M); Expenditures, $154,364; Total giving, $75,000; Grants to individuals, 12 grants totaling $75,000 (high: $6,000, low: $3,000).
Fields of interest: Science; Engineering/technology; Protestant agencies & churches.
Type of support: Scholarships—to individuals.
Application information: Applications accepted. Application form required.
Deadline(s): Apr.
Additional information: Application must include the names of references, one of whom must be the minister of the applicant's church. Students must be Protestants, and may reapply for scholarships.
EIN: 046004390

4316
Marion and Jasper Whiting Foundation
c/o Rice, Heard & Bigelow, Inc.
50 Congress St., Ste. 1025
Boston, MA   02109-4002   (617) 227-1782
Contact: Robert G. Bannish, Tr.

Foundation type: Public charity
Purpose: Travel and training grants to college and university professors.
Financial data: Year ended 10/31/2011. Assets, $3,358,455 (M); Expenditures, $141,616; Total giving, $116,007.
Fields of interest: College; University.
Type of support: Fellowships; Travel grants.

Application information: Applications accepted. Application form not required.
Initial approach: Proposal
Deadline(s): Jan. 29
Final notification: Mar.
Applicants should submit the following:
1) Letter(s) of recommendation
2) Budget Information
3) Curriculum vitae
Additional information: The three letters of recommendation should be sent directly to the foundation by the writers.
EIN: 046147345

4317
Edna May Whittemore Trust
c/o Eastern Bank
605 Broadway, 42nd Fl.
Saugus, MA   01906-3200   (781) 581-4276
Contact: Leanne Martin

Foundation type: Independent foundation
Purpose: Scholarships to current graduates of secondary schools in Malden, MA for postsecondary education.
Financial data: Year ended 06/30/2012. Assets, $171,804 (M); Expenditures, $10,685; Total giving, $8,000; Grants to individuals, 4 grants totaling $4,000 (high: $1,000, low: $1,000).
Fields of interest: Higher education.
Type of support: Undergraduate support.
Application information: Applications accepted. Application form required.
Deadline(s): June 1
Additional information: Application forms available upon request.
EIN: 046045950

4318
Milton L. Williams Trust
c/o Eastern Bank
605 Broadway, Ste. LF41
Saugus, MA   01906-3200
Contact: Robert W. Welch Esq., Tr.
Application address: 18 Brown St., Salem, MA 01970-3830

Foundation type: Independent foundation
Purpose: Scholarships by nomination only to graduates of high schools in Salem, MA.
Financial data: Year ended 12/31/2012. Assets, $358,003 (M); Expenditures, $23,250; Total giving, $17,000; Grants to individuals, 10 grants totaling $15,250 (high: $2,250, low: $1,000).
Type of support: Support to graduates or students of specific schools; Awards/grants by nomination only; Undergraduate support.
Application information:
Deadline(s): June 1
Additional information: Applicants must be nominated by a high school principal.
EIN: 046016107

4319
Winter Course in Infectious Diseases, Inc.
c/o Beth Israel Deaconess
110 Francis St., Ste. GB
Boston, MA   02215-5563   (303) 407-3411
Application address: c/o Grant Downing Education, 600 Grant St., Ste. 510, Denver, CO 80203

Foundation type: Independent foundation
Purpose: Fellowships for advanced training in infectious diseases for postdoctoral fellows.

Scholarships to individuals to enable them to attend courses in infectious diseases.
Financial data: Year ended 12/31/2012. Assets, $247,142 (M); Expenditures, $184,440; Total giving, $43,500.
Fields of interest: Diseases (rare).
Type of support: Fellowships; Scholarships—to individuals; Postdoctoral support.
Application information: Contact the organization for additional guidelines.
EIN: 201285673

4320
Mr. & Mrs. L. Dexter Woodman Scholarship Fund Inc.
127R Main St.
Essex, MA 01929-0002 (978) 768-3636
URL: http://www.woodmans.com/scholarship/

Foundation type: Company-sponsored foundation
Purpose: Scholarships to graduating seniors from Manchester-Essex Regional High School, MA, or any senior who graduated from Essex Elementary School, MA.
Financial data: Year ended 06/30/2013. Assets, $513,606 (M); Expenditures, $75,833; Total giving, $26,750; Grants to individuals, 12 grants totaling $22,250 (high: $4,000, low: $500).
Type of support: Support to graduates or students of specific schools; Undergraduate support.
Application information: Applications accepted. Application form required.
  Deadline(s): Apr. 3
  Applicants should submit the following:
    1) Financial information
    2) Essay
    3) Letter(s) of recommendation
    4) Transcripts
EIN: 222925975

4321
Woods Hole Oceanographic Institution
266 Woods Hole Rd.
Woods Hole, MA 02543-1050 (508) 289-2252
Contact: Susan K. Avery, Ph.D.
E-mail: information@whoi.edu; URL: http://www.whoi.edu

Foundation type: Public charity
Purpose: Scholarships and fellowships for students enrolled in U.S. colleges and universities pursuing undergraduate, graduate or postdoctoral programs in oceanography.
Publications: Application guidelines; Newsletter.
Financial data: Year ended 12/31/2011. Assets, $497,650,905 (M); Expenditures, $226,559,293; Total giving, $9,549,957; Grants to individuals, totaling $9,549,957.
Fields of interest: Marine science.
Type of support: Fellowships; Research; Scholarships—to individuals.
Application information: Applications accepted.
  Deadline(s): Varies
  Additional information: See web site for additional guidelines.
Program descriptions:
  Guest Student Program: The institution offers an informal internship program in which a limited number of college undergraduates and advanced high-school students enrolled in the Cape Cod area are accepted as guest students at its laboratories on a year-round basis. Students will be placed on a limited based, depending on whether the student's interest and academic background coincide with available openings at the time the application is

received. Appointments are made for periods of up to one year.
  Marine Policy Fellowship Program: Fellowships are available to qualified individuals in the social sciences to apply their training and expertise to the economic, legal, and policy issues that arise from use of the world's oceans at the institution's Marine Policy Center. Fellowships are intended to provide support and experience to research fellows interested in marine policy issues, provide opportunities for interdisciplinary application of social sciences and natural sciences to marine policy problems, and conduct research and convey information necessary for the development of effective local, national, and international ocean policy. The field of economics, law, statistics, public policy, natural resources management, and international relations are preferred, but strong applications from other relevant fields are welcome.
  Ocean Science Journalism Fellowship Program: This program provides an intensive one-week program for science communicators interested in learning more about the interdisciplinary fields of oceanography and ocean engineering. Fellows gain access to new research findings and fundamental background information in engineering, marine biology, geology and geophysics, marine chemistry and geochemistry, and physical oceanography. Applications will be accepted from professional writers, producers, and editors working for print, broadcasting, radio, and internet media.
  Postdoctoral Fellowships: Postdoctoral fellowships are available to qualified individuals for research opportunities at the institution.
  Postdoctoral Scholar Program: Eighteen-month postdoctoral scholar awards of up to $55,000 each are offered annually to recipients of new or recent doctorates in the fields of chemistry, engineering, geology, geophysics, mathematics, meteorology, oceanography, physics, and biology. Awards are designed to further the education and training of the applicant, with primary emphasis placed on the individual's research promise. Eligible applicants must have received their doctoral degree within the past two to three years, and have a command of the English language.
  Summer Student Fellowship: These fellowships provide an opportunity to work on a project related to oceanography, in collaboration with their sponsors, that span a vast spectrum of topics and will provide meaningful results. Fellowships have the opportunity to work with institution researchers and graduate students, attend a series of talks and seminars, and participate in data collection and sampling methods with advanced oceanographic technology and instruments. Fellowships will be awarded to undergraduate students who have completed their junior or senior year at colleges or universities, and are studying in any field of science or engineering (including, but not limited to, biology, chemistry, engineering, geology, geophysics, mathematics, meteorology, physics, oceanography, and marine policy). Students must at least have a tentative interest in the ocean sciences, oceanographic engineering, mathematics, or marine policy; persons from under-represented groups (African-American/Black, Asian-American, Chicano/Mexican-American/Puerto Rican/other Hispanic, Native American, Alaska Native, and Native Hawaiian) are encouraged to apply for special consideration to the institution's Minority Fellowship program.
EIN: 042105850

4322
Worcester Community Action Council, Inc.
484 Main St., 2nd Fl.
Worcester, MA 01608-1893 (508) 754-1176
Contact: Jill C. Dagilis, Exec. Dir.
FAX: (508) 754-0203; E-mail: jdagilis@wcac.net; URL: http://www.wcac.net

Foundation type: Public charity
Purpose: Grants to low-income residents of the Worcester, MA area.
Financial data: Year ended 09/30/2011. Assets, $4,052,590 (M); Expenditures, $24,326,996; Total giving, $12,742,084; Grants to individuals, totaling $12,400,516.
Fields of interest: Economically disadvantaged.
Type of support: Grants for special needs.
Application information:
  Initial approach: Letter
  Additional information: Contact foundation for full eligibility requirements.
EIN: 042382160

4323
Greater Worcester Community Foundation, Inc.
370 Main St., Ste. 650
Worcester, MA 01608-1738 (508) 755-0980
Contact: For grants: Pam Kane, Sr. Prog. Off.; Donor Services: Kelly A. Stimson, Dir., Donor Svcs.; Ann T. Lisi, C.E.O.; For scholarships: Beckley W. Schowalter, Scholarship Coord.
FAX: (508) 755-3406;
E-mail: donorservices@greaterworcester.org;
URL: http://www.greaterworcester.org

Foundation type: Community foundation
Purpose: Scholarships to graduating high school seniors of Worcester County, MA for attendance at an accredited college or university.
Publications: Application guidelines; Annual report; Financial statement; Grants list; Newsletter.
Financial data: Year ended 12/31/2012. Assets, $124,690,268 (M); Expenditures, $7,684,053; Total giving, $5,320,132; Grants to individuals, 358 grants totaling $573,924.
Fields of interest: Higher education; Scholarships/financial aid.
Type of support: Scholarships—to individuals; Support to graduates or students of specific schools; Undergraduate support.
Application information: Applications accepted. Application form required. Application form available on the grantmaker's web site. Interview required.
  Initial approach: Application
  Send request by: Online
  Copies of proposal: 2
  Deadline(s): Mar. 10
  Final notification: Recipients notified in June
  Applicants should submit the following:
    1) SAT
    2) GPA
    3) Resume
    4) Essay
    5) Transcripts
    6) Letter(s) of recommendation
    7) Financial information
  Additional information: Contact your school's guidance office for application information. See web site for additional guidelines.
Program description:
  Scholarships: The foundation offers many scholarships for local students to attend college. Awards are made through an annual, competitive selection process that takes place from Mar.

through June. Each scholarship fund has special criteria established by donors. The qualifications of each applicant will be matched accordingly. The amount of money for each award varies, from $250 to $5,000, depending on the size of the fund and the criteria set by the donors. Many of the awards are renewable.
EIN: 042572276

4324
World Computer Exchange, Inc.
936 Nantasket Ave.
Hull, MA   02045-1453
Contact: Timothy Anderson, Pres.
E-mail: info@worldcomputerexchange.org;
URL: http://www.worldcomputerexchange.org/

Foundation type: Public charity
Purpose: Assistance with low-cost donated working, used computer for use in developing countries to connect poor youth to the internet.
Financial data: Year ended 06/30/2011. Assets, $720,754 (M); Expenditures, $115,521; Total giving, $191. In-kind gifts amount not specified.
Fields of interest: Education.
Type of support: In-kind gifts.
Application information: Applications not accepted.
> *Additional information:* See web site for additional information on donated computers in the developing countries.
Program description:
> *Empowering Girls Education:* Schools are equipped with computers and teachers are trained how to use the internet to improve learning via experimental, interactive, multi-country projects delivers real and sustainable results. Working together with schools, libraries, and Partner organizations ensures that girls have access to the opportunities, skills and understanding of the internet. The potential of giving access to computers and internet technologies to engage and motivate, especially when tied to education, is limitless. Children can learn new skills, teachers can design new and previously unimaginable curricula and the broader community has a resource for their socioeconomic development.
EIN: 043529016

4325
Wurtman Ner David Foundation, Inc.
(formerly Wurtman Foundation)
c/o Robert Finkel
60 Wallnut St., 4th Fl.
Wellesley, MA   02481
URL: http://www.rikma.org.il/foundation.php

Foundation type: Operating foundation
Purpose: Fellowships for rabbinical students and other community leaders-in-training for study in Israel and the U.S.
Financial data: Year ended 06/30/2012. Assets, $9,635 (M); Expenditures, $2,673; Total giving, $0.
Fields of interest: Jewish agencies & synagogues.
Type of support: Fellowships.
Application information: Applications accepted. Application form required.
> *Send request by:* Mail
> *Applicants should submit the following:*
> 1) Curriculum vitae
> 2) Essay
> 3) Photograph
EIN: 650881769

4326
Xeric Foundation
351 Pleasant St.
PMB 214
Northampton, MA   01060-3900   (413) 585-0671
E-mail: xericgrant@aol.com; URL: http://www.xericfoundation.org/

Foundation type: Independent foundation
Purpose: Financial assistance to self-publishing comic book creators in the U.S. and Canada.
Financial data: Year ended 09/30/2013. Assets, $3,712,994 (M); Expenditures, $192,350; Total giving, $151,561; Grants to individuals, 13 grants totaling $47,702 (high: $6,985, low: $857).
Fields of interest: Drawing.
Type of support: Publication; Grants for special needs.
Application information: Application form required. Application form available on the grantmaker's web site.
> *Initial approach:* Letter
> *Copies of proposal:* 6
> *Deadline(s):* Jan. 31 and July 31
> *Applicants should submit the following:*
> 1) Work samples
> 2) Resume
> 3) Proposal
> 4) Financial information
> *Additional information:* Applicant must be a citizen or permanent resident currently living in either country.
EIN: 223149258

4327
The Yard, Inc.
P.O. Box 405
Chilmark, MA   02535-0405   (508) 645-9662
Contact: David R. White, Exec. Dir.
FAX: (508) 645-9677;
E-mail: info@dancetheyard.org; E-mail For David R. White: drw@dancetheyard.org; URL: http://www.dancetheyard.org

Foundation type: Public charity
Purpose: Residencies to choreographers and dancers specializing in contemporary dance.
Publications: Application guidelines.
Financial data: Year ended 09/30/2012. Assets, $2,173,128 (M); Expenditures, $472,680.
Fields of interest: Dance; Choreography.
Type of support: Residencies; Stipends.
Application information: Application form required.
> *Initial approach:* Letter or e-mail
> *Deadline(s):* Oct. 31
> *Applicants should submit the following:*
> 1) Photograph
> 2) SASE
> 3) Resume
> 4) Letter(s) of recommendation
> *Additional information:* Application should also include $20 application fee, and VHS tape of recent work.
Program description:
> *Residencies:* The organization offers two four-week residences that provide dance artists with housing, work space, stipends, technical and administrative support, artistic mentoring, concert performances of new work, and the time and freedom to explore their craft without interruption or outside obligation. Two residencies are available under this program. The Professional Dance Company Residency is open to established and emerging companies that have been working together professionally for a minimum of three years; artists of color are especially encouraged to

apply. The Bessie Schonberg Individual Choreographers' Residency allows four independent choreographers and eight dancers to nurture their talent and creativity at the organization's headquarters in Martha's Vineyard.
EIN: 237348937

4328
Alden N. Young Trust
1500 Worcester Rd., Ste. F
Framingham, MA   01702-8984   (603) 552-3373
Contact: Nancy S. Smith, Tr.
Application address: 2676 Wakefield Rd., Wakefield, NH 03872, tel.: (603) 522-3373

Foundation type: Independent foundation
Purpose: Scholarships to residents of Wakefield, NH, pursuing higher education.
Financial data: Year ended 12/31/2012. Assets, $2,437,755 (M); Expenditures, $249,499; Total giving, $225,000; Grants to individuals, 27 grants totaling $121,332 (high: $8,000, low: $150).
Fields of interest: Higher education.
Type of support: Undergraduate support.
Application information: Applications accepted. Application form required.
> *Deadline(s):* None
> *Additional information:* Application forms available at local high schools, libraries and Rev. Dr. Smith.
EIN: 026117755

4329
Youth Opportunities Upheld, Inc.
81 Plantation St.
Worcester, MA   01604-3069   (508) 849-5600
Contact: Maurice Boisvert M.A., C.E.O. and Pres.
FAX: (508) 849-5617;
E-mail: boisvertm@youinc.org; URL: http://www.youinc.org

Foundation type: Public charity
Purpose: Foster care stipends to parents and emergency assistance primarily to residents of central MA.
Publications: Annual report; Financial statement; Newsletter.
Financial data: Year ended 06/30/2011. Assets, $15,841,146 (M); Expenditures, $30,848,961.
Fields of interest: Foster care; Economically disadvantaged.
Type of support: Grants for special needs; Stipends.
Application information:
> *Initial approach:* Letter
EIN: 237112665

4330
Angela M. Zampogna Scholarship Fund
c/o Enterprise Bank
222 Merrimack St.
Lowell, MA   01852   (978) 632-8558
Contact: Raymond F. LaFond, Tr.
Application address: 333 Betty Spring Rd., Gardner, MA 01440-2411, tel.: (978) 632-8558

Foundation type: Independent foundation
Purpose: Scholarships to graduates of Gardner High School, MA for postsecondary education.
Financial data: Year ended 12/31/2012. Assets, $488,285 (M); Expenditures, $34,374; Total giving, $27,000; Grants to individuals, 54 grants totaling $27,000 (high: $500, low: $500).
Fields of interest: Higher education.

Type of support: Support to graduates or students of specific schools; Undergraduate support.
Application information: Application form required.
Deadline(s): Varies

Additional information: Application should include transcript.
EIN: 223193009

MICHIGAN

4331
Frances H. Abbott Memorial Foundation
P.O. Box 3636
Grand Rapids, MI   49501-3636
Application address: c/o Riverside-Brookfield High School, Attn.: Beth Augustine, 160 Ridgewood Rd., Riverside, IL 60546, tel.: (708) 442-7500

Foundation type: Independent foundation
Purpose: Scholarships for graduating seniors from Riverside-Brookfield High School, IL.
Financial data: Year ended 12/31/2011. Assets, $0 (M); Expenditures, $12,582; Total giving, $7,000; Grants to individuals, 2 grants totaling $7,000 (high: $3,500, low: $3,500).
Type of support: Support to graduates or students of specific schools; Undergraduate support.
Application information: Applications accepted.
> *Deadline(s):* First Tues. in May

EIN: 366672535

4332
ACI Foundation
(formerly Concrete Research & Education Foundation, also known as American Concrete Institute Foundation)
38800 Country Club Dr.
Farmington Hills, MI   48333   (248) 848-3778
FAX: (248) 848-3701;
E-mail: scholarships@concrete.org; URL: http://www.concrete.org/

Foundation type: Public charity
Purpose: Fellowships and graduate scholarships to students who are pursuing a course of study in the concrete field.
Financial data: Year ended 12/31/2011. Assets, $4,382,033 (M); Expenditures, $416,665; Total giving, $96,503; Grants to individuals, totaling $83,503.
Fields of interest: Engineering school/education; Business/industry.
Type of support: Fellowships; Graduate support.
Application information: Applications accepted.
> *Deadline(s):* Oct. 7
> *Additional information:* See web site for additional guidelines.

Program descriptions:
> *ACI Scholarship Program:* The foundation provides $3,000 scholarships for graduate study in the field of concrete. The awards include the ACI-W. R. Grace Scholarship, V. Mohan Malhotra Scholarship, Kumar Mehta Scholarship, Katharine and Bryant Mather Scholarship, ACI Bertold E. Weinberg Scholarship, and ACI Scholarship.
> *ACI Student Fellowship Program:* The purpose of the program is to identify, attract, and develop outstanding professionals for productive careers in the concrete field. This fellowship is offered to high-potential undergraduate and graduate students in engineering, construction management, and other appropriate curricula who are identified by the ACI-Member Faculty. The fellowship can have a nominal term of up to two academic years, renewed annually, and may extend through graduate study. Annual renewal will be subject to renomination and reapplication. These awards are granted based on the availability of contributions received. ACI will also award an additional ACI Student Fellowship named the Charles Pankow Foundation ACI Student Fellowship. Awardees are required to, as a

condition of acceptance, agree to, and serve, at least one internship period (ten to twelve weeks) working in a construction environment with challenging assignments. This internship is to be served the summer before the academic award year.

EIN: 382986800

4333
Allegan County Community Foundation
(formerly Allegan County Foundation)
524 Marshall St.
Allegan, MI   49010-1632   (269) 673-8344
Contact: Theresa Bray, Exec. Dir.
FAX: (269) 673-8745;
E-mail: info@alleganfoundation.org; Additional e-mail: theresa@gmail.com; URL: http://www.alleganfoundation.org

Foundation type: Community foundation
Purpose: Scholarships to students of Allegan County, MI.
Publications: Annual report; Financial statement; Grants list.
Financial data: Year ended 12/31/2012. Assets, $15,449,871 (M); Expenditures, $789,365; Total giving, $486,176.
Type of support: Scholarships—to individuals; Undergraduate support.
Application information: Application form required. Application form available on the grantmaker's web site.
> *Initial approach:* Letter or e-mail
> *Send request by:* Mail
> *Deadline(s):* Varies
> *Applicants should submit the following:*
> 1) Transcripts
> 2) Letter(s) of recommendation
> 3) GPA
> 4) Essay

EIN: 386189947

4334
Allegan County Resource Development Committee, Inc.
323 Water St.
Allegan, MI   49010-1325   (269) 673-5472
FAX: (269) 673-3795;
E-mail: cfarnsworth@acrdc.org; URL: http://www.acrdc.org

Foundation type: Public charity
Purpose: Emergency assistance to families of Allegan county, MI, with food, clothing, education, shelter, rent, and utilities.
Financial data: Year ended 09/30/2011. Assets, $639,547 (M); Expenditures, $5,860,584; Total giving, $1,567,982; Grants to individuals, totaling $1,567,982.
Fields of interest: Human services; Economically disadvantaged.
Type of support: Emergency funds; In-kind gifts.
Application information: Applications accepted.
> *Additional information:* Application is required for some assistance. Contact the agency for eligibility determination.

EIN: 381790220

4335
Allen Scholarship Trust
P.O. Box 3636
Grand Rapids, MI   49501-3636   (800) 795-4115

Foundation type: Independent foundation

Purpose: Scholarships to residents of Lake County, IN who are college bound or already in college.
Financial data: Year ended 12/31/2012. Assets, $525,119 (M); Expenditures, $32,092; Total giving, $25,000; Grants to individuals, 25 grants totaling $25,000 (high: $1,000, low: $1,000).
Type of support: Scholarships—to individuals; Undergraduate support.
Application information: Applications accepted. Application form required.
> *Initial approach:* Letter
> *Deadline(s):* Mar. 15
> *Additional information:* Applicants must show high scholastic achievement, good citizenship and character.

EIN: 266010234

4336
Alliance for Gifted Children
2200 Fuller Ct., Ste. 1101B
Ann Arbor, MI   48105-2381   (734) 995-0999
Contact: David Klimek Ph.D., Pres.

Foundation type: Independent foundation
Purpose: Financial assistance for psychological therapy for children, including parent and teacher consultations, in Ann Arbor, MI only.
Financial data: Year ended 12/31/2011. Assets, $1 (M); Expenditures, $31,222; Total giving, $0.
Fields of interest: Mental health, counseling/support groups.
Type of support: Grants to individuals.
Application information: Applications not accepted.
> *Additional information:* Unsolicited requests for funds not considered or acknowledged.

EIN: 383555369

4337
The Amy Foundation
P.O. Box 16091
Lansing, MI   48901-6091   (517) 323-6233
E-mail: amyfoundtn@aol.com; URL: http://www.amyfound.org/

Foundation type: Independent foundation
Purpose: Awards to authors of published articles on biblical interpretations of topical social issues.
Publications: Informational brochure; Newsletter.
Financial data: Year ended 12/31/2012. Assets, $64,139 (M); Expenditures, $155,565; Total giving, $36,400; Grants to individuals, 16 grants totaling $36,400 (high: $10,000, low: $1,000).
Fields of interest: Literature; Religion.
Type of support: Awards/prizes.
Application information:
> *Final notification:* Applicants notified May 1
> *Additional information:* The foundation contributes only to preselected individuals. Unsolicited requests for funds not considered or acknowledged.

Program description:
> *Amy Writing Awards:* The award recognizes creative, skillful writing that presents in a sensitive, thought-provoking manner the biblical position on issues affecting the world today. To be eligible, articles must be published in a secular publication. The author should present biblical truth as quoted from an accepted and popular edition of the Bible such as the New International Version, The Living Bible, the King James, or the Revised Standard Version. The article should deal with the Bible's position on current and provocative issues such as divorce, moral values, family, abortion, and addiction to drugs and alcohol. In addition to content, articles will be judged on their persuasive

power, the author's skill in relating the Bible to contemporary issues, and the author's sensitivity in relating the biblical position to the search for the meaning of life.
EIN: 237044543

4338
Ann Arbor Area Community Foundation
(formerly Ann Arbor Area Foundation)
301 N. Main St., Ste. 300
Ann Arbor, MI 48104-1296 (734) 663-0401
Contact: For grants: Jillian Rosen, Prog. Off.
FAX: (734) 663-3514; E-mail: info@aaacf.org;
URL: http://www.aaacf.org

Foundation type: Community foundation
Purpose: Scholarships to residents of the Washtenaw County, MI, area for higher education.
Publications: Application guidelines; Annual report (including application guidelines); Newsletter; Program policy statement.
Financial data: Year ended 12/31/2011. Assets, $57,032,280 (M); Expenditures, $3,524,685; Total giving, $2,306,043. Scholarships—to individuals amount not specified.
Fields of interest: Music; Higher education; Athletics/sports, training; Women.
Type of support: Employee-related scholarships; Scholarships—to individuals; Undergraduate support; Camperships.
Application information: Applications accepted. Application form required. Application form available on the grantmaker's web site.
   Initial approach: E-mail
   Send request by: On-line
   Deadline(s): Apr. 1
   Applicants should submit the following:
      1) GPA
      2) Letter(s) of recommendation
      3) Transcripts
   Additional information: See web site for a complete listing of scholarship funds and applications, eligibility criteria and required materials.
Program description:
   Scholarship Funds: The foundation manages 44 scholarship funds for area students to attend an accredited college or university. Each scholarship has its own list of criteria and application requirements. See web site for additional information.
EIN: 386087967

4339
Ann Arbor Film Festival
217 N. First St.
Ann Arbor, MI 48104-2432 (734) 995-5356
FAX: (734) 995-5396; E-mail: info@aafilmfest.org;
Application address: P.O. Box 8232, Ann Arbor, MI 48107-8232; URL: http://aafilmfest.org

Foundation type: Public charity
Purpose: Awards to winners of the Ann Arbor Film Festival, held in MI.
Publications: Informational brochure (including application guidelines); Newsletter.
Financial data: Year ended 05/31/2012. Assets, $168,405 (M); Expenditures, $421,804; Total giving, $17,828; Grants to individuals, totaling $17,828.
Fields of interest: Film/video.
Type of support: Awards/prizes.
Application information: Applications accepted. Application form required. Application form available on the grantmaker's web site.

Initial approach: E-mail
Deadline(s): Nov. 15
Additional information: Application should include application fee and synopsis.
Program descriptions:
   Between The Lines Award Best Gay/Lesbian Film: This $500 award honors the film that best deals with gay/lesbian issues.
   Chris Frayne Award Best Animated Film: This $1,000 award is given for the best animated film in the festival in memory of Chris Frayne, a key participant in the festival's early years, whose spirit and approach was reminiscent of his cartoon characters.
   Doug Wandrei Award Best Lighting Design: This $500 award recognizes the most creative use of lighting in a film in which mood and atmosphere of the environment are greatly enhanced through lighting design.
   Griot Editorial Best Editing Award: This $500 award is given to a film entry that demonstrates outstanding creativity and technical excellence in the art of motion picture editing.
   Gus Van Sant Best Experimental Film Award: This $1,000 award goes to the film that best represents the use of experimental processes, forms, and topics.
   Isabella Liddell Art Award: This award of $400 is given to the film(s) that best deal(s) with women's issues.
   Kodak/Film Craft Lab Award for Best Cinematography: This award is for the film that demonstrates the highest excellence and creativity in cinematography. Award is for $1,500 worth of 16mm or 35mm film stock donated by Kodak, with the processing donated by Film Craft Lab.
   Lawrence Kasdan Award Best Narrative Film: This $1,000 award is given to recognize works which make use of the film medium's unique ability to convey striking and original stories.
   Marvin Felheim Award Special Jury Prize: This $500 prize is awarded to a work of film art that extends the range of subject matter traditionally dealt with in the film medium, while at the same time transcending standard genre categorization.
   Michael Moore Award Best Documentary Film: This $1,000 award is given for the best documentary film in the festival.
   Michigan Vue Magazine Award Best Michigan Filmmaker: This award of $500 is given to support and encourage the local filmmaking community by rewarding excellence in a Michigan-produced film within any genre.
   Peter Wilde Award Most Technically Innovative Film: This award of $500 goes to the film that most respects the integrity of the projected image and celebrates the indelible beauty of metallic silver-based images.
   Prix DeVarti Funniest Film: Awards $1,000 to the funniest film in the festival in memory of Dominick and Alice DeVarti.
   The EMPA Work Life Award (Employee Motivation Performance Assessment): This award of $1,200 goes to the film that best addresses issues that pertain to careers, the workplace, job hunting, employment, co-workers, job responsibilities, or the impact of employment on the individual's personal life.
   The Ken Burns Best of the Festival Award: This top award of $3,000 recognizes the filmmaker with the most outstanding entry award, and the film that best represents the artistic and creative standards of the festival.
   Tio's Red Hot & Spicy Award: This $500 award is awarded to any film considered "red hot and spicy" based on form, flavor, or content.
   Tom Berman Most Promising Filmmaker Award: This award of $1,000 supports a young filmmaker

that the Awards Jury expects will make a significant contribution to the art of film in the course of his/her filmmaking career.
   Vicki Honeyman Award for Best 16mm Film: This $500 award is intended for the 16mm film that are technically challenging, innovative, quirky, and unique, and that demonstrates a strong respect and passion for film as an art form.
EIN: 382379836

4340
Arts Council of Greater Kalamazoo
359 S. Kalamazoo Mall, Ste. 203
Kalamazoo, MI 49007-4842 (269) 342-5059
FAX: (269) 342-6531;
E-mail: info@kalamazooarts.org; Additional tel. (re-granting programs): (269) 342-5059;
URL: http://www.kalamazooarts.org

Foundation type: Public charity
Purpose: Grants to local artists in Kalamazoo County, MI, for innovative projects.
Publications: Application guidelines; Grants list; Informational brochure; Informational brochure (including application guidelines); Program policy statement (including application guidelines).
Financial data: Year ended 09/30/2011. Assets, $288,677 (M); Expenditures, $922,982; Total giving, $365,415; Grants to individuals, totaling $52,550.
Fields of interest: Arts, artist's services; Arts; Aging; Disabilities, people with; Minorities; Native Americans/American Indians; Economically disadvantaged.
Type of support: Program development.
Application information: Applications not accepted.
   Additional information: Contact council for current application deadline/guidelines. Unsolicited requests for funds not considered or acknowledged.
Program description:
   Arts Fund of Kalamazoo County: This program awards approximately $60,000 annually to promote the continuing high standards of artistic achievement in the Kalamazoo community. The program functions on three levels: for program support for Kalamazoo County arts organizations with budgets over $300,000 to develop special art programs involving persons from rural, ethnic, minority, or tribal traditions; for operational support for Kalamazoo County arts organizations with annual operating budgets under $300,000; and for independent creation of new work or completion of work in progress, internship with an established artist or organization, or arts career development for individual artists residing in Kalamazoo County who may apply for up to $2,000.
EIN: 386121183

4341
Avondale Foundation
2940 Waukegan St.
Auburn Hills, MI 48326-3264 (248) 537-6041
Contact: Tom DelPup, Pres.
E-mail: avondalefoundation@avondale.k12.mi.us;
E-Mail for Tom DelPup: tjdelpup@ameritech.net;
URL: http://www.avondalefoundation.org/

Foundation type: Public charity
Purpose: Awards and grants to students and teachers in the Avondale School District, MI.
Publications: Application guidelines.
Financial data: Year ended 06/30/2012. Assets, $69,521 (M); Expenditures, $56,565; Total giving, $52,293.

Fields of interest: Higher education.
Type of support: Scholarships—to individuals; Awards/prizes.
Application information: Applications accepted. Application form required.
  Additional information: Contact the Avondale School District for additional application information.
EIN: 383039178

4342
The Howard Baker Foundation
c/o Paul J. Gambka, C.P.A.
2817 S. Milford Rd., No. 100
Highland, MI 48357-4900
Scholarship application address: Office of Scholarship and Financial Aid, Wayne State University, Welcome Center, 42 W. Warren, 3rd Fl., Detroit, MI 48202, tel.: (313) 577-3378

Foundation type: Independent foundation
Purpose: Scholarships to City of Detroit residents in financing their education at Wayne State University, majoring in nursing or in natural science.
Publications: Financial statement.
Financial data: Year ended 09/30/2012. Assets, $481,768 (M); Expenditures, $294,907; Total giving, $123,366.
Fields of interest: Nursing school/education; Science; Minorities.
Type of support: Grants to individuals; Scholarships—to individuals; Graduate support; Undergraduate support; Grants for special needs; Camperships; Project support.
Application information: Applications accepted. Interview required.
  Initial approach: Letter
  Send request by: Mail
  Copies of proposal: 1
  Deadline(s): None
  Applicants should submit the following:
    1) Pell Grant
    2) Proposal
    3) Letter(s) of recommendation
    4) GPA
    5) ACT
  Additional information: Applicant must demonstrate financial need.
EIN: 383083465

4343
John Ball Zoological Society
1300 W. Fulton St.
P.O. Box 2506
Grand Rapids, MI 49504-6100 (616) 336-4301
Contact: Brenda Stringer, Exec. Dir.
E-mail: info@johnballzoosociety.org; Email for Brenda Stringer: bstringer@johnballzoosociety.org; tel. for Brenda Stringer: (616) 336-4303;
URL: http://www.johnballzoosociety.org

Foundation type: Public charity
Purpose: Grants for wild animal preservation and conservation projects world-wide.
Publications: Application guidelines.
Financial data: Year ended 12/31/2011. Assets, $13,187,879 (M); Expenditures, $1,721,232; Total giving, $71,593; Grants to individuals, 9 grants totaling $15,619. Subtotal for grants to individuals: 9 grants totaling $15,619.
Fields of interest: Research; Animals/wildlife.
Type of support: Research.
Application information: Applications accepted. Application form required. Application form available on the grantmaker's web site.

Initial approach: Application
Deadline(s): Mar. 4 for Wildlife Conservation Fund
Applicants should submit the following:
  1) Letter(s) of recommendation
  2) Curriculum vitae
Program description:
  Wildlife Conservation Grants: Grants, generally ranging from $500 to $2,500, will be awarded to conservation-based efforts around the world that promote the understanding and endangerment of rare, threatened, and endangered animals and their habitats, and that support zoological research that will directly benefit captive animal management. Grants will be awarded that: enhance and/or assist wild animal preservation (both native and exotic, and threatened and endangered) and their habitat management; enhance and/or improve captive animal management, including environmental design; and assist in the development of education programming.
EIN: 386076879

4344
Baraga County Community Foundation
100 Hemlock St.
P. O. Box 338
Baraga, MI 49908 (906) 353-7898
Contact: Gordette Luetz, Exec. Dir.
FAX: (906) 353-7896; E-mail: baragacf@up.net;
URL: http://www.baragacountyfoundation.org/

Foundation type: Community foundation
Purpose: Scholarships to Baraga County, MI high school students for higher education at accredited colleges or universities.
Financial data: Year ended 12/31/2011. Assets, $855,853 (M); Expenditures, $66,598; Total giving, $2,150; Grants to individuals, totaling $2,150.
Fields of interest: Higher education.
Type of support: Scholarships—to individuals.
Application information: Applications accepted. Application form required.
  Initial approach: Application
  Send request by: Mail
  Additional information: Application should include transcripts. See web site for additional information. Scholarship applications are available at Baraga County area schools guidance counselor offices and students are also notified of scholarship availability through the local area schools.
EIN: 383198122

4345
Baraga-Houghton-Keweenaw Community Action Agency, Inc.
926 Dodge St.
Houghton, MI 49931-1944 (906) 482-5528
Contact: Jean M. Laberge, Exe. Dir.
FAX: (906) 482-5512

Foundation type: Public charity
Purpose: Emergency assistance for utility, transportation, food and shelter for residents of Baraga, Houghton, and Keweenaw counties, MI.
Financial data: Year ended 09/30/2011. Assets, $473,229 (M); Expenditures, $3,571,826.
Fields of interest: Human services, emergency aid.
Type of support: Emergency funds.
Application information:
  Initial approach: Telephone
  Additional information: Contact agency for eligibility requirements.
EIN: 381800879

4346
Shelley & Terry Barr Foundation
29600 Northwestern Hwy., Ste. 102
Southfield, MI 48034-1016

Foundation type: Independent foundation
Purpose: Scholarships only to graduates of Grand Rapids Central High School, MI, and Rogers High School, Wyoming, MI.
Financial data: Year ended 12/31/2010. Assets, $12,095 (M); Expenditures, $35,829; Total giving, $35,000; Grants to individuals, totaling $35,000.
Type of support: Support to graduates or students of specific schools; Undergraduate support.
Application information: Contact foundation for current application guidelines.
EIN: 382258156

4347
Barry Community Foundation
231 S. Broadway
Hastings, MI 49058-1835 (269) 945-0526
Contact: Bonnie Hildreth, Pres.
FAX: (269) 945-0826; E-mail: info@barrycf.org;
URL: http://www.barrycf.org

Foundation type: Community foundation
Purpose: Scholarships to students in Barry County, MI to attend college, graduate school, vocational or technical school.
Publications: Application guidelines; Annual report; Informational brochure; Newsletter.
Financial data: Year ended 06/30/2012. Assets, $18,490,625 (M); Expenditures, $1,226,924; Total giving, $729,433; Grants to individuals, 55 grants totaling $106,900.
Fields of interest: Vocational education, post-secondary; Higher education.
Type of support: Scholarships—to individuals; Graduate support; Undergraduate support.
Application information: Applications accepted. Application form available on the grantmaker's web site.
  Send request by: On-line
  Deadline(s): Mar. 15
  Additional information: See web site for additional application guidelines. All applicants must use the foundation's Scholarship eGRANT application system. School districts include,Thomapple Kellogg, Lake Odessa, Hastings Area, Maple Valley, Delton Kellogg, and Home School Barry County Christian.
EIN: 383246131

4348
Basilica of St. Adalbert Foundation
654 Davis Ave. N.W.
Grand Rapids, MI 49504-5104
Contact: R. Louis Stasker, Pres.

Foundation type: Independent foundation
Purpose: Scholarships to student parishioners of St. Adalbert's Basilica, Grand Rapids, MI, for attendance at Catholic elementary schools or Catholic high schools.
Financial data: Year ended 06/30/2013. Assets, $427,884 (M); Expenditures, $37,891; Total giving, $37,746; Grants to individuals, 9 grants totaling $19,660 (high: $2,800, low: $1,000).
Fields of interest: Catholic agencies & churches.
Type of support: Precollege support.
Application information: Applications accepted.
  Initial approach: Letter

Additional information: Contact foundation for complete application guidelines.
EIN: 382685451

4349
Battle Creek Community Foundation
(formerly Greater Battle Creek Foundation)
1 Riverwalk Ctr.
34 W. Jackson St.
Battle Creek, MI   49017-3505   (269) 962-2181
Contact: Brenda L. Hunt, C.E.O.
FAX: (269) 962-2182;
E-mail: bccf@bccfoundation.org; URL: http://www.bccfoundation.org/

Foundation type: Community foundation
Purpose: Scholarships to residents of the greater Battle Creek, MI, area, for attendance at colleges and universities in the U.S.
Publications: Application guidelines; Annual report; Biennial report (including application guidelines); Financial statement; Grants list; Informational brochure; Newsletter; Program policy statement.
Financial data: Year ended 03/31/2013. Assets, $105,736,262 (M); Expenditures, $11,000,947; Total giving, $8,528,657. Scholarships—to individuals amount not specified.
Fields of interest: Higher education; Scholarships/financial aid.
Type of support: Scholarships—to individuals; Support to graduates or students of specific schools; Undergraduate support.
Application information: Applications accepted. Application form required. Application form available on the grantmaker's web site.
Initial approach: Application
Send request by: Online
Deadline(s): Apr. 1
Applicants should submit the following:
1) SAT
2) Photograph
3) Transcripts
4) Letter(s) of recommendation
5) GPA
6) Financial information
7) Essay
8) ACT
Additional information: See web site for a complete list of programs.
Program description:
Scholarships: The foundation has over 70 scholarships available for Battle Creek area residents seeking postsecondary education. Eligibility for each scholarship is based on several criteria, including high school, GPA, area of study and/or the educational institution you plan to attend. Each scholarship has its own unique criteria. See web site for additional information.
EIN: 382045459

4350
Bay Area Community Foundation
Pere Marquette Depot
1000 Adams St., Ste. 200
Bay City, MI   48708-5994   (989) 893-4438
Contact: Eileen A. Curtis, C.E.O. and Pres.
FAX: (989) 893-4448;
E-mail: bacfnd@bayfoundation.org; URL: http://www.bayfoundation.org

Foundation type: Community foundation
Purpose: Scholarships to residents and graduates of high schools in Bay County, MI.
Publications: Annual report; Financial statement; Grants list; Informational brochure; Newsletter.

Financial data: Year ended 12/31/2012. Assets, $41,282,876 (M); Expenditures, $2,742,059; Total giving, $1,376,361; Grants to individuals, 389 grants totaling $496,359.
Fields of interest: Print publishing; Performing arts; History/archaeology; Business school/education; Medical school/education; Nursing school/education; Students, sororities/fraternities; Physical therapy; Home economics; Recreation; Race/intergroup relations; Science; Economics; Native Americans/American Indians; Men.
Type of support: Employee-related scholarships; Graduate support; Technical education support; Undergraduate support.
Application information: Applications accepted. Application form available on the grantmaker's web site.
Deadline(s): First Mon. in Mar.
Applicants should submit the following:
1) Essay
2) Letter(s) of recommendation
3) FAFSA
Additional information: See web site for program descriptions.
EIN: 382418086

4351
The Bay Harbor Foundation
750 Bay Harbor Dr.
Bay Harbor, MI   49770-8056   (231) 439-2700
Contact: Candace Fitzsimons, Exec. Dir.
FAX: (231) 439-2701;
E-mail: info@bayharborfoundation.org; URL: http://www.bayharborfoundation.org

Foundation type: Community foundation
Purpose: Scholarships to students of Bay Harbor, MI enrolled full-time in either a two or four year university or college and are employees of a Bay Harbor, MI business or children/grandchildren of an employee.
Publications: Application guidelines; Grants list.
Financial data: Year ended 12/31/2012. Assets, $325,674 (M); Expenditures, $295,578; Total giving, $137,373; Grants to individuals, 30 grants totaling $61,000.
Fields of interest: Higher education.
Type of support: Scholarships—to individuals.
Application information: Applications accepted. Application form required. Application form available on the grantmaker's web site.
Initial approach: Application
Send request by: Mail
Copies of proposal: 5
Deadline(s): July 16
Final notification: Recipients notified in Aug.
Applicants should submit the following:
1) Financial information
2) Photograph
3) FAFSA
4) Transcripts
5) Letter(s) of recommendation
6) Essay
Additional information: Awards are a minimum of $2000, with $4000 being the maximum amount. Funds are paid directly to the educational institution on behalf of the students. See web site for additional application information.
EIN: 371491024

4352
William Beaumont Hospital
16500 W. Twelve Mile Rd.
Southfield, MI   48076-2975   (248) 423-2459
Contact: Gene Michalski, Pres. and C.E.O.
URL: http://www.beaumonthospitals.com

Foundation type: Public charity
Purpose: Stipends for students pursuing a career in the medical field.
Financial data: Year ended 12/31/2011. Assets, $2,704,700,180 (M); Expenditures, $2,122,063,387; Total giving, $23,733,390; Grants to individuals, 429 grants totaling $23,589,819.
Fields of interest: Medical school/education.
Type of support: Stipends.
Application information: Applications accepted.
Additional information: Contact the organization for additional guidelines.
EIN: 381459362

4353
Bedford Community Foundation
(formerly Bedford Foundation)
7276 Jackman Rd., Ste. C
Temperance, MI   48182   (734) 854-1722
Contact: Walt Wilburn, Pres.
E-mail: info@bedfordcommunityfoundation.com;
Mailing Address: P. O. Box 54, Lambertville, MI 48144; URL: http://www.bedfordcommunityfoundation.com

Foundation type: Community foundation
Purpose: Awards scholarships to Bedford Township and surrounding area high school students for higher education.
Financial data: Year ended 03/31/2012. Assets, $888,201 (M); Expenditures, $103,036; Total giving, $63,897; Grants to individuals, 33 grants totaling $16,700.
Fields of interest: Higher education.
Type of support: Scholarships—to individuals; Undergraduate support.
Application information: Applications accepted. Application form required. Application form available on the grantmaker's web site.
Initial approach: Application
Send request by: Mail
Deadline(s): Apr. 4
Applicants should submit the following:
1) Essay
2) Letter(s) of recommendation
3) SAT
4) ACT
5) Transcripts
Additional information: Application should also include a copy of acceptance letter. See web site for additional guidelines.
EIN: 383544941

4354
John & Nesbeth Bees Scholarship Foundation
328 S. Saginaw St., M/C 002072
Flint, MI   48502-1923   (989) 776-7368
Contact: Helen James
Application address: c/o Citizens Bank, N.A. Attn.: Helen James, Wealth Mgmt., 101 N. Washington Ave., Saginaw, MI 48607-1207, tel.: (989) 776-7368

Foundation type: Independent foundation
Purpose: Scholarships to residents of Saginaw County, MI.

Financial data: Year ended 12/31/2012. Assets, $623,559 (M); Expenditures, $33,094; Total giving, $20,000; Grants to individuals, 20 grants totaling $20,000 (high: $1,000, low: $1,000).
Type of support: Scholarships—to individuals.
Application information: Applications accepted. Application form required.
Deadline(s): May 1
EIN: 386601371

4355
Don & Iva M. Bellinger Scholarship Fund
328 S. Saginaw St., M/C 001065
Flint, MI   48502   (989) 776-7368
Contact: Helen James
Application address: 101 N. Washington Ave., Saginaw, MI 48607, tel.: (989) 776-7368

Foundation type: Independent foundation
Purpose: Scholarships to students attending the nursing program at Saginaw Valley State University, MI.
Financial data: Year ended 12/31/2012. Assets, $1,114,576 (M); Expenditures, $60,879; Total giving, $41,000; Grants to individuals, 41 grants totaling $41,000 (high: $1,500, low: $500).
Fields of interest: Nursing school/education.
Type of support: Scholarships—to individuals; Support to graduates or students of specific schools.
Application information: Applications accepted. Application form required.
Deadline(s): Jan. 31
EIN: 386615679

4356
Samuel L. Bemis Scholarship Fund
P.O. Box 3636
Grand Rapids, MI   49501-3636   (802) 257-0356

Foundation type: Independent foundation
Purpose: Scholarships to female graduating seniors at Brattleboro Union High School, VT.
Financial data: Year ended 12/31/2011. Assets, $1,176,584 (M); Expenditures, $68,239; Total giving, $51,572.
Fields of interest: Women.
Type of support: Support to graduates or students of specific schools; Undergraduate support.
Application information: Applications accepted. Application form required.
Initial approach: Letter or telephone
Deadline(s): May 10
Additional information: Contact fund for current application guidelines.
EIN: 367112890

4357
Berrien Community Foundation, Inc.
2900 S. State St., Ste. 2E
Saint Joseph, MI   49085-2467   (269) 983-3304
Contact: Lisa Cripps-Downey, Pres.
FAX: (269) 983-4939;
E-mail: bcf@BerrienCommunity.org; Additional e-mail: bcf@BerrienCommunity.org; URL: http://www.BerrienCommunity.org

Foundation type: Community foundation
Purpose: Scholarships to Berrien County, MI, students who intend to pursue a higher education.
Publications: Financial statement; Informational brochure (including application guidelines); Occasional report.
Financial data: Year ended 12/31/2012. Assets, $26,823,838 (M); Expenditures, $2,879,539;

Total giving, $2,679,827; Grants to individuals, 90 grants totaling $97,500 (high: $5,000).
Fields of interest: Higher education.
Type of support: Scholarships—to individuals.
Application information: Applications accepted. Application form required. Application form available on the grantmaker's web site.
Send request by: Mail
Copies of proposal: 1
Deadline(s): Mar. 8
Additional information: Additional application information can be found on the foundation's web site each Feb.
EIN: 386057160

4358
Birkenstock Family Foundation
32100 Telegraph Rd., Ste. 200
Bingham Farms, MI   48025-2454

Foundation type: Independent foundation
Purpose: Scholarships for college education only to residents of subdivisions in Howell, MI.
Financial data: Year ended 12/31/2012. Assets, $0 (M); Expenditures, $4,222; Total giving, $2,463; Grants to individuals, 2 grants totaling $2,463 (high: $1,232, low: $1,231).
Type of support: Undergraduate support.
Application information: Applications accepted. Application form required.
Additional information: Contact foundation for current application deadline/guidelines.
EIN: 912119072

4359
Birmingham Student Loan & Scholarship Fund
550 W. Merrill St.
Birmingham, MI   48009-1443   (248) 644-9300

Foundation type: Public charity
Purpose: College scholarships to high school graduates residing withing the Birmingham School District, MI in pursuit of a higher education.
Financial data: Year ended 09/30/2011. Assets, $825,202 (M); Expenditures, $68,485; Total giving, $57,750; Grants to individuals, totaling $57,750.
Fields of interest: Higher education.
Type of support: Scholarships—to individuals.
Application information: Applications accepted.
Additional information: Checks are made payable to both the recipient and the educational institution to ensure the funds are used for educational purposes.
EIN: 386091548

4360
Birtwistle Family Foundation
(formerly Donald B. Birtwistle Foundation)
300 S. Rath Ave., Apt. 25
Ludington, MI   49431   (616) 843-2501
Contact: Joclyn Birtwhistle, Pres.

Foundation type: Independent foundation
Purpose: Scholarships to graduates of the Ludington Area School District, MI, for college and graduate school.
Financial data: Year ended 12/31/2012. Assets, $2,108,971 (M); Expenditures, $83,919; Total giving, $73,400.
Type of support: Support to graduates or students of specific schools; Graduate support; Undergraduate support.

Application information: Application form required.
Deadline(s): Apr. 1 of senior year of high school
Additional information: Applicant should provide a written application with personal academic and professional data.
EIN: 382787567

4361
Bixby Community Health Foundation
818 Riverside Ave.
Adrian, MI   49221-1446

Foundation type: Public charity
Purpose: Scholarships to graduating high school students of Lenawee county, MI pursuing a career in the health care field.
Financial data: Year ended 12/31/2011. Expenditures, $542,047; Total giving, $314,967.
Fields of interest: Health sciences school/education.
Type of support: Scholarships—to individuals.
Application information: Applications accepted. Application form required.
Deadline(s): Mar. 31
Applicants should submit the following:
  1) Transcripts
  2) Letter(s) of recommendation
Program description:
  Scholarships: Scholarships in the amount of $500 to $2,000 to students who live or work in Lenawee county or be a family member of LHA employee pursuing a health care curriculum. Applicant must have a cumulative 3.0 GPA, be of good character, demonstrate continued academic success, and show intent to return to Lenawee county for employment.
EIN: 382691494

4362
Blaske-Hill Foundation
500 S. Main St.
Ann Arbor, MI   48104   (734) 747-7055
Contact: Thomas Blaske, V.P.

Foundation type: Independent foundation
Purpose: Scholarships to graduates of Battle Creek Central, St. Philip, and Niles High Schools, MI.
Financial data: Year ended 02/28/2013. Assets, $339,314 (M); Expenditures, $28,044; Total giving, $24,000; Grants to individuals, 12 grants totaling $24,000 (high: $2,000, low: $2,000).
Type of support: Support to graduates or students of specific schools; Undergraduate support.
Application information: Applications accepted. Application form required.
Initial approach: Letter
Deadline(s): Mar. 15
EIN: 382525817

4363
Blue Cross Blue Shield of Michigan Foundation
(formerly Michigan Health Care Education and Research Foundation/MHCERF)
600 Lafayette E., Ste. Mcx 520
Detroit, MI   48226-2998   (313) 225-8706
Contact: Ira Strumwasser Ph.D., C.E.O. and Exec. Dir.
FAX: (313) 225-7730;
E-mail: foundation@bcbsm.com; Additional tel.: (313) 225-7560; URL: http://www.bcbsm.com/foundation/

Foundation type: Public charity

Purpose: Awards to doctoral and medical students enrolled in MI universities, for the funding of a wide range of health care projects, including applied research, pilot programs or demonstration and evaluation projects. Research support and awards to MI residents who are health and medical researchers. Awards to outstanding senior citizen advocates.

Publications: Application guidelines; Annual report (including application guidelines); Informational brochure (including application guidelines).

Financial data: Year ended 12/31/2011. Assets, $48,632,275 (M); Expenditures, $2,508,366; Total giving, $1,345,356; Grants to individuals, totaling $62,250.

Fields of interest: Medical school/education; Research; Public policy; Health care; Health care; Medical research; Aging; Men.

Type of support: Research; Awards/grants by nomination only; Awards/prizes; Doctoral support.

Application information: Applications accepted. Application form required. Application form available on the grantmaker's web site.

  Initial approach: Letter or telephone
  Deadline(s): Apr. 30 for Student Awards
  Applicants should submit the following:
    1) SASE
    2) Resume
    3) Transcripts
    4) Letter(s) of recommendation
    5) Proposal

Program descriptions:

Excellence in Research Awards for Students: This program identifies and acknowledges Michigan's university students who have made significant contributions to health and health care through applied research in health policy or medical care. Awards are presented to doctoral or medical students for published papers that represent a contribution to health policy or clinical care. Three awards will be given: the first place winner receives $1,000, the second place winner receives $750, and the third place winner receives $500.

Frank J. McDevitt, D.O. Excellence in Research Awards for Health Services, Policy & Clinical Care: This program provides four awards of $10,000 each for research projects in progress or planned by the recipient in the fields of health policy, health services, and clinical care. Proposals should focus on such topics as public health, the financing and organization of health services, population health, reimbursement, or resource allocation. Eligible applicants include Michigan-based researchers with terminal research degrees (e.g. Ph.D. or Dr.PH) and Michigan-based physicians (M.D. or D.O.); separate awards will be offered to physician- and doctoral-level researchers. The financial award will be made to the recipient's 501(c)(3) nonprofit or educational organization, and is unrestricted.

Investigator-Initiated Research Program: This program encourages Michigan-based applied research projects designed to improve health care in the state of Michigan. It does not support basic science or biomedical research, including drug studies or studies using animals. Projects that focus on the quality and cost of health care and appropriate access are considered priority and include: the organization and delivery of health care services; evaluation of new methods or approaches to containing health care costs and providing access to high quality health care; assessment and assurance of quality care; and identification and validation of clinical protocols and evidence-based practice guidelines. Grants are typically in the $50,000 to $75,000 per year range; exceptional projects will be considered for multiyear funding or funding requests in excess of $75,000.

Physician-Investigator Research Award Program: This program is for physicians who have an interest in health and medical care research. The purpose is to provide seed money to physicians to explore the merits of a potential research idea. The proposed project might be in the form of a pilot study, feasibility study, or a small research study. Grants of $10,000 are available for research related to the quality of care, cost, and appropriate access to health and medical care. The program does not support basic science, biomedical research (including drug studies) or studies using animals.

Primary and Clinical Prevention: Addressing the Three Leading Causes of Death in Michigan: Funding of $500,000 is available to eligible Michigan physicians and members of the research community interested in preventing the three leading causes of death in Michigan: heart disease, cancer, and stroke. This program aims to increase the use of evidence-based prevention efforts to improve the health of Michigan residents. Priority will be given to proposals that: target high-risk subgroups of the population (racial, ethnic, and low-income groups in particular); develop clinical prevention efforts based on U.S. Preventive Services Task Force guidelines; and include a cost-effectiveness analysis for the intervention, if applicable, in addition to an evaluation of the effectiveness of the intervention.

Proposal Development Award Program: The award is intended to help Michigan-based nonprofit community organizations develop grant proposals for new health care initiatives. This award of up to $3,500 is available to help nonprofits obtain grant writing resources so they may secure the funding they need to bring creative community-based health care programs to life.

Student Awards Program: The program provides a $3,000 one-year stipend to students for applied research addressing health, health services, or policy. The intent is to support the next generation of applied researchers in health and health care policy and delivery by supporting doctoral and medical student research.

EIN: 382338506

4364

Dr. & Mrs. Edmund T. Bott Foundation, Inc.

1801 14th St.
Wyandotte, MI 48192-3634 (734) 649-2004
Application address: c/o John Clancy

Foundation type: Independent foundation

Purpose: Scholarships to students of Gabriel Richard High School, MI and Wyandotte Catholic Consolidated School, MI for higher education.

Financial data: Year ended 12/31/2011. Assets, $423,482 (M); Expenditures, $64,015; Total giving, $39,500; Grants to individuals, 26 grants totaling $39,500 (high: $2,500, low: $800).

Fields of interest: Education.

Type of support: Support to graduates or students of specific schools.

Application information: Applications accepted. Application form required.

  Deadline(s): Apr. 30
  Additional information: Students must maintain a 2.0 GPA.

EIN: 205068278

4365

Branch County Community Foundation

2 W. Chicago St., Ste. E-1
Coldwater, MI 49036-1602 (517) 278-4517
Contact: Colleen Knight, Exec. Dir.
FAX: (888) 479-8640;
E-mail: info@brcofoundation.org; URL: http://www.brcofoundation.org

Foundation type: Community foundation

Purpose: Scholarships to individuals of Branch County, Colon, or St. Joseph's County, MI, for undergraduate education at colleges and universities in the U.S.

Publications: Application guidelines; Annual report; Financial statement; Informational brochure; Newsletter; Occasional report.

Financial data: Year ended 09/30/2012. Assets, $4,957,523 (M); Expenditures, $602,517; Total giving, $425,689; Grants to individuals, 55 grants totaling $63,550.

Fields of interest: Higher education.

Type of support: Scholarships—to individuals.

Application information: Applications accepted. Application form required. Application form available on the grantmaker's web site.

  Send request by: Mail or e-mail
  Deadline(s): Mar. 14 for paper applications, Mar. 21 for electronic applications
  Applicants should submit the following:
    1) Letter(s) of recommendation
    2) Transcripts
    3) Resume
    4) GPA
    5) Financial information
    6) ACT
  Additional information: See web site for complete scholarship information.

EIN: 383021071

4366

C. William Brenske Scholarship Fund

328 S. Saginaw St., M/C 002072
Flint, MI 48502-1923 (989) 776-7368
Contact: Helen James
Application address: c/o Citizens Bank Wealth Mgmt., NA, 101 N. Washington Ave., Saginaw, MI 48607

Foundation type: Independent foundation

Purpose: Scholarships to residents of Saginaw County, MI, attending Nouvel Catholic Central High School.

Financial data: Year ended 12/31/2012. Assets, $124,972 (M); Expenditures, $6,936; Total giving, $3,200; Grants to individuals, 2 grants totaling $3,200 (high: $2,800, low: $400).

Fields of interest: Higher education.

Type of support: Support to graduates or students of specific schools.

Application information: Applications accepted. Application form required.

  Deadline(s): May 1

EIN: 386568888

4367

Anthony Stephen & Elizabeth E. Brenske Student Loan Fund

328 S. Saginaw St., M/C 001065
Flint, MI 48502-1923 (989) 776-7638
Application address: c/o Helen James, Citizens Bank Wealth Mgmt., N.A., 101 N. Washington Ave., Saginaw, MI 48607

Foundation type: Independent foundation

Purpose: Student loans to residents of Saginaw county, MI for attendance at a Michigan college or university.
Financial data: Year ended 12/31/2012. Assets, $257,286 (M); Expenditures, $6,443; Total giving, $0; Loans to individuals, 7 loans totaling $25,400.
Fields of interest: Higher education.
Type of support: Student loans—to individuals.
Application information: Applications accepted. Application form required.
　Deadline(s): May 1
　Additional information: Contact the fund for additional application information.
EIN: 386568889

4368
The Hilda E. Bretzlaff Foundation, Inc.
1550 N. Milford Rd., Ste. 101
Milford, MI　48381-1058
Contact: Janelle M. Radtke, V.P.
E-mail: jradtke@hebf.org; Additional e-mail: klindbeck@hebf.org; URL: http://www.hebf.org

Foundation type: Independent foundation
Purpose: Scholarships to assist individuals attending educational institutions in the U.S. or England that promote high educational, moral and conservative ideals.
Financial data: Year ended 12/31/2012. Assets, $22,774,256 (M); Expenditures, $1,522,097; Total giving, $986,558; Grants to individuals, 40 grants totaling $130,540 (high: $2,500, low: $500).
Fields of interest: Elementary/secondary education; College; University; Graduate/professional education.
Type of support: Precollege support; Undergraduate support.
Application information: Application form required.
　Initial approach: Through high school, college, or university office
　Deadline(s): May 15
　Applicants should submit the following:
　　1) Letter(s) of recommendation
　　2) Essay
　　3) Transcripts
　Additional information: Application should also include copy of parents' and students' tax returns. Applicant must demonstrate financial need.
EIN: 382619845

4369
Buist Foundation
8650 Byron Center Ave. S.W.
Byron Center, MI　49315-9201　(616) 878-3315
Contact: Brent Brinks, Pres.
URL: http://www.buistelectric.com/company_info/community/buist_foundation.php

Foundation type: Operating foundation
Purpose: Scholarships and tuition assistance to individuals in the MI, area. Financial assistance to indigent residents of the Grand Rapids, MI, area, for utilities and other living expenses.
Publications: Application guidelines.
Financial data: Year ended 12/31/2012. Assets, $70,537 (M); Expenditures, $312,030; Total giving, $311,307.
Fields of interest: Higher education.
Type of support: Scholarships—to individuals; Grants for special needs.
Application information: Applications accepted.
　Initial approach: Letter
　Deadline(s): None

Additional information: Contact the foundation for application information.
EIN: 383314509

4370
Byrne Family Foundation
P.O. Box 200
Rockford, MI　49341　(616) 866-3461
Contact: Arlene Warwick
Application address: 320 Byrne Industrial Dr., Rockford, MI 49341

Foundation type: Independent foundation
Purpose: Scholarships to graduating seniors of Lowell High School, MI, who have maintained a GPA of at least 2.0/4.0 in their last two years of high school.
Financial data: Year ended 12/31/2012. Assets, $42,529 (M); Expenditures, $11,495; Total giving, $10,000; Grants to individuals, 4 grants totaling $10,000 (high: $3,000, low: $1,000).
Fields of interest: Higher education.
Type of support: Scholarships—to individuals; Support to graduates or students of specific schools.
Application information: Applications accepted. Application form required.
　Deadline(s): Apr. 1
　Applicants should submit the following:
　　1) Financial information
　　2) Transcripts
　Additional information: Application should also include work experience, personal and community service information.
EIN: 383574869

4371
Cadillac Area Community Foundation
201 N. Mitchell St., Ste. 101
Cadillac, MI　49601-1859　(231) 775-9911
Contact: Linda L. Kimbel, Exec. Dir.
FAX: (231) 775-8126;
E-mail: cacf@cadillacfoundation.org; URL: http://www.cadillacfoundation.org

Foundation type: Community foundation
Purpose: Scholarships to qualified residents of Cadillac, MI and the four surrounding townships who attended Cadillac Area Public Schools.
Publications: Application guidelines; Annual report; Annual report (including application guidelines); Financial statement; Grants list; Informational brochure; Newsletter; Occasional report; Occasional report (including application guidelines); Program policy statement.
Financial data: Year ended 12/31/2012. Assets, $7,897,763 (M); Expenditures, $269,873; Total giving, $97,566; Grants to individuals, 18 grants totaling $22,900.
Fields of interest: Higher education; Dental school/education; Engineering school/education.
Type of support: Support to graduates or students of specific schools.
Application information: Applications accepted. Application form required. Application form available on the grantmaker's web site.
　Initial approach: Application
　Send request by: Mail or e-mail
　Deadline(s): Mid-Apr.
　Final notification: Recipients notified three months after deadline
　Additional information: See web site for a complete listing of schools.
EIN: 382848513

4372
Canton Community Foundation
50430 School House Rd., Ste. 200
Canton, MI　48187-5910　(734) 495-1200
FAX: (734) 495-1212;
E-mail: info@cantonfoundation.org; Additional e-mail: mmalamis@cantonfoundation.org;
URL: http://www.cantonfoundation.org

Foundation type: Community foundation
Purpose: Scholarships to residents of Canton Township, Plymouth or Plymouth Township, MI for postsecondary education.
Publications: Annual report; Financial statement; Grants list; Informational brochure (including application guidelines); Newsletter.
Financial data: Year ended 06/30/2012. Assets, $1,597,218 (M); Expenditures, $288,043; Total giving, $59,047.
Fields of interest: Higher education; Scholarships/financial aid.
Type of support: Scholarships—to individuals; Undergraduate support.
Application information: Applications accepted. Application form required. Application form available on the grantmaker's web site.
　Initial approach: Application
　Send request by: Mail
　Deadline(s): Mar.
　Final notification: Applicants notified May 1
　Applicants should submit the following:
　　1) GPA
　　2) Financial information
　　3) Letter(s) of recommendation
　　4) Essay
　　5) SAT
　　6) ACT
　　7) Transcripts
　Additional information: See web site for complete listing of scholarships.
Program description:
　Scholarships: The foundation's scholarship program includes financial aid opportunities for students of all ages who are at different points in their educational pursuits as well as a number of different areas of study. Each fall the foundation published its scholarship application for the coming year. See web site for additional information.
EIN: 382898615

4373
Career Alliance, Inc.
(also known as Genesee/Shiawassee Michigan Works!)
711 N. Saginaw St., Ste. 300
Flint, MI　48503-1769　(810) 233-5627
Contact: Alicia Booker, Pres. and C.E.O.
Additional address (Shiawassee County office): 1975 W. Main St., 2nd Fl., Owosso, MI 48867-9311, tel. (989) 729-9599, toll-free tel.: (800) 551-3575; URL: http://www.gsworks.org/

Foundation type: Public charity
Purpose: Tuition assistance to eligible individuals throughout Genesee and Shiawassee counties, MI.
Financial data: Year ended 06/30/2012. Assets, $5,070,777 (M); Expenditures, $22,027,218; Total giving, $17,262,876; Grants to individuals, 270 grants totaling $1,441,261.
Fields of interest: Education; Employment.
Type of support: Scholarships—to individuals.
Application information: Applications accepted.
　Additional information: Contact the organization for additional guidelines.
EIN: 382498451

4374
CareLink Network, Inc.
1333 Brewery Park Blvd,. Ste. 300
Detroit, MI 48207-4544 (313) 656-0000
FAX: (313) 656-2589; E-mail: info@bhpnet.org;
Toll-free tel.: (888) 711-5465; URL: http://
www.bhpnet.org/carelink.asp

Foundation type: Public charity
Purpose: Assistance with healthcare services for individuals diagnosed with mental illness, and children with serious emotional disorders in Wayne County, MI and surrounding areas.
Financial data: Year ended 09/30/2011. Assets, $13,261,671 (M); Expenditures, $123,885,874; Total giving, $118,357,869; Grants to individuals, 63,401 grants totaling $118,357,869.
Fields of interest: Health care; Family services; Human services; Mentally disabled.
Type of support: Grants to individuals.
Application information: Contact the agency for additional information for assistance.
EIN: 383653299

4375
Caring Athletes Team for Children's and Henry Ford Hospitals
(also known as CATCH)
223 Fisher Bldg.
3011 W. Grand Blvd.
Detroit, MI 48202-1601 (313) 876-9399
Contact: Jim Hughes, Exec. Dir.
FAX: (313) 876-9241;
E-mail: jhughes@catchcharity.org; Additional E-mail: info@catchcharity.org; URL: http://
www.catchcharity.org

Foundation type: Public charity
Purpose: Scholarship assistance and awards to Michigan high school seniors who excel in mathematics, science, arts, world studies and vocational-technical studies.
Financial data: Year ended 12/31/2011. Assets, $6,742,066 (M); Expenditures, $948,138; Total giving, $326,760; Grants to individuals, totaling $23,000.
Fields of interest: Education.
Type of support: Scholarships—to individuals.
Application information: Students are selected on the basis of grades, test scores, honors, community involvement and a demonstrated ability in one of the academic areas.
EIN: 382746810

4376
Norman & Ardis Carpenter Scholarship Trust
9957 Cherry Valley S.E.
Caledonia, MI 49316 (616) 891-9961
Contact: Jeff Pettinga
Application address: 7517 Noffke Dr., Caledonia, MI 49316

Foundation type: Independent foundation
Purpose: Scholarships to graduating seniors who are members of Caledonia Christian Reformed Church, MI.
Financial data: Year ended 07/31/2013. Assets, $113,181 (M); Expenditures, $18,185; Total giving, $17,100; Grants to individuals, 17 grants totaling $17,100 (high: $1,100; low: $500).
Fields of interest: Higher education.
Type of support: Scholarships—to individuals.
Application information: Applications accepted. Application form required.
Applicants should submit the following:

1) Essay
2) Letter(s) of recommendation
EIN: 203485260

4377
Central Montcalm Community Foundation
P.O. Box 128
Stanton, MI 48888 (989) 289-2312
Contact: Gale Parr, Pres.
URL: http://www.cmcommunityfoundation.org

Foundation type: Community foundation
Purpose: Scholarships for graduating seniors of Central Montcalm MI, for continuing education at institutions of higher learning.
Publications: Annual report; Informational brochure.
Financial data: Year ended 12/31/2011. Assets, $750,428 (M); Expenditures, $33,352; Total giving, $13,977; Grants to individuals, 9 grants totaling $7,450.
Fields of interest: Higher education.
Type of support: Scholarships—to individuals.
Application information: Applications accepted. Application form required. Application form available on the grantmaker's web site.
Initial approach: Application
Send request by: Online or mail
Deadline(s): Mar. 29
Applicants should submit the following:
1) GPA
2) Resume
3) Letter(s) of recommendation
Additional information: Application should also include a copy of your college acceptance letter. See web site for additional guidelines.
EIN: 383068773

4378
Chang Foundation
807 Asa Gray Dr., Ste. 401
Ann Arbor, MI 48105-2566 (810) 238-4617
Contact: Cheng-Yang Chang M.D., Dir.

Foundation type: Independent foundation
Purpose: Grants and scholarships to students of Taiwan, China with potential and the talent to excel in the field of Chinese traditional art.
Financial data: Year ended 09/30/2012. Assets, $269,078 (M); Expenditures, $15,401; Total giving, $11,400.
Fields of interest: Cultural/ethnic awareness; Folk arts.
Type of support: Grants to individuals; Scholarships—to individuals.
Application information: Applications accepted. Application form required.
Deadline(s): None
Applicants should submit the following:
1) Transcripts
2) Resume
3) Essay
Additional information: Application should also include two works by the student, and to submit within one year after receiving a grant, a letter from one of their instructors/professors in the field of art setting forth the student's progress in the field. The student will be required to submit a short statement as to how the grant/scholarship was used. Students are recommended by their department head.
EIN: 382796315

4379
Charity Motors, Inc.
10431 Grand River Ave.
Detroit, MI 48204-2005 (313) 933-4000
Contact: Gary E. Bowersox, Exec. Dir.; Stephen Hendrix, Mgr., Business Opers.
FAX: (313) 933-3754;
E-mail: gbowersox@charitymotors.org; Toll-free tel.: (888) 908-2277; URL: http://
www.charitymotors.org

Foundation type: Public charity
Purpose: Grants to low-income individuals for transportation costs, primarily in the Detroit, MI and Dallas, TX areas.
Publications: Annual report.
Financial data: Year ended 12/31/2011. Assets, $3,766,094 (M); Expenditures, $8,114,659; Total giving, $5,187,582; Grants to individuals, totaling $4,003,719.
Fields of interest: Economically disadvantaged.
Type of support: Grants for special needs.
Application information:
Initial approach: Letter
EIN: 383251827

4380
Charlevoix County Community Foundation
507 Water St.
P.O. Box 718
East Jordan, MI 49727-9476 (231) 536-2440
FAX: (231) 536-2640; E-mail: info@c3f.org;
URL: http://www.c3f.org

Foundation type: Community foundation
Purpose: Scholarships to high school students of Charlevoix County, MI, public schools.
Publications: Annual report (including application guidelines); Grants list.
Financial data: Year ended 12/31/2011. Assets, $21,993,193 (M); Expenditures, $1,338,490; Total giving, $963,688.
Fields of interest: Education.
Type of support: Scholarships—to individuals.
Application information: Applications accepted. Application form required. Application form available on the grantmaker's web site.
Initial approach: Application
Send request by: Deliver to high school counselor's office
Deadline(s): Mar. 20, unless otherwise indicated
Applicants should submit the following:
1) FAFSA
2) Financial information
3) Essay
4) Resume
5) ACT
6) Transcripts
7) GPA
Additional information: Each scholarship has its own eligibility criteria and guidelines; see web site for complete list of scholarships. You may also contact local high school counselor or the Community Foundation with inquiries.
EIN: 383033739

4381
Lavere Leonard and Gladys Loraine Chase Scholarship Fund
P.O. Box 75000, M/C 3302
Detroit, MI 48275-9413 (734) 930-2413
Contact: Mary Jo Anderle-Moro
Application address: 101 N. Main St., Ste. 100, Ann Arbor, MI 48104-5507

Foundation type: Independent foundation

Purpose: Scholarships to graduates of Jonesville School System who have been residents of Jonesville county, MI for a period of five years.
Financial data: Year ended 10/31/2013. Assets, $810,589 (M); Expenditures, $56,772; Total giving, $46,800; Grants to individuals, 45 grants totaling $46,800 (high: $1,200, low: $750).
Fields of interest: Higher education.
Type of support: Scholarships—to individuals.
Application information: Applications accepted. Application form required.
  Deadline(s): Dec. 31
EIN: 206975298

4382
Chelsea Education Foundation, Inc.
(also known as C.E.F.)
P.O. Box 281
Chelsea, MI 48118-0295 (734) 475-3841
E-mail: president@chelseaeducationfoundation.org
; URL: http://chelseaeducationfoundation.org/

Foundation type: Public charity
Purpose: Scholarships to Chelsea high school students and other residents of the Chelsea School District.
Publications: Application guidelines.
Financial data: Year ended 06/30/2012. Assets, $588,296 (M); Expenditures, $65,090; Total giving, $51,644; Grants to individuals, totaling $31,660.
Fields of interest: Education.
Type of support: Scholarships—to individuals.
Application information: Applications accepted. Application form required. Application form available on the grantmaker's web site.
  Deadline(s): Apr. 12
  Applicants should submit the following:
    1) Transcripts
    2) Letter(s) of recommendation
    3) Essay
  Additional information: Application must be completed online.
EIN: 382953926

4383
Children's Leukemia Foundation of Michigan
5455 Corporate Dr., Ste. 306
Troy, MI 48098-7650 (248) 530-3000
Contact: William D. Seklar, Pres. and C.E.O.
Additional tel. for assistance: Patient Services Dept., (800) 825-2536
FAX: (248) 530-3042;
E-mail: info@leukemiamichigan.org; Toll-free tel.: (800) 825-2536; E-Mail for William D. Seklar: wseklar@leukemiamichigan.org; URL: http://www.leukemiamichigan.org

Foundation type: Public charity
Purpose: Financial assistance to individuals and families who are residents of MI, on coping with leukemia and related disorders. Funds medical research to improve the well-being of patients and their families.
Publications: Annual report; Informational brochure; Newsletter.
Financial data: Year ended 06/30/2012. Assets, $570,216 (M); Expenditures, $976,463; Total giving, $28,088; Grants to individuals, totaling $28,088.
Fields of interest: Leukemia; Family services.
Type of support: Grants for special needs.
Application information: Contact foundation for additional guidelines for assistance.

Program description:
  Financial Assistance: Financial assistance of up to $1,000 per fiscal year for treatment costs for patients with little or no insurance, prescription costs for patients with little or no insurance, travel to and from treatment centers and wigs for head coverings. The Special Needs Funds of up to $500 (separate from the $1,000) covers the expenses that fall through the cracks of traditional financial aid programs (such as lodging, rent/mortgage, auto repairs, child care and other needs)
EIN: 381682300

4384
Clinton Rotary Scholarship Foundation
13091 Bartlett Hwy.
Clinton, MI 49236

Foundation type: Independent foundation
Purpose: Scholarships to seniors of Clinton High School, Clinton, MI for continuing education at accredited colleges or universities.
Financial data: Year ended 06/30/2013. Assets, $0 (M); Expenditures, $7,588; Total giving, $7,500; Grants to individuals, 3 grants totaling $7,500 (high: $2,500, low: $2,500).
Fields of interest: Higher education.
Type of support: Support to graduates or students of specific schools.
Application information: Applications accepted. Application form required. Interview required.
  Applicants should submit the following:
    1) Essay
    2) Photograph
    3) Resume
    4) GPA
  Additional information: Awards criteria are scholastic achievement, community service, extracurricular activity, and continuing education. Recipients are chosen by the senior class as Student of the Month.
EIN: 386150118

4385
The Cold Heading Foundation
(formerly DeSeranno Educational Foundation, Inc.)
21777 Hoover Rd.
Warren, MI 48089-2544

Foundation type: Independent foundation
Purpose: Scholarships primarily to students attending Madonna University.
Financial data: Year ended 12/31/2012. Assets, $24,538,280 (M); Expenditures, $655,624; Total giving, $430,435.
Type of support: Support to graduates or students of specific schools; Undergraduate support.
Application information: Applications not accepted.
EIN: 237005737

4386
Bradford Cole Trust
P.O. Box 75000
Detroit, MI 48275-3302

Foundation type: Independent foundation
Purpose: Scholarships to high school graduates from Carver, MA for higher education.
Financial data: Year ended 12/31/2011. Assets, $85,888 (M); Expenditures, $9,819; Total giving, $6,250.
Fields of interest: Higher education.
Type of support: Scholarships—to individuals.

Application information: Applicants must demonstrate financial need.
EIN: 596829423

4387
Collectors Foundation
141 River's Edge Dr., Ste. 200
Traverse City, MI 49684-3299 (231) 932-6835
Contact: Bob Knechel, Pres. and C.E.O.
FAX: (231) 932-6857;
E-mail: info@collectorsfoundation.org; E-Mail for Bob Knechel : bob@collectorsfoundation.org;
URL: http://www.collectorsfoundation.org

Foundation type: Public charity
Purpose: Scholarships for students to attend accredited colleges that have special automotive or wooden boat programs.
Publications: Annual report; Financial statement; Grants list; Informational brochure; Newsletter; Newsletter (including application guidelines); Program policy statement.
Financial data: Year ended 12/31/2011. Assets, $943,139 (M); Expenditures, $350,478; Total giving, $228,688.
Fields of interest: Engineering/technology.
Type of support: Seed money; Scholarships—to individuals; Technical education support; Project support.
Application information: Applications accepted. Application form required. Application form available on the grantmaker's web site.
  Initial approach: Letter, telephone, or e-mail
  Send request by: Mail, fax or e-mail
  Copies of proposal: 1
  Deadline(s): Jan. 1, Apr. 1., July 1, and Oct. 1
EIN: 202102643

4388
Coller Foundation
35 S. Elk St.
Sandusky, MI 48471 (810) 648-2414
Contact: John Paterson, Pres.

Foundation type: Independent foundation
Purpose: Scholarships to financially needy graduates of high schools in Tuscola and Sanilac counties, MI.
Financial data: Year ended 12/31/2012. Assets, $1,561,562 (M); Expenditures, $85,806; Total giving, $82,000.
Type of support: Support to graduates or students of specific schools; Undergraduate support.
Application information: Applications accepted. Application form required.
  Deadline(s): Mar. 1
EIN: 382832816

4389
Come Together Foundation
(formerly The Pistons-Palace Foundation)
6 Championship Dr.
Auburn Hills, MI 48326-1753 (248) 377-0100
Contact: Dennis Sampier
FAX: (248) 377-0309; URL: http://www.nba.com/pistons/community/come-together-foundation

Foundation type: Company-sponsored foundation
Purpose: Scholarships to K-12 students who submit an essay or short story on sportsmanship and to students in Michigan who demonstrate knowledge of Black history.
Publications: Annual report.

Financial data: Year ended 02/29/2012. Assets, $812,106 (M); Expenditures, $79,646; Total giving, $54,434.
Fields of interest: Scholarships/financial aid; Reading; Athletics/sports, amateur leagues; African Americans/Blacks.
Type of support: Scholarships—to individuals; Awards/prizes.
Application information: Applications accepted. Application form required. Application form available on the grantmaker's web site.
  Deadline(s): Feb. for Know Your Black History
Program descriptions:
  Gift of Reading Scholarship Contest: The foundation, in partnership with Detroit Free Press, annually awards scholarships to K-12 students as part of the "Read to Achieve" tour and online contest. Students submit an essay or short story of up to 2,000 words on the importance of good sportsmanship. Submissions are judged on originality, writing style, grammar, content, and overall message and eight grand-prize winners receive scholarships of up to $2,500 at a Pistons home game.
  Know Your Black History Tour and Contest: The foundation, in partnership with Quicken Loans and Fathead.com, annually hosts a Black history tour with which three students from Detroit schools perform a three-minute interpretation on the importance of knowing your Black history in the art form of their choice. Winners receive scholarships of up to $10,000, a Pistons Flathead wall graphic, four tickets to a Pistons game, and participating schools receive five laptops. The foundation also sponsors an online contest which awards a $2,500 scholarship and tickets to a Piston's home game to a high school student who demonstrates extensive knowledge of Black history. The program is limited to high school students in Michigan.
EIN: 382858649

4390
Community Foundation Alliance of Calhoun County

104 S. Hillsdale St.
P.O. Box 101
Homer, MI 49245-1026 (517) 568-5222
Contact: Email Carol, Admin.
Application address for Youth scholarship: MSU Extension Office, Attn: 4-H Swine Scholarship Committee, 315 W. Green St., Marshall, MI 49068
FAX: (517) 568-5453; E-mail: alliance@cfa-cc.org; URL: http://www.cfa-cc.org/

Foundation type: Public charity
Purpose: Scholarships for nontraditional students residing within Calhoun county, MI who are seeking educational opportunities to take them further. Scholarships for youth of Calhoun county, MI who show determination and leadership abilities.
Publications: Annual report.
Financial data: Year ended 03/31/2012. Assets, $2,651,900 (M); Expenditures, $530,264; Total giving, $311,131; Grants to individuals, totaling $4,600.
Fields of interest: Higher education; Adults; Young adults.
Type of support: Scholarships—to individuals.
Application information: Applications accepted. Application form required. Application form available on the grantmaker's web site.
  Send request by: Mail (Swine Club Scholarship), on-line (Adult Scholarship)
  Deadline(s): Apr. 25 for Adult Scholarship, May 21 for 4-H Swine Club Scholarship
  Additional information: See web site for additional application guidelines.

Program descriptions:
  Calhoun County Adult Scholarship: The program provides scholarships of up to $1,000 each to individuals who reside within Calhoun County, MI, and who are seeking educational opportunities. Eligibility is for adults who have not been enrolled in any full-time educational program for at least six months prior to the application deadline and are in need of additional education and/or technical training to enhance current employment status and/or employability. Scholarships can be applied toward technical training, college education, company-related training/education, and GED. Application should include general and academic information, financial information, essay, and transcript and academic statement.
  Calhoun County Swine Club Scholarship: Two scholarships of $300 will be awarded annually to applicants who must be a member of the Calhoun County 4-H Swine Club. Applicant may not be older than 19 years of age of Jan. 1 of the current year, and must be enrolled as a Calhoun county 4-H youth swine exhibitor for a minimum of four years. Applicant must either be a senior in high school or a high school graduate continuing their education at an accredited institution in the year in which they are applying. Previous recipients are not eligible.
EIN: 043597340

4391
Community Foundation for Muskegon County

(formerly Muskegon County Community Foundation, Inc.)
425 W. Western Ave., Ste. 200
Muskegon, MI 49440-1101 (231) 722-4538
Contact: Chris Ann McGuigan, C.E.O.
FAX: (231) 722-4616; E-mail: grants@cffmc.org; URL: http://www.cffmc.org

Foundation type: Community foundation
Purpose: Scholarships to residents of Muskegon, Oceana, and Mason counties, MI for postsecondary education.
Publications: Application guidelines; Annual report (including application guidelines); Financial statement; Grants list; Informational brochure (including application guidelines); Newsletter.
Financial data: Year ended 12/31/2011. Assets, $113,996,605 (M); Expenditures, $7,233,409; Total giving, $3,994,364.
Fields of interest: Vocational education; Higher education; Scholarships/financial aid.
Type of support: Scholarships—to individuals; Support to graduates or students of specific schools; Undergraduate support.
Application information: Applications accepted. Application form required. Application form available on the grantmaker's web site. Interview required.
  Send request by: Mail
  Deadline(s): Mar. 1
  Applicants should submit the following:
    1) Transcripts
    2) Work samples
    3) GPA
    4) FAFSA
    5) Essay
    6) Curriculum vitae
    7) ACT
  Additional information: See web site for complete listing of scholarships.
Program description:
  Scholarships: The foundation administers over 100 scholarship funds established by donors to provide higher education opportunities for area students. Most awards are for residents of

Muskegon, Manistee, Mason and Oceana counties, though there are scholarships available outside the 4-county service area. Each scholarship has its own unique eligibility requirements, applications are considered and matched with the most appropriate scholarship source via a "single application" method of scholarship selection. See web site for additional information.
EIN: 386114135

4392
Community Foundation for Northeast Michigan

(formerly Northeast Michigan Community Foundation)
100 N. Ripley, Suite F
P.O. Box 495
Alpena, MI 49707-2838 (989) 354-6881
Contact: Barbara Frantz, Exec. Dir.; For Scholarship: Julie Wiesen, Prog. Dir.
Scholarship e-mail: wiesenj@cfnem.org
FAX: (989) 356-3319; E-mail: bfrantz@cfnem.org; URL: http://www.cfnem.org

Foundation type: Community foundation
Purpose: Scholarships to residents of Alpena, Alcona, Montmorency, Preque Isle, Cheboygan, Crawford, Iosco, Ogemalo and Oscoda counties, MI.
Publications: Application guidelines; Annual report; Financial statement; Grants list; Informational brochure; Newsletter; Program policy statement.
Financial data: Year ended 09/30/2012. Assets, $24,243,748 (M); Expenditures, $1,133,535; Total giving, $828,561; Grants to individuals, 242 grants totaling $282,784 (high: $8,000; low: $250).
Type of support: Scholarships—to individuals.
Application information: Applications accepted. Application form required. Application form available on the grantmaker's web site.
  Initial approach: Application
  Send request by: Mail, fax or e-mail
  Copies of proposal: 1
  Deadline(s): Apr. 1
  Final notification: Recipients notified sixty days after deadline
  Applicants should submit the following:
    1) Transcripts
    2) Letter(s) of recommendation
    3) GPA
  Additional information: See web site for specific application guidelines.
EIN: 237384822

4393
Community Foundation for Southeast Michigan

(formerly Community Foundation for Southeastern Michigan)
333 W. Fort St., Ste. 2010
Detroit, MI 48226-3134 (313) 961-6675
Contact: Mariam C. Noland, Pres.; For scholarships: Sally Foster, Scholarship Consultant
Scholarship inquiry e-mail: sfoster@cfsem.org
FAX: (313) 961-2886; E-mail: cfsem@cfsem.org; URL: http://www.cfsem.org

Foundation type: Community foundation
Purpose: Scholarships to individuals in southeastern MI for postsecondary education.
Publications: Application guidelines; Annual report (including application guidelines); Grants list; Informational brochure (including application guidelines); Newsletter.

Financial data: Year ended 12/31/2012. Assets, $655,525,319 (M); Expenditures, $61,026,127; Total giving, $55,775,204.
Fields of interest: Vocational education; Higher education; Scholarships/financial aid.
Type of support: Scholarships—to individuals; Support to graduates or students of specific schools; Undergraduate support.
Application information: Applications accepted. Application form required. Application form available on the grantmaker's web site.
Deadline(s): Varies
Additional information: See web site for complete listing of scholarships.
Program description:
Scholarships: The foundation supports the future of the local region by investing in the education of its young people through scholarship programs. Each scholarship has its own unique set of eligibility criteria, including graduation from a particular high school and plans to pursue of particular fields of study such as liberal arts, chemistry, athletics and medicine. Visit the foundation's web site for more information.
EIN: 382530980

4394
Community Foundation of Greater Flint
500 S. Saginaw St.
Flint, MI 48502 (810) 767-8270
Contact: Kathi Horton, Pres.
FAX: (810) 767-0496; E-mail: info@cfgf.org;
Additional e-mail: khorton@cfgf.org; URL: http://www.cfgf.org

Foundation type: Community foundation
Purpose: Scholarships to individuals from the Flint, MI, area for undergraduate education at American colleges and universities.
Publications: Application guidelines; Annual report; Financial statement; Grants list; Informational brochure; Occasional report; Program policy statement.
Financial data: Year ended 12/31/2012. Assets, $147,222,393 (M); Expenditures, $6,186,537; Total giving, $4,633,003. Scholarships—to individuals amount not specified.
Fields of interest: Music; Performing arts, education; Higher education; Business school/education; Medical school/education; Nursing school/education; Engineering school/education; Social work school/education; Athletics/sports, amateur leagues; Athletics/sports, soccer; Athletics/sports, winter sports; African Americans/Blacks.
Type of support: Scholarships—to individuals; Support to graduates or students of specific schools; Awards/prizes; Graduate support; Technical education support; Undergraduate support.
Application information: Applications accepted. Application form required. Application form available on the grantmaker's web site.
Deadline(s): Varies
Additional information: See web site for a complete listing of scholarships and application guidelines.
Program description:
Scholarships: The foundations administers more than 60 scholarship funds established by donors to primarily benefit students across Genesee County, MI. Scholarships range from small one-time awards to larger multi-year awards. In most cases the scholarships are designated for graduates of particular high schools and typically provide partial support toward the full cost of higher education. Eligibility requirements, deadlines and application

guidelines vary per fund. See web site for additional information.
EIN: 382190667

4395
Community Foundation of Greater Rochester
(formerly Greater Rochester Area Community Foundation)
127 W. University Dr.
Rochester, MI 48308 (248) 608-2804
Contact: Peggy Hamilton, Exec. Dir.
FAX: (248) 608-2826; E-mail: cfound@cfound.org;
URL: http://www.cfound.org

Foundation type: Community foundation
Purpose: Scholarships to graduating high school students in the greater Rochester, MI, area.
Publications: Annual report (including application guidelines); Financial statement; Informational brochure; Newsletter.
Financial data: Year ended 12/31/2012. Assets, $7,257,570 (M); Expenditures, $892,017; Total giving, $235,010; Grants to individuals, 75 grants totaling $97,145.
Fields of interest: Higher education; Scholarships/financial aid.
Type of support: Scholarships—to individuals; Support to graduates or students of specific schools; Undergraduate support.
Application information: Applications accepted. Application form required.
Send request by: Mail or hand deliver
Deadline(s): Mar. 4
Applicants should submit the following:
1) Transcripts
2) Essay
Additional information: Contact foundation for information on specific scholarship programs.
EIN: 382476777

4396
Community Foundation of Monroe County
28 S. Macomb St., Ste. C
Monroe, MI 48161-2176 (734) 242-1976
Contact: Kathleen Russeau, Exec. Dir.
FAX: (734) 242-1234; E-mail: info@cfmonroe.org;
URL: http://www.cfmonroe.org

Foundation type: Community foundation
Purpose: Scholarships to graduates of Monroe County, MI, pursuing careers in technical schools, pre-med, pre-law, journalism, engineering, and computer tech education.
Publications: Application guidelines; Annual report; Financial statement; Grants list; Informational brochure; Newsletter.
Financial data: Year ended 03/31/2013. Assets, $5,952,555 (M); Expenditures, $706,353; Total giving, $116,827; Grants to individuals, 93 grants totaling $48,809.
Fields of interest: Print publishing; Law school/education; Medical school/education; Engineering.
Type of support: Scholarships—to individuals.
Application information: Applications accepted. Application form required. Application form available on the grantmaker's web site.
Initial approach: Application
Send request by: Online
Copies of proposal: 15
Deadline(s): Feb. 21 to high school counselor, Feb 28 to foundation
Applicants should submit the following:
1) Transcripts
2) SAT
3) GPA

4) Essay
5) ACT
Additional information: Each scholarship has its own unique set of eligibility criteria. See web site for a complete listing.
EIN: 382236628

4397
Community Foundation of St. Clair County
516 McMorran Blvd.
Port Huron, MI 48060-3826 (810) 984-4761
Contact: Randy D. Maiers, C.E.O.
FAX: (810) 984-3394;
E-mail: info@stclairfoundation.org; URL: http://www.stclairfoundation.org

Foundation type: Community foundation
Purpose: Scholarships only to students in St. Clair County, MI pursuing a college or vocational education.
Publications: Application guidelines; Annual report; Financial statement; Grants list; Informational brochure; Newsletter.
Financial data: Year ended 12/31/2012. Assets, $35,632,575 (M); Expenditures, $1,758,563; Total giving, $753,914.
Fields of interest: Higher education.
Type of support: Scholarships—to individuals.
Application information: Applications accepted. Application form required. Application form available on the grantmaker's web site.
Initial approach: Application
Copies of proposal: 5
Deadline(s): Mar. 15
Applicants should submit the following:
1) SAT
2) Transcripts
3) Letter(s) of recommendation
4) GPA
5) Financial information
6) Essay
7) ACT
Additional information: See web site for scholarship criteria eligibility.
EIN: 381872132

4398
The Community Foundation of the Holland/Zeeland Area
(formerly Holland Community Foundation, Inc.)
85 E. 8th St., Ste. 110
Holland, MI 49423-3528 (616) 396-6590
Contact: Janet DeYoung, C.E.O.; Elizabeth Kidd, Dir., Grantmaking
FAX: (616) 396-3573; E-mail: info@cfhz.org;
URL: http://www.cfhz.org

Foundation type: Community foundation
Purpose: Scholarships to graduates of the Holland-Zeeland School District, MI for postsecondary education.
Publications: Application guidelines; Annual report; Financial statement; Grants list; Informational brochure; Newsletter; IRS Form 990 or 990-PF printed copy available upon request.
Financial data: Year ended 12/31/2012. Assets, $48,409,622 (M); Expenditures, $5,342,564; Total giving, $4,037,907; Grants to individuals, 168 grants totaling $398,186.
Fields of interest: Higher education; Scholarships/financial aid.
Type of support: Employee-related scholarships; Scholarships—to individuals; Support to graduates or students of specific schools; Undergraduate support.

Application information: Applications accepted. Application form required.

> *Send request by:* On-line
> *Deadline(s):* Mar. 1
> *Final notification:* Recipients notified in May
> *Applicants should submit the following:*
> 1) Class rank
> 2) GPA
> 3) Letter(s) of recommendation
> 4) SAR
> 5) Essay
> 6) Transcripts
> 7) ACT
> 8) Financial information
> 9) FAFSA
> *Additional information:* Each scholarship has its own unique eligibility criteria.

EIN: 386095283

4399

Community Foundation of the Upper Peninsula

(formerly Upper Peninsula Community Foundation Alliance)
2420 1st. Ave S., Ste. 101
Escanaba, MI   49829-1309   (906) 789-5972
Contact: Gary LaPlant, Exec. Dir.; Debra Millican, Off. Mgr.
FAX: (906) 786-9124; E-mail: glaplant@cfup.org;
Additional e-mail: dmillican@cfup.org; URL: http://www.cfup.org

Foundation type: Community foundation
Purpose: Scholarships to graduating seniors of the Upper Peninsula, MI area for continuing education at colleges, universities or vocational schools.
Publications: Application guidelines; Annual report; Financial statement; Informational brochure; Informational brochure (including application guidelines).
Financial data: Year ended 12/31/2012. Assets, $22,158,613 (M); Expenditures, $2,351,657; Total giving, $1,109,977; Grants to individuals, 65 grants totaling $134,971.
Fields of interest: Vocational education, post-secondary; Higher education.
Type of support: Technical education support; Undergraduate support.
Application information: Applications accepted. Application form required.

> *Initial approach:* Letter
> *Send request by:* Mail, fax, or e-mail
> *Deadline(s):* Apr. 1
> *Applicants should submit the following:*
> 1) GPA
> 2) Essay
> 3) ACT
> 4) Transcripts
> 5) Proposal
> 6) Letter(s) of recommendation
> 7) Financial information

EIN: 383227080

4400

Community Network Services, Inc.

38855 Hills Tech Dr., Ste. 200
Farmington Hills, MI   48331-3428   (248) 994-8001
Contact: Michael Garrett, Pres.
FAX: (248) 994-8005; Toll-free tel.: (Farmington Hills area) (800) 615-0411; Toll-free tel.: (Waterford area) (800) 273-0258; URL: http://www.cnsmi.org

Foundation type: Public charity

Purpose: Financial assistance to individuals with support in areas of housing, pharmacy, transportation and other needed services in the Oakland County area of southeastern, MI.
Publications: Newsletter.
Financial data: Year ended 09/30/2011. Assets, $3,424,991 (M); Expenditures, $32,115,941; Total giving, $465,796; Grants to individuals, totaling $465,796.
Fields of interest: Mental health, counseling/support groups; Mentally disabled.
Type of support: Grants for special needs.
Application information: Applications not accepted.

> *Additional information:* Unsolicited requests for funds not considered or acknowledged.

EIN: 431969008

4401

The Louis Cunningham Scholarship Foundation

21411 Civic Center Dr., Ste. 206
Southfield, MI   48076-3950   (248) 263-7680
Contact: Louis E. Cunningham, Treas.

Foundation type: Independent foundation
Purpose: Scholarships to individuals for study with tuition, books, room and board at institutions of higher learning.
Financial data: Year ended 12/31/2011. Assets, $125,048 (M); Expenditures, $4,198; Total giving, $3,000; Grants to individuals, 2 grants totaling $3,000 (high: $2,500, low: $500).
Fields of interest: Higher education; Scholarships/financial aid.
Type of support: Scholarships—to individuals.
Application information: Applications accepted. Application form required.

> *Deadline(s):* Spring
> *Additional information:* Application should include transcripts.

EIN: 383197360

4402

Dana Foundation

1 Village Center Dr.
Van Buren Township, MI   48111   (419) 887-5141
Contact: Joe Stancati, Secy.
Application address: P.O. Box 1000, Maumee, OH 43537, Tel.: (419) 887-5141

Foundation type: Company-sponsored foundation
Purpose: Scholarships only to children of employees of the Driveshaft division of the Dana Corporation.
Financial data: Year ended 03/31/2013. Assets, $72,134 (M); Expenditures, $445,299; Total giving, $439,726.
Type of support: Employee-related scholarships.
Application information: Applications accepted.

> *Deadline(s):* None
> *Additional information:* Contact foundation for current application guidelines.

Company name: Dana Corporation
EIN: 346544909

4403

Opal Dancey Memorial Foundation

c/o Plante Moran Trust
P.O. Box 307
Southfield, MI   48037-0307   (866) 846-3600
Contact: Susan Dudas, V.P. and Secy.
Application Address: 217 Traditions Dr., Alpharetta, GA 30004
E-mail: applicants@opaldanceygrants.org;
URL: http://www.opaldanceygrants.org

Foundation type: Independent foundation
Purpose: Grants to students seeking a Master of Divinity degree who will serve in pulpit ministry, and who have lived in a Great Lakes state.
Financial data: Year ended 10/31/2012. Assets, $1,973,038 (M); Expenditures, $136,041; Total giving, $105,000; Grants to individuals, totaling $105,000.
Fields of interest: Theological school/education.
Type of support: Grants to individuals.
Application information: Applications accepted. Application form available on the grantmaker's web site.

> *Send request by:* Online
> *Deadline(s):* April 15
> *Final notification:* Applicant notified early July

Program description:

> *Scholarship Program:* Grants are awarded to applicants who hold an undergraduate degree from an accredited university or college. Applicant must be a full time student, and plan to attend an accredited theological seminary located within the Great Lakes Region or plan to attend Asbury Theological Seminary. Applicant must be a resident of the Great Lakes Region, have been a resident for at least two years of a Great Lakes state and plan to attend an accredited theological seminary outside of the region.

EIN: 386361282

4404

Henry & Sidney T. Davenport Educational Trust

(formerly Henry & Sidney T. Davenport Educational Fund)
P.O. Box 75000, MC 7874
Detroit, MI   48275-7874

Foundation type: Independent foundation
Purpose: Student loans to financially needy residents of Nash or Edgecombe county, NC, who are U.S. citizens.
Financial data: Year ended 06/30/2013. Assets, $790,564 (M); Expenditures, $14,497; Total giving, $0.
Fields of interest: Higher education; Economically disadvantaged.
Type of support: Student loans—to individuals.
Application information: Applications accepted. Application form required.

> *Send request by:* Mail
> *Deadline(s):* June 1
> *Applicants should submit the following:*
> 1) SAT
> 2) ACT
> 3) FAFSA
> 4) Transcripts

EIN: 237422939

4405
Delta College Foundation
1961 Delta Rd.
University Center, MI 48710-0001 (989) 686-9224
Contact: Pamela N. Clark, Exec. Dir.
FAX: (989) 667-2212;
E-mail: foundation@delta.edu; URL: http://www.delta.edu/foundation.aspx

Foundation type: Public charity
Purpose: College scholarships to students of the Bay City, MI area for continuing education at accredited colleges or universities. Financial assistance to individuals to help with utilities, shelter, rent, medical expenses and other special needs.
Publications: Application guidelines.
Financial data: Year ended 06/30/2012. Assets, $5,157,323 (M); Expenditures, $1,864,078; Total giving, $1,579,467; Grants to individuals, totaling $30,460.
Type of support: Scholarships—to individuals; Grants for special needs.
EIN: 382274366

4406
Delta Dental Foundation
(formerly Delta Dental Fund)
P.O. Box 30416
Lansing, MI 48909-7916 (517) 349-6000
Contact: Penelope K. Majeske Ph.D., Vice-Chair.
Application address: P.O. Box 293, Okemos, MI 48805-0293, tel.: (517) 347-5333, fax: (517) 347-5320,
e-mail: DeltaDentalFund@deltadentalmi.com
E-mail: ddfund@ddpmi.com; URL: http://www.deltadentalmi.com/About/Giving-Back/Delta-Dental-Foundation.aspx

Foundation type: Public charity
Purpose: Scholarships and awards to deserving students of IN, MI, and OH pursuing a career in dentistry.
Publications: Application guidelines; Biennial report (including application guidelines).
Financial data: Year ended 12/31/2011. Assets, $37,489,864 (M); Expenditures, $1,514,443; Total giving, $1,097,319; Grants to individuals, totaling $154,469.
Fields of interest: Dental school/education.
Type of support: Research; Scholarships—to individuals; Awards/prizes.
Application information: Applications accepted. Application form required.
 Send request by: Mail
 Deadline(s): Apr. 15
 Additional information: See web site for additional application guidelines.
Program descriptions:
 Dental Master's Thesis Award Program: This program is intended to encourage thesis research that is of direct relevance to the costs or outcomes of dental care. The award offers up to $3,000 to cover costs associated with conducting master's thesis research.
 Scholarships and Student Leadership Awards: Awards and scholarships to students who demonstrate excellent academic and leadership skills, and who exhibit a passion for dentistry. Two students from each dental school in MI, OH, and IN are awarded a foundation scholarship and one graduating dental student from each school is awarded a Student Leadership Award. Recipients are selected by the dean of their school of dentistry.
EIN: 382337000

4407
Detroit Golf Club Caddie Scholarship Foundation
201 W. Big Beaver Rd., Ste. 1020
Troy, MI 48084

Foundation type: Independent foundation
Purpose: Scholarships toward college tuition to caddies at the Detroit Golf Club, MI.
Financial data: Year ended 12/31/2012. Assets, $271,937 (M); Expenditures, $50,724; Total giving, $48,177; Grants to individuals, 25 grants totaling $48,177 (high: $2,000, low: $996).
Fields of interest: Higher education.
Type of support: Scholarships—to individuals.
Application information: Applications not accepted.
 Additional information: Unsolicited requests for funds not considered or acknowledged.
EIN: 300023878

4408
Dickinson Area Community Foundation
(formerly Dickinson County Area Community Foundation)
333 S. Stephenson Ave., Ste. 204
Iron Mountain, MI 49801-2942 (906) 774-3131
Contact: Tamara Juul, Exec. Dir.
FAX: (906) 774-7640; E-mail: dcacf@uplogon.com;
Additional e-mail: tjuul@uplogon.com; URL: http://www.dickinsonareacommunityfoundation.org

Foundation type: Community foundation
Purpose: Scholarships to nursing students in Dickinson County, MI, and surrounding MI and WI communities.
Publications: Application guidelines; Annual report; Financial statement; Grants list.
Financial data: Year ended 12/31/2012. Assets, $6,402,362 (M); Expenditures, $208,516; Total giving, $77,725; Grants to individuals, 61 grants totaling $60,015.
Fields of interest: Nursing school/education; Scholarships/financial aid.
Type of support: Undergraduate support.
Application information: Application form required.
 Deadline(s): Mar. 15
 Applicants should submit the following:
  1) Essay
  2) Transcripts
  3) Letter(s) of recommendation
 Additional information: Contact foundation for current application deadline/guidelines.
EIN: 383218990

4409
Domino's Pizza Partners Foundation
30 Frank Lloyd Wright Dr.
Ann Arbor, MI 48106-0997 (734) 930-3297
E-mail: partners@dominos.com; Toll-free fax: (800) 253-8182; URL: http://www.dominosbiz.com/Biz-Public-EN/Site+Content/Secondary/About+Dominos/Community/

Foundation type: Public charity
Purpose: Assistance to Domino's Pizza team members in time of special need or tragedy as a result of natural disaster, unexpected afflictions, on-the-job accidents, and other emergencies.
Financial data: Year ended 12/31/2011. Assets, $3,627,285 (M); Expenditures, $1,209,264; Total giving, $850,382; Grants to individuals, totaling $850,382.
Type of support: Emergency funds; Employee-related welfare; Grants for special needs.

Application information: Applications not accepted.
 Additional information: Contributes only through employee-related emergency grants. Unsolicited requests for funds not considered or acknowledged.
Company name: Domino's Pizza, Inc.
EIN: 581703733

4410
The Dow Chemical Company Foundation
2030 Dow Ctr.
Midland, MI 48674-0001
Contact: R.N. "Bo" Miller, Pres. and Exec. Dir.
FAX: (989) 636-3518; E-mail: bomiller@dow.com;
URL: http://www.dow.com/company/citizenship/

Foundation type: Company-sponsored foundation
Purpose: Provides financial assistance to employees of Dow Chemical Co. and their resident dependents in the event of a federally-declared natural disaster.
Financial data: Year ended 12/31/2012. Assets, $15,017,322 (M); Expenditures, $22,154,634; Total giving, $22,154,105.
Type of support: Emergency funds; Employee-related welfare.
Application information: Applications accepted. Application form not required.
 Initial approach: Letter or telephone
 Send request by: Mail
 Copies of proposal: 1
 Deadline(s): None
 Final notification: Recipients notified within four to six weeks after application
Company name: The Dow Chemical Company
EIN: 382314603

4411
Earhart Foundation
2200 Green Rd., Ste. H
Ann Arbor, MI 48105-1569 (734) 761-8592
Contact: Ingrid A. Gregg, Pres.
FAX: (734) 761-2722

Foundation type: Independent foundation
Purpose: Fellowship research grants to individuals who have distinguished themselves professionally, in such disciplines as government/politics, economics, religion, philosophy, history, sociology, law/legal history and English. Graduate fellowships by nomination only.
Publications: Annual report (including application guidelines).
Financial data: Year ended 12/31/2012. Assets, $23,360,564 (M); Expenditures, $6,727,570; Total giving, $5,282,611. Grants to individuals amount not specified.
Fields of interest: Humanities; Research; Political science.
Type of support: Publication; Fellowships; Research; Graduate support.
Application information: Applications accepted. Application form not required.
 Initial approach: Letter
 Send request by: Mail
 Copies of proposal: 1
 Deadline(s): Not less than 120 days before commencement of projected work period
 Final notification: Recipients notified in four months after receipt of application
 Applicants should submit the following:
  1) Resume
  2) Proposal
  3) Curriculum vitae
  4) Budget Information

Additional information: Applications must include personal history, three- to five-page description of proposed research, intended end use or publication of research, abstract of approximately one single-spaced page, budget, time schedule, list of five references, and statement about applications pending elsewhere.

Program descriptions:

Fellowship Research Grants: Fellowship research grants are awarded upon direct application to individuals who have already established themselves professionally. Such persons must be associated or affiliated with educational or research institutions and the effort supported should lead to the advancement of knowledge through teaching, lecturing, and publication. The applications evaluated must include: 1) curriculum vitae; 2) a full description of the proposed research - three to five pages are sufficient; 3) an abstract of approximately one page (single-spaced); 4) the intended end use or publication; 5) a budget and time schedule; 6) a list of five referees with addresses; and 7) a statement about applications pending elsewhere. Each award is for a specific purpose and progress is monitored.

H.B. Earhart Fellowships: Fellowships are awarded to move talented individuals through graduate study in optimum time to embark upon careers in college or university teaching or in research. Awards are made to graduate students nominated by faculty sponsors whose participation is invited annually. The sponsors also monitor performance. Direct applications from candidates or from non-invited sponsors are not accepted.

EIN: 386008273

4412
Easter Seals of Michigan, Inc.

2399 E. Walton Blvd.
Auburn Hills, MI 48326-1955 (248) 475-6400
Contact: Brent L. Wirth, Pres. and C.E.O.
Toll-free tel.: (800) 75-SEALS; URL: http://www.essmichigan.org

Foundation type: Public charity
Purpose: Medical, dental, and hospital payment assistance to mentally or physically disabled individuals in MI. Also mental health support services to disabled adults and children in MI, including transitional and post-adjudication services.
Financial data: Year ended 09/30/2011. Assets, $8,402,404 (M); Expenditures, $35,962,853; Total giving, $8,607,481; Grants to individuals, totaling $8,607,481.
Fields of interest: Offenders/ex-offenders, transitional care; Offenders/ex-offenders, services; Independent living, disability; Human services; Disabilities, people with; Economically disadvantaged.
Type of support: Grants for special needs.
Application information: Contact foundation or see web site for detailed program and application information.
EIN: 381402860

4413
C. K. Eddy Family Memorial Fund

c/o Citizens Bank Wealth Mgmt., N.A.
328 S. Saginaw St., M/C 001065
Flint, MI 48502-1926
Application address: c/o Helen James, Trust Off., Citizens Bank Wealth Mgmt., N.A., 101 N.

Washington Ave., Saginaw, MI 48607-1207, tel.: (989) 776-7368

Foundation type: Independent foundation
Purpose: Student loans to financially needy individuals who have been residents of Saginaw County, MI, for at least one year prior to application deadline, and are or will be attending colleges in MI.
Publications: Application guidelines.
Financial data: Year ended 06/30/2013. Assets, $16,182,714 (M); Expenditures, $825,782; Total giving, $579,300; Loans to individuals, 17 loans totaling $67,000.
Fields of interest: Higher education; Scholarships/financial aid.
Type of support: Student loans—to individuals.
Application information: Applications accepted. Application form required.
  Deadline(s): May 1
  Applicants should submit the following:
    1) Transcripts
    2) ACT
    3) SAT
    4) GPA
    5) Financial information
    6) Essay
  Additional information: Applicant must have a 2.0 GPA and financial need.
EIN: 386040506

4414
Evereg-Fenesse Educational Society

28302 Cypress Ct.
Farmington Hills, MI 48331-2996

Foundation type: Independent foundation
Purpose: Scholarships to students attending Armenian day schools, and to full-time undergraduate or graduate students of Armenian descent pursuing their undergraduate, Master's or Doctoral degree.
Financial data: Year ended 07/31/2013. Assets, $866,503 (M); Expenditures, $11,775; Total giving, $11,440; Grants to individuals, 51 grants totaling $11,000.
International interests: Armenia.
Type of support: Graduate support; Precollege support; Undergraduate support.
Application information: Application form required.
  Deadline(s): Dec. 15
  Additional information: Standard application forms available from, and submitted to, designated local chapter representatives.
EIN: 136154468

4415
H. T. Ewald Foundation

15450 E. Jefferson, Ste. 180
Grosse Pointe Park, MI 48230 (313) 821-1278
Contact: Judith Ewald, Pres.
Application address: 18450 E. Jefferson, Ste. 180, Grosse Pointe, MI 48230; URL: http://www.ewaldfoundation.org

Foundation type: Independent foundation
Purpose: Undergraduate scholarships to high school seniors who are residents of the metropolitan Detroit, MI, area.
Publications: Informational brochure (including application guidelines).
Financial data: Year ended 12/31/2012. Assets, $2,845,863 (M); Expenditures, $237,220; Total giving, $137,574; Grants to individuals, 30 grants totaling $99,700 (high: $4,000, low: $2,000).
Fields of interest: Higher education.
Type of support: Undergraduate support.

Application information: Applications accepted. Application form required.
  Initial approach: Letter or telephone
  Deadline(s): Mar. 1
  Applicants should submit the following:
    1) SAT
    2) ACT
    3) Transcripts
    4) Photograph
    5) Letter(s) of recommendation
  Additional information: Application must also include biography; Interviews required for finalists only.
EIN: 386007837

4416
Fabri-Kal Foundation

600 Plastics Pl.
Kalamazoo, MI 49001-4882 (269) 385-5050
Contact: Robert P. Kittredge, Pres.
URL: http://www.fabri-kal.com/why-fabri-kal/foundation/

Foundation type: Company-sponsored foundation
Purpose: Scholarships for higher education to children of employees of Fabri-Kal Corporation, primarily in MI, PA and SC.
Publications: Application guidelines; Grants list.
Financial data: Year ended 12/31/2012. Assets, $4,789 (M); Expenditures, $824,554; Total giving, $824,534; Grants to individuals, 73 grants totaling $655,535.
Fields of interest: Higher education.
Type of support: Employee-related scholarships.
Application information: Applications not accepted.
  Additional information: Unsolicited requests for funds not considered or acknowledged.
Company name: Fabri-Kal Corporation
EIN: 237003366

4417
Fallen and Wounded Soldier Fund

P.O. Box 33099
Bloomfield Hills, MI 48303-0003 (734) 779-4512
Contact: Tino Del Signore, Chair.
E-mail: contact@fwsf.org; Additional tel.: (734) 462-0770; URL: http://www.fwsf.org

Foundation type: Public charity
Purpose: Financial assistance with living expense to Michigan-based soldiers and their families who serve and protect the U.S.
Financial data: Year ended 12/31/2011. Assets, $242,138 (M); Expenditures, $105,656; Total giving, $93,664; Grants to individuals, totaling $53,664.
Fields of interest: Military/veterans' organizations.
Type of support: Grants for special needs.
Application information: Applications not accepted.
  Additional information: Unsolicited requests for funds not considered or acknowledged. Assistance only for soldiers and their families of MI.
EIN: 204882017

4418
John E. Fetzer Institute, Inc.
(formerly John E. Fetzer Foundation, Inc.)
9292 West KL Ave.
Kalamazoo, MI 49009-9398
Contact: Thomas F. Beech, C.E.O. and Pres.
FAX: (269) 372-2163; E-mail: info@fetzer.org;
URL: http://www.fetzer.org

Foundation type: Operating foundation
Purpose: Research grants to individuals for the exploration of the integral relationships among the body, mind and spirit.
Publications: Informational brochure; Newsletter; Occasional report; Program policy statement.
Financial data: Year ended 06/30/2013. Assets, $462,945,654 (M); Expenditures, $29,760,405; Total giving, $1,029,621.
Fields of interest: Biology/life sciences; Gerontology; Social sciences.
Type of support: Research.
Application information: Applications not accepted.
Additional information: Unsolicited requests for funds not considered or acknowledged.
EIN: 386052788

4419
Flint Cultural Center Corporation, Inc.
1310 E. Kearsley St.
Flint, MI 48503-1851 (810) 237-7333
FAX: (810) 237-7335;
E-mail: info@TheWhiting.com; URL: http://www.flintculturalcenter.com

Foundation type: Public charity
Purpose: Scholarships for dancers to attend a four-week summer program at the Joffrey Midwest Workshop in Flint, MI.
Publications: Informational brochure.
Financial data: Year ended 06/30/2012. Assets, $27,522,173 (M); Expenditures, $6,852,133; Total giving, $87,050; Grants to individuals, totaling $29,550.
Fields of interest: Performing arts centers; Dance; Ballet.
Type of support: Scholarships—to individuals.
Application information: Scholarships are awarded on a merit-only basis. Contact foundation for further application and program information.
EIN: 386089075

4420
Gerald R. Ford Foundation
303 Pearl St., N.W.
Grand Rapids, MI 49504-5343 (616) 254-0396
Contact: For Journalism Prize: Joseph S. Calvaruso, Exec. Dir.
Additional tel.: (616) 254-0373, e-mail address: barbara.mcgregor@nara.gov (Prizes); Contact Helmi Raaska, c/o Gerald R. Ford Presidential Library, 1000 Beal Ave., Ann Arbor, MI 48109-2114, tel.: (734) 205-0555, e-mail address: helmi.raaska@nara.gov (Travel).
FAX: (616) 254-0403;
E-mail: ford@38foundation.org; URL: http://www.geraldrfordfoundation.org

Foundation type: Public charity
Purpose: Grants to journalists for reporting on the presidency or national defense, to individuals for distinguished public service, and to individuals for research at the Gerald R. Ford Library.
Publications: Application guidelines; Informational brochure.

Financial data: Year ended 12/31/2011. Assets, $31,630,897 (M); Expenditures, $1,684,401; Total giving, $49,760; Grants to individuals, 39 grants totaling $49,760. Subtotal for research: 29 grants totaling $31,760. Subtotal for internship funds: 8 grants totaling $8,000. Subtotal for awards/prizes: 2 grants totaling $10,000.
Fields of interest: Print publishing; Political science; American studies.
Type of support: Research; Awards/prizes; Travel grants.
Application information: Applications accepted. Application form required. Application form available on the grantmaker's web site.
Copies of proposal: 1
Deadline(s): Mar. 8 for Journalism Prize, Mar. 15 and Sept. 15 for Research Travel Grants
Applicants should submit the following:
1) Letter(s) of recommendation
2) Proposal
3) Curriculum vitae
Additional information: See web site for complete application guidelines.
Program descriptions:
Gerald R. Ford Foundation Research Travel Grant: Grants of up to $2,000 each are available to support research in the holdings of the Gerald R. Ford Presidential Library.
Gerald R. Ford Journalism Prizes: This program awards two $5,000 prizes for distinguished reporting by journalists covering the presidency or national defense. The competition is restricted to print journalism; journalists may apply directly or be nominated by others.
EIN: 382368003

4421
Henry Ford Health System
1 Ford Pl., 5F
Detroit, MI 48202-3450 (313) 876-8714
URL: http://www.henryford.com/

Foundation type: Public charity
Purpose: Financial assistance to eligible employees and to eligible volunteers and retirees of Henry Ford Health System, MI who, due to a catastrophe cannot afford basic necessities.
Publications: Annual report.
Financial data: Year ended 12/31/2011. Assets, $1,874,131,097 (M); Expenditures, $2,236,526,717; Total giving, $3,060,609; Grants to individuals, 1,008 grants totaling $855,848. Subtotal for in-kind gifts: 877 grants totaling $658,024. Subtotal for grants to individuals: 131 grants totaling $197,824.
Fields of interest: Human services.
Type of support: Employee-related welfare; Grants for special needs.
Application information: Applications not accepted.
Additional information: Eligible employees receive assistance of up to $1,500, volunteers and retirees receive up to $500. Unsolicited requests for funds not considered or acknowledged.
EIN: 381357020

4422
William C. Ford, Jr. Scholarship Program
1901 Saint Antoine St., 6th Fl.
Ford Field
Detroit, MI 48226-2310
Application address: c/o Scholarship America, Att.: William C. Ford, P.O. Box 297, Saint Peter, MN 56082-0297, tel.: (800) 537-4180

Foundation type: Independent foundation
Purpose: Scholarships to the children of full-time Ford employees who will be enrolled as a sophomore in college.
Financial data: Year ended 12/31/2011. Assets, $1,188,015 (M); Expenditures, $332,176; Total giving, $313,500; Grants to individuals, 209 grants totaling $313,500 (high: $1,500, low: $1,500).
Fields of interest: Higher education.
Type of support: Employee-related scholarships; Scholarships—to individuals.
Application information: Application form required.
Deadline(s): July 1
Additional information: Application forms are available from Scholarship America. Applications must include a college transcript from the student's freshman year.
EIN: 202462203

4423
Foster Family Foundation
P.O. Box 437
St. Clair, MI 48079-0437

Foundation type: Independent foundation
Purpose: Scholarships to deserving high school students of St. Clair Michigan for attendance at colleges or universities.
Financial data: Year ended 12/31/2011. Assets, $321,201 (M); Expenditures, $50,419; Total giving, $46,000; Grants to individuals, 18 grants totaling $46,000 (high: $6,000, low: $1,000).
Fields of interest: Education.
Type of support: Scholarships—to individuals.
Application information: Contact foundation for application guidelines.
EIN: 203439954

4424
Foster Foundation
(formerly Foster Welfare Foundation)
P.O. Box 3636
Grand Rapids, MI 49501-3636
Contact: Karly Johns, Exec. Dir.
Application address: 581 Alta Dale S.E., Ada, MI 49301

Foundation type: Independent foundation
Purpose: Scholarships to financially needy students with demonstrated academic aptitude attending accredited colleges in Kent County, MI.
Financial data: Year ended 04/30/2013. Assets, $40,094 (M); Expenditures, $32,203; Total giving, $22,500; Grants to individuals, 23 grants totaling $22,500 (high: $1,500, low: $500).
Type of support: Support to graduates or students of specific schools; Undergraduate support.
Application information: Applications accepted.
Deadline(s): Feb. 1
Additional information: Application should include four letters of recommendation.
EIN: 380831533

4425
Foundation for Birmingham Senior Residents
2121 Midvale St.
Birmingham, MI 48009 (248) 203-5270

Foundation type: Independent foundation
Purpose: Loans to senior residents of Birmingham, MI, for minor home repairs who are homeowners 60 years of age or older with financial need.

Financial data: Year ended 12/31/2012. Assets, $397,927 (M); Expenditures, $23,130; Total giving, $19,700.
Fields of interest: Aging.
Type of support: Loans—to individuals.
Application information: Application form required.
  Additional information: Contact the foundation for application guidelines.
EIN: 382507882

4426
Foundation for Saline Area Schools
P. O. Box 5
Saline, MI 48176-0005 (734) 429-5922
Contact: Cheryl Hoeft, Pres.
FAX: (734) 429-8025;
E-mail: superdeb@gmail.com; URL: http://www.supportfsas.org/

Foundation type: Public charity
Purpose: Grants to teachers in Saline, MI, for projects and programs aimed at enhancing the quality of education and educational opportunities.
Publications: Application guidelines.
Financial data: Year ended 12/31/2011. Assets, $356,505 (M); Expenditures, $96,343; Total giving, $87,408.
Fields of interest: Education.
Type of support: Grants to individuals.
Application information: Applications accepted. Application form required. Application form available on the grantmaker's web site.
  Deadline(s): Mid-Oct.
  Final notification: Recipients notified in Nov.
  Additional information: Upon receipt of a grant, the recipient will have approximately 60 days to purchase all materials and/or supplies to carry out the idea/project.
Program description:
  Teaching Grants: These grants, of up to $1,000, are designed to get resources quickly into classrooms to support innovative ideas and project proposed by Saline-area educators that cannot be funded by the school's budget.
EIN: 382733854

4427
Four County Community Foundation
(formerly Four County Foundation)
231 E. St. Clair
P.O. Box 539
Almont, MI 48003-0539 (810) 798-0909
Contact: Janet Bauer, Pres. and C.E.O.; For grants: Ross Moore, Prog. Asso.
FAX: (810) 798-0908; E-mail: info@4ccf.org;
URL: http://www.4ccf.org

Foundation type: Community foundation
Purpose: Scholarships to high school students of southeast Lapeer, northwest Macomb, northeast Oakland, and southwest St. Clair counties, MI.
Publications: Application guidelines; Annual report; Informational brochure.
Financial data: Year ended 12/31/2012. Assets, $10,948,995 (M); Expenditures, $520,036; Total giving, $278,682; Grants to individuals, 159 grants totaling $121,395.
Fields of interest: Higher education.
Type of support: Scholarships—to individuals; Support to graduates or students of specific schools; Undergraduate support.
Application information: Applications accepted. Application form required.
  Deadline(s): Apr. 1 for FCCF Scholarship, varies for others
  Final notification: Applicants notified in July

Applicants should submit the following:
  1) Essay
  2) Transcripts
  3) Letter(s) of recommendation
Additional information: Applications are available at your high school counselor's office. See web site for a complete listing of available scholarships per school district.
Program description:
  Scholarships: The foundation manages multiple scholarship funds available to high school students of the Four County community service area for higher education. Some post-graduate scholarships are also available. Each fund has unique eligibility requirements and application forms. See web site for additional information.
EIN: 382736601

4428
Frankenmuth Community Foundation
(formerly Greater Frankenmuth Area Community Foundation)
P.O. Box 386
Frankenmuth, MI 48734-0386 (989) 284-4674
Contact: Stephen C. List, Exec. Dir.; For grants: Scott Zimmer, Treas.
E-mail: steve@frankenmuthcommunityfoundation.org; URL: http://www.frankenmuthfoundation.org

Foundation type: Community foundation
Purpose: Scholarships to graduates of the Frankenmuth School District, MI pursuing a college education.
Publications: Application guidelines; Informational brochure.
Financial data: Year ended 12/31/2012. Assets, $5,694,325 (M); Expenditures, $422,154; Total giving, $366,256; Grants to individuals, totaling $17,300.
Fields of interest: Higher education.
Type of support: Scholarships—to individuals; Support to graduates or students of specific schools; Undergraduate support.
Application information: Applications accepted. Application form required. Application form available on the grantmaker's web site.
  Additional information: Students should contact their school's guidance counselors.
Program description:
  Scholarships: The foundation currently offers 15 scholarship funds which were created to offer assistance to Frankenmuth students pursuing a college education. Eligibility requirements vary, and may be based on abilities in specific areas such as athletics and mathematics. Interested students should visit the foundation's web site and see their counselors at Frankenmuth High School for additional information and application.
EIN: 382140032

4429
Fraser Area Educational Foundation
33466 Garfield Rd.
Fraser, MI 48026-1892 (586) 879-2201

Foundation type: Public charity
Purpose: Scholarships to graduates of Fraser High School, MI.
Financial data: Year ended 06/30/2012. Assets, $51,261 (M); Expenditures, $19,548; Total giving, $17,867.
Type of support: Support to graduates or students of specific schools; Undergraduate support.
Application information: Applications accepted. Application form required.
  Deadline(s): Mar. 6

Applicants should submit the following:
  1) ACT
  2) Letter(s) of recommendation
  3) Transcripts
Additional information: Applications are available at the office of the guidance counselor.
EIN: 382785496

4430
Edwin R. Fredericksen Scholarship Fund
P.O. Box 3636
Grand Rapids, MI 49501-3636 (815) 233-3628

Foundation type: Independent foundation
Purpose: Scholarships to graduates of Riverside-Brookfield High School for attendance at technical college or trade school education.
Financial data: Year ended 12/31/2012. Assets, $721,323 (M); Expenditures, $76,084; Total giving, $64,500.
Fields of interest: Vocational education, post-secondary.
Type of support: Support to graduates or students of specific schools.
Application information: Applications accepted. Application form required.
  Deadline(s): May 1
  Additional information: Application available from high school.
EIN: 206956670

4431
Fremont Area Community Foundation
(formerly The Fremont Area Foundation)
4424 W. 48th St.
P.O. Box B
Fremont, MI 49412-8721 (231) 924-5350
Contact: Carla A. Roberts, Pres. and C.E.O.; For grants: Todd Jacobs, V.P., Community Investment; For scholarships: Robin Cowles, Scholarship and Donor Svcs. Mgr.
E-mail for scholarship inquiries: rcowles@tfacf.org
FAX: (231) 924-5391; E-mail: info@tfacf.org;
URL: http://www.tfacf.org

Foundation type: Community foundation
Purpose: Scholarships to graduates of high schools in Newaygo, Lake, Mecosta & Osceolay County, MI.
Publications: Application guidelines; Annual report; Grants list; Informational brochure; Newsletter.
Financial data: Year ended 12/31/2012. Assets, $188,094,887 (M); Expenditures, $9,572,607; Total giving, $8,330,639; Grants to individuals, 529 grants totaling $720,832 (high: $5,000, low: $125, average grant: $500-$1,500).
Fields of interest: Design; Teacher school/education; Theological school/education; Health sciences school/education; Scholarships/financial aid; Agriculture; Athletics/sports, school programs; Athletics/sports, basketball; Protestant agencies & churches.
Type of support: Scholarships—to individuals; Support to graduates or students of specific schools; Awards/prizes; Undergraduate support.
Application information: Applications accepted. Application form available on the grantmaker's web site.
  Initial approach: Application
  Send request by: On-line
  Deadline(s): Mar. 1
  Applicants should submit the following:
    1) Transcripts
    2) Resume
    3) GPA
    4) Financial information
    5) FAFSA

6) Essay
7) Budget Information
8) ACT
Additional information: See web site for additional information.
EIN: 381443367

4432
Galesburg-Augusta Community Schools Foundation

(formerly Galesburg-Augusta Education Foundation)
1076 N. 37th St.
Galesburg, MI   49053   (269) 484-2000

Foundation type: Operating foundation
Purpose: Scholarships to graduates from Galesburg-Augusta Community Schools, MI, for continued education. Grants to teachers for concepts that enhance education in the school district.
Publications: Informational brochure.
Financial data: Year ended 06/30/2012. Assets, $29,412 (M); Expenditures, $23,105; Total giving, $22,039; Grants to individuals, 22 grants totaling $16,850 (high: $2,500, low: $300).
Fields of interest: Higher education.
Type of support: Support to graduates or students of specific schools; Undergraduate support.
Application information: Applications accepted. Application form required.
  Deadline(s): Jan. 15 for Scholarships
  Applicants should submit the following:
    1) Transcripts
    2) Resume
    3) Essay
EIN: 383082334

4433
The Genesis Program Inc.

c/o Daniel R. Slate
P.O. Box 9
Fremont, MI   49412-0009   (231) 924-6890
Contact: Dorothy Paris

Foundation type: Operating foundation
Purpose: Interest free loans to individuals to aid in mortgage financing who are residents of Newaygo County, MI and surrounding counties.
Financial data: Year ended 12/31/2012. Assets, $93,340 (M); Expenditures, $4,399; Total giving, $0.
Fields of interest: Business/industry.
Type of support: Loans—to individuals.
Application information: Application form required.
  Initial approach: Letter
  Deadline(s): None
  Additional information: Loan application should include cash flow projections, business plan, personal tax returns and personal financial statements.
EIN: 383305718

4434
The Gerber Foundation

(formerly The Gerber Companies Foundation and The Gerber Baby Food Fund)
4747 W. 48th St., Ste. 153
Fremont, MI   49412-8119   (231) 924-3175
Contact: Catherine A. Obits, Prog. Mgr.
FAX: (231) 924-7906; E-mail: tgf@ncresa.org; Additional e-mail (Catherine A. Obits): cobits@ncresa.org; URL: http://www.gerberfoundation.org

Foundation type: Independent foundation

Purpose: Scholarships to Newaygo and Muskegon, MI county high school seniors for attendance at accredited colleges or universities, vocational or technical training program.
Publications: Application guidelines; Annual report (including application guidelines); Grants list; Program policy statement.
Financial data: Year ended 12/31/2013. Assets, $74,314,600 (M); Expenditures, $4,116,500; Total giving, $3,511,300; Grants to individuals, 70 grants totaling $302,018 (high: $9,200, low: $2,300).
Fields of interest: Higher education; Scholarships/financial aid.
Type of support: Scholarships—to individuals; Undergraduate support.
Application information: Applications accepted. Application form required. Application form available on the grantmaker's web site.
  Initial approach: E-mail
  Send request by: On-line and mail
  Copies of proposal: 1
  Deadline(s): Feb. 28
  Applicants should submit the following:
    1) Essay
    2) GPA
    3) Letter(s) of recommendation
  Additional information: Application available on the foundation web site or from the foundation office.
Program descriptions:
  Daniel Gerber, Sr. Medallion Scholarship: This scholarship was created for students graduating from one of the five school districts in Newaygo County, MI, and was established to recognize and honor academic excellence among graduating seniors. Students must have a GPA of 3.71 or higher to apply (higher of weighted or unweighted). The scholarship provides $9,200, in aggregate, to be applied to tuition, fees, and books over the course of the student's undergraduate studies.
  The Gerber Foundation Merit Scholarship: This scholarship was established to recognize academic achievement among graduating seniors from Newaygo and Muskegon Counties in MI. Students must have a GPA of 3.70 or below to apply. The scholarship provides $2,300 to be applied to tuition, fees, and books for a course of study at a postsecondary institution.
EIN: 386068090

4435
Ruby L. Gibbs Charitable Trust

328 S. Saginaw St., M/C 001065
Flint, MI   48502   (989) 834-2271
Contact: Pam Washburn
Application addresses: Ovid-Elsie High School, 8989 E. Colony Rd., Elsie, MI 48831,

Foundation type: Independent foundation
Purpose: Scholarships to students of Arthur Hill High School, MI, who will be attending an accredited college in MI and students of Ovid-Elsie High School, MI, attending a college in central MI.
Financial data: Year ended 12/31/2012. Assets, $1,252,814 (M); Expenditures, $69,570; Total giving, $48,372; Grants to individuals, 15 grants totaling $31,700 (high: $10,000, low: $800).
Type of support: Support to graduates or students of specific schools; Undergraduate support.
Application information: Applications accepted. Application form required.
  Deadline(s): May 1
EIN: 386658848

4436
Herbert & Florence Gilles Scholarship Trust

328 S. Saginaw St., M/C 001065
Flint, MI   48502   (989) 797-6000
Contact: Oscar Mendoza
Application address: C/o Saginaw Area Catholic Schools, 5376 State St., Saginaw, MI 48608. Tel.: (989) 797-6000

Foundation type: Independent foundation
Purpose: Scholarships only to students at Nouvel Catholic Central High School, MI.
Financial data: Year ended 12/31/2012. Assets, $173,015 (M); Expenditures, $11,273; Total giving, $5,900; Grants to individuals, 6 grants totaling $5,900 (high: $1,235, low: $706).
Type of support: Support to graduates or students of specific schools; Undergraduate support.
Application information: Applications accepted. Application form required.
  Deadline(s): Second Mon. in May
EIN: 386738557

4437
The Gilmore Foundation

c/o Fifth Third Bank
P.O. Box 3636
Grand Rapids, MI   49501-3636

Foundation type: Independent foundation
Purpose: Financial assistance to extremely low-income residents of the Kalamazoo, MI, area who are unable to care for themselves due to physical limitations or advanced age.
Financial data: Year ended 12/31/2012. Assets, $57,654 (M); Expenditures, $51,914; Total giving, $49,274; Grants to individuals, 5 grants totaling $49,274 (high: $13,870, low: $5,035).
Fields of interest: Aging; Disabilities, people with; Economically disadvantaged.
Type of support: Grants for special needs.
Application information: Applications not accepted.
EIN: 386052803

4438
Irving S. Gilmore International Keyboard Festival

359 S. Kalamazoo Mall, Ste. 101
Kalamazoo, MI   49007-4843   (269) 342-1166
Contact: William C. Richardson, Pres.
FAX: (269) 342-0968; Toll-free tel.: (800) 347-4266; URL: http://www.thegilmore.org/festival/

Foundation type: Public charity
Purpose: Awards by nomination only to exceptional pianists who demonstrate the talent and drive to become successful concert artists.
Publications: Newsletter.
Financial data: Year ended 08/31/2011. Assets, $4,262,626 (M); Expenditures, $1,384,730; Total giving, $80,741; Grants to individuals, 12 grants totaling $80,741. Subtotal for scholarships—to individuals: 8 grants totaling $890. Subtotal for awards/prizes: 3 grants totaling $77,500.
Fields of interest: Music.
Type of support: Awards/grants by nomination only; Foreign applicants; Awards/prizes.
Application information: Applications not accepted.
Program descriptions:
  Gilmore Artist Award: Awards $300,000 every four years to an exceptional pianist who, regardless of age or nationality, is a superb pianist and

profound musician, who desires and can sustain a career as a major international concert artist, and whose developing career can be enhanced by the Award's money and prestige.

Gilmore Young Artist Award: This program awards $15,000 every two years, as well as $10,000 to commission a new piano composition for which the artist will have exclusive performance rights for one year, to a promising young American pianist who is 22 years old or younger. Nominations are made by leaders in the field of music, and nominees are not told of their inclusion in the non-competitive selection process.

EIN: 382868071

4439
Sheldon Glaser Trust

P.O. Box 3636
Grand Rapids, MI   49501-3636   (815) 233-3628
Contact: Cheryl Lessman, Tr.
*Aplplication Address:*101 W. Stephenson St.
Freeport,IL 61032

Foundation type: Independent foundation
Purpose: Scholarships to students enrolled at a qualifying educational institution that qualifies as a public charity, primarily in Lena, IL.
Financial data: Year ended 12/31/2012. Assets, $221,674 (M); Expenditures, $18,867; Total giving, $12,000.
Fields of interest: Higher education.
Type of support: Scholarships—to individuals.
Application information: Application form required.
  Deadline(s): Mar.
EIN: 367074441

4440
Gleaner Life Insurance Society
Scholarship Foundation

5200 W. U.S. Hwy. 223
Adrian, MI   49221-9461   (517) 263-2244
FAX: (517) 265-7745;
E-mail: scholarships@gleanerlife.org; Additional tel.: (800) 992-1894; URL: http://www.gleanerlife.org/PreviewNewsMore.aspx?NewsArticleID=352

Foundation type: Operating foundation
Purpose: Scholarships only to members of the society and their family members.
Publications: Application guidelines; Informational brochure.
Financial data: Year ended 06/30/2012. Assets, $737,684 (M); Expenditures, $50,993; Total giving, $48,489; Grants to individuals, 4 grants totaling $48,489 (high: $41,000; low: $1,000).
Fields of interest: Fraternal societies (501(c)(8)).
Type of support: Scholarships—to individuals.
Application information: Application form required. Application form available on the grantmaker's web site.
  Deadline(s): Mar. 1
  Applicants should submit the following:
    1) Transcripts
    2) Letter(s) of recommendation
EIN: 383006741

4441
Glen Arbor Art Association

P.O. Box 305
Glen Arbor, MI   49636-0305   (231) 334-6112
Contact: Peg McCarty, Exec. Dir.
E-mail: info@glenarborart.org; URL: http://www.glenarborart.org

Foundation type: Public charity
Purpose: Residencies to visiting artists specializing in writing, visual arts, photography, sculpture, fiber arts, ceramics, music, philosophy, and creative research.
Publications: Application guidelines; Newsletter.
Financial data: Year ended 12/31/2011. Assets, $332,301 (M); Expenditures, $146,397.
Fields of interest: Visual arts; Photography; Sculpture; Ceramic arts; Music.
Type of support: Residencies.
Application information: Applications accepted.
  Initial approach: Letter
  Send request by: Mail
  Copies of proposal: 1
  Deadline(s): Mar. 1 for Artists-in-Residence Program
  Applicants should submit the following:
    1) Work samples
    2) SASE
    3) Resume
    4) Proposal
  Additional information: Visual artists should send at least five photos of current work.
EIN: 382886660

4442
David Goodrich College Education Fund

P.O. Box 3636
Grand Rapids, MI   49501-3636   (989) 834-2271
Contact: Wayne Petroelje
Application address: c/o Elsie Area Supt. of Schools, 8989 E. Colony Rd., Elsie, MI 48831-9724, tel. (989) 834-2271

Foundation type: Independent foundation
Purpose: Scholarships to financially needy students living within a four-mile radius of Ovid, MI, who have high scholastic averages.
Financial data: Year ended 12/31/2012. Assets, $644,291 (M); Expenditures, $39,805; Total giving, $31,541.
Type of support: Scholarships—to individuals.
Application information: Applications accepted.
  Deadline(s): May 1
EIN: 386658237

4443
Beatrice I. Goss Educational
Testamentary Trust

P.O. Box 3636
Grand Rapids, MI   49501-3636   (800) 795-4115
Application address: c/o Beatrice Goss Scholarship Trust, 38 Fountain Sq. Pl., Cincinnati, OH 45263

Foundation type: Independent foundation
Purpose: Scholarships to residents of Marshall County, IN, for higher education.
Financial data: Year ended 09/30/2013. Assets, $146,770 (M); Expenditures, $11,892; Total giving, $6,000; Grants to individuals, 12 grants totaling $6,000 (high: $500; low: $500).
Type of support: Undergraduate support.
Application information: Application form required.
  Deadline(s): Mar. 15
  Additional information: Contact foundation for current application guidelines.
EIN: 356361029

4444
Grand Haven Area Community
Foundation, Inc.

1 S. Harbor Dr.
Grand Haven, MI   49417-1385   (616) 842-6378
Contact: Holly Johnson, Pres.; For grants: Beth Larson, Dir., Grants and Progs.
FAX: (616) 842-9518; E-mail: bpost@ghacf.org; URL: http://www.ghacf.org

Foundation type: Community foundation
Purpose: Scholarships to residents of northwest Ottawa County, MI, including the City of Grand Haven, Grand Haven Township, the Village of Spring Lake, Spring Lake Township, the City of Ferrysburg, and Robinson Township.
Publications: Application guidelines; Annual report (including application guidelines); Financial statement; Informational brochure (including application guidelines); Newsletter; Program policy statement.
Financial data: Year ended 12/31/2011. Assets, $46,499,148 (M); Expenditures, $3,200,912; Total giving, $2,575,162; Grants to individuals, 178 grants totaling $179,264.
Fields of interest: Higher education; Scholarships/financial aid.
Type of support: Scholarships—to individuals; Undergraduate support.
Application information: Applications accepted. Application form required. Application form available on the grantmaker's web site.
  Initial approach: Application
  Send request by: Online
  Deadline(s): Mar. 1
  Final notification: Applicants notified between May and June
  Applicants should submit the following:
    1) FAFSA
    2) Transcripts
    3) Financial information
    4) SAR
  Additional information: See web site for additional information.
Program description:
  Scholarship Program: Scholarships are awarded on a competitive basis which considers financial need, academic achievement, and personal and career goals. Each scholarship has it's own unique set of eligibility criteria. An internal process exists for scholarship selection based on questions answered in the body of the application, however, if you wish, you may address specific scholarships in the essay section of the application. See web site for additional information.
EIN: 237108776

4445
Grand Rapids Community Foundation

(formerly The Grand Rapids Foundation)
185 Oakes Street SW
Grand Rapids, MI   49503-4219   (616) 454-1751
Contact: Diana R. Sieger, President; For grant inquiries: Shavon Doyle, Grants Admin.
Scholarship contact: Ruth Bishop, tel.: (616) 454-1751, ext. 103,
e-mail: rbishop@grfoundation.org
FAX: (616) 454-6455;
E-mail: grfound@grfoundation.org; URL: http://www.grfoundation.org

Foundation type: Community foundation
Purpose: Scholarships to residents of Kent, Ottawa and surrounding counties (Greater Grand Rapids), and select awards to other state residents.
Publications: Annual report; Informational brochure; Newsletter.

Financial data: Year ended 06/30/2012. Assets, $244,475,151 (L); Expenditures, $15,550,105; Total giving, $11,022,722; Grants to individuals, 584 grants totaling $844,250.
Fields of interest: Arts education; Performing arts, education; Higher education; Business school/education; Law school/education; Health sciences school/education; Scholarships/financial aid; Race/intergroup relations.
Type of support: Employee-related scholarships; Scholarships—to individuals; Support to graduates or students of specific schools; Undergraduate support; Postgraduate support; Camperships.
Application information: Applications accepted. Application form required. Application form available on the grantmaker's web site.
  Initial approach: Application
  Send request by: Online
  Deadline(s): Apr. 1
  Final notification: Applicants notified by June 1
  Applicants should submit the following:
    1) ACT
    2) Transcripts
    3) Letter(s) of recommendation
    4) GPA
    5) Essay
    6) Financial information
  Additional information: See web site for complete listing of scholarships.
EIN: 382877959

4446
Grand Rapids Urban League
745 Eastern Ave., S.E.
Grand Rapids, MI 49503-5544 (616) 245-2207
FAX: (616) 245-6510;
E-mail: info@grurbanleague.org; URL: http://grurbanleague.org

Foundation type: Public charity
Purpose: Assistance to minorities and the disadvantaged in the Grand Rapids, MI area with child care, housing, employment, education and other special needs to become self-sufficient.
Financial data: Year ended 12/31/2011. Assets, $375,176 (M); Expenditures, $875,368; Total giving, $305,953; Grants to individuals, 9,559 grants totaling $305,953. Subtotal for grants to individuals: 9,559 grants totaling $305,953.
Fields of interest: Minorities; African Americans/Blacks; Economically disadvantaged.
Type of support: Grants for special needs.
Application information: Contact the league for eligibility determination.
EIN: 381359259

4447
Grand Traverse Regional Community Foundation
250 E. Front St., Ste. 310
Traverse City, MI 49684-2552 (231) 935-4066
Contact: Phil Ellis, Exec. Dir.; For grants: Gina Limbocker, Grantmaking and Prog. Assoc.
FAX: (231) 941-0021; E-mail: info@gtrcf.org; Grant application e-mail: glimbocker@gtrcf.org; URL: http://www.gtrcf.org

Foundation type: Community foundation
Purpose: Scholarships to students in Antrim, Benzie, Grand Traverse, Kalkaska and Leelanau counties, MI for postsecondary education.
Publications: Annual report; Informational brochure; Newsletter.
Financial data: Year ended 12/31/2012. Assets, $51,932,338 (M); Expenditures, $2,430,791;

Total giving, $1,805,370; Grants to individuals, 148 grants totaling $131,349.
Fields of interest: Higher education.
Type of support: Scholarships—to individuals; Undergraduate support.
Application information: Applications accepted. Application form required. Application form available on the grantmaker's web site.
  Initial approach: Application
  Send request by: Mail
  Deadline(s): Spring
  Additional information: Scholarships are offered to students based on a variety of criteria, including planned major, high school participation, academic achievement, financial need, and more. Each scholarship has its own set of eligibility criteria and guidelines. See web site for a complete listing.
EIN: 383056434

4448
Gratiot County Community Foundation
168 E. Center St.
P.O. Box 248
Ithaca, MI 48847-0248 (989) 875-4222
Contact: Tina M. Travis, Exec. Dir.
FAX: (989) 875-0016;
E-mail: gccf@gratiotfoundation.org; URL: http://www.gratiotfoundation.org

Foundation type: Community foundation
Purpose: Scholarships to students of Gratiot County, MI pursuing an education at institutions of higher learning.
Publications: Application guidelines; Annual report; Informational brochure; Newsletter.
Financial data: Year ended 09/30/2012. Assets, $9,175,826 (M); Expenditures, $1,745,520; Total giving, $257,552.
Fields of interest: Higher education.
Type of support: Scholarships—to individuals; Graduate support; Undergraduate support.
Application information: Applications accepted. Application form required. Application form available on the grantmaker's web site.
  Initial approach: Application
  Send request by: Mail
  Deadline(s): Mar. 11
  Final notification: Applicants notified in Apr.
  Applicants should submit the following:
    1) Essay
    2) SAT
    3) SAR
    4) Transcripts
    5) GPA
    6) ACT
  Additional information: Eligibility criteria varies per scholarship. See web site for a complete listing.
EIN: 383087756

4449
Gratiot Physicians Foundation
121 N. Pine River Rd.
Ithaca, MI 48847 (989) 875-5111
Application Address: Gratiot Phisicians Foundation, 121 N Pine Rd., Ithaca, MI 48847

Foundation type: Operating foundation
Purpose: Scholarships to residents of Gratiot county, or within Gratiot hospital's service area who are accepted to a professional school for training in one of the many various branches of health care such as medical or nursing school, podiatry, physical therapy, x-ray or ultrasound technology.

Financial data: Year ended 12/31/2012. Assets, $193,127 (M); Expenditures, $630; Total giving, $0.
Fields of interest: Medical school/education; Nursing school/education.
Type of support: Scholarships—to individuals.
Application information: Applications accepted. Application form required.
  Deadline(s): None
EIN: 383571320

4450
Great Lakes Castings Corporation Foundation
800 N. Washington Ave.
Ludington, MI 49431-2724 (231) 843-2501
Contact: Carol Henke, Tr.

Foundation type: Company-sponsored foundation
Purpose: Scholarships to high school graduates from Ludington, MI, area school districts.
Financial data: Year ended 12/31/2012. Assets, $960,945 (M); Expenditures, $33,659; Total giving, $27,980; Grants to individuals, 12 grants totaling $16,500 (high: $1,500; low: $750).
Type of support: Undergraduate support.
Application information: Applications accepted.
  Initial approach: Letter or telephone
  Deadline(s): Apr. 1 of applicant's senior year of high school or college for scholarships
  Additional information: Application must outline personal, academic, and professional data.
EIN: 382250546

4451
Greenville Area Community Foundation
(formerly Greenville Area Foundation)
101 N. Lafayette St.
Greenville, MI 48838-1853 (616) 754-2640
Contact: Alison Barberi, C.E.O.; For grants: Amy O'Brien, Dir., Grants and Comms.
E-mail: alison@gacfmi.org; URL: http://www.gacfmi.org

Foundation type: Community foundation
Purpose: Scholarships to graduating seniors of Greenville, Lakeview, Montabella, and Tri County MI high schools. Financial assistance to a college or university-bound adult resident of the Lakeview Community.
Publications: Application guidelines; Annual report; Financial statement; Grants list; Informational brochure; Informational brochure (including application guidelines); Newsletter.
Financial data: Year ended 12/31/2012. Assets, $22,246,132 (M); Expenditures, $1,733,444; Total giving, $1,353,562; Grants to individuals, totaling $142,875.
Fields of interest: Higher education.
Type of support: Scholarships—to individuals; Support to graduates or students of specific schools; Undergraduate support.
Application information: Applications accepted.
  Final notification: Applicants notified in Spring
  Additional information: Contact local high school counseling offices for scholarship information. Contact GACF Program Administrator for further information about the Lincoln Family Adult Scholarship Fund. See web site for additional information.
EIN: 382899657

4452
Guardian Industries Educational Foundation
2300 Harmon Rd.
Auburn Hills, MI 48326-1714 (609) 771-7878

Foundation type: Company-sponsored foundation
Purpose: Scholarships to children of full-time employees of Guardian Industries and its U.S. subsidiaries for attendance at accredited two- and four-year colleges, vocational and technical schools, and hospital schools of nursing in the U.S.
Financial data: Year ended 12/31/2012. Assets, $81,521 (M); Expenditures, $802,069; Total giving, $776,800; Grants to individuals, 195 grants totaling $776,800 (high: $4,000, low: $2,000).
Fields of interest: Vocational education; Nursing school/education.
Type of support: Employee-related scholarships; Technical education support; Undergraduate support.
Application information: Application form required.
　Deadline(s): Nov. 30
　Additional information: Application should include SAT scores.
Company name: Guardian Industries
EIN: 382707035

4453
Mary L. Gumaer Scholarship Foundation
P.O. Box 3636
Grand Rapids, MI 49501-3636 (989) 862-5820

Foundation type: Independent foundation
Purpose: Scholarships to graduating seniors of Ovid-Elsie High School, MI with at least a 2.5 GPA, and entering college as a full time student.
Financial data: Year ended 12/31/2012. Assets, $273,798 (M); Expenditures, $18,425; Total giving, $13,481.
Fields of interest: Higher education.
Type of support: Support to graduates or students of specific schools.
Application information: Applications accepted. Application form required.
　Deadline(s): May 1
　Additional information: Applications available at high school.
EIN: 386751392

4454
Habitat for Humanity of Kent County, Inc.
425 Pleasant St., S.W.
Grand Rapids, MI 49503-4959 (616) 774-2431
FAX: (616) 774-4120; URL: http://habitatkent.org/

Foundation type: Public charity
Purpose: Financial assistance to indigent residents of Kent County, MI, for the payment of utilities, food, clothing and shelter.
Financial data: Year ended 06/30/2012. Assets, $14,833,523 (M); Expenditures, $6,222,638.
Type of support: Grants for special needs.
Application information: Unsolicited requests for funds not considered.
EIN: 382527968

4455
Hammel-Delangis Scholarship Trust
c/o Northern Michigan Bank And Trust
1502 W. Washington St.
Marquette, MI 49855 (906) 779-2610

Foundation type: Independent foundation

Purpose: Scholarships to graduates of Iron Mountain High School, MI pursuing a four year degree in a health related field in optometry, medicine, nursing or similar course or instruction.
Financial data: Year ended 09/30/2013. Assets, $62,718 (M); Expenditures, $3,116; Total giving, $1,630; Grant to an individual, 1 grant totaling $1,630.
Fields of interest: Medical school/education; Nursing school/education; Health sciences school/education.
Type of support: Support to graduates or students of specific schools; Undergraduate support.
Application information: Application form required.
　Deadline(s): Apr. 25
　Applicants should submit the following:
　　1) Letter(s) of recommendation
　　2) Transcripts
　　3) ACT
EIN: 386513191

4456
Harbor Springs Educational Foundation
P.O. Box 844
Harbor Springs, MI 49740-0844
Contact: Frank Shumway, Pres.

Foundation type: Public charity
Purpose: Scholarships to graduating seniors of Harbor Springs High School, MI for higher education at colleges or universities.
Fields of interest: Higher education.
Type of support: Support to graduates or students of specific schools.
Application information: Students are selected by a committee of instructors. Scholarship is based on need and family income.
EIN: 383458936

4457
George Harding Scholarship Fund
507 S. Grand Ave.
Lansing, MI 48933 (517) 485-3600
Contact: Betty Kirkey

Foundation type: Independent foundation
Purpose: Scholarships to MI residents who are full-time students, enrolled in a four-year out-of-state or MI college or university, and pursuing finance-related degrees. Scholarships are available for the junior and senior year of college, or first year of graduate school. Recipients must maintain MI residency and an overall GPA of 3.0 or higher.
Financial data: Year ended 12/31/2012. Assets, $63,204 (M); Expenditures, $13,821; Total giving, $0.
Fields of interest: Business school/education; Economics.
Type of support: Graduate support; Undergraduate support.
Application information: Application form required.
　Send request by: Mail
　Deadline(s): July 15
　Additional information: Application must include transcript.
EIN: 382527040

4458
HCC Foundation
2113 N. White Birch Dr.
Mears, MI 49436-9434 (616) 928-9120
Contact: Ned Timmer
Application address: 301 Hoover Blvd., Holland, MI 49423

Foundation type: Operating foundation
Purpose: Scholarships to residents of Holland, MI.
Financial data: Year ended 12/31/2012. Assets, $0 (M); Expenditures, $270; Total giving, $0.
Type of support: Undergraduate support.
Application information:
　Initial approach: Letter
　Additional information: Contact foundation for application requirements.
EIN: 061660898

4459
The Heat and Warmth Fund
(also known as THAW)
607 Shelby, Ste. 400
Detroit, MI 48226-1848 (313) 226-9465
Contact: Susan Sherer, C.E.O.
FAX: (313) 963-2777; E-mail: info@thawfund.org; Toll-free tel.: (800) 866-8429; E-mail For Susan Sherer: ssherer@thawfund.org; URL: http://www.thawfund.org

Foundation type: Public charity
Purpose: Assistance to low income individuals and families of Michigan with energy assistance during crisis.
Publications: Application guidelines.
Financial data: Year ended 06/30/2012. Assets, $10,191,135 (M); Expenditures, $10,904,700; Total giving, $8,602,975; Grants to individuals, totaling $8,602,975.
Fields of interest: Human services; Economically disadvantaged.
Type of support: Grants for special needs.
Application information:
　Initial approach: Telephone
　Additional information: Applicant must have proof of household income, which must be at or below 200 percent of the current Federal Poverty Level guidelines, must have a valid Michigan drivers license or State ID, and applicant must pay unauthorized usage charges. All energy assistance payments are made directly to the vendors. Contact the agency for eligibility determination or see web site for additional information.
EIN: 382646924

4460
Hebert Memorial Scholarship Fund
c/o Kim M. Gardey
100 Harrow Ln.
Saginaw, MI 48638-6095
Application address: c/o Saginaw Community Foundation, 100 S. Jefferson, Ste. 201, Saginaw, MI 48607, tel.: (989) 755-0545
E-mail: info@saginawfoundation.org

Foundation type: Independent foundation
Purpose: Scholarships to deserving individuals pursuing studies at a college or university of their choice.
Financial data: Year ended 12/31/2012. Assets, $1,974,149 (M); Expenditures, $172,686; Total giving, $150,000; Grants to individuals, 50 grants totaling $150,000 (high: $3,000, low: $3,000).
Fields of interest: Higher education.
Type of support: Scholarships—to individuals.
Application information: Applications accepted. Application form required.
　Deadline(s): Feb. 1
　Applicants should submit the following:
　　1) Letter(s) of recommendation
　　2) Transcripts
　Additional information: Applicants must be residents of Saginaw county, MI, and have

maintained at least a 3.0 GPA during their four year high school education.

EIN: 262764191

4461
Maurice and Virginia Hecht Scholarship Fund

328 S. Saginaw St., MC 001065
Flint, MI   48502-1923   (810) 237-4186
Contact: Melissa Hendges

Foundation type: Independent foundation
Purpose: Scholarships to graduates of Burr Oak High School, MI for continuing education at institutions of higher learning.
Financial data: Year ended 03/31/2013. Assets, $203,018 (M); Expenditures, $14,933; Total giving, $8,432; Grants to individuals, 8 grants totaling $8,432 (high: $1,054, low: $1,054).
Fields of interest: Higher education.
Type of support: Support to graduates or students of specific schools; Undergraduate support.
Application information: Applications accepted.
  Initial approach: Letter
  Deadline(s): None
  Applicants should submit the following:
    1) Letter(s) of recommendation
    2) Financial information
  Additional information: Application should also include a list of academic and nonacademic achievements and goals from the superintendent and principal of Burr Oak High School.
EIN: 382923150

4462
The George and Lucile Heeringa Foundation

P.O. Box 9016
Holland, MI   49422-9016

Foundation type: Independent foundation
Purpose: Scholarships to western MI area high school students for higher education.
Financial data: Year ended 12/31/2012. Assets, $775,278 (M); Expenditures, $31,322; Total giving, $27,250; Grants to individuals, 36 grants totaling $25,250 (high: $1,500, low: $250).
Type of support: Undergraduate support.
Application information: Applications not accepted.
  Additional information: Unsolicited requests for funds not considered or acknowledged.
EIN: 383024217

4463
Hemophilia Foundation of Michigan

1921 W. Michigan Ave.
Ypsilanti, MI   48197-4816   (734) 544-0015
Contact: Ivan C. Harner FACHE, Exec. Dir.
FAX: (734) 544-0095; E-mail: hfm@hfmich.org;
Toll-free tel.: (800) 482-3041; URL: http://
www.hfmich.org

Foundation type: Public charity
Purpose: Scholarships to individuals in the bleeding disorder community to defray the cost of higher education. Financial aid to consumers in a temporary financial emergency.
Publications: Application guidelines; Annual report.
Financial data: Year ended 12/31/2011. Assets, $2,650,757 (M); Expenditures, $2,167,416; Total giving, $953,847. Emergency funds amount not

specified. Scholarships—to individuals amount not specified.
Fields of interest: Higher education; Hemophilia.
Type of support: Emergency funds; Research; Scholarships—to individuals.
Application information: Applications accepted. Application form required. Application form available on the grantmaker's web site.
  Initial approach: Application
  Send request by: Mail
  Deadline(s): Mar. 22 for Academic Scholarships
  Final notification: Recipients notified in Apr. for scholarships
  Additional information: See web site for additional guidelines.
Program descriptions:
  Academic Scholarships: The foundation annually provides two scholarship awards of $2,500 each to individuals within the bleeding disorder community who reside in Michigan. Applicants should be seeking a higher education through a college, university, or trade school.
  Financial Aid: Emergency financial assistance is available to consumers who find themselves in a temporary financial emergency. Funds can be accessed for such items as food, utility bills, rent, and car repair for individuals whose bleeding disorder impacts their income. Assistance is dependent on the severity of the need, and the ability of the applicant to change his/her financial standing.
EIN: 381905673

4464
Elizabeth A. Herdegen Trust

P.O. Box 75000
Detroit, MI   48275-3302   (416) 486-6959
Application address: c/o Taylor Statten Camps, 28 Longwood, Don Mills, Ontario, Canada M4S 2X5

Foundation type: Independent foundation
Purpose: Camperships to financially needy individuals aged seven to seventeen.
Financial data: Year ended 12/31/2011. Assets, $124,460 (M); Expenditures, $9,553; Total giving, $6,898; Grant to an individual, 1 grant totaling $6,898.
Fields of interest: Children/youth, services; Economically disadvantaged.
Type of support: Precollege support.
Application information:
  Deadline(s): Feb. 15
  Additional information: Contact foundation for current application guidelines.
EIN: 386461176

4465
F. W. & Elsie Heyl Science Scholarship Fund

1200 Academy St.
Kalamazoo, MI   49006-3268   (269) 337-7103
Contact: For Kalamazoo College applicants: Dr. Diane R. Kiino, Exec. Dir.; For WMU Bronson School of Nursing applicants: Dr. Marie Gates
E-mail: dkiino@kzoo.edu; URL: http://
www.kzoo.edu/heyl/

Foundation type: Public charity
Purpose: Scholarships to high school seniors from Kalamazoo Public Schools and seniors from other high schools or home school programs for studies in the sciences and nursing for attendance at Kalamazoo College or the WMU Bronson School of Nursing. Fellowships to graduates of Kalamazoo College for attendance at Yale University pursuing Chemistry-related studies.

Publications: Application guidelines.
Financial data: Year ended 12/31/2011. Assets, $34,811,036 (M); Expenditures, $1,525,029; Total giving, $1,425,491. Scholarships—to individuals amount not specified.
Fields of interest: Higher education; Nursing school/education; Science.
Type of support: Fellowships; Scholarships—to individuals; Support to graduates or students of specific schools.
Application information: Applications accepted. Application form required. Interview required.
  Deadline(s): Dec. 1 for Scholarships
  Applicants should submit the following:
    1) SAT
    2) GPA
    3) ACT
  Additional information: Payments are made directly to the educational institution on behalf of the students. See web site for additional application guidelines.
Program description:
  Scholarships: Scholarships to high school seniors from Kalamazoo Public Schools (as well as seniors from other high schools or home school programs) who will earn certificates of completion from the Kalamazoo Area Math and Science Center (KAMSC). Scholarships will be used to allow recipients to attend Kalamazoo College, Western Michigan University Bronson School of Nursing, or Yale University. Applicants must have a high school GPA of at least 3.5, have an SAT verbal score greater than 500 and an SAT math score greater than 550 (or an ACT composite score greater than 25), demonstrate a challenging high school curriculum that includes one year each of biology, chemistry, and physics, and four years of math, an interest in science, math, or nursing (as demonstrated by their choice of classes and activities outside of the classroom), strong writing skills, and strong teacher evaluations.
EIN: 386194019

4466
Hillier Scholarship Fund of Evart

142 N. Main St.
Evart, MI   49631-5104   (231) 734-5563
Contact: Lynn Salinas, Treas.
Application address: P.O. Box 608, Evart, MI 49631-0608

Foundation type: Operating foundation
Purpose: Scholarships to qualified graduating seniors of Evart High School, MI for continuing education at accredited colleges or universities.
Financial data: Year ended 12/31/2012. Assets, $169,525 (M); Expenditures, $5,077; Total giving, $1,500; Grants to individuals, 2 grants totaling $1,500 (high: $750, low: $750).
Fields of interest: Higher education.
Type of support: Scholarships—to individuals; Support to graduates or students of specific schools.
Application information: Applications accepted.
  Deadline(s): Mar. 15
  Additional information: Graduating seniors with a 3.0 GPA receives a letter of application.
EIN: 383299844

4467
Hillsdale County Community Foundation
2 S. Howell St.
P.O. Box 276
Hillsdale, MI 49242-0276 (517) 439-5101
Contact: Sharon E. Bisher, Exec. Dir.
FAX: (517) 439-5109; E-mail: info@abouthccf.org;
Additional e-mail: s.bisher@abouthccf.org;
URL: http://www.abouthccf.org

Foundation type: Community foundation
Purpose: Scholarships to local students and
residents of Hillsdale County, MI pursuing higher
education.
Publications: Application guidelines; Annual report;
Financial statement; Informational brochure
(including application guidelines); Newsletter.
Financial data: Year ended 09/30/2012. Assets,
$11,594,701 (M); Expenditures, $858,874; Total
giving, $482,777; Grants to individuals, totaling
$196,830.
Fields of interest: Higher education.
Type of support: Scholarships—to individuals.
Application information: Applications accepted.
Application form required.
Deadline(s): Mar. 1
Final notification: Applicants notified in June
Applicants should submit the following:
　　1) Financial information
　　2) Transcripts
　　3) Letter(s) of recommendation
　　4) Essay
　　5) SAR
Additional information: See web site for
　　additional application guidelines.
EIN: 383001297

4468
Home and Building Association
Foundation
(formerly Greater Grand Rapids Home Builders
Association Foundation, also known as HBA
Foundation)
3959 Clay Ave., S.W.
Wyoming, MI 49548
Application Address: c/o Home and Building
Association Foundation, Attn.: Foundation Director

Foundation type: Independent foundation
Purpose: Scholarships to students residing in Kent,
Eastern Ottawa, Montcalm or Ionia counties, MI,
who are pursuing a career related to the building
industry.
Publications: Application guidelines; Annual report;
Newsletter.
Financial data: Year ended 12/31/2012. Assets,
$204,569 (M); Expenditures, $24,672; Total
giving, $5,500.
Fields of interest: Housing/shelter, development.
Type of support: Scholarships—to individuals.
Application information: Application form required.
Application form available on the grantmaker's web
site.
Initial approach: Telephone or e-mail
Deadline(s): Mar. 14
Applicants should submit the following:
　　1) Transcripts
　　2) Letter(s) of recommendation
EIN: 382836920

4469
Charles & Alda Horgan Charitable Trust
328 S. Saginaw St., MC 001065
Flint, MI 48502 (989) 776-7368
Contact: Helen James
Application address: C/o Firstmerit Bank, N.A., 101
N. Washington Ave., MC 332021, Saginaw, MI
48607

Foundation type: Independent foundation
Purpose: Scholarships to residents of Saginaw
Township, MI for postsecondary education.
Financial data: Year ended 09/30/2013. Assets,
$1,152,460 (M); Expenditures, $66,219; Total
giving, $49,200; Grants to individuals, 12 grants
totaling $19,200 (high: $1,600, low: $1,600).
Type of support: Scholarships—to individuals.
Application information: Applications accepted.
Application form required.
Initial approach: Letter
Deadline(s): July 1
Additional information: Recipients must maintain
　　a GPA of at least 2.5 and display ambition and
　　leadership skills.
EIN: 386661683

4470
Hospitalers Committee of Detroit
Commandery No. 1 Knights Templar
500 Temple Ave.
Detroit, MI 48201-2659

Foundation type: Independent foundation
Purpose: Scholarships to individuals, primarily in
Detroit, MI.
Financial data: Year ended 12/31/2012. Assets,
$9,720 (M); Expenditures, $138,550; Total giving,
$64,500.
Type of support: Scholarships—to individuals.
Application information: Applications accepted.
Application form required.
Initial approach: Letter
EIN: 383476671

4471
Hovarter Scholarship Fund Trust
(formerly Leon & Audrey Hovarter Scholarship Fund
Trust, also known as Donald R. France)
P.O. Box 247
Marcellus, MI 49067-0247 (269) 646-5345
Contact: Donald France, Tr.

Foundation type: Independent foundation
Purpose: Scholarships to graduates of Marcellus
High School, MI, who will attend an accredited
university, college or community college in the state
of MI.
Financial data: Year ended 12/31/2012. Assets,
$381,788 (M); Expenditures, $45,212; Total
giving, $25,650; Grants to individuals, 19 grants
totaling $23,650 (high: $2,500, low: $500).
Application information: Applications accepted.
Application form required.
Deadline(s): Apr. 15
Applicants should submit the following:
　　1) Transcripts
　　2) Essay
　　3) Letter(s) of recommendation
EIN: 616309487

4472
M & H Howe Scholarship Fund
(formerly Marjorie W. Howe & Howard C. Howe
Scholarship Trust, also known as M. & H. Howe
Scholarship Trust)
P.O. Box 3636
Grand Rapids, MI 49501-3636 (800) 795-4115

Foundation type: Independent foundation
Purpose: Scholarships to students at Waukegan
High School, IL.
Financial data: Year ended 12/31/2012. Assets,
$746,782 (M); Expenditures, $96,071; Total
giving, $78,959; Grants to individuals, 20 grants
totaling $78,959 (high: $13,334, low: $1,000).
Type of support: Scholarships—to individuals;
Support to graduates or students of specific
schools.
Application information: Application form required.
Interview required.
Deadline(s): Apr. 1
Applicants should submit the following:
　　1) Class rank
　　2) Transcripts
　　3) SAT
　　4) GPA
　　5) Letter(s) of recommendation
　　6) ACT
EIN: 364005689

4473
Hudson-Webber Foundation
333 W. Fort St., Ste. 1310
Detroit, MI 48226-3149
Contact: Katy Locker, V.P., Programs
FAX: (313) 963-2818; URL: http://
www.hudson-webber.org

Foundation type: Independent foundation
Purpose: Grants to qualified employees and former
employees of the J.L. Hudson Company
("Hudsonians") and their dependents for
assistance and professional counseling, primarily
in MI.
Publications: Application guidelines; Financial
statement; Grants list.
Financial data: Year ended 12/31/2012. Assets,
$167,077,561 (M); Expenditures, $9,365,966;
Total giving, $7,118,032. Grants to individuals
amount not specified.
Fields of interest: Human services.
Type of support: Grants to individuals;
Employee-related welfare.
Application information: Contributes only to J.L.
Hudson employees, unsolicited requests for funds
not considered or acknowledged.
Program description:
Hudsonian Assistance and Counseling Program:
The program provides a professional counselor to
assist eligible J.L. Hudson Co. employees and
ex-employees and their dependents who are
seeking help with personal crises. This counselor
offers referral to public agencies and private
resources. When financial assistance is a
necessary component of crisis resolution, and
when personal or family resources, outside
commercial resources, and/or assistance available
through community, charitable, or public resources
is unavailable or inadequate, the program's
counselor may apply for a grant from the foundation
on the individual's behalf.
EIN: 386052131

4474
Human Development Commission
429 Montague Ave.
Caro, MI 48723-1921 (989) 673-4121
Contact: Lori Offenbecher, Exec. Dir.
FAX: (989) 673-2031; E-mail: keithp@hdc-caro.org;
Additional address (Sanilac County office): 227 N.
Elk St., P.O. Box 207, Sandusky, MI 48471-1106,
tel.: (989) 673-4121, fax: (989) 673-2031;
additional address (Huron County office): 150
Nugent Rd., Bad Axe, MI 48413-8705, tel.: (810)
648-4497, fax: (810) 648-5422; additional
address (Lapeer County office): 1559 Imlay City
Rd., Lapeer, MI 48446-3175, tel.: (810) 664-7133,
fax: (810) 664-2649; e-mail for Lori Offenbecher:
lorio@hdc-caro.org; URL: http://www.hdc-caro.org

Foundation type: Public charity
Purpose: Emergency assistance to eligible
low-income individuals within the counties of Huron,
Lapeer, Sanilac and Tuscola, MI, with housing,
utilities, transportation, food, and clothing.
Publications: Annual report.
Financial data: Year ended 09/30/2011. Assets,
$4,820,438 (M); Expenditures, $13,970,620;
Total giving, $2,216,600; Grants to individuals,
9,115 grants totaling $2,216,600. Subtotal for
grants for special needs: 5,678 grants totaling
$1,297,698. Subtotal for in-kind gifts: 3,437
grants totaling $918,902.
Fields of interest: Human services.
Type of support: Grants for special needs.
Application information:
  Initial approach: Telephone
EIN: 381792679

4475
Humane Society of Macomb Foundation, Inc.
11350 22 Mile Rd.
Utica, MI 48317 (586) 731-9210
Contact: Shirley Burgess, Dir.

Foundation type: Independent foundation
Purpose: Scholarships, primarily to MI residents, to
study veterinary medicine.
Financial data: Year ended 12/31/2012. Assets,
$1,292,591 (M); Expenditures, $72,970; Total
giving, $70,200; Grants to individuals, 8 grants
totaling $21,200 (high: $6,500, low: $750).
Fields of interest: Veterinary medicine.
Type of support: Scholarships—to individuals.
Application information: Application form not
required.
  Additional information: Contact foundation for
  current application deadline/guidelines.
EIN: 383183238

4476
Paul A. Humbert Scholarship Trust
P.O. Box 3636
Grand Rapids, MI 49501-3636 (574) 842-3391

Foundation type: Independent foundation
Purpose: Scholarships to students or graduates of
Culver Community School Corp., IN.
Financial data: Year ended 06/30/2013. Assets,
$543,885 (M); Expenditures, $11,079; Total
giving, $3,320; Grants to individuals, 4 grants
totaling $3,320 (high: $990, low: $350).
Type of support: Support to graduates or students
of specific schools; Undergraduate support.
Application information: Application form required.
  Deadline(s): Apr. 15
EIN: 356505726

4477
Huron County Community Foundation
1160 S. Van Dyke Rd.
P.O. Box 56
Bad Axe, MI 48413 (989) 269-2850
FAX: (989) 269-8209;
E-mail: hccf@huroncounty.com; URL: http://
www.huroncountycommunityfoundation.org/

Foundation type: Community foundation
Purpose: Scholarships to individuals in Huron
County, MI for higher education at accredited
institutions.
Publications: Annual report.
Financial data: Year ended 09/30/2012. Assets,
$2,839,509 (M); Expenditures, $124,425; Total
giving, $56,265; Grants to individuals, 34 grants
totaling $31,550.
Fields of interest: Higher education; Scholarships/
financial aid.
Type of support: Scholarships—to individuals;
Undergraduate support.
Application information: Applications accepted.
Application form required. Application form
available on the grantmaker's web site.
  Initial approach: Application
  Deadline(s): Varies
  Applicants should submit the following:
    1) SAR
    2) Transcripts
    3) Resume
  Additional information: See web site for eligibility
  criteria, application form, and complete listing
  of scholarships.
EIN: 383160009

4478
Theodore Huss, Sr. and Elsie Endert Huss Memorial Fund
328 S. Saginaw St., M/C 001065
Flint, MI 48502 (989) 776-7368
Contact: Helen James
Application address: Citizens Bank, 101 N.
Washington Ave., Saginaw, MI 48607

Foundation type: Independent foundation
Purpose: Scholarships to full-time undergraduate
students of Saginaw County, MI.
Financial data: Year ended 12/31/2012. Assets,
$369,850 (M); Expenditures, $19,715; Total
giving, $11,000; Grants to individuals, 11 grants
totaling $11,000 (high: $1,000, low: $1,000).
Fields of interest: Higher education.
Type of support: Undergraduate support.
Application information: Application form required.
  Deadline(s): June 1
EIN: 386476850

4479
I Have a Dream Foundation - Port Huron
5538 Lakeshore Rd.
Fort Gratiot, MI 48059-2813

Foundation type: Independent foundation
Purpose: Scholarships to economically
disadvantaged graduating students attending high
schools in the Port Huron, MI, area for college
tuition, room and board, and summer school.
Financial data: Year ended 06/30/2012. Assets,
$1,301 (M); Expenditures, $39,153; Total giving,
$38,194; Grants to individuals, 6 grants totaling
$38,194 (high: $12,203, low: $2,984).
Fields of interest: Higher education; Economically
disadvantaged.
Type of support: Support to graduates or students
of specific schools; Grants for special needs.

Application information: Applications accepted.
  Deadline(s): None
EIN: 383193498

4480
Ilitch Charities, Inc.
(formerly Ilitch Charities for Children, Inc.)
2211 Woodward Ave.
Detroit, MI 48201-3400 (313) 983-6340
Contact: Anne Marie Krappmann, V.P.; for
Scholarship: Kimberly Haranczak, Mgr.
URL: http://www.ilitchcharitiesforchildren.com

Foundation type: Public charity
Purpose: Scholarships to residents of the
metropolitan Detroit, MI, area who plan to attend
college or university.
Publications: Application guidelines.
Financial data: Year ended 12/31/2011. Assets,
$3,437,177 (M); Expenditures, $1,222,162; Total
giving, $796,823; Grants to individuals, 41 grants
totaling $160,229. Subtotal for grants to
individuals: grants totaling $92,493. Subtotal for
in-kind gifts: grants totaling $67,736.
Fields of interest: Higher education; Athletics/
sports, amateur leagues; Recreation.
Type of support: Undergraduate support.
Application information: Applications accepted.
Application form required. Application form
available on the grantmaker's web site.
  Deadline(s): Apr. 15
  Applicants should submit the following:
    1) Essay
    2) Transcripts
    3) SAT
    4) Letter(s) of recommendation
    5) ACT
Program description:
  Little Caesars AAA Hockey Scholarship Program:
  The program honors an outstanding high school
  male and female (19 and under) athlete and
  provides each of them with a $2,500 scholarship
  toward the college of their choice.
EIN: 383548144

4481
International Development Fund for Higher Education
615 N. Fox Hills Dr.
Bloomfield Hills, MI 48304-1313 (248)
335-0774
Contact: Dr. Venkateswarlu Jasti, Pres.

Foundation type: Public charity
Purpose: Scholarships to poor and deserving
students in Andhra Pradesh, India.
Publications: Annual report; Financial statement;
Grants list.
Financial data: Year ended 12/31/2011. Assets,
$119,315 (M); Expenditures, $42,011; Total
giving, $42,000.
Fields of interest: Economically disadvantaged.
Type of support: Undergraduate support.
Application information: Application form not
required.
  Send request by: Mail
  Deadline(s): Dec. 31
  Final notification: Applicants notified in one
  month
  Applicants should submit the following:
    1) Letter(s) of recommendation
EIN: 382305676

4482
Ironwood Area Scholarship Foundation
650 E. Ayer St.
Ironwood, MI 49938-2206 (906) 932-1550

Foundation type: Public charity
Purpose: Scholarships to graduates of Ironwood Area School District, MI.
Financial data: Year ended 06/30/2012. Assets, $1,108,558 (M); Expenditures, $11,778.
Type of support: Support to graduates or students of specific schools.
Application information:
  Initial approach: Letter
  Additional information: Contact foundation for current application deadline/guidelines.
EIN: 382822183

4483
Italian American Delegates, Inc.
15985 Canal Rd., Ste. 5
Clinton Township, MI 48038-5021 (586) 228-5800
Contact: Salvatore Ventimiglia, Pres.

Foundation type: Public charity
Purpose: Assistance to the disadvantaged of the Detroit, MI metropolitan area, especially those of Italian-American heritage children and senior citizens.
Financial data: Year ended 10/31/2011. Assets, $29,565 (M); Expenditures, $42,725; Total giving, $39,500; Grants to individuals, totaling $39,500.
Fields of interest: Children; Aging; Economically disadvantaged.
Type of support: Grants for special needs.
Application information: Applications not accepted.
  Additional information: Unsolicited requests for funds not considered or acknowledged.
EIN: 382840038

4484
Jackson Community Foundation
(formerly The Jackson County Community Foundation)
1 Jackson Sq.
100 East Michigan Ave., Ste. 308
Jackson, MI 49201-1406 (517) 787-1321
FAX: (517) 787-4333; E-mail: jcf@jacksoncf.org;
URL: http://www.jacksoncf.org/

Foundation type: Community foundation
Purpose: Scholarships primarily to students in Jackson County, MI pursuing higher education.
Publications: Application guidelines; Annual report (including application guidelines); Grants list; Newsletter.
Financial data: Year ended 12/31/2012. Assets, $19,724,146 (M); Expenditures, $1,471,578; Total giving, $993,884; Grants to individuals, 69 grants totaling $160,000.
Fields of interest: Education.
Type of support: Support to graduates or students of specific schools; Undergraduate support.
Application information: Applications accepted. Application form required. Application form available on the grantmaker's web site.
  Initial approach: Application
  Send request by: Online, mail
  Copies of proposal: 1
  Deadline(s): Mar. 1
  Applicants should submit the following:
    1) Transcripts
    2) SAT
    3) Letter(s) of recommendation

4) GPA
5) Financial information
6) Essay
7) Budget Information
8) ACT
Additional information: See web site for complete program and application information.
EIN: 386070739

4485
Corwill and Margie Jackson Foundation, Co.
P.O. Box 75000
Detroit, MI 48275-7874 (231) 843-1883
Contact: David J. Hall, Pres.
Application address: 6954 W. Jackson Rd., Ludington, MI 49341

Foundation type: Independent foundation
Purpose: Scholarships to high school seniors in Mason County, MI, for the first year of college. Four-year awards are also given.
Financial data: Year ended 12/31/2012. Assets, $2,152,467 (M); Expenditures, $145,178; Total giving, $108,600; Grants to individuals, 49 grants totaling $108,600 (high: $6,000, low: $500).
Type of support: Support to graduates or students of specific schools; Undergraduate support.
Application information: Applications accepted. Application form required.
  Send request by: Application should include transcript
  Deadline(s): May 1
EIN: 386064502

4486
Michael Jeffers Memorial Education Fund
328 S. Saginaw St., M/C 001065
Flint, MI 48502-1923
Application address: c/o Citizens Bank, N.A., Wealth Mgmt., Attn.: Helen James, 101 N. Washington Ave., Saginaw, MI 48607, tel.: (989) 776-7368

Foundation type: Independent foundation
Purpose: Educational loans to residents of Saginaw, MI, who are ages 16 to 19 and have an economic need.
Financial data: Year ended 12/31/2012. Assets, $7,503,935 (M); Expenditures, $397,070; Total giving, $280,700; Loans to individuals, 21 loans totaling $80,700.
Fields of interest: Higher education.
Type of support: Student loans—to individuals.
Application information: Applications accepted. Application form required.
  Deadline(s): June 1 for renewals, June 15 for new loans
  Additional information: Selection is based on need.
EIN: 383431990

4487
Paul T. & Frances B. Johnson Foundation
P.O. Box 203
Benzonia, MI 49616-0203 (231) 882-4681

Foundation type: Independent foundation
Purpose: Scholarships and honoraria to graduating students attending high schools in Grand Traverse, Leelanau, and Benzie counties, MI.
Financial data: Year ended 06/30/2013. Assets, $3,821,899 (M); Expenditures, $175,141; Total giving, $160,600; Grants to individuals, 72 grants totaling $130,600 (high: $8,000, low: $800).

Type of support: Support to graduates or students of specific schools; Undergraduate support.
Application information: Application form required. Interview required.
  Deadline(s): May 1
  Applicants should submit the following:
    1) Transcripts
    2) FAFSA
EIN: 383382755

4488
George W. & Sadie Marie Juhl Scholarship Fund
P.O. Box 309
Coldwater, MI 49036-0309
Application Address: c/o Mary Guthrie, 51 W. Pearl St., Coldwater, MI 49036, tel.:(517) 279-5503

Foundation type: Independent foundation
Purpose: Scholarships to students residing in Branch County, MI, to attend schools of higher education in MI.
Financial data: Year ended 03/31/2013. Assets, $2,663,470 (M); Expenditures, $191,521; Total giving, $163,564; Grants to individuals, 82 grants totaling $163,564 (high: $2,000, low: $1,564).
Fields of interest: Vocational education.
Type of support: Scholarships—to individuals.
Application information: Applications accepted. Application form required.
  Initial approach: Contact local high school
  Deadline(s): None
  Additional information: Forms are available at each high school in Branch County.
EIN: 386372257

4489
Junior League of Lansing, Michigan
1231 Michigan Ave., Ste. 204
East Lansing, MI 48823-2060 (517) 324-8716
FAX: (517) 324-3735; E-mail: office@jllansing.org;
URL: http://www.jllansing.org/

Foundation type: Public charity
Purpose: Scholarships to outstanding men and women in the greater Lansing, MI area for postsecondary education.
Publications: Application guidelines.
Financial data: Year ended 06/30/2012. Assets, $792,005 (M); Expenditures, $103,080; Total giving, $29,409; Grants to individuals, totaling $2,000.
Fields of interest: Higher education.
Type of support: Scholarships—to individuals.
Application information: Applications accepted. Application form required. Application form available on the grantmaker's web site.
  Deadline(s): Mar. 15
  Additional information: Application should include transcripts. Application by nomination only. See web site for additional guidelines.
Program description:
  Scholarships: Each year, the league awards scholarships of $1,000 each to recognize men and women who have demonstrated outstanding commitment to their community and voluntarism. Eligible applicants must be committed to academic excellence, be involved in community service and volunteerism, and be enrolled in an educational institution for the award year.
EIN: 381601529

4490
Junior League of Saginaw Valley

5800 Gratiot Rd., Ste. 104
Saginaw, MI 48638-6090 (989) 790-3763
Contact: LeAnne Iamurri, Pres.
E-mail: communityimpact@jlsv.org; E-Mail for
LeAnne Iamurri: president@jlsv.org; URL: http://
jlsv.org/

Foundation type: Public charity
Purpose: Scholarships to outstanding
college-enrolled women in Saginaw, Bay, or Midland
counties, MI with at least a 2.5 GPA pursuing an
undergraduate degree or vocational training.
Publications: Application guidelines.
Financial data: Year ended 05/31/2012. Assets,
$209,189 (M); Expenditures, $58,597; Total
giving, $9,739. Scholarships—to individuals
amount not specified.
Fields of interest: Vocational education,
post-secondary; Higher education; Young adults,
female.
Type of support: Scholarships—to individuals.
Application information: Applications accepted.
Initial approach: Telephone
Deadline(s): Feb.
Final notification: Applicants notified the first
week of May
Additional information: Contact the organization
for additional guidelines.
Program description:
Scholarships: Two scholarships of $500 each are
awarded annually to college-enrolled women who
reside in Saginaw, Bay or Midland counties, and
who have at least a 2.5 GPA. Applicants are
evaluated on community service, financial need,
and scholastic record.
EIN: 381513320

4491
Kadant Johnson, Inc. Scholarship
Foundation

(formerly Johnson Corporation Scholarship
Foundation)
805 Wood St.
Three Rivers, MI 49093-1053
Application address: Three Rivers High School
Guidance Office, 700 Sixth Ave., Three Rivers, MI
49093
Application address: 700 6th Ave., Three Rivers, MI
49093

Foundation type: Company-sponsored foundation
Purpose: Scholarships to graduates of Three Rivers
High School, MI who plan to attend a MI institution
of higher learning to pursue studies in engineering,
dentistry, nursing, medicine, teaching, or science.
Financial data: Year ended 06/30/2012. Assets,
$206 (M); Expenditures, $10,800; Total giving,
$10,800; Grants to individuals, totaling $10,800.
Fields of interest: Dental school/education;
Medical school/education; Nursing school/
education; Teacher school/education; Engineering
school/education; Science.
Type of support: Support to graduates or students
of specific schools; Undergraduate support.
Application information:
Initial approach: Letter
EIN: 386098327

4492
Kalamazoo Communities in Schools
Foundation

(formerly Kalamazoo Public Education Foundation)
125 W. Exchange Pl.
Kalamazoo, MI 49007-5094 (269) 337-1601
Contact: Pamela Kingery, Exec. Dir.
FAX: (269) 385-5806; Pam Kingery E-mail :
pkingery@ciskalamazoo.org; URL: http://
www.ciskalamazoo.org/

Foundation type: Public charity
Purpose: Scholarships primarily to minorities of the
Kalamazoo, MI, area, for teaching education.
Grants to Kalamazoo public school, MI, teachers for
programs to benefit students.
Publications: Application guidelines; Grants list.
Financial data: Year ended 06/30/2012. Assets,
$2,253,705 (M); Expenditures, $2,778,457; Total
giving, $32,696; Grants to individuals, totaling
$32,696.
Fields of interest: Arts education; Visual arts;
Higher education; Teacher school/education;
Minorities; African Americans/Blacks.
Type of support: Grants to individuals;
Scholarships—to individuals; Undergraduate
support.
Application information: Application form required.
Deadline(s): Apr. for Scholarships, Oct. for Grants
Applicants should submit the following:
1) Transcripts
2) Letter(s) of recommendation
Additional information: See web site for
additional guidelines on scholarships and
grants.
Program descriptions:
McCaslin Scholarships: Scholarships of at least
$500 are awarded annually to students upon
graduation from a Kalamazoo public high school
and enrollment at an accredited two or four-year
college. Applicant must be African-American, must
demonstrate potential for successful completion of
high school and an accredited two or four-year
college or university curriculum. Applicant must
show financial need.
Mini Grants for Educators: Grants to any
Kalamazoo Public School employee for projects
directly and actively involving students. Applicants
may apply for grants up to $750. Grant recipients
will be required to furnish a report at the end of the
project which must contain an evaluation of the
project and an itemized financial accounting
including receipts for purchases/services.
EIN: 382873188

4493
Kalamazoo Community Foundation

(formerly Kalamazoo Foundation)
151 S. Rose St., Ste. 332
Kalamazoo, MI 49007-4775 (269) 381-4416
Contact: For grants: Kari Benjamin, Community
Investment Asst.
FAX: (269) 381-3146; E-mail: info@kalfound.org;
URL: http://www.kalfound.org

Foundation type: Community foundation
Purpose: Scholarships to students from Kalamazoo
and Van Buren county high schools, Kalamazoo, MI.
Publications: Application guidelines; Annual report;
Financial statement; Grants list; Informational
brochure; Informational brochure (including
application guidelines); Newsletter; Quarterly
report.
Financial data: Year ended 12/31/2012. Assets,
$343,972,044 (M); Expenditures, $18,905,346;
Total giving, $15,722,579. Scholarships—to
individuals amount not specified.

Fields of interest: Vocational education,
post-secondary; Higher education; Scholarships/
financial aid.
Type of support: Scholarships—to individuals;
Support to graduates or students of specific
schools; Undergraduate support.
Application information: Applications accepted.
Application form required. Application form
available on the grantmaker's web site.
Send request by: On-line, mail, hand deliver
Deadline(s): Mar. 31 for most scholarships
Final notification: Applicants notified by June
Applicants should submit the following:
1) FAFSA
2) Letter(s) of recommendation
3) Transcripts
4) SAT
5) ACT
Additional information: See web site for a
complete listing of scholarships and
application guidelines.
Program description:
Scholarship Funds: The foundation administers
various scholarships funds for area students to
attend college, or a trade or technical school. Each
scholarship has its own unique set of application
requirements and eligibility criteria, which may
include attendance at a specific high school,
academic achievement, involvement in sports,
financial need, and particular fields of study such
as medicine, psychology, social justice and
mathematics. All scholarships may be used for
tuition and fees, room and board, books,
transportation and personal expenses associated
with the cost of education. Students must be U.S.
citizens or permanent residents to apply. See web
site for additional information.
EIN: 383333202

4494
Kalamazoo Symphony Orchestra

359 S. Kalamazoo Mall, Ste. 100
Kalamazoo, MI 49007-4843 (269) 349-7759
FAX: (269) 349-9229; URL: http://
www.kalamazoosymphony.com

Foundation type: Public charity
Purpose: Scholarships to students who are string
players in the greater Kalamazoo, MI area.
Financial data: Year ended 05/31/2012. Assets,
$15,792,053 (M); Expenditures, $2,339,880;
Total giving, $1,399.
Fields of interest: Orchestras.
Type of support: Scholarships—to individuals.
Application information: Contact foundation for
eligibility criteria.
EIN: 386005710

4495
Ryan Michael Kay Scholarship Foundation

4820 Leonard Ct.
West Bloomfield, MI 48322-2207

Foundation type: Independent foundation
Purpose: Scholarships to graduating students of W.
Bloomfield High School, MI pursuing a
postsecondary education.
Financial data: Year ended 09/30/2012. Assets,
$0 (M); Expenditures, $41,310; Total giving,
$39,670.
Fields of interest: Higher education.
Type of support: Support to graduates or students
of specific schools.
Application information: Applications accepted.
Application form required.
Deadline(s): May 10

Applicants should submit the following:
1) Transcripts
2) Essay
Additional information: The scholarship is a one-time $5,000 award, and student must have an overall GPA of 3.0. Essay can either be written or video.
EIN: 320102123

4496
Kellogg Company 25-Year Employees Fund, Inc.
c/o Kellogg Co.
1 Kellogg Sq.
P.O. Box 3599
Battle Creek, MI   49016-3599   (269) 961-2000
Contact: Timothy S. Knowlton, Co-Pres.

Foundation type: Company-sponsored foundation
Purpose: Supplemental living expense grants to financially needy individuals who have been employed by Kellogg Company or any of its subsidiaries for at least 25 years or who are spouses of such a person.
Financial data: Year ended 12/31/2012. Assets, $64,524,389 (M); Expenditures, $3,929,759; Total giving, $3,691,544; Grants to individuals, 165 grants totaling $1,219,544 (high: $36,529, low: $189).
Fields of interest: Economically disadvantaged.
Type of support: Employee-related welfare.
Application information: Applications not accepted.
Additional information: Unsolicited requests for funds not considered or acknowledged.
Company name: Kellogg Company
EIN: 386039770

4497
W. K. Kellogg Foundation
1 Michigan Ave. E.
Battle Creek, MI   49017-4005   (269) 968-1611
Fellowship application URL: http://www.wkkf.org/leadership
URL: http://www.wkkf.org

Foundation type: Independent foundation
Purpose: Fellowships to merging and established leaders for leadership development with a focus on improving conditions for vulnerable children.
Publications: Annual report; Financial statement; Grants list.
Financial data: Year ended 08/31/2013. Assets, $8,155,292,105 (M); Expenditures, $347,270,256; Total giving, $259,898,647.
Fields of interest: Leadership development.
Type of support: Fellowships.
Application information: Applications accepted. Application form required. Application form available on the grantmaker's web site. Interview required.
Send request by: On-line
Deadline(s): Jan.
Final notification: Recipients notified in Mar.
Additional information: Applicants must be 23 years old or older. Participants selected beyond the initial application phase will move on to the second and final round, where they will interview with WKKF selection committee members.
Program description:
Community Leadership Network Fellowship: The fellowship targets individuals who can be transformative social change agents in their communities so that vulnerable children and their families can achieve optimal health and well-being,

academic achievement and financial security. Embedded in this effort are the foundation's two approaches to all its work: community and civic engagement and racial equity and healing. Selected fellow will spend three years honing leadership skills and sharing their experiences with a cohort of developing leaders. A total of 100 fellows will be equitably selected from the foundation's U.S. priority places - Michigan, Mississippi, New Mexico and New Orleans - and will do their work from there. Another 20 fellows will be selected to function as a national cohort whose work will focus on racial healing and equity.
EIN: 381359264

4498
C.L. Kelly Charitable Trust
P.O. Box 7500
Detroit, MI   48275-7874   (252) 467-4743
Contact: Sharon Stephens
Application address: 130 S. Frankin St., Rocky Mount, NC 27804-5707

Foundation type: Independent foundation
Purpose: Student loans to U.S. citizens who are residents of Halifax County, NC.
Financial data: Year ended 01/31/2013. Assets, $1,791,727 (M); Expenditures, $79,648; Total giving, $51,548.
Type of support: Student loans—to individuals.
Application information: Applications accepted. Application form required.
Initial approach: Letter
Deadline(s): June 15
EIN: 566218777

4499
Keweenaw Community Foundation
236 Quincy St.
Hancock, MI   49930-1817   (906) 482-9673
Contact: Barbara Rose, Exec. Dir.
FAX: (906) 482-9679; E-mail: mail@k-c-f.org;
URL: http://www.k-c-f.org/
Alternate URL: http://www.k-c-f.org

Foundation type: Community foundation
Purpose: Scholarships to residents of Houghton and Keweenaw Counties, MI.
Publications: Annual report; Financial statement; Informational brochure; Occasional report; IRS Form 990 or 990-PF printed copy available upon request.
Financial data: Year ended 03/31/2012. Assets, $5,395,803 (M); Expenditures, $269,864; Total giving, $89,150; Grants to individuals, totaling $6,693.
Type of support: Undergraduate support.
Application information: Applications accepted. Application form required.
Initial approach: Letter
Additional information: Scholarship applications are available to be picked up in person. See web site for additional information.
EIN: 383223079

4500
Kiwanis Club of Shorewood Foundation
21055 E. 12 Mile Rd.
Roseville, MI   48066-2205   (586) 772-0100

Foundation type: Public charity
Purpose: Scholarships to individuals of St. Clair Shores, MI for higher education.

Financial data: Year ended 09/30/2011. Assets, $109,338 (M); Expenditures, $8,393; Total giving, $7,000.
Fields of interest: Higher education.
Type of support: Scholarships—to individuals.
Application information: Contact foundation for guidelines.
EIN: 383544978

4501
Kiwanis Foundation of Harbor Springs
P.O. Box 485
Harbor Springs, MI   49740-0485   (231) 526-9342

Foundation type: Public charity
Purpose: Scholarships to graduates of the Harbor Springs School District, MI.
Financial data: Year ended 09/30/2012. Assets, $341,094 (M); Expenditures, $22,036; Total giving, $20,923.
Type of support: Support to graduates or students of specific schools; Undergraduate support.
Application information: Applications accepted. Application form required.
Initial approach: Letter
Additional information: Contact foundation for full eligibility requirements.
EIN: 382577262

4502
Verne O. & Dorothy M. Kling Scholarship
P.O. Box 7500, MC 7874
Detroit, MI   48275-7874

Foundation type: Independent foundation
Purpose: Scholarships to members of the Protestant Church, preferably those who reside in Shelby County, IN. Secondary consideration is given in order of preference to Protestants residing anywhere within IN, MI, and in other states of the U.S.
Financial data: Year ended 06/30/2013. Assets, $12,523 (M); Expenditures, $5,400; Total giving, $1,500.
Fields of interest: Protestant agencies & churches.
Type of support: Scholarships—to individuals.
Application information: Applications accepted.
Initial approach: Letter
Deadline(s): Apr. 1
Applicants should submit the following:
1) Transcripts
2) Letter(s) of recommendation
3) Financial information
Additional information: Application must also include a list of extracurricular activities.
EIN: 386302950

4503
Edward M. and Henrietta M. Knabusch Scholarship Foundation
c/o Monroe Bank & Trust
102 E. Front St.
Monroe, MI   48161-2162   (734) 242-2068

Foundation type: Independent foundation
Purpose: Undergraduate scholarships to graduating high school seniors who are children of La-Z-Boy, Inc. employees.
Publications: Annual report.
Financial data: Year ended 12/31/2011. Assets, $1,960,297 (M); Expenditures, $63,086; Total giving, $40,000; Grants to individuals, 40 grants totaling $40,000 (high: $1,000, low: $1,000).

Fields of interest: Higher education; Scholarships/ financial aid.
Type of support: Employee-related scholarships.
Application information: Applications accepted. Application form required.
   Deadline(s): None
   Applicants should submit the following:
      1) Transcripts
      2) GPA
      3) Financial information
      4) Letter(s) of recommendation
      5) SAT
      6) ACT
   Additional information: Payments are made to the educational institution on behalf of the students. All students must be accepted at an accredited college or university, and must reapply on an annual basis provided they maintain a minimum GPA of 3.0.
EIN: 383450698

4504
Robert & Margaret Koch Bomarko Founders Scholarship Fund
P.O. Box 3636
Grand Rapids, MI   49501-3636

Foundation type: Independent foundation
Purpose: Scholarships for attendance at Ancilla College to graduates of the Argos, Bremen, Culverd, Laville, Plymouth or Triton school corporations, IN, and to employees of BoMarko, Plymouth, IN.
Financial data: Year ended 09/30/2013. Assets, $106,485 (M); Expenditures, $9,238; Total giving, $4,954.
Type of support: Employee-related scholarships; Support to graduates or students of specific schools; Undergraduate support.
Application information: Applications accepted. Application form required.
   Deadline(s): Apr. 15
   Applicants should submit the following:
      1) Transcripts
      2) SAT
      3) Financial information
Company name: BoMarko
EIN: 351781577

4505
The Kohn-Bancroft Family Foundation
3389 Linco Rd.
Stevensville, MI   49127-9725   (269) 465-5757

Foundation type: Independent foundation
Purpose: Scholarships to employees of Supreme Casting, Inc. and their spouses and dependents for higher education.
Financial data: Year ended 12/31/2012. Assets, $739,556 (M); Expenditures, $52,098; Total giving, $51,248; Grants to individuals, 5 grants totaling $26,818 (high: $16,069, low: $115).
Fields of interest: Higher education.
Type of support: Employee-related scholarships; Scholarships—to individuals.
Application information: Applications accepted. Application form required.
   Deadline(s): May 1 and Oct. 1
EIN: 383537827

4506
Cmdr. and Mrs. Robert Krause Foundation
132 State St.
Harbor Beach, MI   48441-1203
Application address: c/o Harbor Beach Community School, 42 S. 5th St., Harbor Beach, MI 48441-1309, tel.: (989) 479-3261

Foundation type: Independent foundation
Purpose: Scholarships to graduates of Harbor Beach Community School, MI, to attend a postsecondary institution.
Financial data: Year ended 12/31/2011. Assets, $663,004 (M); Expenditures, $60,641; Total giving, $32,600; Grants to individuals, 46 grants totaling $32,600 (high: $1,000, low: $400).
Fields of interest: Higher education.
Type of support: Support to graduates or students of specific schools.
Application information: Applications accepted. Application form required.
   Deadline(s): End of Apr.
   Additional information: Application should include GPA.
EIN: 527317516

4507
L & L Educational Foundation
160 McLean Dr.
Romeo, MI   48065-4919   (586) 336-1608
Contact: Peggy Domenick-Muscat, Pres.
FAX: (586) 336-1635;
E-mail: edfoundation@llproducts.com; URL: http://foundationcenter.org/grantmaker/landl

Foundation type: Operating foundation
Purpose: Grants to employees and family of employees of L&L Products, Inc. to support adult postsecondary educational efforts specifically undertaken to prepare for a future career or to enhance a current career.
Financial data: Year ended 12/31/2012. Assets, $9,319,779 (M); Expenditures, $385,757; Total giving, $348,409; Grants to individuals, 101 grants totaling $347,409 (high: $9,000, low: $343).
Fields of interest: Education.
Type of support: Employee-related scholarships.
Application information: Applications accepted. Application form required. Application form available on the grantmaker's web site.
   Deadline(s): Apr. 1
   Additional information: Eligible employees must have at least one year of employment seniority by the application deadline. Former employees must have left the company due to death, disability, or retirement. Application should include transcripts.
EIN: 382785121

4508
William T. Laflin Scholarship Fund, Inc.
3226 Arthur Rd.
Remus, MI   49340-9541   (989) 967-2016

Foundation type: Independent foundation
Purpose: Scholarships to graduates of Chippewa Hills School District, MI.
Financial data: Year ended 12/31/2012. Assets, $79,366 (M); Expenditures, $2,334; Total giving, $2,000; Grants to individuals, 3 grants totaling $2,000 (high: $1,000, low: $500).
Type of support: Support to graduates or students of specific schools.
Application information: Applications accepted. Application form required.

   Additional information: Application must include proof of college acceptance.
EIN: 381579001

4509
The Helen Laidlaw Foundation
314 Newman St.
East Tawas, MI   48730-1214   (989) 362-4447

Foundation type: Independent foundation
Purpose: Scholarships to MI residents for the study of health care.
Financial data: Year ended 12/31/2012. Assets, $421,423 (M); Expenditures, $29,922; Total giving, $15,000; Grants to individuals, 15 grants totaling $15,000 (high: $1,500, low: $500).
Fields of interest: Health care.
Type of support: Scholarships—to individuals.
Application information: Applications accepted. Application form required.
   Deadline(s): Mar. 1
   Applicants should submit the following:
      1) FAF
      2) Transcripts
      3) Resume
      4) GPA
      5) Financial information
EIN: 382901107

4510
Lakeland Health Foundation, Niles
(formerly Pawating Health Foundation)
1234 Napier Ave.
St. Joseph, MI   49085-2112   (800) 968-0115
Contact: Robert Habicht, Chair.
E-mail: dburghart@lakelandregional.org;
URL: http://www.lakelandhealth.org/body.cfm?xyzpdqabc=0&id=742&action=detail&ref=57

Foundation type: Public charity
Purpose: Scholarships primarily to individuals in MI pursuing a career in a health care-related field and who are in need of tuition assistance.
Publications: Application guidelines.
Financial data: Year ended 09/30/2011. Assets, $1,580,789 (M); Expenditures, $150,580; Total giving, $106,817; Grants to individuals, 15 grants totaling $15,057.
Fields of interest: Health sciences school/ education.
Type of support: Scholarships—to individuals.
Application information: Contact foundation for current application deadline/guidelines.
EIN: 383130558

4511
Lansing Art Gallery, Inc.
119 N. Washington Sq.
Lansing, MI   48933-1703   (517) 374-6400
Contact: Catherine Allswede-Babcock, Exec. Dir.
FAX: (517) 374-6385;
E-mail: lansingartgallery@yahoo.com; URL: http://www.lansingartgallery.org

Foundation type: Public charity
Purpose: Scholarships and prizes to Lansing, MI, artists who win the juried art competition.
Financial data: Year ended 06/30/2012. Assets, $207,685 (M); Expenditures, $150,670.
Fields of interest: Visual arts.
Type of support: Awards/prizes; Undergraduate support.
Application information: Applications accepted.
   Additional information: Contact foundation for current application deadline/guidelines.

Program descriptions:

Art Scholarship Alert: This program is a juried art exhibition and scholarship competition for grades 9 through 12, from over twenty Lansing area communities. This program is designed to give recognition and financial assistance for outstanding art students, encourage artistic growth, and provide an opportunity to participate as artists in a professional setting. Students are required to submit a portfolio of five original works of art to be juried by a team of professional artists and educators. Acceptance to the exhibition is determined by the consistency of excellence in each portfolio (not each individual piece) and is judged exclusively within its own grade level.

Sara Jane Venable Scholarship: To qualify for this $1,000 award the student must demonstrate an exceptional record of achievement and involvement in the visual arts and prove a commitment to advanced study, write an essay for review, and present a portfolio of artwork including slides. A special panel of jurors selects one senior each year to receive this prestigious award.
EIN: 381889973

4512
Lapeer County Community Foundation
(formerly Lapeer County Community Fund)
264 Cedar St.
Lapeer, MI   48446   (810) 664-0691
Contact: Ashley White, Exec. Dir.
E-mail: awhite@lapeercountycommunityfoundation.
org; URL: http://
www.lapeercountycommunityfoundation.org/

Foundation type: Community foundation
Purpose: Scholarships to individuals and graduating seniors of Lapeer County, MI for postsecondary education.
Publications: Application guidelines; Annual report; Grants list; Informational brochure; Newsletter; Program policy statement.
Financial data: Year ended 12/31/2012. Assets, $8,096,455 (M); Expenditures, $682,654; Total giving, $480,600; Grants to individuals, 45 grants totaling $63,950 (high: $3,000, low: $500).
Fields of interest: Higher education.
Type of support: Scholarships—to individuals; Support to graduates or students of specific schools; Graduate support; Undergraduate support.
Application information: Applications accepted. Application form required. Application form available on the grantmaker's web site. Interview required.
Initial approach: Application
Deadline(s): Mar. 31, varies for others
Applicants should submit the following:
   1) SAT
   2) Transcripts
Additional information: Students may contact their guidance counselors for application information. See web site for a complete list of scholarships.
EIN: 201271563

4513
Daisy Harder LaVictoire Memorial Scholarship
7254 Michigan Ave.
Pigeon, MI   48755-5145   (989) 453-2097
Contact: Robert Smith, Tr.
Application address: 6136 W. Pigeon Rd., Pigeon, MI 48755, tel.: (989) 453-2097

Foundation type: Independent foundation

Purpose: Scholarships to graduating students from Elkton, Pigeon or Bay Port, MI, attending Laker High School.
Financial data: Year ended 03/31/2013. Assets, $242,480 (M); Expenditures, $3,504; Total giving, $774; Grants to individuals, 5 grants totaling $774 (high: $194, low: $97).
Type of support: Support to graduates or students of specific schools; Undergraduate support.
Application information: Applications accepted. Application form required.
Deadline(s): Mar. 31
EIN: 386629469

4514
Leelanau Township Community Foundation, Inc.
104 Wing St.
P.O. Box 818
Northport, MI   49670-0818   (231) 386-9000
Contact: Joan Moore, Exec. Dir.
FAX: (231) 386-9000;
E-mail: director@leelanaufoundation.org;
URL: http://www.leelanaufoundation.org

Foundation type: Community foundation
Purpose: Scholarships to local students in the Leelanau township, MI area pursuing a higher education.
Publications: Annual report; Newsletter.
Financial data: Year ended 12/31/2012. Assets, $3,760,430 (M); Expenditures, $227,221; Total giving, $145,600; Grants to individuals, 15 grants totaling $39,500.
Fields of interest: Higher education.
Type of support: Scholarships—to individuals.
Application information: Applications accepted. Application form required. Application form available on the grantmaker's web site.
Deadline(s): Mar. 30
Additional information: See web site for a listing of scholarship programs and criteria.
EIN: 386060138

4515
The Legion Foundation
1750 S. Telegraph Rd., Ste. 301
Bloomfield Hills, MI   48302-0179   (248) 253-1100
Contact: James E. Mulvoy Esq., Pres.
FAX: (248) 253-1142;
E-mail: mulvoy@thelegionfoundation.org;
URL: http://www.thelegionfoundation.org/Pages/default.aspx

Foundation type: Independent foundation
Purpose: Scholarships and grants for personal, physical and spiritual development, in order to facilitate and encourage the study and maintenance of Christian faith in the secular world.
Financial data: Year ended 12/31/2011. Assets, $9,516,813 (M); Expenditures, $981,132; Total giving, $712,520; Grants to individuals, 45 grants totaling $519,020 (high: $60,901, low: $225).
Fields of interest: Christian agencies & churches; Religion.
Type of support: Scholarships—to individuals.
Application information: Applications accepted. Application form required.
Deadline(s): June 30
Additional information: Financial need is not a factor in evaluating applicants. Scholarships will be paid directly to the educational institution.
EIN: 383330588

4516
Lenawee Community Foundation
(formerly Tecumseh Community Fund Foundation)
603 N. Evans St.
P.O. Box 142
Tecumseh, MI   49286-1166   (517) 423-1729
Contact: Suann D. Hammersmith, C.E.O.
FAX: (517) 424-6579;
E-mail: shammersmith@ubat.com; URL: http://www.lenaweecommunityfoundation.com/

Foundation type: Community foundation
Purpose: Scholarships to students in the Lenawee MI, area for continuing education at accredited colleges or universities.
Publications: Application guidelines; Annual report (including application guidelines); Grants list; Informational brochure; Newsletter.
Financial data: Year ended 09/30/2012. Assets, $18,965,901 (M); Expenditures, $1,549,432; Total giving, $1,263,323; Grants to individuals, 114 grants totaling $83,255.
Fields of interest: Higher education.
Type of support: Scholarships—to individuals.
Application information: Contact the foundation for eligibility requirements.
EIN: 386095474

4517
Lighthouse Emergency Services, Inc.
46156 Woodward Ave.
P.O. Box 430598
Pontiac, MI   48342-5033   (248) 920-6000
E-mail: info@lighthouseoakland.org; URL: http://www.lighthouseoakland.org/

Foundation type: Public charity
Purpose: Emergency assistance to underprivileged individuals and families of Northern Oakland county, MI, with food, clothing, shelter and other needs.
Financial data: Year ended 06/30/2012. Assets, $531,404 (M); Expenditures, $2,443,727; Total giving, $1,491,723; Grants to individuals, 10,440 grants totaling $485,166.
Fields of interest: Human services.
Type of support: Emergency funds.
Application information:
Initial approach: Telephone
Program description:
Assistance Program: The organization provides various emergency services to residents of Oakland county, MI. The programs offered are for senior citizens, physically challenged individuals, individuals in short-term crisis situations, individuals in need of special medical assistance, and the homeless.
EIN: 383327797

4518
Lions of Michigan Service Foundation, Inc.
5730 Executive Dr.
Lansing, MI   48911-5301   (517) 887-6640
Contact: Chad McCann, Exec. Dir.
FAX: (517) 887-6642; E-mail: info@lmsf.net;
Additional email: administration@lmsf.net;
URL: http://www.lmsf.net

Foundation type: Public charity
Purpose: Grants to uninsured and underinsured MI residents in order to provide for medical care and services, especially for the treatment of sight and hearing impairments.
Financial data: Year ended 06/30/2012. Assets, $1,445,604 (M); Expenditures, $384,533; Total

giving, $211,017; Grants to individuals, totaling $170,632.
Fields of interest: Health care; Safety/disasters; Disabilities, people with; Blind/visually impaired; Deaf/hearing impaired.
Type of support: Emergency funds; Grants to individuals; Grants for special needs.
Application information: Applications accepted. Application form required.
  Initial approach: Letter
  Send request by: Mail
  Deadline(s): Contact foundation for current application deadline
  Final notification: Applicants notified 10 days after board meeting
  Additional information: Contact local Lions Club for complete application information.
EIN: 382537921

4519
The Earle and Elsie Little Scholarship Trust

c/o Monroe Bank & Trust
102 E. Front St.
Monroe, MI 48161-2162 (734) 242-2734

Foundation type: Independent foundation
Purpose: Scholarships primarily to MI residents for undergraduate studies in an accredited MI college or university.
Financial data: Year ended 12/31/2011. Assets, $331,730 (M); Expenditures, $23,700; Total giving, $19,000; Grants to individuals, 14 grants totaling $19,000 (high: $2,000, low: $1,000).
Type of support: Undergraduate support.
Application information: Applications accepted.
  Initial approach: Letter
EIN: 386729055

4520
Lutheran Child & Family Service of Michigan, Inc.

6019 W. Side Saginaw Rd.
P.O. Box 48
Bay City, MI 48707-0048 (989) 686-7650
E-mail: information@lcfsmi.org; Toll-free tel.: (800) 625-7650

Foundation type: Public charity
Purpose: Specific assistance to individuals and families of MI with foster care, residential care, adoption, counseling and other services.
Financial data: Year ended 12/31/2011. Assets, $15,960,337 (M); Expenditures, $18,332,929; Total giving, $2,635,077; Grants to individuals, 2,271 grants totaling $2,635,077.
Fields of interest: Substance abuse, services; Children/youth, services; Adoption; Foster care; Family services; Family services, adolescent parents; Family services, counseling.
Type of support: Grants for special needs.
Application information: Contact the agency for eligibility determination.
EIN: 381359524

4521
M & M Area Community Foundation

1101 11th Ave., Ste. 2
P.O. Box 846
Menominee, MI 49858-0846 (906) 864-3599
Contact: Lisa K. Bayerl, Off. Mgr.
FAX: (906) 864-3657;
E-mail: info@mmcommunityfoundation.org;
URL: http://www.mmcommunityfoundation.org

Foundation type: Community foundation
Purpose: Scholarships to graduating seniors from Nenominee, MI, and Marinette county WI, high schools.
Publications: Annual report; Financial statement; Grants list; Informational brochure; Newsletter.
Financial data: Year ended 12/31/2012. Assets, $6,890,983 (M); Expenditures, $548,255; Total giving, $212,254; Grants to individuals, 47 grants totaling $63,875.
Fields of interest: Education.
Type of support: Scholarships—to individuals.
Application information: Applications accepted. Application form required. Application form available on the grantmaker's web site.
  Initial approach: Letter of intent
  Send request by: E-mail
  Copies of proposal: 1
  Applicants should submit the following:
    1) Proposal
    2) Budget Information
  Additional information: See web site for full list of programs and additional information.
EIN: 383264725

4522
Make-A-Wish Foundation of Michigan

2300 Genoa Business Pk. Dr., Ste. 290
Brighton, MI 48114-7369 (800) 622-9474
FAX: (734) 994-8025;
E-mail: wish@michigan.wish.org; URL: http://www.wishmich.org

Foundation type: Public charity
Purpose: Giving limited to terminally-ill children throughout MI.
Publications: Application guidelines.
Financial data: Year ended 08/31/2011. Assets, $3,481,221 (M); Expenditures, $6,031,689; Total giving, $3,186,148; Grants to individuals, 279 grants totaling $3,186,148.
Type of support: In-kind gifts; Grants for special needs.
Application information: Applications accepted. Application form required. Application form available on the grantmaker's web site.
  Deadline(s): None
Program description:
  Grants: The foundation provides support to children throughout Michigan with life-threatening conditions who would like to make their wishes come true. Eligible applicants must be between the ages of 2 1/2 and 18 years old, be diagnosed with a life-threatening medical condition (as determined by their physician and based on the standards set forth by the Make-a-Wish Foundation of America); the foundation grants wishes to qualified children regardless of race, ethnic background, religion, or financial status.
EIN: 382505812

4523
Marquette Area Public Schools Education Foundation

1201 W. Fair Ave.
Marquette, MI 49855-2668 (906) 225-5320
URL: http://www.mapsnet.org/Home.aspx

Foundation type: Public charity
Purpose: Scholarships to students in the Marquette, MI, Public Schools area.
Publications: Application guidelines; Grants list.
Financial data: Year ended 06/30/2012. Assets, $872,035 (M); Expenditures, $39,930; Total giving, $34,091; Grants to individuals, totaling $17,574.

Fields of interest: Education.
Type of support: Scholarships—to individuals.
Application information: Applications accepted.
  Initial approach: Letter
EIN: 382972673

4524
Marquette County Community Foundation

(formerly Marquette Community Foundation)
401 E. Fair Ave.
P.O. Box 37
Marquette, MI 49855-2951 (906) 226-7666
Contact: Gail Anthony, C.O.O.
FAX: (906) 226-2104; E-mail: mcf@chartermi.net;
URL: http://www.mqt-cf.org

Foundation type: Community foundation
Purpose: Scholarships to individuals from the Marquette County, MI, area, for undergraduate education at U.S. colleges and universities.
Publications: Application guidelines; Annual report; Financial statement; Informational brochure; Newsletter; Program policy statement; Program policy statement (including application guidelines).
Financial data: Year ended 12/31/2011. Assets, $10,756,226 (M); Expenditures, $756,502; Total giving, $371,261; Grants to individuals, 41 grants totaling $33,031.
Fields of interest: Music (choral); Higher education; Teacher school/education; Scholarships/financial aid.
Type of support: Scholarships—to individuals; Precollege support; Undergraduate support.
Application information: Applications accepted. Application form required. Application form available on the grantmaker's web site.
  Initial approach: Letter, telephone, or e-mail
  Copies of proposal: 6
  Deadline(s): Apr. 15
  Applicants should submit the following:
    1) Transcripts
    2) Letter(s) of recommendation
    3) GPA
    4) Essay
EIN: 382826563

4525
Marshall Community Foundation

(formerly Marshall Civic Foundation)
614 Homer Rd.
Marshall, MI 49068-1966 (269) 781-2273
Contact: Sherry Anderson, Exec. Dir.
FAX: (269) 781-9747; E-mail: info@marshallcf.org;
URL: http://www.marshallcf.org

Foundation type: Community foundation
Purpose: Scholarships to residents of Calhoun County, MI, for higher education.
Publications: Application guidelines; Annual report; Informational brochure.
Financial data: Year ended 09/30/2012. Assets, $10,567,997 (M); Expenditures, $810,503; Total giving, $649,147; Grants to individuals, totaling $649,147.
Fields of interest: Higher education.
Type of support: Scholarships—to individuals.
Application information: Applications accepted. Application form required. Application form available on the grantmaker's web site. Interview required.
  Initial approach: Application
  Deadline(s): Mar. 1
  Applicants should submit the following:
    1) Transcripts
    2) FAF
    3) Letter(s) of recommendation

4) Essay
Additional information: Students may contact their high school guidance counselors for application information. See web site for a complete listing of scholarships.
EIN: 237011281

4526
Marcus K. Martin Scholarship
(formerly Gertrude E. Martin Trust)
P.O. Box 75000
Detroit, MI 48275-3302

Foundation type: Independent foundation
Purpose: Scholarships to graduates of Santa Cruz High School, CA, for continuing education at institutions of higher learning.
Financial data: Year ended 12/31/2011. Assets, $88,271 (M); Expenditures, $9,425; Total giving, $5,000; Grant to an individual, 1 grant totaling $5,000.
Fields of interest: Higher education.
Type of support: Scholarships—to individuals; Support to graduates or students of specific schools.
Application information: Applications accepted. Application form required.
Additional information: Contact scholarship committee for application information.
EIN: 946113526

4527
Matrix Human Services
(formerly MetroMatrix Human Services)
120 Parsons St.
Detroit, MI 48201-2002 (313) 831-1000
Contact: Marcella Wilson Ph.D., Pres. and C.E.O.
FAX: (313) 831-4634;
E-mail: inquiries@matrixhs.org; URL: http://www.matrixhumanservices.org

Foundation type: Public charity
Purpose: Assistance to the Detroit, MI, metropolitan community, its families, and individuals of all ages.
Publications: Annual report.
Financial data: Year ended 09/30/2011. Assets, $4,963,820 (M); Expenditures, $16,513,694; Total giving, $554,041; Grants to individuals, totaling $60,073.
Fields of interest: Human services.
Type of support: Grants for special needs.
Application information: Applications not accepted.
Additional information: Unsolicited requests for funds not considered or acknowledged.
EIN: 381358015

4528
Lorraine D. Matson Trust
P.O. Box 75000, MC 9413
Detroit, MI 48275-9413

Foundation type: Independent foundation
Purpose: Scholarships to graduates of Avondale High School and to members of the Auburn Hills Presbyterian Church, MI.
Financial data: Year ended 11/30/2013. Assets, $184,452 (M); Expenditures, $14,007; Total giving, $9,300.
Fields of interest: Protestant agencies & churches.
Type of support: Support to graduates or students of specific schools; Undergraduate support.

Application information: Application form required.
Deadline(s): Jan. 1 to Apr. 1
EIN: 386523330

4529
McCurdy Memorial Scholarship Foundation
49 W. Michigan Ave.
Battle Creek, MI 49017-3603 (269) 962-9591
Contact: Michael Jordan

Foundation type: Independent foundation
Purpose: Undergraduate scholarships to residents of Calhoun County, MI.
Financial data: Year ended 12/31/2012. Assets, $763,538 (M); Expenditures, $48,404; Total giving, $38,450; Grants to individuals, 32 grants totaling $38,450 (high: $1,500, low: $700).
Fields of interest: Higher education; Scholarships/financial aid.
Type of support: Undergraduate support.
Application information: Application form required. Interview required.
Deadline(s): Mar. 31
Additional information: Awards are made on the basis of excellence in scholastic and other activities and are renewable contingent upon the continuance of above-average work in college. Approximately six to eight new awards are available each year.
EIN: 381687120

4530
R. S. McPherson Trust
328 S. Saginaw St., M/C 001065
Flint, MI 48502

Foundation type: Independent foundation
Purpose: Giving to assist crippled and afflicted children of Clinton or Gration counties, MI. Recipients are determined by the county courts.
Financial data: Year ended 12/31/2012. Assets, $273,863 (M); Expenditures, $13,190; Total giving, $8,510.
Fields of interest: Children/youth; Economically disadvantaged.
Type of support: Grants to individuals.
Application information: Applications not accepted.
EIN: 386140246

4531
MEEMIC Foundation for the Future of Education
1685 N. Opdyke Rd.
Auburn Hills, MI 48326-2656
E-mail: foundation@meemic.com; URL: http://www.meemicfoundation.com/

Foundation type: Company-sponsored foundation
Purpose: Mini-grants of up to $2,500 awarded to MI educators in support of innovative programs that enhance curriculum.
Publications: Application guidelines; Grants list.
Financial data: Year ended 12/31/2012. Assets, $1,855,596 (M); Expenditures, $118,475; Total giving, $104,853; Grants to individuals, 112 grants totaling $104,853 (high: $2,500, low: $154).
Fields of interest: Education.
Type of support: Awards/prizes.

Application information: Applications accepted. Application form required. Application form available on the grantmaker's web site.
Deadline(s): June 30
Final notification: Applicants notified in July
EIN: 383048526

4532
Allen H. and Nydia Meyers Foundation
(formerly Allen H. Meyers Foundation)
P.O. Box 100
Tecumseh, MI 49286 (734) 649-5840
URL: http://www.meyersfoundation.org/

Foundation type: Independent foundation
Purpose: Scholarships to Lenawee County, MI, graduating high school seniors from Lenawee County High School, pursuing careers in aviation, aerospace science, engineering, biology, chemistry, natural sciences, medicine and nursing.
Financial data: Year ended 04/30/2013. Assets, $675,459 (M); Expenditures, $36,751; Total giving, $35,000; Grants to individuals, 12 grants totaling $35,000 (high: $5,000, low: $2,500).
Fields of interest: Medical school/education; Nursing school/education; Engineering school/education; Science; Physical/earth sciences; Space/aviation; Chemistry; Biology/life sciences.
Type of support: Scholarships—to individuals; Support to graduates or students of specific schools.
Application information: Applications accepted. Application form required. Application form available on the grantmaker's web site. Interview required.
Initial approach: Telephone
Send request by: Online
Deadline(s): Mar. 9
Additional information: Scholarships are only for graduating seniors of Lenawee county students. Unsolicited requests for funds not considered or acknowledged.
EIN: 386143278

4533
Michigan Accountancy Foundation
5480 Corporate Dr., Ste. 200
Troy, MI 48098-2642 (248) 267-3700
Application address: c/o MAF Accounting Scholarship Prog., P.O. Box 5068, Troy, MI 48007-5068
FAX: (248) 267-3737; E-mail: macpa@michcpa.org; URL: http://www.michcpa.org/Content/home.aspx

Foundation type: Public charity
Purpose: Scholarships to current accounting majors enrolled in a MI college or university, to fund their fifth graduate year.
Publications: Application guidelines.
Financial data: Year ended 06/30/2012. Assets, $367,023 (M); Expenditures, $116,848; Total giving, $91,500; Grants to individuals, totaling $91,500.
Fields of interest: Business school/education.
Type of support: Graduate support.
Application information: Applications accepted. Application form required. Application form available on the grantmaker's web site.
Initial approach: Letter
Deadline(s): Jan. 31
Final notification: Mar. 15
Applicants should submit the following:
1) Letter(s) of recommendation
2) Resume
3) Transcripts
EIN: 386090334

4534
Michigan Agri-Business Association Educational Trust Fund

(also known as Michigan Agri-Dealers Educational Trust)
1501 Northshore Dr.
East Lansing, MI 48823   (517) 336-0223
URL: http://www.miagbiz.org/

Foundation type: Independent foundation
Purpose: Scholarships to students in MI pursuing advanced education and degrees related to agri-business and grain elevator management.
Financial data: Year ended 12/31/2012. Assets, $507,366 (M); Expenditures, $24,725; Total giving, $15,475; Grants to individuals, 31 grants totaling $15,475 (high: $675, low: $275).
Fields of interest: Agriculture.
Type of support: Scholarships—to individuals.
Application information: Application form required.
  Initial approach: Letter
  Deadline(s): None
  Applicants should submit the following:
    1) Financial information
    2) Transcripts
  Additional information: Application should also include references, student affairs participation and personal qualities of leadership, personality, and citizenship.
EIN: 382086180

4535
Michigan Dental Foundation

c/o Lori Kleinfelt
3657 Okemos Rd., Ste. 200
Okemos, MI 48864-3927   (517) 372-9070
URL: http://www.smilemichigan.com/ Default.aspx?alias=www.smilemichigan.com/ foundation

Foundation type: Public charity
Purpose: Scholarships to dental, dental hygiene and dental assisting students in MI.
Publications: Application guidelines.
Financial data: Year ended 12/31/2011. Assets, $1,439,671 (M); Expenditures, $140,921; Total giving, $40,865; Grants to individuals, totaling $40,865.
Fields of interest: Dental care.
Type of support: Undergraduate support.
Application information: Applications accepted. Application form required. Application form available on the grantmaker's web site.
  Initial approach: Letter
  Send request by: Mail
  Deadline(s): Feb. 15 for dental assisting students; Nov. 15 for dental and dental hygiene students
  Applicants should submit the following:
    1) Transcripts
    2) Financial information
    3) Letter(s) of recommendation
  Additional information: Application should also include a biographical sketch.
EIN: 383421257

4536
Michigan Education Association Scholarship Fund

1216 Kendale Blvd.
P. O. Box 2573
East Lansing, MI 48826-2573   (517) 332-6551
Contact: Steven B. Cook, Pres.
Toll-free tel.: (800) 292-1934; URL: http://www.mea.org

Foundation type: Public charity
Purpose: Scholarships to graduates of Michigan public high schools for attendance at MI public community/junior college, four year degree-granting institution or vocational training institutions.
Publications: Application guidelines.
Financial data: Year ended 08/31/2012. Assets, $1,172,686 (M); Expenditures, $53,436; Total giving, $35,600; Grants to individuals, totaling $35,600.
Fields of interest: Higher education.
Type of support: Support to graduates or students of specific schools.
Application information: Applications accepted. Application form required.
  Deadline(s): Feb. 11
  Applicants should submit the following:
    1) Transcripts
    2) SAT
    3) Resume
    4) Letter(s) of recommendation
    5) GPA
    6) ACT
  Additional information: Applicants attending the following private institutions are also eligible to apply: Baker College-Flint/Owosso; University of Detroit-Mercy; Davenport University-Eastern Region Campus; Adrian College; Finlandia University; Albion College; and Kendall College of Art and Design of Ferris State University. Applications are available from local affiliates of the MEA, UniServ offices or high school counseling offices. Fax or e-mail applications are not accepted.
EIN: 383285500

4537
Michigan Elks Association Charitable Grant Fund

150 Woodrow Ave. S.
Battle Creek, MI 49015-3044   (616) 962-8593
Application address: c/o Michigan Elks Lodge, P.O. Box 2006, 1200 Harmonia Rd., Battle Creek, MI 49015. tel.: (616) 962-8593

Foundation type: Independent foundation
Purpose: Scholarships to physically disabled students who are residents of MI for attendance at colleges and universities.
Financial data: Year ended 03/31/2013. Assets, $426,957 (M); Expenditures, $68,665; Total giving, $60,000; Grants to individuals, 30 grants totaling $60,000 (high: $2,000, low: $2,000).
Fields of interest: Disabilities, people with.
Type of support: Scholarships—to individuals.
Application information: Application form required.
  Deadline(s): Jan. 31
  Additional information: Application must include financial and academic information; Applications should be made to individual Elk Lodges.
EIN: 382599208

4538
Michigan Gateway Community Foundation

(formerly Buchanan Area Foundation)
111 Days Ave.
Buchanan, MI 49107-1609   (269) 695-3521
Contact: Robert N. Habicht, C.E.O. and Pres.
FAX: (269) 695-4250; E-mail: info@mgcf.org;
URL: http://www.mgcf.org

Foundation type: Community foundation

Purpose: Scholarships to high school seniors of the Buchanan, MI area for degree or certificate programs in any field of study.
Publications: Application guidelines; Annual report; Financial statement; Informational brochure; Newsletter.
Financial data: Year ended 03/31/2013. Assets, $7,729,400 (M); Expenditures, $522,236; Total giving, $228,341; Grants to individuals, totaling $720.
Fields of interest: Higher education; Scholarships/financial aid.
Type of support: Scholarships—to individuals; Support to graduates or students of specific schools; Undergraduate support.
Application information: Applications accepted. Application form required. Application form available on the grantmaker's web site.
  Initial approach: Application
  Send request by: Mail
  Copies of proposal: 2
  Deadline(s): Mar. 14
  Final notification: Applicants notified by June 15
  Applicants should submit the following:
    1) Letter(s) of recommendation
    2) Financial information
    3) Transcripts
    4) Class rank
    5) SAT
    6) GPA
    7) ACT
  Additional information: Application should also include a personal statement describing your educational plans. Some interviews required.
EIN: 382180730

4539
Michigan Masonic Charitable Foundation

(formerly Michigan Masonic Home Charitable Foundation)
1200 Wright Ave.
Alma, MI 48801-1133   (989) 466-4339
Contact: Keith Bankwitz, Dir., Philanthropy
FAX: (989) 466-4340; Tel. for Keith Bankwitz: (800) 994-7400 ext. 3802, e-mail: kbankwitz@michiganmasonsfoundation.org;
URL: http://www.michiganmasonsfoundation.org/

Foundation type: Public charity
Purpose: Scholarships to graduating high school seniors and undergraduate students of MI, for attendance at an accredited college, university, trade or vocational school.
Publications: Application guidelines.
Financial data: Year ended 03/31/2012. Assets, $112,610,859 (M); Expenditures, $5,889,739; Total giving, $4,523,438.
Fields of interest: Higher education.
Type of support: Scholarships—to individuals.
Application information: Applications accepted. Application form required. Application form available on the grantmaker's web site.
  Deadline(s): May 1
  Applicants should submit the following:
    1) Transcripts
    2) SAT
    3) Letter(s) of recommendation
    4) GPA
    5) ACT
  Additional information: Students should contact a Michigan Masonic lodge in their area if they are interested in applying for a scholarship.
EIN: 383266089

4540
Michigan Minority Business Development Council, Inc.
3011 W. Grand Blvd., Ste. 230
Detroit, MI 48202-3042 (313) 873-3200
FAX: (313) 873-4783; E-mail: mail@mmbdc.com;
URL: http://www.mmbdc.com

Foundation type: Public charity
Purpose: Scholarships to minority students residing in Michigan for undergraduate education.
Publications: Application guidelines; Newsletter.
Financial data: Year ended 12/31/2011. Assets, $4,126,371 (M); Expenditures, $2,469,088.
Fields of interest: Media/communications; Business school/education; Computer science; Engineering; Minorities.
Type of support: Scholarships—to individuals; Undergraduate support.
Application information: Application form required. Interview required.
> *Deadline(s):* Apr.
> *Applicants should submit the following:*
> 1) Photograph
> 2) Transcripts
> 3) Resume
> 4) Essay
> *Additional information:* Applicant must show proof of citizenship and ethnicity.

Program description:
> *Scholarships:* Scholarships of $2,000 each are available annually to ten students with junior or senior standing who are attending an accredited Michigan-based college or university with a degree focus in engineering, computer science, business (accounting), administration, or communications. Eligible recipients must have a GPA of 2.5 or higher, be a member of a minority group (as defined by the National Minority Supplier Development Council: African-American, Hispanic-American, Native-American, Asian-Pacific American, or Asian-Indian American), and demonstrate involvement in community activities while enrolled.
EIN: 382292187

4541
Joseph & Lottie Michner Educational Foundation
P.O. Box 274
Jackson, MI 49204-0274 (517) 788-9280
Contact: Julius J. Hoffman, Dir.

Foundation type: Independent foundation
Purpose: Scholarships to students attending Lumen Christi High School, Jackson, MI.
Financial data: Year ended 12/31/2011. Assets, $378,323 (M); Expenditures, $23,777; Total giving, $22,783.
Fields of interest: Secondary school/education.
Type of support: Support to graduates or students of specific schools.
Application information: Applications accepted. Application form required.
> *Initial approach:* Letter
> *Deadline(s):* Apr. 30
> *Additional information:* Applications are available at the high school or will be mailed upon request.
EIN: 382346759

4542
Midland Area Community Foundation
(formerly Midland Foundation)
76 Ashman Cir.
Midland, MI 48640 (989) 839-9661
Contact: For grants: Nancy Money, Prog. Off.
FAX: (989) 839-9907;
E-mail: info@midlandfoundation.org; Additional tel: (800) 906-9661; Grant application e-mail: nmoney@midlandfoundation.org; URL: http://www.midlandfoundation.org

Foundation type: Community foundation
Purpose: Scholarships to high school seniors or college students, as well as for adults of Midland or Gladwin county, MI who are resuming undergraduate study or who are retraining to enter the job market.
Publications: Application guidelines; Annual report; Grants list; Informational brochure; Newsletter.
Financial data: Year ended 12/31/2012. Assets, $73,391,036 (M); Expenditures, $3,481,841; Total giving, $2,346,665; Grants to individuals, 151 grants totaling $334,281.
Fields of interest: Vocational education; Higher education; Scholarships/financial aid.
Type of support: Scholarships—to individuals; Support to graduates or students of specific schools; Undergraduate support.
Application information: Applications accepted. Application form available on the grantmaker's web site.
> *Initial approach:* Application
> *Send request by:* Online
> *Deadline(s):* Mar. 1
> *Applicants should submit the following:*
> 1) Financial information
> 2) GPA
> 3) SAT
> 4) ACT
> 5) Transcripts
> *Additional information:* Scholarships are paid directly to the educational institutions on behalf of the students. See web site for a complete listing of scholarship funds.

Program description:
> *Scholarships:* The foundation administers several scholarships to individuals who seek higher education. For purposes of the scholarship program, applicants must be a legal resident of either Midland or Gladwin County for at least a year, a current high school senior graduating from a Midland or Gladwin County high school, or a college student who is a Midland or Gladwin County resident and moved out of the county only for the specific purpose of going away to college. Students may apply to up to five scholarships. See web site for additional information.
EIN: 382023395

4543
Howard Miller Foundation
860 E. Main Ave.
Zeeland, MI 49464-0301

Foundation type: Independent foundation
Purpose: Scholarships to children of Howard Miller Clock Co. employees for undergraduate education.
Financial data: Year ended 12/31/2012. Assets, $16,131,543 (M); Expenditures, $682,026; Total giving, $613,500; Grants to individuals, totaling $27,500.
Type of support: Employee-related scholarships.
Application information: Applications not accepted.
> *Additional information:* Unsolicited requests for funds not considered or acknowledged.

Company name: Howard Miller Clock Company
EIN: 382137226

4544
Helen Lancaster Minton Educational Fund
P.O. Box 75000
Detroit, MI 48275-7874 (252) 467-4743
Contact: Sharon Stephens
Application address: 130 S. Franklin St., Rocky Mount, NC 27802

Foundation type: Independent foundation
Purpose: Scholarships to students of Nash and Edgecombe counties, NC, for attendance at North Carolina Wesleyan College.
Financial data: Year ended 03/31/2013. Assets, $670,148 (M); Expenditures, $39,397; Total giving, $28,250.
Fields of interest: Higher education; Scholarships/financial aid.
Type of support: Support to graduates or students of specific schools; Undergraduate support.
Application information: Application form required.
> *Deadline(s):* May 1
> *Applicants should submit the following:*
> 1) Photograph
> 2) SAT
> 3) Transcripts
> *Additional information:* Application should also include handwritten personal statement and outline of high school activities.
EIN: 566180453

4545
The Morey Foundation
P.O. Box 374
Winn, MI 48896-0374
Application address: c/o Lon Morey, Pres., P.O. Box 1000, Winn, MI 48896-1000, tel.: (989) 866-2381

Foundation type: Independent foundation
Purpose: Scholarships to students at Central Michigan University.
Financial data: Year ended 12/31/2012. Assets, $33,297,951 (M); Expenditures, $1,957,998; Total giving, $1,382,766.
Type of support: Support to graduates or students of specific schools.
Application information: Applications accepted. Application form required.
> *Deadline(s):* Mar. 15.
EIN: 382965346

4546
James K. Morrill Scholarship Fund
P.O. Box 3636
Grand Rapids, MI 49501-3636 (413) 534-2020

Foundation type: Independent foundation
Purpose: Scholarships to graduating female students of Holyoke High School, MA.
Financial data: Year ended 12/31/2012. Assets, $1,170,683 (M); Expenditures, $69,893; Total giving, $51,867; Grants to individuals, 8 grants totaling $40,878 (high: $5,962, low: $4,617).
Fields of interest: Women.
Type of support: Support to graduates or students of specific schools; Undergraduate support.
Application information: Application form required.
> *Deadline(s):* May 10
> *Additional information:* Applications available in guidance office.
EIN: 367112892

4547
Mount Clemens Regional Health Care Foundation

(formerly M. C. G. Foundation)
1000 Harrington Blvd.
Mount Clemens, MI 48043-2920 (586) 493-8000
E-mail: desmith@mcrmc.org; Mailing address: 1000 Harrington Blvd., Mt. Clemens, MI 48043-2920; URL: http://www.mcrmc.org/foundation

Foundation type: Public charity
Purpose: Scholarships to employees of Mt. Clemens Regional Medical Center pursuing a health-related career.
Financial data: Year ended 09/30/2011. Assets, $7,208,887 (M); Expenditures, $868,504; Total giving, $126,963; Grants to individuals, 8 grants totaling $11,960.
Fields of interest: Health sciences school/education.
Type of support: Scholarships—to individuals.
Application information: Applicant will remain a student in good standing with a "B" average or better and agrees that during and/or upon completion of his/her training, will apply to become a full time employee of MCGH.
EIN: 382578873

4548
Mount Pleasant Area Community Foundation

(formerly Mount Pleasant Community Foundation)
306 S. Univ.
P.O. Box 1283
Mount Pleasant, MI 48804-1283 (989) 773-7322
Contact: Amanda Schafer, Exec. Dir.
FAX: (989) 773-1517; E-mail: info@mpacf.org; URL: http://www.mpacf.org

Foundation type: Community foundation
Purpose: Scholarships primarily to residents of Isabella County, MI.
Publications: Application guidelines; Annual report; Financial statement; Grants list; Informational brochure; Newsletter; IRS Form 990 or 990-PF printed copy available upon request.
Financial data: Year ended 12/31/2012. Assets, $12,636,443 (M); Expenditures, $705,715; Total giving, $319,324; Grants to individuals, 65 grants totaling $66,405.
Fields of interest: Higher education.
Type of support: Scholarships—to individuals; Support to graduates or students of specific schools; Graduate support; Undergraduate support.
Application information: Application form available on the grantmaker's web site.
> Send request by: Mail
> Copies of proposal: 5
> Deadline(s): Mar.
> Applicants should submit the following:
> 1) Transcripts
> 2) GPA
> 3) Essay
> 4) ACT
> Additional information: See web site for additional guidelines.
EIN: 382951873

4549
National Kidney Foundation of Michigan, Inc.

1169 Oak Valley Dr.
Ann Arbor, MI 48108-9674 (734) 222-9800
Contact: Daniel M. Carney, Pres. and C.E.O.
Scholarship inquiry e-mail: jherzog@nkfm.org
FAX: (734) 222-9801; E-mail: info@nkfm.org; URL: http://www.nkfm.org

Foundation type: Public charity
Purpose: Emergency funds as one time grants to individuals of MI, suffering from kidney disease. Scholarships available to individuals of MI, with kidney failure, for continuing education.
Financial data: Year ended 06/30/2012. Assets, $8,024,261 (M); Expenditures, $5,261,439; Total giving, $12,350; Grants to individuals, totaling $12,350.
Fields of interest: Higher education; Kidney research.
Type of support: Emergency funds; Research; Scholarships—to individuals; Grants for special needs.
Application information: Applications accepted. Application form required. Application form available on the grantmaker's web site.
> Send request by: Mail or fax
> Deadline(s): May 1 for Scholarship
> Additional information: For scholarship, application should include transcript, application appraisal form, and name and address of school to which award will be applied.
Program descriptions:
> Luann Scheppelmann-Eib Emergency Fund: This fund provides a one-time grant of up to $100 for non-medical needs of people with kidney disease. Payments are made directly to vendors, not individuals. See web site for additional information.
> Swartz/Ferriter Scholarships: This program awards $500 to people with kidney failure for continuing education. The awards are paid directly to the educational institution on behalf of the students. See web site for additional information.
EIN: 381559941

4550
National Multiple Sclerosis Society Michigan Chapter, Inc.

21311 Civic Ctr. Dr.
Southfield, MI 48076-3911 (248) 351-2190
Contact: Cynthia Zagieboylo, Pres. and C.E.O.
FAX: (248) 350-0029; E-mail: info@mig.nmss.org; Toll-free tel.: (800) 344-4867; URL: http://www.nationalmssociety.org/chapters/MIG/index.aspx

Foundation type: Public charity
Purpose: Grants to individuals in MI afflicted with multiple sclerosis, for medical equipment.
Publications: Annual report; Newsletter.
Financial data: Year ended 09/30/2012. Assets, $2,832,134 (M); Expenditures, $3,073,586; Total giving, $105,233; Grants to individuals, totaling $105,233.
Fields of interest: Multiple sclerosis research.
Type of support: Grants for special needs.
Application information: Applications accepted. Application form required.
> Initial approach: Telephone
> Deadline(s): None
EIN: 381410476

4551
Donald E. and Margaret L. Nelson Scholarship Fund

W9473 H. Lucas Dr.
Iron Mountain, MI 49801-9409 (906) 542-9281
Application address: c/o North Dickinson County School, Attn.: Daniel J. Nurmi, Principal, W6588 M-69, Felch, MI 49831-8890

Foundation type: Independent foundation
Purpose: Scholarships to graduates of North Dickinson County School, Felch, MI in pursuit of a higher education.
Financial data: Year ended 12/31/2011. Assets, $167,607 (M); Expenditures, $7,865; Total giving, $7,750; Grants to individuals, totaling $7,750.
Fields of interest: Higher education.
Type of support: Scholarships—to individuals.
Application information: Applications accepted. Application form required.
> Deadline(s): Apr. 1
> Additional information: Applications available from North Dickinson County School.
EIN: 382731508

4552
The New Common School Foundation

6861 E. Nevada St., Ste. 300
Detroit, MI 48234-2968 (313) 368-8580
Contact: W. Clark Durant, Pres.

Foundation type: Public charity
Purpose: Scholarships to urban students at two local private schools in Detroit, MI, who are academically talented or need tuition assistance.
Financial data: Year ended 12/31/2011. Assets, $16,486,530 (M); Expenditures, $1,802,551; Total giving, $1,270,821; Grants to individuals, totaling $44,002.
Fields of interest: Education; Economically disadvantaged.
Type of support: Scholarships—to individuals.
Application information: Applications not accepted.
> Additional information: Unsolicited requests for funds not accepted.
EIN: 383326860

4553
The New Day Foundation for Families

1174 Miners Run
P.O. Box 81252
Rochester, MI 48306-4801 (248) 330-0471
Contact: Gine Kell Spehn, Dir.
URL: http://www.foundationforfamilies.com

Foundation type: Public charity
Purpose: Financial assistance for young families of Michigan who have lost a parent due to cancer.
Financial data: Year ended 12/31/2011. Assets, $95,171 (M); Expenditures, $63,765; Total giving, $17,396; Grants to individuals, totaling $17,396.
Fields of interest: Cancer; Human services.
Type of support: Grants for special needs.
Application information: Applications accepted. Application form required. Application form available on the grantmaker's web site.
> Initial approach: Application
> Send request by: Mail
> Deadline(s): None
> Additional information: Application should include medical, and financial information.
EIN: 260609040

4554
Newaygo County Community Services
6308 S. Warner Ave.
P.O. Box 149
Fremont, MI   49412-9279   (231) 924-0641
Contact: Beverly Cassidy, C.E.O.
FAX: (231) 924-5594; E-mail: info@nccsweb.org;
Toll-free tel.: (800) 379-0221; URL: http://
www.nccsweb.org

Foundation type: Public charity
Purpose: Grants to residents of Newaygo County,
MI, for child care, food, housing and other
assistance.
Publications: Annual report; Financial statement.
Financial data: Year ended 12/31/2011. Assets,
$6,623,205 (M); Expenditures, $8,585,347; Total
giving, $4,858,229; Grants to individuals, totaling
$4,858,229.
Fields of interest: Food services; Housing/shelter;
Children/youth, services.
Type of support: Grants for special needs.
Application information: Contact the organization
for application guidelines.
EIN: 386158533

4555
Newaygo Public Schools Educational Advancement Foundation
360 S. Mill St.
Newaygo, MI   49337

Foundation type: Independent foundation
Purpose: Scholarships to residents of Newaygo, MI,
for higher education.
Financial data: Year ended 06/30/2010. Assets,
$0 (M); Expenditures, $22,080; Total giving,
$20,400; Grants to individuals, 14 grants totaling
$20,400 (high: $9,000, low: $400).
Type of support: Undergraduate support.
Application information: Application form required.
Deadline(s): Apr. 1
Applicants should submit the following:
1) GPA
2) Financial information
Additional information: Application must also
include character information and career
choice.
EIN: 382989275

4556
Sara L. Nieman Scholarship Fund
c/o Argus Corp.
12540 Beech Daly
Redford, MI   48239-2469   (313) 937-2900
Contact: Sandra K. Nieman, Pres.
Application address: 1012 Kensington, Grosse
Pointe Pk., MI 48230-1403

Foundation type: Operating foundation
Purpose: Scholarships to graduates of Dearborn
MI, pursuing postsecondary education.
Financial data: Year ended 12/31/2012. Assets,
$33,078 (M); Expenditures, $5,130; Total giving,
$4,000; Grants to individuals, 4 grants totaling
$4,000 (high: $1,000, low: $1,000).
Fields of interest: Higher education.
Type of support: Scholarships—to individuals.
Application information: Applications accepted.
Application form required.
Deadline(s): May
Applicants should submit the following:
1) Resume
2) Transcripts
3) Financial information

Additional information: Scholarships are in the
amount of $1,00 each, per year for four years.
EIN: 383570934

4557
Dr. William F. and Mabel E. Nill Foundation, Inc.
41700 Hayes Rd., Ste. A
Clinton TWP, MI   48038   (586) 286-6505
Contact: Wayne Stewart, Dir.

Foundation type: Independent foundation
Purpose: Scholarships to individuals attending
medical and law school, and assistance to needy
families in MI.
Financial data: Year ended 12/31/2012. Assets,
$718,260 (M); Expenditures, $82,226; Total
giving, $37,680.
Fields of interest: Law school/education; Medical
school/education; Economically disadvantaged.
Type of support: Research; Scholarships—to
individuals; Grants for special needs.
Application information: Contact foundation for
eligibility criteria.
EIN: 383546563

4558
Amos Nordman Foundation Charitable Trust
(also known as Amos Nordman Charitable Trust)
P.O. Box 1242
Muskegon, MI   49443   (231) 766-3660

Foundation type: Independent foundation
Purpose: Scholarships to individuals attending
colleges and universities in the Muskegon, MI,
area.
Financial data: Year ended 12/31/2012. Assets,
$326,958 (M); Expenditures, $40,699; Total
giving, $8,500.
Fields of interest: Higher education; Scholarships/
financial aid.
Type of support: Support to graduates or students
of specific schools; Undergraduate support.
Application information: Applications accepted.
Application form required.
Deadline(s): Mar. 1
Additional information: Applicant must
demonstrate financial need.
EIN: 237251583

4559
Northeast Michigan Community Service Agency, Inc.
2375 Gordon Rd.
Alpena, MI   49707-4627   (989) 356-3474
FAX: (989) 354-5909; E-mail: contact@nemcsa.org;
Toll-free tel.: (866) 484-7077; URL: http://
www.nemcsa.org

Foundation type: Public charity
Purpose: Financial assistance to indigent residents
of northeastern MI, for weatherization, utilities and
living expenses.
Publications: Annual report.
Financial data: Year ended 09/30/2011. Assets,
$7,162,577 (M); Expenditures, $47,360,583;
Total giving, $17,889,392; Grants to individuals,
totaling $13,018,101. Subtotal for grants to
individuals: 28,439 grants totaling $8,694,742.
Type of support: Grants for special needs.
Application information:
Initial approach: Letter

Additional information: Contact the agency for
complete eligibility requirements.
EIN: 381873461

4560
Northern Michigan Hospital Foundation
360 Connable Ave.
Petoskey, MI   49770-2272   (231) 487-3500
E-mail: foundation@northernhealth.org;
URL: http://www.nmh-foundation.org

Foundation type: Public charity
Purpose: Hospital bill financial assistance to
indigent patients at McLaren-Northern Michigan
Hospital who do not qualify for Medicaid.
Financial data: Year ended 12/31/2011. Assets,
$19,281,341 (M); Expenditures, $7,937,423;
Total giving, $6,473,719; Grants to individuals,
16,745 grants totaling $251,923.
Fields of interest: Hospitals (general); Health care,
patient services; Economically disadvantaged.
Type of support: Grants for special needs.
Application information: Applications accepted.
Application form required.
Initial approach: Tel.
Applicants should submit the following:
1) Financial information
Additional information: Call 231.487.4760 for
eligibility guidelines.
EIN: 382445611

4561
Northville Community Foundation
18600 Northville Rd., Ste. 275
Northville, MI   48168   (248) 374-0200
Contact: Shari Peters, Pres.
FAX: (248) 374-0403;
E-mail: ncfmanager@gmail.com; URL: http://
mayburyfarm.org/

Foundation type: Community foundation
Purpose: Scholarships to high school seniors of the
Northville School District, MI for continuing
education at institutions of higher learning.
Financial data: Year ended 12/31/2011. Assets,
$597,960 (M); Expenditures, $207,112; Total
giving, $7,700; Grants to individuals, totaling
$1,500.
Fields of interest: Higher education.
Type of support: Scholarships—to individuals.
Application information: Applications accepted.
Application form required. Application form
available on the grantmaker's web site.
Initial approach: Application
Send request by: Mail
Deadline(s): Apr. 1
Applicants should submit the following:
1) Letter(s) of recommendation
2) Transcripts
3) GPA
4) Essay
Additional information: Selection is based on
volunteer work within the community,
maintain a 3.8 GPA, and a 50 word essay on
the importance of volunteerism in the
community. Contact your guidance counselor
for application information.
EIN: 383361844

4562
Northville Educational Foundation
501 W. Main St., Rm. 211
Northville, MI 48167-1576   (248) 344-8458
Contact: Jennifer Pearson
E-mail: nef@northvilleedfoundation.org;
URL: http://www.northvilleedfoundation.org/

Foundation type: Public charity
Purpose: Grants to Norville Public School teachers of MI, to provide funding for innovative educational opportunities. Assistance for students lacking financial resources for school activities/events.
Financial data: Year ended 06/30/2012. Assets, $1,854,906 (M); Expenditures, $281,889; Total giving, $194,153; Grants to individuals, totaling $10,538.
Fields of interest: Education.
Type of support: Grants to individuals; Grants for special needs.
Application information: Applications accepted. Application form required.
  Send request by: On-line and mail
  Deadline(s): Dec.
  Final notification: Applicants notified Jan. for grants
  Additional information: Application should include budget information. See web site for additional application guidelines.
EIN: 383503644

4563
Northwest Michigan Human Services, Inc.
3963 Three Mile Rd.
Traverse City, MI 49686-9164   (231) 947-3780
FAX: (231) 947-4935; E-mail: mgordon@nmhsa.org

Foundation type: Public charity
Purpose: Financial assistance to indigent residents of northwest lower MI, for home weatherization, housing/shelter, heat, utilities and medication.
Financial data: Year ended 09/30/2011. Assets, $4,032,110 (M); Expenditures, $22,711,809; Total giving, $8,354,709; Grants to individuals, totaling $8,041,152.
Type of support: Grants for special needs.
Application information:
  Initial approach: Letter or e-mail
  Additional information: Contact the organization for application guidelines.
EIN: 382027389

4564
Novi Educational Foundation
25345 Taft Rd.
Novi, MI 48374-2423   (248) 449-1203
FAX: (248) 449-1219

Foundation type: Public charity
Purpose: Scholarships to students of the Novi Community School District, MI, to broaden and enrich their experiences.
Publications: Informational brochure.
Financial data: Year ended 06/30/2012. Assets, $655,299 (M); Expenditures, $91,684; Total giving, $74,530.
Type of support: Support to graduates or students of specific schools; Precollege support.
Application information: Applications not accepted.
  Additional information: Unsolicited requests for funds not considered or acknowledged.
EIN: 382665305

4565
Novi Parks Foundation
P.O. Box 1169
Novi, MI 48376-1169   (248) 250-2943
Application address: 45175 W. Ten Mile Rd., Novi, MI 48375-3006, Attn: Evie Watt, Exec. Secty., tel.: (248) 735-5611, fax: (248) 347-3286
FAX: (248) 474-6659; E-mail: info@noviparks.org; URL: http://www.noviparks.com/

Foundation type: Public charity
Purpose: Scholarships to residents of Novi, MI to attend recreational events.
Publications: Application guidelines.
Financial data: Year ended 12/31/2011. Assets, $592,077 (M); Expenditures, $25,633; Total giving, $11,000.
Fields of interest: Parks/playgrounds.
Type of support: Scholarships—to individuals.
Application information: Applications accepted. Application form required.
  Send request by: Mail
  Deadline(s): None
Program description:
  Parks, Recreation, and Forestry Scholarship: The organization awards up to $500 per family, per year, in scholarships that enable children to partake in recreational outdoor activities. Eligible applicants will be able to verify one or more years of residency in Novi (driver's license, state ID, property tax statement, or City of Novi water bill are all acceptable proof), furnish proof of income (W-2 form), provide transportation to and from all programs, classes, and events that are being subsidized by the organization, and be able to cover any additional fees associated with the programs, classes, and events. The organization reserves the right to adjust the maximum amount for scholarships based on annual funding levels. Scholarship may be rescinded and restitution of any fees mandated if scholarship information is falsified. The scholarship will be valid for four months from the date of approval.
EIN: 200902251

4566
Oakland Livingston Human Service Agency
196 Cesar E. Chavez Ave.
P.O. Box 430598
Pontiac, MI 48343-0598   (248) 209-2600
Contact: Irene Onderchanin, Chair.
Additional tel.: (248) 542-5860 for Oakland County South Office, or (517) 546-8500 for Livingston County Office, e-mail address for Livingston county: livingston@olhsa.org
FAX: (248) 209-2645; E-mail: info@olhsa.org; URL: http://www.olhsa.org

Foundation type: Public charity
Purpose: Emergency assistance to low income individuals including the elderly and disabled of Oakland and Livingston counties, MI to become self-sufficient. Assistance includes food, utilities, shelter, prescription assistance and other special needs.
Publications: Annual report; Informational brochure.
Financial data: Year ended 12/31/2011. Assets, $5,896,360 (M); Expenditures, $40,794,730; Total giving, $15,890,122; Grants to individuals, totaling $11,278,199.
Fields of interest: Human services; Aging; Disabilities, people with; Economically disadvantaged.
Type of support: Grants for special needs.

Application information: Some programs require applications. Services are available based on funding and local availability. Contact the agency for eligibility determination.
EIN: 381785665

4567
Oakwood Healthcare, Inc.
15500 Lundy Pkwy.
Dearborn, MI 48126-2778   (313) 586-5052
URL: http://www.oakwood.org

Foundation type: Public charity
Purpose: Scholarships to employees of Oakwood Healthcare pursuing a career in the healthcare field. Assistance to employees in their greatest time of need due to personal crisis or catastrophic event. Stipends provided to medical residents.
Financial data: Year ended 12/31/2011. Assets, $1,028,254,726 (M); Expenditures, $1,099,655,037; Total giving, $11,311,943; Grants to individuals, 355 grants totaling $11,145,104.
Fields of interest: Health sciences school/education.
Type of support: Scholarships—to individuals; Grants for special needs; Stipends.
Application information: Applications not accepted.
  Additional information: Unsolicited requests for funds not considered or acknowledged. Assistance only for Oakwood Healthcare employees.
EIN: 381405141

4568
Old Newsboys Goodfellow Fund of Detroit
P.O. Box 44444
Detroit, MI 48244-0444   (586) 775-6139
Contact: Sari Klok Schneider, Exec. Dir.
FAX: (586) 775-6173;
E-mail: sarigoodfellows@wowway.com; URL: http://www.detroitgoodfellows.org/

Foundation type: Public charity
Purpose: Services dedicated to the welfare of Detroit metro area underprivileged children by offering Christmas gift packages, shoe and dental vouchers, camp and educational scholarships.
Financial data: Year ended 01/31/2013. Assets, $5,405,370 (M); Expenditures, $1,452,430; Total giving, $1,175,415; Grants to individuals, totaling $1,175,415.
Fields of interest: Children/youth; Youth; Economically disadvantaged.
Type of support: In-kind gifts.
Application information:
  Initial approach: Letter
  Additional information: Contact foundation for eligibility criteria.
EIN: 386061491

4569
The Ontonagon Area Scholarship Foundation
P.O. Box 92
Ontonagon, MI 49953-0092   (906) 884-4963 ext. 2
E-mail: marilyn@oasd.k12.mi.us; URL: http://scholarship.oasd.k12.mi.us/index.htm

Foundation type: Public charity
Purpose: Scholarships to graduates of Ontonagon Area High School, MI.
Publications: Application guidelines; Grants list.

Financial data: Year ended 05/31/2012. Assets, $133,417 (M); Expenditures, $216,464; Total giving, $15,250.
Type of support: Support to graduates or students of specific schools.
Application information:
  Initial approach: Letter
  Deadline(s): Apr. 4
  Additional information: Application should include transcript.
EIN: 383525614

4570
The Optimist Club Foundation
P.O. Box 891
Clarkston, MI 48347-0891

Foundation type: Public charity
Purpose: Oratory scholarships for residents of the Clarkston, MI area.
Financial data: Year ended 09/30/2012. Assets, $87,554 (M); Expenditures, $117,134; Total giving, $117,134.
Type of support: Undergraduate support.
Application information:
  Initial approach: Letter
  Additional information: Contact foundation for eligibility criteria.
EIN: 383373756

4571
Otsego County Community Foundation
123 W. Main St.
P.O. Box 344
Gaylord, MI 49734 (989) 731-0597
Contact: For grants: Dana Bensinger, Exec. Dir.
FAX: (989) 448-8377;
E-mail: contact@otsegofoundation.org; Grant inquiry e-mail: dana@otsegofoundation.org; URL: http://www.otsegofoundation.org

Foundation type: Community foundation
Purpose: Scholarships to students from Otsego County, MI or students who attend an Otsego County High School pursuing higher education.
Publications: Annual report.
Financial data: Year ended 12/31/2012. Assets, $3,295,819 (M); Expenditures, $205,484; Total giving, $99,398; Grants to individuals, 14 grants totaling $10,726.
Fields of interest: Higher education.
Type of support: Scholarships—to individuals; Support to graduates or students of specific schools.
Application information: Applications accepted. Application form required. Application form available on the grantmaker's web site.
  Initial approach: Application
  Send request by: Mail or hand-deliver
  Deadline(s): Mar. 15
  Applicants should submit the following:
    1) ACT
    2) SAT
    3) GPA
    4) Letter(s) of recommendation
    5) Transcripts
  Additional information: Each scholarship has its own set of eligibility criteria. See web site for a complete listing.
EIN: 383216235

4572
Pardee Cancer Treatment Fund of Bay County
c/o County Michigan
P.O. Box 541
Bay City, MI 48707-0541 (989) 891-8815
Contact: Carol Wells

Foundation type: Operating foundation
Purpose: Payment of medical bills for cancer patients who are residents of Bay County, MI.
Publications: Annual report.
Financial data: Year ended 09/30/2013. Assets, $0 (M); Expenditures, $203,082; Total giving, $186,276.
Fields of interest: Health care; Cancer.
Type of support: Grants for special needs.
Application information: Applications accepted. Application form not required. Interview required.
  Initial approach: Telephone
  Deadline(s): None
  Additional information: Applications by in-person visit with list of expenses incurred and other financial information.
EIN: 382877951

4573
Henry & Louise Parker Scholarship Trust
P.O. Box 75000
Detroit, MI 48275-3302

Foundation type: Independent foundation
Purpose: Scholarships to graduating students of Santa Cruz High School, CA and Soquel High School, CA.
Financial data: Year ended 12/31/2011. Assets, $215,693 (M); Expenditures, $17,367; Total giving, $12,000; Grants to individuals, 2 grants totaling $12,000 (high: $6,000, low: $6,000).
Fields of interest: Higher education.
Type of support: Support to graduates or students of specific schools; Undergraduate support.
Application information: Applications not accepted.
  Additional information: Recipients are chosen by a scholarship committee made up of the principals of Santa Cruz, and Soquel high schools. Unsolicited requests for funds not considered or acknowledged.
EIN: 946347991

4574
Rosa L. Parks Scholarship Foundation, Inc.
c/o The Detroit News
P.O. Box 950
Detroit, MI 48231-3124 (313) 222-2538
E-mail: info@rosaparksscholarship.org;
URL: http://www.rosaparksscholarshipfoundation.org

Foundation type: Public charity
Purpose: Scholarships to MI high school seniors who hold close to the legacy of Rosa Parks, while demonstrating academic skills, community involvement, and economic need.
Financial data: Year ended 04/30/2012. Assets, $93,388 (M); Expenditures, $88,273; Total giving, $80,000; Grants to individuals, 40 grants totaling $80,000 (high: $2,000, low: $2,000).
Fields of interest: Higher education; Civil/human rights.
Type of support: Scholarships—to individuals; Undergraduate support.

Application information: Applications accepted. Application form required. Application form available on the grantmaker's web site.
  Initial approach: Letter
  Send request by: Mail
  Deadline(s): Mar. 1
  Applicants should submit the following:
    1) GPA
    2) Transcripts
    3) SAT
    4) Letter(s) of recommendation
    5) Financial information
    6) Essay
    7) ACT
Program description:
  Scholarships: The foundation offers one-year, non-renewable scholarships of up to $2,000 each to graduating Michigan high school seniors. Winners are selected on the basis of scholarship, leadership and dedication to the civil rights principles of Rosa L. Parks, whose historic stand against racial prejudice in 1955 has brought her national recognition. Eligible applicants must be seniors attending a public or private high school in Michigan who anticipates graduating by Aug. of his/her application year and has a GPA of 2.5 or above.
EIN: 382339613

4575
Paulsen Trust
521 Curvebrook S.E.
Kentwood, MI 49548 (520) 751-7897
Contact: Nelson R. Allen, Tr.
Application address: 2121 Pantano Rd., No. 267, Tucson, AZ 85710-6119, tel.: (520) 751-7897

Foundation type: Independent foundation
Purpose: Scholarships to graduating high school seniors in MI pursuing their studies at accredited Michigan institutions of higher learning.
Financial data: Year ended 12/31/2012. Assets, $183,180 (M); Expenditures, $9,901; Total giving, $9,000; Grants to individuals, 6 grants totaling $9,000 (high: $1,500, low: $1,500).
Fields of interest: Vocational education, post-secondary; Higher education.
Type of support: Scholarships—to individuals.
Application information: Applications accepted. Application form required.
  Deadline(s): May 1
Program description:
  Scholarship: Scholarships range from $1,000 to $2,000 to high school seniors for postsecondary learning skills, trade, career opportunities and/or updates, business, non-degree programs, associate degrees and/or advanced college work. Scholarships are distributed annually to approximately two to six students.
EIN: 386537948

4576
Pennock Foundation
1009 W. Green St.
Hastings, MI 49058-1790 (269) 948-3122
Contact: Matthew J. Thompson
Scholarship tel.: (269) 948-3125
FAX: (269) 945-4130;
E-mail: jdalman@pennockhealth.com; URL: http://www.pennockhealth.com/foundation/index.html

Foundation type: Public charity
Purpose: Scholarships to qualified students of Hastings, MI pursuing a career in various health care fields.
Financial data: Year ended 09/30/2011. Assets, $5,300,936 (M); Expenditures, $667,300; Total

giving, $572,449; Grants to individuals, 25 grants totaling $81,471.
Fields of interest: Nursing school/education; Health sciences school/education.
Type of support: Scholarships—to individuals; Undergraduate support; Grants for special needs.
Application information: Applications accepted. Application form required.
Initial approach: Telephone
Additional information: See web site for additional guidelines.
Program description:
Doris I. Cappon Scholarship: This scholarship provides funds to qualified students for schooling. A service commitment is required. Applicants must also provide a personal statement, have a GPA of 2.75 (on a 4.0 scale) for the last two years, provide official documentation as proof of acceptance into an approved program, go through an interview process, and commit to working at Pennock for at least two years after the degree is obtained.
EIN: 382713275

4577
Petoskey-Harbor Springs Area Community Foundation
616 Petoskey St., Ste. 203
Petoskey, MI 49770-2779 (231) 348-5820
Contact: David L. Jones, Exec. Dir.; For grants: Sara Ward, Prog. Off.
Application inquiry e-mail: sward@phsacf.org
FAX: (231) 348-5883; *E-mail:* info@phsacf.org;
URL: http://www.phsacf.org

Foundation type: Community foundation
Purpose: Scholarships to individuals residing in the Emmet County, MI, area for undergraduate education at institutions in the U.S.
Publications: Application guidelines; Annual report; Financial statement; Grants list; Informational brochure.
Financial data: Year ended 03/31/2012. Assets, $28,459,934 (M); Expenditures, $1,103,975; Total giving, $754,595; Grants to individuals, 20 grants totaling $25,750.
Fields of interest: Vocational education, post-secondary; Business school/education; Law school/education; Medical school/education; Nursing school/education; Engineering school/education; Health sciences school/education; Formal/general education; Mathematics; Computer science; Science.
Type of support: Support to graduates or students of specific schools; Technical education support; Undergraduate support.
Application information: Applications accepted. Application form required. Application form available on the grantmaker's web site.
Initial approach: Telephone
Send request by: Mail
Copies of proposal: 8
Deadline(s): Mar. 26
Final notification: Applicants notified 60 days after receipt of application
Applicants should submit the following:
1) Transcripts
2) ACT
3) Essay
4) Financial information
5) Letter(s) of recommendation
Additional information: Most scholarship applications require a $5 fee. See web site for complete scholarship and program information.
Program description:
Scholarships: The foundation currently administers more than 40 scholarship funds,

mostly for graduating high school seniors from Dare County, Currituck County, and Ocracoke. In addition to scholarships for local, college-bound seniors, the foundation also manages several scholarship endowments targeting College of The Albemarle students, including the need-based Milton A. Jewell Trade and Technical Scholarship program for continuing education students. These applications are handled by the College of The Albemarle, contact the College for details.
EIN: 383032185

4578
Roger S. Phelps Scholarship Trust
P.O. Box 75000
Detroit, MI 48275-3302

Foundation type: Independent foundation
Purpose: Scholarships to graduates of Antioch Senior High School and San Lorenzo Valley High School, CA for undergraduate studies at accredited colleges or universities.
Financial data: Year ended 12/31/2011. Assets, $246,947 (M); Expenditures, $18,812; Total giving, $13,100; Grants to individuals, 2 grants totaling $13,100 (high: $8,800; low: $4,300).
Fields of interest: Higher education.
Type of support: Scholarships—to individuals; Support to graduates or students of specific schools.
Application information: Contact scholarship committee for application guidelines.
EIN: 946087426

4579
Plumbers and Pipefitters Local No. 333 Scholarship Plan
5405 S. Martin Luther King Jr. Blvd.
Lansing, MI 48911-3543 (517) 784-7500

Foundation type: Public charity
Purpose: Scholarships to residents of Jackson, MI.
Financial data: Year ended 06/30/2012. Assets, $45,302 (M); Expenditures, $31,675; Total giving, $28,500.
Type of support: Undergraduate support.
Application information: Contact foundation for complete application deadline/guidelines.
EIN: 386191955

4580
The Pokagon Fund, Inc.
821 E. Buffalo St.
New Buffalo, MI 49117-1522 (269) 469-9322
Contact: Mary L. Dunbar, Exec. Dir.
E-mail address for scholarships:
scholarships@pokagonfund.org
E-mail: info@pokagonfund.org; *URL:* http://www.pokagonfund.org/

Foundation type: Company-sponsored foundation
Purpose: Scholarships to graduating high school seniors from River Valley or New Buffalo High Schools; adults who are full-time residents of New Buffalo, Chikaming or Three Oaks Township; and to members of the Pokagon Tribe for higher education.
Publications: Application guidelines; Annual report (including application guidelines); Financial statement; Grants list.
Financial data: Year ended 06/30/2012. Assets, $10,129,849 (M); Expenditures, $3,519,027; Total giving, $3,191,126. Scholarships—to individuals amount not specified.
Fields of interest: Vocational education, post-secondary; Higher education.

Type of support: Scholarships—to individuals; Support to graduates or students of specific schools.
Application information: Applications accepted. Application form required. Application form available on the grantmaker's web site.
Initial approach: Application
Send request by: Mail or e-mail
Copies of proposal: 1
Deadline(s): Mar. 15
Final notification: Applicants notified in May
Applicants should submit the following:
1) SAT
2) Pell Grant
3) GPA
4) Financial information
5) FAFSA
6) Essay
7) Letter(s) of recommendation
8) Transcripts
Additional information: Applications should also include a copy of the vocational/technical school or university/college acceptance letter, a copy of applicant's and parent's 1040 tax return, and a one-page mini autobiography. The scholarship will be paid directly to educational institution on behalf of the student.
Program descriptions:
Pokagon Adult Scholarship: The foundation award scholarships to adult members of the Pokagon Tribe and their non-tribal relatives living in Dowagiac or South Bend.
Pokagon Fund Children's Vision Program: The foundation, in partnership with the New Buffalo Lion's Club, provides free eye exams and glasses to children between 9 months through 6th grade in Harbor Country. See web site, http://www.newbuffalolions.org/ for additional information.
Scholarships: The fund awards college scholarships to graduating high school seniors from River Valley or New Buffalo High Schools. The fund awards $2,500 per year for study at a two-year vocational or technical school (total $5,000), and $2,500 per year for study at a four-year college or university (total $10,000). Scholarships are renewable if the student maintains a 3.0 GPA. Applicants must be residents of the townships of New Buffalo, Chikaming, or Three Oaks, and the cities and villages within those townships.
EIN: 300130499

4581
John Polakovic Charitable Trust
32100 Telegraph Rd., Ste. 200
Bingham Farms, MI 48025-2454
Contact: Patricia Bowman, Tr.
Application address: 7916 Greenview Terr. Ct., Charlotte, NC 28277

Foundation type: Independent foundation
Purpose: Scholarships to individuals attending J. Sterling Morton high schools in Berwyn, Cicero and Stickney IL, for undergraduate education.
Financial data: Year ended 12/31/2011. Assets, $98,193 (M); Expenditures, $4,240; Total giving, $1,500; Grant to an individual, 1 grant totaling $1,500.
Type of support: Support to graduates or students of specific schools; Undergraduate support.
Application information: Applications accepted. Application form required.
Initial approach: Letter
Additional information: Application should include high school academic information.
EIN: 386390004

4582
Jennifer Gordon Polan Foundation
27816 Lakehills Dr.
Franklin, MI 48025-1787   (248) 626-2231
Contact: Jesse N. Polan, Tr.

Foundation type: Independent foundation
Purpose: Scholarships to residents of the Birmingham, MI area for higher education.
Financial data: Year ended 12/31/2011. Assets, $17,602 (M); Expenditures, $600; Total giving, $0.
Fields of interest: Education.
Type of support: Undergraduate support.
Application information: Applications accepted. Application form required.
  Initial approach: Letter
  Deadline(s): May 1
EIN: 383540779

4583
Rachor Family Foundation, Ltd.
(formerly Michael Garry Rachor Professional School Scholarship Fund, Ltd.)
P.O. Box 320100
Flint, MI 48532-0002

Foundation type: Independent foundation
Purpose: Scholarships to students pursuing an education in professional school or graduate school leading to an advanced degree.
Financial data: Year ended 12/31/2012. Assets, $2,667,896 (M); Expenditures, $138,961; Total giving, $125,500.
Fields of interest: Higher education.
Type of support: Scholarships—to individuals.
Application information: Application form required.
  Initial approach: Letter.
  Applicants should submit the following:
    1) Transcripts
    2) Letter(s) of recommendation
    3) GPA
    4) Financial information
    5) Essay
  Additional information: Application must also include references.
EIN: 383264828

4584
The Raval Education Foundation Inc.
1004 Browns Lake Rd.
Jackson, MI 49203-5669   (517) 414-3400
Contact: Harish Rawal, Pres.

Foundation type: Independent foundation
Purpose: Scholarships to graduates of Jackson High School, MI for postsecondary education.
Financial data: Year ended 12/31/2012. Assets, $8,943 (M); Expenditures, $26,021; Total giving, $26,000; Grants to individuals, 8 grants totaling $9,000 (high: $2,000, low: $1,000).
Fields of interest: Higher education.
Type of support: Support to graduates or students of specific schools; Undergraduate support.
Application information:
  Initial approach: Letter
  Deadline(s): None
EIN: 383624064

4585
Recreational Boating Industries Educational Foundation
32398 Five Mile Rd.
Livonia, MI 48154-6109   (734) 261-0123
Contact: John Ropp, Dir.

Foundation type: Independent foundation
Purpose: Scholarships to permanent residents of MI pursuing a career in the recreational boating industry, including marketing, service, facilities design for boat stores and marinas, and manufacturing.
Financial data: Year ended 12/31/2011. Assets, $55,558 (M); Expenditures, $19,145; Total giving, $9,450; Grants to individuals, 14 grants totaling $9,450 (high: $1,000, low: $500).
Fields of interest: Recreation; Marine science.
Type of support: Undergraduate support.
Application information:
  Initial approach: Letter
  Deadline(s): Apr. 20
  Additional information: Application should outline financial need and academic and work-related performance.
EIN: 382704909

4586
Region 3b Area Agency on Aging
200 Michigan Ave. W. Ste. 102
Battle Creek, MI 49017-3632   (269) 966-2450
Contact: Karla Fales, Exec. Dir.
FAX: (269) 966-2493; E-mail: lmiller@region3b.org; Toll Free Tel.: (800)-626-6719; URL: http://www.region3b.org/

Foundation type: Public charity
Purpose: Care services to elderly residents of MI's Barry, Branch, Calhoun, Kalamazoo, Berrien, Cass, Van Buren and St. Joseph counties.
Financial data: Year ended 09/30/2011. Assets, $4,539,425 (M); Expenditures, $14,472,443; Total giving, $9,517,017; Grants to individuals, totaling $9,517,017.
Fields of interest: Aging, centers/services; Aging.
Type of support: In-kind gifts.
Application information: Applications accepted.
  Initial approach: Telephone
  Additional information: Eligibility requirements include must be financially eligible for Medicaid, gross (total of all income before any bills are paid and deductions taken) income for applicant cannot exceed $2,163 per month, medically eligible for long term care, must require a waiver service.
EIN: 383013931

4587
C. M. & A. A. Reid Charitable & Student Loan
328 S. Saginaw St., M/C 001065
Flint, MI 48502-1923   (989) 776-7368
Contact: Helen James
Application address: C/O Firstmerit, N.A., 101 N. Washington St., Saginaw, MI 48607

Foundation type: Independent foundation
Purpose: Student loans to residents of Saginaw County, MI, who are between the ages of 15 and 30.
Financial data: Year ended 08/31/2013. Assets, $646,437 (M); Expenditures, $14,310; Total giving, $0.
Fields of interest: Education.
Type of support: Student loans—to individuals.
Application information: Application form required.
  Deadline(s): June 1
EIN: 386347006

4588
Walter and May Reuther Memorial Fund
(formerly Reuther Memorial Fund)
P.O. Box 75000
Detroit, MI 48275-3462

Foundation type: Independent foundation
Purpose: Scholarships for the study of educational services in the fields of labor, human relations, and the betterment of mankind.
Financial data: Year ended 12/31/2012. Assets, $998,791 (M); Expenditures, $68,203; Total giving, $62,186; Grants to individuals, 21 grants totaling $18,258 (high: $2,000, low: $75).
Type of support: Undergraduate support.
Application information: Applications accepted.
  Initial approach: Letter
  Additional information: Applicant must be a member, or be the dependent of a member of the UAW or of some other labor organization or be a student in an accredited educational institution; Contact organization for further application guidelines.
EIN: 237067164

4589
Sigurd & Jarmila Rislov Foundation
206 S. Main St., Ste. 218
Ann Arbor, MI 48103-5408
Contact: Sue Ann Savas, Secy.
URL: http://www.rislovfoundation.org

Foundation type: Independent foundation
Purpose: Scholarships for classical music education to exceptional classical musicians, including vocalists.
Financial data: Year ended 12/31/2012. Assets, $998,687 (M); Expenditures, $89,605; Total giving, $65,000.
Fields of interest: Music; Music composition.
Type of support: Scholarships—to individuals.
Application information: Applications accepted.
  Initial approach: Letter
  Applicants should submit the following:
    1) Transcripts
    2) Resume
  Additional information: Application should also include evidence of current enrollment in a university or educational program, a written career plan narrative, and a CD of a short performance.
EIN: 931247286

4590
Rochester Area Neighborhood House, Inc.
1234 Inglewood
Rochester, MI 48307-1517   (248) 651-5836
Contact: Linda Riggs, Exec. Dir.
FAX: (248) 651-5310;
E-mail: ranhranh@sbcglobal.net; E-Mail for Linda Riggs: director@ranh.org; URL: http://www.ranh.org

Foundation type: Public charity
Purpose: Financial assistance for low to moderate income individuals and families of Oakland county, MI, with food, shelter, clothing and transportation. A $2,500 scholarship is awarded to one outstanding high school student for the Junior Ambassador Program.
Financial data: Year ended 12/31/2011. Assets, $270,177 (M); Expenditures, $531,337; Total giving, $336,913; Grants to individuals, totaling $336,913.
Fields of interest: Youth; Aging; Economically disadvantaged.

Type of support: Scholarships—to individuals; Grants for special needs.
Application information: Applications accepted. Application form required.
Deadline(s): Apr. 15 for Scholarship
Additional information: Contact the organization for eligibility requirements for assistance. Application for scholarship can be obtained from any area high school guidance office or the Rochester Area Neighborhood House.
EIN: 381956214

4591
Otto & Helen Roethke Scholarship Fund
328 S. Saginaw St., MC 001065
Flint, MI 48502 (517) 797-4815
Contact: Mercedes Perez
Application address: Arthur Hill Scholarship Selection, 3115 Mackinaw St., Saginaw, MI 48602

Foundation type: Independent foundation
Purpose: Scholarships to Arthur High School, MI, graduates attending the University of Michigan with consideration given to students pursuing a major in English.
Financial data: Year ended 07/31/2013. Assets, $131,074 (M); Expenditures, $4,656; Total giving, $1,700; Grant to an individual, 1 grant totaling $1,700.
Fields of interest: Higher education.
Type of support: Support to graduates or students of specific schools.
Application information: Applications accepted. Application form required.
Deadline(s): May 1
EIN: 386720940

4592
Roscommon County Community Foundation
701 Lake St.
P.O. Box 824
Roscommon, MI 48653 (989) 275-3112
Contact: Mary Fry, Pres. and C.E.O.
FAX: (989) 275-3112;
E-mail: rococofo@yahoo.com; URL: http://www.roscommoncountycommunityfoundation.org

Foundation type: Community foundation
Purpose: College scholarships to residents of Roscommon County, MI for higher education at accredited institutions.
Publications: Application guidelines; Annual report; Annual report (including application guidelines); Financial statement; Grants list; Informational brochure; Newsletter.
Financial data: Year ended 12/31/2012. Assets, $6,189,935 (M); Expenditures, $313,659; Total giving, $138,211; Grants to individuals, 50 grants totaling $118,419.
Fields of interest: Higher education; Scholarships/financial aid.
Type of support: Scholarships—to individuals; Undergraduate support.
Application information: Applications accepted. Application form required. Application form available on the grantmaker's web site.
Initial approach: Application
Deadline(s): Varies
Additional information: See web site for eligibility criteria and application forms per scholarship.
EIN: 383612480

4593
Rotary Club of Lowell Community Foundation
P.O. Box 223
Lowell, MI 49331-0223 (616) 676-0891

Foundation type: Public charity
Purpose: Scholarships to residents of Lowell, MI.
Financial data: Year ended 12/31/2011. Assets, $151,317 (M); Expenditures, $61,910; Total giving, $41,944.
Type of support: Undergraduate support.
Application information: Contact foundation for eligibility requirements.
EIN: 383563288

4594
Royal Oak Foundation for Public Education
707 Girard
Royal Oak, MI 48073-3648 (248) 588-5050
Contact: Anne Redmond
E-mail: secretary@rofoundation.org; email for Anne Redmond: redmonda@royaloakschools.com; URL: http://www.rofoundation.org

Foundation type: Public charity
Purpose: Grants to teachers at Royal Oak, MI, public schools for programs in their classroom or school.
Financial data: Year ended 12/31/2011. Assets, $316,143 (M); Expenditures, $26,359; Total giving, $24,637.
Fields of interest: Education.
Type of support: Program development; Grants to individuals.
Application information: Applications not accepted.
Additional information: Contributes only to preselected individuals.
EIN: 383147156

4595
Rudy Scholarship Fund
(also known as Rudy Scholarship)
P.O. Box 3636
Grand Rapids, MI 49501-3636 (847) 526-6611
Application address: c/o Wauconda School District, Attn.: Daniel Cole, Supt., 555 N. Main St., Wauconda, IL 60084-1299, tel.: (847) 526-6611

Foundation type: Independent foundation
Purpose: Scholarships to graduating students of Wauconda High School, IL.
Financial data: Year ended 12/31/2011. Assets, $486,710 (M); Expenditures, $26,660; Total giving, $20,000.
Type of support: Support to graduates or students of specific schools; Undergraduate support.
Application information: Application form required.
Deadline(s): Apr. 1
Additional information: Application should include proof of registration to an accredited two- or four-year college or university. Recipients must be in the upper 25 percent of their graduating classes, participate in at least one extracurricular activity during their four years in high school and maintain good citizenship and attendance record. Students attending two-year colleges should have the intent of continuing his/her education at a four-year college or university.
EIN: 367168424

4596
Clara A. Ruf Scholarship Trust
515 Christy Dr.
St. Charles, MI 48655-1428 (989) 652-9945
Contact: Robert F. Loomis, Chair.
Application Adddress: 207 S. Saginaw, Saint Charles, MI 48655

Foundation type: Independent foundation
Purpose: Scholarships to graduates of St. Charles High School, MI for postsecondry education.
Financial data: Year ended 12/31/2012. Assets, $79,075 (M); Expenditures, $7,005; Total giving, $4,000; Grants to individuals, 4 grants totaling $4,000 (high: $1,000, low: $1,000).
Fields of interest: Higher education.
Type of support: Support to graduates or students of specific schools; Undergraduate support.
Application information: Applications accepted.
Initial approach: Letter
Deadline(s): None
EIN: 382587560

4597
Saginaw Community Foundation
1 Tuscola, Ste. 100
Saginaw, MI 48607-1282 (989) 755-0545
Contact: Renee S. Johnston, C.E.O.
FAX: (989) 755-6524;
E-mail: info@saginawfoundation.org; URL: http://www.saginawfoundation.org

Foundation type: Community foundation
Purpose: Scholarships to area students of Saginaw, MI pursuing undergraduate studies, vocational training or graduate school and for nontraditional students.
Publications: Application guidelines; Annual report (including application guidelines); Newsletter; Occasional report.
Financial data: Year ended 12/31/2012. Assets, $41,787,699 (M); Expenditures, $3,550,088; Total giving, $1,208,239; Grants to individuals, totaling $334,592.
Fields of interest: Higher education.
Type of support: Scholarships—to individuals; Undergraduate support.
Application information: Applications accepted. Application form required. Application form available on the grantmaker's web site.
Send request by: Online
Copies of proposal: 2
Deadline(s): Feb. 1
Final notification: Recipients notified by May 1
Applicants should submit the following:
    1) Photograph
    2) Transcripts
    3) Proposal
    4) Letter(s) of recommendation
    5) GPA
    6) Financial information
    7) FAFSA
    8) Essay
    9) ACT
Additional information: Each scholarship has its own unique eligibility criteria. See web site for a complete listing.
EIN: 382474297

4598
Burl E. Salisbury Memorial Scholarship Fund

c/o Southern Michigan Bank & Trust
P.O. Box 309
Coldwater, MI   49036-0309   (517) 279-5503
Contact: Mary Guthrie, Trust Off., Southern Michigan Bank & Trust

Foundation type: Independent foundation
Purpose: Educational loans to students who graduated from Bronson High School, MI and attending college.
Financial data: Year ended 04/30/2012. Assets, $279,470 (M); Expenditures, $43,078; Total giving, $33,000.
Fields of interest: Higher education.
Type of support: Support to graduates or students of specific schools; Undergraduate support.
Application information: Application form required.
Initial approach: Letter
Deadline(s): May 1
Applicants should submit the following:
1) Class rank
2) Transcripts
3) GPA
4) Financial information
5) ACT
EIN: 386429664

4599
Sanilac County Community Foundation

47 Austin St.
P.O. Box 307
Sandusky, MI   48471-0307   (810) 648-3634
Contact: Joan Nagelkirk, Exec. Dir.
FAX: (810) 648-4418;
E-mail: director@sanilaccountycommunityfoundatio n.org; Additional e-mail: joan@clearideas.biz;
URL: http://www.sanilaccountycommunityfoundation.org

Foundation type: Community foundation
Purpose: Scholarships to graduating high school seniors of Sanilac County, MI for higher education.
Publications: Annual report; Financial statement; Grants list; Informational brochure; Informational brochure (including application guidelines); Program policy statement.
Financial data: Year ended 12/31/2011. Assets, $3,631,077 (M); Expenditures, $273,209; Total giving, $172,899; Grants to individuals, 80 grants totaling $58,489.
Fields of interest: Higher education.
Type of support: Support to graduates or students of specific schools; Undergraduate support.
Application information:
Deadline(s): June 1 and Dec. 1
Additional information: Students must show proof of registration at a college or university in order to receive their money. See web site for a listing of various scholarships.
EIN: 383204484

4600
Scears Foundation of Akron Michigan

c/o Jan Holik
998 N. Graf Rd.
Caro, MI   48723-9682

Foundation type: Independent foundation
Purpose: Scholarships to graduates of Tuscola county, MI for continuing education at institutions of higher learning.

Financial data: Year ended 12/31/2012. Assets, $0 (M); Expenditures, $14,352; Total giving, $14,352.
Fields of interest: Education.
Type of support: Scholarships—to individuals.
Application information: Contact the foundation for additional guidelines.
EIN: 383593135

4601
The A. Paul and Carol C. Schaap Foundation

c/o Comerica Bank
500 Woodward Ave., 21st Fl.
Detroit, MI   48226-3416   (313) 222-3304

Foundation type: Independent foundation
Purpose: Scholarships to Michigan residents pursuing a career in theological study.
Financial data: Year ended 12/31/2012. Assets, $5,583,957 (M); Expenditures, $882,933; Total giving, $824,795.
Fields of interest: Theological school/education.
Type of support: Scholarships—to individuals.
Application information:
Initial approach: Letter
Additional information: Selection is based on applicants who demonstrate a promise for pastoral leadership through his or her academic excellence, leadership ability, interpersonal relationship skills, theologically inspired creatively, and Christian vision.
EIN: 207097647

4602
Scholarship Fund of Flint Plumbing & Pipefitting Industry

6525 Centurion Dr.
Lansing, MI   48917-9275   (810) 720-5243
Contact: Mike Tomaszewski, Tr.

Foundation type: Company-sponsored foundation
Purpose: Scholarships to undergraduate students who are sons and daughters of active or deceased members of Flint Plumbing and Pipefitting Industry.
Financial data: Year ended 04/30/2013. Assets, $12,045 (M); Expenditures, $18,724; Total giving, $17,000; Grants to individuals, 17 grants totaling $17,000 (high: $1,000, low: $1,000).
Fields of interest: Higher education.
Type of support: Employee-related scholarships; Scholarships—to individuals.
Application information: Applications not accepted.
Additional information: Unsolicited requests for funds not considererd or acknowledged.
Company name: Flint Association of Plumbing and Mechanical Contractors, Inc.
EIN: 386522581

4603
Elizabeth Schultheiss Foundation

223 E. Grand River Ave.
Willliamston, MI   48895   (517) 655-1700
Contact: Paul T. Joseph, Tr.

Foundation type: Independent foundation
Purpose: Scholarships for students of Michigan for attendance at an accredited four year college or university.
Financial data: Year ended 12/31/2012. Assets, $1,640 (M); Expenditures, $14,000; Total giving, $13,400; Grants to individuals, 3 grants totaling $13,400 (high: $5,000, low: $3,400).

Fields of interest: Higher education.
Type of support: Scholarships—to individuals.
Application information: Applications accepted.
Deadline(s): Aug. 1
Additional information: Application should include transcript and a letter.
EIN: 205894065

4604
Shelby Community Foundation

P.O. Box 183181
Shelby Township, MI   48318-3181   (586) 909-5305
Contact: Linda Stout, Exec. Dir.
E-mail: contactus@shelbycommunityfoundation.co m; URL: http://shelbycommunityfoundation.com

Foundation type: Community foundation
Purpose: Awards scholarships to graduating high school seniors of Shelby Township, MI for attendance at community colleges and trade schools.
Publications: Annual report; Informational brochure; Newsletter.
Financial data: Year ended 12/31/2012. Assets, $660,234 (M); Expenditures, $72,704; Total giving, $43,947; Grants to individuals, 14 grants totaling $13,000.
Fields of interest: Vocational education, post-secondary; Higher education.
Type of support: Scholarships—to individuals.
Application information: Applications accepted. Application form required. Application form available on the grantmaker's web site.
Initial approach: Application
Send request by: Mail
Deadline(s): Apr. 1
Applicants should submit the following:
1) Transcripts
2) Financial information
3) Essay
Additional information: See web site for additional information.
EIN: 383341102

4605
Shiawassee Community Foundation

(formerly Shiawassee Foundation)
217 N. Washington St., Ste. 104
P.O. Box 753
Owosso, MI   48867-0753   (989) 725-1093
Contact: Carol Soule, Exec. Dir.
FAX: (989) 729-1358;
E-mail: shiafdn@michonline.net; URL: http://www.shiawasseecommunityfoundation.org/

Foundation type: Community foundation
Purpose: Scholarships to residents of Shiwassee County, MI for continuing education at institutions of higher learning.
Publications: Annual report; Newsletter.
Financial data: Year ended 09/30/2012. Assets, $4,873,819 (M); Expenditures, $181,570; Total giving, $96,097; Grants to individuals, 76 grants totaling $52,712.
Fields of interest: Higher education; Scholarships/financial aid.
Type of support: Scholarships—to individuals; Support to graduates or students of specific schools; Undergraduate support.
Application information: Applications accepted. Application form required. Application form available on the grantmaker's web site.

Initial approach: Application
Deadline(s): Mar. 14
Final notification: Applicants notified during May and June
Applicants should submit the following:
1) Letter(s) of recommendation
2) SAR
3) FAFSA
4) Transcripts
5) Resume
6) Essay
Additional information: Scholarship and grant amounts vary from year to year. See web site for a complete listing of scholarships and application guidelines.
EIN: 383285624

4606
Bill and Vi Sigmund Foundation

P.O. Box 1128
Jackson, MI 49204-1128 (517) 784-5464
Contact: Carolyn M. Pratt, Secy.
E-mail: sigmundfoundation@sbcglobal.net;
URL: http://www.sigmundfoundation.org

Foundation type: Independent foundation
Purpose: Scholarships to graduating high school seniors, students enrolled in college as full or part-time students or adult residents of Jackson and Lenawee counties, MI pursuing a career in nursing and aviation.
Publications: Application guidelines; Grants list.
Financial data: Year ended 12/31/2012. Assets, $10,287,234 (M); Expenditures, $648,514; Total giving, $587,425; Grants to individuals, totaling $337,125.
Fields of interest: Higher education; Nursing school/education; Space/aviation.
Type of support: Scholarships—to individuals.
Application information: Applications accepted. Application form required.
Send request by: Mail
Deadline(s): Apr. 15
Final notification: Applicants notified mid-July
Applicants should submit the following:
1) Transcripts
2) SAT
3) Letter(s) of recommendation
4) Financial information
5) ACT
6) Essay
Additional information: Application should also include a copy of the last two most recent family tax returns. Application sent by e-mail or hand delivery are not accepted.
EIN: 300002491

4607
Skandalaris Family Foundation

c/o Robert J. Skandalaris
1030 Doris Rd.
Auburn Hills, MI 48326-2613 (248) 220-2004
College Scholarship tel.: (248) 220-2004, fax: (248) 220-2038
FAX: (248) 220-2038;
E-mail: info@skandalaris.com; URL: http://www.skandalaris.com

Foundation type: Independent foundation
Purpose: College scholarships to students primarily of Michigan pursuing any chosen course of study at an accredited college or university in the U.S.
Financial data: Year ended 12/31/2012. Assets, $225,268 (M); Expenditures, $282,598; Total giving, $263,394; Grants to individuals, 131 grants totaling $263,394 (high: $2,500, low: $394).

Fields of interest: Higher education.
Type of support: Undergraduate support.
Application information:
Deadline(s): Apr. 15 for previous recipients, May 1 for re-applicants and first time applicants
Additional information: See web site for additional guidelines.
EIN: 383394567

4608
Chester J. & Angela M. Skrocki Foundation

c/o David Terrell
3787 Holiday Village Rd.
Traverse City, MI 49686-3915

Foundation type: Independent foundation
Purpose: Scholarships to individuals of the Traverse City, MI area for higher education at colleges, institutes and universities.
Financial data: Year ended 12/31/2012. Assets, $581,952 (M); Expenditures, $44,914; Total giving, $21,250.
Fields of interest: Higher education.
Type of support: Scholarships—to individuals.
Application information: Applicants are selected by the supported parishes.
EIN: 383708874

4609
Jean M. R. Smith Foundation

P.O. Box 42
Bad Axe, MI 48413-0042 (989) 860-8169
Contact: Rosemary Esch, V.P. and Exec. Dir.

Foundation type: Independent foundation
Purpose: Scholarships primarily to graduating students attending Huron County, MI, high schools for postsecondary education.
Financial data: Year ended 12/31/2012. Assets, $7,246,464 (M); Expenditures, $552,941; Total giving, $444,810; Grants to individuals, 40 grants totaling $179,312 (high: $7,500, low: $318).
Fields of interest: Higher education.
Type of support: Support to graduates or students of specific schools; Undergraduate support.
Application information: Applications accepted. Application form required.
Deadline(s): April 1
Applicants should submit the following:
1) ACT
2) Letter(s) of recommendation
3) Transcripts
EIN: 383323030

4610
Society for Research in Child Development, Inc.

(also known as SRCD)
2950 S. State St., Ste. 401
Ann Arbor, MI 48104-6773 (734) 926-0600
FAX: (734) 926-0601; E-mail: info@srcd.org;
URL: http://www.srcd.org

Foundation type: Public charity
Purpose: Fellowships for scholars in a variety of fields who are interested in child development research. Promotes interdisciplinary study in the development of children, facilitates communication between researchers across fields and encourages the application of findings.
Publications: Application guidelines.

Financial data: Year ended 06/30/2012. Assets, $11,134,832 (M); Expenditures, $3,844,686; Total giving, $25,000.
Fields of interest: Child development, services.
Type of support: Fellowships; Research; Stipends.
Application information: Applications accepted. Application form required. Application form available on the grantmaker's web site. Interview required.
Initial approach: Application
Deadline(s): Dec.
Applicants should submit the following:
1) Letter(s) of recommendation
2) Curriculum vitae
3) Essay
Additional information: Applicant must have a doctoral-level degree in any discipline to apply.
Program descriptions:
Congressional Fellowships in Child Development: This program is designed to provide greater interaction between the developmental research community and Congress. Fellows spend one year working as a legislative assistant on the staff of a congressional committee, on the staff of a member of Congress, or in a congressional support agency that works directly for members or committees of Congress. Fellows may participate in such activities as drafting and preparing legislation, preparing or assisting in Congressional hearings, or preparing briefs and speeches. Fellowships begin at $74,872 and are determined by experience and federal government pay scale.
Frances Degen Horowitz Millennium Scholars Program: This program, developed as a vehicle to encourage and support undergraduates from underrepresented groups to pursue graduate work in child development and other related disciplines, aims to increase the numbers of underrepresented minority students pursuing careers in fields of child development through association with and participation in the society. Participants will partner with junior and senior mentors to help provide educational and professional development. Benefits of participating in the program include participation at society meeting and special events, compensation for travel to Boston, transportation to and from hotel and airport, hotel accommodations, and some meal support.
Harold Stevenson Travel Award: This award will provide travel funds to attend the society's biennial meeting to scholars from countries with low-income economies and lower- and upper-middle-income economies as specified by the World Bank Country Classifications. To qualify, applicants must be participating in an accepted submission and be a citizen and resident of one of these countries. Both professional staff and students are available.
Jacob Foundation International Travel Award: This award supports attendance at the society's biennial meeting, and is available to a presenter or an accepted submission focusing on adolescence. Awardees must be a scholar residing in Central or Eastern Europe, Russia, or a developing nation as defined by United Nations' criteria. Awards are typically made to scholars who have received their Ph.D. degree or equivalent within the past seven years.
Outstanding Doctoral Dissertation Awards: This $500 honorarium is given for a dissertation completed in the previous year this is unusually noteworthy.
SECC Dissertation Funding Research Awards: Up to five awards of up to $2,000 each will be given to research dissertations and proposals that display the strong potential to contribute to the field of human development. Eligible applicants must be graduate students in a field related to human

development, in good standing with their university, and must have their dissertation proposals approved by their advisor; applicants must also be members of the society. Submissions should be in the proposal stage; money is to be used for research costs or professional development related to the proposed dissertation project.

SRCD International Travel Award: Funding to be applied towards travel expenses for the society's biennial meeting is available to primary or secondary presenters on an accepted submission on any aspect of child development, who reside outside the U.S. and who have received their Ph.D. degree or equivalent within the past several years.

SRCD Student Travel Awards: Funding, to be applied towards travel expenses for the society's biennial meeting, is available to the first author(s) of an accepted submission and a student society member at the time of submission and registration. This award may be applied to expenses as determined by the recipient.
EIN: 356005842

4611
Society of Manufacturing Engineers Education Foundation
(also known as SME Education Foundation)
1 SME Dr.
P.O. Box 930
Dearborn, MI 48128-2408 (313) 425-3300
Contact: Bart A. Aslin, C.E.O.
FAX: (313) 425-3411; E-mail: foundation@sme.org;
E-mail for Bart A. Aslin: baslin@sme.org; Telephone for Bart A. Aslin: (313) 425-3302; URL: http://www.smeef.org

Foundation type: Public charity
Purpose: Scholarships to graduating high school seniors, current undergraduates and masters or doctoral degree students pursuing degrees in manufacturing and related fields at two-year and four-year colleges.
Publications: Application guidelines; Annual report; Grants list; Program policy statement.
Financial data: Year ended 12/31/2011. Assets, $18,428,842 (M); Expenditures, $2,480,803; Total giving, $1,219,356; Grants to individuals, 253 grants totaling $593,013.
Fields of interest: Literature; Engineering school/education; Education; Engineering/technology; Engineering; Minorities.
International interests: Canada.
Type of support: Research; Scholarships—to individuals; Support to graduates or students of specific schools; Awards/prizes; Graduate support; Technical education support; Undergraduate support.
Application information: Application form required. Application form available on the grantmaker's web site.
Initial approach: Telephone
Deadline(s): Feb. 1.
Additional information: Application should be completed online. See web site for listing of additional programs.
Program descriptions:
Albert E. Wischmeyer Memorial Scholarship Award: Supports two scholarships of $2,000 each. Applicants must be residents of western New York state (west of Interstate 81), and graduating high school seniors or current undergraduate students enrolled in an accredited degree program in manufacturing engineering, manufacturing engineering technology, or mechanical technology. Applicants must plan to attend a college or university in Wisconsin and have an overall minimum GPA of 2.5; preference will be given to

applicants living in Milwaukee, Ozaukee, Washington, and Waukesha counties, followed by applicants who reside in the rest of the state.

Alvin & June Sabroff Manufacturing Engineering Scholarship: This scholarship recognizes, encourages, and assists a promising student who wants to pursue a career in manufacturing engineering. Eligible applicants must be U.S. citizens who are seeking a bachelor's degree in manufacturing engineering, technology, or a closely-related field at an accredited public or private college or university in the U.S. or Canada; eligible applicants must also possess a minimum GPA of 3.0 (on a 4.0 scale). First preference will be given to applicants planning to attend a college or university in Ohio.

Chapter 105 - Memphis, Les Segar Memorial Scholarship: This scholarship is available to a student seeking an associate's degree or bachelor's degree in manufacturing engineering, industrial engineering, manufacturing technology, or a closely-related field of study. Eligible applicants must have an overall minimum GPA of 3.0 (on a 4.0 scale). First preference will be given to applicants who reside in Tennessee; second preference will be given to applicants seeking their education at the University of Memphis; and third preference will be given to scholarship applicants seeking their education at a college or university within Tennessee.

Chapter 116 - Kalamazoo - Roscoe Douglas Scholarship: Scholarships are available to full-time undergraduates students enrolled at Western Michigan University. Applicants must have completed a minimum of 30 college credit hours, be seeking a career in manufacturing engineering or manufacturing engineering technology, and must possess an overall minimum GPA of 3.0.

Chapter 198 - Downriver Detroit/Chapter 79 Ann Arbor Area Scholarship: Scholarships are available to full-time students seeking an associate's degree, bachelor's degree, or graduate degree in manufacturing, mechanical, or industrial technology at an accredited public or private college or university in Michigan, who have a minimum GPA of 2.5. First preference will be given to applicants who are a child or grandchild of a current SME Downriver Chapter No. 198 member or Ann Arbor Area Chapter No. 79 member; preference will then be given to SME student members of student chapters that SME Downriver Chapter No. 198 or Ann Arbor Area Chapter No. 79 members sponsor, followed by scholarship applicants who reside within the state of Michigan and applicants planning to attend a college or university in Michigan.

Chapter 311 - Tri-City Scholarship: Scholarships are available to students seeking a bachelor's degree in manufacturing engineering, industrial engineering, manufacturing engineering technology, or a closely-related field of study. Eligible applicants must have a GPA of 3.0 or better on a 4.0 scale; first preference will be given to scholarship applicants who are residents of Michigan, while second preference will be given to applicants seeking their education from a college or university in Michigan.

Chapter 4 - Lawrence A. Wacker Memorial Award: Scholarships are available for students seeking a bachelor's degree in manufacturing or mechanical/industrial engineering, and who have a minimum grade point average of 3.0. Preference will be given to scholarship applicants who are Chapter 4 members, their spouses, and/or their children or grandchildren, followed by applicants who reside in Milwaukee, Ozaukee, Washington, and Waukesha counties; then preference will be given to applicants planning on attending a four-year program at an

accredited public or private college or university in Wisconsin.

Chapter 52 - Wichita Scholarship: Scholarships are available to individuals seeking an associate's degree, bachelor's degree, or graduate degree in manufacturing/mechanical/industrial engineering, engineering technology, or industrial technology at an accredited public or private college or university in Kansas, Oklahoma, or Missouri. Applicants must possess an overall minimum GPA of 2.5. First preference will be given to scholarship applicants who are a child, grandchild, or relative of a current SME Wichita Chapter No. 52 member; second preference will then be given to applicants who reside within the states of Kansas, Oklahoma or Missouri, followed by applicants planning to attend a college or university in Kansas.

Chapter 6 - Fairfield County Scholarship: Scholarships are available to full-time undergraduate students who are enrolled in a degree program in manufacturing engineering, technology, or a closely-related field in the United States or Canada, and who possess a minimum GPA of 3.0. Preference is given, but not limited, to residents and/or students residing in the eastern part of the United States.

Chapter 63 - Portland James E. Morrow Scholarship: This scholarship provides support to a child of a current member of SME Chapter 63 - Portland who plans to pursue a career in manufacturing (or a closely-related field). Eligible applicants must have an overall minimum GPA of 2.5 (on a 4.0 scale); preference will be given to a child, grandchild, or step-child of a current Chapter 63 member.

Chapter 63 - Portland Uncle Bud Scholarship: Scholarships are available to students who wish to pursue a career in manufacturing (or a closely-related field). Eligible applicants must have an overall minimum GPA of 2.5 (on a 4.0 scale). First preference will be given to children, grandchildren, or step-children of current Chapter 63 members; second preference will be given to SME student chapter members in Oregon or southwest Washington; third preference will be given to students planning to attend a school in Oregon or southwest Washington; and fourth preference will be given to applicants residing within Oregon or Washington.

Chapter 67 - Phoenix Scholarship: Scholarships are available to high school seniors who plan on enrolling, or current full-time students who are enrolled, in a manufacturing engineering technology, manufacturing technology, industrial technology, or closely-related program at an accredited college or university in Arizona. Applicants must possess a minimum GPA of 2.5, and must maintain it if they wish to continue their eligibility for the scholarship in subsequent years.

Chapter 77 - Denver Scholarship: This scholarship is available to a student who is seeking an associate's or bachelor's degree in manufacturing or industrial engineering, manufacturing technology, or a closely-related field of study. Eligible applicants must possess an overall minimum GPA of 2.5 (on a 4.0 scale). First preference will be given to scholarship applicants from Colorado; second preference will be given to applicants who plan to attend a college or university in Colorado.

Chapter 93 - Albuquerque Scholarship: This scholarship is available to entering freshmen or undergraduate students who plan to pursue a bachelor's degree in manufacturing engineering or a related field at an accredited college or university in New Mexico. Applicants must possess an overall minimum GPA of 2.5 on a 4.0 scale. First preference will be given to scholarship applicants who are children, grandchildren, or step-children of a current Chapter 93 member; second preference will be given to students attending a New Mexico university; third preference will be given to applicants residing within the state of New Mexico; fourth preference will be given to scholarship applicants who are planning to attend an engineering college or university located in New Mexico; and fifth preference will be given to scholarship applicants pursuing an associate's degree.

Clarence & Josephine Myers Scholarship: Scholarships are available to individuals seeking an associate, bachelor, or graduate degree in manufacturing, mechanical, or industrial engineering in Indiana, and who have a minimum GPA of 3.0. Preference will be given to students who are planning on or are currently attending a college or university in Indiana, students who attend Arsenal Technological High School in Indianapolis, SME student members of SME Chapter 37-sponsored chapters, or applicants who are a child or grandchild of a current SME Chapter 37 member.

Connie and Robert T. Gunter Scholarship Award Fund: This fund provides one scholarship of $1,200 to a full-time undergraduate with at least a 3.5 GPA enrolled in a manufacturing engineering or technology degree program at a selected school in Georgia.

E. Wayne Kay Community College Scholarship: This program provides two scholarships of $1,000 each to full-time entering freshmen or sophomore undergraduate students at a two-year community college, trade school, or other two-year degree-granting institution which offers programs in manufacturing or a closely-related field, and who have fewer than 60 college credit hours. Applicants must have at least a 3.0 GPA.

E. Wayne Kay High School Scholarship: The program provides scholarships to graduating high-school seniors in their senior year who commit to enroll in a manufacturing engineering or technology program at an accredited college or university as a full-time freshman in the current summer or fall semester. Applicants must possess an overall minimum GPA of 3.0.

Future Leaders of Manufacturing Scholarships: Ten $1,000 scholarships are available to SME Student Chapter members who are full-time students pursuing a degree in manufacturing engineering, engineering technology, industrial technology, or related majors. Eligible individuals must be a member of an SME Student Chapter and must be nominated by the chapter's faculty advisor.

Lucile B. Kaufman Women's Scholarship Fund: This fund provides two scholarships of $1,500 for full-time female undergraduates with at least a 3.0 GPA who are enrolled in a degree program in manufacturing engineering or technology in the U.S. or Canada.

SME Education Foundation Family Scholarship: This program provides a scholarship valued at up to $20,000 annually to a child or grandchild of an SME member. This scholarship is renewable for a total of four years, contingent upon continuing excellent academic performance. One-year scholarship awards of $5,000 to two individuals are also provided. Applicants must have an overall minimum GPA of 3.0, a minimum SAT score of 1000, and/or ACT score of 21.

William E. Weisel Scholarship Fund: This fund provides one $2,000 scholarship to a full-time undergraduate with a minimum 3.5 GPA who is enrolled in an engineering or technology degree program, and who seeks a career in robotics or automated systems use in manufacturing, or robotics used in the medical field.
EIN: 382746841

4612
Society of St. Vincent de Paul - Detroit
3000 Gratiot Ave.
Detroit, MI   48207-2334   (313) 393-2930
Contact: William D. Brazier, Exec. Dir.
FAX: (313) 393-2978; E-mail: execdir@svdpdet.org;
Toll-free tel.: (877) 788-4623; URL: http://www.svdpdet.org

Foundation type: Public charity
Purpose: Financial assistance to individuals and families of southeast Michigan with food, clothing, energy assistance, dental expense to those who lack insurance, access to affordable basic dental care, and other special needs.
Publications: Annual report.
Financial data: Year ended 09/30/2011. Assets, $8,674,198 (M); Expenditures, $11,095,656; Total giving, $3,882,172; Grants to individuals, totaling $3,673,752.
Fields of interest: Human services; Economically disadvantaged.
Type of support: Grants for special needs.
Application information:
   Initial approach: Telephone
   Additional information: Contact the agency for eligibility determination.
EIN: 381359592

4613
Sojourner Foundation
P.O. Box 2011
Southfield, MI   48037-2011
Contact: Brenda Scoggins, Grants/Corporate Giving Committee
E-mail: sojournerfound@sbcglobal.net; Tel./fax: (248) 723-5778; URL: http://sojournerfoundation.org

Foundation type: Public charity
Purpose: Grants of up to $5,000 to fund projects designed to enable southeastern MI women and girls to participate more fully in society.
Publications: Application guidelines; Grants list; Informational brochure; Newsletter.
Financial data: Year ended 12/31/2012. Assets, $6,210 (M); Expenditures, $13,654; Total giving, $10,000.
Fields of interest: Civil/human rights, women; Adults, women.
Type of support: Program development.
Application information: Applications accepted. Application form required. Application form available on the grantmaker's web site.
   Initial approach: Letter
   Deadline(s): Dec. 14
   Final notification: Mar. 15
EIN: 382477123

4614
The Sonneveldt Foundation
18042 Wildwood Springs Pkwy.
Spring Lake, MI   49456-9048   (616) 847-0801
Contact: Carol A. Sonneveldt, Pres.

Foundation type: Independent foundation
Purpose: Scholarships to graduating seniors primarily from MI for postsecondary education.
Financial data: Year ended 12/31/2011. Assets, $599,835 (M); Expenditures, $44,112; Total giving, $21,750.
Fields of interest: Higher education.
Type of support: Scholarships—to individuals.
Application information: Applications accepted. Application form required.
   Deadline(s): None

Applicants should submit the following:
   1) Transcripts
   2) Letter(s) of recommendation
   3) Financial information
   4) Essay
Additional information: Awards are paid directly to the educational institution on behalf of the student.
EIN: 382835613

4615
Southeastern Michigan Chapter NECA Educational and Research Foundation
2735 Bellingham
Troy, MI   48099

Foundation type: Independent foundation
Purpose: Scholarship to employees and relatives of employees of SMC/NECA.
Financial data: Year ended 12/31/2012. Assets, $493,029 (M); Expenditures, $42,748; Total giving, $34,392.
Type of support: Employee-related scholarships.
Application information: Applications accepted. Application form required.
   Initial approach: Letter
   Deadline(s): Apr. 15
   Additional information: Contact foundation for further program information.
EIN: 300134735

4616
Southfield Community Foundation
25630 Evergreen Rd.
Southfield, MI   48075-1769   (248) 796-4190
Contact: Raquel Robinson, Exec. Dir.
FAX: (248) 796-4195; E-mail: info@scfmi.org;
URL: http://www.scfmi.org

Foundation type: Community foundation
Purpose: Scholarships for youth from the Southfield and Lathrup Village, MI, area achieve their highest aspirations for the future.
Publications: Annual report; Financial statement; Grants list; IRS Form 990 or 990-PF printed copy available upon request.
Financial data: Year ended 06/30/2012. Assets, $1,620,281 (M); Expenditures, $194,013; Total giving, $43,545; Grants to individuals, totaling $3,500.
Fields of interest: Higher education.
Type of support: Scholarships—to individuals; Undergraduate support.
Application information: Applications accepted. Application form required. Application form available on the grantmaker's web site.
   Initial approach: Application
   Send request by: Mail
   Deadline(s): Apr. 30
   Applicants should submit the following:
   1) Letter(s) of recommendation
   2) Transcripts
   Additional information: Each scholarship has its own unique set of eligibility requirements and application guidelines. See web site for a complete listing.
EIN: 382918048

4617
Southwest Michigan Community Action Agency
185 E. Main St., Ste. 200
Benton Harbor, MI   49022-4432   (269)
925-9077
FAX: (269) 925-9271; E-mail: contact@smcaa.com;
URL: http://www.smcaa.com

Foundation type: Public charity
Purpose: Assistance to low-income individuals of
southwest, MI, counties of Berrien, Cass, and Van
Buren with food, clothing, shelter, transportation
and other special needs.
Publications: Financial statement; Informational
brochure.
Financial data: Year ended 09/30/2011. Assets,
$1,466,566 (M); Expenditures, $7,827,025.
Fields of interest: Human services; Economically
disadvantaged.
Type of support: Grants for special needs.
Application information: Contact agency for
information on assistance.
EIN: 382415106

4618
Southwest Michigan Rehab Foundation
3 Heritage Oak Lake
Battle Creek, MI   49015-4262   (269) 969-0974
Application address: 100 Peets Cove, Battle Creek,
MI 49015

Foundation type: Independent foundation
Purpose: Payment of medical equipment expenses
for patient rehabilitation to financially needy
residents of the greater Calhoun County, MI, area
only. Recipient's income must not exceed two and
one-half times the poverty rate.
Publications: Informational brochure.
Financial data: Year ended 12/31/2012. Assets,
$1,831,407 (M); Expenditures, $106,060; Total
giving, $91,957; Grants to individuals, totaling
$66,557.
Fields of interest: Physical therapy; Health care;
Economically disadvantaged.
Type of support: Grants for special needs.
Application information: Applications accepted.
Application form required. Interview required.
  Initial approach: Letter
  Send request by: Mail or fax
  Copies of proposal: 1
  Deadline(s): Fri. before monthly meeting
  Final notification: Recipients notified in 30 days
  Additional information: Application should
    include financial information and doctor's
    prescription.
EIN: 382939930

4619
Sparrow Foundation
(formerly Sparrow Hospital Memorials and
Endowment Foundation)
1110 E. Michigan Ave.
Lansing, MI   48912-1811   (517) 364-5680
FAX: (517) 364-5698;
E-mail: foundation@sparrow.org; Mailing address:
P.O. Box 30480, Lansing, MI 48909-7980;
URL: http://www.sparrow.org/foundation

Foundation type: Public charity
Purpose: Assistance to employees of Sparrow
Health System, MI who are experiencing personal
hardship, including payment for rent, mortgage,
utilities, and other special needs.
Financial data: Year ended 12/31/2011. Assets,
$12,182,449 (M); Expenditures, $2,922,553;

Total giving, $1,438,682; Grants to individuals,
159 grants totaling $96,033.
Fields of interest: Human services.
Type of support: Emergency funds; Grants to
individuals.
Application information: Applications not
accepted.
EIN: 386100687

4620
Spectrum Human Services, Inc.
28303 Joy Rd.
Westland, MI   48185-5524   (734) 458-8736
FAX: (734) 458-8836;
E-mail: info@spectrumhuman.org; URL: http://
www.spectrumhuman.org

Foundation type: Public charity
Purpose: Services by referral only for at-risk
populations in MI. Populations served include
delinquent and abused youth, recently incarcerated
individuals, foster and adoptive families, and those
who are disabled.
Publications: Annual report; Newsletter.
Financial data: Year ended 12/31/2011. Assets,
$6,507,311 (M); Expenditures, $4,881,655.
Fields of interest: Children, services; Family
services; Residential/custodial care, half-way
house; Human services; Disabilities, people with;
Offenders/ex-offenders.
Type of support: Grants for special needs.
Application information: Applications not
accepted.
  Additional information: Contact foundation or
    visit their web site for detailed program
    information.
EIN: 510154248

4621
Peter and Evelyn Speerstra Scholarship Fund Trust
P.O. Box 3636
Grand Rapids, MI   49501-3636   (616) 897-4125
Contact: Barbara Pierce
Application address: Lowell High School, 750
Foreman, Lowell, MI 49331

Foundation type: Independent foundation
Purpose: Scholarships to graduates of the Lowell,
MI, Public School District for study at colleges,
universities, and technical schools.
Financial data: Year ended 02/28/2013. Assets,
$219,270 (M); Expenditures, $16,447; Total
giving, $10,800; Grants to individuals, 19 grants
totaling $10,800 (high: $600, low: $500).
Fields of interest: Vocational education.
Type of support: Support to graduates or students
of specific schools; Technical education support;
Undergraduate support.
Application information: Application form required.
  Deadline(s): Apr. 1
  Additional information: Application must include
    transcripts and a statement of educational
    goals.
EIN: 386480250

4622
The Sphinx Organization
(formerly Concert Competitions & Musical
Development, Inc.)
400 Renaissance Ctr., Ste. 2550
Detroit, MI   48243-1679   (313) 877-9100
Contact: Aaron P. Dworkin, Pres.
FAX: (313) 877-0164;
E-mail: info@sphinxmusic.org; E-Mail for Aaron P.
Dworkin: aaronpd@sphinxmusic.org; URL: http://
www.sphinxmusic.org

Foundation type: Public charity
Purpose: Prizes and scholarships to
African-American and Latino classical music
students who are winners of the annual Sphinx
Competition.
Publications: Application guidelines.
Financial data: Year ended 12/31/2011. Assets,
$1,724,576 (M); Expenditures, $2,570,252; Total
giving, $11,600; Grants to individuals, totaling
$11,600.
Fields of interest: Orchestras; Minorities; African
Americans/Blacks; Hispanics/Latinos.
Type of support: Awards/prizes; Undergraduate
support.
Application information: Applications accepted.
Application form required.
  Send request by: Mail
  Deadline(s): Nov. 15
  Additional information: Application must include
    a copy of birth certificate, biography and
    photo, $35 application fee, and audition
    tape/CD.
Program description:
  Sphinx Competition: This competition offers
  young African-American and Latino classical string
  players a chance to compete under the guidance of
  an internationally-renowned panel of judges, and to
  perform with established professional musicians in
  a competition setting. The competition works to
  encourage, develop, and recognize classical music
  talent in the Black and Latino communities.
  Eighteen semifinalists will travel to Detroit and Ann
  Arbor, Michigan to compete in semifinal and finals
  divisions, prizes range from $2,000 to $10,000. In
  addition, all semifinalists will receive a Sphinx
  Assistance Music Fund scholarship, in partnership
  with the American Symphony Orchestra League,
  which they can apply toward their musical
  development.
EIN: 383283759

4623
St. John Vianney Foundation
(formerly St. John Vianney Educational Foundation)
4101 Clyde Park Ave., S.W.
Wyoming, MI   49509-4033   (616) 534-5449
Contact: John Armendarez, Pres.

Foundation type: Public charity
Purpose: Scholarships to students at St. John
Vianney School, MI, based on financial aid.
Financial data: Year ended 09/30/2012. Assets,
$1,538,273 (M); Expenditures, $72,196; Total
giving, $46,068.
Type of support: Support to graduates or students
of specific schools; Precollege support.
Application information:
  Initial approach: Letter
  Additional information: Contact foundation for
    complete eligibility requirements.
EIN: 382700546

4624
St. Joseph Kiwanis Foundation
P.O. Box 378
St. Joseph, MI   49085   (269) 983-0531
Contact: Jonathan B. Sauer, Treas.
E-mail: emeny@parrett.net; URL: http://
sjkiwanis.org/programs_events.htm

Foundation type: Independent foundation
Purpose: Scholarships to students from Lakeshore
High School, St. Joseph High School, and Lake
Michigan Catholic High School, all in MI.
Financial data: Year ended 12/31/2012. Assets,
$540,330 (M); Expenditures, $18,481; Total
giving, $12,000; Grants to individuals, 18 grants
totaling $12,000 (high: $1,000, low: $250).
Fields of interest: Higher education; Scholarships/
financial aid.
Type of support: Support to graduates or students
of specific schools; Undergraduate support.
Application information: Applications accepted.
Application form required. Interview required.
Applicants should submit the following:
   1) Financial information
   2) Photograph
Additional information: Application must also
  include two references and personal
  statement.
EIN: 386117678

4625
St. Mary's of Michigan Foundation
(formerly St. Mary's Hospital Foundation)
800 S. Washington Ave.
Saginaw, MI   48601-2551   (989) 907-8000
Contact: Karen Stiffler, Exec. Dir.
FAX: (989) 907-8737;
E-mail: foundation@stmarysofmichigan.org; E-Mail
for Karen Stiffler: KStiffler@stmarysofmichigan.org;
URL: http://www.stmarysofmichigan.org/
giving_and_giving_back/foundation/index.php

Foundation type: Public charity
Purpose: Scholarships for individuals affiliated with
St. Mary's of Michigan who wish to pursue further
educational opportunities.
Publications: Application guidelines.
Financial data: Year ended 06/30/2011. Assets,
$13,931,216 (M); Expenditures, $997,848; Total
giving, $361,944.
Fields of interest: Higher education.
Type of support: Scholarships—to individuals.
Application information: Applications accepted.
Application form required.
Deadline(s): May 18
Additional information: A 500-word statement
  stating reasons for pursuing scholarships
  must accompany applications.
Program descriptions:
Beverly Kremin Scholarship: The foundation
awards this $3,000 scholarship annually to up to
two high school seniors who are pursuing a degree
in an allied health care field and whose parent(s)
is/are associates of St. Mary's of Michigan.
Dr. Raana Akbar Scholarship: A $1,500 is
awarded annually to women enrolled in or accepted
for enrollment in a full-time undergraduate or
graduate academic program in a healthcare-related
field. Applicants must have a GPA of 2.5 or higher.
EIN: 382246366

4626
Sterling Heights Community Foundation
P.O. Box 7023
Sterling Heights, MI   48311-7023   (586)
446-2489
FAX: (586) 276-4065;
E-mail: foundation@sterling-heights.net;
URL: http://
www.sterlingheightscommunityfoundation.org

Foundation type: Community foundation
Purpose: Scholarships to Sterling Heights, MI high
school students planning to enter college or
residents currently enrolled at a college or
university.
Publications: Annual report.
Financial data: Year ended 12/31/2012. Assets,
$529,077 (M); Expenditures, $39,561; Total
giving, $29,713.
Fields of interest: Higher education.
Type of support: Undergraduate support.
Application information: Applications accepted.
Application form required. Application form
available on the grantmaker's web site.
Initial approach: Application
Send request by: Mail
Deadline(s): Mar. 16
Applicants should submit the following:
   1) Letter(s) of recommendation
   2) Transcripts
Additional information: See web site for
  application form and guidelines.
EIN: 383004613

4627
Stewart Management Group Charitable Foundation
31850 Ford Rd.
Garden City, MI   48135   (734) 458-5273
Contact: Gordon L. Stewart, Pres.

Foundation type: Independent foundation
Purpose: Scholarships by recommendation only to
students of Westland and Garden City, MI.
Financial data: Year ended 11/30/2012. Assets,
$211,002 (M); Expenditures, $6,134; Total giving,
$5,455; Grants to individuals, 10 grants totaling
$5,455 (high: $1,000, low: $455).
Fields of interest: Higher education.
Type of support: Awards/grants by nomination only;
Undergraduate support.
Application information: Applications not
accepted.
Additional information: Applicants must be
  recommended by the selection committee at
  their school. Unsolicited requests for funds
  not considered or acknowledged.
EIN: 383189964

4628
Olive A. Stokes Scholarship Trust
P.O. Box 75000 MC 7874
Detroit, MI   48275-7874   (252) 467-4743
Contact: Sharon Stephens
Application Address: c/o Sharon Stephens, 1305 S
Franklin, Rocky Mount NC. 27804

Foundation type: Independent foundation
Purpose: Scholarships to residents of Nash or
Edgecombe counties, NC, with at least a C+ GPA
and who are U.S. citizens.
Financial data: Year ended 09/30/2012. Assets,
$483,350 (M); Expenditures, $30,320; Total
giving, $22,000.
Fields of interest: Education.
Type of support: Scholarships—to individuals.

Application information: Applications accepted.
Deadline(s): June 1
EIN: 316646001

4629
Sturgis Area Community Foundation
(formerly Sturgis Foundation)
310 N. Franks Ave.
Sturgis, MI   49091-1259   (269) 659-8508
Contact: LeeAnn McConnell, Chair.
FAX: (269) 659-4539;
E-mail: sacf@sturgisfoundation.org; URL: http://
www.sturgisfoundation.org

Foundation type: Community foundation
Purpose: Scholarships primarily to residents of St.
Joseph, MI, for postsecondary education.
Publications: Application guidelines; Annual report;
Financial statement; Grants list; Informational
brochure; Informational brochure (including
application guidelines); Newsletter.
Financial data: Year ended 03/31/2013. Assets,
$22,352,377 (M); Expenditures, $740,009; Total
giving, $458,226; Grants to individuals, totaling
$65,719.
Fields of interest: Higher education.
Type of support: Scholarships—to individuals;
Camperships.
Application information: Applications accepted.
Application form required. Application form
available on the grantmaker's web site.
Send request by: Mail
Copies of proposal: 10
Deadline(s): Last Fri. in Mar. for general
  scholarships
Final notification: Applicants for general
  scholarships notified by the first week in June
Applicants should submit the following:
   1) SAR
   2) Transcripts
   3) Letter(s) of recommendation
   4) GPA
   5) FAFSA
   6) Essay
   7) ACT
Additional information: Checks are sent directly
  to the educational institution on behalf of the
  students.
EIN: 383649922

4630
Tahquamenon Education Foundation
P.O. Box 482
Newberry, MI   49868-0482   (906) 293-3045
FAX: (906) 293-3410; E-mail: teflil@lighthouse.net

Foundation type: Public charity
Purpose: Scholarships to graduating seniors of the
Tahquamenon Area School, MI, for undergraduate
education.
Publications: Newsletter.
Financial data: Year ended 06/30/2012. Assets,
$465,354 (M); Expenditures, $56,458; Total
giving, $27,500; Grants to individuals, 27 grants
totaling $27,500 (high: $2,000, low: $500).
Type of support: Support to graduates or students
of specific schools.
Application information: Contact foundation for
current application deadline/guidelines.
EIN: 382744932

4631
Tamer Foundation
1222 Balfour St.
Grosse Pointe Park, MI 48230-1020

Foundation type: Independent foundation
Purpose: Scholarships to residents of MI for higher education, and grants for religious development.
Financial data: Year ended 04/30/2013. Assets, $8,426,913 (M); Expenditures, $510,147; Total giving, $391,698; Grants to individuals, 35 grants totaling $256,118 (high: $12,000, low: $3,571).
Fields of interest: Higher education; Religion.
Type of support: Grants to individuals; Scholarships—to individuals.
Application information: Contact foundation for additional application information.
EIN: 382679633

4632
Tassell-Wisner-Bottrall Foundation
(formerly The Leslie E. Tassell Foundation)
c/o Fifth Third Bank
111 Lyon St. N.W.
Grand Rapids, MI 49501-3636
Application address: c/o Joyce Wisner, 3439 Quiggle Ave. S.E., Ada, MI 49301-9237

Foundation type: Independent foundation
Purpose: Scholarships to residents of MI to attend schools in MI.
Financial data: Year ended 12/31/2012. Assets, $7,627,815 (M); Expenditures, $427,500; Total giving, $349,050; Grants to individuals, 32 grants totaling $71,513 (high: $25,000, low: $1,500).
Type of support: Undergraduate support.
Application information: Applications accepted. Application form required.
   Initial approach: Letter
   Deadline(s): None
EIN: 383186818

4633
H. Taylor Trust Scholarship Trust
c/o Century Bank & Trust
100 W. Chicago St.
Coldwater, MI 49036-1807
Contact: Alicia Cole, Trust Off.

Foundation type: Independent foundation
Purpose: Scholarships to individuals for higher education who are residents of Branch County, MI.
Financial data: Year ended 12/31/2012. Assets, $2,470,397 (M); Expenditures, $144,170; Total giving, $125,564; Grants to individuals, 63 grants totaling $125,564 (high: $2,000, low: $1,564).
Fields of interest: Higher education.
Type of support: Scholarships—to individuals.
Application information: Applications accepted. Application form required.
   Deadline(s): Mar.
   Applicants should submit the following:
      1) ACT
      2) Budget Information
      3) Essay
      4) Financial information
      5) GPA
      6) Letter(s) of recommendation
      7) Resume
   Additional information: Submit application to high school guidance counselor.
EIN: 326030259

4634
Temple-Krick YFU Scholarship Fund, Inc.
214 Katherine Way
Dexter, MI 48103-6170

Foundation type: Independent foundation
Purpose: Scholarships to high school students residing in MI who have been accepted to participate in Youth For Understanding, an international student exchange program.
Financial data: Year ended 01/31/2013. Assets, $0 (M); Expenditures, $5,794; Total giving, $5,698.
Fields of interest: International exchange, students.
Type of support: Exchange programs; Precollege support.
Application information: Applications accepted. Interview required.
   Initial approach: Letter
   Deadline(s): None
EIN: 382808315

4635
Carl and Elinor Glyn Thom Charitable Foundation
1625 W. Big Beaver, Ste. C
Troy, MI 48084

Foundation type: Independent foundation
Purpose: Scholarships to residents of MI for higher education.
Financial data: Year ended 12/31/2012. Assets, $1,356,211 (M); Expenditures, $64,412; Total giving, $28,000; Grants to individuals, 14 grants totaling $28,000 (high: $2,000, low: $2,000).
Type of support: Scholarships—to individuals.
Application information: Applications not accepted.
EIN: 383105784

4636
Russ Thomas Scholarship Fund
3707 W. Maple St., Ste. 13
Bloomfield Hills, MI 48301-3212 (313) 216-4050
Contact: John Thomas, Tr.

Foundation type: Independent foundation
Purpose: Undergraduate scholarships to residents of the greater Detroit, MI, area who are graduating high school seniors.
Financial data: Year ended 11/30/2012. Assets, $886,805 (M); Expenditures, $95,894; Total giving, $82,000; Grants to individuals, 23 grants totaling $82,000 (high: $5,500, low: $1,500).
Type of support: Scholarships—to individuals; Undergraduate support.
Application information: Applications accepted.
   Initial approach: Letter
   Deadline(s): None
EIN: 382984958

4637
Three Rivers Area Community Foundation
(formerly Three Rivers Community Foundation)
333 W. Michigan Ave.
P.O. Box 453
Three Rivers, MI 49093 (269) 273-1632
Contact: For grants and scholarships: Melissa J. Bliss, Admin.
FAX: (269) 273-3132;
E-mail: melissa@threeriversfoundation.com;
URL: http://threeriversfoundation.com

Foundation type: Community foundation
Purpose: Scholarships to students from St. Joseph County, MI for higher education.
Publications: Annual report; Informational brochure; IRS Form 990 or 990-PF printed copy available upon request.
Financial data: Year ended 12/31/2012. Assets, $2,937,536 (M); Expenditures, $69,743; Total giving, $35,421; Grants to individuals, 22 grants totaling $18,950.
Fields of interest: Higher education; Nursing school/education.
Type of support: Scholarships—to individuals; Undergraduate support.
Application information: Applications accepted. Application form required. Application form available on the grantmaker's web site.
   Initial approach: Application
   Send request by: Mail
   Deadline(s): Apr. 25
   Final notification: Applicants notified mid-May
   Additional information: See web site for application forms and eligibility requirements per scholarship.
EIN: 382051672

4638
Thresholds, Inc.
1225 Lake Dr. S.E.
Grand Rapids, MI 49506-1656 (616) 445-0960
Contact: Tom Ferch, Pres. and C.E.O.
FAX: (616) 774-0328; E-mail: main@threshnet.org;
URL: http://threshnet.org/

Foundation type: Public charity
Purpose: Grants to indigent individuals in the Grand Rapids, MI, area.
Financial data: Year ended 09/30/2012. Assets, $4,115,001 (M); Expenditures, $15,255,512; Total giving, $5,818,935; Grants to individuals, 549 grants totaling $5,818,935.
Fields of interest: Economically disadvantaged.
Type of support: Grants for special needs.
Application information: Applications not accepted.
   Additional information: Unsolicited requests for funds not considered or acknowledged.
EIN: 382063018

4639
The Tiscornia Foundation, Inc.
505 Pleasant St., Ste. 301
Saint Joseph, MI 49085 (269) 983-4711
Contact: James W. Tiscornia, V.P.
FAX: (269) 983-6959

Foundation type: Independent foundation
Purpose: Scholarships to graduating seniors of Northern Berrien County, MI high schools.
Publications: Annual report (including application guidelines).
Financial data: Year ended 12/31/2012. Assets, $3,140,576 (M); Expenditures, $137,389; Total giving, $53,500.
Fields of interest: Higher education; Scholarships/financial aid.
Type of support: Support to graduates or students of specific schools.
Application information: Applications accepted. Application form not required.
   Initial approach: Letter
   Send request by: Mail
   Copies of proposal: 4
   Deadline(s): Apr. 1
   Final notification: Recipients notified 90 days after receipt of application

Applicants should submit the following:
1) Photograph
2) Letter(s) of recommendation
3) GPA
EIN: 381777343

4640
Travelers Aid Society of Metropolitan Detroit
30th Fl. Cadillac Twr.
65 Cadillac Square
Detroit, MI   48226-1900   (313) 926-6740
FAX: (313) 962-3609;
E-mail: info@travelersaiddetroit.org; URL: http://
www.travelersaiddetroit.org

Foundation type: Public charity
Purpose: Emergency and crisis assistance to
residents of the Detroit metropolitan area, MI, who
are unemployed, in transition, homeless, runaways
and victims of domestic violence.
Publications: Annual report.
Financial data: Year ended 06/30/2012. Assets,
$1,009,478 (M); Expenditures, $3,730,333; Total
giving, $1,922,780; Grants to individuals, totaling
$1,922,780.
Fields of interest: Economically disadvantaged.
Type of support: Grants for special needs.
Application information:
Initial approach: Letter
Additional information: Contact the society for
further information.
EIN: 381358052

4641
Otto Trinklein Educational Trust
328 S. Saginaw St., M/C 002072
Flint, MI   48502-1923   (989) 652-9955
Application address: c/o Frankenmuth High School,
Attn.: Donald J. Zoeller, 525 E. Genesee St.,
Frankenmuth, MI 48734-1139

Foundation type: Independent foundation
Purpose: Scholarships to graduates of
Frankenmuth, MI, public schools.
Financial data: Year ended 12/31/2012. Assets,
$151,815 (M); Expenditures, $8,052; Total giving,
$3,600; Grants to individuals, 3 grants totaling
$3,600 (high: $1,200, low: $1,200).
Type of support: Support to graduates or students
of specific schools; Undergraduate support.
Application information: Applications accepted.
Application form required.
Initial approach: Letter
Deadline(s): May 1
EIN: 386040607

4642
Blanche Barr Trone Scholarship Trust
20152 E. Ave. N.
Battle Creek, MI   49017-9707

Foundation type: Independent foundation
Purpose: Scholarships to financially needy high
school graduates of the Battle Creek, MI, area.
Preference is shown to those studying pharmacy, or
other medical fields.
Financial data: Year ended 12/31/2012. Assets,
$444,431 (M); Expenditures, $18,888; Total
giving, $14,000; Grants to individuals, 14 grants
totaling $14,000 (high: $1,000, low: $1,000).
Fields of interest: Medical school/education;
Pharmacy/prescriptions.
Type of support: Undergraduate support.

Application information: Application form required.
Deadline(s): June
Applicants should submit the following:
1) Transcripts
2) Financial information
Additional information: Application must also
include three personal and educational
references, and parents' tax return. Awards
are a maximum of $1,000 to an individual.
EIN: 386500164

4643
Trudell Scholarship Trust
c/o First National Bank & Trust Co.
P.O. Box 370
Iron Mountain, MI   49801   (906) 779-2259

Foundation type: Independent foundation
Purpose: Scholarships to students who are
residents of Dickinson county, MI or any of its
surrounding counties for attendance at Bay De Noc
College in Iron Mountain, MI.
Financial data: Year ended 12/31/2011. Assets,
$132,799 (M); Expenditures, $8,387; Total giving,
$6,480; Grants to individuals, 5 grants totaling
$6,480 (high: $1,800, low: $740).
Fields of interest: Higher education.
Type of support: Support to graduates or students
of specific schools.
Application information: Applications accepted.
Application form required.
Deadline(s): Varies
Additional information: Applicant must
demonstrate financial need.
EIN: 726230453

4644
Jeremiah Tumey Fund
(also known as Jeremiah Tumey & Grand Lodge)
c/o Comerica Bank
P.O. Box 75000
Detroit, MI   48275-3302

Foundation type: Independent foundation
Purpose: Grants to economically disadvantaged
members of Masons or their spouses in MI.
Financial data: Year ended 12/31/2011. Assets,
$144,948 (M); Expenditures, $8,621; Total giving,
$6,000; Grants to individuals, 2 grants totaling
$3,000 (high: $1,500, low: $1,500).
Fields of interest: Economically disadvantaged.
Type of support: Grants for special needs.
Application information: Applications not
accepted.
Additional information: Unsolicited requests for
funds not considered or acknowledged.
EIN: 386043299

4645
Berndine MacMullen Tuohy-University of Michigan Student Loan Fund
120 Cypress St.
Manistee, MI   49660-1753
URL: http://www.umclubs.com

Foundation type: Independent foundation
Purpose: Student loans to residents of Manistee,
Mason, Wexford, and Benzie counties, MI, who
have attended the University of Michigan for at least
one year.
Financial data: Year ended 12/31/2012. Assets,
$1,206,062 (M); Expenditures, $103,566; Total
giving, $84,200; Grants to individuals, 3 grants
totaling $84,200 (high: $33,400, low: $24,800).
Fields of interest: Higher education.

Type of support: Support to graduates or students
of specific schools; Undergraduate support.
Application information: Applications accepted.
Application form required.
Deadline(s): None
EIN: 382528185

4646
Tuscola County Community Foundation
317 S. State St.
P.O. Box 534
Caro, MI   48723-0534
Contact: Ken Micklash, Exec. Dir.
E-mail: tccf534@centurytel.net; Tel/fax: (989)
673-8223; URL: http://
www.tuscolacountycommunityfoundation.org

Foundation type: Community foundation
Purpose: Scholarships to graduating seniors from
Tuscola County, MI pursuing higher education at
accredited colleges or universities.
Publications: Application guidelines; Annual report;
Financial statement; Grants list; Informational
brochure; Newsletter.
Financial data: Year ended 12/31/2012. Assets,
$8,533,076 (M); Expenditures, $541,875; Total
giving, $339,776; Grants to individuals, 70 grants
totaling $106,050.
Fields of interest: Higher education; Scholarships/
financial aid.
Type of support: Support to graduates or students
of specific schools; Undergraduate support.
Application information: Applications accepted.
Application form required. Application form
available on the grantmaker's web site.
Initial approach: Application
Send request by: Mail
Copies of proposal: 6
Deadline(s): Feb. 1 and Oct. 1
Final notification: Recipients notified three
months after deadline
Applicants should submit the following:
1) ACT
2) Letter(s) of recommendation
3) Transcripts
Additional information: See web site for
additional information.
EIN: 383351315

4647
UAW-Ford National Programs
151 West Jefferson Ave.
P.O. Box 33009
Detroit, MI   48232-5009   (313) 392-7100
Contact: Jimmy Settles, Co.-Chair. and Co.-Pres.
URL: http://www.uawford.com

Foundation type: Public charity
Purpose: Scholarships to Ford and Visteon
employees who have graduated from high school or
obtained their GED and have been accepted for a
post-secondary or post-graduate degree program,
or a career specific vocational training program. The
program is administered by Scholarship America.
Publications: Newsletter.
Financial data: Year ended 12/31/2011. Assets,
$29,344,949 (M); Expenditures, $25,457,434;
Total giving, $1,167,077; Grants to individuals,
totaling $1,167,077.
Type of support: Employee-related scholarships.
Application information: Applications accepted.
Initial approach: Letter
Company names: Ford Motor Company; Visteon
Corporation
EIN: 382416006

4648
UAW-GM Center for Human Resources
200 Walker St.
Detroit, MI 48207-4229   (313) 324-5290
Contact: Diana Tremblay, Co-Pres
URL: https://www.uawgmjas.org/j/

Foundation type: Public charity
Purpose: Financial assistance to current or former employees of General Motors to attend licensed or accredited schools (including colleges, universities, proprietary schools, and vocational schools).
Publications: Application guidelines.
Financial data: Year ended 12/31/2011. Assets, $120,867,134 (M); Expenditures, $59,227,800; Total giving, $5,801,187; Grants to individuals, totaling $5,801,187.
Type of support: Employee-related scholarships.
Application information: Applications accepted.
Initial approach: Letter
Additional information: Contact foundation for eligibility criteria.
Company name: General Motors Company
EIN: 383211550

4649
United Arts Council of Calhoun County
(also known as Calhoun County Arts Council)
131 E. Colubia Ave., Ste. 211
P.O. Box 1079
Battle Creek, MI 49015   (269) 245-2522
Contact: Sherri Douglas, Exec. Dir.
FAX: (269) 441-2707;
E-mail: Douglas@calhouncountyarts.org;
URL: http://www.artsandindustrycouncil.org

Foundation type: Public charity
Purpose: Grants to residents of Calhoun County, MI, for the development of creative industries.
Publications: Application guidelines; Annual report; Grants list; Informational brochure.
Financial data: Year ended 06/30/2012. Assets, $396,132 (M); Expenditures, $85,243. Grants to individuals amount not specified.
Fields of interest: Arts.
Type of support: Program development; Conferences/seminars; Seed money; Project support.
Application information: Applications accepted. Application form required. Application form available on the grantmaker's web site.
Initial approach: Application
Send request by: Mail
Copies of proposal: 4
Applicants should submit the following:
  1) Work samples
  2) Resume
  3) Proposal
  4) Photograph
  5) Letter(s) of recommendation
  6) Financial information
  7) Curriculum vitae
  8) Budget Information
Additional information: See web site for additional guidelines.
Program descriptions:
Artist Microloan: These funds are intended for individual artists seeking funding for personal or "for profit" art related endeavors. Microloans are backed by the CCAC and obtained through OMNI Family Credit Union. Recipients are required to be members of OMNI Family Credit Union. Microloans must be repaid under the terms set jointly between the CCAC and OMNI. Loans are up to $1,000.
Artist Stipend: These funds are awarded to individual artists seeking funding for projects with

social value benefitting the Calhoun County Community. Amount of the award is $1,000.
EIN: 386091848

4650
United Communities Foundation
2647 E Mill Hwy.
Rogers City, MI 49779   (989) 734-7412
Application address: c/o Anne Belanger, 6442 Beach Dr., Rogers City, MI 49709, tel:. (989) 734-7412
E-mail: amarloweproductions@yahoo.com

Foundation type: Operating foundation
Purpose: Scholarships to individuals of MI, with future goals and objectives within the arts industry.
Financial data: Year ended 12/31/2012. Assets, $112,108 (M); Expenditures, $2,403; Total giving, $2,155.
Fields of interest: Arts education.
Type of support: Scholarships—to individuals.
Application information: Applications accepted.
Initial approach: Letter
Send request by: Mail
Deadline(s): May 1
Additional information: Letter must address future goals.
EIN: 331106471

4651
United Way of Midland County
220 W. Main St., Ste. 100
Midland, MI 48640-5184   (989) 631-3670
FAX: (989) 832-5524;
E-mail: answers@unitedwaymidland.org; E-Mail for Ann Fillmore: afillmore@unitedwaymidland.org;
URL: http://www.unitedwaymidland.org/

Foundation type: Public charity
Purpose: Grants to needy residents of Midland County, MI.
Financial data: Year ended 12/31/2011. Assets, $11,178,129 (M); Expenditures, $6,009,955; Total giving, $4,727,445; Grants to individuals, totaling $709,523.
Fields of interest: Economically disadvantaged.
Type of support: Grants for special needs.
Application information:
Initial approach: Letter
Additional information: Contact foundation for eligibility requirements.
EIN: 381434224

4652
United Way of St. Clair County
1723 Military St.
Port Huron, MI 48060-5934   (810) 985-8169
Contact: Lonnie Stevens, Exec. Dir.
FAX: (810) 982-7202;
E-mail: uwsccadm@sbcglobal.net; E-Mail for Lonnie Stevens: lstevens@uwstclair.org; URL: http://uwstclair.org/

Foundation type: Public charity
Purpose: Grants for healthcare and basic human services to residents of St. Clair County, MI.
Financial data: Year ended 03/31/2013. Assets, $4,082,540 (M); Expenditures, $1,341,258; Total giving, $872,032; Grants to individuals, totaling $100,336.
Fields of interest: Economically disadvantaged.
Type of support: Grants for special needs.
Application information: Applications accepted.
Initial approach: Letter

Additional information: Contact foundation for eligibility criteria.
EIN: 381357996

4653
Universal Forest Products Education Foundation
(formerly Universal Companies, Inc. Education Foundation)
2801 E. Beltline Ave. N.E.
Grand Rapids, MI 49525-9680
Contact: Nancy DeGood, Dir.

Foundation type: Company-sponsored foundation
Purpose: Scholarships to employees of Universal Forest Products, Inc. and its subsidiaries who have 12 months of seniority prior to June 1st of the scholarship year, and to their natural and adopted children under the age of 25 for postsecondary education at community colleges, junior colleges or four-year colleges and universities.
Financial data: Year ended 12/31/2012. Assets, $624,696 (M); Expenditures, $36,578; Total giving, $34,000; Grants to individuals, 42 grants totaling $34,000 (high: $1,500, low: $500).
Fields of interest: Vocational education.
Type of support: Employee-related scholarships.
Application information: Application form required.
Initial approach: Letter or telephone
Deadline(s): May 31
Final notification: Notice of all grants will be given by July 15
Applicants should submit the following:
  1) Letter(s) of recommendation
  2) Essay
Company name: Universal Forest Products, Incorporated
EIN: 382945715

4654
W. E. Upjohn Unemployment Trustee Corp.
(also known as W.E. Upjohn Institute for Employment Research)
300 S. Westnedge Ave.
Kalamazoo, MI 49007-4630   (269) 343-5541
Contact: Richard Wyrwa, Publications and Mktg. Mgr.
FAX: (269) 343-3308;
E-mail: webmaster@upjohninstitute.org;
URL: http://www.upjohninstitute.org

Foundation type: Public charity
Purpose: Research grants to professional social scientists who have earned a Ph.D., or the equivalent, for studies on the causes, effects, prevention, and alleviation of unemployment.
Publications: Application guidelines; Newsletter; Program policy statement.
Financial data: Year ended 12/31/2011. Assets, $141,159,755 (M); Expenditures, $16,252,215; Total giving, $7,407,927; Grants to individuals, totaling $265,892.
Fields of interest: Research; Social sciences.
Type of support: Research.
Application information: Applications accepted. Application form not required.
Initial approach: Three-page summary of project
Send request by: Mail
Copies of proposal: 8
Deadline(s): Feb. 1
Additional information: Application should include curriculum vitae.

Program descriptions:

Dissertation Award: This program awards up to $2,000 for the best Ph.D. dissertation on employment-related issues, with up to two honorable mention awards of $1,000 also given. The awards are meant to further the support and conduct of policy-relevant research on issues related to employment, unemployment, and social insurance programs. Dissertations may come from any academic discipline, but must have a substantial policy thrust; submissions will be evaluated on policy relevance, technical quality of the research, and presentation.

Policy Research Grants: This program offers two types of grants: Research Grants and Mini-Grants. Research Grants are intended to produce papers and briefs that should be suitable for publication in a peer-reviewed journal, and carry an award f up to $10,000. Mini-Grants, of up to $5,000, are awarded to untenured junior faculty who are within six years of earning their Ph.D. degree, and are intended to provide flexibility to meet special funding needs that, without support, would impede researchers from pursuing the project. Recipients are expected to write a research paper that would be submitted to a peer-reviewed journal, to prepare a synopsis of the research for consideration as an article in the institute's newsletter Employment Research, and to enter the paper in the institute's Working Paper series. Topics of interest include, but are not limited to: vulnerable groups, such as immigrants, older workers, and youths; 'jobless recovery' causes and consequences; structural and cyclical unemployment; sectoral adjustments (automobiles, finance, real estate, etc.); entrepreneurship, including self-employment and job creation; workforce programs; UI extension and consequences; finance and labor markets; housing, migration, and regional adjustments; state and local budgets and employments; and compensation.
EIN: 381360419

4655
Homer J. Van Hollenbeck Foundation
13231 23 Mile Rd.
Shelby Township, MI 48315
Contact: Stefan Wanczyk, Pres.

Foundation type: Independent foundation
Purpose: Scholarships to Macomb County, MI, area high school seniors who are financially needy and have at least a 2.5 GPA. Scholarships are limited to $2,000 per year, with a maximum total award of $6,000 per student.
Financial data: Year ended 12/31/2012. Assets, $1,006,219 (M); Expenditures, $68,636; Total giving, $65,000; Grants to individuals, 26 grants totaling $65,000 (high: $2,500, low: $2,500).
Type of support: Support to graduates or students of specific schools; Undergraduate support.
Application information: Application form required.
  Deadline(s): May 31
  Additional information: Application must include letter of recommendation. Contact foundation for current application guidelines.
EIN: 383085929

4656
Dr. Lavern and Betty VanKley Educational Foundation
351 W. Main St.
Zeeland, MI 49464-2082   (616) 403-2763
Contact: Thomas Vankley, Tr.
Application address: 351 W. Main St., Zeeland, MI 49464

Foundation type: Independent foundation
Purpose: Student loans to members and children of members of the First Reformed Church of Zeeland, MI.
Financial data: Year ended 12/31/2012. Assets, $415,837 (M); Expenditures, $4,997; Total giving, $31,880; Grants to individuals, 14 grants totaling $31,880 (high: $12,500, low: $5).
Fields of interest: Protestant agencies & churches.
Type of support: Student loans—to individuals.
Application information: Applications not accepted.
  Additional information: Unsolicited requests for funds not considered or acknowledged.
EIN: 386500707

4657
Veteran's Haven, Inc.
4924 Wayne Rd.
Wayne, MI 48184-3200   (734) 728-0527
FAX: (734) 728-1278;
E-mail: vetshaven@earthlink.net; URL: http://www.vetshaveninfo.org/haven.htm

Foundation type: Public charity
Purpose: Assistance of basic necessities to military veterans in need.
Financial data: Year ended 12/31/2012. Assets, $524,542 (M); Expenditures, $160,311.
Fields of interest: Military/veterans; Economically disadvantaged.
Type of support: Grants for special needs.
Application information:
  Initial approach: Telephone or e-mail
  Additional information: Contact foundation for complete eligibility requirements.
EIN: 383176960

4658
Vetowich Family Foundation
c/o William Felosak
26026 Telegraph Rd., Ste. 200
Southfield, MI 48034-2560   (248) 355-5151

Foundation type: Independent foundation
Purpose: Soccer scholarships, by nomination only, to individuals residing in the Southfield, MI, area.
Financial data: Year ended 08/31/2012. Assets, $305,352 (M); Expenditures, $9,031; Total giving, $6,553.
Fields of interest: Athletics/sports, soccer.
Type of support: Awards/grants by nomination only; Undergraduate support.
Application information: Applications not accepted.
  Additional information: Unsolicited requests for funds not considered or acknowledged.
EIN: 386750824

4659
The Vomberg Foundation
c/o Olivet College
320 S. Main St.
Olivet, MI 49076-9406   (269) 749-9364

Foundation type: Independent foundation

Purpose: Scholarships to financially needy high school seniors who are residents of Eaton County, MI.
Financial data: Year ended 12/31/2012. Assets, $684,575 (M); Expenditures, $38,992; Total giving, $33,000.
Type of support: Undergraduate support.
Application information: Applications accepted. Application form required. Interview required.
  Deadline(s): Dec. 1
  Additional information: Application must include high school transcript.
EIN: 386072845

4660
Waterford Foundation for Public Education
P.O. Box 300681
Waterford, MI 48330-0681   (248) 673-9898
E-mail: wsdfoundation1984@gmail.com;
URL: http://www.waterford.k12.mi.us/wfpe/

Foundation type: Public charity
Purpose: Scholarships to graduates of Waterford public high schools, MI. Grants to teachers of the Waterford School District, MI, to fund educational enrichment programs.
Publications: Annual report; Financial statement; Informational brochure.
Financial data: Year ended 06/30/2012. Assets, $1,112,831 (M); Expenditures, $32,904; Total giving, $7,210; Grants to individuals, 5 grants totaling $6,000.
Fields of interest: Elementary/secondary education.
Type of support: Support to graduates or students of specific schools; Project support.
Application information: Applications accepted. Application form available on the grantmaker's web site.
  Initial approach: Letter
  Deadline(s): Mar. 1 for scholarships; Mar. 31 for grants to teachers
  Additional information: Scholarship applications should include essay, letter of recommendation, and transcripts. Applications for grants to teachers should include a proposal; contact foundation for further program information. See web site for additional application guidelines.
EIN: 382528009

4661
John W. and Rose E. Watson Foundation
c/o Tri-Star Trust Bank
1004 N. Michigan Ave.
Saginaw, MI 48602-4325
Application address: c/o Jean Seman, 5800 Weiss St., Saginaw, MI 48602, tel.: (989) 792-2011

Foundation type: Independent foundation
Purpose: Scholarships to Saginaw County, MI, residents graduating from Catholic high schools.
Financial data: Year ended 12/31/2012. Assets, $7,433,357 (M); Expenditures, $410,824; Total giving, $331,500; Grants to individuals, 92 grants totaling $227,500 (high: $25,000, low: $25,000).
Fields of interest: Higher education; Catholic agencies & churches.
Type of support: Scholarships—to individuals.
Application information: Applications accepted. Application form required.
  Deadline(s): One month prior to beginning of academic year

Additional information: Applications can be obtained from Citizens Bank Wealth Management, N.A.
EIN: 386091611

4662
Wayne-Metropolitan Community Action Agency
2121 Biddle Ave., Ste. 102
Wyandotte, MI 48192-4064 (734) 246-2280
FAX: (734) 246-2288;
E-mail: info@waynemetro.org; URL: http://www.waynemetro.org

Foundation type: Public charity
Purpose: Financial assistance to low-income individuals of Wayne county, MI, with adequate housing, job placement assistance, and after school tutoring for at-risk youth.
Financial data: Year ended 09/30/2011. Assets, $8,862,210 (M); Expenditures, $27,740,869; Total giving, $3,649,928; Grants to individuals, 11,037 grants totaling $1,388,960.
Fields of interest: Human services; Economically disadvantaged; Homeless.
Type of support: Grants for special needs.
Application information: Contact the agency for eligibility criteria.
EIN: 381976979

4663
Lorna A. Welch Charitable Foundation
P.O. Box 390
Flushing, MI 48433-0390
Contact: James Wood
Application address: 121 E. Main St., Flushing, MI 48433-2023

Foundation type: Operating foundation
Purpose: Scholarships to graduating seniors from Flushing High School, MI for postsecondary education.
Financial data: Year ended 12/31/2011. Assets, $535,468 (M); Expenditures, $531; Total giving, $30,000; Grants to individuals, 6 grants totaling $30,000 (high: $5,000, low: $5,000).
Fields of interest: Higher education.
Type of support: Support to graduates or students of specific schools; Undergraduate support.
Application information:
   Deadline(s): Feb. 1
   Additional information: Applicant must have a 3.7 GPA, participate in extracurricular activities and perform community service. Applicant must be a resident from the city of Flushing or Flushing Township Michigan.
EIN: 383553903

4664
Leon Wells Trust
c/o Monroe Bank & Trust
102 E. Front St.
Monroe, MI 48161-2162 (734) 242-2734

Foundation type: Independent foundation
Purpose: Scholarships by nomination only to financially needy graduating seniors who are residents of Dundee or Summerfield townships, Monroe County, MI.
Financial data: Year ended 05/31/2012. Assets, $289,104 (M); Expenditures, $12,084; Total giving, $7,500; Grants to individuals, 15 grants totaling $7,500 (high: $560, low: $400).

Type of support: Support to graduates or students of specific schools; Awards/grants by nomination only; Undergraduate support.
Application information: Application form required.
   Deadline(s): May 1
   Applicants should submit the following:
      1) Transcripts
      2) Financial information
   Additional information: Application must include an affidavit of residency; Application forms are available from the qualifying high school, and are to be submitted to the high school principal. Scholarships are renewable for up to four years.
EIN: 386146348

4665
Whaley Children's Center, Inc.
1201 N. Grand Traverse St.
Flint, MI 48503-1312 (810) 234-3603
Contact: Kevin Roach, Pres.
FAX: (810) 232-3416;
E-mail: info@whaleychildren.org; URL: http://www.whaleychildren.org/

Foundation type: Public charity
Purpose: Specific assistance to children and families of Flint, MI who have been victims of severe abuse and neglect.
Financial data: Year ended 12/31/2011. Assets, $6,547,925 (M); Expenditures, $3,686,262; Total giving, $136,991; Grants to individuals, totaling $136,991.
Fields of interest: Child abuse; Sexual abuse; Family services.
Type of support: Grants for special needs.
Application information: See the Center's web site for additional information.
EIN: 381358235

4666
Whirlpool Foundation
2000 N. M-63, MD 3106
Benton Harbor, MI 49022 (269) 923-5580
Contact: Candice Garman, Communty Rels. Mgr.
FAX: (269) 925-0154;
E-mail: whirlpool_foundation@whirlpool.com; Tel. for Candice Garman: (269) 923-5584; URL: http://www.whirlpoolcorp.com/responsibility/building_communities/whirlpool_foundation.aspx

Foundation type: Company-sponsored foundation
Purpose: Scholarships to children of employees of the Whirlpool Corporation.
Financial data: Year ended 12/31/2012. Assets, $587,136 (M); Expenditures, $14,143,109; Total giving, $13,804,448. Employee-related scholarships amount not specified.
Fields of interest: Scholarships/financial aid.
Type of support: Employee-related scholarships.
Application information: Applications not accepted.
   Additional information: Unsolicited requests for funds not considered or acknowledged.
Program description:
   Whirlpool Foundation Sons and Daughters Scholarship Program: The foundation awards college scholarships to the children of employees of Whirlpool and its subsidiaries in the U.S. and Canada. The foundation awards four-year $16,000 scholarships, one-time honor awards of $2,500, and one-time incentive awards of $1,000.
Company name: Whirlpool Corporation
EIN: 386077342

4667
The John and Elizabeth Whiteley Foundation
c/o Hubbard Law Firm
5801 W. Michigan Ave.
Lansing, MI 48917 (517) 886-7176
Contact: Donald B. Lawrence, Pres.
Application address: P.O. Box 80507, Lansing, MI 48908-0857
FAX: (517) 886-1080

Foundation type: Independent foundation
Purpose: Scholarships to financially needy and deserving students from Ingham, Eaton and Clinton counties, MI.
Financial data: Year ended 12/31/2011. Assets, $1,525,900 (M); Expenditures, $72,676; Total giving, $36,000; Grants to individuals, 20 grants totaling $19,500 (high: $1,000, low: $500).
Fields of interest: Business school/education.
Type of support: Undergraduate support.
Application information: Applications accepted. Application form required.
   Deadline(s): May 1
   Applicants should submit the following:
      1) Letter(s) of recommendation
      2) Transcripts
      3) Financial information
   Additional information: Application must also include letter of admission from college or university applicant is attending.
EIN: 381558108

4668
Wigginton Educational Foundation
c/o Fifth Third Bank
233 Washington Ave.
Grand Haven, MI 49417 (616) 842-6760
Contact: Lisa Danicek, Treas.
Application address: 1415 S., Beechtree, Grand Heven, MI 49417, tel.: 616-842-6760

Foundation type: Independent foundation
Purpose: Scholarships to worthy, financially needy residents of school districts in Ottawa and Muskegon counties, MI, and in the city of Grand Haven, MI.
Financial data: Year ended 12/31/2012. Assets, $399,332 (M); Expenditures, $21,726; Total giving, $15,699; Grants to individuals, 120 grants totaling $15,699 (high: $1,390, low: $12).
Fields of interest: Higher education.
Type of support: Scholarships—to individuals.
Application information: Applications accepted. Application form required.
   Initial approach: Letter or telephone
   Deadline(s): None
   Applicants should submit the following:
      1) Transcripts
      2) Financial information
   Additional information: Applicant must include name of college attending or will be attending.
EIN: 382388277

4669
George & Emily Harris Willard Trust
3 W. Vanburen St.
Battle Creek, MI 49017-3009

Foundation type: Public charity
Purpose: Care and aid to underprivileged children residing within the city of Battle Creek, MI and attending the public schools therein.
Financial data: Year ended 06/30/2012. Assets, $925,538 (M); Expenditures, $32,565; Total giving, $29,820.

Fields of interest: Economically disadvantaged.
Type of support: Grants for special needs; Camperships.
Application information: Contact the trust for additional information.
EIN: 386053144

4670
Wilson Scholarship Fund

(formerly Rodney B. Wilson Scholarship Fund)
c/o Citizens Bank Wealth Management, N.A.
328 S. Saginaw St., M/C 001065
Flint, MI 48502-1923 (989) 227-4023
Application address: c/o St. John's Public High School, Attn.: Janet Thelen, P.O. Box 230, St. Johns, MI 48879-0230

Foundation type: Independent foundation
Purpose: Scholarships to graduates of St. Johns Public High School, MI who are in the upper one-third of their class.
Financial data: Year ended 12/31/2012. Assets, $316,754 (M); Expenditures, $33,782; Total giving, $28,000; Grants to individuals, 14 grants totaling $28,000 (high: $3,000, low: $1,000).
Fields of interest: Higher education.
Type of support: Support to graduates or students of specific schools.
Application information: Applications accepted. Application form required.
Deadline(s): Apr. and Aug.
Additional information: Applicant must maintain good citizenship and character. Applications available at high school.
EIN: 386619088

4671
John J. Winkler Memorial Trust

c/o David Halperin
1742 Westridge Rd.
Ann Arbor, MI 48105-4903 (734) 647-5884
Application Address: 3187 Angel Hall, Ann Arbor, MI 48109

Foundation type: Independent foundation
Purpose: Grant awards for essays on a neglected or marginal topic in the field of classical studies.
Financial data: Year ended 05/31/2012. Assets, $26,944 (M); Expenditures, $2,821; Total giving, $2,000; Grants to individuals, 2 grants totaling $2,000 (high: $1,000, low: $1,000).
Type of support: Awards/prizes.
Application information: Applications accepted. Application form not required.
Deadline(s): Apr. 1
EIN: 776062330

4672
Winship Memorial Scholarship Foundation

c/o Comerica Bank, Trust Div.
49 W. Michigan Ave.
Battle Creek, MI 49017-3603 (269) 966-6344

Foundation type: Independent foundation
Purpose: Scholarships to graduates of Battle Creek, MI, area public high schools.
Publications: Application guidelines; Annual report; Informational brochure.
Financial data: Year ended 12/31/2011. Assets, $3,285,261 (M); Expenditures, $208,315; Total giving, $130,400; Grants to individuals, 72 grants totaling $130,400 (high: $4,200, low: $500).
Fields of interest: Higher education; Scholarships/financial aid.

Type of support: Support to graduates or students of specific schools; Undergraduate support.
Application information: Application form required. Interview required.
Deadline(s): Nov. 15
Additional information: Contact foundation for applications guidelines.
EIN: 386092543

4673
Evelyn and Ronald Wirick Foundation

504 Maple Dr.
Morenci, MI 49256
Contact: Ralph Ferris, Tr.

Foundation type: Operating foundation
Purpose: Scholarships to graduates of schools in the Morenci, MI area for higher education.
Financial data: Year ended 12/31/2012. Assets, $1,180,876 (M); Expenditures, $44,862; Total giving, $21,600; Grants to individuals, 16 grants totaling $21,600 (high: $1,350, low: $1,350).
Type of support: Support to graduates or students of specific schools; Undergraduate support.
Application information: Applications accepted.
Deadline(s): None
EIN: 382700421

4674
World Medical Relief, Inc.

11745 Rosa Parks Blvd.
Detroit, MI 48206-1269 (313) 866-5333
Contact: George V. Samson, Pres. and C.E.O.
FAX: (313) 866-5588;
E-mail: info@worldmedicalrelief.org; URL: http://www.worldmedicalrelief.org

Foundation type: Public charity
Purpose: Specific assistance to low income individuals of Metropolitan Detroit, MI with medical prescriptions, durable medical equipment or medical supplies. Medical assistance also, to underprivileged people around the world.
Publications: Annual report; Financial statement; Informational brochure; Newsletter; Occasional report; Program policy statement.
Financial data: Year ended 12/31/2011. Assets, $2,285,358 (M); Expenditures, $20,881,819; Total giving, $19,990,700; Grants to individuals, 56,594 grants totaling $3,846,255.
Fields of interest: Medical care, community health systems; Economically disadvantaged.
Type of support: Grants for special needs.
Application information: Individuals are screened to determine if they qualify for assistance based on funder criteria. Individuals complete a one-page application listing medications and the physicians who prescribe them.
Program description:
Prescription Program: Individuals with an income of less than $21,780 and couples with an income of less than $29,420, who are older than 18 and have no prescription insurance coverage and live in Michigan, may be eligible for assistance in covering the cost of their prescriptions.
EIN: 381575570

4675
Wyandotte Public Schools Scholarship Foundation

(formerly Wyandotte Public Schools Foundation, also known as WPS Scholarship Foundation)
P.O. Box 412
Wyandotte, MI 48192 (734) 759-5000
Application address: C/o.High School Principal,540 Elireika Rd.,Cuyandette MI 4819, tel.: 734-759-5000

Foundation type: Operating foundation
Purpose: Scholarships to students graduating from Wyandotte, MI, public high schools.
Financial data: Year ended 06/30/2010. Assets, $509,910 (M); Expenditures, $73,604; Total giving, $69,620; Grants to individuals, 100 grants totaling $69,620 (high: $2,500, low: $150).
Fields of interest: Higher education.
Type of support: Support to graduates or students of specific schools.
Application information: Applications accepted. Application form required.
Deadline(s): Apr. 28
Additional information: Application forms are available from qualifying high schools.
EIN: 382898957

4676
Yankama Feed the Children Charitable Foundation

601 S. Shore Dr.
Battle Creek, MI 49014-5440

Foundation type: Independent foundation
Purpose: Grants to economically disadvantaged individuals for food and other basic necessities.
Financial data: Year ended 12/31/2011. Assets, $3,974 (M); Expenditures, $1,525; Total giving, $500; Grants to individuals, 2 grants totaling $500 (high: $300, low: $200).
Fields of interest: Food services; Human services; Economically disadvantaged.
Type of support: Grants for special needs.
Application information: Applications accepted.
Additional information: Contact foundation for current application deadline/guidelines.
EIN: 383219667

4677
Coleman A. Young Foundation

2111 Woodward Ave., Ste. 600
Detroit, MI 48201-3473 (313) 962-2200
Contact: Claudette Y. Smith Ph.D., Exec. Dir.
FAX: (313) 962-2208; E-mail: info@cayf.org;
URL: http://www.cayf.org

Foundation type: Public charity
Purpose: Scholarships to graduating seniors who are residents of Detroit, MI, planning to attend an accredited, Historically-Black College/University, or an accredited four-year college or university in MI.
Publications: Application guidelines; Annual report; Financial statement; Informational brochure (including application guidelines); Newsletter.
Financial data: Year ended 12/31/2011. Assets, $1,472,206 (M); Expenditures, $592,659; Total giving, $90,475; Grants to individuals, totaling $90,475.
Fields of interest: Higher education; African Americans/Blacks.
Type of support: Undergraduate support.
Application information: Applications accepted. Application form required. Application form available on the grantmaker's web site. Interview required.

Copies of proposal: 1
Deadline(s): Mar. 13
Final notification: Semi-finalists notified Apr. 30, Finalists notified no later than May 5
Applicants should submit the following:
1) Resume
2) SAT
3) Letter(s) of recommendation
4) Financial information
5) Essay

6) ACT
Additional information: Application should also include statement of need declaration, W-2 and federal tax return, or statement of welfare, proof of residence.

Program description:
Scholarships: Scholarship recipients receive a $20,000 award payable in annual increments of up to $5,000. Students must be graduates from a Detroit high school during the award year and plan to pursue a degree in an area of emphasis for the CAYF including Liberal Arts, Education, Economics, Finance, Engineering, and Science. Student must have a cumulative GPA of 2.5 or better. Funds must be used to pay for expenses related to attending college including tuition, fees, room and board, books and transportation.
EIN: 382400801

MINNESOTA

4678
3-H Farms Charitable Foundation
c/o Trust Tax Services
P.O. Box 64713
Saint Paul, MN 55164-0713 (320) 693-2424
Application address: c/o Guidance Office, 901
Gilman Ave. N., Litchfield, MN 55355

Foundation type: Independent foundation
Purpose: Scholarships to students from Litchfield, MN, for study in the fields of health or agriculture.
Financial data: Year ended 06/30/2013. Assets, $132,469 (M); Expenditures, $10,147; Total giving, $6,000; Grants to individuals, 3 grants totaling $6,000 (high: $2,000; low: $2,000).
Fields of interest: Health sciences school/education; Formal/general education.
Type of support: Scholarships—to individuals.
Application information: Applications accepted. Application form required.
EIN: 416466247

4679
Abbott Northwestern Hospital Foundation
P.O. Box 43
Minneapolis, MN 55440-0043 (612) 863-4126
FAX: (612) 863-2833;
E-mail: anwfoundation@allina.com; URL: http://www.abbottnorthwestern.com/ahs/anw.nsf/page/foundation

Foundation type: Public charity
Purpose: Scholarships to students of Minneapolis Roosevelt School, MN who demonstrate academic excellence for postsecondary education.
Publications: Annual report; Newsletter.
Financial data: Year ended 12/31/2011. Assets, $73,598,883 (M); Expenditures, $8,141,585; Total giving, $6,443,535; Grants to individuals, totaling $12,773.
Fields of interest: Higher education.
Type of support: Scholarships—to individuals.
Application information: Contact the foundation for additional information.
EIN: 043643816

4680
Ada Scholarship Foundation Inc.
702 E. 1st Ave.
Ada, MN 56510 (218) 784-5300
Application address: Ada Borup High School, 604 W. Thorpe Ave., Ada, MN 56510

Foundation type: Independent foundation
Purpose: Scholarships to high school seniors of Ada-Borup High School, MN for higher education.
Financial data: Year ended 05/31/2013. Assets, $2,484,888 (M); Expenditures, $135,116; Total giving, $113,100; Grants to individuals, 84 grants totaling $113,100 (high: $2,000, low: $300).
Fields of interest: Higher education.
Type of support: Support to graduates or students of specific schools.
Application information: Applications accepted. Application form required.
Deadline(s): Apr.
Applicants should submit the following:
   1) GPA
   2) Class rank
   3) Transcripts

Additional information: Application should also include three letters of reference, extracurricular activities, community service and work activities.
EIN: 411566681

4681
Adams Educational Fund Inc.
P.O. Box 1012
Willmar, MN 56201-1012 (320) 214-2919
Contact: Brett Aamot, Treas.
E-mail: baamot@cdscpa.com

Foundation type: Independent foundation
Purpose: Loans to graduates of the Willmar School System, MN, and surrounding areas. Maximum loan is $1,000 per year for four years.
Financial data: Year ended 12/31/2012. Assets, $316,895 (M); Expenditures, $8,289; Total giving, $0.
Type of support: Student loans—to individuals; Support to graduates or students of specific schools; Undergraduate support.
Application information: Applications accepted. Application form required.
Initial approach: Telephone
Deadline(s): None
EIN: 416038636

4682
The Affinity Plus Federal Credit Union Foundation
175 W. Lafayette Rd.
St. Paul, MN 55107-1488
E-mail: foundation@affinityplus.org; URL: http://www.affinityplus.org/additionalresources/foundation/aboutfoundation.aspx

Foundation type: Independent foundation
Purpose: Scholarships to high school graduates or returning students from the metropolitan St. Paul, MN area.
Financial data: Year ended 12/31/2011. Assets, $580,649 (M); Expenditures, $44,629; Total giving, $29,500.
Fields of interest: Higher education.
Type of support: Undergraduate support.
Application information: Applications accepted. Application form required.
Deadline(s): Jan. 31
Final notification: Applicants notified by Mar. 30
EIN: 411974262

4683
AgStar Fund for Rural America
1921 Premier Dr.
P.O. Box 4249
Mankato, MN 56002-4249 (952) 997-1255
Contact: Melanie Olson
Additional tel.: (507) 345-5656
E-mail: Melanie.Olson@Agstar.com; URL: http://www.agstar.com/enhancingamerica/fundforruralamerica/Pages/default.aspx

Foundation type: Corporate giving program
Purpose: Scholarships to high school seniors residing in areas of AgStar company operations who wishes to pursue a major related to agricultural or rural studies and to high school seniors who already have a background in agricultural or rural studies and plan to continue their education in any field of study. Scholarships to junior or third year students who are interested in agricultural financing or agricultural-related careers.

Publications: Application guidelines; Grants list; Informational brochure.
Fields of interest: Higher education; Formal/general education; Agriculture; Rural studies.
Type of support: Scholarships—to individuals; Undergraduate support.
Application information: Applications accepted. Application form required. Application form available on the grantmaker's web site.
Initial approach: Application
Send request by: Mail
Deadline(s): Apr. 1 for high school seniors, Jan. 14 for AgStar Scholars
Applicants should submit the following:
   1) Resume
   2) Essay
   3) Transcripts
   4) Letter(s) of recommendation
Program descriptions:
AgStar Scholars Program: AgStar, in partnership with the University of Minnesota - St. Paul and the University of Wisconsin - River Valley, supports students in their third year of college who are interested in agricultural financing or agricultural-related careers. The program includes a $2,000 scholarship; an orientation session; guest lectures by AgStar executives; a rural or agriculture-related research project to be completed by the scholar and presented to AgStar and university representatives; and a paid internship with AgStar. Applicants must have a GPA of 3.0 or better.
High School Senior Scholarships: AgStar annually awards fifteen $1,000 college scholarships to high school seniors pursuing agriculture-related degrees and five $1,000 scholarships to high school seniors with an agricultural or rural background who plan to continue their education in any field of study. Applicants must live in a AgStar service area and have GPA of 3.0 or higher. Applicants are selected based on academic achievement, leadership characteristics, and community involvement. Preference will be given to children of parents who are client of AgStar Financial Services, ACA.

4684
Alumnae Association of the College of St. Teresa Scholarship Fund
(also known as Teresan Scholarship Fund)
357 Gould St.
Winona, MN 55987 (507) 454-2930

Foundation type: Independent foundation
Purpose: Scholarships to residents of Winona, MN, who are Catholic school undergraduates in the upper 25 percent of their class.
Financial data: Year ended 12/31/2012. Assets, $1,089,511 (M); Expenditures, $57,927; Total giving, $34,975; Grants to individuals, 72 grants totaling $34,975 (high: $750, low: $300).
Type of support: Undergraduate support.
Application information:
Initial approach: Letter
Additional information: Contact foundation for current application deadline/guidelines.
EIN: 411688308

4685
Marshall H. and Nellie Alworth Memorial Fund

402 Alworth Bldg.
306 W. Superior St., Ste. 402
Duluth, MN 55802-5017   (218) 722-9366
Contact: Patty Salow Downs, Exec. Dir.
E-mail for scholarship questions and recent IRS 1040 forms: alworth@cpinternet.com; Additional URL: http://www.futurestakeflight.com
FAX: (218) 529-3760;
E-mail: alworth@alworthscholarship.org;
URL: http://www.alworthscholarship.org/

Foundation type: Independent foundation
Purpose: Scholarships to graduating high school seniors from Aitkin, Beltrami, Carlton, Cass, Cook, Crow Wing, Lake, Itasca, Koochiching, and St. Louis counties MN for postsecondary education.
Publications: Application guidelines; Informational brochure; Informational brochure (including application guidelines).
Financial data: Year ended 06/30/2013. Assets, $6,343,449 (M); Expenditures, $112,974; Total giving, $18,650; Grants to individuals, totaling $18,650.
Fields of interest: Architecture; Medical school/education; Nursing school/education; Engineering school/education; Research; Veterinary medicine; Animals/wildlife; Genetic diseases and disorders; Biomedicine; Neuroscience; Agriculture; Physical/earth sciences; Mathematics; Physics; Geology; Engineering/technology; Computer science; Biology/life sciences; Botany; Science.
Type of support: Graduate support; Undergraduate support.
Application information: Applications accepted. Application form required. Application form available on the grantmaker's web site.
  Send request by: On-line
  Copies of proposal: 1
  Deadline(s): Jan. 15
  Applicants should submit the following:
    1) Transcripts
    2) Essay
    3) GPA
    4) Letter(s) of recommendation
    5) Financial information
    6) ACT
    7) Class rank
  Additional information: Application forms available from high school counselors in northern, MN. See web site for additional guidelines.
EIN: 410797340

4686
American Brain Foundation

201 Chicago Ave.
Minneapolis, MN 55415-1126   (612) 928-6100
E-mail: foundation@aan.com; Toll-free tel.: (866) 770-7570; URL: https://www.curebraindisease.org/

Foundation type: Public charity
Purpose: Grants to neurologists and clinical investigators interested in clinical research in the field of neurology.
Publications: Application guidelines.
Financial data: Year ended 12/31/2011. Assets, $8,797,416 (M); Expenditures, $3,685,624; Total giving, $1,802,950; Grants to individuals, totaling $7,900.
Fields of interest: Neuroscience; Neuroscience research.
Type of support: Fellowships; Research.

Application information: Applications accepted. Application form required. Application form available on the grantmaker's web site.
  Initial approach: Application
  Deadline(s): Oct. 1 for Training Fellowships and Development Awards, July for Lawrence M. Bass Stroke Research Postdoctoral Fellowship
  Applicants should submit the following:
    1) Budget Information
    2) Curriculum vitae
    3) Proposal
    4) Letter(s) of recommendation
  Additional information: Contact foundation for further eligibility criteria.
Program descriptions:
  AHA/ASA/ABF Lawrence M. Brass M.D. Stroke Research Postdoctoral Fellowships: The fellowships are two-year awards at a level of $65,000 per year to support a postdoctoral fellow with a preference for trainees in vascular neurology, stroke, neurocritical care, or outcomes research. Applicants must hold an MD, PhD, DO, DM or equivalent doctoral degree at the time of award activation and have no more than five years postdoctoral research training. MDs must have completed their residency within the past five years.
  Clinician Scientist Development Awards: In conjunction with the Amyotrophic Lateral Sclerosis (ALS) Association, a three-year award is available to support research into drug discovery and the development of therapies that will effectively treat ALS, and to recognize the importance of good clinical research in encouraging young investigators in clinical studies. Awards consist of an annual salary of $75,000, plus a $5,000 institutional award. Eligible applicants must be a neurologist interested in an academic career in clinical research; applicants must hold an M.D., D.O., or equivalent clinical degree from an accredited institution, and must be licensed to practice medicine in the U.S. Applicants must also have competed residency training but be less than seven years from completion of their residency when funding begins.
  Health Policy Research Fellowship: This fellowship program is designed to prepare neurologists for an academic career in health policy research. The selected fellow will obtain a master's degree at the George Washington University School of Public Health and Health Services while continuing clinical rotations. Graduates will be prepared to enter an academic or research career in health policy, and course work will include biostatistics, epidemiology, health policy analysis, health economics, and health policy research design. The fellow also will gain experience working in a congressional, federal, or executive government office. The fellow will receive a stipend of $102,500 a year for two years. The stipend will cover all related costs and expenses, with no separate reimbursement to the fellow. In addition to the stipend, George Washington University will contribute 90 percent of the fellow's master's program tuition.
  Practice Research Training Fellowship: One two-year fellowship is available to support training in clinical practice research (defined as clinical research that evaluates the translation of evidence into best clinical practice). This may include the evaluation of health services, quality of care, implementation of proven therapies, physician performance, or patient adherence. Fellowships are for $55,000 per year for two years, plus $10,000 per year for tuition to support formal education in clinical research methodology at the applicant's institution or elsewhere. Eligible applicants must be academy members who have completed residency

or a post-doctoral fellowship (for a Ph.D.) within the past five years.
EIN: 411717098

4687
American Composers Forum

332 Minnesota St., Ste. E-145
St. Paul, MN 55101-1300   (651) 228-1407
Contact: John Nuechterlein, Pres. and C.E.O.
FAX: (651) 291-7978;
E-mail: mail@composersforum.org; E-Mail for John Nuechterlein: jnuechterlein@composersforum.org;
URL: http://www.composersforum.org/

Foundation type: Public charity
Purpose: Fellowships and grants to composers to support their creative work.
Publications: Application guidelines; Annual report; Newsletter.
Financial data: Year ended 06/30/2011. Assets, $7,420,355 (M); Expenditures, $1,821,743; Total giving, $416,687; Grants to individuals, totaling $291,500.
Fields of interest: Music composition; Religion, interfaith issues.
Type of support: Fellowships; Grants to individuals; Residencies; Loans—to individuals.
Application information: Applications accepted. Application form required.
  Initial approach: Telephone or e-mail
  Deadline(s): Vary
Program descriptions:
  Continental Harmony: Developed in partnership with the National Endowment for the Arts, this program takes the form of community-designed and managed composer residencies, culminating in premieres of new works. For more information visit http://www.continentalharmony.org.
  Encore: The program encourages performers, individuals, and ensembles to add newly-created works by living composers to their repertoires. It also aims to assist composers in securing premiere and post-premiere performances that are vital to building a career. While not a commissioning program and not expected to fully finance performances, this program acts as an incentive to build new partnerships between performers and composers. By offering an opportunity for performers to work directly with the composer and helping compensate players for the time and effort required to undertake a new piece, the program will ensure that new works continue to reach a variety of audiences. The program makes grants from $500 to $2,500 to performers and ensembles to present a work at least three times during an 18-month period. Joint applications may be initiated by composers or performers, may be submitted at any time, and are reviewed on a twice-yearly basis. Composers and performers must be based in different geographic areas of the U.S. For more information, contact Craig Carnahan at ccarnahan@composersforum.org.
  Faith Partners Residency Program: This program funds two-year-long composer residencies in three consortia, in both urban and rural settings. Each consortium consists of two congregations of different faiths. Each composer creates a total of six works during the course of the residency: three to be shared by all members of the consortium, and one for each consortium member individually. Each composer receives $10,000. Forum members in the upper Midwest of the U.S. may apply.
  Finale National Composition Contest: Awarded in partnership with MakeMusic, Inc. and the chamber music ensemble eighth blackbird, this competition will award cash prizes to composers of chamber music for outstanding compositions commissioned

specifically for eighth blackbird. Eligible applicants may be of any age, but must be U.S. residents; pieces must be between eight and ten minutes long, and scored for the instrumentation unique to the six members of eighth blackbird (flute, clarinet, violin/viola, cello, percussion, and piano)

First Nations Composer Initiative Common Ground Grant: The initiative is dedicated to serving the needs of American Indian/Alaska Native/First Nations/indigenous makers of new music throughout Indian country. The program also provides Native musical artists with the opportunity to enrich their work through contact with a variety of communities, makes Native musical artists more visible to underserved communities and/or larger non-Native cultural institutions, and assists Native artists in collaboration with non-Native arts organizations in building audiences, thereby increasing demand for their work. Individual awards will range from $500 to $7,500.

Jerome Fund for New Music: Grants of up to $7,000 are available to emerging composers from Minnesota or the five boroughs of New York City, or emerging composers living elsewhere who partner with Minnesota performers, to support the creation of new musical works in all genres. Eligible artists must be 'emerging' composers (artists at an early stage of their careers, with as-yet little peer recognition, no national reputation, and limited professional opportunities)

McKnight Composer Fellowships: These $25,000 fellowships are intended to reward artistic excellence and support composers who have reached a critical point in their career development. The unrestricted portion of the grant may be used for any purpose, such as "buying" compositional time, the acquisition of equipment, travel, and private study. Funds for optional, self-designed community projects enable composers to work outside the conventional new-music orbit for at least 25 days. Residencies in schools and rural areas, with neighborhood organizations or in any other setting where the composer acts as facilitator, and educator are especially encouraged.

McKnight Visiting Composer Program: Each year, this program underwrites a Minnesota residency of two months or longer for two non-Minnesota composers, including $14,000 fellowships. While in residence, the visiting fellow collaborates on a project with Minnesota performing, presenting, and/or community organizations. The program encourages interaction with a variety of audiences, including rural populations and students; the selection process favors projects that promise to have considerable impact on the host community. Applications with detailed descriptions of the proposed residency activities are reviewed by a three-member panel. Visiting composers should complete their projects within one year of receiving the award.

Recording Assistance Program: Through this program, forum members enter into a collaboration with the forum to produce and distribute a compact disc of their work on the Innova Recordings label. The forum makes a low-interest loan (six percent APR) available to composers to record their music.

Welcome Christmas Carol Contest: This annual contest is open to composers of all ages. The theme of the contest changes yearly, but winners always receive a $1,000 prize and the chance to see their carol premiered in the Welcome Christmas concerts.
EIN: 237452688

4688
American Finnish Workers Society
Memorial Educational Trust
c/o Trust Tax Services
P.O. Box 64713
St. Paul, MN   55164-0713   (218) 262-0422

Foundation type: Independent foundation
Purpose: Scholarships and interest-free loans to students of Hibbing, MN, high schools.
Financial data: Year ended 12/31/2012. Assets, $89,171 (M); Expenditures, $4,468; Total giving, $0.
Type of support: Support to graduates or students of specific schools; Undergraduate support.
Application information: Application form required.
  Deadline(s): None
  Additional information: Application form, information and materials available from superintendent of schools, Hibbling, MN.
EIN: 416018271

4689
American Indian Family and Children
Services, Inc.
25 Empire Dr.
St. Paul, MN   55103-1856   (651) 223-8526
FAX: (651) 223-8529; E-mail: staff@aifacs.org;
Toll-free tel.: (866) 568-2892; Additional address (McGregor office): P.O. Box 40, McGregor, MN 55760-0040, tel.: (218) 768-2892, fax: (218) 768-2894; URL: http://www.aifacs.org/

Foundation type: Public charity
Purpose: Foster care is provided for American Indian children primarily in the St. Paul, MN area and northern MN.
Financial data: Year ended 12/31/2011. Assets, $481,463 (M); Expenditures, $1,533,409; Total giving, $979,391; Grants to individuals, totaling $979,391.
Fields of interest: Foster care; Family services; Native Americans/American Indians.
Type of support: Grants for special needs.
Application information: Payments are distributed to various foster parents depending on the number of children they are supporting. Contact the agency for additional guidelines.
EIN: 411740864

4690
Anderson Center for Interdisciplinary
Studies, Inc.
163 Tower View Dr.
P.O. Box 406
Red Wing, MN   55066-1108   (651) 388-2009
FAX: (651) 388-5538;
E-mail: info@andersoncenter.com; URL: http://www.andersoncenter.org

Foundation type: Public charity
Purpose: Short term residencies to artists, writers, scientists and scholars in the U.S. and abroad so that they may work on their indiviudal projects.
Publications: Application guidelines; Annual report.
Financial data: Year ended 06/30/2012. Assets, $4,818,141 (M); Expenditures, $433,842.
Fields of interest: Literature; Arts.
Type of support: Residencies.
Application information: Applications accepted. Application form required. Application form available on the grantmaker's web site.
  Copies of proposal: 5
  Deadline(s): Feb. 1 and Mar. 1
  Final notification: Applicants notified 30 to 45 days after application deadline

Applicants should submit the following:
  1) Resume
  2) SASE
  3) Work samples
  Additional information: See web site for work sample guidelines.
Program descriptions:
Emerging Artists and Writers Fellowship Program: Emerging artists and writers from New York City and Minnesota are eligible for residency-fellowships of two weeks to one month, which includes room, board, workspace, travel expenses, and a weekly stipend.
Residency Program: Awards residencies to artists, writers, and scholars from the United States and abroad, that include meals and lodging at the center. The residencies are for two weeks to one month, during which time resident-fellows are expected to work on a clearly defined project and to make a substantive contribution to the community in the form of talk, class, or performance of their work. No monetary support is given.
EIN: 411792770

4691
Harold C. Anderson Educational Trust
305 Ochre St., W.
Comfrey, MN   56019-0098   (507) 877-3491
Contact: Allen Hoffmann, Tr.

Foundation type: Operating foundation
Purpose: Scholarships to graduates of Comfrey High School, MN, for higher education.
Financial data: Year ended 12/31/2011. Assets, $215,959 (M); Expenditures, $4,279; Total giving, $3,500; Grants to individuals, 7 grants totaling $3,500 (high: $500; low: $500).
Fields of interest: Higher education.
Type of support: Support to graduates or students of specific schools; Undergraduate support.
Application information: Applications accepted. Application form required.
  Initial approach: Letter
  Deadline(s): None
EIN: 416325121

4692
Anodyne Artist Company
825 Carleton St.
Saint Paul, MN   55114-1618   (651) 642-1684
Contact: Mary Pendergast, Exec. Dir.
E-mail: anodyneart@aol.com

Foundation type: Public charity
Purpose: Studio space to handicapped and non-traditional artists residing in the St. Paul, MN area, who specialize in visual and performing arts.
Financial data: Year ended 06/30/2012. Assets, $15,098 (M); Expenditures, $329,130.
Fields of interest: Visual arts; Performing arts; Disabilities, people with.
Type of support: Residencies.
Application information:
  Initial approach: Letter and telephone
  Additional information: Contact foundation for further information.
EIN: 411951094

4693
The Arrowhead Regional Arts Council
1301 Rice Lake Rd., Ste. 111
Duluth, MN 55811-2702 (218) 722-0952
Contact: Robert DeArmond, Exec. Dir.
FAX: (218) 722-4459; E-mail: info@aracouncil.org;
Toll-free tel.: (800) 569-8134; URL: http://
www.aracouncil.org

Foundation type: Public charity
Purpose: Grants to artists in Aitkin, Carlton, Cook, Itasca, Koochiching, Lake and St. Louis counties, MN.
Publications: Application guidelines; Annual report; Biennial report; Financial statement; Grants list; Informational brochure; Newsletter.
Financial data: Year ended 06/30/2012. Assets, $115,402 (M); Expenditures, $745,492; Total giving, $518,990; Grants to individuals, totaling $145,425.
Fields of interest: Arts.
Type of support: Fellowships; Residencies; Travel grants; Project support.
Application information: Applications accepted. Application form required. Application form available on the grantmaker's web site.
Initial approach: Letter, telephone or e-mail
Send request by: Mail or in person
Copies of proposal: 1
Deadline(s): Varies
Final notification: Six to eight weeks
Applicants should submit the following:
1) Budget Information
2) Proposal
3) Resume
4) Work samples
Program descriptions:
McKnight/ARAC Quick Start Opportunity Grants: Grants of up to $500 are available to artists and/or arts organizations that would enable applicants to take advantage of goal-affirming arts activities that come up with little advance notice. Examples of possible quick start opportunities might include, but are not limited to: workshop, performance, or exhibition expenses arising at an untimely moment; fees for opportunities that provide career training in the arts; an immediate need for equipment and/or repair to facilitate an arts-related project; or an unexpected or unanticipated presenting activity. Applicants (whether individuals or organizations) must reside in Aitkin, Cook, Carlton, Itasca, Koochiching, Lake, or St. Louis counties; in addition, organizations must be registered as federally-designated nonprofits within the state of Minnesota, and have 501(c)(3) status or be an accredited school or unit of government.
Small Capital Grants for Individual Artists and Arts Organizations: This program provides up to $1,500 to support nonprofit arts organizations or individual artists in projects and endeavors related to the building, programming, equipment, and/or service needs of artists in the Arrowhead region. Grants are intended to allow organizations and individuals to purchase equipment needed to execute programming and services, make small repairs or alterations to facilities, and/or facilitate the advancement of artistic careers. Grants may be used to: purchase computers, software, and other appropriate office equipment; upgrade computers and software for organizational or artistic purposes; engage in web site development for career or organizational enhancement; purchase specialty equipment directly related to an artistic endeavor; purchase microphones, boom stands, and other sound equipment; upgrade a light board and sound equipment, or purchase lighting gels; purchase a dance floor; purchase art tables and other studio equipment; and make improvements to a

non-profit-owned facility (including addressing accessibility for people with disabilities, repairing windows and insulating a building against the weather, fixing plumbing/heating/electrical wiring in a building, and purchasing lighting and exhibition equipment for a new gallery space). Eligible applicants must be individual artists or arts organizations based in Aitkin, Cook, Carlton, Itasca, Koochiching, Lake, or St. Louis counties. Organizations must also: be legally incorporated and registered as a nonprofit in the state of Minnesota; be a regional arts organization administratively independent of state or national affiliation; and have total verifiable operating cash expenses of no more than $150,000 for each of the two most recently completed fiscal years. Applicants must secure a 10 percent cash match.
EIN: 411358639

4694
Artist Relief Fund
1301 Rice Lake Rd., Ste. 111
Duluth, MN 55811-2702 (218) 722-0952
FAX: (218) 722-4459;
E-mail: info@artistrelieffund.org; Toll-free tel.: (800) 569-8134; E-mail for Erika Mock: erikam@discover-net.net; URL: http://
www.artistrelieffund.org

Foundation type: Public charity
Purpose: Emergency grants of up to $1,500 to artists in northeastern MN and northwestern WI who find themselves, due to unexpected and career-threatening loss of income, in immediate need of financial assistance.
Publications: Application guidelines; Program policy statement.
Fields of interest: Arts, artist's services.
Type of support: Grants for special needs.
Application information: Applications accepted. Application form required. Application form available on the grantmaker's web site.
Initial approach: Application
Send request by: Mail or e-mail
Copies of proposal: 1
Deadline(s): 15th of each month
Final notification: Applicants notified in about one week
Applicants should submit the following:
1) Resume
2) Proposal
3) Financial information
4) Curriculum vitae
5) Budget Information
EIN: 203445751

4695
Royale B. and Eleanor M. Arvig Memorial Scholarship Fund
(formerly Royale B. Arvig Memorial Scholarship Fund)
160 2nd Ave. S.W.
Perham, MN 56573-1409

Foundation type: Independent foundation
Purpose: Scholarships to graduating high school seniors from specific MN school districts for further education at a college, university, vocational-technical school, or other postsecondary educational organization.
Financial data: Year ended 12/31/2012. Assets, $408,789 (M); Expenditures, $51,117; Total giving, $51,000; Grants to individuals, 67 grants totaling $51,000 (high: $1,500, low: $750).
Fields of interest: Vocational education.
Type of support: Undergraduate support.

Application information:
Initial approach: Letter
Additional information: Contact fund for current application deadline/guidelines.
EIN: 411574208

4696
Hobey Baker Memorial Award Foundation
13033 Ridgedale Dr., Ste. 195
Minnetonka, MN 55305 (612) 615-4229
Contact: Jill Wagner, Exec. Dir.
E-mail: 4hobeybaker@gmail.com; URL: http://
www.hobeybaker.com

Foundation type: Public charity
Purpose: Awards to players on each high school team who show exemplary character and sportsmanship. Awards also to full time students attending an accredited NCAA college or university and completed 50 percent or more of the season.
Financial data: Year ended 06/30/2012. Assets, $99,486 (M); Expenditures, $187,483.
Fields of interest: Athletics/sports, winter sports.
Type of support: Awards/prizes.
Application information: Students must demonstrate academic achievement and sportsmanship.
EIN: 411721288

4697
The Bakken
(formerly Bakken Library of Electricity in Life)
3537 Zenith Ave. S.
Minneapolis, MN 55416
Contact: David Rhees, Exec. Dir.
FAX: (612) 927-7265; E-mail: info@thebakken.org;
E-Mail for David Rhees: rhees@thebakken.org;
URL: http://www.thebakken.org

Foundation type: Public charity
Purpose: Research grants and fellowships to individuals for work related to science, technology, medicine, and other related fields.
Financial data: Year ended 12/31/2011. Assets, $9,274,786 (M); Expenditures, $2,210,844; Total giving, $9,013; Grants to individuals, totaling $9,013.
Fields of interest: Medical research; Research; Engineering/technology.
Type of support: Fellowships; Research; Travel grants.
Application information:
Deadline(s): Apr. 19 for Summer Graduate Fellowship; none for Research Travel Grants
Additional information: Application by letter outlining proposed research , including C.V. and two letters of recommendation; See web site for further application information.
Program descriptions:
Research Travel Grants: Provides grants of up to a maximum of $500 (domestic) and $750 (foreign) to be used to help to defray the expenses of travel, subsistence, and other direct costs of conducting research at The Bakken. The minimum period of residence is one week.
Visiting Research Fellowship: These fellowships provide up to a maximum of $1,500 to be used to help to defray the expenses of travel, subsistence, and other direct costs of conducting research at The Bakken. The minimum period of residence is two weeks. Preference is given to researchers who are interested in collaborating for a day or two during their research visit with The Bakken on exhibits or other programs.
EIN: 510175508

4698
Matt Birk's HIKE Foundation, Inc.
574 Prairie Ctr. Dr., No. 287
Eden Prairie, MN 55344-7930
FAX: (859) 360-6087;
E-mail: jeff.ginn@legacymg.net; URL: http://
www.hikefoundation.org

Foundation type: Public charity
Purpose: Scholarships to at-risk Twin Cities
children from elementary school through college
with educational opportunities needed to excel in
the classroom and in life.
Financial data: Year ended 12/31/2011. Assets,
$73,525 (M); Expenditures, $202,229; Total
giving, $134,025.
Fields of interest: Education.
Type of support: Scholarships—to individuals.
Application information: See web site for additional
guidelines.
EIN: 300119375

4699
Blacklock Nature Sanctuary
P.O. Box 426
Moose Lake, MN 55767-0426 (218) 485-0478
Contact: Craig Blacklock
E-mail: craig@blacklockgallery.com; URL: http://
www.blacklocknaturesanctuary.org

Foundation type: Public charity
Purpose: Fellowships and residencies to MN
artists.
Publications: Application guidelines.
Financial data: Year ended 12/31/2011. Assets,
$888,654 (M); Expenditures, $23,029.
Fields of interest: Visual arts; Performing arts;
Literature; Arts; Women.
Type of support: Residencies.
Application information: Applications accepted.
Application form available on the grantmaker's web
site.
  Initial approach: Application
  Deadline(s): Jan. 30
  Applicants should submit the following:
    1) Essay
    2) Resume
  Additional information: Eligible applicants must
    send samples of work. See web site for
    specific application guidelines.
Program descriptions:
  Emerging Artists Fellowships: These fellowships,
  supported by the Jerome Foundation, annually offer
  five two-week opportunities for emerging artists in
  the visual arts (including painting, sculpting,
  printmaking, photography, fiber, media,
  environmental arts, video, or interdisciplinary
  studies), literary arts (including fiction or creative
  non-fiction writing, poetry, playwriting, or
  screenwriting), and performing arts (composition,
  choreography, spoken-word performance, etc.).
  Emerging artists can work alone, in collaboration,
  or with a mentor (defined as an established or
  mid-career artist). Eligible applicants must be
  professional emerging artists who are at least 21
  years of age, not currently enrolled in a B.F.A.
  program, and residents of Minnesota for at least
  one year. Fellowships are accompanied by a
  $1,000 stipend to cover food or supplies.
  *Nadine Blacklock Nature Photography Fellowship
  for Women:* One month-long residency is available
  for a woman nature photograph, with the hope of
  giving recognition to both the resident and al women
  working in the nature photography genre, and
  allowing them access to the subject matter of the
  sanctuary. No stipend is available for the
  fellowship; however, the photographer will have free

use of sanctuary land and studios, as well as
housing and access to property located on Lake
Superior. Eligible applicants must be at least 21
years of age, and not currently enrolled in a B.F.A.
program.
EIN: 411794361

4700
Charles K. Blandin Foundation
(formerly The Blandin Foundation)
100 N. Pokegama Ave.
Grand Rapids, MN 55744-2739 (218)
326-0523
Contact: James Hoolihan, Pres.
FAX: (218) 327-1949;
E-mail: info@blandinfoundation.org; Additional tel.:
(877) 882-2257; URL: http://
www.blandinfoundation.org

Foundation type: Independent foundation
Purpose: Scholarships for undergraduate and
vocational study to recent graduates of high
schools in Itasca County, MN. Candidates must be
under the age of 25 as of Sept. 1 of the effective
school year.
Publications: Financial statement; Informational
brochure (including application guidelines).
Financial data: Year ended 12/31/2012. Assets,
$404,340,951 (M); Expenditures, $19,311,216;
Total giving, $11,594,701; Grants to individuals,
575 grants totaling $814,498 (high: $3,399, low:
$350).
Fields of interest: Vocational education.
Type of support: Support to graduates or students
of specific schools; Technical education support;
Undergraduate support.
Application information: Application form required.
Interview required.
  Initial approach: Telephone
  Deadline(s): May 1
  Applicants should submit the following:
    1) SAR
    2) FAFSA
  Additional information: Application should also
    include a copy of parents' or independent
    students' 1040 income tax form.
Program description:
  Blandin Educational Awards Program: Since
  1956, this program has given over 11,500 awards
  totaling more than $12.9 million which have been
  given to college-bound students from Itasca County
  to attend post-secondary institutions that best
  meet their needs. Awards are based on financial
  need and are for educational expenses for one
  academic year of full-time study at any accredited
  post-high school educational program, except
  graduate or professional school.
EIN: 416038619

4701
Bottemiller Family Foundation
(formerly Homecrest Foundation)
13995 42nd Ave. N.
Plymouth, MN 55446-3826 (218) 640-1428
Contact: Donald L. Bottemiller, Tr.

Foundation type: Company-sponsored foundation
Purpose: One college scholarship to a senior at
Wadena High School in Wadena, MN. Also, college
scholarships to children of employees of
Homecrest Industries.
Publications: Annual report.
Financial data: Year ended 07/31/2013. Assets,
$124,169 (M); Expenditures, $11,640; Total
giving, $11,600; Grants to individuals, 2 grants
totaling $1,000 (high: $500, low: $500).

Type of support: Employee-related scholarships;
Support to graduates or students of specific
schools.
Application information:
  Initial approach: Letter
  Deadline(s): None
  Additional information: Contact foundation for
    eligibility criteria.
Company name: Homecrest Industries, Inc.
EIN: 411550750

4702
**Sister Thea Bowman Black Catholic
Educational Foundation**
4870 Woodridge Dr.
Hermantown, MN 55811 (218) 263-4865
Contact: Mary Lou Jennings, Exec. Dir.
E-mail: marylouj11@aol.com; URL: http://
www.cermusa.francis.edu/
sistertheabowmanfoundation/index.htm

Foundation type: Public charity
Purpose: Scholarships to students who are of
African-American descent for attendance at the
Catholic university of his or her choice.
Financial data: Year ended 06/30/2012. Assets,
$64,405 (M); Expenditures, $107,994; Total
giving, $95,648.
Fields of interest: Higher education; African
Americans/Blacks; Economically disadvantaged.
Type of support: Scholarships—to individuals.
Application information: Applications accepted.
Application form required.
  Additional information: Applicant must
    demonstrate financial need and must show a
    willingness to help others and to give of
    themselves. Contact the foundation for
    additional application information.
Program description:
  Scholarships: Scholarships are designed to
  awaken a hope in Black students who have been
  conditioned by poverty. This awakening comes as
  an opportunity to receive a quality education at one
  of the many Catholic institutions of higher
  education around the country. Scholarship awards
  range from $2,500 to $5,000. These funds are
  available on a year-by-year basis as donations are
  received by the governing board of the foundation.
  Scholarships are available to high school students
  who are transitioning to college. Scholarship
  awards will be applied toward tuition, on-campus
  room and board, and books.
EIN: 030322037

4703
The Bridge for Runaway Youth, Inc.
1111 W. 22nd St.
Minneapolis, MN 55405-2705 (612) 377-8800
Contact: Dan Pfarr, Exec. Dir.
FAX: (612) 377-6426;
E-mail: info@bridgeforyouth.org; E-Mail for Dan
Pfarr: d.pfarr@bridgeforyouth.org; URL: http://
www.bridgeforyouth.org

Foundation type: Public charity
Purpose: Emergency need and support to youth and
their families in crisis with shelter and support in
the Minneapolis, Minnesota area.
Publications: Annual report; Newsletter.
Financial data: Year ended 12/31/2011. Assets,
$7,907,982 (M); Expenditures, $2,981,548; Total
giving, $66,812; Grants to individuals, totaling
$66,812.
Fields of interest: Economically disadvantaged.
Type of support: Grants for special needs.

Application information: Contact the organization for information on assistance.
EIN: 410983062

4704

The Herb Brooks Foundation

1700 105th Ave. N.E.
Blaine, MN   55449-4500   (763) 785-5601
Contact: Skip Peltier, Exec. Dir.
E-mail: speltier@mnsports.org; URL: http://www.herbbrooksfoundation.com

Foundation type: Public charity
Purpose: Scholarships to the most qualified players to attend Minnesota hockey camps who represents the values, characteristics and traits on and off the ice.
Financial data: Year ended 12/31/2011. Assets, $1,131,240 (M); Expenditures, $209,516.
Fields of interest: Camps.
Type of support: Scholarships—to individuals.
Application information: Players must be nominated; forms can be obtained from student school's web site. See foundation web site for additional guidelines.
EIN: 411493766

4705

Bush Foundation

101 5th St. East, Ste. 2400
St. Paul, MN   55101-1898   (651) 227-0891
Contact: Kelly M. Kleppe, Dir., Prog. Opers.
FAX: (651) 297-6485;
E-mail: info@bushfoundation.org; URL: http://www.bushfoundation.org

Foundation type: Independent foundation
Purpose: Fellowships to residents of MN, ND, and SD.
Publications: Annual report; Financial statement; Informational brochure; Occasional report.
Financial data: Year ended 12/31/2012. Assets, $780,000,000 (M); Expenditures, $33,086,000; Total giving, $20,362,449; Grants to individuals, 98 grants totaling $1,566,509 (high: $67,313, low: $500).
Fields of interest: Leadership development.
Type of support: Fellowships.
Application information: Applications accepted. Application form required. Application form available on the grantmaker's web site.
   Initial approach: Letter, telephone, e-mail or web site
   Send request by: Online
   Deadline(s): Varies
   Applicants should submit the following:
      1) Resume
      2) Work samples
      3) Budget Information
      4) Essay
      5) Financial information
      6) GPA
      7) Letter(s) of recommendation
      8) Proposal
   Additional information: Students are ineligible for fellowships. See web site for specific eligibility requirements.
Program description:
   Bush Fellowship Program: The program provides individuals with opportunities to demonstrate and improve their capacity for leadership as they learn by doing. The work of the fellowship is to combine opportunities for personal development with opportunities to effectively engage with others to create positive change within their communities. Funding ranges from $50,000 to $100,000.

Applicant must be a U.S. citizen or permanent resident, 24 years old at the time of the application deadline, must have lived at least one continuous year immediately prior to the application deadline in either MN, ND, SD or one of the 23 sovereign nations that share geography with the states and cannot have previously received a Bush Fellowship, Bush Artist Fellowship, Bush Leadership Fellowship, Bush Medical Fellowship or Enduring Vision Award. See web site for additional information.
EIN: 416017815

4706

The Camargo Foundation

5959 Centerville Rd., Ste. 220
North Oaks, MN   55127
E-mail: apply@camargofoundation.org; URL: http://www.camargofoundation.org

Foundation type: Operating foundation
Purpose: Fellowships to scholars, visual artists, photographers, video artists, filmmakers, media artists, composers and writers to stay at the foundation's study center in Cassis, France.
Financial data: Year ended 12/31/2011. Assets, $18,816,439 (M); Expenditures, $881,583; Total giving, $6,055; Grants to individuals, 11 grants totaling $6,055 (high: $1,000, low: $250).
Fields of interest: Media/communications; Film/video; Visual arts; Photography; Music composition; Literature.
Type of support: Fellowships; Residencies; Stipends.
Application information: Applications accepted. Application form required. Application form available on the grantmaker's web site.
   Deadline(s): Jan. 15
   Applicants should submit the following:
      1) Curriculum vitae
      2) Work samples
      3) Resume
      4) Proposal
      5) Letter(s) of recommendation
   Additional information: Application should also include project description; See web site for further application information.
Program description:
   Residential Grants: The program provides free housing, reference library, darkroom, artist's studio, music composition studio, and a $3,500 stipend. A visa is required for a stay in France of more than three months. Residential grants last from three to four months.
EIN: 132622714

4707

Ben & Verna Carson Scholarship Fund

c/o Frandsen Bank & Trust Co.
100 N. Minnesota St.
New Ulm, MN   56073-1730   (507) 233-4800

Foundation type: Independent foundation
Purpose: Scholarships to graduates or residents of the Gibbon-Fairfax-Winthrop School District, MN pursuing a course of education in teaching.
Financial data: Year ended 12/31/2012. Assets, $185,397 (M); Expenditures, $16,437; Total giving, $14,000.
Fields of interest: Teacher school/education.
Type of support: Support to graduates or students of specific schools.
Application information: Applications accepted. Application form required.
   Deadline(s): Apr. 16
   Applicants should submit the following:

   1) Essay
   2) Transcripts
   Additional information: Application forms are available at the Career Center Office at GFW High School.
EIN: 876257731

4708

Catholic Charities of St. Paul and Minneapolis

1200 2nd Ave. S.
Minneapolis, MN   55403-2513   (651) 204-8500
Contact: Timothy Marx, C.E.O.
FAX: (651) 664-8555;
E-mail: timothy.marx@cctwincities.org; URL: http://www.cctwincities.org

Foundation type: Public charity
Purpose: Emergency assistance to individuals and families in need throughout the Twin Cities, MN area.
Financial data: Year ended 06/30/2011. Assets, $62,655,680 (M); Expenditures, $39,027,794; Total giving, $2,838,505; Grants to individuals, totaling $2,793,005.
Fields of interest: Children; Adults; Economically disadvantaged.
Type of support: Grants for special needs.
Application information:
   Initial approach: Telephone
   Additional information: See web site for additional guidelines.
EIN: 411302487

4709

CentraCare Health Foundation

1406 6th Ave. N.
St. Cloud, MN   56303-1900   (320) 240-2810
Contact: Mark Larkin, Exec. Dir.
FAX: (320) 255-6691;
E-mail: foundation@centracare.com; Toll-free tel.: (800) 835-6652, ext. 52810; E-Mail for Mark Larkin: larkinm@centracare.com; URL: http://www.centracare.com/foundation/

Foundation type: Public charity
Purpose: Awards and scholarships to individuals affiliated with St. Cloud Hospital who are seeking further education.
Publications: Application guidelines.
Financial data: Year ended 06/30/2012. Assets, $43,739,615 (M); Expenditures, $10,073,368; Total giving, $7,810,907; Grants to individuals, totaling $90,773.
Fields of interest: Medical school/education; Nursing school/education; Scholarships/financial aid.
Type of support: Grants to individuals.
Application information:
   Initial approach: Submit application
   Deadline(s): May 13 for St. Cloud Hospital School of Nursing Alumni Scholarship; July 10 for Dr. William Held Scholarships
   Applicants should submit the following:
      1) Letter(s) of recommendation
      2) Essay
      3) Transcripts
Program descriptions:
   Dr. William Held Scholarships: This scholarship is intended to aid students who have successfully completed their first year of the radiologic technology program at the St. Cloud Hospital School of Radiologic Technology. One student each year is awarded a $500 scholarship. Eligible applicants must: be enrolled full-time, in good academic standing, and completing their first year

in the St. Cloud Hospital School of Radiologic Technology Program; and plan to continue a second year there as a full-time student.

Spirit of Caring Award: This award recognizes collaborative efforts to improve people's health through education, intervention, or service. The award carries with it a $5,000 prize.

St. Cloud Hospital School of Nursing Alumni Scholarship: These scholarships support nursing education and recruitment of viable candidates into the profession through financial assistance. Eligible applicants include graduates of St. Cloud Hospital School of Nursing who are seeking to further their education or earn a specialty degree within the field of nursing, and family members (children and/or grandchildren) of St. Cloud Hospital School of Nursing Alumni. Eligible applicants must be enrolled in an undergraduate or technical program in the nursing field, maintain a GPA of at least 3.0, and demonstrate involvement in alumni association, community, and/or school activities. Applications will be accepted regardless of geographic location or residence.
EIN: 411855173

4710
Central Minnesota Arts Board

220 4th Ave. N.
P.O. Box 458
Foley, MN 56329-8441 (320) 968-4290
Contact: Leslie LeCuyer, Exec. Dir.
FAX: (320) 968-4291;
E-mail: media@centralmnartsboard.org; Toll-free tel.: (866)-345-7140; E-Mail for Leslie LeCuyer: director@centralmnartsboard.org; URL: http://www.centralmnartsboard.org

Foundation type: Public charity
Purpose: Awards to outstanding individual artists residing in Benton, Sherburne, Stearns and Wright counties, MN, as well as scholarships to graduating high school seniors in the region for those who want to further their education in the arts.
Publications: Application guidelines; Newsletter.
Financial data: Year ended 06/30/2013. Assets, $507,054 (M); Expenditures, $858,297; Total giving, $645,152; Grants to individuals, totaling $94,988.
Fields of interest: Arts education; Visual arts; Performing arts; Music; Performing arts, education; Literature.
Type of support: Scholarships—to individuals; Awards/prizes.
Application information: Applications accepted. Application form required. Application form available on the grantmaker's web site.
  Initial approach: Letter or telephone
  Send request by: Mail
  Copies of proposal: 8
  Deadline(s): Mar
  Applicants should submit the following:
    1) Transcripts
    2) SASE
    3) Work samples
  Additional information: Applications must include an artist statement. Letter(s) of recommendation required for high school scholarships.
Program descriptions:
  Individual Artist Awards: These awards are intended to recognize, reward, and encourage outstanding individual artists in central Minnesota. Up to four awards ranging of $3,000 each will be awarded annually to talented area artists. Awards may be used any way the artist wishes.
  Project Grants: These grants are a funding vehicle for any board-approved art activity

sponsored by a tax-exempt organization or educational institution in Benton, Sherburne, Stearns, or Wright counties. The purpose of the grant is to advance the artistic development of the applicant organization, audience, and the artists involved in the project; to explore new ways of providing collaborative and participatory artistic activities; to further arts education; to allow a regional organization to host artists and arts activities not provided by the hosting organization; and to provide and enrich after-school and summer arts educational programming. Matching grants of up to $4,500 with a 30 percent match for any one project or not more than $4,500 in any one grant round for arts focused activities.
  Scholarships: These are designed to help graduating high school seniors who want to further their education in the areas of music, dance, literature, visual arts, and performance art. These are one-time, monetary awards, and the amounts awarded will be determined each year based on the board's determination of the overall quality of the applicant pool. The typical range has been $1,000 to $2,000 each.
EIN: 411349992

4711
Central Minnesota Community Foundation

101 S. 7th Ave., Ste. 100
Saint Cloud, MN 56301 (320) 253-4380
Contact: Steven R. Joul, Pres.; For grants: Susan Lorenz, Dir., Community Progs.
FAX: (320) 240-9215;
E-mail: info@communitygiving.org; URL: http://www.communitygiving.org

Foundation type: Community foundation
Purpose: Scholarships primarily to individuals residing in the St. Cloud, MN, area for undergraduate education at U.S. colleges and universities.
Publications: Application guidelines; Annual report; Informational brochure; Newsletter.
Financial data: Year ended 06/30/2012. Assets, $74,790,077 (M); Expenditures, $5,437,648; Total giving, $3,937,494; Grants to individuals, 55 grants totaling $164,106.
Fields of interest: Higher education.
Type of support: Undergraduate support.
Application information: Applications accepted. Application form required. Application form available on the grantmaker's web site.
  Send request by: Online
  Deadline(s): Varies
  Applicants should submit the following:
    1) Transcripts
    2) SAT
    3) Letter(s) of recommendation
    4) GPA
    5) Financial information
    6) Essay
    7) ACT
  Additional information: Application eligibility and guidelines vary with each scholarship. See web site for additional information.
EIN: 363412544

4712
Child Care Choices, Inc.

2901 Clearwater Rd.
St. Cloud, MN 56301-5950 (320) 251-5081
FAX: (320) 654-8650;
E-mail: providercare@childcarechoices.net;
URL: http://www.childcarechoices.net/

Foundation type: Public charity
Purpose: Supports MN child care providers by offering them the opportunity to apply for funding to help with supplies and equipment, training and professional development, and start up assistance.
Financial data: Year ended 09/30/2011. Assets, $922,164 (M); Expenditures, $7,209,776; Total giving, $5,999,482; Grants to individuals, totaling $5,999,482.
Fields of interest: Early childhood education; Day care.
Type of support: Grants to individuals.
Application information: Applications accepted. Application form required.
  Initial approach: Tel.
  Additional information: Grant funds are limited and are awarded on a competitive basis to qualified child care providers and programs. Grants recipients are required to complete additional trainings based on the amount awarded. For providers in Benton, Sherburne, Stearns, and Wright Counties, call Tina at 800-292-5437.
EIN: 411321820

4713
Stanley & Marvel Chong Foundation

c/o John M. Ratelle
6804 Brittany Rd.
Edina, MN 55435

Foundation type: Independent foundation
Purpose: Scholarships to individuals for higher education in MN and OR.
Financial data: Year ended 12/31/2012. Assets, $1,651,155 (M); Expenditures, $110,626; Total giving, $78,305.
Type of support: Scholarships—to individuals.
Application information: Unsolicited requests for funds not considered or acknowledged.
EIN: 363411371

4714
Christian Fellowship Foundation of the Peace United Church of Christ

1503 2nd Ave., N.E.
Rochester, MN 55906

Foundation type: Independent foundation
Purpose: Scholarships to students of MN, enrolled in an accredited, degree-granting high school or undergraduate college or vocational program.
Financial data: Year ended 12/31/2011. Assets, $330,331 (M); Expenditures, $45,336; Total giving, $35,000.
Fields of interest: Theological school/education; Social work school/education; Health sciences school/education.
Type of support: Scholarships—to individuals.
Application information: Application form required.
  Deadline(s): Mar. 15
  Final notification: Recipients notified by May
  Applicants should submit the following:
    1) Transcripts
    2) Financial information
  Additional information: Recipients must provide the committee with the full name and address of the postsecondary institution he or she will be attending. Payment is made directly to the educational institution on behalf of the student.
EIN: 410694748

4715
CHS Foundation
5500 Cenex Dr.
Inver Grove Heights, MN   55077-1733   (800) 814-0506
Contact: William J. Nelson, Pres.
Contact for scholarships: Jennifer Thatcher, Mgr., tel.: (800) 814-0506 ext. 3
FAX: (651) 355-5073;
E-mail: info@chsfoundation.org; URL: http://www.chsfoundation.org

Foundation type: Company-sponsored foundation
Purpose: Scholarships to graduating high school seniors to study agriculture at a two or four-year college. Scholarships to first-year agricultural students attending two-year colleges.
Publications: Application guidelines; Informational brochure; Program policy statement.
Financial data: Year ended 12/31/2012. Assets, $33,914,988 (M); Expenditures, $3,284,739; Total giving, $2,722,357.
Fields of interest: Higher education; Public education.
Type of support: Scholarships—to individuals.
Application information: Applications accepted. Application form required. Application form available on the grantmaker's web site.
Send request by: Online
Deadline(s): Apr. 1
Applicants should submit the following:
1) Transcripts
2) GPA
3) Essay
Program descriptions:
High School Scholarship Program: The foundation awards 50 $1,000 scholarships to graduating high school students entering into an agricultural field of study at a two or four-year college. Applicant must U.S. citizen or permanent resident.
Two-Year Scholarship Program: The foundation annually awards 25 $1,000 college scholarships to first-year college students at two-year institutions studying an agricultural-related major. Student must be a U.S. citizen or permanent resident.
EIN: 416025858

4716
Clearway Minnesota
2 Appletree Sq., Ste. 400
8011 34th Ave. S.
Minneapolis, MN   55425-1883   (952) 767-1400
Contact: David J. Willoughby M.A., C.E.O.
FAX: (952) 767-1422; Toll-free tel.: (866) 243-2337; URL: http://www.clearwaymn.org

Foundation type: Public charity
Purpose: Research funds to reduce exposure to secondhand smoke and disparities in exposure to secondhand smoke across defined populations and locations in Minnesota.
Publications: Application guidelines; Annual report; Newsletter.
Financial data: Year ended 06/30/2012. Assets, $101,658,125 (M); Expenditures, $14,453,633; Total giving, $5,080,368; Grants to individuals, totaling $54,603.
Fields of interest: Smoking.
Type of support: Research.
Application information:
Initial approach: Tel.
Deadline(s): Feb. 10 for letter of intent, Mar. 26 for application
Additional information: Call Megan Whittet at 952-767-1415 for eligibility criteria.
EIN: 411921094

4717
Columbia Heights High School Alumni Scholarship Foundation
4111 Central Ave. N.E., Ste. 206S
Columbia Heights, MN   55421-2953   (651) 788-1605
Contact: Vernon Hoium, Pres.

Foundation type: Independent foundation
Purpose: Scholarships to students from Columbia Heights High School, MN, for study at an accredited college or university.
Financial data: Year ended 06/30/2013. Assets, $346,476 (M); Expenditures, $40,730; Total giving, $30,000; Grants to individuals, 4 grants totaling $30,000 (high: $7,500, low: $7,500).
Fields of interest: Higher education.
Type of support: Support to graduates or students of specific schools.
Application information: Applications accepted. Application form required.
Deadline(s): Feb. 1
Additional information: Applications available from the high school counseling office.
EIN: 411890675

4718
Community Action of Minneapolis
505 E. Grant St., Ste. 100
Minneapolis, MN   55404-1411   (612) 348-8858
Contact: William J. Davis, Pres. and C.E.O.
FAX: (612) 348-9384; URL: http://www.campls.org

Foundation type: Public charity
Purpose: Assistance to low-income residents of Minneapolis, MN, in areas of weatherization, energy assistance, self-sufficiency, food and clothing.
Financial data: Year ended 06/30/2012. Assets, $2,749,827 (M); Expenditures, $10,716,946; Total giving, $3,374,554; Grants to individuals, totaling $3,374,554.
Fields of interest: Human services, emergency aid.
Type of support: Grants for special needs.
Application information: Application form required.
Initial approach: Telephone
Additional information: Application must include copy of most recent heating and electric bill, and income documentation.
EIN: 411739467

4719
Community Action Partnership of Ramsey and Washington Counties
450 Syndicate St., N.
St. Paul, MN   55104-4107   (651) 645-6445
FAX: (651) 645-2253; URL: http://www.caprw.org

Foundation type: Public charity
Purpose: Assistance to low-income families who are residents of Ramsey and Washington counties, MN, with housing, utilities, food, transportation and other assistance.
Publications: Newsletter.
Financial data: Year ended 09/30/2011. Assets, $9,598,777 (M); Expenditures, $25,307,360; Total giving, $1,059,925; Grants to individuals, totaling $992,657.
Fields of interest: Economically disadvantaged.
Type of support: Grants for special needs.
Application information: Applications accepted.
Additional information: Contact the agency for eligibility determination. Some assistance require an application.
EIN: 410883443

4720
Concordia College Corporation
901 S. 8th St.
Moorhead, MN   56562-0001   (218) 299-4206
URL: http://www.concordiacollege.edu/directories/offices-services/vocation-church-leadership/college-corporation/

Foundation type: Public charity
Purpose: Scholarships and grants to qualified students of Concordia College, MN to help with tuition costs.
Financial data: Year ended 04/30/2012. Assets, $285,976,307 (M); Expenditures, $115,284,827; Total giving, $32,839,081; Grants to individuals, 2,578 grants totaling $32,839,081.
Fields of interest: Higher education; College.
Type of support: Scholarships—to individuals.
Application information: Applications accepted. Application form required.
Additional information: Selection is based on academic achievement, financial need and other standards. See web site for additional guidelines.
EIN: 410693977

4721
Cornucopia Art Center, Inc.
103 Parkway Ave. N.
P.O. Box 152
Lanesboro, MN   55949-9796   (507) 467-2446
E-mail: info@lanesboroarts.org; E-Mail for John Davis : executive@lanesboroarts.org; URL: http://www.lanesboroarts.org

Foundation type: Public charity
Purpose: Residencies to emerging artists, primarily in the disciplines of sculpture, painting, poetry, and writing.
Publications: Application guidelines; Annual report.
Financial data: Year ended 12/31/2011. Assets, $364,804 (M); Expenditures, $248,717; Total giving, $400.
Fields of interest: Sculpture; Painting; Literature.
Type of support: Residencies.
Application information: Application form required.
Initial approach: E-mail
Deadline(s): June 30
Applicants should submit the following:
1) SASE
2) Work samples
3) Proposal
Additional information: Application must also include references and artist statement.
Program description:
Lanesboro Residency Program: Offers four 4-week residencies to emerging artists each year. Artists from all disciplines are encouraged to apply, though primary consideration will be given to emerging sculptors, painters, poets, and writers (please note: applicants must reside in the USA). Housing, studio space and stipend are provided. Artists will further their work while spending a minimum of 6 to 8 hours per week working in the community to promote and expand opportunities for learning, enrichment, and meaning in the lives of people within the community.
EIN: 411731338

4722
James M. Cox Foundation
c/o Trust Tax Svcs.
P.O. Box 64713
St. Paul, MN 55164-0713 (402) 488-1951
Contact: Norman A. Otto, Pres.
Application address: 1500 Kingston Rd., Lincoln, NE
68506, tel.: (402) 488-1951

Foundation type: Company-sponsored foundation
Purpose: Scholarships by nomination only to
residents of the eastern-most third of NE.
Publications: Application guidelines.
Financial data: Year ended 12/31/2012. Assets,
$2,099,880 (M); Expenditures, $181,786; Total
giving, $143,500.
Type of support: Awards/grants by nomination only;
Undergraduate support.
Application information: Applications accepted.
Application form not required.
  Initial approach: Letter
  Send request by: Mail
  Copies of proposal: 1
  Deadline(s): Apr. 15
  Final notification: Response to application is May
  Applicants should submit the following:
    1) FAFSA
    2) Letter(s) of recommendation
  Additional information: Contact foundation for
    current application guidelines.
EIN: 470719195

4723
Frances Bane Crockett and H. Paul Crockett Scholarship Trust
(formerly Frances Crockett Trust)
5224 17th Ave. S.
Minneapolis, MN 55417
Application address: c/o West Hancock High
School, Attn.: Principal's Office, 420 9th Ave. S.W.,
Britt, IA 50423-1157

Foundation type: Independent foundation
Purpose: Scholarships to graduating seniors of the
Britt school system, IA.
Financial data: Year ended 12/31/2012. Assets,
$309,423 (M); Expenditures, $16,100; Total
giving, $15,000; Grants to individuals, 10 grants
totaling $15,000 (high: $1,500, low: $1,500).
Fields of interest: Higher education.
Type of support: Scholarships—to individuals;
Support to graduates or students of specific
schools.
Application information: Application form required.
  Deadline(s): Prior to school ending
  Additional information: Application can be
    obtained from high school principals office;
    Recommendations per school principal.
EIN: 416446873

4724
Crosslake Ideal Scholarship Fund Inc.
P.O. Box 725
Crosslake, MN 56442-0725
Contact: Rita Ewert

Foundation type: Operating foundation
Purpose: Scholarships to graduating students from
Crosslake and Ideal Corners, MN area high schools.
Financial data: Year ended 03/31/2013. Assets,
$160,460 (M); Expenditures, $4,329; Total giving,
$4,300; Grants to individuals, 7 grants totaling
$4,300 (high: $700, low: $500).
Fields of interest: Vocational education,
post-secondary; Higher education; Business
school/education.

Type of support: Scholarships—to individuals;
Support to graduates or students of specific
schools.
Application information: Applications accepted.
Application form required.
  Initial approach: Application
  Deadline(s): 10 days prior to commencement
    "award night"
  Applicants should submit the following:
    1) GPA
    2) Financial information
Program description:
  Scholarship Program: Scholarships range from
  $500 to $1,500 to Crosslake and Ideal Corners
  students graduating from area high schools.
  Mission Townships students graduating from
  Pequot Lakes High School or Pine River-Backus
  High School may also apply for these scholarships.
  Applicant must demonstrate financial need,
  involvement in school and community activities,
  determination to succeed in one's chosen field,
  strong leadership and good sound citizenship.
  Applicant must apply for College, Vo-Tech or
  Business College as a full-time student.
EIN: 411636618

4725
Daggett Scholarship Fund, Inc.
P.O. Box 158
Frazee, MN 56544-0158

Foundation type: Independent foundation
Purpose: Undergraduate scholarships to high
school seniors of MN.
Financial data: Year ended 08/31/2010. Assets,
$207,949 (M); Expenditures, $11,845; Total
giving, $10,500; Grants to individuals, 7 grants
totaling $10,500 (high: $1,500, low: $1,500).
Type of support: Undergraduate support.
Application information: Applications not
accepted.
  Additional information: Contributes only to
    pre-selected individuals. Unsolicited
    applications not accepted.
EIN: 410901977

4726
Greater Denfeld Foundation, Inc.
c/o Trust Tax Svcs.
P.O. Box 64713
St. Paul, MN 55164-0713 (218) 723-2894

Foundation type: Public charity
Purpose: Scholarships to graduates of Denfeld High
School, MN, for higher education.
Financial data: Year ended 04/30/2011. Assets,
$5,757,269 (M); Expenditures, $243,007; Total
giving, $204,850; Grants to individuals, totaling
$204,850.
Type of support: Support to graduates or students
of specific schools; Undergraduate support.
Application information: Applications accepted.
Application form required.
  Deadline(s): Jan. 6
  Additional information: Application forms
    available through high school counselors.
EIN: 237182610

4727
Laurel Dietrick-Parks Foundation
528 Marshall Ave.
St. Paul, MN 55102-1721
Contact: David D. Jones, Treas.

Foundation type: Independent foundation

Purpose: Scholarships for high school graduates
and/or post-high school students from low-income
households in the MN area.
Financial data: Year ended 12/31/2012. Assets,
$228,825 (M); Expenditures, $51,308; Total
giving, $51,277.
Fields of interest: Higher education.
Type of support: Scholarships—to individuals.
Application information: Applications accepted.
  Initial approach: Letter
  Deadline(s): Ongoing
EIN: 411722426

4728
Dolan Media Foundation
222 S. 9th St., Ste. 2300
Minneapolis, MN 55402-3363
Contact: Scott J. Pollei, Dir.

Foundation type: Company-sponsored foundation
Purpose: Emergency assistance to individuals in
the MN area, who are victims of domestic abuse,
tornado damage and home foreclosure.
Financial data: Year ended 12/31/2012. Assets,
$11,191 (M); Expenditures, $1,745; Total giving,
$1,720; Grant to an individual, 1 grant totaling
$1,720.
Fields of interest: Domestic violence; Safety/
disasters; Human services.
Type of support: Emergency funds.
Application information: Applications accepted.
  Initial approach: Letter
  Deadline(s): None
EIN: 204000022

4729
Duluth Superior Area Community Foundation
Zeitgeist Arts Building
222 E. Superior St., Ste. 302
Duluth, MN 55802 (218) 726-0232
Contact: Holly C. Sampson, Pres.; For scholarships:
David Hammer, Scholarship Off.
Scholarship application e-mail:
dhammer@dsacommunityfoundation.com
FAX: (218) 726-0257;
E-mail: info@dsacommunityfoundation.com; Grant
application e-mail:
grantsinfo@dsacommunityfoundation.com;
URL: http://www.dsacommunityfoundation.com

Foundation type: Community foundation
Purpose: Scholarships to residents of Douglas and
Bayfield counties, WI, and Koochiching, Itasca, St.
Louis, Lake, Cook, Carlton, and Aitkin counties in
northeastern MN, for attendance at colleges or
technical schools.
Publications: Application guidelines; Annual report;
Grants list; Informational brochure (including
application guidelines); Newsletter.
Financial data: Year ended 12/31/2012. Assets,
$53,678,765 (M); Expenditures, $2,900,014;
Total giving, $1,860,658; Grants to individuals,
138 grants totaling $261,012.
Fields of interest: Vocational education,
post-secondary; Higher education.
Type of support: Scholarships—to individuals;
Support to graduates or students of specific
schools; Technical education support;
Undergraduate support.
Application information: Applications accepted.
Application form required. Application form
available on the grantmaker's web site. Interview
required.

Additional information: See web site for complete listing of scholarship funds, application forms and guidelines.

Program description:

Scholarships: The foundation administers over 50 scholarship funds to help high school students living in Northeastern Minnesota and Northwestern Wisconsin pursue their educational goals. While most scholarships are open to students pursuing a degree in any subject, some scholarships are for students pursuing a degree in a specific subject area such as arts, law enforcement or education. There are a few scholarships for vocational training schools. Each scholarship has unique eligibility requirements and application guidelines. See web site for additional information.

EIN: 411429402

4730

ECMC Foundation

(formerly ECMC Group Holdings Foundation)
1 Imation Pl., Bldg. 2
Oakdale, MN   55128-3422   (651) 221-0566
Contact: March Kessler, Exec. Dir.
FAX: (651) 325-3065;
E-mail: info@ecmcfoundation.org; URL: http://www.ecmcfoundation.org

Foundation type: Public charity
Purpose: Scholarships for low-income, first-generation college bound students of OR, VA and CT pursuing higher education.
Financial data: Year ended 12/31/2011. Assets, $47,897,705 (M); Expenditures, $64,184,404; Total giving, $62,984,750; Grants to individuals, totaling $699,750.
Fields of interest: Higher education.
Type of support: Scholarships—to individuals.
Application information: Students at designated, underserved schools are chosen to participate in the program. Contact the foundation for additional guidelines.

Program description:

ECMC Scholars Program: This program provides a rigorous two-year mentoring program for high school juniors and seniors at select schools in Connecticut, Oregon, and Virginia, with the goal of providing them with scholarships for college. Each student is chosen to participate in the program by their potential, not necessarily the best test scores or grades. The program gives students extra support during their junior and senior years, and pairs students with mentors who help them build strong study and social skills. Successful scholars will be awarded $4,000 for their first year of college, and $2,000 for their second year of college.
EIN: 411990628

4731

Ecolab Foundation

(also known as Ecolab Industry Foundation)
370 Wabasha St. N.
St. Paul, MN   55102-1323   (651) 225-3427
Contact: Kris J. Taylor, V.P.
FAX: (651) 225-3193;
E-mail: ecolabfoundation@ecolab.com; Additional tel.: (651) 293-2259; URL: http://www.ecolab.com/our-story/our-company/community-involvement

Foundation type: Company-sponsored foundation
Purpose: Grants to teachers for the enhancement of their curriculum by providing more exciting, challenging or accessible ways to learn.
Publications: Application guidelines.

Financial data: Year ended 12/31/2012. Assets, $11,538,974 (M); Expenditures, $5,094,052; Total giving, $4,764,127. Grants to individuals amount not specified.
Fields of interest: Education.
Type of support: Grants to individuals.
Application information: Applications accepted. Application form required.
Initial approach: E-mail
Deadline(s): Spring
Additional information: This program is only available in 13 communities across the nation, where Ecolab employees live.

Program description:

Visions for Learning: Through the Visions for Learning program, the foundation awards grants of up to $3,000 to teachers to enhance their curriculum by providing more exciting, challenging, and accessible ways to learn. The program is designed to increase understanding of academic content, raise student achievement, and emphasize the connection between school and life.
EIN: 411372157

4732

Ecotrust Foundation

c/o Peter Vaughan
1976 Sheridan Ave. S.
Minneapolis, MN   55405-2211

Foundation type: Independent foundation
Purpose: Fellowships by nomination only to individuals whose activities demonstrate durable qualities of leadership to improve the social, economic, political and environmental conditions in their homelands.
Financial data: Year ended 12/31/2012. Assets, $1,606,233 (M); Expenditures, $253,318; Total giving, $252,800.
Fields of interest: Environment, land resources; Environment; Native Americans/American Indians.
Type of support: Fellowships; Awards/grants by nomination only; Awards/prizes.
Application information:
Deadline(s): Sept. 31
EIN: 411735062

4733

Ely-Winton Hospital Scholarship Trust

c/o Trust Tax Serivces
P.O. Box 64713
Saint Paul, MN   55164-0713   (218) 365-6166
Contact: Terrence Merfeld
Application address: c/o Supt. of Schools, ISD No. 694, 601 Harvey St., Ely, MN 55731

Foundation type: Independent foundation
Purpose: Scholarships to graduates of Ely High School, MN, pursuing medical-related fields of study.
Financial data: Year ended 07/31/2013. Assets, $409,599 (M); Expenditures, $25,576; Total giving, $19,000; Grants to individuals, 9 grants totaling $19,000 (high: $3,500; low: $1,500).
Fields of interest: Medical school/education; Public health school/education; Health sciences school/education.
Type of support: Support to graduates or students of specific schools; Undergraduate support.
Application information: Applications accepted. Application form required.
Deadline(s): Oct. 31
EIN: 416045814

4734

Engen Seminary Student Scholarship Assistance Trust

c/o Trust Tax Services
P.O. Box 64713
St. Paul, MN   55164-0713   (605) 895-2670
Contact: Lori Hope, Dir.
Application address: P.O. Box 400, Presho, SD 57568-0400, tel.: (605) 895-2670

Foundation type: Independent foundation
Purpose: Scholarships for seniors and alumni to attend any accredited postsecondary institution. Preference is given to members of Kennebec Lutheran Church, Kennebec Community, Lyman City Parish and Lyman High School, SD.
Financial data: Year ended 12/31/2012. Assets, $1,661,678 (M); Expenditures, $124,962; Total giving, $81,182.
Fields of interest: Higher education.
Type of support: Scholarships—to individuals.
Application information: Applications accepted. Application form required.
Deadline(s): Last day of Apr. for seniors; June 15 for alumni
EIN: 460343956

4735

Catherine Ernst Memorial Educational Trust Fund

1815 9th Ave. SE
St. Cloud, MN   56304   (320) 252-7839
Contact: Charles Ernst, Tr.

Foundation type: Independent foundation
Purpose: Scholarships only to descendants of Catherine Ernst.
Financial data: Year ended 12/31/2011. Assets, $1,054,649 (M); Expenditures, $55,451; Total giving, $52,750; Grants to individuals, 19 grants totaling $52,750 (high: $5,000; low: $500).
Type of support: Scholarships—to individuals.
Application information: Applications accepted. Application form required.
Initial approach: Letter or telephone
Deadline(s): Aug. 31
EIN: 416307139

4736

Family Housing Fund

Midwest Plaza W., Ste. 1825
801 Nicollet Mall
Minneapolis, MN   55402-2530   (612) 375-9644
Contact: Thomas P. Fulton, Pres.
FAX: (612) 375-9648; E-mail: miko@fhfund.org;
URL: http://www.fhfund.org/

Foundation type: Public charity
Purpose: Grants and loans to assist in providing affordable housing for low and moderate income individuals and families in the seven county area of Minneapolis and St. Paul, MN.
Publications: Annual report.
Financial data: Year ended 12/31/2011. Assets, $72,156,907 (M); Expenditures, $10,554,586; Total giving, $4,979,997; Grants to individuals, totaling $5,000.
Fields of interest: Housing/shelter, home owners.
Type of support: Grants to individuals; Loans—to individuals.
Application information: Applications accepted.
Additional information: Only projects developed or approved by the cities of the seven county area of Minneapolis and St. Paul are supported.
EIN: 411380923

4737
Farmers Union Marketing & Processing Foundation
P.O. Box 319
Redwood Falls, MN 56283-0319
Contact: Dwight Bassingthwaite, Pres.

Foundation type: Company-sponsored foundation
Purpose: Scholarships to Farmers Union members and their children to pursue higher education in the field of agricultural production and management. Scholarships to children of employees of FUMPA for higher education.
Publications: Annual report; Informational brochure.
Financial data: Year ended 06/30/2013. Assets, $2,726,717 (M); Expenditures, $406,470; Total giving, $308,172; Grants to individuals, 5 grants totaling $8,000 (high: $1,500, low: $1,000).
Fields of interest: Higher education; Management/technical assistance; Agriculture.
Type of support: Employee-related scholarships.
Application information: Applications not accepted.
  Additional information: Unsolicited requests for funds not considered or acknowledged.
Program descriptions:
  David Morman Scholarship: The foundation annually awards scholarships to children of FUMPA employees to attend an accredited two or four year college, university, or technical program for any field of study. FUMPA is an association made up of five companies including Central Bi-Products, Northland Choice, Midwest Grease, and Pet Care Systems.
  FUMP Stanley Moore Scholarship: The foundation awards $1,000 scholarships to Farmers Union members and their children who plan to pursue agricultural study at an institute of higher education. Recipients are selected based on academic record, social and community involvement, personal/professional goals, and applicants involvement with the Farmers Union.
Company name: Farmers Union Marketing & Processing Association
EIN: 311634460

4738
The Five Wings Arts Council
121 4th St. NE
P.O. Box 118
Staples, MN 56479-2398 (218) 895-5660
Contact: Mark Turner, Exec. Dir.
FAX: (218) 895-5660; E-mail: mark.fwac@arvig.net;
Toll-free tel.: (877) 654-2166; URL: http://www.fwac.org

Foundation type: Public charity
Purpose: Grants to individual artists working in visual, literary, or performing arts for short term opportunities. Scholarships to area high school students in grades 9 through 12 who demonstrate high motivation to work in the arts.
Publications: Newsletter.
Financial data: Year ended 06/30/2012. Assets, $187,583 (M); Expenditures, $477,614; Total giving, $354,120; Grants to individuals, totaling $43,195.
Fields of interest: Visual arts; Performing arts; Dance; Theater.
Type of support: Grants to individuals; Scholarships—to individuals.
Application information: Applications accepted. Application form required. Interview required.
  Deadline(s): Jan. 15, May 15 and Sept. 15 for Individual Artist; Ongoing for Scholarship
  Additional information: Scholarship application must include letter of recommendation and writing samples if literary artist. Individual artist application must include work samples, photos, electronic images, videos, recordings and other sample work. See web site for additional application guidelines.
Program descriptions:
  Individual Artist Grant: Grants up to $1,000 are available for apprentices who are still learning the basics but serious in their pursuit of a particular arts discipline. Artisan artists are emerging artists who will benefit from a project that will take them to the next level as a working artist. They may apply for up to $2,000. Master artists may be nominated by anyone (other than themselves) and, if chosen by a review board, will receive a cash stipend of $5,000 and other benefits. Artists who at least 18 years of age working in the visual, literary, or performing arts, and who are requesting support for short-term opportunities (not routine work in progress) are eligible to apply if they are residents of Cass, Crow Wing, Todd, Morrison or Wadena counties.
  Student Artist Mentor Grants: Scholarships are awarded to rural high school students of Todd, Morrison, Wadena, Cass and Crow Wing counties in grades 9 to 12 who demonstrate high motivation to work in the arts. The program serves to supplement the arts education in the region's schools by providing the opportunity to study a chosen art field with a regional practicing artist.
EIN: 411994039

4739
Harry Foley Scholarship Foundation
P.O. Box 418
Winnebago, MN 56098-0418 (507) 526-3201
Contact: Allen Cue, Tr.
Application address: Blue Earth Area Schools, 1125 N. Grove St., Blue Earth, MN 56013, tel.: (507) 526-3201

Foundation type: Operating foundation
Purpose: Scholarships to resident students of the Winnebago School District, MN.
Financial data: Year ended 12/31/2012. Assets, $182,834 (M); Expenditures, $4,792; Total giving, $3,856; Grants to individuals, 12 grants totaling $3,856 (high: $536, low: $170).
Type of support: Support to graduates or students of specific schools; Undergraduate support.
Application information: Application form required.
  Deadline(s): Apr. 1
  Additional information: Application must include all relevant data to allow trustees to establish financial need.
EIN: 411499816

4740
Forecast Public Artworks
2300 Myrtle Ave.,Ste. 160
Saint Paul, MN 55114-1843 (651) 641-1128
Contact: Jack Becker, Exec. Dir. and Prin.
FAX: (651) 641-1983;
E-mail: info@forecastpublicart.org; Toll-free tel.: (800) 627-3529; e-mail for Jack Becker: jack@forecastpublicart.org; URL: http://forecastpublicart.org/

Foundation type: Public charity
Purpose: Grants to MN artists for the development and production of public art.
Publications: Application guidelines; Informational brochure; Informational brochure (including application guidelines); Newsletter; Program policy statement (including application guidelines).
Financial data: Year ended 12/31/2011. Assets, $632,672 (M); Expenditures, $671,845; Total giving, $62,996; Grants to individuals, totaling $62,996.
Fields of interest: Arts, artist's services; Arts.
Type of support: Research; Grants to individuals; Project support.
Application information: Applications accepted. Application form required. Application form available on the grantmaker's web site.
  Initial approach: Telephone
  Send request by: Mail or e-mail
  Copies of proposal: 5
  Deadline(s): Nov. 15
  Final notification: Recipients notified in three months
  Applicants should submit the following:
    1) Budget Information
    2) Curriculum vitae
    3) Essay
    4) Proposal
    5) Resume
    6) Work samples
Program description:
  Public Art Annual Grant Program: Grants are awarded to emerging Minnesota artists in all disciplines and are available in three categories: Research and Development Stipends ($2,000), Public Projects (up to $7,000) and University Avenue Commissions (varies). Stipends fund development and design of public art installations and activities. Public Projects grants fund production costs and artist fees for publicly-accessible temporary or permanent works in Minnesota.
EIN: 411361351

4741
Foundation for Anesthesia Education and Research
200 1st St. S.W., WF6-674
Rochester, MN 55905-0002 (507) 266-6866
Contact: Denham S. Ward, Pres. and C.E.O.
FAX: (507) 284-0291; URL: http://www.faer.org

Foundation type: Public charity
Purpose: Grants to individuals for clinical research related to anesthesia care and perioperative medicine.
Publications: Annual report; Newsletter.
Financial data: Year ended 12/31/2011. Assets, $20,225,969 (M); Expenditures, $2,788,443; Total giving, $1,889,793. Grants to individuals amount not specified.
Fields of interest: Anesthesiology research.
Type of support: Research; Postdoctoral support.
Application information: Applications accepted. Application form required. Application form available on the grantmaker's web site.
  Initial approach: Telephone
  Send request by: On-line
  Copies of proposal: 3
  Deadline(s): Feb. 15 for Mentored Research Training Grants, Research in Education Grant, Research Fellowship Grant
  Final notification: Recipients notified by May 15 for Mentored Research Training Grants, Research in Education Grant and Research Fellowship Grant
Program descriptions:
  Medical Student Programs: The program provides fellowships to medical students with an interest in anesthesiology and research, FAER aims to expand the scientific talent in academic anesthesiology. Funding is for support over a summer or a year in focusing on research, training in scientific methods

and techniques, and learning how to incorporate research into a medical career.

Research Fellowship Grant: The grant is a one-year, $75,000 award for anesthesiology trainees after the CA-1 year. The RFG is awarded in conjunction with clinical training in an anesthesiology residency or fellowship program.

Resident Scholar Program: The program provides selected anesthesiology residents with the opportunity to attend the American Society of Anesthesiologists annual meeting each year. The scholars participate in activities at the annual meeting including workshops, scientific sessions, exhibits and refresher courses.

EIN: 521494164

4742

Joe Francis Scholarship Foundation

P.O. Box 50625
Minneapolis, MN 55405-0625 (651) 769-1757
FAX: (651) 459-8371;
E-mail: kimlarsonmn@gmai.com; URL: http://www.joefrancis.com

Foundation type: Independent foundation
Purpose: Scholarships to individuals for professional training in hairstyling and cosmetology.
Publications: Application guidelines.
Financial data: Year ended 12/31/2012. Assets, $838,252 (M); Expenditures, $49,214; Total giving, $25,000; Grants to individuals, 25 grants totaling $25,000 (high: $1,000, low: $1,000).
Fields of interest: Vocational education.
Type of support: Scholarships—to individuals.
Application information: Applications accepted. Application form required. Application form available on the grantmaker's web site.
> *Send request by:* Mail or fax
> *Copies of proposal:* 1
> *Deadline(s):* June 1
> *Final notification:* Applicant notified in three months

EIN: 411778518

4743

Franconia Sculpture Park

29836 St. Croix Trail
Franconia, MN 55074-9743 (651) 257-6668
E-mail: info@franconia.org; Additional telephone/fax: (651) 465-3701; E-mail For John Hock: johnhock@franconia.org; URL: http://www.franconia.org

Foundation type: Public charity
Purpose: Residencies to sculpture, installation and 3-D multimedia artists for the creation of a project in a public outdoor setting.
Publications: Application guidelines.
Financial data: Year ended 12/31/2012. Assets, $1,574,399 (M); Expenditures, $498,770; Total giving, $26,500; Grants to individuals, totaling $26,500.
Fields of interest: Media/communications; Sculpture.
Type of support: Residencies.
Application information: Applications accepted.
> *Initial approach:* Letter or e-mail
> *Deadline(s):* Feb. 9 for FSP/Jerome Fellowship Artist
> *Applicants should submit the following:*
> 1) SASE
> 2) Resume
> *Additional information:* Application must also include slides of recent work, sketch or

drawing of proposal, laser prints, budget, and residency date preferences.
Program description:
> *Franconia/Jerome Fellowship Grants:* Approximately 10 artists are invited to create work in a public outdoor setting which can last from three days to three months. Eligible applicants must be U.S. residents whose work falls within the area of sculpture, installation, and/or 3-D multi-media; applicants must not be enrolled in a degree-seeking program, either part-time or full-time, at any institution of higher learning during the year in which he/she is applying. Financial assistance range from $3,000 to $5,000.

EIN: 411843609

4744

Don Franz Broadcast Journalism Scholarship Trust

15 1th St. S.E. Ste.220
Rochester, MN 55904-5584 (507) 282-2335
Contact: Tim Melin, Trust Off.

Foundation type: Independent foundation
Purpose: Scholarship awards to journalism students in Minnesota.
Financial data: Year ended 12/31/2011. Assets, $418,544 (M); Expenditures, $42,736; Total giving, $30,000; Grants to individuals, 6 grants totaling $30,000 (high: $5,000, low: $5,000).
Fields of interest: Journalism school/education.
Type of support: Scholarships—to individuals.
Application information: Applications accepted. Application form not required.
EIN: 206727005

4745

Fredrikson & Byron Foundation

200 South 6th St., Ste. 4000
Minneapolis, MN 55402-1425 (612) 492-7000
Scholarship e-mail: glarson@fredlaw.com
FAX: (612) 492-7077;
E-mail: jkoneck@fredlaw.com; URL: http://www.fredlaw.com/firm/foundation.html

Foundation type: Public charity
Purpose: Scholarships to first year minority law students in the U.S.
Publications: Application guidelines.
Financial data: Year ended 05/31/2012. Assets, $136,138 (M); Expenditures, $442,309; Total giving, $440,954; Grants to individuals, totaling $10,000.
Fields of interest: Law school/education; Minorities.
Type of support: Scholarships—to individuals.
Application information: Applications accepted. Application form required. Application form available on the grantmaker's web site.
> *Send request by:* Mail or online
> *Deadline(s):* Mar. 31
> *Applicants should submit the following:*
> 1) Letter(s) of recommendation
> 2) Transcripts
> 3) Resume
> *Additional information:* Application should also include one writing sample form your first-year legal writing course.

Program description:
> *Minority Scholarship Program:* This program sponsors educational opportunities for currently-enrolled, first-year law students of diverse backgrounds by providing one $10,000 scholarship.

EIN: 237401456

4746

The Gallagher Foundation

c/o Gerald R. Gallagher
3890 Wells Fargo Ctr.
90 S. 7th St.
Minneapolis, MN 55402-3903
URL: http://www.gallagherfoundation.org/

Foundation type: Independent foundation
Purpose: Scholarships to individuals for college tuition, room, board and travel expenses.
Financial data: Year ended 12/31/2012. Assets, $5,544,283 (M); Expenditures, $810,113; Total giving, $629,007.
Fields of interest: College; Scholarships/financial aid.
International interests: Mexico; South Africa; Turkey.
Type of support: Undergraduate support.
Application information: Applications not accepted.
> *Additional information:* Scholarships only to pre-selected individuals; unsolicited requests for funds not considered or acknowledged.

EIN: 412019884

4747

Fanny S. Gilfillan Memorial, Inc.

P.O. Box 68
Morgan, MN 56266 (507) 637-4050
Application address: Redwood County Human Svcs., P.O. Box 27, Redwood Falls, MN 56283

Foundation type: Independent foundation
Purpose: Medical assistance to needy residents of Redwood County, MN, who are otherwise unable to pay, yet who are ineligible for government-sponsored medical assistance programs.
Financial data: Year ended 12/31/2012. Assets, $963,338 (M); Expenditures, $15,171; Total giving, $10,973; Grants to individuals, 21 grants totaling $10,973 (high: $1,230, low: $95).
Fields of interest: Health care.
Type of support: Grants for special needs.
Application information: Applications accepted. Application form required.
> *Deadline(s):* None
> *Additional information:* Applicant must demonstrate financial need. Application forms available at Redwood County Human Services.

EIN: 410892731

4748

Charles D. Gilfillan Paxton Memorial Foundation

511 Morten Dr.
Redwood Falls, MN 56283-9800 (507) 627-5752
Contact: Francis Uhelenkamp, Secy.-Treas.

Foundation type: Independent foundation
Purpose: Grants for medical assistance to residents of Paxton Township, MN who are otherwise unable to pay their medical bills and do not qualify for government assistance.
Financial data: Year ended 12/31/2011. Assets, $22,262 (M); Expenditures, $10,278; Total giving, $6,357; Grants to individuals, 10 grants totaling $5,650 (high: $1,000, low: $150).
Fields of interest: Hospitals (general); Human services; Economically disadvantaged.
Type of support: Grants for special needs.

Application information: Applications accepted. Application form required.
   Deadline(s): None
EIN: 416023986

4749
Helen Gough Foundation Trust
c/o Trust Tax Services
P.O. Box 64713
St. Paul, MN   55164-0713   (701) 627-4112
Contact: Martha Hunter
Application Address: c/o 404 Frontage Rd., New Town, ND 58763

Foundation type: Independent foundation
Purpose: Scholarships to enrolled members of the three affiliated tribes of the Fort Berthold Reservation, ND.
Financial data: Year ended 12/31/2012. Assets, $556,131 (M); Expenditures, $41,175; Total giving, $25,162.
Fields of interest: Native Americans/American Indians.
Type of support: Undergraduate support.
Application information: Application form required.
   Initial approach: Letter
   Deadline(s): June 1
   Additional information: Applications can be obtained by contacting the local high school counselor's office, Fort Berthold, ND.
EIN: 456014772

4750
Grand Rapids Area Community Foundation
350 N.W. First Ave., Ste. E
Grand Rapids, MN   55744-2756   (218) 999-9100
Contact: Chris Fulton, Exec. Dir.; For grants: Sarah Copeland, Dir., Grants and Progs.
FAX: (218) 999-7430; E-mail: info@gracf.org; URL: http://www.gracf.org

Foundation type: Community foundation
Purpose: Scholarships to high school graduates of Grand Rapids and Itasca, MN, for higher education.
Publications: Application guidelines; Annual report (including application guidelines); Financial statement; Informational brochure; Newsletter; IRS Form 990 or 990-PF printed copy available upon request.
Financial data: Year ended 12/31/2011. Assets, $12,330,429 (M); Expenditures, $1,301,182; Total giving, $896,090.
Fields of interest: Higher education.
Type of support: Scholarships—to individuals; Support to graduates or students of specific schools; Undergraduate support.
Application information: Applications accepted. Application form required. Application form available on the grantmaker's web site.
   Send request by: Online
   Copies of proposal: 1
   Deadline(s): Mar. 15
   Applicants should submit the following:
     1) Essay
     2) Letter(s) of recommendation
     3) GPA
     4) ACT
   Additional information: See web site for complete listing of scholarships.
EIN: 411761590

4751
Grannis-Martin Memorial Foundation
c/o Bob Lange
189 Logan Pkwy., N.E.
Fridley, MN   55432-3041

Foundation type: Independent foundation
Purpose: Scholarships to prospective clergy in the United Methodist Church.
Financial data: Year ended 12/31/2011. Assets, $137,410 (M); Expenditures, $4,534; Total giving, $4,500; Grants to individuals, 3 grants totaling $4,500 (high: $1,500, low: $1,500).
Fields of interest: Theological school/education; Protestant agencies & churches.
Type of support: Scholarships—to individuals; Undergraduate support.
Application information: Applications accepted. Application form required.
   Deadline(s): None
   Applicants should submit the following:
     1) Letter(s) of recommendation
     2) Financial information
EIN: 411378657

4752
The Virginia A. Groot Foundation
(formerly Candice B. Groot Foundation)
10750 55th Pl. N.
Plymouth, MN   55442-1930   (763) 550-9003
Application address: P.O. Box 1050, Evanston, IL 60203-1050
E-mail: virginia@virginiaagrootfoundation.org; URL: http://www.virginiaagrootfoundation.org

Foundation type: Independent foundation
Purpose: Grants to artists who have exceptional talent and demonstrated ability in ceramic sculpture or sculpture.
Financial data: Year ended 12/31/2011. Assets, $260,455 (M); Expenditures, $72,298; Total giving, $47,500; Grants to individuals, 4 grants totaling $47,500 (high: $17,500, low: $5,000).
Fields of interest: Sculpture; Ceramic arts.
Type of support: Grants to individuals.
Application information: Applications accepted. Application form required. Application form available on the grantmaker's web site.
   Send request by: Mail
   Deadline(s): Mar. 1
   Final notification: Recipients notified by May 1
   Additional information: Applicants must submit up to 20 digital images of their work on a CD.
Program description:
   Artist Grants: Each year the foundation offers three grants (up to $35,000, $10,000, $5,000) to artists who may be at any stage of career development, from emerging through mature. Applicants must be 21 years of age or older at the time of the application deadline. Students enrolled or attending, either full-time or part-time, any institution of higher learning, are not eligible to apply. Teachers are eligible if their program plans are for their development as artists rather than as teachers. The grant is not for the support of continued academic training.
EIN: 411570531

4753
Hansen Scholarship Trust
1650 Riverpointe Ct.
Anoka, MN   55303   (763) 576-8596
Contact: Juanita McKeever, Tr.

Foundation type: Independent foundation

Purpose: Scholarships to student athletes of Washington High School, Sioux Falls, SD pursuing a teaching education.
Financial data: Year ended 12/31/2012. Assets, $54,765 (M); Expenditures, $5,249; Total giving, $4,800.
Fields of interest: Teacher school/education; Athletics/sports, school programs.
Type of support: Support to graduates or students of specific schools.
Application information: Applications accepted. Application form required.
   Deadline(s): May 15
   Applicants should submit the following:
     1) Letter(s) of recommendation
     2) Essay
   Additional information: Application should also include proof of enrollment.
EIN: 466094569

4754
Harvard Club of Minnesota Foundation
1730 Clifton Pl., Ste. 103
Minneapolis, MN   55403

Foundation type: Independent foundation
Purpose: Scholarships to MN students to attend Harvard University, MA.
Financial data: Year ended 06/30/2013. Assets, $524,773 (M); Expenditures, $16,743; Total giving, $12,273.
Type of support: Support to graduates or students of specific schools.
Application information: Applications accepted.
   Additional information: Contact school's financial aid office for current application deadline/guidelines.
EIN: 416083667

4755
Hastings Family Service
121 E. 3rd St.
Hastings, MN   55033-1211   (651) 437-7134
Additional tel.: (651) 480-4128; URL: http://www.hastingsfamilyservice.org

Foundation type: Public charity
Purpose: Emergency financial assistance to indigent individuals residing in Hastings, MN. Support includes funds for basic needs such as food, clothing, and shelter.
Financial data: Year ended 12/31/2011. Assets, $1,916,302 (M); Expenditures, $1,521,181; Total giving, $401,666.
Fields of interest: Pharmacy/prescriptions; Food services; Housing/shelter, expense aid; Children/youth, services; Family services; Senior continuing care; Utilities.
Type of support: Emergency funds; Grants to individuals; Grants for special needs.
Application information:
   Initial approach: Letter, telephone, or e-mail
   Additional information: Contact foundation for application and program information.
Program descriptions:
   Clothes Closet: The program makes available clean, seasonal, and carefully-inspected used clothing and household items at no cost to those in need.
   Emergency Assistance and Referrals Program: The program allots grants to individuals and families in emergency situations. Grants include assistance with housing, utility and car related expenses, and prescriptions. Assistance in the form of vouchers is also offered for such items as

dairy, baby food/formula, diapers, and gas for getting to school, work or medical appointments.

Emergency Grants Program: The program allots emergency grants to families in financial crisis faced with eviction, utility shut-off, transportation problems, housing, school- or job-related expenses, or lack of funds for medical prescriptions.

Food Shelf Program: Provides groceries to people in need of emergency or short-term assistance. Supplies last three to five days; participants receive a voucher to a local grocery store for perishables.

Furniture Bank Program: The program matches requests with offers of donated furniture by arranging to transfer furniture items between donors and recipients.

Holiday Assistance Program: The program provides food, clothing, gifts and toys to those in need at Christmas.

Just Friends Program: The program endeavors to help people with needs that are often outside of their physical capabilities because of illness, age, disability, or life circumstances. Services provided include: daily/weekly phone call support, mentoring support (one-on-one relationship building), rides to medical appointments and other necessary outings, light housekeeping, yard work, meals, emergency childcare, shopping, and carpentry and repairs. All services are extended to each recipient free of charge.

Meals on Wheels Program: The program provides hot meals to the elderly and homebound on a daily basis by distributing meals tailored to individual nutritional needs as set forth by the client's doctor.

School Assistance Program: The program makes available supplies for children at all grade levels in need. Scholarship assistance is available for pre-school and other specialized classes. The program also provides emergency aid, such as furniture and limited assistance with transportation along with financial assistance in purchasing specialized baby formula or diapers for those in need.

EIN: 237083534

4756
HealthEast Foundation
1690 University Ave., Ste. 250
St. Paul, MN   55104-3729   (651) 232-4990
Contact: Joan Pennington, System Dir., Devel.
FAX: (651) 232-4834;
E-mail: jpennington@healtheast.org; URL: http://www.plan.gs/Home.do?orgId=1043

Foundation type: Public charity
Purpose: Crisis grant assistance for HealthEast employees experiencing catastrophic financial difficulties. Scholarships to HealthEast employees who wish to pursue an education in the health care field, and scholarship to their children, and teen volunteers pursuing postsecondary education.
Financial data: Year ended 08/31/2011. Assets, $14,490,024 (M); Expenditures, $5,808,186; Total giving, $3,999,692; Grants to individuals, totaling $87,262.
Fields of interest: Higher education; Health care.
Type of support: Emergency funds; Scholarships—to individuals.
Application information: Applications not accepted.
  Additional information: Unsolicited requests for funds not considered or acknowledged.
EIN: 411602044

4757
Patrick Henry High School Foundation
4320 Newton Ave. N.
Minneapolis, MN   55412-1150   (612) 521-3370
Contact: Ann Kaari, Treas.
Application address: 2502 Victory Memorial Dr., Minneapolis, MN 55412-1030

Foundation type: Independent foundation
Purpose: Scholarships to graduating students from Patrick Henry High School, MN for attendance only at Minnesota colleges or universities or those states within reciprocal agreements with Minnesota or traditional Black Colleges nationwide.
Financial data: Year ended 12/31/2012. Assets, -$11,315 (M); Expenditures, $19,586; Total giving, $8,655; Grants to individuals, 8 grants totaling $8,655 (high: $1,500, low: $500).
Fields of interest: Higher education.
Type of support: Support to graduates or students of specific schools; Undergraduate support.
Application information: Application form required.
  Deadline(s): Feb. or Mar.
  Additional information: Application can be obtained from school counselors or career center staff.
EIN: 411970958

4758
Higher Education Consortium for Urban Affairs, Inc.
2233 University Ave. W., Ste. 210
St. Paul, MN   55114-1629   (651) 287-3300
FAX: (651) 659-9421; E-mail: hecua@hecua.org;
E-Mail for Jenny Keyser: jkeyser@hecua.org;
URL: http://www.hecua.org

Foundation type: Public charity
Purpose: Scholarships to students enrolled in HECUA programs.
Financial data: Year ended 06/30/2012. Assets, $846,545 (M); Expenditures, $1,873,846; Total giving, $54,490; Grants to individuals, totaling $17,690.
Fields of interest: Urban studies; African Americans/Blacks; Economically disadvantaged.
Type of support: Scholarships—to individuals.
Application information: Applications accepted.
  Deadline(s): Apr. 15 and Nov. 15
  Applicants should submit the following:
    1) SAR
    2) Financial information
    3) Letter(s) of recommendation
    4) Essay
Program descriptions:
  Scholarship for Racial Justice: Students of color who are currently enrolled at a HECUA member school are eligible for a $4,000 scholarship to be used to start a program committed to undoing institutionalized racism in higher education.
  Scholarship for Social Justice: Two $1,500 scholarships will be awarded to first generation college students, students from low-income families, and students of color who are enrolling in HECUA semester programs.
  Scholarships for Community Engagement: $750 awards for semester-long programs, and $250 to short-term programs, will be made each term to students who have worked for social change and whose future goals will be strengthened by a HECUA semester program. Students must have applied to a HECUA program in order to be eligible.
EIN: 410968262

4759
Highpoint Center for Printmaking
912 W. Lake St.
Minneapolis, MN   55408-2857   (612) 871-1326
E-mail: info@highpointprintmaking.org; URL: http://www.highpointprintmaking.org

Foundation type: Public charity
Purpose: Residencies to emerging printmaking artists residing in MN.
Publications: Application guidelines.
Financial data: Year ended 12/31/2011. Assets, $2,821,747 (M); Expenditures, $676,151.
Fields of interest: Visual arts.
Type of support: Residencies.
Application information: Applications accepted. Application form required. Application form available on the grantmaker's web site.
  Initial approach: E-mail
  Deadline(s): July 16
  Final notification: Applicants notified in Aug.
  Applicants should submit the following:
    1) Work samples
    2) Resume
    3) SASE
  Additional information: Application must also include slides of recent work, letter of intent, and slide list.
EIN: 411977650

4760
Hmong National Development, Inc.
1075 Arcde St.
St. Paul, MN   55106-3213
E-mail: info@hndinc.org; Additional tel.: (202) 797-9106; URL: http://www.hndinc.org

Foundation type: Public charity
Purpose: Scholarships to Hmong students who show academic excellence and leadership qualities in their chosen field of study.
Publications: Application guidelines.
Financial data: Year ended 12/31/2011. Assets, $18,691 (M); Expenditures, $238,397.
Fields of interest: Education.
Type of support: Scholarships—to individuals.
Application information: Contact the organization for additional information.
Program description:
  HND Scholarships: One-time scholarships are available for students of Hmong descent to support and encourage their educational development, and to assist them in achieving important roles as leaders in their chosen profession and promoting a stronger presence of Hmong in academia and in the professional community. Eligible students must be of Hmong descent with residency in the U.S., who are enrolled full-time in an accredited college, university, or graduate degree program.
EIN: 521804060

4761
Hoffman & McNamara Foundation
1368 Feather Stone Ct.
Hastings, MN   55033-9179

Foundation type: Independent foundation
Purpose: Scholarships to residents of Hastings, MN.
Financial data: Year ended 12/31/2012. Assets, $367,116 (M); Expenditures, $15,377; Total giving, $15,343; Grants to individuals, 3 grants totaling $6,234 (high: $2,834, low: $1,700).
Type of support: Undergraduate support.
Application information: Applications not accepted.

Additional information: Unsolicited requests for funds not considered or acknowledged.
EIN: 411894440

4762

Orson A. & Minnie E. Hull Educational Foundation

c/o Trust Tax Services
P.O. Box 64713
St. Paul, MN 55164-0713
Contact: Thomas Farrell
Application address: c/o Hull Educational Fdn., P.O. Box 1, Minneapolis, MN 55418 (612) 810-3585

Foundation type: Independent foundation
Purpose: Scholarships to graduating seniors from Johnson High School and Harding High School, St. Paul, MN.
Financial data: Year ended 06/30/2013. Assets, $4,677,032 (M); Expenditures, $214,858; Total giving, $135,265.
Fields of interest: Higher education; Scholarships/financial aid.
Type of support: Support to graduates or students of specific schools; Undergraduate support.
Application information: Applications accepted. Application form required.
Final notification: Recipients notified by May 1
Additional information: Applications must be submitted to and approved by school counselors.
EIN: 416019516

4763

IFP Minnesota Center for Media Arts

(formerly IFP Minneapolis/St. Paul)
2446 University Ave. W., Ste. 100
St. Paul, MN 55114-1740 (651) 644-1912
FAX: (651) 644-5708; E-mail: info@ifpmn.org; Additional E-mail: word@ifpmn.org; URL: http://www.ifpmn.org/

Foundation type: Public charity
Purpose: Support for artists who create screenplays, film, video, and photography in the Midwest.
Publications: Application guidelines.
Financial data: Year ended 12/31/2011. Assets, $649,211 (M); Expenditures, $769,630.
Fields of interest: Film/video; Arts, artist's services.
Type of support: Fellowships; Fiscal agent/sponsor.
Application information: Applications accepted. Application form required. Application form available on the grantmaker's web site.
Additional information: Application form for Fiscal Sponsorship program available online. See web site for McKnight Fellowship guidelines.
Program descriptions:
Fiscal Sponsorship: This sponsorship program is designed to assist media artists who are members of the Center to seek and receive grants and/or contributions from sources which require a federal exempt tax status (i.e., a non-profit organizational status). Eligible participants must be individual-level members of the Center in good standing, and currently reside in and have been residing in the state of Minnesota for the past twelve months.
Fresh Filmmakers Production Grants: In partnership with ETS Pictures and the Twin Cities-based production community, stipends of $1,000 each will be made available to filmmakers who have been making films for no more than five years, for a short narrative film of ten minutes or

less. Recipients will also receive mentorships and logistical support. Applicants must be members of IFP Minnesota and current residents of Minnesota or western Wisconsin (including Buffalo, Chippewa, Dunn, Eau Claire, Pepin, Pierce, St. Croix, and Trempeleau counties). Full-time students are ineligible to apply, though part-time students are eligible.
McKnight Artist Fellowships for Filmmakers: Supported by the McKnight Foundation and administered by the Center, this program provides two $25,000 fellowships to honor the professional and artistic accomplishments of mid-career Minnesota artists working in the medium of film/video, as demonstrated by two examples of completed, original works in any of the genres and formats of narrative, documentary, experimental, or animation, in feature or short lengths. Applicants must be current Minnesota residents who have resided in the state continuously for a minimum of one full year before the application deadline.
McKnight Artist Fellowships for Screenwriters: Supported by the McKnight Foundation and administered by the Center, two $25,000 fellowships will be made available to honor the professional and artistic accomplishments of Minnesota artists writing for the screen, as demonstrated by one completed feature-length screenplay. This program recognizes these mid-career screenwriters by providing financial assistance, professional encouragement, and recognition. Applicants must be current Minnesota residents who have resided in the state continuously for a minimum of one full year before the application deadline.
EIN: 411594894

4764

Initiative Foundation

(formerly Central Minnesota Initiative Fund)
405 1st St., S.E.
Little Falls, MN 56345-3007 (320) 632-9255
Contact: Kathy Gaalswyk, Pres.
FAX: (320) 632-9258; E-mail: info@ifound.org; Additional tel: (877) 632-9255; Grant inquiry e-mail: grants@ifound.org; Additional e-mail: kgaalswyk@ifound.org; URL: http://www.ifound.org

Foundation type: Community foundation
Purpose: Scholarships to high school seniors who reside in the 14-county area of Benton, Cass, Chisago, Crow Wing, Isanti, Kanabec, Mille Lacs, Morrison, Pine, Sherburne, Stearns, Todd, Wadena, and Wright, MN.
Publications: Application guidelines; Annual report; Grants list; Informational brochure; Program policy statement; Quarterly report.
Financial data: Year ended 12/31/2011. Assets, $47,762,113 (M); Expenditures, $4,444,204; Total giving, $1,602,405; Grants to individuals, totaling $304,049.
Type of support: Undergraduate support.
Application information: Applications accepted. Application form required. Application form available on the grantmaker's web site.
Initial approach: Telephone
Send request by: Mail
EIN: 363451562

4765

Interfaith Outreach and Community Partners

(also known as IOCP)
1605 County Rd. 101 N.
Plymouth, MN 55447-2708 (763) 489-7500
FAX: (763) 489-7510; E-mail: info@iocp.org; E-Mail for LaDonna Hoy: lhoy@iocp.org; URL: http://www.iocp.org

Foundation type: Public charity
Purpose: Assistance to low-income families, children and individuals of Hamel, Long Lake, Medicine Lake, Medina, Minnetonka Beach, Orono, Plymouth, and Wayzata, MN, with food, clothing, shelter, transportation, medical and dental assistance.
Publications: Annual report; Newsletter.
Financial data: Year ended 03/31/2012. Assets, $9,990,903 (M); Expenditures, $5,781,873; Total giving, $3,750,440; Grants to individuals, totaling $3,750,440.
Fields of interest: Human services, transportation; Human services, emergency aid.
Type of support: Emergency funds; Grants for special needs.
Application information:
Initial approach: Telephone
EIN: 363482724

4766

Intermedia Arts Minnesota, Inc.

2822 Lyndale Ave. S.
Minneapolis, MN 55408-2108 (612) 871-4444
Contact: Theresa Sweetland, Exec. and Artistic Dir.
FAX: (612) 871-6927;
E-mail: info@intermediaarts.org; E-mail for Daniel Gumnit: daniel@intermediaarts.org; E-mail for Theresa Sweetland: Theresa@IntermediaArts.org; URL: http://www.intermediaarts.org

Foundation type: Public charity
Purpose: Grants and services to artists to create and participate in meaningful civic dialogue. Residencies to artists working in visual, performing, literary, interdisciplinary, music, and media, based in the Twin Cities.
Publications: Application guidelines; Annual report.
Financial data: Year ended 06/30/2012. Assets, $1,257,062 (M); Expenditures, $789,428; Total giving, $18,950; Grants to individuals, totaling $18,950.
Fields of interest: Cultural/ethnic awareness; Film/video; Arts, artist's services.
Type of support: Residencies; Project support; Fiscal agent/sponsor.
Application information: Applications accepted.
Initial approach: Letter
Deadline(s): Feb. 25 for Beyond the Pure Fellowships, May 31 for VERVE Grants
Final notification: Recipients notified Apr. 30 for Beyond the Pure Fellowships
Program descriptions:
Artist-in-Residence Program: This program offers support to community-engaged artists who actively seek to engage sustained community participation and foster positive social changes as part of their artistic process. Support is open to Twin Cities-based artists working in any of the following disciplines: visual, performing, literary, interdisciplinary, music, and media. The organization will support one artist per residency period, which may last from six to 18 months; resident artists are granted free 24-hour access to non-living studio space in the organization's gallery, as well as a residency stipend.

Beyond the Pure Fellowships for Writers: This program awards grants of up to $4,000 for four to six emerging Minnesota writers each year, to support their creation and production of new artistic works and contribute to their professional development. Eligible individuals must be legal residents of Minnesota for at least twelve months prior to the application deadline who work in poetry, fiction or creative nonfiction and have not published more than two full-length books with a publishing house.

Fiscal Sponsorship: Fiscal sponsorship services are available to artists or groups of artists for non-commercial projects that are consistent with the organization's mission. Services include: use of the organization's nonprofit status as a grant-receiving entity; administration of funds for the project; acknowledgment of all grants and contributions on organization letterhead; and grant review from development and business personnel in preparing fundraising plans and application packages. Five percent of all monies received by the fiscal sponsee will be retained.

VERVE Grants for Spoken Word Artists: Grants of up to $4,000 are available to emerging Minnesota spoken word poets who are ready to achieve their next level of artistic success, and who are interested in developing their abilities to become artistic leaders in their communities. Recipients will spend twelve months supporting one another as they complete their grant projects and work to achieve their next level of artistic success. Eligible applicants must be legal residents of Minnesota for at least twelve months prior to the application deadline. Applicant must not be a full time student and work must be spoken word poetry. Applicant must have been a spoken word poet for longer than six months.
EIN: 411226945

4767
Intertech Foundation
1575 Thomas Center Dr.
Eagan, MN 55122-2642
Contact: Ryan McCabe, Secy.
FAX: (651) 846-5666;
E-mail: Foundation@intertech.com; Additional tel.: (651) 994-8558; URL: http://www.intertech-inc.com/Foundation/Foundation.aspx

Foundation type: Company-sponsored foundation
Purpose: Grants to MN families with terminally ill children in need of financial assistance. Applicants must be or have been a resident of Ronald McDonald House in Minneapolis.
Publications: Application guidelines.
Financial data: Year ended 12/31/2012. Assets, $120,694 (M); Expenditures, $9,683; Total giving, $8,948.
Fields of interest: Health care.
Type of support: Grants for special needs.
Application information:
 Initial approach: Letter
 Additional information: Individuals may receive up to two grants per year.
EIN: 200498817

4768
Italian American Club Foundation, Inc.
2221 Central Ave. N.E.
Minneapolis, MN 55418-3707   (612) 781-0625

Foundation type: Public charity

Purpose: Scholarships to MN residents. Italian heritage is a consideration, but individuals of all backgrounds may apply.
Financial data: Year ended 06/30/2012. Assets, $980,357 (M); Expenditures, $205,621; Total giving, $151,800; Grants to individuals, totaling $151,800.
Type of support: Undergraduate support.
Application information: Applications accepted. Application form required.
 Applicants should submit the following:
  1) Letter(s) of recommendation
  2) Transcripts
  3) Financial information
 Additional information: Application should also include school and community activities.
EIN: 411440206

4769
Clive T. Jaffray Employees Trust
c/o Trust Tax Services
P.O. Box 64713
St. Paul, MN 55164-0713   (612) 303-3208
Contact: Sarah S. Godfrey
Application address: 800 Nicollet Mall, Minneapolis, MN 55402

Foundation type: Independent foundation
Purpose: Financial assistance to employees of U.S. Bank, N.A. for extraordinary expenses due to illness or other emergencies, primarily in MN.
Financial data: Year ended 12/31/2012. Assets, $127,807 (M); Expenditures, $18,758; Total giving, $11,424.
Type of support: Employee-related welfare.
Application information:
 Initial approach: Letter
 Deadline(s): None
EIN: 416015737

4770
Vernon & Leoma Jenniges Education Trust
P.O. Box 126
Springfield, MN 56087   (507) 723-4234
Contact: Paul Pieschel, Tr.
Application address: 101 N Marshall, Springfield, MN 56087

Foundation type: Operating foundation
Purpose: Scholarships to students from the Springfield School District, MN, for postsecondary education.
Financial data: Year ended 12/31/2012. Assets, $428,662 (M); Expenditures, $78,850; Total giving, $73,069; Grants to individuals, 29 grants totaling $73,069 (high: $62,444, low: $200).
Type of support: Support to graduates or students of specific schools; Undergraduate support.
Application information: Applications accepted. Application form required.
 Deadline(s): None
EIN: 416325986

4771
Jerome Foundation
400 Sibley St., Ste. 125
St. Paul, MN 55101-1928   (651) 224-9431
Contact: Cynthia A. Gehrig, Pres.
FAX: (651) 224-3439; E-mail: info@jeromefdn.org; Toll-free tel.: (800) 995-3766 (MN and New York City only); URL: http://www.jeromefdn.org

Foundation type: Independent foundation
Purpose: Grants for film and video production artists residing in New York City, NY, and the state of MN. Travel and study grants for artists in dance, literature, media arts, music, theater, and the visual arts residing in MN and New York City.
Publications: Application guidelines; Financial statement; Grants list; Informational brochure (including application guidelines).
Financial data: Year ended 04/30/2013. Assets, $87,591,859 (M); Expenditures, $4,205,965; Total giving, $3,164,455; Grants to individuals, 62 grants totaling $516,424 (high: $30,000, low: $810).
Fields of interest: Film/video; Visual arts; Dance; Theater; Music; Literature.
Type of support: Travel grants; Project support.
Application information: Applications accepted. Application form required. Application form available on the grantmaker's web site.
 Initial approach: Letter, telephone, or e-mail
 Send request by: Online preferred or mail
 Copies of proposal: 1
 Deadline(s): Varies
 Final notification: Recipients notified in four to five months
 Applicants should submit the following:
  1) Work samples
  2) Resume
  3) Proposal
  4) Curriculum vitae
  5) Budget Information
Program descriptions:
 General Program: This is the foundation's largest program. It is open to not-for-profit arts organizations and to fiscal sponsors applying on behalf of artists for the creation, development, and production of new works by emerging artists in New York City and Minnesota. See web site for additional guidelines.
 Minnesota Film and Video: This program is for individual film and video artists who are MN residents, and work in the genres of experimental, narrative, animation, and documentary production. The program does not support installation, new media, or interactive work, which are subsidized in other foundation programs, commercial, industrial, informational, or educational work.
 New York City Film and Video: This program is for individual film and video artists who reside within the five boroughs of New York City, and who work in the genres of experimental, narrative, animation and documentary production. The program does not support installation, new media or interactive work, which are subsidized in other foundation programs, or commercial, industrial, informational or educational work. See web site for additional information.
 Travel and Study Grant Program: This program awards grants to emerging artists who create new work, rotating the eligible disciplines in alternating years. (See web site for current disciplines). Minnesota-based executive and program administrators working for not-for-profit arts organizations are also eligible to apply. The program supports such activities as research leading to the creation of new work, the development of collaborations, participation in specific training programs, time for reflection and individualized study, investigating artistic work outside of Minnesota or New York City, and dialogue on aesthetic issues. This program does not support the production of new work or the acquisition of teaching credentials.
EIN: 416035163

4772
Jewish Family & Childrens Service of Minneapolis
13100 Wayzata Blvd., Ste. 400
Minnetonka, MN 55305-1821 (952) 546-0616
FAX: (952) 593-1778; E-mail: jfcs@jfcsmpls.org;
URL: http://www.jfcsmpls.org/

Foundation type: Public charity
Purpose: Scholarships to individuals of MN, for postsecondary education. Camp scholarships for Jewish youths of MN, to participate in various summer experiences. Interest-free loans to individuals of the Twin Cities Jewish community.
Publications: Application guidelines.
Financial data: Year ended 08/31/2011. Assets, $15,124,907 (M); Expenditures, $8,214,783; Total giving, $1,729,075; Grants to individuals, totaling $1,695,328.
Fields of interest: Higher education.
Type of support: Camperships; Scholarships—to individuals; Loans—to individuals.
Application information: Applications accepted.
Send request by: Mail for postsecondary scholarship
Deadline(s): Mar. 15 for Camp Scholarship, Mar. 31 for Postsecondary Scholarship
Final notification: Applicants notified by Apr. 30 for Camp Scholarship
Additional information: Application should include three letters of recommendation and most recent transcript for postsecondary scholarship. See web site for additional guidelines for camp scholarship.
Program description:
Jewish Free Loan Program: The organization helps members of the Twin Cities Jewish community who face unexpected financial challenges by helping them secure interest-free loans of up to $7,500.
EIN: 410693860

4773
Lloyd K. Johnson Foundation
130 W. Superior St., Ste. 710
Duluth, MN 55802-4035 (218) 726-9000
Contact: Joan Gardner-Goodno, Exec. Dir.
FAX: (218) 726-9002;
E-mail: jgardner@lloydkjohnsonfoundation.org;
URL: http://www.lloydkjohnsonfoundation.org/

Foundation type: Independent foundation
Purpose: Scholarships to assist graduating seniors who have a minimum GPA of 2.0 at Cook County High School in Grand Marais, Minnesota to continue their education at Lake Superior College in Duluth, Minnesota.
Publications: Application guidelines; Annual report; Grants list.
Financial data: Year ended 12/31/2012. Assets, $19,999,830 (M); Expenditures, $1,133,046; Total giving, $911,157. Scholarships—to individuals amount not specified.
Fields of interest: Higher education.
Type of support: Scholarships—to individuals.
Application information: Applications accepted. Application form required. Application form available on the grantmaker's web site.
Initial approach: Application
Deadline(s): Apr.
Final notification: Applicants notified May 7
Applicants should submit the following:
1) Transcripts
2) Letter(s) of recommendation
3) SAR
4) FAFSA

Additional information: Students must submit a copy of their acceptance letter from Lake Superior College along with their Lloyd K. Johnson post-Secondary School Scholarship Application. Visit the Cook County High School Guidance counselor or the Lloyd K. Johnson Foundation administrative office.
EIN: 510180842

4774
The Jostens Foundation, Inc.
3601 Minnesota Dr., Ste. 400
Minneapolis, MN 55435-5281 (952) 830-3235
Contact: Teresa Olson
E-mail: foundation@jostens.com; URL: http://www.jostens.com/misc/aboutus/about_jostens_cp_foundation.html

Foundation type: Company-sponsored foundation
Purpose: Scholarships to high school seniors who are full-time dependents of a Jostens employee or sales representative for higher education.
Publications: Application guidelines; Informational brochure (including application guidelines); Program policy statement.
Financial data: Year ended 12/31/2012. Assets, $119,451 (M); Expenditures, $580,802; Total giving, $567,357.
Fields of interest: Higher education; Scholarships/financial aid.
Type of support: Employee-related scholarships.
Application information: Applications not accepted.
Additional information: Unsolicited requests for funds not considered or acknowledged.
Program description:
Josten Scholarships: The foundation awards $2,000 college scholarships to dependents of full-time employees and independent sales representatives of Jostens. Winners are eligible for an additional three-year $2,500 scholarship. Recipients are selected based on outstanding community service, academic achievement, and leadership.
Company name: Jostens, Inc.
EIN: 411280587

4775
Victor E. and Hazel V. Kohl Educational Foundation
c/o Trust Tax services
P.O. Box 64713
St. Paul, MN 55164-0713 (573) 684-2017

Foundation type: Independent foundation
Purpose: Scholarships to graduating seniors of Wellsville-Middletown R-1 High School, MO, for higher education.
Financial data: Year ended 08/31/2013. Assets, $171,348 (M); Expenditures, $12,839; Total giving, $8,000.
Fields of interest: Higher education.
Type of support: Scholarships—to individuals.
Application information: Applications accepted.
Additional information: Application information available from Wellsville-Middletown schools.
EIN: 200263331

4776
Ida C. Koran Trust
c/o Ecolab Inc.
370 Wabasha St. N
St. Paul, MN 55102-1323 (651) 293-2392
FAX: (651) 452-0485;
E-mail: Sue@idakorantrust.org; URL: http://idakoran.com/

Foundation type: Independent foundation
Purpose: Academic financial assistance for dependent children of Ecolab associates and retirees for postsecondary education. One time financial relief through loans and grants to employees of Ecolab, Inc., MN.
Publications: Application guidelines.
Financial data: Year ended 12/31/2012. Assets, $40,961,033 (M); Expenditures, $2,180,808; Total giving, $1,638,753; Grants to individuals, totaling $1,638,753; Loans to individuals, totaling $424,350.
Fields of interest: Vocational education, post-secondary; Higher education; Human services.
Type of support: Employee-related scholarships; Employee-related welfare.
Application information: Applications accepted.
Deadline(s): Feb. for academic assistance
Final notification: Applicants notified in May for academic assistance
Additional information: Application should include a transcript for academic assistance. Applicants must demonstrate financial need. Unsolicited requests for funds not considered or acknowledged.
Program descriptions:
Academic Assistance: Assistance range from a minimum of $2,000 to a maximum of $10,000. Awards are renewable to qualifying students for up to three years or until graduation, whichever comes first. Financial need and academic performance will be considered in determining the size of each award.
Hardship Assistance: Assistance is determined on a case-by-case basis, and is available in the form of low interest loans or grants for urgent, time-sensitive financial needs resulting from an unplanned event. Applicant must be a current employee of Ecolab or a retiree of Ecolab with at least 12 months of continuous service.
EIN: 416124022

4777
Lake Region Arts Council, Inc.
133 S. Mill St.
Fergus Falls, MN 56537-2578 (218) 739-5780
FAX: (218) 739-0296;
E-mail: lrac4@charterinternet.com; Toll-free tel. (in MN): (800) 262-2787; URL: http://www.lrac4.org/

Foundation type: Public charity
Purpose: Fellowships and grants to artists and students living in the MN counties of Becker, Clay, Douglas, Grant, Otter Tail, Pope, Stevens, Traverse and Wilkin.
Publications: Application guidelines; Annual report; Informational brochure; Newsletter.
Financial data: Year ended 06/30/2013. Assets, $218,501 (M); Expenditures, $588,559; Total giving, $329,273; Grants to individuals, totaling $42,010.
Fields of interest: Arts.
Type of support: Fellowships; Grants to individuals.
Application information: Applications accepted. Application form required.
Initial approach: Letter, telephone, or e-mail
Send request by: Mail

Copies of proposal: 1
Deadline(s): Varies
Applicants should submit the following:
1) Work samples
2) Resume
3) Proposal
4) Budget Information
Program descriptions:
Artist Mentor Program: This program offers an opportunity for students, grades 9 to 11, to study with a professional in the student's area of artistic interest. Eligible students must be residents of the council's service area.
Career Development Grants: The program provides deserving artists with grants of up to $1,200 for specific projects that contribute directly to their growth and development as professionals.
LRAC/McKnight Fellowship: This program provides deserving artists with significant financial support that enables them to further their work and their contribution to their communities. It is intended to recognize, reward and encourage outstanding individual artists in the region.
Small Grants for Individual Artists: Awards of up to $500 each are available to enable individual artists residing in the region to take advantage of artistic opportunities.
EIN: 411430764

4778
The Lakeland Group Foundation, Inc.
5735 Lindsay St.
Minneapolis, MN 55422-4655
URL: http://www.lakelandcompanies.com/

Foundation type: Company-sponsored foundation
Purpose: Scholarships to employees of Lakeland Engineering Equipment Co., Inc., primarily in MN.
Financial data: Year ended 01/31/2013. Assets, $362,434 (M); Expenditures, $24,978; Total giving, $23,500; Grants to individuals, 5 grants totaling $5,000 (high: $1,000, low: $1,000).
Fields of interest: Engineering school/education.
Type of support: Employee-related scholarships.
Application information: Contact foundation for current application deadline/guidelines.
Company name: Lakewood Engineering Equipment Company, Incorporated
EIN: 411738234

4779
Land O'Lakes Foundation
P.O. Box 64150
St. Paul, MN 55164-0150
Contact: Lydia Botham, Exec. Dir.
E-mail: mlatkins-sakry@landolakes.com;
URL: http://www.foundation.landolakes.com/

Foundation type: Company-sponsored foundation
Purpose: Scholarships to graduate students studying the dairy sciences at Iowa State University, South Dakota State University, the University of Minnesota, Twin Cities, and the University of Wisconsin, Madison.
Publications: Application guidelines; Annual report; Grants list; Informational brochure (including application guidelines); IRS Form 990 or 990-PF printed copy available upon request.
Financial data: Year ended 12/31/2012. Assets, $10,546,206 (M); Expenditures, $3,134,989; Total giving, $2,848,785.
Fields of interest: Formal/general education; Agriculture.
Type of support: Scholarships—to individuals; Support to graduates or students of specific schools; Graduate support.

Application information: Application form required. Application form available on the grantmaker's web site.
Initial approach: Application
Deadline(s): May 2
Applicants should submit the following:
1) Financial information
2) Essay
3) Letter(s) of recommendation
4) Transcripts
Additional information: Applications should include a personal history and a plan of study and research for the advanced degree.
Program description:
John Brandt Memorial Scholarships: The foundation awards $25,000 scholarships to graduate students pursuing a program of study leading to a master's or doctorate degree in dairy cattle nutrition, genetics, physiology or management, or the manufacturing, processing or marketing of milk and dairy products. Students must be enrolled at and accepted into one of the four required universities, Iowa State University, South Dakota State University, the University of Minnesota, Twin Cities, or the University of Wisconsin, Madison.
EIN: 411864977

4780
Winthrop and Frances Lane Foundation
c/o Trust Tax Services
P.O. Box 64713
St. Paul, MN 55164-0713
Application address: c/o US Bank, N.A., 525 N. 132nd St., Omaha, NE 68154, tel.: (402) 963-2156

Foundation type: Independent foundation
Purpose: Scholarships to students at Creighton University School of Law, NE, and University of Nebraska College of Law.
Financial data: Year ended 12/31/2012. Assets, $3,099,462 (M); Expenditures, $288,669; Total giving, $245,500.
Fields of interest: Law school/education.
Type of support: Support to graduates or students of specific schools; Graduate support.
Application information: Applications accepted. Application form required.
Deadline(s): None
Applicants should submit the following:
1) Class rank
2) Financial information
3) GPA
Additional information: Application must also include LSAT scores.
EIN: 470581778

4781
Law Review Inc.
6950 France Ave. S., Ste. 100
Edina, MN 55435-2024

Foundation type: Operating foundation
Purpose: Financial assistance and free legal assistance to the poor and disadvantaged including legal immigrants of Hennepin county, MN.
Financial data: Year ended 12/31/2012. Assets, $43,099 (M); Expenditures, $2,461; Total giving, $2,370.
Fields of interest: Immigrants/refugees; Economically disadvantaged.
Type of support: Grants for special needs.
Application information: Applications not accepted.
EIN: 411809929

4782
Geraldine N. Lemieux Charitable Trust
31114 Bluff Ridge Trail
Grand Rapids, MN 55744-6465 (218) 327-1567
Contact: Jack B. Velzen, Tr.

Foundation type: Independent foundation
Purpose: Scholarships to qualified African Americans, Native Americans, and Hispanic students of Risen Christ Catholic School, MN for post primary education at a Catholic Twin City area private school.
Financial data: Year ended 12/31/2013. Assets, $32,343 (M); Expenditures, $14,728; Total giving, $14,000; Grants to individuals, 7 grants totaling $14,000 (high: $2,000, low: $2,000).
Fields of interest: Education; African Americans/ Blacks; Hispanics/Latinos; Native Americans/ American Indians.
Type of support: Support to graduates or students of specific schools.
Application information: Applications accepted. Application form required. Interview required.
Deadline(s): Apr. 1
Applicants should submit the following:
1) Transcripts
2) Letter(s) of recommendation
Additional information: Application should also include a personal statement stating why they should receive the scholarship.
Program description:
Scholarship Program: Partial scholarships are provided to qualified African American, Native American, and Hispanic students of Risen Christ School to continue their post primary education. The scholarships are for $1,500 per school year and is renewable each after the first year, if renewal criteria are met, for an additional three years of high school at a Catholic Twin City area private school. Applicant must have maintained a "C" or better average in primary grades.
EIN: 416461599

4783
The Charles A. and Anne Morrow Lindbergh Foundation
(also known as Lindbergh Foundation)
2150 3rd Ave. N., Ste. 310
Anoka, MN 55303-2200 (763) 576-1596
Contact: Yolanka Wulff, Pres. and C.E.O. and Exec. Dir.
FAX: (763) 576-1664;
E-mail: info@lindberghfoundation.org; Mailing Address: P. O. Box 11429, Bainbridge Island, Wa, 98110; E-Mail for Yolanka Wulff: ywulff@lindberghfoundation.org; URL: http:// www.lindberghfoundation.org

Foundation type: Public charity
Purpose: Grants for research and educational projects that address the balance between technology and the environment.
Publications: Application guidelines; Annual report; Grants list; Informational brochure; Newsletter.
Financial data: Year ended 12/31/2011. Assets, $571,355 (M); Expenditures, $395,759; Total giving, $60,954.
Fields of interest: Health sciences school/ education; Natural resources; Energy; Animals/ wildlife, preservation/protection; Institute; Biomedicine research; Agriculture; Research; Space/aviation; Engineering/technology; Population studies.
Type of support: Program development; Research; Foreign applicants.

Application information: Applications accepted. Application form required. Application form available on the grantmaker's web site.

Initial approach: Letter

Copies of proposal: 7

Deadline(s): 2nd Thurs. of June

Final notification: Recipients notified by Apr. 15

Applicants should submit the following:
1) Letter(s) of recommendation
2) Curriculum vitae
3) Budget Information

Additional information: Application should also include statement, project summary, methodology, list of personnel, and two endorsers' reports. E-mail applications are accepted as long as paper copies, if required, are also filed.

Program description:

Lindbergh Grants Program: This program provides grants of up to $10,580 annually to men and women whose individual initiative and work in a wide spectrum of disciplines furthers the foundation's vision of a balance between the advance of technology and the preservation of the natural/human environment.

EIN: 132882090

4784
The Loft, Inc.

(also known as The Loft Literary Center)
1011 Washington Ave. S., Ste. 200
Minneapolis, MN 55415-1278 (612) 215-2575
Contact: Jocelyn Hale, Exec. Dir.
FAX: (612) 215-2576; E-mail: loft@loft.org; E-Mail for Jocelyn Hale: jhale@loft.org; URL: http://www.loft.org

Foundation type: Public charity

Purpose: Fellowships, awards, and prizes to MN writers of fiction, poetry, creative nonfiction, and children's literature.

Publications: Application guidelines; Annual report; Grants list.

Financial data: Year ended 08/31/2011. Assets, $4,200,837 (M); Expenditures, $2,011,981; Total giving, $153,000; Grants to individuals, totaling $153,000.

Fields of interest: Literature.

Type of support: Publication; Fellowships; Awards/prizes.

Application information:

Initial approach: Telephone

Send request by: Mail

Deadline(s): Vary

Additional information: Contact foundation for complete program details. Some programs have entry fees.

Program descriptions:

McKnight Artist Fellowships: Each year, this program awards five $25,000 fellowships to one writer of children's literature and four writers of creative prose (four in poetry in alternate years) to provide Minnesota writers of demonstrated ability with an opportunity to work for a concentrated period of time on their writing. The awards include publication in an anthology, a public reception, and a reading or other writing-related activity (depending on the award). Winners are selected by out-of-state judges on the basis of anonymous manuscript submissions.

Minnesota Emerging Writers Grants: This program offers up to $9,000 to emerging writers to help advance them toward the next stage of their careers.

EIN: 411297735

4785
Lutheran Community Foundation

625 4th Ave. S., Ste. 1500
Minneapolis, MN 55415-1624 (612) 340-4110
Contact: Chris D. Andersen, Exec. Dir.
FAX: (612) 340-4109; E-mail: contact@thelcf.org; Toll-free tel.: (800) 365-4172; URL: http://www.thelcf.org

Foundation type: Public charity

Purpose: Scholarships to Lutherans, people attending a Lutheran college, and for those studying Lutheran professional ministry or professional lay ministry.

Publications: Application guidelines.

Financial data: Year ended 12/31/2011. Assets, $246,502,070 (M); Expenditures, $13,252,806; Total giving, $10,792,014.

Fields of interest: Protestant agencies & churches.

Type of support: Undergraduate support.

Application information:

Initial approach: E-mail

Deadline(s): Apr. 15 for Norman Krueger American Legion Memorial Scholarship; Apr. 17 for St. Paul Lutheran Church

Program descriptions:

Lutheran Community Foundation Scholarship: These scholarships work to benefit Lutheran students who are members of congregations that hold active organizational endowment funds at the foundation. Eligible applicants must: be a high school graduating senior and a member of a congregation that holds and active foundation organizational fund; demonstrate financial need (applicants must also submit a FAFSA Student Aid Report); plan to attend an accredited Lutheran-affiliated college or university on a full-time basis; and be in good academic standing, with a minimum 3.5 GPA on a 4.0 grading system.

Norman Krueger American Legion Memorial Scholarship: Provides one scholarship of $900 to a graduating high school senior residing in the American Legion Sixth District (Calumet, Fond du Lac, Green Lake, Manitowoc, Marquette and Winnebago counties). Scholarships are awarded on the basis of merit and need and directly made to the institution of higher learning and student after certification of enrollment and acceptance is sent to the scholarship committee.

The Immanuel Evangelical Lutheran Church of North Minneapolis Scholarship: Scholarships are awarded to eligible candidates pursuing a career in professional ministry or professional lay ministry.

The Silverdale Lutheran Church Scholarship: Awards two scholarships in the amounts of $4,000 for a recipient attending a four-year college or university, and $2,000 for a recipient attending a two-year community college or vocational/technical school.

The St. Paul Lutheran Church Scholarship: The scholarship program benefits Lutheran students residing in Lycoming County, Pennsylvania.

The Tulare County Lutheran Scholarship Program for Graduate and Professional Education: Scholarships are awarded to Lutheran students residing in Tulare County. Eligible applicants must be currently enrolled in, or seeking enrollment at, an accredited graduate or professional school; preference will be given to former recipients of the foundation's Scholarship Program for Undergraduates.

The Tulare County Lutheran Scholarship Program for Undergraduates: The scholarships are awarded to high school seniors planning to attend a Lutheran college or university, and to full-time students currently enrolled as an undergraduate in a Lutheran college or university.

EIN: 411802412

4786
Lutheran Social Service of Minnesota

2485 Como Ave.
St. Paul, MN 55108-1445 (651) 642-5990
FAX: (651) 969-2360;
E-mail: mpeterso@lssmn.org; Toll-free tel.: (800) 582-5260; URL: http://www.lssmn.org

Foundation type: Public charity

Purpose: Financial assistance to indigent residents of MN, to help pay for medical services and utilities.

Publications: Annual report; Financial statement; Newsletter.

Financial data: Year ended 09/30/2011. Assets, $75,478,142 (M); Expenditures, $87,447,187; Total giving, $5,221,576; Grants to individuals, totaling $4,613,484.

Type of support: Grants for special needs.

Application information:

Initial approach: Letter

Additional information: Contact the agency for further application guidelines.

EIN: 410872993

4787
Carol E. MacPherson Memorial Scholarship Fund

64 Appleby Hall, 128 Pleasant Ave. S
Minneapolis, MN 55455 (612) 625-6039
Application address: Women's Center

Foundation type: Independent foundation

Purpose: Scholarships for 28-year-old or older female residents of MN, with a five year gap in their education, in a degree program at the University of Minnesota.

Financial data: Year ended 06/30/2012. Assets, $1,015,948 (M); Expenditures, $56,945; Total giving, $46,000; Grants to individuals, 14 grants totaling $46,000 (high: $6,000, low: $2,000).

Fields of interest: Women.

Type of support: Support to graduates or students of specific schools.

Application information: Interview required.

Initial approach: Letter

Deadline(s): Apr. 15

EIN: 510180046

4788
Mahube Community Council

1125 West River Rd.
P.O. Box 747
Detroit Lakes, MN 56502-0747 (218) 847-1385
Contact: Leah Pigatti, Exec. Dir.
FAX: (218) 847-1388; E-mail: dloffice@mahube.org; E-mail for Leah Pigatti: lpigatti@mahube.org; URL: http://www.mahube.org

Foundation type: Public charity

Purpose: Emergency assistance to low-income and elderly persons of Mahnomen, Hubbard, and Becker counties, MN, with food, shelter, and energy assistance.

Publications: Annual report.

Financial data: Year ended 09/30/2011. Assets, $8,431,818 (M); Expenditures, $12,305,978; Total giving, $5,342,537; Grants to individuals, totaling $5,342,537.

Fields of interest: Family services; Aging; Economically disadvantaged; Homeless.

Type of support: Grants for special needs.

Application information: Applications accepted.

Additional information: Applicants must provide proof of income.

EIN: 416049474

4789
Mankato Area Foundation, Inc.
1560 Adams St., Ste. 2
Mankato, MN 56001-3574 (507) 389-4583
Contact: Nancy Zallek
FAX: (507) 389-4581;
E-mail: info@mankatoareafoundation.com;
URL: http://www.mankatoareafoundation.org

Foundation type: Community foundation
Purpose: Scholarship funds for current high school seniors from the Mankato, MN area, pursuing postsecondary education.
Publications: Annual report; Informational brochure (including application guidelines).
Financial data: Year ended 06/30/2012. Assets, $3,558,631 (M); Expenditures, $321,048; Total giving, $122,000; Grants to individuals, 11 grants totaling $18,500.
Fields of interest: Higher education.
Type of support: Scholarships—to individuals; Undergraduate support.
Application information: Applications accepted. Application form required. Application form available on the grantmaker's web site.
> *Deadline(s):* Varies
> *Additional information:* Each scholarship has its own unique set of eligibility criteria and guidelines. See web site for a complete listing.
EIN: 410011094

4790
Masonic Benevolence
923 Upper Valley Dr.
Blue Earth, MN 56013 (507) 526-3680
Contact: William Olson, Dir.

Foundation type: Independent foundation
Purpose: Scholarships to residents of MN affiliated with the Grand Lodge of Masons.
Financial data: Year ended 12/31/2012. Assets, $197,984 (M); Expenditures, $8,785; Total giving, $8,760; Grants to individuals, 8 grants totaling $7,500 (high: $1,000, low: $500).
Fields of interest: Fraternal societies.
Type of support: Undergraduate support.
Application information: Applications accepted.
> *Initial approach:* Letter
> *Additional information:* Application should include description of college and/or career goals.
EIN: 411993844

4791
Mayo Clinic
(formerly Mayo Clinic Rochester)
200 1st St. S.W.
Rochester, MN 55905-0001 (507) 284-2511
FAX: (507) 538-7802; URL: http://www.mayoclinic.org/rochester/

Foundation type: Public charity
Purpose: Research grants, medical assistance to indigent residents of MN, and financial assistance to transplant patients and their families.
Financial data: Year ended 12/31/2011. Assets, $7,570,727,549 (M); Expenditures, $3,413,595,379; Total giving, $125,503,964; Grants to individuals, totaling $4,271,189.
Fields of interest: Health care.
Type of support: Research; In-kind gifts; Grants for special needs.
Application information:
> *Initial approach:* Letter

Additional information: Contact the clinic for eligibility criteria.
EIN: 416011702

4792
Mayo Clinic - St. Mary's Hospital
(formerly St. Mary's Hospital of Rochester)
1216 2nd St., S.W.
Rochester, MN 55902-1906 (507) 538-1297
URL: http://www.mayoclinic.org/saintmaryshospital/

Foundation type: Public charity
Purpose: Short term financial assistance to employees experiencing temporary hardship, and nursing scholarships to employees of Mayo Clinic - St. Mary's Hospital and their dependents to offset the cost of tuition, books or other expenses.
Financial data: Year ended 12/31/2011. Assets, $649,597,613 (M); Expenditures, $800,428,612; Total giving, $72,640; Grants to individuals, totaling $51,500.
Fields of interest: Nursing school/education; Human services.
Type of support: Grants to individuals; Scholarships—to individuals.
Application information: Applications accepted.
EIN: 410944601

4793
The McKnight Endowment Fund for Neuroscience
710 2nd St. S., Ste. 400
Minneapolis, MN 55401-2290 (612) 333-4220
Contact: Kathleen Rysted
FAX: (612) 332-3833;
E-mail: emaler@mcknight.org; URL: http://www.mcknight.org/neuroscience

Foundation type: Operating foundation
Purpose: Grants for medical research in the neurosciences, especially as it pertains to memory and to a clearer understanding of diseases affecting memory and its biological substrates.
Publications: Application guidelines.
Financial data: Year ended 12/31/2012. Assets, $8,037 (M); Expenditures, $3,492,831; Total giving, $2,966,958; Grants to individuals, 35 grants totaling $2,966,958 (high: $100,000, low: $25,000).
Fields of interest: Brain disorders; Neuroscience research.
Type of support: Research; Awards/prizes.
Application information: Application form required.
> *Initial approach:* Letter of intent
> *Deadline(s):* Varies
> *Additional information:* Letters of intent should not exceed two pages. See web site for additional guidelines.
Program descriptions:
> *McKnight Memory and Cognitive Disorders Awards:* Each year this program offers up to four awards, each providing $100,000 per year for three years. These awards support innovative efforts to solve the problems of neurological and psychiatric diseases, especially those related to memory and cognition. They encourage research aimed at translating laboratory discoveries about the brain and nervous system into diagnoses and therapies to improve human health. Collaborative projects between basic and clinical neuroscientists are welcomed, as are proposals that help link basic with clinical neuroscience.
> *McKnight Scholar Awards:* These awards encourage neuroscientists in the early stages of their careers to focus on disorders of learning and

memory. The awards support young scientists who hold a M.D. and/or Ph.D. degree, who have completed formal postdoctoral training, and who demonstrate a commitment to neuroscience. The fund especially seeks applicants working on problems that, if solved at the basic level, would have immediate and significant impact on clinically relevant issues. Up to six McKnight Scholars are selected each year to receive three years' support of $75,000. Funds may be used in any way that will facilitate development of the Scholar's research program, but not indirect costs.
> *McKnight Technological Innovations in Neuroscience Award:* These awards support scientists working on new and unusual approaches to understanding brain function. The program seeks to advance and enlarge the range of technologies available to the neurosciences. It does not support research based primarily on existing techniques. The fund is especially interested in how technology may be used or adapted to monitor, manipulate, analyze, or model brain function at any level, from the molecular to the entire organism. Collaborative and cross-disciplinary applications are invited. Awards are up to $100,000 per year for two years. Up to four awards are given each year. Funds may be used toward a variety of research activities but not the recipient's salary.
EIN: 411563321

4794
The McKnight Foundation
710 S. 2nd St., Ste. 400
Minneapolis, MN 55401-2290 (612) 333-4220
Contact: Kate Wolford, Pres.
FAX: (612) 332-3833; E-mail: info@mcknight.org;
URL: http://www.mcknight.org

Foundation type: Independent foundation
Purpose: Awards to MN artists in recognition of their artistic excellence and significant impacts on the state's cultural life over several decades. Awards by nomination only to residents of MN who are direct-care personnel with minimum public recognition and minimum financial remuneration.
Publications: Application guidelines; Annual report; Financial statement; Grants list; Informational brochure; Newsletter; Occasional report.
Financial data: Year ended 12/31/2012. Assets, $2,063,472,860 (M); Expenditures, $112,560,597; Total giving, $85,114,992. Awards/prizes amount not specified.
Fields of interest: Arts; Human services.
Type of support: Awards/grants by nomination only; Awards/prizes.
Application information:
> *Initial approach:* Letter
> *Deadline(s):* Mar. 31 for Artist Awards; July 7 for Human Services
> *Additional information:* Individual applications not accepted; Completion of formal nomination required for named programs.
Program descriptions:
> *McKnight Distinguished Artist Award:* The McKnight Distinguished Artist Award recognizes a Minnesota artist for artistic excellence as well as significant impact on the state's cultural life over several decades. One artist is honored with this $50,000 award each year. The award celebrates the achievements and contributions of a generation of artists who, individually and collectively, have laid the foundation for the wealth of arts activity Minnesotans currently enjoy. Although these artists have been working in the state throughout their lives, their role in Minnesota's vital artistic tradition as well as their own accomplishments often are overlooked as time goes on. In recognizing them,

the award will help document Minnesota's cultural history. The award is the newest component of the foundation's long-standing support for individual artists. Artists in all disciplines - including ceramics, dance, film, literature, music, theater, and visual arts - whose careers have made a substantial impact on the arts in Minnesota may be nominated. Artists must have worked in Minnesota over a span of decades, although they need not reside in Minnesota when nominated. Those from Minnesota who achieved their primary successes elsewhere, however, are not eligible. No one may receive the award more than once. No posthumous awards will be made. Send your nomination via e-mail to Kristen Marx, Arts Program Admin., kmarx@mcknight.org.

Virginia McKnight Binger Awards in Human Service: Each year the foundation recognize up to six Minnesotans who have demonstrated an exceptional personal commitment to helping others in their communities but who have received little or no public recognition. Each receives $10,000 and is honored at a ceremony in late summer. See web site for nomination deadlines. Nominations may be submitted online, or a nomination form can be printed from the foundation's web site and submitted via postal mail.
EIN: 410754835

4795
Methodist Hospital

6500 Excelsior Blvd.
St. Louis Park, MN   55426-4702   (952) 993-5000
URL: http://www.parknicollet.com/methodist/

Foundation type: Public charity
Purpose: Scholarship assistance to Park Nicollet Methodist Hospital volunteers who have provided exceptional service and are interested in furthering their education.
Financial data: Year ended 12/31/2010. Assets, $659,774,758 (M); Expenditures, $472,445,469; Total giving, $5,033,519; Grants to individuals, totaling $15,000.
Fields of interest: Education.
Type of support: Scholarships—to individuals.
Application information: Applications accepted.
EIN: 410132080

4796
Roy E. and Merle Meyer Foundation

P.O. Box 385573
Minneapolis, MN   55438-5573   (651) 385-4603
Contact: Beth Kelly
Application address: c/o Red Wing Central High School, Guidance Office, 154 Tower View Dr., Red Wing, MN 55066-1134

Foundation type: Independent foundation
Purpose: Scholarships to Red Wing Central High School, MN, seniors who intend to pursue a career in the sciences.
Financial data: Year ended 12/31/2012. Assets, $52,641 (M); Expenditures, $3,693; Total giving, $3,600; Grants to individuals, 3 grants totaling $3,600 (high: $1,200, low: $1,200).
Fields of interest: Higher education; Science.
Type of support: Scholarships—to individuals; Support to graduates or students of specific schools.
Application information: Applications accepted.
Applicants should submit the following:
    1) ACT
    2) SAT
    3) GPA

Additional information: Application should also include a list of extracurricular activities. Students should contact their guidance counselor for application information.
EIN: 416078887

4797
Minnesota American Legion, Auxiliary & The Sons of The American Legion Brain Science Foundation

(formerly Minnesota American Legion Auxiliary Brain Science Foundation)
20 W. 12th St., State Veterans Bldg., Ste. 300A
St. Paul, MN   55155   (651) 291-1800
Contact: Jim Kellogg, Pres.
URL: http://www.mnlegion.org/

Foundation type: Independent foundation
Purpose: Scholarships for the investigation of brain and brain related disease.
Financial data: Year ended 12/31/2012. Assets, $998,629 (M); Expenditures, $64,703; Total giving, $52,453; Grants to individuals, 3 grants totaling $12,000 (high: $10,000, low: $1,000).
Fields of interest: Brain research.
Type of support: Scholarships—to individuals.
Application information: Contact the foundation for application guidelines.
EIN: 411577513

4798
Minnesota Business Partnership

3530 IDS Ctr.
Minneapolis, MN   55402-2100   (612) 370-0840
Application e-mail: angie.scheib@mnbp.com
FAX: (612) 334-3086;
E-mail: jim.bartholomew@mnbp.com; URL: http://www.mnbp.com/

Foundation type: Public charity
Purpose: Grants to MN public school teachers for the development of programs that focus on science, technology, engineering and math (STEM) education.
Publications: Application guidelines.
Financial data: Year ended 08/31/2011. Assets, $860,970 (M); Expenditures, $2,498,804; Total giving, $719,488.
Fields of interest: Education.
Type of support: Grants to individuals.
Application information: Applications accepted. Application form required. Application form available on the grantmaker's web site.
Initial approach: Proposal
Send request by: Online
Deadline(s): Mar. 30
Additional information: See web site for additional guidelines.
Program description:
Qwest Teachers and Technology Grant Program: The program, sponsored by CenturyLink and administered by the Minnesota Business Partnership Education Foundation, works to improve E-12 education by recognizing teachers who are finding innovative ways to apply technology in the classroom to improve student achievement, increasing awareness of how other teachers are using technology in the classroom, and modeling best practices of technology integration in the classroom. The program will consider grant requests up to $7,500, with special consideration given to proposals that focus on science, technology, engineering and math (STEM) education. To be eligible, the applicant must be a teacher in a Minnesota public school which must be located in the CenturyLink service area (the school

does not need to be a CenturyLink customer). The school must be open and operating for at least one year prior to applying for the grant, and neither the teacher nor school must have received a grant in the past year.
EIN: 411317465

4799
Minnesota Center for Book Arts

(also known as MCBA)
1011 Washington Ave. S., Ste. 100
Minneapolis, MN   55415-1279   (612) 215-2520
Contact: Jeff Rathermel, Exec. Dir.
FAX: (612) 215-2545;
E-mail: mcba@mnbookarts.org; E-Mail for Jeff Rathermel: jrathermel@mnbookarts.org;
URL: http://www.mnbookarts.org

Foundation type: Public charity
Purpose: Residencies to emerging printmaking, papermaking and bookbinding artists residing in MN.
Publications: Application guidelines.
Financial data: Year ended 04/30/2012. Assets, $255,476 (M); Expenditures, $775,405.
Fields of interest: Arts.
Type of support: Residencies.
Application information: Applications accepted. Application form required. Application form available on the grantmaker's web site.
Initial approach: Letter
Send request by: Mail
Deadline(s): Oct. 1, Feb. 1, June 1 for Artist-In-Residence Program, Sept. 5 for MCBA/Jerome Foundation Book Arts Mentorship Program
Applicants should submit the following:
    1) Budget Information
    2) Resume
    3) Proposal
Additional information: Application should also include artist statement.
Program descriptions:
Artists-in-Residence Program (AIR): This program is designed to support selected artists by providing resources, space, and equipment to assist in the creation and promotion of their work. Residencies may be short-term (two to weeks) are designed for research, skill building, and/or work on a single phase of a new or ongoing project, and include a stipend of $2,500, or long-term (two to three months) are designed for production of a new work, and include a $2,000 housing allowance, a $2,500 stipend, and a $1,000 materials budget, for a total grant of $5,500. Studios and equipment are available to facilitate work in papermaking, printing, and bookbinding. Participation in the program is based on the artistic merit of proposed projects as well as the degree to which artists further the center's artistic vision.
MCBA/Jerome Foundation Book Arts Fellowship: This program allows Minnesota artists of diverse disciplines, including printers, papermakers, binders, painters, sculptors, poets, photographers, and essayists, to explore the book as a vehicle for personal expression. Fellowships are open to artists of all disciplines interested in exploring the book form; fellows receive project funding, studio and equipment use, artistic support from center staff and artists, and a one-year center membership. This is a biennial program, application materials are released in late summer of odd years.
MCBA/Jerome Foundation Book Arts Mentorship: This mentorship is an artist development program aimed at introducing book arts to emerging artists whose primary medium is in another discipline. Mentorships will be awarded to six emerging artists

selected from the following disciplines: literary arts (poetry, spoken word, fiction, and creative nonfiction); visual arts (drawing, painting, photography, sculpture, mixed media, and new media); music (composing); film/video (filmmakers, animation), theater (playwriting), and dance (choreography). Selected artists will receive $1,500 for the purchase of materials and to supplement living or travel costs, three months of basic book arts training at the center, free tuition to participate in up to three workshops offered by the center through its regular adult education schedule (artist pays material fees), the ability to meet regularly with a mentor and attend master classes that provide contextual and historical foundations for book arts, one year's membership to the center, and recognition through a culminating exhibition held in the center's main gallery.
EIN: 411455905

4800
Minnesota Licensed Family Child Care Association, Inc.

1821 University Ave. W., Ste. 324-S
St. Paul, MN 55104-2874 (651) 636-1989
Contact: Katy Chase, Exec. Dir.
FAX: (651) 636-9146;
E-mail: orderinfo@MLFCCA.org; Toll-free tel.: (800)-652-9704; E-Mail for Katy Chase: katy.chase@mlfcca.org; URL: http://www.mlfcca.org/

Foundation type: Public charity
Purpose: Support services for family child care providers in Minnesota.
Financial data: Year ended 09/30/2011. Assets, $377,453 (M); Expenditures, $3,314,703; Total giving, $2,618,549; Grants to individuals, totaling $2,618,549.
Fields of interest: Children, services.
Type of support: Grants for special needs.
Application information: Contact association for additional information.
EIN: 416152641

4801
Minnesota Medical Foundation

200 Oak St. S.E., Ste. 300
Minneapolis, MN 55455-2030 (612) 624-3333
FAX: (612) 625-4305; E-mail: mmf@mmf.umn.edu;
Toll-free tel.: (800) 775-2187; URL: http://www.mmf.umn.edu/

Foundation type: Public charity
Purpose: Scholarships and grants to individual faculty and students of the University of Minnesota Academic Health Center, to support their educational goals.
Publications: Application guidelines; Annual report; Newsletter.
Financial data: Year ended 06/30/2013. Assets, $0 (M); Expenditures, $510,668,529; Total giving, $502,716,337; Grants to individuals, totaling $72,580.
Application information: Applications accepted.
Program descriptions:
Medical School Grants: Research and equipment grants are awarded to University of Minnesota Medical School faculty for basic and clinical research. Priority is given to new faculty who are establishing a research program, to established faculty exploring new areas of research, and for interim support. Support is given to startup funding for new investigations, equipment funding, bridge funding during a grant lapse, emergency funding, or support for faculty whose research focus has

changed. Eligibility is limited to departmental faculty who hold full-time salaried positions in the University of Minnesota Medical School at the rank of assistant professor or above.
Medical School Scholarships: Scholarships are available to graduate students enrolled in medical programs at the University of Minnesota. Scholarships are awarded through the financial aid offices at both the Twin Cities and Duluth campuses; eligibility is determined through a standard nationwide financial aid application process.
Research Grants: Grants are available to University of Minnesota Medical School students who are pursuing innovative research in basic and clinical research. First-year students are eligible for $3,000 grants for eight weeks of research during the summer after year one; third- and fourth-year students are eligible for $4,000 grants for twelve weeks of research.
School of Public Health Scholarships: Financial awards are given each fall to incoming graduate students enrolled in medical programs at the University of Minnesota. Applicants who wish to be considered for an award must submit a scholarship form with their application materials.
EIN: 416027707

4802
Minnesota Ovarian Cancer Alliance

(also known as MOCA)
4604 Chicago Ave.
Minneapolis, MN 55407-3513 (612) 822-0500
Contact: Kathleen Gavin, Exec. Dir.
FAX: (612) 825-1140;
E-mail: kgavin@mnovarian.org; URL: http://www.mnovarian.org
Additional URL: http://www.ovaryact.org

Foundation type: Public charity
Purpose: Research grants to individuals for ovarian cancer research projects conducted in MN that support better treatment and a cure. Also, scholarships for oncology nurses to attend ovarian cancer conferences.
Publications: Annual report; Informational brochure; Newsletter.
Financial data: Year ended 12/31/2012. Assets, $1,577,212 (M); Expenditures, $1,158,805; Total giving, $690,000; Grants to individuals, totaling $690,000.
Fields of interest: Cancer; Cancer research.
Type of support: Research; Scholarships—to individuals; Awards/prizes.
Application information: Applications accepted. Application form required. Application form available on the grantmaker's web site.
Initial approach: Application
Send request by: Mail, fax or e-mail
Deadline(s): Varies
Applicants should submit the following:
1) Letter(s) of recommendation
2) Curriculum vitae
3) Budget Information
EIN: 411960449

4803
Minnesota P.E.O. Home Fund

2711 Chestnut Ave.
Minneapolis, MN 55405 (612) 377-0843
Contact: Barbara Zielinski, Admin.

Foundation type: Public charity
Purpose: Grants to individuals who are aged, infirmed, or indigent and are in need of housing,

medical treatment and other basic necessities throughout MN.
Financial data: Year ended 03/31/2013. Assets, $1,515,513 (M); Expenditures, $152,761; Total giving, $142,126; Grants to individuals, totaling $142,126.
Fields of interest: Aging; Economically disadvantaged.
Type of support: Grants for special needs.
Application information: Applications accepted.
Additional information: Contact the fund for additional information.
EIN: 411223084

4804
Minnesota Power Foundation

30 W. Superior St.
Duluth, MN 55802-2191
Contact: Peggy Hanson, Secy.
E-mail: mhanson@mnpower.com; URL: http://www.mnpowerfoundation.org/

Foundation type: Company-sponsored foundation
Purpose: Scholarships to high school seniors in areas of Minnesota Power company operations for college, university, or vocational education. Scholarships to students at selected schools who are in their second year of study in an engineering or business related field.
Publications: Application guidelines.
Financial data: Year ended 12/31/2012. Assets, $1,238,481 (M); Expenditures, $1,008,111; Total giving, $983,948.
Fields of interest: Vocational education; Higher education; Environment; Business/industry; Engineering/technology.
Type of support: Scholarships—to individuals; Undergraduate support.
Application information: Applications accepted. Application form required. Application form available on the grantmaker's web site.
Send request by: E-mail
Deadline(s): Jan. 14 for Community Involvement Scholarships, Feb. 1 for New Generation Scholarships
Final notification: Applicants notified in Apr.
Applicants should submit the following:
1) Photograph
2) Letter(s) of recommendation
3) Essay
4) Transcripts
Program descriptions:
Community Involvement Scholarship Program: The foundation awards 20 $2,500 scholarships to high school seniors residing in Minnesota Power's service territory. The award is based on student's involvement in the community through volunteer activities, and financial need.
New Generation Scholarships: The foundation awards $1,000 college scholarships to students in the second year of an Associate Degree program and $2,500 scholarships to students in the junior or senior year of a Bachelor Degree program at selected universities. Associate degree students must study electrical or mechanical maintenance, electric technology, environmental water quality, industrial technology, engineering, electrical lineworker technology, electrical construction and maintenance, wind energy, or business, accounting, or finance. Bachelor Degree students must study engineering, economics, teaching including math, science, or industrial education, accounting, business or finance, information technology, or environmental science. Students must have a GPA of 3.0.
EIN: 562560595

4805
Minnesota Section PGA Foundation
c/o Bob Bush
12800 Bunker Prairie Rd.
Coon Rapids, MN 55448-1445 (612) 754-0820
Contact: Jon Tollette, Exec. Dir.
URL: http://www.minnesotapga.com/
foundation.php

Foundation type: Public charity
Purpose: College scholarships to junior golfers to continue their education beyond high school.
Financial data: Year ended 12/31/2011. Assets, $956,915 (M); Expenditures, $34,151; Total giving, $30,150; Grants to individuals, 21 grants totaling $21,000.
Fields of interest: Higher education; Athletics/sports, golf.
Type of support: Scholarships—to individuals.
Application information: Applications accepted.
Additional information: Scholarship recipients must provide documentation or current grades and enrollment at a university, by producing class schedule before any payment is made to the university. Applicants must be 18 years old or younger.
EIN: 411810679

4806
Minnesota Valley Action Council, Inc.
706 N. Victory Dr.
Mankato, MN 56001-4804 (507) 345-6822
E-mail: lynn@mnvac.org; Toll-Free Tel.: (800) 767-7139; URL: http://www.mnvac.org

Foundation type: Public charity
Purpose: Assistance to low income individuals and families of south central Minnesota with utility, weatherization, employment, housing and other special needs.
Publications: Application guidelines; Newsletter.
Financial data: Year ended 03/31/2012. Assets, $7,432,587 (M); Expenditures, $19,595,482; Total giving, $9,286,849; Grants to individuals, totaling $8,349,731.
Fields of interest: Human services; Economically disadvantaged.
Type of support: Grants for special needs.
Application information: Applications accepted. Application form required.
Send request by: Mail for Energy Assistance
Deadline(s): May 31 for Energy Assistance
Additional information: Applications for Energy Assistance are available on the web site. See web site for eligibility determination for other assistance.
EIN: 416050353

4807
Minnesota Zoo Foundation
13000 Zoo Blvd.
Apple Valley, MN 55124-4621 (952) 431-9200
Contact: Melissa Lindsay, Exec. Dir.
E-mail address for internship: mnzoo@state.mn.us
FAX: (952) 431-9300; E-mail: info@mnzoo.org; Toll Free tel. : (800)-366-7811; URL: http://mnzoo.org/

Foundation type: Public charity
Purpose: Internships for junior and senior students of MN, with learning experiences to further their zoological or public service careers.
Financial data: Year ended 06/30/2012. Assets, $4,199,270 (M); Expenditures, $4,196,478; Total giving, $3,105,959; Grants to individuals, totaling $21,237.
Fields of interest: Higher education.

Type of support: Internship funds.
Application information: Applications accepted. Application form required.
Send request by: E-mail
Deadline(s): Mar. 31 for summer internship, Dec. 1 for spring internship
Applicants should submit the following:
1) Transcripts
2) Resume
Additional information: Student intern must be receiving academic credit from, or fulfilling an academic requirement for an accredited educational institution.
EIN: 510147653

4808
Miracle-Ear Children's Foundation
5000 Cheshire Pkwy. N.
Plymouth, MN 55446-4103 (763) 268-4000
Contact: Jenni Hargraves
URL: http://www.miracle-ear.com/childrenrequest.aspx

Foundation type: Company-sponsored foundation
Purpose: Contributions of hearing aids to hearing-impaired children ages 16 and younger from families with income levels which do not allow them to receive public support.
Financial data: Year ended 12/31/2012. Assets, $15,907 (M); Expenditures, $55,636; Total giving, $55,636.
Fields of interest: Children/youth, services; Disabilities, people with.
Type of support: Grants for special needs.
Application information: Applications accepted. Application form required. Application form available on the grantmaker's web site.
Deadline(s): None
Additional information: Application must also include a dated, recent audiogram and medical clearance.
EIN: 411677967

4809
Miracles of Mitch Foundation
P.O. Box 0878
Chanhassen, MN 55317-878 (952) 361-9600
Contact: Mike Krance, Exec. Dir.
FAX: (952) 400-8838;
E-mail: rmsassoc@usinternet.com; URL: http://www.miraclesofmitchfoundation.org

Foundation type: Public charity
Purpose: Grants and other assistance to families of children struggling with cancer within the state of MN.
Financial data: Year ended 09/30/2012. Assets, $525,072 (M); Expenditures, $855,146; Total giving, $380,171; Grants to individuals, totaling $380,171.
Fields of interest: Cancer; Children.
Type of support: Grants for special needs.
Application information:
Initial approach: Telephone or e-mail
Send request by: Fax
Additional information: Families should contact their Social Worker for help with forms to apply for a grant.
EIN: 562384527

4810
Jack Moon Scholarship Foundation
c/o Wells Fargo Bank, N.A.
230 W. Superior St., 5th Fl.
Duluth, MN 55802-1916
Application address: c/o Wells Fargo Wealth Mgmt. Minnesota Scholarship Programs, Attn.: Scholarship Mgmt. Svcs., 1 Scholarship Way, St. Peter, MN 56082, tel.: (507) 931-1682

Foundation type: Independent foundation
Purpose: Scholarships to graduating high school students of Denfeld High School, MN for attendance at accredited vocational or trade schools in Minnesota, Wisconsin or Michigan.
Financial data: Year ended 12/31/2012. Assets, $5,069,387 (M); Expenditures, $386,261; Total giving, $169,428; Grants to individuals, 60 grants totaling $169,428 (high: $7,500; low: $2,500).
Fields of interest: Vocational education, post-secondary.
Type of support: Support to graduates or students of specific schools.
Application information: Applications accepted. Application form required.
Deadline(s): Jan. 15
Applicants should submit the following:
1) Transcripts
2) Letter(s) of recommendation
Additional information: Scholarship is based on financial need, academic achievement, serious purpose and likelihood to succeed. Application forms are available from the high school guidance department.
EIN: 202403787

4811
National Multiple Sclerosis Society, Minnesota Chapter
200 12th Ave. S.
Minneapolis, MN 55415-1222 (612) 335-7900
FAX: (612) 335-7997; E-mail: info@mssociety.com; Toll-Free tel.: (800) 582-5296; URL: http://www.nationalmssociety.org/chapters/mnm/index.aspx

Foundation type: Public charity
Purpose: Scholarships to residents of MN with multiple sclerosis. Grants for medical equipment and emergency needs are also given.
Publications: Annual report; Newsletter.
Financial data: Year ended 09/30/2011. Assets, $5,012,483 (M); Expenditures, $7,406,146; Total giving, $787,263; Grants to individuals, totaling $525,790.
Fields of interest: Multiple sclerosis.
Type of support: Scholarships—to individuals; Grants for special needs.
Application information: Contact foundation for application guidelines.
EIN: 410790658

4812
New York Mills Arts Retreat
24 N. Main Ave.
P.O. Box 246
New York Mills, MN 56567-4318 (218) 385-3339
Contact: Jamie Robertson, Exec. Dir.
FAX: (218) 385-3366; E-mail: info@kulcher.org; URL: http://www.kulcher.org

Foundation type: Public charity
Purpose: Residencies to artists, primarily to residents of MN and New York City, NY.
Publications: Application guidelines.

Financial data: Year ended 12/31/2011. Assets, $239,110 (M); Expenditures, $144,006.
Fields of interest: Sculpture; Arts; African Americans/Blacks.
Type of support: Residencies; Stipends.
Application information: Application form required.
  Initial approach: E-mail
  Send request by: Mail
  Copies of proposal: 5
  Deadline(s): Apr. 1 and Oct. 1
  Applicants should submit the following:
    1) SASE
    2) Letter(s) of recommendation
    3) Work samples
    4) Resume
  Additional information: Application should also include biography.
Program description:
  Arts Retreat Program: This program provides artists with dedicated time for creative exploration and development, while providing a unique taste of life in rural Minnesota. Artists are given two to six weeks in which to immerse themselves in their artwork, as well as a fully-furnished house.
EIN: 411690163

4813
North Suburban Community Foundation
3422 Chandler Road
Shoreview, MN 55126-3914   (651) 633-3623

Foundation type: Community foundation
Purpose: Awards college scholarships to high school seniors from donor-designated funds.
Financial data: Year ended 06/30/2012. Assets, $893,755 (M); Expenditures, $107,891; Total giving, $100,813; Grants to individuals, 8 grants totaling $5,000.
Application information: Recipients are selected by broad-based committees based on merit and need.
EIN: 411408909

4814
Northern Clay Center
2424 Franklin Ave. E.
Minneapolis, MN 55406-1027   (612) 339-8007
Contact: Emily Galusha, Exec. Dir.; Sarah Millfelt, Dir., Artists' Grants
FAX: (612) 339-0592;
E-mail: nccinfo@northernclaycenter.org;
URL: http://www.northernclaycenter.org

Foundation type: Public charity
Purpose: Project grants and fellowships to ceramic artists, primarily to MN residents, NYC and elsewhere.
Publications: Application guidelines; Annual report; Newsletter.
Financial data: Year ended 12/31/2011. Assets, $3,725,413 (M); Expenditures, $1,625,657; Total giving, $101,726; Grants to individuals, totaling $101,726.
Fields of interest: Ceramic arts.
Type of support: Fellowships; Residencies; Project support.
Application information: Applications accepted. Application form required. Application form available on the grantmaker's web site.
  Initial approach: Application
  Copies of proposal: 1
  Deadline(s): Feb. for Project Grants, Mar. for Fellowships
  Final notification: Recipients notified in approximately six weeks
  Applicants should submit the following:
    1) Work samples

2) Curriculum vitae
    3) SASE
    4) Resume
    5) Budget Information
Program descriptions:
  Anonymous Potter Studio Fellowship Program: This program supports an emerging potter through the provision of single private studio space for a 12-month period (valued at $2,200). In addition, the fellowship includes ongoing opportunities to teach adult and children's classes through the center's education program. Fellowships provide an opportunity to develop his/her body of work, experiment with various techniques and processes, and participate in center workshops and lectures. Eligible applicants must have completed all formal undergraduate academic training by the start of the grant period, who are not currently enrolled full- or part-time in a degree-granting institution (including B.A., M.F.A., or a teaching certification program), and who are not employed full-time as a ceramics teacher at the college level.
  Fogelberg Studio Fellowship Program: Fellowship awards of $3,000 each are available to provide emerging ceramic artists an opportunity to be in residence for one year at the center, where they can develop their own work as well as exchange ideas and knowledge with other ceramic artists. Eligible applicants must be established clay artists who have completed all formal undergraduate academic training by the start of the grant period, who are not currently enrolled full- or part-time in a degree-granting institution (including B.A., M.F.A., or a teaching certification program), and who are not employed full-time as a ceramics teacher at the college level.
  Jerome Project Grants: This program provides three grants of $6,000 each to Minnesota ceramic artists at relatively early stages in their careers, as they accomplish short-term, specific objects. Projects may include, but are not limited to: experimenting with new techniques and materials; working on studying with a mentor; purchasing equipment to facilitate an aesthetic or technical investigation; providing studio time, studio rental, supplies, and technical support; collaborations between ceramic artists and artists working in other media; education or exhibition opportunities; and travel. Eligible applicants must be clay artists who have completed all formal academic training by the start of the grant period, who are not enrolled either full- or part-time in degree-granting institutions (including B.A., M.F.A., and teaching certification programs), who are not employed full-time as ceramics teachers at the college level, and who have lived in Minnesota for at least six months prior to the application deadline.
  McKnight Artist Fellowships for Ceramic Artists: Two grants of $25,000 each are annually awarded to strengthen and enhance Minnesota's artistic community by providing recognition and direct financial support for mid-career ceramic artists. Fellowships are intended to significantly advance the work of Minnesota ceramic artists whose work is of exceptional artistic merit, who have already proven their abilities, and are at a career stage that is beyond emerging. Awarded may be used for, but are not limited to, supplementing living or travel costs, purchasing materials and equipment, experimenting with new materials and techniques, and collaborating with other artists. Eligible applicants must: be residents of Minnesota who have lived in the state for at least one year prior to the application deadline; be primarily a ceramic artist (either functional or sculptural); have completed all formal academic training and may not be enrolled either full- or part-time in school; provide evidence of professional achievement over a period

of at least five years, through inclusion in major regional or national museum or gallery exhibitions, juried or invitational craft shows, or receipt of other awards, grants, or fellowships; and demonstrate that their work has a sustained level of accomplishment, commitment, and excellence.
  McKnight Artist Residencies for Ceramic Artists: This program provides grants of $5,000 each to provide national and international mid-career individual ceramic artists an opportunity to be in residence for three months at the center, where they can develop their own work and, at the same time, exchange ideas and knowledge with Minnesota ceramic artists. In addition to grant support, artists will be provided with studio space, as well as a glaze and firing allowance, and an additional $300 honorarium. Eligible applicants must be ceramic artists (either functional or sculptural) who are not residents of Minnesota, who have completed all formal academic training, and who may not be enrolled either full- or part-time in school.
EIN: 411616650

4815
Northern Coop Foundation
P.O. Box 52
Wadena, MN 56482

Foundation type: Independent foundation
Purpose: Scholarships to students of MN enrolled in a postsecondary course related to cooperative principles.
Financial data: Year ended 09/30/2013. Assets, $205,617 (M); Expenditures, $3,089; Total giving, $3,000; Grants to individuals, 3 grants totaling $3,000 (high: $1,000, low: $1,000).
Fields of interest: Higher education.
Type of support: Scholarships—to individuals.
Application information: Applications accepted. Application form required.
  Initial approach: Application
  Send request by: Mail
  Deadline(s): Mar. 1
EIN: 363258840

4816
Northern Star Council, Boy Scouts of America, Inc.
(formerly Indianhead/Viking Council, Boy Scouts of America, Inc.)
393 Marshall Ave.
Saint Paul, MN 55102-1717   (763) 231-7201
Contact: John Andrews, C.E.O.
FAX: (763) 231-7202; Toll-free tel.: (877) 231-7276; URL: http://www.northernstarbsa.org

Foundation type: Public charity
Purpose: Scholarships to graduating seniors who have attained the rank of Eagle Scout for attendance at an accredited college or university for higher education.
Publications: Annual report; Informational brochure; Newsletter.
Financial data: Year ended 12/31/2011. Assets, $30,546,694 (M); Expenditures, $13,714,449; Total giving, $386,894; Grants to individuals, totaling $340,544.
Fields of interest: Higher education; Boy scouts.
Type of support: Scholarships—to individuals.
Application information: Applications accepted. Application form required.
  Deadline(s): Jan. 30
  Final notification: Recipients notified Mar.16
  Applicants should submit the following:
    1) Transcripts

2) SAT
3) Letter(s) of recommendation
4) ACT
5) Financial information
Additional information: Applicant must demonstrate leadership ability in Scouting and a strong record of participation in activities outside of Scouting, and a brief statement of 50 to 100 words entitled "What receiving this Eagle Scout Scholarship would mean to me"
EIN: 203000282

4817
Northwest Minnesota Foundation (NWMF)

201 3rd St. N.W.
Bemidji, MN 56601 (218) 759-2057
Contact: For grants: Nate Dorr, Grants Off.
FAX: (218) 759-2328; E-mail: info@nwmf.org;
Additional tel. for MN residents: (800) 659-7859;
Grant request e-mail: nated@nwmf.org;
URL: http://www.nwmf.org

Foundation type: Community foundation
Purpose: Support to entrepreneurs to encourage business development in the northwestern MN, region.
Publications: Application guidelines; Annual report; Grants list; Informational brochure; Newsletter.
Financial data: Year ended 06/30/2012. Assets, $48,212,224 (M); Expenditures, $4,336,767; Total giving, $1,788,505; Grants to individuals, 151 grants totaling $204,650 (high: $3,000, low: $100).
Fields of interest: Agriculture; Business/industry.
Type of support: Program development; Seed money; Scholarships—to individuals.
Application information: Applications accepted. Application form required.
Initial approach: E-mail
Send request by: Mail or online
Copies of proposal: 2
Final notification: Applicants notified within two to three weeks
Additional information: Contact the foundation for additional application guidelines.
EIN: 411556013

4818
C.P. & Irene Olson Trust

1100 W. St. Germain St.
St. Cloud, MN 56301

Foundation type: Independent foundation
Purpose: Scholarships to individuals who are residents of Burke, Renville, Ward or Bottineau counties, ND.
Financial data: Year ended 12/31/2012. Assets, $244,433 (M); Expenditures, $16,050; Total giving, $12,000; Grants to individuals, 15 grants totaling $12,000 (high: $800, low: $800).
Fields of interest: Higher education.
Type of support: Undergraduate support.
Application information: Applications accepted.
Initial approach: Letter
Deadline(s): None
Additional information: Request for scholarship should be sent to the Scholarship Committee.
EIN: 456076668

4819
Joyce L. Osborn Scholarship Trust

P.O. Box 64713 - Trust Tax Servcies
St. Paul, MN 55164-0713 (507) 285-7927
Application address: c/o High School Counselors, Rochester Area High Schools, Rochester, MN 55902

Foundation type: Independent foundation
Purpose: Scholarships to Rochester, MN, high school graduates to attend colleges and universities in the U.S.
Financial data: Year ended 12/31/2012. Assets, $169,926 (M); Expenditures, $7,504; Total giving, $4,000; Grants to individuals, 4 grants totaling $4,000 (high: $1,000, low: $1,000).
Fields of interest: Higher education.
Type of support: Support to graduates or students of specific schools; Undergraduate support.
Application information: Applications accepted. Application form required.
Deadline(s): Apr. 1
Additional information: Application should include transcript.
EIN: 416293028

4820
Page Education Foundation

P.O. Box 581254
Minneapolis, MN 55458-1254 (612) 332-0406
Contact: Carolyn Jones, Dir., Admin.
FAX: (612) 332-0403; E-mail: info@page-ed.org;
Application address: P.O. Box 581254, Minneapolis, MN 55458-1254; URL: http://www.page-ed.org

Foundation type: Public charity
Purpose: Grants to graduating MN high school students of color for postsecondary education to attend colleges, universities and technical schools within MN.
Publications: Application guidelines; Annual report; Newsletter.
Financial data: Year ended 06/30/2011. Assets, $3,311,935 (M); Expenditures, $1,099,936; Total giving, $757,411; Grants to individuals, 568 grants totaling $757,411.
Fields of interest: Vocational education, post-secondary; Higher education; Minorities.
Type of support: Grants to individuals; Undergraduate support.
Application information: Applications accepted. Application form required. Application form available on the grantmaker's web site.
Send request by: Mail
Deadline(s): May 1
Applicants should submit the following:
1) Financial information
2) Letter(s) of recommendation
3) Transcripts
4) Essay
Additional information: Application should also include a copy of parents' most recent federal tax return, SSI benefits, MFIP/welfare benefits or other income statement. Grants must be renewed every year.
Program description:
Grants: Grants are available to Minnesota youth of color who want to pursue their dreams through postsecondary education. Eligible applicants must be students of color who are graduates of a Minnesota high school and who are enrolled full-time in a postsecondary educational institution in Minnesota. Applicants must be willing to complete a minimum of 50 hours for a

service-to-children project. Awards range in value from $1,000 to $2,500.
EIN: 363605013

4821
Patterson Foundation

(formerly Patterson Dental Foundation)
1031 Mendota Heights Rd.
St. Paul, MN 55120-1419 (651) 686-1929
Contact: Admin.
E-mail: information@pattersonfoundation.net;
URL: http://www.pattersonfoundation.net

Foundation type: Independent foundation
Purpose: Scholarships for dependents of Patterson Dental Co. employees. the program is administered through Scholarship America.
Publications: Application guidelines; Grants list; Informational brochure (including application guidelines).
Financial data: Year ended 12/31/2012. Assets, $16,890,021 (M); Expenditures, $981,875; Total giving, $796,755.
Type of support: Employee-related scholarships.
Application information: Applications accepted.
Initial approach: Letter
EIN: 743076772

4822
Hans and Thora Petraborg Educational Trust Fund

46 2nd Ave Se.
Aitkin, MN 56431 (218) 927-2115
Contact: Bernie Novak, Tr.
Application address: Aitkin Schools, Aitkin, MN 56431

Foundation type: Operating foundation
Purpose: Interest-free loans to graduates of Aitkin High School, MN, for higher education.
Financial data: Year ended 12/31/2011. Assets, $364,134 (M); Expenditures, $39,363; Total giving, $39,262; Grants to individuals, 32 grants totaling $39,262 (high: $3,000, low: $562).
Type of support: Student loans—to individuals; Support to graduates or students of specific schools; Undergraduate support.
Application information: Applications accepted. Application form required.
Deadline(s): None
Additional information: Application forms available upon request.
EIN: 411360435

4823
The John T. Petters Foundation

3101 Old Highway 8
Roseville, MN 55113-1072 (952) 405-9144
Contact: Robert D. Lawson, Exec. Dir.
E-mail: info@johntpettersfoundation.org

Foundation type: Public charity
Purpose: Scholarship support to undergraduate students wishing to study abroad, especially in the field of business.
Publications: Application guidelines.
Financial data: Year ended 12/31/2011. Assets, $1,972,090 (M); Expenditures, $275,993; Total giving, $40,000.
Fields of interest: Business school/education.
Type of support: Scholarships—to individuals.
Application information: Applications accepted. Application form required. Application form available on the grantmaker's web site.
Deadline(s): Sept. 30

Applicants should submit the following:
1) Letter(s) of recommendation
2) Transcripts
3) Essay

Program description:

Scholarships: Scholarships, generally averaging $5,000 each, will be made available to students who wish to study abroad as part of their educational experience. Eligible applicants must be attending an accredited college or university in the U.S. as an undergraduate student, and must be applying, or have been accepted, into a study abroad program eligible for credit by the student's accredited institution. Scholarships are primarily for students who are looking to study business internationally; students from all disciplines are welcome to apply, but all awarded scholarships must be used toward international programs that have some business element, which must be shown in the application.

EIN: 200881450

4824
Philanthrofund Foundation

1409 Willow St., Ste. 210
Minneapolis, MN 55403-3293   (612) 870-1806
Contact: Kate Eubank, Exec. Dir.
FAX: (612) 871-6587;
E-mail: info@pfundonline.org; Toll-free tel.: (800) 435-1402; URL: http://www.pfundonline.org

Foundation type: Public charity
Purpose: Scholarships to individuals who are from, or are attending school in MN, for higher education.
Publications: Application guidelines; Annual report; Financial statement; Grants list; Newsletter.
Financial data: Year ended 06/30/2012. Assets, $1,017,765 (M); Expenditures, $756,918; Total giving, $147,900.
Fields of interest: Higher education; Voluntarism promotion; LGBTQ.
Type of support: Scholarships—to individuals; Support to graduates or students of specific schools; Graduate support; Undergraduate support; Doctoral support.
Application information: Applications accepted. Application form required. Application form available on the grantmaker's web site.
Initial approach: Letter
Send request by: Mail
Copies of proposal: 2
Deadline(s): Feb. 1
Final notification: Recipients will be notified in three months
Applicants should submit the following:
1) Transcripts
2) Letter(s) of recommendation
3) GPA
Program description:
Scholarships: The foundation provides scholarships for students enrolled in GED, trade schools, colleges and universities and those who show a commitment to serving and leading GLBTA communities. Scholarship amounts generally range from $2,000 to $5,000 with one $10,000 scholarship available.
EIN: 363567019

4825
The Vernon J. Pick Foundation

5815 W. Main St.
Maple Plain, MN 55359-9363
Contact: Frederick A. Pick, Pres. and Dir.
Application address: 8136 Long Lake Dr. N.E., Bemidji, MN 56601-7025

Foundation type: Independent foundation
Purpose: Scholarships to MN high school seniors majoring in science or engineering.
Financial data: Year ended 12/31/2011. Assets, $681,666 (M); Expenditures, $30,127; Total giving, $15,000; Grants to individuals, 2 grants totaling $5,000 (high: $2,500, low: $2,500).
Fields of interest: Engineering school/education; Science.
Type of support: Undergraduate support.
Application information: Applications accepted. Application form required.
Deadline(s): Mar. 1
EIN: 411733851

4826
PLUS Foundation

5353 Wayzata Blvd., Ste.600
Minneapolis, MN 55416-1340   (952) 746-2590
FAX: (952) 746-2599;
E-mail: info@plusfoundation.org; Toll-free tel.: (800) 845-0778; URL: http://www.plusfoundation.org/

Foundation type: Public charity
Purpose: Four-year college scholarships to members, corporate sponsor employees and their families. Grants for the study of insurance.
Publications: Annual report.
Financial data: Year ended 12/31/2012. Assets, $1,218,755 (M); Expenditures, $451,445; Total giving, $199,014; Grants to individuals, totaling $42,028.
Fields of interest: Business school/education.
Type of support: Scholarships—to individuals; Graduate support.
Application information: Application form required. Application form available on the grantmaker's web site.
Initial approach: Letter
Deadline(s): Mar. 15
EIN: 411903374

4827
The Polaris Foundation

2100 Hwy. 55
Medina, MN 55340-9770
URL: http://www.polaris.com/en-us/company/2012/polaris-foundation.aspx

Foundation type: Company-sponsored foundation
Purpose: Disaster relief grants to employees of Polaris Industries, Inc.
Publications: Application guidelines; Program policy statement.
Financial data: Year ended 12/31/2012. Assets, $717,844 (M); Expenditures, $442,031; Total giving, $440,910.
Type of support: Emergency funds; Employee-related welfare.
Application information: Application form required.
Deadline(s): None
Company name: Polaris Industries, Inc.
EIN: 411828276

4828
Prairie Lakes Regional Arts Council

105 22nd Ave., N.E., Ste. A
Waseca, MN 56093-2930   (507) 833-8721
Contact: Brenda Byron, Exec. Dir.
FAX: (507) 833-8799;
E-mail: plrac@hickorytech.net; Toll-free tel.: (800) 298-1254; URL: http://www.plrac.org

Foundation type: Public charity

Purpose: Grants to professional and emerging artists in the nine county area of south central MN.
Publications: Application guidelines; Newsletter.
Financial data: Year ended 06/30/2012. Assets, $200,591 (M); Expenditures, $493,541; Total giving, $323,547; Grants to individuals, totaling $54,000.
Fields of interest: Visual arts; Performing arts; Literature.
Type of support: Fellowships; Grants to individuals.
Application information: Applications accepted. Application form required. Application form available on the grantmaker's web site.
Initial approach: Telephone or e-mail
Deadline(s): Varies
Applicants should submit the following:
1) Letter(s) of recommendation
2) Work samples
3) SASE
4) Resume
5) Budget Information
Additional information: All proposals must be submitted on the official application form and signed by the artist. See web site for additional application guidelines.
Program descriptions:
Arts and Cultural Heritage Grant: This program awards grants, ranging from $3,500 to $6,500, in three categories: arts programming and arts access (supporting Minnesota artists and arts organizations in creating, producing, and presenting high-quality arts activities; overcoming barriers to accessing the arts; and instilling the arts into the community and public life), arts education (supporting life-long learning and appreciation of the arts, including support to K-12 activities that enhance, but not replace, school arts curricula), and arts and cultural heritage festivals (for arts festivals and activities that represent the diverse ethnic and cultural arts traditions, including folk and traditional artists and arts organizations). Applications will be accepted from Minnesota-based, non-profit tax-exempt 501(c)(3) arts organizations, as well as non-profit community groups, units of government, and non-parochial schools that are sponsoring an arts activity in dance, literature, media arts, music, theater, and visual arts.
PLRAC/McKnight Emerging Artist Grants: Grants of $1,000 each are available to provide financial support to developing artists committed to advancing their work and careers. Applicants may work in any discipline (including, but not limited to, literature, music, theater, and visual art), but must be emerging artists in their formative stages of development.
PLRAC/McKnight Fellowship Grant: Grants of $3,000 each are available to professional mid-career artists with financial support that enables them to further their work and their contribution to their communities. Grants are intended to recognize, reward, and encourage outstanding individual artists in the region. Fellowship recipients are expected to demonstrate professional achievement in their disciplines (including, but not limited to, juried exhibitions, performances, and publications), and must be beyond the 'emerging' or 'beginning' stage in their careers.
Small Arts Project Grants: Grants, ranging from $200 to $1,200, are available to nonprofit tax-exempt (501(c)(3)) arts organizations, community groups, public organizations, or units of government that produce or sponsor arts activities. Applicants must demonstrate a 50-percent cash (or in-kind) match.
Youth Scholarship/Mentorship Grant: Grants of $300 each are available to provide selected

students in grades 7-12 the opportunity to study their chosen art with a practicing professional artist or attend an arts workshop, series of classes, or special training opportunity. Scholarships can also be used to take lessons or pay fees to a nonprofit arts organization serving youth.
EIN: 411761756

4829
Pro-Choice Resources
250 3rd Ave. N., Ste. 625
Minneapolis, MN 55401-1677 (612) 825-2000
Web site for grants and loans:
www.prochoiceresources.org
FAX: (612) 825-0159;
E-mail: pcr@birdsandbees.org; URL: http://prochoiceresources.org/

Foundation type: Public charity
Purpose: Grants, interest-free loans and resources to teens and women who choose abortion but are unable to afford them.
Publications: Annual report; Newsletter.
Financial data: Year ended 06/30/2012. Assets, $77,289 (M); Expenditures, $512,692; Total giving, $34,590; Grants to individuals, totaling $34,590.
Fields of interest: Youth, pregnancy prevention; Family services, adolescent parents; Pregnancy centers; Women, centers/services.
Type of support: Grants to individuals; Loans—to individuals.
Application information:
   Initial approach: Telephone
   Additional information: Contact foundation for further program information.
EIN: 410971333

4830
Charles E. Proshek Foundation
P.O. Box 64713, Trust Tax Services
St. Paul, MN 55164-0713 (612) 313-5189
Contact: Benjamin Webster
Application address: c/o U.S. Bank, N.A. 200 S.6th St. EP-MN-L9PT, Minneapolis, MN 55402

Foundation type: Independent foundation
Purpose: Scholarships to students living in Czechoslovakia, Yugoslavia, or Poland studying to be medical doctors, nurses or any advanced medical research field for study at the University of Minnesota, Twin Cities Campus.
Financial data: Year ended 12/31/2012. Assets, $500,704 (M); Expenditures, $28,286; Total giving, $21,138.
Fields of interest: Medical school/education; Nursing school/education.
International interests: Poland; Slovakia; Yugoslavia.
Type of support: Research; Scholarships—to individuals.
Application information:
   Initial approach: Letter
   Deadline(s): None
   Additional information: Scholarships are paid directly to the University.
EIN: 416245266

4831
Providers Choice, Inc.
10901 Red Circle Dr., Ste. 100
Minnetonka, MN 55343-9300 (952) 944-7010
FAX: (952) 944-7011;
E-mail: provider@providerschoice.com; Toll-free

tel.: (800) 356-5983; Mailing address: P. O. Box 390813, Minneapolis, MN 55439-0813;
URL: http://www.providerschoice.com

Foundation type: Public charity
Purpose: Assistance to child care providers throughout MN, and to promote child care as a profession.
Financial data: Year ended 09/30/2012. Assets, $2,324,188 (M); Expenditures, $25,759,384; Total giving, $22,424,580; Grants to individuals, 4,658 grants totaling $22,424,580.
Fields of interest: Food services; Day care; Children/youth.
Type of support: Grants to individuals.
Application information: Applications accepted.
   Additional information: Contact the agency for additional information.
EIN: 363347057

4832
Mark R. Pryor Foundation
P.O. Box 889
Winona, MN 55987 (507) 454-4124
Contact: Jean M. Pryor, V.P.
Application address: P.O. Box 534, Onalaska, WI 54650

Foundation type: Independent foundation
Purpose: Scholarships to students who are residents of Winona, MN for tuition, fees, books, laboratory materials, and room and board.
Financial data: Year ended 12/31/2012. Assets, $640,213 (M); Expenditures, $58,203; Total giving, $50,952.
Fields of interest: Higher education.
Type of support: Scholarships—to individuals.
Application information: Application form required.
   Initial approach: Letter
   Deadline(s): Vary
   Additional information: Application should include a letter of recommendation from an educator or other community leader. Payments are made directly to the institution on behalf of applicant.
EIN: 411637603

4833
Rahr Foundation
800 W. 1st Ave.
Shakopee, MN 55379-1148 (952) 496-7003
Contact: Frederick W. Rahr, Pres.
FAX: (952) 496-7055; E-mail: mtech@rahr.com

Foundation type: Company-sponsored foundation
Purpose: Scholarships only to children of employees of Rahr Malting Company and its affiliates.
Financial data: Year ended 12/31/2012. Assets, $4,201,075 (M); Expenditures, $267,871; Total giving, $173,500.
Fields of interest: Higher education.
Type of support: Employee-related scholarships.
Application information: Applications not accepted.
   Additional information: Unsolicited requests for funds not considered or acknowledged.
EIN: 396046046

4834
Thomas M. Redmond Foundation
2001 Killebrew Dr., Ste.400
Minneapolis, MN 55421
Contact: Daniel A. Boeckermann, Tr.

Foundation type: Independent foundation
Purpose: Scholarships to children of employees of Wolf Springs Ranches, Inc., of Westcliffe, CO.
Financial data: Year ended 12/31/2011. Assets, $33,009 (M); Expenditures, $4,640; Total giving, $2,180; Grant to an individual, 1 grant totaling $2,180.
Fields of interest: Education.
Type of support: Employee-related scholarships.
Application information: Applications accepted.
   Initial approach: Letter
   Deadline(s): Feb. 28
   Additional information: Letter should include educational background, achievements and financial need factors.
EIN: 411767070

4835
Redwood Area Communities Foundation, Inc.
P.O. Box 481
Redwood Falls, MN 56283-0127 (507) 637-4004
FAX: (507) 637-4082;
E-mail: radc@redwoodfalls.org; URL: http://www.radc.org

Foundation type: Independent foundation
Purpose: Loans and scholarships to needy students graduating from high schools in the Redwood County, MN, area.
Financial data: Year ended 12/31/2011. Assets, $2,590,391 (M); Expenditures, $2,352,020; Total giving, $322,307.
Fields of interest: Vocational education; College; Mathematics; Science.
Type of support: Student loans—to individuals; Undergraduate support.
Application information: Applications accepted. Application form required. Application form available on the grantmaker's web site.
   Initial approach: Letter, telephone or e-mail
   Deadline(s): Feb. 15 for Grefe Scholarship, May 10 for Ehlers Student Fund
   Applicants should submit the following:
     1) ACT
     2) Transcripts
     3) Letter(s) of recommendation
   Additional information: Application must also include photocopy of parents' tax form and proof of enrollment. See web site for additional application information.
Program descriptions:
   Dr. Ray and Joan Grefe Scholarship Fund: The fund provides $5,000 scholarships to two high school seniors who will major in math or natural sciences in college, and have three years of math or natural science course work in high school. Applications will be accepted from individuals living within or attending school within the following MN counties: Brown, Chippewa, Cottonwood, Jackson, Lac Qui Parle, Lincoln, Lyon, Martin, Murray, Nobles, Pipestone, Redwood, Renville, Rock, Watonwan, and Yellow Medicine. Scholarships will be made on the basis of need, character, and academic ability, and are renewable for up to four years.
   Martin and Winifred Ehlers Student Fund: The fund provides $5,000 scholarships to two high school seniors who will major in math or natural sciences in college, and have three years of math or natural science course work in high school. Applications will be accepted from individuals living within or attending school within the following MN counties: Brown, Chippewa, Cottonwood, Jackson, Lac Qui Parle, Lincoln, Lyon, Martin, Murray, Nobles, Pipestone, Redwood, Renville, Rock,

Watonwan, and Yellow Medicine. Scholarships will be made on the basis of need, character, and academic ability, and are renewable for up to four years.

EIN: 363611923

4836
Region 2 Arts Council
426 Bemidji Ave.
Bemidji, MN 56601-3139 (218) 751-5447
Contact: Terri Widman, Exec. Dir.
E-mail: terriwidman@r2arts.org; Toll-free tel.: (800) 275-5447: E-Mail For Terri Widman: terriwidman@r2arts.org; URL: http://www.r2arts.org

Foundation type: Public charity
Purpose: Project grants to artists who reside in the MN counties of Beltrami, Clearwater, Hubbard, Lake of the Woods and Mahnomen.
Publications: Application guidelines; Biennial report; Newsletter.
Financial data: Year ended 06/30/2012. Assets, $106,704 (M); Expenditures, $389,747; Total giving, $227,462; Grants to individuals, totaling $43,408.
Fields of interest: Arts.
Type of support: Publication; Grants to individuals; Residencies; Travel grants; Project support.
Application information: Applications accepted. Application form required. Application form available on the grantmaker's web site.
> *Initial approach:* Telephone or e-mail
> *Send request by:* Mail or hand-delivered
> *Copies of proposal:* 1
> *Deadline(s):* Varies
> *Final notification:* Recipients notified in four to six weeks
> *Applicants should submit the following:*
> 1) Work samples
> 2) Resume
> 3) Proposal
> 4) Curriculum vitae
> 5) Budget Information

Program descriptions:
> *Anishinaabe Grants for Individual Artists:* Grants of up to $1,000 are available for American Indian artists residing in Beltrami, Clearwater, Hubbard, Lake of the Woods, Mahnomen, Becker, Roseau, Itasca, and Cass counties, to produce artistic work or for a creative opportunity. Eligible applicants must be at least 18 years of age and be a resident of Minnesota.
> *Arts and Cultural Heritage Grants:* Grants, ranging from $3,000 to $6,000, are available to support artists, arts organizations, nonprofit groups (including schools, youth groups, etc.), cultural heritage groups, and local governments in the council's service area. Grants are available in three categories: arts and arts access (these grants will support artists and arts organizations to produce high-quality arts activities, overcome barriers to accessing arts activities, and instill the arts into community and public life); arts education (projects that support lifelong learning in the arts through artist residencies in schools, after-school programs, adult art classes and workshops, and trips for youth to visit art museums, performances, and other art activities); and arts and cultural heritage (projects that represent regional and statewide ethnic and cultural arts traditions, including arts and music festivals, performances, folk art classes, or other cultural activities)
> *Arts Project Grants:* Grants of up to $1,500 are available to 501(c)(3) nonprofit organizations, community groups, schools, units of government, and organizations applying under a fiscal sponsor

to supports arts projects within Beltrami, Clearwater, Hubbard, Lake of the Woods, and Mahnomen counties. Support will be provided for: putting together an exhibit, performance, or workshop; sponsoring a 'pre-packaged' arts performance or exhibit, hosting an artist-in-residence at a school, or planning or consulting assistance to an arts organization.
> *Individual Artist Grants:* This program provides grants of up to $1,000 for artists who show serious commitment to creative growth and career advancement. Grants are intended to help with expenses associated with the exhibition, performance, or production of a specific creative work or educational opportunity; provide support for an established artist who wishes to mentor an exceptional student artist; and provide support for projects involving collaborations between two or more artists. Artists must reside in Beltrami, Clearwater, Hubbard, Lake of the woods, and Mahnomen counties.
> *R2AC/McKnight Career Development Fellowship Award:* Two grants of $6,000 each will be awarded yearly to provide a significant career development experience to individual artists in Beltrami, Clearwater, Hubbard, Mahnomen, and Lake of the Woods counties. Grants will provide funding for artists to support experiences that facilitate depth and advancement in artistic careers, and intend to assist the region's most talent artists in furthering and innovating their work. Funding can be used for exploring new directions or continuing works in progress, production costs and materials, taking time to engage in collaborative or community projects, non-credited educational experiences that further the artist's career, and embarking on travel or research in order to fulfill artistic goals. Artists applying for this fellowship must be at least 21 years of age and be working in their field of choice for at least five years (excluding student work and exhibits)

EIN: 411390021

4837
Regions Hospital Foundation
8170 33rd Ave. S.
P.O. Box 1309
Minneapolis, MN 55440-1309 (952) 883-6584
Contact: Keevan Kosidowski, Exec. Dir
E-mail: rhf@healthpartners.com; URL: http://www.regionshospital.com/rh/foundation/index.html

Foundation type: Public charity
Purpose: Nursing scholarships for current employees of Regions Hospital, MN pursuing higher education in the health care field.
Publications: Occasional report.
Financial data: Year ended 12/31/2011. Assets, $21,286,560 (M); Expenditures, $15,538,893; Total giving, $12,330,688; Grants to individuals, 17 grants totaling $16,500.
Fields of interest: Nursing school/education.
Type of support: Scholarships—to individuals.
Application information: Applications accepted.
> *Additional information:* Applicant must be a current RN who is in a bachelor's, master's or Ph.D. program with a nursing/health focus, and a nurse who is planning to continue his/her employment with Regions in the future.

EIN: 411888902

4838
Restless Legs Syndrome Foundation, Inc.
1530 Greenview Dr., S.W., Ste. 210
Rochester, MN 55902-4327 (507) 287-6465
Contact: Georgianna Bell, Exec. Dir.
FAX: (507) 287-6312;
E-mail: info@willis-ekbom.org; E-mail For Georgianna Bell: bell@willis-ekbom.org; URL: http://www.rls.org

Foundation type: Public charity
Purpose: Research grants to postdoctoral candidates for basic and clinical research studies of restless leg syndrome.
Publications: Annual report; Financial statement; Grants list; Informational brochure; Newsletter.
Financial data: Year ended 09/30/2012. Assets, $454,173 (M); Expenditures, $584,694; Total giving, $50,000.
Fields of interest: Medical specialties research.
Type of support: Research.
Application information: Application form required.
> *Initial approach:* Letter of intent
> *Send request by:* E-mail
> *Copies of proposal:* 1
> *Deadline(s):* Dec. 1 for letter of intent; Feb. 1 for full proposal
> *Applicants should submit the following:*
> 1) Budget Information
> 2) Proposal

Program description:
> *Research Grants:* The foundation awards two to five grants of $20,000 to $35,000 each for one year of basic and clinical research studies of restless legs syndrome (RLS). Grants are available for both basic and clinical research; preference will be given to proposals that focus on epidemiology (ascertaining the prevalence and incidence of RLS), neurophysiology, dopaminergic regulation of movements in individuals with RLS, developing strategies for identifying the genes responsible for RLS, examining the role of iron metabolism in RLS, and studying the effects of Circadian rhythms in individuals with RLS. Proposals are especially encouraged from promising postdoctoral candidates, or fellows working under the direction of established investigators on topics of potential relevance to RLS.

EIN: 561784846

4839
Louis A. Roberg Endowment Trust
P.O. Box 682
Litchfield, MN 55355 (320) 693-3289

Foundation type: Independent foundation
Purpose: Scholarships and loans to financially needy graduating seniors residing in Meeker, McLeod, or Kandiyohi counties, MN, and graduating from one of six participating high schools, to attend agricultural and vocational schools located anywhere, and public colleges and universities in MN.
Financial data: Year ended 09/30/2013. Assets, $1,151,548 (M); Expenditures, $81,158; Total giving, $54,000.
Fields of interest: Vocational education; Agriculture.
Type of support: Scholarships—to individuals; Support to graduates or students of specific schools.
Application information: Application form required.
> *Deadline(s):* Apr.
> *Applicants should submit the following:*
> 1) Class rank
> 2) Letter(s) of recommendation
> 3) Financial information

4) Essay

Additional information: Scholarships and loans are based on financial need, scholastic ability and achievement, extracurricular participation, community service, and likelihood of success in chosen field. Grants are renewable.

EIN: 416223072

4840
Rochester Area Foundation
400 S. Broadway, Ste. 300
Rochester, MN 55904   (507) 282-0203
Contact: JoAnn Stomer, Pres.
FAX: (507) 282-4938;
E-mail: raf-info@rochesterarea.org; URL: http://www.rochesterarea.org

Foundation type: Community foundation
Purpose: Scholarships to individuals from the greater Rochester, MN area from funds held by schools at the foundation.
Publications: Application guidelines; Annual report; Informational brochure (including application guidelines); Newsletter.
Financial data: Year ended 12/31/2011. Assets, $38,004,741 (M); Expenditures, $3,035,858; Total giving, $1,486,568.
Fields of interest: Higher education; Scholarships/financial aid.
Type of support: Scholarships—to individuals; Undergraduate support.
Application information: Applications accepted.
EIN: 416017740

4841
The Rosen Family Foundation, Inc.
P.O. Box 933
Fairmont, MN   56031-0933

Foundation type: Company-sponsored foundation
Purpose: Scholarships to young adults for postseconday education to pursue careers of interest to Rosen's Diversified Inc.
Financial data: Year ended 12/31/2012. Assets, $1,494,919 (M); Expenditures, $12,296; Total giving, $12,130.
Fields of interest: Higher education; Scholarships/financial aid; Agriculture; Food services; Mathematics; Engineering.
Type of support: Scholarships—to individuals.
Application information: Contact the foundation for additional guidelines.
Program description:
  Rosen's Diversified Inc.'s Scholarship Program: The foundation awards college scholarships to students who plan to pursue careers in agriculture, food science, animal and agricultural science, engineering, or marketing. Recipients are selected based on leadership, civic and extracurricular activities, academics, and community service.
EIN: 412054672

4842
The Saint Paul Foundation
101 Fifth St. E., Ste. 2400
St. Paul, MN   55101   (651) 224-5463
Contact: Carleen K. Rhodes, C.E.O.
FAX: (651) 224-8123;
E-mail: inbox@saintpaulfoundation.org; Additional tel.: (800) 875-6167; Additional e-mail: ckr@saintpaulfoundation.org; URL: http://saintpaulfoundation.org

Foundation type: Community foundation

Purpose: Scholarships to residents of MN, primarily in the Saint Paul area for postsecondary education.
Publications: Application guidelines; Financial statement; Grants list; Newsletter.
Financial data: Year ended 12/31/2012. Assets, $695,259,473 (M); Expenditures, $92,525,679; Total giving, $77,615,019; Grants to individuals, 1,623 grants totaling $1,828,469.
Fields of interest: Higher education; Scholarships/financial aid; Health care; Human services.
Type of support: Scholarships—to individuals; Support to graduates or students of specific schools; Undergraduate support; Grants for special needs.
Application information: Applications accepted.
  Initial approach: Telephone or e-mail
  Deadline(s): Varies
  Additional information: See web site for a complete list of scholarship programs and guidelines.
Program description:
  Scholarship Funds: The foundation administers many scholarships established by donors. Most scholarships are for graduating seniors planning to enroll in a post-secondary educational institution the next succeeding academic year. Each scholarship has its own unique set of eligibility criteria, including but not limited to county of residence, extra-curricular activities and particular fields of study. See web site for additional information.
EIN: 416031510

4843
Sampson Family Foundation
50 Parkview Ln.
P.O. Box 698
Hector, MN   55342-1058

Foundation type: Independent foundation
Purpose: Scholarships primarily to residents of MN in pursuit of a higher education at accredited colleges and universities.
Financial data: Year ended 12/31/2011. Assets, $265,960 (M); Expenditures, $66,013; Total giving, $61,758.
Fields of interest: Higher education.
Type of support: Scholarships—to individuals.
Application information: Contact foundation for application guidelines.
EIN: 411681957

4844
Floy Gilman Scheidler Scholarship Foundation, Inc.
1201 Tall Pine Ln., Ste. 1
Cloquet, MN   55720-3797   (218) 879-6784

Foundation type: Independent foundation
Purpose: Scholarships for tuition and books for students who pursue a postsecondary education the the fields of communications and/or business.
Financial data: Year ended 12/31/2012. Assets, $469,488 (M); Expenditures, $34,677; Total giving, $16,000; Grants to individuals, 11 grants totaling $16,000 (high: $2,000, low: $1,000).
Fields of interest: Media/communications; Higher education; Business school/education.
Type of support: Scholarships—to individuals.
Application information: Applications accepted. Application form required.
  Deadline(s): First business day of the first week in Mar.
  Applicants should submit the following:
    1) Letter(s) of recommendation
    2) Essay

Additional information: Applicants must submit a hand written essay of no more than 500 words, why he or she qualifies as a candidate and what he or she intends to do with his or her education.
EIN: 411925664

4845
Scholarship America
(formerly Citizens' Scholarship Foundation of America)
1 Scholarship Way
P.O. Box 297
St. Peter, MN   56082-1693
FAX: (507) 931-1682;
E-mail: development@scholarshipamerica.org; Toll-free tel.: (800) 279-2083; URL: http://www.scholarshipamerica.org

Foundation type: Public charity
Purpose: Scholarships to students at a wide variety of postsecondary institutions in the U.S.
Publications: Annual report (including application guidelines); Newsletter.
Financial data: Year ended 06/30/2011. Assets, $176,046,357 (M); Expenditures, $162,637,168; Total giving, $149,817,439; Grants to individuals, 66,011 grants totaling $146,829,214. Subtotal for scholarships—to individuals: 66,465 grants totaling $147,869,723.
Fields of interest: Vocational education, post-secondary; Higher education; Disasters, 9/11/01.
Type of support: Scholarships—to individuals; Undergraduate support.
Application information: Applications accepted.
  Additional information: See web site for additional information.
Program descriptions:
  Dollars for Scholars: The program mobilizes and unites local citizens and encourages local students to reach for and achieve their educational goals. Through this program, communities connect young people with caring and supportive adults; positive connections produce the high expectations and strong motivation that all students need to succeed in school and in life.
  Dreamkeepers Emergency Financial Aid Program: The program addresses the high dropout rates of community college students when faced with an unexpected crisis. Average grants are $523, and are most commonly used for housing, utilities, meals, transportation, car repairs, and child care.
  Families of Freedom Scholarship Fund: The sole purpose of this fund is to provide financial assistance for postsecondary education to the spouses and children of individuals killed in the Sept. 11, 2001 terrorist attacks. Visit http://www.familiesoffreedom.org/ for more information.
  Target Field Trips Grant Program: Administered in conjunction with Target Corporation, this program awards grants for field trip-related costs, such as transportation, ticket fees, resource material, and supplies. The program is open to educational professionals who are at least 18 years old and employed by an accredited K-12 public, private, or charter school in the U.S. that maintains 501(c)(3) or 509(a)(1) tax-exempt status. Educators, teachers, principals, paraprofessionals, or classified staff of these institutions must be willing to plan and execute a field trip that will provide a demonstrable learning experience for students. Funds may be used for visits to art, science, and cultural museums; community service or civics projects; career enrichment opportunities; and other events or activities away from school facilities. See http://sites.target.com/site/en/

company/page.jsp?contentId=WCMP04-039156 for more information.
EIN: 042296967

4846
Scott-Carver-Dakota Cap Agency, Inc.
712 Canterbury Rd.
Shakopee, MN 55379-1840 (952) 496-2125
Contact: Carolina Bradpiece, Pres. and C.E.O.
FAX: (952) 402-9815; E-mail: info@capagency.org;
URL: http://www.capagency.org/

Foundation type: Public charity
Purpose: Services to indigent residents of Scott, Carver and Dakota counties, MN, such as home weatherization, home energy assistance, food supplies, school supplies, and meals for the elderly.
Financial data: Year ended 09/30/2011. Assets, $7,041,518 (M); Expenditures, $13,135,228; Total giving, $5,392,159; Grants to individuals, totaling $5,392,159.
Fields of interest: Economically disadvantaged.
Type of support: In-kind gifts.
Application information:
  Initial approach: Letter
  Additional information: Contact foundation for eligibility guidelines.
EIN: 410903890

4847
Second Harvest Heartland
1140 Gervais Ave.
St. Paul, MN 55109-2020 (651) 484-5117
Contact: Rob Zeaske, C.E.O.
FAX: (651) 484-1064; Toll-free tel.: (888) 339-3663; Additional address (Minneapolis office): 3100 California St., N.E., Minneapolis, MN 55418-1808, tel.: (651) 209-7980, fax: (612) 789-0125; URL: http://www.2harvest.org/site/PageServer

Foundation type: Public charity
Purpose: Emergency assistance to individuals and families in need throughout southern MN and western WI.
Publications: Annual report; Financial statement.
Financial data: Year ended 09/30/2012. Assets, $19,658,291 (M); Expenditures, $113,111,482; Total giving, $97,283,744; Grants to individuals, totaling $6,291,928.
Fields of interest: Human services; Economically disadvantaged.
Type of support: In-kind gifts; Grants for special needs.
Application information: Contact the agency for eligibility determination.
EIN: 237417654

4848
Second Harvest North Central Food Bank, Inc.
P.O. Box 5130
Grand Rapids, MN 55744-5130 (218) 326-4420
E-mail: susan@secondharvestncfb.com;
URL: http://www.secondharvestncfb.com

Foundation type: Public charity
Purpose: Giving limited food assistance for the needy in north-central MN.
Financial data: Year ended 12/31/2011. Assets, $2,214,925 (M); Expenditures, $5,863,872; Total giving, $4,845,347; Grants to individuals, totaling $1,869,111.

Fields of interest: Food services.
Type of support: In-kind gifts.
Application information: Applications not accepted.
EIN: 411782776

4849
Semcac, Inc.
204 S. Elm St.
P.O. Box 549
Rushford, MN 55971-0549 (507) 864-7741
FAX: (507) 864-2440;
E-mail: semcac@semcac.org; URL: http://www.semcac.org

Foundation type: Public charity
Purpose: Assistance to low-income families, the elderly, and disabled of Dodge, Fillmore, Freeborn, Houston, Mower, Steel, and Winona counties, MN, with emergency food and shelter, health services, housing, energy assistance, weatherization and other needs.
Financial data: Year ended 09/30/2011. Assets, $4,670,079 (M); Expenditures, $14,347,838; Total giving, $4,446,986; Grants to individuals, totaling $4,446,986.
Fields of interest: Human services; Aging; Disabilities, people with; Economically disadvantaged.
Type of support: Emergency funds; Grants for special needs.
Application information: Applications accepted.
  Initial approach: Telephone
EIN: 410907135

4850
Dennis K. and Vivian D. Siemer Foundation Inc.
751 Summit Ave.
Mankato, MN 56001-2717 (507) 387-2039
Contact: Dennis K. Siemer, Pres.

Foundation type: Independent foundation
Purpose: Scholarships to students of the Mankato, MN area for postsecondary education.
Financial data: Year ended 12/31/2011. Assets, $91,108 (M); Expenditures, $4,069; Total giving, $4,000.
Fields of interest: Higher education.
Type of support: Undergraduate support.
Application information: Applications accepted.
  Initial approach: Letter
  Deadline(s): None
EIN: 411957558

4851
Walter & Anna Soneson Scholarship Fund Trust
c/o Trust Tax Services
P.O. Box 64713
Saint Paul, MN 55164-0713 (218) 723-2914
Application address: P.O. Box 161077, Duluth, MN 55816-1077

Foundation type: Independent foundation
Purpose: Scholarships for high school seniors in Duluth, MN, with a 2.5 GPA who will attend college in MN, MI, IA, IN, IL, WI, ND or SD.
Financial data: Year ended 12/31/2012. Assets, $710,631 (M); Expenditures, $42,887; Total giving, $31,875; Grants to individuals, 13 grants totaling $31,875 (high: $3,250, low: $1,500).
Type of support: Support to graduates or students of specific schools; Undergraduate support.

Application information: Application form required.
  Deadline(s): Fall of senior year in high school
  Additional information: Applications available through Duluth high school counselors.
EIN: 416018233

4852
South St. Paul Educational Foundation
521 Marie Ave.
South Saint Paul, MN 55075-2049 (651) 457-9440
Contact: Cari Vujovich, Exec. Dir.
FAX: (651) 552-5586;
E-mail: foundation@sspps.org; URL: http://www.sspef.com/

Foundation type: Public charity
Purpose: Scholarships to graduating high school seniors in South St. Paul Public School District No. 6, MN.
Publications: Annual report.
Financial data: Year ended 06/30/2012. Assets, $4,435,712 (M); Expenditures, $523,720; Total giving, $324,265; Grants to individuals, totaling $324,265.
Type of support: Scholarships—to individuals.
Application information: Application form required.
  Deadline(s): Feb.
EIN: 411494597

4853
South Washington County Scholarship Committee
944 Portland Ave.
Saint Paul Park, MN 55071-1507

Foundation type: Operating foundation
Purpose: Scholarships to individuals attending Park High School, MN, and Woodbury High School, MN for higher education.
Financial data: Year ended 12/31/2012. Assets, $44,048 (M); Expenditures, $18,069; Total giving, $18,000; Grants to individuals, 12 grants totaling $18,000 (high: $1,500, low: $1,500).
Type of support: Support to graduates or students of specific schools; Undergraduate support.
Application information: Applications accepted. Application form required.
  Deadline(s): May 1
  Additional information: Applications available from high school counselors at Woodbury and Park high schools.
EIN: 411433314

4854
The Southeastern Minnesota Arts Council, Inc.
1610 14th St., N.W., Ste. 206
Rochester, MN 55901-7683 (507) 281-4848
FAX: (507) 281-8373; E-mail: staff@semac.org;
URL: http://www.semac.org

Foundation type: Public charity
Purpose: Grants to established and emerging artists in southeastern MN to advance and further their work and careers.
Publications: Application guidelines; Grants list; Informational brochure; Newsletter.
Financial data: Year ended 06/30/2011. Assets, $271,396 (M); Expenditures, $806,804; Total giving, $598,772.
Fields of interest: Visual arts; Arts.
Type of support: Grants to individuals.

Application information: Applications accepted. Application form required. Application form available on the grantmaker's web site.

Send request by: Mail
Copies of proposal: 2
Deadline(s): Feb. 1 for McKnight Individual Artist Grants; within thirty days of start date for Opportunity Grants
Applicants should submit the following:
1) Resume
2) Proposal
3) Budget Information
Additional information: Application should also include optional work samples. See web site for additional application information.

Program descriptions:

McKnight Individual Artist Grants: Grants are available to individual artists in the southeastern Minnesota community to encourage the development of entirely original work by both emerging artists and established artists. Such works can include original literary or dramatic scripts, musical compositions, choreographies, visual artist creations, and interdisciplinary works. Works must be earmarked for a public showcasing via publication, performance, or exhibition, in conjunction with a nonprofit arts organization. Grants ranging from $200 to $2,500 will be awarded to emerging artists, while established artists are eligible for grants of up to $5,000.

Opportunity Grants: These grants provide assistance to artists, nonprofit organizations, and schools or educational institutions in southeastern Minnesota for 'sudden' projects that enable them to take advantage of opportunities that arise with little advance notice. Grant proposals of up to $250 will be considered.
EIN: 411417579

4855
Southern Theater Foundation
1420 Washington Ave. S.
Minneapolis, MN 55454-1038   (612) 340-0155
Contact: Damon Runnals, Ger. Mgr.
URL: http://www.southerntheater.org

Foundation type: Public charity
Purpose: Collaboration for emerging artists in the Minnesota area, and the five boroughs of New York City to commission works involving original music, new media and multiple art forms.
Publications: Application guidelines.
Financial data: Year ended 08/31/2012. Assets, $239,893 (M); Expenditures, $155,086.
Fields of interest: Performing arts.
Type of support: Fellowships; Project support.
Application information:
Deadline(s): Sept. 2 intent to apply, Mar. 22 final application
Applicants should submit the following:
1) Work samples
2) SASE
3) Resume
4) Proposal
Additional information: Application should also include one DVD, and 20 minutes of work sample from at least three different works.
Program descriptions:
Electric Eyes: New Music & Media Festival: This festival is intended to encourage collaboration across disciplines and is seeking to commission works involving original music, new media, and multiple art forms. Up to five full- or partial-evening works (with a duration lasting from ten minutes up to a full evening) will be selected to receive a commission fee ($2,500 to $5,000 each) and support services. The festival takes place from late

May to early June, and grant recipients must be available for those dates.

McKnight Artist Fellowships for Choreographers and Dancers: The program annually awards three $25,000 fellowships to dancers and three $25,000 fellowships to choreographers who reside in Minnesota. Fellowships provide recognition and financial support for mid-career choreographers and dancers. The program is designed to award artists whose work is of exceptional artist merit, who have created a substantial body of work over a period of time, and are at a career stage that is beyond emerging. This program is supported by the McKnight Foundation.
EIN: 411313132

4856
Southwest Minnesota Housing
Partnership
2401 Broadway Ave., Ste. 4
Slayton, MN 56172-1167   (507) 836-1608
Contact: Rick Goodemann, C.E.O.
FAX: (507) 836-8866;
E-mail: maureenc@swmhp.org; E-Mail for Rick Goodemann : rickg@swmhp.org; URL: http://www.swmhp.org

Foundation type: Public charity
Purpose: Financial assistance to low-income individuals and families of southwestern, MN with home ownership, and home purchase assistance.
Financial data: Year ended 12/31/2011. Assets, $31,496,344 (M); Expenditures, $7,830,029; Total giving, $2,379,767; Grants to individuals, totaling $2,379,767.
Fields of interest: Housing/shelter, home owners; Housing/shelter.
Type of support: Grants to individuals.
Application information: Applications accepted.
Additional information: Applicants should contact the partnership for additional information.
EIN: 411721815

4857
Southwest Minnesota Private Industry
Council, Inc.
Lyon County Courthouse, 3rd Fl.
607 W. Main St.
Marshall, MN 56258-3021   (507) 537-6236
Contact: Juanita Lauritsen
E-mail: info@swmnpic.org; Toll-free tel.: (800) 818-9295; URL: http://www.swmnpic.org

Foundation type: Public charity
Purpose: Assistance for adults and youth to help them become self-sufficient individuals in the southwestern, MN area.
Publications: Annual report; Newsletter.
Financial data: Year ended 06/30/2011. Assets, $1,449,823 (M); Expenditures, $4,441,403; Total giving, $1,639,135; Grants to individuals, totaling $1,576,353.
Fields of interest: Youth; Adults; Economically disadvantaged.
Type of support: Grants for special needs.
Application information: Application form required. Application form available on the grantmaker's web site.
Additional information: Applications for youth programs are available from local school counselors, teachers, county family service agencies probation officers or the local Workforce Center. See web site for additional information.
EIN: 411487964

4858
Southwest MN Arts and Humanities
Council
114 N. 3rd St.
P. O. Box 55
Marshall, MN 56258-2099   (507) 537-1471
Contact: Greta Murray, Exec. Dir.
E-mail: smahcinfo@iw.net; Toll-free tel.: (800)-622-5284; URL: http://www.smahc.org

Foundation type: Public charity
Purpose: Grants to professional and emerging artists of southwestern, MN to create and promote the arts and humanities in their communities.
Publications: Application guidelines.
Financial data: Year ended 06/30/2012. Assets, $602,037 (M); Expenditures, $629,956; Total giving, $378,681; Grants to individuals, totaling $61,954.
Fields of interest: Humanities; Arts, artist's services.
Type of support: Grants to individuals.
Application information: Applications accepted. Application form required. Application form available on the grantmaker's web site.
Initial approach: Telephone or e-mail
Deadline(s): Varies
Applicants should submit the following:
1) Work samples
2) SASE
3) Resume
Additional information: See web site for additional application information.
Program descriptions:
Art Study for Youth Grants: This program provides up to $500 to aid southwestern Minnesota artists in grades K-12 to study their chosen art (including dance, literature, media arts, music, theater, and visual arts) with a practicing professional artist, and/or attend an arts workshop, series of classes, or special training opportunity.
Prairie Disciple Award: This $500 award acknowledges and honors an individual who has been instrumental in promoting the arts in southwestern Minnesota. Preference is given to teachers and educators.
Prairie Star Award: A $5,000 award will be given to honor a distinguished artist whose work and activities have best exemplified standing leadership and vision to southwestern Minnesota's artistic community.
SMAHC/McKnight Individual Artist Development Grant Program: The program provides $1,500 to aid emerging southwestern Minnesota artists at the early stages of their career development.
SMAHC/McKnight Individual Artist Established Career Grants Program: The program provides up to $7,000 to aid established career artists in the advanced stages of their career development.
EIN: 416168522

4859
Springboard for the Arts
308 Prince St., Ste. 270
St. Paul, MN 55101-1437   (651) 292-4381
FAX: (651) 292-4315;
E-mail: info@springboardforthearts.org;
URL: http://www.springboardforthearts.org

Foundation type: Public charity
Purpose: Emergency relief funds for area artists living in MN to cover unexpected catastrophic events such as unpaid bills, theft, fire, flood and health emergency. Grants for individual artists seeking fiscal sponsorship.
Publications: Annual report; Newsletter.

Financial data: Year ended 06/30/2011. Expenditures, $1,032,665; Total giving, $4,374; Grants to individuals, 12 grants totaling $4,374. Fiscal agent/sponsor amount not specified. Emergency funds amount not specified.
Fields of interest: Arts, artist's services; Human services.
Type of support: Emergency funds; Fiscal agent/sponsor.
Application information: Applications accepted. Application form available on the grantmaker's web site.
 Send request by: Online
 Additional information: See web site for fiscal sponsorship guidelines.
Program descriptions:
 Emergency Relief Fund: The fund was established to meet the emergency needs of artists who find themselves in need of immediate monies to cover an expense due to loss from fire, theft, a health emergency, or other catastrophic, career-threatening events. Artists may access up to $500 to meet unexpected "emergency" expenses.
 Fiscal Sponsorship/Agency: The program provides fiscal sponsorship for art groups who are not ready to become a nonprofit, so that they can manage their financial affairs professionally. A non-refundable application fee of $95 must be paid before an application can be considered. Eligible applicants must be arts-related and fit with the organization's mission.
EIN: 411690483

4860
St. Paul College Club, Inc. - AAUW Scholarship Trust
990 Summit Ave.
St. Paul, MN   55105-3033   (651) 227-4477
Contact: Silvey Barge, Chair.

Foundation type: Independent foundation
Purpose: Scholarships limited to area high school seniors in MN attending an AAUW approved college or university.
Financial data: Year ended 06/30/2012. Assets, $1,142,160 (M); Expenditures, $109,073; Total giving, $104,000.
Type of support: Undergraduate support.
Application information: Applications accepted. Application form required.
 Deadline(s): Mar. 15
 Additional information: Applications available from area high school counseling offices.
EIN: 411373110

4861
A. L. Steinke Perpetual Scholarship
c/o Trust Tax Services
P.O. Box 64713
St. Paul, MN   55164-0713   (612) 303-3232
Contact: Donna Mohr
Application Address: 800 Nicollet Mall, Minneapolis, MN 55402, tel.: (612) 303-3232

Foundation type: Independent foundation
Purpose: Scholarships to financially needy students who have completed four years of regular high school in Pipestone County, MN.
Financial data: Year ended 12/31/2011. Assets, $1,050,206 (M); Expenditures, $64,232; Total giving, $49,575.
Fields of interest: Higher education; Scholarships/financial aid; Economically disadvantaged.
Type of support: Scholarships—to individuals; Support to graduates or students of specific schools.

Application information: Applications accepted.
 Initial approach: Letter
 Deadline(s): None
EIN: 416045691

4862
Dr. W. C. Stillwell Foundation
c/o Dr. Philip Wold
25 Browns Ct.
Mankato, MN   56001   (507) 345-6151
Contact: Dr. John Hoines, Secy.
Application address: 1630 Adams St., Mankato, MN 56001

Foundation type: Operating foundation
Purpose: Four-year scholarships to full-time medical students who are/were originally from one of 22 selected counties in the southcentral and southwestern, MN areas.
Financial data: Year ended 12/31/2012. Assets, $743,279 (M); Expenditures, $37,835; Total giving, $35,490; Grants to individuals, 7 grants totaling $35,490 (high: $5,070, low: $5,070).
Fields of interest: Medical school/education.
Type of support: Graduate support.
Application information: Application form required.
 Initial approach: Letter
 Deadline(s): July 1
 Applicants should submit the following:
  1) Transcripts
  2) Letter(s) of recommendation
  3) Financial information
EIN: 411423785

4863
Sun Country Airlines Foundation
1300 Mendota Hts. Rd.
Mendota Heights, MN   55120-1128

Foundation type: Company-sponsored foundation
Purpose: Scholarships to employees and their dependents of Sun Country Airlines for higher education.
Financial data: Year ended 12/31/2012. Assets, $3,308 (M); Expenditures, $26,542; Total giving, $26,500.
Fields of interest: Education.
Type of support: Employee-related scholarships.
Application information: Applications accepted. Application form required.
 Deadline(s): July 1
 Applicants should submit the following:
  1) FAFSA
  2) Transcripts
  3) SAT
  4) ACT
  5) Essay
 Additional information: Unsolicited requests for funds not considered or acknowledged.
Company name: MN Airlines, LLC
EIN: 470943188

4864
Target Corporation Contributions Program
c/o C.R. Comms. Mgr.
1000 Nicollet Mall
Minneapolis, MN   55403-2530   (612) 338-0085
E-mail: Community.Relations@target.com;
URL: https://corporate.target.com/corporate-responsibility

Foundation type: Corporate giving program

Purpose: Grants to college students under the age of 25, who are active in community service. Grants of up to $1,000 for teachers to fund field trips.
Publications: Application guidelines; Grants list.
Fields of interest: Elementary/secondary education; Higher education; Teacher school/education; Education.
Type of support: Grants to individuals; Scholarships—to individuals; Undergraduate support.
Application information: Applications accepted. Application form required. Application form available on the grantmaker's web site.
 Initial approach: Letter
 Additional information: Applications are available on the foundation's web site beginning in the fall of each school year. See web site for further program information.

4865
Thorbeck Foundation, Inc.
48987 U.S. State Hwy. 92
Gonvick, MN   56644

Foundation type: Operating foundation
Purpose: Scholarships to graduates of high schools in the northern Clearwater County, MN, area, to attend four-year colleges and universities.
Financial data: Year ended 12/31/2012. Assets, $208,396 (M); Expenditures, $10,780; Total giving, $10,000; Grants to individuals, 10 grants totaling $10,000 (high: $1,000, low: $1,000).
Type of support: Support to graduates or students of specific schools; Undergraduate support.
Application information: Applications not accepted.
EIN: 363487775

4866
Three Rivers Community Action, Inc.
1414 N. Star Dr.
Zumbrota, MN   55992-1091   (507) 732-7391
Contact: Michael Thorsteinson, Exec. Dir.
FAX: (507) 732-8547; Toll Free Tel.: (800)-277-8418; URL: http://www.threeriverscap.org

Foundation type: Public charity
Purpose: Financial assistance to low-income individuals and families in the tri-county area in southeastern, MN, with food, clothing, shelter, transportation, education, energy assistance and affordable housing.
Financial data: Year ended 09/30/2011. Assets, $9,825,129 (M); Expenditures, $9,934,435; Total giving, $4,490,670; Grants to individuals, 139 grants totaling $3,571,380.
Fields of interest: Human services.
Type of support: Grants for special needs.
Application information: Applications accepted.
 Initial approach: Telephone
EIN: 410906178

4867
Thrivent Financial For Lutherans
625 Fourth Ave. S.
Minneapolis, MN   55415-1624   (612) 844-7143
E-mail: mail@thrivent.com; URL: http://www.thrivent.com

Foundation type: Public charity
Purpose: Emergency needs to individuals for disaster, education, food/hunger, health/medical, rent, utilities, and other needs.

Financial data: Year ended 12/31/2011. Assets, $8,471,354 (M); Expenditures, $77,008,570; Total giving, $70,230,195; Grants to individuals, 5,185 grants totaling $20,189,157.
Fields of interest: Family services; Human services.
Type of support: Emergency funds.
Application information: Applications accepted.
> *Additional information:* Contact the organization for assistance. Some assistance may require an application.
EIN: 510200276

4868
Harlan R. Thurston Foundation
420 E. Main St., Ste. 203
Anoka, MN   55303-2530   (763) 421-0960

Foundation type: Independent foundation
Purpose: Student loans to graduates of Anoka-Hennepin Independent School District No. 11, MN, for undergraduate study.
Financial data: Year ended 12/31/2011. Assets, $941,955 (M); Expenditures, $50,185; Total giving, $5,000.
Type of support: Student loans—to individuals; Support to graduates or students of specific schools; Undergraduate support.
Application information: Applications accepted. Application form required.
> *Deadline(s):* Contact foundation for deadline.
> *Additional information:* Applications are accepted at published or posted times as funds are available .
EIN: 416043390

4869
Tiwahe Foundation
(formerly American Indian Family Empowerment Program)
2801 21st Ave. S., Ste. 132F
Minneapolis, MN   55407   (612) 722-0999
Contact: Kelly Drummer, Pres. and C.E.O.
E-mail application: lapple@tiwahefoundation.org
FAX: (612) 879-0613;
E-mail: info@tiwahefoundation.org; *URL:* http://www.tiwahefoundation.org/

Foundation type: Public charity
Purpose: Grants to American Indian individuals or families in the St. Paul, MN area pursuing professional, educational, or cultural opportunities.
Publications: Application guidelines.
Financial data: Year ended 12/31/2012. Assets, $1,085,045 (M); Expenditures, $255,263; Total giving, $90,123; Grants to individuals, 38 grants totaling $90,123.
Fields of interest: Native Americans/American Indians.
Type of support: Grants to individuals.
Application information: Applications accepted. Application form required.
> *Send request by:* Mail or e-mail
> *Deadline(s):* Jan. 6, May 6, and Sept. 6
> *Final notification:* Recipients notified Feb. 28/29, June 30, and Oct. 30
> *Applicants should submit the following:*
> 1) Letter(s) of recommendation
> 2) Budget Information
> 3) Essay
> *Additional information:* Application should also include proof of tribal enrollment or lineage, copy of birth certificate, if required, school registration confirmation (if applying educational, or a business plan. Hand delivered or faxed applications are not

accepted. See web site for additional guidelines.
Program description:
> *Grants:* Grants between $500 to $2,500 are available to Native Americans who wish to pursue further educational opportunities. Applicants must be 18 years of age, and provide evidence of their proactive involvement in their community and a list of goals for how they will further better their community.
EIN: 264377588

4870
Tozer Foundation, Inc.
1213 1/2 5th Ave. S.
Stillwater, MN   55082-5813   (651) 439-1530
FAX: (651) 430-2112;
E-mail: info@TozerFoundation.com; *URL:* http://www.tozerfoundation.com

Foundation type: Independent foundation
Purpose: Scholarships to graduating high school students of Pine, Kanabec, or Washington counties, MN for attendance at accredited colleges or universities.
Publications: Application guidelines.
Financial data: Year ended 10/31/2012. Assets, $24,247,405 (M); Expenditures, $1,454,050; Total giving, $1,179,875. Scholarships—to individuals amount not specified.
Fields of interest: Higher education.
Type of support: Scholarships—to individuals; Support to graduates or students of specific schools.
Application information: Applications accepted. Application form required. Application form available on the grantmaker's web site.
> *Send request by:* Mail
> *Deadline(s):* Mar. 1
> *Applicants should submit the following:*
> 1) Letter(s) of recommendation
> 2) SAT
> 3) ACT
> 4) Transcripts
> 5) FAFSA
> *Additional information:* Candidates must apply for scholarships through selected high schools. Checks are sent directly to the educational institution on behalf of the students. See web site for additional application guidelines.
EIN: 416011518

4871
Tri-County Hospital, Inc.
415 Jefferson St. N.
Wadena, MN   56482-1264   (218) 631-3510
Contact: Joel Beiswenger, Pres. and C.E.O.
E-mail: lisa.reddick@tricountyhospital.org;
URL: http://www.tricountyhospital.org/index.aspx

Foundation type: Public charity
Purpose: Scholarships for students form Tri-County Health Care, MN service area pursuing healthcare careers.
Financial data: Year ended 12/31/2011. Assets, $34,283,217 (M); Expenditures, $46,448,354; Total giving, $3,437,980; Grants to individuals, 68 grants totaling $46,685. Subtotal for scholarships—to individuals: 10 grants totaling $12,500. Subtotal for grants to individuals: 58 grants totaling $34,185.
Fields of interest: Health care.
Type of support: Scholarships—to individuals.

Application information: Applications accepted. Application form required. Application form available on the grantmaker's web site.
> *Send request by:* Mail
> *Deadline(s):* Vary
> *Additional information:* See web site for additional application guidelines.
Program descriptions:
> *Auxillary Scholarship:* One $500 scholarship is awarded annually to encourage and promote qualified individuals from the hospital's service area to pursue a health care career. Applicant must be entering the second year of schooling, has a minimum cumulative GPA on a 4.0 scale, participates in community activities and express or exhibit a financial need.
> *Bernadine Marquardt and Margaret Prindle Scholarship:* One $2,000 scholarship will assist a Tri-County health Care (TCHC) employee in fulfilling their educational goals. Applicant must be in good standing, demonstrate leadership ability, initiative and active participation in work, volunteerism and/or community activities, and has a GPA of at least a 2.5 on a 4.0 scale or the equivalent, or meets the minimum GPA requirements established for the college or university's academia if it is higher.
> *Davis Family Nursing Scholarship:* The $2,500 scholarship will assist nursing students in an accredited program. Recipients are selected using a blind selection process from the eligibility criteria. A student must be from the TCHC service area pursuing a nursing degree and plan to seek employment in the TCHC service area after graduating.
> *Frances E. Raatikka Scholarship:* This $2,500 scholarship will assist a third or fourth year nursing student in an accredited Bachelor of Science Nursing program. One recipient is selected each year, determined by award availability, from the eligibility criteria.
> *High School Scholarship:* Six $1,000 scholarships are awarded annually to graduating high school seniors in the Tri-county Health Care service area from Bertha-Hewitt, Wadena-Deer Creek, New York Mills, Henning, Sebeka, Menahga or Verndale. Applicant must have a minimum high school cumulative GPA of 3.0 on a 4.0 scale, and pursuing a health related career.
> *Jim Lawson Scholarship:* This $1,000 scholarship is awarded to encourage and promote qualified individuals from the hospital's service area to pursue an advanced or graduate level health care career.
> *Larry Mayer Scholarship:* A $1,000 scholarship is awarded annually to encourage qualified individuals to pursue a health care career in the field of Radiologic Technology. Two recipients are selected annually, using a blind selection process from the eligibility criteria.
EIN: 410713913

4872
Trinity Lutheran Scholarship Fund
950 N. Hwy. 95
Bayport, MN   55003-1014
Contact: Robert Eiselt, Chair.
Application address: 115 N. 4th St., Stillwater, MN 55082

Foundation type: Operating foundation
Purpose: Scholarships to residents of Stillwater, MN who have been baptized at, confirmed by and be members of Trinity Lutheran Church of Stillwater, MN.
Financial data: Year ended 12/31/2011. Assets, $123,697 (M); Expenditures, $19,986; Total

giving, $18,000; Grants to individuals, 18 grants totaling $18,000 (high: $1,000, low: $1,000).
Fields of interest: Education; Christian agencies & churches.
Type of support: Undergraduate support.
Application information: Applications accepted. Application form required.
Applicants should submit the following:
1) Transcripts
2) Letter(s) of recommendation
Additional information: Application should also include a personal letter.
EIN: 416464201

4873
The Two Feathers Endowment
c/o St. Paul Foundation/SpectruTrust
55 Fifth St. E., Ste. 600
Saint Paul, MN 55101-1718 (651) 224-5463
Contact: Carolina Bradpiece, Dir., SpectrumTrust
URL: http://www.saintpaulfoundation.org/

Foundation type: Public charity
Purpose: Scholarships to Minnesota residents of Native American descent to further their education.
Publications: Application guidelines.
Fields of interest: Scholarships/financial aid; Education; Native Americans/American Indians.
Type of support: Scholarships—to individuals.
Application information: Applications accepted. Application form required. Application form available on the grantmaker's web site.
Deadline(s): July 1
Applicants should submit the following:
1) Letter(s) of recommendation
2) Essay
3) Transcripts
4) Financial information
5) FAF
Additional information: All scholarship applicants must be Minnesota residents who can provide (and submit) proof of being a lineal descendent of a federally-recognized tribe; applicants must also be full time students at recognized postsecondary institutions.
Program descriptions:
Richard W. Tanner Scholarship Endowment: Grants of $1,000 each are available to college juniors and seniors who meet application requirements, to offset college costs for the upcoming academic year. Awards are not based on financial need.
Two Feathers Endowment American Indian Scholarship: Scholarships of $1,000 each will be awarded to qualified applicants, to be used for the upcoming academic year. Awards are based on financial need.
Two Feathers Endowment Health Initiative: Grants of $5,000 each are available to qualified applicants who are enrolled in a health-related field of study, to be used for the upcoming academic year. Awards are based on financial need.

4874
United Hospital Foundation
333 N. Smith Ave.
Saint Paul, MN 55102-2344 (651) 241-8022
FAX: (651) 241-5420; URL: http://www.unitedhospital.com/ahs/united.nsf/page/foundation

Foundation type: Public charity
Purpose: Support to nurses who are furthering their education leading to degrees in nursing, and to support education for advancing nursing practice at United Hospital in St. Paul. Assistance to United

Hospital employees in catastrophic need, or who desire to attend educational conferences.
Publications: Annual report; Newsletter.
Financial data: Year ended 12/31/2011. Assets, $41,168,909 (M); Expenditures $10,239,316; Total giving, $8,937,165; Grants to individuals, totaling $35,180.
Fields of interest: Nursing school/education.
Type of support: Undergraduate support; Grants for special needs.
Application information:
Initial approach: Letter
Additional information: Contact foundation for further application guidelines.
EIN: 237420998

4875
United Jewish Fund and Council
(also known as The United Jewish Fund and Council of St. Paul)
790 Cleveland Ave., Ste. 227
St. Paul, MN 55116-3859 (651) 690-1707
Contact: Eli Skora, Exec. Dir.
FAX: (651) 690-0228; URL: http://www.jewishminnesota.org

Foundation type: Public charity
Purpose: Scholarships to help community members experience Jewish camp, higher education and Israel, in the St. Paul, MN area.
Publications: Application guidelines; Annual report; Informational brochure; Newsletter.
Financial data: Year ended 04/30/2012. Assets, $12,259,952 (M); Expenditures, $3,309,511; Total giving, $2,203,574; Grants to individuals, totaling $147,543.
Fields of interest: Education; Jewish agencies & synagogues.
Type of support: Scholarships—to individuals.
Application information: Applications accepted.
Send request by: Online or mail
Deadline(s): Varies
Additional information: See web site for additional guidelines.
Program descriptions:
Higher Education Scholarships: The organization offers three annual scholarship funds, ranging from $250 to $1,500 but scholarships may differ from year to year, for undergraduate and graduate students seeking two-year, four-year, graduate and professional degrees. Scholarships are awarded based on financial need, scholastic performance, and who possess Jewish identity and community involvement. Students of all ages are eligible, including those who have just graduated from high school and are starting their first year of higher education, and adults returning to school. Scholarship recipients must carry a full-time course load of 12 credits, or nine credits if working more than 20 hours per week.
Israel Experience Scholarship: The organization offers scholarships to Jewish children and young adults, ages 13 to 22. Scholarship awards are limited to 25 percent of the program cost or a maximum of $750, whichever is greater. Applicants planning their first trip to Israel will receive priority.
Jay and Esther, Gary and Alise Goldberger Family Scholarship: The scholarship provides funding for the benefit of St. Paul Jewish community families who have children ages 12 months to 18 years old with school district or medically diagnosed Autism Spectrum Disorder. Selection is based on family need and income and completion of the application.
The E. David Fischman Scholarship: The scholarship provides opportunities for Israeli students to pursue a doctorate in political science, law or economics in the U.S. The E. David Fischman

Scholarship will not be awarded for the 2012-2013 academic year. Continue to check web site for updated information on the scholarship.
The Edward Hoffman Scholarship Fund: The program monetarily assists people attending colleges or universities, with preference given to those in Minnesota.
The Jewish Camp Scholarships: The program offers need-based scholarships to help local youth participating in Jewish residential summer camps. Eligible applicants must demonstrate their affiliation with Judaism, reside in the East Metro area and/or be a member of a St. Paul synagogue, the St. Paul Jewish Community Center, or the Talmud Torah of St. Paul, and demonstrate financial need.
EIN: 410693887

4876
UnitedHealthcare Children's Foundation
MN017-W400
P.O. Box 41
Minneapolis, MN 55440-0041 (952) 992-4459
E-mail: customerservice@uhccf.org; Toll-free tel.: (800) 328-5979, ext. 24459; URL: http://www.uhccf.org

Foundation type: Public charity
Purpose: Grants to families to help pay for child health care services such as speech therapy, physical therapy, occupational therapy sessions, prescriptions, and medical equipment such as wheelchairs, orthotics, and eyeglasses.
Publications: Application guidelines; Informational brochure.
Financial data: Year ended 12/31/2011. Assets, $9,720,389 (M); Expenditures, $3,087,756; Total giving, $2,577,507; Grants to individuals, totaling $2,577,507.
Fields of interest: Medical care, community health systems; Health care, insurance; Health care; Children/youth, services; Insurance, providers; Children/youth; Economically disadvantaged.
Type of support: Program development; Grants for special needs.
Application information:
Initial approach: Letter
Deadline(s): None
Additional information: Contact foundation for further eligibility guidelines.
Program description:
Grants Program: Grants are available to provide financial assistance for families who have children with medical needs not covered or not fully covered by their commercial health benefit plan. Eligible applicants must be sixteen years old or younger and live in the U.S.; and must be covered by a commercial health benefit plan (as defined by the foundation) and limits for the requested service are either exceeded, or no coverage is available and/or the co-payments are a serious financial burden on the family. Amount awarded to an individual within a 12-month period is limited to either $5,000 or 85 percent of the fund balance, whichever amount is less; awards to any one individual are limited to a lifetime maximum of $7,500. Grant applications requesting assistance for dental or orthodontic treatment unrelated to a serious medical condition are excluded from grant consideration.
EIN: 522177891

4877
University of Minnesota Foundation
200 Oak St. S.E., Ste. 500
McNamara Alumni Ctr.
Minneapolis, MN 55455-2010 (612) 624-3333
Nomination tel.: (612) 624-1234,
e-mail: siehlprz@umn.edu
FAX: (612) 625-4305; E-mail: giving@umn.edu;
Toll-free tel.: (800) 775-2187; URL: http://
www.giving.umn.edu/foundation/index.html

Foundation type: Public charity
Purpose: Awards and prizes by nomination only to individuals of MN, who have made extraordinary contributions toward producing food and ending hunger.
Publications: Annual report; Financial statement.
Financial data: Year ended 06/30/2012. Assets, $1,744,419,146 (M); Expenditures, $138,780,368; Total giving, $115,023,453; Grants to individuals, totaling $50,000.
Fields of interest: Agriculture/food.
Type of support: Awards/grants by nomination only; Awards/prizes.
Application information: Application form required.
Initial approach: Telephone or e-mail
Deadline(s): Jan.
Additional information: Self nominations and nominations of relatives are not accepted.
Program description:
Siehl Prize for Excellence in Agriculture: Each laureate receives a monetary award of $50,000 and a beautiful granite and glass sculpture. The nominee(s) must currently reside or must have resided in Minnesota for at least five years or hold a degree from the University of Minnesota. The nomination should be submitted in one of three categories: knowledge (teaching, research and outreach); production agriculture; or agribusiness.
EIN: 416042488

4878
The Valspar Foundation
P.O. Box 1461
Minneapolis, MN 55440-1461
Contact: Gwen Leifeld
URL: http://www.valsparglobal.com/corp/about/valspar_foundation.jsp

Foundation type: Company-sponsored foundation
Purpose: Scholarships to children of employees of the Valspar Corporation to pursue higher education as full-time students.
Financial data: Year ended 09/30/2012. Assets, $527,409 (M); Expenditures, $1,063,300; Total giving, $1,061,875.
Fields of interest: Higher education.
Type of support: Employee-related scholarships.
Application information: Applications not accepted.
Additional information: Unsolicited requests for funds not considered or acknowledged.
Company name: The Valspar Corporation
EIN: 411363847

4879
Vermilion Community College Foundation
1900 E. Camp St.
Ely, MN 55731 (218) 235-2166
Contact: Gil Knight, Pres.
E-mail: p.zupancich@vcc.edu; URL: http://www.vcc.edu/foundation-alumni/

Foundation type: Public charity
Purpose: Scholarships to individuals attending Vermillion Community College, MN.

Financial data: Year ended 06/30/2012. Assets, $597,702 (M); Expenditures, $52,402; Total giving, $32,020; Grants to individuals, totaling $32,020.
Type of support: Support to graduates or students of specific schools.
Application information: Applications accepted. Application form required. Application form available on the grantmaker's web site.
Initial approach: Letter
Deadline(s): Mar. 4
Applicants should submit the following:
1) Letter(s) of recommendation
2) Financial information
3) Transcripts
Additional information: See web site for complete list of programs.
EIN: 411351691

4880
Volunteers Enlisted to Assist People
9728 Irving Ave. S.
Bloomington, MN 55431-2625 (952) 888-9616
Contact: Susan Russell Freeman, Exec. Dir.
FAX: (952) 881-8322; URL: http://www.veapvolunteers.org/

Foundation type: Public charity
Purpose: Emergency financial assistance for housing, utilities, car repairs, and other economic essentials to indigent residents of Bloomington, Richfield, Edina and South Minneapolis, MN. Also available are food deliveries, emergency bus passes and gas cards.
Financial data: Year ended 12/31/2011. Assets, $2,039,884 (M); Expenditures, $5,683,129; Total giving, $4,519,142; Grants to individuals, totaling $4,519,142.
Fields of interest: Economically disadvantaged.
Type of support: In-kind gifts; Grants for special needs.
Application information:
Initial approach: Tel.
Additional information: To speak with a licensed social worker about eligibility criteria, call 952.888.9616 x 133.
EIN: 416175999

4881
Volunteers of America
7625 Metro Blvd.
Minneapolis, MN 55439-3053 (952) 945-4000
FAX: (952) 945-4100; URL: http://www.voamn.org/

Foundation type: Public charity
Purpose: Financial support and other in-kind assistance to individuals and families throughout MN with food, clothing, shelter, medical, dental and hospital expenses, and other special needs.
Publications: Annual report; Newsletter.
Financial data: Year ended 06/30/2011. Assets, $25,739,320 (M); Expenditures, $40,471,037; Total giving, $3,772,902; Grants to individuals, totaling $3,772,902.
Fields of interest: Human services; Economically disadvantaged.
Type of support: Emergency funds; In-kind gifts; Grants for special needs.
Application information: Contact the agency for additional information for support.
EIN: 411554078

4882
VSA Minnesota
(formerly VSA arts of Minnesota)
528 Hennepin Ave., Ste. 305
Minneapolis, MN 55403-1810 (612) 332-3888
Contact: Craig Dunn, Exec. Dir.
FAX: (612) 305-0132; E-mail: info@vsaartsmn.org;
TTD/TTY: (612) 332-3888; TTD/TTY (greater MN): (800) 801-3883; URL: http://www.vsaartsmn.org/

Foundation type: Public charity
Purpose: Grants to Minnesota-based artists with disabilities.
Publications: Application guidelines; Newsletter.
Financial data: Year ended 09/30/2012. Assets, $315,831 (M); Expenditures, $422,444; Total giving, $177,653; Grants to individuals, totaling $177,653.
Fields of interest: Visual arts; Performing arts; Literature; Arts; Disabilities, people with.
Type of support: Grants to individuals.
Application information: Applications accepted. Application form required. Application form available on the grantmaker's web site.
Initial approach: Letter, telephone, or e-mail
Copies of proposal: 1
Deadline(s): None
Final notification: Recipients notified in six weeks
Applicants should submit the following:
1) Resume
2) Work samples
3) Proposal
Additional information: Application should include artist statements.
Program descriptions:
Artist-in-Residence Grant Program: This program works to enhance creative expression and personal development through arts experiences for Minnesota-area students with disabilities and their peers who would otherwise have limited access to these opportunities. Residency projects are scheduled according to available funding, location of requests, and teaching artist ability, but will generally provide from $500 to $1,250. Eligible applicants include any public or private school (kindergarten to grade 12), or organizations serving as an alternative education site for special education students (kindergarten to age 21) in the state of Minnesota. Residencies require a minimum of 15 students receiving educational support through an IEP/504 Plan, each of whom must receive at least five direct contact hours each with teaching assistants.
Project Grants for Emerging Artists with Disabilities: Grants are available to Minnesota-based individuals with disabilities who are working to establish a career in their arts medium. Applicants may enter one of these broad areas of arts: visual arts (including sculpture, painting, photography, drawing, mixed media, film/video, computer graphics, fiber arts, jewelry, and printmaking); performance (including music, theater, dance, spoken word, and comedy); writing (including essays, short stories, plays, poetry, and screenplays); and multi-media works. Grants are intended to fund travel or time to research, complete, and present new work; the professional documentation of new work; the purchase of supplies, equipment, or artist services; workshops, conferences, or mentoring for professional development; and studio, theater, or other space rental to produce or present work.
EIN: 363440452

4883
Ross Wagner Foundation
103 Mensing Way
Cannon Falls, MN 55009-1143 (507) 263-3957
Contact: Nancy Vandergon, Secy.-Treas.
E-mail: info@rosswagnerfoundation.org;
URL: http://www.rosswagnerfoundation.org/

Foundation type: Independent foundation
Purpose: Scholarships to students majoring in civil, aeronautical, mechanical, electrical, aerospace, biomedical and chemical engineering in the U.S. and Canada. Students seeking degrees in chemistry and physics may also apply.
Financial data: Year ended 09/30/2012. Assets, $1,400,956 (M); Expenditures, $215,655; Total giving, $199,980; Grants to individuals, 13 grants totaling $199,980 (high: $43,400, low: $1,685).
Fields of interest: Higher education; Engineering school/education.
Type of support: Scholarships—to individuals.
Application information: Applications accepted. Application form required.
> *Initial approach:* E-mail
> *Send request by:* Mail
> *Deadline(s):* Feb. 1
> *Applicants should submit the following:*
> 1) Transcripts
> 2) SAT
> 3) ACT
> *Additional information:* See web site for additional guidelines.

EIN: 208983294

4884
Wallin Education Partners
(formerly Northstar Partners Scholarship Fund)
5200 Willson Rd., Ste. 209
Minneapolis, MN 55424-1343 (952) 345-1920
FAX: (952) 345-1930;
E-mail: wallin.staff@wallinpartners.org; Additional e-mail: info@wallinpartners.org; URL: http://www.wallinfoundation.org

Foundation type: Operating foundation
Purpose: Scholarships to high school graduates of MN from low and moderate income families for attendance at accredited four year colleges or universities in MN, WI, IA, ND, SD or one of the Historically Black Colleges and Universities.
Financial data: Year ended 06/30/2013. Assets, $0 (M); Expenditures, $2,687,900; Total giving, $1,830,681; Grants to individuals, totaling $1,830,681.
Fields of interest: Higher education.
Type of support: Support to graduates or students of specific schools.
Application information: Applications accepted. Application form required. Application form available on the grantmaker's web site.
> *Send request by:* Online
> *Applicants should submit the following:*
> 1) Essay
> 2) GPA
> 3) Transcripts
> 4) Letter(s) of recommendation
> 5) ACT
> *Additional information:* See web site for partnering high school and eligible college or university, and additional guidelines.

Program description:
> *Scholarship:* Scholarships are up to $16,000 for four years ($4,000 per year) to high potential students with financial need. Applicant must be a senior at a partnering high school with a family taxable income of $75,000 or less with low to

moderate assets, have an unweighted GPA of 3.0 or above, composite ACT score of 19 or above, and apply to at least one eligible college or university.

EIN: 208505156

4885
J.A. Wedum Foundation
2615 University Ave. S.E.
Minneapolis, MN 55414-3207
Contact: Jay J. Portz, Pres.
FAX: (612) 789-4044; E-mail: jayportz@wedum.org;
URL: http://www.wedum.org

Foundation type: Independent foundation
Purpose: Student aid primarily to residents of the Midwest, with preference to those living in or near Alexandria, MN.
Publications: Annual report; Informational brochure.
Financial data: Year ended 12/31/2012. Assets, $158,283,160 (M); Expenditures, $38,923,549; Total giving, $1,204,378.
Fields of interest: Education.
Type of support: Scholarships—to individuals.
Application information: Application form required.
> *Deadline(s):* None
> *Additional information:* Application should include resume of academic qualifications.

EIN: 416025661

4886
Welshons Family Scholarship Trust
c/o Minnesota Fiduciary Services Inc.
999 Westview Dr.
Hastings, MN 55033 (651) 438-9777

Foundation type: Independent foundation
Purpose: College scholarships to Hastings High School graduates for continuing their education at accredited colleges or universities.
Financial data: Year ended 12/31/2012. Assets, $221,949 (M); Expenditures, $20,297; Total giving, $15,000; Grants to individuals, 6 grants totaling $15,000 (high: $3,500, low: $1,500).
Application information: Applications accepted. Application form required.
> *Deadline(s):* None
> *Applicants should submit the following:*
> 1) Class rank
> 2) GPA
> 3) Financial information
> 4) Essay

EIN: 416287586

4887
Wenger Foundation
P.O. Box 142
Navarre, MN 55392-0142 (952) 471-3667
Contact: Wendy Dankey, Exec. Dir.

Foundation type: Company-sponsored foundation
Purpose: Scholarships to juniors and seniors from Minnesota pursuing a degree in music education.
Financial data: Year ended 12/31/2012. Assets, $8,451,686 (M); Expenditures, $313,960; Total giving, $277,185.
Fields of interest: Music.
Type of support: Undergraduate support.
Application information: Applications not accepted.
> *Additional information:* Awards are determined by financial aid officers at each college and university. Contributes only to preselected

individuals, unsolicited requests for funds not considered or acknoweldged.
EIN: 411436658

4888
Western Minnesota Masonic Foundation
101 S. 1st St., Ste. 50
Montevideo, MN 56265-1572
Contact: Ralph Lunde, Secy.

Foundation type: Operating foundation
Purpose: Scholarships to graduates of Montevideo High School, MN, for attendance at colleges or universities in the United States.
Financial data: Year ended 12/31/2012. Assets, $132,733 (M); Expenditures, $8,886; Total giving, $8,750; Grants to individuals, 4 grants totaling $8,750 (high: $2,500, low: $1,250).
Type of support: Support to graduates or students of specific schools; Undergraduate support.
Application information: Applications accepted. Application form required.
> *Deadline(s):* Apr. 1
> *Additional information:* Application should include class rank and anticipated college major.

EIN: 411570211

4889
Whiteside Scholarship Fund Trust
(formerly Robert B. and Sophia Whiteside Scholarship Fund)
c/o U.S. Bank, N.A., Trust Tax Svcs.
P.O. Box 64713
St. Paul, MN 55164-0713

Foundation type: Independent foundation
Purpose: Scholarships to graduates of Duluth, MN, high schools.
Financial data: Year ended 12/31/2012. Assets, $3,709,871 (M); Expenditures, $740,930; Total giving, $552,000; Grants to individuals, 35 grants totaling $552,000 (high: $147,000, low: $3,000).
Fields of interest: College; Scholarships/financial aid.
Type of support: Support to graduates or students of specific schools; Undergraduate support.
Application information: Applications accepted. Application form required. Interview required.
> *Deadline(s):* Fall of senior year in high school
> *Additional information:* Application through local high school counselors.

Program description:
> *Whiteside Scholarship Program:* Applicants are interviewed and selected by a scholarship committee in the spring of their senior year. Awards are renewable for up to four years providing recipients maintain at least a 3.0 GPA.

EIN: 411288761

4890
Amherst H. Wilder Foundation
451 Lexington Pkwy. N.
St. Paul, MN 55104-4636 (651) 280-2000
FAX: (651) 280-3471;
E-mail: maykao.hang@wilder.org; Tel. for Maykao Y. Hang : (651)-280-2122; URL: http://www.wilder.org

Foundation type: Public charity
Purpose: Grants to assist poor, sick, disadvantaged and otherwise needy residents of the St. Paul, MN area.
Publications: Annual report.

Financial data: Year ended 06/30/2011. Assets, $237,929,773 (M); Expenditures, $43,058,041; Total giving, $1,643,522; Grants to individuals, totaling $1,568,183.
Fields of interest: Economically disadvantaged.
Type of support: Grants for special needs.
Application information:
  Initial approach: Letter
  Additional information: Contact foundation for complete eligibility requirements.
EIN: 410693889

4891
Oscar and Mary Wildey Mitchell Scholarship Fund

(formerly Oscar Mitchell, Jr. Trust Scholarship Fund)
c/o Wells Fargo Bank Fiduciary Tax
230 W. Superior St., 5th Fl.
Duluth, MN 55802

Foundation type: Independent foundation
Purpose: Scholarships to graduating seniors of public, private, or home schools in Carlton, Cloquet, Duluth, Esko, Hermantown, Proctor, Two Harbors, and Wrenshall high schools, Minnesota for study at any accredited private college or any branch of the University of Minnesota.
Publications: Informational brochure.
Financial data: Year ended 06/30/2013. Assets, $2,933,644 (M); Expenditures, $147,683; Total giving, $96,350; Grants to individuals, 26 grants totaling $96,350 (high: $4,100, low: $2,050).
Fields of interest: Education.
Type of support: Support to graduates or students of specific schools; Undergraduate support.
Application information: Application form required.
  Deadline(s): Jan. 15
  Applicants should submit the following:
    1) Letter(s) of recommendation
    2) Financial information
    3) Essay
  Additional information: Application forms available from the guidance department of each participating high school; All forms must be submitted to the student's counselor by the announced date.
EIN: 416148927

4892
Winona State University Foundation

175 W. Mark St.
P.O. Box 5838
Winona, MN 55987-0838   (507) 457-5000
FAX: (507) 457-5620;
E-mail: csieracki@winona.edu; TTY: (877)-627-3848; URL: http://www.winona.edu/foundation

Foundation type: Public charity
Purpose: Scholarships for students at Winona State University, MN.
Publications: Application guidelines.
Financial data: Year ended 06/30/2012. Assets, $31,871,685 (M); Expenditures, $3,041,247; Total giving, $2,201,317; Grants to individuals, totaling $920,544.
Fields of interest: Higher education.
Type of support: Scholarships—to individuals; Support to graduates or students of specific schools.
Application information: Applications accepted.
  Send request by: Online
  Deadline(s): May 3
  Applicants should submit the following:
    1) Financial information
    2) Essay
    3) GPA
  Additional information: Recipients are selected by the foundation scholarship committee.
EIN: 237079002

4893
Winslow Foundation

5301 W. Highwood Dr.
Edina, MN 55436-1222
Contact: Penny Winslow, Pres.

Foundation type: Independent foundation
Purpose: Scholarships to financially disadvantaged minorities attending North High School, MN, only.
Financial data: Year ended 12/31/2012. Assets, $1,468 (M); Expenditures, $6,050; Total giving, $4,000; Grants to individuals, 4 grants totaling $4,000 (high: $1,000, low: $1,000).
Fields of interest: Minorities.

Type of support: Support to graduates or students of specific schools.
Application information: Applications accepted.
  Initial approach: Letter
  Deadline(s): None
  Additional information: Application must outline financial need and educational background.
EIN: 411670398

4894
The Woman's Club of Minneapolis

410 Oak Grove St.
Minneapolis, MN 55403-3294   (612) 813-5300
FAX: (612) 813-5336;
E-mail: Frontdesk@womansclub.org; URL: http://www.womansclub.org

Foundation type: Public charity
Purpose: Scholarship to a female student for attendance at the University of Minnesota Graduate School and to women students at the Minneapolis Community and Technical College.
Publications: Application guidelines; Grants list.
Financial data: Year ended 04/30/2013. Assets, $6,839,124 (M); Expenditures, $3,216,964; Total giving, $47,000.
Fields of interest: Higher education; Human services; Community/economic development.
Type of support: Scholarships—to individuals; Support to graduates or students of specific schools; Grants for special needs.
Application information: See web site for additional application information.
Program description:
  Scholarships: The club annually awards a $5,000 scholarship to a female student in the University of Minnesota Graduate School, and three $1,000 scholarships to women students at the Minneapolis Community and Technical College.
EIN: 410618870

MISSISSIPPI

4895
AJFC Community Action Agency

1038A N. Union St.
Natchez, MS 39120-2875 (601) 442-8681
Contact: Sandra Sewell, Exec. Dir.
FAX: (601) 442-9572; E-mail: rhill@cableone.net;
E-mail For Brenda Letcher: bletcher@cableone.net;
URL: http://www.ajfccommunityaction.org

Foundation type: Public charity
Purpose: Emergency and financial assistance to low- and moderate-income individuals and families in the nine-county area of MS with affordable housing, food, shelter, energy, child care, and other special needs.
Financial data: Year ended 01/31/2012. Assets, $13,214,173 (M); Expenditures, $10,289,086; Total giving, $1,797,363; Grants to individuals, totaling $1,797,363.
Fields of interest: Economically disadvantaged.
Type of support: Emergency funds; Grants for special needs.
Application information: Contact the agency for eligibility determination. The nine county area includes, Adams, Clairborne, Copiah, Franklin, Jefferson, Lawrence, Lincoln, Amite and Wilkinson.
Program description:
Individual Development Account (Promise) Program: The agency provides a matching-savings-account program designed to help low-income families and individuals save money for home ownership, education, and business capitalization. Eligible applicants must have a household income of less than 200 percent of federal poverty guidelines, show documentation of employment, and have a household net worth of $10,000 or less.
EIN: 640442959

4896
Bacot/Jolly McCarty Foundation, Inc.

(formerly Bacot Foundation, Inc.)
P.O. Box 1442
Pascagoula, MS 39568-1442 (228) 934-1338
Contact: Todd Trenchard, Exec. Dir.
FAX: (228) 934-1342;
E-mail: todd.trenchard@mandmbank.com;
URL: http://www.bacotmccarty.org/

Foundation type: Public charity
Purpose: Scholarships to worthy individuals of Jackson county and South Mississippi with special needs pursuing a higher education.
Financial data: Year ended 10/31/2012. Assets, $1,149,141 (M); Expenditures, $526,104; Total giving, $358,586.
Fields of interest: Education.
Type of support: Scholarships—to individuals.
Application information: Contact the foundation for additional guidelines.
EIN: 640620054

4897
D.A. Biglane Foundation

P.O. Box 966
Natchez, MS 39121-0966 (601) 445-7000
Contact: James M. Biglane, Mgr.
Application address: 75 Melrose-Montebello Pkwy., Natchez, MS 39120

Foundation type: Independent foundation

Purpose: Scholarship loans only to residents of the Natchez, MS, area.
Financial data: Year ended 12/31/2012. Assets, $2,183,466 (M); Expenditures, $128,252; Total giving, $98,909; Grants to individuals, 12 grants totaling $72,000 (high: $9,000, low: $2,500).
Type of support: Student loans—to individuals.
Application information: Applications accepted. Application form required.
  Deadline(s): None
  Additional information: Application must include transcripts and financial information.
EIN: 646028044

4898
John M. & Elizabeth Beeman Bleuer
Scholarship Fund

P.O. Box 289
Biloxi, MS 39533-0289 (228) 374-2100
Contact: Mildred B. Page, Tr.
Application address: 759 Vieux Marche Mall, Biloxi, MS 39530

Foundation type: Operating foundation
Purpose: Scholarships to qualified high school seniors residing in Biloxi, MS.
Publications: Informational brochure (including application guidelines).
Financial data: Year ended 12/31/2011. Assets, $1,876,044 (M); Expenditures, $84,433; Total giving, $63,000.
Type of support: Scholarships—to individuals.
Application information: Applications accepted. Application form required.
  Send request by: Mail
  Deadline(s): Mar. 31
  Final notification: Recipients notified after Apr. 15
  Applicants should submit the following:
    1) Photograph
    2) Letter(s) of recommendation
    3) SAT
    4) Transcripts
    5) Essay
    6) Financial information
    7) ACT
    8) GPA
  Additional information: Contact fund for current application guidelines.
EIN: 646197850

4899
The Box Project, Inc.

315 Losher St., Ste. 100
Hernando, MS 38632-2124 (662) 449-5002
Contact: Sue Patneaude, Exec. Dir.
FAX: (662) 449-5006; E-mail: info@boxproject.org;
Toll-free tel.: (800)-268-9928; URL: http://www.boxproject.org

Foundation type: Public charity
Purpose: Grants for necessities and emergency funds to families living in rural poverty in MS, ME, Appalachia, and Native American reservations in FL and SD.
Publications: Application guidelines; Annual report; Financial statement; Newsletter (including application guidelines).
Fields of interest: Economically disadvantaged.
Type of support: Emergency funds; Grants for special needs.
Application information: Contact foundation for eligibility requirements.
EIN: 060854618

4900
C Spire Wireless Foundation

1018 Highland Colony Pkwy., Ste. 360
Ridgeland, MS 39157 (601) 355-1522
Contact: Beth C. Byrd, Exec. Dir.
URL: http://www.cspire.com/company_info/about/programs/foundation.jsp

Foundation type: Company-sponsored foundation
Purpose: Grants to individuals who have suffered losses due to Hurricane Katrina.
Publications: Application guidelines.
Financial data: Year ended 12/31/2012. Assets, $109,038 (M); Expenditures, $656,316; Total giving, $597,000.
Fields of interest: Disasters, Hurricane Katrina.
Type of support: Grants to individuals.
Application information: Applications accepted. Application form required.
  Deadline(s): None
  Additional information: Application should include documents that substantiate the amount of loss due to Hurricane Katrina.
EIN: 203426826

4901
Care Consistency Foundation, Inc.

7761 Meadow Cir.
Meridian, MS 39305-8913 (601) 483-9556

Foundation type: Public charity
Purpose: Grants to individuals in the MS, area to acquire medical equipment such as vans lifts, special computers and specialized equipment for use by handicapped persons. Scholarships to qualying individuals for higher education.
Financial data: Year ended 12/31/2011. Assets, $9,693,765 (M); Expenditures, $253,124; Total giving, $151,089; Grants to individuals, 8 grants totaling $17,434.
Fields of interest: Education; Disabilities, people with.
Type of support: Scholarships—to individuals; Grants for special needs.
Application information: Applications accepted.
  Additional information: Applying for scholarshup funds may require an application. Contact the foundation for additional information.
EIN: 640730846

4902
Community Foundation of Greater
Jackson

(formerly Greater Jackson Foundation)
525 E. Capitol St., Ste. 5B
Jackson, MS 39201-2702 (601) 974-6044
Contact: Jane Alexander, C.E.O.
FAX: (601) 974-6045;
E-mail: info@cfgreaterjackson.org; URL: http://www.cfgreaterjackson.org

Foundation type: Community foundation
Purpose: Scholarships to students for higher education in LA and MS.
Publications: Application guidelines; Annual report; Financial statement; Informational brochure; Newsletter; Occasional report.
Financial data: Year ended 03/31/2012. Assets, $28,150,528 (M); Expenditures, $2,478,582; Total giving, $1,910,690; Grants to individuals, 175 grants totaling $90,177.
Fields of interest: Media/communications; Vocational education, post-secondary; Higher education; Business school/education; Engineering school/education; Journalism school/education; Education.

Type of support: Scholarships—to individuals; Support to graduates or students of specific schools; Awards/prizes; Undergraduate support.
Application information: Applications accepted. Application form required. Application form available on the grantmaker's web site.
Initial approach: Application
Send request by: Mail
Copies of proposal: 1
Deadline(s): Varies
Final notification: Recipients notified within 90 days
Applicants should submit the following:
1) Letter(s) of recommendation
2) SAT
3) GPA
4) Financial information
5) ACT
EIN: 640845750

4903
CREATE Foundation
(formerly Create Christian Research Education Action Technical Enterprise, Inc.)
213 W. Main St.
Tupelo, MS 38802-3941 (662) 844-8989
Contact: Michael K. Clayborne, Pres.
FAX: (662) 844-8149;
E-mail: info@createfoundation.com; Mailing address: P.O. Box 1053, Tupelo, MS 38802-1053; E-Mail for Michael K. Clayborne: mike@createfoundation.com; URL: http://www.createfoundation.com

Foundation type: Community foundation
Purpose: Scholarships to graduating students attending Tupelo High School, MS, and Baldwin High School in Lee County, MS.
Publications: Application guidelines; Annual report; Informational brochure; Newsletter.
Financial data: Year ended 12/31/2012. Assets, $65,353,647 (M); Expenditures, $5,904,551; Total giving, $4,462,511; Grants to individuals, 180 grants totaling $146,906.
Fields of interest: Higher education.
Type of support: Support to graduates or students of specific schools; Undergraduate support.
Application information: Contact individual schools for current application deadline/guidelines.
EIN: 237248582

4904
The Carl and Virginia Day Trust
P.O. Box 1018
Yazoo City, MS 39194-1018
Contact: Rosemary Knox; Melba Mood
Application address: 104 S. Main, Yazoo City, MS 39194

Foundation type: Independent foundation
Purpose: Interest-free student loans to residents of MS who are under 25 years old, have a 2.0 GPA, and attend MS schools.
Publications: Annual report; Financial statement.
Financial data: Year ended 12/31/2012. Assets, $2,660,334 (M); Expenditures, $64,856; Total giving, $250,650; Grants to individuals, 214 grants totaling $250,650 (high: $1,250, low: $900).
Fields of interest: Education.
Type of support: Student loans—to individuals; Undergraduate support.
Application information:
Deadline(s): July 4 for fall loans and Nov. 4 for spring loans
Additional information: Application by letter, including statement of school planning to

attend, age, transcripts, state of residence, parents' financial statements and four references.
EIN: 640386095

4905
Danny M. Dunnaway Foundation
P.O. Box 545
Brookhaven, MS 39602-0545

Foundation type: Independent foundation
Purpose: Grants to domestic and foreign missionaries with whom a working relationship has been developed over the years.
Financial data: Year ended 12/31/2012. Assets, $30,962 (M); Expenditures, $53,962; Total giving, $52,460; Grants to individuals, 7 grants totaling $48,380 (high: $33,100, low: $390).
Fields of interest: Christian agencies & churches; Religion.
International interests: Global Programs.
Type of support: Grants for special needs.
Application information: Applications not accepted.
EIN: 640847778

4906
East Mississippi Development Corporation
c/o Meridian Community College
910 Hwy. 19 N.
Meridian, MS 39307-5801

Foundation type: Operating foundation
Purpose: Loans to individuals for high-risk and minority business enterprises in East MS.
Financial data: Year ended 12/31/2012. Assets, $184,921 (M); Expenditures, $725,308; Total giving, $0.
Fields of interest: Housing/shelter, expense aid.
Type of support: Loans—to individuals.
Application information: Applications accepted. Application form available on the grantmaker's web site.
Initial approach: Letter
Deadline(s): Varies
Additional information: Applicant for loan approval must submit financial statements, residential appraisal, equifax reports, deeds, certificate of title, truth and lending disclosure and certificate of participation documents from the bank which is participating in the loan to be made.
EIN: 640773932

4907
Feild Co-Operative Association Inc.
4400 Old Canton Rd., Ste. 170
Jackson, MS 39211-5982 (601) 713-2312
Contact: Cindy May, Secy.
FAX: (601) 713-2314; *Application address:* P.O. Box 5054, Jackson, MS 39296; URL: http://www.feildstudentloans.org

Foundation type: Independent foundation
Purpose: Student loans to MS residents who are undergraduate juniors or seniors, or graduate students at accredited colleges and universities.
Publications: Application guidelines; Informational brochure.
Financial data: Year ended 12/31/2012. Assets, $19,180,701 (M); Expenditures, $868,467; Total giving, $572,200; Loans to individuals, totaling $352,000.
Fields of interest: Higher education.

Type of support: Graduate support; Undergraduate support.
Application information: Applications accepted. Application form required. Interview required.
Initial approach: Letter
Deadline(s): Six to eight weeks before each semester begins
Applicants should submit the following:
1) Letter(s) of recommendation
2) Transcripts
3) Financial information
4) Photograph
Additional information: Application must also include student's employment history.
Program description:
Loan Program: Loans are made to supplement other funds available to students, but never to cover all expenses. The maximum loan amount is $3,000 per calendar year, for a total of no more than $9,000 over a three-year period. Students of good character who have satisfactorily completed two years of college work, graduate students, and students in special fields may apply for loans. Students must show evidence of financial need, and promise of social and financial responsibility. Application should be made for only one year at a time. Loans are made at six percent interest. First payment on account is due no later than three months from date of graduation or withdrawal from college for any reason, military or otherwise. Loan repayment schedule is not less than $50 per month if loan is less than $2,500.
EIN: 640155700

4908
Franks Foundation
P.O. Box 250
Booneville, MS 38829-0250

Foundation type: Independent foundation
Purpose: Scholarships to individuals in the First Congressional District of MS, for higher education.
Financial data: Year ended 12/31/2012. Assets, $2,748,809 (M); Expenditures, $26,024; Total giving, $10,800; Grants to individuals, 35 grants totaling $10,800 (high: $400, low: -$400).
Fields of interest: Higher education.
Type of support: Scholarships—to individuals; Undergraduate support.
Application information: Applications accepted. Application form required.
Deadline(s): 30 days prior to start of semester
Additional information: Applicants should contact the college or university for application.
EIN: 640845922

4909
Gulf Coast Community Foundation
11975 Seaway Rd., Ste. B-150
Gulfport, MS 39503 (228) 897-4841
Contact: Ashley Bryan, Cont.
FAX: (228) 897-4843; E-mail: abryan@mgccf.org; URL: http://www.mgccf.org

Foundation type: Community foundation
Purpose: Scholarships to residents of George, Hancock, Harrison, Jackson, Pearl River, and Stone counties, MS pursuing higher education.
Publications: Application guidelines; Annual report; Financial statement; Informational brochure; Newsletter; Occasional report.
Financial data: Year ended 06/30/2013. Assets, $19,624,158 (M); Expenditures, $6,693,684; Total giving, $5,743,673; Grants to individuals, 511 grants totaling $164,750.
Fields of interest: Higher education.

Type of support: Scholarships—to individuals; Undergraduate support.
Application information: Applications accepted. Application form required. Application form available on the grantmaker's web site.
    Initial approach: Telephone or application
    Send request by: Mail
    Deadline(s): Spring
    Additional information: Eligibility requirements vary, see web site for additional application guidelines.
EIN: 570908490

4910
Mary Kirkpatrick Haskell Scholarship Foundation, Inc.
1608 Highland Dr.
Amory, MS 38821-8742 (662) 257-9673

Foundation type: Independent foundation
Purpose: Scholarships for graduating high school seniors of Monroe county, MS for attendance at a Mississippi university.
Financial data: Year ended 09/30/2011. Assets, $240,697 (M); Expenditures, $46,095; Total giving, $42,300. Scholarships—to individuals amount not specified.
Fields of interest: Higher education.
Type of support: Scholarships—to individuals.
Application information: Applications accepted. Application form required.
    Initial approach: Letter
    Additional information: The foundation announces through the local schools when applications for graduating seniors are accepted.
EIN: 640813608

4911
Mary & Annie Hazard Memorial Foundation
916 College St.
Columbus, MS 39701 (662) 328-3088
Contact: Eulalie H. Davis, Tr.

Foundation type: Independent foundation
Purpose: Scholarships to individuals attending Mississippi University for Women or Belhaven College, MS.
Financial data: Year ended 12/31/2011. Assets, $156,948 (M); Expenditures, $7,125; Total giving, $4,000; Grants to individuals, 3 grants totaling $4,000 (high: $2,000, low: $1,000).
Fields of interest: Women.
Type of support: Support to graduates or students of specific schools; Undergraduate support.
Application information: Application form required.
    Deadline(s): Prior to the beginning of the semester
    Additional information: Forms are available from eligible schools.
EIN: 646024825

4912
The Lexington Foundation
P.O. Box 445
Lexington, MS 39095-0445
Application address: c/o Carolyn Mirick, 102 Andrews St., Lexington, MS 39095; tel.: (622) 834-2488

Foundation type: Independent foundation
Purpose: Grants to residents of MS for medical, educational and emergency support.

Financial data: Year ended 12/31/2012. Assets, $1,205,566 (M); Expenditures, $261,812; Total giving, $203,809; Grants to individuals, 237 grants totaling $124,195 (high: $16,725, low: $50).
Fields of interest: Education; Health care; Safety/disasters; Economically disadvantaged.
Type of support: Emergency funds; Grants for special needs.
Application information: Applications accepted. Application form required.
    Initial approach: Letter
    Deadline(s): None
    Additional information: Recipients based entirely on need.
EIN: 640912814

4913
Katrina Overall McDonald Memorial Scholarship Fund
142 Lakewood Dr.
Waveland, MS 39576-4319

Foundation type: Independent foundation
Purpose: Scholarships by nomination only to graduates of Bay High School in Bay St. Louis, MS.
Financial data: Year ended 12/31/2012. Assets, $309,742 (M); Expenditures, $49,101; Total giving, $46,500; Grants to individuals, 6 grants totaling $16,500 (high: $3,000, low: $1,500).
Type of support: Support to graduates or students of specific schools; Awards/grants by nomination only; Undergraduate support.
Application information: Applications not accepted.
    Additional information: Recipients are selected from a list of nominees submitted by the school faculty committee.
EIN: 640725975

4914
Mississippi Bar Foundation, Inc.
P.O. Box 2168
Jackson, MS 39225-2168 (601) 948-4471
Contact: Larry Houchins, Secy.-Treas.; Angie Cook
FAX: (601) 355-8635; URL: http://www.msbar.org/programs-affiliates/ms-bar-foundationiolta.aspx

Foundation type: Public charity
Purpose: Emergency assistance to MS lawyers and their families. Scholarships for vocational/technical education to graduating seniors who are the children of deceased or incapacitated MS lawyers.
Publications: Annual report.
Financial data: Year ended 07/31/2011. Assets, $1,793,570 (M); Expenditures, $976,231; Total giving, $789,364; Grants to individuals, totaling $51,250.
Fields of interest: Vocational education; Human services, emergency aid.
Type of support: Scholarships—to individuals; Grants for special needs.
Application information: Application form required. Application form available on the grantmaker's web site.
    Deadline(s): May 1 for scholarships
    Applicants should submit the following:
     1) FAF
     2) Financial information
     3) Letter(s) of recommendation
     4) Transcripts
    Additional information: Scholarship applications must also include proof of the parent's death or injury.

Program descriptions:
  Kid's Chance of Mississippi Scholarship Fund: Scholarships for vocational/technical school to students who have had a parent killed or permanently and totally disabled on the job. Applicants must be Mississippi residents between the ages of 17 and 23. The scholarship is good for one year, but recipients may apply each year of school as long as they make satisfactory academic progress. In addition, applicants must demonstrate substantial financial need.
  Lawyers Emergency Assistance Fund: The program designed to financially assist lawyers or their families suffering from financial hardship as a result of a catastrophic injury or illness to a lawyer.
EIN: 646029087

4915
Mississippi Society of Certified Public Accountants Foundation
306 Southhampton Row
Ridgeland, MS 39157-2042 (601) 856-4244
URL: http://www.ms-cpa.org/foundation.asp

Foundation type: Independent foundation
Purpose: Grants to senior college students majoring in accounting or working toward a Masters degree in accounting who are residents of MS.
Financial data: Year ended 06/30/2012. Assets, $499,002 (M); Expenditures, $20,612; Total giving, $19,000; Grants to individuals, 11 grants totaling $19,000 (high: $2,000, low: $1,000).
Fields of interest: Business school/education; Business/industry.
Type of support: Graduate support; Undergraduate support.
Application information: Applications accepted. Application form required.
    Deadline(s): July 1
    Additional information: Applications provided in MS colleges and universities.
EIN: 646038540

4916
Mobile Medical Mission Hospital, Inc.
78 Grandview Cir.
Brandon, MS 39047-7398 (601) 829-2377
Contact: Samuel O. Massey, Jr. M.D.

Foundation type: Independent foundation
Purpose: Scholarships to financially needy individuals pursuing health care education.
Financial data: Year ended 10/31/2012. Assets, $959,612 (M); Expenditures, $133,279; Total giving, $66,608.
Fields of interest: Health sciences school/education.
Type of support: Undergraduate support.
Application information:
    Deadline(s): None
    Additional information: Recipients must volunteer ten percent of their time to low-income areas.
EIN: 581348941

4917
The Herman and Hazel Owen Foundation
425 Eubanks Dr.
Columbus, MS 39702-8885 (662) 328-2785
Contact: Marjorie Robertson, Secy.-Treas.
Application address: 490 Eubanks Dr., Columbus, MS 39702

Foundation type: Independent foundation

Purpose: Welfare assistance to indigent residents of Lowndes County, MS, and to individuals residing within 50 miles of Columbus, MS, for medical expenses.
Financial data: Year ended 01/31/2013. Assets, $1,036,097 (M); Expenditures, $60,119; Total giving, $39,187.
Fields of interest: Health care; Economically disadvantaged.
Type of support: Grants for special needs.
Application information: Applications accepted.
  Initial approach: Letter
  Deadline(s): None
  Additional information: Application should include biographical and financial information.
EIN: 640601824

4918
Phillips Foundation
P.O. Box 471
Columbus, MS 39703-0471
Application address: c/o Betty Miller, 116 5th St. N., Columbus, MS 39701, tel.: (662) 327-8401

Foundation type: Operating foundation
Purpose: General welfare grants primarily to economically disadvantaged residents of Lowndes County, MS, for medical, surgical, pharmaceutical and hospital expenses other than doctors' bills or surgical fees.
Financial data: Year ended 12/31/2011. Assets, $4,409,575 (M); Expenditures, $194,528; Total giving, $151,358; Grants to individuals, totaling $151,358.
Type of support: Grants for special needs.
Application information: Applications accepted. Application form required.
  Additional information: Application should include referral.
EIN: 646020136

4919
Pine Family Foundation
1121 Del Norte Cr.
Pascagoula, MS 39581

Foundation type: Independent foundation
Purpose: Scholarships and grants to support research towards the cure of Alzheimer's and other incurable diseases.
Financial data: Year ended 12/31/2012. Assets, $995,819 (M); Expenditures, $115,000; Total giving, $100,000; Grants to individuals, 2 grants totaling $100,000 (high: $50,000, low: $50,000).
Fields of interest: AIDS research; Alzheimer's disease research.
Type of support: Research.
Application information: Applications accepted. Application form required.
  Deadline(s): Mar. 15
Program description:
  Research Program: Grants and scholarships are awarded to researchers and graduate students who are working toward a cure for Alzheimer's and other diseases. Applying for a scholarship, ($500 to $2,500), applicants must be engaged in active research towards the cure of Alzheimer's or AIDS, be working on a graduate degree, submit a letter from the supervising professor, a personal resume, a letter detailing how funds are to be used, designate a person to oversee the spending of funds, and submit a progress report and final report. Applying for a grant, ($500 to $10,000), applicants must conduct research on Alzheimer's or AIDS, use no more than five percent of funds for administrative purposes, submit a letter detailing

how funds are to be used, designate a person to oversee the spending of funds, and submit a progress report and final report.
EIN: 742697612

4920
Allen B. Puckett, Jr. Family Foundation
P.O. Box 9630
Columbus, MS 39705 (662) 328-4931
Contact: Allen B. Puckett III, Tr.

Foundation type: Independent foundation
Purpose: Grants to needy individuals residing in MS for general welfare and medical expenses.
Financial data: Year ended 12/31/2012. Assets, $165,160 (M); Expenditures, $23,934; Total giving, $22,153; Grants to individuals, 17 grants totaling $13,595 (high: $4,000, low: $150).
Fields of interest: Economically disadvantaged.
Type of support: Grants for special needs.
Application information: Applications accepted.
  Final notification: Within 90 days
  Additional information: Individuals should include a summary of qualifications for the charitable award and circumstances regarding financial need. Applications are accepted by mail only.
EIN: 640732703

4921
Homer Skelton Charitable Foundation
4555 Spring Meadow Way N.
Olive Branch, MS 38654-8133
Contact: Homer D. Skelton, Tr.

Foundation type: Independent foundation
Purpose: Scholarships to individuals for higher education. Financial assistance to individuals of TN for child care.
Financial data: Year ended 12/31/2011. Assets, $3,226,581 (M); Expenditures, $330,539; Total giving, $328,453. Grants to individuals amount not specified.
Fields of interest: Higher education; Day care.
Type of support: Scholarships—to individuals; Grants for special needs.
Application information: Applications accepted.
  Initial approach: Letter
  Additional information: Contact the foundation for eligibility determination.
EIN: 621578268

4922
St. Vincent de Paul Community Pharmacy, Inc.
P.O. Box 1228
Biloxi, MS 39533-1228 (228) 374-4860
Contact: Jill Roth; Samuel J. Burke, Exec. Dir.
E-mail: t_pavlov@svdp-pharmacy.com; URL: http://www.svdprx.org

Foundation type: Public charity
Purpose: Assistance to disadvantaged persons on the Mississippi Gulf Coast with prescription medicines, free of charge.
Publications: Annual report; Informational brochure; Newsletter.
Financial data: Year ended 12/31/2011. Assets, $722,431 (M); Expenditures, $1,542,454. Grants for special needs amount not specified.
Fields of interest: Economically disadvantaged.
Type of support: Grants for special needs.
Application information: Applications accepted.
  Initial approach: Telephone
  Additional information: Applicant must demonstrate that he or she cannot afford his

or her medicine. Applicant must have photo ID, proof of income and proof of coverage. Contact the group or see web site for eligibility requirements.
EIN: 640891772

4923
Mr. & Mrs. E. H. Sumners Foundation
c/o Regions Bank
P.O. Box 23100
Jackson, MS 39225-3100 (601) 354-8458

Foundation type: Public charity
Purpose: Scholarships to students of Attala, Carroll, Choctaw, Montgomery and Webster counties, MS for postsecondary education.
Financial data: Year ended 12/31/2012. Assets, $59,875,858 (M); Expenditures, $3,704,548; Total giving, $3,154,119. Scholarships—to individuals amount not specified.
Fields of interest: Higher education.
Type of support: Scholarships—to individuals; Undergraduate support.
Application information: Applications not accepted.
  Additional information: Payments are made directly to the educational institution on behalf of the students. Unsolicited requests for funds not considered or acknowledged.
EIN: 646167983

4924
Louise W. Thalheimer Charitable Trust
P.O. Box 937
Greenwood, MS 38935-0937

Foundation type: Independent foundation
Purpose: Financial assistance for indigent individuals of Greenwood, MS for medical expense.
Financial data: Year ended 12/31/2012. Assets, $113,211 (M); Expenditures, $1,549; Total giving, $12,210; Grants to individuals, 26 grants totaling $12,210 (high: $7,751, low: $11).
Fields of interest: Economically disadvantaged.
Type of support: Grants for special needs.
Application information: Applications accepted.
  Deadline(s): None
  Additional information: Applications received from individuals through referrals from medical professionals and are screened by the trustees.
EIN: 237208414

4925
The University of Southern Mississippi Foundation
118 College Dr., Ste. 5210
Hattiesburg, MS 39406-0001 (601) 266-5210
Contact: Bob Pierce, Exec. Dir.
FAX: (601) 266-5735;
E-mail: foundation@usm.edu; Toll-free tel.: (888) 338-2876; E-mail for Bob Pierce: bob.pierce@usm.edu; URL: http://www.usm.edu/foundation/

Foundation type: Public charity
Purpose: Scholarships for students at the University of Southern Mississippi for higher education.
Financial data: Year ended 06/30/2012. Assets, $98,276,680 (M); Expenditures, $11,321,410; Total giving, $8,791,674; Grants to individuals, totaling $4,450.
Fields of interest: Higher education.

Type of support: Support to graduates or students of specific schools.
Application information: Applications accepted.
  Initial approach: Telephone
  Deadline(s): Varies
  Additional information: See web site for a listing of available annual and endowed scholarships.
EIN: 646022505

4926
Yates Emergency Relief Foundation
P.O. Box 456
Philadelphia, MS 39350-0456 (601) 656-5411
Contact: Carolyn Y. Voyles, Pres.

Foundation type: Public charity
Purpose: Financial assistance to employees of W.G. Yates & Sons Construction Company who have suffered a substantial loss due to a tragedy.
Fields of interest: Human services, emergency aid.
Type of support: Employee-related welfare.
Application information:
  Initial approach: Letter
  Additional information: Contact foundation for eligibility criteria.
EIN: 203449198

MISSOURI

4927
African Methodist Episcopal Church Fifth District Economic Development Fund
4144 Lindell Blvd., Ste. 216
St. Louis, MO 63108-2932 (314) 534-3064

Foundation type: Public charity
Purpose: Scholarships to students residing in the 5th District of St. Louis, MO.
Financial data: Year ended 09/30/2011. Assets, $1,433,968 (M); Expenditures, $113,739; Total giving, $5,416.
Fields of interest: Higher education.
Type of support: Scholarships—to individuals.
Application information: Applications accepted. Application form required. Interview required.
Applicants should submit the following:
1) Letter(s) of recommendation
2) GPA
3) Financial information
4) Essay
Additional information: Application should also include three references.
EIN: 431127614

4928
Agriculture Future of America
906 Grand Ave., Ste. 915
P.O. Box 414838
Kansas City, MO 64141-4838 (816) 472-4232
Contact: K.Russell Weathers, Pres. and C.E.O.
FAX: (816) 472-4239; E-mail: afa@agfuture.org;
E-mail For K.Russell Weathers:
russell.weathers@agfuture.org; URL: http://www.agfuture.org

Foundation type: Public charity
Purpose: Scholarships to students for attendance at postsecondary institutions pursuing a degree in agriculture-related fields.
Publications: Annual report; Grants list.
Financial data: Year ended 02/28/2012. Assets, $2,445,484 (M); Expenditures, $1,665,793; Total giving, $293,645; Grants to individuals, totaling $293,645.
Fields of interest: Agriculture/food.
Type of support: Scholarships—to individuals.
Application information: Applications accepted. Application form required. Application form available on the grantmaker's web site.
Initial approach: Application
Deadline(s): Varies
Additional information: See web site for additional application guidelines.
Program descriptions:
AFA Leader and Academic Scholarship: A $2,600 scholarship is awarded to high school seniors enrolling in agriculture related degree programs. Preference is given to applicants with strong leadership and community involvement background, and financial need. $1,000 of the award must be used to attend the AFA Leaders Conference.
National Association of Farm Broadcasting Foundation Scholarship: A $4,000 and $5,000 scholarship is awarded to students pursuing a career in agricultural communications. Recipients also receive an expense paid trip to the National NAFB Convention.
EIN: 431759425

4929
Alpha Delta Kappa Foundation
1615 W. 92nd St.
Kansas City, MO 64114-3210 (816) 363-5525
Contact: Janice M. Estell, Exec. Admin.
FAX: (816) 363-4010;
E-mail: headquarters@alphadeltakappa.org;
Toll-free tel.: (800) 247-2311; URL: http://www.alphadeltakappa.org

Foundation type: Public charity
Purpose: Scholarships to female educators who are non-US citizens living outside of the U.S., for study at American colleges and universities. Financial assistance to teachers of GA or those preparing to teach.
Financial data: Year ended 05/31/2012. Assets, $3,776,659 (M); Expenditures, $370,335; Total giving, $249,268; Grants to individuals, totaling $150,872.
Fields of interest: Teacher school/education; Leadership development; Women.
Type of support: Foreign applicants; Undergraduate support.
Application information: Application form required.
Initial approach: Letter, telephone, fax or e-mail
Deadline(s): May 30 for Melba Priestley Scholarship, Jan. 1 for International Teacher Education
Final notification: Recipients notified July 15 for Melba Priestley Scholarship
Program descriptions:
International Teacher Education: Provides scholarships of $10,000 to foreign students for one-year study in American colleges and universities. Applicants must be single, female, have at least one year college background, and be living outside the U.S. at the time of application.
Melba Priestley Scholarship for Georgia Residents: This $1,500 scholarship is awarded to a qualified college junior, senior, or graduate student preparing for a career in education. The scholarships is awarded in odd-numbered years only. Applications are available at http://www.alphadeltakappa.org/MP_Scholarship.
EIN: 431280111

4930
Alpha Phi Omega National Service Fraternity
14901 E. 42nd St.
Independence, MO 64055-4778 (816) 373-8667
Contact: Bob London, Exec. Dir.
FAX: (816) 373-5975; URL: http://www.apo.org

Foundation type: Public charity
Purpose: Scholarships to fraternity members and travel assistance for conventions and for leadership sessions.
Publications: Application guidelines.
Financial data: Year ended 07/30/2011. Assets, $6,374,369 (M); Expenditures, $1,630,972; Total giving, $41,692; Grants to individuals, 66 grants totaling $41,692. Subtotal for travel grants: 18 grants totaling $5,692. Subtotal for scholarships—to individuals: 48 grants totaling $36,000.
Fields of interest: Higher education; Students, sororities/fraternities.
Type of support: Scholarships—to individuals; Travel grants.
Application information: Applications accepted. Application form available on the grantmaker's web site.
Initial approach: Application
Deadline(s): May 1 for John Mack National Scholarship

Applicants should submit the following:
1) Letter(s) of recommendation
Additional information: Application should include letters of recommendation.
Program description:
John Mack National Scholarship: Scholarships (of at least $500 each) are available to members of the fraternity who are enrolled at a college or university for the upcoming school year, and who are pursuing classes leading to a college or university degree. Eligible applicants must demonstrate a history of volunteerism and unselfish service to others, and demonstrate significant participation and leadership in extracurricular activities to benefit individuals in need, or charitable or humanitarian organizations.
EIN: 440562039

4931
American Institute of Architects St. Louis Scholarship Fund
(formerly St. Louis Chapters American Institute of Architects Scholarship Fund, also known as AIA St. Louis Scholarship Fund)
911 Washington Ave., Ste. 100
St. Louis, MO 63101-1214 (314) 621-3484
E-mail: chapter@aia-stlouis.org; E-Mail for Michelle C. Swatek: mswatek@aia-stlouis.org; URL: http://www.aia-stlouis.org

Foundation type: Public charity
Purpose: Scholarships to St. Louis, MO, regional students in their third, fourth or fifth year of architectural studies at an accredited architectural school, and support for graduate architectural studies.
Publications: Application guidelines; Grants list.
Financial data: Year ended 12/31/2011. Assets, $2,777,985 (M); Expenditures, $109,042; Total giving, $88,762.
Fields of interest: Architecture.
Type of support: Support to graduates or students of specific schools; Undergraduate support; Postgraduate support.
Application information: Applications accepted. Interview required.
Initial approach: Telephone
Deadline(s): Vary
Applicants should submit the following:
1) Essay
2) Transcripts
3) Letter(s) of recommendation
Program descriptions:
George E. Kassabaum Scholarship: This program provides scholarships to graduate students at the Washington University School of Architecture. The maximum annual award is $1,500. Applicant must be nominated by faculty member. Deadline Feb. 15.
Ranft Scholarship: Students in their fifth year of study or graduate studies are eligible for these scholarships. Maximum awards are: Washington University $12,000; Drury College $6,500; University of Kansas $6,500; Kansas State University $6,500. Candidates must be nominated by faculty member. Deadline Feb. 15.
St. Louis Chapter Award: The award is offered to third, fourth, and fifth year of undergraduate or graduate studies to St. Louis metropolitan residents to attend any accredited school of architecture. Deadline June 1.
The Masonry Institute, Bricklayers Local No. 1 of MO and the Mason Contractors Association Scholarship: This program is offered during the third, fourth, and fifth year of undergraduate study, and for graduate study at an accredited architectural school. Eligibility is limited to students in Lincoln, Crawford, Franklin, Jefferson, St.

Charles, St. Louis, St. Louis City and Warren counties. Deadline June 1.

Wischmeyer Scholarship: This scholarship is for fourth and fifth year students at the University of Kansas, Kansas State University, and Drury College, on a rotating basis, are eligible for awards of up to $3,000. Applicant must be nominated by faculty member. Deadline Feb. 15.
EIN: 436060703

4932
American Society of Newspaper Editors Foundation
209 Reynolds Journalism Institute
Missouri School of Journalism
Columbia, MO   65211-0001   (573) 884 2405
Application address: The Poynter Institute, 801 3rd St. S., St. Petersburg, FL 33701, tel.: (727) 821-9494
FAX: (703) 453-1133; E-mail: asne@asne.org;
URL: http://www.asne.org/

Foundation type: Public charity
Purpose: Awards to recognize excellence in writing in American and Canadian daily newspapers and eligible wire services.
Publications: Application guidelines.
Financial data: Year ended 06/30/2012. Assets, $2,564,007 (M); Expenditures, $2,128,726; Total giving, $731,250; Grants to individuals, 23 grants totaling $11,250.
Fields of interest: Print publishing; Literature.
Type of support: Awards/prizes.
Application information: Applications accepted. Application form required.
   Initial approach: Telephone
   Send request by: Mail
   Deadline(s): Feb. 1
   Additional information: Application by fax or e-mail not accepted.
Program descriptions:
   Batten Medal: This award of $2,500 recognizes individual achievement in public-service journalism. Five to ten articles may be submitted for consideration.
   Community Service Photojournalism Award: Awards $1,000 in recognition of a body of work that contributes to an improvement or heightened awareness in the community through photography.
   Distinguished Writing Awards: These awards are designed to foster, recognize, and reward excellence in writing in American and Canadian daily newspapers and eligible wire services. Content may be great events or small happenings. Entries will be judged on the basis of language, style, precision or word usage, structure, descriptive power, narrative skill, etc. Four $1,000 awards will be given per year for work done in these categories: 1) Non-Deadline Writing: focuses on writing not accomplished on deadline (except commentary), from any section of the newspaper. This category may include investigative and news-related material as well as any features material - profiles, interviews, trend stories, lifestyle, travel, etc; 2) Commentary/Column Writing: encompasses any writing that expresses a personal point of view - columns and other forms of journalism opinion; 3) Editorial Writing: deals with editorials, signed or unsigned, written by one individual, that speak for the newspaper; and 4) Local Accountability Reporting: focuses on news and feature writing that holds important local institutions accountable for their actions. A minimum of three and a maximum of five articles will be accepted.
   Freedom Forum/ASNE Award for Distinguished Writing on Diversity: This $2,500 award recognizes writing that helps a community understand and

better appreciate its racial, ethnic, and religious diversity. One to three articles may be submitted for consideration.
   Jesse Laventhol Prizes for Deadline News Reporting: This award is designed to foster, recognize, and reward excellence in writing in American and Canadian daily newspapers and eligible wire services. Content may be great events or small happenings. In particular, these prizes are awarded for breaking news events covered under deadline pressure. Entries will be evaluated in terms of descriptive power and literary style, depth and breadth of reporting, timeliness, completeness, and perspective. $10,000 awards are given to either individual or a team. One to three articles may be submitted in this category.
   Online Storytelling: This $1,000 award recognizes excellence in the use of digital tools to tell new stories. Judges will consider strong writing, narrative skill, engaging graphical and visual elements, and compelling audio.
EIN: 239935413

4933
Etta Mae Anderson Trust
P.O. Box 446
New London, MO   63459-0446
Contact: John W. Briscoe, Tr.
Application address: 423 S. Main St., New London, MO 63459-1403

Foundation type: Independent foundation
Purpose: Scholarships to full time students who are residents of Ralls county, MO for continuing their education at accredited colleges or universities.
Financial data: Year ended 12/31/2011. Assets, $380,927 (M); Expenditures, $32,021; Total giving, $27,500.
Fields of interest: Higher education.
Type of support: Scholarships—to individuals.
Application information: Applications accepted. Application form required.
   Applicants should submit the following:
      1) Transcripts
      2) SAT
      3) ACT
   Additional information: Application must also include evaluation form completed by school administrator or counselor.
EIN: 436596084

4934
Arch Coal Foundation
1 Cityplace Dr., Ste. 300
St. Louis, MO   63141   (704) 332-8880
Contact: Donald Bernstein, Pres.
Contact for Teacher Achievement Awards: archteacherawards@gmail.com

Foundation type: Company-sponsored foundation
Purpose: Scholarships to dependents of employees of Arch Coal, Inc. and awards to classroom teachers in recognition of outstanding achievement in grade school through high school education in UT, WY, and WV in areas of company operations.
Publications: Application guidelines; Grants list.
Financial data: Year ended 12/31/2012. Assets, $2,552,601 (M); Expenditures, $1,585,959; Total giving, $179,316.
Type of support: Employee-related scholarships; Awards/prizes.
Application information: Applications not accepted.
   Additional information: Unsolicited requests for funds not considered or acknowledged.

Company name: Arch Coal, Inc.
EIN: 203980901

4935
Baptist-Trinity Lutheran Legacy Foundation
6675 Holmes Rd., Ste. 470
Kansas City, MO   64131-1118   (816) 276-7555
FAX: (816) 926-2261; E-mail: becky@btllf.org;
URL: http://www.btllf.org

Foundation type: Public charity
Purpose: Scholarships to individuals currently pursuing a nursing or respiratory therapy undergraduate or graduate degree. Emergency assistance to individuals for medical needs in the greater Kansas City, MO area.
Publications: Application guidelines.
Financial data: Year ended 12/31/2011. Assets, $35,279,199 (M); Expenditures, $1,752,053; Total giving, $898,263; Grants to individuals, totaling $669,664.
Fields of interest: Nursing school/education; Economically disadvantaged.
Type of support: Emergency funds; Scholarships—to individuals; Graduate support; Undergraduate support.
Application information: Application form required. Application form available on the grantmaker's web site. Interview required.
   Initial approach: Telephone for medical assistance
   Deadline(s): May 1 for Trinity Lutheran School of Nursing Alumnae Scholarship, May 15 for L.A. Hollinger, M.D. Scholarship
   Additional information: Application forms available online, or at the foundation for scholarships. Applicants must provide official transcripts and three references. For medical assistance, applicant must provide picture IDs, Social Security cards, proof of income of everyone in household and proof of address for past 30 days.
Program descriptions:
   L.A. Hollinger, M.D. Scholarship: This scholarship is awarded to individuals who are currently pursuing a nursing or respiratory therapy undergraduate or graduate degree at Johnson Community College or the University of Kansas. Eligible applicants must have a cumulative GPA of 2.5.
   Trinity Lutheran School of Nursing Alumnae Scholarship: This fund assists those pursuing a career in nursing (such as undergraduate, advanced degree, etc.) who need financial assistance. Eligible students must: be currently enrolled in an accredited RN school of nursing or higher-education nursing program; have completed at least one semester at an accredited school; be a full- or part-time student; and have a cumulative GPA of at least 2.5.
EIN: 237432481

4936
George and Hazel Barber Scholarship Trust
c/o F&M Bank and Trust Co.
P.O. Box 938
Hannibal, MO   63401-0938   (573) 221-6424

Foundation type: Independent foundation
Purpose: Scholarships only to graduating seniors in Marion County, MO, and Pike County, IL.
Financial data: Year ended 12/31/2012. Assets, $375,735 (M); Expenditures, $17,710; Total giving, $6,000; Grants to individuals, 12 grants totaling $6,000 (high: $500; low: $500).

Type of support: Support to graduates or students of specific schools; Undergraduate support.
Application information: Application form required. Interview required.
  Deadline(s): Apr. 10
  Additional information: Application must be notarized.
EIN: 237214882

4937
Harold W. and Emily K. Beattie Scholarship Trust Fund
P.O. Box 1119
St. Joseph, MO 64502

Foundation type: Independent foundation
Purpose: Scholarships to graduates of Savannah, MO, high schools who are in the top ten percent of their classes.
Financial data: Year ended 12/31/2012. Assets, $1,133,184 (M); Expenditures, $65,134; Total giving, $54,250.
Type of support: Scholarships—to individuals.
Application information: Applications not accepted.
  Additional information: Unsolicited requests for funds not considered or acknowledged.
EIN: 436355648

4938
Louis E. Bell Charitable Trust
P.O. Box 387
St. Louis, MO 63166-0387   (816) 364-7245
Contact: Bill Titcomb
Application address: c/o US Bank, N.A. 415 Francis St., St. Joseph, MO 64501

Foundation type: Independent foundation
Purpose: Scholarships to graduates of Atchinson County, MO, public high schools.
Financial data: Year ended 12/31/2012. Assets, $99,180 (M); Expenditures, $8,771; Total giving, $3,900.
Type of support: Support to graduates or students of specific schools.
Application information: Applications accepted. Application form required.
  Deadline(s): None
  Applicants should submit the following:
    1) Photograph
    2) Transcripts
    3) SAT
    4) GPA
    5) ACT
  Additional information: Applications should also include extracurricular activities, employment history, financial and family information, students and parents' tax return, and three references.
EIN: 436406133

4939
Frank C. and Georgia M. Bentley Charitable Trust
P.O. Box 3357
Springfield, MO 65808   (417) 887-8547
Application Address: Bentley Trust, 2041 E Briar, Springfield, MO 65804

Foundation type: Independent foundation
Purpose: Financial assistance to individuals residing in Springfield, MO, who are over 60 years of age.

Financial data: Year ended 12/31/2012. Assets, $1,812,488 (M); Expenditures, $147,142; Total giving, $100,874; Grants to individuals, 105 grants totaling $100,874 (high: $4,327, low: $71).
Fields of interest: Aging.
Type of support: Grants for special needs.
Application information: Applications accepted. Application form required.
  Initial approach: Telephone
  Deadline(s): None
EIN: 436050610

4940
Bolivar Educational Advancement Foundation
P.O. Box 117
Bolivar, MO 65613-0117   (417) 326-5261

Foundation type: Public charity
Purpose: Scholarships to students of the Bolivar Missouri R-1 school district for higher education.
Financial data: Year ended 12/31/2011. Assets, $1,164,793 (M); Expenditures, $41,357; Total giving, $34,485; Grants to individuals, totaling $34,485.
Fields of interest: Education.
Type of support: Scholarships—to individuals.
Application information: Contact the foundation for guidelines as the scholarships have different requirements.
EIN: 431589841

4941
Boys Hope Girls Hope Affiliates
12120 Bridgeton Sq. Dr.
Bridgeton, MO 63044-2607   (314) 298-1250
Contact: Paul A. Minorini, Pres. and C.E.O.
FAX: (314) 298-1251; E-mail: hope@bhgh.org;
URL: http://www.boyshopegirlshope.org

Foundation type: Public charity
Purpose: Scholarships to high school seniors who have completed the Boys Hope Girls Hope residential program.
Publications: Annual report; Financial statement.
Financial data: Year ended 06/30/2012. Assets, $29,940,766 (M); Expenditures, $13,536,292; Total giving, $2,215,719; Grants to individuals, totaling $2,215,719.
Fields of interest: Children/youth, services; Foster care; Children/youth.
Type of support: Undergraduate support.
Application information: Applications not accepted.
  Additional information: Unsolicited requests for funds not considered or acknowledged.
EIN: 431209928

4942
Boys Hope Girls Hope National
12120 Bridgeton Sq. Dr.
Bridgeton, MO 63044-2607   (314) 298-1250
FAX: (314) 298-1251; Toll-free tel.:(877) 878-4673; URL: http://www.boyshopegirlshope.org

Foundation type: Public charity
Purpose: Financial assistance for college tuition, books, room and board only to students who have "graduated" from the Boys Hope Girls Hope program or program of their affiliates.
Publications: Annual report; Newsletter.
Financial data: Year ended 06/30/2011. Assets, $16,122,533 (M); Expenditures, $2,878,370;

Total giving, $568,557; Grants to individuals, 102 grants totaling $242,861.
Fields of interest: Higher education.
International interests: Brazil; Guatemala; Mexico; Peru.
Type of support: Scholarships—to individuals; Undergraduate support.
Application information: Applications not accepted.
  Additional information: Scholarships and financial assistance only to children recommended to the program. Unsolicited requests for funds not considered or acknowledged.
EIN: 510182614

4943
Claude Brey and Ina L. Brey Memorial Endowment Fund
P.O. Box 387
Saint Louis, MO 63166-0387   (913) 795-2287
Application address: c/o Pat West, 11540 Co Rd., No. 1095, Mound City, KS 66056

Foundation type: Independent foundation
Purpose: Scholarships to fourth-degree Kansas Grange members to attend colleges and accredited trade schools.
Financial data: Year ended 04/30/2013. Assets, $96,796 (M); Expenditures, $6,572; Total giving, $3,000.
Fields of interest: Vocational education; Agriculture, farm bureaus/granges.
Type of support: Technical education support; Undergraduate support.
Application information: Application form required. Interview required.
  Deadline(s): Apr. 15
  Additional information: Contact local Grange chapter for application forms.
EIN: 486187137

4944
Dan Broida/Sigma-Aldrich Scholarship Fund, Inc.
3050 Spruce St.
St. Louis, MO 63103-2530

Foundation type: Operating foundation
Purpose: Scholarships for the study of science to children of employees of Sigma-Aldrich Corp. or its subsidiaries in MO.
Financial data: Year ended 03/31/2012. Assets, $935,279 (M); Expenditures, $130,030; Total giving, $105,750.
Fields of interest: Science.
Type of support: Employee-related scholarships.
Application information: Applications not accepted.
  Additional information: Deadline Apr. 10. Children of officers and directors of Sigma-Aldrich Corp. are ineligible. Unsolicited requests for funds not considered or acknowledged.
Company name: Sigma-Aldrich Corporation
EIN: 431253095

4945
Margaret G. Buckner Scholarship Trust
P.O. Box 625
Marshall, MO 65340-0625   (660) 886-3408
Contact: William G. Buckner

Foundation type: Operating foundation

Purpose: Scholarships to students in Saline County, MO, for higher education to become trained health care providers in the Saline County, MO, area.
Financial data: Year ended 12/31/2012. Assets, $987,991 (M); Expenditures, $88,187; Total giving, $74,450; Grants to individuals, 25 grants totaling $74,450 (high: $9,000, low: $1,000).
Fields of interest: Health care.
Type of support: Undergraduate support.
Application information: Applications accepted. Application form required.
  Deadline(s): None
  Applicants should submit the following:
    1) Financial information
    2) Transcripts
    3) SAT
    4) ACT
EIN: 431735027

4946
Build-A-Bear Workshop Foundation, Inc.
1954 Innerbelt Business Center Dr.
Saint Louis, MO   63114-5760   (314) 423-8000
Contact: Tina Klocke, Pres.
E-mail: giving@buildabear.com; URL: http://www.buildabear.com/shopping/contents/content.jsp?catid=400002&id=700012

Foundation type: Public charity
Purpose: Prizes to winners of the Huggable Heroes competition, which is a contest for kids ages 7-18 who demonstrate extraordinary service to their local communities.
Publications: Application guidelines.
Financial data: Year ended 12/31/2011. Assets, $1,273,986 (M); Expenditures, $1,215,075; Total giving, $1,175,883.
Fields of interest: Youth development, centers/clubs; Youth development, community service clubs; Youth development; Volunteer services.
Type of support: Awards/prizes.
Application information: Application form required. Application form available on the grantmaker's web site.
  Initial approach: Letter or telephone
  Send request by: Mail or online
  Deadline(s): Feb. 27
  Additional information: Application must include a description of the project. See web site for complete application guidelines.
Program description:
  Huggable Heroes: A 'Huggable Hero' is a young person 18 years of age or under seeking to make a difference in their neighborhood, school, or community. Each year Build-A-Bear Workshop honors twelve 'Huggable Heroes' chosen from the U.S. and Canada for their outstanding community service.
EIN: 331007188

4947
The Burkhalter Educational Fund
c/o Patricia A. Capps
23 Lynns Ct.
Louisiana, MO   63353

Foundation type: Independent foundation
Purpose: Scholarships to students living in the area serviced by First Baptist Church, Louisiana, MO for higher education.
Financial data: Year ended 12/31/2012. Assets, $19,806 (M); Expenditures, $4,038; Total giving, $1,000; Grant to an individual, 1 grant totaling $1,000.

Fields of interest: Vocational education, post-secondary; Higher education.
Type of support: Scholarships—to individuals.
Application information: Application form required.
  Deadline(s): June 15
  Applicants should submit the following:
    1) Transcripts
    2) Financial information
  Additional information: Application should include parents' tax return. Completed applications must be returned to the Louisiana RII High School guidance counselor.
EIN: 431228710

4948
Butler Manufacturing Company Foundation
1540 Genessee St.
P.O. Box 419917
Kansas City, MO   64141-0917   (816) 968-3208
FAX: (816) 627-8993

Foundation type: Company-sponsored foundation
Purpose: Scholarships only to children of full-time employees of Butler Manufacturing Company, and its wholly-owned subsidiaries. Hardship grants to financially needy employees who are retirees of the Butler Manufacturing Co. and their dependents, who reside in IL, MO and TX.
Publications: Application guidelines; Informational brochure (including application guidelines).
Financial data: Year ended 06/30/2013. Assets, $6,181,903 (M); Expenditures, $433,657; Total giving, $352,152.
Fields of interest: Education; Economically disadvantaged.
Type of support: Employee-related scholarships; Employee-related welfare.
Application information: Application form required.
  Initial approach: Telephone
  Deadline(s): Feb.
  Additional information: Applications available at human resources offices at all company locations; Scholarships are paid directly to the student's academic institution.
Program descriptions:
  Butler Manufacturing Employee Program: The foundation awards grants to employees of Butler Manufacturing Co. and its wholly-owned subsidiaries who are in financial distress because of serious illness, accidents, or loss or damage to property from weather or fire.
  Scholarship Program: The foundation annually awards eight four-year $2,500 college scholarships to children of full-time employees of Butler Manufacturing and its wholly-owned subsidiaries. Awards are based on academic achievement, financial need, personal characteristics, and future promise.
Company name: Butler Manufacturing Company
EIN: 440663648

4949
Ina Calkins Trust
1200 Main St., 14 Fl.
P.O. Box 219119
Kansas City, MO   64121-9119
Contact: Spence Heddens, Bank of America
URL: http://www.calkinsboard.org

Foundation type: Independent foundation
Purpose: Scholarships to residents of Kansas City, MO. in the areas of education, medicine and welfare.

Financial data: Year ended 12/31/2012. Assets, $6,028,651 (M); Expenditures, $235,060; Total giving, $176,200.
Type of support: Scholarships—to individuals.
Application information: Application form required.
  Deadline(s): Oct. 2
  Additional information: Application by letter of no more than three pages, including appropriate attachments.
EIN: 526994869

4950
Hubert Campbell Charitable Foundation
(also known as Jerry Campbell)
801 Lafayette St.
St. Joseph, MO   64503-2499   (816) 279-6354

Foundation type: Operating foundation
Purpose: Scholarships to individuals in the St. Joseph, MO area.
Financial data: Year ended 12/31/2011. Assets, $821,675 (M); Expenditures, $43,113; Total giving, $42,000; Grants to individuals, 11 grants totaling $42,000 (high: $6,000, low: $1,500).
Type of support: Undergraduate support.
Application information: Applications accepted.
  Deadline(s): Apr. 1
EIN: 431904656

4951
Cape Girardeau Public School Foundation
301 N. Clark
Cape Girardeau, MO   63702-0399   (573) 651-0555
E-mail: director@capeschools.org

Foundation type: Public charity
Purpose: Grants to PreK-12 teachers of the Cape Girardeau Public School District #63, MO for innovative learning in the classroom.
Publications: Application guidelines; Grants list.
Financial data: Year ended 12/31/2011. Assets, $871,166 (M); Expenditures, $81,323; Total giving, $6,719.
Fields of interest: Education.
Type of support: Grants to individuals.
Application information: Applications accepted. Application form required. Application form available on the grantmaker's web site.
  Initial approach: Proposal
  Send request by: E-mail
  Deadline(s): Mar. 1
  Final notification: Applicants notified between Mar. 30 and Apr. 15
EIN: 431666808

4952
Cardinal Glennon Childrens Hospital Foundation
3800 Park Ave.
St. Louis, MO   63110   (314) 577-5605
Contact: Dan Buck, Exec. Dir.
E-mail: dan_buck@ssmhc.com; URL: http://glennon.org/

Foundation type: Public charity
Purpose: Hospital bill financial assistance to patients of Cardinal Glennon Children's Medical Center, MO, who are without insurance, underinsured, ineligible for a government program or otherwise unable to pay for medically necessary care.
Financial data: Year ended 12/31/2011. Assets, $63,299,406 (M); Expenditures, $8,546,404;

Total giving, $5,823,205; Grants to individuals, totaling $24,765.
Fields of interest: Hospitals (general); Health care, patient services; Economically disadvantaged.
Type of support: Grants for special needs.
Application information: Applications accepted. Application form required. Application form available on the grantmaker's web site.
   Initial approach: E-mail
   Final notification: 30 days
   Applicants should submit the following:
     1) Financial information
   Additional information: For queries, email financialaid@ssmhc.com. Application should include checking & savings account statements, verification of income, last year's federal tax return or non-filing letter, verification of monthly expense and Medicaid or Medicare denial/approval.
EIN: 431754347

4953

Clinton J. Carr Foundation Inc.

P.O. Box 1547
Lebanon, MO   65536   (417) 718-0311
Contact: Jill Carr

Foundation type: Independent foundation
Purpose: Scholarships to high school graduates who reside in MO.
Financial data: Year ended 07/31/2013. Assets, $2,164,172 (M); Expenditures, $84,051; Total giving, $68,250.
Type of support: Undergraduate support.
Application information: Application form required.
   Deadline(s): Contact high school for current application deadline
   Applicants should submit the following:
     1) SAT
     2) ACT
     3) GPA
     4) Essay
   Additional information: Applications are submitted to the foundation through participating high schools.
EIN: 431534880

4954

Central Missoui Community Action

(formerly Central Missouri Counties Human Development Corporation)
807B N. Providence Rd.
Columbia, MO   65203-4359   (573) 443-8706
Contact: Darin Pries, Exec. Dir.
FAX: (573) 499-9198; *URL:* http://www.showmeaction.org/

Foundation type: Public charity
Purpose: Grants to needy individuals residing in Audrain, Boone, Callaway, Cole, Cooper, Howard, Moniteau, and Osage counties, MO, to help with rental utilities, and weatherization assistance.
Financial data: Year ended 09/30/2011. Assets, $5,127,412 (M); Expenditures, $19,149,672; Total giving, $3,212,331; Grants to individuals, totaling $3,212,331.
Type of support: Grants for special needs.
Application information:
   Initial approach: Letter
EIN: 430835026

4955

Chesed V'Emet The Avigdor Ben Yosef Family Foundation

7915 Big Bend Blvd.
Saint Louis, MO   63119-2703   (314) 952-6061
Contact: Claudia Perreault, Mgr.
Application address: P.O. Box 440148, Saint Louis, MO 63144

Foundation type: Independent foundation
Purpose: Grants to individuals primarily in MO and Israel for Jewish education.
Financial data: Year ended 12/31/2012. Assets, $118,636 (M); Expenditures, $102,041; Total giving, $100,486.
Fields of interest: Jewish agencies & synagogues.
Type of support: Scholarships—to individuals.
Application information: Applications accepted. Application form not required.
   Deadline(s): None
   Additional information: Contact foundation for current application guidelines.
EIN: 320048095

4956

Child Day Care Association of Saint Louis

4236 Lindell Blvd., Ste. 300
St. Louis, MO   63108-2948   (314) 531-1412
Contact: John Daley, Interim Exec. Dir.
FAX: (314) 531-4184; *E-mail:* info@childcarestl.org; *URL:* http://www.childcarestl.org

Foundation type: Public charity
Purpose: Grants for reimbursement to enable child care providers of St. Louis, MO to attend workshops. Incentives for child care providers participating in programs to enhance child care quality.
Financial data: Year ended 12/31/2011. Assets, $788,435 (M); Expenditures, $5,835,102; Total giving, $40,164; Grants to individuals, totaling $40,164.
Fields of interest: Children/youth, services.
Type of support: Grants to individuals.
Application information: Applications accepted.
   Additional information: Grants are based on eligibility for participation in various programs and completion of programs.
EIN: 430953838

4957

Clarkson Eyecare Foundation

18141 Edgewood Cir.
Wildwood, MO   63038   (636) 227-2600
FAX: (636) 200-4020;
E-mail: tpeel@clarksoneyecare.com; *URL:* http://www.theclarksoneyecarefoundation.org

Foundation type: Public charity
Purpose: Eye care service is provided to uninsured, underprivileged low income individuals in the St. Louis, MO area.
Publications: Application guidelines; Occasional report.
Financial data: Year ended 12/31/2011. Assets, $233,600 (M); Expenditures, $131,826; Total giving, $540.
Fields of interest: Economically disadvantaged.
Type of support: Grants for special needs.
Application information: Applications accepted. Application form required. Application form available on the grantmaker's web site.
   Initial approach: Letter
   Copies of proposal: 1
   Deadline(s): None
   Final notification: Recipients notified in one week

Additional information: Application must include proof of income.
EIN: 200265693

4958

William L. Clay Scholarship & Research Fund

6023 WaterMan Blvd.
P.O. Box 4693
St. Louis, MO   63112
E-mail: info@wlcsrf.org; *URL:* http://www.wlcsrf.org/

Foundation type: Independent foundation
Purpose: Scholarships to high school seniors who are residents of the First Congressional District of MO for continuing education at institutions of higher learning.
Financial data: Year ended 12/31/2012. Assets, $577,133 (M); Expenditures, $136,841; Total giving, $82,341; Grants to individuals, 32 grants totaling $79,841 (high: $6,000, low: $500).
Fields of interest: Scholarships/financial aid.
Type of support: Undergraduate support.
Application information: Application form required. Interview required.
   Send request by: Mail
   Deadline(s): Jan. 15 for Washington University, Mar. 1 for all others
   Final notification: Recipients notified by June 30
   Applicants should submit the following:
     1) SAT
     2) ACT
     3) Letter(s) of recommendation
     4) Transcripts
   Additional information: Application should also include personal statement, a copy of parents' most recent tax return, and a copy of your voter registration card.
EIN: 431288222

4959

Bernard & Anna Clayton Scholarship Trust

c/o HNB National Bank
100 N. Main St.
Hannibal, MO   63401-3537   (573) 221-0050

Foundation type: Independent foundation
Purpose: Scholarships to residents of the A.D. Stowell School attendance area of Hannibal, MO, School District No. 60, for study at colleges and technical schools.
Financial data: Year ended 12/31/2011. Assets, $359,173 (M); Expenditures, $23,230; Total giving, $18,300; Grants to individuals, 2 grants totaling $18,300 (high: $12,200, low: $6,100).
Fields of interest: Vocational education.
Type of support: Support to graduates or students of specific schools; Technical education support; Undergraduate support.
Application information: Application form required.
   Deadline(s): May
EIN: 431652040

4960

William & Hannah Cohen Foundation

714 Elkington Ln.
Saint Louis, MO   63132   (954) 747-3393
Contact: Paula Polsyn
Application Address: 2541 N. Nob Hill Rd., 301, Sunrise, FL 33322

Foundation type: Operating foundation
Purpose: College scholarship to students for higher education.

Financial data: Year ended 03/31/2013. Assets, $268,353 (M); Expenditures, $7,343; Total giving, $4,750; Grants to individuals, 4 grants totaling $4,750 (high: $1,250, low: $1,000).
Fields of interest: Higher education.
Type of support: Scholarships—to individuals.
Application information: Applications accepted. Application form required.
> *Deadline(s):* May or June
> *Applicants should submit the following:*
> 1) Transcripts
> 2) Letter(s) of recommendation
EIN: 226085831

4961
College Club of St. Louis
3 Media Dr.
St. Louis, MO 63146 (314) 997-1610
Contact: Ann Anderson
Application address: 3 Valley View Pl., St. Louis, MO 63124

Foundation type: Independent foundation
Purpose: Scholarships to female graduates of high schools in St. Louis County, MO. Recipients must have a GPA of at least 3.0.
Financial data: Year ended 05/31/2013. Assets, $1,388,856 (M); Expenditures, $98,175; Total giving, $63,000; Grants to individuals, 11 grants totaling $63,000 (high: $6,000, low: $3,000).
Type of support: Undergraduate support.
Application information: Applications accepted. Application form required.
> *Deadline(s):* Jan. 31
> *Applicants should submit the following:*
> 1) GPA
> 2) Essay
> 3) ACT
> 4) SAT
> 5) Class rank
EIN: 436031163

4962
Community Action of St. Louis County, Inc.
2709 Woodson Rd.
Overland, MO 63114-4817 (314) 863-0015
FAX: (314) 863-1252; E-mail: info@caastlc.org;
URL: http://www.caastlc.org/

Foundation type: Public charity
Purpose: Assistance to indigent residents of St. Louis, MO, in the form of utility help, home weatherization, and temporary emergency housing.
Financial data: Year ended 09/30/2011. Assets, $3,716,626 (M); Expenditures, $11,133,140; Total giving, $6,645,844; Grants to individuals, totaling $6,645,844.
Fields of interest: Economically disadvantaged.
Type of support: In-kind gifts.
Application information:
> *Initial approach:* Letter
> *Additional information:* Contact foundation for eligibility criteria.
EIN: 237037248

4963
Community Foundation of the Ozarks
(formerly Community Foundation, Inc.)
425 E. Trafficway
Springfield, MO 65806-1121 (417) 864-6199
Contact: Bridget Dierks, Dir., Nonprofit Svcs.; For scholarships: Judith Billings, Scholarship Coord.
FAX: (417) 864-8344;
E-mail: mlemmon@cfozarks.org; Mailing address: P.O. Box 8960, Springfield, MO, 65801; Additional tel.: (888) 266-6815; URL: http:// www.cfozarks.org

Foundation type: Community foundation
Purpose: Scholarships to graduating high school seniors and to students currently enrolled in an accredited college or university, and for post-graduate study in the Missouri Ozarks areas.
Publications: Application guidelines; Annual report (including application guidelines); Financial statement; Informational brochure; Newsletter.
Financial data: Year ended 06/30/2013. Assets, $225,287,783 (M); Expenditures, $26,736,890; Total giving, $22,331,261. Scholarships—to individuals amount not specified.
Fields of interest: Vocational education; Teacher school/education; Students, sororities/ fraternities; Athletics/sports, training; Chemistry; Mathematics; Physics; Government/public administration; Military/veterans' organizations.
Type of support: Internship funds; Scholarships—to individuals; Support to graduates or students of specific schools; Awards/prizes; Technical education support; Undergraduate support.
Application information: Applications accepted. Application form required.
> *Initial approach:* Letter
> *Deadline(s):* None
> *Additional information:* See web site for complete program and application information.
EIN: 237290968

4964
Community Housing Network
2600 E. 12th St.
Kansas City, MO 64127-1321 (816) 482-5744
Contact: John Sandner, Exec. Dir.
FAX: (816) 482-5749;
E-mail: info@communityhousingnet.org

Foundation type: Public charity
Purpose: Assistance to the mentally disabled with affordable housing in the Kansas City, MO, metro area.
Financial data: Year ended 06/30/2012. Assets, $113,476 (M); Expenditures, $2,083,840.
Fields of interest: Independent housing for people with disabilities; Mentally disabled.
Type of support: Grants for special needs.
Application information: Applications accepted. Application form required.
> *Additional information:* Applicants must prove that they are disabled and meet the income criteria. Included in the package must be copy of birth certificate, copy of social security card, proof of income for everyone living in the dwelling, and criminal background check.
EIN: 431645335

4965
Concerned Christians for the Community, Inc.
P.O. Box 445
Chillicothe, MO 64601-0445 (660) 646-1555

Foundation type: Public charity

Purpose: Specific assistance to needy elderly for supportive services in addition to food, shelter and clothing.
Financial data: Year ended 06/30/2012. Assets, $536,962 (M); Expenditures, $356,660.
Fields of interest: Aging; Economically disadvantaged.
Type of support: Grants for special needs.
Application information: Contact the organization for further information.
EIN: 237193767

4966
John Byron Corbin Charitable Trust
P.O. Box 550
Nevada, MO 64772 (417) 667-4412
Contact: Don Hutchison C.P.A., Tr.

Foundation type: Independent foundation
Purpose: Scholarships to U.S. citizens who are graduating high school seniors within 50 miles of Nevada, MO or Waurika, OK.
Financial data: Year ended 12/31/2012. Assets, $2,971,039 (M); Expenditures, $224,966; Total giving, $102,455; Grants to individuals, 93 grants totaling $102,454 (high: $1,750, low: $350).
Type of support: Undergraduate support.
Application information: Applications accepted. Application form required.
> *Deadline(s):* Apr. 30
> *Additional information:* Application should include a brief resume of personal and academic qualifications.
EIN: 436250034

4967
Covington Memorial Scholarship Fund
106 W. Stoddard St.
Dexter, MO 63841-1653 (573) 614-1000
Contact: Corey Mouser, Tr.
Application address: c/o Dexter High School, MO 63841

Foundation type: Independent foundation
Purpose: Scholarships to graduates of Dexter High School or Bloomfield High School, MO for higher education at accredited institutions.
Financial data: Year ended 12/31/2011. Assets, $0 (M); Expenditures, $4,308; Total giving, $4,000; Grants to individuals, 8 grants totaling $4,000 (high: $750, low: $250).
Fields of interest: Higher education.
Type of support: Scholarships—to individuals; Support to graduates or students of specific schools.
Application information: Applications accepted.
> *Initial approach:* Letter
> *Deadline(s):* None
> *Additional information:* Scholarships are renewable provided student maintains satisfactory grades.
EIN: 431201123

4968
Lester E. Cox Medical Centers
1423 N. Jefferson Ave.
Springfield, MO 65802-1917 (417) 269-8811
Contact: Robert H. Bezanson, Pres. and C.E.O.
URL: http://www.coxhealth.com

Foundation type: Public charity
Purpose: Scholarships to students of the Springfield, MO area pursuing a career in nursing and other health related field.

Financial data: Year ended 09/30/2011. Assets, $1,009,866,577 (M); Expenditures, $910,557,384; Total giving, $1,705,898; Grants to individuals, totaling $1,123,059.
Fields of interest: Nursing school/education.
Type of support: Scholarships—to individuals.
Application information: Scholarship is awarded based on need and academic performance.
EIN: 440577118

4969
Coxhealth Foundation
3525 S. National Ave., Ste. 204
Springfield, MO 65807-7315 (417) 269-7150
E-mail: lisa.alexander@coxhealth.com

Foundation type: Public charity
Purpose: Scholarships to students at Cox College of Nursing and Health Sciences based on achievement and need. Specific assistance to individuals in areas of medical, dental, family and other needs.
Financial data: Year ended 09/30/2011. Assets, $19,127,219 (M); Expenditures, $2,399,325; Total giving, $2,361,096; Grants to individuals, totaling $1,575,399.
Fields of interest: Nursing school/education; Human services.
Type of support: Scholarships—to individuals; Grants for special needs.
Application information: Applications accepted.
Additional information: Assistance for patients need a recommendation from a physician/care worker/patient clinician to verify need.
EIN: 436810485

4970
Craft Alliance
6640 Delmar Blvd.
St. Louis, MO 63130-4503 (314) 725-1177
Contact: Boo McLoughlin, Exec. Dir.
Application address: 501 N. Grand Blvd., St. Louis, MO 63103
FAX: (314) 725-2068;
E-mail: boo.mcloughlin@craftalliance.org;
URL: http://www.craftalliance.org

Foundation type: Public charity
Purpose: Residencies to emerging and mid-career artists by providing them with free work space, access to a built-in audience and an opportunity to exhibit and sell their work.
Financial data: Year ended 06/30/2012. Assets, $901,831 (M); Expenditures, $1,314,743.
Fields of interest: Ceramic arts.
Type of support: Residencies.
Application information: Applications accepted. Application form required.
Deadline(s): Feb. 14
Final notification: Recipients notified in Mar.
Applicants should submit the following:
1) SASE
2) Resume
3) Letter(s) of recommendation
Additional information: Application should also include ten images of recent work (completed within the last two years) in one of the three available areas: small metals, ceramics or fiber, artist statement, letter of intent and a non-refundable $25 application fee.
Program description:
Residency Program: Residencies in clay, metal, and fibers are available for three, nine and twelve months. Each artist receive a 180 square foot rent-free space equipped with internet access and all associated utilities are absorbed by Craft

Alliance. Artists are responsible for their own housing and living expenses as well as costs of materials associated with producing their work. While there is no stipend offered in the residency program, selected artists will be compensated for classes they teach and may apply for job openings at Craft Alliance. Artists are expected to work a minimum of approximately five hours per week on Craft Alliance Education Center studio maintenance and be present as monitors for open studio sessions.
EIN: 431022226

4971
Roy Creasey Trust
108 N. Jefferson St.
Mexico, MO 65265-2765

Foundation type: Independent foundation
Purpose: Scholarships to residents of Mexico, MO.
Financial data: Year ended 12/31/2012. Assets, $721,689 (M); Expenditures, $55,446; Total giving, $42,446.
Type of support: Undergraduate support.
Application information: Applications not accepted.
Additional information: Unsolicited requests for funds not considered or acknowledged.
EIN: 436247042

4972
Delta Area Economic Opportunity Corporation
99 Skyview Rd.
Portageville, MO 63873-9180 (573) 379-3851
FAX: (573) 379-5935; E-mail: pturley@daeoc.com;
Toll-free tel.: (800) 748-8320; URL: http://www.daeoc.org

Foundation type: Public charity
Purpose: Rent and utility assistance to low income individuals and families of Dunklin, Mississippi, New Madrid, Pemiscot, Scott, and Stoddard counties, MO.
Financial data: Year ended 12/31/2011. Assets, $10,150,327 (M); Expenditures, $18,702,569; Total giving, $2,619,002; Grants to individuals, totaling $2,619,002.
Fields of interest: Human services; Community/economic development.
Type of support: Emergency funds; Grants to individuals.
Application information: Applicants must meet the income eligibility guidelines. Contact the corporation for eligibility determination.
EIN: 430834206

4973
Delta Phi Benefit Fund, Inc.
483 Airport Rd.
Ferguson, MO 63135-1929
Contact: Daniel Wentz, Secy.-Treas.

Foundation type: Independent foundation
Purpose: Scholarships to active members of Delta Phi Tau at the University of Illinois.
Financial data: Year ended 10/31/2011. Assets, $120,201 (M); Expenditures, $188; Total giving, $0.
Fields of interest: Higher education.
Type of support: Scholarships—to individuals.
Application information:
Initial approach: Letter
Deadline(s): Apr. and Oct.

Additional information: Application must include status in Delta Phi and GPA.
EIN: 376027993

4974
Demolay Foundation, Inc.
10200 N.W. Ambassador Dr.
Kansas City, MO 64153-1367 (816) 891-8333
Contact: Jeffery C. Kitsmiller Sr., Exec. Dir.
Toll-free tel.: (800) 336-6529; URL: http://www.demolay.org/giving/foundation.php

Foundation type: Public charity
Purpose: Scholarships to Demolay members for undergraduate and postgraduate education.
Financial data: Year ended 12/31/2011. Assets, $4,407,793 (M); Expenditures, $137,621; Total giving, $22,000; Grants to individuals, totaling $22,000.
Fields of interest: Higher education; Dental school/education; Medical school/education; Men; Young adults, male.
Type of support: Scholarships—to individuals; Graduate support; Undergraduate support.
Application information: Application form required.
Initial approach: E-mail
Deadline(s): Apr. 1
Additional information: Application must include two letters of recommendation and two reference letters. Awards are based on academic achievement, progress and need.
Program description:
Frank S. Land Fellow Program: Applicant must be an active member of DeMolay to be eligible for one of the several $1,000 scholarships awarded each year. Applicants must be under 21 years old.
EIN: 430893446

4975
McDavid Dental Educational Trust
(formerly G. N. and Edna McDavid Dental Education Trust)
P.O. Box 387
Saint Louis, MO 63166-0387

Foundation type: Independent foundation
Purpose: Student loans to residents of MO attending an accredited dental school in MO. Preference given to residents of Madison County, MO.
Financial data: Year ended 12/31/2012. Assets, $1,939,356 (M); Expenditures, $376,509; Total giving, $306,000.
Fields of interest: Dental school/education.
Type of support: Graduate support.
Application information: Applications accepted. Application form required. Interview required.
Additional information: Forms available from Student Financial Aid office of accredited MO dental schools.
EIN: 436192984

4976
Dodd Foundation
2220 E. Circle Dr.
Saint Joseph, MO 64505

Foundation type: Independent foundation
Purpose: Scholarships primarily to residents of the St. Joseph, MO, area.
Financial data: Year ended 06/30/2012. Assets, $9,273 (M); Expenditures, $198; Total giving, $0.
Type of support: Scholarships—to individuals.
Application information:
Deadline(s): May 15

Applicants should submit the following:
1) Financial information
2) Photograph
3) Transcripts
Additional information: Unsolicited applications not considered or acknowledged.
EIN: 436048719

4977
Ray & Rosetta Doerhoff Scholarship Trust
P.O. Box 6
St. Elizabeth, MO   65075   (573) 493-2277
Contact: Bert Doerhoff, Tr.

Foundation type: Independent foundation
Purpose: Scholarships to graduating seniors at St. Elizabeth Public School, MO.
Financial data: Year ended 03/31/2013. Assets, $9 (M); Expenditures, $0; Total giving, $0.
Type of support: Support to graduates or students of specific schools; Undergraduate support.
Application information:
Initial approach: Letter
Deadline(s): Apr.
Additional information: Contact foundation for current application guidelines.
EIN: 431565655

4978
Clifford Doolin Foundation, Inc.
c/o Nelson Dinsmore
104 S. Rice
Meadville, MO   64659-0157

Foundation type: Independent foundation
Purpose: Scholarships to residents of MO for higher education.
Financial data: Year ended 12/31/2012. Assets, $491,171 (M); Expenditures, $24,832; Total giving, $23,822; Grants to individuals, 26 grants totaling $13,000 (high: $500; low: $500).
Type of support: Scholarships—to individuals.
Application information: Applications not accepted.
Additional information: Unsolicited requests for funds not considered or acknowledged.
EIN: 431573474

4979
Bruce V. Drowns Educational Foundation
c/o UMB Bank
P.O. Box 415044, M/S 1020307
Kansas City, MO   64141-6692

Foundation type: Independent foundation
Purpose: Scholarships to financially needy students and graduates of Benton High School, St. Joseph, MO.
Financial data: Year ended 06/30/2013. Assets, $1,200,646 (M); Expenditures, $36,709; Total giving, $23,650; Grants to individuals, 28 grants totaling $23,650 (high: $2,000; low: $300).
Type of support: Scholarships—to individuals; Support to graduates or students of specific schools; Graduate support; Technical education support; Undergraduate support.
Application information: Application form required.
Deadline(s): Apr. 1
EIN: 436371635

4980
Mary Frances Dunlop Scholarship Trust
c/o HNB National Bank
100 N. Main St.
Hannibal, MO   63401   (573) 267-3397

Foundation type: Independent foundation
Purpose: Scholarships to needy high school graduates who reside in Ralls County, MO. for assistance in obtaining a college or university education.
Financial data: Year ended 12/31/2011. Assets, $60,666 (M); Expenditures, $5,304; Total giving, $3,200.
Fields of interest: Scholarships/financial aid.
Type of support: Undergraduate support.
Application information: Applications accepted. Application form available on the grantmaker's web site.
Additional information: Application forms, supplied by the awards committee, may be obtained from the superintendent of Mark Twain High School.
EIN: 436116557

4981
Hazel C. Ebert Memorial Fund
c/o Commerce Bank, N.A.
P.O. Box 419248
Kansas City, MO   64141-6248
Contact: Kenneth Niemeyer
Application address: c/o Dean, School of Veterinary Medicine, University of Missouri-Columbia, Columbia, MO 65211

Foundation type: Independent foundation
Purpose: Scholarships to third- and fourth-year veterinary medicine students at the University of Missouri-Columbia who have financial need and academic potential.
Financial data: Year ended 12/31/2011. Assets, $621,827 (M); Expenditures, $37,214; Total giving, $28,832; Grants to individuals, 4 grants totaling $28,832 (high: $7,208; low: $7,208).
Fields of interest: Veterinary medicine.
Type of support: Scholarships—to individuals; Support to graduates or students of specific schools.
Application information: Applications accepted. Application form required. Interview required.
Initial approach: Letter
EIN: 431260509

4982
William Edgar Charitable Foundation
P.O. Box 387
St. Louis, MO   63166   (314) 505-8204
Contact: Carol Eaves

Foundation type: Independent foundation
Purpose: Scholarships to graduates of Ironton High School, Iron County, MO.
Publications: Application guidelines; Informational brochure (including application guidelines).
Financial data: Year ended 06/30/2012. Assets, $3,598,056 (M); Expenditures, $217,867; Total giving, $147,850.
Fields of interest: Scholarships/financial aid.
Type of support: Scholarships—to individuals; Support to graduates or students of specific schools; Awards/grants by nomination only; Technical education support; Undergraduate support.
Application information: Applications accepted. Application form required.
Initial approach: Letter

Send request by: Mail
Copies of proposal: 5
Deadline(s): Feb. 15
Applicants should submit the following:
1) Transcripts
2) Class rank
3) GPA
4) SAT
5) ACT
Additional information: Application must also include the most relevant standardized test that is applicable to an applicant's chosen avenue of further education and verification of graduation or impending graduation from Ironton High School, MO. scholarships are paid directly to the colleges or universities.
EIN: 436829350

4983
Educational Foundation of Alpha Gamma Rho
10101 N. Ambassador Dr.
Kansas City, MO   64153-1395   (816) 891-9200
Contact: James Ferrell, Dir., Devel.
FAX: (816) 891-9401;
E-mail: AGR@AlphaGammaRho.org; E-Mail for James Farrell : james@alphagammarho.org;
URL: http://www.alphagammarho.org/foundation

Foundation type: Public charity
Purpose: Scholarships to undergraduate and graduate members of Alpha Gamma Rho.
Publications: Application guidelines; Annual report.
Financial data: Year ended 06/30/2012. Assets, $4,547,307 (M); Expenditures, $1,318,489; Total giving, $911,347; Grants to individuals, totaling $616,347.
Fields of interest: Students, sororities/fraternities.
Type of support: Undergraduate support.
Application information: Applications accepted. Application form required.
Initial approach: Letter or telephone
Deadline(s): Apr. 30
Applicants should submit the following:
1) GPA
2) Essay
3) Transcripts
Additional information: Contact foundation for additional guidelines.
Program description:
FFA Scholarships: One $1,000 scholarships to an FFA member who is an undergraduate or plans to attend a four-year institution with an accredited college of agriculture is available.
EIN: 366158409

4984
Educational Foundation of the Missouri Society of Certified Public Accountants, Inc.
540 Maryville Ctr. Dr., Ste. 200
P. O. Box 419041
St. Louis, MO   63141-5830   (314) 997-7966
Contact: Peter C. Sharamitaro C.P.A., Pres.
FAX: (314) 997-2592;
E-mail: scholarships@mocpa.org; Toll-free tel.: (800) 264-7966; Mailing Address: P.O. Box 958868, St. Louis, MO 63195-8868; URL: http://www.mocpa.org/member-resources/awards-program

Foundation type: Public charity
Purpose: Scholarships of $500 to $1,000 to residents of MO, who are enrolled in a MO college studying accounting.

Financial data: Year ended 06/30/2012. Assets, $356,914 (M); Expenditures, $1,803,371; Total giving, $29,750; Grants to individuals, totaling $29,750.
Fields of interest: Business school/education.
Type of support: Undergraduate support.
Application information: Applications accepted. Application form required. Application form available on the grantmaker's web site.
  Initial approach: E-mail
  Deadline(s): Jan. 15
  Applicants should submit the following:
    1) ACT
    2) SAT
    3) Transcripts
    4) Essay
  Additional information: Applicants must provide proof of enrollment.
EIN: 237028488

4985
Emerson Charitable Trust
8000 W. Florissant Ave.
P.O. Box 4100
St. Louis, MO 63136-8506
URL: http://www.emerson.com/en-US/about_emerson/company_overview/pages/emerson_charitable_trust.aspx

Foundation type: Company-sponsored foundation
Purpose: Scholarships only to children of employees of Emerson Electric Company, St. Louis, MO.
Publications: Corporate giving report.
Financial data: Year ended 09/30/2012. Assets, $20,263,890 (M); Expenditures, $27,610,954; Total giving, $27,575,141.
Type of support: Employee-related scholarships.
Application information:
  Deadline(s): Jan. 1
Company name: Emerson Electric Company
EIN: 526200123

4986
Employees Emergency Aid Fund of Boeing St. Louis
(also known as EFAF)
c/o UMB Bank, N.A.
P.O. Box 415044 M/S 1020307
Kansas City, MO 64141-6692   (314) 232-7256
Contact: Angela Most
Application address: c/o P.O. Box 516, St. Louis. MO 63166

Foundation type: Independent foundation
Purpose: Grants to employees of Boeing Co. for emergency assistance.
Financial data: Year ended 12/31/2012. Assets, $11,738 (M); Expenditures, $2,148; Total giving, $2,135; Grants to individuals, 2 grants totaling $2,135 (high: $1,105, low: $1,030).
Type of support: Grants for special needs.
Application information: Applications accepted. Application form required.
  Initial approach: Telephone
  Deadline(s): None
Company name: Boeing Company
EIN: 431554300

4987
Epilepsy Foundation of Missouri and Kansas
4406 St. Vincent Ave.
St. Louis, MO 63119-3729   (314) 781-4909
E-mail: epilepsy@stl-epil.org; Additional address (Kansas City office): 6400 Prospect Ave., Ste. 300B, Kansas City, MO 64132-4103, tel.: (816) 444-2800; URL: http://old.epilepsyfoundation.org/local/stlouis/

Foundation type: Public charity
Purpose: Medication assistance to individuals in KS and MO suffering from epilepsy.
Publications: Annual report.
Financial data: Year ended 06/30/2012. Assets, $224,870 (M); Expenditures, $538,665; Total giving, $7,280; Grants to individuals, totaling $4,000.
Fields of interest: Human services.
Type of support: Grants for special needs.
Application information: Applications accepted.
  Additional information: Payments for medication are made on behalf of individuals.
EIN: 436048869

4988
ESCO Technologies Foundation
9900A Clayton Rd.
St. Louis, MO 63124-1186   (314) 213-7277
Contact: for Scholarship: Kathleen Lowrey, Chair.
E-mail: info@escotechnologiesfoundation.org;
URL: http://www.escotechnologiesfoundation.org/

Foundation type: Public charity
Purpose: Scholarships to college-age children of U.S. ESCO Technologies Inc. employees, enrolled and accepted at accredited technical schools, colleges, universities or graduate schools. Emergency assistance is also available to employees of ESCO Technologies Inc. and its subsidiaries.
Financial data: Year ended 09/30/2012. Assets, $347,029 (M); Expenditures, $257,852; Total giving, $257,800; Grants to individuals, totaling $26,000.
Fields of interest: Vocational education, post-secondary; Higher education.
Type of support: Emergency funds; Employee-related scholarships.
Application information: Applications accepted. Application form required.
  Initial approach: E-mail
  Additional information: Contact the foundation for additional application guidelines.
Program description:
  Scholarship Program: The foundation awards scholarships to college-age children of U.S. ESCO Technologies Inc. employees. Candidates must be enrolled for a minimum of 12 hours and accepted at an accredited technical school, college, university, or graduate school. Selection criteria include community involvement, academics, work experience, participation in the arts, and sports activities.
EIN: 203192719

4989
LaVerna Evans Teacher's Scholarship Trust
135 N. Meamec, 3rd Fl.
Clayton, MO 63105
Application address: 600 Smiley Ofallon, IL 62269

Foundation type: Independent foundation

Purpose: Scholarships to graduates of O'Fallon Township High School, IL, who intend to become elementary or secondary education teachers.
Financial data: Year ended 12/31/2012. Assets, $262,013 (M); Expenditures, $10,870; Total giving, $5,000; Grants to individuals, 5 grants totaling $5,000 (high: $1,000, low: $1,000).
Fields of interest: Teacher school/education.
Type of support: Support to graduates or students of specific schools.
Application information: Applications accepted. Application form required.
  Deadline(s): Contact local high school superintendent for deadline
EIN: 371179974

4990
William Pablo Feraldo Memorial Fund
c/o U.S. Bank, N.A.
P.O. Box 387
St. Louis, MO 63166-0387
Contact: Angela Pearson

Foundation type: Independent foundation
Purpose: Renewable scholarships to male high school graduates residing in the St. Louis, MO, area, for undergraduate education.
Financial data: Year ended 12/31/2012. Assets, $14,041,530 (M); Expenditures, $474,998; Total giving, $324,259.
Fields of interest: Men.
Type of support: Undergraduate support.
Application information: Application form required.
  Deadline(s): Feb. 1
  Applicants should submit the following:
    1) Transcripts
    2) Letter(s) of recommendation
    3) Financial information
  Additional information: Application must include a copy of student's or parent's tax return. Contact foundation for current application guidelines.
EIN: 436019398

4991
Ross D. Ferris Charitable Trust
108 N. Jefferson St.
Mexico, MO 65265-2765   (573) 581-3773
Application address: c/o Ross D. Ferris Scholarship Committee, Attn.: Superintendent Mexico School, District 59, Mexico, MO 65265

Foundation type: Independent foundation
Purpose: Scholarships to graduates of Mexico High School, MO who are in the upper 10 percent of his or her graduating class pursuing a course of study in the physical science, mathematics, or engineering field.
Financial data: Year ended 12/31/2011. Assets, $36,358 (M); Expenditures, $12,730; Total giving, $6,250; Grants to individuals, 3 grants totaling $6,250 (high: $2,500, low: $1,250).
Fields of interest: Higher education.
Type of support: Scholarships—to individuals; Support to graduates or students of specific schools.
Application information: Applications accepted. Application form required.
  Deadline(s): Apr. 1
  Additional information: Applications are available from Mexico High School guidance office.
EIN: 436506730

4992
Morris Fingersh Scholarship Fund
(formerly Morris Fingersh Charitable Trust Fund)
c/o UMB Bank, N.A.
P.O. Box 415044 M/S 1020307
Kansas City, MO 64141-6692 (816) 860-7711

Foundation type: Independent foundation
Purpose: Scholarships to students attending the Hyman Brand Hebrew Academy in Overland Park, KS.
Financial data: Year ended 03/31/2013. Assets, $256,470 (M); Expenditures, $18,607; Total giving, $15,260.
Fields of interest: Elementary school/education; Secondary school/education; Jewish agencies & synagogues.
Type of support: Scholarships—to individuals; Support to graduates or students of specific schools.
Application information: Applications accepted. Application form not required.
  Initial approach: Letter
  Deadline(s): June 1
EIN: 510214040

4993
The Dred and Lula Finnell Trust
c/o Norman Bentley
117 E. Tom St.
Keytesville, MO 65261-1244 (660) 288-3237

Foundation type: Independent foundation
Purpose: Scholarships to high school graduates from Keytesville Township School District, MO.
Financial data: Year ended 12/31/2012. Assets, $2,585,370 (M); Expenditures, $100,611; Total giving, $69,165; Grants to individuals, 35 grants totaling $42,947 (high: $1,550, low: $697).
Type of support: Support to graduates or students of specific schools; Undergraduate support.
Application information:
  Deadline(s): Last Fri. in June for fall semester and last Fri. in Nov. for spring semester.
  Additional information: Contact trust for current application guidelines.
EIN: 431589370

4994
Foundation of Metropolitan Community College
3200 Broadway St.
Kansas City, MO 64111-2408 (816) 604-1195
Contact: Kent Huyser, Exec. Dir.
FAX: (816) 759-1408;
E-mail: mcc.foundation@mcckc.edu; E-Mail for Kent Huyser: Kent.Huyser@mcckc.edu; URL: http://mcckc.edu/foundation

Foundation type: Public charity
Purpose: Scholarships to students attending the Junior College District of Metropolitan Kansas City, MO for continuing education.
Financial data: Year ended 06/30/2012. Assets, $7,355,416 (M); Expenditures, $1,568,116; Total giving, $1,222,429; Grants to individuals, totaling $287,167.
Fields of interest: College (community/junior).
Type of support: Scholarships—to individuals.
Application information: Applications accepted. Application form required.
  Additional information: Application forms can be obtained form the financial aid offices at each of the Metropolitan Community Colleges' member campus.
EIN: 510181875

4995
Ed French Charitable Foundation Inc.
12 Elm Tree Dr.
Mexico, MO 65265 (573) 473-2290
Contact: Ruby Hamlett, Secy.-Treas.

Foundation type: Independent foundation
Purpose: Undergraduate scholarships to individuals who are residents of Ranges 6 and 7 in Audrain County, MO.
Financial data: Year ended 06/30/2013. Assets, $2,300,114 (M); Expenditures, $150,750; Total giving, $119,100; Grants to individuals, 44 grants totaling $109,500 (high: $2,500, low: $2,000).
Type of support: Undergraduate support.
Application information: Applications accepted. Application form required.
  Deadline(s): June 1
EIN: 431393163

4996
A.E. Robert Friedman PDCA Scholarship Fund
2316 Millpark Dr.
Maryland Heights, MO 63043
URL: http://www.pdca.org/

Foundation type: Independent foundation
Purpose: Scholarships to deserving graduating high school seniors, and must be no more than 26 years old for attendance at a postsecondary educational institution as an undergraduate or graduate student.
Financial data: Year ended 12/31/2012. Assets, $340,684 (M); Expenditures, $15,771; Total giving, $15,000; Grants to individuals, 5 grants totaling $15,000 (high: $3,000, low: $3,000).
Fields of interest: Vocational education, post-secondary; College (community/junior); College; University.
Type of support: Scholarships—to individuals; Postgraduate support.
Application information:
  Deadline(s): Aug. 15
  Applicants should submit the following:
    1) Transcripts
    2) Letter(s) of recommendation
    3) Essay
  Additional information: Applicant must be nominated by an active PDCA member in good standing to be considered for the award. Selection is also based on character, and financial need.
EIN: 541605077

4997
Ruth Perrin Fues Memorial Scholarship Fund
c/o St. Clair County State Bank
P.O. Box 539
Osceola, MO 64776-0539 (417) 646-8128
Contact: Kirk Sibley

Foundation type: Independent foundation
Purpose: Scholarships to high school graduates residing in Osceola, MO, or St. Clair County, MO.
Financial data: Year ended 12/31/2012. Assets, $233,107 (M); Expenditures, $3,822; Total giving, $1,914; Grants to individuals, 3 grants totaling $1,914 (high: $638, low: $638).
Type of support: Support to graduates or students of specific schools; Undergraduate support.
Application information: Applications accepted. Application form required.
  Deadline(s): May 15

Additional information: Application must include short statement, extracurricular and work experience, and two references.
EIN: 431788109

4998
Esther A. and Bruce S. Gibbs Charitable Trust
c/o CB&T
P.O Box 70
Rock Port, MO 64482 (660) 744-5333
Contact: Jerry Moore; Kymm Nuckolls

Foundation type: Independent foundation
Purpose: Scholarships to graduating seniors of Atchison County, MO for postsecondary education.
Financial data: Year ended 12/31/2012. Assets, $1,665,491 (M); Expenditures, $92,638; Total giving, $53,375; Grants to individuals, 35 grants totaling $53,375 (high: $1,525, low: $1,525).
Fields of interest: Higher education.
Type of support: Scholarships—to individuals.
Application information: Applications accepted. Application form not required.
  Deadline(s): None
  Additional information: Contact trust for current application guidelines.
EIN: 436370943

4999
Gift of Hope, Inc.
15366 US Hwy. 160
Forsyth, MO 65653-8107 (417) 546-8062
FAX: (417) 546-6433;
E-mail: info@giftofhopeinc.org; URL: http://www.giftofhopeinc.org

Foundation type: Public charity
Purpose: Scholarships and assistance to needy individuals and families of Taney County, MO.
Financial data: Year ended 01/31/2013. Assets, $75,635 (M); Expenditures, $149,286; Total giving, $15,963.
Fields of interest: Higher education; Economically disadvantaged.
Type of support: Scholarships—to individuals; Grants for special needs.
Application information: Contact the organization for eligibility criteria.
EIN: 431612944

5000
The Gilbert Foundation
(formerly The W. A. Gilbert Family Foundation)
609 S. Warson Rd.
St. Louis, MO 63124

Foundation type: Independent foundation
Purpose: Scholarships to natural or legally adopted children of employees of Landscape Brands, Inc., and Upbeat, Inc. or any child of a former employee who received a grant in the immediate preceding year.
Financial data: Year ended 12/31/2012. Assets, $1,073,842 (M); Expenditures, $174,125; Total giving, $161,162; Grant to an individual, 1 grant totaling $1,385.
Fields of interest: Higher education.
Type of support: Employee-related scholarships.
Application information: Applications accepted. Application form required.
  Deadline(s): May
  Applicants should submit the following:
    1) Transcripts
    2) GPA

3) ACT
4) Essay
5) SAT
6) Letter(s) of recommendation
Additional information: Unsolicited requests for funds not considered or acknowledged. Scholarships only for employee children.
EIN: 431730251

5001

Goetze Educational Foundation Inc.
P.O. Box 414630
Kansas City, MO 64141 (660) 785-4130
URL: http://www.goetzefoundation.com

Foundation type: Independent foundation
Purpose: College scholarships to students enrolled at Truman State University, MO for higher education.
Financial data: Year ended 06/30/2013. Assets, $227,848 (M); Expenditures, $14,397; Total giving, $6,525; Grants to individuals, 17 grants totaling $5,900 (high: $500, low: $300).
Fields of interest: Higher education.
Type of support: Scholarships—to individuals.
Application information: Applications accepted. Application form required.
Deadline(s): Early Sept. and Mar.
Additional information: Applications are available from the director of financial aid.
EIN: 430907602

5002

Gorman Foundation
612 Spirit Dr.
Saint Louis, MO 63005
Contact: Kelly Y. Crowell
Application address: c/o Missouri University of Science and Technology, Office of the Director, G-1 Parker Hall, Rola, MO 64501-0249

Foundation type: Operating foundation
Purpose: Scholarships to residents of St. Louis, MO, who graduated from high schools located in the city of St. Louis, and who will pursue an undergraduate and/or graduate education in engineering at the University of Missouri—Rolla.
Financial data: Year ended 06/30/2013. Assets, $528,651 (M); Expenditures, $37,514; Total giving, $26,250; Grants to individuals, totaling $26,250.
Fields of interest: Engineering school/education.
Type of support: Support to graduates or students of specific schools; Graduate support; Undergraduate support.
Application information: Application form required.
Send request by: Mail
Deadline(s): Contact foundation for current application deadline
Additional information: For further information contact the specific school relating to your application.
EIN: 431377593

5003

William T. & Frances D. Grant Foundation
c/o UMB Bank
P.O. Box 415044, M/S 1020307
Kansas City, MO 64141-6692

Foundation type: Independent foundation
Purpose: Scholarships to individuals, primarily in the Kansas City, MO, area for undergraduate education.

Financial data: Year ended 12/31/2012. Assets, $2,343,338 (M); Expenditures, $109,122; Total giving, $80,883.
Type of support: Undergraduate support.
Application information: Applications not accepted.
Additional information: Unsolicited requests for funds not considered or acknowledged.
EIN: 446010325

5004

The Greater Lee's Summit Healthcare Foundation
c/o Greater Kansas City Community Foundation
P.O. Box 571
Lee's Summit, MO 64063-0571
E-mail for scholarship: scholarship@lshealthcare.org
E-mail: info@lshealthcare.org; *URL:* http://www.lshealthcare.org/

Foundation type: Public charity
Purpose: Scholarships to students in the Lee's Summit, MO area pursuing a career in the healthcare industry.
Publications: Application guidelines.
Financial data: Year ended 12/31/2011. Assets, $2,326,428 (M); Expenditures, $147,540; Total giving, $132,425; Grants to individuals, 9 grants totaling $40,000 (high: $5,000, low: $1,284).
Fields of interest: Medical school/education; Nursing school/education; Health care.
Type of support: Scholarships—to individuals.
Application information: Applications accepted. Application form required. Application form available on the grantmaker's web site.
Send request by: Mail or e-mail
Deadline(s): Mar. 1
Final notification: Applicants notified in Apr.
Applicants should submit the following:
1) Essay
2) Transcripts
3) Letter(s) of recommendation
Additional information: Funds are paid directly to the educational institution on behalf of the students. See web site for additional application guidelines.
Program description:
Scholarships: The foundation awards multiple scholarships of up to $5,000 to support individuals whose academic studies lead to a career in a medical or healthcare discipline. Scholarships will support studies in medicine, nursing, pharmacy, physical therapy, radiology technology, and other allied healthcare fields. Eligible applicants must have lived in Lee's Summit for a period of at least five years, or have graduated from an area high school (students must be able to present supporting documentation upon request), have completed studies in his/her chosen healthcare field, including completing his/her undergraduate degree and being accepted to a medical school. Applicant must have at least a 3.0 GPA on a 4.0 scale.
EIN: 431341459

5005

Allen P. & Josephine B. Green Foundation
c/o Greater Kansas City Community Foundation
1055 Broadway, Ste. 130
Kansas City, MO 64105-1595 (816) 627-3420
Contact: Matthew Fuller, Mgr., Community Investment, Greater Kansas City Community Foundation
FAX: (816) 268-3420;
E-mail: greenfoundation@gkccf.org; *URL:* http://www.greenfdn.org

Foundation type: Independent foundation
Purpose: Scholarships of $7,500 to graduates of Mexico High School in MO.
Publications: Application guidelines; Annual report (including application guidelines); Grants list.
Financial data: Year ended 12/31/2012. Assets, $10,748,762 (M); Expenditures, $612,946; Total giving, $505,000; Grants to individuals, 4 grants totaling $20,000 (high: $5,000, low: $5,000).
Fields of interest: Higher education.
Type of support: Support to graduates or students of specific schools; Undergraduate support.
Application information: Applications accepted. Application form required.
Initial approach: Application
Copies of proposal: 1
Deadline(s): Jan. 15
Final notification: Recipients notified in two months
Applicants should submit the following:
1) SAT
2) Transcripts
3) GPA
4) ACT
5) Financial information
6) Essay
7) Curriculum vitae
Additional information: Applications available at Mexico High School. Application and attachments should be submitted to the high school counselor.
EIN: 436030135

5006

Green Hills Community Action Agency
(also known as GHCAA)
1506 Oklahoma Ave.
P.O. Box 278
Trenton, MO 64683-0278 (660) 359-3907
FAX: (660) 359-6619; *URL:* http://www.ghcaa.org

Foundation type: Public charity
Purpose: Assist low-income individuals and families, of Caldwell, Daviess, Grundy, Harrison, Linn, Livingston, Mercer, Putnam, and Sullivan counties, MO, with health care, human services, affordable housing, home repair, employment and job skills, and other basic needs.
Financial data: Year ended 09/30/2011. Assets, $7,300,042 (M); Expenditures, $6,780,378; Total giving, $2,001,015; Grants to individuals, totaling $2,001,015.
Fields of interest: Housing/shelter, repairs; Human services; Economically disadvantaged.
Type of support: Grants for special needs.
Application information: Applications accepted.
EIN: 430828205

5007

Griffin Family Foundation, Inc.
100 N. Jefferson St.
Mexico, MO 65265-3786 (573) 581-5280
Contact: Dan K. Erdel, Tr.

Foundation type: Independent foundation
Purpose: Scholarships to residents of MO, with emphasis on Mexico, Moberly and Springfield counties.
Financial data: Year ended 12/31/2012. Assets, $5,125,736 (M); Expenditures, $213,189; Total giving, $171,133.
Fields of interest: Higher education.
Type of support: Scholarships—to individuals; Undergraduate support.
Application information: Applications accepted.
Initial approach: Letter or telephone
Deadline(s): Varies
Additional information: Contact foundation for additional application guidelines.
EIN: 431822804

5008
Growing Family Foundation, Inc.
3613 Mueller Rd.
Saint Charles, MO   63301-8003   (636) 946-5115
Contact: Cindy Looser

Foundation type: Company-sponsored foundation
Purpose: Grants by nomination only by providing financial gifts to needy families who have experienced recent births.
Publications: Application guidelines.
Financial data: Year ended 12/31/2012. Assets, $103,828 (M); Expenditures, $16,986; Total giving, $16,900; Grants to individuals, 84 grants totaling $16,900 (high: $900, low: $50).
Fields of interest: Children, services; Economically disadvantaged.
Type of support: Grants for special needs.
Application information: Application form required.
Deadline(s): Varies
Additional information: Application must be completed and submitted online by a professional healthcare provider. Grants are based on individual need and amount of available funding.
EIN: 431877493

5009
Anna M. Guilander Scholarship Trust
c/o First Bank Wealth Management
135 N. Meramec 3rd Fl.
Clayton, MO   63105-3751

Foundation type: Independent foundation
Purpose: Scholarships for graduating seniors of Jersey Community Unit School District 100 high school for attendance at a college, university or trade school.
Financial data: Year ended 09/30/2013. Assets, $5,759,052 (M); Expenditures, $327,112; Total giving, $272,112; Grants to individuals, 37 grants totaling $272,112 (high: $52,580, low: $2,000).
Fields of interest: Higher education.
Type of support: Scholarships—to individuals.
Application information: Applications accepted. Application form required.
Deadline(s): None
Applicants should submit the following:
1) Transcripts
2) Financial information
3) Essay
4) ACT
5) SAT
6) Letter(s) of recommendation
Additional information: Application should also include school/community involvement.
EIN: 271847433

5010
Edna Haddad Welfare Trust Fund
7215 Creveling Dr.
Saint Louis, MO   63130-4124   (314) 727-1155
Contact: Evelyn B. Goldberg, Tr.

Foundation type: Independent foundation
Purpose: Scholarships to residents of MO, pursuing higher education.
Financial data: Year ended 03/31/2013. Assets, $236,674 (M); Expenditures, $12,324; Total giving, $11,038; Grants to individuals, 3 grants totaling $11,038 (high: $5,600, low: $1,133).
Fields of interest: Higher education.
Type of support: Scholarships—to individuals.
Application information: Applications accepted. Application form required.
Additional information: Contact fund for application form. Send self-addressed stamped envelope.
EIN: 431434151

5011
Hall Family Foundation
P.O. Box 419580, Dept. 323
Kansas City, MO   64141-6580   (816) 274-8516
FAX: (816) 274-8547; URL: http://www.hallfamilyfoundation.org

Foundation type: Independent foundation
Purpose: Scholarships only to children of employees of Hallmark Cards, Inc., to finance their college education.
Publications: Annual report; Grants list; Informational brochure (including application guidelines).
Financial data: Year ended 12/31/2012. Assets, $822,884,571 (M); Expenditures, $44,501,891; Total giving, $35,685,608; Grants to individuals, 328 grants totaling $245,250 (high: $750, low: $750).
Fields of interest: Higher education.
Type of support: Employee-related scholarships.
Application information: Applications not accepted.
Additional information: Contributes only to children of Hallmark Cards; unsolicited requests for funds not considered or acknowledged.
Program description:
Scholarships: Scholarships only to children of employees of Hallmark Cards, Inc.
EIN: 446006291

5012
Helen and June Hamilton Teachers Scholarship Fund
P.O. Box 387
St. Louis, MO   63166-0387   (217) 753-7362
Contact: Mary Jo Janessen
Application address: US Bank, N.A., P.O. Box 19264, Springfield, IL 62794, tel.: (217) 753-7362

Foundation type: Independent foundation
Purpose: Loans to high school graduates who are residents of Sangamon County, IL.
Financial data: Year ended 08/31/2012. Assets, $210,712 (M); Expenditures, $4,246; Total giving, $250.
Fields of interest: Higher education; Graduate/professional education.
Type of support: Student loans—to individuals; Graduate support; Undergraduate support.
Application information: Applications accepted. Application form required.

Additional information: Loan applications available at U.S. Bank. Applicants must be between the ages 16 and 25. Loans are to be used for college or graduate and professional schools.
EIN: 376325303

5013
Dale Irwin Hayes Scholarship Fund
P.O. Box 387
St. Louis, MO   63166-0387   (573) 341-4282
Application address: c/o University of Missouri-Rolla, G-1 Parker Hall Rolla, MO 65409-0250

Foundation type: Independent foundation
Purpose: Scholarships of at least $2,000 to students enrolled at the University of Missouri-Rolla, with priority given to students at the undergraduate level to study engineering or a related subject. Students should demonstrate financial need.
Financial data: Year ended 09/30/2013. Assets, $1,119,815 (M); Expenditures, $77,707; Total giving, $46,000.
Fields of interest: Engineering school/education.
Type of support: Support to graduates or students of specific schools; Undergraduate support.
Application information: Application form required.
Initial approach: Letter or telephone
Additional information: Contact fund for current application deadline/guidelines.
EIN: 436619759

5014
J. L. & D. A. Hays Memorial Scholarship Trust
111 E. Miller St.
Jefferson City, MO   65101-2959

Foundation type: Independent foundation
Purpose: Scholarships to students of Van-Far School District No. 1, MO for postsecondary education.
Financial data: Year ended 12/31/2012. Assets, $343,617 (M); Expenditures, $18,702; Total giving, $15,000.
Fields of interest: Higher education.
Type of support: Support to graduates or students of specific schools.
Application information: Applications accepted.
Additional information: Students should contact their guidance counselor for scholarship guidelines.
EIN: 436877605

5015
Helias Foundation, Inc.
P.O. Box 694
1106 Swifts Hwy.
Jefferson City, MO   65102-0694   (573) 635-3808
Contact: Marti Dupuis, Exec. Dir.
FAX: (573) 634-3205;
E-mail: info@heliasfoundation.org; E-Mail for Marti Dupuis: mdupuis@heliasfoundation.org;
URL: http://www.heliasfoundation.org

Foundation type: Public charity
Purpose: Scholarships to Helias Catholic High School students of central Missouri for higher education.
Financial data: Year ended 08/31/2011. Assets, $5,382,083 (M); Expenditures, $397,904; Total

giving, $160,154; Grants to individuals, totaling $22,700.
Fields of interest: Higher education.
Type of support: Scholarships—to individuals.
Application information: Applications not accepted.
   Additional information: Unsolicited requests for funds not considered or acknowledged. Scholarship is only for Helias High School students.
EIN: 431064064

5016
Leonard W. & Helen L. Hester Student Memorial Trust
1626 Hedges Plz.
Nevada, MO 64772-4260 (417) 667-3057
Contact: David Swearingen, Tr.
Application address: P.O. Box 388 Nevada, MO 64772

Foundation type: Independent foundation
Purpose: Scholarships for higher education to members of farm families in Vernon and Cedar counties, MO, seeking degrees in medicine, nursing, dentistry, veterinary medicine, teaching, or missionary studies.
Financial data: Year ended 12/31/2011. Assets, $1,550,909 (M); Expenditures, $46,140; Total giving, $32,000; Grants to individuals, 21 grants totaling $32,000 (high: $3,000, low: $1,000).
Fields of interest: Dental school/education; Medical school/education; Nursing school/ education; Teacher school/education; Theological school/education; Veterinary medicine.
Type of support: Scholarships—to individuals.
Application information: Application form required.
   Send request by: Mail
   Deadline(s): Jan. 5 for spring and summer semesters, June 15 for fall semester
   Applicants should submit the following:
     1) Class rank
     2) Financial information
     3) Transcripts
     4) SAT
     5) Letter(s) of recommendation
     6) GPA
     7) ACT
   Additional information: Application should also include a list of extracurricular activities, and a copy of you and your parents' tax forms.
EIN: 436478437

5017
Florence Hirsch Educational Endowment Fund
P.O. Box 1119
St. Joseph, MO 64501 (816) 671-4000
Application address: St. Joseph School District, 925 Felix, St. Joseph, MO 64501

Foundation type: Independent foundation
Purpose: Scholarships for St. Joseph, MO, residents attending four-year colleges.
Financial data: Year ended 12/31/2012. Assets, $1,155,502 (M); Expenditures, $88,420; Total giving, $68,000; Grants to individuals, 44 grants totaling $68,000 (high: $3,000, low: $1,000).
Type of support: Undergraduate support.
Application information: Applications accepted. Application form required.
   Deadline(s): None
EIN: 436068192

5018
Bonnie L. Holmes Scholarship Fund
P.O. Box 146
Mount Vernon, MO 65712-8314 (417) 466-7585
Application address: Mt. Vernon High School, 400 W. Highway 174, Mt. Vernon, MO 65712

Foundation type: Independent foundation
Purpose: Scholarships to financially needy students attending Mt. Vernon High School, MO.
Financial data: Year ended 12/31/2011. Assets, $157,133 (M); Expenditures, $14,320; Total giving, $13,600; Grants to individuals, 12 grants totaling $13,600 (high: $1,200, low: $1,000).
Fields of interest: Higher education.
Type of support: Scholarships—to individuals.
Application information: Applications accepted. Application form required.
   Deadline(s): Apr. 15
   Applicants should submit the following:
     1) Class rank
     2) Essay
     3) Financial information
     4) ACT
     5) SAT
   Additional information: Application should also include a list of extracurricular activities, work experience and awards received.
EIN: 431603665

5019
Larry Hughes Foundation
12455 Bennett Springs Ct.
Saint Louis, MO 63146
E-mail: hughesv5252@sbcglobal.net

Foundation type: Public charity
Purpose: Financial assistance to families of organ donors and recipients in the St. Louis, MO area with burial expenses, rent and mortgage payments.
Financial data: Year ended 12/31/2011. Assets, $5,352 (M); Expenditures, $3,824.
Type of support: Grants for special needs.
Application information: Contact the foundation for additional information.
EIN: 431899617

5020
Helen Huss Charitable Trust
P.O. Box 189
Salisbury, MO 65281-0189 (660) 388-6145
Contact: Ray Widmer, Tr.

Foundation type: Independent foundation
Purpose: Scholarships to graduates of Salisbury High School, MO, for higher education.
Financial data: Year ended 12/31/2012. Assets, $122,707 (M); Expenditures, $43,298; Total giving, $43,000; Grants to individuals, 20 grants totaling $43,000 (high: $4,000, low: $1,000).
Type of support: Support to graduates or students of specific schools.
Application information: Applications accepted. Application form required.
   Deadline(s): None
   Additional information: Application forms available from the high school's guidance counselor.
EIN: 436766144

5021
Harold J. Hutchins Foundation Fund
P.O. Box 387
St. Louis, MO 63166-0387 (270) 575-5334
Contact: James C. Acton
Application address: 201 N. ELM , Centralia, IL 62801, tel.: (270) 575-5334

Foundation type: Independent foundation
Purpose: Scholarship loans to graduates of Mount Vernon High School, IL, for undergraduate study.
Financial data: Year ended 09/30/2013. Assets, $170,719 (M); Expenditures, $12,351; Total giving, $8,000; Grants to individuals, 8 grants totaling $8,000 (high: $1,000, low: $1,000).
Fields of interest: Higher education; Education.
Type of support: Student loans—to individuals; Support to graduates or students of specific schools.
Application information: Application form required. Interview required.
EIN: 376235717

5022
C. P. and Dorthea Hutchinson Foundation, Inc.
P.O. Box 620
Chillicothe, MO 64601-0620

Foundation type: Independent foundation
Purpose: Scholarships to high school graduates of Livingston county, MO, pursuing higher education.
Financial data: Year ended 12/31/2011. Assets, $1,128,660 (M); Expenditures, $63,608; Total giving, $50,000; Grants to individuals, 9 grants totaling $25,000 (high: $2,500, low: $2,500).
Fields of interest: Higher education.
Type of support: Scholarships—to individuals.
Application information: Applications accepted.
   Deadline(s): None
   Additional information: Students should contact their guidance counselors for application information.
EIN: 320126518

5023
Greater Kansas City Community Foundation
(formerly The Greater Kansas City Community Foundation and Affiliated Trusts)
1055 Broadway, Ste. 130
Kansas City, MO 64105-1595 (816) 842-0944
Contact: Deborah L. Wilkerson, C.E.O.
Tel. for scholarship info.: (816) 842-7444, e-mail inquiries: scholarship@gkccf.org
FAX: (816) 842-8079; *E-mail:* info@gkccf.org;
URL: http://www.gkccf.org

Foundation type: Community foundation
Purpose: Awards to residents of the greater Kansas City, MO, area for pre-school, middle school, high school, grade school, collegiate undergraduate and collegiate graduate scholarships as well as extracurricular and camp scholarships.
Publications: Annual report; Financial statement; Informational brochure; Newsletter.
Financial data: Year ended 12/31/2012. Assets, $1,636,468,707 (M); Expenditures, $229,340,887; Total giving, $226,808,114.
Fields of interest: Elementary/secondary education; Early childhood education; Higher education; Graduate/professional education; Nursing school/education; Teacher school/ education; Education, services.
Type of support: Scholarships—to individuals; Support to graduates or students of specific

schools; Graduate support; Precollege support; Undergraduate support; Camperships.
Application information: Applications accepted. Application form available on the grantmaker's web site.
  Initial approach: E-mail
  Deadline(s): Varies
  Additional information: Contact the foundation for additional guidelines.
EIN: 431152398

5024
Greater Kansas City Football Coaches Association
(also known as G.K.C.F.C.A.)
c/o Brian Johnston
2621 S.W., 9th Terr.
Lee's Summit, MO 64064

Foundation type: Independent foundation
Purpose: Scholarships to Kansas City, MO area senior high school football players for continuing education at institutions of higher learning.
Financial data: Year ended 12/31/2012. Assets, $0 (M); Expenditures, $64,742; Total giving, $21,000.
Fields of interest: Higher education; Athletics/sports, football.
Type of support: Scholarships—to individuals.
Application information: Applications not accepted.
  Additional information: Scholarships are only for the football players. Unsolicited requests for funds not considered or acknowledged.
EIN: 431575634

5025
Ewing Marion Kauffman Foundation
4801 Rockhill Rd.
Kansas City, MO 64110-2046 (816) 932-1000
Contact: Barbara Pruitt, Dir., Comms.
FAX: (816) 932-1100; E-mail: info@kauffman.org;
URL: http://www.kauffman.org

Foundation type: Independent foundation
Purpose: Fellowships to Ph.D. students who are completing a dissertation relating to entrepreneurship. Awards also for research in entrepreneurship.
Publications: Application guidelines; Annual report; Financial statement; Grants list; Newsletter.
Financial data: Year ended 12/31/2012. Assets, $1,880,334,000 (M); Expenditures, $85,487,000; Total giving, $28,443,000.
Fields of interest: Business/industry.
Type of support: Fellowships; Research.
Application information: Applications accepted. Application form available on the grantmaker's web site.
  Deadline(s): Sept. 14 for Kauffman Dissertation Fellowship
  Additional information: See web site for additional application information.
Program descriptions:
  Ewing Marion Kauffman Prize Medal for Distinguished Research in Entrepreneurship: The prize was established to inspire promising young scholars to contribute new insight into the field of entrepreneurship. The Medal, which includes a $50,000 prize, is awarded annually to one scholar under age 40 whose research has made a significant contribution to the literature in entrepreneurship.
  Junior Faculty Fellowship in Entrepreneurship Research: The Kauffman Foundation will award up to five Junior Faculty Fellowship grants to junior

faculty members whose research has the potential to make significant contributions to the body of literature about entrepreneurship. Each fellow's university will receive a grant of $35,000 over two years to support the research activities of the fellow. Nominees must be tenured or tenure-track junior faculty members at accredited U.S. institutions of higher education who received a Ph.D. or equivalent doctoral degree.
EIN: 436064859

5026
Gene Kauffman Scholarship Foundation, Inc.
P.O. Box 113
Princeton, MO 64673-0113
Contact: Angela Ormsby, Pres.

Foundation type: Independent foundation
Purpose: Scholarships to unmarried female non-smokers who have graduated from a Mercer County, MO, high school for attendance at a MO college.
Financial data: Year ended 06/30/2012. Assets, $3,258 (M); Expenditures, $245,155; Total giving, $239,000; Grants to individuals, 66 grants totaling $239,000 (high: $5,549, low: $555).
Fields of interest: Women.
Type of support: Support to graduates or students of specific schools; Undergraduate support.
Application information: Application form required.
  Initial approach: Letter
  Deadline(s): Contact foundation for current application deadline
  Applicants should submit the following:
    1) FAFSA
    2) GPA
EIN: 431825689

5027
Kelly Family Charitable Foundation
P.O. Box G
Troy, MO 63379-0167

Foundation type: Independent foundation
Purpose: Scholarships to eighth grade graduates of Holy Rosary Catholic School in Warrenton, MO, for attendance at St. Francis Borgia Regional High School, Washington, MO, or St. Dominic High School, O'Fallon, MO.
Financial data: Year ended 08/31/2013. Assets, $9,196 (M); Expenditures, $205; Total giving, $0.
Fields of interest: Secondary school/education; Scholarships/financial aid.
Type of support: Support to graduates or students of specific schools; Precollege support.
Application information: Applications not accepted.
  Additional information: Unsolicited requests for funds not considered or acknowledged.
EIN: 436685888

5028
Arthur Kennett Educational Fund
P.O. Box 387
Saint Louis, MO 63166-0387 (314) 298-0566
Contact: James B. Gerdes, Tr.
Application address: 3554 Bostons Farms Dr., Bridgeton, MO 63044-3123

Foundation type: Independent foundation
Purpose: Scholarships to financially needy high school seniors and graduates of secondary schools in St. Louis County, MO, who are U.S. citizens with

demonstrated ability to succeed in postsecondary work. Scholarships are for one academic year only.
Financial data: Year ended 06/30/2013. Assets, $543,958 (M); Expenditures, $37,029; Total giving, $16,320; Grants to individuals, 24 grants totaling $16,320 (high: $680, low: $680).
Type of support: Support to graduates or students of specific schools; Undergraduate support.
Application information: Applications accepted. Application form required.
  Initial approach: Letter or telephone
  Applicants should submit the following:
    1) Transcripts
    2) Letter(s) of recommendation
    3) Essay
  Additional information: Contact foundation for current application deadline/guidelines.
EIN: 436517200

5029
William Toben King Educational Trust
320 Robidoux Ctr.
St. Joseph, MO 64501-1736
Application address: c/o Commerce Trust Company, Att.: Lori Boyer, St. Joseph, MO 64501, tel.: (816) 236-5751

Foundation type: Independent foundation
Purpose: Scholarships only to high school graduates of Andrew and Buchanon counties, MO, for higher education based on financial need and academic merit.
Financial data: Year ended 09/30/2012. Assets, $7,626,472 (M); Expenditures, $345,686; Total giving, $265,940.
Type of support: Scholarships—to individuals.
Application information: Applications accepted. Application form required.
  Deadline(s): June 1
  Additional information: Application should include student's and parents' tax returns, extracurricular activities, work experience, detailed financial information, GPA, ACT or P-ACT scores, transcripts, guidance counselor's recommendation and signature, and one additional reference letter.
EIN: 431582893

5030
John E. Kirschner Educational Trust
P.O. Box 11356
Clayton, MO 63105-0156 (816) 236-5751
Application address: c/o The Commerce Trust Co., Attn.: Lori Boyer, P.O. Box 1119, St. Joseph, MO 64502

Foundation type: Independent foundation
Purpose: Scholarships to members of the Zion United Church of Christ of St. Joseph, MO pursuing careers in religion, religious services, social work, education, and ministry. Scholarships for students graduating from the St. Joseph Public School System, MO, and to students attending Missouri Western State College.
Financial data: Year ended 09/30/2013. Assets, $1,474,899 (M); Expenditures, $94,753; Total giving, $67,536.
Fields of interest: Higher education; Theological school/education; Social work school/education; Christian agencies & churches; Religion.
Type of support: Scholarships—to individuals; Support to graduates or students of specific schools; Undergraduate support.
Application information: Applications accepted. Application form required.
  Deadline(s): June 1

Additional information: Application can be obtained from Commerce Bank NA.

EIN: 436385089

5031
Ray & Mary Klapmeyer Grandview High School Foundation

c/o UMB Bank, N.A.
P.O Box 415044 M/S 1020307
Kansas City, MO 64141-6692
Contact: Sara Barrows

Foundation type: Independent foundation
Purpose: Scholarships to students graduating from Grandview High School, MO.
Financial data: Year ended 02/28/2013. Assets, $103,564 (M); Expenditures, $4,249; Total giving, $2,500.
Type of support: Support to graduates or students of specific schools; Undergraduate support.
Application information: Applications accepted. Application form required.
    Deadline(s): Mar. 31
    Applicants should submit the following:
        1) Letter(s) of recommendation
        2) Photograph
EIN: 237382733

5032
Lake Area Civic Association, Inc.

680 W. Hwy. 54
Camdenton, MO 65020-9012

Foundation type: Independent foundation
Purpose: Scholarships to students of Camden County, MO, high schools for higher education.
Financial data: Year ended 09/30/2012. Assets, $193,678 (M); Expenditures, $9,607; Total giving, $9,074.
Fields of interest: Higher education.
Type of support: Scholarships—to individuals.
Application information: Application form required.
    Initial approach: Through a Camden County, MO high school.
    Deadline(s): Apr. 30
EIN: 431273132

5033
Della Lamb Community Services

(formerly Della C. Lamb Neighborhood House)
500 Woodland Ave.
Kansas City, MO 64106-9908 (816) 842-8040
FAX: (816) 842-7727;
E-mail: jakers@dellalamb.org; URL: http://www.dellalamb.org

Foundation type: Public charity
Purpose: Emergency assistance to needy residents of Kansas City, MO.
Financial data: Year ended 12/31/2011. Assets, $4,506,697 (M); Expenditures, $12,850,285; Total giving, $692,827; Grants to individuals, totaling $692,827.
Fields of interest: Human services.
Type of support: Grants for special needs.
Application information: Applications accepted.
    Initial approach: Letter
EIN: 440549931

5034
H. K. Lange Charitable Trust

1 Angelica St.
Saint Louis, MO 63147-3401 (314) 241-9531
Contact: Richard W. Stegmann, Tr.

Foundation type: Independent foundation
Purpose: Scholarships primarily to residents of MO.
Financial data: Year ended 12/31/2011. Assets, $13,096 (M); Expenditures, $6,000; Total giving, $6,000; Grants to individuals, 4 grants totaling $6,000 (high: $1,500, low: $1,500).
Type of support: Scholarships—to individuals.
Application information: Applications accepted. Application form not required.
    Deadline(s): None
    Additional information: Contact foundation for current application guidelines.
EIN: 431327794

5035
Leader Foundation

8077 Maryland Ave.
Clayton, MO 63105 (314) 863-7733
Contact: Robert Epstein, Secy.
Application address: 1 N. Brentwood Blvd., Ste. 1000, Clayton, MO 63105 Tel.: (314) 863-7733

Foundation type: Independent foundation
Purpose: Financial assistance to needy former employees, and their dependents, of Stix, Baer & Fuller.
Financial data: Year ended 01/31/2013. Assets, $562,708 (M); Expenditures, $130,563; Total giving, $106,352; Grants to individuals, totaling $106,352.
Type of support: Employee-related welfare.
Application information: Applications accepted.
    Initial approach: Letter
    Deadline(s): None
EIN: 436036864

5036
The Liebling Foundation for Worthy Students

(also known as The Liebling Foundation)
P.O. Box 387
St. Louis, MO 63166 (816) 364-7235
Contact: Shannon Moore
Application address: US Bank, N.A., P.O. Box 308, St. Joseph, MO 64501; tel.: (816) 364-7245

Foundation type: Independent foundation
Purpose: Scholarships to students of the St. Joseph, MO, school district for higher education.
Financial data: Year ended 12/31/2012. Assets, $873,611 (M); Expenditures, $53,523; Total giving, $39,275.
Type of support: Scholarships—to individuals; Support to graduates or students of specific schools.
Application information: Application form required.
    Initial approach: Letter or telephone
    Deadline(s): None
    Applicants should submit the following:
        1) Photograph
        2) Essay
        3) Letter(s) of recommendation
    Additional information: Application must also include federal tax returns.
EIN: 431722158

5037
Lord Educational Fund

P.O. Box 387
Saint Louis, MO 63166 (217) 287-1830
Contact: Deborah Jostes
Application address: c/o U.S. Bank, N.A., 108 W. Market St., Taylorville, IL 62568-0350, Tel:(217) 287-1830

Foundation type: Independent foundation
Purpose: Scholarships to graduates of Taylorville Senior High School, IL, and graduates from any other high school who reside at Kemmerer Village Specialized Foster Home in Assumption, IL. Recipients may attend college, vocational, or business schools.
Financial data: Year ended 09/30/2013. Assets, $2,936,547 (M); Expenditures, $143,314; Total giving, $94,000; Grants to individuals, 42 grants totaling $94,000.
Fields of interest: Vocational education; Business school/education.
Type of support: Technical education support; Undergraduate support.
Application information: Application form required.
    Additional information: Application must include financial statement and projected costs; Interviews required for finalists.
EIN: 510175613

5038
Pearl Lowrie Student Loan Fund

c/o HNB Bank, N.A.
100 N. Main St.
Hannibal, MO 63401-3537 (573) 221-3675
Application addresses: c/o Hannibal LaGrange College, Financial Aid Office, 2800 Palmyra Rd., Hannibal, MO 63401; c/o Central Methodist College, 411 Central Methodist Sq., Fayette, MO 65248

Foundation type: Independent foundation
Purpose: Student loans to financially needy local students attending Hannibal-LaGrange College, Culver-Stocton College or Central Methodist College, MO.
Financial data: Year ended 12/31/2011. Assets, $512,001 (M); Expenditures, $45,984; Total giving, $37,615.
Type of support: Student loans—to individuals; Support to graduates or students of specific schools.
Application information: Applications accepted.
    Deadline(s): None
    Additional information: Application forms can be obtained from the financial aid office of the respective colleges.
EIN: 436029573

5039
Charles Lyons Memorial Foundation, Inc.

P.O. Box 236
Lexington, MO 64067-0236 (660) 259-6151

Foundation type: Independent foundation
Purpose: Scholarships to graduates of Lafayette County, MO, high schools who are residents of the county, for postsecondary education at accredited colleges, universities or trade schools.
Financial data: Year ended 12/31/2012. Assets, $578,929 (M); Expenditures, $63,237; Total giving, $49,700; Grants to individuals, 35 grants totaling $49,700 (high: $2,000, low: $1,300).
Fields of interest: Vocational education, post-secondary; Higher education; Scholarships/financial aid.

Type of support: Undergraduate support.
Application information: Application form required.
Deadline(s): Apr. 1
Applicants should submit the following:
1) Financial information
2) Class rank
3) SAT
4) GPA
5) ACT
6) Photograph
7) Transcripts
Additional information: Application should also include two references.
EIN: 436056850

5040
Make-A-Wish Foundation of Metro St. Louis, Inc.
600 Kellwood Pkwy.
Chesterfield, MO 63017-5806 (314) 918-9474
Contact: Luann Bott, Pres. and C.E.O.
FAX: (314) 918-8690;
E-mail: info@stlouis.wish.org; Toll-free tel.: (800) 548-5058; E-mail for Luann Bott: lbott@mo.wish.org; URL: http://stlouis.wish.org

Foundation type: Public charity
Purpose: Granting wishes to children primarily of St. Louis, MO who are suffering with life-threatening medical conditions.
Publications: Financial statement; Informational brochure.
Financial data: Year ended 08/31/2012. Assets, $2,826,575 (M); Expenditures, $3,643,106; Total giving, $2,025,232; Grants to individuals, totaling $2,025,232.
Fields of interest: Human services; Children.
Type of support: Grants for special needs.
Application information:
Initial approach: Referral
Additional information: Children must be referred to the foundation and determined to be eligible for a wish between the ages of 2 1/2 and 18 by their physician. Contact foundation for additional guidelines.
EIN: 431550697

5041
Edward Mallinckrodt, Jr. Foundation
7701 Forsyth Blvd., Ste. 1100
St. Louis, MO 63103-1823 (314) 955-3136
Contact: Oliver M. Langenberg, Chair. and Treas.

Foundation type: Independent foundation
Purpose: Grants for advancing knowledge in the various fileds of clinical and laboratory medical research.
Publications: Annual report.
Financial data: Year ended 09/30/2012. Assets, $36,491,572 (M); Expenditures, $2,042,405; Total giving, $1,880,000; Grants to individuals, 28 grants totaling $1,880,000.
Fields of interest: Medical research.
Type of support: Research.
Application information: Applications accepted. Interview required.
Initial approach: Proposal
Deadline(s): None
Applicants should submit the following:
1) Budget Information
2) Proposal
Additional information: Annual grants range in the $50,000 to $75,000 level, not to exceed $100,000. A grant is made on the assumption that the recipient will use the funds for the purpose indicated in the

applications while serving on the faculty of the same institution as at the time the application is made. Contact the foundation for additional guidelines.
EIN: 436030295

5042
Joe L. Mann, Jr. Memorial Fund
15 Lakeview Dr.
Lexington, MO 64067 (660) 259-2277
Contact: Joe Aull, Tr.
Application address: 629 Plz., Marshall, MO 65340

Foundation type: Independent foundation
Purpose: Scholarships to individuals who reside in Lafayette County, MO for continuing education at accredited colleges or universities.
Financial data: Year ended 12/31/2012. Assets, $544,529 (M); Expenditures, $3,542; Total giving, $1,000; Grant to an individual, 1 grant totaling $1,000.
Fields of interest: Higher education.
Type of support: Undergraduate support.
Application information: Applications accepted.
Deadline(s): Apr. 20
Additional information: Application should include transcripts.
EIN: 431204485

5043
Louis and Temple Marsch Charitable Trust
P.O. Box 387
St. Louis, MO 63166-0387 (217) 753-7362
Contact: Mary Jo Janssen
Application address: 205 S. 5th St., P.O. Box 19264, Springfield, IL 62794-9264, tel.: (217) 753-7362

Foundation type: Independent foundation
Purpose: Scholarships to high school graduates from specific geographical areas of southern IL, pursuing engineering or scientific fields of study on a full-time basis.
Financial data: Year ended 06/30/2013. Assets, $945,143 (M); Expenditures, $53,459; Total giving, $32,800.
Fields of interest: Engineering school/education; Science.
Type of support: Scholarships—to individuals.
Application information: Applications accepted. Application form required.
Initial approach: Letter or telephone
Deadline(s): Apr. 1
Applicants should submit the following:
1) Transcripts
2) Letter(s) of recommendation
Additional information: See program description for a list of counties and townships from which recipients are chosen. Application should also include acceptance letter from university.
Program description:
Scholarship Fund: Recipients must be from one of the following locales in southern IL: Christian, Montgomery, or Macoupin counties; the townships of Auburn, Pawnee, Divernon, Rochester, and Mechanicsburg in Sangamon County; or the townships of Moweaqua, Flat Branch, or Shelbyville in Shelby County. Generally five to fifteen new recipients are chosen each year. Students must be enrolled on a full-time basis, pursue an education in engineering or a scientific field, and maintain at least a "C" average. Verified transcripts of courses taken and grades received are required during scholarship funding. The Board must be notified of any change in circumstances.
EIN: 376129244

5044
Loy Crump Martin Charitable Trust
720 E. Broadway
Columbia, MO 65201

Foundation type: Independent foundation
Purpose: Scholarships to students of Southern Boone High School, Ashland, MO.
Financial data: Year ended 09/30/2013. Assets, $1,235,929 (M); Expenditures, $84,125; Total giving, $61,500.
Type of support: Support to graduates or students of specific schools.
Application information: Applications not accepted.
Additional information: Unsolicited requests for funds not considered or acknowledged.
EIN: 436589909

5045
Joseph W. Martino Trust
P.O. Box 387
St. Louis, MO 63166-0387 (800) 313-1305
Contact: Patricia Tyus

Foundation type: Independent foundation
Purpose: Scholarships to members and children of members of the Boys Club of St. Louis, MO, or the B.P.O.E. Lodge, No. 9.
Financial data: Year ended 11/30/2012. Assets, $733,456 (M); Expenditures, $42,499; Total giving, $27,488.
Fields of interest: Boys clubs; Men.
Type of support: Scholarships—to individuals.
Application information: Applications accepted. Application form required.
Deadline(s): None
EIN: 436274479

5046
Mother Joseph Rogan Marymount Foundation
43 Rio Vista
Saint Louis, MO 63124 (636) 391-6248
Contact: Christopher Imbs, Dir.
Application address: 100 S. 4th St., Ste. 800, Saint Louis, MO 63102

Foundation type: Independent foundation
Purpose: Scholarships to financially needy high school students and student loans to college and university students. Applicants must be U.S. citizens and residents of greater St. Louis, MO.
Financial data: Year ended 06/30/2012. Assets, $1,128,038 (M); Expenditures, $47,270; Total giving, $40,000.
Type of support: Student loans—to individuals; Undergraduate support.
Application information: Applications accepted.
Deadline(s): None
Additional information: Application by letter outlining financial need.
EIN: 237418805

5047
William E. McElroy Charitable Foundation
P.O. Box 387
St. Louis, MO 63166-0387 (217) 753-7362
Contact: Mary Jo Janssen
Application Address: US Bank N.A. , P.O. Box 19264Springfield, IL 62794-9264 Tel.: (217) 753-7362

Foundation type: Independent foundation

Purpose: Scholarships to boys graduating from high schools in Sangamon County, IL.
Financial data: Year ended 07/31/2012. Assets, $3,562,773 (M); Expenditures, $182,249; Total giving, $139,879.
Fields of interest: Higher education; Young adults, male.
Type of support: Support to graduates or students of specific schools; Undergraduate support.
Application information: Application form required.
  Initial approach: Letter or telephone
  Deadline(s): None
  Applicants should submit the following:
    1) SAT
    2) Letter(s) of recommendation
    3) ACT
EIN: 376306920

5048
Arthur B. and Anna F. McGlothlan Trust
P.O. Box 387
St. Louis, MO 63166-0387 (816) 364-7235
Contact: Shanon Moore
Application address: c/o U.S. Bank, N.A., 415 Francis St., St. Joseph, MO 64501-1715

Foundation type: Independent foundation
Purpose: Scholarships to graduates of St. Joseph, MO, area high schools who will attend a church-related or -affiliated college.
Financial data: Year ended 06/30/2013. Assets, $260,286 (M); Expenditures, $13,717; Total giving, $8,588; Grants to individuals, 25 grants totaling $8,588 (high: $500, low: $250).
Fields of interest: Theological school/education; Christian agencies & churches.
Type of support: Support to graduates or students of specific schools; Undergraduate support.
Application information: Applications accepted. Application form required.
  Deadline(s): Apr. 1
  Applicants should submit the following:
    1) Letter(s) of recommendation
    2) Photograph
    3) Transcripts
    4) GPA
    5) Financial information
  Additional information: Contact foundation for current application deadline/guidelines.
EIN: 446009610

5049
Paul & Regina Meyer Scholarship Trust
1517 E., Bradford Pkwy.
Springfield, MO 65804 (417) 890-7770
Contact: Sumer Tripp
Application address: c/o Trust Company of the Ozarks, Springfield MO, 65804

Foundation type: Independent foundation
Purpose: Scholarships to graduates of Sikeston High School, MO, for higher education at a MO institution.
Financial data: Year ended 03/31/2013. Assets, $1,546,624 (M); Expenditures, $88,336; Total giving, $71,485; Grants to individuals, totaling $71,485.
Type of support: Support to graduates or students of specific schools; Undergraduate support.
Application information: Application form required.
  Deadline(s): Apr. 1
EIN: 436721837

5050
MFA Foundation
201 Ray Young Dr.
Columbia, MO 65201-3568
Contact: Larna Lavelle, Secy.-Treas.
URL: http://www.mfafoundation.com/

Foundation type: Company-sponsored foundation
Purpose: Scholarships to graduating high school seniors of MO, for attendance at any accredited college or university to pursue any course of study and reside in areas where MFA agencies operate.
Publications: Application guidelines; Informational brochure.
Financial data: Year ended 06/30/2012. Assets, $14,438,601 (M); Expenditures, $856,372; Total giving, $775,987; Grants to individuals, 336 grants totaling $643,086 (high: $2,000, low: $500).
Fields of interest: Higher education; Scholarships/financial aid; Agriculture.
Type of support: Scholarships—to individuals; Undergraduate support.
Application information: Applications accepted. Application form required.
  Deadline(s): Mar. 15
  Applicants should submit the following:
    1) Photograph
    2) Class rank
  Additional information: Students should contact their guidance counselor for application forms.
Program description:
  Scholarships: The foundation awards college scholarships of $2,000 to high school seniors located in areas of MFA agency operations planning to study agriculture or other fields of study that benefit rural life. Recipients are selected based on applicant's participation and leadership in school, church, and community, the applicants reputation for good citizenship and moral character, applicant's financial need, sources of income, and willingness to work, and the applicant's academic progress.
EIN: 436026877

5051
MHA Center for Education
P.O. Box 60
Jefferson Cty, MO 65102-0060 (573) 893-3700
Contact: Herb B. Kuhn, Pres.

Foundation type: Public charity
Purpose: Healthcare scholarships to residents of MO.
Financial data: Year ended 12/31/2011. Assets, $30,659,956 (M); Expenditures, $2,829,285; Total giving, $1,487,750; Grants to individuals, totaling $518,640.
Fields of interest: Nursing school/education.
Type of support: Undergraduate support.
Application information: Applications not accepted.
  Additional information: Unsolicited requests for funds not considered or acknowledged.
EIN: 430898947

5052
MICDS Scholarship Fund
(formerly Mary Institute Scholarship Fund)
101 N. Warson Rd.
St. Louis, MO 63124-1399 (314) 995-7410

Foundation type: Public charity
Purpose: Scholarships for students attending Mary Institute and St. Louis Country Day School.

Financial data: Year ended 06/30/2012. Assets, $5,692,234 (M); Expenditures, $327,496; Total giving, $286,980.
Fields of interest: Education.
Type of support: Scholarships—to individuals; Support to graduates or students of specific schools.
Application information: Applications not accepted.
  Additional information: Unsolicited requests for funds not considered or acknowledged. Scholarships only for students attending MICDS.
EIN: 431220528

5053
Mid-America Arts Alliance
2018 Baltimore Ave.
Kansas City, MO 64108-1914 (816) 421-1388
Contact: Mary Kennedy McCabe, Exec. Dir.
FAX: (816) 421-3918; E-mail: info@maaa.org;
URL: http://www.maaa.org

Foundation type: Public charity
Purpose: Individual assistance to artists in the mid-America region (Arkansas, kansas, Missouri, Nebraska, Oklahoma and Texas) in an effort to expand their skills and knowledge in the arts.
Publications: Application guidelines.
Financial data: Year ended 06/30/2011. Assets, $4,715,497 (M); Expenditures, $4,179,148; Total giving, $595,245; Grants to individuals, totaling $14,000.
Fields of interest: Arts, artist's services; Arts.
Type of support: Grants to individuals.
Application information: Applications accepted. Application form available on the grantmaker's web site.
  Send request by: On-line
  Applicants should submit the following:
    1) Resume
    2) Budget Information
  Additional information: See web site for additional guidelines.
Program description:
  Professional Development Support Program: This program supports arts-based professionals and artists across the M-AAA region (Arkansas, Kansas, Missouri, Nebraska, Oklahoma and Texas). Professional development is supported through this grant program which reimburses up to $1,000 for expenses incurred thought activities that professionally enhance business acumen and expand skills and knowledge in the arts. applicant must be at least 21 years of age, have lived in the M-AAA region full-time for at least two years prior to applying and intend to remain a regional resident during the entire grant period, have not received a professional Development Support/Travel Stipend Grant in the previous fiscal year, and be in good standing with M-AAA, with no overdue or delinquent reports and/or grant documents.
EIN: 237303693

5054
Miles Educational Foundation
P.O. Box 387
Saint Louis, MO 63166-0387 (314) 505-8136
Contact: Jill Forbes, Trust Off., U.S. Bank, N.A.

Foundation type: Independent foundation
Purpose: Scholarships to graduates of Doniphan High School, MO for attendance at accredited colleges or universities.

Financial data: Year ended 12/31/2011. Assets, $640,227 (M); Expenditures, $46,069; Total giving, $30,000.
Type of support: Support to graduates or students of specific schools; Undergraduate support.
Application information:
 Initial approach: Letter or telephone
 Additional information: Contact foundation for additional information.
EIN: 436072185

5055
Minnesouri Scholarship Foundation
800 W. 47th St., Ste. 430
Kansas City, MO 64112-1246

Foundation type: Independent foundation
Purpose: Scholarships to employees of the Minnesouri Homes Association and their children in Miltona, MN and members of the surrounding community enrolled in four-year postsecondary courses of study. Some scholarships may be awarded for postsecondary technical studies.
Financial data: Year ended 12/31/2011. Assets, $15,725 (M); Expenditures, $15,038; Total giving, $15,000; Grants to individuals, 15 grants totaling $15,000 (high: $1,000, low: $1,000).
Fields of interest: Vocational education, post-secondary; Higher education.
Type of support: Employee-related scholarships.
Application information: Applications accepted. Application form required. Interview required.
 Additional information: Applicant must demonstrate need. Unsolicited requests for funds not considered or acknowledged.
EIN: 431929305

5056
Missouri Bar Foundation
326 Monroe
P. O. Box 119
Jefferson City, MO 65102-1069 (573) 635-4128
FAX: (573) 635-2811; E-mail: mobar@mobar.org;
URL: http://www.mobar.org/About_Us/
Information/Missouri_Bar_Foundation/
Missouri_Bar_Foundation.htm

Foundation type: Public charity
Purpose: Financial support for needy women members of the Missiouri Bar and/or needy dependents or deceased members. Awards to individuals who have helped improve the state's justice system.
Financial data: Year ended 12/31/2011. Assets, $2,167,874 (M); Expenditures, $201,031; Total giving, $141,647; Grants to individuals, totaling $16,111.
Fields of interest: Law school/education; Women.
Type of support: Awards/prizes; Grants for special needs.
Application information: Applications not accepted.
 Additional information: Unsolicited requests for funds not considered or acknowledged.
EIN: 446011930

5057
Missouri Federation of Music Clubs
c/o Duane D. Langley
1203 Whispering Pines Dr.
St. Louis, MO 63146-4541 (314) 878-2193
Contact: Arsene Burton, Recording Secy.
URL: http://www.missourifmc.com

Foundation type: Public charity
Purpose: College scholarships for students of Missouri, pursuing a degree in music.
Financial data: Year ended 06/30/2010. Assets, $187,019 (M); Expenditures, $38,973; Total giving, $11,625; Grants to individuals, totaling $9,950.
Fields of interest: Arts education; Music.
Type of support: Scholarships—to individuals.
Application information: Applications accepted. Application form required.
 Deadline(s): Feb. 14
 Additional information: Application should include Junior Festival entries.
Program description:
 Scholarship: Scholarship range from $200 to $1,000 for students 18 years old or under as of Mar. 1, senior year in high school. Applicant must be a U.S. citizen or provide a birth certificate or naturalization certificate. Student must have participated in District IVB Festivals for a minimum of five years, including the current year, and must have completed college application and acceptance letter from the college, and be a music major.
EIN: 436216278

5058
Missouri Ozarks Community Action, Inc.
306 S. Pine St.
P.O. Box 69
Richland, MO 65556-0069 (573) 765-3263
FAX: (573) 765-4426; Toll-free tel.: (800) 876-3264; URL: http://www.mocaonline.org

Foundation type: Public charity
Purpose: Assistance to low-income residents of Camden, Crawford, Gasconade, Laclede, Maries, Miller, Phelps, and Pulaski counties, MO, with transportation, housing, education, food, shelter, and utility.
Financial data: Year ended 01/31/2013. Assets, $2,996,818 (M); Expenditures, $9,540,792; Total giving, $3,132,140; Grants to individuals, totaling $3,132,140.
Fields of interest: Economically disadvantaged.
Type of support: Grants for special needs.
Application information: Contact agency for information on assistance.
EIN: 430837331

5059
Missouri State University Foundation
300 S. Jefferson St., Ste. 100
Springfield, MO 65806-2211 (417) 836-4143
FAX: (417) 836-6886;
E-mail: foundation@missouristate.edu;
URL: http://www.missouristatefoundation.org/

Foundation type: Public charity
Purpose: Scholarship support to students at Missouri State University for continuing education.
Publications: Annual report.
Financial data: Year ended 06/30/2011. Assets, $117,027,132 (M); Expenditures, $15,311,859; Total giving, $14,547,113; Grants to individuals, totaling $1,599,021.
Fields of interest: Higher education.
Type of support: Scholarships—to individuals; Technical education support; Undergraduate support.
Application information: Applications accepted. Application form required. Application form available on the grantmaker's web site.
 Send request by: On-line
 Deadline(s): Mar. 1

Additional information: See web site for additional application guidelines.
EIN: 431234200

5060
Missouri Valley Community Action Agency
1415 S. Odell
Marshall, MO 65340-3144 (660) 886-7476
FAX: (660) 886-5868; E-mail: info@mvcaa.net;
URL: http://www.mvcaa.net/

Foundation type: Public charity
Purpose: Assistance to low-income people, targeting the physically disadvantaged, the elderly and children of Carroll, Chariton, Johnson, Lafayette, Pettis, Ray and Saline counties, MO, with affordable housing, energy and rental assistance, weatherization, head start programs and other needs.
Financial data: Year ended 08/31/2011. Assets, $4,953,145 (M); Expenditures, $10,457,904; Total giving, $2,416,844; Grants to individuals, totaling $2,416,844.
Fields of interest: Human services; Children; Aging; Disabilities, people with.
Type of support: Grants for special needs.
Application information: Applications accepted.
 Initial approach: Telephone
EIN: 430837257

5061
NASB Foundation, Inc.
(formerly North American Savings Bank Foundation, Inc.)
12498 S. 71 Hwy.
Grandview, MO 64030 (816) 765-2200
Contact: Christine Schaben

Foundation type: Operating foundation
Purpose: Scholarships to graduating seniors in communities where North American Savings Bank, F.S.B. conducts business, for attendance at any public college, community college, or accredited trade school within the state of MO.
Financial data: Year ended 09/30/2013. Assets, $0 (M); Expenditures, $59,594; Total giving, $58,875; Grants to individuals, 25 grants totaling $58,875 (high: $5,000, low: $125).
Fields of interest: Vocational education, post-secondary; College (community/junior); College.
Type of support: Scholarships—to individuals; Support to graduates or students of specific schools.
Application information: Applications accepted. Application form required.
 Applicants should submit the following:
  1) Essay
  2) Letter(s) of recommendation
  3) Transcripts
 Additional information: Applicant must demonstrate need. Applications available through high school administrators.
EIN: 431796549

5062
National Children's Cancer Society, Inc.
1 S. Memorial Dr., Ste. 800
St. Louis, MO 63102-2439 (314) 241-1600
Contact: Mark Stolze, Pres. and C.E.O.
FAX: (314) 241-1996; Toll-free tel.: (800) 532-6459; URL: http://
www.nationalchildrenscancersociety.org

Foundation type: Public charity
Purpose: Financial assistance for children with cancer and their families.
Publications: Application guidelines; Annual report; Informational brochure; Newsletter.
Financial data: Year ended 09/30/2012. Assets, $4,110,737 (M); Expenditures, $22,799,245; Total giving, $15,249,828; Grants to individuals, totaling $2,977,853.
Fields of interest: Health care, patient services; Health care; Cancer.
Type of support: Grants for special needs.
Application information: Application form required. Interview required.
　　Initial approach: Letter
　　Send request by: Mail
　　Additional information: Application for assistance must be accompanied by a letter of support from a hospital professional. See web site for additional guidelines.
Program descriptions:
　　Beyond the Cure Scholarship Program: This program provides scholarships to childhood cancer survivors who have demonstrated the ability to overcome the difficult challenges of cancer with determination and motivation.
　　Financial Assistance: The organization provides financial assistance to families of children who have been diagnosed with cancer, to assist in lodging, meals, transportation, health insurance costs, and medical expenses not otherwise covered by insurance.
EIN: 371227890

5063
Robert L. Nichols, Jr. Scholarship Foundation

1 S. Main, Ste. 1
Webb City, MO　64870

Foundation type: Independent foundation
Purpose: Scholarships to graduating seniors of Terrell High School, TX.
Financial data: Year ended 12/31/2012. Assets, $207,616 (M); Expenditures, $10,716; Total giving, $10,000; Grants to individuals, 2 grants totaling $10,000 (high: $5,000, low: $5,000).
Fields of interest: Women.
Type of support: Support to graduates or students of specific schools; Undergraduate support.
Application information: Applications accepted. Application form required. Interview required.
　　Deadline(s): Contact foundation for current application deadline
EIN: 756081322

5064
North Central Missouri College Foundation, Inc.

1301 Main St.
Trenton, MO　64683-1824　(660) 359-2263
Contact: Jeff Crowley

Foundation type: Public charity
Purpose: College scholarships for students to attend North Central Missouri College, Trenton, MO.
Financial data: Year ended 06/30/2012. Assets, $3,176,327 (M); Expenditures, $1,018,560; Total giving, $913,070; Grants to individuals, totaling $60,550.
Fields of interest: Higher education.
Type of support: Scholarships—to individuals; Support to graduates or students of specific schools.

Application information: Applications accepted. Application form required.
　　Additional information: Scholarships are awarded to students who are in good standing. Contact the foundation for additional guidelines.
EIN: 431423040

5065
North East Community Action Corporation

16 N. Court St.
P.O. Box 470
Bowling Green, MO　63334-0470　(573) 324-2231
Contact: Don Patrick, Pres. and C.E.O.
FAX: (573) 324-3960; E-mail: necac@necac.org; Toll-free tel.: (800) 735-2466; TDD: (800) 735-2966; URL: http://www.necac.org

Foundation type: Public charity
Purpose: Assistance to disadvantaged low-income elderly, youth, handicapped individuals and families in the twelve county area of Lewis, Lincoln, Macon, Marion, Monroe, Montgomery, Pike, Ralls, Randolph, Shelby, St. Charles and Warren, MO, with housing assistance, utilities, medical, dental, hospital expenses, and other needs.
Financial data: Year ended 09/30/2011. Assets, $17,048,896 (M); Expenditures, $15,725,340; Total giving, $3,917,762; Grants to individuals, totaling $3,917,762.
Fields of interest: Human services; Youth; Aging; Disabilities, people with; Economically disadvantaged.
Type of support: Grants for special needs.
Application information:
　　Initial approach: Telephone
EIN: 431017571

5066
The North Platte Foundation

P.O. Box 68
Dearborn, MO　64439-0068
Contact: Jimmy Paden, Pres.
Application address: c/o North Platte High School, Attn.: Ms. Babcock, 212 W. 6th St., Dearborn, MO 64439-9400, tel.: (816) 450-3344

Foundation type: Public charity
Purpose: Scholarships to graduating seniors in the North Platte R-I, MO school district.
Financial data: Year ended 06/30/2012. Assets, $167,767 (M); Expenditures, $15,300; Total giving, $15,300; Grants to individuals, totaling $15,300.
Fields of interest: Higher education.
Type of support: Support to graduates or students of specific schools; Undergraduate support.
Application information: Applications accepted. Application form required.
　　Deadline(s): Apr. 5
　　Additional information: Application available in school guidance office.
EIN: 431725048

5067
Northeast Missouri Area Agency on Aging

815 N. Osteopathy St.
Kirksville, MO　63501-1367　(660) 665-4682
URL: http://www.nemoaaa.com

Foundation type: Public charity
Purpose: Services for older persons throughout northeast MO, to help them to maintain maximum independence and dignity in a home environment. Examples of services include transportation, legal

services, personal care, and medication management.
Financial data: Year ended 06/30/2011. Assets, $568,562 (M); Expenditures, $3,281,332; Total giving, $2,969,799.
Fields of interest: Aging.
Type of support: In-kind gifts.
Application information:
　　Initial approach: Letter
　　Additional information: Contact foundation for eligibility criteria.
EIN: 430995687

5068
Orscheln Industries Foundation Inc.

P.O. Box 280
Moberly, MO　65270-0280　(660) 263-4900
Contact: R. Brent Bradshaw
Application address: P.O. Box 266, Moberly, MO 65270

Foundation type: Company-sponsored foundation
Purpose: Scholarships to graduates of Cairo, Higbee, Madison, Moberly, and Westran high schools, of Randolph County, MO. A limited number of scholarships go to children of Orschein employees.
Publications: Application guidelines.
Financial data: Year ended 09/30/2012. Assets, $18,934,299 (M); Expenditures, $698,391; Total giving, $628,813; Grants to individuals, totaling $82,250.
Fields of interest: Higher education.
Type of support: Employee-related scholarships; Support to graduates or students of specific schools.
Application information: Applications accepted. Application form required. Interview required.
　　Deadline(s): Apr. 1
　　Applicants should submit the following:
　　　1) ACT
　　　2) SAT
　　　3) GPA
　　　4) Transcripts
Program description:
　　Orscheln Industries Foundation Scholarships: The foundation awards college scholarships to graduating seniors from Cairo, Higbee, Madison, Moberly, and Western High Schools in Randolph County, MO. Applicants must have of a GPA of 3.5 and excel in academic achievement and leadership ability. The award consists of $500 per semester to assist the student in meeting educational expenses. A limited number of college scholarships are also awarded to dependent children of full-time employees of Orscheln and affiliated companies.
Company name: Orscheln Group
EIN: 237115623

5069
Ozarks Area Community Action Corporation

215 S. Barnes Ave.
Springfield, MO　65802-2204　(417) 862-4314
Contact: Carl Rosenkranz, Exec. Dir.
FAX: (417) 864-3499;
E-mail: crosenkranz@oacac-caa.org; Tel. for Carl Rosenkranz : (417)-864-3492; URL: http://www.oacac-caa.org

Foundation type: Public charity
Purpose: Assistance to low-income individuals and families of Barry, Christian, Dade, Dallas, Greene, Lawrence, Polk, Stone, Taney and Webster counties in southwest MO, for energy, housing, and family planning needs.

Financial data: Year ended 09/30/2011. Assets, $5,716,617 (M); Expenditures, $30,628,653.
Fields of interest: Economically disadvantaged.
Type of support: Grants for special needs.
Application information: Applications accepted.
EIN: 430836672

5070
Thomas M. Paul Memorial Trust
P.O. Box 387
Saint Louis, MO   63166   (816) 364-7245
Contact: Bill Titcomb
Application address: U.S. Bank, N.A., c/o Bill Titcomb, P.O. Box 398, St. Joseph, MO 64501, tel.: (816) 364-7245

Foundation type: Independent foundation
Purpose: Scholarships to students of Missouri Western State College who have graduated from St. Joseph, MO, high schools and who are preparing for careers in the medical field.
Financial data: Year ended 12/31/2012. Assets, $890,113 (M); Expenditures, $55,731; Total giving, $40,500.
Fields of interest: Medical school/education.
Type of support: Support to graduates or students of specific schools; Undergraduate support.
Application information: Application form required.
> *Initial approach:* Telephone
> *Deadline(s):* Prior to semester registration
> *Applicants should submit the following:*
>> 1) Letter(s) of recommendation
>> 2) Financial information
>> 3) Photograph
>> 4) Class rank
>> 5) Transcripts
>> 6) SAT
>> 7) GPA
>> 8) ACT

EIN: 436009612

5071
Peculiar Charitable Foundation
P.O. Box 331
Peculiar, MO   64078-0331
Contact: Mary Catherine Dobson, Dir.
Application address: P.O. Box 347, Raymore, MO 64083

Foundation type: Independent foundation
Purpose: Scholarships to worthy high school seniors of Cass County public high schools, MO for full time attendance at any four year accredited college or university.
Financial data: Year ended 12/31/2012. Assets, $5,777,141 (M); Expenditures, $345,358; Total giving, $304,200.
Fields of interest: Higher education.
Type of support: Scholarships—to individuals.
Application information: Applications accepted. Application form required.
> *Deadline(s):* Mar. 27
> *Applicants should submit the following:*
>> 1) Class rank
>> 2) SAT
>> 3) Resume
>> 4) GPA
>> 5) ACT
>> 6) Essay
> *Additional information:* Application should also include two letters of reference.

EIN: 436077697

5072
People to People International
911 Main St., Ste. 2110
Kansas City, MO   64105-5305   (816) 531-4701
Contact: Mary Eisenhower, Pres. and C.E.O.
FAX: (816) 561-7502; E-mail: ptpi@ptpi.org;
URL: http://www.ptpi.org

Foundation type: Public charity
Purpose: Scholarships to students for higher education who are involved in any of the organization's programs.
Publications: Application guidelines; Newsletter.
Financial data: Year ended 12/31/2011. Assets, $4,688,028 (M); Expenditures, $4,578,115; Total giving, $115,246; Grants to individuals, totaling $41,278.
Fields of interest: Elementary/secondary education; Secondary school/education; Higher education.
Type of support: Scholarships—to individuals.
Application information: Applications accepted. Application form required. Application form available on the grantmaker's web site.
> *Send request by:* Online
> *Deadline(s):* Varies
> *Applicants should submit the following:*
>> 1) Financial information
>> 2) Transcripts
>> 3) Letter(s) of recommendation
>> 4) Essay

Program descriptions:
Global Youth Forum Scholarship: This scholarship awards full or partial tuition for the organization's annual conference for student leaders, the Global Youth Forum. Eligible applicants must be between the ages of 13 and 18, and must not yet have graduated from high school. Scholarships are awarded based on the quality of work presented in the application, as well as financial need.
James & Eunice Doty PTPI/Congressional Award Scholarship: This scholarship provides an outstanding middle or high school student (excluding high school seniors) with an opportunity to attend the organization's Global Youth Forum. Awards include all program fees and airfare. Applicants must be recipients of a Congressional Award (bronze, silver, or gold), currently be a middle or high school student who is in good academic standing, and demonstrate maturity, well-rounded interests, and financial need.
Joyce C. Hall College Scholarship: Up to five scholarships of $2,000 each are available to organization participants, to support study at a college or university. Applicants must have participated in one of the organization's programs (Student Ambassador Program, Student or University Chapter Programs, School and Classroom Program, or Global Youth Forum); applicants must also be current organizations members who are enrolled as a high-school senior or full-time college or university student with a 3.0 GPA (on a 4.0 scale). Funds may be used to pay tuition, books, and supplies.
Mary Jean Eisenhower Partner in Peace Scholarship: This annual scholarship recognizes students' accomplishments in peace-building, international understanding, and year-long involvement with their community. Applicants must be current organization members (ages 13 to 18) who exemplify the organization's mission of peace through understanding. Recipients will receive paid registration to attend the organization's annual conference, the Global Youth Forum, or equivalent funds toward university tuition/books (if a graduating senior)

EIN: 440659517

5073
Pi Beta Phi Foundation
1154 Town & Country Commons Dr.
Town and Country, MO   63017-8200   (636) 256-1357
Contact: Teri Champion, Exec. Dir.
FAX: (636) 256-8124; E-mail: fndn@pibetaphi.org;
E-Mail for Teri Champion: teri@pibetaphi.org;
URL: http://www.pibetaphifoundation.org

Foundation type: Public charity
Purpose: Scholarships and fellowships to Phi Beta Phi Fraternity members. Financial assistance also to indigent alumnae.
Publications: Application guidelines.
Financial data: Year ended 06/30/2012. Assets, $10,885,363 (M); Expenditures, $1,944,481; Total giving, $1,024,376; Grants to individuals, totaling $403,998.
Fields of interest: Fraternal societies; Women; Young adults, female.
Type of support: Undergraduate support; Grants for special needs.
Application information: Applications accepted. Application form required. Application form available on the grantmaker's web site.
> *Initial approach:* See foundation web site for requirements
> *Applicants should submit the following:*
>> 1) Letter(s) of recommendation
>> 2) Resume
>> 3) FAFSA
>> 4) Financial information

Program descriptions:
Alumnae Continuing Education Scholarship: This program awards scholarships to a dues-paying alumna member of Pi Beta Phi Fraternity who is planning a course of study to enhance career qualifications at a career, vocational, or technical school, as well as at a college or university. Applicants must have been out of school for more than two academic years, have a 3.0 minimum undergraduate or graduate GPA, and have a record of service to Pi Beta Phi, campus, and community.
Emma Harper Turner Fund: The foundation provides one-time grants or monthly stipends on a confidential basis to alumnae in dire financial need, to alumnae continuing their education due to extreme circumstances, and for the education expenses of collegians who have experienced a life change that jeopardizes their ability to stay in school.
Graduate Fellowship: The foundation awards fellowships to due-paying alumnae members of Pi Beta Phi fraternity. Applicants must be planning full-time graduate work in a chosen field at an accredited college, university, or technical/professional school. Applicants must have no more than four academic years prior to application year, a 3.0 minimum undergraduate or graduate GPA, and a record of service to Pi Beta Phi, campus, and community.
Sign of the Arrow Melissa Scholarship: The primary criterion for this award is outstanding community service. Applicants must have senior class standing during the year in which the award is made, be a full time student, have a minimum cumulative GPA of 3.1, and meet all other undergraduate requirements.
Undergraduate Scholarship: The foundation awards academic undergraduate scholarships to Phi Beta Phi Fraternity members. Applicants must have a 3.0 minimum GPA (Canadian students a 70 percent GPA) and a record of service to Pi Beta Phi, campus, and community.

EIN: 431542735

5074
PKD Foundation
(formerly Polycystic Kidney Research Foundation)
8330 Ward Pkwy., Ste. 510
Kansas City, MO 64114-2027 (816) 931-2600
Contact: Jackie Hancock, C.E.O.
FAX: (816) 931-8655;
E-mail: pkdcure@pkdcure.org; Toll-free tel.: (800)
PKD-CURE; URL: http://www.pkdcure.org

Foundation type: Public charity
Purpose: Grants and fellowships to investigators for research for the cause, treatment, and cure of polycystic kidney disease.
Publications: Annual report; Financial statement; Informational brochure; Newsletter.
Financial data: Year ended 06/30/2012. Assets, $2,409,330 (M); Expenditures, $6,931,107; Total giving, $1,425,167.
Fields of interest: Kidney research.
Type of support: Conferences/seminars; Fellowships; Research; Grants to individuals; Foreign applicants; Postdoctoral support.
Application information: Applications accepted. Application form required. Application form available on the grantmaker's web site.
  Initial approach: Application form
  Send request by: Mail or e-mail
  Deadline(s): Jan. 15 for Translational Research Program; Mar. 1, Sept. 1, and Dec. 1 for Bridge Grants; Aug. 15 for Research Grants and Fellowships; Sept. 1 for Young Investigator Grant
  Final notification: Recipients notified in four months
  Applicants should submit the following:
    1) Proposal
    2) Financial information
    3) Curriculum vitae
    4) Budget Information
EIN: 431266906

5075
John Williams Poillon Memorial Scholarship Trust
c/o UMB Bank, N.A.
P.O. Box 415044 M/S 1020307
Kansas City, MO 64141-6692

Foundation type: Independent foundation
Purpose: Scholarships to graduating high school seniors who are dependents of a member of the military forces assigned to military reservation at Fort Leavenworth, KS, within the last eighteen months, and to dependents of current civilian employees of Fort Leavenworth, KS.
Financial data: Year ended 12/31/2012. Assets, $133,745 (M); Expenditures, $7,544; Total giving, $4,500.
Fields of interest: Higher education; Military/veterans.
Type of support: Undergraduate support.
Application information: Applications accepted. Application form required.
  Deadline(s): Last business day of Apr.
  Additional information: Applicant must be accepted to an accredited institution of higher learning.
EIN: 486125025

5076
Edwin M. Porter Educational Fund
P.O. Box 387
St. Louis, MO 63166

Foundation type: Independent foundation

Purpose: Scholarships to students from the Bowling Green R-1 School District, MO, for postsecondary education.
Financial data: Year ended 03/31/2013. Assets, $268,375 (M); Expenditures, $16,550; Total giving, $9,650; Grants to individuals, totaling $9,650.
Fields of interest: Higher education.
Type of support: Support to graduates or students of specific schools; Undergraduate support.
Application information: Applications accepted. Application form required.
  Deadline(s): None
  Additional information: Application forms are available from the guidance counselor and principal of Bowling Green high schools, MO.
EIN: 436225390

5077
Queen of Peace Center
325 N. Newstead Ave.
St. Louis, MO 63108-2707 (314) 531-0511
Contact: Lara Pennington, Exec. Dir.
FAX: (314) 652-2637;
E-mail: lpennington@ccstl.org; E-Mail For Lara Pennington: lpennington@ccstl.org; URL: http://www.qopcstl.org

Foundation type: Public charity
Purpose: Grants for food, shelter, clothing, and other expenses to chemically-dependent women and their families who are clients at the Queen of Peace Center, St. Louis, MO.
Financial data: Year ended 06/30/2012. Assets, $6,830,611 (M); Expenditures, $7,266,099; Total giving, $2,137,748; Grants to individuals, totaling $2,137,748.
Fields of interest: Substance abuse, treatment; Women.
Type of support: Grants for special needs.
Application information: Contact foundation for eligibility requirements.
EIN: 431528548

5078
Ray-Carroll Scholarship Fund
(formerly Ray-Carroll County Grain Growers Scholarship Fund, Inc.)
P.O. Box 158
Richmond, MO 64085-0158 (816) 776-2291
Contact: Mike Nordwald

Foundation type: Company-sponsored foundation
Purpose: Scholarships to graduating seniors residing in the Ray-Carroll Cooperative service area to attend colleges in MO. Scholarships must be used within two years of graduation from high school.
Financial data: Year ended 08/31/2013. Assets, $158,085 (M); Expenditures, $15,710; Total giving, $14,550; Grants to individuals, 30 grants totaling $14,550 (high: $500, low: $500).
Type of support: Undergraduate support.
Application information: Applications accepted. Application form required.
  Deadline(s): Six weeks after application form is sent out
  Additional information: Application should include teacher evaluation, transcripts, a statement of plans, goals, and the college to be attended.
EIN: 431244005

5079
Harry Bertram Reynolds Trust
P.O. Box 387
Saint Louis, MO 63166 (270) 575-5334
Contact: James Acton
Application address: 201 N. Elm, Centralia, IL 62801

Foundation type: Independent foundation
Purpose: Scholarships to residents of Jefferson County, IL, for high school, trade school, and higher education.
Financial data: Year ended 12/31/2012. Assets, $69,513 (M); Expenditures, $5,729; Total giving, $2,700.
Fields of interest: Vocational education; Higher education.
Type of support: Technical education support; Precollege support; Undergraduate support.
Application information: Applications accepted. Application form required. Interview required.
  Initial approach: In person
  Deadline(s): None
EIN: 376027000

5080
Ronald McDonald House Charities of Kansas City, Inc.
(formerly Ronald McDonald House Charities of the Heart of America, Inc.)
2502 Cherry St.
Kansas City, MO 64108-2751 (816) 842-8321
Contact: Holly Buckendahl, C.E.O. and Exec. Dir.
FAX: (816) 842-7033; E-mail: info@rmhckc.org;
E-Mail For Holly Buckendahl: hbuckendahl@rmhckc.org; URL: http://www.rmhckc.org

Foundation type: Public charity
Purpose: Emergency housing to families whose children are receiving care for a serious illness or injury at a Kansas City, MO area hospital or treatment facility.
Financial data: Year ended 12/31/2011. Assets, $14,164,618 (M); Expenditures, $2,190,344.
Fields of interest: Human services; Children/youth; Terminal illness, people with; Economically disadvantaged.
Type of support: In-kind gifts.
Application information:
  Initial approach: Letter
  Additional information: Contact the charity for eligibility criteria.
EIN: 431190760

5081
Darrik S. Sabada Memorial Scholarship Foundation
1432 Westbrooke Ter. Dr.
Ballwin, MO 63021-7577 (636) 225-6054
Contact: David Sabada
URL: http://www.a-mrazek.com/tournament/mission.htm

Foundation type: Public charity
Purpose: Scholarships by nomination only to MO eighth graders looking to attend private high school and MO graduating high school seniors looking to attend college who have financial need.
Financial data: Year ended 12/31/2011. Assets, $436,006 (M); Expenditures, $62,374; Total giving, $56,500.
Type of support: Awards/grants by nomination only.
Application information: Applications not accepted.

Additional information: Unsolicited requests for funds not considered or acknowledged.
EIN: 431870059

5082
Greater Saint Louis Community Foundation
(formerly St. Louis Community Foundation)
319 N. 4th St., Ste. 300
Saint Louis, MO 63102-1906 (314) 588-8200
Contact: For scholarships: Amy B. Murphy, Dir., Scholarships and Donor Svcs.
Scholarship inquiry e-mail: amurphy@stlouisgives.org
FAX: (314) 588-8088;
E-mail: info@stlouisgives.org; URL: http://www.stlouisgives.org

Foundation type: Community foundation
Purpose: Scholarships to residents of the St. Louis, MO, metropolitan area for attendance at colleges in IL and MO.
Publications: Informational brochure.
Financial data: Year ended 03/31/2013. Assets, $219,377,679 (M); Expenditures, $35,980,434; Total giving, $33,338,981. Scholarships—to individuals amount not specified.
Fields of interest: Higher education; Scholarships/financial aid.
Type of support: Employee-related scholarships; Scholarships—to individuals; Support to graduates or students of specific schools; Undergraduate support.
Application information: Applications accepted. Application form required. Application form available on the grantmaker's web site.
> *Send request by:* On-line
> *Deadline(s):* Vary
> *Additional information:* See web site for a complete listing of scholarships.
EIN: 436023126

5083
Frank and Elizabeth Schafer Scholarship Fund
P.O. Box 387
Saint Louis, MO 63166 (573) 437-2174

Foundation type: Independent foundation
Purpose: Scholarships to graduates of Owensville High School, MO, pursuing two- or four-year college degrees, graduate degrees, or professional studies.
Financial data: Year ended 06/30/2013. Assets, $528,284 (M); Expenditures, $37,225; Total giving, $22,500; Grants to individuals, 31 grants totaling $22,500 (high: $1,000, low: $500).
Fields of interest: Higher education.
Type of support: Support to graduates or students of specific schools; Graduate support; Undergraduate support; Postgraduate support.
Application information: Applications accepted. Application form required. Interview required.
> *Applicants should submit the following:*
> 1) Transcripts
> 2) Letter(s) of recommendation
> *Additional information:* Application can be obtained from the Supt. of schools.
Program description:
> *Scholarships:* Scholarships are renewable and are limited to $5,000 per year per student. Recipients must carry a course load of at least 12 credits and maintain at least a 2.7 GPA.
EIN: 436294428

5084
The Scholarship Foundation of St. Louis
8215 Clayton Rd.
St. Louis, MO 63117-1107 (314) 725-7990
FAX: (314) 725-5231; E-mail: info@sfstl.org;
URL: http://www.sfstl.org

Foundation type: Public charity
Purpose: Interest-free educational loans and grants to postsecondary students of the St. Louis, MO, metropolitan area, who do not have the financial means to fulfill their educational means.
Financial data: Year ended 12/31/2012. Assets, $34,086,622 (M); Expenditures, $5,129,540; Total giving, $3,580,166; Grants to individuals, totaling $3,580,166.
Fields of interest: Higher education.
Type of support: Grants to individuals; Student loans—to individuals.
Application information: Applications accepted. Application form required.
> *Deadline(s):* Apr. 15 and Nov. 15
> *Applicants should submit the following:*
> 1) Transcripts
> 2) SAT
> 3) SAR
> 4) Letter(s) of recommendation
> 5) GPA
> 6) Financial information
> 7) Essay
> 8) ACT
EIN: 436031234

5085
Schowengerdt Family Scholarship Fund
12555 Manchester Rd.
St. Louis, MO 63131-3710
Application address: c/o Scholarship Committee, P.O. Box 786, Warrenton, MO 63383-0786

Foundation type: Independent foundation
Purpose: Scholarships to graduating high school seniors of MO to attend the University of Missouri-Columbia.
Financial data: Year ended 12/31/2012. Assets, $367,694 (M); Expenditures, $25,286; Total giving, $18,060; Grants to individuals, totaling $18,060.
Fields of interest: Higher education.
Type of support: Support to graduates or students of specific schools; Undergraduate support.
Application information: Applications accepted.
> *Additional information:* Students should contact their guidance counselor for additional application information.
EIN: 376318007

5086
A.J. Schwartze Linn High School Scholarship Fund Trust I
P.O. Box 779
Jefferson City, MO 65102-0779

Foundation type: Independent foundation
Purpose: Scholarships to graduates of Linn High School, MO, for higher education. Recipients must be in the top 20 percent of their graduating class.
Financial data: Year ended 12/31/2012. Assets, $418,349 (M); Expenditures, $49,234; Total giving, $42,490; Grants to individuals, 15 grants totaling $42,490 (high: $8,151, low: $43).
Type of support: Support to graduates or students of specific schools; Undergraduate support.

Application information: Application form required. Interview required.
> *Deadline(s):* Contact trust for current application deadline
> *Additional information:* Application must include essay.
EIN: 436816359

5087
A. J. Schwartze Scholarship Fund Trust
P.O. Box 779
Jefferson City, MO 65102
Application address: c/o Supt. Osage County R-III School Dist., P.O. Box 37, 143 E. Main St., Westphalia, MO 65085, tel.: (573) 455-2375

Foundation type: Independent foundation
Purpose: Scholarships to graduates of Fatima High School, MO, who are in the top twenty percent of their class.
Financial data: Year ended 12/31/2012. Assets, $303,506 (M); Expenditures, $66,166; Total giving, $60,742.
Type of support: Support to graduates or students of specific schools; Undergraduate support.
Application information: Applications accepted.
> *Deadline(s):* Apr. 1
> *Additional information:* Applications are to be completed by the student and returned to the High School Counselor for additional information requested by the trust from the High School.
EIN: 436550546

5088
A.J. Schwartze Scholarship Fund Trust II
P.O. Box 779
Jefferson City, MO 65102

Foundation type: Independent foundation
Purpose: Scholarships to graduates of Fatima High School, MO, ranking in the upper third of their graduating class who plan to attend a university, college, or vocational/technical school in MO.
Financial data: Year ended 12/31/2012. Assets, $189,836 (M); Expenditures, $96,212; Total giving, $91,540; Grants to individuals, 40 grants totaling $91,540 (high: $2,397, low: $2,180).
Type of support: Support to graduates or students of specific schools; Technical education support; Undergraduate support.
Application information: Applications accepted. Application form required.
> *Initial approach:* Letter
> *Deadline(s):* Mar. 15
EIN: 436685932

5089
A.J. Schwartze Trust - Chamois High School I
P.O. Box 779
Jefferson City, MO 65102-0779
Application address: c/o Chamois High School, Attn.: Superintendent, 616 S. Poplar St., Chamois, MO 65024-2649

Foundation type: Independent foundation
Purpose: Scholarships to students of Chamois High School, MO, for higher education.
Financial data: Year ended 12/31/2011. Assets, $516,837 (M); Expenditures, $55,795; Total giving, $48,905; Grants to individuals, 15 grants totaling $48,905 (high: $9,530, low: $68).
Fields of interest: Higher education.
Type of support: Scholarships—to individuals.

Application information: Applications accepted. Application form required. Interview required.
Initial approach: Contact scholarship selection committee
Applicants should submit the following:
1) Essay
Additional information: Students must be in the top 20 percent of the graduating class, be a person of good citizenship, and intend to further their education on a full-time basis at an institution of higher learning in Missouri.
EIN: 436837620

5090
A. J. Schwartze Trust - Chamois High School II
P.O. Box 779
Jefferson City, MO   65102
Application address: Chamois High School, Osage County R-I School Dist., 614 S. Poplar St., Chamois, MO 65024-2649

Foundation type: Independent foundation
Purpose: Scholarships to students in the top thirty-three and one-third percent of the graduating class of a high school of the Osage County R-I School District in Chamois, MO for higher education.
Financial data: Year ended 12/31/2012. Assets, $588,661 (M); Expenditures, $45,251; Total giving, $36,616; Grants to individuals, 16 grants totaling $36,616 (high: $2,397, low: $2,180).
Fields of interest: Higher education.
Type of support: Scholarships—to individuals.
Application information: Applications accepted. Application form required. Interview required.
Applicants should submit the following:
1) Class rank
2) SAT
3) ACT
4) GPA
5) Letter(s) of recommendation
6) Essay
Additional information: Applicant must be of good citizenship, and good moral character.
EIN: 436837621

5091
A. J. Schwartze Trust - Scholarship Fund III
P.O. Box 779
Jefferson City, MO   65102-0779
Application address: c/o Osage County R-III School Dist., Attn.: Supt., P.O. Box 37, 143 E. Main St., Westphalia, MO 65085-9717

Foundation type: Independent foundation
Purpose: Scholarships only to students in the top 20 percent of their graduating class at Fatima High School, Westphalia, MO.
Financial data: Year ended 12/31/2012. Assets, $391,448 (M); Expenditures, $61,778; Total giving, $55,226; Grants to individuals, 18 grants totaling $55,226 (high: $9,520, low: $767).
Fields of interest: Higher education.
Type of support: Support to graduates or students of specific schools; Undergraduate support.
Application information: Applications accepted. Application form required. Interview required.
Applicants should submit the following:
1) Transcripts
2) Essay
Additional information: Applicant must be of good citizenship, and good moral character.
EIN: 436804089

5092
A. J. Schwartze Trust - Scholarship Fund IV
P.O. Box 779
Jefferson City, MO   65102

Foundation type: Independent foundation
Purpose: Scholarships to graduating high school seniors of Fatima High School of Westphalia, MO, for attendance at accredited colleges or universities.
Financial data: Year ended 12/31/2012. Assets, $207,475 (M); Expenditures, $93,942; Total giving, $89,143; Grants to individuals, 39 grants totaling $89,143 (high: $2,397, low: $2,180).
Fields of interest: Higher education.
Type of support: Support to graduates or students of specific schools; Undergraduate support.
Application information: Applications accepted. Application form required. Interview required.
Applicants should submit the following:
1) Transcripts
2) Essay
Additional information: Students must be in the top thirty-three and one-third percent of the graduating class to be eligible for the scholarship.
EIN: 436804090

5093
A. J. Schwartze Trust Helias High School Scholarship Fund
P.O. Box 779
Jefferson City, MO   65102

Foundation type: Independent foundation
Purpose: Scholarships to graduating students attending Helias High School, MO, enrolled in a four year degree granting program at a college or university or a degree from a vocational/technical school.
Financial data: Year ended 12/31/2012. Assets, $105,656 (M); Expenditures, $57,269; Total giving, $53,028.
Fields of interest: Vocational education, post-secondary; Higher education.
Type of support: Support to graduates or students of specific schools.
Application information: Applications accepted. Application form required.
Applicants should submit the following:
1) Letter(s) of recommendation
2) Transcripts
3) Essay
EIN: 436700316

5094
A. J. Schwartze Trust Helias High School Scholarship Fund II
P.O. Box 779
Jefferson City, MO   65102-0779

Foundation type: Independent foundation
Purpose: Scholarships to graduating seniors of Helias High School, MO, for higher education.
Financial data: Year ended 12/31/2011. Assets, $140,466 (M); Expenditures, $50,202; Total giving, $47,430; Grants to individuals, 23 grants totaling $47,430 (high: $2,010, low: $2,010).
Fields of interest: Vocational education, post-secondary; Higher education.
Type of support: Support to graduates or students of specific schools; Undergraduate support.
Application information: Applications accepted. Application form required. Interview required.
Applicants should submit the following:

1) Transcripts
2) Letter(s) of recommendation
3) Essay
Additional information: Students should contact their school's guidance counselor for application information.
EIN: 436804088

5095
A. J. Schwartze Trust Helias High School Scholarship Fund III
P.O. Box 779
Jefferson City, MO   65102-0779
Application address: c/o Helias High School, Attn.: Scholarship Comm., 1305 Swifts Hwy., Jefferson City, MO 65101-2557

Foundation type: Independent foundation
Purpose: Scholarships to graduates of Helias High School, MO, for undergraduate education primarily at MO colleges, universities, or vocational/technical school in MO.
Financial data: Year ended 12/31/2012. Assets, $421,253 (M); Expenditures, $37,984; Total giving, $30,715; Grants to individuals, 16 grants totaling $30,714 (high: $9,530, low: $61).
Fields of interest: Vocational education, post-secondary; Higher education.
Type of support: Support to graduates or students of specific schools; Undergraduate support.
Application information: Applications accepted. Application form required.
Initial approach: Letter
Applicants should submit the following:
1) Transcripts
2) Letter(s) of recommendation
3) Essay
Additional information: Selection is based on good citizenship and good moral character.
EIN: 436837622

5096
A.J. Schwartze Trust Linn High School Scholarship Fund Trust II
P.O. Box 779
Jefferson City, MO   65102-0779

Foundation type: Independent foundation
Purpose: Scholarships to graduates of Linn High School, MO, for higher education.
Financial data: Year ended 12/31/2012. Assets, $346,634 (M); Expenditures, $88,421; Total giving, $82,386; Grants to individuals, 36 grants totaling $82,386 (high: $2,397, low: $2,180).
Fields of interest: Vocational education, post-secondary; Higher education.
Type of support: Support to graduates or students of specific schools; Undergraduate support.
Application information: Applications accepted. Application form required.
Applicants should submit the following:
1) Transcripts
2) Letter(s) of recommendation
3) Essay
Additional information: Students must be in the top thirty-three and one-third percent of the graduating class of a high school of the Osage County R-II School District in Linn, MO in order to be eligible for the scholarship.
EIN: 436816360

5097
Scottish Rite Foundation of Missouri, Inc.

3633 Lindell Blvd.
St. Louis, MO 63108-3301 (314) 533-5557
URL: http://moscottishrite.org/foundation/

Foundation type: Public charity
Purpose: Undergraduate scholarships to deserving individuals of MO, attending an accredited college or university and pursuing a bachelor's degree. Financial assistance for medical, dental, and personal needs to children who would otherwise have to do without the treatment or benefit.
Financial data: Year ended 12/31/2011. Assets, $7,457,644 (M); Expenditures, $509,706; Total giving, $391,004; Grants to individuals, totaling $75,966.
Fields of interest: Higher education; Children; Economically disadvantaged.
Type of support: Scholarships—to individuals; Undergraduate support; Grants for special needs.
Application information: Applications accepted. Application form required.
> *Deadline(s):* Mar. 1 for Scholarships
> *Additional information:* Students seeking renewal scholarship must complete and return an application each year.

Program description:
> *Scholarships:* The foundation awards scholarships to residents of Missouri who are undergraduate full-time students, carrying at least twelve academic hours per semester. Eligible recipients must have graduated from an accredited high school, and must have been accepted in a four-year accredited Missouri college or university, leading to a bachelor's degree.

EIN: 436033388

5098
Sertoma, Inc.

1912 E. Meyer Blvd.
Kansas City, MO 64132-1141 (816) 333-8300
Contact: Steven Murphy, Secy.
FAX: (816) 333-4320;
E-mail: infosertoma@sertomahq.org; URL: http://www.sertoma.org/

Foundation type: Public charity
Purpose: Undergraduate and graduate scholarships to students who are deaf or hard-of-hearing, or students studying pathology and audiology.
Publications: Application guidelines; Annual report.
Financial data: Year ended 06/30/2012. Assets, $10,980,357 (M); Expenditures, $2,280,230.
Fields of interest: Speech/hearing centers; Pathology; Disabilities, people with.
Type of support: Scholarships—to individuals; Graduate support; Undergraduate support.
Application information: Applications accepted. Application form required. Application form available on the grantmaker's web site.
> *Copies of proposal:* 2
> *Deadline(s):* Mar. 30 for Communicative Disorders Scholarship Program; May 1 for Deaf and Hard of Hearing Scholarship
> *Applicants should submit the following:*
> 1) Transcripts
> 2) Letter(s) of recommendation
> 3) GPA
> *Additional information:* Recipients notified in June.

Program descriptions:
> *Communicative Disorders Scholarships:* Scholarships of $1,000 each are awarded annually to full-time students pursuing master's or doctorate degrees in audiology and speech language

pathology at accredited institutions. Applicants must be citizens residents of the U.S. and have at least a 3.2 cumulative GPA.
> *Deaf and Hard of Hearing Scholarships:* Scholarships of $1,000 each are awarded to full-time students with documented hearing loss (minimum 40dB hearing loss) for bachelor's degree-study at a U.S. college or university. Applicants must be citizens or permanent residents of the U.S. and have a 3.2 cumulative GPA.

EIN: 630655922

5099
Shelter Insurance Foundation

1817 W. Broadway
Columbia, MO 65218-0001 (573) 214-4324
Contact: Joe L. Moseley, V.P. and Secy.

Foundation type: Company-sponsored foundation
Purpose: Scholarships to high school seniors and to students who are children of employees or agents of Shelter Insurance. Grants also to individuals who have demonstrated excellence in selected fields and to a graduate of the Missouri School for the Deaf.
Financial data: Year ended 06/30/2012. Assets, $12,701,387 (M); Expenditures, $1,357,894; Total giving, $589,157; Grants to individuals, 3 grants totaling $487,525 (high: $364,500).
Fields of interest: Education.
Type of support: Employee-related scholarships; Grants to individuals; Scholarships—to individuals; Grants for special needs.
Application information: Applications accepted. Application form required.
> *Deadline(s):* Varies for Agent Scholarship Program
> *Additional information:* Agent Scholarship Program is limited to schools sponsored by a Shelter Insurance agent. Contact foundation or particpating school for application form for Agent Scholarship Program.

Program descriptions:
> *Agent Scholarship Program:* The foundation annually awards $1,500 college scholarships to graduating high school seniors in communities where there is a Shelter Mutual Insurance Company agent who participates in the program. The award is selected based on scholastic achievement, participation and leadership in school and community activities, citizenship and moral character, and educational goals.
> *F.V. Heinkel Award:* The foundation awards $2,000 grants to individuals and organizations that have demonstrated excellence in any area of science, medical research, health, education, history, athletics, or any other field designated by the foundation's board of directors. The award is named in honor of Shelter Insurance Companies' founder and first chairman.
> *William H. Lang Vocational Excellence Award:* The foundation annually honors an outstanding vocational-education graduate of Missouri School for the Deaf (MSD). The award is presented at commencement ceremonies and includes a $500 savings bond.

Company name: Shelter Mutual Insurance Company
EIN: 431224155

5100
Chris A. Skillman Scholarship Fund

P.O. Box 380
Platte City, MO 64079-0380
Application address: John W. Coots, Jr., P.O. Box 368, Platte City, MO 64079

Foundation type: Independent foundation
Purpose: Student loans to deserving and needy students of Platte County, MO for continuing education.
Financial data: Year ended 12/31/2011. Assets, $482,517 (M); Expenditures, $44,468; Total giving, $42,700; Loans to individuals, 5 loans totaling $12,000.
Fields of interest: Higher education.
Type of support: Student loans—to individuals.
Application information: Applications accepted. Application form required.
> *Initial approach:* Letter or telephone
> *Deadline(s):* None
> *Final notification:* Applicants notified within two months
> *Additional information:* Application should include a resume.

EIN: 436188683

5101
Mace C. Smith and Dee Smith Memorial Scholarship Fund

c/o Wood Huston Bank
P.O. Box 40
Marshall, MO 65340 (660) 886-6825
URL: https://www.woodhuston.com/

Foundation type: Independent foundation
Purpose: Scholarships to graduates of Sweet Springs High School, MO for postsecondary education.
Financial data: Year ended 12/31/2012. Assets, $268,784 (M); Expenditures, $15,284; Total giving, $11,941; Grants to individuals, 12 grants totaling $11,941 (high: $1,641, low: $600).
Fields of interest: Higher education.
Type of support: Support to graduates or students of specific schools; Undergraduate support.
Application information: Applications accepted. Application form required.
> *Initial approach:* Letter or telephone
> *Deadline(s):* Vary
> *Additional information:* Contact foundation for application guidelines.

EIN: 436455069

5102
Soldwedel Foundation

P.O. Box 11356
Clayton, MO 63105-0156 (309) 477-4216
Contact: Paula Davis
Application Address: 320 Stadium Dr., Pekin IL 61554

Foundation type: Independent foundation
Purpose: Scholarships to financially needy Pekin High School, IL, graduates who meet certain field of study and academic expectations for study at a college or university.
Financial data: Year ended 09/30/2013. Assets, $345,538 (M); Expenditures, $20,701; Total giving, $16,000; Grants to individuals, 5 grants totaling $16,000 (high: $4,000, low: $2,000).
Type of support: Support to graduates or students of specific schools; Undergraduate support.
Application information: Applications not accepted.

Additional information: Application form can be obtained from guidance counselor. Unsolicited requests for funds not considered or acknowledged.

EIN: 376296318

5103
Ralph & Bernice Sprehe Scholarship Trust
P.O. Box 387
Saint Louis, MO 63166

Foundation type: Independent foundation
Purpose: Scholarships to individuals who are members of the parish of St. Mary's Roman Catholic Church in Centralia, IL who are graduates of Centralia High School, IL, and who are enrolled in Kaskaskia College, IL. Occasionally, scholarship recipients may also be members of any Roman Catholic Church in Marion County, IL.
Financial data: Year ended 01/31/2013. Assets, $754,785 (M); Expenditures, $58,313; Total giving, $48,218.
Fields of interest: Higher education; Catholic agencies & churches.
Type of support: Support to graduates or students of specific schools; Undergraduate support.
Application information: Applications not accepted.
Additional information: Giving only to preselected individuals. Unsolicited requests for funds not considered or acknowledged.
EIN: 371369459

5104
St. Louis Carpenters District Council Scholarship Fund, Inc.
c/o Scholarship Comm.
1401 Hampton Ave.
St. Louis, MO 63139-3159 (314) 644-4800
Contact: Terry Nelson, Pres.
E-mail: jjensen@carpdc.org

Foundation type: Public charity
Purpose: Scholarships to high school seniors who are dependents of members in good standing of the Carpenters' District Council of Greater St. Louis, MO.
Publications: Application guidelines.
Financial data: Year ended 12/31/2012. Assets, $37,312 (M); Expenditures, $43,723; Total giving, $43,500.
Fields of interest: Higher education.
Type of support: Scholarships—to individuals.
Application information: Application form required.
Initial approach: Letter or telephone
Deadline(s): Feb. 24
Additional information: Payments are made directly to the educational institution for tuition, books or fees on behalf of the student.
Program description:
The St. Louis Carpenter Scholarship: Thirty scholarships of $500 each are available to students in the graduating class of a high school, or its related equivalent, who is a dependent of a member in good standing of the United Brotherhood of Carpenters of St. Louis, Missouri and Vicinity. Scholarships are renewable for up to three additional years, provided that the student maintains a semester GPA of 2.5 or better, and maintains full-time status (minimum of 12 credit hours) for each of the Fall and Spring semesters consecutively.
EIN: 431812440

5105
St. Louis Community Foundation, Inc.
(also known as Greater Saint Louis Community Foundation)
319 N. 4th St., Ste. 300
Saint Louis, MO 63102-1906 (314) 588-8200
Contact: Amelia A.J. Bond, Pres. and C.E.O.
FAX: (314) 588-8088; E-mail: dluckes@gstlcf.org;
E-Mail for Amelia A. J. Bond:
abond@stlouisgives.org; URL: http://www.gstlcf.org

Foundation type: Public charity
Purpose: The foundation provides scholarships to individuals in the St. Louis, MO metropolitan area through various funds.
Financial data: Year ended 03/31/2012. Assets, $116,190,175 (M); Expenditures, $17,491,047; Total giving, $16,223,733; Grants to individuals, totaling $1,110,212.
Fields of interest: Higher education.
Type of support: Student aid/financial aid; Scholarships—to individuals; Student loans—to individuals.
Application information: Applications accepted. Application form required. Application form available on the grantmaker's web site.
Copies of proposal: 1
Deadline(s): Mar. 30 for Zimmer Family Scholarships, Apr. 15 for all other scholarships
Applicants should submit the following:
1) FAF
2) FAFSA
3) Letter(s) of recommendation
4) Transcripts
Additional information: Scholarship funds use a common application format. See web site for additional guidelines.
EIN: 431758789

5106
St. Louis Public Schools Foundation
801 N. 11th St., Fl. 3
Saint Louis, MO 63101-1015 (314) 436-2025
Contact: C. Christopher Lee, Exec. Dir.
FAX: (314) 436-7081;
E-mail: clee@slpsfoundation.org; URL: http://www.slpsfoundation.org

Foundation type: Public charity
Purpose: College scholarships to students for the St. Louis City Public Schools for continuing education. Awards and prizes to teachers and principals of St. Louis Public Schools.
Financial data: Year ended 06/30/2011. Assets, $642,955 (M); Expenditures, $571,105; Total giving, $440,513.
Fields of interest: Education.
Type of support: Scholarships—to individuals; Awards/prizes.
Application information: Students' application should include transcripts. Scholarships are monitored by proof of enrollment for renewal. Principals and teachers are nominated for selection of awards.
EIN: 431813849

5107
St. Marys Health Center Jefferson City Missouri Foundation
100 St. Marys Medical Plz.
Jefferson City, MO 65101-1602 (573) 761-7000
Contact: Bev Stafford, Dir.; For Scholarships: Dianne Lowry, Devel. and Fdn. Coord.
E-mail: Dianne_Lowry@ssmhc.com
Additional tel.: (573) 761-7197; URL: http://www.lethealingbegin.com/Foundation/Pages/default.aspx

Foundation type: Public charity
Purpose: Scholarships for students seeking an educational degree pursuing careers in nursing and other allied health care professions; also, financial and in-kind assistance to patients in need.
Financial data: Year ended 12/31/2011. Assets, $4,148,863 (M); Expenditures, $92,809; Total giving, $51,322; Grants to individuals, totaling $13,300.
Fields of interest: Nursing school/education; Health care.
Type of support: Employee-related scholarships; Scholarships—to individuals.
Application information: Applications accepted. Application form required.
Initial approach: Telephone or e-mail
Program descriptions:
Scholarship Fund: The foundation provides scholarships to students and employees pursuing education in health care professions.
St. Mary's Medication Assistance Fund: The foundation provides medication support (both in cash and in-kind) when patients are in financial need.
EIN: 431575307

5108
James & Cecile Steven Scholarship Trust
P.O. Box 1119
St. Joseph, MO 64502-1119 (816) 236-5700
Contact: Lori Boyer
Application address: c/o The Commerce Trust Company, 328 Felix, P.O. Box 1119, St. Joseph, MO 64502 Tel.: (816) 236-5700

Foundation type: Independent foundation
Purpose: Scholarships to financially needy high school students from Buchanan and Andrew Counties, MO, for undergraduate education.
Financial data: Year ended 06/30/2013. Assets, $178,532 (M); Expenditures, $13,909; Total giving, $8,450; Grants to individuals, 16 grants totaling $8,450 (high: $1,000, low: $250).
Fields of interest: Higher education.
Type of support: Scholarships—to individuals.
Application information: Application form required.
Send request by: Mail
Deadline(s): Mar. 15
Applicants should submit the following:
1) Class rank
2) Letter(s) of recommendation
3) Financial information
4) GPA
5) Transcripts
Additional information: Application should also include income tax form for both parents and student for current and previous tax years.
EIN: 436633578

5109
Stowers Institute for Medical Research
(also known as Stowers Medical Institute)
1000 E. 50th St.
Kansas City, MO   64110-2262   (816) 926-4000
Contact: David Chao, Pres. and C.E.O.
FAX: (816) 926-2000; E-mail: info@stowers.org;
URL: http://www.stowers.org/

Foundation type: Public charity
Purpose: Grants and fellowships to undergraduate, graduate and postdoctoral students pursuing a career in the biomedical field.
Financial data: Year ended 12/31/2011. Assets, $475,896,618; Expenditures, $72,060,275; Total giving, $1,151,122; Grants to individuals, totaling $1,151,122.
Fields of interest: Biomedicine; Medical research; Science.
Type of support: Fellowships; Research; Postdoctoral support; Graduate support; Undergraduate support.
Application information: Applications accepted. Application form required.
> *Deadline(s):* Feb. 1 for Undergraduate Stowers Summer Scholars
> *Final notification:* Applicants notified early Apr. for undergraduate students
> *Additional information:* Application should include a curriculum vitae and bibliography for postdoctoral candidates. Two letters of recommendation from advisors, and an official transcript for undergraduate students. See web site for additional guidelines.

EIN: 202993509

5110
Ernest and Lillian Swanson Memorial Scholarship Trust
341 6th St.
Farmington, MO   63640   (314) 323-4430
Contact: Kris Corey, V.P
Application address: 1503 Main St., Ste. 291, Grandview, MO 64030

Foundation type: Operating foundation
Purpose: Scholarships to MO residents attending accredited universities or community colleges enrolled in a degree program of botany, plant genetics, or a related field.
Publications: Application guidelines.
Financial data: Year ended 12/31/2012. Assets, $297,467 (M); Expenditures, $11,970; Total giving, $5,300; Grants to individuals, 4 grants totaling $5,300 (high: $2,500, low: $300).
Fields of interest: Botany.
Type of support: Graduate support; Undergraduate support.
Application information: Applications accepted. Application form required.
> *Initial approach:* Application
> *Copies of proposal:* 1
> *Deadline(s):* Mar. 1
> *Applicants should submit the following:*
>   1) Transcripts
>   2) Letter(s) of recommendation
>   3) GPA
>   4) Financial information
> *Additional information:* Applications can be obtained from accredited community colleges or universities.

EIN: 431713377

5111
Gerald Swope Trust
P.O. Box 387
St. Louis, MO   63166-0387   (877) 228-0197
Contact: Kimberly Weiss
Application address: 7th and Washington, St. Louis, MO 63101, tel.: (877) 228-0197

Foundation type: Independent foundation
Purpose: Scholarships to graduates of St. Louis, MO, city or county high schools for postsecondary education.
Financial data: Year ended 09/30/2012. Assets, $403,448 (M); Expenditures, $23,498; Total giving, $20,000.
Fields of interest: Higher education.
Type of support: Support to graduates or students of specific schools; Undergraduate support.
Application information: Applications accepted.
> *Initial approach:* Letter
> *Deadline(s):* None

EIN: 436019071

5112
Tension Envelope Foundation
c/o ED Cockrell
819 E. 19th St.
Kansas City, MO   64108-1781   (816) 471-3800
Contact: William Berkley, Dir.

Foundation type: Company-sponsored foundation
Purpose: Scholarships to employees of Tension Envelope Corporation, and their dependents.
Financial data: Year ended 11/30/2012. Assets, $1,642,303 (M); Expenditures, $346,265; Total giving, $335,970.
Type of support: Employee-related scholarships.
Application information: Applications not accepted.
> *Additional information:* Unsolicited requests for funds not considered or acknowledged.

Company name: Tension Envelope Corporation
EIN: 446012554

5113
The Donald E. Thompson Family Charitable Foundation
P.O. Box G
Troy, MO   63379   (636) 528-7001
Contact: David W. Thompson, Tr.

Foundation type: Independent foundation
Purpose: Scholarships to individuals residing in the Lincoln county, MO, area for undergraduate education.
Financial data: Year ended 12/31/2011. Assets, $416,005 (M); Expenditures, $92,966; Total giving, $89,336; Grants to individuals, 41 grants totaling $70,225 (high: $3,000, low: $1,000).
Fields of interest: Higher education.
Type of support: Undergraduate support.
Application information: Application form required.
> *Deadline(s):* None
> *Applicants should submit the following:*
>   1) Transcripts
>   2) Financial information
> *Additional information:* Application should also include references.

EIN: 436816074

5114
Rabbi Samuel Thurman Educational Foundation Inc.
15332 Braefield Dr.
Chesterfield, MO   63017-1832   (314) 290-5720

Foundation type: Operating foundation
Purpose: Scholarships to individuals in St. Louis, MO, pursuing higher education.
Financial data: Year ended 05/31/2013. Assets, $209,258 (M); Expenditures, $12,199; Total giving, $12,000.
Fields of interest: Higher education.
Type of support: Scholarships—to individuals.
Application information: Applications accepted. Application form required.
> *Deadline(s):* None

EIN: 431063744

5115
The Tilles Fund
(formerly Rosalie Tilles Nonsectarian Charity Fund)
c/o U.S. Bank, N.A
The Private Client Reserve, Attn.: Carol Eaves, Mail Loc: SL-MO-CTCS
10 N. Hanley Rd.
Clayton, MO   63105-3426   (314) 505-8204
Contact: Garth Silvey, V.P.
Application information: Carol Eaves, tel.: (314) 418-8391; URL: http://www.thetillesfund.org

Foundation type: Independent foundation
Purpose: Scholarships to recent high school graduates who are residents of the city or county of St. Louis, MO, and who have been nominated by their financial aid officers, to attend colleges and universities in MO.
Publications: Application guidelines.
Financial data: Year ended 06/30/2013. Assets, $12,930,390 (M); Expenditures, $586,763; Total giving, $490,183; Grants to individuals, totaling $341,783.
Fields of interest: Higher education; Scholarships/financial aid.
Type of support: Scholarships—to individuals; Awards/grants by nomination only; Undergraduate support.
Application information: Application form required.
> *Copies of proposal:* 7
> *Deadline(s):* May 1
> *Applicants should submit the following:*
>   1) SAT
>   2) ACT
> *Additional information:* The foundation is not currently accepting new scholar applications. See web site for updates.

Program description:
> *The Tilles Fund for Full-Tuition Undergraduate Scholarships:* Scholarships are awarded to residents of St. Louis, MO, to attend MO universities and colleges. Applicants must be first-year students directly out of high school. Scholarships are renewable for four years and cover full tuition, provided a 3.0 cumulative GPA is maintained for the semester. Transcripts must be provided after each semester to verify compliance with the GPA criteria. Recipients are chosen by the student financial aid officer or scholarship coordinator at the student's school. The officer must submit the name of one scholar and one alternate to the Tilles Trustees for selection. Recipients are selected on the basis of secondary school academic record, class rank, test scores, major academic interest, extracurricular activity, and financial need (based on previous year's family income and parent(s) occupation(s)

EIN: 436020833

5116
Martin L. & Mary Ellen Tompkins & John A. Tompkins Trust
P.O. Box 388
Nevada, MO   64772-0388   (417) 667-3057
Contact: David J. Swearingen, Tr.

Foundation type: Independent foundation
Purpose: Scholarships to graduating seniors of Vernon County high schools, MO, to attend the School of Agriculture at the University of Missouri at Columbia, MO.
Financial data: Year ended 12/31/2011. Assets, $161,788 (M); Expenditures, $5,996; Total giving, $5,250; Grants to individuals, totaling $5,250.
Fields of interest: Agriculture.
Type of support: Support to graduates or students of specific schools; Undergraduate support.
Application information: Applications accepted.
Initial approach: Letter
Additional information: Application must include name of parents, their occupation and financial condition, transcript, and what the applicant plans to do after graduation.
EIN: 436121395

5117
Esther L. Trotter Charitable Trust
P.O. Box 387
Saint Louis, MO   63166-0387
Application address: c/o J. Douglas Hauser, P.O. Box 308, St. Joseph, MO 64502-0308, tel.: (417) 625-3264

Foundation type: Independent foundation
Purpose: Grants to St. Joseph or Buchanan County, MO, residents who are physically handicapped and require educational assistance at any academic level. Grants may be used for tuition, specialized equipment, transportation costs, and/or other items related to the individual's educational pursuits.
Financial data: Year ended 10/31/2011. Assets, $0 (M); Expenditures, $166,255; Total giving, $162,550.
Fields of interest: Vocational education; Disabilities, people with.
Type of support: Grants for special needs.
Application information: Applications accepted. Application form required.
Deadline(s): June 1
Additional information: Application must include description of handicap from physician, and parents' or student's tax return.
EIN: 436436638

5118
Truman Heartland Community Foundation
(formerly Independence Community Foundation)
4200 Little Blue Parkway, Ste. 340
Independence, MO   64057-8303   (816) 836-8189
Contact: Elizabeth A. McClure, Dir., Progs. and Rels.
FAX: (816) 836-8898; E-mail: thomson@thcf.org;
Additional e-mail: mcclure@thcf.org; URL: http://www.thcf.org

Foundation type: Community foundation
Purpose: Scholarships to graduating seniors, undergraduate and graduate school students of eastern Jackson county, MO pursuing various fields of study.
Publications: Application guidelines; Annual report; Informational brochure; Newsletter.
Financial data: Year ended 12/31/2011. Assets, $27,529,375 (M); Expenditures, $3,998,297;

Total giving, $3,092,814; Grants to individuals, 212 grants totaling $213,279.
Fields of interest: Higher education; Graduate/professional education.
Type of support: Scholarships—to individuals; Support to graduates or students of specific schools; Graduate support; Undergraduate support.
Application information: Applications accepted. Application form required. Application form available on the grantmaker's web site.
Deadline(s): Varies
Additional information: Eligibility criteria varies per scholarship fund, see web site for additional application guidelines.
EIN: 431482136

5119
UniGroup Incorporated Scholarship
1 United Dr., Ste. R-3
Fenton, MO   63026-2535

Foundation type: Operating foundation
Purpose: Undergraduate scholarships to the children of employees of UniGroup, Inc. and its affiliated companies in MO.
Financial data: Year ended 12/31/2012. Assets, $159,891 (M); Expenditures, $66,399; Total giving, $62,000; Grants to individuals, 18 grants totaling $62,000 (high: $5,000, low: $3,000).
Type of support: Employee-related scholarships.
Application information: Applications accepted. Application form required.
Deadline(s): Feb. 20
EIN: 431806966

5120
United Services Community Action Agency
6323 Manchester Ave.
Kansas City, MO   64133-4717   (816) 358-6868
FAX: (816) 358-0143;
E-mail: tgillespie@unitedservicescaa.org;
URL: http://www.uscaa.info/

Foundation type: Public charity
Purpose: Financial assistance to indigent residents of Jackson, Clay and Platte counties, MO, to help with utilities, housing, clothing and emergency food needs.
Financial data: Year ended 09/30/2011. Assets, $3,434,329 (M); Expenditures, $6,947,834; Total giving, $4,591,530; Grants to individuals, totaling $4,591,530.
Type of support: Grants for special needs.
Application information:
Initial approach: Telephone
Additional information: Contact the agency for more information on program requirements.
EIN: 431197168

5121
United Way of Greater St. Louis, Inc.
910 N. 11th St.
Saint Louis, MO   63101-1018   (314) 421-0700
E-mail: info@stl.unitedway.org; URL: http://www.stl.unitedway.org

Foundation type: Public charity
Purpose: Assistance to needy residents of MO and St. Clair, Clinton, Randolph, Monroe, Madison, Jersey, Greene, Calhoun, and Macoupin counties, IL.
Publications: Annual report; Newsletter.

Financial data: Year ended 06/30/2012. Assets, $76,047,550 (M); Expenditures, $73,995,926; Total giving, $61,868,118; Grants to individuals, totaling $6,233,486.
Fields of interest: Human services; Economically disadvantaged.
Type of support: In-kind gifts; Grants for special needs.
Application information: Applications accepted.
Initial approach: Telephone or letter
Additional information: Contact the agency for eligibility criteria.
EIN: 430714167

5122
Urban League of Metropolitan St. Louis, Inc.
3701 Grandel Sq.
St. Louis, MO   63108-3627   (314) 615-3600
Contact: Brenda Wrench, C.O.O.
FAX: (314) 531-4822;
E-mail: bwrench@urbanleague-stl.org; URL: http://www.ulstl.org

Foundation type: Public charity
Purpose: Scholarships to students from the St. Louis, MO, metropolitan area, to support their college education and career goals; assistance is also provided to individuals with housing and other emergency needs.
Publications: Application guidelines; Newsletter.
Financial data: Year ended 12/31/2011. Assets, $10,495,011 (M); Expenditures, $23,108,816; Total giving, $8,212,707; Grants to individuals, totaling $8,212,707.
Fields of interest: Higher education; Education; Human services.
Type of support: Scholarships—to individuals; Grants for special needs.
Application information: Applications accepted. Application form required.
Initial approach: Submit application
Deadline(s): Feb. 18 for Scholarships
Applicants should submit the following:
1) Essay
2) Photograph
3) Letter(s) of recommendation
4) Financial information
5) Transcripts
Program description:
Scholarships: The league awards scholarships to students from the St. Louis metropolitan area to support their college education and career goals. Awardees are selected based on their academic achievement, community service, character, and financial need. Eligible applicants must: be a U.S. citizen and a resident of the St. Louis metropolitan area; be a high school graduate; be between the ages of 17 and 22 years old; have a 2.0 or better grade point average; be accepted to an accredited college or university; and have participated in at least 60 hours of a community/volunteer activity.
EIN: 430653605

5123
Ward Educational Scholarship
(formerly Ward Educational Trust)
c/o First Bank Wealth Management
135 N. Meramec Ave., 3rd Fl.
Clayton, MO   63105-3751

Foundation type: Independent foundation
Purpose: Scholarships to individuals residing within ten miles of Pleasant Hill, IL for continuing education at institutions of higher learning.

Financial data: Year ended 12/31/2011. Assets, $171,800 (M); Expenditures, $5,931; Total giving, $2,760; Grants to individuals, 2 grants totaling $2,760 (high: $1,840, low: $920).
Fields of interest: Higher education.
Type of support: Scholarships—to individuals.
Application information:
　Initial approach: Letter
　Deadline(s): None
EIN: 431835410

5124
West Central Missouri Community Action Agency, Inc.
106 W. 4th St.
P.O. Box 125
Appleton City, MO　64724-1402　(660) 476-2185
FAX: (660) 476-5529; E-mail: info@wcmcaa.org; E-Mail for Amos E. Jackson: ajackson@wcmcaa.org; URL: http://www.wcmcaa.org

Foundation type: Public charity
Purpose: Utility, housing, weatherization and other special needs to indigent residents of the west central area of MO.
Financial data: Year ended 08/31/2011. Assets, $24,364,162 (M); Expenditures, $24,696,679; Total giving, $6,183,426; Grants to individuals, totaling $6,183,426.
Fields of interest: Economically disadvantaged.
Type of support: Grants for special needs.
Application information: Applications not accepted.
　Additional information: Unsolicited requests for funds not considered or acknowledged.
Program descriptions:
　Housing Choice Voucher Program: The program provides the opportunity for low-income individuals and families to live in decent, safe, and sanitary housing. For more information about the program, call housing at (660) 476-2184 or e-mail housing@wcmcaa.org.
　In-Home Services Program: The program enables elderly persons to remain in their homes while

receiving the care and attention they need. For more information about the program, call (660) 476-2138 or send an e-mail to wchealth@iland.net.
　Women's Health Services Program: The program provides confidential and personalized care at affordable prices. Services include breast and pelvic examinations, pap smears, fertility counseling, birth control, and contraceptive counseling.
EIN: 430838410

5125
Windsor High School Master Scholarship Endowment Fund, Inc.
405 E. Benton St.
P.O. Box 261
Windsor, MO　65360-1307　(660) 647-2125

Foundation type: Public charity
Purpose: Scholarships for postsecondary education to deserving students who are graduates of Windsor High School in Windsor, MO.
Financial data: Year ended 12/31/2011. Assets, $274,162 (M); Expenditures, $8,902; Total giving, $8,515.
Fields of interest: Higher education.
Type of support: Support to graduates or students of specific schools.
Application information: Applications not accepted.
　Additional information: Unsolicited requests for funds not considered or acknowledged.
EIN: 431414822

5126
Judson Young Memorial Educational Foundation
100 W. 4th St.
P.O. Box 459
Salem, MO　65560　(573) 729-3137
Contact: Geriann C. Ball, Secy.

Foundation type: Independent foundation

Purpose: Student loans to graduates in the Salem, MO, area. Preference is given to graduates of Salem High School, MO.
Financial data: Year ended 12/31/2011. Assets, $4,002,943 (M); Expenditures, $220,784; Total giving, $160,250.
Type of support: Support to graduates or students of specific schools; Undergraduate support.
Application information: Applications accepted. Application form required.
　Copies of proposal: 2
　Deadline(s): Aug. 15 for fall term, Dec. 15 for winter term, and May 15 for summer term
EIN: 436061841

5127
Young Men's Christian Association of Greater St. Louis
1528 Locust St.
St. Louis, MO　63103-1816　(314) 436-1177
FAX: (314) 436-1901;
E-mail: metro@ymcastlouis.org; URL: http://www.ymcastlouis.org

Foundation type: Public charity
Purpose: Financial assistance to individuals and families of greater St. Louis, MO who cannot afford membership. Also, scholarships to individuals at all branches.
Financial data: Year ended 12/31/2011. Assets, $119,035,510 (M); Expenditures, $57,386,075; Total giving, $2,512,427; Grants to individuals, totaling $2,410,427.
Fields of interest: Education; Economically disadvantaged.
Type of support: Scholarships—to individuals; Grants for special needs.
Application information: Applications accepted. Application form required. Application form available on the grantmaker's web site.
　Final notification: Applicants are notified within two weeks of receipt of application
　Additional information: Applications for financial assistance are available at any branch service center.
EIN: 430653616

MONTANA

5128
Allegiance Benefit Foundation, Inc.
2806 S. Garfield St.
Missoula, MT   59801-7733   (406) 721-2222

Foundation type: Independent foundation
Purpose: Scholarships to students of MT pursuing a degree at an accredited college or university.
Financial data: Year ended 12/31/2011. Assets, $52,885 (M); Expenditures, $32,340; Total giving, $31,495; Grants to individuals, 3 grants totaling $15,000 (high: $5,000, low: $5,000).
Fields of interest: Higher education.
Type of support: Scholarships—to individuals.
Application information: Applications accepted. Application form required.
  Deadline(s): None
  Additional information: Applicant must demonstrate financial need, and have a C+ GPA.
EIN: 201430196

5129
Ashcraft Foundation Inc.
2437 Eastridge Dr.
Billings, MT   59102-2896

Foundation type: Independent foundation
Purpose: Scholarships to individuals for undergraduate support, primarily in MT.
Financial data: Year ended 09/30/2013. Assets, $31 (M); Expenditures, $14,035; Total giving, $13,500; Grants to individuals, 14 grants totaling $13,500 (high: $1,000, low: $500).
Type of support: Undergraduate support.
Application information: Application form not required.
  Initial approach: Letter
  Deadline(s): None
  Additional information: Contact foundation for current application guidelines.
EIN: 810472889

5130
Charles M. Bair Memorial Trust
c/o U.S. Bank, N.A.
P.O. Box 30678
Billings, MT   59115-0001
FAX: (406) 657-8034;
E-mail: penny.doak@usbank.com; URL: http://www.charlesmbairtrusts.org/scholarship.html

Foundation type: Independent foundation
Purpose: Scholarships to high school graduates who have lived in as well as attended school in Meagher or Wheatland counties, MT for undergraduate studies at an accredited college, university or trade school.
Financial data: Year ended 01/31/2013. Assets, $9,627,035 (M); Expenditures, $731,040; Total giving, $661,432; Grants to individuals, totaling $661,432.
Fields of interest: Vocational education, post-secondary; Higher education.
Type of support: Support to graduates or students of specific schools; Undergraduate support.
Application information: Applications accepted. Application form required.
  Send request by: Mail
  Deadline(s): Mar. 15
  Applicants should submit the following:

1) SAT
2) ACT
3) Letter(s) of recommendation
4) Essay
5) Transcripts
6) Financial information
  Additional information: Selection is based on academic achievement, moral character, financial need, and extracurricular activities. See web site for additional application guidelines.
EIN: 810370774

5131
Beartooth Billings Clinic Foundation
(formerly Beartooth Hospital & Health Center Foundation)
2525 N. Broadway Ave.
P.O. Box 1290
Red Lodge, MT   59068-9222   (406) 446-0610
Contact: Sara Urbanik, Exec. Dir.
URL: http://www.beartoothbillingsclinic.org/Foundation.aspx

Foundation type: Public charity
Purpose: Scholarships to graduating seniors of Carbon County High School, MT pursuing a career in the health care field. Scholarships to Beartooth employees who wish to refine or increase their skills and knowledge in the medical field.
Financial data: Year ended 12/31/2011. Assets, $1,675,251 (M); Expenditures, $232,779; Total giving, $125,056; Grants to individuals, totaling $6,000.
Fields of interest: Vocational education, post-secondary; Nursing school/education; Health sciences school/education.
Type of support: Employee-related scholarships; Scholarships—to individuals.
Application information: Applications accepted. Application form required. Application form available on the grantmaker's web site. Interview required.
  Send request by: Mail
  Deadline(s): Mar. 1
  Final notification: Applicants notified in May
  Applicants should submit the following:
    1) Transcripts
    2) Letter(s) of recommendation
    3) Essay
  Additional information: See web site for additional guidelines.
Program description:
  High School Senior Scholarship: The Dr. James and Juanita Kane Scholarship Fund offers assistance to high school students pursuing a career in a rural healthcare field. Applicants must be a Montana or Wyoming resident. Scholarships range from $1,000 to $2,000.
EIN: 810484562

5132
Benefis Healthcare Foundation, Inc.
1101 26th St., S.
P.O. Box 7008
Great Falls, MT   59406-7008   (406) 455-5840
Contact: John H. Goodnow, Exec. Dir.
FAX: (406) 455-4821;
E-mail: foundation@benefis.org; Toll-free tel.: (800) 544-7798; URL: http://www.benefisfoundation.org

Foundation type: Public charity
Purpose: Scholarships to individuals pursuing further education in the healthcare industry, as well as grants to individuals in need throughout central Montana.

Publications: Annual report; Financial statement; Newsletter.
Financial data: Year ended 12/31/2011. Assets, $21,120,652 (M); Expenditures, $1,013,898; Total giving, $744,449; Grants to individuals, totaling $173,450.
Application information: Applications accepted. Application form available on the grantmaker's web site.
  Initial approach: Application
  Deadline(s): Varies
Program descriptions:
  Darlene Glantz Skees Memorial Nursing Scholarship: Scholarships of up to $2,500 are available to individuals actively delivering patient care the opportunity to obtain an associate's degree or B.S. in nursing. Applicants must be a current full-time, part-time, or registry employee of Benefis Healthcare, have a minimum of two years' experience in the field of healthcare, have been an employee of Benefis Healthcare for at least one year, maintain a 2.75 GPA, and take a minimum of nine credits per semester.
  Healthcare Scholarship Program: Scholarships are available for current Benefis Healthcare employees and college students with the desire to obtain or advance in healthcare education or certification. Up to $2,500 per semester is available. Applicants must have been accepted into an accredited nursing program or other approved allied healthcare program and be pursuing a degree or certification in a specific skill set, be in good academic standing (with a GPA of 2.75 or higher), take a minimum of nine credits per semester, and be eligible for employment at Benefis Healthcare (and sign a Work Commitment Agreement)
  Jane M. Buckman Husted Nursing Scholarship: This scholarship provides up to $1,000 for books and tuition to an A.D.N. or R.N. student who is pursuing a B.S.N. The scholarship carries a work commitment to Benefis Healthcare upon graduation.
  Margaret Wynn Memorial Nursing Scholarship: Scholarships of up to $2,500 are available to licensed Practical Nurses, Certified Nursing Assistants, or Emergency Medical Technicians who wish to further their education in the nursing or health care field. Applicants must be a current member of Benefis Healthcare or one of its subsidiaries, must maintain a 3.0 GPA, and must take a minimum of nine credits per semester. Scholarship funding is renewable.
  Mercy Flight Memorial Scholarships: These scholarships provide assistance for books and tuition to deserving students attending an accredited school in Montana. The Darcy Dengel Nursing Scholarship is available to B.S.N. or master's degree students, while the Paul Erickson Paramedic Scholarship is available to students assisting a paramedic program.
  Smith and Van Orsdel Nursing Scholarship: Scholarships are available to Montana State University, Bozeman (MSU) nursing students enrolled in the MSU degree program at Great Falls Extended Campus. Applicants must: have attained junior or higher status and be actively seeking either a bachelor of science or a master of science degree; have an accumulated GPA of 2.75 or higher; and demonstrate leadership abilities, sound clinical performance, and service to the community, the college of nursing, and/or the healthcare profession. Scholarship funding is renewable.
  Terry L. Jackson, M.D. Memorial Scholarship: This scholarship provides support to students interested in becoming a physical therapy assistant. Eligible applicants must be students at Montana State University College of Technology,

Great Falls who are enrolled in its Physical Therapy Assistant program.
EIN: 810480587

5133
Bottrell/Dolan Family Foundation
P.O. Box 80745
Billings, MT 59108-0745   (406) 652-8328
Contact: James Bennett, Treas.
Application address: P.O. Box 80284, Billings, MT 59108-0284

Foundation type: Independent foundation
Purpose: Scholarships to graduating high school seniors from Montana and North Dakota who intend to attend college in Montana and North Dakota.
Financial data: Year ended 12/31/2011. Assets, $1,118 (M); Expenditures, $10,917; Total giving, $9,500; Grants to individuals, 10 grants totaling $9,500 (high: $3,000, low: $500).
Type of support: Scholarships—to individuals; Undergraduate support.
Application information: Applications accepted.
   Initial approach: Letter
   Deadline(s): Aug. 1
EIN: 450453811

5134
Archie Bray Foundation
2915 Country Club Ave.
Helena, MT 59602-9240   (406) 443-3502
Contact: Steven Young Lee, Resident Artist Dir.
FAX: (406) 443-0934;
E-mail: archiebray@archiebray.org; Contact inf. for Steven Young Lee: tel.: (406) 443-3502 ext. 12, e-mail: steve@archiebray.org; URL: http://www.archiebray.org

Foundation type: Public charity
Purpose: Fellowships and scholarships to clay artists based on merit and future promise. Residencies that offer free studio space are also available.
Financial data: Year ended 12/31/2011. Assets, $3,834,610 (M); Expenditures, $1,307,763.
Fields of interest: Ceramic arts.
Type of support: Fellowships; Scholarships—to individuals; Residencies.
Application information: Applications accepted. Application form required. Application form available on the grantmaker's web site.
   Initial approach: Letter, telephone, fax or e-mail.
   Deadline(s): Feb. 1 for fellowships; Mar. 1 for Artist-in-Residence program
   Applicants should submit the following:
      1) Resume
      2) Letter(s) of recommendation
      3) Work samples
      4) Essay
Program descriptions:
   Artist-in-Residence Program: Studio space is provided free to residents. There are eleven year-round studios. Residencies range from a few months to up to two years. New residents are chosen once a year in Mar.
   Fellowships: The foundation awards four fellowships: the Taunt Fellowship, the Lilian Fellowship, the Matsutani Fellowship, and the Lincoln Fellowship. Each fellowship provides $5,000 to a ceramic artist who demonstrates merit and exceptional promise for a one-year, non-renewable residency at the foundation.
   The Bill and Stirling Sage Scholarship: Provides an $800 annual scholarship for a ceramic artist between the ages of 18 and 35 who demonstrates

merit and exceptional promise for a three-month summer residency at the foundation.
   The Eric Myhre Resident Scholarship: Provides a $750 annual scholarship for a ceramic artist who demonstrates merit and exceptional promise for a three month summer residency at the foundation.
EIN: 810284022

5135
Marshall and Mary Brondum Special Assistance Foundation, Inc.
P.O. Box 3106
Missoula, MT 59806-3106   (406) 549-4148

Foundation type: Independent foundation
Purpose: Financial assistance to needy residents primarily from the northwestern U.S.
Financial data: Year ended 03/31/2013. Assets, $3,720,048 (M); Expenditures, $144,536; Total giving, $101,226; Grants to individuals, 29 grants totaling $86,726 (high: $25,145).
Fields of interest: Health care; Human services.
Type of support: Grants for special needs.
Application information: Application form required.
   Deadline(s): 45 days prior to quarterly meetings in Apr., July, Oct. and Jan.
   Additional information: Application should include a brief description of purpose and need.
EIN: 363700887

5136
George M. & Florence M. Clarkson Scholarship Foundation
P.O. Box 1299
Polson, MT 59860-1299   (406) 883-8813
Contact: Kirk Fulford

Foundation type: Independent foundation
Purpose: Scholarships to seniors and graduates of Polson High School, MT, for study at any accredited college, university, or technical or vocational training school.
Financial data: Year ended 12/31/2011. Assets, $195,483 (M); Expenditures, $11,623; Total giving, $9,000.
Fields of interest: Vocational education.
Type of support: Support to graduates or students of specific schools; Technical education support; Undergraduate support.
Application information: Applications accepted. Application form required.
   Deadline(s): Apr. 1
   Applicants should submit the following:
      1) Transcripts
      2) Letter(s) of recommendation
      3) FAF
EIN: 363802270

5137
The Clay Studio of Missoula
1106 Hawthorne St., Ste. A
Missoula, MT 59802-2336   (406) 543-0509
E-mail: fire@theclaystudioofmissoula.org;
URL: http://www.theclaystudioofmissoula.org

Foundation type: Public charity
Purpose: Studio space to independent artists to pursue their strengths in clay whether it is sculptural, functional, or experimental for two, four, and six months.
Publications: Newsletter.
Financial data: Year ended 12/31/2011. Assets, $56,346 (M); Expenditures, $104,886.

Fields of interest: Ceramic arts.
Type of support: Residencies.
Application information: Applications accepted. Application form required. Application form available on the grantmaker's web site.
   Initial approach: Letter of intent
   Deadline(s): Ongoing
   Applicants should submit the following:
      1) Work samples
      2) Resume
      3) SASE
      4) Letter(s) of recommendation
   Additional information: Application must also include five to ten high quality slides and $10 application fee.
Program description:
   Artist-In-Residence: The residency program provides an independent artist a space to pursue their strengths in clay, whether that is sculptural, functional, or experimental. Residents are paid to teach community classes at the studio.
EIN: 810523194

5138
Jack Creek Preserve Foundation, Inc.
P.O. Box 3
Ennis, MT 59729   (406) 995-7550
Contact: Jon S. Fossel, Pres.
URL: http://www.jackcreekpreserve.org/

Foundation type: Independent foundation
Purpose: Scholarships to graduating seniors of any Madison county high school, MT for postsecondary education.
Financial data: Year ended 09/30/2012. Assets, $13,299,787 (M); Expenditures, $124,859; Total giving, $3,900; Grants to individuals, 10 grants totaling $3,900 (high: $1,000, low: $50). Subtotal for awards/prizes: grants totaling $400 (high: $400, low: $0).
Fields of interest: Higher education.
Type of support: Support to graduates or students of specific schools; Undergraduate support.
Application information: Applications accepted.
   Deadline(s): Spring
   Additional information: Application available at all Madison county high schools.
EIN: 202214684

5139
Cut Bank Elks Lodge Charitable Corp.
118 E. Main St.
Cut Bank, MT 59427-2956

Foundation type: Independent foundation
Purpose: Scholarships to MT students in their second, third or fourth year of postsecondary education who are members of the Cut Bank Elks Lodge, No. 1632, or whose spouse, parent, or grandparent is a member thereof for the past three years.
Financial data: Year ended 12/31/2011. Assets, $0 (M); Expenditures, $11,841; Total giving, $8,000; Grants to individuals, 19 grants totaling $8,000 (high: $500, low: $150).
Fields of interest: Fraternal societies.
Type of support: Undergraduate support.
Application information: Application form required.
   Deadline(s): June 30
EIN: 810495546

5140
Jim & Doris Daley Scholarship Foundation
P.O. Box 343
Somers, MT 59932
Contact: Guidance Counselor
Application address: Flathead High School And
Glacier High School,Kalispell,MT 59901

Foundation type: Operating foundation
Purpose: Scholarships to financially qualified
graduates of Flathead High School, MT for
attendance at a MT school of higher learning.
Financial data: Year ended 12/31/2012. Assets,
$809,616 (M); Expenditures, $50,000; Total
giving, $50,000; Grants to individuals, 10 grants
totaling $50,000 (high: $5,000, low: $5,000).
Fields of interest: Higher education.
Type of support: Support to graduates or students
of specific schools; Undergraduate support.
Application information: Application form required.
  Deadline(s): Apr. 1
  Additional information: Application available at
    the guidance counselor's office.
EIN: 810533021

5141
Dayton Foundation
c/o Brenner Averett & Co., PC
P.O. Box 1049
Sidney, MT 59270-1049 (406) 433-8600
Contact: Robert Goss
Application address: 121 S. Central Ave., Sidney,
MT 59270-4123

Foundation type: Independent foundation
Purpose: Scholarship to residents of Sidney, MT.
Financial data: Year ended 12/31/2012. Assets,
$251,401 (M); Expenditures, $28,512; Total
giving, $23,975; Grants to individuals, 4 grants
totaling $10,000 (high: $4,000, low: $2,000).
Type of support: Scholarships—to individuals.
Application information: Applications accepted.
Application form not required.
  Deadline(s): None
EIN: 810376620

5142
District 7 Human Resources Development Council
7 N. 31st St.
Billings, MT 59101-2114 (406) 247-4732
FAX: (406) 248-2943; E-mail: info@hrdc7.org;
Additional address: 501 North Center Ave., Hardin,
MT 59034, tel.: (406) 665-3500, fax: (406)
665-1395; URL: http://www.hrdc7.org/

Foundation type: Public charity
Purpose: Assistance to individuals and families in
MT with emergency food, and housing, employment
and energy assistance, and other special needs.
Scholarships to help families and individuals pay for
postsecondary education or job-training.
Financial data: Year ended 06/30/2012. Assets,
$3,014,704 (M); Expenditures, $7,801,872; Total
giving, $2,592,114; Grants to individuals, totaling
$2,564,584.
Fields of interest: Vocational education,
post-secondary; Higher education; Economically
disadvantaged.
Type of support: Scholarships—to individuals;
Grants for special needs.
Application information: Applications accepted.
Application form required.
  Deadline(s): June 30 for scholarships
  Additional information: Scholarship funds are
    paid directly to the educational institution on

behalf of the students. See web site for
eligibility determination for assistance.
Program description:
  Scholarship Program: Scholarships to students
of Big Horn, Carbon, Stillwater, Sweet Grass, or
Yellowstone County, MT to help pay for
postsecondary education. Scholarships vary from
$500 to $2,000 and covers tuition, books, and
required supplies at an eligible educational
institution. Applicants must be 18 years or older,
have a source of earned income (not currently
receiving TANF, SSI/SSDI), have a minor child
currently living at home, have household gross
income not exceeding 185 percent of the Federal
Poverty Level, be in good academic standing and
currently enrolled in postsecondary education or a
training program.
EIN: 810300207

5143
District XI Human Resource Council, Inc.
1801 S. Higgins Ave.
Missoula, MT 59801-5763 (406) 728-3710
Contact: James Morton, Exec. Dir. and C.E.O.
E-mail: hrcxi@montana.com; URL: http://
www.hrcxi.org/

Foundation type: Public charity
Purpose: Assistance to low income individuals and
families of Missoula, MT with energy costs,
housing, and other special needs.
Financial data: Year ended 06/30/2012. Assets,
$14,378,148 (M); Expenditures, $4,803,864;
Total giving, $1,801,634; Grants to individuals,
totaling $1,698,398.
Fields of interest: Housing/shelter; Human
services.
Type of support: Grants for special needs.
Application information: Applications accepted.
Application form required.
  Additional information: See web site for
    additional application guidelines or contact
    the agency for eligibility determination.
EIN: 810332017

5144
Henry Elm Trust
101 S. Central Ave.
Sidney, MT 59270-4123 (406) 433-8600
Contact: Garth Kallevig, Tr.

Foundation type: Independent foundation
Purpose: Scholarships to graduating seniors of
Richland County, MT.
Financial data: Year ended 12/31/2012. Assets,
$540,969 (M); Expenditures, $94,264; Total
giving, $82,502; Grants to individuals, 22 grants
totaling $82,502 (high: $8,018, low: $478).
Type of support: Support to graduates or students
of specific schools; Undergraduate support.
Application information: Applications not
accepted.
  Additional information: Unsolicited requests for
    funds not considered or acknowledged.
EIN: 237418092

5145
Fergus Electric Cooperative, Inc.
84423 U.S. Hwy. 87
Lewistown, MT 59457-2058 (406) 538-3465
FAX: (406) 538-7391;
E-mail: ferguselectric@ferguselectric.coop;
URL: http://www.ferguselectric.coop

Foundation type: Public charity

Purpose: Scholarships to members of Montana
Electric Cooperative's Association who plan to
attend a university or vocational technical school.
Publications: Newsletter.
Financial data: Year ended 12/31/2011. Assets,
$37,691,718 (M); Expenditures, $21,899,879.
Fields of interest: Vocational education,
post-secondary; Higher education.
Type of support: Scholarships—to individuals.
Application information: Applications accepted.
Application form required. Application form
available on the grantmaker's web site.
  Initial approach: Application
  Deadline(s): Jan. 31
  Applicants should submit the following:
    1) Letter(s) of recommendation
    2) ACT
    3) SAT
    4) Transcripts
Program description:
  Scholarships: Each year, the foundation offers
two $500 scholarships to qualified students whose
parents are cooperative members and whose
cooperative belongs to the Montana Electric
Cooperative's Association (MECA). Eligible
applicants must be a member of a Montana electric
cooperative, and must either be a graduating high
school senior with plans to attend a university or
vocational technical school, or an undergraduate
college student.
EIN: 810134746

5146
Flathead Educational Foundation
P. O. Box 759
Kalispell, MT 59903-0759 (406) 752-6644
Contact: Dan Johns, Pres.
Application address: c/o Jerry J. James, P.O. Box
7130, Kalispell, MT 59904, tel.: (406) 752-5202

Foundation type: Public charity
Purpose: Scholarships to graduating students
attending high school in Flathead County, MT for
postsecondary education.
Financial data: Year ended 12/31/2011. Assets,
$2,240,062 (M); Expenditures, $151,798; Total
giving, $130,000; Grants to individuals, totaling
$130,000.
Fields of interest: Higher education; Scholarships/
financial aid.
Type of support: Support to graduates or students
of specific schools; Undergraduate support.
Application information: Applications accepted.
  Applicants should submit the following:
    1) Financial information
    2) SAR
    3) FAFSA
  Additional information: Preference is given to
    students who are both worthy and needy.
EIN: 816013249

5147
Melvin Gay Citizenship Incentive Trust
P.O. Box 2309
Great Falls, MT 59403 (406) 761-4645

Foundation type: Independent foundation
Purpose: Citizenship awards to students of Hardin
High School, Hardin, MT.
Financial data: Year ended 06/30/2013. Assets,
$145,770 (M); Expenditures, $9,950; Total giving,
$7,050; Grants to individuals, 47 grants totaling
$7,050 (high: $150, low: $150).
Fields of interest: Higher education.
Type of support: Support to graduates or students
of specific schools; Awards/prizes.

Application information:
Deadline(s): Apr. 1
Additional information: Recommendations are made by a three person advisory committee.
EIN: 363626365

5148
Gebhardt Scholarship Foundation
P.O. Box 724
Roundup, MT   59072-0724   (406) 323-1564
Contact: Kelly N. Gebhardt, Tr.

Foundation type: Independent foundation
Purpose: Scholarships to high school students from certain areas in Montana pursuing education beyond the high school level.
Financial data: Year ended 12/31/2011. Assets, $1,098,455 (M); Expenditures, $54,755; Total giving, $52,000; Grants to individuals, 30 grants totaling $52,000 (high: $5,500, low: $500).
Fields of interest: Vocational education, post-secondary; Higher education.
Type of support: Scholarships—to individuals.
Application information: Applications accepted. Application form required.
Deadline(s): Apr. 1
Applicants should submit the following:
1) Transcripts
2) Financial information
3) Essay
Additional information: Recipients are selected based on need, ambition and scholastic capabilities. Application must also include three non-family character references.
EIN: 816080867

5149
Geyser Public School - Strand
c/o Geyser School District
P.O. Box 70
Geyser, MT   59447-0070   (406) 735-4368

Foundation type: Independent foundation
Purpose: Scholarships to Geyser Public School graduating students for continuing education.
Financial data: Year ended 06/30/2013. Assets, $222,785 (M); Expenditures, $13,930; Total giving, $13,000; Grants to individuals, 13 grants totaling $13,000 (high: $2,000, low: $500).
Fields of interest: Higher education.
Type of support: Scholarships—to individuals.
Application information: Applications accepted. Application form required.
Deadline(s): Apr. 15
Additional information: Scholarship awards are based on academic performance.
EIN: 841422401

5150
Groskinsky Foundation
34851 CR 120Z
Sidney, MT   59270-6402
Application address: c/o Anne Groskinski, 12102 Highway 16, Sidney, MT 59270

Foundation type: Independent foundation
Purpose: Scholarships to residents of Sidney, MT.
Financial data: Year ended 09/30/2012. Assets, $151,781 (M); Expenditures, $233,693; Total giving, $229,885; Grants to individuals, 8 grants totaling $7,050 (high: $1,000, low: $50).
Type of support: Undergraduate support.
Application information: Applications not accepted.

Additional information: Unsolicited requests for funds not considered.
EIN: 810372197

5151
The H2 Brensdal Scholarship Fund Trust
P.O. Box 52
Jefferson City, MT   59638-0052   (406) 933-5493
Contact: Bruce Brensdal, Tr.

Foundation type: Operating foundation
Purpose: Scholarships to high school graduates for attendance at institutions of higher learning.
Financial data: Year ended 12/31/2011. Assets, $272,724 (M); Expenditures, $13,189; Total giving, $12,500; Grants to individuals, 13 grants totaling $12,500 (high: $1,000, low: $500).
Fields of interest: Higher education.
Type of support: Scholarships—to individuals.
Application information: Applications accepted. Application form required.
Deadline(s): Feb.
Applicants should submit the following:
1) Transcripts
2) SASE
3) Financial information
Additional information: Applicant must demonstrate need, show determination to complete course of study, academics, community service and two letters of reference.
EIN: 810525472

5152
Arnold E. Haack Scholarship Trust
c/o First Interstate Bank, N.A.
P.O. Box 5010
Great Falls, MT   59403-5010

Foundation type: Independent foundation
Purpose: Scholarship awards to graduates or graduating seniors of Hobson High School, Montana.
Financial data: Year ended 03/31/2013. Assets, $137,642 (M); Expenditures, $7,652; Total giving, $6,990; Grants to individuals, 14 grants totaling $6,990 (high: $850, low: $300).
Type of support: Support to graduates or students of specific schools; Undergraduate support.
Application information:
Initial approach: Letter
Deadline(s): Apr. 1
EIN: 841387370

5153
Ruby E. Hanson Charitable Trust
100 W. Laurel
Plentywood, MT   59254-1647   (406) 765-1212
Contact: Steven Howard, Tr.

Foundation type: Operating foundation
Purpose: Scholarships to graduating seniors of Plentywood or Scobey High School, MT in pursuit of a higher education.
Financial data: Year ended 12/31/2012. Assets, $0 (M); Expenditures, $22,881; Total giving, $21,000; Grants to individuals, 21 grants totaling $21,000 (high: $1,000, low: $1,000).
Fields of interest: Higher education.
Type of support: Support to graduates or students of specific schools.
Application information: Applications accepted. Application form required.
Deadline(s): Apr. 15

Applicants should submit the following:
1) Transcripts
2) SAR
3) Essay
EIN: 746525100

5154
Dorris Harbert Scholarship Foundation
P.O. Box 1299
Polson, MT   59860-1299   (406) 883-8813
Contact: Kirk Fulford

Foundation type: Independent foundation
Purpose: Scholarships to high school seniors and graduates of Polson, Montana High School for attendance at any accredited college, university, technical or vocational training school.
Financial data: Year ended 12/31/2011. Assets, $323,525 (M); Expenditures, $20,245; Total giving, $16,000.
Fields of interest: Higher education.
Type of support: Support to graduates or students of specific schools; Graduate support; Technical education support; Undergraduate support.
Application information: Applications accepted. Application form required.
Deadline(s): Apr. 1
Applicants should submit the following:
1) Letter(s) of recommendation
2) Transcripts
Additional information: Applications must also include a Financial Aid Form and three references, with only one associated with a Montana high school.
EIN: 810519264

5155
Hawkins Scholarship Foundation
c/o Davidson Trust Co.
P.O. Box 2309
Great Falls, MT   59403-2309   (406) 791-7325

Foundation type: Independent foundation
Purpose: Scholarships to graduating students of Flathead County High Schools, MT.
Financial data: Year ended 12/31/2011. Assets, $3,639,743 (M); Expenditures, $191,729; Total giving, $154,250; Grants to individuals, 173 grants totaling $154,250 (high: $1,000, low: $750).
Fields of interest: Higher education.
Type of support: Support to graduates or students of specific schools; Undergraduate support.
Application information: Applications accepted. Application form required.
Deadline(s): Before graduation
Applicants should submit the following:
1) Class rank
2) GPA
EIN: 816018444

5156
The Heisey Foundation
c/o U.S. Bank, N.A.
P.O. Box 5000
Great Falls, MT   59403-5000

Foundation type: Independent foundation
Purpose: Awards by nomination only to students attending specific public and parochial schools in the Great Falls, MT, trade area.
Financial data: Year ended 12/31/2012. Assets, $5,876,453 (M); Expenditures, $257,960; Total giving, $225,040.
Fields of interest: Education.

Type of support: Support to graduates or students of specific schools; Awards/grants by nomination only; Awards/prizes.
Application information: Applications not accepted.
   Additional information: Applications are accepted by nomination only.
EIN: 816009624

5157
E. A. Hinderman Scholarship Memorial
P.O. Box 236
Whitefish, MT   59937   (406) 862-8600
Application address: Hinderman Scholarship Committee, Guidance Counselor, Whitefish, MT 59937

Foundation type: Independent foundation
Purpose: Scholarships to financially needy graduating high school seniors of Whitefish High School, MT, pursuing higher education.
Financial data: Year ended 12/31/2012. Assets, $914,534 (M); Expenditures, $39,628; Total giving, $38,250; Grants to individuals, 9 grants totaling $38,250 (high: $9,000, low: $750).
Fields of interest: Higher education.
Type of support: Support to graduates or students of specific schools; Undergraduate support.
Application information: Applications accepted.
   Initial approach: Letter
   Deadline(s): Apr. 30
   Additional information: Application should include high school transcript and college application.
EIN: 810392053

5158
Horsman Foundation
c/o Davidson Trust Co.
P.O. Box 2039
Great Falls, MT   59403-2309   (406) 751-3504

Foundation type: Independent foundation
Purpose: Scholarships to financially needy graduates of Flathead High School, MT, who are planning to attend an accredited four-year program of higher education.
Financial data: Year ended 09/30/2013. Assets, $562,388 (M); Expenditures, $133,956; Total giving, $121,525; Grants to individuals, 6 grants totaling $121,525 (high: $56,040, low: $1,449).
Type of support: Support to graduates or students of specific schools; Undergraduate support.
Application information: Application form required.
   Deadline(s): May
   Additional information: Application information packet available at guidance counselor's office.
EIN: 810520094

5159
Hurst-Sorenson Memorial Fund
P.O. Box 428
Stanford, MT   59479-0428   (406) 566-2238
Contact: Mike Zacher, Tr.
Application address: 103 Central Ave., Stanford, MT 59479-0000

Foundation type: Independent foundation
Purpose: Scholarships to graduates of Stanford High School, MT, who attend Protestant universities or vocational or technical schools.
Financial data: Year ended 06/30/2013. Assets, $645,373 (M); Expenditures, $10,253; Total

giving, $7,210; Grants to individuals, 22 grants totaling $7,210 (high: $496, low: $6).
Fields of interest: Vocational education; Vocational education, post-secondary; Protestant agencies & churches.
Type of support: Support to graduates or students of specific schools; Undergraduate support.
Application information: Applications accepted.
   Initial approach: Letter of application including name of school planning to attend
   Deadline(s): July 1
EIN: 810372356

5160
Interbel Education Foundation
P.O. Box 648
Eureka, MT   59917   (406) 889-3311
URL: http://www.interbel.com/

Foundation type: Company-sponsored foundation
Purpose: Scholarships to students with a parent or guardian who is, or has been, a member of InterBel Telephone Cooperative, MT, for two of the past five years.
Financial data: Year ended 12/31/2012. Assets, $124,571 (M); Expenditures, $8,946; Total giving, $8,000; Grants to individuals, 8 grants totaling $8,000 (high: $1,500, low: $750).
Type of support: Scholarships—to individuals.
Application information: Applications accepted. Application form required.
   Additional information: Contact foundation for application form.
EIN: 363684131

5161
Jarecki Foundation
28517 Rocky Pt Rd.
Polson, MT   59860-1299   (406) 883-2248

Foundation type: Independent foundation
Purpose: Scholarships to financially-needy individuals studying range management at Montana State University.
Financial data: Year ended 12/31/2011. Assets, $28,443 (M); Expenditures, $31,969; Total giving, $33,022.
Type of support: Support to graduates or students of specific schools.
Application information: Applications accepted. Application form required.
   Initial approach: Letter
   Deadline(s): None
EIN: 816070700

5162
Mike Venner Memorial Scholarship Fund, Inc.
307 Galaxy Dr.
Butte, MT   59701-3917   (406) 782-0484
Contact: Mike Fisher, Scholarship Committee Lead
Scholarship inquiry e-mail: golf@mikevennermemorial.com
E-mail: quinn3464@bresnan.net; URL: http://www.mikevennermemorial.com/contact.php

Foundation type: Public charity
Purpose: Scholarships to graduating high school seniors from Southwest Montana high schools, MT for attendance at accredited colleges or universities.
Financial data: Year ended 12/31/2011. Assets, $93,248 (M); Expenditures, $18,101; Total giving, $7,500; Grants to individuals, 4 grants totaling $7,500 (high: $2,500, low: $1,250).

Fields of interest: Higher education.
Type of support: Scholarships—to individuals.
Application information: Applications accepted. Application form required. Application form available on the grantmaker's web site.
   Send request by: Mail
   Deadline(s): May
   Applicants should submit the following:
      1) Transcripts
      2) Essay
Program description:
   Scholarships: This scholarship is available to all graduating seniors from southwest Montana high schools. Applicants must plan to attend a two or four year accredited college or university, or be accepted into a post-secondary apprenticeship or training program that has been recognized and approved by the scholarship committee.
EIN: 770672868

5163
Montana Community Foundation
1 N. Last Chance Gulch, Ste. 1
Helena, MT   59624-1145   (406) 443-8313
FAX: (406) 442-0482; E-mail: info@mtcf.org; Mailing address: P.O. box 1145, Helena, MT 59624-1145; URL: http://www.mtcf.org

Foundation type: Community foundation
Purpose: Scholarships to students of MT pursuing higher education at accredited institutions.
Publications: Financial statement; Newsletter.
Financial data: Year ended 06/30/2012. Assets, $59,658,108 (M); Expenditures, $4,674,299; Total giving, $2,567,904. Scholarships—to individuals amount not specified.
Fields of interest: Higher education.
Type of support: Support to graduates or students of specific schools; Undergraduate support.
Application information: Applications accepted. Application form required. Application form available on the grantmaker's web site.
   Initial approach: Application
   Send request by: Online
   Deadline(s): Varies
   Additional information: Scholarship awards range between $500 to $5,000. See web site for eligibility criteria and application guidelines per scholarship type.
EIN: 810450150

5164
Montana State University Billings Foundation
1500 University Dr.
Billings, MT   59101-0245   (406) 657-2244
Contact: Marilynn Miller, Pres. and C.E.O.
FAX: (406) 657-1600;
E-mail: foundation@msubillings.edu; URL: http://www.msubillings.edu/foundation/

Foundation type: Public charity
Purpose: Scholarships to students at Montana State University - Billings.
Publications: Annual report; Financial statement; Newsletter.
Financial data: Year ended 06/30/2012. Assets, $22,968,945 (M); Expenditures, $2,981,723; Total giving, $1,950,827.
Type of support: Employee-related scholarships; Support to graduates or students of specific schools; Undergraduate support; Grants for special needs.
Application information: Applications accepted. Application form required. Application form available on the grantmaker's web site.

Send request by: Mail or e-mail
Copies of proposal: 1
Deadline(s): Jan. 15 for Chancellor's
 Scholarship; Feb. 1 for all others
Final notification: Applicants notified in three to
 four months
Additional information: See web site for complete
 program listings.
EIN: 810301477

5165
The Mountain West Track & Field Club, Inc.

2 Corporate Way
Missoula, MT 59808

Foundation type: Operating foundation
Purpose: Awards by nomination only to athletes residing in MT who have completed their NCAA eligibility, to provide competitive and educational opportunities.
Financial data: Year ended 08/31/2013. Assets, $18,854 (M); Expenditures, $240,114; Total giving, $115,550; Grants to individuals, 5 grants totaling $115,550 (high: $44,550, low: $5,000).
Fields of interest: Athletics/sports, training.
Type of support: Awards/grants by nomination only; Awards/prizes.
Application information: Applications not accepted.
 Additional information: Eligibility and acceptance
 is by invitation only.
EIN: 810459511

5166
Stella M. Nelson Nadeau & Louise E. Nelson Scholarship Foundation

(formerly Stella M. Nelson Nadeau & Louise E. Nelson Senft Scholarship Foundation)
c/o Davidson Trust Co.
P.O. Box 2309
Great Falls, MT 59403-2309 (406) 791-7325

Foundation type: Independent foundation
Purpose: Scholarships to graduates of Flathead High School, MT for postsecondary education.
Financial data: Year ended 12/31/2011. Assets, $94,382 (M); Expenditures, $12,964; Total giving, $10,500; Grants to individuals, 6 grants totaling $10,500 (high: $3,000, low: $1,000).
Type of support: Support to graduates or students of specific schools.
Application information: Application form required.
 Deadline(s): Mid-Apr.
 Applicants should submit the following:
 1) GPA
 2) SAT
 3) Letter(s) of recommendation
 4) ACT
 5) Essay
EIN: 816087287

5167
National Forest Foundation

Fort Missoula Rd., Bldg. 27, Ste. 3
Missoula, MT 59804-7254 (406) 542-2805
Contact: William J. Possiel, Pres.; Adam Liljeblad, Dir., Conservation Awards
FAX: (406) 542-2810;
E-mail: bpossiel@nationalforests.org; Contact inf. for Adam Liljeblad: tel.: (406) 542-2805, ext. 12, e-mail: aliljeblad@natlforests.org; URL: http://www.nationalforests.org/

Foundation type: Public charity
Purpose: Cash awards for innovative market-based solutions to natural resource issues benefitting U.S. National Forests and Grasslands. $75,000 cash award to the winning submission and a $25,000 cash award to the first runner-up in the final stage of the competition.
Publications: Annual report; Newsletter.
Financial data: Year ended 09/30/2011. Assets, $14,864,877 (M); Expenditures, $8,356,952; Total giving, $6,210,755.
Fields of interest: Environment, forests.
Type of support: Awards/prizes.
Application information: Applications accepted.
 Initial approach: Pre-proposal
 Deadline(s): June 16
 Additional information: See web site for eligibility
 criteria. Questions can be sent to
 barrettprize@nationalforests.org.
EIN: 521786332

5168
Fred L. Robinson Fund

P.O. Box 910
Malta, MT 59538-0910

Foundation type: Independent foundation
Purpose: Scholarships to Phillips County, MT, high school seniors pursuing higher education.
Financial data: Year ended 12/31/2013. Assets, $6,000 (M); Expenditures, $6,000; Total giving, $6,000; Grant to an individual, 1 grant totaling $6,000.
Fields of interest: Higher education.
Type of support: Support to graduates or students of specific schools; Undergraduate support.
Application information: Applications accepted. Application form available on the grantmaker's web site.
 Initial approach: Letter
 Deadline(s): Jan. 15
 Additional information: Students should contact
 their guidance counselors for additional
 application guidelines.
EIN: 237079421

5169
Rocky Mountain Elk Foundation, Inc.

5705 Grant Creek Rd.
P.O. Box 8249
Missoula, MT 59808-9394 (406) 523-4500
FAX: (404) 523-4550; E-mail: info@rmef.org;
Toll-free tel.: (800) 225-5355; URL: http://www.rmef.org

Foundation type: Public charity
Purpose: Scholarships to college juniors and seniors with wildlife-related majors.
Publications: Application guidelines; Annual report.
Financial data: Year ended 12/31/2011. Assets, $54,068,544 (M); Expenditures, $54,445,324; Total giving, $4,000; Grants to individuals, totaling $4,000.
Fields of interest: Animals/wildlife, preservation/protection.
Type of support: Scholarships—to individuals.
Application information: Applications accepted. Application form required. Application form available on the grantmaker's web site.
 Deadline(s): Mar. 1
 Applicants should submit the following:
 1) Letter(s) of recommendation
 2) Essay
Program description:
 Wildlife Leadership Awards: Ten $2,000
 undergraduate scholarship awards are given to

junior- and senior-year college students in recognized U.S. or Canadian wildlife programs with at least one semester or two quarters remaining in their degree programs. Previous recipients are ineligible. Applicants must be enrolled as a full-time student for the following fall semester/quarter. Recipients also receive free one-year memberships to the foundation.
EIN: 810421425

5170
Mars & Verna Rolfson Scholarship Trust

P.O. Box 1299
Polson, MT 59860-1299 (406) 883-8813
Contact: Kirk Fulford

Foundation type: Independent foundation
Purpose: Scholarships to high school seniors and graduates of Polson High School, MT, for higher education or Vocational/Technical training.
Financial data: Year ended 12/31/2011. Assets, $500,626 (M); Expenditures, $27,223; Total giving, $21,000.
Fields of interest: Vocational education, post-secondary; Higher education.
Type of support: Support to graduates or students of specific schools; Undergraduate support.
Application information: Application form required.
 Deadline(s): Apr. 1
 Applicants should submit the following:
 1) Letter(s) of recommendation
 2) Transcripts
 3) FAF
EIN: 363677368

5171
The Sacred Portion Children's Outreach, Inc.

7104 Bristol Ln.
Bozeman, MT 59715-8356 (406) 586-5773
Contact: Craig Druckenmiller, Pres.
E-mail: info@sacredportion.org; URL: http://www.sacredportion.org

Foundation type: Public charity
Purpose: Interest free loans and grants to help families with the cost of adoption of children.
Financial data: Year ended 12/31/2011. Assets, $404,335 (M); Expenditures, $302,845; Total giving, $114,004; Grants to individuals, totaling $2,200.
Fields of interest: Adoption.
Type of support: Grants to individuals; Loans—to individuals.
Application information: See web site for additional guidelines.
EIN: 810393190

5172
Louise E. Senft Scholarship Foundation

c/o Davidson Trust Co.
P.O. Box 2309
Great Falls, MT 59403-2309 (406) 791-7325
Application Address: 8 3rd St. N., Great Falls, MT 59903

Foundation type: Independent foundation
Purpose: Scholarships to graduates of Sandpoint High School, ID for attendance at accredited colleges or universities.
Financial data: Year ended 12/31/2011. Assets, $122,487 (M); Expenditures, $10,703; Total giving, $8,000; Grants to individuals, 8 grants totaling $8,000 (high: $1,000, low: $1,000).

Type of support: Support to graduates or students of specific schools.
Application information: Applications accepted. Application form required.
  Initial approach: Letter
  Deadline(s): Mid-Apr.
  Additional information: Contact guidance counselor for further application information.
EIN: 816090522

5173
Shields Valley Foundation Inc.
P.O. Box 308
Clyde Park, MT   59018-0308   (406) 578-2535
Contact: Lisa Held
Application address: P.O. Box 131, Wilsall, MT 59086

Foundation type: Independent foundation
Purpose: Scholarships to graduates of Shields Valley High School, MT, for attendance at an institution of the Montana University System.
Financial data: Year ended 12/31/2012. Assets, $61,252 (M); Expenditures, $20,591; Total giving, $20,130; Grants to individuals, 8 grants totaling $19,500 (high: $4,000, low: $2,000).
Type of support: Support to graduates or students of specific schools.
Application information: Applications accepted. Application form required. Interview required.
  Initial approach: Letter
  Deadline(s): Late Mar. and early May
  Additional information: Application must include high school transcript. Applicant must meet academic standards during each term of higher education to continue to receive the scholarship.
EIN: 810504746

5174
Student Assistance Foundation
2500 Broadway
Helena, MT   59601-4901   (406) 495-7800
Contact: Kelly Chapman, Exec. V.P.
FAX: (406) 495-7852;
E-mail: kcresswell@safmt.org; Toll-free tel.: (877) 265-4463; URL: http://www.smartaboutcollege.org

Foundation type: Public charity
Purpose: Foster Care Education and Training Vouchers only to foster youth ages 16 to 23 who are residents of MT to cover the cost of attending a postsecondary institution.
Publications: Annual report; Financial statement; Newsletter.
Financial data: Year ended 06/30/2012. Assets, $13,791,458 (M); Expenditures, $18,398,693; Total giving, $1,650,498; Grants to individuals, totaling $182,237.
Fields of interest: Higher education; Youth, services.
Type of support: Scholarships—to individuals; Undergraduate support.
Application information: Applications accepted. Application form required. Application form available on the grantmaker's web site.
  Initial approach: Application
  Send request by: Mail for Vouchers, on-line for Circle of Success
  Copies of proposal: 1
  Deadline(s): Jan. 15 and July 15 for Vouchers, Mar. 15 for Circle of Success Grants
  Final notification: Recipients notified Apr. 15 for Circle of Success
  Applicants should submit the following:

1) Transcripts
2) GPA
3) Financial information
4) FAFSA
Additional information: See web site for additional guidelines.
EIN: 810527529

5175
Rudy Suden Scholarship Trust Fund
c/o First Interstate Bank Montana
P.O. Box 5010
Great Falls, MT   59403-5010

Foundation type: Independent foundation
Purpose: Scholarships to graduates and graduating seniors of Denton High School, MT, or Stanford High School, MT for postsecondary education.
Financial data: Year ended 03/31/2012. Assets, $2,022,635 (M); Expenditures, $103,549; Total giving, $93,354; Grants to individuals, 52 grants totaling $93,354 (high: $2,877, low: $877).
Fields of interest: Vocational education, post-secondary; Higher education.
Type of support: Support to graduates or students of specific schools; Technical education support; Undergraduate support.
Application information: Application form required.
  Deadline(s): Apr. 1
  Applicants should submit the following:
  1) Class rank
  2) Letter(s) of recommendation
  3) Transcripts
  4) GPA
  5) Financial information
EIN: 816063733

5176
Svarre Foundation
c/o Robert Goss
101 S. Central Ave.
Sidney, MT   59270   (406) 433-8600
Contact: Robert Goss

Foundation type: Independent foundation
Purpose: Scholarships to residents of Richland County, MT in pursuit of a higher education at accredited institutions.
Financial data: Year ended 12/31/2012. Assets, $415,334 (M); Expenditures, $43,843; Total giving, $33,375; Grants to individuals, 5 grants totaling $10,000 (high: $2,000, low: $2,000).
Fields of interest: Higher education.
Type of support: Scholarships—to individuals.
Application information: Applications accepted. Application form required.
  Initial approach: Request application
  Applicants should submit the following:
  1) Transcripts
  2) Resume
  Additional information: Application must also include the purpose of the grant and reason needed.
EIN: 816013673

5177
Lloyd D. Sweet Education Foundation
P.O. Box 638
Chinook, MT   59523
URL: http://www.sweetscholarship.com/

Foundation type: Independent foundation
Purpose: Scholarships only to graduates of Chinook High School, MT, who maintain at least a 2.0 GPA and carry at least 12 college credits.

Financial data: Year ended 12/31/2012. Assets, $2,540,194 (M); Expenditures, $115,665; Total giving, $81,850; Grants to individuals, 46 grants totaling $81,850 (high: $4,150, low: $500).
Type of support: Support to graduates or students of specific schools; Undergraduate support.
Application information: Applications accepted. Application form required. Application form available on the grantmaker's web site.
  Send request by: Mail
  Deadline(s): Mar. 1
  Applicants should submit the following:
  1) Essay
  2) ACT
  3) Transcripts
  4) Letter(s) of recommendation
EIN: 237131688

5178
George & Blanche Taber Educational Trust
(formerly George and Blanche Taber Scholarship Trust)
P.O. Box 1299
Polson, MT   59860-1299   (406) 883-8831

Foundation type: Independent foundation
Purpose: Scholarship awards to graduates of high schools in Wheatland County, MT.
Financial data: Year ended 12/31/2011. Assets, $69,953 (M); Expenditures, $3,750; Total giving, $1,000.
Type of support: Undergraduate support.
Application information: Applications accepted. Application form required.
  Initial approach: Letter
  Deadline(s): Apr. 1
  Applicants should submit the following:
  1) Letter(s) of recommendation
  2) FAF
  3) Transcripts
EIN: 363718835

5179
Harry and Minerva Townley Educational Trust
P.O. Box 313
Wibaux, MT   59353-0313
Contact: Connie J. Chaffee, Tr.
Application address: P.O. Box 124, Wibaux, MT 59353-0124

Foundation type: Independent foundation
Purpose: Scholarships to graduating seniors of Wibaux County High School, MT, pursuing higher education.
Financial data: Year ended 12/31/2011. Assets, $237,239 (M); Expenditures, $14,025; Total giving, $12,750; Grants to individuals, 20 grants totaling $12,750 (high: $1,000, low: $250).
Fields of interest: Higher education.
Type of support: Support to graduates or students of specific schools; Undergraduate support.
Application information: Applications accepted. Application form required.
  Deadline(s): May 1
  Applicants should submit the following:
  1) Transcripts
  2) Financial information
  3) ACT
  Additional information: Applicants may apply for funds for the first five years after high school graduation and must be enrolled full time to qualify for awards.
EIN: 816082126

5180
Treacy Company

(also known as Treacy Foundation)
P.O. Box 1479
Helena, MT 59624-1479 (406) 443-3549
Contact: Kimmy Skiftun, Exec. Dir.
FAX: (406) 443-6183;
E-mail: kimmy@treacyfoundation.org; URL: http://www.treacyfoundation.org/

Foundation type: Independent foundation
Purpose: Scholarships to financially needy freshmen and sophomore college students who are residents of ID, MT and ND.
Publications: Application guidelines; Annual report.
Financial data: Year ended 12/31/2012. Assets, $37,358,279 (M); Expenditures, $1,616,774; Total giving, $1,158,555; Grants to individuals, totaling $125,000.
Fields of interest: College; Scholarships/financial aid.
Type of support: Scholarships—to individuals.
Application information: Application form required.
Initial approach: Letter
Send request by: Mail
Deadline(s): May 1
Applicants should submit the following:
1) Photograph
2) Letter(s) of recommendation
3) Transcripts
Additional information: Grants are paid directly to the institution to be applied to the student's account. Scholarships are not offered to junior, senior or graduate college students.
EIN: 810270257

5181
Peggy L. Unrau Scholarship Foundation

P.O. Box 1299
Polson, MT 59860-1299 (406) 883-8831
Contact: Kirk Fulford

Foundation type: Independent foundation
Purpose: Scholarships to graduating seniors of Polson High School, MT for attendance at any accredited college, university, technical or vocational training school.
Financial data: Year ended 12/31/2011. Assets, $410,680 (M); Expenditures, $25,437; Total giving, $20,000.
Fields of interest: Higher education.
Type of support: Support to graduates or students of specific schools.
Application information: Applications accepted. Application form required.
Send request by: Mail
Deadline(s): Apr. 1
Applicants should submit the following:
1) Letter(s) of recommendation
2) Class rank
3) GPA

4) Transcripts
5) Financial information
Additional information: Application should also include three references.
EIN: 836051706

5182
Dennis & Phyllis Washington Foundation, Inc.

(formerly Dennis R. Washington Foundation, Inc.)
P.O. Box 16630
Missoula, MT 59808-6630 (406) 523-1300
Contact: Mike Halligan, Exec. Dir.
URL: http://www.dpwfoundation.org/

Foundation type: Company-sponsored foundation
Purpose: Scholarships to Montana residents who plan to attend the select universities in Montana and scholarships to spouses and children of employees of Washington Companies to pursue education. Graduate scholarships to State and National Horatio Alger Scholar Alumni.
Publications: Application guidelines; Program policy statement.
Financial data: Year ended 12/31/2012. Assets, $499,978,077 (M); Expenditures, $5,299,198; Total giving, $3,759,769.
Fields of interest: Higher education; Native Americans/American Indians.
Type of support: Fellowships; Employee-related scholarships; Scholarships—to individuals; Support to graduates or students of specific schools; Graduate support; Undergraduate support.
Application information: Applications accepted. Application form required. Application form available on the grantmaker's web site. Interview required.
Initial approach: Letter
Deadline(s): Apr. 1 for Dennis R. Washington Achievement Scholarship, Apr. 15 for Horatio Alger Montana Undergraduate Scholarship Program
Final notification: Applicants notified in six weeks
Applicants should submit the following:
1) Essay
2) Transcripts
3) Letter(s) of recommendation
4) GPA
Program descriptions:
Dennis and Phyllis Washington Native American Graduate Fellowship: The foundation awards a graduate fellowship of up to $10,000 to a member of a Montana Native American Tribe who is accepted into a Master's or Doctoral Degree program at the Graduate School of The University of Montana or Montana State University. The program is administered by the graduate school admissions office at Montana State University and The University of Montana.

Dennis R. Washington Achievement Scholarship: The foundation annually awards scholarships of up to $30,000 for up to 3 years to State and National Horatio Alger Scholar Alumni who have exhibited integrity and perseverance in overcoming personal adversity and who is working towards a post-graduate degree in education.

Helen B. Miller Horatio Alger Scholarship: The foundation awards college scholarships to students who attend Montana State University, demonstrate financial need, and demonstrate the ability to overcome adversity in their young lives. The program is administered by Montana State University.

Horatio Alger Montana Undergraduate Scholarship Program: The foundation annually awards 50 $10,000 college scholarships to Montana high school seniors planning to attend The University of Montana, The University of Montana-Western, The University of Montana-Missoula College of Technology, Helena College of Technology of the University of Montana, or Montana Tech of the University of Montana. The scholarship was expanded to include Montana State University and its affiliate campuses.

Washington Companies Employee Family Scholarship Program: The foundation awards college scholarships of up to $8,000 to children or spouses of employees who are attending an accredited university, college, vocational technical school, community college of technology, or trade school. Employees must work full-time within an eligible Washington Company.
Company name: The Washington Corporations
EIN: 363606913

5183
Yellowstone Boys and Girls Ranch Foundation, Inc.

2050 Overland Ave.
Billings, MT 59102-6453 (406) 656-8772
Contact: Kurt Alme J.D., Pres.
Toll-free tel.: (800) 879-0850; URL: http://www.yellowstonefoundation.org/

Foundation type: Public charity
Purpose: Scholarships to Yellowstone boys and girls for post high school education or training with tuition, books and supplies.
Publications: Newsletter.
Financial data: Year ended 06/30/2012. Assets, $69,051,251 (M); Expenditures, $3,594,428; Total giving, $1,939,440.
Fields of interest: Vocational education, post-secondary; Higher education.
Type of support: Scholarships—to individuals.
Application information: Contact the foundation for eligibility requirements.
EIN: 810419905

NEBRASKA

5184
Alegent Health-Immanuel Medical Center
6901 N. 72nd St.
Omaha, NE 68122-1799 (402) 572-2121
Contact: Cliff A. Robertson, Pres. and C.E.O.
URL: http://www.alegent.com/body.cfm?id=52

Foundation type: Public charity
Purpose: Scholarships to employees of Immanuel Medical Center for continuing education for personal growth and/or professional development. Financial assistance to patients with demonstrated inability to pay for medical services.
Financial data: Year ended 06/30/2012. Assets, $617,826,265 (M); Expenditures, $244,688,156; Total giving, $21,877,790; Grants to individuals, totaling $21,861,512.
Fields of interest: Education; Economically disadvantaged.
Type of support: Employee-related scholarships; Grants for special needs.
Application information: Patients should complete an application form and provide financial information. Employees applying for scholarships, payments are made directly to the institution upon receipt of statement of costs.
EIN: 470376615

5185
All Our Kids Inc. Foundation
1004 Farnam St., Ste. 200
Omaha, NE 68102 (402) 930-3003

Foundation type: Public charity
Purpose: Scholarships for disadvantaged students from the greater Omaha metro area for attendance at colleges, universities or trade schools in NE, IA, or the greater U.S.
Financial data: Year ended 12/31/2011. Assets, $5,159,533 (M); Expenditures, $162,691; Total giving, $112,899; Grants to individuals, totaling $77,899.
Fields of interest: Vocational education, post-secondary; Higher education.
Type of support: Scholarships—to individuals.
Application information: Applications accepted. Application form required.
  Additional information: The scholarship is for tuition, books and housing. Scholarship is paid directly to the educational institution on behalf of the students. Contact the foundation for additional application guidelines.
EIN: 300206686

5186
Bemis Center for Contemporary Arts, Inc.
724 S. 12th St.
Omaha, NE 68102-3202 (402) 341-7130
Contact: Adam Price, Exec. Dir.
Contact for Artist Residency Program: Heather Johnson, Residency Mgr., tel.: (402) 341-7130, ext. 12, e-mail: heather@bemiscenter.org
FAX: (402) 341-9791;
E-mail: info@bemiscenter.org; URL: http://www.bemiscenter.org

Foundation type: Public charity
Purpose: Residencies to visual artists for a period of three to six months.
Financial data: Year ended 12/31/2011. Assets, $4,403,814 (M); Expenditures, $1,433,175; Total giving, $12,562; Grants to individuals, totaling $12,562.
Fields of interest: Visual arts; Disabilities, people with.
Type of support: Residencies.
Application information: Applications accepted. Application form available on the grantmaker's web site.
  Send request by: Online
  Deadline(s): Sept. 30 and Feb. 28
  Applicants should submit the following:
    1) Work samples
    2) Curriculum vitae
    3) Resume
  Additional information: Application fee of $40 is required. Applicant must be able to speak and understand English. See web site for complete program guidelines.
Program description:
  Residencies: The center provides well-equipped studio spaces, living accommodations and monthly stipends to 36 artists per year. Three month residencies allow artists time to reflect, research and take risks. Spaces range from 860 to 2,400 square feet. The center's facilities are designed to foster creativity and the productive exchange of ideas.
EIN: 470653927

5187
Bran Inc.
4205 N. 101st St.
Omaha, NE 68134 (402) 397-9785
Contact: Ray Weinberg, Pres.
URL: http://www.bran-inc.org

Foundation type: Operating foundation
Purpose: Scholarships to undergraduate students enrolled at accredited universities or colleges in NE.
Financial data: Year ended 06/30/2013. Assets, $316,191 (M); Expenditures, $139,374; Total giving, $23,500; Grants to individuals, 26 grants totaling $23,500 (high: $1,500, low: $500).
Fields of interest: Higher education.
Type of support: Undergraduate support.
Application information: Applications accepted.
  Deadline(s): None
  Additional information: Apply through the school's scholarship office, including name of school, status and GPA.
EIN: 363449742

5188
Fred A. Bryan College Students Fund
c/o Wells Fargo Bank Nebraska, N.A.
1919 Douglas St. 2nd Fl. Mac N8000-027
Omaha, NE 68102-1317 (888) 730-4933

Foundation type: Independent foundation
Purpose: Scholarships to male graduates of high schools in South Bend, IN, with preference given to those who have been Boy Scouts in good standing for a period of two years at some time prior to application.
Financial data: Year ended 12/31/2012. Assets, $243,383 (M); Expenditures, $11,994; Total giving, $6,500.
Fields of interest: Boy scouts; Men; Young adults, male.
Type of support: Support to graduates or students of specific schools; Undergraduate support.
Application information: Application form required.
  Initial approach: Letter
  Applicants should submit the following:
    1) FAF
    2) Transcripts
    3) GPA
    4) Class rank
    5) Letter(s) of recommendation
  Additional information: Nomination application should also include IQ rating, attendance record, school activity record and, if a Boy Scout, a copy of Scout Record. Contact foundation for current application deadline/guidelines.
EIN: 356012911

5189
BryanLGH Foundation
1600 S. 48th St.
Lincoln, NE 68506-1299 (402) 481-8605
Contact: Bob Ravenscroft, V.P., Advancement and C.D.O
FAX: (402) 481-8459;
E-mail: bob.ravenscroft@bryanhealth.org;
URL: http://www.bryanlgh.com/contactthefoundation

Foundation type: Public charity
Purpose: Scholarship to students of NE pursuing an education in the health science field who would otherwise be unable to pursue their educational and professional goals.
Financial data: Year ended 05/31/2012. Assets, $12,762,233 (M); Expenditures, $569,495; Total giving, $418,349; Grants to individuals, totaling $182,423.
Fields of interest: Health sciences school/education.
Type of support: Scholarships—to individuals.
Application information: Applications accepted. Application form available on the grantmaker's web site.
  Additional information: Application must be completed on-line. See web site for additional application information.
EIN: 237005720

5190
The Susan Thompson Buffett Foundation
(formerly The Buffett Foundation)
222 Kiewit Plz.
Omaha, NE 68131-3302
Contact: Allen Greenberg, Pres.
Tel. for scholarship information: (402) 943-1383
E-mail: scholarships@stbfoundation.org;
URL: http://www.buffettscholarships.org

Foundation type: Independent foundation
Purpose: Scholarships to residents of NE to attend NE public colleges and universities.
Financial data: Year ended 12/31/2012. Assets, $2,384,070,265 (M); Expenditures, $374,616,566; Total giving, $367,167,893; Grants to individuals, totaling $21,073,377.
Fields of interest: Public education; Elementary/secondary education; Higher education.
Type of support: Scholarships—to individuals; Awards/grants by nomination only; Awards/prizes; Undergraduate support.
Application information: Application form required. Application form available on the grantmaker's web site.
  Deadline(s): Feb. 1 for scholarships
  Additional information: Scholarships are based on financial need. Prizes by nomination only to winners of the Alice Buffett Outstanding Teacher Award, held in NE. The foundation only responds to questions about scholarships and awards. See web site for additional information.

Program descriptions:

Outstanding Teacher Awards: Teaching awards are made to outstanding certified teachers in the Omaha public school system (K-12) with a minimum of two years teaching experience. The program provides 15 awards annually, $10,000 per recipient. Teachers must be nominated by members of the community. Individual applications are not accepted.

Scholarship Program: The scholarships can be used to cover expenses related to attending college (e.g. tuition and fees, housing, books). The amount of the scholarship is reviewed each year and adjusted accordingly to accommodate increases or decreases in college-going costs. The foundation initiated the William H. Thompson Scholars Learning Communities. Students who receive the scholarship and will be attending either University of Nebraska-Omaha, University of Nebraska-Lincoln or University of Nebraska-Kearney will be part of this Learning Community.

EIN: 476032365

5191
Art & Clara Butts Scholarship Foundation
P.O. Box 577
Burwell, NE   68823-0577
Contact: Joan Vodenhal

Foundation type: Independent foundation
Purpose: Scholarships to residents of Garfield County, NE, and the surrounding area.
Financial data: Year ended 06/30/2013. Assets, $188,615 (M); Expenditures, $10,359; Total giving, $8,000; Grants to individuals, 8 grants totaling $8,000 (high: $1,000, low: $1,000).
Type of support: Scholarships—to individuals.
Application information: Applications accepted. Application form required.
  Deadline(s): June 1
  Applicants should submit the following:
    1) Letter(s) of recommendation
    2) Transcripts
  Additional information: Application should also include a college application letter.
EIN: 362899308

5192
The CEDARS Home for Children Foundation, Inc.
6601 Pioneers Blvd., Ste. 2
Lincoln, NE   68506-5260   (402) 434-5437
Contact: James R. Blue, Pres. and C.E.O.
FAX: (402) 437-8833; E-mail: info@cedars-kids.org;
URL: http://www.cedarskids.org

Foundation type: Public charity
Purpose: Scholarships to former participants of CEDARS Home for Children programs in the Lincoln, NE area.
Publications: Annual report.
Financial data: Year ended 06/30/2012. Assets, $25,300,501 (M); Expenditures, $2,524,415; Total giving, $1,163,103.
Fields of interest: Higher education.
Type of support: Scholarships—to individuals.
Application information: Applications accepted. Application form required. Application form available on the grantmaker's web site. Interview required.
  Initial approach: Application
  Deadline(s): Apr. 1
  Applicants should submit the following:
    1) SAR
    2) Letter(s) of recommendation
    3) Essay

Program description:

CEDARS Scholarships: Scholarships up to $1,000 are available to individuals who have previously received services from the CEDARS Home for Children, to be used towards their postsecondary education. Eligible applicants must have obtained their high school diploma or G.E.D., and be eligible for federal Pell Grants. Applicants may re-apply on an annual basis.
EIN: 476024881

5193
Cozad Public Schools Foundation
P.O. Box 540
Cozad, NE   69130

Foundation type: Independent foundation
Purpose: Scholarships to residents of Cozad, NE for higher education.
Financial data: Year ended 08/31/2013. Assets, $870,830 (M); Expenditures, $103,405; Total giving, $102,033; Grants to individuals, 18 grants totaling $35,550 (high: $5,000, low: $200).
Fields of interest: Higher education.
Type of support: Scholarships—to individuals.
Application information: Applications accepted.
  Initial approach: Letter
  Deadline(s): None
EIN: 470688549

5194
William E. & Rose Marie Davis Foundation
2391 Davis Mountain Ln.
Omaha, NE   68112-5159   (402) 455-9035
E-mail: davisfnd@aol.com

Foundation type: Independent foundation
Purpose: Scholarships to high school graduates or GED recipients, primarily in NE, for higher education.
Financial data: Year ended 12/31/2012. Assets, $548,781 (M); Expenditures, $45,461; Total giving, $35,640.
Fields of interest: Higher education; Scholarships/financial aid.
Type of support: Scholarships—to individuals.
Application information: Applications accepted. Application form required. Interview required.
  Initial approach: Telephone
  Send request by: Mail
  Copies of proposal: 1
  Deadline(s): May 1
  Applicants should submit the following:
    1) Transcripts
    2) SAT
    3) Letter(s) of recommendation
    4) ACT
  Additional information: Application should also include essay of no more than 300 words about experiences and/or potential as a leader. Recipients must maintain at least a 2.2 cumulative GPA. Scholarships are renewable.
EIN: 911787066

5195
Doniphan-Trumbull Public School Foundation
(formerly Doniphan/Trumbull Educational Foundation)
P.O. Box 300
Doniphan, NE   68832-0300   (402) 845-2282

Foundation type: Independent foundation

Purpose: Scholarships primarily to residents of NE for higher education.
Financial data: Year ended 12/31/2011. Assets, $205,635 (M); Expenditures, $3,920; Total giving, $3,300; Grants to individuals, 5 grants totaling $3,300 (high: $900, low: $500).
Fields of interest: Higher education.
Type of support: Scholarships—to individuals.
Application information:
  Deadline(s): Apr. 30
EIN: 470778534

5196
The Dressage Foundation, Inc.
1314 O St., Ste. 305
Lincoln, NE   68508-1424   (402) 434-8585
Contact: Clay Teske, Pres. and C.E.O.
FAX: (402) 436-3053;
E-mail: info@dressagefoundation.org; URL: http://www.dressagefoundation.org

Foundation type: Public charity
Purpose: Scholarships and grants to individuals for study and training in Dressage.
Publications: Application guidelines; Informational brochure.
Financial data: Year ended 12/31/2011. Assets, $2,092,853 (M); Expenditures, $408,803; Total giving, $208,542; Grants to individuals, totaling $149,026.
Fields of interest: Athletics/sports, equestrianism.
Type of support: Scholarships—to individuals.
Application information: Applications accepted. Application form required.
  Initial approach: Telephone
  Deadline(s): Vary
  Additional information: See web site for complete program information.
Program descriptions:

Amanda Ward Legacy Fund: This fund provides an annual award of $1,000 to the highest-scoring junior/young rider at 3rd-level and above, at the New England Dressage Association Fall Festival.

Anne L. Barlow Ramsay Annual Grant: This $25,000 grant is available to successful American competitors at Prix St. George or higher to train and compete in Europe. Successful applicants will demonstrate an ability to be an ambassador for the American-bred horse in Europe.

Carol Lavell Advanced Dressage Prize: This $25,000 prize is used to provide coaching and training to a talented, committed, qualified rider whose plan is to reach and excel at the elite, international standards of high performance Dressage.

Carol Lavell Gifted Fund: The fund provides up to nine scholarships of $1,000 to adult amateur riders so that they may spend more time training with their horse.

Cheryl Finke Developing Rider Fund for CenterLine Dressage (IL): The fund awards scholarships to help provide education training for riders who are members of CenterLine Dressage (IL) and are riding at Fourth Level and above.

Continuing Education for Dressage Instructors: Founded by Maryal Barnett, the program offers five annual grants of $1,000 each to USDF GMOs for Instructor education and five annual grants of up to $1,500 to individuals pursuing Instructor Certification.

Major Anders Lindgren Scholarship: Two $2,000 and one $6,000 scholarships are available annually from the foundation to help an individual study abroad to improve his/her teaching and training of Dressage. Talented and successful Dressage instructors, especially those in the USDF certified pool (training through Fourth Level), are eligible to apply.

Renee Isler Dressage Support Fund: This fund helps applicants to the United States Dressage Federation FEI Junior/Young Rider Clinic Series, who are in need of financial assistance in order to attend, if qualified and accepted by the federation. Nine grants of up to $800 each are available each year.

Trip Harting Fund: One $500 grant is available annually to a current or graduate rider with a Pony Club rating of B or A to assist in attending the United States Dressage Foundation's "L" Education or Instructor Certification programs.

USDF Region 9 Teaching Excellence Award: This $5,000 award recognizes excellence in teaching Dressage by a USDF Region 9 Dressage Instructor.

Young Rider Olympic Dream Program: The program takes four top young American dressage riders to Europe for a two week introduction to European dressage. Applications are accepted from USDF Young Riders, 16-21 years of age, and 22 year-old graduates of the Advanced Young Rider Program, who are riding at Fourth Level or above.
EIN: 363670953

5197
EducationQuest Foundation
(formerly Foundation for Educational Funding, Inc.)
P.O. Box 82552
Lincoln, NE 68501-2552 (402) 479-6735
Contact: Liz Fieselman, Pres. and C.E.O.
FAX: (402) 479-6658;
E-mail: info@educationquest.org; Additional address: 1300 O St., Lincoln, NE 68508; Toll-free tel.: (800) 303-3745; URL: http://www.educationquest.org/

Foundation type: Public charity
Purpose: Scholarships by nomination only to low-income NE residents attending colleges and universities in NE. Some scholarships also to high school guidance counselors.
Financial data: Year ended 09/30/2011. Assets, $13,710,499 (M); Expenditures, $1,338,146; Total giving, $1,284,535.
Fields of interest: Economically disadvantaged.
Type of support: Awards/grants by nomination only; Undergraduate support.
Application information: See web site for further program and application information.
Program description:
Reaching Your Potential Scholarship Program: Students who face significant obstacles to higher education are the target of this need-based, renewable scholarship program which provides scholarships between $2,500 and $6,000. Applicants are referred to the program by statewide community agencies and colleges. This scholarship is not available to the general public, students must be referred by a college financial aid office.
EIN: 470606382

5198
The Winifred, Ruth, Frances & Dorothy Edwards Foundation, Inc.
6443 Glenwood Rd.
Omaha, NE 68132-1844 (402) 556-4769
Contact: Gerald L. Adcock, V.P. and Dir.

Foundation type: Independent foundation
Purpose: Scholarships to individuals in IA and NE for higher education, with preference given to students of the behavioral sciences.
Financial data: Year ended 12/31/2013. Assets, $1,271,515 (M); Expenditures, $76,813; Total

giving, $62,000; Grants to individuals, 46 grants totaling $62,000 (high: $3,000, low: $1,000).
Fields of interest: Psychology/behavioral science.
Type of support: Scholarships—to individuals.
Application information: Applications accepted. Application form required.
Deadline(s): Jan. 10 and June 10
Additional information: Application must include transcript and references.
EIN: 470623166

5199
Elliott-Hemingford Scholarship Foundation
(formerly Hemingford Scholarship Foundation)
803 Box Butte Ave.
Alliance, NE 69301 (308) 487-3327
Contact: Ramona Hucke
Application address: P.O. Box 217, Hemingford, NE 69348; tel.: (308) 487-3327

Foundation type: Independent foundation
Purpose: Scholarships to graduates of Hemingford High School, NE, in their second, third, or fourth year of college.
Financial data: Year ended 07/31/2011. Assets, $723,586 (M); Expenditures, $45,337; Total giving, $42,928; Grants to individuals, 24 grants totaling $42,928 (high: $3,047, low: $858).
Type of support: Support to graduates or students of specific schools; Undergraduate support.
Application information: Application form required.
Initial approach: Letter
Deadline(s): June 15
Additional information: Application must include recommendations, scholastic standing, and financial need.
EIN: 363504495

5200
Jeffrey Wallace Ellis Trust
c/o McDermott & Miller PC
P.O. Box 1317
Hastings, NE 68902-1317 (216) 498-3914
Contact: Lloyd H. Ellis, Jr., Pres. and Dir.
Application address: 32250 Woodsdale Ln., Solon, OH 44139, tel.: (216) 498-3914

Foundation type: Independent foundation
Purpose: Graduate and advanced study scholarships in professional arts, sciences, or equivalent fields to NE residents. Applicants must rank in the upper ten percent of their undergraduate classes to qualify.
Financial data: Year ended 12/31/2012. Assets, $2,542,483 (M); Expenditures, $140,723; Total giving, $111,500.
Fields of interest: Arts; Science.
Type of support: Graduate support; Postgraduate support.
Application information: Applications accepted.
Initial approach: Letter or telephone
Deadline(s): None
Applicants should submit the following:
   1) Letter(s) of recommendation
   2) Transcripts
Additional information: Application must also include GMAT or equivalent scores and description of extracurricular activities.
EIN: 363494704

5201
Harland and Genevieve Emerson Foundation
c/o Wells Fargo, Trust Tax Department
1919 Douglas St., 2nd Fl., MAC N8000-027
Omaha, NE 68102-1317 (515) 697-4300
Contact: James E. Van Werden, Tr.
Application address: 1009 Main St., P.O. Box 99, Adel, IA 50003, tel:(515) 697-4300

Foundation type: Independent foundation
Purpose: Loans to graduates of Adel-Minburn-Desoto High School, IA, to attend college, university, trade or business school.
Financial data: Year ended 09/30/2013. Assets, $924,106 (M); Expenditures, $59,744; Total giving, $9,875; Grants to individuals, 23 grants totaling $9,875 (high: $750, low: $250).
Fields of interest: Vocational education, post-secondary; Higher education; Business school/education.
Type of support: Student loans—to individuals; Support to graduates or students of specific schools; Undergraduate support.
Application information: Application form required.
Initial approach: Letter
Deadline(s): Apr. 15 and Dec. 1
Applicants should submit the following:
   1) Transcripts
   2) Essay
Additional information: Application must also include the tax returns from the last three years of the parent and student. Loans cover college expenses.
EIN: 426543700

5202
The Federated Church of Columbus Foundation, Inc.
2704 15th St.
Columbus, NE 68601-4935

Foundation type: Independent foundation
Purpose: Scholarships to residents of Columbus, NE, for higher education.
Financial data: Year ended 12/31/2011. Assets, $766,819 (M); Expenditures, $44,115; Total giving, $39,000.
Fields of interest: Scholarships/financial aid.
Type of support: Undergraduate support.
Application information: Applications accepted. Application form required.
Deadline(s): June 15
Additional information: Application should include most recent transcripts; scholarships are renewable.
EIN: 470818736

5203
Bruce M. Fellman Charitable Foundation Trust
809 N. 96th St.
Omaha, NE 68114 (402) 392-1800
Contact: Howard Kooper, Tr.

Foundation type: Independent foundation
Purpose: Scholarships to financially needy individuals pursuing an undergraduate degree who reside in Omaha, NE and surrounding areas.
Financial data: Year ended 12/31/2011. Assets, $404,751 (M); Expenditures, $22,036; Total giving, $21,000; Grants to individuals, 21 grants totaling $21,000 (high: $1,000, low: $1,000).
Fields of interest: Education.
Type of support: Undergraduate support.
Application information: Application form required.

Initial approach: Letter
Deadline(s): Apr. 1
Applicants should submit the following:
1) Transcripts
2) Letter(s) of recommendation
3) GPA
Additional information: Applicant must demonstrate financial need.
EIN: 476146480

5204
The Foundation for Lincoln Public Schools
3801 S. 14th St.
PO Box 82889
Lincoln, NE 68502-5340 (402) 436-1612
Contact: Sharon Wherry, Pres.
FAX: (402) 436-1692; E-mail: foundation@lps.org;
URL: http://www.foundationforlps.org

Foundation type: Public charity
Purpose: Memorial scholarships to high school seniors of Lincoln, NE to further their education at colleges or universities.
Publications: Annual report; Informational brochure; Newsletter.
Financial data: Year ended 08/31/2012. Assets, $7,285,307 (M); Expenditures, $1,365,172; Total giving, $778,058; Grants to individuals, totaling $163,900.
Fields of interest: Higher education.
Type of support: Fellowships; Scholarships—to individuals; Graduate support.
Application information: Applications accepted. Application form required.
Copies of proposal: 1
Deadline(s): Varies
Applicants should submit the following:
1) Letter(s) of recommendation
2) Financial information
3) Essay
Additional information: Contact foundation for eligibility requirements and application information for the various scholarships administered by the foundation.
Program descriptions:
Helen Krieger Outstanding Healthcare Provider Award: An award of $1,000 is given to recognize a healthcare provider who has made a significant contribution to the lives of students and families by providing excellence in healthcare and healthcare education.
John Prasch Health and Physical Fitness Award: An award of $1,000 is given to recognize an educator each year who has made a significant contribution to students' lives by promoting health and physical fitness.
Marie Bourke Leadership Award: An annual award of $1,000 is given to recognize an outstanding principal in the Lincoln Public Schools. Principals honored by the award demonstrate outstanding levels of leadership and continuous improvement in student achievement and development.
Nebraska Heart Institute Outstanding Science Educator Award: An award of $1,000 will be given to a Lincoln Public Schools science educator who has made significant contributions to students' lives in the classroom and beyond.
R.L. Fredstrom Leadership Award: An award of $1,000 is given to recognize outstanding leadership or potential for leadership in the Lincoln Public Schools.
Russwood Chrysler Outstanding Science Educator Award: Awards of $1,000 are given to recognize Lincoln Public Schools educators who demonstrate excellence in science education.
State Farm Insurance Companies Outstanding Educator Award: An award of $1,000 is given to

Lincoln Public Schools educators who motivate students to reach their full potential in the classroom and beyond. To be eligible for nominations, educators must have worked for Lincoln Public Schools for three or more years.
EIN: 363490560

5205
Fremont Area Community Foundation
1005 E. 23rd St., Ste. 2
P.O. Box 182
Fremont, NE 68025-4932 (402) 721-4252
Contact: Jessica Janssen, Exec. Dir.
FAX: (402) 721-9359;
E-mail: info@facfoundation.org; URL: http://www.facfoundation.org

Foundation type: Community foundation
Purpose: Scholarships to residents of Fremont, NE, and surrounding communities.
Publications: Application guidelines; Annual report; Informational brochure (including application guidelines); Newsletter.
Financial data: Year ended 06/30/2012. Assets, $14,338,572 (M); Expenditures, $1,938,057; Total giving, $1,546,904.
Fields of interest: Higher education.
Type of support: Technical education support; Undergraduate support.
Application information: Applications accepted. Application form required. Application form available on the grantmaker's web site.
Send request by: Mail or fax
Copies of proposal: 1
Deadline(s): Apr. 1
Applicants should submit the following:
1) Transcripts
2) Resume
3) Letter(s) of recommendation
4) GPA
5) FAFSA
6) Essay
7) ACT
Additional information: Applications submitted through area high school guidance counselors. See web site for additional information.
EIN: 470629642

5206
Genesis Foundation, Inc.
3223 N. 45th St.
Omaha, NE 68104-3713
Contact: Robert K. Gjere, Pres., Treas., and Exec. Dir.

Foundation type: Independent foundation
Purpose: Scholarships to young Christians residing in urban Omaha, NE, who are pursuing theological education. Major emphasis for determining eligibility will be given to their living environments, financial need, other available resources, and commitment to the ministry.
Financial data: Year ended 12/31/2012. Assets, $4,527,076 (M); Expenditures, $212,301; Total giving, $100,500.
Fields of interest: Theological school/education.
Type of support: Undergraduate support.
Application information: Applications accepted. Application form required. Interview required.
Deadline(s): Contact foundation for current application deadlines
Applicants should submit the following:
1) Financial information
2) Essay
EIN: 470799762

5207
Girl Scouts - Homestead Council
8230 Beechwood Dr.
Lincoln, NE 68510
Contact: Fran Marshall, C.E.O.
FAX: (402) 476-0966;
E-mail: HomesteadInfo@girlscoutsnebraska.org;
Toll-free tel.: (800) 487-2578; E-Mail for Fran Marshall: fmarshall@girlscoutsnebraska.org;
URL: http://girlscoutsnebraska.org/

Foundation type: Public charity
Purpose: Provides financial assistance for girls and adults who want to participate in the Girl Scouts program, removing financial barriers that may prevent participation. Funds go towards dues, uniforms, program resources, special activities and training.
Publications: Application guidelines.
Financial data: Year ended 09/30/2011. Assets, $12,925,211 (M); Expenditures, $6,040,286.
Fields of interest: Girl scouts; Girls.
Type of support: Grants to individuals.
Application information: Applications accepted. Application form required. Application form available on the grantmaker's web site.
EIN: 470432299

5208
Good Neighbor Community Center, Inc.
2617 Y St.
Lincoln, NE 68503-1750 (402) 477-4173
Contact: Sheila Schlisner, Exec. Dir.
FAX: (402) 477-4174; E-mail: tom@gncclincoln.org;
E-Mail for Sheila Schlisner : sheila@gncclincoln.orgTel. for Sheila Schlisner : (402)-477-4173 Ext. 104; URL: http://gncclincoln.org/

Foundation type: Public charity
Purpose: Provides basic and emergency needs such as food, clothing and household items to low-income individuals and families.
Publications: Newsletter.
Financial data: Year ended 06/30/2012. Assets, $74,578 (M); Expenditures, $3,246,036; Total giving, $3,022,020; Grants to individuals, totaling $3,022,020.
Fields of interest: Human services.
Type of support: Grants to individuals.
Application information: Applications not accepted.
EIN: 200391739

5209
Good Samaritan Hospital Foundation
111 W. 31st St.
Kearney, NE 68847 (308) 865-2700
Contact: Randy DeFreece, Pres. and Exec. Dir.
FAX: (308) 865-2933; Additional tel.: (308) 865-2703; URL: http://bur-ms-sm6-03a.medseek.com/websitefiles/chigshs10027/body.cfm?id=421

Foundation type: Public charity
Purpose: Scholarships to residents of Good Samaritan Health Systems' primary or secondary service county area, or who are attending an educational institution in this area, for health-related education.
Publications: Annual report; Informational brochure; Newsletter; Occasional report.
Financial data: Year ended 06/30/2012. Assets, $10,295,927 (M); Expenditures, $2,332,961; Total giving, $1,711,299.
Fields of interest: Health care.

Type of support: Undergraduate support.
Application information: Applications accepted.
Application form required. Application form
available on the grantmaker's web site.
 Send request by: Mail
 Deadline(s): June 1
 Applicants should submit the following:
  1) Essay
  2) Transcripts
  3) Letter(s) of recommendation
 Additional information: Application should also
  include two letters of recommendation
  verification of enrollment.
EIN: 470659443

5210
Grand Island Community Foundation, Inc.
1811 W. 2nd St., Ste. 480
Grand Island, NE 68803 (308) 381-7767
Contact: Tammy Morris M.S., C.E.O.
FAX: (308) 384-4069; E-mail: info@gicf.org;
URL: http://www.gicf.org

Foundation type: Community foundation
Purpose: Scholarships to individuals residing in
Central Nebraska for higher education.
Publications: Application guidelines; Annual report;
Annual report (including application guidelines);
Financial statement; Grants list; Informational
brochure; Informational brochure (including
application guidelines); Newsletter; Occasional
report.
Financial data: Year ended 12/31/2012. Assets,
$7,077,774 (M); Expenditures, $763,287; Total
giving, $499,132; Grants to individuals, 66 grants
totaling $499,132.
Fields of interest: Higher education; Scholarships/
financial aid.
Type of support: Scholarships—to individuals;
Support to graduates or students of specific
schools; Graduate support; Undergraduate
support.
Application information: Applications accepted.
Application form required. Application form
available on the grantmaker's web site.
 Send request by: Online
 Copies of proposal: 1
 Deadline(s): Feb. 19
Program description:
 Scholarships: The foundation manages over 20
scholarship funds that have been established by
caring donors who have a commitment to higher
education and wish to provide opportunities and
assistance to students who want to further their
education. Scholarship amounts typically range
from $100 to $10,000. The actual amount of any
given scholarship award can vary from year to year
due to fluctuations in investment returns and in the
number of qualified applications received. The
foundation determines, on a yearly basis, the
number of scholarship awards and the amount
awarded from each scholarship fund. Most
scholarships are awarded to graduating high school
students for undergraduate education, some
non-traditional student scholarships are also
available. Each scholarship fund has unique
eligibility requirements.
EIN: 476032570

5211
H.H. Red and Ruth Nelson Foundation
302 S. 36th St.
Omaha, NE 68131-3827

Foundation type: Public charity

Purpose: Awards to outstanding teachers or
counselors in the Council Bluffs and Lewis Central
School Districts, Omaha, NE.
Financial data: Year ended 12/31/2011. Assets,
$1,259,948 (M); Expenditures, $164,282; Total
giving, $106,958. Awards/prizes amount not
specified.
Type of support: Awards/grants by nomination only;
Awards/prizes.
Application information: Awards are by nomination
only.
Program description:
 Excellence in Teaching Award: This award honors
outstanding teachers and counselors from the
Council Bluffs and Lew Central School Districts.
Award recipients are chosen based on their
knowledge, skills, and abilities (both inside and
outside the classroom) that benefit both young
people and the Omaha community. Teachers will
receive a $5,000 check each, a specifically
designed trophy and public recognition.
EIN: 911876884

5212
Hamilton Community Foundation, Inc.
1216 L St.
P.O. Box 283
Aurora, NE 68818-2016 (402) 694-3200
Contact: Sidney L. Widga, Treas.
FAX: (402) 694-6160

Foundation type: Community foundation
Purpose: Scholarships to residents of Hamilton
County, NE for continuing education at accredited
colleges or universities.
Publications: Annual report.
Financial data: Year ended 12/31/2012. Assets,
$12,819,535 (M); Expenditures, $917,306; Total
giving, $803,492; Grants to individuals, 112 grants
totaling $234,628.
Fields of interest: Education.
Type of support: Scholarships—to individuals.
Application information: Application form required.
 Initial approach: Letter
EIN: 476038289

5213
Albert G. and Bernice F. Hansen
Charitable Foundation
12165 W. Center Rd., Ste. 56
Omaha, NE 68144-3974
Contact: Robert Roh, Tr.

Foundation type: Independent foundation
Purpose: Scholarships to students graduating from
high schools in Chase, Dundy, Frontier, Hayes,
Hitchcock and Red Willow counties, NE, for
postsecondary education.
Financial data: Year ended 12/31/2012. Assets,
$4,979,363 (M); Expenditures, $285,865; Total
giving, $203,458; Grants to individuals, 20 grants
totaling $78,800 (high: $4,000, low: $2,800).
Fields of interest: Higher education.
Type of support: Scholarships—to individuals.
Application information: Applications accepted.
 Initial approach: Letter
 Deadline(s): None
 Additional information: Application must outline
  financial need and qualifications.
EIN: 363847506

5214
Hapke Educational Fund
c/o Wells Fargo Bank, N.A.
1919 Douglas St., 2nd Fl.
Omaha, NE 68102-1310
Contact: Sue Wiele
Application address: c/o Sue Wiele, 2511 W. 60th
St., Davenport, IA 52806

Foundation type: Independent foundation
Purpose: Scholarships to graduates of high schools
in Davenport, IA, for study at accredited four-year
colleges in the U.S.
Financial data: Year ended 05/31/2011. Assets,
$0 (M); Expenditures, $18,473; Total giving,
$10,000; Grants to individuals, 2 grants totaling
$10,000 (high: $5,000, low: $5,000).
Type of support: Support to graduates or students
of specific schools.
Application information: Applications accepted.
Application form required.
 Initial approach: Letter
 Send request by: Mail
 Deadline(s): Mar. 19
 Applicants should submit the following:
  1) Essay
  2) SAR
  3) Photograph
  4) GPA
  5) ACT
  6) FAFSA
  7) Transcripts
EIN: 426344503

5215
Hastings Community Foundation, Inc.
800 W. 3rd St. Ste. 232
Hastings, NE 68901 (402) 462-5152
Contact: Susan Poppe, Office Mgr.; Stephanie Bliss,
Admin. Asst.
FAX: (402) 462-5171; E-mail: hcf@inebraska.com;
Mailing address: P.O. Box 703, Hastings, NE
68902-0703; URL: http://
www.hastingscommunityfoundation.org/

Foundation type: Community foundation
Purpose: Scholarships to graduating seniors of
Hastings, NE and Adams County, NE.
Publications: Application guidelines; Annual report;
Grants list; Informational brochure; Informational
brochure (including application guidelines);
Newsletter; Occasional report.
Financial data: Year ended 12/31/2012. Assets,
$8,227,061 (M); Expenditures, $426,433; Total
giving, $359,084; Grants to individuals, 37 grants
totaling $23,000.
Fields of interest: Higher education.
Type of support: Scholarships—to individuals;
Support to graduates or students of specific
schools; Undergraduate support.
Application information: Applications accepted.
Application form required.
EIN: 363569968

5216
The Hawks Foundation
1044 N. 115th St., Ste. 400
Omaha, NE 68154-4410 (402) 691-9500
Contact: Rhonda Hawks, Tr.

Foundation type: Independent foundation
Purpose: Scholarships primarily to Omaha, NE,
area residents.
Financial data: Year ended 12/31/2012. Assets,
$82,003,672 (M); Expenditures, $3,681,078;
Total giving, $3,051,612.

Fields of interest: Scholarships/financial aid.
Type of support: Scholarships—to individuals.
Application information: Applications accepted. Application form required.
> *Deadline(s):* None
> *Applicants should submit the following:*
>   1) Transcripts
>   2) ACT
> *Additional information:* Applicants must be high school graduates enrolled or in the process of being enrolled full-time in an accredited institution of higher learning. In addition, they must have maintained at least a 2.8 cumulative GPA.

EIN: 476194021

5217
Hay Springs School-Community Foundation

P.O. Box 81
Hay Springs, NE 69347-0081 (308) 638-7127
FAX: (308) 638-7201;
E-mail: foundation@hsscfoundation.org;
URL: http://www.hsscfoundation.org

Foundation type: Public charity
Purpose: Scholarships to individuals in the Hay Springs, NE area for postsecondary education.
Financial data: Year ended 12/31/2012. Assets, $789,002 (M); Expenditures, $241,305; Total giving, $0.
Fields of interest: Higher education.
Type of support: Scholarships—to individuals; Undergraduate support.
Application information: Applications accepted.
> *Additional information:* Contact the foundation for additional guidelines.

EIN: 710897086

5218
Elmer E. Hester - Dundy County Public Schools Foundation

P.O. Box 33
Benkelman, NE 69021-0033 (308) 423-2214
Contact: Elmer Case, Pres.

Foundation type: Independent foundation
Purpose: Scholarships to high school graduates of Dundy County, NE, for higher education.
Financial data: Year ended 12/31/2012. Assets, $3,733,710 (M); Expenditures, $212,066; Total giving, $149,354.
Fields of interest: Education.
Type of support: Support to graduates or students of specific schools.
Application information: Applications accepted. Application form required.
> *Initial approach:* Letter
> *Deadline(s):* July 31
> *Additional information:* Contact foundation for application procedures.

EIN: 476026486

5219
Higher Education Trust

(formerly Trust for Higher Education of Graduates of Accredited Fillmore County, Nebraska High Schools)
896 G. St.
P.O. Box 313
Geneva, NE 68361
Contact: Evelyn M. Volkmer, V.P.

Foundation type: Independent foundation

Purpose: Scholarships to students of Fillmore County, NE, high schools for higher education in NE.
Publications: Annual report.
Financial data: Year ended 11/30/2012. Assets, $295,515 (M); Expenditures, $24,102; Total giving, $21,000; Grants to individuals, 23 grants totaling $21,000 (high: $1,750, low: $750).
Type of support: Support to graduates or students of specific schools; Undergraduate support.
Application information: Application form required.
> *Deadline(s):* Contact foundation for current application deadline
> *Applicants should submit the following:*
>   1) Class rank
>   2) GPA
>   3) Essay

EIN: 237159935

5220
Home Instead Senior Care Disaster Relief Foundation

13323 California St.
Omaha, NE 68154-5241 (402) 498-4466
Contact: Paul Hogan

Foundation type: Independent foundation
Purpose: Financial assistance to Home Instead Senior Care Network members affected by natural disasters.
Financial data: Year ended 12/31/2012. Assets, $69,375 (M); Expenditures, $750; Total giving, $0.
Fields of interest: Aging.
Type of support: Emergency funds.
Application information:
> *Initial approach:* Letter
> *Applicants should submit the following:*
>   1) Financial information
> *Additional information:* Application must include documentation supporting the financial need and an itemized description of how the monies will be used.

EIN: 043826630

5221
Jewish Federation of Omaha, Inc.

333 S. 132nd St.
Omaha, NE 68154-2106 (402) 334-8200
Additional tel.: (402) 334-6445
FAX: (402) 334-1330; URL: http://www.jewishomaha.org

Foundation type: Public charity
Purpose: Leadership awards and prize money to youth in the Omaha, NE metropolitan area for leadership qualities in rendering service to the Jewish and general community.
Publications: Informational brochure.
Financial data: Year ended 06/30/2011. Assets, $35,624,997 (M); Expenditures, $25,107,934; Total giving, $4,097,401; Grants to individuals, 561 grants totaling $451,379. Subtotal for scholarships—to individuals: 169 grants totaling $296,223. Subtotal for grants to individuals: 392 grants totaling $42,450.
Fields of interest: Youth development, community service clubs; Youth development; Jewish agencies & synagogues.
Type of support: Awards/prizes.
Application information:
> *Initial approach:* Tel.
> *Additional information:* Contact foundation for eligibility criteria.

EIN: 470384659

5222
Johnson Student Scholarship & Loan Foundation

P.O. Box 248
Ord, NE 68862-0248
Contact: Lana Kruml, Chairperson
Application address: c/o Ord High School, Attn.: Lana Kruml, Chairperson, Selection Comm., 1800 K. St., Ord, NE 68862-1357

Foundation type: Independent foundation
Purpose: Loans for higher education to graduating seniors of Ord public high schools, NE.
Financial data: Year ended 11/30/2012. Assets, $243,192 (M); Expenditures, $13,927; Total giving, $11,000.
Type of support: Student loans—to individuals; Support to graduates or students of specific schools; Undergraduate support.
Application information: Application form required.
> *Deadline(s):* May 1

EIN: 470606386

5223
Kearney Area Community Foundation

412 W. 48th St., Ste. 12
Kearney, NE 68845 (308) 237-3114
Contact: Judi Sickler, Exec. Dir.
FAX: (308) 237-9845;
E-mail: kacf@kearneyfoundation.org; Mailing address: P.O. Box 1694, Kearney, NE 68848;
Additional e-mail: judi@kearneyfoundation.org;
URL: http://www.kearneyfoundation.org

Foundation type: Community foundation
Purpose: Scholarships to students from the Kearney, NE area for higher education.
Publications: Application guidelines; Grants list.
Financial data: Year ended 12/31/2012. Assets, $9,598,323 (M); Expenditures, $7,247,265; Total giving, $4,388,637; Grants to individuals, totaling $54,139.
Fields of interest: Vocational education, post-secondary; Higher education.
Type of support: Scholarships—to individuals; Support to graduates or students of specific schools; Undergraduate support.
Application information: Applications accepted. Application form required. Application form available on the grantmaker's web site.
> *Send request by:* Mail
> *Deadline(s):* Varies
> *Additional information:* Each scholarship has its own unique eligibility criteria. See web site for additional guidelines and application forms.

EIN: 470786586

5224
Peter Kiewit Foundation

1125 S. 103rd St., Ste. 500
Omaha, NE 68124-6022 (402) 344-7890
Contact: Lyn Wallin Ziegenbein, Exec. Dir.
FAX: (402) 344-8099; URL: http://www.peterkiewitfoundation.org/

Foundation type: Independent foundation
Purpose: Undergraduate scholarships only to high school students in the Omaha, NE—Council Bluffs, IA, area, specifically Douglas and Sarpy counties, NE, and Pottawattamie County, IA. Grants also to NE teachers for excellence in classroom teaching.
Publications: Application guidelines; Annual report; Informational brochure (including application guidelines).
Financial data: Year ended 06/30/2013. Assets, $397,287,545 (M); Expenditures, $14,845,364;

Total giving, $10,895,438; Grants to individuals, totaling $1,088,750.
Fields of interest: Education.
Type of support: Undergraduate support.
Application information: Application form required.
  Initial approach: Letter or telephone
  Deadline(s): Jan. 1
EIN: 476098282

5225
Killen Scholarship Trust
c/o Wells Fargo Bank, N.A., Trust Tax Dept.
1919 Douglas St., 2nd Fl., MACN8000-027
Omaha, NE 68102-1317

Foundation type: Independent foundation
Purpose: Scholarships to residents of Ely, MN.
Financial data: Year ended 12/31/2013. Assets, $386,957 (M); Expenditures, $21,262; Total giving, $14,000; Grants to individuals, 8 grants totaling $14,000 (high: $1,750, low: $1,750).
Type of support: Undergraduate support.
Application information: Applications not accepted.
  Additional information: Unsolicited requests for funds not accepted.
EIN: 416211303

5226
Robert H. and Dorothy G. Kooper Charitable Foundation Trust
809 N. 96th St.
Omaha, NE 68114-2498   (402) 392-1800
Contact: Howard M. Kooper, Tr.

Foundation type: Independent foundation
Purpose: Scholarships to individuals for higher education.
Financial data: Year ended 12/31/2011. Assets, $144,500 (M); Expenditures, $12,289; Total giving, $11,500; Grants to individuals, 21 grants totaling $11,500 (high: $1,000, low: $500).
Fields of interest: Higher education.
Type of support: Scholarships—to individuals.
Application information: Application form required.
EIN: 911816704

5227
Leslie Scholarship Fund
c/o Wells Fargo Bank, N.A.
1919 Douglas St., 2nd Fl., MACN8000-027
Omaha, NE 68102-1317

Foundation type: Independent foundation
Purpose: Scholarships to individuals for attendance at OH universities.
Financial data: Year ended 07/31/2013. Assets, $202,015 (M); Expenditures, $14,963; Total giving, $8,750; Grants to individuals, 2 grants totaling $8,750 (high: $7,000, low: $1,750).
Type of support: Undergraduate support.
Application information: Application form required.
  Additional information: Contact foundation for current application deadline/guidelines.
EIN: 346566216

5228
Lexington Community Foundation
607 N. Washington St.
P.O. Box 422
Lexington, NE 68850-1915   (308) 324-6704
Contact: Jacqueline Berke, Exec. Dir.
E-mail: lexfoundation@windstream.net;
URL: http://www.lexfoundation.org

Foundation type: Community foundation
Purpose: Scholarships to graduating high school seniors at Lexington High School, NE, for higher education.
Publications: Application guidelines; Annual report; Financial statement; Grants list; Informational brochure; Newsletter; Program policy statement.
Financial data: Year ended 12/31/2012. Assets, $7,104,616 (M); Expenditures, $722,440; Total giving, $372,578; Grants to individuals, 61 grants totaling $38,800.
Fields of interest: Higher education; Engineering school/education; Scholarships/financial aid; Computer science.
Type of support: Scholarships—to individuals; Support to graduates or students of specific schools; Undergraduate support.
Application information: Applications accepted. Application form required. Application form available on the grantmaker's web site.
  Copies of proposal: 1
  Deadline(s): Varies
  Applicants should submit the following:
    1) Transcripts
    2) Resume
    3) Letter(s) of recommendation
    4) GPA
    5) Financial information
    6) Essay
    7) ACT
  Additional information: See web site for complete list of scholarship programs.
EIN: 470794760

5229
Lincoln Community Foundation, Inc.
(formerly Lincoln Foundation, Inc.)
215 Centennial Mall S., Ste. 100
Lincoln, NE 68508-1813   (402) 474-2345
Contact: For grants: Sarah Peetz, V.P., Community Outreach
FAX: (402) 476-8523; E-mail: lcf@lcf.org;
URL: http://www.lcf.org

Foundation type: Community foundation
Purpose: Scholarships for graduating seniors of Lincoln, NE for postsecondary education.
Publications: Application guidelines; Annual report; Grants list; Informational brochure (including application guidelines); Newsletter; Program policy statement.
Financial data: Year ended 12/31/2011. Assets, $63,437,945 (M); Expenditures, $6,025,270; Total giving, $4,026,777. Scholarships—to individuals amount not specified.
Fields of interest: Higher education.
Type of support: Scholarships—to individuals; Support to graduates or students of specific schools.
Application information: Applications accepted. Application form required. Application form available on the grantmaker's web site.
  Send request by: Online
  Deadline(s): Mar. 31
  Applicants should submit the following:
    1) Financial information
    2) Letter(s) of recommendation
    3) Transcripts

    4) Essay
  Additional information: Criteria for each scholarship varies. See web site for a complete listing.
EIN: 470458128

5230
Merle Loessin Memorial Scholarship Trust
c/o Wells Fargo Bank, N.A., Trust Tax Dept.
1919 Douglas St., 2nd Fl. MACN8000-027
Omaha, NE 68102-1317

Foundation type: Independent foundation
Purpose: Scholarships primarily to SD residents.
Financial data: Year ended 12/31/2013. Assets, $162,209 (M); Expenditures, $3,734; Total giving, $0.
Type of support: Scholarships—to individuals.
Application information: Applications not accepted.
  Additional information: Unsolicited requests for funds not considered or acknowledged.
EIN: 916423024

5231
Lutheran Family Services of Nebraska, Inc.
124 S. 24th St., Ste. 230
Omaha, NE 68102-1226   (402) 342-7038
FAX: (402) 342-6408;
E-mail: rhenrichs@lfsneb.org; URL: http://www.lfsneb.org

Foundation type: Public charity
Purpose: Counseling, job training, education, and employment preparation to indigent residents of NE. Assistance to local residents in need following natural and man-made disasters. Also, legal assistance to refugees, immigrants and asylees of NE.
Publications: Annual report.
Financial data: Year ended 12/31/2011. Assets, $4,191,876 (M); Expenditures, $15,636,659; Total giving, $494,524; Grants to individuals, totaling $494,524.
Fields of interest: Immigrants/refugees; Economically disadvantaged.
Type of support: Emergency funds; In-kind gifts.
Application information:
  Initial approach: Letter
  Additional information: Contact foundation for eligibility criteria.
EIN: 237267972

5232
Harry & Winnie McNay Educational Trust
c/o Great Western Bank
P.O. Box 4070
Omaha, NE 68104-0070   (641) 774-4700
Contact: Jodi Briggs
Application Address: Great Western Bank, 201 Main St., Chariton, IA 50049

Foundation type: Independent foundation
Purpose: Low-interest student loans to residents of Lucas County, IA.
Financial data: Year ended 06/30/2012. Assets, $743,495 (M); Expenditures, $16,147; Total giving, $0.
Type of support: Student loans—to individuals.
Application information: Applications accepted. Application form required.
  Additional information: Application must include financial information.
EIN: 426252638

5233
Merrick Foundation, Inc.
1532 17th Ave.
P.O. Box 206
Central City, NE   68826   (308) 946-3707
Contact: Chuck Griffith, Exec. Dir.; Michelle Carroll, Acct.
E-mail: merrickfoundation@gmail.com; URL: http://www.merrick-foundation.org

Foundation type: Community foundation
Purpose: Scholarships to graduating high school students in the Merrick county, NE, area, and to individuals whose permanent address is in Merrick county and graduated from a Merrick county high school within the last five years.
Publications: Annual report; Financial statement.
Financial data: Year ended 10/31/2012. Assets, $13,519,850 (M); Expenditures, $786,528; Total giving, $552,873; Grants to individuals, 128 grants totaling $59,238.
Fields of interest: Higher education.
Type of support: Emergency funds; Scholarships—to individuals; Support to graduates or students of specific schools; Undergraduate support; Camperships.
Application information: Applications accepted. Application form required. Application form available on the grantmaker's web site.
   Initial approach: Telephone or e-mail
   Send request by: Mail
   Copies of proposal: 6
   Deadline(s): 1st Mon. of each month except Dec.
   Final notification: Recipients notified 30 to 60 days after receipt of application
   Applicants should submit the following:
      1) Transcripts
      2) Photograph
      3) Letter(s) of recommendation
      4) GPA
      5) Essay
   Additional information: See web site for additional information.
EIN: 476024770

5234
Mid-Nebraska Community Foundation, Inc.
120 N. Dewey
P.O. Box 1321
North Platte, NE   69101   (308) 534-3315
Contact: Eric Seacrest, Exec. Dir.
FAX: (308) 534-6117; E-mail: mncf@hamilton.net; URL: http://www.midnebraskafoundation.org

Foundation type: Community foundation
Purpose: Scholarships to individuals in Custer, Dawson, Frontier, Hayes, Keith, Lincoln, Logan, McPherson and Perkins counties, NE, for postsecondary education.
Publications: Application guidelines; Annual report; Financial statement; Informational brochure; Occasional report.
Financial data: Year ended 05/31/2012. Assets, $19,520,620 (M); Expenditures, $1,015,268; Total giving, $772,973; Grants to individuals, 155 grants totaling $179,781.
Fields of interest: Higher education.
Type of support: Grants to individuals; Scholarships—to individuals.
Application information: Applications accepted. Application form required.
   Deadline(s): End of Feb. for Scholarships, Oct. 15, Jan. 15 and Apr. 15 for Teachers Grants
   Additional information: Applications are generally available through area high school

counselors, except for non-traditional students and students already in college.
EIN: 470604965

5235
Midwest Foundaton for Higher Education
3800 S. 48th St.
Lincoln, NE   68506-4386   (402) 486-2502
Contact: Harvey Meier, Cont.
E-mail: advance@ucollege.edu

Foundation type: Public charity
Purpose: Scholarships to students enrolled at Union College in Lincoln, NE.
Publications: Informational brochure; Occasional report.
Financial data: Year ended 12/31/2012. Assets, $9,267,990 (M); Expenditures, $314,796; Total giving, $314,796; Grants to individuals, totaling $314,796.
Type of support: Support to graduates or students of specific schools.
Application information: Applications not accepted.
   Additional information: Unsolicited requests for funds not considered.
EIN: 470698086

5236
Morrison Education Foundation
(formerly Morrison Education Foundation)
c/o Wells Fargo Bank, N.A., Trust Tax Dept.
1919 Douglas St., 2nd Fl., MACN8000-027
Omaha, NE   68102-1317

Foundation type: Independent foundation
Purpose: Scholarships to individuals in Morrison, IL, for higher education.
Financial data: Year ended 12/31/2012. Assets, $776,459 (M); Expenditures, $29,026; Total giving, $19,400.
Type of support: Scholarships—to individuals.
Application information: Applications not accepted.
   Additional information: Unsolicited requests for funds not considered or acknowledged.
EIN: 363583712

5237
Nebraska Academy of Sciences
302 Morill Hall
14th and U Sts.
Lincoln, NE   68588-0339
E-mail: nebacad@unl.edu; URL: http://www.neacadsci.org

Foundation type: Independent foundation
Purpose: Grants to residents of NE, with priority given to research into the basic sciences, travel to educational and scientific conferences, and formal and informal K-20 science education.
Financial data: Year ended 12/31/2012. Assets, $1,245,093 (M); Expenditures, $187,237; Total giving, $64,457; Grants to individuals, 17 grants totaling $30,287 (high: $9,187, low: $100).
Fields of interest: Science.
Type of support: Grants to individuals.
Application information: Applications accepted. Application form required. Application form available on the grantmaker's web site.
   Initial approach: Application
   Send request by: E-mail
   Deadline(s): None
   Applicants should submit the following:
      1) Budget Information

   2) Proposal
   Additional information: See web site for additional information.
EIN: 470445712

5238
Nebraska Cattlemen Research and Education Foundation
1010 Lincoln Mall, Ste. 101
Lincoln, NE   68508-2833   (402) 475-2333
Contact: for Scholarships: Lee Weide
Additional tel. for scholarships: Jana Jensen (308) 588-6299
FAX: (402) 475-0822; E-mail: nc@necattlemen.org; URL: http://www.nebraskacattlemen.org/default.php

Foundation type: Public charity
Purpose: Scholarships to high school seniors or college students of NE for attendance at any college or university, vocation or trade school in NE pursuing a career in an agriculture field of study.
Financial data: Year ended 06/30/2012. Assets, $1,229,094 (M); Expenditures, $148,853; Total giving, $91,551; Grants to individuals, totaling $31,500.
Fields of interest: Vocational education, post-secondary; Higher education; Agriculture.
Type of support: Scholarships—to individuals.
Application information: Applications accepted. Application form required. Application form available on the grantmaker's web site.
   Initial approach: Telephone
   Send request by: Mail
   Deadline(s): Mar. 1
   Applicants should submit the following:
      1) Class rank
      2) ACT
      3) Photograph
      4) Transcripts
      5) SAT
      6) GPA
      7) Letter(s) of recommendation
      8) Essay
   Additional information: Payments are made directly to the educational institution on behalf of the students. Selection is based on academic achievement, beef industry involvement, and goals and quality of application. See web site for additional guidelines.
EIN: 476057097

5239
Nebraska Community Foundation
3833 S. 14th St.
P.O. Box 83107
Lincoln, NE   68501-3107   (402) 323-7330
Contact: Jeffrey G. Yost, Pres. and C.E.O.
FAX: (402) 323-7349;
E-mail: info@nebcommfound.org; URL: http://www.nebcommfound.org

Foundation type: Community foundation
Purpose: College scholarships for Nebraska students for higher education at accredited institution.
Publications: Annual report; Financial statement; Informational brochure; Newsletter; Occasional report; Program policy statement.
Financial data: Year ended 06/30/2012. Assets, $78,664,829 (M); Expenditures, $24,460,826; Total giving, $172,231; Grants to individuals, totaling $172,231.
Fields of interest: Higher education.
Type of support: Scholarships—to individuals.

Application information: Applications accepted. Application form required.

Additional information: Scholarship funds are paid directly to the educational institution on behalf of the student.

EIN: 470769903

5240

Nebraska Friends of Foster Children Foundation

P.O. Box 541034
Omaha, NE   68131-0142   (402) 659-5879
Contact: Liz Hruska, Pres.
URL: http://www.ne-friends.org/

Foundation type: Public charity
Purpose: Grants to current and former children under the age of 21 of NE who are wards of the state.
Financial data: Year ended 06/30/2011. Assets, $36,608 (M); Expenditures, $33,075; Total giving, $28,187.
Fields of interest: Children/youth, services; Foster care.
Type of support: Grants for special needs.
Application information: Applications accepted. Application form required.

Deadline(s): None
EIN: 363926272

5241

Nebraska Independent Film Projects

(also known as NIFP)
P.O. Box 80205
Lincoln, NE   68501-0205
Contact: Jeremy Bishop, Pres.
E-mail: president@nifp.org; URL: http://www.nifp.org

Foundation type: Public charity
Purpose: Support to Nebraska filmmakers through a fiscal sponsorship program.
Publications: Application guidelines.
Fields of interest: Film/video.
Type of support: Fiscal agent/sponsor.
Application information:

Initial approach: Download fiscal sponsorship application form and return via regular mail
Additional information: Applicant must apply for membership to organization before being considered for fiscal sponsorship.

Program description:

Fiscal Sponsorship: Fiscal sponsorship is available to members of NIFP. Eligible applicants must be producing a film or video project that is non-commercial in nature (not being undertaken by a producer for a third party that has agreed to pay the producer for their services), and must be imaginative contributions to the film and video art form. The applicant must retain creative control of the proposed production and must own the copyright to the program. A five percent fiscal agent fee for any money granted through the organization to sponsored projects is charged to NIFP.
EIN: 470753318

5242

The Nebraska Medical Center

987400 Nebraska Medical Ctr.
Omaha, NE   68198-7450   (402) 552-2000
Contact: Janette Garvin, Recording Secy.
Toll-Free Tel.: (800) 922-0000; URL: http://www.nebraskamed.com

Foundation type: Public charity
Purpose: Financial assistance to patients for medication and other medical expenses.
Financial data: Year ended 06/30/2012. Assets, $797,174,434 (M); Expenditures, $802,668,135; Total giving, $114,453,911; Grants to individuals, totaling $45,676,864.
Fields of interest: Health care.
Type of support: Emergency funds; Grants for special needs.
Application information: Financial assistance is for those who qualify. Contact the center for eligibility criteria.
EIN: 911858433

5243

Nebraska Medical Foundation, Inc.

233 S. 13th St., Ste. 1200
Lincoln, NE   68508-2091   (402) 474-4472
Contact: Dale Mahlman, Pres.
E-mail: nebmed@nebmed.org; URL: http://www.nebmed.org/template.aspx?id=286

Foundation type: Public charity
Purpose: Scholarships to students attending a Nebraska university for higher education.
Publications: Application guidelines.
Financial data: Year ended 01/31/2012. Assets, $1,336,367 (M); Expenditures, $81,028; Total giving, $47,500; Grants to individuals, totaling $47,500.
Type of support: Undergraduate support.
Application information: Application form required.

Initial approach: E-mail or letter
Deadline(s): Apr. 10
Additional information: Contact university for application guidelines.
EIN: 476036827

5244

Nebraska Methodist Hospital Foundation

8401 W. Dodge Rd., Ste. 225
Omaha, NE   68114-3415   (402) 354-4825
Contact: Cynthia S. Peacock, Pres. and C.E.O.
FAX: (402) 354-4868;
E-mail: cyndy.peacock@nmhs.org; URL: http://www.methodisthospitalfoundation.org

Foundation type: Public charity
Purpose: Provides assistance to employees of Methodist Health System who are students at Nebraska Methodist College of Nursing, and administers a nursing loan forgiveness program to retain staff at Nebraska Methodist Hospital.
Publications: Annual report; Newsletter.
Financial data: Year ended 12/31/2011. Assets, $99,490,504 (M); Expenditures, $17,943,246; Total giving, $15,984,982; Grants to individuals, totaling $380,256.
Fields of interest: Nursing school/education.
Type of support: Computer technology; Employee-related scholarships; Scholarships—to individuals; Support to graduates or students of specific schools.
Application information: Applications accepted.

Initial approach: Contact foundation
EIN: 470595345

5245

Nebraska Wesleyan University Theta Chi Scholarship Fund Inc.

5509 T St.
Lincoln, NE   68509   (402) 760-2758
Contact: Kale Burdick, Pres.

Foundation type: Independent foundation
Purpose: College scholarships to members of Theta Chi Fraternity at Nebraska Wesleyan University for higher education.
Financial data: Year ended 12/31/2012. Assets, $70,152 (M); Expenditures, $6,750; Total giving, $6,450; Grants to individuals, 17 grants totaling $6,450 (high: $500, low: $150).
Fields of interest: Higher education; Students, sororities/fraternities.
Type of support: Scholarships—to individuals.
Application information: Applications accepted. Application form required.

Deadline(s): First week of Fall
Additional information: Application available upon request.
EIN: 470706299

5246

Nelnet Foundation

121 S. 13th St., Ste. 201
Lincoln, NE   68508-1911
URL: http://www.nelnet.com/overview.aspx?id=1052&path=nel.cor.nap.cm#corp

Foundation type: Company-sponsored foundation
Purpose: Scholarships to high school seniors or individuals who have passed the GED within the past six months.
Publications: Application guidelines.
Financial data: Year ended 12/31/2012. Assets, $6,757,696 (M); Expenditures, $2,225,499; Total giving, $1,374,144.
Fields of interest: Higher education.
Type of support: Scholarships—to individuals.
Application information: Applications accepted. Application form required.

Initial approach: Letter
Deadline(s): Mar. 31
Applicants should submit the following:
1) Class rank
2) Transcripts
3) SAT
4) Financial information
5) ACT
Additional information: Applicants are selected based on financial need, class rank, high school grades, and ACT/SAT scores. Funds are sent directly to the education institution on behalf of the students.
EIN: 202202134

5247

Darold A. Newblom Foundation

1208 Laramie Ave.
Alliance, NE   69301   (308) 762-4693
Contact: Wally A. Seiler, Treas.
Tel: (308) 762-4693

Foundation type: Independent foundation
Purpose: Scholarships to residents of Box Butte and Dawes counties, NE.
Financial data: Year ended 12/31/2012. Assets, $227,308 (M); Expenditures, $13,975; Total giving, $8,900.
Type of support: Scholarships—to individuals.
Application information: Application form required.

Deadline(s): Mar. 1
Applicants should submit the following:
1) Transcripts
2) Letter(s) of recommendation
3) Essay
EIN: 363696589

5248
Frank J. & Joe E. Novak Scholarship Foundation
P.O. Box 248
Ord, NE 68862-0248

Foundation type: Independent foundation
Purpose: Scholarships to graduates of Ord High School, NE for continuing education at accredited colleges, universities or accredited trade school.
Financial data: Year ended 12/31/2013. Assets, $684,690 (M); Expenditures, $35,427; Total giving, $35,000; Grants to individuals, 7 grants totaling $35,000 (high: $5,000, low: $5,000).
Fields of interest: Vocational education, post-secondary; Higher education.
Type of support: Scholarships—to individuals; Support to graduates or students of specific schools.
Application information: Applications accepted. Application form required. Interview required.
  Deadline(s): Apr. 1
  Applicants should submit the following:
    1) Financial information
    2) Transcripts
    3) Letter(s) of recommendation
    4) Essay
  Additional information: Applicant must demonstrate financial need.
Program description:
  Scholarship: Scholarships in the amount of $5,000 are awarded to needy and worthy graduates with preference to residents of Valley county for tuition, college room and board (on campus housing only), books, or college fees. Scholarships will be awarded to those with demonstrated motivation toward completion of the chosen course of study.
EIN: 223877964

5249
OEA Foundation, Inc.
4202 S. 57th St.
Omaha, NE 68137-1349 (402) 346-0400
Contact: Mary Moberg, Pres.
FAX: (402) 346-8410; URL: http://omahaoea.org/allied-organizations/oea-foundation-scholarships/

Foundation type: Public charity
Purpose: Various scholarships to graduates of Omaha public schools, NE.
Publications: Application guidelines.
Financial data: Year ended 08/31/2012. Assets, $4,879,155 (M); Expenditures, $374,235; Total giving, $354,350; Grants to individuals, totaling $354,350.
Type of support: Undergraduate support.
Application information: Applications accepted. Application form required. Application form available on the grantmaker's web site.
  Initial approach: Letter
  Deadline(s): Varies
  Applicants should submit the following:
    1) Transcripts
    2) Photograph
    3) Letter(s) of recommendation
    4) GPA
    5) Financial information
    6) ACT
  Additional information: See web site for complete program listing.
EIN: 470488295

5250
Omaha Schools Foundation
3215 Cuming St.
Omaha, NE 68131-2000 (402) 557-2045
E-mail: Toba.Cohen-Dunning@ops.org; URL: http://www.omahaschoolsfoundation.org/

Foundation type: Public charity
Purpose: Scholarships to graduating seniors of Omaha, NE for post-secondary education at accredited colleges or universities.
Financial data: Year ended 12/31/2011. Assets, $2,090,136 (M); Expenditures, $9,032,567; Total giving, $574,695; Grants to individuals, totaling $574,695.
Fields of interest: Higher education.
Type of support: Scholarships—to individuals.
Application information: Unsolicited applications not accepted.
EIN: 363301526

5251
Omaha Volunteers for Handicapped Children
10842 John Galt Blvd.
Omaha, NE 68137

Foundation type: Independent foundation
Purpose: Scholarships to individuals in Omaha, NE, who are pursuing careers in the education or care of handicapped children.
Financial data: Year ended 12/31/2011. Assets, $254,238 (M); Expenditures, $375; Total giving, $0.
Fields of interest: Education, special; Teacher school/education; Disabilities, people with.
Type of support: Undergraduate support.
Application information: Applications accepted. Application form required.
  Initial approach: Letter or telephone
  Deadline(s): July 15
  Additional information: Application must also include transcripts and acceptance to institution.
EIN: 363958269

5252
Oregon Trail Community Foundation, Inc.
115 W. Railway St.
P.O. Box 1344
Scottsbluff, NE 69361-1344 (308) 635-3393
Contact: Bev Overman, Exec. Admin.
FAX: (308) 635-3393; E-mail: info@otcf.org; URL: http://www.otcf.org

Foundation type: Community foundation
Purpose: Scholarships to individuals from the Scottsbluff, NE, area for undergraduate education at American colleges and universities.
Publications: Grants list; Informational brochure (including application guidelines); Newsletter.
Financial data: Year ended 12/31/2012. Assets, $3,408,473 (M); Expenditures, $401,459; Total giving, $273,371; Grants to individuals, 33 grants totaling $47,700.
Fields of interest: Vocational education; Higher education.
Type of support: Scholarships—to individuals; Support to graduates or students of specific schools; Undergraduate support.
Application information: Applications accepted. Application form required. Application form available on the grantmaker's web site.
  Deadline(s): Varies

Additional information: See web site for complete listing of scholarships.
EIN: 470596705

5253
Patton Scholarship Trust
c/o Wells Fargo Bank, N.A.
1919 Douglas St.,2nd Fl., MACN8000-027
Omaha, NE 68102-1317

Foundation type: Independent foundation
Purpose: Scholarships to graduating seniors of Twin Lakes High School, IN for continuing education at accredited colleges or universities.
Financial data: Year ended 02/28/2013. Assets, $306,704 (M); Expenditures, $15,841; Total giving, $9,000.
Fields of interest: Higher education.
Type of support: Support to graduates or students of specific schools.
Application information: Application form required.
  Deadline(s): Mar. 1
EIN: 356570391

5254
People's City Mission
110 Q St.
P.O. Box 80636
Lincoln, NE 68501-0636 (402) 475-1303
Contact: Pastor Tom Barber, Exec. Dir.
URL: http://peoplescitymission.org

Foundation type: Public charity
Purpose: Provides safe and secure temporary housing and assistance to homeless individuals in the Lincoln, NE area for women, men, children and families.
Publications: Newsletter.
Financial data: Year ended 12/31/2011. Assets, $4,352,149 (M); Expenditures, $10,846,076; Total giving, $7,331,075; Grants to individuals, totaling $7,331,075.
Fields of interest: Human services; Economically disadvantaged.
Type of support: Grants for special needs.
Application information: Contact the mission for additional information.
EIN: 470376896

5255
Phelps County Community Foundation, Inc.
504 4th Ave.
Holdrege, NE 68949 (308) 995-6847
Contact: Vickie Klein, Exec. Dir.; For scholarships: Lacy Chapman, Prog. Assoc.
E-mail for L. Chapman: lcpccf@phelpsfoundation.org
FAX: (308) 995-2146;
E-mail: vlpccf@phelpsfoundation.org; URL: http://www.phelpsfoundation.org

Foundation type: Community foundation
Purpose: Scholarships to residents and former residents of south-central NE, including Phelps County and the surrounding area.
Publications: Application guidelines; Financial statement; Grants list; Informational brochure; Newsletter.
Financial data: Year ended 06/30/2013. Assets, $13,843,311 (M); Expenditures, $1,017,991; Total giving, $777,580; Grants to individuals, 82 grants totaling $175,359.
Fields of interest: Higher education; Scholarships/financial aid.

Type of support: Scholarships—to individuals; Support to graduates or students of specific schools; Undergraduate support.
Application information: Applications accepted. Application form required. Application form available on the grantmaker's web site.
  Initial approach: Letter, telephone or e-mail
  Send request by: On-line and by mail, or in person
  Copies of proposal: 1
  Deadline(s): Feb. 18
  Final notification: Recipients notified in two months
  Applicants should submit the following:
    1) Photograph
    2) Transcripts
    3) SAT
    4) Proposal
    5) Letter(s) of recommendation
    6) GPA
    7) FAFSA
    8) Essay
    9) ACT
  Additional information: See web site for a complete listing of scholarships and application guidelines.
Program description:
  Scholarship Program: The foundation manages many scholarship funds, using one scholarship application form to determine the eligibility of nearly all scholarships. Most scholarships are based upon financial need and scholastic ability. All scholarships of the Phelps County Community Foundation are administered according to the following guidelines: Recipients must be enrolled in an accredited, tax-exempt college, university, technical, or vocational school; awards will be for the purposes of tuition and fees, books, supplies and equipment required for coursework; awards will be paid directly to the student's school after the foundation has received verification of enrollment notification from the school. Scholarship amounts vary.
EIN: 510189077

5256
Regional West Foundation
2 W. 42nd St.
Scottsbluff, NE 69361-4602 (308) 630-1485
E-mail: knutsos@rwmc.net; Tel. for Shelley Knutson: (308) 630-2244; URL: http://www.rwmc.net/RegionalWestFoundation

Foundation type: Public charity
Purpose: Scholarships to residents of NE for health care-related study.
Financial data: Year ended 12/31/2011. Assets, $7,189,564 (M); Expenditures, $477,683; Total giving, $263,207; Grants to individuals, totaling $47,495.
Fields of interest: Hospitals (general).
Type of support: Scholarships—to individuals.
Application information: Applications accepted. Application form required.
  Additional information: Contact foundation for current application deadline/guidelines.
EIN: 237171022

5257
The Grace O. & Harry D. Riley Foundation
936 S. 111th Plz.
Omaha, NE 68154-3306 (402) 554-6505
Application addresses: c/o Randolph High School, Attn.: Scholarship Comm., 207 N. Pierce St., Randolph, NE 68771-5514, tel.: (402) 337-0252, or c/o Omaha North High School, Attn.: Scholarship

Comm., 4323 N. 37th St., Omaha, NE 68111-2264, tel.: (402) 554-6506

Foundation type: Independent foundation
Purpose: Scholarships to high school students of Randolph High School, NE and Omaha North High School, NE for higher education.
Financial data: Year ended 12/31/2011. Assets, $465 (M); Expenditures, $227,697; Total giving, $226,545; Grants to individuals, totaling $226,545.
Type of support: Support to graduates or students of specific schools; Undergraduate support.
Application information: Application form required.
  Deadline(s): Apr.1.
EIN: 470697802

5258
Lois E. Riss Trust
c/o Wayne Kjeldgaard & Frank Kjeldaard
P.O. Box 257
Big Springs, NE 69122-0257 (308) 889-3118
Contact: Wayne Kjeldgaard, Tr.; Franklin Kjeldgaard, Tr.

Foundation type: Independent foundation
Purpose: Scholarships to high school seniors and graduates of high schools in the cities of Big Springs, Chappell, Brule, Ogallala, Lewellen, and Oshkosh, NE, and Julesburg, Sedgwick and Ovid, CO for higher education.
Financial data: Year ended 12/31/2011. Assets, $447,133 (M); Expenditures, $32,593; Total giving, $21,850; Grants to individuals, 16 grants totaling $9,750 (high: $1,500, low: $1,000).
Fields of interest: Higher education.
Type of support: Scholarships—to individuals.
Application information: Applications accepted.
  Initial approach: Letter
  Deadline(s): None
  Additional information: Application must include ambitions, objectives and references.
EIN: 476199355

5259
Cecil Mae Schmoker Trust
c/o Wells Fargo Bank, N.A.
1919 Douglas St., 2nd Fl.
Omaha, NE 68102-1317

Foundation type: Independent foundation
Purpose: Scholarships to high school seniors who reside in Webster County, IA.
Financial data: Year ended 12/31/2012. Assets, $841,879 (M); Expenditures, $35,073; Total giving, $25,194; Grants to individuals, 21 grants totaling $17,550 (high: $2,000, low: $250).
Type of support: Scholarships—to individuals.
Application information: Applications not accepted.
  Additional information: Unsolicited requests for funds not considered or acknowledged.
EIN: 426446089

5260
Sherman County Community Foundation, Inc.
611 O. St.
P.O. Box 310
Loup City, NE 68853-8003 (308) 745-0720
Contact: Rich Peters, Treas.; For grants: Mark Eurek
FAX: (308) 745-1655; URL: http://www.shercofoundation.org

Foundation type: Community foundation

Purpose: Awards scholarships to graduates of Sherman County area high schools for higher education.
Financial data: Year ended 12/31/2012. Assets, $36,359 (M); Expenditures, $31,883; Total giving, $30,372.
Application information: Applications accepted. Application form required.
  Initial approach: Application
  Send request by: Return application to high school counselor
  Deadline(s): Apr. 8
  Applicants should submit the following:
    1) Essay
    2) Letter(s) of recommendation
    3) Transcripts
  Additional information: See web site for complete listing of scholarships.
EIN: 470732031

5261
Simon Educational Irrevocable Trust Foundation
c/o Wells Fargo Bank, N.A.
1919 Douglas St., 2nd Fl., MAC N8000-027
Omaha, NE 68102-1317

Foundation type: Independent foundation
Purpose: Scholarships to graduating seniors from South Bend Community School Corporation high schools and non-public high schools located in South Bend, IN.
Financial data: Year ended 12/31/2011. Assets, $236,415 (M); Expenditures, $13,997; Total giving, $9,000.
Fields of interest: Higher education; Scholarships/financial aid.
Type of support: Support to graduates or students of specific schools; Undergraduate support.
Application information: Applications accepted. Application form required.
  Initial approach: Letter
  Deadline(s): Mar. 1
  Applicants should submit the following:
    1) FAF
    2) GPA
    3) Class rank
    4) SAT
    5) Transcripts
  Additional information: Applications are available in student's guidance counselor's office.
EIN: 356012970

5262
The Steinhart Foundation, Inc.
601 Central Ave., Ste. 105
Nebraska City, NE 68410-2468 (402) 873-3285
Contact: Leta Harshman, Pres.

Foundation type: Independent foundation
Purpose: Scholarships to residents of the Nebraska City, NE area for postsecondary education.
Financial data: Year ended 12/31/2012. Assets, $8,416,003 (M); Expenditures, $531,004; Total giving, $399,120.
Type of support: Undergraduate support.
Application information: Applications accepted.
  Additional information: Contact foundation for current application guidelines.
EIN: 476025185

5263
Clifton Strengths Institute
(formerly The Clifton Institute)
1001 Gallup Dr.
Omaha, NE 68102-4222 (402) 938-6220
Contact: Mary C. Rechmeyer, Pres.

Foundation type: Operating foundation
Purpose: Scholarships for academic advancement, including the Clifton Strengths Prize, awarded every other year, which recognizes significant advances in the science and practice of strengths-based psychology, education, and leadership.
Financial data: Year ended 12/31/2012. Assets, $3,177,956 (M); Expenditures, $147,922; Total giving, $10,355.
Fields of interest: Research; Higher education; Leadership development.
Type of support: Scholarships—to individuals; Awards/prizes.
Application information: Candidates are nominated by three non-related sources who will be asked to complete a structured evaluation form to determine the merits of the work to be considered for the award.
Program description:
The Clifton Strengths Prize: The Clifton Strengths Prize is awarded every other year to individuals or teams whose exemplary work has advanced the science and/or practice of strengths-based psychology, education, and leadership. Each Clifton Strengths Laureate will deliver a public keynote address, contribute three brief white papers to the Clifton Strengths School, and contribute to strengths-related instruction or mentoring activities for strengths scholars. The amount of the prize is $250,000.
EIN: 400002257

5264
The Stueven Charitable Foundation
5251 W. Husker Hwy.
Alda, NE 68810-9610
Contact: Delbert G. Stueven, Pres.

Foundation type: Independent foundation
Purpose: Scholarships are limited to residents or individuals attending high schools in Hall county, NE.
Financial data: Year ended 12/31/2011. Assets, $675,186 (M); Expenditures, $30,836; Total giving, $28,000; Grants to individuals, 30 grants totaling $28,000 (high: $1,000, low: $500).
Fields of interest: Education.
Type of support: Scholarships—to individuals.
Application information: Application form required.
  Deadline(s): Feb. 15
  Applicants should submit the following:
    1) Transcripts
    2) Letter(s) of recommendation
    3) Essay
  Additional information: Application must also include extracurricular activities and a support letter from parent or guardian.
EIN: 470732885

5265
Harry B. Sweet Foundation, Inc.
145 E. 4th St.
Superior, NE 68978

Foundation type: Independent foundation
Purpose: Scholarships to residents or graduates of high schools in Smith, Jewell, and Republic counties, KS, or Nuckolls County, NE. Award must

be used for tuition and other college-related expenses.
Financial data: Year ended 12/31/2011. Assets, $364,884 (M); Expenditures, $16,585; Total giving, $14,500; Grants to individuals, 19 grants totaling $14,500 (high: $1,000, low: $500).
Type of support: Support to graduates or students of specific schools; Undergraduate support.
Application information: Application form required.
  Deadline(s): Feb. 1
  Applicants should submit the following:
    1) Transcripts
    2) Letter(s) of recommendation
  Additional information: Application should be sent through counselor, not directly to the foundation.
EIN: 470634034

5266
Tri-Valley Medical Foundation
304 Nelson
P.O. Box 488
Cambridge, NE 69022-3592 (308) 697-1520
Contact: Beth Siegfried, Exec. Dir.
E-mail: foundation@trivalleyhealth.com;
URL: http://trivalleyhealth.com/

Foundation type: Public charity
Purpose: College scholarships to qualified students pursuing a degree in the medical profession.
Financial data: Year ended 04/30/2012. Assets, $2,135,178 (M); Expenditures, $940,641; Total giving, $857,177; Grants to individuals, totaling $17,400.
Fields of interest: Medical school/education.
Type of support: Scholarships—to individuals.
Application information: Applications accepted. Application form required.
  Deadline(s): Apr. 15
  Additional information: Application should include a copy of your transcript.
EIN: 470739522

5267
UNMC Physicians
988101 Nebraska Medical Ctr.
Omaha, NE 68198-8101 (402) 559-9800
Contact: Cory D. Shaw, Exec. V.P. and C.E.O.
Toll-free tel.: (888) 898-8662; URL: http://www.unmcphysicians.com

Foundation type: Public charity
Purpose: Assistance to individuals of Nebraska who are unable to pay for medically necessary healthcare services.
Financial data: Year ended 06/30/2012. Assets, $126,343,283 (M); Expenditures, $220,300,510; Total giving, $46,570,240; Grants to individuals, 4,787 grants totaling $6,013,670. Subtotal for in-kind gifts: 4,787 grants totaling $6,013,670.
Fields of interest: Health care; Economically disadvantaged.
Type of support: Emergency funds; In-kind gifts.
Application information: Applications accepted.
  Additional information: Application forms determine your ability for pay for services. Patients must demonstrate an inability to pay for services.
EIN: 470785575

5268
Wabash County Scholarship Trust
c/o Wells Fargo Bank, N.A.
1919 Douglas St., 2nd Fl.
Omaha, NE 68102-1310 (800) 352-3705
Contact: Jennifer Stensland
Application address: C/o. Wells Fargo Bank, 625 Marquette Ave., Minneapolis, MN 55402, tel.: (800) 352-3705

Foundation type: Independent foundation
Purpose: Scholarships to high school seniors or graduates who plan to enroll or students who are already enrolled in a full time undergraduate course of study at an accredited two year or four year college, university, or vocational/technical school.
Financial data: Year ended 12/31/2011. Assets, $878,383 (M); Expenditures, $62,654; Total giving, $42,562.
Fields of interest: Vocational education, post-secondary; Higher education.
Type of support: Scholarships—to individuals.
Application information: Applications accepted. Application form required.
  Send request by: Mail
  Deadline(s): Mar. 1
  Final notification: Applicants notified early May
  Additional information: Application should include transcripts. The scholarship is administered by Scholarship Management Services.
EIN: 356735235

5269
Wake Charitable Foundation
203 S. 6th St.
Seward, NE 68434

Foundation type: Independent foundation
Purpose: Scholarships to NE graduates of Seward High School in Seward, East Butler High School in Brainard, Aquinas High School in David City, and Centennial High School in Utica.
Financial data: Year ended 12/31/2012. Assets, $2,467,788 (M); Expenditures, $95,501; Total giving, $82,000; Grants to individuals, 25 grants totaling $25,000 (high: $1,000, low: $1,000).
Fields of interest: Higher education.
Type of support: Support to graduates or students of specific schools; Undergraduate support.
Application information: Applications accepted. Application form required.
  Deadline(s): Apr.
  Applicants should submit the following:
    1) GPA
    2) Financial information
  Additional information: Application forms can be obtained from the guidance office or principals of the respective high schools. Applicant must demonstrate financial need.
EIN: 476038985

5270
Charles & Alberta Walther Scholarship Fund
c/o Wells Fargo Bank Nebraska, N.A.
13330 California No. 100
Omaha, NE 68154

Foundation type: Independent foundation
Purpose: Scholarships to dependent children of Omaha, NE, firefighters for attendance in college or vocational school programs.
Financial data: Year ended 12/31/2012. Assets, $170,661 (M); Expenditures, $10,939; Total giving, $7,500.

Fields of interest: Vocational education, post-secondary; Disasters, fire prevention/control.
Type of support: Scholarships—to individuals.
Application information: Application form required.
  Deadline(s): Mar. 1
  Additional information: Scholarship program is administered by Scholarship America.
EIN: 470806637

5271
The Weller Foundation, Inc.
P.O. Box 636
Atkinson, NE   68713-0636   (402) 925-2803

Foundation type: Independent foundation
Purpose: Scholarships to financially needy high school graduates residing in the NE counties of Boyd, Brown, Garfield, Holt, Keya Paha, and Rock, and Gregory county in SD (graduates of Fairfax/Bonesteel High School only).
Publications: Application guidelines.
Financial data: Year ended 10/31/2012. Assets, $8,949,641 (M); Expenditures, $540,856; Total giving, $388,400; Grants to individuals, 140 grants totaling $388,400 (high: $5,050, low: $600).
Fields of interest: Vocational education, post-secondary; College (community/junior); Nursing school/education.
Type of support: Support to graduates or students of specific schools; Technical education support; Undergraduate support.
Application information: Application form required.
  Deadline(s): Apr. 1 and Nov. 1 for new applicants, June 1 and Nov. 1 for renewal applicants
  Final notification: Applicants notified after July 1 for fall applicants and Dec. 1 for spring applicants
  Additional information: Application should include financial information. Each grant is awarded for a period of two semesters or their equivalent. No student will receive more than two full grants with the exception of a person in an approved nursing program. See application for a listing of approved schools.
EIN: 470611350

5272
West Point Community Foundation
P.O. Box 65
West Point, NE   68788-0065
Contact: Cleo Toelle, Treas.
E-mail: westpointcommunityfoundation@yahoo.com; URL: http://wpcommunityfoundation.com/

Foundation type: Community foundation
Purpose: Scholarships to qualified graduating seniors from area high schools of West Point, NE for continuing education.
Publications: Informational brochure.
Financial data: Year ended 12/31/2011. Assets, $1,187,580 (M); Expenditures, $17,820; Total giving, $17,800; Grants to individuals, 7 grants totaling $5,000.
Fields of interest: Higher education.
Type of support: Scholarships—to individuals; Support to graduates or students of specific schools.
Application information: Applications accepted. Application form required. Application form available on the grantmaker's web site.

Initial approach: Application
Send request by: Mail
Deadline(s): Mar. 14
Additional information: Each scholarship has its own unique eligibility criteria. See web site for a complete listing.
EIN: 363819725

5273
Wilson Foundation
c/o Scott Trusdale
P.O. Box 540
Cozad, NE   69130-0540   (308) 784-2212

Foundation type: Independent foundation
Purpose: Scholarships to residents of Cozad, NE, who are employed and in financial need to complete college.
Financial data: Year ended 12/31/2012. Assets, $1,767,821 (M); Expenditures, $95,859; Total giving, $69,284.
Type of support: Undergraduate support.
Application information:
  Initial approach: Letter
EIN: 911818834

5274
Warren and Velda Wilson Foundation
c/o John F. Farrell, Well Fargo Bank, N.A.
747 N. Burlington Ave.
Hastings, NE   68901-4421

Foundation type: Independent foundation
Purpose: Scholarships to individuals residing in the Hastings, NE, area for undergraduate education.
Financial data: Year ended 12/31/2012. Assets, $11,557,646 (M); Expenditures, $873,894; Total giving, $608,925.
Type of support: Undergraduate support.
Application information: Application form required.
  Deadline(s): Apr. 24
  Additional information: Contact foundation for current application guidelines.
EIN: 470741012

5275
Hester C. Wood Trust
c/o Wells Fargo Bank N.A.
1919 Douglas St., 2nd Fl., MAC N8000-027
Omaha, NE   68102-1317
Application address: c/o First Presbyterian Church, 102 W. Main St., Peru IN 46970

Foundation type: Independent foundation
Purpose: Scholarships to Graduates of Peru High School, IN who are active members of the First Presbyterian Church of Peru, for postsecondary education.
Financial data: Year ended 12/31/2012. Assets, $0 (M); Expenditures, $95,526; Total giving, $90,008.
Fields of interest: Higher education; Christian agencies & churches.
Type of support: Support to graduates or students of specific schools.
Application information: Applications accepted. Application form required.
  Applicants should submit the following:

1) Transcripts
2) Letter(s) of recommendation
3) GPA
EIN: 356021042

5276
World-Herald Goodfellows Charities, Inc.
1314 Douglas St., Ste. 125
Omaha, NE   68102-1811   (402) 444-1388
E-mail: goodfellows@owh.com; URL: http://www.omaha.com/section/owh02

Foundation type: Public charity
Purpose: Food certificates and other emergency assistance to financially needy individuals and families primarily in western NE.
Financial data: Year ended 02/28/2013. Assets, $751,626 (M); Expenditures, $554,357; Total giving, $554,357; Grants to individuals, totaling $554,357.
Fields of interest: Economically disadvantaged.
Type of support: Emergency funds; Grants for special needs.
Application information: Interview required.
  Additional information: Applicants must be referred by local partnering or human services agencies.
EIN: 476000559

5277
York Community Foundation
603 N. Lincoln Ave.
York, NE   68467-4240   (402) 362-5531
Contact: Donna Bitner, Exec. Dir.
E-mail: ycf@yorkchamber.net; URL: http://www.yorkcommunityfoundation.org/index.html

Foundation type: Community foundation
Purpose: Scholarships to students in the York, NE, area, for higher education.
Financial data: Year ended 09/30/2012. Assets, $4,935,535 (M); Expenditures, $485,548; Total giving, $406,410; Grants to individuals, 61 grants totaling $148,500.
Fields of interest: Higher education; Scholarships/financial aid.
Type of support: Undergraduate support.
Application information: Applications accepted. Application form required. Application form available on the grantmaker's web site.
  Applicants should submit the following:
  1) Financial information
  2) Letter(s) of recommendation
  3) SAT
  4) ACT
  Additional information: Students should contact their guidance counselor for additional application information. See web site for additional guidelines.
Program description:
  Scholarships: The foundation administers twenty scholarship funds to students in the York area. The scholarship program consists of separate scholarship funds created by individuals, families or organizations who wish to provide opportunities to students to further their education. The donors have established criteria for the administration of their scholarships which are consistent with the foundation's scholarship policy.
EIN: 363324526

NEVADA

5278
A Charitable Foundation
2657 Windmill Pkwy., Ste. 220
Henderson, NV 89014 (702) 248-8184

Foundation type: Independent foundation
Purpose: Scientific research grants to individuals with emphasis on Brazil.
Financial data: Year ended 12/31/2012. Assets, $5,636,231 (M); Expenditures, $232,900; Total giving, $172,450; Grant to an individual, 1 grant totaling $36,000.
International interests: Brazil.
Type of support: Research.
Application information: Application form not required.
> *Initial approach:* Brief proposal
> *Copies of proposal:* 1
> *Deadline(s):* Contact foundation for application deadline/guidelines.

EIN: 880375802

5279
Berner Educational Trust No. 2
P.O. Box 5940
Stateline, NV 89449-5940
E-mail: info@bernerscholarship.org; *URL:* http://www.bernerscholarship.org

Foundation type: Independent foundation
Purpose: Scholarship to graduating students from high schools in northern Nevada for continuing education at institutions of higher learning.
Publications: Application guidelines.
Financial data: Year ended 12/31/2012. Assets, $20,814,752 (M); Expenditures, $2,244,741; Total giving, $1,606,040; Grants to individuals, 90 grants totaling $1,606,040 (high: $58,635, low: $385).
Fields of interest: Vocational education, post-secondary; Higher education.
Type of support: Scholarships—to individuals.
Application information: Applications accepted. Application form required. Application form available on the grantmaker's web site.
> *Initial approach:* Application
> *Send request by:* Mail
> *Deadline(s):* Mar. 29
> *Applicants should submit the following:*
>   1) Letter(s) of recommendation
>   2) ACT
>   3) SAT
>   4) Transcripts
>   5) Resume
> *Additional information:* Application should also include a signed FERPA form. See web site for complete application guidelines.

EIN: 201799697

5280
Caring 4 Kids Foundation
(formerly Corps of Compassion)
7231 S. Eastern Ave., Ste. 254
Las Vegas, NV 89119-0451 (702) 544-1400
Contact: David S. Sullivan, Pres.
E-mail: admin@caring4kidsfoundation.org; Mailing address: 7231 S. Eastern Ave., Ste. 254, Las Vegas, NV 89119-0451; *URL:* http://www.caring4kidsfoundation.org/

Foundation type: Public charity

Purpose: Grants providing relief and support to disaster victims in the United States. Also provides food and educational opportunities to poor and at-risk children.
Financial data: Year ended 06/30/2010. Assets, $23,201 (M); Expenditures, $124,959.
Fields of interest: Safety/disasters.
Type of support: Emergency funds.
Application information: Applications not accepted.
> *Additional information:* Unsolicited requests for funds not accepted.

EIN: 203435764

5281
Catholic Charities of Southern Nevada
1501 Las Vegas Blvd. N.
Las Vegas, NV 89101-1120 (702) 385-2662
Contact: Thomas A. Roberts, Co-Pres. and C.E.O.
FAX: (702) 384-0677; *URL:* http://www.catholiccharities.com/

Foundation type: Public charity
Purpose: Asssistance to indigent residents of southern NV in the form of emergency food, clothing, hygiene items, diapers/baby goods, and school supplies.
Financial data: Year ended 06/30/2012. Assets, $20,206,423 (M); Expenditures, $19,464,432; Total giving, $6,316,982; Grants to individuals, totaling $6,034,208.
Fields of interest: Economically disadvantaged.
Type of support: In-kind gifts.
Application information:
> *Initial approach:* Tel.
> *Additional information:* For food pantry entrance, please bring Nevada ID, social security card, and proof of residence.

EIN: 880059425

5282
Community Foundation of Western Nevada
1885 S. Arlington Ave., Ste. 103
Reno, NV 89509-3370 (775) 333-5499
Contact: Margaret Stewart, Comms. Dir.; For scholarships: Tracy Turner Ph.D., Prog. Off.
FAX: (775) 333-5487; *E-mail:* info@cfwnv.org; Additional e-mail: mstewart@cfwnv.org;
URL: http://www.cfwnv.org

Foundation type: Community foundation
Purpose: Scholarships to residents of Western Nevada for higher education.
Publications: Application guidelines; Annual report; Financial statement; Informational brochure; Newsletter.
Financial data: Year ended 12/31/2012. Assets, $66,094,688 (M); Expenditures, $8,155,527; Total giving, $5,916,488. Scholarships—to individuals amount not specified.
Fields of interest: Elementary/secondary education; Higher education.
Type of support: Scholarships—to individuals; Support to graduates or students of specific schools; Graduate support; Undergraduate support.
Application information: Applications accepted. Application form available on the grantmaker's web site.
> *Initial approach:* Telephone
> *Deadline(s):* Vary
> *Additional information:* See web site for a complete listing of scholarship funds and application.

Program description:
> *Scholarships:* The foundation offers a wide variety of scholarships from pre-schoolers to seniors in high school preparing to graduate and attend college, students who have already graduated from high school, or students who are already enrolled in college. Some scholarships available for graduate school as well. All scholarships have their own unique eligibility requirements, and may vary by age, sex, school and location of residence. Learn more about each scholarship fund and search for opportunities for which you may qualify on the foundation's web site.

EIN: 880370179

5283
The Nicholas & Dorothy Cummings Foundation
4781 Caughlin Pkwy.
Reno, NV 89509
URL: http://thecummingsfoundation.org/

Foundation type: Independent foundation
Purpose: Research grants to professional psychotherapists who are studying behavioral health treatment, primarily in CA and NV.
Financial data: Year ended 12/31/2011. Assets, $62,716 (M); Expenditures, $289,419; Total giving, $50,000; Grants to individuals, totaling $50,000.
Fields of interest: Medical specialties research.
Type of support: Research.
Application information: Applications not accepted.
> *Additional information:* Unsolicited requests for funds not considered or acknowledged.

EIN: 880321190

5284
Davidson Institute for Talent Development
9665 Gateway Dr., Ste. B
Reno, NV 89521-8997
E-mail: info@davidsongiften.org; *URL:* http://www.davidsongifted.org

Foundation type: Operating foundation
Purpose: Giving for the support of gifted students.
Publications: Application guidelines; Annual report; Informational brochure.
Financial data: Year ended 06/30/2013. Assets, $3,226,843 (M); Expenditures, $4,947,634; Total giving, $487,470; Grants to individuals, 105 grants totaling $477,470 (high: $45,000, low: $20).
Fields of interest: Education, gifted students; Scholarships/financial aid.
Type of support: Fellowships; Scholarships—to individuals.
Application information: Applications accepted. Application form required. Application form available on the grantmaker's web site.
> *Deadline(s):* Mar. 25 for Davidson Fellows Scholarship; Monthly for the Davidson Young Scholars
> *Additional information:* Faxed or e-mailed applications are not accepted. See web site for further application instructions.

Program descriptions:
> *Davidson Fellows Scholarships:* The program awards scholarships of $50,000, $25,000 and $10,000 to extraordinary young people under the age of 18 who have completed a significant piece of work. Application categories are Mathematics, Science, Literature, Music, Technology, Philosophy

and Outside the Box. Application information available on the foundation web site.

Davidson Young Scholars: The Young Scholars Program provides free services designed to nurture and support members of an underserved population, profoundly gifted young people. Students and their parents are assisted in the areas of educational advocacy, social and emotional development, talent development and peer connections. Services can help students draw upon their unique skills, talents and interests to maximize their educational potential and make a difference in the lives of others. Applicants must be 5- to 18-years old (applicants must not be older than 16 at the time of application). Application information available on foundation web site.
EIN: 880427864

5285
Alexander Dawson Foundation
4045 S. Spencer St., Ste. 312
Las Vegas, NV 89119-5248 (702) 733-7880
Contact: Lamar K. Cloud, Exec. Dir.

Foundation type: Public charity
Purpose: Scholarships to students attending co-educational prepatory schools in NV and CO.
Financial data: Year ended 06/30/2012. Assets, $213,221,066 (M); Expenditures, $34,344,732; Total giving, $3,073,380; Grants to individuals, totaling $3,073,380.
Fields of interest: Education.
Type of support: Scholarships—to individuals.
Application information: Applications accepted. Application form required.
Additional information: Applicant must demonstrate financial need.
EIN: 226044616

5286
DiRienzo Foundation, Inc.
4735 Saddlehorn Dr.
Reno, NV 89511-6756 (775) 853-8962
Contact: Margaret A. DiRienzo, Pres.

Foundation type: Operating foundation
Purpose: Grants and scholarships to low income individuals who are striving to improve their life conditions from tragedy or misfortune by pursuing career education or training.
Financial data: Year ended 12/31/2012. Assets, $183,722 (M); Expenditures, $17,192; Total giving, $17,000; Grants to individuals, 2 grants totaling $11,000 (high: $10,000, low: $1,000).
Fields of interest: Higher education.
Type of support: Grants to individuals; Scholarships—to individuals.
Application information: Applications accepted. Application form required.
Additional information: Applicant should provide personal and financial information as well as an explanation of how the applicant is improving him/herself.
EIN: 311393435

5287
The Frank M. Doyle Foundation, Inc.
3495 Lakeside Dr., No. 34
Reno, NV 89509-4841 (775) 829-1972
FAX: (775) 829-1974;
E-mail: FMDFoundation@aol.com; URL: http://www.frankmdoyle.org

Foundation type: Operating foundation

Purpose: Scholarships to high school graduates of the Huntington Beach Union High School District and Huntington Beach Adult High School in CA, as well as students and graduates of community colleges in Coastline, Cypress, Fullerton, Golden West, Irvine Valley, Orange Coast, Saddleback, Santa Ana, or Santiago Canyon, CA. Scholarships also to students and graduates of the Washoe County School District or Washoe Adult High School in NV.
Publications: Application guidelines.
Financial data: Year ended 08/31/2013. Assets, $69,711,491 (M); Expenditures, $4,259,601; Total giving, $3,426,930; Grants to individuals, 409 grants totaling $1,043,757 (high: $10,000, low: $67).
Fields of interest: Vocational education, post-secondary; Higher education.
Type of support: Scholarships—to individuals; Support to graduates or students of specific schools; Graduate support; Technical education support; Undergraduate support; Postgraduate support; Doctoral support.
Application information: Application form required. Application form available on the grantmaker's web site.
Send request by: Mail
Deadline(s): Mar. 1
Final notification: Applicants notified in May
Applicants should submit the following:
1) SAR
2) Transcripts
3) Letter(s) of recommendation
4) Essay
Additional information: See web site for additional guidelines.
EIN: 880372802

5288
The Foundation for Social Equity
1350 E. Flamingo Rd., Ste. 13B
P.O. Box 346
Las Vegas, NV 89119-5263 (702) 992-0277
E-mail: applications@foundationforsocialequity.com; URL: http://www.foundationforsocialequity.com

Foundation type: Independent foundation
Purpose: Scholarships and grants for medical assistance to financially needy individuals.
Financial data: Year ended 12/31/2012. Assets, $102,436 (M); Expenditures, $15,082; Total giving, $12,000; Grants to individuals, 3 grants totaling $12,000 (high: $8,000, low: $1,500).
Fields of interest: Higher education; Health care; Economically disadvantaged.
Type of support: Undergraduate support; Grants for special needs.
Application information: Applications accepted. Application form required. Application form available on the grantmaker's web site.
Additional information: Application should include financial information. Scholarship application should also include personal narrative.
EIN: 752986747

5289
The Holder Family Foundation
c/o H. Randolf Holder, Jr.
120 Country Club Dr.
Incline Village, NV 89451 (775) 887-0588

Foundation type: Independent foundation
Purpose: Scholarships primarily to residents of Sonora, CA.

Financial data: Year ended 12/31/2012. Assets, $7,590 (M); Expenditures, $6,300; Total giving, $6,000; Grants to individuals, 9 grants totaling $5,000 (high: $1,000, low: $500).
Type of support: Undergraduate support.
Application information:
Initial approach: Letter
Deadline(s): None
EIN: 880475661

5290
A. G. and Hattie Odell Kirchner Educational Scholarship Trust
1695 Meadow Wood Ln., Ste.100
Reno, NV 89502-6573 (559) 891-1934
Contact: Robert Kirchner, Tr.
Application address: 1404 Burnham St., Selma, CA 93662

Foundation type: Independent foundation
Purpose: Scholarships to individuals for continuing their education at accredited institutions of higher learning.
Financial data: Year ended 12/31/2012. Assets, $69,825 (M); Expenditures, $28,700; Total giving, $24,250.
Fields of interest: Higher education.
Type of support: Scholarships—to individuals.
Application information: Applications accepted.
EIN: 880387137

5291
Michelle Korfman Scholarship Foundation
806 Buchanan Blvd.
Boulder City, NV 89005-2130

Foundation type: Independent foundation
Purpose: Scholarships to graduating seniors of Boulder City High School, NV for college tuition.
Financial data: Year ended 12/31/2011. Assets, $37,640 (M); Expenditures, $7,180; Total giving, $500; Grant to an individual, 1 grant totaling $500.
Fields of interest: Higher education.
Type of support: Scholarships—to individuals; Support to graduates or students of specific schools.
Application information: Application form required.
Deadline(s): Mar. 1
Additional information: Applications available from high school.
EIN: 880199046

5292
Sumi Laetz Fund Inc.
6693 Turina Rd.
Las Vegas, NV 89146

Foundation type: Independent foundation
Purpose: Scholarships primarily to residents of Las Vegas, NV.
Financial data: Year ended 12/31/2013. Assets, $222,221 (M); Expenditures, $8,151; Total giving, $8,000; Grants to individuals, totaling $8,000.
Type of support: Scholarships—to individuals.
Application information: Applications not accepted.
Additional information: Unsolicited requests for funds not considered or acknowledged.
EIN: 880347440

5293
A. Marchionne Foundation for Scientific Study of Human Relations

(formerly A. Marchionne Foundation for Scientific Study)
844 Entrada Ridge Ave.
Henderson, NV   89012

Foundation type: Independent foundation
Purpose: Research grants for the study of scientific study of human relationships.
Financial data: Year ended 12/31/2012. Assets, $1,885,553 (M); Expenditures, $82,837; Total giving, $20,000.
Fields of interest: Psychology/behavioral science.
Type of support: Research.
Application information: Applications not accepted.
   Additional information: Unsolicited requests for funds not considered or acknowledged.
EIN: 141826951

5294
Miracle Flights For Kids

2764 N. Green Valley Pkwy., Ste. 115
Green Valley, NV   89014-2120   (702) 261-0494
Contact: William P. McGee, V.P., Admin.
FAX: (702) 261-0497;
E-mail: wpmcgee@miracleflights.org; Toll-free tel.: (800) 359-1711; URL: http://www.miracleflights.org

Foundation type: Public charity
Purpose: Grants for air transportation for seriously ill children and their families to receive proper medical care and get second opinions.
Financial data: Year ended 04/30/2012. Assets, $1,486,020 (M); Expenditures, $2,355,090; Total giving, $965,323.
Fields of interest: Health care; Children.
Type of support: Grants for special needs.
Application information: Applications accepted.
   Initial approach: Telephone
   Additional information: See web site for complete program guidelines.
EIN: 880209952

5295
Nevada Community Foundation, Inc.

1635 Village Center Circle, Ste. 160
Las Vegas, NV   89134   (702) 892-2326
Contact: Gian Brosco, Pres.
FAX: (702) 892-8580; E-mail: info@nevadacf.org;
URL: http://www.nevadacf.org

Foundation type: Community foundation
Purpose: Scholarships to students of NV for higher education. Financial assistance to Nevada residents with food, clothing, utility, rent/mortgage assistance and other special needs.
Publications: Application guidelines; Annual report; Financial statement; Grants list.
Financial data: Year ended 06/30/2012. Assets, $29,804,819 (M); Expenditures, $3,188,892; Total giving, $2,232,341.
Fields of interest: Higher education; Scholarships/financial aid; Economically disadvantaged.
Type of support: Scholarships—to individuals; Support to graduates or students of specific schools; Awards/prizes; Grants for special needs.
Application information: Applications accepted. Application form required. Application form available on the grantmaker's web site.
   Initial approach: E-mail
   Additional information: The foundation has partnered with the Public Education

Foundation to administer a variety of Scholarship funds. E-mail Jane Ramos at jane.ramos@nevadacf.org for inquiry of scholarship program or visit www.thepef.org If you are inquiring about a specific scholarship program please contact.
EIN: 880241420

5296
Nevada Women's Fund

770 Smithridge Dr., Ste. 300
Reno, NV   89502-0708   (775) 786-2335
Contact: Isabelle Rodriguez Wilson, Pres. and C.E.O.
FAX: (775) 786-8152;
E-mail: info@nevadawomensfund.org; URL: http://www.nevadawomensfund.org

Foundation type: Public charity
Purpose: Scholarships to women residing in NV. Preference is given to Northern NV students, and those at the University of Nevada and its community college system.
Publications: Application guidelines; Grants list; Informational brochure; Newsletter.
Financial data: Year ended 12/31/2012. Assets, $2,943,151 (M); Expenditures, $581,370; Total giving, $284,858; Grants to individuals, totaling $117,108.
Fields of interest: Higher education; Women.
Type of support: Support to graduates or students of specific schools; Graduate support; Technical education support; Undergraduate support; Doctoral support.
Application information: Application form required. Application form available on the grantmaker's web site.
   Initial approach: E-mail or telephone
   Deadline(s): Last Fri. in Feb.
EIN: 942860375

5297
The Elwood and Stephanie Norris Foundation

8617 Canyon View Dr.
Las Vegas, NV   89117-5737
Contact: Elwood Norris, Tr.
Application address: 16101 Blue Crystal Trl., Poway, CA 92064-3178

Foundation type: Independent foundation
Purpose: Grants to support science, technology and invention through education and entrepreneurial endeavors.
Financial data: Year ended 12/31/2011. Assets, $2,581 (M); Expenditures, $37,848; Total giving, $37,000.
Fields of interest: Education; Science.
Type of support: Grants to individuals; Scholarships—to individuals.
Application information: Applications accepted. Application form required.
EIN: 202462445

5298
NV Energy Charitable Foundation

(formerly NV Energy Foundation)
P.O. Box 10100
Reno, NV   89520-3150   (775) 834-5642
Contact: Mary Simmons, Secy.
Application address for Southern Nevada: NV Energy, Powerful Partnership Scholarship - M/S 15, P.O. Box 98910, Las Vegas, NV 89151; Northern Nevada: NV Energy, Powerful Partnership

Scholarship, Community Foundation of Western Nevada, 1885 South Arlington Ave., Ste. 103, Reno, NV 89509
E-mail: Communitynorth@nvenergy.com;
URL: http://www.nvenergy.com/community/funding/sprfoundation/

Foundation type: Company-sponsored foundation
Purpose: Scholarships to high school seniors and home schooled students in NV Energy's northern service territory, high school seniors from a Clark County high school, and to a home schooled student in Clark County.
Publications: Application guidelines; Informational brochure (including application guidelines); Program policy statement.
Financial data: Year ended 12/31/2012. Assets, $6,886,115 (M); Expenditures, $4,027,816; Total giving, $4,027,600.
Fields of interest: Higher education.
Type of support: Scholarships—to individuals; Support to graduates or students of specific schools.
Application information: Applications accepted. Application form required. Application form available on the grantmaker's web site.
   Initial approach: Application
   Send request by: Mail
   Deadline(s): Mar. 1
   Applicants should submit the following:
      1) Transcripts
      2) Resume
      3) Letter(s) of recommendation
      4) GPA
      5) Financial information
      6) Essay
   Additional information: Applications should also include evidence of enrollment at an institution of higher education, a personal statement outlining career goals and aspirations, a 100 to 300 word essay explaining why community service is important. See web site for additional guidelines.
Program description:
   Powerful Partnerships High School Scholarship: The foundation annually awards $1,000 scholarships to high school seniors attending school or homeschooled in NV Energy's northern and southern service territory. The scholarship is based on demonstrated leadership, academic achievement, financial need, and 20 hours of community service. In southern Nevada application forms are available through Clark County School District. In northern Nevada application forms are available through the Community Foundation of Western Nevada.
EIN: 880244735

5299
Mary Orcutt Memorial Foundation

(formerly Mary Orcutt Memorial Scholarship Foundation)
2509 Bohr Rd.
Carson City, NV   89706   (775) 246-6240

Foundation type: Independent foundation
Purpose: Scholarships to graduates of Dayton High School, NV for higher education.
Financial data: Year ended 12/31/2013. Assets, $68,280 (M); Expenditures, $20,151; Total giving, $18,399; Grants to individuals, 5 grants totaling $17,606 (high: $4,725; low: $2,500).
Fields of interest: Higher education.
Type of support: Support to graduates or students of specific schools.

Application information: Applications accepted. Application form required.

Deadline(s): Apr. 15

EIN: 880380539

5300
Reno Rodeo Foundation

500 Ryland St., Ste. 200
Reno, NV 89502-1676 (775) 322-9875
Contact: Marie Baxter, Exec. Dir.
FAX: (775) 825-6411;
E-mail: info@renorodeofoundation.org; URL: http://www.renorodeofoundation.org

Foundation type: Public charity
Purpose: Undergraduate and graduate scholarship to rural Nevada high schools students for attendance at the University of Nevada pursuing medical and vererinary degrees.
Financial data: Year ended 07/31/2011. Assets, $1,398,342 (M); Expenditures, $331,926; Total giving, $135,718; Grants to individuals, totaling $37,000.
Fields of interest: Higher education.
Type of support: Scholarships—to individuals.
Application information: Applications accepted. Application form required.

Additional information: Application should include official transcripts and other test scores. See web site for additional application guidelines.

Program descriptions:

Bob & Kristen Tallman/Reno Rodeo Foundation Scholarship: Awards a $2,500 annual scholarship to a graduate of a of rural Nevada high schools who attends the University of Nevada, Reno and declares a major in the College of Agriculture, Biotechnology, Natural Resources or the College of Science specific to a Pre-Vet or Pre-Med degree or declares a major in the Colleges of Business, Education, or Nursing. Recipient must have an overall high school GPA of 3.0 and maintain a GPA of 3.0 and take a minimum of 12 credits per semester. Recipient receives $1,250 per semester, for a total annual scholarship of $2,500.

Reno Rodeo Foundation Scholarship: Awards a $2,000 scholarship annually to up to 20 graduates of rural Nevada high schools who attend the University of Nevada, Reno and declare a major in the College of Agriculture, Biotechnology, Natural Resources or the College of Science specific to Pre-Vet or Pre-Med degrees or declare a major in the Colleges of Business, Education, or Nursing. Recipients must have an overall high school GPA of 3.0 and maintain a GPA of 3.0 and take a minimum of 12 credits per semester. Each of the 20 recipients receive $1,000 per semester, for a total annual scholarship of $2,000. Once a student is selected to receive the scholarship, that student keeps it for four years.

EIN: 880230538

5301
Renown Health Foundation

(formerly Washoe Medical Foundation, Inc.)
c/o Tax Treasury Z-5
1155 Mill St.
Reno, NV 89502-1576 (775) 982-4100
FAX: (775) 982-5565; URL: http://www.renown.org/homepage.cfm?id=109&oTopID=109

Foundation type: Public charity
Purpose: Scholarships to nursing students in Nevada accepted into an accredited nursing program.
Publications: Annual report; Informational brochure.
Financial data: Year ended 06/30/2011. Assets, $14,160,054 (M); Expenditures, $1,233,027; Total giving, $912,788; Grants to individuals, totaling $67,580.
Fields of interest: Nursing school/education.
Type of support: Scholarships—to individuals.
Application information: Applications accepted.

Additional information: Selection criteria is based on scholastic abilities and attendance.

EIN: 942972749

5302
Nicole Snyder Memorial Fund, Inc.

c/o John and Patti Snyder
1407 Selkirk Cir.
Gardnerville, NV 89460-8886

Foundation type: Independent foundation
Purpose: Scholarships to graduating students of Douglas High School pursuing their studies at any level of postsecondary education.
Financial data: Year ended 12/31/2011. Assets, $14,324 (M); Expenditures, $7,537; Total giving, $7,012.
Fields of interest: Higher education; Athletics/sports, school programs.
Type of support: Support to graduates or students of specific schools.
Application information: Applications accepted. Application form required.

Send request by: Mail or hand delivered
Deadline(s): Apr. 7
Applicants should submit the following:
  1) Letter(s) of recommendation
  2) Transcripts
  3) GPA
  4) Essay
Additional information: Applications are available in the Douglas High School scholarship office.

EIN: 830429292

5303
United Way of Southern Nevada

5830 W. Flamingo Rd.
Las Vegas, NV 89139-7114 (702) 892-2300
E-mail: info@uwsn.org; URL: http://www.uwsn.org

Foundation type: Public charity
Purpose: Grants to needy individuals in southern NV.
Publications: Multi-year report; Newsletter.
Financial data: Year ended 06/30/2011. Assets, $11,963,605 (M); Expenditures, $34,791,580; Total giving, $6,693,794; Grants to individuals, totaling $916,699.
Fields of interest: Economically disadvantaged.
Type of support: Grants for special needs.
Application information:

Initial approach: Letter
Additional information: Contact foundation for complete eligibility requirements.

EIN: 880071328

5304
Western Shoshone Scholarship Foundation

905 W. Main St.
Elko, NV 89803-2774 (775) 748-1258
Contact: Katie Neddenriep

Foundation type: Independent foundation
Purpose: Scholarships to eligible students in the U.S. for university and college education, and vocational and technical training.
Financial data: Year ended 12/31/2012. Assets, $2,631,513 (M); Expenditures, $288,002; Total giving, $288,000; Grants to individuals, 89 grants totaling $288,000 (high: $6,000, low: $1,500).
Fields of interest: Vocational education, post-secondary; College (community/junior); University; Graduate/professional education.
Type of support: Scholarships—to individuals; Graduate support; Technical education support; Undergraduate support.
Application information: Applications accepted. Application form required.

Initial approach: Telephone
Send request by: Mail
Deadline(s): July
Applicants should submit the following:
  1) Essay
  2) Transcripts
Additional information: Application should also include a personal statement, copy of registration for upcoming term reflecting enrollment for a minimum of 11 credits (not exceeding 50 percent of credits on-line), and evidence of Tribal affiliation.

EIN: 364663132

NEW HAMPSHIRE

5305
American Ground Water Trust
50 Pleasant St.
Concord, NH 03301-4073 (603) 228-5444
Contact: Andrew Stone, Exec. Dir.
FAX: (603) 228-6557; E-mail: trustinfo@agwt.org;
E-Mail for Andrew Stone: astone@agwt.org;
URL: http://www.agwt.org

Foundation type: Public charity
Purpose: Scholarships to high school seniors for attendance at accredited colleges or universities pursuing a career in the ground water industry.
Publications: Application guidelines.
Financial data: Year ended 12/31/2011. Assets, $41,003 (M); Expenditures, $463,488; Total giving, $6,500; Grants to individuals, totaling $6,500.
Fields of interest: Environment, water resources.
Type of support: Scholarships—to individuals.
Application information: Applications accepted. Application form required. Application form available on the grantmaker's web site.
> *Send request by:* Mail
> *Deadline(s):* June 1
> *Final notification:* Applicants will be notified by the end of Aug.
> *Applicants should submit the following:*
> 1) Transcripts
> 2) Letter(s) of recommendation
> 3) GPA
> 4) Essay
> *Additional information:* See web site for additional application guidelines.
Program descriptions:
> *Amtrol, Inc. Scholarship:* Up to $1,500 is awarded to a high-school senior intending to pursue a career in a ground water-related field.
> *BAROID Scholarship:* The scholarship is awarded to a high-school senior intending to pursue a career in a ground water-related field. The scholarship award is $2,000.
> *Thompson M. Stetson Scholarship:* A scholarship award in the amount of $2,000 will be awarded to a high-school senior intending to pursue a career in a ground water field. The scholarship is only for a student attending a college or university located west of the Mississippi River.
EIN: 237244958

5306
The Ayer Scholarship Trust
P.O. Box 96
Plymouth, NH 03264-0096 (603) 536-2520
Contact: Ross V. Deachman, Tr.
Application address: 66 Main St., Plymouth, NH 03264-1451

Foundation type: Independent foundation
Purpose: Scholarships to individuals of Plymouth, NH for continuing education at institutions of higher learning.
Financial data: Year ended 12/31/2012. Assets, $777,749 (M); Expenditures, $23,026; Total giving, $13,000; Grants to individuals, 5 grants totaling $13,000 (high: $3,000, low: $2,000).
Fields of interest: Higher education.
Type of support: Scholarships—to individuals.
Application information: Applications accepted.
> *Initial approach:* Letter
> *Deadline(s):* None

Additional information: Contact the trust for additional application guidelines.
EIN: 020526252

5307
The Bean Foundation
265 Old Dublin Rd.
Peterborough, NH 03458 (603) 532-8311

Foundation type: Company-sponsored foundation
Purpose: Scholarships to individuals showing financial need who reside in the Jaffrey, NH, area.
Financial data: Year ended 12/31/2012. Assets, $981,970 (M); Expenditures, $104,026; Total giving, $102,700; Grants to individuals, 2 grants totaling $4,500 (high: $4,000, low: $500).
Type of support: Scholarships—to individuals.
Application information: Application form not required.
> *Initial approach:* Letter
> *Additional information:* Contact foundation for eligibility requirements.
EIN: 026005330

5308
Jasper W. & Catherine L. Blandin Scholarship Trust
P.O. Box 477
Concord, NH 03302-0477 (603) 823-7411
Application Address: c/o Profile High School, 691 Profile Rd., Bethlehem, NH 03574

Foundation type: Independent foundation
Purpose: Scholarships to graduating high school seniors who are residents of Easton, Sugar Hill, Franconia or Bethlehem, NH, pursuing a career in the health-related field.
Financial data: Year ended 12/31/2012. Assets, $542,962 (M); Expenditures, $33,595; Total giving, $26,100; Grants to individuals, 24 grants totaling $26,100 (high: $2,500, low: $500).
Fields of interest: Higher education; Health sciences school/education.
Type of support: Scholarships—to individuals.
Application information: Applications accepted. Application form required.
> *Initial approach:* Letter or telephone
> *Additional information:* Students must have academic standard of excellence, and participated in athletic activities. Application available upon request.
EIN: 026123358

5309
E. Dante Bogni Trust
P.O. Box 477
Concord, NH 03302-0477 (802) 860-5553

Foundation type: Independent foundation
Purpose: Scholarships to graduating seniors of Montpelier High School, VT, and Spaulding High School, VT, for higher education in the study of science or math.
Financial data: Year ended 12/31/2012. Assets, $870,309 (M); Expenditures, $62,048; Total giving, $48,750; Grants to individuals, 8 grants totaling $48,750 (high: $11,000, low: $1,000).
Fields of interest: Mathematics; Science.
Type of support: Support to graduates or students of specific schools; Undergraduate support.
Application information: Applications accepted.
> *Deadline(s):* None
EIN: 036044565

5310
Blanche A. Bruce Trust
95 Market St.
Manchester, NH 03101-1933 (603) 699-4140
Contact: Richard Thorner Esq., Tr.

Foundation type: Independent foundation
Purpose: Scholarships to NH residents enrolled at colleges or universities for higher education.
Financial data: Year ended 06/30/2013. Assets, $2,271,118 (M); Expenditures, $108,537; Total giving, $79,000; Grants to individuals, 9 grants totaling $19,000 (high: $3,000, low: $1,500).
Fields of interest: Higher education.
Type of support: Scholarships—to individuals.
Application information: Applications accepted. Application form not required.
> *Deadline(s):* June
> *Additional information:* Application must demonstrate financial need, merit, community service and academic achievement.
EIN: 026014968

5311
Abraham Burtman Charity Trust
P.O. Box 608
Dover, NH 03820-4103 (603) 742-2332
Contact: Paul R. Cox Esq., Tr.

Foundation type: Independent foundation
Purpose: Undergraduate scholarships to financially needy NH residents.
Financial data: Year ended 12/31/2012. Assets, $1,370,678 (M); Expenditures, $91,835; Total giving, $74,000.
Type of support: Undergraduate support.
Application information: Application form required.
> *Initial approach:* Letter
> *Deadline(s):* May 10
> *Applicants should submit the following:*
> 1) Financial information
> 2) SAR
EIN: 026004364

5312
The Butler Foundation
(formerly Neslab Charitable Foundation)
c/o Charter Trust Co.
90 N. Main St.
Concord, NH 03301-4915 (603) 224-1350

Foundation type: Independent foundation
Purpose: Scholarships to children of employees of NES labs for higher education.
Financial data: Year ended 12/31/2012. Assets, $9,055,546 (M); Expenditures, $603,725; Total giving, $483,307.
Fields of interest: Natural resources.
Type of support: Scholarships—to individuals.
Application information:
> *Deadline(s):* None
> *Applicants should submit the following:*
> 1) Transcripts
> 2) Essay
EIN: 222701588

5313
Francis Earl and Edwina Jones Clarke Trust
P.O. Box 477
Concord, NH 03302-0477 (802) 773-6820
Contact: Justin Baker
Application address: c/o Christ the King Church, 66 S. Main St., Rutland, VT 05701

Foundation type: Independent foundation
Purpose: Scholarships to graduating students of Rutland County School District, VT for attendance at institutions of higher learning.
Financial data: Year ended 12/31/2012. Assets, $509,122 (M); Expenditures, $32,582; Total giving, $24,370; Grants to individuals, 15 grants totaling $24,370 (high: $6,958, low: $185).
Fields of interest: Higher education.
Type of support: Scholarships—to individuals.
Application information: Applications accepted. Application form required.
   Deadline(s): None
   Applicants should submit the following:
      1) Class rank
      2) Transcripts
      3) Letter(s) of recommendation
   Additional information: Applicants must have attended school at Rutland County School District for three years and must be under age 21.
EIN: 036072967

5314
George T. Cogan Trust
P.O. Box 477
Concord, NH   03302-0477

Foundation type: Independent foundation
Purpose: Scholarships to male students who have resided in Portsmouth, NH, for at least four years prior to graduation from either Portsmouth High School, NH, or St. Thomas Aquinas High School, NH.
Financial data: Year ended 12/31/2012. Assets, $471,011 (M); Expenditures, $29,389; Total giving, $18,000; Grants to individuals, 21 grants totaling $18,000 (high: $1,000, low: $500).
Fields of interest: Higher education; Men.
Type of support: Support to graduates or students of specific schools; Undergraduate support.
Application information: Applications not accepted.
   Additional information: Unsolicited requests for funds not considered or acknowledged.
EIN: 026019789

5315
Community Action Program Belknap & Merrimack Counties, Inc.
2 Industrial Park Dr.
P.O. Box 1016
Concord, NH   03302-1016   (603) 225-3295
Contact: Ralph Littlefield, Exec. Dir.
FAX: (603) 228-1898; *URL:* http://www.bm-cap.org/index.html

Foundation type: Public charity
Purpose: Grants up to $300 to indigent households in Belknap-Merrimack Counties in NH once in a 24 month period that will be applied toward utility bills. Fuel and electric, and transportation assistance is also available.
Financial data: Year ended 02/28/2012. Assets, $11,235,025 (M); Expenditures, $27,659,774; Total giving, $4,905,881; Grants to individuals, totaling $4,905,881.
Fields of interest: Economically disadvantaged.
Type of support: In-kind gifts; Grants for special needs.
Application information:
   Initial approach: Tel.
   Additional information: Contact foundation for eligibility criteria.
EIN: 020270376

5316
Concord Hospital Associates
250 Pleasant St.
Concord, NH   03301-7560   (603) 228-1193

Foundation type: Public charity
Purpose: Scholarships to employees of Concord Hospital, NH for continuing education.
Financial data: Year ended 09/30/2011. Assets, $382,400 (M); Expenditures, $236,477; Total giving, $22,500; Grants to individuals, totaling $2,500.
Fields of interest: Education.
Type of support: Scholarships—to individuals.
Application information: Scholarship selection is based on need.
EIN: 020237260

5317
John K. and Thirza F. Davenport Foundation
P.O. Box 477
Concord, NH   03302-0477   (508) 398-2293
Contact: Dewitt Davenport
Application address: 20 N. Main St., South Yarmouth, MA 02664,tel.: 508-398-2293

Foundation type: Independent foundation
Purpose: Scholarships to students of the arts who are residents of Barnstable County, MA.
Financial data: Year ended 06/30/2013. Assets, $736,857 (M); Expenditures, $25,348; Total giving, $19,850.
Fields of interest: Arts education.
Type of support: Scholarships—to individuals.
Application information: Applications accepted. Application form required.
   Initial approach: Letter
   Deadline(s): None
EIN: 222647795

5318
Dodge Scholarship Trust for Girls
(formerly Adelaide Dodge Scholarship Trust)
95 Market St.
Manchester, NH   03101-1933   (603) 669-4140
Contact: Richard Thorner Esq., Tr.

Foundation type: Independent foundation
Purpose: Scholarships to female graduates of Manchester High School Central NH for higher education.
Financial data: Year ended 12/31/2011. Assets, $388,526 (M); Expenditures, $30,440; Total giving, $24,000; Grants to individuals, 8 grants totaling $24,000 (high: $3,000, low: $3,000).
Fields of interest: Higher education; Women.
Type of support: Scholarships—to individuals; Support to graduates or students of specific schools.
Application information: Applications accepted. Application form required.
   Deadline(s): May 15
EIN: 020439653

5319
V. Faith Edmunds Scholarship Trust
P.O. Box 477
Concord, NH   03302   (802) 888-4600

Foundation type: Independent foundation
Purpose: Scholarships to students at People's Academy in Morrisville, VT, for higher education.
Financial data: Year ended 12/31/2012. Assets, $109,770 (M); Expenditures, $7,828; Total giving,

$5,000; Grants to individuals, 9 grants totaling $5,000 (high: $600, low: $500).
Type of support: Support to graduates or students of specific schools; Undergraduate support.
Application information: Application form not required.
   Deadline(s): None
   Additional information: Scholarships up to $1,000 per year for a maximum of four years of study.
EIN: 946443878

5320
Mary E. Elliott Trust
93 Woodland Dr.
Contoocook, NH   03229-2533   (603) 746-5729

Foundation type: Independent foundation
Purpose: Grants to economically disadvantaged citizens of Contoocook and Hopkinton, NH.
Financial data: Year ended 12/31/2012. Assets, $637,253 (M); Expenditures, $32,167; Total giving, $26,525; Grants to individuals, 7 grants totaling $26,525 (high: $10,495, low: $1,200).
Fields of interest: Economically disadvantaged.
Type of support: Grants for special needs.
Application information: Applications not accepted.
   Additional information: The town of Hopkinton advises trustees of needy residents.
EIN: 026010880

5321
Fond Rev. Edmond Gelinas Inc.
39 Carpenter St.
Manchester, NH   03104-2206   (603) 578-6788
Contact: Donald N. Fournier, Pres. and Secy.

Foundation type: Operating foundation
Purpose: Scholarships to NH students who are Catholic and of French or Canadian ancestry.
Financial data: Year ended 12/31/2011. Assets, $178,985 (M); Expenditures, $11,375; Total giving, $9,800; Grants to individuals, 22 grants totaling $9,800 (high: $650, low: $200).
Fields of interest: Higher education; Catholic agencies & churches.
International interests: Canada; France.
Type of support: Scholarships—to individuals; Undergraduate support.
Application information: Application form required.
   Deadline(s): June 1
   Applicants should submit the following:
      1) Letter(s) of recommendation
      2) Photograph
      3) Transcripts
      4) Financial information
EIN: 020262914

5322
Foundation for Seacoast Health
100 Campus Dr., Ste. 1
Portsmouth, NH   03801-5892   (603) 422-8200
Contact: Debra S. Grabowski, Exec. Dir.
FAX: (603) 422-8207;
E-mail: ffsh@communitycampus.org; *URL:* http://www.ffsh.org

Foundation type: Independent foundation
Purpose: Scholarships of $1,000 to $5,000 to students in health-related fields who have been residents of one of the following communities for at least two years: Greenland, New Castle, Newington, North Hampton, Portsmouth, and Rye, NH; Eliot, Kittery, and York, ME.

Publications: Annual report; Financial statement; Newsletter.
Financial data: Year ended 12/31/2012. Assets, $44,348,114 (M); Expenditures, $2,892,559; Total giving, $733,040; Grants to individuals, 7 grants totaling $10,000 (high: $2,500, low: $1,000).
Fields of interest: Medical school/education; Health sciences school/education.
Type of support: Scholarships—to individuals; Graduate support; Undergraduate support.
Application information: Applications not accepted.
   Additional information: Unsolicited applications not accepted.
Program descriptions:
   Edwina Foye Award for Outstanding Graduate Student: This scholarships is awarded to a graduate student who is a resident in one of the nine towns in the foundation area. The individual selected for this award must be pursuing a career in health and demonstrate outstanding academic achievement and personal accomplishments.
   Steven Cutter Award for Outstanding Graduate Student: A special award is made at the foundation's annual meeting in April to an outstanding undergraduate student who is a resident in one of the nine towns in the foundation area and who is pursuing a health-related field of study. For eligibility requirements, see foundation web site.
EIN: 020386319

5323
Hazel Chase Gifford Fund
P.O. Box 477
Concord, NH   03302-0477

Foundation type: Independent foundation
Purpose: Scholarships to residents of Yarmouth, MA, who are students of Dennis/Yarmouth Regional High School.
Financial data: Year ended 10/31/2013. Assets, $301,853 (M); Expenditures, $25,406; Total giving, $20,000; Grants to individuals, 20 grants totaling $20,000 (high: $1,000, low: $1,000).
Fields of interest: Higher education.
Type of support: Support to graduates or students of specific schools; Undergraduate support.
Application information: Application form required.
   Deadline(s): Apr. 15
   Additional information: Applications can be obtained from Dennis-Yarmouth Regional High School.
EIN: 046208360

5324
George B. Green Scholarship Trust
180 Locust St.
Dover, NH   03820-4033   (603) 749-5535
Contact: William Tanguay, Tr.

Foundation type: Independent foundation
Purpose: Scholarships to financially needy students residing in Barrington, NH, to pursue undergraduate degrees. Preference given to studies in the fields of nursing, forestry or medicine at colleges and universities.
Financial data: Year ended 12/31/2011. Assets, $795,945 (M); Expenditures, $40,892; Total giving, $36,800; Grants to individuals, 48 grants totaling $36,800 (high: $3,500, low: $200).
Fields of interest: Medical school/education; Nursing school/education; Environment, forests.
Type of support: Undergraduate support.

Application information: Application form required.
   Deadline(s): May
   Applicants should submit the following:
      1) Transcripts
      2) SAR
      3) Letter(s) of recommendation
EIN: 223208678

5325
Abbie M. Griffin Educational Fund
378 Main St.
Nashua, NH   03060-5046   (603) 881-5633
Contact: William M. Prizer III Tr.

Foundation type: Independent foundation
Purpose: Scholarships to graduating high school seniors who are residents of Merrimack, NH.
Financial data: Year ended 06/30/2013. Assets, $331,914 (M); Expenditures, $16,600; Total giving, $9,000; Grants to individuals, 5 grants totaling $9,000 (high: $1,800, low: $1,800).
Type of support: Undergraduate support.
Application information: Applications not accepted.
   Additional information: Unsolicited requests for funds not considered or acknowledged.
EIN: 026021466

5326
Abbie M. Griffin Hospital Fund
378 Main St.
Nashua, NH   03060-5046   (603) 881-5633
Contact: William M. Prizer III, Tr.

Foundation type: Independent foundation
Purpose: Grants to financially needy residents of Merrimack, NH, for the payment of hospital bills.
Financial data: Year ended 06/30/2013. Assets, $374,065 (M); Expenditures, $19,542; Total giving, $11,220; Grants to individuals, 4 grants totaling $11,220 (high: $3,653, low: $2,072).
Fields of interest: Health care.
Type of support: Grants for special needs.
Application information: Applications accepted.
   Initial approach: Letter
   Deadline(s): None
EIN: 026021464

5327
Dorothy S. Hastings Student Aid Fund
(also known as Hastings Student Aid Fund)
P.O. Box 477
Concord, NH   03302-0477   (802) 860-5553

Foundation type: Independent foundation
Purpose: Scholarships to residents of Barton, VT.
Financial data: Year ended 03/31/2013. Assets, $444,612 (M); Expenditures, $21,439; Total giving, $13,472; Grants to individuals, 16 grants totaling $13,472 (high: $842, low: $842).
Type of support: Support to graduates or students of specific schools; Undergraduate support.
Application information: Applications accepted. Application form required.
   Initial approach: Letter
   Deadline(s): July 15
   Additional information: Application must include high school transcripts.
EIN: 036048694

5328
Hitchcock Foundation
1 Medical Ctr. Dr.
Lebanon, NH   03756-1000   (603) 653-1231
Contact: Jennifer Kitchel Reining
E-mail: Jennifer.K.Reining@Hitchcock.org;
URL: http://www.dhmc.org/hitchcock_foundation.cfm

Foundation type: Public charity
Purpose: Grants, loans, and awards to persons with a formal affiliation to Dartmouth-Hitchcock Medical Center or Dartmouth College for research and for general health programs.
Financial data: Year ended 06/30/2012. Assets, $21,638,519 (M); Expenditures, $5,446,097; Total giving, $324,457; Grants to individuals, totaling $324,457.
Fields of interest: Medical research.
Type of support: Fellowships; Research; Student loans—to individuals.
Application information: Applications accepted. Application form required. Application form available on the grantmaker's web site.
   Initial approach: Application
   Deadline(s): Feb. 12 for Helmut Schumann Fellowship; Mar. 15 for Student Research Award; Mar. 29, Aug. 11, and Dec. 1 for Research Grants
   Additional information: See web site for additional guidelines.
Program descriptions:
   Helmut Schumann Fellowship: The fellowship was developed to encourage teaching and patient care that is intended to promote healthful living. Mr. Schumann wished to provide a means to "find new and more effective ways to help patients to stay well or become well again, to live better and longer lives, and to be happier human beings"
   Research Grants: Research grants fund and of the broad areas of biomedical research, including basic, translational, clinical, and/or population-based studies. Persons with a formal affiliation with Dartmouth-Hitchcock Medical Center or Dartmouth College are eligible. Residents, Dartmouth Medical School students and Dartmouth College graduate and undergraduate students are invited to apply in conjunction with faculty member.
   Revolving Loan Fund: Loans are restricted to full-time Residents and Fellows in hospitals affiliated with the Dartmouth Hitchcock Medical Center. Loans to an individual will not exceed $2,000 and will be made only for essential expenses incidental to the period of training. Applicants with combined credit card and charge card debt in excess of $5,000 must arrange for credit counseling prior to the approval of a loan application and a distribution of funds from the Resident's Revolving Loan Fund.
   Student Research Award: The purpose of this award is to recognize academic excellence, to increase awareness of research opportunities, to encourage students to enter the field of biomedical research and to reward the best project with a cash prize. The award is designed to support a research project of a Dartmouth Medical School student, working in conjunction with an established faculty investigator at Dartmouth-Hitchcock Medical Center or Dartmouth College, during an elective period. The award of up to $1,500 is for the purchase of equipment and/or supplies, and for such other authorized expenses as may be necessary to carry out this project. The award winner will receive a $500 cash prize and may also apply for an additional supplemental award of up to $500 to cover expenses to present the results of the research at a national meeting.
EIN: 020222139

5329

Hubbard Farms Charitable Foundation
P.O. Box 505
Walpole, NH   03608-0505   (603) 756-3311
Contact: Jane F. Kelly, Secy.

Foundation type: Company-sponsored foundation
Purpose: Scholarships to financially needy students in the fields of poultry science, genetics, and other life sciences.
Publications: Application guidelines.
Financial data: Year ended 12/31/2012. Assets, $1,035,286 (M); Expenditures, $58,610; Total giving, $55,700.
Fields of interest: Genetic diseases and disorders; Agriculture, livestock issues; Science.
Type of support: Scholarships—to individuals.
Application information:
   Initial approach: Letter
   Additional information: Contact foundation for current application guidelines.
EIN: 026015114

5330

Hunt Community, Inc.
10 Allds St.
Nashua, NH   03060-4777   (603) 882-6511
Contact: Dr. Elliot Lasky, Chair.
FAX: (603) 598-1431;
E-mail: info@huntseniorliving.org; Toll-free tel.: (888) 258-4868; URL: http://www.huntcommunity.org

Foundation type: Public charity
Purpose: Scholarships for employees or employee dependents of Nashua, NH pursuing higher education at accredited colleges or universities in the U.S. Assistance with housing, long term care and other needs to the elderly in Nashua, NH.
Financial data: Year ended 04/30/2013. Assets, $41,128,792 (M); Expenditures, $8,733,322; Total giving, $39,709; Grants to individuals, totaling $39,709.
Fields of interest: Higher education; Aging.
Type of support: Employee-related scholarships; Grants for special needs.
Application information: Applications not accepted.
   Additional information: For scholarship, employees must be successfully employed for a minimum of six continuous months and establish a good working relationship. The dependent must qualify for admission to the educational program for which the scholarship would be used. Employee dependent must be less than 24 years old on date of the award.
EIN: 020369906

5331

William & Glenna James Scholarship Fund
P.O. Box 477
Concord, NH   03302-0477   (802) 860-5420
Application address: c/o TD Banknorth, N.A., IM Group, 89 Merchants Row, Rutland, VT 05701-5904, tel.: (802) 786-4154

Foundation type: Independent foundation
Purpose: Scholarships to residents of Proctor, VT, to attend the University of Vermont.
Financial data: Year ended 12/31/2012. Assets, $502,081 (M); Expenditures, $28,678; Total giving, $22,000; Grants to individuals, 7 grants totaling $22,000 (high: $4,000, low: $2,000).
Type of support: Support to graduates or students of specific schools; Graduate support; Undergraduate support.

Application information: Applications accepted. Application form required.
   Initial approach: Letter
   Deadline(s): None
   Additional information: Application must include statement of financial need.
EIN: 036064491

5332

The Krempels Brain Injury Foundation
(formerly 2001 Brain Injury Support Fund, Inc.)
100 Campus Dr., Ste. 24
Portsmouth, NH   03801-5892   (603) 433-9821
E-mail: grants@krempelsfoundation.org;
URL: http://www.krempelsfoundation.org/

Foundation type: Public charity
Purpose: Financial assistance to New Hampshire residents who suffered severe traumatic brain injury, brain tumor, or stroke, and to families of NH children who have had a brain injury.
Publications: Application guidelines; Newsletter.
Financial data: Year ended 06/30/2012. Assets, $495,469 (M); Expenditures, $420,184; Total giving, $782; Grants to individuals, totaling $782.
Fields of interest: Disabilities, people with.
Type of support: Grants for special needs.
Application information: Applications accepted. Application form required.
   Deadline(s): None
   Additional information: Application should include medical and financial information. Applications are accepted from the New Hampshire Brain Injury Association, families and friends of survivors, hospitals, rehab facilities, social workers, and therapists.
Program description:
   Family Support Emergency Grant: Individuals and families in financial need whose lives have been affected by brain injury can receive financial assistance for daily activities made more difficult due to brain injury.
EIN: 020499997

5333

La Napoule Art Foundation
799 South St.
Portsmouth, NH   03801-5420   (603) 436-3040
Application address for residency: Art Residencies, La Napoule Art Foundation, Chateau de La Napoule, 1 Avenue Henry Clews, 06210 Mandelieu - La Napoule, France
FAX: (603) 430-0025; E-mail: lnaf@clews.org; URL: http://www.chateau-lanapoule.com/

Foundation type: Public charity
Purpose: Residencies to emerging and established artists of different nationalities and disciplines.
Publications: Application guidelines.
Financial data: Year ended 12/31/2011. Assets, $2,171,731 (M); Expenditures, $1,295,321.
Fields of interest: Film/video; Visual arts; Design; Performing arts; Music composition; Literature.
Type of support: Exchange programs; Residencies.
Application information: Applications accepted. Application form required.
   Initial approach: Letter
   Send request by: Mail
   Deadline(s): July 1
   Final notification: Applicants notified two months prior to the start of the residency
   Applicants should submit the following:
      1) Work samples
      2) SASE
      3) Resume
      4) Letter(s) of recommendation

Additional information: Application must also include $20 nonrefundable fee. See web site for additional application information.
Program description:
   Residencies: The foundation awards residencies in all disciplines: dance, design, film, literature, music, theatre, and visual and performing arts. Residents are selected on the basis of a record of excellence and commitment. Applications may be submitted by groups (including music, theatre, and dance ensembles) and individuals; no monetary support is given.
EIN: 135638284

5334

Ladies Charitable Society of Keene
P.O. Box 271
Keene, NH   03431-0271
Contact: Jane Pitts, Treas.

Foundation type: Independent foundation
Purpose: Scholarships to students of Keene, NH, public schools and residents of Keene, NH, to attend institutions within the NH University system, or NH vocational-technical colleges.
Financial data: Year ended 12/31/2011. Assets, $754,789 (M); Expenditures, $34,162; Total giving, $28,200.
Fields of interest: Vocational education.
Type of support: Technical education support; Undergraduate support.
Application information: Applications accepted. Application form required.
   Initial approach: Letter
   Deadline(s): May 1
EIN: 026007047

5335

Lakes Region Scholarship Foundation
DeCamp Ctr.
14 Country Club Rd.
Gilford, NH   03249-6907   (603) 527-3533
Contact: Joan M. Cormier, Exec. Dir.
E-mail: scholarship@metrocast.net; Mailing address: P.O. Box 7312, Gilford, NH 03247-7312; URL: http://www.lrscholarship.org

Foundation type: Public charity
Purpose: Scholarships to graduating high school students and residents of Laconia High School, Gilford High School or Belmont High School in New Hampshire.
Publications: Application guidelines; Annual report; Annual report (including application guidelines).
Financial data: Year ended 12/31/2011. Assets, $4,297,573 (M); Expenditures, $326,723; Total giving, $253,260; Grants to individuals, totaling $253,260.
Type of support: Support to graduates or students of specific schools; Undergraduate support.
Application information: Applications accepted. Application form required.
   Deadline(s): Apr. 15
   Applicants should submit the following:
      1) GPA
      2) Transcripts
   Additional information: Application must also include parents income tax forms, and a nonrefundable $15 application fee.
Program description:
   Scholarships: The foundation awards scholarships to graduates of Laconia High School, Gilford High School, and Belmont High School, as well as legal residents of Laconia, Gilford, and Belmont, to further their educational goals.
EIN: 026012236

5336
Lela M. Lancaster Trust
P.O. Box 575
Laconia, NH   03247-0575
Application address: c/o Lakes Region Scholarship
Foundation, P.O. Box 100, Laconia, NH
03247-0100

Foundation type: Independent foundation
Purpose: Scholarship awards to residents of
Gilford, Gilmanton, Laconia, and Sanbornton, NH
through the selection process of the Lakes Region
Scholarship Foundation.
Financial data: Year ended 05/31/2010. Assets,
$184,021 (M); Expenditures, $7,824; Total giving,
$6,200.
Fields of interest: Scholarships/financial aid;
Education.
Type of support: Scholarships—to individuals;
Undergraduate support.
Application information: Applications accepted.
  Deadline(s): None
  Additional information: Some preference is
    shown to applicants from Gilford, NH, the
    town where Lela M. Lancaster resided.
EIN: 026036769

5337
Lavoie Foundation
P.O. Box 12
Barnstead, NH   03218-0012   (603) 435-7583
Contact: Patricia Sanborn, Dir.

Foundation type: Independent foundation
Purpose: Financial assistance to economically
disadvantaged individuals, primarily in NH, for
medical expenses, rent, and some scholarships.
Financial data: Year ended 12/31/2011. Assets,
$2,039,193 (M); Expenditures, $114,415; Total
giving, $86,787.
Fields of interest: Education; Health care;
Economically disadvantaged.
Type of support: Scholarships—to individuals;
Grants for special needs.
Application information: Applications accepted.
  Initial approach: Letter
  Deadline(s): None
EIN: 020502244

5338
Raymond & Lorraine Letourneau
Educational Foundation
292 South St.
Portsmouth, NH   03801   (802) 864-5058
Contact: Raymond Letourneau
Application address: P.O. Box 276, Burlington, VT
05401, (802) 864-5058

Foundation type: Independent foundation
Purpose: Scholarships to Burlington, VT, residents.
Financial data: Year ended 12/31/2012. Assets,
$241,545 (M); Expenditures, $16,321; Total
giving, $11,665; Grants to individuals, 3 grants
totaling $11,665 (high: $4,000, low: $3,665).
Type of support: Scholarships—to individuals.
Application information: Applications accepted.
  Send request by: Mail
  Deadline(s): None
  Final notification: Notification before end of
    school year
  Applicants should submit the following:
    1) Financial information
    2) Resume
EIN: 030277007

5339
Linwood Educational Trust Fund, Inc.
c/o Jane Fournier
P.O. Box 1391
Lincoln, NH   03251-1391

Foundation type: Independent foundation
Purpose: Scholarships to graduates of Linwood
Public High School, Lincoln, NH.
Financial data: Year ended 06/30/2012. Assets,
$150,439 (M); Expenditures, $21,116; Total
giving, $20,250; Grants to individuals, 17 grants
totaling $20,250 (high: $2,000, low: $500).
Type of support: Support to graduates or students
of specific schools.
Application information: Applications accepted.
  Initial approach: Letter
EIN: 020474928

5340
Lyman Fund, Inc.
7 Riverwoods Dr.
Exeter, NH   03833   (413) 863-9026
Contact: Stephen Cobb, Clerk
Application address: 179 Ave. A, 2nd Fl., Turners
Falls, MA 01376,
e-mail: scobb.homeopath@verison.net

Foundation type: Independent foundation
Purpose: Scholarships to individuals seeking to
pursue their spiritual journeys, with preference to
members of the Religious Society of Friends in the
U.S.
Financial data: Year ended 06/30/2013. Assets,
$873,695 (M); Expenditures, $44,613; Total
giving, $35,275; Grants to individuals, 14 grants
totaling $35,275 (high: $3,000, low: $1,000).
Fields of interest: Education; Religion.
Type of support: Scholarships—to individuals;
Travel grants.
Application information: Application form required.
  Initial approach: Telephone
  Copies of proposal: 7
  Deadline(s): Apr. 1 and Oct. 1
  Applicants should submit the following:
    1) Resume
    2) Letter(s) of recommendation
    3) Photograph
    4) Financial information
    5) Essay
    6) Budget Information
  Additional information: Application should also
    include a brief statement of proposal, spiritual
    journey and a personal statement.
EIN: 020471515

5341
MacDowell Colony, Inc.
100 High St.
Peterborough, NH   03458-2442   (603)
924-3886
Contact: Cheryl Young, Exec. Dir.
FAX: (603) 924-9142;
E-mail: admissions@macdowellcolony.org;
Additional E-mail: info@macdowellcolony.org;
URL: http://www.macdowellcolony.org

Foundation type: Public charity
Purpose: Residencies for architecture, film/video
arts, interdisciplinary arts, literature, music
composition, theatre, and visual arts and those
collaborating on creative works. Travel and Writers'
aid grants are also offered.
Publications: Application guidelines; Annual report;
Informational brochure; Newsletter.

Financial data: Year ended 03/31/2012. Assets,
$34,667,114 (M); Expenditures, $3,322,825;
Total giving, $80,000; Grants to individuals,
totaling $74,250.
Fields of interest: Film/video; Visual arts;
Architecture; Music composition; Literature.
Type of support: Foreign applicants; Residencies;
Travel grants.
Application information: Application form required.
Application form available on the grantmaker's web
site.
  Send request by: Online
  Deadline(s): Jan. 15, Apr. 15 and Sept. 15
  Final notification: Applicants are notified
    approximately 10 weeks after applicable
    deadline
  Additional information: Application must include
    work samples and one reference form
    completed. A nonrefundable processing fee of
    $30 (U.S.) is required with each application.
    See web site for additional guidelines.
Program description:
  MacDowell Fellowships: Residencies of up to
eight weeks are available at the colony's facility in
Peterborough, NH to artists, providing time and
space in which to create lasting works of the
imagination. Both artists with professional standing
in their fields and emerging artists are eligible for
residencies. Artists from all backgrounds and
disciplines are eligible to apply. Need-based
stipends and travel grants are available to help
cover expenses that continue to accrue while away
(such as rent, utilities, and childcare), lost income,
and the cost of transportation to NH.
EIN: 131592242

5342
Manchester Community Music School
2291 Elm St.
Manchester, NH   03104-2213   (603) 644-4548
Contact: Jeanine Tousignant, C.E.O.
FAX: (603) 644-4507;
E-mail: info@mcmusicschool.org; URL: http://
www.mcmusicschool.org

Foundation type: Public charity
Purpose: Financial assistance for music education
to qualified students of the Manchester, NH area,
based on merit and need.
Publications: Application guidelines.
Financial data: Year ended 08/31/2011. Assets,
$1,245,071 (M); Expenditures, $1,121,654; Total
giving, $76,134; Grants to individuals, totaling
$76,134.
Fields of interest: Music.
Type of support: Grants for special needs.
Application information: Application form required.
Application form available on the grantmaker's web
site.
  Initial approach: Telephone
  Send request by: Mail
  Deadline(s): June 15 for returning students, Aug.
    15 for new students
  Additional information: Application should
    include proof of total family income and most
    recent income tax form. A registration fee of
    $30 per student, $60 maximum per family.
    See web site for additional guidelines.
Program description:
  Financial Aid: The school provides financial aid to
students with demonstrated need and a
commitment to learn. Aid amounts will be based on
household income, family size, and financial
obligations. Consideration will also be given to
families in the event of emergencies, illness, job
loss, or other extenuating circumstances.
EIN: 020376586

5343
Viola G. Manuel Trust
P.O. Box 477
Concord, NH   03302-0477   (508) 255-1510

Foundation type: Independent foundation
Purpose: Scholarships to graduating students of
Nauset Regional High School, North Eastham, MA.
Financial data: Year ended 06/30/2013. Assets,
$470,410 (M); Expenditures, $27,688; Total
giving, $20,000; Grants to individuals, 20 grants
totaling $20,000 (high: $1,000; low: $1,000).
Type of support: Support to graduates or students
of specific schools; Undergraduate support.
Application information: Applications accepted.
Application form required.
> *Deadline(s):* May 1
> *Additional information:* Applications available
> from the high school guidance department.

EIN: 046555836

5344
Mary R. Martin Trust 1
c/o Thomas Bickford
P.O. Box 1739
Wolfeboro, NH   03894-1739
Contact: G. Thomas Bickford, Tr.

Foundation type: Independent foundation
Purpose: Assistance with bills and living expenses
to economically disadvantaged residents of
Wolfeboro, NH.
Financial data: Year ended 12/31/2012. Assets,
$414,131 (M); Expenditures, $14,818; Total
giving, $7,502; Grants to individuals, 33 grants
totaling $7,502 (high: $300, low: $43).
Fields of interest: Economically disadvantaged.
Type of support: Grants for special needs.
Application information: Applications accepted.
Interview required.
> *Initial approach:* Letter
> *Copies of proposal:* 1
> *Deadline(s):* None

EIN: 026009373

5345
Mary R. Martin Trust No. 2
c/o G. Thomas Bickford
P.O. Box 1739
Wolfeboro, NH   03894
Contact: Thomas G Bickford

Foundation type: Independent foundation
Purpose: Scholarships to worthy boys and girls
whose parents are residents of Wolfeboro, NH
needing assistance to obtain an education.
Financial data: Year ended 12/31/2012. Assets,
$545,490 (M); Expenditures, $18,105; Total
giving, $6,646.
Fields of interest: Economically disadvantaged.
Type of support: Graduate support; Undergraduate
support.
Application information: Applications accepted.
Application form required.
> *Copies of proposal:* 1
> *Deadline(s):* June 30

EIN: 026009374

5346
The McIninch Scholarship Fund
P.O. Box 477
Concord, NH   03302-0477

Foundation type: Independent foundation

Purpose: Scholarships to graduates of Manchester
High School, NH, for study at four-year colleges and
universities.
Financial data: Year ended 12/31/2012. Assets,
$1,564,636 (M); Expenditures, $99,736; Total
giving, $75,000; Grants to individuals, 15 grants
totaling $75,000 (high: $5,000, low: $5,000).
Type of support: Support to graduates or students
of specific schools; Undergraduate support.
Application information: Applications not
accepted.
> *Additional information:* Application forms
> available from Manchester High School
> principal. Unsolicited requests for funds not
> considered or acknowledged.

EIN: 026076262

5347
Money for Women Barbara Deming Memorial Fund, Inc.
P.O. Box 309
Wilton, NH   03086   (603) 654-6446
Contact: Susan Pliner, Exec. Dir.
URL: http://www.demingfund.org

Foundation type: Independent foundation
Purpose: Grants to individual feminist women in the
arts whose work in some way focuses upon women.
Publications: Application guidelines; Informational
brochure; Newsletter.
Financial data: Year ended 07/31/2013. Assets,
$117,780 (M); Expenditures, $36,368; Total
giving, $16,500; Grants to individuals, 19 grants
totaling $16,500 (high: $1,000, low: $500).
Fields of interest: Visual arts; Literature; Arts,
artist's services; Civil/human rights, minorities;
Civil/human rights, women; Women's studies;
Minorities; Women; LGBTQ.
Type of support: Grants to individuals.
Application information: Applications accepted.
Application form required.
> *Initial approach:* Letter
> *Send request by:* Mail
> *Deadline(s):* June 30 for Poetry and Nonfiction,
> Dec. 31 for Visual Art, Mixed Genre, and
> Fiction
> *Final notification:* Recipients notified
> approximately five months after the deadline
> *Applicants should submit the following:*
> 1) SASE
> 2) Budget Information
> 3) Resume
> 4) Work samples
> *Additional information:* Application should also
> include a $20 processing fee.

Program description:
> *Artist Grants:* The fund provides small grants to
> individual feminists active in the following
> categories of the arts, visual art, mixed genre,
> fiction, poetry, and nonfiction. The work of these
> women speaks for peace and social justice and in
> some way sheds light upon the condition of women
> or enhances self-realization. Applicants must be
> citizens of the U.S. or Canada. The fund does not
> give grants in the areas of dance, theater (play
> scripts, performance art), film (screenplays), video
> or music. It does not give loans or money for
> educational assistance toward work on dissertation
> projects or research (except to be used in writing a
> book), or grants for business projects or funds for
> self-publication. It also does not give emergency
> money to people in need. The fund has two granting
> cycles each year.

EIN: 510176956

5348
Moore Center Services, Inc.
195 McGregor St., Ste. 400
Manchester, NH   03102-3709   (603) 206-2700
E-mail: info@moorecenter.org; *URL:* http://
www.moorecenter.org

Foundation type: Public charity
Purpose: Specific assistance to developmentally
disabled individuals of Auburn, Bedford, Candia,
Goffstown, Hooksett, Londonderry, Manchester,
and New Boston in the greater Manchester, NH
area, with food, shelter, clothing, medical, dental,
hospital expenses and transportation.
Publications: Newsletter.
Financial data: Year ended 06/30/2012. Assets,
$12,130,941 (M); Expenditures, $37,605,688;
Total giving, $1,536,261; Grants to individuals,
totaling $1,536,261.
Fields of interest: Human services; Disabilities,
people with.
Type of support: Grants for special needs.
Application information: Contact agency for
information on assistance.
EIN: 020261136

5349
William A. Morse Fund
P.O. Box 477
Concord, NH   03302-0477   (802) 860-5420
Application address: c/o TD Bank, N.A., Attn.: Paul
Smith, 89 Merchants Bow, Rutland, VT 05701

Foundation type: Independent foundation
Purpose: Financial assistance to residents from
Brattleboro, Williamsville, South Newfane, or
Newfane, VT, and to children under 16 years of age
needing temporary assistance.
Financial data: Year ended 12/31/2011. Assets,
$306,778 (M); Expenditures, $12,396; Total
giving, $4,893; Grants to individuals, totaling
$4,893.
Fields of interest: Human services; Children/youth;
Economically disadvantaged.
Type of support: Grants for special needs.
Application information: Applications accepted.
Application form required.
> *Deadline(s):* None
> *Additional information:* Preference is given to
> those residing in each area for two years or
> more.

EIN: 036004778

5350
Alice E. Morton Memorial Trust
c/o TD Bnk
P.O. Box 477
Concord, NH   03302

Foundation type: Independent foundation
Purpose: College scholarships to financially needy
graduates of Bellows Free Academy, St. Albans, VT
pursuing higher education.
Financial data: Year ended 12/31/2011. Assets,
$121,846 (M); Expenditures, $7,886; Total giving,
$4,000; Grants to individuals, 8 grants totaling
$4,000 (high: $500, low: $500).
Fields of interest: Higher education.
Type of support: Support to graduates or students
of specific schools; Undergraduate support.
Application information: Applications accepted.
Application form required.
> *Deadline(s):* May 1
> *Additional information:* Application must include
> financial information.

EIN: 036005300

5351
Moving Company Dance Center
76 Railroad St.
Keene, NH 03431-3744 (603) 357-2100
Contact: Reagan Messer, Exec. Dir.
E-mail: info@moco.org; URL: http://www.moco.org

Foundation type: Public charity
Purpose: Scholarships to individuals or groups in the Monadnock region, NH, who demonstrate financial need to explore and experience dance, movement arts, visual arts, and theater.
Publications: Annual report.
Financial data: Year ended 08/31/2011. Assets, $958,690 (M); Expenditures, $1,170,904; Total giving, $23,258; Grants to individuals, totaling $23,258.
Fields of interest: Scholarships/financial aid.
Type of support: Scholarships—to individuals.
Application information: Application form required. Application form available on the grantmaker's web site.
> *Initial approach:* Telephone
> *Deadline(s):* Aug. 6 for fall, Jan. 2 for spring, May 8 for summer
EIN: 020514391

5352
New Hampshire Bar Foundation
(also known as NH Bar Foundation)
2 Pillsbury St., Ste. 300
Concord, NH 03301-3502 (603) 224-6942
Contact: Jeannine McCoy, Exec. Dir.
FAX: (603) 224-2910;
E-mail: info@nhbarfoundation.org; URL: http://www.nhbarfoundation.org

Foundation type: Public charity
Purpose: Student loans for attorneys who work for legal agencies serving low-income clients in the New Hampshire area.
Publications: Annual report; Newsletter.
Financial data: Year ended 05/31/2012. Assets, $1,641,256 (M); Expenditures, $1,175,095; Total giving, $977,316.
Fields of interest: Law school/education.
Type of support: Student loans—to individuals.
Application information: Applications accepted. Application form required.
> *Additional information:* Applicants employed by NHLA, LARC, DRC, or Pro Bono, full time or part time with outstanding law school loans are eligible. See web site for additional guidelines.
Program description:
> *Loan Forgiveness Program:* This program provides law school assistance, in the form of forgivable loans, to help legal service providers recruit and maintain a diverse body of highly-qualified staff attorneys. This program is currently open to all attorneys employed by New Hampshire Legal Assistance, Legal Advice and Referral Center, Disabilities Rights Center, and NH Pro Bono Referral Program.
EIN: 020333762

5353
New Hampshire Charitable Foundation
37 Pleasant St.
Concord, NH 03301-4005 (603) 225-6641
Contact: Kate Merrow, V.P., Prog.; For scholarships: Norma Daviault, Student Aid Asst.
Scholarship inquiry e-mail: nd@nhcf.org
FAX: (603) 225-1700; E-mail: info@nhcf.org; URL: http://www.nhcf.org

Foundation type: Community foundation
Purpose: Scholarships, fellowships, and student loans to NH residents pursuing undergraduate or graduate study at accredited colleges, universities, and vocational schools. Two programs open to out-of-state applicants in Vermont or Maine.
Publications: Application guidelines; Annual report; Financial statement; Grants list; Informational brochure; Informational brochure (including application guidelines); Newsletter; Program policy statement.
Financial data: Year ended 12/31/2012. Assets, $508,157,557 (M); Expenditures, $37,536,193; Total giving, $30,529,068; Grants to individuals, 1,741 grants totaling $4,965,256.
Fields of interest: Vocational education, post-secondary; Higher education.
Type of support: Fellowships; Scholarships—to individuals; Student loans—to individuals; Technical education support.
Application information: Applications accepted. Application form required. Application form available on the grantmaker's web site.
> *Send request by:* Online
> *Deadline(s):* Varies
> *Additional information:* See web site for complete listing of scholarships.
Program description:
> *Statewide Student Aid Program:* A variety of support is offered through the foundation's scholarship and loan programs. The foundation administers more than 350 separate funds established by individuals, families, organizations, and businesses to provide scholarships for education beyond high school. Funding priorities include: 1) closing the gap for those with financial need; 2) enabling access for low-income and minority students to higher education; 3) encouraging skill and knowledge acquisition that can be shared with the community; and 4) recognizing good work. Each scholarship and loan has its own unique eligibility criteria. See web site for additional information.
EIN: 026005625

5354
New Hampshire Food Industries Education Foundation
(formerly Food Industry Scholarship Fund of New Hampshire)
110 Stark St.
Manchester, NH 03101-1934 (603) 669-9333
Contact: John Dumais, Secy.-Treas.
URL: http://www.grocers.org

Foundation type: Independent foundation
Purpose: Scholarships to employees or family members of employees of food stores that are members of NH Retail Grocers Assn.
Financial data: Year ended 12/31/2012. Assets, $194,847 (M); Expenditures, $110,175; Total giving, $54,000; Grants to individuals, 56 grants totaling $54,000 (high: $1,000; low: $500).
Fields of interest: Business/industry.
Type of support: Employee-related scholarships.
Application information: Application form required.
> *Deadline(s):* Contact foundation for application guidelines
Company name: New Hampshire Retail Grocers Assn. member food stores
EIN: 020433248

5355
New Hampshire Humanities Council, Inc.
117 Pleasant St.
Concord, NH 03301-3852 (603) 224-4071
Contact: Deborah Watrous, Exec. Dir.
FAX: (603) 224-4072; E-mail: dwatrous@nhhc.org; URL: http://www.nhhc.org

Foundation type: Public charity
Purpose: Film and media awards to NH residents for projects including documentary film, video, television, and radio, at any stage of development and production.
Publications: Application guidelines; Annual report; Informational brochure; Newsletter; Program policy statement.
Financial data: Year ended 10/31/2012. Assets, $2,779,974 (M); Expenditures, $1,158,045; Total giving, $164,562.
Fields of interest: Film/video; Television; Radio.
Type of support: Awards/prizes.
Application information: Applications accepted. Application form required.
> *Initial approach:* Telephone
> *Deadline(s):* Vary
> *Applicants should submit the following:*
> 1) Proposal
> 2) Budget Information
> *Additional information:* See web site for current application guidelines.
EIN: 020317350

5356
New London Service Organization, Inc.
P.O. Box 42
New London, NH 03257

Foundation type: Operating foundation
Purpose: Scholarships to individuals from New London, NH, to attend U.S. colleges and universities.
Financial data: Year ended 12/31/2011. Assets, $773,303 (M); Expenditures, $29,846; Total giving, $25,983; Grants to individuals, 9 grants totaling $14,983 (high: $3,000, low: $983).
Fields of interest: Education.
Type of support: Scholarships—to individuals.
Application information: Applications accepted. Application form required.
> *Deadline(s):* None
> *Additional information:* Application must include personal history, academic record, future goals, and resume.
EIN: 026007487

5357
Avis M. Nye Charitable Trust
95 Market St.
Manchester, NH 03101-1933 (603) 669-3454
Contact: Richard Thorner Esq., Tr.

Foundation type: Independent foundation
Purpose: Scholarships to high school graduates of New Hampshire pursuing liberal arts at NH non-denominational colleges or universities.
Financial data: Year ended 12/31/2011. Assets, $79,928 (M); Expenditures, $9,263; Total giving, $5,000; Grant to an individual, 1 grant totaling $5,000.
Fields of interest: Arts; Higher education.
Type of support: Scholarships—to individuals.
Application information: Applications accepted. Application form required.
> *Deadline(s):* End of school year
EIN: 020509966

5358
Robert & Joyce Oberkotter Family Foundation
P.O. Box 45
Newport, NH   03773-0045   (603) 863-8088

Foundation type: Independent foundation
Purpose: Scholarships to seniors at Fall Mountain High School, NH; Kearsage High School, NH; Lebanon High School, NH; The Oliverian School, NH; Stevens High School, NH; Newport High School, NH; Mount Royal Academy, NH; Kimball Union Academy, NH; Mascoma Valley Regional High School, NH; Mid-Vermont Christian School, VT; or Windsor High School, VT.
Financial data: Year ended 06/30/2012. Assets, $9,307,906 (M); Expenditures, $519,983; Total giving, $475,000.
Type of support: Support to graduates or students of specific schools; Undergraduate support.
Application information: Applications accepted. Application form required.
   Send request by: Mail
   Deadline(s): Feb. 12
   Final notification: Recipients notified on or about Apr. 9
   Applicants should submit the following:
      1) Essay
      2) Letter(s) of recommendation
      3) Transcripts
EIN: 820577634

5359
Our House for Girls, Inc.
576 Central Ave.
Dover, NH   03820-3431   (603) 742-2963
FAX: (603) 749-0487;
E-mail: ourhouseinc@comcast.net; URL: http://www.ourhouseforgirls.org/

Foundation type: Public charity
Purpose: Financial assistance to indigent female adolescents residing at the foundation's group home facility in NH, for medical, dental, hospital, and living expenses.
Financial data: Year ended 12/31/2011. Assets, $428,950 (M); Expenditures, $508,110.
Type of support: Grants for special needs.
Application information: Applications not accepted.
   Additional information: Unsolicited requests for funds not considered or acknowledged.
EIN: 020328076

5360
Parkland Medical Center Nursing Memorial Scholarship Fund
11 King Edward Dr.
Londonderry, NH   03053   (603) 434-2193
Contact: Barbara Bernard, Pres.

Foundation type: Independent foundation
Purpose: College scholarships to area high school students of NH, who plan to pursue a nursing career.
Financial data: Year ended 03/31/2013. Assets, $1,229 (M); Expenditures, $4,075; Total giving, $4,000; Grants to individuals, 4 grants totaling $4,000 (high: $1,000, low: $1,000).
Fields of interest: Nursing school/education.
Type of support: Scholarships—to individuals.
Application information: Applications accepted.
   Initial approach: Letter
   Deadline(s): None

Additional information: Applicant must include personal and academic information.
EIN: 020471944

5361
Plan NH - The Foundation for Shaping the Built Environment
56 Middle St., 2nd Fl.
P.O. Box 1105
Portsmouth, NH   03802-1105   (603) 452-7526
Contact: Robin H. LeBlanc, Exec. Dir.
E-mail: info@planNH.org; Toll-free tel.: (800) 721-7526; URL: http://www.plannh.com

Foundation type: Public charity
Purpose: Scholarships and fellowships to outstanding students of NH pursuing a career in built environment at an accredited two or four year college or university or trade school.
Publications: Newsletter.
Financial data: Year ended 06/30/2013. Assets, $33,678 (M); Expenditures, $101,204.
Fields of interest: Visual arts; Vocational education, post-secondary; Higher education; Landscaping; Environmental education; Science; Engineering.
Type of support: Fellowships; Scholarships—to individuals; Graduate support; Undergraduate support.
Application information: Applications accepted. Application form required. Application form available on the grantmaker's web site. Interview required.
   Send request by: E-mail
   Deadline(s): Apr. 4
   Applicants should submit the following:
      1) Transcripts
      2) SAT
      3) Essay
   Additional information: A $10 application fee should also be included. See web site for additional guidelines.
EIN: 223019910

5362
John & Anna Newton Porter Foundation
P.O. Box 325
Alton Bay, NH   03810-0325   (603) 875-3060
Contact: Douglas Latham, Chair.

Foundation type: Public charity
Purpose: Scholarships for children from disadvantaged backgrounds to attend Camp Kavaiya in NH.
Financial data: Year ended 12/31/2011. Assets, $2,438,379 (M); Expenditures, $1,022,856; Total giving, $48,085; Grants to individuals, totaling $48,085.
Fields of interest: Camps.
Type of support: Camperships.
Application information: Applications accepted. Application form required. Interview required.
   Applicants should submit the following:
      1) Letter(s) of recommendation
      2) Financial information
EIN: 026034452

5363
Helene Ramsaye Medical Trust
P.O. Box 477
Concord, NH   03302-0477

Foundation type: Independent foundation
Purpose: Grants to individuals pursuing courses and attending seminars in the health care field.

Financial data: Year ended 12/31/2012. Assets, $1,515,926 (M); Expenditures, $48,498; Total giving, $0.
Fields of interest: Health care.
Type of support: Grants to individuals.
Application information: Unsolicited requests for funds not accepted.
EIN: 226333204

5364
Helene Ramsaye Scholarship Trust
P. O. Box 477
Concord, NH   03302-0477   (201) 422-6130
Application address: c/o Weehawken High School, Attn.: Ramsaye College Scholarship Committee, Weehawken, NJ 07086

Foundation type: Independent foundation
Purpose: College scholarships for graduating students of Weehawken High School, NJ for higher education in the areas of science and language arts to peer leadership and journalism.
Financial data: Year ended 12/31/2012. Assets, $1,607,028 (M); Expenditures, $38,036; Total giving, $17,500; Grants to individuals, 9 grants totaling $17,500 (high: $5,000, low: $1,000).
Fields of interest: Print publishing; Language/linguistics; Higher education; Science.
Type of support: Scholarships—to individuals; Support to graduates or students of specific schools.
Application information: Contact the trust for additional guidelines.
EIN: 226333205

5365
The Randolph Foundation
P.O. Box 283
Gorham, NH   03581-0283   (603) 466-3850
Application address: c/o Trisha Ouellette, 597 Durand Rd., Randolph, New Hampshire 03593, tel.: (603) 466-3670
E-mail: cmcdowell@ne.rr.com; URL: http://www.randolphfoundationnh.org/

Foundation type: Public charity
Purpose: Scholarships to high school seniors who are residents of Randolph, NH, for postsecondary education.
Publications: Application guidelines; Annual report; Newsletter.
Financial data: Year ended 06/30/2012. Assets, $572,785 (M); Expenditures, $33,898; Total giving, $5,000.
Fields of interest: Higher education.
Type of support: Scholarships—to individuals.
Application information: Applications accepted. Application form required. Application form available on the grantmaker's web site.
   Initial approach: Letter or telephone
   Send request by: Mail
   Copies of proposal: 1
   Deadline(s): Aug. 1 and Jan. 15
   Final notification: Recipients notified in one week.
   Applicants should submit the following:
      1) Transcripts
      2) GPA
Program description:
   Scholarships: The foundation annually awards scholarships to eligible Randolph residents to pursue their studies at the post-secondary level. Recipients will be awarded a base scholarship of $1,200 annually ($600 per semester) for a full-time course of undergraduate study, not to exceed four years. Beginning at the second turn of the first year

of study, recipients whose GPA is 3.5 for that semester will receive $750 to be used for the following semester. Graduate students receive a flat scholarship of $900 annually for a full time course of graduate study not to exceed three years. Eligible applicants must maintain a cumulative GPA of at least 2.0 to maintain scholarship support.
EIN: 026009502

5366
Rockingham County Community Action, Inc.
4 Cutts St.
Portsmouth, NH   03801-4500   (603) 431-2911
FAX: (603) 431-2916; E-mail: info@rcaction.org;
Toll-free tel.: (800)-556-9300; URL: http://www.rcaction.org/

Foundation type: Public charity
Purpose: Financial assistance to low income and elderly residents of Rockingham County, NH, for the payment of rent, mortgage, electricity, fuel, or other basic necessities for households facing evictions, foreclosures, utility terminations, lack of fuel, or other emergencies.
Financial data: Year ended 06/30/2011. Assets, $2,334,084 (M); Expenditures, $11,214,598; Total giving, $5,597,609; Grants to individuals, totaling $5,597,609.
Type of support: Grants for special needs.
Application information:
 Initial approach: Letter or e-mail
 Additional information: Contact the organization for application guidelines.
EIN: 020268379

5367
Scots' Charitable Society of Boston
c/o Douglas Kilgore
1465 Hooksett Rd. Ste. 102
Hooksett, NH   03106
Contact: Joseph Macleod
Application address: 16 Imperial Ct., Westborough, MA 01581

Foundation type: Independent foundation
Purpose: Assistance to Scots or people of Scottish decent living in or around the greater Boston, MA area.
Financial data: Year ended 10/31/2012. Assets, $1,880,817 (M); Expenditures, $130,824; Total giving, $71,800.
Fields of interest: Higher education; Economically disadvantaged.
International interests: Scotland.
Type of support: Technical education support; Undergraduate support; Grants for special needs.
Application information: Applications accepted.
 Initial approach: Letter
 Deadline(s): Prior to commencement of school year
EIN: 046040091

5368
Skrungloo Farms, Inc.
18 Centre St.
Concord, NH   03301-6315   (603) 225-7170

Foundation type: Operating foundation
Purpose: Scholarships to residents of NH. Priority is given to students from Sanwich, Center Harbor, Moultonboro, Carroll County, and Belknap County, NH.
Financial data: Year ended 12/31/2012. Assets, $2,145,890 (M); Expenditures, $135,403; Total

giving, $79,250; Grants to individuals, 56 grants totaling $79,250 (high: $5,000, low: $500).
Type of support: Graduate support; Technical education support; Undergraduate support.
Application information: Applications accepted. Application form required.
 Initial approach: Letter
 Send request by: Mail
 Deadline(s): Mar. 1
 Applicants should submit the following:
  1) FAFSA
  2) Letter(s) of recommendation
  3) Transcripts
EIN: 020524940

5369
Jason C. Somerville Trust
c/o John & Nancy Stevenson
P.O. Box 299
Bethlehem, NH   03574-0299

Foundation type: Independent foundation
Purpose: Scholarships for full-time study to residents of Bethlehem, NH, who attended Profile High School for four years and graduated.
Financial data: Year ended 12/31/2012. Assets, $1,435,095 (M); Expenditures, $126,662; Total giving, $112,500; Grants to individuals, 42 grants totaling $112,500 (high: $4,000, low: $1,000).
Fields of interest: Higher education; Scholarships/financial aid.
Type of support: Support to graduates or students of specific schools; Undergraduate support.
Application information: Applications accepted. Application form required. Interview required.
 Applicants should submit the following:
  1) Pell Grant
  2) Financial information
  3) Transcripts
  4) SAT
 Additional information: Application must also include PSAT scores and FAS from the college. Contact foundation for current application deadline/guidelines.
EIN: 026033716

5370
The Stickney Educational Trust
P.O. Box 101
Twin Mountain, NH   03595-0101   (603) 846-5725
Contact: George E. Brodeur, Sr., Tr.

Foundation type: Independent foundation
Purpose: Scholarships to individuals of Twin Mountain, NH for undergraduate study at accredited colleges or universities.
Financial data: Year ended 12/31/2012. Assets, $133,749 (M); Expenditures, $5,430; Total giving, $5,000; Grants to individuals, 5 grants totaling $5,000 (high: $1,000, low: $1,000).
Fields of interest: Higher education.
Type of support: Scholarships—to individuals.
Application information: Application form required.
 Deadline(s): July 31
 Additional information: Application must include name of school or university applicant will be attending.
EIN: 026088650

5371
Strafford County Community Action Committee, Inc.
P.O. Box 160
Dover, NH   03821-0160   (603) 516-8130
Contact: Betsey Andrews Parker, Exec. Dir.
FAX: (603) 516-8140;
E-mail: cap@co.strafford.nh.us; URL: http://www.straffcap.org

Foundation type: Public charity
Purpose: Financial and emergency assistance to low-income and disadvantaged individuals and families of Strafford county, NH, with food, housing, utilities, healthcare, quality child care and other special need.
Financial data: Year ended 12/31/2011. Assets, $2,445,673 (M); Expenditures, $8,997,760; Total giving, $3,746,599; Grants to individuals, totaling $3,746,599.
Fields of interest: Human services; Economically disadvantaged.
Type of support: Grants for special needs.
Application information: Applications accepted.
 Additional information: Contact the committee for additional information on eligibility.
EIN: 020268636

5372
Tri-County Community Action Program, Inc.
30 Exchange St.
Berlin, NH   03570-1911   (603) 752-7001
FAX: (603) 752-7607; E-mail: admin@tccap.org;
Toll Free Tel.: (800)-552-4617; URL: http://www.tccap.org

Foundation type: Public charity
Purpose: Emergency assistance with utilities, fuel, weatherization and other support to indigent residents of Coos, Carroll and Grafton counties, NH.
Financial data: Year ended 06/30/2011. Assets, $8,846,281 (M); Expenditures, $23,051,417; Total giving, $7,274,834; Grants to individuals, totaling $7,274,834.
Type of support: Grants for special needs.
Application information:
 Initial approach: Letter
 Additional information: Contact the organization for application guidelines.
EIN: 020267404

5373
U.S. Foundation for the Inspiration & Recognition Science & Technology
200 Bedford St
Manchester, NH   03101-1132   (603) 666-3906
Toll-Free Tel.: (800) 871-8326; URL: http://www.usfirst.org/

Foundation type: Public charity
Purpose: College scholarships to students, primarily in the fields of mathematics and technology.
Publications: Application guidelines; Annual report; Newsletter.
Financial data: Year ended 06/30/2012. Assets, $33,081,122 (M); Expenditures, $47,875,532; Total giving, $18,073,319; Grants to individuals, totaling $10,000.
Fields of interest: Higher education; Mathematics; Engineering/technology; Computer science.
Type of support: Scholarships—to individuals; Graduate support.

Application information: Applications accepted. Application form required. Application form available on the grantmaker's web site.
> *Deadline(s):* Varies
> *Additional information:* See web site for additional guidelines.

Program description:
> *Scholarships:* The foundation provides a wide variety of scholarships to juniors, seniors, and post graduates who are studying at various colleges and universities throughout the U.S. Most (but not all) scholarships are reserved for students studying math, engineering, computer sciences, or any other technology-related field.
EIN: 222990908

5374
Union Leader Charitable Fund, Inc.
100 William Loeb Dr.
P.O. Box 9555
Manchester, NH   03108-9555
Contact: Katie McQuaid

Foundation type: Independent foundation
Purpose: Scholarships to individuals who are residents of NH for at least two years for attendance at a postsecondary institution pursuing a career in journalism.
Financial data: Year ended 12/31/2012. Assets, $107,569 (M); Expenditures, $9,975; Total giving, $6,000; Grants to individuals, 2 grants totaling $6,000 (high: $3,000, low: $3,000).
Fields of interest: Journalism school/education.
Type of support: Scholarships—to individuals.
Application information: Applications accepted. Application form required.
> *Deadline(s):* Mar. 1
> *Applicants should submit the following:*
> 1) Transcripts
> 2) Letter(s) of recommendation
> 3) Essay
> *Additional information:* Applicant must have proof of acceptance and/or enrollment in the postsecondary program within one year of the award.
EIN: 204354509

5375
William Vanderhout Trust
P.O. Box 477
Concord, NH   03302-0477   (508) 255-1505
Application Address: c/o Principal Nauset Regional High School,P.O Box 1887, North Eastham, MA 02654

Foundation type: Independent foundation
Purpose: Scholarships to graduates of Nauset Regional High School, North Eastham, MA, residing in the towns of Brewster, Eastham, Orleans, and Wellfleet, MA, to attend accredited colleges.
Financial data: Year ended 07/31/2013. Assets, $1,372,691 (M); Expenditures, $85,475; Total

giving, $55,000; Grants to individuals, 5 grants totaling $55,000 (high: $15,000, low: $10,000).
Type of support: Support to graduates or students of specific schools; Undergraduate support.
Application information: Applications accepted.
> *Initial approach:* Letter
> *Deadline(s):* Apr. 15
EIN: 046753154

5376
Walpole Village District Nursing
Association
P.O. Box 74
Walpole, NH   03608-0074   (603) 756-9265
Contact: Estelle Burr, Pres.
Application address: P.O. Box 479, Walpole, NH 03608, tel.: (603) 756-9265

Foundation type: Independent foundation
Purpose: Scholarships to graduates of Fall Mountain Regional High School, NH and are in the nursing program pursuing a nursing career.
Financial data: Year ended 01/31/2012. Assets, $145,746 (M); Expenditures, $10,299; Total giving, $7,400; Grants to individuals, 8 grants totaling $7,400 (high: $925, low: $925).
Fields of interest: Higher education.
Type of support: Scholarships—to individuals; Support to graduates or students of specific schools.
Application information: Applications accepted. Application form required.
> *Deadline(s):* None
> *Additional information:* Contact the association for further application information.
EIN: 020262942

5377
Eleanor White Trust
P.O. Box 477
Concord, NH   03302-0477   (802) 446-2378
Contact: Richard Smith, Tr.
Application address: 69 Church St., Wallingford, VT 05773, tel.: (802) 446-2378

Foundation type: Independent foundation
Purpose: Scholarships to residents of Fair Haven, VT, for attendance at technical schools, colleges, and universities.
Financial data: Year ended 12/31/2012. Assets, $390,896 (M); Expenditures, $37,604; Total giving, $28,500; Grants to individuals, 9 grants totaling $28,500 (high: $5,000, low: $2,000).
Fields of interest: Vocational education, post-secondary; Higher education.
Type of support: Technical education support; Undergraduate support.
Application information: Application form required.
> *Deadline(s):* Apr. 11

Additional information: Application must include Student Aid Report.
EIN: 036004915

5378
John R. Wilson Scholarship Trust
P.O. Box 477
Concord, NH   03302-0477   (802) 860-5553
Application address: c/o 4 Bennington Area High Schools, Bennington, VT 05201

Foundation type: Independent foundation
Purpose: Scholarships by school recommendation only to female students from Bennington County high schools, VT.
Financial data: Year ended 12/31/2012. Assets, $421,802 (M); Expenditures, $19,840; Total giving, $13,000; Grants to individuals, 6 grants totaling $13,000 (high: $3,000, low: $1,000).
Fields of interest: Scholarships/financial aid; Women.
Type of support: Support to graduates or students of specific schools; Awards/grants by nomination only; Undergraduate support.
Application information: Application form required.
> *Deadline(s):* May 1
> *Additional information:* Scholarship recipients must be nominated by their respective high schools. Individual applications not accepted.
EIN: 036016072

5379
Alice M. & Samuel Yarnold Scholarship
Trust
402 State St.
Portsmouth, NH   03802-4480
Contact: Stephen H. Roberts, Tr.

Foundation type: Independent foundation
Purpose: Scholarships to financially needy postsecondary students in the fields of nursing, medicine, and social work, who are NH residents.
Financial data: Year ended 12/31/2011. Assets, $640,279 (M); Expenditures, $45,529; Total giving, $39,500; Grants to individuals, 23 grants totaling $39,500 (high: $3,000, low: $1,000).
Fields of interest: Vocational education; Medical school/education; Nursing school/education; Human services.
Type of support: Technical education support; Undergraduate support.
Application information: Applications accepted. Application form required.
> *Deadline(s):* May 1
> *Applicants should submit the following:*
> 1) Financial information
> 2) Transcripts
> 3) Letter(s) of recommendation
> 4) FAFSA
> 5) Essay
EIN: 020476417

NEW JERSEY

5380
A Place For Us - Atlantic County Womens Center
1201 New Rd., Ste. 240
Linwood, NJ 08221-1154 (609) 601-9925
Contact: Claudia Ratzlaff, C.E.O.
FAX: (609) 601-2975; E-mail: webinfo@acwc.org;
E-mail for Claudia Ratzlaff:
claudia.ratzlaff@acwc.org; URL: http://
www.acwc.org

Foundation type: Public charity
Purpose: Assistance with emergency shelter for victims and their families of domestic violence, counseling and crisis intervention for victims of sexual assault and abuse, in the Linwood, NJ area.
Publications: Newsletter.
Financial data: Year ended 09/30/2012. Assets, $1,726,687 (M); Expenditures, $4,978,884.
Fields of interest: Abuse prevention; Domestic violence; Sexual abuse.
Type of support: Grants for special needs.
Application information: Contact the center for assistance. See web site for additional information.
EIN: 510244563

5381
Adelphic Educational Fund, Inc.
c/o George McKelvey Co.
529 Washingt
Sea Girt, NJ 08750-2904 (860) 685-3882
Contact: Erhard F. Konerding
*Application address:*10 Yellow Cir., Middletown, CT 06459-0001

Foundation type: Independent foundation
Purpose: Scholarships and student loans to financially needy undergraduate students at Wesleyan University, CT. Recipients are chosen on the basis of financial need and scholastic aptitude.
Financial data: Year ended 04/30/2013. Assets, $1,258,625 (M); Expenditures, $51,016; Total giving, $35,236.
Type of support: Student loans—to individuals; Support to graduates or students of specific schools; Undergraduate support.
Application information: Applications accepted. Application form required. Interview required.
  Initial approach: Letter
  Deadline(s): Oct. 1
EIN: 066023615

5382
David Akers Kicks for Kids, Inc.
P.O. Box 321
Voorhees, NJ 08043-0321 (856) 625-2046
FAX: (856) 809-1168;
E-mail: rose@davidakerskicksforkids.org

Foundation type: Public charity
Purpose: Emergency assistance to children and families in need in the Philadelphia, PA area.
Financial data: Year ended 12/31/2011. Assets, $14,101 (M); Expenditures, $139,286; Total giving, $86,928; Grants to individuals, totaling $28,455.
Fields of interest: Human services.
Type of support: Emergency funds; Grants for special needs.

Application information: Contact the organization for information to obtain assistance.
EIN: 611400383

5383
American Friends of Even Yisroel Charitable Foundation
25 Dakota St.
Passaic, NJ 07055-3331
Contact: Mitchell Lisker

Foundation type: Independent foundation
Purpose: Grants for members for religious study, in the NJ area.
Financial data: Year ended 12/31/2012. Assets, $2,572 (M); Expenditures, $259,636; Total giving, $217,126; Grants to individuals, 30 grants totaling $217,126 (high: $7,200, low: $7,200).
Fields of interest: Theological school/education.
Type of support: Grants to individuals.
Application information: Applications accepted.
  Deadline(s): None
  Additional information: Application should include a personal narrative and reasons for joining an education group. Unsolicited requests for funds not considered or acknowledged.
EIN: 137173269

5384
American Hungarian Foundation
300 Somerset St.
P.O. Box 1084
New Brunswick, NJ 08901-2248 (732) 846-5777
Contact: August J. Molnar, Pres.
FAX: (732) 249-7033;
E-mail: info@ahfoundation.org; URL: http://
www.ahfoundation.org

Foundation type: Public charity
Purpose: Scholarships to students of Hungarian descent for higher education.
Financial data: Year ended 06/30/2011. Assets, $2,289,084 (M); Expenditures, $460,502.
International interests: Hungary.
Type of support: Undergraduate support.
Application information:
  Initial approach: Letter.
  Deadline(s): Contact foundation for current application deadline
  Additional information: Application by letter must detail academic and personal achievement and interest in Hungarian studies. Application must also include three references and any other sources that have been contacted for financial assistance.
EIN: 366085165

5385
American Society of Transplantation
15000 Commerce Pkwy., Ste. C
Mount Laurel, NJ 08054-2212 (856) 439-9986
Contact: Libby McDannell, Exec. Dir.
FAX: (856) 439-9982; E-mail: info@myAST.org;
E-Mail for Libby McDannell:
emcdannell@myAST.org; URL: http://www.a-s-t.org

Foundation type: Public charity
Purpose: Research grants to individuals in the field of transplantation.
Publications: Application guidelines.
Financial data: Year ended 12/31/2011. Assets, $13,732,131 (M); Expenditures, $4,257,849;

Total giving, $916,289; Grants to individuals, totaling $846,461.
Fields of interest: Health care; Surgery; Surgery research.
Type of support: Research; Grants to individuals.
Application information: Applications accepted. Application form required.
  Deadline(s): Apr. 1 and Oct. 1 for RO1 Bridge Grant; Dec. 14 for Faculty and Fellowship Grants
  Additional information: Awards are based on relative strength of the applicant's research and training plan, the environment for training provided by the sponsor, and the potential for the applicant's career development if awarded the fellowship. See web site for complete program listing.
Program descriptions:
  Faculty and Fellowship Grants: The AST supports a wide range of basic and clinical research topics. Research topics that involve under-represented areas including minorities, women and pediatrics are strongly encouraged. The AST also encourages applications from women and minority researchers (as defined by the NIH). Individuals applying for the Faculty Grants must be active members of the AST by the application deadline. Individuals applying for the Fellowship Grants must be sponsored by an AST member.
  Physician Scientist Training Grant: This three year grant ($30,000/year) is intended to cover graduate trainee's support, travel to the American Transplant Congress and other relevant expenses. This grant does not cover indirect institutional costs.
  RO1 Bridge Grant: The grant provides bridge funding for investigators who are between independent NIH Research Grants (e.g. from RO1 to RO1 and/or North American equivalent), and whose new application was scored, but not funded. Applicant must hold an M.D. or Ph.D. (or equivalent) degree. Applicant must be an active member of the AST at the time of application. Grant award is $50,000.
EIN: 421182936

5386
The Ammonius Foundation
(formerly A.M. Monius Institute, Inc.)
375 Metuchen Rd.
South Plainfield, NJ 07080
E-mail: rd@ammonius.org; URL: http://
www.ammonius.org

Foundation type: Independent foundation
Purpose: Prizes to winners of an essay competition for younger scholars in the field of metaphysics. Grants also to leading philosophers for research on key metaphysical concerns.
Financial data: Year ended 12/31/2012. Assets, $834,979 (M); Expenditures, $632,971; Total giving, $0.
Fields of interest: Science; Physics.
Type of support: Research; Awards/prizes.
Application information:
  Initial approach: Letter or e-mail
  Send request by: Online
  Deadline(s): Jan. 30
  Applicants should submit the following:
    1) Proposal
    2) Curriculum vitae
  Additional information: Application inquiries for the Younger Scholar Prize should be addressed to Dean Zimmerman, Editor, at dwzimmer@rci.rutgers.edu.
Program descriptions:
  Research Grant: Applicant must have attained a Ph.D. or equivalent degree and have published an

article in Journal of Philosophy, The Philosophical Review, Mind, The Monist, Nous, and/or The Review of Metaphysics. Applicant also must submit a research proposal of not more than three typed pages which demonstrates a detailed knowledge of the work.

Younger Scholar Prize: The program awards an $8,000 prize to scholars who are within ten years of receiving a Ph.D. or students who are currently enrolled in a graduate program. Essays should generally be between 7,500 and 15,000 words. Longer essays may be considered, but authors must seek prior approval by providing the Editor with an abstract and word count prior to submission. The winner will be determined by a committee of members of the editorial board of Oxford Studies in Metaphysics.
EIN: 223840808

5387
Anyone Can Fly Foundation, Inc.
127 Jones Rd.
Englewood, NJ   07631   (201) 816-1374
Contact: Barbara F. Wallace, Secy.
E-mail: enquiries@anyonecanflyfoundation.org;
URL: http://www.anyonecanflyfoundation.org

Foundation type: Independent foundation
Purpose: Grants to professional scholars, educators, art historians and teachers for research, writing, and teaching about the Master Artists of the African Diaspora to both adults and kids.
Financial data: Year ended 12/31/2012. Assets, $46,497 (M); Expenditures, $36,927; Total giving, $2,000; Grant to an individual, 1 grant totaling $2,000.
Fields of interest: Arts education; Literature.
Type of support: Research; Grants to individuals.
Application information: Applications accepted. Application form required.
> *Send request by:* Mail
> *Deadline(s):* Feb. 28
> *Additional information:* See foundation web site for additional information.
EIN: 223762980

5388
The Arc of Bergen and Passaic Counties, Inc.
223 Moore Ave.
Hackensack, NJ   07601-7402   (201) 343-0322
Contact: Kathy Walsh, Pres. and C.E.O.
FAX: (201) 343-0401; E-mail: arc@arcbp.com;
URL: http://www.arcbergenpassaic.org

Foundation type: Public charity
Purpose: Assistance to individuals of Bergen and Passaic counties, NJ with mental retardation and other developmental disabilities and their families.
Publications: Annual report; Informational brochure; Newsletter.
Financial data: Year ended 06/30/2012. Assets, $8,586,334 (M); Expenditures, $15,595,652.
Fields of interest: Disabilities, people with; Mentally disabled.
Type of support: Grants for special needs.
Application information: Contact the organization for eligibility determination.
EIN: 221620254

5389
ARCH Foundation
6 W. Belt
Wayne, NJ   07470-6806   (973) 305-5022
Contact: Donald Nerz, Treas.
Additional application addresses: P.O. Box 220908, Charlotte, NC 29222-0908, tel.: (877) 393-9071, Fax: (877) 229-1421; URL: http://www.archfoundation.com/

Foundation type: Operating foundation
Purpose: Assistance with the birth control medication Mirena to economically disadvantaged people who live below the federal poverty level and have no insurance coverage.
Publications: Application guidelines.
Financial data: Year ended 12/31/2012. Assets, $14,241 (M); Expenditures, $11,158,843; Total giving, $11,000,400; Grants to individuals, totaling $11,000,400.
Fields of interest: Pharmacy/prescriptions; Health care; Women; Economically disadvantaged.
Type of support: Grants to individuals; Grants for special needs.
Application information: Applications accepted. Application form available on the grantmaker's web site.
> *Initial approach:* Application
> *Send request by:* Fax or Mail
> *Deadline(s):* None
> *Additional information:* Application should include financial information, and must be completed in part by a healthcare provider.
EIN: 221231236

5390
The Edward Thatcher Astle Memorial Scholarship Foundation
24 West St.
P.O. Box 182
Annandale, NJ   08801-3052   (908) 735-5339
Contact: David Olekna, Tr.

Foundation type: Independent foundation
Purpose: Scholarships to high school seniors from central NJ who are U.S. citizens, have at least a "B" average, and require financial assistance to attend college or trade school.
Financial data: Year ended 04/30/2013. Assets, $709,511 (M); Expenditures, $62,664; Total giving, $42,180.
Fields of interest: Vocational education; Higher education.
Type of support: Technical education support; Undergraduate support.
Application information: Application form required. Interview required.
> *Deadline(s):* Mar. 19
> *Additional information:* Application must include tax return and written recommendation from the guidance department or a teacher. Applications available from the foundation.
Program description:
> *Scholarship Program:* Scholarships of $6,000 are awarded annually to graduating seniors. There are no restrictions on areas of study that applicants must pursue. However, recipients will be selected based on the importance of the area of study to society. Applicants over 18 years of age must be registered to vote in NJ. Candidates must have shown that they are willing to help pay for their education by working during the summer or after school hours. If a student leaves college or trade school during the school year, any unused scholarship funds must be donated to the college or trade school's general scholarship fund. Individuals who have known drug involvement or

involvement in unlawful activities are discouraged from applying.
EIN: 222817002

5391
Atlantic County Medical Society Scholarship Fund
P.O. Box 581
Somers Point, NJ   08244-2363   (609) 926-3488
Contact: Suzane Syed

Foundation type: Independent foundation
Purpose: Scholarships to medical students who are residents of Atlantic County, NJ.
Financial data: Year ended 04/30/2013. Assets, $369,370 (M); Expenditures, $22,750; Total giving, $20,250; Grants to individuals, 13 grants totaling $20,250 (high: $2,000, low: $1,000).
Fields of interest: Medical school/education.
Type of support: Graduate support.
Application information: Applications accepted. Application form required.
> *Deadline(s):* Mid-June
> *Additional information:* Application should include tax return, MCAT scores, college and medical school grades, letter of acceptance, and statement of marital status. Applicant must be a U.S. citizen.
EIN: 237024987

5392
Atlanticare Regional Medical Center, Inc.
1925 Pacific Ave.
Atlantic City, NJ   08401-6713   (609) 652-1000
URL: http://www.atlanticare.org/

Foundation type: Public charity
Purpose: The Charity Care program is designed to help indigent NJ patients of AtlantiCare that are not eligible for the insurances offered through the Health Insurance Marketplace or have a balance after their insurance has paid.
Publications: Annual report.
Fields of interest: Health care; Economically disadvantaged.
Type of support: Grants for special needs.
Application information: Applications accepted. Application form required. Application form available on the grantmaker's web site.
> *Initial approach:* Letter or in-person
> *Applicants should submit the following:*
> 1) Financial information
> *Additional information:* Eligibility is based upon income and assets on the day of service. The program does not cover physician fees.
EIN: 210634549

5393
The Avoda Club of Atlantic County
P. O. Box 3120
Margate City, NJ   08402-0120   (609) 822-4493

Foundation type: Public charity
Purpose: Scholarships to Jewish graduates of Atlantic County, NJ, high schools for undergraduate education.
Financial data: Year ended 12/31/2011. Assets, $787,593 (M); Expenditures, $91,479; Total giving, $60,000; Grants to individuals, totaling $60,000.
Fields of interest: Higher education.
Type of support: Support to graduates or students of specific schools; Undergraduate support.

Application information: Applications accepted. Application form required. Interview required.
  Deadline(s): Mar. 1
  Applicants should submit the following:
    1) Photograph
    2) Financial information
    3) Transcripts
    4) SAT
  Additional information: Students should contact their guidance counselor for application information.
EIN: 226085397

5394
Leslie Bartell Scholarship Foundation Inc.
c/o Leonard J. Krieger, Jr., C.P.A.
49 Roberts Rd.
Clark, NJ   07066-2722   (732) 382-0910

Foundation type: Independent foundation
Purpose: Scholarships to graduating seniors of Johnson High School, NJ, who are residents of Clark, NJ for attendance at a four-year college.
Financial data: Year ended 08/31/2013. Assets, $355,105 (M); Expenditures, $42,890; Total giving, $39,500; Grants to individuals, 4 grants totaling $39,500 (high: $12,500, low: $2,000).
Fields of interest: Higher education.
Type of support: Scholarships—to individuals; Support to graduates or students of specific schools; Undergraduate support.
Application information: Applications accepted.
  Initial approach: Letter
  Deadline(s): May
  Additional information: Application should include a transcript and activity participation.
EIN: 223504274

5395
Bass Memorial Foundation, Inc.
(formerly Ruth Bass Memorial Foundation)
P.O. Box 392
Maplewood, NJ   07040-0392   (973) 763-9723
E-mail: thebassfoundation@gmail.com;
URL: http://thebassfoundation.org/content/

Foundation type: Public charity
Purpose: Scholarship for the benefit of a Columbia high school student of Maplewood, NJ who is in financial need, and demonstrates a commitment to community service. Assistance with food, clothing, toys and care to those less fortunate in the greater NJ area.
Financial data: Year ended 12/31/2011. Assets, $155,761 (M); Expenditures, $148,804; Total giving, $81,428; Grants to individuals, totaling $2,773.
Fields of interest: Higher education; Economically disadvantaged.
Type of support: Scholarships—to individuals; Grants for special needs.
Application information: Applications accepted.
  Additional information: Contact the foundation for information on assistance.
EIN: 223207547

5396
Belleville Foundation Inc.
c/o Al Schmidt
61 Hill St.
Belleville, NJ   07109-1504   (973) 450-3500
Contact: Deborah Perry
Application address: c/o Belleville High School, Passaic Ave., Passaic, NJ 07109

Foundation type: Independent foundation
Purpose: Scholarships to graduating students of Belleville High School, NJ who have shown an aptitude for continuing their education at accredited institutions of higher learning.
Financial data: Year ended 12/31/2012. Assets, $193,631 (M); Expenditures, $7,951; Total giving, $4,000; Grants to individuals, 4 grants totaling $4,000 (high: $1,000, low: $1,000).
Fields of interest: Higher education.
Type of support: Support to graduates or students of specific schools.
Application information: Applications accepted. Application form required.
  Deadline(s): Apr. 15
  Applicants should submit the following:
    1) Class rank
    2) SAT
    3) Financial information
  Additional information: Application should also include character/personal reference and extracurricular activities.
EIN: 226000099

5397
Edwin J. Berkowitz Scholarship Foundation Inc.
c/o J.E. Berkowitz, L.P.
P.O. Box 427
Pedricktown, NJ   08067   (856) 456-7800

Foundation type: Company-sponsored foundation
Purpose: Scholarships to eligible employees and children of eligible employees of J.E. Berkowitz, L.P. for continuing education at higher institutions.
Financial data: Year ended 09/30/2012. Assets, $29,662 (M); Expenditures, $10,000; Total giving, $10,000; Grants to individuals, 6 grants totaling $10,000.
Fields of interest: Higher education; Scholarships/financial aid.
Type of support: Employee-related scholarships.
Application information: Applications not accepted.
  Additional information: Unsolicited requests for funds not considered or acknowledged.
Company name: J. E. Berkowitz, L.P.
EIN: 223402191

5398
Bernards Area Scholarship Assistance, Inc.
P.O. Box 7037
Bedminster, NJ   07921   (908) 470-9352
Contact: Bea Daggett, Pres.
Application address: 96 Deer Ridge Rd. Basking Ridge, NJ 07920, tel.: 908-470-9352

Foundation type: Independent foundation
Purpose: Scholarships to residents of the Bernardsville/Basking Ridge, NJ, area who demonstrate academic ability and financial need.
Financial data: Year ended 06/30/2013. Assets, $36,628 (M); Expenditures, $3,226; Total giving, $3,000; Grants to individuals, 2 grants totaling $3,000 (high: $2,000, low: $1,000).
Type of support: Scholarships—to individuals.
Application information: Applications accepted. Application form required.
  Deadline(s): Feb. 15
  Applicants should submit the following:
    1) Financial information
    2) Transcripts
EIN: 222590097

5399
The Russell Berrie Foundation
300 Frank W. Burr Blvd., Bldg. East, 7th Fl.
Teaneck, NJ   07666-6704   (201) 928-1880
Contact: Ruth Salzman, C. E. O
E-mail: inquiry@rbfdtn.org; URL: http://www.russellberriefoundation.org

Foundation type: Independent foundation
Purpose: Awards to NJ residents who have made a difference in the well-being of society.
Financial data: Year ended 12/31/2012. Assets, $215,018,834 (M); Expenditures, $21,536,292; Total giving, $18,532,935; Grants to individuals, 12 grants totaling $173,888 (high: $35,000, low: $5,000).
Fields of interest: Social sciences.
Type of support: Awards/prizes.
Application information: Application form required.
  Additional information: Awards are by nomination only. Contact foundation for application guidelines.
Program description:
  Russ Berrie Award for Making a Difference: The award celebrates New Jersey's unsung heroes-everyday people whose extraordinary volunteer efforts have made a real difference in the lives of others. Created in 1997, the annual award program honors nineteen individuals who have performed outstanding community service or an act of heroism. The unsung heroes are chosen from a pool of several hundred nominees and awards the top three with cash prizes of $50,000, $35,000 and $25,000. Eight other finalists are distinguished with cash prizes of $5,000.
EIN: 222620908

5400
Beth Medrash Govoha of Lakewood, Inc.
601 Private Way
Lakewood, NJ   08701-2754

Foundation type: Public charity
Purpose: Scholarships and stipends to rabbinical students for higher education.
Financial data: Year ended 12/31/2011. Assets, $25,071,203 (M); Expenditures, $4,305,852; Total giving, $736,027.
Fields of interest: Higher education.
Type of support: Scholarships—to individuals.
Application information: Students are recommended by the faculty and the financial aid office of the school.
EIN: 223839462

5401
The Dr. William J. Bicket Memorial Scholarship Fund Inc.
22 Abernethy Dr.
Trenton, NJ   08618

Foundation type: Independent foundation
Purpose: Scholarships to graduates of the Trenton, NJ, public school system to attend accredited four-year colleges in the following year.
Financial data: Year ended 04/30/2013. Assets, $159,434 (M); Expenditures, $4,906; Total giving, $3,750; Grants to individuals, 3 grants totaling $3,750 (high: $1,500, low: $750).
Type of support: Support to graduates or students of specific schools; Undergraduate support.
Application information: Applications not accepted.
  Additional information: Contact foundation for current application deadline/guidelines.

Unsolicited requests for funds not considered or acknowledged.
EIN: 226049584

5402
BLSJ Scholarship Foundation
114 Haddontown Ct.
Cherry Hill, NJ 08034-3699 (856) 616-8460
Contact: Richard Van Osten, Treas.

Foundation type: Independent foundation
Purpose: Scholarships to qualified high school graduates who live in or attend school in Burlington, Camden, Gloucester, Salem, Cumberland, Cape May or Atlantic counties, NJ for attendance at accredited colleges or universities pursuing a course of study related to the fields of real estate development and construction.
Financial data: Year ended 07/31/2013. Assets, $127,828 (M); Expenditures, $6,214; Total giving, $5,500; Grants to individuals, 4 grants totaling $5,500 (high: $2,500, low: $1,000).
Fields of interest: Vocational education, post-secondary; Engineering/technology.
Type of support: Scholarships—to individuals.
Application information: Applications accepted. Application form required. Application form available on the grantmaker's web site. Interview required.
> *Deadline(s):* Apr. 8
> *Applicants should submit the following:*
> 1) Letter(s) of recommendation
> 2) Transcripts
> 3) SAT
> 4) Financial information
> 5) Essay
> *Additional information:* Application should also include academic achievement, work experience and community service. Applications can be obtained from the school guidance counselors.

Program description:
> *Scholarship Program:* Scholarships ranging up to $2,000 is awarded to students attending qualified trade school programs as well as junior and four year colleges or universities. The study fields include, but are not limited to, air conditioning, plumbing and heating technology, architecture, civil engineering, construction management, CAD drafting, landscape architecture, real estate marketing and surveying. As long as the recipient is successfully pursuing his or her course of study, he or she may reapply for a scholarship each year.
EIN: 521847644

5403
B'nai Brith Food Industry Lodge Foundation Inc
c/o Steve Piller
12 Canterbury Ct.
Warren, NJ 07059 (973) 376-7550
Contact: Steven Piller, Tr.

Foundation type: Operating foundation
Purpose: Scholarships to food industry students.
Financial data: Year ended 12/31/2011. Assets, $504,795 (M); Expenditures, $25,563; Total giving, $24,500; Grants to individuals, 6 grants totaling $10,000 (high: $2,000, low: $1,000).
Type of support: Scholarships—to individuals.
Application information: Applications accepted.
EIN: 223223678

5404
Vincent M. Boland, Jr. Memorial Scholarship Fund
280 Burnt Meadow Rd.
Ringwood, NJ 07456-1113
Contact: Vincent Boland, Tr.

Foundation type: Operating foundation
Purpose: College scholarships for north Jersey, NJ, students for postsecondary education.
Financial data: Year ended 03/31/2012. Assets, $41,024 (M); Expenditures, $25; Total giving, $0.
Fields of interest: Higher education.
Type of support: Scholarships—to individuals.
Application information: Applications accepted. Application form required.
> *Deadline(s):* Apr. 30
> *Additional information:* Contact the fund for application forms.
EIN: 223831791

5405
The Brookdale Foundation
300 Frank W. Burr Blvd., No. 13
Teaneck, NJ 07666-6703

Foundation type: Independent foundation
Purpose: Fellowships to encourage emerging leaders in the field of aging.
Financial data: Year ended 06/30/2013. Assets, $4,562,407 (M); Expenditures, $174,295; Total giving, $106,264.
Fields of interest: Aging.
Type of support: Fellowships.
Application information:
> *Initial approach:* Letter
> *Deadline(s):* Nov. 6
Program descriptions:
> *Relatives as Parents Program (RAPP):* The Relatives as Parents Program (RAPP) was initiated in 1996. It is designed to encourage and promote the creation or expansion of services for grandparents and other relatives who have taken on the responsibility of surrogate parenting due to the absence of the parents. The program awards seed grants of $10,000 over a two-year period in three categories: local, regional, and state public agencies. Currently RAPP provides extensive services, primarily to relative caregivers caring for children outside the foster care system, in 44 States, the District of Columbia, and Puerto Rico. As part of the foundation's sponsorship of RAPP, it conducts its National Orientation and Training Conference and provide technical assistance through site bulletins, a listserv, its annual newsletter, conference calls and webchats to facilitate opportunities for networking and information exchange.
> *The Brookdale Leadership in Aging Fellowship Program:* For over twenty years, the Brookdale Foundation Group has been committed to training the next generation of experts in geriatrics and gerontology. In 1985, it began its Brookdale National Fellowship Program, which sought out those with the professional experience, capacity and potential to become leaders in the field of aging. The original Fellowship program ended in 2003, but after some retooling was revived in 2007 as the Brookdale Leadership in Aging Fellowship Program. This program continues to foster leaders in aging and each year brings together past & current fellows to network and exchange ideas.
> *The Brookdale National Group Respite Program:* Since 1989, the Brookdale National Group Respite Program has awarded seed grants to organizations to develop and implement social model group respite programs. These day programs have served

thousands of elders with Alzheimer's disease or related dementia and their family caregivers. In addition to group respite, the development of programs for people with Early Memory Loss (EML) is also supported through this grant initiative. The goals of the program are: to offer opportunities for persons with Alzheimer's disease or a related dementia to engage in a program of meaningful social and recreational activities in a secure and supportive setting in order to maximize their cognitive and social abilities, and to provide relief and support to family members and other primary caregivers of individuals with Alzheimer's disease or a related dementia.
EIN: 136076863

5406
The Samuel & Esther Buchalter Foundation, Inc.
897 Frelinghuysen Ave.
Newark, NJ 07114 (973) 242-2900
Contact: Gilbert Buchalter, Tr.

Foundation type: Company-sponsored foundation
Purpose: Scholarships to employees or dependents of employees of Pharmaceutical Innovations.
Financial data: Year ended 12/31/2012. Assets, $229,097 (M); Expenditures, $15,482; Total giving, $11,925; Grants to individuals, 12 grants totaling $4,925 (high: $1,000, low: $175).
Type of support: Employee-related scholarships.
Application information: Applications accepted. Application form required.
> *Initial approach:* Letter
> *Deadline(s):* None
> *Additional information:* Contact foundation for application guidelines.
Company name: Pharmaceutical Innovations, Inc.
EIN: 223269458

5407
Burlington County Community Action Program
718 Rte. 130 S.
Burlington, NJ 08016-1276 (609) 386-5800
FAX: (609) 386-7380;
E-mail: stownsend@bccap.org; URL: http://www.bccap.org

Foundation type: Public charity
Purpose: Financial assistance to indigent residents of Burlington County, NJ, for home repairs when faced with life-threatening situations in their homes (i.e. no heat, water or cooking utilities)
Publications: Annual report; Financial statement; Newsletter.
Financial data: Year ended 02/28/2012. Assets, $7,684,602 (M); Expenditures, $20,147,570; Total giving, $8,851,201; Grants to individuals, totaling $8,851,201.
Type of support: Grants for special needs.
Application information: Applications accepted. Application form required.
> *Initial approach:* Telephone
> *Additional information:* Contact foundation for application guidelines.
EIN: 221804209

5408
Gertrude Butts Memorial Fund, Inc.
31 Mulberry St.
Newark, NJ 07102-5202 (973) 622-4306
Contact: Linda Curtiss, Tr.

Foundation type: Independent foundation
Purpose: Scholarships to destitute, orphaned, and half-orphaned children in the Diocese of Newark, NJ, for higher education. General welfare support to children of urban clergy in NJ.
Financial data: Year ended 12/31/2011. Assets, $2,073,183 (M); Expenditures, $101,000; Total giving, $101,000; Grants to individuals, 3 grants totaling $19,000 (high: $7,000, low: $6,000).
Fields of interest: Christian agencies & churches.
Type of support: Undergraduate support; Grants for special needs.
Application information: Applications accepted. Application form required.
Deadline(s): None
Additional information: Scholarships are renewable; Contact foundation for current application guidelines.
EIN: 226043630

5409
Francis L. Calvi Memorial Foundation
14 S. California Ave.
Atlantic City, NJ 08401-6413 (609) 345-0151
Contact: George Brestle, Tr.

Foundation type: Company-sponsored foundation
Purpose: Scholarships only to employees and children of employees of Calvi Electric Company, residing in the NJ jurisdiction of Local No. 211.
Financial data: Year ended 12/31/2012. Assets, $162,221 (M); Expenditures, $12,199; Total giving, $12,000; Grants to individuals, 7 grants totaling $12,000 (high: $2,500, low: $1,000).
Type of support: Employee-related scholarships.
Application information: Applications not accepted.
Additional information: Unsolitcted requests for funds not considered or acknowledged.
Company name: Calvi Electric Company
EIN: 222769316

5410
Camden County Hero Scholarship Fund - 200 Club, Inc.
c/o Muriel Mansmann
191 White Horse Pike
Berlin, NJ 08009-2021 (856) 768-9656
Contact: Muriel Mansmann, Secy.

Foundation type: Public charity
Purpose: Scholarships to spouses and children of Camden County, NJ, firefighters and law enforcement officers who lost their lives or became disabled in the line of duty. Scholarships are for attendance at colleges, junior colleges, or postsecondary vocational schools. Some work-related continuing education grants for firefighters and officers are also available. Selection is based on need, scholarship, character, and extracurricular activities.
Financial data: Year ended 09/30/2012. Assets, $569,840 (M); Expenditures, $105,327; Total giving, $14,416; Grants to individuals, totaling $14,416.
Fields of interest: Vocational education; Adult/continuing education; Crime/law enforcement, police agencies; Disasters, fire prevention/control.
Type of support: Technical education support; Undergraduate support.
Application information: Applications accepted.
Initial approach: Letter
Deadline(s): None

Additional information: Letter should be in written proposal form and accepted on a case by case basis.
EIN: 226105887

5411
Camp Arcadia Scholarship Foundation
c/o Anne Fritts
Box 225
New Vernon, NJ 07976-9707 (973) 538-5409

Foundation type: Public charity
Purpose: Scholarships for summer camp to enable girls whose families could not otherwise afford the expense to attend summer camp.
Financial data: Year ended 12/31/2011. Assets, $780,106 (M); Expenditures, $134,605; Total giving, $97,290; Grants to individuals, 24 grants totaling $97,290. Subtotal for camperships: 24 grants totaling $97,290.
Fields of interest: Camps; Girls.
Type of support: Scholarships—to individuals.
Application information: Contact the foundation for further information.
EIN: 222806682

5412
Capezio/Ballet Makers Dance Foundation, Inc.
1 Campus Rd.
Totowa, NJ 07512-1201
Contact: Jane Remer, Exec. Dir.
E-mail: dfiorenzi@balletmakers.com; URL: http://www.capezio.com/all-access/dance-foundation/

Foundation type: Company-sponsored foundation
Purpose: Awards by nomination only to individuals who contribute to the public awareness of dance.
Publications: Application guidelines; Grants list.
Financial data: Year ended 12/31/2011. Assets, $635 (M); Expenditures, $70,000; Total giving, $70,000; Grant to an individual, 1 grant totaling $10,000.
Fields of interest: Dance.
Type of support: Awards/grants by nomination only; Awards/prizes.
Application information: Applications not accepted.
Program description:
Capezio Dance Award: Through the Capezio Dance Award, the foundation annually awards $10,000 to an individual, company, or organization that has made a significant contribution to American dance. Candidates must be nominated from a group indentified by the trustees and the award is presented at a ceremony honoring the awarded.
EIN: 136161198

5413
Catholic Charities - Diocese of Metuchen
319 Maple St.
Perth Amboy, NJ 08861-4101 (732) 324-8200
FAX: (732) 826-3549; E-mail: admin@ccdom.org;
URL: http://www.ccdom.org

Foundation type: Public charity
Purpose: Emergency assistance to individuals in need throughout Essex, Hunterdon, Middlesex, Monmouth, Morris, Somerset, Sussex, Union, and Warren counties, NJ.
Publications: Annual report.
Financial data: Year ended 06/30/2011. Assets, $25,715,407 (M); Expenditures, $39,959,048;

Total giving, $3,775,801; Grants to individuals, 25,853 grants totaling $3,208,606.
Fields of interest: Children/youth, services; Family services; Economically disadvantaged.
Type of support: Emergency funds; In-kind gifts.
Application information: See web site or contact the Catholic charity for eligibility determination.
EIN: 222423496

5414
Catholic Charities, Diocese of Trenton
383 W. State St.
P.O. Box 1423
Trenton, NJ 08618-5705
FAX: (609) 394-0732; E-mail: info@cctrenton.org;
Toll-free tel.: (800) 642-0218; URL: http://www.catholiccharitiestrenton.org

Foundation type: Public charity
Purpose: Financial assistance for qualified individuals and families in the Trenton, NJ area with rent and mortgage payments, utility assistance, medication and other special needs.
Publications: Annual report; Newsletter.
Financial data: Year ended 12/31/2011. Assets, $27,432,783 (M); Expenditures, $42,960,862; Total giving, $4,599,093; Grants to individuals, totaling $4,599,093.
Fields of interest: Economically disadvantaged.
Type of support: Grants for special needs.
Application information: Contact organization for eligibility determination.
EIN: 210634494

5415
Catholic Christmas Campaign, Inc.
(formerly Catholic Christmas Crusade)
18 Cove Rd.
Moorestown, NJ 08057-3310
Contact: William J. Begley, Pres.

Foundation type: Independent foundation
Purpose: Grants to indigent individuals and families in the Burlington County, NJ, area.
Financial data: Year ended 11/30/2013. Assets, $65,050 (M); Expenditures, $12,672; Total giving, $12,663.
Fields of interest: Economically disadvantaged.
Type of support: Grants for special needs.
Application information:
Initial approach: Telephone or letter
Deadline(s): None
EIN: 222763910

5416
Center of Theological Inquiry
50 Stockton St.
Princeton, NJ 08540-6813 (609) 683-4797
Contact: William Storrar, Exec. Dir.
FAX: (609) 683-4030; E-mail: cti@ctinquiry.org;
URL: http://www.ctinquiry.org

Foundation type: Public charity
Purpose: Research fellowships to further the conversation between theology and natural science.
Publications: Application guidelines; Informational brochure; Newsletter.
Financial data: Year ended 06/30/2012. Assets, $19,454,515 (M); Expenditures, $1,353,823; Total giving, $22,500; Grants to individuals, totaling $22,500.
Fields of interest: Science; Christian agencies & churches.
Type of support: Fellowships.

Application information: Applications accepted. Application form required.
  Initial approach: Proposal
  Send request by: Online
  Deadline(s): Nov. 30 for Inquiry on Religious Experience & Moral Identity
  Additional information: See web site for additional guidelines.
Program description:
  An Inquiry on Evolution & Human Nature: With support from the John Templeton Foundation, eight research fellowships of up to $70,000 and two postdoctoral fellowships of $40,000 are offered to research scholars who welcome the dialogue between theology and science. Proposals should explore how the explosion of new research in evolutionary biology, psychology, and anthropology is challenging and changing understandings of human nature and development, not least in relation to religion and theological accounts of the human condition.
EIN: 222212290

5417
Cerebral Palsy International Research Foundation, Inc.
(formerly The United Cerebral Palsy Research and Educational Foundation, Inc.)
186 Princeton Hightstown Rd., Bldg. 4, 2nd Fl.
Princeton Junction, NJ 08550-1668 (609) 452-1200
Grant application e-mail: grants@cpirf.org
FAX: (609) 452-1201; E-mail: cpirf@cpirf.org;
URL: http://www.cpirf.org

Foundation type: Public charity
Purpose: Research grants to investogators for the cause, cure and evidence based care for those with cerebral palsy and related developmental disabilities.
Publications: Financial statement; Informational brochure.
Financial data: Year ended 09/30/2011. Assets, $4,066,643 (M); Expenditures, $1,393,565; Total giving, $778,286.
Fields of interest: Cerebral palsy research; Disabilities, people with.
Type of support: Research; Grants to individuals.
Application information: Applications accepted.
  Initial approach: Letter of Intent
  Send request by: On-line
  Deadline(s): Jan. 15 for Letter of Intent, and Mar. 1 for Proposals for Hausman Award and Research Grant Program
  Additional information: See web site for additional application guidelines.
Program descriptions:
  Ethel & Jack Hausman Clinical Research Scholars Award: The award is in the amount of $75,000 per year for up to three years assists institutions in the United States to recruit promising clinician-investigators early in their careers and to help in their establishment as focal points for scholarly activities in areas of direct relevance to cerebral palsy and related developmental brain disorders. Candidates for the award must either be citizens of the United States or have permanent residency status. The award funds will be used to conduct clinical research and educational program relevant to cerebral palsy and related developmental brain disorders. The clinical research program can be patient based or a combined laboratory-patient endeavor. Candidates for the award will have completed their formal clinical, graduate, and/or fellowship training.
  Research Grant Program: The foundation provides funding for pilot studies on research

important to the prevention, cure, and treatment of cerebral palsy, including improvement in the quality of life of persons with disabilities due to cerebral palsy. This broad research agenda includes basic, clinical and applied research in the biomedical and bioengineering sciences. Grants are awarded on a competitive basis taking into account scientific merit, scientific and clinical significance and relevance to cerebral palsy. Grants are generally awarded for up to two years at a maximum of $50,000 a year.
EIN: 136093337

5418
The Chakrabarti Foundation
1288 Rte. 73 S., Ste. 401
Mount Laurel, NJ 08054-2237
Contact: Srimati Chakrabarti, Pres.

Foundation type: Independent foundation
Purpose: Scholarships to children and stepchildren of employees of Polymer Products, Inc.; Crystal, Inc.-PMC; Lenco, Inc.-PMC; PMC Film Canada, Inc.; The PMC Group; or any company acquired by the PMC Group or Dr. or Mrs. Chakrabarti.
Financial data: Year ended 12/31/2012. Assets, $11,718 (M); Expenditures, $20,024; Total giving, $20,000; Grants to individuals, 13 grants totaling $20,000 (high: $14,000, low: $500).
Type of support: Employee-related scholarships.
Application information: Applications accepted. Application form required.
  Deadline(s): Apr. 30
  Applicants should submit the following:
    1) Essay
    2) Transcripts
EIN: 251735900

5419
Chatham Kiwanis Scholarship Fund
P.O. Box 422
Chatham, NJ 07928-0422 (973) 635-2000

Foundation type: Independent foundation
Purpose: Scholarships to graduating seniors of Chatham High School, NJ, for higher education.
Financial data: Year ended 09/30/2013. Assets, $171,445 (M); Expenditures, $16,743; Total giving, $16,000; Grants to individuals, 8 grants totaling $16,000 (high: $2,000, low: $2,000).
Fields of interest: Business school/education; Teacher school/education; Natural resources; Youth development; Volunteer services; Voluntarism promotion; Leadership development.
Type of support: Support to graduates or students of specific schools; Undergraduate support.
Application information: Application form required.
  Deadline(s): Feb. 27
  Applicants should submit the following:
    1) Transcripts
  Additional information: Contact foundation for complete program listing. Applications available at Chatham High School.
EIN: 237438319

5420
Child and Family Resources, Inc.
111 Howard Blvd., Ste. 201
Mount Arlington, NJ 07856-1315 (973) 398-1730
FAX: (973) 398-0319; URL: http://www.childandfamily-nj.org

Foundation type: Public charity

Purpose: Child care assistance and referral assistance, violence and abuse prevention, professional development assistance to professionsl in the child care field to eligible families in the New Jersey, area.
Financial data: Year ended 09/30/2011. Assets, $579,571 (M); Expenditures, $3,918,022; Total giving, $3,094,454; Grants to individuals, totaling $3,094,454.
Fields of interest: Children, services.
Type of support: Grants for special needs.
Application information: Applications accepted.
  Additional information: Financial reimbursement/ direct payment for services to eligible clients. Contact the agency for additional information.
EIN: 221985526

5421
Child Care Connection, Inc.
1001 Spruce St., Ste. 201
Trenton, NJ 08638-3957 (609) 989-7770
Contact: Clayton E. Chandler III, Pres.
FAX: (609) 989-8060;
E-mail: mail@childcareconnection-nj.org;
URL: http://www.childcareconnection-nj.org/

Foundation type: Public charity
Purpose: Child care assistance for low-income working parents for children age birth through 13 years in the Mercer county, NJ area.
Publications: Newsletter.
Financial data: Year ended 06/30/2012. Assets, $2,412,913 (M); Expenditures, $9,053,821; Total giving, $6,797,089; Grants to individuals, totaling $6,797,089.
Fields of interest: Early childhood education; Day care.
Type of support: Grants for special needs.
Application information: Applications accepted. Application form required.
  Send request by: Online, mail, or fax
  Additional information: Application should include proof of income.
EIN: 222698190

5422
Child Care Resources of Monmouth County, Inc.
(formerly Child Care Services of Monmouth County, Inc.)
3301 C Ste. Route 66 W.
P.O. Box 1234
Neptune, NJ 07754-1234 (732) 918-9901
Contact: Kim Perrelli, Exec. Dir.
FAX: (732) 918-9902; E-mail: info@ccrnj.org; E-mail For Kim Perrelli: kperrelli@ccrnj.org; E-mail FOr Richard Hall: rhall@ccrnj.org; URL: http://www.ccrnj.org

Foundation type: Public charity
Purpose: Childcare subsidies for eligible working families in Monmouth County, NJ.
Financial data: Year ended 09/30/2012. Assets, $1,671,033 (M); Expenditures, $4,755,466; Total giving, $2,968,912; Grants to individuals, totaling $2,968,912.
Fields of interest: Day care; Children, services; Family services; Children/youth; Economically disadvantaged.
Type of support: Grants for special needs.
Application information: Applications accepted. Application form required. Application form available on the grantmaker's web site.
  Initial approach: Telephone
  Send request by: Mail
  Deadline(s): Rolling

Additional information: Contact charity for further application and program information.
EIN: 223276972

5423
Children's Foundation for the Arts, Inc.
(formerly Ira B. Brown Foundation, Inc.)
500 Rte. 17 S.
Hasbrouck Heights, NJ 07604 (201) 288-5301
Contact: Maria Beerman, Exec. Dir.
URL: http://www.childrensfoundationforthesrts.org

Foundation type: Operating foundation
Purpose: Grants to children under the age of 17 who have been emotionally deprived due to a lack of a relationship with a grandparent, and who have exhibited artistic, musical, dramatic, scientific, mathematic, or other similar capacity, skill, or talent. Primarily to residents of NY, NJ, and TX.
Publications: Annual report; Informational brochure; Newsletter.
Financial data: Year ended 08/31/2013. Assets, $778,972 (M); Expenditures, $195,203; Total giving, $48,200; Grants to individuals, 103 grants totaling $48,200 (high: $750, low: $250).
Fields of interest: Music; Arts.
Type of support: Grants to individuals.
Application information: Applications accepted. Application form required. Interview required.
Deadline(s): Dec. 31
EIN: 223329717

5424
The Chubb Foundation
15 Mountain View Rd.
Warren, NJ 07059-6711
Scholarship address: c/o R & R Consultants, Attn.: Roger Lehecka, P.O. Box 250861, Columbia University Station, New York, NY 10025

Foundation type: Company-sponsored foundation
Purpose: Scholarships only to qualified relatives of employees of the Chubb Group Insurance Co., including Chubb and Son, Inc., the Colonial Life Insurance Company of America, and the Chubb Corp.
Financial data: Year ended 12/31/2012. Assets, $19,651,936 (M); Expenditures, $933,473; Total giving, $867,000; Grants to individuals, 315 grants totaling $867,000 (high: $7,000).
Fields of interest: Higher education.
Type of support: Employee-related scholarships.
Application information:
Send request by: On-line
Deadline(s): Dec. 31
EIN: 226058567

5425
The CJ Foundation for SIDS, Inc.
c/o HUMC - WFAN Pediatric Ctr.
30 Prospect Ave.
Hackensack, NJ 07601-1914 (201) 996-5111
Contact: Linda Tantawi, Exec. Dir.
FAX: (201) 996-5326; E-mail: info@cjsids.org;
Toll-free tel.: (888) 825-7437; URL: http://www.cjsids.com

Foundation type: Public charity
Purpose: Grants to researchers specializing in Sudden Infant Death Syndrome (SIDS).
Publications: Application guidelines; Grants list; Newsletter.
Financial data: Year ended 12/31/2011. Assets, $1,581,194 (M); Expenditures, $1,259,082; Total giving, $416,566.

Type of support: Research.
Application information: Applications accepted.
Initial approach: Telephone or e-mail
Additional information: See web site for complete program information.
EIN: 223280254

5426
Clayton Kiwanis Scholarship Foundation
c/o F. Gordon Myers
293 Clayton Ave.
Monroeville, NJ 08343-2652 (856) 881-4800
Contact: James J. Gaglianone, Chair.
Application address: c/o Doughty's Furniture, Inc., N. Delsea Dr., Clayton, NJ 08312

Foundation type: Independent foundation
Purpose: Scholarships to graduating seniors of Clayton High School, NJ for continuing education at institutions of higher learning.
Financial data: Year ended 12/31/2012. Assets, $90,273 (M); Expenditures, $10,600; Total giving, $10,000; Grants to individuals, 6 grants totaling $10,000 (high: $2,000, low: $1,000).
Fields of interest: Higher education.
Type of support: Support to graduates or students of specific schools.
Application information: Applications accepted. Application form required.
Deadline(s): May 15
Additional information: Applications available form guidance counselor.
EIN: 237251289

5427
The Cooper Foundation
1 Cooper Plz.
Camden, NJ 08103-1461 (856) 382-6502
Contact: Susan Bass Levin, Pres. and C.E.O.
E-mail: forman-gail@cooperhealth.edu; E-Mail for Susan Bass Levin : basslevin-susan@cooperhealth.eduTel. for Susan Bass Levin : (856)-342-2222; URL: http://www.cooperhealth.org/content/Foundation.htm

Foundation type: Public charity
Purpose: A $1,000 college scholarship annually to one outstanding student of Brimm Medical Arts High School, NJ. Also, a program available to students from Camden City high schools to work in paid internship positions at Cooper University Hospital.
Financial data: Year ended 12/31/2011. Assets, $25,222,122 (M); Expenditures, $2,372,507; Total giving, $2,266,100.
Fields of interest: Health care.
Type of support: Internship funds; Undergraduate support.
Application information:
Initial approach: Letter
Additional information: Contact foundation for eligibility criteria.
EIN: 222213715

5428
Costume Society of America, Inc.
(also known as CSA)
390 Amwell Rd., Ste. 402
Hillsborough, NJ 08844 (908) 359-1471
FAX: (908) 450-1118;
E-mail: national.office@costumesocietyamerica.com; URL: http://www.costumesocietyamerica.com

Foundation type: Public charity

Purpose: Fellowships, awards and scholarships are provided to individuals for excellence in costume design.
Publications: Application guidelines.
Financial data: Year ended 06/30/2012. Assets, $469,936 (M); Expenditures, $246,750; Total giving, $24,231; Grants to individuals, totaling $2,000.
Fields of interest: Design.
Type of support: Grants to individuals; Awards/prizes.
Application information: Applications accepted. Application form not required. Application form available on the grantmaker's web site.
Initial approach: Letter, fax or e-mail
Send request by: Mail
Deadline(s): Varies
Applicants should submit the following:
1) Photograph
2) Resume
3) Letter(s) of recommendation
4) Proposal
5) Curriculum vitae
6) Budget Information
Additional information: See web site for additional guidelines.
Program descriptions:
Adele Filene Travel Award: This $500 award is given annually on a competitive basis to society members currently enrolled as students to assist the cost of presenting oral research papers or research exhibit at a CSA national Symposium. Applicant must be full time undergraduate or graduate university student. Deadline Mar. 1.
CSA Travel Research Grants: The grant assists an individual non-student member of the society in traveling to collections for research purposes. The $1,500 grants are for travel to any library, archive, museum, or other collection or site to further an on-going research project. The grants are not limited to academic study, nor to those with academic affiliations. Recipients are encouraged to present their research to CSA members at either a regional meeting or a National CSA Symposium. Deadline Sept. 1.
Millia Davenport Publication Award: The author of this award receives $500, a certificate, and an invitation to speak at the annual Symposium of the CSA the following year. The award recognizes excellence in scholarship in the study of costume and to promote research and publication on costume. It is awarded to a published book or exhibition catalog that makes a significant contribution to the study of costume, reflects original thought and exceptional creativity, and draws on appropriate research methods and techniques. Nominations may be made by anyone and should be in the form of a letter. Deadline Jan. 15.
Stella Blum Student Research Grant: This $2,000 grant is awarded to assist the research of current undergraduate or graduate student who is a member of the CSA and working in the field of North American costume. Applicant must be a student matriculating, at the time of their funded research, in a degree granting program at an accredited institution. An additional travel component of up to $500 is awarded as a stipend to allow the recipient to present the completed research at a National Symposium. Deadline May 1.
EIN: 237362574

5429
J. Fletcher Creamer & Son Scholarship Foundation
101 E. Broadway
Hackensack, NJ 07601-6832
Contact: Estelle R. Marafino, Tr.

Foundation type: Company-sponsored foundation
Purpose: Scholarships to children and grandchildren of current employees of J. Fletcher Creamer & Son, Inc., Creamer Bros., Inc., and Signs of Safety, exclusive of these companies' owners.
Financial data: Year ended 11/30/2012. Assets, $2,055 (M); Expenditures, $10,105; Total giving, $10,000; Grants to individuals, 4 grants totaling $10,000 (high: $2,500, low: $2,500).
Type of support: Employee-related scholarships.
Application information: Applications accepted. Application form required.
  Deadline(s): Mar. 1
Company names: J. Fletcher Creamer & Son, Incorporated; Creamer Bros., Incorporated; Signs of Safety
EIN: 222870454

5430
Croatian Relief Services, Inc.
225 Anderson Ave.
P. O. Box 355
Fairview, NJ 07022-1401 (201) 945-4891
FAX: (201) 941-1344; E-mail: frgio@aol.com; Toll Free Tel. : (800)-932-4340; URL: http://www.croatianrelief.org

Foundation type: Public charity
Purpose: International relief at sites of natural disasters, political strife and war.
Financial data: Year ended 09/30/2012. Assets, $565,689 (M); Expenditures, $850,269; Total giving, $591,748.
Fields of interest: International relief.
International interests: Africa; Bosnia and Herzegovina; Central America; Croatia; Haiti.
Type of support: Grants to individuals.
Application information: Applications not accepted.
EIN: 223203653

5431
William H. & Sadie R. Cutter Trust Fund, Inc.
P.O. Box 310
Summit, NJ 07902-0310 (908) 273-5730

Foundation type: Independent foundation
Purpose: Scholarships to students of Summit High School, Summit, NJ, and Woodbridge High School, Woodbridge, NJ for postsecondary education.
Financial data: Year ended 12/31/2012. Assets, $525,933 (M); Expenditures, $24,821; Total giving, $12,250; Grants to individuals, 8 grants totaling $7,250 (high: $1,500, low: $500).
Fields of interest: Higher education.
Type of support: Support to graduates or students of specific schools; Undergraduate support.
Application information: Application form required.
  Initial approach: Letter
  Deadline(s): Mar. 31
  Applicants should submit the following:
    1) Transcripts
    2) Resume
EIN: 237096467

5432
D'Annunzio Family Foundation Inc.
136 Central Ave.
Clark, NJ 07066-1142 (732) 574-1300
Contact: Michael A. D'Annunzio, Pres.

Foundation type: Company-sponsored foundation
Purpose: Scholarships to family members of a deceased or injured construction worker, in the Bethlehem, PA metropolitan area.
Financial data: Year ended 12/31/2011. Assets, $4,378 (M); Expenditures, $0; Total giving, $0.
Type of support: Undergraduate support.
Application information: Applications not accepted.
  Additional information: Unsolicited requests for funds not considered or acknowledged.
EIN: 352305027

5433
Diabetes Foundation, Inc.
(also known as DFI)
13 Sunflower Ave.
Paramus, NJ 07652-3700 (201) 444-0337
Contact: Roberta Schmidt, Exec. Dir.
FAX: (201) 444-5580;
E-mail: info@diabetesfoundationinc.org; Toll-free tel.: (800) 633-3160; URL: http://www.diabetesinnj.org

Foundation type: Public charity
Purpose: Financial assistance to people with diabetes, and their families by providing education and funding research.
Financial data: Year ended 06/30/2012. Assets, $388,217 (M); Expenditures, $449,473; Total giving, $165,566; Grants to individuals, totaling $145,566.
Fields of interest: Diabetes; Human services.
Type of support: Grants for special needs.
Application information: Contact foundation for information on assistance.
EIN: 223551926

5434
Dirshu International, Inc.
212 2nd St., Ste. 404B
Lakewood, NJ 08701-3424
Contact: Ahron Gobioff, Tr.

Foundation type: Independent foundation
Purpose: Awards based on exam scores to individuals primarily in the NJ area, and abroad for religious education.
Financial data: Year ended 01/31/2013. Assets, $69,567 (M); Expenditures, $2,742,102; Total giving, $1,179,736; Grants to individuals, totaling $1,029,791.
Fields of interest: Theological school/education.
Type of support: Grants to individuals.
Application information: Applications accepted.
  Deadline(s): None
  Additional information: The tests are administered in the U.S. Canada, Israel and other countries.
EIN: 261870154

5435
Dow Jones News Fund, Inc.
(formerly Dow Jones Newspaper Fund, Inc.)
P.O. Box 300
Princeton, NJ 08543-0300 (609) 452-2820
Contact: Richard S. Holden, Exec. Dir.
FAX: (609) 520-5804; E-mail: djnf@dowjones.com; URL: https://www.newsfund.org/

Foundation type: Independent foundation
Purpose: Monetary awards by nomination only to high school journalism students. Scholarships by nomination only to minority high school seniors who attend the High School Journalism Workshop for Minorities or students of teachers selected through the High School Journalism Teacher of the Year Program. Fellowships to high school journalism teachers and newspaper advisors; scholarships and internships to college sophomores, juniors, seniors, and graduate students.
Publications: Application guidelines; Annual report; Grants list.
Financial data: Year ended 12/31/2011. Assets, $22,397 (M); Expenditures, $477,100; Total giving, $359,801; Grants to individuals, 44 grants totaling $42,500 (high: $1,000, low: $500).
Fields of interest: Print publishing; Education; Minorities.
Type of support: Fellowships; Internship funds; Awards/grants by nomination only; Awards/prizes; Precollege support; Undergraduate support.
Application information:
  Initial approach: Letter
  Deadline(s): July 31 for Special Awards Program and Sept. 1 for Summer Workshops Writing Competition
  Additional information: Completion of formal nomination required for the Special Awards program and The Summer Workshops Writing Competition; Individual applications not accepted; Grants awarded to recipient's school. Some programs require attendance at Dow Jones workshops for fellowships.
EIN: 136021439

5436
DRC Sannam Forum, Inc.
664 Orchard St.
Oradell, NJ 07649-1436 (201) 803-7664
Contact: Man Won Chun, Pres.

Foundation type: Independent foundation
Purpose: Scholarships to underprivileged and indigent individuals in the U.S. and Korea.
Financial data: Year ended 12/31/2011. Assets, $19,803 (M); Expenditures, $15,875; Total giving, $15,800.
Fields of interest: Economically disadvantaged.
International interests: South Korea.
Type of support: Scholarships—to individuals.
Application information: Applications accepted. Application form required.
  Initial approach: Application
  Send request by: Mail
  Deadline(s): Contact foundation for current deadline
  Applicants should submit the following:
    1) Transcripts
    2) Letter(s) of recommendation
  Additional information: Application should also include the student's vision statement.
EIN: 223681726

5437

Easter Seals of New Jersey, Inc.
25 Kennedy Blvd., Ste. 600
East Brunswick, NJ   08816-2010   (732)
257-6662
Contact: Brian J. Fitzgerald, Pres. and C.E.O.
FAX: (732) 257-7373; TTY/TDD: (732) 545-1317;
URL: http://nj.easterseals.com

Foundation type: Public charity
Purpose: Assistance to individuals with disabilities or special needs and their families of NJ, in overcoming physical, social and economic barriers.
Publications: Informational brochure.
Financial data: Year ended 08/31/2012. Assets, $20,129,374 (M); Expenditures, $99,366,406; Total giving, $33,985,907; Grants to individuals, totaling $33,985,907.
Fields of interest: Human services; Disabilities, people with.
Type of support: Grants for special needs.
Application information: Contact the organization for additional information.
EIN: 221508591

5438

Eastern Star Charity Foundation of New Jersey, Inc.
111 Findern Ave.
Bridgewater, NJ   08807-3100   (908) 725-0222

Foundation type: Public charity
Purpose: Scholarships and student loans to members of the Eastern Star of NJ. Grants to economically disadvantaged members of the Eastern Star of NJ.
Financial data: Year ended 05/31/2012. Assets, $974,442 (M); Expenditures, $227,920; Total giving, $197,939; Grants to individuals, totaling $108,930.
Fields of interest: Education; Human services; Economically disadvantaged.
Type of support: Scholarships—to individuals; Student loans—to individuals; Grants for special needs.
Application information: Applications accepted. Application form required. Interview required.
Deadline(s): Contact foundation for deadline
Applicants should submit the following:
1) Letter(s) of recommendation
2) ACT
3) SAT
EIN: 221613650

5439

Eden Autism Services Foundation, Inc.
(formerly Eden Institute Foundation)
2 Merwick Rd.
Princeton, NJ   08540-5711   (609) 987-0099
Contact: Melinda McAleer, C.D.O.
Application address: c/o Aileen Kornblatt, Eden Autism Services/ Clayton Center, 2031 Old Trenton Rd., West Windsor, NJ 08550,tel.: (609) 426-8658,
e-mail: aileen.kornblatt@edenservices.org
FAX: (609) 987-1346;
E-mail: foundation@edenservices.org; URL: http://edenautism.org/donors-2/about/

Foundation type: Public charity
Purpose: Scholarships to graduating high school seniors and to college sophomores or juniors pursuing special education careers.
Publications: Annual report.

Financial data: Year ended 06/30/2012. Assets, $22,146,490 (M); Expenditures, $3,174,721; Total giving, $1,116,271.
Fields of interest: Education, special; Higher education; Autism.
Type of support: Scholarships—to individuals.
Application information: Applications accepted. Application form required. Application form available on the grantmaker's web site.
Deadline(s): Apr. 18 for Alexis Kate Teachers Scholarship, Apr. 8 for Eden Foundation Scholarship
Applicants should submit the following:
1) Transcripts
2) Letter(s) of recommendation
3) GPA
4) Essay
Additional information: Scholarship support is provided to students living in the communities in which Eden operates its facilities. See web site for additional guidelines.
Program descriptions:
Alexis Kate Special Education Teachers Scholarship: A $500 annual scholarship is presented to a worthy college sophomore or junior who has declared a special education major and has also demonstrated extracurricular commitment to the field.
Eden Institute Foundation Scholarship: This $1,000 scholarship is offered to qualified graduating high school seniors who have made a commitment to pursue special education or a related discipline as their major field of study in college.
EIN: 224215005

5440

Embrace Kids Foundation
121 Somerset St.
The Edith and Martin Stein Bldg. of Hope
New Brunswick, NJ   08901-1945   (732)
247-5300
Contact: Glenn Jenkins, Exec. Dir.
FAX: (732) 247-5768;
E-mail: info@embracekids.org; E-mail For Glenn Jenkins: glenn@embracekids.org; URL: http://www.embracekids.org

Foundation type: Public charity
Purpose: Emergency assistance to families of children with cancer or blood disorders in NY and NJ. Scholarships to foundation program participants.
Financial data: Year ended 12/31/2012. Assets, $1,551,335 (M); Expenditures, $1,352,963; Total giving, $496,767; Grants to individuals, totaling $206,767.
Fields of interest: Education; Health care; Cancer; Children.
Type of support: Scholarships—to individuals; Grants for special needs.
Application information: Contact the foundation for eligibility determination.
Program descriptions:
Embrace Kids/Front and Center Scholarship Fund: This program provides scholarships to all current and former patients of foundation programs. The scholarship awards are paid directly to their school by Embrace Kids.
Emergency Assistance: The foundation provides emergency assistance to families of children suffering from cancer or blood disorders who live in the New York/New Jersey metropolitan area. Assistance is available for utility bills (gas, electric, phone, etc.), rent/mortgage payments, assistance

with babysitters, and transportation to and from clinics and other medical appointments.
EIN: 223092432

5441

Essex County Bar Foundation
470 Martin Luther King, Jr. Blvd., Ste. B01
Newark, NJ   07102-1734   (973) 622-6207

Foundation type: Public charity
Purpose: Scholarships to financially needy students attending Rutgers University School of Law, NJ, or Seton Hall University School of Law, NJ.
Publications: Newsletter.
Financial data: Year ended 05/31/2012. Assets, $295,351 (M); Expenditures, $78,462; Total giving, $6,000; Grants to individuals, totaling $6,000.
Fields of interest: Law school/education; Disabilities, people with.
Type of support: Graduate support.
Application information: Applications accepted. Application form required. Interview required.
Initial approach: Letter or telephone
Deadline(s): Apr. 25
Program description:
Scholarships: Scholarships are available to students entering Rutgers-Newark School or Seton Hall University of Law.
EIN: 221661299

5442

Everly Scholarship Fund Inc.
c/o John R. Lolio, Esq, Sherman Silver
308 Harper Dr., Ste. 200
Moorestown, NJ   08057-3245

Foundation type: Independent foundation
Purpose: Undergraduate scholarships to graduates of high schools in southern NJ.
Financial data: Year ended 03/31/2012. Assets, $2,601,077 (M); Expenditures, $185,748; Total giving, $151,876.
Type of support: Support to graduates or students of specific schools; Undergraduate support.
Application information: Application form required.
Initial approach: Letter or telephone
Deadline(s): None
Applicants should submit the following:
1) SAT
2) GPA
EIN: 223161410

5443

Excelsior Scottish Rite Bodies Charity Fund, Inc.
315 White Horse Pike
West Collingswood, NJ   08107   (856) 854-1991
Application address: Scottish Rite Temple, Attn: Secretary's Office

Foundation type: Independent foundation
Purpose: Scholarships to residents of Atlantic, Burlington, Camden, Cape May, Cumberland, Gloucester, Ocean, or Salem counties, NJ who are sons and daughters of any living or deceased Master Freemason.
Publications: Application guidelines.
Financial data: Year ended 07/31/2013. Assets, $2,018,944 (M); Expenditures, $144,789; Total giving, $131,568.
Fields of interest: Fraternal societies.
Type of support: Undergraduate support.

Application information: Applications accepted. Application form required.
Deadline(s): Apr. 1
Applicants should submit the following:
1) Resume
2) Transcripts
Additional information: Application must also include information on scholastic honors, extracurricular and community activities, hobbies, family background, and anticipated course of study. This scholarship is $2,000 per year, for up to four years, and may be used for undergraduate education.
EIN: 222917990

5444
Family Outreach Foundation
5 Wilson St.
Mendham, NJ   07945-1403

Foundation type: Independent foundation
Purpose: Medical assistance to financially needy children.
Financial data: Year ended 12/31/2012. Assets, $100,211 (M); Expenditures, $58,967; Total giving, $52,271; Grants to individuals, 28 grants totaling $50,897 (high: $5,000, low: $375).
Fields of interest: Medical care, outpatient care; Children; Economically disadvantaged.
Type of support: Grants for special needs.
Application information: Applications accepted. Application form required.
Initial approach: Letter
Additional information: Application must state child's medical condition and purpose of contribution.
EIN: 223788982

5445
First Brokers Good Samaritan Fund
Harborside Financial Ctr.
Plz. 5, Ste. 1500
Jersey City, NJ   07311   (212) 513-4466

Foundation type: Independent foundation
Purpose: Grants primarily to individuals affected by September 11, 2001. Support also to economically disadvantaged individuals for payment of medical bills and other needs.
Financial data: Year ended 12/31/2012. Assets, $230,607 (M); Expenditures, $52,560; Total giving, $45,000; Grants to individuals, 2 grants totaling $15,000 (high: $10,000, low: $5,000).
Fields of interest: Human services; Economically disadvantaged.
Type of support: Grants for special needs.
Application information: Applications accepted.
Initial approach: Letter
Deadline(s): None
EIN: 137298341

5446
Margaret and Thomas Flynn Scholarship Fund
c/o Roberta A. Jones , ESQ
155 U.S. Hwy. 46, Plz. II
Wayne, NJ   07470

Foundation type: Independent foundation
Purpose: Scholarships to individuals residing in Hewitt, NJ, for higher education.
Financial data: Year ended 12/31/2012. Assets, $0 (M); Expenditures, $7,212; Total giving, $4,000; Grants to individuals, 2 grants totaling $4,000 (high: $2,000, low: $2,000).

Type of support: Scholarships—to individuals.
Application information: Applications not accepted.
Additional information: Unsolicited requests for funds not considered or acknowledged.
EIN: 226690913

5447
FMI Scholarship Foundation, Inc.
(formerly Franklin Mutual Insurance Scholarship Foundation, Inc.)
P.O. Box 400
Branchville, NJ   07826-0400

Foundation type: Company-sponsored foundation
Purpose: Scholarships to high school students of Sussex, NJ, for postsecondary education.
Financial data: Year ended 12/31/2012. Assets, $25,000 (M); Expenditures, $70,780; Total giving, $69,000; Grants to individuals, 30 grants totaling $69,000 (high: $3,000, low: $500).
Fields of interest: Higher education.
Type of support: Undergraduate support.
Application information: Unsolicited requests for funds not considered or acknowledged.
EIN: 223394738

5448
Charles Le Geyt Fortescue Fund
c/o IEEE Foundation
445 Hoes Ln.
Piscataway, NJ   08854-4141   (732) 562-3842
URL: http://www.ieee.org/index.html

Foundation type: Independent foundation
Purpose: Scholarship to a first-year full time graduate student for work in the field of electrical engineering at an engineering school of recognized standing in the U.S.
Financial data: Year ended 12/31/2012. Assets, $381,198 (M); Expenditures, $24,372; Total giving, $20,000.
Fields of interest: Engineering.
Type of support: Graduate support.
Application information: Applications accepted. Application form required.
Deadline(s): Nov. 15
EIN: 256030358

5449
Foundation for the Art Renewal Center, Inc.
100 Markley St.
Port Reading, NJ   07064
URL: http://www.artrenewal.org

Foundation type: Operating foundation
Purpose: Scholarships to artists for attendance at an approved program, whose work reflects classical technique. Awards also to winners of the organization's Annual Open Competition.
Financial data: Year ended 12/31/2012. Assets, $651,878 (M); Expenditures, $173,468; Total giving, $44,609.
Fields of interest: Painting; Art history.
Type of support: Graduate support; Undergraduate support.
Application information: Applications accepted. Application form required. Application form available on the grantmaker's web site.
Send request by: E-mail
Deadline(s): May
Applicants should submit the following:
1) Curriculum vitae
2) Letter(s) of recommendation

3) Work samples
4) Essay
Additional information: Application should also include biography. See web site for further application information.
EIN: 043598440

5450
Alexia Foundation for World Peace, Inc.
P.O. Box 87
Bloomingdale, NJ   07403
URL: http://www.alexiafoundation.org

Foundation type: Independent foundation
Purpose: Scholarships for students to study photojournalism at Syracuse University in London, England. Awards to professional photographers whose photojournalism projects further cultural understanding and promote world peace.
Financial data: Year ended 12/31/2011. Assets, $543,045 (M); Expenditures, $102,968; Total giving, $36,000; Grants to individuals, 9 grants totaling $28,000 (high: $12,000, low: $500).
Fields of interest: Print publishing; Photography.
Type of support: Awards/prizes; Undergraduate support; Travel grants.
Application information:
Initial approach: E-mail
Copies of proposal: 1
Deadline(s): Feb. 1 for Student Competition, Jan. 18 for Professional Competition
Applicants should submit the following:
1) Work samples
2) Proposal
3) Essay
4) Resume
Additional information: Application by proposal of up to 750 words, including project resume, three references, and portfolio of up to 20 photographs; See web site for further application information and to submit proposal.
Program descriptions:
Professional Alexia Grants: The foundation offers this professional grant to enable a photographer to have the financial ability to produce a substantial picture story that furthers the foundation's goals of promoting world peace and cultural understanding. Recipient will receive $15,000 for the production of the proposed project.
Student Alexia Grants: The foundation helps to provide the financial ability for students to improve their knowledge and skills of photojournalism and to increase their own knowledge and understanding of other cultures by providing scholarships to study photojournalism at Syracuse University in London, England.
EIN: 223114228

5451
Friends of Marty Wilson
(formerly Marty Wilson Scholarship Fund)
c/o John T. Reed
505 Cape Island Ct.
Egg Harbor Township, NJ   08234-7273   (609) 646-3000

Foundation type: Independent foundation
Purpose: Scholarship to one male and one female Holy Spirit High School student-athlete to assist with their financial needs in pursuit of a college degree.
Financial data: Year ended 12/31/2011. Assets, $10,157 (M); Expenditures, $1,529; Total giving, $1,500; Grant to an individual, 1 grant totaling $1,500.

Fields of interest: Higher education.
Type of support: Support to graduates or students of specific schools.
Application information: Applications accepted. Application form required.
> *Deadline(s):* Apr. 16
> *Final notification:* Applicants notified by May 20
> *Additional information:* Application should include a transcript and a copy of parents' and applicant's income tax return.

EIN: 223228665

5452

The Giants Foundation, Inc.

Giants Stadium
50 Rte. 120
East Rutherford, NJ   07073-2131   (201) 935-8111
Contact: Allison Stangeby, Exec. Dir.
E-mail: Stangeby@giants.nfl.net; For GameOn! Grant Program: c/o Allison Stangeby, Community Rels. Dept., tel.: (201) 939-1673; URL: http://www.giants.com/Community.asp

Foundation type: Company-sponsored foundation
Purpose: Grants to recreational or high school NY or NJ football coaches for team costs.
Publications: Application guidelines; Annual report.
Financial data: Year ended 12/31/2012. Assets, $274,851 (M); Expenditures, $450,363; Total giving, $437,000.
Fields of interest: Athletics/sports, football.
Type of support: Program development; Project support.
Application information: Applications accepted. Application form not required.
> *Initial approach:* Proposal
> *Copies of proposal:* 1
> *Deadline(s):* Oct. 1st through Dec. 31 each year
> *Applicants should submit the following:*
>   1) Budget Information
>   2) Financial information

Program description:
> *GameOn! Grant Program:* The foundation awards grants of up to $2,500 to recreational and high school football coaches on behalf of local youth football teams. Grants may be used for football equipment purchases, football uniforms, insurance costs, and transportation to games for children.

EIN: 223183916

5453

Glen Rock Unified Scholarship Council, Inc.

(formerly Glen Rock High School Unified Scholarship Council, Inc.)
400 Hamilton Ave.
Glen Rock, NJ   07452

Foundation type: Operating foundation
Purpose: Scholarships to seniors at Glen Rock High School, NJ, for attendance at accredited colleges, universities, and training programs.
Financial data: Year ended 06/30/2010. Assets, $0 (M); Expenditures, $1,809; Total giving, $1,400.
Fields of interest: Vocational education; Higher education.
Type of support: Support to graduates or students of specific schools; Undergraduate support.
Application information:
> *Initial approach:* Letter
> *Deadline(s):* June

EIN: 226053789

5454

The Robert J. Glushko and Pamela Samuelson Foundation

P.O. Box 1501, NJ2-130-03-31
Pennington, NJ   08534-1501

Foundation type: Independent foundation
Purpose: Awards and prizes to an individual or collaborative team making a significant contemporary contribution to the theoretical foundations of human cognition.
Financial data: Year ended 02/28/2013. Assets, $121,334 (M); Expenditures, $102,740; Total giving, $100,000.
Fields of interest: Science.
Type of support: Awards/grants by nomination only; Awards/prizes.
Application information:
> *Deadline(s):* Jan. 12
> *Additional information:* Nomination materials should include a three-page statement of nomination, a complete curriculum vitae and copies of up to five of the nominee's relevant publications.

Program description:
> *Rumelhart Prize in Cognitive Science:* The prize consists of a hand-crafted, custom bronze medal, a certificate, a citation of the awardee's contribution, and a monetary award of $100,000. The foundation sponsors the Rumelhart Prize in Cognitive Science which is awarded annually by the Cognitive Science Society. Web site for awards: http://rumelhartprize.org.

EIN: 943357746

5455

Ruth Estrin Goldberg Memorial for Cancer Research

c/o Greenberg & Co.
P. O. Box 194
Springfield, NJ   07081-0194   (732) 574-8848
Contact: Rhoda Goodman
Mailing address for Rhoda Goodman: 653 Colonial Arms Rd., Union, NJ 07803-7605; Tel. for Rhoda Goodman: (908) 686-5508

Foundation type: Public charity
Purpose: Grants for cancer research to individuals who work in NY, NJ or PA.
Publications: Occasional report.
Financial data: Year ended 05/31/2010. Assets, $39,240 (M); Expenditures, $39,011; Total giving, $36,000.
Fields of interest: Cancer; Cancer research.
Type of support: Research.
Application information: Applications accepted. Application form required.
> *Initial approach:* Letter or telephone
> *Send request by:* Mail
> *Copies of proposal:* 12
> *Deadline(s):* May 1
> *Final notification:* Applicants notified at the end of June
> *Applicants should submit the following:*
>   1) Work samples
>   2) Proposal

EIN: 226029605

5456

Trooper Scott Gonzalez Memorial Scholarship Fund

12 Belmont Ct.
Pittstown, NJ   08867   (908) 238-5207
Contact: Maureen Gonzalez Pres.

Foundation type: Independent foundation

Purpose: Scholarships to family members of NJ state troopers, as well as NJ residents interested in entering the field of law enforcement.
Financial data: Year ended 12/31/2012. Assets, $164,899 (M); Expenditures, $78,109; Total giving, $62,000; Grant to an individual, 1 grant totaling $62,000.
Fields of interest: Crime/law enforcement.
Type of support: Undergraduate support.
Application information: Applications accepted. Application form required.
> *Initial approach:* Letter
> *Applicants should submit the following:*
>   1) Essay
> *Additional information:* Contact foundation for eligibility criteria.

EIN: 223591586

5457

Lauren Catuzzi Grandcolas Foundation

65 Merrywood Ln.
Short Hills, NJ   07078
URL: http://www.lcgfoundation.org/grants.htm

Foundation type: Independent foundation
Purpose: Scholarships to graduating high school female pursuing higher education at accredited colleges or universities.
Financial data: Year ended 12/31/2012. Assets, $161,920 (M); Expenditures, $37,187; Total giving, $35,500.
Fields of interest: Higher education.
Type of support: Scholarships—to individuals.
Application information: Applications accepted. Application form required. Interview required.
> *Deadline(s):* Apr. 15
> *Applicants should submit the following:*
>   1) Letter(s) of recommendation
>   2) Essay
> *Additional information:* Applicants must demonstrate academic achievement, commitment to physical activity, community involvement and show a strong sense of independence.

EIN: 760692927

5458

Raven Leigh Grande Memorial Foundation, Inc.

P.O. Box 339
Park Ridge, NJ   07656-0339   (845) 753-5084
Contact: Kim T. Grande, V.P.

Foundation type: Independent foundation
Purpose: Scholarships to graduates of Park Ridge High School, NJ, who will be majoring in education or the performing arts in college.
Financial data: Year ended 12/31/2011. Assets, $136,405 (M); Expenditures, $6,810; Total giving, $5,250.
Fields of interest: Performing arts; Teacher school/education.
Type of support: Support to graduates or students of specific schools.
Application information: Applications accepted. Application form required.
> *Deadline(s):* June 30

EIN: 010782787

5459
Greater Community Educational Foundation, Inc.
1455 Valley Rd.
Wayne, NJ 07470-2089 (973) 305-8506
Contact: Anthony M. Bruno, Jr., Pres.
Application address: 1195 Hamburg Tpke., Wayne, NJ 07470

Foundation type: Company-sponsored foundation
Purpose: College scholarships to students who show proof of admission for freshman year of college and proof for the ensuing three years of education.
Financial data: Year ended 12/31/2011. Assets, $164,230 (M); Expenditures, $15,630; Total giving, $15,500; Grants to individuals, 7 grants totaling $15,500 (high: $3,500, low: $1,250).
Fields of interest: Higher education.
Type of support: Scholarships—to individuals.
Application information: Applications accepted. Application form required.
  Deadline(s): The calendar year preceding applicant's first year of college
  Additional information: Application must include an essay.
EIN: 223705689

5460
Frank and Louise Groff Foundation
c/o Susan Rechel
15 Whitehall Rd.
Monroe, NJ 08831 (609) 235-9318
Contact: Susan Rechel
URL: http://www.groff-foundation.org/

Foundation type: Independent foundation
Purpose: Scholarships to graduates of Red Bank National Regional High School, graduates from any public high school in Monmouth County, NJ or graduates from any public school in NJ pursuing a career in nursing or medicine.
Publications: Application guidelines.
Financial data: Year ended 06/30/2013. Assets, $379,666 (M); Expenditures, $23,157; Total giving, $6,700; Grants to individuals, 9 grants totaling $6,700 (high: $1,000, low: $500).
Fields of interest: Medical school/education; Nursing school/education.
Type of support: Support to graduates or students of specific schools; Undergraduate support.
Application information: Applications accepted. Application form required. Interview required.
  Deadline(s): Mar. 15
  Applicants should submit the following:
    1) Transcripts
    2) Financial information
  Additional information: Application available at Monmouth County, NJ, public high schools. Selection is based on financial need.
EIN: 237082026

5461
The Gruenberg Foundation
50 N. Franklin Tpke., Ste. 206
Hohokus, NJ 07423-1562 (201) 652-0404

Foundation type: Independent foundation
Purpose: Scholarships to high school seniors who attend Tri-State University, IN, as undergraduates, are U.S. citizens, and have been residents of Ridgewood, NJ, for four years.
Financial data: Year ended 09/30/2013. Assets, $6,229,144 (M); Expenditures, $321,957; Total giving, $107,343; Grants to individuals, 18 grants totaling $107,343 (high: $15,000, low: $1,650).

Type of support: Support to graduates or students of specific schools; Undergraduate support.
Application information: Applications accepted.
  Initial approach: Letter or telephone
  Deadline(s): Mar. 1
EIN: 223381175

5462
William F. Grupe Foundation, Inc.
c/o TD Banknorth
1500 U.S. Hwy. 202, Ste. 201
Basking Ridge, NJ 07920-1646
Contact: Barbara Driscoll, Secy.

Foundation type: Independent foundation
Purpose: Medical, nursing, and paramedical scholarships only to needy residents of Bergen, Essex, and Hudson counties, NJ, planning to practice within the state.
Publications: Application guidelines.
Financial data: Year ended 12/31/2012. Assets, $968,273 (M); Expenditures, $74,965; Total giving, $49,000.
Fields of interest: Medical school/education; Nursing school/education.
Type of support: Graduate support; Undergraduate support.
Application information: Applications accepted. Application form required.
  Deadline(s): Mar. 1
EIN: 226094704

5463
Paul Gubitosi Charitable Fund Inc.
5 Joshua Dr.
Hillsborough, NJ 08844

Foundation type: Operating foundation
Purpose: Scholarships to residents of the Hillsborough, Somerset county NJ area for higher education.
Financial data: Year ended 12/31/2012. Assets, $4,119 (M); Expenditures, $57,224; Total giving, $32,650.
Type of support: Scholarships—to individuals.
Application information: Unsolicited requests for funds not accepted.
EIN: 810547982

5464
The Jen Hale Memorial Foundation, Inc.
P.O. Box 1400
Voorhees, NJ 08043-1400 (856) 768-1330
Contact: Barry J. Hale, Tr.

Foundation type: Independent foundation
Purpose: Scholarships to graduating seniors from Eastern Regional High School, NJ and local high schools for attendance at colleges or universities.
Financial data: Year ended 12/31/2011. Assets, $113,403 (M); Expenditures, $55,521; Total giving, $55,000; Grant to an individual, 1 grant totaling $2,500.
Fields of interest: Higher education.
Type of support: Support to graduates or students of specific schools; Undergraduate support.
Application information: Applications accepted. Application form required.
  Deadline(s): May 1
  Applicants should submit the following:
    1) SAT
    2) Essay

Additional information: Applicant must demonstrate financial need, academic and other achievements.
EIN: 311703194

5465
Kevin J. Hannaford, Sr. Foundation Inc.
P.O. Box 113
Basking Ridge, NJ 07920-0113 (908) 221-1825
URL: http://www.kevinhannaford.org

Foundation type: Independent foundation
Purpose: Scholarships to residents of Bernards Township, NJ, and Bernardsville, NJ, who have lost a parent.
Financial data: Year ended 12/31/2012. Assets, $271,044 (M); Expenditures, $80,150; Total giving, $29,000; Grants to individuals, 9 grants totaling $23,000 (high: $3,000, low: $1,000).
Type of support: Undergraduate support.
Application information: Applications accepted. Application form required. Application form available on the grantmaker's web site.
  Deadline(s): Apr. 15
EIN: 341982414

5466
Harness Horsemen International Foundation, Inc.
319 High St.
Burlington, NJ 08016

Foundation type: Independent foundation
Purpose: Scholarships to a son or daughter of a full-time Standardbred groom or the son or daughter of a member of a Harness Horsemen International affiliated association.
Financial data: Year ended 12/31/2012. Assets, $26,589 (M); Expenditures, $4,609; Total giving, $4,000; Grants to individuals, 2 grants totaling $4,000 (high: $2,000, low: $2,000).
Fields of interest: Higher education; Scholarships/financial aid.
Type of support: Undergraduate support.
Application information: Applications accepted. Application form required.
  Initial approach: Letter
  Deadline(s): June 1
  Applicants should submit the following:
    1) Photograph
    2) SAT
    3) ACT
    4) Essay
    5) Transcripts
    6) Letter(s) of recommendation
Program description:
  Jerome L. Hauck Scholarship: A $4,000 college scholarship at $1,000 per school year for students who have demonstrated exceptional scholarship, citizenship, and leadership, have completed high school or its equivalent and is entering college for the first time. Character and personality traits are also reviewed in the selection process, and financial need is a consideration as well.
EIN: 061182260

5467
Health and Welfare Fund Local 456
c/o I. E. Shaffer & Co.
830 Bear Tavern Rd.
West Trenton, NJ 08628-1020

Foundation type: Public charity

Purpose: Medical insurance reimbursements to members of Local 456.
Financial data: Year ended 12/31/2011. Assets, $16,498,714 (M); Expenditures, $20,631,920; Total giving, $19,899,315; Grants to individuals, totaling $19,899,315.
Fields of interest: Insurance, providers.
Type of support: Grants for special needs.
Application information: Applications not accepted.
EIN: 222317253

5468
Hemophilia Association of New Jersey

197 Route 18 S., Ste. 206 N.
P. O. Box 16
East Brunswick, NJ   08816-1440   (732) 249-6000
Contact: Elena Bostick, Exec. Dir.
FAX: (732) 249-7999; E-mail: hemnj@comcast.net; E-mail For Elena Bostick: ebostick@comcast.net; URL: http://www.hanj.org

Foundation type: Public charity
Purpose: Scholarships to students of NJ presently enrolled in an accredited institution of academic and/or vocational higher learning or those beginning a formal program in the fall.
Financial data: Year ended 06/30/2012. Assets, $4,009,983 (M); Expenditures, $1,875,611; Total giving, $600,087.
Fields of interest: Vocational education, post-secondary; Higher education; Hemophilia.
Type of support: Scholarships—to individuals.
Application information: Applications accepted. Application form not required.
> *Additional information:* Selection is based on financial need and/or academic ability. Contact the association for additional scholarship opportunities.

Program description:
> *Scholarships:* A $1,500 scholarship for full time undergraduate students is renewable for up to three additional years, while enrolled in college or trade school. $2,000 scholarships, renewable for up to one year, are available to full-time graduate students with hemophilia. Part time graduate students taking six credit hours per semester for two semesters (fall/winter, spring/summer) will apply for $1,000 scholarship, renewable for three additional years. Applicants must submit a present grade transcript, proof of enrollment at a college or trade school and a brief letter of accomplishment and future plans. Grade point standing of 2.5 or better is needed to apply.

EIN: 221964188

5469
Adelaide Hollander Scholarship Foundation, Inc.

1201 New Rd., Ste. 204
Linwood, NJ   08221   (609) 927-1177
Application address: c/o Bacharach Institute for Rehabilitation, 61 W. Jimmie Leeds Rd., Pomona, NJ 08240-0723, tel.: (609) 927-1177

Foundation type: Operating foundation
Purpose: Scholarships to children of regular full-time employees of the Bacharach Institute for Rehabilitation for full time study at an accredited college or university.
Financial data: Year ended 12/31/2012. Assets, $2,208 (M); Expenditures, $14,176; Total giving, $14,000; Grants to individuals, 14 grants totaling $14,000 (high: $1,000, low: $1,000).
Fields of interest: Higher education.

Type of support: Employee-related scholarships.
Application information: Applications accepted. Application form required.
> *Deadline(s):* June 30
> *Applicants should submit the following:*
> 1) Essay
> 2) Letter(s) of recommendation
> 3) Transcripts
> *Additional information:* Scholarships are paid directly to the institution on behalf of the recipient.

EIN: 223217578

5470
Pauline Hollander Scholarship Fund for Registered Nurses Inc.

1201 New Rd., Ste. 204
Linwood, NJ   08221-1154   (609) 927-1177
Application address: 61 W. Jimmie Leeds Rd., Pomona, NJ 082400723 Tel:(609) 927-1177

Foundation type: Independent foundation
Purpose: Scholarships to residents of Atlantic County, NJ pursuing a Registered Nursing degree program in Atlantic county, NJ.
Financial data: Year ended 12/31/2011. Assets, $16,391 (M); Expenditures, $13,179; Total giving, $13,000.
Fields of interest: Nursing school/education.
Type of support: Scholarships—to individuals.
Application information: Applications accepted. Application form required.
> *Deadline(s):* June 30
> *Applicants should submit the following:*
> 1) Transcripts
> 2) Letter(s) of recommendation
> 3) Essay

EIN: 223229943

5471
The Jeffrey S. Holman Foundation

1 Centennial Sq.
Haddonfield, NJ   08033-2332
Application address: c/o Frank R. Demmerly, Jr., Archer & Greiner PC, P.O. Box 3000, Haddonfield, NJ 08033, tel.: (856) 354-3100

Foundation type: Independent foundation
Purpose: Scholarship/loans to graduating seniors of Haddonfield Memorial High School, NJ, for higher education.
Financial data: Year ended 12/31/2012. Assets, $2,361,949 (M); Expenditures, $141,206; Total giving, $137,613; Grants to individuals, 79 grants totaling $137,613 (high: $4,000, low: $598).
Fields of interest: Higher education.
Type of support: Student loans—to individuals; Support to graduates or students of specific schools.
Application information: Applications accepted. Application form required.
> *Initial approach:* Letter
> *Deadline(s):* Apr. 15
> *Applicants should submit the following:*
> 1) Transcripts
> 2) SAT
> 3) Financial information
> 4) Essay

EIN: 223351283

5472
Honeywell Corporate Giving Program

(formerly AlliedSignal Inc. Corporate Giving Program)
101 Columbia Rd.
Morristown, NJ   07962-2245
URL: http://www.honeywell.com/sites/hhs

Foundation type: Corporate giving program
Purpose: Grants to middle school (grades 6-8) math and science teachers to attend a five-day program at the U.S. Space and Rocket Center in Huntsville, AL. Grants to middle and high school science and social studies teachers to attend a four-day institute on ecosystems.
Publications: Application guidelines.
Fields of interest: Teacher school/education; Environmental education; Environment; Safety/disasters; Science; Space/aviation; Mathematics.
Type of support: Grants to individuals; Travel grants; Stipends.
Application information: Applications accepted. Application form required.
> *Initial approach:* Application
> *Send request by:* Mail or e-mail
> *Deadline(s):* June for Honeywell Institute for Ecosystems Education
> *Additional information:* Application should include an essay. See website for additional guidelines.

Program descriptions:
> *Honeywell Educators @ Space Academy:* Honeywell, in partnership with the U.S. Space and Rocket Center, annually awards 100 scholarships to middle school science and math teachers to attend a five-day program of intensive classroom, laboratory, and training time focusing on space science and space exploration at the U.S. Space and Rocket Center in Huntsville, Alabama.
> *Honeywell Institute for Ecosystems Foundation:* Honeywell, in partnership with the New Jersey Audubon Society, Montezuma Audubon Center, Onondaga Audubon Society, and the Maryland Science Center, awards stipends and scholarships to middle and high school science and social studies teachers to attend a four-day institute in August to learn about ecosystems. The institute is designed to teach education techniques to integrate environmental science into curriculums.

5473
Irving Louis Horowitz Foundation for Research in Social Policy

1247 State Rd., Rte. 206
Princeton, NJ   08540-1619   (609) 921-1479
Contact: Mary E. Curtis, Chair.
URL: http://www.horowitz-foundation.org/

Foundation type: Independent foundation
Purpose: Research grants to individuals for work in major areas of the social sciences.
Financial data: Year ended 03/31/2013. Assets, $3,570,971 (M); Expenditures, $93,275; Total giving, $81,069.
Fields of interest: Social sciences; Anthropology/sociology; Economics; Psychology/behavioral science; Political science; Urban studies.
Type of support: Research.
Application information: Applications accepted. Application form required. Application form available on the grantmaker's web site.
> *Initial approach:* Letter, e-mail or website
> *Send request by:* E-mail (preferred) or mail
> *Deadline(s):* Jan. 31
> *Final notification:* Recipients notified in May
> *Applicants should submit the following:*
> 1) Proposal

2) Curriculum vitae
3) Budget Information
Additional information: See foundation web site for complete application guidelines.
EIN: 311612153

5474
Houton Scholarship Foundation
300 Central Ave.
Egg Harbor Township, NJ 08234-8327 (609) 513-2727
Contact: Mina Houton Salartash, Tr.
URL: http://www.houtan.org/

Foundation type: Independent foundation
Purpose: Scholarships to students who have an interest in pursuing a course of study in Iranian culture and a working knowledge of the Farsi language or a willingness to learn.
Financial data: Year ended 12/31/2011. Assets, $250,865 (M); Expenditures, $40,117; Total giving, $35,624.
International interests: Iran.
Type of support: Scholarships—to individuals.
Application information: Applications accepted. Application form required.
Deadline(s): None
EIN: 223655423

5475
Herbert J. and Geneva S. Hull Scholarship Fund, Inc.
28 Hillside Ave.
Newton, NJ 07860-1202

Foundation type: Independent foundation
Purpose: Scholarships to residents of Sussex County, NJ, who are preparing for a career in conservation or environmental science through full-time postsecondary education.
Financial data: Year ended 12/31/2012. Assets, $453,586 (M); Expenditures, $20,500; Total giving, $20,500.
Fields of interest: Natural resources; Animals/wildlife, preservation/protection.
Type of support: Undergraduate support.
Application information: Application form required. Interview required.
Deadline(s): May 15
Applicants should submit the following:
1) Transcripts
2) Letter(s) of recommendation
Additional information: Application should also include letter outlining citizenship, scholarship, and career potential in conservation.
EIN: 223173661

5476
IEEE Foundation, Inc.
445 Hoes Ln.
Piscataway, NJ 08854-4141 (732) 981-3435
Contact: Karen Galuchie, Dir. Foundation Operations
FAX: (732) 981-9019;
E-mail: foundation-office@ieee.org; URL: http://www.ieeefoundation.org

Foundation type: Public charity
Purpose: Awards by nomination only to technical professionals for exceptional achievements and outstanding contributions that have made a lasting impact on technology, society and the engineering profession.

Publications: Application guidelines; Annual report; Financial statement; Grants list; Informational brochure; Newsletter.
Financial data: Year ended 12/31/2012. Assets, $36,983,423 (M); Expenditures, $4,155,093; Total giving, $3,040,448; Grants to individuals, totaling $379,791.
Fields of interest: Engineering school/education; Engineering.
Type of support: Fellowships; Scholarships—to individuals; Awards/grants by nomination only; Awards/prizes; Travel grants.
Application information: Application form required.
Initial approach: Letter or e-mail
Additional information: See web site for additional information.
EIN: 237310664

5477
The Infinity Foundation, Inc.
66 Witherspoon St.
Princeton, NJ 08542 (609) 683-0548
Contact: Rajiv Malhotra, Pres. and Treas.
E-mail: mail@infinityfoundation.com; URL: http://www.infinityfoundation.com

Foundation type: Independent foundation
Purpose: Research grants for scientific purposes to individuals, in the U.S., England, and India.
Financial data: Year ended 06/30/2013. Assets, $3,568,444 (M); Expenditures, $214,084; Total giving, $34,581; Grants to individuals, 7 grants totaling $34,042 (high: $17,083, low: $349).
Type of support: Research.
Application information:
Initial approach: Proposal
Additional information: Contact foundation for current application guidelines.
EIN: 223339826

5478
Ingersoll-Rand Charitable Foundation
1 Centennial Ave.
Piscataway, NJ 08854-3921
Contact: Misty Zelent
URL: http://company.ingersollrand.com/ircorp/en/discover-us/our-company/community-relations/ingersoll-rand-foundation.html

Foundation type: Company-sponsored foundation
Purpose: Grants to individuals affected by Hurricane Katrina.
Financial data: Year ended 12/31/2012. Assets, $592,010 (M); Expenditures, $3,007,471; Total giving, $2,933,306.
Fields of interest: Disasters, Hurricane Katrina.
Type of support: Emergency funds; Grants to individuals.
Application information: Applications not accepted.
Additional information: Unsolicited requests for funds not considered.
EIN: 202045897

5479
Abdol H. Islami, M.D. Foundation Inc.
(formerly Comprehensive Medical Review Course, Inc.)
c/o Susann Islami Donohue
35 Morris Dr.
Princeton, NJ 08540
Contact: Susann Islami Do No Hue

Foundation type: Independent foundation

Purpose: Scholarships to NJ residents for the study of medicine and related fields.
Financial data: Year ended 12/31/2012. Assets, $2,591,174 (M); Expenditures, $130,558; Total giving, $110,000; Grants to individuals, 24 grants totaling $110,000 (high: $15,000, low: $3,000).
Fields of interest: Medical school/education.
Type of support: Scholarships—to individuals.
Application information: Applications accepted. Application form required.
Deadline(s): Apr. 20
EIN: 222111419

5480
George Jackson Scholarship Foundation
(formerly George Jackson Trust)
c/o Peapack Gladstone Bank
500 Hills Dr., Ste 300
P.O. Box 7037
Bedminster, NJ 07921 (908) 719-4360

Foundation type: Independent foundation
Purpose: Scholarships to students of Sussex County high schools, NJ, who are also residents of Sussex County.
Financial data: Year ended 12/31/2011. Assets, $1,205,230 (M); Expenditures, $135,715; Total giving, $121,000; Grants to individuals, totaling $121,000.
Type of support: Support to graduates or students of specific schools; Undergraduate support.
Application information: Application form required.
Additional information: Contact guidance departments for application and deadlines.
EIN: 226474357

5481
Johnson & Johnson Patient Assistance Foundation, Inc.
(formerly Janssen Ortho Patient Assistance Foundation, Inc.)
1 Johnson & Johnson Plz.
New Brunswick, NJ 08933-0001
Contact: Denise Sitarikev, V.P.
FAX: (888) 526-5168; E-mail: dsitarik@jnj.com;
Application address: Patient Assistance Program, P.O. Box 221857, Charlotte, NC 28222-1857; Additional tel.: (866) 317-2775, (800) 652-6227; URL: http://www.jjpaf.org/

Foundation type: Operating foundation
Purpose: Grants of pharmaceutical products to needy individuals who lack prescription drug coverage.
Publications: Application guidelines; Informational brochure.
Financial data: Year ended 12/31/2012. Assets, $69,921,484 (M); Expenditures, $628,527,654; Total giving, $611,680,261; Grants to individuals, 152,000 grants totaling $611,680,261.
Fields of interest: Health care; Human services; Economically disadvantaged.
Type of support: Grants for special needs.
Application information: Applications accepted. Application form required.
Initial approach: Application
Send request by: Mail or fax
Deadline(s): None
Additional information: Application must be completed and signed, accompanied by proof of income and a HIPAA release form signed by patient. Application should include most recent tax return.
EIN: 311520982

5482
Barbara Piasecka Johnson Foundation
c/o BJP Holding Corp.
4519 Province Line Rd.
Princeton, NJ 08540-6627 (609) 688-1030
Contact: Christopher Piasecka, Treas.

Foundation type: Independent foundation
Purpose: Fellowships to graduate, doctoral, and postgraduate students who are Polish or of Polish descent.
Financial data: Year ended 12/31/2012. Assets, $4,766,082 (M); Expenditures, $71,177; Total giving, $63,424; Grants to individuals, 6 grants totaling $58,424 (high: $23,864, low: $3,923).
Fields of interest: Arts, artist's services; Research.
International interests: Poland.
Type of support: Program development; Research; Foreign applicants; Graduate support; Postgraduate support; Doctoral support.
Application information: Application form required.
Initial approach: Letter or telephone
Deadline(s): Mar. 30 and Sept. 1
Additional information: Contact foundation for current application guidelines.
EIN: 510201795

5483
Joint Council No. 73 Scholarship Fund
(also known as Josephine Provenzano Scholarship Fund)
150 Morris Ave.
Springfield, NJ 07081 (973) 467-9100

Foundation type: Independent foundation
Purpose: Scholarships of up to $750 per semester to children of Joint Council No. 73 members in NJ to attend four-year colleges.
Financial data: Year ended 12/31/2011. Assets, $582,398 (M); Expenditures, $41,756; Total giving, $37,000; Grants to individuals, 28 grants totaling $37,000 (high: $1,500, low: $1,000).
Fields of interest: Labor unions/organizations.
Type of support: Undergraduate support.
Application information: Applications accepted. Application form required.
Deadline(s): Apr. 1
Applicants should submit the following:
1) Letter(s) of recommendation
2) Transcripts
3) SAT
EIN: 226017773

5484
Justice Lodge No. 285 F. & A. M., Educational Trust
348 S. Main St.
Pleasantville, NJ 08232 (609) 484-9800
Application address: 1520 S. Main St., Pleasantville, NJ 08232

Foundation type: Operating foundation
Purpose: Scholarships to relatives of members of NJ 23rd Masonic District Encompassing Atlantic County.
Financial data: Year ended 12/31/2012. Assets, $611,056 (M); Expenditures, $26,395; Total giving, $25,833; Grants to individuals, 10 grants totaling $25,833 (high: $7,000, low: $875).
Fields of interest: Fraternal societies.
Type of support: Scholarships—to individuals.
Application information: Application form required.
Additional information: Contact trust for complete application guidelines.
EIN: 222857778

5485
The Walter S. Kapala Scholarship Trust
P.O. Box 1501, NJ2-130-03-31
Pennington, NJ 08534-1501

Foundation type: Independent foundation
Purpose: Scholarships to graduating high school seniors attending public high schools in the towns of Hartford, West Hardford or Plainfield, NJ entering a four-year college or university.
Financial data: Year ended 12/31/2012. Assets, $127,299 (M); Expenditures, $6,690; Total giving, $5,000.
Fields of interest: Higher education.
Type of support: Scholarships—to individuals.
Application information: Applications accepted. Application form required.
Deadline(s): May 1
Applicants should submit the following:
1) Class rank
2) SAT
3) ACT
4) Essay
Additional information: Applicant must demonstrate financial need and academic excellence.
EIN: 066446026

5486
Kennedy Health System, Inc.
(formerly Kennedy Health Care Foundation, Inc.)
2201 Chapel Ave. W.
Cherry Hill, NJ 08002-2020 (856) 488-6500
Contact: Martin A. Bieber, Pres. and C.E.O.
E-mail: infokennedy@kennedyhealth.org;
URL: http://www.kennedyhealth.org

Foundation type: Public charity
Purpose: Scholarships primarily to children of regular, full-time, or part-time associates of Kennedy Health System who have completed at least one year of service.
Financial data: Year ended 12/31/2011. Assets, $15,634,206 (M); Expenditures, $542,132; Total giving, $59,304; Grants to individuals, totaling $52,804.
Fields of interest: Health sciences school/ education.
Type of support: Undergraduate support.
Application information:
Applicants should submit the following:
1) Essay
2) Transcripts
Additional information: Application should also include list of extracurricular activities.
EIN: 222442036

5487
Kessler Foundation
300 Executive Dr., Ste. 70
West Orange, NJ 07052-3327 (973) 324-8362
Application e-mail address:
jstoumbos@kesslerfoundation.org
FAX: (973) 324-8373;
E-mail: info@kesslerfoundation.org; URL: http://www.kesslerfoundation.org

Foundation type: Public charity
Purpose: Awards to individuals who demonstrate excellence in supporting and advocating for people with physical disabilities.
Publications: Application guidelines; Annual report.
Financial data: Year ended 12/31/2011. Assets, $213,838,717 (M); Expenditures, $17,244,222; Total giving, $2,776,283.

Fields of interest: Medical care, rehabilitation; Disabilities, people with.
Type of support: Awards/prizes.
Application information: Applications accepted. Application form available on the grantmaker's web site.
Send request by: Mail or online
Deadline(s): Dec. 14 for Joel A. DeLisa Award
Final notification: Recipients notified in Mar.
Applicants should submit the following:
1) Letter(s) of recommendation
2) Curriculum vitae
Program description:
Joel A. DeLisa, M.D. Award for Excellence in Research and Education in the Field of Physical Medicine and Rehabilitation: One $50,000 annual award will recognize a leader and role model in the field of physical medicine and rehabilitation, particularly as it relates to the translation of research and education to patient care. Eligible nominees must demonstrate significant accomplishments in the domains of publications, funding, program development, education and training, service, and leadership. Award applicants must be nominated by a second party who can attest to the individual's qualifications.
EIN: 311562134

5488
Kiwanis Club of Cape May Foundation, Inc.
P.O. Box 124
Cape May, NJ 08204 (609) 884-8888

Foundation type: Operating foundation
Purpose: Scholarships to college bound students of Cape May, NJ for continuing education at accredited colleges or universities.
Financial data: Year ended 09/30/2011. Assets, $49,981 (M); Expenditures, $75,519; Total giving, $40,879.
Fields of interest: Higher education.
Type of support: Scholarships—to individuals.
Application information: Applications accepted.
Initial approach: Letter
Deadline(s): End of senior year
Additional information: Application should include high school records and college invoices.
EIN: 223734672

5489
Janet H. and C. Harry Knowles Foundation, Inc.
(also known as Knowles Science Teaching Foundation (KSTF))
1000 N. Church St.
Moorestown, NJ 08057-1764 (856) 608-0001
Contact: Angelo Collins Ph.D., Exec. Dir
FAX: (856) 608-0008; E-mail: info@kstf.org;
URL: http://www.kstf.org

Foundation type: Operating foundation
Purpose: Fellowships to young men and women in the U.S. with degrees in science or mathematics to become professional high school teachers. Support includes tuition assistance, stipends, and mentoring.
Publications: Annual report; Informational brochure; Occasional report.
Financial data: Year ended 05/31/2012. Assets, $71,700,153 (M); Expenditures, $6,268,425; Total giving, $1,167,446; Grants to individuals, 193 grants totaling $1,057,446 (high: $18,154, low: $37).
Fields of interest: Science; Mathematics.

Type of support: Fellowships; Graduate support.
Application information: Applications accepted.
Application form required. Application form
available on the grantmaker's web site.
  Initial approach: Application
  Send request by: On-line
  Copies of proposal: 1
  Deadline(s): 2nd Tues. in Jan.
  Final notification: Applicants notified two months
    after receipt of application
  Applicants should submit the following:
    1) Curriculum vitae
    2) Essay
    3) GPA
    4) Letter(s) of recommendation
    5) Transcripts
  Additional information: Applicants for Teaching
    Fellowship should have a degree in science,
    mathematics or engineering. See web site for
    further eligibility guidelines.
Program descriptions:
  Alumni Program: This program provides
continued activities for teaching fellows after
fellowship to enhance teacher leaders skills.
  Teaching Fellowships: Awarded to young men and
women with degrees in mathematics and science
who want to teach high school. Support lasts 5
years.
EIN: 010485964

5490
K. Kiki Konstantinos Scholarship Foundation
P. O. Box 685
Medford, NJ   08055-0685   (856) 983-0870
Contact: Steven Zeuli, Chair.

Foundation type: Public charity
Purpose: Scholarships to high school seniors of
Lenape School District, NJ for continuing education.
Financial data: Year ended 12/31/2012. Assets,
$191,046 (M); Expenditures, $24,665; Total
giving, $24,000.
Fields of interest: Higher education.
Type of support: Scholarships—to individuals.
Application information: Contact high school
guidance office for application information.
EIN: 521822371

5491
Judith Kirsch Kovach Memorial Trust
P.O. Box 3074
Allwood Station, NJ   07012   (908) 930-7358

Foundation type: Independent foundation
Purpose: Scholarships to Edison High School, NJ,
seniors based on the display of courage and
perseverance in the face of adversity.
Financial data: Year ended 12/31/2011. Assets,
$22,497 (M); Expenditures, $10,000; Total giving,
$10,000; Grants to individuals, 2 grants totaling
$10,000 (high: $5,000, low: $5,000).
Type of support: Support to graduates or students
of specific schools; Undergraduate support.
Application information: Applications not
accepted.
  Additional information: Recipients are chosen by
    Edison High School Administration.
    Unsolicited requests for funds not considered
    or acknowledged.
EIN: 226503902

5492
KPMG Disaster Relief Fund
3 Chestnut Ridge Rd.
Montvale, NJ   07645-1842   (201) 307-7763
Contact: Bernard J. Milano, Pres.
URL: http://www.kpmgcampus.com/whykpmg/
ci_disaster.shtml

Foundation type: Public charity
Purpose: Grants to partners and employees of
KPMG to assist in responding to an immediate
financial need and/or permanent financial loss
resulting from a natural disaster.
Financial data: Year ended 06/30/2012. Assets,
$1,188,025 (M); Expenditures, $710,330; Total
giving, $693,155; Grants to individuals, totaling
$63,500.
Fields of interest: Safety/disasters.
Type of support: Emergency funds; Grants to
individuals.
Application information: Applications accepted.
  Additional information: Grants only available to
    employees of KPMG LLP.
Company name: KPMG LLP
EIN: 223263347

5493
The KPMG Foundation
(formerly The KPMG Peat Marwick Foundation)
3 Chestnut Ridge Rd.
Montvale, NJ   07645-0435   (201) 307-7932
Contact: Tara Perino, Dir.
*Application address for Minority Accounting Doctoral
Scholarships:* KPMG Foundation, Doctoral
Scholarship Prog., c/o Joanne Berry
FAX: (201) 624-7763;
E-mail: us-kpmgfoundation@kpmg.com;
URL: http://www.kpmgfoundation.org

Foundation type: Company-sponsored foundation
Purpose: Scholarships to full-time doctoral
students of accounting who are African-American,
Hispanic-American, or Native American.
Publications: Application guidelines; Annual report;
Grants list.
Financial data: Year ended 06/30/2012. Assets,
$4,892,000 (L); Expenditures, $8,935,597; Total
giving, $8,212,856.
Fields of interest: Business school/education;
Minorities; African Americans/Blacks; Hispanics/
Latinos; Native Americans/American Indians.
Type of support: Scholarships—to individuals;
Doctoral support.
Application information: Applications accepted.
Application form required. Application form
available on the grantmaker's web site.
  Initial approach: Application
  Send request by: Mail
  Copies of proposal: 1
  Deadline(s): May 1
  Final notification: Recipients notified May 15
  Applicants should submit the following:
    1) Resume
    2) Transcripts
  Additional information: Applications should also
    include proof of matriculation.
Program description:
  Minority Accounting Doctoral Scholarships: The
foundation awards five-year $10,000 graduate
scholarships to minority doctoral accounting
students. The program is designed to increase the
completion rate among African-American,
Hispanic-American, and Native American doctoral
students. The scholarship is eligible for annual
renewal. Cumulative total scholarship amount may
not exceed $50,000.
EIN: 136262199

5494
John C. Lasko Foundation
P.O. Box 1501, NJ2-130-03-31
Pennington, NJ   08534-1501
Contact: Clint Blair
Application address: P.O. Box 339 Belleville, MI
48111; tel.: (734) 699-3400

Foundation type: Independent foundation
Purpose: Awards to individuals through
scholarships, fellowships, internships, prizes and
loans to encourage and further the education of
employees of Republic Die & Tool Co., as well as
their children.
Financial data: Year ended 12/31/2012. Assets,
$107,957,818 (M); Expenditures, $6,538,752;
Total giving, $5,706,500.
Fields of interest: Higher education.
Type of support: Fellowships; Internship funds;
Scholarships—to individuals; Student loans—to
individuals; Awards/prizes.
Application information: Applications accepted.
Interview required.
  Additional information: Applications are solicited
    through communications to employees.
    Grantees are selected based on prior
    academic performance, recommendations,
    financial need and test performance.
EIN: 276173297

5495
Stephanie E. Laucius Educational and Charitable Foundation
c/o Joanne Jensen
P.O. Box 4099
Brick, NJ   08723   (908) 415-7159
Contact: Stephanie E. Laucius

Foundation type: Independent foundation
Purpose: Scholarships to graduating high school
seniors for undergraduate education.
Financial data: Year ended 12/31/2012. Assets,
$1,063,003 (M); Expenditures, $34,053; Total
giving, $31,000; Grants to individuals, 12 grants
totaling $31,000 (high: $3,500, low: $1,000).
Type of support: Undergraduate support.
Application information: Application form required.
  Initial approach: Letter
  Deadline(s): Apr. 15
  Applicants should submit the following:
    1) Transcripts
EIN: 521947741

5496
LearningAlly
(formerly Recording for the Blind & Dyslexic)
20 Roszel Rd.
Princeton, NJ   08540-6206   (609) 520-8010
Contact: for Awards: Andrew Friedman, Pres. and
C.E.O.
Tel. and e-mail for M. Greenwald: (609) 243-7087,
e-mail: mgreenwald@rfbd.org
FAX: (609) 987-8116;
E-mail: custserv@learningally.org; Toll-free tel.:
(800) 221-4792; URL: http://www.rfbd.org

Foundation type: Public charity
Purpose: Awards to blind or visually impaired high
school seniors and college seniors in recognition of
their scholastic achievement.
Publications: Annual report.
Financial data: Year ended 06/30/2012. Assets,
$45,474,088 (M); Expenditures, $25,790,152;
Total giving, $56,000; Grants to individuals,
totaling $56,000.

Fields of interest: Higher education; Blind/visually impaired.
Type of support: Awards/prizes.
Application information: Applications accepted. Application form required. Application form available on the grantmaker's web site.
  Deadline(s): Mar. 1
  Applicants should submit the following:
    1) Transcripts
    2) Letter(s) of recommendation
    3) Essay
  Additional information: Application should also include honors, achievements and community activities.
EIN: 131659345

5497
Legal Services of New Jersey, Inc.
P.O. Box 1357
Edison, NJ 08818-1357 (732) 572-9100
E-mail: legalhelp@lsnj.org; Toll-free tel.: (888) 576-5529; URL: http://www.lsnj.org

Foundation type: Public charity
Purpose: Legal assistance to low-income residents of NJ in all topics of civil matters.
Publications: Occasional report.
Financial data: Year ended 12/31/2011. Assets, $7,338,498 (M); Expenditures, $35,468,202; Total giving, $17,077,194; Grants to individuals, totaling $14,048.
Fields of interest: Legal services; Economically disadvantaged.
Type of support: In-kind gifts.
Application information:
  Initial approach: Letter
  Additional information: Applicants are subject to a financial eligibility screening and other routine intake procedures.
EIN: 222059939

5498
Life Saving Benevolent Association of New York
c/o SCI
118 Export St.
Newark, NJ 07114 (917) 207-2311
Contact: Julie Vroon

Foundation type: Independent foundation
Purpose: Awards for life-saving heroism at sea and for training in seamanship, primarily to individuals living in NY.
Financial data: Year ended 12/31/2012. Assets, $517,335 (M); Expenditures, $46,327; Total giving, $8,500; Grants to individuals, 14 grants totaling $8,500 (high: $750, low: $500).
Fields of interest: Disasters, search/rescue; Military/veterans' organizations.
Type of support: Awards/prizes.
Application information: Applications accepted. Application form required.
  Initial approach: Letter
  Deadline(s): Dec.
Program description:
  Awards Program: The association awards medals, pins, and sums of money to those individuals whose courage, skill, and seamanship saved a human life on the sea or any navigable waters (or lakes connected therewith). The association also gives medals and monetary awards to encourage training in seamanship, lifeboat work, methods of rescue in the water, and resuscitation.
EIN: 136104148

5499
The Raymond Lukenda Educational & Scholarship Foundation Inc.
61 Queen Anne Dr.
Basking Ridge, NJ 07920
Contact: Robert R. Stanicki Esq.
Apllication address: 1435 Raritan Rd., Clark, NJ 07066

Foundation type: Independent foundation
Purpose: Scholarships to NJ residents entering high school or college.
Financial data: Year ended 12/31/2012. Assets, $391 (M); Expenditures, $32,945; Total giving, $32,000; Grants to individuals, 12 grants totaling $32,000 (high: $3,000, low: $500).
Type of support: Scholarships—to individuals.
Application information: Applications accepted. Application form required.
  Deadline(s): June 30
EIN: 200123479

5500
Madison Scholarship Committee
78 Lincoln Ave.
Florham Park, NJ 07932
Contact: Robert Newhouse, Pres.

Foundation type: Independent foundation
Purpose: Scholarships only to graduates of Madison High School, NJ.
Financial data: Year ended 06/30/2013. Assets, $78,137 (M); Expenditures, $28,072; Total giving, $26,000; Grants to individuals, 18 grants totaling $26,000 (high: $2,000, low: $1,000).
Type of support: Support to graduates or students of specific schools; Undergraduate support.
Application information: Applications accepted. Application form required. Interview required.
  Deadline(s): Feb. 15
EIN: 226100079

5501
Varoon Mahajan Memorial Trust, Inc.
154 Vacarro Dr.
Cresskill, NJ 07626
Contact: Manjit S. Bains Dr., C.E.O. and Pres.
Application address: 1544 Huyler Landing Rd., Cresskill, NJ 07626

Foundation type: Independent foundation
Purpose: Awards to individuals who have or will have medical training at accredited medical institutions in the U.S., and who demonstrate a strong interest in promoting the advancement of medical care in India and the U.S.
Financial data: Year ended 06/30/2013. Assets, $57,016 (M); Expenditures, $752; Total giving, $0.
Fields of interest: Medical school/education.
International interests: India.
Type of support: Graduate support.
Application information: Applications accepted. Application form required.
  Deadline(s): None
  Additional information: Contact trust for current application guidelines.
EIN: 133387669

5502
Stephen F. McCready Scholarship Fund
P.O. Box 1501, NJ2-130-03-31
Pennington, NJ 08534-101

Foundation type: Independent foundation

Purpose: Student loans for higher education with preference given to Marion County, FL, residents who are attending theological seminaries or who have otherwise indicated intentions of entering full-time Christian service.
Financial data: Year ended 12/31/2012. Assets, $532,399 (M); Expenditures, $29,770; Total giving, $19,748.
Fields of interest: Theological school/education; Christian agencies & churches.
Type of support: Student loans—to individuals.
Application information: Applications accepted. Application form required.
  Initial approach: Loan application
  Deadline(s): June 1 for fall term and Dec. 1 for winter term
EIN: 596577844

5503
Dorothea van Dyke McLane Association
120 John St.
Princeton, NJ 08542-3121 (609) 924-9713
URL: http://www.dorotheashouse.org/

Foundation type: Independent foundation
Purpose: Scholarships to graduates of secondary schools in the Princeton, NJ, area, based on academic ability and financial need.
Financial data: Year ended 12/31/2012. Assets, $4,249,100 (M); Expenditures, $242,580; Total giving, $102,500.
Type of support: Support to graduates or students of specific schools; Undergraduate support.
Application information: Applications accepted.
  Initial approach: Letter
  Deadline(s): None
EIN: 216000849

5504
Merck Institute for Science Education, Inc.
P.O. Box 100, WS2F-96
Whitehouse Station, NJ 08889-0100
Contact: Carlo Parravano, Exec. Dir.
E-mail: contactus@mise.org; URL: http://www.merckresponsibility.com/giving-at-merck/education/

Foundation type: Company-sponsored foundation
Purpose: Scholarships and fellowships to outstanding African-American students pursuing studies and research careers in biological and chemical sciences.
Financial data: Year ended 12/31/2012. Assets, $0 (M); Expenditures, $2,616,833; Total giving, $1,057,700.
Fields of interest: Science; Biology/life sciences.
Type of support: Fellowships; Research; Postdoctoral support; Graduate support; Undergraduate support.
Application information: Applications accepted. Application form available on the grantmaker's web site.
  Send request by: Online
  Deadline(s): Varies
  Additional information: Applicants for the UNCF/Merck Science Initiative should contact the United Negro College Fund at: http://umsi.uncf.org/.
Program description:
  The UNCF/Merck Science Initiative (UMSI): The institute, in partnership with the United Negro College Fund, provides scholarships, fellowships, and mentoring to outstanding African-American students pursuing studies and careers in the field of biological and chemical sciences. Awards are

made at the undergraduate, graduate, and post-doctoral levels and ranges from $25,000 up to $92,000.
EIN: 223208944

5505
Merck Patient Assistance Program, Inc.
1 Merck Dr.
P.O. Box 100, Ste. WSF-96
Whitehouse Station, NJ 08889-0100 (800) 727-5400
URL: http://www.merckresponsibility.com/focus-areas/access-to-health/community-investment/patient-assistance-program/home.html

Foundation type: Operating foundation
Purpose: Financial assistance to provide Merck medication to economically disadvantaged individuals lacking prescription drug coverage when a physician has determined that a Merck product may be appropriate.
Financial data: Year ended 12/31/2012. Assets, $11,101,394 (M); Expenditures, $520,507,909; Total giving, $520,507,909; Grants to individuals, totaling $520,507,909.
Fields of interest: Economically disadvantaged.
Type of support: Grants for special needs.
Application information: Applications accepted. Application form required. Application form available on the grantmaker's web site.
  Initial approach: Application
  Send request by: Mail
  Deadline(s): None
EIN: 010575520

5506
Fern Michaels Foundation, Inc.
10 Wildwood Ave.
Livingston, NJ 07039
Contact: Michael Kuczkir, Tr.
Application address: c/o Michael Kuczkir, 8695 Dorchester Rd., North Charleston, SC 29420

Foundation type: Independent foundation
Purpose: Scholarships to students from households that make less than $25,000 income.
Financial data: Year ended 12/31/2011. Assets, $14,117 (M); Expenditures, $28,080; Total giving, $27,925; Grants to individuals, 2 grants totaling $22,925 (high: $15,516, low: $7,409).
Type of support: Undergraduate support.
Application information: Applications accepted.
  Additional information: Contact foundation for current application deadline/guidelines.
EIN: 223233929

5507
Middlesex County Medical Society Foundation
P.O. Box 215
Edison, NJ 08818-0215 (732) 257-6800
Contact: Leticia V. De Castro M.D., Pres.
URL: http://mcmsfoundation.shutterfly.com/

Foundation type: Independent foundation
Purpose: Scholarships to individuals who have been residents of Middlesex County, NJ, for at least five years for the study of medicine, nursing, or pharmacology at an accredited school.
Financial data: Year ended 09/30/2012. Assets, $318,178 (M); Expenditures, $17,102; Total giving, $11,000; Grants to individuals, 7 grants totaling $11,000 (high: $2,500, low: $500).

Fields of interest: Medical school/education; Nursing school/education; Pharmacy/prescriptions.
Type of support: Scholarships—to individuals.
Application information: Applications accepted. Application form required.
  Initial approach: Telephone
  Send request by: Mail
  Deadline(s): Mar. 15 for continuing students, Apr. 15 for new students
  Applicants should submit the following:
    1) Letter(s) of recommendation
    2) Transcripts
    3) Financial information
  Additional information: Application should also include proof of enrollment. See web site for additional guidelines.
EIN: 221767843

5508
Sadie H. Miller Trust
P.O. Box 980, 10 S. Main St.
Elmer, NJ 08318-4178
Application address: c/o Arthur P. Schlick High School, Attn.: Guidance Office, 718 Centerton Rd., Pittsgrove, NJ 08318-3945, tel.: (856) 358-2054

Foundation type: Independent foundation
Purpose: Scholarships to graduates of Schalick High School, Pittsgrove, NJ.
Financial data: Year ended 12/31/2011. Assets, $194,674 (M); Expenditures, $8,660; Total giving, $6,000.
Type of support: Support to graduates or students of specific schools; Undergraduate support.
Application information: Applications accepted. Application form required.
  Deadline(s): Varies
  Additional information: Forms available from high school guidance office.
EIN: 226625423

5509
Kasser Mochary Family Foundation Corp.
26 Park St.
Montclair, NJ 07042-3434 (973) 744-4470
Contact: Mary V. Mochary, Mgr.

Foundation type: Independent foundation
Purpose: Scholarships to students at Israeli public school K.B. Beit Haemek for the Aryanl Prize.
Financial data: Year ended 05/31/2013. Assets, $2,682,718 (M); Expenditures, $32,338; Total giving, $5,000.
Fields of interest: Jewish agencies & synagogues.
Type of support: Support to graduates or students of specific schools; Foreign applicants.
Application information: Applications accepted.
  Initial approach: Letter or telephone
  Additional information: Formal application must be filed through the applicant's school.
EIN: 237043288

5510
Montclair Fund for Educational Excellence, Inc.
22 Valley Rd.
Montclair, NJ 07042-2709 (973) 509-4021
Contact: Lois Whipple, Exec. Dir.
FAX: (973) 509-4098; E-mail: info@mfee.org;
URL: http://www.mfee.org/

Foundation type: Public charity

Purpose: Grants to Montclair, NJ Public School faculty to promote educational excellence.
Publications: Application guidelines.
Financial data: Year ended 06/30/2012. Assets, $1,055,785 (M); Expenditures, $572,105; Total giving, $424,365; Grants to individuals, totaling $424,365.
Fields of interest: Education.
Type of support: Grants to individuals.
Application information: Applications accepted. Application form required. Application form available on the grantmaker's web site.
  Send request by: E-mail
  Deadline(s): Oct. 26
  Final notification: Recipients notified in Dec.
  Additional information: Application should include a budget.
Program descriptions:
  Educational Excellence Grants: This program works to fund projects proposed by Montclair Public Schools faculty and staff for classroom projects, curriculum innovation, and projects that promote academic achievement and student-well-being. Grants may be funded in amounts up to $1,000, and may be awarded to teachers, teacher teams, administrators, other school staff, and parent organizations.
  Greenwald Professional Development Grants: Grants of up to $600 are available to cover tuition and fees associated with the program in question. Grants are awarded to teachers, teachers teams, administrators, other school staff and parent organizations.
  Turner Social and Emotional Learning Grants: Grants may be funded in amounts up to $1,000 to teachers, teacher teams, administrators, other school staff, and parent organizations.
EIN: 061320335

5511
Moorestown Education Foundation
803 N. Stanwick Rd.
Moorestown, NJ 08057-2147 (856) 778-6600
Contact: Lynn Shugars

Foundation type: Operating foundation
Purpose: Scholarships to graduating seniors of Moorestown High School, NJ for postsecondary education.
Financial data: Year ended 12/31/2012. Assets, $939,551 (M); Expenditures, $163,707; Total giving, $68,535; Grants to individuals, 47 grants totaling $68,353 (high: $4,500, low: $100).
Fields of interest: Higher education.
Type of support: Support to graduates or students of specific schools; Undergraduate support.
Application information: Applications accepted. Application form required.
  Deadline(s): Apr. 30
  Additional information: Application can be obtained from Moorestown High School.
EIN: 222699954

5512
The Morello Foundation
1631 Whispering Woods Way
Vineland, NJ 08361
Contact: Judith Browne, Tr.

Foundation type: Operating foundation
Purpose: Scholarships primarily to residents of the Vineland, NJ, area pursuing higher education.
Financial data: Year ended 12/31/2012. Assets, $369,395 (M); Expenditures, $17,818; Total giving, $14,667; Grants to individuals, 5 grants totaling $14,667 (high: $4,000, low: $2,000).

Fields of interest: Higher education.
Type of support: Scholarships—to individuals.
Application information: Applications accepted.
Applicants should submit the following:
   1) Financial information
   2) Transcripts
Additional information: Contact the foundation for additional application guidelines.
EIN: 237051152

5513
NARM Scholarship Foundation, Inc.
9 Eves Dr., Ste. 120
Marlton, NJ 08053-3138 (856) 596-1801
Contact: Rachelle Friedman, Chair.
Pat Daly's contact: (856) 596-1608,
e-mail: daly@narm.com
FAX: (856) 596-3268; E-mail: daly@narm.com;
URL: http://www.narm.com/

Foundation type: Public charity
Purpose: Scholarships for employees, children and spouses of employees of NARM member companies, pursuing higher education at an accredited college or university.
Financial data: Year ended 09/30/2012. Assets, $412,155 (M); Expenditures, $106,427; Total giving, $68,000.
Fields of interest: Higher education.
Type of support: Scholarships—to individuals.
Application information: Applications accepted. Application form required.
Send request by: Online
Deadline(s): Mar. 1
Final notification: Applicants notified mid-Apr.
Applicants should submit the following:
   1) Photograph
   2) Transcripts
   3) SAT
   4) Financial information
   5) ACT
Additional information: Scholarship payments are made directly to the educational institution on behalf of the students.
EIN: 236427333

5514
National Football League Alumni, Inc.
1 Washington Pk.
1 Washington St., 14th Fl.
Newark, NJ 07102-3140 (954) 630-2100
FAX: (862) 772-0277;
E-mail: katie.hilder@nflalumni.org; Toll-free tel.: (877) 258-6635; additional address (Ft. Lauderdale office): 3696 N. Federal Hwy., Ste. 202, Fort Lauderdale, FL 33308-6262, toll-free tel. (FL only): (800) 878-5437, fax: (862) 772-0277;
URL: https://www.nflalumni.org/

Foundation type: Public charity
Purpose: Assistance to former professional football athletes experiencing financial hardship for medical expense.
Publications: Application guidelines.
Financial data: Year ended 12/31/2010. Assets, $1,616,058 (M); Expenditures, $3,788,700; Total giving, $1,578,503; Grants to individuals, totaling $17,599.
Fields of interest: Athletics/sports, professional leagues.
Type of support: Grants to individuals.
Application information: Application form required.
Send request by: Online
Deadline(s): None
Additional information: Applications are considered on a case-by-case basis.

Program description:
Financial Assistance: The organization provides monetary grants to qualified National Football League (NFL) alumni who are experiencing financial hardships, including grants to eligible players who need financial assistance in paying for the cost of Player Care Plan programs (such as joint replacement, spine treatment, or neurological care). Eligible applicants must be former NFL players, with at least two credited seasons of NFL play (both spouses and children are also eligible for care), and must meet financial qualifications. Preference will be given to first-time applicants.
EIN: 591782262

5515
New Jersey Council on the Arts
225 W. State St., 4th Fl.
Trenton, NJ 08608-1001 (609) 292-6130
FAX: (609) 989-1440;
E-mail: feedback@sos.state.nj.us; Mailing address: P.O. Box 306, Trenton, NJ 08625-0306;
URL: http://nj.gov/state/njsca/index.html

Foundation type: Public charity
Purpose: Grants to NJ-based artists to continue to work, and to develop links with their communities.
Publications: Application guidelines.
Fields of interest: Arts, services; Arts, artist's services; Arts.
Type of support: Grants to individuals.
Application information: Applications accepted. Application form required. Application form available on the grantmaker's web site.
Initial approach: Application
Deadline(s): Varies
Additional information: See web site for additional guidelines.
Program descriptions:
Artists and Communities Grants: Administered as a co-sponsored project of the Mid-Atlantic Arts Foundation, these grants help underwrite the expenses of artist residencies both in New Jersey and the surrounding mid-Atlantic states, with the object being to place an artist in a community setting and engage that community in a creative process that illuminates how artistic creativity can meet community needs. New Jersey artists may go into residence at a site in New Jersey or in another state.
Folk Arts Apprenticeships: The council provides grants to individuals to encourage cultural communities to continue passing on their valued art forms in traditional settings, by providing stipends of up to $3,000 to master folk artists and craftspersons that can help apprentices develop greater skills. Priority will be given to applicants that represent endangered arts (including arts that help to preserve endangered languages that are disappearing due to lack of master artists, materials, or marketable means to attract the general public or the community's youth population), community-based initiatives (arts that are valuable to communities, but are not likely involved in professional individual networks or taught in a formal or institutional process), and communities and art forms not previously represented by grants.
Individual Artist Fellowship Grants: The council awards fellowships (ranging from $6,500 to $12,000) to practicing professional New Jersey artists to enable them to pursue their artistic goals. Artists may use fellowship awards to pursue work in their artistic discipline, including purchasing supplies, studying in a workshop situation, renting studio space, or otherwise freeing their time. Eligible applicants include artists who are

permanent residents of the state of New Jersey, artists who have not received a fellowship in the fast five years, and artists who are not matriculated students in a graduate, undergraduate, or high school program at the time of application or award.

5516
New Jersey Health Foundation, Inc.
120 Albany St., Twr. II, Ste. 850
New Brunswick, NJ 08901-2126 (908) 731-6601
Contact: James M. Golubieski, Pres.
E-mail: jgolubieski@njhf.org; URL: http://www.njhealthfoundation.org

Foundation type: Public charity
Purpose: Grants to researchers at Rutgers Biomedical Health Sciences and The Rutgers Cancer Institute of New Jersey. Grants to researchers with promising ideas that may lead to developing patents or intellectual property.
Financial data: Year ended 06/30/2011. Assets, $159,397,143 (M); Expenditures, $7,455,295; Total giving, $4,710,857.
Fields of interest: Biomedicine; Biomedicine research.
Type of support: Research.
Application information: Applications accepted. Application form required. Application form available on the grantmaker's web site.
Initial approach: Letter
Deadline(s): May 19 - July 18
Additional information: See web site for eligibility criteria.
EIN: 030430873

5517
New Jersey Motor Truck Association Scholarship Fund
160 Tices Ln.
East Brunswick, NJ 08816-2016 (732) 254-5000
Contact: Jennifer Blazovic
E-mail: bsala@njmta.org; URL: http://www.njmta.org/

Foundation type: Independent foundation
Purpose: Scholarships to children of New Jersey employees of NJMTA members who seek to pursue a college education at an accredited college.
Financial data: Year ended 12/31/2012. Assets, $43,548 (M); Expenditures, $5,495; Total giving, $3,000.
Fields of interest: Vocational education, post-secondary; Higher education.
Type of support: Scholarships—to individuals; Undergraduate support.
Application information: Applications accepted. Application form required. Application form available on the grantmaker's web site.
Deadline(s): May 18
Final notification: Applicants notified in June
Applicants should submit the following:
   1) Financial information
   2) SAT
   3) ACT
   4) GPA
   5) Transcripts
   6) Class rank
Additional information: Funds are paid directly to the named institution on behalf of the students.
Program description:
Scholarship Program: Scholarships to NJ residents who are dependent children, age 23 and under, of a full-time NJ-based employee of a NJMTA

member in good standing. Scholarships are made on academic potential, financial need and unusual circumstances regardless of race, creed, gender, disability, religion or national origin. Scholarship awards are $1,000 for undergraduate study only at an accredited two-year or four-year college or university or at an accredited vocational/technical institution.

EIN: 222300922

5518
New Jersey Osteopathic Education Foundation

1 Distribution Way, Ste. 201
Monmouth Junction, NJ 08852-3001 (732) 940-9000
Contact: Ira Monka, Chair.
FAX: (732) 940-8899; E-mail: njaops@njosteo.com; URL: http://www.njosteo.com/

Foundation type: Independent foundation
Purpose: Scholarships to NJ residents accepted into their first year at any approved college of osteopathic medicine.
Financial data: Year ended 12/31/2011. Assets, $590,004 (M); Expenditures, $72,864; Total giving, $53,317; Grants to individuals, 5 grants totaling $21,000 (high: $5,000, low: $3,000).
Fields of interest: Nerve, muscle & bone research.
Type of support: Doctoral support.
Application information: Applications accepted. Application form required. Application form available on the grantmaker's web site. Interview required.
> *Deadline(s):* Apr. 30
> *Applicants should submit the following:*
> 1) Essay
> 2) Financial information
> 3) Transcripts
> 4) Letter(s) of recommendation
> *Additional information:* Application should also include four references, MCAT scores and last year's tax return. See web site for further information.

Program description:
Scholarship Program: The foundation offers scholarships to New Jersey residents who will be entering their first year of study at a college of osteopathic medicine. Approximately five scholarships are awarded each year. Each scholarship recipient must agree to become a member of the New Jersey Association of Osteopathic Physicians and Surgeons, and the American Osteopathic Association.
EIN: 226088562

5519
New Jersey Performing Arts Center, Corp.

(also known as NJPAC)
1 Center St.
Newark, NJ 07102-4501 (973) 642-8989
Tel. for Scholarships: (973) 353-8009
E-mail: artseducation@njpac.org; Toll-free tel.: (888) 466-5722; URL: http://www.njpac.org

Foundation type: Public charity
Purpose: Scholarships to high school and college students who attend NJPAC's professional arts training programs, and demonstrate the potential to become leading arts professionals.
Publications: Application guidelines; Newsletter.
Financial data: Year ended 06/30/2012. Assets, $201,342,305 (M); Expenditures, $31,134,958; Total giving, $124,059; Grants to individuals, totaling $124,059.

Fields of interest: Arts education; Performing arts; Music; Music ensembles/groups.
Type of support: Scholarships—to individuals.
Application information: Applications accepted.
> *Initial approach:* Letter, telephone or e-mail
> *Deadline(s):* Apr. 1 for Star-Ledger Scholarship for the Performing Arts
> *Applicants should submit the following:*
> 1) Essay
> 2) Resume
> 3) SAT
> 4) Letter(s) of recommendation
> 5) Transcripts

Program descriptions:
Jeffrey Carollo Music Scholarship: The foundation offers scholarships to students in grades eleven and under who study classical piano, vocals, and instrumental music. Comprehensive training includes private lessons, music theory, and ensembles during two private lessons per week (after school, in the evenings, and/or on Saturdays) at the Newark School of the Arts. Scholarships pay for one lesson per week, with the second to be paid for by the student. Additional scholarship support may be available to those in extreme financial need.

Star-Ledger Scholarship for the Performing Arts: Each year, three merit-based scholarships are awarded for either $40,000 ($10,000 per year for four years) or $20,000 ($5,000 per year for four years) to identify, cultivate, and train gifted college bound Newark high school seniors who demonstrate the potential to become leading arts professionals. Scholarships are available for students proficient in vocal music, instrumental music, acting, or dance, and are intended to support a four-year education leading to the completion of a degree from an accredited undergraduate institution. Eligible applicants must be seniors who attend a Newark high school and who permanently reside in Newark. Students should have an overall academic GPA of at least 2.5, though extremely talented individuals with a GPA of less than 2.5 may be considered.
EIN: 222889703

5520
New Jersey Press Foundation

840 Bear Tavern Rd., Ste. 305
West Trenton, NJ 08628-1019
Contact: John J. O'Brien, Dir.
FAX: (609) 406-0300; E-mail: jjobrien@njpa.org; URL: http://www.njpa.org/foundation/

Foundation type: Public charity
Purpose: Scholarships and internship opportunities to outstanding New Jersey high school seniors and college/university students pursuing a degree in journalism.
Publications: Application guidelines.
Financial data: Year ended 12/31/2011. Assets, $1,701,254 (M); Expenditures, $260,478; Total giving, $19,500; Grants to individuals, 4 grants totaling $19,000. Subtotal for scholarships—to individuals: grants totaling $11,000. Subtotal for grants to individuals: grants totaling $8,000.
Fields of interest: Journalism school/education.
Type of support: Internship funds; Scholarships—to individuals.
Application information: Applications accepted. Application form required. Application form available on the grantmaker's web site.
> *Deadline(s):* Jan. 31 for Isaac Roth Media/ Business Internships, Feb. 15 for Bernard Kilgore Memorial Scholarship, Mar. 28 for Richard Drukker Memorial Scholarship, Dec. 31 for Mac Borg New Media Internship and Newspaper Internship Program

Applicants should submit the following:
> 1) Work samples
> 2) Transcripts
> 3) Letter(s) of recommendation

Program descriptions:
Bernard Kilgore Memorial Scholarship: Awarded in conjunction with the Garden State Scholastic Press Association, a $5,000 scholarship is available to an outstanding New Jersey high school senior who wishes to major in journalism. Applicants must have at least two years of experience on their high school newspaper, and have at least three samples of writing published in their high school or community newspaper, and have at least a 3.0 GPA.

Isaac Roth Media/Business Internships: A paid summer internship is available to a college student who is interested in pursuing a career in media business, circulation, or distribution. One applicant will be selected to receive an internship to work in the business, circulation, or distribution office of a New Jersey Press Association member newspaper or media company. Recipients will receive a salary of $350 per week for six weeks. Eligible applicants include students who attend New Jersey colleges or who are New Jersey residents currently enrolled at other U.S. colleges.

Mac Borg New Media Internship: This paid summer internship to a college student who is interested in pursuing a journalism career and who wants to explore new ways of communicating with readers. Eligible applicants include students who attend New Jersey colleges, or who are New Jersey residents currently enrolled at other U.S. colleges. One college student will be selected to receive an internship to work in the newsroom of a New Jersey Press Association member newspaper or media company. The recipient will receive a salary of $350 per week for six weeks.

Newspaper Internship Program: The foundation offers paid summer internships to students attending New Jersey colleges (or New Jersey residents currently enrolled at other U.S. colleges), who are interested in pursuing journalism careers. Interns are selected to work in newsrooms of New Jersey Press Association members, and receive a salary of $400 per week for eight weeks.

Richard Drukker Memorial Scholarship: This $2,000 scholarship will be available to a Montclair State University journalism students, and/or who is on the staff of The Montclarion. Students who received a New Jersey Press Foundation scholarship or internship last year are not eligible for this year's Drukker scholarship.
EIN: 226071765

5521
New Jersey State Bar Foundation

1 Constitution Sq.
New Brunswick, NJ 08901-1500 (732) 249-5000
Contact: Angela C. Scheck, Exec. Dir.
FAX: (732) 828-0034; URL: http://www.njsbf.org

Foundation type: Public charity
Purpose: Awards scholarships to worthy students entering their second or third year at a New Jersey law school, as well as awards fellowships to attorneys in positions that primarily relate to public education about the law, legal aid to the poor and the improvement in the administration of justice.
Publications: Application guidelines.
Financial data: Year ended 06/30/2012. Assets, $14,436,364 (M); Expenditures, $4,321,556; Total giving, $401,811; Grants to individuals, totaling $12,571.
Fields of interest: Law school/education.

Type of support: Fellowships; Scholarships—to individuals.
Application information: Applications accepted. Application form available on the grantmaker's web site.
  Additional information: Scholarship applications are available at the beginning of the second semester at the financial aid offices of the New Jersey law schools. Fellowship application is available on foundation web site. See web site for additional guidelines.
Program descriptions:
  Fellowship Program: The foundation offers fellowships to New Jersey-based attorneys in positions that primarily relate to public education about the law, legal aid to the poor, and the improvements in the administration of justice. Fellowships support programs focused on serving the legal needs of inner-city residents, which allow the fellow to directly represent clients and supervises law student representation of clients to the clinic.
  Law School Scholarship Program: The foundation awards scholarships to worthy students entering their second or third year at Rutgers University School of Law-Rutgers, Rutgers University School of Law-Camden, and Seton Hall University School of Law. Named scholarships include the Wallace Vail Scholarship (given to the candidate who achieves the highest academic performance among the three law schools), the Labor Law Scholarship (given to a student wishing to enter the field of labor law), the Sonia Morgan Scholarship (given to a female law student), and the Abram D. and Maxine H. Londa Scholarship (gives to a student living in Union County)
EIN: 226074475

5522
New Jersey State Elks Association Special Children's Committee, Inc.
P.O. Box 1596
Woodbridge, NJ 07095-1596 (732) 326-1300

Foundation type: Public charity
Purpose: Scholarships to handicapped college students residing in NJ.
Financial data: Year ended 03/31/2012. Assets, $11,114,295 (M); Expenditures, $790,613; Total giving, $19,129; Grants to individuals, totaling $19,129.
Fields of interest: Higher education; Disabilities, people with.
Type of support: Scholarships—to individuals.
Application information:
  Initial approach: Letter
  Additional information: Contact foundation for further application information.
EIN: 221522929

5523
New Jersey State Firemen's Association
1700 Galloping Hill Rd.
Kenilworth, NJ 07033-1303 (908) 620-1871
Contact: George H. Heflich Sr., Pres.
FAX: (908) 620-1874; E-mail: georgeh@njsfa.com; Additional tel.: (973) 677-9296; Toll-free tel.: (800) 852-0137; URL: http://www.njstatefiremensrelief.com/

Foundation type: Public charity
Purpose: Financial assistance to indigent firefighters residing in NJ, and to NJ firefighters injured, incapacitated, or killed in the performance of their duty.

Financial data: Year ended 06/30/2012. Assets, $58,336,731 (M); Expenditures, $30,403,073; Total giving, $27,636,767; Grants to individuals, totaling $7,599,623.
Type of support: Grants for special needs.
Application information:
  Initial approach: Letter
  Additional information: Applicants should contact their local relief association.
EIN: 221153991

5524
New World Gospel Mission, Inc.
272 8th Ave.
Palisades Park, NJ 07650

Foundation type: Independent foundation
Purpose: Scholarships to individuals, primarily on the East Coast of the US and in Toronto, Canada.
Financial data: Year ended 12/31/2011. Assets, $756,999 (M); Expenditures, $33,307; Total giving, $10,919; Grants to individuals, 17 grants totaling $10,919 (high: $1,000, low: $491).
International interests: Canada.
Type of support: Scholarships—to individuals.
Application information: Applications not accepted.
EIN: 113325506

5525
The Newark Museum Association
49 Washington St.
Newark, NJ 07102-3109 (973) 596-6550
Contact: Stephen McKenzie, Mgr.; Paul Robeson Awards: Patricia Faison, Mktg. Assoc.
E-mail: webmaster@newarkmuseum.org;
URL: http://www.newarkmuseum.org

Foundation type: Public charity
Purpose: Prizes to winners of the Newark Museum's Paul Robeson Awards and honorariums through an artist-in-residence program.
Publications: Application guidelines; Newsletter.
Financial data: Year ended 12/31/2011. Assets, $68,267,558 (M); Expenditures, $17,376,790.
Fields of interest: Film/video; Arts, artist's services; African Americans/Blacks.
Type of support: Awards/prizes; Stipends.
Application information: Application form required.
  Initial approach: Telephone
  Deadline(s): Feb. 20 for Robeson Award and July 18 for Artist-in-Residence program
  Additional information: For the Robeson Awards, application should include a $35 entry fee, and film in VHS or DVD.
Program descriptions:
  Adolf Konrad Artist-in-Residence Program: Each year, the association offers three artists the opportunity to use the museum's professional facilities to create new work. The museum consists of three studios: one for weaving, fiber, textiles, and related areas of study; one for fine metals and enameling; and one open for a variety of disciplines. Artists working in any area of the visual arts will be provided with five weeks; stipends of $1,300 will be paid to selected artists.
  Paul Robeson Awards: During even numbered years, this biennial competition recognizes outstanding, original, non-commercial ('independent') films over which the filmmaker had control of the finished piece. Videotapes, DVDs, and films released in the 16mm format, including narratives, documentaries, experimental, and animated works are accepted. Applications are accepted in February of the competition year. Cash prizes are awarded at the judges' discretion.

Awards are extended, and entries are screened for the public, during The Newark Museum's Annual Newark Black Film Festival that is presented during the summer from June to August each summer.
EIN: 221487275

5526
The Charlotte W. Newcombe Foundation
35 Park Pl.
Princeton, NJ 08542-6918 (609) 924-7022
Contact: Thomas N. Wilfrid Ph.D., Exec. Dir.
FAX: (609) 252-1773;
E-mail: twilfrid@newcombefoundation.org;
Additional e-mail: info@newcombefoundation.org;
URL: http://www.newcombefoundation.org

Foundation type: Independent foundation
Purpose: Scholarhips to students with physical, medical, learning, and psychological handicaps. Partial tuition, internship and special expense scholarships to women 25 and older who have completed half the credits required for their degrees. Fellowships in the humanities and social sciences are also provided to encourage original and significant study of ethical and religious values in all areas of human endeavor. These programs are administered by the Woodrow Wilson National Fellowship Foundation.
Publications: Informational brochure; Program policy statement.
Financial data: Year ended 12/31/2012. Assets, $47,794,700 (M); Expenditures, $2,712,532; Total giving, $2,119,725.
Fields of interest: Physically disabled; Mentally disabled; Minorities; Women; Adults, women.
Type of support: Fellowships; Scholarships—to individuals.
Application information: Applications not accepted.
  Additional information: Unsolicited requests for funds are not accepted.
Program descriptions:
  Newcombe Doctoral Dissertation Fellowships: These encourage original and significant study of ethical and religious values in all areas of human endeavor. Awards are based on a rigorous national competition administered by the Woodrow Wilson National Fellowship Foundation. See foundation web site for application information.
  Newcombe Scholarships for Mature Women: Colleges and universities receive grants from the foundation for scholarship aid to women over the age of twenty-five who have earned at least sixty credits towards a bachelor's degree. (The foundation now permits but does not require recipient institutions to extend Newcombe Scholarships to mature men students who meet the eligibility standards outlined in the foundation's policy guiding selection of Newcombe Scholars.) Each funded institution is responsible for selection of recipients and scholarship administration according to the foundation's guidelines. Campus committees of counselors, faculty members and financial aid officers review applications, award scholarships and report to the foundation.
  Newcombe Scholarships for Students with Disabilities: These support completion of degrees by students with disabilities who need financial assistance at selected colleges and universities. See foundation web site for further information and current list of schools.
  Special Scholarship Endowment Grants: These support completion of degrees by economically disadvantaged students at a select group of institutions. The foundation awards grants to selected institutions, not to individual students. Each funded institution selects scholarship

recipients and administers the scholarship program according to institutional and foundation policies. See foundation web site for further information.
EIN: 232120614

5527
North Jersey Media Group Foundation, Inc.
P.O. Box 75
Hackensack, NJ 07602-9192 (973) 569-7681
Contact: Jenifer A. Borg, Pres.
FAX: (973) 569-7268

Foundation type: Public charity
Purpose: Short-term assistance to those who have suffered losses due to natural disasters, medical illness or injury, or personal reasons to residents of Bergen, Essex, Hudson, Morris, Passaic, Sussex, and Union counties in NJ.
Publications: Application guidelines.
Financial data: Year ended 12/31/2011. Assets, $672,849 (M); Expenditures, $484,216; Total giving, $449,609.
Fields of interest: Safety/disasters.
Type of support: Grants for special needs.
Application information: Applications accepted. Application form required.
    Initial approach: Letter
    Deadline(s): Jan. 1, Apr. 1, Aug. 1, and Oct. 1
    Additional information: Contact foundation for eligibility criteria.
Program description:
    Compassion Fund: The fund assists individuals or families in northern New Jersey who are impacted by an immediate personal crisis. The fund's purpose is to provide short-term assistance to those who have suffered losses due to natural causes (e.g. fire, flood, hurricane), medical illness or injury, or personal reasons. In order to qualify for donations from the fund, an individual must currently reside in Bergen, Essex, Hudson, Morris, Passaic, Sussex, or Union counties in New Jersey.
EIN: 352165636

5528
Northwest New Jersey Community Action Program, Inc.
(also known as NORWESCAP)
350 Marshall St.
Phillipsburg, NJ 08865-3273 (908) 454-7000
Contact: Terry Newhard, C.E.O. and Exec.Dir.
FAX: (908) 859-0729; E-mail: info@norwescap.org; URL: http://www.norwescap.org

Foundation type: Public charity
Purpose: Assistance to low-income individuals, families, and the elderly of Hunterdon, Morris, Passaic, Somerset, Sussex, and Warren counties, NJ, with childcare, energy, food, affordable housing, home repairs, and other services.
Financial data: Year ended 08/31/2011. Assets, $6,325,063 (M); Expenditures, $28,399,536; Total giving, $7,547,418; Grants to individuals, totaling $7,547,418.
Fields of interest: Human services; Aging; Economically disadvantaged.
Type of support: Grants for special needs.
Application information: Application form required.
    Initial approach: Telephone
EIN: 221777156

5529
Novartis Patient Assistance Foundation, Inc.
1 Health Plz.
USEH 701-441
East Hanover, NJ 07936-1080 (800) 277-2254
Application address: P.O. Box 66531, St. Louis, MO 63166-6556; fax: (866) 470-1750; URL: http://www.pharma.us.novartis.com/about-us/our-patient-caregiver-resources/index.shtml

Foundation type: Company-sponsored foundation
Purpose: Financial assistance to provide Novartis medication to economically disadvantaged individuals lacking prescription drug coverage.
Publications: Application guidelines.
Financial data: Year ended 12/31/2012. Assets, $31,616,576 (M); Expenditures, $459,661,136; Total giving, $452,745,445; Grants to individuals, totaling $452,745,445.
Fields of interest: Economically disadvantaged.
Type of support: Grants for special needs.
Application information: Applications accepted. Application form required. Application form available on the grantmaker's web site.
    Initial approach: Application
    Send request by: Mail, fax or online
    Deadline(s): None
    Additional information: Applications should include a copy of the applicants most recent federal tax return. Faxed applications must be sent from a physician's office. Application address varies per medication requested. URL: https://www.npcpapportal.com/ for additional information.
EIN: 262502555

5530
O'Brien's Irish Angel Endowment Fund
c/o Sovereign Trust Co.
1886 Hinds Road, Ste. 2
Toms River, NJ 08753-8199 (732) 255-5000
Contact: Barbara Kannheiser

Foundation type: Public charity
Purpose: Scholarships to one male or one female graduating student of Toms River High School, NJ for attendance at a college or university, or vocational/technical school.
Financial data: Year ended 12/31/2012. Assets, $58,699 (M); Expenditures, $3,280; Total giving, $2,500.
Fields of interest: Vocational education, post-secondary; Higher education.
Type of support: Scholarships—to individuals; Support to graduates or students of specific schools.
Application information: Applications not accepted.
    Additional information: Unsolicited requests for funds not considered or acknowledged. Application only for Toms River High School graduates.
EIN: 226819669

5531
Simone O'Leary Foundation
108 Hill Hollow Rd.
South Plainfield, NJ 07080-1621 (908) 769-0351
Contact: Simone O'Leary, Dir.

Foundation type: Independent foundation
Purpose: Scholarships to graduating high school seniors of NJ for full time undergraduate course of study at an accredited two or four year college,

university, or vocational/technical school in the U.S.
Financial data: Year ended 12/31/2012. Assets, $5,321 (M); Expenditures, $11,209; Total giving, $5,500; Grants to individuals, 11 grants totaling $5,500 (high: $500, low: $500).
Fields of interest: Vocational education, post-secondary; Higher education.
Type of support: Scholarships—to individuals.
Application information: Applications accepted. Application form required.
    Send request by: Mail
    Deadline(s): Apr. 1
    Additional information: Selection is based on academic achievement, goals and aspirations, demonstrate leadership, participation in community service, high school activities, and work experience.
EIN: 204918545

5532
Henry and Carolyn Sue Orenstein Foundation, Inc.
c/o Henry Orenstein
35 Smull Ave.
Caldwell, NJ 07006-5011

Foundation type: Independent foundation
Purpose: Grants to Jewish families and elderly individuals for food, medical supplies, and other needs. Grants also for medical research.
Financial data: Year ended 12/31/2012. Assets, $4,472,919 (M); Expenditures, $889,299; Total giving, $887,669.
Fields of interest: Jewish agencies & synagogues; Aging.
Type of support: Research; Grants for special needs.
Application information: Applications not accepted.
    Additional information: Unsolicited requests for funds not considered or acknowledged.
EIN: 222806030

5533
The Ostberg Foundation, Inc.
87 Ruckman Rd.
Alpine, NJ 07620-1098
Contact: Christine Dineen

Foundation type: Independent foundation
Purpose: Financial aid to elderly and ill individuals, regardless of country of residence.
Financial data: Year ended 11/30/2012. Assets, $443,750 (M); Expenditures, $169,991; Total giving, $163,905.
Fields of interest: Aging; Disabilities, people with; Economically disadvantaged; Homeless.
International interests: Africa; Europe; Haiti.
Type of support: Foreign applicants; Grants for special needs.
Application information: Applications accepted. Application form required.
    Deadline(s): None
    Additional information: Grants to individuals made by referral from social service agencies.
EIN: 132963335

5534
Paper Mill Playhouse
22 Brookside Dr.
Millburn, NJ 07041-1610 (973) 379-4343
E-mail: info@papermill.org; URL: http://www.papermill.org

Foundation type: Public charity
Purpose: Scholarships to outstanding graduating seniors from a NJ high school participating in the Rising Star Awards production studying theater in college, and to students planning to continue their studies in technical theater.
Publications: Application guidelines.
Financial data: Year ended 06/30/2011. Assets, $8,844,159 (M); Expenditures, $14,326,606; Total giving, $6,500; Grants to individuals, 7 grants totaling $6,500.
Fields of interest: Dance; Music; Performing arts, education.
Type of support: Scholarships—to individuals.
Application information: Applications accepted. Application form available on the grantmaker's web site.
  Deadline(s): Apr. 20
  Applicants should submit the following:
    1) Transcripts
    2) Letter(s) of recommendation
    3) GPA
    4) Essay
  Additional information: Application should also include proof of acceptance to a college or university. Students must be nominated by their teachers and/or administrators from their district.
Program description:
  Rising Star Award Scholarships: As a component of the organization's Rising Star Awards, four $1,000 cash awards will be given to outstanding individual students who have participated in the awards program and who plan to continue studying theater in college. An additional $1,000 scholarship, sponsored by Scaramouche Costumes LLC, will be awarded to students continuing their studies in technical theater. Applicants must have participated in theatrical activities throughout the majority of their high school career.
EIN: 221550515

5535
Winston E. Parker Scholarship Foundation
(formerly Winston E. Parker Scholarship Fund)
P.O. Box 105
Moorestown, NJ   08057
Contact: Richard Decou

Foundation type: Independent foundation
Purpose: Scholarships to full-time college juniors, seniors, and graduate students studying arboriculture, forestry, ornamental horticulture, or related fields.
Publications: Informational brochure.
Financial data: Year ended 12/31/2011. Assets, $374,665 (M); Expenditures, $26,939; Total giving, $20,000.
Fields of interest: Higher education; Environment, forests; Horticulture/garden clubs; Biology/life sciences.
Type of support: Scholarships—to individuals.
Application information: Application form not required. Interview required.
  Deadline(s): None
  Additional information: Applicants from Rotary Districts 7500 and 7640 (southern NJ) are preferred. The fund is administered by the Rotary Club of Moorestown, NJ. Selection is based on academic performance, financial need, and residency in the counties of Atlantic, Burlington, Camden, Cape May, Cumberland, Gloucester, or Salem, NJ.
EIN: 223069120

5536
Charles K. Payne Scholarship Fund, Inc.
P.O. Box 125
Butler, NJ   07405-0125

Foundation type: Independent foundation
Purpose: Scholarships to high school graduates from Bloomingdale and Kinnelon areas in NJ.
Financial data: Year ended 12/31/2012. Assets, $316,587 (M); Expenditures, $20,184; Total giving, $16,000; Grants to individuals, 16 grants totaling $16,000 (high: $1,000, low: $1,000).
Fields of interest: Higher education.
Type of support: Undergraduate support.
Application information: Application form required.
  Deadline(s): Apr. 15
  Additional information: Contact fund to request an application.
EIN: 226207012

5537
Penn Jersey Youth Umpires School, Inc.
c/o Alan H. Schorr
5 Split Rock Dr.
Cherry Hill, NJ   08003-1220   (856) 874-9090

Foundation type: Public charity
Purpose: Scholarships to undergraduate students in NJ for higher education.
Financial data: Year ended 01/31/2012. Assets, $560,311 (M); Expenditures, $53,870; Total giving, $43,701; Grants to individuals, totaling $36,083.
Fields of interest: Recreation.
Type of support: Scholarships—to individuals; Awards/prizes.
Application information: Scholarships are awarded based on performance in scrabble, crossword, and chess competitions at Penn Jersey Youth Umpires School.
EIN: 222430620

5538
The People Technology Foundation, Inc.
25 Chatham Rd.
Summit, NJ   07901   (908) 665-5940
Contact: Frank J. Ponzio, Pres.

Foundation type: Operating foundation
Purpose: Paid internship opportunities to Eastern Europeans, with emphasis on individuals from Romania, who want to gain experience in the computer field by working as an intern in the U.S. for a summer.
Financial data: Year ended 12/31/2012. Assets, $23,276 (M); Expenditures, $19,516; Total giving, $7,700; Grant to an individual, 1 grant totaling $1,200.
Fields of interest: Computer science.
International interests: Romania.
Type of support: Internship funds.
Application information: Contact foundation for application guidelines.
EIN: 223273424

5539
Peters Valley Craftsman, Inc.
19 Kuhn Rd.
Layton, NJ   07851-2004   (973) 948-5200
Contact: Jimmy Clark, Exec. Dir.
FAX: (973) 948-0011; E-mail: pv@warwick.net;
URL: http://www.petersvalley.org/index.cfm

Foundation type: Public charity

Purpose: Scholarships to college students to attend the Center's workshops and classes; tuition scholarships to art teachers for attendance at the Center's workshops; and residencies to artists specializing in blacksmithing, ceramics, fine metals, photography, surface design, weaving and woodworking.
Publications: Application guidelines.
Financial data: Year ended 09/30/2011. Assets, $192,264 (M); Expenditures, $587,682.
Fields of interest: Folk arts; Arts education; Visual arts; Ceramic arts; Arts; Secondary school/education; Teacher school/education.
Type of support: Scholarships—to individuals; Precollege support; Undergraduate support; Residencies; Workstudy grants.
Application information: Application form required.
  Initial approach: E-mail
  Deadline(s): Apr. 1
  Applicants should submit the following:
    1) Letter(s) of recommendation
    2) Resume
    3) Work samples
    4) Essay
Program descriptions:
  Guest Artist Residencies: From the beginning of Nov. to the end of Apr., the organization provides residency opportunities for practicing artists. These residencies may be one or two months in duration, and provide a heated room and access to a heated studio, except blacksmithing, for a monthly fee (currently $500). Materials and food are the responsibility of the participant but all houses are equipped with fully-functional kitchens.
  High School Student Scholarships: The center will award four full-tuition workshop scholarships to high school students, in order to learn new craft skills or enhance existing ones. Eligible applicants must be at least 17 years of age; at least two scholarships are reserved for New Jersey students.
  Summer Studio Assistantships: Assistantships are available in each of the Valley's eight studios: blacksmithing, ceramics, fine metals, fibers, surface fibers, structure, wood, photography, and special topics. Assistantship positions generally run the length of the summer workshop season (May to Sept.), but may vary from studio to studio as some departments prefer to split the summer between two or more assistants. Assistants live at Peters Valley and work in the studio, on average, 35 hours per week. Responsibilities include, but are not limited to, maintaining the studio, welcoming and preparing for incoming students and instructors, etc. In exchange, assistants are provided with room and board as well as workshop and exhibition opportunities.
  Tuition Scholarships for Art Teachers: Each year, the center offers tuition scholarships to four art teachers, with one each being awarded in the following categories: elementary, middle/junior-high, high, and other (which may include special arts programs). Recipients will receive one-half off of workshop tuition for a workshop of their choice. Recipients will be responsible for all associated costs, such as the balance of tuition, material fees, and room and board (if needed)
  Tuition Scholarships for College Students: Scholarship opportunities are available to college students who reflect a strong need and desire to further develop their skills and understanding of craft media. Recipients will receive one-half off of the workshop tuition for a single workshop; based on availability, students will also receive a bed in the center's youth-hostel-style dorm at no charge. Recipients must work two hours per workshop day for the center (including housekeeping, kitchen, and/or maintenance)

Work Exchange Scholarship Program: Each year, the center offers a very limited number of work-exchange scholarships during the summer workshop season, with the hopes of provide students who might otherwise not have funds the opportunity to pursue their artistic education. Recipients will be required to work eight hours of supervised work (scraping, painting, mowing, hauling garbage, etc.), and will receive one day of workshop tuition in return.
EIN: 221920050

5540
John P. Peterson Foundation
P.O. Box 164
Park Ridge, NJ   07656   (201) 203-6225
Contact: James Burnes, Tr.

Foundation type: Independent foundation
Purpose: Undergraduate scholarships to high school seniors in NJ and the greater NY/NJ metropolitan area who are financially needy or who have a mental or physical disability to further their education at a college, university or an accredited trade or professional school of their choice.
Financial data: Year ended 12/31/2012. Assets, $1,661,079 (M); Expenditures, $117,619; Total giving, $92,000; Grants to individuals, 19 grants totaling $91,000 (high: $12,000, low: $1,000).
Fields of interest: Vocational education, post-secondary; Higher education; Physically disabled; Mentally disabled.
Type of support: Undergraduate support.
Application information: Application form required.
Applicants should submit the following:
    1) Letter(s) of recommendation
    2) Transcripts
    3) SAR
    4) Essay
Additional information: Application should include summary of extracurricular activities, community service, student government, clubs, sports, efforts towards self supporting yourself and estimate of school costs.
EIN: 222147375

5541
Edward Pinson Scholarship Foundation
900 E. Pine St.
P.O. Box 863
Millville, NJ   08332-0863   (856) 327-5656
Contact: Phillip Van Embden Esq.

Foundation type: Independent foundation
Purpose: Scholarships to individuals from Cumberland County, NJ for attendance at accredited colleges or universities.
Financial data: Year ended 12/31/2012. Assets, $656,924 (M); Expenditures, $46,673; Total giving, $32,750; Grants to individuals, 40 grants totaling $32,750 (high: $2,000, low: $500).
Fields of interest: Higher education.
Type of support: Scholarships—to individuals.
Application information: Applications accepted. Application form required.
Send request by: Mail or in person
Deadline(s): Apr. 16
Applicants should submit the following:
    1) Resume
    2) Letter(s) of recommendation
    3) Transcripts
EIN: 223552984

5542
Polonsky Brothers Foundation
P.O. Box 2412
Westfield, NJ   07091   (908) 789-9690
Contact: Andrea Taylor, Treas.
Application address: 525 Clifton St., Westfield, NJ 07090; URL: http://projectepic.org/

Foundation type: Operating foundation
Purpose: Scholarships to disadvantaged urban youths who are high school juniors in selected schools in NJ and NY to help cover tuition, books, travel, and fees for summer educational enrichment programs.
Financial data: Year ended 12/31/2011. Assets, $10,751 (M); Expenditures, $96,075; Total giving, $81,160.
Fields of interest: Youth, services.
Type of support: Scholarships—to individuals.
Application information: Applications accepted. Application form required.
Deadline(s): None
Program description:
Scholarship Program: The program selects high school juniors from preselected public high schools in NY or NJ for summer enrichment programs. The foundation hopes that this experience will stimulate the student in his senior year to apply for college placement.
EIN: 136169593

5543
Portuguese-American Scholarship
Foundation
P.O. Box 3848
Union, NJ   07083-1890   (973) 522-3808
URL: http://www.americo.net/vivaportugal/nj/org/pasf/index.htm

Foundation type: Public charity
Purpose: Scholarships to New Jersey high school seniors of Portuguese ancestry pursuing a bacherlor's degree.
Publications: Application guidelines.
Financial data: Year ended 12/31/2011. Assets, $338,042 (M); Expenditures, $81,029; Total giving, $64,000.
Fields of interest: Higher education.
Type of support: Scholarships—to individuals.
Application information: Applications accepted. Application form required.
Initial approach: Letter
Deadline(s): Mar. 15
Additional information: Applicants must demonstrate financial need.
Program description:
Scholarships: Scholarships of $8,000 each are available to New Jersey students of Portuguese ancestry who wish to further their postsecondary school education and gain greater access to a better way of life. Eligible applicants must be New Jersey high school seniors that are Portuguese-born or that have a parent or grandparent that is Portuguese-born, and who have a GPA of B or better.
EIN: 237017106

5544
Frank C. Poucher & Lillian S. Poucher
Memorial Fund
1777 New Rd.
Linwood, NJ   08221   (609) 343-7300
Contact: Laurie Carter
Application address: 1400 N. Albany Ave., Atlantic City, NJ 08401

Foundation type: Independent foundation

Purpose: Scholarships to financially needy students of the Atlantic County Vocational and/or Atlantic City, NJ public school systems.
Financial data: Year ended 12/31/2012. Assets, $1,124,948 (M); Expenditures, $70,103; Total giving, $62,250; Grants to individuals, 43 grants totaling $62,250 (high: $2,000, low: $1,000).
Type of support: Support to graduates or students of specific schools; Technical education support; Undergraduate support.
Application information: Applications accepted. Application form required.
Deadline(s): None
EIN: 223579083

5545
A. A. Previti Foundation
(formerly A.A. Previti Family Charitable Foundation, Inc.)
4030 Ocean Heights Ave.
Egg Harbor Township, NJ   08234-7505   (609) 927-1177
Contact: Andrew Preveti, Pres.
Application address: c/o Andrew Previti, P.O. Box 52, Somers Point, NJ 08244-0052

Foundation type: Operating foundation
Purpose: Scholarships to graduates of Florham Park, NJ, area high schools for undergraduate education.
Financial data: Year ended 12/31/2011. Assets, $508,265 (M); Expenditures, $35,194; Total giving, $30,000.
Type of support: Support to graduates or students of specific schools.
Application information: Applications accepted. Application form not required.
Initial approach: Letter
Deadline(s): None
Additional information: Applicants should submit a brief resume of academic qualifications.
EIN: 223633945

5546
Princeton Area Community Foundation,
Inc.
(formerly The Princeton Area Foundation, Inc.)
15 Princess Rd.
Lawrenceville, NJ   08648-2301   (609) 219-1800
Contact: Nancy W. Kieling, Pres.
FAX: (609) 219-1850; E-mail: info@pacf.org;
URL: http://www.pacf.org

Foundation type: Community foundation
Purpose: Scholarships to residents of Mercer, Monmouth, and Ocean counties, NJ, for higher education.
Publications: Application guidelines; Annual report; Grants list; Informational brochure; Newsletter.
Financial data: Year ended 12/31/2012. Assets, $88,395,021 (M); Expenditures, $7,565,242; Total giving, $6,525,163; Grants to individuals, 39 grants totaling $145,896.
Fields of interest: Higher education; Teacher school/education; Health sciences school/education.
Type of support: Scholarships—to individuals; Support to graduates or students of specific schools; Undergraduate support.
Application information: Applications accepted. Application form required. Application form available on the grantmaker's web site.
Initial approach: Application

Copies of proposal: 1
Deadline(s): Mar. 1
Final notification: Recipients notified within six weeks
Applicants should submit the following:
1) Transcripts
2) SAR
3) SAT
4) Letter(s) of recommendation
5) GPA
6) Financial information
7) Essay
Additional information: See web site for a complete listing of scholarship funds.
Program description:
Scholarship Funds: The foundation administers several scholarships to graduating high school residents of the Greater Mercer County area who are entering four-year colleges or universities. Each scholarship has its own unique eligibility requirements, such as attendance at a particular high school, or to pursue particular fields of study, such as education or the allied health profession. See web site for additional information.
EIN: 521746234

5547
Prudential Financial, Inc. Corporate Giving Program

c/o Prudential Financial, Inc., Comm. Resources
751 Broad St.
Newark, NJ 07102-3714
Contact: Mary O'Malley, V.P., Local Initiatives; Scharron N. Little, Contribs. Mgr.
Application address for Spirit of Community Awards: Prudential Spirit of Community Awards, State-Level Judging Comm., One Scholarship Way, P.O. Box 297, St. Peter, MN 56082, e-mail: spirit@prudential.com
FAX: (973) 802-3345;
E-mail: scharron.little@prudential.com;
URL: http://www.prudential.com/community

Foundation type: Corporate giving program
Purpose: Awards to secondary and middle school students for excellence in volunteerism.
Fields of interest: Youth, services; Volunteer services; Young adults.
Type of support: Awards/prizes.
Application information: Applications accepted.
Initial approach: Letter
Send request by: Online
Deadline(s): Nov. 6
Additional information: See web site for additional guidelines.
Program description:
Prudential Spirit of Community Awards: Through the Prudential Spirit of Community Awards program, Prudential annually awards two $1,000 grants to middle level and secondary school students in each state, Washington, DC, and Puerto Rico for outstanding volunteer service to their communities. Ten national winners receive an additional $5,000.

5548
PSEG Foundation, Inc.

(formerly Public Service Electric and Gas Company Foundation, Inc.)
80 Park Plz., 10C
Newark, NJ 07102-4109 (973) 430-7842
Contact: Marion C. O'Neill, Mgr., Corp. Contribs.
FAX: (973) 297-1480;
E-mail: marion.oneill@pseg.com; Additional tel.: (973) 430-5874; URL: http://pseg.com/info/community/nonprofit/foundation.jsp

Foundation type: Company-sponsored foundation
Purpose: Project grants to teachers who can successfully link their students' understanding of science, mathematics, computer science, and/or technology concepts with an enthusiasm and appreciation for the environment.
Publications: Application guidelines; Corporate report; Newsletter (including application guidelines).
Financial data: Year ended 12/31/2012. Assets, $31,919,220 (M); Expenditures, $6,500,893; Total giving, $6,341,914.
Fields of interest: Elementary school/education; Education; Environmental education.
Type of support: Program development; Project support.
Application information: Applications accepted. Application form required. Application form available on the grantmaker's web site.
Initial approach: Application
Send request by: Mail
Deadline(s): June 24
Final notification: Applicants notified in Oct.
EIN: 223125880

5549
Puffin Foundation, Ltd.

20 Puffin Way
Teaneck, NJ 07666-4167
Contact: Gladys Miller-Rosenstein, Exec. Dir.
Application address: c/o Gladys Miller-Rosenstein, Exec. Dir., 20 Puffin Way, Teaneck, NJ 07666-4111; URL: http://www.puffinfoundation.org

Foundation type: Independent foundation
Purpose: Grants to emerging artists in the U.S. in the areas of video/film, fine arts, dance, and public interest.
Publications: Application guidelines.
Financial data: Year ended 12/31/2012. Assets, $12,466,688 (M); Expenditures, $2,614,568; Total giving, $1,922,046.
Fields of interest: Cultural/ethnic awareness; Film/video; Photography; Performing arts; Music; Literature; Arts, artist's services; Arts.
Type of support: Seed money; Grants to individuals; Awards/prizes; Project support.
Application information: Applications accepted. Application form required.
Initial approach: Letter
Send request by: Mail
Copies of proposal: 1
Deadline(s): See foundation web site for current deadline
Applicants should submit the following:
1) Budget Information
2) Letter(s) of recommendation
3) Proposal
4) Resume
5) Work samples
Additional information: See web site for additional application guidelines.
EIN: 133155489

5550
Christopher Reeve Foundation

636 Morris Tpke., Ste. 3A
Short Hills, NJ 07078-2608 (973) 379-2690
Contact: Peter Wilderotter, Pres. and C.E.O.
FAX: (973) 912-9433;
E-mail: info@christopherreeve.org; Toll-free tel.: (800) 225-0292; URL: http://www.christopherreeve.org
Additional URL: http://www.apacure.org/

Foundation type: Public charity
Purpose: Research grants to investigators for the study and development of effective therapies for paralysis associated with spinal cord injury and other central nervous system disorders.
Publications: Application guidelines; Annual report; Newsletter.
Financial data: Year ended 12/31/2011. Assets, $10,972,420 (M); Expenditures, $15,600,939; Total giving, $8,256,262.
Fields of interest: Spine disorders research; Neuroscience research.
Type of support: Program development; Fellowships; Research; Postdoctoral support.
Application information: Applications accepted. Application form required. Application form available on the grantmaker's web site.
Send request by: Mail or online
Deadline(s): June 15 and Dec. 15
Additional information: See web site for additional guidelines.
Program description:
Individual Research Grants: This program supports investigator-initiated research on a variety of fronts, including axon growth and guidance, remyelination, cellular replacement, rehabilitation, and neuroprotection. Applications will be accepted from those with a Ph.D., M.D., or other equivalent professional degree, employed at a qualifying research institution; established scientists, young investigators who have completed a postdoctoral fellowship within the last five years, and current postdoctoral fellows may serve as principal investigators. Two-year awards are available for senior scientists and young investigators with a maximum funding level of $75,000 per year, while postdoctoral fellowships are available with a maximum funding level of $60,000 per year.
EIN: 222939536

5551
Rigorous Educational Assistance for Deserving Youth Foundation, Inc.

(also known as READY Foundation, Inc.)
310 South St.
Morristown, NJ 07960

Foundation type: Independent foundation
Purpose: Tuition assistance for postsecondary training to students in Newark, NJ, who have been in the program prior to 1997.
Financial data: Year ended 09/30/2013. Assets, $205,579 (M); Expenditures, $2,730; Total giving, $0.
Fields of interest: Education.
Type of support: Undergraduate support.
Application information: Applications not accepted.
Additional information: Unsolicited requests for funds not considered or acknowledged.
EIN: 222815535

5552
Robustelli Family Foundation

c/o Jonathan Robustelli
118 St. Nicholas Ave.
South Plainfield, NJ 07080 (908) 753-8080
Contact: Stacy Robustelli

Foundation type: Company-sponsored foundation
Purpose: Scholarships to high school students of South Plainfield and Mt. Holly areas, NJ.
Financial data: Year ended 12/31/2011. Assets, $125,261 (M); Expenditures, $14,745; Total giving, $14,695; Grants to individuals, 5 grants totaling $12,695 (high: $5,000, low: $195).

Fields of interest: Higher education.
Type of support: Scholarships—to individuals.
Application information:
  Deadline(s): End of Nov.
  Additional information: Applications accepted through Vision 2000 Foundation and Rancosas Valley high school.
EIN: 223341755

5553
The Mary Therese Rose Fund
33 Wolfe Dr.
Wanaque, NJ 07465-1026 (973) 835-5772
E-mail: jackcrilly@hotmail.com; URL: http://www.marythereserose.org/
Foundation type: Public charity
Purpose: Grants for medical expenses for pediatric patients care for at the Valley Hospital Center for Family Wellness and Child Development, NJ.
Financial data: Year ended 12/31/2011. Assets, $74,747 (M); Expenditures, $83,253; Total giving, $68,083; Grants to individuals, totaling $68,083.
Fields of interest: Children; Disabilities, people with.
Type of support: Grants for special needs.
Application information: Applications not accepted.
  Additional information: Unsolicited requests for funds not considered or acknowledged.
EIN: 200964551

5554
Rowan University Foundation, Inc.
201 Mullica Hill Rd.
Glassboro, NJ 08028-1700 (856) 256-4097
Contact: R.J. Tallarida, Jr., Exec. Dir.
FAX: (856) 256-4437;
E-mail: contact@rufoundation.org; E-Mail for R.J. Tallarida : tallarida@rowan.edu; Tel. for R.J. Tallarida: (856)-256-5413; URL: http://www.rufoundation.org
Foundation type: Public charity
Purpose: Scholarships to students at Rowan University, NJ.
Financial data: Year ended 06/30/2012. Assets, $150,342,866 (M); Expenditures, $8,148,464; Total giving, $7,900,670; Grants to individuals, totaling $1,227,417.
Type of support: Support to graduates or students of specific schools.
Application information: Contact foundation for current application deadline/guidelines.
EIN: 222482802

5555
S. Rubenstein Family Foundation, Inc.
170 E. Main St.
Rockaway, NJ 07866-3530
Contact: David F. Miller, Pres.
Foundation type: Independent foundation
Purpose: Grants for qualified graduating high school students primarily in northern and central NJ who are referred by their high schools.
Financial data: Year ended 10/31/2013. Assets, $3,247,496 (M); Expenditures, $103,486; Total giving, $88,236.
Fields of interest: Higher education.
Type of support: Support to graduates or students of specific schools.
Application information: Applications accepted.
  Deadline(s): Mar. 31
EIN: 223279029

5556
Ryu Family Foundation, Inc.
186 Parish Dr.
Wayne, NJ 07470-6009 (973) 692-9696
Contact: Gerald J. Suh, Exec. Dir.
FAX: (973) 692-0999; URL: http://www.seolbong.org/
Foundation type: Operating foundation
Purpose: Scholarships to U.S. citizens or permanent residents of Korean ancestry who are legal residents of ten northeastern states and who will study at a legally approved college or university in any one of the northeastern states.
Financial data: Year ended 06/30/2012. Assets, $1,196,417 (M); Expenditures, $74,818; Total giving, $43,300; Grants to individuals, 21 grants totaling $42,000 (high: $2,000; low: $2,000).
Fields of interest: Higher education; Asians/Pacific Islanders.
Type of support: Scholarships—to individuals; Graduate support.
Application information: Applications accepted. Application form required.
  Deadline(s): Nov. 4
  Applicants should submit the following:
    1) Resume
    2) FAFSA
    3) Letter(s) of recommendation
    4) Transcripts
    5) Essay
  Additional information: Application should also include a copy of you and/or your parent's tax return. Applications sent by e-mail or fax are not accepted.
Program description:
  Seol Bong Scholarship: Applicants must be full-time students working toward an advanced degree at an approved institution of higher education in CT, DE, ME, MA, NH, NJ, NY, PA, RI, or VT. Applicants must also be residents of one of the aforementioned states and have at least a 3.5 GPA. Students may repeatedly be allowed to receive the RFF scholarship grant, if qualified.
EIN: 223319101

5557
Saddle River Valley Lions Charities, Inc.
P.O. Box 333
Saddle River, NJ 07458-0333 (201) 825-3358
Foundation type: Public charity
Purpose: Scholarships primarily to legally blind residents of Bergen County, NJ.
Financial data: Year ended 06/30/2012. Assets, $93,046 (M); Expenditures, $76,477; Total giving, $75,315. Scholarships—to individuals amount not specified.
Fields of interest: Higher education; Disabilities, people with.
Type of support: Scholarships—to individuals; Undergraduate support.
Application information: Applications accepted.
  Additional information: Funds are paid directly to the educational institution on behalf of the students. Contact the foundation for additional application guidelines.
EIN: 222051734

5558
Saint Barnabas Development Foundation
95 Old Short Hills Rd.
West Orange, NJ 07052-1008 (973) 322-4330
Contact: Hoda Blau, Exec. Dir.
FAX: (973) 322-4346;
E-mail: foundation@sbhcs.com; URL: http://www.saintbarnabasfoundation.org
Foundation type: Public charity
Purpose: Scholarships primarily to students pursuing a healthcare-related field in NJ. Grants for medical expenses to needy residents of NJ.
Financial data: Year ended 12/31/2011. Assets, $58,315,555 (M); Expenditures, $5,215,917; Total giving, $3,330,936; Grants to individuals, totaling $82,684.
Fields of interest: Health care.
Type of support: Undergraduate support; Grants for special needs.
Application information: Contact foundation for eligibility requirements.
EIN: 222378422

5559
Sanofi Foundation for North America
(formerly Sanofi-aventis Patient Assistance Foundation)
55 Corporate Dr.
Bridgewater, NJ 08807-2855 (888) 847-4877
FAX: (888) 847-1797; E-mail: nacsr@sanofi.com; Application address: P.O. Box 222138, Charlotte, NC 28222-2138; URL: http://www.sanofifoundation-northamerica.org/
Foundation type: Company-sponsored foundation
Purpose: Prescription drugs to individuals who fall below the federal poverty level and who have no prescription reimbursement coverage. Applicants must also be ineligible for third party medication payments.
Publications: Application guidelines.
Financial data: Year ended 12/31/2012. Assets, $2,559,174 (M); Expenditures, $284,044,399; Total giving, $284,044,399; Grants to individuals, totaling $280,485,036.
Fields of interest: Pharmacy/prescriptions; Economically disadvantaged.
Type of support: Grants for special needs.
Application information: Applications accepted.
  Initial approach: Telephone
  Send request by: Mail
  Deadline(s): None
  Additional information: Application should include physician's certification of patient's medical and financial needs.
EIN: 431614543

5560
The Scholarship Foundation
P.O. Box 2211
Cherry Hill, NJ 08034-0165
Application address: Bernard T. Cote, Pres., 307 Provincetown Rd., Cherry Hill, NJ 08034, tel.: (856) 616-9311
Foundation type: Independent foundation
Purpose: Scholarships to students for attendance at accredited colleges or universities.
Financial data: Year ended 12/31/2012. Assets, $144,275 (M); Expenditures, $2,305,697; Total giving, $2,256,545; Grants to individuals, totaling $105,750.
Fields of interest: Higher education.
Type of support: Scholarships—to individuals.

Application information: Application form required.
Deadline(s): Apr. 30
Applicants should submit the following:
1) Class rank
2) Letter(s) of recommendation
3) GPA
Additional information: Application should also include participation in extra-curricular activities, non-salaried involvement in community activities, part or full-time paid work, as well as a written statement of desire for a college education.
EIN: 521560429

5561
Scotch Plains Fanwood Scholarship Foundation

P. O. Box 123
Fanwood, NJ   07023-0123   (908) 889-6625
Contact: Mary Ball Cappio, Pres.

Foundation type: Public charity
Purpose: Scholarships to graduates of Scotch Plains-Fanwood High School, NJ.
Financial data: Year ended 12/31/2011. Assets, $557,939 (M); Expenditures, $111,115; Total giving, $105,710; Grants to individuals, totaling $105,710.
Type of support: Support to graduates or students of specific schools; Undergraduate support.
Application information: Applications accepted. Application form required.
Initial approach: Letter
Deadline(s): Mar. 1
Applicants should submit the following:
1) Letter(s) of recommendation
2) Transcripts
EIN: 226105926

5562
George & Helen Segal Foundation

136 Davidson's Mill Rd.
North Brunswick, NJ   08902-4747
Contact: Susan Kutliroff, Secy.-Treas.
FAX: (732) 821-5877;
E-mail: segalfoundation@comcast.net; Application address for New Jersey Photographers: 357 Shawn Pl., North Brunswick, NJ 08902; URL: http://www.segalfoundation.org

Foundation type: Independent foundation
Purpose: Grants to NJ photographers who are over the age of 21, and who are not students.
Publications: Grants list; Informational brochure.
Financial data: Year ended 06/30/2013. Assets, $19,085,822 (M); Expenditures, $1,861,862; Total giving, $1,294,900.
Fields of interest: Photography.
Type of support: Grants to individuals.
Application information: Applications accepted. Application form required. Application form available on the grantmaker's web site.
Initial approach: Letter
Send request by: Mail
Deadline(s): Oct. 15
Final notification: Recipients notified by Mar. 1
Applicants should submit the following:
1) Resume
2) Work samples
Additional information: Application should include a current resume. See web site for application guidelines.
EIN: 223744151

5563
Several Sources Foundation, Inc.

P. O. Box 157
Ramsey, NJ   07446-1289   (201) 825-7277
Contact: Kathy Difiore, Pres.
E-mail: mail@severalsourcesfd.org; URL: http://www.severalsourcesfd.org

Foundation type: Public charity
Purpose: Shelter, food, and clothing in the New York City metropolitan area for mothers and their babies, and for poor inner-city children who are "at-risk" or afflicted with AIDS.
Fields of interest: AIDS; Children/youth, services; Women.
Type of support: Grants for special needs.
Application information: Applications accepted throughout the year; Contact foundation for current application guidelines.
EIN: 222368937

5564
Shoshana Foundation Inc.

66 Willow Ave.
Hackensack, NJ   07601-3001   (201) 861-6579
Contact: Flavia Gale, Pres.
Application address: 444 Central Park W., New York, NY 10025

Foundation type: Independent foundation
Purpose: Scholarships by nomination only to deserving young singers who are assisted in establishing their career in the U.S. and abroad.
Financial data: Year ended 12/31/2011. Assets, $550,481 (M); Expenditures, $68,406; Total giving, $60,305.
Fields of interest: Music.
Type of support: Awards/grants by nomination only.
Application information:
Deadline(s): None
Additional information: Recipients are chosen on academic merit and by each institution. Contact foundation for further information.
EIN: 133317859

5565
William A. & Mary A. Shreve Foundation

25 Abe Voorhees Dr.
Manasquan, NJ   08736   (732) 223-8484
Contact: Peter Broege Esq., Tr.

Foundation type: Independent foundation
Purpose: Scholarships primarily to students in Manasquan, NJ for postsecondary education.
Financial data: Year ended 12/31/2012. Assets, $568,082 (M); Expenditures, $47,483; Total giving, $29,150; Grants to individuals, 15 grants totaling $27,900 (high: $5,000, low: $400).
Fields of interest: Higher education.
Type of support: Scholarships—to individuals.
Application information:
Deadline(s): None
Additional information: Contact foundation for additional application guidelines.
EIN: 226054057

5566
Siemens Foundation

170 Wood Ave. S.
Iselin, NJ   08830-2704   (877) 822-5233
FAX: (732) 590-1252;
E-mail: foundation.us@siemens.com; URL: http://www.siemens-foundation.org

Foundation type: Company-sponsored foundation

Purpose: Scholarships and awards to students in recognition of achievement in mathematics and science through AP exams, competitions, and research projects.
Publications: Application guidelines; Program policy statement.
Financial data: Year ended 09/30/2012. Assets, $54,853,788 (M); Expenditures, $7,861,552; Total giving, $1,577,623; Grants to individuals, totaling $745,800.
Fields of interest: Elementary/secondary education; Education, gifted students; Higher education; Environment; Science; Chemistry; Mathematics; Physics; Engineering/technology; Science.
Type of support: Scholarships—to individuals; Awards/prizes.
Application information: Applications accepted. Application form required. Application form available on the grantmaker's web site.
Send request by: On-line
Deadline(s): Sept. 30 for the Siemens Competition, Mar. 4 for Siemens We Can Change the World Challenge
Program descriptions:
Siemens Competition in Math, Science, and Technology: The foundation, in partnership with Discovery Education, fosters individual growth for high school students who are willing to undertake individual or team research projects in science, mathematics, engineering, and technology. Scholarships for winning projects range from $1,000 for regional finalists and up to $100,000 for national winners. See web site: http://www.discoveryeducation.com/siemenscompetition/ for additional information.
Siemens Awards for Advanced Placement: The foundation awards scholarships of $2,000 to students with the greatest number of scores of 5 on AP exams taken in grades 9, 10, and 11 in each of the 50 states and two national winners are awarded a $5,000 scholarship. Eligible exams are Biology, Calculus BC, Chemistry, Computer Science A, Environmental Science, Physics C: Mechanics, Physics C: Electricity and Magnetism, and Statistics. The College Board identifies eligible students for Siemens Foundation.
Siemens We Can Change the World Challenge: The foundation awards grants and prizes to students in grades K-12 who uses the fundamentals of scientific methods to address environmental problems in their own backyard. Students, while working with a teacher or mentor, researches, creates green solutions, and shares their results with other students nationwide. Prizes include a grant to the participants school, savings bonds, an appearance on Planet Green, a presentation at the United Nations, a Discovery trip, a pocket video camera, and a Siemens We Can Change the World Challenge green prize pack. See web site: http://www.wecanchange.com/ for additional information.
EIN: 522136074

5567
The Rosanne H. Silbermann Foundation, Inc.

c/o M. Steven Silbermann
23 Camelot Dr.
Livingston, NJ   07039-5126

Foundation type: Independent foundation
Purpose: Grants to individuals for medical research in cell biology and ophthalmology.
Financial data: Year ended 12/31/2012. Assets, $10,785,457 (M); Expenditures, $567,659; Total giving, $550,000.

Fields of interest: Biomedicine; Medical research.
Type of support: Research.
Application information: Applications not accepted.
>   *Additional information:* Unsolicited requests for funds not considered or acknowledged.
EIN: 223578791

5568
The Thomas J. and Rita T. Skeuse Scholarship Fund Inc.
115 Rte. 202-31 S.
Ringoes, NJ 08551

Foundation type: Company-sponsored foundation
Purpose: Scholarships to employees of Reagent and Chemical Research, Inc., NJ.
Financial data: Year ended 12/31/2012. Assets, $6,048 (M); Expenditures, $10,000; Total giving, $10,000; Grants to individuals, 5 grants totaling $10,000 (high: $2,500, low: $1,250).
Type of support: Employee-related scholarships.
Application information: Unsolicited requests for funds not considered or acknowledged.
Company name: Reagent Chemical and Research, Incorporated
EIN: 223741423

5569
Charles C. Smith Educational Foundation
c/o Lori Fitzgibbon
P.O. Box 310
Washington, NJ 07882

Foundation type: Independent foundation
Purpose: Scholarships to high school seniors in Washington township and North Hunterdon county, NJ.
Financial data: Year ended 12/31/2011. Assets, $149,654 (M); Expenditures, $16,815; Total giving, $16,250; Grants to individuals, 8 grants totaling $16,250 (high: $2,500, low: $1,250).
Fields of interest: Higher education.
Type of support: Scholarships—to individuals.
Application information: Applications accepted. Application form required.
>   *Deadline(s):* Apr. 1
EIN: 222186867

5570
The Harold B. and Dorothy A. Snyder Foundation
331 Newman Springs Rd., Bldg. 1, No. 143
Red Bank, NJ 07701-5688
Application address: P.O. Box 671, Moorestown, NJ 08057-0671; URL: http://www.snyderfoundation.com/.

Foundation type: Independent foundation
Purpose: Scholarships to Union County, NJ, residents for attendance at an accredited college or university in Union county, NJ pursuing an undergraduate degree in nursing, special education or construction management, or a graduate pursuing a degree/vocation in the ministry.
Financial data: Year ended 09/30/2012. Assets, $9,435,549 (M); Expenditures, $535,915; Total giving, $312,500. Scholarships—to individuals amount not specified.
Fields of interest: Education, special; Nursing school/education; Theological school/education; Engineering.
Type of support: Graduate support; Undergraduate support.

Application information: Applications accepted. Application form required. Application form available on the grantmaker's web site. Interview required.
>   *Send request by:* Mail, on-line or e-mail
>   *Deadline(s):* Mar.
>   *Applicants should submit the following:*
>   1) Transcripts
>   2) Essay
>   *Additional information:* Application should also include copies of your parents' and your current tax returns. Preference is given to applicants who are in their junior or senior years. See web site for additional guidelines.
EIN: 222316043

5571
The Society for Organizing Charity of the City of Salem, New Jersey, Inc.
c/o P. Olejarski
209 Princeton Ave.
National Park, NJ 08063 (856) 853-1941

Foundation type: Operating foundation
Purpose: Emergency aid and assistance, including medical expenses, to economically disadvantaged individuals residing in Salem, NJ.
Financial data: Year ended 12/31/2012. Assets, $631,230 (M); Expenditures, $39,015; Total giving, $35,630.
Fields of interest: Economically disadvantaged.
Type of support: Grants for special needs.
Application information: Applications accepted.
>   *Initial approach:* Letter
>   *Deadline(s):* None
EIN: 216015103

5572
Southpole Foundation Inc.
222 Bridge Plz. S.
Fort Lee, NJ 07024-5712
E-mail: contact@khymfoundation.org; URL: http://www.khymfoundation.org/

Foundation type: Independent foundation
Purpose: Scholarships to promising students in the Tri-State area for attendance at select community colleges.
Financial data: Year ended 12/31/2012. Assets, $4,795,901 (M); Expenditures, $299,157; Total giving, $243,000.
Fields of interest: Higher education.
Type of support: Support to graduates or students of specific schools.
Application information: Students are selected based on merit and financial need.
EIN: 200471235

5573
The Summit Area Public Foundation
P.O. Box 867
Summit, NJ 07902-0867 (908) 277-1422
Contact: Barbara Bunting, Treas.
FAX: (908) 277-3042; E-mail: info@sapfnj.org; Grant inquiry e-mail: grants@sapfnj.org; URL: http://www.sapfnj.org

Foundation type: Community foundation
Purpose: Scholarships to graduating high school seniors living in or around Summit, NJ for higher education.
Publications: Application guidelines; Grants list; Informational brochure.

Financial data: Year ended 12/31/2012. Assets, $13,706,082 (M); Expenditures, $743,899; Total giving, $656,164.
Fields of interest: Higher education.
Type of support: Awards/grants by nomination only.
Application information: Applications not accepted.
>   *Additional information:* The foundation does not accept unsolicited applications. Candidates are nominated by high school guidance departments or by the foundation's scholarship committee.
EIN: 221948007

5574
Summit Home for Children Chesebrough Foundation
480 Morris Ave.
Summit, NJ 07901

Foundation type: Independent foundation
Purpose: Scholarships and financial assistance to individuals in the greater summit, NJ area to defray educational, medical and other expenses.
Financial data: Year ended 12/31/2011. Assets, $277,204 (M); Expenditures, $7,020; Total giving, $3,250.
Fields of interest: Higher education; Human services.
Type of support: Scholarships—to individuals; Grants for special needs.
Application information:
>   *Initial approach:* Letter
>   *Additional information:* Contact foundation for guidelines.
EIN: 226063803

5575
Jane and Tom Tang Foundation for Education, Inc.
c/o RRBB & Co.
111 Dunnell Rd., Ste. 100
Maplewood, NJ 07040

Foundation type: Operating foundation
Purpose: Scholarships primarily to Chinese students.
Financial data: Year ended 12/31/2012. Assets, $174,675 (M); Expenditures, $21,992; Total giving, $14,500.
Fields of interest: Medical school/education.
Type of support: Graduate support; Doctoral support.
Application information: Applications not accepted.
>   *Additional information:* Unsolicited requests for funds not considered or acknowledged.
EIN: 223693816

5576
Tavitian Foundation Inc.
c/o Syncsort Inc.
50 Tice Blvd.
Woodcliff Lake, NJ 07677-7654

Foundation type: Independent foundation
Purpose: Scholarships primarily to individuals who are natural or descendants of an Armenian or Eastern European parent, grandparent, or great-grandparent.
Financial data: Year ended 12/31/2012. Assets, $28,390,498 (M); Expenditures, $2,785,184; Total giving, $2,514,800.
International interests: Armenia; Eastern Europe.

Type of support: Scholarships—to individuals; Undergraduate support.
Application information: Applications not accepted.
Additional information: Recipients may use their award at any approved institution for any course of study. Recipients are selected on the basis of standardized test scores, recommendations, financial need, and personal interviews, and strong preference to those of Armenian or Eastern European descent. Unsolicited requests for funds not considered or acknowledged.
EIN: 521939275

5577
Terplan Family Foundation, Inc.
25 Summit Ave.
Hackensack, NJ 07601-1262 (201) 487-0881

Foundation type: Independent foundation
Purpose: Scholarship to a deserving young Hungarian artist or musician not older than 35 years old to study at Montclair State University, NJ.
Financial data: Year ended 12/31/2012. Assets, $10,276 (M); Expenditures, $57,387; Total giving, $23,093; Grants to individuals, 3 grants totaling $23,093 (high: $20,093, low: $1,000).
Fields of interest: Arts education; Higher education.
International interests: Hungary.
Type of support: Scholarships—to individuals; Support to graduates or students of specific schools; Foreign applicants.
Application information: Application form required.
Deadline(s): Oct. 1 Fall semester
Additional information: Application should include a certified copy of the student status, curriculum vitae and language certificate.
EIN: 223789231

5578
The Townsend Foundation, Inc.
58 Holly Oak Dr.
Voorhees, NJ 08043-1538 (856) 772-9570
Contact: John Langan, Mgr.

Foundation type: Operating foundation
Purpose: Scholarships to full- and part-time Bachelor's and Associates students enrolled in a developmental reading or writing course.
Financial data: Year ended 12/31/2012. Assets, $329,507 (M); Expenditures, $188,453; Total giving, $126,420.
Fields of interest: Adult education—literacy, basic skills & GED.
Type of support: Undergraduate support.
Application information: Applications accepted.
Initial approach: E-mail
Deadline(s): None
Additional information: Contact foundation for additional application guidelines.
EIN: 223435514

5579
Ethel C. Townsend Scholarship Fund
c/o Berkeley College
P.O. Box 440
Little Falls, NJ 07424-0440

Foundation type: Independent foundation
Purpose: Scholarships primarily to students from NY, NJ, and CT for postsecondary education.
Financial data: Year ended 06/30/2011. Assets, $87,132 (M); Expenditures, $26,379; Total giving,

$26,333; Grants to individuals, 25 grants totaling $26,333 (high: $3,500, low: $300).
Type of support: Scholarships—to individuals.
Application information: Applications not accepted.
Additional information: Unsolicited requests for funds not considered or acknowledged.
EIN: 237028890

5580
Trial Lawyers Foundation for Youth Education
c/o Bank of America, N.A.
P.O. Box 1525
Pennington, NJ 08534 (361) 387-5999
Application address: Robstown High School, Financial Aid Office, 609 Hwy. 44, Robstown, TX 78380

Foundation type: Independent foundation
Purpose: Scholarships to full-time students graduating from Robstown High School, TX.
Financial data: Year ended 12/31/2012. Assets, $1,171,716 (M); Expenditures, $57,586; Total giving, $31,250; Grants to individuals, 62 grants totaling $31,250 (high: $1,000, low: $250).
Type of support: Support to graduates or students of specific schools; Undergraduate support.
Application information: Applications accepted. Application form required.
Deadline(s): Mar. 13
Applicants should submit the following:
1) Essay
2) SAT
3) ACT
4) Transcripts
5) Letter(s) of recommendation
Additional information: Application should also include list of extracurricular activities and community service.
EIN: 866267254

5581
Tri-County Community Action Agency, Inc.
110 Cohansey St.
Bridgeton, NJ 08302-1922 (856) 451-6330
Contact: Albert Kelly, C.E.O.
FAX: (856) 455-7288; Toll Free Tel.:
(800)-457-3188; URL: http://www.tricountycaa.org

Foundation type: Public charity
Purpose: Assistance and other services to help indigent residents of Cumberland, Gloucester and Salem counties in southern NJ meet the basic needs of daily living.
Financial data: Year ended 06/30/2011. Assets, $10,806,067 (M); Expenditures, $33,898,022.
Fields of interest: Economically disadvantaged.
Type of support: In-kind gifts; Grants for special needs.
Application information:
Initial approach: Letter
Additional information: Contact the agency for eligibility determination.
EIN: 221942357

5582
Union County CPA Scholarship Fund
c/o Philip J. Kinzel, CPA
195 Fairfield Ave.
West Caldwell, NJ 07006-6419

Foundation type: Independent foundation

Purpose: Scholarships to Union County, NJ, residents majoring in accounting.
Financial data: Year ended 05/31/2012. Assets, $0 (M); Expenditures, $12,563; Total giving, $12,200; Grants to individuals, 3 grants totaling $4,500 (high: $1,500, low: $1,500).
Fields of interest: Business school/education.
Type of support: Scholarships—to individuals.
Application information: Applications not accepted.
Additional information: Unsolicited requests for funds not considered or acknowledged.
EIN: 222377473

5583
Union Mutual Foundation
82 N. Summit St., No. 2
Tenafly, NJ 07670-1018 (201) 569-8180

Foundation type: Public charity
Purpose: Scholarships primarily to residents of NY and NJ.
Financial data: Year ended 12/31/2011. Assets, $947,878 (M); Expenditures, $284,888; Total giving, $58,000; Grants to individuals, totaling $58,000.
Type of support: Scholarships—to individuals.
Application information:
Initial approach: Letter
Additional information: Contact foundation for eligibility information.
EIN: 237358092

5584
United States Equestrian Team Foundation, Inc.
1040 Pottersville Rd.
P.O. Box 35
Gladstone, NJ 07934-2053 (908) 234-1251
FAX: (908) 234-0670; URL: http://www.uset.com

Foundation type: Public charity
Purpose: Grants to individuals representing the United States in the Olympic games, Pan American games and other international competitions for training, preparation and financing.
Financial data: Year ended 12/31/2011. Assets, $15,457,189 (M); Expenditures, $4,414,541; Total giving, $2,144,613; Grants to individuals, totaling $49,613.
Fields of interest: Athletics/sports, equestrianism.
Type of support: Grants to individuals.
Application information: Individuals are determined by planning committees and subcommittees. Riders at certain levels of training are evaluated by their competing record, how long they have been competing, what they have done during their riding career, and what they will do in the future pertaining to this career. Contact foundation for current application guidelines.
EIN: 221668879

5585
United Way of Bergen County
6 Forest Ave.
Paramus, NJ 07652-5241 (201) 291-4050
Contact: Thomas M. Toronto, Pres. and C.E.O.
FAX: (201) 291-0681;
E-mail: info@bergenunitedway.org; Toll-free tel.:
(888) 340-8929; E-Mail for Thomas M. Toronto:
ttoronto@bergenunitedway.org; URL: http://
www.bergenunitedway.org

Foundation type: Public charity

Purpose: Assistance with urgent financial needs such as utility bills when faced with shut-off, medication and healthcare costs for those without insurance, and mortgage and rent payments to prevent eviction or foreclosure, to needy residents of Bergen County, NJ.
Financial data: Year ended 03/31/2012. Assets, $13,266,887 (M); Expenditures, $10,712,811; Total giving, $9,184,926; Grants to individuals, totaling $398,154.
Fields of interest: Economically disadvantaged.
Type of support: Grants for special needs.
Application information:
  Initial approach: Telephone
  Deadline(s): None
  Additional information: Contact foundation for eligibility requirements.
EIN: 226028959

5586
United Way of Greater Union County, Inc.
33 W. Grand St.
Elizabeth, NJ   07202-1449   (908) 353-7171
FAX: (908) 353-6310; E-mail: info@uwguc.org;
Additional address (Summit office): 71 Summit Ave., Summit, NJ 07901-3690; URL: http://www.uwguc.org/

Foundation type: Public charity
Purpose: Emergency assistance for low and moderate income individuals and families in need in Union County, NJ, with utility and rental assistance.
Publications: Annual report; Newsletter.
Financial data: Year ended 08/31/2011. Assets, $4,705,095 (M); Expenditures, $6,527,589; Total giving, $4,273,723; Grants to individuals, 172 grants totaling $86,733.
Fields of interest: Economically disadvantaged.
Type of support: Emergency funds; Grants for special needs.
Application information: Contact the organization for eligibility determination.
EIN: 221904427

5587
United Way of Hudson County
857 Bergen Ave.
Jersey City, NJ   07306-4405   (201) 434-2625
FAX: (201) 434-8643;
E-mail: contact@unitedwayhudson.org; E-mail for Daniel Altilio: daltilio@unitedwayofhc.org;
URL: http://www.unitedwayofhc.org

Foundation type: Public charity
Purpose: Rental assistance to individuals and families in need in Hudson County, NJ.
Publications: Informational brochure; Newsletter.
Financial data: Year ended 12/31/2011. Assets, $1,836,968 (M); Expenditures, $4,895,564; Total giving, $2,364,082; Grants to individuals, totaling $1,356,720.
Fields of interest: Human services; Economically disadvantaged.
Type of support: Grants to individuals; Grants for special needs.
Application information: Individual rents are paid directly to landlords. Contact the organization for eligibility criteria.
EIN: 221487218

5588
United Way of North Essex
60 S. Fullerton Ave.
Montclair, NJ   07042-2632   (973) 746-4040
Contact: John Franklin, C.E.O.
FAX: (973) 746-6207; E-mail: uwne@uwne.org;
E-Mail for John Franklin:
John.Franklin@UnitedWayNNJ.org; URL: http://www.uwne.org

Foundation type: Public charity
Purpose: Financial assistance for rent, utility payments, and pharmaceutical bills for indigent individuals and families in the North Essex, NJ, area. Also, emergency financial assistance to victims of Hurricane Katrina who relocated to the North Essex, NJ, area from New Orleans, LA.
Financial data: Year ended 06/30/2010. Assets, $3,535,690 (M); Expenditures, $1,056,786; Total giving, $345,706; Grants to individuals, totaling $28,747.
Fields of interest: Economically disadvantaged.
Type of support: Emergency funds; Grants for special needs.
Application information:
  Initial approach: Letter
  Additional information: Contact foundation for eligibility requirements.
EIN: 221772825

5589
The Valley Hospital Auxiliary
223 N. Van Dien Ave.
Ridgewood, NJ   07450-2726   (201) 447-8135
E-mail: webinfo@valleyhealth.com; URL: http://www.valleyhealth.com/valley_hospital_auxillary.aspx?id=792

Foundation type: Public charity
Purpose: Scholarships to graduating seniors residing or enrolled in high schools in the Valley Hospital's service area, NJ, who are interested in a career in a health-related field.
Financial data: Year ended 06/30/2011. Assets, $262,809 (M); Expenditures, $452,345; Total giving, $445,000.
Fields of interest: Medical school/education; Nursing school/education.
Type of support: Undergraduate support.
Application information: Contact foundation for complete application guidelines.
EIN: 226059984

5590
Scott Van Doren Memorial Scholarship Fund
60 Deerhill Rd.
Lebanon, NJ   08833

Foundation type: Operating foundation
Purpose: Four-year scholarships to wrestlers at North Hunterdon High School, Annandale, NJ, for postsecondary education.
Financial data: Year ended 06/30/2012. Assets, $70,156 (M); Expenditures, $9,028; Total giving, $9,000; Grants to individuals, 5 grants totaling $9,000 (high: $4,000, low: $500).
Fields of interest: Athletics/sports, training.
Type of support: Support to graduates or students of specific schools; Undergraduate support.
Application information: Applications not accepted.
  Additional information: Unsolicited requests for funds not considered or acknowledged.
EIN: 223117696

5591
Van Doren Scholarship Trust 008963
(formerly Peter Ellis Van Doren Scholarship Fund)
P.O. Box 7037
Bedminster, NJ   07921

Foundation type: Independent foundation
Purpose: Scholarships to graduating seniors who are residents of Somerset County, NJ, with preference to the boroughs of Peapack and Gladstone.
Financial data: Year ended 12/31/2012. Assets, $770,434 (M); Expenditures, $50,039; Total giving, $39,000; Grants to individuals, 26 grants totaling $39,000 (high: $3,500, low: $500).
Type of support: Support to graduates or students of specific schools; Undergraduate support.
Application information: Application form required.
  Additional information: Forms are available at all public and private secondary school guidance departments in Somerset County, NJ.
EIN: 226666043

5592
Virtua Health Foundation, Inc.
401 Rt. 73 N.
50 Lake Ctr. Dr., Ste. 301
Marlton, NJ   08053-3248   (856) 355-0830
FAX: (856) 355-0831; E-mail: vhf@virtua.org;
URL: http://www.virtua.org/about/foundation/default.aspx

Foundation type: Public charity
Purpose: Scholarships to students at the Helene Fuld School of Nursing in Camden county, NJ. Grants to individuals for disaster relief such as house fires or catastrophic illness.
Publications: Newsletter.
Financial data: Year ended 12/31/2011. Assets, $65,747,184 (M); Expenditures, $6,468,384; Total giving, $3,207,295; Grants to individuals, totaling $292,668.
Fields of interest: Higher education; Safety/disasters.
Type of support: Scholarships—to individuals; Grants for special needs.
Application information: Applications accepted. Application form required.
  Additional information: Applicant must demonstrate financial need and have a GPA of 2.5 or higher to be eligible for scholarships.
EIN: 043722352

5593
Wei Family Private Foundation
359 Centre St., Ste. 2
Nutley, NJ   07110-2791
Application address: P.O. Box 14, Glen Rock, NJ 07452-0014, e-mail: admin@wfpf888.org
E-mail: info@wfpf888.org; URL: http://wfpf888.org/

Foundation type: Independent foundation
Purpose: Scholarships to students of Chinese heritage with high academic credentials pursuing a degree in Science or Engineering or Mathematics at Oregon State University or an Electrical Engineering graduate degree at Columbia University.
Financial data: Year ended 12/31/2012. Assets, $4,068,043 (M); Expenditures, $195,913; Total giving, $165,166; Grants to individuals, 14 grants totaling $165,166 (high: $43,333, low: $2,000).
Fields of interest: Science; Mathematics; Engineering; Asians/Pacific Islanders.

Type of support: Scholarships—to individuals; Support to graduates or students of specific schools; Graduate support.
Application information: Applications accepted. Application form required. Application form available on the grantmaker's web site. Interview required.
> *Send request by:* Mail or e-mail
> *Deadline(s):* Apr. 1
> *Applicants should submit the following:*
> 1) GPA
> 2) Letter(s) of recommendation
> 3) Transcripts
> 4) Resume
> 5) Curriculum vitae
> *Additional information:* See web site for additional application guidelines.
EIN: 264525149

5594
The Harold Wetterberg Foundation
89 Headquarters Plz.
Morristown, NJ 07960
Contact: Gene R. Korf Esq., Secy.
Application address for veterinary graduate education scholarships: Academic and Student Affairs Program Specialist, Association of American Veterinary Medical Colleges, 1101 Vermont Ave., NW, Ste. 301, Washington, DC 20005-3539

Foundation type: Independent foundation
Purpose: Scholarships to current or former residents of NJ who are enrolled in postgraduate education in veterinary medicine. Consideration will also be given to veterinary medical students enrolled in the second or third year of the professional DVM curriculum.
Financial data: Year ended 12/31/2012. Assets, $1,945,371 (M); Expenditures, $266,159; Total giving, $210,000.
Fields of interest: Medical school/education.
Type of support: Graduate support; Postgraduate support.
Application information: Applications accepted. Application form required.
> *Send request by:* Mail
> *Deadline(s):* Mar. 19
> *Final notification:* Recipients notified in July
> *Applicants should submit the following:*
> 1) GPA
> 2) Transcripts
> 3) Letter(s) of recommendation
> 4) Essay
> *Additional information:* Application should also include four letters of reference. The scholarship is administered by the American Association of Veterinary Medical Colleges.
EIN: 226042915

5595
WheatonArts and Cultural Center
(formerly Wheaton Village, Inc.)
1501 Glasstown Rd.
Millville, NJ 08332-1568 (856) 825-6800
Contact: Susan Gogan, Pres. and Exec. Dir.
FAX: (856) 825-2410;
E-mail: mail@wheatonarts.org; Toll-free tel.: (800) 998-4552; URL: http://www.wheatonarts.org

Foundation type: Public charity
Purpose: Fellowships to artists specializing in glass.
Publications: Informational brochure (including application guidelines).
Financial data: Year ended 06/30/2011. Assets, $5,001,925 (M); Expenditures, $3,001,790.

Fields of interest: Arts.
Type of support: Fellowships.
Application information: Application form required.
> *Deadline(s):* Sept. 20
> *Applicants should submit the following:*
> 1) Essay
> 2) Resume
> 3) Letter(s) of recommendation
> *Additional information:* Application should include ten slides of work, and a brief biographical statement.
Program description:
> *CGCA Fellowship Program:* This professional-level program provides focused and self-directed artists working in glass with a concentrated period of time to work alongside their peers. Fellows work toward a common goal of advancing their careers through the perfection or refinement of techniques needed to develop a new or expanded body of work. The program is an environment where facilities, equipment, and a technical orientation are provided; however, technical assistance is not on hand.
EIN: 221849118

5596
White Beeches Country Club Caddy Scholarship Fund, Inc.
c/o White Beeches Golf & Country Club, Inc.
70 Haworth Dr.
Haworth, NJ 07641

Foundation type: Independent foundation
Purpose: Scholarships to caddies at the White Beeches Country Club, NJ for postsecondary education.
Financial data: Year ended 12/31/2011. Assets, $2,722 (M); Expenditures, $18,956; Total giving, $14,250; Grants to individuals, 14 grants totaling $14,250 (high: $1,500, low: $750).
Fields of interest: Athletics/sports, golf.
Type of support: Undergraduate support.
Application information: Interview required.
EIN: 222918973

5597
Howard Whitfield Foundation
P.O. Box 336
Red Bank, NJ 07701-0336

Foundation type: Independent foundation
Purpose: Scholarships to graduating seniors of Red Bank Regional High School, NJ. Graduates from public schools in Monmouth County, NJ, are eligible for awards as funds permit. Six types of scholarships are awarded by the foundation: medical, legal, commercial, liberal arts, religious, and journalism.
Financial data: Year ended 12/31/2012. Assets, $221,289 (M); Expenditures, $17,994; Total giving, $12,850; Grant to an individual, 1 grant totaling $12,850.
Fields of interest: Print publishing; Higher education; Law school/education.
Type of support: Support to graduates or students of specific schools.
Application information: Applications accepted. Application form required.
> *Deadline(s):* May 1
> *Additional information:* Application and financial statement forms are available from the guidance offices of all public schools in Monmouth County, NJ.
EIN: 210593879

5598
The Wight Foundation, Inc.
60 Park Pl., 17th Fl.
Newark, NJ 07102-5511 (973) 824-1195
FAX: (973) 824-1199;
E-mail: Wightfoundation@wightfoundation.org;
URL: http://www.wightfoundation.org

Foundation type: Independent foundation
Purpose: Scholarships by nomination only for private high school education at specific boarding schools to residents of the greater Newark, NJ, area. Students currently in the seventh grade who attend public, private, or parochial schools are eligible.
Publications: Informational brochure (including application guidelines); Newsletter.
Financial data: Year ended 12/31/2011. Assets, $11,743,941 (M); Expenditures, $1,535,049; Total giving, $381,107; Grants to individuals, 65 grants totaling $259,072 (high: $9,290, low: $90).
Fields of interest: Secondary school/education.
Type of support: Support to graduates or students of specific schools; Awards/grants by nomination only; Precollege support.
Application information: Interview required.
> *Deadline(s):* For preliminary applications Jan. 25; approved students are sent final applications, which are due Feb. 15
> *Applicants should submit the following:*
> 1) SAT
> 2) Letter(s) of recommendation
> 3) Essay
> *Additional information:* Application must also include report from the School and Student Services for Financial Aid (SSS); Students must apply directly to the foundation.
Program description:
> *Wight Scholarship Program:* To qualify, students must maintain a "B" average and score above grade level in standardized tests in reading, language, and math. Scholars are expected to complete 20 hours of community service annually in the greater Newark area. All finalists must compete in STEP, a 14-month enrichment program taught by Wight Foundation alumni, which prepares them for the boarding school experience. The following boarding schools participate in the program: Blair Academy, NJ; Canterbury School, CT; Cheshire Academy, CT; Episcopal High School, VA; George School, PA; Hill School, PA; Kent School, CT; Lawrenceville School, NJ; Marvelwood School, CT; Miss Porter's School, CT; Peddie School, NJ; Perkiomen School, PA; Phillip Exeter Academy, NH; Purnell School, NJ; Solebury School, PA; South Kent School, CT; St. Andrew's School, DE; St. Paul's School, NH; St. Timothy's School, MD; Stoneleigh-Burnham School, MA; Taft School, CT; Trinity-Pawling School, NY; Westminster School, CT; Westover School, CT; Westtown School, PA.
EIN: 222743349

5599
The Wiley Foundation, Inc.
c/o D. Wiley, Wiley & Sons
111 River St.
Hoboken, NJ 07030-5773
Contact: Deborah E. Wiley, Chair.; Alicia Baldo, Secy.
URL: http://www.wileyfoundation.org

Foundation type: Company-sponsored foundation
Purpose: Prizes by nomination only to exceptional Ph.D. and M.D. scientists whose research has set the standard for excellence in the biomedical field.
Publications: Application guidelines; Grants list.

Financial data: Year ended 04/30/2012. Assets, $1,065,382 (M); Expenditures, $105,969; Total giving, $86,001; Grants to individuals, 5 grants totaling $36,001 (high: $11,667, low: $500).
Fields of interest: Biomedicine; Science.
Type of support: Research; Awards/grants by nomination only; Awards/prizes.
Application information: Application form available on the grantmaker's web site.
> Copies of proposal: 4
> Deadline(s): July 31
> Additional information: Nominations for the Wiley Prize in Biomedical Sciences should be submitted by someone other than the nominee. More than one nomination can be made from the same organization. Nominations should include letters of support from colleagues familiar with the nominee's work and a curriculum vitae.

Program description:
> *Wiley Prize in Biomedical Sciences:* Through the Wiley Prize in Biomedical Sciences program, the foundation annually awards one $35,000 grant to a Ph.D. or M.D. scientist who has opened new fields of research or advanced novel concepts or their applications in a particular biomedical discipline. The award recognizes a specific contribution or series of contributions that demonstrate the nominee's leadership in the development of research concepts or their clinical application.
> **EIN:** 134163744

5600
The Woodrow Wilson National Fellowship Foundation

5 Vaughn Dr., Ste. 300
Princeton, NJ 08540-6313 (609) 452-7007
Contact: Beverly Sanford, Secy.
FAX: (609) 452-0066;
E-mail: communications@woodrow.org; Application address: P.O. Box 5281, Princeton, NJ 08543-5281; URL: http://www.woodrow.org

Foundation type: Public charity
Purpose: Awards and fellowships in a variety of areas to qualified individuals. Fellowships and grants to individuals in various disciplines. Grants to artists for social, cultural or educational projects.
Publications: Annual report; Newsletter.
Financial data: Year ended 06/30/2014. Assets, $36,185,833 (M); Expenditures, $20,452,425; Total giving, $11,346,104; Grants to individuals, totaling $10,175,523.
Fields of interest: Humanities; Language (foreign); Arts; Health care; Children/youth, services; International affairs; Business/industry; Ethics; Social sciences; Anthropology/sociology; Women's studies; Government/public administration; Leadership development; Religion; Women.
Type of support: Program development; Fellowships; Internship funds; Graduate support; Undergraduate support; Doctoral support.
Application information: Applications accepted. Application form required. Application form available on the grantmaker's web site.
> Initial approach: Proposal for artist grants; Letter or telephone for other programs
> Deadline(s): Feb. 12 for artist grants; For other programs contact foundation for current application deadlines.
> Additional information: Applications for artist grants may be submitted by e-mail via publicscholarship@woodrow.org with appropriate attachments.

Program descriptions:
> *Charlotte W. Newcombe Doctoral Dissertation Fellowships:* Awards fellowships of $24,000 to

Ph.D. and Th.D. candidates in the final year of a humanities or social sciences dissertation that explores ethical or religious values within the candidates' discipline. Grants to individuals through competitive application process.
> *Doris Duke Conservation Fellowship:* Fellowships for graduate students who are already enrolled in multidisciplinary master's programs at partner universities, and who are committed to careers as practicing conservationists. Fellows are selected by participating universities; only students currently enrolled in environmental programs at these participating universities are eligible to apply.
> *Leonore Annenberg Teaching Fellowships:* Awards fellowships of $30,000 for master's-degree preparation of secondary-level teachers committed to teach in high-need schools. Specified institutions only; grants to individuals through institutions' application process only.
> *Mellon Mays Undergraduate Fellowship Dissertation Grants:* Grants of up to $20,000 are available to graduate students who have participated in the Mellon Mays Undergraduate Fellowship Program. Grants provide graduate students at the critical juncture of completing their graduate degrees with support to spend a year finishing the writing of their dissertation.
> *Mellon Mays Undergraduate Fellowship Travel and Research Grants:* These grants, available to graduate students who have participated in the Mellon Mays Undergraduate Fellowship Program, provide eligible graduate students with the financial means to complete their research prior to the start of dissertation writing. Funding of up to $5,000 is available for one summer or one semester of travel and/or research support; awards are based on the scholarly merit of individual applications received.
> *Millicent C. Macintosh Fellowship for Recently Tenured Faculty:* This fellowship provides a $15,000 stipend to support especially promising faculty who demonstrate a deep commitment to excellent teaching and scholarship in the humanities, and who are exceptional citizens of their academic community. The fellowship is specifically intended for recently-tenured faculty who would benefit from additional time and resources to continue their scholarly work, but whose family and other obligations make it difficult for them to be away from their homes for extended periods of time.
> *The Thomas R. Pickering Foreign Affairs Fellowship Program:* Fellowships for talented college sophomores interested in international affairs and in careers in the U.S. Foreign Service. Preference is given to groups historically underrepresented in the Foreign Service and to qualified applicants with financial need. Sponsored by the Department of State, the fellowship includes junior and senior year scholarships, attendance at a junior year, seven-week summer institute for preparation for graduate school, participation in two summer internships in the State Department, and graduate funding at a school of international affairs. Applicants accepted into the program incur the obligation of four and one-half years as Foreign Service Officers in the Department of State. Grants to individuals through competitive application process only.
> *The Thomas R. Pickering Graduate Foreign Affairs Fellowship Program:* Fellowships for individuals in the first year of a two-year full-time master's degree program related to international affairs who are interested in careers in the U.S. Foreign Service. Women and members of minority groups historically underrepresented in the Foreign Service and students with financial need are encouraged to apply. Tuition, living stipend, and books are paid during the first and second year of graduate study,

and fellows participate in one domestic and one overseas internship within the State Department. Fellows incur a contractual obligation of three years of service in an appointment as a Foreign Service Officer.
> *Woodrow Wilson Doctoral Dissertation Fellowships in Women's Studies:* Awards fellowships of $3,000 to Ph.D. candidates in the final year of humanities or social sciences dissertation that explores issues of women and gender. Grants to individuals through competitive application process only.
> **EIN:** 210703075

5601
The Winn Feline Foundation

(formerly Robert H. Winn Foundation for Cat Research, Inc.)
355 Cornell St.
Wyckoff, NJ 07481 (201) 275-0624
Contact: Maureen Walsh, C.E.O.
FAX: (877) 933-0939;
E-mail: winn@winnfelinehealth.org; Application address: c/o Janet Wolf, 293 Landing Rd., Newport, NJ 08345-2021, tel.: (856) 447-9787, e-mail: winnfeline@aol.com; E-mail for Maureen Walsh: mwalsh@winnfelinehealth.org; URL: http://www.winnfelinehealth.org

Foundation type: Public charity
Purpose: Research grants to advance veterinary knowledge in all areas of feline health.
Publications: Application guidelines; Annual report; Grants list; Informational brochure; Newsletter; Occasional report; Program policy statement.
Financial data: Year ended 04/30/2012. Assets, $2,200,545 (M); Expenditures, $540,281; Total giving, $324,710; Grants to individuals, totaling $37,219.
Fields of interest: Animal welfare; Veterinary medicine.
Type of support: Research.
Application information: Applications accepted. Application form not required.
> Deadline(s): Varies
> Applicants should submit the following:
> 1) Proposal
> 2) Curriculum vitae
> 3) Budget Information
> **EIN:** 237138699

5602
WKBJ Partnership Foundation

(formerly The Made in Dover Foundation)
50 Smith Rd.
Denville, NJ 07834-9405 (973) 328-0303
Contact: Bob Howitt, Pres.
FAX: (973) 328-0388

Foundation type: Operating foundation
Purpose: Scholarships to financially disadvantaged students residing in Dover, NJ for higher education.
Financial data: Year ended 12/31/2012. Assets, $1,609,619 (M); Expenditures, $1,050,813; Total giving, $922,687; Grants to individuals, 92 grants totaling $665,248 (high: $24,050, low: $300).
Fields of interest: Economically disadvantaged.
Type of support: Undergraduate support.
Application information: Applications accepted.
> Initial approach: Letter
> Deadline(s): None
> **EIN:** 223000244

5603

Woman's Club of Westfield, Inc.

P.O. Box 2428
Westfield, NJ 07091-2428
Contact: Anita Smith

Foundation type: Independent foundation
Purpose: Scholarships to students from Westfield High School, NJ for higher education.
Financial data: Year ended 05/31/2012. Assets, $0 (M); Expenditures, $77,640; Total giving, $46,900.
Fields of interest: Education.
Type of support: Support to graduates or students of specific schools; Undergraduate support.
Application information: Applications accepted. Application form required.
  Initial approach: Application
  Deadline(s): Mar. 15
EIN: 221585838

5604

Woodbridge Rotary Scholarship Foundation, Inc.

605 King Georges Post Rd.
Fords, NJ 08863-1812

Foundation type: Operating foundation
Purpose: Scholarships to residents of Woodbridge Township, NJ for postsecondary education at an accredited college, university, trade school, or other educational institution.
Financial data: Year ended 06/30/2011. Assets, $841,778 (M); Expenditures, $54,647; Total giving, $44,000; Grants to individuals, totaling $44,000.
Fields of interest: Vocational education, post-secondary; Higher education.
Type of support: Scholarships—to individuals.
Application information: Applications accepted. Application form required.
  Deadline(s): Apr. 15
  Applicants should submit the following:
    1) Financial information
    2) Class rank
    3) Transcripts
    4) SAT
    5) GPA
  Additional information: Application should also include character reference from a teacher, guidance counselor, or principal.
EIN: 222925024

5605

Wound Ostomy Continence Nurses Foundation

15000 Commerce Pkwy., Ste. C
Mount Laurel, NJ 08054-2212 (856) 439-0500
E-mail: wocn_info@wocn.org; Toll-free tel.: (888) 224-9626; URL: https://www.wocnfoundation.org/

Foundation type: Public charity
Purpose: Scholarships to deserving individuals working within the wound, ostomy and continence nursing specialty.
Financial data: Year ended 12/31/2011. Assets, $388,453 (M); Expenditures, $256,504; Total giving, $107,108; Grants to individuals, totaling $107,108.
Fields of interest: Nursing school/education; Medical specialties research.
Type of support: Scholarships—to individuals.
Application information: Applications accepted. Application form available on the grantmaker's web site.
  Send request by: Online
  Deadline(s): May 1 and Nov. 1
  Additional information: Application should include recommendations. See web site for accredited and advanced scholarship criteria.
EIN: 330883148

5606

The Leonard Young Memorial Foundation

179 Chestnut Ridge Rd.
Saddle River, NJ 07458-2810

Foundation type: Independent foundation
Purpose: Financial assistance to cancer patients and their families, primarily of NJ, to pay for psychological counseling to help them cope with the illness.
Financial data: Year ended 12/31/2011. Assets, $255,860 (M); Expenditures, $24,453; Total giving, $15,000.
Fields of interest: Mental health, counseling/support groups; Cancer.
Type of support: Grants for special needs.
Application information:
  Initial approach: Letter
  Additional information: Contact foundation for additional guidelines.
EIN: 223006817

5607

Edward B. Zahn FFA Scholarship Trust at the Iola High School

c/o Richard W. Zhan
P.O. Box 2318
Long Beach Island, NJ 08008-2318 (620) 365-4715
Contact: David Grover
Application Address: c/o Principal Iola High School, 300 E. Jackson Ave., KS 66749

Foundation type: Independent foundation
Purpose: Scholarships to Lola High School FFA members to pursue postsecondary training in the agricultural field, KS.
Financial data: Year ended 12/31/2010. Assets, $82,474 (M); Expenditures, $10,069; Total giving,

$10,000; Grants to individuals, 9 grants totaling $10,000 (high: $2,000, low: $500).
Fields of interest: Formal/general education.
Type of support: Support to graduates or students of specific schools; Undergraduate support.
Application information: Applications accepted. Application form required.
  Deadline(s): None
  Applicants should submit the following:
    1) Class rank
    2) GPA
    3) ACT
EIN: 486327729

5608

Zipf Memorial Scholarship Foundation, Inc.

c/o Charles Komar
10 Buttonwood Ln.
Rumson, NJ 07760

Foundation type: Independent foundation
Purpose: Scholarships to students pursuing a degree in supply chain management, material management or another business-related field. Applicants should have a 3.0 GPA and membership (individually or through an immediate family member) in the National Association of Purchasing Management of the Lehigh Valley, Inc.
Financial data: Year ended 12/31/2012. Assets, $240,397 (M); Expenditures, $10,000; Total giving, $10,000; Grants to individuals, 5 grants totaling $10,000 (high: $2,000, low: $2,000).
Type of support: Scholarships—to individuals.
Application information: Applications accepted.
  Deadline(s): Dec. 1
EIN: 201002355

NEW MEXICO

5609

A Room of Her Own Foundation
P.O. Box 778
Placitas, NM 87043-0778 (505) 867-5373
Contact: Darlene Chandler Bassett, Pres.
E-mail: info@aroomofherownfoundation.org;
URL: http://www.aroomofherownfoundation.org

Foundation type: Public charity
Purpose: Awards to female writers or female visual artists to pursue their chosen artistic endeavors.
Publications: Application guidelines; Informational brochure; Newsletter; Occasional report.
Financial data: Year ended 12/31/2012. Assets, $87,170 (M); Expenditures, $83,160; Total giving, $9,100.
Fields of interest: Visual arts; Literature; Arts.
Type of support: Conferences/seminars; Publication; Grants to individuals; Awards/prizes; Project support.
Application information: Applications accepted. Application form required. Application form available on the grantmaker's web site.
> *Initial approach:* Application
> *Copies of proposal:* 1
> *Deadline(s):* July 31 for Orlando Prizes for Short Fiction
> *Additional information:* See web site for additional guidelines.

Program descriptions:
> *Gift of Freedom Award:* The program awards up to $50,000, every two years, to one qualified female writer (fiction, creative nonfiction, or poetry) and biennial retreats for committed women writers providing writing workshops and practical publishing help. Acceptable genres for this award are poetry, playwriting, creative nonfiction, and fiction. Eligible applicants must be citizens or legal residents of the U.S., who will be residing in the U.S. during the entire two-year grant period.
> *Orlando Prizes:* Awards four $1,000 prizes twice yearly to an outstanding unpublished work of poetry, nonfiction, 'sudden' or 'flash' fiction, and short fiction.

EIN: 850475649

5610

Albuquerque Community Foundation
624 Tijeras Ave., NW
Albuquerque, NM 87102 (505) 883-6240
Contact: For grants: Nancy Johnson, Prog. Dir.
FAX: (505) 883-3629;
E-mail: foundation@albuquerquefoundation.org;
URL: http://www.albuquerquefoundation.org

Foundation type: Community foundation
Purpose: Scholarships and financial aid awards to graduating high school seniors who are residents of NM for higher education. Scholarships available to students already in college.
Publications: Annual report (including application guidelines); Financial statement; Grants list; Newsletter.
Financial data: Year ended 12/31/2011. Assets, $53,405,526 (M); Expenditures, $3,811,337; Total giving, $2,211,285; Grants to individuals, totaling $138,133.
Fields of interest: Higher education; Engineering school/education; Continuing education; Scholarships/financial aid; Athletics/sports, soccer; Science; Mathematics.

Type of support: Scholarships—to individuals; Support to graduates or students of specific schools; Undergraduate support.
Application information: Applications accepted. Application form required. Application form available on the grantmaker's web site.
> *Send request by:* Mail
> *Deadline(s):* Varies
> *Additional information:* See web site for complete listing of scholarship programs, application guidelines and deadlines.

Program description:
> *Student Aid:* The foundation has twelve separate scholarship and student aid programs to help New Mexico students attain their educational goals. Each program was established by a donor with individual interests and priority areas. They represent the broad diversity of the generous individuals who care about education and believe it is the best way to give back to future generations. For this reason, requirements vary for each program. Scholarships are based totally or partially on the student's academic and/or personal merit while financial aid awards are based on the student's financial need. See web site for additional information.

EIN: 850295444

5611

American Indian Graduate Center, Inc.
3701 San Mateo N.E.
Albuquerque, NM 87110-1230 (505) 881-4584
FAX: (505) 884-0427; E-mail: sam@aigcs.org;
Toll-free tel.: (800) 628-1920; URL: http://www.aigcs.org

Foundation type: Public charity
Purpose: Fellowships and loans to Native American and Alaskan Native students enrolled full time in accredited colleges or universities in the U.S. seeking graduate and professional degrees.
Publications: Application guidelines; Annual report; Informational brochure; Newsletter.
Financial data: Year ended 06/30/2013. Assets, $3,531,319 (M); Expenditures, $2,558,890; Total giving, $1,821,464; Grants to individuals, totaling $1,821,464.
Fields of interest: Graduate/professional education; Asians/Pacific Islanders; Native Americans/American Indians.
Type of support: Fellowships; Student loans—to individuals; Graduate support; Postgraduate support.
Application information: Applications accepted. Application form required.
> *Deadline(s):* Vary
> *Additional information:* Students must be enrolled in a federally recognized tribe or have one quarter Indian blood. See web site for additional information and eligibility requirements.

EIN: 850222386

5612

American Indian Graduate Center Scholars
(also known as AIGC Scholars)
3701 San Mateo N.E. Ste. 200
Albuquerque, NM 87110-1217 (505) 881-4584
Contact: P. Deloria, Dir.
FAX: (505) 884-0427; E-mail: web@aigcs.org;
Toll-free tel.: (800)-628-1920; URL: http://www.aigcs.org

Foundation type: Public charity

Purpose: Scholarships to American Indian and Alaska native graduate students for continuing education at institutions of higher learning.
Financial data: Year ended 06/30/2012. Assets, $1,882,462 (M); Expenditures, $10,537,797; Total giving, $9,504,657; Grants to individuals, totaling $9,504,657.
Fields of interest: Higher education; Native Americans/American Indians.
Type of support: Graduate support; Undergraduate support.
Application information: Applications accepted. Application form required.
> *Deadline(s):* Vary
> *Additional information:* Applicant must demonstrate financial need. Contact foundation or see web site for additional application guidelines.

EIN: 850477062

5613

B.F. Foundation
c/o David Chase
766 Calle del Resplandor
Santa Fe, NM 87505-5988
E-mail: dchase@vestor.com

Foundation type: Independent foundation
Purpose: Undergraduate scholarships primarily to AZ residents who are U.S. citizens and enrolled full-time at Northern Arizona University. Continuing education students at Arizona State University who are AZ residents and U.S. citizens may also be eligible.
Financial data: Year ended 12/31/2012. Assets, $4,028,150 (M); Expenditures, $315,782; Total giving, $178,400.
Fields of interest: Adult/continuing education.
Type of support: Support to graduates or students of specific schools; Undergraduate support.
Application information: Applications not accepted.
> *Additional information:* Unsolicited requests for funds not considered or acknowledged.

EIN: 366141070

5614

Mary Anne Berliner Foundation Trust
P.O. Box AA
Artesia, NM 88211-7526 (575) 748-8005
Application Address: c/o First American Bank

Foundation type: Independent foundation
Purpose: Scholarships to students residing in southeast NM for undergraduate and graduate education.
Financial data: Year ended 12/31/2011. Assets, $1,007,170 (M); Expenditures, $65,144; Total giving, $50,600; Grants to individuals, 24 grants totaling $50,600 (high: $2,525, low: $750).
Fields of interest: Education.
Type of support: Graduate support; Undergraduate support.
Application information: Applications accepted. Application form required.
> *Deadline(s):* Mar. 15
> *Applicants should submit the following:*
> 1) Essay
> 2) Letter(s) of recommendation
> 3) Financial information

EIN: 856122581

5615
Border Art Residency
3125 Hwy. 28
Anthony, NM 88021   (915) 533-4020
Contact: Kimber McCarden Foster, Pres.
E-mail: info@borderartresidency.com; URL: http://www.borderartresidency.com

Foundation type: Public charity
Purpose: Residency to artists for the disciplines of painting, conceptual art, installation and electronic media.
Publications: Newsletter.
Financial data: Year ended 12/31/2012. Assets, $18,772 (M); Expenditures, $21,520; Total giving, $6,500.
Fields of interest: Painting; Drawing.
Type of support: Residencies.
Application information: Contact the residency program for application deadlines.
Program description:
  Border Art Residency: This program offers a ten-month residency program for the disciplines of painting, drawing, conceptual art, installation, and electronic media at the organization's Mesilla Valley studio. Rent, utilities, repairs/maintenance, appliances, utensils, and laundry facilities are included.
EIN: 742840847

5616
Carlsbad Foundation, Inc.
114 S. Canyon St.
Carlsbad, NM 88220-5733   (505) 887-1131
Contact: Jim Harrison, Exec. Dir.

Foundation type: Community foundation
Purpose: Scholarships to students living in the Carlsbad, NM area paid directly to state universities.
Publications: Annual report (including application guidelines); Newsletter.
Financial data: Year ended 06/30/2013. Assets, $25,018,128 (M); Expenditures, $1,526,960; Total giving, $310,240; Grants to individuals, totaling $56,290.
Fields of interest: Higher education.
Type of support: Scholarships—to individuals; Support to graduates or students of specific schools; Undergraduate support.
Application information: Applications accepted. Application form required.
  Applicants should submit the following:
    1) Transcripts
  Additional information: Contact foundation for scholarship information.
EIN: 850206472

5617
Kit Carson Electric Education Foundation Inc
P.O. Box 578
Taos, NM 87571   (575) 758-2258
Contact: Thomas Tafoya, Pres.

Foundation type: Company-sponsored foundation
Purpose: Scholarships to high school seniors whose parents are members of the Kit Carson Electric Cooperative, Inc. and reside within the service area of the cooperative.
Publications: Application guidelines; Grants list.
Financial data: Year ended 12/31/2012. Assets, $66,701 (M); Expenditures, $10,643; Total giving, $6,000; Grants to individuals, 12 grants totaling $6,000.
Fields of interest: Higher education.

Type of support: Scholarships—to individuals.
Application information: Applications accepted. Application form required. Application form available on the grantmaker's web site.
  Initial approach: Application
  Send request by: Mail
  Deadline(s): Apr. 15
  Final notification: Recipients notified in 30 days
  Applicants should submit the following:
    1) Transcripts
    2) Letter(s) of recommendation
  Additional information: Applicants must provide an original class schedule from the college or school they will be attending before funds can be released.
Program description:
  Kit Carson Electric Education Foundation Scholarship: The foundation annually awards one-time scholarships to high school seniors who are children of members of the Kit Carson Electric Cooperative service area. Applicants are selected based on character, academic achievement, demonstration of a degree plan, and willingness to pursue higher education.
EIN: 311578049

5618
Catching the Dream
8200 Mountain Rd., N.E., Ste. 203
Albuquerque, NM 87110-7856   (505) 262-2351
FAX: (505) 262-0534; E-mail: nscholarsh@aol.com;
URL: http://www.catchingthedream.org

Foundation type: Public charity
Purpose: Scholarships to Native American students for attendance at a four year accredited college or university.
Financial data: Year ended 06/30/2012. Assets, $738,718 (M); Expenditures, $466,451; Total giving, $267,757; Grants to individuals, totaling $267,757.
Fields of interest: Higher education; Native Americans/American Indians.
Type of support: Scholarships—to individuals.
Application information: Applications accepted. Application form required.
  Initial approach: Telephone or e-mail
  Send request by: Mail
  Deadline(s): Apr. 15 for Fall semester, Sept. 15 for Spring semester
  Applicants should submit the following:
    1) Photograph
    2) SAT
    3) ACT
    4) Transcripts
    5) Essay
    6) Letter(s) of recommendation
    7) Financial information
  Additional information: See web site for additional application guidelines.
Program description:
  Scholarship Program: Scholarships ranging from $500 to $5,000 are awarded on merit to students attending or planning to attend a college or university full-time who are at least one-quarter or more degree American Indian, and be an enrolled member of a U.S. tribe. Study must be at the college level, and can range from bachelor's degrees to postdoctoral study.
EIN: 850360858

5619
Central New Mexico Electric Education Foundation
P.O. Box 157
Mountainair, NM 87036-0157   (505) 832-4483
Contact: Dolores Jones
Application address: P.O. Box 669, Moriarty, NM 87035, tel.: (505) 832-4483

Foundation type: Company-sponsored foundation
Purpose: Scholarships to members and the children of members of Central New Mexico Electric Cooperative, NM.
Publications: Application guidelines; Grants list.
Financial data: Year ended 12/31/2012. Assets, $116,784 (M); Expenditures, $4,539; Total giving, $2,250; Grants to individuals, 8 grants totaling $2,250 (high: $500, low: $250).
Type of support: Undergraduate support.
Application information: Applications accepted. Application form required.
  Initial approach: Letter
  Deadline(s): Feb. 1
  Applicants should submit the following:
    1) Essay
    2) GPA
    3) Transcripts
    4) Letter(s) of recommendation
  Additional information: Application address: P.O. Box 669, Moriarty, NM 87035, tel.: (505) 847-1024.
EIN: 850366030

5620
Central Valley Electric Education Foundation
P.O. Box 230
Artesia, NM 88211-0230   (505) 746-3571
Contact: Mike Anderson

Foundation type: Company-sponsored foundation
Purpose: Scholarships to members, or children of members, of the Central Valley Electric Cooperative, Inc. to attend NM colleges and universities.
Publications: Application guidelines.
Financial data: Year ended 12/31/2012. Assets, $1,340,767 (M); Expenditures, $127,546; Total giving, $127,000; Grants to individuals, 87 grants totaling $117,000 (high: $3,000, low: $1,000).
Fields of interest: Higher education.
Type of support: Scholarships—to individuals.
Application information: Applications accepted. Application form required. Application form available on the grantmaker's web site.
  Initial approach: Application
  Send request by: Mail
  Deadline(s): Apr. 15
  Final notification: Applicants notified in 60 days
  Applicants should submit the following:
    1) Photograph
    2) Letter(s) of recommendation
    3) Transcripts
  Additional information: Applicant must maintain a 2.5 GPA on a 4.0 scale, and be of good character.
EIN: 850323120

5621
Chase Foundation
510 Texas Ave.
Artesia, NM 88210-2041   (575) 746-4610
Contact: Richard Price, Exec. Dir.
E-mail: richardprice@chasefoundation.com;
Additional e-mail: info@chasefoundation.com;

Additional Contact: Ginny Bush, Assoc. Dir., e-mail: GinnyBush@chasefoundation.com; URL: http://www.chasefoundation.com

Foundation type: Company-sponsored foundation
Purpose: Scholarships to graduating seniors of Artesia High School, NM and to dependents of employees of Mack Energy Corporation, Chase Farms, Deerhorn Aviation employed outside Artesia, NM and attend select colleges and universities in the U.S.
Publications: Application guidelines; Grants list.
Financial data: Year ended 12/31/2012. Assets, $43,095,024 (M); Expenditures, $2,630,880; Total giving, $2,089,375.
Fields of interest: Higher education.
Type of support: Employee-related scholarships; Support to graduates or students of specific schools; Graduate support.
Application information: Applications accepted. Application form required. Application form available on the grantmaker's web site.
  Send request by: Online
  Deadline(s): Apr. 24 for scholarships for graduating AHS students, June 9 for scholarships for 5th year college seniors
  Applicants should submit the following:
    1) Transcripts
    2) SAT
    3) GPA
    4) FAFSA
    5) ACT
  Additional information: Awards will be paid directly to the educational institution on behalf of the student. See web site for participating colleges and universities.
Company name: Chase Oil Corporation
EIN: 367466258

5622

Clovis Community College Foundation, Inc.

417 Schepps Blvd.
Clovis, NM 88101-8345 (505) 769-4994
Contact: Natalie Daggett, Exec. Dir.
FAX: (907) 272-5060;
E-mail: stephanie.spencer@clovis.edu

Foundation type: Public charity
Purpose: College scholarships to students of Clovis Community College, MN for higher education.
Financial data: Year ended 06/30/2012. Assets, $2,103,567 (M); Expenditures, $28,781; Total giving, $25,363; Grants to individuals, totaling $25,363.
Fields of interest: College (community/junior).
Type of support: Support to graduates or students of specific schools.
Application information: Applications accepted. Application form required.
EIN: 742849118

5623

Columbus Electric Scholarship, Inc.

P.O. Box 631
Deming, NM 88031-0631 (575) 546-8838
URL: http://www.columbusco-op.org/Education/scholarship.cfm

Foundation type: Company-sponsored foundation
Purpose: Scholarships to members and the children of members of Columbus Electric Cooperative attending college in AZ or NM.
Financial data: Year ended 12/31/2012. Assets, $4,111 (M); Expenditures, $5,001; Total giving,

$5,000; Grants to individuals, 14 grants totaling $5,000 (high: $500, low: $250).
Type of support: Undergraduate support.
Application information: Applications accepted. Application form required.
  Initial approach: Letter
  Send request by: Mail
  Deadline(s): June 30 for fall semester; Dec. 31 for spring semester
  Applicants should submit the following:
    1) Transcripts
    2) Letter(s) of recommendation
    3) Essay
EIN: 850373471

5624

Community Foundation of Southern New Mexico

301 S. Church St., Ste. H
Las Cruces, NM 88001 (575) 521-4794
Contact: Luan Wagner Burn Ph.D., Exec. Dir.
E-mail: luan@cfsnm.org; URL: http://www.cfsnm.org

Foundation type: Community foundation
Purpose: College scholarships to graduating seniors of southern New Mexico for continuing education at accredited institutions.
Publications: Annual report; Financial statement.
Financial data: Year ended 12/31/2012. Assets, $13,902,672 (M); Expenditures, $1,415,729; Total giving, $561,090. Scholarships—to individuals amount not specified.
Fields of interest: Higher education; Journalism school/education; Adults, women.
Type of support: Scholarships—to individuals.
Application information: Applications accepted. Application form required. Application form available on the grantmaker's web site.
  Initial approach: Application
  Send request by: E-mail, fax, or mail
  Deadline(s): Apr. 4 for most scholarships; Apr. 30 for SpringBoard! and Over the Rainbow scholarships
  Additional information: See web site for application form and guidelines.
EIN: 850455682

5625

The Community Pantry

P.O. Box 520
Gallup, NM 87305-0520 (505) 726-8068
Contact: John Sakasitz, Pres.
URL: http://thecommunitypantry.org/

Foundation type: Public charity
Purpose: Emergency food assistance to indigent residents of Northwestern New Mexico.
Financial data: Year ended 12/31/2011. Assets, $696,188 (M); Expenditures, $4,945,958; Total giving, $4,257,353; Grants to individuals, totaling $4,257,353.
Fields of interest: Food banks.
Type of support: In-kind gifts.
Application information:
  Initial approach: Tel.
  Additional information: Contact foundation for eligibility criteria.
EIN: 850460193

5626

Continental Divide Electric Education Foundation

P.O. Box 1087
Grants, NM 87020-1087
Contact: Corina Sandoval
URL: http://www.cdec.coop/content/scholarships

Foundation type: Company-sponsored foundation
Purpose: Undergraduate scholarships to active members, or the immediate family of active members, of Continental Divide Electric Cooperative, Inc. to attend accredited colleges and universities in AZ and NM.
Publications: Application guidelines.
Financial data: Year ended 12/31/2012. Assets, $4,010,053 (M); Expenditures, $253,630; Total giving, $211,500; Grants to individuals, 141 grants totaling $211,500 (high: $1,500, low: $1,500).
Fields of interest: Higher education; Scholarships/financial aid.
Type of support: Undergraduate support.
Application information: Applications accepted. Application form required. Application form available on the grantmaker's web site.
  Initial approach: Application
  Send request by: Mail
  Deadline(s): May 1
  Applicants should submit the following:
    1) Letter(s) of recommendation
    2) Transcripts
  Additional information: Grants of up to $3,000 are awarded and recipients must maintain a 2.5 GPA in order for the scholarship to be renewed beyond the first semester. Letters of recommendation should state why the applicant is college material and needs financial assistance.
EIN: 850365720

5627

ENMR Education Foundation

(formerly ENMR Telephone Education Foundation)
P.O. Box 1947
Clovis, NM 88102-1947 (575) 389-5100

Foundation type: Company-sponsored foundation
Purpose: Scholarships to active members receiving landline telephone service from ENMR Telephone Cooperative and their immediate families and dependents, who wish to attend an institution of higher learning.
Publications: Application guidelines; Informational brochure; Program policy statement.
Financial data: Year ended 12/31/2012. Assets, $2,217,112 (M); Expenditures, $130,122; Total giving, $117,545; Grants to individuals, 73 grants totaling $68,950 (high: $1,600, low: $500).
Fields of interest: Higher education; Scholarships/financial aid.
Type of support: Scholarships—to individuals.
Application information: Applications accepted. Application form required. Application form available on the grantmaker's web site.
  Initial approach: Download application form and mail to foundation
  Deadline(s): 30 days prior to the academic year enrollment period
  Applicants should submit the following:
    1) FAFSA
    2) SAT
    3) ACT
    4) Essay
    5) Letter(s) of recommendation
    6) GPA
    7) Transcripts

Program description:

Committed to Excellence Endowment Fund Scholarships: Through the Committed to Excellence Endowment Fund, the foundation awards $1,000 scholarships to high school seniors and returning college students. Applicants must hold a membership in the Cooperative and reside within one of the ENMR Telephone Cooperative exchange areas. High school applicants must have a 19 ACT score or a 1350 SAT score and returning college students must have a cumulative GPA of 2.5 or higher.

EIN: 850385194

5628
ENMR-Plateau Corporate Giving Program

c/o Office of Public Affairs
P.O. Box 1947
Clovis, NM 88102-1947   (575) 389-4241
Address for Higher Education Grant Program:
ENMR-Plateau Telecommunications, P.O. Box 1947, 7111 N. Prince St., Clovis, NM 88102
FAX: (575) 389-5255; E-mail: jrj@plateautel.com;
URL: http://www.enmr.com/donations.asp

Foundation type: Corporate giving program
Purpose: Scholarships to a member of the ENMR telephone cooperative or is the dependent of a cooperative member who is in good standing pursuing a career in allied health or medical services.
Publications: Application guidelines.
Fields of interest: Higher education; Scholarships/financial aid.
Type of support: Scholarships—to individuals; Graduate support; Undergraduate support.
Application information: Applications accepted. Application form required. Application form available on the grantmaker's web site.
  Initial approach: Application
  Send request by: Mail
  Deadline(s): None
  Additional information: Candidates who met eligibility and selection criteria will be selected on a first come, first served basis.

Program description:
Higher Education Grant Program: ENMR-Plateau awards grants of up to $3,200 to undergraduate and graduate students who are members of the telephone cooperative or is the dependent of a cooperative member. The program is designed to off-set the costs of higher education including costs such as tuition, books, fees, temporary housing, or other educational expenses. All applicants must be employed while either residing full-time or working full-time in one or more of the telephone exchanges served by EMNR-Plateau.

5629
Farmers' Electric Education Foundation

P.O. Box 550
Clovis, NM 88102-0550   (505) 762-4466
Contact: Thom Moore
E-mail: thom@fecnm.org; URL: http:// fecnm.coopwebbuilder.com/content/ farmers-electric-education-foundation

Foundation type: Company-sponsored foundation
Purpose: Scholarships to members of Farmers' Electric Cooperative, Inc. of NM, and their immediate families.
Publications: Application guidelines; Grants list.
Financial data: Year ended 12/31/2012. Assets, $829,969 (M); Expenditures, $38,568; Total giving, $37,500; Grants to individuals, 50 grants totaling $37,500 (high: $750, low: $750).

Fields of interest: Vocational education; Higher education; Scholarships/financial aid; Government/public administration.
Type of support: Conferences/seminars; Precollege support; Undergraduate support.
Application information: Applications accepted. Application form required. Application form available on the grantmaker's web site.
  Initial approach: Application
  Send request by: Mail or e-mail
  Deadline(s): Feb. 1
  Final notification: Applicants notified in 60 days
  Applicants should submit the following:
    1) GPA
    2) Transcripts
    3) Letter(s) of recommendation
    4) Essay

Program descriptions:
Farmers' Electric Education Foundation Scholarship Fund: The foundation annually awards one-time scholarships of $500 to $750 to active members and the immediate family of active members receiving services from Farmers' Electric Cooperative. Applicants must plan to attend a vocational school, technical school, college, or university and maintain a 2.5 GPA.
Youth Tour: The foundation annually sponsors a contest for high school seniors who are dependents of active members of the cooperative to attend the Government In Action Youth Tour in Washington, DC held in June. The foundation selects two individuals a year and selection is based on series of questions and essay response. Farmers' Electric provides transportation, lodging, meals, and tour expenses.
EIN: 850348498

5630
Finis Heidel Trust

5130 N. Baggett Dr.
Hobbs, NM 88241-0165   (575) 392-8827
Contact: Vikki Arnwine, Tr.

Foundation type: Independent foundation
Purpose: Scholarships to graduating seniors of Lea County high schools, NM, for higher education.
Financial data: Year ended 12/31/2011. Assets, $1,518,107 (M); Expenditures, $87,455; Total giving, $63,000; Grants to individuals, 39 grants totaling $63,000 (high: $2,000, low: $1,000).
Fields of interest: Vocational education, post-secondary; Higher education.
Type of support: Technical education support; Undergraduate support.
Application information: Application form required.
  Deadline(s): Mar.
  Applicants should submit the following:
    1) GPA
    2) Photograph
    3) Financial information
    4) Essay
    5) Class rank
    6) Transcripts
    7) SAT
    8) ACT
  Additional information: Scholarships will be paid directly to the educational institution on behalf of the students. Applicants must be residents of New Mexico.
EIN: 856117343

5631
Robert W. Hamilton Foundation

P.O. Box 898
Alamogordo, NM 88311
Contact: Marion Ledford, Pres./Dir.

Foundation type: Independent foundation
Purpose: Scholarships to graduating seniors who are residents of Otero County, NM pursuing postsecondary education.
Financial data: Year ended 12/31/2012. Assets, $0 (M); Expenditures, $36,703; Total giving, $33,000; Grants to individuals, 31 grants totaling $33,000 (high: $2,000, low: $500).
Fields of interest: Higher education.
Type of support: Support to graduates or students of specific schools; Undergraduate support.
Application information: Application form required.
  Deadline(s): Apr. 1
  Additional information: Applicants must be New Mexico residents. Application forms available upon request.
EIN: 850466070

5632
John Y. & Willie Mae Helm Scholarship Fund

c/o First National Bank of SF
P.O. Box 609
Santa Fe, NM 87504-0609   (505) 662-4351
Contact: Lori Whitley, Secy.-Treas.
Application address: c/o Los Alamos Medical center, 3917 W. Rd. Ste.D, Los Alamos, NM 87544
Tel:(505) 662-4351

Foundation type: Independent foundation
Purpose: Scholarships to medical students who are or have been residents of Los Alamos County, NM.
Financial data: Year ended 01/31/2013. Assets, $294,496 (M); Expenditures, $21,670; Total giving, $15,500; Grants to individuals, 9 grants totaling $15,500 (high: $3,500, low: $500).
Fields of interest: Medical school/education.
Type of support: Graduate support.
Application information:
  Initial approach: Letter or telephone
  Deadline(s): July 31
  Additional information: Applications by letter outlining background, extracurricular activities, career goals, and transcripts.
EIN: 856108694

5633
Jemez Mountains Electric Foundation

(also known as Jemez Mountains Electric Foundation)
P.O. Box 128
Espanola, NM 87532-0128

Foundation type: Company-sponsored foundation
Purpose: Scholarships to high school students residing within the Jemez Mountains Electrical Cooperative service area.
Financial data: Year ended 12/31/2012. Assets, $527,307 (M); Expenditures, $34,285; Total giving, $23,000; Grants to individuals, 26 grants totaling $23,000 (high: $1,000, low: $500).
Fields of interest: Higher education.
Type of support: Scholarships—to individuals.
Application information: Application form required.
  Initial approach: Letter or telephone
  Deadline(s): Apr. 1
  Applicants should submit the following:
    1) SAT
    2) Essay
    3) Transcripts
    4) Letter(s) of recommendation
    5) GPA
    6) FAFSA
    7) ACT
  Additional information: Parents must have resided within the cooperative's service area

for a minimum period of one year and must have been members or patrons for that period of time.
EIN: 237022094

5634
Laguna Education Foundation, Inc.
P.O. Box 645
Laguna, NM 87026-0645 (505) 552-6377
FAX: (502) 552-6398;
E-mail: lagunaedfoundation@gmail.com;
URL: http://www.lagunaedfoundation.org

Foundation type: Public charity
Purpose: Scholarships to undergraduate and graduate students of New Mexico for attendance at a regionally accredited post secondary institution in the U.S.
Publications: Application guidelines.
Financial data: Year ended 06/30/2012. Assets, $491,777 (M); Expenditures, $159,166; Total giving, $23,685; Grants to individuals, totaling $23,685.
Fields of interest: Higher education.
Type of support: Scholarships—to individuals; Graduate support; Undergraduate support.
Application information: Applications accepted. Application form required. Application form available on the grantmaker's web site.
  Send request by: Mail
  Deadline(s): May
  Applicants should submit the following:
    1) Essay
    2) SAT
    3) GPA
    4) ACT
  Additional information: See web site for additional guidelines for undergraduate and graduate scholarships.
EIN: 311711693

5635
Lannan Foundation
313 Read St.
Santa Fe, NM 87501-2628 (505) 986-8160
Contact: Ruth Simms, Cont.
FAX: (505) 986-8195; E-mail: info@lannan.org;
Additional contact information (for Ruth Simms): Fax: (505) 954-5143, e-mail: ruth@lannan.org;
URL: http://www.lannan.org

Foundation type: Independent foundation
Purpose: Awards to writers writing in the English language, and grants to visual artists from indigenous communities promoting cultural freedom.
Financial data: Year ended 12/31/2012. Assets, $217,897,171 (M); Expenditures, $10,264,920; Total giving, $5,274,486; Grants to individuals, 17 grants totaling $2,617,500 (high: $110,000, low: $25,000).
Fields of interest: Visual arts; Literature.
Type of support: Program development; Publication; Awards/grants by nomination only; Awards/prizes.
Application information: Applications not accepted.
  Additional information: Unsolicited requests for funds not considered or acknowledged.
Program descriptions:
  Art Program: The goals of this funding area are to support the creativity of exceptional contemporary artists, foster serious criticism and discussion of contemporary art, and to bring new and experimental works of art to a wide audience. The program also includes the Acquisition and

Exhibition programs. The Acquisition and Gift program enables the foundation to collect the work of contemporary artists as well as making gifts of their work to museums and other public institutions. The Exhibition program was established to support the creation of new work and to give greater exposure to contemporary artists.
  Literary Program: The purpose of the program is to support the creation of exceptional poetry and prose written originally in the English language and to increase the audience for contemporary literature. The foundation honors writers whose work reflects and changes our understanding of the world. Applications and nominations for literary awards or fellowships are not accepted.
EIN: 366062451

5636
Lea County Electric Education Foundation
P.O. Box 1447
Lovington, NM 88260-1447 (575) 396-3631
URL: http://www.lcecnet.com/

Foundation type: Company-sponsored foundation
Purpose: Scholarships to members receiving electric service from Lea County Electric Cooperative, Inc. and their dependents, who attend recognized NM and TX institutions.
Publications: Application guidelines.
Financial data: Year ended 12/31/2012. Assets, $1,112,450 (M); Expenditures, $128,775; Total giving, $131,500; Grants to individuals, 72 grants totaling $131,500 (high: $7,000, low: $1,000).
Fields of interest: Higher education.
Type of support: Undergraduate support.
Application information: Applications accepted. Application form required. Application form available on the grantmaker's web site.
  Initial approach: Application
  Send request by: Mail or online
  Deadline(s): 2nd Friday in Jan.
  Final notification: Applicants notified May 1
  Applicants should submit the following:
    1) Letter(s) of recommendation
    2) Essay
Program description:
  Scholarship Program: The foundation annually awards 65 scholarships to active members and dependents of Lea County Electric Cooperative. The foundation awards $1,000 per semester up to a maximum of eight semesters. Recipients must reside in the Lea County Electric territory, maintain a 2.50 GPA, and attend an accredited school in New Mexico or Texas.
EIN: 850351147

5637
Leaco Rural Telephone Education Foundation
220 W. Broadway
Hobbs, NM 88240-6004 (505) 370-5010
URL: http://www.leaco.net/

Foundation type: Company-sponsored foundation
Purpose: Scholarships to active members and the immediate family members of active members of Leaco Rural Telephone Cooperative in NM.
Publications: Application guidelines.
Financial data: Year ended 12/31/2012. Assets, $42,680 (M); Expenditures, $2,500; Total giving, $2,500; Grants to individuals, 5 grants totaling $2,500 (high: $500, low: $500).
Type of support: Undergraduate support.
Application information:
  Initial approach: Letter

Additional information: Application address: c/o C. Gene Samberson, 311 N. 1st St., P.O. Drawer 1599, Lovington, NM 88260.
EIN: 856120669

5638
Los Alamos National Laboratory Foundation
1112 Plaza del Norte
Espanola, NM 87532-3216 (505) 753-8890
FAX: (505) 753-8915;
E-mail: info@lanlfoundation.org; URL: https://www.lanlfoundation.org

Foundation type: Public charity
Purpose: Scholarships to Northern New Mexico high school students to attend the college of their choice.
Publications: Application guidelines.
Financial data: Year ended 12/31/2011. Assets, $62,934,827 (M); Expenditures, $7,254,339; Total giving, $3,078,466; Grants to individuals, totaling $353,256.
Fields of interest: Higher education.
Type of support: Scholarships—to individuals.
Application information: Applications accepted. Application form required. Application form available on the grantmaker's web site.
  Send request by: Online
  Deadline(s): Jan. 17
  Applicants should submit the following:
    1) Photograph
    2) Letter(s) of recommendation
    3) Essay
    4) Transcripts
    5) SAT
    6) GPA
    7) ACT
  Additional information: See web site for additional guidelines.
Program description:
  Los Alamos Employees' Scholarship Fund (LAESF): The fund provides scholarships that support the best and brightest students in northern New Mexico who are pursuing undergraduate degrees in fields serving the Los Alamos Laboratory and the region. Awards are based on academic performance, leadership potential, and career goals relevant to laboratory or local community needs. Financial need, diversity, and regional representation are integral components of the selection process.
EIN: 742853972

5639
J. F Maddox Foundation
P.O. Box 2588
Hobbs, NM 88241-2588 (575) 393-6338
Contact: Robert J. Reid, Secy. and Exec. Dir.; For Scholarships: Cassie Ater, Scholarship Coord.
Physical address and address for Scholarship applications: 220 W. Broadway St., Ste. 200, Hobbs, NM 88240
E-mail: bobreid@jfmaddox.org; URL: http://www.jfmaddox.org/

Foundation type: Independent foundation
Purpose: Scholarships only to high school students who are residents of Lea County, NM.
Publications: Grants list.
Financial data: Year ended 12/31/2012. Assets, $245,058,304 (M); Expenditures, $15,582,079; Total giving, $8,662,696; Grants to individuals, 26 grants totaling $197,006 (high: $46,833, low: $75).
Fields of interest: Higher education.

Type of support: Scholarships—to individuals; Undergraduate support.
Application information: Applications accepted. Application form required. Application form available on the grantmaker's web site. Interview required.

Initial approach: Application
Send request by: Online or mail
Copies of proposal: 1
Deadline(s): June 30
Final notification: Recipients notified by Sept. 15
Applicants should submit the following:
1) Class rank
2) Transcripts
3) SAT
4) Letter(s) of recommendation
5) GPA
6) Essay
7) ACT
Additional information: Application should also include a copy of birth certificate or certificate of citizenship. See web site for application form and specific instructions.
Program description:
Jack Maddox Distinguished Scholarship Program: The scholarship program awards five scholarships to high school juniors in Lea County, New Mexico, each year. The five young scholars chosen will receive a scholarship for undergraduate study. One scholarship will cover the costs of undergraduate tuition, required texts, lab, other required fees, and room and board to the college or university of the scholar's choice in the continental United States. The remaining four scholarships will provide each Maddox Scholar with $20,000 ($5,000 per year for four years) for undergraduate study at the college or university of the scholar's choice in the continental United States .
EIN: 756023767

5640
The New Mexico Community Foundation

502 W. Cordova, Ste. 1
Santa Fe, NM 87505 (505) 820-6860
Contact: For scholarships: Denise Gonzales, Dir., Community Philanthropy
Scholarship inquiry e-mail: dgonzales@nmcf.org
FAX: (505) 820-7860; E-mail: info@nmcf.org;
Additional address: 2015 Mountain Rd., NW, Albuquerque, NM 87104, tel.: (505) 821-6735; URL: http://www.nmcf.org

Foundation type: Community foundation
Purpose: Scholarships to students of New Mexico pursuing higher education.
Publications: Annual report; Newsletter; Occasional report.
Financial data: Year ended 12/31/2011. Assets, $22,132,404 (M); Expenditures, $11,158,078; Total giving, $8,752,768. Scholarships—to individuals amount not specified.
Fields of interest: Higher education.
Type of support: Scholarships—to individuals; Support to graduates or students of specific schools.
Application information: Applications accepted. Application form required.
Deadline(s): Varies
Additional information: See web site for a complete listing of scholarships.
EIN: 850311210

5641
Otero County Electric Education Foundation

P.O. Box 227
Cloudcroft, NM 88317-0227 (575) 682-2521

Foundation type: Independent foundation
Purpose: Scholarships to active members of Otero County Electric Cooperative and to their immediate families to attend recognized NM institutions of higher education.
Financial data: Year ended 12/31/2011. Assets, $992,977 (M); Expenditures, $53,245; Total giving, $49,300; Grants to individuals, 48 grants totaling $49,300 (high: $1,700, low: $500).
Fields of interest: Higher education.
Type of support: Undergraduate support.
Application information: Application form required.
Deadline(s): Mar. 4
Final notification: Applicants notified within 60 days
Applicants should submit the following:
1) SAT
2) ACT
3) Transcripts
4) Letter(s) of recommendation
Program description:
Scholarship: The foundation awards a one-year, $1,700 scholarship, $850 to be paid at the start of each semester on confirmation that the applicant has maintained at least a 2.5 GPA on a 4.0 scale, and is a full-time student. Applicants must be of good character, demonstrate a coherent degree plan, and a willingness to pursue a course of higher learning. Economic need of the applicant is given secondary consideration. Recipients must reapply each year.
EIN: 850374112

5642
Penasco Valley Telephone Education Foundation

4011 W. Main St.
Artesia, NM 88210-9566 (575) 748-1241
URL: http://www.pvt.com/about/community/scholarships/

Foundation type: Company-sponsored foundation
Purpose: Scholarships to members of Penasco Valley Telephone Cooperative and dependents of active members of the Cooperative for higher education.
Publications: Application guidelines.
Financial data: Year ended 12/31/2012. Assets, $593,684 (M); Expenditures, $62,981; Total giving, $37,500; Grants to individuals, 32 grants totaling $37,500 (high: $1,500, low: $750).
Fields of interest: Higher education.
Type of support: Scholarships—to individuals.
Application information: Applications accepted. Application form required. Application form available on the grantmaker's web site.
Initial approach: Application
Send request by: Mail
Deadline(s): Mar. 1
Applicants should submit the following:
1) Photograph
2) Letter(s) of recommendation
3) Transcripts
4) Essay
Additional information: Applications are also available at high schools as well as through the foundation.
EIN: 850422272

5643
The Peninsula Foundation

1512 Pacheco St., Ste. D-203
Santa Fe, NM 87505-5111 (505) 986-6874

Foundation type: Independent foundation
Purpose: Scholarships to graduating seniors at Menominee High School, MI for higher education.
Financial data: Year ended 12/31/2011. Assets, $11,558 (M); Expenditures, $10,848; Total giving, $10,000; Grants to individuals, 4 grants totaling $10,000 (high: $2,500, low: $2,500).
Fields of interest: Higher education.
Type of support: Support to graduates or students of specific schools; Undergraduate support.
Application information: Applications accepted. Application form required.
Deadline(s): Feb. 1
Applicants should submit the following:
1) Transcripts
2) Letter(s) of recommendation
3) Essay
Additional information: Contact the guidance department for application forms.
EIN: 742028228

5644
PRMC-Clovis Hospital Auxiliary

(formerly Presbyterian Healthcare Services)
P.O. Box 26666
Albuquerque, NM 87125-6666 (505) 923-6101

Foundation type: Public charity
Purpose: Scholarships to high school graduates of Curry county, NM pursuing a degree in medical, technical, or other fields pertaining to health care; also, indigent transportation and emergency funding given to patients in need.
Financial data: Year ended 12/31/2011. Assets, $1,948,674,842 (M); Expenditures, $1,266,392,139; Total giving, $1,453,652; Grants to individuals, totaling $404,428.
Fields of interest: Medical school/education.
Type of support: Scholarships—to individuals.
Application information: Applications accepted. Application form required.
Send request by: Mail
Copies of proposal: 1
Deadline(s): July 1
Final notification: 60 days after receipt of application
Applicants should submit the following:
1) Transcripts
2) Letter(s) of recommendation
Additional information: Application must also include two character references; applicant must maintain a "C" average.
Program description:
Scholarship Program: The organization provides scholarships to students seeking degrees in the medical profession.
EIN: 850105601

5645
Roosevelt County Electric Education Foundation

P.O. Box 389
Portales, NM 88130-0389 (575) 356-4491
Contact: Robin Inge
E-mail: inger@rcec.coop; URL: http://www.rcec.org

Foundation type: Company-sponsored foundation
Purpose: Scholarships to members and their immediate families who receive services from Roosevelt County Electric Cooperative, Inc.
Publications: Application guidelines; Grants list.

Financial data: Year ended 12/31/2012. Assets, $628,632 (M); Expenditures, $28,613; Total giving, $23,500; Grants to individuals, 46 grants totaling $23,500 (high: $1,000, low: $500).
Fields of interest: Higher education.
Type of support: Scholarships—to individuals.
Application information: Applications accepted. Application form required.
> *Deadline(s):* Jan. 31, Dec. 2 for Government in Action Youth Tour
> *Applicants should submit the following:*
> 1) Essay
> 2) ACT
> 3) Letter(s) of recommendation
> 4) Transcripts
> *Additional information:* Selections are made by the foundation scholarship selection committee.

Program descriptions:
> *Government in Action Youth Tour:* The foundation awards scholarships to sophomore and junior students who are dependents of members of the Roosevelt County Electric Cooperative. Students are asked to submit a 500 word essay on various cooperative topics, and 2 students are chosen to represent the cooperative on an all expense paid trip to Washington, DC for the Government in Action Youth Tour. The trip includes visits to famous landmarks, the U.S. Senate, the House of Representatives, and a visit to the Congressional Representative from their district.
> *Scholarships:* The foundation awards college scholarships to members and dependents of the Roosevelt County Electric Cooperative. The program is designed to assist individuals to further their education, knowledge, and skills to be better prepared to participate in the future employment marketplace. Applicants should be in the current year graduating class or an accredited public or private high school, home schooled or have obtained a New Mexico GED or equivalent. This one year scholarship will be awarded on the basis of funds available and the applicant's eligibility. Applicant must maintain at least a 2.5 GPA on a 4.0 scale and must demonstrate acceptable standards of citizenship and character.

EIN: 850350615

5646
Roosevelt County Rural Telephone Education Foundation
P.O. Box 867
Portales, NM   88130   (575) 226-2255

Foundation type: Company-sponsored foundation
Purpose: Scholarships to active members and immediate family members of Roosevelt County Rural Telephone Cooperative in Roosevelt County, NM.
Financial data: Year ended 12/31/2012. Assets, $252,152 (M); Expenditures, $7,749; Total giving, $7,000; Grants to individuals, 14 grants totaling $7,000 (high: $500, low: $500).
Fields of interest: Higher education.
Type of support: Undergraduate support.
Application information: Applications accepted. Application form required.
> *Initial approach:* Letter
> *Deadline(s):* Feb. 6
> *Applicants should submit the following:*
> 1) Class rank
> 2) Letter(s) of recommendation
> 3) GPA
> 4) Essay
> 5) ACT
> *Additional information:* Contact foundation for application guidelines.

Company name: Roosevelt County Rural Telephone Cooperative, Inc.
EIN: 850452616

5647
Sacramento Mountain Scholarship Fund, Inc.
P.O. Box 900
Artesia, NM   88211-0900   (505) 748-1471
Contact: Lester Rinderknecht, Tr.

Foundation type: Independent foundation
Purpose: Scholarships to graduates of Weed or Cloudcroft High Schools, NM, with a GPA above 2.5, to attend an accredited educational institution.
Financial data: Year ended 12/31/2011. Assets, $580,982 (M); Expenditures, $23,057; Total giving, $21,950; Grants to individuals, 41 grants totaling $21,950 (high: $1,200, low: $200).
Type of support: Support to graduates or students of specific schools; Undergraduate support.
Application information: Applications accepted. Application form required.
> *Deadline(s):* Apr. 1

EIN: 850347084

5648
Santa Fe Art Institute
(also known as SFAI)
1600 St. Michael's Dr.
Santa Fe, NM   87505-7615   (505) 424-5050
FAX: (505) 424-5051; E-mail: info@sfai.org; Mailing address: P.O. Box 24044, Santa Fe, NM 87502-0447; E-Mail For Sanjit Sethi: ssethi@sfai.org; URL: http://www.sfai.org

Foundation type: Public charity
Purpose: Residencies to emerging and mid-career artists for the duration of one to three months. Scholarships are also available for writers, based on financial need.
Publications: Application guidelines; Grants list.
Financial data: Year ended 12/31/2011. Assets, $5,028,949 (M); Expenditures, $794,601.
Fields of interest: Literature; Arts; Safety/disasters.
Type of support: Scholarships—to individuals; Residencies; Stipends.
Application information: Application form required. Application form available on the grantmaker's web site.
> *Initial approach:* Letter or telephone
> *Deadline(s):* July 5 and Dec. 31
> *Applicants should submit the following:*
> 1) SASE
> 2) Letter(s) of recommendation
> 3) Curriculum vitae
> *Additional information:* Application should also include $35 processing fee; see web site for additional application information.

Program descriptions:
> *Emergency Relief Residencies:* This program provides a respite to artists affected by the horrors of political, social, or natural disasters with living space and studios to professional artists, writers and crafts people.
> *Residency Program:* The institute provides residencies for artists and writers, that focuses on the professional experience of the artist, the quality of their past work, and their potential to produce quality work. Residencies can last from one to three months; residents are housed in handsomely-appointed rooms with private baths and studio spaces, allowing them to pursue

creative projects without interruption. Residents receive $1,000 per month, for up to three months.
EIN: 850404277

5649
Santa Fe Community Foundation
501 Halona St.
Santa Fe, NM   87505   (505) 988-9715
Contact: Brian T. Byrnes, C.E.O. and Pres.; Donor-Advised Funds and Grants Contact: Christa Coggins, V.P., Community Philanthropy
FAX: (505) 988-1829;
E-mail: foundation@santafecf.org; Mailing address: P.O. Box 1827, Sante Fe, NM 87504-1827; Workshop registration e-mail: workshops@santafecf.org; URL: http://www.santafecf.org

Foundation type: Community foundation
Purpose: Scholarships to low-income students of Santa Fe, Rio Arriba, Taos, San Miguel, Los Alamos or Mora county, NM.
Publications: Annual report; Informational brochure (including application guidelines); Newsletter.
Financial data: Year ended 12/31/2012. Assets, $57,212,049 (M); Expenditures, $6,325,123; Total giving, $3,916,552.
Fields of interest: Higher education; Economically disadvantaged.
Type of support: Scholarships—to individuals; Undergraduate support; Grants for special needs.
Application information: Applications accepted. Application form required. Application form available on the grantmaker's web site.
> *Deadline(s):* Apr. 18
> *Final notification:* Applicants notified late June
> *Applicants should submit the following:*
> 1) FAFSA
> 2) Transcripts
> 3) Letter(s) of recommendation
> 4) Essay
> *Additional information:* Application should also include a letter of acceptance from a college, and a copy of financial aid letter. Applications are available at all high school counselors and college financial aid offices in Northern New Mexico.

EIN: 850303044

5650
School for Advanced Research on the Human Experience
(formerly School of American Research)
P.O. Box 2188
Santa Fe, NM   87504-2188   (505) 954-7200
Contact: David E. Stuart, Interim Pres.
FAX: (505) 954-7214; E-mail: info@sarsf.org; E-mail for David E. Stuart: stuart@sarsf.org; URL: http://www.sarweb.org

Foundation type: Public charity
Purpose: Fellowships to Native American artists, and to Native American scholars. A prize is also available to an author of a book that exemplifies outstanding scholarship and writing in anthropology.
Publications: Application guidelines; Annual report; Informational brochure.
Financial data: Year ended 06/30/2012. Assets, $31,543,563 (M); Expenditures, $3,540,808; Total giving, $309,322; Grants to individuals, totaling $238,957.
Fields of interest: Arts; Anthropology/sociology; Native Americans/American Indians; Women.
Type of support: Fellowships; Awards/prizes.

Application information:

Initial approach: E-mail

Deadline(s): Jan. 15 for Native Artist Fellowships; Dec. 15 for Summer Fellowships; Nov. 1 for all others

Program descriptions:

Anne Ray Fellowship: One fellowship is available for an established Native American scholar, working in the humanities, arts, or the sciences, who has a commitment to providing mentorship to recent graduates or graduate students. In addition to working on their own research, scholars serve as mentors to two interns working at the Indian Arts Research Center. Fellows receive a $40,000 stipend, as well as housing and office space.

Arroyo Hondo Grants Program: The school periodically awards grants to advanced students or scholars interested in using its Arroyo Hondo archaeological collection as part of their own research.

Campbell Fellowship for Women Scholar-Practitioners from Developing Nations: One six-month fellowship is available for a female postdoctoral social scientist from a developing nation whose work addresses women's economic and social empowerment in that nation. The program is intended to advance the scholarly careers of women social scientists from the developing world, and to support research that identifies the causes of gender equality inequity in the developing world and that proposes practical solutions for promoting women's economic and social empowerment. Recipients are awarded a $4,500-per-month stipend, housing and office space, travel and library resource funds, and health insurance.

Henry Luce Foundation Resident Scholar Fellowship: One nine-month fellowship is available for a postdoctoral Asian or American scholar whose research focuses on East Asia or Southeast Asia. Applicants must be either U.S. citizens or permanent residents, or residents of one of the following nations: Brunei, Burma/Myanmar, Cambodia, China, East Timor, Indonesia, Hong Kong, Japan, Korea, Laos, Malaysia, Mongolia, Philippines, Singapore, Taiwan, Thailand, and Vietnam. Applicants must also be pursuing research in one of the following social sciences or humanities: anthropology, economics, education, geography, history, languages, law, linguistics, philosophy, political science, psychology, religion, social work, or sociology. Fellows receive a $40,000 stipend, as well as housing and office space.

J. Staley Prize: This $10,000 award recognizes innovative works that go beyond traditional frontiers and dominant schools of thought in anthropology, and add new dimensions to the understanding of the human species.

Katrin H. Lamon Fellowship: One fellowship is available for a Native American scholar, either pre- or post-doctoral, working in either the humanities or the social sciences. Fellows receive a $40,000 stipend ($30,000 for Ph.D. candidates), as well as housing and office space.

National Endowment for the Humanities Fellowship: One nine-month fellowship is available for a postdoctoral scholar whose project relates to the humanities. Eligible applicants must be U.S. citizens or have resided in the U.S. for three years. Fellows receive a $40,000 stipend, as well as housing and office space.

Native Artist Fellowships: Awarded in conjunction with the Indian Arts Research Center, this program offers four artist-in-residence fellowships annually to advance the work of mature and emerging Native artists. Fellowships are intended to support diverse creative disciplines (including sculpture,

performance, basketry, painting, printmaking, digital art, mixed media, photography, pottery, writing, and film and video). Each fellowship include a monthly stipend, housing, studio space, a supplies allowance, and travel reimbursement to and from the school. Named fellowships under this program include: the Ron and Susan Dubin Native Artist Fellowship (dedicated to supporting traditional Native artistry); the Rollin and Mary Ella King Native Artist Fellowship (dedicated to preserving the Southwest's extensive artistic heritage, and intended for Native artists from Arizona, Colorado, New Mexico, and Utah, who work in the visual arts); SAR Indigenous Writer-in-Residence Fellowship (designed to support the literary arts); and Eric and Barbara Dobkin Native Artist Fellowship for Women (encouraging the creativity and growth of indigenous women artists working in any media)

Prize for Outstanding Public Education and Outreach in Archaeology: This program offers an annual prize for an outstanding public education or outreach program that brings archaeological knowledge about the past to inform issues and problems of the present. The award seeks to stimulate innovative archaeological and historical scholarship that is relevant to issues of contemporary concern, such as sustainability, immigration, human responses to climate change, ethnic relations, war and peace, technological change, and other issues facing contemporary societies. The prize is accompanied by a $5,000 cash prize.

Summer Fellowships: These fellowships are awarded to five or six scholars in anthropology and related fields to pursue research or writing projects that promote the understanding of human behavior, culture, society, and the history of anthropology. Both humanistically- and scientifically-oriented scholars are encouraged to apply; summer scholars are provided with a small stipend, a rent-free apartment and office on campus, an allowance account, library support, and other benefits. Named scholarships under this program include: the Ethel-Jane Westfeldt Bunting Fellowship (up to three fellowships for scholars in the social sciences, humanities, or arts); William Y. and Nettie K. Adams Fellowship in the History of Anthropology (a summer scholar fellowship to a scholar, either pre- or post-doctoral, whose proposed work focused on the history of anthropology); the Cotsen Fellowship in Archaeology; and the Christopher Smeall Fellowship in Anthropological Linguistics.

Weatherhead Fellowship: Two fellowships are available for either Ph.D. candidates or scholars with doctorates whose work is either humanistic or social-scientific in nature. Fellows receive a $40,000 stipend ($30,000 for Ph.D. candidates), and housing and office space.

EIN: 850125045

5651

The Simon Charitable Foundation

524 Don Gaspar Ave.
Santa Fe, NM 87505-2626 (505) 982-0733, Ext. 5
FAX: (505) 212-0101; E-mail: susan@simoncf.org; URL: http://simoncf.org

Foundation type: Independent foundation

Purpose: Scholarships to students of NM enrolled in a designated Simon Scholar High School for postsecondary education.

Financial data: Year ended 06/30/2012. Assets, $353,634 (M); Expenditures, $1,366,689; Total giving, $340,086; Grants to individuals, totaling $163,586.

Fields of interest: Higher education.

Type of support: Scholarships—to individuals; Support to graduates or students of specific schools.

Application information: Applications accepted. Application form required.

Applicants should submit the following:
1) Photograph
2) Transcripts
3) Letter(s) of recommendation
4) Essay

Additional information: Application should also include parents income tax form. Designated schools are Sante Fe High School, Capital High School, Albuquerque High School, West Mesa High School and South Valley Academy. Unsolicited requests for funds not considered or acknowledged.

EIN: 273309123

5652

Southwestern Association for Indian Arts, Inc.

(also known as SWAIA)
P.O. Box 969
Santa Fe, NM 87504-0969 (505) 983-5220
Contact: Dale Tingey, Exec. Dir.
FAX: (505) 983-7647; E-mail: info@swaia.org; URL: http://www.swaia.org/fellowship.php

Foundation type: Public charity

Purpose: Fellowships to emerging and established Native American artists, primarily in the southwest.

Publications: Application guidelines; Newsletter; Newsletter (including application guidelines).

Financial data: Year ended 12/31/2012. Assets, $480,613 (M); Expenditures, $1,465,196; Total giving, $19,000; Grants to individuals, 8 grants totaling $19,000.

Fields of interest: Visual arts; Arts; Native Americans/American Indians.

Type of support: Fellowships.

Application information: Applications accepted. Application form required. Application form available on the grantmaker's web site.

Initial approach: Application form

Deadline(s): Varies

Final notification: Recipients notified in two months

Applicants should submit the following:
1) Work samples
2) Resume
3) Essay
4) Budget Information

Program description:

Fellowship Program: The purpose of the program is to encourage American Indian artists, 18 years and older, to reach their full artistic potential by providing funds to help advance their artistic careers. The fellowship is intended to further the professional development of working artists, including portfolio development. The current fellowship award is $5,000.

EIN: 850212504

5653

SPARX/Lorenzo Antonio Foundation

P.O. Box 36389
Albuquerque, NM 87176
E-mail: SLAFoundation.org@gmail.com; URL: http:// www.sparxlorenzoantoniofoundation.org/

Foundation type: Operating foundation

Purpose: Scholarships to graduating seniors of New Mexico high schools for postsecondary education.

Financial data: Year ended 12/31/2012. Assets, $217,703 (M); Expenditures, $178,990; Total giving, $20,000; Grants to individuals, 16 grants totaling $20,000 (high: $3,000, low: $500).
Fields of interest: Higher education.
Type of support: Support to graduates or students of specific schools; Technical education support; Undergraduate support.
Application information: Applications accepted. Application form required. Application form available on the grantmaker's web site.
Initial approach: Letter
Deadline(s): Mar. 12
Applicants should submit the following:
  1) Financial information
  2) Letter(s) of recommendation
  3) Transcripts
Program descriptions:
Scholarship to Benefit APS and Albuquerque ENLACE Public High School Students: Scholarships to graduating seniors of a public high school in Albuquerque, NM, with a high school cumulative GPA of 2.5 or higher and plan to enroll full-time at the University of New Mexico. Scholarship is for $4,000.
Scholarship to Benefit New Mexico High School Students Who Plan to Attend ITT Technical Institute: Scholarships to graduating seniors of a NM high school who plan to enroll as full-time students at the ITT Technical Institute, Albuquerque, NM, and have a high school cumulative GPA of 2.5 or higher. Scholarship is worth $2,500.
Scholarship to Benefit New Mexico Public High School Students: Scholarships to graduating seniors of a public high school in NM, have a high school cumulative GPA of 2.5 or higher and plan to enroll full-time at a two or four year college of your choice. Scholarship is worth up to $2,000.
Scholarship to Benefit New Mexico Public High School Students Who Plan to Attend UNM: Scholarships to graduating seniors of a NM public high school who plan to enroll as full-time students at the University of New Mexico, NM, and have a high school cumulative GPA of 2.5 or higher. Scholarship is worth up to $4,000.
EIN: 331018724

5654
Springer Electric Cooperative Education Foundation
P.O. Box 698
Springer, NM 87747-0698
Contact: Don Schutz, Pres.
URL: http://www.springercoop.com

Foundation type: Company-sponsored foundation
Purpose: Scholarships to high school graduates who are dependents of members of Springer Electric Cooperative in NM.
Financial data: Year ended 12/31/2012. Assets, $276,427 (M); Expenditures, $12,200; Total giving, $12,200; Grants to individuals, 15 grants totaling $12,200 (high: $1,000, low: $500).
Fields of interest: Higher education.
Type of support: Undergraduate support.
Application information: Applications accepted. Application form required.
Initial approach: Application
Deadline(s): Feb.
Applicants should submit the following:
  1) Transcripts
  2) SAT
  3) Essay
  4) ACT
Additional information: Application should also include two letters of reference from a

teacher, counselor or an employer. Contact the foundation for additional information.
EIN: 850366101

5655
SUMMA Foundation
600 Valverde S.E.
Albuquerque, NM 87108-3466 (505) 277-4423
Contact: Dr. Edl Schamiloglu, Pres.
FAX: (505) 277-1439; E-mail: edl@ece.unm.edu;
URL: http://www.ece.unm.edu/summa/index.htm

Foundation type: Public charity
Purpose: Fellowships to graduate students pursuing a Ph.D. in the study of electromagnetics. Also, grants for travel funds for individuals to attend an electromagnetics symposium.
Publications: Application guidelines.
Financial data: Year ended 06/30/2011. Assets, $146,608 (M); Expenditures, $52,678; Total giving, $39,240.
Fields of interest: Science.
Type of support: Fellowships; Travel grants.
Application information: Applications accepted.
Deadline(s): Feb. 1
Applicants should submit the following:
  1) Letter(s) of recommendation
  2) Proposal
EIN: 237299352

5656
Taos Community Foundation
114 Des Georges Ln.
P.O. Box 1925
Taos, NM 87571-1925 (575) 737-9300
Contact: Elizabeth Crittenden-Palacios, Foundation Dir.
FAX: (575) 751-7130; E-mail: info@taoscf.org;
URL: http://www.taoscf.org

Foundation type: Community foundation
Purpose: Scholarships to high school graduates residents of Taos, NM for postsecondary education.
Publications: Annual report; Financial statement; Grants list; Informational brochure; Newsletter.
Financial data: Year ended 06/30/2012. Assets, $6,503,900 (M); Expenditures, $1,001,604; Total giving, $457,712. Scholarships—to individuals amount not specified.
Fields of interest: Vocational education, post-secondary; Higher education; Hispanics/Latinos.
Type of support: Scholarships—to individuals; Undergraduate support.
Application information: Applications accepted. Application form required. Application form available on the grantmaker's web site.
Initial approach: Application
Send request by: Mail or hand-deliver
Deadline(s): Apr. 16
Applicants should submit the following:
  1) Transcripts
  2) Class rank
  3) Resume
  4) SAT
  5) ACT
  6) Essay
Additional information: Eligibility requirements and application guidelines vary per scholarship type. See web site for additional guidelines.
Program description:
Friedman Family Scholarship: The scholarship is available to graduating seniors in Taos County for students pursuing advancement of higher education. The scholarship is available to those

applying to four year colleges and universities as well as two year vocational/trade schools. The award is $1,000 and is renewable for up to three years if a 3.0 GPA is maintained.
EIN: 850425147

5657
Viles Foundation, Inc.
c/o Bank of America, N.A.
PO Box 1117
Las Vegas, NM 87701-1117 (575) 387-2260

Foundation type: Independent foundation
Purpose: Scholarships to financially needy residents of San Miguel and Mora counties, NM, for attendance at colleges, universities, and vocational-technical schools.
Financial data: Year ended 12/31/2012. Assets, $58,886 (M); Expenditures, $65,971; Total giving, $61,750; Grants to individuals, 38 grants totaling $61,750 (high: $2,900, low: $800).
Fields of interest: Vocational education; Residential/custodial care; Women.
Type of support: Technical education support; Undergraduate support.
Application information: Applications accepted.
Initial approach: Letter
Deadline(s): Apr.
Additional information: Application must include transcript.
EIN: 856011506

5658
Whited Foundation
P.O. Box 1771
Raton, NM 87740-1771 (505) 445-2768
Contact: Mark Morris, Dir.
E-mail: parkavemark@bacavalley.com

Foundation type: Independent foundation
Purpose: Music or art scholarships to students of Raton High School, NM.
Publications: Annual report.
Financial data: Year ended 12/31/2011. Assets, $1,300,357 (M); Expenditures, $132,064; Total giving, $112,838.
Fields of interest: Music; Arts.
Type of support: Scholarships—to individuals.
Application information: Applications accepted. Application form required.
Initial approach: Letter
Send request by: Mail
Copies of proposal: 5
Deadline(s): None
Final notification: Recipients notified in three months
Applicants should submit the following:
  1) Transcripts
  2) SAT
  3) Resume
  4) Letter(s) of recommendation
  5) GPA
  6) Curriculum vitae
  7) Budget Information
  8) ACT
EIN: 850446414

5659
The Woodson Foundation
200 W. Marcy, Ste. 129
Santa Fe, NM 87501
Contact: Mark Kriendier Nelson

Foundation type: Independent foundation

Purpose: Awards to New Mexico artists and scholars for lifetime achievement.
Financial data: Year ended 12/31/2012. Assets, $11,625 (M); Expenditures, $5,000; Total giving, $5,000; Grant to an individual, 1 grant totaling $5,000.
Fields of interest: Arts, artist's services.
Type of support: Awards/prizes.
Application information:
  Initial approach: Letter
  Deadline(s): None
  Additional information: Contact the foundation for additional guidelines.
EIN: 450533589

5660
The Helene Wurlitzer Foundation of New Mexico
P.O. Box 1891
Taos, NM 87571-1891   (575) 758-2413
Contact: Michael Knight, Exec. Dir.
FAX: (575) 758-2559; URL: http://www.wurlitzerfoundation.org/

Foundation type: Operating foundation
Purpose: Residencies to creative (not interpretive) artists in all media for rent- and utilities-free housing in Taos, NM.
Financial data: Year ended 03/31/2012. Assets, $4,001,431 (M); Expenditures, $224,917; Total giving, $69,950; Grants to individuals, 2 grants totaling $2,000 (high: $1,000, low: $1,000).
Fields of interest: Arts, artist's services.
Type of support: Residencies.
Application information: Applications accepted. Application form required. Application form available on the grantmaker's web site.
  Initial approach: Letter
  Deadline(s): Jan. 18
  Final notification: Artists notified June 1
  Additional information: Application should include sample of work and description of project.
Program description:
  Residency Program: The foundation was established to encourage and stimulate creative work in the humanities, arts, and allied fields through the provision of rent- and utilities-free

housing in Taos, NM. The eleven houses are used for a period of three months and provide residents with a peaceful setting in which to pursue their creative endeavors.
EIN: 850128634

NEW YORK

5661
A Child Waits Foundation
c/o Ota, L.P.
1 Manhattanville Rd.
Purchase, NY 10577
E-mail: cnelson@achildwaits.org; Application address: c/o Cynthia and Randolph Nelson, 1136 Barker Rd., Ste. 12, Pittsfield, MA 01201, tel.: (413) 499-7859; URL: http://www.achildwaits.org

Foundation type: Operating foundation
Purpose: Low-interest loans to eligible families to help with the cost of adoption. Also, grants to families for adopting older or special-needs children.
Financial data: Year ended 12/31/2012. Assets, $2,697,884 (M); Expenditures, $441,606; Total giving, $315,733; Grants to individuals, 63 grants totaling $228,241 (high: $9,090, low: $1,388).
Fields of interest: Adoption.
Type of support: Loans—to individuals.
Application information: Applications accepted. Application form required.
> *Initial approach:* Letter, telephone, or e-mail
> *Copies of proposal:* 1
> *Deadline(s):* Ongoing
> *Applicants should submit the following:*
> 1) Photograph
> 2) Letter(s) of recommendation
> 3) Financial information
> 4) Budget Information
> *Additional information:* Application must also include copies of previous two years tax returns, most recent pay stub, copy of drivers license and a $20 application processing fee. Loan is based on financial need. See web site for additional guidelines or contact foundation.
EIN: 133978652

5662
AAAA Foundation, Inc.
c/o AAAA, Inc.
1065 Ave. of the Americas, 16th Fl.
New York, NY 10018-0174 (212) 682-2500
FAX: (212) 682-8391; URL: http://www.aaaa.org/careers/scholarships/Pages/default.aspx

Foundation type: Public charity
Purpose: Scholarships to people of color and to women for undergraduate and graduate education leading towards media, art, and advertising careers.
Financial data: Year ended 12/31/2012. Assets, $785,380 (M); Expenditures, $285,485; Total giving, $199,680. Scholarships—to individuals amount not specified.
Fields of interest: Media/communications; Scholarships/financial aid; Minorities; Asians/Pacific Islanders; African Americans/Blacks; Hispanics/Latinos; Native Americans/American Indians; Women.
Type of support: Graduate support; Undergraduate support.
Application information: Application form required.
> *Additional information:* See web site for additional application information.
EIN: 133949950

5663
Academy of American Poets, Inc.
75 Maiden Ln., Ste. 901
New York, NY 10038-4610 (212) 274-0343
Contact: C.J. Evans, Awards Coord.
FAX: (212) 274-9427; E-mail: academy@poets.org; URL: http://www.poets.org

Foundation type: Public charity
Purpose: Fellowships and prizes by nomination only, with the exception of the Walt Whitman Prize, to American poets at all stages of their careers.
Publications: Application guidelines; Annual report; Financial statement; Informational brochure; Newsletter.
Financial data: Year ended 06/30/2012. Assets, $8,245,557 (M); Expenditures, $1,754,681; Total giving, $192,000; Grants to individuals, totaling $192,000.
Fields of interest: Literature.
Type of support: Publication; Fellowships; Awards/grants by nomination only; Awards/prizes.
Application information: Applications not accepted.
> *Additional information:* Awards by nomination only.
Program descriptions:
> *Academy Fellowship:* Under this program, an annual fellowship of $25,000 is awarded to an American poet for distinguished poetic achievement.
> *Harold Morton Landon Translation Award:* This $1,000 award recognizes a published translation of poetry from any language into English. A noted translator chooses the winning book. Books must be submitted in the year in which they are published.
> *James Laughlin Award:* This award is given to recognize and support a poet's second book. The winning poet is awarded a cash prize of $5,000, and the academy purchases copies of the book for distribution to its members. Only manuscripts already under contract with publishers will be considered.
> *Lenore Marshall Poetry Prize:* This $25,000 award recognizes the most outstanding book of poetry published in the U.S. in the previous year.
> *Raiziss/de Palchi Translation Award:* This award recognizes outstanding translations into English of modern Italian poetry through a $5,000 book prize, a $20,000 fellowship, and a residency at the American Academy in Rome. This award is given in even-numbered years; self-published books are not accepted.
> *Wallace Stevens Prize:* The award carries a stipend of $100,000, and is given to an individual who has shown outstanding and proven mastery in the art of poetry.
> *Walt Whitman Award:* This award brings first-book publication, $5,000, and a residency at the Vermont Studio Center to an American poet who has not yet published a book of poetry. The winning manuscript, chosen by an eminent poet, is published by Louisiana State University Press. The academy purchases copies of the book for distribution to its members.
EIN: 131879953

5664
ACMP Foundation
1133 Broadway No. 810
New York, NY 10010-8046 (212) 645-7424
Contact: Daniel Nimetz, Exec. Dir.
FAX: (212) 741-2678; E-mail: office@acmp.net; URL: http://www.acmp.net

Foundation type: Public charity
Purpose: Grants to amateur musicians who meet regularly in groups to hire professional coaches.
Publications: Application guidelines; Grants list; Occasional report; Program policy statement.
Financial data: Year ended 07/31/2012. Assets, $7,424,583 (M); Expenditures, $182,158; Total giving, $63,618; Grants to individuals, totaling $7,734.
Fields of interest: Music ensembles/groups.
Type of support: Grants to individuals.
Application information: Applications not accepted.
> *Additional information:* Unsolicited requests for funds not considered or acknowledged.
Program descriptions:
> *Home Coaching Program:* This program is intended to encourage amateur musicians who meet regularly to engage professional coaches in order to improve their rehearsal techniques, musical insight, and to exchange musical ideas. The foundation provides up to 50 percent of the coach's fee. Participants must be members of ACMP (Associated Chamber Music Players) Associated Chamber Music Players, Inc.
> *Special Initiatives:* Projects or events that further the aims of ACMP but do not fall within the other grant programs offered by the foundation are considered on an individual basis. Examples include funds to establish a database of contemporary chamber music, seed money to initiate an amateur component at a major European festival, or subsidy to scan and digitize out-of-print chamber music at the Sibley Music Library for public downloading via the internet.
EIN: 954437773

5665
Actors Fund of America
729 7th Ave., 10th Fl.
New York, NY 10019-6895 (212) 221-7300
FAX: (212) 764-0238; Toll-free tel.: (800) 221-7303; URL: http://www.actorsfund.org

Foundation type: Public charity
Purpose: Scholarships to entertainment industry professionals who have financial need, are enrolled in a degree or certificate program, and who demonstrate significant work history in entertainment and the performing arts. Emergency assistance grants to entertainment industry professionals for essentials such as food, rent and medical care.
Publications: Annual report; Informational brochure; Newsletter.
Financial data: Year ended 12/31/2011. Assets, $54,040,116 (M); Expenditures, $27,124,839; Total giving, $3,491,428; Grants to individuals, 3,046 grants totaling $2,521,525.
Fields of interest: Performing arts; Arts, artist's services.
Type of support: Scholarships—to individuals; Grants for special needs.
Application information: Applications accepted.
> *Initial approach:* Telephone or e-mail
> *Additional information:* Contact foundation for complete eligibility requirements.
EIN: 131635251

5666
Emma J. Adams Memorial Fund, Inc.
328 Eldert Ln.
Brooklyn, NY 11208

Foundation type: Independent foundation
Purpose: Grants to aid the indigent elderly through a church-sponsored meals program and ecumenical

medical care, also limited, nonrecurring grants to elderly individuals who are agency, medically or professionally-sponsored residing in the greater New York, NY, metropolitan area.
Publications: Application guidelines.
Financial data: Year ended 12/31/2012. Assets, $2,493,720 (M); Expenditures, $145,218; Total giving, $60,565; Grants to individuals, 9 grants totaling $60,565 (high: $11,650, low: $1,575).
Fields of interest: Aging; Economically disadvantaged.
Type of support: Grants for special needs.
Application information: Applications accepted. Interview required.
> *Initial approach:* Letter
> *Deadline(s):* None
> *Additional information:* Application should include financial information.
EIN: 136116503

5667
Adirondack Foundation
(formerly Adirondack Community Trust)
2284 Saranac Ave.
P.O. Box 288
Lake Placid, NY   12946   (518) 523-9904
Contact: Cali Brooks, Exec. Dir.; For grants: Andrea Grout, Prog. Off.
FAX: (518) 523-9905;
E-mail: info@generousact.org; Grant inquiry e-mail: andrea@generousact.org; URL: http://www.generousact.org

Foundation type: Community foundation
Purpose: Scholarships to graduating seniors, college or graduate students in the Adirondack, NY region to pursue their education at institutions of higher learning.
Publications: Annual report; Financial statement; Grants list; Informational brochure; Newsletter.
Financial data: Year ended 06/30/2012. Assets, $30,832,731 (M); Expenditures, $2,889,127; Total giving, $2,456,365; Grants to individuals, 66 grants totaling $834,868.
Fields of interest: Higher education.
Type of support: Support to graduates or students of specific schools.
Application information: Applications accepted. Application form available on the grantmaker's web site.
> *Initial approach:* Application
> *Send request by:* Mail
> *Deadline(s):* Spring; specific deadline dates vary for each scholarship
> *Additional information:* See web site for complete listing of scholarships.
EIN: 161535724

5668
Adirondack Scholarship Foundation
P.O. Box 97
Willsboro, NY   12996-0097   (518) 963-7656
Contact: Peter Levine, Pres.
E-mail: info@pokomac.com; URL: http://www.adkscholarship.org/

Foundation type: Public charity
Purpose: Camp scholarships to deserving families of children for camping experience in the Adirondacks, NY.
Financial data: Year ended 12/31/2011. Assets, $438,272 (M); Expenditures, $59,405; Total giving, $53,100; Grants to individuals, totaling $53,100.
Type of support: Camperships.
Application information: Applications accepted.

> *Additional information:* Application should include financial information and two references from the child's teachers.
EIN: 222303625

5669
AEC Electrical Scholarship & Educational Fund Corporation
36-36 33rd St., Ste. 402
Long Island City, NY   11106   (718) 752-0800

Foundation type: Independent foundation
Purpose: Scholarships to graduating students of New York City high schools who have been accepted at a college or university in an engineering major.
Financial data: Year ended 12/31/2011. Assets, $173,424 (M); Expenditures, $104,073; Total giving, $50,329; Grants to individuals, 18 grants totaling $50,329 (high: $7,000, low: $1,000).
Fields of interest: Engineering school/education; Scholarships/financial aid.
Type of support: Scholarships—to individuals.
Application information: Applications accepted. Application form required.
> *Initial approach:* Letter
> *Deadline(s):* May 15
> *Additional information:* Recipient selected by school committee.
EIN: 132946603

5670
Aero Cares, Inc.
112 W. 34th St., 22nd Fl.
New York, NY   10120-2400   (201) 508-5549
URL: http://www.aeropostalecareers.com/community.asp

Foundation type: Public charity
Purpose: Emergency financial assistance to employees of Aeropostale, Inc., and their immediate families during times of extreme financial hardship and/or need resulting from a personal tradegy such as death in the family, catastrophic medical claim, fire, flood, earthquake and other disasters.
Financial data: Year ended 12/31/2012. Assets, $603,235 (M); Expenditures, $279,970; Total giving, $252,489; Grants to individuals, totaling $252,489.
Fields of interest: Safety/disasters; Human services.
Type of support: Emergency funds; Grants for special needs.
Application information: Applications accepted. Application form required.
> *Additional information:* Assistance for Aeropostale, Inc. employees only. Unsolicited requests for funds not considered or acknowledged.
EIN: 272040286

5671
AFS-USA, Inc.
(also known as American Field Service - USA, Inc.)
1 Whitehall St., 2nd Fl.
New York, NY   10004-2109   (212) 299-9000
FAX: (212) 299-9090; E-mail: afsinfo@afs.org;
Toll-free tel.: (800) 237-4636; URL: http://www.afsusa.org/usa_en/home

Foundation type: Public charity
Purpose: Scholarships to students participating in the AFS international exchange program who are in financial need.

Financial data: Year ended 12/31/2011. Assets, $17,567,775 (M); Expenditures, $34,759,195; Total giving, $6,471,261; Grants to individuals, totaling $1,643,499.
Fields of interest: Scholarships/financial aid; International exchange, students.
Type of support: Scholarships—to individuals.
Application information: Applications accepted. Application form required.
> *Initial approach:* Letter or telephone
> *Deadline(s):* Varies
> *Applicants should submit the following:*
> 1) Financial information
> 2) GPA
> 3) Essay
> *Additional information:* Application must also include parents tax forms, and demonstrate financial need. Applicant must have a strong record of academic commitment and community involvement.
Program descriptions:
> *AFS Family Award:* Members of former or current AFS host families, AFS returnees and their siblings, children of current AFS volunteers, and descendants of AFS ambulance drivers are eligible for a $200 award towards study abroad programs.
> *AFS Global Leaders Scholarship Program:* The organization provides scholarship for academic semesters, summer semesters, and up to a full academic year of study abroad for high school students. Current award ranges are $200 to $1,500. Families who qualify typically have household incomes under $55,000.
> *Congress-Bundestag Youth Exchange Scholarships:* The organization partners with the U.S. Department of State to offer 50 full scholarships for a year of study in Germany. Students must be between the ages of 15 and 18, with a strong interest in Germany and a GPA of at least 3.0. Previous study of the German language not required. Student must reside in Connecticut, D.C., Delaware, Massachusetts, Maryland, Maine, New Hampshire, New Jersey, New York, Ohio, Pennsylvania, Rhode Island, or Vermont.
> *Scholarships by State:* Additional need-based scholarships are available to high school students wishing to study abroad for up to one year. Scholarships could cover up to 90 percent of program cost, but vary depending on state and financial need.
> *YES Abroad Scholarship:* The Kennedy-Lugar Youth Exchange and Study (YES) Abroad Program provides 50 full scholarships to American high school students, ages 15 to 18, to study for up to one year in Egypt, Ghana, India, Indonesia, Malaysia, Mali, Morocco, Oman, Thailand, and Turkey.
EIN: 391711417

5672
The AFTRA Foundation Inc.
c/o SAG-AFTRA
260 Madison Ave., 7th Fl.
New York, NY   10016-2401   (212) 863-4315
Contact: Shelby Scott, Pres.
E-mail: aftrafoundation@sagaftra.org; URL: http://www.sagaftra.org/aftrafoundation

Foundation type: Public charity
Purpose: Scholarships to members of the Screen Actors Guild-American Federation of Television and Radio Artists (SAG-AFTRA) and their dependents. Emergency benefit funds for supporting members in need.
Financial data: Year ended 04/30/2012. Assets, $2,424,694 (M); Expenditures, $323,926; Total giving, $250,817.

Fields of interest: Arts education; Higher education; Journalism school/education.
Type of support: Emergency funds; Scholarships—to individuals.
Application information: Applications accepted. Application form required. Application form available on the grantmaker's web site.

> *Send request by:* Mail
> *Deadline(s):* May 1
> *Final notification:* Applicants notified in June for Heller scholarship
> *Applicants should submit the following:*
> 1) Financial information
> 2) Transcripts
> 3) Essay
> 4) Letter(s) of recommendation
> *Additional information:* See web site for additional application guidelines.

Program description:

> *George Heller Memorial Scholarship:* Up to fifteen scholarships, of up to $2,500 each, are available to members of the Screen Actors Guild-American Federation of Television and Radio Artists (SAG-AFTRA) and their dependents for academic study in any field, including broadcast journalism and labor relations, or for professional training in the arts. Eligible applicants must have been members of SAG-AFTRA in good standing for at least five years; applicants will be evaluated on academic excellence, financial need, and acceptance/enrollment in a university, professional school, or other accredited institution of higher education.

EIN: 133904351

5673
Athas Zaharis Agoriani Trust
58-29 213th St.
Bayside, NY   11364   (718) 423-1732
Contact: John Zaharis, Tr.

Foundation type: Independent foundation
Purpose: Grants to indigent residents of the town of Agoriani in Sparta, Greece. Grants are given for rent, repairs, student aid, the disabled, and general support.
Financial data: Year ended 12/31/2011. Assets, $123,532 (M); Expenditures, $41,677; Total giving, $38,901.
Fields of interest: Disabilities, people with; Economically disadvantaged.
Type of support: Foreign applicants; Grants for special needs.
Application information: Applications not accepted.

> *Additional information:* Unsolicited requests for funds not considered or acknowledged.

EIN: 112801980

5674
Agudath Israel of America, Inc.
42 Broadway, 14th Fl.
New York, NY   10004-1617   (212) 797-9000
Contact: Labish Becker, Exec. Dir.

Foundation type: Public charity
Purpose: Grants to needy individuals and families for educational purpose, food, medical assistance, summer camps and other purposes.
Financial data: Year ended 08/31/2012. Assets, $26,726,142 (M); Expenditures, $18,774,154; Total giving, $3,971,802; Grants to individuals, totaling $5,171.
Fields of interest: Education; Jewish agencies & synagogues; Economically disadvantaged.
Type of support: Grants for special needs.

Application information: Applications accepted.

> *Additional information:* Contact the organization for additional guidelines.

EIN: 135604164

5675
AIG Foundation, Inc.
c/o Linda Sabo
175 Water Street, 20th Floor
New York, NY   10038

Foundation type: Company-sponsored foundation
Purpose: Scholarships to dependents of employees of American International Group, Inc.
Publications: Corporate giving report.
Financial data: Year ended 12/31/2012. Assets, $3,394 (M); Expenditures, $1,728,281; Total giving, $1,461,140; Grants to individuals, totaling $1,461,140.
Fields of interest: Higher education.
Type of support: Employee-related scholarships.
Application information: Applications not accepted.

> *Additional information:* Unsolicited requests for funds not considered or acknowledged.

Company name: American International Group, Inc.
EIN: 203713472

5676
Alvin Ailey Dance Foundation, Inc.
(formerly Dance Theatre Foundation, Inc.)
405 W. 55th St., 9th Ave.
New York, NY   10019-4402   (212) 405-9000
Contact: Bennett Rink, Exec. Dir.
FAX: (212) 405-9004; URL: http://www.alvinailey.org

Foundation type: Public charity
Purpose: Financial assistance for talented young dancers for attendance at The Ailey School, NY.
Financial data: Year ended 06/30/2012. Assets, $156,824,391 (M); Expenditures, $34,552,103; Total giving, $1,501,633; Grants to individuals, totaling $1,501,633.
Fields of interest: Dance.
Type of support: Scholarships—to individuals; Support to graduates or students of specific schools.
Application information: Students must maintain satisfactory academic progress in all their classes for assistance. Contact the foundation for additional guidelines.

Program description:

> *Scholarship Fund:* Scholarships are awarded to students ages 15 to 21, to ensure that the most talented students can attend The Ailey School regardless of economic ability. Students enrolled in the program receive comprehensive technique classes, performance opportunities and support service that enable them to develop into versatile and expressive dancers, well prepared for the rigors of a professional career. More than 70 percent of the scholarship recipients are from minority groups.

EIN: 132584273

5677
Edward Albee Foundation, Inc.
14 Harrison St.
New York, NY   10013-2842
E-mail: info@albeefoundation.org; URL: http://www.albeefoundation.org

Foundation type: Operating foundation
Purpose: Residencies to sculptors, visual artists and writers for four to six weeks.

Publications: Application guidelines.
Financial data: Year ended 12/31/2011. Assets, $2,373,735 (M); Expenditures, $111,832; Total giving, $0. No monetary support given for residencies.
Fields of interest: Visual arts; Sculpture; Theater (playwriting); Literature.
Type of support: Residencies.
Application information: Applications accepted. Application form required.

> *Initial approach:* Letter
> *Send request by:* Mail
> *Deadline(s):* Mar. 1 and before Feb. 15 for international applicants
> *Applicants should submit the following:*
> 1) Work samples
> 2) Resume
> 3) Letter(s) of recommendation

Program description:

> *Residencies:* The foundation maintains the William Flanagan Memorial Center for Creative Persons where talented sculptors, visual artists, and writers may receive a grant for a free room in order to allow them to work free from financial pressure. Applicants for grants of a room are recommended by well-known persons in the arts as well as by application. The residency period is from mid-May to mid-Oct. Residencies can be either four week or six week periods depending on availability.

EIN: 136168827

5678
Albion High School Alumni Foundation
P.O. Box 345
Albion, NY   14411-0345   (585) 589-4477
URL: http://www.albionalumni.org

Foundation type: Operating foundation
Purpose: Scholarships to students or alumni of Albion High School, NY.
Financial data: Year ended 12/31/2012. Assets, $424,505 (M); Expenditures, $40,269; Total giving, $14,000.
Type of support: Support to graduates or students of specific schools; Precollege support; Undergraduate support.
Application information: Applications accepted. Application form required.

> *Deadline(s):* Mid-Apr.
> *Applicants should submit the following:*
> 1) Essay
> 2) Transcripts
> *Additional information:* Application should also include list of school and community activities.

EIN: 222925068

5679
John Alexander Memorial Scholarship Fund
3 Sarnowski Dr.
Glenville, NY   12302

Foundation type: Independent foundation
Purpose: Scholarships to residents of Schenectady County, NY, attending a law school in NY.
Financial data: Year ended 12/31/2012. Assets, $534,082 (M); Expenditures, $29,023; Total giving, $22,927; Grants to individuals, 15 grants totaling $22,927 (high: $1,529, low: $1,528).
Fields of interest: Law school/education.
Type of support: Graduate support.
Application information: Applications accepted.

> *Initial approach:* Letter

Additional information: Application must outline financial need and professional objectives.
EIN: 146111436

5680
All Stars Project, Inc.
543 W. 42nd St.
New York, NY 10036-6216 (212) 941-9400
Contact: Gabrielle Kurlander, Pres. and C.E.O.
Toll-free tel.: (800) 435-7453; URL: http://www.allstars.org

Foundation type: Public charity
Purpose: Scholarships to individuals residing in New York, NY, for undergraduate education.
Publications: Application guidelines; Newsletter.
Financial data: Year ended 12/31/2012. Assets, $19,461,322 (M); Expenditures, $7,653,728; Total giving, $12,441.
Fields of interest: Higher education.
Type of support: Scholarships—to individuals.
Application information: Applications accepted. Application form required. Interview required.
EIN: 133148295

5681
Allegany County Area Foundation, Inc.
6807 Route 19 N., Ste. 180
Crossroads Center
Belmont, NY 14813 (585) 808-8444
Contact: Patricia Oliver, Scholarship Coord.
E-mail: director@alleganycountyareafoundation.org;
Additional tel.: (585) 365-2319; Additional e-mail: oliverpa@yahoo.com; URL: http://www.alleganycountyareafoundation.org

Foundation type: Community foundation
Purpose: Scholarships to residents of Allegany County, NY pursuing postsecondary education.
Publications: Application guidelines; Annual report; Informational brochure.
Financial data: Year ended 04/30/2013. Assets, $7,743,250 (M); Expenditures, $237,004; Total giving, $126,650; Grants to individuals, totaling $126,650.
Fields of interest: Higher education.
Type of support: Undergraduate support.
Application information: Applications accepted. Application form required. Application form available on the grantmaker's web site.
Send request by: Mail or online
Deadline(s): Mar. 1
Applicants should submit the following:
  1) Transcripts
  2) Letter(s) of recommendation
  3) Essay
Additional information: See web site for a complete program listing.
EIN: 222506596

5682
Alliance for Young Artists and Writers, Inc.
(also known as Scholastic Art & Writing Awards)
557 Broadway
New York, NY 10012-3962 (212) 343-6100
FAX: (212) 389-3939;
E-mail: info@artandwriting.org; E-mail for Virginia McEnerney: vmcenerney@artandwriting.org;
URL: http://www.artandwriting.org

Foundation type: Public charity
Purpose: Awards and scholarships to young artists and writers for creative works of art and writing.

Publications: Annual report; Grants list.
Financial data: Year ended 06/30/2012. Assets, $3,477,793 (M); Expenditures, $3,173,122; Total giving, $420,835; Grants to individuals, totaling $394,585.
Fields of interest: Visual arts; Literature.
International interests: Canada.
Type of support: Scholarships—to individuals; Awards/prizes.
Application information:
  Initial approach: E-mail
  Deadline(s): Vary
  Additional information: See web site for additional guidelines.
Program descriptions:
  AMD Game Changer Award: In partnership with the AMD Foundation, two top students will receive $1,000 awards for their video game designs, a laptop, and up to $2,500 toward professional development activities.
  ASAP Awards: Awards to students in grades 7 through 11 to receive partial to full tuition scholarships to attend summer art and writing programs offered by colleges, camps, and nonprofit organizations. Students must have earned a Gold Key (for either Art or Writing) in the Scholastic Art & Writing Awards. Students must come from a low income household (under $40,000 per year)
  B.I.G. Awards: The alliance will provide $500 scholarships to two artists and two writers for each grade level (7 through 12) in the Scholastic Art and Writing Awards. These scholarships will be chosen from national Gold Medals across all categories.
  Creativity and Citizenship Award: Teens are encouraged to submit their works of art and writing that address contemporary social issues important to them. Three winners will be selected to receive $1,000 scholarships. Select works will be included in the National Scholastic Art & Writing Awards Teen Exhibition. This special award is presented in collaboration with the National Constitution Center in Philadelphia.
  Distinguished Portfolio Teacher Award: Thirty $250 awards are presented to sponsoring teachers of Distinguished Portfolio Medalists.
  New York Life Award: Teens are encouraged to submit their works of art and writing that deal with loss and bereavement for the opportunity to earn recognition as part of this special award sponsored by the New York Life Foundation. Six winners will be selected to receive $1,000 scholarships.
  Ovation Inspired Teaching Award: Two $1,000 awards will be given to the teachers with the most outstanding group of student submissions: one for art, and one for writing.
  Portfolio Gold Teacher Award: Awards of $1,000 each are presented to sponsoring teachers of Art and Writing Portfolio Gold Medalists.
  The Scholastic Art & Writing Awards: The awards are national in scope and administered by the alliance. The process begins across the country as young artists and writers in grades 7 through 12 submit creative works of art and writing to a network of affiliate programs of the alliance who share the alliance's vision to inspire the next generation of artists and writers.
  Undergraduate Tuition Scholarships: Fifteen $10,000 scholarships are available to graduating seniors who earn Portfolio Gold Medals in art, photography, general writing, and nonfiction categories. An additional 30 seniors will earn Distinguished Achievement Awards of $1,000 each.
EIN: 133780998

5683
Alpha Psi of Chi Psi Educational Trust
c/o William W. Huling, Jr.
328 Snyder Hill Rd.
Ithaca, NY 14850 (607) 255-2075
Contact: John L. Neuman, Chair. and Pres.
Application address: 1077 Taughannock Blvd., Ithaca, NY 14850

Foundation type: Operating foundation
Purpose: Scholarships to members of Chi Psi Fraternity who demonstrate financial need.
Financial data: Year ended 05/31/2013. Assets, $0 (M); Expenditures, $14,888; Total giving, $10,000.
Fields of interest: Higher education; Students, sororities/fraternities.
Type of support: Scholarships—to individuals.
Application information: Applications accepted. Application form required. Interview required.
  Deadline(s): Apr. 30
  Additional information: Applicant must show academic achievement, service to the fraternity and service to the Cornell community.
EIN: 156021424

5684
Alumni Association of Hunter College
695 Park Ave., Rm. E-1314A
New York, NY 10021-5024

Foundation type: Independent foundation
Purpose: Scholarships for students of Hunter College, NY.
Financial data: Year ended 06/30/2011. Assets, $662,425 (M); Expenditures, $94,227; Total giving, $81,197.
Type of support: Support to graduates or students of specific schools; Undergraduate support.
Application information: Applications not accepted.
  Additional information: Unsolicited requests for funds not considered or acknowledged.
EIN: 130452366

5685
Alzheimer's Drug Discovery Foundation
(also known as V.G.I.F.)
57 W. 57th St., Ste. 904
New York, NY 10019-2822 (212) 935-2402
Contact: Howard Fillit M.D., Exec. Dir.
FAX: (212) 935-2408;
E-mail: info@alzdiscovery.org; URL: http://www.alzdiscovery.org

Foundation type: Public charity
Purpose: Research grants for the discovery and development of drugs to prevent, treat, and cure Alzheimer's disease and cognitive aging.
Publications: Application guidelines; Annual report.
Financial data: Year ended 12/31/2011. Assets, $7,707,145 (M); Expenditures, $5,761,641; Total giving, $5,521,875.
Fields of interest: Alzheimer's disease research.
Type of support: Research.
Application information:
  Initial approach: Letter
  Deadline(s): None
  Additional information: Contact foundation for further application guidelines.
EIN: 201082179

5686

America-Israel Cultural Foundation, Inc.
1140 Broadway, Ste. 304
New York, NY   10001   (212) 557-1600
Contact: David Homan, Exec. Dir.
FAX: (212) 557-1611; E-mail: admin@aicf.org;
URL: http://www.aicf.org

Foundation type: Public charity
Purpose: Grants and scholarships to talented students in Israel and abroad who bring theater, music, and fine arts to towns, villages and settlements in Israel.
Publications: Application guidelines; Informational brochure; Newsletter.
Financial data: Year ended 12/31/2011. Assets, $5,920,788 (M); Expenditures, $2,173,294; Total giving, $858,232; Grants to individuals, totaling $141,263.
Fields of interest: Performing arts.
International interests: Israel.
Type of support: Grants to individuals; Scholarships—to individuals.
Application information: Contact the foundation for eligibility determination.
Program description:
   The Sharett Scholarship Fund: The fund provides assistance to Israeli students who demonstrate significant talent and potential. Students are awarded tuition scholarships annually in five creative and performing arts disciplines: music, dance, theatre, visual arts, and film and television.
EIN: 131664048

5687

American Academy in Berlin
14 E. 60th St., Ste. 604
New York, NY   10022-7130   (212) 588-1755
Contact: Dr. Gary Smith, Exec. Dir.
FAX: (212) 588-1758;
E-mail: nyoffice@americanacademy.de; E-mail For Gary Smith: gs@americanacademy.de; URL: http://www.americanacademy.de

Foundation type: Public charity
Purpose: Fellowships for scholars of the fine arts, scholarly disciplines and professional fields to study at the American Academy in Berlin, Germany.
Publications: Application guidelines; Newsletter.
Financial data: Year ended 06/30/2012. Assets, $37,672,257 (M); Expenditures, $6,230,524; Total giving, $540,681.
Fields of interest: Film/video; Sculpture; Drawing; Theater; Opera; Music (choral); Art history; Arts.
International interests: Germany.
Type of support: Fellowships; Exchange programs.
Application information: Applications accepted. Application form required. Application form available on the grantmaker's web site.
   Send request by: Mail
   Copies of proposal: 6
   Deadline(s): Oct.
   Applicants should submit the following:
      1) Work samples
      2) Curriculum vitae
      3) Proposal
Program description:
   Fellowships: Each year, the academy welcomes about 22 scholars, artists, and professionals who wish to engage in independent study in Berlin for an academic semester or, in very rare cases, for an entire academic year. The prizes have been awarded to scholars working in a variety of disciplines, including history, political science, literature, economics, German studies, art history, musicology, anthropology, law, and linguistics, as well as to writers, composers, and visual artists.

Academy alumni also include public policy experts, journalists, and critics. Benefits include a stipend ranging from $3,500 to $5,000 per month of residency, round-trip airfare, and an apartment with partial board at the Hans Arnhold Center, a historic lakeside villa in the Wannsee district of Berlin. Fellows are expected to be in residence during the entire period of award, that is, for a full semester. Short term fellowships of six to eight weeks are only available for the Bosch Fellows in Public Policy.
EIN: 521726273

5688

American Academy in Rome
7 E. 60th St.
New York, NY   10022-1001   (212) 751-7200
FAX: (212) 751-7220; E-mail: info@aarome.org;
URL: http://www.aarome.org

Foundation type: Public charity
Purpose: Fellowships for emerging artists and scholars in the early or middle stages of their careers, for a duration of six or eleven months.
Publications: Application guidelines; Newsletter.
Financial data: Year ended 08/31/2011. Assets, $124,148,000 (M); Expenditures, $12,560,296; Total giving, $888,259; Grants to individuals, totaling $855,259.
Fields of interest: Visual arts.
Type of support: Fellowships; Awards/prizes.
Application information: Applications accepted. Application form required.
   Initial approach: Letter, telephone or e-mail
   Deadline(s): Nov. 1
   Applicants should submit the following:
      1) Letter(s) of recommendation
      2) SASE
      3) Resume
      4) Proposal
      5) Curriculum vitae
   Additional information: Application should also include a $30 application fee for one application, $40 if submitting two or more applications. Applications postmarked Nov. 2 through Nov. 15 require a $60 application fee if submitting one application and $75 if submitting two or more applications. Interviews may be required.
Program description:
   Rome Prize Fellowship: This prize is awarded to thirty emerging artists and scholars in the early or middle stages of their careers who represent the highest standard of excellence in the arts and humanities. Fellows are chosen from the disciplines of architecture, design, historic preservation and conservation, landscape architecture, literature (awarded only by nomination through the American Academy of Arts and Letters), musical composition, visual arts, ancient studies, medieval studies, renaissance and early modern studies, and modern Italian studies. The prize provides a stipend, meals, a bedroom with private bath, and a study or studio. Those with children under 18 live in partially subsidized apartments nearby. Winners of six-month and eleven-month fellowships receive stipends of $15,000 and $27,000, respectively. Applicants must be U.S. citizens at the time of application.
EIN: 131623881

5689

American Academy of Arts and Letters
(formerly American Academy & Institute of Arts and Letters)
633 W. 155th St.
New York, NY   10032-7501   (212) 368-5900
Contact: Virginia Dajani, Exec. Dir.
FAX: (212) 491-4615;
E-mail: academy@artsandletters.org; URL: http://www.artsandletters.org

Foundation type: Operating foundation
Purpose: Prizes to artists, architects, writers, and composers who are not members of the Academy, for exceptional artistic achievement. Candidates for prizes must be nominated by members.
Publications: Informational brochure.
Financial data: Year ended 12/31/2012. Assets, $81,869,068 (M); Expenditures, $3,127,265; Total giving, $889,100; Grants to individuals, 95 grants totaling $889,100 (high: $70,000, low: $250).
Fields of interest: Theater (musical); Arts.
Type of support: Awards/grants by nomination only; Awards/prizes.
Application information: Applications accepted. Application form required. Application form available on the grantmaker's web site.
   Copies of proposal: 1
   Deadline(s): Nov. 1
   Additional information: With the exception of the Richard Rodgers Awards in Musical Theater, applications for awards or financial assistance are not accepted. Recipients notified in Mar.
Program descriptions:
   Awards and Prizes: These awards subsidize workshops, readings, and productions of original musical theatre works in nonprofit, off-Broadway theatres. Winners receive an allowance for personal expenses during production.
   The Richard Rogers Awards for Workshops, Readings, And Productions: These awards subsidize workshops, readings, and productions of original musical theatre works in nonprofit, off-Broadway theatres. Winners receive an allowance for personal expenses during production.
EIN: 130429640

5690

American Australian Association, Inc.
50 Broadway, Ste. 2003
New York, NY   10004-3813   (212) 338-6860
FAX: (212) 338-6864;
E-mail: information@aaanyc.org; URL: http://www.americanaustralian.org

Foundation type: Public charity
Purpose: Fellowships to Australian and American students for post graduate studies and research.
Financial data: Year ended 12/31/2011. Assets, $11,157,441 (M); Expenditures, $4,579,184; Total giving, $599,409; Grants to individuals, 7 grants totaling $188,600.
Fields of interest: Nerve, muscle & bone diseases.
Type of support: Fellowships; Research.
Application information: Applications accepted. Application form required.
   Deadline(s): Apr. 15 for Australia to U.S. Fellowship, Oct. 31 U.S. to Australia Fellowship
   Additional information: See web site for additional guidelines.
Program descriptions:
   APSA Congressional Fellowships: For nine months, a select political scientist, journalist, federal executive, or international scholar will gain

hands-on understanding of the legislative process by serving on congressional staffs. Fellows receive a monthly stipend of $3,800 for ten months, $2,150 for program-related international travel, $160 for books, and additional travel expenses for the visit to the Canadian Parliament and one trip to the district office of their respective Congress member. Applicants must be Australian citizens.

Australia to U.S.A. Fellowships: The association awards individual fellowships for advanced study in the U.S. of up to $30,000 each year. The fellowships build on existing strong social and economic partnerships and foster intellectual exchange between the U.S. and Australia. Fields of study supported by the fellowship include science, technology, sustainability, pediatrics, neuroscience, geology/geophysics, conservation, biopharmaceuticals, medicine, and engineering. Research/study must be at the graduate or postgraduate level. Proof of acceptance into a U.S. educational institution is required. Applicant must be an Australian citizen or permanent resident.

Corporate Fellowships: Corporate fellowships are offered in specific fields of science, health, safety, environment, technology, pediatrics, and sustainability to American and Australian researchers.

U.S.A. to Australia Fellowships: The association awards individual fellowships for advanced study in Australia of up to $30,000 each year. The fellowships build on existing strong social and economic partnerships and foster intellectual exchange between the U.S. and Australia. Fields of study supported by the fellowship include life sciences, oceanography/marine sciences, stem cell research, mining, medicine, and engineering. Research/study must be at the graduate or postgraduate level. Proof of acceptance into an Australian educational institution is required. Applicant must be a U.S. citizen or permanent resident.

EIN: 136151807

5691
American Council for Learned Societies
633 3rd Ave. 8th Fl.
New York, NY 10017-6795 (212) 697-1505
ACLS on-line fellowship application: ofa.acls.org
FAX: (212) 949-8058; URL: http://www.acls.org/

Foundation type: Public charity
Purpose: Fellowships and stipends to postdoctoral scholars and graduate students throughout the world to support programs of research and for educational and cultural exchange programs.
Financial data: Year ended 06/30/2012. Assets, $138,677,713 (M); Expenditures, $22,760,388; Total giving, $15,506,154; Grants to individuals, 110 grants totaling $3,659,962.
Fields of interest: Humanities; Social sciences.
Type of support: Fellowships; Exchange programs; Postdoctoral support; Graduate support; Stipends.
Application information: Applications accepted. Application form available on the grantmaker's web site.
   Send request by: On-line
   Deadline(s): Sept.
   Final notification: Recipients notified early Feb.
   Additional information: See web site for additional application guidelines.
Program descriptions:
   ACLS Collaborative Research Fellowships: The aim of this fellowship program is to offer small teams of two or more scholars the opportunity to collaborate intensively on a single, substantive project. The fellowships are for a total period of up to 24 months, to be initiated between July 1, 2014

and Sept.1, 2016, and provide up to $60,000 in salary replacement for each collaborator as well as up to $20,000 in collaboration funds.
   ACLS Digital Innovation Fellowships: The aim of this program is to provide scholars the means to pursue intellectually significant projects that deploy digital technologies intensively and innovatively. ACLS will award up to six Digital Innovation Fellowships in this competition year. Each fellowship carries a stipend of up to $60,000 towards an academic year's leave and provides for project costs of up to $25,000.
   ACLS Fellowship Program: This program is geared to all applicants with concentration in humanities and social sciences. The fellowships are intended as salary replacement to help scholars devote six to twelve continuous months to full-time research and writing which should ultimately result with a major piece of scholarly work. Additionally, the stipend is set at three levels based on academic rank, up to $35,000 for Assistant Professor and career equivalent, up to $45,000 for Associate Professor and career equivalent, and up to $65,000 for full Professor and career equivalent. ACLS will determine the level based on the candidate's rank or career status as of the application deadline date.
EIN: 131851145

5692
American Council of Learned Societies
(also known as ACLS)
633 3rd Ave., Ste. 8C
New York, NY 10017-6795 (212) 697-1505
FAX: (212) 949-8058; E-mail: grants@acls.org;
URL: http://www.acls.org

Foundation type: Public charity
Purpose: Fellowships and grants to American and international scholars for advanced research and study in the humanities and social sciences.
Publications: Application guidelines; Annual report; Occasional report.
Financial data: Year ended 06/30/2011. Assets, $140,761,136 (M); Expenditures, $23,867,809; Total giving, $15,986,940; Grants to individuals, 129 grants totaling $4,128,606.
Fields of interest: Architecture; Performing arts; Humanities; Language (foreign); Literature; Philosophy/ethics; Social sciences; Economics; Psychology/behavioral science; International studies.
International interests: Albania; Bulgaria; China; Czech Republic; Eastern Europe; Estonia; Hungary; Latvia; Lithuania; Poland; Romania; Slovakia; Yugoslavia.
Type of support: Fellowships; Research; Scholarships—to individuals; Foreign applicants; Postdoctoral support; Graduate support; Travel grants; Doctoral support; Stipends.
Application information: Applications accepted. Application form required.
   Initial approach: Letter, e-mail or fax
   Deadline(s): Varies
   Additional information: See web site for additional application guidelines.
Program descriptions:
   ACLS Collaborative Research Awards: Awards of up to $140,000 are available to support collaborative research in the humanities and related social sciences, by offering teams of two or more scholars the opportunity to collaborate intensively on a single, substantive project. The fellowships are for a total of up to 24 months. Up to $35,000 for assistant professor, up to $40,000 for associate professor, and up to $60,000 for full professor, as well as $20,000 in collaboration

funds (which may be used for such purposes as travel, materials, or research assistance).
   ACLS Digital Innovation Fellowships: This program supports digitally-based research projects in all disciplines of the humanities and humanities-related social sciences. It is hoped that projects of successful applicants will help advance digital humanistic scholarship by broadening understanding of its nature and exemplifying the robust infrastructure necessary for creating further such works. Fellowships are intended to support an academic year dedicated to work on a major scholarly project that takes a digital form. Eligible applicants must have a Ph.D. conferred prior to the application deadline, in any field of the humanities or the humanistic social sciences. Each fellowship carries a stipend of up to $60,000 towards an academic year's leave and provides for project costs of up to $25,000.
   ACLS Fellowships: Provides awards to individual scholars at the postdoctoral level to pursue research in the humanities and social sciences. The program offers up to $65,000 for full professor and career equivalent, $45,000 for associate professor and career equivalent, and $35,000 for assistant professor and career equivalent, for six to twelve months of research leave between July and February. Fellowships include residencies at the New York Public Library.
   ACLS Public Fellows: Recent Ph.Ds from the humanities and humanistic social sciences will be placed in two-year staff positions at partnering organizations in government and the non-profit sector. Stipends of $50,000 to $65,000 per year is provided, depending on position.
   African Humanities Program: This program provides grants to sustain individuals doing exemplary work, so as to ensure continued future leadership in the humanities, in sub-Saharan Africa. Awards are made for projects in various fields, including history, archaeology, literature, linguistics, film studies, art history and studies of the performing arts, ethnographic and cultural studies, gender studies, philosophy, and religious studies. Eligible applicants must be residents of a country in sub-Saharan Africa and have a current affiliation at an institution in Ghana, Nigeria, South Africa, Tanzania, or Uganda.
   American Research in the Humanities in China: Grants of up to $50,400 are available to scholars in the humanities and humanities-related social sciences who have received a Ph.D. or its equivalent by the time of application. Fellowships are from four months to one year of continuous research in China. Applicants must submit a carefully-formulated research proposal that reflects an understanding of the present Chinese academic and research environment. The proposal should include a persuasive statement of the need to conduct the research in China. Support is offered to specialists in all fields of the humanities and humanities-related social sciences, and is not limited to China scholars.
   Charles A. Ryskamp Research Fellowships: Provides $64,000, plus $2,500 for research and travel, to provide time and resources to enable advanced assistant professors in the humanities and related social sciences to conduct their research under optimal conditions.
   Comparative Perspectives on Chinese Culture and Society: This program awards funds in support of planning meetings, workshops, and/or conferences leading to publication of scholarly volumes. The program will support collaborative work of three types of grants, up to $25,000 will be offered to support formal research conferences intended to produce significant new research published in a conference volume, grants of $10,000 to $15,000

will be offered for support of workshops or seminars, designed to informally facilitate new research on newly available or inadequately researched problems, data, or texts, and grants of up to $6,000 will be offered for one-day meetings to plan conferences or workshops, or for less structured explorations, e.g., brainstorming sessions.

East European Studies Programs: This program provides funds to help develop expertise in the U.S. needed for broad knowledge and analysis of developments in Albania, Bosnia and Herzegovina, Bulgaria, Croatia, Czech Republic, Estonia, Hungary, Kosovo, Latvia, Lithuania, Macedonia, Montenegro, Poland, Romania, Serbia, Slovakia, and Slovenia. Components of the program include: Dissertation Fellowships in East European Studies (up to $18,000 to support field work, archival investigations, or dissertation writing); Early-Career Postdoctoral Fellowships in East European Studies (up to $25,000 to support postdoctoral research and writing in East European studies in all disciplines of the humanities and social sciences); Conference Grants (up to $25,000 to support formal research conferences that intend to produce significant new research on Eastern Europe publishable in a conference volume); Travel Grants (grants ranging from $1,000 to $2,000 to support travel for presentation of papers at scholarly conferences); Language Grants to Individuals for Summer Study (grants of up to $2,500 to support intensive summer study of Albanian, Bosnian-Croatian-Serbian, Bulgarian, Czech, Estonian, Hungarian, Latvian, Lithuanian, Macedonian, Polish, Romanian, Slovak, or Slovene); and Research on Heritage Speakers of Eastern European Languages (a grant of up to $20,000 to an individual or collaborative team for a research project on heritage speakers of an eastern European language in the U.S.)

Frederick Burkhardt Residential Fellowships for Recently Tenured Scholars: These fellowships are open to scholars engaged in long-term, unusually ambitious projects in the humanities and related social sciences. Appropriate fields of specialization include, but are not limited to, archaeology, anthropology, art history, economics, geography, history, language and literature, law, linguistics, musicology, philosophy, political science, psychology, religion, and sociology. Proposals in the social science fields listed above are eligible only if they employ predominantly humanistic approaches. Proposals in interdisciplinary and cross-disciplinary studies are welcome, as are proposals focused on any geographic region or any cultural or linguistic group. Each fellowship carries a stipend of $75,000.

Henry Luce Foundation/ACLS Dissertation Fellowship Program in American Art: Ten fellowships of $25,000 each are available for a one-year term for the current academic year to postgraduate students who are engaging in dissertation research in art history. The fellowships may be carried out in residence at the fellow's home institution, abroad, or at another appropriate site for research. They may not be used to defray tuition costs or be held concurrently with any other major fellowship or grant. An applicant must be a candidate for a Ph.D. to be granted by a department of art history in the U.S. The applicant's dissertation must be focused on a topic in the history or visual arts of the U.S., and applicants must have U.S. citizenship or permanent residency.

Mellon/ACLS Dissertation Completion Fellowships: This program provides stipends of $25,000, plus funds for research costs of up to $3,000 and for university fees of up to $5,000, to assist graduate students in the humanities and related social sciences in the last year of Ph.D.

dissertation writing. Eligible applicants must be Ph.D. candidates in a humanities or social science department in the U.S. (applicants from other departments may be eligible if their project is in the humanities or related social sciences, and their principal dissertation supervisor holds an appointment in a humanities field or related social science field), have all requirements for the Ph.D. except the dissertation completed before beginning fellowship tenure, and be no more than six years in the degree program.

Mellon/ACLS Recent Doctoral Recipients Fellowships: This program provides a $30,000 stipend to help assist young scholars in the humanities and related social sciences in the first or second year following completion of the Ph.D. Eligible applicants are limited to scholars who have been awarded Mellon/ACLS Dissertation Completion Fellowships in the prior year's competition, alternates selected in the prior year's Mellon/ACLS competition, and those awarded other dissertation fellowships of national stature that require applicants to complete their dissertations within a specific period.
EIN: 131851145

5693
American Federation for Aging Research, Inc.
(also known as AFAR)
55 W. 39th St., 16th Fl.
New York, NY 10018-0541 (212) 703-9977
Contact: Stephanie Lederman, Exec. Dir.; For Research: Odette van der Willik
E-mail address for individual grants contact: grants@afar.org
FAX: (212) 977-0330; E-mail: info@afar.org;
Toll-free tel.: (888) 582-2327; URL: http://www.afar.org

Foundation type: Public charity
Purpose: Fellowships, scholarships, and research grants for the study of aging.
Publications: Application guidelines; Annual report; Grants list; Informational brochure; Newsletter; Occasional report.
Financial data: Year ended 12/31/2012. Assets, $34,846,814 (M); Expenditures, $9,501,739; Total giving, $6,993,830; Grants to individuals, totaling $235,078.
Fields of interest: Geriatrics; Geriatrics research; Gerontology.
International interests: Ireland; Israel; United Kingdom.
Type of support: Fellowships; Research; Grants to individuals; Postdoctoral support; Doctoral support.
Application information: Applications accepted. Application form required. Application form available on the grantmaker's web site.
  Initial approach: Letter or e-mail
  Send request by: E-mail
  Copies of proposal: 1
  Deadline(s): Varies
  Applicants should submit the following:
    1) Proposal
    2) Letter(s) of recommendation
    3) GPA
    4) Essay
    5) Curriculum vitae
    6) Budget Information
Program descriptions:
AFAR/Pfizer Innovations in Aging Research Award: In conjunction with Pfizer, Inc., twelve $200,000 two-year awards will be given to promising junior faculty wanting to start highly-innovative projects focused on the basic

biology of aging and its relationship to human disease.

Ellison Medical Foundation/AFAR Postdoctoral Fellows in Aging Research Program: The program addresses the current concerns about an adequate funding base for postdoctoral fellows (both MDs and PhDs) who conduct research in the fundamental mechanisms of aging. Postdoctoral fellows at all levels of training are eligible for up to fifteen one-year fellowships, ranging from $46,346 (for first-year fellows) to $60,492 (for fellows with more than seven years of training), will be awarded. Up to $7,850 of the award may be requested for such expenses as research supplies, equipment, health insurance, and travel to scientific meetings.

Ellison Medical Foundation/AFAR Senior Postdoctoral Fellows Research Program: The program encourages and furthers the careers of postdoctoral fellows (both MDs and PhDs) in the fundamental mechanisms of aging. Postdoctoral fellows at all levels of training are eligible. Up to fifteen one-year fellowships ranging from $47,114 for first-year fellow to $55,670 for a fellow with five years of training. Of the award, up to $7,850 may be requested for expenses such as research supplies, equipment, health insurance and travel to scientific meetings.

Glenn/AFAR Breakthrough in Gerontology Awards: This initiative provides timely support to a small number of pilot research programs that may be of relatively high risk but which offer significant promise of yielding transforming discoveries in the fundamental biology of aging. Applicants must, at the time they submit their proposal, be full-time faculty members at the rank of assistant professor or higher. Projects that focus on genetic controls associated with aging and longevity, on delay of aging by pharmacological agents or dietary means, or which elucidate the mechanisms by which alterations in hormones, anti-oxidant defenses, or repair processes promote longevity are all within the intended scope of this competition. Projects that focus on specific diseases or assessment of healthcare strategies will receive lower priority, unless the research plan makes clear and direct connections to fundamental issues in the biology of aging. Studies of invertebrates, mice, human clinical materials, or cell lines are eligible. Two two-year awards will be made, at the level of $200,000 ($100,000 per year for two years), of which up to eight percent may be used for institutional overhead.

Julie Martin Mid-Career Awards in Aging Research: This program, administered in conjunction with The Ellison Medical Foundation, provides funding to outstanding mid-career scientists who propose new directions of high importance to biological gerontology. The proposed research must be conducted at any type of nonprofit setting in the U.S. The applicant must be an associate professor who was promoted to that position (with or without tenure) after Dec. 1, 2010. Applicants who are employees in the NIH Intramural program are not eligible to apply. Two four-year awards of $500,000 each will be made, at the level of $125,000 per year. In addition, up to 10 percent ($50,000) may be requested for administrative/indirect costs.

Medical Student Training in Aging Research (MSTAR) Program: This program provides medical students, early in their training, with an enriching experience in aging-related research and geriatrics, under the mentorship of top experts in the field, and introduces students to research and academic experiences that they might not otherwise have had during medical school. Students participate in an eight- to twelve-week structured research, clinical, and didactic program in geriatrics, appropriate to their level of training and interests, at one of seven national training centers across the country. Participants must be allopathic or osteopathic medical students in good standing, who will have successfully completed one year of medical school at a U.S. institution by June of the application year. The stipend level is approximately $1,748 per month. The actual amounts will vary based on the specific appointment period of individual students.

Research Grants: These grants are provided to junior faculty (M.D.s and Ph.D.s) to conduct research that will serve as the basis for longer term research efforts. Supported investigators study a broad range of biomedical and clinical topics including the causes of cellular senescence, the role of estrogen in the development of osteoporosis, the effects of nutrition and exercise on the aging process, and much more. The major goal of this program is to assist in the development of the careers of junior investigators committed to pursuing careers in the field of aging research. Approximately ten grants of up to $100,000 over one or two years will be awarded.
EIN: 133045282

5694
American Foundation for Aging Research
c/o Dr. Paul Agris
Life Sciences Research Bldg., Rm. 1076
Albany, NY 12222-0100 (518) 437-4448
Contact: Mary Beth Hollman, Prog. Asst.
E-mail: afar@agingresearchfoundation.org;
URL: http://www.americanagingresearch.org

Foundation type: Public charity
Purpose: Grants to undergraduate, graduate or pre-doctoral students conducting cellular, molecular or genetic research on aging or age related illnesses such as alzheimer's, diabetes and cancer.
Publications: Application guidelines; Annual report; Grants list; Informational brochure; Newsletter.
Financial data: Year ended 12/31/2011. Assets, $0 (M); Expenditures, $413.
Fields of interest: Alzheimer's disease; Biomedicine; Cancer research; Leukemia research; Diabetes research.
Type of support: Research.
Application information: Applications accepted. Application form required. Application form available on the grantmaker's web site.
> *Initial approach:* Letter or e-mail
> *Applicants should submit the following:*
>   1) Transcripts
>   2) Proposal
>   3) Letter(s) of recommendation
> *Additional information:* See web site for further application procedures.
Program description:
Awards: Funding of up to $2,000 is available to undergraduate, graduate, or pre-doctoral students enrolled in degree programs at colleges or universities in the U.S., and who are studying the effects of aging in one of the following subject areas: molecular and cellular biology; immunobiology; cancer research; neurobiology; biochemistry; molecular biophysics; genomics; and proteomics. Awards include up to $500 to undergraduates, $1,000 to graduates, and $500 for neurological cancer research and graduate research; applicants from North Carolina will be eligible for specific grant opportunities from GlaxoSmithKline.
EIN: 431217061

5695
American Foundation for Suicide Prevention
120 Wall St., 29nd Fl.
New York, NY 10005-3904 (212) 363-3500
Contact: Robert T. Gebbia, C.E.O.
Application e-mail: grants@afsp.org
FAX: (212) 363-6237; E-mail: info@afsp.org;
Toll-free tel.: (888) 333-2377; E-mail For Robert T. Gebbia:rgebbia@afsp.org; URL: http://www.afsp.org

Foundation type: Public charity
Purpose: Research grants for investigators to increase understanding of the causes of suicide and factors related to suicide risk, or to test treatments and other interventions designed to prevent suicide.
Publications: Application guidelines; Annual report; Newsletter.
Financial data: Year ended 06/30/2012. Assets, $5,876,043 (M); Expenditures, $9,222,406; Total giving, $1,212,099.
Fields of interest: Suicide; Psychology/behavioral science.
Type of support: Fellowships; Research; Postdoctoral support; Doctoral support.
Application information: Applications accepted. Application form required. Application form available on the grantmaker's web site.
> *Initial approach:* Telephone or e-mail
> *Send request by:* Online
> *Deadline(s):* Nov. 15
> *Additional information:* See web site for additional application guidelines.
Program descriptions:
Linked Standard Research Grants: Grants of up to $225 over two years are awarded to investigators at any level performing research involving three or more unique sites.
Pilot Grants: Grants of up to $30,000 over one or two years are awarded to investigators at any level, these grants provide seed funding for new projects that have the potential to lead to larger investigations and they typically entail feasibility studies rather than hypothesis-driven research.
Postdoctoral Research Fellowships: Fellowships for up to $104,000 over two years are awarded to investigators who have received a Ph.D., M.D., or other doctoral degree within the preceding six years and have not had more than three years of fellowship support. Fellows receive a stipend $46,000 per year with an institutional allowance of $6,000 per year.
EIN: 133393329

5696
American Foundation for the Blind
(also known as AFB)
2 Penn Plz., Ste. 1102
New York, NY 10121-1100 (212) 502-7600
Contact: Carl R. Augusto, Pres. and C.E.O.
FAX: (212) 502-7777; E-mail: afbinfo@afb.net;
Toll-free tel.: (800) 232-5463; URL: http://www.afb.org

Foundation type: Public charity
Purpose: Undergraduate and graduate scholarships to legally blind and visually impaired individuals.
Publications: Application guidelines; Annual report; Informational brochure; Newsletter.
Financial data: Year ended 06/30/2012. Assets, $40,745,456 (M); Expenditures, $11,209,478; Total giving, $68,500; Grants to individuals, totaling $19,000.

Fields of interest: Eye diseases; Disabilities, people with.
Type of support: Graduate support; Undergraduate support.
Application information: Applications accepted. Application form required. Application form available on the grantmaker's web site.
> *Deadline(s):* Apr. 30
> *Applicants should submit the following:*
>   1) SAR
>   2) Essay
>   3) Transcripts
>   4) Letter(s) of recommendation
> *Additional information:* Application must also include proof of acceptance into college or program and official evidence of legal blindness.
Program descriptions:
Delta Gamma Foundation Memorial Scholarship: Awards one $1,000 scholarship to an undergraduate or graduate student who is legally blind and of good character, has exhibited academic excellence, and is studying in the field of rehabilitation and/or education of persons who are visually impaired or blind. Applicant must be a U.S. citizen.
Ferdinand Torres AFB Scholarship: Provides one $1,500 scholarship to a full-time post-secondary student who is legally blind and who presents evidence of economic need. Applicant need not be a U.S. citizen but must reside in the U.S. Preference is given to applicants residing in the New York metropolitan area, and new immigrants to the U.S.
Gladys C. Anderson Memorial Scholarship: A $1,000 scholarship is available to a female undergraduate or graduate student studying classical or religious music.
Karen D. Carsel Memorial Scholarship: Provides one $500 grant to a full-time graduate student who is legally blind and who presents evidence of economic need. Applicant must be a U.S. citizen.
R.L. Gillette Scholarship: Two $1,000 scholarships are available to women enrolled in a full-time four-year undergraduate degree program in literature or music.
Rudolph Dillman Memorial Scholarship: Provides four grants of $2,500 each to undergraduate and graduate students who are legally blind and studying in the field of rehabilitation and/or education of persons who are visually impaired or blind. One of the four grants requires for the students to present evidence of economic need. Applicant must be a U.S. citizen.
EIN: 135562161

5697
The American Friends of Needy Israeli Sephardic Children
c/o Ventura Corp.
512 7th Ave.
New York, NY 10018-1761 (212) 391-0170

Foundation type: Public charity
Purpose: Grants to Sephardic Israeli children who come from economically disadvantaged families. Recipients must be residents of Israel, of Sephardic extraction, and come from a family that earns no more than $300 per week.
Financial data: Year ended 12/31/2011. Assets, $0 (M); Expenditures, $1,100.
Fields of interest: Economically disadvantaged.
Type of support: Foreign applicants; Grants for special needs.
Application information: Applications accepted.
> *Additional information:* Contact foundation for current application deadline/guidelines.
EIN: 133180929

5698
American Geriatrics Society, Inc.
40 Fulton St., 18th Fl.
New York, NY 10038-1850 (212) 308-1414
FAX: (212) 832-8646;
E-mail: info@americangeriatrics.org; URL: http://
www.americangeriatrics.org

Foundation type: Public charity
Purpose: Development awards by nomination only
to young faculty in certain specialties within
geriatrics.
Publications: Annual report; Financial statement;
Newsletter.
Financial data: Year ended 12/31/2011. Assets,
$5,852,537 (M); Expenditures, $7,144,527; Total
giving, $982,101; Grants to individuals, totaling
$153,520.
Fields of interest: Surgery; Anesthesiology
research; Geriatrics research; Medical research;
Orthopedics research.
Type of support: Program development;
Conferences/seminars; Publication; Research;
Awards/grants by nomination only; Awards/prizes.
Application information: Applications accepted.
Application form required. Application form
available on the grantmaker's web site.
 Initial approach: Letter, telephone, fax or e-mail
 Deadline(s): Dec. 9, Mar. 4 for Residents
 Program
Program descriptions:
 *Dennis W. Jahnigen Career Development Scholars
 Awards:* The program offers two-year career
 development awards to support junior faculty in the
 specialties of anesthesiology, emergency
 medicine, general surgery, gynecology,
 ophthalmology, orthopaedic surgery,
 otolaryngology, physical medicine and
 rehabilitation, thoracic surgery, and urology. The
 award is intended to allow individuals to initiate and
 ultimately sustain a career in research and
 education in the geriatrics aspects of his/her
 discipline. To be eligible, a candidate must be a
 physician who is a U.S. citizen or permanent
 resident, be certified or board eligible to practice in
 one of the program's targeted specialties, and have
 a primary academic appointment in a U.S.
 institution in one of the targeted specialty
 departments. Each grant will provide two-year
 support of $75,000 per year for salary and fringe
 benefits and/or the costs of doing research. Each
 scholar's institution must provide a minimum
 match of $25,000 per year.
 Edward Henderson Student Award: A $500 travel
 stipend to attend the AGS annual meeting is
 awarded to a student interested in pursuing a
 career in geriatrics who has demonstrated
 excellence in the field.
 Merck/AGS New Investigator Award: A $1,500
 award is available to junior investigators in
 medicine, nursing, social work, pharmacy,
 dentistry, psychology, physical or occupational
 therapy with a faculty appointment of no more than
 five years, or, if a visiting scholar, no more than five
 years since the completion of post-graduate
 training.
 Nascher/Manning Award: Travel expenses to
 attend the society's annual meeting to recognize an
 individual with distinguished, life-long achievement
 in clinical geriatrics, including medicine, psychiatry,
 and all other relevant disciplines.
 *Outstanding Scientific Achievement for Clinical
 Investigation Award:* The foundation provides travel
 expenses to attend the society's annual meeting to
 recognize outstanding achievement in clinical
 research addressing healthcare problems of older
 adults by an investigator who is actively involved in
 direct patient care. The award targets mid-career
 clinician-investigators actively involved in geriatric

patient care who have accomplished meritorious
clinical research and who have transitioned beyond
the career development stage of their research
career. Ideal candidates include individuals who
have achieved an associate professor rank, or who
has been awarded an RO1-type grant (or its
equivalent). Applicants should be residents of the
U.S. or Canada and have graduated from
professional/graduate school.
 Scientist-in-Training Research Award: A $500
travel stipend to attend the society's annual
meeting is awarded to a pre-doctoral candidate
from a range of disciplines, including psychology,
gerontology, epidemiology, etc. who submitted the
most outstanding abstract for the society's annual
meeting. Abstracts are chosen based on originality,
scientific merit, and relevance of the research.
EIN: 131950856

5699
American Indonesian Cultural and Educational Foundation, Inc.
c/o Carl Morelli
380 Lexington Ave., Ste. 4400
New York, NY 10168 (212) 972-1100

Foundation type: Independent foundation
Purpose: University scholarships to citizens of
Indonesia with genuine financial need and a
superior academic record for study in the U.S.
Preference is given to individuals at the graduate
level.
Publications: Annual report.
Financial data: Year ended 12/31/2012. Assets,
$1,347,760 (M); Expenditures, $102,850; Total
giving, $44,250; Grants to individuals, 24 grants
totaling $44,250 (high: $3,000, low: $250).
Fields of interest: International exchange,
students.
Type of support: Foreign applicants; Graduate
support.
Application information: Applications accepted.
Application form required.
 Initial approach: Letter
 Deadline(s): May 15 and Nov. 15
 Applicants should submit the following:
 1) Transcripts
 2) Letter(s) of recommendation
EIN: 237055841

5700
The American Jewish Committee
165 E. 56th St.
New York, NY 10022-2709 (212) 751-4000
Contact: David Harris, Exec. Dir.
Fellowship e-mail address: fellowship@ajc.org
FAX: (212) 891-1450; E-mail: pr@ajc.org;
URL: http://www.ajc.org

Foundation type: Public charity
Purpose: Fellowships to individuals for developing
their skills as future leaders in the areas of
international and domestic politics, diplomacy,
public relations, and management throughout the
world.
Publications: Application guidelines; Annual report;
Occasional report.
Financial data: Year ended 12/31/2011. Assets,
$125,816,370 (M); Expenditures, $42,203,285;
Total giving, $387,660; Grants to individuals,
totaling $1,000.
Fields of interest: Political science.
Type of support: Fellowships.
Application information: Applications accepted.
Application form available on the grantmaker's web
site.

 Initial approach: Application
 Send request by: Online
 Deadline(s): Feb. 15
 Final notification: Applicants notified Mid-Mar.
 Applicants should submit the following:
 1) Letter(s) of recommendation
 2) Transcripts
 3) Resume
 4) Essay
 Additional information: Application should also
 include a short (one or two page) writing
 sample or excerpt of a larger paper, preferably
 on a topic of political, social, ethical, or
 specifically Jewish interest.
Program description:
 AJC Goldman Fellowship Program: This program
is designed to develop future leaders in the areas
of international and domestic politics, diplomacy,
public relations, and management, and gives
participants the unique opportunity to work for a
period of nine weeks full-time (or longer part-time)
at offices throughout the world. Fellows work closely
with supervisors in a mentor relationship with
senior personnel to learn about strategy, advocacy,
and the development and implementation of
programming. Fellows may also spend part of their
time developing an independent project with the
offices to which they are assigned. Eligible
applicants include undergraduates in their junior or
senior years, and students in graduate and
professional schools. Fellows receive a $3,000
stipend for the program, plus major travel
expenses.
EIN: 135563393

5701
The American Jewish Joint Distribution Committee, Inc.
711 3rd Ave.
New York, NY 10017-4014 (212) 687-6200
E-mail: info@jdc.org; URL: http://www.jdc.org

Foundation type: Public charity
Purpose: Fellowships to individuals who wish to
participate in work-study programs throughout the
world.
Publications: Application guidelines.
Financial data: Year ended 12/31/2012. Assets,
$483,793,948 (M); Expenditures, $305,853,172;
Total giving, $253,790,469.
Fields of interest: International relief; Jewish
agencies & synagogues.
Type of support: Fellowships.
Application information: Applications accepted.
Application form available on the grantmaker's web
site.
 Initial approach: E-mail
 Deadline(s): Dec. 20 Letter of Intent for The Ralph
 I. Goldman Fellowship, varies for Roslyn Z.
 Wolf Cleveland-JDC Fellowship
 Additional information: See web site for
 additional guidelines.
Program descriptions:
 Roslyn Z. Wolf Cleveland-JDC Fellowship: In
partnership with the Jewish Federation of
Cleveland, this program provides an opportunity for
a select individual to spend one year abroad,
making a significant difference in the lives of
members of an overseas Jewish community. One
fellow will be chosen annually to help an isolated or
reemerging Jewish community develop programs to
educate youth, care for the elderly, and/or train
future leaders. Prospective fellows can be any age
but must be college graduates, and should possess
a strong Jewish background, teaching or group work
experience, exceptional leadership skills, and the

ability to quickly adapt to the unique culture of the local community.

The Ralph I. Goldman Fellowship: The program awards one person annually a one-of-a-kind, paid, professional developemnt opportunity to live and work in overseas locations where JDC is active and engage with the inner workings of the world's largest Jewish humanitarian aid organization. The Fellowship will have a transformational impact on international Jewish life and the Fellow's understanding of complex global Jewish issues.
EIN: 131656634

5702
American Liver Foundation
39 Broadway, Ste. 2700
New York, NY   10006-3054   (212) 668-1000
FAX: (212) 483-8179;
E-mail: info@liverfoundation.org; Toll-free tel.: (800) 465-4837; URL: http://www.liverfoundation.org

Foundation type: Public charity
Purpose: Scholarships and grants to young scientists to stimulate research into the cause, treatment, prevention and cure of liver disease.
Publications: Application guidelines; Annual report; Financial statement; Grants list.
Financial data: Year ended 09/30/2011. Assets, $5,096,471 (M); Expenditures, $8,216,744; Total giving, $956,250; Grants to individuals, 10 grants totaling $125,000. Subtotal for grants to individuals: 1 grant totaling $62,500.
Fields of interest: Liver research.
Type of support: Research; Awards/prizes.
Application information: Applications accepted. Application form required. Application form available on the grantmaker's web site.
  Send request by: On-line
  Deadline(s): Oct.
  Final notification: Recipients notified in Mar.
  Additional information: See web site for additional application information and eligibility determination.
Program descriptions:
  Liver Scholar Award: The foundation provides young scientists with support for their research to bridge the gap between completion of research training and attainment of status as an independent research scientist. The additional research experience provided by this award is intended to enable them to successfully compete for research awards from national sources, particularly National Institutes of Health. Eligible applicants must be sponsored by a public or private nonprofit institution accredited in the U.S., Canada, or Mexico engaged in health care and health-related issues; and must apply within the first three years of his/her first faculty appointment (including prior appointments in universities outside of North America) and commence the award within the first four years of faculty appointment. Funding is awarded over three years in the amount of $225,000.
  Postdoctoral Research Fellowship Awards: The program seeks to help in the professional development of individuals with research potential who require additional training and experience in preparation for a career of independent liver research. This award provide $12,500 for one year.
  PSC Seed Grant Award: This grant provides support for a faculty member at any level to initiate a project that address a novel and important research related to pancreatic stelate cells. Proposed investigations may involve basic, clinical, or translational research; awards support investigational work related, but not limited to, pathophysiological studies, clinical trials and

applications, or assessment of new diagnostic and/or therapeutic modalities. Funding is provided in the amount of $100,000 over two years; annual review will depend on scientific progress, verification of faculty status, and other received or pending research funding. Eligible applicants must be sponsored by a public or private nonprofit institution accredited in the U.S., Canada, or Mexico engaged in health care and health-related research, and must have a full-time faculty appointment at any level.
EIN: 362883000

5703
American Museum of Natural History
79th St. at Central Park W.
New York, NY   10024-5193   (212) 769-5100
Contact: Ellen V. Futter, Pres.
E-mail: grants@amnh.org; URL: http://www.amnh.org

Foundation type: Public charity
Purpose: Grants, fellowships, and internships to undergraduate students, graduate students, and doctorate practitioners for research and study in the areas of zoology, paleozoology, anthropology, astrophysics, and earth and planetary sciences.
Financial data: Year ended 06/30/2012. Assets, $1,132,976,753 (M); Expenditures, $188,087,953; Total giving, $2,829,528; Grants to individuals, totaling $1,085,825.
Fields of interest: Museums (natural history); History/archaeology; Research; Graduate/ professional education; International exchange, students; Science; Physical/earth sciences; Astronomy; Space/aviation; Physics; Geology; Biology/life sciences; Anatomy (human); Anatomy (animal); Science; Anthropology/sociology.
Type of support: Fellowships; Internship funds; Research; Grants to individuals; Graduate support.
Application information: Applications accepted. Application form required. Application form available on the grantmaker's web site.
  Initial approach: Letter, telephone, or e-mail
  Deadline(s): Vary
  Applicants should submit the following:
    1) Proposal
    2) Transcripts
    3) Resume
    4) GPA
    5) Letter(s) of recommendation
    6) Budget Information
    7) Essay
  Additional information: See web site for application procedures and deadlines.
Program descriptions:
  AMNH Comparative Biology Ph.D. Program: This accelerated program, designed for students to complete their degrees in four years, typically provides full financial support.
  Annette Kade Graduate Student Fellowship Program: This program will allow museum graduate students to spend 3 months during the year at a selected university in France or Germany and would also allow 2 French and German students to come to the U.S. for 3 months.
  Anthropology Internship Program: Internships for undergraduates and graduates to work on projects relating to the collections or to the ongoing research interests of curatorial staff in the museum or in the field. The Museum's collections and current research interests include North, South, and Mesoamerican archaeology and ethnology; Asian, African and Pacific ethnology; and Human Biology. In addition to Curatorial Research, internships can be considered in collections management, archives, and conservation. Internships are offered

for periods ranging from three months to one year depending on the project. Grants provide monthly stipends for periods of two months to one year.
  Fellowship in Evolutionary Primatology: Fellows conduct research on primates, or studies of living or fossil mammals linked to ecosystems that include primates, and contribute actively to the broader NYCEP community through participation in a NYCEP research internship, course, and seminar.
  Gerstner Scholars Program: Funded by the Gerstner Family Foundation, the program encourages and supports groundbreaking research in biology, with an emphasis on genomics, including such topics as microbes, mammals, invertebrates, marine life, and computational biology.
  Graduate Student Fellowship Program: These fellowships offer stipend and health benefits to Ph.D. candidates training in those scientific disciplines practiced at the museum. The student must gain admission to one of four universities participating in this Program, and apply to and be approved by the museum.
  Postdoctoral Research Fellowship Program: The program provides training to postdoctoral investigators and established scientists to carry out a specific project within a limited time period, usually over two years. Fellows are expected to be in residence at the Museum.
  Research Experiences for Undergraduates Program: This program offers summer internships to qualified undergraduate students. Students participate actively as researchers on projects with museum scientists in evolutionary biology or in physical sciences. Students must be U.S. citizens enrolled as an undergraduate in a university or college at the time of application.
  Research Fellowship in Museum Anthropology: The fellowship provides support to a postdoctoral researcher to carry out a specific project for a two-year period, which will involve teaching one graduate-level course per year at the Bard Graduate Center. Housing and a stipend are provided.
EIN: 136162659

5704
American Parkinson's Disease Association
135 Parkinson Ave.
Staten Island, NY   10305-1946
Contact: Leslie A. Chambers, Pres. and C.E.O.
FAX: (718) 981-4399;
E-mail: apda@apdaparkinson.org; Toll-free tel.: (800) 223-2732; URL: http://www.apdaparkinson.org

Foundation type: Public charity
Purpose: Research grants and fellowships to doctors, medical students, and new investigators for the study of Parkinson's disease.
Publications: Application guidelines; Annual report; Grants list; Informational brochure; Newsletter.
Financial data: Year ended 08/31/2011. Assets, $10,058,121 (M); Expenditures, $7,959,866; Total giving, $3,186,919.
Fields of interest: Nerve, muscle & bone research.
Type of support: Fellowships; Research.
Application information: Applications accepted. Application form required. Application form available on the grantmaker's web site.
  Initial approach: Telephone
  Send request by: E-mail
  Copies of proposal: 3
  Deadline(s): Dec. 31 for Medical Students Summer Fellowships; Mar. 1 for all other programs

Additional information: See web site for complete program information.
EIN: 131962771

5705
American Psychoanalytic Association
309 E 49th St.
New York, NY 10017-1601 (212) 752-0450
FAX: (212) 593-0571; E-mail: info@apsa.org;
URL: http://www.apsa.org/

Foundation type: Public charity
Purpose: Fellowships to early career psychiatrist, psychologist, social worker, and academic conducting research in the field of psychoanalysis.
Financial data: Year ended 08/31/2012. Assets, $5,269,046 (M); Expenditures, $2,782,745; Total giving, $104,765; Grants to individuals, 19 grants totaling $15,065.
Fields of interest: Social sciences; Psychology/behavioral science.
Type of support: Fellowships.
Application information: Applications accepted. Application form required. Application form available on the grantmaker's web site.
  Send request by: Mail
  Deadline(s): Feb. 10
  Applicants should submit the following:
    1) Letter(s) of recommendation
    2) Curriculum vitae
  Additional information: Application should also include a personal statement. See web site for specific eligibility requirements.

Program description:
  Fellowship Program: The program encourages interest and involvement in psychoanalysis among the future leaders, researchers and educators of mental health and academia. Early-career psychiatrists, psychologists, social workers and academics are eligible to apply for the Fellowship. All qualified applicants receive a psychoanalyst mentor with whom they meet to discuss their interest in psychoanalytic ideas and how they may apply to their work. Additionally, fellows are offered the opportunity to present their work at biannual meetings.
EIN: 131685533

5706
American Skin Association, Inc.
6 E. 43rd St., 28th Fl.
New York, NY 10017-4605 (212) 889-4858
Contact: Kathleen Reichert, Exec. V.P.
FAX: (212) 889-4959;
E-mail: info@americanskin.org; Toll-free tel.: (800) 499-7546; URL: http://www.americanskin.org

Foundation type: Public charity
Purpose: Grants to researchers in the field of skin disease at major institutions in the country.
Publications: Application guidelines; Financial statement; Grants list; Newsletter.
Financial data: Year ended 12/31/2011. Assets, $1,678,320 (M); Expenditures, $1,217,650; Total giving, $369,250; Grants to individuals, totaling $369,250.
Fields of interest: Skin disorders research.
Type of support: Research; Awards/prizes.
Application information: Application form required. Application form available on the grantmaker's web site.
  Deadline(s): Sept. 15 for Medical Student Grants, Quality of Life/Health Services/Outcome Study Grants, Research Grants, and Research Scholar Awards; Dec. 6 for all others

  Applicants should submit the following:
    1) Letter(s) of recommendation
    2) Resume
Program descriptions:
  David Martin Carter Mentor Award: This award honors a member of the dermatology community who embodies the following criteria: superior achievement in clinical and/or basic dermatological research; long-term involvement as a visionary developer of clinical and/or basic science research fellows; a pattern of long-term career advice and support for colleagues, including former research fellows; and personal characteristics meriting the trust, respect, and emulation of colleagues. Awards include an honorarium, to be presented at the annual meeting of the Society for Investigative Dermatology.
  Medical Student Grants Targeting Melanoma and Skin Cancer: Up to five grants of $7,000 each will be available to medical students working actively in the areas of melanoma and skin cancer. Eligible applicants must be working actively in areas related to dermatology. Funds may be used to support a new or ongoing research/clinical investigation project. A second year of funding may be requests upon receipt and review of a final progress report and re-application.
  Public Policy and Medical Education Award: Awards are available that recognize those outstanding medical specialists whose contributions to public policy or medical education have significantly advanced the specialty of dermatology.
  Quality of Life/Health Services/Outcome Study Grants: One to two grants of $15,000 each will be given to outstanding projects that target quality of life, health services, or outcome studies. Eligible applicants must be working actively in areas related to dermatology; funds may be used for support of a new or ongoing research/clinical investigation project, with preference given to applicants without prior knowledge who in their formative stage of their career, or who are undergoing a mid-career research change.
  Research Achievement Awards: These awards recognize meritorious contribution to cutaneous biology and medicine, and honor established physician-scientists in the U.S. and around the world whose innovative work is making an impact on the lives of those who suffer from psoriasis, autoimmune/inflammatory skin disorders, skin cancer/melanoma, vitiligo, and pigment cell disorders.
  Research Grants: Grants of $15,000 each will be available to support disease-specific research targeting the following disorders: childhood skin diseases/disfigurement; psoriasis/inflammatory skin diseases; skin cancer; melanoma; and vitiligo/pigment cell disorders. Eligible applicants must be working actively in areas related to dermatology; funds may be used for support of a new or ongoing research/clinical investigation project, with preference given to applicants without prior funding who are in the formative stages of their career, or who are undergoing a mid-career research change.
  Research Scholar Awards: An award of $60,000 is available to foster the career development of a young research investigator working at the level of instructor through associate professor, in the field of dermatology and cutaneous biology. Eligible applicants must have a strong career goal within the field of dermatology, and be dedicated to the furtherance of knowledge concerning skin disorders; research must be focused on new discoveries in the basic and clinical sciences, which should have current or potential impact on the understanding and treatment of a skin disease. Preference will be given to applicants under 45

years of age, with a rank of instructor or institutional equivalent up through associate professor; first preference will be given to those working in a department or division of dermatology, while second preference will be given to those who show evidence of a close working relationship with dermatology.
EIN: 133401320

5707
American Society of Journalists and Authors Charitable Trust
(formerly The Llewellyn Miller Fund of the American Society of Journalists and Authors Charitable Trust, also known as Writers Emergency Assistance Fund)
1501 Broadway
New York, NY 10036-5505 (212) 997-0947

Foundation type: Independent foundation
Purpose: Relief assistance to financially needy, established established freelance writers who, because of advanced age, illness, disability, a natural disaster, or an extraordinary professional crisis, are unable to work.
Financial data: Year ended 06/30/2013. Assets, $257,966 (M); Expenditures, $259,802; Total giving, $6,460; Grants to individuals, 3 grants totaling $6,460.
Fields of interest: Print publishing; Literature; Aging; Disabilities, people with.
Type of support: Grants for special needs.
Application information: Applications accepted. Application form required. Application form available on the grantmaker's web site.
  Applicants should submit the following:
    1) Curriculum vitae
    2) Financial information
    3) Work samples
  Additional information: Application must also include explanation or proof of hardship.
Program description:
  Writers Emergency Assistance Fund: This fund of the American Society of Journalists and Authors was established to help needy writers who have demonstrated their professionalism over a sustained period of years, but who have no pension from a former employer on which to rely. It also helps younger writers of demonstrated professionalism who have become disabled and thus unable to earn a living, or who are caught up in an extraordinary professional crisis such as a lawsuit. This fund is for professional writers only.
EIN: 136625578

5708
American Theatre Wing, Inc.
570 7th Ave., Ste. 501
New York, NY 10018-1639 (212) 765-0606
Contact: Heather A. Hitchens, Exec. Dir.
FAX: (212) 307-1910;
E-mail: mailbox@americantheatrewing.org;
URL: http://americantheatrewing.org/grants/

Foundation type: Public charity
Purpose: Grants to outstanding young professional composers/lyricists/librettists.
Publications: Application guidelines; Grants list.
Financial data: Year ended 09/30/2012. Assets, $7,532,579 (M); Expenditures, $1,457,607; Total giving, $112,500; Grants to individuals, totaling $12,500.
Fields of interest: Theater (musical).
Type of support: Grants to individuals.
Application information: Applications accepted. Application form required. Application form available on the grantmaker's web site.

Initial approach: Application
Send request by: Mail or hand deliver
Copies of proposal: 3
Deadline(s): Sept. 9 for Jonathan Larson Grants
Applicants should submit the following:
   1) Work samples
   2) Curriculum vitae
   3) Letter(s) of recommendation
Additional information: See web site for detailed
   application guidelines.

Program description:
Jonathan Larson Grants: These grants are intended to honor and recognize emerging musical theater artists, including composers, lyricists, and librettists who work in musical theatre. Grant awards are based on merit, and are intended for those artists with a demonstrated commitment and dedication to a career in musical theatre. Applicants must include samples of work from at least one complete work of musical theatre (including book, music, and lyrics). Individuals may apply, but must demonstrate work done as a composer/lyricist/librettist; collaborative teams may apply together, but the work represented must include contributions of a composer, lyricist, and librettist.
EIN: 131893906

5709
The American Turkish Society, Inc.
3 Dag Hammarskjold Plz.
New York, NY 10017-2322 (212) 583-7614
Contact: Selen Ucak, Exec. Dir.
Additional contact: Dee Kayalar Polat, Dir. Prog.,
e-mail: d.kayalar@americanturkishsociety.org
FAX: (212) 583-7615;
E-mail: info@americanturkishsociety.org;
URL: http://www.americanturkishsociety.org

Foundation type: Public charity
Purpose: Grants to elementary and secondary school teachers in the U.S. to develop projects and classroom activities about Turkey.
Publications: Application guidelines; Annual report.
Financial data: Year ended 12/31/2011. Assets, $5,156,019 (M); Expenditures, $391,383; Total giving, $54,796; Grants to individuals, totaling $17,028.
Fields of interest: Education.
Type of support: Grants to individuals.
Application information:
   Initial approach: Proposal
   Deadline(s): Nov. 27
   Final notification: Applicants notified Dec. 13
   Applicants should submit the following:
      1) Proposal
      2) Curriculum vitae
      3) Budget Information
   Additional information: Application should also
      include a letter of support from the teacher's
      school. See web site for additional guidelines.
Program description:
Curriculum Development Grants: This program offers funds of up to $2,500 to elementary and second school teachers to develop innovative curricula, projects, and other classroom activities about Turkey. Grants are intended to cover the costs of research, materials, speakers, and other expenses incurred by the school or the teacher.
EIN: 131978281

5710
American-Italian Cancer Foundation
112 E. 71st St., Ste. 2B
New York, NY 10021-5034 (212) 628-9090
FAX: (212) 517-6089;
E-mail: info@americanitaliancancer.org;
URL: http://www.americanitaliancancer.org

Foundation type: Public charity
Purpose: Grants and fellowships to physicians and researchers in the fight against cancer through research, training, and education in the U.S. and Italy.
Publications: Application guidelines; Annual report; Financial statement; Informational brochure; Newsletter.
Financial data: Year ended 06/30/2011. Assets, $3,758,650 (M); Expenditures, $1,873,012; Total giving, $920,000; Grants to individuals, totaling $100,000.
Fields of interest: Cancer research.
Type of support: Conferences/seminars; Fellowships; Research; Awards/prizes.
Application information: Applications accepted. Application form required. Application form available on the grantmaker's web site.
   Initial approach: Telephone or e-mail
   Send request by: Mail
   Deadline(s): Mar. 31
   Final notification: Applicants notified by July 1
   Applicants should submit the following:
      1) Proposal
      2) Curriculum vitae
      3) Letter(s) of recommendation
EIN: 133035711

5711
The American-Scandinavian Foundation
58 Park Ave., 38th St.
New York, NY 10016-3007 (212) 779-3587
Contact: Edward P. Gallagher, Pres. and C.E.O.
E-mail: info@amscan.org; URL: http://www.amscan.org

Foundation type: Public charity
Purpose: Fellowships and grants to U.S. citizens or permanent residents for study in Scandinavian countries. Fellowships also for U.S. citizens or permanent residents to study the arts in Scandinavia.
Publications: Application guidelines; Annual report; Newsletter.
Financial data: Year ended 06/30/2012. Assets, $46,548,242 (M); Expenditures, $5,413,666; Total giving, $751,163; Grants to individuals, totaling $726,413.
Fields of interest: Arts.
Type of support: Fellowships; Research; Foreign applicants; Awards/prizes; Postdoctoral support; Graduate support; Postgraduate support; Travel grants; Doctoral support; Project support.
Application information: Applications accepted. Application form required. Application form available on the grantmaker's web site.
   Send request by: Mail
   Deadline(s): Vary
   Applicants should submit the following:
      1) Transcripts
      2) Proposal
      3) Letter(s) of recommendation
      4) Curriculum vitae
      5) Budget Information
   Additional information: Include fifteen copies of application and of project statement. See web site for additional application information.

Program descriptions:
Awards for Study in Scandinavia: Fellowships of up to $23,000 and grants of up to $5,000 are available to individuals to pursue research or study in one or more Scandinavian countries for up to one year, in any academic discipline. Grants will be awarded primarily to post-graduate scholars, professionals, and candidates in the arts to carry out research or study visits of one to three months' duration; fellowships are intended to support a year-long stay, with priority being given to candidates at the graduate level for dissertation study or research. Applicants must have a well-defined research or study project that makes a stay in Scandinavia essential, be U.S. citizens or permanent residents, and have completed their undergraduate education by the start of their project in Scandinavia. Proficiency in one or more Scandinavian languages is required.
Birgit Nilsson Opera Competition: The prize is awarded periodically to an outstanding young American singer on the verge of an international career.
Fellowships and Grants for Advanced Study or Research in America: The foundation offers over $500,000 in funding to Scandinavians to undertake study or research programs, usually at the graduate level, in the United States for up to one year. Applicants must be citizens of Denmark, Finland, Iceland, Norway or Sweden.
Translation Prize: This $2,000 prize encourages the English translation of Scandinavian literature of the last two centuries.
Visiting Lectureships: Funding of $25,000 ($20,000 teaching/research stipend and $5,000 travel stipend) is available to U.S. colleges and universities to host a visiting lecturer from Norway or Sweden. Awards are for appointments of one semester, and should be in the area of contemporary studies with an emphasis on one of five areas: public policy, conflict resolution, environmental studies, multiculturalism, and healthcare. Lecturers must be Norwegian or Swedish citizens and scholars/experts in a field appropriate to the host department or program.
EIN: 131623897

5712
America's Future Through Academic Progress, Inc.
P.O. Box 312
South Salem, NY 10590

Foundation type: Operating foundation
Purpose: Academic assistance to individuals primarily in the NY area, in pursuit of a higher education.
Financial data: Year ended 12/31/2011. Assets, $144,311 (M); Expenditures, $155,501; Total giving, $90,500; Grants to individuals, 3 grants totaling $30,000 (high: $10,000, low: $10,000).
Fields of interest: Higher education.
Type of support: Scholarships—to individuals.
Application information: Applications accepted.
   Additional information: Contact the organization
      for additional guidelines.
EIN: 133562338

5713
Carolann K. Andrews Charitable Foundation
25 Woodcrest Dr.
Batavia, NY 14020-2721 (585) 343-2480
Application addresses: Batavia High School
Guidance Office, 39 Washington Ave., Batavia, NY

14020, tel.: (585) 343-2480; Notre Dame High School Guidance Office, 73 Union St., Batavia, NY 14020, tel.: (585) 343-2783

Foundation type: Operating foundation
Purpose: Scholarships to graduating seniors of Batavia High School or Notre Dame High School of Batavia, NY, pursuing a career in elementary education.
Financial data: Year ended 12/31/2011. Assets, $210,974 (M); Expenditures, $8,111; Total giving, $4,500; Grants to individuals, 5 grants totaling $3,500 (high: $1,000, low: $500).
Fields of interest: Higher education; Teacher school/education.
Type of support: Scholarships—to individuals; Support to graduates or students of specific schools.
Application information: Applications accepted. Application form required.
  Deadline(s): May 25
  Applicants should submit the following:
    1) Transcripts
    2) Essay
  Additional information: Application should also include community and school activities. Students should contact their guidance counselor for additional guidelines.
EIN: 161552802

5714
Angle Educational Trust

(formerly Faerie L. Angle Educational Trust)
1 M&T Plz., 8th Fl.
Buffalo, NY 14203

Foundation type: Independent foundation
Purpose: Scholarships only to law students who are residents of Franklin County, PA.
Financial data: Year ended 12/31/2012. Assets, $556,067 (M); Expenditures, $11,263; Total giving, $4,600; Grants to individuals, 2 grants totaling $4,600 (high: $2,600, low: $2,000).
Fields of interest: Law school/education.
Type of support: Graduate support.
Application information: Applications accepted. Application form required.
  Deadline(s): May 1
  Additional information: Request application form from the trust.
EIN: 256365680

5715
Animal Welfare Trust

141 Halstead Ave., Ste. 301
Mamaroneck, NY 10543-2652 (914) 381-6177
Contact: Brad Goldberg, Pres.
E-mail for internships: ali@animalwelfaretrust.org
FAX: (914) 381-6176;
E-mail: email@animalwelfaretrust.org; Mailing and application address: P.O. Box 737, Mamaroneck, NY 10543; URL: http://fdnweb.org/awt/

Foundation type: Operating foundation
Purpose: Grants to students to fund independent animal-related research projects, and grants to fund otherwise unpaid internship positions within established animal-related organizations.
Publications: Application guidelines; Grants list.
Financial data: Year ended 12/31/2012. Assets, $4,225,279 (M); Expenditures, $481,551; Total giving, $293,150; Grants to individuals, 4 grants totaling $25,000 (high: $10,000, low: $5,000).
Fields of interest: Animal welfare.
Type of support: Internship funds.
Application information: Applications accepted.

Initial approach: E-mail
Deadline(s): Apr. 30
Applicants should submit the following:
  1) Essay
  2) Transcripts
  3) Resume
  4) Letter(s) of recommendation
Additional information: Application by letter. See web site for further program guidelines.
Program description:
  Student Internship Grant Program: The foundation seeks to make a meaningful contribution to animal welfare by encouraging students to work on projects that facilitate positive reform for animals. This Program was created to fund independent student research projects or provide funding to otherwise unpaid internship positions within established animal-related organizations. The foundation's primary areas of focus are factory farming and farm animal welfare issues, pro-vegetarian campaigns and humane education. See Trust web site for complete information.
EIN: 134131408

5716
Aperture Foundation

547 W. 27th St., 4th Fl.
New York, NY 10001-5511 (212) 505-5555
FAX: (212) 598-4015; E-mail: info@aperture.org;
URL: http://www.aperture.org

Foundation type: Public charity
Purpose: Awards to photographers whose work has been created within the past five years and hasn't been widely seen in major publications or exhibition venues.
Publications: Newsletter.
Financial data: Year ended 12/31/2011. Assets, $8,373,001 (M); Expenditures, $5,087,911.
Fields of interest: Photography.
Type of support: Awards/prizes.
Application information: Applications accepted.
  Deadline(s): July
  Final notification: Recipients notified by Dec. 1
  Applicants should submit the following:
    1) Curriculum vitae
    2) Resume
    3) Work samples
  Additional information: Application must also include a statement of up to 250 words about your work, 15 images with title/caption information, and a $25 entry fee payable during online entry process. Entrants must be current, paid subscribers of Aperture magazine.
Program description:
  Aperture Portfolio Prize: A first prize of $3,000 is awarded to the winner of the foundation's international photography competition. The first-prize winner and three runners-up will be featured on Aperture's web site (for approximately a year). Winners also will be announced in Aperture's e-newsletter. Entrants must be current, paid subscribers of Aperture magazine.
EIN: 133120824

5717
Armenian General Benevolent Union

55 E. 59th St.
New York, NY 10022-1112 (212) 319-6383
FAX: (212) 319-6507; E-mail: agbuwb@agbu.org;
URL: http://www.agbu.org

Foundation type: Public charity

Purpose: Scholarships to gifted young Armenian full time students of Armenian descent enrolled in competitive academic institutions around the world.
Publications: Biennial report; Newsletter.
Financial data: Year ended 12/31/2011. Assets, $211,648,007 (M); Expenditures, $22,943,264; Total giving, $13,969,158; Grants to individuals, totaling $137,823.
Fields of interest: Performing arts; Higher education; Theological school/education.
Type of support: Fellowships; Scholarships—to individuals; Graduate support; Undergraduate support; Postgraduate support.
Application information: Applications accepted. Application form required.
  Deadline(s): Apr. 1 and May 15
  Additional information: See web site for more information on eligibility.
Program descriptions:
  AGBU Fellowships: Grants awarded annually to graduate and postgraduate students of Armenian descent who are residents/citizens of the Unites States or Armenia, enrolled in highly competitive colleges/universities in the U.S.
  AGBU Heritage Scholar Grants: One-time grant awarded to one college-bound high school senior graduating from each of the three AGBU high schools in the United States.
  AGBU International Scholarships: Grants awarded annually to full time undergraduate students and some graduate students of Armenian descent (excluding citizens of Armenia studying in Armenia), enrolled in recognized colleges in their countries of residence.
  AGBU Performing Arts Fellowships: Grants to full time undergraduate and graduate students of Armenian descent worldwide (excluding citizens of Armenia studying in Armenia) who are pursuing studies in the field of performing arts, enrolled in recognized colleges and universities worldwide.
  AGBU Religious Studies Fellowships: Grants awarded annually to full time graduate students of Armenian descent worldwide (excluding citizens of Armenia studying in Armenia) who are pursuing religious studies (e.g., priesthood, church youth directors)
  Scholarship Program: The program offers financial assistance to full-time students of Armenian descent from 25 countries and five continents, enrolled in competitive academic institutions.
EIN: 135600421

5718
The Art Bridge Association, Inc.

670 White Plains Rd., No. 224
Scarsdale, NY 10583
E-mail: artbridgea@aol.com; URL: http://www.artbridgeassociation.org

Foundation type: Operating foundation
Purpose: Grants, services and information to artists creating within the independent film and theatre communities.
Financial data: Year ended 12/31/2010. Assets, $0 (M); Expenditures, $14,505; Total giving, $0.
Fields of interest: Film/video; Theater; Theater (musical); Music; Arts, artist's services.
Type of support: Project support; Fiscal agent/sponsor.
Application information: Applications accepted.
  Initial approach: Letter or telephone
  Copies of proposal: 1
  Deadline(s): Jan. 15th for Musical Composition and May 15 for Theater proposals and Short films

Additional information: Contact the association for grant guideline procedures. There is a $15 fee for grant submissions. Grants are given every other year in the areas of film, music, and theater.

Program description:

Fiscal Sponsorship: Through this program, artists from any state can secure donations and grants under the association's non-profit umbrella. This allows tax deductibility for the contribution and tax exempt status for the artist.

EIN: 133929084

5719
Art in General, Inc.
79 Walker St.
New York, NY 10013-3523 (212) 219-0473
Contact: Anne J. Barlow, Exec. Dir.
FAX: (212) 219-0511;
E-mail: info@artingeneral.org; URL: http://www.artingeneral.org

Foundation type: Public charity
Purpose: Residencies for artists to emphasize the growth and development of contemporary art through the presentation of their work.
Financial data: Year ended 07/31/2011. Assets, $689,918 (M); Expenditures, $773,611.
Fields of interest: Visual arts.
Type of support: Residencies.
Application information: Applications accepted. Application form required.
Initial approach: Letter
Applicants should submit the following:
  1) Curriculum vitae
  2) Resume
Additional information: Application should include ten slides, artist statement, and project outline.

Program descriptions:

Artist Residency Program: The program provides artists with the opportunity to create work in a new context and to meet and interact with art communities and audiences in New York City and abroad. The program offers artists in residence an honorarium and accommodations for a six- to nine-week residency period, and materials to create new work.

New Commissions Program: Through this program the organization commissions 6-8 artists each year to create a challenging new work that would otherwise not be realized. Selected artists create new projects in any medium or form - from painting to sculpture to performance to video to other, perhaps undefined, types of art or interdisciplinary work. The organization works closely with the artists to help them develop their work from idea to final form and releases a publication highlighting the project with critical texts and documentation.

EIN: 133472869

5720
Art Matters, Inc.
P.O. Box 311
Prince St. Sta.
New York, NY 10012-0006
Contact: Sacha Yanow, Prog. Dir.
E-mail: info@artmattersfoundation.org; URL: http://www.artmattersfoundation.org/

Foundation type: Independent foundation
Purpose: Grants and fellowships to artists who make work intending to break ground aesthetically and socially.

Financial data: Year ended 12/31/2012. Assets, $73,996 (M); Expenditures, $289,578; Total giving, $176,400; Grants to individuals, 38 grants totaling $158,400 (high: $8,000, low: $300).
Fields of interest: Visual arts; Performing arts.
Type of support: Fellowships; Grants to individuals.
Application information: Applications not accepted.
Additional information: Applications by invitation only. Unsolicited requests for funds not considered or acknowledged.

Program description:

Grant Program: Grants of $3,000 to $10,000 to U.S. artists for projects that are socially engaged with a focus on local, national and/or global concerns. Art Matters funds individuals, collectives and collaborative teams working all visual media including experimental performance, and film.
EIN: 133271577

5721
Art Omi International Arts Center
(formerly Art/Omi, Inc.)
55 15th Ave., 15th Fl.
New York, NY 10003-4398 (212) 206-6170
Contact: Ruth Adams, Admin. Dir.
FAX: (212) 206-6023; E-mail: info@artomi.org;
E-Mail for Ruth Adams: director@artomi.org;
URL: http://www.artomi.org

Foundation type: Public charity
Purpose: Fellowships and residencies to visual artists, writers and musicians.
Publications: Application guidelines; Informational brochure; Newsletter.
Financial data: Year ended 12/31/2011. Assets, $29,106,878 (M); Expenditures, $1,157,132.
Fields of interest: Visual arts; Music; Literature.
International interests: Global Programs.
Type of support: Fellowships; Residencies.
Application information: Applications accepted. Application form required.
Deadline(s): Feb. 1 for visual artists, Nov. 30 for writers, May 1 for musicians
Additional information: See web site for complete application guidelines.

Program descriptions:

Art OMI International Artists Residency: Each year thirty visual artists from around the world are selected to create new work, develop discourse and collaborations with their peers, exhibit their work to the public, and advance their careers in New York City and internationally. Artists are given room, board, and studio space free of charge for a three-week period each July. Participants are responsible for transportation and material costs, and are asked to donate a work of art created during the residency to the Art Omi Foundation Collection.

Ledig House International Writer's Residency: Writers and translators from all fields are encouraged to apply for a residency lasting anywhere from one week to two months. Up to twenty writers per session (ten at a given time) are awarded fellowships, the cost of which depends on the length of the stay. All meals are provided.

Music/OMI International Residency Program: The program invites applicants from all musical disciplines who wish to broaden their artistic horizons and engage actively with other musicians for two and a half weeks. Full room and board is provided. Applicants are required to participate in a public concert at the conclusion of the program.
EIN: 133641616

5722
Art Students League of New York
215 W. 57th St.
New York, NY 10019-2104 (212) 247-4510
Contact: Ira Goldberg, Exec. Dir.
FAX: (212) 541-7024;
E-mail: info@artstudentsleague.org; URL: http://www.theartstudentsleague.org

Foundation type: Public charity
Purpose: Scholarships to students attending classes at the Art Students League of New York with financial need.
Publications: Informational brochure; Newsletter.
Financial data: Year ended 05/31/2012. Assets, $52,623,856 (M); Expenditures, $7,923,376; Total giving, $104,874; Grants to individuals, totaling $104,874.
Fields of interest: Arts.
Type of support: Scholarships—to individuals.
Application information: Contact foundation for complete application guidelines.
EIN: 131844837

5723
The ArtCouncil, Inc.
111 Front St., Ste. 210
Brooklyn, NY 11201-1007 (212) 727-2233
Contact: Carolyn Ramo, Exec. Dir.
FAX: (212) 352-9979; E-mail: info@artadia.org;
E-mail for Carolyn Ramo: carolyn@artadia.org;
URL: http://www.artadia.org

Foundation type: Public charity
Purpose: Grants to visual artists who demonstrate exceptional promise from the San Francisco Bay Area, CA, Los Angeles, CA, Chicago, IL, Houston, TX, Atlanta, GA, Boston, MA.
Publications: Application guidelines.
Financial data: Year ended 09/30/2012. Assets, $143,150 (M); Expenditures, $407,523.
Fields of interest: Visual arts.
Type of support: Grants to individuals; Awards/prizes; Residencies.
Application information: Applications accepted. Application form required. Application form available on the grantmaker's web site.
Send request by: On-line
Deadline(s): Mar. 23
Final notification: Applicants notified late Apr.
Applicants should submit the following:
  1) Work samples
  2) Resume
  3) Curriculum vitae
Additional information: Application should also include artist's statement and eight images of artwork and/or details, or video/media/sound. See web site for additional guidelines.

Program description:

Artadia Award: The award provides financial support, critical validation, and broader public exposure for artists across the country. Awards ranging from $3,000 to $15,000 are unrestricted, and can be used however the artist sees fit. Cash awards are granted in the participating cities of the San Francisco Bay area, Los Angeles, Chicago, greater Atlanta, Houston, and Boston on a rotating basis.
EIN: 911877238

5724

Artis Contemporary Israeli Art Fund, Inc.

(also known as Artis)
401 Broadway Ste. 803
New York, NY 10013-3027 (212) 285-0960
Contact: Tali Cherizli, Prog. Mgr.
E-mail: info@artiscontemporary.org; URL: http://
www.artiscontemporary.org/

Foundation type: Public charity
Purpose: Grants for artists from Israel seeking
cultural exchange and dialogue with the
international art world.
Financial data: Year ended 12/31/2011. Assets,
$609,445 (M); Expenditures, $675,910; Total
giving, $230,154; Grants to individuals, 8 grants
totaling $26,500.
Fields of interest: Arts, artist's services; Arts.
Type of support: Grants to individuals.
Application information: Applications accepted.
Application form required.
   Send request by: E-mail
   Deadline(s): Oct. 9 for Artist Grant Program
   Applicants should submit the following:
      1) Resume
      2) Curriculum vitae
      3) Budget Information
   Additional information: See web site for
      additional information.
Program descriptions:
   Artist Research Trips to Israel: The organization
   hosts international museum directors, curators,
   writers and art professionals for weeklong cultural
   research trips to Israel.
   Exhibition Grant Program: This program funds
   opportunities for promising and established artists
   to further to further cultural exchange and access
   to contemporary art from Israel by supporting
   projects outside it. Grants are awarded on a project
   basis to organizations and individual artists. The
   organization prioritizes high impact, high visibility
   solo or group projects that reach broad audiences
   outside of Israel.
   Israeli Artists Fund at Columbia University: The
   organization provides annual scholarships in
   support of MFA students accepted and/or enrolled
   in the Visual Arts Program at Columbia University.
   Beyond the traditional scholarship funding model
   support includes curatorial and gallery
   introductions, press and promotional opportunities,
   as well as artist lectures and community building
   events.
EIN: 264184988

5725

Artists Fellowship Inc.

c/o Salmagundi Club
47 5th Ave.
New York, NY 10003-4303 (212) 255-7740,
ext. 216
E-mail: info@Artistsfellowship.org; URL: http://
artistsfellowship.org

Foundation type: Independent foundation
Purpose: Emergency aid to American professional
visual artists and their families for relief of financial
distress due to disability, age, or bereavement.
Preference is shown to those living in the U.S.
Financial data: Year ended 10/31/2013. Assets,
$4,883,603 (M); Expenditures, $300,738; Total
giving, $234,303; Grants to individuals, 66 grants
totaling $234,303 (high: $23,500, low: $500).
Fields of interest: Visual arts; Arts, artist's
services.
Type of support: Grants for special needs.

Application information: Applications accepted.
Application form required. Application form
available on the grantmaker's web site.
   Deadline(s): None
   Applicants should submit the following:
      1) Financial information
      2) SASE
      3) Work samples
   Additional information: Application should also
      include a tax return, copies of medical
      expenses and a letter detailing the need for
      financial assistance.
EIN: 136122134

5726

Arts & Cultural Council for Greater Rochester, Inc.

277 N. Goodman St.
Rochester, NY 14607-1123
Contact: David B. Semple, Dir., Devel.
FAX: (585) 473-4051;
E-mail: mfutter@artsrochester.org; Telephone for
Jennifer Watson (585) 473-4000, Ext. 206; e-mail:
jwatson@artsrochester.org; URL: http://
www.artsrochester.org

Foundation type: Public charity
Purpose: Grants to artists in all disciplines who are
residents of Rochester, NY.
Publications: Application guidelines; Annual report;
Grants list; Newsletter.
Financial data: Year ended 12/31/2011. Assets,
$490,496 (M); Expenditures, $546,805; Total
giving, $97,485; Grants to individuals, totaling
$11,475.
Fields of interest: Arts.
Type of support: Stipends; Project support.
Application information:
   Initial approach: Letter or telephone
   Deadline(s): Feb., May, and Sept. for Strategic
      Opportunity Stipends, Nov. for
      Decentralization Individual Artist Grants
   Additional information: Contact Council for
      application guidelines or consult Web site for
      additional information.
Program descriptions:
   Education Through the Arts Grants: Matching
   funds of up to $5,000 to support in-school arts in
   education programming. Programs must combine
   the arts and at least one non-arts subject.
   Fiber Arts Program: In partnership with the
   Genesee Valley Quilt Club, the program provides
   grants of up to $500 for project that further the craft
   of fiber arts and engage the community. Projects
   may involve any fiber art, with priority consideration
   for quilting.
   *NYSCA Decentralization Grants (Individual Artist
   Project):* Grants of $2,000 are awarded for Monroe
   County artists for the creation of new work with
   public input to creative process.
   Strategic Opportunity Stipends (SOS): $200 to
   $1,500 stipends are given to artists in all media to
   take advantage of opportunities that may benefit
   their work or career development.
EIN: 222309669

5727

The Arts Center of the Capital Region

265 River St.
Troy, NY 12180-3215 (518) 273-0552
FAX: (518) 273-4591;
E-mail: info@theartscenter.cc; E-Mail for
Christopher Marblo: chris@artscenteronline.org;
URL: http://www.artscenteronline.org

Foundation type: Public charity

Purpose: Grants to artists to take advantage of
unique career opportunities in an eleven county
region of the Capital District.
Publications: Application guidelines; Grants list.
Financial data: Year ended 06/30/2012. Assets,
$3,870,651 (M); Expenditures, $1,226,781; Total
giving, $91,000; Grants to individuals, totaling
$10,800.
Fields of interest: Media/communications; Visual
arts; Theater; Music; Literature; Arts.
Type of support: Grants to individuals.
Application information: Application form required.
Application form available on the grantmaker's web
site.
   Deadline(s): Sept. 28, Feb. 1, and May 24
   Applicants should submit the following:
      1) Resume
      2) Budget Information
   Additional information: Unsolicited application
      not accepted.
Program descriptions:
   Arts>Expertise: An Artist's Marketing Clinic:
   One-on-one 20-minute consultations with artist
   consultants are available to artists. The sessions
   provide insight regarding best practices for
   professional careers and how to apply for shows,
   grants, residencies, and gallery exhibitions.
   Sessions are not designed to critique the content
   of artwork, but rather to give feedback on the work's
   professional presentation.
   Strategic Opportunity Stipends: In collaboration
   with the New York Foundation for the Arts, this
   program is designed to help individual artists of all
   disciplines within the Capital Region take
   advantage of unique opportunities that will
   significantly benefit their work or career. Artists may
   request stipends from $200 to $1,500.
EIN: 141484756

5728

Arts Council for Wyoming County

31 S. Main St.
P.O. Box 249
Perry, NY 14530-1521 (585) 237-3517
Contact: Jacqueline Hoyt, Exec. Dir.
FAX: (585) 237-6385; E-mail: info@artswyco.org;
E-Mail for Jacqueline Hoyt : hoyt@artswyco.org;
URL: http://www.artswyco.org

Foundation type: Public charity
Purpose: Grants of up to $500 available to
artistically gifted and talented Wyoming County High
School students, NY.
Publications: Application guidelines; Newsletter.
Financial data: Year ended 12/31/2011. Assets,
$238,906 (M); Expenditures, $215,925; Total
giving, $21,622.
Fields of interest: Visual arts.
Type of support: Support to graduates or students
of specific schools.
Application information: Applications accepted.
Application form required. Application form
available on the grantmaker's web site.
   Initial approach: E-mail
   Deadline(s): May 1
   Final notification: Applicants will be notified
      within six weeks after the deadline
   Applicants should submit the following:
      1) Letter(s) of recommendation
      2) Transcripts
      3) Work samples
Program description:
   Balus Grants: Through this program, the council
   makes grants of up to $500 available to artistically
   gifted and talented Wyoming County High School
   students.
EIN: 161065245

5729
Arts Engine, Inc.
145 W. 24th St., 3th Fl.
New York, NY 10011-7329   (646) 230-6368
Contact: Steven Mendelsohn, Exec. Dir.
FAX: (646) 230-6388; E-mail: info@artsengine.net;
E-mail for Kibra Yohannes: kibra@artsengine.net;
URL: http://www.artsengine.net

Foundation type: Public charity
Purpose: Support to independent filmmakers for film, video or multimedia projects.
Financial data: Year ended 12/31/2011. Assets, $394,268 (M); Expenditures, $2,450,356; Total giving, $1,334,486.
Fields of interest: Film/video; Arts, artist's services.
Type of support: Fiscal agent/sponsor.
Application information: Application form required. Application form available on the grantmaker's web site.
Initial approach: Submit fiscal sponsorship application package by mail
Deadline(s): None
Final notification: Applicants notified in two to four weeks
Applicants should submit the following:
1) Work samples
2) Proposal
Additional information: Application should also include a $50 application fee, a treatment, and a script.
Program description:
Fiscal Sponsorship: The program is available for individuals unaffiliated with a 501(c)(3) organization who are working on a high-quality film, video, or multimedia project. A 6 percent service commission of all funds made payable to Arts Engine, Inc., is charged. Eligible applicants must be a U.S. citizen with a Social Security number or have a production company with a U.S. federal identification number. Evaluation criteria include: relevance of the subject matter; whether the project meets the mission of Arts Engine, Inc.; budgeting that is realistic for the project; fundraising ability of the project director and his/her identification of potential appropriate sources of funding for the project; experience of key project personnel associated with the project and their feasibility of completing the project; and distribution potential of the completed project.
EIN: 134129275

5730
ArtsConnection
520 8th Ave., Ste. 321
New York, NY 10018-8906   (212) 302-7433
Contact: for Programs: Carol Rice, Dir., Programs
FAX: (212) 302-1132;
E-mail: artsconnection@artsconnection.org;
URL: http://www.artsconnection.org

Foundation type: Public charity
Purpose: Grants and scholarships for art class to New York City public school students in grades 6 through 12 for achievement in visual arts.
Publications: Annual report; Newsletter.
Financial data: Year ended 08/31/2011. Assets, $2,065,568 (M); Expenditures, $3,326,997; Total giving, $39,950; Grants to individuals, totaling $39,950.
Fields of interest: Arts education; Performing arts, education.
Type of support: Program development; Grants to individuals; Residencies.
Application information: Student work is submitted by visual arts teachers.

Program description:
Student Art Program: This program connects young artist from New York City public schools with corporate partners through exhibitions of student artwork. Each year, a theme is identified and a call is sent out to art teachers in middle and high schools across New York City. Through a selection process, exhibitions of student artwork are curated and then installed in corporate sponsor art spaces for one year. Gift certificates for art supplies are awarded to each student and their teachers to support their continued artistic development.
EIN: 132953240

5731
The ASCAP Foundation
1 Lincoln Plz.
New York, NY 10023-7142   (212) 621-6219
Contact: Colleen McDonough, Dir.; Julie Lapore, Prog. Mgr.
FAX: (212) 595-3342;
E-mail: info@ascapfoundation.com; URL: http://www.ascapfoundation.org

Foundation type: Public charity
Purpose: Awards to aspiring and established composers, songwriters, and lyricists.
Publications: Application guidelines; Annual report; Informational brochure; Newsletter.
Financial data: Year ended 12/31/2011. Assets, $8,081,675 (M); Expenditures, $1,532,282; Total giving, $825,265; Grants to individuals, totaling $212,175.
Fields of interest: Theater (musical); Orchestras; Music composition.
Type of support: Awards/grants by nomination only; Awards/prizes.
Application information: Applications accepted. Application form required. Application form available on the grantmaker's web site.
Initial approach: Letter of inquiry
Copies of proposal: 1
Deadline(s): Aug. 1
Program descriptions:
Boosey and Hawkes Young Composer Award Honoring Aaron Copland: This award is presented each year to a senior at LaGuardia High School of Music & Art & Performing Arts in New York City for excellence in music composition.
Charlotte V. Bergen Scholarship: This scholarship is awarded to the top Morton Gould Young Composer, age 18 or under, to be used for music study at an accredited college or music conservatory.
David Rose Scholarship: This scholarship is awarded to a college-level student who is an ASCAP member working toward a career in scoring for film and/or television, and who is participating in ASCAP's Television and Film Scoring Workshop in Los Angeles.
Fellowship for Film Scoring & Composing at Aspen: This program assists aspiring film and television composers with full fellowships to study film scoring and composition at the Aspen Music Festival and School summer session. Aspen Music Festival and School administers the application and selection process.
Fran Morgenstern Davis Scholarships: These awards are presented annually to two full-time students at the Manhattan School of Music, one in jazz composition and the other to a musical theater major. Recipients must demonstrate the potential to produce creative and original work as well as financial need.
Frederick Loewe Scholarship: This scholarship is presented annually to a student of musical theater

composition at the Tisch School of the Arts at New York University.
Harold Adamson Lyric Award: The award is presented annually to aspiring lyricists who participate in an ASCAP or ASCAP Foundation workshop in the musical theater, pop and/or country genres.
Harold Arlen Film & TV Award: This award is presented to an outstanding participant from the annual ASCAP Television & Film Scoring Workshop in Los Angeles. Recipients are chosen by nomination only.
Henry Mancini Music Scholarship: This scholarship, administered in conjunction with the Henry Mancini Summer Institute, enables music composition students to attend the institute.
Ira Gershwin Scholarship: This scholarship is presented annually to a junior-year orchestra member at LaGuardia High School of Music & Art & Performing Arts in New York City.
Irving Berlin Summer Camp Scholarship: This scholarship makes the summer music camp experience possible for a young music creator who may not otherwise have the opportunity, and is awarded through summer camps selected by the foundation.
Irving Caesar Scholarship: This scholarship is presented with the goal of providing an enjoyable and meaningful experience to young people, with an emphasis on the economically disadvantaged.
Jamie Deroy and Friends Award: This award is presented to an ASCAP songwriter whose work has been of a high and consistent level of professionalism.
John Denver Music Camp Scholarship Program: This scholarship affords young students the opportunity to attend the Perry-Mansfield Performing Arts School and Camp in Colorado.
Leiber & Stoller Music Scholarships: This program provides two scholarships to young aspiring songwriters, musicians, and vocalists for studying at accredited music schools. One scholarship is awarded to an incoming freshman at Berklee College of Music in Boston; the second recipient is recommended by the Young Musicians Foundation in Los Angeles.
Leon Brettler Award: This award is presented annually to an outstanding songwriter-performer participating in a Nashville Songwriter Workshop. Recipients are chosen by nomination only.
Life in Music Award: This award, which recognizes the efforts of veteran music creators who have made significant contributions to the music culture of the U.S., is presented each year to up to three ASCAP writer members, each one representing a different musical genre. Recipients are chosen by nomination only.
Livingston & Evans Music Scholarship: This program supports aspiring songwriters and musicians through the Young Musicians Foundation in Los Angeles.
Louis Armstrong Award Honoring W.C. Handy: Two scholarships will be awarded to junior year students at Mount Vernon High School based on abilities in jazz performance and composition.
Louis Armstrong Scholarship: This scholarship is presented to a jazz composition student at the Aaron Copland School of Music at Queens College/City University of New York.
Louis Armstrong Scholarship at the University of New Orleans: Provides talented jazz musicians who have limited financial resources the opportunity to study music in a formal academic environment at the University of New Orleans.
Louis Dreyfus Warner/Chappell City College Scholarship Honoring George and Ira Gershwin: This scholarship provides the opportunity to study music in a formal academic environment to a talented B.A.

or B.F.A. student jazz musician at City College, CUNY.

Max Dreyfus Scholarship: This scholarship, given to a composer of musical theater, is presented to a student at NYU's Tisch School of the Arts.

Michael Masser Scholarship: This scholarship supports the educational advancement, professional training, and development of a student of any age demonstrating outstanding talent in the arts. Recipients are chosen by nomination only.

Morton Gould Young Composer Awards: These awards provide up to $30,000 to encourage talented young composers in all musical genres. Eligible applicants must be citizens or permanent residents of the U.S. who have not reached their 30th birthday by Jan. 1 of the year following the application year. Original concert music of any style will be considered; works which have previously earned awards or prizes in any other national competition, and arrangements of previously-composed work, are ineligible.

Richard Rodgers Award: This annual award recognizes a veteran composer or lyricist of musical theater for a lifetime of achievement. Application are accepted by nomination only.

Rudolf Nissim Prize: This program awards cash prizes of $5,000 annually to an ASCAP member composer for an orchestral work written for a large ensemble requiring a conductor, and which has not been performed professionally. Supplementary funds are also available to recipients to support costs of rehearsals to the ensemble scheduling the first professional performance of prize-winning compositions.

Rudy Perez Scholarship: This award is presented to an aspiring Latino songwriter who demonstrates both the potential to produce creative and original work and financial need. One scholarship is presented annually on a rotating basis to a student attending one of the following schools: Conservatorio de Musica de Puerto Rico, The Juilliard School, Los Angeles County High School for the Arts, the University of Miami, and the University of Texas at San Antonio.

Sammy Cahn Award: This cash award is given each year to a promising lyricist from the foundation's Songwriter Workshops. Recipients are chosen by nomination only.

Steve Kaplan TV and Film Studies Scholarship: This scholarship is presented annually to an aspiring film and television composer participating in the foundation's Television and Film Scoring Workshop in Los Angeles.

Young Jazz Composer Awards: In conjunction with the Gibson Foundation, up to $25,000 is available to encourage talented young jazz composers who write original music. Eligible applicants must be citizens or permanent residents of the U.S., or enrolled students with student visas, who have not reached their 30th birthday by Dec. 31 of the application year. Applications must include the notated score of one composition, a CD or cassette of the composition submitted, and composer biographical information.
EIN: 510181769

5732
The Ashley and Sierra Memorial
Scholarship Fund, Inc.
c/o Community Foundation of Orange & Sullivan
30 Scott's Corners Dr., Suite 202
Montgomery, NY 12549-2262 (845) 769-9393
Application address: c/o Joseph Kenny, P.O. Box 303, Monticello, NY 12701-0303; URL: http://www.ashleysierra.org/index.htm

Foundation type: Public charity

Purpose: Scholarships to graduating seniors of Monticello High School, NY for attendance at an accredited college or university.
Publications: Application guidelines.
Financial data: Year ended 12/31/2011. Assets, $97,185 (M); Expenditures, $2,650.
Fields of interest: Vocational education, post-secondary; Higher education.
Type of support: Scholarships—to individuals.
Application information: Applications accepted. Application form required. Application form available on the grantmaker's web site.
  Deadline(s): May 15
  Applicants should submit the following:
    1) Essay
    2) Financial information
    3) Class rank
    4) GPA
  Additional information: Application can be obtained from the guidance office at the high school. Scholarship payments are made directly to the educational institution on behalf of the students.
Program description:
  Scholarships: Two scholarships of $1,000 each are awarded each year to deserving graduating seniors in the Monticello Central School District, with the goal of encouraging well-rounded scholarship and vocational aptitude geared to service of others and the ever-changing needs of society. Eligible applicants must be graduating seniors who reside within the territorial limits of the Monticello Central School District, have a GPA of 3.2 or above, and have maintained a safe driving record during their high school years.
EIN: 201890997

5733
The Asia Society
725 Park Ave.
New York, NY 10021-5088 (212) 288-6400
FAX: (212) 517-8315; E-mail: info@asiaoc.org;
Toll-free tel.: (888) 275-2742; URL: http://www.asiasociety.org

Foundation type: Public charity
Purpose: Prizes awarded annually to a writer who has produced the best example of journalism about Asia in print or online during the calendar year. Awards to young winners of an essay contest that address social or economic issues.
Publications: Application guidelines.
Financial data: Year ended 06/30/2012. Assets, $98,303,024 (M); Expenditures, $30,745,615; Total giving, $2,122,753.
Fields of interest: Print publishing; Economics; International studies; Young adults, female; Young adults, male.
International interests: Asia.
Type of support: Awards/prizes.
Application information:
  Initial approach: Letter or e-mail
  Deadline(s): Mar. 1, and June 12 for Youth Prize
  Additional information: Contact foundation for application guidelines and complete program information.
Program descriptions:
  Goldman Sachs Foundation Prizes for Excellence in International Education: This program awards high-school students who demonstrate an in-depth understanding of key issues in international affairs and the global economy with scholarship prizes of up to $10,000 each. Elementary, middle, and high schools, as well as school districts and states departments are eligible for grants of $25,000 for programs that engage students in learning about other world regions, cultures, and languages. U.S.

programs that have developed outstanding programs that use media/technology to educate students or teacher about world regions, cultures, and languages are also eligible to receive a $25,000 grant.
  Osborn Elliot Prize for Excellence in Journalism in Asia: Criteria for the $10,000 prize include the impact of the work, its originality, creativity, depth of research, and educational value in informing the public about Asia. An independent jury of distinguished writers, award-winning journalists, and Asia-hands will review nominations for the prize from both media organizations and journalists. All nominations or direct applications are limited to one per organization or journalist. For the purposes of this award, "Asia" is defined by the Asia Society, comprising countries from Iran eastward to and including Australia and New Zealand. It does not include the Arab Middle East.
EIN: 133234632

5734
Asian Cultural Council
6 W. 48th St., 12th Fl.
New York, NY 10036-1802 (212) 843-0403
Contact: Dawn Byrnes, Mgr., Comms.
Application address: application@accny.org
FAX: (212) 843-0343; E-mail: acc@accny.org; Fax for D. Byrnes: (212) 843-0343; URL: http://www.asianculturalcouncil.org

Foundation type: Public charity
Purpose: Fellowships and grants to Asian artists, scholars, and specialists to conduct research, study, receive specialized training, undertake observation tours, or pursue creative activity in the U.S. Americans seeking aid to undertake activities in Asia are also eligible to apply.
Publications: Application guidelines; Annual report; Grants list; Informational brochure; Newsletter.
Financial data: Year ended 12/31/2011. Assets, $29,701,119 (M); Expenditures, $6,000,216; Total giving, $1,639,500; Grants to individuals, totaling $93,000.
Fields of interest: Cultural/ethnic awareness; Film/video; Visual arts; Architecture; History/archaeology; Arts; International studies.
International interests: Japan.
Type of support: Grants to individuals; Awards/prizes.
Application information: Applications accepted.
  Initial approach: Letter of inquiry
  Send request by: On-line
  Deadline(s): Nov. 1
  Additional information: See web site for complete program information.
Program descriptions:
  Grants to Individuals: Grants provide support to Asian individuals to conduct research, study, receive specialized training, undertake observation tours, or pursue non-commercial creative activity in the United States or among the countries of Asia in the visual and performing arts. Grant recipients are expected to return to their home countries at the conclusion of the fellowship period, using the training or experience acquired during their grant to fulfill professional responsibilities in their countries of origin. Support is not provided for undergraduate study, individual performance tours, or activities conducted by individuals within their own countries. Applicants seeking support to pursue graduate degrees in the U.S. must obtain tuition assistance from other sources. Grants are typically no more than $8,000 for a six-month duration. Americans seeking support to undertake activities in Asia are also eligible to apply.

John D. Rockefeller Third Award: Awards of $35,000 each are awarded to individuals from Asia or the U.S. who has made a significant contribution to the international understanding, practice, or study of the visual or performing arts of Asia. Candidates must be nominated by artists, scholars, and others professionally involved in Asian art and culture. Recipients are selected by council trustees in consultation with various specialists in the candidates' fields, as well as with qualified individuals having firsthand knowledge of the nominees' professional activities and accomplishments. The award enables recipients to pursue work in some aspect of the arts of Asia through international travel and research. Individuals from Asia and the United States who are active in any field of the visual or performing arts of Asia, whether affiliated with an institution or working independently, are eligible for award consideration.
EIN: 133018822

5735
Associated Medical Schools of New York
1270 Ave. of the Americas, Ste. 606
New York, NY   10020-1903   (212) 218-4610
Contact: Jo Wiederhorn, Pres. and C.E.O.
FAX: (212) 218-4278; E-mail: info@amsny.org;
E-mail For Jo Wiederhorn: jowiederhorn@amsny.org;
URL: http://www.amsny.org

Foundation type: Public charity
Purpose: Stipends to cover living expenses to qualified students while attending the University at Buffalo, SUNY School of Medicine and Biomedical Sciences, NY.
Financial data: Year ended 06/30/2012. Assets, $2,535,451 (M); Expenditures, $3,412,245; Total giving, $2,220,908; Grants to individuals, totaling $579,087.
Fields of interest: Medical school/education.
Type of support: Support to graduates or students of specific schools; Stipends.
Application information: Contact participating school for application information.
Program description:
Post-Baccalaureate Program: This program works to expand the pool of underrepresented minority, educationally- and economically-disadvantaged students in medicine by supporting a baccalaureate program. The program provides up to 25 students with formal mentoring, advising, and a tailored curriculum at the University at Buffalo - SUNY School of Medicine and Biomedical Sciences. Qualifying students are referred to the program through the admissions process at participating medical schools Albany Medical College, Albert Einstein College of Medicine, New York College of Osteopathic Medicine, New York Medical College, Stony Brook University Medical Center, SUNY Downstate Medical Center, SUNY Upstate Medical University, University at Buffalo - SUNY School of Medicine and Biomedical Sciences, and University of Rochester School of Medicine and Dentistry.
EIN: 136214887

5736
The Astraea Lesbian Foundation for Justice, Inc.
(formerly ASTRAEA, National Lesbian Action Foundation)
116 E. 16th St., 7th Fl.
New York, NY   10003-2112   (212) 529-8021
Contact: J. Bob Alotta, Exec. Dir.
FAX: (212) 982-3321;
E-mail: info@astraeafoundation.org; URL: http://www.astraeafoundation.org

Foundation type: Public charity
Purpose: Grants to emerging lesbian writers and visual artists. Scholarships to female undergraduates at a City University of New York school.
Publications: Application guidelines; Annual report; Grants list; Informational brochure; Newsletter.
Financial data: Year ended 06/30/2012. Assets, $10,175,205 (M); Expenditures, $3,704,719; Total giving, $1,369,547; Grants to individuals, totaling $32,600.
Fields of interest: Visual arts; Literature; Women; LGBTQ.
Type of support: Support to graduates or students of specific schools; Awards/prizes; Undergraduate support.
Application information: Applications accepted. Application form required.
Initial approach: Letter, telephone, or e-mail
Deadline(s): Vary
Program descriptions:
Astraea Visual Arts Fund: The fund aims to recognize the work of contemporary lesbian artists by providing support to those who show artistic merit and whose art and perspective reflect a commitment to the foundation's mission and efforts to promote lesbian visibility and social justice. The fund awards three $2,500 cash awards to lesbian visual artists, including bisexual and queer-identified women who also identify as part of lesbian communities. Winners must agree to be publicly acknowledged as lesbian artists and agree to have their art work publicized. Applicants must be U.S. residents, and submit slides of current original works of art produced within the last three years in the following categories only: sculpture, painting in any medium, print, drawing, work on paper, or mixed media. Art with an audio component is judged on visual content alone (such samples should stand alone competitively). Students currently enrolled in an arts degree granting program or its equivalent at the time of application are not eligible to apply.
Lesbian Writers Fund: The fund supports the work of emerging lesbian poets and fiction writers within the U.S. To be eligible for an award, applicants must be a lesbian-identified writer of poetry and/or fiction who resides in the U.S. Applicants should have published at least one piece of writing (in any genre) in a newspaper, magazine, journal, anthology, or professional web publication; and should have not published more than one book, including a chapbook, in any subject or genre with a publisher. First-place awardees and two runners-up in the poetry and fiction categories will receive cash awards ($10,000 for the awardee and $1,500 for runners-up). At least one grant will be awarded to a lesbian writer who is based west of the Mississippi.
Margot Karle Scholarship: This scholarship is available to lesbian undergraduates in the City University of New York (CUNY) system who demonstrate social activism and financial need.
EIN: 132992977

5737
Athanasiades Cultural Foundation, Inc.
30-96 42nd St.
Astoria, NY   11103-3031   (718) 278-3014

Foundation type: Independent foundation
Purpose: Scholarships to individuals in NY for higher education. Grants to needy individuals for medical expenses and general welfare, primarily in NY.
Financial data: Year ended 12/31/2010. Assets, $2,652,895 (M); Expenditures, $72,178; Total giving, $21,240; Grants to individuals, 39 grants totaling $21,240.
Fields of interest: Higher education; Health care; Economically disadvantaged.
Type of support: Scholarships—to individuals; Grants for special needs.
Application information: Applications accepted.
Initial approach: Letter
Deadline(s): Last Fri. of Oct. for Scholarship
Additional information: Application should include transcript for scholarship.
EIN: 133614414

5738
The Doctor Theodore A. Atlas Foundation, Inc.
543 Cary Ave.
Staten Island, NY   10310-1942
Contact: Kathy Zito, Exec. Dir.
E-mail: info@dratlasfoundation.com; Tel./fax: (718) 980-7037; URL: http://www.dratlasfoundation.com

Foundation type: Public charity
Purpose: Scholarships and grants to worthy individuals based on scholastic potential, community service, athletic achievement and economic need.
Publications: Grants list.
Financial data: Year ended 12/31/2011. Assets, $719,483 (M); Expenditures, $492,795; Total giving, $174,124.
Fields of interest: Higher education.
Type of support: Scholarships—to individuals.
Application information: Applications accepted.
Initial approach: Letter
Program descriptions:
George Horowitz Scholarship: Scholarships of $5,000 to amateur boxers attending or about to attend college to be used for tuition, room, board, and books.
John Garand Rowan "Admiral" Scholarship: Scholarships of $2,500 to one male and one female graduating senior of Curtis High School, NY, with records of academic achievement, community service, and financial need. Special attention is given to applicants who are involved in the Curtis Naval Junior Reserve Officer Training Program (NJROTC)
EIN: 134012789

5739
Audio Engineering Society Educational Foundation, Inc.
(also known as AES Educational Foundation, Inc.)
60 E. 42nd St., Ste. 2520
New York, NY   10165-0009
Contact: Donald Puluse, Pres.

Foundation type: Independent foundation
Purpose: Graduate scholarships to talented students in the U.S. and abroad, who are preparing to enter the audio engineering profession and related fields.

Publications: Application guidelines.
Financial data: Year ended 12/31/2011. Assets, $438,218 (M); Expenditures, $50,022; Total giving, $45,000; Grants to individuals, 9 grants totaling $45,000 (high: $5,000, low: $5,000).
Fields of interest: Engineering.
Type of support: Graduate support.
Application information: Application form required. Application form available on the grantmaker's web site.

Initial approach: Letter
Send request by: Mail
Deadline(s): May 15
Additional information: Application should include two letters of recommendation. Payments are made directly to the educational institution on behalf of the students.

Program description:

Scholarship Program: Scholarship are granted on an international basis to students who have completed an undergraduate degree, have demonstrated their commitment to audio engineering or a related field, and have been accepted or are awaiting acceptance to a graduate degree program leading to a master's or higher degree, or an internationally recognized equivalent. Application may be renewed once upon successful completion of at least one year of graduate study.
EIN: 112664807

5740
Jean B. Authier Trust
c/o Paul Walter, Jr.
P.O. Box 718
New Lebanon, NY 12125-0718 (570) 296-1850

Foundation type: Independent foundation
Purpose: Scholarships to graduating seniors of Delaware Valley High School, PA, or Dieruff High School, PA, with ambitions to become an accomplished chef and are enrolled or will enroll in a culinary arts program.
Financial data: Year ended 12/31/2011. Assets, $947,358 (M); Expenditures, $73,735; Total giving, $40,172.
Type of support: Support to graduates or students of specific schools.
Application information: Applications not accepted.

Additional information: Contact trust for additional application guidelines.
EIN: 256820083

5741
The Authors League Fund
31 E. 32nd St., 7th Fl.
New York, NY 10016-5509 (212) 268-1208
Contact: Isabel A. Howe, Exec. Dir.
FAX: (212) 564-5363;
E-mail: staff@authorsleaguefund.org; URL: http://www.authorsleaguefund.org

Foundation type: Independent foundation
Purpose: Loans, which do not have to be repaid, to professional writers and dramatists who find themselves in financial need because of medical or health-related problems, temporary loss of income or other misfortune.
Financial data: Year ended 12/31/2012. Assets, $6,245,062 (M); Expenditures, $335,329; Total giving, $197,356; Loans to individuals, totaling $172,000.
Fields of interest: Literature.
Type of support: Loans—to individuals.

Application information: Applications accepted. Application form required.

Send request by: Mail or fax
Deadline(s): None
Additional information: Application should include financial information.
EIN: 131966496

5742
Autism Science Foundation
28 W. 39th St., Ste. 502
New York, NY 10018-2177 (212) 391-3913
Contact: Casey Gold, Operations Mgr.
FAX: (212) 391-3954;
E-mail: contactus@autismsciencefoundation.org;
E-mail for Casey Gold: cgold@autismsciencefoundation.org; URL: http://www.autismsciencefoundation.org/

Foundation type: Public charity
Purpose: Grants to scientists for the discovery in the causes of autism and the development of better treatments. Travel grants to individuals affected with autism to attend a conference on autism research.
Publications: Application guidelines; Newsletter.
Financial data: Year ended 12/31/2011. Assets, $288,440 (M); Expenditures, $448,193; Total giving, $273,923; Grants to individuals, totaling $28,923.
Fields of interest: Autism research.
Type of support: Grants to individuals; Travel grants.
Application information: Applications accepted.

Initial approach: Proposal for Research, letter for Travel Grant
Deadline(s): Nov. for Research Grant
Final notification: Recipients notified in Mar. for Research and Travel Grant
Additional information: See web site for additional guidelines.

Program descriptions:

IMFAR Travel Grants: Grants of $1,000 each are available to send a limited number of parents of children with autism, individuals with autism, special education teachers, and other stakeholders to attend the foundation's annual International Meting for Autism Research. Awards can be used for registration, travel, accommodations, meals, and other directly-related expenses, including childcare or special accommodations to enable individuals with autism to participate.

Pre- and Post-Doctoral Training Awards: The foundation awards scholarships to graduate students, medical students, and post-doctoral fellows interested in pursuing careers in basic and clinical research relevant to autism spectrum disorders. Proposed training must be scientifically linked to autism and may be broadened to include training in a closely-related area of scientific research, including (but not limited to) human behavior across the lifespan (language, learning, communication, social functioning, epilepsy, sleep, and repetitive disorders), neurobiology (anatomy, development, and neuroimaging), pharmacology, neuropathology, human genetics/genomics, immunology, molecular and cellular mechanisms, studies employing model organisms and systems, and studies of treatment and service delivery. Predoctoral students are eligible for a $25,000 stipend (not including tuition reimbursement), plus a maximum $1,000 allowance to support registration and travel for the student to attend the International Meeting for Autism Research. Postdoctoral students are eligible for a $35,000 stipend, plus a maximum $1,000 allowance to support registration and travel for the postdoctoral

fellow to attend the International Meeting for Autism Research.
EIN: 264522309

5743
Autism Speaks
1 E. 33 Rd. Ste., 4th Fl.
New York, NY 10016-5675 (212) 252-8584
FAX: (212) 252-8676;
E-mail: contactus@autismspeaks.org; Additional address (Princeton office): 1060 State Rd., 2nd Fl., Princeton, NJ 08540-1446, tel.: (609) 228-7310, fax: (609) 430-9163, addl. fax: (609) 430-9505; additional address (Los Angeles office): 6330 San Vicente Blvd., Ste. 401, Los Angeles, CA 90048-5464, tel.: (323) 549-0500, fax: (323) 549-0547; URL: http://www.autismspeaks.org

Foundation type: Public charity
Purpose: Emergency support to individuals and families affected by autism. Fellowship and research opportunities for doctoral and postdoctoral researchers in autism.
Publications: Application guidelines.
Financial data: Year ended 12/31/2011. Assets, $22,705,993 (M); Expenditures, $56,711,411; Total giving, $17,742,139; Grants to individuals, 182 grants totaling $79,050. Subtotal for grants for special needs: 182 grants totaling $79,050.
Fields of interest: Autism; Autism research.
Type of support: Emergency funds; Fellowships; Research; Awards/prizes.
Application information: Applications accepted. Application form required. Application form available on the grantmaker's web site.

Initial approach: Application
Deadline(s): Varies

Program descriptions:

Dennis Weatherstone Predoctoral Fellowship Program: This program works to provide highly-qualified candidates with exceptional research training opportunities broadly related to the study of autism spectrum disorders (ASD). General areas of research include: behavioral, psychosocial, and/or educational challenges; family issues; language/communication issues; environmental factors; epidemiology and public health; health services research; genetics and/or genomics; health services research; medical/psychiatric comorbidities; biomedical and/or pharmacological interventions; developmental biology; neuroscience; physiology/anatomy; and technology development. Priority will be given to applications that address: understanding environmental risk factors and their interaction with genetic susceptibility to enable prevention and improve diagnosis and treatment; discovery of biomarkers that can improve risk assessment and subtype stratification that will allow for an individualized approach to treatment; improving quality of life through more effective medicines, behavioral interventions, and technologies; enhancing diagnosis and treatment of underserved and under-studied populations, including nonverbal persons with ASD, ethnically-diverse and/or low-resource communities, and those with medical co-morbidities; and the dissemination and implementation of evidence-based clinical practices to the broader worldwide community. Fellowships are for two years and include an annual $29,500 award (a $22,100 stipend plus a $7,400 annual allowance). Eligible applicants must be an enrolled student in a program leading to a research doctorate (such as a Ph.D. or Sc.D., or a combined degree such as an M.D./Ph.D.) in an academic department of an accredited university or health/medical institution; prior to application, applicants must also have identified a mentor for their fellowship (who has a Ph.D. and/or M.D. or equivalent degree, and who is a scientific investigator with an academic or research institutional appointment).

Suzanne and Bob Wright Trailblazer Award Program: This award will support highly novel "out of the box" autism-relevant research that opens new avenues to understanding the causes, diagnosis, subtyping, prevention, treatments, and cure of autism spectrum disorders. The project is not required to have preliminary data but should have a sound rational supporting its need and be considered risky. Applying investigators must hold full-time tenured or tenure-track faculty appointments (or equivalent full-time non-tenure track appointments) at accredited academic, medical, or research institutions; applicants also should have a demonstrated track record of research experience relevant to the project. Awards are limited to a period of 12 months and for up to $10,000 total (inclusive of 10 percent indirect costs).

Translational Postdoctoral Fellowship: The program supports promising and well-qualified postdoctoral scientists pursuing training in translational research of autism spectrum disorders. Successful applicants will have a project that bridges basic laboratory research and behavioral or biomedical clinical research, and a training plan that includes mentoring in both basic and clinical research environments. The fellowship includes a stipend between $38,000 and $50,000 and a $10,000 annual allowance for two years. Candidates must have a M.D. or Ph.D. and cannot have more than five years of postdoctoral experience at the commencement of the award.
EIN: 202329938

5744
Avery Scholarship Foundation
P.O. Box 772
Livingston Manor, NY   12758-0772

Foundation type: Independent foundation
Purpose: Scholarships to graduating seniors of Livingston Manor High School, NY, for undergraduate education at a four-year college.
Financial data: Year ended 12/31/2012. Assets, $541,467 (M); Expenditures, $28,172; Total giving, $27,500; Grants to individuals, 6 grants totaling $27,500 (high: $5,000, low: $2,500).
Type of support: Support to graduates or students of specific schools; Undergraduate support.
Application information: Applications accepted. Application form required.
    Deadline(s): May 1
    Additional information: Application form is available from the school's guidance department.
EIN: 141798357

5745
Avon Foundation for Women
(formerly Avon Foundation, also known as Avon Products Foundation, Inc.)
777 3rd Ave., 2nd Fl.
New York, NY   10017-1401   (212) 282-5000
Contact: Carol Kurzig, Pres.
E-mail: info@avonfoundation.org; E-mail For Carolyn Ricci: carolyn.ricci@avonfoundation.org;
URL: http://www.avonfoundation.org

Foundation type: Public charity
Purpose: Bridge funding to scientists with innovative concepts in breast cancer while they

develop the pilot data necessary to seek funding from larger sources. Awards to pursue projects to better the lives of women (of all ages) in the United States.
Publications: Application guidelines; Annual report; Financial statement; Grants list; Informational brochure; Newsletter.
Financial data: Year ended 12/31/2012. Assets, $35,104,686 (M); Expenditures, $59,596,256; Total giving, $33,154,275. Scholarships—to individuals amount not specified.
Fields of interest: Cancer; Cancer research; Breast cancer research; Women; Girls; Adults, women; Young adults, female.
Type of support: Research; Employee-related scholarships; Scholarships—to individuals; Awards/prizes.
Application information: Applications accepted. Application form required. Application form available on the grantmaker's web site.
    Additional information: See web site for additional guidelines.
Program descriptions:
    James E. Preston Community Service Scholarship: The foundation annually awards one four-year $5,000 college scholarship to a dependent child of a full-time employee of Avon who demonstrates outstanding community service experience that is deemed most exemplary.
    Scholarship Program for Children of Associates: One scholarship of $12,000, paid in installments of $3,000 over a four-year period, is available to dependent children of a current, regular, full-time U.S. or Puerto Rico associate.
    Scholarship Program for Representatives: The foundation awards full-time and part-time college scholarships, ranging from $1,500 to $2,500, to representatives of Avon.
EIN: 136128447

5746
Babylon Breast Cancer Coalition, Inc.
100 Montauk Hgwy.
Copiague, NY   11726-4915   (631) 893-4110
FAX: (631) 539-8862;
E-mail: bbccest1993@aol.com; URL: http://www.babylonbreastcancer.org

Foundation type: Public charity
Purpose: Scholarships to graduating high school seniors for higher education, whose parent or legal guardian has had a past or present diagnosis of breast cancer and, who reside within the Township of Babylon, NY.
Publications: Application guidelines; Newsletter.
Financial data: Year ended 12/31/2011. Assets, $235,168 (M); Expenditures, $208,069; Total giving, $13,065; Grants to individuals, totaling $5,965.
Fields of interest: Higher education; Breast cancer; Women.
Type of support: Support to graduates or students of specific schools; Technical education support; Undergraduate support.
Application information: Applications accepted. Application form required.
    Deadline(s): Apr. 15
    Additional information: Application should include an essay. Application can be obtained from your high school guidance counselors.
Program description:
    Scholarship Program: Scholarships of $1,000 each are awarded annually to Babylon Township high school seniors who have had a parent or legal guardian with a personal breast cancer history. Scholarship candidates must write an essay describing how breast cancer has affected their life,

and must have plans to attend college or an accredited vocational school immediately after high school graduation; applicants must also have legal residence within the township of Babylon.
EIN: 113191035

5747
Victor A. Bacile Scholarship Fund
c/o Vincent Corana
227 Mill St.
Poughkeepsie, NY   12601-3026

Foundation type: Independent foundation
Purpose: Scholarships to qualified individuals in the Poughkeepsie, NY area who are registered full time students in the second, third or fourth year of study at an accredited college or university.
Financial data: Year ended 12/31/2012. Assets, $127,567 (M); Expenditures, $9,735; Total giving, $8,000; Grants to individuals, 4 grants totaling $8,000 (high: $2,000, low: $2,000).
Fields of interest: Higher education.
Type of support: Scholarships—to individuals.
Application information: Applications accepted.
    Send request by: On-line
    Deadline(s): Sept. 15
    Applicants should submit the following:
        1) Photograph
        2) Transcripts
        3) Essay
EIN: 141730868

5748
Daisy S. Bacon Scholarship Fund
P.O. Box 209
Port Washington, NY   11050-3737
Contact: Carmine Matina

Foundation type: Independent foundation
Purpose: Scholarships to residents of Port Washington, NY, who have demonstrated high academic standards, character, and financial need, and who are seeking a college degree.
Financial data: Year ended 12/31/2012. Assets, $269,307 (M); Expenditures, $14,388; Total giving, $3,000; Grants to individuals, 4 grants totaling $3,000 (high: $1,000, low: $500).
Type of support: Scholarships—to individuals.
Application information: Applications accepted. Application form required. Interview required.
    Initial approach: Letter
    Deadline(s): Dec. 31
    Applicants should submit the following:
        1) Letter(s) of recommendation
        2) Financial information
EIN: 116386052

5749
The Bagby Foundation for the Musical Arts, Inc.
501 5th Ave., Ste. 801
New York, NY   10017-7893   (212) 986-6094
Contact: J. Andrew Lark, Exec. Dir.

Foundation type: Independent foundation
Purpose: Music study grants based on talent and need to residents of NY. Grants for pensions and emergency aid to aged needy individuals who have aided the world of music.
Financial data: Year ended 12/31/2011. Assets, $1,854,006 (M); Expenditures, $156,382; Total giving, $68,295; Grants to individuals, 5 grants totaling $66,295 (high: $8,900, low: $935).
Fields of interest: Music; Performing arts, education; Aging.

Type of support: Grants to individuals; Grants for special needs.
Application information: Applications accepted.
   Initial approach: Letter
   Deadline(s): None
EIN: 131873289

5750
Jessie H. Baker Educational Fund
c/o NBT Bank, N.A.
52 S. Broad St.
Norwich, NY   13815   (716) 566-3027

Foundation type: Independent foundation
Purpose: Scholarships to graduates of high schools in Broome County, NY.
Financial data: Year ended 08/31/2013. Assets, $2,567,477 (M); Expenditures, $134,478; Total giving, $106,862; Grants to individuals, 105 grants totaling $106,862 (high: $4,968, low: $237).
Type of support: Undergraduate support.
Application information: Applications accepted.
   Deadline(s): None
   Applicants should submit the following:
      1) Letter(s) of recommendation
      2) Essay
      3) Transcripts
      4) Financial information
EIN: 222478098

5751
The George Balanchine Foundation, Inc.
David H. Koch Theater
20 Lincoln Ctr.
New York, NY   10023-6913   (212) 799-3196
FAX: (212) 496-7124;
E-mail: information@balanchine.org; URL: http://www.balanchine.org

Foundation type: Public charity
Purpose: Support to dancers participating in The Interpretive Archives of George Balanchine and The Balanchine Essays programs, as well as occasional grants to individuals working on projects related to the foundation's mission.
Publications: Informational brochure.
Financial data: Year ended 12/31/2012. Assets, $144,618 (M); Expenditures, $141,784.
Fields of interest: Dance; Choreography.
Type of support: Program development.
Application information: Unsolicited applications not accepted for most grants.
EIN: 133180628

5752
Ballet Hispanico of New York, Inc.
167 W. 89th St.
New York, NY   10024-1904   (212) 362-6710
Contact: Lee Koonce, Exec. Dir.
FAX: (212) 362-7809;
E-mail: info@ballethispanico.org; E-Mail for Lee Koonce: lkoonce@ballethispanico.org; URL: http://www.ballethispanico.org

Foundation type: Public charity
Purpose: Scholarships to students at the Ballet Hispanico School of Dance, NY.
Financial data: Year ended 06/30/2012. Assets, $13,447,681 (M); Expenditures, $4,912,658; Total giving, $163,323; Grants to individuals, totaling $163,323.
Fields of interest: Dance; Performing arts, education.
Type of support: Scholarships—to individuals.

Application information: Applications accepted. Application form required. Application form available on the grantmaker's web site.
   Additional information: Contact foundation for current application deadline/guidelines.
EIN: 132685755

5753
James S. Barton Jr. Emerging Artist Fund
P.O. Box 601
Pleasant Valley, NY   12601
Contact: Peter C. Geertz, Tr.

Foundation type: Independent foundation
Purpose: Scholarships to graduates of Arlington High School, Lagrangeville, Rhinebeck High School, or Dutchess Community College, Poughkeepsie, New York.
Financial data: Year ended 06/30/2013. Assets, $275,346 (M); Expenditures, $16,188; Total giving, $15,000; Grants to individuals, 14 grants totaling $15,000 (high: $2,000, low: $1,000).
Fields of interest: Higher education.
Type of support: Scholarships—to individuals; Support to graduates or students of specific schools.
Application information: Applications accepted.
   Deadline(s): Apr. 30
EIN: 200657169

5754
Baseball Assistance Team
245 Park Ave., 34th Fl.
New York, NY   10167-0002   (212) 931-7800
FAX: (212) 949-5433; E-mail: BAT@mlb.com;
Toll-free tel.: (866) 605-4594; URL: http://www.baseballassistanceteam.com

Foundation type: Public charity
Purpose: Grants to former Major League Baseball players, employees, and their families for living expenses and other financial needs.
Publications: Informational brochure; Newsletter.
Financial data: Year ended 12/31/2011. Assets, $12,316,238 (M); Expenditures, $2,298,518; Total giving, $2,006,406; Grants to individuals, totaling $1,749,668.
Fields of interest: Athletics/sports, baseball.
Type of support: Employee-related welfare.
Application information: Applications accepted. Application form required. Application form available on the grantmaker's web site.
   Additional information: Contact foundation for current application deadline/guidelines.
Company name: Major League Baseball
EIN: 133355155

5755
Bath Rotary Student Fund, Inc.
P.O. Box 648
Bath, NY   14810   (607) 776-1489
Contact: Richard McCandless, Chair.
Application address: 7186 Peach St. Bath, NY 14810

Foundation type: Independent foundation
Purpose: Students loans to high school graduates from the greater Bath, New York, area.
Financial data: Year ended 12/31/2012. Assets, $190,330 (M); Expenditures, $10,537; Total giving, $0.
Fields of interest: Higher education.
Type of support: Student loans—to individuals.
Application information: Applications accepted.

Initial approach: Letter
Deadline(s): None
Additional information: Applicant must state need and institution attending. $4,000 maximum loan per student.
EIN: 161109902

5756
The Bay and Paul Foundations, Inc.
(formerly Josephine Bay Paul and C. Michael Paul Foundation, Inc.)
17 W. 94th St., 1st Fl.
New York, NY   10025-7116   (212) 663-1115
Contact: Frederick Bay, C.E.O. and Pres.
FAX: (212) 932-0316;
E-mail: info@bayandpaulfoundations.org;
URL: http://www.bayandpaulfoundations.org

Foundation type: Independent foundation
Purpose: Awards by nomination only to researchers in the biodiversity conservation field.
Publications: Application guidelines.
Financial data: Year ended 12/31/2012. Assets, $71,635,854 (M); Expenditures, $5,489,268; Total giving, $3,473,026.
Fields of interest: Natural resources; Biology/life sciences.
Type of support: Awards/grants by nomination only; Awards/prizes.
Application information: Applications not accepted.
   Additional information: Unsolicited applications not accepted.
EIN: 131991717

5757
Beacon of Learning Foundation
c/o Sacks Press & Lacher
600 3rd Ave., 18th Fl.
New York, NY   10016   (212) 541-1264
Contact: Karin J. Barkhorn Esq.
Application address: c/o Bryan Cave, 1290 Ave. of Americas, New York, NY 10104

Foundation type: Independent foundation
Purpose: Scholarships to individuals in the U.S. and abroad for higher education.
Financial data: Year ended 12/31/2012. Assets, $45,544 (M); Expenditures, $452,066; Total giving, $441,091; Grants to individuals, 9 grants totaling $232,916 (high: $53,446, low: $12,334).
Fields of interest: Higher education.
Type of support: Scholarships—to individuals.
Application information: Applications accepted. Application form required.
   Initial approach: Telephone
   Deadline(s): None
   Applicants should submit the following:
      1) Letter(s) of recommendation
      2) Transcripts
   Additional information: Contact the foundation for additional guidelines.
EIN: 272520016

5758
James Beard Foundation, Inc.
167 W. 12th St.
New York, NY   10011-8201   (212) 675-4984
Contact: Susan Ungaro, Pres.
E-mail address for individuals:
scholarships@jamesbeard.org
FAX: (212) 645-1438;
E-mail: info@jamesbeard.org; Toll-free tel.: (800) 362-3273; URL: http://www.jamesbeard.org

Foundation type: Public charity
Purpose: Scholarships to high school seniors or graduates who plan to enroll or are already enrolled at least part-time at a licensed or accredited culinary school seeking to further their careers in the culinary arts.
Publications: Application guidelines; Newsletter.
Financial data: Year ended 03/31/2012. Assets, $2,800,103 (M); Expenditures, $6,735,483; Total giving, $240,218; Grants to individuals, totaling $168,955.
Type of support: Scholarships—to individuals.
Application information: Applications accepted. Application form required.
> *Deadline(s):* May
> *Applicants should submit the following:*
> 1) Letter(s) of recommendation
> 2) GPA
> 3) Financial information
> *Additional information:* Applicant selection is based on past academic performance and future potential, leadership and participation in school and community activity, work experience, statement of career and educational aspirations and goals.
EIN: 132752108

5759
The James Gordon Bennett Memorial Corporation
c/o Pamela Gubitosi
620 8th Ave.
New York, NY 10018-1618

Foundation type: Independent foundation
Purpose: Scholarships to children of journalists who have worked in New York, NY, on a daily newspaper for 10 years or more. Pecuniary aid to needy journalists or their dependents who have been employees for 10 or more years of a New York, NY, daily newspaper.
Financial data: Year ended 12/31/2012. Assets, $5,016,933 (M); Expenditures, $242,615; Total giving, $209,750; Grants to individuals, totaling $95,300.
Fields of interest: Print publishing.
Type of support: Employee-related scholarships; Employee-related welfare.
Application information: Applications not accepted.
> *Additional information:* Unsolicited requests for funds not considered or acknowledged.
EIN: 136150414

5760
Herbert Berger Scholarship Foundation
30 Seguine Ave.
Staten Island, NY 10309-3721 (301) 365-3065
Contact: Shelby Jacoby
Application address: 7420 Westlake Terr, Bethesda, MD 20817, tel.:(301) 365-3065

Foundation type: Independent foundation
Purpose: College scholarship to graduates of Tottenville High School, Staten Island, NY for higher education.
Financial data: Year ended 12/31/2011. Assets, $25,820 (M); Expenditures, $5,267; Total giving, $5,000; Grant to an individual, 1 grant totaling $5,000.
Fields of interest: Higher education.
Type of support: Support to graduates or students of specific schools.

Application information: Applications can be obtained from the principal of the high school. Scholarship is based on merit.
EIN: 136939674

5761
The Tyler Berntsen Memorial Foundation
1 Wall St.
New York, NY 10286
URL: http://www.tylerberntsenfoundation.org

Foundation type: Independent foundation
Purpose: Scholarships to graduates of Chatham High School, NY for college attendance.
Financial data: Year ended 12/31/2012. Assets, $0 (M); Expenditures, $12,167; Total giving, $12,000; Grants to individuals, 2 grants totaling $12,000 (high: $6,000, low: $6,000).
Fields of interest: Higher education.
Type of support: Scholarships—to individuals.
Application information: Applications accepted. Application form required.
EIN: 200131098

5762
Bibliographical Society of America, Inc.
P.O. Box 1537
Lenox Hill Sta.
New York, NY 10021-0043 (212) 734-2500
E-mail: bsa@bibsocamer.org; Tel./FAX: (212) 452-2710; URL: http://www.bibsocamer.org

Foundation type: Public charity
Purpose: Fellowships and awards to applicants for various studies relating to bibliographical inquiries as well as research in the history of books and publishing.
Publications: Application guidelines.
Financial data: Year ended 12/31/2012. Assets, $3,017,740 (M); Expenditures, $218,825; Total giving, $28,300; Grants to individuals, totaling $28,300.
Fields of interest: Literature.
Type of support: Fellowships; Research; Awards/prizes; Stipends.
Application information: Applications accepted. Application form required. Application form available on the grantmaker's web site.
> *Initial approach:* E-mail
> *Deadline(s):* Sept. 1 for Justin G. Schiller Prize; Dec. 1 for Fellowship; Sept. 1, 2008 for William L. Mitchell Prize
> *Applicants should submit the following:*
> 1) Proposal
> 2) Curriculum vitae
> 3) Letter(s) of recommendation
> *Additional information:* See web site for additional awards information and guidelines.
Program descriptions:
> *Fellowship Program:* The annual short-term fellowship program supports bibliographical inquiry as well as research in the history of the book trades and in publishing history. The program awards fellows a stipend of up to $3,000 per month in support of travel, living and research expenses.
> *New Scholars Program:* The program gives new scholars an opportunity to present unpublished research and to acquaint members of the society with new work on bibliographical topics. The society seeks to identify scholars who are new to the field of bibliography, broadly defined to include any research that deals with the creation, production, publication, distribution, and reception of texts as material objects. New scholars selected for the panel receive a subvention of $600 toward the cost

of travel to the annual meeting and a year's complimentary membership to the society.
> *The Justin G. Schiller Prize for Bibliographical Work in Pre-20th Century Children's Books:* The Schiller Prize awards a cash award of $2,000 and a year's membership in the society to the winner. Submissions for the prize may concentrate on any children's book printed before the year 1901 in any country or any language, but must be written in English. They should be based on investigations into bibliography and printing history broadly conceived and should focus on the physical aspects of the book as historical evidence for studying topics such as history of book publication, production, distribution, collecting or reading.
> *The St. Louis Mercantile Library Prize in American Bibliography:* Awarded every three years, the prize bring a cash award of $2,000 and a year's membership in the Society to researchers who concentrate on some aspect of American history and culture in territories that now comprise the United States. Projects should involve research in bibliography and printing history broadly conceived and focus on the book as historical evidence for studying topics such as the history of book production, publication, distribution, collecting, or reading. Studies of the printing, publishing, and allied trades, as these relate to American history and literature, are also welcome.
> *The William L. Mitchell Prize for Research on Early British Serials:* The prize serves as an encouragement to scholars engaged in bibliographical scholarship on 18th-century periodicals published in English or in any language but within the British Isles and its colonies and former colonies. The winner of the prize receives a cash award of $1,000 and a year's membership in the society.
EIN: 131632509

5763
Margaret T. Biddle Trust Twelfth
(formerly Margaret T. Biddle Paragraph Twelfth Trust)
c/o Cullen and Dykman
100 Quentin Roosevelt Blvd., Ste. 402
Garden City, NY 11530-4850

Foundation type: Independent foundation
Purpose: Financial assistance to needy persons or dependent members of the immediate families of such persons, who have been in the employment of the decedent.
Financial data: Year ended 12/31/2012. Assets, $293,718 (M); Expenditures, $21,844; Total giving, $16,500; Grant to an individual, 1 grant totaling $16,500.
Type of support: Grants for special needs.
Application information: Applications not accepted.
> *Additional information:* Unsolicited requests for funds not considered or accepted.
EIN: 136066488

5764
Big Guy Foundation, Inc.
312 Feeks Ln.
P.O. Box 203
Mill Neck, NY 11765 (516) 671-0746
Contact: Susan Altamore Carusi, Exec. V.P.

Foundation type: Operating foundation
Purpose: Scholarships to indigent residents of NY for attendance at schools in NY.
Financial data: Year ended 12/31/2012. Assets, $75,520 (M); Expenditures, $978,459; Total

giving, $978,169; Grants to individuals, 110 grants totaling $816,023 (high: $29,424, low: $225).
Type of support: Undergraduate support.
Application information: Applications not accepted.
  Additional information: Unsolicited requests for funds not considered or acknowledged.
EIN: 542118808

5765
James Hubert Blake Scholarship Trust
(also known as Eubie Blake Scholarship Fund)
c/o Beldock, Levine & Hoffman, LLP
99 Park Ave., Ste. 1600
New York, NY   10016   (212) 490-0400

Foundation type: Independent foundation
Purpose: Scholarships to instrumental music students, particularly those who intend to be musical performers (i.e. "working musicians"). Special consideration given for individuals studying American ragtime piano. Scholarship funds are paid directly to the school.
Financial data: Year ended 03/31/2013. Assets, $683,077 (M); Expenditures, $77,215; Total giving, $56,000; Grants to individuals, 15 grants totaling $56,000 (high: $7,500, low: $1,000).
Fields of interest: Music; Performing arts, education.
Type of support: Undergraduate support.
Application information: Applications accepted. Application form required.
  Deadline(s): Apr. 30 and Nov. 30
  Applicants should submit the following:
    1) Work samples
    2) Transcripts
    3) Financial information
    4) Letter(s) of recommendation
  Additional information: Application must also include proof of admission or enrollment at an educational institution. Work sample must be a recorded cassette tape or compact disc (30-minute maximum) of the applicant's recent musical performance(s).
EIN: 136836085

5766
Marion Tyler Blake Trust
c/o Beldock, Levine & Hoffman, LLP
99 Park Ave., Ste. 1600
New York, NY   10016-1503   (212) 490-0400
Contact: Elliot L. Hoffman, Tr.

Foundation type: Independent foundation
Purpose: Scholarships to students pursuing their study in music, particularly those interested in fostering greater interest in traditional American ragtime piano studies.
Financial data: Year ended 03/31/2013. Assets, $168,074 (M); Expenditures, $16,638; Total giving, $14,750; Grants to individuals, 4 grants totaling $14,750 (high: $4,000, low: $3,500).
Fields of interest: Music; Performing arts, education.
Type of support: Scholarships—to individuals; Awards/grants by nomination only; Undergraduate support.
Application information: Applications accepted. Application form required.
  Initial approach: Letter
  Send request by: Mail
  Deadline(s): Apr. 30 and Nov. 30
  Applicants should submit the following:
    1) Letter(s) of recommendation
    2) Financial information
    3) Transcripts

Additional information: Applications should also include proof of admission or enrollment at an educational institution, a personal statement and a recorded cassette tape or compact disc of most recent musical performance(s).
Program description:
  Eubie Blake Scholarship Fund: All candidates are nominated by preselected professors of music. Only participants in studies of instrumental music who are preparing for careers as instrumental performing artists are considered. Preference may be shown to applicants who are interested in traditional American ragtime piano studies. Selection criteria include demonstrated musical talent and ability, motivation, and financial need. Grants are $1,500 or $3,000 per student per year. The scholarship is renewable.
EIN: 136836084

5767
Blarney Fund Education Trust
c/o Bell & Company LLP
350 5th Ave., Ste. 7412
New York, NY   10118-7412   (310) 838-5011
Contact: Michael Emmet Walsh, Tr.
Scholarship address: P.O. Box 214, Swanton, VT 05488, tel.: (310) 838-5011

Foundation type: Independent foundation
Purpose: Scholarships to graduating seniors of Bellows Free Academy and Missisquoi Valley Union High School, Franklin County, VT, who are entering or pursuing a two-year or four-year college degree program.
Financial data: Year ended 05/31/2013. Assets, $311,559 (M); Expenditures, $33,010; Total giving, $33,000.
Fields of interest: Education.
Type of support: Support to graduates or students of specific schools; Undergraduate support.
Application information: Applications accepted.
  Deadline(s): May
  Additional information: Contact trust for current application guidelines.
EIN: 036051035

5768
James J. Bloomer Charitable Trust
c/o Chemung Canal Trust Co.
P.O. Box 1522
Elmira, NY   14902-1522

Foundation type: Independent foundation
Purpose: Scholarships to residents of Elmira, NY, who are members of St. Anthony and St. Patrick parishes, for attendance at Catholic colleges and universities in the U.S.
Financial data: Year ended 12/31/2011. Assets, $224,072 (M); Expenditures, $13,730; Total giving, $10,234; Grants to individuals, 7 grants totaling $10,234 (high: $1,462, low: $1,462).
Fields of interest: Catholic agencies & churches.
Type of support: Undergraduate support.
Application information: Applications accepted. Interview required.
  Additional information: Contact foundation for current application deadline/guidelines.
EIN: 166022129

5769
Marlin E. Blosser Trust
1 M&T Plz., 8th Fl.
Buffalo, NY   14203-2309

Foundation type: Independent foundation

Purpose: Scholarships to graduates of Carlisle High School, PA, for higher education.
Financial data: Year ended 12/31/2012. Assets, $244,163 (M); Expenditures, $14,664; Total giving, $10,500.
Fields of interest: Vocational education, post-secondary.
Type of support: Support to graduates or students of specific schools; Technical education support.
Application information: Applications not accepted.
  Additional information: Unsolicited requests for funds not considered or acknowledged.
EIN: 256579913

5770
Blue Mountain Center
P.O. Box 109
Blue Mountain Lake, NY   12812-0109
E-mail: bmc@bluemountaincenter.org; URL: http://www.bluemountaincenter.org

Foundation type: Operating foundation
Purpose: Residencies to writers, visual artists and composers for a period of four weeks. Awards to a promising young journalists or essayists.
Financial data: Year ended 12/31/2012. Assets, $15,454,197 (M); Expenditures, $803,296; Total giving, $15,000; Grant to an individual, 1 grant totaling $5,000.
Fields of interest: Print publishing; Literature.
Type of support: Awards/prizes; Residencies.
Application information: Applications accepted.
  Initial approach: Letter
  Send request by: Mail
  Deadline(s): Feb. 2 for Residency; July 1 for the Margolis Award
  Applicants should submit the following:
    1) SASE
    2) Work samples
  Additional information: Application must also include a $20 application fee for residency.
Program descriptions:
  Residency Program: Residencies are for four weeks, usually between mid-June and Sept. Fourteen to fifteen residents are selected for each session. Spouses may apply separately, and each applicant will be evaluated as an individual. Residents are permitted to attend a maximum of two out of every four years.
  The Richard J. Margolis Award: A one-month residency with a $5,000 prize is given annually to a promising new journalist or essayist whose work recalls Richard Margolis' warmth, humor, and concern for social issues. There should be at least two examples of the writer's work (published or unpublished, 30 pages maximum) and a short biographical note including a description of his or her current and anticipated work.
EIN: 222370485

5771
BMI Foundation, Inc.
7 World Trade Ctr.
250 Greenwich St.
New York, NY   10007-0030   (615) 401-2411
Contact: Porfirio Pina, Pres.
E-mail: info@bmifoundation.org; URL: http://www.bmifoundation.org

Foundation type: Public charity
Purpose: Awards and scholarships to young songwriters and composers. Awards, commissions, and fellowships to music composers.
Publications: Application guidelines; Informational brochure.

Financial data: Year ended 06/30/2011. Assets, $2,401,413 (M); Expenditures, $231,385; Total giving, $202,521; Grants to individuals, totaling $202,521.

Fields of interest: Theater (musical); Music; Music composition; Education; Women.

Type of support: Fellowships; Support to graduates or students of specific schools; Awards/grants by nomination only; Awards/prizes; Undergraduate support.

Application information:
Initial approach: E-mail
Deadline(s): Vary
Additional information: See web site for complete program information.

Program descriptions:
BMI Student Composer Awards: The program is a competition for young composers of classical music. Awards are made on an annual basis for compositions submitted by students actively engaged in the study of music, and all works are judged under pseudonyms.

Boudleaux Bryant Commissions: This program funds the creation of new chamber works by former winners of the BMI Student Composer Awards. Awarded on a regular basis, these commissions were established through the generosity of the family and friends of the late celebrated songwriter, Boudleaux Bryant. For each commission, the BMI Foundation chooses a prominent contemporary music performer or organization and they in turn select a former BMI Student Composer Award-winning composer to write the commissioned work. This program is by invitation only, no applications accepted.

Carlos Surinach Commissions: This program funds the creation of new works by former winners of the BMI Student Composer Awards. Established by a generous bequest from the late classical composer Carlos Surinach, the program identifies orchestras, chamber music groups and classical soloists with a strong record of performing contemporary music. For each commission, the selected performer or organization chooses a former BMI Student Composer Award-winning composer and premieres the commissioned work. This program is by invitation only, no applications accepted.

Charlie Parker Jazz Composition Prize: This prize is awarded annually to the best new work created in the BMI Jazz Composers Workshop. The winner is awarded a $3,000 commission to write a new work to be premiered at the following year's showcase concert.

Harriette Schiff Roth Scholarship: The scholarship consists of an award to a female student at or graduate of Jackson Memorial High School, NJ, for the purpose of assisting in paying for voice lessons either under private tutelage or at a college, university or music school. The scholarship is by invitation only, no applications accepted.

Jean Pratt Scholarship: The scholarship is given annually to a music student in Coffeyville Community College in Coffeyville, Kansas.

Jerry Bock Musical Theatre Award: The award is given to a project developed in the BMI Lehman Engel Musical Theatre Workshop. The award is a $2,000 grant split between the composer and lyricist of the project.

Jerry Harrington Musical Theatre Award: The award is presented annually to a writer in each of the BMI Lehman Engel Musical Theatre Workshop groups: First Year ($500), Second Year ($600), Advanced ($1,000) and Librettist ($500). Awardees are selected by the moderators of the workshop groups.

John Lennon Scholarship Program: The program recognizes young songwriters working in any genre, between the ages of 17 and 24. Three scholarships with prizes totaling $20,000 will be awarded to the best original songs submitted to the competition. Entries are solicited from applicants who are either a member of the National Association for Music Education/MENC collegiate chapter in their school, or who are a current student or alumnus/alumna of one of the following schools: University of Alabama, Appalachian State University, Bard College, Belmont University, Berklee College of Music, Birmingham-Southern College, Brown University, University of California Los Angeles, California State University Northridge, Carnegie Mellon University, Catawba College, University of Cincinnati, City College of New York, Clark Atlanta University, Colorado State University, University of Colorado Boulder, Columbia College (Chicago), DePaul University, Drexel University, Elmhurst College, Emory University, University of Florida, Florida State University, Full Sail, Georgia State University, Harvard University, University of Houston, Hunter College, University of Idaho, Indiana University, Ithaca College, Lehigh University, Loyola University (New Orleans), University of Memphis, University of Miami, University of Michigan, Michigan State University, Middle Tennessee State University, Millikin University, New England Conservatory, New York University, University of North Alabama, University of North Carolina Chapel Hill, University of North Texas, Northwestern University, Oberlin College, Purchase College (SUNY), University of Southern California, University of Texas at Austin, University of Utah, Vanderbilt University, Wilkes Community College, and Yale University.

Lionel Newman Conducting Scholarship: The scholarship gives young conductors the opportunity to work for a three-year period with the Los Angeles Young Musicians Foundation Debut Orchestra. This includes not only the opportunity to work with well-known conductors but to conduct works independently.

Milton Adolphus Award: This award is given on an annual basis to a student at the LaGuardia High School of Music and Art in New York City for excellence in jazz improvisation. The award is by nomination only, no applications accepted.

peermusic Latin Scholarship: This annual competition awards a $5,000 scholarship for the best song or instrumental work in any Latin genre. The competition is open to songwriters and composers who are current students at colleges and universities located in the U.S. and Puerto Rico. Applicants must be between the ages of 16 and 24. All words and music must be original.

Robert Sherman Scholarship: This $1,000 scholarship is awarded each year to a talented student composer studying musical theatre.

Theodora Zavin Scholarship: The scholarship is presented annually to a graduating senior musician at LaGuardia High School of Music and Art & Performing Arts in New York City.

Women's Music Commission: The classical music competition for women composers ages 20 through 30 who are citizens or permanent resident of the United States offers the winning composer $5,000 commission to create a new work. For each competition, the Foundation partners with a different world class performer, ensemble or presenter, who presents the premiere performance. Entries are judged under pseudonyms.

Woody Guthrie Fellowship Program: In cooperation with the Woody Guthrie Foundation, the foundation offers short-term fellowships to support scholarly use of the Woody Guthrie Archives Research Collection. A limited number of fellowships will be selected annually with a value of up to $2,500 per recipient to help defray travel to New York City and residence expenses for the duration of the fellowship. The length of the fellowship will depend on the applicant's research proposal, but is normally limited from one to six months.
EIN: 133249311

5772
The Bogliasco Foundation, Inc.
10 Rockefeller Plz. 16th Fl.
New York, NY 10020
E-mail: info@bfny.org; URL: http://www.bfny.org

Foundation type: Operating foundation

Purpose: Residential fellowships at the Liguria Study Center in Bogliasco, Italy, for individuals doing creative or scholarly work in the arts and humanities.

Financial data: Year ended 06/30/2012. Assets, $1,529,981 (M); Expenditures, $1,481,489; Total giving, $16,000; Grants to individuals, 6 grants totaling $16,000 (high: $3,000, low: $2,000).

Fields of interest: Film/video; Visual arts; Architecture; Dance; Theater; Music; History/archaeology; Language (classical); Literature; Philosophy/ethics; Landscaping.

Type of support: Fellowships; Residencies.

Application information: Applications accepted. Application form required. Application form available on the grantmaker's web site.
Initial approach: Letter or e-mail
Copies of proposal: 1
Deadline(s): Jan. 15 for the fall/winter semester and Apr. 15 for the winter/spring semester
Applicants should submit the following:
1) Work samples
2) Letter(s) of recommendation
3) Curriculum vitae
Additional information: Application should also include a project description.

Program description:
Bogliasco Fellowships: Fellowships are granted to qualified persons for residencies at the Liguria disciplines of archaeology, architecture, classics, dance, film or video, history, landscape architecture, literature, music, philosophy, theater, and visual arts. An approved project is presumed to lead to the completion of a major work followed by publication, performance, production, or exhibition. Fellowships are scheduled during the two semesters of the academic year, and usually have a duration of either one month or a half semester.
EIN: 133632296

5773
The Giorgio Bon Charitable Trust
25-84 Steinway St.
Astoria, NY 11103-3706

Foundation type: Independent foundation

Purpose: Scholarships to individuals for tuition and/or board for higher education.

Financial data: Year ended 12/31/2010. Assets, $0 (M); Expenditures, $76,313; Total giving, $72,311.

Fields of interest: Higher education.

Type of support: Scholarships—to individuals.

Application information: Applications not accepted.
Additional information: Unsolicited requests for funds not considered or acknowledged.
EIN: 336331514

5774
The Bone Marrow Foundation, Inc.
515 Madison Ave., Ste. 1130
New York, NY 10022 (212) 838-3029
FAX: (212) 223-0081;
E-mail: thebmf@bonemarrow.org; Toll-free tel.:
(800) 365-1336; URL: http://www.bonemarrow.org

Foundation type: Public charity
Purpose: Grants to bone marrow transplant patients for medical and other related expenses.
Publications: Newsletter.
Financial data: Year ended 12/31/2012. Assets, $399,256 (M); Expenditures, $625,813; Total giving, $261,735; Grants to individuals, totaling $261,735.
Fields of interest: Nerve, muscle & bone diseases.
Type of support: Grants for special needs.
Application information: Application form required.
Initial approach: Telephone or e-mail
Additional information: Contact your physician, nurse coordinator or social worker for an application.
Program description:
Patient Aid Program: This program covers the cost for donor searches, compatibility testing, bone marrow procurement, medication, transportation, housing expenses and many other ancillary costs associated with a transplant. The application requires information about diagnosis, treatment, financial status information from the social worker and physician. The social worker must be contacted to apply for the Patient Aid Program grant. Applications are only accepted from affiliated institutions. See Web site for affiliated centers.
EIN: 133674198

5775
Bonei Olam, Inc.
1755 46th St.
Brooklyn, NY 11204-1270 (718) 252-1212
URL: http://www.boneiolam.org

Foundation type: Public charity
Purpose: Assistance towards the cost of fertility related treatments to Jewish individuals. Interest-free loans are also available for treatments.
Publications: Informational brochure.
Financial data: Year ended 12/31/2011. Assets, $1,180,893 (M); Expenditures, $6,282,468; Total giving, $4,089,183; Grants to individuals, totaling $3,739,183.
Fields of interest: Reproductive health, fertility; Family services; Jewish agencies & synagogues.
Type of support: Grants for special needs; Loans— to individuals.
Application information:
Initial approach: Tel.
Additional information: Contact foundation for eligibility criteria.
EIN: 113473757

5776
Walter & Cecile Borchert Scholarship Fund
1100 Wehrle Dr., 2nd Fl.
Amherst, NY 14221 (716) 842-5506

Foundation type: Independent foundation
Purpose: Scholarships to graduating seniors of Fayetteville-Manlius High School, NY, and Skaneateles High School, NY, for undergraduate education.

Financial data: Year ended 02/28/2013. Assets, $670,905 (M); Expenditures, $29,364; Total giving, $20,000.
Type of support: Support to graduates or students of specific schools; Undergraduate support.
Application information: Applications accepted.
Initial approach: Letter
Deadline(s): None
Applicants should submit the following:
1) Resume
2) FAFSA
3) Essay
Additional information: Application should also include financial aid information. Students apply through high school Career Centers.
EIN: 166384392

5777
Bossak-Heilbron Charitable Foundation, Inc.
c/o Shulman, Jones & Co.
287 Bowman Ave.
Purchase, NY 10577 (914) 967-5828
Contact: Jane Heilbron, Pres. and Treas.
Application address: 720 Milton Rd., Rye, NY, 10580, tel.:(914) 967-5828

Foundation type: Independent foundation
Purpose: Project grants primarily to residents of WA and NY in the performing arts, especially dance.
Publications: Application guidelines.
Financial data: Year ended 10/31/2013. Assets, $1,552,195 (M); Expenditures, $61,918; Total giving, $53,200; Grants to individuals, 5 grants totaling $9,500 (high: $3,000, low: $1,000).
Fields of interest: Dance.
Type of support: Program development; Grants to individuals; Awards/prizes.
Application information: Applications accepted. Application form required.
Initial approach: Letter
Copies of proposal: 3
Applicants should submit the following:
1) Work samples
2) Proposal
EIN: 133862827

5778
Robert T. & Beatrice V. Bowman Scholarship Trust
1 M T Plz., 8th Fl.
Buffalo, NY 14203

Foundation type: Independent foundation
Purpose: Scholarships to graduates of South Western High School, PA, who are residents of Penn, Manheim, or West Manheim townships, PA.
Financial data: Year ended 12/31/2012. Assets, $549,784 (M); Expenditures, $33,181; Total giving, $27,000.
Type of support: Support to graduates or students of specific schools; Undergraduate support.
Application information: Applications not accepted.
Additional information: Unsolicited requests for funds not considered or acknowledged.
EIN: 237684863

5779
The Brackett Foundation
P.O. Box 8
Hamilton, NY 13346-0008 (315) 824-3435
Contact: Thomas Brackett, C.E.O.
E-mail: tomb@twcny.rr.com; URL: http://brackett.colgate.edu/

Foundation type: Public charity
Purpose: Educational support to refugees, hill tribe people and displaced persons from Burma pursuing their education in Thailand and India.
Publications: Annual report; Financial statement; Informational brochure; Newsletter.
Financial data: Year ended 12/31/2012. Assets, $691,445 (M); Expenditures, $279,566; Total giving, $267,094.
Fields of interest: Elementary school/education; Secondary school/education; International relief; Immigrants/refugees.
Type of support: Foreign applicants; Undergraduate support; Grants for special needs.
Application information: Applications not accepted.
Additional information: Unsolicited requests for funds not considered.
Program description:
Special Needs Grants: This grant supports projects directed by target population to provide elementary schools (where there are no schools) and boarding houses (to bring children from remote villages to areas providing schools) and to supplement teacher's salaries.
EIN: 161523586

5780
Lorraine M. And Eugene P. Brady Memorial Scholarship Trust
P.O. Box 456
Lockport, NY 14095 (716) 439-6422
Application address: 250 Linco Ln.Ave.,Lockport,NY 14094, tel.: (716) 439-6422

Foundation type: Independent foundation
Purpose: Scholarships to graduates of Lockport School District, NY, who do not qualify for financial aid but would otherwise be unable to attend the college of their choice.
Financial data: Year ended 12/31/2011. Assets, $285,563 (M); Expenditures, $25,155; Total giving, $17,750; Grants to individuals, 27 grants totaling $17,750 (high: $3,000, low: $250).
Type of support: Support to graduates or students of specific schools; Undergraduate support.
Application information: Applications accepted. Application form required.
Deadline(s): Nov. 30
EIN: 166411714

5781
Joel Braverman Foundation, Inc.
1609 Ave. J
Brooklyn, NY 11230-3711
Contact: Joel Wolowelsky, Mgr.
Application address: Yeshivah of Flatbush

Foundation type: Operating foundation
Purpose: Scholarships to graduates of the Yeshiva of Flatbush Joel Braverman High School in Brooklyn, NY, for one year of study at universities or yeshivas in Israel.
Financial data: Year ended 07/31/2013. Assets, $314,143 (M); Expenditures, $2,159; Total giving, $11,733; Grants to individuals, 4 grants totaling $11,733 (high: $10,000, low: $400).

Fields of interest: Theological school/education; Jewish agencies & synagogues.
Type of support: Support to graduates or students of specific schools; Undergraduate support.
Application information: Applications accepted. Interview required.
Initial approach: Letter
Deadline(s): None
EIN: 116036594

5782
Breast Cancer Help, Inc.
32 Park Ave.
Bay Shore, NY 11706-6027 (631) 675-9003
E-mail: breastcancerinc@optonline.net;
URL: http://www.breastcancerhelpinc.org

Foundation type: Public charity
Purpose: Scholarships to Long Island, NY high school students, who have had a parent, legal guardian or have been themselves, diagnosed with breast cancer, pursuing higher education.
Publications: Informational brochure; Newsletter.
Financial data: Year ended 12/31/2012. Assets, $526,533 (M); Expenditures, $146,747; Total giving, $2,000; Grants to individuals, totaling $2,000.
Fields of interest: Higher education; Breast cancer.
Type of support: Scholarships—to individuals.
Application information: Applications accepted. Application form required.
Send request by: Mail
Deadline(s): Apr. 30
Applicants should submit the following:
1) Letter(s) of recommendation
2) Essay
Additional information: Application should also include acceptance letter from college, university or accredited vocational school, and a physician's letter supporting a cancer diagnosis.
Program description:
Lorraine Pace College Scholarship Program: This one time scholarship of $2,000 is provided to residents of Bay Shore, Islip, Brentwood, Deer Park, North Babylon, Babylon, West Babylon or West Islip, NY diagnosed with breast cancer. Applicant must have been accepted to and plan to attend a two or four year college or university or accredited vocational school upon graduation, and be a U.S. citizen or permanent resident of the U.S.
EIN: 113199345

5783
The Breast Cancer Research Foundation, Inc.
60 E. 56th St., 8th Fl.
New York, NY 10022-3343 (646) 497-2600
Contact: Margaret Mastrianni, Deputy Dir.
FAX: (646) 497-0890; E-mail: bcrf@bcrfcure.org;
Toll-free tel.: (866) 346-3228; URL: http://www.bcrfcure.org

Foundation type: Public charity
Purpose: Grants to individuals engaged in innovative breast cancer research.
Publications: Annual report; Financial statement; Grants list; Informational brochure; Newsletter.
Financial data: Year ended 06/30/2012. Assets, $60,066,003 (M); Expenditures, $45,439,688; Total giving, $40,000,000.
Fields of interest: Breast cancer; Medical research.
Type of support: Research; Grants to individuals; Awards/prizes.
Application information: Applications not accepted.

Additional information: Proposals accepted by invitation of the Medical Advisory Board only.
Program description:
Grants: Grants averaging $250,000 are made to enable brilliant minds to pursue some of their most creative theories. Grants are meant to cover the period extending from Oct. 1 to Sept. 30, with two progress reports due over the year. Grants are paid in two installments, the second of which is contingent upon the board's approval of the organization's progress report.
EIN: 133727250

5784
The Eric Breindel Memorial Foundation, Inc.
c/o Hogan Lovells US LLp, Attn.: HMT
875 3rd Ave.
New York, NY 10022-6225

Foundation type: Independent foundation
Purpose: Scholarships in the form of a prize award to the winners of 2 editorial awards.
Financial data: Year ended 12/31/2011. Assets, $4,005 (M); Expenditures, $44,237; Total giving, $30,000; Grants to individuals, 2 grants totaling $30,000 (high: $20,000, low: $10,000).
Fields of interest: Journalism school/education.
Type of support: Grants to individuals.
Application information: Applications accepted.
Deadline(s): None
Additional information: Two copies should be submitted. The original article with the name and date of the publication, or a photocopy of each. The second copy must be submitted on 8 1/2 x 11 white paper, which can be taken directly from the computer or typewriter. Submissions may be editorials, columns or newstories. "Letters to the Editor" are not eligible for consideration.
EIN: 133995665

5785
Brewster Education Foundation, Inc.
P. O. Box 320
Brewster, NY 10509-0320 (845) 279-5051
E-mail for Teachers' grants: grants@bef.og
E-mail: info@bef.org; URL: http://www.bef.org

Foundation type: Public charity
Purpose: Scholarships to graduating students attending high school in the Brewster Central School District, NY. Grants to teachers of the Brewster Central School District, NY, to develop innovative educational programs.
Publications: Application guidelines; Financial statement; Informational brochure.
Financial data: Year ended 06/30/2012. Assets, $530,060 (M); Expenditures, $83,194; Total giving, $64,983; Grants to individuals, totaling $64,983.
Fields of interest: Education.
Type of support: Program development; Support to graduates or students of specific schools; Awards/prizes; Undergraduate support.
Application information: Applications accepted. Application form required.
Send request by: Online, mail or hand deliver
Deadline(s): Jan. 20 for Grant Program
Additional information: See web site for complete program information.
Program descriptions:
Grant Program: This program provides grants to educators within the Brewster school system, who wish to enact unique, innovative, and/or creative projects of a significant nature. Projects that are not

normally funded through the regular school budget process will be considered. Preference will be given to projects utilizing a team approach at a grade level, multi-grade level, or departmental level, or that use an interdisciplinary approach, with a successful project benefiting the greatest number of students.
June H. Weigelt Memorial Scholarship: A $500 scholarship is given to a Brewster High School yearbook staff member who is voted 'most valuable to production' each year by the yearbook staff and advisor.
EIN: 222553348

5786
Marion Brill Scholarship Foundation, Inc.
P.O. Box 480
Ilion, NY 13357-0480 (315) 894-9033
Contact: Laurie Landry, Secy.

Foundation type: Operating foundation
Purpose: Scholarships to residents of Ilion, NY, who are also graduates of Ilion High School, NY.
Financial data: Year ended 06/30/2013. Assets, $275,110 (M); Expenditures, $16,642; Total giving, $12,000; Grants to individuals, 12 grants totaling $12,000 (high: $1,600, low: $500).
Type of support: Support to graduates or students of specific schools.
Application information: Application form required.
Deadline(s): Apr. 15
Additional information: Application should include financial aid forms. High school seniors should also include a transcript and a college letter of acceptance.
EIN: 222373170

5787
E. Brink Trust Scholarship Fund
c/o Alliance Bank, N.A.
160 Main St.
Oneida, NY 13421-1629

Foundation type: Independent foundation
Purpose: Scholarships to male graduates of Union-Endicott High School, NY, for higher education.
Financial data: Year ended 12/31/2012. Assets, $852,904 (M); Expenditures, $51,120; Total giving, $41,102; Grants to individuals, 20 grants totaling $41,102 (high: $2,085, low: $1,500).
Fields of interest: Men.
Type of support: Support to graduates or students of specific schools; Undergraduate support.
Application information: Applications not accepted.
Additional information: Unsolicited requests for funds not considered or acknowledged.
EIN: 166076060

5788
The Bristol-Myers Squibb Patient Assistance Foundation, Inc.
345 Park Ave.
New York, NY 10154-0004 (800) 736-0003
FAX: (866) 736-1611; Application address: P.O. Box 220769, Charlotte, NC 28222-0769;
URL: http://www.bmspaf.org/index.html

Foundation type: Operating foundation
Purpose: Financial assistance for prescription medicines to indigent patients who have no private prescription drug insurance and who are not eligible for prescription drug coverage through Medicaid or other government programs.

Publications: Application guidelines; Informational brochure.
Financial data: Year ended 12/31/2012. Assets, $18,684,630 (M); Expenditures, $562,094,036; Total giving, $548,857,548; Grants to individuals, totaling $548,857,548.
Fields of interest: Economically disadvantaged.
Type of support: Grants for special needs.
Application information: Applications accepted. Application form required. Application form available on the grantmaker's web site.
  Initial approach: Letter or telephone
  Deadline(s): None
  Additional information: Applications must be completed by the patient and a healthcare provider. Applicants must attach a photocopy of the annual household income, including Federal tax form (1040), social security income (SSA 1099), pension, interest, retirement, or child support, if applicable.
EIN: 223622487

5789
Broadcasters Foundation of America
(formerly Broadcasters Foundation, Inc.)
125 W. 55th St., 21st Fl.
New York, NY 10019-5366
E-mail: info@thebfoa.org; URL: http://www.broadcastersfoundation.org/

Foundation type: Independent foundation
Purpose: Financial assistance to needy members of the broadcast industry.
Publications: Newsletter.
Financial data: Year ended 12/31/2012. Assets, $4,823,818 (M); Expenditures, $1,742,209; Total giving, $698,600; Grants to individuals, 68 grants totaling $698,600 (high: $18,000, low: $1,000).
Fields of interest: Media/communications; Print publishing.
Type of support: Grants for special needs.
Application information: Applications accepted. Application form required.
  Initial approach: Letter
  Deadline(s): None
  Additional information: Grants are paid directly to the individual, for his or her general welfare. The foundation does not pay any bills directly.
EIN: 131975618

5790
Broadway Cares/Equity Fights AIDS
165 W. 46th St., Ste. 1300
New York, NY 10036-2508 (212) 840-0770
Contact: Tom Viola, Exec. Dir.
FAX: (212) 840-0551;
E-mail: info@broadwaycares.org; URL: http://www.broadwaycares.org/

Foundation type: Public charity
Purpose: Emergency financial assistance to women in the entertainment industry who are coping with critical health concerns such as breast, cervical and ovarian cancers, domestic violence, chemical dependency, mental health issues, and other critical conditions.
Publications: Application guidelines; Annual report; Financial statement; Informational brochure; Newsletter.
Financial data: Year ended 09/30/2011. Assets, $1,821,846 (M); Expenditures, $16,564,922; Total giving, $9,320,200; Grants to individuals, totaling $7,500.
Fields of interest: Arts, artist's services.
Type of support: Grants for special needs.

Application information:
  Initial approach: Email
  Additional information: Contact foundation for further details.
EIN: 133458820

5791
Brockway Foundation for the Needy of the Village and Township of Homer, New York
P.O. Box 121
Homer, NY 13077 (607) 749-3382

Foundation type: Independent foundation
Purpose: Financial assistance only to needy residents of the Homer, NY, area.
Financial data: Year ended 12/31/2012. Assets, $541,772 (M); Expenditures, $29,428; Total giving, $22,925; Grants to individuals, 8 grants totaling $21,925 (high: $3,250, low: $1,400).
Fields of interest: Economically disadvantaged.
Type of support: Grants for special needs.
Application information: Applications accepted.
  Initial approach: Letter
  Deadline(s): None
EIN: 156021436

5792
The Charles R. Bronfman Prize Foundation
110 E. 59th St., 26th Fl.
New York, NY 10022 (212) 931-0127
Contact: Jeffrey Solomon, Pres.
URL: http://www.thecharlesbronfmanprize.com

Foundation type: Independent foundation
Purpose: Awards by nomination to an individual or team who has made significant humanitarian contribution for the betterment of the world.
Financial data: Year ended 12/31/2012. Assets, $3,768,424 (M); Expenditures, $601,220; Total giving, $105,000; Grant to an individual, 1 grant totaling $100,000.
Fields of interest: Human services, personal services.
Type of support: Awards/grants by nomination only; Awards/prizes.
Application information: Application form available on the grantmaker's web site.
  Initial approach: Telephone or e-mail
  Send request by: Mail
  Deadline(s): Jan. 13
  Applicants should submit the following:
    1) Resume
    2) Curriculum vitae
  Additional information: Completion of formal nomination only. Nomination letter should include three additional letters of reference. Application should also include copy of birth certificate or passport page.
Program description:
  The Charles R. Bronfman Prize: An award of $100,000 to an individual or team under 50 years of age whose humanitarian work has contributed to the betterment of the world. The candidates must be nominated, must exhibit excellence in their chosen field, and must inspire, through his/her work, the next generations of Jews.
EIN: 043612920

5793
Bronx Council on the Arts
1738 Hone Ave.
Bronx, NY 10461-1486 (718) 931-9500
Contact: Bill Aguado, Pres. and Exec. Dir.
FAX: (718) 409-6445; E-mail: info@bronxarts.org;
URL: http://www.bronxarts.org

Foundation type: Public charity
Purpose: Grants and fellowships to artists working in literary, media, performing, and visual arts who are residents of the Bronx, NY.
Publications: Application guidelines; Annual report; Financial statement; Informational brochure.
Financial data: Year ended 06/30/2011. Assets, $1,496,893 (M); Expenditures, $1,526,907.
Fields of interest: Visual arts; Theater (playwriting); Literature.
Type of support: Fellowships; Grants to individuals.
Application information: Applications accepted. Application form required.
  Initial approach: Letter or telephone
  Deadline(s): Jan. 23 for BRIO
  Additional information: See web site for further application guidelines.
Program descriptions:
  Arts Fund: Grant of up to $5,000 are available to Bronx-based arts organization and artists with new public projects that have not taken place due to lack of funding or projects already scheduled for which additional funds would have a significant impact.
  Arts-in-Education Grants: The foundation provides funds for artists and organizations to work in Bronx schools.
  Bronx Recognizes Its Own (BRIO): 25 grants of $3,000 each are provided to literary, media, performing, and visual artists who live in the Bronx, NY. Winners must complete a one-time public service activity to receive their complete award.
  Bronx Writers' Center Fellowship: The foundation provides fellowship opportunities for two literary artists to receive a $5,000 grant.
  Chapter One: The foundation provides opportunities for emerging novelists to share their work with an audience, while emphasizing the importance of a strong first chapter. Winners receive a $1,000 honorarium.
EIN: 132601303

5794
The Bronx Museum of the Arts
1040 Grand Concourse
Bronx, NY 10456-3999
Contact: Holly Block, Exec. Dir.
FAX: (718) 681-6181;
E-mail: aim@bronxmuseum.org; URL: http://www.bronxmuseum.org/

Foundation type: Public charity
Purpose: Support to emerging visual artists from the New York metropolitan area.
Financial data: Year ended 06/30/2011. Assets, $3,349,169 (M); Expenditures, $2,332,370.
Fields of interest: Visual arts.
Type of support: Project support.
Application information: Application form required.
  Initial approach: Telephone or e-mail
  Deadline(s): June 30
  Applicants should submit the following:
    1) SASE
    2) Resume
  Additional information: Application must also include artist statement, 8-10 35mm slides, and $10 application fee.
Program description:
  Artist in the Marketplace (AIM): This program provides professional development opportunities to

emerging artists in the greater New York metropolitan area. The program comprises a twelve-week seminar program offered to artists annually in the fall and the spring, culminating with an annual group exhibition and accompanying catalogue. The program is limited to 36 artists each year (18 for the fall semester and 18 for the spring)
EIN: 132709368

5795
Bronx Shepherds Restoration Corporation
1932 Washington Ave.
Bronx, NY   10457-4317   (718) 299-0500
Contact: Ted Jefferson, Exec. Dir.
FAX: (718) 299-1512;
E-mail: info@bronxshepherds.org; URL: http://www.bronxshepherds.org

Foundation type: Public charity
Purpose: Assistance to low to moderate income families of the Bronx, NY with affordable housing, and energy conservation. Scholarships to graduating high school seniors who have been accepted into college.
Financial data: Year ended 12/31/2011. Assets, $5,595,200 (M); Expenditures, $7,341,177.
Fields of interest: Higher education; Economically disadvantaged.
Type of support: Scholarships—to individuals; Grants for special needs.
Application information: Contact the corporation for additional information.
EIN: 133013030

5796
Brooklyn Architects Scholarship Foundation, Inc.
41 2nd St.
Brooklyn, NY   11231-4801   (718) 625-7233

Foundation type: Public charity
Purpose: Scholarships to college students studying architecture at accredited institutions of higher learning.
Financial data: Year ended 12/31/2011. Assets, $43,471 (M); Expenditures, $14,980; Total giving, $10,000.
Fields of interest: Architecture.
Type of support: Scholarships—to individuals.
Application information: Contact the foundation for additional information.
EIN: 113684284

5797
The Brooklyn Arts Council
(also known as BAC)
55 Washington St., Ste. 218
Brooklyn, NY   11201-1074   (718) 625-0080
Contact: Ella J. Weiss, Pres.
FAX: (718) 625-3294;
E-mail: bac@brooklynartscouncil.org; E-Mail for Ella J. Weiss: ejweiss@brooklynartscouncil.org

Foundation type: Public charity
Purpose: Giving primarily to artists in the Brooklyn, NY, area to promote and sustain the arts.
Publications: Informational brochure (including application guidelines); Newsletter.
Financial data: Year ended 06/30/2011. Assets, $1,130,366 (M); Expenditures, $2,455,163; Total giving, $366,164; Grants to individuals, totaling $157,963.
Fields of interest: Arts, artist's services.
Type of support: Fiscal agent/sponsor.
Application information: Applications accepted.

Additional information: Contact foundation for current application deadline/guidelines.
Program descriptions:
Artist-Community Collaboration Award: Support is available to individual artists to support the creation and presentation of new work, in which the artist engages the Brooklyn community in the creative process. Applications are accepted in the categories of visual arts/photography/crafts, film/video/media, and design/architecture.
DCA Regrant Program: Funding is available to nonprofits and individuals to support high-quality arts projects in all disciplines that reach the Brooklyn public and enrich the cultural life of the borough.
Fiscal Sponsorship Program: The Brooklyn Arts Council provides fiscal sponsorship to individual artists or groups of artists to allow them to raise funds for a specific project, or to small arts organizations allowing them to operate and raise funds during the period in which they are applying for their non-profit status. Those interested should write a request describing the proposed project, the background of the artist(s), and/or an organizational description and mission statement. Proposals are considered as they are received. If the council agrees to sponsor an individual or organization a formal fiscal sponsorship letter is written.
EIN: 237072915

5798
Brooklyn Arts Exchange, Inc.
(also known as BAX)
421 5th Ave., 3rd Fl.
Brooklyn, NY   11215-3315   (718) 832-0018
Contact: Marya Warshaw, Exec. Dir.
FAX: (718) 832-9189; E-mail: info@bax.org; E-Mail for Marya Warshaw: marya@bax.org; URL: http://www.bax.org

Foundation type: Public charity
Purpose: Residencies to dance and theater artists residing in New York, NY.
Publications: Grants list; Newsletter.
Financial data: Year ended 06/30/2011. Assets, $424,223 (M); Expenditures, $985,542.
Fields of interest: Dance; Theater.
Type of support: Residencies.
Application information: Applications accepted. Application form required. Application form available on the grantmaker's web site. Interview required.
Initial approach: Letter, telephone or e-mail
Send request by: Mail
Copies of proposal: 6
Deadline(s): Contact foundation for current application deadline
Final notification: Applicants notified by May 15
Applicants should submit the following:
1) Proposal
2) Resume
3) SASE
4) Work samples
Program descriptions:
Artist in Residence Program: Exceptional artists are provided with an artistic home base for one two-year period, giving them a tangible sense of permanence and place. Resident artists have the use of four spaces suitable for theater, dance, and performance work; and are offered up to 200 hours of free rehearsal space, a stipend, formal presentations of new works and works in progress, and administrative and technical support.
Space Grant Program: The program is designed to give Brooklyn based choreographers, playwrights, and multi-disciplinary artists the

opportunity to create new work in a setting that is conducive to working deeply and exploring new territory. Awards are between 70 hours of free space in one of the organization's four spaces, and are granted one time per year; hours must be used in a selected three month period.
EIN: 113071458

5799
Broome County Arts Council, Inc.
81 State St., Ste. 501
Binghamton, NY   13901-4703   (607) 723-4620
Contact: Sharon Ball, Exec. Dir.
FAX: (607) 723-2232;
E-mail: information@bcartscouncil.com;
URL: http://www.bcartscouncil.com

Foundation type: Public charity
Purpose: Grants to artists residing in Broome County, NY to provide high-quality arts programming or an arts project for their community.
Publications: Application guidelines; Informational brochure.
Financial data: Year ended 12/31/2011. Assets, $311,013 (M); Expenditures, $388,403; Total giving, $271,000; Grants to individuals, totaling $10,300.
Fields of interest: Arts.
Type of support: Program development.
Application information: Applications accepted. Application form required. Application form available on the grantmaker's web site.
Initial approach: Telephone
Send request by: Mail or in person
Copies of proposal: 8
Deadline(s): Jan. 15
Final notification: Applicants notified in two months
EIN: 161279751

5800
Brown Brothers Harriman & Co. Undergraduate Fund
140 Broadway, Tax-117
New York, NY   10005-1108

Foundation type: Company-sponsored foundation
Purpose: Scholarships to children of employees of The Brown Brothers Harriman & Co., based on scholastic ability and financial need.
Financial data: Year ended 07/31/2012. Assets, $1,356,748 (M); Expenditures, $101,650; Total giving, $84,250; Grants to individuals, 25 grants totaling $84,250 (high: $5,850, low: $1,000).
Type of support: Employee-related scholarships; Undergraduate support.
Application information: Applications accepted. Application form required.
Deadline(s): May 1
Applicants should submit the following:
1) Transcripts
2) SAT
Additional information: Applications distributed to employees only.
Company name: Brown Brothers Harriman & Co., The
EIN: 136169140

5801
The Arch and Bruce Brown Foundation
16 Sterling Pl
Brooklyn, NY   11217

Foundation type: Independent foundation

Purpose: Grants and awards to writers whose work is based on Gay and Lesbian lifestyle in a positive manner.
Financial data: Year ended 12/31/2012. Assets, $0 (M); Expenditures, $7,653; Total giving, $4,000.
Fields of interest: Theater (playwriting); Literature.
Type of support: Awards/prizes.
Application information: Applications accepted.
  Deadline(s): Nov.30
  Additional information: Application must include a complete manuscript, a piano-vocal score or full score, a demo tape, a screenplay, treatment or prospectus, and a SASE.
Program description:
  Writers Awards: Awards are granted to writers in three rotating disciplines: Theatre, Full-length Fiction, and Short Stories. All works submitted must present the gay and lesbian lifestyle in a positive manner and be based on, or inspired by, a historic person, culture, event or work of art. Awards are $1,000 and are not limited to a single writer.
EIN: 133782849

5802
Buffalo Sabres Alumni Association
c/o Robert Travis
45 Bryant Woods N.
Amherst, NY 14228-3600 (716) 630-2400
Contact: Robert Travis, Treas. and Dir.
Scholarship address: The Buffalo Sabres Alumni Scholarship Program, c/o Buffalo Sabres Alumni Assoc., First Niagara Ctr., 1 Seymour H. Knox III Plz., Buffalo, NY 14203
URL: http://www.sabresalumni.com/

Foundation type: Independent foundation
Purpose: Scholarships to graduating high school seniors of Western New York (within the 716 and 585 area codes) and Southern Ontario (within the 905 area code) for postsecondary education.
Financial data: Year ended 12/31/2012. Assets, $544,185 (M); Expenditures, $1,282,422; Total giving, $623,020. Scholarships—to individuals amount not specified.
Fields of interest: Higher education; Scholarships/financial aid.
Type of support: Scholarships—to individuals.
Application information: Applications accepted. Application form required. Application form available on the grantmaker's web site.
  Initial approach: Application
  Send request by: Mail
  Deadline(s): July 1
  Final notification: Recipients notified on or about Aug. 29
  Applicants should submit the following:
    1) Essay
    2) GPA
    3) Transcripts
Program description:
  Buffalo Sabres Alumni Scholarship Program: Scholarships are available to legal residents of Western New York (within the 716 and 585 area codes) and Southern Ontario, Canada (within the 905 area code) who are, or will be, high school seniors graduating in the spring of current year who plan to, and do, enroll in a full-time undergraduate course of study at an accredited college or university in the U.S. or Canada for the fall term of the next school year.
EIN: 161356116

5803
Buffalo Urban League, Inc.
15 Genesee St.
Buffalo, NY 14203-1405 (716) 250-2400
Contact: Brenda W. McDuffie, Pres. and C.E.O.
FAX: (716) 854-8960; *URL:* http://www.buffalourbanleague.org

Foundation type: Public charity
Purpose: Scholarships to students residing in the Buffalo, NY, area for undergraduate and graduate education.
Publications: Annual report; Newsletter.
Financial data: Year ended 03/31/2012. Assets, $1,200,427 (M); Expenditures, $3,484,731; Total giving, $63,804; Grants to individuals, totaling $63,804.
Type of support: Graduate support; Undergraduate support.
Application information: Applications accepted. Application form required. Application form available on the grantmaker's web site. Interview required.
  Deadline(s): Contact foundation for current application deadline
  Final notification: Applicants notified before June 26
  Applicants should submit the following:
    1) Letter(s) of recommendation
    2) Transcripts
    3) SAR
    4) Financial information
    5) Essay
  Additional information: Application should also include college acceptance letter.
EIN: 160743940

5804
Elizabeth Roosa Buisch Memorial Scholarship Fund
1 Steuban Sq.
Hornell, NY 14843-1699

Foundation type: Independent foundation
Purpose: Scholarships to graduating seniors of Hornell High School, NY.
Financial data: Year ended 12/31/2012. Assets, $238,837 (M); Expenditures, $19,439; Total giving, $15,000; Grants to individuals, 2 grants totaling $5,000 (high: $2,500, low: $2,500).
Fields of interest: Scholarships/financial aid.
Type of support: Support to graduates or students of specific schools; Awards/grants by nomination only; Undergraduate support.
Application information: Contact foundation for current application deadline/guidelines.
EIN: 161501166

5805
Belle C. Burnett Foundation
P.O. Box 573
Salem, NY 12865-0573 (518) 854-6010
Application address: c/o Salem Central School, Attn.: Guidance Office, E. Broadway, Salem, NY 12865-1301

Foundation type: Independent foundation
Purpose: Scholarships to graduating seniors from Salem Central High School, NY.
Financial data: Year ended 12/31/2011. Assets, $124,319 (M); Expenditures, $7,105; Total giving, $5,500; Grants to individuals, 4 grants totaling $5,500 (high: $2,000, low: $1,000).
Type of support: Support to graduates or students of specific schools; Undergraduate support.

Application information: Application form required.
  Deadline(s): Jan. 1 through June 1
EIN: 146018940

5806
The Burrows Little Falls Foundation
501 W. Main St.
Little Falls, NY 13365-1829 (315) 823-2300
Contact: Carolyn Zaklukiewicz, Tr.

Foundation type: Operating foundation
Purpose: Scholarships to individuals of Little Falls, NY for higher education.
Financial data: Year ended 12/31/2011. Assets, $3,691,668 (M); Expenditures, $176,101; Total giving, $148,287.
Fields of interest: Education.
Type of support: Scholarships—to individuals.
Application information: Applications accepted.
  Initial approach: Letter
  Deadline(s): None
EIN: 223059155

5807
The Buttonwood Foundation, Inc.
c/o Louis Sternbach & Co. LLP
11 Wall St., 21st Fl.
New York, NY 10005-1905
Contact: Jose W. Noyes, Pres.

Foundation type: Public charity
Purpose: Scholarships, grants and honorarium to qualifying college students of New York Stock Exchange families for postsecondary education.
Financial data: Year ended 12/31/2011. Assets, $6,345,708 (M); Expenditures, $271,093; Total giving, $198,105; Grants to individuals, totaling $198,105.
Fields of interest: Education.
Type of support: Grants to individuals; Scholarships—to individuals.
Application information: Applications not accepted.
  Additional information: Unsolicited requests for funds not considered or acknowledged.
EIN: 136163559

5808
Henry Calman Trust
c/o Alliance Bank, N.A.
160 Main St.
Oneida, NY 13421-1629

Foundation type: Independent foundation
Purpose: Scholarships to students attending The Juilliard School, NY for continuing education in the arts.
Financial data: Year ended 12/31/2012. Assets, $529,454 (M); Expenditures, $27,747; Total giving, $19,830; Grant to an individual, 1 grant totaling $19,830.
Fields of interest: Performing arts, education.
Type of support: Support to graduates or students of specific schools.
Application information: Applications not accepted.
  Additional information: Unsolicited requests for funds not considered or acknowledged.
EIN: 562604194

5809
Camera News, Inc.
545 8th Ave., 10th Fl.
New York, NY 10018-4307 (212) 947-9277
FAX: (212) 594-6417; E-mail: twn@twn.org; e-mail for Dorothy Thigpen: dorothy@twn.org; URL: http://www.thirdworldnewsreel.org

Foundation type: Public charity
Purpose: Workshops for emerging film and video makers for people of color for a duration of six months.
Financial data: Year ended 02/28/2012. Assets, $330,534 (M); Expenditures, $558,038; Total giving, $207,589; Grants to individuals, totaling $24,529.
Fields of interest: Film/video; Arts, artist's services; Minorities; African Americans/Blacks.
Type of support: Project support; Fiscal agent/sponsor.
Application information: Application form required. Interview required.
  Initial approach: Letter
  Deadline(s): Jan. 15
  Applicants should submit the following:
    1) Resume
    2) Letter(s) of recommendation
  Additional information: Faxed or e-mail applications are not accepted.
Program description:
  Fiscal Sponsorship: The organization serves as a fiscal sponsor of independent film and electronic media productions, as well as artistic, educational, and cultural projects emphasizing people of color and their concerns. The organization provides consultation and limited access to its own administrative, financial, and technical resources.
EIN: 132624257

5810
Ruth Camp Campbell Charitable Trust
(formerly Ruth Camp McDougall Charitable Trust)
140 Broadway, 5th Fl.
New York, NY 10005-1101 (212) 493-8000
Application address: c/o Brown Brothers Harriman Trust Co., N.A., 227 W. Trade St., Ste. 2100, Charlotte, NC 28202

Foundation type: Independent foundation
Purpose: Scholarships to residents of VA, with preference to Southampton, Sussex, Surrey, Isle of Wight, Nansemond and Greenville counties.
Financial data: Year ended 12/31/2012. Assets, $13,418,990 (M); Expenditures, $759,507; Total giving, $629,299.
Type of support: Undergraduate support.
Application information: Applications accepted.
  Initial approach: Letter
  Deadline(s): None
  Additional information: Contact foundation for current application guidelines.
EIN: 546162697

5811
Camphill Foundation
285 Hungry Hollow Rd.
Chestnut Ridge, NY 10977-6329 (845) 517-2776
FAX: (845) 517-2779; E-mail: info@camphillfoundation.org; URL: http://camphillfoundation.org/

Foundation type: Public charity
Purpose: Research and professional development support to individuals focusing on developmental disability-related research, especially as it relates to self-sustainment and agriculture.
Publications: Application guidelines; Financial statement; Informational brochure; Newsletter; Occasional report.
Financial data: Year ended 05/31/2012. Assets, $8,364,530 (M); Expenditures, $523,007; Total giving, $227,025.
Fields of interest: Agriculture; Human services; Disabilities, people with.
Type of support: Program development; Fellowships; Grants to individuals.
Application information: Applications accepted. Application form required.
  Initial approach: Proposal
  Deadline(s): Feb. 1 (proposal)
  Final notification: Applicant notified July 1
Program descriptions:
  Professional Development Scholarships: Scholarship grants are available to those who work with or care for individuals with developmental, cognitive, and psychological disabilities. Grants are available for internships, workshops, and classes at institutions approved by the foundation.
  Research Fellowships: The foundation administers research fellowships to further the application of sustainable agriculture, social therapy, arts-based approaches, and shared living. Applicants must be master's thesis or doctoral dissertation candidates. Fellowships are also awarded to scholars or practitioners in such fields as sociology, psychology, and agriculture for publishing and conference paper presentations that advance these models.
EIN: 236421082

5812
Cancer Care, Inc.
275 7th Ave., 22nd Fl.
New York, NY 10001-6754 (212) 712-8400
Contact: Patricia J. Goldsmith, C.E.O.
FAX: (212) 712-8495; E-mail: info@cancercare.org; Toll-free tel.: (800) 813-4673; URL: http://www.cancercare.org

Foundation type: Public charity
Purpose: Financial assistance to individuals affected by cancer, for treatment-related costs such as medication, transportation, homecare, and childcare.
Publications: Annual report; Financial statement; Informational brochure; Newsletter.
Financial data: Year ended 06/30/2012. Assets, $22,832,102 (M); Expenditures, $18,576,570; Total giving, $5,678,587; Grants to individuals, totaling $5,633,860.
Fields of interest: Cancer.
Type of support: Emergency funds; Grants for special needs.
Application information:
  Initial approach: Letter
  Additional information: Contact foundation for further information.
EIN: 131825919

5813
Cancer Research Institute, Inc.
1 Exchange Plz.
55 Broadway, Ste. 1802
New York, NY 10006-3724 (212) 688-7515
Contact: Jill O'Donnell-Tormey, C.E.O.
FAX: (212) 832-9376;
E-mail: info@cancerresearch.org; Toll-free tel.: (800) 992-2623; e-mail for Jill O'Donnell-Tormey: jtormey@cancerresearch.org; URL: http://www.cancerresearch.org

Foundation type: Public charity
Purpose: Funding and fellowships to individuals for basic research in cancer immunology, immunotherapies, and other therapeutic areas that are synergistic with immunotherapy.
Publications: Application guidelines; Annual report; Financial statement; Grants list; Informational brochure; Newsletter; Program policy statement.
Financial data: Year ended 06/30/2012. Assets, $51,037,681 (M); Expenditures, $16,035,693; Total giving, $10,893,566.
Fields of interest: Immunology; Cancer research.
Type of support: Fellowships; Research; Postdoctoral support; Graduate support.
Application information: Applications accepted. Application form required. Application form available on the grantmaker's web site.
  Initial approach: Letter or e-mail
  Deadline(s): Varies
  Applicants should submit the following:
    1) Proposal
    2) Letter(s) of recommendation
    3) Curriculum vitae
  Additional information: Applications should be sent by either mail or e-mail.
Program descriptions:
  Investigator Award Program: Awards tenured-tracked assistant professors $50,000 a year for a period of four years to undertake their first independent investigations.
  Postdoctoral Fellowship Program: Fellowships are awarded for up to three years. The stipend for new fellows is $45,000 for the first year, $47,000 for the second, and $49,000 for the third. A yearly allowance of $1,500 is provided to the host institution to help meet expenses for research supplies, travel to scientific meetings, and health insurance incurred on behalf of the fellow.
  William B. Coley Award for Distinguished Research in Basic and Tumor Immunology: This award is given to one or more scientists for outstanding achievements in the field of basic immunology and cancer immunology. Awardees receive an honorary medal and a $5,000 prize.
EIN: 131837442

5814
Cantor Fitzgerald Relief Fund
199 Water St.
New York, NY 10038 (212) 829-4770
Contact: Edith Lutnick Esq., Exec. Dir.
Additional tel.: (866) 339-0947 for grant application
FAX: (212) 829-4895; E-mail: info@cantorrelief.org; URL: http://www.cantorrelief.org/

Foundation type: Public charity
Purpose: Financial assistance to individuals and families in connection with disaster relief for childcare, tuition, housing, and living expenses.
Financial data: Year ended 12/31/2011. Assets, $15,169,922 (M); Expenditures, $12,382,969; Total giving, $11,991,998; Grants to individuals, totaling $3,810,432.
Fields of interest: Mental health, counseling/support groups; Disasters, 9/11/01; Disasters, Hurricane Katrina; Children, services.
Type of support: Emergency funds; Grants to individuals; Grants for special needs.
Application information: Applications accepted. Application form required.
  Initial approach: Telephone
  Additional information: Contact the fund for grant applications and further information.
EIN: 134189179

5815

Jasmine L. Cantor Foundation, Inc.

201 W. 3rd St., Ste. 205
Jamestown, NY 14701-4972 (716) 664-3906
Contact: Eddy Cantor

Foundation type: Public charity
Purpose: Scholarships to the top ten graduates of Jamestown High School, NY, to attend four-year colleges.
Financial data: Year ended 12/31/2012. Assets, $195,020 (M); Expenditures, $16,058; Total giving, $14,000.
Type of support: Support to graduates or students of specific schools; Undergraduate support.
Application information: Application form not required.
  Initial approach: Letter
EIN: 161287432

5816

Career Transition For Dancers

c/o C&T Newhouse Ctr. for Dancers
165 W. 46th St., Ste. 701
New York, NY 10036-2501
Contact: Alexander J. Dube, Exec. Dir.
FAX: (212) 764-0343;
E-mail: info@careertransition.org; URL: http://www.careertransition.org

Foundation type: Public charity
Purpose: Scholarships to current and former dancers for education, career transitions, and entrepreneurial endeavors.
Publications: Application guidelines; Annual report; Informational brochure; Newsletter.
Financial data: Year ended 12/31/2011. Assets, $2,876,947 (M); Expenditures, $1,614,297; Total giving, $451,492; Grants to individuals, totaling $346,863.
Fields of interest: Dance; Scholarships/financial aid.
Type of support: Seed money; Grants to individuals; Scholarships—to individuals; Support to graduates or students of specific schools; Graduate support; Technical education support; Undergraduate support.
Application information: Applications accepted. Application form required.
  Initial approach: Telephone
  Copies of proposal: 1
  Deadline(s): See web site for deadlines
  Applicants should submit the following:
    1) Financial information
    2) Essay
  Additional information: Recipients notified in four to six weeks.
Program descriptions:
  Caroline H. Newhouse Scholarship Fund: Grants of up to $2,000 may be awarded for educational scholarships, retraining programs, and seed money central to fledgling business endeavors.
  Sono Osata Scholarship Program: Assists dancers in meeting the substantial financial commitment that comes with the pursuit of a graduate-level degree by providing $5,000 scholarships for fields other than performance dance.
EIN: 133488203

5817

Careers through Culinary Arts Program, Inc.

(also known as C-CAP)
250 W. 57th St., Ste. 2015
New York, NY 10107-2006 (212) 974-7111
Contact: Susan Robbins, Pres.
FAX: (212) 974-7117; E-mail: info@ccapinc.org;
URL: http://www.ccapinc.org

Foundation type: Public charity
Purpose: Scholarships to public high school students pursuing a career in the food service industry.
Publications: Financial statement; Newsletter.
Financial data: Year ended 06/30/2012. Assets, $2,364,023 (M); Expenditures, $4,928,615; Total giving, $3,216,604; Grants to individuals, totaling $3,216,604.
Fields of interest: Home economics.
Type of support: Scholarships—to individuals.
Application information: Applications accepted. Application form required. Interview required.
  Send request by: Mail or hand delivered
  Applicants should submit the following:
    1) Transcripts
    2) Letter(s) of recommendation
    3) Essay
  Additional information: Students are selected by their teachers based on class attendance, performance, and their overall academic record, and in an annual culinary competition.
Program description:
  C-CAP Cooking Competition for Scholarships: The program provides awards and scholarships ranging from $1,000 to full tuition by providing an opportunity for motivated youth who wish to pursue a career in a culinary- or hospitality-related field. Individuals participate in a cooking competition where students prepare memorized recipes to be judged by local industry professionals. Winners of local competitions then move on to a national, final cooking competition. Participants include juniors and seniors from any participating program high school who have completed at least one culinary, cooking, or home economics class. Only seniors who pass the preliminary competition are eligible to continue on to the final competition. C-CAP operates in the following locations: New York; Los Angeles, CA; Chicago, IL; Philadelphia, PA; Hampton Roads, VA; Prince George's County, MD; and AZ.
EIN: 133662917

5818

Carnegie Fund for Authors

1 Old Country Rd.
Carle Place, NY 11514 (516) 877-2141
Contact: Barbara Magalnick, Trustee
E-mail: magalnick@gmail.com

Foundation type: Independent foundation
Purpose: Emergency assistance to financially needy writers who have commercially published at least one book of reasonable length.
Financial data: Year ended 12/31/2012. Assets, $1,098,379 (M); Expenditures, $32,248; Total giving, $14,500; Grants to individuals, 3 grants totaling $14,500 (high: $7,500, low: $2,000).
Fields of interest: Literature.
Type of support: Grants for special needs.
Application information: Applications accepted.
  Initial approach: Letter
  Deadline(s): None
  Applicants should submit the following:
    1) Financial information
    2) Curriculum vitae
  Additional information: Application should also include the author's credited titles with publication details. The applicant must state why assistance is needed. Acceptable bases for a grant would be medical emergency or other temporary situation requiring financial aid.
Program description:
  Emergency Grant: The grant offers applicants financial emergency as a result of illness or injury to self, spouse, or dependent child, or some other misfortune that has placed the applicant in pressing, substantial, and verifiable need. The fund does not make loans or grants to permit an applicant to complete a projected or unfinished work for publication. The work must be published by a traditional publisher. If the applicant paid to have the work published, the work is not eligible.
EIN: 136084244

5819

Milton Carpenter Foundation, Inc.

P.O. Box 9
Claryville, NY 12725 (845) 985-2372
Contact: Arlene Stoffel, Dir.

Foundation type: Independent foundation
Purpose: Scholarships to financially needy students of northern Westchester and Putnam counties, NY, whose families have been affected by chemical dependency.
Publications: Informational brochure (including application guidelines).
Financial data: Year ended 12/31/2012. Assets, $563,603 (M); Expenditures, $106,577; Total giving, $77,089; Grants to individuals, 66 grants totaling $77,089 (high: $2,500, low: $250).
Fields of interest: Higher education; Substance abuse, treatment; Alcoholism.
Type of support: Scholarships—to individuals; Undergraduate support.
Application information: Applications accepted. Application form required. Application form available on the grantmaker's web site. Interview required.
  Send request by: E-mail
  Deadline(s): Feb. 1
  Final notification: Recipients notified May 15
  Applicants should submit the following:
    1) FAFSA
    2) Essay
    3) Financial information
    4) Letter(s) of recommendation
    5) Transcripts
    6) SAT
    7) ACT
  Additional information: Application by nomination letter. Application should also include verification of chemically dependency in the immediate family, copy of parents' federal tax forms, acceptance letters. See web site for additional guidelines.
EIN: 061102502

5820

Carrier & Bryant Distributors' Educational Foundation

(formerly William A. Blees Educational Foundation)
Carrier Pkwy., Bldg. TR4
P.O. Box 4808
Syracuse, NY 13221-4808 (800) 722-2577

Foundation type: Independent foundation
Purpose: Scholarships to employees and children of employees in the HVAC industry for attendance at four-year colleges and universities.

Financial data: Year ended 07/31/2013. Assets, $153,327 (M); Expenditures, $42,524; Total giving, $37,500; Grants to individuals, 25 grants totaling $37,500 (high: $1,500, low: $1,500).
Type of support: Employee-related scholarships; Undergraduate support.
Application information: Application form required.
Deadline(s): May 31
Applicants should submit the following:
1) ACT
2) SAT
3) Class rank
4) Transcripts
Additional information: Applications available from Carrier dealers. Application address: c/o Matt Richardson, P.O. Box 770728, Lakewood, OH 44107.
EIN: 161153992

5821

The Carter Burden Center for the Aging, Inc.

(formerly The Burden Center for the Aging, Inc.)
1484 1st Ave., 2nd Fl.
New York, NY 10075-2304 (212) 879-7400
Contact: William J. Dionne, Exec. Dir.
FAX: (212) 879-9864; E-mail: info@burdencntr.org; E-mail For William J. Dionne: dionnew@carterburdencenter.org; URL: http://www.burdencenter.org

Foundation type: Public charity
Purpose: Assistance to elderly residents of the Upper East Side, New York, area with food, clothing, shelter, and emergency financial assistance.
Financial data: Year ended 06/30/2012. Assets, $5,483,385 (M); Expenditures, $3,768,476.
Fields of interest: Human services; Aging.
Type of support: Grants for special needs.
Application information: Seniors age 60 and older are offered a variety of services throughout the Upper East Side.
EIN: 237129499

5822

Carver Scholarship Fund, Inc.

75 W. 125th St.
New York, NY 10027-4512 (212) 876-4747
Contact: Richard T. Greene, Chair.

Foundation type: Company-sponsored foundation
Purpose: Scholarships to residents of the New York, NY, area.
Publications: Informational brochure.
Financial data: Year ended 12/31/2010. Assets, $278,225 (M); Expenditures, $24,900; Total giving, $15,000.
Type of support: Scholarships—to individuals.
Application information: Contact fund for current application deadline/guidelines.
EIN: 133277661

5823

Catholic Charities Community Services, Archdiocese of New York

1011 1st Ave., 11th Fl.
New York, NY 10022-4112 (212) 371-1000
Contact: Rachel Barett, Dir., Corp. and Fdn. Rels.
Toll-free tel.: (888) 744-7900; URL: http://www.catholiccharitiesny.org

Foundation type: Public charity
Purpose: Social services are provided to individuals and families throughout New York City boroughs of

Manhattan, the Bronx and Staten Island, and the Lower Hudson Valley counties of Westchester, Rockland, Orange, Sullivan, Putnam, Ulster and Dutchess. Grants provided for economic need, limited primarily to eviction prevention, utility shut-off prevention and others on an individual basis.
Publications: Annual report; Newsletter.
Financial data: Year ended 08/31/2011. Assets, $16,515,622 (M); Expenditures, $37,770,313; Total giving, $3,205,148; Grants to individuals, totaling $3,146,133.
Fields of interest: Human services.
Type of support: Grants for special needs.
Application information:
Deadline(s): None
Additional information: Giving is need based and income driven. See web site for highlights of CCCS services.
EIN: 135562185

5824

Catholic Guardian Society and Home Bureau

1011 1st Ave., 10th Fl.
New York, NY 10022-4112 (212) 371-1000
FAX: (212) 758-5892; E-mail: info@cgshb.org; URL: http://www.cgshb.org/

Foundation type: Public charity
Purpose: Specific assistance to individuals and families in the New York area with residential and related services, educational and medical support services, and other special needs.
Financial data: Year ended 06/30/2012. Assets, $31,452,065 (M); Expenditures, $83,298,079; Total giving, $20,110,345; Grants to individuals, totaling $20,110,345.
Fields of interest: Adoption; Foster care; Youth, services; Residential/custodial care; Disabilities, people with; Mentally disabled.
Type of support: Grants for special needs.
Application information: Contact the society for guidelines on services.
EIN: 135562186

5825

Catholic Teachers Association of the Diocese of Brooklyn, Inc.

191 Joralemon St.
Brooklyn, NY 11201-4306 (718) 852-6565
Contact: Edward Rice, Pres.

Foundation type: Public charity
Purpose: Scholarships and study grants to NY members based on merit and need.
Financial data: Year ended 06/30/2012. Assets, $31,991 (M); Expenditures, $27,224; Total giving, $14,500.
Fields of interest: Association; Formal/general education; Catholic agencies & churches.
Type of support: Scholarships—to individuals.
Application information: Contact foundation for current application deadline/guidelines.
EIN: 111687465

5826

Cattaraugus Region Community Foundation

(formerly Greater Olean Community Foundation)
120 N. Union St.
Olean, NY 14760-2735 (716) 372-4433
Contact: Karen Niemic Buchheit, Exec. Dir.; Ryan Michelle Wilcox, Asst. Exec. Dir.
FAX: (716) 372-7912;
E-mail: foundation@cattfoundation.org; Additional e-mail: karen@cattfoundation.org; URL: http://www.cattfoundation.org

Foundation type: Community foundation
Purpose: Scholarships to high school students and home schooled students of Cattaraugus county of southwestern New York.
Publications: Application guidelines; Annual report; Financial statement; Newsletter.
Financial data: Year ended 12/31/2012. Assets, $10,358,800 (M); Expenditures, $593,872; Total giving, $405,307; Grants to individuals, totaling $79,523.
Fields of interest: Higher education; Scholarships/financial aid.
Type of support: Scholarships—to individuals; Undergraduate support.
Application information: Applications accepted. Application form required. Application form available on the grantmaker's web site.
Deadline(s): Apr. 1
Final notification: Applicants notified within two months
Applicants should submit the following:
1) Essay
2) Transcripts
3) FAFSA
Additional information: See web site for a listing of scholarships and eligibility criteria or see your school's guidance counselor.
EIN: 161468127

5827

Cave Canem Foundation, Inc.

20 Jay St., Ste. 310-A
Brooklyn, NY 11201-8322 (718) 858-0000
FAX: (718) 858-0002;
E-mail: cavecanempoets@aol.com; URL: http://www.cavecanempoets.org

Foundation type: Public charity
Purpose: Prizes to African American writers who have not had a full-length book of poetry published by a professional press.
Publications: Application guidelines; Annual report; Informational brochure (including application guidelines).
Financial data: Year ended 12/31/2012. Assets, $65,340 (M); Expenditures, $360,902.
Fields of interest: Literature; African Americans/Blacks.
Type of support: Awards/prizes.
Application information:
Initial approach: Letter
Deadline(s): Apr. 30
Additional information: A $15 non-refundable entry fee is required. Application should include two copies of a single manuscript.
Program description:
Poetry Prize: Awards $1,000 to an African American poet with excellent manuscripts who have not yet found a publisher for their book. The prize includes publication of their manuscript by the University of Pittsburgh Press, 15 copies of the book and a feature reading.
EIN: 133932909

5828
CDS International, Inc.
440 Park Ave. S., 2nd Fl.
New York, NY 10016-8012 (212) 497-3500
Contact: Rob Fenstermacher, Pres. and C.E.O.
FAX: (212) 497-3535; E-mail: info@cdsintl.org;
URL: http://www.cdsintl.org

Foundation type: Public charity
Purpose: Fellowships to professionals with graduate degrees in business administration, economics, journalism and mass communication, law, political science or public affairs to work in Germany.
Publications: Annual report; Informational brochure; Newsletter.
Fields of interest: Media/communications; Print publishing; Business/industry; Economics; Political science; Law/international law; Administration/regulation.
Type of support: Fellowships; Internship funds; Exchange programs.
Application information:
Initial approach: Letter or e-mail.
Deadline(s): Oct. 15 for Robert Bosch Fellowship, Dec. 1 for Alfa Fellowship and Congress-Bundestag Youth Exchange for Young Professionals
Additional information: See web site for additional guidelines.
Program descriptions:
Alfa Fellowship Program: The program is a high-level professional development exchange program placing qualified American citizens in work assignments at leading Russian organizations in the fields of business, economics, journalism, law, public policy, and government. The program includes language training, seminar programs, and extended professional work experience. Fellows receive stipends, travel, housing, and insurance.
Congress-Bundestag Youth Exchange for Young Professionals: Provides a 12-month work-study program for 75 Americans in Germany in the agricultural, business, technical, and vocational fields. Program provides full-year scholarship, living stipend, round-trip transatlantic flight, and program related travel costs in Germany.
Robert Bosch Fellowship Program: Fellowships for 20 young American professionals in Germany with graduate degrees in business administration, economics, journalism and mass communication, law, political science or public affairs/policy. Over the course of a nine-month program the Fellows complete two work phases at leading German institutions, both customized to each fellow's professional expertise, and attend three seminars with key decision-makers from the public and private sectors, taking place across Europe. Fellows receive a monthly stipend of EUR 2,000 and financial support for accompanying spouse and children, including 50 percent of travel costs, supplemental living stipend, health insurance, and limited funding for language training.
EIN: 136275141

5829
CEC ArtsLink, Inc.
291 Broadway, 12th Fl.
New York, NY 10007 (212) 643-1985
FAX: (212) 643-1996; E-mail: info@cecartslink.org;
URL: http://www.cecartslink.org

Foundation type: Public charity
Purpose: Residencies to contemporary and traditional creative artists and arts managers for a duration of five weeks from 30 countries in Central/Eastern Europe, Russia and Eurasia.

Publications: Application guidelines; Grants list; Newsletter.
Financial data: Year ended 12/31/2011. Assets, $871,892 (M); Expenditures, $1,273,299; Total giving, $245,536; Grants to individuals, totaling $81,400.
Fields of interest: Performing arts; Literature.
International interests: Asia; Eastern Europe; Europe; Russia.
Type of support: Grants to individuals; Residencies.
Application information: Applications accepted. Application form required. Application form available on the grantmaker's web site.
Deadline(s): Nov.
Applicants should submit the following:
1) Curriculum vitae
2) Letter(s) of recommendation
3) Resume
4) Work samples
Additional information: Application must also include audio or video tapes. Work samples must be no more than five years old.
Program descriptions:
ArtsLink Projects: This program supports artists and arts managers from eligible countries for project grants to carry out self-directed projects in the United States. ArtsLink accepts applications from contemporary and traditional creative artists working in the performing, design, media, literary, and visual arts as well as arts managers at independent, nonprofit and government organizations working in these disciplines. Arts managers must be affiliated with an organization in the non-commercial sector. Artists seeking to work with commercial firms are ineligible. Applicants must be citizens of, and currently reside in, an eligible country. The award amount request must not exceed $5,000, regardless of the number of people planning to travel to the U.S. for the project.
ArtsLink Residencies: This program places artists and arts managers from Central/Eastern Europe, Russia and Eurasia ("ArtsLink Fellows") at U.S. arts organizations for five-week residencies. Opportunities will be provided to pursue artistic and/or professional collaborations that will enrich and enhance artistic work; establish mutually beneficial exchange of ideas and expertise with U.S. artists and organizations and with colleagues from Central Europe, Russia, and Eurasia; deepen understanding of a particular artistic expression that is related to artistic work; create new work that draws inspiration from interaction with artists and arts professionals in the U.S.; and expand professional arts management skills through work with U.S. organizations.
Independent Projects: This project awards up to $5,000 to support artists and arts managers from Central/Eastern Europe, Russia and Eurasia who plan to undertake projects in the United States. Applicants must have a letter of invitation from a U.S. nonprofit organization in order to apply for this award.
EIN: 132531695

5830
Center for Alternative Media and Culture
c/o AGS
200 Park Ave. S., 8th Fl.
New York, NY 10003-1503 (212) 768-4500
Contact: Frank Selvaggi

Foundation type: Independent foundation
Purpose: Scholarships to Flint, MI, area students. Grants to filmmakers whose projects focus on civil justice issues.

Financial data: Year ended 12/31/2012. Assets, $207,149 (M); Expenditures, $32,360; Total giving, $22,401.
Fields of interest: Film/video.
Type of support: Program development; Grants to individuals; Scholarships—to individuals.
Application information:
Initial approach: Letter
Deadline(s): None
Additional information: Contact foundation for current application deadline/guidelines.
EIN: 382415253

5831
Center for Architecture Foundation
(formerly New York Foundation for Architecture, Inc.)
536 LaGuardia Pl.
New York, NY 10012-1401 (212) 358-6133
Contact: Rick Bell, Exec. Dir.
FAX: (212) 696-5022;
E-mail: info@cfafoundation.org; E-mail for Erin McCluskey: emccluskey@cfafoundation.org;
URL: http://www.cfafoundation.org

Foundation type: Public charity
Purpose: Scholarships to residents of NY enrolled in architecture programs at New York City colleges and universities. Grants to individuals in the U.S. in the architecture field.
Publications: Application guidelines; Informational brochure.
Financial data: Year ended 12/31/2011. Assets, $2,540,674 (M); Expenditures, $679,544; Total giving, $18,000; Grants to individuals, totaling $18,000.
Fields of interest: Architecture.
Type of support: Scholarships—to individuals; Awards/prizes; Precollege support.
Application information: Applications accepted. Application form available on the grantmaker's web site.
Initial approach: Letter
Send request by: Mail
Copies of proposal: 1
Deadline(s): Feb. 1 for Arnold W. Brunner Grant; Mar. 15 for Women's Auxiliary Eleanor Allwork Scholarship; Nov. 1 for Stewardson Keef LeBrun Travel Grant
Final notification: Recipients notified in two to three months for scholarships
Additional information: Students are nominated by the Dean or Chair for scholarships. Application should include work samples, letter(s) of recommendation and curriculum vitae. Application forms are required for grants.
Program descriptions:
Arnold W. Brunner Grant: Merit-based scholarships (of up to $10,000) are available to support architectural students with demonstrated financial need. Applicants must be seeking their first degree in an National Architecture Accrediting Board (NAAB)-accredited school within the State of New York.
Center for Architecture Foundation Design Scholarships: Awards of up to $5,000 each are available to support deserving students studying architecture, design, engineering, planning, or a related discipline in an accredited school within New York State.
Stewardson Keef LeBrun Travel Grant: Grants of up to $15,000 each are available to further the personal and professional development of an architect in his/her early or mid-career through travel. Travel plans should be focused on a selected topic of interest to the individual, rather than a part

of a larger humanitarian or institutional endeavor. Eligible applicants must be U.S. citizens with a degree in architecture, as well as a full-time practitioner (either licensed or unlicensed)

Women's Auxiliary Eleanor Allwork Scholarship: Merit-based scholarships (of up to $10,000) are available to support architectural students with demonstrated financial need. Applicants must be seeking their first degree in an National Architecture Accrediting Board (NAAB)-accredited school within the state of New York.

EIN: 223047700

5832
Center for Book Arts, Inc.
28 W. 27th St., 3rd Fl.
New York, NY 10001-2609 (212) 481-0295
Contact: Virginia Bartow; Sarah Nicholls, Programs Mgr.
E-mail: info@centerforbookarts.org; Toll-free fax: (866) 708-8994; URL: http://www.centerforbookarts.org

Foundation type: Public charity
Purpose: Residencies to writers and artists who practice the craft of bookmaking, all of whom are residents of NY.
Publications: Application guidelines.
Financial data: Year ended 12/31/2011. Assets, $582,517 (M); Expenditures, $561,460; Total giving, $50,233; Grants to individuals, totaling $50,233.
Fields of interest: Arts.
Type of support: Residencies; Stipends.
Application information:
Initial approach: Telephone or e-mail
Deadline(s): Oct. 1
Additional information: Application must include resume, personal statement and 10 slides of recent work. See web site for complete application guidelines.
Program descriptions:
Sally R. Bishop Faculty Fellowship: The recipient of this award will create a limited edition book and will teach a workshop at The Center during a six-week residency. The residency includes travel expenses, housing, materials, a $1,500 stipend, studio space, and an assistant.
Stein Family Scholarship fo the Advanced Study of Book Arts: Awards two scholarships to artists to further their study and career in book arts.
Workspace Grants for New York Emerging Artists: This program includes studio space, a $500 stipend, materials budget, and a reception and presentation of artist's work.
EIN: 132842726

5833
The Center for Jewish History, Inc.
15 W. 16th St.
New York, NY 10011-6301 (212) 294-8301
URL: http://www.cjh.org

Foundation type: Public charity
Purpose: Fellowships and scholarships to qualified doctoral candidates in accredited institutions to conduct research in the field of Jewish studies.
Publications: Application guidelines.
Financial data: Year ended 12/31/2011. Assets, $56,316,109 (M); Expenditures, $7,260,318; Total giving, $120,710; Grants to individuals, totaling $120,710.
Fields of interest: History/archaeology; Jewish agencies & synagogues.
Type of support: Fellowships; Research.

Application information: Applications accepted. Application form required.
Send request by: Mail or e-mail
Deadline(s): Oct. 15 for Joseph S. Steinberg Fellowship, Dec. 15 for NEH Fellowship and Prins Foundation Post-Doctoral Fellowships, Feb. 1 for Graduate Research Fellowship and Prins Foundation Fellowship for Senior Scholars, None for Undergraduate Fellowship
Additional information: See web site for additional guidelines.
Program descriptions:
Graduate Research Fellowship: Fellowship opportunities are available to Ph.D. candidates to support original research using the collections at the center. Fellowships carry a stipend of up to $14,000 for one year; preference will be given to applicants who draw on library and archival resources of more than one of the center's partners. Applicants are expected to have completed all requirements for their doctoral degree except for the dissertation; applicants must also spend a minimum of two days per week at the Lillian Goldman Reading Room, using, archived and library resources, and deliver at least one lecture based on his or her research.
Joseph S. Steinberg Emerging Jewish Filmmaker Fellowship: Grants of up to $5,000 are available to undergraduate and graduate emerging filmmakers working on topics related to modern Jewish history. Awards are designed to help further existing projects, or to start new projects, whose subject matter is in line with the collections housed at the center. Recipients are expected to present finished works, or works in progress, to a public audience at the center.
NEH Fellowship for Senior Scholars: Awarded in conjunction with the National Endowment for the Humanities, this fellowship supports original research at the center in the humanities, including but not limited to Jewish studies, Russian and East European studies, American studies, Germanic studies, musicology, linguistics, anthropology, sociology, and history. Applications are welcome from college and university faculty in any field who have completed a Ph.D. more than six years prior to the start of the fellowship, and whose research will benefit considerably from consultation with center materials. Fellowships carry a stipend of up to $50,400 for a period of one academic year.
Prins Foundation Fellowship for Senior Scholars: This 12-month fellowship is for senior scholars from outside the U.S. who seek permanent teaching and research positions. The fellowship is for scholars who has held the Ph.D. for at least six years and will be provided with an annual living stipend of $75,000 as well as a relocation stipend of up to $15,000 for a period of one academic year.
Prins Foundation Post-Doctoral Fellowship for Emigrating Scholars: One-year stipends of $35,000 each are available to foreign scholars who are at the beginning of their careers, and who seek permanent teaching and research positions in North America, to conduct original research at the center's Lillian Goldman Reading Room. Fellows are expected to conduct original research at the center, deliver at least one lecture based on the research conducted, actively participate in the scholarly community at the center, and submit a report upon completion of the fellowship describing the experience.
Undergraduate Research Fellowship: Fellowship awards of up to $1,000 are available to advanced undergraduate students currently enrolled at North American universities, to carry out research in the archives and libraries of the center and its partner institutions. This fellowship is specifically designed for third- and fourth-year undergraduates preparing

theses or other major projects in Jewish history and related fields. Fellowship awards are intended to be used for travel and lodging while using the center.
EIN: 133863344

5834
The Center for Photography of Woodstock, Inc.
59 Tinker St.
Woodstock, NY 12498-1236 (845) 679-9957
FAX: (845) 679-6337; E-mail: info@cpw.org;
URL: http://cpw.org/

Foundation type: Public charity
Purpose: Fellowships to photographers and artists who use photography and reside in NY State. Residency to emerging artists of color working in the photographic arts.
Publications: Application guidelines; Informational brochure; Program policy statement.
Financial data: Year ended 09/30/2011. Assets, $256,611 (M); Expenditures, $399,651.
Fields of interest: Visual arts; Photography.
Type of support: Fellowships; Residencies.
Application information: Applications accepted.
Initial approach: Letter
Deadline(s): Sept. 16 for Fellowships
Final notification: Recipients notified in Oct. for Fellowships
Additional information: See web site for additional guidelines.
Program descriptions:
Photographers' Fund Fellowships: One $2,500 fellowship is granted to a regional artist who use the photographic process and reside in one of the following New York State counties: Albany, Clinton, Columbia, Delaware, Dutchess, Essex, Franklin, Fulton, Greene, Hamilton, Montgomery, Orange, Otsego, Putnam, Rensselaer, Saratoga, Schenectady, Schoharie, Sullivan, Ulster, Warren, and Washington. Proof of residency is required, together with an artist statement and bio, and a portfolio of ten prints.
Woodstock A-I-R Residency Program: Awards seven residencies for artists of color and one "critical studies residency" for a curator/critic of color. Residents receive 24/7 access to workspace facilities (including black & white darkroom, digital imaging stations, and library), critical and technical support, stipend for food and travel, and honoraria.
EIN: 141592639

5835
Center for Social Inclusion
150 Broadway, Ste. 303
New York, NY 10038-4350 (212) 248-2785
FAX: (212) 248-6409; E-mail: info@thecsi.org;
URL: http://www.centerforsocialinclusion.org

Foundation type: Public charity
Purpose: Fellowships to community leaders of color who wish to take a sabbatical to focus on other issues.
Publications: Application guidelines; Annual report; Newsletter; Occasional report.
Financial data: Year ended 12/31/2012. Assets, $2,634,567 (M); Expenditures, $1,264,834; Total giving, $175,000; Grants to individuals, 5 grants totaling $125,000.
Fields of interest: Civil/human rights; Community/economic development.
Type of support: Fellowships.
Application information: Applications accepted. Application form required. Application form

available on the grantmaker's web site. Interview required.

> *Deadline(s):* Apr. 5 for Alston Bannerman Leadership Initiative
> *Applicants should submit the following:*
> 1) Letter(s) of recommendation
> 2) Essay
> 3) Curriculum vitae

Program description:

Alston Bannerman Sabbatical Fellowship: This fellowship program honors and supports longtime organizers of color by giving them the resources to take time out for reflection and renewal. Fellows will each receive $25,000 to take sabbaticals for three months or more. Eligible applicants must: be a person of color; have more than ten years of community organizing experience; be committed to social change work in communities of color; and live in the U.S., Puerto Rico, Guam, American Samoa, or the U.S. Virgin Islands. Priority will be given to applicants who: attack the root causes of inequity by organizing those affected to take collective strategic action; challenge the systems that perpetuate injustice and effect institutional and structural change; acknowledge the cultural values of the community; create accountable participatory structures in which community members have decision-making power; and contribute to building a movement for social change by making connections among issues, developing alliances with other constituencies, and collaborating with other organizations. Both paid and unpaid leaders are eligible to apply; fellowship recipients will be required to stop their day-to-day work activities for at least three consecutive months and devote that time to activities that are substantially different from their normal routine.

EIN: 900686577

5836
The Central National-Gottesman Foundation

3 Manhattanville Rd.
Purchase, NY 10577-2110
Contact: Christine Royer
Application address: 417 Riverside Dr., New York, NY 10025

Foundation type: Company-sponsored foundation
Purpose: Scholarships to children of full-time employees of Central National Gottesman or Lindenmeyr Divisions for full-time study leading to a B.A. degree, or the equivalent.
Financial data: Year ended 12/31/2012. Assets, $20,946,946 (M); Expenditures, $1,004,970; Total giving, $795,572; Grants to individuals, 26 grants totaling $552,418 (high: $62,738, low: $3,485).
Type of support: Employee-related scholarships; Undergraduate support.
Application information: Applications not accepted.

> *Additional information:* Unsolicited requests for funds not considered or acknowledged.

Company name: Central National Gottesman Division
EIN: 133047546

5837
Central New York Community Foundation, Inc.

431 East Fayette St., Ste. 100
Syracuse, NY 13202 (315) 422-9538
Contact: Peter A. Dunn, C.E.O.; For grants: Olive Sephuma, Dir., Community Grantmaking
FAX: (315) 471-6031; E-mail: peter@cnycf.org; Grant inquiry e-mail: olive@cnycf.org; URL: http://www.cnycf.org

Foundation type: Community foundation
Purpose: Provides scholarships to area students of Onondaga or Madison county, NY through various funds.
Publications: Annual report (including application guidelines); Informational brochure (including application guidelines); Newsletter.
Financial data: Year ended 03/31/2013. Assets, $143,992,070 (M); Expenditures, $10,847,470; Total giving, $8,337,264.
Fields of interest: Higher education.
Type of support: Scholarships—to individuals.
Application information: Applications accepted.

> *Additional information:* See foundation web site for listing of various scholarship funds and restrictions.

EIN: 150626910

5838
CFDA Foundation, Inc.

65 Bleecker St., 11 Fl.
New York, NY 10018-9250 (212) 302-1821
Contact: Steven Kolb, C.E.O.
E-mail: info@cfda.com; URL: http://cfda.com/

Foundation type: Public charity
Purpose: Financial awards to one or more aspiring fashion designers.
Publications: Application guidelines.
Financial data: Year ended 12/31/2011. Assets, $21,557,963 (M); Expenditures, $5,147,713; Total giving, $2,070,373; Grants to individuals, totaling $45,000.
Fields of interest: Design; Business school/education.
Type of support: Awards/prizes.
Application information: Applications accepted. Application form required. Application form available on the grantmaker's web site. Interview required.

> *Deadline(s):* Varies
> *Additional information:* Application should include a 350-word biographical statement and affirm his/her eligibility, and three to five references. Selection is based on the exceptional talent they have already demonstrated in fashion design and their capacity for future distinction in the fashion industry.

Program description:

CFDA/Vogue Fashion Fund: This fund is intended to support the next generation of American fashion designers by annually selecting three emerging fashion designers who receive business mentoring from an established team of fashion industry professionals, in areas such as business planning, marketing, sourcing, production, and exporting, and funding to encourage and enable them to pursue their own independent design plan. One winner will be selected and receive $300,000, two runners-up will receive $100,000 each. Eligible applicants must be in business for a minimum of two consecutive years, be a designer of demonstrable talent (i.e., have garnered substantial and recent editorial coverage, and have support from key retailers), and have professional staff (paid or

volunteer) that can devote the time and effort required to accomplish the stated aims of the applicant's design career plans.
EIN: 237371666

5839
Chamber Music America

243 5th Ave.
UPS Box 458
New York, NY 10016-8703 (212) 242-2022
Contact: Margaret M. Lioi, C.E.O.
FAX: (646) 430-5667;
E-mail: info@chamber-music.org; URL: http://www.chamber-music.org

Foundation type: Public charity
Purpose: Grants and awards to individuals performing in chamber music ensembles, who are members of the Chamber Music America organization.
Publications: Application guidelines; Financial statement; Grants list; Informational brochure; Newsletter.
Financial data: Year ended 06/30/2012. Assets, $10,078,136 (M); Expenditures, $2,448,304; Total giving, $733,680; Grants to individuals, totaling $291,050.
Fields of interest: Music; Music ensembles/groups; Music composition.
Type of support: Conferences/seminars; Awards/prizes; Residencies.
Application information: Applications accepted. Application form required.

> *Send request by:* Mail or hand deliver
> *Deadline(s):* Mar. 8 for New Jazz Works: Commissioning and Ensemble Development, Nov. 1 for Residency Partnership Program
> *Applicants should submit the following:*
> 1) Work samples
> 2) Budget Information
> *Additional information:* See web site for additional guidelines.

Program descriptions:

Cleveland Quartet Award: Established in recognition of the Cleveland Quartet's enduring legacy in the areas of chamber music performance and education, this biennial award is presented to an exceptional young string quartet. Candidates are nominated confidentially and selected by a panel with expertise in quartet teaching, performance, and presenting.

CMA/FACE French American Jazz Exchange Program: Co-sponsored with the French Embassy and the French American Cultural Exchange (FACE), this program fosters collaborative projects that unite French and American jazz artists in both France and the U.S. Projects may include (but are not limited to) composition, touring, recording, and audience-development activities. Public performance is required, with the understanding that jazz speaks to diverse populations and experiencing music together bridges differences. Grants range from $5,000 to $12,000. French and American citizens or legal residents are encouraged to apply.

CMAcclaim: This award honors an individual chamber musician, ensemble, or organization for achievements in chamber music that have had a significant impact on a community at the local or regional level. The award celebrates diversity of musical styles and genres, race and gender, types of audience served, and geographic location.

Residency Partnership Program: This program supports non-traditional partnerships among ensembles, presenters, and community-based organizations, with the goal of bringing live ensemble music to urban, rural, and suburban audiences across the United States. Short-term residency projects (three to nine activities taking place over at least three days within a month) will receive grants ranging from $2,500 to $6,000 each. Extended residency projects (ten or more activities taking place over more than one month and up to one year) will receive grants of from $5,000 to $12,000 each. Applicants and program participants (organizing and performing partners) must be organization members at the time of application, and be based in the United States. In addition, an annual residency grant is available for a string quartet that applies to the program.

Richard J. Bogomolny National Service Award: The award recognizes those individuals who have had a profound and lasting impact on the chamber music field.

EIN: 132934575

5840
Chaminade Development Fund, Inc.
Jackson Ave. and Emory Rd.
Mineola, NY   11501   (516) 742-5555

Foundation type: Public charity
Purpose: Tuition assistance for students of Chaminade High School, NY.
Financial data: Year ended 06/30/2012. Assets, $31,871,416 (M); Expenditures, $3,098,923; Total giving, $2,238,287.
Type of support: Support to graduates or students of specific schools.
Application information:
Initial approach: Letter
Additional information: Contact the fund for eligibility criteria.
EIN: 237069462

5841
chashama, Inc.
675 3rd Ave.
New York, NY   10017-5704   (212) 391-8151
Contact: Anita Durst, Artistic Dir.; Adarsh Alphons, Genl. Mgr.
FAX: (212) 391-8153;
E-mail: chashama@chashama.org; URL: http://www.chashama.org

Foundation type: Public charity
Purpose: Residencies, technical support, administrative support, and stipends to performing and visual artists residing in the New York, NY metropolitan area.
Publications: Informational brochure.
Financial data: Year ended 06/30/2013. Assets, $379,354 (M); Expenditures, $816,170.
Fields of interest: Film/video; Visual arts; Performing arts.
Type of support: Residencies; Stipends.
Application information: Applications accepted. Application form required. Application form available on the grantmaker's web site.
Initial approach: Telephone
Send request by: Mail
Copies of proposal: 1
Deadline(s): Varies
Final notification: Recipients notified in one to six months
Applicants should submit the following:
1) Work samples
2) Proposal
3) Budget Information
EIN: 133862422

5842
Chautauqua Region Community
Foundation, Inc.
418 Spring St.
Jamestown, NY   14701-5332   (716) 661-3390
Contact: Randall J. Sweeney, Exec. Dir.; For grant and scholarship inquiries: Lisa W. Lynde, Prog. Off.
Scholarship inquiries e-mail: llynde@crcfonline.org; Kids First Mini-Grants
e-mail: jdiethrick@crcfonline.org
FAX: (716) 488-0387;
E-mail: rsweeney@crcfonline.org; URL: http://www.crcfonline.org

Foundation type: Community foundation
Purpose: Scholarships to graduates of 18 school districts in the Chautauqua County, NY, area, as well as Allegheny and Cattaraugus counties, NY.
Publications: Application guidelines; Annual report (including application guidelines); Informational brochure; Newsletter.
Financial data: Year ended 12/31/2012. Assets, $68,078,179 (M); Expenditures, $2,830,133; Total giving, $1,994,144; Grants to individuals, 634 grants totaling $689,119.
Fields of interest: Arts education; Music; Performing arts, education; Business school/education; Medical school/education; Nursing school/education; Education; Engineering/technology.
Type of support: Scholarships—to individuals; Support to graduates or students of specific schools; Graduate support; Undergraduate support.
Application information: Applications accepted. Application form required. Application form available on the grantmaker's web site.
Send request by: On-line
Deadline(s): June 2
Final notification: Applicants notified in Nov.
Applicants should submit the following:
1) Transcripts
2) SAT
3) GPA
4) Financial information
5) FAFSA
6) Essay
7) ACT
Additional information: See web site for a complete listing of scholarship funds.
Program description:
Scholarships: The foundation administers over 100 scholarship funds to provide financial assistance to area students for higher education. Many are for students interested in specific subjects, such as music, art, nursing, education, business, and engineering. Almost all awards are for undergraduate college study, although a few awards are made to graduate students, primarily for medical education. Some awards are given to graduates of specific schools. See web site for additional information.
EIN: 161116837

5843
Chenango County Medical Society & The
Otsego County Medical Society
c/o NBT Bank, N.A.
52 S. Broad St.
Norwich, NY   13815   (315) 735-2204
Contact: Kathleen E. Dyman, Exec. V.P.
Application address: 4311 Middle Settlement Rd., New Hartford, NY 13413

Foundation type: Independent foundation

Purpose: Scholarships to residents of Chenango or Otsego counties, NY, who are attending medical or osteopathic school.
Financial data: Year ended 04/30/2013. Assets, $313,024 (M); Expenditures, $27,227; Total giving, $17,500; Grants to individuals, 5 grants totaling $17,500 (high: $6,000, low: $1,500).
Fields of interest: Medical school/education.
Type of support: Scholarships—to individuals.
Application information: Applications accepted. Application form required.
Deadline(s): July 1
Additional information: Application must include essay.
EIN: 237325443

5844
Chesed Avrhom Hacohn Foundation
201 Edward Curry Ave., Ste. 2014
Staten Island, NY   10314   (718) 668-3874
Application address: 5312 17th Ave., Brooklyn, NY 11201; tel.: (718) 568-3874

Foundation type: Independent foundation
Purpose: Educational grants for rabbinical scholars for religious studies in Israel.
Financial data: Year ended 12/31/2012. Assets, $245,905 (M); Expenditures, $126,689; Total giving, $89,000; Grants to individuals, 14 grants totaling $89,000 (high: $13,400, low: $2,200).
Fields of interest: Theological school/education; Jewish agencies & synagogues.
International interests: Israel.
Type of support: Postgraduate support.
Application information: Applications accepted. Application form required.
Deadline(s): Apr. 1
Additional information: Application should include qualifications and other pertinent personal data.
Program description:
Awards Program: The Crown of Torah Award and The Diadem of Jurisprudence Award were established to assist individuals to become rabbis, teachers, and leaders. Each award recipient receives $25,000. Recipients study for five years under the supervision of Roshei Yeshiva and great rabbis. The recipient of The Crown of Torah Award studies the Talmud, Rashi, Tosefos, the Ri'f, and the Ro'sh intensively. The recipient of The Diadem of Jurisprudence Award studies the Laws of Shabbos in Orach Chayim; the Laws of that which is Forbidden and that which is Permitted; Ritual Cleanliness and Interest in Yoreh Deah; and the Laws of Judges in Choshen Hamishpat. He must aspire to be ordained with the Ordination of Scholars according to the Torah, and to be accepted to the glorious position of a righteous judge. At the end of the five-year program, they will be examined on the Talmudic and other knowledge that they acquired during the entire period.
EIN: 116313080

5845
Chest and Foundation of the Fur Industry
of the City of New York, Inc.
40 W. 37 St., Ste. 1700
New York, NY   10018-7102   (212) 760-9343

Foundation type: Public charity
Purpose: Grants to economically disadvantaged former members of the fur industry.
Financial data: Year ended 12/31/2012. Assets, $47,426 (M); Expenditures, $34,154; Total giving, $28,960; Grants to individuals, totaling $24,960.
Fields of interest: Economically disadvantaged.

Type of support: Grants for special needs.
Application information: Contact foundation for current application deadline/guidelines.
EIN: 135631505

5846
Children for Children
(also known as GenerationOn)
281 Park Ave. S., 6th Fl.
New York, NY   10010-6125   (917) 746-8182
Contact: Maggie Jones, Exec. Dir.
E-mail: info@generationon.org; URL: http://www.generationon.org

Foundation type: Public charity
Purpose: Grants to New York City public school teachers who lack materials and resources needed to educate their students.
Publications: Application guidelines; Annual report; Informational brochure; Newsletter.
Financial data: Year ended 09/30/2011. Assets, $2,340,800 (M); Expenditures, $218.
Fields of interest: Public education.
Type of support: Grants to individuals.
Application information: Applications accepted. Application form required. Application form available on the grantmaker's web site.
> *Initial approach:* Telephone or e-mail
> *Send request by:* Mail or e-mail
> *Copies of proposal:* 1
> *Deadline(s):* None
> *Applicants should submit the following:*
>> 1) Resume
>> 2) Letter(s) of recommendation
>> 3) Curriculum vitae
>> 4) Budget Information
> *Additional information:* Application should include a letter, budget information and a description of the school.

EIN: 133880287

5847
Children of China Pediatrics Foundation
Rockefeller Center Station
P.O. Box 5594
New York, NY   10185-5594
Contact: Regina Palumbo, Pres.
E-mail: info@chinapediatrics.org; URL: http://www.chinapediatrics.org/

Foundation type: Public charity
Purpose: Medical treatment for children with disabilities and deformities living in Chinese orphanages only.
Financial data: Year ended 12/31/2011. Assets, $470,958 (M); Expenditures, $251,395; Total giving, $34,800.
Fields of interest: Children/youth, services; Children; Disabilities, people with; Physically disabled; Asians/Pacific Islanders; Economically disadvantaged.
Type of support: Foreign applicants.
Application information:
> *Initial approach:* Letter
> *Additional information:* Contact foundation for eligibility criteria.

EIN: 134014724

5848
Children's Aid Association of Amsterdam, NY
P.O. Box 327
Amsterdam, NY   12010   (518) 829-9900
Contact: Geraldine DeNovio
Application address: 188 Country Club Ln., Fort Johnson, NY 12070

Foundation type: Operating foundation
Purpose: Scholarships to financially needy, single high school seniors or graduates of Montgomery County, NY, to attend accredited colleges.
Financial data: Year ended 05/31/2013. Assets, $1,313,860 (M); Expenditures, $115,525; Total giving, $92,275.
Fields of interest: Higher education; Scholarships/financial aid; Economically disadvantaged.
Type of support: Scholarships—to individuals; Undergraduate support.
Application information: Applications accepted. Application form required. Interview required.
> *Send request by:* Mail
> *Deadline(s):* June 27
> *Additional information:* Application should include financial information.

EIN: 141340035

5849
Children's Aid Society
105 E. 22nd St.
New York, NY   10010-5493   (212) 949-4800
Contact: Richard R. Buery, Jr., Pres. and C.E.O.
URL: http://www.childrensaidsociety.org

Foundation type: Public charity
Purpose: Emergency and support funds to underserved children and their families in New York, NY.
Publications: Annual report; Financial statement; Newsletter.
Financial data: Year ended 06/30/2011. Assets, $292,097,486 (M); Expenditures, $110,987,761; Total giving, $3,698,790; Grants to individuals, totaling $3,698,790.
Fields of interest: Higher education; Scholarships/financial aid; Youth development, services; Volunteer services.
Type of support: Undergraduate support.
Application information: Contact foundation for current application deadline/guidelines.
Program description:
> *CAS Scholarship Program:* Provides scholarships to students from the community centers and schools to help with the financial burdens of higher education and allow deserving youth to attend college.

EIN: 135562191

5850
Children's Scholarship Fund
8 W. 38th St., 9th Fl.
New York, NY   10018-6229   (212) 515-7100
FAX: (212) 515-7111;
E-mail: info@scholarshipfund.org; E-mail For Darla Romfo: dromfo@scholarshipfund.org; URL: http://www.scholarshipfund.org

Foundation type: Public charity
Purpose: Tuition assistance to economically disadvantaged children for attendance at private elementary and parochial schools.
Publications: Annual report; Financial statement; Informational brochure; Newsletter.
Financial data: Year ended 08/31/2012. Assets, $14,797,235 (M); Expenditures, $25,289,912;

Total giving, $23,473,142; Grants to individuals, totaling $17,190,183.
Fields of interest: Elementary school/education; Economically disadvantaged.
Type of support: Grants to individuals.
Application information: Applications accepted. Application form available on the grantmaker's web site.
> *Additional information:* Applications are accepted for scholarships in some cities. See web site for listing city listings.

EIN: 134002189

5851
Children's Tumor Foundation
(formerly National Neurofibromatosis Foundation, Inc.)
95 Pine St., 16th Fl.
New York, NY   10005-3904   (212) 344-6633
Contact: John Risner, Pres.
For research grants: Kim Hunter-Schaedle, Ph.D., Chief Scientific Off., tel.: (212) 344-6633 ext. 231, e-mail: khunter-schaedle@ctf.org
FAX: (212) 747-0004; E-mail: info@ctf.org; Toll Free Tel.: (800)-323-7938 for research grants: Annette Bakker, Ph.D., Chief Scientific Officer, tel.: (212) 344-6633 ext. 7029, e-mail: abakker@ctf.org; URL: http://www.ctf.org

Foundation type: Public charity
Purpose: Research grants to scientists for the development of therapies and cures for neurofibromatosis type 1 (NF1), neurofibromatosis type 2 (NF2), schwannomatosis and related disorders.
Publications: Application guidelines; Annual report; Financial statement; Informational brochure; Newsletter.
Financial data: Year ended 12/31/2011. Assets, $9,102,033 (M); Expenditures, $8,148,587; Total giving, $3,401,857.
Fields of interest: Nerve, muscle & bone diseases; Nerve, muscle & bone research.
Type of support: Research.
Application information: Applications accepted. Application form required. Application form available on the grantmaker's web site.
> *Initial approach:* Letter or e-mail
> *Applicants should submit the following:*
>> 1) Letter(s) of recommendation
>> 2) Proposal
>> 3) Budget Information
> *Additional information:* See web site for application guidelines and complete program listing.

EIN: 132298956

5852
Chinese Staff and Workers Association, Inc.
P.O. Box 130401
New York, NY   10013-0995   (212) 334-2333
Contact: Wing Lam, Exec. Dir.
FAX: (212) 334-1974; E-mail: cswa@cswa.org; URL: http://www.cswa.org

Foundation type: Public charity
Purpose: Financial assistance to indigent members of the Chinese Staff and Workers' Association.
Financial data: Year ended 06/30/2012. Assets, $3,557,678 (M); Expenditures, $435,887.
Type of support: Grants for special needs.
Application information:
> *Initial approach:* Letter

Additional information: Contact foundation for further information.
EIN: 133015932

5853
Cinereach Ltd.
126 5th Ave., 5th Fl.
New York, NY   10011-5606   (212) 727-3224
FAX: (212) 727-3282;
E-mail: grants@cinereach.org; Reach Film Fellowship e-mail: info@thereachfilmfellowship.org; Additional e-mail: info@cinereach.org; URL: http://www.cinereach.org/

Foundation type: Operating foundation
Purpose: Fellowships to early-career filmmakers who have studied film at the undergraduate or graduate level, or are self-taught with the equivalent level of experience.
Publications: Application guidelines; Grants list.
Financial data: Year ended 06/30/2012. Assets, $4,108,680 (M); Expenditures, $3,195,200; Total giving, $372,306.
Fields of interest: Film/video.
Type of support: Fellowships.
Application information: Applications accepted. Application form available on the grantmaker's web site. Interview required.
   Send request by: Online
   Additional information: See web site for additional guidelines.
Program description:
   Reach Film Fellowships: The foundation is in the process of developing a new Fellowships program. See foundation web site for updates in this matter.
EIN: 202946241

5854
Adam Cirillo Scholarship Foundation
5 Morse Ave.
Staten Island, NY   10314   (718) 698-3947
Contact: Patricia Cuzzocrea, Dir.

Foundation type: Independent foundation
Purpose: An annual scholarship to a graduating member of the football team at Brooklyn Technical High School, NY, who is outstanding in academics, football and character.
Financial data: Year ended 12/31/2012. Assets, $693,369 (M); Expenditures, $43,073; Total giving, $20,000; Grants to individuals, 4 grants totaling $20,000 (high: $8,000; low: $4,000).
Fields of interest: Higher education; Athletics/sports, football.
Type of support: Support to graduates or students of specific schools.
Application information: Applications accepted. Application form required.
   Deadline(s): Mar. 1
EIN: 133844881

5855
Cirio Foundation, Inc.
c/o Flanagan & Co.
60 E. 42nd St., Ste. 1536
New York, NY   10165

Foundation type: Operating foundation
Purpose: Scholarships to young minority students for continuing education at accredited colleges or universities.
Financial data: Year ended 12/31/2012. Assets, $459,651 (M); Expenditures, $203,428; Total giving, $117,548; Grants to individuals, totaling $117,548.

Fields of interest: Higher education; Minorities.
Type of support: Scholarships—to individuals.
Application information: Applications not accepted.
   Additional information: Unsolicited requests for funds not considered or acknowledged.
EIN: 133729580

5856
The City College 21st Century Foundation, Inc.
138th St., Convent Ave.
New York, NY   10031-9101   (212) 650-7125
Contact: Rachelle D. Butler, Exec. Dir.

Foundation type: Public charity
Purpose: Scholarships to entering freshman, transfer and graduate students for attendance at the City College of New York, NY.
Financial data: Year ended 06/30/2011. Assets, $157,191,535 (M); Expenditures, $11,452,579; Total giving, $3,947,673; Grants to individuals, totaling $3,466,362.
Fields of interest: Higher education.
Type of support: Support to graduates or students of specific schools.
Application information: Applications accepted. Application form required. Application form available on the grantmaker's web site.
   Initial approach: Letter
   Deadline(s): Varies
   Applicants should submit the following:
      1) SAT
      2) ACT
      3) Essay
      4) Transcripts
      5) Letter(s) of recommendation
   Additional information: Selection is based on academic merit. Scholarships are paid either directly to the student or to the educational institution.
Program descriptions:
   Alumni Association Economics Department Scholarships: The foundation awards funds, prizes, and internships to qualified students in the economics department of City College of New York.
   Mellon Mays Undergraduate Fellowships: Awards a stipend of $1,000 per semester, support of $3,000 for summer research following sophomore and junior years, and repayment of up to $10,000 in undergraduate or graduate loans to minority students who desire to matriculate in a Ph.D. program and pursue a career in research and teaching at the college or university level.
   Rudin Research Fellowships: Awards $2,500 stipends to biomedical students to undertake at least 250 hours of research that is mentored by a faculty member of the Sophie Davis Program.
   Zitrin Foundation Scholarships: Awards $5,000 to juniors or seniors in the Student Support Services Program (SSSP) to tutor and mentor other SSSP students and help with SSSP activities.
EIN: 133850823

5857
City Parks Foundation
830 5th Ave.
New York, NY   10065-7001   (212) 360-1399
Contact: Alison Tocci, Pres.
FAX: (212) 360-8283;
E-mail: info@cityparksfoundation.org; E-mail for Alison Tocci: atocci@cityparksfoundation.org; URL: http://www.cityparksfoundation.org

Foundation type: Public charity

Purpose: Grants to art presenters and groups to produce works in New York City.
Financial data: Year ended 03/31/2012. Assets, $35,081,325 (M); Expenditures, $12,842,247; Total giving, $90,780.
Fields of interest: Arts, artist's services.
Type of support: Grants to individuals.
Application information: Applications accepted. Application form required. Application form available on the grantmaker's web site.
   Initial approach: Application
   Send request by: E-mail for LOI, mail or hand delivered for application
   Copies of proposal: 7
   Deadline(s): Dec. 16 for LOI, Feb. 17 for application
   Final notification: Recipients notified within four to eight weeks
   Applicants should submit the following:
      1) Work samples
      2) Proposal
      3) Letter(s) of recommendation
      4) Curriculum vitae
      5) Budget Information
   Additional information: See web site for additional guidelines.
EIN: 133561657

5858
The Civil Service Employees Association, Inc.
143 Washington Ave.
Albany, NY   12210-2303   (518) 257-1000
URL: https://cseany.org/

Foundation type: Public charity
Purpose: Scholarship and tuition assistance for CSEA members and members children.
Financial data: Year ended 09/30/2011. Assets, $113,685,090 (M); Expenditures, $129,419,059; Total giving, $4,574,383; Grants to individuals, totaling $4,574,383.
Fields of interest: Education.
Type of support: Employee-related scholarships.
Application information: Members must provide proof of attendance and grades for reimbursement for courses taken.
EIN: 140479613

5859
The Clark Foundation
1 Rockefeller Plz., 31st Fl.
New York, NY   10020-2102   (212) 977-6900
Contact: Doug Bauer, Exec. Dir.

Foundation type: Independent foundation
Purpose: Grants for medical and convalescent care to financially needy individuals who are primarily patients at the Mary Imogene Bassett Hospital in Cooperstown, NY.
Publications: Application guidelines; Program policy statement.
Financial data: Year ended 12/31/2012. Assets, $471,369,685 (M); Expenditures, $28,693,172; Total giving, $17,511,410.
Fields of interest: Nursing home/convalescent facility; Health care.
Type of support: Grants for special needs.
Application information: Interview required.
   Initial approach: Letter
EIN: 135616528

5860
The Royce W. Clark Memorial Trust
P.O. Box 389
Walton, NY 13856 (607) 865-4126

Foundation type: Independent foundation
Purpose: Scholarships to graduates of Walton Central School District #1, NY, for undergraduate education.
Financial data: Year ended 12/31/2012. Assets, $162,257 (M); Expenditures, $2,845; Total giving, $1,460; Grants to individuals, 3 grants totaling $1,460 (high: $560, low: $400).
Fields of interest: Higher education.
Type of support: Support to graduates or students of specific schools; Undergraduate support.
Application information: Applications accepted.
> *Initial approach:* Letter
> *Deadline(s):* May 31
> *Additional information:* Contact the trust for additional application information.
EIN: 166333418

5861
Clinton Community College Foundation, Inc.
136 Clinton Point Dr.
Plattsburgh, NY 12901-6002 (518) 562-4125
FAX: (518) 562-4380; URL: http://www.clinton.edu/alumni/aboutfoundation.cxml

Foundation type: Public charity
Purpose: Scholarships to students attending Clinton Community College, NY for higher education.
Financial data: Year ended 08/31/2011. Assets, $3,732,743 (M); Expenditures, $314,068; Total giving, $36,486; Grants to individuals, totaling $36,486.
Fields of interest: College (community/junior).
Type of support: Support to graduates or students of specific schools.
Application information: Applications accepted. Application form required.
> *Send request by:* Fax, or mail
> *Deadline(s):* Apr. 24
> *Additional information:* Application must be typed and be submitted to the financial aid office by the due date.
EIN: 146097944

5862
CNN Heroes
1 Time Warner Ctr.
New York, NY 10019-6038
URL: http://www.cnnheroes.com

Foundation type: Corporate giving program
Purpose: Awards by nomination only to individuals in the U.S. and abroad who have done remarkable deeds in their communities and beyond.
Publications: Application guidelines; Grants list.
Fields of interest: Environment; Health care; Civil/human rights; Community/economic development; Children.
Type of support: Awards/grants by nomination only; Awards/prizes.
Application information: Application form required. Application form available on the grantmaker's web site.
> *Send request by:* Online
> *Deadline(s):* Aug. 31 for 2011, Aug. 1 for 2012
> *Additional information:* Nominations submitted by mail will not be accepted. Self nominations are not accepted.

Program description:
> *CNN Heroes Awards Program:* Awards to individuals in the U.S. and abroad who are making a difference in their communities and beyond, who are at least thirteen years of age or older as of Nov. 25, 2010, and some portion of the nominee's activities must have taken place on Nov. 25, 2010 or be ongoing. Each finalist will receive $50,000 and the winner will receive $250,000. Nominees cannot have previously been selected as a CNN Hero Finalist or Winner.

5863
Cogar Foundation, Inc.
1001 Broad St.
Utica, NY 13501-1545 (315) 866-0300

Foundation type: Independent foundation
Purpose: Scholarships to Herkimer County High School, NY, students and to Herkimer County Community College graduates.
Financial data: Year ended 12/31/2011. Assets, $663,342 (M); Expenditures, $39,005; Total giving, $33,557.
Type of support: Support to graduates or students of specific schools; Undergraduate support.
Application information: Applications accepted. Application form required.
> *Deadline(s):* 1st quarter of the year.
> *Applicants should submit the following:*
> 1) Transcripts
> 2) Financial information
EIN: 237035415

5864
Deo B. Colburn Education Foundation
P.O. Box 824
Lake Placid, NY 12946-0824
Contact: Margaret E. Doran, Treas.

Foundation type: Independent foundation
Purpose: Scholarships to residents of school districts of northeast portions of the Adirondack Park in northern NY for attendance at colleges, universities, and technical schools.
Financial data: Year ended 06/30/2013. Assets, $5,849,145 (M); Expenditures, $303,847; Total giving, $257,250; Grants to individuals, 277 grants totaling $257,250 (high: $1,500, low: $500).
Fields of interest: Higher education.
Type of support: Technical education support; Undergraduate support.
Application information: Applications accepted. Application form required.
> *Deadline(s):* Apr. 15
> *Applicants should submit the following:*
> 1) Class rank
> 2) Resume
> 3) Transcripts
> 4) GPA
> *Additional information:* Application forms available after Feb. 1. Application must also include copy of financial aid award letter and a handwritten statement of future plans.
EIN: 222777121

5865
Coleman Student Fund, Inc.
P.O. Box 284
Trumansburg, NY 14886

Foundation type: Independent foundation
Purpose: Interest-free student loans to graduates of Trumansburg Central School District,

Trumansburg, NY, for study at the undergraduate level.
Financial data: Year ended 07/31/2013. Assets, $193,106 (M); Expenditures, $304; Total giving, $0.
Fields of interest: Higher education.
Type of support: Student loans—to individuals; Support to graduates or students of specific schools; Undergraduate support.
Application information: Applications accepted. Interview required.
> *Deadline(s):* May 31
> *Applicants should submit the following:*
> 1) Transcripts
> 2) Letter(s) of recommendation
> *Additional information:* Application should also include a copy of letter of acceptance from the college to be attended. Applicant must demonstrate financial need.
EIN: 222387137

5866
College Art Association
(formerly College Art Association of America, Inc.)
50 Broadway, 21st Fl.
New York, NY 10004 (212) 691-1051
Contact: Linda Downs, Exec. Dir. and C.E.O.
FAX: (212) 627-2381;
E-mail: nyoffice@collegeart.org; Additional e-mail: fellowship@collegeart.org; URL: http://www.collegeart.org

Foundation type: Public charity
Purpose: Fellowships limited to M.F.A., and Ph.D. students studying art and art history. Grants to support publication of manuscripts in the history of art and related subjects.
Publications: Application guidelines; Biennial report; Financial statement; Grants list; Informational brochure; Newsletter.
Financial data: Year ended 06/30/2012. Assets, $9,537,023 (M); Expenditures, $4,856,481; Total giving, $86,800; Grants to individuals, totaling $35,000.
Fields of interest: Visual arts; Art history.
Type of support: Fellowships; Awards/grants by nomination only; Awards/prizes; Graduate support; Doctoral support.
Application information: Application form required.
> *Initial approach:* Letter, telephone, or e-mail
> *Deadline(s):* Varies
> *Additional information:* See web site for additional guidelines.
Program descriptions:
> *Alfred H. Barr, Jr. Award:* The award is presented to the author or authors of an especially distinguished catalogue in the history of art, published in the English language under the auspices of a museum, library, or collection, Catalogues of public or private collections or significant portions thereof and exhibition catalogues are eligible. Awards are by nomination only. Deadline July 31.
> *Art Journal Award:* The award is presented to the author of the most distinguished contribution, article, interview, conversation, portfolio, review, or any other text or visual project published in Art Journal during the previous calendar year. Awards by nomination only. Deadline Aug. 31.
> *Arthur Kingsley Porter Prize:* The award seeks to encourage high scholarly standards among younger members of the profession. The prize is awarded for a distinguished article published in The Art Bulletin during the previous calendar year by a scholar of any nationality who is under the age of 35 or who has received the doctorate not more than ten years before acceptance of the article for

publication. Awards by nomination only. Deadline Aug. 31.

Artist Award for a Distinguished Body of Work: A peer award given to an artist for exceptional work through exhibitions, presentations, or performances. The award is presented to a living artist or national or international stature and must tie him or her to an exceptional recent exhibition. Awards by nomination only. Deadline Aug. 31.

CAA/Heritage Preservation Award for Distinction in Scholarship and Conservation: The award is presented for an outstanding contribution by one or more persons who, individual or jointly, have enhanced understanding of art through the application of knowledge and experience in conservation, art history, and art. Awards by nomination only. Deadline Aug. 31.

Charles Rufus Morey Book Award: The award honors an especially distinguished book in the history of art, published in the English language. Preference is given to books, including catalogues raisonnes, by a single author, but major publications in the form of articles or group studies may be included. Publication of documents or inventories unless specifically in the context of an exhibition, are also eligible. Awards by nomination only. Deadline July 31.

Distinguished Artist Award for Lifetime Achievement: The award celebrates the career of an artist who, among other distinctions, has demonstrated particular commitment to his or her work throughout a long career and has had an important impact nationally and internationally on the field. Awards by nomination only. Deadline Aug. 31.

Distinguished Lifetime Achievement Award for Writing on Art: The award celebrates the career of an author of note, and includes art criticism, art history, art biography, and/or art theory. The award is presented to an author who, among other distinctions, has demonstrated particular commitment to his or her work throughout a long career and has had an impact, nationally or internationally, on the field. Awards by nomination. Deadline Aug. 31.

Distinguished Teaching of Art Award: The award is presented to an individual who has been actively engaged in teaching art for most of his/her career. This award is presented to an artist of distinction who has developed a philosophy or technique of instruction based on his or her experience as an artist; has encouraged his or her students to develop their own individual abilities; and/or has made some contribution to the body of knowledge loosely called theory and understood as embracing technical, material, aesthetic, and perceptual issues. Awards by nomination only. Deadline Aug. 31.

Distinguished Teaching of Art History Award: The award is presented to an individual who has been actively engaged in teaching art history for most of his or her career. Awards by nomination only. Deadline Aug. 31.

Frank Jewett Mather Award: The award for art journalism is awarded for significant published art criticism that has appeared in publication in a one-year period beginning Sept. 1 through Aug. 31. The award may be given for work that originated before the indicated period provided that such work extends into that award period. Awards by nomination only. Deadline Aug. 31.

Millard Meiss Publication Grants: Grants for the purpose of subsidizing book length scholarly manuscripts in the history of art and related subjects that have been accepted by a publisher on their merits, but cannot be published in the most desirable form without a subsidy. Deadline Oct. 1.

Professional Development Fellowships: Supports promising artists and art historians who are enrolled in M.F.A. and Ph.D. programs nationwide by offering support of $5,000 to each fellow to aid various aspects of their work from job-search expenses or purchasing materials for the studio. Fellows and honorable mentions also receive a free one-year membership to CAA and complimentary registration to the Annual Conference. Deadline Sept. 30.

Travel Grants for the Annual Conference: Travel grants for graduate students in art history and studio art and to international artists and scholars. A limited number of $150 travel grants are available to advanced Ph.D. and M.F.A. graduate students as partial reimbursement of travel expense to attend the conference. Students must be current CAA members and successful applicants will also receive a complimentary conference registration. Deadline Sept. 23.

Wyeth Publication Grant: The Wyeth Foundation for American Art supports the publication of books on American art, art created in the United State, Canada, and Mexico prior to 1970. Grants support books on the history of America Art, visual studies, and related subjects that have been accepted by a publisher on their merits but cannot be published in the most desirable form without a subsidy. Deadline Oct. 1.
EIN: 131671148

5867
College Careers Fund of Westchester, Inc.
190 E. Post Rd., 3rd Fl.
P.O. Box 1530
White Plains, NY 10602-1530 (914) 576-3000
Contact: Peter Adams, Pres.
FAX: (914) 576-3001; E-mail: ccareers@aol.com;
Mailing address: P.O. Box 1530, White Plains, NY 10602-1530; URL: http://www.collegecareersny.org

Foundation type: Public charity
Purpose: Scholarships to economically disadvantaged young people for higher education in combination with unique counseling services.
Fields of interest: Economically disadvantaged.
Type of support: Undergraduate support.
Application information: Contact fund for current application guidelines.
EIN: 132628725

5868
Joseph Collins Foundation
c/o Willkie Farr & Gallagher
787 7th Ave.
New York, NY 10019-7099

Foundation type: Independent foundation
Purpose: Grants only to students with inadequate resources, for attendance at accredited medical schools in states east of or contiguous to the Mississippi River, in sums not exceeding $10,000. Grants also for tuition to needy second through fourth year undergraduate medical students on the recommendation of medical school authorities.
Publications: Annual report; Program policy statement.
Financial data: Year ended 06/30/2013. Assets, $23,909,544 (M); Expenditures, $1,788,992; Total giving, $1,640,000; Grants to individuals, 82 grants totaling $1,640,000 (high: $20,000, low: $20,000).

Fields of interest: Medical school/education; Mental health, treatment; Neuroscience; Psychology/behavioral science.
Type of support: Graduate support; Undergraduate support.
Application information: Applications accepted. Application form required.
Initial approach: Letter
Deadline(s): Mar.
Additional information: Selection is based on financial need, scholastic record and standing, and evidence of good moral character. Students must stand in the upper half of their class, intend to specialize in neurology or psychiatry, or to become a general practitioner, and have outside cultural interests. Application must be obtained from the medical school authorities.
EIN: 136404527

5869
Tom Collins/Chris Panatier 9/11 Memorial Foundation, Inc.
50 Jericho Tpke., Ste. 109
Jericho, NY 11753-1014
E-mail: info@tccpmemorialfoundation.org;
URL: http://www.tccpmemorialfoundation.org/

Foundation type: Public charity
Purpose: Scholarships provided annually to two students currently attending Half Hollow Hills High School East, Dix Hills, New York for higher education.
Financial data: Year ended 12/31/2010. Assets, $63,310 (M); Expenditures, $31,597; Total giving, $26,600.
Fields of interest: Higher education.
Type of support: Support to graduates or students of specific schools.
Application information: Applicants must demonstrate strong leadership skills, promote positive attitudes, show integrity, compassion and have a financial need.
EIN: 331056681

5870
Columbia University-Presbyterian Hospital School of Nursing Alumni Association
480 Mamaroneck Ave.
Harrison, NY 10528-1621 (914) 481-5787
FAX: (914) 481-5788; E-mail: info@cuphsonaa.org;
URL: http://www.cuphsonaa.org

Foundation type: Public charity
Purpose: Scholarships and research grants to students or graduates of the Columbia University School of Nursing, NY.
Publications: Informational brochure; Newsletter.
Financial data: Year ended 06/30/2012. Assets, $6,234,884 (M); Expenditures, $289,464; Total giving, $122,234; Grants to individuals, totaling $122,234.
Fields of interest: Graduate/professional education; Nursing school/education.
Type of support: Research; Grants to individuals; Scholarships—to individuals; Support to graduates or students of specific schools.
Application information: Application form required. Application form available on the grantmaker's web site.
Initial approach: Letter, telephone or e-mail
Send request by: Mail or fax
Deadline(s): Mar. 1
Applicants should submit the following:

1) Curriculum vitae
2) Transcripts
Additional information: Application should also include letter of acceptance from school, two letters of professional reference plus one personal, and a personal statement of 500 words or less.

Program description:
Scholarships: Scholarships are available to members of the association. Undergraduate scholarships are given to the most qualified undergraduate students at Columbia University School of Nursing; graduate scholarships are distributed by the association directly to qualified alumni applicants.
EIN: 131681281

5871
Columbus Citizens Foundation, Inc.
8 E. 69th St.
New York, NY 10021-4906 (212) 249-9923
Contact: David J. Iommarini, Exec. Dir.
FAX: (212) 737-4413;
E-mail: ccf@columbuscitizens.org; E-Mail for David J. Lommarini: diommarini@columbuscitizens.org; URL: http://www.columbuscitizensfd.org

Foundation type: Public charity
Purpose: Scholarships to students of Italian heritage in elementary school, high school, and college pursuing higher education.
Publications: Application guidelines; Annual report; Informational brochure.
Financial data: Year ended 12/31/2011. Assets, $16,200,931 (M); Expenditures, $3,753,057; Total giving, $1,821,377; Grants to individuals, totaling $1,306,878.
Fields of interest: Elementary school/education; Secondary school/education; College.
Type of support: Scholarships—to individuals.
Application information: Applications accepted. Application form required. Application form available on the grantmaker's web site. Interview required.
Deadline(s): Feb.
Final notification: Applicants notified approximately one month after all interviews
Additional information: See web site for additional application guidelines.
Program descriptions:
College Scholarships: This fund helps young men and women of Italian descent to pursue their career dreams by helping to fund their post-secondary education. Students who are of Italian descent with a GPA of 3.0 (85% or B) or higher who are from households where the total gross income does not exceed $25,000 per capita are eligible. Only seniors in high school who will enter college as freshmen the following fall are eligible to apply. Students who are already in college are NOT eligible for scholarships.
Franco Zeffirelli Scholarship for the Arts: This fund supports graduate-level students of Italian descent who have shown talent and a commitment to the arts, a field overlooked by many organizations that support education. Recipients are selected by a private committee.
High School Scholarships: Students who are of Italian descent with a GPA of 3.0 (85% or B) or higher who are from households where the total gross income does not exceed $20,000 per capita are eligible. Only 8th graders who will enter high school the following fall are eligible to apply. Students who are already in high school are NOT eligible for scholarships.
EIN: 136118967

5872
The Commonwealth Fund
1 E. 75th St.
New York, NY 10021-2692
Contact: Andrea C. Landes, V.P., Grants Mgmt.
FAX: (212) 606-3500; E-mail: info@cmwf.org; E-mail for questions from grant applicants: grants@cmwf.org; URL: http://www.commonwealthfund.org

Foundation type: Independent foundation
Purpose: Health policy fellowships to junior health policy researchers or practitioners from the United Kingdom, Australia, and New Zealand for research and training in the U.S., and also fellowships for the study of public policy in New Zealand.
Publications: Annual report; Annual report (including application guidelines); Financial statement; Grants list; Informational brochure; Newsletter; Occasional report; Program policy statement.
Financial data: Year ended 06/30/2013. Assets, $702,204,618 (M); Expenditures, $48,738,642; Total giving, $29,564,183; Grants to individuals, totaling $2,380,423.
Fields of interest: Public policy; Health care; Research.
International interests: New Zealand.
Type of support: Fellowships; Research; Foreign applicants; Travel grants.
Application information: Application form required.
Initial approach: Letter, telephone, or e-mail
Deadline(s): Sept. 1 for Harkness Fellowships
Applicants should submit the following:
1) Proposal
2) Letter(s) of recommendation
3) Curriculum vitae
Additional information: Application must include statement of professional objectives; Interviews required for short listed candidates; Application guidelines are also available on Web site.
EIN: 131635260

5873
Community Arts Partnership of Tompkins County, Inc.
171 E. State St., PMB 107
Ithaca, NY 14850-4351 (607) 273-5072
Contact: John Spence, Exec. Dir.
FAX: (607) 273-4816; E-mail: info@artspartner.org; E-mail For John Spence: director@artspartner.org; URL: http://www.artspartner.org

Foundation type: Public charity
Purpose: Grants to individual artists in Ithaca and Tompkins County, NY, for the development of arts in the community.
Publications: Application guidelines; Newsletter.
Financial data: Year ended 12/31/2011. Assets, $183,385 (M); Expenditures, $404,574; Total giving, $57,400.
Fields of interest: Arts, artist's services.
Type of support: Grants to individuals.
Application information: Applications accepted. Application form required. Application form available on the grantmaker's web site.
Deadline(s): Oct. 11 for Artist in Community Grants, Oct. 12 for CAP Artist Fellowships, Nov. 15 for Artist/Teacher Partnership Grants
Program descriptions:
Artist in Community Grants: Formerly CAP II, the grant program awards amount of $1,500 to $2,500 each to Tompkins County artists. Grants support the creation of new work of artists whose interaction with communities is an integral part of their art-making.

Artist/Teacher Partnership Grants: Formerly LCB grants, the program is designed to assist schools in developing and implementing visual and performing arts residencies that are integrated into the core curriculum. Grants are available for teacher/teaching artist partnerships in multi-day school residencies.
CAP Fellowships for Artists: $1,000 fellowships to artists are available each year to help advance their careers. Five awards will be distributed to residents of Tompkins County who have lived continuously in the county from 10/1/09 through the present. Artists must be 18 years of age or older and not be currently enrolled in a graduate or undergraduate degree program.
EIN: 161384455

5874
Community Development Corporation of Long Island, Inc.
2100 Middle Country Rd., Ste. 300
Centereach, NY 11720-3578 (631) 471-1215
FAX: (631) 471-1210; E-mail: info@cdcli.org; Additional address (Nassau County): 54 W. Merrick Rd., Freeport, NY 11520-3710, tel.: (516) 867-7727, fax: (516) 867-9398; URL: http://www.cdcli.org

Foundation type: Public charity
Purpose: Rental housing assistance payments to low and moderate income families and grants to low income homeowners to ensure their homes are energy efficient. Low interest home improvement loans to eligible homeowners of Long Island, NY.
Publications: Annual report.
Financial data: Year ended 10/31/2011. Assets, $15,211,361 (M); Expenditures, $69,804,419; Total giving, $60,671,268; Grants to individuals, totaling $60,671,268.
Fields of interest: Housing/shelter, rehabilitation; Housing/shelter, home owners.
Type of support: Grants for special needs; Loans—to individuals.
Application information: Applications accepted. Application form required.
Additional information: Contact the corporation for eligibility requirements.
EIN: 112221341

5875
Community Foundation for Greater Buffalo
726 Exchange St., Ste. 525
Buffalo, NY 14210 (716) 852-2857
Contact: For grants: Darren Penoyer, Prog. Off.; Clotilde Perez-Bode Dedecker, C.E.O.
FAX: (716) 852-2861; E-mail: mail@cfgb.org; Grant inquiry e-mail: darrenp@cfgb.org; URL: http://www.cfgb.org

Foundation type: Community foundation
Purpose: Scholarships to current residents of Allegany, Cattaraugus, Chautauqua, Erie, Genesee, Niagara, Orleans, and Wyoming, NY for full time study at an accredited school in the U.S.
Publications: Application guidelines; Annual report; Biennial report; Financial statement; Grants list; Newsletter; Occasional report.
Financial data: Year ended 12/31/2011. Assets, $209,558,554 (M); Expenditures, $12,862,227; Total giving, $9,954,560; Grants to individuals, 1,698 grants totaling $1,915,048.
Fields of interest: Higher education.
Type of support: Scholarships—to individuals.
Application information: Applications accepted. Application form required.

Initial approach: Application
Send request by: Online
Deadline(s): Mar.
Final notification: Applicants notified in July
Additional information: Application should
include a transcript, and applicants must
complete the FAFSA.
EIN: 222743917

5876
The Community Foundation for South Central New York, Inc.

520 Columbia Dr., Ste. 100
Johnson City, NY 13790-0000 (607) 772-6773
FAX: (607) 722-6752; E-mail: cfscny@stny.rr.com;
URL: http://www.cfscny.org
Additional URL: http://www.donorswhocare.org/

Foundation type: Community foundation
Purpose: Scholarships limited to residents of
Broome, Chenango, Delaware, Otsego and Tioga
counties, NY for postsecondary education.
Publications: Application guidelines; Annual report;
Financial statement; Grants list; Informational
brochure; Newsletter.
Financial data: Year ended 12/31/2012. Assets,
$18,120,027 (M); Expenditures, $1,292,456;
Total giving, $744,440; Grants to individuals, 7
grants totaling $9,000 (high: $5,000, low: $250).
Fields of interest: Higher education.
Type of support: Scholarships—to individuals.
Application information: Applications accepted.
Additional information: Scholarship payments are
made directly to the educational institution on
behalf of the student. Contact the foundation
for additional guidelines.
EIN: 161512085

5877
The Community Foundation for the Greater Capital Region, Inc.

6 Tower Pl.
Albany, NY 12203-3725 (518) 446-9638
Contact: For grants: Jackie Mahoney, V.P., Progs.
FAX: (518) 446-9708; E-mail: info@cfcr.org;
Pre-application submission e-mail:
jmahoney@cfgcr.org; URL: http://www.cfgcr.org

Foundation type: Community foundation
Purpose: Scholarships to students at high schools
in the NY Capital Region for higher education.
Publications: Application guidelines; Annual report;
Financial statement; Informational brochure;
Newsletter.
Financial data: Year ended 12/31/2012. Assets,
$58,388,566 (M); Expenditures, $4,971,233;
Total giving, $3,902,076. Scholarships—to
individuals amount not specified.
Fields of interest: Higher education.
Type of support: Scholarships—to individuals;
Support to graduates or students of specific
schools; Undergraduate support.
Application information: Applications accepted.
Application form required. Application form
available on the grantmaker's web site.
Deadline(s): Apr. through May
Additional information: Eligibility criteria and
application procedures for each scholarship
differ. See web site for guidelines on each
fund.
EIN: 141505623

5878
The Community Foundation of Elmira-Corning and the Finger Lakes, Inc.

(formerly The Community Foundation of the
Chemung County Area and Corning Community
Foundation)
301 S. Main St.
Horseheads, NY 14845 (607) 739-3900
Contact: Randi Hewit, Pres.; Sara Palmer, Dir.,
Grants and Comms.
E-mail: rlh@communityfund.org; Additional e-mail:
sep@communityfund.org; URL: http://
www.communityfund.org

Foundation type: Community foundation
Purpose: Scholarships only to residents of
Chemung, Steuben, and Schuyler counties, NY.
Publications: Application guidelines; Annual report
(including application guidelines); Financial
statement.
Financial data: Year ended 06/30/2013. Assets,
$39,755,545 (M); Expenditures, $2,014,843;
Total giving, $1,327,606; Grants to individuals,
96 grants totaling $213,650.
Fields of interest: Research; Formal/general
education; Secondary school/education;
Vocational education; Higher education; College
(community/junior); Business school/education;
Law school/education; Nursing school/education;
Social work school/education; Disasters, fire
prevention/control; Athletics/sports, training;
Athletics/sports, school programs; Athletics/
sports, baseball; Human services; Volunteer
services; Business/industry; Science; Engineering;
Christian agencies & churches; Physically disabled;
Women; Economically disadvantaged.
Type of support: Grants to individuals;
Scholarships—to individuals; Support to graduates
or students of specific schools; Awards/prizes;
Graduate support; Undergraduate support.
Application information: Applications accepted.
Application form required. Application form
available on the grantmaker's web site.
Initial approach: Application
Send request by: Mail
Copies of proposal: 1
Deadline(s): Feb. 17
Applicants should submit the following:
1) ACT
2) Essay
3) Financial information
4) GPA
5) Letter(s) of recommendation
6) Resume
7) SAT
8) Transcripts
Additional information: Scholarship information
and applications are sent out at the end of
Oct. to each high school guidance counselor
in the foundation's catchment area for high
school seniors; for adult scholarships, see
web site for application forms and guidelines.
Program description:
Scholarship Funds: Individuals, families and
companies have established funds at the
foundation for educational scholarships so that
deserving neighbors can attend college or acquire
job skills. Most scholarships are for graduating high
school seniors to attend an accredited college or
university; some awards are available for adults
seeking to further their education. Each scholarship
has unique eligibility requirements; see web site for
additional information.
EIN: 161100837

5879
The Community Foundation of Herkimer & Oneida Counties, Inc.

(formerly Utica Foundation, Inc.)
1222 State St.
Utica, NY 13502-4728 (315) 735-8212
Contact: Margaret O'Shea, C.E.O. and Pres.
FAX: (315) 735-9363;
E-mail: info@foundationhoc.org; Telephone (for
grants): 315-735-8212; URL: http://
www.foundationhoc.org

Foundation type: Community foundation
Purpose: Scholarships to residents of Herkimer and
Oneida counties, NY.
Publications: Application guidelines; Annual report;
Financial statement; Newsletter.
Financial data: Year ended 12/31/2012. Assets,
$101,339,408 (M); Expenditures, $4,282,999;
Total giving, $2,189,578.
Type of support: Undergraduate support.
Application information:
Initial approach: Letter
Additional information: Contact foundation for
complete eligibility requirements.
EIN: 156016932

5880
Community Foundation of Orange County, Inc.

(formerly Community Foundation of Orange and
Sullivan, Inc.)
30 Scott's Corner Dr., Ste. 202
Montgomery, NY 12549-2262 (845) 769-9393
Contact: Karen VanHouten Minogue, C.E.O.
FAX: (845) 769-9391; E-mail: admin@cfoc-ny.org;
Additional e-mail: vanhouten@cfoc-ny.org;
URL: http://www.cfoc-ny.org

Foundation type: Community foundation
Purpose: Provides scholarships to students in
Orange and Sullivan counties, NY through various
funds.
Publications: Annual report; Financial statement;
Grants list; Informational brochure; Newsletter.
Financial data: Year ended 06/30/2012. Assets,
$7,625,870 (M); Expenditures, $765,992; Total
giving, $364,304; Grants to individuals, 82 grants
totaling $95,346.
Fields of interest: Higher education.
Type of support: Scholarships—to individuals.
Application information: Applications accepted.
EIN: 061551843

5881
Community Foundations of the Hudson Valley

80 Washington St., Ste. 201
Poughkeepsie, NY 12601-2316 (845)
452-3077
Contact: Andrea L. Reynolds, C.E.O.; For grants:
Jennifer Killian, Dir., Progs.
FAX: (845) 452-3083; E-mail: cfdc@cfdcny.org;
Additional E-mail: areynolds@cfdcny.org; Grant
inquiry e-mail: jkillian@cfhvny.org; URL: http://
www.cfdcny.org

Foundation type: Community foundation
Purpose: Scholarships to Dutchess County, NY,
residents. Grants to pre-kindergarten through 12th
grade public, private, and parochial school teachers
in Dutchess County, NY, for special projects and
professional development.
Publications: Application guidelines; Annual report;
Newsletter; IRS Form 990 or 990-PF printed copy
available upon request.

Financial data: Year ended 06/30/2012. Assets, $33,258,296 (M); Expenditures, $2,869,704; Total giving, $1,900,351; Grants to individuals, totaling $239,050.
Fields of interest: Scholarships/financial aid; Education.
Type of support: Program development; Scholarships—to individuals.
Application information: Applications accepted. Application form required. Application form available on the grantmaker's web site.
   Initial approach: Application
   Deadline(s): Apr. 1
   Applicants should submit the following:
      1) Letter(s) of recommendation
      2) FAFSA
      3) SAR
      4) Transcripts
   Additional information: Elibility requirements vary per scholarship fund; see web site for complete listing of scholarships.
EIN: 237026859

5882
Community Mayors, Inc.
9728 3rd Ave., Ste. 632
Brooklyn, NY   11209-7742   (908) 268-9016
Contact: Hon. Florence Thristino, Exec. Secy.
FAX: (718) 238-2036;
E-mail: kids@communitymayors.org; Additional tel.: (718) 439-3401; URL: http://www.communitymayors.org

Foundation type: Public charity
Purpose: Recreational therapy to children with special needs in the New York City metropolitan area.
Financial data: Year ended 03/31/2012. Assets, $59,529 (M); Expenditures, $183,501; Total giving, $134,230; Grants to individuals, totaling $134,230.
Fields of interest: Recreation; Children; Disabilities, people with.
Type of support: Grants to individuals.
Application information:
   Initial approach: Letter
   Additional information: Contact foundation for eligibility criteria.
EIN: 116077795

5883
Community Service Society of New York
105 E. 22nd St.
New York, NY   10010-5413   (212) 254-8900
Contact: David R. Jones, Pres. and C.E.O.
Additional tel.: (212) 614-5484 for Social Services Dept.
FAX: (212) 614-5515; E-mail: info@cssny.org;
E-Mail for David R. Jones: djones@cssny.org;
URL: http://www.cssny.org

Foundation type: Public charity
Purpose: Emergency financial assistance to needy families and individuals and those facing a temporary crisis in New York City, NY.
Publications: Annual report; Occasional report.
Financial data: Year ended 06/30/2012. Assets, $158,753,030 (M); Expenditures, $22,580,592; Total giving, $242,415; Grants to individuals, totaling $191,397.
Fields of interest: Human services; Economically disadvantaged.
Type of support: Emergency funds; Grants for special needs.
Application information: Interview required.
   Initial approach: Telephone

Additional information: Contact the agency for additional information.
EIN: 135562202

5884
Conference on Jewish Material Claims Against Germany
1359 Broadway, Rm. 2000
New York, NY   10018-7102   (646) 536-9100
FAX: (212) 679-2126; E-mail: info@claimscon.org;
URL: http://www.claimscon.org

Foundation type: Public charity
Purpose: Support to individual victims of the Holocaust, and their families with compensation and restitution payments.
Publications: Financial statement; Grants list.
Financial data: Year ended 12/31/2012. Assets, $966,798,749 (M); Expenditures, $774,500,408; Total giving, $715,243,756; Grants to individuals, totaling $58,335,455.
Fields of interest: Aging; Crime/abuse victims.
Type of support: Grants to individuals.
Application information: Applications accepted. Application form required.
   Additional information: Contact the organization or see web site for additional guidelines.
Program descriptions:
   Article 2 Fund: This program provides monthly payments of 300 euros, an amount that has increased over the years, and is paid in quarterly installments. The fund is limited to individuals who were incarcerated in a concentration camp, were imprisoned for at least three months in a ghetto as defined by the German government, were hiding for at least six to twelve months under inhumane condition without access to the outside world in German Nazi occupied territory or in Nazi satellite states (Nazi instigation), lived illegally under false identity or with false papers for at least six to twelve months under inhumane conditions in German Nazi occupied territory or in Nazi satellite states (Nazi instigation)
   Hardship Fund: Compensation in the form of a one-time payment of 2,556 euros is limited to Jewish Nazi victims who are alive at the time of filing the application. Heirs are not eligible to file and application. The fund is open to residents of all Eastern European countries, including the Baltic States.
   Orphans Fund: Nazi victims living in former Soviet bloc countries in Eastern Europe who were born in 1928 or later, and were orphaned due to Nazi persecution (both parents were killed due to persecution), may be eligible for a one-time payment of 2,556 euros.
EIN: 131677841

5885
John Confort Foundation Trust
c/o Martin L. Riker
100 Summit Lake Dr., Ste. 205
Valhalla, NY   10595-1362
Contact: Patricia Finn
Application address: 30-15 149th St., Flushing, NY 11354

Foundation type: Independent foundation
Purpose: Scholarships to high school seniors and eighth-grade students who are dependent children of Confort & Co., Inc. employees in good standing with at least two years of service. Scholarships also to qualified students who are unrelated to employees, but are recommended by employees.
Financial data: Year ended 12/31/2012. Assets, $16,872 (M); Expenditures, $89,340; Total giving,

$85,479; Grants to individuals, 21 grants totaling $50,579 (high: $5,000, low: $1,250).
Fields of interest: Secondary school/education; Higher education.
Type of support: Employee-related scholarships; Undergraduate support.
Application information: Application form required.
   Deadline(s): Mar. 15
   Applicants should submit the following:
      1) Transcripts
      2) SAR
      3) FAFSA
      4) SAT
      5) Letter(s) of recommendation
      6) GPA
   Additional information: Application should also include parents' tax return.
EIN: 137053704

5886
The Corning Museum of Glass
1 Museum Way
Corning, NY   14830-2253   (800) 732-6845
FAX: (607) 974-8470;
E-mail: whitehoudb@cmog.org; URL: http://www.cmog.org

Foundation type: Operating foundation
Purpose: Grants to foster scholarly research in the history of glassmaking.
Publications: Annual report; Newsletter.
Financial data: Year ended 12/31/2012. Assets, $36,897,511 (M); Expenditures, $40,904,960; Total giving, $35,000; Grants to individuals, 2 grants totaling $10,000 (high: $5,000, low:. $5,000).
Fields of interest: Visual arts; Arts.
Type of support: Research; Residencies.
Application information: Applications accepted. Application form required. Application form available on the grantmaker's web site.
   Initial approach: Application
   Send request by: Mail
   Deadline(s): Feb. 1 for Rakow Grant for Glass Research, Feb. 1 and Oct. 31 for Residencies
   Applicants should submit the following:
      1) Budget Information
      2) Proposal
      3) Letter(s) of recommendation
      4) Resume
   Additional information: Proposals for residencies should include 10 slides or digital images on CD of applicants work.
Program descriptions:
   Rakow Grant for Glass Research: Corning Museum of Glass awards grants of up to $10,000 to foster research in the history of glass and glassmaking. Special preference is given to projects that will bring researchers to Corning to study the museum's collections or to use its library. Projects are selected based on merit, the nature and contribution to glass studies, and the ability of the applicant to accomplish the goals as stated. Grants may be used to cover travel, living expenses, or other expenditures necessary to conduct the research or to publish it.
   Residency Programs: Corning Museum of Glass offers an artist-in-residence and researcher-in-residence program at the Studio. Artists and researchers are invited to spend a month at The Studio to explore glass art or expand on their current bodies of work. The residency offers transportation, room and board, basic supplies, and the facility will be made available whenever classes are not in session. Residencies are held in March, April, May, October, and November.
EIN: 160764349

5887
Corporation for Relief of Widows & Children of Clergymen of the Protestant Episcopal Church in NY
445 5th Ave.
New York, NY 10016-0109 (212) 592-6416

Foundation type: Public charity
Purpose: Financial assistance to widows and children of deceased Protestant Episcopal clergymen in NY.
Financial data: Year ended 08/31/2011. Assets, $15,441,779 (M); Expenditures, $490,700; Total giving, $422,200; Grants to individuals, totaling $422,200.
Fields of interest: Protestant agencies & churches.
Type of support: Grants for special needs.
Application information: Applications not accepted.
  Additional information: Unsolicited requests for funds not considered or acknowledged.
EIN: 237279145

5888
The Corporation of Yaddo
312 Union Ave.
P.O. Box 395
Saratoga Springs, NY 12866-6420 (518) 584-0746
Contact: Elaina Richardson, Pres.
FAX: (518) 584-1312;
E-mail: erichardson@yaddo.org; Additional address (New York City office): 20 W. 44th St., 4th Fl., Ste. 408, New York, NY 10036-6603, tel.: (212) 307-7685, fax: (212) 307-9663; URL: http://www.yaddo.org

Foundation type: Public charity
Purpose: Residencies to professional writers, visual artists, composers, choreographers, performance artists, and film and video artists.
Publications: Application guidelines; Annual report; Informational brochure (including application guidelines); Newsletter.
Financial data: Year ended 12/31/2011. Assets, $38,442,709 (M); Expenditures, $2,897,035.
Fields of interest: Film/video; Visual arts; Choreography; Music composition; Performing arts (multimedia); Literature.
International interests: Global Programs.
Type of support: Foreign applicants; Residencies.
Application information: Application form required. Application form available on the grantmaker's web site.
  Initial approach: Telephone, e-mail or fax
  Deadline(s): Jan. 1 and Aug. 1
  Applicants should submit the following:
    1) Work samples
    2) Resume
  Additional information: Application must also include references.
Program description:
  Residencies: Residencies are available for artists who are working at the professional level in their field. Applications will be considered from artists and small groups (two to three individuals) of artists who work in the following fields: literature (including fiction, nonfiction, poetry, drama, translation, and librettos); visual arts (including painting, drawing, sculpture, printmaking photography, mixed media, and installation art); music composition; performance and media (including choreography, performance art, sound art, and multi-media installations); and film and video (including narrative, documentary and experimental films, animation, and screenplays)
EIN: 141343055

5889
The Correspondents Fund
c/o The New York Times
620 8th Ave.
New York, NY 10018
Contact: Barbara Baumgarten
URL: http://correspondentsfund.org/

Foundation type: Independent foundation
Purpose: Grants for temporary emergency aid to individuals and their spouses and children who have served in the U.S. press, television, radio, news, film, and related organizations within or outside the U.S., or who have served the foreign press or other foreign news organizations.
Financial data: Year ended 04/30/2013. Assets, $610,686 (M); Expenditures, $152,286; Total giving, $145,500.
Fields of interest: Media/communications; Film/video; Television; Print publishing; Human services, emergency aid.
Type of support: Grants for special needs.
Application information: Applications accepted.
  Deadline(s): None
  Additional information: Applications by letter, including details of circumstances for which aid is being requested.
EIN: 136100568

5890
Cortland College Foundation, Inc.
Brockway Hall, Rm. 312
Cortland, NY 13045-2499 (607) 753-2518
Contact: Kimberly Pietro, V.P.
FAX: (607) 753-5448;
E-mail: cortlandcollegefoundation@cortland.edu;
E-Mail for Raymond D. Franco: raymond@em.cortland.edu; Tel. for Raymond D. Franco: (607) 753-2518; URL: http://www.cortland.edu/foundation/

Foundation type: Public charity
Purpose: Merit and need-based scholarships to deserving students who cannot afford the cost of a private college, for continuing education at SUNY Cortland.
Financial data: Year ended 06/30/2012. Assets, $27,882,491 (M); Expenditures, $2,079,539; Total giving, $601,826; Grants to individuals, totaling $601,826.
Fields of interest: Higher education.
Type of support: Support to graduates or students of specific schools.
Application information: Students selected for the scholarships will be notified in their letter of admission. There is no application process for incoming students. See web site for a complete listing of scholarship programs.
EIN: 160979814

5891
William Henry Cosby, Jr. and Camille Olivia Cosby Foundation, Inc.
c/o Patterson Belknapp Webb & Tyler LLP
1133 Ave. of the Americas, Ste. 2200
New York, NY 10036-6710

Foundation type: Independent foundation
Purpose: Scholarships by nomination only to financially needy students enrolled in selected colleges and universities in the U.S., primarily in NY and PA, on the basis of academic achievement.
Financial data: Year ended 06/30/2012. Assets, $3,803 (M); Expenditures, $41,457; Total giving, $38,842.

Type of support: Awards/grants by nomination only; Undergraduate support.
Application information: Applications not accepted.
  Additional information: Recipients are nominated by selected educational institutions that the foundation has invited to participate in the program.
EIN: 133408842

5892
Theresa Costa Scholarship Fund
c/o NBT Bank, N.A.
52 S. Broad St.
Norwich, NY 13815

Foundation type: Independent foundation
Purpose: Scholarships for higher education, primarily in Schuyler County, NY.
Financial data: Year ended 02/28/2013. Assets, $283,696 (M); Expenditures, $18,620; Total giving, $14,755.
Type of support: Scholarships—to individuals.
Application information: Applications not accepted.
  Additional information: Unsolicited requests for funds not considered or acknowledged.
EIN: 166417356

5893
Council of Community Services of New York State, Inc.
(also known as CCSNYS)
272 Broadway
Albany, NY 12204-2737 (518) 434-9194
FAX: (518) 434-0392; E-mail: dmack@ccsnys.org;
Application address: International Charitable Initiative, Inc., c/o Council of Community Services of New York State, Inc., 272 Broadway, Albany, NY 12204-2737; URL: http://www.ccsnys.org

Foundation type: Public charity
Purpose: Fiscal sponsorship to individuals with projects supporting the nonprofit sector.
Publications: Application guidelines; Annual report.
Financial data: Year ended 12/31/2011. Assets, $1,667,600 (M); Expenditures, $2,689,853.
Type of support: Fiscal agent/sponsor.
Application information: Contact the organization for application guidelines.
Program description:
  Fiscal Sponsorship Program: Fiscal sponsorship opportunities are available that provide unincorporated groups, projects, or coalitions with an alternative to managing the day-to-day administrative and accounting responsibilities with volunteers or limited staff capacity. The council provides use of its legal and tax-exempt status, prepares required financial reports for funders, manages contracts and subcontracts, deposits grant funds and cash receipts into a segregated account system, handles payments and cash disbursements, prepares monthly financial statements, and records donations and gifts; human resources and administrative services are also available. Eligible applicants must have a minimum of $1,000,000 in general liability insurance to cover all activities carried on by the organization. Reimbursement to the council is made according to a fixed schedule; the council also retains interest on any funds covered by the fiscal sponsorship arrangement.
EIN: 141343047

5894
Council on the Arts & Humanities for Staten Island

(also known as COAHSI)
1000 Richmond Terr.
Staten Island, NY 10301-1114 (718) 447-3329
Contact: Melanie Franklin Cohn, Exec. Dir.
FAX: (718) 442-8572;
E-mail: info@statenislandarts.org; E-Mail for
Melanie Franklin Cohn :
mcohn@statenislandarts.org; URL: http://
www.statenislandarts.org

Foundation type: Public charity
Purpose: Grants to individual Staten Island artists
of all disciplines for the creation of new work.
Publications: Application guidelines; Financial
statement; Grants list; Newsletter.
Financial data: Year ended 06/30/2012. Assets,
$380,013 (M); Expenditures, $662,089; Total
giving, $208,256; Grants to individuals, totaling
$163,656.
Fields of interest: Folk arts; Film/video; Visual arts;
Performing arts; Arts.
Type of support: Grants to individuals.
Application information: Applications accepted.
Application form required. Application form
available on the grantmaker's web site.
  Send request by: Mail
  Deadline(s): Oct. 15
  Applicants should submit the following:
    1) Letter(s) of recommendation
    2) Budget Information
    3) Work samples
    4) Proposal
  Additional information: Applicants must attend a
    workshop. Fax, e-mail or applications on disk
    or CD or in any other format are not accepted.
    See web site for current application deadline/
    guidelines.
Program descriptions:
  Encore Grants: Grants of $750 to $3,000 are
  available for community projects in the arts and
  humanities, awarded to Staten Island nonprofit
  organizations and individuals with nonprofit fiscal
  sponsors who have not previously received a
  council grant.
  Grants for the Arts: Grants of $750 to $3,000 are
  available for community projects in the arts and
  humanities, awarded to Staten Island nonprofit
  organizations and individuals with nonprofit fiscal
  sponsors who have not previously received a
  council grant.
  Original Work Grant: Grants of $2,125 for Staten
  Island individual artists for all disciplines to create
  new work. Artists who have received an Original
  Work grant in the last five years are not eligible.
  Artists must be 18 years old. Artists who are
  enrolled in high school or university degree
  programs or trade school certificate programs are
  not eligible.
EIN: 133713211

5895
The Covenant Foundation

1270 Ave. of the Americas, Ste. 304
New York, NY 10020-1702 (212) 245-3500
Contact: Harlene Winnick Appelman, Exec. Dir.
FAX: (212) 245-0619; E-mail: info@covenantfn.org;
E-Mail for Harlene Winnick Appelman :
harlene@covenantfn.org; URL: http://
www.covenantfn.org

Foundation type: Public charity
Purpose: Awards by nomination only to outstanding
educators in the U.S. and Canada who perform
exceptional work in any form of Jewish education.

Publications: Application guidelines; Grants list;
Informational brochure; Program policy statement.
Financial data: Year ended 12/31/2011. Assets,
$2,435,611 (M); Expenditures, $3,109,110; Total
giving, $1,387,828; Grants to individuals, totaling
$198,000.
Fields of interest: Secondary school/education;
Theological school/education; Education; Jewish
agencies & synagogues.
Type of support: Grants to individuals; Awards/
prizes.
Application information: Application form required.
  Initial approach: Letter or telephone
  Deadline(s): Dec. 2 for nominations, Dec. 16 for
    supporting materials
  Additional information: Nomination packets
    available after Sept.; Formal nomination form
    required should include biographical
    information, three letters of support,
    statement of motivation, and statement of
    purpose; Recipients notified in May; See
    program description for additional
    information.
Program description:
  Covenant Grants: A maximum of ten grants of up
  to $50,000 are awarded annually to creative Jewish
  educators to develop and implement outstanding
  approaches to Jewish education that are potentially
  replicable in other settings. Grants may also be
  awarded for the dissemination of programs that are
  especially effective. All institutions, agencies, and
  organizations actively involved in transmitting
  Jewish heritage in the United States and Canada
  are eligible to apply.
EIN: 363722029

5896
William and Dorothy Cox Foundation

c/o James Fantigrossi
1105 S. Creek Dr.
Webster, NY 14580 (585) 218-9860

Foundation type: Independent foundation
Purpose: Scholarships by nomination only to
students at secondary schools in the western NY
Section V athletic zone.
Financial data: Year ended 12/31/2011. Assets,
$204,501 (M); Expenditures, $12,416; Total
giving, $12,000; Grants to individuals, 6 grants
totaling $12,000 (high: $4,500, low: $500).
Type of support: Awards/grants by nomination only;
Undergraduate support.
Application information:
  Initial approach: Letter
  Additional information: Contact foundation for
    current nomination deadline/guidelines;
    Nomination by letter from nominee's high
    school principal, including recommendation
    letters from student's athletic coach and
    community leader who can attest to
    nominee's character and Christian values.
EIN: 161353302

5897
William J. Cox Memorial Fund

9600 Main St., Ste. 3
Clarence, NY 14031-2093

Foundation type: Independent foundation
Purpose: Grants and scholarships to individuals
and their families employed in the forest products
industry.
Financial data: Year ended 12/31/2011. Assets,
$581,203 (M); Expenditures, $25,959; Total
giving, $22,764; Grants to individuals, 9 grants
totaling $22,764 (high: $4,500, low: $764).

Fields of interest: Higher education.
Type of support: Grants to individuals;
Scholarships—to individuals.
Application information: Applications not
accepted.
  Additional information: Unsolicited requests for
    funds not considered or accepted.
EIN: 161494319

5898
Creative Capital Foundation

65 Bleecker St., 7th Fl.
New York, NY 10012-2420 (212) 598-9900
Contact: Sean Elwood, Dir., Grantmaking and Artists
Svcs.; For MAP Fund: Moira Brennan, Prog. Dir.
FAX: (212) 598-4934;
E-mail: info@creative-capital.org; Contact info. for
MAP Fund: 73 Spring St., Ste. 401, New York, NY
10012-5801, tel.: (212) 226-1677, Fax: (212)
226-7665, E-mail: mapinfo@mapfund.org, URL:
http://www.mapfund.org; Contact info for Arts
Writers Grant Program: tel.: (212) 598-0140, URL:
www.artswriters.org; URL: http://
www.creative-capital.org/

Foundation type: Public charity
Purpose: Grants to artists pursuing projects in five
disciplines, Emerging Fields, Film/Video, Literature,
Performing Arts and Visual Arts.
Publications: Application guidelines; Biennial
report; Financial statement; Grants list.
Financial data: Year ended 06/30/2012. Assets,
$15,447,607 (M); Expenditures, $8,169,110;
Total giving, $4,661,203; Grants to individuals,
totaling $1,720,724.
Fields of interest: Media/communications; Film/
video; Visual arts; Performing arts; Theater; Music;
Performing arts (multimedia).
Type of support: Project support.
Application information: Applications accepted.
Application form required. Application form
available on the grantmaker's web site.
  Deadline(s): Mar. 1
  Final notification: Recipients notified in Jan.
  Applicants should submit the following:
    1) Resume
    2) Proposal
    3) Budget Information
  Additional information: See web site for
    additional application guidelines.
Program descriptions:
  Grants: Grants of up to $10,000 are available to
  artists working in one or more disciplines. Emerging
  fields may include architecture/design, digital arts,
  gaming, interdisciplinary, new genres and sound
  art. Literature may include fiction, genre-defying
  literary work, nonfiction and poetry. Performing Arts
  may include dance, dance-theater, experimental
  music performance, interdisciplinary, multimedia
  performance, music-theater, non-traditional opera,
  performance art, puppetry, spoken word and
  theater. The focus is on the live performing arts.
  Eligible applicants must be U.S. citizens or
  permanent legal residents who are at least 25
  years old, and who are working artists with at least
  five years of professional experience.
  *Grants in Emerging Fields, Innovative Literature,
  and Performing Arts:* This program supports artists
  pursuing adventurous and imaginative work in the
  performing and visual arts, film/video, innovative
  literature, and emerging fields. Grants will be made
  to artists who are deeply engaged with their art
  forms, articulate a case for bold originality in their
  work, demonstrate a rigorous commitment to their
  craft, have potential for significant artistic and
  cultural impact, and understand the professional
  landscape of their field. Grants will be awarded in

three categories: Emerging Fields (digital arts, gaming, sound art, architecture, design, interdisciplinary projects, and new genres); Innovative Literature (poetry, fiction, nonfiction, and genre-defying literary work); and Performing Arts (dance, music theater, experimental music performance, non-traditional opera, spoken word, theater/performance art, puppetry, and interdisciplinary projects). In addition, artists who receive grants from the foundation can be eligible for artist retreat opportunities. Eligible applicants must be U.S. citizens or permanent legal residents who are at least 25 years old and with at least five years of professional artist experience; collaborative projects and works by collectives are also accepted. Organizations that are chosen can receive grant support of up to $76,000 for the life-cycle of the grant.
EIN: 311605982

5899
Crohn's & Colitis Foundation of America, Inc.
386 Park Ave. S., 17th Fl.
New York, NY   10016-8804   (800) 932-2423
Contact: Richard J. Geswell, Pres. and C.E.O.
FAX: (212) 779-4098; E-mail: info@ccfa.org;
Toll-free tel.: (800) 923-2423; URL: http://www.ccfa.org

Foundation type: Public charity
Purpose: Research grants for the prevention and cure of Crohn's disease and ulcerative colitis.
Publications: Application guidelines; Annual report; Financial statement; Informational brochure.
Financial data: Year ended 12/31/2011. Assets, $23,007,692 (M); Expenditures, $49,604,872; Total giving, $15,624,591.
Fields of interest: Medical school/education; Digestive disorders research.
Type of support: Fellowships; Research; Awards/prizes; Postdoctoral support; Graduate support.
Application information: Applications accepted. Application form required. Application form available on the grantmaker's web site.
Initial approach: Telephone
Copies of proposal: 2
Deadline(s): Jan 14 and July 1 for Senior Research, Research Fellowship Award and Career Development Awards; Mar. 15 for Student Research Fellowship Awards.
Applicants should submit the following:
1) Proposal
2) Letter(s) of recommendation
3) Curriculum vitae
4) Budget Information
Additional information: Application must also include one disk or CD.
Program descriptions:
Career Development Awards: Awards of up to $90,000 per year for a maximum of three years are offered to encourage the development of individuals with research potential to help them prepare for a career of independent basic and/or clinical investigation in the area of inflammatory bowel disease. Individuals who are already well-established in the field of IBD research are not considered eligible for this award. Applicants must be employed by an institution (public non-profit, private non-profit or government) engaged in health care and/or health related research within the U.S. Research is not restricted by citizenship; however, proof of legal work status is required. Applicant must hold an M.D., Ph.D. or equivalent. Candidates holding M.D. degrees must have five years of post doctoral experience, two years of which must be documented research experience relevant to IBD.

Generally, the candidates must not be in excess of ten years beyond the attainments of the doctoral degree. Applicants holding Ph.D.s must have at least two years of documented post-doctoral research relevant to IBD.
Research Fellowship Awards: Awards of up to $58,250 per year for a maximum of three years are offered to encourage the development of individuals with research potential to help them prepare for a career of independent basic and/or clinical investigation in the area of Crohn's disease and ulcerative colitis. Individuals who are already well-established in the field of IBD research are not considered eligible for this award. Applicants must be employed by an institution (public non-profit, private non-profit, or government) engaged in health care and/or health-related research within the U.S. Research is not restricted by citizenship; however, proof of legal work status is required. Applicant must hold an M.D., Ph.D. or equivalent. Candidates holding M.D. degrees must have two years of post doctoral experience, one year of which must be documented research experience relevant to IBD. Applicants holding Ph.D.s must have at least one year of documented post-doctoral research relevant to IBD.
Scientific Conferences and Workshops Awards: The foundation provides financial support ranging from $5,000 to $10,000 for conferences related to inflammatory bowel disease. Selection criteria include: the relevance of the proposal to IBD research; scientific merit of proposals; and the excellence of the investigator and the research environment. Awards are made payable to the applicant's institution.
Senior Research Award: This award seeks to provide established researchers with funds to generate sufficient preliminary data to become competitive for funds from other sources, such as the National Institutes of Health (NIH). Applicants must hold an M.D., Ph.D., or equivalent degree, and must be employed by an institution (public non-profit, private non-profit or government) engaged in health care and/or health related research. Applicants must have attained independence from his/her mentor; eligibility is not restricted by citizenship or geography. The award will fund $128,700 per year for a maximum of three years.
Student Research Fellowship Awards: This program offers financial support for students to spend time performing research on topics relevant to inflammatory bowel disease for a minimum of ten weeks. The foundation hopes to stimulate research interest in the areas of Crohn's disease or ulcerative colitis. Candidates may be undergraduate, medical or graduate students (not yet engaged in thesis research) in accredited North American institutions. Candidates may not hold similar salary support from other agencies. Up to 16 awards will be available for full-time research with a mentor investigating a subject relevant to IBD. Mentors may not be a relative of the applicant and may not work in their lab. The mentor must be a faculty member who directs a research project highly relevant to the study of IBD at an accredited institution. Awards will be payable to the institution, not the individual; awards will be given in the amount of $2,500 (excluding indirect costs)
EIN: 136193105

5900
The William Nelson Cromwell Foundation for the Research of the Law and Legal

History of the Colonial Period of the U.S.A.
c/o Sullivan & Cromwell, LLP
125 Broad St.
New York, NY   10004-2498

Foundation type: Independent foundation
Purpose: Project and publication support to individuals for research on American legal history with emphasis on the Colonial and early Federal periods.
Financial data: Year ended 11/30/2012. Assets, $3,199,012 (M); Expenditures, $174,148; Total giving, $125,559; Grants to individuals, 9 grants totaling $60,559 (high: $26,237, low: $2,500).
Fields of interest: History/archaeology; Law/international law.
Type of support: Program development; Publication; Research.
Application information: Applications accepted. Application form not required.
Initial approach: Letter
Deadline(s): Nov. 15
EIN: 136068485

5901
Crouse Health Foundation, Inc.
(formerly Crouse Irving Memorial Foundation, Inc.)
736 Irving Ave.
Syracuse, NY   13210-1622   (315) 470-7702
FAX: (315) 470-5645;
E-mail: CrouseFoundation@crouse.org;
URL: http://www.crouse.org/aboutus/foundation.html

Foundation type: Public charity
Purpose: Grants to employees of Crouse Health Hospital, NY who have experienced catastrophic circumstances. Also, scholarships to attend Crouse Hospital's School of Nursing.
Financial data: Year ended 12/31/2011. Assets, $20,238,968 (M); Expenditures, $3,262,017; Total giving, $2,570,716; Grants to individuals, totaling $63,661.
Fields of interest: Hospitals (general).
Type of support: Employee-related scholarships.
Application information:
Initial approach: Letter
Deadline(s): Apr. 15 for scholarships
Final notification: July
Applicants should submit the following:
1) Class rank
2) SAT
3) Financial information
4) GPA
EIN: 161035427

5902
Cuban Artists Fund, Inc.
10 Park Avenue, Ste. 12 A
New York, NY   10003-3263   (212) 352-3460
Contact: Carlos Pomares, Exec. Dir.
FAX: (212) 352-3467;
E-mail: info@cubanartistsfund.org; URL: http://www.cubanartistsfund.org

Foundation type: Public charity
Purpose: Grants to Cuban-born artists around the world, and to artists of Cuban descent based in the U.S. The fund supports a limited number of artists' residencies at the Vermont Studio Center.
Publications: Application guidelines; Newsletter.
Financial data: Year ended 12/31/2012. Assets, $63,850 (M); Expenditures, $124,715.
Fields of interest: Visual arts; Performing arts; Music; Literature; Arts; Hispanics/Latinos.

Type of support: Grants to individuals; Residencies.
Application information: Applications accepted. Application form required. Application form available on the grantmaker's web site.

   Send request by: Mail or on-line
   Deadline(s): Sept. 1
   Applicants should submit the following:
     1) Work samples
     2) Letter(s) of recommendation
     3) Resume
     4) Budget Information
   Additional information: Applicants should also submit a cover letter (no more than two to three pages) about his/her work in general and the proposed project; a biography, print recognition of work (including catalogs, clippings, or written documentation of work in journals, magazines, or newspaper articles, submitted in .jpg or .pdf format). Contact the fund for additional information for the Vermont Studio Center Residencies.

Program description:
   Grants: Grants, ranging from $5,000 to $7,000, are available to Cuban artists living outside of Cuba, as well as artists of Cuban descent living in the U.S., who work in the disciplines of visual arts, performance art, literature, and music. Artists must demonstrate artistic ability and recognition, and be able to document a career in the arts; projects must also show additional sources of actual and potential sources of funding.
EIN: 134005473

5903
Cultural Resources Council of Syracuse & Onondaga County

411 Montgomery St.
Syracuse, NY 13202-2930 (315) 435-2155
Contact: Artist Grants: Mark J. Wright, Prog. Dir.
FAX: (315) 435-2160;
E-mail: sbutler@mycnyarts.org; URL: http://www.arts4ed.org/

Foundation type: Public charity
Purpose: Grants to individual artists in Cortland, Onondaga, and Oswego counties, NY, to support the development of new work.
Publications: Application guidelines.
Financial data: Year ended 06/30/2012. Assets, $910,163 (M); Expenditures, $1,002,687; Total giving, $683,557.
Fields of interest: Arts, artist's services.
Type of support: Grants to individuals.
Application information: Application form required. Application form available on the grantmaker's web site.

   Initial approach: Telephone
   Send request by: Mail
   Copies of proposal: 4
   Deadline(s): See web site for current application deadline
   Applicants should submit the following:
     1) Budget Information
     2) Financial information
     3) Work samples
     4) Resume
   Additional information: Application must also include income tax form.

Program description:
   Individual Artist Grants: Grants of $1,000 each are awarded to artists in Cortland, Herkimer, Madison, Oneida, Onondaga, and Oswego counties who work in the visual, performing, literary, and media arts, and who wish to carry out creative projects that strengthen the connection between working artists and their community. Grants can be used for: the creation of art in public places; the

creation of new music, choreography, or plays for public performance; or the creation and public dissemination of film or video works. Eligible applicants must be at least eighteen years of age.
EIN: 150625350

5904
The Nathan Cummings Foundation

475 10th Ave., 14th Fl.
New York, NY 10018-9715 (212) 787-7300
Contact: Simon Greer, C.E.O. and Pres.
FAX: (212) 787-7377;
E-mail: contact@nathancummings.org; URL: http://www.nathancummings.org

Foundation type: Independent foundation
Purpose: Fellowships to individuals for one year to pursue a social or economic objective.
Publications: Annual report; Financial statement; Grants list; Newsletter; Occasional report; Program policy statement.
Financial data: Year ended 12/31/2012. Assets, $407,948,470 (M); Expenditures, $27,252,765; Total giving, $18,799,000. Fellowships amount not specified.
Fields of interest: Arts; Environment.
Type of support: Fellowships.
Application information: Applications accepted. Application form available on the grantmaker's web site. Interview required.

   Initial approach: Proposal
   Send request by: On-line
   Deadline(s): Sept. 14 for short applications, Oct. 19 for long applications
   Final notification: Recipients notified in Dec.
   Additional information: Semi-finalists participate in skype interviews. Finalists make presentations to Board.

Program description:
   The Nathan Cummings Foundation Fellowship: The program provides three individuals with $100,000 each to pursue a social or economic justice objective over one year. The proposed projects must demonstrate exceptional vision and relate to at least one of the foundation's focus areas: a) Inequality and/or b) Climate Change. And use at least one of the foundation's four approaches: 1) Arts and Culture; 2) Constituency Building; 3) Disruptive Ideas and 4) Religious Traditions and Contemplative Practices. The fellowship requires a yearlong commitment to work in the foundation's office. It is advisable to live within commuting distance of New York City. See web site for application and additional information. You may contact: Fellowship@nathancummings.org.
EIN: 237093201

5905
Cunningham Dance Foundation, Inc.

130W 56th St., Ste. 707
New York, NY 10019 (212) 255-8240
Contact: Keith Butler, Dir., Devel.
E-mail: bradley@merce.org

Foundation type: Public charity
Purpose: Scholarships to students in the field of dance and music.
Financial data: Year ended 06/30/2013. Assets, $0 (M); Expenditures, $11,185.
Fields of interest: Dance; Music.
Type of support: Scholarships—to individuals.
Application information: Scholarships are awarded on the basis of the student's performance such as attendance, motivation and skills.
EIN: 132502177

5906
Cure Childhood Cancer Association

200 Westfall Rd.
Rochester, NY 14620-4636 (585) 473-0180
Contact: Brian Wirth, Exec. Dir.
FAX: (585) 473-0201;
E-mail: curemn@rochester.rr.com; E-mail For Brian Wirth: brian.wirth@curekidscancer.com;
URL: http://www.curekidscancer.com

Foundation type: Public charity
Purpose: Financial assistance to families coping with childhood cancer or chronic blood disorders.
Financial data: Year ended 06/30/2012. Assets, $412,140 (M); Expenditures, $345,582.
Fields of interest: Cancer; Pediatrics; Family services.
Type of support: Grants for special needs.
Application information:

   Initial approach: Letter
   Additional information: Contact foundation for eligibility criteria.
EIN: 510215037

5907
Curran Music Scholarship Fund

(also known as Gertrude D. Curran Trust f/b/o Curran Music School)
c/o Alliance Bank, N.A.
160 Main St.
Oneida, NY 13421-1629

Foundation type: Independent foundation
Purpose: Music scholarships to residents of Utica, NY who are or were students of Proctor High School or other schools of the Utica, NY public school system.
Financial data: Year ended 12/31/2012. Assets, $200,297 (M); Expenditures, $10,201; Total giving, $8,555; Grants to individuals, 7 grants totaling $8,555 (high: $1,557, low: $771).
Fields of interest: Music.
Type of support: Support to graduates or students of specific schools; Undergraduate support.
Application information: Applications not accepted.

   Additional information: Unsolicited requests for funds not considered or acknowledged.
EIN: 156015514

5908
Dactyl Foundation for the Arts & Humanities, Inc.

c/o Victoria N. Alexander
64 Grand St.
New York, NY 10013-2267 (646) 329-5398
E-mail: email@dactyl.org; URL: http://www.dactyl.org/

Foundation type: Operating foundation
Purpose: Residencies to artists and scholars in the New York, area with living accommodations and work space.
Financial data: Year ended 12/31/2010. Assets, $90,226 (M); Expenditures, $65,963; Total giving, $0.
Fields of interest: Arts.
Type of support: Residencies.
Application information: Contact foundation for additional information.
Program description:
   Artist/Scholar in Residence Program: Artists and scholars are offered living accommodations and limited working space for either the summer, fall, or spring term. With housing provided residents are better able to focus on their artistic or scholarly

pursuits. Residency is onsite at the foundation in SoHo. Recipients may apply for renewals up to one year.
EIN: 133915372

5909
Daiwa Securities America Foundation
Financial Sq., 32 Old Slip, 14th Fl.
New York, NY 10005-3504 (212) 612-7000
Contact: Gary Mass, Dir.
E-mail: christine.shapiro@daiwausa.com

Foundation type: Company-sponsored foundation
Purpose: Scholarships to children of employees of Daiwa Securities America, Inc. and its U.S. affiliates. Awards are renewable and limited to $2,500 per semester, or $5,000 per year for eligible high school seniors.
Financial data: Year ended 02/28/2013. Assets, $421,446 (M); Expenditures, $20,799; Total giving, $20,000; Grants to individuals, 4 grants totaling $20,000 (high: $5,000, low: $5,000).
Type of support: Employee-related scholarships.
Application information: Application form required.
Deadline(s): Nov. 30
Applicants should submit the following:
1) Letter(s) of recommendation
2) Transcripts
3) SAT
4) Essay
Additional information: Applicant must submit three letters of recommendation.
Company name: Daiwa Securities America Inc.
EIN: 133637516

5910
Dance Films Association, Inc.
252 Java St. Ste. 333
Brooklyn, NY 11222 (347)505-8649
Contact: Christy Park, Exec. Dir.
E-mail: info@dancefilms.org; E-Mail for Christy Park: christy@dancefilms.org; URL: http://www.dancefilms.org

Foundation type: Public charity
Purpose: Assistance to young choreographers and film makers in New York, through festivals, publications, workshops and other resources.
Financial data: Year ended 06/30/2012. Assets, $260,410 (M); Expenditures, $184,175.
Fields of interest: Film/video; Dance; Arts, artist's services.
Type of support: Awards/prizes; Fiscal agent/sponsor.
Application information: Contact the association for additional guidelines.
Program descriptions:
Fiscal Sponsorship: The association serves as a fiscal sponsor for its member filmmakers, upon acceptance of their proposals. It offers support developing ideas, proposals, and feedback on works-in-progress.
Post Production Grants: Members may apply for post-production funding once a year. Only films that have completed shooting and are in production will be considered.
Susan Braun Award: The association awards grants to emerging choreographers living in one of the five boroughs of New York City, to create a short film and/or adapt a stage choreography for the camera with a young filmmaker. The award will provide cash support from a team of mentors. Entries are judged on the strength of the choreography and their vision for how the choreography would be adapted for the camera.
EIN: 136125002

5911
Dance Theater Workshop, Inc.
(also known as New York Live Arts)
219 W. 19th St.
New York, NY 10011-4001 (212) 691-6500
Contact: Jean Davidson, C.E.O.
FAX: (212) 633-1974;
E-mail: info@newyorklivearts.org; Additional e-mail for Richert Schnorr: richert@dtw.org; URL: http://www.newyorklivearts.org/

Foundation type: Public charity
Purpose: Support to independent contemporary artists to advance dance and live performance.
Publications: Application guidelines.
Financial data: Year ended 06/30/2012. Assets, $13,164,260 (M); Expenditures, $6,208,354.
Fields of interest: Dance; Arts, artist's services.
Type of support: Grants to individuals; Residencies; Fiscal agent/sponsor.
Application information:
Initial approach: Contact to request acceptance in the Fiscal Sponsorship Program and schedule enrollment meeting
Program descriptions:
Creative Residencies for Artists: This program works to address the critical need for commissions, rehearsal space, and technical residencies, in support of the creative process. All artists creating new work through this program will be given either a five-day technical residency in the theater, or 100 hours of free rehearsal time in the program's participating studios, as well as a stipend. Artists will also have the opportunity to work with an advisor who provides constructive criticism as well as an outside perspective on new material generated during the residency.
DTW Commissioning Fund: The fund commissions new works by artists at all stages of their careers, and provides individualized and comprehensive support (such as fiscal sponsorship and strategic advisement)
Fiscal Sponsorship Program: The organization offers through this program a simple and affordable way for independent artists and companies to raise tax-deductible donations and apply for grants. Through sponsorship, members are able to raise the money they need to produce their work, pay their performers and collaborators, and thereby contribute to the growing ecology of dance and performance in New York and beyond. The organization deducts a 6 percent fee. There is a $100 annual fee to participate in the program.
EIN: 136206608

5912
Josiah H. Danforth Memorial Fund
c/o NBT Bank, N.A.
52 S. Broad St.
Norwich, NY 13815-1646 (518) 725-0653

Foundation type: Independent foundation
Purpose: Grants to residents of Fulton County, NY for health care expenses.
Financial data: Year ended 12/31/2011. Assets, $574,800 (M); Expenditures, $33,788; Total giving, $27,044.
Fields of interest: Health care.
Type of support: Grants for special needs.
Application information: Applications accepted. Application form required.
Deadline(s): None
Additional information: Maximum annual amount of grant per recipient is limited to $500. Contact the fund for application forms.
EIN: 146023489

5913
Dante Foundation of Nassau County, Inc.
235 E. Jericho Tpke.
Mineola, NY 11501-2032 (516) 746-2350

Foundation type: Public charity
Purpose: Scholarships to deserving students of Italian decent to further their education.
Financial data: Year ended 12/31/2011. Assets, $74,582 (M); Expenditures, $84,998; Total giving, $64,200; Grants to individuals, totaling $51,000.
Fields of interest: Higher education.
International interests: Italy.
Type of support: Scholarships—to individuals.
Application information: Applications accepted. Interview required.
Initial approach: Letter
EIN: 112843055

5914
Taraknath Das Foundation
276 Riverside Dr.
New York, NY 10025-5204 (212) 666-4282
Contact: Leonard A. Gordon, V.P.

Foundation type: Independent foundation
Purpose: Scholarships to Indian graduate students, scholars, writers, and researchers who are studying in the U.S. and have completed one year of study in the U.S.
Financial data: Year ended 05/31/2013. Assets, $433,565 (M); Expenditures, $35,068; Total giving, $26,500; Grants to individuals, 4 grants totaling $21,000 (high: $6,000, low: $5,000).
Fields of interest: Literature; International exchange, students.
Type of support: Foreign applicants; Graduate support.
Application information: Application form required.
Deadline(s): Aug. 1
Applicants should submit the following:
1) Transcripts
2) Letter(s) of recommendation
Additional information: Application should also include a photocopy of the applicant's passport.
EIN: 136161284

5915
Daughters of the Cincinnati
20 W. 44th St., Ste. 508
New York, NY 10036-6603 (212) 991-9945
URL: http://daughters1894.org/

Foundation type: Independent foundation
Purpose: Scholarships to high school seniors who are daughters of career commissioned officers (on active duty, retired, or deceased) in the United States military.
Financial data: Year ended 12/31/2012. Assets, $2,484,651 (M); Expenditures, $228,947; Total giving, $65,500; Grants to individuals, 18 grants totaling $65,500 (high: $5,000, low: $2,000).
Fields of interest: Military/veterans' organizations; Young adults, female.
Type of support: Undergraduate support.
Application information: Applications accepted. Application form required.
Deadline(s): Mar. 15
Applicants should submit the following:
1) Transcripts
2) Financial information
3) SAT
4) Letter(s) of recommendation
5) ACT
EIN: 136096069

5916
The Davidson Krueger Foundation
5002 2nd Ave.
Brooklyn, NY 11232-4320

Foundation type: Independent foundation
Purpose: Scholarships to children of FL and NY employees of Davidson Pipe Supply Co., Inc., for higher education.
Financial data: Year ended 11/30/2012. Assets, $661,740 (M); Expenditures, $49,825; Total giving, $35,900.
Type of support: Employee-related scholarships.
Application information:
  Initial approach: Letter
  Deadline(s): Mar. 15
  Additional information: Application must include transcripts.
Company name: Davidson Pipe Supply Co., Incorporated
EIN: 116005674

5917
Jerome Lowell De Jur Trust
c/o City College Fund
Convent Ave. & 138th St.
New York, NY 10031

Foundation type: Independent foundation
Purpose: Awards for qualified City College of New York students for creative writing.
Financial data: Year ended 06/30/2011. Assets, $84,864 (M); Expenditures, $7,424; Total giving, $6,000; Grants to individuals, 2 grants totaling $6,000 (high: $3,000, low: $3,000).
Fields of interest: Literature; Education.
Type of support: Awards/prizes.
Application information:
  Initial approach: Manuscript
  Deadline(s): Apr. 1
EIN: 136223537

5918
Josephine De Karman Scholarship Trust
2 Court Sq., 8th Fl.
Long Island City, NY 11120-0001

Foundation type: Independent foundation
Purpose: Fellowships to students in any discipline, including international students, who are currently enrolled in a university or college located within the United States.
Financial data: Year ended 12/31/2012. Assets, $2,787,733 (M); Expenditures, $222,094; Total giving, $174,000; Grants to individuals, 18 grants totaling $174,000 (high: $11,000, low: $7,000).
Fields of interest: Education.
Type of support: Fellowships.
Application information: Applications not accepted.
  Additional information: Unsolicited requests for funds not considered or acknowledged.
EIN: 956019527

5919
Dedalus Foundation, Inc.
3 Columbus Cir.
New York, NY 10019-1903
Contact: Richard Rubin, Chair.
E-mail: grants@dedalusfoundation.org; URL: http://www.dedalusfoundation.org

Foundation type: Operating foundation
Purpose: Graduate fellowships by nomination only to aid students of painting and/or sculpture, or

those preparing a dissertation on some aspect of the modernist tradition. Fellowship to an art historian, critic, or curator pursuing a project related to the study of modern art and modernism.
Publications: Application guidelines.
Financial data: Year ended 12/31/2012. Assets, $55,739,228 (M); Expenditures, $4,632,325; Total giving, $779,250; Grants to individuals, 29 grants totaling $171,000.
Fields of interest: Arts education; Visual arts; Museums (art); Art history; Higher education.
Type of support: Fellowships; Graduate support; Doctoral support.
Application information: Applications accepted.
  Initial approach: Letter
  Copies of proposal: 1
  Deadline(s): Oct. 1 for Senior Fellowships, Dec. 1 for Dissertation Fellowships, Dec. 15 for Robert Motherwell Book Award, and Exhibition Catalogue Award, Jan. 15 for MFA Fellowships
  Additional information: See web site for specific program criteria.
Program descriptions:
  Exhibition Catalogue Award: The foundation's Exhibition Catalogue Award is an annual prize of $20,000 given to the author or authors of an outstanding exhibition catalogue published in 2013 that makes a significant contribution to the scholarship of modern art or modernism. This award is given in addition to, and as the complement of, the Robert Motherwell Book Award. E-mail: cataward@dedalusfoundation.org.
  Ph.D. Dissertation Fellowship: The foundation's Dissertation Fellowship is awarded annually to a Ph.D. candidate at a university in the United States who is working on a dissertation related to modern art and modernism. The fellowship carries a stipend of $20,000. Candidacy for the fellowship is by nomination only. Each September, doctoral art history programs throughout the country are invited to nominate one candidate. Candidates should have completed all of their coursework, and be focused primarily on researching and writing their dissertation. Nominees need not be U.S. citizens. E-mail inquiries: fellowships@dedalusfoundation.org.
  Senior Fellowship Program: The foundation's Senior Fellowship program is intended to encourage and support critical and historical studies of modern art and modernism. Under this program, fellowships are awarded to writers and scholars who have demonstrated their abilities through previous accomplishments and who are not currently matriculated for academic degrees. Applicants must be citizens of the United States. Fellowship stipends vary according to the needs of the specific project, with a maximum of $30,000. E-mail inquiries: fellowships@dedalusfoundation.org.
  The Robert Motherwell Book Award: The Robert Motherwell Book Award is given annually and carries a prize of $20,000 awarded to the author of an outstanding publication in the history and criticism of modernism in the arts, including the visual arts, literature, music and the performing arts. Nominations are normally made by publishers, and the winner is chosen by a panel of distinguished scholars and writers. E-mail: bookaward@dedalusfoundation.org.
EIN: 133091704

5920
Brian A. Dellomo Scholarship Foundation
55 Lakeland Rd.
Staten Island, NY 10314-2505

Foundation type: Independent foundation

Purpose: Scholarship awards for male residents of Staten Island, NY to attend Catholic high schools.
Financial data: Year ended 12/31/2011. Assets, $1,126 (M); Expenditures, $7,095; Total giving, $6,820.
Fields of interest: Elementary/secondary education; Men.
Type of support: Support to graduates or students of specific schools.
Application information: Applications not accepted.
  Additional information: Unsolicited requests for funds not considered or acknowledged.
EIN: 134076626

5921
The Gladys Krieble Delmas Foundation
275 Madison Ave., 33rd Fl.
New York, NY 10016-1101 (212) 687-0011
Contact: Rachel Kimber, Fdn. Admin.
FAX: (212) 687-8877; E-mail: info@delmas.org;
URL: http://www.delmas.org

Foundation type: Independent foundation
Purpose: Predoctoral and postdoctoral grants for research in Venice and the Veneto, Italy.
Publications: Application guidelines; Financial statement; Grants list.
Financial data: Year ended 12/31/2012. Assets, $42,979,324 (M); Expenditures, $1,897,458; Total giving, $1,350,083; Grants to individuals, 32 grants totaling $172,223 (high: $19,900, low: $1,800).
Fields of interest: Architecture; Theater; Music; Art history; History/archaeology; Literature; Science; Economics; Political science; Law/international law.
International interests: Italy.
Type of support: Fellowships; Research; Postdoctoral support; Travel grants.
Application information: Applications accepted. Application form required. Application form available on the grantmaker's web site.
  Initial approach: Letter
  Send request by: Mail
  Copies of proposal: 7
  Deadline(s): Dec. 15 for Venetian Scholars Program
  Final notification: Recipients notified by Apr. 1
  Applicants should submit the following:
    1) Curriculum vitae
    2) Budget Information
    3) Letter(s) of recommendation
    4) Proposal
  Additional information: Application should also include a statement of proficiency in the necessary languages.
Program description:
  Venetian Research Program: This program awards four types of support to individuals: 1) Grants for Independent Research on Venetian History and Culture are pre-doctoral and post-doctoral grants for travel and residence in Venice and the Veneto. The grants support historical research on Venice, the former Venetian empire, and contemporary Venice; 2) Grants for Venetian Research in European Libraries and Archives outside Venice allow scholars who have already received and accepted a Delmas grant for work in Venice and the Venito to apply for a one-time grant of $3,000, for one month only, to work on Venetian materials in other European libraries and archives; 3) Publication Assistance supports publications to help make possible the dissemination of work accomplished through Delmas Grants for Independent Research; and 4) Grants for Organizations in Support of Venetian

Scholarship and Culture which awards grants to organizations for projects aimed at broadening understanding of Venetian history and culture, including the preservation of scholarly resources relating to Venice.
EIN: 510193884

5922
Democracy Matters Institute, Inc.
P.O. Box 157
Hamilton, NY   13346-0157
Tel./fax: (315) 824-4306; URL: http://www.democracymatters.org

Foundation type: Public charity
Purpose: High school fellowships and paid college internships are provided to students who display a talent and passion for political organization.
Publications: Newsletter.
Financial data: Year ended 08/31/2012. Assets, $506,070 (M); Expenditures, $199,097.
Fields of interest: Reform; Public affairs, citizen participation.
Type of support: Fellowships; Internship funds.
Application information: Applications accepted. Application form required.
  Initial approach: E-mail
  Send request by: Online
  Deadline(s): June
  Additional information: Applicants should e-mail a cover letter and resume to apply. See web site for additional information.
Program description:
  Campus Intern Program: The program offers a paid internship of $500 per semester to college students with a commitment to social change and some organizing experience.
EIN: 161609711

5923
Diamond Blackfan Anemia Foundation
P.O. Box 1092
West Seneca, NY   14224-3666   (716) 674-2818
Application address: c/o Dawn Baumgardner, Pres., DBAF, 20 Tracy Lynn Ln., West Seneca, NY 14224; Proposal email address: Steven R. Ellis, PhD, Research Dir., DBAF, srellis@louisville.edu
E-mail: dbafoundation@juno.com; URL: http://www.dbafoundation.org

Foundation type: Public charity
Purpose: Grants for investigators to further research on Diamond Blackfan Anemia (DBA) to find a cure for this disorder.
Publications: Application guidelines; Newsletter.
Financial data: Year ended 12/31/2011. Assets, $295,818 (M); Expenditures, $222,556; Total giving, $201,728.
Type of support: Research; Postdoctoral support.
Application information: Applications accepted. Application form available on the grantmaker's web site.
  Initial approach: Proposal
  Send request by: Mail and email
  Deadline(s): None
  Additional information: Funds are sent directly to institutions on behalf of the investigators.
EIN: 161459422

5924
Dorothy Dickinson Trust
c/o NBT Bank, N.A.
52 S. Broad St.
Norwich, NY   13815-1646   (607) 337-6193

Foundation type: Independent foundation
Purpose: Grants to residents of Bainbridge, NY, for assistance with medical bills.
Publications: Application guidelines.
Financial data: Year ended 10/31/2013. Assets, $183,466 (M); Expenditures, $10,887; Total giving, $8,274.
Fields of interest: Health care.
Type of support: Grants for special needs.
Application information: Applications accepted. Application form required.
  Copies of proposal: 1
  Deadline(s): None
  Additional information: Application must include medical bill.
EIN: 166130872

5925
Dieu Donne Papermill
(also known as Dieu Donne)
315 W. 36th St., Ste. 101
New York, NY   10018-6404   (212) 226-0573
Contact: Kathleen Flynn, Exec. Dir.
Additional tel. (for workspace application only): (212) 226-0573
FAX: (212) 226-6088;
E-mail: kflynn@dieudonne.org; URL: http://www.dieudonne.org

Foundation type: Public charity
Purpose: Residencies to New York State emerging and mid-career artists to create new work in handmade paper.
Publications: Application guidelines.
Financial data: Year ended 06/30/2012. Assets, $2,321,142 (M); Expenditures, $892,788.
Fields of interest: Visual arts; Arts.
Type of support: Residencies.
Application information: Applications accepted. Application form required. Application form available on the grantmaker's web site.
  Initial approach: Telephone or e-mail
  Deadline(s): Jan. 15
  Applicants should submit the following:
    1) SASE
    2) Resume
  Additional information: Application must also include 10 slides of current work. Online applications accepted when posted on web site. Dieu Donne only accepts online applications and only for the Emerging Artist Workspace Program. Unsolicited requests for funds not accepted.
Program descriptions:
  Lab Grant Program: This residency program is designed to provide mid-career artists with the opportunity to work in-depth for an extended period of time at the papermill in order to produce landmark work in hand papermaking. Each artist will receive a $1,200 honorarium, twelve days of full technical assistance on the main wet-floor studio, all papermaking materials, and the option to present an exhibition at the Dieu Donne Gallery.
  Workspace Program: The purpose of the program is to give emerging artists the opportunity to produce new projects in handmade paper. New York State emerging artists from all disciplines are invited to explore the applications of paper as a visual art medium. Three artists will be selected and will receive a $700 honorarium, advance preparation of materials, and professional assistance during a seven-day collaboration.
EIN: 222814886

5926
Direct Marketing Educational Foundation
1120 Avenue of the Americas, 14th Fl.
New York, NY   10036-6700   (212) 768-7277
Contact: Terri L. Bartlett, Pres.
FAX: (212) 790-1561;
E-mail: tlbartlett@directworks.org; URL: http://www.directworks.org

Foundation type: Public charity
Purpose: Scholarships and doctoral support to students in the U.S. who wish to focus on marketing.
Publications: Application guidelines.
Financial data: Year ended 06/30/2011. Assets, $9,023,159 (M); Expenditures, $837,625. Scholarships—to individuals amount not specified. Doctoral support amount not specified.
Fields of interest: Higher education; Business school/education.
Type of support: Scholarships—to individuals; Doctoral support.
Application information: Applications accepted. Application form required.
  Initial approach: Application
  Deadline(s): Apr. 30 for letter of intent and June 1 for full proposal for DMEF Shankar-Spiegel Award, May 31 for Scholarships
  Applicants should submit the following:
    1) Resume
    2) Transcripts
Program descriptions:
  DMEF Shankar-Spiegel Award for the Best Dissertation Proposal in Direct/Interactive Marketing: This program provides awards to marketing Ph.D. candidates worldwide who have successfully completed their comprehensive preliminary exams as certified by the chair(s) of their dissertation. Doctoral candidates in disciplines other than marketing are encouraged to apply (computer science, economics, management science, organizational psychology, statistics, advertising and communications, strategy, management and organization, information systems, and other relevant disciplines whose developments help advance the understanding of direct/interactive marketing). Funds are intended to support research and data collection, and to support recipients in their dissertation progress. The winner will receive a $3,000 award, while honorable mention recipients (if any are named) will receive $1,500.
  Scholarship Awards: Scholarships to U.S. citizens or permanent residents who are enrolled in an accredited four-year undergraduate institution as a graduate student, and who demonstrate a commitment to pursuing a career in direct/interactive marketing (applicants should have taken one or more courses focused on direct marketing, interactive marketing, e-mail marketing, electronic marketing, mobile marketing, social marketing, business-to-business marketing, not-for-profit marketing, database marketing, customer relationship marketing, or integrated marketing communications). See web site for the named scholarships under this program.

5927
Division A Education and Scholarship Fund
(formerly Local 758 S & E Fund)
709 8th Ave.
New York, NY   10036-6902   (212) 245-8100

Foundation type: Independent foundation

Purpose: Scholarships to members and dependents of Local 758, Service Employee International Union.
Financial data: Year ended 06/30/2013. Assets, $233,263 (M); Expenditures, $58,087; Total giving, $58,500.
Type of support: Scholarships—to individuals.
Application information: Applications accepted.
  Initial approach: Letter
  Deadline(s): None
  Applicants should submit the following:
    1) Transcripts
    2) Essay
  Additional information: Applications should also include social security number.
EIN: 134181778

5928
Do Something, Inc.
24-32 Union Sq. E., 4th Fl.
New York, NY 10003-3201   (212) 254-2390
Contact: Steve Buffone, Chair.
FAX: (212) 522-1307;
E-mail: grants@dosomething.org; URL: http://www.dosomething.org

Foundation type: Public charity
Purpose: Grants to young people who submit proposals to solve local problems that deal with community building, health and environment.
Publications: Application guidelines.
Financial data: Year ended 12/31/2011. Assets, $7,910,735 (M); Expenditures, $3,841,290; Total giving, $406,395; Grants to individuals, totaling $176,795.
Fields of interest: Youth development; Volunteer services; Voluntarism promotion.
Type of support: Program development; Awards/prizes; Undergraduate support.
Application information: Applications accepted. Application form required. Application form available on the grantmaker's web site.
  Initial approach: Letter or telephone
  Deadline(s): Vary
  Applicants should submit the following:
    1) Essay
    2) Letter(s) of recommendation
    3) Proposal
  Additional information: See web site for additional application guidelines.
Program descriptions:
  Do Something Awards: Formerly the BR!CK Awards, this award honors individuals under the age of 25 who are leaders in creating change in and improving their communities and the world. Four award winners will receive $10,000. One grand prize winner will be selected from the group of nine winners and will receive $100,000. Each winner has the option of receiving up to $5,000 as an educational scholarship. Eligible applicants must be permanent residents or citizens of the U.S. or Canada, and must be 25 years of age or under.
  Do Something Club Startup Grants: Grants of up to $250 will be made available to groups of five individuals or more who wish to start a Do Something group, and who register with the organization and start at least one project that works to improve relationships between youth and the community.
  Scholarships: Scholarship amounts vary, and are awarded to young people ages 25 and under for their involvement in improving their community. Scholarships are awarded for various activities that change frequently. See web site for a list of currently funded activities and additional information.

  Seed Grants: $500 grants are awarded on a weekly basis to help young people ages 25 and under start a community action project.
EIN: 133720473

5929
James Doherty Scholarship Fund
1 Ct. Sqr., 29th Fl.
Long Island City, NY 11120

Foundation type: Independent foundation
Purpose: Scholarships to Cretin-Derham High School, MN, students.
Financial data: Year ended 07/31/2011. Assets, $824,524 (M); Expenditures, $46,816; Total giving, $39,974.
Fields of interest: Education.
Type of support: Scholarships—to individuals; Support to graduates or students of specific schools.
Application information: Applications not accepted.
  Additional information: Unsolicited requests for funds not considered or acknowledged.
EIN: 416257985

5930
Angelo Donghia Foundation, Inc.
c/o Levy Sonet & Siegel, LLP
630 3rd Ave., 23rd Fl.
New York, NY 10017-6731

Foundation type: Independent foundation
Purpose: Scholarships to interior design students entering their final year of a degree-awarding program.
Financial data: Year ended 12/31/2012. Assets, $18,487,363 (M); Expenditures, $1,053,534; Total giving, $805,325.
Fields of interest: Design.
Type of support: Scholarships—to individuals.
Application information: Applications not accepted.
  Additional information: Unsolicited requests for funds not considered or acknowledged.
EIN: 133523056

5931
DonorsChoose.org
(formerly DonorsChoose, Inc.)
213 W. 35th St., 2nd Fl. E.
New York, NY 10001-1903   (212) 239-3615
FAX: (212) 239-3619; URL: http://www.donorschoose.org

Foundation type: Public charity
Purpose: Project grants to public school teachers, particularly in underfunded schools that otherwise would not have the resources to support the proposed project.
Financial data: Year ended 06/30/2012. Assets, $23,256,651 (M); Expenditures, $36,277,463.
Fields of interest: Fund raising/fund distribution; Elementary school/education; Secondary school/education.
Type of support: Grants to individuals; Project support.
Application information: Applications accepted. Application form required. Application form available on the grantmaker's web site.
  Send request by: Online
  Deadline(s): None
  Applicants should submit the following:
    1) Proposal
    2) Essay

    3) Budget Information
Program description:
  DonorsChoose Grants: Project grants are funded by concerned individuals who search for projects to support at the organization's web site. The organization administers all contact between the school and the donors. Public school teachers create student project proposals on the organization's web site (consisting of writing a one-page essay and listing the exact resources needed). Individual donors then visit the web site and search for projects that they would like to fund. Once interest is identified, the organization contacts the school principal, alerting him/her of the funded project. Within the next week, the organization forwards the donor an "e-thank-you" from the teacher, which notes the date by which the donor can expect his/her full feedback package. The organization purchases the student materials and ships items directly to the school along with a disposable camera, guidelines for preparing feedback packages, and a stamped envelope in which to enclose the feedback.
EIN: 134129457

5932
Dove Givings Foundation
222 Purchase St.
P.O. Box 316
Rye, NY 10580-2101   (914) 460-4040
Contact: Kevin J. Heneghan, Secy.-Treas.

Foundation type: Operating foundation
Purpose: Financial assistance to needy children and families.
Financial data: Year ended 12/31/2012. Assets, $2,630,979 (M); Expenditures, $776,010; Total giving, $758,427; Grants to individuals, 26 grants totaling $262,899 (high: $25,000, low: $1,000).
Fields of interest: Children/youth, services; Family services; Christian agencies & churches; Economically disadvantaged.
Type of support: Grants for special needs.
Application information: Applications accepted.
  Initial approach: Letter
  Deadline(s): None
  Additional information: Letter should include a written request detailing circumstances and needs.
EIN: 133795957

5933
Downtown Community Television Center, Inc.
87 Lafayette St.
New York, NY 10013-4410   (212) 966-4510
Contact: Jon Alpert, Pres. and Co-Exec. Dir.
Application e-mail: clarivel@dctvny.org
FAX: (212) 226-3053; E-mail: info@dctvny.org;
E-mail for Jon Alpert: jonny@dctvny.org;
URL: http://www.dctvny.org

Foundation type: Public charity
Purpose: Assistance to underserved individuals from low income and minority communities who cannot otherwise afford a media arts education.
Publications: Application guidelines.
Financial data: Year ended 12/31/2011. Assets, $3,255,480 (M); Expenditures, $2,444,926; Total giving, $43,775; Grants to individuals, totaling $9,139.
Fields of interest: Film/video; Television.
Type of support: Fellowships.
Application information: Applications accepted. Application form required.
  Deadline(s): Mar. 12

Applicants should submit the following:
1) Transcripts
2) Essay
Additional information: See web site for additional guidelines.

Program description:
PRO-TV Media Fellowship: This program is available to eight high-school juniors and seniors in the New York City area. It is designed to cultivate young men and women into mature, articulate, and accomplished media artists. Recipients must be able to take classes at the center twice a week for two years, and will receive a stipend along with food and transportation money and use of center facilities.
EIN: 132742777

5934
Dramatists Guild Fund, Inc.
1501 Broadway
New York, NY 10036-5601 (212) 391-8384
Contact: Rachel Routh, Exec. Dir.
FAX: (212) 202-4093;
E-mail: rrouth@dramatistsguild.com; URL: http://www.dramatistsguildfund.org/

Foundation type: Independent foundation
Purpose: Grants-in-aid are made to needy U.S. playwrights who have had their works produced or published. Applicants are asked to restrict requests to their immediate needs.
Publications: Informational brochure.
Financial data: Year ended 12/31/2011. Assets, $3,237,395 (M); Expenditures, $622,428; Total giving, $226,272; Grants to individuals, 37 grants totaling $48,222 (high: $3,000, low: $400).
Fields of interest: Theater (playwriting); Literature.
Type of support: Grants for special needs.
Application information: Applications accepted. Application form required.
Initial approach: Letter, telephone, or e-mail
Send request by: Mail
Copies of proposal: 1
Deadline(s): None
Final notification: Applicants are notified of decision within two weeks
EIN: 136144932

5935
The Camille and Henry Dreyfus Foundation, Inc.
555 Madison Ave., 20th Fl.
New York, NY 10022-3301 (212) 753-1760
Contact: Mark J. Cardillo Ph.D., Exec. Dir.
E-mail: admin@dreyfus.org; URL: http://www.dreyfus.org

Foundation type: Independent foundation
Purpose: Grants by nomination only to young faculty members in chemistry, biochemistry, and chemical engineering departments of academic institutions in the U.S.
Financial data: Year ended 12/31/2012. Assets, $93,637,833 (M); Expenditures, $4,803,372; Total giving, $2,909,464; Grants to individuals, totaling $2,837,592.
Fields of interest: Science; Chemistry.
Type of support: Awards/grants by nomination only.
Application information: Application form required.
Initial approach: Nomination letter
Send request by: On-line
Deadline(s): See foundation web site for current deadlines
Additional information: See web site for additional application guidelines.

Program descriptions:
ACS Award for Encouraging Disadvantages Students into Careers in the Chemical Sciences: This award recognizes significant accomplishments by individuals in stimulating students, underrepresented in the profession, to elect careers in the chemical sciences and engineering. The award consists of $5,000 and a certificate. A grant of $10,000 will also be made to an eligible non-profit institution, designated by the recipient, to strengthen its activities in meeting the objectives of the award. Nominees for the award may come from any professional setting: academia, industry, government, or other independent facility.
ACS Award for Encouraging Women into Careers in the Chemical Sciences: This program recognizes significant accomplishments by individuals who have stimulated or fostered the interest of women in chemistry, promoting their professional development as chemists or chemical engineers. The award consists of $5,000 and a certificate. A grant of $10,000 will also be made to an eligible non-profit institution, designated by the recipient, to strengthen its activities in meeting the objectives of the award. Nominees for the award may come from any professional setting: academia, industry, government, or other independent facility.
Camille Dreyfus Teacher-Scholar Awards Program: This program supports the research and teaching careers of talented young faculty in the chemical sciences. Based on institutional nominations, the program provides discretionary funding to faculty at an early stage in their careers. Criteria for selection include an independent body of scholarship attained within the first five years of their appointment as independent researchers, and a demonstrated commitment to education, signaling the promise of continuing outstanding contributions to both research and teaching. The program provides an unrestricted research grant of $75,000.
Dreyfus Prize in the Chemical Sciences: The prize, to be awarded biennially, will consist of a citation, a medal, and a monetary award of $250,000. The prize will be awarded to an individual in a selected area of chemistry to recognize exceptional and original research that has advanced the field in a major way. The first Dreyfus Prize will be awarded in the field of materials chemistry, honoring the accomplishments of the Dreyfus brothers, Camille and Henry. The prize is open to individuals, both domestically and internationally. There is no restriction on the number of nominees from a given institution, nor is institutional approval required.
Henry Dreyfus Teacher-Scholar Awards Program: This program supports the research and teaching careers of talented young faculty in the chemical sciences at undergraduate institutions. The program is based on nominations which provides discretionary funding to faculty at an early stage in their careers. Awardees are typically in departments that do not grant a doctoral degree. Nominees must hold a full time tenure-track academic appointment, be after the fourth and not after the twelfth years of their independent academic careers, and be engaged in research in teaching primarily with undergraduates. The award provides a $60,000 unrestricted research grant. Of the total amount, $5,000 is to be allocated for departmental expenses associated with research and education.
Postdoctoral Program in Environmental Chemistry: This program seeks to further the development of scientific leadership in the field of environmental chemistry, and provides a principal investigator with an award of $120,000 over two years to appoint a Postdoctoral Fellow in environmental chemistry. The program is open to all academic and other not-for-profit organizations in all

U.S. States, Districts, and Territories. Applications are accepted from principal investigators that have well-established research efforts in environmental science or engineering. These research activities need not be located in traditional departments in the chemical sciences, and collaboration across departments and institutions is encouraged.
Senior Scientist Mentor Program: Emeritus faculty who maintain active research programs in the chemical sciences may apply for one of a limited number of awards that will allow undergraduates to do research under their guidance. Successful applicants are expected to be closely engaged in a mentoring relationship with undergraduate students. The program provides a $20,000 award over two years, intended mostly for undergraduate stipends. Modest research support is also allowed. Funds are normally expended over a period of three years after notification of an award.
EIN: 135570117

5936
Druckenmiller Foundation
c/o Duquesne Capital Mgmt.
40 W. 57th St., 25th Fl.
New York, NY 10019-4001 (212) 404-1150

Foundation type: Independent foundation
Purpose: Undergraduate scholarships to students who have caddied for at least two seasons at Oakmont Country Club in PA.
Financial data: Year ended 11/30/2012. Assets, $866,525,510 (M); Expenditures, $42,830,143; Total giving, $42,236,422; Grants to individuals, 34 grants totaling $211,422 (high: $13,500, low: $1,750).
Fields of interest: Athletics/sports, golf.
Type of support: Undergraduate support.
Application information: Application form required.
Initial approach: Letter or telephone
Send request by: Mail
Deadline(s): July 1
Applicants should submit the following:
1) Essay
2) Financial information
3) Letter(s) of recommendation
4) Transcripts
Additional information: Scholarships are paid directly to the educational institution on behalf of the students.

Program description:
Oakmont Scholarship: Scholarships for college students who have caddied at Oakmont Country Club during the past year. Scholarships are available for a maximum of five years of college but are not for graduate school.
EIN: 133735187

5937
George Duffy Foundation
c/o Cordovano
1 Claire Pass
Saratoga Springs, NY 12866-7505 (518) 993-2738
Contact: Norma Jean Clark, Tr.
Application Address: 22 Gilbert Ave., Fort Plain, NY 13339 Tel.: (518) 993-2738

Foundation type: Independent foundation
Purpose: Scholarships to graduates of Canajoharie High School, Fort Plain High School, and St. Johnsville High School, Montgomery County, NY, for study in a medical or health-related field.
Publications: Informational brochure.
Financial data: Year ended 12/31/2012. Assets, $2,892,048 (M); Expenditures, $174,633; Total

giving, $130,900; Grants to individuals, 39 grants totaling $130,900 (high: $3,850, low: $1,925).
Fields of interest: Medical school/education; Health sciences school/education.
Type of support: Support to graduates or students of specific schools; Undergraduate support.
Application information: Application form required.
Initial approach: Letter
Send request by: Mail
Deadline(s): July 15
Final notification: Recipients are notified by Aug. 1
Applicants should submit the following:
1) Letter(s) of recommendation
2) Transcripts
Additional information: Application should also include a copy of the acceptance letter from the college.
EIN: 146016445

5938
Doris Duke Charitable Foundation
650 5th Ave., 19th Fl.
New York, NY 10019-6108 (212) 974-7000
FAX: (212) 974-7590; URL: http://www.ddcf.org

Foundation type: Independent foundation
Purpose: Supports physician-scientists in the U.S. at different stages of their careers and innovative and multidisciplinary approaches to clinical research conducted with human subjects. Grants for projects selected through the RFP process are then made to non-profit medical institutions on behalf of individual investigators or project directors.
Financial data: Year ended 12/31/2012. Assets, $1,726,653,990 (M); Expenditures, $95,724,516; Total giving, $77,659,983.
Fields of interest: Medical school/education; Heart & circulatory research; Medical research.
Type of support: Fellowships; Research; Awards/grants by nomination only; Postdoctoral support.
Application information: Application form required. Application form available on the grantmaker's web site.
Initial approach: Proposal
Deadline(s): Vary
Program descriptions:
Arts Program- Performing Artists Initiative: This is a special initiative of the Doris Duke Charitable Foundation (DDCF), providing pioneering support to individual artists while adding $50 million to the foundation's substantial existing commitment to contemporary dance, jazz, theatre and related interdisciplinary work. Over the course of ten years, the three-part Performing Artists Initiative will provide awards to more than 200 artists, as well as a range of dance companies, theaters and presenters. Unlike other grants, the new DDCF fellowships will not be project based. Instead, they will give artists flexible and unrestricted multi-year support, enabling them to take creative risks, explore new ideas and pay for important needs such as healthcare. The third sub-initiative will support artist residencies designed to increase demand for jazz, theatre, contemporary dance and related interdisciplinary work at nonprofit arts organizations. See foundation web site for specific award categories.
Clinical Scientist Development Award: The program provides grants to junior physician-scientists to facilitate their transition to independent clinical research careers. It was created to provide mentored research funding to early career physician-scientist faculty to enable their transition to independence. All applicants are required to complete a web-based questionnaire

assessing their eligibility to apply for this award. If eligibility criteria are met, applicants will be automatically directed to the web-based pre-proposal form. It is strongly suggested that potential applicants see the foundation web site to review the Request for Applications page prior to accessing the eligibility questionnaire.
Distinguished Clinical Scientist Award: The program recognizes outstanding mid-career physician-scientists who are applying the latest scientific advances to the prevention, diagnosis, treatment, and cure of disease, and enables them to mentor the next generation of physician-scientists conducting clinical research. Distinguished Clinical Scientist Awards provide grants of up to $1.5 million over five to seven years. New grants are not currently being offered. To be notified of future competitions, sign up for the Medical Research Program's mailing on program's web page.
EIN: 137043679

5939
Dungannon Foundation, Inc.
c/o CPI Assocs., Inc.
32 E. 57th St., 14th Fl.
New York, NY 10022-2513 (212) 421-6600
Contact: Elizabeth R. Rea, Pres.

Foundation type: Operating foundation
Purpose: Awards only to North American short story writers who have made a significant contribution to the short story form.
Financial data: Year ended 12/31/2012. Assets, $20,980 (M); Expenditures, $266,777; Total giving, $226,465; Grant to an individual, 1 grant totaling $30,000.
Fields of interest: Literature.
Type of support: Awards/grants by nomination only; Awards/prizes.
Application information:
Deadline(s): None
Additional information: Nominees are selected by a jury of three unrelated and independent experts.
EIN: 133312300

5940
Agatha Durland Foundation
(formerly The Visiting Nurse Association of Rye, Inc.)
c/o Miscimarra
9 George Langeloh Ct.
Rye, NY 10580 (914) 967-5679
Contact: Lauren Miscimarra, Pres.

Foundation type: Independent foundation
Purpose: Scholarships only to residents of Rye, NY, pursuing degrees in medicine, nursing, or related fields.
Financial data: Year ended 12/31/2012. Assets, $427,987 (M); Expenditures, $54,072; Total giving, $50,900; Grants to individuals, 23 grants totaling $22,600 (high: $1,500, low: $500).
Fields of interest: Medical school/education; Nursing school/education; Health sciences school/education.
Type of support: Scholarships—to individuals.
Application information: Applications accepted. Application form required. Interview required.
Deadline(s): Apr. 15
Additional information: Application forms available at all Rye public and parochial schools.
EIN: 131825945

5941
Dutchess County Arts Council, Inc.
9 Vassar St.
Poughkeepsie, NY 12601-3211 (845) 454-3222
FAX: (845) 454-6902;
E-mail: info@artsmidhudson.org; URL: http://www.artsmidhudson.org

Foundation type: Public charity
Purpose: Fellowships to Dutchess and Ulster county, NY residents who are in the developmental phase of a career as a creative artist.
Publications: Grants list.
Financial data: Year ended 12/31/2011. Assets, $177,555 (M); Expenditures, $550,574; Total giving, $167,125; Grants to individuals, totaling $2,000.
Fields of interest: Music composition.
Type of support: Fellowships.
Application information: Application form required. Application form available on the grantmaker's web site.
Initial approach: Telephone
Deadline(s): July
Applicants should submit the following:
1) Resume
2) Work samples
Additional information: Application should also include proof of residency and one audio CD. See web site for additional information.
Program description:
Individual Artists' Fellowship: The fellowship provides support to individuals living in Dutchess County, NY, who are in the developmental phase of a career as a creative artist. Awards are geared toward supporting artists' career development, rather than project support.
EIN: 146035153

5942
Herbert T. Dyett Foundation, Inc.
1002 N. George St.
Rome, NY 13440-3414 (315) 337-3617
Contact: James P. Kehoe, Jr., Secy.
Application Address: 218 N., Washington St., Rome NY, 13440

Foundation type: Independent foundation
Purpose: Scholarships for the first two years of college only to financially needy graduating seniors at Rome Free Academy and Rome Catholic High School, both in Rome, NY. Applicants must have attended the schools for two years prior to graduation and rank in the top third of their classes.
Financial data: Year ended 12/31/2011. Assets, $1,621,688 (M); Expenditures, $65,878; Total giving, $59,385; Grants to individuals, 62 grants totaling $59,385 (high: $1,250, low: $625).
Fields of interest: Scholarships/financial aid.
Type of support: Support to graduates or students of specific schools; Undergraduate support.
Application information: Applications accepted. Application form required. Interview required.
Additional information: Scholarships are awarded on the basis of financial need, personality, character, leadership, citizenship, and health.
EIN: 166041857

5943
Dysautonomia Foundation, Inc.
315 W. 39th St., Ste. 701
New York, NY 10018-1469 (212) 279-1066
Contact: David Brenner, Exec. Dir.
FAX: (212) 279-2066;
E-mail: info@familialdysautonomia.org;
URL: http://www.familialdysautonomia.org

Foundation type: Public charity
Purpose: Grants to researchers and scientists for the study of causes, treatments, and cures of Familial Dysautonomia.
Financial data: Year ended 12/31/2011. Assets, $4,116,432 (M); Expenditures, $1,616,096; Total giving, $986,656.
Fields of interest: Nerve, muscle & bone research.
Type of support: Research; Grants to individuals.
Application information: Applications accepted.
Initial approach: Proposal
Applicants should submit the following:
1) Proposal
2) Curriculum vitae
EIN: 136145280

5944
Dystrophic Epidermolysis Bullosa Research Association of America, Inc.
(also known as DebRA of America)
16 E. 41st St., 3rd Fl.
New York, NY 10017-7212 (212) 868-1573
E-mail: staff@debra.org; Toll-free tel.: (866) 332-7276; URL: http://www.debra.org

Foundation type: Public charity
Purpose: Emergency funds to individuals and families whose lives have been affected by epidermolysis bullosa.
Publications: Application guidelines; Newsletter.
Financial data: Year ended 12/31/2011. Assets, $931,446 (M); Expenditures, $696,374.
Fields of interest: Diseases (rare) research.
Type of support: Emergency funds; Grants to individuals.
Application information: Applications accepted. Application form required. Application form available on the grantmaker's web site.
Initial approach: Application
Deadline(s): None
Program description:
Family Crisis Fund: The fund seeks to alleviate some of the financial burden of un-reimbursed costs of medical supplies, other comforting aids, or procedures for people with epidermolysis bullosa.
EIN: 112519726

5945
Eagleton War Memorial Scholarship Fund
P.O. Box 980
Bridgehampton, NY 11932-0980
Application address: c/o Bridgehampton High School, Attn.: Supt. of Schools, 2685 Montauk Hwy., P.O. Box 3021, Bridgehampton, NY 11932-3021

Foundation type: Independent foundation
Purpose: Scholarships to graduating seniors of Bridgehampton High School, NY with financial need.
Financial data: Year ended 12/31/2012. Assets, $204,074 (M); Expenditures, $5,929; Total giving, $3,000; Grants to individuals, 3 grants totaling $3,000 (high: $1,000, low: $1,000).
Type of support: Support to graduates or students of specific schools; Undergraduate support.

Application information:
Initial approach: Letter
Deadline(s): June 1
EIN: 237149864

5946
Harrison Earl & Frances Smith Scholarship
c/o Chemung Canal Trust Co.
P.O. Box 152
Elmira, NY 14902-1522 (607) 271-3900
Application Address: c/o Board of Education, Elmira Heights C, 100 Robinhood Ave., Elmira, NY 14903
Application Address: c/o Board of Education, Elmira Heights C, 100 Robinhood Ave., Elmira, NY 14903

Foundation type: Independent foundation
Purpose: Scholarships to graduates of Thomas A. Edison High School, Elmira, NY for postsecondary education.
Financial data: Year ended 12/31/2012. Assets, $70,996 (M); Expenditures, $4,584; Total giving, $3,324; Grants to individuals, 5 grants totaling $3,224 (high: $2,224, low: $250).
Fields of interest: Higher education.
Type of support: Support to graduates or students of specific schools; Undergraduate support.
Application information: Contact fund for additional guidelines.
EIN: 166038545

5947
Caspar S. Early Memorial Scholarship Trust
1 M T Plz., 8th Fl.
Buffalo, NY 14203

Foundation type: Independent foundation
Purpose: Scholarships to individuals who are members of first United Church of Christ.
Financial data: Year ended 12/31/2012. Assets, $116,052 (M); Expenditures, $8,262; Total giving, $7,000.
Fields of interest: Higher education.
Type of support: Scholarships—to individuals.
Application information: Applications accepted.
Deadline(s): Apr. 30
Additional information: Applications available at First United Church of Christ or M&T Bank. Unsolicited requests for funds not considered or acknowledged.
EIN: 236957202

5948
East Williston Teachers' Association Scholarship Foundation
c/o The Wheatley School
11 Bacon Rd.
Old Westbury, NY 11568-1502 (516) 333-1233

Foundation type: Operating foundation
Purpose: Scholarships to graduating seniors of The Wheatley School, NY, who have maintained a GPA of 3.0 or better and have a desire to become public school teachers.
Financial data: Year ended 12/31/2011. Assets, $53,160 (M); Expenditures, $21,757; Total giving, $8,500; Grants to individuals, 3 grants totaling $8,500 (high: $3,000, low: $2,500).
Fields of interest: Teacher school/education.
Type of support: Support to graduates or students of specific schools.
Application information:
Applicants should submit the following:

1) Transcripts
2) Letter(s) of recommendation
3) Essay
EIN: 113321870

5949
Eastern New York Youth Soccer Association Inc.
53 N. Park Ave., Ste. 103
Rockville Centre, NY 11570-4111 (516) 766-0849
FAX: (516) 678-7411;
E-mail: enyoffice@enysoccer.com; Toll-Free Tel.: (888) 536-9972; URL: http://www.enysoccer.com/

Foundation type: Public charity
Purpose: Scholarships to high school soccer players throughout eastern NY, pursuing higher education.
Publications: Application guidelines.
Financial data: Year ended 06/30/2012. Assets, $2,140,239 (M); Expenditures, $2,372,827; Total giving, $74,872; Grants to individuals, totaling $33,872.
Fields of interest: Higher education; Athletics/sports, soccer.
Type of support: Scholarships—to individuals.
Application information: Applications accepted. Application form available on the grantmaker's web site. Interview required.
Initial approach: Application
Send request by: Mail
Deadline(s): June 1
Applicants should submit the following:
1) Essay
2) Transcripts
3) Resume
EIN: 112590396

5950
The Annie Eaton Society, Inc.
c/o Suzanne May
500 E. 83rd St., Ste. 9J
New York, NY 10028-7245 (212) 734-8695

Foundation type: Public charity
Purpose: Awards child care grants to graduate students in social work.
Financial data: Year ended 07/31/2012. Assets, $769,643 (M); Expenditures, $37,824; Total giving, $30,750; Grants to individuals, totaling $20,000.
Fields of interest: Human services; Day care.
Type of support: Grants for special needs.
Application information: Applications not accepted.
EIN: 136112113

5951
Fred Ebb Foundation
40 W. 20th St., 11th Fl.
New York, NY 10011-4211
Application address: c/o Roundabout Theatre, 231 W. 39th St., Ste. 1200, New York, NY 10018
E-mail: info@fredebbfoundation.org; URL: http://www.fredebbfoundation.org

Foundation type: Operating foundation
Purpose: Grants to composers/lyricists wishing to create works for the musical theatre.
Financial data: Year ended 12/31/2012. Assets, $27,821,621 (M); Expenditures, $1,542,112; Total giving, $1,350,000; Grant to an individual, 1 grant totaling $50,000.

Fields of interest: Theater (musical).
Type of support: Grants to individuals; Awards/prizes.
Application information: Application form required.
  Send request by: Mail or hand deliver
  Deadline(s): June 30
  Additional information: Applicants must include a CD of up to four songs for one or more musical theater pieces, with typewritten lyrics and a description of the dramatic content for each song. Only musical theater work will be considered. No individual may appear on more than one application. See web site for additional guidelines.
Program description:
  Fred Ebb Award: The award recognizes excellence in musical theatre songwriting, by a songwriter or songwriting team that has not yet achieved significant commercial success. The award is meant to encourage and support aspiring songwriters to create new works for the musical theatre. The prize includes a $50,000 award. In addition to the monetary prize the foundation will produce a one-night-only showcase of winner's work.
EIN: 202184998

5952
Echoing Green
(formerly Echoing Green Foundation)
494 8th Ave., 2nd Fl.
New York, NY   10001-2519   (212) 689-1165
Contact: Cheryl L. Dorsey, Pres.
FAX: (212) 689-9010;
E-mail: info@echoinggreen.org; URL: http://www.echoinggreen.org

Foundation type: Public charity
Purpose: Fellowships to visionary leaders who want to start their own organization to create lasting social change.
Publications: Application guidelines; Annual report; Financial statement; Grants list; Informational brochure; Newsletter; Occasional report.
Financial data: Year ended 06/30/2011. Assets, $5,784,569 (M); Expenditures, $3,752,192; Total giving, $913,638.
Fields of interest: Leadership development.
Type of support: Program development; Conferences/seminars; Seed money; Fellowships.
Application information: Application form required. Application form available on the grantmaker's web site. Interview required.
  Deadline(s): Dec. 2
  Additional information: See web site for further application and program information.
Program description:
  Echoing Green Fellowship: All areas of public service are eligible for consideration for this seed money, including the environment, arts, education, youth service, civil and human rights, and community and economic development. Research projects, staff positions, and positions to implement another individual's or an organization's idea are not eligible for support. Fellows receive up to $90,000 ($80,000 for individuals and $90,000 for partnerships of two people) in seed funding and technical support over two years to turn their innovative ideas into sustainable social change organizations.
EIN: 133424419

5953
Dr. Robert Eckert Memorial Fund
P.O. Box 389
Walton, NY   13856   (607) 865-4126
Application address: National Bank, Attn: President, Delaware Country

Foundation type: Independent foundation
Purpose: Scholarships to residents of the town of Colchester, NY, which includes Roscoe Central school and Downsville school districts, NY.
Financial data: Year ended 12/31/2011. Assets, $792,487 (M); Expenditures, $38,066; Total giving, $24,734; Grants to individuals, 27 grants totaling $24,734 (high: $3,375, low: $250).
Type of support: Scholarships—to individuals; Support to graduates or students of specific schools.
Application information: Applications accepted.
  Initial approach: Letter
  Deadline(s): None
EIN: 166280587

5954
Educational Foundation for the Fashion Industries
227 W. 27th St.
New York, NY   10001-5902   (212) 217-7820

Foundation type: Public charity
Purpose: Scholarships and awards for students of the Fashion Institute of Technology of NY.
Financial data: Year ended 06/30/2011. Assets, $37,291,999 (M); Expenditures, $5,444,519; Total giving, $2,837,754; Grants to individuals, totaling $1,371,948.
Fields of interest: Higher education.
Type of support: Scholarships—to individuals.
Application information: Applications accepted. Application form required.
  Additional information: Grants to the individuals are based on both need and merit. Scholarship payments are applied directly to the student accounts.
EIN: 135675757

5955
Virgil & Jane Peck Ehle Scholarship Foundation
(formerly Virgil and Jane Peck Ehle Scholarship Trust Fund)
c/o NBT Bank, N.A.
52 S. Broad St.
Norwich, NY   13815-1646   (518) 775-5205

Foundation type: Independent foundation
Purpose: Scholarships to graduating students of Gloversville High School, Gloversville, NY for postsecondary education.
Financial data: Year ended 10/31/2013. Assets, $234,434 (M); Expenditures, $12,454; Total giving, $10,858; Grants to individuals, 2 grants totaling $10,858 (high: $5,429, low: $5,429).
Fields of interest: Higher education.
Type of support: Support to graduates or students of specific schools.
Application information: Applications accepted.
  Deadline(s): May 31
  Additional information: Applications available upon request and must include parents financial statement.
EIN: 146128271

5956
Charles and Anna Elenberg Foundation, Inc.
2720 Ave. J.
Brooklyn, NY   11210

Foundation type: Independent foundation
Purpose: Scholarships to financially needy students of Hebrew faith, who are attending high school or college, with preference given to orphans. No grants to married students.
Financial data: Year ended 06/30/2012. Assets, $769,585 (M); Expenditures, $39,050; Total giving, $27,500; Grants to individuals, totaling $17,500 (high: $5,000, low: $2,500).
Fields of interest: Residential/custodial care; Jewish agencies & synagogues.
Type of support: Precollege support; Undergraduate support.
Application information: Applications not accepted.
  Additional information: Unsolicited requests for funds not considered or acknowledged.
EIN: 116042334

5957
The Elizabeth Foundation for the Arts
323 W. 39th St., 3rd Fl.
New York, NY   10018   (212) 563-5855
FAX: (212) 563-1875; E-mail: info@efancy.org; URL: http://www.efanyc.org

Foundation type: Public charity
Purpose: Grants and support to professional visual artists through the foundation's programs.
Financial data: Year ended 12/31/2011. Assets, $8,613,326 (M); Expenditures, $1,618,019; Total giving, $15,500; Grants to individuals, totaling $15,500.
Fields of interest: Visual arts; Sculpture; Arts; Aging.
Type of support: Fellowships.
Application information: Application form required.
  Initial approach: Letter
  Send request by: Online
  Deadline(s): Dec. 16 for EFA Studio Program
  Final notification: Recipients notified Mar. 1 for Studio Program
  Additional information: See web site for additional guidelines.
Program descriptions:
  EFA Project Space Program: Formerly known as the EFA Gallery, the EFA Project Space is currently exploring how to expand the vision of what a "gallery" can be, with the hope of creating a new model for sites of interaction, creativity, community building, and growth in the arts.
  EFA Studio Program: This program provides artists with a developed studio practice and career experience. Applicants cannot be in a college or university degree-granting program. Certain types of work cannot be accommodated for practical reasons, including large or heavy sculptures, some types of metal work, and work involving high noise levels or fire risk. Applications are judged solely on the quality of the work as presented. Visual artists working in all forms of media are eligible.
  Robert Blackburn Printmaking Workshop Program: The fellowships are aimed at providing any artist with the ability to complete short and long-term printmaking related projects. Fellows will be able to pursue aesthetic and conceptual goals in a professional, co-operative printmaking workspace. The fellowships are designed to allow for the full realization and completion of a specific project during the fellowship period, encouraging individual artists to develop their craft and

connections to the NY fine art and printmaking community. Artists with little or no printmaking experience are permitted to apply for the RBPMW Project Fellowships. Artists with limited experience will be required to take educational courses at RBPMW.

EIN: 061313662

5958

The Thomas R. Elsasser Scholarship Fund

204 E. 23rd St.
New York, NY 10010-4628 (212) 683-4832
Contact: Stephen Cassidy, Co-Chair.

Foundation type: Public charity
Purpose: Scholarships and grants are provided for the family members of New York City firefighters who died outside the line of duty as active members of the FDNY. Funds are used to help cover medical costs, housing, tuition and other expenses.
Financial data: Year ended 07/31/2011. Assets, $3,669,070 (M); Expenditures, $532,133; Total giving, $498,206; Grants to individuals, totaling $498,206.
Fields of interest: Education; Human services.
Type of support: Grants to individuals; Scholarships—to individuals.
Application information: Applications not accepted.
EIN: 133661508

5959

The Ensemble Studio Theatre, Inc.

549 W. 52nd St.
New York, NY 10019-5012 (212) 247-4982
Contact: Paul A. Slee, Exec. Dir.
FAX: (212) 664-0041;
E-mail: info@ensemblestudiotheatre.org; E-Mail for Paul A. Slee: slee@ensemblestudiotheatre.org;
URL: http://www.ensemblestudiotheatre.org

Foundation type: Public charity
Purpose: Commission awards to artists, composers and choreographers whose winning proposals evolve into works presented at the Theater's First Light Festival.
Publications: Application guidelines.
Financial data: Year ended 06/30/2012. Assets, $1,215,912 (M); Expenditures, $1,346,434.
Fields of interest: Performing arts; Arts.
Type of support: Awards/prizes.
Application information:
Initial approach: Letter, fax or e-mail
Send request by: E-mail (preferred) or mail
Copies of proposal: 1
Deadline(s): Nov. 1
Additional information: Application should include a one- or two-page description or a simple outline/synopsis of the project, and a resume or biography for new commissions. See web site for additional guidelines.
Program description:
EST/Alfred P. Sloan Foundation Science and Technology Project: This project is designed to stimulate artists to create credible and compelling work exploring the worlds of science and technology and to challenge the existing stereotypes of scientists and engineers in the popular imagination. Each season, the project commissions and develops new works and then presents the results. Commissions will be awarded to individuals, groups, and creative teams for full-length and one-act plays and musicals. The project is open to a broad range of topics relevant to the issues, people, ideas, processes, leading-edge discoveries, inventions, and/or

history of the 'hard' sciences and technology. Works about psychology, human behavior, medical conditions, victims of disease, and science fiction will not be considered. Commissions between $1,000 and $10,000 each are available for script proposals; rewrite commissions of between $1,000 and $5,000 each are available for existing scripts.
EIN: 237150345

5960

Episcopal Actors Guild of America, Inc.

1 E. 29th St., Guild Hall
New York, NY 10016-7405 (212) 685-2927
Contact: Karen A. Lehman, Exec. Dir.
FAX: (212) 685-8793; E-mail: info@actorsguild.org;
URL: http://www.actorsguild.org

Foundation type: Public charity
Purpose: Emergency assistance to professional performing artists pursuing an established and ongoing career in the performing arts in the New York City area, with food, clothing, shelter, utility, medical, dental, hospital expenses and other special needs. Some scholarship is also provided for the study of performing arts and playwrights.
Financial data: Year ended 03/31/2012. Assets, $1,495,329 (M); Expenditures, $243,221; Total giving, $78,242; Grants to individuals, totaling $78,242.
Fields of interest: Arts, artist's services; Education; Human services.
Type of support: Emergency funds; Scholarships—to individuals; Grants for special needs.
Application information: Application form required. Interview required.
Initial approach: Telephone
Additional information: Checks are sent directly to vendors on behalf of the recipient. See web site for additional guidelines.
Program descriptions:
Emergency Aid Relief Program: Grants of up to $750 to qualified applicants for medical expense, rent, utilities, transportation and other needs. Applicant must be a professional performing artist pursuing a career in the performing arts and must show proof of an ongoing and sustained professional career.
The Thomas Barbour Memorial Playwright's Award: This program awards $500 to an up-and-coming or established playwright.
The Thomas Barbour Memorial Scholarships and Awards Program: A variety of scholarships are available through this program to provide at least $1,000 per year to qualified individuals attending the American Academy of Dramatic Arts, or to theater arts students attending the University of Missouri. Named scholarships include the Vinton Freedley Memorial Scholarship, the Tessa Kosta Scholarship, the Claire Harris Strakosch Memorial Scholarship, the Lon C. Clark Scholarship, the Peter Harris/Ted Tiller Memorial Scholarship, and the George C. Scott Memorial Scholarship.
EIN: 135563397

5961

Episcopal Church Foundation

815 2nd Ave.
New York, NY 10017-4503 (212) 697-2858
Contact: Donald V. Romanik, Pres.
FAX: (212) 297-0142;
E-mail: all@episcopalfoundation.org; Toll-free tel.: (800) 697-2858; E-mail for Donald V. Romanik: Donald@EpiscopalFoundation.org; URL: http://www.episcopalfoundation.org

Foundation type: Public charity
Purpose: Fellowships to individuals pursuing a doctoral degree with the intention of working in theological education, and to individuals engaged in ministries at the community or congregational level that will change individuals, groups or communities in positive ways.
Publications: Annual report; Newsletter.
Financial data: Year ended 12/31/2011. Assets, $173,119,177 (M); Expenditures, $3,427,175; Total giving, $147,000; Grants to individuals, totaling $97,000.
Fields of interest: Protestant agencies & churches.
Type of support: Fellowships; Doctoral support.
Application information:
Send request by: Mail
Deadline(s): Mar. 15
Final notification: Applicants notified in May
Applicants should submit the following:
1) Essay
2) Curriculum vitae
3) Resume
4) Transcripts
5) Letter(s) of recommendation
Additional information: Applicants must be nominated. See web site for complete application information.
EIN: 131776448

5962

Epsilon Association Charitable Trust

c/o Sciarabba, Walker & Co., LLP
200 E. Buffalo St.
Ithaca, NY 14850 (607) 272-5550
Contact: William Chen

Foundation type: Independent foundation
Purpose: Scholarships to members of the Epsilon Chapter of Sigma Phi at Cornell University, NY.
Financial data: Year ended 05/31/2012. Assets, $108,436 (M); Expenditures, $21,833; Total giving, $500; Grant to an individual, 1 grant totaling $500.
Type of support: Support to graduates or students of specific schools.
Application information: Applications accepted.
Additional information: Contact foundation for current application deadline/guidelines.
EIN: 166076130

5963

ESA Foundation

(also known as Entertainment Software Association Fdn.)
317 Madison Ave., 22nd Fl.
New York, NY 10017-5207 (917) 522-3250
FAX: (917) 522-3258;
E-mail: esafinfo@theesa.com; URL: http://www.theesa.com/foundation/

Foundation type: Public charity
Purpose: Scholarships to help women and minority students who are looking to pursue study in Computer & Video Game Arts. Scholarships also to graduating high school seniors.
Publications: Application guidelines; Grants list.
Financial data: Year ended 03/31/2012. Assets, $3,679,829 (M); Expenditures, $1,914,415; Total giving, $1,547,678.
Fields of interest: Higher education; Computer science; Minorities; Women.
Type of support: Scholarships—to individuals.
Application information: Applications accepted. Application form required. Application form available on the grantmaker's web site.
Send request by: Online

Copies of proposal: 1
Deadline(s): Varies
Program descriptions:
Challenge Grants: Three prizes will be awarded to the most innovative entries, in the amounts of $40,000, $20,000 and $15,000, to be used toward implementing the proposed lesson. The awards will be based on the originality and creativity of lesson plans that reflect the contributions that games make to a child's learning. Applicants should submit lesson plans, submissions and other proposals incorporating existing computer and video games into school curricula. The goal is to harness the excitement and energy of playing video games into positive, measurable outcomes that advance children's education and learning experiences.
Scholarship Program: Up to fifteen scholarships of $3,000 each are available to assist women and minority students who plan to continue their education in fields supporting video game development, graphic design, computer science, animation or programming, digital entertainment, or software engineering. Scholarships are available for full-time study at accredited four-year colleges and universities. Up to fifteen scholarships of $3,000 each are also available to assist high school seniors who have been accepted to a four-year college or university and who plan to pursue a degree leading to a career in video game development.
EIN: 061582325

5964
The Eshe Fund
P.O. Box 65
Madison Sq. Station
New York, NY 10159-0065 (212) 744-4276
Contact: Henry H. Steiner, Secy.
URL: http://www.eshefund.org/

Foundation type: Independent foundation
Purpose: Grants for biomedical research, primarily in CT, MA and MO.
Financial data: Year ended 08/15/2012. Assets, $5,975,316 (M); Expenditures, $110,013; Total giving, $106,562.
Fields of interest: Biomedicine research.
Type of support: Research.
Application information: Applications accepted.
Initial approach: Letter
Deadline(s): None
Additional information: Contact foundation for application guidelines.
EIN: 133247309

5965
Boomer Esiason Foundation
(formerly Boomer Esiason Heroes Foundation)
483 10th Ave., Ste. 300
New York, NY 10018-1136 (646) 292-7930
Contact: David B. Rimington, Pres.
FAX: (646) 344-7945; E-mail: info@esiason.org; Additional address: 200 B Armstrong Rd., Garden City Park, NY 11040-5339, tel.: (516) 746-0077, fax: (516) 746-4437; URL: http://www.esiason.org

Foundation type: Public charity
Purpose: Scholarships and grants to people with cystic fibrosis, and to their families for expenses that are not covered by their insurance.
Publications: Application guidelines.
Financial data: Year ended 03/31/2012. Assets, $5,278,804 (M); Expenditures, $4,727,726; Total giving, $2,021,992; Grants to individuals, 140 grants totaling $359,050.

Fields of interest: Higher education; Cystic fibrosis.
Type of support: Grants to individuals; Scholarships—to individuals; Grants for special needs.
Application information: Applications accepted. Application form required. Application form available on the grantmaker's web site.
Initial approach: Application
Send request by: Mail
Deadline(s): Varies
Additional information: See web site for additional guidelines for scholarships and grants.
Program descriptions:
BEF Scholarship Program: Scholarships ranging from $500 to $2,500 are available to assist cystic fibrosis patients pursuing undergraduate and graduate degrees. Scholarships will be awarded on the basis of financial need, academic accomplishments, scholastic ability, character, leadership potential, and service to the community. Grants are made directly to the academic institution to assist in covering the cost of tuition and fees. Applicants must show proof from a physician of their cystic fibrosis diagnosis and therapy routine.
Bonnie Strangio Education Scholarship: This program grants $500 to $1,000 scholarships to a person living with cystic fibrosis who has an upbeat personality and "can-do" attitude, and shows a tremendous passion for life in achieving their goals despite battling cystic fibrosis.
Exercise for Life Athletic Scholarship Program: This program provides awards to scholar-athletes to assist cystic fibrosis high-school senior athletes pursuing undergraduate degrees, with the goal of improving the quality of life for and increasing the lifespan of all cystic fibrosis patients through the power of daily physical exercise. One male and one female scholar-athlete will be presented with a $10,000 grant, to assist in covering costs associated with receiving an undergraduate education.
Gunnar Esiason Scholarship: This scholarship is awarded annually to a student living with cystic fibrosis or who has an immediate family member with CF. He or she also must already be admitted or enrolled at Boston College and qualify for financial aid by demonstrating financial need, as determined by the University's Office of Financial Aid. The scholarship amount is $10,000.
Jerry Cahill You Cannot Fail Scholarship: This scholarship is a component of the You Cannot Fail program and honors exceptional student-athletes with cystic fibrosis who don't let the disease get in their way of living lives filled with purpose, passion, optimism and courage. These energetic young adults also understand that exercise is the key to living, breathing and succeeding with CF, so they have embraced physical activity as part of their everyday routine. The scholarship will be awarded annually, beginning in 2013, to one male and one female student. Grants in the amount of $5,000 are made directly to an academic institution to assist in covering the cost of tuition and fees.
Rimington Trophy Scholarship: This scholarship is awarded to recognize individuals who are living, breathing and succeeding with cystic fibrosis. Applicants must have cystic fibrosis and demonstrate scholastic ability, character, leadership, service to the community, need for financial assistance and daily compliance to CF therapy. Awards range from $1,000 to $2,000.
Rosemary Quigley Memorial Scholarship: $500 to $2,000 scholarships will be awarded to students with cystic fibrosis who are pursuing undergraduate or graduate degrees with a clear sense of life goals, and whose commitment to living life to the fullest

despite the challenges of living with cystic fibrosis is exemplary.
Sacks for CF Scholarship: $3,000 to $10,000 undergraduate and graduate scholarships will be awarded to recipients living with cystic fibrosis based on scholastic ability, character, leadership potential, service to the community, and demonstrated commitment to maintaining a healthy lifestyle. Total funding for the program is based on the number of quarterbacks who are sacked during NFL regular seasons games.
Scholarship of the Arts: $500 to $1,000 scholarships are available to students who promote communication through creativity in video, painting, sketching, and sculpture. Eligible applicants must submit a photo of the art entry being considered for the award.
Transplant Grant Program: The program is designed to help families cover expenses that are not covered by their insurance. Possible expenses to the recipient and family include, but are not limited to patient and family transportation costs for evaluation, surgery, and clinic visits after transplant, and housing, food, and living expenses associated with relocation to the transplant site. Grant recipients are required to provide a copy of official receipts to the Foundation for all expenses covered by the grant. BEF makes grant donations directly to institutions to pay for expenses directly related to the transplant grant, such as housing. BEF does not pay grant money directly to the individual applicant.
EIN: 113142753

5966
Estonian Relief Committee, Inc.
243 E. 34th St.
New York, NY 10016-4852 (212) 685-7467
Contact: Endel Reinpoid, Pres.

Foundation type: Public charity
Purpose: Giving primarily to Estonian individuals and families in need. Some support also for scholarships.
Financial data: Year ended 12/31/2011. Assets, $1,032,293 (M); Expenditures, $140,909; Total giving, $104,788; Grants to individuals, totaling $16,620.
Fields of interest: Human services.
Type of support: Scholarships—to individuals; Grants for special needs.
Application information:
Initial approach: Letter
Additional information: Contact foundation for current application information.
EIN: 135576607

5967
Experimental Television Center, Ltd.
109 Lower Fairfield Rd.
Newark Valley, NY 13811-3215 (607) 687-4341
Contact: Ralph Hocking, Dir.
FAX: (607) 687-4341;
E-mail: etc@experimentaltvcenter.org; URL: http://www.experimentaltvcenter.org

Foundation type: Public charity
Purpose: Awards and residencies to NY artists to support the creation of new media work.
Financial data: Year ended 06/30/2012. Assets, $340,415 (M); Expenditures, $89,663.
Fields of interest: Film/video; Arts, artist's services; Arts.
Type of support: Awards/prizes; Residencies; Fiscal agent/sponsor.

Application information: Application form required.
Initial approach: Letter
Deadline(s): Mar. 15 for Finishing Funds, July 15 and Dec. 15 for Residencies
Additional information: Full-time students not eligible.

Program descriptions:
Finishing Funds: The program provides support to New York State artists for the completion of works of moving-image and sonic art (audio, film, video, new media and web-based forms). Awards range from $500 to $2,500.

Presentation Funds: The program supports in-person presentations by electronic media and film artists at nonprofit organizations in the state.

Residencies: About 45 artists each year are awarded residencies which offer instruction, work space, and access to facilities. The program provides an estimated $50,000 of services to these artists each year. Each artist pays a $100 residency fee.
EIN: 160993211

5968
The Explorers Club
46 E. 70th St.
New York, NY   10021-4928   (212) 628-8383
Contact: Alan H. Nichols, Pres.
FAX: (212) 288-4449;
E-mail: cthompson@explorers.org; E-mail for Lorie Karnath: president@explorers.org; URL: http://www.explorers.org

Foundation type: Public charity
Purpose: Grants and awards to individuals to promote the scientific exploration of land, sea, air, and space by supporting research and education in the physical, natural, and biological sciences.
Publications: Application guidelines; Newsletter.
Financial data: Year ended 06/30/2011. Assets, $8,048,949 (M); Expenditures, $1,541,728; Total giving, $165,950; Grants to individuals, totaling $165,950.
Fields of interest: Arts, artist's services; Physical/earth sciences; Biology/life sciences.
Type of support: Research; Grants to individuals.
Application information: Applications accepted. Application form required. Application form available on the grantmaker's web site.
Send request by: Mail
Deadline(s): Oct. 15 for Eddie Bauer Grants, Nov. 8 for Student Grants

Program descriptions:
Eddie Bauer Grants: This program is funding two significant grants for research and exploration, The Explorers Club - Eddie Bauer Youth Grant of $25,000 is awarded to one or more eligible applicant with valid student I.D. for work in climate change, preservation and sustainability, consistent with the mission of The Explorers Club. The Explorers Club - The Eddie Bauer Grant for Expeditions of $25,000 is used to fund one or more eligible expeditions relating to climate change, preservation and sustainability, consistent with the mission of the Explorers Club.

Scott Pearlman Field Awards: Grants of up to $1,500 are made to professional artists, writers, photographers, filmmakers, and journalists in support of scientific expeditions. The awards are meant to provide scientific expeditions with professional, reproduction quality materials for the publication and dissemination of the work through print and electronic media.

Student Grants: The grants are awarded to students conducting individual scientific or exploration research projects through their respective schools with a supervising instructor.

Exploration Fund, for graduate, post-graduate, doctorate and early career post-doctoral students, provides grants in support of exploration and field research for those who are just beginning their research careers. Awards typically range from $500 to $2,500. A few awards may be granted up to a $5,000 award level.
EIN: 131866795

5969
Exploring the Arts, Inc.
16 W. 23rd St., 4th Fl.
New York, NY   10010-5262   (646) 745-9123
FAX: (646) 810-9199; URL: http://exploringthearts.org/

Foundation type: Public charity
Purpose: College scholarships to graduating seniors for attendance at four year colleges pursuing arts education. Scholarships to rising 11th and 12th graders to study at pre-college summer arts programs for teens. Financial support for teachers' innovative, arts-related class projects.
Publications: Newsletter.
Financial data: Year ended 06/30/2012. Assets, $3,854,174 (M); Expenditures, $2,200,187; Total giving, $349,411; Grants to individuals, totaling $349,411.
Fields of interest: Arts education.
Type of support: Grants to individuals; Scholarships—to individuals.
Application information: Applications accepted. Application form required.
Additional information: Tuition assistance for high school seniors is paid directly to the educational institution on behalf of the students. Contact the organization for additional guidelines.

Program descriptions:
Apprenticeship Program: Supported in part by an award from the National Endowment for the Arts, this program places students as apprentices with professional artists and as interns at arts organizations and cultural institutions during after-school, weekend, and summer hours. Participating students additionally receive one-on-one mentorship from program staff and partake in group meetings and field trips with fellow students in the program.

Tony Bennett College Scholarship: The organization awards scholarships to graduating seniors to help pay for their freshman year at four-year colleges and conservatories.
EIN: 134069251

5970
The Eyebeam Atelier
540 W. 21st St.
New York, NY   10011-2812   (212) 937-6580
Contact: Patricia Jones, Exec. Dir.
FAX: (212) 937-6582; E-mail: info@eyebeam.org;
E-Mail for Patricia Jones: pat@eyebeam.org;
URL: http://www.eyebeam.org

Foundation type: Public charity
Purpose: Residencies and fellowships to artists for multi-disciplinary projects.
Financial data: Year ended 06/30/2011. Assets, $239,238 (M); Expenditures, $1,414,372.
Fields of interest: Visual arts; Engineering/technology.
Type of support: Fellowships; Residencies; Stipends.

Application information: Applications accepted. Application form required. Application form available on the grantmaker's web site.
Deadline(s): Vary
Applicants should submit the following:
1) Proposal
2) Resume
Additional information: Application must also include timeline.

Program descriptions:
Fellowships: Fellowships are offered in the R&D OpenLab, the Production Lab and the Education Lab. The focus of the fellowships varies depending on the tools and skills available and the creative objectives and philosophy of each Lab. The program duration is for 11 months, running from October to August. Fellows are selected from an open call. International applicants are welcome to apply. Fellows receive a $30,000 stipend and health benefits during their stay.

Residencies: Artists, hackers, designers, engineers and creative technologists are invited to apply to be residents at Eyebeam, to work for six months on projects or research of artistic endeavor or creative expression. The ideal resident has experience working with and generating innovative technological art and/or creative technology projects and has a passion for interdisciplinary exchange. Residents will be selected from an open call, based on the work being proposed, the availability of the necessary tools and skills to support them, and in consideration of the overarching research themes and activities of the organization. Residents receive 24/7 access to Eyebeam's Chelsea facility in New York City, including equipment and technical expertise from Eyebeam staff and fellows, a $5,000 honorarium, the potential for collaborative exchange with other residents as well as support from interns. The program term is approximately from September to February and March to August with the potential for extension and/or re-application.
EIN: 133952075

5971
Ezer M'Zion, Inc.
1281 49th St.
Brooklyn, NY   11219-3055   (718) 853-8400
FAX: (718) 989-8589;
E-mail: office@ezermizionusa.org; URL: http://www.ezermizion.org/

Foundation type: Public charity
Purpose: Grants to individuals in Israel for medical expenses.
Publications: Newsletter.
Financial data: Year ended 12/31/2011. Assets, $528,197 (M); Expenditures, $3,553,118; Total giving, $2,599,196.
Fields of interest: Health care.
International interests: Israel.
Type of support: Foreign applicants; Grants for special needs.
Application information: Contact foundation for current application deadline/guidelines.
EIN: 133660421

5972
Katherine & George Fan Foundation
163 Cedar Ln.
Ossining, NY   10562   (212) 757-4760
Contact: George Fan, Pres. and Secy.

Foundation type: Independent foundation
Purpose: Scholarships awarded to individuals of Chinese descent in pursuit of a higher education.

Financial data: Year ended 08/31/2013. Assets, $154,130 (M); Expenditures, $155,166; Total giving, $154,000.
Fields of interest: Higher education.
Type of support: Scholarships—to individuals.
Application information: Applications accepted.
  Deadline(s): None
  Additional information: Contact foundation for application guidelines.
EIN: 133784702

5973
Fantasy Fountain Fund Inc.
1674 Broadway 6th Fl.
New York, NY   10019   (212) 586-4300

Foundation type: Operating foundation
Purpose: Scholarships to art students of NY, currently studying art at educational institutions.
Financial data: Year ended 10/31/2013. Assets, $30,814 (M); Expenditures, $207,180; Total giving, $49,172; Grants to individuals, 19 grants totaling $8,726 (high: $3,500, low: $18).
Fields of interest: Arts.
Type of support: Scholarships—to individuals.
Application information: Applications accepted.
  Deadline(s): Vary
  Additional information: Contact the fund for additional information.
EIN: 133356903

5974
Charles D. Farber Memorial Foundation, Inc.
200 E. 61st St., Ste. 34A
New York, NY   10065-8575   (212) 371-5683

Foundation type: Independent foundation
Purpose: Grants to residents of FL and NY in financial distress caused by illness, indigence and/or other unfortunate circumstances.
Financial data: Year ended 12/31/2012. Assets, $2,789,263 (M); Expenditures, $227,298; Total giving, $220,640.
Type of support: Grants for special needs.
Application information:
  Initial approach: Letter
  Deadline(s): None
EIN: 237017599

5975
Elizabeth Farmen Trust for St. Mark's Church
1 HSBS Ctr., 23rd Fl.
Buffalo, NY   14203-2885

Foundation type: Independent foundation
Purpose: Scholarships to members of St. Mark's Episcopal Church, NY, for undergraduate education at U.S. universities.
Financial data: Year ended 11/30/2012. Assets, $1,070,362 (M); Expenditures, $69,177; Total giving, $50,461.
Fields of interest: Education.
Type of support: Undergraduate support.
Application information: Contact trust for current application guidelines.
EIN: 527044240

5976
The Fashion Group Foundation, Inc.
8 W. 40th St., 7th Fl.
New York, NY   10018-2276   (212) 302-5511
Contact: Margaret Hayes, Pres.
FAX: (212) 302-5533; E-mail: info@fgi.org;
URL: http://www.fgi.org

Foundation type: Public charity
Purpose: Scholarships to students for tuition to colleges or universities to further their education in the fashion design industry.
Financial data: Year ended 12/31/2011. Assets, $51,206 (M); Expenditures, $14,214; Total giving, $9,025.
Fields of interest: Design.
Type of support: Scholarships—to individuals.
Application information: Contact the foundation for eligibility criteria.
EIN: 136161608

5977
Father Murphy Scholarship Fund
c/o Stephen Oberst
P. O. Box 64823
Rochester, NY   14624-4533   (585) 247-5650
Contact: Gary Prokop

Foundation type: Public charity
Purpose: Scholarships for financially needy high school students in Rochester, NY to attend Catholic high school.
Financial data: Year ended 06/30/2012. Assets, $705,395 (M); Expenditures, $59,960; Total giving, $52,635.
Fields of interest: Secondary school/education.
Type of support: Scholarships—to individuals; Support to graduates or students of specific schools.
Application information: Application form required.
  Initial approach: Letter.
  Deadline(s): Mar. 31.
  Additional information: Applications only accepted from students currently in grades eight through eleven during the first quarter of the year.
EIN: 161351291

5978
FDNY Foundation
9 Metrotech Ctr., Rm. 5E-10
Brooklyn, NY   11201-5431   (718) 999-0779
Contact: Jean O'Shea, Exec. Dir.
FAX: (718) 999-7124;
E-mail: contact@fdnyfoundation.org; URL: http://www.fdnyfoundation.org/

Foundation type: Public charity
Purpose: College scholarships to active FDNY fire officers and firefighters who plan to take one or more courses during the academic year.
Publications: Annual report; Financial statement.
Financial data: Year ended 06/30/2012. Assets, $10,808,269 (M); Expenditures, $4,804,153; Total giving, $1,145,198; Grants to individuals, totaling $63,220.
Type of support: Scholarships—to individuals.
Application information: Applications accepted. Application form required.
  Deadline(s): Mar. 31
  Additional information: Application should include an essay no more than 250 words. Unsolicited requests for funds not considered or acknowledged.
EIN: 112632404

5979
Federation of Protestant Welfare Agencies, Inc.
(also known as FPWA)
281 Park Ave. S.
New York, NY   10010-6102   (212) 777-4800
Contact: Jennifer Jones Austin, C.E.O. and Exec. Dir.
FAX: (212) 533-8792; E-mail: info@fpwa.org; E-Mail for Jennifer Jones Austin: jjaustin@fpwa.org;
URL: http://www.fpwa.org

Foundation type: Public charity
Purpose: Financial and emergency assistance to the needy in the New York metropolitan area, and limited giving to clients of FPWA member agencies. Also, scholarships to disadvantaged youth who have overcome adversity and demonstrate academic excellence.
Publications: Application guidelines; Annual report; Informational brochure; Newsletter.
Financial data: Year ended 12/31/2011. Assets, $37,761,138 (M); Expenditures, $5,413,528; Total giving, $772,411; Grants to individuals, totaling $645,768.
Fields of interest: Higher education; Human services; Aging.
Type of support: Scholarships—to individuals; Awards/grants by nomination only; Stipends; Camperships.
Application information: Application form required. Application form available on the grantmaker's web site.
  Send request by: Mail or fax
  Copies of proposal: 1
  Deadline(s): Apr. 20 for Scholarships
  Applicants should submit the following:
    1) Letter(s) of recommendation
    2) Essay
  Additional information: Applicant must demonstrate financial need, and will be notified in late May. For emergency assistance, contact agency for additional guidelines. Unsolicited application not accepted.
EIN: 135562220

5980
Federman Scholarship Fund
1 M T Plz., 8th Fl.
Buffalo, NY   14203   (716) 882-1166
Contact: Peter Fleischmann, Dir.
Application address: 787 Delaware Ave., Buffalo, NY 14209

Foundation type: Independent foundation
Purpose: Scholarships to residents of Erie County, NY, who are members of the Jewish faith.
Financial data: Year ended 12/31/2012. Assets, $239,270 (M); Expenditures, $15,004; Total giving, $12,500; Grants to individuals, 11 grants totaling $12,500 (high: $2,000, low: $500).
Fields of interest: Jewish agencies & synagogues.
Type of support: Scholarships—to individuals.
Application information: Applications accepted.
  Deadline(s): None
  Additional information: Contact trust for current application guidelines.
EIN: 166223968

5981
Enrico Fermi Educational Fund
c/o Maddalena
13 Ann Marie Pl.
Yonkers, NY   10703-1117   (914) 478-9305
Contact: Rosalin Mariani
Application address: 445 Broadway, Hastings on Hudson, NY 10706.

Foundation type: Operating foundation
Purpose: Scholarships and awards to Italian-American high school students in Yonkers, NY.
Financial data: Year ended 06/30/2013. Assets, $271,031 (M); Expenditures, $49,546; Total giving, $30,000; Grants to individuals, 3 grants totaling $30,000 (high: $10,000, low: $10,000).
Fields of interest: Arts education; Science.
International interests: Italy.
Type of support: Undergraduate support.
Application information: Application form required.
  Initial approach: Letter
  Deadline(s): Feb. 1
  Applicants should submit the following:
    1) GPA
    2) FAF
    3) Resume
EIN: 136159001

5982
Fight for Sight, Inc.
381 Park Ave. S., Ste. 809
New York, NY   10016-8806   (212) 679-6060
Contact: Arthur Makar, Exec. Dir.
FAX: (212) 679-4466;
E-mail: info@fightforsight.com; URL: http://www.fightforsight.com

Foundation type: Public charity
Purpose: Research fellowships studies in ophthalmology, vision, or related sciences.
Publications: Application guidelines; Annual report; Financial statement; Grants list; Informational brochure; Newsletter.
Financial data: Year ended 12/31/2011. Assets, $2,765,165 (M); Expenditures, $664,706; Total giving, $284,000.
Fields of interest: Eye research.
Type of support: Fellowships; Postdoctoral support; Graduate support; Undergraduate support.
Application information: Applications accepted.
  Initial approach: Letter
  Send request by: Online
  Deadline(s): Feb. 1
  Final notification: Recipients notified by June
  Additional information: See web site for additional guidelines.
Program descriptions:
  Grants-In-Aid: This program funds pilot projects of investigators who have limited or no research funding with grants of up to $20,000. Novel experiments in areas of priority interest are especially encouraged. Applications are rarely considered from residents, post-doctoral fellows, or senior investigators with other means of support for research. Awards are used to help defray costs of personnel (excluding the applicant), equipment, and consumable supplies. Travel costs are generally not supported.
  Post-Doctoral Fellowships: These fellowships of up to $20,000 support individuals interested in pursuing academic or clinical research careers in ophthalmology or vision-related science. Eligibility is limited to those who are within three years of the awarding of their doctorate. Clinical research fellows are required to spend at least 50 percent of their effort on their research, while basic

researchers are expected to devote full time to their project. The department is expected to supplement awards with institutional funds, providing the combined total does not exceed the PGY5 level per annum.
  Summer Student Fellowships: Student fellowships are available to undergraduates, medical students, and graduate students from the U.S. or Canada interested in conducting an 8- to 12-week project in an area of interest to the organization. The research project must take place under the direction of a sponsor with expertise in vision or eye-related research. Students accepting the stipend of $2,100 may not receive funding from other sources.
EIN: 237085732

5983
Figliolia Foundation Trust
45 Broadway St.
New York, NY   10006   (212) 635-0760
Contact: George J. Figliolia, Tr.

Foundation type: Company-sponsored foundation
Purpose: Scholarships to individuals recommended by a Builders Group employee for high school and higher education.
Financial data: Year ended 12/31/2011. Assets, $131,659 (M); Expenditures, $1,778; Total giving, $0.
Fields of interest: Secondary school/education; Higher education.
Type of support: Employee-related scholarships; Scholarships—to individuals.
Application information: Applications accepted. Application form required.
  Send request by: Mail
  Applicants should submit the following:
    1) SAR
    2) FAFSA
    3) Financial information
    4) Transcripts
    5) SAT
    6) Letter(s) of recommendation
    7) ACT
  Additional information: Applicants must be recommended by a Builders Group employee.
EIN: 133922569

5984
The James Marston Fitch Charitable Foundation
232 E. 11th St.
New York, NY   10003-7301   (212) 252-6809
Contact: Frederick Bland, Chair.
E-mail: info@fitchfoundation.org; URL: http://www.fitchfoundation.org

Foundation type: Independent foundation
Purpose: Grants for the research and/or execution of preservation-related projects in the fields of historic preservation, architecture, landscape architecture, urban design, environmental planning, architectural history or the decorative arts.
Publications: Application guidelines.
Financial data: Year ended 12/31/2012. Assets, $542,675 (M); Expenditures, $63,030; Total giving, $26,833; Grants to individuals, 5 grants totaling $26,833 (high: $10,000, low: $1,750).
Fields of interest: Historic preservation/historical societies.
Type of support: Research.
Application information:
  Initial approach: Proposal

  Copies of proposal: 7
  Deadline(s): Contact foundation for current application deadline
  Applicants should submit the following:
    1) Letter(s) of recommendation
    2) Budget Information
    3) Curriculum vitae
  Additional information: Application must also include brief project description, schedule of work, and past and present grants received.
Program descriptions:
  Fitch Mid-Career Grants: The foundation awards research grants of up to $15,000 to mid-career professionals who have an academic background, professional experience, and an established identity in historic preservation or related fields including, architecture, landscape architecture, urban design, environmental planning, architectural history, and the decorative arts. See foundation web site for application guidelines.
  Richard L. Blinder Award: The award of up to $15,000 is given biennially for the best proposal exploring the preservation of an existing structure, complex of buildings, or genre of building type.
EIN: 133993856

5985
William J. Fitzpatrick Memorial Scholarship Fund
1 M & T Plz. 8th Fl.
Buffalo, NY   14203-1205

Foundation type: Independent foundation
Purpose: Scholarships to graduates of York Catholic High School, PA, for higher education in the field of engineering or scientific studies related to engineering.
Financial data: Year ended 12/31/2011. Assets, $218,724 (M); Expenditures, $15,224; Total giving, $11,375.
Fields of interest: Engineering school/education.
Type of support: Support to graduates or students of specific schools; Undergraduate support.
Application information: Application form required.
  Deadline(s): Mar. 1
EIN: 236692323

5986
FJC - A Foundation of Philanthropic Funds
(formerly The Foundation for the Jewish Community)
520 8th Ave., 20th Fl.
New York, NY   10018-4167   (212) 714-0001
FAX: (212) 714-0303; E-mail: fjc@fjc.org; Toll-free tel.: (888) 448-3352; E-mail For Leonard Glickman: Glickman@FJC.org; URL: http://www.fjc.org

Foundation type: Public charity
Purpose: Scholarships to individuals.
Publications: Application guidelines; Financial statement; Newsletter.
Financial data: Year ended 03/31/2012. Assets, $216,454,124 (M); Expenditures, $30,822,023; Total giving, $29,447,214; Grants to individuals, 855 grants totaling $4,412,706. Subtotal for grants to individuals: 855 grants totaling $36,400 (high: $10).
Type of support: Fiscal agent/sponsor.
Application information: Applications accepted.
  Initial approach: Telephone or e-mail
  Deadline(s): None
  Final notification: Four to six weeks after application
  Additional information: See web site for further application information.
EIN: 133848582

5987
Fondation Sante
c/o Stelios Papadopoulos
3 Somerset Dr. S.
Great Neck, NY   11020-1821   (516) 487-5654
URL: http://www.fondationsante.org

Foundation type: Independent foundation
Purpose: Scholarships to outstanding high school graduates who have demonstrated exceptional academic performance in high school.
Financial data: Year ended 12/31/2012. Assets, $590,217 (M); Expenditures, $313,825; Total giving, $127,714.
Fields of interest: Higher education.
Type of support: Scholarships—to individuals.
Application information: Applications accepted.
> *Applicants should submit the following:*
> 1) Letter(s) of recommendation
> 2) Curriculum vitae
> *Additional information:* Application should also include a statement (no longer than one page) describing interests and desired field of study. Applicant must demonstrate financial need and be fluent in English.
EIN: 522285411

5988
The Food Allergy Initiative, Inc.
515 Madison Ave., Ste. 1912
New York, NY   10022-5403   (212) 207-1974
Contact: Robert Pacenza, Exec. Dir.
FAX: (917) 338-5130;
E-mail: info@foodallergyinitiative.org; URL: http://www.foodallergyinitiative.org

Foundation type: Public charity
Purpose: Research grants for projects relevant to food allergy, conducted by established investigators who hold an MD, PhD or equivalent, and are employed by a public nonprofit, private nonprofit or government institution engaged in health care and/or health-related research.
Publications: Application guidelines; Financial statement; Informational brochure; Occasional report.
Financial data: Year ended 12/31/2011. Assets, $8,954,358 (M); Expenditures, $8,484,611; Total giving, $4,469,649; Grants to individuals, totaling $181,667.
Fields of interest: Allergies; Allergies research.
Type of support: Research.
Application information: Applications accepted. Application form required. Application form available on the grantmaker's web site.
> *Initial approach:* Proposal
> *Send request by:* Mail or e-mail
> *Deadline(s):* None
> *Applicants should submit the following:*
> 1) Budget Information
> 2) Proposal
> *Additional information:* See web site for complete application information.
EIN: 133905508

5989
Food for Thought Endowment Fund, Inc.
130 Washington Ave.
Albany, NY   12210   (518) 434-1900
Application address: Food Industry Alliance of NYS, Inc.

Foundation type: Independent foundation
Purpose: Scholarships to students who will attend educational institutions pursuing careers relating to the food industry.

Financial data: Year ended 12/31/2012. Assets, $2,093 (M); Expenditures, $14,692; Total giving, $7,500; Grants to individuals, 5 grants totaling $7,500 (high: $1,500, low: $1,500).
Fields of interest: Education; Agriculture/food.
Type of support: Scholarships—to individuals.
Application information: Application form required.
> *Deadline(s):* Mar.
> *Additional information:* Application should include the applicant's vision of the future of the food industry and the role he/she contemplates playing in it through his/her career choice.
EIN: 223293055

5990
Olga Forrai Foundation Inc.
c/o Metis Group LLC
14 Penn Plz., Ste. 1800
New York, NY   10122   (212) 861-4590
Contact: Robert M. Walsh, Treas.
Application address: 1540 York Ave., New York, NY 10028, tel.: (212) 861-4590

Foundation type: Independent foundation
Purpose: Grants to singers and music conductors who are residents of New York City, to study and perform.
Financial data: Year ended 12/31/2012. Assets, $473,013 (M); Expenditures, $37,114; Total giving, $19,040; Grants to individuals, 4 grants totaling $19,040 (high: $6,540, low: $1,000).
Fields of interest: Music.
Type of support: Scholarships—to individuals.
Application information: Applications accepted.
> *Initial approach:* Letter
> *Deadline(s):* None
EIN: 133182161

5991
Foundation for Accounting Education, Inc.
3 Park Ave.
New York, NY   10016-5902   (212) 719-8300
Contact: Joanne S. Barry, Exec. Dir.
URL: http://fae.org/

Foundation type: Public charity
Purpose: Scholarships to students attending a college or university in NY who are planning to enter the accounting profession.
Financial data: Year ended 05/31/2012. Assets, $2,478,730 (M); Expenditures, $5,438,580; Total giving, $126,240; Grants to individuals, totaling $126,240.
Fields of interest: Business school/education.
Type of support: Undergraduate support.
Application information: Applications accepted. Application form required.
> *Additional information:* Applications are provided by each participating school's campus ambassador.
EIN: 237171151

5992
The Foundation for AIDS Research, Inc.
(also known as amfAR & AIDS Research Foundation & American Foundation for AIDS Research)
120 Wall St., 13th Fl.
New York, NY   10005-3902   (212) 806-1600
Contact: Kent Cozad
FAX: (212) 806-1601; E-mail: grants@amfar.org;
Additional address: 1150 17th St., N.W., Ste. 406, Washington, DC 20036-4622, tel.: (202)

331-8600, fax: (202) 331-8606; URL: http://www.amfar.org

Foundation type: Public charity
Purpose: Research grants for the study of HIV/AIDS, particularly in developing countries.
Publications: Application guidelines; Annual report; Financial statement; Informational brochure; Newsletter; Occasional report; Program policy statement.
Financial data: Year ended 09/30/2011. Assets, $38,004,315 (M); Expenditures, $26,110,413; Total giving, $6,694,401. Grants to individuals amount not specified.
Fields of interest: AIDS research.
Type of support: Research; Postdoctoral support; Travel grants.
Application information: Application form available on the grantmaker's web site.
> *Deadline(s):* Sept. 27 for Targeted Biomedical Research
> *Additional information:* See web site for additional application guidelines.
Program descriptions:
> *Fellowship Grants:* These grants encourage the postdoctoral (M.D., Ph.D., or equivalent) investigator with limited experience in the field to advance a career in HIV/AIDS research. The applicant's interest in a career in HIV/AIDS will be demonstrated by previous relevant work at the postdoctoral fellow or instructor level and will be carefully evaluated. The fellowship applicant must be sponsored by an experienced investigator who: is qualified to oversee the proposed research; has successfully supervised postdoctoral fellows; and is typically at the associate professor level or higher. Fellows and sponsors must be affiliated with the same nonprofit institution. Fellowship grants provide up to $45,000 for personnel costs per year for two years, $20,000 for supplies (total $110,000), and an additional $3,636 to support transportation, registration, and lodging for participation in professional development activities, as designed by the foundation (following discussion with fellow) after an award is made, plus up to 10 percent for indirect costs. Fellowships are awarded for two years and may not be renewed for additional funding.
> *Mathilde Krim Fellowships in Basic Biomedical Research:* Fellowships provide support for talented new researchers in their ongoing HIV research and facilitate his or her transition to a productive and independent long-term career in the HIV/AIDS biomedical research field. Up to $125,000 is available to researchers who possess a research or clinical doctorate and who have no more than four years of postdoctoral training.
> *Targeted Biomedical Research Project Awards:* Projects that research topics relevant to exploring the mechanisms for HIV persistence and the potential for HIV eradication are eligible for research grants of up to $180,000 in total costs including indirect costs of up to 20 percent of direct costs. Research grant funding is for a one-year period. Principal investigators must hold a doctoral degree and be affiliated with a nonprofit research institution. It is not required that principal investigators hold a faculty-level position.
EIN: 133163817

5993
Foundation for Arts Initiatives
(formerly American Center Foundation)
770 Broadway, 2nd Fl.
New York, NY   10003-9557
URL: http://www.ffaiarts.net/

Foundation type: Independent foundation

Purpose: Grants by nomination only to curators and other arts professionals to enable them to travel and pursue research around the world.
Financial data: Year ended 08/31/2012. Assets, $19,486,492 (M); Expenditures, $808,363; Total giving, $359,000.
Type of support: Awards/grants by nomination only.
Application information: Applications not accepted.
Additional information: Unsolicited requests for funds not considered.
Program description:
Fund for Arts Research: The program encourages emerging and independent curators and other arts professionals to develop projects that are consistent with the American Center Foundation's mission of supporting under-recognized talents, risk-taking projects, and experimental thinking. Candidates are selected for award consideration by the Board of the American Center Foundation after being identified by Board members and by outside nominators who are invited to submit names. There is no application or interview process and candidates are not informed of their nomination in order to preserve the objectivity of the selection process.
EIN: 986000319

5994
Foundation for Child Development
295 Madison Ave., 40th Fl.
New York, NY 10017-6304 (212) 867-5777
Contact: Mark Bogosian, Comms. and Grants Off.
Program e-mail: ysp@fcd-us.org
FAX: (212) 867-5844; E-mail: info@fcd-us.org;
URL: http://www.fcd-us.org

Foundation type: Independent foundation
Purpose: Fellowships to scholars with doctoral degrees for policy- and practice-relevant research on the development and learning needs of the nation's young children growing up under conditions of poverty and low-income.
Publications: Annual report; Grants list; Informational brochure; Newsletter; Occasional report; Program policy statement.
Financial data: Year ended 03/31/2013. Assets, $99,997,180 (M); Expenditures, $5,158,021; Total giving, $2,515,945. Fellowships amount not specified.
Fields of interest: Education; Children, services; Immigrants/refugees.
Type of support: Fellowships; Research.
Application information: Application form not required.
Initial approach: E-mail
Send request by: On-line
Deadline(s): Early May for Letter of Intent, early July for full proposals
Additional information: See web site for additional guidelines.
Program description:
Young Scholars Program: This program supports policy- and practice-relevant research on the development and learning needs of the nation's young children growing up under conditions of poverty and low-income. The foundation believes that early learning is a solid first step towards lifelong development and that promoting research in this area, conducted in a holistic and culturally sensitive manner, will help address the disparities in children's outcomes. This program encourages applications from scholars who are: 1) from historically disadvantaged or underrepresented groups, (e.g. first-generation college graduates, and those from low-income communities); and 2) scholars who represent a variety of disciplines and

methods, given that mental, physical, health, social, economic, institutional, and community factors impact early learning and child development. Eligible researchers will have received their doctoral degrees (e.g., Ph.D., J.D., Ed.D., Psy.D., M.D.) within seven years of application submission, ten years for physician applicants.
EIN: 131623901

5995
Foundation for Contemporary Arts
820 Greenwich St.
New York, NY 10014-5134 (212) 807-7077
Contact: Stacy T. Stark, Exec. Dir.
FAX: (212) 807-7177;
E-mail: info@contemporary-arts.org; URL: http://www.foundationforcontemporaryarts.org

Foundation type: Public charity
Purpose: Grants by nomination only to outstanding or unusually promising artists working in the areas of dance, music/sound, performance art/theater, poetry, and the visual arts.
Publications: Application guidelines; Grants list.
Financial data: Year ended 12/31/2012. Assets, $16,038,596 (M); Expenditures, $1,386,148; Total giving, $692,000; Grants to individuals, totaling $492,000.
Fields of interest: Visual arts; Performing arts; Dance; Theater; Music; Literature; Arts, artist's services.
Type of support: Emergency funds; Grants to individuals; Awards/prizes; Awards/grants by nomination only;
Application information: Applications not accepted.
Additional information: See web site for nomination information.
Program description:
Emergency Grants: Grants are made for unexpected expenses when projects are close to completion or for sudden work-related opportunities. Requests are often made from artists who are "emerging" and not widely recognized and have few other sources of financial support. Applicants are asked to write a letter describing the project or opportunity, the timeliness of the situation and how a specific amount would help accomplish the goal. A project budget is also requested. Grants are available on an as-needed basis throughout the year and the foundation responds to requests on a timely basis. Grants are small, and generally range between $200 and $2,000. Applicants must be living, working and paying taxes in the U.S. Applicants may not reapply for three years from the date of a past award and may only receive a maximum of two grants during their lifetime. Requests should be emailed to: grants@contemporary-arts.org and addressed to the Emergency Grants panel.
EIN: 131978163

5996
The Foundation for Health in Aging, Inc.
40 Fulton St., 18th Fl.
New York, NY 10118-0801 (212) 308-1414
Contact: Jennie Chin Hansen, C.E.O.
FAX: (212) 832-8646;
E-mail: info.amger@americangeriatrics.org;
Toll-free tel.: (800) 563-4916; Email For Jenie Chin Hansen: jhansen@americangeriatrics.org;
URL: http://www.healthinaging.org

Foundation type: Public charity

Purpose: Grants to develop or support research initiatives in the field of geriatrics and, in particular, help reduce disability and frailty and improve the quality of life for all older adults.
Publications: Application guidelines.
Financial data: Year ended 12/31/2011. Assets, $347,953 (M); Expenditures, $301,160; Total giving, $136,900; Grants to individuals, totaling $49,400.
Fields of interest: Health care; Geriatrics; Aging.
Type of support: Research; Grants to individuals.
Application information: Applications accepted. Application form required. Application form available on the grantmaker's web site.
Initial approach: Application
Deadline(s): Rolling for Williams Scholars
Program descriptions:
Hartford Geriatrics Health Outcomes Research Scholars Award Program: Awarded in conjunction with the John A. Hartford Foundation, this program supports physician-scientists committed to improving the health care of older adults with a two-year, $200,000 research grant, helping to bridge the critical transition from junior faculty to independent researcher. Eligible researchers must: have an M.D. or D.O. degree; hold a full-time faculty appointment at the level of assistant professor for no longer than two years at the time the grant becomes effective. Applicants must also have primary sponsors who are committed to providing guidance and collaboration throughout the course of the proposed project. This program will not be accepting applications for the 2012 cycle.
Student Researcher Fund: This fund provides students from all disciplines with funding to enable them to attend and participate in the annual meeting of the American Geriatrics Society where students present their work through poster sessions as well as interact with nationally known faculty.
T. Franklin Williams Research Scholars Award Program: This $100,000 grant, paid over two years, is given annually to an academic, junior faculty geriatrician (within four years of their first faculty appointment) who is conducting research on older patients that has applicability to the care provided by sub-specialists of internal medicine. Eligible applicants must: have an M.D. or D.O. degree; be within four years of their first faculty appointment at the time the grant becomes effective; be an internal medicine geriatrician who has completed all of the requirements to be eligible to sit for a Certificate of Added Qualifications by the time the award commences; and be sponsored by at least two academics who are committed to providing guidance and collaboration throughout the course of the proposed project (with one representing geriatrics and the other a subspecialty of internal medicine)
EIN: 311622556

5997
Foundation for Independent Artists, Inc.
246 W. 38th St., Fl. 4
New York, NY 10018-5805 (212) 278-8111
E-mails for fiscal sponsorship: Msg@aol.com, annan@pentacle.org

Foundation type: Public charity
Purpose: Residencies to individual dancers for the creation of new work, as well as a fiscal sponsor program open to members on a yearly or project basis by invitation only.
Financial data: Year ended 06/30/2012. Assets, $114,309 (M); Expenditures, $213,548.
Fields of interest: Dance.

Type of support: Residencies; Fiscal agent/sponsor.
Application information: Applications not accepted.
   Additional information: Unsolicited applications for residencies or fiscal sponsorship not accepted.
Program description:
   Fiscal Sponsorship: Provides an umbrella to individual dancers and companies through fiscal sponsorship.
EIN: 133082845

5998
Foundation for Italian Art and Culture
112 E. 71st St., Ste. 1B
New York, NY 10021-5034 (212) 980-1755
Contact: Alain Elkann, Pres.
E-mail: info@fiacfoundation.org; URL: http://www.fiacfoundation.org

Foundation type: Public charity
Purpose: Awards by nomination only to two leading individuals who excel in activities relating to all aspects of Italian culture, one from the USA and the other from Italy.
Financial data: Year ended 12/31/2011. Assets, $320,650 (M); Expenditures, $119,444.
Fields of interest: Arts.
International interests: Italy.
Type of support: Awards/grants by nomination only; Awards/prizes.
Application information: Applications not accepted.
   Additional information: Nominations for the Italian award will be made by the Foundation's US advisory board, and the American award by the Italian advisory board. Nominations can be made by mail and/or telephone by contacting the foundation's cultural director.
EIN: 320081843

5999
Foundation for Jewish Philanthropies, Inc.
2640 N. Forest Rd., Ste. 200
Getzville, NY 14068-1573 (716) 204-1133
Contact: Peter Fleischmann, C.E.O.
FAX: (716) 204-1129;
E-mail: peter@jewishphilanthropies.org; Toll Free Tel.: (877) 933-6369; URL: http://www.jewishphilanthropies.org

Foundation type: Public charity
Purpose: Interest-free loans and/or grants to undergraduate and graduate Jewish students who have attended high school or are residing in either Erie or Niagara county in New York State. Financial assistance for high school and college students to travel and study in Israel.
Financial data: Year ended 12/31/2011. Assets, $115,368,960 (M); Expenditures, $9,346,220; Total giving, $4,616,962; Grants to individuals, totaling $113,527.
Fields of interest: Higher education.
Type of support: Graduate support; Undergraduate support; Travel grants.
Application information: Applications accepted. Application form required.
   Deadline(s): Mar. 15 for Israel Scholarships
   Additional information: Assistance is based on financial need. See web site for additional application information.
Program descriptions:
   Academic Scholarships: The foundation administers a limited amount of scholarship funds that are available on an annual basis to provide

financial aid to undergraduate and graduate students to help meet the escalating costs of higher education. Scholarships are awarded in the form of interest/free loans and/or in the form of outright grants.
   Israel Scholarships: The foundation administers a limited amount of financial assistance for high school and college students to travel and study in Israel. Students participating in approved programs will be eligible for the upcoming summer based upon financial need. Scholarships will be awarded from individual endowment funds, which have been established by donors for this special purpose.
EIN: 166023261

6000
The Foundation of Advocacy for Mental Health, Inc.
(also known as The Mental Health Foundation)
P.O. Box 322
Albany, NY 12201-0322
Proposal inquiry email: MHFgrants2014@gmail.com
E-mail: info@mentalhealthfoundation.net;
URL: http://www.mentalhealthfoundation.net

Foundation type: Public charity
Purpose: Grants to individuals that support educational campaigns and other initiatives to improve understanding of mental illness and ensure access to quality care.
Publications: Application guidelines; Informational brochure.
Financial data: Year ended 12/31/2012. Assets, $217,521 (M); Expenditures, $71,794; Total giving, $28,450. Grants to individuals amount not specified.
Fields of interest: Mental health, disorders.
Type of support: Grants to individuals.
Application information: Applications accepted. Application form not required.
   Initial approach: Proposal
   Send request by: On-line
   Copies of proposal: 1
   Deadline(s): Jan.
   Final notification: Applicants notified of proposal receipt within 20 days
   Additional information: Application should include a budget proposal. Project proposals must be four to eight pages. See web site for additional guidelines.
Program description:
   It's Okay to Talk About It Grants: Grants between $1,000 and $10,000 are available to organizations or individuals who create programs that support peer to peer initiatives to encourage young people to confront their mental health challenges. Payment of grants will be issued with one-half of the total grant amount at award announcement, and one-half of total grant amount at mid-point of the project's duration/work plan.
EIN: 141802500

6001
Foundation of the Alumnae Association of the Mount Sinai Hospital School of Nursing, Inc.
1 Gustave Levy Pl.
P.O. Box 1143
New York, NY 10029-6504 (212) 289-5575
Contact: Joan Cropley, Secy.-Treas.

Foundation type: Independent foundation
Purpose: Scholarship to registered professional nurses from the NY area, pursuing postgraduate studies in nursing and related fields only.

Financial data: Year ended 09/30/2013. Assets, $104,745 (M); Expenditures, $28,630; Total giving, $23,054; Grants to individuals, 12 grants totaling $18,054 (high: $3,000, low: $454).
Fields of interest: Nursing school/education.
Type of support: Scholarships—to individuals; Postgraduate support.
Application information: Applications accepted.
   Initial approach: Letter or telephone
   Deadline(s): Apr. 15
   Additional information: Contact the association for additional application information.
EIN: 136096777

6002
Foundation of The National Student Nurses Association, Inc.
45 Main St., Ste. 606
Brooklyn, NY 11201-1099 (718) 210-0705
Contact: for Scholarships: Lauren Sperle
FAX: (718) 210-0710; E-mail: nsna@nsna.org;
URL: http://www.nsna.org/foundationscholarships.aspx

Foundation type: Public charity
Purpose: Scholarships to qualified undergraduate and graduate students in pursuit of a nursing career.
Publications: Application guidelines; Annual report.
Financial data: Year ended 05/31/2012. Assets, $4,360,361 (M); Expenditures, $1,087,412; Total giving, $705,481.
Fields of interest: Nursing school/education.
Type of support: Graduate support; Undergraduate support.
Application information: Applications accepted. Application form required. Application form available on the grantmaker's web site.
   Initial approach: Letter, telephone or e-mail
   Send request by: Mail
   Deadline(s): Jan. 16
   Final notification: Recipients notified in Mar.
   Applicants should submit the following:
      1) Transcripts
      2) Resume
   Additional information: A non-refundable $10 processing fee must accompany each application. High school students are not eligible. See web site for additional application information.
EIN: 133123125

6003
Foundation of the State University of New York At Binghamton, Inc.
P.O. Box 6005
Binghamton, NY 13902-6005 (607) 777-4015
URL: http://www2.binghamton.edu/giving/index.html

Foundation type: Public charity
Purpose: Scholarships and grants to deserving students of Binghamton University, NY.
Financial data: Year ended 06/30/2012. Assets, $91,066,257 (M); Expenditures, $10,717,243; Total giving, $7,580,097; Grants to individuals, totaling $2,301,013.
Fields of interest: Higher education.
Type of support: Scholarships—to individuals; Support to graduates or students of specific schools.
Application information: Applications not accepted.
   Additional information: Unsolicited requests for funds not considered or acknowledged.

Scholarships only for Binghamton University students.
EIN: 166053710

6004
Fountain House, Inc.
425 W. 47th St.
New York, NY 10036-2304 (212) 582-0340
Contact: Kenneth J. Dudek, Pres.
Application inquiry: slieblich@fountainhouse.org
FAX: (212) 265-5482; URL: http://www.fountainhouse.org/

Foundation type: Public charity
Purpose: Scholarships to Fountain House members/staff of NY, pursuing higher education.
Financial data: Year ended 06/30/2012. Assets, $38,922,718 (M); Expenditures, $17,182,779; Total giving, $185,219; Grants to individuals, totaling $51,757.
Fields of interest: Vocational education; Education.
Type of support: Scholarships—to individuals.
Application information: Applications accepted. Application form required. Application form available on the grantmaker's web site.
   Additional information: Application should include a short essay. Payments of up to $500 twice a year for members attending school.
EIN: 131624009

6005
The Four Oaks Foundation, Inc.
c/o BCRS Associates
77 Water St., 9th Fl.
New York, NY 10005-3701

Foundation type: Operating foundation
Purpose: Grants to young artists in New York, NY.
Financial data: Year ended 10/31/2011. Assets, $4,369,601 (M); Expenditures, $89,346; Total giving, $71,000.
Fields of interest: Performing arts.
Type of support: Grants to individuals.
Application information: Applications not accepted.
   Additional information: Unsolicited requests for funds not considered or acknowledged.
EIN: 133225336

6006
Michael J. Fox Foundation for Parkinson's Research
Grand Central Stn.
P.O. Box 4777
New York, NY 10163-4777 (800) 708-7644
E-mail: research@michaeljfox.org; URL: http://www.michaeljfox.org

Foundation type: Public charity
Purpose: Research grants to investigators for the study and eventual cure of Parkinson's disease.
Publications: Application guidelines; Grants list; Informational brochure; Newsletter.
Financial data: Year ended 12/31/2011. Assets, $95,542,240 (M); Expenditures, $65,638,981; Total giving, $53,857,613. Research amount not specified.
Fields of interest: Parkinson's disease; Parkinson's disease research.
Type of support: Research; Awards/prizes.
Application information:
   Initial approach: Letter
   Additional information: See web site for additional guidelines.

Program descriptions:
Rapid Response Innovation Awards: The goal of this program is to rapidly support innovative research focused on the cause of and cure for Parkinson's disease (PD). In particular, the foundation is eager to fund high-risk, high-reward projects tackling critical scientific roadblocks that, if successful, can open new avenues for PD therapy development. The program is designed to support projects with little to no existing preliminary data, but that have the potential to significantly impact understanding or treatment of Parkinson's disease.
Research Grants: Awards grants to investigators with scientific interests and demonstrated success in the development, culture, and manipulation of individual cell lines. The intent is to develop cell lines that will benefit researchers in their understanding of the causes of Parkinson's disease, to aid them in the developing of appropriate models relevant to understanding and treating the disease, and to assist them in developing innovative strategies to prevent, limit, or reverse the process of neuronal degeneration in Parkinson's disease.
Target Validation Initiative: The initiative will award up to $2 million in grants for investigator-initiated projects seeking to demonstrate that modulation of a specific cellular target (such as a gene or protein) results in a PD-relevant therapeutic response in an appropriate whole-animal mammalian model of Parkinson's disease. In particular, the initiative will target efforts that could lead to treatments for the symptoms of the disease, including both motor and non-motor symptoms such as cognitive dysfunction, autonomic dysfunction, sleep disorders, and depression. Also of interest are treatments that could be used to protect or restore degenerating neurons, or that can address complications of current PD treatments such as involuntary movements (dyskinesias). Applicants may request a project period of up to two years and a total budget of $250,000. See web site for application instructions.
EIN: 134141945

6007
Fractured Atlas Productions, Inc.
248 W. 35th St., Ste. 1202
New York, NY 10001-2505 (212) 277-8020
Contact: Adam Natale, Dir., Member Svcs.
FAX: (212) 277-8025;
E-mail: support@fracturedatlas.org; URL: http://www.fracturedatlas.org

Foundation type: Public charity
Purpose: Funding, services and support to emerging artists in all disciplines.
Publications: Annual report.
Financial data: Year ended 08/31/2011. Assets, $4,138,598 (M); Expenditures, $9,606,426; Total giving, $6,593,746; Grants to individuals, totaling $6,593,746.
Fields of interest: Arts, artist's services; Arts.
Type of support: Fiscal agent/sponsor.
Application information: Applications accepted. Application form required.
   Deadline(s): Last day of each month
   Final notification: Applicants notified on or before the 15th of each month
   Additional information: See web site for additional guidelines.
Program description:
   Fiscal Sponsorship: The organization provides fiscal sponsorship for artists and arts organizations nationwide and in every discipline. Sponsored

artists are regranted all contributed funds, minus a six percent administrative handling charge.
EIN: 113451703

6008
Franklin Furnace Archive, Inc.
80 Arts/The James E. Davis Arts Bldg.
80 Hanson Pl., Ste. 301
Brooklyn, NY 11217-1506 (718) 398-7255
Contact: Angel Nevarez, Prog. Coord.
E-mail for applications:
proposals@franklinfurnace.org
FAX: (718) 398-7256;
E-mail: ljtrooper@yahoo.co.uk; URL: http://www.franklinfurnace.org

Foundation type: Public charity
Purpose: Residencies and grants to emerging performance artists.
Publications: Application guidelines; Annual report; Newsletter.
Financial data: Year ended 07/31/2012. Assets, $492,089 (M); Expenditures, $446,790.
Fields of interest: Visual arts; Performing arts.
Type of support: Awards/prizes; Residencies; Stipends.
Application information: Applications accepted. Application form required. Application form available on the grantmaker's web site.
   Initial approach: E-mail
   Send request by: E-mail preferred; Mail visual support material
   Copies of proposal: 1
   Deadline(s): Apr. 1
   Final notification: Recipients notified in four months
   Applicants should submit the following:
      1) Work samples
      2) SASE
      3) Budget Information
      4) Resume
   Additional information: Application must also include 100 word summary of proposed work and video/support materials.
Program descriptions:
   Franklin Furnace Fund: The fund supports emerging performance artists and works in New York that engage the internet as an art medium and/or venue. Grants range from $2,000 to $10,000.
   Future of the Present: This area funds the creation of "live art on the Internet," works which engage the internet as an art medium and/or venue. Grants range from $2,000 to $5,000.
EIN: 132879766

6009
French-American Foundation
28 W. 44th St., Ste. 1420
New York, NY 10036-7410 (212) 829-8800
Contact: Charles Kolb, Pres.
FAX: (212) 829-8810;
E-mail: info@frenchamerican.org; E-mail for Charles Kolb: ckolb@frenchamerican.org; URL: http://www.frenchamerican.org

Foundation type: Public charity
Purpose: Prizes to translators of French prose work into English. Prizes and fellowships to journalists who concentrate on immigration issues.
Publications: Application guidelines; Biennial report; Newsletter; Occasional report.
Financial data: Year ended 12/31/2011. Assets, $2,942,789 (M); Expenditures, $1,791,536; Total giving, $40,000; Grants to individuals, totaling $40,000.

Fields of interest: Language (foreign); Literature.
International interests: France.
Type of support: Awards/prizes.
Application information: Applications accepted.
Application form available on the grantmaker's web
site.
  Initial approach: Application
  Deadline(s): Aug. 19 for Immigration Journalism
    Awards
  Additional information: See web site for
    additional guidelines.
Program descriptions:
  Immigration Journalism Fellowship: This program
is open to journalists of all nationalities working in
all forms of media (web, print, documentary,
photography, etc.), in French or in English, with an
interest in immigration and integration. The
foundation seeks to support meaningful, visionary
stories on under-reported topics with a strong social
justice component and with the potential to
advance public debate on the issue. All types of
stories (local, global, cultural, economic, etc.) will
be considered. Those selected will receive up to
$10,000 each for their work to be completed over
a four- to six-month period.
  Journalism Award: Awarded in conjunction with
the Ford Foundation, this award specifically honors
excellence in the coverage of immigration and
integration issues worldwide. The foundation will
recognize the work of two journalists, one based in
Europe, the other in North America with a monetary
award for best immigration reporting and will be
invited to attend and speak at the foundation's
Immigration Journalism Award Ceremony. Eligible
applicants include journalists of any nationality who
focus on questions of immigration and integration,
work submitted for consideration must be in English
or French, and was published by a U.S. or European
media.
  Translation Prize: The foundation along with the
support of the Florence Gould Foundation, has
awarded annual translation prizes for the best
translation from French to English in fiction and
non-fiction.
EIN: 132847092

6010
Friars National Association Foundation, Inc.
57 E. 55th St.
New York, NY 10022-3205 (212) 751-7272
Contact: Michael Gyure, Exec. Dir.
FAX: (212) 355-0217; URL: http://
www.friarsclub.com/

Foundation type: Public charity
Purpose: Grants and scholarships to deserving
deserving students of NY, studying the performing
arts.
Financial data: Year ended 06/30/2012. Assets,
$2,222,723 (M); Expenditures, $694,474; Total
giving, $316,301; Grants to individuals, totaling
$316,301.
Fields of interest: Performing arts.
Type of support: Grants to individuals;
Scholarships—to individuals.
Application information: Applications accepted.
Application form required.
  Additional information: Grants and scholarships
    are based on financial need,
    accomplishments and/or factors supporting
    documentation provided with the
    applications. Contact the foundation for
    additional guidelines.
EIN: 132906649

6011
The Frick Collection
1 E. 70th St.
New York, NY 10021-4981 (212) 288-0700
Contact: Ian Wardropper, Dir.
Application e-mail: center@frick.org
FAX: (212) 628-4417; E-mail: info@frick.org;
URL: http://www.frick.org/

Foundation type: Public charity
Purpose: Grants to researchers into the history of
collecting art.
Publications: Application guidelines.
Financial data: Year ended 06/30/2012. Assets,
$270,629,014 (M); Expenditures, $27,395,694;
Total giving, $82,500; Grants to individuals,
totaling $82,500.
Fields of interest: Museums (history); Historic
preservation/historical societies.
Type of support: Fellowships; Postdoctoral support;
Graduate support.
Application information: Applications accepted.
Application form required. Application form
available on the grantmaker's web site.
  Initial approach: Letter
  Send request by: Mail or e-mail
  Deadline(s): Feb. 15
  Final notification: Recipients notified Mar. 1
  Applicants should submit the following:
    1) Proposal
    2) Curriculum vitae
  Additional information: Faxed applications are
    not accepted.
Program description:
  Research Fellowships in the History of Collecting:
The center offers short-term junior fellowships (of
eight to ten weeks), for graduate and pre-doctoral
students, senior fellowships (of eight to ten weeks),
for post-doctoral and senior scholars, and long-term
(four to five months) fellowship opportunities to
research projects that utilize its collection.
Proposals may address wide-ranging aspects of the
history of collecting in the U.S., from colonial times
to the present, and may focus on individual
collectors, dealers, developments, or trends in the
art market. Fellowships range from $5,000 (for
junior scholars) to $10,000 (for senior scholars),
with a limited amount of $25,000 scholarships for
long-term projects. Applicants may come from the
academic or museum worlds, or from other relevant
professional backgrounds. They may be full- or
part-time students, full- or part-time employees, or
independent art historians, historians, and/or
curators.
EIN: 131624012

6012
Friends of Hama'ayan Institution Inc.
c/o Paul Schwartz, C.P.A.
222 W. 83rd St.
New York, NY 10024 (718) 633-9082
Contact: Mordechai Krashinsky, Secy.
Application address: c/o Jacob Paskesz, 1353 56th
St., Brooklyn, NY 11219

Foundation type: Independent foundation
Purpose: Scholarships to residents of Israel for
postgraduate rabbinic and Talmudic research
related to Talmudic jurisprudence.
Financial data: Year ended 12/31/2012. Assets,
$108,581 (M); Expenditures, $43,789; Total
giving, $45,750; Grants to individuals, 21 grants
totaling $45,750 (high: $2,600, low: $1,000).
Fields of interest: Research; Jewish agencies &
synagogues.
International interests: Israel.

Type of support: Research; Scholarships—to
individuals; Foreign applicants; Postgraduate
support.
Application information:
  Initial approach: Letter
  Deadline(s): None
EIN: 112686188

6013
Friends of the Mauritshuis, Inc.
866 United Nations Plz., Ste. 437
New York, NY 10017-1822 (212) 336-1556
Contact: Mirelle Mosler, Pres.

Foundation type: Public charity
Purpose: Grants to American art students for the
study of Dutch Masters.
Financial data: Year ended 12/31/2011. Assets,
$170,075 (M); Expenditures, $178,859; Total
giving, $165,015.
Fields of interest: Arts.
Type of support: Grants to individuals.
Application information: Contact the organization
for additional information.
EIN: 133118418

6014
Fund for the City of New York, Inc.
121 Ave. of the Americas, 6th Fl.
New York, NY 10013-1590 (212) 925-6675
Contact: Mary McCormick, Pres.
FAX: (212) 925-5675;
E-mail: mmccormick@fcny.org; URL: http://
www.fcny.org

Foundation type: Public charity
Purpose: Public service awards by nomination only
to career public servants in New York City
government.
Publications: Application guidelines; Informational
brochure.
Financial data: Year ended 09/30/2011. Assets,
$60,361,290 (M); Expenditures, $42,710,961;
Total giving, $7,323,538; Grants to individuals,
totaling $92,500.
Fields of interest: Teacher school/education;
Community/economic development; Science;
Mathematics; Leadership development.
Type of support: Awards/grants by nomination only;
Awards/prizes.
Application information:
  Send request by: Online
  Additional information: See web site for
    additional nomination guidelines.
Program descriptions:
  *Sloan Awards for Excellence in Teaching Science
and Mathematics:* The awards recognize creative
New York City high school mathematics and science
teachers who achieve superb results and inspire
young people to pursue careers in science and
mathematics. Each year, seven awards are given.
Each teacher receives $5,000 and the school's
science or mathematics department receives
$2,500 to be used to strengthen their program. A
teacher must be a New York City high school math
or science teacher for at least five years, must
teach at least four periods a day, and must
demonstrate excellence in teaching and achieving
results. Teachers are chosen based on student
achievement, progress, and outcomes; teaching
style and effectiveness; innovation and creativity in
the classroom environment; extracurricular
mathematics or science activities for students;
success in motivating students with diverse or
special backgrounds; use of technology where
appropriate; promotes mathematics and science

inside and outside the school; and encouraging students to pursue careers in science and mathematics, including teaching.

Sloan Public Service Awards: This program annually honors six civil servants whose work performance and commitment to the public transcend not merely the ordinary but the extraordinary, day after day and year after year. In honoring these winners, the fund also acknowledges the contributions of the many thousands of dedicated public servants who, with integrity and devotion, perform the work that keep New York City running.

EIN: 132612524

6015
Joseph N. Gaffney Foundation, Inc.
c/o Citrin Cooperman & Co., LLP
529 5th Ave., 4th Fl.
New York, NY   10017-4608
Contact: Mary E. Gaffney, Chair.
Application address: 4312 S.E. Frazier Ct., Stuart, FL 34997-5680, tel.: (202) 434-5000

Foundation type: Independent foundation
Purpose: Scholarships to graduating seniors of Mendham High School, NJ for attendance at institutions of higher learning.
Financial data: Year ended 12/31/2011. Assets, $396,835 (M); Expenditures, $43,746; Total giving, $36,000. Scholarships—to individuals amount not specified.
Fields of interest: Higher education.
Type of support: Support to graduates or students of specific schools; Undergraduate support.
Application information:
   Deadline(s): Vary
   Additional information: Students should submit statement as to why they are seeking a grant, and submit financial aid form to support their statement need.
EIN: 522131182

6016
The Sal Gargiulo Local 12 Scholarship Fund
(formerly Heat & Frost Insulators Local 12 Officers Scholarship Fund)
35-53 24th St.
Long Island City, NY   11106   (718) 784-3456

Foundation type: Operating foundation
Purpose: Scholarship awards to active Local 12 members or retirees receiving a Local 12 pension in NY and NJ.
Financial data: Year ended 12/31/2012. Assets, $202,971 (M); Expenditures, $360,606; Total giving, $2,500; Grant to an individual, 1 grant totaling $2,500.
Type of support: Undergraduate support.
Application information:
   Initial approach: Letter
   Deadline(s): Dec. 7
EIN: 113440178

6017
Gavin Scholarship Trust
(formerly Ora & Bernard Gavin Scholarship Trust)
c/o Bernard Gavin
201 N. Union St.
Olean, NY   14760

Foundation type: Independent foundation

Purpose: Educational assistance to residents of the greater Olean area, Cattaraugas, county, NY for postsecondary education.
Financial data: Year ended 12/31/2012. Assets, $778,584 (M); Expenditures, $18,357; Total giving, $8,156; Grants to individuals, 8 grants totaling $8,156 (high: $1,250, low: $687).
Fields of interest: Education.
Type of support: Scholarships—to individuals.
Application information: Applications accepted. Application form required.
   Deadline(s): Spring
EIN: 136779926

6018
Arthur J. Gavrin Foundation Inc.
1865 Palmer Ave., Ste. 108
Larchmont, NY   10538-3037

Foundation type: Independent foundation
Purpose: Scholarships to graduating students from New Rochelle High School, NY, pursuing higher education.
Financial data: Year ended 12/31/2012. Assets, $344,368 (M); Expenditures, $26,120; Total giving, $26,000; Grants to individuals, 11 grants totaling $26,000 (high: $4,000, low: $1,000).
Fields of interest: Higher education.
Type of support: Support to graduates or students of specific schools; Undergraduate support.
Application information: Applications accepted.
   Deadline(s): Apr. 15
   Applicants should submit the following:
     1) ACT
     2) SAT
     3) Transcripts
   Additional information: Application should include statement of need and personal and family history, and college and career goals.
EIN: 136265245

6019
General Israel Orphan Home for Girls Jerusalem, Inc.
132 Nassau St., Ste. 725
New York, NY   10038-2400   (212) 267-7222
FAX: (212) 385-3441; E-mail: info@gioh.org;
Toll-free tel.: (888) 203-7222; URL: http://www.gioh.org

Foundation type: Public charity
Purpose: Grants to provide assistance to past and present students of the orphan home.
Publications: Newsletter.
Financial data: Year ended 12/31/2011. Assets, $2,185,054 (M); Expenditures, $1,592,719; Total giving, $510,000.
Fields of interest: Adoption; Foster care.
International interests: Israel.
Type of support: Grants for special needs.
Application information: Applications not accepted.
   Additional information: Unsolicited requests for funds not considered or acknowledged.
EIN: 135640819

6020
The Genesee Community College Foundation, Inc.
One College Rd.
Batavia, NY   14020-9703   (585) 345-6809
Contact: Richard Ensman, Exec. Dir.

Foundation type: Public charity

Purpose: Scholarships to students who are residents of Genesee, Livingston, Orleans or Wyoming counties, NY for attendance at Genesee Community College.
Financial data: Year ended 08/31/2011. Assets, $3,179,452 (M); Expenditures, $608,205; Total giving, $408,379. Scholarships—to individuals amount not specified.
Fields of interest: College (community/junior).
Type of support: Scholarships—to individuals; Support to graduates or students of specific schools.
Application information: Applications accepted. Application form required.
   Deadline(s): Mar. 1 for fall semester, Dec. 1 for spring semester
   Additional information: Application should include an essay.
EIN: 222704305

6021
Genesee Valley Council on the Arts
4 Murray Hill Dr.
Mount Morris, NY   14510-1122   (585) 243-6785
Contact: Chris Norton, Exec. Dir.
FAX: (585) 243-6787;
E-mail: info@livingstonarts.org; E-mail For Chris Norton: chris@livingstonarts.org; URL: http://livingstonarts.org/

Foundation type: Public charity
Purpose: Grants to artists who are residents of Livingston County, NY.
Publications: Application guidelines; Annual report; Newsletter.
Financial data: Year ended 06/30/2012. Assets, $39,803 (M); Expenditures, $167,868; Total giving, $33,002; Grants to individuals, totaling $10,140.
Fields of interest: Media/communications; Visual arts; Performing arts; Literature; Arts.
Type of support: Grants to individuals.
Application information: Applications accepted. Application form required. Application form available on the grantmaker's web site.
   Initial approach: Telephone
   Send request by: Mail or hand delivery
   Copies of proposal: 1
   Deadline(s): Third Wed. in Oct. for Individual Artists Grants, third Wed. in May and Nov. for Dick Smith Grant
   Final notification: Applicants notified by mid-Dec. for Individual Artists Grants, and within one month following the deadline for Dick Smith Grant
   Applicants should submit the following:
     1) Transcripts
     2) Work samples
     3) SASE
     4) Resume
     5) Letter(s) of recommendation
   Additional information: Applicants must attend a grant writing/information seminar. See web site for additional application guidelines.
Program descriptions:
   Dick Smith Young Artists Grants: This program works to develop high school juniors and seniors who are serious about developing their artistic talents. Any junior or senior who resides in Livingston County is eligible to apply for up to $500 to pursue a special extra-curricular opportunity in his or her artistic discipline. Awards are granted twice a year for opportunities in creative writing, dance, music, theatre, or visual arts (including film, video and computer art).
   Individual Art Grants: The program provides awards to individual artists annually for the creation

of new work with a community component. The program looks for proposals of high artistic merit, which directly benefit the community and involve the members of the community in the artistic process. Projects may include site-specific works, installations and any artistic process in which the community participates directly. Visual, literary, media, and performing artists may apply. Artists must reside in Livingston county and have done so for at least six months prior to the application deadline and must be 18 years of age or older.
EIN: 237171154

6022
Sergeant Philip German Memorial Foundation
1 M & T Plz., 8th Fl.
Buffalo, NY 14203 (717) 852-3011
Contact: Diane Rimer

Foundation type: Independent foundation
Purpose: Scholarships to children of veterans living in Cumberland and Dauphin counties, PA.
Financial data: Year ended 12/31/2012. Assets, $1,348,435 (M); Expenditures, $81,365; Total giving, $65,100.
Fields of interest: Military/veterans' organizations.
Type of support: Undergraduate support.
Application information: Application form required.
  Deadline(s): June 10
  Additional information: Contact foundation for current application guidelines.
EIN: 236745697

6023
Daniel & Flavia Gernatt Family Foundation
Richardson Rd.
Collins, NY 14034-9709

Foundation type: Independent foundation
Purpose: Financial assistance to economically disadvantaged families in Collins, North Collins and Gowanda, NY.
Financial data: Year ended 12/31/2012. Assets, $2,932,715 (M); Expenditures, $178,237; Total giving, $148,450.
Type of support: Grants for special needs.
Application information: Applications accepted. Application form required.
  Deadline(s): None
  Additional information: Contact foundation for current application guidelines.
EIN: 222914177

6024
Alice & Murray Giddings Foundation
c/o Albina Evans
P.O. Box 182
Chatham, NY 12037-0182 (518) 555-1212

Foundation type: Independent foundation
Purpose: Scholarships to graduating high school seniors from the public school systems in Columbia County, NY for higher education.
Financial data: Year ended 12/31/2011. Assets, $0 (M); Expenditures, $51,105; Total giving, $37,654; Grants to individuals, 14 grants totaling $37,654 (high: $5,000, low: $500).
Fields of interest: Higher education.
Type of support: Support to graduates or students of specific schools; Undergraduate support.
Application information: Applications accepted. Application form required.
  Deadline(s): Mar. 1
  Applicants should submit the following:

1) Transcripts
2) Letter(s) of recommendation
Additional information: Students should contact their guidance departments of their respective schools for application guidelines.
EIN: 141781248

6025
Conrad H. and Anna Belle Gillen Scholarship Fund
(formerly Conrad H. and Anna Belle Gillen Trust Fund)
c/o NBT Bank, N.A.
52 S. Broad St.
Norwich, NY 13815-1646 (518) 863-7000

Foundation type: Independent foundation
Purpose: Scholarships to current year high school graduates residing in Fulton County, NY, attending Gloversville High School, Northville Central School, Johnstown High School, Mayfield Central School, or Broadalbin-Perth School, NY, with preference for graduates pursuing an education in the field of ministry, priesthood or christian work.
Publications: Application guidelines.
Financial data: Year ended 12/31/2011. Assets, $299,727 (M); Expenditures, $17,604; Total giving, $13,250; Grants to individuals, 24 grants totaling $13,250 (high: $1,000, low: $500).
Fields of interest: Higher education; Theological school/education.
Type of support: Scholarships—to individuals; Support to graduates or students of specific schools.
Application information: Application form required.
  Deadline(s): May 15
  Applicants should submit the following:
    1) Financial information
    2) Transcripts
    3) Letter(s) of recommendation
  Additional information: Scholarships are $500 per year for up to four years. Applications must be submitted to guidance director of eligible high schools.
EIN: 146016128

6026
James P. & Ruth C. Gillroy Foundation Inc.
c/o E. Grainger
480 Mamaroneck Ave.
Harrison, NY 10528 (914) 698-8670

Foundation type: Independent foundation
Purpose: Undergraduate scholarships primarily to residents of the five boroughs of the City of New York.
Publications: Application guidelines.
Financial data: Year ended 05/31/2013. Assets, $1,254,877 (M); Expenditures, $42,784; Total giving, $27,750.
Fields of interest: Higher education.
Type of support: Scholarships—to individuals; Undergraduate support.
Application information: Applications accepted.
  Initial approach: Letter
  Deadline(s): At least two months prior to the date payment is due the college
  Additional information: Application should include a secondary school transcript and college transcript (if applicable), a statement of extracurricular activities and educational goals, the name and address of the college to be attended, the courses to be undertaken, the anticipated total annual expenses, and how these expenses are to be met.
EIN: 237129473

6027
Girl Scout Council of Greater New York, Inc.
43 W. 23rd St., 7th Fl.
New York, NY 10010-4218 (212) 645-4000
Contact: Barbara Murphy, C.E.O.
FAX: (212) 645-4599; E-mail: info@gscgny.org; Toll Free : (800)-478-7248; URL: http://www.girlscoutsnyc.org

Foundation type: Public charity
Purpose: Scholarships for young women in the greater New York area to pursue higher education.
Publications: Annual report.
Financial data: Year ended 09/30/2011. Assets, $6,760,281 (M); Expenditures, $5,653,381; Total giving, $233,624; Grants to individuals, totaling $233,624.
Fields of interest: Girl scouts.
Type of support: Scholarships—to individuals.
Application information: Applications accepted.
  Additional information: Applicants must participate in a specific class and completing assigned course work, submitting an application and essay or project, and/or an interview.
EIN: 131624014

6028
Girls Incorporated
120 Wall St., 3rd Fl.
New York, NY 10005-3904 (212) 509-2000
FAX: (212) 509-8708;
E-mail: communications@girlsinc.org; Toll-free tel.: (800)-374-4475; URL: http://www.girlsinc.org

Foundation type: Public charity
Purpose: Scholarships to outstanding high school women to pursue secondary education at any accredited two- or four-year college or university.
Publications: Annual report; Informational brochure.
Financial data: Year ended 03/31/2012. Assets, $21,325,375 (M); Expenditures, $7,231,654; Total giving, $1,183,619; Grants to individuals, totaling $195,703.
Fields of interest: Women.
Application information: Applications accepted.
  Applicants should submit the following:
    1) Transcripts
    2) Letter(s) of recommendation
    3) Essay
EIN: 131915124

6029
Louis and Florence Glasgow Foundation
c/o NBT Bank, N.A.
52 S. Broad St.
Norwich, NY 13815 (607) 334-1600
Application address: c/o Norwich Highscholl Att: Guidance, 89 Midland Dr., Norwich,NY 13815

Foundation type: Independent foundation
Purpose: Scholarships to graduating seniors of Norwich High School, NY, for higher education.
Financial data: Year ended 12/31/2012. Assets, $349,238 (M); Expenditures, $18,079; Total giving, $15,400.
Type of support: Support to graduates or students of specific schools; Undergraduate support.
Application information: Application form required.
  Deadline(s): May 1
  Additional information: Application can be obtained from guidance office and must include a transcript. Applicant must show ability to successfully pursue further studies,

have good moral character, average or better grades through high school and have a pleasant personality.
EIN: 237304980

6030
The Glaucoma Foundation, Inc.
80 Maiden Ln., Ste. 700
New York, NY 10038-4778   (212) 285-0080
Contact: Scott R. Christensen, Pres. and C.E.O.
FAX: (212) 651-1888;
E-mail: info@glaucomafoundation.org; URL: http://www.glaucomafoundation.org

Foundation type: Public charity
Purpose: Grants to scientists and doctors conducting research to improve the lives of glaucoma patients.
Publications: Application guidelines; Annual report; Financial statement; Newsletter.
Financial data: Year ended 12/31/2011. Assets, $3,715,160 (M); Expenditures, $1,303,415; Total giving, $190,712.
Fields of interest: Eye diseases; Institute; Eye research.
Type of support: Research.
Application information: Applications accepted. Application form required. Application form available on the grantmaker's web site.
Initial approach: Letter or telephone
Copies of proposal: 6
Deadline(s): Mar. 1 and Sept. 1
Applicants should submit the following:
1) Budget Information
2) SASE
3) Curriculum vitae
4) Proposal
Program description:
Research Grants: Provides funding in two specific areas relating to glaucoma: investigations in optic nerve rescue and restoration, and molecular genetics. Grants are awarded for a one-year period and are renewable. Initial grant funding for a one-year period is limited to a maximum of $40,000. The principal investigator may apply for a renewal for up to $50,000, based upon research findings from the initial grant research.
EIN: 133174839

6031
Charles G. Glazer Scholarship Fund
1 M & T Plz., 8th Fl.
Buffalo, NY 14203

Foundation type: Independent foundation
Purpose: Scholarships to graduates of James Buchanan High School, PA.
Financial data: Year ended 12/31/2012. Assets, $52,928 (M); Expenditures, $53,226; Total giving, $51,900.
Type of support: Support to graduates or students of specific schools; Undergraduate support.
Application information: Application form required.
Deadline(s): Apr. 1
EIN: 236485096

6032
The Glens Falls Foundation
237 Glen St.
Glens Falls, NY 12801   (518) 761-7350
Contact: D. Michael Niles, Business Admin.
FAX: (518) 798-8620;
E-mail: administrator@glensfallsfoundation.org;
URL: http://www.glensfallsfoundation.org

Foundation type: Community foundation
Purpose: Scholarships to residents of Warren, Washington, and Saratoga counties, NY, to attend Dartmouth College, NH or Harvard University, MA. Medical scholarships are also available.
Publications: Application guidelines; Annual report; Informational brochure.
Financial data: Year ended 12/31/2011. Assets, $13,336,425 (M); Expenditures, $539,695; Total giving, $441,610; Grants to individuals, 80 grants totaling $140,228 (high: $12,000, low: $75).
Fields of interest: Higher education; Medical school/education.
Type of support: Scholarships—to individuals; Support to graduates or students of specific schools; Undergraduate support.
Application information: Applications accepted. Application form required. Application form available on the grantmaker's web site.
Send request by: Mail or e-mail
Deadline(s): May 15 for Harry B. Pulver Scholarship, The fourth Friday in June for Medical Scholarships
Final notification: Recipients notified by July 24 for medical scholarships
Applicants should submit the following:
1) Essay
2) Letter(s) of recommendation
3) Transcripts
Additional information: See web site for application forms and guidelines per scholarship type.
Program descriptions:
Harry B. Pulver Scholarships: Through a bequest of Harry Brereton Pulver, the foundation provides scholarships to area students attending Dartmouth College or Harvard University as undergraduates. The scholarships are for a maximum of four years and each scholar will be eligible to receive $2,000 a year for four years. Applicants must be of good moral character, good academic proficiency, and have financial need.
Medical Scholarships: The foundation's Gilberto and Lennetta Pesquera Fund offers scholarship grants for medical education on an annual basis to assist qualified men and women who have graduated from local area schools and have successfully completed the first year of medical school. The current amount for each grant is $4,000 per year. These grants are restricted to tuition, fees, books and supplies. The payments are remitted directly to the educational institution for credit to the student's account.
EIN: 146036390

6033
Global Jewish Assistance and Relief Network
511 Ave. of the Americas, Ste. 18
New York, NY 10011-8436   (212) 868-3636
Contact: Rabbi Eliezer Avtzon, Exec. Dir.
FAX: (212) 868-7878; E-mail: info@gjarn.org;
Additional address: 1485 Union St., Brooklyn, NY 11213-4447; E-mail for Rabbi Eliezer Avtzon: director@globaljewish.org; URL: http://www.globaljewish.org/

Foundation type: Public charity
Purpose: Assistance to individuals and families with food, homes, scholarships and medical assistance.
Financial data: Year ended 12/31/2010. Assets, $221,525 (M); Expenditures, $720,089; Total giving, $379,099; Grants to individuals, totaling $36,681.
Fields of interest: Human services; Economically disadvantaged.

Type of support: Grants for special needs.
Application information: Applications not accepted.
Additional information: Individuals needs are evaluated before disbursing funds. Contact the agency for additional information.
EIN: 113095240

6034
Andrew Glover Youth Program
100 Ctr. St., Rm. 1541
New York, NY 10013-4308   (212) 349-6381
Contact: Angel Rodriguez, Exec. Dir.
FAX: (212) 349-6388; E-mail: info@agyp.org;
URL: http://www.agyp.org

Foundation type: Public charity
Purpose: Grants, counseling and other services are provided to youths in trouble with the law as an alternative to incarceration.
Publications: Annual report.
Financial data: Year ended 12/31/2011. Assets, $1,891,347 (M); Expenditures, $1,022,714; Total giving, $20,199; Grants to individuals, totaling $20,199.
Fields of interest: Crime/violence prevention, youth; Youth development.
Type of support: Grants to individuals.
Application information: Applications not accepted.
EIN: 133267496

6035
Rita & Herbert Z. Gold Charitable Trust
P.O. Box 319
Rockville Centre, NY 11570

Foundation type: Independent foundation
Purpose: Scholarships to students of South Side High School, Rockville Centre, NY, who started school in the Head Start program.
Financial data: Year ended 12/31/2011. Assets, $315,020 (M); Expenditures, $11,283; Total giving, $10,183; Grants to individuals, 6 grants totaling $10,183 (high: $3,000, low: $1,000).
Type of support: Scholarships—to individuals; Support to graduates or students of specific schools.
Application information: Applications not accepted.
Additional information: Unsolicited requests for funds not considered or acknowledged.
EIN: 116465852

6036
Sam & Adele Golden Foundation for the Arts
237 Bell Rd.
New Berlin, NY 13411-3616

Foundation type: Company-sponsored foundation
Purpose: Fellowships and residencies to professional artists, 25 years of age or older, working in paint who demonstrate exceptional creative ability.
Financial data: Year ended 12/31/2012. Assets, $2,122,928 (M); Expenditures, $123,943; Total giving, $0.
Fields of interest: Painting.
Type of support: Fellowships; Residencies.
Application information: Applications accepted. Application form available on the grantmaker's web site.
Initial approach: Application for residencies
Send request by: Online

Copies of proposal: 1
Deadline(s): Oct. 29 for residencies
Applicants should submit the following:
1) Resume
2) Letter(s) of recommendation
Additional information: Golden Foundation
Fellowships are administered through Atlantic
Center for the Arts, Bemis Center for
Contemporary Art, Headlands Center for the
Arts, and the Vermont Studio Center. See web
site for application and additional information.

Program description:
The Exploratory Residency: The foundation
awards artist residencies to assist the professional
visual artist in discovering the innovative use of new
materials and technologies. Residencies are four
weeks in length and includes a range of acrylic and
oil paints and mediums, custom and experimental
acrylic products, an introduction to the Golden Artist
Colors laboratories and manufacturing facilities,
consultations with paint technicians, 24/7 access
to open studio space, and a private apartment.
EIN: 161523983

6037
Goldstein Family Foundation
6 Vincent Rd.
Spring Valley, NY 10977-3829

Foundation type: Independent foundation
Purpose: Scholarships to Jewish residents of NY,
primarily in Brooklyn. General welfare grants to
Jewish indigent individuals residing in NY, primarily
in Brooklyn.
Financial data: Year ended 12/31/2011. Assets,
$1,595,661 (M); Expenditures, $64,789; Total
giving, $58,841; Grants to individuals, 8 grants
totaling $58,841 (high: $20,000, low: $110).
Type of support: Undergraduate support; Grants for
special needs.
Application information:
Initial approach: Letter
Additional information: Contact foundation for
further information.
EIN: 020581239

6038
Good News Foundation of Central New York, Inc.
10475 Cosby Manor Rd.
Utica, NY 13502-1205 (315) 735-6210

Foundation type: Operating foundation
Purpose: Scholarships to students at seven
Catholic schools in NY.
Financial data: Year ended 12/31/2012. Assets,
$20,921,187 (M); Expenditures, $845,711; Total
giving, $106,270.
Fields of interest: Christian agencies & churches.
Type of support: Scholarships—to individuals.
Application information: Applications not
accepted.
Additional information: Unsolicited requests for
funds not considered or acknowledged.
EIN: 161421215

6039
Cora A. Goodell and Menzo W. Goodell Scholarship Endowment Trust
245 Main St.
P.O. Box 430
Oneonta, NY 13820-2502

Foundation type: Independent foundation

Purpose: College scholarship to assist one student
with tuition cost from Worcester Central High to
attend Hartwick College, NY.
Financial data: Year ended 12/31/2012. Assets,
$125,992 (M); Expenditures, $1,840; Total giving,
$0.
Fields of interest: Higher education.
Type of support: Scholarships—to individuals;
Support to graduates or students of specific
schools.
Application information: Applications not
accepted.
Additional information: Unsolicited requests for
funds not considered or acknowledged.
EIN: 166272694

6040
Goshen Rotary Scholarship Foundation
c/o J. Goodreds
162 Merriewold Rd.
Forestburgh, NY 12777 (845) 794-2230

Foundation type: Public charity
Purpose: Scholarships to graduating high school
students of the Goshen School District in NY.
Publications: Application guidelines; Annual report;
Informational brochure.
Financial data: Year ended 06/30/2012. Assets,
$429,577 (M); Expenditures, $18,620; Total
giving, $18,250.
Fields of interest: Higher education.
Type of support: Scholarships—to individuals.
Application information:
Applicants should submit the following:
1) Resume
2) SAT
3) Transcripts
4) Work samples
5) GPA
6) Financial information
7) Essay
8) ACT
Additional information: Applicant must
demonstrate financial need. All applications
must go through the guidance department.
Program description:
Goshen Rotary Club Scholarship Program: This
program works to encourage well-rounded
scholarship and aptitude geared toward service to
others and the ever-changing needs of society.
Scholarships ranging from $300 to $1,500 are
available to students who reside in the territorial
limits of the Goshen School District, are able to
demonstrate financial need, and give evidence as
to ability, commitment, and personal initiative
toward achieving his/her goals and those of the
Rotary.
EIN: 061352671

6041
Adolph and Esther Gottlieb Foundation, Inc.
380 West Broadway
New York, NY 10012-5115 (212) 226-0581
Contact: Sanford Hirsch, Exec. Dir.
FAX: (212) 274-1476;
E-mail: shirsch@gottliebfoundation.org;
URL: http://www.gottliebfoundation.org

Foundation type: Independent foundation
Purpose: Grants to painters, sculptors, and
printmakers who have at least 20 years of
experience in a mature phase of their art.
Emergency assistance to qualified artists whose
needs are the result of an unexpected, catastrophic
event.

Publications: Application guidelines; Informational
brochure.
Financial data: Year ended 06/30/2013. Assets,
$32,911,466 (M); Expenditures, $1,244,487;
Total giving, $548,500; Grants to individuals, 33
grants totaling $548,500.
Fields of interest: Visual arts; Sculpture; Design;
Painting; Arts, artist's services.
Type of support: Emergency funds; Grants for
special needs.
Application information: Applications accepted.
Application form required.
Initial approach: Letter for individual support,
telephone for emergency grant
Send request by: Mail
Copies of proposal: 1
Deadline(s): Dec. 15 for Individual Support
Applicants should submit the following:
1) Work samples
2) Essay
3) SASE
4) Financial information
Additional information: See web site for
additional application guidelines.
Program descriptions:
Emergency Grants: Grants of up to $15,000 is
given as one-time assistance for a specific
emergency such as fire, flood, or emergency
medical need. An artist must be able to
demonstrate a minimum involvement of ten years
in a mature phase of his or her work. Artists must
work in the disciplines of painting, sculpture or
printmaking.
Individual Support Grants: Twelve grants are
awarded each year to encourage artists who have
dedicated their lives to developing their art,
regardless of their level of commercial success.
Artist must show their primary involvement has
been with their artistic goals, regardless of other
personal or financial responsibilities. Artists must
work in the disciplines of painting, sculpture, or
printmaking.
EIN: 132853957

6042
The Grand Marnier Foundation
c/o Elise Aubespin-Seignolle
183 Madison Ave. 15th Fl.,Ste.1504
New York, NY 10016 (212) 323-3085
Contact: Elise Aubespin Seignolle

Foundation type: Company-sponsored foundation
Purpose: Fellowships to students at select schools
to study French civilization and culture.
Financial data: Year ended 12/31/2012. Assets,
$5,155,025 (M); Expenditures, $302,797; Total
giving, $210,000.
Fields of interest: Cultural/ethnic awareness.
Type of support: Fellowships; Graduate support.
Application information: Contact the foundation for
additional information.
EIN: 133258414

6043
Grandma Brown Foundation Inc.
P.O. Box 230
Mexico, NY 13114-0230 (315) 963-7221
Contact: Sandra L. Brown, Tr.

Foundation type: Company-sponsored foundation
Purpose: Scholarships primarily to residents of the
Syracuse, NY area, who plan on attending
institutions of higher learning in NY.
Financial data: Year ended 12/31/2011. Assets,
$277,778 (M); Expenditures, $23,127; Total

giving, $21,500; Grants to individuals, 4 grants totaling $9,000 (high: $2,500, low: $2,000).
Type of support: Undergraduate support.
Application information: Applications accepted.
   Initial approach: Letter or telephone
   Additional information: Contact foundation for eligibility criteria.
EIN: 166052275

6044
Nancy Graves Foundation, Inc.
c/o Hecht and Co., P.C.
622 3rd. Ave.
New York, NY 10017
E-mail: mail@nancygravesfoundation.org;
URL: http://www.nancygravesfoundation.org

Foundation type: Operating foundation
Purpose: Grants by nomination only to visual artists who wish to master a technique, medium, or discipline that is different from the one in which he or she is primarily recognized.
Publications: Grants list.
Financial data: Year ended 09/30/2012. Assets, $9,628,549 (M); Expenditures, $302,155; Total giving, $10,000; Grants to individuals, 2 grants totaling $10,000 (high: $5,000, low: $5,000).
Fields of interest: Visual arts.
Type of support: Awards/grants by nomination only.
Application information: Applications not accepted.
   Additional information: Unsolicited requests for funds not considered or acknowledged.
EIN: 133885307

6045
Grayson-Jockey Club Research Foundation
40 E. 52nd St.
New York, NY 10022-5911 (212) 521-5327
Contact: Edward L. Bowen, Pres.
FAX: (212) 371-6123;
E-mail: contactus@grayson-jockeyclub.org;
Application address: 821 Corporate Dr., Lexington, KY 40503, tel.: (859) 224-2850, fax: (859) 224-2853; URL: http://www.grayson-jockeyclub.org

Foundation type: Public charity
Purpose: Grants to investigators for conducting equine-related scientific research.
Publications: Annual report; Newsletter.
Financial data: Year ended 12/31/2011. Assets, $18,177,178 (M); Expenditures, $1,398,965; Total giving, $848,934. Grants to individuals amount not specified.
Fields of interest: Animal welfare.
Type of support: Research; Grants to individuals.
Application information: Applications accepted. Application form available on the grantmaker's web site.
   Send request by: Mail
   Deadline(s): Nov. 1
   Final notification: Recipient notified late Feb. or early Mar.
   Additional information: See web site for additional guidelines.
Program description:
   Storm Cat Research Career Advancement Grant: The program is intended to promote development of promising investigators by providing a one year salary supplement of $15,000. This program is restricted to one award per year. The applicant must be working under the supervision of a tenured faculty member who is responsible for directing the post-graduate fellowship experience. The long-term

goal of this annual program is to spur development of potential career researchers by allowing post-graduate and post-residency students to further their experience with techniques and general research methods in areas under investigation by their institutions. Preference is given to post-residency fellows and Ph.D. students nearing completing of their program with a record of publication and production.
EIN: 616031750

6046
The Griffin Foundation, Inc.
(formerly Mordechai Weisz Private Foundation, Inc.)
c/o Morris Werner Law Offices
155 N. Main St.
New City, NY 10956-3845

Foundation type: Operating foundation
Purpose: Financial assistance for basic food and shelter needs to large families living at or below poverty level in New City, NY.
Financial data: Year ended 10/31/2010. Assets, $636 (M); Expenditures, $860; Total giving, $0.
Type of support: Grants for special needs.
Application information: Applications not accepted.
   Additional information: Unsolicited requests for funds not considered.
EIN: 201960245

6047
Thomas V. Guarino Family Foundation
247 Scotchtown Rd.
Goshen, NY 10924-5023 (845) 294-6127
Contact: Thomas V. Guarino, Pres.

Foundation type: Independent foundation
Purpose: Scholarships to graduates of Goshen Central School District, NY.
Financial data: Year ended 12/31/2011. Assets, $215,776 (M); Expenditures, $27,650; Total giving, $27,100; Grants to individuals, 4 grants totaling $6,000 (high: $2,000, low: $1,000).
Type of support: Support to graduates or students of specific schools; Undergraduate support.
Application information:
   Initial approach: Letter
   Deadline(s): May 1
EIN: 061617207

6048
The Guenther Scholarship Fund
1 Steuben Sq.
Hornell, NY 14843-1699

Foundation type: Independent foundation
Purpose: Scholarships to graduating seniors of Hornell High School District, NY, pursuing a college, university, technical and similiar advanced education and training.
Financial data: Year ended 12/31/2012. Assets, $634,280 (M); Expenditures, $42,915; Total giving, $40,000; Grants to individuals, 20 grants totaling $40,000 (high: $2,000, low: $2,000).
Fields of interest: Vocational education, post-secondary; Higher education.
Type of support: Support to graduates or students of specific schools; Undergraduate support.
Application information: Applications accepted.
   Additional information: Student must demonstrate financial need, have an acceptable scholastic record, and prove outstanding citizenship and demonstrate

such traits as leadership, capability and perceptiveness.
EIN: 222314303

6049
The Harry Frank Guggenheim Foundation
25 W. 53rd St., 16th Fl.
New York, NY 10019-5401 (646) 428-0971
Contact: Staff
FAX: (646) 428-0981; E-mail: info@hfg.org;
URL: http://www.hfg.org

Foundation type: Operating foundation
Purpose: Grants for doctoral and postdoctoral research in behavioral, social, and biological sciences, with the aim of providing a better understanding of dominance, aggression, and violence. Dissertation fellowship support in the same field is also available.
Publications: Application guidelines; Multi-year report; Occasional report.
Financial data: Year ended 12/31/2012. Assets, $58,474,110 (M); Expenditures, $4,041,582; Total giving, $1,299,902; Grants to individuals, 29 grants totaling $575,933 (high: $41,000, low: $1,588).
Fields of interest: Crime/violence prevention; Science; Social sciences; Psychology/behavioral science.
Type of support: Fellowships; Research; Postdoctoral support; Doctoral support.
Application information: Applications accepted. Application form required. Application form available on the grantmaker's web site.
   Send request by: Mail
   Deadline(s): Feb. 1 for Dissertation Fellowships, Aug. 1 for Research Grants
   Applicants should submit the following:
      1) Budget Information
      2) Curriculum vitae
      3) Letter(s) of recommendation
      4) Proposal
   Additional information: See web site for additional guidelines.
Program descriptions:
   Dissertation Fellowships: Ten or more dissertation fellowships are awarded each year to graduate students who will complete the writing of the dissertation within the award year. These fellowships of $20,000 each are designed to contribute to the support of the doctoral candidate to enable him or her to complete the thesis in a timely manner. Applications are evaluated in comparison with each other and not in competition with the postdoctoral research proposals. Applicants may be citizens of any country and studying at colleges or universities in any country.
   Research Grants: The foundation welcomes proposals from any of the natural and social sciences and the humanities that promise to increase understanding of the causes, manifestations, and control of violence, aggression, and dominance. The foundation awards research grants to individuals for individual projects in the range of $15,000 to $40,000 a year for periods of one or two years. Applicants may be citizens of any country, while almost all recipients of the research grant possess a Ph.D., M.D., or equivalent degree, there are no formal degree requirements for the grant. The grant may not be used to support research undertaken as part of the requirements for a graduate degree.
EIN: 136043471

6050
John Simon Guggenheim Memorial Foundation
90 Park Ave.
New York, NY   10016-1302   (212) 687-4470
Contact: Edward Hirsch, Pres.
FAX: (212) 697-3248; E-mail: fellowships@gf.org;
URL: http://www.gf.org

Foundation type: Independent foundation
Purpose: Fellowships to published authors, exhibited artists, researchers, and others in the arts, humanities, social sciences, and natural sciences.
Publications: Application guidelines; Annual report; Financial statement; Informational brochure (including application guidelines).
Financial data: Year ended 12/31/2012. Assets, $238,109,536 (M); Expenditures, $16,867,864; Total giving, $8,069,150; Grants to individuals, 325 grants totaling $8,069,150 (high: $55,000, low: $5,000).
Fields of interest: Humanities; Literature; Arts; Research; Mathematics; Social sciences.
Type of support: Fellowships.
Application information: Applications accepted. Application form required. Application form available on the grantmaker's web site.
Initial approach: Letter
Send request by: Online
Copies of proposal: 1
Deadline(s): Sept. 15
Final notification: Recipients notified in six months
Applicants should submit the following:
1) Resume
2) Letter(s) of recommendation
3) Work samples
4) Proposal
Program description:
Fellowships to Assist Research and Artistic Creation: Fellowships are awarded through three annual competitions: two open to citizens and permanent residents of the United States and Canada, and the other open to citizens and permanent residents of Latin America and the Caribbean. The fellowships will be awarded by the trustees upon nominations made by a selection committee. The fellowships are awarded to men and women who have already demonstrated exceptional capacity for productive scholarship or exceptional creative ability in the arts. The foundation consults with distinguished scholars and artists regarding the accomplishments and promise of the applicants and presents this evidence to the selection committee. Guggenheim Fellowships are grants to selected individuals made for a minimum of six months and a maximum of twelve months. Since the purpose of the program is to help provide fellows with blocks of time in which they can work with as much creative freedom as possible, grants are made freely. No special conditions attach to them, and Fellows may spend their grant funds in any manner they deem necessary to their work. The United States IRS, however, does require the foundation to ask for reports from its Fellows at the end of their Fellowship terms. Guggenheim Fellowships are not scholarships, and they are not available to those who seek to complete their training either as undergraduate, graduate, or part-time students. They are also not intended for immediate postgraduate work. The amounts of the grants will be adjusted to the needs of the fellows, considering their other resources and the purpose and scope of their plans. Members of the teaching profession receiving sabbatical leave on full or part salary are eligible for appointment, as are holders of other

fellowships and of appointments at research centers. For the United States and Canadian competition: completed applications must be submitted by the candidates themselves no later than Sept. 15. For the Latin American and Caribbean competition: completed applications must be submitted by the candidates themselves no later than Dec. 1. The board of trustees has instructed the selection committee to recommend only individuals who have not previously had the foundation's support. Fellowship in the field of Constitutional Studies was created in 2007.
EIN: 135673173

6051
Gunglach Scholarship Trust
1 M.T. Plz., 8th Fl.
Buffalo, NY   14203

Foundation type: Independent foundation
Purpose: Scholarships to residents of York, PA.
Financial data: Year ended 12/31/2012. Assets, $174,908 (M); Expenditures, $4,927; Total giving, $4,500; Grants to individuals, 8 grants totaling $4,500 (high: $1,000, low: $500).
Type of support: Undergraduate support.
Application information: Applications not accepted.
Additional information: Unsolicited requests for funds not accepted.
EIN: 166203833

6052
The Gunk Foundation
99 Sayre Rd.
Westport, NY   12993
URL: http://www.gunk.org

Foundation type: Independent foundation
Purpose: Grants to individual artists for work that seeks out new topics, new spaces and new forms for public art.
Financial data: Year ended 12/31/2012. Assets, $187,977 (M); Expenditures, $48,038; Total giving, $0.
Fields of interest: Arts.
Type of support: Program development; Grants to individuals.
Application information: Applications accepted. Application form available on the grantmaker's web site.
Initial approach: Letter
Deadline(s): Apr. 30
Additional information: Application must include examples of previous work (on slide sheet, one to two videos, CD-roms or DVDs).
EIN: 141777559

6053
Starr Hacker Memorial Scholarship Fund
350 Daniel St.
Lindenhurst, NY   11757-3547
Contact: Daniel Giordano, Tr.
Application address: 300 Charles St., Lindenhurst, NY 11757-3545

Foundation type: Independent foundation
Purpose: Scholarships to graduates of Lindenhurst High School, NY, who show distinction in English and/or Drama. Applicants must have an average of at least 85 percent in English.
Financial data: Year ended 11/20/2012. Assets, $249,012 (M); Expenditures, $9,343; Total giving, $8,400; Grants to individuals, 4 grants totaling $8,400 (high: $2,100, low: $2,100).

Type of support: Support to graduates or students of specific schools; Undergraduate support.
Application information: Interview required.
Deadline(s): Nov. 19
Applicants should submit the following:
1) Letter(s) of recommendation
2) Essay
Additional information: Finalists announced Dec. 3; Finalists will submit a written piece or a dramatic audition by Jan. 7; Recipients announced Feb. 4.
EIN: 112487557

6054
The Richard and Mica Hadar Foundation
(formerly The Hadar Foundation)
400 E. 84th St.
New York, NY   10028-5606   (212) 832-9797
Contact: Richard Hadar, Co-Chair.
URL: http://www.hadarfoundation.org

Foundation type: Operating foundation
Purpose: Scholarships by nomination to selected students from high schools specializing in the arts, and have been accepted into a college program.
Financial data: Year ended 12/31/2012. Assets, $3,444,519 (M); Expenditures, $353,946; Total giving, $176,510; Grants to individuals, 6 grants totaling $13,060 (high: $7,500, low: $40).
Fields of interest: Visual arts; Performing arts.
Type of support: Awards/grants by nomination only.
Application information: Applicant must be in need of financial assistance, and have demonstrated ability in either the performing, literary or visual arts. Application forms and nominators' forms available from the foundation.
EIN: 133721350

6055
James T. Hambay Foundation
1 M&T Plz., 8th Fl.
Buffalo, NY   14203   (716) 842-5506
Contact: Diane Rimer

Foundation type: Independent foundation
Purpose: Medical expense assistance to blind, physically disabled, and economically disadvantaged children under the age of 18, who reside in Dauphin, Cumberland, York, Lebanon and Perry counties, PA.
Financial data: Year ended 12/31/2012. Assets, $2,117,851 (M); Expenditures, $161,532; Total giving, $120,000.
Fields of interest: Health care; Children/youth, services; Disabilities, people with; Economically disadvantaged.
Type of support: Grants for special needs.
Application information: Application form required.
Initial approach: Letter
Send request by: Mail
Deadline(s): None
Applicants should submit the following:
1) Proposal
2) Financial information
EIN: 236243877

6056
Ralph Dean & Evelyn Peake Harby Scholarship Fund
P.O. Box 389
Walton, NY   13856-0389   (607) 865-4126

Foundation type: Independent foundation
Purpose: Scholarships to students of Walton Central High School, NY.

Financial data: Year ended 12/31/2012. Assets, $297,846 (M); Expenditures, $7,523; Total giving, $3,750; Grants to individuals, 4 grants totaling $3,750 (high: $1,500, low: $750).
Type of support: Support to graduates or students of specific schools; Precollege support.
Application information: Applications accepted. Application form required.
  Initial approach: Letter
  Deadline(s): July 31
EIN: 166210926

6057
Harden Foundation
8550 Mill Pond Way
Mc Connellsville, NY   13401   (315) 245-1000
Contact: David Harden, Dir.

Foundation type: Independent foundation
Purpose: Scholarships for children of employees of Harden Furniture Company, primarily in NY.
Financial data: Year ended 12/31/2012. Assets, $790,228 (M); Expenditures, $56,436; Total giving, $38,834; Grants to individuals, 39 grants totaling $29,750 (high: $1,000, low: $750).
Type of support: Employee-related scholarships.
Application information: Applications accepted.
  Deadline(s): None
  Additional information: Applications by letter, detailing need.
Company name: Harden Furniture Company
EIN: 156017586

6058
Harvestworks, Inc.
596 Broadway, Ste. 602
New York, NY   10012-3210   (212) 431-1130
FAX: (212) 606-3286;
E-mail: carolp@harvestworks.org; URL: http://www.harvestworks.org

Foundation type: Public charity
Purpose: Residencies to young artists living in New York, NY, for the creation of a new work of art that incorporates interactive technologies into the concept, design and presentation.
Publications: Application guidelines; Grants list; Informational brochure.
Financial data: Year ended 06/30/2012. Assets, $73,166 (M); Expenditures, $379,683; Total giving, $77,148; Grants to individuals, totaling $77,148.
Fields of interest: Media/communications; Film/video; Visual arts; Music.
Type of support: Residencies.
Application information: Application form required.
  Initial approach: E-mail
  Deadline(s): May 1
  Applicants should submit the following:
    1) Work samples
    2) SASE
    3) Resume
  Additional information: Application should also include description of project.
Program description:
  New Works Residencies: The program offers commissions of up to $4,000 to make new work in their state of the art digital media facility. New works may include multiple channel audio or video installations, interactive performance systems, data visualization or projects involving hardware hacking, circuit bending or custom built interfaces, as well as projects that use the web. Emerging artists and artists of color are encouraged to apply. Students who are currently enrolled in a university are not eligible. AIR recipients from the past two

years are not eligible to apply . Applicants must reside in the U.S.
EIN: 132891159

6059
HASTAGA Foundation
P.O. Box 248
Broadalbin, NY   12025-0248   (518) 461-4552
Contact: James B. Longwell, Jr.
URL: http://www.hastaga.org/

Foundation type: Operating foundation
Purpose: Grant to residents of Lombok, Indonesia for education and assistance with living standards.
Financial data: Year ended 12/31/2012. Assets, $8,973 (M); Expenditures, $35,154; Total giving, $26,582; Grants to individuals, 5 grants totaling $26,582 (high: $8,000, low: $4,000).
International interests: Indonesia.
Type of support: Grants for special needs.
Application information: Applications accepted.
  Initial approach: Letter
  Deadline(s): None
  Additional information: Letter should include contact information and educational plans.
EIN: 204338717

6060
The Haven Foundation
c/o Marks Paneth & Shron
685 3rd Ave., 5th Fl.
New York, NY   10017-8401   (212) 503-8800
Contact: Robert Lyons
URL: http://www.thehavenfdn.org

Foundation type: Independent foundation
Purpose: Grants to freelance professional writers and artists experiencing career-threatening illness, accident, natural disaster or other emergency or personal catastrophe.
Publications: Application guidelines.
Financial data: Year ended 12/31/2012. Assets, $12,983,347 (M); Expenditures, $322,939; Total giving, $280,793; Grants to individuals, 33 grants totaling $280,793 (high: $25,000, low: $500).
Fields of interest: Arts, artist's services.
Type of support: Grants to individuals.
Application information: Applications accepted. Application form required.
  Additional information: See web site for additional guidelines.
EIN: 204356938

6061
The Havens Relief Fund Society
475 Riverside Dr., Rm. 1940
New York, NY   10115-0023
Contact: Allison S. McDermott, Exec. Dir.
E-mail: info@havensfund.org; URL: http://www.havensfund.org

Foundation type: Operating foundation
Purpose: Financial assistance to needy residents of greater New York City with food, clothing, rent, utilities, health care and other special needs.
Financial data: Year ended 12/31/2012. Assets, $26,114,200 (M); Expenditures, $1,339,081; Total giving, $753,518; Grants to individuals, totaling $753,518.
Fields of interest: Economically disadvantaged.
Type of support: Emergency funds; Awards/grants by nomination only; Grants for special needs.
Application information: Unsolicited applications not accepted.

Program description:
  Assistance Program: Funds are distributed to Almoners, appointed by the foundation, who are responsible for distributing them to individuals who meet the Havens guidelines and are residents of New York City.
EIN: 135562382

6062
The Hawley Foundation for Children
P.O. Box 1017
Saratoga Springs, NY   12866-0837   (518) 587-0207
Contact: Pam Farrell, Dir.
URL: http://hawleyfoundation.org/

Foundation type: Independent foundation
Purpose: Scholarships to graduates of high schools in Saratoga Springs, NY, for undergraduate or vocational study. Camperships are also available.
Financial data: Year ended 12/31/2013. Assets, $2,376,304 (M); Expenditures, $125,948; Total giving, $106,350; Grants to individuals, 3 grants totaling $6,000 (high: $2,000, low: $2,000).
Fields of interest: Vocational education.
Type of support: Support to graduates or students of specific schools; Technical education support; Undergraduate support.
Application information: Applications accepted. Application form required. Interview required.
  Deadline(s): May 1
  Additional information: Application should FAF or FSS form and parents' or guardians' income tax form.
EIN: 141340069

6063
Charles O. and Elsie Haynes Trust
1410 County Hwy. 48
Oneonta, NY   13820   (607) 432-4605
Contact: Thomas J. Trelease, Mgr.

Foundation type: Operating foundation
Purpose: Scholarships to students residing in the Charlotte Valley Central School District, Davenport, NY for attendance at an institution of higher learning.
Financial data: Year ended 12/31/2012. Assets, $422,330 (M); Expenditures, $19,351; Total giving, $18,055; Grants to individuals, 10 grants totaling $14,500 (high: $2,000, low: $500).
Type of support: Scholarships—to individuals.
Application information: Application form required.
  Initial approach: Letter
  Send request by: Mail or in person
  Deadline(s): June 2
  Applicants should submit the following:
    1) Transcripts
    2) GPA
    3) Financial information
    4) Essay
  Additional information: Application must also include a copy of students' and parents' income tax returns and a copy of last two college semester tuition bills if you are currently attending college.
EIN: 222429332

6064
Health Insurance Plan of Greater New York

(also known as EmblemHealth, Inc.)
55 Water St., 11th Fl.
New York, NY   10041-0004
Toll-free tel.: (800) 447-7187; URL: http://
www.emblemhealth.com

Foundation type: Public charity
Purpose: Health care coverage for members.
Publications: Annual report.
Financial data: Year ended 12/31/2012. Assets,
$2,211,939,156; Expenditures, $4,905,852,884.
Fields of interest: Association; Health care;
Community/economic development.
Type of support: Grants for special needs.
Application information: Applications not
accepted.
EIN: 131828429

6065
Hearing Health Foundation

(formerly Deafness Research Foundation)
363 Seventh Ave., 10th Fl.
New York, NY   10001-3904   (212) 257-6140
Contact: Andrea Kardonsky Boidman, Exec. Dir.
E-mail: info@hearinghealthfoundation.org; Toll-free
tel.: (866) 454-3924; TTY: (888) 435-6104;
URL: http://www.drf.org

Foundation type: Public charity
Purpose: Research grants to third-year medical
students for the study of hearing and balance.
Publications: Application guidelines; Annual report;
Financial statement; Grants list; Informational
brochure; Informational brochure (including
application guidelines); Newsletter; Program policy
statement.
Financial data: Year ended 09/30/2011. Assets,
$4,144,752 (M); Expenditures, $1,962,192; Total
giving, $609,250.
Fields of interest: Ear, nose & throat research;
Medical research.
Type of support: Research; Grants to individuals;
Graduate support.
Application information: Applications accepted.
Application form required. Application form
available on the grantmaker's web site.
   Initial approach: E-mail
   Send request by: Online
   Deadline(s): Dec. 1
   Final notification: Recipients notified in June
   Applicants should submit the following:
      1) Resume
      2) Proposal
   Additional information: See web site for
      additional guidelines.
Program description:
   DRF Centurion Clinical Research Award: In
partnership with the American Academy of
Otolaryngology - Head and Neck Surgery's CORE
Grants Program, a one-year grant of $50,000 is
available for clinical research in the hearing and
balance sciences. Research can involve human
participants and may be directed toward diagnosis,
epidemiology, genetics, clinical pathophysiology,
and treatment. Eligible applicants include those
holding an M.D., Ph.D., or equivalent degrees, and
a faculty or post-doctoral appointment in the U.S.
EIN: 131882107

6066
Hemophilia Association of New York, Inc.

13 W. 33rd St., Ste. 11D
New York, NY   10001   (212) 682-5510
Contact: Linda E. Mugford, Exec. Dir.
FAX: (212) 983-1114; E-mail: hany@bestweb.net;
URL: http://www.hemophilia-newyork.org/

Foundation type: Public charity
Purpose: Grants to researchers for the study of
hemophilia and related congenital blood disorders.
Financial data: Year ended 06/30/2012. Assets,
$2,688,478 (M); Expenditures, $694,721; Total
giving, $143,483; Grants to individuals, totaling
$143,483.
Fields of interest: Hemophilia; Hemophilia
research.
Type of support: Research; Grants to individuals.
Application information: Applications accepted.
   Initial approach: Telephone or e-mail
EIN: 135650955

6067
Henry Street Settlement

265 Henry St.
New York, NY   10002-4808   (212) 766-9200
Contact: David Garza, Exec. Dir.
FAX: (212) 505-8329; E-mail: info@henrystreet.org;
Residency application address: c/o Abrons Art
Center, Attn: Artist-In-Residence Workspace Prog.,
466 Grand St., New York, NY 10002-4804;
additional tel.: (212) 598-0400; URL: http://
www.henrystreet.org

Foundation type: Public charity
Purpose: Scholarships to New York City residents
aged 6-14 to attend Henry Street Settlement
summer camps. Also, awards of studio space only
to painters, printmakers, sculptors, installation
artists and a clay artist, all of whom are residents
of New York City.
Publications: Application guidelines; Financial
statement.
Financial data: Year ended 06/30/2012. Assets,
$44,138,133 (M); Expenditures, $30,515,341;
Total giving, $141,005.
Fields of interest: Visual arts; Sculpture; Painting;
Camps.
Type of support: Awards/prizes; Residencies;
Camperships.
Application information: Application form required.
   Initial approach: Telephone
   Deadline(s): May 1 for Artist Awards
   Applicants should submit the following:
      1) Financial information
      2) Resume
      3) Letter(s) of recommendation
   Additional information: Health and immunization
      records required for Scholarships. Application
      must also include artist statement, slides of
      work, and references.
Program descriptions:
   Artist-in-Residence Workspace Program: The
program provides free studio space for one year,
starting in late September, to eight New York City
visual artists. Among the artists selected for the
program are painters, printmakers, sculptors, or
installation artists, who work in a shared
workspace. In addition, a clay artist works in a
separate shared space adjacent to the
settlement's ceramics workshop.
   Youth Scholarships: Each year, the settlement
awards a number of need-based scholarships to
current and former youth program participants who
are entering or attending colleges and universities.
The scholarships serve to supplement the
students' book costs and expenses during the

academic year, as well as to recognize the
achievements of "Henry Street Kids" as they
embark on their next life phase.
EIN: 131562242

6068
Hereditary Disease Foundation

3960 Broadway, 6th Fl.
New York, NY   10032-1543   (212) 928-2121
Contact: Carl D. Johnson Ph.D., Exec. Dir.
FAX: (212) 928-2172;
E-mail: curehd@hdfoundation.org; URL: http://
www.hdfoundation.org

Foundation type: Public charity
Purpose: Grants, fellowships, and awards for
research leading to the treatment and cure of
Huntington's disease.
Publications: Application guidelines; Grants list;
Newsletter.
Financial data: Year ended 12/31/2011. Assets,
$9,436,673 (M); Expenditures, $2,092,861; Total
giving, $680,948; Grants to individuals, totaling
$554,547.
Fields of interest: Genetic diseases and disorders
research.
Type of support: Fellowships; Awards/grants by
nomination only; Awards/prizes; Postdoctoral
support.
Application information:
   Initial approach: Letter
   Send request by: E-mail
   Deadline(s): Feb. 15, June 15 and Oct. 15
   Applicants should submit the following:
      1) Proposal
      2) Budget Information
Program descriptions:
   Basic Research Grants Program: The program
provides funding for promising new directions in HD
research. Grants are generally for one year only and
are considered seed money. It is hoped that other
sources of research support will provide follow-on
funding for successful projects. The maximum
award for research grants is $50,000.
   *John J. Wasmuth Postdoctoral Fellowship
Program:* The program provides support for
post-graduate training in research relevant to curing
HD for up to two years. Awards are based on a scale
which includes all university fringe benefits plus
$8,000 for supplies. The scale is based on years
of experience since applicants attained their Ph.D.
and stipends range from $40,500 to $56,000.
   Lieberman Award: The award is presented to a
successful applicant whose research is highly
relevant to understanding the cause and treatment
of HD. An award can be funded for two years for up
to $75,000 per year. Applications are not accepted
for this award.
   Milton Wexler Postdoctoral Fellowship Award: The
award is presented to a postdoctoral fellow whose
proposed research is innovative and highly relevant
to curing Huntington's disease. Areas of interest
include trinucleotide expansions, animal models,
gene therapy, neurobiology and development of the
basal ganglia, cell survival and death, and
intercellular signaling in striatal neurons.
Applications are not accepted for the award.
EIN: 237376197

6069
Irvin E. Herr Foundation

1 MT Plz., 8th Fl.
Buffalo, NY   14203   (716) 842-5506

Foundation type: Independent foundation

Purpose: Scholarships to graduating high school seniors in Cumberland, Dauphin, Northumberland, and Perry counties, PA.
Financial data: Year ended 12/31/2012. Assets, $417,382 (M); Expenditures, $26,570; Total giving, $21,000.
Type of support: Support to graduates or students of specific schools; Undergraduate support.
Application information: Contact foundation for application guidelines.
EIN: 222550087

6070
Grove W. and Agnes M. Hinman Charitable Foundation
P.O. Box 209
Hamilton, NY   13346-0209   (315) 824-2292
Contact: Susan Schapiro, Tr.
Application address: 30 Broad St., Hamilton, NY 13346

Foundation type: Independent foundation
Purpose: Scholarships to students in the Morrisville-Eaton, Hamilton, and Madison, NY, school districts.
Financial data: Year ended 04/30/2013. Assets, $602,760 (M); Expenditures, $51,716; Total giving, $41,800; Grants to individuals, 34 grants totaling $32,000 (high: $1,500, low: $500).
Type of support: Support to graduates or students of specific schools; Undergraduate support.
Application information: Applications accepted. Application form required.
 Additional information: Applications accepted after May 1.
EIN: 237194828

6071
Hirth Family Foundation, Inc.
c/o J. Popper
192 Lexington Ave.
New York, NY   10016

Foundation type: Independent foundation
Purpose: Scholarships to residents of CT to attend any college or university in CT.
Financial data: Year ended 12/31/2012. Assets, $178,507 (M); Expenditures, $53,666; Total giving, $40,752.
Type of support: Undergraduate support.
Application information: Applications not accepted.
 Additional information: Unsolicited requests for funds not considered or acknowledged.
EIN: 651179388

6072
Hispanic Federation
55 Exchange Pl., 5th Fl.
New York, NY   10005-3303   (212) 233-8955
Contact: Lillian Rodriguez Lopez, Pres.
FAX: (212) 233-8996;
E-mail: info@hispanicfederation.org; Additional address: 1522 K St., N.W., Ste. 1130, Washington D.C. 20005-1225; tel.: (202) 842-0236;
URL: http://www.hispanicfederation.org

Foundation type: Public charity
Purpose: Emergency financial assistance to individuals and families of the Latino community.
Publications: Annual report; Financial statement; Informational brochure; Newsletter.
Financial data: Year ended 12/31/2011. Assets, $7,643,194 (M); Expenditures, $4,281,221; Total giving, $590,331.

Fields of interest: Human services; Hispanics/Latinos.
Type of support: Emergency funds; Grants for special needs.
Application information:
 Initial approach: E-mail
 Additional information: Contact organization on guidelines for assistance.
EIN: 133573852

6073
Historical Research Foundation, Inc.
c/o Sanford Becker & Co.
1430 Broadway, 6th Fl.
New York, NY   10018-3308   (212) 313-9386
Contact: Frances Bronson, Secy.
Application address: c/o National Review, 215 Lexington Ave., New York, NY 10016-6023

Foundation type: Independent foundation
Purpose: Grants for historic and philosophic research and studies.
Financial data: Year ended 12/31/2011. Assets, $23,839 (M); Expenditures, $0; Total giving, $0.
Fields of interest: History/archaeology; Philosophy/ethics.
Type of support: Research.
Application information: Applications accepted.
 Initial approach: Letter
 Additional information: Application must include an informal description of the project, time of completion, and results anticipated.
EIN: 136059836

6074
J. M. Hodges Educational Fund Trust
201 N. Union St.
Olean, NY   14760

Foundation type: Independent foundation
Purpose: Student loans to high school students within a ten-mile radius of Olean, NY.
Financial data: Year ended 12/31/2012. Assets, $316,721 (M); Expenditures, $18,899; Total giving, $14,170; Grants to individuals, 13 grants totaling $14,170 (high: $1,405, low: $821).
Fields of interest: Education.
Type of support: Student loans—to individuals.
Application information: Applications not accepted.
 Additional information: Contributes only to preselected individuals. Unsolicited requests for funds not considered or acknowledged.
EIN: 166136464

6075
Valeria E. Hoffert Scholarship Trust
One M&T Plz., 8th Fl.
Buffalo, NY   14203   (716) 842-5506
Contact: Diane M. Rimer

Foundation type: Independent foundation
Purpose: Scholarships to graduates of Reading Senior High School, PA.
Financial data: Year ended 12/31/2012. Assets, $1,100,499 (M); Expenditures, $63,335; Total giving, $51,000.
Type of support: Support to graduates or students of specific schools; Undergraduate support.
Application information: Applications not accepted.
 Additional information: Unsolicited requests for funds not considered or acknowledged.
EIN: 237763256

6076
Holland Lodge Foundation Inc.
c/o Holland Lodge Foundation Inc.
71 W. 23rd St., Ste. 701
New York, NY   10010-4174   (212) 675-0323

Foundation type: Independent foundation
Purpose: Relief grants to the elderly and young, primarily in New York, NY.
Financial data: Year ended 09/30/2013. Assets, $1,837,197 (M); Expenditures, $84,663; Total giving, $36,250; Grant to an individual, 1 grant totaling $3,000.
Fields of interest: Children/youth, services; Aging.
Type of support: Grants for special needs.
Application information: Applications accepted.
 Deadline(s): None
 Additional information: Applications should outline financial need and reason for assistance.
EIN: 136126132

6077
Home for Contemporary Theater and Art
145 6th Ave.
New York, NY   10013-1548   (212) 647-0202
Contact: Kristin Marting, Exec. Dir.
E-mail for Basil Twist: dreammusic@here.org
FAX: (212) 647-0257; E-mail: info@here.org; E-mail for Kristin Marting: kristin@here.org; URL: http://www.here.org

Foundation type: Public charity
Purpose: Residencies to writers, performers, composers, directors, designers, puppeteers, dancers and singers in the live performance arts.
Publications: Application guidelines.
Financial data: Year ended 08/31/2011. Assets, $4,205,066 (M); Expenditures, $1,572,142.
Fields of interest: Film/video; Design; Performing arts; Performing arts centers; Dance; Theater; Music composition; Literature.
Type of support: Residencies.
Application information: Interview required.
 Initial approach: Proposal for Dream Music
 Deadline(s): Fall for HERE Artist Residency Program
 Applicants should submit the following:
  1) Resume
  2) Work samples
 Additional information: Application should also include, biography, artist statement, and project outline.
Program description:
 Dream Music Puppetry Program: This program provides performance opportunities to puppet artists, and encourages multidisciplinary collaboration to develop new puppetry techniques.
EIN: 133449416

6078
Howard Memorial Fund
1920 Mott Ave.
Far Rockaway, NY   11691-4111

Foundation type: Independent foundation
Purpose: Scholarships for undergraduate and technical studies to young high school graduates of the City of New York including Nassau and Suffolk counties.
Financial data: Year ended 06/30/2012. Assets, $963,564 (M); Expenditures, $50,679; Total giving, $43,500.
Fields of interest: Vocational education, post-secondary; Higher education.

Type of support: Technical education support; Undergraduate support.
Application information: Applications accepted. Application form required.
> *Initial approach:* Letter
> *Send request by:* Mail
> *Deadline(s):* Apr. 30
> *Applicants should submit the following:*
>   1) Financial information
>   2) Letter(s) of recommendation
>   3) Transcripts
>   4) Essay
> *Additional information:* Application should also include verification of U.S. citizenship, and copy of W-2 or other documents.

Program description:
Scholarship: Scholarships are awarded to disadvantaged students whose academic averages may not qualify them for other scholarships, but who have the potential to pursue a bona fide course of study, either academic or vocational, at a college or professional institution. Applicants must be accepted by a school of their choice and demonstrate financial need. The grants may be used for tuition, books or living expenses. Scholarships are renewable.
EIN: 136161770

6079
J.E. Howe Educational Fund Trust
201 N. Union St.
Olean, NY   14760

Foundation type: Independent foundation
Purpose: Student loans to Olean, NY area high school students for education assistance.
Financial data: Year ended 12/31/2012. Assets, $281,542 (M); Expenditures, $19,413; Total giving, $15,034; Grants to individuals, 23 grants totaling $15,034 (high: $3,204, low: $1,067).
Fields of interest: Higher education.
Type of support: Student loans—to individuals.
Application information: Applications accepted.
> *Initial approach:* Letter
> *Deadline(s):* May 30
EIN: 166031953

6080
Hudson River Foundation for Science & Environmental Research
17 Battery Pl., Ste. 915
New York, NY   10004-1114   (212) 483-7667
FAX: (212) 924-8325; E-mail: info@hudsonriver.org;
URL: http://www.hudsonriver.org

Foundation type: Public charity
Purpose: Fellowships and research and travel grants restricted to projects for the study of the Hudson River.
Publications: Application guidelines.
Financial data: Year ended 12/31/2011. Assets, $36,162,055 (M); Expenditures, $3,928,532; Total giving, $1,584,736; Grants to individuals, totaling $37,100.
Fields of interest: Research; Environment, water resources.
Type of support: Research; Graduate support; Undergraduate support; Travel grants; Doctoral support.
Application information: Applications accepted. Application form required.
> *Initial approach:* Letter or telephone
> *Send request by:* Online
> *Deadline(s):* Feb. 14 for Polgar Fellowship, Mar. 21 for Graduate Fellowship,
> *Applicants should submit the following:*

1) Proposal
2) Curriculum vitae
3) Budget Information
Program descriptions:
Hudson River Graduate Fellowships: Awards up to four full-time research fellowships to advanced graduate students conducting research on the Hudson River system. Fellowships awarded to doctoral students will consist of a stipend consistent with the policy of the student's institution, in an amount of up to $15,000 for one year, and an incidentals research budget of up to $1,000. A fellowship awarded to a master's level student will include a stipend consistent with the policy of the student's graduate institution, of up to $11,000 for one year, and an incidentals research budget of up to $1,000.
Tibor T. Polgar Fellowships: Provides a summer grant of up to $3,800 per fellowship and limited research funds to eight undergraduate or graduate college students to conduct research on the Hudson River. The objectives of the program are to gather important information on all aspects of the River and to train students in conducting estuarine studies and public policy research. Each fellow must be sponsored by a primary advisor who will receive a stipend of $500.
EIN: 133089956

6081
Human Growth Foundation
997 Glen Cove Ave., Ste. 5
Glen Head, NY   11545-1593
Contact: D. Costa, Exec. Dir.
FAX: (516) 671-4055; E-mail: hgf1@hgfound.org;
Toll-free tel.: (800) 451-6434; URL: http://www.hgfound.org

Foundation type: Public charity
Purpose: Research grants to doctors for the study on human growth and its disorders.
Publications: Application guidelines.
Financial data: Year ended 12/31/2011. Assets, $266,922 (M); Expenditures, $236,181.
Fields of interest: Research.
Type of support: Research; Postdoctoral support.
Application information:
> *Initial approach:* Letter
> *Send request by:* E-mail
> *Deadline(s):* May 15 for Letter of Intent, Sept. 1 for Full Grant Application
> *Final notification:* Recipients notified Nov. 15
> *Additional information:* Contact the foundation for additional eligibility criteria.

Program description:
Small Grants Program: The foundation provides grants for the investigation of human growth and its disorders. Grants are for postdoctoral research only. The foundation will only consider topics relevant to human growth and development, including but not limited to areas of biology, psychosocial studies, and nutrition, with special consideration given to chondrodystrophies. Amounts awarded will be $10,000 to $15,000 each. No part of the grant shall be used toward administrative overhead. The foundation requires a synopsis of the research to be submitted in the following year.
EIN: 160913012

6082
Humanas, Inc.
69 West 9th St., 12G
New York, NY   10011
Contact: Herbert Gstalder, Dir.

Foundation type: Operating foundation
Purpose: College scholarships to students for attendance at colleges or universities in New York for books, fees and other incidental expenses exclusive of tuition and board.
Financial data: Year ended 12/31/2012. Assets, $31,551 (M); Expenditures, $23,411; Total giving, $22,500.
Fields of interest: Higher education.
Type of support: Scholarships—to individuals.
Application information: Applications accepted.
> *Initial approach:* Letter
> *Deadline(s):* Aug. 31
> *Additional information:* Application should state college or university student is or will be attending, course of study, amount of grant required, and number of semesters.
EIN: 133132602

6083
Humanitas Scholarship Trust
c/o Henry M. Tausig
233 W. 77th St., Ste. 8G
New York, NY   10024   914-723-4476
Contact: H. Stephen Lieb, Secy.
Application address: 233 Nelson Rd., Scarsdale, NY 10583

Foundation type: Independent foundation
Purpose: Scholarships to worthy, qualified students in the New York area for continuing education at accredited colleges or universities.
Financial data: Year ended 12/31/2012. Assets, $0 (M); Expenditures, $30,916; Total giving, $30,500.
Fields of interest: Higher education.
Type of support: Scholarships—to individuals.
Application information: Applications accepted. Application form required.
> *Deadline(s):* May 15
> *Additional information:* Application should include school transcript and a copy of 1040 tax form.
EIN: 133123849

6084
Hunter Douglas Foundation Inc.
1 Blue Hill Plz.
Pearl River, NY   10965-3104   (845) 664-7000
Contact: Kathy O'Keefe

Foundation type: Operating foundation
Purpose: Scholarships to children of employees of Hunter Douglas, Inc. and its subsidiaries, primarily in NJ.
Financial data: Year ended 12/31/2012. Assets, $92,844 (M); Expenditures, $625,996; Total giving, $622,250; Grants to individuals, 87 grants totaling $197,250 (high: $5,000, low: $500).
Fields of interest: Higher education.
Type of support: Employee-related scholarships.
Application information: Applications not accepted.
> *Additional information:* Unsolicited requests for funds not considered or acknowledged.
EIN: 223694713

6085
Hunter's Hope Foundation, Inc.
P.O. Box 643
6368 W. Quaker St.
Orchard Park, NY   14127-0643   (716) 667-1200
E-mail: info@huntershope.org; Toll-free tel.: (877) 984-4673; URL: http://www.huntershope.org

Foundation type: Public charity
Purpose: Assistance to families with children undergoing treatment with Krabbe disease in Durham, NC. Grants for research that will identify new treatments, therapies and ultimately a cure for Krabbe disease and other leukodystrophies.
Publications: Annual report; Grants list; Newsletter; Program policy statement.
Financial data: Year ended 12/31/2011. Assets, $872,419 (M); Expenditures, $989,634; Total giving, $218,537; Grants to individuals, 40 grants totaling $61,537.
Fields of interest: Leukemia research.
Type of support: Grants to individuals; Grants for special needs.
Application information: Contact the foundation for additional guidelines.
EIN: 161552315

6086

Huntington's Disease Society of America, Inc.

505 8th Ave., Ste. 902
New York, NY   10018-6588   (212) 242-1968
Contact: Louise Vetter, C.E.O.
FAX: (212) 239-3430; E-mail: hdsainfo@hdsa.org;
Toll-free tel.: (800) 345-4372; E-mail For Louise Vetter: lvetter@hdsa.org; URL: http://www.hdsa.org

Foundation type: Public charity
Purpose: Research grants and fellowships to investigators for research on Huntington's disease.
Publications: Application guidelines; Annual report; Financial statement; Grants list; Informational brochure; Newsletter.
Financial data: Year ended 09/30/2011. Assets, $2,685,966 (M); Expenditures, $5,979,017; Total giving, $1,015,600.
Fields of interest: Genetic diseases and disorders research.
Type of support: Fellowships; Research; Grants to individuals.
Application information: Applications accepted. Application form required. Application form available on the grantmaker's web site.
  Initial approach: E-mail
  Send request by: E-mail
  Copies of proposal: 1
  Deadline(s): July 1
  Final notification: Recipients notified Oct. 15
  Applicants should submit the following:
    1) Letter(s) of recommendation
    2) Essay
    3) Curriculum vitae
    4) Budget Information
Program descriptions:
  Coalition For The Cure Grants: Grants provide funding for Huntington disease investigation and research. Average grants are $150,000 for one year and are renewable.
  Fellowship Awards: Awards $40,000 to young postdoctoral investigators in the early stages of their careers. Awards are for one year. Fellows who have demonstrated sufficient progress are eligible to apply for a second and final year of funding.
  Research Grants: Grants provide seed monies of up to $50,000 to all investigators for a one-year period in support of basic or clinical research. Grants are not renewable but investigators can apply for another grant.
EIN: 133349872

6087

Mary J. Hutchins Foundation, Inc.

c/o TCC Group
31 W. 27th St., 4th Fl.
New York, NY   10001-6914

Foundation type: Independent foundation
Purpose: Welfare assistance to economically disadvantaged individuals, primarily in the New York, NY, metropolitan area.
Financial data: Year ended 12/31/2012. Assets, $33,646,113 (M); Expenditures, $1,725,267; Total giving, $1,502,925.
Fields of interest: Economically disadvantaged.
Type of support: Grants for special needs.
Application information: Applications not accepted.
  Additional information: Unsolicited requests for funds not considered or acknowledged.
EIN: 136083578

6088

The Edmund Niles Huyck Preserve Inc.

P.O. Box 189
Rensselaerville, NY   12147-0188
Contact: Chad Jemison, Exec. Dir.
URL: http://www.huyckpreserve.org/

Foundation type: Independent foundation
Purpose: Grants to students and senior investigators working toward advanced degrees, postdoctoral students or professional scientists. Research grants are also awarded each year to scientists wishing to work at the preserves.
Financial data: Year ended 12/31/2011. Assets, $2,227,866 (M); Expenditures, $378,278; Total giving, $22,050; Grants to individuals, 6 grants totaling $22,050 (high: $10,000, low: $500).
Fields of interest: Research; Biology/life sciences; Botany.
Type of support: Research; Postdoctoral support; Postgraduate support; Doctoral support.
Application information:
  Initial approach: Letter
  Deadline(s): Feb. 1
  Applicants should submit the following:
    1) Budget Information
    2) Curriculum vitae
EIN: 141338387

6089

IBM International Foundation

(formerly IBM South Africa Projects Fund)
New Orchard Rd.
Armonk, NY   10504-1709
Contact: Judy Chin, Fdn. Mgr.
E-mail for IBM Fellowship Grants:
phdfellow@us.ibm.com
URL: http://www.ibm.com/ibm/responsibility/

Foundation type: Company-sponsored foundation
Purpose: Fellowships to students pursuing a Ph.D. in areas of interest to IBM.
Financial data: Year ended 12/31/2012. Assets, $193,326,732 (M); Expenditures, $23,839,105; Total giving, $21,618,005. Fellowships amount not specified.
Fields of interest: Engineering/technology; Computer science; Engineering; Science.
Type of support: Fellowships; Awards/grants by nomination only; Doctoral support.
Application information: Application form required. Application form available on the grantmaker's web site.
  Deadline(s): Sept. 22 to Nov. 2

Additional information: Applicants must be enrolled full-time in a college or university Ph.D. program and must have competed at least one year of doctoral study. Applicants must be nominated by a faculty member.
Program description:
  IBM Fellowship Grants: The foundation awards Ph.D. fellowships to students with an interest in solving problems that are important to IBM. Academic disciplines and areas of study are computer science and engineering, electrical and mechanical engineering, physical sciences including chemistry, material sciences, and physics, mathematical sciences including analytics, statistics, operations research, and optimization, business sciences including financial services, risk management, marketing, communications, and learning/knowledge management, and service science, management, and engineering (SSME). Ph.D. fellowships include a stipend for one academic year and Ph.D. Fellows are paired with an IBM mentor according to their technical interests. The program is by nomination only.
EIN: 133267906

6090

ID Identifying Discourse, Inc.

P.O. Box 638
New York, NY   10008-0631   (518) 429-3458
E-mail: Info@identifyingdiscourse.org; URL: http://identifyingdiscourse.org

Foundation type: Public charity
Purpose: Scholarships to students who wish to study at Mouly Ismail University or other universities throughout Morocco.
Publications: Application guidelines.
Fields of interest: Higher education.
Type of support: Scholarships—to individuals; Support to graduates or students of specific schools.
Application information: Applications accepted. Application form required. Application form available on the grantmaker's web site. Interview required.
  Applicants should submit the following:
    1) Letter(s) of recommendation
    2) Essay
  Additional information: Applicants must demonstrate financial need.
Program description:
  Caaff Scholarship: This scholarship, awarded three times per year, is available to four students who display promise and excellence in English language studies, community organizing, math/economics, history/humanities, culture/sociology, and law/government. Scholarships are awarded to university freshman students of financial need who live outside of Meknes, and need to travel into Meknes to study at Moulay Ismail University and other universities throughout Morocco.
EIN: 455231803

6091

Illuminating Engineering Society

(formerly Illuminating Engineering Society of North America)
120 Wall St., 17th Fl.
New York, NY   10005-3904   (212) 248-5000
Contact: William Hanley, Exec. V.P.
FAX: (212) 248-5017; E-mail: ies@ies.org;
Additional Fax: (212)-248-5018; URL: http://www.iesna.org

Foundation type: Public charity

Purpose: Provides scholarships to those studying illumination engineering, and awards to individuals displaying excellence in the field.
Publications: Application guidelines.
Financial data: Year ended 06/30/2012. Assets, $15,622,989 (M); Expenditures, $5,510,707; Total giving, $81,891; Grants to individuals, totaling $69,391.
Fields of interest: Higher education.
Type of support: Scholarships—to individuals; Awards/prizes.
Application information: Applications accepted.
  Additional information: See society web site for individual program information.
Program descriptions:
  Besal Lighting Education Fund: The Besal Lighting Education Fund has awarded over $500,000 in scholarships to students from accredited schools throughout the United States. Established in honor of the late Robert J. Besal, the fund aspires to encourage talented and committed students to pursue a career in the lighting industry. The scholarship fund is merit based, and as such it is currently determined completely by academic excellence. Students on campuses that have qualified as Besal campuses can apply through their university's Besal Liaison.
  Howard Brandston Student Lighting Design Grant: The grant is intended to encourage and recognize students who have demonstrated exceptional professional promise through the presentation of an original and ingenious solution to a supplied design problem. The award comprises a plaque and a check in the amount of $1,000. To be eligible to enter this competition, applicants must be enrolled as full-time students in an approved academic degree program.
  Richard Kelly Grant: The purpose of the grants is to recognize and encourage creative thought and activity in the use of light. Cash award(s) will be granted to the person(s) who preserve and carry forth Richard Kelly's ideals, enthusiasm and reverence for light. Applicants must demonstrate accomplishment as well as the potential to contribute to the art and science of illumination. Proposed, completed, and on-going work involving light may be submitted and should clearly illustrate the way in which the conceptual or applied use of light in new and innovative ways is used to solve or better understand a problem.
  Robert E. Thunen Memorial Scholarships: Applications for scholarships may be submitted by full-time (junior, senior, or graduate) students in an accredited four-year college or university located in northern California, Nevada, Oregon or Washington who desire to study illumination as a career. Typically, at least two $2,500 grants are made each academic year.
  Young Professionals Scholarship Fund: A minimum of four awards (one from each of the Society's Regions) of $1,000 each will be granted each year to emerging professionals (individuals working in the lighting profession for five or fewer years) and students in their junior or senior year of undergraduate studies or enrolled in a graduate program. All awardees must be a member of the IES. The grant will offset some of the costs of travel and lodging; the conference fee will be waived. Scholarships will be awarded to applicants who show evidence of a commitment to the lighting profession, leadership abilities, and potential for future involvement in the IES.
EIN: 131767038

6092

Independent Feature Project, Inc.

(also known as IFP)
68 Jay St., Rm. 425
Brooklyn, NY 11201-8361 (212) 465-8200
Contact: Joana Vicente, Exec. Dir.
FAX: (212) 465-8525; E-mail: mbyrd@ifp.org;
URL: http://www.ifp.org

Foundation type: Public charity
Purpose: Grants and support services to independent filmmakers.
Publications: Application guidelines.
Financial data: Year ended 02/28/2012. Assets, $1,080,411 (M); Expenditures, $4,216,614; Total giving, $2,196,604; Grants to individuals, totaling $2,196,604.
Fields of interest: Film/video; Arts, artist's services.
Type of support: Grants to individuals; Fiscal agent/sponsor.
Application information: Applications accepted. Application form required.
  Initial approach: Letter
  Deadline(s): Sept. 1 and Mar. 1; none for Fiscal Sponsorship
  Additional information: An application fee of $50 is required for the Fiscal Sponsorship Program. See web site for additional application information.
Program descriptions:
  Fiscal Sponsorship: The organization's Minneapolis, New York, and Seattle branches offer fiscal sponsorship opportunities for individuals and organizations that do not have 501(c)(3) status, but would still like to solicit and receive funds from outside sources. The organization charges up to 6 percent of all monies received as an administrative fee. Eligible projects must be considered 'non-commercial' works (able to be financed by personal funds, donations, grants, corporate sponsorships, in-kind donations, etc., but not by offering investment for profit), and must fall into one of the following categories: be documentary films, other works of nonfiction, or experimental films; be films of any length produced by first-time filmmakers or students; and fictions works with proposed budgets not exceeding Tier 1 of the International Alliance of Theatrical Stage Employers' National Agreement.
  The Anthony Radziwill Documentary Fund: Provides grants to emerging and established documentary filmmakers in the form of development funds (seed money) for specific new projects. The fund seeks to provide an additional much-needed source of funding for independent non-fiction filmmakers at the earliest stage of new work, traditionally a difficult point at which to secure funding.
EIN: 133118525

6093

Independent Production Fund, Inc.

(also known as IPF)
200 Central Park S., 12F
New York, NY 10019-1442 (212) 221-6310
Contact: Alvin H. Perlmutter, Dir.
FAX: (212) 302-1854; E-mail: info@ipfmedia.org;
E-Mail for Alvin H. Permutter: ahp@ipfmedia.org;
URL: http://www.ipfmedia.org

Foundation type: Public charity
Purpose: Fiscal sponsorship to individuals with documentary projects.
Publications: Application guidelines.
Financial data: Year ended 01/31/2013. Assets, $1,187,674 (M); Expenditures, $254,695.

Fields of interest: Film/video; Television.
Type of support: Fiscal agent/sponsor.
Application information: Applications accepted.
  Initial approach: Submit a fiscal sponsor proposal packet
  Copies of proposal: 1
  Deadline(s): None
  Final notification: 3 to 4 weeks after receipt of application
  Additional information: There is a $50 non-refundable application fee.
Program description:
  Fiscal Sponsorship: The organization offers fiscal sponsorship to a limited number of documentary projects each year that it believes will make a strong positive impact. Fiscal sponsorship allows individual filmmakers and for-profit production companies to become eligible for foundation, corporate, and government grants which require 501(c)(3) tax-exempt status, and to accept tax deductible donations from individuals. Once accepted into the fiscal sponsorship program, applicants may submit their film proposal to various funding sources under the fund's nonprofit umbrella. Fiscal sponsorships are currently closed.
EIN: 133455677

6094

John N. Insall Foundation for Orthopaedics Inc.

270 Madison Ave., 17th Fl.
New York, NY 10016-0601
Application address: c/o Kathy Lenhardt, Insall Scott Kelly Institute, 210 E. 64th St., 4th Fl., New York, NY 10065-7471, tel.: (212) 434-4340, e-mail: klenhardt@iskinstitute.com

Foundation type: Independent foundation
Purpose: Fellowships to applicants who have completed (within 5 years) either an Adult Reconstruction Knee Fellowship or Sports Medicine Fellowship.
Financial data: Year ended 06/30/2013. Assets, $2,559,563 (M); Expenditures, $226,208; Total giving, $217,336.
Fields of interest: Orthopedics.
Type of support: Fellowships.
Application information: Applications accepted. Application form required. Application form available on the grantmaker's web site.
  Initial approach: Application
  Send request by: On-line
  Deadline(s): Oct. 1
  Applicants should submit the following:
    1) Curriculum vitae
    2) Letter(s) of recommendation
    3) Photograph
  Additional information: The photograph which must be submitted with application should be 2" x 2." Only two letters of recommendation are required. One sponsor should be an orthopaedic surgeon who is familiar with the applicant's work during their residency or fellowship, and the other from an orthopaedic surgeon who is familiar with the applicant's work. See online application form for specific requirements.
Program description:
  John N. Insall Travelling Fellowship: A group of four international candidates will be selected to travel to various Knee Society locations for this one-month program in Oct. of each year. Applicants must have completed either an Adult Reconstruction Knee Fellowship or Sports Medicine Fellowship.
EIN: 134167179

6095
Institute of International Education, Inc.
809 United Nations Plz., 9th Fl.
New York, NY 10017-3380 (212) 883-8200
Contact: Allan E. Goodman, Pres. and C.E.O.;
Margot Steinberg, Dir., Indiv. Giving
FAX: (212) 984-5501; E-mail: msteinberg@iie.org;
URL: http://www.iie.org

Foundation type: Public charity
Purpose: Grants to U.S. students, teachers, professionals and scholars to study, teach, lecture, and conduct research in foreign countries, and to foreign individuals to engage in similar activities in the U.S.
Publications: Application guidelines; Annual report; Grants list; Informational brochure.
Financial data: Year ended 09/30/2012. Assets, $21,415,344; Expenditures, $386,452,876; Total giving, $277,979,921; Grants to individuals, totaling $175,008,171.
Fields of interest: Visual arts; Architecture; Performing arts; Literature; Education.
Type of support: Exchange programs; Postdoctoral support; Graduate support; Undergraduate support; Postgraduate support; Travel grants; Workstudy grants; Doctoral support.
Application information: Applications accepted. Application form required. Application form available on the grantmaker's web site.
> *Send request by:* Online
> *Deadline(s):* Varies
> *Additional information:* See web site for additional application guidelines.

Program descriptions:
Benjamin A. Gilman International Scholarship Program: The program offers awards for undergraduate study abroad and was established by the International Academic Opportunity Act of 2000. This scholarship provides awards for U.S. undergraduate students who are receiving Federal Pell Grant funding at a two-year or four-year college or university to participate in study abroad programs worldwide. The program aims to diversify the kinds of students who study abroad and the countries and regions where they go by supporting undergraduates who might otherwise not participate due to financial constraints. Award amounts vary depending on the length of study and student need with the average award being approximately $4,000.

Boren Scholars and Fellows: Boren Scholars and Fellows represent a variety of academic backgrounds, but all are interested in studying less commonly taught languages, including but not limited to Arabic, Chinese, Korean, Portuguese, Russian, and Swahili. Boren Scholarships provide up to $20,000 to U.S. undergraduate students to study abroad in areas of the world that are critical to U.S. interests and underrepresented in study abroad, including Africa, Asia, Central and Eastern Europe, Eurasia, Latin America, and the Middle East. Boren Fellowships provide up to $30,000 to U.S. graduate students to add an important international and language component to their graduate education through specialization in area study, language study, or increased language proficiency. Boren Fellowships support study and research in areas of the world that are critical to U.S. interests.

Dissertation Fellowship in Population, Reproductive Health, and Economic Development: Sponsored by the William and Flora Hewlett Foundation, the program will provide fellows with stipends to support tuition and research expenses. The objective of the Fellowship is to produce sound evidence on the role of population and reproductive health in economic development that could be incorporated into national and international

economic planning and decision making. Research that focuses on one of the following themes will be given priority: 1) the impact of reproductive health on women's economic empowerment, particularly as measured by economic outcomes at the household and individual levels; and 2) relationships between reproductive health/family planning (including population policies and dynamics) and macroeconomic outcomes in countries. Applicants should be currently enrolled in Ph.D. programs in either sub-Saharan Africa, the United States, or Canada, and should have completed their coursework by the start of the fellowship. Students in economics, geography, population studies, and epidemiology are especially encouraged to apply. Fellowship recipients will be awarded a maximum of $20,000 per year (depending on tuition, research expenses, and cost of living) for a total of two years to cover expenses incurred while working on their dissertation.

Fulbright U.S. Student Program: Awards grants annually to Americans the opportunity to study and conduct research in other nations. Recipients aim to increase mutual understanding among nations through educational and cultural exchange while serving as catalysts for long-term leadership development. Grants generally provide funding for roundtrip travel, maintenance for one academic year, limited health benefits and full or partial tuition. Travel-only grants are also available to limited countries. Applicants must be U.S. citizens at the time of application and hold a bachelor's degree by the beginning of the grant period but will not have a doctoral degree by the deadline and who is thinking of studying, assistant-teaching English, or conducting research abroad. The program offers grants in nearly all fields and disciplines, including the sciences, professional fields and Creative and Performing Arts.

Whitaker International Fellows and Scholars Program: The program is a funding opportunity for emerging U.S. leaders in biomedical engineering to build collaborative ties with individuals and institutions overseas. This program is open to U.S.-based biomedical engineers who are graduating seniors, graduate students, post-docs or early-career professionals. Applicants should be either currently-enrolled or no more than three years from their most recent degree. Award benefits include maintenance allowance, airfare, accident and sickness insurance, partial tuition reimbursement (Fellows only), and access to grantee events, as well as membership in an elite alumni resource network.
EIN: 131624046

6096
InterExchange, Inc.
161 6th Ave.
New York, NY 10013-1205 (212) 924-0446
Contact: Christine La Monica-Lunn, Exec. Dir.
FAX: (212) 924-0575;
E-mail: info@interexchange.org; URL: http://www.interexchange.org

Foundation type: Public charity
Purpose: Grants to individuals for cross-culutral awareness through work and volunteer exchange programs.
Publications: Application guidelines.
Financial data: Year ended 12/31/2011. Assets, $29,932,027 (M); Expenditures, $10,678,203; Total giving, $42,055; Grants to individuals, totaling $42,055.
Fields of interest: International exchange, students.
Type of support: Grants to individuals.

Application information: Applications accepted. Application form required. Application form available on the grantmaker's web site. Interview required.
> *Send request by:* Mail
> *Deadline(s):* Approximately eight weeks prior to program start date for Working Abroad Grant, Mar. 15, July 15 and Oct. 15 for Christianson Grant
> *Final notification:* Recipients notified two to three weeks after receipt of application for Working Abroad Grant, and six to eight weeks after each grant deadline for Christianson Grant
> *Applicants should submit the following:*
> 1) Resume
> 2) Letter(s) of recommendation
> 3) Essay
> *Additional information:* Application should also include a $50 application fee for Christianson Grant. See web site for additional guidelines.

Program descriptions:
Christianson Grant: This program provides grants to young Americans who wish to help further cultural awareness through meaningful work abroad experiences. Grants, ranging from $2,500 to $10,000, are available to applicants who have sought out and arranged their own programs. Proposed programs must be at least six months in length and emphasize a work component. Applicants must be U.S. citizens or legal permanent residents between the ages 18 and 28.

Working Abroad Grant: Grants of $1,500 each are available to applicants who show a high level of commitment to their chosen Working Abroad program. Preference is given toward applicants with limited or no previous international travel experience. Applicants must be U.S. citizens or legal permanent residents between the ages of 18 and 28.
EIN: 133449415

6097
International Center of Photography
1114 Ave. of the Americas at 43rd. Str.
New York, NY 10036-7701 (212) 857-0001
Contact: Mark Lubell, Exec. Dir.
FAX: (212) 857-0090; E-mail: info@icp.org;
URL: http://www.icp.org

Foundation type: Public charity
Purpose: Educational grants and scholarships to photographers and artists who demonstrate financial need at the International Center of Photography, NY.
Publications: Newsletter.
Financial data: Year ended 06/30/2012. Assets, $36,550,642 (M); Expenditures, $18,045,366; Total giving, $602,488; Grants to individuals, totaling $602,488.
Fields of interest: Photography.
Type of support: Scholarships—to individuals.
Application information: Applications accepted. Application form required.
> *Applicants should submit the following:*
> 1) Transcripts
> 2) Resume
> *Additional information:* Application must also include statement of purpose, portfolio, three letters of reference, and a $75 nonrefundable application fee.
EIN: 237412428

6098
International Council of Shopping Centers Educational Foundation, Inc.

1221 Ave. of the Americas, 41st Fl.
New York, NY 10020-1099 (646) 728-3628
FAX: (212) 589-5555; E-mail: icsc@icsc.org;
URL: http://www.icsc.org/foundation/index.php

Foundation type: Public charity
Purpose: Scholarships to members of ICSC to further their career in the retail real estate industry.
Publications: Application guidelines.
Financial data: Year ended 12/31/2011. Assets, $4,164,127 (M); Expenditures, $225,284; Total giving, $149,050.
Fields of interest: Business school/education.
Type of support: Scholarships—to individuals; Foreign applicants; Travel grants.
Application information: Applications accepted. Application form required. Application form available on the grantmaker's web site.
> *Deadline(s):* Mar. 15
> *Applicants should submit the following:*
>   1) Essay
>   2) Resume
>   3) Letter(s) of recommendation
>   4) Curriculum vitae
> *Additional information:* See web site for additional application information.
Program descriptions:
> *Charles Grossman Graduate Scholarships:* Two $10,000 scholarships are available to full-time graduate students who have selected retail real estate as their career path. Eligible recipients must also be ICSC members.
> *Harold E. Eisenberg Foundation Scholarship:* This scholarship covers tuition, enrollment fees, textbooks, workbooks, airfare, and hotel accommodations for an individual to attend the John T. Riordan School for Professional Development. Areas of concentration include management, marketing, and leasing at a technical or strategic level.
> *ICSC CenterBuild Scholarship:* A scholarship will be made available annually to a graduate student enrolled in its Master of Real Estate Development program, or an undergraduate student majoring in planning, architecture, interior design, construction management, engineering, landscape architecture, or real estate development.
> *John T. Riordan Professional Education Scholarship:* This scholarship covers enrollment feels, textbooks, workbooks, airfare, and hotel accommodations for a recipient to attend the John T. Riordan School for Professional Development. Available areas of concentration include management, marketing, and leasing at a technical or strategic level; and development, design, and construction at a technical level. Applicants may be new to retail real estate and looking to expand his or her knowledge of management, marketing, leasing or development, or design and construction. Eligible applicants must be members of the International Council of Shopping Centers (ICSC), employed by a member company in good standing, and be actively employed in the retail real estate industry for a minimum of one year and/or a recent graduate of a college or university with an emphasis in real estate.
> *Schurgin Family Foundation Scholarship:* This program provides a $5,000 scholarship to an undergraduate student who is studying retail real estate, real estate development, or shopping center leasing. Applicants for this scholarship must demonstrate academic excellence, as the scholarship is intended to help qualified students pursue an education that will lead them into productive careers in commercial real estate.

> *Undergraduate Real Estate Award:* Twenty-five awards of $1,000 are provided annually to juniors and seniors enrolled in a collegiate undergraduate real estate program who demonstrate exceptional potential for a career in retail real estate.
EIN: 133525440

6099
International Fellowships Fund

(also known as IFF)
809 United Nations Plz.
New York, NY 10017-3503 (212) 883-8200
Contact: Joan Dassin, Exec. Dir.
FAX: (212) 984-5594; URL: http://www.fordifp.org

Foundation type: Public charity
Purpose: Fellowships to individuals from Africa, Asia, Latin America, the Middle East, and Russia for up to three years of graduate-level study.
Publications: Informational brochure.
Financial data: Year ended 09/30/2012. Assets, $35,157,969 (M); Expenditures, $15,609,790; Total giving, $13,199,253; Grants to individuals, totaling $429,719.
Fields of interest: Graduate/professional education; Human services; Leadership development.
Type of support: Fellowships; Foreign applicants; Graduate support.
Application information: Applications not accepted.
> *Additional information:* The fund is no longer accepting new applicants. It's work will conclude in 2013.
Program description:
> *International Fellows Program:* Fellows are expected to use this education to become leaders in their respective fields, furthering development in their own countries and greater economic and social justice worldwide. Fellows may enroll in master's or doctoral programs and may pursue any academic discipline or field of study that is consistent with the interests of the Ford Foundation. Fellows receive placement guidance and may enroll in any university in the world to which they can gain admission up to approximately one year following selection. Funds are available for short-term pre-academic training, test and application fees, tuition and related fees, living expenses, health insurance, books, computer, travel, language training, professional development, and leadership development.
EIN: 134162722

6100
International Print Center New York

508 W. 26th St., Rm. 5A
New York, NY 10001-5538 (212) 989-5090
FAX: (212) 989-6069; E-mail: contact@ipcny.org;
URL: http://www.ipcny.org

Foundation type: Public charity
Purpose: Project support to artists and publishers at all stages of their careers in printmaking.
Financial data: Year ended 12/31/2011. Assets, $330,459 (M); Expenditures, $450,198.
Fields of interest: Print publishing.
Type of support: Project support.
Application information: Application form required.
> *Initial approach:* Letter
> *Send request by:* Mail
> *Deadline(s):* Sept. 14 for New Prints Progam
> *Applicants should submit the following:*
>   1) Work samples
>   2) SAT

> *Additional information:* See web site for complete application guidelines.
EIN: 133837466

6101
International Rescue Committee, Inc.

122 E. 42nd St.
New York, NY 10168-1289 (212) 551-3000
Contact: George Rupp, Pres. and C.E.O.
FAX: (212) 551-3179;
E-mail: fundraising@theirc.org; URL: http://www.theirc.org

Foundation type: Public charity
Purpose: Financial and emergency assistance for displaced people and victims of violent conflict.
Publications: Annual report; Financial statement; Newsletter.
Financial data: Year ended 09/30/2011. Assets, $195,269,065 (M); Expenditures, $386,464,097; Total giving, $154,092,887; Grants to individuals, totaling $21,480,093.
Type of support: Emergency funds; Grants for special needs.
Application information: Contact foundation for eligibility criteria.
EIN: 135660870

6102
International Sephardic Education Foundation

135 W. 29th St., Ste. 303
New York, NY 10001-5124 (212) 683-7772
Contact: Janice G. Stolar, Exec. Dir.
FAX: (212) 683-7779; E-mail: isefadmin@isef.org;
URL: http://www.isef.org

Foundation type: Public charity
Purpose: Scholarships and educational projects to students in the U.S. and Israel.
Publications: Annual report.
Financial data: Year ended 09/30/2011. Assets, $5,698,701 (M); Expenditures, $3,321,465; Total giving, $2,517,529.
Fields of interest: Higher education.
Type of support: Scholarships—to individuals; Postdoctoral support; Graduate support.
Application information: Applications accepted. Interview required.
> *Additional information:* Applicants are awarded scholarships based on financial need, academic merit, and community service. Contact foundation for eligibility criteria.
EIN: 132909403

6103
The Intrepid Fallen Heroes Fund

(also known as Armed Forces Family Survivors Fund)
1 Intrepid Sq.
W. 46th St. and 12th Ave.
New York, NY 10036-1007 (212) 957-7020
Contact: David Winters, Pres.
FAX: (212) 957-1989;
E-mail: mkrause@fallenheroesfund.org; Toll-free tel.: (800) 340-HERO; E-mail for David Winters: dwinters@fallenheroesfund.org; URL: http://www.fallenheroesfund.org

Foundation type: Public charity
Purpose: Grants to both military personnel in the U.S. and the United Kingdom who have been injured in operation in Iraq or Afghanistan.
Publications: Financial statement.

Financial data: Year ended 04/30/2012. Assets, $24,659,594 (M); Expenditures, $840,765; Total giving, $226,250.
Fields of interest: Military/veterans.
Type of support: Grants for special needs.
Application information: Applications not accepted.
Additional information: Unsolicited application for funds not considered.
EIN: 200366717

6104
Inwood House
320 E. 82nd St.
New York, NY   10028-4102   (212) 861-4400
Contact: Linda Lausell Bryant, Exec. Dir.
FAX: (212) 535-3775;
E-mail: info@inwoodhouse.com; E-Mail for Linda Lausell Bryant: llbryant@inwoodhouse.com;
URL: http://www.inwoodhouse.com

Foundation type: Public charity
Purpose: Scholarships to high school seniors, full-time college students, and students enrolled in an accredited vocational training program. Scholarships on a limited basis for students pursuing a graduate degree program.
Publications: Application guidelines.
Financial data: Year ended 06/30/2011. Assets, $20,367,838 (M); Expenditures, $10,804,969.
Fields of interest: Higher education; Family services, adolescent parents; Residential/custodial care, group home.
Type of support: Scholarships—to individuals.
Application information: Applications accepted. Application form required.
Deadline(s): Apr.
Final notification: Applicants notified late spring or early summer
Applicants should submit the following:
  1) Transcripts
  2) SAR
  3) SAT
  4) Resume
  5) Letter(s) of recommendation
  6) FAFSA
  7) Essay
  8) ACT
Additional information: Application should also include acceptance letter from the school the applicant plans to attend. Finalists may be interviewed.
Program description:
Inwood House Scholarship Fund: The fund assists young people ready to attend college and other advanced learning programs with money for applications, tuition, books, transportation, special housing, and child care needs. Applicants must have participated meaningfully in an Inwood House program.
EIN: 135562254

6105
IRT Foundation
4611 12th Ave., Apt. 2E
Brooklyn, NY   11219-2514   (718) 435-1759
Contact: Rachela Tauber, Tr.

Foundation type: Independent foundation
Purpose: Scholarships to needy individuals in Brooklyn, NY, for higher education.
Financial data: Year ended 02/28/2013. Assets, $99,298 (M); Expenditures, $55,926; Total giving, $55,186.
Fields of interest: Higher education; Economically disadvantaged.

Type of support: Undergraduate support.
Application information:
Initial approach: Letter
Deadline(s): None
Applicants should submit the following:
  1) Letter(s) of recommendation
Additional information: Application must include description of activities.
EIN: 113576037

6106
Ivy Foundation of Suffolk-Nassau
1258 Waterview Dr.
Rockville Centre, NY   11570-3428
Contact: Hazel Brandon Palmore, Pres.
Application address: c/o Mrs. Eva R. Denton, 6 Maple Dr., Roosevelt, NY 11575, tel.: (516) 868-8830

Foundation type: Public charity
Purpose: Scholarships to African-American and other minority students who are residents of Long Island, NY pursuing undergraduate study at an accredited two or four year college.
Financial data: Year ended 12/31/2011..
Fields of interest: Minorities; African Americans/Blacks.
Type of support: Undergraduate support.
Application information: Interview required.
Initial approach: Letter
Deadline(s): Mar.
Applicants should submit the following:
  1) SAT
  2) ACT
  3) Essay
  4) Letter(s) of recommendation
Additional information: Scholarship awards are based on scholastic achievement, and school and community services. Applicant must have achieved a GPA of 85 or better.
EIN: 113551213

6107
Amelia G. Jachym Scholarship Fund
P.O. Box 3236, 24 E. 3rd St.
Jamestown, NY   14701

Foundation type: Independent foundation
Purpose: Scholarships to graduating seniors in the top 20 percent of their class at Pine Valley Central School, South Dayton, NY.
Financial data: Year ended 08/31/2013. Assets, $189,712 (M); Expenditures, $21,436; Total giving, $20,000; Grants to individuals, 5 grants totaling $20,000 (high: $5,000, low: $2,500).
Fields of interest: Higher education; Scholarships/financial aid.
Type of support: Scholarships—to individuals; Support to graduates or students of specific schools; Undergraduate support.
Application information: Applications accepted.
Additional information: Applicants must contact the guidance counselor of Pine Valley Central School. Unsolicited requests for funds not considered or acknowledged.
EIN: 112599257

6108
The Rona Jaffe Foundation
21 Wildwood Dr.
Dix Hills, NY   11746-6039

Foundation type: Independent foundation
Purpose: Grants to writers to support them in their works.

Financial data: Year ended 09/30/2012. Assets, $39,544,112 (M); Expenditures, $2,826,103; Total giving, $2,111,780; Grants to individuals, 6 grants totaling $180,000 (high: $30,000, low: $30,000).
Fields of interest: Print publishing; Literature.
Type of support: Awards/prizes.
Application information: Applications not accepted.
Additional information: Unsolicited requests for funds not considered or acknowledged.
EIN: 133383860

6109
JAM Anonymous Foundation, Inc.
(formerly The Dakota Foundation, Inc.)
c/o CAB
950 3rd Ave., 20th Fl.
New York, NY   10022-2705
Application address: c/o Nancy B. Mulheren, Rumson Mgmt., 95 Ave. of Two Rivers, Rumson, NJ 07760-1703, tel.: (732) 450-0488

Foundation type: Independent foundation
Purpose: Scholarships to residents of Rumson or Fair Haven, NJ who have completed high school in these municipalities with average grades (B- to C).
Financial data: Year ended 10/31/2012. Assets, $17,441 (M); Expenditures, $1,337,918; Total giving, $1,335,224; Grants to individuals, 7 grants totaling $125,520 (high: $48,905, low: $2,120).
Type of support: Scholarships—to individuals.
Application information: Applications accepted.
Additional information: Contact foundation for current program guidelines.
Program description:
College Scholarship Program: The foundation sponsors a college scholarship program which includes tuition, fees, room, and board for 4 years, as long as the student maintains a 2.0 average. In order to be nominated, the student must be a resident of Rumson or Fair Haven, NJ, (at least through the high school years), with average grades from B- to C. The student's financial needs are evidenced by a FAFSA report. The program is searching for "late bloomers" who lack encouragement to attend college, who may have fallen through the cracks or who may have had a life-altering experience, and who are willing to attend college outside of New Jersey.
EIN: 222621688

6110
Jandon Foundation
c/o Donald Cecil
3 Stratford Rd.
Harrison, NY   10528-1115
Scholarship address: Jandon Scholars Program, c/o Westchester County Board of Legislators, 148 Maritine Ave., 8th Fl., White Plains, NY 10601, tel.: (914) 995-8620, fax: (914) 995-3884, e-mail: maml@westchestergov.com
URL: http://jandonfoundation.org/

Foundation type: Independent foundation
Purpose: The foundation awards 15 scholarships to low-income academic achievers who are graduating seniors from a Westchester County, NY, public high school, and will attend a 4-year accredited university and obtain a bachelor's degree.
Publications: Application guidelines.
Financial data: Year ended 12/31/2012. Assets, $11,974,872 (M); Expenditures, $562,759; Total giving, $581,129.
Fields of interest: Higher education.
Type of support: Scholarships—to individuals.

Application information: Applications accepted. Application form required. Application form available on the grantmaker's web site.
  Initial approach: Application
  Deadline(s): See foundation web site for current deadline
  Applicants should submit the following:
    1) Curriculum vitae
    2) Letter(s) of recommendation
    3) GPA
    4) Financial information
    5) SAT
    6) Transcripts
    7) ACT
    8) Essay
  Additional information: Applicants must also provide a W-2 for each employed adult with whom they have resided for the past 12 months. In addition, a complete copy of the tax return on which the applicant was claimed as a dependent should also be included.
EIN: 136199442

6111
Jay's World Childhood Cancer Foundation
813 Blue Ridge Rd.
Medford, NY 11763-1205   (516) 671-0852

Foundation type: Public charity
Purpose: College scholarship to children who are either cured of cancer, in remission or able to attend college while undergoing treatment.
Publications: Application guidelines.
Financial data: Year ended 12/31/2011. Assets, $49,015 (M); Expenditures, $23,418.
Fields of interest: Cancer; Children/youth.
Type of support: Scholarships—to individuals.
Application information: Applications accepted. Application form required.
  Send request by: Mail
  Deadline(s): Apr.
  Additional information: Application should include high school transcript, a letter from the oncologist and a copy of family's most recent 1040 tax form. Applicant must be a resident of New York State.
EIN: 113391002

6112
Jazz Foundation of America, Inc.
322 W. 48th St., 6th Fl.
New York, NY 10036-1308   (212) 245-3999
E-mail: info@jazzfoundation.org; E-Mail for Wendy Oxenhorn: Wendy@jazzfoundation.org; URL: http://jazzfoundation.org/

Foundation type: Public charity
Purpose: Emergency assistance to jazz artists with medical, financial, and career development needs.
Publications: Newsletter.
Financial data: Year ended 06/30/2012. Assets, $2,564,563 (M); Expenditures, $2,159,489.
Fields of interest: Music; Human services.
Type of support: Emergency funds; Grants for special needs.
Application information: Applications accepted. Application form required.
  Initial approach: Telephone or e-mail
  Send request by: Fax or mail.
  Copies of proposal: 1
  Deadline(s): None
  Final notification: Two or three days after receipt of application
  Applicants should submit the following:
    1) Work samples
    2) Resume

    3) Financial information
    4) Budget Information
Program descriptions:
  Housing Fund: Emergency funds are available to help pay rents and mortgages for jazz musicians living in New York City and throughout the South, to prevent foreclosures and keep legendary artists from homelessness.
  Musicians' Emergency Fund: The fund supports jazz and blues musicians in crisis and prevents eviction and homelessness by paying rents, mortgages, utilities, and basic needs; pro bono medical and legal services are also available.
EIN: 133631523

6113
Scott Jenkins Fund
c/o Caroline Jenkins, Community Bank Systems, Inc.
245 Main St.
Oneonta, NY 13820-2502   (607) 432-2532

Foundation type: Independent foundation
Purpose: Scholarships by nomination only to students of State University of New York College at Oneonta.
Financial data: Year ended 06/30/2013. Assets, $469,368 (M); Expenditures, $31,863; Total giving, $26,625; Grants to individuals, 79 grants totaling $26,625 (high: $500, low: -$500).
Fields of interest: Higher education; Formal/general education; Minorities; Economically disadvantaged.
Type of support: Program development; Support to graduates or students of specific schools; Awards/grants by nomination only; Foreign applicants; Undergraduate support.
Application information: Scholarships granted by nomination only.
Program descriptions:
  Scott-Jenkins Foreign Student Scholarships: These scholarships are open to any foreign student who is matriculated at the college. Grants pay for room, board, and/or maintenance costs for students living on campus. Applicants must be recommended by the Dir. of International Education by Aug. 1. Recipients are chosen by Aug. 15.
  Scott-Jenkins Foreign Study Scholarships: These scholarships are open to any financially needy full-time matriculated State University of New York College at Oneonta student in a foreign study program sponsored by the State University or Hartwick College. Scholarships cover program costs over and above those which are not covered by financial aid, but not to exceed $500 per student. Candidates are identified by the Dir. of International Education and the Financial Aid Office, and recommended to the selection committee by Apr. 1 for summer, May 1 for fall, and Dec. 1 for spring. Recipients are chosen by May 1 for summer, June 1 for fall, and Jan. 3 for spring.
  Scott-Jenkins Memorial Scholarship: These scholarships are open to minority students of State University of New York College at Oneonta. Recipients must be in good academic standing and in financial need. Candidates are identified by the Office of Special Programs and the Financial Aid Office, and recommended to the selection committee by May 1. Recipients are chosen by June 1. Scholarships are renewable.
  Scott-Jenkins Work-Grants: These grants are open to any full-time matriculated student. Grants of $750 are paid to financially needy students who work a minimum of 11 hours per week on average for 30 weeks. Interested students must be

recommended to the selection committee by Aug. 1. Recipients are chosen by Aug. 15.
EIN: 166183805

6114
Melvin H. & Thelma N. Jenkins Scholarship Fund
1 M & T Plz., 8th Fl.
Buffalo, NY 14203   (716) 842-5506
Application address: Ann L. Rich, c/o M&T Trust Co., 1 South Centre St., Pottsville, PA 17901, tel.: (570) 628-9270

Foundation type: Independent foundation
Purpose: Scholarships to graduates of Minersville Area High School, PA for attendance at accredited colleges or universities.
Financial data: Year ended 12/31/2011. Assets, $912,797 (M); Expenditures, $56,250; Total giving, $44,000; Grants to individuals, 45 grants totaling $44,000 (high: $2,500, low: $250).
Fields of interest: Higher education.
Type of support: Support to graduates or students of specific schools.
Application information: Application form required.
  Deadline(s): Feb. 15
  Additional information: Application available at Minersville Area High School, and application must include transcripts and verification of school activities.
EIN: 256373763

6115
Jewish Association for Services for the Aged
(also known as JASA)
247 W. 37th St.
New York, NY 10018-3406   (212) 273-5272
Contact: David M. Warren, Pres.
E-mail: help@jasa.org; URL: http://www.jasa.org

Foundation type: Public charity
Purpose: Specific assistance to older adults of all backgrounds from Manhattan, Queens, Brooklyn, the Bronx, Nassau and Suffolk counties, NY, with housing and other services.
Publications: Newsletter.
Financial data: Year ended 06/30/2012. Assets, $24,226,748 (M); Expenditures, $37,851,832.
Fields of interest: Human services; Aging.
Type of support: Grants for special needs.
Application information:
  Initial approach: Letter
EIN: 132620896

6116
Jewish Children's Home of Rochester, New York
c/o Jewish Family Service
441 East Ave.
Rochester, NY 14607-1998   (585) 461-0115
Contact: Barbara A. Connor, Secy.

Foundation type: Operating foundation
Purpose: Scholarships to undergraduate college students whose grants are paid to Jewish Family Services of New York which distributes the awards.
Financial data: Year ended 12/31/2012. Assets, $55,661 (M); Expenditures, $5,957; Total giving, $5,700; Grants to individuals, 5 grants totaling $5,700 (high: $1,400, low: $650).
Fields of interest: Education; Jewish agencies & synagogues.
Type of support: Undergraduate support.

Application information: Applications accepted.
Initial approach: Letter
Deadline(s): None
EIN: 166040408

6117
Jewish Education Service of North America, Inc.
(also known as JESNA)
318 W. 39th St., 5th Fl.
New York, NY   10018-1655   (212) 284-6950
FAX: (212) 284-6951; E-mail: info@jesna.org;
URL: http://www.jesna.org

Foundation type: Public charity
Purpose: Financial assistance to outstanding Jewish educators.
Financial data: Year ended 06/30/2012. Assets, $3,602,999 (M); Expenditures, $3,447,502; Total giving, $48,000; Grants to individuals, totaling $48,000.
Fields of interest: Human services; Jewish agencies & synagogues; Economically disadvantaged.
Type of support: Grants for special needs.
Application information:
  Deadline(s): May 11 for Grinspoon-Steinhardt Awards for Excellence in Jewish Education
  Additional information: Contact foundation for further program information.
Program description:
  Grinspoon-Steinhardt Awards for Excellence in Jewish Education: These awards of up to $1,000 are designed to recognize early childhood to grade 12 teachers in communities across North America who have made a commitment to the field of Jewish education. Applicants must demonstrate exceptional achievement and serve as a role model in Jewish education; have a minimum of three years' experience in the field; teach at least six hours per week in a Jewish day school or other formal Jewish educational setting (educators can fulfill the hour requirement in more than one institution); and be classroom-based in the fields of early childhood education, day-school teachers, or congregational school teachers. Awards are to be used for professional development opportunities.
EIN: 131628141

6118
Jewish Family Service of Rochester, Inc.
441 E. Ave.
Rochester, NY   14607-1932   (585) 461-0110
FAX: (585) 461-9658;
E-mail: bwolfgram@jfsrochester.org; URL: http://www.jfsrochester.org

Foundation type: Public charity
Purpose: Financial assistance to low-income individuals and families of Rochester, NY with transportation, food, transportation, housing, utilities and other special needs. Interest-free loans and scholarships to qualified individuals. Internship for graduate and undergraduate students.
Publications: Annual report; Newsletter.
Financial data: Year ended 06/30/2012. Assets, $857,125 (M); Expenditures, $1,330,172; Total giving, $148,114; Grants to individuals, totaling $148,114.
Fields of interest: Vocational education, post-secondary; Higher education; Jewish agencies & synagogues; Economically disadvantaged.
Type of support: Internship funds; Scholarships—to individuals; Grants for special needs; Loans—to individuals.
Application information: Applications accepted.

Send request by: Mail
Deadline(s): June 30 for Scholarship, May 1 for Internship
Additional information: See web site for additional guidelines.
Program descriptions:
  Emergency Family Assistance Services: Assistance includes food cupboard with a non-perishable food items, food vouchers and bus tokens. These services are available to Jewish and non-Jewish individuals.
  Hebrew Free Loans: Interest-free loans to Jewish individuals in need. Loans are from $100 to $1,000. A plan to repay loan within one year is required.
  Scholarships: Undergraduate scholarships are available to Jewish youth in Monroe County be helped in meeting their educational and vocational goals. Applicants must explore and exhaust all community and personal financial resources, must be Jewish, and have legal residence in area served by the agency. Priority is given to descendants of residents of the Jewish Children's Homes as well as to those who face financial hardships paying for college.
  The Morris and Ruth Malett Summer Internship: The paid internship job is awarded to a college student whose area of academic interest is in Judaic studies, human services or a field relevant to the work of Jewish Family Service. Graduate and undergraduate students may apply.
EIN: 160743059

6119
The Jewish Foundation for the Righteous, Inc.
305 7th Ave., 19th Fl.
New York, NY   10001-6008   (212) 727-9955
Contact: Stanlee Joyce Stahl, Exec. V.P.
FAX: (212) 727-9956; E-mail: jfr@jfr.org; E-mail for Stanlee Joyce Stahl: sstahl@jfr.org; URL: http://www.jfr.org

Foundation type: Public charity
Purpose: Financial assistance to non-Jews who rescued Jews during the Holocaust, living in Eastern Europe.
Financial data: Year ended 12/31/2011. Assets, $7,575,265 (M); Expenditures, $3,575,773; Total giving, $1,998,226; Grants to individuals, 26 grants totaling $28,471.
Fields of interest: Human services; Aging.
Type of support: Grants for special needs.
Application information: Applications accepted.
  Additional information: Application should include complete address, rescue story, description of rescuer's present living conditions, copy of rescuer's most recent pension statement, identity card or passport, copy of the Yad Vashem diploma, maiden name of the rescuer's mother, name(s) of the Jews rescued, is rescuer in contact with the Jewish survivor(s) and if the survivor is still alive, when was the last time the rescuer saw the survivor.
Program description:
  Rescuer Support Program: Rescuers receive awards in U.S. dollars three times during the year for funds to cover the costs of food, home heating, fuel, medical care, medication, and emergency needs. The foundation also awards a small grant, upon request, to help defray funeral expenses, and also provides one-time grants for the purchase of food during the Christmas holiday season to rescuers living in Poland and other Eastern European countries. The foundation currently

provides monthly financial assistance to more than 750 aged and needy rescuers living in 22 countries.
EIN: 133807016

6120
The Jewish Guild for the Blind
15 W. 65th St.
New York, NY   10023-6601   (212) 769-6200
Contact: for Scholarship: Alan R. Morse Ph.D., Pres. and C.E.O.
Tel. for G. Rovins: (212) 769-7801,
e-mail: guildscholar@jgb.org
FAX: (212) 769-6266; E-mail: info@jgb.org; Toll-free tel.: (800) 284-4422; URL: http://www.jgb.org

Foundation type: Public charity
Purpose: Scholarships to college bound high school students who are legally blind for higher education at accredited colleges or universities.
Publications: Application guidelines; Annual report; Newsletter.
Financial data: Year ended 12/31/2011. Assets, $133,376,133 (M); Expenditures, $47,718,012; Total giving, $215,000; Grants to individuals, totaling $165,000.
Fields of interest: Higher education; Blind/visually impaired.
Type of support: Scholarships—to individuals; Awards/prizes.
Application information: Applications accepted. Application form required. Application form available on the grantmaker's web site.
  Deadline(s): Sept. 15
  Final notification: Recipients notified by mid Dec.
  Applicants should submit the following:
    1) Transcripts
    2) Letter(s) of recommendation
    3) SAT
    4) ACT
Program descriptions:
  Alfred W. Bressler Prize in Vision Science: This $43,500 award recognizes a professional in the field of vision science whose leadership, research, and service have resulted in important advancements in the treatment of eye disease or rehabilitation of persons with vision lost. Eligible applicants must be established professionals in the field of vision sciences whose contributions have advanced vision care, the treatment of eye disease, or the rehabilitation of persons with visual disabilities or blindness, and whose further work is expected to contribute significantly.
  GuildScholar Award: Twelve to sixteen scholarships of $15,000 each are available to college-bound high school students who are legally blind. Applications will be accepted from students at the end of their junior year, with recipients selected and scholarships awarded the following academic year.
EIN: 131623854

6121
The Jockey Club Foundation
40 E. 52nd St., 15th Fl.
New York, NY   10022-5911
Contact: Nancy Kelly, Secy.
E-mail: contactus@tjcfoundation.org; URL: http://www.tjcfoundation.org

Foundation type: Independent foundation
Purpose: Relief assistance to financially needy individuals who are licensed and legitimately connected with thoroughbred breeding and racing.
Financial data: Year ended 12/31/2012. Assets, $7,788,584 (M); Expenditures, $516,829; Total

giving, $361,738; Grants to individuals, 77 grants totaling $333,083 (high: $15,600, low: $900).
Fields of interest: Athletics/sports, equestrianism.
Type of support: Grants for special needs.
Application information: Applications accepted.
Initial approach: Letter
EIN: 136124094

6122
Louis August Jonas Foundation, Inc.
152 Madison Ave., Ste. 2400
New York, NY   10016-5424   (212) 686-1930
Contact: Judith R. Fox, Exec. Dir.
FAX: (212) 981-3722; E-mail: contact@lajf.org;
Toll-free tel: (800)-262-0136; E-mail for Judith R. Fox: jfox@lajf.org; URL: http://www.lajf.org

Foundation type: Public charity
Purpose: Scholarships, a summer leadership program for teenagers from more than 25 different countries. Scholarships for alumni requiring financial assistance for completion of postsecondary education. Grants for alumni pursuing humanitarian-oriented projects.
Publications: Application guidelines; Annual report; Newsletter.
Financial data: Year ended 09/30/2011. Assets, $11,238,540 (M); Expenditures, $1,551,864; Total giving, $19,400; Grants to individuals, totaling $19,400.
Fields of interest: Education.
Type of support: Camperships; Grants to individuals; Scholarships—to individuals.
Application information: Applications accepted. Application form required.
Send request by: Online
Deadline(s): Feb. 1 for U.S. Camper Scholarship
Applicants should submit the following:
1) Transcripts
2) Essay
Additional information: Application should also include personal and family information, and two references. See web site for additional application guidelines.
Program description:
International Scholarship Program: The foundation operates a full scholarship, international, summer program for teenagers selected for their character and leadership potential. The foundation brings together a diverse group of extraordinary, highly motivated young people from twenty-five countries to participate in seven weeks of programming carefully designed to promote personal growth, leadership skills, a service ethic, and intercultural understanding.
EIN: 141387863

6123
Joukowsky Family Foundation
620 Park Ave., 5th Fl.
New York, NY   10065-6561   (212) 355-3151
Contact: Nina J. Koprulu, Pres. and Dir.
FAX: (212) 355-3147; URL: http://www.joukowsky.org

Foundation type: Independent foundation
Purpose: Scholarships to individuals enrolled in degree-granting programs in institutions of higher education.
Publications: Grants list; IRS Form 990 or 990-PF printed copy available upon request.
Financial data: Year ended 10/31/2012. Assets, $17,671,447 (M); Expenditures, $2,046,154; Total giving, $1,661,123.
Type of support: Scholarships—to individuals; Undergraduate support.

Application information: Applications accepted. Application form not required.
Initial approach: Letter
Copies of proposal: 1
Deadline(s): None
Final notification: Applicants are notified of decision within 2-4 weeks
Applicants should submit the following:
1) Transcripts
2) Proposal
3) Financial information
EIN: 133242753

6124
Journeys End Refugee Services, Inc.
2495 Main St., Ste. 317
Buffalo, NY   14214-2152   (716) 882-4963
Contact: Molly Short, Exec. Dir.
FAX: (716) 882-4977; E-mail: bbc@jersbuffalo.org; E-mail for Molly Short: mshort@jersbuffalo.org; tel. for Molly Short: (716) 882-4963, ext. 215; URL: http://www.jersbuffalo.org/index.php/about

Foundation type: Public charity
Purpose: Financial assistance and support for refugees settling in the Buffalo, NY area with food, clothing, housing, transportation, medical and other special needs.
Financial data: Year ended 12/31/2011. Assets, $620,381 (M); Expenditures, $2,016,264; Total giving, $559,729; Grants to individuals, 336 grants totaling $199,269.
Fields of interest: Immigrants/refugees.
Type of support: Grants for special needs.
Application information: Applications not accepted.
Additional information: Unsolicited requests for funds not considered or acknowledged.
EIN: 161242203

6125
Ernest L. & Florence L. Judkins Scholarship Fund
3 Sarnowski Dr.
Glenville, NY   12302

Foundation type: Independent foundation
Purpose: Scholarships to students of Schenectady, NY for attendance at an accredited college or university.
Financial data: Year ended 09/30/2013. Assets, $152,929 (M); Expenditures, $6,298; Total giving, $5,506.
Fields of interest: Higher education.
Type of support: Scholarships—to individuals.
Application information: Applications not accepted.
Additional information: Applicants should contact the fund for application guidelines.
EIN: 146015967

6126
Just Imagine Making Miracles Yours
9 Buenta Way
P. O. Box 477
Purdys, NY   10578-1409   (914) 619-5576
Contact: Gina Arena, Pres.
FAX: (914) 277-8120;
E-mail: info@jimmyfoundation.org; URL: http://www.jimmyfoundation.org

Foundation type: Public charity
Purpose: Financial assistance to families of children 18 years of age and under who are residents of Westchester and Putnam counties, NY,

suffering with life threatening illness, disease, or injuries.
Financial data: Year ended 12/31/2011. Assets, $18,905 (M); Expenditures, $61,553; Total giving, $29,810; Grants to individuals, totaling $29,810.
Fields of interest: Human services; Children/youth; Economically disadvantaged.
Type of support: Grants for special needs.
Application information: Contact the foundation for additional information on eligibility.
Program description:
Grants: The organization provides grants to families residing in Westchester and Putnam counties, New York, who are in financial need and have minors 18 years old and under with life threatening illness, diseases, or injuries. Assistance includes transportation, non-insured medical costs, food, medical resources and other needs.
EIN: 203664630

6127
Juvenile Diabetes Research Foundation International
26 Broadway
New York, NY   10004-1703   (212) 479-7551
Contact: Jeffrey Brewer, Pres. and C.E.O.
FAX: (212) 785-9595; E-mail: info@jdrf.org; Toll-free tel.: (800) 533-2873; URL: http://www.jdrf.org

Foundation type: Public charity
Purpose: Grants and fellowships for the study of juvenile (Type 1) diabetes.
Publications: Annual report; Informational brochure; Newsletter.
Financial data: Year ended 06/30/2012. Assets, $187,007,468 (M); Expenditures, $205,351,840; Total giving, $110,071,078.
Fields of interest: Diabetes research.
Type of support: Program development; Research; Awards/prizes; Postdoctoral support; Doctoral support.
Application information: Applications accepted. Application form required. Application form available on the grantmaker's web site.
Initial approach: Telephone or e-mail.
Deadline(s): Jan. 15 and Aug. 15.
Additional information: Letter of intent required for Special Grants.
Program descriptions:
Career Development Awards: The award provides up to $150,000 a year for a total of five years. The awards provide salary and research support for exceptional scientists in research related to diabetes who are beginning their careers as junior faculty. These prestigious awards provide support during the crucial first five years as an independent investigator.
Early Career Patient-Oriented Diabetes Research Award: Awards up to $150,000 per year for five years to support promising physicians or clinical doctoral recipients who pursue a career in patient-oriented, diabetes-related clinical investigation. These awards are made in the late stages of training and include the support for recipients to transition to independent faculty or research appointments.
Innovative Grants: Grants of up to $110,000, including up to 10% for indirect costs, support highly-innovative basic and clinical research still at the developmental stage.
Postdoctoral Fellowships: Fellowships provide $43,240 to $57,568 per year for three years. The fellowships provide crucial training support to M.D. or PhD recipients who will focus on research related to diabetes. Emphasis is placed on postdoctoral fellows whose focus is in clinical research. These

awards are highly competitive and are focused toward recruiting outstanding junior scientists.
EIN: 231907729

6128
The Edward Kane Guardian Life Welfare Trust
(formerly The Guardian Life Welfare Trust)
7 Hanover Sq., Ste. H21-L
New York, NY 10004-2616
URL: http://www.guardianlife.com/
AboutGuardian/CompanyOverview/
CorporateCitizenship/
EdwardKaneGuardianWelfareTrust/index.htm

Foundation type: Company-sponsored foundation
Purpose: Grants and loans to needy employees of the Guardian Life Insurance Company, for catastrophic events when no other resources are available.
Financial data: Year ended 12/31/2012. Assets, $436,543 (M); Expenditures, $116,166; Total giving, $115,172; Grants to individuals, 55 grants totaling $115,172 (high: $7,500, low: $400).
Type of support: Emergency funds.
Application information: Applications not accepted.
  Additional information: Contributes only through employee grants and loans.
Company name: The Guardian Life Insurance Company of America
EIN: 136197206

6129
Lazare and Charlotte Kaplan Foundation
c/o Rouis & Co., LLP
P.O. Box 209
Wurtsboro, NY 12790-0209 (845) 439-5252
Contact: Leon Siegel, Pres. and Treas.
Application address: P.O. Box 456, Livingston Manor, N.Y. 12758-0456 tel: (845) 439-5252

Foundation type: Independent foundation
Purpose: Scholarships to high school graduates and postsecondary students of Livingston Manor School District. Priority is given to Livingston Manor School district students, followed by Town of Rockland residents.
Financial data: Year ended 12/31/2011. Assets, $1,288,398 (M); Expenditures, $86,771; Total giving, $68,532.
Fields of interest: Higher education.
Type of support: Undergraduate support.
Application information: Applications accepted.
  Initial approach: Letter
EIN: 136193153

6130
Kassenbrock Brothers Memorial Scholarship Fund, Inc.
c/o Colabella Co.
1444 86th St.
Brooklyn, NY 11228-3429 (718) 234-0190
Contact: Mary Ann Walsh, Admin.

Foundation type: Public charity
Purpose: Scholarships to college bound high school seniors in the Bay Ridge, Brooklyn, NY area who have demonstrated outstanding community service.
Financial data: Year ended 01/31/2013. Assets, $68,012 (M); Expenditures, $41,978; Total giving, $40,050.
Fields of interest: Higher education.

Type of support: Scholarships—to individuals.
Application information: Selection criteria is based on outstanding character and good scholarship.
EIN: 237183877

6131
Irfan Kathwari Foundation Inc.
1875 Palmer Ave.
Larchmont, NY 10538-3053 (203) 743-8438
E-mail: kathwarifoundation@gmail.com

Foundation type: Independent foundation
Purpose: Scholarships to children of Ethan Allen employees.
Financial data: Year ended 06/30/2011. Assets, $6,027,688 (M); Expenditures, $302,716; Total giving, $240,394; Grants to individuals, 45 grants totaling $36,708.
Type of support: Employee-related scholarships; Undergraduate support.
Application information: Application form required.
  Initial approach: Letter
  Deadline(s): None
  Additional information: Contact foundation for current application guidelines.
Company name: Ethan Allen
EIN: 133681135

6132
Hanna Kaupp Foundation
c/o Pompeyo R. Realuyo, Esq.
358 5Th.Ave., Ste. 301
New York, NY 10001 (056) 421-1507
Contact: Nancy Valdez
Application address:c/o Sorsogon PNB Branch, Rizal St., Sorsogon City

Foundation type: Operating foundation
Purpose: Scholarships to students attending Bicol University, School of Nursing, and are from the Philippines.
Financial data: Year ended 06/30/2013. Assets, $1,189,736 (M); Expenditures, $122,294; Total giving, $92,756.
Type of support: Support to graduates or students of specific schools.
Application information:
  Initial approach: Letter
  Deadline(s): Mar. 31
EIN: 470945214

6133
Charles and Pauline Kautz Foundation
c/o Rouis and Co., LLP
P.O. Box 209
Wurtsboro, NY 12790-0209
Application address: c/o Robert Curtis, Tr., P.O. Box 18, Obernberg, NY 12767, tel.: (845) 482-6064

Foundation type: Independent foundation
Purpose: Scholarships to graduates of the former Delaware Valley Central School District to continue their education at a higher institution.
Financial data: Year ended 12/31/2011. Assets, $2,854,341 (M); Expenditures, $297,799; Total giving, $236,925; Grants to individuals, totaling $236,925.
Type of support: Support to graduates or students of specific schools; Undergraduate support.
Application information:
  Deadline(s): May 1
  Additional information: Applications available through the Guidance Dept. of Delaware Valley High School.
EIN: 141579429

6134
Ezra Jack Keats Foundation, Inc.
450 14th St.
Brooklyn, NY 11215
URL: http://www.ezra-jack-keats.org

Foundation type: Independent foundation
Purpose: Awards to outstanding new writers and new illustrators of picture books for children age 9 and under.
Financial data: Year ended 12/31/2012. Assets, $4,531,613 (M); Expenditures, $506,087; Total giving, $52,195.
Fields of interest: Literature; Children.
Type of support: Awards/prizes.
Application information:
  Deadline(s): Dec. 30 for New Writer Award, Dec. 31 for New Illustrator Award
  Additional information: Writers and illustrators must have had no more than three books published. A cash award of $1,000 and a medallion will be presented to the winning author. See web site for additional guidelines.
EIN: 237072750

6135
Keren Keshet - The Rainbow Foundation
1015 Park Ave.
New York, NY 10028-0904
Contact: Linda Sakacs, Secy.

Foundation type: Independent foundation
Purpose: Occasional grants for research purposes.
Financial data: Year ended 12/31/2012. Assets, $233,526,369 (M); Expenditures, $28,566,377; Total giving, $22,313,494; Grants to individuals, 3 grants totaling $50,351 (high: $30,000, low: $9,017).
Fields of interest: Jewish agencies & synagogues; Economically disadvantaged.
International interests: Israel.
Type of support: Research; Grants for special needs.
Application information: Applications not accepted.
  Additional information: Unsolicited requests for fund not considered or acknowledged.
EIN: 134069592

6136
Keren Tifereth Yisroel Foundation
c/o Yehuda Braun
41 White St.
New York, NY 10013-3549 (212) 219-3944

Foundation type: Independent foundation
Purpose: Scholarships to graduates of Sinai Academy, NY, to study the Torah in Israel.
Financial data: Year ended 06/30/2012. Assets, $91,347 (M); Expenditures, $59,979; Total giving, $54,216.
Fields of interest: Jewish agencies & synagogues.
International interests: Israel.
Type of support: Support to graduates or students of specific schools.
Application information: Applications accepted.
  Initial approach: Proposal
EIN: 311662769

6137
Kidney & Urology Foundation of America, Inc.

2 W. 47th St., Ste. 401
New York, NY 10036-3339 (212) 629-9770
Contact: Sam Giarrusso, Pres.
FAX: (212) 629-5652;
E-mail: info@kidneyurology.org; Toll-free tel.: (800) 633-6628; additional address (New Jersey office): 63 W. Main St., Ste. G, Freehold, NJ 07728-2141, tel.: (732) 866-4444; URL: http://www.kidneyurology.org

Foundation type: Public charity
Purpose: Grants to institutions and individuals for research and study regarding kidney disease. Scholarships and achievement awards for kidney and urology patients enabling them to live productively with renal and urologic disease.
Financial data: Year ended 06/30/2012. Assets, $98,083 (M); Expenditures, $418,959.
Fields of interest: Kidney diseases.
Type of support: Grants to individuals; Scholarships—to individuals.
Application information: See web site for additional guidelines.
Program descriptions:
Bright Star Recognition Award: This award recognizes kidney and urologic patients and their family members for their courage, strength, determination, generosity of spirit, and kindness. Recipients can be of any age; parents, grandparents, other family members, community members, and healthcare staff can be nominated as well if they make a significant contribution to the life of kidney/urology patients. The award consists of a certificate, a $250 grant to the recipient and a grant of $500 to the medical facility's patient service fund.
Covelli Achievement Award: This award encourages school-age patients with kidney or urologic diseases to master life skills and focus on their education. This award is for children in elementary, middle, or high school. The awards, of up to $500, will be available for patients with kidney or urologic diseases (ages 6-18) for the following: most improved grades; mastering a subject; outstanding academic performance - The nominee has received good to excellent grades overall; achievement in life skills (developing confidence, communications, interpersonal relations, self-discipline and other skills which mark maturity and will assist him or her in living a productive life; and effort (extending himself or herself to mature and develop academically in areas such as school attendance, participation in educational activities and events, independent study, reading, and practice of fundamentally important and useful skills). Financial need will not be used as a criteria in selecting recipients. All nominees will receive a certificate recognizing their achievements.
Fellowhips and Awards in Nephrology and Urology: The foundation provides fellowships and awards in nephrology and urology to support the training and development of new researchers who will advance the knowledge and understanding of kidney, urologic and hypertensive diseases, and ultimately the search for treatment and cures for these diseases.
New Day Education and Rehabilitation Award: This award, of up to $1,500, is given to 6 adults (25 years and older) with kidney or urologic disease who are attending or returning to school to complete a degree or obtain a professional certification; learn a new job skill or change careers, or seek physical rehabilitation to allow the nominee to return to a productive lifestyle which could include improved ability to carry out activities of daily living, volunteerism, or pursuing a vocation or career. Candidates should be motivated to take charge of their own lives and to improve their ability to be productive members of their communities. Grants will be based on financial need, evidence of prior achievements, and the ability to maintain a minimum C average.
EIN: 131777413

6138
Charles & Lucille King Family Foundation, Inc.

1212 Avenue of the Americas, 7th Fl.
New York, NY 10036-1600 (212) 682-2913
Contact: Michael Donovan, Educational Dir.; Karen E. Kennedy, Asst. Educational Dir.
E-mail: kingscholarships@aol.com; URL: http://www.kingfoundation.org

Foundation type: Independent foundation
Purpose: Tuition scholarships to television and film undergraduate students residing in the United States who are juniors or seniors and demonstrate academic excellence, financial need, and professional potential.
Publications: Application guidelines; Informational brochure (including application guidelines).
Financial data: Year ended 12/31/2012. Assets, $1,207,068 (M); Expenditures, $418,636; Total giving, $251,910.
Fields of interest: Film/video.
Type of support: Support to graduates or students of specific schools; Undergraduate support.
Application information: Applications accepted. Application form required. Application form available on the grantmaker's web site.
Initial approach: Letter
Send request by: Mail
Deadline(s): Mar. 15
Applicants should submit the following:
  1) Essay
  2) Financial information
  3) GPA
  4) Letter(s) of recommendation
  5) Transcripts
Additional information: Applications can be downloaded from web site between Sept. 1 and Apr. 1.
Program descriptions:
The King Family Foundation Undergraduate Scholarship Program: The King Family Foundation Undergraduate Scholarship Program awards up to $7,000 in scholarships to undergraduate students majoring in television, film, and related media fields. Applicants must demonstrate academic ability, financial need and professional potential.
The King Family Foundation/NYU Heinemann Award: The King Family Foundation/NYU Heinemann Award is an annual $10,000 award given to an outstanding film/video senior undergraduate at New York University. (Contact NYU directly for information about this award)
The King Family Foundation/NYU Post Production Award: The King Family Foundation/NYU Post Production Award, in honor of the late Roger King, is an annual $10,000 award toward the completion of an outstanding film/video by a graduate student in the MFA Program at New York University. (Contact NYU directly for information about this award)
The King Family Foundation/UCLA Post Production Award: The King Family Foundation/UCLA Post Production Award is an annual $10,000 award toward the completion of an outstanding film/video project by a graduate student in the MFA program at the University of California, Los Angeles. (Contact UCLA directly for information about this award)
The King Family Foundation/USC Post Production Award: The King Family Foundation/USC Post Production Award is an annual $10,000 award toward the completion of an outstanding film/video project by a graduate student in the MFA program at the University of Southern California. (Contact USC directly for information about this award)
EIN: 133489257

6139
George Leech King-St. Ferdinand College Scholarship Foundation

(formerly Ray Tyo-St. Ferdinand College Scholarship Foundation)
1 M & T Plz., 8th Fl.
Buffalo, NY 14203 (716) 842-5506

Foundation type: Independent foundation
Purpose: Scholarships to financially needy graduates of Harrisburg Diocesan high schools in PA who will be attending Catholic colleges and universities for undergraduate study.
Financial data: Year ended 12/31/2012. Assets, $1,799,945 (M); Expenditures, $92,735; Total giving, $84,000.
Fields of interest: Catholic agencies & churches.
Type of support: Undergraduate support.
Application information: Application form required.
Applicants should submit the following:
  1) Transcripts
  2) Financial information
  3) Essay
EIN: 236508132

6140
The Kleban Foundation, Inc.

c/o Marks Paneth & Shron, LLP
685 3rd Ave.
New York, NY 10017
Application address: c/o Kleban Award Coordinator, New Dramatists, 424 W. 44th St., New York, NY 10036, tel.: (212) 757-6960, ext.75
URL: http://www.newdramatists.org/kleban_award.htm

Foundation type: Independent foundation
Purpose: Support to promising theatrical lyricists and librettists.
Publications: Application guidelines.
Financial data: Year ended 06/30/2013. Assets, $3,027,920 (M); Expenditures, $347,343; Total giving, $250,000; Grants to individuals, 5 grants totaling $250,000 (high: $50,000, low: $50,000).
Fields of interest: Music.
Type of support: Grants to individuals.
Application information: Applications accepted.
Initial approach: Letter
Deadline(s): Application must be postmarked by Sept. 15
Final notification: Spring
Additional information: Selection is made by a panel of theatrical lyricists and librettists. Any individual who has previously won the Kleban Award or any individual whose work has been performed on the Broadway stage for a cumulative period of two years prior to the date of the application is ineligible. See web site for additional information.
Program description:
Kleban Prize In Musical Theatre: This award is given annually to both a librettist and a lyricist. The amount is $100,000 to each recipient payable in two annual installments of $50,000. Applicants must meet either of the following criteria: 1) A work by the applicant has previously been produced on a stage or in a workshop performance or 2) the

applicant is or has been a member or an associate of a professional musical workshop or theater group, i.e., ASCAP, BMI Theater Workshop or the Dramatists Guild Musical Theater Development Program.
EIN: 133490882

6141
A. M. Kleeman, Jr. Scholarship Fund
212 Dolson Ave.
Middletown, NY 10940-6541 (845) 987-3050
Contact: Raymond Bryant Ph.D.
Application address: P.O. Box 595 Warwick, NY 10990, tel.: (845) 987-3050

Foundation type: Independent foundation
Purpose: Scholarships to students who graduated from Central School District No. 1 in Warwick and Chester, Orange County, NY.
Financial data: Year ended 05/31/2013. Assets, $240,236 (M); Expenditures, $5,797; Total giving, $2,400; Grants to individuals, 3 grants totaling $2,400 (high: $800, low: $800).
Type of support: Support to graduates or students of specific schools; Undergraduate support.
Application information: Applications accepted. Application form required.
Deadline(s): None
EIN: 133586537

6142
The Klein-Kaufman Family Foundation
134 W. Hills Rd.
Huntington Station, NY 11746-3140

Foundation type: Company-sponsored foundation
Purpose: Welfare assistance to employees of W&K Management Corp. who are residents of Suffolk County, NY.
Financial data: Year ended 02/28/2013. Assets, $11,408 (M); Expenditures, $0; Total giving, $0.
Type of support: Employee-related welfare.
Application information: Applications not accepted.
Additional information: Unsolicited requests for funds not considered or acknowledged.
Company name: W & K Management Corporation
EIN: 113185247

6143
The Esther A. & Joseph Klingenstein Fund, Inc.
125 Park Ave., Ste. 1700
New York, NY 10017-5529 (212) 492-6195
Contact: Andrew D. Klingenstein, Pres.; Kathleen Pomerantz, V.P.
FAX: (212) 492-7007;
E-mail: kathleen.pomerantz@klingenstein.com;
URL: http://www.klingfund.org

Foundation type: Independent foundation
Purpose: Fellowships to young investigators in the early stages of their careers engaged in basic or clinical research that may lead to a better understanding of neurological and psychiatric disorders.
Publications: Informational brochure.
Financial data: Year ended 09/30/2013. Assets, $91,013,473 (M); Expenditures, $1,726,374; Total giving, $721,681.
Fields of interest: Mental health, disorders; Neuroscience; Neuroscience research.
Type of support: Fellowships; Research.
Application information: Application form required.
Initial approach: Letter or telephone

Send request by: Online
Deadline(s): Jan. 10
Additional information: Application should include three letters of recommendation. Fellows must obtain approval before accepting awards from other foundations.
EIN: 136028788

6144
The Klingenstein Third Generation Foundation
c/o Tanton Collp
125 Park Ave., Ste. 1700
New York, NY 10017-5529
Contact: Sally Klingenstein Martell, Exec. Dir.
E-mail: info@ktgf.org; URL: http://www.ktgf.org

Foundation type: Independent foundation
Purpose: Fellowships to study child and adolescent depression, as well as Attention Deficit Hyperactivity Disorder (ADHD). Investigators must hold a Ph.D. and/or an M.D. degree, and have completed all research training, including post-doctoral training.
Financial data: Year ended 09/30/2012. Assets, $6,205,413 (M); Expenditures, $416,218; Total giving, $255,922.
Fields of interest: Research; Mental health, treatment; Mental health, disorders; Depression; Medical research.
Type of support: Fellowships.
Application information: Applications not accepted.
Additional information: Send an e-mail requesting addition to the mailing list for fellowship announcements. Unsolicited applications are not accepted. Fellowship nominations are solicited by invitation only. Applications for funding outside of fellowship programs not accepted.
Program description:
Research Fellowship Program: The foundation awards two or three fellowships for each program per year. Fellows receive an award of $30,000 per year for two years. The fellowship supports recent graduates who have demonstrated outstanding promise and are eager to continue in an academic research career. In the fall of each year, the foundation sends an invitation to the department heads of a group of institutions, asking for the nomination of candidates.
EIN: 133732439

6145
Kosciuszko Foundation, Inc.
15 E. 65th St.
New York, NY 10065-6501 (212) 734-2130
Contact: Prof. John Micgiel, Pres. and Exec. Dir.
Address in Poland: ul. Nowy Swiat 4, Rm. 118, 03-921 Warszawa, tel.: (48) (22) 21-7067
FAX: (212) 628-4552; E-mail: thekf@aol.com;
E-Mail for John Micgiel: jsm@thekf.org; URL: http://www.thekf.org

Foundation type: Public charity
Purpose: Scholarships for Americans of Polish descent and study/research programs for Americans in Poland, and grants also to Polish individuals who reside permanently in Poland for study in the U.S.
Publications: Annual report; Informational brochure (including application guidelines); Newsletter.
Financial data: Year ended 06/30/2012. Assets, $33,801,414 (M); Expenditures, $2,099,357; Total giving, $603,828; Grants to individuals, totaling $559,704.

Fields of interest: Music; International exchange, students.
International interests: Canada; Poland.
Type of support: Fellowships; Research; Foreign applicants; Graduate support; Undergraduate support; Postgraduate support; Residencies; Travel grants.
Application information: Application form required.
Initial approach: Letter
Deadline(s): Oct. 15 for applications or re-applications
Additional information: Interviews required for Polish individuals who are permanent residents of Poland for study in the US.
Program descriptions:
Dr. Marie E. Zakrzewski Medical Scholarship: Provides one $3,500 scholarship to a young woman of Polish ancestry for her first, second, or third year of medical studies at an accredited school of medicine in the United States.
Fellowships and Grants for Polish Citizens: The foundation annually awards a number of fellowships/grants to Poles for advanced study/research or teaching at universities and other institutions of higher learning in the United States. The foundation provides a cost-of-living stipend, which includes transatlantic travel, housing allowance, health and accident insurance coverage, and, when warranted, domestic travel. There is no allowance for dependents (spouse or child) support. Awardees are solely responsible for all expenses of accompanying dependents.
Graduate Study and Research in Poland Scholarship: Award in conjunction with the Polish Ministry of Education and Sports, this scholarship supports graduate-level research at universities in Poland by American graduate students and university faculty members Research projects may be conducted at any Polish university or institution under the jurisdiction of the Polish Ministry of Education and Sports. The grant provides a stipend for dormitory housing and living expenses; transportation to and from Poland is not included, nor is tuition to attend classes at Polish universities.
Massachusetts Federation of Polish Women's Clubs Scholarships: These $1,250 scholarships provide funding to qualified students for the student's second, third, or fourth year of undergraduate studies in the United States.
Polish American Club of North Jersey Scholarships: These $500 to $2,000 scholarships are awarded to qualified students for full-time undergraduate and graduate studies at accredited colleges and universities in the United States. Scholarships are renewable.
Polish National Alliance of Brooklyn, USA, Inc. Scholarships: These $2,000 scholarships provide funding to qualified undergraduate students for full-time studies at accredited colleges and universities in the United States.
Tomaszkiewicz-Florio Scholarships: Scholarships are available for studies at the Jagiellonian University. The scholarship covers the cost of program fees of a 3-week session (program fees include the cost of tuition, a shared room, three meals per day and sightseeing). It does not include fees for single rooms, registration, scholarship application fee, optional add-ons and extra nights. In order to apply for a scholarship, the applicant must meet all program eligibility requirements, be a full-time high school senior or undergraduate student. You must be a US citizen of Polish descent or Polish citizen with legal US permanent residency status and have a cumulative GPA of 3.0 or higher to compete for a scholarship.
Tuition Scholarships: Scholarships, ranging from $1,000 to $7,000, support American students of

Polish descent for full-time graduate studies in the United States, the Center for European Studies at Jagiellonian University - Cracow, and English Schools of Medicine in Poland.

Year Abroad Scholarship Program: This scholarship supports semester- and year-long Polish language studies with funding from the Polish Ministry of Education and Sports. Studies take place at the Center of Polish Language and Culture in the World, Jagiellonian University - Cracow. The scholarship includes acceptance to the program, a tuition waiver, and a stipend for housing and living expenses; airfare to and from Poland is not included.
EIN: 131628179

6146
Koussevitzky Music Foundation, Inc.
254 W. 31st St., 15th Fl.
New York, NY   10001-2813   (212) 461-6956
Contact: James M. Kendrick, Secy.
Application address: 611 Pennsylvania Ave. S.E., No. 118, Washington, DC 20003-4303, tel.: (202) 707-5503, fax: (202) 707-0621
FAX: (212) 810-4567;
E-mail: info@koussevitzky.org; URL: http://www.koussevitzky.org/

Foundation type: Independent foundation
Purpose: Commissions based on merit to composers of serious music who are over 25 years of age, have completed formal conservatory studies or have a B.A. from a recognized conservatory, college, or university, or demonstrated equivalent, and whose music has been published, recorded, and/or performed in public, and are sponsored by a performing organization. Composers who received commission during the past ten years are ineligible.
Publications: Application guidelines; Informational brochure (including application guidelines).
Financial data: Year ended 12/31/2012. Assets, $1,310,001 (M); Expenditures, $134,248; Total giving, $76,250; Grants to individuals, 10 grants totaling $76,250 (high: $12,500, low: $6,250).
Fields of interest: Music; Music composition.
Type of support: Grants to individuals.
Application information: Application form required. Application form available on the grantmaker's web site.
   Send request by: Mail
   Deadline(s): Mar. 1
   Applicants should submit the following:
      1) Work samples
      2) SASE
EIN: 046128361

6147
The Scott S. Krueger Memorial Foundation, Inc.
11 Ranch Trail Ct.
Orchard Park, NY   14127-3061   (716) 209-6222
Application address: c/o Orchard Park High School, Attn.: Guidance Dept., 4040 Baker Rd., Orchard Park, NY 14127-2052

Foundation type: Independent foundation
Purpose: Scholarships to seniors at Orchard Park High School, NY, for higher education.
Financial data: Year ended 12/31/2011. Assets, $752,340 (M); Expenditures, $88,721; Total giving, $80,000; Grants to individuals, 8 grants totaling $80,000 (high: $10,000, low: $10,000).
Type of support: Support to graduates or students of specific schools; Undergraduate support.
Application information:
   Deadline(s): Feb.

Additional information: Contact foundation for current application guidelines.
EIN: 161599236

6148
Barbara L. Kuhlman Foundation, Inc.
335 Rt. 41
Willet, NY   13863   (607) 656-9037
Application address: c/o Barbara L. Kulman, P.O. Box 30, Greene, NY 13778, tel.: (607) 656-9037

Foundation type: Independent foundation
Purpose: Scholarships to students whose area of study is the fiber arts.
Financial data: Year ended 12/31/2011. Assets, $1,936,670 (M); Expenditures, $100,236; Total giving, $53,420.
Fields of interest: Arts education; Visual arts.
Type of support: Undergraduate support.
Application information:
   Initial approach: Letter or telephone
   Deadline(s): None
EIN: 202199944

6149
L.H. Foundation, Inc.
Rte. 202
P.O. Box 600
Lincolndale, NY   10540-0600   (914) 248-7474

Foundation type: Public charity
Purpose: Scholarships to residents of Lincoln Hall, NY.
Financial data: Year ended 06/30/2011. Assets, $26,609,625 (M); Expenditures, $908,077; Total giving, $771,007; Grants to individuals, totaling $59,542.
Fields of interest: Housing/shelter, rehabilitation; Children, services; Residential/custodial care; Residential/custodial care, group home.
Type of support: Scholarships—to individuals.
Application information: Applications accepted. Application form required.
   Applicants should submit the following:
      1) Letter(s) of recommendation
      2) Essay
EIN: 133330145

6150
La Unidad Latina Foundation
132 E. 43rd St., Ste. 358
New York, NY   10017-4019   (718) 768-8891
E-mail: info@lulfoundation.org; URL: http://www.lulfoundation.org/

Foundation type: Public charity
Purpose: Scholarships for worthy and needy Hispanic students pursuing a bachelor's or master's degree at an accredited four year college or university.
Financial data: Year ended 06/30/2011. Assets, $31,431 (M); Expenditures, $7,982; Total giving, $7,000; Grants to individuals, totaling $7,000.
Fields of interest: Education; Hispanics/Latinos.
Type of support: Scholarships—to individuals; Graduate support; Undergraduate support.
Application information: Applications accepted. Application form required. Application form available on the grantmaker's web site.
   Send request by: Mail
   Deadline(s): Feb. 15 and Oct. 15
   Applicants should submit the following:
      1) Transcripts
      2) Letter(s) of recommendation
      3) Essay

Program description:
   Scholarships: Educational scholarships are awarded to Hispanic students on a competitive basis ranging from $250 to $1,000. Applicants must reside in the U.S., must be currently enrolled in a Bachelor's degree, Master of Arts, Master of Science, Master of Public Administration/Policy, Master of Social Work, Master of Education, or Master of Divinity program. Applicant must complete at least one full-time year of study for undergraduate applicants, and at least one full-time semester of study for graduate applicants. Undergraduate applicants should have a cumulative GPA above 2.8 out of a 4.0 GPA scale.
EIN: 522268102

6151
Laboratory Institute of Merchandising Fashion Education Foundation, Inc.
(also known as LIM Fashion Education Foundation, Inc.)
12 E. 53rd St.
New York, NY   10022-5208   (212) 752-1530
FAX: (212) 750-3452; E-mail: sfs@LIMCollege.edu; URL: http://www.limcollege.edu/financial-aid/1597.aspx

Foundation type: Public charity
Purpose: Scholarships for new, and continuing students entering their third year attending the Laboratory Institute of Merchandising College, NY.
Financial data: Year ended 06/30/2013. Assets, $1,098,598 (M); Expenditures, $137,257; Total giving, $72,300; Grants to individuals, totaling $72,300.
Fields of interest: Higher education; Business school/education.
Type of support: Support to graduates or students of specific schools.
Application information: Applications accepted. Application form required.
   Deadline(s): Mar. 1
   Additional information: Selection is based on high academic achievement and character.
EIN: 132934035

6152
Emory and Ilona E. Ladany Foundation Inc.
P.O. Box 6
Merrick, NY   11566-0006
Contact: Andrew S. Erderly, Pres. and Treas.
Application address: 12 Ranch Pl., Merrick, Ny 11566

Foundation type: Independent foundation
Purpose: Grants to young American artists.
Financial data: Year ended 10/31/2013. Assets, $0 (M); Expenditures, $90,971; Total giving, $74,061; Grants to individuals, 3 grants totaling $2,200 (high: $2,000, low: $100).
Fields of interest: Arts, artist's services.
Type of support: Grants to individuals.
Application information:
   Deadline(s): None
   Additional information: Application by submission of a sample portfolio.
EIN: 133448832

6153
Albert and Mary Lasker Foundation, Inc.
110 E. 42nd St., Ste. 1300
New York, NY 10017-8532   (212) 286-0222
Contact: Maria Freire Ph.D., Pres.
Scholars inquiry: Charles R. Dearolf, Ph.D., Asst.
Dir. for Intramural Research, National Institutes of
Health, Bldg. 1, Rm. 152, Bethesda, MD 20892,
e-mail: laskerScholar@nih.gov
FAX: (212) 286-0924;
E-mail: info@laskerfoundation.org; URL: http://
www.laskerfoundation.org

Foundation type: Operating foundation
Purpose: Awards by nomination only to scientists,
physicians, and public servants who have made
major advances in the understanding, diagnosis,
treatment, cure, and prevention of human disease.
Publications: Application guidelines.
Financial data: Year ended 12/31/2012. Assets,
$66,678,481 (M); Expenditures, $3,383,575;
Total giving, $750,215.
Fields of interest: Public health; Health care;
Biomedicine research; Medical research; Science.
Type of support: Research; Awards/grants by
nomination only; Awards/prizes.
Application information: Application form required.
  Deadline(s): June 24 for Clinical Research
    Scholars
Program description:
  The Lasker Clinical Research Scholars Program:
The program supports the research activities during
the early stage careers of independent clinical
researchers, and also offers the opportunity for a
unique bridge between the NIH intramural and
extramural research communities and contains two
phases. The first phase, the scholars will receive
appointments for up to five to seven years as
tenure-track investigators within the NIH Intramural
Research Program with independent research
budgets. The second phase, successful scholars
will be eligible to apply for up to five years of NIH
support for their research at an extramural research
facility, or the scholar can be considered to remain
as in investigator within the intramural program.
EIN: 131680062

6154
LD Resources Foundation, Inc.
31 East 32nd St., Ste. 607
New York, NY 10016-5509   (646) 701-0000
Contact: Zahavit Paz, Exec. Dir.
FAX: (212) 444-1061; E-mail: zpaz@ldrfa.org; E-mail
for Abby Biggs Smith: abby@ldrfa.org; URL: http://
www.ldrfa.org

Foundation type: Public charity
Purpose: Financial assistance to students with
learning disabilities to accommodate their learning
needs.
Publications: Application guidelines.
Financial data: Year ended 07/31/2011. Assets,
$100,129 (M); Expenditures, $36,118. Awards/
prizes amount not specified.
Fields of interest: College; Graduate/professional
education; Disabilities, people with.
Type of support: Computer technology.
Application information: Applications accepted.
Application form required. Application form
available on the grantmaker's web site.
  Deadline(s): Feb. 12
  Applicants should submit the following:
    1) Essay
    2) FAFSA
  Additional information: Applicants must provide
    proof of diagnosis of learning disability and
    proof of college registration.

Program descriptions:
  LD Resources Foundation Recognition Award:
This award honors those who have assisted other
students in dealing with the challenges of learning
disabilities. This award is not based on financial
need.
  LiveScribe Award: This tool allows the user to
capture words, diagrams, scribbles, symbols, and
audio. It syncs audio to what is written so that the
user can write less and listen more. Tapping
something on your notes, the tool will replay the
audio recording from that time.
  Voice Recognition Award: This tool makes it
easier for anyone to use their computer as it types
what the user is speaking. This tool eliminates the
challenge of writing for students with learning
disabilities.
EIN: 134186250

6155
Le Rosey Foundation
c/o N.B. Zoullas Securities
555 Madison Ave., 17th Fl.
New York, NY 10022-4731

Foundation type: Independent foundation
Purpose: Scholarships to individuals by nomination
only.
Financial data: Year ended 12/31/2011. Assets,
$532,842 (M); Expenditures, $1,174; Total giving,
$0.
Fields of interest: Higher education.
Type of support: Scholarships—to individuals;
Awards/grants by nomination only.
Application information: Applications not
accepted.
  Additional information: Unsolicited requests for
    funds not considered or acknowledged.
EIN: 311502618

6156
League of American Orchestras
(formerly American Symphony Orchestra League)
33 W. 60th St., 5th Fl.
New York, NY 10023-7905   (212) 262-5161
Contact: Jesse Rosen, Pres. and C.E.O.; For
Fellowship: Michael Lawrence, Prog. Dir.
Tel. for fellowship (646) 822-4037, e-mail:
mlawrence@symphony.org
FAX: (212) 262-5198;
E-mail: league@symphony.org; URL: http://
www.americanorchestras.org/

Foundation type: Public charity
Purpose: Scholarships to gifted, young
African-American and Latino musicians who intend
to pursue professional careers in American
symphonies or orchestras.
Publications: Application guidelines.
Financial data: Year ended 09/30/2012. Assets,
$8,908,362 (M); Expenditures, $6,269,773; Total
giving, $95,871; Grants to individuals, totaling
$43,371.
Fields of interest: Music; Orchestras; African
Americans/Blacks.
Type of support: Fellowships; Scholarships—to
individuals.
Application information: Application form required.
Application form available on the grantmaker's web
site.
  Initial approach: E-mail
  Deadline(s): Sept. 28 for American Conducting
    Fellows Program
  Applicants should submit the following:
    1) Resume
    2) Essay

  Additional information: Application must also
    include a video (VHS or DVD) containing three
    contrasting pieces, and a $50 nonrefundable
    application fee.
Program description:
  *Bank of America Awards for Excellence in
Orchestra Education:* The awards are designed to
honor excellence, identify best practices, and share
information about outstanding programs with the
league's member orchestras. The program is
available only to American Symphony Orchestra
League member orchestras. The program's current
focus is partnerships with elementary schools
serving underserved children. The programs must
include the following elements: no fewer than six
in-school events per class per year; at least one
event per year involving the full orchestra; no fewer
than five classes per year involved; professional
development for teachers; professional
development for musicians; clearly defined goals
(can be artistic, academic, or both); evidence of
achievement of goals; involvement of parents,
though not a requirement, would be an additional
positive element. The program must have been in
place for a minimum of three seasons in order to
be eligible for consideration.
EIN: 237300636

6157
Leary Firefighters Foundation
594 Broadway, Ste. 409
New York, NY 10012-3234   (212) 343-0240
Contact: Margaret A Grant, Exec. Dir.
FAX: (212) 343-1762; URL: http://
www.learyfirefighters.org/

Foundation type: Public charity
Purpose: Grants to the families of firefighters who
have perished or been injured in the line of duty.
Publications: Annual report.
Financial data: Year ended 12/31/2011. Assets,
$321,687 (M); Expenditures, $252,084; Total
giving, $43,940.
Fields of interest: Disasters, fire prevention/
control; Disasters, 9/11/01.
Type of support: Grants for special needs.
Application information:
  Initial approach: E-mail or letter.
  Additional information: Contact foundation for
    further application information.
EIN: 134125074

6158
Legacy Heritage Fund Limited
(formerly KBRK, Inc.)
c/o Hertz, Herson & Co., LLP
477 Madison Ave., 10th Fl.
New York, NY 10022-5841   (212) 686-7160

Foundation type: Independent foundation
Purpose: Fellowships to exceptional university
graduates in North America, Europe and Israel who
embark upon a year-long internship in governmental
or major non-governmental non-for-profit
organizations.
Financial data: Year ended 06/30/2012. Assets,
$34,579,400 (M); Expenditures, $1,838,528;
Total giving, $501,160.
International interests: Canada; Europe; Israel.
Type of support: Fellowships; Stipends.
Application information: Applications not
accepted.
  Additional information: Contributes only to
    preselected individuals through the Legacy
    Heritage Program. Unsolicited requests for
    funding not considered or acknowledged.

Program description:

Legacy Heritage Fellowships: The program strives to encourage young adults to select a career in public service and to foster the development of a global community of outstanding leaders. The program awards fellowships to exceptional university graduates in North America, Europe and Israel who embark upon a year-long internship in governmental or major non-governmental nonprofit organizations. Mentored by senior executives in the organization where the fellow was placed and informed by specially designed educational seminars, the Legacy Heritage Fellows develop leadership skills and receive specialized training in international affairs, public service and public policy. The fellows are expected to continue on to graduate school and thereafter assume leadership positions in the public sector where they will be involved in public policy.
EIN: 134077801

6159
Manfred & Anne Lehmann Foundation
910 5th Ave., Ste.11A
New York, NY 10021
URL: http://www.manfredlehmann.com/

Foundation type: Independent foundation
Purpose: Research grants to scholars of Jewish history, primarily in NY.
Financial data: Year ended 09/30/2013. Assets, $1,743,806 (M); Expenditures, $129,171; Total giving, $18,535.
Fields of interest: History/archaeology; Jewish agencies & synagogues.
Type of support: Research.
Application information: Applications accepted. Interview required.
  Initial approach: Letter
EIN: 132918194

6160
The Leukemia & Lymphoma Society, Inc.
(formerly The Leukemia & Lymphoma Society of America, Inc.)
1311 Mamaroneck Ave., Ste. 310
White Plains, NY 10605-5221   (914) 949-5213
Contact: Louis J. DeGennaro Ph.D., Pres. and C.E.O.
FAX: (914) 949-6691; E-mail: infocenter@lls.org;
Toll-Free Tel.: (800) 955-4572; URL: http://www.lls.org

Foundation type: Public charity
Purpose: Grants for research on leukemia and related diseases.
Publications: Application guidelines; Annual report (including application guidelines); Grants list; Informational brochure; Program policy statement.
Financial data: Year ended 06/30/2012. Assets, $223,445,924 (M); Expenditures, $292,394,514; Total giving, $115,731,627; Grants to individuals, totaling $49,018,526.
Fields of interest: Cancer research; Leukemia research.
Type of support: Fellowships; Research; Doctoral support.
Application information: Applications accepted.
  Initial approach: Letter
  Send request by: On-line
  Deadline(s): Varies
  Additional information: See web site for additional application guidelines.
Program descriptions:
Career Development Program: The program supports fundamental research in genetics, molecular and cell biology, molecular pharmacology, molecular virology, and immunology. The program also encompasses translational research directly relevant to the improved treatment or diagnosis of leukemia, lymphoma, myeloma and, where applicable, to prevention. The awards (Scholar, Scholar in Clinical Research, Special Fellow, Special Fellow in Clinical Research, and Fellow) provide stipends to investigators, allowing them to devote themselves to research bearing on leukemia, lymphoma, and myeloma.

New Idea Award: This program is intended to support academic researchers with innovative therapy ideas that are substantially different from current standard treatments and may advance to clinical testing in the short term. It is anticipated that each project funded through the program will be unique and represent a high-risk, potentially high-reward opportunity. Grants will support initial exploration of untested but potentially transformative research ideas and treatment approaches. Applicants must succinctly describe the innovative idea/approach and a method for testing it within one year to receive the award. Upon completion of the one-year grant period, applicants will be evaluated on the extent to which their concept has been substantiated by initial testing, and promising projects may be selected for extended funding. Grants in the amount of up to $100,000 will be awarded for a one year grant period.

Specialized Center of Research Program: This program was established to encourage multidisciplinary research focused on the prevention, diagnosis, or treatment of leukemia, lymphoma, or myeloma. The program requires synergy among at least three research programs that may be supported by scientific core laboratories. The program permits an application for a competitive renewal of the grant after five years, depending on the progress shown. The program is organized to encourage the interaction of complementary sciences and the linkage of basic sciences to a translational research program. The center's maximal annual total cost, direct and indirect, cannot exceed $1.25 million. The aggregate costs over five years cannot exceed $6.25 million. The direct costs, if justified by the aggregate budget, may be up to $1.042 million per year. The indirect or institutional costs cannot exceed 20 percent of the direct costs per year.

Translational Research Program: This program supports research in the development of small molecules for in vivo proof of concept studies in disease-relevant animal models for hematological malignancies. Proposals should include strong scientific rationale for a new drug target in a hematological malignancy, provide information to assess existing intellectual property or the potential for novel chemical space, and demonstrate or explain how a screening assay can be developed to accommodate a high volume of compounds or indicate how a tractable lead compound can be further developed. Grant amounts will be determined on a project-by-project basis.
EIN: 135644916

6161
Harvey R. Lewis Foundation, Inc.
31 S. Bayles Ave.
Port Washington, NY 11050-3708
Contact: Robert Brady Sr., Fdn. Mgr.

Foundation type: Operating foundation
Purpose: Undergraduate and graduate scholarships to residents of Port Washington, NY.
Financial data: Year ended 06/30/2013. Assets, $1,316,733 (M); Expenditures, $139,146; Total giving, $85,000.
Type of support: Graduate support; Undergraduate support.
Application information: Applications accepted.
  Initial approach: Letter
  Deadline(s): None
  Applicants should submit the following:
    1) Financial information
    2) Transcripts
  Additional information: Applications should also include description of extracurricular activities.
EIN: 112630467

6162
Light Work Visual Studies, Inc.
316 Waverly Ave.
Syracuse, NY 13210-2437   (315) 443-1300
Contact: Jeffrey Hoone, Exec. Dir.
FAX: (315) 443-9516; E-mail: info@lightwork.org;
URL: http://www.lightwork.org

Foundation type: Public charity
Purpose: Residencies to U.S. and international artists working in photography and related media.
Publications: Grants list.
Financial data: Year ended 06/30/2012. Assets, $898,505 (M); Expenditures, $413,372; Total giving, $2,500; Grants to individuals, totaling $2,500.
Fields of interest: Photography.
Type of support: Residencies.
Application information: Applications accepted. Application form not required.
  Initial approach: Telephone or e-mail
  Send request by: Mail
  Copies of proposal: 1
  Deadline(s): Rolling
  Applicants should submit the following:
    1) SASE
    2) Resume
  Additional information: Applications must include artist statement, and 20 examples of recent work. Recipients notified in three to four months.
Program description:
Artist-in-Residence Program: Every year, the facility invites between twelve and fifteen artists to come to Syracuse to devote one month to creative projects. Residencies include a $4,000 stipend, a furnished artist apartment, 24-hour access to darkroom and digital facilities, and staff support. Participants are expected to use their month to pursue their own projects, though they are not obligated to teach at the facility.
EIN: 237385641

6163
Lighthouse International
111 E. 59th St.
New York, NY 10022-1202   (212) 821-9200
Contact: Mark G. Ackermann, Pres. and C.E.O.
FAX: (212) 821-9707; E-mail: sca@lighthouse.org;
Toll-free tel.: (800) 829-0500; URL: http://www.lighthouse.org

Foundation type: Public charity
Purpose: Scholarships to partially-sighted or blind students. Awards for eye research, and to partially-sighted or blind employees who have overcome their vision limitations by achieving gainful employment.
Publications: Annual report; Informational brochure; Newsletter.

Financial data: Year ended 12/31/2011. Assets, $90,471,699 (M); Expenditures, $26,862,020; Total giving, $102,000; Grants to individuals, totaling $102,000.

Fields of interest: Education; Eye diseases; Disabilities, people with; Blind/visually impaired.

Type of support: Research; Scholarships—to individuals; Awards/grants by nomination only; Awards/prizes; Graduate support; Undergraduate support.

Application information:

Initial approach: Telephone or e-mail

Additional information: See web site for additional guidelines.

Program descriptions:

Career Awards: This award recognizes exceptional employees who are blind or partially sighted and have successfully overcome their vision limitations by achieving gainful employment. In addition, the awards acknowledge employers who demonstrate that people with impaired vision are a vital part of the workforce. The winning employee and self-employed individual will each receive a $1,000 prize.

Pisart Vision Award: This award of $30,000 is given by nomination only to people who have made a noteworthy contribution to the prevention, cure, or treatment of severe vision impairment or blindness. The award is open to citizens of any country.

Scholarship Awards: The awards are designed to reward excellence, recognize accomplishments and help students who are blind or partially sighted achieve their goals. Awards are divided into three categories: College-bound Award, Undergraduate Award, and Graduate Award, and each carries a $5,000 prize.

EIN: 131096620

6164

Lincoln Center for the Performing Arts, Inc.

(also known as Lincoln Center, Inc.)
70 Lincoln Ctr. Plz.
New York, NY 10023-6583 (212) 875-5000
URL: http://www.lincolncenter.org

Foundation type: Public charity

Purpose: Scholarships and awards to individuals for attendance at The Juilliard School, NY.

Publications: Annual report; Financial statement; Occasional report.

Financial data: Year ended 06/30/2012. Assets, $717,729,133 (M); Expenditures, $154,282,450; Total giving, $8,144,553; Grants to individuals, totaling $83,900.

Fields of interest: Performing arts, education.

Type of support: Support to graduates or students of specific schools; Undergraduate support.

Application information:

Initial approach: Letter

Additional information: Application by nomination only. Individuals may not apply directly.

EIN: 131847137

6165

Gerda Lissner Foundation, Inc.

15 E. 65th St., 4th Fl.
New York, NY 10065-6501 (212) 826-6100
Contact: Stephen DeMaio, Pres.
FAX: (212) 826-0366;
E-mail: mail@gerdalissner.com; URL: http://www.gerdalissner.org

Foundation type: Independent foundation

Purpose: Grants on an international basis for professional development to young operatic singers.

Publications: Application guidelines.

Financial data: Year ended 12/31/2012. Assets, $9,427,251 (M); Expenditures, $911,826; Total giving, $325,520; Grants to individuals, 50 grants totaling $185,000 (high: $15,000, low: $2,000).

Fields of interest: Music; Opera.

Type of support: Grants to individuals.

Application information: Applications accepted. Application form required. Application form available on the grantmaker's web site.

Initial approach: Application

Deadline(s): Contact foundation for application deadline.

Additional information: Auditions required.

EIN: 133566516

6166

Living Archives, Inc.

262 W. 91st St.
New York, NY 10024-1125 (212) 496-9195
Contact: D.A. Pennebaker, Pres.
E-mail: living.archives@gmail.com

Foundation type: Public charity

Purpose: Support only through a fiscal sponsor program to artists for film production in NY.

Publications: Annual report.

Financial data: Year ended 10/31/2011. Assets, $50,534 (M); Expenditures, $479,782; Total giving, $435,127; Grants to individuals, totaling $435,127.

Fields of interest: Film/video; Performing arts; Arts, artist's services.

Type of support: Fiscal agent/sponsor.

Application information: Contact foundation for application information.

Program description:

Fiscal Sponsorship: Living Archives acts as a conduit for funds raised for projects deemed suitable for its support. The program provides only services to filmmakers. There is no application fee but .08 percent of the funding must be returned to the organization to cover expenses incurred.

EIN: 132896424

6167

George London Foundation for Singers, Inc.

460 W. 49th St.
New York, NY 10019-7240 (212) 956-2809
Contact: Maria Bedo, Exec. Dir.
FAX: (212) 956-2817;
E-mail: info@georgelondon.org; URL: http://www.georgelondon.org

Foundation type: Public charity

Purpose: Grants and awards to promising young singers in the U.S. and Canada to help them further their careers in opera and the concert stage.

Publications: Application guidelines.

Financial data: Year ended 06/30/2012. Assets, $767,437 (M); Expenditures, $291,828; Total giving, $88,000; Grants to individuals, totaling $88,000.

Fields of interest: Opera.

Type of support: Awards/prizes.

Application information: Applications accepted. Application form required. Application form available on the grantmaker's web site.

Deadline(s): Jan. 14

Additional information: Application should include a photograph, a recent Letter of Endorsement from someone familiar with your professional qualifications, and a list of four arias in contrasting styles and languages which they will present at audition.

Program description:

Awards: Six Career Awards of $10,000 each and six Encouragement Grants of $1,000 each are given yearly to U.S. or Canadian citizens under the age of 35, and must have performed at least one professional engagement. Honorable mentions of $500 will got to all finalists who do not receive an award. Winners will be required to supply proof of citizenship and age.

EIN: 133576839

6168

Long Island Caddie Scholarship Fund, Inc.

114 Old Country Rd., Ste. LL80
Mineola, NY 11501-4420 (516) 746-1015
Contact: Douglas Vergith, Exec. Dir.
FAX: (516) 746-3032;
E-mail: stephens@longislandgolf.org; E-mail For Douglas Vergith: dougv@longislandgolf.org;
URL: http://www.longislandgolf.org

Foundation type: Public charity

Purpose: Scholarships to qualified caddies who work at golf courses in Nassau and Suffolk counties, NY for attendance at an accredited college, university, or trade school.

Financial data: Year ended 10/31/2012. Assets, $341,251 (M); Expenditures, $194,999; Total giving, $163,500; Grants to individuals, totaling $160,500.

Fields of interest: Vocational education, post-secondary; Higher education; Athletics/sports, golf.

Type of support: Scholarships—to individuals.

Application information: Applications accepted. Application form required. Interview required.

Deadline(s): June 15

Applicants should submit the following:

1) Photograph

2) Transcripts

3) SAR

4) SAT

5) FAFSA

6) ACT

Additional information: Applicant must demonstrate scholastic ability, be of outstanding character, integrity and leadership.

EIN: 136166011

6169

Charles Looney Memorial Fund

c/o Grand Lodge
71 W. 23rd St.
New York, NY 10010-4102
Contact: Frank S. Grado, Tr.

Foundation type: Independent foundation

Purpose: Provides grants for residents of NY facing financial hardship.

Financial data: Year ended 12/31/2012. Assets, $433,981 (M); Expenditures, $22,831; Total giving, $19,200; Grants to individuals, 3 grants totaling $5,850 (high: $4,850, low: $500).

Type of support: Grants for special needs.

Application information: Applications accepted. Application form not required.

Initial approach: Letter

Deadline(s): None

Additional information: Application should include detailed information setting forth reasons charitable assistance is required.

EIN: 132937671

6170
L'Oreal USA, Inc. Corporate Giving Program

(formerly Cosmair, Inc. Corporate Giving Program)
575 5th Ave.
New York, NY 10017-2422 (212) 984-4894
Contact: Rebecca Caruso, Exec. V.P., Corp. Comms.
FAX: (212) 984-4564; Application address for Fellowships: c/o AAS, Attn: Yolanda George, Education and Human Resources, 120 New York Ave., NW, Washington, DC 20005; URL: http://www.lorealusa.com/_en/_us/html/our-company/as-a-corporate-citizen.aspx?

Foundation type: Corporate giving program
Purpose: Fellowships to outstanding women scientists and awards to women for their volunteer work and contributions to the community.
Publications: Application guidelines.
Fields of interest: Cancer research; Research; Biology/life sciences; Women.
Type of support: Fellowships; Research; Grants to individuals; Awards/grants by nomination only; Foreign applicants; Awards/prizes.
Application information: Application form required. Application form available on the grantmaker's web site.
  Send request by: Mail for Women in Science, online for Women of Worth
  Deadline(s): Dec. 13 for U.S. Women in Science, June 30 for International Women in Science, June 30 for Women of Worth
  Final notification: Recipients notified Oct. for Women of Worth
Program descriptions:
  L'Oreal Fellowships for Women In Science: Through the L'Oreal Fellowships for Women in Science program, the company annually awards grants to U.S.-based postdoctoral associates involved with life and physical/material sciences, engineering, technology, computer science, mathematics, immunology, chemistry, earth science, and medical research. The company also awards grants to 15 international postdoctoral associates whose projects have been accepted by a reputable institution outside their home county. The program is designed to raise awareness of the contribution of women to the sciences; and identify exceptional female researchers to serve as role models for younger generations.
  Women of Worth: L'Oreal Paris, a division of L'Oreal USA, annually honors 10 women who are making a difference in their communities through volunteerism. The company awards $5,000 to each honorees charity of choice; a $5,000 matching donation is made in their name to the Ovarian Cancer Research Fund; and one national nominee selected by online public vote will also receive an additional $25,000 for their cause. The program is administered by Points of Light Institute.

6171
The Lucille Lortel Foundation, Inc.

322 8th Ave., 21st. Fl.
New York, NY 10001-6763 (212) 924-2817
FAX: (212) 9890036; E-mail: jshubart@lortel.org; URL: http://www.lortel.org/

Foundation type: Independent foundation
Purpose: Fellowships to emerging and experienced playwrights living in the NY Tri-state area promoting artistic careers.
Financial data: Year ended 06/30/2012. Assets, $30,688,664 (M); Expenditures, $1,223,351; Total giving, $643,452.
Fields of interest: Theater (playwriting).

Application information: Application by nomination only. Self nomination not accepted.
EIN: 133036521

6172
Lower East Side Printshop, Inc.

306 W. 37th St., 6th Fl.
New York, NY 10018-4605 (212) 673-5390
Contact: Dusica Kirjakovic, Exec. Dir.
FAX: (212) 979-6493; E-mail: info@printshop.org; E-Mail for Dusica Kirjakovic: dusica@printshop.org; URL: http://www.printshop.org

Foundation type: Public charity
Purpose: Fellowships to artists who practice the art of printmaking.
Publications: Application guidelines.
Financial data: Year ended 06/30/2013. Assets, $258,553 (M); Expenditures, $698,803.
Fields of interest: Arts.
Type of support: Fellowships; Residencies.
Application information:
  Initial approach: Letter or e-mail
  Deadline(s): None
  Additional information: Contact foundation for current application guidelines.
Program description:
  Keyholder Residency Program: Offers emerging artists free 24-hour access to its professional printmaking facilities to develop new work and foster their artistic careers. Residencies are free and one year long, starting on Apr. 1 and Oct. 1, and they take place in the Artists' Studio, including the solvent/etching area and the darkroom.
EIN: 132812419

6173
Lower Manhattan Cultural Council, Inc.

(also known as LMCC)
125 Maiden Ln., 2nd Fl.
New York, NY 10038-4912 (212) 219-9401
Contact: Sam Miller, Pres.
FAX: (212) 219-2058; E-mail: info@lmcc.net; E-mail for Kay Takeda: ktakeda@lmcc.net; URL: http://www.lmcc.net

Foundation type: Public charity
Purpose: Grants to artists who are residents of the borough of Manhattan, New York, and residencies in New York City open to artists throughout the world.
Publications: Application guidelines; Financial statement; Grants list; Informational brochure; Newsletter.
Financial data: Year ended 06/30/2012. Assets, $6,706,448 (M); Total giving, $521,698; Grants to individuals, totaling $521,698.
Fields of interest: Visual arts; Photography; Sculpture; Painting; Performing arts (multimedia); Arts, artist's services.
International interests: France.
Type of support: Program development; Grants to individuals; Residencies; Project support.
Application information: Applications accepted. Application form required. Application form available on the grantmaker's web site.
  Initial approach: Letter or telephone
  Deadline(s): Jan. 19 for Workspace Residency
  Applicants should submit the following:
    1) Work samples
    2) SASE
    3) Resume
    4) Proposal
  Additional information: Application should include printed materials, and biography. See

web site for additional application information.
Program description:
  Boroughwide Grants: Fund for Creative Communities: The fund supports small and midsized non-profit organizations that provide high-quality local arts programs by increasing access to arts and cultural activities in neighborhoods throughout Manhattan and encouraging new arts activities in communities where the need exists. Grants of up to $5,000 are awarded to non-profit organizations and to artists partnering with a community-based organization or applying through a fiscal sponsor, for arts projects with a public component that will benefit Manhattan communities.
EIN: 237348782

6174
Lozynskyj Foundation

c/o Askold S. Lozynskyj
225 E. 11th St.
New York, NY 10003-7316 (212) 677-2790
Contact: Bohdhan Chaban, V.P.
Application address: c/o Bohdan Chaban, 25 Saint Marks Pl., New York, NY 10003-7836, tel.: (212) 677-2790

Foundation type: Operating foundation
Purpose: Scholarships to students of the Ukraine attending a university in the Ukraine.
Financial data: Year ended 12/31/2011. Assets, $398,427 (M); Expenditures, $10,532; Total giving, $8,000; Grants to individuals, 5 grants totaling $8,000 (high: $1,600, low: $1,600).
Fields of interest: Higher education.
Type of support: Support to graduates or students of specific schools.
Application information: Applications accepted.
  Initial approach: Letter
  Deadline(s): None
EIN: 311616242

6175
The Henry Luce Foundation, Inc.

51 Madison Ave., 30th Fl.
New York, NY 10010-1603 (212) 489-7700
Contact: Michael Gilligan, Pres.
FAX: (212) 581-9541; E-mail: hlf1@hluce.org; URL: http://www.hluce.org

Foundation type: Independent foundation
Purpose: Fellowships by institutional nomination only to American citizens with a bachelor's degree who are no more than 29 years of age as of Sept. 1 of the year they enter the program.
Publications: Biennial report (including application guidelines); Grants list; Program policy statement.
Financial data: Year ended 12/31/2012. Assets, $764,393,011 (M); Expenditures, $41,694,946; Total giving, $30,658,138; Grants to individuals, totaling $570,535.
Fields of interest: International studies.
International interests: Asia.
Type of support: Fellowships; Internship funds; Awards/grants by nomination only.
Application information: Applications not accepted.
  Additional information: Individual applications not accepted. Awards based on nominations submitted by 75 participating colleges and universities. Unsolicited requests for funds not considered or acknowledged.
Program description:
  Luce Scholars Program: Relying on a network of 75 colleges and universities for nominees, this

program enables 15 to 18 Americans under age 30, who have earned a bachelor's degree, who are not Asian specialists to spend one year in East or Southeast Asia in internship positions under the guidance of leading Asian professionals. The foundation administers the program with cooperation from the Asia Foundation, which arranges placements for the scholars and provides administrative support during the program year.
EIN: 136001282

6176
Georges Lurcy Charitable and Educational Trust

1633 Broadway, 32nd Fl.
New York, NY 10019-6708
Contact: Seth E. Frank, Tr.

Foundation type: Independent foundation
Purpose: Fellowships to graduate students at American colleges and universities to study in France and to graduate students of French colleges and universities to study in the U.S.
Financial data: Year ended 06/30/2012. Assets, $26,606,098 (M); Expenditures, $1,457,875; Total giving, $1,062,400.
Fields of interest: International exchange, students.
International interests: France.
Type of support: Fellowships; Exchange programs; Awards/grants by nomination only; Foreign applicants; Graduate support.
Application information: Applications not accepted.
> *Additional information:* Fellowship applicants from America must be recommended by their universities. Applicants from France must apply to the Franco-American Commission for Educational Exchange using the commission's application. Unsolicited requests for funds not considered or acknowledged.

EIN: 136372044

6177
Marc Lustgarten Pancreatic Cancer Foundation

1111 Stewart Ave.
Bethpage, NY 11714-3533 (516) 803-2304
Contact: Kerri Kaplan, Exec. Dir.
FAX: (516) 803-2303; Toll-free tel.: (866) 789-1000; URL: http://www.lustgartenfoundation.org/

Foundation type: Public charity
Purpose: Research grants for the study of pancreatic cancer.
Publications: Application guidelines; Annual report; Newsletter.
Financial data: Year ended 12/31/2011. Assets, $33,576,010 (M); Expenditures, $8,102,402; Total giving, $6,001,054.
Fields of interest: Cancer research.
Type of support: Research.
Application information:
> *Initial approach:* Letter
> *Deadline(s):* Sept. 12 (concept proposals) and Oct. 31 (full proposals) for Innovator Awards; none for Correlative Studies Awards Program
> *Additional information:* Contact foundation for further eligibility guidelines.

Program descriptions:
> *Correlative Studies Award Program:* Awarded in conjunction with the National Cancer Institute's Cancer Therapy Evaluation Program (CTEP), this program will fund selected correlative research

applications directly linked to a CTEP-sponsored clinical trial of novel therapeutics for pancreatic cancer. Proposals must be focused on pancreatic ductal adenocarcinoma studies, and must be based on strong and testable hypotheses. Eligible projects for funding include, but are not limited to: phenotypic or genotypic alterations that correlate with response to therapy; phenotypic or genotypic alterations that explain the development of therapy resistance; phenotypic or genotypic alterations related to prognosis; studies that determine if test agents reach their cellular targets; studies that define the mechanisms of action of test agents in target tissues; early surrogate markers of later clinical responses; phenotypic or genotypic alterations that may be used for risk assessment, early detection, or prognosis; characterization of immune response with association to new immunotherapies for prevention or treatment; defining and targeting specific signal transduction pathways and populations of cells for therapy; or evaluation of accessible sites for monitoring changes occurring in less accessible sites (for example, the oral cavity as a surrogate site for cells in the pancreas)
> *Innovator Awards Program:* This program provides a one-year, $100,000 award to fund novel, 'out-of-the-box' concepts in both translational and basic research. Applicants must hold an M.D. or Ph.D. and an independent, faculty-level position with or without tenure at the time of review; proposed investigations must be conducted at a university, hospital, or research institution possessing non-profit status.

EIN: 311611837

6178
Lymphatic Research Foundation

40 Garvies Point Rd.
Glen Cove, NY 11542-2887 (516) 625-9675
Contact: William Repicci, Exec. Dir.
FAX: (516) 625-9410;
E-mail: lrf@lymphaticresearch.org; URL: http://www.lymphaticresearch.org

Foundation type: Public charity
Purpose: Research grants and fellowships to young investigators to find effective treatments and cures for lymphatic diseases, lymphedma and related disorders.
Publications: Application guidelines; Newsletter.
Financial data: Year ended 12/31/2011. Assets, $1,139,343 (M); Expenditures, $528,390; Total giving, $133,500; Grants to individuals, totaling $133,500.
Fields of interest: Medical research.
Type of support: Fellowships.
Application information: Applications accepted.
> *Initial approach:* Nomination
> *Deadline(s):* Jan. 31
> *Additional information:* See web site for additional application guidelines.

Program description:
> *Postdoctoral Fellowship Awards Program:* This program is to expand and strengthen the pool of outstanding junior investigators in the field of lymphatic research. The awards will support investigators who have recently received their doctorates, a critical point in career development when young scientists choose their lifelong research focus.

EIN: 582404527

6179
Lymphoma Research Foundation

115 Broadway, Ste. 1301
New York, NY 10006-1901 (212) 349-2910
Contact: Elizabeth Thompson, C.E.O.
FAX: (212) 349-2886;
E-mail: researchgrants@lymphoma.org; Toll-free tel.: (800) 235-6848; URL: http://www.lymphoma.org

Foundation type: Public charity
Purpose: Fellowships for research that will result in better, safer treatments and cures for lymphomas. Awards by nomination only to researchers for lymphoma research.
Publications: Annual report; Financial statement; Grants list; Informational brochure; Newsletter.
Financial data: Year ended 06/30/2012. Assets, $15,125,491 (M); Expenditures, $11,179,163; Total giving, $3,884,315; Grants to individuals, totaling $152,470.
Fields of interest: Cancer research; Diagnostic imaging research.
Type of support: Program development; Fellowships; Research; Awards/grants by nomination only; Awards/prizes.
Application information: Application form required.
> *Initial approach:* Letter or telephone
> *Send request by:* Online
> *Deadline(s):* Aug. 26 for Fellowship and Award
> *Final notification:* Recipients notified in Nov.
> *Additional information:* See web site for additional guidelines.

Program descriptions:
> *Clinical Investigator Career Development Award:* The organization funds training of clinicians who will participate in developing new therapeutics and diagnostic tools for lymphoma. Clinicians will be trained to design and administer clinical studies and to take on primary responsibility for trial design, protocol development, IRB submission, and publication. A career development plan and the commitment of a mentor are required as part of the grant application. Up to three awards will be given annually, each at a maximum of $75,000 per year for three years. Applicants must be licensed in the U.S. or Canada.
> *Post-Doctoral Fellowships:* Up to ten of these two-year awards will be given to applicants interested in pursuing careers in lymphoma. Each award offers $50,000 in the first year and $55,000 in the second year. Research may be laboratory- or clinic-based, and may include (but is not limited to) focus on etiology, immunology, genetics, therapies, or transplants. Results and conclusions must be clearly relevant to the treatment, diagnosis, or prevention of Hodgkin and/or non-Hodgkin lymphoma. Applicants must hold an M.D., Ph.D., or equivalent degree and must remain affiliated with a U.S.- or Canada-based institution for the duration of the award. Citizenship is not required. Applicants must have completed two years of fellowship, or not more than two years as a junior faculty instructor or assistant professor at the start of the award period.

EIN: 954335088

6180
Cornelius T. & Elizabeth Lynch Scholarship Fund

(formerly Cornelius T. & Elizabeth Lynch Scholarship Trust)
1100 Wehrle Dr. 2nd Fl.
Amherst, NY 14221

Foundation type: Independent foundation

Purpose: Scholarships to graduates of Geneva High School, NY, and LaSalle High School, Niagara Falls, NY.
Financial data: Year ended 03/31/2013. Assets, $201,335 (M); Expenditures, $11,942; Total giving, $9,000; Grants to individuals, 6 grants totaling $9,000 (high: $1,500, low: $1,500).
Type of support: Support to graduates or students of specific schools; Undergraduate support.
Application information: Applications accepted.
Deadline(s): None
Additional information: Contact fund for current application guidelines.
EIN: 166014594

6181
Mary W. MacKinnon Fund
c/o Community Bank
245 Main St.
P.O. Box 430
Oneonta, NY   13820   (607) 432-1700

Foundation type: Independent foundation
Purpose: Medical, hospital, rehabilitation, and nursing home expenses paid for elderly and economically disadvantaged residents of Sidney, NY.
Financial data: Year ended 12/31/2012. Assets, $2,382,869 (M); Expenditures, $103,563; Total giving, $85,628.
Fields of interest: Medical care, in-patient care; Medical care, outpatient care; Medical care, rehabilitation; Aging; Economically disadvantaged.
Type of support: Grants for special needs.
Application information: Applications accepted. Application form required.
Copies of proposal: 1
Deadline(s): None
Additional information: Requests for assistance must be submitted through a doctor or hospital on behalf of the patient and include financial information; Applications should be sent by mail or fax.
EIN: 237234921

6182
MADRE, Inc.
121 W. 27th St., Ste. 301
New York, NY   10001-6207   (212) 627-0444
Contact: Yifat Susskind, Exec. Dir.
FAX: (212) 675-3704; E-mail: madre@madre.org;
URL: http://madre.org

Foundation type: Public charity
Purpose: Support to individuals through an internship program addressing issues of human rights, women's rights, and/or peace/peace education.
Publications: Newsletter.
Financial data: Year ended 12/31/2011. Assets, $2,557,888 (M); Expenditures, $2,105,678; Total giving, $505,816.
Fields of interest: Education; Reproductive health; Family services; Human services; Women.
Type of support: Stipends; Fiscal agent/sponsor.
Application information: Applications accepted.
Deadline(s): Mar. 15, July 15, and Nov 15 for Internship
Additional information: Application for the internship program should include a cover letter and resume addressed to the Internship Coordinator.
Program description:
Internship Program: This program provides a great way to gain work experience and support's MADRE's work with women and families worldwide.

Internships come with a $15 a day stipend and require a time commitment of 15 hours a week for at least three months. Internships take place at the MADRE Manhattan office.
EIN: 133280194

6183
Magnum Cultural Foundation
P.O. Box 300
New York, NY   10276-0300
E-mail: info@magnumfoundation.org; URL: http://magnumfoundation.org

Foundation type: Public charity
Purpose: Financial support to outstanding photographers for documenting issues world wide.
Financial data: Year ended 12/31/2011. Assets, $760,806 (M); Expenditures, $646,187; Total giving, $81,435; Grants to individuals, totaling $81,435.
Fields of interest: Photography; Arts, artist's services.
Type of support: Grants to individuals; Awards/grants by nomination only; Awards/prizes.
Application information: Applications not accepted.
Additional information: Nominations by invitation only.
Program descriptions:
Emergency Fund: The foundation provides emergency funding to experienced photographers with a commitment to documenting social issues, working long-term, and engaging with an issue over time. Projects address critical global issues that have not received the attention they deserve, or budding crises that are still over the horizon. Each year, a diverse group of photography professionals nominate 100 professional photographers to submit proposals; an independent editorial board then selects ten to twenty photographs to support, based on the strength of their proposals and the importance of the issues they propose to present. Photographers retain the copyright to their work and can distribute it widely, either through traditional or new media (and in collaboration with other nonprofits or non-governmental organizations, if desired)
Emerging Photographer Award: This $10,000 prize supports ongoing work by a young documentary photographer nominated by an online community.
Inge Morath Award: Awarded in conjunction with the IM Foundation, this award gives a $5,000 prize to a female photographer under the age of 30, to support the completion of a long-term documentary project.
EIN: 450573269

6184
Maidstone Foundation, Inc.
1225 Broadway, 9th Fl.
New York, NY   10001-4309   (212) 889-5760
Contact: Duncan Whiteside, Pres.
E-mail: maidstoneduncan@aol.com; Tel./fax: (212) 889-5760; additional E-mail: president@maidstonefdn.org; URL: http://maidstonefdn.org/home.html

Foundation type: Public charity
Purpose: Grants to Russian families who are residents of Queens, NY with disabled family members.
Financial data: Year ended 06/30/2011. Assets, $423,718 (M); Expenditures, $851,059; Total giving, $5,140; Grants to individuals, totaling $5,140.

Fields of interest: Disabilities, people with.
Type of support: Grants for special needs.
Application information: Applications accepted. Application form required.
Initial approach: Letter or telephone
Send request by: Mail
Copies of proposal: 1
Deadline(s): None
Final notification: Recipients notified in six months
EIN: 112718381

6185
The Malevich Society
2 Park Ave., 21st Fl.
New York, NY   10016   (212) 592-1400
Contact: Lawrence M. Kaye, Secy.
E-mail: malevichsociety@hotmail.com

Foundation type: Independent foundation
Purpose: Research and publication grants primarily to Russian and Spanish individuals for work relating to the history and memory of the Russian artist Kazimir Malevich.
Financial data: Year ended 12/31/2012. Assets, $934,566 (M); Expenditures, $18,455; Total giving, $0.
Fields of interest: Arts.
International interests: Russia.
Type of support: Publication; Research; Foreign applicants.
Application information: Applications accepted. Application form required. Application form available on the grantmaker's web site.
Deadline(s): Sept. 30
Applicants should submit the following:
   1) Letter(s) of recommendation
   2) Budget Information
   3) Proposal
   4) Work samples
   5) Curriculum vitae
Additional information: Application should also include a bibliography.
EIN: 134181214

6186
Manhattan Neighborhood Network
(also known as Manhattan Community Access Corporation)
537 W. 59th St.
New York, NY   10019-1006   (212) 757-2670
Contact: Daniel Coughlin, Exec. Dir.
FAX: (212) 757-1603; URL: http://www.mnn.org

Foundation type: Public charity
Purpose: Project grants and travel grants to producers of successful cablecasts on Manhattan Neighborhood Network (MNN), NY.
Publications: Application guidelines; Financial statement; Newsletter.
Financial data: Year ended 12/31/2011. Assets, $22,827,010 (M); Expenditures, $4,778,311.
Fields of interest: Film/video; Television; Print publishing; Community/economic development; Computer science.
Type of support: Program development; Conferences/seminars; Project support.
Application information: Application form required.
Deadline(s): Oct. 15
Program descriptions:
Advanced Facilities Grant: Producers with successful cablecast of minimum two quarters of series programming or three specials on MNN to his/her credit may apply for subsidized use of advanced postproduction facilities in Manhattan. The program created must be cablecast on MNN

when completed. Applicants must have the appropriate certificate of training for use of the facilities requested. Applications must include a clear description of the work to be done, the number of hours needed, how the work will improve the quality of the program, and other resources available.

Alliance for Community Media Conference Travel Grant: This program supports travel, accommodations, and registration at the Alliance's conference for producers with successful cablecast of a minimum of two quarters of series programming or two specials on MNN to their credit. Applicants with recommendation from at least one MNN staff member increase their chances for support. Recipients must submit reports after the conference and may be asked to participate on video crews at the conference.

Community Event Coverage: Support is provided to producers interested in coverage of community events for cablecast on MNN. Events include organized events such as parades, ethnic celebrations, street fairs, performances, etc. Events should be outdoors and admission free and open to the public. Special consideration will be given to the level of organization in the production and to the subject treatment. All applicants must have successful cablecast of minimum one quarter of series programming or two specials on MNN to his/her credit. MNN certification is required in appropriate categories if MNN facilities are to be used in production.

Community Media Grants: Awards range from $5,000 to $30,000 for a maximum of three years. Organizations must be Manhattan-based, serving Manhattan residents.

New Technologies Program: Support is available to producers with successful cablecast of a minimum one quarter of series programming or one special on MNN to his/her credit and to other producers by special consideration of MNN, for innovative use of new technologies of community media in the production of MNN programming. Possible technologies include Internet, video streaming, teleconferencing, public projection, and electronic signage. Special attention will be given to projects which bridge various forms of community media. Projects will be judged on creativity, reproducibility, and community accessibility. MNN certification in appropriate categories is required if MNN facilities are to be used. In addition, the applicant must demonstrate a working knowledge of the design and implementation of the technology to be utilized.

Process of Dialogue Program: Producers with successful cablecast of a minimum of one quarter of series programming or two specials on MNN to their credit may apply for funding for programs which employ innovative use of video and MNN programming to establish dialogue between diverse or conflicting communities, interest groups, or philosophies. The end product should be the quality of the interaction between the groups involved, with the video being a medium of expression or documentation of the process. MNN certification in appropriate categories is required if MNN facilities are to be used.

Program Enhancement Grant: These grants may be used to add enhancements to a video program by producers who have a successful cablecast of a minimum one quarter of series programming on MNN to their credit. Eligible activities include: production of roll-in and/or credit video for series programs; production of video promos for use on MNN and/or other Time Warner cable channels; production of short-form pieces of 15 seconds to five minutes in length for fill between full-length programs; design and purchase of set materials or studio backdrops; express studio enhancements; rights to copyrighted music by local artists; or other approved enhancements.

Thematic Grants: Grants of up to $2,000 each are available to producers for the production of programming in predetermined themes around key cultural spaces and activities often overlooked in MNN programming. Projects may be documentaries, talk shows, or narrative pieces. To be eligible, producers must have successful cablecast of minimum of one quarter of series programming or two specials on MNN to his/her credit. MNN certification in appropriate categories is required if MNN facilities are to be used in production.
EIN: 133625426

6187
Rema Hort Mann Foundation, Inc.
155 Hudson St., Ground Fl.
New York, NY   10013-2138   (212) 966-8444
Contact: Quang Bao, Exec. Dir.
FAX: (212) 966-8453;
E-mail: rhmfoundation@gmail.com; URL: http://www.remahortmannfoundation.org

Foundation type: Public charity
Purpose: Grants by nomination only to cancer patients, primarily in the New York, NY metropolitan area, to pay for expenses relating to medical and emotional well-being. Grants also by nomination only to emerging artists, primarily in NY.
Financial data: Year ended 12/31/2011. Assets, $670,334 (M); Expenditures, $275,338; Total giving, $119,676.
Fields of interest: Visual arts; Cancer.
Type of support: Awards/grants by nomination only; Grants for special needs.
Application information: All grants are by nomination only. Contact foundation for guidelines.
EIN: 133879538

6188
March of Dimes Foundation
(formerly March of Dimes Birth Defects Foundation)
1275 Mamaroneck Ave.
White Plains, NY   10605-5201   (914) 428-7100
Contact: Richard Mulligan, C.O.O. and Exec. V.P.
FAX: (914) 997-4560;
E-mail: researchgrants@marchofdimes.com;
Additional tel.: (914) 997-4555; Additional e-mail: mkatz@marchofdimes.com; URL: http://www.marchofdimes.com

Foundation type: Public charity
Purpose: Research grants by nomination only to investigators specializing in birth defects.
Publications: Application guidelines; Annual report; Financial statement; Grants list; Informational brochure; Newsletter.
Financial data: Year ended 12/31/2011. Assets, $156,180,805 (M); Expenditures, $207,290,112; Total giving, $29,903,909; Grants to individuals, totaling $135,000.
Fields of interest: Genetic diseases and disorders; Genetic diseases and disorders research.
Type of support: Research.
Application information: Application form available on the grantmaker's web site.
Deadline(s): Sept. 15.
Additional information: Completion of formal nomination required, including curriculum vitae; Nomination form available on web site.
Program description:
Basil O'Connor Starter Scholar Research Awards: Provides up to $75,000 per year for two years for technical assistance and supplies that may be needed by young scientists who are ready to begin independent research after completing postdoctoral training. Funding is limited to those holding recent faculty appointments at the instructor or assistant professor level.
EIN: 131846366

6189
Clara A. March Scholarship Fund
78 Bryant St.
Buffalo, NY   14209
Application address: c/o NYU Medical School, Attn.: Dennis A. Nadler, 40 Biomedical Bldg., SUNY, Buffalo, NY 14214

Foundation type: Independent foundation
Purpose: Scholarships and loans to medical students attending the State University of New York at Buffalo.
Publications: Annual report.
Financial data: Year ended 12/31/2011. Assets, $1,477,191 (M); Expenditures, $65,403; Total giving, $50,000.
Fields of interest: Medical school/education.
Type of support: Student loans—to individuals; Support to graduates or students of specific schools.
Application information: Applications accepted.
Initial approach: Letter
Deadline(s): None
Additional information: Applicant must demonstrate financial need.
EIN: 166119078

6190
Marine Corps-Law Enforcement Foundation, Inc.
10 Rockefeller Ctr., Rm. 1007
New York, NY   10020-1903   (877) 606-1775
Contact: Pete Haas, Pres.
FAX: (212) 332-2998; E-mail: info@mc-lef.org;
URL: http://www.mc-lef.org

Foundation type: Public charity
Purpose: Scholarships to children of active reserve and former Marines and to children of persons associated with the federal law enforcement especially those killed in the line of duty.
Publications: Newsletter.
Financial data: Year ended 12/31/2011. Assets, $12,295,601 (M); Expenditures, $3,187,294; Total giving, $3,047,120; Grants to individuals, totaling $3,047,120.
Fields of interest: Association.
Type of support: Scholarships—to individuals.
Application information: Unsolicited applications not accepted.
EIN: 223357410

6191
John Michael Marino Foundation, Inc.
223 Main St.
Port Washington, NY   11050   (516) 767-2600
Contact: Salvatore R. Zimbardi, Treas.

Foundation type: Independent foundation
Purpose: Scholarships to graduating high school students in the Port Washington, NY area for continuing education at institutions of higher learning.
Financial data: Year ended 12/31/2012. Assets, $233,884 (M); Expenditures, $23,354; Total giving, $18,225; Grants to individuals, 16 grants totaling $11,300 (high: $1,000, low: $100).

Fields of interest: Higher education.
Type of support: Scholarships—to individuals.
Application information: Applications accepted.
EIN: 113351080

6192
Glenn L. Martin Foundation
c/o Fiduciary Trust Co.
600 5th Ave.
New York, NY 10020 (212) 632-4088

Foundation type: Independent foundation
Purpose: Financial assistance to retired employees of the Martin Marietta Corporation, MD, who are suffering hardship.
Financial data: Year ended 12/31/2011. Assets, $2,476,497 (M); Expenditures, $113,988; Total giving, $85,000; Grants to individuals, 5 grants totaling $85,000 (high: $17,000, low: $17,000).
Type of support: Employee-related welfare.
Application information: Applications not accepted.
    Additional information: Unsolicited requests for funds not considered or acknowledged.
Company name: Martin Marietta Corporation
EIN: 136086736

6193
David M. Martin Trust Fund
c/o SG Kall
3522 James St., Ste. 101
Syracuse, NY 13206-2351
Contact: Sheldon G. Kall, Tr.

Foundation type: Independent foundation
Purpose: Loans only to Jewish students living in the central NY area.
Financial data: Year ended 09/30/2013. Assets, $0 (M); Expenditures, $19,403; Total giving, $15,000.
Fields of interest: Jewish agencies & synagogues.
Type of support: Student loans—to individuals.
Application information:
    Initial approach: Letter
    Deadline(s): 3 months prior to college semester
EIN: 166385390

6194
Mashomack Foundation
c/o Anthony J. Morabito
2 Dover Ct.
Rochester, NY 14624

Foundation type: Independent foundation
Purpose: Scholarships to worthy college students of Rochester, NY for study at educational institutions.
Financial data: Year ended 11/30/2012. Assets, $2,270,862 (M); Expenditures, $135,222; Total giving, $114,000.
Fields of interest: Higher education.
Type of support: Undergraduate support.
Application information: Contact foundation for eligibility criteria.
EIN: 237120560

6195
MasterCard Incorporated Corporate Giving Program
2000 Purchase St.
Purchase, NY 10577-2405
URL: http://www.mastercard.com/corporate/responsibility/corporate-philanthropy.html

Foundation type: Corporate giving program
Purpose: Scholarships to dependent children of MasterCard employees for higher education.
Publications: Application guidelines; Informational brochure.
Fields of interest: Higher education.
Type of support: Employee-related scholarships.
Application information: Applications not accepted.
    Additional information: Unsolicited requests for funds not considered or acknowledged.
Program description:
    MasterCard Scholarship Program: MasterCard awards $5,000 college scholarships to 10 children of employees of the company. The program is designed to encourage academic excellence and to help employees of MasterCard meet the cost of their children's undergraduate college education.
Company name: MasterCard Incorporated

6196
Israel Matz Foundation
14 E. 4th St., Ste. 403
New York, NY 10012-1141 (212) 673-8142
Contact: RH Arfa, Tr.
E-mail: info@imfoundation.net; URL: http://www.imfoundation.net

Foundation type: Independent foundation
Purpose: Relief assistance to economically disadvantaged Hebrew writers, scholars, public workers, and their dependents in Israel and the U.S.
Financial data: Year ended 12/31/2011. Assets, $1,393,031 (M); Expenditures, $178,385; Total giving, $44,100; Grants to individuals, 8 grants totaling $22,500 (high: $6,300, low: $1,000).
International interests: Israel.
Type of support: Grants for special needs.
Application information:
    Initial approach: Letter
    Deadline(s): None
    Applicants should submit the following:
    1) Curriculum vitae
    2) Letter(s) of recommendation
    Additional information: Application must include purpose of request.
EIN: 136121533

6197
The Mayday Fund
c/o SPG
127 W. 26th St., Ste. 800
New York, NY 10001-6869 (212) 366-6970
Contact: Christina Spellman, Exec. Dir.
Application fax: (301) 654-1589,
e-mail: ghertz@burnesscommunications.com
FAX: (212) 366-6979;
E-mail: inquiry@maydayfund.org; URL: http://www.maydayfund.org/

Foundation type: Independent foundation
Purpose: Fellowships for physicians, nurses, pharmacists, social workers, scientists, and legal scholars in the pain management community to go beyond their own professional pursuits to become advocates and leaders for change in the management of pain.
Publications: Annual report; Financial statement; Grants list.
Financial data: Year ended 12/31/2012. Assets, $24,459,869 (M); Expenditures, $1,812,304; Total giving, $1,212,733.
Fields of interest: Health care; Formal/general education; Biomedicine research; Pathology research.

Type of support: Program development; Fellowships; Research; Travel grants.
Application information: Applications accepted. Application form required. Application form available on the grantmaker's web site. Interview required.
    Send request by: E-mail or fax
    Deadline(s): July 1
    Applicants should submit the following:
    1) Proposal
    2) Curriculum vitae
    3) Essay
    Additional information: Application should also include a letter approving your participation in the program from your immediate supervisor or chairperson. See web site for additional guidelines.
Program description:
    Mayday Pain & Society Fellowship: The initiative trains physicians, nurses, pharmacists, social workers, basic, translational and clinical scientists, policy experts, and legal scholars in the pain management community to go beyond their own professional pursuits to become thought leaders and advocates for change in the pain field in the U.S. and Canada. The Fellowship seeks those applicants who have the capacity, time and passion to become active advocates in the field, and foresee significant impact from their efforts to improve the lives of people in pain.
EIN: 133645438

6198
The Mayer Foundation
300 E. 74th St.
New York, NY 10021-3746
URL: http://foundationcenter.org/grantmaker/mayer/

Foundation type: Independent foundation
Purpose: Scholarships to high school, college or graduate school students to complete their education in the field and school of their choice. Economic relief grants to needy individuals who are distressed or suffering as a result of poverty, low-income or lack of financial resources.
Financial data: Year ended 12/31/2012. Assets, $267,803 (M); Expenditures, $59,614; Total giving, $59,000; Grants to individuals, 22 grants totaling $52,000 (high: $2,500, low: $1,000).
Fields of interest: Higher education; Human services; Economically disadvantaged.
Type of support: Scholarships—to individuals; Grants for special needs.
Application information: Applications accepted.
    Initial approach: Letter
    Copies of proposal: 1
    Deadline(s): None
    Additional information: A proposal is required for economic relief grant. See web site for additional information.
Program description:
    Mayer Scholarship: Scholarships range from $2,500 to $5,000 per year to students with sufficient academic ability, show good character and exhibit need for financial assistance. Scholarship may be used for tuition, fees, books, supplies, and, room and board. Scholarships are renewed annually provided the student is not on academic or disciplinary probation.
EIN: 020569535

6199
The McCaddin-McQuirk Foundation, Inc.
c/o O'Connor Davies Munns & Dobbins, LLP
60 E. 42nd St.
New York, NY 10165-0006 (212) 935-8619
Contact: John Eager, Pres.
Application address: P.O. Box 5001, New York, NY
10185; tel.: (212) 935-8619

Foundation type: Independent foundation
Purpose: Scholarships to students who wish to
become priests, deacons, catechists or lay
teachers of the Roman Catholic Church in the U.S.
or elsewhere.
Financial data: Year ended 12/31/2011. Assets,
$4,223,459 (M); Expenditures, $116,108; Total
giving, $96,800.
Fields of interest: Theological school/education;
Catholic agencies & churches.
Type of support: Scholarships—to individuals.
Application information: Applications accepted.
　Initial approach: Letter
　Deadline(s): Dec. 1
EIN: 136134444

6200
The Penny McCall Foundation, Inc.
408 E. 79th St., Ste. 5D
New York, NY 10075
E-mail: info@pennymccallfoundation.org;
URL: http://www.pennymccallfoundation.org

Foundation type: Independent foundation
Purpose: Grants by nomination only to U.S. citizens
for research of the visual arts. Awards are given
biennially.
Financial data: Year ended 12/31/2012. Assets,
$971,282 (M); Expenditures, $135,127; Total
giving, $0.
Fields of interest: Research; Visual arts.
Type of support: Research; Awards/grants by
nomination only; Awards/prizes.
Application information: Applications not
accepted.
　Additional information: Candidates are
　nominated by an anonymous committee
　selected by the board.
EIN: 133376289

6201
The McConnell Scholarship Foundation
(formerly The Lynn E. and Mattie G. McConnell
Foundation and Scholarship Fund)
72 S. Main St.
Canandaigua, NY 14424

Foundation type: Independent foundation
Purpose: Scholarships to graduates of Prattsburg,
NY Central School.
Financial data: Year ended 12/31/2012. Assets,
$167,294 (M); Expenditures, $11,920; Total
giving, $8,640.
Type of support: Scholarships—to individuals;
Support to graduates or students of specific
schools.
Application information: Application form required.
　Deadline(s): May 15
　Additional information: Application must include
　financial information.
EIN: 166237917

6202
Anne O'Hare McCormick Memorial Fund, Inc.
c/o Newswomen's Club
15 Gramercy Park S.
New York, NY 10003-1705
E-mail: mccormickscholarship@hotmail.com

Foundation type: Independent foundation
Purpose: Scholarships to women who are U.S.
citizens and have been accepted to the Columbia
University Graduate School of Journalism, NY.
Publications: Application guidelines.
Financial data: Year ended 12/31/2012. Assets,
$242,162 (M); Expenditures, $17,015; Total
giving, $15,000; Grants to individuals, 3 grants
totaling $15,000 (high: $5,000, low: $5,000).
Fields of interest: Print publishing; Women.
Type of support: Support to graduates or students
of specific schools; Graduate support.
Application information: Applications accepted.
Application form required. Application form
available on the grantmaker's web site.
　Initial approach: Letter
　Send request by: Online, mail or hand delivery
　Deadline(s): May 23
　Applicants should submit the following:
　　1) Resume
　　2) Letter(s) of recommendation
　　3) Financial information
　　4) Essay
　Additional information: Selection of scholarship
　recipients is based on financial need,
　academic background, and the fund's
　assessment of the individual's potential for
　contributing to journalism in either broadcast
　or print media. Prior experience in the field is
　not necessary.
EIN: 136144221

6203
Joseph F. McCrindle Foundation
(formerly The Henfield Foundation)
c/o Patterson, Belknap, Webb & Tyler, LLP
1133 Avenue of the Americas, Ste. 2200
New York, NY 10036-6710

Foundation type: Independent foundation
Purpose: Awards for excellence in creative writing
to full time students at colleges and universities in
the U.S.
Financial data: Year ended 12/31/2012. Assets,
$5,051,587 (M); Expenditures, $3,831,095; Total
giving, $3,508,317.
Fields of interest: Literature.
Type of support: Awards/prizes.
Application information: Applications not
accepted; unsolicited requests for funds not
considered or acknowledged.
EIN: 136112779

6204
McGee Trust
1 M&T Plz., 8th Fl.
Buffalo, NY 14203

Foundation type: Independent foundation
Purpose: Scholarships to Fannett Metal High
School graduates for continuing education at
accredited colleges or universities.
Financial data: Year ended 12/31/2012. Assets,
$202,529 (M); Expenditures, $13,142; Total
giving, $7,650.
Fields of interest: Higher education.
Type of support: Scholarships—to individuals.
Application information: Applications accepted.

　Initial approach: Letter
　Deadline(s): May 1
　Additional information: Letter must state
　educational background.
EIN: 251222910

6205
Margaret A. McGrath Charitable Foundation Scholarship Fund
P.O. Box 287
Brockport, NY 14420 (585) 637-7170
Contact: Richard Dollard, Exec. Dir.
URL: http://frontiernet.net

Foundation type: Independent foundation
Purpose: Scholarships to individuals who are
residents of the town of Sweden or Hamlin, NY,
enrolled or accepted at an accredited college or
university with a major in elementary education or
business.
Financial data: Year ended 12/31/2012. Assets,
$2,489,632 (M); Expenditures, $150,478; Total
giving, $52,000; Grants to individuals, 20 grants
totaling $52,000 (high: $4,000, low: $1,000).
Fields of interest: Elementary school/education;
Business school/education.
Type of support: Scholarships—to individuals.
Application information: Applications accepted.
Application form required.
　Deadline(s): Mar. 1
　Applicants should submit the following:
　　1) Transcripts
　　2) Resume
　　3) Letter(s) of recommendation
　　4) Financial information
　Additional information: Applicant must
　demonstrate financial need.
EIN: 206228522

6206
Melville House Inc.
330 Willis Ave.
Roslyn Heights, NY 11577

Foundation type: Independent foundation
Purpose: Scholarships and periodic awards to
college students who display financial need.
Financial data: Year ended 06/30/2013. Assets,
$1,620,492 (M); Expenditures, $51,531; Total
giving, $37,600.
Type of support: Awards/prizes; Undergraduate
support.
Application information: Applications not
accepted.
　Additional information: Unsolicited requests for
　funds not considered or acknowledged.
EIN: 112289338

6207
Memorial Foundation for Jewish Culture, Inc.
50 Broadway, 34th Fl.
New York, NY 10004-1607 (212) 425-6606
Contact: Profismar Schorch, Pres.
FAX: (212) 425-6602; *E-mail:* office@mfjc.org;
URL: http://www.mfjc.org

Foundation type: Public charity
Purpose: Scholarships and fellowships to Jewish
scholars for leadership positions in Jewish culture.
Financial data: Year ended 09/30/2011. Assets,
$24,926,842 (M); Expenditures, $1,901,904;
Total giving, $679,408; Grants to individuals,
totaling $132,000.

Fields of interest: Jewish agencies & synagogues.
Type of support: Fellowships; Scholarships—to individuals; Doctoral support.
Application information: Applications accepted. Application form required.
  Initial approach: Letter or e-mail
  Deadline(s): Oct. 31 for International Fellowships in Jewish Studies, and International Doctoral Scholarship for Studies Specializing in Jewish Fields, Nov. 31 for International Scholarship Program for Community Service
Program descriptions:
  International Doctoral Scholarship for Studies in Specializing in Jewish Fields: Grants ranging up to $10,000 per year are awarded to graduate students specializing in a Jewish field who are officially enrolled or registered in a doctoral program at a recognized university. Only applicants who have had their dissertation approved can apply.
  International Fellowships in Jewish Studies: Grants ranging up to $10,000 are awarded to qualified scholars, researchers, and artists who possess the knowledge and experience to formulate and implement a project in a field of Jewish specialization.
  International Scholarship Program for Community Service: Scholarships are awarded to well-qualified individuals to train for careers in the rabbinate, Jewish education, social work, and as religious functionaries (e.g., shohatim, mohalim) in diaspora Jewish communities in need of such personnel. Individuals planning to serve in the United States, Canada, and Israel are excluded from this program.
EIN: 136209691

6208
Laura's Galik Memorial Scholarship
(formerly Laura Schriber Gallik Memorial Scholarship Fund)
P.O. Box 389
Walton, NY 13856-0389 (607) 865-4126

Foundation type: Independent foundation
Purpose: Scholarships to graduates of Walton Central High School, NY for postsecondary education.
Financial data: Year ended 12/31/2012. Assets, $216,585 (M); Expenditures, $6,047; Total giving, $4,500; Grants to individuals, 4 grants totaling $4,500 (high: $2,000, low: $500).
Fields of interest: Higher education.
Type of support: Support to graduates or students of specific schools; Undergraduate support.
Application information: Applications accepted.
  Initial approach: Letter or telephone
  Deadline(s): Apr.
EIN: 161406866

6209
Merchant and Ivory Foundation, Ltd.
c/o Merchant Ivory Productions
250 W. 57th St., Ste. 1825
New York, NY 10107-1803 (212) 582-8049
E-mail: foundation@merchantivory.com;
URL: http://www.merchantivory.com/foundation.html

Foundation type: Public charity
Purpose: Grants to artists in the visual and performing arts and to further the preservation and awareness of art and cinema.
Fields of interest: Visual arts; Performing arts.
Type of support: Grants to individuals.
Application information: Applications accepted.
  Initial approach: Contact foundation
EIN: 133607890

6210
MetLife Foundation
1095 Ave. of the Americas
New York, NY 10036-6797 (212) 578-6272
Contact: A. Dennis White, C.E.O. and Pres.
FAX: (212) 578-0617;
E-mail: metlifefoundation@metlife.com;
URL: https://www.metlife.com/metlife-foundation/

Foundation type: Company-sponsored foundation
Purpose: Awards to individuals for recognition of outstanding medical research in Alzheimer's disease. Scholarships to children of associates of MetLife, administered by the National Merit Scholarship Corp. Residencies for artists who conduct programs for museums and communities.
Publications: Annual report (including application guidelines); Corporate giving report (including application guidelines); Financial statement.
Financial data: Year ended 12/31/2012. Assets, $168,418,066 (M); Expenditures, $41,832,441; Total giving, $41,107,662.
Fields of interest: Visual arts; Arts; Alzheimer's disease research.
Type of support: Research; Employee-related scholarships; Awards/prizes.
Application information:
  Initial approach: Letter
EIN: 132878224

6211
The Metropolitan Museum of Art
1000 5th Ave.
New York, NY 10028-0198 (212) 535-7710
FAX: (212) 396-5168;
E-mail: education.grants@metmuseum.org;
URL: http://www.metmuseum.org/en/research/internships-and-fellowships/fellowships

Foundation type: Public charity
Purpose: Fellowships to graduate students and postdoctoral researchers who specialize in art history, archaeology or art conservation.
Financial data: Year ended 06/30/2011. Assets, $3,324,866,332 (M); Expenditures, $345,356,939; Total giving, $1,459,262; Grants to individuals, 69 grants totaling $1,359,794. Subtotal for fellowships: 75 grants totaling $1,459,262.
Fields of interest: Visual arts; Art conservation; Museums (art); Art history; Arts; International exchange, arts; International exchange, students; Science.
International interests: Asia; France; Germany; Greece; Italy.
Type of support: Fellowships; Internship funds; Research; Awards/prizes; Graduate support; Postgraduate support.
Application information:
  Initial approach: Letter or e-mail
  Deadline(s): Vary
  Applicants should submit the following:
   1) Transcripts
   2) Resume
Program descriptions:
  Andrew W. Mellon Postdoctoral Curatorial Fellowship: A postdoctoral curatorial fellowship is offered for curatorial training and scholarly research. The fellow is fully integrated into one of the Museum's curatorial departments and exposed to the full range of curatorial work. This two-year fellowship is available to eligible individuals who demonstrate scholarly excellence as well as a strong commitment to the curatorial profession. Fellows receive an annual salary of $46,590 plus research and travel expenses up to $6,000.

Art History Fellowships: The museum offers annual resident fellowships in art history to qualified graduate students at the pre-doctoral level as well as to postdoctoral researchers. Projects should relate to the museum's collections. The fields of research for art history candidates include: Asian art; arts of Africa, Oceania, and the Americas; antiquities; arms and armor; costumes; drawings and illuminated manuscripts; paintings; photographs; prints; sculpture; textiles; and Western art. Some art history fellowships are also available for students whose projects involve firsthand examination of paintings in major European collections. Fellowships generally cannot be given for projects involving exhibitions to be organized and installed during the fellowship period. The number of fellowships awarded depends upon the funds available; the stipend amount for one year is $40,000 for senior fellows and $30,000 for pre-doctoral fellows, with up to an additional $5,000 for travel. Senior fellowships are intended for those who hold a Ph.D. on the date of application and for well-established scholars.

Conservation and Scientific Research Fellowships: The museum offers annual resident fellowships in conservation to qualified graduate students at the pre-doctoral level as well as to postdoctoral researchers. Fellowship applications for short-term research for senior museum conservators are also considered. Projects should relate to the museum's collections. The fields of research for conservation candidates include: paintings; paper; photographs; objects (including sculpture, metalwork, glass, ceramics, furniture and archaeological objects); textiles; musical instruments; costumes; and scientific research. It is desirable that applicants for the conservation fellowship program should have reached an advanced level of experience or training. All fellowship recipients will be expected to spend the fellowship in residence in the department with which they are affiliated. The stipend amount for one year is $40,000 to $30,000 with up to an additional $5,000 for travel.

Research Scholarship in Photograph Conservation: A two-year term with the museum, with the possibility of renewal for a third year, is available to qualified individuals interested in working on-site in the photograph conservation lab of the Sherman Fairchild Center for Works on Paper and Photograph Conservation. The scholar is expected to carry out independent research related to issues of historic and contemporary processes, preservation, analysis, or treatment of photographs and to participate in the collection- and exhibition-related activities of the Photograph Conservation Department. The scholar's term follows the academic calendar, with successful candidates beginning in September. Scholars may apply during the second year of their tenure for an extension to a third year. The stipend amount is $40,000 per year, plus a $3,000 travel allowance.
EIN: 131624086

6212
Metropolitan Opera Association, Inc.
30 Lincoln Ctr., Rm. 419
New York, NY 10023-7103 (212) 799-3100
Contact: Nadia Hashim; Maureen Thomas
FAX: (212) 870-4524;
E-mail: mthomas@mail.metopera.org; URL: http://www.metopera.org

Foundation type: Public charity
Purpose: Awards and scholarships to gifted singers in furthering their careers.
Publications: Annual report.

Financial data: Year ended 07/31/2011. Assets, $410,745,269 (M); Expenditures, $320,966,882; Total giving, $583,760; Grants to individuals, totaling $583,760.
Fields of interest: Opera.
Type of support: Awards/prizes.
Application information:
Initial approach: Letter
Program descriptions:
Lindemann Young Artist Development Program: The program identifies and educates the most gifted young American singers and coach/accompanists for performances not only at The Met, but also with opera companies throughout the country. To meet the individual needs of each young artist, the program provides specialized training in music, language and dramatic coaching from The Met's own artistic staff and invited master teachers. Along with an annual stipend for living expenses, the program also funds private lessons with approved teachers from outside the Met staff. In addition, program participants have access to rehearsals for all Metropolitan Opera productions. Participants are offered a position with the program for a period of one year with second and third year options held by The Met. During this period, the artist performs only at The Met or outside engagements approved by the Artistic Director.
National Council Auditions Program: This program is designed to discover promising young opera singers and assist in the development of their careers. The auditions are held annually in fifteen Regions of the United States and Canada. The auditions are administered by National Council members and volunteers in each region. The jury will award up to five Grand Winner awards of $15,000 each. The concert is broadcast nationwide on The Metropolitan Opera Radio Network. The remaining National Finalists will receive $5,000 each, and those singers who were National Semi-Finalists, but did not advance to the National Finals will be given $1,500 to further their studies.
EIN: 131624087

6213
Stella E. Metzger Scholarship Fund
1 M&T Plz., 8th Fl.
Buffalo, NY   14203   (716) 842-5506

Foundation type: Independent foundation
Purpose: Scholarships to financially needy graduates of Lebanon High School, PA, who have outstanding academic records.
Financial data: Year ended 01/31/2013. Assets, $65,563 (M); Expenditures, $4,417; Total giving, $2,500.
Type of support: Support to graduates or students of specific schools; Undergraduate support.
Application information: Applications accepted.
Initial approach: Letter
Additional information: Application must also include academic record and statement of financial need.
EIN: 236853062

6214
Dr. Jose Antonio Mijangos, Jr. Foundation
13 Stonegate Ln.
Pittsford, NY   14534-1913

Foundation type: Independent foundation
Purpose: Medical scholarships to men and women who aspire to serve others with compassion and a commitment to excellence.

Financial data: Year ended 12/31/2011. Assets, $332,721 (M); Expenditures, $15,084; Total giving, $11,826.
Fields of interest: Medical school/education.
Type of support: Scholarships—to individuals; Support to graduates or students of specific schools.
Application information: Only students entering the top 25-ranked medical schools in the country as well as the University of Rochester are eligible. Winners of the scholarship are chosen for their academic strength, passion for medicine, and a demonstration of strong ethical and moral character.
EIN: 141942917

6215
Yvar Mikhashoff Trust for New Music
c/o Jan & Diane Williams
152 Russell St.
Buffalo, NY   14214   (415) 624-4120
Application address: c/o Dr. Amy Williams, Competition Coord., Yvar Mikhashoff Trust for New Music, 204 S. Atlantic Ave., Pittsburgh, PA 15224, e-mail: amy@mikhashofftrust.org
E-mail: info@mikhashofftrust.org; URL: http://www.mikhashofftrust.org

Foundation type: Independent foundation
Purpose: Grants for the support of composers, performers and presenters of New Music for young professionals.
Financial data: Year ended 12/31/2012. Assets, $288,054 (M); Expenditures, $15,174; Total giving, $9,000.
Fields of interest: Music; Music composition.
Type of support: Grants to individuals; Awards/prizes.
Application information: Applications accepted.
Copies of proposal: 1
Deadline(s): Nov. 15
Final notification: Winners announced in Jan.
Additional information: Application for the competition must be submitted jointly by both the pianist and composer. See web site for additional guidelines.
EIN: 161466808

6216
The Millay Colony for the Arts, Inc.
454 E. Hill Rd.
P.O. Box 3
Austerlitz, NY   12017-2208   (518) 392-3103
Contact: Caroline Crumpacker, Exec. Dir.
E-mail: apply@millaycolony.org; E-mail for Caroline Crumpacker: director@millaycolony.org;
URL: http://www.millaycolony.org

Foundation type: Public charity
Purpose: Residencies to writers, composers, visual artists, and filmmakers/video artists.
Publications: Application guidelines.
Financial data: Year ended 12/31/2011. Assets, $1,278,111 (M); Expenditures, $293,966.
Fields of interest: Film/video; Visual arts; Music composition; Literature.
Type of support: Foreign applicants; Residencies.
Application information: Application form required.
Initial approach: E-mail
Deadline(s): Oct. 1
Applicants should submit the following:
1) Work samples
2) SASE
Additional information: Application should also include project description. See web site for complete program guidelines.

Program description:
Residency Program: Residents are offered free housing, food, and studio space for a one month period. Six residents are selected for each month between the months of Apr. and Nov.
EIN: 141556850

6217
Thomas and Lois Mills Scholarship Trust
c/o NBT Bank, N.A.
52 S. Broad St.
Norwich, NY   13815

Foundation type: Independent foundation
Purpose: Scholarships to students at Gowanda Central School, Gowanda, NY.
Financial data: Year ended 06/30/2013. Assets, $520,629 (M); Expenditures, $32,571; Total giving, $24,196; Grants to individuals, 29 grants totaling $24,196 (high: $835, low: $834).
Type of support: Support to graduates or students of specific schools; Awards/grants by nomination only; Undergraduate support.
Application information: Applications not accepted.
EIN: 166136606

6218
The Joan Mitchell Foundation, Inc.
c/o Carolyn Somers
545 W. 25th St., 15th Fl.
New York, NY   10001-5501   (212) 524-0100
FAX: (212) 524-0101;
E-mail: info@joanmitchellfoundation.org;
URL: http://www.joanmitchellfoundation.org/

Foundation type: Independent foundation
Purpose: Grants to artists and sculptors to further their careers.
Financial data: Year ended 12/31/2012. Assets, $234,765,443 (M); Expenditures, $6,997,063; Total giving, $1,767,918; Grants to individuals, 70 grants totaling $851,800 (high: $15,000, low: $4,800).
Fields of interest: Visual arts; Sculpture; Painting; Arts.
Type of support: Grants to individuals; Stipends.
Application information: Applications not accepted.
Additional information: Application by nomination only, unsolicited requests for funds not considered or acknowledged.
Program descriptions:
Emergency Program: The foundation provides emergency support to visual artists working in the mediums of painting, sculpture, and/or drawing, who have suffered significant losses after natural or manmade disasters that have affected their community. Artists who have been negatively impacted due to catastrophic situations of this nature can apply to the foundation for funding.
MFA Grant Program: This annual grant of $15,000 is awarded to assist fifteen painters and sculptors who will receive their MFA degrees. The grants are given in recognition to artistic quality to artists chosen from a body of candidates put forth by nominators from MFA programs across the U.S. The award assists in furthering the recipient's artistic career and their transition from academic to professional studio work.
Painters and Sculptors Grant Program: This Program awards $25,000 to twenty-five artists through a nomination process. Nominators across the country are invited to recommend artists, at any stage in their career, who are currently under-recognized for their creative achievements,

and whose practice would significantly benefit from the grant.
EIN: 113161054

6219
The Mitsui U.S.A. Foundation
200 Park Ave.
New York, NY 10166-0001
URL: http://www.mitsui.com/us/en/index.html

Foundation type: Company-sponsored foundation
Purpose: Scholarships to children of employees of Mitsui & Co. (U.S.A.). Scholarships also to students in the Business and Liberal Arts Program (BALA) undergoing undergraduate studies at Queens College, NY, and the Weissman Center for International Business undergoing MBA studies at Baruch College, NY. The scholarships are administered by Queens College and Baruch College.
Publications: Informational brochure.
Financial data: Year ended 03/31/2013. Assets, $15,865,446 (M); Expenditures, $925,023; Total giving, $772,000.
Type of support: Employee-related scholarships; Support to graduates or students of specific schools.
Application information: Applications not accepted.
Additional information: Unsolicited requests for funds not considered.
Company name: Mitsui & Co. (U.S.A.), Inc.
EIN: 133415220

6220
Modest Needs Foundation
115 E. 30th St., Fl. 1
New York, NY 10016-7302 (212) 463-7042
Contact: Keith P. Taylor, Pres.
E-mail: general.questions@modestneeds.org;
URL: http://www.modestneeds.org

Foundation type: Public charity
Purpose: Grants to individuals and families in New York and Canada, who encounter temporary financial crisis through no immediate fault of their own.
Publications: Application guidelines; Financial statement; Informational brochure; Newsletter.
Financial data: Year ended 12/31/2011. Assets, $1,487,333 (M); Expenditures, $1,378,835; Total giving, $616,832; Grants to individuals, totaling $616,832.
Fields of interest: Human services.
Type of support: Grants to individuals.
Application information: Applications accepted. Application form available on the grantmaker's web site.
Send request by: On-line
Additional information: Applicants must be at least 18 years of age, legal resident of the U.S. or Canada, ingend to apply for assistance either for yourself, or for a person living in your home, and your household has at least one active bank account. See web site for additional application guidelines.
Program descriptions:
Independent Living Grants: Grants are made by remitting payment to a creditor for an expense on behalf of persons who are permanently unable to work but who nevertheless are living independently on the limited income to which they are entitled - their retirement income, or their permanent disability income.
Self-Sufficiency Grants: Grants are made to a creditor for an expense on behalf of an otherwise

self-sufficient individual or family for a relatively small, emergency expense which the individual or family could not have anticipated or prepared for.
EIN: 470863430

6221
Mohawk Valley Community Action Agency, Inc.
1721 Black River Blvd.
Rome, NY 13440-2447 (315) 624-9930
FAX: (315) 624-9931; E-mail: info@mvcaa.com; Additional address (Utica office): 5 Johnson Pk., Utica, NY 13501-4426, tel.: (315) 624-0821, fax: (315) 624-0827; additional address (Herkimer office): 401 E. German St., Herkimer, NY 13350-1046, tel.: (315) 866-0030, fax: (315) 866-2523; URL: http://www.mvcaa.com

Foundation type: Public charity
Purpose: Assistance to homeless individuals, and financial assistance to prevent homelessness to families in Oneida and Herkimer counties, NY.
Financial data: Year ended 07/31/2012. Assets, $2,629,842 (M); Expenditures, $17,085,850.
Fields of interest: Housing/shelter, homeless.
Type of support: Grants for special needs.
Application information: Contact agency for information on assistance.
EIN: 160918009

6222
Monahan-Laighton Memorial Fund
(formerly Margaret B. Monahan and Alberta W. Laighton Memorial Fund)
One Memorial Ave.
P.O. Box 668
Pawling, NY 12564-0788 (845) 855-5900
Contact: David Daniels

Foundation type: Independent foundation
Purpose: Grants to economically disadvantaged individuals residing in Pawling, NY, town and village, primarily for medical expenses.
Financial data: Year ended 12/31/2011. Assets, $510,324 (M); Expenditures, $30,326; Total giving, $28,350.
Fields of interest: Economically disadvantaged.
Type of support: Emergency funds; Grants for special needs.
Application information: Application form not required.
Initial approach: Letter or telephone
Additional information: Applicants must demonstrate financial need. Contact foundation for current application guidelines.
EIN: 146022154

6223
Monroe 2 Orleans Educational Foundation, Inc.
3599 Big Ridge Rd.
Spencerport, NY 14559-1709 (585) 349-9009
URL: http://www.monroe2boces.org/about.cfm?subpage=791

Foundation type: Public charity
Purpose: Scholarships to students of NY State in non-traditional programs pursuing higher education. Scholarships to qualified graduates pursuing careers working with special needs students.
Financial data: Year ended 06/30/2012. Assets, $1,229,623 (M); Expenditures, $77,037; Total giving, $47,500; Grants to individuals, totaling $47,500.

Fields of interest: Vocational education, post-secondary; Higher education.
Type of support: Scholarships—to individuals.
Application information: Applications accepted. Application form required.
Send request by: Mail
Deadline(s): Mar. 14
Applicants should submit the following:
1) Transcripts
2) Letter(s) of recommendation
3) Essay
Additional information: School districts include Brockport, Churchville-Chili, Gates Chili, Greece, Hilton, Holley, Kendall, Spencerport and Wheatland-Chili, NY. See web site for additional application information.
Program description:
Scholarship: Approximately twelve scholarships of up to $5,000 are awarded to students who, by choice or circumstance, are in non-traditional or alternative programs, students who are coping with disabilities, students who have chosen to study a skilled trade, or students who are earning their GED. Scholarship awards must be used within two years. Recipients are chosen based on circumstance and merit.
EIN: 562354704

6224
The Douglas Moore Fund for American Opera, Inc.
c/o Gordon Ostrowski
120 Claremont Ave.
New York, NY 10027 (515) 520-2191
Contact: Michael Ching
Application address: 2019 Ashmore Dr., Ames, IA 50014

Foundation type: Independent foundation
Purpose: Fellowship to an emerging American composer or librettist.
Financial data: Year ended 12/31/2012. Assets, $57,458 (M); Expenditures, $29,374; Total giving, $24,000; Grant to an individual, 1 grant totaling $24,000.
Fields of interest: Opera; Performing arts, education.
Type of support: Fellowships.
Application information: Applications accepted. Application form required.
Deadline(s): Nov.
Applicants should submit the following:
1) Letter(s) of recommendation
2) Essay
Additional information: Contact the fund for additional application guidelines.
EIN: 061633557

6225
John E. Morgan Foundation, Inc.
c/o Bessemer Trust
630 5th Ave.
New York, NY 10111-0100
Application address: c/o James R. Zigmant, Treas., P.O. Box 349, Tamaqua, PA 18252-0349

Foundation type: Independent foundation
Purpose: Educational scholarships to individuals in the Tamaqua, PA, area.
Financial data: Year ended 12/31/2012. Assets, $63,315,197 (M); Expenditures, $3,141,831; Total giving, $2,941,460; Grants to individuals, totaling $286,459.
Fields of interest: Education.
Type of support: Scholarships—to individuals.

Application information:
EIN: 562290010

6226

Morgan Stanley Foundation, Inc.

(formerly Morgan Stanley Foundation)
c/o Community Affairs
1585 Broadway, 23rd Fl.
New York, NY   10036-8200   (212) 296-3600
FAX: (646) 519-5460;
E-mail: whatadifference@morganstanley.com;
E-mail for Richard B. Fisher Scholarship Program:
richardbfisherprogram@morganstanley.com;
URL: http://www.morganstanley.com/
globalcitizen/ms_foundation.html

Foundation type: Company-sponsored foundation
Purpose: Scholarships and internships to minority
students in their junior year to pursue a career in
the financial services industry.
Publications: Application guidelines; Corporate
giving report.
Financial data: Year ended 12/31/2012. Assets,
$55,817,750 (M); Expenditures, $9,937,056;
Total giving, $9,937,056.
Fields of interest: Scholarships/financial aid;
Education; Business/industry; Minorities.
Type of support: Internship funds; Scholarships—
to individuals.
Application information: Applications accepted.
Application form required.
Initial approach: E-mail
Deadline(s): Varies
Applicants should submit the following:
    1) GPA
    2) Letter(s) of recommendation
    3) Essay
    4) Transcripts
    5) Resume
Program description:
    Morgan Stanley Scholarship Initiatives: The
foundation supports students and faculty in
minority and underserved communities through
scholarships, fellowships, and internships at the
undergraduate and graduate level. Through the
Richard B. Fisher Scholars Program, the foundation
awards $7,500 scholarships to underrepresented
undergraduate minority students for academic
achievement and a paid summer internship at
Morgan Stanley in Global Wealth Management or
National Sales. Applicants must be in their junior
year of college, have a 3.2 GPA, and have desire to
build a career in the financial services industry.
EIN: 261226280

6227

Alan Morton Foundation

93 Thompson Blvd.
Greenport, NY   11944-3107

Foundation type: Operating foundation
Purpose: Scholarships for disadvantaged
individuals of NY with special needs. Emergency
assistance for individuals of NY in crisis and need,
and to those with HIV/AIDS.
Financial data: Year ended 08/31/2012. Assets,
$18,141 (M); Expenditures, $170,117; Total
giving, $169,000; Grants to individuals, 3 grants
totaling $34,000 (high: $15,000, low: $4,000).
Fields of interest: Education; Disabilities, people
with; AIDS, people with.
Type of support: Emergency funds; Scholarships—
to individuals; Grants for special needs.
Application information: Applications accepted.

Additional information: Contact foundation for
additional guidelines.
EIN: 133295743

6228

Movement Research, Inc.

55 Ave. C
New York, NY   10009-6855   (212) 598-0551
FAX: (212) 633-1974;
E-mail: info@movementresearch.org; Additional
tel.: (212) 539-2611; E-mail For Barbara Bryan:
director@movementresearch.org; URL: http://
www.movementresearch.org

Foundation type: Public charity
Purpose: Residencies to dance and performance
artists.
Publications: Informational brochure; Newsletter.
Financial data: Year ended 06/30/2012. Assets,
$348,266 (M); Expenditures, $584,307.
Fields of interest: Performing arts; Dance.
Type of support: Residencies.
Application information: Applications accepted.
Application form required.
    Initial approach: E-mail, telephone or letter
    Deadline(s): Mar. 31
    Applicants should submit the following:
        1) SASE
        2) Work samples
        3) Resume
        4) Proposal
    Additional information: Applications must also
    include an artistic statement.
Program descriptions:
    Artist-in-Residence (A.I.R.) Program: The program
provides a space in which artists can experiment
and create work. Artists at any stage of creative
development and who reflect a range of directions
and approaches to making work are encouraged to
apply. Artists receive commission support, access
to subsidized and free rehearsal space, the
opportunity to moderate at least one open
performance, teach or take classes/workshops,
serve on studies project panels, write for the
organization's publications, and serve on peer
selection panels.
    Movement Research Exchange: Intensive
residency program meant to spur exchange of ideas
amongst individual choreographers from different
areas and countries. Enables artists to travel.
EIN: 133041403

6229

The Moving Image, Inc.

209 W. Houston St.
New York, NY   10014-4837   (212) 727-8110
Contact: Karen Cooper, Pres.
FAX: (212) 627-2471;
E-mail: filmforum@filmforum.org; URL: http://
www.filmforum.org

Foundation type: Public charity
Purpose: Fiscal sponsorship to filmmakers for
project support.
Financial data: Year ended 06/30/2012. Assets,
$9,514,452 (M); Expenditures, $4,691,441.
Fields of interest: Fund raising/fund distribution;
Film/video.
Type of support: Project support; Fiscal agent/
sponsor.
Application information: Applications accepted.
Application form required.
    Additional information: Applicants must submit a
    one-page synopsis of the film, biographies of
    the principals (director, writer, producer) and
    the name of the individual/entity that will be

responsible for receiving the funds. Contact
foundation for further program information.
Program description:
    Fiscal Sponsorship: Fiscal sponsorship is
available to filmmakers in support of their projects,
allowing individuals to solicit and receive
tax-deductible donations from individuals and gifts
from foundations in support of a specific project,
without having to create a 501(c)(3) nonprofit
corporation. The organization retains 5 percent of
all funds received on the filmmaker's behalf for this
service.
EIN: 510175953

6230

Kenneth Muhlenbruck Foundation, Inc.

c/o Henry Blizzard
1301 Nottingham Rd.
Jamesville, NY   13078

Foundation type: Independent foundation
Purpose: Scholarships to students of New York
State for continuing education at institutions of
higher learning.
Financial data: Year ended 12/31/2012. Assets,
$538,878 (M); Expenditures, $13,329; Total
giving, $10,000; Grant to an individual, 1 grant
totaling $10,000.
Fields of interest: Higher education.
Type of support: Scholarships—to individuals.
Application information: Applications accepted.
    Initial approach: Letter
    Additional information: Contact the foundation for
    eligibility criteria.
EIN: 320143947

6231

Musicians Emergency Fund Inc.

P.O. Box 1256, FDR Sta.
New York, NY   10150-1256
Contact: Marie Ashdown, Exec. Dir.

Foundation type: Independent foundation
Purpose: Financial aid and assistance programs for
elder classical music artists and musicians who
find themselves in crisis.
Financial data: Year ended 08/31/2012. Assets,
$2,167,187 (M); Expenditures, $220,722; Total
giving, $119,557; Grants to individuals, 11 grants
totaling $53,586 (high: $15,291, low: $100).
Fields of interest: Arts, artist's services.
Type of support: Emergency funds.
Application information: Applications accepted.
    Initial approach: Letter
    Deadline(s): None
EIN: 131635273

6232

Musicians Emergency Relief Fund-Local 802

322 W. 48th St.
New York, NY   10036   (212) 245-4802
Contact: Augustino Gagliardi, Tr.

Foundation type: Operating foundation
Purpose: Financial assistance to local 802 sick,
distressed, or economically disadvantaged
musicians and their families.
Publications: Application guidelines; Financial
statement; Program policy statement.
Financial data: Year ended 12/31/2011. Assets,
$91,663 (M); Expenditures, $159,379; Total
giving, $93,259; Grants to individuals, 10 grants
totaling $4,254 (high: $585, low: $161).

Fields of interest: Music; Disabilities, people with; Economically disadvantaged.
Type of support: Grants for special needs.
Application information: Applications accepted. Interview required.
> *Additional information:* Members of local 802 must be in good standing and be a member for a minimum of two years or a pensioner.

EIN: 136222619

6233
Musicians Foundation, Inc.
875 6th Ave., Ste. 2303
New York, NY 10001-3507 (212) 239-9137
Contact: B.C. Vermeersch, Exec. Dir.
FAX: (212) 239-9138;
E-mail: info@musiciansfoundation.org; URL: http://www.musiciansfoundation.org

Foundation type: Public charity
Purpose: Emergency financial assistance to professional musicians and their families.
Publications: Application guidelines.
Financial data: Year ended 04/30/2012. Assets, $3,066,290 (M); Expenditures, $241,444; Total giving, $140,162; Grants to individuals, totaling $140,162.
Fields of interest: Music.
Type of support: Emergency funds; Grants for special needs.
Application information: Applications accepted. Application form required. Application form available on the grantmaker's web site.
> *Initial approach:* Letter
> *Send request by:* Mail or fax
> *Copies of proposal:* 1
> *Deadline(s):* None
> *Applicants should submit the following:*
> 1) Financial information
> 2) Curriculum vitae
> 3) Budget Information

EIN: 131790739

6234
Myasthenia Gravis Foundation of America, Inc.
355 Lexington Ave., 15th Fl.
New York, NY 10017-6603
Contact: Tor Holtan, C.E.O.
FAX: (212) 370-9047;
E-mail: mgfa@myasthenia.org; Toll-free tel.: (800) 541-5454; URL: http://www.myasthenia.org

Foundation type: Public charity
Purpose: Awards to individuals in the U.S. or Canada for research on myasthenia gravis.
Publications: Application guidelines; Annual report; Financial statement; Grants list; Informational brochure; Newsletter.
Financial data: Year ended 12/31/2012. Assets, $5,772,122 (M); Expenditures, $1,192,029; Total giving, $330,086.
Fields of interest: Medical school/education; Nursing school/education; Myasthenia gravis; Myasthenia gravis research.
International interests: Global Programs.
Type of support: Awards/prizes; Postdoctoral support; Graduate support; Doctoral support.
Application information: Application form required. Application form available on the grantmaker's web site.
> *Send request by:* Online
> *Copies of proposal:* 9
> *Deadline(s):* Oct. 1 for Clinician-Scientist Award
> *Final notification:* Recipients notified in Jan. for Clinician-Scientist Award

> *Additional information:* See web site for additional guidelines.

Program descriptions:
> *Clinician-Scientist Development Three-Year Award:* This award supports a clinician scientist's research related to Myasthenia Gravis. The award aims to recognize the importance of good clinical research and encourage young investigators in clinical studies. This three-year award consists of an annual salary of $75,000 and $5,000 in educational expenses, per year. Only direct costs are funded by this award.
> *Dr. John Newsom-Davis Award for Neurology Residents-in-Training:* This award provides neurology residents-in-training (registrars, residents, or fellows) to attend scientific or clinical meetings related to myasthenia gravis (MG). Awards will be given to residents who wish to present MG-related research at a recognized professional event or gathering, such as the foundation's annual Scientific Session. Other funding considerations may include travel and lodging for a resident to attend a meeting that might significantly further his or her understanding of MG and related autoimmune diseases.

EIN: 135672224

6235
Mycenaean Foundation
c/o The Millburn Corporation
1270 Avenue of the Americas
New York, NY 10020
Contact: Mr. Philip Betancourt, Pres. and Secy.-Treas.
Application address: c/o Institute for Aegean Prehistory, 3550 Market St., Ste. 100, Philadelphia, PA 19104

Foundation type: Independent foundation
Purpose: Grants to individuals to promote interest in Mycenaean research.
Financial data: Year ended 12/31/2012. Assets, $413,178 (M); Expenditures, $39,702; Total giving, $24,000; Grant to an individual, 1 grant totaling $24,000.
Fields of interest: History/archaeology.
International interests: Greece.
Type of support: Research.
Application information: Applications accepted.
> *Initial approach:* Letter
> *Deadline(s):* None

EIN: 436070522

6236
The N Foundation, Inc.
c/o Citrin
709 Westchester Ave.
White Plains, NY 10604

Foundation type: Independent foundation
Purpose: Scholarships to graduating high school seniors of Larchmont, NY pursuing postsecondary education.
Financial data: Year ended 08/31/2013. Assets, $0 (M); Expenditures, $12,000; Total giving, $12,000; Grants to individuals, 15 grants totaling $12,000 (high: $800, low: $800).
Fields of interest: Higher education.
Type of support: Scholarships—to individuals.
Application information: Applications accepted.
> *Additional information:* Contact the foundation for additional application information.

EIN: 133361672

6237
NAACP Legal Defense and Education Fund, Inc.
40 Rector St., 5th Fl.
New York, NY 10013-2815 (212) 965-2200
Contact: Sherrilyn Ifill, Pres.
E-mail: ldaniels@naacpldf.org; URL: http://www.naacpldf.org

Foundation type: Public charity
Purpose: Scholarships to undergraduate and law students.
Publications: Application guidelines; Annual report; Financial statement; Informational brochure (including application guidelines); Newsletter.
Financial data: Year ended 06/30/2012. Assets, $35,098,865 (M); Expenditures, $15,541,541; Total giving, $2,493,149; Grants to individuals, totaling $335,000.
Fields of interest: Law school/education; African Americans/Blacks.
Type of support: Graduate support; Undergraduate support.
Application information: Application form required.
> *Initial approach:* Letter
> *Deadline(s):* Apr. 30 for Lehman Education Fund, Mar. 31 for Warren Legal Training Program
> *Final notification:* July 31 for the Warren Legal Training Program; Aug. 1 for the Herbert Lehman Education Fund
> *Additional information:* Applications for The Herbert Lehman Education Fund may be requested between Nov. 1 and Mar. 31; Applications for The Earl Warren Legal Training Program may be requested between Nov. 1 and Feb.

Program descriptions:
> *Earl Warren Civil Rights Training Scholarships::* Scholarships are awarded each year to 15 to 20 new students whose community involvement activities and leadership qualities demonstrate outstanding potential for training as civil rights and public interest attorneys. Awards are limited to U.S. citizens; preference will be given to students who are entering their first year of full-time study. The scholarships are in the amount of $3,000. They are renewable, provided funds are available and the student remains in good standing and fulfills all program requirements.
> *Earl Warren Shearman & Sterling Scholarships:* Scholarships are awarded annually to talented African-American students who are entering law school. Each $15,000 grant includes a $13,500 scholarship and a $1,500 allowance to meet the costs of attending the fund's yearly Civil Rights Institute. Scholarships are renewable for the second and third years of law school, provided the scholar maintains an acceptable academic record and makes normal progress toward obtaining a law degree within three consecutive academic years.
> *Herbert Lehman Educational Program:* These scholarships, in the amount of $2,000, are awarded to students who are entering college for the first time and who will be attending a four-year college as a full-time student. They are renewable if the recipient remains in good academic and social standing and program funds remain available. Awards generally do not exceed four years.

EIN: 131655255

6238
NARSAD Research Institute, Inc.
90 Park Ave., 16th Fl.
New York, NY 10016 (646) 681-4888
Contact: Jeffrey Borenstein M.D., Pres. and C.E.O.
E-mail: info@bbrfoundation.org; Toll-Free Tel.: (800) 829-8289; URL: http://bbrfoundation.org/

Foundation type: Public charity
Purpose: The foundation supports efforts to alleviate the suffering of mental illness by awarding grants that will lead to advances and breakthroughs in scientific research.
Financial data: Year ended 12/31/2012. Assets, $2,513,753 (M); Expenditures, $1,000,000; Total giving, $1,000,000.
Fields of interest: Mental health, disorders; Depression; Schizophrenia; Medical research.
Type of support: Grants to individuals.
Application information: Applications accepted. Application form available on the grantmaker's web site.
  Send request by: Online
  Deadline(s): Sept. 15
  Final notification: Recipients notified in Mar.
  Applicants should submit the following:
    1) Proposal
    2) Curriculum vitae
    3) Budget Information
  Additional information: See web site for additional guidelines.
Program description:
  Young Investigator Grant: The grant provides support for the most promising young scientists conducting neurobiological research. One and two year awards up to $30,000 per year are provided to enable promising investigators to either extended research fellowship training or begin careers as independent research faculty. Basic and/or clinical investigators are supported, but research must be relevant to serious psychiatric disorders such as schizophrenia, mood disorders, anxiety disorders, or child and adolescent psychiatric disorders.
  EIN: 113401438

6239
NARSAD: The World's Leading Charity Dedicated to Mental Health Research
(formerly National Alliance for Research on Schizophrenia and Depression, also known as Brain and Behavior Research Foundation)
90 Park Ave., 16th Fl.
New York, NY   10016   (646) 681-4888
FAX: (516) 487-6930;
E-mail: info@bbrfoundation.org; Toll-Free Tel.: (800) 829-8289; URL: http://www.narsad.org

Foundation type: Public charity
Purpose: Research grants to scientists at all stages of their careers for neurobiological research, specifically severe psychiatric brain and behavior disorders.
Publications: Application guidelines; Annual report; Financial statement; Grants list; Informational brochure; Newsletter.
Financial data: Year ended 12/31/2012. Assets, $28,754,847 (M); Expenditures, $17,116,774; Total giving, $13,818,632; Grants to individuals, totaling $115,000.
Fields of interest: Schizophrenia; Neuroscience; Neuroscience research.
Type of support: Fellowships; Research; Awards/prizes; Postdoctoral support.
Application information: Applications accepted. Application form required. Application form available on the grantmaker's web site.
  Send request by: Online
  Deadline(s): Jan. 25 for Young Investigator Awards, Mar. 5 for Independent Investigator Grants, June 1 for Lieber Prize, Goldman-Rakic Prize, Colvin Prize, and Ruane Prize, Sept. 15 for Young Investigator Grant
  Applicants should submit the following:
    1) Proposal
    2) Budget Information

    3) Curriculum vitae
  Additional information: See web site for additional guidelines.
Program descriptions:
  Distinguished Investigator Grant: This program provides support for experienced investigators (full professor or equivalent) conducting neurobiological and behavioral research. A one-year award of $100,000 is provided for established scientists pursuing innovative projects in diverse areas of neurobiological research.
  Freedman Award for Outstanding Basic Research: A $1,000 award is given to honor a pioneer in biological psychiatry, who has distinguished him/herself through outstanding basic science research.
  Goldman-Rakic Prize for Cognitive Neuroscience Research: An award of $40,000 is annually given to recognize excellence in neurobiological research at the cellular, physiological, or behavioral levels that may lead to a greater understanding of underlying psychiatric or neurological disease. Eligible individuals must be nominated.
  Independent Investigator Grants: These grants provide support for investigators during the critical period between the initiation of research and the receipt of sustained funding. A two-year award of up to $50,000 per year (maximum of $100,000 for two years) is provided to scientists at the associate professor level or equivalent, who are pursuing new, innovative directions in neurobiological research. The program is intended to facilitate innovative research opportunities by supporting basic, as well as translational and/or clinical, investigators; however, research must be relevant to understanding, treating, and preventing such serious psychiatric disorders as schizophrenia, mood disorders, anxiety disorders, and child/adolescent disorders. Eligible applicants must have a doctoral-level degree (M.D., Ph.D., or equivalent) and have received, as primary investigators, competitive research support at a national level (such as from the National Institutes of Health, the National Science Foundation, or other foundation support)
  Joy and William Ruane Prize for Childhood Psychiatric Disorders: An award of $50,000 is available to an outstanding scientist carrying out research on the causes, pathophysiology, treatment, or prevention of severe child psychiatric illness. The scientist to be recognized is one who gives particular promise for advancing the understanding of psychotic, affective, or other severe psychiatric disorders having their onset in childhood or adolescence. Contributions may be for clinical research or relevant basic science. Eligible individuals must be nominated.
  Klerman Award for Outstanding Clinical Research: This $1,000 award honors outstanding achievements in clinical research by young investigators.
  Lieber Prize for Schizophrenia Research: This prize of $50,000 is awarded to a research scientist who has made distinguished contributions to the understanding of schizophrenia, and is meant to reward past achievement and provide further incentive for an outstanding working scientist to continue to do exceptional research into the causes, prevention, and treatment of schizophrenia. Eligible applicants must be nominated.
  Sidney R. Baer, Jr. Prize for Schizophrenia Research: This award of $40,000 is given to one recipient on a yearly basis, selected by the current year's Lieber Prize for Schizophrenia Research winner. The prize is intended to support the recipient's important work in schizophrenia.

  Young Investigator Grant: This program provides support for the most promising young scientists conducting neurobiological research. One- and two-year awards of up to $30,000 per year are provided to enable promising investigators to either extend research fellowship training, or begin careers as independent research faculty. Eligible applicants must have a doctoral-level degree (e.g., M.D., Ph.D., Psy.D., etc.) and already be employed in research training, or be in a faculty or independent research position. Awards are intended to support postdoctoral fellows, instructors, and assistant professors (or equivalent). Pre-doctoral students or investigators at the rank of associate professor or equivalent are not eligible.
  EIN: 311020010

6240
National Academy Foundation
218 W. 40th St., 5th Fl.
New York, NY   10018-1592   (212) 635-2400
Contact: J.D. Hoye, Pres.
FAX: (212) 635-2409; E-mail: jdhoye@naf.org;
URL: http://www.naf.org

Foundation type: Public charity
Purpose: Scholarships to students enrolled in an Academy in their senior year and have a minimum GPA of 3.0.
Publications: Application guidelines.
Financial data: Year ended 12/31/2011. Assets, $10,467,092 (M); Expenditures, $13,407,365; Total giving, $247,908; Grants to individuals, totaling $35,500.
Fields of interest: Higher education.
Type of support: Scholarships—to individuals.
Application information: Application form required. Application form available on the grantmaker's web site.
  Applicants should submit the following:
    1) Letter(s) of recommendation
    2) Essay
  Additional information: Letter of recommendation must be from a teacher, Academy Director, or internship employer.
  EIN: 133480246

6241
National Action Council for Minorities in Engineering, Inc.
(also known as NACME)
440 Hamilton Ave., Ste. 302
White Plains, NY   10601-1813   (914) 539-4010
Contact: Irving Pressley McPhail, Pres. and C.E.O.
FAX: (914) 539-4032; E-mail: info@nacme.org;
URL: http://www.nacme.org

Foundation type: Public charity
Purpose: Scholarships and fellowships to minority undergraduate engineering students. Awards and prizes to high school seniors who have demonstrated excellence in pre-college math and science.
Publications: Annual report; Financial statement; Newsletter.
Financial data: Year ended 08/31/2011. Assets, $13,954,244 (M); Expenditures, $4,340,797; Total giving, $1,642,239; Grants to individuals, totaling $1,642,239.
Fields of interest: Engineering school/education; Environment; Mathematics; Science; Minorities; African Americans/Blacks; Hispanics/Latinos; Native Americans/American Indians.

Type of support: Fellowships; Internship funds; Awards/prizes; Undergraduate support; Workstudy grants.
Application information: Applications accepted. Application form required.
   Deadline(s): Vary
   Additional information: Applicants must be U.S. citizens or permanent residents. See web site for further application and program information.
Program descriptions:
   Phillip D. Reed Undergraduate Endowment Fellowship: This award is designed to increase access to careers in this area among African American, Latino, and American Indian students. The award provides $5,000 payable for up to three years. Undergraduate students may apply during the second semester of the sophomore year. Applicants must have a GPA of 3.0 and a demonstrated interest in environmental engineering.
   Pre-Engineering Student Scholarship Program: This award is a financial support program that encourages and recognizes high academic achievement of students interested in pursuing a corporate career in a construction-related engineering discipline. The award is accompanied by internship and mentoring opportunities. The scholarship provides up to $2,500 over two years to engineering students from underrepresented minority population groups majoring in a construction-related engineering field. Students may apply during their second semester in the sophomore year.
   STEM Innovation Grant Program: Awards five $1,000 grants to teachers in inner-city communities to assist with funding for projects that make students aware of the excitement and opportunity to be found in the field of engineering - turning theoretical classroom lessons into real-world applications that bring science, technology, engineering, and math (STEM) concepts to life.
   The Bechtel Undergraduate Fellowship Award: This award is a financial support program that encourages and recognizes high academic achievement of students interested in pursuing a corporate career in a construction-related engineering discipline. The award is accompanied by internship and mentoring opportunities. The scholarship provides up to $2,500 over two years to engineering students from underrepresented minority population groups majoring in a construction-related engineering field. Students may apply during their second semester in the sophomore year.
EIN: 521190664

6242
National Alliance for Musical Theatre, Inc.
(also known as NAMT)
520 8th Ave., Ste. 301
New York, NY   10018-8614   (212) 714-6668
Contact: Betsy King Militello, Exec. Dir.
FAX: (212) 714-0469; E-mail: info@namt.org; E-mail for Betsy King Militello: betsy@namt.org; URL: http://www.namt.org

Foundation type: Public charity
Purpose: Residencies to writers who are writing musical theatre and those who are producing new musicals in regional theatres around the country.
Publications: Application guidelines.
Financial data: Year ended 04/30/2012. Assets, $366,794 (M); Expenditures, $660,428; Total giving, $48,000.
Fields of interest: Theater (musical).

Type of support: Grants to individuals; Residencies.
Application information: Applications not accepted.
   Additional information: Applicant must be a member of the National Alliance for Musical Theater to apply. Unsolicited requests for funds not considered or acknowledged.
EIN: 133441160

6243
The National Arts Club
15 Gramercy Park S.
New York, NY   10003-1705   (212) 475-3424
Contact: Dianne B. Bernhard, Pres.
URL: http://www.nationalartsclub.org

Foundation type: Public charity
Purpose: Awards and scholarships by nomination only to artists, writers and singers.
Financial data: Year ended 06/30/2011. Assets, $4,361,537 (M); Expenditures, $2,591,007; Total giving, $13,733; Grants to individuals, totaling $13,733.
Fields of interest: Theater (playwriting); Music; Literature.
Type of support: Awards/grants by nomination only; Awards/prizes.
Application information: Applications not accepted.
   Additional information: Unsolicited requests for funds not considered or acknowledged.
EIN: 135265900

6244
The National Association of Asian Professionals, Inc.
P.O. Box 2628
New York, NY   10163   (646) 389-9199
Application e-mail: scholarship@naaap.org
E-mail: info@naaap.org; URL: http://www.naaap.org/

Foundation type: Public charity
Purpose: College scholarships to outstanding Asian Americans pursuing higher education.
Publications: Application guidelines.
Financial data: Year ended 12/31/2012. Assets, $38,678 (M); Expenditures, $24,621; Total giving, $600.
Fields of interest: Higher education; Asians/Pacific Islanders.
Type of support: Scholarships—to individuals.
Application information: Applications accepted. Application form required.
   Send request by: E-mail
   Deadline(s): Dec.
   Applicants should submit the following:
     1) Financial information
     2) GPA
     3) Essay
   Additional information: Preference will be given to individuals who are at least one quarter Asian by heritage.
EIN: 133348321

6245
National Cancer Center, Inc.
88 Sunnyside Blvd.
Plainview, NY   11803-1507   (516) 349-0610
Contact: Regina English, Exec. Dir.

Foundation type: Public charity
Purpose: Fellowships for research into the causes and cure of cancer.

Financial data: Year ended 03/31/2012. Assets, $1,395,256 (M); Expenditures, $2,589,514; Total giving, $448,000.
Fields of interest: Cancer research.
Type of support: Fellowships; Research.
Application information: Contact foundation for current application deadline/guidelines.
EIN: 131919715

6246
National Child Labor Committee
1501 Broadway, Ste. 1908
New York, NY   10036-5600   (212) 840-1801
Contact: Jeffrey Newman, Pres. and Exec. Dir.
FAX: (212) 768-0963;
E-mail: info@nationalchildlabor.org; URL: http://www.nationalchildlabor.org

Foundation type: Public charity
Purpose: Awards to those who have made a commitment to the well-being, growth, and development of youth.
Publications: Application guidelines.
Financial data: Year ended 12/31/2011. Assets, $47,047 (M); Expenditures, $237,330.
Fields of interest: Youth; Young adults.
Type of support: Awards/prizes.
Application information:
   Initial approach: Letter
   Deadline(s): Oct. 23
Program description:
   Lewis Hine Awards for Service to Children and Youth: These awards recognize the outstanding work being done on behalf of children and youth by individuals in the community. Ten recipients (five professionals and five volunteers) will be awarded for their unheralded and exceptional service to young people in a variety of fields (including health, welfare, education, and recreation) with a $1,000 award.
EIN: 135562999

6247
National Council of Jewish Women - New York Section
241 W. 72nd St.
New York, NY   10023-2703   (212) 687-5030
FAX: (212) 799-7283; E-mail: info@ncjwny.org; URL: http://www.ncjwny.org

Foundation type: Public charity
Purpose: Scholarships to physically challenged students attending college in an undergraduate or graduate program in the New York Metropolitan area.
Publications: Application guidelines; Informational brochure.
Financial data: Year ended 06/30/2012. Assets, $5,999,983 (M); Expenditures, $1,833,119; Total giving, $7,000; Grants to individuals, 7 grants totaling $7,000. Subtotal for scholarships—to individuals: 7 grants totaling $7,000.
Fields of interest: Higher education; Disabilities, people with.
Type of support: Scholarships—to individuals; Graduate support; Undergraduate support.
Application information: Applications accepted. Application form required.
   Send request by: Mail
   Deadline(s): Apr. 17
   Applicants should submit the following:
     1) Transcripts
     2) Essay
   Additional information: Application should also include two references.

Program description:

The Jackson-Stricks Scholarship Fund: This one time scholarship provides financial aid to students with physical challenges, for academic study or vocational training that leads to independent living.
EIN: 131624132

6248
National Down Syndrome Society
666 Broadway, 8th Fl.
New York, NY 10012-2317 (212) 460-9330
Contact: Jules Greenwald, V.P.
FAX: (212) 979-2873; E-mail: info@ndss.org;
Toll-free tel.: (800) 221-4602; URL: http://www.ndss.org

Foundation type: Public charity
Purpose: Research grants for the study of Down syndrome, and financial assistance to young adults with Down syndrome.
Publications: Informational brochure.
Financial data: Year ended 03/31/2012. Assets, $4,208,275 (M); Expenditures, $2,200,589; Total giving, $10,111; Grants to individuals, totaling $10,111.
Fields of interest: Down syndrome; Down syndrome research.
Type of support: Research; Grants for special needs.
Application information: Applications accepted. Application form required. Application form available on the grantmaker's web site.
> *Initial approach:* Telephone
> *Deadline(s):* June for Joshua O'Neill and Zeshan Tabani Enrichment Fund

Program descriptions:

Charles J. Epstein Research Award: The award provides seed money in grants, ranging from $5,000 to $35,000, to scientists and clinicians who seek to gain a better understanding of Down syndrome, thereby helping to improve the lives of individuals born with this genetic condition. Research awards are given in either basic or applied research, including sensory motor function, aging, health care, genetics, language, cognition, and behavior.

Joshua O'Neill and Zeshan Tabani Enrichment Fund: Through this fund, the society provides financial assistance to young adults with Down syndrome who wish to continue to enrich their lives by enrolling in postsecondary programs or taking enrichment classes that will help them to enrich life through employment, independent living skills, life skills or another way. Grants of up to $1,000 are available.
EIN: 132992567

6249
National Eating Disorders Association
165 W. 46th St., Ste. 402
New York, NY 10036-2522 (212) 575-6200
Contact: Lynn S. Grefe, Pres. and C.E.O.
FAX: (212) 575-1650;
E-mail: info@nationaleatingdisorders.org;
URL: http://www.nationaleatingdisorders.org

Foundation type: Public charity
Purpose: Grants of up to $10,000 are available to promising new scientists to advance eating disorder research.
Publications: Annual report; Informational brochure; Newsletter.
Financial data: Year ended 04/30/2012. Assets, $1,842,296 (M); Expenditures, $2,171,040; Total giving, $13,187; Grants to individuals, totaling $13,187.

Fields of interest: Eating disorders.
Type of support: Research.
Application information:
> *Initial approach:* Letter
> *Deadline(s):* Jan. 2 for Young Investigator Grants
> *Final notification:* May 30

EIN: 133444882

6250
The National Hemophilia Foundation
116 W. 32nd St., 11th Fl.
New York, NY 10001-3212 (212) 328-3700
Contact: Val Bias, C.E.O.
FAX: (212) 328-3777; E-mail: info@hemophilia.org;
Toll-free tel.: (800) 424-2634; URL: http://www.hemophilia.org

Foundation type: Public charity
Purpose: Grants to scientists for the cures of inherited bleeding disorders and the prevention and treatment of their complications through education, advocacy, and research.
Publications: Financial statement; Program policy statement.
Financial data: Year ended 12/31/2011. Assets, $13,060,987 (M); Expenditures, $10,878,241; Total giving, $657,896; Grants to individuals, totaling $657,896.
Fields of interest: Hemophilia research.
Type of support: Fellowships; Research.
Application information: Applications accepted. Application form required.
> *Initial approach:* Telephone, letter or e-mail
> *Deadline(s):* Vary
> *Additional information:* See web site for additional application guidelines.

Program descriptions:

Career Development Awards: Provides up to three awards, of $70,000 per year for up to three years, for projects that advance bleeding disorders research by promoting development of infrastructural resources and innovative studies by established investigators. Candidates must hold an M.D., Ph.D., or equivalent degree, and be an assistant professor (or equivalent) with up to six years experience since completion of training.

Clinical Fellowship Program: This fellowship is intended to increase the number of skilled clinicians committed to providing comprehensive care for individuals with bleeding and clotting disorders and to prepare candidates for academic careers. The program is designed for licensed physicians who are seeking hands-on training in bleeding and clotting disorders care and research. Training will take place in qualified hemophilia/thrombophilia treatment centers in the United States.

Judith Graham Pool Postdoctoral Research Fellowship Program: Provides up to four fellowships per year of $42,000 each for hemophilia research to investigators early in their careers. Fellowships are awarded through professional or graduate schools or research institutions. Applicants must enter the program from a doctoral, postdoctoral, internship, or residency-training program, and have completed their doctoral training. Established investigators or faculty members are not eligible.

Nursing Excellence Fellowship: Provides a fellowship of up to $13,500 for one year to 18 months to a registered nurse currently employed or interested in bleeding disorders care to conduct nursing research or clinical projects. Endorsement by a federally funded hemophilia treatment center is recommended. Only registered nurses from an accredited nursing school enrolled in a graduate nursing program or practicing hemophilia nursing care may apply.

Physical Therapy Excellence Fellowship: Provides $5,000 to improve physical therapy care of bleeding disorders. Applicants should be physical therapists currently working with bleeding disorder patients.

Social Work Excellence Fellowship: Provides one fellowship of up to $10,000 to a social worker interested in bleeding disorders care for conducting psychosocial research or a clinical project of benefit to the bleeding disorders community. Applicants must meet one of the following criteria: be an M.S.W. from an accredited school of social work; be a student in a D.S.W. program; or have a master's degree in a related field and be licensed by the state to practice as a masters level clinical social worker and work in a bleeding disorder program.
EIN: 135641857

6251
National Kidney Foundation, Inc.
30 E. 33rd St., Ste. 1100
New York, NY 10016-5337 (212) 889-2210
FAX: (212) 689-9261; E-mail: info@kidney.org;
Toll-free tel.: (800) 622-9010; URL: http://www.kidney.org

Foundation type: Public charity
Purpose: Research grants and fellowships to young physician scientists for training assistance in kidney disease. Scholarships and patient assistance to persons with kidney disease.
Publications: Application guidelines; Annual report; Newsletter; Occasional report.
Financial data: Year ended 06/30/2011. Assets, $23,274,999 (M); Expenditures, $50,568,381; Total giving, $3,750,987; Grants to individuals, totaling $3,750,987. Subtotal for grants for special needs: 2,781 grants totaling $1,582,623. Subtotal for scholarships—to individuals: 18 grants totaling $24,354. Subtotal for research: 105 grants totaling $3,168,663.
Fields of interest: Medical school/education; Kidney diseases; Kidney research; Diabetes research; Medical research.
International interests: Singapore.
Type of support: Fellowships; Research; Grants to individuals; Awards/prizes; Postdoctoral support; Postgraduate support; Travel grants.
Application information: Applications accepted. Application form available on the grantmaker's web site.
> *Additional information:* Application should include letter(s) of recommendation.

Program descriptions:

NKF/KDOQI Research Fellowships: This program is designed to provide training opportunities in epidemiology, biostatistics, translational research, health systems research, and/or health outcomes research, and to prepare young kidney investigators to address the gaps in knowledge identified in the process of developing Kidney Disease Outcomes Quality Initiative (KDOQI) Clinical Practice Guidelines. Eligible applicants must: have completed four years, but not more than four-and-a-half years, of research training (in addition to clinical training) beyond a doctoral degree (M.D., Ph.D., D.O., or its equivalent); must have received their last doctoral degree no more than ten years after submission of proposals; and must not have, or have had at any time, a faculty position at the level of assistant professor at any academic institution.

NKF/Mitsubishi Tanabe Pharma Corporation Fellowship for the Study of Uremia: Awarded in conjunction with the Mitsubishi Tanabe Pharma Corporation, this program is designed to stimulate investigation of the uremic state in humans, with the hopes of improving the understanding of the physiologic mechanisms underlying disease progression and symptom manifestation, and the association of these symptoms with the initiation of dialysis. Proposals should relate to one of the following topics: mechanisms of uremia in humans; progression in stage 4-5 chronic kidney disease (CKD), and how uremic toxins may contribute to progression; isolation and characterization of uremic toxins, methods for assessing patient-reported outcomes in stage 4-5 CKD; and impact of uremia on cardiometabolic function (e.g., oxidative stress, endothelic function, and insulin resistance)

Research Fellowships: This program works to foster the training of young and new investigators who demonstrate the potential to make contributions to the understanding and cure of kidney diseases. Both basic and clinical research activities will be funded. Eligible applicants must: have completed four years, but not more than four-and-a-half years, of research training (in addition to clinical training) beyond a doctoral degree (M.D., Ph.D., D.O., or its equivalent); must have received their last doctoral degree no more than ten years after submission of proposals; and must not have, or have had at any time, a faculty position at the level of assistant professor at any academic institution. Recipients will receive $50,000 per year.

Young Investigator Grants: This program works to support research in the fields of nephrology, urology, and related disciplines by individuals who have completed fellowship training and who hold junior faculty positions at university-affiliated medical centers in the U.S. Applications will be considered from individuals who will have completed research training in nephrology, urology, or closely-related fields prior to the start of the grant award and who intend to pursue research directly related to these areas.
EIN: 131673104

6252
National Medical Fellowships, Inc.
347 5th Ave., Ste. 510
New York, NY   10016   (212) 483-8880
Contact: Franca Gaudio, C.O.O.; Melissa Brito, Prog. Coord.
FAX: (212) 483-8897; E-mail: info@nmfonline.org; E-mail for Franca Gaudio: fgaudio@nmfonline.org; E-Mail for Melissa Brito: mbrito@nmfonline.org; URL: http://www.nmfonline.org/

Foundation type: Public charity
Purpose: Scholarships to medical students in the U.S. Fellowships and awards to minority medical students by nomination or recommendation by medical school deans.
Publications: Application guidelines; Informational brochure; Informational brochure (including application guidelines); Newsletter; Program policy statement.
Financial data: Year ended 06/30/2010. Assets, $1,363,996 (M); Expenditures, $1,516,236; Total giving, $521,800; Grants to individuals, totaling $451,000.
Fields of interest: Medical school/education; Minorities; African Americans/Blacks.
Type of support: Scholarships—to individuals; Awards/grants by nomination only; Awards/prizes.
Application information: Applications accepted. Application form required. Application form available on the grantmaker's web site.
  Initial approach: Letter, telephone, or e-mail
  Final notification: Recipients notified in six months

Applicants should submit the following:
  1) Resume
  2) Financial information
  3) Curriculum vitae
  4) Letter(s) of recommendation
  5) Essay
  6) Transcripts
Program descriptions:
  Franklin C. McLean Award: One award is presented annually to a senior student in recognition of outstanding academic achievement, leadership, and community service. The award includes a certificate of merit and $3,000 stipend.
  Hugh J. Andersen Memorial Scholarships: Up to five scholarships are annually presented to Minnesota residents enrolled in any accredited U.S. medical school, or students attending Minnesota medical schools. The scholarship includes a certificate of merit and $2,500 stipend.
  Irving Graef Memorial Scholarship: This two-year scholarship is presented annually to a third-year student and recognizes outstanding academic achievement, leadership, and community service. The scholarship is renewable in the fourth year if the award winner continues in good academic standing. One new scholarship is awarded annually; this honor includes a certificate of merit and annual renewable stipend of $2,000.
  Metropolitan Life Foundation Awards Program for Academic Excellence in Medicine: These need-based scholarships are awarded annually to second- through fourth-year underrepresented medical students in recognition of outstanding academic achievement and leadership. Seventeen awardees will receive a one-time award of $4,000 each.
  National Medical Association Special Awards Programs: The association annually recognizes and rewards African-American medical students for extraordinary accomplishments, academic excellence, leadership, and potential for outstanding contributions to medicine. The awards include the JNMA Awards for Medical Journalism, which recognize demonstrated skill in journalism and academic achievement; the Patti LaBelle Award; and the NMA Emerging Scholar Awards, presented for outstanding academic achievement, exceptional leadership and community service.
  Ralph W. Ellison Prize: One prize is presented annually; the honor includes a certificate of merit and a $500 stipend.
  William and Charlotte Cadbury Award: This award is presented annually to a senior medical student in recognition of outstanding academic achievement, leadership and community service. The designated Cadbury Scholar is honored during the annual meeting of the Association of American Medical Colleges. The award includes a certificate of merit and $2,000 stipend.
EIN: 362125449

6253
National Multiple Sclerosis Society
733 3rd Ave.
New York, NY   10017-3288   (212) 986-3240
Contact: Cynthia Zagieboylo, Pres. and C.E.O.
FAX: (212) 986-7981;
E-mail: cynthia.zagieboylo@nmss.org; Toll-free tel.: (800) 344-4867; URL: http://www.nationalmssociety.org

Foundation type: Public charity
Purpose: Research and research fellowship grants to support scientific studies or investigation for the eventual cure of multiple sclerosis.

Publications: Application guidelines; Annual report; Financial statement; Informational brochure; Newsletter; Program policy statement.
Financial data: Year ended 09/30/2012. Assets, $78,420,407 (M); Expenditures, $101,141,538; Total giving, $39,839,720; Grants to individuals, totaling $1,283,537.
Fields of interest: Multiple sclerosis; Multiple sclerosis research.
Type of support: Research.
Application information: Applications accepted. Application form required. Application form available on the grantmaker's web site.
  Initial approach: Letter or telephone
  Deadline(s): Early Feb., early Oct. for Research Grants; June 1 and Dec. 1 for McFarlin Travel Awards or NMSS Postdoctoral Fellows; Sept. 1 for Career Transition preliminary application; Nov. 1 for Dystel Prize for MS Research; Aug. for all others
  Additional information: See web site for specific grant deadlines.
Program descriptions:
  Career Transition Fellowship: Awards approximately $550,000 over five years to support a two-year period of advanced postdoctoral training in MS research and the first three years of research support in a new faculty appointment. Applicants must hold a doctoral degree (M.D., Ph.D., or equivalent) and must be in a research-oriented postdoctoral training program at an academic, government, or nonprofit research institution.
  Dale McFarlin Travel Awards for NMSS Postdoctoral Fellows: Stipends, ranging from $1,000 to $1,500, will be made available to society fellows to attend a scientific meeting pertinent to their research project and multiple sclerosis. Stipends are intended to help defray costs of travel and lodging expenses and meeting registration fees.
  Daniel Haughton Senior Faculty Awards: This award will be granted to established MS investigators seeking support for specialized training in a field which they are not currently expert, inasmuch as such training will enhance their capacity to conduct research related to multiple sclerosis. This award can also be used for sabbatical support for qualified individuals.
  Harry Weaver Neuroscience Scholar Awards: A limited number of awards will be offered to highly-qualified candidates who have concluded their research training and begun academic careers as independent investigators in an area related to multiple sclerosis. Awards are designed to provide salary and grant support for a five-year period, thus permitting the awardee to establish competence in his/her chosen research area. Eligible applicants must hold a doctoral degree (M.D., Ph.D., or equivalent) and have sufficient research training at the postdoctoral level to be capable of independent research; individuals who have already conducted independent research for more than five years after postdoctoral training are ineligible.
  Health Care Delivery and Policy Grants: Investigators funded by this program study issues of health care access and quality to improve care for people with MS, including current priorities in the organization, funding, quality, outcomes, and costs of MS care. This program aims to provide results that can be influential in improving government and private-sector policies, service, and benefit programs nationwide. Each year, contract requests-for-proposals are distributed, with an invitation to prospective applicants to submit brief letters-of-intent; program priorities generally change every year.
  John Dystel Prize for Multiple Sclerosis Research: This $15,000 prize recognizes outstanding

contributions to research in the understanding, treatment, or prevention of multiple sclerosis.

Mentor-Based Postdoctoral Fellowship in Rehabilitation Research: These fellowships support mentors and institutions that provide training of postdoctoral fellows in research related to multiple sclerosis rehabilitation, which may serve to advance the mission of the society. This program provides support for a mentor-institution combination, which is responsible for the recruitment, selection, and training of postdoctoral fellows to pursue a career in rehabilitation research applied to multiple sclerosis and similar disorders. Eligible mentors must hold a faculty appointment at an accredited institution, and have adequate research funding and support to provide an appropriate training environment for a postdoctoral fellow; eligible fellows must have up to (but not more than) 36 months of previous postdoctoral training, and must hold or be candidates for a Ph.D., M.D., or equivalent degree.

National MS Society Scholarship Program: Awards range in amount from $1,000 to $3,000. Recipients are chosen based on financial need, an academic record that shows the applicant is able to succeed in his or her chosen area. Applicant must be a U.S. citizen or legal resident who plan to enroll in an undergraduate course of study at an accredited two-or four-year college, university, or vocational/technical school within the U.S. Applicants must be enrolled in at least six credit hours per semester in course work leading to a degree, license, or certificate.

Postdoctoral Fellowships: Funding of up to $50,000 per year for up to three years is available toward the support of training of postdoctoral fellows in studies related to multiple sclerosis, which may serve to advance the mission of the society. Fellowships will be offered to unusually promising recipients of M.D., Ph.D., or equivalent degrees when it appears that the program of training to be supported by the grant will enhance the likelihood that the trainee will perform meaningful and independent research relevant to multiple sclerosis in the future, and obtain a suitable position which will enable them to do so. Eligible applicants must have no more than three years of previous postdoctoral training.

Ralph I. Straus Award for Multiple Sclerosis: This prize honors outstanding research in multiple sclerosis and related fields.

Research Grants: Funding is available for the support of studies related to multiple sclerosis, which may serve in any way to advance the mission of the society. Both fundamental and applied studies, non-clinical or clinical in nature, including projects in patient management, care, and rehabilitation, are eligible for funding. Funding may be used for salaries for professional and nonprofessional personnel (up to $51,036 per year), patient costs, permanent equipment, consumable supplies, travel, other expenditures not included in the above categories, and indirect costs (of up to 10 percent of total request)

Sylvia Lawry Physician Fellowship Award for Training in MS Clinical Trials: Funding of up to $65,000 per year is available for individuals with an M.D. or equivalent medical degree to acquire formal training, under the tutelage of an established investigator, in key elements associated with conducting clinical trials in MS, including (but not limited to) design of study protocols, recruitment of patients, power calculations, randomization procedures, use of controls, identification of appropriate entrance and exclusions criteria, identification of primary and secondary outcome measures, maintenance and assessment of blinding, informed consent, safety monitoring and

evaluation, and data access and statistical analysis. Eligible applicants must have received an M.D. or equivalent medical degree from an accredited institution, must be licensed to practice medicine in the U.S., and must have completed (in whole or in part) training in a medical specialty related to multiple sclerosis.
EIN: 135661935

6254
National Sculpture Society, Inc.
c/o American Numismatic Society
75 Varick St., 11th Fl.
New York, NY   10013
Contact: Gwen Pier, Exec. Dir.
URL: http://www.nationalsculpture.org

Foundation type: Operating foundation
Purpose: Grants and scholarships to encourage the creation and appreciation of sculpture throughout the U.S.
Publications: Financial statement; Informational brochure (including application guidelines).
Financial data: Year ended 12/31/2012. Assets, $9,968,923 (M); Expenditures, $620,358; Total giving, $25,150; Grants to individuals, 13 grants totaling $19,150 (high: $5,000, low: $100).
Fields of interest: Arts education; Sculpture.
Type of support: Grants to individuals; Scholarships—to individuals; Awards/prizes.
Application information: Application form not required. Application form available on the grantmaker's web site.
    Initial approach: Letter
    Copies of proposal: 1
    Deadline(s): June 1 for Scholarship, Sept. 30 for Alex J. Ettl Grant and Henry Hering Award
    Additional information: See web site for additional guidelines.
Program descriptions:
    Alex J. Ettl Grant: The unrestricted prize of $4,000 is awarded annually to a figurative or realist sculptor who has demonstrated a commitment to sculpting and outstanding ability in his or her body of work. The grant is for a mature body or work, sculpture created in workshop or instructional settings should not be submitted.
    Henry Hering - Art and Architecture Award: The award is presented as the occasion warrants for outstanding collaboration between architect, owner and sculptor in the distinguished use of sculpture in an architectural project. The jury is looking for excellence in an architectural project in which the architect collaborated with the sculptor and the owner or a site. The winning entry will receive three medals and three hand-lettered citations, one each for architect, owner and sculptor.
    Scholarships: Four scholarships of $2,000 each are available for students of sculpture. The work is inspired by nature or figurative or realist sculpture. The educational institution the student attends must be an accredited U.S. institution. Scholarships are paid directly to the academic institution through which the student applies.
    The Dexter Jones Award: The award is an unrestricted prize of $5,000 presented annually to an emerging sculptor for an outstanding work of sculpture in bas-relief. Each competitor must be an emerging sculptor, between the ages of 18 and 39. Applicants must be U.S. citizens or residents with a social security number. The use of figurative or realist sculpture is of greatest interest.
EIN: 131656673

6255
National Urban Fellows, Inc.
(also known as NUF, Inc.)
102 W. 38th St., Ste. 700
New York, NY   10018-3613   (212) 730-1700
Contact: Miguel A. Garcia, Jr., Prog. Dir.
FAX: (212) 730-1823; E-mail: mgarciajr@nuf.org;
URL: http://www.nuf.org

Foundation type: Public charity
Purpose: Fellowships for mid-career men and women to the School of Public Affairs at Bernard Baruch College, NY.
Publications: Application guidelines; Annual report; Occasional report.
Financial data: Year ended 09/30/2011. Assets, $2,836,254 (M); Expenditures, $4,398,144; Total giving, $1,217,087; Grants to individuals, totaling $1,217,087.
Type of support: Fellowships.
Application information: Applications accepted. Application form required. Application form available on the grantmaker's web site.
    Initial approach: Application
    Deadline(s): Varies
    Applicants should submit the following:
        1) Transcripts
        2) Resume
        3) Letter(s) of recommendation
        4) Essay
    Additional information: See web site for additional guidelines.
Program description:
    National Urban Fellows Program: The program is a 14-month, full-time graduate program comprised of two semesters of academic course work and a nine-month mentorship, leading to a Master of Public Administration (MPA) degree from the Bernard M. Baruch College School of Public Affairs at the City University of New York. Following graduation, fellows will be able to effect positive changes in communities nationally and internationally, contributing their newly-acquired leadership skills to public service for the betterment of communities and the nation. Fellows receive a $25,000 stipend, health insurance, a book allowance, relocation and travel reimbursement, and full payment of tuition, in addition to their ongoing personal and professional development.
EIN: 237404350

6256
NCCC Foundation, Inc.
Eugene Dswenson
3111 Saunders Settlement Rd.
Sanborn, NY   14132-9487   (718) 614-6222
URL: http://www.niagaracc.suny.edu/foundation/

Foundation type: Public charity
Purpose: Scholarships for students attending Niagara County Community College, NY, pursuing their educational goals.
Financial data: Year ended 08/31/2011. Assets, $6,775,568 (M); Expenditures, $726,651; Total giving, $279,149; Grants to individuals, totaling $279,149.
Fields of interest: College (community/junior).
Type of support: Scholarships—to individuals; Support to graduates or students of specific schools.
Application information: Applications accepted. Application form required.
    Send request by: On-line
    Deadline(s): Oct.
    Applicants should submit the following:
        1) Transcripts
        2) Letter(s) of recommendation

3) Essay

Additional information: Application should also include career goals, and extracurricular or community service activities. See web site for additional guidelines and a listing of scholarships.

EIN: 161315885

6257
Needham September 11th Scholarship Fund

c/o Needham & Company, LLC
445 Park Ave.
New York, NY   10022-2606   (212) 705-0293
Contact: Kathleen Mumma

Foundation type: Company-sponsored foundation
Purpose: Scholarships to dependents of victims of the World Trade Center attacks for a private secondary and/or college-level education.
Financial data: Year ended 12/31/2012. Assets, $1,146,027 (M); Expenditures, $72,166; Total giving, $65,000; Grants to individuals, 12 grants totaling $65,000 (high: $12,000, low: $2,500).
Fields of interest: Disasters, 9/11/01.
Type of support: Undergraduate support.
Application information: Applications accepted. Application form required. Application form available on the grantmaker's web site.
  Initial approach: E-mail
  Applicants should submit the following:
    1) Transcripts
    2) Essay
    3) Financial information
    4) GPA
Company name: Needham & Company, LLC
EIN: 134196881

6258
The Netherland-America Foundation, Inc.

82 Wall St., Ste. 709
New York, NY   10005-3613   (212) 825-1221
Contact: Angela Molenaar, Exec. Dir.
FAX: (212) 825-9105; E-mail: info@TheNAF.org;
E-mail for Angela Molenaar:
amolenaar@theNAF.org; URL: http://www.thenaf.org

Foundation type: Public charity
Purpose: Fellowships and educational loans to graduate and postgraduate students in the Netherlands and the U.S. Grants to young, beginning and aspiring visual and performing artists in the Netherlands and the U.S.
Publications: Application guidelines; Annual report; Financial statement; Grants list; Newsletter; Program policy statement.
Financial data: Year ended 12/31/2012. Assets, $4,641,649 (M); Expenditures, $821,801; Total giving, $327,618; Grants to individuals, totaling $115,079.
Fields of interest: Visual arts; Performing arts.
International interests: Netherlands.
Type of support: Fellowships; Graduate support; Postgraduate support.
Application information: Applications accepted. Application form not required. Application form available on the grantmaker's web site.
  Initial approach: Application for educational support and letter of inquiry for the arts
  Send request by: Mail
  Copies of proposal: 8
  Deadline(s): Mar. 1, May 1, Sept. 1, and Dec. 1 for educational support and Feb. 1, May 1, Aug. 1, and Nov. 1 for the arts
  Applicants should submit the following:

1) Transcripts
2) Resume
3) Letter(s) of recommendation
4) GPA
5) Curriculum vitae
6) Budget Information
Additional information: Application should also include eight proposals and work samples for the arts. No application form required for the arts. One proposal is required for educational support.
EIN: 132989216

6259
Netzach Foundation

156 W. 56th St., Ste. 1701
New York, NY   10019

Foundation type: Independent foundation
Purpose: Grants to individuals for religious and literary tutoring, and general welfare.
Financial data: Year ended 03/31/2013. Assets, $4,432,953 (M); Expenditures, $24,734; Total giving, $1,000.
Fields of interest: Education, services; Jewish agencies & synagogues; Religion.
Type of support: Scholarships—to individuals; Grants for special needs.
Application information: Applications not accepted.
  Additional information: Unsolicited requests for funds not considered or acknowledged.
EIN: 136967224

6260
New Alternatives for Children, Inc.

37 W. 26th St., 6th Fl.
New York, NY   10010-1006   (212) 696-1550
Contact: Arlene Goldsmith Ph.D., Exec. Dir.
FAX: (212) 696-1602;
E-mail: info@newalternativesforchildren.org;
URL: http://www.nac-inc.org

Foundation type: Public charity
Purpose: Specific assistance to children with medical disabilities and/or chronic illnesses, and their families, living in the five boroughs of New York City. Families must be enrolled as agency clients.
Publications: Annual report; Newsletter.
Financial data: Year ended 06/30/2012. Assets, $4,152,025 (M); Expenditures, $16,985,811.
Fields of interest: Adoption; Foster care; Family resources and services, disability.
Type of support: Grants for special needs.
Application information: Applications not accepted.
  Additional information: Unsolicited requests for funds not considered or acknowledged.
EIN: 133149298

6261
New England Society in the City of Brooklyn

c/o David Goodrich
155 Congress St.
Brooklyn, NY   11201-6103
Contact: Harrison M. Davis III
Application address: 175 Adams St., Apt. 1G, Brooklyn, NY 11201-; URL: http://www.newenglandsociety.org/

Foundation type: Independent foundation
Purpose: Scholarships for undergraduate full time students for attendance either at a preparatory

school or college in New England, or Prep school located in Brooklyn or Long Island, New York.
Publications: Application guidelines; Program policy statement.
Financial data: Year ended 12/31/2012. Assets, $631,935 (M); Expenditures, $45,807; Total giving, $34,500.
Fields of interest: Secondary school/education; Higher education.
Type of support: Scholarships—to individuals.
Application information: Applications accepted. Application form required. Interview required.
  Initial approach: Letter or telephone
  Send request by: Mail or e-mail
  Applicants should submit the following:
    1) SAT
    2) Financial information
  Additional information: Application should also include at least two references. Permanent residence within the borough of Brooklyn or Long Island is required throughout the period the scholarship is in effect.
EIN: 116036708

6262
New Music USA, Inc.

90 John St., No. 312
New York, NY   10038-3243   (212) 645-6949
Contact: Ed Harsh, Pres. and C.E.O.
E-mail: info@newmusicusa.org; URL: https://www.newmusicusa.org/

Foundation type: Public charity
Purpose: Financial assistance to musicians in the early stages of their careers.
Financial data: Year ended 06/30/2012. Assets, $19,643,796 (M); Expenditures, $2,512,377; Total giving, $910,726; Grants to individuals, 4 grants totaling $232,975 (high: $74,975, low: $15,000).
Fields of interest: Music.
Type of support: Grants to individuals; Grants for special needs.
Application information: Applications accepted. Application form required.
  Additional information: Contact the organization for additional application guidelines.
Program descriptions:
  Composer Assistance Program: This program aims to help composers offset costs associated with live premieres and public readings of new or significantly revised works. Supported expenses include copying costs; score and part extraction and reproduction; travel and lodging; costs for obtaining copyrighted material; and more. The maximum one-time grant is $5,000. Most grants are between $1,000 and $3,000.
  MetLife Creative Connections Program: This program provides support for composers to participate in public activities related to specific performances of their original music. By supporting the composer's interaction with audiences, performers, arts organizations, and local communities, the program aims to increase public awareness and enhance the creative artist's role in society. Applicants may request amounts ranging from $250 to $3,500, to be made payable directly to the composer. The program supports approximately three hundred composers working with approximately one hundred and fifty organizations annually. The average award is close to $500 per composer.
  Music Alive: This program, administered in partnership with the League of American Orchestras, offers financial and administrative support for composer-in-residence positions with orchestral ensembles.

Van Lier Fellowships: The purpose of the Fellowship is to provide financial support for young composers in the early stages of their careers, working in any style of music or sound art. Funds can be used for any purpose including the creation of new work, the purchasing of music/tech equipment, travel, or research and development. The Fellowship is open to African-American and Latin-American composers thirty-two years of age or younger. The applicant must be a full-time resident of New York City (any borough) and show financial need. The applicant must not be enrolled in a degree-granting program at the time of application (i.e. no students). The one-year fellowship award is $7,000. Additional monetary support of $1,000 will be provided if the composer develops and participates in an educational outreach program with students and/or youth groups during the time of their fellowship.
EIN: 130432981

6263
New Visions for Public Schools, Inc.
(formerly Fund for New York City Public Education)
320 W. 13th St.
New York, NY 10014-1200 (212) 645-5110
Contact: Robert L. Hughes, Pres.
Online address for teachers:
www.fundforteachers.org
FAX: (212) 645-7409;
E-mail: jgreenberg@newvisions.org; URL: http://www.newvisions.org

Foundation type: Public charity
Purpose: Scholarships to graduating high school seniors from New Visions schools, NY for attendance at an accredited four-year college or university. Fellowships for summer learning for New York City teachers.
Publications: Annual report; Informational brochure.
Financial data: Year ended 06/30/2011. Assets, $40,056,133 (M); Expenditures, $17,996,168; Total giving, $2,963,434; Grants to individuals, totaling $1,585,252.
Fields of interest: Secondary school/education; Charter schools; Higher education.
Type of support: Fellowships; Scholarships—to individuals; Support to graduates or students of specific schools.
Application information: Applications accepted.
Send request by: Online
Deadline(s): Feb. 1 for scholarships, Mar. for summer fellowship
Additional information: Application for scholarships should include an essay, two letters of recommendation and a transcript. See web site for additional application guidelines.
Program descriptions:
Funds for Teachers: New Visions for Public Schools has collaborated with Fund for Teachers, a nonprofit organization committed to recognizing outstanding and dedicated teachers across the U.S. Applicants must teach in a 9th through 12th grade classroom, have a minimum of three years of classroom teaching experience by June, spend at least 50 percent of a full-time position in the classroom, and commit to teaching in the NYC public school system for the school year, following completion of the project. Teachers can apply for grants of up to $7,500 for an individual with a project in Asia, $5,000 for an individual with a project elsewhere, or $10,000 for those applying as a team (in all locations).
New Visions Scholarship Fund: The fund awards up to $20,000 over four years of full-time graduate

study for students who have demonstrated exceptional academic achievement, leadership, strong character, and financial need. Applicants must be U.S. citizens or legal permanent residents.
EIN: 133538961

6264
The New World Foundation
666 West End Ave.
New York, NY 10025-7357 (212) 249-1023
Contact: Colin Greer, Pres.
FAX: (212) 472-0508; E-mail: info@newwf.org;
URL: http://www.newwf.org

Foundation type: Public charity
Purpose: Fellowships to those nominated or employed by qualified, tax-exempt organizations.
Publications: Biennial report (including application guidelines); Financial statement.
Financial data: Year ended 09/30/2011. Assets, $33,876,147 (M); Expenditures, $16,428,171; Total giving, $13,136,047.
Fields of interest: Education; Health care; AIDS; AIDS research; Human services; Children/youth, services; Minorities/immigrants, centers/services; International peace/security; Arms control; Race/intergroup relations; Civil/human rights; Community/economic development; Research; Minorities.
Type of support: Program development; Conferences/seminars; Seed money; Fellowships; Awards/grants by nomination only.
Application information: Applications not accepted.
EIN: 131919791

6265
New York Academy of Medicine
1216 5th Ave., 103rd St.
New York, NY 10029-5202 (212) 822-7200
Contact: Gerard Lebeda
URL: http://www.nyam.org/

Foundation type: Public charity
Purpose: Grants to researchers to further their studies in neurology, urology, microbiology, dentistry, and cardiovascular disease, primarily in NY.
Publications: Annual report; Grants list; Newsletter.
Financial data: Year ended 12/31/2011. Assets, $101,052,606 (M); Expenditures, $19,588,458; Total giving, $906,317; Grants to individuals, totaling $445,731.
Fields of interest: Medical research.
Type of support: Fellowships; Awards/prizes.
Application information: Applications accepted. Application form required. Application form available on the grantmaker's web site.
Initial approach: Letter
Deadline(s): Jan. 16 for Elsberg Fellowship; Jan. 23 for Hoar Fellowship; Jan. 30 for Valentine Research Grants; Feb. 6 for Glorney-Raisbeck Fellowships; Feb. 13 for Beer Research Fellowship; Feb. 20 for Glorney-Raisbeck Student Grants; Mar. 21 for Rogers Fellowship
Final notification: May 2nd for David E. Rogers Fellowship
Additional information: Contact foundation for further eligibility requirements and current deadlines for programs without specific deadlines.
Program descriptions:
Audrey and William H. Helfand Fellowship in the History of Medicine and Public Health: This program

supports research using the academy's library resources (for at least four weeks) for scholarly study on the history of medicine and public health. Proposals are accepted from anyone, regardless of citizenship, academic discipline, or academic status; preference will be given to those whose research will take advantage of resources that are uniquely available at the academy, individuals at the early stages of their career, and applications which include an emphasis on the use of visual materials held within the academy collections and elsewhere. Each fellow receives a stipend of $5,000 to support travel, lodging, and incidental expenses.
Charles A. Elsberg Fellowship in Neurological Surgery: This fellowship supports research training in the specialty of neurological surgery for individuals who have completed, or will shortly complete, accredited residency training in neurological surgery; and who intend to use research training for continued development of an academic career in this field. Eligible applicants must have, or will have, completed an accredited neurological surgery residency program by June of the application year, and whose career direction suggests eligibility for subsequent research support; candidates must be at the start of their academic careers, having completed their residency training within the past year or two, and must also be board-certified or eligible for certification by the beginning of the grant period. Fellowships are awarded for up to $50,000.
Dr. Steve Miller Humanism in Medicine Lecture, supported by the Arnold P. Gold Foundation: This fund provides an annual lecture and award, as well as education and research opportunities, that demonstrate an investigate new ways of teaching human, social, and cultural dimensions of illness, health, and health care. In addition, the fund offers mini-grants to support work by medical students, curriculum development, and research in humanism by students, residents, and young faculty members.
Edward N. Gibbs Memorial Lecture and Award in Nephrology: This prize is awarded to a physician in practice in the U.S. for the best original work in the etiology, pathology, and treatment of diseases of the kidney. Nominations are sought from physician-scientists who have dedicated their careers to advances in nephrology or are presently making cutting-edge discoveries in the field. Eligible candidates must hold an M.D. degree and be citizens of the U.S.; recipients will be awarded a $7,500 honorarium, as well as reimbursement for travel expenses associated with the lecture.
Ferdinand C. Valentine Fellowship for Research in Urology: Up to four grants of $3,500 each are available for students pursuing a research project seeking better understanding of the causes, prevention, and treatment of cardiovascular disease, with an additional $500 in lab support (to be paid to the laboratory or department at which the student will conduct the research). Funding will be provided for research projects lasting between ten and twelve weeks in the summer of the application year, preferably between the first and second years of medical school, but medical students in any year of their education may apply. Preference will be given to M.D. candidates attending medical school or conducting research in the greater New York area (including New York City, Long Island, Westchester County, or New Jersey); projects outside the greater New York area will be considered if a mentor who is located within the greater New York area is identified. Candidates must be U.S. citizens, permanent residents of the U.S., or authorized to work in the U.S. for the period of time covered by the proposal award.

Gladys Brook Internship: This internship is designed to provide an opportunity for interested individuals for training in book and paper conservation. Internships include: examining and applying book and paper conservation principles; understanding the steps in determining conservation needs; learning which materials and structures are appropriate for use in repairing, binding, and storing rare and fragile materials; and executing agreed-upon conservation treatments. Eligible applicants must: have some experience in the field of bookbinding and/or book conservation, and possess a desire to gain expertise through hands-on work in a functioning conservation laboratory; have aesthetic appreciation and the manual dexterity to work with delicate and fragile materials; and have student or working visas (if they are not U.S. citizens). Internships are accompanied by a $5,000 stipend.

Mary and David Hoar Fellowship in the Prevention and Treatment of Hip Fracture: The fellowship offers a two-year, $100,000 grant in support of clinical, epidemiologic and health services research in the prevention and treatment of hip fractures. Candidates must hold an MD, PhD, or equivalent degree and must conduct their research in a supervised program in the greater New York area.

Millie and Richard Brock Lecture, Award, and Visiting Professorship in Pediatrics: This award sponsors a nationally-recognized leader in pediatrics to engage in a one- to two-day visiting professorship at a New York-area pediatrics training program, to deliver an annual lecture, and to receive an award for distinguished contributions to pediatrics. Professorships should be part of a program that includes a grand rounds lecture, as well as teaching interactions with medical students, pediatric residents, fellows, and members of the attending staff. Lectures must address issues concerned with providing care for underserved children; suggested topics include, but are not restricted to, childhood nutrition, HIV/AIDS, substance abuse, child abuse, asthma, violence, and environmental issues such as lead poisoning. Awards include a $1,000 honorarium and all expenses for travel, lodging, and meals.

Paul Klemperer Fellowship in the History of Medicine: This fellowship supports research using the academy's library resources for scholarly study of the history of medicine. Applications will be accepted from anyone, regardless of citizenship, academic discipline, or academic status; preference will be given to those whose research will take advantage of resources that are uniquely available at the academy, and individuals in the early stages of their careers. Fellows receive a $5,000 stipend to support travel, lodging, and incidental expenses.
EIN: 131656674

6266
New York City "Bravest" Scholarship Fund
225 Broadway, Ste. 401
New York, NY 10007-3001   (212) 293-9300
Contact: Alexander Hagan, Pres.
FAX: (212) 292-1560;
E-mail: administrator@ufoa.org; URL: http://www.ufoa.org

Foundation type: Public charity
Purpose: Scholarships to children of fire officers and firefighters of the New York City Fire Department who have died while on active duty.
Financial data: Year ended 12/31/2011. Assets, $2,459,844 (M); Expenditures, $168,551.

Fields of interest: Disasters, fire prevention/control.
Type of support: Emergency funds; Employee-related scholarships.
Application information: Applications accepted. Application form required.
  Deadline(s): May 1
EIN: 134055458

6267
New York City Police Foundation, Inc.
555 5th Ave., 15th Fl.
New York, NY 10017-2416   (212) 751-8170
Contact: Susan L. Birnbaum, Pres. and C.E.O.
FAX: (212) 750-7616;
E-mail: info@nycpolicefoundation.org; URL: http://www.nycpolicefoundation.org

Foundation type: Public charity
Purpose: Scholarships to eligible police officers and their family members based on financial need and academic excellence who are employed with the NYPD.
Publications: Annual report; Financial statement; Grants list; Informational brochure; Program policy statement.
Financial data: Year ended 06/30/2012. Assets, $15,388,445 (M); Expenditures, $7,420,469; Total giving, $2,840,837; Grants to individuals, totaling $125,550.
Fields of interest: Crime/law enforcement, police agencies; Crime/law enforcement.
Type of support: Employee-related scholarships.
Application information: Applications not accepted.
  Additional information: Unsolicited applications not accepted.
Company name: New York City Police Department
EIN: 132711338

6268
The New York Classical Club
c/o Susanna McFadden, Fordham University
113 W. 60th St., No. LL423
New York, NY 10023   (212) 636-7739
Contact: Susana McFadden, Secy.
Application Address: c/o Fordham University, 60th St. 423 New Yorl, NY 10023
E-mail: ctorigian@gmail.com; URL: http://www.nyclassicalclub.org/

Foundation type: Independent foundation
Purpose: Scholarships, fellowships and prizes to individuals in the classical disciplines.
Financial data: Year ended 03/31/2013. Assets, $328,512 (M); Expenditures, $28,569; Total giving, $13,605; Grants to individuals, 18 grants totaling $13,605 (high: $4,500, low: $100).
Fields of interest: Language (classical); Education.
International interests: Greece; Italy.
Type of support: Fellowships; Scholarships—to individuals; Awards/prizes.
Application information: Applications accepted. Application form required.
  Send request by: Mail
  Deadline(s): Jan. 15 for Rome/Athens Summer Scholarships, Feb. 1 for President's Grant, Mar. 1 for Phyllis Winquist Tuition Assistance
  Additional information: See web site for additional guidelines.
Program descriptions:
Phyllis Winquist Tuition Assistance Awards: The award supports candidates who are taking courses to acquire or improve skills in teaching Latin or Ancient Greek in grades 7-12. Candidates must be paid members of the NYCC at the time of applying

and during the twelve months of the funded period. They must either be teaching Classics in grades 7-12 or show clear indication of doing so in the near future.

President's Grant: Grants of $500 to $1,000 are available to support projects promoting interest in classical antiquity in the New York area. Applicants must be current NY Classical Club members.

Rome/Athens Summer Scholarships: Scholarships of up to $5,000 are available for Club members toward the cost of study in the summer session of the American Academy in Rome, the American School of Classical Studies at Athens, or the Paideia Institute for study in Greece and/or Rome. All members in the third consecutive year of paid membership in the Club are eligible to apply for the award, although preference is given to secondary school teachers and graduate students.
EIN: 133970766

6269
The New York Community Trust
909 3rd Ave., 22nd Fl.
New York, NY 10022-4752   (212) 686-0010
Contact: For grant inquiries: Mary Gentile, Exec. Asst., Grants and Special Projects
FAX: (212) 532-8528; E-mail: aw@nyct-cfi.org; Tel. for grant inquiries: (212) 686-0010, ext. 554; URL: http://www.nycommunitytrust.org

Foundation type: Community foundation
Purpose: Fellowships to New York City's disadvantaged young people who are seriously dedicated to a career in the arts.
Publications: Application guidelines; Annual report; Financial statement; Grants list; Informational brochure (including application guidelines); Newsletter; Occasional report; Program policy statement (including application guidelines).
Financial data: Year ended 12/31/2012. Assets, $2,147,925,714 (M); Expenditures, $148,327,384; Total giving, $135,740,478. Fellowships amount not specified.
Fields of interest: Music; Music composition; Arts; Minorities; African Americans/Blacks; Hispanics/Latinos; Economically disadvantaged.
Type of support: Fellowships; Awards/prizes.
Application information: Applications accepted. Application form required.
  Initial approach: Application
  Deadline(s): Apr. 30
  Additional information: See web site for additional information.
Program description:
Edward and Sally Van Lier Arts Fellowships: The Edward and Sally Van Lier Fund of The New York Community Trust provides support for talented, culturally diverse, economically disadvantaged young people who are seriously dedicated to a career in the arts. This round of grants will provide assistance to arts organizations in all disciplines to help individual artists at the post-college level make the transition from formal training to professional careers. Grants of one to two years will be awarded to a small number of arts organizations to sponsor two or more artist fellowships. The purpose of the fellowships is to enable young artists to achieve a significant professional credit that can lead to future career opportunities. Grants will range up to a maximum of $60,000 for each organization, depending upon the number and size of fellowships covered. The amount that the fund will contribute to an individual fellowship will be up to $10,000 a year. See web site for additional information.
EIN: 133062214

6270
New York Library Association

6021 State Farm Rd.
Guilderland, NY   12084-9503   (518) 432-6952
FAX: (518) 427-1697; E-mail: info@nyla.org;
Toll-free tel.: (800) 252-6952; URL: http://
www.nyla.org

Foundation type: Public charity
Purpose: Scholarships to enable interested and deserving students to pursue a Master's Degree in Library Science at an ALA-accredited library school in New York State.
Publications: Application guidelines.
Financial data: Year ended 06/30/2011. Assets, $1,896,833 (M); Expenditures, $386,197.
Fields of interest: Libraries/library science.
Type of support: Graduate support.
Application information: Applications accepted. Application form required. Application form available on the grantmaker's web site.
Initial approach: E-mail
Deadline(s): Aug. 31 for Mary Bobinski Innovative Public Library Director Award; Sept. 2 for NYLA-Dewey Fellowship Award; Sept. 30 for NYLA-Dewey Scholarship Award
Final notification: Recipients notified Dec. 1
Additional information: Application should include letter(s) of recommendation.
Program descriptions:
Mary Bobinski Innovative Public Library Director Award: This $1,200 prize is given annually to a public library directors who, during the past two years, developed or implemented an innovative program leading to an increase in financial support and/or usage of their library by: demonstrating the value and importance of their public library to community leaders and local government officials; enhancing the image of the public library through an innovative public relations program publicizing the resources and services in multiple media formats; developing new programs and services to attract users and non-users; and demonstrate evidence of success.
NYLA-Dewey Fellowship Award: Awards of up to $1,000 are available to eligible applicants to attend the association's annual conference. Eligible applicants must have at least five years' experience as a library, a record of accomplishment in the library profession, and involvement in activities to advance the library community. In addition to the cash award, each fellow will receive a $100 gift certificate to use at the association's store.
NYLA-Dewey Scholarship Award: A $1,000 award will be given to enable an interested and deserving student to pursue a master's degree in library science in an American Library Association (ALA)-accredited library school in New York State. Eligible applicants must: be a full- or part-time student, or be accepted into an ALA-accredited library school or school of information science located in New York State; and have maintained at least a B average during the semester preceding the award (transcripts must be provided to receive payment). Awards are intended to cover tuition costs and related expenses; in addition, the winner will receive free attendance at the association's annual conference.
EIN: 141407060

6271
The New York Public Library Astor, Lenox and Tilden Foundations

(also known as The New York Public Library)
188 Madison Ave., 5th Fl.
New York, NY   10016-4314   (212) 592-7403
Contact: Paul Leclerc, Pres. and C.E.O.
URL: http://www.nypl.org

Foundation type: Public charity
Purpose: Research grant and fellowships to writers and scholars in the fields of humanities, social sciences, and black studies.
Publications: Annual report.
Financial data: Year ended 06/30/2011. Assets, $1,332,730,535 (M); Expenditures, $270,634,964; Total giving, $1,100,249; Grants to individuals, totaling $1,100,249.
Fields of interest: Humanities; Literature; Historical activities; Libraries/library science.
Type of support: Fellowships; Research.
Application information: Application form required.
Deadline(s): Sept. 29 for Scholars and Writers, and Dec. 1 for Scholars-in-Residence Program
Program descriptions:
Dorothy and Lewis B. Cullman Center for Scholars and Writers: The center hosts an international fellowship program open to people whose work will benefit directly from access to the collections at the Humanities and Social Sciences Library, including academics, independent scholars, and creative writers (including novelists, playwrights, and poets). The center appoints 15 fellows a year for a nine-month term at the library, from September through May. In addition to working on their own projects, fellows engage in an ongoing exchange of ideas within the center and in public forums throughout the library. Fellows receive a stipend of $50,000 to $55,000, an office, a computer, and full access to the library's physical and electronic resources. Fellows work at the center for the duration of the fellowship term.
Schomburg Center Scholars-in-Residence Program: The program assists those scholars and professionals whose research in the black experience can benefit from extended access to the center's resources. Fellowships funded by the center will allow recipients to spend six months or a year in residence with access to resources at the Schomburg Center and other centers of The New York Public Library. The program encourages research and writing on black history and culture, facilitates interaction among participating scholars, and provides wide-spread dissemination of findings through lectures, publications, and colloquia and seminars. It encompasses projects in African, Afro-American, and Afro-Caribbean history and culture. Fellowships are awarded for continuous periods of six or twelve months at the Schomburg Center with maximum stipends of $25,000 for six months and $50,000 for twelve months. Fellows are expected to be in continuous residence at the Schomburg Center and to participate in the intellectual life of the program.
EIN: 131887440

6272
New York State 4-H Foundation, Inc.

248 Grant Ave., Ste. II-A
Auburn, NY   13021-1495   (315) 702-8242
Contact: Linda L. Henley, Exec. Dir.
FAX: (607) 255-0788;
E-mail: nys4-hfoundation@nys4hfoundation.org;
E-mail for Linda L. Henley:
lindah@nys4hfoundation.org; URL: http://
www.nys4hfoundation.org/

Foundation type: Public charity
Purpose: Scholarships to New York 4-H members for their accomplishments as a result of experiences with the club, and to support future educational goals.
Publications: Application guidelines; Annual report.
Financial data: Year ended 12/31/2011. Assets, $1,119,164 (M); Expenditures, $335,421; Total giving, $103,983; Grants to individuals, totaling $10,000.
Fields of interest: Higher education; Young adults.
Type of support: Undergraduate support.
Application information:
Initial approach: Application
Deadline(s): Feb. 15 for Opportunity Scholarships
Program description:
Opportunity Scholarships: Scholarships, ranging from $1,000 to $5,000, are available to 4-H members between 17 and 21 years of age, a member of a 4-H affiliate based in New York state, or have participated in a Cornell Cooperative Extension 4-H Youth Development Program for at least one year, be enrolled in a university, college, or technical school, and have a current GPA of at least 2.0 on a 4.0 scale.
EIN: 146021395

6273
New York Stem Cell Foundation, Inc.

178 Columbus Ave., No. 237064
New York, NY   10023-5001   (212) 787-4111
Contact: Susan L. Solomon, C.E.O.
E-mail: info@nyscf.org; URL: http://www.nyscf.org

Foundation type: Public charity
Purpose: Fellowships and research grants for human embryonic stem cell research and somatic cell nuclear transfer.
Publications: Application guidelines.
Financial data: Year ended 06/30/2011. Assets, $49,802,989 (M); Expenditures, $10,299,460; Total giving, $2,289,496. Grants to individuals amount not specified.
Fields of interest: Genetic diseases and disorders research; Medical research; Hematology research.
Type of support: Fellowships; Research.
Application information: Applications accepted. Application form required.
Deadline(s): Jan. 18 for Postdoctoral Fellowships, Mar. 22 for Innovator Awards for Early Career Investigators
Additional information: See web site for additional application guidelines.
Program description:
Innovator Awards Program for Early Career Investigators: This award provides $1.5 million over five years to researchers based at accredited academic institutions from throughout the world for the use of exploring the basic biology and translational potential of stem cells. The goal is to foster bold and innovative science with the potential to transform the field of stem cell research, and advance the understanding and use of stem cells for the treatment of human disease. Applicant must have completed one or more of the following degrees: MD, PhD, or DPhil, be within five years of starting a faculty (professorship) or comparable position at the start of the award, demonstrated ability to independently supervise staff and research, have a publication record containing articles that are innovative and high impact, and have demonstrated or strategized true innovation from translation of basic science to a clinical setting.
EIN: 202905531

6274
The New York Stock Exchange Fallen Heroes Fund
c/o Tax Dept.
11 Wall St.
New York, NY   10005-1916
Contact: Steve Wheeler
URL: https://nyse.nyx.com/

Foundation type: Company-sponsored foundation
Purpose: Grants to surviving spouses and/or children of New York City police officers and firefighters killed in the line of duty. Assistance to families of police officers of the Port Authority of New York and New Jersey who lost their lives in the line of duty in the 9/11 attacks.
Publications: IRS Form 990 or 990-PF printed copy available upon request.
Financial data: Year ended 12/31/2012. Assets, $2,498,598 (M); Expenditures, $127,000; Total giving, $127,000.
Fields of interest: Crime/law enforcement, police agencies; Disasters, fire prevention/control; Disasters, 9/11/01; Safety/disasters.
Type of support: Grants to individuals.
Application information: Applications not accepted.
> *Additional information:* Unsolicited requests for funds not considered or acknowledged.

EIN: 134048148

6275
The New York Times Company Foundation Inc.
620 8th Ave., 17th Fl.
New York, NY   10018-1618
URL: http://www.nytco.com/social-responsibility/college-scholarship-program/
Additional URL: http://www.nytimes.com/scholarship

Foundation type: Company-sponsored foundation
Purpose: Scholarships to New York City high school seniors who have overcome financial, racial, ethnic, language or other difficulties.
Financial data: Year ended 12/31/2011. Assets, $252,090 (M); Expenditures, $419,253; Total giving, $68,640.
Fields of interest: Higher education; Scholarships/financial aid.
Type of support: Scholarships—to individuals.
Application information: Applications accepted. Application form required.
> *Deadline(s):* Oct. 27
> *Additional information:* Applications are available from principals and college counselors.

Program description:
> *New York Times College Scholarship Program:* The foundation annually awards four-year college scholarships of up to $7,500 to six New York City public high school students who have overcome exceptional hardship including financial, racial, ethnic, language, or other obstacles to achieve excellence. Preference is given to students whose parents did not graduate from a four-year college or university. The award includes a summer internship at the New York Times, educational and job counseling, mentoring, cultural and civic activities, and a laptop computer.

EIN: 136066955

6276
The New York Times Neediest Cases Fund, Inc.
620 8th Ave.
New York, NY   10018-1618   (212) 556-7019
Contact: Michael Golden, Pres.
FAX: (212) 730-0927; Toll-free tel.: (800) 381-0075; URL: http://www.nytimes.com/neediest

Foundation type: Public charity
Purpose: The fund seeks to give direct assistance to troubled children, families, and elders in the New York City metropolitan area.
Financial data: Year ended 02/28/2012. Assets, $48,180,864 (M); Expenditures, $8,406,094; Total giving, $8,359,847; Grants to individuals, totaling $224,797.
Fields of interest: Economically disadvantaged.
Type of support: Grants for special needs.
Application information: Applications not accepted.
> *Additional information:* Unsolicited requests for funds not considered.

EIN: 136066063

6277
New York Women in Film & Television, Inc.
(also known as NYWIFT)
6 E. 39th St., Ste. 1200
New York, NY   10016-0112   (212) 679-0870
Contact: Terry Lawler, Exec. Dir.
FAX: (212) 679-0899; E-mail: info@nywift.org; URL: http://www.nywift.org

Foundation type: Public charity
Purpose: Grants to professional women in film, television, and new media. Also, financial assistance to second-year female graduate film students at Columbia University, New York Universities, and the City College of New York, as well as a Fiscal Sponsorship program available to members.
Publications: Application guidelines.
Financial data: Year ended 06/30/2012. Assets, $314,660 (M); Expenditures, $730,659; Total giving, $29,079; Grants to individuals, totaling $21,579.
Fields of interest: Media/communications; Film/video; Television; Women.
Type of support: Emergency funds; Grants to individuals; Scholarships—to individuals; Support to graduates or students of specific schools; Awards/prizes; Fiscal agent/sponsor.
Application information: Application form required. Application form available on the grantmaker's web site.
> *Initial approach:* Letter
> *Deadline(s):* July 8 for film award, Nov. for grants, None for fiscal sponsorship
> *Applicants should submit the following:*
>   1) Proposal
>   2) Budget Information
> *Additional information:* University students are nominated by faculty at their respective institutions for the scholarship fund.

Program descriptions:
> *Fiscal Sponsorship Program:* Through its fiscal sponsorship program, the organization accepts tax-deductible contributions for nonprofit film and video projects being made by its members. The primary purpose of projects must be to support educational, artistic, or charitable purposes. There is no application fee; the fund takes an administrative fee of 7 percent for the first

$100,000 raised and 5 percent for any funds over $100,000.
> *Scholarship Fund:* The fund provides financial assistance to second-year female students enrolled in graduate film programs at Columbia University, New York University, and The City College of New York.

EIN: 132983705

6278
New York-Presbyterian Fund, Inc.
525 E. 68th St.
P.O. Box 156
New York, NY   10065-4870   (212) 297-4356

Foundation type: Public charity
Purpose: Emergency assistance for patients at The New York-Presbyterian Hospital, NY.
Financial data: Year ended 12/31/2011. Assets, $1,830,211,183 (M); Expenditures, $153,226,735; Total giving, $66,946,270; Grants to individuals, totaling $1,205,244.
Fields of interest: Health care; Economically disadvantaged.
Type of support: Emergency funds.
Application information: Applications not accepted.
> *Additional information:* Unsolicited requests for funds not considered or acknowledged.

EIN: 133160356

6279
Samuel I. Newhouse Foundation, Inc.
c/o Advance Finance Group LLC
1440 Broadway, 12th Fl.
New York, NY   10018-2301   (212) 588-2200
Contact: Steven Markovits

Foundation type: Independent foundation
Purpose: Awards to artists with disabilities in recognition of their artistic merit.
Financial data: Year ended 10/31/2012. Assets, $95,860,756 (M); Expenditures, $12,313,482; Total giving, $11,742,031; Grants to individuals, 9 grants totaling $60,000 (high: $10,000, low: $4,000).
Fields of interest: Disabilities, people with.
Type of support: Awards/prizes.
Application information: Applications accepted.
> *Initial approach:* Letter
> *Deadline(s):* None
> *Additional information:* Nominees must be artists of professional standing and have a disability as recognized by the Americans with Disability Act of 1990.

EIN: 116006296

6280
NLN Foundation for Nursing Education
61 Broadway, 33rd Fl.
New York, NY   10006-2800   (212) 812-0348
Contact: Beverly Malone Ph.D, R.N., C.E.O.
FAX: (212) 812-0392; E-mail: foundation@nln.org; Toll-free tel.: (800) 699-1656; URL: http://www.nlnfoundation.org

Foundation type: Public charity
Purpose: Scholarships to students in doctoral and graduate nursing education programs who identify as underrepresented minorities.
Publications: Application guidelines.
Financial data: Year ended 12/31/2011. Assets, $1,174,359 (M); Expenditures, $636,528; Total giving, $79,474; Grants to individuals, totaling $79,474.

Fields of interest: Nursing school/education; Minorities.
Type of support: Graduate support; Doctoral support.
Application information: Applications accepted. Application form required.
  Initial approach: Letter
  Deadline(s): Aug. 10 for Minority Faculty Preparation Scholarship
Program descriptions:
  Dissertation Scholarships for Nursing Education Scholars: The program provides financial assistance to doctoral candidates in nursing education programs who are working on dissertations focusing on nursing education research. Four awards will be given in the amount of $2,500 each. Awardees will use the funds to offset dissertation expenses.
  Minority Faculty Preparation Scholarship: The program provides financial support to students in graduate nursing education programs who identify as underrepresented minorities and are preparing for the nurse faculty role. Two scholarships will be awarded in the amount of $5,000 each. Eligible candidates include men and women who are of African American, Hispanic, Native American, Native Alaskan, Arab or Asian decent; Caucasian men are also eligible.
EIN: 753032867

6281
Nok Charitable Organization, Inc.
(also known as NOK Foundation, Inc.)
c/o Quest Partners LLC
126 E. 56th St., 19th Fl.
New York, NY   10022-3613
E-mail: info@nokfoundation.com; URL: http://www.nokfoundation.com/

Foundation type: Independent foundation
Purpose: Awards scholarships to promote and encourage: 1) The study of Yoga at reputable schools in India; 2) to study Zen meditation in a three-month training program at a New York monastery; 3) to participate in an intensive week-long Zen retreat.
Publications: Informational brochure.
Financial data: Year ended 12/31/2012. Assets, $0 (M); Expenditures, $326,948; Total giving, $213,586.
Fields of interest: Spirituality.
Type of support: Scholarships—to individuals.
Application information: Applications not accepted.
EIN: 020654795

6282
Robert J. Nolan Foundation, Inc.
82 Glenwood Ave.
Queensbury, NY   12804-3127   (518) 792-4900
Contact: Michael Borgos, Pres.

Foundation type: Independent foundation
Purpose: Scholarships to high school students from the greater Glen Falls, NY area participating in varsity athletic teams with the intention of participating in organized athletic teams and endeavors at the undergraduate and/or graduate level.
Financial data: Year ended 09/30/2013. Assets, $894,942 (M); Expenditures, $52,758; Total giving, $37,500; Grants to individuals, 10 grants totaling $37,500 (high: $5,000, low: $2,500).
Fields of interest: Higher education; Athletics/sports, school programs.

Type of support: Scholarships—to individuals; Graduate support; Undergraduate support.
Application information: Applications accepted. Application form required.
  Deadline(s): May
  Applicants should submit the following:
    1) Financial information
    2) Class rank
    3) Essay
    4) Letter(s) of recommendation
    5) Transcripts
    6) SAR
  Additional information: Application can be obtained from the guidance office.
EIN: 222826285

6283
St. Thomas Knights/Maureen Nolan Memorial Fund
(formerly Shoppers Village/Maureen Nolan Memorial Fund)
1980 Washington St.
Merrick, NY   11566-3052

Foundation type: Independent foundation
Purpose: Scholarships to high school students who are members of St. Thomas the Apostle Parish, West Hempstead, NY, or of West Hempstead School District No. 27.
Financial data: Year ended 07/31/2013. Assets, $58,452 (M); Expenditures, $14,050; Total giving, $14,000; Grants to individuals, 16 grants totaling $14,000 (high: $1,500, low: $500).
Fields of interest: Christian agencies & churches.
Type of support: Scholarships—to individuals.
Application information: Application form required.
  Deadline(s): Nov. 25
EIN: 112617929

6284
North Fork Women for Women Fund, Inc.
P. O. Box 804
Greenport, NY   11944-0804   (631) 477-8464
Contact: Debra Roth, Pres.
E-mail: info@nfwfwf.net

Foundation type: Public charity
Purpose: Grants for health care costs and crisis situations to lesbians residing on the North Fork of Long Island, NY.
Publications: Application guidelines; Annual report; Informational brochure; Newsletter.
Financial data: Year ended 12/31/2012. Assets, $288,795 (M); Expenditures, $36,774; Total giving, $53,562.
Fields of interest: Health care; Women; LGBTQ.
Type of support: Grants for special needs.
Application information: Applications accepted. Application form required. Application form available on the grantmaker's web site.
  Send request by: Mail
  Deadline(s): None
Program description:
  Grants: Emergency funds are available to self-identified lesbians who reside full-time (either year-round or seasonally) on the North Fork of Long Island (from Riverhead Township to Orient Point and Shelter Island), for out-of-pocket medical expenses, such as mammograms, other diagnostic tests, annual physicals, health insurance co-payments, dental and eye care, physical therapy, and medication.
EIN: 113116020

6285
North Shore Animal League America, Inc.
25 Davis Ave.
Port Washington, NY   11050-3701   (516) 883-7575
URL: http://www.nsalamerica.org

Foundation type: Public charity
Purpose: Scholarships to qualified veterinary scholars at the following institutions: Purdue University, Tuskegee University, Cornell University, Michigan State University, Oregon State University, Tufts University, and the Animal Medical Center.
Financial data: Year ended 12/31/2011. Assets, $24,192,776 (M); Expenditures, $31,912,001; Total giving, $171,714; Grants to individuals, totaling $1,714.
Fields of interest: Veterinary medicine.
Type of support: Undergraduate support.
Application information: Applications not accepted.
  Additional information: Unsolicited requests for funds not considered.
EIN: 111666852

6286
Northern Chautauqua Community Foundation, Inc.
212 Lake Shore Dr. W.
Dunkirk, NY   14048-1436   (716) 366-4892
Contact: Diane Hannum, Exec. Dir.
FAX: (716) 366-3905;
E-mail: info@nccfoundation.org; Grant application e-mail: grants@nccfoundation.org; Additional e-mail: dhannum@nccfoundation.org; URL: http://www.nccfoundation.org

Foundation type: Community foundation
Purpose: Scholarships to high school graduates of over 15 high schools in northern Chautauqua County, NY.
Publications: Application guidelines; Annual report (including application guidelines); Financial statement; Newsletter.
Financial data: Year ended 12/31/2012. Assets, $19,439,061 (M); Expenditures, $585,935; Total giving, $338,122; Grants to individuals, totaling $146,423.
Type of support: Undergraduate support.
Application information:
  Initial approach: Letter or telephone
  Deadline(s): Varies
EIN: 161271663

6287
Northern New York Community Foundation, Inc.
(formerly Watertown Foundation, Inc.)
120 Washington St., Ste. 400
Watertown, NY   13601-3330   (315) 782-7110
Contact: Rande S. Richardson, Exec. Dir.
FAX: (315) 782-0047; E-mail: info@nnycf.org;
Additional e-mail: rande@nnycf.org; URL: http://www.nnycf.org

Foundation type: Community foundation
Purpose: Scholarships to legal residents of Jefferson and Lewis counties, NY, who are enrolled as full-time undergraduate students at accredited institutions in the U.S.
Publications: Annual report; Grants list; Newsletter.
Financial data: Year ended 12/31/2011. Assets, $39,154,062 (M); Expenditures, $2,289,115; Total giving, $1,549,255; Grants to individuals, totaling $734,122.

Fields of interest: Higher education.
Type of support: Scholarships—to individuals; Support to graduates or students of specific schools; Undergraduate support.
Application information: Applications accepted. Application form required. Application form available on the grantmaker's web site. Interview required.
Send request by: Mail or hand delivered
Deadline(s): Apr. 1
Final notification: Recipients notified Aug. 1
Applicants should submit the following:
1) ACT
2) SAT
3) Transcripts
4) Essay
Additional information: See web site for complete scholarship listings and application forms. Applications are also available at local high school guidance offices and the Jefferson Community College Financial Aid office.
Program description:
Scholarships: The foundation administers multiple scholarship funds to high school seniors for their freshman year in college or technical school, college sophomores for their junior year and non-traditional students for any year in college or technical school. Each scholarship has unique eligibility requirements, including but not limited to awards for students in specific school districts, engineering, mathematics, nursing and liberal arts majors, and students who have experienced personal or family hardships.
EIN: 156020989

6288
Northrup Educational Foundation Inc.
331 N. Glen Ave.
Watkins Glen, NY 14891 (606) 535-7438
Contact: Marilyn W. Cross, Secy.-Treas.

Foundation type: Independent foundation
Purpose: Interest-free student loans to college students in good standing who have resided in Schuyler County, NY, for ten years. Awards to the students with the highest ACT and SAT scores from Watkins Glen Central School and Odessa-Montour Central School, NY.
Financial data: Year ended 08/31/2013. Assets, $420,966 (M); Expenditures, $10,543; Total giving, $2,000; Grants to individuals, 2 grants totaling $2,000 (high: $1,000, low: $1,000).
Fields of interest: Higher education.
Type of support: Student loans—to individuals; Support to graduates or students of specific schools; Undergraduate support.
Application information: Applications accepted. Application form required.
Deadline(s): June 10
Final notification: Recipients notified by July 15
Applicants should submit the following:
1) SAT
2) ACT
Additional information: Application should also include statement of ten-year residency in Schuyler County, other tuition resources, unpaid debts, and grades from prior year.
EIN: 156020359

6289
The Norwegian Children's Home Association of New York, Inc.
P.O. Box 280104
Brooklyn, NY 11228-0104 (718) 238-4326
Contact: Ruth Santoro, Pres.

Foundation type: Independent foundation
Purpose: Scholarships to students who are of at least 25 percent Norwegian ancestry, or who have a significant Norwegian affiliation, for higher education.
Financial data: Year ended 12/31/2011. Assets, $3,395,960 (M); Expenditures, $213,674; Total giving, $159,490.
Fields of interest: Higher education.
International interests: Norway.
Type of support: Undergraduate support.
Application information:
Initial approach: Letter
Deadline(s): Mar. 16
EIN: 111666853

6290
NYS Fraternal Order of Police Foundation
(formerly NYS Fraternal Order of Police Empire State Foundation)
911 Police Plz.
Empire St. Lodge
Hicksville, NY 11801-1000 (516) 433-4455
Contact: Charles J. Caputo, Pres.
E-mail: nysfop@nysfop.org; Toll-Free No.: (888) 610-2239; E-Mail For Charlie Caputo: CharlieC@nysfop.org; URL: http://www.nysfop.org

Foundation type: Public charity
Purpose: Scholarships to high school seniors residing in NY to pursue a higher education. Financial assistance also to family members of police officers killed in the line of duty in NY.
Publications: Application guidelines; Financial statement.
Financial data: Year ended 12/31/2011. Assets, $31,080 (M); Expenditures, $107,747.
Fields of interest: Higher education; Crime/law enforcement, police agencies.
Type of support: Undergraduate support; Grants for special needs.
Application information: Applications accepted. Application form required.
Deadline(s): May 3 for Scholarships
Additional information: Contact foundation for additional information for financial assistance.
EIN: 113207296

6291
Jeanette Odasz Trust
3 Sarnowski Dr.
Schenectady, NY 12302

Foundation type: Independent foundation
Purpose: Scholarships to graduates of Niskayuna High School, Linton High School, Mount Pleasant High School, and Mononasen High School, NY, for music education.
Financial data: Year ended 12/31/2012. Assets, $102,153 (M); Expenditures, $2,670; Total giving, $1,950; Grants to individuals, 3 grants totaling $1,950 (high: $650, low: $650).
Fields of interest: Higher education.
Type of support: Support to graduates or students of specific schools; Undergraduate support.
Application information:
Initial approach: Letter
Deadline(s): June 1
EIN: 146105337

6292
Oneida Savings Bank Charitable Foundation
P.O. Box 240
Oneida, NY 13421-1607 (315) 363-2000
Contact: Eric E. Stickels, Dir.

Foundation type: Company-sponsored foundation
Purpose: The foundation awards college scholarships to residents living in areas surrounding branch offices of the Oneida Financial Corporation. The program is administered by Scholarship America, Inc.
Financial data: Year ended 12/31/2012. Assets, $1,547,678 (M); Expenditures, $140,150; Total giving, $136,498.
Type of support: Undergraduate support.
Application information: Applications not accepted.
Additional information: Unsolicited requests for funds not considered.
EIN: 161561680

6293
Ontario Children's Foundation
(formerly Ontario Children's Home)
P.O. Box 82
Canandaigua, NY 14424-0082
Application address for education assistance: c/o Jane Wheeler, 4160 W. Lake Rd., Canadaigua, NY 14424, e-mail: jwheele4@rochester.rr.com
URL: http://ontariochildrensfoundation.org

Foundation type: Independent foundation
Purpose: Student loans to residents of Ontario County, NY, who are under the age of 21. Grants restricted to children under 21 years of age in Ontario County, NY, for child day care, youth organization membership, medical and dental expenses, day camp, field trips, and participation in the Special Olympics.
Financial data: Year ended 09/30/2013. Assets, $3,770,687 (M); Expenditures, $198,692; Total giving, $174,248.
Fields of interest: Education; Children/youth, services; Day care; Disabilities, people with.
Type of support: Student loans—to individuals; Grants for special needs.
Application information: Interview required.
Initial approach: Letter
Deadline(s): Mar. 15 for loans
Additional information: Ineligible applications will not be considered or acknowledged.
EIN: 166028318

6294
Open Society Institute
224 W. 57th St.
New York, NY 10019-3212 (212) 548-0600
Contact: Inquiry Mgr.
FAX: (212) 548-4600; Baltimore, MD office: 201 N. Charles St., Ste. 1300, Baltimore, MD 21201, tel.: (410) 234-1091; Washington, DC office: 1730 Pennsylvania Ave. N.W., 7th fl., Washington, DC 20006, tel.: 202-721-5600; URL: http://www.opensocietyfoundations.org/

Foundation type: Operating foundation
Purpose: Scholarships to students from Burma, Central and Eastern Europe, and the former Soviet Union to study at postsecondary institutions in the U.S. and Europe. Fellowships to individuals for research, program support, and professional development. Support to photographers for documentary exhibitions, and whose work

addresses a variety of social justice and human rights issues.

Publications: Annual report; Informational brochure; Newsletter; Program policy statement.

Financial data: Year ended 12/31/2012. Assets, $685,871,435 (M); Expenditures, $586,306,761; Total giving, $455,863,798; Grants to individuals, 862 grants totaling $9,998,480 (high: $120,020, low: $79).

Fields of interest: Film/video; Print publishing; Photography; Humanities; Higher education; Graduate/professional education; Social work school/education; Education; Public policy; Reform; Legal rights; International exchange, students; International exchange; International economic development; Community development, neighborhood development; Social sciences; Leadership development; Minorities; Economically disadvantaged.

Type of support: Program development; Fellowships; Scholarships—to individuals; Foreign applicants; Graduate support; Undergraduate support.

Application information: Applications accepted. Application form not required. Interview required.

 Deadline(s): Varies
 Additional information: Completion of formal application required for Soros Justice Fellows and Palliative Care Fellowships. See web site or contact foundation for detailed application information and additional programs.

Program descriptions:

Baltimore Community Fellowships: The fellowships were established to assist individuals wishing to apply their education and professional experiences to serve marginalized communities. The goals of these fellowships are to encourage public and community service careers, expand the number of mentors and role models available to youth in inner-city neighborhoods, and promote entrepreneurial initiatives that empower communities to increase opportunities and improve the quality of life for their residents.Up to 10 individuals are awarded a Community Fellowship to implement innovative projects that seek to improve the circumstances and capacity of an underserved community in Baltimore City. Applicants may apply for a fellowship either: 1) to work under the auspices of a nonprofit organization in Baltimore City; or 2) independently. Deadline: Mar. 21.

Documentary Photography Project: The project's Audience Engagment Grants supports photographers to take an existing body of work on a social justice or human rights issue and devise an innovative way of using that work as a catalyst for social change. Projects should combine existing bodies of work with programming or tools that give viewers a deeper, more nuanced understanding of issues and empower them to participate in the process of improving their own or others' realities. Projects should also include a partnership between a photographer and an organization that combines expertise in documentary photography with experience working on the topic or community the project addresses. Five to eight grants of $5,000 to $30,000 are awarded.

Faculty Development Fellowship Program: Each year, for up to three years, participants from Armenia, Azerbaijan, Georgia, Kazakhstan, Kyrgyzstan, Moldova, Mongolia, Tajikistan, and Uzbekistan at a U.S. university and one semester teaching at their home universities. Deadline Apr. 19.

Georgia Program for Education Professionals: The program offers fellowships for graduate study in the United States leading to a master's degree in education. Competition is merit based, and selection is made on the basis of academic

excellence, professional aptitude, leadership potential in the field of specialization, and proven commitment to support the reform of the Georgian educational system. Applicants must be a legal resident of Georgia at the time of application and be willing upon completing the program to accept employment at a position designated by the Georgian Ministry of Education and Science (MoES) for a period of up to three years, in addition to other criteria.

International Pain Policy: This fellowship provides candidates with the knowledge and skills necessary to develop and implement a project to improve the availability of pain medications for pain relief and palliative care in their country. It is intended for health professionals (e.g. oncologists, AIDS clinicians, pain and palliative care physicians), health care administrators, managers, policy experts, or lawyers from low or middle income countries with an interest in drug policy advocacy to improve availability of opioid analgesics for pain relief and palliative care. Two-year awards will be made to either the institution or to the fellow directly.

Moving Walls: Moving Walls is an exhibition series that features in-depth and nuanced explorations of human rights and social issues. It recognizes the brave and difficult work that photographers undertake globally in their documentation of complex social and political issues. Any emerging or veteran photographer who has completed a body of work on a human rights or social justice issue may apply.

Open Society Fellowships: The fellowships supports individuals who are developing innovative solutions to pressing open society challenges. The fellowship program seeks applicants eager to communicate original and provocative ideas to a broad audience, as well as to shape policy and inspire critical debate among activists, intellectuals, decision makers, and the public. It is open to journalists, activists, academics, and public policy practitioners from around the world.Full-time fellows based in the United States will receive a stipend of $80,000 or $100,000, depending on work experience, seniority, and current income. In evaluating each proposal, the selection committee weighs three factors: the applicant, the topic of the project, and the work product. For more information please contact: OSFellows@sorosny.org.

Social Work Fellowship Program: The program supports individuals from Jordan, Kyrgyzstan and Tajikistan to complete a two year graduate program in social work at an American University. The program is designed to provide training in social work to implement reform, create policy and foster the development of social work in the participating countries. Upon the conclusion of the fellowship, participants return home to apply their new knowledge in practice. The participating host universities are Columbia University and Washington University in St. Louis .

Soros Fellowships: Awards one- and two-year stipends for the following: 1) Media Fellowship: Awards up to $3,000 for one year to journalists working in print, photography, radio and documentary film; 2) Senior Fellowship: Awards $45,000 - $60,000 for one year to support activists, lawyers, academics and community leaders; 3) Soros Justice Advocacy Fellowships: Awards a one-time payment of $1,200 for relocation costs, a stipend of $37,500, a $2,000 professional development budget, a $2,500 health insurance budget, and $6,000 to help with graduate school loan debt per year for two years to outstanding individuals in law, organizing, public health, public policy, and other disciplines.

Undergraduate Exchange Program: The program supports students from Albania, Kosovo, and Ukraine (studying in Dnipropetrovsk, Donetsk, Kharkiv, Kherson, Luhansk, Mykolaiv, Odessa, Poltava, Sumy, or Zaporizhia only) in the United States for one-year of non-degree academic studies and service learning and one subsequent year in their home country leading a community service project of their own design. Applicants must be a citizen and resident of Albania, Kosovo, or Ukraine as well as be enrolled as a second-year student at a university in one of these countries to be eligible and be studying American Studies, Art History, Classical Studies, Cultural Anthropology, Economic Theory*, Fine or Performing Arts, History, International Relations, Journalism, Law, Literature and Languages, Philosophy, Political Science, Sociology, or Women's or Gender Studies. Deadline: Dec. 1.

EIN: 137029285

6295
Open Space Institute
1350 Broadway, Ste. 201
New York, NY 10018-0983 (212) 290-8200
Contact: Tally Blumberg, Sr. V.P., Progs.
FAX: (212) 244-3441; E-mail: tblumberg@osiny.org;
URL: http://www.osiny.org

Foundation type: Public charity

Purpose: Grants for land conservation planning and applied research. Grantees should have sufficient GIS capacity to complete projects. Catalyst grants will range from $7,500 to $25,000 per project. Projects should be completed within one year of the grant award, with focus within Maine, New Hampshire, and Vermont, with a smaller amount of funding available in Massachusetts.

Financial data: Year ended 12/31/2011. Assets, $11,761,751 (M); Expenditures, $10,919,832; Total giving, $8,093,970.

Fields of interest: Physical/earth sciences; Biology/life sciences; Botany; Science.

Type of support: Research.

Application information: Applications accepted. Application form required. Application form available on the grantmaker's web site.

 Initial approach: E-mail
 Deadline(s): July 8
 Additional information: All applications must be submitted through OSI's online application form.

EIN: 521053406

6296
OPERA America
330 7th Ave., 16th Fl.
New York, NY 10001-5010 (212) 796-8620
Contact: Marc A. Scorca, Pres. and C.E.O.
FAX: (212) 796-8631;
E-mail: frontdesk@operaamerica.org; URL: http://www.operaamerica.org

Foundation type: Public charity

Purpose: Stipends for travel to members to help offset the cost of transportation and accomodations to attend annual meetings.

Publications: Application guidelines; Annual report; Informational brochure; Newsletter.

Financial data: Year ended 06/30/2012. Assets, $15,346,715 (M); Expenditures, $3,780,627; Total giving, $259,582; Grants to individuals, totaling $35,582.

Fields of interest: Opera.

Type of support: Stipends.

Application information: Applications accepted. Application form required.

> *Deadline(s):* June 15
> *Final notification:* Applicants are notified of award within 48 hours of receipt of request in order to facilitate the completion of travel plan.
> *Additional information:* Members must register to take part in forum meetings, and applications are included in the Forum registration forms. Applicants must contact the appropriate staff member. See web site for additional application guidelines.

Program description:

> *Forum Travel Stipends:* Stipends go to members in good standing who are invited to participate in one or more Forums and who live more that 150 miles from New York City may request subsidy of up to $250. Stipends will be awarded in the order in which requests are received until funds allocated for each Forum are expended. Only one stipend will be awarded per company for each Forum.

EIN: 203520577

6297

The Opera Foundation, Inc.

(formerly The American Berlin Opera Foundation, Inc.)
712 5th Ave., 32nd Fl.
New York, NY   10019-4108   (212) 664-8843
FAX: (212) 664-8415;
E-mail: gala@operafoundation.org; URL: http://www.operafoundation.org

Foundation type: Public charity
Purpose: Scholarships to young American singers to study and perform in Berlin, Germany, or Turin, Italy, and thereafter to pursue career opportunities in Europe.
Publications: Application guidelines.
Financial data: Year ended 06/30/2011. Assets, $72,999 (M); Expenditures, $79,877; Total giving, $50,779; Grants to individuals, 4 grants totaling $50,779.
Fields of interest: Opera; Performing arts, education.
International interests: Germany; Italy.
Type of support: Scholarships—to individuals.
Application information: Applications accepted. Application form required. Application form available on the grantmaker's web site.

> *Initial approach:* Letter
> *Send request by:* Mail
> *Deadline(s):* Jan. 18
> *Applicants should submit the following:*
> 1) Photograph
> 2) Letter(s) of recommendation
> *Additional information:* Audition required. Application should also include copy of birth certificate, green card, or passport, and a non-refundable $40 application fee.

Program description:

> *Scholarship Competition:* This program awards up to four scholarships and stipends of $16,000 each and travel expenses of $1,300, for a ten-month training opportunity at one of Europe's three most prestigious opera companies; the Deutsche Oper in Berlin, Germany, the Teatro Regio Torino in Turin, Italy, and the Bayerische Staatsoper in Munich, Germany. Scholarships are open to American citizens or permanent residents between the ages of 18 and 30 who are at the beginning of their professional singing careers. Selected candidates will be invited to participate in New York auditions.

EIN: 133377138

6298

Opportunities for Broome, Inc.

5 W. State St.
Binghamton, NY   13901-2520   (607) 723-6493
Contact: Mark Silvanic, Exec. Dir.
FAX: (607) 723-6497;
E-mail: msilvanic@ofbonline.org; E-mail for Mark Silvanic: msilvanic@ofbonline.org; URL: http://www.ofbonline.org/

Foundation type: Public charity
Purpose: Financial assistance to indigent residents of Broome County, NY to help with living expenses.
Financial data: Year ended 12/31/2011. Assets, $8,196,985 (M); Expenditures, $3,136,328; Total giving, $850; Grants to individuals, totaling $850.
Type of support: Grants for special needs.
Application information: Applications not accepted.

> *Additional information:* Unsolicited requests for funds not considered.

EIN: 160903802

6299

Opportunities for Chenango, Inc.

44 W. Main St.
P.O. Box 470
Norwich, NY   13815-0470   (607) 334-7114
Contact: Wayne Viera, Exec. Dir.
FAX: (607) 336-6958; URL: http://www.ofcinc.org

Foundation type: Public charity
Purpose: Services to indigent residents of Chenango County, NY in the form of home repair, energy assistance, literacy programs, financial counseling, and job training.
Publications: Financial statement.
Financial data: Year ended 12/31/2011. Assets, $3,332,004 (M); Expenditures, $6,507,168.
Fields of interest: Economically disadvantaged.
Type of support: In-kind gifts.
Application information:

> *Initial approach:* Letter
> *Additional information:* Contact foundation for eligibility criteria.

EIN: 160909190

6300

The Oyster Bay Sailing Foundation

P. O. Box 720
Oyster Bay, NY   11771-0720   (917) 828-7251
Contact: J. Anthony Reaper, Pres.
E-mail: vonet@pb.net

Foundation type: Public charity
Purpose: Grants to individuals for training and preparation for local, regional, national, world or Olympic sailing events.
Financial data: Year ended 12/31/2012. Assets, $40,054 (M); Expenditures, $67,399; Total giving, $54,629.
Fields of interest: Athletics/sports, water sports; Athletics/sports, amateur competition; Athletics/sports, Olympics.
Type of support: Grants to individuals.
Application information: Applications should include a sailing resume and sailing plan.
EIN: 112839663

6301

Parapsychology Foundation, Inc.

P.O. Box 1562
New York, NY   10021   (212) 628-1550
Contact: Eileen Coly, Chair.
Application address: 308 Front St., Greenport, NY 11944; URL: http://www.parapsychology.org

Foundation type: Operating foundation
Purpose: Research and scholarship grants for study in parapsychology including clairvoyance, clairaudience, telepathy, precognition, retrocognition, psychokinesis, poltergeist, out-of-body experiences, spontaneous phenomena, mediumship, survival, psychology, psychiatry, unorthodox healing, altered states of consciousness, hypnosis, drugs, and dreams.
Publications: Application guidelines; Annual report (including application guidelines); Informational brochure; Informational brochure (including application guidelines); Newsletter.
Financial data: Year ended 12/31/2011. Assets, $320,277 (M); Expenditures, $831,901; Total giving, $3,000; Grant to an individual, 1 grant totaling $3,000.
Fields of interest: Psychology/behavioral science.
Type of support: Research; Scholarships—to individuals.
Application information: Applications accepted. Application form required.

> *Initial approach:* Letter
> *Copies of proposal:* 2
> *Deadline(s):* Vary
> *Additional information:* See web site for complete program information.

EIN: 131677742

6302

Ron Parham Fund for Scholastic Excellence

c/o J. Traub
30 E. 65th St., Ste. 13B
New York, NY   10021

Foundation type: Operating foundation
Purpose: Scholarships to individuals based on academic excellence.
Financial data: Year ended 12/31/2011. Assets, $26,340 (M); Expenditures, $7,551; Total giving, $2,900; Grants to individuals, 2 grants totaling $2,900 (high: $2,500, low: $400).
Fields of interest: Higher education.
Type of support: Scholarships—to individuals.
Application information: Applications accepted.

> *Initial approach:* Letter
> *Deadline(s):* Dec.

EIN: 133749141

6303

Pauline R. Parker Charitable Trust

c/o Chemung Canal Trust Company
P.O. Box 152
Elmira, NY   14902-1522

Foundation type: Independent foundation
Purpose: Scholarships and student loans to Broome County, NY residents under 25 years of age, attending Broome Community College or State University of New York at Binghamton.
Financial data: Year ended 12/31/2011. Assets, $259,656 (M); Expenditures, $15,753; Total giving, $9,942.
Fields of interest: Higher education.
Type of support: Student loans—to individuals; Support to graduates or students of specific schools.

Application information: Application form required.
Deadline(s): None
Additional information: Application should include financial information. The maximum grant or loan amount is $2,500 per student.
EIN: 166095226

6304
The Parodneck Foundation for Self-Help, Housing & Community Development, Inc.
(formerly The Consumer-Farmer Foundation, Inc.)
121 6th Ave., Ste. 501
New York, NY   10013-1510   (212) 431-9700
Contact: Carlton Collier, Exec. Dir.
FAX: (212) 431-9783;
E-mail: info@parodneckfoundation.org;
URL: http://www.parodneckfoundation.org

Foundation type: Public charity
Purpose: Loan programs for senior citizens in the New York City metropolitan area who are in danger of losing their homes.
Publications: Application guidelines; Annual report; Financial statement; Informational brochure; Newsletter.
Financial data: Year ended 12/31/2011. Assets, $15,426,301 (M); Expenditures, $1,120,087.
Fields of interest: Housing/shelter, home owners; Aging; Economically disadvantaged.
Type of support: Grants for special needs.
Application information: Applications accepted. Application form available on the grantmaker's web site. Interview required.
Additional information: Applicants must provide proof of age (copy of birth certificate, pension or social security documentation, driver's license, or passport), proof of current personal and rental income for all members of the household, copies of both sides of the filed deed, and copies of any mortgages and/ or satisfaction of mortgages.
Program description:
Senior Citizen Homeowner Assistance Program (SCHAP): This program provides financial assistance to senior citizen homeowners who are living in physically-deteriorated housing, or who are in danger of losing their homes to foreclosure. The program provides no- and low-interest loans and extensive technical assistance to qualified seniors, allowing them to retain their homes, improve their living conditions, and avoid financial insolvency, displacement, and/or loss of independence. Eligible applicants must reside in any of the five boroughs of the city of New York, be at least 60 years old, and have been an owner-occupant of a one- to four-family home for at least two years.
EIN: 112229635

6305
William G. & Rhoda B. Partridge Memorial Scholarship Fund
c/o NBT Bank, N.A.
52 S. Broad St.
Norwich, NY   13815   (607) 337-6497

Foundation type: Independent foundation
Purpose: Scholarships to graduates of Northville High School or residents of Edinburg in Saratoga County, NY to pursue a medical degree.
Publications: Application guidelines.
Financial data: Year ended 06/30/2013. Assets, $809,423 (M); Expenditures, $51,931; Total giving, $41,500; Grants to individuals, 9 grants totaling $41,500 (high: $10,000, low: $1,250).

Fields of interest: Medical school/education.
Type of support: Support to graduates or students of specific schools; Undergraduate support.
Application information: Applications accepted. Application form required.
Initial approach: Letter or telephone
Deadline(s): May 15
EIN: 141597911

6306
Pasteur Foundation
420 Lexington Ave., Ste. 1654
New York, NY   10170-1699   (212) 599-2050
Contact: Caitlin Hawke, Exec. Dir.
Application address for Fellowships: Attn: Mr. Claude Parsot, Director Delegue a l'Enseignement, Institut Pasteur, 28 rue du Docteur Roux, 75724 Paris Cedex 15, France
FAX: (212) 599-2047; E-mail: pasteurus@aol.com;
URL: http://www.pasteurfoundation.org

Foundation type: Public charity
Purpose: Fellowships to U.S. postdoctoral researchers to work in laboratories at the Institut Pasteur, Paris for the prevention and treatment of infectious diseases. Summer internship for U.S. undergraduate students for research at the Institut Pasteur, Paris.
Publications: Application guidelines; Newsletter.
Financial data: Year ended 12/31/2011. Assets, $3,031,625 (M); Expenditures, $3,645,929; Total giving, $3,422,467.
Fields of interest: Diseases (rare) research; Biomedicine research; Medical research; Biology/ life sciences.
International interests: France.
Type of support: Fellowships; Internship funds; Research.
Application information: Applications accepted. Application form required.
Deadline(s): Sept. 23 for Post-Doctoral Fellowship Program; Dec. for Undergraduate Internship Program
Final notification: Applicants for Internships are notified in Feb.
Additional information: The fellowship program is for American citizens and does not apply to candidates already in France.
Program descriptions:
Post-Doctoral Fellowship Program: In collaboration with the Institut Pasteur, the program aims to bring U.S. post-doctoral researchers to work in Institut Pasteur Laboratories in Paris. The fellowships are $70,000 ($55,000 fellowship plus $15,000 bench fees to support the research) per year for a term of three years and are not renewable. Financing for the second and third years is contingent upon positive annual review by the host lab head. Candidates are expected to commit to a three-year stay.
Undergraduate Internship Program: This program provides U.S. undergraduates with a rare opportunity to conduct summer research at the Institut Pasteur, with the goal of encouraging students in the pursuit of a scientific career and exposing them to an international laboratory experience. During the internships, interns carry out research supervised by a lab mentor; applicants should be eager to engage with a different culture, and self-sufficient enough to arrange travel and secure housing in Paris. Eligible applicants must: be undergraduates with an excellent academic record and a strong interest in biosciences and biomedical research (prior lab experience is highly recommended); have completed three full years (six semesters) of college course work by the time the internship commences; and not have received an

undergraduate degree at the time of application. Interns will receive a living allowance of $400 per week (with a maximum of $4,000 awarded); travel and housing are not paid by this program, but a $500 subsidy is provided and intended to defray costs of travel and requisite insurance.
EIN: 136018861

6307
Pathfinder Village Foundation, Inc.
3 Chenango Rd.
Edmeston, NY   13335-2314   (607) 965-8377
Contact: William Cole, Chair.

Foundation type: Public charity
Purpose: Scholarships to residents of the Village, in the Edmeston, NY area with down syndrome who are in need of financial assistance.
Financial data: Year ended 12/31/2011. Assets, $7,328,905 (M); Expenditures, $1,182,965; Total giving, $903,142; Grants to individuals, totaling $90,171.
Fields of interest: Disabilities, people with.
Type of support: Scholarships—to individuals.
Application information: Contact the foundation for additional guidelines.
EIN: 222516331

6308
Nicholas Patterson Perpetual Fund
P.O. Box 214
Kenmore, NY   14217   (716) 885-6361
Contact: Frederick B. Cohen, Tr.
E-mail: pattersonfund@aol.com; Application Address:c/o Frederick Cohen, P.O. Box 1018, Hamburg NY.14075-1018

Foundation type: Independent foundation
Purpose: Scholarships to residents of Erie County, NY, for college and graduate school.
Financial data: Year ended 12/31/2012. Assets, $411,668 (M); Expenditures, $32,544; Total giving, $24,000; Grants to individuals, 10 grants totaling $20,000 (high: $2,000, low: $2,000).
Fields of interest: Higher education.
Type of support: Graduate support; Undergraduate support.
Application information: Applications accepted.
Initial approach: Letter
Copies of proposal: 5
Deadline(s): May 15
Applicants should submit the following:
1) Letter(s) of recommendation
2) Financial information
3) Transcripts
EIN: 222806714

6309
James Bradley Peace Foundation Inc.
(formerly Sons of Iwo Jima, Inc.)
c/o Eisikovic
1430 Broadway
New York, NY   10018
URL: http://www.jamesbradley.com/jbpf/

Foundation type: Company-sponsored foundation
Purpose: Scholarships to high school students to study in China and Japan. The program is administered by Youth for Understanding USA.
Publications: Newsletter.
Financial data: Year ended 12/31/2011. Assets, $52,025 (M); Expenditures, $28,698; Total giving, $24,250.
International interests: China; Japan.
Type of support: Undergraduate support.

Application information: Applications not accepted.
  Additional information: Contributes only to preselected individuals.
EIN: 392008597

6310
Pearson Charitable Foundation
1330 Avenue of the Americas, 7th Fl.
New York, NY 10019-5400 (212) 641-6689
Contact: Shaheda Sayed, Secy.
E-mail: info@pearsonfoundation.org; URL: http://www.pearsonfoundation.org/

Foundation type: Public charity
Purpose: Scholarships and awards to outstanding college students who work to improve their communities while completing their undergraduate studies.
Publications: Application guidelines.
Financial data: Year ended 12/31/2011. Assets, $4,774,167 (M); Expenditures, $19,568,579; Total giving, $4,556,019.
Fields of interest: Higher education.
Type of support: Awards/prizes; Undergraduate support.
Application information: Applications accepted. Application form required. Application form available on the grantmaker's web site.
  Deadline(s): Mar. 18 for Pearson Prize for Higher Education
  Final notification: Recipients notified in June
Program descriptions:
  Pearson Fellowship for Social Innovation: This fellowship supports exemplary young leaders around the globe who are using their ingenuity, passion, and energy to build better lives for themselves and their communities. Two International Fellows will be named and receive a $5,000 award to help launch their project, while 10 addition fellows will receive a $1,000 award; all fellows will also receive one-on-one mentoring from experienced social innovators who consult with them as they implement their project plans.
  Pearson Prize for Higher Education: This prize celebrates students who are giving back to their college communities by providing cash awards to seventy students in recognition of their academic achievements and their commitment to their local communities. The prize recognizes students who have been attending a two- or four-year school, completed at least one year in college, and demonstrated leadership in community service. Twenty National Fellows will be named and awarded a two-year cash prize of $10,000; fifty Community Fellows will be chosen and receive a $500 award.
EIN: 113690722

6311
Dr. Abel E. Peck Memorial Fund
P.O. Box 389
Walton, NY 13856 (607) 865-4116
Application address: c/o Walton Central High School, Attn.: Guidance Dept., Walton, NY 13856

Foundation type: Independent foundation
Purpose: Scholarships to students of Walton Central School District No. 1, NY.
Financial data: Year ended 11/30/2013. Assets, $819,885 (M); Expenditures, $21,927; Total giving, $16,212; Grants to individuals, 4 grants totaling $16,212 (high: $4,500, low: $3,712).
Fields of interest: Higher education.
Type of support: Scholarships—to individuals; Support to graduates or students of specific schools.

Application information: Application form required.
  Initial approach: Letter
  Deadline(s): Apr. 1
  Additional information: Application available upon request from Walton Central School District guidance department.
EIN: 166254479

6312
PEN American Center, Inc.
588 Broadway, Ste. 303
New York, NY 10012-5246 (212) 334-1660
Contact: Suzanne Nossel, Exec. Dir.; Meghan Kyle-Miller, Devel. Assoc.
Additional e-mail: awards@pen.org
FAX: (212) 334-2181; E-mail: pen@pen.org; Additional E-Mail: info@pen.org; E-Mail for Linda Morgan: linda@pen.org; E-Mail for Suzanne Nossel: snossel@pen.org; URL: http://www.pen.org

Foundation type: Public charity
Purpose: Awards by nomination only to writers, translators, editors, and book critics in various categories. Also, emergency assistance to published writers and editors for unexpected financial crises and HIV/AIDS-related emergencies.
Publications: Application guidelines.
Financial data: Year ended 06/30/2011. Assets, $2,823,685 (M); Expenditures, $3,133,085; Total giving, $277,288; Grants to individuals, totaling $208,161.
Fields of interest: Print publishing; Literature; International human rights.
Type of support: Awards/grants by nomination only; Awards/prizes.
Application information: Application form required.
  Initial approach: Letter or telephone
  Deadline(s): Vary
Program descriptions:
  Beyond Margins Award: The award confers five $1,000 prizes upon authors of color. The program invites submission of book-length writings by authors of color, published in the United States during the current calendar year.
  Freedom-to-Write Awards: Under this program, the PEN/Katherine Anne Porter First Amendment Award of $10,000 is given to an American who has courageously striven to safeguard the right to free expression. In addition, the program awards one PEN/Barbara Goldsmith Freedom-to-Write Award of $10,000 to a foreign writer who is in prison or in danger as a consequence of their work. Applications for both awards are by nomination only.
  PEN Award for Poetry in Translation: The $3,000 award recognizes book-length translations of poetry from any language into English published during the current calendar year.
  PEN Translation Prize: The program offers a $3,000 award to honor book-length translations from any language into English published during the current calendar year.
  PEN Writers Fund: The program provides grants and loans to published professional literary writers or editors with serious financial difficulties.
  PEN/Jacqueline Bograd Weld Award: This program provides a $10,000 award to a distinguished biography published in the United States during the previous two calendar years.
  PEN/John Kenneth Galbraith Award for Nonfiction: The program offers a biennial prize of $10,000 to the author of a distinguished book of general nonfiction possessing notable literary merit.
  PEN/Laura Pels Awards for Drama: Two playwrights are selected for the following honors: a specially commissioned art object will be presented

to a master American dramatist, in recognition of his or her body of work; and a cash prize of $7,500 will be awarded to an American playwright in mid-career, whose literary achievements are vividly apparent in the rich and striking language of his or her work. In both cases, honorees are writers working indisputably at the highest level of achievement. Nominations are not accepted.
  PEN/Nabokov Award: This award of $20,000 celebrates the accomplishments of a living author whose body of work represents achievement in a variety of literary genres, and is of enduring originality and consummate craftsmanship. Applications are by nomination only.
  PEN/Nora Magid Award: This biennial award of $2,500 honors a magazine editor whose high literary standards and taste have, throughout his or her career, contributed significantly to the excellence of the publication he or she edits.
  PEN/Osterweil Award for Poetry: The program offers a grant award of $5,000 to recognize the high literary character of the published work to date of a new and emerging American poet of any age and the promise of further literary achievement. Applications are by nomination only.
  PEN/Phyllis Naylor Working Writer Fellowship: This fellowship of $5,000 is offered annually to an author of children's or young-adult fiction who is in financial need, and who has published at least two books, and no more than five, during the past ten years. Applications are by nomination only.
  PEN/Robert Bingham Fellowship for Writers: The fellowship ($35,000 a year for two consecutive years) honors exceptionally talented fiction writers whose debut work represents distinguished literary achievement and suggests great promise.
  PEN/Saul Bellow Award: This award of $40,000 is given to a distinguished living American author of fiction whose body of work in English possesses qualities of excellence, ambition, and scale of achievement over a sustained career which place him or her in the highest rank of American literature. Applications are by nomination only.
  PEN/Voelcker Award for Poetry: This biennial award of $5,000 is presented to an American poet whose distinguished and growing body of work to date represents a notable and accomplished presence in American literature.
  Translation Fund Grants: These grants aim at increasing the number and quality of literary translations published in English. The amount of the grant will vary from $2,000 to $10,000, depending on the nature and length of the project and the number of proposals deemed worthy of support during a given year.
EIN: 133447888

6313
The Performance Zone, Inc.
75 Maiden Ln., Ste. 906
New York, NY 10038 (212) 691-6969
Contact: Jennifer Wright Cook, Exec. Dir.
FAX: (212) 255-2053; E-mail: audra@thefield.org; E-mail For Jennifer Wright Cook: jennifer@thefield.org; URL: http://www.thefield.org

Foundation type: Public charity
Purpose: Support to independent performing artists on a completely non-exclusive basis.
Financial data: Year ended 12/31/2012. Assets, $651,171 (M); Expenditures, $2,889,263; Total giving, $2,212,920; Grants to individuals, totaling $2,212,920.
Fields of interest: Performing arts; Arts, artist's services.
Type of support: Residencies; Fiscal agent/sponsor.

Application information: Applications accepted. Application form required. Application form available on the grantmaker's web site.
Initial approach: Telephone or e-mail
Deadline(s): May 12 for Artward Bound, Aug. 17 for Field Artist Residency
Final notification: Recipients notified Aug. 31 for FAR residency
Program descriptions:
Field Artist Residencies (FAR): The Field Artist Residency supports the creative endeavors of performing artists working with movement as they work toward an upcoming production. The program aims to alleviate the financial and logistical burden of the 'space chase' so that artists can focus on their creative process. The Emerging Artist Residency offers performing artists a supportive structure of resources and guidance to allow them to delve more fully into their creative work. A group of seven artists will be selected to develop their work through workshops with fellow resident artists to discuss their projects and career development, and to exchange feedback on their work. A showcase performance concludes the program.
Sponsored Artist Program: The program enables independent performing artists to receive contributions and grants to help make their artistic and career goals a reality. See web site, http://www.thefield.org/t-Sponsored_Artist_Program.aspx for additional information.
EIN: 133357408

6314
Petra Foundation Charitable Trust
115 S. Oxford St., Ste. 575
Brooklyn, NY 11217 (212) 665-6673
Contact: Robin Templeton, Exec. Dir.
Application address: c/o Muriel Morisey Spence, Chair., Award Comm., P.O. Box 11579, Washington, DC 20008-0779, tel.: (202) 364-8964
FAX: (212) 864-4924;
E-mail: info@petrafoundation.org; E-mail for Robin Templeton: robin@petrafoundation.org;
URL: http://petrafoundation.org/

Foundation type: Public charity
Purpose: Grants and fellowships to individuals to promote research, teaching and education in the areas of civil rights, human rights and social justice.
Financial data: Year ended 03/31/2012. Assets, $140,630 (M); Expenditures, $233,075; Total giving, $30,000; Grants to individuals, totaling $30,000.
Fields of interest: International human rights; Civil/human rights, advocacy.
Type of support: Awards/grants by nomination only; Awards/prizes.
Application information:
Send request by: Mail or e-mail
Deadline(s): Feb. 21
Additional information: Awards are by nomination only. See web site for additional guidelines and nomination form.
EIN: 046603552

6315
Pfizer Patient Assistance Foundation, Inc.
235 E. 42nd St.
New York, NY 10017-5703 (866) 706-2400
Application address: Pfizer Connection to Care Prog., P.O. Box 66585, St. Louis, MO 63166; Pfizer MAINTAIN, P.O. Box 66549, St. Louis, MO 63166; Tel. for Sharing the Care Prog.: (800) 984-1500; Tel. for Pfizer Bridge Prog.: (800) 645-1280;

URL: http://www.pfizerhelpfulanswers.com/pages/misc/Default.aspx

Foundation type: Operating foundation
Purpose: Assistance with medication to uninsured, underinsured patients, and economically disadvantaged patients in need through health centers, hospitals, and healthcare providers.
Publications: Application guidelines; Informational brochure.
Financial data: Year ended 12/31/2012. Assets, $17,817,709 (M); Expenditures, $528,618,809; Total giving, $515,726,553; Grants to individuals, totaling $410,301,026.
Fields of interest: Pharmacy/prescriptions; Economically disadvantaged.
Type of support: Grants for special needs.
Application information: Applications accepted. Application form available on the grantmaker's web site.
Initial approach: Application
Send request by: Mail
Deadline(s): None
Additional information: Patient assistance is administered through Pfizer Helpful Answers, a joint program of Pfizer, Inc. and the Pfizer Patient Assistance Foundation. Applications should include proof of income and must be signed by a health physician.
Program descriptions:
Connection to Care: Through Connection to Care, the foundation provides free Pfizer medicines to individuals through healthcare providers. Applicants should have no prescription coverage or should qualify for hardship assistance. The program includes a 90-day supply of medicine that is shipped directly to healthcare provider's office.
First Resource: The foundation provides reimbursement support services and patient assistance to help patients gain access to select Pfizer medicines. The program also provides free medicine and co-payment assistance to patients with prescription coverage who are having financial difficulties.
Pfizer Bridge Program: Through the Pfizer Bridge Program, the foundation provides reimbursement support services and patient assistance for the Pfizer medications Genotropin and Somavert. Applicants must be uninsured or underinsured, have no prescription coverage, and meet the household income guidelines.
RSVP: Through Reimbursement Solutions, Verification, and Payment HELPline, the foundation offers reimbursement support services and patient assistance for select Pfizer medicines. The program also provides free medicine and co-payment assistance to patients with prescription coverage who are having financial difficulties.
Sharing the Care: Through Sharing the Care, the foundation partners with federally qualified health centers and Disproportionate Share hospitals to provide free medicine to eligible uninsured patients across the country.
EIN: 261437283

6316
Philippe Foundation, Inc.
c/o Philippe Investment Mgmt., Inc.
1 Penn Plz., Ste. 1628
New York, NY 10119
Contact: Beatrice Philippe, Pres.; Alain Philippe, V.P.

Foundation type: Independent foundation
Purpose: Grants primarily for cancer research to French and American physicians and scientists. Living and travel expenses and supplemental

support are also given to recipients of research grants.
Publications: Application guidelines.
Financial data: Year ended 12/31/2012. Assets, $6,257,006 (M); Expenditures, $625,238; Total giving, $574,157.
Fields of interest: Medical research.
International interests: France.
Type of support: Research; Exchange programs; Travel grants.
Application information: Applications accepted.
Initial approach: Letter
Deadline(s): One month before end of quarter
Applicants should submit the following:
1) Budget Information
2) Resume
3) Letter(s) of recommendation
Additional information: Application must be sent in triplicate and may be written in either English or French.
EIN: 136087157

6317
Poetry Society of America
15 Gramercy Park
New York, NY 10003-1705 (212) 254-9628
Contact: Alice Quinn, Exec. Dir.
FAX: (212) 673-2352; URL: http://www.poetrysociety.org

Foundation type: Public charity
Purpose: Awards honoring excellence in poetry by new and established poets.
Publications: Application guidelines.
Financial data: Year ended 06/30/2012. Assets, $3,171,565 (M); Expenditures, $470,120.
Fields of interest: Literature.
Type of support: Awards/prizes.
Application information:
Send request by: Mail
Copies of proposal: 2
Deadline(s): Dec. 22
Additional information: See web site for complete list of programs.
EIN: 136019220

6318
The Pollock-Krasner Foundation, Inc.
863 Park Ave.
New York, NY 10075-0380 (212) 517-5400
Contact: Caroline Black, Prog. Off.
FAX: (212) 288-2836; E-mail: grants@pkf.org;
E-mail for application-related questions: grantapplication@pkf.org; URL: http://www.pkf.org

Foundation type: Independent foundation
Purpose: Grants based on financial need as well as merit to talented painters, sculptors, and artists who work on paper (including printmakers) in the U.S. and abroad, to further their artistic pursuits.
Publications: Application guidelines; Annual report; Informational brochure (including application guidelines).
Financial data: Year ended 06/30/2012. Assets, $56,416,156 (M); Expenditures, $4,502,367; Total giving, $2,039,900.
Fields of interest: Visual arts; Sculpture; Design; Painting; Arts, artist's services.
Type of support: Awards/grants by nomination only; Foreign applicants; Awards/prizes; Grants for special needs.
Application information: Application form required.
Initial approach: Letter
Deadline(s): None
Applicants should submit the following:
1) Resume

2) Curriculum vitae

Additional information: Application must include a biographical record, ten slides of current work, and a cover letter stating the purpose of the grant and the amount requested.

Program descriptions:

Lee Krasner Awards: Lee Krasner Awards are based on the same criteria as all regular Pollock-Krasner grants, but are given in recognition of a lifetime of artistic achievement. This honor is a tribute to and recognition of artists with long and distinguished careers. This award is by nomination only.

Special Needs Grant: Financial assistance to individual working artists of established ability through the generosity of the late Lee Krasner, one of the leading abstract expressionist painters and widow of Jackson Pollock. The foundation welcomes nominations and applications from painters, sculptors, graphic, mixed media, and installation artists of artistic merit. There is no age or geographic limitation. The foundation does not give grants to commercial artists, photographers, video artists, filmmakers, craft-makers, or students who are not or have not been working artists. Grants are not awarded as scholarships or for tuition reimbursements. Grants are intended for a one-year period. Legitimate expenditures relating to work, living, and medical care are considered, as is emergency assistance. Grants are not made for past debts, legal fees, the purchase of real estate, moves to other cities, or to pay for installations or projects ordered by others. Both recipients and those refused grants may reapply in 12 months.

EIN: 133255693

6319
The Generoso Pope Foundation
(formerly The Pope Foundation)
1 Generoso Pope Pl.
Tuckahoe, NY   10707   (914) 793-7777
Contact: David Pope, C.E.O.
FAX: (914) 793-7748; URL: http://www.gpfny.org

Foundation type: Independent foundation
Purpose: Scholarships for higher education for students who are residents of Westchester, NY, possess a minimum GPA of 3.0, who have competitive SAT scores, and are active in community service.
Financial data: Year ended 12/31/2012. Assets, $13,142,767 (M); Expenditures, $2,386,061; Total giving, $1,007,967.
Fields of interest: Higher education.
Type of support: Scholarships—to individuals.
Application information: Applicant must also be of at least 50 percent Italian heritage.
EIN: 136096193

6320
The Population Council, Inc.
1 Dag Hammarskjold Plz.
New York, NY   10017-2203   (212) 339-0500
FAX: (212) 756-6052;
E-mail: pubinfo@popcouncil.org; URL: http://www.popcouncil.org

Foundation type: Public charity
Purpose: Fellowships to population specialists, biomedical specialists, biomedical researchers, and those studying reproductive biology and immunology.
Publications: Annual report; Newsletter.
Financial data: Year ended 12/31/2011. Assets, $135,947,611 (M); Expenditures, $85,080,839;

Total giving, $11,206,273; Grants to individuals, totaling $746,410.
Fields of interest: Reproductive health; Population studies.
Type of support: Fellowships.
Application information: Applications not accepted.

Additional information: Unsolicited requests for funds not considered or acknowledged.

Program descriptions:

Fred H. Bixby Fellowship Program: The fellowship program seeks to expand opportunities for recently trained population specialists and biomedical specialists and biomedical researchers. The program is a ten-year program, beginning in Jan. 2007. The program is highly competitive and offers a limited number of fellowships each year. The fellowships allow citizens of developing countries to work with experienced mentors in the council's network of offices. Fellows work on projects in the following program areas: HIV and AIDS; Reproductive Health; Poverty; and Gender and Youth.

Reproductive Biology and Immunology Postdoctoral Fellowship: The council offers fellowships to persons who wish to pursue advanced study in reproductive biology and immunology. Fellows train in the laboratories of the council's Center for Biomedical Research. Fundamental biomedical research leads to innovative technical advances that will become the reproductive health products of the future. By its nature, this basic research is highly technical and under rapid change. There is an ongoing need in council laboratories for highly skilled scientists who have been trained in modern medical science or in biomolecular research. In turn, young scientists from around the world need guidance and outstanding facilities to foster their transition to careers as independent investigators in the United States or in their home countries. The postdoctoral training program in reproductive biology and immunology at the council was designed to fulfill these complementary needs.

EIN: 131687001

6321
Ralph B. Post Trust
c/o NBT Bank, N.A.
52 S. Broad St.
Norwich, NY   13815
Application address: c/o Post Memorial Scholarship Fund, NBT Bank, N.A., 241 Main St., Ste. 200, Buffalo, NY 14203, tel.: (716) 566-3032

Foundation type: Independent foundation
Purpose: Scholarships to women who are residents of the Village of Ballston Spa, NY majoring in nursing, laboratory technology or cytology.
Financial data: Year ended 09/30/2013. Assets, $2,128,388 (M); Expenditures, $207,403; Total giving, $184,274; Grants to individuals, 33 grants totaling $184,274 (high: $21,323, low: $625).
Fields of interest: Nursing school/education; Biology/life sciences; Women.
Type of support: Scholarships—to individuals.
Application information:
Deadline(s): None
EIN: 146052967

6322
The Philip E. Potter Foundation
6 Ford Ave.
Oneonta, NY   13820-1818   (607) 432-6720
Contact: Anne T. Wolek, Fdn. Mgr.

Foundation type: Independent foundation
Purpose: Scholarships primarily to graduates of Oneonta High School in Oneonta, NY.
Financial data: Year ended 10/31/2012. Assets, $10,078,367 (M); Expenditures, $453,178; Total giving, $299,750; Grants to individuals, 364 grants totaling $299,750 (high: $1,750, low: $250).
Type of support: Support to graduates or students of specific schools; Undergraduate support.
Application information: Application form required.
Deadline(s): May 15
Additional information: Application must include high school evaluation form and financial information; Application forms available from local high school and foundation office.
EIN: 166169167

6323
Stephen J. Potter Memorial Foundation, Inc.
c/o John McDonald
P.O. Box 391
Ticonderoga, NY   12883
Application Address: c/o Scholarship to Ticonderoga High School, Attn: Principal, Calkins Pl., Ticonderoga, NY. 12883

Foundation type: Independent foundation
Purpose: Scholarships to graduating seniors of Ticonderoga High School, NY for higher education.
Financial data: Year ended 09/30/2012. Assets, $506,469 (M); Expenditures, $35,972; Total giving, $24,000; Grants to individuals, 22 grants totaling $24,000 (high: $1,500, low: $750).
Type of support: Support to graduates or students of specific schools; Undergraduate support.
Application information: Applications accepted. Application form required.
Deadline(s): Apr. 1
EIN: 146016858

6324
Preferred Mutual Insurance Company Foundation
c/o NBT Bank, N.A.
52 S. Broad St.
Norwich, NY   13815-1646   (800) 333-7642
Contact: Kecia Burton
E-mail: info@pminsco.com

Foundation type: Company-sponsored foundation
Purpose: Scholarships to students in Chenango, Delaware, and Otsego counties, NY for postsecondary education.
Financial data: Year ended 12/31/2012. Assets, $999,187 (M); Expenditures, $60,034; Total giving, $59,195; Grants to individuals, 11 grants totaling $22,040 (high: $2,500, low: $500).
Fields of interest: Higher education.
Type of support: Scholarships—to individuals.
Application information: Applications accepted. Application form required. Interview required.
Deadline(s): Apr. 12
Additional information: Selection is based on academic performance.
EIN: 226423721

6325
Prescott Fund for Children & Youth, Inc.
521 5th Ave.
New York, NY   10175-1799

Foundation type: Independent foundation

Purpose: Scholarships to high school graduates in the New York area for attendance at colleges or universities.
Financial data: Year ended 12/31/2012. Assets, $1,232,447 (M); Expenditures, $154,116; Total giving, $68,884.
Fields of interest: Higher education.
Type of support: Scholarships—to individuals.
Application information: Award is based on academic achievement and need. Contact trust for application guidelines.
EIN: 131674446

6326
William Pressman Co. Trust
1100 Wehrle Dr., 2nd Fl.
Amherst, NY   14221
Contact: Charles R. Dashiell, Jr. Esq., Tr.
Application Address: P.O. Box 138, Salisbury, MD 21803, Tel.: (717) 852-3011

Foundation type: Independent foundation
Purpose: Scholarships to graduates of Wicomico High School, Wicomico Junior High, and Parkside High School, all in MD, who participated in their school's marching and concert bands throughout high school, and continue in both the marching and concert bands in college.
Financial data: Year ended 06/30/2013. Assets, $350,810 (M); Expenditures, $24,196; Total giving, $17,355.
Fields of interest: Music.
Type of support: Undergraduate support.
Application information:
   Deadline(s): None
EIN: 521885294

6327
Price Chopper's Golub Foundation
(formerly Golub Foundation)
461 Nott St.
Schenectady, NY   12308-1812   (518) 356-9450
FAX: (518) 374-4259; Application address: P.O. Box 1074, Schenectady, NY 12301; Additional tel.: (877) 877-0870; URL: http://www.pricechopper.com/community/golub-foundation

Foundation type: Company-sponsored foundation
Purpose: Scholarships to residents of areas served by Price Chopper Supermarkets, including upstate NH, NY, MA, PA, VT, and northwestern CT, who are entering two- or four-year colleges or graduate schools in NY, MA, PA, VT, NH, or CT.
Publications: Application guidelines; Informational brochure (including application guidelines).
Financial data: Year ended 03/31/2013. Assets, $153,951 (M); Expenditures, $1,196,043; Total giving, $1,111,914.
Fields of interest: Research; Health care; Business/industry; Computer science; Minorities; Asians/Pacific Islanders; African Americans/Blacks; Hispanics/Latinos; Native Americans/American Indians.
Type of support: Employee-related scholarships; Graduate support; Undergraduate support.
Application information: Applications accepted. Application form required. Application form available on the grantmaker's web site. Interview required.
   Initial approach: Application
   Send request by: Online
   Deadline(s): Mar. 15
   Final notification: Recipients notified by May 22
   Applicants should submit the following:
      1) Essay

2) Transcripts
3) SAT
4) Letter(s) of recommendation
Additional information: Application must include an original essay of less than 1,000 words on why the foundation should award the scholarship. Graduate scholarship applicants must also supply GRE and/or LSAT or MCAT test scores, if applicable. See program descriptions for further limitations.
Program descriptions:
   Computer Studies Scholarship: The foundation annually awards one $8,000 college scholarship to a graduating high school senior who has demonstrated scholastic ability and is planning to enter the computer sciences, computer information systems, electronic arts, or graphic design field.
   Founder's Scholarships: The foundation annually awards two $8,000 college scholarships to graduating high school seniors who have demonstrated outstanding leadership and scholastic abilities.
   Graduate or Professional School Scholarship: The foundation annually awards one $4,000 scholarship to a graduating college senior or college graduate who has demonstrated scholastic ability.
   Junior College Transfer Scholarship: The foundation annually awards one $4,000 college scholarship to a graduating community or junior college student or community or junior college graduate who has demonstrated scholastic ability.
   Lewis Golub Scholarship for Entrepreneurial Sprit: The foundation annually awards one $8,000 college scholarship to a graduating high school senior who has demonstrated scholastic ability and entrepreneurial sprit.
   Lotte Meers Memorial Scholarship for Educators: The foundation annually awards one $8,000 college scholarship to a graduating high school senior who has demonstrated scholastic ability and has chosen to enter the field of education.
   Tillie Golub-Schwartz Memorial Scholarship for Minorities: The foundation annually awards one $8,000 college scholarship to a minority graduating high school senior who has shown a commitment to humanity through demonstrated activities in school, community, or religious organizations.
   Two-Year Health Care Scholarship: The foundation annually awards a $2,000 college scholarship to a graduating high school senior planning to study health care at a degree-granting community or junior college.
   Two-Year Scholarship: The foundation annually awards a $2,000 college scholarship to a graduating high school senior planning to attend a degree-granting community or junior college.
Company name: Golub Corporation
EIN: 222341421

6328
PricewaterhouseCoopers Charitable Foundation, Inc.
(formerly Coopers & Lybrand Foundation)
300 Madison Ave.
New York, NY   10017-6232   (813) 348-7725
URL: http://www.pwc.com/us/en/about-us/corporate-responsibility/corporate-responsibility-report-2011/community/charitable-foundation.jhtml

Foundation type: Public charity
Purpose: Assistance to PwC employees and their families facing financial difficulties in their own personal lives as a result of health emergencies, property losses, loss of a family member or other challenging situations.

Financial data: Year ended 09/30/2011. Assets, $16,564,273 (M); Expenditures, $2,661,257; Total giving, $2,092,719; Grants to individuals, totaling $432,124.
Fields of interest: Disasters, floods; Safety/disasters.
Type of support: Employee-related welfare; Grants for special needs.
Application information: Applications not accepted.
   Additional information: Unsolicited requests for funds not considered or acknowledge. Assistance only for PwC employees and their families.
EIN: 136116238

6329
Princess Grace Foundation - U.S.A.
150 E. 58th St., 25th Fl.
New York, NY   10155-0002   (212) 317-1470
Contact: Toby E. Boshak, Exec. Dir.
FAX: (212) 317-1473; E-mail: grants@pgfusa.org; Additional e-mail: info@pgfusa.org; URL: http://www.pgfusa.org

Foundation type: Public charity
Purpose: Scholarships, apprenticeships, and fellowships to emerging artists in the fields of theater, dance, playwriting, and film who are U.S. citizens or permanent residents.
Publications: Application guidelines; Annual report; Financial statement; Grants list; Newsletter.
Financial data: Year ended 12/31/2011. Assets, $15,165,973 (M); Expenditures, $2,031,464; Total giving, $793,151; Grants to individuals, totaling $793,151.
Fields of interest: Film/video; Performing arts; Dance; Choreography; Theater; Theater (playwriting).
Type of support: Fellowships; Grants to individuals; Scholarships—to individuals; Awards/grants by nomination only.
Application information: Applications accepted. Application form required. Application form available on the grantmaker's web site.
   Initial approach: Letter
   Copies of proposal: 1
   Deadline(s): Apr. 1 for theater and playwriting, Apr. 30 for dance performance and dance choreography
   Final notification: Recipient notified July 31 for Theater, Dance Performance and Dance Choreography
   Applicants should submit the following:
      1) SASE
      2) Resume
      3) Letter(s) of recommendation
      4) Work samples
   Additional information: See web site for additional application information.
Program description:
   JustFilms Documentary Award: Made possible by the Ford Foundation, the award seeks to identify and support voices that tell authentic and powerful stories from or about underrepresented communities. These funds will be awarded to help support social justice documentary thesis projects of students in undergraduate/graduate programs and final projects of individuals participating in production programs at media arts centers. Grants will be made in accordance with the applicants' thesis/final project budgets. Candidates from colleges and universities must be full-time students or matriculated but have not yet completed their thesis films, have completed at least one film as director, be the director of the proposed thesis film,

and be a United States citizen or be able to demonstrate proof of permanent resident status.
EIN: 232218331

6330
Professional Horsemen's Scholarship Fund
c/o Ann Grenci
202 Old Sleepy Hollow Rd.
Pleasantville, NY 10570 (914) 769-1493
Application address: 20 Via Del Corso, Palm Beach Gardens, FL 33418

Foundation type: Operating foundation
Purpose: Scholarships to members of the Professional Horsemen's Association for higher education.
Financial data: Year ended 12/31/2011. Assets, $147,986 (M); Expenditures, $17,000; Total giving, $17,000; Grants to individuals, 18 grants totaling $17,000 (high: $1,000, low: $500).
Type of support: Scholarships—to individuals.
Application information: Application form required.
  Initial approach: Letter or telephone
  Deadline(s): July 1
  Additional information: Application must include letter outlining financial need and proof of professional membership in Professional Horsemen's Association.
EIN: 066086137

6331
Professional Women Photographers, Inc.
119 W. 72nd St., Ste. 223
New York, NY 10023-3201 (212) 794-0251
Contact: Beth Portnoi-Shaw, Pres.
For Student Awards: Patricia Gilman, Dir., tel.: (212) 362-7435, e-mail: beyondthelens42@yahoo.com
E-mail: info@pwponline.org; URL: http://www.pwponline.org

Foundation type: Public charity
Purpose: Awards to young women enrolled in a New York City high school with an enthusiasm for photography, in addition to a fiscal sponsorship program for members of the organization.
Publications: Application guidelines.
Financial data: Year ended 06/30/2012. Assets, $99,460 (M); Expenditures, $62,962.
Fields of interest: Photography; Young adults, female.
Type of support: Awards/prizes; Fiscal agent/sponsor.
Application information: Application form required. Application form available on the grantmaker's web site.
  Initial approach: Letter or e-mail for fiscal sponsorship program
  Deadline(s): Varies
  Applicants should submit the following:
    1) Work samples
    2) SASE
    3) Letter(s) of recommendation
Program descriptions:
  Fiscal Sponsorship: The organization provides its members the opportunity to use it as a fiscal sponsor, to gain access to funds that might not normally be available to individuals.
  Student Awards: These awards are given to young women enrolled in a New York City public high school, with an enthusiasm for and talent in photography. There are two categories for submission: 9th and 10th grade, and 11th and 12th grade. One $1,000 first prize in each category

will be awarded, as well as two $500 second prizes and two third prizes of $250 each.
EIN: 133163521

6332
Project A.L.S., Inc.
3960 Broadway, Ste. 420
New York, NY 10032-1543 (212) 420-7382
Contact: Meredith Estess, Pres.
FAX: (212) 781-3241; E-mail: info@projectals.org;
Toll-free tel.: (800)-603-0270; URL: http://www.projectals.org

Foundation type: Public charity
Purpose: Specific assistance to researchers for the treatment and cure of the disease known as Amyotrophic Lateral Sclerosis (ALS).
Publications: Annual report; Financial statement; Informational brochure; Newsletter.
Financial data: Year ended 07/31/2011. Assets, $2,731,589 (M); Expenditures, $5,087,250; Total giving, $3,008,032.
Fields of interest: Brain research.
Type of support: Research.
Application information:
  Initial approach: Letter or telephone
EIN: 134019464

6333
Project Dream Foundation
P.O. Box 8005
Rock Hill, NY 12775
E-mail: info@projectdreamfoundation.org;
URL: http://www.projectdreamfoundation.org

Foundation type: Independent foundation
Purpose: Scholarships to deserving young men and women of the Monticello Central School District, NY pursuing a higher education at a college of their choice.
Financial data: Year ended 12/31/2010. Assets, $131,864 (M); Expenditures, $17,860; Total giving, $1,100.
Fields of interest: Higher education.
Type of support: Scholarships—to individuals; Support to graduates or students of specific schools.
Application information: Selection is based on students who have overcome adversity and are in financial need, and to students who have exemplified dedicated excellence in athletics, community service, art and/or music, or peer leadership and support.
EIN: 203916575

6334
Project Home Again Foundation
c/o Bryan Cave LLP
1290 Ave. of the Americas
New York, NY 10104
Application address: P.O. Box 851008, New Orleans, LA 70185-1008; tel.: (866) 550-4742;
URL: http://www.projecthomeagain.net

Foundation type: Operating foundation
Purpose: Grants to low and moderate income families in New Orleans, LA, who, due to Hurricane Katrina, own homes that are uninhabitable in Gentilly (Planning District 6) in Orleans Parish.
Publications: Application guidelines.
Financial data: Year ended 03/31/2012. Assets, $13,529,442 (M); Expenditures, $3,489,039; Total giving, $948,320; Grants to individuals, 38 grants totaling $948,320 (high: $31,600, low: $18,000).

Fields of interest: Housing/shelter; Disasters, Hurricane Katrina; Economically disadvantaged.
Type of support: Emergency funds.
Application information: Applications accepted. Application form required. Application form available on the grantmaker's web site.
  Initial approach: Application
  Additional information: Applicants must meet family size and income requirements. Contact foundation for additional guidelines.
EIN: 208733214

6335
Project Renewal, Inc.
200 Varick St., 9th Fl.
New York, NY 10014-4810 (212) 620-0340
Contact: Mitchell Netburn, Pres. and C.E.O.
E-mail: careers@projectrenewal.org; URL: http://www.projectrenewal.org

Foundation type: Public charity
Purpose: Financial assistance to homeless residents of New York, NY, particularly those suffering from addiction or mental illness.
Publications: Annual report.
Financial data: Year ended 06/30/2012. Assets, $36,361,398 (M); Expenditures, $48,578,422; Total giving, $61,977.
Fields of interest: Substance abuse, services; Mental health, treatment; Disabilities, people with; Homeless.
Type of support: Grants for special needs.
Application information: Contact the organization for additional information.
EIN: 132602882

6336
Provident Bank Charitable Foundation
400 Rella Blvd.
Montebello, NY 10901-4241
URL: http://www.providentbanking.com/foundation_Mission.cfm

Foundation type: Operating foundation
Purpose: Scholarships to high school seniors from Rockland, Orange, Ulster, Sullivan, Putnam, Dutchess, and Westchester counties, NY, and Bergen County, NJ, who are attending a college in one of those counties and have completed at least 40 hours of community service over the last two years.
Publications: Application guidelines; Annual report.
Financial data: Year ended 12/31/2010. Assets, $3,600,486 (M); Expenditures, $154,080; Total giving, $140,491.
Type of support: Undergraduate support.
Application information: Applications accepted. Application form required. Application form available on the grantmaker's web site.
  Deadline(s): May 1
  Final notification: Recipients notified in June
  Applicants should submit the following:
    1) Essay
    2) Letter(s) of recommendation
  Additional information: Application should also include a college acceptance letter.
EIN: 321013899

6337
Public Interest Law Foundation at Columbia

(formerly Columbia Foundation for Public Interest Law, also known as PILF)
435 W. 116 St.
New York, NY 10027-7201 (212) 854-5917
Contact: Maggie Maurone, V.P., Community Grants;
For Fellowships: Kim Zafran, Dir., Pub. Svc.
Fellowships
FAX: (212) 854-8873;
E-mail: pilf.grants@gmail.com; URL: http://www.columbia.edu/cu/pilf/

Foundation type: Public charity
Purpose: Fellowships to provide supplementary support for Columbia Law School, NY, students engaged in public interest law summer internships.
Publications: Application guidelines; Grants list; Newsletter.
Financial data: Year ended 01/31/2010. Assets, $217,974 (M); Expenditures, $50,000; Total giving, $50,000. Scholarships—to individuals amount not specified.
Fields of interest: Legal services, public interest law.
Type of support: Fellowships; Internship funds; Graduate support.
Application information: Applications accepted. Application form required.
  Initial approach: Telephone or e-mail
  Deadline(s): Dec. 5
  Applicants should submit the following:
    1) Curriculum vitae
    2) Budget Information
    3) Letter(s) of recommendation
  Additional information: Proposals must be a maximum of ten double-spaced typed pages. Application must also include a project description and timetable.
Program description:
  Student Fellowships: The foundation provides stipends to Columbia Law School students engaging in public interest legal work over the summer. The grants allow the students to accept internships at nonprofit organizations and government agencies that do not have the resources to pay summer legal interns.
EIN: 133007632

6338
Public Media, Inc.

521 E. 14th St., Ste. 4F
New York, NY 10009 (917) 608-7427
Contact: Eugene N. Aleinikoff, Exec. Dir.
E-mail: pubmediainc@aol.com; URL: http://www.publicmediainc.org

Foundation type: Public charity
Purpose: Grants and support to independent film producers for the production of documentary films.
Publications: Financial statement; Occasional report.
Financial data: Year ended 06/30/2012. Assets, $110,854 (M); Expenditures, $48,851; Total giving, $38,763.
Fields of interest: Film/video; Arts, artist's services.
Type of support: Grants to individuals; Fiscal agent/sponsor.
Application information: Applications accepted. Application form not required.
  Initial approach: Letter or e-mail
  Send request by: Mail

Copies of proposal: 1
Deadline(s): None
Final notification: 2-3 weeks after receipt of application
Applicants should submit the following:
  1) Budget Information
  2) Curriculum vitae
  3) Proposal
Program description:
  Fiscal Sponsorship: The organization assists independent video- and film-makers who qualify for a foundation or corporate grant or individual donation, for which the donor requires the recipient to have nonprofit status under 501(c)(3) of the U.S. Internal Revenue Code. The organization charges a 5 percent administrative fee for all monies received.
EIN: 132839977

6339
Puerto Rican Bar Association Scholarship Fund, Inc.

c/o Church Street Station
303 Park Ave. S., Ste. 1405
New York, NY 10010-3601 (212) 313-5458
Contact: Rosevelie M. Morales, Pres.
URL: http://www.prba.net/

Foundation type: Public charity
Purpose: Scholarships to first- or second-year Latino law students who are in a JD program at an American Bar Association-approved law school. Students working towards their L.L.M. may not apply. Third-year evening law students are also eligible.
Publications: Application guidelines.
Financial data: Year ended 12/31/2012. Assets, $79,430 (M); Expenditures, $43,716; Total giving, $27,000.
Fields of interest: Law school/education; Hispanics/Latinos.
Type of support: Graduate support.
Application information: Applications accepted. Application form required. Application form available on the grantmaker's web site.
  Send request by: Mail
  Deadline(s): Mar. 14
  Final notification: Recipients notified in Apr.
  Applicants should submit the following:
    1) Letter(s) of recommendation
    2) Financial information
    3) Resume
    4) Transcripts
  Additional information: Application should also include a personal statement.
EIN: 061016586

6340
Queens College Foundation, Inc.

65-30 Kissena Blvd., Kiely Hall, Rm. 1306
Flushing, NY 11367-1575 (718) 997-3920
Contact: Laurie F. Dorf, Exec. Dir.
FAX: (718) 997-3924;
E-mail: qc_foundation@qc.cuny.edu; URL: http://qcpages.qc.cuny.edu/QCF/index.php

Foundation type: Public charity
Purpose: Scholarships to students of Queens College, NY.
Financial data: Year ended 06/30/2012. Assets, $47,690,601 (M); Expenditures, $6,178,401; Total giving, $1,681,719; Grants to individuals, totaling $1,681,719.
Type of support: Support to graduates or students of specific schools.

Application information:
  Initial approach: Letter
  Additional information: Contact the Office of Honors and Scholarships.
EIN: 116080521

6341
Queens Council on the Arts, Inc.

37-11 35th Ave, Entrance on 37th St.
Astoria, NY 11101 (347) 505-3010
Contact: Hoong Yee Lee Krakauer, Exec. Dir.
FAX: (718) 647-5036;
E-mail: qca@queenscouncilarts.org; URL: http://www.queenscouncilarts.org

Foundation type: Public charity
Purpose: Grants and technical assistance to artists who are residents of the borough of Queens, NY.
Publications: Application guidelines; Annual report; Grants list; Informational brochure (including application guidelines); Newsletter.
Financial data: Year ended 06/30/2012. Assets, $743,704 (M); Expenditures, $983,566; Total giving, $437,471; Grants to individuals, totaling $437,471.
Fields of interest: Folk arts; Visual arts; Dance; Theater.
Type of support: Program development; Awards/prizes; Project support.
Application information: Applications accepted. Application form available on the grantmaker's web site.
  Initial approach: E-mail, telephone, in-person
  Send request by: Online
  Copies of proposal: 11
  Deadline(s): Oct. 5
  Final notification: Recipients notified in eight weeks
  Applicants should submit the following:
    1) Resume
    2) Work samples
    3) Proposal
    4) Budget Information
  Additional information: Applications by mail are not accepted.
Program descriptions:
  New York City Department of Cultural Affairs Greater New York Arts Development Fund: Grants of up to $2,000 to individuals who are residents of Queens, NY and must be 18 years of age. Applicants must work in any literary and performing art including, but not limited to, dance, music, theater, fiction and nonfiction literature, poetry, playwriting, spoken word, and folk arts. All individual artists are encouraged to apply, including those that represent various ethnic, social, and geographic areas. Collaborations is accepted and will be reviewed as one project.
  New York State Council on the Arts Decentralization Program for Individual Artists: Grants of up to $2,500 are available to support Queens-based individual artists to create new work directly involving the community. The artist must engage his or community through active participation in the creation and/or production of the project. The grant is specifically intended to fund projects in any visual arts discipline, including but not limited to: fiber, folk arts/traditional, graphics, media arts - film/video, painting, photography, printmaking, sculpture. Artist must be at least 18 years of age.
EIN: 112219193

6342
The Radius Foundation, Inc.
101 Central Park W., Ste. 2D-E
New York, NY 10023-4250
URL: http://radiusfoundation.org/

Foundation type: Operating foundation
Purpose: Grants to individuals for research of and publications about Islam.
Financial data: Year ended 12/31/2013. Assets, $186,488 (M); Expenditures, $66,890; Total giving, $18,736; Grants to individuals, 4 grants totaling $18,736 (high: $11,000, low: $500).
Fields of interest: Islam.
Type of support: Publication; Research.
Application information: Applications not accepted.
> *Additional information:* Unsolicited requests for funds not considered or acknowledged.

EIN: 760723998

6343
Rainforest Alliance, Inc.
233 Broadway, 28th Fl.
New York, NY 10279 (212) 677-1900
FAX: (212) 677-2187; E-mail: info@ra.org; Toll-free tel.: (888) MY-EARTH; URL: http://www.rainforest-alliance.org

Foundation type: Public charity
Purpose: Fellowships for research of the ecological, social and business challenges for successful non-timber forest product enterprises in Latin America.
Publications: Application guidelines.
Financial data: Year ended 06/30/2012. Assets, $18,613,190 (M); Expenditures, $40,723,740; Total giving, $3,241,513.
Fields of interest: Natural resources; Environment, forests.
International interests: Latin America.
Type of support: Fellowships; Research.
Application information: Applications accepted. Application form not required.
> *Applicants should submit the following:*
> 1) Letter(s) of recommendation
> 2) Proposal
> 3) Curriculum vitae
> 4) Budget Information
> *Additional information:* Contact foundation for current application deadline/guidelines.

Program description:
Kleinhans Fellowship: This fellowship supports research to better understand and improve the impacts of non-timber forest product (NTFP) harvest and marketing on rural livelihoods and tropical forest ecosystems in Latin America. A successful application will outline the need for research, its potential applications, and its likely impact on local communities and forest ecosystems. Applications for projects conducted in the Peten region of Guatemala or southern Mexico are especially encouraged. The fellowship provides a grant of $15,000 per year, for two years. Fellowships are not intended to subsidize academic tuition and fees, nor will it cover costs of purchasing transport vehicles, or unnecessary or unreasonable equipment.
EIN: 133377893

6344
Randon House Foundation, Inc.
(formerly Bertelsmann Foundation U.S., Inc.)
1745 Broadway
New York, NY 10019-4305
Contact: Melanie Fallon-Houska

Foundation type: Company-sponsored foundation
Purpose: Scholarships to graduating seniors of New York City public high schools.
Financial data: Year ended 12/31/2012. Assets, $21,736 (M); Expenditures, $238,279; Total giving, $111,500; Grants to individuals, 70 grants totaling $111,500 (high: $10,000, low: $500).
Fields of interest: Music; Literature.
Type of support: Undergraduate support.
Application information: Applications accepted. Application form required.
> *Deadline(s):* Mar. 1
> *Additional information:* Applicants are required to submit original literary compositions.

EIN: 133777740

6345
Alexander and Cassia Rau Trust
1 M&T Plz., 8th Fl.
Buffalo, NY 14203 (717) 845-8023
Application address: c/o St. Mark's Lutheran Church Council, Attn: Pres., 700 E. Market St., York, PA 17403-1607, tel.: (717) 845-8023

Foundation type: Independent foundation
Purpose: Student loans to members of St. Mark's Lutheran Church in PA, for higher education,.
Financial data: Year ended 12/31/2012. Assets, $312,808 (M); Expenditures, $19,137; Total giving, $14,000; Loan to an individual, 1 loan totaling $14,000.
Fields of interest: Higher education.
Type of support: Student loans—to individuals.
Application information:
> *Deadline(s):* None
> *Additional information:* Applications available from the Church Council.

EIN: 236417951

6346
Reaching Up, Inc.
c/o Citrin Cooperman and Co., LLP
529 5th Ave.
New York, NY 10017-4608 (212) 827-0660

Foundation type: Public charity
Purpose: Assistance to individuals employed in the mental retardation rehabilitation field with job and salary advancement through education.
Financial data: Year ended 12/31/2011. Assets, $89,140 (M); Expenditures, $103,390; Total giving, $15,250; Grants to individuals, totaling $15,250.
Fields of interest: Education, special; Education.
Type of support: Grants to individuals.
Application information: Contact the organization for additional information.
EIN: 133577206

6347
Realty Foundation of New York
551 5th Ave., Ste. 415
New York, NY 10176-0415
FAX: (212) 949-9319; E-mail: pfrfny@aol.com

Foundation type: Independent foundation
Purpose: Scholarships for full-time undergraduate and graduate-level study to employees and children of employees of the foundation's member firms in the real estate industry in the five boroughs of New York City. Assistance to financially needy employees of the real estate industry in the five boroughs of New York City.
Publications: Informational brochure.

Financial data: Year ended 06/30/2013. Assets, $2,300,263 (M); Expenditures, $581,994; Total giving, $321,350; Grants to individuals, 121 grants totaling $321,350 (high: $30,000, low: $300).
Fields of interest: Higher education; Business/industry; Community development, real estate; Economically disadvantaged.
Type of support: Employee-related scholarships; Scholarships—to individuals; Employee-related welfare; Undergraduate support.
Application information: Application form required.
> *Initial approach:* Letter or telephone
> *Deadline(s):* None
> *Additional information:* Application for scholarships should include letter(s) of recommendation and FAF. Application for employee-related welfare should include financial information and letter(s) of recommendation.

Program descriptions:
Charles B. Benenson Scholarship Program: The program is available to employees and children of employees of the member firms of the foundation Board of Directors. The program is available to college-bound students only. Applications should be requested from the foundation after acceptance to college.
Harry Helmsley Financial Aid Program: Awards financial aid to needy members of the real estate community for at least 3 years who hold a current license. Applications and interviews are required.
EIN: 136016622

6348
The REBNY Foundation Inc.
570 Lexington Ave.
New York, NY 10022-6837 (212) 532-3100
Contact: Angela Pinsky, Exec. Dir.

Foundation type: Independent foundation
Purpose: Financial assistance primarily to the homeless of New York, NY.
Financial data: Year ended 06/30/2012. Assets, $775,036 (M); Expenditures, $486,564; Total giving, $208,523.
Fields of interest: Housing/shelter, development; Economically disadvantaged; Homeless.
Type of support: Grants for special needs.
Application information:
> *Initial approach:* Letter
> *Deadline(s):* None
> *Additional information:* Letter should detail reason for assistance requested.

EIN: 133317104

6349
John A. Reddington Scholarship Fund & Trust
1221 Pittsford-Victor Rd.
Pittsford, NY 14534-3819 (585) 586-6900

Foundation type: Operating foundation
Purpose: Scholarships to students in NY who are attending or planning to attend Catholic school or college.
Financial data: Year ended 08/31/2013. Assets, $571,129 (M); Expenditures, $38,006; Total giving, $28,600; Grants to individuals, 192 grants totaling $28,600 (high: $3,667, low: $63).
Fields of interest: Higher education; Catholic agencies & churches.
Type of support: Precollege support; Undergraduate support.
Application information: Application form required.
> *Deadline(s):* Apr. 30

Additional information: Recipients must demonstrate a financial need using criteria normally utilized by institutions to which admission is sought.
EIN: 161555796

6350
Peter S. Reed Foundation, Inc.
(formerly The Concrete Foundation, Inc.)
125 Watts St., 2nd Fl.
New York, NY 10013 (212) 966-1507
Contact: Arne Svenson, Pres.

Foundation type: Independent foundation
Purpose: Grants to talented and needy artists in the performing, visual, and literary arts.
Financial data: Year ended 06/30/2012. Assets, $1,912,241 (M); Expenditures, $149,206; Total giving, $108,000; Grants to individuals, 24 grants totaling $105,000 (high: $6,600, low: $2,600).
Type of support: Grants to individuals.
Application information: Applications accepted. Application form required.
  Deadline(s): Apr. 1
EIN: 133036536

6351
The Reinhardt Family Scholarship Trust
1207 Delaware Ave.
Buffalo, NY 14209-1401 (716) 537-2131
Application address:c/o Selection Committee Holland Central, 103 Canada St., Holland, NY 14080

Foundation type: Independent foundation
Purpose: Scholarships to students of Holland Central High School, NY for attendance at a two or four year college or university.
Financial data: Year ended 12/31/2012. Assets, $112,171 (M); Expenditures, $13,454; Total giving, $10,500; Grants to individuals, 6 grants totaling $10,500 (high: $2,500, low: $1,000).
Fields of interest: Higher education.
Type of support: Support to graduates or students of specific schools; Undergraduate support.
Application information: Applications accepted. Application form required.
  Deadline(s): None
  Additional information: Applications available from high school.
EIN: 161512484

6352
Floyd J. Reinhart Memorial Scholarship Foundation
524 Maple Ave.
Saratoga Springs, NY 12866-5540 (518) 306-5261
Contact: Richard J. Cordovano, Tr.

Foundation type: Independent foundation
Purpose: Scholarships to current graduates of Canajoharie, Fort Plain, and St. Johnsville high schools, all in Montgomery County, NY.
Financial data: Year ended 06/30/2013. Assets, $2,458,936 (M); Expenditures, $102,966; Total giving, $86,000; Grants to individuals, 52 grants totaling $86,000 (high: $4,000, low: $1,000).
Type of support: Support to graduates or students of specific schools; Undergraduate support.
Application information: Applications accepted.
  Additional information: Contact foundation for current application deadline/guidelines.
EIN: 141605307

6353
Rental Assistance Corporation of Buffalo
470 Franklin St.
Buffalo, NY 14202-1302 (716) 882-0063
Contact: Mary Shine, Exec. Dir.
FAX: (716) 882-9512; Additional fax: (716) 886-3790; URL: http://racbny.org/

Foundation type: Public charity
Purpose: Rental assistance to low income families and elderly, or handicapped or disabled individuals in need in Buffalo, NY.
Financial data: Year ended 06/30/2012. Assets, $4,561,138 (M); Expenditures, $28,054,511; Total giving, $24,932,061; Grants to individuals, 5,000 grants totaling $24,932,061.
Fields of interest: Housing/shelter, expense aid; Housing/shelter; Economically disadvantaged.
Type of support: Emergency funds.
Application information: Applications accepted.
  Additional information: Some assistance require an application for eligibility. See web site for additional guidelines.
EIN: 161337423

6354
Research Foundation of The City University of New York
230 W. 41st St., 7th Fl.
New York, NY 10036-7207 (212) 417-8300
Contact: Richard F. Rothbard, Pres.
E-mail: questions@rfcuny.org; URL: http://www.rfcuny.org

Foundation type: Public charity
Purpose: Scholarships and fellowships to undergraduate and graduate students attending City University of New York, NY. Funds for research and creative projects to all permanent full-time faculty members of City University of New York, NY.
Publications: Annual report; Financial statement.
Financial data: Year ended 06/30/2012. Assets, $285,371,545 (M); Expenditures, $448,930,039; Total giving, $27,095,873; Grants to individuals, totaling $27,095,873.
Fields of interest: University.
Type of support: Research; Support to graduates or students of specific schools.
Application information:
  Initial approach: Letter or e-mail
  Deadline(s): Jan. 15
  Final notification: Applicants notified Apr. 15
  Additional information: Scholarships based on various sets of criteria established by the restricted projects and by type of awards listed in the CUNY catalogue. Application for CUNY Research Program must include a proposal. Contact foundation for program descriptions and application procedures.
Program description:
  Professional Staff Congress-City University of New York (PSC-CUNY) Research Award Program: Funding for research and creative project are available to all permanent full-time staff members within the CUNY system, with emphasis on junior members of the faculty (defined as those at the rank of untenured associate professor, assistant professor, instructor, or lecturer). Eligible proposals must involve original research or creative activates, headed by a principal investigator. Applications will be evaluated on the scholarly/creative merit of the project, the ability of the applicant to perform such work successfully, and the potential for the research to be awarded funding from external agencies or attain national or international prominence.
EIN: 131988190

6355
The Gordon A. Rich Memorial Foundation
1 Madison Ave., 10th Fl.
New York, NY 10010-3603 (212) 325-2227
E-mail: info@gordonrich.org; URL: http://www.gordonrich.org

Foundation type: Public charity
Purpose: Scholarships to qualified high school students who demonstrate financial need and whose parents or guardians work in the financial services industry. The program is administered by Scholarship America.
Publications: Application guidelines.
Financial data: Year ended 12/31/2011. Assets, $3,803,194 (M); Expenditures, $382,844; Total giving, $210,830; Grants to individuals, totaling $210,830.
Type of support: Undergraduate support.
Application information: Applications accepted. Application form required.
  Initial approach: Letter
  Deadline(s): Feb. 10
  Applicants should submit the following:
    1) SAT
    2) ACT
    3) Transcripts
    4) Financial information
    5) Essay
    6) Curriculum vitae
Program description:
  Scholarships: The foundation awards up to five scholarships per year to support the higher education goals of exceptionally-qualified high school students whose parents or guardians have, or had, a career in the financial services industry. Eligible applicants must: be graduating high-school seniors who are enrolling as full-time first-year students in pursuit of a four-year bachelor's degree at an accredited college or university in the U.S.; demonstrate financial need; and have a minimum GPA of 3.5 (on a 4.0 scale) and rank in the top 20 percent of their class. Scholarships of up to $12,500 are awarded, renewable for up to four years; all scholarships recipients become eligible for the Parkman Prize, which awards an additional $5,000 to the scholar with the highest GPA in each academic year.
EIN: 030385929

6356
Jackie Robinson Foundation, Inc.
1 Hudson Sq.
75 Varick St., 2nd Fl.
New York, NY 10013-1917 (212) 290-8600
FAX: (212) 290-8081;
E-mail: general@jackierobinson.org; Additional address: 550 S. Hope St., Ste. 2300, Los Angeles, CA 90071-2678, tel.: (213) 330-7726, fax: (213) 330-7526; URL: http://www.jackierobinson.org

Foundation type: Public charity
Purpose: Four-year college scholarships to financially needy minority students who are high school graduates.
Publications: Application guidelines; Biennial report; Financial statement; Informational brochure.
Financial data: Year ended 06/30/2012. Assets, $20,590,081 (M); Expenditures, $6,817,943; Total giving, $1,146,331; Grants to individuals, 207 grants totaling $1,146,331.
Fields of interest: Higher education; Minorities.
Type of support: Undergraduate support.
Application information: Applications accepted.

Send request by: Online
Deadline(s): Mar. 15
Final notification: Applicants notified June 1
Applicants should submit the following:
1) Transcripts
2) SAT
3) ACT
4) Letter(s) of recommendation
Additional information: See web site for additional application guidelines.

Program description:
Scholarship Program: Scholarships of up to $7,500 are available to minority high-school students who demonstrate leadership potential and financial need, in order to attend an accredited four-year college or university of their choice. Eligible applicants must be U.S. citizens who have a minimum SAT score of 1,000 (or a composite ACT score of 21), and who plan to attend an accredited and approved four-year institution within the U.S.
EIN: 132896345

6357
Rochester Area Community Foundation
500 East Ave.
Rochester, NY 14607-1912 (585) 271-4100
Contact: For grants: Mary Harstein, Prog. Admin.; Edward Doherty, V.P., Community Progs.; For scholarships: Lori Banning, Scholarship and Grants Admin.
Scholarship inquiry tel.: (585) 341-4357
FAX: (585) 271-4292; E-mail: edoherty@racf.org;
URL: http://www.racf.org

Foundation type: Community foundation
Purpose: Scholarships and fellowships primarily to residents of Genesee, Livingston, Monroe, Ontario, Orleans, Seneca, Wayne, and Yates counties, NY.
Publications: Annual report (including application guidelines); Biennial report (including application guidelines); Financial statement; Grants list; Informational brochure; Newsletter; Program policy statement.
Financial data: Year ended 03/31/2013. Assets, $271,283,243 (M); Expenditures, $24,765,181; Total giving, $21,154,364. Fellowships amount not specified. Scholarships—to individuals amount not specified.
Fields of interest: Higher education.
Type of support: Employee-related scholarships; Scholarships—to individuals; Support to graduates or students of specific schools; Graduate support; Technical education support; Undergraduate support.
Application information: Applications accepted. Application form required. Application form available on the grantmaker's web site.
Initial approach: Application
Send request by: Mail
Copies of proposal: 1
Deadline(s): Varies
Applicants should submit the following:
1) Transcripts
2) SAT
3) SAR
4) Resume
5) Letter(s) of recommendation
6) GPA
7) Financial information
8) FAF
9) Essay
10) ACT
Additional information: Recipients are chosen by specified educational institutions. Application process is handled by the high schools

involved. See web site for complete program listing.
EIN: 237250641

6358
Rochester Area Community Foundation Initiatives, Inc.
500 E. Ave.
Rochester, NY 14607-1912 (585) 271-4100
Contact: Adam McFadden, Exec. Dir.
Tel. for L. Banning: (585) 341-4357,
e-mail: lbanning@racf.org
FAX: (585) 271-4292; E-mail: amcfadden@racf.org;
URL: http://racf.org

Foundation type: Public charity
Purpose: College scholarships for students from Genesee, Livingston, Monroe, Ontario, Orleans, Seneca, Wayne, and Yates counties, NY pursuing higher education.
Publications: Application guidelines; Annual report.
Financial data: Year ended 03/31/2012. Assets, $490,625 (M); Expenditures, $1,207,615; Total giving, $378,042; Grants to individuals, totaling $24,645.
Fields of interest: Higher education.
Type of support: Scholarships—to individuals; Support to graduates or students of specific schools.
Application information: Applications accepted. Application form required.
Deadline(s): Varies
Additional information: The foundation administers more than 100 different scholarships funds to help students further their education. Many scholarship offered by the foundation have very specific requirements, while others are more general interest. See web site for additional guidelines.
EIN: 800024332

6359
The Rockefeller Foundation
420 5th Ave.
New York, NY 10018-2702 (212) 869-8500
URL: http://www.rockefellerfoundation.org/

Foundation type: Independent foundation
Purpose: Awards to recognize two living individuals whose creative vision for the urban environment has significantly contributed to the vibrancy and variety of New York City. Residencies to composers, novelists, playwrights, poets, video/filmmakers, and visual artists to work on their projects in Italy.
Publications: Annual report (including application guidelines); Financial statement; Grants list.
Financial data: Year ended 12/31/2012. Assets, $3,695,617,868 (M); Expenditures, $203,195,149; Total giving, $135,082,747; Grants to individuals, 8 grants totaling $196,989 (high: $50,000, low: $11,400).
Fields of interest: Film/video; Visual arts; Theater (playwriting); Music; Music composition; Literature; Arts; Urban/community development.
Type of support: Awards/prizes; Residencies.
Application information:
Initial approach: Letter
Deadline(s): Dec. 11 for residencies
Additional information: Contact foundation for further eligibility requirements.
Program descriptions:
Bellagio Center Residency Programs: The residency program offers a serene setting conducive to focused, goal-oriented work, and the unparalleled opportunity to establish new

connections with fellow residents from a stimulating array of disciplines and geographies. 1) The writing residency is for university and think tank-based academics, researchers, professors, and scientists working in any discipline. The program typically offers one-month residencies for no more than 12 residents at a time. Individuals based at a university or a think tank in any discipline and from any part of the world are welcome to apply. To ensure an intellectually diverse and stimulating environment, the program welcomes projects from all academic disciplines. 2) The arts and literary arts residencies are for composers, fiction and non-fiction writers, playwrights, poets, video/filmmakers, and visual artists who share in the foundation's mission of promoting the well-being of humankind and whose work is inspired by or relates to global or social issues. The program typically offers one-month stays for about three to five artists at a time. Artists of significant achievement from any country are welcome to apply. 3) The practitioner residencies are open to professionals in fields and institutions relevant to the foundation's work. The Center has a strong interest in proposals that align with the foundation's mission to expand opportunities and to strengthen resilience for poor or vulnerable people, in particular projects relevant to the foundation's core issue areas. The foundation works on global health; climate change resilience; urbanization; social and economic security; and food, water, and housing. The program seeks practitioner applicants with demonstrated leadership qualities and the capacity to contribute to the intellectual life at the center. See web site for application guidelines.
Jane Jacobs Medal: In 2007, the year after the visionary urban activist Jane Jacobs died, the foundation launched the Jane Jacobs annual award to honor her work. This medal reaffirms the foundation's commitment to New York City by recognizing those whose creative uses of the urban environment build a more diverse, dynamic and equitable city. Medals are awarded to two living persons whose accomplishments represent Jane Jacobs' principles and practices in action in New York City. The selection of the winners and allocation of the prize money-totaling $200,000-are decided by the members of a medal selection jury. The first award recognizes leadership and lifetime contribution. The second award recognizes new ideas and activism. Together the medalists represent the creativity, innovation and dynamism of New York City.
EIN: 131659629

6360
Ronald McDonald House Charities of Central New York, Inc.
1100 E. Genesee St.
Syracuse, NY 13210-1808 (315) 476-1027
Contact: Beth M. Trunfio, Exec. Dir.
FAX: (315) 476-5022;
E-mail: house@cnyronaldmcdonaldhouse.org;
E-mail For Beth M. Trunfio:
btrunfio@cnyronaldmcdonaldhouse.org;
URL: http://www.cnyronaldmcdonaldhouse.org

Foundation type: Public charity
Purpose: Emergency housing to families whose children are receiving care for a serious illness or injury at an area hospital or treatment facility in central NY or northern PA.
Financial data: Year ended 12/31/2011. Assets, $9,081,331 (M); Expenditures, $868,193.
Fields of interest: Human services; Children/youth; Children; Youth; Terminal illness, people with; Economically disadvantaged.

Type of support: In-kind gifts.
Application information:
Initial approach: Letter
Additional information: Contact the charity for eligibility criteria.
EIN: 222371193

6361
The Roothbert Fund Inc.
475 Riverside Dr., Rm. 1830
New York, NY 10115-0107 (212) 870-3116
E-mail: mail@roothbertfund.org; URL: http://www.roothbertfund.org

Foundation type: Independent foundation
Purpose: Graduate and undergraduate scholarships to students who are motivated by spiritual values, with preference to those considering teaching as a profession.
Publications: Application guidelines; Annual report; Informational brochure.
Financial data: Year ended 12/31/2012. Assets, $4,328,202 (M); Expenditures, $224,746; Total giving, $145,000; Grants to individuals, 50 grants totaling $145,000 (high: $4,000, low: $1,500).
Fields of interest: Research; Formal/general education.
Type of support: Scholarships—to individuals.
Application information: Applications accepted. Application form required. Application form available on the grantmaker's web site.
Initial approach: Letter
Send request by: Mail
Copies of proposal: 1
Deadline(s): Feb. 1
Final notification: Applicant notified in two months
Applicants should submit the following:
1) Letter(s) of recommendation
2) Essay
3) Photograph
4) Transcripts
Additional information: Application must also include SAT and/or GRE scores, personal statement, references; Interviews are held during Mar. of each year at fund headquarters in New York City and currently also in Washington, DC, Philadelphia, PA, and New Haven, CT.
EIN: 136162570

6362
Susan W. Rose Fund for Music, Inc.
200 Madison Ave., 5th Fl.
New York, NY 10016

Foundation type: Independent foundation
Purpose: Assistance to young, professional, classical musicians who have potential for excellence and are financially needy.
Financial data: Year ended 12/31/2011. Assets, $5,333 (M); Expenditures, $13,000; Total giving, $13,000.
Fields of interest: Music; Scholarships/financial aid.
Type of support: Grants to individuals.
Application information: Applications accepted. Application form required. Interview required.
Applicants should submit the following:
1) Essay
2) Transcripts
3) Letter(s) of recommendation
4) Financial information
EIN: 133808182

6363
Herman & Lenore Rottenberg Foundation
c/o Spitz & Greenstein, C.P.A.
494 8th Ave., Ste. 806
New York, NY 10001 (212) 889-7776
Contact: Herman Rottenberg, Chair. and Pres.
Application address: 115 Central Park W., New York, NY 10023

Foundation type: Independent foundation
Purpose: Grants to individuals, primarily in NY, to talented young performing artists for assistance in helping them achieve their goals which brought them to New York City.
Financial data: Year ended 01/31/2012. Assets, $2,225,855 (M); Expenditures, $177,392; Total giving, $168,025.
Type of support: Grants to individuals.
Application information: Applications accepted.
Initial approach: Letter
Deadline(s): None
Additional information: Letter should include complete background information.
EIN: 136132611

6364
Royal Oak Foundation
35 W. 35th St., Ste. 1200
New York, NY 10001-2205 (212) 480-2889
FAX: (212) 785-7234;
E-mail: general@royal-oak.org; Toll-free tel.: (800) 913-6565; E-mail for Sean E. Sawyer: ssawyer@royal-oak.org; URL: http://www.royal-oak.org

Foundation type: Public charity
Purpose: Fellowships and scholarships for Americans who wish to learn more about the National Trust and the rich heritage of Great Britain.
Publications: Application guidelines; Financial statement; Grants list; Informational brochure; Newsletter.
Financial data: Year ended 12/31/2011. Assets, $5,090,639 (M); Expenditures, $1,817,109; Total giving, $360,050; Grants to individuals, totaling $500.
Fields of interest: Architecture; Design; Landscaping.
International interests: United Kingdom.
Type of support: Fellowships; Scholarships—to individuals; Travel grants.
Application information: Applications accepted.
Deadline(s): None
Additional information: See web site for additional guidelines.
Program descriptions:
The Attingham Summer School Scholarship: This scholarship is a highly regarded intensive three-week residential educational program in the English countryside devoted to the study of British historic houses. Since its foundation in 1952, many scholars, curators, architects, and designers from the U.S. have participated each year.
The Damaris Horan Prize: The prize is awarded biennially to provide talented Americans with a serious interest in landscaping history and gardening, a chance to experience the National Trust first-hand.
EIN: 237349380

6365
Damon Runyon Cancer Research Foundation
(formerly Cancer Research Fund of the Damon Runyon-Walter Winchell Foundation)
1 Exchange Plz.
55 Broadway, Ste. 302
New York, NY 10006-3738 (212) 455-0500
Contact: Lorraine W. Egan, Exec. Dir.; Toby Falk, Devel. Admin.
FAX: (212) 455-0509;
E-mail: info@damonrunyon.org; Additional tel.: (212) 455-0520 (awards); E-mail for Toby Falk: toby.falk@drcrf.org; URL: http://www.damonrunyon.org

Foundation type: Public charity
Purpose: Fellowships to postdoctoral scientists and MDs pursuing cancer research.
Publications: Application guidelines; Annual report; Newsletter.
Financial data: Year ended 06/30/2012. Assets, $107,113,018 (M); Expenditures, $15,244,420; Total giving, $11,771,648.
Fields of interest: Cancer research.
Type of support: Fellowships; Research; Postdoctoral support.
Application information: Applications accepted. Application form required. Application form available on the grantmaker's web site.
Deadline(s): Mar. 1 for Damon Runyon Clinical Investigator Award, Mar. 15 and Aug. 15 for Damon Runyon Fellowship Award, June 1 for pre-proposals and Sept. 1 for full proposals for Innovation Awards, July 16 for Dale F. Frey Award for Breakthrough Scientists
Applicants should submit the following:
1) Letter(s) of recommendation
2) Proposal
3) Curriculum vitae
Program descriptions:
Dale F. Frey Award for Breakthrough Scientists: This award identifies the nation's top postdoctoral fellows and provides funding that enables them to complete their training under the mentorship of a leading senior scientist and encourages them to follow their own bold ideas. The funds are intended to be flexible and can be used for a variety of scientific needs including the awardee's salary, salaries for professional and technical personnel, equipment, supplies, and other miscellaneous items required to conduct the research. Funds may also be used to defray the cost of the recipient's healthcare benefits. The award is $100,000 paid over one year and must be expended within two years of the initial award date.
Damon Runyon Clinical Investigator Award: This award supports young physician-scientists conducting patient-oriented cancer research, with the hopes of increasing the number of physicians capable of moving seamlessly between the laboratory and the patient's bedside in search of breakthrough treatments. Awards of up to $450,000, for up to three years, will be awarded, to be used for a variety of scientific needs (including the investigator's stipend and/or fringe benefits, salaries for professional and technical personnel, special equipment, supplies, and other miscellaneous items required to conduct the proposed research. Eligible applicants must be U.S. citizens or permanent legal residents, be nominated by his/her institution, have received an M.D. or M.D./Ph.D. degree from an accredited institution and be board-eligible; currently hold, or be in the process of securing, a tenure-track position at his/her institution, and apply in conjunction with a mentor who is established in the field of clinical translational cancer research,

cancer prevention, and/or epidemiology, and can provide the critical guidance needed during the period of the award. In addition to the awards, the foundation will retire up to $100,000 of any medical school debt still owed by the awardee. Third-year grant recipients are also eligible for up to two years of additional funding under the Damon Runyon Clinical Investigator Award Continuation Grant.

Damon Runyon Fellowship Award: This award provides early career scientists with resources to further hone their cancer research skills and explore their own ideas while working with mentors in top universities and cancer research centers. Applicants must have completed one or more of the following degrees or its equivalent, M.D., Ph.D., M.D./Ph.D., D.D.S., and/or D.V.M. Candidates must apply for the fellowship under the guidance of a sponsor capable of providing mentorship to the fellow. Awards are made to institutions for the support of the fellow under direct supervision of the sponsor. The award provides a stipend of $50,000 per year for three years for Level I funding, and $60,000 per year for three years for Level II funding. (Physician-scientists who have completed their residencies, clinical training, and are board eligible will receive Level II funding.) The award may not be used for institutional overhead or indirect costs. Fellows also receive an annual $2,000 expense allowance for educational and scientific expenses. Approximately thirty new fellows are selected each year.

Damon Runyon-Rachleff Innovation Award: This award program is designed to provide support for the next generation of exceptionally creative thinkers with 'high risk/high reward' ideas that have the potential to significantly impact the understanding of, and/or approaches to, the prevention, diagnosis, or treatment of cancer. Awards of up to $450,000, for up to three years, will be awarded to provide funding to extraordinary career researchers who have an innovative new idea but lack sufficient preliminary data to obtain traditional funding. Eligible applicants must: be conducting independent research at a U.S.-based research institution; belong to one of three categories (tenure-track assistant professors, clinical instructors/senior clinical fellows, and distinguished fellows); and demonstrate that they have the necessary access to resources and infrastructure needed to conduct the proposed research.
EIN: 131933825

6366
Russian Children's Welfare Society, Inc.
200 Park Ave. S., Ste. 1508
New York, NY   10003-1503   (212) 473-6263
FAX: (212) 473-6301; E-mail: main@rcws.org;
Toll-free tel.: (888) 732-7297; URL: http://
www.rcws.org

Foundation type: Public charity
Purpose: Grants to economically disadvantaged children of Russian descent, both in Russia and in other countries. Also, scholarships to orphans in Russia.
Publications: Grants list.
Financial data: Year ended 12/31/2011. Assets, $4,379,776 (M); Expenditures, $1,301,811; Total giving, $853,207; Grants to individuals, totaling $5,900.
Fields of interest: Children/youth, services; Economically disadvantaged.
International interests: Russia; South America.
Type of support: Grants for special needs.
Application information: Contact foundation for current application guidelines. Russian families in

New York are visited by the foundation's volunteers, who gather applications.
EIN: 135562332

6367
Rye Rotary Foundation Inc.
c/o F.J. Larusso
P.O. Box 736
Harrison, NY   10528   (914) 967-4927
Contact: Robert Praid, Pres.
Application address: PO Box 404, Rye, NY 10580, tel.: (914) 967-4927

Foundation type: Independent foundation
Purpose: Scholarships to graduates of Rye High School, Rye, NY, for higher education.
Financial data: Year ended 09/30/2013. Assets, $107,242 (M); Expenditures, $21,330; Total giving, $21,000; Grants to individuals, 14 grants totaling $21,000 (high: $2,000, low: $1,000).
Fields of interest: Higher education.
Type of support: Support to graduates or students of specific schools; Undergraduate support.
Application information: Application form required.
   Initial approach: Letter
   Deadline(s): None
   Additional information: Selection is based on leadership, academic achievement, and financial need.
EIN: 133041401

6368
S.B.H. Community Service Network, Inc.
(formerly Sephardic Bikur Holim & Ma'oz La'ebyon)
425 Kings Hwy.
Brooklyn, NY   11223-1629   (718) 787-1100
Contact: Douglas Balin, Exec. Dir.
FAX: (718) 787-9598;
E-mail: contactus@sbhonline.org; URL: http://
www.sbhonline.org/

Foundation type: Public charity
Purpose: Financial assistance to indigent Sephardic residents of Brooklyn, NY, for food, shelter, clothing, and medical bills.
Financial data: Year ended 12/31/2011. Assets, $13,647,962 (M); Expenditures, $5,825,321; Total giving, $1,620,521; Grants to individuals, totaling $1,405,521.
Fields of interest: Jewish agencies & synagogues; Economically disadvantaged.
Type of support: Grants for special needs.
Application information: Applications accepted. Application form required. Application form available on the grantmaker's web site.
   Initial approach: Telephone
   Send request by: Mail, fax, or in person
EIN: 237406410

6369
The Saagny Foundation, Inc.
277 N. Ave., Lower Level
New Rochelle, NY   10801   (201) 505-9550
Contact: Rhonda Blum, Chair.
URL: http://www.saagny.org

Foundation type: Public charity
Purpose: Scholarships to individuals in pursuit of a higher education at accredited colleges and universities.
Financial data: Year ended 07/31/2012. Assets, $178,602 (M); Expenditures, $26,281; Total giving, $10,000.
Fields of interest: Higher education.
Type of support: Scholarships—to individuals.

Application information: Applications accepted.
EIN: 113306978

6370
Sakhi for South Asian Women
Greeley Sq. Sta.
P.O. Box 20208
New York, NY   10014-0710   (212) 714-9153
Contact: Tiloma Jayasinghe, Exec. Dir.
FAX: (646) 398-8498; E-mail: contactus@sakhi.org;
E-Mail for Tiloma Jayasinghe:
tiloma.jayasinghe@sakhi.org; URL: http://
www.sakhi.org

Foundation type: Public charity
Purpose: Scholarships to domestic abuse victims of South Asian descent to further educational and professional advancement.
Financial data: Year ended 06/30/2012. Assets, $247,769 (M); Expenditures, $754,614; Total giving, $18,136; Grants to individuals, totaling $18,136.
Fields of interest: Domestic violence; Asians/Pacific Islanders; Women.
Type of support: Scholarships—to individuals.
Application information: Applications not accepted.
   Additional information: Unsolicited requests for funds not considered or acknowledged.
EIN: 133593806

6371
Constance Saltonstall Foundation for the Arts, Inc.
435 Ellis Hollow Creek Rd.
Ithaca, NY   14850-9677   (607) 539-3146
Contact: Lesley D. Williamson, Prog. Dir.
FAX: (607) 539-3147; E-mail: info@saltonstall.org;
URL: http://www.saltonstall.org

Foundation type: Operating foundation
Purpose: Residencies to photographers, visual artists and writers who are NY State residents age 21 or older.
Publications: Application guidelines; Informational brochure; Newsletter.
Financial data: Year ended 09/30/2012. Assets, $5,356,669 (M); Expenditures, $217,997; Total giving, $11,250; Grants to individuals, 20 grants totaling $10,000 (high: $500, low: $500).
Fields of interest: Photography; Painting; Literature; Arts, artist's services; Arts.
Type of support: Seed money; Residencies.
Application information: Applications accepted. Application form required.
   Send request by: Mail
   Deadline(s): Jan. 14
   Applicants should submit the following:
      1) Letter(s) of recommendation
      2) Work samples
      3) Resume
   Additional information: Application should also include a one-page statement and a $25 application fee.
Program description:
   Residency: The residency competition is open to legal residents of New York State (all counties). Artists who are selected for residencies must commit to spending four weeks at the Colony. Artists who wish to apply for more than one artistic category must make complete and separate applications for each category.
EIN: 161481219

6372
Samaritan Hospital School of Nursing Alumni Association Charitable Foundation
2215 Burdett Ave.
Troy, NY   12180

Foundation type: Independent foundation
Purpose: Scholarships to graduates of the Samaritan Hospital School of Nursing, NY or must have been associated with the School of Nursing in some capacity.
Financial data: Year ended 12/31/2011. Assets, $98,209 (M); Expenditures, $5,587; Total giving, $3,000; Grants to individuals, 5 grants totaling $3,000 (high: $600, low: $600).
Fields of interest: Nursing school/education.
Type of support: Scholarships—to individuals.
Application information: Applications accepted. Application form required.
> *Deadline(s):* None
> *Additional information:* Contact the foundation for additional guidelines.

EIN: 141684557

6373
The Sandy Hill Foundation
15 Boulevard
Hudson Falls, NY   12839-1001   (518) 791-3490
Contact: Nancy Juckett Brown, Tr.
Scholarship application address: P.O. Box 607, Williston, VT 05495,
e-mail: njbrown@sandyhillfoundation.org

Foundation type: Independent foundation
Purpose: Scholarships to qualifying young men and women from designated local area schools of the greater Hudson Falls, NY, area with tuition, fees, books, room and board and other college expense.
Financial data: Year ended 08/31/2013. Assets, $8,355,434 (M); Expenditures, $520,184; Total giving, $447,779; Grants to individuals, 44 grants totaling $88,000 (high: $2,000, low: $2,000).
Fields of interest: Higher education.
Type of support: Scholarships—to individuals.
Application information: Applications accepted. Application form required.
> *Deadline(s):* Apr. 1
> *Applicants should submit the following:*
> 1) Transcripts
> 2) Letter(s) of recommendation
> 3) Essay
> *Additional information:* Application should also include standardized test results, and a copy of page 1 of parents' Federal Tax Return Form 1040, which can be mailed separately, or submitted in a sealed envelope with application. School academic record which must be provided by applicant's guidance counselor, may be mailied under a separate cover.

EIN: 146018954

6374
Saranac Lake Voluntary Health Association, Inc.
75 Main St., Ste. 2
Saranac Lake, NY   12983-5737   (518) 891-0910
Contact: Brenda Reeve

Foundation type: Operating foundation
Purpose: Grants for dental assistance to students attending schools in the Saranac Lake School District, NY, and for visiting nurse services for the elderly in Saranac Lake, NY.

Financial data: Year ended 03/31/2013. Assets, $3,701,392 (M); Expenditures, $249,677; Total giving, $131,751; Grants to individuals, 3 grants totaling $66,320.
Fields of interest: Dental care; Health care, home services; Aging.
Type of support: Grants for special needs.
Application information: Applications not accepted.

EIN: 150532253

6375
Saratoga County Economic Opportunity Council
40 New St.
P.O. Box 5120
Saratoga Springs, NY   12866-6046   (518) 587-3158
Contact: Julie Hoxsie, Exec. Dir.
FAX: (518) 580-9293;
E-mail: info@saratogaeoc.org; E-Mail for Julie Hoxsie: j.hoxsie@saratogaeoc.org; URL: http://www.saratogaeoc.org

Foundation type: Public charity
Purpose: Assistance to low-income individuals in communities of Saratoga county, NY, to help themselves become economically self-sufficient.
Publications: Newsletter.
Financial data: Year ended 12/31/2011. Assets, $3,678,785 (M); Expenditures, $12,566,805; Total giving, $1,484,414; Grants to individuals, totaling $1,484,414.
Fields of interest: Economically disadvantaged.
Type of support: Grants for special needs.
Application information:
> *Initial approach:* Telephone

EIN: 237438457

6376
Sawyer Scholarship Foundation
51 Sullivan St.
P.O. Box 209
Wurtsboro, NY   12790   (845) 482-6064
Contact: Ruth Brustman, Tr.
Application address: P.O. Box 18, Obernburg, NY 12767-0018 Tel.: (845) 482-6064

Foundation type: Independent foundation
Purpose: Scholarships to qualified graduates of the former Delaware Valley Central School District, NY for postsecondary education.
Financial data: Year ended 12/31/2011. Assets, $104,791 (M); Expenditures, $36,944; Total giving, $36,550.
Fields of interest: Higher education.
Type of support: Scholarships—to individuals.
Application information: Applications accepted.
> *Initial approach:* Letter
> *Deadline(s):* May 15

EIN: 136113938

6377
Scalp and Blade Scholarship Trust
1 M&T Plz., 8th Fl.
Buffalo, NY   14203   (716) 848-7581
Application address: c/o Scalp and Blade,164 Cayuga Rd., Cheektowaga NY 14225

Foundation type: Independent foundation
Purpose: Scholarships to male students graduating from high schools in Erie County, NY, who plan to attend schools outside Erie and Niagara counties. Scholarships are up to $750 annually for eligible applicants.

Financial data: Year ended 12/31/2012. Assets, $413,461 (M); Expenditures, $27,801; Total giving, $22,000; Grants to individuals, 10 grants totaling $22,000 (high: $3,250, low: $1,000).
Fields of interest: Higher education; Men.
Type of support: Scholarships—to individuals.
Application information: Applications accepted.
> *Deadline(s):* May 31
> *Additional information:* Interviews granted upon request. Contact Erie County, NY, high school guidance counselors or principals for current application guidelines.

EIN: 166020842

6378
Scarsdale Foundation
P.O. Box 542
Scarsdale, NY   10583-0542   (914) 472-2311
Contact: Richard Toder, Pres.
E-mail: scarsdalefoundation@gmail.com;
URL: http://scarsdalefoundation.org/

Foundation type: Public charity
Purpose: Scholarships to high school seniors who attend Scarsdale High School and summer camp scholarships to Scarsdale residents. Financial assistance to employees of Scarsdale Union Free School District, NY.
Publications: Financial statement.
Financial data: Year ended 06/30/2012. Assets, $1,728,835 (M); Expenditures, $110,941; Total giving, $106,009; Grants to individuals, totaling $106,009.
Fields of interest: Education.
Type of support: Support to graduates or students of specific schools; Employee-related welfare; Undergraduate support; Camperships.
Application information: Application form required.
> *Initial approach:* Telephone or letter.
> *Deadline(s):* June 1 for scholarships, camperships
> *Applicants should submit the following:*
> 1) Transcripts
> 2) GPA
> 3) Financial information
> 4) FAFSA
> *Additional information:* For employee assistance contact foundation for eligibility requirements.

EIN: 136103826

6379
Robert Schalkenbach Foundation, Inc.
90 John St., Ste. 501
New York, NY   10038
URL: http://www.schalkenbach.org/

Foundation type: Operating foundation
Purpose: Grants to individuals for academic projects related to the economic and social justice ideals of Henry George. Projects may focus upon urban or rural landscapes.
Financial data: Year ended 06/30/2012. Assets, $15,034,301 (M); Expenditures, $739,055; Total giving, $0.
Fields of interest: Research; Economics; Political science; Urban studies; Research.
Type of support: Publication; Research.
Application information: Applications accepted. Application form required. Application form available on the grantmaker's web site.
> *Initial approach:* E-mail
> *Deadline(s):* Quarterly
> *Applicants should submit the following:*
> 1) Work samples
> 2) Resume
> 3) Proposal

4) Curriculum vitae
5) Budget Information
Additional information: See web site for further application information.
EIN: 131656331

6380
The Schechter Foundation
c/o Shirley Schechter
33 Garden Rd.
Scarsdale, NY   10583-2105
E-mail: schechtertenrock@aol.com

Foundation type: Independent foundation
Purpose: Scholarships to graduate students studying occupational and physical therapy, as well as other graduate programs in health care and related fields.
Financial data: Year ended 12/31/2012. Assets, $397,766 (M); Expenditures, $44,018; Total giving, $7,000.
Fields of interest: Physical therapy; Health care.
Type of support: Graduate support.
Application information: Applications accepted. Application form required.
  Initial approach: Letter
  Deadline(s): July 1
  Applicants should submit the following:
    1) Photograph
    2) Transcripts
    3) FAF
    4) Financial information
    5) SAT
    6) Resume
    7) Letter(s) of recommendation
    8) Essay
  Additional information: Application should also include statement of financial need, goals, academic evaluation form, and signed copy of applicant or parents' most recent tax return.
EIN: 133157311

6381
Jane I Schenck Fund 003490
(formerly Jane Schenck Estate Trust)
c/o NBT Bank, N.A.
52 S. Broad St.
Norwich, NY   13815-1646   (607) 656-4161
Application addresses: c/o Supt., Greene Central School, Greene, NY 13778, c/o Supt., Afton Central School, Afton, NY 13730

Foundation type: Independent foundation
Purpose: Loans for higher education to graduates of Greene and Afton Central Schools, NY.
Financial data: Year ended 06/30/2012. Assets, $195,172 (M); Expenditures, $6,973; Total giving, $3,000; Grants to individuals, 2 grants totaling $3,000 (high: $1,500, low: $1,500).
Fields of interest: Higher education.
Type of support: Student loans—to individuals; Support to graduates or students of specific schools.
Application information: Applications accepted. Application form required.
  Deadline(s): May 31
  Additional information: Application available at Greene Central School, NY or Afton Central School, NY.
EIN: 166052404

6382
The Schenectady Foundation
376 Broadway, Fl. 2
Schenectady, NY   12305   (518) 393-9500
Contact: Robert A. Carreau, Secy.
E-mail: info@schenectadyfoundation.org;
URL: http://www.schenectadyfoundation.org

Foundation type: Community foundation
Purpose: Scholarships to graduating seniors of high schools in Schenectady County, NY, pursuing a teaching career.
Publications: Application guidelines; Annual report; Grants list; Informational brochure.
Financial data: Year ended 12/31/2012. Assets, $18,112,931 (M); Expenditures, $1,217,918; Total giving, $1,163,978. Scholarships—to individuals amount not specified.
Fields of interest: Teacher school/education.
Type of support: Scholarships—to individuals; Undergraduate support.
Application information: Applications accepted. Application form required. Application form available on the grantmaker's web site.
  Deadline(s): Apr. 2
  Additional information: Application should include a letter of recommendation from a class teacher and a personal letter explaining why you are interested in a teaching career.
Program description:
  Anna Hudson Erbacher Scholarships: This scholarship is intended to support students who share a passion to teach. The scholarship is $2,500 per year, and is awarded for a total of four years subject to continued qualification. The foundation generally awards one or two new scholarships each year. See web site for additional information.
EIN: 146019650

6383
Leopold Schepp Foundation
551 5th Ave., Ste. 3000
New York, NY   10176-3201   (212) 692-0191
URL: http://www.scheppfoundation.org

Foundation type: Independent foundation
Purpose: Scholarships to students who are U.S. citizens enrolled on a full-time basis at accredited colleges and universities. Only one member of a family may apply at the same time. Four-year undergraduate scholarships to individuals under 30, graduate scholarships to individuals under 40, and a limited number of postdoctoral fellowships to individuals in the arts, literature, medicine, and oceanography.
Financial data: Year ended 02/28/2013. Assets, $10,125,550 (M); Expenditures, $862,772; Total giving, $344,500; Grants to individuals, 57 grants totaling $344,500 (high: $8,500; low: $1,000).
Fields of interest: Literature; Arts; Medical school/education; Public health; Marine science.
Type of support: Grants to individuals; Scholarships—to individuals; Awards/prizes; Graduate support; Undergraduate support; Doctoral support.
Application information: Applications accepted. Application form required. Application form available on the grantmaker's web site. Interview required.
  Initial approach: Letter
  Deadline(s): Contact foundation for current application deadline.
  Applicants should submit the following:
    1) Transcripts
    2) Letter(s) of recommendation
    3) GPA

4) Financial information
5) Essay
6) Curriculum vitae
7) Budget Information
8) SASE
Additional information: Applications distributed to eligible students. Lists close when a sufficient number of applications have been completed and received for committee decisions.
Program description:
  Schepp Foundation Scholarships: Scholarships are awarded to U.S. citizens of character and ability who have insufficient means to obtain or complete their formal education and who are already enrolled in college or preparing for graduate study. Preference is given to those with goals that show promise of future usefulness to society. Those who have only the doctoral dissertation to complete may not apply. A limited number of grants are made for independent study and research beyond the doctoral level to individuals in the fields of literature, the arts, oceanography, and medicine (including public health) upon the recommendation of a recognized institution. Research likely to improve the general welfare of humankind is particularly favored and encouraged.
EIN: 135562353

6384
Kathryn Schiffner Music Fund
1 M.T. Plz. 8th Fl.
Buffalo, NY   14203   (610) 376-3395
Application address: P.O. Box 14835, Reading, PA 19612. Tel.: (610) 376-3395

Foundation type: Independent foundation
Purpose: Scholarships to graduating seniors in the Reading/Berks, PA county area pursuing a major in voice or piano to further a career in music.
Financial data: Year ended 12/31/2011. Assets, $141,103 (M); Expenditures, $10,439; Total giving, $7,800.
Fields of interest: Music.
Type of support: Scholarships—to individuals.
Application information:
  Initial approach: Letter
  Deadline(s): None
  Additional information: Applicant must have been accepted to a college or university, or qualified music school.
EIN: 256641692

6385
Helen M. Schiffner Scholarship Fund
1 M.T. Plaza, 8th Fl.
Buffalo, NY   14203   (610) 374-4031
Application address: Wyomissing Area High School, 630 Evans Ave., Wyomissing, PA 19610, tel.: (610) 374-4031

Foundation type: Independent foundation
Purpose: Scholarships to the Wyomissing Area High School, PA, male and female graduates with the highest academic standing.
Financial data: Year ended 12/31/2011. Assets, $143,740 (M); Expenditures, $8,840; Total giving, $6,200.
Fields of interest: Higher education.
Type of support: Support to graduates or students of specific schools; Undergraduate support.
Application information: Applications accepted.
  Deadline(s): None
  Additional information: Application must include transcripts.
EIN: 256641691

6386
Scholarship and Welfare Fund of the Alumni Association of Hunter College, Inc.
695 Park Ave., Ste. 1314E
New York, NY 10065 (212) 772-4092
Contact: Ruofan Li, Exec. Dir.
E-mail: scholarship.welfare@hunter.cuny.edu

Foundation type: Public charity
Purpose: Scholarships to undergraduate and graduate students attending Hunter College, NY who otherwise might not be able to complete their education.
Financial data: Year ended 05/31/2012. Assets, $21,620,321 (M); Expenditures, $1,382,213; Total giving, $1,209,661; Grants to individuals, totaling $1,209,661.
Type of support: Support to graduates or students of specific schools.
Application information:
Initial approach: Letter
Applicants should submit the following:
1) Financial information
2) GPA
Additional information: Contact the college's financial aid office for further information.
EIN: 131809290

6387
Scholarship Association of Fort Plain Inc.
c/o D. Dutcher
52 Garfield St.
P.O. Box 65
Fort Plain, NY 13339-0065 (518) 993-4000

Foundation type: Independent foundation
Purpose: Scholarships to graduating seniors of Fort Plain High School, NY for postsecondary education.
Financial data: Year ended 04/30/2013. Assets, $0 (M); Expenditures, $16,396; Total giving, $0.
Fields of interest: Higher education.
Type of support: Support to graduates or students of specific schools.
Application information: Applications accepted. Application form required.
Additional information: Application forms available from the school's administrative office.
EIN: 146026454

6388
Scott-Jenkins Fund
c/o Community Bank Systems, Inc.
245 Main St.
Oneonta, NY 13820 (607) 432-2532
Application address: SUCO, Financial Aid Office, Netzer Administration Building, Oneonta, NY 13820

Foundation type: Independent foundation
Purpose: Scholarships and work-grants to students attending State University of New York College at Oneonta.
Financial data: Year ended 06/30/2013. Assets, $885,563 (M); Expenditures, $61,318; Total giving, $51,811; Grants to individuals, 112 grants totaling $51,811 (high: $622, low: $189).
Fields of interest: Education; International exchange, students; Minorities.
Type of support: Support to graduates or students of specific schools; Foreign applicants; Undergraduate support; Workstudy grants.
Application information: Application form required.
Additional information: Students should contact the financial aid office at the school.

Program descriptions:
Scott-Jenkins Foreign Student Scholarships: The scholarship is available for any foreign student matriculated at the college to be used for room and board or maintenance expenses in a campus residence hall. Candidates must be recommended by the Director of International Education.
Scott-Jenkins Foreign Study Scholarships: Available to students in a foreign study program sponsored by State University of New York College at Oneonta, or Hartwick College. The scholarship covers the program costs over and above those which are not already covered by financial aid, but not to exceed $500 per student. Candidates are recommended by the Director of International Education and the Financial Aid Office.
Scott-Jenkins Memorial Scholarship: This renewable scholarship is for full time minority students at the College in good academic standing. Candidates are recommended by the Office of Special Programs and the Financial Aid Office. Students must be in financial need as determined by the Financial Aid office.
Scott-Jenkins Work-Grants: This scholarship is for any full time matriculated student eligible for these work-grants of $750 each who work a minimum of 11 hours per week on average for 30 weeks. Students will be paid every two weeks for hours worked the previous two weeks. Students must be in financial need determined by the Financial Aid office.
EIN: 166199427

6389
Scotts Miracle-Gro Foundation
c/o Rob McMahon
800 Port Washington Blvd.
Port Washington, NY 11050-3720

Foundation type: Independent foundation
Purpose: Scholarships to children enrolled in the Miracle-Gro Kids Program in Columbus, OH. Awards by nomination only to community gardeners and teachers integrating gardening into their curriculum.
Financial data: Year ended 12/31/2012. Assets, $36,098 (M); Expenditures, $470,321; Total giving, $469,000.
Fields of interest: Volunteer services; Horticulture/garden clubs; Environment, beautification programs; Youth development, adult & child programs.
Type of support: Scholarships—to individuals; Awards/grants by nomination only; Awards/prizes.
Application information:
Initial approach: Letter; telephone for nominations only
Deadline(s): Dec. 2 for awards by nomination only
Additional information: Scholarship applicants should contact foundation for additional application information. Nomination only awards, each winner will receive a cash prize and public recognition for their work. Each of two finalists in each category will receive a $2,500 cash prize and public recognition for their work.
Program descriptions:
Miracle-Gro Kids Program: This program salutes volunteers working in an urban area who have successfully used community gardening to address the various challenges of an inner-city neighborhood.
Scotts Classroom Gardner of the Year: This program salutes elementary through high school teachers who have integrated a school gardening program into their curriculum.
Scotts Community Beautification Gardner of the Year: This program salutes volunteers who have

helped beautify a main street, park or neighborhood within their city limits, and in the process significantly contributed to community pride.
Scotts Good Neighbor Gardner of the Year: This program salutes gardeners who donate produce to feed the hungry in their own communities.
Scotts Urban Gardner of the Year: This program salutes volunteers working in an urban area who have successfully used community gardening to address the various challenges of an inner-city neighborhood.
EIN: 311799491

6390
Sculpture Space, Inc.
12 Gates St.
Utica, NY 13502-3414 (315) 724-8381
Contact: Monika Burczyk, Exec. Dir.
FAX: (315) 797-6639;
E-mail: info@sculpturespace.org; URL: http://www.sculpturespace.org

Foundation type: Public charity
Purpose: Residencies to professional artists whose focus is sculpture.
Publications: Application guidelines; Annual report; Informational brochure; Newsletter.
Financial data: Year ended 06/30/2012. Assets, $326,058 (M); Expenditures, $198,146.
Fields of interest: Sculpture.
Type of support: Residencies.
Application information: Application form required.
Initial approach: Letter, telephone, fax, or e-mail
Deadline(s): Dec. 1
Final notification: Feb.
Applicants should submit the following:
1) SASE
2) Resume
3) Letter(s) of recommendation
Additional information: Application must also include slides of work and project description.
Program description:
Residency Program: Twenty artists are annually chosen to participate in the organization's residency program, which take place between September and August, and which last for up to four months. Artists receive 24-hour access to studio space; residents must provide their own materials, specialized tools, and assistants. Residents also receive a $2,000 stipend, to be used toward expenses; free housing and a $100 transportation stipend are available for New York State artists.
EIN: 222197162

6391
SculptureCenter
44-19 Purves St.
Long Island City, NY 11101-2907 (718) 361-1750
FAX: (718) 786-9336;
E-mail: info@sculpture-center.org; URL: http://www.sculpture-center.org

Foundation type: Public charity
Purpose: Residencies to artists for the creation of new work on-site for exhibition.
Financial data: Year ended 08/31/2011. Assets, $3,340,601 (M); Expenditures, $1,030,025.
Fields of interest: Sculpture.
Type of support: Awards/prizes.
Application information: Applications accepted.
EIN: 131669204

6392
Selfhelp Community Services Foundation, Inc.
(formerly United Help, Inc.)
520 8th Ave., 5th Fl.
New York, NY 10018-8915
Contact: Raymond V.J. Schrag, Pres.
Toll-fee tel.: (866) 735-1234; URL: http://www.selfhelp.net

Foundation type: Public charity
Purpose: Scholarships to survivors of the Holocaust and their families, primarily in NY.
Financial data: Year ended 06/30/2011. Assets, $4,934,081 (M); Expenditures, $124,614; Total giving, $95,000.
Fields of interest: Jewish agencies & synagogues.
Type of support: Undergraduate support.
Application information:
  Initial approach: Letter
  Additional information: Contact foundation for current application deadline/guidelines.
EIN: 135654450

6393
Ronald Seltzer Memorial Scholarship Foundation
30 S. Brewster Ln.
Bellport, NY 11713 (631) 286-8849
Contact: Regina Seltzer, Pres.

Foundation type: Independent foundation
Purpose: Scholarship to outstanding students of the graduating class of Bellport High School, New York.
Financial data: Year ended 11/30/2012. Assets, $9,135 (M); Expenditures, $5,797; Total giving, $5,000; Grants to individuals, 6 grants totaling $5,000 (high: $2,500, low: $500).
Fields of interest: Higher education.
Type of support: Support to graduates or students of specific schools.
Application information: Applications accepted. Application form required.
  Deadline(s): None
  Additional information: Applications can be obtained from the principal.
EIN: 112457979

6394
Seneca Diabetes Foundation
726 Exchange, Ste. 500
Buffalo, NY 14210 (716) 626-3064
Contact: Barry E. Snyder, Chair.
Application address: c/o Lucille White, P.O. Box 309, Irving, NY 14081, fax: (716) 532-6272
URL: http://www.senecadiabetesfoundation.org

Foundation type: Public charity
Purpose: Scholarships to young members of the Seneca Nation pursuing higher education in the health and human services fields.
Publications: Application guidelines.
Financial data: Year ended 12/31/2011. Assets, $1,779,647 (M); Expenditures, $183,327; Total giving, $98,200; Grants to individuals, totaling $45,000.
Fields of interest: Nursing school/education; Health sciences school/education.
Type of support: Scholarships—to individuals.
Application information: Applications accepted. Application form required.
  Send request by: Mail
  Deadline(s): June 25
  Final notification: Applicants notified by July 13
  Applicants should submit the following:

1) Transcripts
2) Letter(s) of recommendation
Additional information: Application should also include proof of enrollment in the Seneca Nation of Indians.
Program descriptions:
  The Barry and Deanna Snyder, Sr. Chairman's Scholarship: Three scholarships of $10,000 each, payable over two years, are available to members of the Seneca nation who wish to pursue a college/university degree in the health or social sciences professions. Priority will be given to students who have experience in leadership positions.
  The Geraldine Memmo Scholarship: A $5,000 scholarship will be awarded to a student who shows interest in Seneca Nation and/or Native American history, and who demonstrates knowledge about their rich and diverse heritage.
  The Ruth Goode Scholarship: A $5,000 scholarship is available to a member of the Seneca Nation who wishes to pursue a college/university degree in the nursing profession.
EIN: 203214056

6395
J. D. Shatford Memorial Trust
c/o JPMorgan Chase Bank, N.A.
270 Park Ave., 16th Fl.
New York, NY 10017-2014
E-mail: connie.a.brandeis@JPMorgan.com;
Application address: c/o Advisory Committee, P.O. Box 192, Hubbards, Nova Scotia B0J 1T0; e-mail: info@jdshatfordmemorialtrust.org; URL: http://fdnweb.org/shatford

Foundation type: Independent foundation
Purpose: Scholarships to residents of Hubbards, Nova Scotia, Canada.
Publications: Grants list; Informational brochure.
Financial data: Year ended 12/31/2012. Assets, $6,613,571 (M); Expenditures, $370,363; Total giving, $288,474.
Type of support: Foreign applicants; Graduate support; Undergraduate support.
Application information: Application form required. Application form available on the grantmaker's web site.
  Deadline(s): Last Fri. in July
  Additional information: Scholarship should include proof of age, proof of acceptance at an institution of higher education and a transcript.
EIN: 136029993

6396
The Lois and Samuel Silberman Fund, Inc.
c/o Alan Holzer
909 3rd Ave.
New York, NY 10022-4731 (212) 686-0010
Contact: Lorie A. Slutsky, Pres.
E-mail: srd@nyct-cfi.org; URL: http://www.socialservicegrants.org

Foundation type: Public charity
Purpose: Grants for professionals in the field of social work education and practice leading to publication in professional journals.
Publications: Application guidelines; Grants list.
Financial data: Year ended 12/31/2011. Assets, $3,511 (M); Expenditures, $7,734,974; Total giving, $7,692,074.
Fields of interest: Human services.
Type of support: Grants to individuals.
Application information: Applications accepted. Application form available on the grantmaker's web site.

Initial approach: Application
Deadline(s): Apr. 29
Final notification: Recipients notified May 31
Applicants should submit the following:
  1) Proposal
  2) Budget Information
Program description:
  Faculty Grant Program: The fund awards grants, on a competitive basis, to applicants whose research and publications hold promise for making significant contributions to social work knowledge and service delivery. Eligible applicants must be full-time faculty at Council of Social Work Education (CSWE)-accredited M.S.W. programs. Priority will be given to projects that have direct applicability to social work policy and practice, and/or is likely to impact graduate social work education. Projects that are primarily conceptual or theoretical will be considered in rare instances where relevance to practice, policy, or social work education can be clearly delineated.
EIN: 136097931

6397
Silver Shield Foundation, Inc.
870 United Nations Plz., 1st Fl.
New York, NY 10017-1822 (212) 832-1100
Contact: K.C. Fuchs, C.O.O.
FAX: (212) 832-1102;
E-mail: kcfuchs@silvershieldfoundation.org;
Toll-free tel.: (800) 811-4692; E-Mail for William G. Walters: bw10022@gmail.com; URL: http://www.silvershieldfoundation.org

Foundation type: Public charity
Purpose: Scholarships to surviving dependents of New York City police officers and firefighters in New York, New Jersey and Connecticut State Troopers and members of other law enforcement agencies within an approximate 50 mile radius of the borough of Manhattan, NY are also eligible.
Publications: Annual report; Informational brochure.
Financial data: Year ended 12/31/2011. Assets, $3,518,885 (M); Expenditures, $501,672; Total giving, $171,040; Grants to individuals, totaling $171,040.
Type of support: Employee-related scholarships; Awards/grants by nomination only; Undergraduate support.
Application information: Applications not accepted.
  Additional information: The foundation will contact the surviving family following official notice of relative's death.
EIN: 133120746

6398
The Skadden Fellowship Foundation, Inc.
(formerly Skadden, Arps, Slate, Meagher & Flom Fellowship Foundation)
360 Hamilton Ave.
White Plains, NY 10601-1811 (212) 735-2956
Contact: Susan Butler Plum, Secy.
FAX: (917) 777-2956;
E-mail: susan.plum@skadden.com; Application address: Skadden Fellowship Program, 4 Times Sq., Rm. 29-218, New York, NY 10036; URL: http://www.skaddenfellowships.org/

Foundation type: Company-sponsored foundation
Purpose: Fellowships to graduating law students and outgoing judicial clerks who want to work in the public interest for organizations that provide civil legal services to the poor, the elderly, the disabled, and those deprived of their civil rights or human

rights. Grants to former Skadden Fellows who want to undertake new initiatives on behalf of their clients.

Publications: Application guidelines.

Financial data: Year ended 12/31/2011. Assets, $9,588,665 (M); Expenditures, $4,029,309; Total giving, $3,477,658; Grants to individuals, 16 grants totaling $59,773 (high: $11,681, low: $200).

Fields of interest: Law school/education; International human rights; Civil/human rights, advocacy; Civil/human rights; Leadership development.

Type of support: Fellowships; Grants to individuals.

Application information: Applications accepted. Application form required. Interview required.

  Initial approach: Application for fellowships, letter for Grants

  Send request by: Mail

  Deadline(s): Oct. 7 for Fellowships, Jan. 15 and July 15 for Flom Memorial Incubator Grants

  Final notification: Recipients notified by Dec. 6 for fellowships

  Applicants should submit the following:

    1) Essay

    2) Resume

    3) Transcripts

    4) Letter(s) of recommendation

  Additional information: Fellowship applications should also include commitment letter from the potential sponsoring organization and copy of the institution's 501(c)(3) tax-exempt letter. Letters for Flom Memorial Incubator Grants should describe the applicants career trajectory, the inspiration for the project, and the proposed plan for grant funds.

Program description:

  Flom Memorial Incubator Grants: The foundation awards $10,000 grants to support creative novel projects undertaken by former Skadden Fellows engaged in public interest work. Proposed projects should identify an evolving need in the community the Fellow serves. Projects can be used to fund outreach to a new population in need of a particular type of service, develop a website to facilitate communication with clients or potential clients, translate materials or brochures into multiple foreign languages, or pilot an innovative approach to a long-standing problem.

EIN: 133455231

6399
Joan Skahan Memorial Fund

c/o NBT Bank, N.A.
52 S. Broad St.
Norwich, NY   13815-6073

Foundation type: Independent foundation

Purpose: Scholarships by nomination only to graduating seniors at Whitesboro Central School, Marcy, NY.

Financial data: Year ended 10/31/2013. Assets, $58,192 (M); Expenditures, $4,417; Total giving, $2,500; Grant to an individual, 1 grant totaling $2,500.

Fields of interest: Higher education.

Type of support: Support to graduates or students of specific schools; Awards/grants by nomination only.

Application information: Application form required.

  Deadline(s): Mid-May for faculty nominations

  Additional information: Recipients are chosen by a committee at Whitesboro High School.

EIN: 166238801

6400
Skaneateles Central School Endowment Foundation

(formerly Skaneateles Central School Endowment Foundation)
1 M & T Plz., 8th Fl.
Buffalo, NY   14203   (717) 852-3011
Contact: Philip D. D' Angelo, Dir.
Application address: 8 Calemad St., Auburn, NY 13021

Foundation type: Independent foundation

Purpose: Scholarships to graduating seniors of Skaneateles Central High School, NY who have attended for a minimum of two years prior to graduation.

Financial data: Year ended 12/31/2012. Assets, $927,911 (M); Expenditures, $47,696; Total giving, $37,000.

Type of support: Support to graduates or students of specific schools; Undergraduate support.

Application information: Scholarship is based on academic standing, character, ability and need.

EIN: 166076528

6401
The Skin Cancer Foundation, Inc.

149 Madison Ave., Ste. 901
New York, NY   10016-8713   (212) 725-5176
Contact: Mary Stine, Exec. Dir.
FAX: (212) 725-5751; *E-mail:* info@skincancer.org;
URL: http://www.skincancer.org

Foundation type: Public charity

Purpose: Research grants to dermatology residents, fellows, and young faculty for basic research, clinical studies, and educational programs related to skin cancer.

Publications: Annual report; Informational brochure; Newsletter.

Financial data: Year ended 12/31/2011. Assets, $7,950,875 (M); Expenditures, $5,962,489.

Fields of interest: Cancer research; Skin disorders research.

Type of support: Research.

Application information: Applications accepted. Application form required. Application form available on the grantmaker's web site.

  Initial approach: Letter of intent

  Send request by: Mail

  Copies of proposal: 6

  Deadline(s): Oct. 3

  Final notification: Applicants notified by Nov.

  Applicants should submit the following:

    1) Essay

    2) Curriculum vitae

Program description:

  Research Grants: The foundation awards grants, ranging from $10,000 to $25,000, to pilot research projects related to skin cancer. Priority will be given to basic research and clinical studies that address improved methods of prevention, detection, and treatment of skin cancer. Researchers are invited to submit applications for one-year projects to be conducted within the dermatology departments of medical institutions within the U.S.

EIN: 132948778

6402
Skowhegan School of Painting & Sculpture

200 Park Ave. S., Ste. 1116
New York, NY   10003-1503   (212) 529-0505
FAX: (212) 473-1342;
E-mail: mail@skowheganart.org; *URL:* http://www.skowheganart.org

Foundation type: Public charity

Purpose: Provides a nine-week summer residency for emerging visual artists with studio space and technical support in Skowhegan, ME.

Publications: Application guidelines; Newsletter; Program policy statement.

Financial data: Year ended 12/31/2011. Assets, $15,141,403 (M); Expenditures, $1,816,296; Total giving, $226,266; Grants to individuals, totaling $226,266.

Fields of interest: Visual arts.

Type of support: Residencies.

Application information: Applications accepted. Application form required. Application form available on the grantmaker's web site.

  Send request by: Online

  Copies of proposal: 1

  Deadline(s): Feb. 1

  Final notification: Recipients notified in Apr.

Program description:

  Financial Assistance: The school provides financial assistance, in the hopes that artists chosen to participate in its program can attend regardless of their financial status. Applicants are asked to request a financial aid amount. Some will be able to pay most or all of the cost of the program, while others may only be able to pay a small amount. Awards are based on individual requests, and are meant to cover tuition, room, and board, to those who provide evidence of financial need. Assistance for other living expense or materials are not provided.

EIN: 010263908

6403
Sky Rink Winter Games Training Facilities, Inc.

c/o Chelsea Piers
Pier 62, Ste. 300
New York, NY   10011-1015   (212) 336-6839
Contact: Krista Bugenhagen

Foundation type: Independent foundation

Purpose: Scholarships to New York City children who do not have the financial resources for youth hockey and figure skating programs.

Financial data: Year ended 08/31/2011. Assets, $792,936 (M); Expenditures, $104,242; Total giving, $87,748; Grants to individuals, totaling $87,748.

Fields of interest: Athletics/sports, winter sports.

Type of support: Scholarships—to individuals.

Application information: Application form required.

  Deadline(s): End of Sept. for Fall/Winter, end of Mar. for Spring, beginning May for Summer

  Additional information: Application should include financial information and reason for the need of the scholarship.

EIN: 133550784

6404
Alfred P. Sloan Foundation

630 5th Ave., Ste. 2550
New York, NY   10111-0242   (212) 649-1649
Contact: Paul L. Joskow, Pres.
FAX: (212) 757-5117; *URL:* http://www.sloan.org

Foundation type: Independent foundation
Purpose: Fellowships by nomination only to regular faculty members in chemistry, physics, computer science, mathematics, economics, and neuroscience at colleges and universities in the U.S. and Canada.
Publications: Application guidelines; Annual report; Grants list; Informational brochure (including application guidelines); IRS Form 990 or 990-PF printed copy available upon request.
Financial data: Year ended 12/31/2012. Assets, $1,734,238,378 (M); Expenditures, $99,583,363; Total giving, $76,720,974; Grants to individuals, 139 grants totaling $6,737,574 (high: $50,000, low: $6,881).
Fields of interest: Higher education; Neuroscience; Science; Chemistry; Mathematics; Physics; Computer science; Biology/life sciences; Economics.
Type of support: Fellowships; Research.
Application information:
 Deadline(s): Sept. 15 for Sloan Research Fellowships, Oct. 15 for Sloan Industry Center Fellowships.
 Additional information: Completion of formal nomination required. Individual applications not accepted.
Program description:
 Sloan Research Fellowships: This program seeks to stimulate fundamental research by early-career scientists and scholars of outstanding promise. Its two-year fellowships are awarded yearly to 126 researchers in recognition of distinguished performance and a unique potential to make substantial contributions to their field. Candidates are required: a) to hold a Ph.D. (or equivalent) in chemistry, computer science, economics, mathematics, computational and evolutionary molecular biology, neuroscience, ocean sciences, physics or in a related interdisciplinary field; b) be members of the regular teaching faculty (i.e., tenure track) of a degree-granting college or university in the United States or Canada; and c) be no more than six years from completion of the most recent Ph.D. or equivalent as of the year of their nomination (some exceptions are made in special circumstances). Candidates must be nominated by department heads or other senior researchers. Direct applications are not accepted. The deadline is Sept. 15. For nomination and other information visit the foundation's website.
EIN: 131623877

6405

Smack Mellon Studios, Inc.

92 Plymouth St.
Brooklyn, NY 11201-1002 (718) 834-8761
Contact: Kathleen Gilrain, Exec. Dir.
FAX: (718) 834-5233;
E-mail: info@smackmellon.org; URL: http://smackmellon.org/

Foundation type: Public charity
Purpose: Residencies and stipends for artists to work in Brooklyn, NY.
Financial data: Year ended 12/31/2011. Assets, $338,325 (M); Expenditures, $319,408.
Fields of interest: Media/communications; Film/video; Visual arts.
Type of support: Stipends.
Application information: Applications accepted. Application form required. Application form available on the grantmaker's web site.
 Initial approach: E-mail or telephone
 Send request by: Mail
 Deadline(s): Contact foundation for current application deadline

Applicants should submit the following:
 1) Work samples
 2) Resume
 3) Letter(s) of recommendation
 4) SASE
Additional information: Application must also include artist statement.
Program description:
 Smack Mellon Artist Studio Program: The program offers free studio space to eligible artists for a one-year period. The program provides artists working in all visual arts media a free private studio space and a $5,000 fellowship (dependent upon funding). The program does not provide living space. Artists also have access to shared facilities that include a fabrication shop, 2 G5 workstations for video editing, DVD burner and CD read/write capabilities, 2 emacs, flatbed and slide scanners, DVD players, projectors and monitors, wireless Internet access and technical support.
EIN: 113375393

6406

W. Eugene Smith Memorial Fund, Inc.

c/o Redux Pict -M.Saba
11 Hanover Sq., 26th Fl.
New York, NY 10005

Foundation type: Company-sponsored foundation
Purpose: Competitive prizes for photojournalists whose work is based on a humanistic theme.
Publications: Application guidelines; Grants list.
Financial data: Year ended 02/28/2013. Assets, $46,484 (M); Expenditures, $41,374; Total giving, $30,000; Grants to individuals, 3 grants totaling $30,000 (high: $20,000, low: $5,000).
Fields of interest: Print publishing; Photography.
Type of support: Awards/prizes.
Application information: Application form required.
 Initial approach: Letter
 Send request by: Mail
 Deadline(s): June 1
 Applicants should submit the following:
 1) Work samples
 2) Resume
 3) Proposal
 Additional information: Finalists submit a comprehensive photographic portfolio in Aug.
Company name: Nikon Inc.
EIN: 133060631

6407

Harry E. and Florence W. Snayberger Memorial Foundation

(also known as Snayberger Memorial Foundation)
c/o M&T Bank
1100 Wehrle Dr., 2nd Fl.
Amherst, NY 14221-7748 (716) 842-5506
Contact: Carolyn Bernatonis, Trust Dept.
E-mail: cbernatonis@mtb.com

Foundation type: Independent foundation
Purpose: Scholarships to financially needy residents of Schuylkill County, PA, for undergraduate, graduate, and vocational study.
Financial data: Year ended 03/31/2013. Assets, $4,259,364 (M); Expenditures, $225,626; Total giving, $187,800; Grants to individuals, 92 grants totaling $151,900 (high: $1,700, low: $200).
Fields of interest: Vocational education; Education.
Type of support: Scholarships—to individuals; Graduate support; Technical education support; Undergraduate support.
Application information: Applications accepted. Application form required.
 Send request by: Mail

Copies of proposal: 1
Deadline(s): Last working day in Feb.
Final notification: Applicants notified mid-Sept.
Additional information: Applications can be picked up at any M&T Bank branch. Applicants for graduate study must be under 25 years of age.
EIN: 232056361

6408

Sir John Soanes Museum Foundation, Inc.

1040 1st Ave., No. 311
New York, NY 10022-2991 (212) 223-2012
Contact: Chas A. Miller III, Exec. Dir.
E-mail: info@soanefoundation.com; URL: http://www.soanefoundation.com

Foundation type: Public charity
Purpose: Fellowships for graduate students in art, architecture, interior design and the decorative arts to study works at Sir John Soane's Museum in London, England.
Publications: Application guidelines.
Financial data: Year ended 12/31/2012. Assets, $1,327,852 (M); Expenditures, $546,061; Total giving, $35,000; Grants to individuals, totaling $10,000.
Fields of interest: Architecture; Design; Museums (art).
Type of support: Fellowships; Travel awards.
Application information: Applications accepted. Application form required.
 Initial approach: Proposals
 Send request by: Mail
 Deadline(s): Mar. 1
 Final notification: Applicants notified before May
 Additional information: Application should include three letters of recommendation and proof of enrollment in a qualified academic program.
Program description:
 Sir John Soane's Museum Foundation Traveling Fellowship Program: A grant of $5,000 is paid to the awardee and may be allocated as the graduate student sees fit within the scope of the approved project. The applicant must be enrolled in a graduate degree program in the history of art, architecture, the decorative arts, interior design or in a field appropriate to the foundation's purpose. The recipient may be asked by Sir John Soane's Museum Foundation to deliver a talk, at a mutually agreeable time and venue, on a fellowship topic related to Sir John Soane, or Sir John Soane's Museum and its collection.
EIN: 133624437

6409

Social Science Research Council

(also known as SSRC)
1 Pierrepoint Plz., 15th Fl.
Brooklyn, NY 11201-2776 (212) 377-2700
Contact: Gail Kovach, Dir., Admin. Svcs.
FAX: (212) 377-2727; E-mail: info@ssrc.org;
URL: http://www.ssrc.org

Foundation type: Public charity
Purpose: Fellowships to students at specific schools for interdisciplinary research and training. Fellowships and grants to social science scholars and advanced students for interdisciplinary research. Prizes awarded for promising dissertation work to recipients of fellowships from an ACLS/SSRC sponsored program.
Publications: Application guidelines; Informational brochure; Newsletter.

Financial data: Year ended 06/30/2011. Assets, $35,011,192 (M); Expenditures, $19,852,752; Total giving, $5,196,868; Grants to individuals, 348 grants totaling $1,921,909.
Fields of interest: Humanities; Language (foreign); Arts; Adult/continuing education; Environment; Crime/violence prevention; International peace/security; International affairs; Urban/community development; Community/economic development; Computer science; Social sciences; Economics; Psychology/behavioral science; Political science; Social sciences, interdisciplinary studies; Minorities; Immigrants/refugees.
International interests: Japan.
Type of support: Fellowships; Research; Support to graduates or students of specific schools; Awards/prizes; Postdoctoral support; Graduate support; Residencies; Doctoral support; Stipends.
Application information: Applications accepted. Application form required.
  Deadline(s): Vary
  Additional information: Applicants for fellowships must contact their school for application guidelines. See web site for additional programs, and guidelines.
Program descriptions:
  Abe Fellowships for Journalists: This program, administered in partnership with the Japan Foundation Center for Global Partnership, is designed to encourage in-depth coverage of topics of pressing concern to the U.S. and Japan through individual short-term policy-related projects. Applicants are invited to submit proposals on the themes of traditional and non-traditional approaches to security and diplomacy, global and religious economic issues, and social and cultural issues. Eligible applicants must be citizens of the U.S. or Japan with at least five years of professional journalistic experience in newspapers, magazines, wire services, and on-line news organizations (including freelancing). The program provides support for six weeks in Japan or the U.S. The maximum stipend is $25,600, which includes one roundtrip air ticket, $500 to prepare for overseas fieldwork, and support for interpretation based on requests.
  CETI Summer Institute Grants: This program is designed to strengthen research capacity and incubate cross-disciplinary collaboration through a week-long intensive program, at which participants are introduced to key conceptual and methodological approaches to environment and health from across the disciplines, analyze and critique previous research, and provide feedback on developing research proposals.
  Drugs, Security and Democracy Fellowship: This fellowship supports a minimum of three and a maximum of twelve months of postdoctoral and dissertation-level research on drug policy, citizen security, and democratic governance as well as associated topics. Fellowship research must address the theme of drugs and at least one of the other two themes of security and democracy in Latin America or the Caribbean. These topics may include but should not be limited to political economy, anti-democratic strategies used by communities or states, legal frameworks and analyses, the impact on vulnerable groups, and the role of elites. Eligible applicants must either be graduate students at the dissertation stage, or recent Ph.D. recipients (within seven years). The program strongly encourages citizens and residents of Latin America and the Caribbean to apply.
  Eurasia Fellowship Program: Funding is available for researchers focusing on the Russian empire, the Soviet Union, and the new states of Eurasia. Research related to the non-Russian states, regions, and peoples (including Armenia,

Azerbaijan, Belarus, Georgia, Kazakhstan, Kyrgyzstan, Moldova, Tajikistan, Turkmenistan, Ukraine, and Uzbekistan) is particularly encouraged. Eligible researchers can apply for one of three types of fellowships: Pre-Dissertation Awards (up to $4,000 for initial field assessments, including archival exploration, preliminary interviews, and other forms of feasibility studies related to their dissertations); Dissertation Development Awards ($22,000 for one year for graduate students who have obtained ABD status and are looking to complete their dissertation); and Post-Doctoral Research Fellowships (up to $33,000 to early-career scholars who have been awarded their Ph.D. within the last five years, to support the furthering of the work initiated in their dissertations or the launching of their first post-dissertation research project)
  FORHEAD Annual Conference: This annual conference provides an opportunity for researchers from different disciplines to share the findings of their recent work with colleagues; officials from relevant government agencies and non-governmental organizations are also invited to attend.
  Japan Society for the Promotion of Science (JSPS) Fellowship: This program provides recent Ph.D. recipients and ABDs with opportunities to conduct research in Japan under the leadership of a host researcher. Under this program, fellows are encouraged to advance their own research and, at the same time, closely collaborate with young Japanese researchers and contribute to Japanese research communities. Applications are welcome from all social science and humanities disciplines and need not be explicitly related to the study of Japan; applicants must also have U.S. citizenship or permanent residency status.
  Korean Studies Dissertation Workshop: This program seeks to create a sustained network of advanced graduate students and faculty by providing the opportunity to give and receive critical feedback on dissertations in progress through attendance at an annual summer workshop. Funding covers participants' travel (in most cases), lodging, and meals. Eligible participants include full-time advanced graduate students, regardless of citizenship, who are enrolled at U.S or Canadian institutions; special consideration will be given to students from universities that are not major Korean studies institutions.
  Next Generation Social Sciences in Africa: Doctoral Dissertation Completion Fellowship: This program offers fellowships to support the advancement of social science faculty toward the completion of doctoral degrees, and to promote the next generation of social science research in Ghana, Nigeria, South Africa, Tanzania, and Uganda. The fellowship offers a one-year leave from teaching responsibilities and a stipend of up to $15,000 to permit the completion of a dissertation that advances research on peace, security, and development topics. Eligible applicants must be citizens of and reside in a sub-Saharan African country while holding a current faculty position at an accredited college or university in Ghana, Nigeria, South Africa, Tanzania, or Uganda; must have a master's degree; and must be working toward completion of the doctoral degree.
  Next Generation Social Sciences in Africa: Doctoral Dissertation Proposal Fellowship: Short-term research costs of up to $3,000 are available to support the advancement of social science faculty toward the completion of their doctoral degrees, and to promote next-generation social science research in Ghana, Nigeria, South Africa, Tanzania, and Uganda. Eligible applicants must be citizens of and reside in a sub-Saharan African country, while holding a current faculty

position at an accredited college or university in Ghana, Nigeria, South Africa, Tanzania, or Uganda; eligible applicants must also be admitted to a graduate program but have yet to undertake dissertation research.
  Next Generation Social Sciences in Africa: Doctoral Dissertation Research Fellowship: Grants of up to $15,000 are available to support the advancement of social science faculty toward the completion of doctoral degrees, and to promote the next generation of social science research in Ghana, Nigeria, South Africa, Tanzania, and Uganda. All applicants must be citizens of and reside in a sub-Saharan African country while holding a current faculty position at an accredited college or university in Ghana, Nigeria, South Africa, Tanzania, or Uganda.
  Rachel Tanur Memorial Prize for Visual Sociology: The prize honor the memory of Rachel Tanur by encouraging students to incorporate visual elements in their study and understanding of Sociology. First prize is $2,500, second prize is $1,500, and third prize is $500. Graduate and undergraduate students of Sociology are eligible.
EIN: 131325070

6410

Societe des Professeurs Francais en Amerique

(formerly Societe des Professeurs Francais en Amerique)
1101 Ave. of the Americas, 11th Fl.
New York, NY 10016
Application address: Marandon Scholarships, SPFFA

Foundation type: Independent foundation
Purpose: Scholarships to researchers, graduate and undergraduate students, and high school students studying French in the U.S., France, or Quebec, Canada.
Publications: Grants list; Informational brochure.
Financial data: Year ended 12/31/2012. Assets, $3,280,567 (M); Expenditures, $229,471; Total giving, $179,626; Grants to individuals, 27 grants totaling $174,400 (high: $10,000, low: $200).
Fields of interest: Language (foreign); International exchange, students.
International interests: France.
Type of support: Research; Graduate support; Precollege support; Undergraduate support; Travel grants.
Application information:
  Deadline(s): Dec. 15
  Applicants should submit the following:
    1) Transcripts
    2) Resume
    3) Proposal
    4) Letter(s) of recommendation
  Additional information: Contact the organization for additional application information.
EIN: 133150248

6411

Society for the Relief of Women & Children

c/o McLaughlin & Stern
260 Madison Ave., 18th Fl.
New York, NY 10016-2404

Foundation type: Independent foundation
Purpose: Grants to women in New York, NY, who after leading productive lives, are unable, because of circumstances beyond their control, to adequately support themselves.

Financial data: Year ended 10/31/2012. Assets, $2,924,830 (M); Expenditures, $137,251; Total giving, $102,959; Grants to individuals, 48 grants totaling $102,959 (high: $4,800, low: $159).
Fields of interest: Women.
Type of support: Awards/grants by nomination only; Grants for special needs.
Application information: Individual applications not accepted; Grants made only on recommendation of church or a social service agency.
EIN: 136161272

6412
Society of Cosmetic Chemists
120 Wall St., Ste. 2400
New York, NY 10005-4088 (212) 668-1500
FAX: (212) 668-1504; E-mail: SCC@scconline.org;
E-mail for Doreen Scelso: dscelso@scconline.org;
URL: http://www.scconline.org

Foundation type: Public charity
Purpose: Fellowships and awards to students of cosmetic science.
Publications: Newsletter.
Financial data: Year ended 08/31/2011. Assets, $2,048,628 (M); Expenditures, $1,726,810.
Fields of interest: Science.
Type of support: Fellowships; Awards/prizes; Graduate support.
Application information:
  Deadline(s): Feb. 1
  Additional information: See web site for additional guidelines.
Program descriptions:
  Allan B. Black Award, sponsored by Presperse, Inc.: A scroll and honorarium are annually awarded for the best paper on make-up technology either presented at an annual meeting or seminar, or published in the Journal of Cosmetic Science, the Official Journal of the Society of Cosmetic Chemists.
  Des Goddard Award, sponsored by Arch Personal Care Products: A scroll and honorarium are awarded annually for the most innovative paper on the topic of Polymer Science related to cosmetics or personal care presented at the previous Annual Scientific Meeting or Seminar or published in the Journal.
  Frontier of Science Award Lecture, sponsored by Cosmetic and Toiletries Magazine: This award presents an honorarium to a speaker who has achieved national or international stature in the scientific community, for delivering a lecture at the society's Annual Scientific Meeting.
  Hans Schaeffer Award, sponsored by Arch Personal Care Products: A scroll and honorarium are awarded annually for the most innovative paper presented at the society's annual meeting, or a society seminar.
  Henry Maso Keynote Award Lecture: A certificate and honorarium is given to a speaker to present at the Annual Scientific Seminar of the Society.
  Joseph P. Ciaudelli Award, sponsored by Croda, Inc.: A scroll and honorarium are awarded annually for the best article appearing in the Journal of Cosmetic Science on the subject of hair care technology.
  Keynote Award Lecture, sponsored by Ruger Chemical Corporation: An honorarium given to a speaker who has achieved exceptional national or international stature in the scientific community, for delivering a lecture at the Annual Scientific Meeting.
  Literature Award: The society awards a scroll and honorarium to the author or authors of scientific papers in basic research judged to be an outstanding contribution to cosmetic science and technology.

SCC Award, sponsored by Rhodia Novecare: A scroll and honorarium are awarded for the best paper presented at the society's annual scientific meeting.
  SCC Award, sponsored by The HallStar Company: A scroll and honorarium are awarded for the Best Paper that makes the greatest scientific contribution to knowledge in the field of protecting against, or ameliorating damage to human skin caused by exposure to UV radiation presented at the society's Annual Scientific Seminar.
  Shaw Mudge Award, sponsored by BASF Corporation: A scroll and honorarium are awarded for the best paper presented at the society's annual scientific seminar.
EIN: 131976655

6413
Society of Kastorians Omonoia, Inc.
150-28 14th Ave.
Whitestone, NY 11357 (718) 746-4505
FAX: (718) 746-4506;
E-mail: kastorians@kastoria.us; URL: http://www.kastoria.us/en/

Foundation type: Operating foundation
Purpose: Scholarships to financially needy individuals in NJ and NY, who are of Kastorian, Greek or Macedonian descent, for higher education.
Financial data: Year ended 12/31/2011. Assets, $4,680,149 (M); Expenditures, $530,580; Total giving, $127,478; Grants to individuals, 28 grants totaling $127,478.
Fields of interest: Higher education.
International interests: Greece; Macedonia.
Type of support: Undergraduate support.
Application information: Applications accepted.
  Initial approach: Letter
  Deadline(s): Aug. 31
  Additional information: Application must include academic achievements, schools attended and all academic and professional goals.
EIN: 133000517

6414
Socrates Sculpture Park
32-01 Vernon Blvd.
P.O. Box 6259
Long Island City, NY 11106-4925 (718) 956-1819
Contact: John Hatfield, Exec. Dir.
Application address for Public Art Residency: Washington Projects for the Arts, 2023 Massachusetts Ave., NW, Washington, DC 20036, tel.: (202) 234-7103
FAX: (718) 626-1533;
E-mail: info@socratessculpturepark.org; E-mail for John Hatfield: jh@socratessculpturepark.org;
URL: http://www.socratessculpturepark.org

Foundation type: Public charity
Purpose: Grants to emerging artists who are residents of New York in need of financial assistance.
Publications: Application guidelines.
Financial data: Year ended 12/31/2011. Assets, $1,245,722 (M); Expenditures, $817,316; Total giving, $147,375; Grants to individuals, totaling $147,375.
Fields of interest: Sculpture.
Type of support: Fellowships; Grants to individuals.
Application information: Applications accepted. Application form required. Application form available on the grantmaker's web site.

Initial approach: Proposal
Deadline(s): Jan. 24 for Emerging Artist Fellowship and Open Space; Apr. 23 for Public Art Residency Program
Applicants should submit the following:
  1) SASE
  2) Resume
  3) Proposal
Additional information: Application should also include 10 35mm slides, slide script, and five color laser copies, photographs, or digital prints of previous artwork. Artists are encouraged to visit the park before submitting an application. See web site for additional guidelines.
Program descriptions:
  Emerging Artist Fellowship: Fellowship recipients are granted financial support in the amount of $5,000, a two- to six-month residency in the organization's outdoor studio, and access to facilities, materials, equipment and technical assistance to create a work for the park's annual Emerging Artist Fellowship Exhibition. Fellowships are awarded to artists who are not yet well established, and must be New York State residents in need of financial assistance.
  Public Art Residency Program: Awarded in conjunction with the Washington Project for the Arts and the DC Commission on the Arts and Humanities, this program provides a residency opportunity to instruct and inform artists about practical and conceptual issues related to the creation of public art. Through this program, artists will learn the fundamentals of developing a proposal for public art work, identifying sources for materials and funding of projects, and accessing a support network for technical assistance and future opportunities related to creating and presenting art in the public realm. One artist who resides in the District of Columbia will be selected to receive a two- to three-month paid residency and exhibition opportunity at the park, and will receive financial support in the amount of $4,5000 ($2,500 production grant plus $2,000 living/travel stipend), a residency in the park's outdoor studio, and access to facilities, materials, equipment, and technical assistance. The selected artist will also be given (by SSP) limited administrative assistance to conduct additional fundraising for his/her project, procure in-kind support, and pursue future commissions, residencies, and placement for his/her work. The selected artist will have to make his/her own living and travel arrangements.
EIN: 113066597

6415
Gerald B. Solomon Freedom Foundation Inc.
P.O. Box 1246
South Glens Falls, NY 12803-1246

Foundation type: Independent foundation
Purpose: Scholarships for higher education to Eagle Scouts who have achieved the gold star award and who reside in the Glens Falls, NY, area.
Financial data: Year ended 08/31/2013. Assets, $429,681 (M); Expenditures, $13,878; Total giving, $11,250; Grants to individuals, 41 grants totaling $10,250 (high: $250, low: $250).
Fields of interest: Boy scouts.
Type of support: Scholarships—to individuals.
Application information: Applications not accepted.
  Additional information: Unsolicited requests for funds not considered or acknowledged.
EIN: 223246773

6416
Paul & Daisy Soros Fellowships for New Americans

(formerly Paul & Daisy Soros Foundation)
400 W. 59th St., 4th Fl.
New York, NY   10019-1105   (212) 547-6926
Contact: For fellowships: Carmel Geraghty, Prog. Off.
FAX: (212) 548-4623;
E-mail: pdsoros_fellows@sorosny.org; URL: http://www.pdsoros.org

Foundation type: Independent foundation
Purpose: Fellowships to graduate students who are new Americans for study in any graduate program.
Publications: Application guidelines; Informational brochure; Newsletter.
Financial data: Year ended 12/31/2012. Assets, $48,405,686 (M); Expenditures, $4,382,955; Total giving, $3,364,625; Grants to individuals, 86 grants totaling $2,401,386 (high: $57,500, low: $5,000).
Fields of interest: Education; Immigrants/refugees.
Type of support: Fellowships; Graduate support.
Application information: Applications accepted. Application form required. Application form available on the grantmaker's web site.
  Initial approach: E-mail
  Send request by: Online or e-mail
  Copies of proposal: 1
  Deadline(s): Nov. 1
  Final notification: Applicants notified Jan. 1
  Applicants should submit the following:
    1) Essay
    2) Letter(s) of recommendation
    3) Transcripts
    4) Resume
  Additional information: Application should include proof of eligibility for fellowship. See web site for further information.
EIN: 137057096

6417
The E. Leo and Louise F. Spain Scholarship Foundation

c/o Behan Communications
86 Glen St.
Glens Falls, NY   12801-4433   (518) 793-1029
Contact: Mark L. Behan, Secy.

Foundation type: Independent foundation
Purpose: Scholarships to worthy or needy students of St. Mary's Academy, Glens Falls, NY, or to students from other schools in the same locality.
Financial data: Year ended 09/30/2012. Assets, $94,910 (M); Expenditures, $4,958; Total giving, $3,600; Grants to individuals, 7 grants totaling $3,600 (high: $1,000, low: $200).
Fields of interest: Higher education.
Type of support: Scholarships—to individuals; Support to graduates or students of specific schools.
Application information: Applications accepted. Application form required.
  Initial approach: Letter
  Additional information: Award is for one year only. Unsolicited requests for funds not considered or acknowledged.
EIN: 133354188

6418
The Sparkplug Foundation

Park West Finance Station
P.O. Box 20956
New York, NY   10025-0016   (877) 866-8285
FAX: (877) 866-8285;
E-mail: info@sparkplugfoundation.org; URL: http://www.sparkplugfoundation.org/

Foundation type: Independent foundation
Purpose: Grants to individuals for art education or music projects.
Financial data: Year ended 12/31/2012. Assets, $6,986,278 (M); Expenditures, $455,869; Total giving, $319,982.
Fields of interest: Arts education; Music.
Type of support: Project support.
Application information: Application form available on the grantmaker's web site.
  Initial approach: Telephone inquiry required
  Send request by: Mail
  Copies of proposal: 1
  Deadline(s): See web site for current application deadline
  Applicants should submit the following:
    1) Proposal
    2) Curriculum vitae
    3) Budget Information
  Additional information: Few grants to individuals are given, especially those without fiscals sponsors.
EIN: 331033952

6419
Spartan Masonic Educational Foundation

c/o Baldwin Masonic Temple
754 Prospect Pl.
Baldwin, NY   11510-3208   (516) 223-3809
Contact: Edward Callaghan, Treas.
Application address: 576 Ashland Ave., Baldwin, NY 11510, tel.: 516-223-3809

Foundation type: Independent foundation
Purpose: Scholarships to children of members of the Spartan Masonic Lodge, Baldwin, NY.
Financial data: Year ended 12/31/2012. Assets, $280,399 (M); Expenditures, $16,432; Total giving, $10,500; Grants to individuals, 14 grants totaling $10,500 (high: $1,000, low: $500).
Type of support: Undergraduate support.
Application information: Applications accepted.
  Initial approach: Letter
  Deadline(s): Apr. 30
  Additional information: Contact foundation for current application guidelines.
EIN: 237118957

6420
Spencer Educational Foundation, Inc.

1065 Ave. of the Americas, 13th Fl.
New York, NY   10018-0713   (212) 286-9292
Contact: Angela Sabatino, Prog. Mgr.
FAX: (212) 655-6044; E-mail: asabatino@rims.org;
Additional e-mail for Angela Sabatino:
asabatino@spencered.org; URL: http://www.spencered.org

Foundation type: Public charity
Purpose: Scholarships to undergraduate, graduate, and doctoral students pursuing a career related to risk management.
Publications: Application guidelines; Annual report; Informational brochure; Newsletter.
Financial data: Year ended 12/31/2011. Assets, $6,604,782 (M); Expenditures, $947,718; Total

giving, $565,850; Grants to individuals, totaling $393,350.
Fields of interest: Business school/education.
Type of support: Internship funds; Scholarships—to individuals; Graduate support.
Application information: Applications accepted. Application form required. Application form available on the grantmaker's web site.
  Initial approach: Letter, telephone, or e-mail
  Send request by: Mail or e-mail
  Copies of proposal: 1
  Deadline(s): Jan. 30
  Applicants should submit the following:
    1) Letter(s) of recommendation
    2) Curriculum vitae
    3) Transcripts
    4) GPA
    5) Resume
    6) Essay
Program descriptions:
Allied World Assurance Company (AWAC) Scholarships: A $5,000 scholarship is available to a full-time undergraduate student who wishes to continue his/her education in risk management.
Anita Benedetti Memorial Scholarship: A $10,000 scholarship is awarded to a female graduate student who wishes to continue her education in risk management.
Dante Petrizzo Memorial Scholarship: This $5,000 scholarship will be awarded to a full-time undergraduate student in Connecticut, New Jersey, or New York who wishes to pursue further study in risk management.
Dr. Ellen Thrower Scholarship: A $5,000 scholarship is awarded to a full-time undergraduate student attending St. John's University who wishes to continue his/her education in risk management studies.
E.J. Leverett Memorial Scholarship (Atlanta Chapter): This $5,000 scholarship will be awarded to a Georgia full-time undergraduate student who wishes to continue his/her education in risk management studies.
FM Global Scholarships: Two scholarships of $5,000 each will be awarded to full-time undergraduate students to aid in pursuing further studies in risk management.
General Fund Scholarships: Each year the foundation awards scholarships to full-time undergraduate students pursuing coursework in risk management, insurance, and related disciplines. Scholarships of $5,000 each will be awarded to junior- and senior-level undergraduate students, while scholarships of $10,000 each will be awarded to graduate and pre-dissertation Ph.D. students. Eligible applicants must demonstrate career objectives in risk management, a 3.0 grade point average or higher, relevant work experience, and leadership skills.
John T. Lockton Memorial Scholarships: Up to ten awards of $5,000 each are available to full-time undergraduate risk management/insurance and business administration majors.
Joseph P. Holwerda Memorial Scholarship: A $5,000 scholarship will be awarded to a full-time undergraduate student who wishes to pursue further coursework in risk management.
Liberty Mutual Group Scholarships: Four scholarships of $5,000 each are available to full-time undergraduate students who wish to continue their education in risk management.
RIMS Atlanta Chapter Scholarship: A $5,000 scholarship is given to a Georgia full-time undergraduate student who wishes to continue his/her studies in risk management.
RIMS Chicago Chapter Scholarship: A $5,000 scholarship is available to a full-time undergraduate student attending a college or university in Illinois,

Indiana, Iowa, Michigan, or Wisconsin who wishes to continue his/her studies in risk management.

RIMS Dallas/Ft. Worth Scholarship: A $5,000 scholarship will be awarded to a permanent resident of Texas who is pursuing full-time undergraduate work in the field of risk management.

Royal & SunAlliance/Douglas Barlow Scholarship: A $7,500 scholarship is awarded to an individual with a high GPA who is currently pursuing full-time undergraduate study in risk management.

September 11th Memorial Scholarship: A $5,000 award will be given to a full-time undergraduate student who is pursuing his/her studies in risk management, and who exemplifies outstanding leadership abilities.

Thomas Regan Memorial/RIMS New York Chapter Scholarships: A $5,000 award will be given to a permanent resident in Connecticut, New Jersey, or New York who is currently pursuing full-time undergraduate work in risk management.

William J. Clagnaz ACE USA Memorial Scholarship: A $5,000 scholarship is awarded to a permanent resident of New York City (including any of the five boroughs) who is pursuing full-time undergraduate study in risk management.

XL Capital Group/Ian R. Heap Memorial Scholarship: A $5,000 award is given to a full-time undergraduate student who is pursuing his/her education in risk management studies.

Zurich Financial Services Scholarship: A $5,000 award will be given to a full-time undergraduate student who is pursuing his/her coursework in the field of risk management studies.

EIN: 581420617

6421
The Sperry Fund
99 Park Ave., Ste. 2220
New York, NY 10016-1601
Contact: Thomas L. Parkinson Ph.D., Prog. Dir.
Scholarship program URL: http://foundationcenter.org/grantmaker/beinecke/index.html, tel.: (610) 395-5560,
e-mail: BeineckeScholarship@earthlink.net
FAX: (610) 625-7919

Foundation type: Independent foundation
Purpose: Scholarships to college juniors who are U.S. citizens and are nominated by the presidents or deans of accredited colleges and universities, primarily in NY.
Publications: Informational brochure.
Financial data: Year ended 06/30/2013. Assets, $16,710,206 (M); Expenditures, $1,041,824; Total giving, $833,274; Grants to individuals, totaling $578,274.
Fields of interest: Higher education; Graduate/professional education; Scholarships/financial aid.
Type of support: Awards/grants by nomination only; Undergraduate support.
Application information: Applications not accepted.
Additional information: College or university must be invited to nominate an applicant. Unsolicited requests for funds not considered or acknowledged.
Program description:
Beinecke Memorial Scholarships: A Beinecke Scholar receives a total of $34,000 in support of his or her graduate education. The initial payment of $4,000 is awarded directly to the student prior to entering graduate school. This award is intended to offset the costs associated with the graduate application process and to pay for travel expenses directly related to the start of graduated school. While in graduate school, a Beinecke Scholar will

receive an additional $30,000 in support. These funds are awarded as a supplement to support provided by the graduate school and the award may be spread over up to five years to comply with institutional limits on the total amount of a student's annual award. In the absence of institutional support or limits, scholars may receive a maximum award of $15,000 per year. These funds are sent directly to the financial aid officer of the institution where the student is enrolled and disbursed in accordance with the scholarship policy of the academic institution. See program web site for additional information and guidelines.
EIN: 136114308

6422
Sponsors for Educational Opportunity, Inc.
55 Exchange Pl., Ste. 601
New York, NY 10005-3301 (212) 979-2040
Contact: William A. Goodloe, Pres. and C.E.O.
E-mail: seoinfo@seo-usa.org; URL: http://www.seo-usa.org/

Foundation type: Public charity
Purpose: Scholarships to highly motivated students of color from underserved public high schools in New York City, NY.
Financial data: Year ended 08/31/2012. Assets, $21,386,071 (M); Expenditures, $7,862,647; Total giving, $263,072; Grants to individuals, totaling $228,072.
Fields of interest: Minorities.
Type of support: Undergraduate support.
Application information: Applications accepted.
Initial approach: Letter
Applicants should submit the following:
1) Financial information
2) Transcripts
Additional information: Contact foundation for current application deadline/guidelines.
EIN: 132578670

6423
Squeaky Wheel
(also known as Buffalo Media Resources, Inc.)
712 Main St.
Buffalo, NY 14202-1720 (716) 884-7172
Contact: Jax Deluca, Exec. Dir.
FAX: (716) 886-1619; E-mail: office@squeaky.org;
URL: http://www.squeaky.org

Foundation type: Public charity
Purpose: Residencies for mid-career experimental filmmakers who are interested in "crossing the digital divide" but lack access and training.
Publications: Application guidelines.
Financial data: Year ended 08/31/2012. Assets, $91,954 (M); Expenditures, $234,061.
Fields of interest: Film/video.
Type of support: Residencies; Fiscal agent/sponsor.
Application information: Applications accepted. Application form required. Application form available on the grantmaker's web site.
Initial approach: Application
Deadline(s): July 16 for Artist-in-Residence Program
Additional information: Application should include work samples.
Program descriptions:
Artist-in-Residence Program: This program annually provides equipment and facility access to four emerging medial artists in the western New York region. Artists-in-residence receive 100 hours of free access to film, digital, or video labs, as well

as five days' rental of film/video production equipment, one free workshop of choice (during the term of residency), and a $100 honorarium upon completion of the residency. During the term of residency, participants must volunteer five hours per month (thirty hours total) at the organization during events or open lab hours, participate in group meetings, and show their new work created during the residency. Eligible applicants must reside in Allegany, Cattaraugus, Chautauqua, Erie, Genesee, Orleans, Niagara, Wyoming, Monroe, Wayne, Livingston, and Ontario counties, and must not be enrolled in an educational facility during the term of residency.

Fiscal Sponsorships: The center provides project sponsorship for its members to federal, state, and municipal granting agencies. The center also sponsors granting workshops and provides grantwriting materials and information to local artists.

International Media Artist/Filmmaker Residency: The organization provides a four-week program to media artists and filmmakers from around the world who are interested in learning new technologies (film or digital) useful for their practice. The residency offers one month of access to 16mm production/post-production systems, film hand-processing facilities, a computer lab with multimedia programs, video/film cameras, and other access to production-related equipment; residents will also receive accommodations, travel, and a $1,000 artist's stipend.
EIN: 222970899

6424
St. Elmo Foundation
(formerly Delta Phi Educational Fund, Inc.)
P.O. Box 1170
Pearl River, NY 10965-0570 (845) 735-3278
FAX: (845) 732-7430;
E-mail: st.elmo@deltaphi.org; Application address: P.O. Box 81521, Athens, GA 30608-1521;
URL: http://www.deltaphifraternity.org/?page=sefound

Foundation type: Public charity
Purpose: Scholarships to qualified Delta Phi members and other students enrolled in a full-time undergraduate or graduate educational program. Some grants also to members, students, and faculty or staff for special projects.
Publications: Application guidelines.
Financial data: Year ended 12/31/2011. Assets, $2,072,519 (M); Expenditures, $79,944; Total giving, $28,250; Grants to individuals, totaling $13,000.
Fields of interest: Higher education.
Type of support: Scholarships—to individuals; Graduate support; Undergraduate support.
Application information: Applications accepted. Application form required. Application form available on the grantmaker's web site.
Initial approach: Telephone
Program descriptions:
R. Kendall Nottingham Chapter Leader Awards: This award recognizes undergraduate and associate members of Delta Phi Fraternity who have played a significant role in the success of their undergraduate chapters, taking on significant and sustained leadership responsibility at the chapter level. Awards of up to $1,000 (in the form of book stipends) will be given annually to one chapter with less than 25 active brothers, and two chapters with 25 active brothers or more. An award of up to $3,000 will be given if there is an exceptional candidate who merits additional recognition.

William P. Carey Scholarships: These awards support undergraduate, associate, and alumni members of Delta Phi Fraternity in need of financial support for their academic studies. First-time awards of up to $225 will be given to support the purchasing of books or other incidental expenses; other awards, ranging from $225 to $2,500, will be given to support demonstrated financial need on the part of members of the fraternity. Eligible applicants must be members of the fraternity in good standing.
EIN: 136170013

6425
St. George's Society of New York
216 E. 45th St., Ste. 901
New York, NY   10017-3304   (212) 682-6110
Contact: John Shannon, Exec. Dir.
FAX: (212) 682-3465;
E-mail: info@stgeorgessociety.org; URL: http://www.stgeorgessociety.org

Foundation type: Operating foundation
Purpose: Financial assistance to elderly or infirm natives of the United Kingdom or the British Commonwealth and their children, who find themselves in need, trouble, sickness, or other adversity in the New York metropolitan area. Scholarships also to assist deserving British and Commonwealth Students enrolled at Lehman College, part of CUNY, in the Bronx with university expenses.
Publications: Application guidelines; Annual report; Informational brochure; Newsletter.
Financial data: Year ended 12/31/2012. Assets, $11,798,622 (M); Expenditures, $1,662,342; Total giving, $834,388; Grants to individuals, 91 grants totaling $499,755.
Fields of interest: Aging.
International interests: United Kingdom.
Type of support: Grants to individuals; Foreign applicants; Grants for special needs.
Application information: Applications accepted. Application form required.
   Initial approach: Letter
   Copies of proposal: 1
   Deadline(s): None
   Additional information: Applications should include financial information, proof of need and British background.
Program description:
   St. George's Society Scholarship Program: To assist deserving British and Commonwealth Students enrolled at Lehman College, part of CUNY, in the Bronx with university expenses. See web site for additional information and scholarship policies.
EIN: 237426425

6426
St. Luke's Nurses' Benefit Fund
P.O. Box 250892, Columbia Sta.
New York, NY   10025   (212) 523-1619
Contact: Carolyn Ciriello, Tr.
URL: http://ww.slhson.org

Foundation type: Independent foundation
Purpose: Grants to graduates of St. Luke's School of Nursing, NY.
Financial data: Year ended 06/30/2012. Assets, $317,655 (M); Expenditures, $14,376; Total giving, $6,641; Grants to individuals, 2 grants totaling $6,641 (high: $3,595, low: $3,046).
Fields of interest: Nursing school/education.
Type of support: Support to graduates or students of specific schools; Undergraduate support.

Application information: Applications accepted. Application form required.
   Deadline(s): None
EIN: 136164433

6427
Dick Stack Memorial Scholarship Fund
209 Southwood Dr.
Vestal, NY   13850

Foundation type: Company-sponsored foundation
Purpose: Scholarships to residents of Broome and Tioga counties, NY.
Financial data: Year ended 09/30/2012. Assets, $101,838 (M); Expenditures, $931; Total giving, $0.
Type of support: Undergraduate support.
Application information: Applications not accepted.
   Additional information: Unsolicited requests for funds not considered or acknowledged.
EIN: 161555913

6428
Stage Directors and Choreographers Foundation
1501 Broadway, Ste. 1701
New York, NY   10036-5653   (212) 391-1070
Contact: Laura Penn, Exec. Dir.
FAX: (212) 302-6195;
E-mail: foundation@sdcweb.org; Toll-free tel.: (800) 541-5204; URL: http://sdcweb.org/index.php?option=com_content&task=view&id=22&Itemid=88#

Foundation type: Public charity
Purpose: Grants to emerging directors and choreographers to observe work of master directors and choreographers.
Publications: Application guidelines.
Financial data: Year ended 06/30/2011. Assets, $420,235 (M); Expenditures, $184,101; Total giving, $71,852; Grants to individuals, totaling $56,852.
Fields of interest: Performing arts.
Type of support: Grants to individuals.
Application information: Applications accepted. Application form required. Application form available on the grantmaker's web site.
   Send request by: Mail or hand deliver
   Deadline(s): June 1
   Final notification: Applicants notified July 15
   Applicants should submit the following:
      1) Resume
      2) Letter(s) of recommendation
   Additional information: Application should also include a one-page statement explaining why an Observership would be beneficial and a $25 application fee. See web site for additional application guidelines.
Program descriptions:
   Observership Program: This program offers early-career directors and choreographers the opportunity to observe the work of master directors and choreographers as they create new productions on Broadway, off-Broadway, and at leading regional theaters across the country. Participants will have the opportunity to observe first-hand the techniques, disciplines, approaches, and insights of master artists as they create new and revive classic productions. Each position includes weekly stipends of $200 to help defray the recipient's expenses during the rehearsal period. Participants will also receive a free one-year membership to the Stage Directors and Choreographers Society.

Zelda Fichandler Award: This award provides an unrestricted grant of $5,000 to an outstanding director or choreographer making an exceptional contribution to the arts through theater work in a particular region of the United States. Anyone may submit a nomination. Nominators need not be SDC Members. Self-nominations are allowed.
EIN: 132570500

6429
Starlight Children's Foundation, NY/NJ/CT
1560 Bdwy., Ste. 600
New York, NY   10036-1525   (212) 354-2878
Contact: Michele Hall-Duncan, Exec. Dir.
FAX: (212) 354-2977; E-mail: info@starlightnyc.org; E-Mail for Michele Hall-Duncan: michele@starlightnyc.org; URL: http://www.starlight-newyork.org

Foundation type: Public charity
Purpose: Assistance to terminally ill children through granting wishes and providing hospital entertainment.
Publications: Annual report; Financial statement; Newsletter.
Financial data: Year ended 03/31/2012. Assets, $3,902,136 (M); Expenditures, $4,651,032; Total giving, $1,114,295.
Type of support: Grants for special needs.
Application information: Applications not accepted.
   Additional information: Unsolicited requests for funds not considered or acknowledged.
EIN: 133442216

6430
The Starr Foundation
399 Park Ave., 17th Fl.
New York, NY   10022-4614   (212) 909-3600
FAX: (212) 750-3536; URL: http://www.starrfoundation.org/

Foundation type: Independent foundation
Purpose: Scholarships to students who are children of employees of C.V. Starr & Co., and Starr International Co.
Publications: IRS Form 990 or 990-PF printed copy available upon request.
Financial data: Year ended 12/31/2012. Assets, $1,273,521,260 (M); Expenditures, $90,160,261; Total giving, $73,536,203.
Type of support: Employee-related scholarships.
Application information: Applications not accepted.
   Additional information: Unsolicited requests for funding not considered or acknowledged.
Program description:
   C.V. Starr Scholarships: The scholarship program has established funds at more than 140 colleges, universities and secondary schools around the world to which it has contributed more than a quarter billion dollars.
EIN: 136151545

6431
Staten Island Ballet Theater, Inc.
3081 Richmond Rd.
Staten Island, NY   10306-1941   (718) 980-0500
E-mail: anbwilson@cs.com

Foundation type: Public charity
Purpose: Scholarships to individuals for ballet arts training at the Staten Island Ballet Theater, NY.

Financial data: Year ended 05/30/2012. Assets, $52,045 (M); Expenditures, $449,023; Total giving, $15,952; Grants to individuals, totaling $15,952.
Fields of interest: Dance; Ballet; Performing arts, education.
Type of support: Scholarships—to individuals.
Application information: Contact foundation for current application deadline/guidelines.
EIN: 133759761

6432
The Statler Foundation
1207 Delaware Ave.
Plaza Suites., No. 222
Buffalo, NY   14209-1458   (716) 852-1104
Contact: Bernard A. Tolbert, Chair.
FAX: (716) 852-3928

Foundation type: Independent foundation
Purpose: Scholarships only to students of hotel management and culinary arts who are residents of Buffalo, NY.
Financial data: Year ended 12/31/2012. Assets, $32,383,893 (M); Expenditures, $2,235,695; Total giving, $1,328,399; Grants to individuals, totaling $628,399.
Fields of interest: Vocational education.
Type of support: Scholarships—to individuals.
Application information: Application form required.
Initial approach: Letter
Deadline(s): Apr. 15
Additional information: Application must include letters of recommendation.
EIN: 131889077

6433
The Statue Foundation, Inc.
c/o Barbara K. Eisold
353 Central Park W.
New York, NY   10025
E-mail: beisold0@gmail.com

Foundation type: Independent foundation
Purpose: Full or partial scholarships for tuition and books for students who are political refugees from abroad and are either in the process of applying for or have been granted asylum in the U.S.
Financial data: Year ended 12/31/2012. Assets, $2,261,064 (M); Expenditures, $190,591; Total giving, $164,165.
Fields of interest: Education; Immigrants/refugees.
Type of support: Scholarships—to individuals.
Application information: Applications accepted. Application form required. Interview required.
Send request by: E-mail
Applicants should submit the following:
1) Transcripts
2) Letter(s) of recommendation
3) Financial information
Additional information: Application should also include a short statement (not exceeding 500 words) describing your interests and goals in regard to education. Tuition will be paid directly to the education institution on behalf of the students.
Program description:
Scholarship Program: Applicants will receive between one third and the total of tuition for one year of course work currently $8,000 to $25,000. Recipients must complete course work with at least a 2.5 GPA. Applicant must have been granted asylum in the United States within the past 10 years (or longer when the applicant is applying for

renewal of the grant) and are presently living either within New York City or its environs.
EIN: 133947134

6434
The Stecher and Horowitz Foundation
119 W. 57th St., Ste. 1401
New York, NY   10019-2401   (212) 581-8380
Contact: Melvin Stecher, Exec. Dir.
FAX: (212) 581-4186;
E-mail: info@stecherandhorowitz.org; URL: http://www.stecherandhorowitz.org

Foundation type: Public charity
Purpose: Awards and prizes for a music competition for young pianists ages 16 to 21 from around the world competing for cash prizes and concert appearances.
Publications: Application guidelines.
Financial data: Year ended 06/30/2012. Assets, $514,232 (M); Expenditures, $469,237; Total giving, $31,000; Grants to individuals, totaling $31,000.
Fields of interest: Music.
Type of support: Awards/prizes.
Application information: Applications accepted. Application form required. Application form available on the grantmaker's web site.
Send request by: Mail
Deadline(s): Dec. 6
Final notification: Applicants notified Mar. 7
Applicants should submit the following:
1) Photograph
2) Letter(s) of recommendation
Additional information: Application should also include a non-refundable $100 application fee. See web site for additional application guidelines.
Program description:
New York International Piano Competition: The competition is dedicated to providing artistic development, educational enhancement, seminars, master classes, and performance opportunities. Twenty-two young pianists, ages 16 to 21, will gather from across the continent for the week-long event. Unique to the competition is the policy of no elimination thus, each contestant will be scheduled to perform in all rounds and be judged by a jury of some of the most distinguished members of the music community. Prizes range from $6,000 to $1,500. In addition to the prizes awarded to winners, each remaining contestant receives a cash award of $1,000.
EIN: 237443019

6435
The Meir and Ruth Stefansky Charitable Trust
3 Roman Blvd.
Monsey, NY   10952-3105

Foundation type: Operating foundation
Purpose: Grants for Jewish scholars to publish their research.
Financial data: Year ended 01/31/2013. Assets, $108,168 (M); Expenditures, $439,136; Total giving, $430,861; Grants to individuals, 2 grants totaling $47,100 (high: $40,000, low: $7,100).
Fields of interest: Jewish agencies & synagogues.
Type of support: Publication.
Application information: Applications not accepted.
Additional information: Unsolicited requests for funds not considered or acknowledged.
EIN: 200699712

6436
The Harold & Mimi Steinberg Charitable Trust
c/o Schulte Roth & Zabel, LLP
919 3rd Ave.
New York, NY   10022-3903   (212) 758-0404

Foundation type: Independent foundation
Purpose: Awards to American playwrights by nomination only through two programs.
Financial data: Year ended 12/31/2012. Assets, $100,757,497 (M); Expenditures, $7,256,630; Total giving, $6,135,666.
Fields of interest: Theater (playwriting).
Type of support: Grants to individuals; Awards/grants by nomination only.
Application information: Applications not accepted.
Additional information: Awards by nomination only. No direct applications accepted.
Program descriptions:
Steinberg Distinguished Playwright Award: This award honors a mid-career playwright whose body of work has already been recognized. With a cash prize of $200,000, it is believed to be the largest award to honor American playwriting. The first award recipient was announced in fall 2008, and the prize is awarded on a biennial basis thereafter. The trust has established an advisory committee of prominent theater professionals to determine the criteria for the awards, nominate playwrights, and select the recipients.
Steinberg Emerging Playwrights Award: Beginning in 2009, the Steinberg Emerging Playwrights Award, awarded biennially, will honor two early career playwrights whose professional work shows great promise. Each recipient will receive a cash prize of $50,000. The trust has established an advisory committee of prominent theater professionals to determine the criteria for the awards, nominate playwrights, and select the recipients.
EIN: 133383348

6437
Evelyn E. Stempfle Scholarship
(formerly Evelyn E. Stempfle Fund Trust)
c/o NBT Bank, N.A.
52 S. Broad St.
Norwich, NY   13815-1699   (518) 725-0671
Application address: c/o Gloversville High School, Attn: Guidance Dir., 234 Lincoln St., Gloversville, NY 12078-1935, tel.: (518) 725-0671

Foundation type: Independent foundation
Purpose: Scholarships to graduates of Gloversville High School, NY pursuing an education in teaching in the field in languages.
Financial data: Year ended 12/31/2012. Assets, $173,881 (M); Expenditures, $9,583; Total giving, $7,500; Grants to individuals, 14 grants totaling $7,500 (high: $1,000, low: $500).
Fields of interest: Teacher school/education.
Type of support: Support to graduates or students of specific schools.
Application information: Applications accepted. Application form required.
Deadline(s): May 15
Applicants should submit the following:
1) Transcripts
2) Financial information
Additional information: Application must also include student and/or parents copy of the latest federal income tax return. Application can be obtained in the school's guidance office.
EIN: 146036979

6438
Stone Quarry Hill Art Park
3883 Stone Quarry Rd.
P.O. Box 251
Cazenovia, NY 13035-8447 (315) 655-3196
Contact: Sarah Webster, Dir.
FAX: (315) 655-5742;
E-mail: office@stonequarryhillartpark.org;
URL: http://www.stonequarryhillartpark.org

Foundation type: Public charity
Purpose: Residencies to established and emerging visual artists for a duration of two to four weeks.
Financial data: Year ended 12/31/2011. Assets, $1,400,731 (M); Expenditures, $217,581.
Fields of interest: Visual arts.
Type of support: Residencies.
Application information: Applications accepted. Application form required.
  Initial approach: Telephone or e-mail
  Send request by: Mail
  Deadline(s): Apr. 1
  Final notification: Recipients notified May 1
  Applicants should submit the following:
    1) SASE
    2) Work samples
    3) Resume
    4) Proposal
Program description:
  Artist-in-Residency Program: The program provides artists with the opportunity to get involved with the community during residency, whether through collaborative projects, working with high school and/or college students, community performances or artist lectures. Residencies typically last from two to four weeks in any month from May through Sept. Artists are provided with a free room with shared bath, cooking and clothes washing facilities, in a communal four bedroom apartment, plus $500 U.S. toward expenses two baths and laundry room. Artists must be at least 21 years of age to apply.
EIN: 161406217

6439
Katherine M. Stoner Trust
1 M & T Plz. 8th Fl.
Buffalo, NY 14203

Foundation type: Independent foundation
Purpose: Grants to undergraduate worthy young men and women for attendance at the nursing school of Franklin County Vo-Tech, PA.
Financial data: Year ended 12/31/2012. Assets, $73,806 (M); Expenditures, $5,904; Total giving, $3,897.
Fields of interest: Vocational education, post-secondary; Nursing school/education.
Type of support: Support to graduates or students of specific schools; Undergraduate support.
Application information: Applications accepted. Application form required.
  Deadline(s): None
  Additional information: A financial need test is required.
EIN: 256266025

6440
Stony Wold-Herbert Fund, Inc.
136 E. 57th St., Rm. 1705
New York, NY 10022-2924 (212) 753-6565
Contact: Cheryl S. Friedman, Exec. Dir.
FAX: (212) 753-6053;
E-mail: director@stonywold-herbertfund.com;
URL: http://www.stonywoldherbertfund.com/

Foundation type: Independent foundation
Purpose: Undergraduate and vocational school scholarships to financially needy students living in the greater New York, NY, area who are at least 16 years old, and who suffer from a documented respiratory or pulmonary problem. Research grants and fellowships to doctors, teachers, and scientific investigators in the greater New York, NY, area working in respiratory and pulmonary fields.
Publications: Application guidelines; Annual report; Informational brochure; Newsletter.
Financial data: Year ended 12/31/2012. Assets, $6,220,071 (M); Expenditures, $451,286; Total giving, $311,108; Grants to individuals, 20 grants totaling $33,008 (high: $3,625, low: $50).
Fields of interest: Vocational education; Lung diseases; Lung research.
Type of support: Fellowships; Research; Technical education support; Undergraduate support.
Application information: Applications accepted. Application form required. Interview required.
  Deadline(s): Oct. 15 for Research Grants and Fellowships
  Additional information: Application for scholarships must include transcripts, letter of recommendation, applicant's medical profile completed by a doctor, proof of residence, W-2 form, and a brief personal history. Application for Research Grants and Fellowships must include references and description of nature and purpose of research. See program descriptions for further application information.
EIN: 132784124

6441
The Studio Museum in Harlem
144 W. 125th St.
New York, NY 10027-4423 (212) 864-4500
FAX: (212) 864-4800;
E-mail: director@studiomuseum.org; URL: http://www.studiomuseum.org

Foundation type: Public charity
Purpose: Residencies to artists of African descent as well as to African American artists.
Publications: Application guidelines; Annual report.
Financial data: Year ended 06/30/2012. Assets, $10,250,604 (M); Expenditures, $5,266,181; Total giving, $110,000; Grants to individuals, totaling $110,000.
Fields of interest: Cultural/ethnic awareness; African Americans/Blacks.
International interests: Africa.
Type of support: Residencies.
Application information: Applications accepted. Application form required.
  Initial approach: Letter
  Deadline(s): Apr. 1
  Applicants should submit the following:
    1) Work samples
    2) SASE
    3) Resume
    4) Letter(s) of recommendation
  Additional information: Application must also include work slides, and artist statement.
Program description:
  Artist in Residence: Awards three emerging artists studio space, a $15,000 fellowship for a period of 12 months, and a $1,000 materials budget. An exhibition of the artist's work will be presented in the Museum's galleries.
EIN: 132590805

6442
Otto Sussman Trust
c/o Boyce
30 Jericho Executive Plz., Ste. 200 W
Jericho, NY 11753-1028
Application address: c/o M. Fleming, P.O. Box 53446, Temple Heights Post Office, Washington, DC 20009

Foundation type: Independent foundation
Purpose: Financial assistance to needy residents of NJ, NY, OK, and PA who are in need due to illness or death in their immediate family or some other unusual or unfortunate circumstance.
Financial data: Year ended 12/31/2012. Assets, $6,212,021 (M); Expenditures, $331,024; Total giving, $267,620; Grants to individuals, 118 grants totaling $267,620 (high: $6,000, low: $371).
Fields of interest: Human services.
Type of support: Grants for special needs.
Application information: Applications accepted. Application form required.
  Initial approach: Letter
  Deadline(s): None
  Additional information: Applicants must be recommended by and submitted through selected educational, medical, social service, or similar entities with whom the trustees has a working relationship.
EIN: 136075849

6443
Timothy Sweitzer Memorial Fund, Inc.
363 County Road Hwy., Ste. 48
Thompson Ridge, NY 10985

Foundation type: Operating foundation
Purpose: Scholarships to graduating seniors from John S. Burke Catholic High School, NY.
Financial data: Year ended 12/31/2012. Assets, $17,961 (M); Expenditures, $0; Total giving, $0.
Type of support: Support to graduates or students of specific schools; Undergraduate support.
Application information: Applications accepted.
  Deadline(s): June 1
  Applicants should submit the following:
    1) Letter(s) of recommendation
    2) Essay
EIN: 061485210

6444
Teach For America
519 8th Ave., 15th Fl.
New York, NY 10018-6404
Contact: Jemina Bernard, Exec. Dir.
FAX: (212) 279-2663; Toll-free tel.: (800) 832-1230; URL: http://www.teachforamerica.org

Foundation type: Public charity
Purpose: Assistance to individuals who complete two years of service with the organization, teaching in a low-income classroom setting.
Publications: Application guidelines; Annual report.
Financial data: Year ended 09/30/2011. Assets, $372,603,252 (M); Expenditures, $218,697,225; Total giving, $4,952,527; Grants to individuals, totaling $4,293,600.
Fields of interest: Education; Economically disadvantaged.
Type of support: Scholarships—to individuals; Postgraduate support.
Application information:
  Initial approach: Application
  Send request by: Online
  Deadline(s): Feb. 4, Aug. 20, Sept. 17, Oct. 27, and Dec. 17 for Education Awards

Additional information: Application should include letter(s) of recommendation.

Program description:

Education Awards: The organization seeks individuals from all backgrounds, majors, and professional experiences who have what it takes to excel as teachers and improve the quality of education for children growing up in low-income communities. Qualities that the organization looks for in potential candidates include: demonstrated past leadership and achievement (achieving ambitious, measurable results in academic, professional, extracurricular, or volunteer settings); perseverance and sustained focus in the face of challenges; strong critical-thinking skills (maintaining accurate linkages between cause and effect and generating relevant solutions to problems); superior organizational ability (planning well, meeting deadlines, and working efficiently); respect for individuals' diverse experiences and working effectively with people from a variety of backgrounds; superior interpersonal skills to motivate and lead others; and a thorough understanding of and desire to work relentlessly in pursuit of the organization's vision. Eligible applicants must have a bachelor's degree from an accredited college or university, have a cumulative undergraduate GPA of 2.5, and be a U.S. citizen, U.S. national, or permanent legal resident. Individuals who complete their term of service receive loan forbearance and an education award of $5,350 at the end of each year of service (up to $10,700 for two years of service) which may be used toward future educational expenses or to repay qualified student loans.
EIN: 133541913

6445
The Teachers Network
c/o Akin Gump Strauss Hauer & Field
1 Bryant Pk.
New York, NY   10036-6728   (212) 872-8011
Contact: Alan Federman
URL: http://www.teachersnetwork.org

Foundation type: Public charity
Purpose: Grants to public school teachers in New York, NY for curriculum projects.
Publications: Application guidelines; Grants list; Newsletter.
Financial data: Year ended 08/31/2012. Assets, $115,621 (M); Expenditures, $93,195.
Fields of interest: Public education; Education.
Type of support: Program development; Awards/prizes.
Application information: Applications accepted. Application form required. Application form available on the grantmaker's web site.
Additional information: Contact network for additional guidelines.
Program description:
Teachnet Grants: These grants are awarded to public school teachers across New York City who demonstrated effective technology integration through an original piece of curriculum that had been classroom-tested.
EIN: 133312788

6446
Teamsters BBYO Scholarship Fund
c/o Martin Adelstein
6 MeadowLark Dr.
West Nyack, NY   10994   (845) 353-0135
Contact: Martin Adelstein, Tr.

Foundation type: Independent foundation

Purpose: Grants to members of B'nai B'rith Youth Organization in the Northeast region to attend B'nai B'rith Youth Organization Summer Programs.
Financial data: Year ended 07/31/2012. Assets, $80,914 (M); Expenditures, $3,932; Total giving, $3,800; Grants to individuals, 15 grants totaling $3,800 (high: $450, low: $150).
Fields of interest: Children/youth, services; Jewish agencies & synagogues.
Type of support: Grants to individuals.
Application information: Application form required.
Deadline(s): Mar. 30
Additional information: Contact fund or nearest B'nai B'rith chapter for current application guidelines.
EIN: 237383406

6447
Fred M. Teel Charitable Trust
c/o NBT Bank, N.A.
52 S. Broad St.
Norwich, NY   13815   (607) 639-8223
Application address: c/o Afton Central School, Attn.: Guidance Dept., 29 Academy St., Afton, NY 13730

Foundation type: Independent foundation
Purpose: Scholarships to graduates of Afton Central School, NY for postsecondary education.
Financial data: Year ended 12/31/2012. Assets, $64,624 (M); Expenditures, $4,957; Total giving, $3,300.
Fields of interest: Higher education.
Type of support: Support to graduates or students of specific schools; Undergraduate support.
Application information: Applications accepted. Application form required. Interview required.
Initial approach: Letter
Deadline(s): May 15
Additional information: Applications obtained through Afton Central school. Letter must include financial status, goals, career to be pursued, and grades.
EIN: 156020508

6448
Theatre Communications Group
520 Eighth Ave., 24th Fl.
New York, NY   10018-4156   (212) 609-5900
Contact: Teresa Eyring, Exec. Dir.
FAX: (212) 609-5901; *E-mail:* grants@tcg.org;
URL: http://www.tcg.org

Foundation type: Public charity
Purpose: Awards to theater directors and designers seeking a career in American nonprofit theater.
Publications: Application guidelines; Annual report.
Financial data: Year ended 06/30/2012. Assets, $10,924,898 (M); Expenditures, $8,510,871; Total giving, $1,441,736; Grants to individuals, totaling $1,441,736.
Fields of interest: Theater; Theater (playwriting).
Type of support: Program development; Awards/prizes; Residencies; Travel grants.
Application information: Application form required.
Deadline(s): Varies
Additional information: See web site for complete application and program information.
Program descriptions:
Alan Schneider Director Award: This award provides a $7,500 cash prize to exceptional directors whose talent has been demonstrated through work in specific regions, but who are not known nationally. Prizes may be used for travel, research, or other activities specifically focused on

the development of the directing craft or related career opportunities.
Bay Area Commissioning Fund: This program aims to establish and/or strengthen ongoing professional relationships with selected arts writers in the San Francisco Bay area, and is designed to bring Bay area theatres and artists to national attention and heighten visibility for the region as a whole. Each writer will receive $2,500 over the course of his or her affiliation. Recipients will maintain regular communication with the American Theatre staff about news and trends in Bay Area theatre, and will complete two articles, one of which will be an in-depth, research-intensive piece.
Fox Foundation Resident Actor Fellowships: Four fellowships per year are available to actors, in order to further their artistic and professional development, to deepen and enrich their relationships with a non-profit theater, and to ensure their professional commitment to live theatre. Awards are given in two categories. The Extraordinary Potential category awards early- to mid-career actors who have completed their training within the last fifteen years and show extraordinary potential with $15,000, with an additional $10,000 available to relieve student loan debt. Applicants in the Distinguished Achievement category will have demonstrated considerable experience in professional theater with a substantial body of work. Winners in this category will receive $25,000. In addition, host theaters of grant recipients in both categories will receive $7,500 to be applied to costs incurred in the actor's residency activities.
Leadership U[niversity] Program: Funded by The Andrew W. Mellon Foundation, this program intends to strengthen the field by developing individuals who are the core and future of theatre. One-on-One grants of $75,000 are available to six talented early-career leaders from all areas of theatre for professional development via mentorships at a TCG Member Theatre, with an additional $5,000 honorarium for their mentor. Up to an additional $10,000 in supplemental funds will be available for one or more of the following: outstanding student loans, approved supplemental activities, and/or life needs. An additional fund of up to $4,500 will be available for mentee and mentor travel costs. Continuing Ed grants of up to $6,000 are awarded to eight mid-career to veteran professionals at TCG Member Theatres for learning opportunities that will advance their leadership skills in areas that include artistic, administrative, educational, and production.
NEA/TCG Career Development Program for Designers: Awards of $25,000 are provided to six exceptionally talented, early-career designers seeking a career in American nonprofit professional theater. This program also gives recipients the opportunity to spend six months developing their designing skills and knowledge of the field by working with senior designers and other freelance or institutionally-based artists.
NEA/TCG Career Development Program for Directors: Awards of $25,000 are provided to six exceptionally talented, early-career directors seeking a career in America's nonprofit theater. The program offers recipients opportunities to spend six months developing their directing skills and expanding their knowledge of the field by working with one or more senior directors and other freelance or institutionally-based artists.
New Generations Program: Future Leaders: In conjunction with the Doris Duke Charitable Foundation and the Andrew W. Mellon Foundation, this program seeks to identify exceptionally talented theatre professionals who will impact the field in a positive way. This program hopes to nurture future leaders in all areas of the theatre

field are mentored by accomplished theatre professionals at a host theatre. $80,000 ($40,000/nine-month period) will be to the theatre in support of an eighteen-month mentorship with an additional $10,000 available to the mentee either to defray outstanding student loan debt or to meet unique costs incurred when an international mentee is selected. Two year grants of $76,000 per theatre will be given to foster these relationships and develop a new generation of leaders through mentorship programs.
EIN: 136160130

6449
Otis A. Thompson Foundation, Inc.
c/o NBT Bank, N.A.
52 S. Broad St.
Norwich, NY   13815-1646   (607) 337-6193

Foundation type: Independent foundation
Purpose: Scholarships to students of high schools in Chenango, Ostego and Delaware counties, NY attending a four-year college or university. Preference may be given to applicants interested in careers in banking or business.
Financial data: Year ended 12/31/2012. Assets, $1,694,477 (M); Expenditures, $92,949; Total giving, $81,250; Grants to individuals, 24 grants totaling $24,000 (high: $1,000, low: $1,000).
Type of support: Undergraduate support.
Application information: Applications accepted. Application form required.
 Deadline(s): Apr. 15
 Additional information: Application should include a list of activities.
EIN: 166046540

6450
Wm. B. Thompson Fund
c/o Cullen and Dykman
100 Quentin Roosevelt Blvd., Ste. 402
Garden City, NY   11530-4850

Foundation type: Independent foundation
Purpose: Grants only to individuals specified in the trust instrument.
Financial data: Year ended 11/30/2012. Assets, $123,133 (L); Expenditures, $9,952; Total giving, $0.
Type of support: Grants for special needs.
Application information: Applications not accepted.
 Additional information: Payments are based upon, among other things, the age, health and income of each such individual and the amount of net income available from the fund. Unsolicited requests for funds not considered or acknowledged.
EIN: 136089682

6451
Charles Thorwelle Foundation
c/o Rouis and Co., LLP
P.O. Box 209
Wurtsboro, NY   12790-0209   (845) 888-5656
Contact: Robert C. Curtis, Tr.
Application address: P.O. Box 18, Obernburg, Ny 12767 tel: (845) 888-5656

Foundation type: Independent foundation
Purpose: Scholarships to graduating seniors of the former Delaware Valley Central School District, Callicoon, NY.

Financial data: Year ended 12/31/2011. Assets, $1,341,687 (M); Expenditures, $91,332; Total giving, $67,878.
Type of support: Support to graduates or students of specific schools; Undergraduate support.
Application information: Applications not accepted.
 Additional information: Contact your school guidance director for additional information. Unsolicited requests for funds not considered or acknowledged.
EIN: 146047928

6452
Thousand Islands Foundation, Inc.
8481 County Rte. 9
Clayton, NY   13624-0001   (315) 686-3428

Foundation type: Operating foundation
Purpose: Scholarships to students from the five high schools in the Clayton, NY area for postsecondary education.
Financial data: Year ended 12/31/2012. Assets, $923,765 (M); Expenditures, $38,857; Total giving, $31,480; Grants to individuals, 21 grants totaling $31,480 (high: $4,000, low: $300).
Type of support: Undergraduate support.
Application information: Applications accepted. Application form required.
 Deadline(s): May 15
 Applicants should submit the following:
  1) Financial information
  2) Letter(s) of recommendation
  3) Transcripts
 Additional information: Students must have attended one of five high schools for at least one year.
EIN: 010628246

6453
THYCA: Thyroid Cancer Survivors' Association, Inc.
P.O. Box 1545
New York, NY   10159-1545
Contact: Gary Bloom, Exec. Dir.
FAX: (630) 604-6078; E-mail: thyca@thyca.org; Toll-free tel.: (877) 588-7904; e-mail for Gary Bloom: execdirector@thyca.org; URL: http://www.thyca.org

Foundation type: Public charity
Purpose: Grants to medical researchers to find the cure for all types of thyroid cancer.
Financial data: Year ended 12/31/2011. Assets, $1,064,255 (M); Expenditures, $397,147; Total giving, $143,750; Grants to individuals, totaling $143,750.
Fields of interest: Medical research.
Type of support: Research; Grants to individuals.
Application information: Applications accepted. Application form required.
 Additional information: Grants are awarded on the basis of scientific merit. The research grants are open to all researchers and institutions worldwide. See web site for additional guidelines.
EIN: 522169434

6454
The Tibet Fund
241 E. 32nd St.
New York, NY   10016-6305   (212) 213-5011
FAX: (212) 213-1219; E-mail: info@tibetfund.org; URL: http://www.tibetfund.org

Foundation type: Public charity
Purpose: Scholarships to Tibetan refugees residing in India, Nepal and Bhutan for two-year Master's Degree programs in the United States.
Publications: Annual report.
Financial data: Year ended 12/31/2011. Assets, $6,855,553 (M); Expenditures, $6,485,839; Total giving, $5,688,264; Grants to individuals, totaling $704,628.
Fields of interest: Education; Immigrants/refugees.
Type of support: Postgraduate support.
Application information: Applications accepted. Application form required. Application form available on the grantmaker's web site.
 Initial approach: E-mail
 Deadline(s): Mar. 31
 Applicants should submit the following:
  1) Transcripts
  2) Photograph
  3) Essay
  4) Resume
 Additional information: Questions regarding the Tibetan Scholarship Program should be sent to Tenzing Choephel Chumeego at tchoephel@tibetfund.org or scholarship@tibet.net.
EIN: 133115145

6455
The Louis Comfort Tiffany Foundation
c/o Artists Space
38 Greene St., 3rd Fl.
New York, NY   10013-2505
Contact: Angela Westwater, Pres.
URL: http://louiscomforttiffanyfoundation.org/

Foundation type: Independent foundation
Purpose: Grants to talented and advanced artists of the fine arts (painting, sculpture, printmaking, photography, video, and craft media), by awarding a limited number of grants biannually.
Financial data: Year ended 12/31/2012. Assets, $5,826,868 (M); Expenditures, $111,986; Total giving, $0.
Fields of interest: Folk arts; Visual arts; Sculpture; Design; Ceramic arts; Arts, artist's services; Arts.
Type of support: Awards/grants by nomination only; Awards/prizes.
Application information: Individual applications not accepted. Awards are by nomination only.
EIN: 131689389

6456
Margaret B. Tilt Scholarship Trust
212 Dolson Ave.
Middletown, NY   10940-6541   (845) 987-3010
Contact: Frank Greenhall

Foundation type: Independent foundation
Purpose: Scholarships to graduates of Warwick Valley Central School District, NY, who are pursuing a bachelor's or master's degree.
Financial data: Year ended 12/31/2011. Assets, $122,586 (M); Expenditures, $3,119; Total giving, $1,175; Grants to individuals, 3 grants totaling $1,175 (high: $400, low: $375).
Type of support: Support to graduates or students of specific schools; Graduate support; Undergraduate support.
Application information: Applications not accepted.
 Additional information: Unsolicited requests for funds not considered or acknowledged.
EIN: 146086361

6457

The Annie Tinker Association for Women, Inc.

(formerly Annie Rensselaer Tinker Memorial Fund)
12 W. 11th St.
New York, NY 10011-8602
Contact: Isabel Spencer
URL: http://www.tinkerfund.org/

Foundation type: Operating foundation
Purpose: The fund encourages the emotional, social, and financial well-being of its beneficiaries. Beneficiaries are women over 65 years of age who are able to live independently and are able to benefit from the interaction with others in the Tinker Fund and their community.
Publications: Informational brochure; Newsletter.
Financial data: Year ended 06/30/2012. Assets, $1,531,749 (M); Expenditures, $221,515; Total giving, $109,035; Grants to individuals, 50 grants totaling $109,035 (high: $4,330, low: $318).
Fields of interest: Arts; Aging; Women; Economically disadvantaged.
Type of support: Grants for special needs.
Application information: Applications accepted. Application form required.
Initial approach: Letter
Deadline(s): None
EIN: 136405671

6458

Topaz Arts, Inc.
55-03 39th Ave.
Woodside, NY 11377-2414 (718) 505-0440
E-mail: info@topazarts.org; Mailing address: P.O. Box 770150, Woodside, NY 11377-0150;
URL: http://www.topazarts.org

Foundation type: Public charity
Purpose: Provides studio space to emerging and established artists for dance, audio and visual arts.
Financial data: Year ended 06/30/2011. Assets, $281,003 (M); Expenditures, $685,198.
Fields of interest: Visual arts; Dance.
Type of support: Residencies.
Application information: Applications accepted. Application form required. Application form available on the grantmaker's web site.
Initial approach: See foundation web site for current application guidelines and deadlines for residencies
Program descriptions:
Outer/Space Creative Residency Program for Artists: The residency provides artists with time and space to investigate and research their process. The residency includes 50 hours of free rehearsal space during a three month period at one of the participating studios. This program is focused on creative development and will include a critical feedback component.
Summer Dance Residency: Each year, four choreographers are selected from an open call. Awardees receive free rehearsal space in the galleries of the museum, a stipend of $500 and a public presentation of their work as part of Passport Fridays music, dance, and film program at QMA.
EIN: 134137551

6459

Tourette Syndrome Association, Inc.
42-40 Bell Blvd.
Bayside, NY 11361-2201 (718) 224-2999
FAX: (718) 279-9596;
E-mail: grantadministrator@tsa-usa.org;
URL: http://www.tsa-usa.org

Foundation type: Public charity
Purpose: Grants and fellowships for researchers to identify the cause and find a cure for persons with Tourette Syndrome.
Publications: Application guidelines; Annual report; Grants list.
Financial data: Year ended 02/28/2012. Assets, $19,992,672 (M); Expenditures, $7,320,687; Total giving, $2,909,446.
Fields of interest: Brain disorders; Medical research.
Type of support: Fellowships; Research; Postdoctoral support.
Application information: Applications accepted. Application form available on the grantmaker's web site.
Deadline(s): Sept. 1 for pre-proposals, Nov. 3 for full grant proposal
Final notification: Recipients notified in Mar.
Program descriptions:
Fellowships: Fellowships of up to $40,000 for one year are available for research on Tourette Syndrome. Candidates must have a M.D., Ph.D., or equivalent. Previous experience in the field of movement disorders is desirable, but not essential. Applicants may reside outside of the U.S.
Research Grants: Grants of up to $75,000 for one year or up to $150,000 for two years are available for research on Tourette Syndrome. Any research study that has the potential to contribute to the understanding of Tourette Syndrome, including genetics, pathogenesis, pathophysiology, clinical treatments, and animal model development, will be considered. Candidates must have a M.D., Ph.D., or equivalent. Previous experience in the field of movement disorders is desirable, but not essential. Applicants may reside outside of the U.S.
EIN: 237191992

6460

Gladys Tozier Memorial Scholarship Trust
One M. T. Plz., 8th Fl.
Buffalo, NY 14203 (716) 842-5506

Foundation type: Independent foundation
Purpose: Scholarships to residents of Lycoming, Elk, and Clearfield counties, PA for postsecondary education.
Financial data: Year ended 12/31/2011. Assets, $336,236 (M); Expenditures, $29,020; Total giving, $24,000.
Type of support: Scholarships—to individuals.
Application information: Applications accepted.
Initial approach: Letter
Deadline(s): None
EIN: 232650705

6461

Trace Foundation
132 Perry St., Ste. 2B
New York, NY 10014-2703 (212) 367-7380
FAX: (212) 367-7383; E-mail: info@trace.org;
URL: http://www.trace.org

Foundation type: Independent foundation
Purpose: Scholarships for individuals pursuing graduate studies in China. Fellowship to individuals with at least a bachelor's degree, and three years work experience in their chosen field.
Publications: Application guidelines; Annual report; Informational brochure; Newsletter; Occasional report.
Financial data: Year ended 12/31/2012. Assets, $1,392,516 (M); Expenditures, $6,072,400; Total giving, $3,391,067.
Fields of interest: Cultural/ethnic awareness; Literature.
Type of support: Fellowships; Research; Scholarships—to individuals; Postgraduate support; Travel grants.
Application information: Applications accepted. Application form required. Application form available on the grantmaker's web site.
Initial approach: Online
Additional information: See web site for additional application guidelines.
Program descriptions:
English Training Bridging Scholarship: This grant provides support to individuals who have recently taken, but failed to pass, their Ph.D. entrance examinations due to problems with English proficiency. The stipend for the one-year domestic scholarship with about 10 quotas per year is offered for a maximum amount of 10,000 RMB.
Postgraduate Bridging Scholarships: This grant provides support for individuals who have taken graduate entrance exams but have failed to be accepted to a graduate program due to a weakness or deficiency in one subject area. The stipend is for up to one year of intensive booster courses, and the individual awards will vary, but will not exceed 10,000 RMB. Applications will be considered from individuals who are graduating from undergraduate programs in the current year, or who have graduated within the past two years. Applicants must provide their scores from their most recent attempt at the graduate entrance exams as soon as they are available. Applicants should specify which subject they need additional training in, and should demonstrate strong performance in all other areas of the graduate exams, particularly in their chosen field of study. Strong preference will be given to those individuals who can demonstrate high levels of Tibetan language proficiency, and to those who are proposing future postgraduate study in fields related to Tibetan medium education. Up to five scholarships in this category will be awarded per year.
Postgraduate Direct Scholarships: This grant provides support to individuals for postgraduate degree studies in the PRC. The stipend for this award is divided into three brackets and offered up to three years. The amount of individual awards will vary, but generally not exceed 8,000RMB per year. Applications will be considered from individuals who are graduating from undergraduate programs in the current year, or who have graduated within the past two years. Applicants should have already taken the graduate entrance exams and be able to provide information about their admission status, including information where their overall score is ranked in the admissions list for their chosen program. Strong preference will be given to those individuals who can demonstrate high levels of Tibetan language proficiency, and who are proposing future postgraduate study in fields related to Tibetan medium education sector and can contribute to its development as their future career directions.
Research Fellowship: This grant is open to professionals, scholars, and artists with the goal of supporting the advancement of knowledge in the fields of social sciences, humanities, and the sciences. Candidates should possess at least a Bachelor's Degree, three years work experience in their chosen field and/or evidence of publications in the chosen field, a high motivation for contributing knowledge and work to Tibetan communities and culture, and proficient language and research skills to enable original and high-quality research work. Awards will be made for up to 12 months in duration for research conducted within China or abroad, or a combination of both. The stipend for the award will cover the cost of

travel, medical/evacuation insurance, certain research activity expenses, and a living stipend for the research period. Research topics must be relevant to the fellowship goal and include: development models, educations systems, minority language issues, modernization versus traditional knowledge, socio-economic studies, tourism, Tibetan medical knowledge, animal husbandry and agricultural policies.
EIN: 137008868

6462
Triangle Arts Association
20 Jay St., Ste. 318
Brooklyn, NY 11201-8322 (718) 858-1260
E-mail: mail@triangleworkshop.org; URL: http://www.triangleworkshop.org

Foundation type: Public charity
Purpose: Residencies to emerging and mid-career international and national visual artists with free studio space.
Publications: Application guidelines.
Financial data: Year ended 08/31/2011. Assets, $39,071 (M); Expenditures, $108,725; Total giving, $900.
Fields of interest: Visual arts.
Type of support: Residencies.
Application information: Applications accepted.
Initial approach: Letter or telephone
Applicants should submit the following:
1) SASE
2) Resume
Additional information: Application should also include artist's statement, three references, and up to 10 images (slides or CD-Rom), or video (DVD only).
EIN: 133209637

6463
Trickle Up Program, Inc.
104 W. 27th St., 12th Fl.
New York, NY 10001-6210 (212) 255-9980
Contact: Daynelle Williams, Office Mgr.
FAX: (212) 255-9974; E-mail: info@trickleup.org;
Toll-free tel.: (866) 246-9980; URL: http://www.trickleup.org

Foundation type: Public charity
Purpose: Grants for people living on less than one dollar a day in developing countries to start a small business.
Publications: Annual report; Newsletter.
Financial data: Year ended 08/31/2012. Assets, $3,729,354 (M); Expenditures, $3,835,110.
Fields of interest: International economic development; Economically disadvantaged.
Type of support: Seed money; Grants to individuals.
Application information:
Initial approach: Letter
Additional information: Contact the organization for additional information.
EIN: 061043042

6464
The Trumansburg Charitable Trust
P.O. Box 368
Trumansburg, NY 14886-0368 (607) 387-5566

Foundation type: Operating foundation
Purpose: Scholarships to graduates of Charles O. Dickerson High School, Trumansburg, NY, pursuing careers as primary or secondary school teachers. Awards to outstanding teachers in the Trumansburg, NY, school system.

Financial data: Year ended 12/31/2011. Assets, $630,734 (M); Expenditures, $21,602; Total giving, $11,000; Grants to individuals, 4 grants totaling $11,000 (high: $5,000, low: $1,000).
Fields of interest: Elementary school/education; Secondary school/education; Teacher school/education; Education.
Type of support: Support to graduates or students of specific schools; Undergraduate support.
Application information: Applications accepted. Application form required.
Deadline(s): Feb. 28 for scholarships; Dec. 31 for teaching awards
EIN: 161422770

6465
Tsadra Foundation
P.O. Box 20192
New York, NY 10014-0710
Advanced Studies Scholarship e-mail: studyscholarship@tsadra.org, Advanced Contemplative Scholarship
e-mail: contemplativescholarship@tsadra.org
E-mail: info@tsadra.org; URL: http://www.tsadra.org

Foundation type: Independent foundation
Purpose: Fellowships to advanced Western students of Tibetan Buddhism. Scholarships to Western Buddhists for in-depth study of Buddhist philosophical literature in the Tibetan language and to Western practitioners of Tibetan Buddhism to pursue long-term contemplative training.
Financial data: Year ended 12/31/2012. Assets, $558,487 (M); Expenditures, $2,296,085; Total giving, $1,479,967; Grants to individuals, totaling $875,050.
Fields of interest: Foundations (private grantmaking); Buddhism.
Type of support: Program development; Publication; Fellowships; Scholarships—to individuals.
Application information: Applications not accepted.
Additional information: Unsolicited requests for funds not considered or acknowledged.
EIN: 137224970

6466
The Richard Tucker Music Foundation
1790 Broadway, Ste. 715
New York, NY 10019-1412 (212) 757-2218
Contact: Peter H. Carwell, Exec. Dir.
FAX: (212) 757-2347;
E-mail: info@richardtucker.org; URL: http://www.richardtucker.org

Foundation type: Public charity
Purpose: Awards and grants by nomination only to American-born opera singers.
Financial data: Year ended 12/31/2010. Assets, $90,108 (M); Expenditures, $522,718; Total giving, $80,000; Grants to individuals, totaling $80,000.
Fields of interest: Opera.
Type of support: Awards/grants by nomination only; Awards/prizes.
Application information: Nominations of all potential candidates are solicited from a national panel of professionals in the field of opera; Auditions required for nominees.
Program descriptions:
Richard Tucker Award: A cash prize of $30,000 is awarded to an American singer poised for the start of a major national and international career. The award recognizes and honors both the

accomplishments as well as the potential for such an artist. In addition to the cash grant, the winner has the opportunity to appear on the annual RTMF Opera Gala, in concert with many of the profession's major stars. The Gala is broadcast live on WQXR in New York City, and is taped for telecast nationally on the PBS network.
Richard Tucker Career Grants: Four Career grant winners are selected each year for unrestricted grants of $10,000 each. Candidates must be 36 years old or younger and should have a fair amount of performing experience in professional companies. The grant has sometimes been followed by the Richard Tucker Award in later years.
Sara Tucker Study Grants: Awarded annually with a cash prize of $5,000. Recipients must be at the start of their professional career, having just completed a conservatory or graduate school program, and the singer may still be at the apprentice level in a company. Ideal candidates have had performing opportunities, but in smaller companies and usually not in major roles.
EIN: 237431029

6467
Isaac H. Tuttle Fund
1155 Park Ave.
New York, NY 10128-1209 (212) 831-0429
Contact: Stephanie A. Raneri, Exec. Dir.
FAX: (212) 426-5684; E-mail: info@tuttlefund.org;
URL: http://www.tuttlefund.org

Foundation type: Independent foundation
Purpose: Direct financial assistance to elderly individuals, 65 years of age or older, who live in Manhattan (New York, NY), with the goal of enabling them to continue living in their own homes so long as they are physically and mentally able to do so.
Publications: Application guidelines; Financial statement.
Financial data: Year ended 12/31/2012. Assets, $42,805,301 (M); Expenditures, $2,267,132; Total giving, $1,220,312; Grants to individuals, totaling $545,312.
Fields of interest: Aging; Economically disadvantaged.
Type of support: Grants for special needs.
Application information: Application form required.
Copies of proposal: 1
Additional information: Applicants must be referred by social service agencies, hospital social work depts., private social workers, or similar organizations; No self-referrals are accepted. Unsolicited applications not accepted or considered.
EIN: 135628325

6468
Maoz Tzur Foundation Inc.
1860 Flatbush Ave.
Brooklyn, NY 11210-4831 (718) 377-8700
Contact: Charles Neiss, Pres.

Foundation type: Independent foundation
Purpose: Grants and scholarships, primarily in Israel, for religious and educational purposes.
Financial data: Year ended 12/31/2012. Assets, $0 (M); Expenditures, $116,114; Total giving, $114,586.
Fields of interest: Jewish agencies & synagogues.
Type of support: Scholarships—to individuals; Stipends.
Application information: Applications not accepted.

Additional information: Unsolicited requests for funds not considered or acknowledged.
EIN: 113423569

6469
UFA Widow's and Children's Fund
204 E. 23rd St
New York, NY   10010-4628   (212) 683-4832
Contact: Joseph Miccio, Recording Secy.
URL: http://www.ufalocal94.org

Foundation type: Public charity
Purpose: Scholarships, memorials, and other financial assistance to surviving dependants of UFA members who passed away in the line of duty. Giving primarily in NY.
Financial data: Year ended 07/31/2011. Assets, $12,818,697 (M); Expenditures, $1,205,167; Total giving, $908,500; Grants to individuals, totaling $908,500.
Fields of interest: Disasters, fire prevention/control.
Type of support: Undergraduate support; Grants for special needs.
Application information: Unsolicited requests for funds not considered or acknowledged.
EIN: 133047544

6470
UJA - Federation of New York
130 E. 59th St.
New York, NY   10022-1302   (212) 980-1000
E-mail: contact@ujafedny.org; *URL:* http://www.ujafedny.org

Foundation type: Public charity
Purpose: Scholarships and fellowships to support children, young adults and adults engaging in Jewish communal life and furthering their own education.
Financial data: Year ended 06/30/2011. Assets, $1,228,189,000 (M); Expenditures, $216,229,000; Total giving, $149,553,000; Grants to individuals, totaling $2,628,000.
Fields of interest: Higher education; Jewish agencies & synagogues; Children; Adults; Young adults.
Type of support: Fellowships; Travel awards; Scholarships—to individuals.
Application information: Applications accepted.
Additional information: See web site for application guidelines and scholarship programs.
EIN: 510172429

6471
Unique Projects, Inc.
246 W. 38th St., 8th Fl.
New York, NY   10018-5805   (212) 278-8111
FAX: (212) 278-8555;
E-mail: salenaw@pentacle.org; *URL:* http://www.pentacle.org

Foundation type: Public charity
Purpose: Grants to artists through a fiscal sponsorship program.
Financial data: Year ended 06/30/2012. Assets, $5,787 (M); Expenditures, $163,850; Total giving, $152,380.
Fields of interest: Performing arts; Dance; Theater (musical).
Type of support: Grants to individuals; Fiscal agent/sponsor.

Application information: Applications accepted. Application form not required.
Initial approach: E-mail
Additional information: Artists must become members and submit a description of his/her project and samples of recent work.
Program description:
Fiscal Sponsorship: The program is designed to connect creative artists to the funding resources needed to make and show work. It functions as a crucial link between artists who are embarking on projects and the individuals, corporations and foundations which are interested in supporting artistic creativity and adventurous work. The organization charges 7.5 percent of monies received for this service.
EIN: 133085289

6472
United Board for Christian Higher Education in Asia
475 Riverside Dr., Ste. 1221
New York, NY   10115-0047   (212) 870-2600
Contact: Jonathan Wolff, Dir., Grants Mgmt.
Scholarship e-mail: aweber@unitedboard.org
FAX: (212) 870-2322;
E-mail: staff@unitedboard.org; *URL:* http://www.unitedboard.org

Foundation type: Public charity
Purpose: Scholarship to selected faculty members of its partner colleges and universities in Asia to study for masters and doctoral degrees.
Publications: Application guidelines; Annual report; Financial statement; Grants list.
Financial data: Year ended 06/30/2011. Assets, $116,164,569 (M); Expenditures, $6,552,067; Total giving, $3,029,160; Grants to individuals, 16 grants totaling $97,154. Subtotal for scholarships—to individuals: 78 grants totaling $466,151. Subtotal for grants for individuals: 16 grants totaling $97,154.
Fields of interest: Education.
Type of support: Scholarships—to individuals; Graduate support; Doctoral support.
Application information: Applications accepted. Application form required. Application form available on the grantmaker's web site.
Initial approach: Proposal
Send request by: E-mail
Deadline(s): Oct.
Additional information: Application should include a detailed budget, letter of acceptance from the hosting institution, goals for purposes of advanced study, stages of proposed study and time frame. See web site for additional application guidelines.
EIN: 135562367

6473
The United Methodist City Society
475 Riverside Dr., Ste. 1922
New York, NY   10115-0001   (212) 870-3084
FAX: (212) 870-3091; *URL:* http://www.umcitysociety.org

Foundation type: Public charity
Purpose: Scholarships to New York City residents who are studying for the ministry or planning to return to the city and work in the service of inner city communities.
Publications: Newsletter.
Financial data: Year ended 12/31/2012. Assets, $24,946,559 (L); Expenditures, $2,696,142; Total giving, $526,176; Grants to individuals, totaling $19,800.

Fields of interest: Christian agencies & churches.
Type of support: Undergraduate support.
Application information: Applications accepted.
Initial approach: Letter
EIN: 135562419

6474
United Neighborhood Houses of New York, Inc.
70 W. 36th St., Ste. 503
New York, NY   10018-8028   (212) 967-0322
Contact: Nancy Wackstein, Exec. Dir.
Scholarship address: smajithia@unhny.org
FAX: (212) 967-0792; E-mail: jziegler@unhny.org; *URL:* http://www.unhny.org/

Foundation type: Public charity
Purpose: Scholarships to college bound graduating high school seniors from settlement houses in New York.
Publications: Annual report; Financial statement; Newsletter; IRS Form 990 or 990-PF printed copy available upon request.
Financial data: Year ended 12/31/2012. Assets, $7,326,160 (M); Expenditures, $3,017,590; Total giving, $631,600; Grants to individuals, totaling $45,400.
Fields of interest: Higher education.
Type of support: Scholarships—to individuals.
Application information: Applications accepted. Application form required.
Additional information: Scholarships are in the amount of $2,000. Contact the organization for eligibility determination.
EIN: 135563409

6475
United Spinal Association, Inc.
7520 Astoria Blvd., Ste. 120
East Elmhurst, NY   11370-1135   (718) 803-3782
FAX: (718) 803-0414;
E-mail: info@unitedspinal.org; Toll-free tel.: (800) 404-2898; *URL:* http://www.unitedspinal.org

Foundation type: Public charity
Purpose: Grants to individuals with spinal cord injuries or disorders.
Publications: Newsletter.
Financial data: Year ended 06/30/2011. Assets, $3,482,145 (M); Expenditures, $18,935,022; Total giving, $179,120.
Fields of interest: Spine disorders; Physically disabled.
Type of support: Grants for special needs.
Application information: Applications accepted.
Initial approach: Letter
Additional information: Contact foundation for eligibility criteria.
EIN: 135612621

6476
United States Fund for UNICEF
125 Maiden Ln.
New York, NY   10038-4912   (212) 686-5522
Contact: Caryl M. Stern, Pres. and C.E.O.
FAX: (212) 779-1670; Toll-free tel: (800)-367-5437; *URL:* http://www.unicefusa.org

Foundation type: Public charity
Purpose: Awards to winners of a greeting card design contest for youth.

Financial data: Year ended 06/30/2012. Assets, $143,789,814 (M); Expenditures, $204,636,266; Total giving, $142,586,140.
Fields of interest: Youth.
Type of support: Awards/prizes.
Application information:
Initial approach: Letter
Deadline(s): Mar. 6
Program description:
Pier 1 Greeting Card Contest: The contest awards one entrant with a winning greeting card design a $5,000 scholarship, and the opportunity to have their design turned into UNICEF's official holiday greeting card. Winners will also receive $500 worth of art supplies for their school; in addition, a 'People's Choice Award' winner, voted on by visitors of Pier 1's official web site, will receive a package of art supplies (worth $500). Eligible applicants must be 14 years old or younger, and must submit an original, hand-drawn design that reflects the theme of the applicant year's contest (which changes every year)
EIN: 131760110

6477
United States Institute for Theatre Technology, Inc.
315 S. Crouse Ave., Ste. 200
Syracuse, NY 13210-1844 (315) 463-6463
Contact: Lea Asbell-Swanger Penn
FAX: (315) 463-6525; E-mail: info@office.usitt.org;
Toll-free tel.: (800) 938-7488; Toll-free fax: (866) 398-7488; URL: http://www.usitt.org/

Foundation type: Public charity
Purpose: Twelve-month fellowships to members in good standing of USITT for research or creative activities in design and/or technology. Grants also to support specific projects in design and/or technology.
Publications: Application guidelines; Newsletter.
Financial data: Year ended 06/30/2012. Assets, $2,903,836 (M); Expenditures, $1,966,562; Total giving, $23,082; Grants to individuals, totaling $23,082.
Fields of interest: Theater.
Type of support: Program development; Fellowships; Project support.
Application information: Applications accepted.
Initial approach: Letter
Deadline(s): Mid-Jan.
Additional information: Contact foundation for eligibility criteria.
EIN: 136216921

6478
United States Merchant Marine Academy Alumni Foundation, Inc.
14 Bond St., Ste. 100
Great Neck, NY 11021 (516) 482-5274
Contact: Jim Tobin, Pres.
For Internship Program: Veronica Barry at the U.S. Merchant Marine Academy at 516-726-5825 or barryv@usmma.edu.
FAX: (516) 482-5308; E-mail: usmmaaf@aol.com;
E-Mail for Jim Tobin: jim.tobin@alumni.usmma.edu;
Tel. for Jim Tobin: (516)-773-5993; URL: http://www.usmmaaf.com/

Foundation type: Public charity
Purpose: Internships to midshipmen, for entry into a Maritime or Transportation Industry management environment. The goal of the program is to increase the midshipman's understanding of management's role in any organization.

Financial data: Year ended 12/31/2011. Assets, $23,979,117 (M); Expenditures, $2,937,215; Total giving, $925,217; Grants to individuals, totaling $75,767.
Fields of interest: Military/veterans.
Type of support: Internship funds.
Application information:
Initial approach: Letter
EIN: 116037948

6479
United States Tennis Association
70 W. Red Oak Ln.
White Plains, NY 10604-3602 (914) 696-7000
Contact: Gordon Smith, Exec. Dir. and C.O.O.
E-mail: grants@usta.com; URL: http://www.usta.com

Foundation type: Public charity
Purpose: Grants and scholarships to individuals to promote and develop the growth of tennis.
Publications: Application guidelines.
Financial data: Year ended 12/31/2011. Assets, $223,316,514 (M); Expenditures, $195,219,826; Total giving, $65,082,654; Grants to individuals, totaling $607,703.
Fields of interest: Athletics/sports, racquet sports.
Type of support: Grants to individuals; Scholarships—to individuals; Awards/prizes.
Application information: See web site for a complete listing of various grants, awards and scholarships.
Program descriptions:
Multicultural Individual Player Grant for National Competition and Training: This program provides funding of up to $10,000 to competitive junior players aspiring to achieve national and/or international rankings. Funding will be based on the success level of the player in the previous year. Eligible applicants must be training and competing in tournaments year-round, and have a history of strong national tournament results.
Multicultural Tennis Teachers Conference and Arthur Ashe Kids Day Moderator Scholarship: This program provides $1,000 in funding to cover expenses for multicultural coaches to attend association Tennis Teachers Conferences, and assist with Arthur Ashe Kids Day.
NJTL Tennis and Leadership Camp Scholarship: These scholarships provide an educational tennis experience for National Junior Tennis League participants who could not otherwise afford such an opportunity. The weeklong session emphasizes character and leadership development, good sportsmanship, physical fitness, proper nutrition, and other healthy attitudes. Applicants must be current NJTL participants who are between 12 and 14 years of age, and whose family demonstrates a financial need.
Okechi Womeodu Scholar Athlete Grant: This program awards two $5,000 grants (one to a male, one to a female) to reward players who work to excel as much in the classroom as in sports. Eligible applicants must be training and competing and tournaments year-round, have a history of strong national tournament results, and a minimum GPA of 3.0.
EIN: 135459420

6480
Univera Community Health, Inc.
205 Park Club Ln.
Buffalo, NY 14221-5239 (716) 504-0560
FAX: (716) 857-6224; Toll-free tel.: (800) 494-2215; URL: http://www.univeracommunityhealth.org

Foundation type: Public charity
Purpose: Assistance with paid benefits to eligible members in Allegany, Cattaraugus, Chautauqua, Erie, and Niagara counties, NY.
Publications: Informational brochure; Newsletter.
Financial data: Year ended 12/31/2011. Assets, $71,574,931 (M); Expenditures, $146,323,013; Total giving, $131,830,589; Grants to individuals, 48,022 grants totaling $131,830,589.
Fields of interest: Health care; Human services.
Type of support: Grants to individuals.
Application information: Applications not accepted.
Additional information: Assistance is only for eligible members.
EIN: 161500379

6481
UrbanGlass
(also known as NYContemporary Glass Center, Inc.)
126 13th St.
Brooklyn, NY 11217-1112 (718) 625-3685
Contact: Cybele Maylone, Exec. Dir.
FAX: (718) 625-3889; E-mail: info@urbanglass.org;
E-mail For Cybele Maylone: Cybele Maylone;
URL: http://www.urbanglass.org

Foundation type: Public charity
Purpose: Fellowships to emerging artists and established artists specializing in glass.
Publications: Application guidelines.
Financial data: Year ended 12/31/2011. Assets, $246,835 (M); Expenditures, $1,372,079.
Fields of interest: Ceramic arts.
Type of support: Fellowships; Foreign applicants.
Application information: Applications accepted. Application form required.
Initial approach: E-mail
Copies of proposal: 2
Deadline(s): May 2 for Fellowship; none for Symonds Scholarships
Final notification: Recipients notified within 45 days for Symonds Scholarships
Applicants should submit the following:
1) Letter(s) of recommendation
2) SASE
3) Resume
4) Proposal
Additional information: Application must also include slides of recent work and a biography.
Program descriptions:
Jerry Raphael Metropolitan Contemporary Glass Group Fellowship: Awarded in conjunction with the Metropolitan Contemporary Glass Group, awards of at least $2,000 are given to glass artists to develop new artwork. Funds may be applied to studio fees for glassblowing, casting, kiln-working, neon, lampworking, stained glass, cold working, and sandblasting; acid etching, technical assistance, and materials are not eligible. Eligible applicants must have a bachelor's of arts degree in glassworking (or its equivalent), a minimum intermediate-level experience with glass, and a demonstrated commitment to glass art.
Pat and Alan Symonds Scholarships: Scholarships of $1,000 each are available to applicants with less than ten years of glassworking experience who wish to take classes at the center. Scholarships cover the cost of classes and studio

rental fees; scholarships are not meant to cover materials or assistance.
EIN: 133098471

6482
USTA Serves - Foundation for Academics. Character. Excellence.
(formerly USTA Tennis and Education Foundation)
70 W. Red Oak Ln.
White Plains, NY 10604-3602 (914) 696-7223
Contact: Karen Ford
FAX: (914) 697-2307;
E-mail: foundation@usta.com; URL: http://www.usta.com/about-usta/usta-serves/

Foundation type: Public charity
Purpose: Scholarships to individuals involved in tennis-related activities for college and university.
Publications: Application guidelines; Annual report; Grants list; Newsletter.
Financial data: Year ended 12/31/2011. Assets, $2,793,299 (M); Expenditures, $1,747,649; Total giving, $1,317,925; Grants to individuals, totaling $397,750.
Fields of interest: Education; Athletics/sports, racquet sports.
Type of support: Scholarships—to individuals; Awards/prizes; Stipends.
Application information: Applications accepted. Application form required. Application form available on the grantmaker's web site.
  Initial approach: Submit application
  Deadline(s): Feb. 5
  Applicants should submit the following:
    1) SAR
    2) FAFSA
    3) Essay
    4) ACT
    5) SAT
    6) Transcripts
    7) Letter(s) of recommendation
    8) Photograph
Program descriptions:
  Dwight F. Davis Memorial Scholarship: A $7,500 scholarship will be awarded over four years to two students who are entering a four-year college or university program. The scholarship is available to high school seniors who have performed with distinction and actively participated in extracurricular activities, community service, and an organized tennis program.
  Dwight Mosley Scholarship Award: A $10,000 scholarship will be awarded over four years to one male and one female student of diverse ethnic backgrounds who are entering a four-year college or university program. The scholarship is available to U.S. Tennis Association-ranked high school seniors of ethnically-diverse heritage who have excelled academically and participated extensively in an organized community tennis program. Applicants must demonstrate sportsmanship on and off the court.
  Eve Craft Education & College Scholarship: A $2,500 scholarship will be awarded to one male and one female student entering a four-year college or university program. The scholarship is available to two high school seniors, one male and one female, who have excelled academically, demonstrated community service, played tennis in an organized program, and who reside in an economically-disadvantaged community.
  Marian Wood Baird Scholarship Award: A scholarship award of $15,000 is available to high school seniors who have excelled academically, demonstrated achievements in leadership, and participated extensively in an organized community tennis program (such as USTA School Tennis, USTA

National Junior Tennis League, USTA Team Tennis, USTA High Performance, or other such qualified programs as determined by the foundation's scholarship committee). Applicants must demonstrate sportsmanship on and off the court.
  Player Incentive Awards: One-time grants of $500 each are available to encourage the development of United States Tennis Association (USTA) youth tennis program participants who demonstrate great potential and a commitment to academic excellence. Grants can be used for such expenses as tournament fees, indoor/winter lessons, summer tennis programs, and/or participation in USTA or other tennis organization programs. Eligible applicants must: currently be enrolled in grades 6 to 199; show financial need for all tennis-related fees; demonstrate a strong commit to academic achievement; and be a middle-school player with high-school varsity team potential, or be a high school varsity player.
  USTA Tennis & Education Foundation College Education Scholarship: A $6,000 scholarship will be awarded over four years to students entering a two or four-year college or university. The scholarship is available to high school seniors who have excelled academically, demonstrated community service and participated in an organized tennis program.
  USTA Tennis & Education USTA T&EF College Textbook Scholarship: A $1,000 scholarship will be awarded to students entering a two- or four-year college or university program. The scholarship provides a one-time award to assist students in purchasing textbooks or supplies.
EIN: 133782331

6483
Utica National Group Foundation, Inc.
c/o Screening Committee Chair.
P.O. Box 530
Utica, NY 13503-0530
Contact: Michael C. Austin, V.P., Corp. Comms.
E-mail: michael.austin@uticanational.com;
URL: http://www.uticanational.com/company/corporatecitizenship.asp

Foundation type: Company-sponsored foundation
Purpose: Scholarships to children of employees of Utica National Insurance Group for higher education.
Publications: Application guidelines; Annual report (including application guidelines).
Financial data: Year ended 12/31/2012. Assets, $5,804,082 (M); Expenditures, $260,251; Total giving, $248,220.
Fields of interest: Higher education.
Type of support: Employee-related scholarships.
Application information: Applications not accepted.
  Additional information: Unsolicited requests for funds not considered or acknowledged.
Company name: Utica Mutual Insurance Company
EIN: 161313450

6484
Van Alen Institute
30 W. 22nd St., 6th Fl.
New York, NY 10010-5816 (212) 924-7000
Contact: Olympia Kazi, Exec. Dir.
FAX: (212) 366-5836; E-mail: vai@vanalen.org;
URL: http://www.vanalen.org

Foundation type: Public charity
Purpose: Fellowships that support advanced research and experimental practice that explores, challenges, and expands conventional definitions of public architecture. Fellows are based at the

institute, where they generate projects on the most significant issues shaping public life and the built environment today. The Institute also sponsors academic, regional and international public design competitions.
Financial data: Year ended 12/31/2011. Assets, $4,652,395 (M); Expenditures, $642,824.
Fields of interest: Architecture.
Type of support: Fellowships.
Application information: Applications accepted. Application form required. Application form available on the grantmaker's web site.
  Initial approach: Letter or email
EIN: 131655152

6485
The Varflex Educational Foundation II
512 W. Court St.
Rome, NY 13440 (315) 685-5690
Contact: Danielle C. LaBeille, Exec. Dir.
Application address: P.O. Box 259, Skaneateles, NY 13152 Tel.: (315) 685-5690

Foundation type: Independent foundation
Purpose: Scholarships to children of employees of the Varflex Corporation, or to graduates of Adirondack High School, Camden High School, New York State School for the Deaf, Oriskany Central School, Rome Catholic High School, Rome Free Academy, Verona-Vernon-Sherrill High School and Westmoreland High School, NY.
Financial data: Year ended 12/31/2011. Assets, $138,830 (M); Expenditures, $28,246; Total giving, $27,000; Grants to individuals, 31 grants totaling $27,000 (high: $1,500, low: $500).
Type of support: Support to graduates or students of specific schools; Undergraduate support.
Application information: Applications accepted. Application form required.
  Initial approach: Letter
  Deadline(s): Apr. 17
  Final notification: Candidates notified on or about June 15
  Applicants should submit the following:
    1) Transcripts
    2) Letter(s) of recommendation
    3) SASE
    4) SAR
EIN: 166552465

6486
Variety Club Foundation of New York, Inc.
505 8th Ave., Ste. 1800
New York, NY 10018-6518 (212) 760-2777
Contact: Katie Goodspeed, Exec. Dir.
Application address: Variety - The Children's Charity of the U.S., 5757 Wilshire Blvd., Ste. 445, Los Angeles, CA 90036
FAX: (212) 760-2779; E-mail: info@varietyny.org;
URL: http://www.varietyny.org

Foundation type: Public charity
Purpose: Grants for children who are 21 years of age and younger who are physically challenged, with medical equipment.
Publications: Application guidelines.
Financial data: Year ended 09/30/2011. Assets, $564,883 (M); Expenditures, $698,253; Total giving, $186,000.
Fields of interest: Economically disadvantaged.
Type of support: Grants for special needs.
Application information: Applications accepted. Application form required. Application form available on the grantmaker's web site.
  Initial approach: Application
  Send request by: Mail

Applicants should submit the following:
1) Budget Information
2) Financial information
Additional information: Assistance is given to those with the greatest financial need.

Program description:
Kids on the Go!: The foundation provides disabled and disadvantaged children gain mobility by providing funding for walkers, wheelchairs, specially designed adaptive bikes, strollers, prosthetic limbs, and other devices.
EIN: 131591127

6487
V-Day
303 Park Ave. S., Ste. 1184
New York, NY 10010-3657 (212) 645-8329
E-mail: info@vday.org; E-Mail For Noelle Colome: noelle@vday.org; URL: http://www.vday.org/home

Foundation type: Public charity
Purpose: Scholarships to girls and young women around the world who would not otherwise have an opportunity for education.
Publications: Annual report.
Financial data: Year ended 06/30/2011. Assets, $5,439,228 (M); Expenditures, $3,249,067; Total giving, $1,141,616; Grants to individuals, totaling $5,000.
Fields of interest: Education; Women; Girls; Economically disadvantaged.
Type of support: Scholarships—to individuals.
Application information: Unsolicited requests for funds not considered or acknowledged. Recipients must agree to give back by working to stop violence against women and girls in their own community.

Program description:
V-Peace Scholarships: Scholarships, ranging from $100 to $5,000, are awarded to individuals who would not otherwise have an opportunity for education and who demonstrate a seeking spirit, a fierce and compassionate nature and exceptional promise as leaders. Funds are used for secondary schooling, college and graduate studies, vocational and leadership training, and such expenses as books, and uniforms, fees and transportation.
EIN: 943389430

6488
A. E. Ventures Foundation, Inc.
114 W. 29th St., 2nd Fl.
New York, NY 10001-5594

Foundation type: Independent foundation
Purpose: Grants by nomination only to mature artists, primarily in NY.
Financial data: Year ended 12/31/2011. Assets, $0 (M); Expenditures, $24,413; Total giving, $18,550; Grants to individuals, 5 grants totaling $18,550 (high: $5,000, low: $2,000).
Fields of interest: Arts.
Type of support: Awards/grants by nomination only.
Application information: Applications not accepted.
Additional information: Nominations from members of Board of Directors only. Unsolicited requests for fund not considered or acknowledged.
EIN: 133999711

6489
Frances S. Viele Scholarship Trust
c/o William Brennan
170 E. 78th St., Ste. 8B
New York, NY 10075-0488

Foundation type: Independent foundation
Purpose: Scholarships to members of Sigma Phi Society.
Financial data: Year ended 05/31/2012. Assets, $2,043,205 (M); Expenditures, $108,700; Total giving, $84,800; Grants to individuals, 63 grants totaling $84,800 (high: $5,000, low: $250).
Fields of interest: Students, sororities/fraternities.
Type of support: Scholarships—to individuals.
Application information: Applications accepted. Application form required.
Applicants should submit the following:
1) Transcripts
2) Essay
3) Financial information
EIN: 953285561

6490
Vietnam Relief Effort
845 United Nations Plz., 90A
New York, NY 10017-3539 (917) 668-2600

Foundation type: Public charity
Purpose: Medical care and disaster relief to individuals in Vietnam.
Financial data: Year ended 12/31/2011. Assets, $166,610 (M); Expenditures, $30,121; Total giving, $8,000.
Type of support: Emergency funds; Grants for special needs.
Application information: Applications not accepted.
Additional information: Unsolicited requests not considered or acknowledged.
EIN: 134095507

6491
The Vilcek Foundation, Inc.
(formerly The Friderika Fischer Foundation)
167 E. 73rd St.
New York, NY 10021-4160 (212) 472-2500
Contact: Rick A. Kinsel, Exec. Dir.
FAX: (212) 472-4720; E-mail: info@vilcek.org; URL: http://www.vilcek.org

Foundation type: Operating foundation
Purpose: Awards to young immigrants who have made outstanding contributions in the fields of biomedical research or the arts and humanities.
Publications: Grants list.
Financial data: Year ended 12/31/2012. Assets, $108,974,493 (M); Expenditures, $4,121,754; Total giving, $516,333; Grants to individuals, 11 grants totaling $280,000 (high: $100,000, low: $5,000).
Fields of interest: Humanities; Arts; Biomedicine research; Immigrants/refugees.
Type of support: Awards/prizes.
Application information:
Initial approach: Letter
Deadline(s): July 11
Additional information: Contact foundation for further eligibility criteria.

Program description:
Vilcek Prize for Creative Promise in Biomedical Science: The foundation will award three prizes of $35,000 each to young foreign-born biomedical scientists who demonstrate outstanding early achievement. Eligible work may be in basic, applied, and/or translational biomedical science. To be

eligible, the applicant must have been born outside the U.S., must not be more than 38 years old, must be a naturalized citizen or permanent resident (green card holder) of the U.S., must have earned a doctoral degree (M.D., Ph.D. or equivalent), and must intend to pursue a professional career in the U.S. The applicant must hold a full-time position in an academic institution or other organization. Eligible positions include the following: Assistant or Associate Professor, Research Scientist or equivalent. The applicant must be directly responsible for the design and execution of the work submitted for consideration. Graduate students and postdoctoral fellows working under supervision of a mentor are not eligible. The applicant must not have been a winner or one of the top four finalists for the Vilcek Prize for Creative Promise in the past. See foundation web site for additional information.
EIN: 510404790

6492
Visual Arts Foundation, Inc.
220 E. 23rd St., Ste. 609
New York, NY 10010-4629 (212) 592-2227
E-mail: president@sva.edu; URL: http://www.visualartsfoundation.org/

Foundation type: Public charity
Purpose: Scholarships and awards to deserving students pursuing courses in the field of art primarily at the School of Visual Arts and grants to emerging and established artists.
Publications: Application guidelines.
Financial data: Year ended 12/31/2011. Assets, $2,063,296 (M); Expenditures, $275,357; Total giving, $230,938; Grants to individuals, totaling $230,938.
Fields of interest: Visual arts.
Type of support: Scholarships—to individuals; Awards/prizes.
Application information: Application form required.
Initial approach: Download application
Deadline(s): Apr. 15

Program description:
Scholarships and Awards: Funding is available to applicants in the School of Visual Arts. Scholarships and awards range from $300 to $25,000, and sometimes award full tuition. Priority is given to upper-classmen.
EIN: 136261474

6493
Visual Studies Workshop, Inc.
31 Prince St.
Rochester, NY 14607-1405 (585) 442-8676
Contact: Staffan Lundback, Pres.
FAX: (585) 442-1992; E-mail: info@vsw.org; URL: http://www.vsw.org/about.php

Foundation type: Public charity
Purpose: Residencies to artists specializing in photography, film, artists' books, digital video and multimedia.
Financial data: Year ended 06/30/2011. Assets, $1,362,828 (M); Expenditures, $383,339.
Fields of interest: Media/communications; Film/video; Visual arts; Photography; Literature.
Type of support: Residencies.
Application information: Applications accepted. Application form required. Application form available on the grantmaker's web site.
Initial approach: Download application form
Copies of proposal: 1
Deadline(s): Oct. 13 for residencies
Applicants should submit the following:

1) SASE
2) Work samples
3) Proposal
Additional information: See web site for further application information.
Program description:
Artists' Residencies: Residencies are project-based and are for a period of up to one month. The organization will provide access to facilities, an honorarium of $1,200, and housing on the premises.
EIN: 160991020

6494
Vocational Foundation, Inc.
7 Times Sq.
New York, NY 10036 (212) 209-4850

Foundation type: Public charity
Purpose: Financial assistance to economically disadvantaged, unemployed youth ages 17 to 21 in the five boroughs of New York City with training programs.
Financial data: Year ended 06/30/2011. Assets, $1,156,835 (M); Expenditures, $2,398,113.
Fields of interest: Economically disadvantaged.
Type of support: Grants for special needs.
Application information: Applications accepted.
Additional information: Contact the foundation for additional guidelines.
EIN: 131878246

6495
Voices Against Brain Cancer Foundation
c/o Darren Port
1375 Broadway, 3rd Fl.
New York, NY 10018-7001 (212) 340-1340
Application email address:
grants@voicesagainstbraincancer.org
FAX: (212) 591-6572;
E-mail: info@voicesagainstbraincancer.org;
URL: http://www.voicesagainstbraincancer.org

Foundation type: Public charity
Purpose: Research grants for the study of brain cancer.
Financial data: Year ended 12/31/2011. Assets, $1,239,634 (M); Expenditures, $1,076,092; Total giving, $624,627.
Fields of interest: Cancer; Cancer research.
Type of support: Research.
Application information: Applications accepted. Application form required. Application form available on the grantmaker's web site.
Initial approach: Letter or email
Deadline(s): Sept. 15
Additional information: See application process on website for eligibility criteria.
EIN: 202872778

6496
Roger L. VonAmelunxen Foundation, Inc.
P.O. Box 660159
Fresh Meadows, NY 11366-0159 (718) 641-4800
Contact: Karen Donnelly, Pres.
FAX: (718) 641-4802;
E-mail: rogerfoundation@aol.com; Mailing Address: P.O. Box 660159; Fresh Meadows, NY 11366;
URL: http://rogerfoundation.org

Foundation type: Public charity
Purpose: Scholarships to children of employees of the U.S. Customs Service for attendance at accredited institutions of higher learning.

Assistance to financially needy and distressed families of U.S. Customs Service employees.
Financial data: Year ended 07/31/2012. Assets, $2,447,343 (M); Expenditures, $522,746; Total giving, $494,904; Grants to individuals, totaling $494,904.
Fields of interest: Economically disadvantaged.
Type of support: Employee-related scholarships; Employee-related welfare.
Application information: Applications accepted.
Initial approach: Letter
Deadline(s): Aug. 1
Additional information: Application must include proof of relationship to U.S. Customs employee.
Company name: U.S. Customs Service
EIN: 112583014

6497
Edwin J. Wadas Foundation, Inc.
c/o Feldman, Domagal and Kupiec
246 Genesse St.
Utica, NY 13502-4325 (315) 732-5158
Contact: Alferd J. Kupiec, Jr., Treas.

Foundation type: Independent foundation
Purpose: Scholarships to graduates of Clinton, New York Mills, Sauquoit, Whitesboro, Whitestown and surrounding school districts, NY.
Financial data: Year ended 12/31/2011. Assets, $2,912,037 (M); Expenditures, $121,563; Total giving, $113,748; Grants to individuals, 37 grants totaling $105,331 (high: $4,065, low: $1,000).
Type of support: Support to graduates or students of specific schools; Undergraduate support.
Application information: Application form required.
Applicants should submit the following:
1) Class rank
2) SAT
3) GPA
EIN: 161361881

6498
Claire Wagner Estate Heinbach-Wagner Trust
c/o Deutsche Bank Trust Co., N.A.
Church St. Sta.
P.O. Box 1297
New York, NY 10008

Foundation type: Independent foundation
Purpose: Scholarships to students at The Albert Einstein College of Medicine of Yeshiva University for medical education, NY.
Financial data: Year ended 12/31/2012. Assets, $1,057,930 (M); Expenditures, $55,634; Total giving, $39,600.
Fields of interest: Medical school/education.
Type of support: Support to graduates or students of specific schools.
Application information: Applications accepted.
Additional information: Contact trust for current application guidelines.
EIN: 136182244

6499
The Marcus Wallenberg Foundation
c/o McDermott, Will & Emery LLP
340 Madison Ave.
New York, NY 10173-1922 (212) 547-5444
URL: http://www.wallenberg.org/

Foundation type: Independent foundation
Purpose: Grants for graduate or undergraduate students pursuing careers in or professionals or

students studying aspects of international trade or business by providing them funds to defray expenses or to provide a stipend or prize to assist in the completion or publication of their studies.
Financial data: Year ended 03/31/2013. Assets, $2,424,937 (M); Expenditures, $158,468; Total giving, $83,500; Grant to an individual, 1 grant totaling $83,500.
Fields of interest: Business school/education; International exchange, students; Business/industry.
International interests: Sweden.
Type of support: Publication; Grants to individuals.
Application information: Applications accepted. Interview required.
Initial approach: Letter
Applicants should submit the following:
1) Letter(s) of recommendation
2) Transcripts
Additional information: Application should also include a complete biographical record, reports on applicant's academic and professional careers, details of applicant's future plans and a list of published works.
Program description:
Grant Program: The program provides grants to individuals enrolled as graduate or undergraduate students, a person participating in a fellowship program, writing program or field research under the auspices of a university, a college graduate working on a book or research paper relating to aspects of international trade or business, a professional or someone employed in international trade or business seeking to further his or her education whether it leads to a degree or not. Grants are renewable for up to four years.
EIN: 133176307

6500
Walton Central School District Trust No. 1
c/o Natl. Bank of Delaware County
P.O. Box 389
Walton, NY 13856-0389 (604) 865-4116
Application Address: c/o Guidance Dept. Walton High School, Stockton Ave., Walton, NY 13856

Foundation type: Independent foundation
Purpose: Scholarships to graduating seniors of Walton Senior High School, NY for postsecondary education.
Financial data: Year ended 12/31/2012. Assets, $111,481 (M); Expenditures, $2,275; Total giving, $1,750; Grants to individuals, 3 grants totaling $1,750 (high: $1,000, low: $250).
Fields of interest: Higher education.
Type of support: Support to graduates or students of specific schools; Undergraduate support.
Application information: Applications accepted. Application form required.
Initial approach: Letter
Deadline(s): Apr. 15
EIN: 166280038

6501
Earl Warren Legal Training Program, Inc.
99 Hudson St., Ste. 1600
New York, NY 10013-2815 (212) 965-2200
Contact: John A. Payton, Pres.
URL: http://www.naacpldf.org/earl-warren-scholarships

Foundation type: Public charity
Purpose: Scholarships to law students who intend to practice civil rights law, as well as to African-American students entering law school.

Financial data: Year ended 06/30/2012. Assets, $632,990 (M); Expenditures, $74,091; Total giving, $34,100; Grants to individuals, totaling $34,100.
Fields of interest: Law school/education; Formal/general education; African Americans/Blacks.
Type of support: Graduate support; Undergraduate support.
Application information:
  Initial approach: Telephone or e-mail
  Send request by: Mail
  Deadline(s): Apr. 30 for Warren Scholarship, Mar. 31 for Lehman Scholarship
  Final notification: Applicants notified by July 31 for Warren and Lehman Scholarships
  Applicants should submit the following:
    1) Letter(s) of recommendation
    2) Essay
  Additional information: Faxed or e-mail applications are not accepted. See web site for additional guidelines.
Program descriptions:
  Earl Warren Scholarships: Scholarships are awarded annually to rising law students whose commitment to social justice reveals outstanding potential for training as civil rights and public interest attorneys. Preference is given to law students entering their first year of full time legal study at an accredited law school. Applicants must be of excellent character and must have a verifiable record of community and school involvement that reveals a clear capacity to work well in diverse settings, must be college graduates, and must be planning to attend a three-year, full time law program at an accredited law school in the U.S. Law students already enrolled in law school are ineligible to apply.
  Herbert Lehman Education Fund Scholarship: Scholarships are awarded to help African-American students of outstanding character who are entering college for the first time or who are beginning their sophomore years in college and who will be attending an accredited four-year college or university as a full time undergraduate student. Applicants must have a demonstrate record of community and school involvement that reveals exceptional leadership potential with a capacity to work well in diverse settings.
EIN: 132695683

6502
Washington County Economic Opportunity Council, Inc.
383 Broadway
Fort Edward, NY 12828-1015 (518) 746-2390
Contact: Claire M. Murphy, Exec. Dir.
URL: http://www.washingtoncountyeoc.com/default.htm

Foundation type: Public charity
Purpose: Assistance to indigent residents of Washington County, NY in the form of food supplies, utility assistance, home weatherization, and elderly transport.
Financial data: Year ended 03/31/2012. Assets, $2,952,560 (M); Expenditures, $6,214,275; Total giving, $5,674,453; Grants to individuals, totaling $5,674,453.
Fields of interest: Economically disadvantaged.
Type of support: In-kind gifts.
Application information:
  Initial approach: Tel.
  Applicants should submit the following:
    1) Financial information
  Additional information: Contact foundation for eligibility criteria.
EIN: 141494402

6503
David Wasserman Scholarship Fund, Inc.
4722 State Hwy. 30
Amsterdam, NY 12010-7430 (518) 843-2800
Contact: Norbert J. Sherbunt, Pres.

Foundation type: Independent foundation
Purpose: Scholarships to undergraduate students residing in Montgomery County, NY for postsecondary education.
Financial data: Year ended 04/30/2012. Assets, $4,312 (M); Expenditures, $22,613; Total giving, $5,250; Grants to individuals, 19 grants totaling $5,250 (high: $300, low: $150).
Fields of interest: Higher education.
Type of support: Undergraduate support.
Application information: Application form required.
  Initial approach: Letter
  Deadline(s): Apr. 15
EIN: 146030181

6504
The Thomas J. Watson Foundation
11 Park Pl., Ste. 1503
New York, NY 10007-2816
FAX: (212) 245-8860; *E-mail:* tjw@tjwf.org;
URL: http://www.watsonfellowship.org

Foundation type: Independent foundation
Purpose: Fellowships by nomination only to graduating seniors of specified colleges and universities for independent study and travel. Nominees must attend one of the specified colleges listed in program description.
Publications: Informational brochure.
Financial data: Year ended 05/31/2012. Assets, $71,472,601 (M); Expenditures, $3,457,329; Total giving, $1,322,572; Grants to individuals, 70 grants totaling $258,801 (high: $9,000, low: $250).
Fields of interest: Education; Leadership development.
Type of support: Fellowships; Awards/grants by nomination only; Undergraduate support; Travel grants.
Application information: Applications accepted. Application form required. Interview required.
  Applicants should submit the following:
    1) Proposal
    2) Essay
    3) Letter(s) of recommendation
    4) Transcripts
    5) Photograph
  Additional information: Individual applications not accepted. Nomination must also include proposed plan of study and personal statement.
Program descriptions:
  Jeannette K. Watson Summer Fellowships: This fellowship program provides internships, mentoring, and enriched educational opportunities to promising New York City undergraduates with the goal of increasing their life choices and developing their capacity to make a difference in their own and others' lives. The program offers fifteen students paid internships for three consecutive summers. The internships will be closely supervised and provide challenging work from which one can learn. In the course of the program, Fellows are encouraged to sample work in at least two of three sectors: nonprofit organizations, government service, and private enterprise. Each internship lasts up to ten weeks. The stipend is $5,000 for the first summer and $6,000 for the second and third summers.
  Thomas J. Watson Fellowship Program: Enables up to 50 college graduates of unusual promise to engage in an initial postgraduate year of independent study and travel abroad. Candidates devise a focused and disciplined plan of travel. The experience is viewed as a break in which they might explore a particular interest, view their lives and American society in greater perspective, and develop a more informed sense of international concern. It is not intended for the Fellows to engage in extended formal study at a foreign university. It is intended to provide Fellows with an opportunity to immerse themselves in cultures other than their own for an entire year. A grant of $25,000 is provided for each Fellow ($35,000 for a Fellow accompanied by a dependent spouse or child). In the selection of Watson Fellows, individuals who demonstrate integrity, strong ethical character, intelligence, the capacity for vision and leadership, and potential for humane and effective participation in the world community are sought. Contact foundation for a complete listing of institutions invited to nominate candidates.
EIN: 136038151

6505
Emma Reed Webster Aid Association, Inc.
13 West Ave.
Holley, NY 14470-1115 (585) 638-6497
Contact: Marylynne Soto

Foundation type: Operating foundation
Purpose: Financial assistance only to indigent individuals and families in Orleans County, NY.
Financial data: Year ended 05/31/2012. Assets, $205,872 (M); Expenditures, $42,283; Total giving, $32,631.
Fields of interest: Economically disadvantaged.
Type of support: Grants for special needs.
Application information: Applications accepted. Application form required.
  Initial approach: Letter
  Deadline(s): None
  Additional information: Application should include a self-addressed stamped envelope. Awards are granted in monthly payments.
EIN: 166031485

6506
The Weeks Family Foundation
5355 Junction Rd.
Lockport, NY 14094-9665 (716) 625-9211
Contact: R. Thomas Weeks, Pres.

Foundation type: Independent foundation
Purpose: Scholarships to graduating seniors in one of the six area school districts of Albion, Barker, Lockport, Newfane, Royalton-Hartland and Starpoint, NY for attendance at any two or four year accredited college or university.
Financial data: Year ended 12/31/2011. Assets, $259,659 (M); Expenditures, $5,101; Total giving, $5,000; Grants to individuals, 5 grants totaling $5,000 (high: $1,000, low: $1,000).
Fields of interest: Higher education.
Type of support: Scholarships—to individuals.
Application information: Applications accepted. Application form required.
  Deadline(s): May 1
  Applicants should submit the following:
    1) Photograph
    2) Transcripts
    3) SAT
    4) Letter(s) of recommendation
    5) ACT
    6) Class rank
    7) Essay

Program description:
Scholarship Program: One student is selected by the foundation for this $1,000 award for up to four years at a two year and/or four year accredited college or university. The scholarship is awarded to an outstanding student, who is of exemplary character and motivation, displaying an impact on his or her peers and the community.
EIN: 222978143

6507
Wegmans Food Markets, Inc. Corporate Giving Program
c/o Contrib. Comm.
1500 Brooks Ave.
Rochester, NY 14603-0844 (585) 328-2550
Contact: Linda Lovejoy, Mgr., Community Rels.
Application addresses: Buffalo, NY: Attn. Theresa Jackson, Buffalo Contrib. Committee, 651 Dick Rd., Depew, NY 14043, tel.: (716) 685-8170; Syracuse: Attn. Evelyn Carter, Syracuse Contrib. Committee, 7519 Oswego Rd., Syracuse, NY 13090, tel.: (315) 546-1110; URL: http://www.wegmans.com/webapp/wcs/stores/servlet/CategoryDisplay?storeId=10052&catalogId=10002&langId=-1&identifier=CATEGORY_532

Foundation type: Corporate giving program
Purpose: Scholarships to employees of Wegmans Food Markets, Inc., in pursuit of a higher education.
Publications: Application guidelines.
Fields of interest: Education; Employment, training; Agriculture/food; Youth development, business; Youth development.
Type of support: Employee-related scholarships; Workstudy grants.
Application information: Applications not accepted.
Additional information: Unsolicited requests for funds not considered or acknowledged.
Program description:
Wegmans Scholarship Program: Wegmans Food Markets annually awards scholarships to employees to pursue their educational goals. Part-time employees are awarded up to $1,500 a year for four years (up to $6,000 total) and full-time employees are awarded up to $2,200 a year for four years (up to $8,800 total). The program is designed to encourage and build the future of employees through strong work performance and academic achievement.
Company name: Wegmans Food Markets, Inc.

6508
Kurt Weill Foundation for Music, Inc.
7 E. 20th St., 3rd Fl.
New York, NY 10003-1106 (212) 505-5240
FAX: (212) 353-9663; E-mail: kwfinfo@kwf.org;
URL: http://www.kwf.org

Foundation type: Operating foundation
Purpose: Grants to individuals for projects which promote greater understanding of the musical works of Kurt Weill, and awards to singing competition winners.
Publications: Application guidelines; Informational brochure; Newsletter.
Financial data: Year ended 12/31/2012. Assets, $26,401,692 (M); Expenditures, $1,326,571; Total giving, $264,350; Grants to individuals, 34 grants totaling $187,350 (high: $15,000, low: $600).
Fields of interest: Music.
Type of support: Program development; Publication; Fellowships; Research; Awards/grants

by nomination only; Awards/prizes; Travel grants; Project support.
Application information: Applications accepted. Application form required.
Initial approach: Letter
Deadline(s): Nov. 1
Final notification: Feb. 1
Additional information: See foundation's web site for complete application guidelines and forms.
EIN: 136139518

6509
Anna L. Weissberger Foundation, Ltd.
c/o DDK Co., LLP
1 Penn Plz., 54th Fl.
New York, NY 10119

Foundation type: Operating foundation
Purpose: Awards to winners of a playwriting contest for residents of NY.
Financial data: Year ended 12/31/2011. Assets, $1,136,618 (M); Expenditures, $33,749; Total giving, $0. Awards/prizes amount not specified.
Fields of interest: Theater (playwriting).
Type of support: Awards/grants by nomination only; Awards/prizes.
Application information: Applications not accepted.
Additional information: Nomination for the award is by invitation only. The recipient of the award will receive a $10,000 grant. Unsolicited requests for funds not considered or acknowledged.
EIN: 132864367

6510
Julia O. Wells Memorial Educational Foundation Inc.
P.O. Box 921
Latham, NY 12110-0921 (518) 482-9292

Foundation type: Independent foundation
Purpose: Scholarships to nurses, and to graduating seniors in the NY State area, who plan to pursue a career in nursing at a two or four year college.
Financial data: Year ended 12/31/2011. Assets, $1,828,508 (M); Expenditures, $78,777; Total giving, $41,250; Grants to individuals, 31 grants totaling $9,500 (high: $500, low: $250).
Fields of interest: Nursing school/education.
Type of support: Scholarships—to individuals.
Application information: Applications accepted.
Applicants should submit the following:
1) Letter(s) of recommendation
2) Essay
Additional information: Contact the foundation for additional guidelines.
EIN: 222921430

6511
Wenner-Gren Foundation for Anthropological Research, Inc.
470 Park Ave. S., 8th Fl.
New York, NY 10016-6818 (212) 683-5000
FAX: (212) 532-1492;
E-mail: inquiries@wennergren.org; URL: http://www.wennergren.org

Foundation type: Operating foundation
Purpose: Research grants, fellowships, and conference grants to scholars holding or enrolled for doctoral degrees in anthropology, for basic or dissertation research in all branches of

anthropology, including cultural/social anthropology, ethnology, biological/physical anthropology, archaeology, anthropological linguistics, and related disciplines concerned with human origins, development, and variation.
Publications: Application guidelines; Annual report; Annual report (including application guidelines); Financial statement; Grants list; Informational brochure.
Financial data: Year ended 12/31/2012. Assets, $162,966,933 (M); Expenditures, $8,487,907; Total giving, $4,679,974; Grants to individuals, 270 grants totaling $4,439,694 (high: $40,000, low: $603).
Fields of interest: History/archaeology; Language/linguistics; Anthropology/sociology.
International interests: Developing Countries.
Type of support: Conferences/seminars; Publication; Fellowships; Research; Awards/prizes; Postdoctoral support; Doctoral support.
Application information: Application form required. Application form available on the grantmaker's web site.
Initial approach: Letter or telephone
Copies of proposal: 5
Deadline(s): May 1 and Nov. 1 for Individual Research Grants; Mar. 1 for Wadsworth International Fellowships; Dec. and June 1 for Conference and International Collaboration Research grants
Final notification: Recipients notified in six to eight months
Additional information: Applications must be initiated at least nine months in advance of date of proposed research for fellowships. Applications should include one on-line copy of the proposal plus 5 hard copies. Unsolicited applications not accepted or considered.
Program descriptions:
Conference and Workshop Grants and International Symposia: The foundation provides conference support in three forms: 1) Conference Grants. Grants for amounts up to $15,000 are available to the organizers of conferences. Priority is given to working conferences that address research issues in anthropology and provide for intensive interaction among participants. To apply for this grant, contact the foundation with a brief description of the planned conference and if eligible, an application will be sent. 2) International Symposium Program. The foundation sponsors and directly administers a limited number of conferences each year under its International Symposium Program. These symposia are intended for topics of broad significance for anthropology. Inquiries concerning the International Symposium Program are initiated with a letter to the president. At least 18 months lead time is required.
Dissertation Fieldwork Grants: Grants of up to $25,000 are awarded to individuals to aid dissertation or thesis research. Application must be made jointly with a thesis advisor or other scholar who will undertake responsibility for supervising the project. Awards are contingent upon the applicant's successful completion of all requirements for the degree other than the dissertation/thesis. Qualified students of all nationalities are eligible. Grants do not cover tuition costs.
Hunt Postdoctoral Fellowships: Fellowships of up to $40,000 are awarded to scholars within ten years of receipt of the doctorate, to aid write-up of research results for publication. Qualified scholars are eligible without regard to nationality or institutional affiliation.
Individual Research Grants: Grants for amounts up to $25,000 are available for basic research in all branches of anthropology. Grants are made to

cover research expenses. The foundation invites projects employing comparative perspectives or integrating two or more subfields of anthropology. The foundation, under this program, offers Dissertation Fieldwork Grants, Post-Ph.D. Grants and Hunt Postdoctoral fellowship awards for writing up research after a Ph.D. is in hand. To download application and guidelines, visit the foundation's Web site. Hunt post-doctoral fellowships provide a maximum of $40,000 for scholars holding a Ph.D for 10 years or less. Money is to provide support for up to 12 months of full-time writing-up of research results.

International Collaborative Research Grants: Grants for amounts up to $35,000 are available to assist anthropological research projects undertaken jointly by two or more academic investigators from different countries. These grants are renewable for a second period of research. The purpose of the program is to encourage collaborations in which the principal investigators bring different and complementary perspectives, knowledge, and/or skills. Applications are evaluated by two main criteria: the quality of the proposed research, and the potential benefits of the collaboration for international anthropology. Projects must be primarily for research. Grants cover research expenses directly related and essential to the project (i.e., travel, living expenses during fieldwork, equipment, supplies, research assistance, expenses of communication between the investigators, and other relevant expenditures). Aid is not provided for salary and/or fringe benefits of applicants, tuition, nonproject personnel, institutional overhead, or institutional support. Applicants should contact the foundation or visit its Web site for application information and program deadlines.

Post-Ph.D. Grants: Grants of up to $25,000 are awarded to individual scholars holding the doctorate or equivalent qualification in anthropology or a related discipline. Qualified scholars are eligible without regard to nationality or institutional affiliation.

The Wadsworth African Fellowships: This program provides support for African students undertaking study leading to a Ph.D. at a South African university that can provide them with international-level training in anthropology (including biological anthropology and archaeology). Currently applications to the University of Witwatersrand or The University of Cape Town are given priority.

Wadsworth International Fellowships: Fellowships are intended for scholars and advanced students from countries in which anthropology or specific subfields of anthropology are underrepresented and who therefore seek additional training to enhance their skills or to develop new areas of expertise in anthropology. The program offers a Predoctoral Fellowship (up to $17,500) for study leading to a Ph.D. Applicants must be prepared to demonstrate: 1) the unavailability of such training in their home country; 2) their provisional acceptance by a host institution that will provide such training; and 3) their intention to return and work in their home country upon completion of their training. The applicant must have a home sponsor who is a member of the institution with which he/she is affiliated in the home country and a host sponsor who is a member of the institution in which the candidate plans to pursue training. The host sponsor must be willing to assume responsibility for overseeing the candidate's training. Because the fellowship is intended as a partnership with the host institution in providing the fellow's training, it is expected that candidates will also be offered support by the host institution.
EIN: 131813827

6512
Westchester Arts Council, Inc.
31 Mamaroneck Ave., 3rd Fl.
White Plains, NY 10601-3328 (914) 428-4220
Contact: Janet T. Langsam, C.E.O.
FAX: (914) 428-4306;
E-mail: website@westarts.com; E-Mail for Janet T. Langsam : jlangsam@ArtsWestchester.org;
URL: http://www.westarts.com

Foundation type: Public charity
Purpose: Grants to artists for the creation of new work in the Westchester county, NY area.
Publications: Application guidelines.
Financial data: Year ended 12/31/2011. Assets, $10,762,518 (M); Expenditures, $3,502,363; Total giving, $1,698,528; Grants to individuals, totaling $501,239.
Fields of interest: Arts.
Type of support: Grants to individuals.
Application information: Applications accepted. Application form required. Application form available on the grantmaker's web site.
  Send request by: Mail
  Deadline(s): Sept.
  Final notification: Recipients notified in Jan.
  Additional information: Applications sent by fax or e-mail are not accepted. See web site for additional guidelines.
Program description:
  Arts Alive Artist Grants Program: Two grants of $2,500 are available to provide direct support to artists to create original new work that incorporates the community as context. Projects must be initiated by the artist. Reflection of the community must be integral to the project and to the creative process. Eligible artists must reside in or own/rent a studio in Westchester County at the time of application and for the duration of the project. Applied arts, such as jewelry making, landscaping, and architecture, are ineligible for funding.
EIN: 132604827

6513
Westchester Community College Foundation, Inc.
75 Grasslands Rd.
Hartford Hall
Valhalla, NY 10595-1693 (914) 606-6600
FAX: (914) 606-6515;
E-mail: wcc.foundation@sunywcc.edu; URL: http://www.sunywcc.edu/aboutwcc/wcc_foundation/foundation.htm

Foundation type: Public charity
Purpose: Scholarships only to beginning or continuing students at Westchester Community College, NY.
Publications: Annual report; Newsletter.
Financial data: Year ended 08/31/2011. Assets, $31,102,302 (M); Expenditures, $3,972,667; Total giving, $2,892,339; Grants to individuals, totaling $1,083,836.
Type of support: Support to graduates or students of specific schools.
Application information: Applications accepted.
  Initial approach: Telephone
  Deadline(s): Apr. 15 for new students; Apr. 1, and Oct. 15 for continuing students
  Additional information: See web site for complete program descriptions and deadlines.
EIN: 237050397

6514
Westchester Golf Association Caddie Scholarship Fund, Inc.
49 Knollwood Rd., Ste. 220
Elmsford, NY 10523-2813 (914) 347-2340
Contact: Ellyn Plato, Dir., Devel.
FAX: (914) 347-2418;
E-mail: info@westchestergolf.org; URL: http://www.westchestergolf.org/

Foundation type: Public charity
Purpose: College scholarships to needy and deserving golf caddies, former caddies and those in service to golf in pursuit of a higher education.
Publications: Application guidelines; Annual report.
Financial data: Year ended 06/30/2012. Assets, $1,832,966 (M); Expenditures, $1,106,151; Total giving, $820,576; Grants to individuals, totaling $820,576.
Fields of interest: Vocational education, post-secondary; Higher education; Athletics/sports, golf.
Type of support: Scholarships—to individuals; Graduate support.
Application information: Application form required.
  Deadline(s): Apr. 30
  Applicants should submit the following:
    1) Photograph
    2) Transcripts
    3) SAR
    4) SAT
    5) Financial information
    6) FAFSA
  Additional information: Application must include applicant and family's most recent income tax return.
Program description:
  WGA Caddie Scholarship Fund: The fund provides need-based financial assistance to qualified caddies and others who work in service to golf, aiding in the pursuit of higher education. Applicants must demonstrate financial need, have applied to or currently attend an accredited school, and have worked a minimum of two seasons in service to golf at a Westchester Golf Association member club.
EIN: 136100835

6515
Westchester Mid Hudson Chapter American Institute of Architects Scholarship Fund
P.O. Box 611
Katonah, NY 10536

Foundation type: Independent foundation
Purpose: Scholarships to students in their final year at an accredited NY school of architecture.
Financial data: Year ended 12/31/2011. Assets, $19,505 (M); Expenditures, $5,525; Total giving, $5,500; Grants to individuals, 7 grants totaling $5,500 (high: $1,500, low: $500).
Fields of interest: Architecture.
Type of support: Undergraduate support.
Application information: Applications not accepted.
  Additional information: Unsolicited requests for funds not accepted or acknowledged.
EIN: 133585407

6516
Peter N. Whitcher Trust
c/o Scolaro
507 Plum St., Ste. 300
Syracuse, NY 13204
Contact: Daniel C. LaBielle, Exec. Dir.
Application address: P.O. Box 259, Skaneateles, NY
13152

Foundation type: Independent foundation
Purpose: Scholarships to eligible sons and
daughters of members and deceased members of
the Iron Workers District Council of Western NY and
vicinity.
Financial data: Year ended 12/31/2012. Assets,
$189,889 (M); Expenditures, $18,691; Total
giving, $7,300.
Fields of interest: Higher education.
Type of support: Scholarships—to individuals.
Application information: Applications accepted.
Application form required. Interview required.
  Initial approach: Letter
  Deadline(s): Feb. 1
  Applicants should submit the following:
    1) Letter(s) of recommendation
    2) Financial information
  Additional information: Application must also
    include extra-curricular activities.
EIN: 112552891

6517
Mrs. Giles Whiting Foundation
(also known as Whiting Foundation)
1133 Ave. of the Americas, 22nd Fl.
New York, NY 10036-6710 (212) 336-2138
Contact: Daniel Reid, Exec. Dir.
E-mail: info@whitingfoundation.org; URL: http://
www.whitingfoundation.org

Foundation type: Independent foundation
Purpose: Awards by nomination only to support
emerging writers.
Financial data: Year ended 11/30/2012. Assets,
$54,247,523 (M); Expenditures, $3,018,089;
Total giving, $2,117,500; Grants to individuals,
16 grants totaling $400,000 (high: $25,000, low:
$25,000).
Fields of interest: Literature.
Type of support: Awards/grants by nomination only;
Awards/prizes.
Application information: Applications not
accepted.
  Additional information: Unsolicited requests for
    funds not considered or acknowledged.
EIN: 136154484

6518
The Helen Hay Whitney Foundation
20 Squadron Blvd., Ste. 630
New City, NY 10956-5247 (845) 639-6799
Contact: Robert Weinberger, Admin. Dir.
FAX: (845) 639-6798; E-mail: hhwf@earthlink.net;
Additional fax: (646) 304-7133; URL: http://
www.hhwf.org/

Foundation type: Independent foundation
Purpose: Support for postdoctoral training in basic
biomedical research through research fellowships
for residents of the United States who are planning
to work in laboratories either in the U.S., Canada,
or abroad, and also to foreign citizens for research
in laboratories in the U.S. only. Fellowships are
awarded to individuals but funds are administered
largely by research institutions. American
citizenship is not required, but foreign nationals are
expected to pursue their research in the U.S.

Publications: Application guidelines; Annual report;
Financial statement; Informational brochure
(including application guidelines).
Financial data: Year ended 12/31/2012. Assets,
$51,969,904 (M); Expenditures, $3,660,183;
Total giving, $2,880,533; Grants to individuals,
59 grants totaling $2,880,533 (high: $54,500,
low: $1,000).
Fields of interest: Institute; Biomedicine research;
Biology/life sciences.
Type of support: Fellowships; Research.
Application information: Application form required.
Application form available on the grantmaker's web
site.
  Send request by: Online
  Deadline(s): Mid-July
  Additional information: See web site for
    additional guidelines.
EIN: 131677403

6519
The Elie Wiesel Foundation for Humanity
555 Madison Ave., 20th Fl.
New York, NY 10022-3301 (212) 490-7788
Contact: Leslie Meyers, Prog. Coord.
FAX: (212) 490-6006;
E-mail: admin@eliewieselfoundation.org;
URL: http://www.eliewieselfoundation.org

Foundation type: Public charity
Purpose: Prizes to full-time undergraduate juniors
and seniors in the U.S. at accredited four-year
colleges and universities during the fall semester
for winning essays on ethics.
Publications: Application guidelines; Annual report;
Informational brochure; Newsletter.
Financial data: Year ended 12/31/2011. Assets,
$5,665,000; Total giving, $430,000; Grants to
individuals, totaling $10,000.
Fields of interest: Philosophy/ethics; Religion.
Type of support: Awards/prizes.
Application information: Application form required.
Application form available on the grantmaker's web
site.
  Initial approach: Letter, telephone or fax
  Deadline(s): 1st. Mon. in Dec.
  Final notification: Recipients are notified in early
    Spring
  Additional information: See web site for
    additional guidelines.
Program description:
  Elie Wiesel Prize in Ethics: The contest is an
  annual competition that challenges college
  students in the U.S. to submit essays on the urgent
  ethical issues that confront them in today's
  complex world. Five prizes are awarded. A first prize
  of $5,000, a second prize of $2,500, a third prize
  of $1,500, and two honorable mentions of $500
  each are awarded to undergraduates who are or will
  be registered as full-time juniors or seniors at
  accredited four-year colleges or universities in the
  U.S. All entries can be in either the formal or
  informal voice, must range from 3,000 to 4,000
  words, and may take the form of an analysis that is
  biographical, historical, literary, philosophical,
  psychological, sociological, or theological. All
  candidates must be sponsored by a faculty
  member.
EIN: 133398151

6520
Wildlife Conservation Society
2300 Southern Blvd.
Bronx, NY 10460-1099 (718) 220-5100
Contact: Steven E. Sanderson, Pres. and C.E.O.
E-mail: gfp@wcs.org; Additional tel.: (718)
741-8197; email for Conservation Leadership
Program Awards: clp@birdlife.org; URL: http://
www.wcs.org

Foundation type: Public charity
Purpose: Grants to support wildlife conservation
field research in Africa, Asia, and Latin America
(including Mexico).
Publications: Application guidelines; Annual report.
Financial data: Year ended 06/30/2011. Assets,
$792,809,108 (M); Expenditures, $206,097,389;
Total giving, $10,854,828; Grants to individuals,
4 grants totaling $54,335. Subtotal for grants to
individuals: 41 grants totaling $703,315 (high:
$6,000). Subtotal for scholarships—to individuals:
3 grants totaling $19,600. Subtotal for research:
10 grants totaling $110,254.
Fields of interest: Animals/wildlife, preservation/
protection.
International interests: Africa; Asia; Latin America;
Mexico.
Type of support: Research; Foreign applicants.
Application information: Applications accepted.
Application form required.
  Deadline(s): Jan. 2 and July 1
  Additional information: Application must include
    proposal, project outline, and abstract.
Program description:
  Graduate Scholarship Program: This program
  provides international standard graduate education
  opportunities to exceptional conservationals from
  Africa, Asia, and Latin American and from North
  American indigenous groups. Named applications
  include the Beinecke African Scholarship,
  Christensen Conservation Leaders Scholarship,
  C.V. Starr Tiger Conservation Fellowship, Robertson
  Big Cat Conservation Fellowship, and Clive Marsh
  Conservation Grant for Field Training. Applications
  are canvassed by WCS-Global Conservation field
  staff; applications without WCS endorsement will
  not be considered.
EIN: 131740011

6521
A. F. Williams Fund for Teachers
(formerly A. F. Williams Fund for Barnard School for
Girls)
1 Court Sq., 8th Fl.
Long Island City, NY 11120

Foundation type: Independent foundation
Purpose: Emergency grants to retired teachers,
primarily in NY.
Financial data: Year ended 12/31/2012. Assets,
$709,158 (M); Expenditures, $51,075; Total
giving, $49,432; Grants to individuals, 4 grants
totaling $49,432 (high: $12,358, low: $12,358).
Type of support: Emergency funds.
Application information: Applications accepted.
Application form not required.
  Initial approach: Letter
  Send request by: Mail
  Deadline(s): Dec. 31.
EIN: 136054008

6522
Windows of Hope Family Relief Fund
c/o Night Sky Holding, LLC
24 W. 57th St., Ste. 504
New York, NY 10019-3918 (212) 300-2596
Contact: Toni A. Nagel-Smith, Exec. Dir.
FAX: (212) 617-4367

Foundation type: Public charity
Purpose: Scholarships and financial assistance to families of the victims of the World Trade Center tragedy who worked in the food, beverage and hospitality professions throughout the entire complex.
Financial data: Year ended 03/31/2012. Assets, $4,087,852 (M); Expenditures, $491,528; Total giving, $407,058.
Fields of interest: Disasters, 9/11/01.
Type of support: Undergraduate support; Grants for special needs.
Application information:
Initial approach: Letter or e-mail
Additional information: Unsolicited requests for funds not considered or acknowledged.
EIN: 134189858

6523
Wine Spectator California Scholarship Foundation
387 Park Ave. S.
New York, NY 10016-8810 (212) 684-4224

Foundation type: Public charity
Purpose: Grants and scholarships to secondary school students to enable them to pursue careers in the wine industry.
Financial data: Year ended 06/30/2012. Assets, $11,640,520 (M); Expenditures, $2,725,778; Total giving, $421,674.
Fields of interest: Vocational education; Business/industry.
Type of support: Graduate support; Doctoral support.
Application information: Contact foundation for current application deadline/guidelines.
EIN: 133129027

6524
Mabel M. Witmer Trust
1 M T Plz., 8th Fl.
Buffalo, NY 14203 (716) 842-5506

Foundation type: Independent foundation
Purpose: Scholarships based on financial need and academic standing, to students from Franklin and Cumberland counties, PA.
Financial data: Year ended 12/31/2011. Assets, $68,709 (M); Expenditures, $5,604; Total giving, $3,600.
Fields of interest: Higher education.
Type of support: Scholarships—to individuals; Technical education support.
Application information: Applications accepted.
Initial approach: Letter
Deadline(s): None
EIN: 256183584

6525
Charles F. Wolf Scholarship Fund
c/o Pagones, Cross & VanTuyl
355 Main St.
Beacon, NY 12508-3020

Foundation type: Independent foundation

Purpose: Scholarships to students accepted to the New York University School of Medicine, NY.
Financial data: Year ended 05/31/2012. Assets, $2,076,025 (M); Expenditures, $215,400; Total giving, $193,000.
Fields of interest: Medical school/education.
Type of support: Support to graduates or students of specific schools; Graduate support.
Application information: Applications not accepted.
Additional information: Unsolicited requests for funds not considered or acknowledged.
EIN: 141580597

6526
Elizabeth Wolf Scholarship Fund
c/o Pagones, Cross & VanTuyl, PC
355 Main St.
Beacon, NY 12508-3020 (845) 838-6900
Contact: Nick Coto
Application address: c/o Beacon High School, Attn.: Mr. Nick Coto, Principal, 101 Matteawan Rd., Beacon, NY 12508-1571, tel.: (914) 838-6950

Foundation type: Independent foundation
Purpose: Scholarships to graduates of Beacon High School, NY.
Financial data: Year ended 05/31/2012. Assets, $47,416 (M); Expenditures, $10,183; Total giving, $7,500; Grants to individuals, 3 grants totaling $7,500 (high: $2,500, low: $2,500).
Type of support: Support to graduates or students of specific schools; Undergraduate support.
Application information: Applications not accepted.
Additional information: Application must include biographical and scholastic information, and references. Unsolicited requests for funds not considered or acknowledged.
EIN: 141580472

6527
Women Make Movies, Inc.
115 W. 29th St., Ste. 1200
New York, NY 10013-2618 (212) 925-0606
FAX: (212) 925-2052; E-mail: info@wmm.com; E-mail For Debra Zimmerman: dzimmerman@wmm.com; URL: http://www.wmm.com/index.asp

Foundation type: Public charity
Purpose: Support for female project directors who are U.S. citizens through a fiscal sponsorship program.
Publications: Application guidelines.
Financial data: Year ended 06/30/2012. Assets, $2,150,794 (M); Expenditures, $3,909,327.
Fields of interest: Film/video; Arts, artist's services.
Type of support: Fiscal agent/sponsor.
Application information: Applications accepted. Application form available on the grantmaker's web site.
Initial approach: Application
Send request by: Mail
Deadline(s): Feb. 15, May 15 and Oct. 15
Program description:
Fiscal Sponsorship: As a fiscal sponsor, the organization acts a non-profit tax-exempt umbrella organization that accepts and administers contributions made to the submitted projects. The organization is legally responsible for the funds received on behalf of fiscally sponsored projects and must insure that the funds are used for charitable activities, as agreed upon between the

donor and recipient, and that the donor reporting requirements are met and in a timely fashion.
EIN: 132740460

6528
Women's Sports Foundation
424 W. 33rd St., Ste. 150
New York, NY 10001-2619 (646) 845-0273
Contact: Kathryn Olson, C.E.O.
FAX: (212) 967-2757;
E-mail: info@womenssportsfoundation.org;
Additional address: Eisenhower Park, 1899 Hempstead Tpke., Ste. 400, East Meadow, NY 11554, tel.: (516) 542-4700, fax: (516) 542-0095; Toll-free tel. (U.S. only): (800)-227-3988;
URL: http://www.womenssportsfoundation.org

Foundation type: Public charity
Purpose: Grants to women and girls achieving certain standards of excellence in the sports related industry.
Publications: Application guidelines; Annual report; Financial statement; Grants list; Informational brochure; Newsletter.
Financial data: Year ended 12/31/2011. Assets, $4,412,110 (M); Expenditures, $5,000,848; Total giving, $334,107; Grants to individuals, 16 grants totaling $53,750.
Fields of interest: Higher education; Athletics/sports, training; Women.
Type of support: Program development; Internship funds; Research; Grants to individuals; Scholarships—to individuals; Awards/prizes; Graduate support; Undergraduate support; Postgraduate support.
Application information:
Send request by: Online
Deadline(s): Sept. 28 for Rusty Kanokogi Fund, June 8 for Travel & Training Fund
Final notification: Applicants notified by Aug. 31 for Travel & Training Fund
Additional information: See web site for additional guidelines.
Program descriptions:
Rusty Kanokogi Fund for the Advancement of U.S. Judo Grant: Grants of up to $5,000 are available to female Judo athletes in need of financial assistance in order to compete at higher levels. Athletes must have successful competitive records as well as the potential to achieve even higher performance levels and rankings. Individuals may request up to $5,000.
Travel and Training Fund: This fund provides direct financial assistance to aspiring athletes who are U.S. citizens or legal residents with successful competitive records who have the potential to achieve even higher performance levels and rankings. Grants will be made available to aspiring elite-level female athletes to help relieve them of the financial burden associated with competing at higher levels and to permit them to concentrate on their training. Applicants will be assessed based on financial need, present and potential level and ranking, lack of support from traditional sources, role of award in continued participation and advancement, potential impact of grant on advancing women in sports, and contribution to greater visibility of female athletes. Priority will be given to those who present a plan for reimbursing the grant in the future, whether financially or otherwise contributing to women's sports.
EIN: 237380557

6529

Women's Studio Workshop, Inc.
722 Binnewater Ln.
P.O. Box 489
Rosendale, NY   12472-0489   (845) 658-9133
Contact: Ann Kalmbach, Exec. Dir.
FAX: (845) 658-9031;
E-mail: info@wsworkshop.org; E-Mail for Ann
Kalmbach: ann@wsworkshop.org; URL: http://
www.wsworkshop.org

Foundation type: Public charity
Purpose: Grants and residencies to printmakers,
papermakers, photographers, and book artists.
Publications: Application guidelines; Informational
brochure; Newsletter; Occasional report.
Financial data: Year ended 06/30/2012. Assets,
$814,125 (M); Expenditures, $516,547.
Fields of interest: Arts, artist's services.
Type of support: Fellowships; Grants to individuals.
Application information: Applications accepted.
Application form required. Application form
available on the grantmaker's web site.
   Initial approach: Letter, telephone or e-mail
   Send request by: Mail
   Copies of proposal: 1
   Deadline(s): Varies
   Final notification: Recipients notified in two
      months
   Applicants should submit the following:
      1) SASE
      2) Budget Information
      3) Letter(s) of recommendation
      4) Proposal
      5) Resume
      6) Work samples
   Additional information: See web site for
      additional application guidelines.
Program descriptions:
   Artists' Book Residency Grants: These residency
grants are designed to enable artists to produce a
limited edition book work at the studio. Residents
receive a stipend of $2,000 to $3,000, a $750
materials stipend, access to studio space for six to
eight weeks, travel costs, and housing.
   Arts Administration Internship: This year-long
internship is available to people considering a
career in arts administration, where they will work
alongside workshop staff attending to the myriad
details that keep an arts organization functioning
smoothly. Internships include housing and a
stipend of $300 per month.
   Arts-in-Education Visiting Artist Project: Awards
$400 per week for up to ten weeks, a $750
materials budget, housing, and unlimited studio
access to two artists for participation in two-month
residencies designed to integrate the creation of an
artist's book while working with young people.
   Ceramics Internship: Internships are available for
young artists interested in functional ceramics.
Interns work closely with the workshop's clay
program coordinator preparing for annual
fundraisers. Internships include hosing and a
stipend of $300 per month.
   *Geraldine R. Dodge Residency Grants for New
Jersey Artists:* Awards residencies to two New Jersey
artists to create a new body of work. These six- to
eight-week residencies include a $2,000 to $3,000
artist's stipend, travel money, housing, and use of
the workshop's studios.
   Joan Snyder Artists Residency: The workshop
offers a six-week residency for women artists
working in the printmaking studio. Residencies
include a $2,100 stipend, $500 toward materials
used during the residency, a travel stipend (of up to
$250), housing, and unlimited studio use.
   *Ora Schneider Residency Grants for Regional
Artists:* This grant supports two
Hudson-Valley-based artists in month-long

residencies in any of the workshop's studios.
Residents receive a $1,500 stipend and unlimited
access to the studio; housing can also be arranged
on a case-by-case basis. Eligible artists must reside
in Greene, Columbia, Delaware, Dutchess, Ulster,
Sullivan, and Orange counties; priority will be given
to artists with experience and a working knowledge
of etching/intaglio/monoprint, letterpress, hand
papermaking, screenprinting, photography, and
ceramics.
   Studio Internships: Three internships are
available to artists, who have the opportunity to work
with workshop staff on projects including
papermaking, book arts, and arts administration.
Internships include housing and a stipend of $300
per month, for up to 12 months. Interns will assist
with the on-going operations of the facility, assist
artists-in-residence with their projects, work with
artist-educators, and participate in the workshop's
Summer Arts Institute classes as studio
assistants.
EIN: 222147463

6530

Woodlawn Foundation, Inc.
56 Harrison St., Ste. 401
New Rochelle, NY   10801-3410
FAX: (914) 632-5502;
E-mail: giving@woodlawnfoundation.org;
URL: http://www.woodlawnfoundation.org/

Foundation type: Public charity
Purpose: Grants to individuals in support of
Catholic Prelature of Opus Dei activities, Harrison,
NY.
Publications: Financial statement; Occasional
report; IRS Form 990 or 990-PF printed copy
available upon request; Program policy statement.
Financial data: Year ended 06/30/2011. Assets,
$36,940,136 (M); Expenditures, $13,945,585;
Total giving, $12,355,754; Grant to an individual,
1 grant totaling $24,448.
Fields of interest: Christian agencies & churches.
Type of support: Program development.
Application information: Applications not
accepted.
   Additional information: Unsolicited requests for
      funds not considered or acknowledged.
EIN: 133055729

6531

**Woori America Bank Scholarship
   Foundation Inc.**
1250 Broadway, 16th Fl.
New York, NY   10001-3701   (212) 244-3000
URL: http://www.wooriamericabank.com/eng/
about/Scholarship.asp

Foundation type: Company-sponsored foundation
Purpose: Scholarships to graduates who are
residents of Woori America Bank Branch operating
area enrolled in a four-year college for higher
education.
Publications: Application guidelines.
Financial data: Year ended 12/31/2012. Assets,
$107,651 (M); Expenditures, $112,328; Total
giving, $100,000; Grants to individuals, 48 grants
totaling $96,000 (high: $2,000, low: $2,000).
Fields of interest: Higher education.
Type of support: Scholarships—to individuals.
Application information: Applications accepted.
Application form required. Application form
available on the grantmaker's web site.
   Deadline(s): Apr. 30
   Final notification: Recipients notified in May
   Applicants should submit the following:

      1) SAT
      2) Transcripts
      3) Essay
   Additional information: Application should also
      include recent family income tax return and
      college acceptance letter.
Program description:
   Scholarships: The foundation awards $2,000
college scholarships to high school graduate
students residing in California, Maryland, New
Jersey, New York, Pennsylvania, Virginia, and
Washington D.C. Applicants must demonstrate
academic excellence, strong leadership, and
financial need.
EIN: 201916285

6532

Working in Support of Education
(also known as W!se)
227 E. 56th St., Ste. 201
New York, NY   10022-3752   (212) 421-2700
Contact: Ms. Phyllis P. Frankfort, Pres. and C.E.O.
FAX: (212) 980-5053; E-mail: info@wise-ny.org;
URL: http://www.wise-ny.org

Foundation type: Public charity
Purpose: Support through fiscal agency services to
individuals and emerging organizations seeking
funds for charitable and educational purposes.
Financial data: Year ended 07/31/2012. Assets,
$1,103,452 (M); Expenditures, $1,983,584.
Type of support: Fiscal agent/sponsor.
Application information: Applications accepted.
   Additional information: Fees for Fiscal Sponsor
      program are very competitive. See web site for
      additional guidelines.
EIN: 134024627

6533

World Federation of Hemophilia - USA
(formerly World Hemophilia Alliance)
911 Central Ave.
PMB 142
Albany, NY   12206-1350   (877) 417-7944
Contact: Mark W. Skinner, Pres.
E-mail: info@wfhusa.org; URL: http://www.wfh.org

Foundation type: Public charity
Purpose: Fellowships to individuals from developing
countries who are physicians or healthcare workers
working in close collaboration with hemophilia
services.
Financial data: Year ended 12/31/2012. Assets,
$405,130 (M); Expenditures, $34,636,571; Total
giving, $34,399,945.
Fields of interest: Hemophilia.
Type of support: Fellowships.
Application information: Applications accepted.
Application form required. Application form
available on the grantmaker's web site.
   Initial approach: Letter
   Deadline(s): June 30 and Dec. 31
   Applicants should submit the following:
      1) Letter(s) of recommendation
      2) Curriculum vitae
   Additional information: Applications should also
      include a recommendation from the National
      Hemophilia Member Organization of the
      applicant's country.
EIN: 161513923

6534
World Hunger Year, Inc.
(also known as WHY)
505 8th Ave., Ste. 2100
New York, NY 10018-6582 (212) 629-8850
Contact: William Ayres, Exec. Dir.
FAX: (212) 465-9274;
E-mail: why@worldhungeryear.org; Toll-free tel:
(800) 548-6479; URL: http://
www.worldhungeryear.org

Foundation type: Public charity
Purpose: Awards to journalists for their coverage of hunger and poverty-related issues.
Publications: Application guidelines; Annual report; Financial statement; Grants list; Informational brochure (including application guidelines); Newsletter.
Financial data: Year ended 03/31/2012. Assets, $2,823,454 (M); Expenditures, $3,098,208; Total giving, $577,009; Grants to individuals, totaling $500.
Fields of interest: Media/communications; International affairs; Poverty studies.
Type of support: Awards/grants by nomination only; Awards/prizes.
Application information: Application form required.
Initial approach: Telephone or e-mail
Deadline(s): Feb. 24
Final notification: Finalists announced in Mar., winners announced in June
Additional information: Application by nomination only. Application fee for one entry, $25; two entries $40; three to five entries, $50.
Program description:
Harry Chapin Media Awards: This program provides awards to encourage, honor, and reward those members of the media who have made significant contributions in bringing the issues of world hunger and poverty to the attention of the public. The awards media categories are: Newspaper, Periodical (magazine, or ezine), TV/Film, New Media, Radio, Photojournalism, and Book. All entries must have appeared in the media between Jan. 1 and Dec. 1 and must be in English. Awards range from $1,000 to $2,500.
EIN: 132805575

6535
Worldstudio Foundation, Inc.
200 Varick St., Ste. 507
New York, NY 10014-7041 (212) 366-1317
Contact: David Sterling, Pres.
FAX: (212) 807-0024; E-mail: info@worldstudio.org;
Additional e-mail: scholarships@worldstudio.org;
URL: http://www.worldstudioinc.com/

Foundation type: Public charity
Purpose: Scholarships and mentoring for minority and disadvantaged undergraduate and graduate students of art, architecture and design, in cooperation with the design/arts industries.
Publications: Application guidelines; Informational brochure; Newsletter.
Financial data: Year ended 12/31/2011. Assets, $114,991 (M); Expenditures, $201,839; Total giving, $78,113; Grants to individuals, totaling $78,113.
Fields of interest: Arts education; Architecture; Design; Arts, artist's services; Arts; Environment; Minorities; Economically disadvantaged.
Type of support: Graduate support; Undergraduate support.
Application information: Application form required. Application form available on the grantmaker's web site.
Deadline(s): Apr. 1

Applicants should submit the following:
1) Photograph
2) Work samples
3) Essay
Additional information: See web site for further guidelines.
Program description:
Worldstudio AIGA Scholarships: Awarded in conjunction with AIGA, the foundation provides scholarships with the aims of increasing diversity in the creative professions, and fostering social and environmental responsibility in the artists, designers, and studios of tomorrow. Awards generally range from $2,000 to $3,000, with a top award of $5,000 available; in addition, honorable mention prizes of up to $500 are also awarded. Eligible applicants must: be citizens of the U.S. or be in possession of a green card; be pursuing an undergraduate or graduate degree in a design or art discipline; have at least a 2.0 GPA; and be planning to matriculate at an accredited college or university in the U.S.
EIN: 133776523

6536
The Kathryn Aguirre Worth Memorial Foundation, Inc.
c/o White & Case LLP
1155 Ave. of the Americas
New York, NY 10036-2787

Foundation type: Independent foundation
Purpose: Scholarships to graduates of the University of Singapore Law Facility to pursue LLM degrees and qualification as US lawyers at accredited US law schools.
Financial data: Year ended 12/31/2011. Assets, $165,072 (M); Expenditures, $15,144; Total giving, $15,000.
Fields of interest: Law school/education.
Type of support: Support to graduates or students of specific schools; Graduate support.
Application information: Applications accepted. Application form required.
Deadline(s): None
EIN: 133983778

6537
Abraham Woursell Foundation
1 Court Sq., 8th Fl.
Long Island City, NY 11120

Foundation type: Independent foundation
Purpose: Literary prizes and fellowships to writers at the University of Vienna, Austria.
Financial data: Year ended 12/31/2012. Assets, $1,812,311 (M); Expenditures, $106,188; Total giving, $77,225.
Fields of interest: Literature.
Type of support: Fellowships; Awards/prizes.
Application information: Contact the foundation for additional guidelines.
EIN: 136140514

6538
Wu Zhong-Yi Scholarship Foundation Inc.
c/o Su Wu
6120 Grand Central Pkwy.
Forest Hills, NY 11375

Foundation type: Independent foundation
Purpose: Scholarships only to individuals at the Ming de School in Liu He, Jiangsu Province, China.

Financial data: Year ended 10/31/2012. Assets, $1,017,581 (M); Expenditures, $63,470; Total giving, $56,250.
Type of support: Scholarships—to individuals; Support to graduates or students of specific schools.
Application information: Applications not accepted.
Additional information: Unsolicited requests for funds not considered or acknowledged.
EIN: 133387111

6539
Yeshiva Endowment Foundation, Inc.
500 W. 185th St.
New York, NY 10033-3201 (212) 960-5470

Foundation type: Public charity
Purpose: Scholarships to students of Yeshiva University, NY.
Financial data: Year ended 06/30/2011. Assets, $33,922,893 (M); Expenditures, $2,159,452; Total giving, $2,119,030.
Type of support: Support to graduates or students of specific schools; Undergraduate support.
Application information: Applications accepted.
Initial approach: Letter
Additional information: Application should include financial information.
EIN: 131790758

6540
Young Women's Leadership Network, Inc.
(formerly The Young Women's Leadership Foundation, Inc.)
322 8th Ave., Ste. 1402
New York, NY 10001-6775 (212) 207-3221
Contact: Anne Adler, Exec. Dir.
FAX: (212) 207-8814; E-mail: info@ywlnetwork.org;
E-mail for Anne Adler: aadler@ywln.org; URL: http://ywlnetwork.org

Foundation type: Public charity
Purpose: Scholarships to high school graduates of New York City to help them defer college costs based on academic performance and need.
Financial data: Year ended 06/30/2012. Assets, $4,870,783 (M); Expenditures, $5,065,550; Total giving, $33,500; Grants to individuals, totaling $33,500.
Fields of interest: Higher education.
Type of support: Scholarships—to individuals.
Application information: See web site for additional guidelines.
EIN: 061517218

6541
Youth Foundation, Inc.
317 Madison Ave., Ste. 824
New York, NY 10017-5257
Contact: Johanna M. Lee
URL: http://fdnweb.org/youthfdn

Foundation type: Independent foundation
Purpose: Scholarships for undergraduate study to high school seniors who are U.S. citizens.
Publications: Application guidelines; Informational brochure; Program policy statement.
Financial data: Year ended 12/31/2012. Assets, $10,444,795 (M); Expenditures, $591,181; Total giving, $358,865; Grants to individuals, 94 grants totaling $320,365 (high: $4,300; low: $1,965).
Fields of interest: College; Scholarships/financial aid.

Type of support: Scholarships—to individuals; Undergraduate support.
Application information: Applications accepted. Application form required.

Initial approach: Letter
Deadline(s): Feb. 28
Final notification: Applicant notified in May
Applicants should submit the following:
1) Letter(s) of recommendation
2) Transcripts
3) SAT
4) SASE
5) GPA
6) Financial information
7) Essay
8) Curriculum vitae
9) ACT
Additional information: Applicant must mail a completed Request for Application Form, a letter of recommendation on letterhead, from a teacher, advisor, principal, or coach, with an SASE, to the foundation by Jan.15 to ensure receipt of the application materials.
EIN: 136093036

6542
Zeta Psi Educational Foundation
15 S. Henry St.
Pearl River, NY   10965-2603   (845) 735-1847
Application e-mail: exec.dir@zetapsi.org
FAX: (845) 735-1989; E-mail: dhunter@zetapsi.org;
URL: http://www.zetapsi.org/foundation/

Foundation type: Public charity
Purpose: Scholarships to eligible students in the U.S. for higher education.
Publications: Application guidelines.
Financial data: Year ended 05/31/2012. Assets, $4,973,190 (M); Expenditures, $686,452; Total giving, $154,029; Grants to individuals, totaling $68,146.
Fields of interest: Higher education; Students, sororities/fraternities.
Type of support: Undergraduate support.
Application information: Application form required. Application form available on the grantmaker's web site.

Send request by: E-mail
Deadline(s): Jan. 21 for Spring semester and Sept. 17 for Fall semester
Additional information: Application should include transcripts.
Program description:

Scholarships: The foundation provides scholarships each year to eligible students in the U.S. Scholarship is generally a one-time per semester award of $500. There is no limit to the number of semesters an individual may apply for and receive an award. In addition, two or three exceptional applicants each semester receive awards ranging from $750 to $2,500.
EIN: 131832953

NORTH CAROLINA

6543
100 Black Men of America, Greater Charlotte Chapter, Inc.
(formerly 100 Black Men of Greater Charlotte, Inc.)
740 W. 5th St., Ste. 206
Charlotte, NC 28202-1408 (704) 375-7300
E-mail: info@100blackmenofcharlotte.org;
URL: http://www.100blackmenofcharlotte.org

Foundation type: Public charity
Purpose: Scholarships to African American students residing in the Charlotte, NC, area, for undergraduate education.
Publications: Annual report; Financial statement; Informational brochure.
Financial data: Year ended 06/30/2012. Assets, $161,956 (M); Expenditures, $281,116.
Fields of interest: Youth development, community service clubs; African Americans/Blacks.
Type of support: Precollege support; Undergraduate support.
Application information: Applications accepted. Application form required. Application form available on the grantmaker's web site.
  Send request by: Mail
  Applicants should submit the following:
    1) Transcripts
    2) Letter(s) of recommendation
    3) Essay
Program descriptions:
  Malcolm Robinson Memorial Community Service Scholarship: Awards $500 to Charlotte-area high school seniors who exhibits solid scholarship and a commitment to community service.
  Movement of Youth Scholarships: Awards $10,000 to African American students with GPAs of at least 3.0, and $3,000 to African American students with GPAs of between 2.0 and 2.9.
EIN: 561795371

6544
Accel Foundation
4209 Lassiter Mill Rd., Apt. 180
Raleigh, NC 27609

Foundation type: Independent foundation
Purpose: Scholarships to college bound high school seniors from Lancaster County, PA, all-county in any sport.
Financial data: Year ended 08/31/2013. Assets, $885,367 (M); Expenditures, $53,058; Total giving, $49,750; Grants to individuals, 8 grants totaling $20,500 (high: $4,000, low: $1,500).
Fields of interest: Higher education; Recreation.
Type of support: Scholarships—to individuals; Undergraduate support.
Application information: Applications accepted. Application form required.
  Deadline(s): May 31
  Additional information: Application can be obtained from Lancaster county guidance counselors and athletic directors.
EIN: 561900007

6545
AIDS Care Service, Inc.
995 W. Northwest Blvd.
Winston-Salem, NC 27101-1215 (336) 777-0116
Contact: Katherine Foster, Pres.
E-mail: jduncan@aidscareservice.org; URL: http://www.aidscareservice.org

Foundation type: Public charity
Purpose: Financial assistance to residents of Forsyth County, NC, who are living with HIV/AIDS.
Publications: Annual report; Newsletter.
Financial data: Year ended 06/30/2011. Assets, $743,397 (M); Expenditures, $947,870.
Type of support: Grants for special needs.
Application information: Applications accepted.
  Initial approach: Letter or e-mail
  Additional information: Contact foundation for eligibility requirements.
EIN: 561717630

6546
Alamance Community College Foundation, Inc.
1247 Jimmy Kerr Rd.
P.O. Box 8000
Graham, NC 27253-8000 (336) 506-4128
FAX: (336) 506-4020; URL: http://www.accfoundation.com

Foundation type: Public charity
Purpose: Scholarships and financial assistance to students of Alamance Community College, NC for higher education.
Publications: Annual report; Financial statement; Newsletter.
Financial data: Year ended 06/30/2012. Assets, $8,289,638 (M); Expenditures, $963,003; Total giving, $872,350; Grants to individuals, totaling $53,833.
Fields of interest: College (community/junior).
Type of support: Support to graduates or students of specific schools.
Application information: Applications accepted. Application form required.
  Additional information: Most scholarships are need-based, a few are merit-based. Contact the foundation for additional guidelines.
EIN: 581511004

6547
Albemarle Smart Start Partnership, Inc.
1403 Parkview Dr.
Elizabeth City, NC 27909-6533 (252) 333-1233
FAX: (252) 333-1201;
E-mail: smartstart@albemarlessp.org; E-Mail for Dr. Denauvo M. Robinson :
drobinson@albemarlessp.org; URL: http://www.albemarlessp.org

Foundation type: Public charity
Purpose: Financial support to parents for childcare through a referral process limited to residents of Camden, Currituck, and Pasqutank counties, NC.
Publications: Newsletter.
Financial data: Year ended 06/30/2012. Assets, $11,805 (M); Expenditures, $2,240,746; Total giving, $755,974; Grants to individuals, totaling $725,489.
Fields of interest: Early childhood education.
Type of support: Grants for special needs.
Application information: Applications accepted.
EIN: 562088109

6548
Iona M. Allen Music Scholarship Fund
c/o Wells Fargo Bank, N.A., Trust Tax Dept.
1 W. 4th St., 4th Fl., MAC D4000-041
Winston Salem, NC 27101-3818 (866) 608-0001
Application address: c/o 4320 Wade Hampton Blvd., Ste. G, Taylors, SC 29687-2223, tel.: (866) 608-0001
URL: http://www.csascholars.org

Foundation type: Independent foundation
Purpose: Scholarships to high school seniors who demonstrate musical aptitude and are residents of one of the following western NC counties: Cherokee, Clay, Graham, Macon, Swain, Haywood, Transylvania, Henderson, Polk, Jackson, Buncombe, and Madison.
Financial data: Year ended 12/31/2013. Assets, $978,233 (M); Expenditures, $56,248; Total giving, $37,000.
Fields of interest: Performing arts, education.
Type of support: Undergraduate support.
Application information: Applications accepted. Application form required. Interview required.
  Initial approach: Letter
  Deadline(s): Varies
  Additional information: See web site for a listing of scholarship programs.
EIN: 586189987

6549
American Dance Festival, Inc.
715 Broad St.
Durham, NC 27705-4833 (919) 684-6402
Contact: Jodee Nimerichter, Exec. Dir.
FAX: (919) 684-5459;
E-mail: adf@americandancefestival.org; Mailing address (Durham office): P.O. Box 90772, Durham, NC 27708-0772; additional address (New York office): 1697 Broadway, Rm. 901, New York, NY 10019-5907, tel.: (212) 586-1925, fax: (212) 397-1196; URL: http://www.americandancefestival.org

Foundation type: Public charity
Purpose: Opportunities for professional journalists interested in refining their skills in writing about dance and analyzing choreography.
Financial data: Year ended 09/30/2011. Assets, $7,174,149 (M); Expenditures, $3,521,160; Total giving, $324,128; Grants to individuals, totaling $324,128.
Fields of interest: Print publishing; Dance; Choreography.
Type of support: Conferences/seminars.
Application information:
  Initial approach: Letter
  Deadline(s): Apr. 2
  Applicants should submit the following:
    1) Work samples
    2) Letter(s) of recommendation
    3) Resume
  Additional information: Applicants must submit a letter specifying reasons for wishing to attend the institute, and three samples of dance criticism.
Program description:
  NEA Arts Journalism Institute for Dance Criticism Scholarships: Supported by the National Endowment for the Arts, this program offers professional print, electronic, radio, and television journalists the opportunity for immersion into one of the world's premiere modern dance festivals with three intensive weeks of performances and seminars, held at Duke University. Participants will attend an extensive range of world-class

performances, write reviews, observe classes, participate in movement sessions, meet with choreographers and other dance professionals, and analyze the role of dance critics in the world of journalism. Scholarships cover the expense of tuition, room, board, transportation, and tickets to performances.
EIN: 060932294

6550
American Institute of Certified Public Accountants
(also known as AICPA)
220 Leigh Farm Rd.
Durham, NC   27707-8110   (919) 402-4500
FAX: (919) 402-4505; E-mail: service@aicpa.org;
URL: http://www.aicpa.org

Foundation type: Public charity
Purpose: Scholarships to students interested in pursuing coursework related to the accounting profession.
Publications: Application guidelines; Annual report.
Financial data: Year ended 07/31/2011. Assets, $206,672,576 (M); Expenditures, $209,750,632; Total giving, $4,052,247; Grants to individuals, totaling $59,906.
Fields of interest: Business school/education; Scholarships/financial aid; Minorities.
Type of support: Fellowships; Scholarships—to individuals; Doctoral support.
Application information: Applications accepted. Application form available on the grantmaker's web site.
   Initial approach: Application
   Deadline(s): Apr. 1
   Final notification: Recipients notified by Aug. 1 for Accountemps Students Scholarship, John L. Carey Scholarship, and Scholarship for Minority Accounting Students
   Applicants should submit the following:
      1) Essay
      2) Letter(s) of recommendation
      3) Transcripts
   Additional information: See web site for additional guidelines.
Program descriptions:
AICPA Fellowship for Minority Doctoral Students: This program awards annual fellowships of $12,000 each to full-time minority accounting scholars who demonstrate significant potential to become accounting educators. Eligible applicants must have applied to a doctoral program and be awaiting word on acceptance, have been accepted into a doctoral program, or already be matriculated in a doctoral program and pursuing appropriate coursework, have a master's degree and/or completed at least three years of full-time experience in the accounting practice, be a minority student of Black/African America, Hispanic/Latino, or Native American ethnicity, be attending school on a full-time basis and plan to remain full-time until attaining one's doctoral degree, and be a U.S. citizen or permanent resident.
AICPA John L. Carey Scholarship: This scholarship program provides financial assistance to liberal arts and non-business degree holders who are pursuing both graduate studies in accounting and CPA licensure. Awards are intended to encourage students with little or no previous accounting experience to consider professional accounting careers. Recipients receive $5,000 for one year. Scholarship aid may be used only for the payment of expenses that directly relate to obtaining an accounting education with tuition, fees, room and board, and/or books and materials only.

AICPA Scholarship for Minority Accounting Students: This program provides financial awards to outstanding minority students to encourage their pursuit of accounting as a major and their ultimate entry into the profession. Recipients will receive individuals awards ranging from $1,500 to $3,000 per year. Scholarship aid may be used only for the payment of expenses that directly relate to obtaining an accounting education, such as tuition, fees, room and board, and/or books and materials only.
AICPA/Accountemps Student Scholarship: This program provides financial assistance to outstanding accounting students who demonstrate potential to become leaders in the CPA profession. Recipients receive $2,500 for one year. Scholarship aid may be used only for the payment of expenses that relate directly to obtaining an accounting education such as tuition, fees, room and board, and/or books and materials only.
EIN: 130432265

6551
American Kennel Club Canine Health Foundation, Inc.
8051 Arco Corporate Dr., Ste. 300
PO Box 900061
Raleigh, NC   27617-3901   (212) 533-7800
FAX: (919) 334-4011; E-mail: info@akcchf.org;
URL: http://www.akcchf.org

Foundation type: Public charity
Purpose: Research grant to investigators to study the causes and origins of canine diseases and afflictions and to formulate effective treatments.
Publications: Application guidelines; Annual report; Grants list; Informational brochure (including application guidelines); Newsletter.
Financial data: Year ended 12/31/2011. Assets, $11,313,575 (M); Expenditures, $3,048,525; Total giving, $1,767,684.
Fields of interest: Animal welfare; Veterinary medicine.
Type of support: Research; Stipends.
Application information: Applications accepted. Application form required.
   Deadline(s): Mar. 1 for Research Grants; at least six months in advance for Education Grants; none for ACORN Research Grants: Small Grants for Quick Results
   Final notification: Sept. for Research Grants
Program descriptions:
ACORN Research Grants: Small Grants for Quick Results: These grants are designed to allow researchers to complete small, relatively short timeframe projects, test research hypotheses, and/or generate preliminary data for possible future grant proposals as larger-scale or longer-term studies. Priority will be given to projects that utilize new genetic technologies, develop improved molecular and diagnostic tools, and provide evidence-based information for breeding decisions; the foundation also funds clinical research on the health of dogs, especially findings with the potential for near-term applicability and positive impact on the health of dogs. Grants of up to $12,000 will be awarded, with an allowance of eight percent for indirect costs.
Education Grants: The foundation funds research and supports canine health scientists and professionals in their efforts to study the causes and origins of canine disease and afflictions in order to formulate effective treatments. Grants are also available for research conferences and meetings where new research is presented and investigators come together to develop new ideas. Grants of up to $5,000 will be awarded.

Research Grants: Grants of at least $12,000 will be made available for canine health research, for both pre-clinical and clinical studies. Proposals will be chosen based on: the significance of health concern through the seriousness of the disease and the potential impact on the lives of dogs; research areas of interest for the foundation and breed clubs; cost benefit of the study; scientific soundness of proposed methods; the humane treatment of dogs with study participation (only with the consent of the owners); the investigator's past performance with research projects and publications in peer-reviewed journals; and current and future portfolio of potential grants. Typically, the foundation has awarded grants between $50,000 and $100,000.
EIN: 133813813

6552
Sherwood Anderson Foundation
5587 Garden Village Way
Greensboro, NC   27410
Contact: David Spear, Co-Pres.
Application address: 264 Tobacco Rd., Madison, NC 27025; URL: https://www.sherwoodandersonfoundation.org

Foundation type: Independent foundation
Purpose: Awards to individuals who are students of journalism and study of American Society and have published at least one book of fiction or a collection of short stories in a major literary or commercial publication.
Financial data: Year ended 12/31/2012. Assets, $581,508 (M); Expenditures, $27,731; Total giving, $20,000; Grant to an individual, 1 grant totaling $20,000.
Fields of interest: Print publishing; Literature.
Type of support: Awards/prizes.
Application information: Applications accepted.
   Send request by: Mail
   Deadline(s): Apr. 1
   Applicants should submit the following:
      1) Work samples
      2) Resume
   Additional information: Application should also include bibliography of works published and $20 application fee.
EIN: 581717970

6553
The Emily B. Andrews Memorial Foundation
401-B S. Green St.
P.O. Box 1329
Morganton, NC   28680   (828) 437-9744
Contact: Patricia O. Ragland, Chair.

Foundation type: Independent foundation
Purpose: Scholarships primarily to students of NC.
Financial data: Year ended 12/31/2011. Assets, $514,603 (M); Expenditures, $111,012; Total giving, $64,700.
Type of support: Undergraduate support.
Application information: Applications accepted.
   Send request by: Mail
   Deadline(s): None
EIN: 561667607

6554
The Arc of Durham County, Inc.
3500 Westgate Dr., Ste. 402
Durham, NC 27707-2534 (919) 493-8141
E-mail: thearcdc@frontier.com; URL: http://
www.thearcofdurhamcounty.org/

Foundation type: Public charity
Purpose: Financial assistance to individuals with developmental disabilities and their families residing in Durham County, NC, for payment of approved expenses.
Financial data: Year ended 06/30/2012. Assets, $345,066 (M); Expenditures, $333,149; Total giving, $47,323; Grants to individuals, totaling $47,323.
Type of support: Grants for special needs.
Application information:
Initial approach: Letter
Additional information: Contact foundation for eligibility requirements.
EIN: 560689237

6555
Area Scholastic Awards Trust Fund
1525 W.W.T. Harris Blvd. D1114-044
Charlotte, NC 28288 (336) 747-8167
Contact: Caroline Beck, Tr.
Application address: 1 W. 4th St., 2nd Fl., Winston-Salem, NC 27101-3818, tel.:(336) 747-8167

Foundation type: Independent foundation
Purpose: Scholarships to graduates of South Williamsport Area School District, PA.
Financial data: Year ended 12/31/2011. Assets, $203,866 (M); Expenditures, $14,261; Total giving, $9,950.
Type of support: Support to graduates or students of specific schools.
Application information: Applications not accepted.
Additional information: Unsolicited requests for funds not considered.
EIN: 237056712

6556
The Edward M. Armfield, Sr. Foundation, Inc.
324 W. Wendover Ave., No. 130
Greensboro, NC 27408-8438
Contact: Melinda W. Oakley

Foundation type: Independent foundation
Purpose: Scholarships to residents of Greensboro, NC, to attend schools in NC.
Financial data: Year ended 12/31/2012. Assets, $60,448,098 (M); Expenditures, $3,334,797; Total giving, $2,220,132; Grants to individuals, totaling $866,500.
Type of support: Undergraduate support.
Application information: Applications not accepted.
Additional information: Unsolicited requests for funds not accepted.
EIN: 562156876

6557
George S. Arnold Trust
1 W. 4th St., D4000-041
Winston Salem, NC 27101 (866) 608-0001

Foundation type: Independent foundation
Purpose: Scholarships to students in Hampshire County, WV, for higher education.

Financial data: Year ended 12/31/2012. Assets, $204,195 (M); Expenditures, $15,552; Total giving, $10,500.
Type of support: Undergraduate support.
Application information: Applications accepted.
Send request by: Mail
Deadline(s): None
EIN: 546191759

6558
Ernest G. Arps Memorial Fund Trust
c/o Trust Tax Dept.
P.O. Box 2907
Wilson, NC 27894-2907 (252) 246-4633

Foundation type: Independent foundation
Purpose: Scholarships to residents of Washington County, NC, to attend four-year colleges.
Financial data: Year ended 09/30/2013. Assets, $801,780 (M); Expenditures, $45,308; Total giving, $30,000; Grants to individuals, 5 grants totaling $30,000 (high: $7,500, low: $3,750).
Fields of interest: Higher education.
Type of support: Scholarships—to individuals.
Application information: Applications accepted. Application form required.
Deadline(s): None
Additional information: Application must include a photograph and demonstrate financial need.
EIN: 566228126

6559
Arts & Science Council
(also known as ASC)
227 W. Trade St., Ste. 250
Charlotte, NC 28202-1675 (704) 333-2272
FAX: (704) 333-2720;
E-mail: asc@artsandscience.org; URL: http://
www.artsandscience.org

Foundation type: Public charity
Purpose: Grants provide individual artists with project support for the enhancement of artistic development.
Publications: Application guidelines; Grants list.
Financial data: Year ended 06/30/2012. Assets, $51,323,022 (M); Expenditures, $15,034,617; Total giving, $11,292,361; Grants to individuals, totaling $51,557.
Fields of interest: Visual arts; Performing arts.
Type of support: Grants to individuals; Project support.
Application information: Applications accepted.
Program descriptions:
ASC Honors: This honor recognizes exceptionally creative, innovative, and inquisitive individuals whose lifetime achievements in the visual, design or performing arts, history, literature or science have distinguished them and have enriched the lives of the citizens of Charlotte-Mecklenburg. Honorees receive a bronze medallion and a cash award of $10,000.
McColl Award: One-time grants of up to $25,000 are available towards the creation of an original work of art or new methods of community art program presentation or delivery. Eligible projects should include as components: a collaborative, cross-disciplinary process; an educational or outreach component; and authentic working partnerships among creative individuals, council affiliates, and partners in the broader community.
Regional Artist Project Grants Program: The program provides individuals with project support for the enhancement of artistic development. Applicants may be either emerging (fewer than ten

years' experience) or established (more than ten years' experience) artists, but in either case must have a record of artistic achievement appropriate to the stage of their career. The maximum grant amount is $5,000.
EIN: 560693436

6560
Artspace
201 E. Davie St.
Raleigh, NC 27601-1869 (919) 821-2787
E-mail address for residency: Lia Newman, lnewman@artspacenc.org
FAX: (919) 821-0383; E-mail: info@artspacenc.org;
E-mail For Mary Poole: mpoole@artspacenc.org;
URL: http://www.artspacenc.org

Foundation type: Public charity
Purpose: Residencies to established visual artists who currently reside in NC.
Publications: Application guidelines; Financial statement; Informational brochure; Newsletter.
Financial data: Year ended 06/30/2013. Assets, $1,571,144 (M); Expenditures, $726,476.
Fields of interest: Visual arts.
Type of support: Residencies.
Application information: Applications accepted.
Initial approach: Letter, telephone or fax
Send request by: Mail
Deadline(s): Oct. 1 for Emerging Artist Residence; Dec. 1 for Summer Residence
Applicants should submit the following:
1) Work samples
2) SASE
3) Letter(s) of recommendation
4) Resume
Additional information: Application must also include artist statement, biography, and a nonrefundable $25 application fee.
Program descriptions:
Regional Emerging Artist in Residence: The program provides emerging visual artists with time and space to explore their work in a supportive, thriving, artistic environment. One artist in his or her early professional career is chosen from a regional pool of applicants. The organization grants two six-month residencies per year in Raleigh, North Carolina. The residency includes a private, rent-free studio with 24-hour access. Each month residents will be presented to the Triangle community during opening receptions and gallery walks. A fully-supported exhibition of the works of the two residents will be mounted at the end of the second residency period.
Summer Artist-In-Residence: The program provides an established artist with a brief studio opportunity to work on a specific project. Each summer, an artist is invited to work in Gallery 1 in an open-studio setting for six to eight weeks. During this time, the artist must teach one adult workshop and one youth class as part of the organization's Summer Arts Program. The residency culminates in a six- to eight-week exhibition of the artist's work in Gallery 1. The intent of this residency is to provide fresh insight about mediums of art and processes of art making that are not common within the organization's community.
EIN: 581450132

6561
Asheville Area Arts Council
346 Depot St.
Asheville, NC 28801-4311 (828) 258-0710
FAX: (825) 252-2787;
E-mail: info@ashevillearts.com; Mailing address:

P.O. Box 507, Asheville, NC 28802-0507; E-mail
For Kitty Love: kitty@ashevillearts.com;
URL: http://www.ashevillearts.com

Foundation type: Public charity
Purpose: Grants to emerging or established artists
who are residents of Buncombe, Madison, Avery,
Yancey, or Mitchell county, NC.
Publications: Application guidelines.
Financial data: Year ended 06/30/2012. Assets,
$224,564 (M); Expenditures, $152,546; Total
giving, $5,000.
Fields of interest: Film/video; Visual arts;
Performing arts; Music; Literature.
Type of support: Grants to individuals.
Application information: Applications accepted.
Application form required. Interview required.
  Deadline(s): Sept. 30 for Regional Artist Project
    Grant
  Applicants should submit the following:
    1) Work samples
    2) Proposal
    3) SASE
    4) Resume
    5) Budget Information
  Additional information: Application must also
    include 10 slides, video tape or DVD (no
    longer than 10 minutes), audio tape or CD (no
    longer than 10 minutes), and twelve pages of
    manuscript.
Program description:
  Regional Artist Project Grant: Conducted in
  coordination with the Toe River Arts Council, the
  Madison County Arts Council, and the Avery County
  Arts Council, this annual grant program provides
  financial support (ranging from $400 to $1,200) to
  developing arts professionals by funding a project
  pivotal to the advancement of careers as artists.
  Artists working in all disciplines are encouraged to
  apply to the program. Applicants must be at least
  18 years old and have been a resident of Avery,
  Buncombe, Madison, Mitchell, or Yancey county as
  of July 1, 2010.
EIN: 581371546

6562
Asheville City Schools Foundation, Inc.
85 Mountain St.
P.O. Box 3196
Asheville, NC 28802-3196 (828) 350-6174
Contact: Kate Pett, Exec. Dir.
FAX: (828) 255-5131; E-mail: acsf@acsf.org; E-mail
For Kate Pett: kate@acsf.org; URL: http://
www.acsf.org

Foundation type: Public charity
Purpose: Scholarships to graduates of Asheville
High School, NC. Grants to teachers of the Asheville
City School system, NC, to fund innovative ideas to
improve education.
Publications: Application guidelines.
Financial data: Year ended 06/30/2012. Assets,
$1,354,913 (M); Expenditures, $534,984; Total
giving, $246,162; Grants to individuals, totaling
$246,162.
Type of support: Program development; Support to
graduates or students of specific schools.
Application information: Applications accepted.
Application form required. Application form
available on the grantmaker's web site. Interview
required.
  Initial approach: Letter
  Copies of proposal: 1
  Deadline(s): Apr. 3 for scholarships
  Additional information: Application available from
    AHS Guidance, ACSF office or download from
    web site. Incomplete applications cannot be

considered. See web site for a complete list
of programs and guidelines.
EIN: 581836982

6563
**Asheville-Buncombe Technical
  Community College Foundation, Inc.**
340 Victoria Rd.
Asheville, NC 28801-4816 (828) 398-7900
Contact: Jayne English, Pres.
Additional e-mail: lcasey@abtech.edu
FAX: (828) 251-6355;
E-mail: ametcalf@abtech.edu; URL: http://
www.abtech.edu/foundation/default.asp

Foundation type: Public charity
Purpose: Scholarships to students enrolled in
Asheville-Buncombe Technical Community College
for continuing education.
Financial data: Year ended 06/30/2013. Assets,
$13,403,343 (M); Expenditures, $860,872; Total
giving, $395,096; Grants to individuals, totaling
$395,096.
Fields of interest: Higher education.
Type of support: Support to graduates or students
of specific schools.
Application information: Applications accepted.
Application form required. Application form
available on the grantmaker's web site.
  Additional information: Scholarships are awarded
    based on financial need and academic
    performance. Application must include three
    letters of reference and must be completed
    online. See web site for additional guidelines.
EIN: 561993458

6564
Robert G. Atkins Educational Trust
c/o Trust Tax Department
P.O. Box 2907
Wilson, NC 27894-2907 (276) 666-3103
Application address: P.O. Box 5228, Martinsville, VA
24115; tel.: (276) 666-3103

Foundation type: Independent foundation
Purpose: Scholarships to students from
Martinsville and Henry counties, VA including
children of officers and employees of Branch
Banking & Trust.
Financial data: Year ended 12/31/2011. Assets,
$868,823 (M); Expenditures, $80,079; Total
giving, $61,500; Grants to individuals, 37 grants
totaling $61,500 (high: $2,000, low: $1,000).
Fields of interest: Education.
Type of support: Employee-related scholarships;
Scholarships—to individuals.
Application information: Applications accepted.
Application form required.
  Deadline(s): None
  Additional information: Scholarships not limited
    to localities if funds are available.
Company name: Branch Banking and Trust
Company
EIN: 546426032

6565
Atlantic Coast Conference
4512 Weybridge Ln.
Greensboro, NC 27407-7876 (336) 854-8787
FAX: (336) 854-8797;
E-mail: feedback@theacc.org; URL: http://
www.theacc.com

Foundation type: Public charity

Purpose: Scholarships to student-athletes who
intend to pursue a graduate degree after
completion of their undergraduate degree.
Financial data: Year ended 06/30/2012. Assets,
$42,021,417 (M); Expenditures, $223,854,779;
Total giving, $203,168,026; Grants to individuals,
totaling $117,500.
Fields of interest: Higher education; Athletics/
sports, amateur competition; Athletics/sports,
professional leagues.
Type of support: Support to graduates or students
of specific schools; Undergraduate support;
Postgraduate support.
Application information: Applications accepted.
  Additional information: Students must
    demonstrate outstanding performance both in
    athletic competition and in the classroom.
EIN: 560599082

6566
**Edward L. Ballard Memorial Scholarship
  Fund**
c/o Wells Fargo Bank, N.A., Trust Tax Dept.
1 W. 4th St., 4th Fl., MAC D4000-041
Winston Salem, NC 27101-3818 (860)
692-7200
Application Address: c/o Wells Fargo Bank, N.A., 10
State House Sq., 2 nd Fl., Hartford, CT 06103

Foundation type: Independent foundation
Purpose: Scholarships only to graduates of
Ridgefield High School, CT.
Financial data: Year ended 09/30/2013. Assets,
$5,268,366 (M); Expenditures, $28,643; Total
giving, $25,000.
Type of support: Support to graduates or students
of specific schools; Undergraduate support.
Application information: Applications accepted.
Application form required.
  Deadline(s): Apr. 15
  Additional information: Forms available at high
    school guidance office and family aid room.
EIN: 066042949

6567
Francis M. Barnes Memorial Trust
P.O. Box 847
Williamston, NC 27892-0847 (252) 792-1799
Contact: Joseph H. Thigpen, Tr.

Foundation type: Independent foundation
Purpose: Scholarships only to residents of Martin
County, North Carolina attending higher education
institutions.
Financial data: Year ended 06/30/2013. Assets,
$2,829,146 (M); Expenditures, $174,644; Total
giving, $105,000; Grants to individuals, 21 grants
totaling $105,000.
Fields of interest: Higher education.
Type of support: Scholarships—to individuals.
Application information: Applications not
accepted.
  Additional information: Qualified applicants are
    identified by school administrators.
    Applications are then submitted to the
    trustees. Unsolicited requests for funds are
    not considered or acknowledged.
EIN: 201533095

6568
R. Aumon & Mary Scott Bass Endowment Fund
c/o Trust Tax Dept.
P.O. Box 2907
Wilson, NC 27894-2907   (703) 533-6253
Contact: Race Drake, Pres.
Application address: 306 Hudson Ave., Staunton, VA 24401, tel.: (703) 533-6253

Foundation type: Independent foundation
Purpose: Scholarships to graduates of Virginia School for the Deaf and the Blind in Staunton, VA, to attend colleges, universities, and technical and vocational schools.
Financial data: Year ended 09/30/2012. Assets, $128,713 (M); Expenditures, $10,772; Total giving, $5,754.
Fields of interest: Vocational education; Disabilities, people with.
Type of support: Support to graduates or students of specific schools; Technical education support; Undergraduate support.
Application information: Applications accepted. Application form required.
   Deadline(s): None
EIN: 541296056

6569
The Bayer Hemophilia Awards Program
c/o Charitable Contribs.
2 T.W. Alexander Dr.
Research Triangle Park, NC 27709-0144
E-mail: programadministrator@bayer-hemophilia-awards.com; URL: http://www.bayer-hemophilia-awards.com

Foundation type: Corporate giving program
Purpose: Research grants for the study of hemophilia.
Publications: Application guidelines.
Fields of interest: Hemophilia; Hemophilia research.
Type of support: Research.
Application information: Applications accepted. Application form required. Application form available on the grantmaker's web site.
   Initial approach: Download letter of intent and e-mail to administrator
   Deadline(s): None of letter of intent, Mar. for full proposals
   Final notification: May
   Applicants should submit the following:
      1) Budget Information
   Additional information: Applicants should submit a Letter of Intent describing the proposed project in 500 words or fewer. A full proposal may be requested at a later date. Individuals receiving support are asked to provide periodic progress reports and a final report.
Program descriptions:
   Caregiver Award: Bayer Biological Products annually awards six grants of up to $25,000 for educational activities in the field of hemophilia for caregivers and allied health professionals who work with hemophilia patients. The award can be used for educational seminars/symposia, mentored experiences, or training workshops.
   Clinical Training Award: Bayer Biological Products annually awards four $100,000 two-year grants to mentored physicians in training for the development of specific clinical expertise in the field of hemophilia and, if desired, research projects in the field of hemostasis.
   Early Career Investigator Award: Bayer Biological Products annually awards five $100,000 two-year grants to junior faculty members for mentored basic

and/or clinical research projects in the bleeding disorders field. Special emphasis is directed toward clinical studies; properties and delivery of clotter factor proteins; assays and models; genetic and epidemiology; and molecular aspects and mechanisms of clotting factor inhibitor formation.
   Special Project Award: Bayer Biological Products annually awards five grants of up to $200,000 for research projects conducted by individuals affiliated with facilities that provide care to hemophilia patients. Special emphasis is directed toward clinical research; basic research; assessment and intervention in psychosocial issues facing patients and their families; and assessment of quality of life and other health economic outcomes in patients with bleeding disorders and the effect of treatment modalities on such outcomes.

6570
John J. and Mildred M. Beattie Scholarship Fund
1525 W WT Harris Blvd. D1114-044
Charlotte, NC 28288

Foundation type: Independent foundation
Purpose: Scholarships to graduates of Lebanon School District, PA, for higher education.
Financial data: Year ended 12/31/2011. Assets, $277,380 (M); Expenditures, $20,708; Total giving, $15,000.
Fields of interest: Higher education.
Type of support: Scholarships—to individuals.
Application information: Applications not accepted.
   Additional information: Contact school guidance office for application information. Unsolicited requests for funds not considered or acknowledged.
EIN: 236851059

6571
Patrick Beaver Scholarship Foundation, Inc.
2425 N. Center St., Ste. 362
Hickory, NC 28601   (828) 325-0655
Contact: Angela B. Simmons, Secy. and Dir.

Foundation type: Independent foundation
Purpose: Scholarships to high school, college, university or graduate students of Catawba and surrounding counties, NC, to attend school in NC.
Financial data: Year ended 08/31/2013. Assets, $1,554,315 (M); Expenditures, $100,434; Total giving, $72,220.
Fields of interest: Scholarships/financial aid.
Type of support: Exchange programs; Graduate support; Technical education support; Undergraduate support.
Application information: Applications accepted. Application form required. Interview required.
   Initial approach: Letter
   Deadline(s): Contact foundation for current application deadline
EIN: 562048446

6572
Bethesda Center for the Homeless, Inc.
930 N. Patterson Ave.
Winston-Salem, NC 27101-1546   (336) 631-5735

Foundation type: Public charity

Purpose: Financial assistance to indigent residents of Winston-Salem, NC, for the payment of medical and living expenses.
Financial data: Year ended 06/30/2011. Assets, $2,674,002 (M); Expenditures, $859,715.
Type of support: Grants for special needs.
Application information:
   Initial approach: Letter
   Additional information: Contact foundation for eligibility requirements.
EIN: 581847103

6573
Better Health of Cumberland County, Inc.
1422 Bragg Blvd.
Fayetteville, NC 28301-4204   (910) 483-7534
Contact: Judy Klinck, Exec. Dir.
FAX: (910) 483-2157;
E-mail: information@betterhealthcc.org;
URL: http://www.betterhealthcc.org

Foundation type: Public charity
Purpose: Emergency financial assistance with health care needs to residents of Cumberland county, NC for prescriptions, vision exams and glasses, medical supplies, travel for medical appointments and other special needs.
Financial data: Year ended 06/30/2012. Assets, $356,674 (M); Expenditures, $338,586; Total giving, $95,828; Grants to individuals, totaling $95,828.
Fields of interest: Health care; Economically disadvantaged.
Type of support: Emergency funds; Grants for special needs.
Application information: Applicant must show proof of residency and demonstrate financial need. Contact the organization for guidelines.
EIN: 582082527

6574
Bicycle Man Community Outreach Center
(formerly Tiffany Pines Community Outreach Center, also known as Bicycleman Community Outreach)
624 Platinum St.
Fayetteville, NC 28311-1825   (910) 822-2034
E-mail: mosesmath624@aol.com; URL: http://www.thebicycleman.com

Foundation type: Public charity
Purpose: Assistance to children who are in need of bicycles and computers in the Cumberland area and surrounding counties, NC.
Publications: Application guidelines.
Financial data: Year ended 06/30/2011. Assets, $29,118 (M); Expenditures, $28,708.
Fields of interest: Children.
Type of support: In-kind gifts.
Application information: Applications accepted.
   Additional information: Contact child's school for application information. The school social worker at the school is the only individual who will accept the application and determine eligibility for the program.
Program description:
   Bicycle Computer Program: The foundation annually gives away bicycles and computers to children in the Cumberland county area. Eligible applicants must be fifteen years and below, and must apply through their school. A family is allowed two bicycles per family once every two years.
EIN: 562210185

6575
Blowing Rock Community Foundation
P.O. Box 525
Blowing Rock, NC 28605-0525 (828) 295-3048
FAX: (828) 295-9576; URL: http://
www.blowingrockcf.org/

Foundation type: Community foundation
Purpose: Scholarships of $1,000 to honor four Blowing Rock students for attendance at community colleges, technical schools, two or four year colleges and universities for higher education.
Financial data: Year ended 12/31/2012. Assets, $1,530,253 (M); Expenditures, $117,311; Total giving, $68,955; Grants to individuals, 18 grants totaling $33,100.
Fields of interest: Higher education; Scholarships/financial aid.
Type of support: Scholarships—to individuals; Undergraduate support.
Application information: Applications accepted. Application form required. Application form available on the grantmaker's web site. Interview required.
  Initial approach: Application
  Send request by: Mail
  Deadline(s): Feb. 15
  Applicants should submit the following:
    1) Essay
    2) Transcripts
    3) SAT
    4) Resume
  Additional information: See web site for application form and eligibility criteria.
EIN: 561515818

6576
T.A. Frank & Sallie Borden Foundation
c/o Wachovia Bank
1 W. 4th St., Ste. 6
Winston Salem, NC 27150 (336) 747-8166

Foundation type: Independent foundation
Purpose: Scholarships and loans to residents of Goldsboro, NC, who are graduating seniors of Goldsboro High School, NC.
Financial data: Year ended 12/31/2012. Assets, $27,500 (M); Expenditures, $660,012; Total giving, $648,812.
Type of support: Support to graduates or students of specific schools; Undergraduate support.
Application information: Applications accepted. Application form required.
  Deadline(s): None
  Additional information: Applications available from principal of Goldsboro High School.
EIN: 566035962

6577
Nelson P. Bowsher Foundation Trust
c/o Wells Fargo Bank, N.A., Trust Tax Dept.
1 W. 4th St., 4th Fl., MAC D4000-041
Winston Salem, NC 27101-3818

Foundation type: Independent foundation
Purpose: Scholarships to financially needy male graduates of Saint Joseph County, IN, high schools to attend colleges and universities.
Financial data: Year ended 12/31/2013. Assets, $563,342 (M); Expenditures, $31,590; Total giving, $22,500.
Fields of interest: Men; Young adults, male.
Type of support: Undergraduate support.
Application information: Applications accepted.
  Initial approach: Letter
  Deadline(s): Mar. 31

Applicants should submit the following:
  1) FAF
  2) GPA
  3) Transcripts
  4) Class rank
  5) Letter(s) of recommendation
Additional information: Application should demonstrate the applicant's creativity, imagination, and originality in any field, and including IQ rating, attendance record, and school activity record.
EIN: 356012966

6578
Boye Scholarship Trust
c/o Wells Fargo Bank, N.A.
1 W. 4th St., 4th fl., MAC D4000-041
Winston Salem, NC 27101-3818

Foundation type: Independent foundation
Purpose: Scholarships to residents of Sacramento County, CA, with preference given to those pursuing agricultural studies.
Financial data: Year ended 06/30/2013. Assets, $616,447 (M); Expenditures, $74,552; Total giving, $63,331.
Fields of interest: Agriculture.
Type of support: Graduate support; Undergraduate support.
Application information: Applications not accepted.
  Additional information: Candidates are identified by teachers and interviews are held to approve funding.
EIN: 946067623

6579
Brandt Scholarship Fund
c/o Wells Fargo Bank, N.A., Trust Tax Dept.
1 W. 4th St., 4th Fl., MAC D4000-041
Winston Salem, NC 27101-3818

Foundation type: Independent foundation
Purpose: Four-year scholarships to graduating seniors of high schools in the southern San Joaquin Valley, CA, area.
Financial data: Year ended 07/31/2013. Assets, $190,471 (M); Expenditures, $10,667; Total giving, $7,000; Grants to individuals, 3 grants totaling $7,000 (high: $2,334, low: $2,333).
Fields of interest: Higher education.
Type of support: Undergraduate support.
Application information: Applications accepted. Application form required.
  Deadline(s): Apr. 15
  Additional information: Applications available from the area high school scholastic committees.
EIN: 956053020

6580
Brewer Foundation Inc.
P.O. Box 7906
Rocky Mount, NC 27804-0906 (252) 443-1333
Contact: Joseph B. Brewer III, Pres.

Foundation type: Company-sponsored foundation
Purpose: Scholarships to residents of NC for continuing education at colleges or universities.
Financial data: Year ended 08/31/2013. Assets, $1,645,395 (M); Expenditures, $66,377; Total giving, $50,900.
Type of support: Undergraduate support.

Application information:
  Initial approach: Letter
  Deadline(s): None
  Additional information: Letter must state purpose and need.
EIN: 560941242

6581
Alton Bridges Memorial Scholarship
P.O. Box 369
Selma, NC 27576-0369 (919) 202-9811
Contact: Alan B. Hewett, Tr.

Foundation type: Independent foundation
Purpose: Scholarships to high school graduates in Wilson County, NC, for higher education.
Financial data: Year ended 12/31/2012. Assets, $244,938 (M); Expenditures, $14,408; Total giving, $10,000; Grants to individuals, 10 grants totaling $10,000 (high: $1,000, low: $1,000).
Type of support: Undergraduate support.
Application information: Applications accepted.
  Send request by: Mail
  Deadline(s): None
EIN: 566486563

6582
The Ruth K. Broad Biomedical Research Foundation, Inc.
512 S. Mangum St., Ste. 400
Durham, NC 27701-3973 (919) 385-3170
FAX: (919) 385-3103;
E-mail: RuthKBroadFoundation@mc.duke.edu;
URL: http://broadfoundation.som.duke.edu/

Foundation type: Public charity
Purpose: Research grants in the neurosciences with a specific focus on investigation that may advance the knowledge or treatment of Alzheimer's disease.
Publications: Application guidelines.
Financial data: Year ended 06/30/2011. Assets, $12,204,875 (M); Expenditures, $524,746; Total giving, $503,049.
Fields of interest: Alzheimer's disease; Alzheimer's disease research; Neuroscience research.
Type of support: Fellowships; Research.
Application information: Applications accepted.
  Deadline(s): Feb. 1
  Applicants should submit the following:
    1) Proposal
    2) Budget Information
    3) Letter(s) of recommendation
    4) Curriculum vitae
Program descriptions:
  Broad Extramural Awards: Two-year grants of up to $90,000 are available to faculty members not affiliated with Duke University for research that may advance the knowledge and/or treatment of Alzheimer's disease. Preference is given to pilot studies that can lead to more conventional funding, as opposed to continuing research.
  Broad Fellowship Awards for Postdoctoral Fellows: A fellowship award is given to an applicant in his/her first or second year of postdoctoral study at Duke University.
  Broad Research Award for Graduate Students: Stipend support, plus tuition and fees, are available to Ph.D. or M.D./Ph.D. candidates at Duke University, who are preferably in their second or third year of study at the time of application. Awards are for a one-year period and require a research report presentation at the foundation's annual board of directors meeting.
  Broad Scholar in the Neurosciences Award: This program provides seed funding (of up to $75,000

per year for two years) to high-priority, high-potential research toward the prevention and cure of neurodegenerative diseases undertaken by a Duke faculty member.

Ruth K. Broad Foundation Medical Fellow in the Neurosciences Award: This award will provide $38,000 to support twelve months of full-time biomedical research training for third-year medical students at Duke University Applicants must be enrolled at the Duke University School of Medicine, and be applying to pursue laboratory-based research (basic or translational, biomedical engineering, etc.) relevant to neurogenerative disease. Awards can be used for tuition, fees, and research allowance.
EIN: 650045051

6583
Aubrey Lee Brooks Foundation
P.O. Box 13663
Research Triangle Park, NC 27709-3663 (919) 549-8614

Foundation type: Public charity
Purpose: Scholarships to graduating high school seniors from a 14-county area of North Carolina.
Financial data: Year ended 06/30/2011. Assets, $26,168,121 (M); Expenditures, $841,688; Total giving, $726,932; Grants to individuals, totaling $726,932.
Fields of interest: Higher education.
Type of support: Scholarships—to individuals; Support to graduates or students of specific schools.
Application information: Applications accepted. Application form required.
   Additional information: Applicant must demonstrate financial need plan to enroll as full time students in a degree-granting program at NC State University, UNC-Chapel Hill or UNC-Greensboro. Contact the organization for additional application guidelines.
EIN: 566044358

6584
Brunswick Family Assistance Agency
4600-8 Main St.
P. O. Box 1551
Shallote, NC 28459-1551 (910) 754-4766
FAX: (910) 755-3313; URL: http:// www.brunswickfamily.org

Foundation type: Public charity
Purpose: Financial assistance to indigent residents of Brunswick County, NC, for utility bills and other living expenses.
Publications: Newsletter.
Financial data: Year ended 12/31/2011. Assets, $347,446 (M); Expenditures, $1,143,456; Total giving, $732,742; Grants to individuals, totaling $732,742.
Type of support: Grants for special needs.
Application information:
   Initial approach: Letter
EIN: 561309961

6585
C.A. Buck Educational Foundation
c/o Wells Fargo Bank, N.A., Trust Tax Dept.
1 W. 4th St., 4th Fl., MAC D4000-041
Winston Salem, NC 27101-3818 (650) 344-3426
Contact: Martin Jerry Magini
Application address: C/o. C.A. Buck Educational Foundation, 316 Burlingame Ave., Burlingame, CA 94010, tel.: (650) 344-3426

Foundation type: Independent foundation
Purpose: Scholarships by nomination only for higher education to financially needy students of San Mateo County, CA, schools.
Financial data: Year ended 11/30/2013. Assets, $506,351 (M); Expenditures, $30,292; Total giving, $20,000.
Type of support: Awards/grants by nomination only; Undergraduate support.
Application information: Applications not accepted.
   Additional information: Selected schools recommend students.
EIN: 946100778

6586
Burke-Weber Memorial Trust
c/o Wells Fargo Bank, N.A.
1 W. 4th St., 4th Fl., MAC D4000-041
Winston Salem, NC 27101-3818

Foundation type: Independent foundation
Purpose: Scholarships to students from Salinas Valley, CA, high schools to study pharmacy.
Financial data: Year ended 11/30/2013. Assets, $268,422 (M); Expenditures, $16,263; Total giving, $10,980.
Fields of interest: Pharmacy/prescriptions.
Type of support: Scholarships—to individuals; Support to graduates or students of specific schools.
Application information: Applications accepted.
   Deadline(s): None
EIN: 946449131

6587
Burlington Industries Foundation
P.O. Box 26540
Greensboro, NC 27415-6540 (336) 379-2903
Contact: Delores C. Sides, Exec. Dir.

Foundation type: Company-sponsored foundation
Purpose: Emergency aid for disaster relief to employees of Burlington Industries and their families residing in NC, SC and VA. The employee must have suffered a severe loss due to a disaster such as a fire or flood. Also, scholarships to North Carolina State University and the University of North Carolina-Greensboro for the children of employees of Burlington Industries.
Publications: Application guidelines.
Financial data: Year ended 09/30/2012. Assets, $1,183,692 (M); Expenditures, $265,423; Total giving, $259,125; Grants to individuals, 4 grants totaling $4,000 (high: $1,000, low: $1,000).
Fields of interest: Disasters, preparedness/ services.
Type of support: Emergency funds; Employee-related welfare.
Application information:
   Initial approach: Telephone or letter
   Deadline(s): None
   Additional information: Interviews granted upon request.

Company name: Burlington Industries, Incorporated
EIN: 566043142

6588
Alice Butler Foundation
(formerly J. D. and Alice Butler Memorial Scholarship Foundation)
c/o Wachovia Bank, N.A.
100 N. Main St., 13th Fl.
Winston-Salem, NC 27150-0001 (754) 322-6691
Contact: Maureen Steinlein
Application address: c/o Scholarship Coord., Deerfield Beach Senior High School, 910 S.W. 15th St., Deerfield Beach, FL 33461
FAX: (754) 322-6676;
E-mail: maureen.steinlein@browardschools.com

Foundation type: Independent foundation
Purpose: Scholarships to graduates of Deerfield Beach Senior High School, FL.
Publications: Application guidelines; Informational brochure.
Financial data: Year ended 08/31/2013. Assets, $9,149,915 (M); Expenditures, $589,327; Total giving, $465,673; Grants to individuals, totaling $465,673.
Type of support: Support to graduates or students of specific schools; Undergraduate support.
Application information: Applications accepted. Application form required. Application form available on the grantmaker's web site.
   Initial approach: Letter
   Send request by: Mail
   Final notification: Four months after receipt of application
   Additional information: Applications are also accepted in Creole and Spanish.
EIN: 596878169

6589
George A. Cady Charity Trust
c/o Wells Fargo Bank, N.A. Trust Tax Dept.
1 W. 4th St., 4th Fl. MAC D4000-041
Winston Salem, NC 27101-3818

Foundation type: Independent foundation
Purpose: Scholarships to graduating seniors from Valley High School, Menlo, WA.
Financial data: Year ended 12/31/2013. Assets, $93,283 (M); Expenditures, $5,460; Total giving, $1,500.
Type of support: Support to graduates or students of specific schools; Undergraduate support.
Application information: Applications accepted. Application form required.
   Deadline(s): First Fri. in May
   Additional information: Application should also include GPA, name of college or university to attend, and future plans. Application information available from Valley High School guidance counselor.
EIN: 916088092

6590
Cancer Services, Inc.
3175 Maplewood Ave.
Winston-Salem, NC 27103-3903 (336) 760-9983
E-mail: csi1955@cancerservicesonline.org;
URL: http://www.cancer-services.com

Foundation type: Public charity

Purpose: Financial assistance to residents of Forsyth, Davie, Stokes and Yadkin counties, NC, to purchase cancer-specific medications or other cancer-related needs.
Publications: Annual report.
Financial data: Year ended 12/31/2011. Assets, $1,140,924 (M); Expenditures, $989,695; Total giving, $276,254; Grants to individuals, totaling $276,254.
Fields of interest: Cancer.
Type of support: Grants for special needs.
Application information: Applications accepted. Application form not required. Interview required.
  Initial approach: Letter or e-mail
  Additional information: Contact foundation for eligibility requirements.
Program description:
  Medical and Financial Assistance: The organization provides monetary assistance to obtain cancer related prescription medications to qualified applicants. A financial interview is required. Applicants must bring proof of household income, monthly expenses, list of medications, insurance cards, most recent tax return, physician's name, and type of cancer and treatment plan.
EIN: 560656375

6591
CarolinaEast Foundation
(formerly Craven Regional Medical Center Foundation)
P.O. Box 1576
New Bern, NC 28563-1576 (252) 633-8247
Contact: Jill Shumate Thompson, Exec. Dir.
FAX: (252) 514-2874;
E-mail: info@carolinaeastfoundation.com;
URL: http://www.carolinaeastfoundation.com/

Foundation type: Public charity
Purpose: Scholarships to residents of Craven, Jones or Pamlico counties, NC enrolled as full time students in an accredited college or university pursuing a nursing career.
Financial data: Year ended 09/30/2011. Assets, $631,381 (M); Expenditures, $90,187; Total giving, $20,200; Grants to individuals, totaling $1,664.
Fields of interest: Nursing school/education.
Type of support: Scholarships—to individuals.
Application information: Applications accepted. Application form required.
  Send request by: Mail
  Deadline(s): Apr. 8
  Applicants should submit the following:
    1) Transcripts
    2) Photograph
    3) Letter(s) of recommendation
  Additional information: Application should also include letter of acceptance.
Program description:
  Joseph Hageman Memorial Nursing Scholarship: The scholarship is awarded annually in the amount of $2,250 for students pursuing a Bachelor of Science degree in Nursing or the Bachelor of Science program with a major in Nursing. A scholarship for those pursuing an Associate of Applied Science degree in Nursing is also available in the amount of $1,500.
EIN: 561991164

6592
John S. Carpenter Trust
1525 West W.T. Harris Blvd., D1114-044
Charlotte, NC 28288-1161 (800) 576-5135

Foundation type: Independent foundation
Purpose: Scholarships to students of Salem High School, NJ or a school affiliated with the Religious Society of Friends for higher education.
Financial data: Year ended 12/31/2012. Assets, $995,483 (M); Expenditures, $78,341; Total giving, $60,746.
Fields of interest: Formal/general education.
Type of support: Undergraduate support.
Application information: Applications accepted.
  Initial approach: Letter
  Deadline(s): None
  Additional information: Contact foundation for application guidelines.
EIN: 226501059

6593
Catawba Valley Community College Foundation
2550 Hwy. 70 S.E.
Hickory, NC 28602-8302 (828) 327-7000
Scholarship information: URL: http://www.cvcc.edu/stud_serv/foundation/presidential.htm
URL: http://www.cvcc.edu/about_us/cvcc_foundation/

Foundation type: Public charity
Purpose: Scholarships to students enrolled at Catawba Valley Community College, NC.
Financial data: Year ended 06/30/2012. Assets, $4,356,366 (M); Expenditures, $766,426; Total giving, $737,965; Grants to individuals, totaling $737,965.
Type of support: Support to graduates or students of specific schools.
Application information: Applications accepted. Application form required.
  Deadline(s): Apr.
EIN: 581598131

6594
James McKeen Cattell Fund
P.O. Box 91050
Durham, NC 27708-0086 (919) 660-5638
Contact: Christina L. Williams, Secy.-Treas.
URL: http://www.cattell.duke.edu

Foundation type: Independent foundation
Purpose: Grants to supplement sabbatical allowances for psychologists teaching at universities in the U.S. and Canada.
Financial data: Year ended 12/31/2012. Assets, $2,405,926 (M); Expenditures, $171,387; Total giving, $88,456; Grants to individuals, 5 grants totaling $88,456 (high: $22,500, low: $9,272).
Fields of interest: Psychology/behavioral science.
Type of support: Fellowships; Sabbaticals.
Application information: Application form required. Application form available on the grantmaker's web site.
  Initial approach: Letter
  Deadline(s): Dec. 10
  Additional information: Application should include two letters of recommendation and a institutional certification. See web site for additional guidelines.
Program description:
  James McKeen Cattell Fund Fellowships: The fellowship provides funds to supplement the regular sabbatical allowance provided by the recipient's home institutions. The maximum award is limited to the lesser of half the recipient's salary for the academic year, an amount less than half salary that will bring the total of the university allowance plus the award up to the individual's normal academic

year salary or a ceiling of $37,500. The awards are available to psychologists who are faculty members at colleges and universities in the U.S. and Canada, and are eligible, according to the regulations of their own institutions for a sabbatical leave or its equivalent.
EIN: 136129600

6595
Center for Craft, Creativity & Design, Inc.
67 Bdwy. St.
P.O. Box 1127
Asheville, NC 28801 (828) 785-1357
Contact: Stephanie Moore, Exec. Dir.
FAX: (828) 785-1372;
E-mail: info@craftcreativitydesign.org; E-Mail for Stephanie Moore:
smoore@craftcreativitydesign.org; URL: http://www.craftcreativitydesign.org

Foundation type: Public charity
Purpose: Research grants and fellowships to advance, expand, and support studio craft in the U.S.
Publications: Application guidelines.
Financial data: Year ended 06/30/2012. Assets, $298,407 (M); Expenditures, $226,876; Total giving, $110,391; Grants to individuals, totaling $78,319.
Fields of interest: Folk arts; Visual arts.
Type of support: Fellowships; Research; Graduate support.
Application information: Applications accepted. Application form required.
  Deadline(s): July 1 for Craft Research Fund
  Final notification: Applicants notified in Oct.
  Applicants should submit the following:
    1) Curriculum vitae
    2) Proposal
    3) Budget Information
  Additional information: Application should also include a bibliography of existing research on the topic, a project description, letters of support, and timeline and schedule.
Program descriptions:
  Craft Research Fund: Grants are available to: support innovative research on artistic and critical issues in craft theory and history; explore the inter-relationship among craft, art, design, and contemporary culture; to foster new cross-disciplinary approaches to scholarship in the in the craft field throughout the U.S.; and advance investigation of neglected questions in U.S. craft history and criticism. Four types of grants are available under this program: Project Grants (of up to $15,000 for research, writing, support documentation, images, or rights to use images or texts, as part of the research yet to be completed); Exhibition Research Grants (of up to $15,000, to support exhibition research related to the goals of the program); Graduate Research Grants (of up to $10,000, to support research related to a thesis or dissertation relating to U.S. studio craft by students enrolled in graduate programs in any accredited college or university); and Travel Grants (of $500 each, awarded to individuals invited to read papers relating to U.S. studio craft at the annual conference of the College Art Association).
  Windgate Fellowships Awards: Ten $15,000 fellowships are awarded to graduating university seniors on the basis of artistic merit, the future promise of the individual's work, and potential for the applicant to make significant contributions to the field of craft.
EIN: 562096677

6596
Joyce A. Chaffer Scholarship Trust
c/o Wells Fargo Bank, N.A.
1 W. 4th St., 4th Fl., MAC D4000-041
Winston Salem, NC   27101-3818

Foundation type: Independent foundation
Purpose: Scholarships for music education to residents of ID and students at ID schools.
Financial data: Year ended 09/30/2013. Assets, $934,550 (M); Expenditures, $67,759; Total giving, $50,000.
Fields of interest: Music; Performing arts, education.
Type of support: Scholarships—to individuals.
Application information:
   Initial approach: Letter
   Deadline(s): Apr. 1
EIN: 826079845

6597
Corabelle Chappell Memorial Fund
1 W. 4th St. D4000-041
Winston Salem, NC   27101   (866) 608-0001
Application address: c/o Center of Scholarship Adm, 4320-G Wade Hampton Blvd. Taylors, SC 29867

Foundation type: Independent foundation
Purpose: Scholarships to financially needy students of Keystone Junior College, PA.
Financial data: Year ended 12/31/2012. Assets, $1,174,058 (M); Expenditures, $73,771; Total giving, $48,800.
Type of support: Support to graduates or students of specific schools; Undergraduate support.
Application information: Applications accepted.
   Initial approach: Letter
   Deadline(s): Apr. 1
   Additional information: Applications must outline financial need.
EIN: 237710777

6598
Cherokee Preservation Foundation, Inc.
71 John Crowe Hill Rd.
P.O. Box 504
Cherokee, NC   28719-0504   (828) 497-5550
Contact: Wanda McCoy, Exec. Asst.
FAX: (828) 497-8929; E-mail: info@cpfdn.org;
Toll-free tel.: (888) 886-8524; URL: http://www.cpfdn.org

Foundation type: Public charity
Purpose: The Jones-Bowman Leadership Award makes financial awards to undergraduate NC college students who are members of the Eastern Band of Cherokee Indians (EBCI) and committed to developing their leadership skills. Each year they participate in the program, Jones-Bowman Fellows receive funding of approximately $4,000 for individual leadership learning plans they develop with their mentor.
Publications: Application guidelines; Annual report; Newsletter.
Financial data: Year ended 09/30/2011. Assets, $14,839,978 (M); Expenditures, $6,681,291; Total giving, $5,318,677; Grants to individuals, totaling $43,403.
Fields of interest: Education; Youth development; Native Americans/American Indians.
Type of support: Fellowships.
Application information: Applications accepted. Application form required. Application form available on the grantmaker's web site.
   Initial approach: E-mail

Additional information: A Jones-Bowman Award nominee must be an enrolled member of the EBCI, be pursuing formal academic study, enrolled in at least six hours of study during each semester of the current academic year or term, and have an acceptance letter from the academic institution he or she will attend or, if a current student, provide a copy of the College or University transcript. A Jones-Bowman Award applicant is required to: Secure 3 letters of recommendation from members of the community who have knowledge of the applicant's potential and capabilities.
EIN: 562272253

6599
Child Care Services Association
1829 E. Franklin St., Bldg. 1000
P.O. Box 901
Chapel Hill, NC   27514-5864   (919) 967-3272
Contact: Susan D. Russell, Pres.
FAX: (919) 967-7683; Additional address (Durham County office): 1201 S. Briggs Ave., Ste. 200, Durham, NC 27703-5076, tel.: (919) 403-6950, fax: (919) 403-6959; (Wake County office): 319 Chapanoke Rd., Ste. 114, Raleigh, NC 27603-3433, tel.: (919) 779-2220, fax: (919) 256-3489; URL: http://www.childcareservices.org

Foundation type: Public charity
Purpose: Payments to child care providers throughout Durham, Orange, and Wake counties, NC. Educational scholarships to child care professionals in the teach early childhood program, support to child care professionals in the teach more at four and infant/toddler programs.
Publications: Annual report; Occasional report.
Financial data: Year ended 06/30/2012. Assets, $8,487,611 (M); Expenditures, $26,433,495; Total giving, $18,891,356; Grants to individuals, 8,575 grants totaling $13,772,237.
Fields of interest: Day care; Children, services.
Type of support: Grants to individuals.
Application information: Applications accepted.
   Additional information: Contact the association for additional guidelines.
EIN: 561514058

6600
Children's Scholarship Fund Charlotte
220 North Tryon St.
Charlotte, NC   28202-2137   (704) 973-4534
FAX: (704) 973-4934; E-mail: lclarke@fftc.org;
URL: http://www.csfcharlotte.org

Foundation type: Public charity
Purpose: Scholarships to economically disadvantaged students in K-8 grade of Mecklenburg county, NC for attendance at independent schools or home school.
Publications: Application guidelines.
Financial data: Year ended 06/30/2011. Assets, $226,818 (M); Expenditures, $79,849. Scholarships—to individuals amount not specified.
Fields of interest: Elementary school/education.
Type of support: Scholarships—to individuals.
Application information: Applications accepted. Application form required.
   Deadline(s): Apr. 30
   Additional information: Application process will be on a first-come, first-served basis.
Program description:
   Scholarships: The fund provides partial scholarships to low-income families in Mecklenburg county who wish to send their children in grades

K-8 to independent schools, or who wish to homeschool their children. Eligible applicants must be at least five years old and entering grades K-8 in the school year applying, and must be transferring from a public school or a homeschooling situation, or starting kindergarten for the school year applying. Applicants must also have a household income that falls within federal free and reduced-meal program guidelines, and must reside in Mecklenburg County. Scholarships range from $500 to $2,500.
EIN: 510462802

6601
Choanoke Area Development Association
120 Sessoms Dr.
P.O. Box 530
Rich Square, NC   27869-0530   (252) 553-4155
Contact: Tyrone Williams, Pres.
FAX: (252) 539-2048; URL: http://www.nc-cada.org/

Foundation type: Public charity
Purpose: Services to indigent residents of Choanoke area, NC, such as home weatherization, emergency home repair, food supplies. Home loans are also available to participants that are in need of down payment assistance with a minimum investment of $750. Eligible participants can receive down payment assistance at twenty percent of the sales price, but not more than $25,000, deferred for the life of the first loan.
Financial data: Year ended 06/30/2012. Assets, $4,048,603 (M); Expenditures, $12,196,949; Total giving, $4,059,756; Grants to individuals, totaling $4,059,756.
Fields of interest: Housing/shelter, services; Housing/shelter, expense aid; Housing/shelter; Economically disadvantaged.
Type of support: In-kind gifts; Loans—to individuals.
Application information:
   Initial approach: Tel.
   Additional information: Contact foundation for eligibility criteria.
EIN: 560841757

6602
Chordoma Foundation
P.O. Box 2127
Durham, NC   27702-2127   (919) 809-6779
FAX: (866) 367-3910; E-mail: josh@chordoma.org;
Toll-free tel.: (866) 367-3910; e-mail for information regarding funding opportunities: grants@chordomafoundation.org; URL: http://www.chordomafoundation.org

Foundation type: Public charity
Purpose: Awards are given to cancer researchers to develop effective treatments and ultimately a cure for chordoma.
Financial data: Year ended 12/31/2011. Assets, $679,814 (M); Expenditures, $607,863; Total giving, $179,321.
Fields of interest: Cancer; Cancer research.
Type of support: Awards/prizes.
Application information: Applications accepted. Application form required.
   Initial approach: Letter
   Deadline(s): Dec. 23 for Prize for New Chordoma Cell Lines
   Additional information: See web site for specific application information.
EIN: 208423943

6603
Gordon H. & Ruth A. Clark Educational Fund
3395 Airport Rd.
PineHurst, NC 28374   (910) 695-3743

Foundation type: Independent foundation
Purpose: Student loans to needy residents of Moore County, NC, to attend a college or institution of higher education.
Financial data: Year ended 06/30/2013. Assets, $735,809 (M); Expenditures, $25,938; Total giving, $24,978; Grants to individuals, 30 grants totaling $24,978 (high: $3,000, low: $18).
Fields of interest: Higher education.
Type of support: Student loans—to individuals.
Application information: Applications accepted. Application form required.
　Initial approach: Letter
　Deadline(s): Apr. 15, Sept. 15, and Jan. 15
　Additional information: Application must be submitted on forms as prescribed by the U.S. Dept. of Education.
EIN: 566045119

6604
Cleft Palate Foundation
1504 E. Franklin St., Ste. 102
Chapel Hill, NC 27514-2820   (919) 933-9044
Contact: Nancy C. Smythe, Exec. Dir.
FAX: (919) 933-9604; E-mail: info@cleftline.org;
Toll-free tel.: (800)-242-5338; URL: http://www.cleftline.org/

Foundation type: Public charity
Purpose: Research grants for investigators studying cleft palate and other craniofacial anomolies. Scholarships to individuals with craniofacial differences.
Publications: Application guidelines.
Financial data: Year ended 06/30/2012. Assets, $1,510,626 (M); Expenditures, $319,078; Total giving, $47,500; Grants to individuals, totaling $47,500.
Fields of interest: Genetic diseases and disorders research.
Type of support: Research; Scholarships—to individuals.
Application information: Applications accepted. Application form required. Application form available on the grantmaker's web site.
　Deadline(s): Jan. 15 for research grants; Mar. 3 for scholarships
　Applicants should submit the following:
　　1) Letter(s) of recommendation
　　2) Transcripts
　　3) Essay
Program descriptions:
CCA/CPF Research Grant: Grants of up to $5,000 per year are available to junior and senior investigators. The purpose of this grant is to promote scientific research about developmental and therapeutic issues related to cleft and craniofacial conditions. The grant is designed for clinical research projects only.
Cleft Lip/Palate and Craniofacial Anomalies Grant: Grants of $10,000 are available to junior and senior investigators to encourage scientific research to evaluate developmental and therapeutic issues relating to cleft lip and palate and other craniofacial anomalies.
College Scholarships for Students with Craniofacial Anomalies: The foundation offers $500 scholarships to a minimum of three full-time undergraduate and/or graduate students with craniofacial anomalies.

David P. Kuehn Speech Scholarship for Students Enrolled in a Communication Sciences and Disorders Program or Related Field: The scholarship provides $500 towards travel expenses to the annual meeting of the American Cleft Palate-Craniofacial Association (ACPA), and $75 for a one year student membership in the ACPA.
DPMF Grant for Nurses: The program exists to assist a nurse who wishes to attend the annual meeting of the American Cleft Palate-Craniofacial Association. The grant pays for registration fees for the meeting and provides $500 for reimbursement of travel costs. Total value of the grant is approximately $1,200. Nurses who devote at least 50 percent of their work time to the care of patients with cleft lip/palate and other craniofacial anomalies and who wish to increase their knowledge of the field are encouraged to apply.
James F. Mulick, D.D.S., M.S., Orthodontic Scholarship Fund: The scholarship provides $500 towards travel expenses to the annual meeting of the American Cleft Palate-Craniofacial Association (ACPA), and $75 for a one year student membership in the ACPA.
Junior Investigators Research Grant: The grant is offered to new investigators (those enrolled in accredited graduate training programs related to the disciplines recognized by the American Cleft Palate-Craniofacial Association; those holding the academic rank of assistant professor or below; or investigators who are no more than five years past their Ph.D or specialty professional training) and has a maximum allocation of $5,000 per year. The purpose of the grant is to: aid in the development of scientific investigators who are committed to problems related to the cleft lip and palate, and other craniofacial abnormalities; and encourage scientific research on problems related to the diagnosis and treatment of cleft lip and palate, and other craniofacial abnormalities.
Karlind T. Moller Cleft/Craniofacial Scholarship for Speech Pathology/Audiology Students: The scholarship provides $500 towards travel expenses to the annual meeting of the American Cleft Palate-Craniofacial Association (ACPA), and $75 for a one year student membership in the ACPA.
Mary J. Hauk, D.D.S., M.P.H. Memorial Scholarship for Dental Residents: The scholarship provides $500 towards travel expenses to the annual meeting of the American Cleft Palate-Craniofacial Association (ACPA), and $75 for a one year student membership in the ACPA.
Samuel Berkowitz, D.D.S., M.S. Long-Term Outcomes Study Award: A $500 award is made annually to the primary author of the article judged to be the best long-term outcomes study published in the Cleft Palate-Craniofacial Journal. The author may be from any discipline represented in the American Cleft Palate-Craniofacial Association, and the article may cover any cleft/craniofacial subject area.
EIN: 251572666

6605
H. Lorens Clements Scholarship
1 W., 4th St. D4000-041
Winston Salem, NC 27101   (336)747-8176
Contact: Wells Fargo Bank

Foundation type: Independent foundation
Purpose: Scholarships to graduates of North Pocono High School in Moscow, PA.
Financial data: Year ended 12/31/2012. Assets, $332,743 (M); Expenditures, $20,940; Total giving, $14,000.
Fields of interest: Higher education.

Type of support: Support to graduates or students of specific schools; Undergraduate support.
Application information: Applications accepted. Interview required.
　Deadline(s): Apr. 1
　Additional information: Selection is based on need and performance.
EIN: 236523865

6606
Cleveland County Partnership for Children, Inc.
312 W. Marion St.
Shelby, NC 28150-5403   (704) 480-5620
Contact: Cathy Taylor, Exec. Dir.
FAX: (704) 480-5625

Foundation type: Public charity
Purpose: Assistance for individuals in the Shelby, NC area with child care and health care, and family support. Scholarship program helps provide affordable, adaptive, inclusive, child care settings and other services for children with special needs.
Publications: Informational brochure.
Financial data: Year ended 06/30/2012. Assets, $178,633 (M); Expenditures, $2,970,074; Total giving, $598,839.
Fields of interest: Libraries/library science; Education; Human services.
Type of support: In-kind gifts; Grants for special needs.
Application information: See web site for additional information.
EIN: 561875246

6607
Coats North American Educational Foundation
(formerly American Thread Educational Foundation, Inc.)
3430 Toringdon Way, Ste. 301
Charlotte, NC 28277-2576   (704) 329-5800

Foundation type: Company-sponsored foundation
Purpose: Scholarships to children of employees of Coats American, Inc., and Coats & Clark, who earn below a certain salary level, primarily in GA, NC, and SC.
Financial data: Year ended 12/31/2012. Assets, $758,148 (M); Expenditures, $60,137; Total giving, $56,993; Grants to individuals, 19 grants totaling $56,993 (high: $4,000, low: $993).
Type of support: Employee-related scholarships.
Application information: Applications not accepted.
　Additional information: Unsolicited requests for funds not considered.
Company name: Coats American, Inc.
EIN: 566093510

6608
The Coffey Foundation, Inc.
P.O. Box 1161
Lenoir, NC 28645-1170
Contact: Harriet Hailey

Foundation type: Independent foundation
Purpose: Scholarships to students who are residents of Caldwell County, NC for attendance at an accredited college or university.
Financial data: Year ended 11/30/2012. Assets, $8,226,168 (M); Expenditures, $534,506; Total giving, $391,250; Grants to individuals, 39 grants totaling $245,000 (high: $8,000, low: $1,000).

Fields of interest: Higher education.
Type of support: Scholarships—to individuals.
Application information: Applications accepted. Application form required.
> *Deadline(s):* Apr. 15
> *Applicants should submit the following:*
> 1) SAT
> 2) Letter(s) of recommendation
> 3) Essay
> 4) ACT
> 5) Transcripts
> 6) Photograph
> *Additional information:* Application forms available at high schools in Caldwell County, NC.

EIN: 566047501

6609
John F. Coffman Scholarship Trust
c/o Wells Fargo Bank, N.A., Trust Tax Dept.
1 W. 4th St., 4th Fl., MAC D4000-041
Winston Salem, NC 27101-3818

Foundation type: Independent foundation
Purpose: Scholarships to graduates of Chehalis, WA, high schools, who are U.S. citizens and demonstrate financial need.
Financial data: Year ended 12/31/2013. Assets, $683,045 (M); Expenditures, $40,348; Total giving, $26,350.
Type of support: Support to graduates or students of specific schools; Undergraduate support.
Application information: Applications accepted. Application form required.
> *Deadline(s):* Within one year of graduation.
> *Additional information:* Application forms available from W.F. West High School.

EIN: 916274936

6610
William Cullen Colburn Memorial Fund
1 W. 4th St., 4th Fl. D4000-041
Winston Salem, NC 27101 (336) 747-8164

Foundation type: Independent foundation
Purpose: Scholarships to residents of Buncombe County, NC, for higher education.
Financial data: Year ended 12/31/2012. Assets, $418,295 (M); Expenditures, $20,882; Total giving, $18,000.
Type of support: Scholarships—to individuals.
Application information: Applications accepted. Application form required. Interview required.
> *Initial approach:* Letter or telephone
> *Deadline(s):* Apr. 1
> *Additional information:* Application must include financial information, honors and awards, and extracurricular, civic, and community activities.

EIN: 566049108

6611
Harold M. Cole Scholarship Trust
130 Applecross Rd.
Pinehurst, NC 28374 (910) 693-2720

Foundation type: Independent foundation
Purpose: Scholarships to financially needy residents of Moore County, NC, or one of the surrounding counties who are attending NC institutions and pursuing undergraduate and graduate accounting degrees.
Financial data: Year ended 03/31/2013. Assets, $1,370,816 (M); Expenditures, $92,976; Total

giving, $69,194; Grants to individuals, 24 grants totaling $69,194 (high: $6,442, low: $189).
Fields of interest: Business school/education.
Type of support: Graduate support; Undergraduate support.
Application information: Applications accepted. Application form required.
> *Initial approach:* Letter or telephone
> *Deadline(s):* June 30
> *Applicants should submit the following:*
> 1) Essay
> 2) Transcripts
> 3) Letter(s) of recommendation
> *Additional information:* Application must also include copies of birth certificate, parents' most recent tax return, and acceptance letter from the college or university.

EIN: 586212292

6612
Community Foundation of Burke County
205 N. King St.
Morganton, NC 28655 (828) 437-7105
Contact: Nancy W. Taylor, Exec. Dir.
FAX: (828) 437-0433;
E-mail: info@cfburkecounty.org; Mailing address: P.O. Box 1156, Morganton, NC 28680;
URL: http://www.cfburkecounty.org

Foundation type: Community foundation
Purpose: Financial assistance to Burke County, NC residents pursuing higher education at accredited institutions.
Publications: Annual report; Informational brochure; Newsletter.
Financial data: Year ended 12/31/2012. Assets, $12,835,403 (M); Expenditures, $878,787; Total giving, $641,404; Grants to individuals, 33 grants totaling $35,950.
Fields of interest: Higher education.
Type of support: Scholarships—to individuals; Support to graduates or students of specific schools.
Application information: Applications accepted. Application form required.
> *Deadline(s):* Varies
> *Additional information:* Scholarships range from $500 to $2,500. Each scholarship fund has unique requirements, see web site for complete listing.

EIN: 562170220

6613
Community Foundation of Gaston County, Inc.
1201 E. Garrison Blvd.
Gastonia, NC 28054 (704) 864-0927
Contact: Ernest W. Sumner, Exec. Dir.; For grants: Elizabeth Biggerstaff, Admin Asst. and Grants Coord.
FAX: (704) 869-0222; E-mail: info@cfgaston.org; Additional e-mail: esumner@cfgaston.org; Grant inquiry e-mail: ebiggerstaff@cfgaston.org;
URL: http://www.cfgaston.org

Foundation type: Community foundation
Purpose: Scholarships to residents of Gaston County, NC, pursuing higher education. Grants for medical expenses only to children under 18 of Gaston County, NC.
Publications: Annual report; Informational brochure; Newsletter.
Financial data: Year ended 12/31/2011. Assets, $124,183,369 (M); Expenditures, $4,381,584; Total giving, $3,652,075. Scholarships—to

individuals amount not specified. Grants for special needs amount not specified.
Fields of interest: Higher education; Scholarships/ financial aid.
Type of support: Scholarships—to individuals; Graduate support; Technical education support; Undergraduate support; Grants for special needs.
Application information: Applications accepted. Application form required. Application form available on the grantmaker's web site. Interview required.
> *Initial approach:* Letter, telephone, or e-mail
> *Send request by:* Mail
> *Copies of proposal:* 1
> *Deadline(s):* Varies for scholarships, none for grants for medical expenses
> *Final notification:* Recipients notified in two to four weeks for scholarships
> *Applicants should submit the following:*
> 1) Essay
> 2) FAFSA
> 3) Financial information
> 4) GPA
> 5) Letter(s) of recommendation
> 6) SAT
> 7) Transcripts
> *Additional information:* Each program has its own specific criteria. See web site for additional information.

EIN: 581340834

6614
Community Foundation of Greater Greensboro, Inc.
(formerly The Foundation of Greater Greensboro, Inc.)
Foundation Place
330 S. Greene St., Ste. 100
Greensboro, NC 27401-2659 (336) 379-9100
Contact: H. Walker Sanders, Pres.; For grants: Kevin Lundy, Prog. Off.
FAX: (336) 378-0725; E-mail: info@cfgg.org;
URL: http://www.cfgg.org

Foundation type: Community foundation
Purpose: Scholarships to students of the greater Greensboro, NC, area.
Publications: Application guidelines; Annual report; Financial statement; Grants list; Informational brochure; Newsletter; Occasional report; Program policy statement.
Financial data: Year ended 12/31/2012. Assets, $146,347,903 (M); Expenditures, $13,463,983; Total giving, $11,534,146. Scholarships—to individuals amount not specified.
Fields of interest: Education.
Type of support: Scholarships—to individuals.
Application information: Applications accepted. Application form required. Application form available on the grantmaker's web site.
> *Copies of proposal:* 1
> *Deadline(s):* Varies
> *Applicants should submit the following:*
> 1) Transcripts
> 2) SAT
> 3) Photograph
> 4) Letter(s) of recommendation
> 5) GPA
> 6) FAFSA
> *Additional information:* See web site for complete program listings.

Program description:
> *Scholarship Program:* Scholarships range from $500 to $10,000 offering financial assistance to individuals pursuing education through various scholarship funds. Individuals are selected on a competitive basis, considering academic and

non-academic factors and demonstrated financial need. The funds target students from areas of interest including performance in high school, high school attended, and academic or career focus.
EIN: 561380249

6615
Community Foundation of Henderson County, Inc.
401 N. Main St., 3rd Fl.
P.O. Box 1108
Hendersonville, NC 28792-4915 (828) 697-6224
Contact: McCray V. Benson, C.E.O.; For grants: Kathryn McConnell, V.P., Philanthropy
FAX: (828) 696-4026; E-mail: info@cfhcforever.org; URL: http://www.cfhcforever.org

Foundation type: Community foundation
Purpose: Scholarships to scholastic achievers and financially needy residents of Henderson County, NC.
Publications: Application guidelines; Annual report; Informational brochure; Newsletter.
Financial data: Year ended 06/30/2012. Assets, $69,187,604 (M); Expenditures, $3,698,138; Total giving, $2,390,793; Grants to individuals, 122 grants totaling $125,787.
Fields of interest: Higher education.
Type of support: Scholarships—to individuals.
Application information: Applications accepted. Application form required.
  Initial approach: Application
  Deadline(s): Mar. 1
  Applicants should submit the following:
    1) SAR
    2) FAFSA
    3) Transcripts
    4) Financial information
    5) SAT
    6) ACT
  Additional information: Applications should include a statement of enrollment from the school. Applications available at high school guidance counselor's office.
Program description:
  Scholarships: The foundation has awarded more than $4 million since 1984 to help individuals pay their college expenses. Scholarship is primarily for students graduating or who have graduated from high schools within Henderson County, N.C. Scholarships are open to graduates of public, private and home schools. See web site for additional information.
EIN: 561330792

6616
The Community Foundation of Western North Carolina, Inc.
4 Vanderbilt Park Dr., Ste. 300
Asheville, NC 28803 (828) 254-4960
Contact: Diane Crisp, Grants Mgr.
FAX: (828) 251-2258; E-mail: crisp@cfwnc.org; Mailing Address: P.O. Box 1888, Asheville, NC 28802-1888; URL: http://www.cfwnc.org

Foundation type: Community foundation
Purpose: Scholarships primarily to western NC students for higher education.
Publications: Application guidelines; Annual report; Financial statement; Newsletter.
Financial data: Year ended 06/30/2012. Assets, $184,694,972 (M); Expenditures, $13,682,166; Total giving, $11,108,547; Grants to individuals, 150 grants totaling $346,150.
Fields of interest: Higher education.

Type of support: Employee-related scholarships; Scholarships—to individuals; Support to graduates or students of specific schools; Undergraduate support.
Application information: Applications accepted. Application form required. Application form available on the grantmaker's web site.
  Initial approach: Application
  Deadline(s): Varies
  Additional information: See web site for application guidelines. Applications also available at local high school guidance offices. Interviews may be required.
Program description:
  Scholarships: The foundation's scholarships are open to North Carolina residents who are public high school seniors, who attend the NC School of Science and Mathematics or the UNC School of the Arts High School or who study in a home school registered with the North Carolina Division of Non-Public Education. There are programs open to private high school students in Buncombe County, and a few programs open to students already in college or who are employees or children of employees of certain area corporations. Applicants must demonstrate financial need (unless otherwise noted), academic achievement or potential, history of active participation in school activities, community service, extracurricular involvement, and/or work experience, and strong moral character; additional eligibility requirements vary per specific programs. See web site for more information.
Company name: Shadowline Inc.
EIN: 561223384

6617
Robert W. Cooke Educational Trust
(formerly Robert W. Cooke Educational Fund)
c/o Wells Fargo Bank, N.A., Trust Tax Dept.
1 W. 4th St., 4th Fl., MAC D4000-041
Winston Salem, NC 27101-3818

Foundation type: Independent foundation
Purpose: Scholarships to graduating seniors of Gilliam County, OR for postsecondary education.
Financial data: Year ended 05/31/2013. Assets, $453,273 (M); Expenditures, $31,838; Total giving, $22,600; Grants to individuals, 38 grants totaling $22,600 (high: $1,130; low: $565).
Fields of interest: Higher education; Scholarships/financial aid.
Type of support: Support to graduates or students of specific schools; Undergraduate support.
Application information: Applications accepted. Application form required.
  Deadline(s): June 30
  Additional information: Applicants must be residents of Gilliam county, OR. Application materials available upon request.
EIN: 936017308

6618
Maxwell M. Corpening, Jr. Memorial Foundation
P.O. Box 2400
Marion, NC 28752-2400 (828) 652-0189
Contact: Terri Laws

Foundation type: Operating foundation
Purpose: Grants for rent, utilities, medicine, and other necessities to financially needy, long-term residents of McDowell County in Marion, NC.
Financial data: Year ended 12/31/2012. Assets, $223,681 (M); Expenditures, $624,230; Total

giving, $606,596; Grants to individuals, totaling $162,444.
Fields of interest: Health care; Housing/shelter, expense aid; Economically disadvantaged.
Type of support: Grants for special needs.
Application information: Applications not accepted.
  Additional information: Unsolicited requests for funds not considered or acknowledged.
EIN: 237201488

6619
R. Cotterel Student Loan Trust
1525 W. WT Harris Blvd. D1114-044
Charlotte, NC 28288 (800) 608-0001

Foundation type: Independent foundation
Purpose: Loans to students for attendance at institutes of higher learning.
Financial data: Year ended 12/31/2011. Assets, $821,915 (M); Expenditures, $51,960; Total giving, $35,914.
Type of support: Student loans—to individuals.
Application information: Applications not accepted.
  Additional information: Unsolicited requests for funds not considered or acknowledged.
EIN: 236907519

6620
Hugh W. Cox Memorial Trust
(formerly Hugh W. Cox Memorial Trust)
c/o Wells Fargo Bank, N.A.
1 W 4th St., 4th fl., MAC D4000-041
Winston Salem, NC 27101-3818

Foundation type: Independent foundation
Purpose: Scholarships to graduating seniors of Prosser High School, WA who are planning to either attend a community college or a trade school or who plan to obtain a certificate or degree in the area of industrial arts.
Financial data: Year ended 09/30/2013. Assets, $125,675 (M); Expenditures, $5,877; Total giving, $2,500.
Fields of interest: Arts; Vocational education, post-secondary; Higher education.
Type of support: Support to graduates or students of specific schools.
Application information: Applications accepted. Application form required.
  Deadline(s): None
EIN: 916368280

6621
Craven Community College Foundation
800 College Ct.
New Bern, NC 28562-4900 (252) 638-7351
Contact: Judy Eurich, Exec. Dir.
E-mail: fndadmin@cravencc.edu; URL: https://www.cravencc.edu/foundation/

Foundation type: Public charity
Purpose: College scholarships to qualified students of Craven Community College, New Bern, NC for continuing education.
Financial data: Year ended 06/30/2012. Assets, $1,940,003 (M); Expenditures, $622,312; Total giving, $407,511; Grants to individuals, totaling $197,732.
Fields of interest: Higher education.
Type of support: Scholarships—to individuals; Support to graduates or students of specific schools.

Application information: Applications accepted. Application form required. Application form available on the grantmaker's web site.

> *Send request by:* On-line
> *Deadline(s):* Mar. 31 for general scholarships
> *Additional information:* Scholarships are based on financial need. See web site for a listing of scholarships.

Program description:

> *Craven Community College Foundation Scholarship Fund:* This program offers financial assistance to qualified students in achieving their dreams. The criteria for scholarships vary. Some are based partly on financial need, while others are based on a student's interest in a specific field or his or her interest in further education and scholastic achievement.

EIN: 591718436

6622
Ethel W. Crawley Memorial Educational Fund
c/o Trust Tax Dept.
P.O. Box 2907
Wilson, NC   27894-2907   (252) 246-4935
Contact: Will Crews
Application address: 223 W. Nash St., Wilson, NC 27893-3801, tel.: (252) 246-4935

Foundation type: Independent foundation
Purpose: Scholarships to individuals who have resided in Halifax County, NC, for at least two years, for higher education.
Financial data: Year ended 12/31/2012. Assets, $3,450,884 (M); Expenditures, $221,279; Total giving, $154,931; Grants to individuals, 16 grants totaling $154,931 (high: $29,094, low: $480).
Type of support: Undergraduate support.
Application information: Application form required.

> *Deadline(s):* Mar. 15
> *Additional information:* Application must include copies of parents' W2 forms. Applications available at local high schools or academy office in Halifax County, NC.

EIN: 566534286

6623
Crisis Control Ministry, Inc.
200 E. Tenth St.
Winston-Salem, NC   27101-1512   (336) 724-7875
E-mail: melliott@crisiscontrol.org; Additional address: 431 W. Bodenhamer St., Kernersville, NC, 27284-2502, tel.: (336) 996-5401; URL: http://crisiscontrol.org

Foundation type: Public charity
Purpose: Financial assistance to indigent residents of Forsyth County, NC, for rent, utilities, and fuel.
Financial data: Year ended 09/30/2011. Assets, $1,091,414 (M); Expenditures, $4,627,864; Total giving, $3,361,039; Grants to individuals, totaling $3,361,039.
Type of support: Grants for special needs.
Application information: Interview required.

> *Initial approach:* Letter
> *Applicants should submit the following:*
> 1) Financial information
> 2) Photograph
> *Additional information:* Contact foundation for eligibility requirements.

EIN: 237348168

6624
Cumberland Community Foundation, Inc.
308 Green St.
P.O. Box 2345
Fayetteville, NC   28301-1703   (910) 483-4449
Contact: Mary M. Holmes, Exec. Dir.
FAX: (910) 483-2905;
E-mail: info@cumberlandcf.org; Additional e-mail: mary@cumberlandcf.org; URL: http://www.cumberlandcf.org

Foundation type: Community foundation
Purpose: Scholarships towards college and technical education to residents of Cumberland County, NC.
Publications: Application guidelines; Annual report; Financial statement; Grants list; Informational brochure; Newsletter; Occasional report; Program policy statement.
Financial data: Year ended 06/30/2012. Assets, $59,203,107 (M); Expenditures, $3,746,211; Total giving, $2,934,345; Grants to individuals, 51 grants totaling $81,500 (high: $4,000, low: $500).
Fields of interest: Higher education; Scholarships/financial aid.
Type of support: Scholarships—to individuals; Support to graduates or students of specific schools; Undergraduate support.
Application information: Applications accepted. Application form required. Application form available on the grantmaker's web site.

> *Initial approach:* Application
> *Send request by:* Online
> *Deadline(s):* Mar. 26
> *Final notification:* Recipients notified in May
> *Applicants should submit the following:*
> 1) ACT
> 2) SAT
> 3) GPA
> 4) Class rank
> 5) Essay
> 6) Financial information
> 7) FAFSA
> 8) Letter(s) of recommendation
> 9) SAR
> 10) Transcripts
> *Additional information:* See web site for a complete listing of scholarships.

Program description:

> *Scholarships:* The foundation administers over 40 scholarship funds established by donors to help residents of the Cumberland area to obtain a higher education. See web site for general eligibility criteria and additional information.

EIN: 581406831

6625
Davie Community Foundation, Inc.
194 Wilkesboro St.
P.O. Box 546
Mocksville, NC   27028-2322   (336) 753-6903
Contact: Jane Simpson, Pres. and C.E.O.
FAX: (336) 753-6904;
E-mail: info@daviefoundation.org; URL: http://www.daviefoundation.org

Foundation type: Community foundation
Purpose: Scholarships to residents of Davie County, NC for higher education.
Publications: Application guidelines; Annual report; Financial statement; Grants list; Informational brochure; Newsletter.
Financial data: Year ended 12/31/2012. Assets, $10,753,669 (M); Expenditures, $588,151; Total giving, $362,359.
Fields of interest: Higher education.

Type of support: Scholarships—to individuals; Support to graduates or students of specific schools; Undergraduate support.
Application information: Applications accepted. Application form required. Application form available on the grantmaker's web site.

> *Send request by:* Mail or in person
> *Copies of proposal:* 1
> *Deadline(s):* Mar. 12 for DCF Scholarship Program; varies for others
> *Applicants should submit the following:*
> 1) FAFSA
> 2) ACT
> 3) SAT
> 4) Transcripts
> *Additional information:* See web site for a complete listing of scholarships and application guidelines.

Program description:

> *Scholarships:* The foundation administers scholarship funds created by donors as well as its own scholarship program to benefit Davie County students. Most scholarships are for students enrolling in a two-year or four-year accredited college/university in North Carolina on a full-time basis. Some scholarships are for students pursuing a specific subject area such as education or nursing. Others have a combined emphasis on academic achievement and financial need. Eligibility guidelines and application deadlines vary per scholarship type.

EIN: 581850531

6626
R.L. Davis Charitable Trust Fund
c/o Durwood Little
P.O. Box 806
Farmville, NC   27828-0806   (252) 753-2000
Contact: Durwood Little, Secy.
Application address: 3729 W. Wilson St., Ste. 6, Farmville, NC 27828-8563, tel.: (252) 315-2870

Foundation type: Independent foundation
Purpose: Medical assistance to financially needy individuals who live within a five-mile radius of Farmville, NC, or on land owned by heirs of R.L. Davis.
Financial data: Year ended 10/31/2012. Assets, $788,211 (M); Expenditures, $34,897; Total giving, $21,561.
Fields of interest: Health care; Economically disadvantaged.
Type of support: Grants for special needs.
Application information: Applications accepted. Interview required.

> *Initial approach:* Telephone
> *Deadline(s):* None
> *Additional information:* Applications must be made in person; Information requested includes the nature of the health problem, extent of financial resources, marital and dependent status, and place of residence.

EIN: 566045863

6627
Charles E. Davis Educational Foundation
c/o Wells Fargo Bank , N.A., Trust Tax Dept.
1 W. 4th St., 4th Fl., MAC D4000-041
Winston Salem, NC   27101-3818
Application address: Sherman Country Scholarship Association

Foundation type: Independent foundation
Purpose: Scholarships to graduates of Sherman County, OR, high schools.

Financial data: Year ended 07/31/2013. Assets, $756,685 (M); Expenditures, $40,829; Total giving, $27,191.
Type of support: Support to graduates or students of specific schools; Undergraduate support.
Application information: Applications accepted. Application form required.
Deadline(s): May 30
EIN: 936170500

6628
Fred D. Davis Memorial Foundation
c/o Wells Fargo Bank, N.A.
1 W. 4th St., 4th Fl., MAC D4000-041
Winston Salem, NC   27101-3818

Foundation type: Independent foundation
Purpose: Scholarships only to Episcopal seminary students in FL for their second year of study.
Financial data: Year ended 08/31/2013. Assets, $706,820 (M); Expenditures, $44,235; Total giving, $31,000.
Fields of interest: Theological school/education; Protestant agencies & churches.
Type of support: Scholarships—to individuals.
Application information: Applications accepted.
Initial approach: Letter
Deadline(s): 30 days prior to semester.
Additional information: Application must show financial need, and include scholastic achievements. Applicants must be recommended by Dean of their Episcopalian seminary.
EIN: 596717509

6629
Emma Fanny Dietrich Trust
c/o B.B. Massagee, III
240 3rd Ave. W.
Hendersonville, NC   28739-4308

Foundation type: Operating foundation
Purpose: Scholarships to male students for post high school education who are graduates of Henderson County, NC high school and are residents of Henderson County, NC.
Financial data: Year ended 12/31/2012. Assets, $1,232,871 (M); Expenditures, $70,502; Total giving, $56,750; Grants to individuals, 28 grants totaling $56,750 (high: $2,700, low: -$1,450).
Fields of interest: Men.
Type of support: Scholarships—to individuals; Support to graduates or students of specific schools.
Application information: Applications accepted. Application form required.
Deadline(s): None
Additional information: Application should include vital statistics, financial need, and explanation of desire for further education.
EIN: 566152201

6630
Dilcher ST LN FD
(formerly Harry J. and Mollie S. Dilcher Student Loan Fund)
1525 W W.T. Harris Blvd., D1114-044
Charlotte, NC   28288

Foundation type: Independent foundation
Purpose: Scholarships to members of The Ashbury Methodist Church in Allentown, PA.
Financial data: Year ended 12/31/2011. Assets, $259,621 (M); Expenditures, $15,330; Total giving, $8,700.

Fields of interest: Protestant agencies & churches.
Type of support: Scholarships—to individuals.
Application information: Applications not accepted.
Additional information: Unsolicited requests for funds not considered or acknowledged.
EIN: 236955204

6631
Howard G. & Nancy C. Dinwiddle Trust
(formerly Nancy Dinwiddle Scholarship Trust)
c/o Wells Fargo Bank, N.A.
1 W. 4th St., 4th Fl. MAC4000-041
Winston Salem, NC   27101-3818

Foundation type: Independent foundation
Purpose: Scholarships to residents of Falbrook, CA for continuing their education at accredited institutions of higher learning.
Financial data: Year ended 10/31/2012. Assets, $458,293 (M); Expenditures, $23,880; Total giving, $14,000.
Fields of interest: Higher education.
Type of support: Scholarships—to individuals.
Application information: Applications accepted.
Initial approach: Letter
Additional information: The program is administered by Scholarship America.
EIN: 946646383

6632
Dixie Foundation, Inc.
1300 National Hwy.
Thomasville, NC   27360-2318   (336) 474-5300

Foundation type: Company-sponsored foundation
Purpose: Undergraduate scholarships to children of Lexington Furniture Industries employees.
Financial data: Year ended 09/30/2013. Assets, $225 (M); Expenditures, $14,024; Total giving, $14,000; Grants to individuals, 6 grants totaling $14,000 (high: $4,000, low: $500).
Type of support: Employee-related scholarships.
Application information: Applications not accepted.
Additional information: Unsolicited request for funds not acknowledged or accepted.
Company name: Lexington Furniture Industries
EIN: 566042530

6633
Durham Arts Council
120 Morris St.
Durham, NC   27701-3230   (919) 560-2709
Contact: Sherry L. Devries, Exec. Dir.
E-mail: receptionist@durhamarts.org; E-mail For Sherry L. DeVries: sldevries@durhamarts.org;
URL: http://www.durhamarts.org

Foundation type: Public charity
Purpose: Grants for emerging artists of Durham, Chatham, Orange, Person and Granville counties, NC.
Publications: Application guidelines.
Financial data: Year ended 06/30/2012. Assets, $520,083 (M); Expenditures, $1,620,784; Total giving, $177,450; Grants to individuals, totaling $23,010.
Fields of interest: Arts, artist's services.
Type of support: Grants to individuals.
Application information: Applications accepted. Application form required.

Send request by: Mail or hand deliver
Deadline(s): Sept. 12
Final notification: Recipients notified by the end of Nov.
Applicants should submit the following:
1) Resume
2) Budget Information
Additional information: Application should also include documentation of your art form. See web site for additional application guidelines.
Program description:
Emerging Artists Grant Program: The program is a project grant program that provides financial support to developing or established professionals by funding a project pivotal to the advancement of their careers as artists. Pivotal projects may happen at different stages of a career, therefore Emerging Artists Grants are not restricted to "unestablished" artists. Individual artists practicing any art form are eligible to apply for a grant. Applicant must be an individual, not a company, group or ensemble, and must be 18 years of age and cannot be currently enrolled in a degree or certificate program in his/her art form at the time of the deadline.
EIN: 560599829

6634
Durham Technical Community College Foundation, Inc.
1637 Lawson St.
Durham, NC   27703-5023   (919) 536-7250
E-mail: RollinsL@durhamtech.edu

Foundation type: Public charity
Purpose: Merit-based and need-based scholarships to students for attendance at Durham Technical Community College, NC, pursuing higher education.
Publications: Annual report; Grants list.
Financial data: Year ended 06/30/2012. Assets, $2,584,849 (M); Expenditures, $202,187; Total giving, $108,287; Grants to individuals, totaling $73,930.
Fields of interest: Higher education.
Type of support: Scholarships—to individuals; Support to graduates or students of specific schools.
Application information: Applications accepted. Application form available on the grantmaker's web site.
Send request by: Online
Deadline(s): Apr. 15
Applicants should submit the following:
1) Transcripts
2) Letter(s) of recommendation
3) Essay
Additional information: Contact the foundation for additional application guidelines.
EIN: 561423848

6635
Fred H. DuVall Scholarship Fund
1525 W. W.T. Harris Blvd., D1114-044
Charlotte, NC   28288-5709   (336) 747-8182
Contact: David Miller
Application address: 1 W. 4th St., Winston Salem, NC 27101, tel.: (336) 747-8182

Foundation type: Independent foundation
Purpose: Scholarships by nomination only to financially needy students residing in Swain City, NC.
Financial data: Year ended 08/31/2013. Assets, $333,840 (M); Expenditures, $17,830; Total giving, $12,000.

Type of support: Scholarships—to individuals; Awards/grants by nomination only.
Application information: Application form required.
Deadline(s): None
EIN: 566415001

6636
The Dale Earnhardt Foundation, Inc.
1675 Dale Earnhardt Hwy., Ste. 3
Mooresville, NC 28115-8330 (704) 662-8000
Contact: Teresa Earnhardt, Chair.
FAX: (704) 663-7945;
E-mail: foundation@dei-zone.com; Toll-free tel.: (877) 334-3253; URL: http://www.daleearnhardtinc.com/foundation/index.php

Foundation type: Public charity
Purpose: Undergraduate scholarships to students interested in motorsports and automotive engineering for attendance at Clemson University, SC. Awards to individuals who can identify a need or problem and have a creative solution.
Financial data: Year ended 12/31/2012. Assets, $3,956,642 (M); Expenditures, $2,125,388; Total giving, $1,981,516; Grants to individuals, totaling $7,000.
Fields of interest: Higher education; Engineering.
Type of support: Support to graduates or students of specific schools; Awards/prizes.
Application information: Applications accepted.
Send request by: Mail for Awards
Deadline(s): Dec. 31 for Awards
Final notification: Recipients notified by Mar. 1 for Awards
Additional information: Students selected to receive the scholarship will be eligible for internships with Dale Earnhardt, Inc.
Program description:
Legend Leadership Award: Grants of $7,000 each are available to individuals who demonstrate creativity and skills to bring bridges across boundaries (geographic, religious, ethnic, and philosophical) and bring together broad and increasingly diverse constituencies.
EIN: 510421279

6637
East Carolina University Foundation, Inc.
2200 S. Charles Blvd., Ste. 1100
Greenville Ctr.
Greenville, NC 27858-5235 (252) 328-9578
Contact: for Scholarships: William F. Clark, Pres.
Bill Clark's tel.: (252) 328-9594,
e-mail: clarkw@ecu.edu
E-mail: give2ecu@ecu.edu; URL: http://www.ecu.edu/ecuf/

Foundation type: Public charity
Purpose: Scholarships to high school graduates of NC who do not have the financial means to attend East Carolina University, NC for postsecondary education.
Publications: Annual report; Financial statement.
Financial data: Year ended 06/30/2012. Assets, $85,547,350 (M); Expenditures, $5,479,602; Total giving, $2,944,849; Grants to individuals, totaling $1,640,836.
Fields of interest: University.
Type of support: Scholarships—to individuals; Support to graduates or students of specific schools.
Application information: Applications accepted. Application form required.
Additional information: Selection is based on financial need and proven academic potential.

Contact the foundation for additional guidelines.
Program description:
Access Scholarship: The scholarship annual award of $5,000 ($2,500 per semester) for students, will cover the cost of instate tuition, fees and books, may be for both on-campus and distance-education students. Scholarship recipients must complete at least 20 hours of volunteer service each year through East Carolina's Volunteer and Service-Learning Center. Students must maintain a minimum 2.5 GPA.
EIN: 566093187

6638
Easter Seals UCP North Carolina and Virginia, Inc.
(formerly Easter Seals UCP North Carolina)
5171 Gleenwood Ave., Ste. 400
Raleigh, NC 27612-3266 (919) 783-8898
FAX: (919) 782-5486;
E-mail: info@nc.eastersealsucp.com; Toll-free tel.: (800) 662-7119; URL: http://nc.easterseals.com

Foundation type: Public charity
Purpose: Assistance in aiding the rehabilitation of NC children and adults with disabilities.
Financial data: Year ended 06/30/2011. Assets, $24,743,581 (M); Expenditures, $85,655,843.
Fields of interest: Family resources and services, disability; Disabilities, people with.
Type of support: Grants for special needs.
Application information:
Initial approach: Letter
Additional information: Contact foundation for eligibility criteria.
EIN: 560670676

6639
Eastern Carolina Human Services Agency, Inc.
P.O. Box 796
Jacksonville, NC 28540-4146
Contact: Daphany Hill, Exec. Dir.
FAX: (910) 347-1237;
E-mail: lgrahamechsa@earthlink.net; URL: http://www.echsainc.com/

Foundation type: Public charity
Purpose: Assistance to low income individuals and families of Onslow and Duplin counties of Jacksonville, NC to help them improve their lives by empowering them to become economically and socially self-sufficient.
Financial data: Year ended 06/30/2012. Assets, $627,185 (M); Expenditures, $5,163,272; Total giving, $3,967,391; Grants to individuals, totaling $3,967,391.
Fields of interest: Economically disadvantaged.
Type of support: Grants for special needs.
Application information: Contact the agency for eligibility determination.
EIN: 566067763

6640
Eastern Catawba Cooperative Christian Ministry, Inc.
(formerly Eastern Catawba Cooperative)
245 E. N St.
Newton, NC 28658-2647 (828) 465-1702
E-mail: ecccmdir@charterinternet.com; Mailing Address: P.O. Box 31, Newton, NC, 28658; E-Mail for Rev. Tony E. Bunton:

executivedirector@ecccm.org; URL: http://www.ecccm.org

Foundation type: Public charity
Purpose: Financial assistance to indigent residents of Catawba County, NC, for utility payments and other living expenses.
Publications: Newsletter.
Financial data: Year ended 12/31/2011. Assets, $1,269,975 (M); Expenditures, $606,734.
Type of support: Grants for special needs.
Application information:
Initial approach: Letter or e-mail
Additional information: Applicants must show photo I.D., a Social Security Card or Green card for everyone in the household, documents showing income and monthly expenses, and a document verifying address.
EIN: 560946753

6641
Eastern Scientific & Education Foundation
1525 W. W.T. Harris Blvd., D1114-044
Charlotte, NC 28288

Foundation type: Independent foundation
Purpose: Grants to individuals for orthopedic research, primarily in PA.
Financial data: Year ended 12/31/2011. Assets, $526,701 (M); Expenditures, $31,672; Total giving, $26,500.
Fields of interest: Orthopedics research.
Type of support: Research.
Application information: Applications accepted. Application form required.
Initial approach: Letter
Deadline(s): Contact foundation for application deadline/guidelines.
Additional information: Application must include financial information.
EIN: 236738070

6642
Eddy Foundation
(formerly Eddy Foundation Charitable Trust)
c/o Wells Fargo Bank, N.A.
1 W. 4th St., 4th Fl., MAC D4000-041
Winston-Salem, NC 27101-3818
Application addresses: For University of Minnesota-Duluth students: Dept. of Communication Sciences and Disorders, University of Minnesota, 221 Bohannon Hall, 10 University Dr., Duluth, MN 55812-2496; For non-University students and special situations: Edwin H. Eddy Foundation Scholarship, Northwest Bank Minnesota North, N.A., Trust Dept., P.O. Box 488, Duluth, MN 55801-0488

Foundation type: Independent foundation
Purpose: Scholarships to full-time college seniors or graduate students studying communication disorders at accredited colleges and universities. Grants also to Duluth, MN, residents, and nonresidents attending the University of Minnesota, Duluth.
Publications: Application guidelines; Informational brochure (including application guidelines); Program policy statement.
Financial data: Year ended 06/30/2013. Assets, $3,228,582 (M); Expenditures, $218,513; Total giving, $164,631.
Fields of interest: Learning disorders research; Disabilities, people with.
Type of support: Scholarships—to individuals; Graduate support; Undergraduate support.

Application information: Applications accepted. Application form required. Interview required.
 Initial approach: Letter
 Deadline(s): July 10
 Final notification: Recipients notified by June 1
 Additional information: Application should include transcripts.
EIN: 416242226

6643
Edgerton Murphy Scholarships Trust
166 J. Howel Rd.
Kenly, NC   27542-9135

Foundation type: Independent foundation
Purpose: Scholarships to financially needy students in Johnston and Wilson counties, NC, for study at an accredited institution.
Financial data: Year ended 09/30/2012. Assets, $218,134 (M); Expenditures, $13,015; Total giving, $8,076; Grants to individuals, 5 grants totaling $8,000 (high: $2,000, low: $1,000).
Fields of interest: Higher education.
Type of support: Scholarships—to individuals; Support to graduates or students of specific schools.
Application information: Applications accepted.
EIN: 561508370

6644
George Walter and Violet C. Edmonds Scholarship Trust
c/o Wells Fargo Bank, N.A.
1 W. 4th St., 4th Fl., MAC D4000-041
Winston Salem, NC   27101-3818   (941) 723-4848

Foundation type: Independent foundation
Purpose: Scholarships only to graduates of Palmetto High School, FL, who are enrolled in junior college or a four-year college or university.
Financial data: Year ended 09/30/2013. Assets, $239,512 (M); Expenditures, $16,918; Total giving, $12,100.
Type of support: Support to graduates or students of specific schools; Undergraduate support.
Application information: Applications accepted.
 Initial approach: Letter
 Applicants should submit the following:
  1) GPA
  2) Financial information
 Additional information: Application must also include college entrance exam scores, and community service.
EIN: 596804593

6645
Elizabeth City Foundation Committee
P.O. Box 574
Elizabeth City, NC   27907-0574

Foundation type: Independent foundation
Purpose: Scholarships only to residents of Elizabeth City and Pasquotank County, NC.
Publications: Financial statement.
Financial data: Year ended 07/31/2012. Assets, $3,162,876 (M); Expenditures, $206,656; Total giving, $162,950.
Type of support: Scholarships—to individuals; Support to graduates or students of specific schools.
Application information: Applications accepted. Application form required.
 Initial approach: Letter

 Send request by: Mail or in person
 Deadline(s): Mar. 15 and Sept. 15
 Additional information: Application forms available at Wachovia Bank and Trust Company and Camden High School.
EIN: 237076018

6646
Ella Mount Burr Trust
c/o Wells Fargo Bank, N.A. Trust Tax Dept.
1 W. 4th St., 4th Fl. MAC D4000-041
Winston Salem, NC   27101-3818   (864) 268-3363

Foundation type: Independent foundation
Purpose: Scholarships to individuals for higher education.
Financial data: Year ended 07/31/2013. Assets, $544,511 (M); Expenditures, $24,702; Total giving, $17,260.
Type of support: Undergraduate support.
Application information: Applications not accepted.
 Additional information: Unsolicited requests for funds not considered or acknowledged.
EIN: 223527315

6647
Rudolph Ellis Gratuity Fund
1 W. 4th St. D4000-041
Winston Salem, NC   27101

Foundation type: Independent foundation
Purpose: Assistance to financially needy families of non-office holding retirees of First Fidelity Bank, PA.
Financial data: Year ended 12/31/2012. Assets, $2,218,047 (M); Expenditures, $151,294; Total giving, $123,500.
Type of support: Scholarships—to individuals.
Application information: Applications not accepted.
 Additional information: Unsolicited requests for funds not considered or acknowledged.
EIN: 236220273

6648
Anna B. and Thomas H. Emerson Trust
c/o Wells Fargo Bank, N.A.
1 W. 4th St., 4th Fl., MAC D4000-041
Winston Salem, NC   27101-3818

Foundation type: Independent foundation
Purpose: Grants to preselected doctors in San Francisco, CA, so that they may provide medical care to arthritis patients.
Financial data: Year ended 09/30/2013. Assets, $437,804 (M); Expenditures, $20,448; Total giving, $12,614.
Fields of interest: Association; Health care, financing; Arthritis.
Type of support: Program development.
Application information: Applications not accepted.
 Additional information: Unsolicited requests for funds not considered or acknowledged.
EIN: 946058560

6649
Environmental Research and Education Foundation
(formerly EIA Research and Education Foundation)
3301 Benson Dr., Ste. 301
Raleigh, NC   27609-7362   (919) 861-6876
Contact: Bryan F. Staley Ph.D., P.E., Pres. and C.E.O.
FAX: (919) 861-6878;
E-mail: foundation@erefdn.org; URL: http://www.erefdn.org

Foundation type: Public charity
Purpose: Scholarships and grants to doctoral candidates in the field of environmental science with an emphasis on the treatment of municipal solid waste.
Publications: Application guidelines; Annual report; Financial statement; Grants list; Informational brochure; Newsletter; Occasional report.
Financial data: Year ended 12/31/2011. Assets, $7,843,775 (M); Expenditures, $1,309,598; Total giving, $604,087; Grants to individuals, totaling $54,817.
Fields of interest: Research; Waste management.
International interests: Global Programs.
Type of support: Graduate support; Postgraduate support.
Application information: Applications accepted. Application form required. Application form available on the grantmaker's web site.
 Initial approach: Application
 Send request by: Mail, fax or e-mail
 Copies of proposal: 1
 Deadline(s): June 1 for scholarships, varies for grants
 Final notification: Recipients notified in Aug. for scholarships
 Applicants should submit the following:
  1) GPA
  2) Essay
  3) Transcripts
  4) Letter(s) of recommendation
 Additional information: Application should also include relevant standardized test scores for scholarships. See web site for additional guidelines.
Program descriptions:
 Grant Awards: Grants ranging from $15,000 to $500,000 are available for research or education in topics pertaining to aspects of solid waste management, including: waste generation rates and composition; waste minimization; collection and transport; sorting, recycling, and remanufacture; disposal options (e.g. landfilling or incineration); waste or energy recovery (e.g. composting, landfill gas to energy); innovations in collection and transportation equipment development; employee health and safety; sustainability of resources; life-cycle assessment of waste management; education of corporate customers in purchasing environmentally-preferable waste services; and development of high school and college educational programs.
 Scholarship Awards: The scholarships recognize graduate students pursuing excellence in solid waste management research and education. Applications will be considered from those are or will be (by the end of the year in which the application is submitted) a full-time master's student, doctoral student, or post-doctoral researcher; and who have a clearly-demonstrated interest in solid waste management research. Awards will be based on academics, professional performance, relevance of one's work to the advancement of solid waste management science, and potential for success. Doctoral and

post-doctoral fellowships are awarded yearly for up to $12,000 each, paid monthly, and are renewable for up to three years. Master's fellowships are awarded for an amount up to $5,000 per year, renewable for a total of two years.
EIN: 521804051

6650
Evans-Moss Fund
c/o Wells Fargo Bank, N.A., Trust Tax Dept.
1 W. 4th St., 4th Fl. MAC D4000-041
Winston Salem, NC 27101-3818 (260) 461-6458

Foundation type: Independent foundation
Purpose: Scholarship assistance to children living in Fort Wayne, IN and/or attending Fort Wayne community schools, that might not otherwise attend college.
Financial data: Year ended 11/30/2013. Assets, $464,825 (M); Expenditures, $24,011; Total giving, $13,150.
Fields of interest: Economically disadvantaged.
Type of support: Undergraduate support.
Application information: Application form required.
  Initial approach: Letter
  Deadline(s): None
  Additional information: Selection is based on scholastic ability and financial need.
EIN: 356332797

6651
Evrytanian Association Velouchi, Inc.
(formerly Evrytanian Association of America)
121 Greenwich Rd., Ste. 212
Charlotte, NC 28211-2313 (704) 366-6571
Contact: Thomas Gorny
FAX: (704) 366-6678;
E-mail: velouchi@bellsouth.net; Toll-free tel.: (800) 307-4795; URL: http://www.velouchiusa.org

Foundation type: Public charity
Purpose: Scholarships to children of Evrytanian origin, based on academic excellence and financial need.
Financial data: Year ended 05/31/2012. Assets, $785,644 (M); Expenditures, $136,889; Total giving, $79,191; Grants to individuals, totaling $28,750.
International interests: Greece.
Type of support: Scholarships—to individuals.
Application information: Applications accepted. Application form required. Application form available on the grantmaker's web site.
  Deadline(s): Apr. 15
  Applicants should submit the following:
    1) Letter(s) of recommendation
    2) Financial information
    3) Transcripts
EIN: 566061036

6652
Kittie M. Fairey Educational Fund
1 W. 4th St., 4th Fl. MAC D4000-041
Winston Salem, NC 27101-3818 (866) 601-0001

Foundation type: Independent foundation
Purpose: Undergraduate scholarships to residents of SC attending a four-year college or university within the state.
Financial data: Year ended 09/30/2013. Assets, $3,004,536 (M); Expenditures, $166,154; Total giving, $118,000.
Type of support: Undergraduate support.

Application information: Application form required.
  Initial approach: Letter
  Additional information: Contact foundation for current application deadline/guidelines.
EIN: 576037140

6653
Freeman E. Fairfield - Meeker Charitable Trust
c/o Wells Fargo Bank, N.A.
1 W. 4th St., 4th Fl., MAC D4000-041
Winston-Salem, NC 27101-3818
Application address: c/o Diane Dunham, P.O. Box 2302, Meeker, CO 81641-2302, tel.: (702) 878-4466

Foundation type: Independent foundation
Purpose: Scholarships to graduates of Meeker High School, CO.
Financial data: Year ended 11/30/2013. Assets, $4,397,241 (M); Expenditures, $222,417; Total giving, $158,642.
Type of support: Support to graduates or students of specific schools; Undergraduate support.
Application information: Applications accepted. Application form not required.
  Deadline(s): None
EIN: 846068906

6654
Philip V. Fava and Nancy Owens D. Fava Scholarship Foundation
(formerly Fava Scholarship Foundation)
1525 W. W.T. Harris Blvd., D1114-044
Charlotte, NC 28288-1161

Foundation type: Independent foundation
Purpose: Scholarships to students attending Blackburn College, IL, Caldwell College, NJ, and Tufts University School of Medicine, MA.
Financial data: Year ended 12/31/2011. Assets, $1,579,357 (M); Expenditures, $98,852; Total giving, $75,000.
Type of support: Support to graduates or students of specific schools.
Application information: Applications not accepted.
  Additional information: Applications are made through institutions. Unsolicited requests for funds not considered or acknowledged.
EIN: 237149743

6655
Percy B. Ferebee Endowment
1525 W. WT Harris Blvd., D1114-044
Charlotte, NC 28288 (866) 608-0001

Foundation type: Independent foundation
Purpose: Scholarships to residents of the NC counties of Cherokee, Clay, Graham, Jackson, Macon, and Swain, and the Cherokee Indian Reservation, for study only at NC colleges and universities.
Publications: Informational brochure (including application guidelines).
Financial data: Year ended 12/31/2011. Assets, $2,963,395 (M); Expenditures, $196,022; Total giving, $148,000.
Fields of interest: Native Americans/American Indians.
Type of support: Scholarships—to individuals.
Application information: Applications accepted. Application form required. Interview required.

Initial approach: Letter
Deadline(s): Feb. 15 for scholarships and Oct. 1 for grants
Additional information: Applications made to high school principals and guidance counselors in the eligible counties.
EIN: 566118992

6656
Ferree Educational & Welfare Fund
P.O. Box 2207
Asheboro, NC 27204-2207 (336) 629-2998
FAX: (336) 629-2040; URL: http://www.ferreefoundation.org/

Foundation type: Independent foundation
Purpose: Student loans, up to $1,000, and scholarships, up to $2,000, to residents of Randolph County, NC, who have a minimum GPA of 2.0.
Financial data: Year ended 12/31/2012. Assets, $2,285,486 (M); Expenditures, $208,377; Total giving, $57,500; Grants to individuals, 28 grants totaling $57,500 (high: $4,000, low: $1,500).
Fields of interest: Scholarships/financial aid.
Type of support: Scholarships—to individuals; Student loans—to individuals.
Application information: Applications accepted. Application form required. Application form available on the grantmaker's web site. Interview required.
  Send request by: Mail
  Deadline(s): May 15
  Final notification: All applicants notified in June
  Additional information: Application must include financial information, letter of acceptance from school to be attended, and personal statement.
EIN: 566062560

6657
First Gaston Foundation, Inc.
(formerly Myers-Ti-Caro Foundation, Inc.)
P.O. Box 2696
Gastonia, NC 28053-2696 (704) 864-9242
Contact: B. Frank Matthews II, Chair.

Foundation type: Independent foundation
Purpose: Scholarships to graduating high school seniors at Gaston County High School, NC pursuing higher education.
Financial data: Year ended 09/30/2013. Assets, $9,928,059 (M); Expenditures, $558,744; Total giving, $417,524; Grants to individuals, 34 grants totaling $127,524 (high: $7,751, low: $647).
Fields of interest: Higher education.
Type of support: Support to graduates or students of specific schools; Undergraduate support.
Application information: Applications accepted. Application form required.
  Deadline(s): None
  Additional information: Application must include extracurricular and civic activities and employment history.
EIN: 560770083

6658
Stuart and Margaret L. Forbes Foundation, Inc.
P.O. Box 1146
Columbus, NC 28722-1146 (828) 254-2254

Foundation type: Independent foundation

Purpose: Scholarships to students at high schools in the Polk County public school system, NC and the Landrum public school system, SC.
Financial data: Year ended 02/28/2013. Assets, $918,337 (M); Expenditures, $64,943; Total giving, $29,000.
Type of support: Support to graduates or students of specific schools; Undergraduate support.
Application information: Applications accepted. Application form required.
  Deadline(s): None
EIN: 562079528

6659
Foundation for Good Business
P.O. Box 26762
Raleigh, NC 27611-6762 (919) 829-1988
Contact: Rufus L. Edmisten, Chair.
E-mail: info@specialsuperkids.com; URL: http://www.specialsuperkids.com/

Foundation type: Public charity
Purpose: Scholarships to deserving students of NC, who come from single-parent or foster homes.
Financial data: Year ended 12/31/2011. Assets, $429,658 (M); Expenditures, $74,946; Total giving, $52,689; Grants to individuals, totaling $52,689.
Fields of interest: Education; Economically disadvantaged.
Type of support: Scholarships—to individuals.
Application information: Applications accepted.
  Additional information: Rewards are for students from fifth through eight grade. Funds are held in trust until the recipients graduate. Students are nominated by their school. The scholarship award is $1,000.
EIN: 561647986

6660
Foundation For The Carolinas
220 N. Tryon St.
Charlotte, NC 28202-3201 (704) 973-4500
Contact: D. Brian Collier, Sr. V.P.; For scholarships: Qiana Austin, V.P., Scholarships, Community Progs. and Civic Leadership
Tel. for Q. Austin: (704) 973-4535,
e-mail: qaustin@fftc.org
E-mail: infor@fftc.org; URL: http://www.fftc.org

Foundation type: Community foundation
Purpose: Scholarships to students residing in the greater Charlotte, NC, area.
Publications: Application guidelines; Annual report (including application guidelines); Newsletter.
Financial data: Year ended 12/31/2012. Assets, $1,016,512,373 (M); Expenditures, $720,798,526; Total giving, $157,713,177. Scholarships—to individuals amount not specified.
Fields of interest: Higher education; Nursing school/education; Scholarships/financial aid; Health care; Children/youth, services; Volunteer services; Engineering/technology; Disabilities, people with; Economically disadvantaged.
Type of support: Employee-related scholarships; Scholarships—to individuals; Support to graduates or students of specific schools; Graduate support; Technical education support; Undergraduate support; Grants for special needs.
Application information: Applications accepted. Application form required. Application form available on the grantmaker's web site. Interview required.
  Initial approach: E-mail

Send request by: Mail
Deadline(s): Mar. 3
Final notification: Applicants notified in June
Additional information: Application should include FAFSA. See web site for a complete listing of scholarship programs.
Program description:
  Scholarships: Grants are provided through numerous scholarship funds managed by the Foundation. The foundation currently administers 108 scholarship programs. Scholarship funds are permanent endowments established by donors, usually in honor or memory of a loved one. See web site for additional information.
EIN: 566047886

6661
A Foundation for Theological Education
312 Blackwell St., Ste. 101
Durham, NC 27701 (919) 613-5323
Contact: L. Gregory Jones, Exec. Dir.
FAX: (919) 613-5333; E-mail: info.afte@gmail.com; URL: http://www.johnwesleyfellows.org/

Foundation type: Public charity
Purpose: Scholarships and fellowship support are available to men and women pursuing Doctoral studies in theology.
Financial data: Year ended 12/31/2011. Assets, $1,710,288 (M); Expenditures, $301,822; Total giving, $162,500; Grants to individuals, totaling $162,500.
Fields of interest: Theological school/education.
Type of support: Doctoral support.
Application information: Candidates are selected for their commitment to Christ and their academic achievements.
EIN: 752382114

6662
The Foundation of Hope for Research and Treatment of Mental Illness
9401 Glenwood Ave.
Raleigh, NC 27617-7514 (919) 781-9255
Contact: Shelley Eure Belk, Exec. Dir.
FAX: (919) 781-9621;
E-mail: walkforhope@walkforhope.com; Email for Shelley Eure Belk: shelley@walkforhope.com; URL: http://www.walkforhope.com/

Foundation type: Public charity
Purpose: Research grants to investigators aimed at discovering the causes, prevention, treatment and cures for mental illness.
Financial data: Year ended 12/31/2011. Assets, $3,281,561 (M); Expenditures, $331,472; Total giving, $118,471; Grants to individuals, totaling $108,471.
Fields of interest: Mental health, disorders.
Type of support: Research.
Application information: Applications accepted.
  Additional information: Contact the foundation for eligibility determination.
EIN: 566246626

6663
Sadie and Hobert Fouts Scholarship Fund
c/o High Point Bank & Trust Co.
P.O. Box 2278
High Point, NC 27261-2278
Contact: Ron Venable, C.F.O.

Foundation type: Independent foundation

Purpose: Scholarships to students from Davidson County, NC, who will be attending Catawba College, NC.
Financial data: Year ended 12/31/2011. Assets, $127,203 (M); Expenditures, $10,386; Total giving, $8,000; Grants to individuals, 2 grants totaling $8,000 (high: $5,000, low: $3,000).
Type of support: Support to graduates or students of specific schools; Undergraduate support.
Application information: Applications accepted.
  Additional information: Contact fund for current application deadline/guidelines.
EIN: 566481132

6664
Mary-Ann Fox Scholarship Trust
1525 W W.T. Harris Blvd., D1114-044
Charlotte, NC 28288

Foundation type: Independent foundation
Purpose: Scholarships to graduates of Lycoming High School or Clinton County High School for attendance at Lock Haven University of Pennsylvania, Pennsylvania State University (including PA College of Technology in Williamsport), Lycoming College or Bucknell University.
Financial data: Year ended 12/31/2012. Assets, $302,690 (M); Expenditures, $16,905; Total giving, $9,750.
Fields of interest: Higher education.
Type of support: Support to graduates or students of specific schools.
Application information: Applications accepted. Application form required.
  Deadline(s): Apr. 8
  Applicants should submit the following:
    1) Transcripts
    2) Financial information
  Additional information: Application should be returned to your guidance counselor or financial aid director.
EIN: 246014594

6665
Frank Family Memorial Scholarship
(formerly Simon Frank Scholarship Fund)
c/o Wells Fargo Bank, N.A. Trust Tax Dept.
1 W. 4th St., 4th Fl. MAC D4000-041
Winston Salem, NC 27101-3818

Foundation type: Independent foundation
Purpose: Scholarships to Homestead High School, Mequon, WI, graduates only.
Financial data: Year ended 12/31/2013. Assets, $2,058,947 (M); Expenditures, $174,328; Total giving, $138,250.
Type of support: Support to graduates or students of specific schools; Undergraduate support.
Application information:
  Deadline(s): None
EIN: 396270979

6666
William G. & Margaret B. Frasier Charitable Foundation
1 W. 4th St., D4000-041
Winston Salem, NC 27101 (866) 608-0001
URL: https://www.csascholars.org/

Foundation type: Independent foundation
Purpose: Scholarships to Baptist ministerial candidates at Southeastern Baptist Theological Seminary and Wake Forest University Divinity School, NC.

Financial data: Year ended 12/31/2012. Assets, $1,541,053 (M); Expenditures, $97,879; Total giving, $68,775.
Fields of interest: Theological school/education; Protestant agencies & churches.
Type of support: Support to graduates or students of specific schools; Undergraduate support.
Application information: Applications not accepted.
  Additional information: Unsolicited requests for funds not considered or acknowledged.
EIN: 566144594

6667
Fund For Human Possibility
P. O. Box 331
Chapel Hill, NC   27514-0331   (919) 967-4387
Contact: R. Terrance Greenlund, Pres.

Foundation type: Public charity
Purpose: Scholarships and grants for high school and college students of NC, for school expenses.
Financial data: Year ended 12/31/2012. Assets, $19,387 (M); Expenditures, $76,971; Total giving, $76,921.
Fields of interest: Higher education.
Type of support: Scholarships—to individuals.
Application information: Applications accepted. Interview required.
  Additional information: Students from single parent families and students who are first generation college students are given priority. Applicant must demonstrate financial need.
EIN: 561868691

6668
The Gaston Arts Council
(formerly United Arts Council of Gaston County)
201 W. Franklin Blvd.
Gastonia, NC   28053-4144   (704) 853-2787
Contact: Jan Jackson, Pres.
FAX: (704) 853-2788; E-mail: uac@gastonarts.org;
Mailing address: P.O. Box 242, Gastonia, NC 28053-0242; URL: http://www.gastonarts.org

Foundation type: Public charity
Purpose: Grants to individuals and groups of artists seeking to further their careers in the arts.
Publications: Application guidelines; Annual report; Financial statement; Grants list; Informational brochure.
Financial data: Year ended 06/30/2011. Assets, $84,349 (M); Expenditures, $190,188; Total giving, $77,592; Grants to individuals, totaling $6,200.
Fields of interest: Arts, artist's services; Arts.
Type of support: Grants to individuals.
Application information: Applications accepted. Application form available on the grantmaker's web site.
  Initial approach: Telephone or e-mail
  Send request by: Online
  Deadline(s): Sept. 20 for Regional Artist Project Grants
  Final notification: Applicants notified in Nov.
  Applicants should submit the following:
    1) Resume
    2) Work samples
Program description:
  Regional Artist Project Grant Program: This program is open to all disciplines, and applicants must be a permanent resident of the region (i.e. have resided for a minimum of twelve months prior to the deadline) of one of the following counties: Cabarrus, Cleveland, Gaston, Iredell, Mecklenburg, Rowan, Rutherford, Union or York, SC. Applicants

must be 18 years of age or older and a U.S. citizen or permanent resident. Applicants and recipients may not enroll in, or be enrolled in, an undergraduate or graduate degree-granting program during the time their funded project is in progress. Grants of up to $2,000 per artist will be awarded.
EIN: 561257449

6669
Gaston College Foundation, Inc.
201 Hwy. 321 S.
Dallas, NC   28034-1402   (704) 922-6511
Contact: Julia Allen, Exec. Dir.
FAX: (704) 922-2329;
E-mail: gcfoundation@gaston.edu; URL: http://www.gaston.edu/aboutus/foundation.php

Foundation type: Public charity
Purpose: Scholarships to students attending Gaston College, NC.
Publications: Application guidelines.
Financial data: Year ended 06/30/2012. Assets, $9,947,513 (M); Expenditures, $1,614,995; Total giving, $290,491; Grants to individuals, totaling $116,933. Subtotal for scholarships—to individuals: grants totaling $116,933.
Fields of interest: College.
Type of support: Support to graduates or students of specific schools.
Application information: Applications accepted. Application form required. Application form available on the grantmaker's web site.
  Send request by: On-line
  Deadline(s): May
Program description:
  Gaston College Foundation Scholarship: The foundation provides scholarships to students who are eligible for admission at Gaston College and have completed a FAFSA.
EIN: 237079454

6670
Gate City Golf Association Foundation, Inc.
P.O. Box 20185
Greensboro, NC   27420
URL: http://www.gatecitygolf.org/home.htm

Foundation type: Operating foundation
Purpose: College scholarships to underprivileged minority students in the Guilford county, NC area for continuing education at accredited colleges or universities.
Financial data: Year ended 12/31/2010. Assets, $7,844 (M); Expenditures, $8,497; Total giving, $8,000; Grants to individuals, 4 grants totaling $8,000 (high: $2,000, low: $2,000).
Fields of interest: Higher education; Minorities; Economically disadvantaged.
Type of support: Scholarships—to individuals.
Application information: Applications accepted. Application form required.
  Deadline(s): Apr.
  Applicants should submit the following:
    1) Transcripts
    2) Letter(s) of recommendation
    3) Essay
EIN: 562247301

6671
Harold C. Gift Scholarship Trust
1525 W. W.T. Harris Blvd. D1114-044
Charlotte, NC   28288   (866) 608-0001
Application address: c/o Center for Scholarship Adm., c/o Sally King, 4320-G Wade Hampton Blvd., Taylors, SC 29687 tel: (866) 608-0001

Foundation type: Independent foundation
Purpose: Scholarship to graduating seniors of Reading High School, in Reading PA, to attend colleges or universities in PA.
Financial data: Year ended 12/31/2012. Assets, $1,653,516 (M); Expenditures, $98,081; Total giving, $72,760.
Type of support: Support to graduates or students of specific schools; Undergraduate support.
Application information: Applications accepted. Application form required.
EIN: 236524243

6672
Edwin Gilbert Trust - Georgetown School Fund
1525 W. W.T. Harris Blvd., D1114-044
Charlotte, NC   28288   (203) 744-5000
Contact: Jim Driscoll III
Application Address: P.O. Box 248, Bethel, CT 06801

Foundation type: Independent foundation
Purpose: Scholarships to individuals living in the area known as the Tenth School District in Redding, Weston, and Wilton, CT.
Financial data: Year ended 12/31/2011. Assets, $492,217 (M); Expenditures, $29,281; Total giving, $18,000; Grants to individuals, totaling $18,000.
Fields of interest: Higher education.
Type of support: Scholarships—to individuals; Support to graduates or students of specific schools.
Application information: Applications accepted. Application form required.
  Initial approach: Letter
  Deadline(s): May 1
  Additional information: Contact the trustee for additional application guidelines.
EIN: 066044834

6673
The Lucille P. and Edward C. Giles Foundation
(formerly The Edward C. Giles Foundation)
2115 Rexford Rd.
Charlotte, NC   28211-5453

Foundation type: Independent foundation
Purpose: Scholarships only to children of employees of Carauster Industries, Inc. and its subsidiaries.
Financial data: Year ended 12/31/2011. Assets, $15,842,305 (M); Expenditures, $1,059,247; Total giving, $848,849.
Type of support: Employee-related scholarships.
Application information: Applications not accepted.
  Additional information: Unsolicited request for funds not considered or acknowledged.
Company name: Carauster Industries, Incorporated
EIN: 581450874

6674
The Clyde O. Ginder Memorial Foundation
c/o Wells Fargo Bank, N.A.
1 W. 4th St., 4th Fl. MAC D4000-041
Winston Salem, NC   27101-3818   (888) 730-4933

Foundation type: Independent foundation
Purpose: Scholarships to high school graduates who are U.S. citizens and members of the Mount Pleasant United Methodist Church in Butler, IN.
Financial data: Year ended 06/30/2013. Assets, $475,498 (M); Expenditures, $18,660; Total giving, $9,900.
Fields of interest: Protestant agencies & churches.
Type of support: Scholarships—to individuals.
Application information: Applications accepted. Application form required.
   Deadline(s): None
   Applicants should submit the following:
      1) Transcripts
      2) Financial information
EIN: 356484641

6675
Girl Scouts Hornets' Nest Council
7007 Idlewild Rd.
Charlotte, NC   28212-5751   (704) 731-6500
Contact: Sally Daley, C.E.O.
FAX: (704) 567-0598;
E-mail: development@hngirlscouts.org; Toll-Free Tel.: (800) 868-0528; E-mail For Sally Daley: sdaley@hngirlscouts.org; URL: http://www.hngirlscouts.org

Foundation type: Public charity
Purpose: Scholarships and financial assistance to graduating Senior Girl Scouts of NC for attendance at institutions of higher learning.
Publications: Application guidelines.
Financial data: Year ended 12/31/2012. Assets, $15,343,402 (M); Expenditures, $3,682,518; Total giving, $119,578; Grants to individuals, totaling $69,578.
Fields of interest: Girl scouts.
Type of support: Scholarships—to individuals.
Application information: Applications accepted. Application form required. Application form available on the grantmaker's web site. Interview required.
   Send request by: Mail or hand delivered
   Deadline(s): Mar. 12
   Final notification: Recipients notified Apr. 30
   Applicants should submit the following:
      1) Class rank
      2) Letter(s) of recommendation
      3) Essay
   Additional information: Applicants must demonstrate academic excellence.
EIN: 560563842

6676
The Giving Hand Foundation, Inc.
4314 Wyo Rd.
Yadkinville, NC   27055-8728   (336) 463-5179
Contact: Alden K. Phillips, Pres.
E-mail: givinghand@yadtel.net; URL: http://www.givinghand.info

Foundation type: Public charity
Purpose: Medical assistance payments for dental services to low-income individuals living in Yadkin County, NC and surrounding areas.
Financial data: Year ended 06/30/2012. Assets, $70,624 (M); Expenditures, $247,548.

Fields of interest: Volunteer services; Health care, clinics/centers; Dental care; Economically disadvantaged.
Type of support: Grants for special needs.
Application information: Contact foundation for further program and application information.
EIN: 562256522

6677
Good Shepherd Foundation Inc.
6244 Hwy., 55 W.
Kinston, NC   28504-7435   (252) 569-3241
Contact: Sue White, Secy.-Treas.

Foundation type: Independent foundation
Purpose: Assistance in paying medical expenses for needy residents of Trent Township, NC.
Financial data: Year ended 11/30/2013. Assets, $16,313 (M); Expenditures, $7,707; Total giving, $5,500; Grants to individuals, 2 grants totaling $5,500 (high: $3,000, low: $2,500).
Fields of interest: Health care.
Type of support: Grants for special needs.
Application information: Applications accepted. Application form required.
   Initial approach: Letter
   Deadline(s): None
EIN: 510175676

6678
Billy Graham Evangelistic Association
1 Billy Graham Pkwy.
Charlotte, NC   28201-0001   (704) 401-2432
Toll-free tel.: (877) 247-2426; URL: http://www.billygraham.org

Foundation type: Public charity
Purpose: Scholarships to pastors, seminary students and Christian leaders to cover cost for evangelistic and discipleship training. Scholarships also to financially needy pastors or church leaders to assist with the cost to attend an evangelistic seminar.
Publications: Annual report.
Financial data: Year ended 12/31/2011. Assets, $199,503,614 (M); Expenditures, $93,738,957; Total giving, $1,425,357; Grants to individuals, totaling $209,495.
Fields of interest: Christian agencies & churches; Religion.
Type of support: Scholarships—to individuals.
Application information: Applications not accepted.
   Additional information: Unsolicited requests for funds not considered or acknowledged.
EIN: 410692230

6679
Gramberg-Millner Scholarship Fund
c/o Wells Fargo Bank N.A. Trust Tax Dept.
1 W. 4th St., 4th Fl. MAC D4000-041
Winston Salem, NC   27101-3818   (605) 394-3896

Foundation type: Independent foundation
Purpose: Scholarships to residents of rural Pennington County in the area west of the Cheyenne River or rural Custer County, SD, who plan to attend a college, university, or nursing school in SD.
Financial data: Year ended 11/30/2013. Assets, $196,782 (M); Expenditures, $8,415; Total giving, $0.
Fields of interest: Nursing school/education.
Type of support: Undergraduate support.
Application information: Application form required.

Applicants should submit the following:
   1) Class rank
   2) GPA
   3) ACT
EIN: 466018116

6680
Stella O. Gray Scholarship Fund
c/o Trust Tax Dept.
P.O. Box 2907
Wilson, NC   27894-2907   (252) 448-2451
Application address: c/o Jones Central High School, Attn.: Principal, 1490 Hwy. 58 S., Trenton, NC 28585-7644, tel.: (252) 448-2451

Foundation type: Independent foundation
Purpose: College scholarship for students of Jones Central High School, residing in Jones County, NC for higher education.
Financial data: Year ended 06/30/2013. Assets, $95,256 (M); Expenditures, $7,115; Total giving, $5,000.
Fields of interest: Higher education.
Type of support: Support to graduates or students of specific schools.
Application information:
   Deadline(s): None
EIN: 566114935

6681
Greensboro Urban Ministry, Inc.
305 W. Lee St.
Greensboro, NC   27406-1240   (336) 271-5959
FAX: (336) 271-5926; E-mail: info@guministry.org; E-mail For Rev. Mike Aiken: aiken@guministry.org; URL: http://greensborourbanministry.org

Foundation type: Public charity
Purpose: Financial assistance to indigent residents of the Guildford County, NC, for living expenses.
Publications: Annual report; Informational brochure; Newsletter.
Financial data: Year ended 06/30/2012. Assets, $10,692,089 (M); Expenditures, $5,227,651; Total giving, $2,408,428; Grants to individuals, totaling $2,408,428.
Type of support: Grants for special needs.
Application information:
   Initial approach: Telephone
   Additional information: Applicant must provide referral from a human service agency, photo ID, Social Security cards for all members of the household, and lease or mortgage verification. Contact foundation for complete eligibility requirements.
EIN: 560890545

6682
The Greater Greenville Foundation, Inc.
625-Suite A, Lynndale Court
P.O. Box 20154
Greenville, NC   27858   (252) 756-8549
Contact: For grants: Charlene Silver, Donor Svcs. Mgr.
FAX: (252) 756-8549;
E-mail: charlene.ggcf@gmail.com; URL: http://www.ggcfnc.org

Foundation type: Community foundation
Purpose: Scholarships to high school students in the greater Greenville, NC area.
Publications: Application guidelines; Financial statement; Grants list; Informational brochure.

Financial data: Year ended 12/31/2012. Assets, $8,107,077 (M); Expenditures, $1,258,143; Total giving, $738,259.
Fields of interest: Higher education.
Type of support: Scholarships—to individuals; Undergraduate support.
Application information: Applications accepted.
   Initial approach: Telephone or e-mail
EIN: 562152669

6683
Virginia S. Grim Educational Fund
c/o Wells Fargo Bank, N.A.
1 W.4th St. 4th Fl.Mac D4000-041
Winston Salem, NC   27101-3818
Application Address: c/o center for Scholarship, 4321 Wade Hampton Blvd.Ste.G Taylors,SG 29687
E-mail: ljenkinscsa@bellsouth.net

Foundation type: Independent foundation
Purpose: Educational loans to students in the Winchester, VA, area only.
Financial data: Year ended 07/31/2013. Assets, $1,059,531 (M); Expenditures, $61,192; Total giving, $43,335.
Type of support: Student loans—to individuals.
Application information: Applications accepted.
Application form required. Interview required.
   Deadline(s): May 1
   Additional information: Application must also include three references, statement form filled out by school, and personal financial statement. Applications are not mailed.
EIN: 546046865

6684
Grimley Scholarship Trust
1525 W. W.T. Harris Blvd. D1114-044
Charlotte, NC   28288   (866) 608-0001

Foundation type: Independent foundation
Purpose: Scholarships to members of the top half graduating class of Kutztown Area High School, PA.
Financial data: Year ended 12/31/2011. Assets, $503,445 (M); Expenditures, $33,501; Total giving, $24,000.
Type of support: Support to graduates or students of specific schools; Undergraduate support.
Application information: Applications not accepted.
   Additional information: Unsolicited requests for funds not considered or accepted.
EIN: 236408183

6685
Mary S. Groff Scholarship Trust
1 W. 4th St., D4000-041
Winston Salem, NC   27101   (717) 684-7500
Application Address: c/o Columbia High School, 901 Ironville Pike St.Columbia, PA 17512

Foundation type: Independent foundation
Purpose: Scholarships to graduates of Columbia High School, PA.
Financial data: Year ended 12/31/2012. Assets, $200,829 (M); Expenditures, $10,784; Total giving, $9,000.
Type of support: Support to graduates or students of specific schools; Undergraduate support.
Application information: Applications not accepted.
   Additional information: Unsolicited requests for funds not considered or acknowledged.
EIN: 236479982

6686
The Beverly W. and Mabel Tudor Grogan Educational Fund
c/o Trust Tax Dept
P.O. Box 2907
Wilson, NC   27894-2907   (276) 694-7137
Contact: Priscilla Diggs
Application address: c/o Patrick County High School, 215 Cougar Ln., Stuart, VA 24171-4519

Foundation type: Independent foundation
Purpose: Scholarships and educational loans to students at Patrick County High School, VA.
Financial data: Year ended 10/31/2012. Assets, $741,132 (M); Expenditures, $31,415; Total giving, $13,500; Grants to individuals, 10 grants totaling $13,500 (high: $2,000, low: $1,000).
Type of support: Support to graduates or students of specific schools; Undergraduate support.
Application information: Applications accepted.
Application form required.
   Deadline(s): Mar. 1
EIN: 541511938

6687
Roland Gross Memorial Scholarship Fund
c/o Wells Fargo Bank, N.A.
1 W.4th St. 4th Fl.Mac D4000-041
Winston Salem, NC   27101-3818

Foundation type: Independent foundation
Purpose: Scholarships to individuals for attendance at University of Nebraska and Hastings College in Nebraska.
Financial data: Year ended 07/31/2013. Assets, $575,009 (M); Expenditures, $54,485; Total giving, $44,628; Grant to an individual, 1 grant totaling $44,628.
Fields of interest: Higher education.
Type of support: Scholarships—to individuals; Support to graduates or students of specific schools.
Application information: Applications not accepted.
   Additional information: Unsolicited requests for funds not considered or acknowledged.
EIN: 396779410

6688
George Grotefend Scholarship Fund
c/o Wells Fargo Bank, N.A., Trust Tax Dept.
1 W. 4th St., 4th Fl., MAC D4000-041
Winston Salem, NC   27101-3818   (530) 225-0330

Foundation type: Independent foundation
Purpose: Graduate and undergraduate scholarships to financially needy students who attended high school in Shasta County, CA.
Financial data: Year ended 04/30/2013. Assets, $1,093,196 (M); Expenditures, $71,988; Total giving, $54,000.
Type of support: Support to graduates or students of specific schools; Graduate support; Undergraduate support.
Application information: Applications accepted.
Application form required.
   Deadline(s): May 1
EIN: 946069688

6689
Simon Guggenheim Scholarship Fund
1525 W. WT Harris Blvd., D1114-044
Charlotte, NC   28288   (866) 608-0001
Tel.: (866) 608-0001

Foundation type: Independent foundation
Purpose: Scholarships to seniors of Central High School in Philadelphia, PA.
Financial data: Year ended 12/31/2011. Assets, $959,854 (M); Expenditures, $44,099; Total giving, $37,000.
Type of support: Support to graduates or students of specific schools; Undergraduate support.
Application information: Applications accepted.
Application form required.
   Deadline(s): None
EIN: 236219173

6690
Guilford Child Development, Inc.
1200 Arlington St.
Greensboro, NC   27406-1421   (336) 378-7700
Contact: C. Robin Britt, Exec. Dir.
FAX: (336) 378-7708;
E-mail: info@guilfordchilddev.org; E-Mail for C. Robin Britt: robinbritt@guilfordchilddev.org;
URL: http://www.guilfordchilddev.org

Foundation type: Public charity
Purpose: Financial assistance to individuals of Guilford county, NC for child care services.
Financial data: Year ended 12/31/2011. Assets, $9,850,349 (M); Expenditures, $17,821,894; Total giving, $2,647,033; Grants to individuals, totaling $2,599,747.
Fields of interest: Day care; Child development, services.
Type of support: Grants for special needs.
Application information: Individuals must show need based on an income evaluation which takes into consideration employment records, child support, and other sources of income that could be used to pay for a child. See web site for additional information.
EIN: 560863474

6691
Tom Haggai and Associates Foundation
(also known as THA Foundation)
200 North Main St., Ste. 200
High Point, NC   27260-5010   (336) 882-0810
Contact: Mary Helen Potts, Exe. Dir.

Foundation type: Public charity
Purpose: Scholarships to non-traditional (or career switcher) students pursuing a teaching career particularly in grades K-6.
Financial data: Year ended 06/30/2012. Assets, $2,578,012 (M); Expenditures, $320,848; Total giving, $262,000.
Fields of interest: Higher education.
Type of support: Scholarships—to individuals.
Application information: Applications accepted.
Application form required. Interview required.
   Deadline(s): Mar. 16
   Applicants should submit the following:
      1) Financial information
      2) Letter(s) of recommendation
      3) GPA
   Additional information: Application should also include proof of being a documented career switcher, evidence that you have been employed in a profession outside of education for at least one year or are still currently employed outside of education and making

the switch, a one page (maximum) statement of financial impact addressing how the scholarship support will make a difference and providing evidence of economic need for the scholarship to continue your education, a one to two page personal statement sharing why you have chosen to become a teacher, your educational goals, and how your personal and professional goals are consistent with those of the foundation.

EIN: 560794896

6692
The Halstead Foundation, Inc.

P.O. Box 9983
Greensboro, NC 27404

Foundation type: Company-sponsored foundation
Purpose: Scholarships to residents of Greensboro, NC, pursuing a career in business.
Financial data: Year ended 12/31/2011. Assets, $1,372,322 (M); Expenditures, $105,495; Total giving, $56,677.
Fields of interest: Business school/education.
Type of support: Scholarships—to individuals.
Application information: Applications accepted.
　Deadline(s): Apr.
　Additional information: Unsolicited requests for
　　funds not considered or acknowledged.
EIN: 581821220

6693
Michael Harasimik Trust

c/o Wells Fargo Bank N.A.
1 W. 4th Fl. MAC D4000-041
Winston Salem, NC 27101-3818 (336) 747-8203

Foundation type: Independent foundation
Purpose: Scholarships to members of St. Vladimer Ukrainian Catholic Church, NJ, attending an institution for higher education.
Financial data: Year ended 03/31/2013. Assets, $1,449,480 (M); Expenditures, $66,191; Total giving, $43,900.
Fields of interest: Higher education; Formal/general education.
Type of support: Scholarships—to individuals.
Application information: Applications accepted.
　Initial approach: Letter
　Deadline(s): None
　Additional information: Application must include
　　transcripts.
EIN: 226362831

6694
Giles Harmon Memorial Scholarship Fund

(formerly Giles Arthur Harmon Memorial Scholarship Fund, Inc.)
600 Tunnel Rd.
Asheville, NC 28805 (828) 298-4253
Contact: Zeb Stroup, Dir.

Foundation type: Independent foundation
Purpose: Scholarships to students from Transylvania county, NC for continuing education in one of the criminal justice related areas at a community college, university or other institution of higher learning.
Financial data: Year ended 12/31/2012. Assets, $78,059 (M); Expenditures, $4,181; Total giving, $4,000; Grant to an individual, 1 grant totaling $4,000.
Fields of interest: Higher education; Formal/general education.

Type of support: Scholarships—to individuals.
Application information: Interview required.
　Additional information: Awards are based on
　　scholastic aptitude, application content, and
　　financial need. Students submit their
　　applications to the board of directors prior to
　　high school graduation through their high
　　school principal's office.
EIN: 581807222

6695
Henrietta Harris and Sable Bernstein Fund

(formerly The Sadie Bernstine and Henrietta Harris Scholarship Fund)
1525 W. WT Harris Blvd., D1114-044
Charlotte, NC 28288-1161

Foundation type: Independent foundation
Purpose: Scholarships to Jewish graduating seniors from Atlantic City High School, NJ.
Financial data: Year ended 09/30/2013. Assets, $1,341,097 (M); Expenditures, $148,029; Total giving, $122,750.
Fields of interest: Jewish agencies & synagogues.
Type of support: Support to graduates or students of specific schools; Undergraduate support.
Application information: Applications not accepted.
　Additional information: Unsolicited requests for
　　funds not considered or acknowledged.
EIN: 226347842

6696
Henderson County Education Foundation, Inc.

P. O. Box 1267
Hendersonville, NC 28793-1267 (828) 698-8884
Contact: Graham R. Fields, Pres.
FAX: (828) 698-8850; E-mail: hcef@bellsouth.net; URL: http://www.hcef.info/

Foundation type: Public charity
Purpose: Scholarships and grants to students and teachers from the Henderson County Public School System, NC for programs and activities.
Publications: Annual report; Informational brochure.
Financial data: Year ended 06/30/2012. Assets, $1,402,261 (M); Expenditures, $334,138; Total giving, $71,772; Grants to individuals, totaling $71,772.
Fields of interest: Higher education; Education.
Type of support: Grants to individuals; Scholarships—to individuals; Support to graduates or students of specific schools.
Application information: Applications accepted.
　Deadline(s): Feb. for Teacher Grants
　Additional information: Scholarship selection is
　　based on need or merit. Each scholarship has
　　its own set of eligibility criteria. See web site
　　for a complete listing of scholarships, and
　　guidelines for teacher grant.
EIN: 581734733

6697
George R. Hess Educational Fund Trust

(also known as Hazel Porter Hess and George R. Hess Educational Trust)
1 W 4th St., D4000-041
Winston Salem, NC 27101 (868) 608-0001
Contact: Sally King
Application Address: c/o Center for Scholarship ADM, 4320 -G Wade Hampton Blvd., Taylors, SC 29867

Foundation type: Independent foundation
Purpose: Scholarships to graduating seniors who have been residents for two years of Loudoun County and Loudoun Valley high schools, VA.
Financial data: Year ended 12/31/2012. Assets, $485,446 (M); Expenditures, $24,225; Total giving, $14,000.
Type of support: Support to graduates or students of specific schools; Undergraduate support.
Application information: Applications accepted.
　Deadline(s): Feb. 15
　Additional information: Application guidelines are
　　available at Loudoun County and Loudoun
　　Valley high schools.
EIN: 546200977

6698
Greater Hickory Cooperative Christian Ministry

31 1st Ave. S.E.
Hickory, NC 28602-3003 (828) 327-0979
FAX: (828) 327-9102; URL: http://www.ccmhickory.com/

Foundation type: Public charity
Purpose: Financial assistance and food distribution to individuals who are eligible, throughout Catawba County, NC. Assistance to unemployed, underemployed and indigent residents with crisis relief, support, and education, as well as health care and food.
Financial data: Year ended 12/31/2011. Assets, $3,875,915 (M); Expenditures, $8,790,238; Total giving, $7,748,294; Grants to individuals, totaling $7,748,294.
Fields of interest: Food services; Family services; Human services, emergency aid; Human services.
Type of support: Emergency funds; In-kind gifts; Grants for special needs.
Application information: Applications accepted. Application form required. Application form available on the grantmaker's web site.
　Initial approach: Submit application
　Deadline(s): None
　Additional information: See web site for
　　additional guidelines.
EIN: 560934855

6699
Helen Reber Hilton Trust

1525 W W.T. Harris Blvd. D1114-044
Charlotte, NC 28288-1161 (866) 608-0001
Application address:
WWW.CSASCHOLARS.ORGTAYLORS, SC 29687

Foundation type: Independent foundation
Purpose: Scholarships to students who are residents of the City of Pottsville, PA, to attend any accredited public or private college, university or other institution for higher education.
Financial data: Year ended 12/31/2011. Assets, $2,044,531 (M); Expenditures, $143,151; Total giving, $112,830.
Fields of interest: Higher education.
Type of support: Scholarships—to individuals.

Application information: Application form required. Application form available on the grantmaker's web site.

> Deadline(s): Mar. 16
> Applicants should submit the following:
> 1) Transcripts
> 2) SAT
> 3) Letter(s) of recommendation
> 4) GPA
> 5) ACT
> Additional information: Application should also include signed copies of parents' 1040 tax form and W2 forms. Applicant must have a minimum cumulative 2.5 GPA on a 4.0 scale. Applicant must demonstrate worthiness and character, and demonstrate some financial need.

EIN: 236279769

6700

Bertram & Alta Heartt Hochmark Scholarship Foundation

(also known as B. A. Hochmark Scholarship Trust)
c/o Wells Fargo Bank, N.A.
1 W. 4th St. 4th Fl. D4000-041
Winston Salem, NC   27101-3818   (406) 883-6351
Application address: Polson High School, 111 14th Ave. E., Polson, MT 59860

Foundation type: Independent foundation
Purpose: Scholarships to graduates of Polson High School, MT.
Financial data: Year ended 10/31/2013. Assets, $266,887 (M); Expenditures, $15,627; Total giving, $11,600.
Type of support: Support to graduates or students of specific schools; Undergraduate support.
Application information: Applications not accepted.

> Additional information: Unsolicited requests for funds not considered or acknowledged.

EIN: 816064383

6701

James M. Hoffman Scholarship Trust

c/o Wells Fargo Bank N.A
1 W. 4th St. 4th Fl. MAC D4000-041
Winston Salem, NC   27101-3818   (866) 601-0001
Application Address: c/o Center for Scholarship Administration, 4230-G Wade Hampton Blvd., Taylors, SC 29687

Foundation type: Independent foundation
Purpose: Scholarships to seniors at Calhoun County, AL, schools.
Publications: Application guidelines.
Financial data: Year ended 09/30/2013. Assets, $153,547 (M); Expenditures, $9,211; Total giving, $6,000.
Type of support: Support to graduates or students of specific schools; Undergraduate support.
Application information: Applications accepted. Application form required.

> Initial approach: Letter
> Deadline(s): Mar.
> Additional information: Application must include a copy of applicant's W-2 form.

EIN: 636077959

6702

Daniel R. Hoover Trust Fund

1525 W. W.T. Harris Blvd.
Charlotte, NC   28288-6732   (866) 608-0001

Foundation type: Independent foundation
Purpose: Scholarships to ministerial students from Cabarrus County, NC, who plan to study the ministry in NC or another southern state.
Financial data: Year ended 12/31/2011. Assets, $947,610 (M); Expenditures, $64,913; Total giving, $47,000.
Fields of interest: Theological school/education; Religion.
Type of support: Scholarships—to individuals.
Application information: Applications accepted. Application form required.

> Deadline(s): May 15
> Applicants should submit the following:
> 1) Financial information
> 2) Essay
> 3) Letter(s) of recommendation
> 4) Transcripts

EIN: 566034863

6703

Horsey Educational Fund Trinity Episcopal

c/o Wells Fargo Bank, N.A. Trust Tax Dept.
1 W. 4th St., 4th Fl. MAC D4000-041
Winston Salem, NC   27101-3818
Contact: John Kempton

Foundation type: Independent foundation
Purpose: Scholarships to members of Trinity Episcopal Cathedral and Embury Methodist Church, IA.
Financial data: Year ended 12/31/2013. Assets, $445,857 (M); Expenditures, $28,638; Total giving, $21,700.
Fields of interest: Higher education; Christian agencies & churches.
Type of support: Scholarships—to individuals.
Application information: Application form required.

> Deadline(s): Mar. 1
> Additional information: Application can be obtained from the church scholarship committee.

EIN: 426468681

6704

Dr. Arthur J. & Helen M. Horvat Foundation

1525 W. WT Harris Blvd., D1114-044
Charlotte, NC   28288-0001
Application address: 4320-G Wade Hampton Blvd., Taylors, SC 29687, tel.: (866) 608-0001.

Foundation type: Independent foundation
Purpose: Scholarships for the study of science to residents of the Duryea, PA, area whose family income is below $30,000. College students must meet criteria for the Dean's List and high school students must be in the top ten percent of their class.
Publications: Informational brochure (including application guidelines).
Financial data: Year ended 12/31/2012. Assets, $5,197,295 (M); Expenditures, $285,748; Total giving, $168,000.
Fields of interest: Science.
Type of support: Scholarships—to individuals.
Application information: Applications accepted.

> Deadline(s): May 15

EIN: 236846849

6705

Housing for New Hope

18 W. Colony Pl., Ste. 250
Durham, NC   27705-7202   (919) 489-6282
FAX: (919) 489-6593; URL: http://www.housingfornewhope.org

Foundation type: Public charity
Purpose: Assistance to homeless people and other persons in crisis of Durham, NC with affordable housing.
Financial data: Year ended 08/31/2011. Assets, $4,299,446 (M); Expenditures, $2,222,208; Total giving, $363,901; Grants to individuals, totaling $363,901.
Fields of interest: Housing/shelter, homeless; Homeless, human services.
Type of support: Grants for special needs.
Application information: Contact the organization for additional information.
EIN: 582089068

6706

Huffman-Cornwell Foundation

1525 W. WT Harris Blvd. D1114-044
Charlotte, NC   28288   (828) 437-5872
Contact: Mary Louise McCombs, Secy.
Application address: P.O. Box 1113, Morganton, NC 28653

Foundation type: Independent foundation
Purpose: Scholarships only to students Burke County High School, NC.
Financial data: Year ended 12/31/2012. Assets, $2,746,522 (M); Expenditures, $168,130; Total giving, $111,000.
Type of support: Support to graduates or students of specific schools; Undergraduate support.
Application information: Applications accepted. Application form required.

> Initial approach: Letter
> Deadline(s): None
> Additional information: Applications available through guidance counselors.

EIN: 566065286

6707

Raymond Hughes Scholarship Fund

(formerly Raymond Hughes Business Scholarship)
10 Hollyberry Ln.
Brevard, NC   28712
URL: http://rhscholarship.googlepages.com/home

Foundation type: Independent foundation
Purpose: Scholarships to students of Enterprise High School, AL, and Slocomb High School, AL, for business education.
Financial data: Year ended 12/31/2013. Assets, $5,754 (M); Expenditures, $3,000; Total giving, $3,000.
Fields of interest: Business school/education.
Type of support: Support to graduates or students of specific schools; Undergraduate support.
Application information: Application form required.

> Deadline(s): Contact schools for current application deadline
> Additional information: Application should include transcripts.

EIN: 582085356

6708
Cedric L. Hughes Scholarship Trust
c/o Wells Fargo N. A. Trust Tax Dept.
1 W 4th St., 4th Fl. MAC D4000-041
Winston Salem, NC   27101-3818   (218)
546-6449
Contact: Earl W. Bedard
Application Address: 200 5th St. Box 1417, Ironton,
MN, 56455.

Foundation type: Independent foundation
Purpose: Scholarships to graduates of
Crosby-Ironton High School, MN, who demonstrate
both an ability to excel and a need for financial
assistance.
Financial data: Year ended 03/31/2013. Assets,
$443,712 (M); Expenditures, $20,908; Total
giving, $13,500.
Type of support: Scholarships—to individuals;
Support to graduates or students of specific
schools.
Application information: Applications accepted.
Application form required.
   Applicants should submit the following:
      1) Transcripts
      2) GPA
      3) Essay
EIN: 416415622

6709
Jim "Catfish" Hunter ALS Foundation
P.O. Box 47
Hertford, NC   27944-0047   (252) 426-5145
Contact: C. Tommy Harrell, Pres.
FAX: (252) 337-7922; URL: http://
catfishfoundation.org/

Foundation type: Public charity
Purpose: Financial assistance to persons living with
ALS (PALS), and/or caregivers providing for PALS.
Publications: Application guidelines.
Financial data: Year ended 12/31/2012. Assets,
$484,554 (M); Expenditures, $9,246; Total giving,
$7,500.
Fields of interest: ALS.
Type of support: Grants for special needs.
Application information: Applications accepted.
Application form required. Application form
available on the grantmaker's web site.
   Send request by: Mail or fax
   Deadline(s): None
   Final notification: Applicants notified one month
      after submission of application
   Additional information: Funding is based on need
      and available resources. Patient's bill will be
      paid directly to the provider.
Program description:
   Patient Assistance: The foundation provides
financial assistance to persons living with ALS
(PALS), and/or caregivers providing for PALS.
Grants are intended to help with medical expenses,
medical equipment, respite care, travel, or other
needs PALS may have (such as home and auto
modifications)
EIN: 562125962

6710
Indian River County Foundation for the
   Elderly
c/o Wachovia Bank, N.A., Wealth Mgmt.
1525 W. W.T. Harris Blvd., D1114-044
Charlotte, NC   28288-1161
Contact: Harry Taylor, Dir.

Foundation type: Public charity

Purpose: Relief assistance only to economically
disadvantaged residents of Indian River County, FL,
who are at least 65 years old.
Financial data: Year ended 12/31/2011. Assets,
$852,737 (M); Expenditures, $34,156; Total
giving, $16,977.
Fields of interest: Aging; Economically
disadvantaged.
Type of support: Grants for special needs.
Application information: Applications accepted.
Application form required.
   Deadline(s): None
   Additional information: All applications must be
      submitted through the Indian River County
      Council of Aging and include financial and
      family information.
EIN: 596214870

6711
Institut Francais d'Amerique
(formerly Institut Francais de Washington)
234 Dey Hall CB 3170 UNC-CH
Chapel Hill, NC   27599-3170
Contact: Catherine A. Maley, Pres.

Foundation type: Independent foundation
Purpose: Fellowships to individuals who are either
in the final stage of their Ph.D. dissertation or who
have held their Ph.D. for no longer than three years.
Publications: Grants list; Informational brochure
(including application guidelines).
Financial data: Year ended 12/31/2012. Assets,
$98,087 (M); Expenditures, $8,248; Total giving,
$5,000; Grants to individuals, 4 grants totaling
$5,000 (high: $1,500, low: $500).
Fields of interest: Art history; History/archaeology;
Language (foreign); Language/linguistics;
Literature; International affairs; Science; Social
sciences; Economics.
International interests: France.
Type of support: Fellowships; Research;
Postdoctoral support; Doctoral support.
Application information: Applications accepted.
Application form not required.
   Initial approach: Letter
   Send request by: Mail
   Deadline(s): Jan. 15
   Applicants should submit the following:
      1) Curriculum vitae
      2) Letter(s) of recommendation
Program description:
   Institut Francais de Washington: Four $1,500
awards for maintenance (not travel) during research
in France for a period of at least one month. French
studies are in the areas of art, economics, history,
history of science, linguistics literature and social
sciences. Upon return the awardees will send a
brief report to the Institut Francais d'Amerique
about their research and what they have completed
in France. All awards are made through the Gilbert
Chinard Research Fellowships, Harmon Chadbourn
Rorison Fellowship and Edouard Morot-Sir
Fellowship in Literature programs.
EIN: 526052929

6712
Insurance Scholarship Foundation of
   America
(formerly National Association of Insurance Women
(International) Education Foundation)
P.O. Box 866
Hendersonville, NC   28793-0866   (828)
890-3328
Contact: Nancy Noe-Nichols, Exec. Dir.
E-mail: foundation@inssfa.org; Toll-free tel.: (866)
379-4732; E-mail for Nancy Noe-Nichols:
nancy@inssfa.org, cell: (904) 571-0124;
URL: http://www.inssfa.org

Foundation type: Public charity
Purpose: Scholarships to college students
preparing for a career in the insurance industry and
for men and women working in the insurance
industry for continued professional studies.
Publications: Application guidelines.
Financial data: Year ended 12/31/2011. Assets,
$186,095 (M); Expenditures, $81,205; Total
giving, $12,546.
Fields of interest: Graduate/professional
education; Business school/education.
Type of support: Scholarships—to individuals;
Undergraduate support.
Application information: Applications accepted.
Application form required. Application form
available on the grantmaker's web site.
   Initial approach: E-mail
   Send request by: Mail
   Copies of proposal: 1
   Deadline(s): Mar. 15 for Spring, Oct. 1 for Fall
   Applicants should submit the following:
      1) Transcripts
      2) Letter(s) of recommendation
      3) Essay
   Additional information: See web site for full
      program descriptions.
Program descriptions:
   Award of Excellence: This award of up to $1,000
recognizes exceptional college scholarship
applicants who demonstrate the qualities
necessary to excel in the insurance industry.
   *Canal Insurance Company Professional
Scholarship:* Scholarships are available to
individuals who have at least three years' insurance
industry employment, are members in good
standing of the National Association of Insurance
Writers, and are engaged in a course of study
designed to improve knowledge and skills in
performing employment responsibilities.
   CPCU Loman Education Foundation Scholarship:
This scholarship, awarded in amounts ranging from
$50 to $1,000, recognizes professional
scholarship applicants who demonstrate the desire
to enhance their career by becoming a CPCU.
Applicants must have a minimum of two years'
employment in the insurance industry.
   Dorris Boden Award of Excellence: This award of
up to $1,000 recognizes outstanding professional
scholarship applicants who demonstrate the
qualities necessary to excel in the insurance
industry.
   Founders Circle Professional Scholarship: This
scholarship, ranging from $1,000 to $2,000,
recognizes exceptional commitment to the
insurance industry. Eligible applicants must have at
least five years of continuous insurance industry
employment, have demonstrated excellence in
educational and career endeavors, and be engaged
in a course of study designed to improve knowledge
and skills in performing employment
responsibilities.
   ISFA College Scholarships: Scholarships, ranging
from $500 to $5,000, are available to candidates
for bachelor's or higher degrees with a major or

minor in insurance, risk management, or actuarial science. Eligible applicants must be currently attending a college or university and be completing or have completed the second year of college; have successfully completed two insurance, risk management, or actuarial science courses having a minimum of three credit hours each; and have achieved at least a 3.0 GPA on a 4.0 scale.

ISFA Professional Scholarship: Scholarships, ranging from $50 to $1,000, are available to individuals who have at least two years of insurance industry employment, and who are engaged in a course of study designed to improve knowledge and skills in performing employment responsibilities. Eligible applicants must have a background that indicates the applicant supports the foundation's mission.

Marsh College Scholarship: Awarded in conjunction with Marsh and McLellan, scholarships ranging from $500 to $5,000 are available to students who are attending a college or university and pursuing a bachelor's or higher degree with a major or minor in insurance, risk management, or actuarial science. Eligible applicants must have successfully completed two insurance, risk management, or actuarial science courses with a minimum of three credit hours each, and have achieved at least a 3.0 GPA on a 4.0 scale.
EIN: 731429257

6713
Interfaith Assistance Ministry, Inc.
210 Ehringhaus St.
P.O. Box 2562
Hendersonville, NC   28793-2562   (828) 697-7029
FAX: (828) 697-7015;
E-mail: interfaith@iam-hc.org; URL: http://iamhendersoncounty.org/

Foundation type: Public charity
Purpose: Financial assistance to indigent residents of Hendersonville, NC, for food, clothing, utilities, medical expenses, and other necessities.
Financial data: Year ended 12/31/2012. Assets, $1,589,228 (M); Expenditures, $812,569; Total giving, $220,467; Grants to individuals, totaling $220,467.
Type of support: Grants for special needs.
Application information:
Initial approach: Letter
Additional information: Contact foundation for complete eligibility requirements.
EIN: 581556963

6714
Inter-Faith Council For Social Service, Inc.
110 W. Main St.
Carrboro, NC   27510-2026   (919) 929-6380
Contact: John Dorward, Exec. Dir.
FAX: (919) 929-3353; E-mail: info@ifcmailbox.org;
E-Mail for John Dorward: jdorward@ifcmailbox.org;
URL: http://www.ifcweb.org

Foundation type: Public charity
Purpose: Emergency and financial assistance to low income individuals of Chapel Hill and Carrboro, NC with basic and necessary services such as food, housing, medical needs and shelter.
Financial data: Year ended 06/30/2012. Assets, $3,361,774 (M); Expenditures, $1,683,541; Total giving, $188,167; Grants to individuals, totaling $188,167.
Fields of interest: Economically disadvantaged.
Type of support: Emergency funds; Grants for special needs.

Application information: Applications accepted.
Additional information: Contact the agency for eligiblity determination. Some services require an application process.
EIN: 591224041

6715
International Burn Foundation of the United States
6915 Ebenezer Church Rd.
Hillsborough, NC   27278-7876   (919) 471-4714
Contact: Jane Boswick-Caffrey, Chair.
URL: http://www.internationalburnfoundation.org

Foundation type: Independent foundation
Purpose: Awards by nomination only to individual investigators to perform research, undertake patient care and treatment and attempt to solve other aspects of the burn problem.
Financial data: Year ended 12/31/2011. Assets, $757,254 (M); Expenditures, $29,959; Total giving, $25,000; Grant to an individual, 1 grant totaling $25,000.
Fields of interest: Institute.
Type of support: Awards/grants by nomination only; Awards/prizes.
Application information: Application form required.
Initial approach: Letter
Deadline(s): Jan.
Additional information: Application should include curriculum vitae, including a list of publications, letter of nomination and two additional letters of support.
Program description:
Tanner-Vandeput-Boswick Burn Prize: The prize is awarded to a person (or persons) who have made an outstanding contribution to any aspect of the burn care field. This could be a specific achievement or might represent a body of work over a period of years. Colleagues may make nominations, or a candidate may make application on their own behalf. The recipient does not have to be a member of the ISBI nor a physician, but be responsible for major advancement of the field of burn care. The prize consists of a gold pin, and a cash award in the amount of approximately $100,000. The prize is presented every four years.
EIN: 742345015

6716
Betty & Ken Isaac Scholarship Foundation, Inc.
3234 Weidner Rd.
Newton, NC   28658-8761   (828) 464-0920
Contact: Betty D. Isaac, V.P.

Foundation type: Independent foundation
Purpose: Scholarships to financially needy residents of Catawba County, NC, who demonstrate an interest in golf to attend a college in NC.
Financial data: Year ended 12/31/2012. Assets, $897,630 (M); Expenditures, $42,051; Total giving, $39,436; Grants to individuals, 7 grants totaling $39,436 (high: $7,500; low: $4,436).
Fields of interest: Higher education; Athletics/sports, golf.
Type of support: Scholarships—to individuals.
Application information: Applications accepted. Application form required.
Deadline(s): Jan. 31
Applicants should submit the following:
1) Letter(s) of recommendation
2) Transcripts
3) SAT

Additional information: Application forms may be obtained from the foundation. Applicant must demonstrate financial need.
EIN: 561875423

6717
Fritz and Lavinia Jensen Foundation
220 N. Tyron St.
Charlotte, NC   28202   (704) 973-4500
Application address: Foundation for the Carolinas
URL: http://www.jensenfoundation.org/

Foundation type: Independent foundation
Purpose: Grants to young aspiring opera singers based on performances at annual competitions.
Financial data: Year ended 06/30/2012. Assets, $2,549,813 (M); Expenditures, $146,490; Total giving, $43,000; Grants to individuals, 15 grants totaling $37,000 (high: $15,000, low: $300).
Fields of interest: Opera.
Type of support: Grants to individuals.
Application information: Applications accepted. Application form required.
Deadline(s): Mar. 15
Additional information: Applicants must include two letters of recommendation from reputable teachers, conductors or coaches. Singers must be between 21 and 35 years of age and must be citizens of the U.S. or permanent residents of the U.S. for at least one year. Singers must have performed in at least one production of a professional opera company.
EIN: 562107412

6718
Marvin A. and Lillie M. Johns Scholarships Foundation
c/o Trust Tax Dept.
P.O. Box 2907
Wilson, NC   27894-2907   (252) 246-4633

Foundation type: Independent foundation
Purpose: Scholarships to students who are residents of Chattooga County, GA.
Financial data: Year ended 12/31/2011. Assets, $275,459 (M); Expenditures, $16,900; Total giving, $12,300.
Fields of interest: Education.
Type of support: Scholarships—to individuals.
Application information: Applications not accepted.
Additional information: Unsolicited requests for funds not considered or acknowledged.
EIN: 581846123

6719
John A. Johnson Scholarship Foundation
c/o Wells Fargo Bank N.A. Trust Tax Dept.
1 W. 4th St., 4th Fl. MAC D4000-041
Winston Salem, NC   27101-3818

Foundation type: Independent foundation
Purpose: Scholarships to residents of MT to attend schools in MT.
Financial data: Year ended 09/30/2013. Assets, $160,471 (M); Expenditures, $9,333; Total giving, $6,000.
Type of support: Undergraduate support.
Application information: Applications not accepted.
Additional information: Unsolicited requests for funds not considered or acknowledged.
EIN: 816060046

6720
Ray and Nell Johnson Scholarship Fund
c/o Wells Fargo Bank, N.A., Trust Tax Dept.
1 W. 4th St., 4th Fl., MAC D4000-041
Winston Salem, NC   27101-3818
Application address: Harlowton High School

Foundation type: Independent foundation
Purpose: Scholarships to graduates of Harlowton High School, MT.
Financial data: Year ended 05/31/2013. Assets, $158,416 (M); Expenditures, $6,134; Total giving, $3,000; Grants to individuals, 2 grants totaling $3,000 (high: $1,750, low: $1,250).
Type of support: Support to graduates or students of specific schools; Undergraduate support.
Application information: Applications accepted.
  Initial approach: Letter
  Deadline(s): First Mon. in May
  Applicants should submit the following:
    1) Transcripts
    2) Financial information
  Additional information: Application must also include current scholarship status, extracurricular activities, educational goals, need for scholarship, and moral character references.
EIN: 816013476

6721
Johnston Community College Foundation, Inc.
245 College Rd.
P.O. Box 2350
Smithfield, NC   27577-2350   (919) 209-2119
Contact: Twyla Casey Wells, Exec. Dir.
FAX: (919) 209-2198;
E-mail: tcwells@johnstoncc.edu; *URL:* http://johnstoncc.edu/foundation/

Foundation type: Public charity
Purpose: Scholarships to selected students attending Johnston Community College, NC for continuing education.
Publications: Newsletter.
Financial data: Year ended 06/30/2013. Assets, $6,258,893 (M); Expenditures, $618,816; Total giving, $561,495; Grants to individuals, totaling $17,826.
Fields of interest: Higher education.
Type of support: Support to graduates or students of specific schools.
Application information: Students are selected by the college through its scholarship committee.
EIN: 581663605

6722
Adora S. Jones Ministerial Trust
c/o Wells Fargo Bank, N.A., Trust Tax Dept.
1 W. 4th St., 4th Fl., MAC D4000-041
Winston Salem, NC   27101-3818

Foundation type: Independent foundation
Purpose: Scholarships to ministerial students of IA, Baptist, Congregational, or Presbyterian denominations for college or seminary education.
Financial data: Year ended 12/31/2013. Assets, $283,553 (M); Expenditures, $14,957; Total giving, $9,000; Grants to individuals, 5 grants totaling $7,500 (high: $1,500, low: $1,500).
Fields of interest: Theological school/education.
Type of support: Scholarships—to individuals.
Application information: Applications accepted.
  Initial approach: Letter
  Deadline(s): Nov. 1

Additional information: Applicant must demonstrate financial need.
EIN: 426506484

6723
Claude R. and Sadie B. Jones Scholarship Foundation
c/o Wells Fargo Bank, N.A.
1 W. 4th St., 4th Fl. MAC D4000-041
Winston Salem, NC   27101-3818

Foundation type: Independent foundation
Purpose: Grants to graduates of Oakridge High School, OR for postsecondary education.
Financial data: Year ended 09/30/2013. Assets, $632,061 (M); Expenditures, $20,010; Total giving, $9,500.
Fields of interest: Higher education.
Type of support: Support to graduates or students of specific schools; Undergraduate support.
Application information: Application form required.
  Deadline(s): Aug. 15
  Additional information: Application should include transcript and proof of enrollment. Application can be obtained from the bank.
EIN: 936055774

6724
Roderick J. & Gertrude B. Jordan Charitable Trust
P.O. Box 448
Murfreesboro, NC   27855-0448   (252) 398-4171
Contact: Mary Etta Flowers, Tr.

Foundation type: Independent foundation
Purpose: Scholarships to high school students who are residents of Northampton County, NC for study at educational institutions of higher learning.
Financial data: Year ended 03/31/2013. Assets, $776,793 (M); Expenditures, $17,570; Total giving, $9,500.
Fields of interest: Higher education.
Type of support: Scholarships—to individuals.
Application information: Application form required.
  Deadline(s): June 1
  Additional information: Applications available from high schools.
EIN: 566302665

6725
The Bessie Noble and Willie Lou Jordan Scholarship Fund
1525 W. W.T. Harris Blvd., D1114-044
Charlotte, NC   28288   (866) 608-0001
Application address: 4230G Wade Hampton Blvd., Taylors, SC 29687-2245, tel.: (866) 608-0001

Foundation type: Independent foundation
Purpose: Scholarships to graduating seniors in Henderson, NC, for higher education.
Financial data: Year ended 12/31/2011. Assets, $1,148,613 (M); Expenditures, $77,464; Total giving, $55,700.
Type of support: Support to graduates or students of specific schools.
Application information: Application form required.
  Deadline(s): Feb. 1
  Applicants should submit the following:
    1) Transcripts
    2) SAT
    3) GPA
    4) Financial information

    5) Essay
EIN: 566487341

6726
Karyae Benevolent Foundation
P.O. Box 33544
Charlotte, NC   28233-3544

Foundation type: Independent foundation
Purpose: Loans, scholarships, and general welfare grants to residents and descendents of residents of Karyae, Greece. Scholarships are to be used for education at universities, colleges, and trade schools. Loans are generally $500 per year.
Financial data: Year ended 12/31/2011. Assets, $422,643 (M); Expenditures, $114,306; Total giving, $105,200; Grants to individuals, 17 grants totaling $8,500 (high: $500, low: $500).
Fields of interest: Vocational education.
Type of support: Scholarships—to individuals; Student loans—to individuals.
Application information: Application form required.
  Deadline(s): Contact foundation for current application deadline
  Additional information: Scholarship application must include letters of recommendation.
EIN: 566058576

6727
H. G. and A. G. Keasbey Memorial Fund
1525 W. W.T. Harris Blvd., D1114-044
Charlotte, NC   28288-0001
Contact: Angela P. Garden
E-mail: Jemjones@rci.rutgers.edu; Additional address: 1701 Market St., Philadelphia, PA 19103, *E-mail:* Jemjones@rci.rutgers.edu

Foundation type: Independent foundation
Purpose: Scholarships to individuals primarily for study in the United Kingdom.
Financial data: Year ended 12/31/2012. Assets, $5,973,861 (M); Expenditures, $286,889; Total giving, $212,738; Grant to an individual, 1 grant totaling $61,314.
International interests: United Kingdom.
Type of support: Scholarships—to individuals.
Application information: Applications not accepted.
  Additional information: Unsolicited requests for funds not considered or acknowledged.
EIN: 236447014

6728
Lorene Lobner Keena Trust
c/o Wells Fargo Bank, N.A., Trust Tax Dept.
1 W. 4th St., 4th Fl., MAC D4000-041
Winston Salem, NC   27101-3818   (916) 816-2284
Application address: Scholarship Committee, 24995 Ben Taylor Rd., Colfax, CA 95713

Foundation type: Independent foundation
Purpose: Scholarships to students of the Placer Joint High School District, CA in pursuit of a higher education at an accredited junior college, college or university.
Financial data: Year ended 08/31/2013. Assets, $463,193 (M); Expenditures, $31,773; Total giving, $23,000.
Type of support: Support to graduates or students of specific schools; Undergraduate support.
Application information: Applications accepted. Application form required.
  Initial approach: Letter
  Deadline(s): Apr. 15

Applicants should submit the following:
1) Transcripts
2) Letter(s) of recommendation
EIN: 946429682

6729
Keep North Carolina Clean and Beautiful, Inc.
P.O. Box 10155
Raleigh, NC 27605-0155 (919) 828-3190
Contact: Robin Nicholson, Pres.
FAX: (919) 828-3028;
E-mail: ncbeautiful@bellsouth.net; URL: http://www.ncbeautiful.org

Foundation type: Public charity
Purpose: Fellowships to students residing in NC for education in environmental studies. Grants to NC K-12 teachers to develop environmental education programs.
Financial data: Year ended 12/31/2011. Assets, $81,415 (M); Expenditures, $110,539; Total giving, $13,279.
Fields of interest: Environmental education.
Type of support: Grants to individuals.
Application information: Applications accepted. Application form available on the grantmaker's web site.
Initial approach: Letter, telephone, or e-mail
Deadline(s): Nov. 11 for Windows of Opportunity Grant
Final notification: Recipients notified Dec. 12 for Windows of Opportunity Grant
Program descriptions:
Undergraduate Scholars Grants: These grants provide $3,000 each to support a student's research and training in environmental studies. Applicants must demonstrate the ability to be innovative, creative, and original in their thinking; understand the global environment picture, North Carolina's place in it, and relate these to their current research; be involved in research related to sustaining the health and beauty of North Carolina's environment; and be a full-time student who will be a rising junior in a North Carolina accredited college or university.
Windows of Opportunity Grants: These grants award up to $1,000 to K-12 teachers in North Carolina to develop educational programs targeted at improving the environment while creating future environment leaders.
EIN: 560932528

6730
Senah C. and C.A. Kent Foundation
1 W. 4th St., D4000-041
Winston Salem, NC 27101 (336) 747-8166
Application address: c/o Kent Foundation Scholarship, 4320-G Wade Hampton Blvd., Taylors, SC 29687

Foundation type: Independent foundation
Purpose: Scholarships to students attending Wake Forest University, North Carolina School of the Arts, Salem College, Winston-Salem College, or Forsyth Technical College, NC.
Financial data: Year ended 12/31/2012. Assets, $1,986,040 (M); Expenditures, $132,082; Total giving, $100,000.
Fields of interest: Vocational education, post-secondary; Higher education.
Type of support: Support to graduates or students of specific schools; Undergraduate support.

Application information: Applications accepted. Application form required.
Deadline(s): Apr. 30
EIN: 566037248

6731
Kimmel & Associates, Inc. Corporate Giving Program
25 Page Ave.
Asheville, NC 28801-2707 (828) 251-9900
URL: http://kimmel.com/mission-values/

Foundation type: Corporate giving program
Purpose: Scholarships to students in the construction industry whose current course of studies, intended course of studies, and past and current affiliation with construction companies indicate a dedication to the construction industry.
Fields of interest: Higher education; Business/industry; Engineering/technology.
Type of support: Scholarships—to individuals; Undergraduate support.
Application information: Scholarship program is currently suspended until further notice. See web site for additional information.
Program description:
Kimmel & Associates Scholarship for Students in Construction: Kimmel annually awards up to 50 $1,000 college scholarships to college students studying construction or a field related to construction. Students must be currently enrolled in an accredited college or university and studying civil engineering, architectural engineering, construction management, construction technology, engineering technology, building construction, building science or another course of studies related to and leading to employment in construction. Preference is shown to students who are enrolled in the above coursework but who are also currently employed with a construction company while they attend school.

6732
Eugene E. Kimmel Scholarship Foundation
c/o Wells Fargo Bank, N.A., Trust Tax Dept.
1 W. 4th St., 4th Fl., MAC D4000-041
Winston Salem, NC 27101-3818 (260) 461-6458
Contact: Jennifer King
Application address: c/o Wells Fargo Bank, P. O. Box 960, Fort Wayne, IN 46801-6632, tel.: (260) 461-6458

Foundation type: Independent foundation
Purpose: Scholarships to graduates of Catholic high schools in Fort Wayne, IN.
Financial data: Year ended 11/30/2013. Assets, $706,582 (M); Expenditures, $38,257; Total giving, $25,600.
Fields of interest: Catholic agencies & churches.
Type of support: Support to graduates or students of specific schools; Undergraduate support.
Application information: Application form required.
Initial approach: Letter
Applicants should submit the following:
1) Financial information
2) Essay
EIN: 311019032

6733
Komarek Charitable Trust
c/o Wells Fargo Bank, N.A. Trust Tax Dept.
1 W. 4th St., 4th Fl., MAC D400-041
Winston Salem, NC 27101-3818

Foundation type: Independent foundation
Purpose: Scholarships to deserving students pursuing careers in the ministry of the Presbyterian and Methodist faiths, and to students at the University of Nebraska College of Medicine.
Financial data: Year ended 05/31/2013. Assets, $1,558,575 (M); Expenditures, $85,034; Total giving, $58,500.
Fields of interest: Medical school/education; Theological school/education; Protestant agencies & churches.
Type of support: Scholarships—to individuals; Awards/grants by nomination only.
Application information: Application should include transcripts. Scholarships are by nomination only. Funds are paid directly to the educational institution on behalf of the students.
EIN: 476141512

6734
Frances Label Memorial Scholarship Trust
1525 W. W.T. Harris Blvd., D1114-044
Charlotte, NC 28288

Foundation type: Independent foundation
Purpose: Scholarships to residents of Winston-Salem, NC.
Financial data: Year ended 12/31/2011. Assets, $117,132 (M); Expenditures, $6,711; Total giving, $5,400.
Type of support: Undergraduate support.
Application information: Applications not accepted.
Additional information: Unsolicited requests for funds not considered.
EIN: 216015823

6735
William B. Lake Foundation
c/o Wells Fargo Bank N.A
1 W 4th St., 4th Fl. MAC D4000-041
Winston Salem, NC 27101-3818 (610) 846-3368
Contact: Elizabeth K. Deegan
Application address: 214 W. Maury St., Chester, PA, 19013

Foundation type: Independent foundation
Purpose: Assistance to residents of Philadelphia, PA, and environs suffering from diseases of the respiratory tract, or pulmonary disease.
Financial data: Year ended 05/31/2013. Assets, $979,738 (M); Expenditures, $68,840; Total giving, $40,176; Grants to individuals, 13 grants totaling $40,176 (high: $7,200, low: $640).
Fields of interest: Lung diseases.
Type of support: Grants for special needs.
Application information: Application form required. Interview required.
Initial approach: Letter
Deadline(s): May 1 and Nov. 1
Additional information: Letter must include full medical details and supporting documents.
EIN: 236266137

6736
Walter Latham Foundation Inc.
c/o Walter Latham
P.O. Box 41023
Greensboro, NC 27404-1023 (336) 545-8062
Contact: Yulonda Smith, Secy.-Treas.

Foundation type: Company-sponsored foundation
Purpose: Scholarships to residents of Greensboro, NC.
Financial data: Year ended 12/31/2011. Assets, $0 (M); Expenditures, $29,339; Total giving, $15,965.
Type of support: Undergraduate support.
Application information:
Initial approach: Letter
EIN: 208573363

6737
Thomas H. and Mary Hadley Conner Leath Foundation
c/o Trust Tax Dept.
P.O. Box 2907
Wilson, NC 27894-2907 (910) 693-2726
Contact: Tonia Wright
Application address: 130 Applecross Rd., Pinehurst, NC 28374

Foundation type: Independent foundation
Purpose: Scholarships to residents of Richmond County, NC, who will attend the University of North Carolina at Chapel Hill, Duke University, NC, or Salem College, NC. Scholarships are renewable.
Financial data: Year ended 07/31/2013. Assets, $2,472,552 (M); Expenditures, $147,365; Total giving, $112,500.
Type of support: Support to graduates or students of specific schools; Undergraduate support.
Application information: Applications accepted. Application form required.
Initial approach: Letter
Deadline(s): None
Applicants should submit the following:
1) Essay
2) Letter(s) of recommendation
3) Transcripts
Additional information: Application must also include copy of the acceptance letter from college or university, and estimate of total costs.
EIN: 566294400

6738
Carol J. Ledward Memorial Scholarship
(formerly J. Dehaven Ledward Memorial Foundation)
c/o Wells Fargo Bank, N.A.
1 W. 4th St., 4th Fl., MAC D4000-041
Winston Salem, NC 27101-3818

Foundation type: Independent foundation
Purpose: Scholarships to law students who are residence of Delaware county, PA for attendance at the University of PA.
Financial data: Year ended 06/30/2013. Assets, $278,939 (M); Expenditures, $14,270; Total giving, $8,000.
Fields of interest: Law school/education.
Type of support: Support to graduates or students of specific schools.
Application information: Applications accepted. Application form required.
Deadline(s): None
Additional information: Application should include financial statements and proof of PA residency.
EIN: 232112337

6739
Lee Industries Educational Foundation, Inc.
210 4th St., N.W.
Conover, NC 28613-3755 (828) 464-8318

Foundation type: Company-sponsored foundation
Purpose: Scholarships to graduating students attending high school in Catawba County, NC, or adjacent counties, who demonstrate financial need. Scholarships also to dependents of Lee employees, Sipe's Orchard Home and the Salvation Army.
Financial data: Year ended 12/31/2012. Assets, $116,448 (M); Expenditures, $31,613; Total giving, $30,600; Grants to individuals, 33 grants totaling $17,600 (high: $1,150, low: $300).
Type of support: Support to graduates or students of specific schools; Undergraduate support.
Application information: Application form required.
Deadline(s): Contact foundation for current application deadline
Applicants should submit the following:
1) Class rank
2) Transcripts
3) SAT
4) Financial information
5) Essay
6) Letter(s) of recommendation
Company name: Lee Industries, Inc.
EIN: 562046037

6740
The Leever Foundation
900 S. Park Pl.
Hendersonville, NC 28791-1906 (203) 927-5997
Contact: Carol O'Donnell
Application address: C/o The Duncannon Group, 45 New Bridge Cir., Cheshire, CT 06410, tel.: (203) 927-5997

Foundation type: Independent foundation
Purpose: Scholarships to children of employees of MacDermid Corporation, CT, at four year accredited institutions of higher learning.
Publications: Application guidelines; Program policy statement.
Financial data: Year ended 12/31/2012. Assets, $10,027,287 (M); Expenditures, $1,177,132; Total giving, $1,067,083.
Fields of interest: Education.
Type of support: Scholarships—to individuals.
Application information: Applications accepted. Application form required.
Initial approach: Letter, or telephone
Send request by: Mail
Copies of proposal: 5
Deadline(s): Mar. 1
Final notification: Recipients notified ten weeks after receipt of application
Applicants should submit the following:
1) FAFSA
2) Transcripts
3) Letter(s) of recommendation
4) GPA
5) Financial information
6) Essay
7) Budget Information
EIN: 223115036

6741
Dorsey S. & Eugenie C. Lenz Foundation
c/o Wells Fargo Bank, N.A., Trust Tax Dept.
1 W. 4th St., 4th Fl., MAC D4000-041
Winston Salem, NC 27101-3818 (800) 352-3705

Foundation type: Independent foundation
Purpose: Scholarships to graduating students attending Big Fork High School, MT.
Financial data: Year ended 12/31/2013. Assets, $267,511 (M); Expenditures, $15,394; Total giving, $10,000.
Type of support: Scholarships—to individuals; Support to graduates or students of specific schools.
Application information: Applications accepted. Application form required.
Deadline(s): Apr. 1
EIN: 816073154

6742
Walter & Hazel Leverenz Trust
(formerly Mr. & Mrs. Walter F. Leverenz Scholarship Trust)
c/o Wells Fargo Bank, N.A.
1 W 4th Fl. Mac D4000-041
Winston Salem, NC 27101-3818
Contact: Deborah Rogers
Application address: c/o Atascadero High School, 1 high school hill, Atascadero, CA 93422

Foundation type: Operating foundation
Purpose: Scholarships to financially needy students graduating from Atascadero High School, CA, to study math, science, or music.
Financial data: Year ended 09/30/2013. Assets, $755,596 (M); Expenditures, $32,794; Total giving, $20,950.
Fields of interest: Music; Performing arts, education; Science; Mathematics.
Type of support: Support to graduates or students of specific schools; Undergraduate support.
Application information: Applications accepted. Application form required.
Deadline(s): Apr. 30
Applicants should submit the following:
1) Transcripts
2) SAT
3) Letter(s) of recommendation
4) ACT
Additional information: The scholarship program is administered by Scholarship America.
EIN: 956721631

6743
The Lion's Pride Foundation, Inc.
P.O. Box 1330
Salisbury, NC 28145-1330 (704) 633-8250
Contact: Gerg Finchum, Pres.
FAX: (704) 656-4162

Foundation type: Public charity
Purpose: Grants to Food Lion, Inc. associates, their immediate family and members of the community in times of hardship.
Financial data: Year ended 12/31/2012. Assets, $891,878 (M); Expenditures, $150,502; Total giving, $127,165; Grants to individuals, totaling $122,165.
Fields of interest: Safety/disasters.
Type of support: Emergency funds; Grants for special needs.
Application information: Applications accepted. Application form required.

Initial approach: Telephone
Deadline(s): None
Program description:
Emergency Assistance Grants: Awards of up to $500 per year are given to individuals who provide sufficient evidence of need (e.g., water, electricity, mortgage bills)
EIN: 561895601

6744
Solon E. & Espie Watts Little Scholarship Loan Fund, Inc.
43 Union St. S.
Concord, NC 28025-5009 (704) 786-8173
Contact: Steve L. Medlin, Pres. and Secy.,-Treas.

Foundation type: Independent foundation
Purpose: Interest-free student loans to graduates of Alexander Central High School, Taylorsville, NC, who have been residents of Alexander County, NC, for at least one year.
Financial data: Year ended 12/31/2012. Assets, $2,522,178 (M); Expenditures, $348,006; Total giving, $174,800; Loans to individuals, 64 loans totaling $174,800.
Type of support: Support to graduates or students of specific schools; Undergraduate support.
Application information: Application form required.
Initial approach: Letter or telephone
Deadline(s): Feb. 15
Additional information: Contact fund for current application guidelines.
EIN: 581491453

6745
James S. & Peggy M. Livingston Educational Trust
c/o Wells Fargo Bank, N.A.
1 W. 4th St., 4th Fl. MAC D4000-041
Winston Salem, NC 27101-3818

Foundation type: Independent foundation
Purpose: Scholarships to graduates of Cedar Rapids, IA, high schools for attendance to an accredited college, university, or junior college.
Financial data: Year ended 10/31/2013. Assets, $185,586 (M); Expenditures, $11,580; Total giving, $7,500; Grants to individuals, 15 grants totaling $7,500 (high: $500, low: $500).
Fields of interest: Higher education; Scholarships/financial aid.
Type of support: Support to graduates or students of specific schools; Undergraduate support.
Application information: Students are recommended by their high school principals.
EIN: 426351732

6746
P. A. & Marie B. Loar Scholarship Foundation
c/o Wells Fargo Bank, N.A.
1 W. 4th St., 4th Fl. MAC D4000-041
Winston Salem, NC 27101-3818
Contact: Greg Snyder
Application address: c/o Silverton High School, 802 Schlador St., Silverton, OR 97381

Foundation type: Independent foundation
Purpose: Student loans to graduates of Silverton High School, OR.
Financial data: Year ended 09/30/2013. Assets, $473,872 (M); Expenditures, $27,090; Total giving, $18,000; Grants to individuals, 29 grants totaling $18,000 (high: $750, low: $500).

Type of support: Support to graduates or students of specific schools; Undergraduate support.
Application information: Applications accepted. Application form required.
Deadline(s): None
EIN: 936041499

6747
Charles B. Loflin Educational Foundation
c/o High Point Bank & Trust Co.
P.O. Box 2278
High Point, NC 27261-2278
Contact: Lisa Foster

Foundation type: Independent foundation
Purpose: Scholarships to former newspaper carriers of The High Point Enterprise, High Point, NC.
Financial data: Year ended 12/31/2012. Assets, $82,409 (M); Expenditures, $6,164; Total giving, $4,100; Grants to individuals, 4 grants totaling $4,100 (high: $1,025, low: $1,025).
Fields of interest: Higher education.
Type of support: Scholarships—to individuals.
Application information: Applications accepted.
Initial approach: Letter
Deadline(s): None
Additional information: Applicant must show financial need.
EIN: 237035432

6748
George and Frances London Educational Foundation
P.O. Box 20389
Raleigh, NC 27619-0389 (919) 787-8880
Contact: David D. Dahl, Tr.

Foundation type: Independent foundation
Purpose: Scholarships to students from specified counties in NC for study at a four-year college or university.
Financial data: Year ended 12/31/2011. Assets, $5,916,953 (M); Expenditures, $370,980; Total giving, $330,000; Grants to individuals, 45 grants totaling $330,000 (high: $7,500, low: $3,750).
Fields of interest: Higher education; Scholarships/financial aid; Volunteer services; Leadership development.
Type of support: Undergraduate support.
Application information: Application form required.
Initial approach: Letter
Deadline(s): Apr. 30
Applicants should submit the following:
1) Class rank
2) Transcripts
3) SAT
4) GPA
Additional information: Nominations shall be solicited from guidance counselors of high schools selected by the trustees. In addition, any interested high school senior from high schools in North Carolina counties may apply on his/her own initiative.
EIN: 582233144

6749
Lowe's Employee Relief Fund
1000 Lowes Blvd., Ste. 2ETA
Mooresville, NC 28117-8520 (704) 758-2009

Foundation type: Public charity
Purpose: Financial assistance to Lowe's employees to help them overcome sudden personal hardship from events including natural disaster,

house fire, family death, medical expenses or other unforeseen events.
Financial data: Year ended 09/30/2011. Assets, $4,470,718 (M); Expenditures, $2,352,647; Total giving, $2,286,079; Grants to individuals, totaling $2,281,300.
Fields of interest: Safety/disasters; Human services, emergency aid.
Type of support: Grants for special needs.
Application information: Applications accepted. Application form required.
Additional information: Individuals must show financial need as a result of a qualifying event.
EIN: 562160955

6750
Lumbee Nation Tribal Programs, Inc.
6984 N.C. Hwy. 711 W.
P.O. Box 2709
Pembroke, NC 28372-2709 (910) 521-7861
E-mail: bbrewer@lumbeetribe.com; *URL:* http://www.lumbeetribe.com/

Foundation type: Public charity
Purpose: Assistance to low income individuals and families of Lumbee Indian households in NC, with housing. Summer camp for boys and girls ages 6 to 18.
Financial data: Year ended 09/30/2011. Assets, $40,743,695 (M); Expenditures, $11,393,150; Total giving, $304,972; Grants to individuals, totaling $304,972.
Fields of interest: Housing/shelter, home owners; Boys & girls clubs.
Type of support: Emergency funds; Camperships; Grants for special needs.
Application information: Applications accepted. Application form required. Application form available on the grantmaker's web site.
Additional information: See web site for additional guidelines.
Program descriptions:
Down Payment Assistance: The program provides housing opportunities for qualified, low-to-moderate income tribal members. This one-time assistance affords tribal families an opportunity to purchase decent, sanitary and safe housing. Down payment assistance in amounts ranging from $4,000 to a maximum amount of $10,000 is available to approved applicants. The amount of assistance is based upon applicant's household income. See web site for eligibility requirements.
Emergency Housing/Rental Assistance: This program provides short-term assistance for displaced victims of burnouts, floods, domestic violence, evictions and other unforeseeable emergencies and/or hardships causing financial difficulty or homelessness. Direct assistance under this program is used to temporarily house applicants who lack available housing resources. Assistance is available for qualified, low-income tribal members who do not have an on-going, chronically delinquent account. See web site for additional requirements.
Emergency Mortgage Assistance: The program provides assistance with mortgage payments to qualified low-income tribal members experiencing a short-term, financial hardship. Assistance is not available to tribal members with an on-going, chronic, delinquent account. See web site for additional requirements.
EIN: 562247884

6751
Walter E. Lundquist Scholarship Foundation

c/o Wells Fargo Bank, N.A.
1 W. 4th St., 4th Fl. MAC D4000-041
Winston Salem, NC 27101-3818 (360)
673-5225

Foundation type: Independent foundation
Purpose: Scholarships to graduates of Kalama High School, WA, who have resided in WA for at least one year.
Financial data: Year ended 03/31/2013. Assets, $738,912 (M); Expenditures, $35,429; Total giving, $24,222; Grants to individuals, 66 grants totaling $24,222 (high: $850, low: $67).
Type of support: Support to graduates or students of specific schools; Undergraduate support.
Application information: Application form required.
   Deadline(s): Apr. 1
   Applicants should submit the following:
      1) Transcripts
      2) Letter(s) of recommendation
      3) Essay
   Additional information: Application must also include a history of employment/volunteer service.
EIN: 936145913

6752
The Turner and Louise Lundy Foundation

(formerly The B-G Foundation)
1 W. 4th St. D4000-041
Winston Salem, NC 27101 (866) 608-0001
Application address: c/o Center for Scholarship Admin, 4320 G-Wade Hampton Blvd., Taylors, NC 29687; URL: http://www.csascholars.org

Foundation type: Independent foundation
Purpose: Scholarships to high school seniors at Brunswick Senior High School of Brunswick county VA, and who are residents of Brunswick county, VA or any municipality therein.
Financial data: Year ended 12/31/2012. Assets, $1,155,412 (M); Expenditures, $65,840; Total giving, $53,626.
Fields of interest: Vocational education, post-secondary; College (community/junior); University.
Type of support: Support to graduates or students of specific schools; Undergraduate support.
Application information: Applications accepted. Application form required.
   Deadline(s): Mar. 1
   Applicants should submit the following:
      1) Transcripts
      2) Letter(s) of recommendation
      3) Essay
   Additional information: Application should also include a copy of parent's federal tax form 1040, and W-2 forms. Applicants must demonstrate high personal character, academic ability and achievement, and financial need. The scholarship is administered by The Center for Scholarship Administration, Inc.
EIN: 541526783

6753
Lutz Foundation, Inc.

780 Oakland Rd.
Spindale, NC 28160 (828) 245-0402
Contact: Jack L. Lutz, Pres.
Application address: 727 E. Main St., Forest City, NC 28043-3235

Foundation type: Independent foundation
Purpose: Scholarship to graduates of Kings Mountain City, Shelby City, Cleveland County, Polk County and Rutherford County, North Carolina, high schools for higher education.
Financial data: Year ended 12/31/2012. Assets, $379,811 (M); Expenditures, $30,553; Total giving, $45,100; Grants to individuals, 32 grants totaling $1,600 (high: $50, low: $50).
Fields of interest: Education.
Type of support: Scholarships—to individuals.
Application information: Applications accepted.
   Additional information: Contact the foundation for application guidelines.
EIN: 561073160

6754
Macon County Care Network

130 Bidwell St.
Franklin, NC 28734-2989 (828) 369-2642
FAX: (828) 369-0274; URL: http://maconcarenet.org/

Foundation type: Public charity
Purpose: Financial assistance to indigent residents of Macon County, NC, for utilities, medication, food, and emergency shelter.
Financial data: Year ended 12/31/2011. Assets, $556,080 (M); Expenditures, $391,754.
Type of support: Grants for special needs.
Application information:
   Initial approach: Letter
   Additional information: Contact foundation for eligibility requirements.
EIN: 581813122

6755
Magdalena School District Gear up Scholarship Trust

c/o Wells Fargo Bank , N.A., Trust Tax Dept.
1 W. 4th St., 4th Fl., MAC D4000-041
Winston Salem, NC 27101-3818

Foundation type: Independent foundation
Purpose: Provides scholarships to low-income students residing in the Magdalena Municipal School District, NM.
Financial data: Year ended 06/30/2013. Assets, $177,106 (M); Expenditures, $24,335; Total giving, $20,800.
Fields of interest: Secondary school/education; Higher education; Economically disadvantaged.
Type of support: Scholarships—to individuals.
Application information: Applications not accepted.
EIN: 206663466

6756
Stanley & Mary Mahalick Scholarship Fund

c/o Wells Fargo Bank, N.A. Trust Tax Dept.
1 W. 4th St., 4th Fl. D4000-041
Winston Salem, NC 27101-3818 (866) 608-0001

Foundation type: Independent foundation
Purpose: Scholarships to residents of Mahanoy area school district who are graduates of Mahanoy Area High School, PA and Marian Catholic High School, PA.
Financial data: Year ended 11/30/2013. Assets, $212,533 (M); Expenditures, $11,482; Total giving, $7,490.
Fields of interest: Higher education.

Type of support: Support to graduates or students of specific schools.
Application information: Applications accepted. Application form required.
   Deadline(s): May
   Applicants should submit the following:
      1) Transcripts
      2) Financial information
      3) Essay
   Additional information: Application must also include notification of college acceptance, and college board scores, if taken.
EIN: 256643477

6757
Albert and Jessie D. Martin Scholarship Trust Fund

115 Coram Ave.
Boonville, NC 27011

Foundation type: Independent foundation
Purpose: Scholarships to graduates of Starmount High School, NC, who are pursuing teaching as a career.
Financial data: Year ended 12/31/2012. Assets, $416,819 (M); Expenditures, $49,704; Total giving, $46,250; Grants to individuals, 20 grants totaling $46,250 (high: $2,500, low: $625).
Fields of interest: Arts; Higher education; Scholarships/financial aid; Education; Volunteer services.
Type of support: Support to graduates or students of specific schools; Awards/grants by nomination only; Undergraduate support.
Application information: Application form required.
   Deadline(s): Apr. 15
   Additional information: Recipients must meet the following criteria to be eligible for scholarship: carry a 3.0 GPA in high school; demonstrate interest in the welfare of others, as evidenced by community and school activities not restricted to student government and athletic organizations; demonstrate ability for divergent thinking and creativity, particularly in writing and other arts; reflect in his/her work an unusual interest and aptitude for a career in education; gained the respect of peers and teachers for personal integrity and effort to live by convictions; and graduated from Boonville Elementary School or the elementary school serving the Boonville community.
EIN: 586241009

6758
Material Handling Educational Foundation, Inc.

8720 Red Oak Blvd., Ste. 201
Charlotte, NC 28217-3996 (704) 676-1190
For scholarships: Donna Varner, dvarner@mhi.org
FAX: (704) 676-1199; E-mail: vwheeler@mhia.org;
URL: http://www.mhia.org/about/mhefi/scholarship

Foundation type: Public charity
Purpose: Scholarships to full time undergraduate or graduate students pursuing an education in materials handling industry.
Financial data: Year ended 12/31/2011. Assets, $699,789 (M); Expenditures, $140,292; Total giving, $99,300; Grants to individuals, totaling $99,300.
Fields of interest: Business school/education; Engineering/technology; Computer science.
Type of support: Scholarships—to individuals; Graduate support; Undergraduate support.

Application information: Applications accepted. Application form available on the grantmaker's web site.

Send request by: Online
Deadline(s): Mar. 15
Applicants should submit the following:
1) Transcripts
2) Letter(s) of recommendation

Program description:

Scholarship Program: The program promotes the study of material handling and seeks to expose as many students as possible to the material handling industry. Students must have completed at least two years of study. Students from two-year postsecondary schools are eligible if they have completed two years of study and have been accepted as transfer students at MHEFI prequalified institutions. All applicants must have a "B" equivalent GPA in postsecondary studies.
EIN: 251303313

6759
James McAllister Christmas Fund
210 Hinsdale Ave.
Fayetteville, NC 28305 (910) 486-3501
Contact: Charles Broadwell, Tr.

Foundation type: Independent foundation
Purpose: Grants to economically disadvantaged black members of the Fayetteville, NC community.
Financial data: Year ended 12/31/2012. Assets, $40,242 (M); Expenditures, $4,603; Total giving, $4,500.
Fields of interest: African Americans/Blacks; Economically disadvantaged.
Type of support: Grants to individuals.
Application information: Applications accepted. Application form not required.
Initial approach: Letter
Deadline(s): None
EIN: 566063083

6760
John S. McClure Trust
1525 W. W.T. Harris Blvd., D11114-044
Charlotte, NC 28288 (866) 608-0001
Application address: c/o Center for Scholarship Admin, Inc., P.O. Box 26311, Richmond, VA 23260

Foundation type: Independent foundation
Purpose: Scholarships to Virginia high school graduates for higher education at accredited colleges or universities.
Financial data: Year ended 12/31/2011. Assets, $678,363 (M); Expenditures, $55,063; Total giving, $40,000.
Fields of interest: Higher education.
Type of support: Scholarships—to individuals.
Application information: Applications accepted.
EIN: 541819359

6761
McColl Center for Visual Arts
721 N. Tryon St.
Charlotte, NC 28202-2221 (704) 332-5535
Contact: Suzanne Fetscher, Pres. and Exec. Dir.
FAX: (704) 377-9808;
E-mail: dmcneil@mccollcenter.org; E-mail For Suzanne Fetscher: sfetscher@mccollcenter.org;
URL: http://www.mccollcenter.org

Foundation type: Public charity
Purpose: Residencies to artists in disciplines of sculpture, painting, technology/media, photography, ceramics, and installation.

Publications: Application guidelines.
Financial data: Year ended 06/30/2012. Assets, $13,935,533 (M); Expenditures, $2,321,264.
Fields of interest: Media/communications; Photography; Sculpture; Painting; Ceramic arts.
Type of support: Residencies.
Application information: Application form required. Application form available on the grantmaker's web site.
Deadline(s): May 3 for Residency, Nov. 2 for Affiliate Artist
Applicants should submit the following:
1) Work samples
2) Resume
3) Proposal
4) Letter(s) of recommendation
5) Essay

Program descriptions:

Affiliate Artists: Affiliate artists are offered studio space, access to the center's supplies, and participation in workshops, open houses, and educational programs. Residencies are for a four month or eleven month period. There is a monthly $175 utility/maintenance fee. Candidates are evaluated on the quality of their work, application essays, and interest in working in a creative environment. Only artists living in Charlotte or within a 50 mile radius are eligible for the Affiliate Program.

Artist-in-Residence Program: The program is open to regional, national, and international artists. Resident artists participate in the center's open houses, artist forums, outreaches, and workshops, and interact with other regional, national, and international artists who are in residence. Artists are provided with a 230- to 819-sq. ft. studio and have twenty-four hour access to the center's facility (including a media lab; machine, metal, and wood shop; dark room; printmaking studio; ceramic studio; and blacksmith shop). In addition to the use of these extraordinary facilities, each artist is given housing accommodations, a travel allowance, $2,000 for materials, and a stipend of $3,300.
EIN: 510195015

6762
Mildred R. McMahan Trust
c/o Wells Fargo Bank, N.A.
1 W. 4th St., 4th Fl., MAC D4000-041
Winston Salem, NC 27101-3818

Foundation type: Independent foundation
Purpose: Scholarships to individuals for continuing education at accredited colleges or universities.
Financial data: Year ended 09/30/2013. Assets, $532,012 (M); Expenditures, $32,230; Total giving, $22,500.
Fields of interest: Higher education.
Type of support: Scholarships—to individuals.
Application information: Contact the trust for application guidelines.
EIN: 596802975

6763
Robert and Janice McNair Educational Foundation
P.O. Box 635
Forest City, NC 28043-0635 (828) 245-4339
Contact: Monica Lee, Exec. Dir.
E-mail: mlee@rcsnc.org; Additional address (Chase High School): 1603 Chase High Rd., Forest City, NC 28043-5679, tel.:(828) 247-8957; E-Mail For Monica Lee: mlee@rcsnc.org; URL: http://www.mcnairedfoundation.org/

Foundation type: Public charity

Purpose: Scholarships and awards to students of Chase High School, NC and East Rutherford High School, NC for postsecondary education.
Financial data: Year ended 06/30/2012. Assets, $15,840,322 (M); Expenditures, $991,301; Total giving, $340,210; Grants to individuals, 74 grants totaling $340,210.
Fields of interest: Higher education.
Type of support: Support to graduates or students of specific schools.
Application information: Applications accepted. Application form required.
Applicants should submit the following:
1) ACT
2) SAT
3) Letter(s) of recommendation
4) FAFSA
Additional information: Students are selected by their teachers, counselors and administrators.
EIN: 581870080

6764
John F. McNair Memorial Fund Trust
1 W. 4th St. D4000-041
Winston Salem, NC 27101 (866) 608-0001
Application Address: c/o Center For Scholarship Admin, 4320-G Wade Hampton Blvd., Taylor, SC 296870031

Foundation type: Independent foundation
Purpose: Scholarships to graduates of public high schools in Laurinburg, NC.
Financial data: Year ended 12/31/2012. Assets, $155,558 (M); Expenditures, $8,521; Total giving, $7,400.
Type of support: Support to graduates or students of specific schools; Undergraduate support.
Application information: Applications accepted. Application form required.
Initial approach: Letter
Deadline(s): None
EIN: 566035967

6765
Dr. Francis McNaught Scholarship Fund
(formerly Grace I. McNaught-Dr. Francis McNaught Scholarship Fund)
c/o Wells Fargo Bank, N.A., Trust Tax Dept.
1 W. 4th St., 4th Fl., MAC D4000-041
Winston Salem, NC 27101-3818
Contact: Margaret Toal
Application address: c/o Wells Fargo Bank, 1740 Broadway Rd., Denver, CO 80274

Foundation type: Independent foundation
Purpose: Loans only to students at the University of Colorado Medical School, CO, who are seeking a doctorate of medicine, or any related degree.
Financial data: Year ended 08/31/2013. Assets, $1,000,863 (M); Expenditures, $17,979; Total giving, $0.
Fields of interest: Medical school/education.
Type of support: Support to graduates or students of specific schools; Graduate support.
Application information: Applications accepted.
Initial approach: Letter
Deadline(s): None
Additional information: Contact university financial aid office for additional application guidelines.
EIN: 846020606

6766
Gertrude L. McRae Scholarship Charity
c/o Wells Fargo Bank, N.A.
1 W. 4th St. 4th Fl. Mac D4000-041
Winston Salem, NC   27101-3818
Application address: c/o Gertrude McRae
Scholarship Comm., Grant County Court
House,Canyon City, OR 97820

Foundation type: Independent foundation
Purpose: Scholarships to graduates of high schools
in Grant County, OR, who have completed one or
more years of college. Secondary preference to
students from Wheeler, Morrow, and Wasco county
high schools, OR.
Financial data: Year ended 06/30/2013. Assets,
$201,268 (M); Expenditures, $6,609; Total giving,
$2,000; Grants to individuals, 10 grants totaling
$2,000 (high: $200, low: $200).
Type of support: Support to graduates or students
of specific schools; Undergraduate support.
Application information: Application form required.
> *Deadline(s):* July 1
> *Additional information:* Application forms
>   available upon request.
EIN: 936097780

6767
MDC, Inc.
307 W. Main St.
Durham, NC   27701-3215   (919) 381-5802
Contact: David Dodson, Pres.
Fellowship contact: Breanna Detwiler, tel.: (919)
968-4531, ext. 371, e-mail bdetwiler@mdcinc.org
E-mail: info@mdcinc.org; URL: http://
www.mdcinc.org

Foundation type: Public charity
Purpose: Fellowships to talented and ambitious
recent college graduates in the South to work for
one year as full time paid staff members at MDC,
Inc.
Publications: Application guidelines; Grants list;
Newsletter.
Financial data: Year ended 06/30/2012. Assets,
$7,153,645 (M); Expenditures, $11,252,877.
Type of support: Fellowships.
Application information: Applications accepted.
Application form required. Application form
available on the grantmaker's web site. Interview
required.
> *Initial approach:* Application
> *Deadline(s):* Feb. 7
Program description:
> *Autry Fellowship Program:* Provides a one-year,
full-time paid position for a recent college graduate
to work at MDC, Inc. Each one-year fellowship will
be centered on a project-specific assignment that
will blend the interests of the fellow with the
program work of MDC during that year. Each fellow
will be assigned a mentor from the staff based on
the project the fellow is undertaking.
EIN: 560894222

6768
Mecklenburg Bar Foundation
1123 S. Church St., Ste. 103
Charlotte, NC   28203-1422   (704) 375-8624
Contact: Nancy M. Roberson, Exec. Dir.
FAX: (704) 333-6209;
E-mail: nroberson@meckbar.org; URL: http://
www.meckbar.org/barfoundation/
barfoundation.cfm

Foundation type: Public charity

Purpose: Summer fellowships to law students of
Mecklenburg county, NC pursuing legal careers in
the nonprofit or government sector.
Publications: Application guidelines.
Financial data: Year ended 06/30/2012. Assets,
$840,173 (M); Expenditures, $306,512; Total
giving, $82,500; Grants to individuals, totaling
$15,000.
Fields of interest: Law school/education.
Type of support: Fellowships.
Application information: Applications accepted.
Application form required.
> *Send request by:* Mail
> *Deadline(s):* Mar.
> *Additional information:* Application should
>   include a resume, personal statement and
>   additional documents the student wishes the
>   committee to review. Applicant must
>   demonstrate good character and suitable
>   academic performance in law school. See web
>   site for additional guidelines.
EIN: 237062151

6769
The Medical Foundation of North Carolina, Inc.
880 M.L.K. Jr. Blvd., C.B., No. 7565
Chapel Hill, NC   27514-2600   (919) 966-1201
FAX: (919) 966-5470; Toll-free tel.: (800)
962-2543; URL: http://
www.medicalfoundationofnc.org

Foundation type: Public charity
Purpose: Scholarships and awards to students at
University of North Carolina Medical School, NC.
Publications: Annual report; Newsletter.
Financial data: Year ended 06/30/2012. Assets,
$213,418,602 (M); Expenditures, $19,971,702;
Total giving, $15,515,510; Grants to individuals,
213 grants totaling $1,541,595.
Fields of interest: Medical school/education.
Type of support: Scholarships—to individuals;
Awards/prizes.
Application information: Applications accepted.
Application form required.
> *Additional information:* Selection is based on
>   need and merit. Contact the foundation for
>   additional guidelines.
EIN: 566057494

6770
Thomas C. Meredith, Jr. Foundation
1 W. 4th St. D4000-041
Winston Salem, NC   27101   (866) 608-0001
E-mail: michael.boyles@wachovia.com

Foundation type: Company-sponsored foundation
Purpose: Scholarships to children of full-time
employees of Consolidated Systems Inc. The
program is administered by the Center for
Scholarship Administration.
Financial data: Year ended 12/31/2012. Assets,
$54,279 (M); Expenditures, $1,924; Total giving,
$0.
Type of support: Employee-related scholarships.
Application information: Applications not
accepted.
> *Additional information:* Unsolicited requests for
>   funds not considered or acknowledged.
Company name: Consolidated Systems, Inc.
EIN: 566455071

6771
Albert & Helen C. Meserve Memorial Fund
c/o Wells Fargo Bank, N.A.
1 W. 4th Fl., MAC D4000-041
Winston-Salem, NC   27101-3818
Application address: c/o Fairfield County FDN, 523
Danbury Rd., Wilton, CT 06897; tel.: 203-834-9393

Foundation type: Independent foundation
Purpose: Scholarships to residents of Bethel,
Bridgewater, Brookfield, Danbury, New Fairfield,
New Milford, Newton, Reading, Ridgefield, and
Sherman, CT.
Financial data: Year ended 08/31/2013. Assets,
$3,819,880 (M); Expenditures, $234,625; Total
giving, $164,000.
Type of support: Scholarships—to individuals.
Application information:
> *Deadline(s):* Oct. 15 and Apr. 15
> *Additional information:* Contact fund for current
>   application guidelines.
EIN: 066254956

6772
Midland Community Club Scholarship Foundation
c/o Wells Fargo Bank, N.A., Trust Tax Dept.
1 W. 4th St., 4th Fl., MAC D4000-041
Winston Salem, NC   27101-3818
Contact: Pat Bustruck
Application address: Franklin Pierce High School,
11002 18th Ave., Tacoma, WA 98445

Foundation type: Independent foundation
Purpose: Scholarships to individuals who attended
Franklin Pierce High School, WA, for four years with
an accumulated GPA of 3.3, demonstrated good
citizenship through participation in student
activities, displayed good moral character and is
planning to attend a four-year college.
Financial data: Year ended 09/30/2013. Assets,
$191,630 (M); Expenditures, $7,253; Total giving,
$3,000.
Type of support: Support to graduates or students
of specific schools; Undergraduate support.
Application information: Applications accepted.
Application form required.
> *Additional information:* Students should contact
>   their school's guidance office.
EIN: 916281184

6773
Military Ex-Prisoners of War Foundation, Inc.
(formerly American Ex-Prisoners of War Service
Foundation, Inc.)
916 Bingham Dr.
Fayetteville, NC   28304-2842   (910) 867-2775
FAX: (910) 867-0339; E-mail: threatt273@aol.com

Foundation type: Public charity
Purpose: Scholarships for children, grandchildren
and great grandchildren of former prisoners of war.
Publications: Application guidelines; Annual report;
Financial statement; Newsletter; Program policy
statement.
Financial data: Year ended 08/31/2010. Assets,
$55,699 (M); Expenditures, $197,502; Total
giving, $161,000.
Fields of interest: Military/veterans.
Type of support: Scholarships—to individuals.
Application information: Applications accepted.
Application form not required.
> *Send request by:* Mail, fax or e-mail
> *Applicants should submit the following:*
>   1) Transcripts

2) SAT
3) Photograph
4) Letter(s) of recommendation
5) GPA
6) Financial information
7) Essay
8) ACT
Additional information: Contact foundation for eligibility requirements.
EIN: 752722738

6774
Daniel R. Miller Trust Fund for Education
1525 W. W.T. Harris Blvd. D1114-044
Charlotte, NC 28288 (866) 608-0001

Foundation type: Independent foundation
Purpose: Scholarships to residents of the following areas in order of preference: Borough of Pinegrove, PA, Township of Pinegrove, PA, and Clear Spring, Washington County, MD.
Financial data: Year ended 12/31/2011. Assets, $581,074 (M); Expenditures, $36,362; Total giving, $26,000.
Type of support: Scholarships—to individuals; Undergraduate support.
Application information: Applications accepted. Application form required.
Deadline(s): June 1
Additional information: Contact foundation for current application guidelines.
EIN: 236246260

6775
Mission Healthcare Foundation, Inc.
890 Hendersonville Rd., Ste. 300
Asheville, NC 28803-1739 (828) 213-1020
Contact: John D. Kimberly, Chair
FAX: (828) 213-1030;
E-mail: missionfoundation@msj.org; Toll-free tel.: (888) 382-5511; mailing address: P.O. Box 5363, Asheville, NC 28813-5363; URL: http://www.missionhospitals.org/foundation

Foundation type: Public charity
Purpose: Support for employees through emergency crises and to provide continuing education for nurses and allied health professionals of Mission Hospital in NC.
Publications: Annual report; Financial statement.
Financial data: Year ended 09/30/2011. Assets, $24,313,109 (M); Expenditures, $12,005,316; Total giving, $9,715,843; Grants to individuals, totaling $80,185.
Fields of interest: Nursing school/education; Health care.
Type of support: Emergency funds; Grants to individuals.
Application information: Applications accepted. Application form required.
Additional information: Payments are made directly to the creditor on behalf of the individuals in crisis situation for basic expenses.
EIN: 561881331

6776
Monger Scholarship Fund
c/o Wells Fargo Bank, N.A.
1 W. 4th St., 4th Fl. MAC D4000-041
Winston Salem, NC 27101-3818 (208) 267-3146
Contact: Don Bartling
Application address: 6577 Main, Ste. 101, Bonner Ferry, ID 83805

Foundation type: Independent foundation
Purpose: Scholarships to graduates of Bonners Ferry High School or Riverside High School who have completed the 8th grade in Boundary County, ID.
Financial data: Year ended 09/30/2013. Assets, $699,992 (M); Expenditures, $36,257; Total giving, $22,400.
Fields of interest: Education.
Type of support: Support to graduates or students of specific schools.
Application information: Application form required.
Deadline(s): Apr. 13
Additional information: Applications available in the counselor's office.
EIN: 916569332

6777
Doris Floyd Moore Scholarship Fund Trust
(formerly J. W. and Doris Floyd Moore Scholarships)
c/o Wells Fargo Bank, N.A.
1 W. 4th St., 4th Fl., MAC D4000-041
Winston Salem, NC 27101-3818
Application Address: c/o JW and Doris F. Moore Scholarship, 4320-G Wade Hampton Blvd. Taylor, SC 29687

Foundation type: Independent foundation
Purpose: Scholarships to worthy high school graduates who are residents of Dillon County, SC, for postsecondary education.
Financial data: Year ended 12/31/2013. Assets, $526,139 (M); Expenditures, $34,221; Total giving, $22,000.
Fields of interest: Higher education.
Type of support: Scholarships—to individuals; Undergraduate support.
Application information: Applications accepted. Application form required.
Deadline(s): Jan. 1
Applicants should submit the following:
1) Essay
2) Transcripts
3) Letter(s) of recommendation
Additional information: Applicant must demonstrate ability in high school.
EIN: 576094970

6778
The Morehead-Cain Foundation
(formerly The John Motley Morehead Foundation)
P.O. Box 690
Chapel Hill, NC 27514-0690 (919) 962-1201
Contact: Charles E. Lovelace, Jr., Exec. Dir.
FAX: (919) 962-1615;
E-mail: moreheadcain@unc.edu; Toll free tel.: (800) 741-9023; URL: http://www.moreheadcain.org/

Foundation type: Independent foundation
Purpose: Undergraduate scholarships by nomination only to high school students in NC and Canada, public schools in Great Britain, and selected secondary schools in the rest of the U.S. to be used for attendance only at the University of North Carolina at Chapel Hill.

Publications: Annual report; Informational brochure.
Financial data: Year ended 06/30/2012. Assets, $181,389,379 (M); Expenditures, $11,339,703; Total giving, $7,058,032; Grants to individuals, 282 grants totaling $5,641,360 (high: $43,207, low: $81).
Fields of interest: Education.
International interests: Canada; England; Ireland; Wales.
Type of support: Support to graduates or students of specific schools; Awards/grants by nomination only; Undergraduate support.
Application information: Application form required. Interview required.
Applicants should submit the following:
1) Photograph
2) Transcripts
3) Letter(s) of recommendation
Additional information: Application must include two-page school form, Contact foundation for additional guidelines.
Program descriptions:
Discovery Fund: Launched in 2008, the fund provides each scholar up to $8,000 in grant funding over the course of four years to delve deeper into personal or professional interests, sharpen skills and to pursue ideas. The fund was designed as a complement to the Summer Enrichment Program. The fund serves to focus and advance the individual scholar's interests, intellectual or creative pursuits, or professional. The fund is optional, for the entire year and must be applied for and approved by a committee of Morehead Alumni.
Morehead-Cain Merit Scholarship Program: The program provides a full four-year scholarship to the University of North Carolina at Chapel Hill that includes: 1) an annual stipend that covers full tuition and all other normal expenses, including student fees, housing, books, supplies, and travel; 2) Laptop computers for all entering freshman; 3) A fully funded, four year Summer Enrichment Program, beginning the summer before the freshman year; 4) Discovery grants of up to $8,000 total over the course of four years at Carolina to be used for education opportunities. The total value of the scholarship over the four years is approximately $80,000 for in-state resdients and $140,000 for out-of-state residents. The scholarship is conferred solely on the basis of merit. Financial need is not considered in the selection. Applicants must be competitive applicants to the University of North Carolina at Chapel. To be selected, the applicant must demonstrate: 1) Moral force of character; 2) Scholarship; 3) Physical Vigor; and 4) Leadership. For more information on nominating or applying, see the foundation web site.
Summer Enrichment Program: Instituted in 1974, this first-of-its-kind program is now the centerpiece of the Morehead-Cain: four summers, fully-funded and strategically designed to broaden perspective, deepen understanding, and accelerate life experience. Scholars receive a stipend each summer to cover all expenses, including travel and housing. The program comprises four diverse, customized experiences and opportunities for scholars to understand more about the world and themselves: 1) Outdoor Leadership: the summer before their freshman year, scholars independently select and participate in one of more than fifty courses offered by Outward Bound or National Outdoor Leadership School (NOLS); 2) Public Service: the second summer directs scholars' attention outward to the needs surrounding them by giving them eight to ten weeks to work full-time in hands-on service to others; 3) International Research: the third summer scatters scholars across the globe to dig into an arena of personal

interest - academic or professional. Scholars customize the summer by choosing either to conduct an independent, in-depth research project or to explore, hands-on, a business or organization through an internship. Lasting anywhere from five to twelve weeks, the International Research summer cultivates and rewards intellectual depth and curiosity; 4) Private Enterprise: the summers culminate with scholars choosing from a wide variety of corporate or government internships. Scholars try on professional life, gaining valuable first-hand experience and personal mentoring from top executives in their field.
EIN: 560599225

6779
Hugh Morson Memorial Scholarship Fund

1 W. 4th St., D4000-041
Winston Salem, NC   27101   (866) 608-0001
Application address: c/o Center for Scholarship Administration, 4230 G. Wade Hampton Blvd., Taylors, SC 29687

Foundation type: Independent foundation
Purpose: Undergraduate scholarships to high school seniors of Raleigh, NC.
Financial data: Year ended 12/31/2012. Assets, $790,922 (M); Expenditures, $45,135; Total giving, $32,500.
Type of support: Support to graduates or students of specific schools; Undergraduate support.
Application information: Application form required.
  Deadline(s): Apr. 30
  Additional information: Applications available through high school guidance offices.
EIN: 237418060

6780
Mountain Projects, Inc.

2251 Old Balsam Rd.
Waynesville, NC   28786-7759   (828) 452-1447
Contact: Patsy Dowling, Exec. Dir.
FAX: (828) 452-9454;
E-mail: info@mountainprojects.org; Additional address: 25 Schulman St., Sylva, NC 28779-8204, tel.: (828) 586-2345, fax: (828) 5869401; URL: http://www.mountainprojects.org

Foundation type: Public charity
Purpose: Home weatherization to indigent residents of Haywood and Jackson Counties, NC, as well as small repairs or improvements to the homes of senior citizens such as minor floor repairs, installation of handrails/ramps, or small appliance replacements.
Publications: Annual report; Newsletter.
Financial data: Year ended 06/30/2012. Assets, $7,315,622 (M); Expenditures, $12,313,105; Total giving, $5,000,208; Grants to individuals, totaling $5,000,208.
Fields of interest: Aging; Economically disadvantaged.
Type of support: In-kind gifts.
Application information:
  Initial approach: Tel.
  Additional information: Contact foundation for eligibility criteria.
EIN: 560849092

6781
Music Maker Relief Foundation, Inc.

224 W. Corbin St.
P.O. Box 1358
Hillsborough, NC   27278-1358   (919) 643-2456
Contact: Timothy Duffy, Pres. and Exec. Dir.
FAX: (888) 238-8592;
E-mail: info@musicmaker.org; URL: http://www.musicmaker.org

Foundation type: Public charity
Purpose: Financial assistance to artists living on extremely small incomes and cannot meet their needs on a continual basis.
Publications: Application guidelines; Newsletter.
Financial data: Year ended 06/30/2012. Assets, $628,713 (M); Expenditures, $608,596; Total giving, $107,162; Grants to individuals, totaling $107,162.
Fields of interest: Music; Economically disadvantaged.
Type of support: Grants for special needs.
Application information: The foundation supports senior American roots musicians over 55 years old.
Program description:
  Musician Sustenance Program: This program provides traditional American musicians who are having trouble making ends meet with emergency funds. The program includes monthly stipends of $50 to $200 per month, meant to provide to artists living on extremely small incomes and emergency one-time grants for medical crises, fire, flood, or other emergencies.
EIN: 133782018

6782
Malcolm W. & Anna G. Myers Scholarship Fund

1525 W. W.T. Harris Blvd., D1114-044
Charlotte, NC   28288-5709   (866) 608-0001
Application address: c/o Wachovia Bank, N.A., Attn: Beth Bradshaw, 100 N. Main St., Winston-Salem, NC 27150, tel.: (336) 732-7206

Foundation type: Independent foundation
Purpose: Scholarships to needy and deserving graduating students from the senior class of Hanover High School or Southwestern High School, PA pursuing a higher education.
Financial data: Year ended 12/31/2011. Assets, $2,644,938 (M); Expenditures, $156,141; Total giving, $115,000; Grants to individuals, totaling $115,000.
Fields of interest: Higher education.
Type of support: Scholarships—to individuals.
Application information: Applications accepted. Application form required.
  Deadline(s): Mar. 28
  Applicants should submit the following:
    1) Transcripts
    2) Letter(s) of recommendation
    3) Financial information
    4) FAFSA
  Additional information: Application can be obtained from the guidance office of both high schools.
Program description:
  Meyers Scholarship: One-time scholarship in the amount of $4,000 is awarded to graduating seniors of the two high schools for tuition, room and board, books or other expenses necessary for the program of study. Applicants must demonstrate a desire to pursue a higher education in colleges or universities in good standing within the continental U.S., likely to succeed as students, and who are likely to make the best citizens of the U.S.
EIN: 237879656

6783
Myers Trust

(formerly Myers Charitable Trust)
c/o Wells Fargo Bank N.A.
1 W. 4th St., 4th Fl., MAC D4000-041
Winston Salem, NC   27101-3818   (563) 383-3440
Contact: Erie Johnson

Foundation type: Independent foundation
Purpose: Scholarships primarily to students from IL, who are seeking a degree in medicine, dentistry, nursing or law in Geneseo, IL School District No. 228.
Financial data: Year ended 12/31/2013. Assets, $1,165,897 (M); Expenditures, $69,860; Total giving, $49,999.
Fields of interest: Dental school/education; Law school/education; Medical school/education; Nursing school/education.
Type of support: Graduate support.
Application information: Applications accepted. Application form required.
  Initial approach: Telephone
EIN: 367233377

6784
National Humanities Center

7 Alexander Dr.
P.O. Box 12256
Research Triangle Park, NC   27709-2256   (919) 549-0661
FAX: (919) 990-8535;
E-mail: lmorgan@nationalhumanitiescenter.org;
URL: http://nationalhumanitiescenter.org/index.htm

Foundation type: Public charity
Purpose: Residential fellowship for advanced study in the humanities.
Publications: Application guidelines; Annual report; Newsletter.
Financial data: Year ended 06/30/2012. Assets, $66,033,236 (M); Expenditures, $5,331,797; Total giving, $1,625,750; Grants to individuals, totaling $1,625,750.
Fields of interest: Humanities.
Type of support: Fellowships.
Application information: Applications accepted. Application form required. Application form available on the grantmaker's web site.
  Initial approach: Letter
  Send request by: Mail
  Copies of proposal: 1
  Deadline(s): Oct. 15
  Applicants should submit the following:
    1) Curriculum vitae
    2) Financial information
    3) Letter(s) of recommendation
  Additional information: Application should also include a short bibliography, a 1,000-word project proposal, and a tentative outline of chapters.
Program description:
  Fellowships: The center offers 40 residential fellowships for advanced study in the humanities each academic year. Eligible applicants must hold doctorate degrees, or equivalent scholarly credentials; young scholars as well as senior scholars are encouraged to apply, but they must have a record of publication, as new Ph.D. recipients should be aware that the center does not normally support the revision of a doctoral dissertation. Scholars are accepted who focus on all fields of the humanities, as well as the natural and social sciences, the arts, the professions, and public life who are engaged in humanistic projects.

Fellowships are individually determined, according to the needs of the fellow and the center's ability to meet them; the center will provide at least half salary, and will cover travel expenses to and from North Carolina for fellows and their dependents.
EIN: 591735367

6785
NC Foundation for Advanced Health Programs, Inc.
2401 Weston Pkwy., Ste. 203
Cary, NC 27513-5596 (919) 821-0485
Contact: for Fellowship: Judy Howell, V.P., Admin.
E-mail for fellowship: judy.howell@ncfahp.org
FAX: (919) 821-9993;
E-mail: maggie.sauer@ncfahp.org; URL: http://www.ncfahp.org/

Foundation type: Public charity
Purpose: Fellowships for up and coming health professionals (clinicians, administrators, and others) who are in the early stages of their careers.
Financial data: Year ended 06/30/2012. Assets, $5,505,552 (M); Expenditures, $2,605,925; Total giving, $15,783; Grants to individuals, totaling $15,783.
Fields of interest: Public health school/education; Health sciences school/education.
Type of support: Fellowships.
Application information: Applications accepted. Application form required. Application form available on the grantmaker's web site. Interview required.
  Initial approach: Proposal
  Send request by: Mail or on-line
  Deadline(s): June 14
  Final notification: Recipients notified Aug. 21
  Applicants should submit the following:
    1) Resume
    2) Letter(s) of recommendation
    3) Curriculum vitae
Program description:
  Fellowship Program: The fellowship of up to $3,000 is for over two years to support approved Fellows' activities, such as educational and training courses, travel, mentoring activities and other approved projects undertaken by Fellows. Applicant must work in a clinical or administrative capacity in a rural and/or other underserved community in NC or with an organization that targets rural/underserved communities. Applicant must demonstrate a strong commitment to underserved populations and primary care, remaining in NC, community service and community-driven care, must demonstrate leadership potential, be sensitive to cultural diversity among client populations in healthcare settings and programs, and must hold realistic expectations about working in rural or other underserved communities and with vulnerable populations.
EIN: 581461316

6786
NC Foundation for Public School Children
700 S. Salisbury St.
Raleigh, NC 27611-7347 (919) 832-3000
FAX: (919) 755-5559;
E-mail: kelvin.spragley@ncae.org; Toll-free tel.: (800) 662-7924; Mailing Address: P.O. Box 27347; Raleigh, NC 27611; URL: https://ncfpsc.org

Foundation type: Public charity
Purpose: Financial support for children of NC with specific needs such as glasses, clothing, shoes, medicine, school supplies and other needs to help them perform better in school.

Publications: Application guidelines.
Financial data: Year ended 06/30/2012. Assets, $433,606 (M); Expenditures, $204,296; Total giving, $24,263; Grants to individuals, totaling $24,263.
Fields of interest: Human services; Economically disadvantaged.
Type of support: Grants for special needs.
Application information: Applications accepted. Application form required.
  Send request by: Online
  Additional information: Assistance will not be given to students 10 days prior to the end of the school year. See web site for additional application requirements.
EIN: 561957977

6787
NC Hospitality Education Foundation
(also known as NC HEF)
6036 6 Forks Rd.
Raleigh, NC 27609-3899 (919) 844-0098
Contact: Lynn Minges, Pres. and C.E.O.
FAX: (919) 844-0190; E-mail: Pauls@ncrla.biz; Toll Free tel.: (800) 582-8750; URL: http://www.ncrla.biz/

Foundation type: Public charity
Purpose: Development grants to faculty and teachers of NC high schools, culinary schools, and colleges pursuing programs in hospitality.
Publications: Application guidelines; Grants list.
Financial data: Year ended 12/31/2012. Assets, $549,104 (M); Expenditures, $150,228; Total giving, $95,565; Grants to individuals, totaling $55,565.
Fields of interest: Business school/education; Business/industry.
Type of support: Grants to individuals.
Application information: Applications accepted. Application form required.
  Send request by: Mail
  Deadline(s): Feb. 8
  Final notification: Applicants notified in Apr.
  Applicants should submit the following:
    1) Budget Information
    2) Letter(s) of recommendation
    3) Essay
Program description:
  Grant Program: Grants, limited to $2,000 per applicant will be awarded to support student development, program development or faculty development. ProStart programs are given preference. This grant is awarded on a competitive basis to qualified applicants and is available to faculty and teachers of NC high schools, culinary schools and colleges and universities.
EIN: 810618683

6788
NC Medical Society Foundation, Inc.
222 N. Person St.
P.O. Box 27167
Raleigh, NC 27611-7167 (919) 833-3836
Contact: Robert W. Seligson, C.E.O.
FAX: (919) 833-2023; Toll-free tel.: (800) 722-1350; URL: http://www.ncmsfoundation.org

Foundation type: Public charity
Purpose: Student loan repayment for professional working in rural areas of North Carolina.
Publications: Newsletter.
Financial data: Year ended 12/31/2011. Assets, $15,162,758 (M); Expenditures, $1,307,569; Total giving, $560,005; Grants to individuals, totaling $483,305.

Fields of interest: Education; Health care.
Type of support: Student loans—to individuals.
Application information: Applications accepted. Application form required. Application form available on the grantmaker's web site.
  Additional information: Application should include a copy of CV and current loan data statements supporting request. Criteria for students to qualify for loans includes working for a practice in an underserved area. Loan amounts are paid directly to the financial institution holding the loan.
EIN: 566088142

6789
Cecelia Hand Nelson and Morgan Hand II Memorial Scholarship Fund
1525 W W.T. Harris Blvd. D1114-044
Charlotte, NC 28288

Foundation type: Independent foundation
Purpose: Scholarships to graduates of Ocean City High School, NJ for postsecondary education.
Financial data: Year ended 07/31/2013. Assets, $1,649,224 (M); Expenditures, $111,337; Total giving, $74,750.
Fields of interest: Higher education.
Type of support: Support to graduates or students of specific schools; Undergraduate support.
Application information: Applications accepted. Application form required.
  Initial approach: Letter
  Deadline(s): None
  Additional information: Contact the fund for application guidelines.
EIN: 237790152

6790
New Penn Motor Express Scholarship Foundation
(formerly Arnold Industries Scholarship Foundation)
1525 W. W.T. Harris Blvd., D1114-044
Charlotte, NC 28288-1161 (717) 274-2521

Foundation type: Company-sponsored foundation
Purpose: Scholarships to children of full-time employees of Arnold Industries and its subsidiaries to support their college education.
Financial data: Year ended 12/31/2010. Assets, $0 (M); Expenditures, $25,584; Total giving, $25,246; Grants to individuals, 15 grants totaling $25,246 (high: $3,000, low: $750).
Fields of interest: Higher education.
Type of support: Employee-related scholarships.
Application information: Applications not accepted.
  Additional information: Unsolicited requests for funds not considered or acknowledged.
Company name: Arnold Industries, Inc.
EIN: 232386384

6791
Howard and Mamie Nichols Scholarship Trust
c/o Wells Fargo Bank, N.A.
1 W. 4th St., 4th Fl., MAC D4000-041
Winston Salem, NC 27101-3818

Foundation type: Independent foundation
Purpose: Scholarships to graduates of high schools in Kern County, CA, for higher education or vocational training. The program is administered by Scholarship America.

Financial data: Year ended 09/30/2013. Assets, $510,065 (M); Expenditures, $36,096; Total giving, $13,337.
Fields of interest: Vocational education, post-secondary; Higher education.
Type of support: Support to graduates or students of specific schools; Technical education support; Undergraduate support.
Application information: Application form required.
  Deadline(s): Mar. 15
  Additional information: Application must include transcripts, confidential statement from an advisor or teacher, and a letter outlining applicant's goals. Applications are available at Kern County, CA, high school offices.
EIN: 956679686

6792
Nickel Producers Environmental Research Association, Inc.
(also known as NiPERA)
2525 Meridian Pkwy., Ste. 240
Durham, NC 27713-5244 (919) 595-1950
Contact: Hudson K. Bates, Exec. Dir.
FAX: (919) 595-1955; E-mail: nipera@nipera.org;
URL: http://www.nipera.org

Foundation type: Independent foundation
Purpose: Research grants for projects that investigate the toxicity of nickel and nickel compounds. Most grants are given over several years.
Publications: Annual report.
Financial data: Year ended 12/31/2012. Assets, $806,659 (M); Expenditures, $3,057,367; Total giving, $1,156,182.
Fields of interest: Environment, pollution control; Environment, toxics; Research; Physical/earth sciences; Chemistry.
Type of support: Research.
Application information:
  Deadline(s): Contact association for application deadline.
  Applicants should submit the following:
    1) Proposal
    2) Budget Information
  Additional information: Applicants are usually preselected by NIPERA; however, unsolicited proposals are accepted. Contact foundation for additional information.
EIN: 133070077

6793
North Carolina A&T University Foundation, Inc.
1601 E. Market St.
Greensboro, NC 27411-0002 (336) 433-5560
FAX: (336) 332-8445; URL: http://www.ncat.edu/~atfound/

Foundation type: Public charity
Purpose: Scholarships to students of North Carolina A&T University, NC.
Publications: Financial statement; Newsletter.
Financial data: Year ended 06/30/2011. Assets, $53,981,240 (M); Expenditures, $2,699,805; Total giving, $758,167; Grants to individuals, totaling $758,167.
Type of support: Support to graduates or students of specific schools.
Application information:
  Initial approach: Letter
EIN: 566075899

6794
North Carolina Academy of Family Physicians Foundation
1303 Annapolis Dr.
Raleigh, NC 27608-2129 (919) 833-2110
Contact: John Rounds, Pres.
Scholarship inquiry, tel.: (800) 872-9482, e-mail: pgraber@ncafp.com
FAX: (919) 833-1801; Mailing address: P.O. Box 10278, Raleigh, NC 27605-0278; URL: http://www.ncafp.com/academy/foundation

Foundation type: Public charity
Purpose: Scholarships to medical students of North Carolina, interested in practicing family medicine.
Publications: Application guidelines.
Financial data: Year ended 12/31/2011. Assets, $1,936,622 (M); Expenditures, $371,159; Total giving, $77,250; Grants to individuals, totaling $77,250.
Fields of interest: Medical school/education.
Type of support: Scholarships—to individuals.
Application information: Applications accepted. Application form required. Application form available on the grantmaker's web site.
  Initial approach: Telephone
  Deadline(s): May
  Additional information: Applicant must demonstrate financial need and interest in the specialty of family medicine.
Program description:
  NCAFP/F Family Medicine Loan/Scholarship Program: The foundation provides scholarships of up to $2,000 to North Carolina medical students seeking careers as family physicians. Scholarships to recipients who do not complete a family medical residency training program will automatically transition into a loan, and will become due when the student has completed all formal medical training (including residencies).
EIN: 561686052

6795
North Carolina Amateur Sports, Inc.
406 Blackwell St., Ste. 120
Durham, NC 27701-3984 (919) 361-1133
FAX: (919) 361-2559; E-mail: ncas@ncsports.org;
URL: http://www.ncsports.org

Foundation type: Public charity
Purpose: Scholarships to participants of the Powerade State Games of NC, for attendance at an institution of higher learning.
Financial data: Year ended 12/31/2012. Assets, $595,400 (M); Expenditures, $938,169; Total giving, $23,415; Grants to individuals, totaling $23,415.
Fields of interest: Athletics/sports, amateur competition.
Type of support: Scholarships—to individuals.
Application information: Applications accepted. Application form required.
  Send request by: Mail
  Deadline(s): July 19
  Final notification: Applicants notified by Oct. 31
  Applicants should submit the following:
    1) GPA
    2) SAT
    3) ACT
    4) Transcripts
    5) Letter(s) of recommendation
  Additional information: Applicant must have excelled academically, athletically, and is active in community service.
EIN: 581527276

6796
North Carolina Community Foundation
4601 Six Forks Rd., Ste. 524
Raleigh, NC 27609-5286 (919) 828-4387
Contact: Jennifer Tolle Whiteside, Pres.; For grants: Sally Migliore, Dir., Community Leadership
FAX: (919) 828-5495;
E-mail: info@nccommunityfoundation.org;
Additional tel.: (800) 201-9533; URL: http://www.nccommunityfoundation.org

Foundation type: Community foundation
Purpose: Scholarships to NC high school students pursuing higher education.
Publications: Application guidelines; Annual report; Financial statement; Grants list; Informational brochure; Newsletter.
Financial data: Year ended 03/31/2013. Assets, $171,218,139 (M); Expenditures, $9,454,598; Total giving, $5,849,110.
Fields of interest: Higher education.
Type of support: Scholarships—to individuals.
Application information: Applications accepted. Application form required. Application form available on the grantmaker's web site.
  Initial approach: Application
  Deadline(s): Varies
  Additional information: Application should include FAFSA. Each scholarship has its own unique eligibility criteria. See web site for a complete listing.
EIN: 581661700

6797
North Carolina Legal Education Assistance Foundation
(also known as NC LEAF)
217 E. Edenton St.
Raleigh, NC 27601-1051 (919) 845-6089
Contact: Esther S. Hall, Exec. Dir.
FAX: (919) 848-9259; E-mail: info@ncleaf.org;
E-mail For Esther S. Hall: ehall@ncleaf.org;
URL: http://www.ncleaf.org

Foundation type: Public charity
Purpose: Loan repayment assistance to recent law school graduates who work in the NC public service sector.
Publications: Application guidelines; Newsletter.
Financial data: Year ended 06/30/2012. Assets, $302,457 (M); Expenditures, $738,612; Total giving, $576,126; Grants to individuals, totaling $576,126.
Fields of interest: Law school/education.
Type of support: Postgraduate support; Loans—to individuals.
Application information: Application form required. Application form available on the grantmaker's web site.
  Initial approach: Letter, telephone or e-mail
  Applicants should submit the following:
    1) Financial information
    2) Essay
  Additional information: Application must also include Employment Certification Forms for the applicant and their domestic partner, Lender Verification forms from all law school loan lenders, and employment history.
Program description:
  Loan Repayment Assistance Program: The program provides for loan deferral in the first three years of public service employment, followed by loan forgiveness for continued public service. To be eligible, applicants must have graduated within the last 10 years from an ABA-accredited law school, be a licensed member in good standing of a state bar,

and work full-time in a law-related public service job in North Carolina.
EIN: 561682398

6798
North Carolina National Guard Association Education Foundation

7410 Chapel Hill Rd.
Raleigh, NC   27607-5047   (919) 851-3390

Foundation type: Public charity
Purpose: Scholarships for NC National Guard members and their families for attendance at accredited colleges and universities.
Financial data: Year ended 06/30/2011. Assets, $603,702 (M); Expenditures, $37,436; Total giving, $17,750; Grants to individuals, totaling $17,750.
Fields of interest: Higher education; Military/ veterans.
Type of support: Scholarships—to individuals.
Application information: Applications accepted. Application form required.
  Additional information: Scholarships are paid directly to the educational institution on behalf of the students. If recipient fails to attend the educational institution, the award is forfeited.
EIN: 237001227

6799
North Carolina Rural Economic Development Center, Inc.

4021 Carya Dr.
Raleigh, NC   27610-2914   (919) 250-4314
Contact: Patrick Woodie, Pres.
FAX: (919) 250-4325;
E-mail: info@ncruralcenter.org; E-mail for Patrick Woodie: pwoodie@ncruralcenter.org; URL: http://www.ncruralcenter.org

Foundation type: Public charity
Purpose: Microenterprise loans to individuals starting or expanding a small business but may not qualify for a bank loan in rural NC communities.
Publications: Application guidelines.
Financial data: Year ended 06/30/2012. Assets, $173,718,148 (M); Expenditures, $61,702,237; Total giving, $53,487,941.
Fields of interest: Community/economic development.
Type of support: Loans—to individuals.
Application information: Applications accepted. Application form required. Application form available on the grantmaker's web site.
  Initial approach: Application
  Send request by: Mail
  Deadline(s): None
  Applicants should submit the following:
    1) Financial information
    2) Budget Information
  Additional information: Applicants must complete a pre-application prior to the application. See web site for additional guidelines.
Program description:
  Microenterprise Loan Program: Loans, ranging from $500 to $25,000, are available to owners and operators of businesses in rural North Carolina or who have definite plans to do so, with the goal of promoting self-employment, small-scale business creation, and economic independence throughout the region. Eligible applicants must have a minimum credit score of 575, with no outstanding judgments or liens. Applicants must also be U.S.

citizens or permanent residents, reside in North Carolina and are at least 18 years of age or older.
EIN: 561552375

6800
North Carolina Science Teacher Association

(also known as NCSTA)
P.O. Box 33478
Raleigh, NC   27636-3478   (919) 771-1226
FAX: (919) 771-1227; URL: http://www.ncsta.org

Foundation type: Public charity
Purpose: Awards and project grants to NC science teachers.
Publications: Newsletter.
Financial data: Year ended 12/31/2011. Assets, $284,485 (M); Expenditures, $158,836; Total giving, $2,600.
Fields of interest: Public education.
Type of support: Awards/prizes; Project support.
Application information: Applications accepted. Application form required. Application form available on the grantmaker's web site.
  Initial approach: Letter
  Deadline(s): Mar. 15, June 15, Sept. 15, and Dec. 15 for Study Grant; May 1 for Innovative Curriculum Support Grant
Program descriptions:
  Innovative Curriculum Support Grant: Association members may apply for funds for supplies, materials, equipment, printing, travel, and other expenses related to an innovative curriculum project involving students in a unique way. These funds are not intended for student travel (such as field trips) or for the personal gain of the project director. A committee will select recipients based on innovation, establishment of need, a realistic plan of action, the ability to replicate, and the number of persons benefited. Two grants of up to $1,000 will be awarded each year.
  Outstanding Student Teacher in Science Award: These awards are presented to recognize undergraduate teacher education students seeking certification from a North Carolina college or university who have demonstrated outstanding ability as well as promise in the teaching of science during the student teaching process. The nominees must have completed student teaching within a year before the award presentation. Three awards may be given: one for elementary grades, one for middle grades, and one for high school. The award will consist of a plaque, one year's membership in the association, and a monetary award.
  Study Grant: All members of the association who are taking study classes, attending conferences, or participating in workshops are eligible for one study grant. The association will pay up to one-half of expenses, not to exceed the amount approved by the association board each year; graduate courses for the purpose of obtaining a degree are not acceptable.
EIN: 561492328

6801
North Carolina Society of Hispanic Professionals, Inc.

8450 Chapel Hill Rd., Ste. 209
Cary, NC   27513-4577   (919) 467-8424
Contact: Marco A. Zarate M.S., Pres.
FAX: (919) 469-1785;
E-mail: mailbox@thencshp.org; URL: http://www.thencshp.org

Foundation type: Public charity

Purpose: Scholarships to recent graduates of NC high schools who are of Hispanic/Latino background and are committed to public service and community development.
Publications: Application guidelines.
Financial data: Year ended 12/31/2012. Assets, $173,555 (M); Expenditures, $310,724; Total giving, $36,500; Grants to individuals, totaling $36,500.
Fields of interest: Higher education; Hispanics/ Latinos.
Type of support: Undergraduate support.
Application information: Applications accepted. Application form required. Application form available on the grantmaker's web site.
  Initial approach: Letter
  Deadline(s): Jan. 15
  Applicants should submit the following:
    1) Essay
    2) Transcripts
    3) Letter(s) of recommendation
    4) GPA
  Additional information: Preference will be given to foreign-born applicants or the native born children of foreign-born parents. Recipients will be chosen based on family economic need, community involvement, academic achievement, volunteerism and leadership.
EIN: 562131090

6802
North Carolina State Grange Foundation, Inc.

1734 Wilkesboro Hwy.
Statesville, NC   28625
URL: http://www.ncgrange.com/NC_State_Grange_Foundation.php

Foundation type: Independent foundation
Purpose: Scholarships to high school seniors or current college students who are residents of NC and members of the Grange.
Financial data: Year ended 12/31/2011. Assets, $7,211 (M); Expenditures, $681; Total giving, $0.
Fields of interest: Higher education.
Type of support: Scholarships—to individuals; Undergraduate support.
Application information: Applications accepted. Application form required. Application form available on the grantmaker's web site.
  Send request by: Mail
  Deadline(s): Apr. 1 for new applicants and June 30 for renewal applicants for NC State Grange Scholarship, Sept. 1 for National GROW Scholarship
  Final notification: Applicants notified Oct. 1 for National GROW Scholarship
  Applicants should submit the following:
    1) Photograph
    2) Letter(s) of recommendation
    3) Transcripts
Program descriptions:
  National Grange GROW Club Scholarship: Scholarships of $1,000 per year are available to NC residents who are members of the Grange for higher education. Scholarships can be renewed up to three times at the undergraduate level (four years total) and four more years for graduate school for a total of eight years of schooling. Applicants must be accepted to a post secondary institution at a two or four year colleges and universities, community colleges or trade schools, and must be able to document active participation in local or State Grange activities.
  NC State Grange Scholarship: Scholarships of $1,000 per year are available to NC residents who are members of the Grange for higher education.

Scholarships can be renewed up to three times at the undergraduate level (four years total) and four more years for graduate school for a total of eight years of schooling. Applicants must be accepted to a post secondary institution at a two or four year colleges and universities, community colleges or trade schools, and must be able to document active participation in local or State Grange activities.
EIN: 562125884

6803
Nucor Foundation
1915 Rexford Rd.
Charlotte, NC 28211-3465   (704) 367-8662
FAX: (704) 943-7199;
E-mail: scholarshipsupport@nucor.com;
URL: https://scholarshipapply.nucor.com/

Foundation type: Company-sponsored foundation
Purpose: Undergraduate and vocational education scholarships to children and stepchildren of employees of Nucor Corporation and scholarships to students pursuing degrees in engineering and metallurgy from communities where Nucor operates.
Financial data: Year ended 12/31/2012. Assets, $157,868 (M); Expenditures, $1,757,988; Total giving, $1,757,048; Grants to individuals, 670 grants totaling $1,757,048 (high: $6,000, low: $197).
Fields of interest: Vocational education; Higher education; Engineering school/education.
Type of support: Employee-related scholarships; Scholarships—to individuals.
Application information: Applications accepted. Application form required. Application form available on the grantmaker's web site.
  Initial approach: Application
  Deadline(s): Mar. 1 for Community Scholarships
  Applicants should submit the following:
    1) SAT
    2) ACT
    3) Class rank
    4) Transcripts
    5) Letter(s) of recommendation
    6) Financial information
Program descriptions:
  Community Scholarships: The foundation awards four-year $3,000 college scholarships to students from areas of Nucor operations to pursue a degree in engineering or metallurgy. Recipients are selected based on personal background, academic abilities, leadership traits, character, and financial need.
  Employee-Related Scholarships: The foundation awards $3,000 undergraduate and vocational education scholarships to children and stepchildren of current or deceased employees of Nucor Corporation. Recipients are selected based on personal background, academic abilities, leadership traits, character, and financial need.
Company name: Nucor Corporation
EIN: 237318064

6804
L.R. Oates Scholarship Fund Trust
1525 W. W.T. Harris Blvd. D1114-044
Charlotte, NC 28288-1161   (866) 608-0001

Foundation type: Independent foundation
Purpose: Student loans to financially needy high school graduates for higher education.
Financial data: Year ended 05/31/2013. Assets, $656,039 (M); Expenditures, $45,828; Total giving, $30,000.
Fields of interest: Higher education.

Type of support: Undergraduate support.
Application information: Applications accepted. Application form required.
  Initial approach: Letter
  Deadline(s): None
  Additional information: Application must also include transcripts and a copy of driver's license.
EIN: 596672364

6805
**Forrest C. & Minnie Less Oates
  Scholarship Trust**
1 W. 4th St. D4000-041
Winston Salem, NC 27101   (205) 621-2351
Application address: c/o First Baptist Church of Pelham, 2867 Pelham Pkwy., Pelhalm, AL 35124

Foundation type: Independent foundation
Purpose: Scholarships to residents of Pelham, AL area who attend or plan to attend a college or university in AL.
Financial data: Year ended 12/31/2012. Assets, $209,060 (M); Expenditures, $14,706; Total giving, $11,000.
Fields of interest: Higher education.
Type of support: Scholarships—to individuals.
Application information: Applications accepted.
  Initial approach: Letter
  Send request by: Mail
  Deadline(s): None
  Additional information: Application should include financial information.
EIN: 636166146

6806
Outer Banks Community Foundation, Inc.
13 Skyline Rd.
Southern Shores, NC 27949   (252) 261-8839
Contact: Lorelei Costa, Exec. Dir.
FAX: (252) 261-0371; E-mail: info@obcf.org;
URL: http://www.obcf.org

Foundation type: Community foundation
Purpose: Scholarships to students and residents of Dare County, NC for higher education.
Publications: Application guidelines; Annual report; Financial statement; Grants list; Informational brochure; Newsletter.
Financial data: Year ended 12/31/2012. Assets, $9,997,620 (M); Expenditures, $714,510; Total giving, $487,985.
Fields of interest: Higher education.
Type of support: Scholarships—to individuals; Undergraduate support.
Application information:
  Deadline(s): Vary
  Additional information: The foundation manages many scholarship funds, each of which has its own criteria for selection, such as academic ability, career choice, financial need, athletic interests, or geographic location. Contact the foundation for specific information about the funds. Unsolicited requests for funds not considered or acknowledged.
EIN: 581516313

6807
The Outreach Center
510 E. Fleming Dr.
P.O. Box 1003
Morganton, NC 28680-5315   (828) 439-8300
FAX: (828) 437-8573; E-mail: outreach@hci.net;
URL: http://www.theoutreachcenter.org

Foundation type: Public charity
Purpose: Provides free adult education, GED preparation, learning-skills training, computer literacy, financial literacy, employment skills education and food distribution to indigent residents of Burke and its surrounding counties in western NC.
Financial data: Year ended 12/31/2011. Assets, $3,349,141 (M); Expenditures, $6,119,426; Total giving, $5,636,750; Grants to individuals, totaling $3,555,262.
Fields of interest: Economically disadvantaged.
Type of support: In-kind gifts.
Application information: Applications not accepted.
  Additional information: Unsolicited requests for funds not considered or acknowledged.
EIN: 562221575

6808
**Peewee and Myrtle Owens Scholarship
  Trust**
(formerly Owens Scholarship Trust Co.)
P.O. Box 2907
Wilson, NC 27894-2907   (252) 399-7700
Application address: c/o Wilson County School, Att.: Dr. Larry Price, 117 N. Tarboro St., Wilson, NC 27893, tel.: (252) 399-7700

Foundation type: Independent foundation
Purpose: Scholarships to graduates of Wilson County, NC, public schools, primarily to those who commit to teach in the Wilson County, NC, public schools for a minimum of four years.
Publications: Application guidelines.
Financial data: Year ended 08/31/2013. Assets, $2,602,334 (M); Expenditures, $162,948; Total giving, $126,000.
Fields of interest: Teacher school/education; Education.
Type of support: Support to graduates or students of specific schools; Undergraduate support.
Application information: Application form required.
  Initial approach: Telephone to request application
  Deadline(s): Apr. 1
  Final notification: High school awards day
  Additional information: Applicants must have at least a 3.0 GPA; Applications available from high school guidance counselors in Wilson County, NC.
EIN: 566532306

6809
Pamlico Partnership for Children, Inc.
702 A Main St.
Bayboro, NC 28515   (252) 745-7850
Contact: Betty W. Blythe, Exec. Dir.
FAX: (252) 745-7860;
E-mail: betty@pamlicopartnership.org; Mailing address: P.O. Box 612, Bayboro, NC 28515-0612; E-Mail for Betty W. Blythe: betty@pamlicopartnership.org; URL: http://www.pamlicopartnership.org

Foundation type: Public charity
Purpose: Financial assistance for eligible working or in-school parents for subsidized child care in Pamlico County, NC.
Financial data: Year ended 06/30/2011. Assets, $23,239 (M); Expenditures, $194,603.
Fields of interest: Early childhood education.
Type of support: Grants for special needs.
Application information:
  Initial approach: Letter

Additional information: Contact foundation for eligibility criteria.
EIN: 561874658

6810
N. J. Pappas Trust I
1525 W. W.T. Harris Blvd., D1114-044
Charlotte, NC   28288   (336) 747-8174
Application address: 1 W., 4th St., 2nd Fl., Winston Salem,NC 27101-3818

Foundation type: Independent foundation
Purpose: Scholarships to residents of Winston-Salem, NC.
Financial data: Year ended 12/31/2012. Assets, $615,685 (M); Expenditures, $41,430; Total giving, $30,000.
Type of support: Undergraduate support.
Application information: Applications not accepted.
   Additional information: Unsolicited requests for funds not considered.
EIN: 236478280

6811
Grace Patch Scholarship Trust
c/o Wells Fargo Bank, N.A.
1 W. 4th St., 4th Fl. MAC D4000-041
Winston Salem, NC   27101-3818

Foundation type: Independent foundation
Purpose: Scholarships to graduates of Sweet Home High School, OR, for education at Linn-Benton Community College in Albany, OR.
Financial data: Year ended 03/31/2013. Assets, $224,372 (M); Expenditures, $12,179; Total giving, $7,500.
Type of support: Support to graduates or students of specific schools; Undergraduate support.
Application information: Applications not accepted.
   Additional information: Unsolicited requests for funds not accepted or considered.
EIN: 936181508

6812
Ola Warren & John W. Patterson, Jr. Scholarship Fund
c/o Wells Fargo Bank, N.A. Trust tax Dept.
1 W. 4th St., 4th Fl. MAC D4000-041
Winston Salem, NC   27101-3818

Foundation type: Independent foundation
Purpose: Scholarships to students for higher education at Campbell or Wake Forest universities, NC.
Financial data: Year ended 12/31/2013. Assets, $923,766 (M); Expenditures, $54,453; Total giving, $38,000; Grants to individuals, 3 grants totaling $38,000 (high: $12,667, low: $12,666).
Fields of interest: Higher education.
Type of support: Support to graduates or students of specific schools; Undergraduate support.
Application information: Applications not accepted.
   Additional information: Unsolicited requests for funds not considered or acknowledged.
EIN: 586314688

6813
Hattie M. Peckitt Scholarship Trust
(formerly Leonard Carlton Peckitt Scholarship Trust)
1 W. 4th St., D4000-041
Winston Salem, NC   27101   (336) 732-6950
Contact: Karolyn Kilpatrick
Application address: Wells Fargo Bank, 100 N. Main St., Winston-Salem, NC 27106

Foundation type: Independent foundation
Purpose: Scholarships for one to four years of study to worthy graduates of Catasauqua High School, PA for attendance at any accredited, public or private, two year or four year college, university, technical college or trade school.
Financial data: Year ended 12/31/2012. Assets, $282,189 (M); Expenditures, $23,359; Total giving, $18,190.
Fields of interest: Vocational education, post-secondary; Higher education.
Type of support: Support to graduates or students of specific schools.
Application information: Selection is based on financial need, academic achievement, and potential to succeed in the student's chosen field. Application can be obtained from the high school. The scholarship is administered by the Center for Scholarship Administration, Inc.
EIN: 236611993

6814
Pediatric Brain Tumor Foundation of the United States, Inc.
(formerly Ride For Kids Foundation, Inc.)
302 Ridgefield Ct.
Asheville, NC   28806-2243   (828) 665-6891
Contact: Dianne Traynor, Chair. and Pres.
FAX: (828) 665-6894; E-mail: research@pbtfus.org;
Toll-free tel.: (800) 253-6530; URL: http://www.pbtfus.org/

Foundation type: Public charity
Purpose: Research grants to investigators for projects that demonstrate the potential to advance basic scientific research in brain tumors, as well as scholarships to individuals diagnosed with malignant and nonmalignant tumors who were younger than 19 at onset.
Publications: Informational brochure; Newsletter.
Financial data: Year ended 12/31/2011. Assets, $6,080,363 (M); Expenditures, $5,882,266; Total giving, $2,035,831; Grants to individuals, totaling $136,518.
Type of support: Fellowships; Research; Scholarships—to individuals.
Application information: Application form required. Application form available on the grantmaker's web site.
   Deadline(s): Aug. 1 for Clinical Research Projects and fellowships
Program descriptions:
   Clinical Fellowships in Pediatric Brain Tumor Research: Supports a junior clinical investigator for two years of research, granting up to $50,000 each year. Applicants should have an appointment at the instructor level, and no higher than the assistant professor level. The grant will be made for a hypothesis-driven clinical research project or correlative laboratory project in the field of pediatric brain tumors. Possible projects include clinical research trials, neuro-imaging research projects, or neuro-psychological quality of life research projects.
   Clinical Pediatric Brain Tumor Research Grants: Supports two years of research granting up to $50,000 each year. Awards will go to hypothesis-driven projects that exhibit high scientific merit. Possible projects include

institutional or collaborative clinical research trials, neuro-psychological quality of life research projects, or correlative translational research with direct clinical application as it relates to patient specimens.
   Scholarship Program: Scholarships are available to students who have been diagnosed at or before the age of 19 with a primary malignant or non-malignant central nervous system brain and/or spinal cord tumor. Awards may be used to cover tuition, fees, and book at any post-secondary institution, including technical schools, vocational schools, junior colleges, and four-year colleges or universities.
EIN: 581966822

6815
Pennsylvania Industrial Chemical
1 W. 4th St., D4000-041
Winston Salem, NC   27101   (800) 576-5135

Foundation type: Independent foundation
Purpose: Scholarships to graduates and graduating seniors of Chester High School, PA.
Financial data: Year ended 12/31/2012. Assets, $1,399,584 (M); Expenditures, $81,298; Total giving, $54,000.
Fields of interest: Higher education.
Type of support: Scholarships—to individuals; Support to graduates or students of specific schools.
Application information:
   Initial approach: Letter
   Deadline(s): Mar. 1
   Final notification: Applicants will be notified after graduation
   Applicants should submit the following:
      1) Essay
      2) Letter(s) of recommendation
      3) ACT
      4) SAT
      5) Class rank
      6) GPA
      7) Transcripts
   Additional information: Application must include personal information, participation in curricular activities and parents' tax forms.
EIN: 236233922

6816
The Perry-Griffin Foundation
P.O. Box 82
Oriental, NC   28571-0082   (252) 249-0227
Contact: Paul Delamar, Secy. and Dir.

Foundation type: Independent foundation
Purpose: Educational loans to individuals in Pamlico and Jones counties, NC, seeking higher education.
Financial data: Year ended 08/31/2013. Assets, $4,692,084 (M); Expenditures, $322,384; Total giving, $83,545; Grants to individuals, 41 grants totaling $83,545 (high: $5,000, low: $350).
Type of support: Student loans—to individuals.
Application information: Applications accepted. Application form required.
   Deadline(s): None
   Applicants should submit the following:
      1) Transcripts
      2) Letter(s) of recommendation
EIN: 560860864

6817
Person County Partnership for Children
111 S. Main St.
Roxboro, NC 27573-5522   (336) 599-3773
Contact: Judy Batten, Exec. Dir.
FAX: (336) 599-3999; E-mail: info@esinc.net;
Mailing address: P.O. Box 1791, Roxboro, NC
27573-1791; E-Mail for Judy Batten:
jbatten@esinc.net; URL: http://
www.personpartnershipforchildren.org

Foundation type: Public charity
Purpose: Financial assistance to residents of
Person County, NC, to help qualifying parents with
the cost of child care.
Publications: Newsletter.
Financial data: Year ended 06/30/2012. Assets,
$281,982 (M); Expenditures, $1,128,108; Total
giving, $804,791; Grants to individuals, totaling
$181,779.
Type of support: Grants for special needs.
Application information:
Initial approach: Letter or e-mail
Additional information: Contact foundation for
current application guidelines.
EIN: 561872882

6818
The Pharmacy Network Foundation, Inc.
P.O. Box 31603
Raleigh, NC 27622-1603   (919) 661-8461
Contact: Jimmy S. Jackson, Secy.-Treas.
Application address: 2015 Navan Ln., Garner, NC
27529

Foundation type: Company-sponsored foundation
Purpose: Scholarships only to students at the
University of North Carolina at Chapel Hill and
Campbell University, NC, who are studying to
become pharmacists.
Financial data: Year ended 12/31/2012. Assets,
$17,179,802 (M); Expenditures, $1,200,171;
Total giving, $820,000.
Fields of interest: Pharmacy/prescriptions.
Type of support: Support to graduates or students
of specific schools; Undergraduate support.
Application information: Applications accepted.
Additional information: Application should
include a two-page essay explaining why
applicant wants to be a retail pharmacist.
EIN: 561690027

6819
Phoenix Challenge Foundation, Inc.
6805 Pleasant Grove Rd.
Waxhaw, NC 28173-8152   (704) 309-3748
Contact: Bettylyn Krafft, Chair.
FAX: (704) 243-2445; URL: http://
www.phoenixchallenge.org

Foundation type: Public charity
Purpose: Scholarships and incentives to high
school and post high school students pursuing a
career in flexography.
Financial data: Year ended 06/30/2012. Assets,
$143,505 (M); Expenditures, $56,152.
Fields of interest: Arts education.
Type of support: Scholarships—to individuals;
Awards/prizes.
Application information: Students are judged in a
competition.
Program description:
High School Competition: The two and a half day
competition includes five areas of rigorous testing
of operating a Flexo press, repress, plate making,
written knowledge, and Flexo math skills. Schools

have the option to bring one or two teams. The first
place team receives medals, and their school
receive a plaque. They will each a $1,000
scholarship along with the "Harper Cup" to display
at their school for one year. The second and third
place teams receive medals and their school
receive a plaque to display. The second place team
each receives a $500 scholarship. Each student
who participates receives a certificate of
participation and well over $100 in
industry-sponsored gifts.
EIN: 571153858

6820
Pitt County Educational Foundation, Inc.
1717 W. 5th St.
Greenville, NC 27834-1601   (252) 830-4223

Foundation type: Public charity
Purpose: Mini-grants and scholarships to teachers
and secondary and post-secondary students in the
Pitt County school system, NC.
Financial data: Year ended 12/31/2011. Assets,
$981,842 (M); Expenditures, $141,267; Total
giving, $109,050; Grants to individuals, totaling
$70,886.
Fields of interest: Elementary/secondary
education.
Type of support: Program development;
Undergraduate support.
Application information:
Initial approach: Letter
EIN: 561540991

6821
The Polk County Community Foundation, Inc.
255 S. Trade St.
Tryon, NC 28782-3707   (828) 859-5314
Contact: Elizabeth Nager, Exec. Dir.; Cathie
Campbell, Grants Mgr.
FAX: (828) 859-6122;
E-mail: foundation@polkccf.org; Additional E-mail:
ccampbell@polkccf.org; URL: http://
www.polkccf.org

Foundation type: Community foundation
Purpose: Scholarships to graduating high school
seniors, and adults returning to school who are
residents of Polk County, NC, Saluda, NC or
Landrum, SC.
Publications: Application guidelines; Annual report;
Financial statement; Informational brochure
(including application guidelines); Occasional
report.
Financial data: Year ended 12/31/2012. Assets,
$43,582,773 (M); Expenditures, $2,025,760;
Total giving, $1,186,813; Grants to individuals,
79 grants totaling $160,698.
Fields of interest: Vocational education,
post-secondary; Higher education.
Type of support: Scholarships—to individuals.
Application information: Applications accepted.
Application form required. Application form
available on the grantmaker's web site.
Initial approach: Telephone, letter, or e-mail
Send request by: Mail or in person
Copies of proposal: 1
Deadline(s): Nov. 5 for high school seniors
Final notification: Applicants notified in two
months
Applicants should submit the following:
1) ACT
2) FAFSA
3) Transcripts
4) SAT

5) Letter(s) of recommendation
6) Financial information
7) Essay
Additional information: See web site for
additional guidelines.
EIN: 510168751

6822
Leslie T. & Frances U. Posey Foundation
c/o Wells Fargo Bank, N.A., Trust Tax Dept.
1 W. 4th St., 4th Fl., MAC D4000-041
Winston Salem, NC 27101-3818   (941)
361-5803

Foundation type: Independent foundation
Purpose: Graduate scholarships for art education,
especially painting and sculpture of the traditional
kind.
Financial data: Year ended 08/31/2013. Assets,
$329,217 (M); Expenditures, $18,570; Total
giving, $12,000.
Fields of interest: Arts education; Sculpture;
Painting; Arts.
Type of support: Graduate support.
Application information: Application form required.
Deadline(s): Mar. 1
Final notification: Apr. 15
Applicants should submit the following:
1) Photograph
2) Essay
Additional information: Application must also
include slides. See foundation web site for
application form and further details.
EIN: 596832335

6823
Edgar and Lois Reich Education Foundation
1 W. 4th St., D4000-041
Winston Salem, NC 27101   (866) 608-0001
Application Address: c/o Center for Scholarship
Admin-Co SA, 4320-G Wade Hampton Blvd.,
Taylors, SC 29687; URL: http://
www.csascholars.org

Foundation type: Independent foundation
Purpose: Scholarships to native born residents of
Forsyth or Davidson counties, NC, pursuing an
undergraduate degree or graduate degree in the
field of education or dental science.
Financial data: Year ended 12/31/2012. Assets,
$510,113 (M); Expenditures, $31,073; Total
giving, $19,574.
Fields of interest: Dental school/education;
Teacher school/education.
Type of support: Graduate support; Undergraduate
support.
Application information: Application form required.
Initial approach: Letter, telephone, e-mail or web
site
Send request by: Mail
Deadline(s): Mar. 14
Applicants should submit the following:
1) GPA
2) Financial information
3) Letter(s) of recommendation
4) Transcripts
Additional information: Application should also
include signed copy of parents' income tax
return and W-2 forms for both parents,
personal statement, and list of academic
honors, leadership positions, and community
service. The scholarship is administered by
the Center for Scholarship Administration, Inc.
EIN: 582245280

6824
Olive Rice Reierson Foundation
c/o Wells Fargo Bank, N.A. Trust Tax Dept.
1 W. 4th St., 4th Fl. MAC D4000-041
Winston Salem, NC   27101-3818   (406)
447-2050

Foundation type: Independent foundation
Purpose: Scholarships to Powell County, MT,
residents for continuing their education at
accredited institutions of higher learning.
Publications: Application guidelines.
Financial data: Year ended 09/30/2013. Assets,
$1,476,749 (M); Expenditures, $84,171; Total
giving, $58,000.
Fields of interest: Higher education.
Type of support: Support to graduates or students
of specific schools; Undergraduate support.
Application information: Application form required.
  Deadline(s): Apr. 1
  Applicants should submit the following:
    1) Transcripts
    2) Essay
  Additional information: Application must also
  include three character references one of
  whom is associated with the applicant's high
  school.
EIN: 363463190

6825
Religious Institutional Finance Corporation of America
(also known as RIFCA)
c/o Brooks Huey
255 Bucahanan St.
Glade Valley, NC   28627   (336) 363-9114
Contact: Brooks T. Huey, Pres.
Application Address: P.O Box 6 Roaring Gap, NC
28668

Foundation type: Independent foundation
Purpose: Scholarships to TN residents based on
need and purpose.
Financial data: Year ended 12/31/2012. Assets,
$146,480 (M); Expenditures, $8,083; Total giving,
$7,020.
Fields of interest: Higher education.
Type of support: Scholarships—to individuals.
Application information: Applications accepted.
Application form required.
  Deadline(s): None
EIN: 621183570

6826
Waldo E. Rennie Scholarship Fund
c/o Wells Fargo Bank, N.A.
1 W. 4th St., 4th Fl. MAC D4000-041
Winston Salem, NC   27101-3818

Foundation type: Independent foundation
Purpose: Loans to financially needy students to
study physics, geology, or engineering at a college
or university which receives its principal support
directly from the state of CO. Recipients must be
pursuing a four-year degree.
Publications: Informational brochure.
Financial data: Year ended 09/30/2013. Assets,
$6,103,232 (M); Expenditures, $77,331; Total
giving, $0.
Fields of interest: Education; Physics; Geology;
Engineering/technology.
Type of support: Student loans—to individuals.
Application information: Application form required.
  Initial approach: Letter
  Deadline(s): None

  Additional information: Contact school's financial
  aid office for application.
EIN: 846138107

6827
Rex Hospital Guild, Inc.
(formerly Korner Gift Shop)
4420 Lake Boone Trail
Raleigh, NC   27607-7505   (919) 784-3114

Foundation type: Public charity
Purpose: Scholarships to high school seniors of NC
pursuing postsecondary in the field of nursing.
Financial data: Year ended 06/30/2012. Assets,
$1,166,884 (M); Expenditures, $177,259; Total
giving, $161,366.
Fields of interest: Nursing school/education.
Type of support: Scholarships—to individuals.
Application information: Applications accepted.
Application form required. Interview required.
  Additional information: Scholarship is paid
  directly to the educational institution on
  behalf of the students.
EIN: 566000865

6828
Z. Smith Reynolds Foundation, Inc.
102 W. 3rd St., Ste. 1110
Winston-Salem, NC   27101-3962   (336)
725-7541
FAX: (336) 725-6069; E-mail: info@zsr.org;
Additional tel.: (800) 443-8319; URL: http://
www.zsr.org

Foundation type: Independent foundation
Purpose: Awards by nomination only to NC
individuals who demonstrate leadership in their
communities. Sabbaticals to leaders of NC
nonprofit organizations.
Publications: Annual report (including application
guidelines); Informational brochure; Informational
brochure (including application guidelines);
Occasional report.
Financial data: Year ended 12/31/2012. Assets,
$16,687,410 (M); Expenditures, $17,965,118;
Total giving, $14,903,958.
Fields of interest: Volunteer services; Nonprofit
management.
Type of support: Awards/grants by nomination only;
Awards/prizes; Grants for special needs.
Application information: Application form available
on the grantmaker's web site.
  Initial approach: Letter or telephone
  Deadline(s): Dec. 1 for Sabbatical Program, June
  1 for Nancy Susan Reynolds Awards
  Additional information: Nomination forms
  required for NSR awards; Completion of
  formal application required for Sabbatical
  program.
Program descriptions:
  Nancy Susan Reynolds Awards: The foundation
  annually honors three unrecognized North
  Carolinians who have shown exceptional qualities
  of community leadership through the Nancy Susan
  Reynolds Awards. Each award is accompanied by a
  $25,000 grant, of which $20,000 is given to
  organizations designated by the award recipient;
  the balance ($5,000) is given to the recipient.
  Nominees for the award must perform valuable
  public service in one of the three following areas: 1)
  Advocacy - This category is for persons whose
  persistence, patience and intelligence have earned
  them the ear of those who make and shape policies
  in the state and its communities; 2) Personal
  Service - This category seeks to recognize people
  who have helped alleviate the condition of some

less-favored group in the community, performed
work which serves as a catalyst for self-respect and
self-sufficiency, and provided special examples of
service which cause others to take more seriously
their responsibilities to people in their communities
and state; and 3) Race Relations - This category
seeks to recognize individuals who have made
significant efforts to encourage communications
and motivate improved relationships between
persons of different racial or ethnic backgrounds,
increased understanding or resolved conflicts
between persons of different racial and ethnic
backgrounds, or helped resolve conflicts created by
racial and ethnic discord, and stimulated action to
eliminate racism.
  Sabbatical Program: The foundation offers up to
  five sabbaticals annually to individuals in paid,
  full-time leadership positions who have served a
  North Carolina nonprofit organization for at least
  three years, two of which were as leaders. The
  sabbaticals are for a three to six month period
  during which the individuals are not working for their
  organization, but instead are engaging in activities
  which offer personal renewal and professional
  growth. Each recipient receives up to $25,000.
  They can do something for themselves, such as
  travel, return to school, or read books they've never
  had time to read. Recipient organizations may
  decide whether or not to keep sabbatical recipients
  on their payroll during the sabbatical. Regardless of
  this decision, the entire award will be paid to the
  recipient.
EIN: 586038145

6829
Richard Richardi Scholarship Trust
c/o IMT Fiduciary Tax
1 W. 4th St., 2nd Fl., D4000
Winston-Salem, NC   27101   (508) 660-7257

Foundation type: Independent foundation
Purpose: Scholarships to graduates of Walpole
High School, MA, who are second-year college
students.
Financial data: Year ended 05/31/2013. Assets,
$2,099,491 (M); Expenditures, $120,001; Total
giving, $69,500; Grants to individuals, 41 grants
totaling $69,500 (high: $3,500, low: $1,000).
Type of support: Support to graduates or students
of specific schools; Undergraduate support.
Application information: Applications not
accepted.
  Additional information: Contributes only to
  preselected individuals.
EIN: 597062049

6830
Robert L. and Shirla B. Richardson Foundation
P.O. Box 2907-Trust Tax Dept.
Wilson, NC   27894-2907   (304) 348-7313
Contact: John Jividen
Application address: c/o John Jividen, 300
Summers St., Charleston, WV 25301-1624,
tel.: (304) 348-7313

Foundation type: Operating foundation
Purpose: Scholarships to graduates of Lincoln High
School, Shinnston, WV for higher education.
Financial data: Year ended 12/31/2011. Assets,
$310,156 (M); Expenditures, $13,462; Total
giving, $7,000.
Fields of interest: Higher education.
Type of support: Support to graduates or students
of specific schools.

Application information: Applications accepted.
  Deadline(s): None
  Additional information: Selection is based on need and SAT score.
EIN: 556143132

6831
The Mary Lynn Richardson Fund
c/o Piedmont Trust Co.
P.O. Box 20124
Greensboro, NC   27420-0124   (336) 274-5471
FAX: (336) 272-8921; E-mail: sgreen@piedfin.com

Foundation type: Independent foundation
Purpose: Provides basic needs for indigent persons and for assistance with their medical expenses.
Publications: Application guidelines.
Financial data: Year ended 12/31/2011. Assets, $6,003,361 (M); Expenditures, $337,496; Total giving, $285,296.
Fields of interest: Human services.
Type of support: Grants to individuals; Grants for special needs.
Application information: Applications accepted.
  Initial approach: Letter
  Deadline(s): Aug. 31
  Additional information: Written proposal with a copy of IRS Determination letter.
EIN: 066025946

6832
Richmond-Pennock Family Scholarship Fund
1525 W. W.T. Harris Blvd. D1114-044
Charlotte, NC   28288   (717) 354-1550

Foundation type: Independent foundation
Purpose: Scholarships to graduates of Garden Spot High School, New Holland, PA, pursuing nursing or dentistry.
Financial data: Year ended 09/30/2013. Assets, $1,621,700 (M); Expenditures, $90,933; Total giving, $68,000.
Fields of interest: Dental school/education; Nursing school/education.
Type of support: Support to graduates or students of specific schools.
Application information: Applications not accepted.
  Additional information: Recipients will be chosen by the High School Awards Committee.
EIN: 236637016

6833
The Riddick Foundation
1 W. 4th St., D4000-041
Winston Salem, NC   27101   (866) 608-0001
Application address: c/o Center for Scholarship Administration, 4320-G Wade Hampton Blvd., Taylors, SC 29687

Foundation type: Independent foundation
Purpose: Scholarships to deserving high school seniors or college students currently enrolled full time at UNC/Chapel Hill and who are residents of North Carolina with preference given first to Bethel, NC, then Pitt County and third to Eastern North Carolina.
Financial data: Year ended 12/31/2012. Assets, $1,072,466 (M); Expenditures, $76,161; Total giving, $60,651.
Fields of interest: Higher education.
Type of support: Support to graduates or students of specific schools.

Application information: Applications accepted. Application form required. Application form available on the grantmaker's web site.
  Initial approach: Letter, telephone, e-mail or web site
  Send request by: Mail or on-line
  Deadline(s): Mar. 28
  Applicants should submit the following:
    1) Transcripts
    2) GPA
  Additional information: Application should also include a personal statement and signed copy of parent's income tax form and W-2 forms. The scholarship is administered by the Center for Scholarship Administration, Inc.
EIN: 256887722

6834
Jean Risley Educational Trust
c/o Wells Fargo Bank, N.A.
1 W. 4th St., 4th Fl. MAC D4000-041
Winston Salem, NC   27101-3818

Foundation type: Independent foundation
Purpose: Student loans to senior-year law students in OR. Preference is given to individuals in Benton, Linn, and Marion counties.
Financial data: Year ended 11/30/2013. Assets, $753,690 (M); Expenditures, $33,366; Total giving, $19,640.
Fields of interest: Law school/education.
Type of support: Loans—to individuals.
Application information: Applications accepted. Application form required.
  Additional information: Application must include transcripts.
EIN: 943117918

6835
Lieutenant Robert Bolenius Ritchie Memorial Fund
1525 W. W.T. Harris Blvd., D1114-044
Charlotte, NC   28288-1161   (866) 608-0001
Application address: 100 North Main St. D4001-130, Winston-Salem, NC 27150-6732, tel.: (336) 732-2523
URL: https://www.csascholars.org/eritchie/index.php

Foundation type: Independent foundation
Purpose: Scholarships to students graduating from public high schools in Lancaster City and County, PA who otherwise would be unable to attend college.
Financial data: Year ended 12/31/2011. Assets, $860,308 (M); Expenditures, $57,317; Total giving, $42,000.
Fields of interest: Higher education.
Type of support: Support to graduates or students of specific schools; Undergraduate support.
Application information: Application form required. Application form available on the grantmaker's web site.
  Send request by: Mail and on-line
  Deadline(s): Feb. 7 for on-line, Feb. 15 by mail
  Applicants should submit the following:
    1) Transcripts
    2) GPA
    3) Essay
    4) ACT
  Additional information: Application should also include a personal statement, a copy of parents' signed income tax form and W-2 forms. The scholarship is administered by the Center for Scholarship Administration, Inc. Payment will be made directly to the college

on behalf of the student. Applicant must demonstrate financial need.
EIN: 236718706

6836
Oscar C. Rixson Foundation, Inc.
P.O. Box 19255
Asheville, NC   28815-1255
Contact: Alan L. Mojonnier, Pres.
E-mail: mojo@asheville.com

Foundation type: Independent foundation
Purpose: Grants to missionaries, teachers, and laymen engaged in the spread of the gospel throughout the world.
Financial data: Year ended 12/31/2012. Assets, $2,792,723 (M); Expenditures, $285,059; Total giving, $227,915; Grants to individuals, 78 grants totaling $48,900 (high: $750, low: $400).
Fields of interest: Christian agencies & churches.
Type of support: Grants to individuals.
Application information: Applications accepted. Application form not required.
  Initial approach: Letter
  Deadline(s): None
  Additional information: Application must include details of use and financial information.
EIN: 136129767

6837
Robeson County Partnership for Children, Inc.
210 E. 2nd St.
Lumberton, NC   28358-5620   (910) 738-6767
Contact: Jessica Lowery, Exec. Dir.
FAX: (910) 738-4379;
E-mail: progdir@rcpartnership4children.org; E-Mail for Jessica Lowery: execdir3@rcpartnership4children.org; URL: http://www.robesonpartnership.org

Foundation type: Public charity
Purpose: Awards to provide teachers, assistant teachers, directors, assistant directors, and family child care providers of Robeson County, NC with salary supplements that are tied to their individual levels of education.
Publications: Application guidelines; Annual report; Informational brochure; Newsletter; Program policy statement; Quarterly report.
Financial data: Year ended 06/30/2011. Assets, $46,055 (M); Expenditures, $2,248,063; Total giving, $1,340,423; Grants to individuals, 19 grants totaling $21,778.
Fields of interest: Early childhood education; Children.
Type of support: Grants to individuals.
Application information:
  Initial approach: Telephone or e-mail
  Deadline(s): Dec. 14
Program description:
  Educational Awards: Awards are intended to provide children with more stable relationships with better-educated teachers by rewarding teacher education and continuity of care. Recipients must work with children in a licensed and registered child care program in Robeson County, and must have an associate's degree or higher in early childhood or be enrolled in at least one college curriculum class (earning at least a grade of C) working toward an associate degree in early childhood. Awards range from $1,150 to $4,050.
EIN: 561940920

6838
A. Robinson Trust f/b/o Scholarship Fund
1525 W. WT Harris Blvd.
Charlotte, NC 28288 (336) 747-8176
Application address: c/o Wells Fargo Bank, 1 W. 4th St., 6th Fl., Winston-Salem, NC 27150

Foundation type: Independent foundation
Purpose: Scholarships to individuals primarily in Ardmore, PA.
Financial data: Year ended 12/31/2011. Assets, $317,320 (M); Expenditures, $21,224; Total giving, $14,700.
Fields of interest: Higher education.
Type of support: Scholarships—to individuals.
Application information: Applications accepted.
   Deadline(s): Apr. 1
EIN: 236421843

6839
Emmet and Mary Robinson Trust Foundation
1525 W. W.T. Harris Blvd., D1114-044
Charlotte, NC 28288-1161 (866) 608-0001
Application address: c/o Center for Scholarship Admin., 4320-G Wade Hampton Blvd. Taylors, SC 29687, tel.: (866) 660-8001

Foundation type: Independent foundation
Purpose: Scholarships to graduating seniors who reside in Wayne county, NC and attend a Wayne County Public High School and intend to pursue a degree in medicine, nursing, agriculture or in the ministry of the Presbyterian and Episcopal Churches.
Financial data: Year ended 12/31/2011. Assets, $738,411 (M); Expenditures, $45,785; Total giving, $32,000.
Fields of interest: Higher education; Medical school/education; Nursing school/education; Theological school/education; Agriculture.
Type of support: Scholarships—to individuals.
Application information: Applications accepted. Interview required.
   Initial approach: Letter
   Deadline(s): Jan. 15
   Applicants should submit the following:
      1) Financial information
      2) Transcripts
      3) SAT
      4) Letter(s) of recommendation
      5) ACT
      6) GPA
   Additional information: Applicant must demonstrate financial need. Application should also include a copy of parents' signed income tax and W2 forms.
EIN: 566582132

6840
John W. Rollison Educational Scholarship Trust
1525 W. W.T. Harris Blvd. D1114-044
Charlotte, NC 28288-5709

Foundation type: Independent foundation
Purpose: Scholarships to worthy students of Franklin and Southampton counties, VA.
Financial data: Year ended 12/31/2012. Assets, $910,620 (M); Expenditures, $58,520; Total giving, $36,850.
Type of support: Scholarships—to individuals.
Application information: Applications accepted. Application form not required.

   Initial approach: Letter
   Deadline(s): None
EIN: 546485419

6841
Freda T. Roof Memorial Scholarship Fund
c/o Wells Fargo Bank, N.A., Trust Tax Dept.
1 W. 4th St., 4th Fl., MAC D4000-041
Winston Salem, NC 27101-3818

Foundation type: Independent foundation
Purpose: Scholarships to financially needy and worthy students in CO obtaining a professional education at nonprofit and accredited colleges and universities in CO.
Financial data: Year ended 12/31/2013. Assets, $1,553,845 (M); Expenditures, $97,395; Total giving, $72,000.
Type of support: Undergraduate support.
Application information:
   Initial approach: Letter
   Deadline(s): None
   Additional information: Students must apply to their school's financial aid office, and not directly to the bank.
EIN: 846016684

6842
Rouch Foundation Charitable Trust
(formerly A. P. and Louise Rouch Boys Foundation)
c/o Wells Fargo Bank, N.A.,Trust Tax Dept.
1 W. 4th St., 4th Fl., MAC D4000-041
Winston Salem, NC 27101-3818 (800) 981-8063

Foundation type: Independent foundation
Purpose: Scholarships to financially needy students attending college in the Twin Falls, ID, area, who are orphaned, poor, or underprivileged, and pursuing undergraduate, vocational, or graduate education.
Financial data: Year ended 12/31/2013. Assets, $205,069 (M); Expenditures, $7,456; Total giving, $2,375.
Fields of interest: Vocational education; Higher education; Economically disadvantaged.
Type of support: Graduate support; Technical education support; Undergraduate support.
Application information: Applications accepted. Application form required.
   Additional information: Awards are paid directly to the educational institution on behalf of the students.
Program description:
   Scholarship Program: The foundation provides college, vocational school, trade school, and university scholarships to high school graduates and individuals who have attained a GED, who are orphaned, poor, or underprivileged. Applicants must have demonstrated ability, industry, and a promise of useful citizenship. The scholarships are awarded on an annual basis for an amount that is approximately equal to the tuition charges for a year at the College of Southern Idaho or the University of Idaho. The foundation grants scholarships only to undergraduate students. However, by unanimous consent, the Advisory Committee may grant scholarships to students seeking advanced degrees, providing that undergraduate work that has been done expeditiously. Each student must submit a grade transcript one month after the conclusion of the academic year. Additional progress reports are encouraged, but not required.
EIN: 826005152

6843
Rowan Helping Ministries
P.O. Box 4026
226 North Long St.
Salisbury, NC 28145-4026 (704) 637-6838
E-mail: rhm@rowanhelpingministries.org; E-Mail For Kyna S. Grubb: kfoster@rhmmail.org; URL: http://www.rowanhelpingministries.org/

Foundation type: Public charity
Purpose: Limited financial assistance to indigent residents of Rowan County, NC, for living expenses.
Financial data: Year ended 06/30/2012. Assets, $5,160,177 (M); Expenditures, $8,540,761; Total giving, $2,076,924; Grants to individuals, 122,863 grants totaling $1,100,051.
Type of support: Grants for special needs.
Application information:
   Initial approach: Letter or telephone
   Additional information: Applicants must present photo ID, proof of income, and proof of crisis or emergency. Contact foundation for complete eligibility requirements.
EIN: 561544532

6844
RSPA Scholarship Foundation, Inc.
(formerly ICRDA/SDA Scholarship Foundation)
10130 Perimeter Pkwy., Ste. 420
Charlotte, NC 28216 (704) 357-3124
URL: http://www.goRSPA.org

Foundation type: Independent foundation
Purpose: Scholarships to children of RSPA member/dealers or children of employees of RSPA member/dealers.
Financial data: Year ended 04/30/2013. Assets, $43,110 (M); Expenditures, $47,589; Total giving, $46,250; Grants to individuals, 31 grants totaling $46,250 (high: $3,000, low: $1,000).
Type of support: Scholarships—to individuals.
Application information: Application form required.
   Deadline(s): June 15
   Applicants should submit the following:
      1) Transcripts
      2) FAF
      3) Essay
   Additional information: Application must also include list of school activities, leadership positions, work experience and awards.
EIN: 364130326

6845
Constance H. Rumbough Trust
(formerly James Hickey Rumbough Fund)
1525 W. W.T. Harris Blvd., D1114-044
Charlotte, NC 28288-1161 (336) 747-8187

Foundation type: Independent foundation
Purpose: Scholarships to residents of Lynchburg, VA, and the immediate surrounding area for higher education or training in a trade, occupation, or for medical care.
Financial data: Year ended 12/31/2011. Assets, $233,898 (M); Expenditures, $17,130; Total giving, $11,050.
Type of support: Scholarships—to individuals.
Application information: Applications accepted. Application form required.
   Initial approach: Letter
   Additional information: Scholarships are awarded on the basis of financial need, character, citizenship, and motivation.
EIN: 546113973

6846
Nancy D. Russell Testamentary Trust
c/o L. Patten Mason
P.O. Box 99
Morehead City, NC   28557-0099

Foundation type: Independent foundation
Purpose: College scholarships to graduating students for attendance at colleges or universities in North Carolina.
Financial data: Year ended 12/31/2011. Assets, $212,107 (M); Expenditures, $9,454; Total giving, $6,875; Grants to individuals, 4 grants totaling $6,875 (high: $2,500, low: $625).
Fields of interest: Higher education.
Type of support: Scholarships—to individuals.
Application information: Contact you schools' guidance office for application information.
EIN: 201117535

6847
S.R.C. Education Alliance
P.O. Box 12053
Research Triangle Park, NC   27709-2053   (919) 941-9400
E-mail: EducationAlliance@src.org; Application e-mail for fellowships and scholarships: apply@src.org; URL: http://www.src.org/program/srcea/

Foundation type: Company-sponsored foundation
Purpose: Fellowships to students and scholarships to women and minorities for post-graduate study in a field relevant to microelectronics and under a GRC-approved research program.
Publications: Application guidelines.
Financial data: Year ended 12/31/2012. Assets, $899,471 (M); Expenditures, $1,615,656; Total giving, $1,301,508; Grants to individuals, 104 grants totaling $742,522 (high: $21,000, low: $122).
Fields of interest: Engineering; Science; Minorities; Women.
Type of support: Fellowships; Scholarships—to individuals; Graduate support.
Application information: Applications accepted. Application form required. Application form available on the grantmaker's web site.
  Initial approach: Application
  Send request by: E-mail
  Deadline(s): Mid-Feb.
  Final notification: Applicants notified in Apr.
  Applicants should submit the following:
    1) Letter(s) of recommendation
    2) Transcripts
  Additional information: Applications should also include Graduate Record Examination (GRE) test scores.
Program descriptions:
  Company-Named Fellowships: The foundation awards company-named fellowships to student applicants from the Graduate Fellowship Program whose proposed research matches a cosponsoring company's research interests. The fellowships are named after the companies who provide matching funding for the program. Fellowship recipients are mentored by an industry advisor and is awarded an internship from the cosponsoring company. Fellowships include the AMD/Mahboob Khan/GRC Fellowship, the Robert M. Burger Fellowship, the Peter Verhofstadt Fellowship, and the International Fellowship.
  Company-Named Scholarships: The foundation awards company-named scholarships to student applicants whose proposed research matches a cosponsoring company's research interests. The scholarships are named after the companies who

provide matching funding for the program. Scholarship recipients are mentored by an industry advisor and is awarded an internship from the cosponsoring company.
  GRC Graduate Fellowship Program: The foundation awards graduate fellowships to encourage academically gifted students to pursue graduate degrees in research areas related to SRC, with emphasis on microelectronics; and to develop a pool of high quality doctoral graduates for member companies and universities. Fellowships provide full tuition, a stipend for up to five years of doctoral study, and a $2,000 annual gift for the student's faculty advisor in support of the student.
  GRC Master's Scholarship Program: The foundation awards scholarships to encourage academically gifted minority students, including women, African-American, Hispanic, and Native American students, to pursue graduate research related to Global Research Collaboration (GRC), with emphasis on microelectronics; and to develop a pool of high quality minority candidates for doctoral study and hire by GRC companies. The scholarship provides full tuition for up to two years of master's level study and a $2,000 unrestricted gift for use by the student's faculty advisor.
EIN: 581807204

6848
Salisbury-Rowan Community Action Agency, Inc.
(formerly Salisbury-Rowan Community Service Council, Inc.)
1300 W. Bank St.
Salisbury, NC   28144-3910   (704) 633-6633
FAX: (704) 633-7814; Mailing address: P.O. Box 631, Salisbury, NC 28145-0631; URL: http://www.srcaa.com/

Foundation type: Public charity
Purpose: Grants to economically disadvantaged individuals, children and families of Rowan, Cabarrus, Davidson, Moore, Montgomery and Stanly counties, NC.
Publications: Application guidelines; Annual report; Financial statement; Informational brochure; Newsletter; Program policy statement.
Financial data: Year ended 10/31/2011. Assets, $1,779,007 (M); Expenditures, $12,142,751. Grants for special needs amount not specified.
Fields of interest: Human services; Economically disadvantaged.
Type of support: Grants for special needs.
Application information: Assistance includes child and family development, youth employment and job training, and weatherization assistance. Contact the agency for eligibility determination.
EIN: 560840196

6849
Samaritan's Purse
P.O. Box 3000
Boone, NC   28607-3000   (828) 262-1980
FAX: (828) 266-1056; E-mail: info@samaritan.org; URL: http://www.samaritanspurse.org/

Foundation type: Public charity
Purpose: Financial assistance to victims of war, poverty, natural disasters, disease, and famine.
Publications: Annual report; Informational brochure; Newsletter.
Financial data: Year ended 12/31/2011. Assets, $280,781,752 (M); Expenditures, $350,183,276; Total giving, $175,948,674; Grants to individuals, totaling $391,712.

Fields of interest: Education; Christian agencies & churches.
Type of support: Emergency funds; Grants for special needs.
Application information: Applications not accepted.
  Additional information: Unsolicited requests for funds not considered or acknowledged.
EIN: 581437002

6850
Sandhills Community Action Program, Inc.
103 Saunders St.
P.O. Box 937
Carthage, NC   28327-0937
Contact: Nina Walker, Exec. Dir.
FAX: (910) 947-5514;
E-mail: Info@sandhillscap.org; URL: http://www.sandhillscap.org/

Foundation type: Public charity
Purpose: Grants for housing assistance and weatherization to economically disadvantaged, handicapped, and elderly residents of Moore, Richmond, Montgomery, and Anson counties, NC.
Financial data: Year ended 06/30/2012. Assets, $1,264,925 (M); Expenditures, $3,134,374; Total giving, $2,009,084; Grants to individuals, totaling $2,009,084.
Fields of interest: Housing/shelter; Human services.
Type of support: Grants for special needs.
Application information: Applications accepted.
  Additional information: Contact foundation for eligibility requirements.
EIN: 560854878

6851
Walter H. Sauvain Trust
(formerly Sauvain Scholarship Fund)
1 W. 4th St., D4000-041
Winston Salem, NC   27101   (866) 608-0011
Application address: c/o Center for Scholarship Administration, P.O.Box 1465 Taylors, SC 29687

Foundation type: Independent foundation
Purpose: Scholarships to graduating students of Lewisburg High School, Lewisburg, PA.
Financial data: Year ended 12/31/2012. Assets, $794,180 (M); Expenditures, $57,237; Total giving, $42,800.
Fields of interest: Higher education.
Type of support: Undergraduate support.
Application information: Applications accepted.
  Deadline(s): Mar. 31
  Additional information: Applicant must demonstrate financial need. Application can be obtained from Lewisburg High School guidance office.
EIN: 236791852

6852
Scholarship Fund for South Carolina State College
c/o Wells Fargo Bank, N.A., Trust Department
1 W. 4th St., 4th Fl., MAC D4000-041
Winston-Salem, NC   27101-3818   (866) 601-0001

Foundation type: Company-sponsored foundation
Purpose: Scholarships to juniors enrolled in the School of Business at South Carolina State College.

The program is administered by the South Carolina Foundation of Independent Colleges.
Financial data: Year ended 10/31/2013. Assets, $69,664 (M); Expenditures, $2,943; Total giving, $2,737.
Type of support: Support to graduates or students of specific schools.
Application information: Applications accepted. Application form required.
  Initial approach: Letter
  Deadline(s): Feb. 1
  Additional information: Application address: c/o South Carolina Foundation of Independent Colleges, P.O. Box 1465, Taylors, SC 29687.
EIN: 586239696

6853
Scholarship Headquarters, Inc.
1390 N. Wesleyan Blvd.
Rocky Mount, NC   27804-1816   (252) 443-9520
Contact: Don Fisher, Dir.

Foundation type: Operating foundation
Purpose: Scholarships and student loans to Christian students in the Rocky Mount, NC, area to attend Christian colleges and universities.
Financial data: Year ended 12/31/2012. Assets, $17,884 (M); Expenditures, $251; Total giving, $0.
Fields of interest: Theological school/education.
Type of support: Undergraduate support.
Application information: Applications accepted. Application form required.
  Initial approach: Letter
  Additional information: Application should include two letters of reference.
EIN: 331038618

6854
Schug Foundation
c/o Peggy Cobb Schug
7013 Erin Ct.
Charlotte, NC   28210-4906   (704) 377-0261
Contact: Phillips M. Bragg
Application address: c/o Bragg Financial Advisors, 1031 S. Caldwell St., Ste. 200, Charlotte, NC, 28203; tel.: (704) 377-0261.

Foundation type: Independent foundation
Purpose: Scholarships to North Carolina residents of Meckenburg, Haywood or Jackson county.
Financial data: Year ended 12/31/2012. Assets, $1,239,953 (M); Expenditures, $182,736; Total giving, $165,347; Grants to individuals, 70 grants totaling $165,347 (high: $7,500, low: $250).
Fields of interest: Education.
Type of support: Scholarships—to individuals.
Application information: Applications accepted. Application form required.
  Deadline(s): Apr. 30
EIN: 566583795

6855
Betty I. and Karl B. Search Scholarship Fund
c/o Wells Fargo Bank, N.A.
1 W. 4th St., 4th Fl., MAC D4000-041
Winston Salem, NC   27101-3818

Foundation type: Independent foundation
Purpose: Scholarships to deserving high school seniors attending either Lake Lehman or Northwest Area High School, PA for full time study at an accredited, public or private two or four year college, university, technical college or trade school.

Financial data: Year ended 12/31/2013. Assets, $538,622 (M); Expenditures, $31,204; Total giving, $20,000.
Fields of interest: Vocational education, post-secondary; Higher education.
Type of support: Support to graduates or students of specific schools.
Application information: Applications accepted. Application form required.
  Send request by: Mail
  Deadline(s): Dec.
  Applicants should submit the following:
    1) Transcripts
    2) Letter(s) of recommendation
    3) GPA
  Additional information: Application should also include a personal statement regarding importance of scholarship, college and/or career plans, and list of academic honors, leadership positions and community service. Scholarship is for college freshman year only, and it's non-renewable.
EIN: 256699396

6856
The Sara Smith Self Foundation, Inc.
1001 W. 4th St.
Winston-Salem, NC   27101-2410   (336) 607-7314
Contact: Robert L. Edwards, Secy.-Treas. and Dir.

Foundation type: Independent foundation
Purpose: Scholarships to students for attendance at University of North Carolina, at Greensboro for continuing education.
Financial data: Year ended 12/31/2011. Assets, $3,452,077 (M); Expenditures, $131,693; Total giving, $94,500.
Fields of interest: Higher education.
Type of support: Support to graduates or students of specific schools.
Application information: Unsolicited requests for funds not considered or acknowledged.
EIN: 203631059

6857
Ben Selling Scholarship Loan Fund
c/o Wells Fargo Bank, N.A.
1 W. 4th St., 4th Fl. MAC D4000-041
Winston Salem, NC   27101-3818

Foundation type: Independent foundation
Purpose: Scholarships to financially needy and worthy students desiring to become students of any college given to Oregon Health Sciences University, Reed College, Portland State University, Portland Community College or Mt. Hood Community College, OR.
Financial data: Year ended 09/30/2013. Assets, $567,459 (M); Expenditures, $10,066; Total giving, $0.
Fields of interest: Higher education.
Type of support: Scholarships—to individuals; Support to graduates or students of specific schools.
Application information: Applications accepted. Application form required.
  Initial approach: Letter
  Additional information: Application should include signed co-signer statement, copy of financial aid, $30 processing fee, previous year transcript and applicant's signature.
EIN: 936017158

6858
Elizabeth Braswell Sheffield Scholarship Fund
P.O. Box 366
Speed, NC   27881

Foundation type: Independent foundation
Purpose: Scholarships to graduating seniors of Tarboro High School, NC enrolled at an accredited college or university.
Financial data: Year ended 12/31/2012. Assets, $150,074 (M); Expenditures, $3,344; Total giving, $2,000; Grant to an individual, 1 grant totaling $2,000.
Fields of interest: Higher education.
Type of support: Support to graduates or students of specific schools.
Application information: Applications accepted. Application form required. Interview required.
  Deadline(s): Apr. 15
  Additional information: Completed applications must be returned to Tarboro high school guidance counselor.
EIN: 566181591

6859
Buck and S.Louise Shelly Scholarship Fund
1525 W W.T. Harris Blvd., D1114-044
Charlotte, NC   28288
Application address: c/o northeast School District Foundation, 41 Harding St.manchester,PA 17345

Foundation type: Independent foundation
Purpose: Scholarships to graduates of Northeast High School for postsecondary education at accredited four year undergraduate college.
Financial data: Year ended 12/31/2012. Assets, $475,891 (M); Expenditures, $30,019; Total giving, $22,000.
Fields of interest: Higher education.
Type of support: Scholarships—to individuals; Undergraduate support.
Application information: Applications accepted. Application form required.
  Deadline(s): June
EIN: 256887904

6860
Sigma Alpha Iota Philanthropies, Inc.
1 Tunnel Rd.
Asheville, NC   28805-1229   (828) 251-0606
FAX: (828) 251-0644; E-mail: nh@sai-national.org; URL: http://www.sigmaalphaiota.org/home/philanthropies/tabid/55/default.aspx

Foundation type: Public charity
Purpose: Scholarships to members of the Sigma Alpha Iota fraternity, and non-members to promote musical development and growth among musical students.
Publications: Application guidelines.
Financial data: Year ended 12/31/2011. Assets, $1,837,973 (M); Expenditures, $374,611.
Fields of interest: Music; Students, sororities/fraternities.
Type of support: Awards/prizes; Graduate support; Undergraduate support; Doctoral support.
Application information: Applications accepted. Application form required. Application form available on the grantmaker's web site.
  Deadline(s): Varies
  Additional information: See web site for additional application guidelines.

Program descriptions:

Alumnae Chapters Project Seed Grants: Four grants of up to $2,500 each are available to Sigma Alpha Iota (SAI) chapters to initiate work on a major project in music that is expected to continue beyond the period of the initial grant (i.e., one year), and become self-sustaining. Proposals will be evaluated on: the potential impact of the project beyond the local level; evidence of potential sustainability of the project in the long term; expressed commitment of the chapter in terms of monetary and 'people' resources; the quality of the overall proposal in terms of clarity, evidence of good planning, and project ideas and goals; and reasonableness/justification of the proposed budget. Eligible chapters must be in good financial standing with the fraternity.

Career Performance Grant in Memory of Verna Ross Orndorff: An annual grant of $5,000 will be awarded to a member of Sigma Alpha Iota (SAI) for the purpose of advancing her career in performance. Depending on the year, grants will be awarded to singers or instrumentalists (piano/harpsichord/organ/percussion or strings/woodwind/brass). Applicants must: have been initiated into SAI while as a college student; must have an undergraduate degree as of the application deadline; be preparing for a concert career and demonstrate career potential; must have had considerable performing experience outside of an academic environment; and must not be under professional management. Eligible singers may also not be older than 35, or instrumentalists no older than 32, as of the application deadline. Funds must be used for advanced study, coaching, or other purposes directly related to the development of a professional performing career.

Doctoral Grant Underwritten by Donna Heiken: A $2,500 grant will be made available to a member of Sigma Alpha Iota who is enrolled in a program leading to a doctoral degree. Dissertations are acceptable in music education, music therapy, musicology, ethnomusicology, theory, psychology of music, or applied research including performance or pedagogy.

Dr. and Mrs. Berge Markarian Scholarship for a Music Industry Internship at Appalachian State University: One $1,000 scholarship will be awarded to a member of Epsilon Theta chapter at Appalachian State University in any music industry area, who is scheduled to do an internship in her chosen field. It can be used for the fall, spring, or summer semester, and will be applied towards the internship tuition at Appalachian State University.

Founders Loan Fund: This loan program provides up to $2,500 at only five percent interest for alumnae and affiliated patronesses to pursue projects related to music or musical study. Programs can include, but are not limited to, continuing studies in music, studies at a major summer music center, private applied music studies or coaching, purchase of a musical instrument, or other expenses for musical activities. Applicant does not have to be a member of an alumnae chapter or a full-time student, but must be in good standing with the Fraternity and have paid National dues.

International Study Grant for Graduate Students: This grant is available for music studies outside of the U.S. for initiated members of Sigma Alpha Iota, who are pursuing advanced studies beyond the bachelor's degree. Grants of $1,500 (for one semester) to $3,000 (for a full academic year) are available.

Jazz Studies Scholarship: A $1,500 scholarship is available to a member of Sigma Alpha Iota who is in good financial standing with the fraternity.

Scholarships must be applied toward study leading to a music degree with an emphasis in jazz studies.

Kennedy Center Internship: The organization makes available a three-month internship for a member of Sigma Alpha Iota at The Institute for Arts Management at the Kennedy Center in Washington, DC during the summer. Interns will be placed in administrative positions dealing with the management, educational, presentational, promotional, and/or technical aspects of the center's operation, depending on the interests and qualifications of the individual intern. Interns will also participate in weekly executive seminar sessions in which they will have an opportunity to learn about all the departments of the center. Eligible applicants may be junior, seniors, graduate students, or graduates out of school for no more than two years, who are in good financial standing with the university. Interns receive a stipend of $225 per week for each week of the internship.

Music Business/Technology Scholarship in Memory of Dorothy Cooke Whinery: This $2,000 scholarship will be made available to a member of Sigma Alpha Iota who is enrolled in an undergraduate degree program in the field of music business or music technology. The degree emphasis may also include music marketing, music business administration, entertainment industry, commercial music, music management, recording industry, or other related fields.

Music Education Scholarship for Graduate Students in Memory of Mabel Biever: A $1,500 scholarship will be awarded to a member of Sigma Alpha Iota who has completed an undergraduate degree in music education, and has been accepted into and/or continuing in an accredited graduate program leading to a masters or doctoral degree in music education. Applicants must be in good standing with the fraternity and have paid national dues; it is preferred that the candidate has had at least one year of teaching experience in a private or public school. Applicants without teaching experience must include a video of student teaching experience and references from her major professor and student teacher advisor.

Music Therapy Scholarship: A $1,500 scholarship is available to an undergraduate or graduate member of Sigma Alpha Iota who has successfully completed a minimum of two years' approved training toward a degree in music therapy. Applicants must be continuing her studies in this field.

Musical Theater Scholarship: A $1,500 scholarship will be made to a member of Sigma Alpha Iota in good standing with the fraternity. Requirements include enrollment in an undergraduate musical theater program, and availability to perform at a Sigma Alpha Iota national convention. Scholarship must be applied toward study leading to a music degree, with an emphasis in musical theater.

Services for Musicians with Special Needs Scholarship: A $1,500 scholarship will be awarded to a member of Sigma Alpha Iota who is enrolled in an undergraduate or graduate degree program in music with a qualifying disability, or to someone pursuing studies to become a teacher or therapist in the field.

Undergraduate Scholarship (in memory of Phyllis Dobbyn Holt): Twelve scholarships of $1,500 each, and three scholarships of $2,000 each, will be made available to Sigma Alpha Iota members who exemplify the ideals of the fraternity and demonstrate financial need, outstanding musical ability, above-average scholarship, potential leadership, and contribution to campus and community life.

EIN: 237391912

6861
Simpson Scholars Trust

(formerly Educational Trust Fund in Memory of J. Lupton Simpson and Marion Porter Simpson, also known as Simpson Education Trust)
1 W 4th St., D4000-041
Winston Salem, NC 27101 (866) 608-0001
Application addresses: c/o Center for Scholarship Admin, 4320-G Wade Hampton Blvd., Taylors, SC 29687

Foundation type: Independent foundation
Purpose: Scholarships to qualified high school graduates from Loudoun County High School, VA or Loudoun Valley High School, VA for higher education.
Financial data: Year ended 12/31/2012. Assets, $680,863 (M); Expenditures, $44,017; Total giving, $30,000.
Fields of interest: Higher education.
Type of support: Support to graduates or students of specific schools.
Application information: Contact your respective schools for application information.
EIN: 546251486

6862
J. E. Sirrine High School Fund
1525 W.W.T. Harris Blvd., Ste. D1114
Charlotte, NC 28262-8522 (336) 747-8182

Foundation type: Public charity
Purpose: Scholarships to high school students of the School District of Greenville, SC county for postsecondary education.
Financial data: Year ended 12/31/2011. Assets, $18,014,430 (M); Expenditures, $1,127,891; Total giving, $845,740. Scholarships—to individuals amount not specified.
Fields of interest: Vocational education, post-secondary; Higher education.
Type of support: Scholarships—to individuals.
Application information: Scholarship selection is based on financial need and academic ability. Contact your school's guidance counselor for additonal application information.
EIN: 576059441

6863
Carole C. and O. Temple Sloan, Jr. Foundation
4900 Falls of Neuse Rd., Ste. 150
Raleigh, NC 27609-5490
Contact: Cheryl Ligon, Tr.

Foundation type: Independent foundation
Purpose: Scholarships and loans to graduating high school seniors, primarily in MT and NC, for higher education.
Financial data: Year ended 12/31/2012. Assets, $16,364,599 (M); Expenditures, $1,216,140; Total giving, $1,089,127.
Type of support: Undergraduate support.
Application information: Applications accepted. Application form required. Interview required.
Additional information: Application must include references.
EIN: 561870844

6864
Smart Start of Buncombe County, Inc.
(formerly Buncombe County Partnership for
Children)
2229 Riverside Dr.
Asheville, NC 28804-9623 (828) 285-9333
Contact: Ron Bradford, Exec. Dir.
FAX: (828) 285-9933;
E-mail: ron@smartstart-buncombe.net; URL: http://
www.smartstart-buncombe.org/

Foundation type: Public charity
Purpose: Scholarships to childcare providers,
directors and students interested in pursuing a
career in early childhood education/care. Funds are
good for early childhood education courses at
Asheville-Buncombe Community College, NC.
Financial data: Year ended 06/30/2011. Assets,
$245,560 (M); Expenditures, $3,979,753; Total
giving, $3,099,077; Grants to individuals, totaling
$700,029.
Fields of interest: Early childhood education.
Type of support: Support to graduates or students
of specific schools.
Application information: Applications accepted.
  Initial approach: Mail, telephone or e-mail
EIN: 561942178

6865
Smart Start Rowan, Inc.
(formerly Rowan Partnership for Children, Inc.)
1839 W. Jake Alexander Blvd.
Salisbury, NC 28147-1144 (704) 630-9085
FAX: (704) 630-6259;
E-mail: jgerstenmier@smartstartrowan.org;
URL: http://www.rowan-smartstart.org

Foundation type: Public charity
Purpose: Grants towards a degree in Early
Childhood Education, to child care professionals
working in licensed child care facilities in Rowan
County, NC.
Publications: Annual report.
Financial data: Year ended 06/30/2012. Assets,
$338,190 (M); Expenditures, $3,169,629; Total
giving, $2,441,803; Grants to individuals, totaling
$13,028.
Fields of interest: Early childhood education; Child
development, education.
Type of support: Grants to individuals.
Application information: Applications not
accepted.
  Additional information: Unsolicited requests for
    funds not considered or acknowledged.
EIN: 561890324

6866
William Harold Smith Charitable Trust
1105 Airport Rd.
Marion, NC 28752-5633 (828) 652-9443
Contact: Matt Smith, Tr.

Foundation type: Independent foundation
Purpose: Scholarships to financially needy
graduates of McDowell High School, NC for
postsecondary education.
Financial data: Year ended 12/31/2012. Assets,
$5,070,411 (M); Expenditures, $311,656; Total
giving, $260,650; Grants to individuals, 89 grants
totaling $260,650 (high: $6,000, low: $400).
Type of support: Support to graduates or students
of specific schools; Undergraduate support.
Application information: Application form required.
  Deadline(s): Apr. 2
  Applicants should submit the following:
    1) Letter(s) of recommendation

  2) Essay
  Additional information: Application must also
    include a list of extracurricular activities and
    copy of parents' and student's tax returns;
    Applications can be obtained from high school
    guidance counselors.
EIN: 566526359

6867
**Winthrop H. Smith Memorial Foundation,
Inc.**
100 N. Tryon St.
Charlotte, NC 28255-4000
Contact: Francine Martin

Foundation type: Independent foundation
Purpose: Grants in aid and loans to needy current
and retired employees of Merrill Lynch & Co. for
emergency relief of personal or family misfortune.
Financial data: Year ended 12/31/2012. Assets,
$2,757,670 (M); Expenditures, $1,374,570; Total
giving, $1,282,560; Grants to individuals, 362
grants totaling $1,282,560 (high: $18,484, low:
$134).
Type of support: Employee-related welfare.
Application information: Contact foundation for
current application deadline/guidelines.
EIN: 136160365

6868
Kathleen A. Smith Scholarship Fund
1 W. 4th St., D4000-041
Winston Salem, NC 27101

Foundation type: Independent foundation
Purpose: Scholarships to graduates of Warren Hills
Regional Senior High School, NJ, for higher
education.
Financial data: Year ended 11/30/2012. Assets,
$236,101 (M); Expenditures, $15,764; Total
giving, $10,300.
Fields of interest: Higher education; Scholarships/
financial aid.
Type of support: Support to graduates or students
of specific schools.
Application information: Applications not
accepted.
  Additional information: Unsolicited requests for
    funds not considered or acknowledged.
EIN: 237773022

6869
The Southern Documentary Fund
(also known as SDF)
762 9th St., Ste. 574
Durham, NC 27705-4803 (919) 308-3714
E-mail: info@southerndocumentaryfund.org;
URL: http://www.southerndocumentaryfund.org

Foundation type: Public charity
Purpose: Support to artists for independent
documentary media projects produced within or
about the American South.
Financial data: Year ended 12/31/2012. Assets,
$134,659 (M); Expenditures, $375,511.
Fields of interest: Media/communications; Film/
video; Arts, artist's services.
Type of support: Fiscal agent/sponsor.
Application information: Applications accepted.
Application form required. Application form
available on the grantmaker's web site.
  Copies of proposal: 1
  Deadline(s): Jan. 15, Apr. 15, July 15, Oct. 15 for
    fiscal sponsorship
  Applicants should submit the following:

  1) Work samples
  2) Proposal
  3) Budget Information
  Additional information: Application should also
    include a $35 application fee; See web site
    for additional application information.
Program description:
  Fiscal Sponsorship: The fund offers fiscal
sponsorship for media projects that are consistent
with SDF's goals and purposes. A 5 percent
administrative fee will be charged to all funds
received for the project; a 7 percent fee will be
assessed to certain projects whose funding comes
from grant sources that require additional reporting
from the SDF.
EIN: 752993148

6870
Abigail L. Spire Foundation, Inc.
312 S. Third St.
Wilmington, NC 28401
Contact: Douglas R. Zieschang, Pres.

Foundation type: Independent foundation
Purpose: Scholarships to individuals for attendance
at Cape Fear Community College, NC, or University
of North Carolina at Wilmington, NC.
Financial data: Year ended 07/31/2013. Assets,
$168,213 (M); Expenditures, $69,943; Total
giving, $65,988; Grants to individuals, 4 grants
totaling $49,788 (high: $16,174, low: $10,524).
Type of support: Support to graduates or students
of specific schools; Undergraduate support.
Application information: Applications accepted.
Application form required.
  Deadline(s): Feb. 28
  Additional information: Contact foundation for
    current application guidelines. Scholarships
    are renewable for a total of four years.
EIN: 562358231

6871
Spivey Scholarship Trust
c/o First Citizens Bank & Trust Dept.
P.O. Box 29522
Raleigh, NC 27626
Contact: Linda F. Hofler
Application address: P.O.Box 1, Box 95, Hobbsville,
NC 27946

Foundation type: Independent foundation
Purpose: Scholarships to seniors of Gates County
High School, NC for attendance at accredited
colleges or universities.
Publications: Annual report.
Financial data: Year ended 11/30/2012. Assets,
$729,514 (M); Expenditures, $41,209; Total
giving, $35,186; Grants to individuals, 4 grants
totaling $35,186 (high: $17,526, low: $637).
Fields of interest: Higher education.
Type of support: Support to graduates or students
of specific schools; Undergraduate support.
Application information: Applications accepted.
Application form required.
  Initial approach: Letter
  Deadline(s): None
EIN: 566235902

6872
James Sprunt Foundation, Inc.

c/o James Sprunt Community College
P.O. Box 398
Kenansville, NC 28349-0398 (910) 296-2416
Contact: Robert Turner, Exec. Dir.; Jeanine
Cavanaugh, Secy.
E-mail: wrturner@jamessprunt.edu; Tel. for Jeanine
Cavanaugh: (910) 296-2417; URL: http://
www.jamessprunt.edu/JSCC_Foundation.html

Foundation type: Public charity
Purpose: Scholarships to high school seniors, and
to students attending James Sprunt Community
College, NC for higher education.
Publications: Newsletter.
Financial data: Year ended 06/30/2012. Assets,
$1,061,040 (M); Expenditures, $53,724; Total
giving, $14,500; Grants to individuals, totaling
$14,500.
Fields of interest: Higher education.
Type of support: Support to graduates or students
of specific schools.
Application information: Applications accepted.
Application form required. Application form
available on the grantmaker's web site.
   Send request by: Mail
   Deadline(s): Mar.
   Final notification: Applicants notified after June
      30
   Additional information: Applicant must maintain
      a cumulative 2.0 GPA and maintain
      enrollment in and complete a minimum of 12
      semester hours each academic semester.
EIN: 237405675

6873
St. Anthony Educational Foundation, Inc.

P.O. Box 4633
Chapel Hill, NC 27515-4633 (919) 294-9387
E-mail: national@stanthonyhall.org; Toll-free tel.:
(888) 580-9349; URL: http://
www.stanthonyhall.org/donations/fund.asp?
id=4135

Foundation type: Public charity
Purpose: Scholarships to members of St. Anthony
Hall, the fraternity of Delta Psi.
Publications: Application guidelines.
Financial data: Year ended 12/31/2011. Assets,
$2,822,844 (M); Expenditures, $215,484; Total
giving, $93,617; Grants to individuals, totaling
$27,549.
Fields of interest: Fraternal societies.
Type of support: Undergraduate support.
Application information:
   Initial approach: Letter or email
   Deadline(s): Nov. 15, Mar. 15
Program description:
   Individual Grants: Proposals for individual grants
   are normally approved only for active undergraduate
   or graduate students. Applicants should be aware
   that the activity to be supported must relate to the
   greater good of a community extending beyond the
   individual. Simple requests to fund a "semester
   abroad" or self-improvement will not be accepted.
   The foundation may approve up to $2,000 from its
   general funds. Local alumni organizations may add
   more as the case may be. Please note that the
   foundation does not cover food or lodging.
EIN: 136103940

6874
Mabel Stagner Charitable Trust

c/o Wells Fargo Bank, N.A.
1 W. 4th Fl., MAC D4000-041
Winston Salem, NC 27101-3818 (800)
352-3705
Application address: c/o Wells Fargo Bank, N.A.,
P.O. Box 20160, Long Beach, CA 90802

Foundation type: Independent foundation
Purpose: Scholarships to graduating seniors of Fort
Bragg High School, CA, for full-time study at a
college or university.
Financial data: Year ended 05/31/2013. Assets,
$156,919 (M); Expenditures, $3,726; Total giving,
$0.
Fields of interest: Higher education.
Type of support: Scholarships—to individuals;
Support to graduates or students of specific
schools.
Application information: Applications accepted.
   Initial approach: Letter
   Deadline(s): None
   Additional information: Recipients must maintain
      at least a 2.0 GPA.
EIN: 956795944

6875
Stambaugh Scholarship Private
Foundation

(formerly William S. & Arthur Stambaugh
Scholarship Fund)
1525 West W.T. Harris Blvd., D1114-044
Charlotte, NC 28288-5709 (866) 601-0001

Foundation type: Independent foundation
Purpose: Scholarships to needy students who are
graduates of Dauphin County High School, NC for
attendance at accredited colleges or universities.
Financial data: Year ended 10/31/2012. Assets,
$318,384 (M); Expenditures, $20,020; Total
giving, $13,000.
Fields of interest: Higher education.
Type of support: Scholarships—to individuals;
Support to graduates or students of specific
schools.
Application information:
   Initial approach: Letter or telephone
   Deadline(s): May 1
   Applicants should submit the following:
      1) Class rank
      2) SAT
      3) GPA
      4) Transcripts
      5) Letter(s) of recommendation
      6) FAFSA
   Additional information: Application should also
      include acceptance letter from accredited
      college or university student will attend.
EIN: 256634174

6876
State Employees Association of North
Carolina Scholarship Fund, Inc.

P.O. Box 27727
Raleigh, NC 27611 (919) 833-6496
Application address: c/o State Employees
Association of NC Scholars
E-mail: mleonard@seanc.org; URL: http://
www.seanc.org/membership/scholarship.aspx

Foundation type: Independent foundation
Purpose: Scholarships for members or the
dependents of state employees who are members
of the State Employees Association of North
Carolina, Inc. (SEANC)

Financial data: Year ended 09/30/2012. Assets,
$326,880 (M); Expenditures, $64,849; Total
giving, $35,000; Grants to individuals, 42 grants
totaling $35,000 (high: $1,000, low: $500).
Type of support: Scholarships—to individuals.
Application information: Applications accepted.
   Initial approach: Letter
   Deadline(s): Apr. 15
EIN: 561436745

6877
State Employees' Credit Union
Foundation

P.O. Box 27665
Raleigh, NC 27611-7665 (919) 839-5000
Contact: G. Mark Twisdale, Exec. Dir.
E-mail: secufoundation@ncsecu.org; Toll free tel.:
(800) 438-1104; URL: http://
www.ncsecufoundation.org

Foundation type: Operating foundation
Purpose: Scholarships to graduating high school
seniors at each traditional public high school and
two charter high schools in NC , and to students
from each community college in NC.
Publications: Application guidelines; Annual report;
Multi-year report.
Financial data: Year ended 06/30/2012. Assets,
$28,689,316 (M); Expenditures, $8,578,996;
Total giving, $8,544,687; Grants to individuals,
1,555 grants totaling $3,872,187.
Fields of interest: Higher education; College
(community/junior).
Type of support: Scholarships—to individuals.
Application information: Applications accepted.
Application form required. Application form
available on the grantmaker's web site.
   Send request by: Mail, fax, or e-mail
   Copies of proposal: 1
   Additional information: Contact your guidance
      counselor or your financial aid office for
      additional information.
Program descriptions:
   Community College Scholarship Program: The
   program establishes two scholarship funds at each
   North Carolina Community College to assist
   students. Preference is given to students with
   parents or guardians and family members who are
   public sector employees who live and work in North
   Carolina.
   *North Carolina Public High School Scholarship
   Program:* The foundation provides this four-year
   scholarship program to assist North Carolina public
   high school students attend college. Each North
   Carolina traditional public high school will receive
   one (1) scholarship valued at $10,000 for a senior
   to attend one of the 16 constituent campuses of
   the University of North Carolina. Preference will be
   to students whose parents or guardians and family
   members are public sector employees who live and
   work in North Carolina. Scholarship recipients in
   good academic standing will be able to receive the
   scholarship up to a maximum of eight (8)
   consecutive semesters at the same university.
   Students selected should not be the recipient of
   other large scholarships.
EIN: 562255292

6878

J. C. Steele, Jr. Scholarship Foundation, Inc.

P.O. Box 1834
Statesville, NC 28687 (704) 872-3681
Contact: John S. Steele, Tr.
Application address: 710 S. Mulberry St.,
Statesville, NC 28677

Foundation type: Operating foundation
Purpose: Scholarships to children of J. C. Steele & Sons, Inc. employees.
Financial data: Year ended 12/31/2012. Assets, $1,814 (M); Expenditures, $8,139; Total giving, $8,000; Grants to individuals, 8 grants totaling $8,000 (high: $1,000, low: $1,000).
Type of support: Employee-related scholarships.
Application information: Application form required.
  Deadline(s): May 17
Company name: J.C. Steele & Sons, Incorporated
EIN: 581530789

6879

Marie Palmer Stewart School Trust

1 W. 4th St. D4000-041
Winston Salem, NC 27101
Application Address: c/o UNC Greensboro, 1500 Spring Garden St., Greensboro, NC 27412

Foundation type: Independent foundation
Purpose: Scholarships to female students of Franklin High School, Franklin, NC, to attend the University of North Carolina at Greensboro. If no one from Franklin High School is eligible, other students from western NC will be considered.
Financial data: Year ended 12/31/2012. Assets, $130,196 (M); Expenditures, $2,885; Total giving, $36.
Fields of interest: Race/intergroup relations; Women.
Type of support: Support to graduates or students of specific schools; Undergraduate support.
Application information: Applications accepted. Interview required.
  Initial approach: Letter
  Deadline(s): None
EIN: 566194108

6880

Stonecutter Foundation, Inc.

230 Spindale St.
Spindale, NC 28160-1604
Contact: Terri C. Barringer, Secy.-Treas.

Foundation type: Company-sponsored foundation
Purpose: Undergraduate student loans to financially needy residents of the Rutherford and Polk County, NC, area.
Financial data: Year ended 03/31/2013. Assets, $9,124,571 (M); Expenditures, $503,973; Total giving, $347,020; Loans to individuals, totaling $13,720.
Type of support: Student loans—to individuals.
Application information: Applications accepted. Application form required.
  Deadline(s): None
  Additional information: Application must include transcripts and proof of acceptance at an institution of higher education.
EIN: 566044820

6881

Lottie D. Stoudenmire Education Fund

c/o Wells Fargo Bank N.A.
1 W 4th St., 4th Fl. MAC D4000-041
Winston Salem, NC 27101-3818

Foundation type: Independent foundation
Purpose: Scholarships to students of all majors at Newberry College, SC, who intend to enter the ministry.
Financial data: Year ended 04/30/2013. Assets, $220,521 (M); Expenditures, $12,581; Total giving, $8,000.
Fields of interest: Theological school/education.
Type of support: Support to graduates or students of specific schools; Undergraduate support.
Application information: Applications accepted.
  Initial approach: Letter
EIN: 576087466

6882

Charles A. Strickland Memorial Fund

1525 W. W.T. Harris Blvd., D1114-044
Charlotte, NC 28288-5709

Foundation type: Independent foundation
Purpose: Scholarships to students, primarily attending Wake Forest University and Duke University, both in NC.
Financial data: Year ended 12/31/2011. Assets, $2,347,722 (M); Expenditures, $137,082; Total giving, $125,400.
Fields of interest: Higher education; University; Scholarships/financial aid.
Type of support: Support to graduates or students of specific schools.
Application information: Applications not accepted.
  Additional information: Unsolicited requests for funds not considered or acknowledged.
EIN: 566050004

6883

Student Action with Farmworkers

(also known as SAF)
1317 W. Pettigrew St.
Durham, NC 27705-4854 (919) 660-3652
Additional info. for fellowship: Laxmi Haynes, National Student Organizer, tel.: (919) 660-3660, e-mail: farmworker_justice@yahoo.com; for scholarship: Rosie Rangel, Migrant Youth Director, e-mail r.rangel@duke.edu
FAX: (919) 681-7600; E-mail: saf-unite@duke.edu; URL: http://www.saf-unite.org

Foundation type: Public charity
Purpose: Fellowships to college students to learn about migrant farmworkers' living and working conditions. Need-based scholarship to an undergraduate student from a farmwork family to attend NC State University.
Publications: Application guidelines; Informational brochure; Newsletter.
Financial data: Year ended 08/31/2012. Assets, $495,388 (M); Expenditures, $627,554; Total giving, $38,250; Grants to individuals, totaling $36,250.
Fields of interest: Public education.
Type of support: Fellowships; Scholarships—to individuals.
Application information: Application form required. Application form available on the grantmaker's web site.
  Initial approach: Application
  Deadline(s): Feb. 11

Program descriptions:
  Into the Fields Summer Internship and Leadership Development Program: The program is a ten-week summer internship and leadership development program that creates opportunities for college students to work for fairness in agricultural industries. Each summer, up to thirty students from diverse backgrounds promote justice for farm workers through full-time work in migrant education programs, rural health clinics, legal services, immigrant assistance organizations, policy and research groups, and with community and labor organizing projects in North and South Carolina.
  Sowing Seeds for Change Fellowship Program: The program provides a summer leadership development opportunity for students in Tennessee, Virginia, Pennsylvania, and New York. The organization trains a small group of bilingual students and prepares them to work with farm worker organizations in their home state. Fellows work towards improvements in farm workers' living and working conditions through legal services, health clinics, and community and labor organizing groups. Eligible applicants must: be current college students or recent graduates (within one year); have an intermediate to advanced knowledge of Spanish; have access to a vehicle for the duration of the program; demonstrate commitment to farmworker justice; and demonstrate previous experience in healthcare, campus activism, community volunteer work with farmworkers, or academic coursework on farmworkers. Preference will be given to students from farmworker families and students form the southeastern U.S.
EIN: 561789014

6884

Chief John Alfred Tahquette Education Trust

(also known as Amy Critzer Trust)
c/o First Citizens Bank
P.O. Box 29522
Raleigh, NC 27626

Foundation type: Independent foundation
Purpose: Scholarships to deserving individuals enrolled in and attend technical schools, colleges or universities located more than 250 miles from Cherokee, NC.
Financial data: Year ended 12/31/2012. Assets, $998,278 (M); Expenditures, $66,128; Total giving, $50,309.
Fields of interest: Vocational education, post-secondary; Higher education.
Type of support: Scholarships—to individuals.
Application information: Applications accepted.
  Initial approach: Letter
  Deadline(s): Mar. 1 June 1, Sept. 1, Dec. 1
EIN: 566529542

6885

Tannenbaum-Sternberger Foundation, Inc.

(formerly Sigmund Sternberger Foundation, Inc.)
324 W. Wendover Ave., Ste. 118
Greensboro, NC 27404-8438 (336) 274-5761
Contact: Robert O. Klepfer, Jr., Exec. Dir.
FAX: (336) 274-5763;
E-mail: bobklepfer@tsfoundation.com; Mailing address: P.O. Box 41199, Greensboro, NC 27404-1199; URL: http://www.TSFoundation.com

Foundation type: Independent foundation
Purpose: Scholarships to children and grandchildren of members of the Revolution Masonic Lodge, Greensboro, NC who are

permanent residents of Guilford County, NC or attend a college located in Guilford County, NC.
Publications: Application guidelines; Grants list.
Financial data: Year ended 03/31/2013. Assets, $16,378,440 (M); Expenditures, $984,473; Total giving, $697,534.
Fields of interest: Higher education.
Type of support: Undergraduate support.
Application information: Applications accepted. Application form required. Application form available on the grantmaker's web site.
   Initial approach: Letter, telephone or e-mail
   Send request by: Online
   Copies of proposal: 1
   Deadline(s): Varies
   Applicants should submit the following:
      1) Transcripts
      2) Letter(s) of recommendation
EIN: 566045483

6886
Tarboro Community Outreach, Inc.
701 Cedar Ln.
P.O. Box 445
Tarboro, NC   27886-0445   (252) 823-8801
Contact: Sr. Mary Ann Czaja, Exec. Dir.
URL: http://www.tcorun.com/about-tarboro-community-outreach

Foundation type: Public charity
Purpose: Grants to residents of Edgecombe County, NC, to pay for utility bills, rent, and prescription drugs. Support also to people in need of food, counseling, or shelter.
Financial data: Year ended 12/31/2011. Assets, $154,183 (M); Expenditures, $880,345.
Fields of interest: Health care; Mental health, counseling/support groups; Housing/shelter; Human services; Poverty studies.
Type of support: Grants for special needs.
Application information: Applications not accepted.
   Additional information: Unsolicited requests for funds not considered.
EIN: 561557200

6887
TASCA
(also known as Taller de Salud Compesina)
P.O. Box 37524
Raleigh, NC   27627-7524
E-mail: info@tascanica.org; *URL:* http://tascanica.org

Foundation type: Independent foundation
Purpose: Scholarships to Nicaraguan public health workers for the study of bioanalysis, epidemiology, clinical and food microbiology, public health, nursing, rural development, and health administration in Nicaragua.
Financial data: Year ended 12/31/2012. Assets, $13,358 (M); Expenditures, $131,805; Total giving, $121,488; Grants to individuals, 56 grants totaling $78,146 (high: $2,950, low: $458).
Fields of interest: Health care.
Type of support: Scholarships—to individuals; Foreign applicants.
Application information: Applications accepted. Application form required.
   Additional information: Priority is given to those working in public health rather than in primary care, and to those from rural communities.
EIN: 561855167

6888
Sally Smith Taylor Trust
396 Vanderbalt Rd.
Binmore Forest, NC   28803-3036

Foundation type: Company-sponsored foundation
Purpose: Scholarships to high school seniors or high school graduates of North Carolina who have demonstrated an interest in science, math and engineering and intend to pursue studies at an educational institution in NC.
Financial data: Year ended 12/31/2012. Assets, $67,836 (M); Expenditures, $1,306; Total giving, $500; Grant to an individual, 1 grant totaling $500.
Fields of interest: Science; Mathematics; Engineering.
Type of support: Scholarships—to individuals.
Application information: Applications accepted.
   Initial approach: Letter
   Applicants should submit the following:
      1) Transcripts
      2) Letter(s) of recommendation
   Additional information: Applicant must maintain a "C" average while enrolled at school to continue to be eligible for a scholarship award.
EIN: 203827822

6889
Dr. Robert A. Team Scholarship Fund
139 W. 1st Ave.
Lexington, NC   27292-4736

Foundation type: Independent foundation
Purpose: Scholarships primarily to residents of Lexington, NC pursuing nursing degrees.
Financial data: Year ended 12/31/2011. Assets, $123,601 (M); Expenditures, $4,419; Total giving, $3,750; Grants to individuals, 5 grants totaling $3,750 (high: $750, low: $750).
Fields of interest: Nursing school/education.
Type of support: Undergraduate support.
Application information: Applications accepted.
   Additional information: Contact foundation for current application deadline/guidelines.
EIN: 561872786

6890
Telamon Corporation
5560 Munsford Rd.
Raleigh, NC   27612-2621   (919) 851-7611
Contact: Richard A. Joanis, Exec.Dir.
FAX: (919) 851-1139; *URL:* http://www.telamon.org/about.aspx

Foundation type: Public charity
Purpose: Assistance to disadvantaged farmworkers and their families, children born into poverty, low-income and elderly residents of rural America, with childcare, employment, housing, education and community development.
Publications: Annual report.
Financial data: Year ended 09/30/2011. Assets, $12,712,139 (M); Expenditures, $60,693,828; Total giving, $6,919,021; Grants to individuals, 8,788 grants totaling $4,046,381.
Fields of interest: Children; Youth; Adults; Aging; Disabilities, people with.
Type of support: Grants to individuals; Grants for special needs.
Application information: See web site for eligibility criteria and additional guidelines.
EIN: 561022483

6891
Harvey Thomas Estate Student Aid Trust
1525 West W.T. Harris Blvd., D1114-044
Charlotte, NC   28288-8522   (336) 747-8175
Application address: c/o Wells Fargo Bank, N.A., 1 West 4th St., D4000-062, Winston-Salem, NC 27101

Foundation type: Independent foundation
Purpose: Student loans to residents of Chester County, PA for postsecondary education.
Financial data: Year ended 09/30/2013. Assets, $1,321,263 (M); Expenditures, $18,768; Total giving, $0.
Fields of interest: Higher education.
Type of support: Student loans—to individuals.
Application information: Applications accepted. Application form required.
   Initial approach: Letter
   Deadline(s): None
   Additional information: Loans are not available for graduate studies.
EIN: 236215693

6892
Thomasville Furniture Industries Foundation
1 W. 4th St. D4000-041
Winston Salem, NC   27101

Foundation type: Company-sponsored foundation
Purpose: Scholarships only to children of employees of Thomasville Furniture Industries, Inc.
Financial data: Year ended 12/31/2012. Assets, $8,716,600 (M); Expenditures, $314,876; Total giving, $248,157.
Fields of interest: Education.
Type of support: Employee-related scholarships.
Application information: Applications not accepted.
   Additional information: Unsolicited requests for funds not considered or acknowledged.
Company name: Thomasville Furniture Industries, Inc.
EIN: 566047870

6893
TD Frank Thomson Scholarships
1 W. 4th St., D4000-041
Winston Salem, NC   27101   (866) 608-0001
Application address: c/o Center for Scholarship Administration, P.O. Box 1465, Taylor, SC 29687

Foundation type: Independent foundation
Purpose: Scholarships to high school seniors who are sons of active, retired, or deceased employees of Conrail, Penn Central, and Amtrak Railroads.
Financial data: Year ended 12/31/2012. Assets, $2,179,821 (M); Expenditures, $80,179; Total giving, $37,500.
Fields of interest: Education.
Type of support: Employee-related scholarships.
Application information: Applications accepted. Application form required.
   Initial approach: Letter
   Deadline(s): Mar. 31
Company names: Conrail; Amtrak; Penn Central Corporation; Pennsylvania Railroad Company; Penn Central Transportation Company
EIN: 236217801

6894
John Shaw and Anna Walters Tillman Scholarship Trust
1870 NC Hwy. 49 S.
Asheboro, NC 27205-9580 (336) 625-6185
Contact: D'Vera Tune, Chair.
Application address: c/o Asheboro High School
Scholarship Comm., Attn: Mitzi W. Graves, Chair.,
1221 S. Park St., Asheboro, NC 27203-6711,
tel.: (336) 625-6185

Foundation type: Independent foundation
Purpose: Scholarships to one male and one female
graduating senior of Asheboro High School, NC, to
further their postsecondary education.
Financial data: Year ended 04/30/2013. Assets,
$145,923 (M); Expenditures, $5,568; Total giving,
$5,000; Grants to individuals, 2 grants totaling
$5,000 (high: $2,500, low: $2,500).
Fields of interest: Higher education.
Type of support: Support to graduates or students
of specific schools.
Application information: Applications accepted.
Application form required.
  Initial approach: Letter
  Deadline(s): Apr. 30
  Additional information: Applicant must
    demonstrate need and show academic
    excellence.
EIN: 561735521

6895
Touchstone Energy Bright Ideas Grant Program
P.O. Box 27306
Raleigh, NC 27611-7306
Contact: Lindsey Listrom
E-mail: lindsey.listrom@ncemcs.com; URL: http://
www.ncbrightideas.com

Foundation type: Corporate giving program
Purpose: Grants to NC K-12 teachers for innovative,
classroom-based projects that would not otherwise
be funded.
Publications: Application guidelines.
Fields of interest: Elementary/secondary
education; Education.
Type of support: Grants to individuals; Project
support.
Application information: Applications accepted.
Application form required. Application form
available on the grantmaker's web site.
  Send request by: Online
  Deadline(s): Aug. 15 for early-birds, Sept. 23
    application deadline (deadline may vary by
    cooperative)
  Final notification: Applicants notified in Nov. and
    Dec.
  Additional information: Teachers who submit
    applications for the early-bird deadline will be
    entered to win a $500 Visa gift card. Support
    is limited to one contribution per teacher
    during any given year. See web site for
    additional guidelines.
Program description:
  Bright Ideas Education Grant Program: North
  Carolina Electric Cooperatives awards grants of up
  to $2,000 to K-12 teachers for innovative
  classroom-based projects. Winning projects must
  involve students directly, achieve clearly defined
  goals and learning objectives, use innovative and
  creative teaching methods, provide ongoing
  benefits to students, and feature measurable
  results that can be evaluated upon completion. This
  program is administered by individual cooperatives
  and award amounts may vary.

6896
Transylvania Community Hospital Foundation, Inc.
P.O. Box 2440
Brevard, NC 28712-2440 (828) 877-4777
Contact: Sharon C. Johnson C.F.R.E., Exec. Dir.
URL: http://www.trhospital.org/foundation/

Foundation type: Public charity
Purpose: Scholarships available to individuals in
NC, for tuition furthering education in the field of
nursing. Financial assistance for prescription
medication for the medically indigent and
underinsured in the Brevard, NC area.
Financial data: Year ended 09/30/2011. Assets,
$8,932,335 (M); Expenditures, $1,562,896; Total
giving, $1,086,431; Grants to individuals, totaling
$32,313.
Fields of interest: Nursing school/education;
Pharmacy/prescriptions.
Type of support: Scholarships—to individuals;
Grants for special needs.
Application information: Payments are made
directly to the pharmacy to cover portions of drug
costs for recipients.
EIN: 561458024

6897
Henrietta S. Treen Fund
1525 W W.T. Harris Blvd., D1114-004
Charlotte, NC 28288 (866) 608-0001
Application address: Center for Scholarship
Administration, P.O. Box 1465 Taylor, SC 29687

Foundation type: Independent foundation
Purpose: Scholarships to students attending
Lafayette College, PA; Lehigh University, PA;
Princeton University, NJ; Temple University, PA; and
the University of Pennsylvania.
Financial data: Year ended 12/31/2011. Assets,
$2,759,395 (M); Expenditures, $185,961; Total
giving, $137,000.
Type of support: Support to graduates or students
of specific schools.
Application information: Applications accepted.
  Additional information: Contact foundation for
    current application deadline/guidelines.
EIN: 236221369

6898
The Triad Health Project
801 Summit Ave.
P.O. Box 5716
Greensboro, NC 27405-7856 (336) 275-1654
Contact: Addison Ore, Exec. Dir.
FAX: (336) 275-2209;
E-mail: info@triadhealthproject.com; Addison Ore
Email: aore@triadhealthproject.com; URL: http://
www.triadhealthproject.com

Foundation type: Public charity
Purpose: Programs and services to individuals
living with HIV/AIDS, and to educate those at risk
and the community about HIV/AIDS. Also, other
assistance include food, clothing and shelter.
Publications: Newsletter.
Financial data: Year ended 06/30/2012. Assets,
$327,837 (M); Expenditures, $1,169,486; Total
giving, $49,345; Grants to individuals, totaling
$49,345.
Fields of interest: AIDS, people with.
Type of support: Grants for special needs.
Application information: Applications not
accepted.
EIN: 581705502

6899
Triangle Community Foundation
324 Blackwell St., Ste. 1220
Durham, NC 27701-3690 (919) 474-8370
Contact: For scholarships: Gina Andersen,
Scholarships and Community Outreach Coord.
Scholarship e-mail: gina@trianglecf.org
FAX: (919) 941-9208; E-mail: info@trianglecf.org;
URL: http://www.trianglecf.org

Foundation type: Community foundation
Purpose: Scholarships to residents of Durham,
Wake, Orange, and Chatham counties, NC for
attendance at accredited colleges or universities.
Publications: Annual report; Newsletter.
Financial data: Year ended 06/30/2012. Assets,
$144,823,851 (M); Expenditures, $15,627,349;
Total giving, $13,351,289.
Fields of interest: Higher education; Medical
school/education; Scholarships/financial aid.
Type of support: Scholarships—to individuals;
Support to graduates or students of specific
schools; Undergraduate support.
Application information: Applications accepted.
Application form required. Application form
available on the grantmaker's web site.
  Initial approach: Varies
  Deadline(s): Varies
  Applicants should submit the following:
    1) Transcripts
  Additional information: See web site for complete
    listing of scholarship funds.
Program description:
  Scholarship Funds: The foundation administers a
  number of endowed and non-endowed scholarship
  funds established by individual donors and
  organizations to assist students in continuing their
  education. Each scholarship has its own set of
  unique eligibility requirements that must be
  reviewed carefully before applying. Most
  scholarships are available for graduating seniors
  entering an accredited college or university, though
  many are seeking students pursuing a degree in
  particular fields of study; visit the foundation's web
  site for detailed information on each of these
  scholarships.
EIN: 561380796

6900
Triangle Family Services, Inc.
3937 Western Blvd.
Raleigh, NC 27606-1936 (919) 821-0790
Contact: Alice Lutz, C.E.O.
FAX: (919) 863-0526; Mailing address: P.O. Box
33393, Raleigh, NC 27636-3393; E-Mail for Alice
Lutz: alutz@tfsnc.org; URL: http://www.tfsnc.org

Foundation type: Public charity
Purpose: Emergency grants to residents of Wake,
Johnston, Durham, Orange, and Chatham counties,
NC, who are in danger of foreclosure or eviction.
Publications: Annual report.
Financial data: Year ended 06/30/2011. Assets,
$1,334,441 (M); Expenditures, $3,230,341; Total
giving, $450,586; Grants to individuals, totaling
$450,586.
Fields of interest: Economically disadvantaged.
Type of support: Grants for special needs.
Application information:
  Initial approach: Telephone or letter
  Additional information: Contact foundation for
    eligibility requirements.
EIN: 560547491

6901
Tri-County Electric Foundation
P.O. Box 130
Dudley, NC 28333-0130   (919) 735-2611

Foundation type: Operating foundation
Purpose: Grants to individuals and families in need of financial assistance for shelter, clothing, food, health care, or other emergencies.
Financial data: Year ended 12/31/2012. Assets, $99,002 (M); Expenditures, $152,264; Total giving, $136,074; Grants to individuals, 29 grants totaling $39,699 (high: $5,000, low: $90).
Type of support: Grants for special needs.
Application information: Applications accepted. Application form required.
  Deadline(s): None
  Additional information: Contact foundation for application form.
EIN: 621838433

6902
Carl W. Troedson Educational Fund
c/o Wells Fargo Bank, N.A.
1W 4th St., 4th fl.,MAC D4000-041
Winston Salem, NC 27101-3118

Foundation type: Independent foundation
Purpose: Scholarships to students of the Morrow County School District, OR.
Financial data: Year ended 06/30/2013. Assets, $529,677 (M); Expenditures, $15,546; Total giving, $6,000; Grants to individuals, 22 grants totaling $6,000 (high: $375, low: $250).
Type of support: Scholarships—to individuals; Support to graduates or students of specific schools.
Application information: Applications accepted. Application form required.
  Deadline(s): First Fri. in May
  Additional information: Forms available from Morrow County School District.
EIN: 936087212

6903
TW National Society Dar, Et Al
(formerly National Society of the Daughters of the American Revolution, North Carolina)
1525 W. W.T. Harris Blvd., D1114-044
Charlotte, NC 28288   (202) 628-1776
Application Address: 1776 D St., Washington, DC 200065392

Foundation type: Independent foundation
Purpose: Scholarships, grants, and academic prizes for fifth grade through high school, college and graduate students from Orange County and parts of Chatham County, NC.
Financial data: Year ended 12/31/2012. Assets, $383,262 (M); Expenditures, $24,259; Total giving, $15,897.
Fields of interest: Elementary/secondary education; Higher education.
Type of support: Scholarships—to individuals.
Application information:
  Initial approach: Letter.
  Deadline(s): Nov. 15
  Additional information: Candidates compose essays and/or prepare projects relating to government and constitutional topics that change annually.
EIN: 566484835

6904
Two Harbors High School Senior Scholarship Fund
c/o Wells Fargo Bank
1W 4th St., 4th fl., MAC D4000-041
Winston Salem, NC 27101-3818

Foundation type: Independent foundation
Purpose: Scholarships to graduates of Two Harbors High School, MN.
Financial data: Year ended 06/30/2013. Assets, $317,913 (M); Expenditures, $18,878; Total giving, $12,985; Grants to individuals, 7 grants totaling $12,985 (high: $1,855, low: $1,855).
Type of support: Support to graduates or students of specific schools; Undergraduate support.
Application information: Application form required.
  Deadline(s): None
EIN: 416395607

6905
Union County Community Arts Council, Inc.
120 N. Main St.
Monroe, NC 28112-4721   (704) 283-2784
Contact: Barbara Faulk, Exec. Dir.
FAX: (704) 283-4460; E-mail: uccac@aol.com;
Mailing address: P.O. Box 576, Monroe, NC 28111-0576; e-mail for Barbara Faulk: barbara@unionarts.org; URL: http://www.unionarts.org

Foundation type: Public charity
Purpose: Grants to Union County, NC-based artists to promote and develop diverse cultural arts programming in Union County.
Publications: Application guidelines.
Financial data: Year ended 06/30/2012. Assets, $508,285 (M); Expenditures, $286,048. Grants to individuals amount not specified.
Fields of interest: Arts, artist's services; Arts.
Type of support: Grants to individuals.
Application information: Applications accepted.
  Additional information: Contact the organization for additional guidelines.
Program description:
  Regional Artists Project Grants: This program provides funds for individuals and groups of unincorporated artists to pursue projects that further enhance their artistic development by attending a professional development experience or purchasing/renting a piece of equipment.
EIN: 581407004

6906
United Arts Council of Catawba County
(formerly Catawba County Council for the Arts, Inc.)
243 3rd Ave. N.E.
P. O. Box 5
Hickory, NC 28601-0005   (828) 324-4906
FAX: (828) 324-4910;
E-mail: artscouncil@artscatawba.org; E-mail For Kathryn T. Greathouse:
KGreathouse@artscatawba.org; URL: http://www.artscatawba.org

Foundation type: Public charity
Purpose: Grants and scholarships to area individuals of Catawba County, NC.
Publications: Application guidelines.
Financial data: Year ended 06/30/2012. Assets, $798,712 (M); Expenditures, $502,624; Total giving, $241,968; Grants to individuals, totaling $18,450.
Fields of interest: Visual arts; Performing arts; Arts; Higher education.

Type of support: Grants to individuals;
Scholarships—to individuals.
Application information: Applications accepted. Application form required. Application form available on the grantmaker's web site.
  Initial approach: Telephone or e-mail
  Deadline(s): Spring for Innovative Artist Project and Barringer Young Artist Award, Sept. for Regional Artist Grants
  Additional information: Students seeking collegiate financial help are not eligible for scholarship.
Program descriptions:
  Edna Bost Barringer Young Artist Award for Performing Arts: A scholarship of $1,000 is available to a student planning to attend college to pursue an arts career. The competition is alternated each year between visual/literary artists and performing artists. This award may be given to an individual or broken into two awards of $500 each.
  Innovative Artist Project Grants: The program offers grants of up to $4,000 to artists and arts organizations of any discipline based in Catawba County for innovative and creative arts projects.
  Regional Artist Grants: Grants of up to $2,000 are available to provide financial support to professional artists of all disciplines and at any stage in their careers. Regardless of the artistic discipline, this program focuses on career development of both the individual and artistic groups.
  Sharon Brown Scholarship: This program provides cultural educational opportunities to students in primary and secondary levels. This grant encourages youth under age 19 who reside or attend school in Catawba County to further their independent cultural studies. The scholarship may be used in the study of music, drama/acting, voice, visual art, dance, writing, historic/genealogy, and architecture/historic preservation. Applicant must either reside or attend an elementary, middle or high school in Catawba county, public, private or home schooled.
  Staff and Board Development Grants: Grants are available to staff and board members of council member organizations (with the exception of public and private school teachers) to attend workshops and conferences that will strengthen their professional skills and expand their capabilities.
EIN: 566065114

6907
United Arts Council of Raleigh and Wake County, Inc.
410 Glenwood Ave., Ste. 170
Raleigh, NC 27603   (919) 839-1498
Contact: Eleanor H. Oakley, Pres. and C.E.O.
FAX: (919) 839-6002;
E-mail: eoakley@unitedarts.org; URL: http://www.unitedarts.org/

Foundation type: Public charity
Purpose: Project grants to artists residing in Wake, Vance, Johnston, Warren and Franklin counties, NC to further their professional development.
Publications: Application guidelines; Annual report; Grants list; Informational brochure.
Financial data: Year ended 06/30/2012. Assets, $798,069 (M); Expenditures, $1,400,925; Total giving, $815,550; Grants to individuals, totaling $148,320.
Fields of interest: Arts.
Type of support: Project support.
Application information: Applications accepted. Application form required. Application form available on the grantmaker's web site.
  Initial approach: Letter

Send request by: Mail or e-mail
Copies of proposal: 1
Deadline(s): Sept. 15
Final notification: Applicants notified in Dec.
Applicants should submit the following:
1) Work samples
2) Proposal
3) Letter(s) of recommendation
4) Financial information
Additional information: No faxed application accepted. See web site for additional guidelines.
Program description:
Regional Artist Grant Project: Provides up to $1,500 to artists pursuing projects that will further their professional development. Individual artists and small unincorporated groups of collaborating artists (e.g., guitar duo, jazz quartet, dance group) who have resided at least in one year in Franklin, Johnston, Vance, Wake or Warren counties are eligible to apply. Artists in all art forms and at all phases of their careers can apply, but must demonstrate a strong record of artistic accomplishment and commitment appropriate to the stage of their career.
EIN: 560770175

6908
United Society of Friends Women Trust
5135 Southland Dr.
Archdale, NC   27263-8028   (317) 839-0773
Contact: Dinah Geiger, Clerk
Application address: 2575 South County Rd. 1050 E., Indianapolis, IN 46231-2373

Foundation type: Independent foundation
Purpose: Scholarships to active Quaker students, primarily for study at a seminary.
Publications: Informational brochure (including application guidelines).
Financial data: Year ended 12/31/2012. Assets, $1,474,173 (M); Expenditures, $62,660; Total giving, $53,700; Grants to individuals, 38 grants totaling $53,700 (high: $27,000, low: $500).
Fields of interest: Higher education; Theological school/education.
Type of support: Scholarships—to individuals.
Application information: Application form required.
Initial approach: Letter
Deadline(s): Apr. 1 and Nov. 1
Additional information: Application forms can be obtained from the trust. Application should include references.
EIN: 237089265

6909
Darryl E. Unruh Foundation, Inc.
44 Wesrhaven Dr.
Asheville, NC   28801   (828) 253-9975
Contact: Grace T. Unruh, Pres. and V.P.
Application Address: C/o grace Unruh, 68 Orange St. Asheville NC. 28801

Foundation type: Operating foundation
Purpose: Scholarships to high school seniors graduating from the City of Asheville, NC, or Buncombe County, NC, school systems, who plan to enroll in a four-year college or university in the North Carolina State University system.
Financial data: Year ended 12/31/2012. Assets, $0 (M); Expenditures, $717; Total giving, $177.
Fields of interest: Higher education; Scholarships/financial aid.
Type of support: Support to graduates or students of specific schools; Undergraduate support.

Application information: Applications accepted. Application form required. Interview required.
Send request by: Mail
Deadline(s): Mar. 15
Applicants should submit the following:
1) Photograph
2) Class rank
3) Transcripts
4) SAT
5) Letter(s) of recommendation
6) GPA
7) ACT
Additional information: Application should also include a 750-word statement of plans, career goals, and reasons for wanting and needing a scholarship.
EIN: 561570954

6910
The V Foundation for Cancer Research
106 Towerview Ct.
Cary, NC   27513-3595   (919) 380-9505
Contact: Nicholas P. Valvano, C.E.O.
FAX: (919) 380-0025; E-mail: info@jimmyv.org;
Toll-free tel.: (800) 454-6698; URL: http://www.jimmyv.org

Foundation type: Public charity
Purpose: Research grants to support researchers at National Cancer Institute-designated facilities and selected institutions.
Publications: Annual report; Financial statement; Grants list; Informational brochure; Newsletter.
Financial data: Year ended 09/30/2012. Assets, $36,782,510 (M); Expenditures, $17,032,307; Total giving, $14,613,141.
Fields of interest: Cancer research.
Type of support: Research.
Application information: Application form not required.
Initial approach: Letter
Applicants should submit the following:
1) Proposal
2) Letter(s) of recommendation
EIN: 133705951

6911
Wake Education Partnership
706 Hillsborough St., Ste. A
Raleigh, NC   27603-1664   (919) 821-7609
FAX: (919) 821-7637;
E-mail: sparrott@wakeedpartnership.org;
URL: http://www.wakeedpartnership.org/

Foundation type: Public charity
Purpose: Grants to full-time Wake County, NC public school classroom teachers, teacher assistants, school psychologists or counselors, social workers, IRTs and media specialists.
Publications: Newsletter.
Financial data: Year ended 06/30/2012. Assets, $243,432 (M); Expenditures, $747,307; Total giving, $86,072; Grants to individuals, totaling $79,072.
Fields of interest: Education.
Type of support: Grants to individuals.
Application information: Applications accepted.
Send request by: Online
Deadline(s): Apr. 13
Final notification: Recipients notified mid-May
Applicants should submit the following:
1) Proposal
2) Budget Information
Additional information: Principals and assistant principals are not eligible.
EIN: 581518182

6912
Wake Technical Community College Foundation, Inc.
(formerly Wake Technical Institute Foundation, Inc.)
9101 Fayetteville Rd.
Raleigh, NC   27603-5696   (919) 866-6250
FAX: (919) 773-9105;
E-mail: foundation@waketech.edu; URL: http://foundation.waketech.edu

Foundation type: Public charity
Purpose: Merit and financial need scholarships for students pursuing an education at Wake Technical Community College, NC.
Publications: Financial statement; Newsletter.
Financial data: Year ended 06/30/2012. Assets, $6,615,179 (M); Expenditures, $2,648,661; Total giving, $418,870; Grants to individuals, totaling $418,870.
Fields of interest: College (community/junior).
Type of support: Scholarships—to individuals; Support to graduates or students of specific schools.
Application information: Applications accepted. Application form required.
Send request by: On-line
Deadline(s): Apr. 30
Additional information: See web site for additional application guidelines and a listing of scholarships.
Program description:
Scholarships: The foundation offers a number of merit and financial need scholarships for students pursuing an education at Wake Technical Community College. Students are highly encouraged to apply for scholarships to help offset the cost of pursuing an education.
EIN: 237017752

6913
Richard Wells Walker Scholarship Fund, Inc.
P.O. Box 585
Oriental, NC   28571-0585

Foundation type: Independent foundation
Purpose: Scholarships to worthy Pamlico County High School, NC students for higher education.
Financial data: Year ended 12/31/2011. Assets, $2,873,387 (M); Expenditures, $126,549; Total giving, $100,000; Grants to individuals, 19 grants totaling $100,000 (high: $10,000, low: $2,500).
Fields of interest: Higher education.
Type of support: Scholarships—to individuals.
Application information: Applications accepted. Application form required. Interview required.
Deadline(s): May
Applicants should submit the following:
1) Transcripts
2) Letter(s) of recommendation
3) FAFSA
Additional information: Application should also include a list of financial aid awards (including any scholarships) you have received and for what you have applied. Application should be returned to the school's guidance office.
EIN: 134222452

6914
Watauga Education Foundation, Inc.
P.O. Box 2658
Boone, NC 28607-2658   (828) 268-1273
Contact: Melanie Bullard, Exec. Dir.
E-mail: info@wataugaeducationfoundation.org;
URL: http://
www.wataugaeducationfoundation.org/

Foundation type: Public charity
Purpose: Scholarships to graduating seniors of Watauga High School, NC for postsecondary education. Scholarships to teachers of Watauga County schools.
Publications: Application guidelines.
Financial data: Year ended 06/30/2012. Assets, $594,864 (M); Expenditures, $102,363; Total giving, $39,334; Grants to individuals, totaling $39,334.
Fields of interest: Education.
Type of support: Scholarships—to individuals.
Application information: Applications accepted. Application form required.
> *Send request by:* Mail
> *Deadline(s):* Mar. 1 for student scholarships, Feb. 15 for teacher scholarships
> *Applicants should submit the following:*
> 1) Class rank
> 2) Transcripts
> 3) Letter(s) of recommendation
> 4) GPA
> 5) Financial information
> 6) Essay
> *Additional information:* See web site for additional guidelines.
Program descriptions:
> *Kate Swift Reese Student Scholarships:* Scholarship in the amount of $1,000 is awarded to a college-bound Watauga High School senior. Student must demonstrate financial need to qualify for scholarship.
> *Price-Deverick Scholarships for Professional Development:* The program awards scholarships to encourage and support teachers in their continuing education efforts. Teachers may apply for financial assistance to obtain renewal credits, to complete certifications or to participate in specialized workshops and training programs. Teachers who are currently employed by and teaching in Watauga County Schools are eligible to apply. Scholarships funds may be used to pay for registration, material fees and out of town travel for classes or workshops. Approximately $4,000 will be awarded.
EIN: 581863113

6915
Grace Margaret Watterson Trust
1525 W. W.T. Harris Blvd. D1114-044
Charlotte, NC 28288-1161   (866) 608-0001
Contact: Sally King
Application address: 4320-G Wade Hampton Blvd., Taylors, SC, 29687 tel: (866) 608-0001

Foundation type: Independent foundation
Purpose: Scholarships to worthy and deserving graduating seniors from high schools in Daytona Beach and Ormond Beach, FL, and Peterborough, Ontario, Canada for attendance at an accredited college or university located in the U.S. or Canada.
Financial data: Year ended 02/29/2012. Assets, $2,217,292 (M); Expenditures, $120,134; Total giving, $86,000.
Fields of interest: Vocational education, post-secondary; Higher education.
Type of support: Support to graduates or students of specific schools.

Application information: Application form required.
> *Deadline(s):* Feb. 26
> *Applicants should submit the following:*
> 1) Letter(s) of recommendation
> 2) Transcripts
> 3) Financial information
> 4) SAT
> 5) ACT
> *Additional information:* Applicant must demonstrate financial need, must submit a personal statement, copy of signed parent's federal income tax form and copies of their W-2 forms. On-line applications are available at: www.wachoviascholars.com. Scholarship is administered by The Center for Scholarship Administration, Inc.
EIN: 596807104

6916
John H. Wellons Foundation, Inc.
(formerly Wellons Foundation, Inc.)
P.O. Box 1254
Dunn, NC 28335-1254   (910) 892-0436

Foundation type: Public charity
Purpose: Student loans for higher education only to local Dunn, NC, students as well as support for needy individuals to cover housing costs.
Financial data: Year ended 12/31/2011. Assets, $10,272,247 (M); Expenditures, $679,879.
Type of support: Student loans—to individuals; Grants for special needs.
Application information: Applications accepted. Application form required.
> *Deadline(s):* None.
EIN: 566061476

6917
Dudley R. West Memorial Foundation Trust
1525 W. W.T. Harris Blvd. D1114-044
Charlotte, NC 28288   (866) 608-0001
Application address: c/o Center for Scholarship P ADM C.O. S.A., 4320-G Wade Hampton Blvd., Taylors, SC 29687

Foundation type: Independent foundation
Purpose: Scholarships to dependent children of employees of Consolidated Systems, Inc. who are under age 25.
Financial data: Year ended 12/31/2011. Assets, $198,295 (M); Expenditures, $19,520; Total giving, $14,500.
Fields of interest: Scholarships/financial aid.
Type of support: Support to graduates or students of specific schools.
Application information: Application form required. Application form available on the grantmaker's web site.
> *Deadline(s):* Feb. 15
> *Applicants should submit the following:*
> 1) Transcripts
> 2) GPA
> 3) Financial information
> *Additional information:* Applicant must demonstrate financial need and show academic achievement.
EIN: 541672687

6918
Western Carolina Community Action, Inc.
220 King Creek Blvd.
P.O. Box 685
Hendersonville, NC 28793-0685   (828) 693-1711
Contact: David White, Exec. Dir.
FAX: (828) 697-4277; URL: http://www.wcca.net/index.html

Foundation type: Public charity
Purpose: Financial assistance to low income individuals or families of Henderson and Transylvania counties, NC to obtain housing rental assistance payments.
Financial data: Year ended 06/30/2011. Assets, $6,663,700 (M); Expenditures, $12,084,364; Total giving, $3,227,529; Grants to individuals, totaling $3,227,529.
Fields of interest: Housing/shelter, owner/renter issues.
Type of support: Grants for special needs.
Application information: Applications accepted. Application form required. Application form available on the grantmaker's web site.
> *Additional information:* Applicant must be very low-income (below 50 percent of area median). They are expected to contribute 30 percent of adjusted monthly income toward and rent and utility expenses. The balance, subject up to established ceilings, is subsidized. Each year the assisted families are re-evaluated to determine whether their incomes still permit them to qualify for assistance under the program and to adjust familily's portion of the rent. Contact the organization for eligibility determination.
EIN: 560846319

6919
Lloyd M. & Doris B. Wiggins Foundation
P.O. Box 1387
Elizabeth City, NC 27906-1387   (252) 338-8021
Contact: Douglas A. Hollowell, Tr.
Application Address: 1880 W. City Dr., Elizabeth City, NC 27906-1387

Foundation type: Independent foundation
Purpose: Scholarships only to residents of Elizabeth City, NC.
Financial data: Year ended 12/31/2011. Assets, $332,008 (M); Expenditures, $60,746; Total giving, $40,512.
Type of support: Undergraduate support.
Application information: Applications not accepted.
> *Additional information:* Unsolicited requests for funds not considered or acknowledged.
EIN: 206244686

6920
Wildacres Retreat
1565 Wildacres Rd.
P.O. Box 280
Little Switzerland, NC 28749-0280   (828) 756-4573
FAX: (828) 756-4586;
E-mail: wildacres@wildacres.org; URL: http://www.wildacres.org

Foundation type: Public charity
Purpose: Residencies to writers, artists, and musicians for a duration of one week.
Publications: Application guidelines.

Financial data: Year ended 12/31/2011. Assets, $2,199,743 (M); Expenditures, $1,296,014.
Fields of interest: Music; Literature; Arts.
Type of support: Residencies.
Application information: Applications accepted. Application form required. Application form available on the grantmaker's web site.
  Send request by: Online submission
Program description:
  The Wildacres Residency Program: Provides 25 one-week residencies available from May through October. The program allows individuals the solitude and inspiration needed to begin or continue work on a project in their particular field. Participants stay in a comfortable, rustic cabin located 1/4 mile from the top of the retreat. They may use the Wildacres facilities and eat in the dining room or prepare their own meals in the cabin kitchen. There is no charge to the participants.
EIN: 237148151

6921
Margaret F. Williams Scholarship Fund
1525 W. W.T. Harris Blvd., D1114-044
Charlotte, NC 28288 (434) 947-8000

Foundation type: Independent foundation
Purpose: Scholarships to graduating seniors of Pitt County High School, NC for attendance as a freshman at East Carolina University, NC.
Financial data: Year ended 12/31/2012. Assets, $256,218 (M); Expenditures, $16,085; Total giving, $11,300.
Fields of interest: Higher education.
Type of support: Scholarships—to individuals; Support to graduates or students of specific schools.
Application information: Applications accepted.
  Deadline(s): Mar. 1
  Additional information: Selection is based on personal character, leadership, scholastic ability and financial need.
EIN: 546107373

6922
John & Mary Wilson Foundation
c/o Wells Fargo Bank Northwest, N.A.
1 W. 4th St., 4th Fl., MAC D4000-041
Winston Salem, NC 27101-3818

Foundation type: Independent foundation
Purpose: Scholarships only to undergraduate or graduate medical students attending the University of Washington.
Financial data: Year ended 12/31/2012. Assets, $6,104,391 (M); Expenditures, $338,889; Total giving, $264,500.
Fields of interest: Medical school/education.
Type of support: Support to graduates or students of specific schools; Graduate support; Undergraduate support.
Application information: Applications accepted. Application form required.
  Initial approach: Letter
  Deadline(s): Contact foundation for application deadline.
EIN: 237425273

6923
The Winston-Salem Foundation
860 W. 5th St.
Winston-Salem, NC 27101-2506
Contact: Scott F. Wierman, Pres.
FAX: (336) 727-0581;
E-mail: info@wsfoundation.org; Toll free tel.: (866) 227-1209; Grant application e-mail: grants@wsfoundation.org; Additional e-mail: swierman@wsfoundation.org; URL: http://www.wsfoundation.org

Foundation type: Community foundation
Purpose: Scholarships primarily to residents of Forsyth County, NC., and for students in the local service area, including Davie, Davidson, Forsyth, Surry, Stokes, Yadkin and Wilkes counties. Grants for teachers in specified areas are also available.
Publications: Application guidelines; Annual report (including application guidelines); Financial statement; Grants list; Informational brochure; Newsletter; Occasional report.
Financial data: Year ended 12/31/2012. Assets, $277,592,363 (M); Expenditures, $24,173,719; Total giving, $20,214,032. Scholarships—to individuals amount not specified.
Fields of interest: Higher education; Scholarships/financial aid.
Type of support: Grants to individuals; Scholarships—to individuals; Student loans—to individuals; Support to graduates or students of specific schools; Undergraduate support.
Application information: Applications accepted. Application form required. Application form available on the grantmaker's web site.
  Initial approach: Application
  Send request by: On-line
  Deadline(s): Apr. for most merit-based scholarships, varies for others
  Additional information: See web site for a complete listing of awards and guidelines.
Program descriptions:
  Student Aid Program: The foundation offers scholarships with more general eligibility criteria, as well as scholarships with more specific criteria, such as those for students attending specific high schools or colleges or those pursuing certain fields of study. Some scholarships entail a one-time award, while many are renewable for three additional years. Additionally, many scholarships are strictly merit-based, while others will also consider family income as a factor. Most scholarships are designated for students attending Forsyth County high schools, but there are also scholarships designated for students who attend high schools in other locations in our service area. Some scholarships allow non-Forsyth County residents who attend a Forsyth County high school to qualify as long as they reside in a county in the Foundation's service area.
  Teacher Grants: Teacher Grants are available in three areas: 1) Forsyth County Teacher Grants: Grants, in amounts of up to $2,500, are available for teachers, guidance counselors, curriculum coordinators, and media coordinators in the Winston-Salem/Forsyth County Schools for various professional growth and enrichment opportunities; 2) Wilkes County C.B. Eller Teaching Awards: Designed to improve the quality of education in Wilkes County by awarding grants for professional growth for public school teachers; and 3) Mt. Airy City Schools, Zach Smith Fund: Provide grant awards designed to improve the quality of education in Mount Airy, NC and may be given annually to public or charter school teachers and/or administrators.
EIN: 566037615

6924
With Love From Jesus Ministries, Inc.
P.O. Box 37713
Raleigh, NC 27627-7713 (919) 233-8010
Contact: Linda Williams, Exec. Dir.
Mailing address: P.O. Box 37713, Raleigh, NC 27627-7713; URL: http://www.withlovefromjesus.org/

Foundation type: Public charity
Purpose: Grants to needy residents of the Raleigh, NC area.
Financial data: Year ended 12/31/2011. Assets, $67,666 (M); Expenditures, $1,798,264; Total giving, $1,474,591; Grants to individuals, totaling $1,450,406.
Fields of interest: Economically disadvantaged.
Type of support: Grants for special needs.
Application information:
  Initial approach: Letter
  Additional information: Contact foundation for complete eligibility requirements.
EIN: 562271441

6925
E. Wolinski Trust f/b/o Notre Dame High School Trust
1525 W. W.T. Harris Blvd. D1114-044
Charlotte, NC 28288-1161 (609) 882-7900
Application address: Notre Dame High School, 601 Lawrence Rd., Lawrenceville, NJ 08648

Foundation type: Independent foundation
Purpose: Scholarships to graduating seniors of Notre Dame High School, NJ accepted into a college or university.
Financial data: Year ended 12/31/2011. Assets, $242,847 (M); Expenditures, $15,043; Total giving, $10,000.
Fields of interest: Higher education.
Type of support: Support to graduates or students of specific schools.
Application information: Applications accepted.
  Deadline(s): Apr. 1
  Additional information: Students must demonstrate financial need.
EIN: 226371904

6926
The Woman's Club of Raleigh, Inc.
3300 Woman's Club Dr.
Raleigh, NC 27612-4825 (919) 782-5599
E-mail: info@womansclubofraleigh.org; URL: http://www.womansclubofraleigh.org

Foundation type: Public charity
Purpose: Scholarships to individuals for attendance at colleges or universities in North Carolina.
Publications: Application guidelines.
Financial data: Year ended 05/31/2012. Assets, $1,313,457 (M); Expenditures, $197,670.
Fields of interest: Higher education; Scholarships/financial aid; Women.
Type of support: Scholarships—to individuals.
Application information: Applications accepted. Application form required. Application form available on the grantmaker's web site. Interview required.
  Initial approach: Application
  Send request by: Mail
  Deadline(s): 1st Wed. in Mar. for WCR Mature Woman Scholarship and WCR Scholarships for High School Seniors, 2nd Wed. in Jan. for Sallie Southall Cotten Scholarship
  Additional information: See web site for additional guidelines for each scholarship.

Program descriptions:
Sallie Southall Cotten Scholarship: The foundation sponsors one applicant annually to apply for the North Carolina-wide scholarship program, which covers all four years of college and is valued at more than $20,000. Applications will be evaluated on academic excellence (applicants must be in the upper 25 percent of their class), evidence of leadership abilities and the potential for success, personal character, a strong desire to serve others, and financial need. Priority will be given to candidates who attend Athens Drive, Broughton, Enloe, Southeast, or Wakefield high schools.
WCR Mature Woman Scholarship: Scholarships, ranging from $250 to $1,500, are available to women who are 30 years of age or older, who are currently enrolled in or who would like to attend (either as a first-time or continuing student) a North Carolina college at the undergraduate level. Applicants must be residents of Wake County.
WCR Scholarships for High School Seniors: Scholarships of $1,000 each are available to public high school seniors who plan to attend a North Carolina college or university. Scholarships under this program include the Ann Collins Scholarship, the Helen Graham Scholarship, and the Lois Fisher Scholarship. Priority will be given to candidates attending Athens Drive, Broughton, Enloe, Southeast, or Wakefield High School.
EIN: 566061486

6927
Women's Aid of Penn Central School IAS
(formerly Women's Aid Scholarship)
1525 W. W.T. Harris Blvd.
Charlotte, NC 28288-5709 (866) 608-0001

Foundation type: Company-sponsored foundation
Purpose: Scholarships to children of employees of Conrail, employees of its predecessor roads (Penn Central or PRR) now employed by Amtrak or Penn Central Corporation, and former employees of Penn Central or PRR who have retired because of age or disability, or who have died.
Financial data: Year ended 12/31/2012. Assets, $1,690,052 (M); Expenditures, $99,041; Total giving, $67,500.
Type of support: Employee-related scholarships.
Application information: Applications not accepted.
Additional information: Scholarship application address: c/o Conrail, 6 Penn Ctr., Rm. 1010, Philadelphia, PA 19102.
Company names: Amtrak; Conrail; Penn Central Corporation; Pennsylvania Railroad Company
EIN: 236232572

6928
Work Family Resource Center, Inc.
530 N. Spring St.
Winston-Salem, NC 27101-3383 (336) 761-5100
Contact: Katura Jackson, Exec. Dir.

Foundation type: Public charity
Purpose: Funds for childcare providers to enhance quality of care, in areas of child development, smart start and food program.
Financial data: Year ended 06/30/2012. Assets, $212,283 (M); Expenditures, $943,127; Total giving, $28,083; Grants to individuals, totaling $28,083.
Fields of interest: Child development, education; Children, services.
Type of support: Grants for special needs.

Application information: Applications accepted.
Initial approach: Telephone
Additional information: Contact the center for additional guidelines.
EIN: 561755762

6929
Wyly Scholarship Fund
c/o Wells Fargo Bank N.A.
1 W. 4th St., 4th Fl., MAC D4000-041
Winston-Salem, NC 27101-3818
Application address: c/o Walhalla High School, Attn.: John Hostetler, 151 Razorback Ln., Walhalla, SC 29691

Foundation type: Independent foundation
Purpose: Full-tuition scholarships to students from Walhalla High School, SC to attend Clemson University and Winthrop University.
Financial data: Year ended 07/31/2013. Assets, $1,682,672 (M); Expenditures, $94,480; Total giving, $63,700.
Fields of interest: Higher education.
Type of support: Support to graduates or students of specific schools; Undergraduate support.
Application information: Application form required.
Deadline(s): Feb. 15
Additional information: Application should include FAF and 1040 tax return; Application forms available from Walhalla High School.
EIN: 570640726

6930
Martha E. Yerkes Scholarship Trust
(formerly Martha E. Yerkes Scholarship Foundation)
1525 W. W.T. Harris Blvd. D1114-044
Charlotte, NC 28288 (866) 608-0001
Application address: c/o Central for Scholarships Adm 4230 - G Wade Hampton Blvd. Taylors, SC 29687; URL: http://www.csascholars.org

Foundation type: Independent foundation
Purpose: Scholarships to high school seniors attending a public high school in Chester County, PA, for attendance at any accredited public or private, two year or four year college, university, technical college or trade school.
Financial data: Year ended 12/31/2011. Assets, $179,609 (M); Expenditures, $8,249; Total giving, $4,000.
Fields of interest: Higher education.
Type of support: Undergraduate support.
Application information:
Deadline(s): Mar. 15
Applicants should submit the following:
  1) Transcripts
  2) SAT
  3) Letter(s) of recommendation
  4) GPA
  5) ACT
Additional information: Applicant must demonstrate academic achievement, financial need, and be morally, mentally and physically worthy. Application should also include a copy of parents' signed income tax form.
EIN: 236441277

6931
John B. & Brownie Young Memorial Fund
c/o BB&T
P.O. Box 2907
Wilson, NC 27894-2907
Scholarship application address: Karen Taber, 230 Frederica St., Owensboro, KY 42301, tel.: (270) 685-4466

Foundation type: Independent foundation
Purpose: Scholarships and awards to unmarried and full-time students in the school districts of Owensboro, Daviess, and McLean counties in KY.
Financial data: Year ended 12/31/2012. Assets, $16,240,918 (M); Expenditures, $1,169,944; Total giving, $1,000,481.
Type of support: Support to graduates or students of specific schools; Undergraduate support.
Application information: Application form required.
Deadline(s): Beginning of college year
Applicants should submit the following:
  1) Transcripts
  2) Essay
  3) Financial information
  4) ACT
  5) GPA
Additional information: Applications available at area high schools.
EIN: 616025137

6932
Young Men's Christian Association of Northwest North Carolina
301 N. Main St., Ste. 1900
Winston-Salem, NC 27101-3890 (336) 777-8055
Contact: Curt Hazelbaker, Pres. and C.E.O.
FAX: (336) 777-6345; E-mail: info@ymcanwnc.org; E-Mail for Curt Hazelbaker: c.hazelbaker@ymcanwnc.org; URL: http://www.ymcanwnc.org

Foundation type: Public charity
Purpose: Grants to residents of NC who are going through financial difficulties for YMCA memberships, programs, child care, and camps; scholarships are also awarded to high-school students who have participated in YMCA-sponsored events.
Publications: Annual report; Financial statement.
Financial data: Year ended 12/31/2011. Assets, $42,266,643 (M); Expenditures, $28,061,602; Total giving, $1,611,358; Grants to individuals, totaling $1,574,108.
Type of support: Grants for special needs.
Application information: Applications accepted. Application form required. Application form available on the grantmaker's web site. Interview required.
Initial approach: Letter
Applicants should submit the following:
  1) Transcripts
  2) SAT
  3) Essay
Additional information: Application should include financial information.
Program description:
Black Achievers Scholarships: Scholarships will be awarded to high-school seniors who have participated in association events within the past year.
EIN: 560530015

6933
Youth Ministry Inc.
332 Briarfield Dr.
Apex, NC 27502 (919) 267-4995
Contact: Matthew Knox, Secy.-Treas.
E-mail: mattfknox@gmail.com

Foundation type: Independent foundation
Purpose: Scholarships to students pursuing biblical and theological studies, prior to their ordination.
Publications: Annual report; Informational brochure.
Financial data: Year ended 12/31/2012. Assets, $11,098 (M); Expenditures, $8,186; Total giving, $7,636; Grants to individuals, 5 grants totaling $7,636 (high: $4,828, low: $150).

Fields of interest: Theological school/education.
Type of support: Graduate support; Undergraduate support.
Application information: Applications accepted.
  Initial approach: Letter
  Deadline(s): None
  Additional information: Application must include academic standing, church affiliation, activities, and financial information.
EIN: 581366662

6934
Zimmerman Scholarship Fund
(formerly Martin H. Zimmerman Scholarship Trust)
1525 W. W.T. Harris Blvd. D1114-044
Charlotte, NC 28288-1161

Foundation type: Independent foundation
Purpose: Scholarships to Pennridge High School graduates or other public school graduates living in the Pennridge, PA, area at the time of graduation.
Financial data: Year ended 06/30/2012. Assets, $450,805 (M); Expenditures, $25,665; Total giving, $19,700.
Type of support: Support to graduates or students of specific schools; Undergraduate support.
Application information: Applications accepted. Application form required.
  Deadline(s): Mar. 15
EIN: 236688479

NORTH DAKOTA

6935
Gabriel J. Brown Trust
112 Ave. E West
Bismarck, ND 58501   (701) 223-5916

Foundation type: Independent foundation
Purpose: Student loans to financially needy residents of ND, for higher education.
Financial data: Year ended 03/31/2013. Assets, $2,855,312 (M); Expenditures, $35,992; Total giving, $0.
Fields of interest: Higher education; Scholarships/financial aid.
Type of support: Student loans—to individuals; Undergraduate support.
Application information: Applications accepted. Application form required.
  Initial approach: Letter or telephone
  Deadline(s): June 15
  Applicants should submit the following:
    1) GPA
    2) Financial information
  Additional information: Forms can be obtained from the trustee.
EIN: 237086880

6936
John A. and Yvonne S. Cronquist Midway Scholarship Trust
P.O. Box 13118
Grand Forks, ND 58208-3118   (701) 795-4532
Contact: Russ Erickson, Chair.

Foundation type: Independent foundation
Purpose: Scholarships only to graduates of Midway High School, ND who show financial need.
Financial data: Year ended 12/31/2012. Assets, $107,075 (M); Expenditures, $6,650; Total giving, $6,500; Grants to individuals, 7 grants totaling $6,500 (high: $1,000, low: $750).
Fields of interest: Higher education.
Type of support: Scholarships—to individuals.
Application information: Applications accepted. Application form required.
  Initial approach: Application
  Deadline(s): None
EIN: 450418794

6937
Dakota Medical Foundation
4152 30th Ave. S., Ste. 102
Fargo, ND 58104-8403   (701) 271-0263
Contact: J. Patrick Traynor, Pres.
FAX: (701) 271-0408;
E-mail: pattraynor@dakmed.org; Toll-free tel.: (877)-977-5770; URL: http://www.dakmed.org

Foundation type: Public charity
Purpose: Financial assistance to qualified students in pursuit of higher education in the health related fields.
Publications: Annual report; Financial statement; Grants list; Newsletter.
Financial data: Year ended 09/30/2011. Assets, $22,224,869 (M); Expenditures, $2,388,521; Total giving, $1,451,906; Grants to individuals, totaling $340,543.
Fields of interest: Higher education.
Type of support: Scholarships—to individuals.

Application information: Contact the foundation for eligibility determination.
EIN: 456012318

6938
Emmons County Sports Alumni, Inc.
240 59th St. S.W.
Hazelton, ND 58544   (701) 782-6871
Contact: Debra Kalberer, Secy.

Foundation type: Independent foundation
Purpose: Scholarships to residents of Emmons County, ND pursuing postsecondary education.
Financial data: Year ended 12/31/2012. Assets, $4,477 (M); Expenditures, $11,374; Total giving, $4,000; Grants to individuals, 2 grants totaling $4,000 (high: $3,000, low: $1,000).
Fields of interest: Higher education.
Type of support: Scholarships—to individuals.
Application information: Applications accepted. Application form required.
  Deadline(s): Apr. 15
EIN: 363442049

6939
Helen R. Ernst Charitable Trust
P.O. Box 160
Devils Lake, ND 58301-0160   (701) 766-1200
Contact: Cheryl Belgarde, Committee Member
Application address: P.O. Box 344, Fort Totten, ND 58335

Foundation type: Independent foundation
Purpose: Scholarships to Native Americans in ND who are members of the Fort Trotten Spirit Lake Nation enrolled or enrolling in an accredited postsecondary institution on a full time basis.
Financial data: Year ended 06/30/2013. Assets, $141,720 (M); Expenditures, $9,888; Total giving, $6,579; Grants to individuals, 8 grants totaling $6,579 (high: $1,234, low: $411).
Fields of interest: Native Americans/American Indians.
Type of support: Scholarships—to individuals.
Application information: Applications accepted. Application form required.
  Deadline(s): July 30
  Additional information: Application must include BIA and Pell grants applied for; Applicants must take a full course load and have a 2.0 GPA.
EIN: 456050423

6940
Fargo-Moorhead Area Foundation
502 1st Ave. N., Ste. 202
Fargo, ND 58102-4804   (701) 234-0756
Contact: For grants and scholarships: Cher Hersrud, Prog. Off.; Darcy Putnam, Admin. Asst.
FAX: (701) 234-9724;
E-mail: lexi@areafoundation.org; Additional grant and scholarship info.: cher@areafoundation.org; URL: http://www.areafoundation.org

Foundation type: Community foundation
Purpose: Scholarship to Fargo-Moorhead, ND area students pursuing various degrees at accredited institutions of higher learning.
Publications: Application guidelines; Annual report; Newsletter; Program policy statement.
Financial data: Year ended 12/31/2012. Assets, $55,942,700 (M); Expenditures, $3,143,377; Total giving, $2,213,801.
Fields of interest: Higher education.
Type of support: Scholarships—to individuals.

Application information: Applications accepted. Application form required.
  Deadline(s): Varies
  Additional information: See web site for a complete listing of scholarship funds and applications guidelines.
EIN: 456010377

6941
Forum Communications Foundation
(also known as Norman Black Foundation)
P.O. Box 2020
Fargo, ND 58107-2020
Contact: Lloyd G. Case, Secy.-Treas.

Foundation type: Independent foundation
Purpose: Grants primarily to residents of Moorhead, MN, and Fargo, ND.
Financial data: Year ended 07/31/2013. Assets, $2,164,957 (M); Expenditures, $40,698; Total giving, $39,500.
Type of support: Scholarships—to individuals.
Application information: Applications accepted.
  Deadline(s): None
EIN: 456012365

6942
Heartland Child Nutrition, Inc.
521 E. Main St.
P.O. Box 1218
Bismarck, ND 58502-1218   (701) 250-0140
FAX: (701) 250-0144;
E-mail: hcn@heartlandnutrition.org; URL: http://www.heartlandnutrition.org/

Foundation type: Public charity
Purpose: Financial assistance to home licensed day care providers for meals provided by the child care providers thought out ND.
Publications: Newsletter.
Financial data: Year ended 09/30/2011. Assets, $314,440 (M); Expenditures, $3,161,517; Total giving, $2,719,718; Grants to individuals, totaling $2,719,718.
Fields of interest: Food services; Human services.
Type of support: Grants for special needs.
Application information: Applications accepted.
  Additional information: Contact the organization for eligibility criteria.
EIN: 450383240

6943
C.F. Martell Memorial Foundation
c/o 1st International Trust Dept.
P.O. Box 1088
Williston, ND 58802-1088   (701) 774-8321

Foundation type: Independent foundation
Purpose: Student loans to residents of Williams and McKenzie counties, ND, for study at trade, technical, and professional schools and colleges in the U.S.
Financial data: Year ended 07/31/2013. Assets, $941,326 (M); Expenditures, $22,575; Total giving, $12,000; Grants to individuals, 4 grants totaling $12,000 (high: $3,000, low: $3,000).
Fields of interest: Vocational education.
Type of support: Technical education support.
Application information: Application form required.
  Deadline(s): July 1
  Applicants should submit the following:
    1) Transcripts
    2) Financial information
  Additional information: Applications available from District Judge of Williams County, County

Judge of McKenzie County, and Pastor of St. Joseph's Church in Williston, ND.
EIN: 456010183

6944
McKenzie County Education Trust
P.O. Box 25
Sharon, ND 58277-0025 (701) 789-1099
Contact: Carolyn Dekker, Tr.

Foundation type: Independent foundation
Purpose: Student loans to residents of McKenzie County, ND, who are under the age of 23.
Financial data: Year ended 12/31/2012. Assets, $210,037; Expenditures, $4,432; Total giving, $3,000; Loan to an individual, 1 loan totaling $3,000.
Type of support: Student loans—to individuals.
Application information:
   Initial approach: Letter
   Deadline(s): June 15
EIN: 311490129

6945
Minot Rotary Scholarship Foundation
1635 15th St. S.E.
Minot, ND 58701-6090

Foundation type: Independent foundation
Purpose: College scholarships to graduating seniors from high school within a 50 mile radius of Minot, North Dakota.
Financial data: Year ended 12/31/2011. Assets, $940 (M); Expenditures, $16; Total giving, $0.
Type of support: Undergraduate support.
Application information:
   Deadline(s): Apr. 15
   Additional information: Considerations for scholarship include demographics, awards won, school activities, scholastic achievements, SAT scores, and employment.
EIN: 363369060

6946
North Dakota Community Foundation
(also known as NDCF)
309 N. Mandan St., Ste. 2
P.O. Box 387
Bismarck, ND 58502-0387 (701) 222-8349
Contact: Kevin J. Dvorak, C.E.O.; Kara Geiger, Devel. Dir.-West; Jordan J. Neufeld, Admin. and Acct.
E-mail: jordan@ndcf.net; URL: http://www.ndcf.net

Foundation type: Community foundation
Purpose: Scholarships for higher education and vocational education to graduates in ND.
Publications: Application guidelines; Annual report; Annual report (including application guidelines); Financial statement; Grants list; Informational brochure; Informational brochure (including application guidelines); Newsletter; Occasional report.
Financial data: Year ended 12/31/2012. Assets, $46,925,453 (M); Expenditures, $2,464,185; Total giving, $1,892,620; Grants to individuals, 306 grants totaling $471,784.
Fields of interest: Vocational education; Higher education.
Type of support: Scholarships—to individuals.
Application information: Application form required.
   Additional information: Applications available through local high school guidance

counselors. Contact foundation for selection criteria.
EIN: 450336015

6947
Dr. Henry Hobert Ruger Trust
P.O. Box 838
Devils Lake, ND 58301-0838 (701) 662-4077
Contact: John T. Traynor, Tr.

Foundation type: Independent foundation
Purpose: Scholarships to needy medical students at the University of North Dakota, Grand Forks, ND.
Financial data: Year ended 12/31/2011. Assets, $951,210 (M); Expenditures, $61,573; Total giving, $35,600; Grants to individuals, 24 grants totaling $26,700 (high: $5,000, low: $300).
Fields of interest: Medical school/education.
Type of support: Support to graduates or students of specific schools; Undergraduate support.
Application information: Application form required. Interview required.
   Deadline(s): Vary
   Additional information: Application should include GPA and at least three references.
EIN: 456071291

6948
Maude M. Schuetze Foundation
c/o American State Bank & Trust Co.
P.O. Box 1446
Williston, ND 58801 (701) 774-4120

Foundation type: Independent foundation
Purpose: Scholarships to high school students who are graduates from Culbertson High School, Westby High School, Plentywood High School, Medicine Lake High School, Froid High School or Bainville High School, MT.
Financial data: Year ended 04/30/2013. Assets, $376,805 (M); Expenditures, $23,686; Total giving, $6,875; Grants to individuals, 40 grants totaling $6,550 (high: $300, low: $150).
Fields of interest: Higher education.
Type of support: Technical education support; Precollege support; Undergraduate support.
Application information: Applications accepted. Application form required.
   Initial approach: Letter
   Deadline(s): Apr. 1
   Applicants should submit the following:
      1) Class rank
      2) Transcripts
      3) Financial information
EIN: 456063398

6949
United Telephone Educational Foundation Inc.
P.O. Box 729
Langdon, ND 58249-0729 (701) 256-5156
Contact: Perry Oster, Secy.-Treas.
URL: http://www.utma.com/

Foundation type: Company-sponsored foundation
Purpose: Scholarships to children of members of United Telephone Mutual Aid Corporation.
Financial data: Year ended 12/31/2012. Assets, $646,764 (M); Expenditures, $40,340; Total giving, $37,000; Grants to individuals, 30 grants totaling $37,000 (high: $4,000, low: $100).
Fields of interest: Scholarships/financial aid.

Type of support: Scholarships—to individuals.
Application information: Applications accepted. Application form required.
   Deadline(s): Mar. 30
Company name: United Telephone Mutual Aid Corporation
EIN: 450414760

6950
University of North Dakota Foundation
3100 University Ave., Stop 8157
Grand Forks, ND 58202-8157 (701) 777-2611
FAX: (701) 777-2416; Toll-free tel.: (800) 543-8764; URL: http://www.undfoundation.org/Page.aspx?pid=632

Foundation type: Public charity
Purpose: Scholarships to students of University of North Dakota, ND.
Financial data: Year ended 06/30/2012. Assets, $246,059,271 (M); Expenditures, $14,902,600; Total giving, $10,554,253.
Type of support: Support to graduates or students of specific schools.
Application information: Applications not accepted.
   Additional information: Unsolicited requests for funds not considered or acknowledged.
EIN: 450348296

6951
VFW Charitable Trust
4605 E. Roundup Rd.
Bismarck, ND 58501
Contact: Wallace Bolte, Tr.

Foundation type: Independent foundation
Purpose: Medical assistance to veterans from ND.
Financial data: Year ended 06/30/2012. Assets, $0 (M); Expenditures, $9,224; Total giving, $7,000; Grants to individuals, 19 grants totaling $7,000 (high: $700, low: $200).
Fields of interest: Health care; Military/veterans' organizations.
Type of support: Grants for special needs.
Application information: Applications accepted.
   Send request by: Mail
   Deadline(s): None
   Additional information: Financial need must be verified by Post Commander.
EIN: 456056378

6952
Frank A. & M. Esther Wenstrom Foundation
c/o American State Bank & Trust Co.
223 Main St.
P.O. Box 1446
Williston, ND 58802-1446 (701) 774-4120
URL: http://www.asbt.com

Foundation type: Independent foundation
Purpose: Scholarships to residents of ND.
Financial data: Year ended 09/30/2012. Assets, $439,870 (M); Expenditures, $23,110; Total giving, $18,000; Grants to individuals, 9 grants totaling $18,000 (high: $1,000, low: $500).
Type of support: Scholarships—to individuals.
Application information: Applications accepted. Application form required.
   Additional information: Application must include college transcript.
EIN: 450447357

OHIO

6953
A Good Day Foundation
414 Walnut St., Ste. 1014
Cincinnati, OH 45202-3913 (513) 651-9333
Contact: T. Hunley

Foundation type: Operating foundation
Purpose: Grants to economically disadvantaged individuals and victims of illness or emergencies, primarily in KY and OH.
Financial data: Year ended 06/30/2013. Assets, $84,221 (M); Expenditures, $433,513; Total giving, $354,001; Grants to individuals, 338 grants totaling $354,001.
Fields of interest: Human services, emergency aid; Human services, victim aid.
Type of support: Grants for special needs.
Application information: Applications not accepted.
   Additional information: Unsolicited requests for
      funds not considered or acknowledged.
EIN: 223885978

6954
Ace Foundation
8919 Rossash Rd.
Cincinnati, OH 45236-1209 (513) 772-4900
Contact: Anthony Munoz, Exec. Dir.
FAX: (513) 772-4911;
E-mail: info@munozfoundation.org; URL: http://www.munozfoundation.org

Foundation type: Public charity
Purpose: Scholarships to youth in the Greater Cincinnati, OH area for attendance at any college or university.
Financial data: Year ended 12/31/2011. Assets, $703,135 (M); Expenditures, $661,862; Total giving, $140,830; Grants to individuals, 38 grants totaling $60,330.
Fields of interest: Higher education.
Type of support: Scholarships—to individuals.
Application information: Applications accepted. Application form required.
   Initial approach: Application
   Deadline(s): Apr. 30
   Additional information: Students applying for this
      scholarship must also attend a high school in
      the Tri-State region, and be enrolled in or
      entering an accredited Tri-State college or
      university.
Program descriptions:
   Anthony Munoz Scholarship Fund: In conjunction with the Cincinnati Scholarship Foundation, this award focuses on supporting youth in the Kentucky, Indiana, and Ohio tri-state area in achieving their dreams of attending a local college or university. Applicants must be a resident of the greater Cincinnati metropolitan area, be attending a college or university in the area, be a graduating high school senior with at least a 2.5 GPA, or at least a composite ACT score of 18.
   Straight "A" Scholarship: Awards are available that recognize students in the greater Cincinnati metropolitan tri-state area who pursue academic excellence and athletic achievement, and play an active role in the community while possessing a strong ambition, a winning attitude, and the ability to overcome adversity. Eighteen Tri-State students, nine male and nine female, will receive the chance to win up to a $5,000 college scholarship. All high

school students with a minimum of a 3.0 GPA and in the Foundation's Impact Region are eligible.
EIN: 300009110

6955
Mary Margaret Ackers Scholarship Trust
3040 West Point Rd., S.E.
Lancaster, OH 43130-8640 (740) 569-3040
Contact: William J. Sitterley, Tr.
E-mail: info@FairfieldCountyScholarships.com;
URL: http://fairfieldcountyscholarships.com/

Foundation type: Independent foundation
Purpose: Scholarships to residents of Fairfield or Hocking County, OH for attendance at accredited four year Ohio colleges or universities.
Financial data: Year ended 05/31/2013. Assets, $309,313 (M); Expenditures, $15,702; Total giving, $12,000; Grants to individuals, 2 grants totaling $12,000 (high: $6,000, low: $6,000).
Fields of interest: Higher education.
Type of support: Support to graduates or students of specific schools; Technical education support; Undergraduate support.
Application information: Applications accepted. Application form required. Application form available on the grantmaker's web site. Interview required.
   Send request by: Mail
   Deadline(s): Mar. 15
   Applicants should submit the following:
      1) Photograph
      2) Transcripts
   Additional information: Applicants must
      demonstrate financial need. See web site for
      additional application guidelines.
Program description:
   Scholarships: Applicants must be residents of Fairfield or Hocking county, OH, and must have attended the last three years of high school, including graduation in said counties. Recipients must maintain a good scholastic record, attend accredited state-supported colleges or universities or technical or vocational schools in OH, be full-time students with a minimum of 15 hours per term and maintain a 2.5 GPA. Applicants need not be recent high school graduates.
EIN: 311327096

6956
Adams Rotary Memorial Fund B
(formerly Charles & Lovie Adams Rotary Memorial Fund B Trust)
c/o KeyBank, N.A.
10 W. 2nd St., 26th Fl.
Dayton, OH 45402
Application Address: 224 N. Main St., Kokomo, IN 46901

Foundation type: Independent foundation
Purpose: Scholarships to high school graduates of Howard County, IN, to study medicine or nursing at any accredited college, university, or nursing school in the U.S.
Financial data: Year ended 12/31/2012. Assets, $371,114 (M); Expenditures, $24,143; Total giving, $20,000; Grants to individuals, 9 grants totaling $20,000 (high: $3,000, low: $1,000).
Fields of interest: Medical school/education; Nursing school/education.
Type of support: Scholarships—to individuals; Support to graduates or students of specific schools.

Application information: Applications accepted. Application form required.
   Deadline(s): Third Friday in Mar.
EIN: 356388193

6957
Lena A. & Paul F. Addison Trust
P.O. Box 630858
Cincinnati, OH 45263-0858 (812) 833-5927

Foundation type: Independent foundation
Purpose: Scholarships to graduating students of Mount Vernon High School, IN, for higher education.
Financial data: Year ended 12/31/2012. Assets, $532,020 (M); Expenditures, $40,344; Total giving, $27,000.
Fields of interest: Education.
Type of support: Support to graduates or students of specific schools; Undergraduate support.
Application information: Application form required.
   Deadline(s): Mar.
   Applicants should submit the following:
      1) Transcripts
      2) Essay
      3) Letter(s) of recommendation
      4) FAFSA
Program description:
   Lena A. and Paul F. Addison Scholarship: Two scholarships are awarded to graduating members of the Mount Vernon Senior High School class. Selection is based on academic achievement, leadership achievement, or future potential in either of these areas. Financial need will also be considered.
EIN: 356639866

6958
Adena Health Foundation
272 Hospital Rd., Ste. 1.
Chillicothe, OH 45601-9031 (740) 779-7528
Contact: Ralph Metzger, Exec. Dir.
E-mail: rmetzger@adena.org; URL: http://www.adena.org/foundation

Foundation type: Public charity
Purpose: Scholarships to south-central Ohio students pursuing a career in the healthcare/medical field. Assistance to indigent hospice patients of Adena Health Systems.
Publications: Application guidelines.
Financial data: Year ended 12/31/2011. Assets, $3,698,376 (M); Expenditures, $1,078,216; Total giving, $833,520; Grants to individuals, 273 grants totaling $135,245.
Fields of interest: Nursing school/education; Health sciences school/education.
Type of support: Scholarships—to individuals.
Application information: Payments for scholarships are made directly to the educational institution on behalf of the students.
Program description:
   Scholarships: There are various scholarships available to students in the south-central Ohio area who wish to further their education in medicine and healthcare. Each scholarship has its own guidelines and criteria. See the web site for a listing of the scholarships.
EIN: 753008742

6959
Agape Minstries, Inc.
1220 E. Spring St.
St. Marys, OH   45885-2405   (419) 394-8700
FAX: (419) 394-6700; E-mail: agape@bright.net;
URL: http://agapeministriesinc.com/

Foundation type: Public charity
Purpose: Assistance to individuals and families in Western Auglaize county, OH with food and clothing in time of disaster or in time of economic hardship. Financial Assistance to individuals and families in emergency need with medical expenses and other special needs.
Financial data: Year ended 12/31/2011. Assets, $1,359,894 (M); Expenditures, $2,773,779; Total giving, $2,436,770; Grants to individuals, totaling $62,688.
Fields of interest: Economically disadvantaged.
Type of support: Grants for special needs.
Application information: Contact the agency for eligibility determination. County includes Minster, New Bremen, New Knoxville and St. Marys, OH.
EIN: 341339704

6960
AGC of Ohio Education Foundation
1755 Northwest Blvd.
Columbus, OH   43212-1638   (614) 486-6446
Contact: Richard Hobbs, Tr.
FAX: (614) 486-6498;
E-mail: educationfoundation@agcohio.com;
URL: http://www.agcohio.com/scholarships.html

Foundation type: Public charity
Purpose: Scholarships to students in the Ohio area, who are U.S. citizens pursuing careers in the construction field.
Publications: Application guidelines; Newsletter.
Financial data: Year ended 12/31/2011. Assets, $387,932 (M); Expenditures, $25,089; Total giving, $21,000; Grants to individuals, totaling $21,000.
Fields of interest: Engineering school/education.
Type of support: Scholarships—to individuals; Support to graduates or students of specific schools.
Application information: Recipients must be in at least their second year of a two-year or four-year college or university degree program. See web site for a complete listing of scholarship programs.
EIN: 311690959

6961
Agnew Foundation
P.O. Box 820
Cambridge, OH   43725-0820   (740) 432-3688
Contact: Kelly Jones Milligan

Foundation type: Independent foundation
Purpose: Scholarships to high school seniors in Guernsey County, OH.
Financial data: Year ended 12/31/2011. Assets, $408,467 (M); Expenditures, $23,342; Total giving, $22,500; Grants to individuals, 23 grants totaling $22,500 (high: $1,000, low: $500).
Type of support: Support to graduates or students of specific schools; Undergraduate support.
Application information: Application form required.
   Deadline(s): May 1
EIN: 316077699

6962
Aikey Foundation
18651 West Dr.
Wellington, OH   44090-2829   (440) 821-3713
Contact: Janice L. Krisko, Exec. Dir.
E-mail: info@aikeyfoundation.org; URL: http://www.aikeyfoundation.org

Foundation type: Independent foundation
Purpose: Scholarships to individuals who are current residents of either the city of Berea, Brookpark, Middleburg Heights, Strongsville or Loraine county, OH for attendance at Kent State University.
Financial data: Year ended 12/31/2012. Assets, $241,498 (M); Expenditures, $34,300; Total giving, $29,191; Grants to individuals, 4 grants totaling $29,191 (high: $9,672, low: $175).
Fields of interest: Teacher school/education.
Type of support: Support to graduates or students of specific schools.
Application information: Applicant must demonstrate financial need.
Program description:
   Ruth M. Aikey Memorial Scholarship: The scholarship pays a full four-year tuition for one new bachelor degree-seeking recipient per year who is or will be attending Kent State University in either their Early Childhood Education or Middle Childhood Education program major. The applicant must currently hold a "B" or 3.0 cumulative CGPA or better and must maintain the CGPA throughout the duration of the scholarship award period. Applicant must be a citizen of the U.S.
EIN: 412085657

6963
AJCA Educational, Youth Activities & Special Awards Fund
6486 E. Main St.
Reynoldsburg, OH   43068   (614) 861-3636

Foundation type: Independent foundation
Purpose: Scholarships for undergraduate or graduate students of NJ pursuing various degrees in the dairy industry.
Financial data: Year ended 12/31/2012. Assets, $182,809 (M); Expenditures, $6,584; Total giving, $6,151; Grants to individuals, 6 grants totaling $6,151 (high: $2,000, low: $261).
Fields of interest: Higher education; Business school/education.
Type of support: Graduate support; Undergraduate support.
Application information: Applications accepted. Application form required.
   Send request by: Mail, fax, or e-mail
   Deadline(s): July 1
   Additional information: Application should include work and education experience, background and extracurricular activities including activities with cattle.
EIN: 550828957

6964
AK Steel Foundation
9227 Centre Pointe Dr.
West Chester, OH   45069-4822   (513) 425-5038
Application address for scholarships: c/o Middletown Community Foundation, 36 Donham Plaza, Middletown, OH 45042, tel.: (513) 424-7369; URL: http://www.mcfoundation.org
URL: http://www.aksteel.com/company/corporate-citizenship/

Foundation type: Company-sponsored foundation
Purpose: Scholarships to the children of employees of AK Steel and to African-American high school seniors attending high schools in Butler and Warren counties, Ohio.
Financial data: Year ended 12/31/2012. Assets, $12,100,389 (M); Expenditures, $2,028,474; Total giving, $1,562,464.
Fields of interest: Scholarships/financial aid; African Americans/Blacks.
Type of support: Employee-related scholarships; Scholarships—to individuals; Undergraduate support.
Application information: Application form required. Application form available on the grantmaker's web site.
   Initial approach: Application
   Send request by: Mail
   Deadline(s): Dec. 31 for Louis F. Cox Memorial AK Steel African-American Scholarships
   Applicants should submit the following:
      1) Transcripts
      2) Class rank
      3) SAT
      4) ACT
   Additional information: All scholarship programs are administered by the Middletown Community Foundation.
Program descriptions:
   AK Steel Sons and Daughters Scholarships: The foundation awards $5,000 college scholarships annually to the children of AK Steel employees. The scholarship is renewable for a maximum of three years, for a total potential scholarship of $20,000. The program is administered by the Middletown Community Foundation.
   Louie F. Cox Memorial AK Steel African-American Scholarships: The foundation awards $5,000 college scholarships annually to African-American high school seniors graduating from schools in Butler and Warren counties, OH. The scholarship is renewable for a maximum of three years, for a total potential scholarship of $20,000. The program is administered by the Middletown Community Foundation. Visit URL: http://www.mcfoundation.org/Available_Scholarships.htm#COX for more information.
Company name: AK Steel Holding Corporation
EIN: 311284344

6965
Akron Community Foundation
195 S. Main St., Ste. 300
Akron, OH   44308   (330) 376-8522
Contact: John T. Petures, Jr., C.E.O.
FAX: (330) 376-0202;
E-mail: acfmail@akroncommunityfdn.org;
URL: http://www.akroncf.org/

Foundation type: Community foundation
Purpose: Scholarships to residents of the Akron, OH area for attendance at accredited colleges or universities.
Publications: Application guidelines; Annual report (including application guidelines); Newsletter.
Financial data: Year ended 03/31/2012. Assets, $140,719,939 (M); Expenditures, $8,425,897; Total giving, $5,983,252. Scholarships—to individuals amount not specified.
Fields of interest: Higher education; Scholarships/financial aid.
Type of support: Scholarships—to individuals; Support to graduates or students of specific schools; Undergraduate support.

Application information: Applications accepted. Application form required.
Deadline(s): Varies
Additional information: Each scholarship fund has a unique set of eligibility criteria and application guidelines. See web site for a complete listing of scholarships funds.
Program description:
Scholarships: The foundation administers a number of scholarship funds established by donors. These funds are usually disbursed annually to specific educational institutions to be used for tuition and/or books. Specific scholarship criteria exist for each award. See web site for additional information.
EIN: 341087615

6966
Akron General Development Foundation
400 Wabash Ave.
Akron, OH   44307-2433   (330) 344-6000
Contact: Karen A. Bozzelli, Pres.
FAX: (330) 344-0068; URL: http://www.akrongeneral.org/portal/page/portal/AGMC_PAGEGROUP/AGMC_PAGE

Foundation type: Public charity
Purpose: Scholarships to children of eligible employees of organizations of the Akron General Health System. Nursing scholarships to students who have graduated from a high school in summit county, OH.
Publications: Application guidelines; Annual report; Newsletter.
Financial data: Year ended 12/31/2011. Assets, $14,426,559 (M); Expenditures, $2,108,255; Total giving, $2,049,175; Grants to individuals, totaling $12,250.
Fields of interest: Higher education; Nursing school/education.
Type of support: Scholarships—to individuals.
Application information: Applications accepted.
Additional information: Unsolicited requests for funds not accepted.
Program descriptions:
AGHS Sons and Daughters Scholarship: Through this program, the foundation promotes higher education with a scholarship opportunity for children of eligible employees of organizations of the Akron General Health System. Scholarships are not limited to any particular trade or field of study.
Akron General Service League's Nurses Scholarship: Through this scholarship, the foundation promotes nursing education in the state of Ohio. Qualified candidates will have graduated from a high school in Summit County, OH, have obtained a minimum of a 3.0 GPA and have applied to and been accepted by one of the seven state funded nursing programs.
EIN: 341127047

6967
Akron Summit Community Action Agency, Inc.
55 E. Mill St.
P.O. Box 2000
Akron, OH   44309-2000   (330) 376-7730
Contact: Malcolm J. Costa, Pres. and C.E.O.
URL: http://www.ascainc.org

Foundation type: Public charity
Purpose: Emergency assistance to low-income individuals and families in need throughout Summit County, OH with food, clothing, household items, rent, utilities and other special needs.
Publications: Annual report.

Financial data: Year ended 12/31/2011. Assets, $4,894,140 (M); Expenditures, $17,363,088; Total giving, $2,614,295; Grants to individuals, totaling $1,108,626.
Fields of interest: Human services; Economically disadvantaged.
Type of support: Emergency funds; Grants for special needs.
Application information: Contact the agency for eligibility determination and additional programs.
EIN: 340965339

6968
Thomas L., Myrtle R., and Eva Alexander Scholarship Fund
c/o Fith Third Bank, Trustee
P.O. Box 630858
Cincinnati, OH   45263-0858

Foundation type: Independent foundation
Purpose: Scholarships to students of Posey County, IN, high schools.
Financial data: Year ended 02/28/2013. Assets, $1,010,088 (M); Expenditures, $68,836; Total giving, $45,000; Grants to individuals, 36 grants totaling $45,000 (high: $2,000, low: $1,000).
Type of support: Scholarships—to individuals; Support to graduates or students of specific schools.
Application information: Applications accepted. Application form required.
Deadline(s): May 1
Additional information: Contact schools for current application guidelines.
EIN: 356333739

6969
Alexander's Future Foundation
P.O. Box 204
Albany, OH   45710-0204   (740) 698-8831

Foundation type: Public charity
Purpose: Scholarships to graduating students of Alexander High School, OH for tuition, books, or fees pursuing a college education.
Financial data: Year ended 12/31/2011. Assets, $605,656 (M); Expenditures, $27,469; Total giving, $27,251; Grants to individuals, totaling $27,251.
Fields of interest: Higher education.
Type of support: Support to graduates or students of specific schools.
Application information: Applications accepted. Application form required. Interview required.
Deadline(s): Apr. 1
Program description:
Scholarships: Scholarships range from $500 to $1,000, awarded to Alexander High School seniors each spring, based on students' financial need, academic achievement and service to the community.
EIN: 311360416

6970
The Bonnie Schatz Allchin Charitable Foundation
6567 Bushnell Rd.
Conneaut, OH   44030   (440) 593-7210
Application address: Conneaut H.S., 381 Mill St., Conneaut, OH 44030

Foundation type: Independent foundation
Purpose: Scholarships to students of OH for higher education at accredited colleges or universities.

Financial data: Year ended 12/31/2012. Assets, $112,218 (M); Expenditures, $19,344; Total giving, $18,500; Grants to individuals, 5 grants totaling $18,500 (high: $12,000, low: $1,000).
Fields of interest: Higher education.
Type of support: Undergraduate support.
Application information: Applications accepted. Application form required.
Initial approach: Letter
EIN: 205898952

6971
The American Electric Power System Educational Trust Fund
c/o AEP Tax Dept.
1 Riverside Plz.
Columbus, OH   43215-2373   (614) 716-1000
Scholarship address: AEP, Human Resources, 1 Riverside Plaza, Columbus, OH 43215

Foundation type: Company-sponsored foundation
Purpose: Undergraduate scholarships to children of employees of American Electric Power Co., Inc.
Publications: Program policy statement.
Financial data: Year ended 02/28/2013. Assets, $5,271,398 (M); Expenditures, $316,144; Total giving, $295,000; Grants to individuals, 125 grants totaling $295,000 (high: $4,500, low: $2,000).
Fields of interest: Higher education.
Type of support: Employee-related scholarships.
Application information: Applications accepted. Application form required.
Deadline(s): First Mon. in Oct.
Company name: American Electric Power Company, Inc.
EIN: 237418083

6972
American Legion Department of Ohio Charities, Inc.
60 Big Run Rd.
P.O. Box 8007
Delaware, OH   43015-9127   (740) 362-7478
FAX: (740) 362-1429;
E-mail: legion@ohiolegion.com; URL: http://www.ohiolegion.com/pages_other/charities.htm

Foundation type: Public charity
Purpose: Scholarships to Ohio high school seniors, Legionnaires, direct descendants of Legionnaires, direct descendants of deceased Legionnaires, and/or surviving spouses or children of deceased U.S. military persons who died on active duty or of injuries received on active duty.
Financial data: Year ended 07/31/2012. Assets, $70,508 (M); Expenditures, $2,993,345; Total giving, $2,934,297. Scholarships—to individuals amount not specified.
Fields of interest: Vocational education, post-secondary; Higher education; Military/veterans.
Type of support: Scholarships—to individuals.
Application information: Applications accepted. Application form required. Application form available on the grantmaker's web site.
Send request by: Mail
Deadline(s): Apr. 15
Additional information: See web site for additional application guidelines.
Program description:
Scholarships: Each year, the organization makes available scholarships of at least $2,000 to deserving students to assist them with the ever-increasing costs associated with higher education. Eligible applicants include high school

seniors, Legionnaires, direct descendants of Legionnaires, direct descendants of deceased Legionnaires, and surviving spouses or children of deceased U.S. military persons who died on active duty or of injuries received on active duty. Applicants will be evaluated on academic achievement through course grades, difficulty of curriculum, scholastic test scores, participation in outside activities, and general impressions by the judging committee. In addition, one applicant will receive a $1,000 Durwand I. Bernhard Scholarship Award, given to a resident of Belmont County, OH.
EIN: 020692968

6973
Dorothy Ames Trust
c/o KeyBank
4900 Tiedeman, OH-01-49-0150
Brooklyn, OH 44144-2302 (866) 238-8650
Contact: Edward Deluccia
Application address: C/o. KeyBank, N.A., 66 S. Pearl St., Albany, NY 12201, tel.: (866) 238-8650

Foundation type: Independent foundation
Purpose: Assistance for hearing-impaired children from the New England states with hearing aids, auditory trainers, and other expenses related to hearing-impairment.
Financial data: Year ended 08/31/2013. Assets, $560,963 (M); Expenditures, $26,495; Total giving, $15,119.
Fields of interest: Children; Deaf/hearing impaired.
Type of support: Grants for special needs.
Application information: Applications accepted.
Initial approach: Letter
Deadline(s): None
Additional information: Application should include parents' most recent tax return, a document showing cost and an audiologist's report.
EIN: 016065594

6974
E. & E. Anderson Scholarship Foundation
c/o Keybank
P.O. Box 10099
Toledo, OH 43699-0099

Foundation type: Independent foundation
Purpose: Scholarships to students, primarily in ME, for higher education.
Financial data: Year ended 12/31/2012. Assets, $469,464 (M); Expenditures, $31,847; Total giving, $19,200.
Type of support: Undergraduate support.
Application information: Applications not accepted.
Additional information: Unsolicited requests for funds not considered or acknowledged.
EIN: 527115055

6975
Olson L. Anderson and Catherine Bastow Anderson Scholarship Trust
41 00 W 150th Street
Cleveland, OH 44135

Foundation type: Independent foundation
Purpose: Scholarships to full-time, on-campus undergraduates with demonstrated financial need who are attending Central Michigan University. Preference will be given to graduates of high schools in Bay County, MI.
Financial data: Year ended 09/30/2011. Assets, $899,872 (M); Expenditures, $104,005; Total

giving, $93,537; Grants to individuals, 20 grants totaling $93,537 (high: $5,536, low: $1,255).
Fields of interest: Scholarships/financial aid.
Type of support: Support to graduates or students of specific schools; Undergraduate support.
Application information: Applications accepted. Application form required.
Initial approach: Letter or telephone
Deadline(s): May 15
Applicants should submit the following:
1) Essay
2) FAFSA
3) Letter(s) of recommendation
EIN: 386345071

6976
Alice A. Andrus Foundation
c/o PNC Bank, N.A.
P.O. Box 94651
Cleveland, OH 44101-4651 (440) 647-3734

Foundation type: Independent foundation
Purpose: Scholarships to graduates of Wellington High School, OH, who are in the top 50 percent of their class.
Financial data: Year ended 10/31/2013. Assets, $447,454 (M); Expenditures, $22,878; Total giving, $18,525; Grant to an individual, 1 grant totaling $18,525.
Fields of interest: Higher education.
Type of support: Support to graduates or students of specific schools; Undergraduate support.
Application information: Applications accepted.
Initial approach: Letter
Deadline(s): Apr. 1
Applicants should submit the following:
1) Class rank
2) Financial information
EIN: 346653271

6977
Annual Emancipation Day Celebration
P.O. Box 511
Gallipolis, OH 45631
URL: http://www.emancipation-day.com

Foundation type: Independent foundation
Purpose: Scholarships to graduating area youth of Gallia county, OH for postsecondary education.
Financial data: Year ended 12/31/2012. Assets, $13,615 (M); Expenditures, $11,409; Total giving, $2,550; Grants to individuals, 6 grants totaling $2,550 (high: $500, low: $350).
Fields of interest: Higher education.
Type of support: Scholarships—to individuals.
Application information: Applications accepted. Application form required.
Send request by: Mail
Deadline(s): Apr. 15
Applicants should submit the following:
1) Transcripts
2) SAT
3) Letter(s) of recommendation
4) GPA
5) Essay
6) ACT
Additional information: Application should also include extracurricluar and school activities.
EIN: 311362400

6978
Arab Student Aid International Corp.
P.O. Box 3546
Dublin, OH 43016-0271 (614) 889-9420
Contact: Dr. Ishaq Al-Qutub, Pres.
FAX: (614) 889-9430;
E-mail: president@arabstudentaid.org; *URL:* http://www.arabstudentaid.org/

Foundation type: Public charity
Purpose: Interest-free loans to students for the Masters and/or Ph.D. programs of Arab citizenship.
Publications: Application guidelines; Informational brochure; Multi-year report; Newsletter; Program policy statement.
Financial data: Year ended 06/30/2012. Assets, $4,069,880 (M); Expenditures, $499,363; Total giving, $372,630.
Fields of interest: Minorities.
Type of support: Program development; Employee-related scholarships; Student loans—to individuals; Foreign applicants; Graduate support; Doctoral support.
Application information: Application form required. Application form available on the grantmaker's web site.
Initial approach: E-mail or fax
Send request by: Mail
Deadline(s): Sept. 1 and Feb. 1
Applicants should submit the following:
1) Work samples
2) Financial information
3) Essay
4) Budget Information
5) ACT
6) Photograph
7) Transcripts
8) Resume
9) Letter(s) of recommendation
10) GPA
11) Curriculum vitae
Additional information: Unsolicited applications not accepted. Incomplete application documents will not be considered.
Program description:
Scholarship Loans: Interest-free loans are available to Arab citizens who are currently enrolled full-time in an accredited school, and who are pursuing a master's degree or Ph.D. Eligible applicants must currently reside in an Arab country (students who are a permanent resident or citizen of a non-Arab country, including those with a dual citizenship, do not qualify), be planning to return to an Arab country to work and serve the community, show evidence of financial need, and have a student visa. Repayment of loans must be secured through two guarantors and must be paid within three years through an installment plan, or at one time.
EIN: 208113798

6979
Ariel Foundation
101 E. Gambier St.
Mount Vernon, OH 43050-3509 (740) 392-0364
Contact: Jan Reynolds, Secy.-Treas.
FAX: (740) 392-0370;
E-mail: jreynolds@ariel-foundation.org; *URL:* http://www.ariel-foundation.org/

Foundation type: Company-sponsored foundation
Purpose: Scholarships to graduating students of Mount Vernon High School, OH to attend a four-year college and study the engineering discipline.
Publications: Application guidelines; Grants list.

Financial data: Year ended 12/31/2012. Assets, $22,663,833 (M); Expenditures, $1,588,591; Total giving, $1,409,517.
Fields of interest: Higher education; Engineering school/education.
Type of support: Scholarships—to individuals; Support to graduates or students of specific schools.
Application information: Applications accepted. Application form required. Application form available on the grantmaker's web site.
  Initial approach: Application
  Send request by: Mail
  Deadline(s): July 7
  Applicants should submit the following:
    1) GPA
    2) Transcripts
    3) Photograph
    4) Letter(s) of recommendation
Program description:
  James P. Buschwald & Tom Rastin Engineering Scholarships: The foundation annually awards $5,000 to students of sophomore status or above who are enrolled at a four-year engineering college in the fields of chemical, electrical, or mechanical engineering. Applicant must be a graduate of Mount Vernon High School, of Mount Vernon, OH, or a resident of Mount Vernon, OH at the time of high school graduation. Applicants are selected based on academic achievement, recommendation from instructors, personal qualities, and financial need.
EIN: 270226408

6980
Ashland County Community Foundation
300 College Ave.
Ashland, OH 44805-3803   (419) 281-4733
Contact: James M. Cutright, Exec. Dir.
FAX: (419) 289-5540;
E-mail: accf@accommunityfoundation.org;
URL: http://www.accommunityfoundation.org

Foundation type: Community foundation
Purpose: Educational loans and scholarships to students of Ashland County high schools who plan matriculation into college prior to the age of 23. Educational loans and scholarships to residents of Ashland county who are U.S. citizens and over the age of 23.
Publications: Application guidelines; Annual report; Grants list; Informational brochure; Newsletter.
Financial data: Year ended 06/30/2012. Assets, $17,879,190 (M); Expenditures, $743,291; Total giving, $473,093; Grants to individuals, totaling $118,615; Loans to individuals, 11 loans totaling $13,200.
Fields of interest: Higher education.
Type of support: Scholarships—to individuals; Student loans—to individuals; Support to graduates or students of specific schools.
Application information: Applications accepted. Application form required. Application form available on the grantmaker's web site.
  Initial approach: Letter, telephone, or e-mail
  Send request by: Mail
  Copies of proposal: 1
  Deadline(s): Apr. 1 and June 15
  Final notification: Recipients notified in one month
EIN: 341812908

6981
The Ashtabula Foundation, Inc.
4510 Collins Blvd., Ste. 6
Ashtabula, OH 44004-6954   (440) 992-6818
URL: http://www.ashtabulafoundation.org

Foundation type: Independent foundation
Purpose: Scholarships to residents of Ashtabula, OH, who are graduates of Ashtabula high schools for attendance at an accredited institution of higher learning.
Publications: Application guidelines; Informational brochure.
Financial data: Year ended 12/31/2012. Assets, $15,984,278 (M); Expenditures, $924,222; Total giving, $703,837.
Fields of interest: Higher education.
Type of support: Support to graduates or students of specific schools; Undergraduate support.
Application information: Applications accepted. Application form required.
  Deadline(s): Last business day of Mar. for Edward J. Harvey Scholarship
  Final notification: Applicants notified at the end of Apr.
  Applicants should submit the following:
    1) Essay
    2) SAR
    3) FAFSA
    4) Pell Grant
    5) Transcripts
  Additional information: Preference is given to students showing financial need and satisfactory academic achievement or ability. Application can be obtain from the foundation or the high school guidance offices.
Program description:
  Edward J Harvey Scholarship Fund: Open to legal residents of Ashtabula, OH, who graduated from a high school in Ashtabula. These $1,000 per year scholarships must be used at accredited institutions by full-time students. Scholarships are renewable but formal request is required each year.
EIN: 346538130

6982
Associated Charities of Findlay, Ohio
1800 N. Blanchard St., Ste. 105
Findlay, OH 45840-4504   (419) 423-2021
Contact: Peggy Wood, Treas.

Foundation type: Independent foundation
Purpose: Emergency financial assistance by referral only to families and individuals living in Findlay, OH, and Hancock County, OH.
Publications: Annual report.
Financial data: Year ended 12/31/2011. Assets, $3,782,230 (M); Expenditures, $192,971; Total giving, $122,993.
Fields of interest: Human services, emergency aid.
Type of support: Awards/grants by nomination only; Grants for special needs.
Application information:
  Deadline(s): None
  Additional information: Applicants must be referred by a social services agency. The majority of aid is given as a result of personal interviews. In extreme cases, aid may be given as a result of a telephone call.
EIN: 346400067

6983
Florence D. Atwood Trust for Brooks Scholarship Fund
c/o KeyBank, N.A.
4900 Tiedeman Rd., OH-01-49-0
Brooklyn, OH 44144-2302
Contact: Kevin Mulligan

Foundation type: Independent foundation
Purpose: Scholarships to financially needy residents of Chazy Central School District, NY, who have attended school in the district and will attend college full-time.
Financial data: Year ended 06/30/2013. Assets, $53,751 (M); Expenditures, $1,919; Total giving, $1,200.
Type of support: Support to graduates or students of specific schools; Undergraduate support.
Application information: Applications accepted.
  Initial approach: Letter
  Deadline(s): Apr. 1
EIN: 222753510

6984
Bud H. Babcock Trust
4077 Clark St.
Willoughby, OH 44094-6141

Foundation type: Operating foundation
Purpose: Scholarships to Willoughby Eastlake School System students for continuing education at accredited institutions of higher learning.
Financial data: Year ended 12/31/2011. Assets, $446,190 (M); Expenditures, $27,251; Total giving, $17,769.
Fields of interest: Higher education.
Type of support: Support to graduates or students of specific schools.
Application information: Applications accepted. Application form required.
  Deadline(s): May 1
  Applicants should submit the following:
    1) Transcripts
    2) Letter(s) of recommendation
  Additional information: Application should also include community activities, extracurricular activities, and awards received.
EIN: 306081202

6985
John E. Bakes Scholarship Trust Fund
c/o PNC Bank, N.A.
P.O. Box 94651
Cleveland, OH 44101-4651

Foundation type: Independent foundation
Purpose: Scholarships to graduating seniors of Switzerland County High School, IN, and Rising Sun High School, IN.
Financial data: Year ended 12/31/2012. Assets, $280,673 (M); Expenditures, $16,022; Total giving, $12,000; Grant to an individual, 1 grant totaling $12,000.
Type of support: Support to graduates or students of specific schools; Undergraduate support.
Application information: Applications not accepted.
  Additional information: Unsolicited requests for funds not considered or acknowledged.
EIN: 356406002

6986
Nellie L. Ball Trust
P.O. Box 106
Wellston, OH   45692   (740) 384-2020
Contact: Peggy Shumate, Treas.

Foundation type: Independent foundation
Purpose: Scholarships to graduates of Wellston High School, OH for attendance at U.S. colleges or universities.
Financial data: Year ended 12/31/2012. Assets, $250,994 (M); Expenditures, $9,317; Total giving, $9,000; Grants to individuals, 3 grants totaling $9,000 (high: $3,000, low: $3,000).
Type of support: Support to graduates or students of specific schools.
Application information: Applications accepted. Application form required.
Deadline(s): Apr. 13
Applicants should submit the following:
1) GPA
2) Financial information
3) Essay
EIN: 316453187

6987
C. Glenn Barber Foundation
P.O. Box 94651
Cleveland, OH   44101-4651
URL: https://www.pnc.com/webapp/unsec/Homepage.do?siteArea=/PNCCorp/PNC/Home/Personal

Foundation type: Independent foundation
Purpose: Scholarships to students who reside in OH for undergraduate education.
Financial data: Year ended 12/31/2012. Assets, $3,108,844 (M); Expenditures, $154,772; Total giving, $148,372.
Type of support: Undergraduate support.
Application information: Applications not accepted.
Additional information: Unsolicited requests for funds not considered or acknowledged.
EIN: 346765153

6988
Barberton Community Foundation
460 W. Paige Ave.
Barberton, OH   44203-2564   (330) 745-5995
Contact: Larry Lallo, Exec. Dir.
FAX: (330) 745-3990;
E-mail: jstephenson@barbertoncf.org; *URL:* http://www.barbertoncf.org

Foundation type: Community foundation
Purpose: Scholarships to graduating seniors for attendance at Barberton High School for at least two years. Scholarships also to residents of the Barberton School District or the City of Barberton, OH.
Publications: Application guidelines; Annual report; Financial statement; Grants list; Informational brochure; Informational brochure (including application guidelines); Newsletter; Quarterly report.
Financial data: Year ended 12/31/2012. Assets, $86,017,062 (M); Expenditures, $4,819,465; Total giving, $3,832,192.
Fields of interest: Higher education.
Type of support: Scholarships—to individuals.
Application information: Applications accepted. Application form required.
Deadline(s): Varies

Additional information: See web site for additional application information.
EIN: 341846432

6989
Raeburn E. Barnes Estate Trust
P.O. Box 499
Sidney, OH   45365-0499
URL: http://www.bright.net

Foundation type: Independent foundation
Purpose: Educational loans to residents of Shelby County, OH or graduates of Shelby County high schools for higher education.
Financial data: Year ended 12/31/2011. Assets, $7,223,423 (M); Expenditures, $167,335; Total giving, $1,000; Loans to individuals, totaling $840,825.
Fields of interest: Higher education.
Type of support: Student loans—to individuals.
Application information: Applications accepted. Application form required.
Initial approach: Letter
Deadline(s): Mar. 31
Additional information: Application available upon request.
EIN: 346639060

6990
Bernard H. Beal Scholarship Foundation
4100 W. 150th St.
Cleveland, OH   44315   (216) 222-9815
Contact: Jane Kleinsmith
Application address: 1900 E. 9th St., Cleveland, OH 44114, tel.: (216) 222-9815

Foundation type: Independent foundation
Purpose: Scholarships to graduates of Millington High School, MI.
Financial data: Year ended 12/31/2012. Assets, $557,772 (M); Expenditures, $26,108; Total giving, $18,800; Grant to an individual, 1 grant totaling $18,800.
Type of support: Support to graduates or students of specific schools; Undergraduate support.
Application information: Application form required.
Send request by: Mail
Deadline(s): Jan. 31
Applicants should submit the following:
1) Essay
2) FAFSA
3) Letter(s) of recommendation
4) SAR
5) Transcripts
EIN: 383381079

6991
L. Carl Bean Scholarship Fund
c/o KeyBank, N.A.
4900 Tiedeman Rd., OH-01-49-0150
Brooklyn, OH   44144-2338   (518) 257-9650

Foundation type: Independent foundation
Purpose: Scholarships to residents of ME for postsecondary education.
Financial data: Year ended 04/30/2013. Assets, $235,566 (M); Expenditures, $12,774; Total giving, $8,800.
Fields of interest: Higher education.
Type of support: Scholarships—to individuals.
Application information: Contact the fund for additional guidelines.
EIN: 016068112

6992
Beane Family Foundation
173 Keswick Dr.
New Albany, OH   43054   (614) 245-8839
Contact: Evan J. Beane, Dir.

Foundation type: Independent foundation
Purpose: Scholarships to residents of IA, primarily in Marshalltown, for higher education.
Financial data: Year ended 12/31/2011. Assets, $1,075,772 (M); Expenditures, $45,270; Total giving, $43,800; Grants to individuals, 5 grants totaling $15,000 (high: $3,000, low: $3,000).
Fields of interest: Higher education.
Type of support: Undergraduate support.
Application information: Applications accepted.
Initial approach: Letter
Send request by: Mail
Deadline(s): None
Additional information: Letter must show need and use of funds.
EIN: 341662821

6993
George C. Beinke Scholarship Fund
4900 Tiedeman Rd., OH-01-49-0150
Brooklyn, OH   44144-2302   (419) 259-8218
Contact: Marilyn Brown
Application address: P.O. Box 10099, Toledo, OH 43699-0099, tel.: (419) 259-8218

Foundation type: Independent foundation
Purpose: Scholarships to financially needy graduates of Lucas County, OH, high schools to attend the University of Toledo.
Financial data: Year ended 08/31/2013. Assets, $525,656 (M); Expenditures, $39,390; Total giving, $32,700.
Fields of interest: Higher education.
Type of support: Support to graduates or students of specific schools; Undergraduate support.
Application information: Application form required.
Initial approach: Letter
Deadline(s): Mar. 1
Additional information: Applicant must demonstrate financial need and scholastic ability.
EIN: 346542089

6994
Belpre Area Community Development Foundation
P. O. Box 731
Belpre, OH   45714-0731
URL: http://www.bacdf.org/

Foundation type: Public charity
Purpose: Scholarships to graduating students of Belpre High School, OH for continuing education at accredited colleges or universities.
Financial data: Year ended 12/31/2012. Assets, $2,443,513 (M); Expenditures, $76,540; Total giving, $61,603; Grants to individuals, totaling $4,750.
Fields of interest: Higher education.
Type of support: Support to graduates or students of specific schools.
Application information: Contact the foundation for additional application guidelines.
EIN: 311315350

6995
Frank F. Bentley Trust
c/o KeyBank, N.A.
4900 Tiedman Rd. OH-01-49-0150
Brooklyn, OH 44144-2302 (330) 399-8801
Contact: John Rossi
Application Address: 185 High St. N.E., Warren, OH 44481

Foundation type: Independent foundation
Purpose: Scholarships to residents of Trumbull County, OH. Preference is given first to orphans, then to persons from foster homes, and then to those from "broken" homes.
Financial data: Year ended 09/30/2013. Assets, $293,380 (M); Expenditures, $20,301; Total giving, $16,000.
Fields of interest: Residential/custodial care.
Type of support: Scholarships—to individuals.
Application information: Applications accepted. Application form required.
  Initial approach: Letter
  Deadline(s): June 30
EIN: 346508762

6996
Berlin Family Educational Foundation
17181 Curry Ln.
Auburn Township, OH 44023-5522 (440) 533-5986

Foundation type: Independent foundation
Purpose: Scholarships to graduating seniors of Willoughby South, Eastlake North, Brush, and Portland Waldorf high schools in Willoughby Hills, OH, or students who are residents of Willoughby Hills, OH. The foundation also awards grants to teachers through its South High School Teacher Grants program.
Financial data: Year ended 12/31/2011. Assets, $1,206,783 (M); Expenditures, $116,335; Total giving, $42,050.
Fields of interest: Education.
Type of support: Support to graduates or students of specific schools; Awards/prizes; Undergraduate support.
Application information: Applications accepted. Application form required.
  Send request by: Proposal must be sent by e-mail
  Copies of proposal: 1 for teacher grants
  Deadline(s): Mid-Feb. for scholarships, Oct. 1 for teacher grants
  Final notification: May for scholarships, teacher grants two weeks after receipt of application
  Additional information: Student's high school guidance office might set an earlier application deadline. Applications for teacher grants must include an estimated list of expenses.
Program description:
  South High School Teacher Grants: Categories considered for grants are: Innovative classroom programs, including materials or technological materials to support the program, other educational programs that enhance the curriculum, attendance at in-service programs or workshops that enhance the curriculum, special programs or assemblies to benefit students and/or teachers.
EIN: 341817284

6997
Bernhard-Wentz Scholarship Fund
P.O. Box 1558, EA4E86
Columbus, OH 43216-1558 (330) 343-7746

Foundation type: Independent foundation
Purpose: Scholarships to graduates of Dover High School, OH.
Financial data: Year ended 12/31/2012. Assets, $1,371,169 (M); Expenditures, $77,157; Total giving, $59,945.
Type of support: Scholarships—to individuals; Support to graduates or students of specific schools; Undergraduate support.
Application information: Applications accepted.
  Deadline(s): June 1
  Additional information: Contact fund for current application guidelines.
EIN: 316334477

6998
The Robert Birr Scholarship Foundation, Inc.
250 W. Main St.
Bellevue, OH 44811-1326 (419) 483-5670
Contact: Glenn Cunningham, Treas.

Foundation type: Independent foundation
Purpose: Scholarships to current high school students or post high school students for continuing his or her education in a technical field not limited to electrical engineering, computer science or physics.
Financial data: Year ended 12/31/2011. Assets, $154,032 (M); Expenditures, $8,109; Total giving, $8,000; Grants to individuals, 8 grants totaling $8,000 (high: $1,000, low: $1,000).
Fields of interest: Engineering school/education; Physics; Computer science.
Type of support: Scholarships—to individuals.
Application information: Applications accepted. Application form required.
  Deadline(s): May 1
EIN: 341940986

6999
Blade Foundation
405 Madison Ave., Ste. 2100
Toledo, OH 43604
Contact: Jodi Miehls, Treas.

Foundation type: Company-sponsored foundation
Purpose: Scholarships to children or legal dependents of full-time Toledo Blade employees with at three years' tenure.
Financial data: Year ended 12/31/2012. Assets, $19,297 (M); Expenditures, $110,598; Total giving, $110,500; Grants to individuals, 2 grants totaling $3,000 (high: $1,500, low: $1,500).
Type of support: Employee-related scholarships.
Application information: Applications accepted. Application form not required.
  Initial approach: Letter
  Deadline(s): Mar. 1
  Additional information: Applicants must submit SAT scores.
Company name: Block Communications, Inc.
EIN: 346559843

7000
Blanchard Valley Health Foundation
1900 S. Main St.
Findlay, OH 45840-1214 (419) 423-4500
Contact: Scott Malaney, C.E.O.
URL: http://www.bvhealthsystem.org/?id=3&sid=3

Foundation type: Public charity
Purpose: Scholarships to individuals within the foundation's service area pursuing a career in nursing.
Publications: Application guidelines.
Financial data: Year ended 12/31/2011. Assets, $8,247,120 (M); Expenditures, $1,557,793; Total giving, $1,036,968; Grants to individuals, totaling $2,000.
Fields of interest: Medical school/education; Nursing school/education.
Type of support: Employee-related scholarships; Scholarships—to individuals; Postgraduate support.
Application information: Applications accepted. Application form required. Application form available on the grantmaker's web site.
  Initial approach: Application
  Send request by: Mail
  Deadline(s): Mar. 31 for Greater Northwest Ohio Diabetes Association Scholarships; Apr. 15 for Findlay Auxiliary Scholarships; May 1 for Karen S. Jones Nursing Certification Scholarship; Apr. 1 for all others
  Applicants should submit the following:
    1) Letter(s) of recommendation
    2) Transcripts
  Additional information: See web site for additional guidelines.
Program descriptions:
  Findlay Auxiliary Scholarships: Scholarships of $1,000 each are available to financially assist a Hancock County area high school senior in pursuing a health-related career. Eligible applicants must be within the top third of their class, be a senior in a Hancock County school, Findlay High School, or St. Wendelin High School, and be sincere about entering a medical field and have definite goals.
  Greater Northwest Ohio Diabetes Association Scholarships: Multiple scholarships, ranging from $500 to $1,000, are available annually to provide financial assistance for furthering the education of persons with diabetes. Eligible applicants must reside in Hancock, Hardin, Putnam, Seneca, Wood, or Wyandot counties, demonstrate medical documentation of a diagnosis of diabetes, and be a high school senior or college student.
  Karen S. Jones Nursing Certification Scholarship: A $500 scholarship is available to Blanchard Valley Health System (BVHS) nurses for a review course and/or certification exam fee. Employee must be an exemplary performer at BVHS.
  Kathleen Higgins Scholarship: Scholarship ranging from $500 to $1,000 are available to individuals who wish to pursue nursing education. Eligible applicants must have a GPA of 3.0 or better, and must have a permanent address in an area served by the foundation. Preference will be given to recipients who demonstrate financial need.
  Maxine Snyder Certification and Masters Preparation Scholarship: Scholarships ranging from $500 to $1,000, will be available to registered nurses who have been employed with Blanchard Valley Health System (BVHS) for at least one year, to continue their nursing education.
  Medical Explorers Post Scholarship: A $1,000 scholarship will be available to seniors attending Hancock County Schools who wish to pursue a nursing or medical education.
  Phyllis Zimber Endowed Scholarship: A $500 scholarship will be awarded to individuals throughout the foundation's service area who wish to pursue their education. Applicants must have a GPA of 3.0 or better, preference will be given to associates of Blanchard Valley Health System (BVHS) or their family members, as well as applicants who demonstrate financial need. Coursework must be for academic credit and count toward a degree in nursing, nursing certification, nurse practitioner, or clinical nurse specialist.

Preference will be given to applicants with an interest in obstetrics.
EIN: 341370522

7001
Lenora Ford and W. Jennings Bland Scholarship Trust
P.O. Box 1621
Coshocton, OH 43812-1511 (740) 622-4248
Contact: Nancy A. Blanchard, Tr.

Foundation type: Independent foundation
Purpose: Scholarships to students of Riverview High School, Ridgewood High School, and Coshocton High School, OH, for undergraduate education.
Financial data: Year ended 12/31/2012. Assets, $292,059 (M); Expenditures, $29,716; Total giving, $12,250; Grants to individuals, 4 grants totaling $12,250 (high: $3,500, low: $1,750).
Fields of interest: Higher education.
Type of support: Support to graduates or students of specific schools; Undergraduate support.
Application information: Application form required.
 Initial approach: Letter or telephone
 Applicants should submit the following:
  1) Transcripts
  2) Resume
  3) Letter(s) of recommendation
EIN: 316430828

7002
Peter J. Blosser Scholarship Trust
(also known as Peter J. Blosser Scholarship Trust)
P.O. Box 6160
Chillicothe, OH 45601-6160 (740) 773-0043
Contact: Peggy Gray
E-mail: Blossertrust@horizonview.net; URL: http://blossertrust.org/Site/Welcome.html

Foundation type: Independent foundation
Purpose: Student loans and scholarships to residents of Ross County, OH for attendance at any accredited college.
Publications: Application guidelines; Annual report; Informational brochure.
Financial data: Year ended 12/31/2011. Assets, $2,223,875 (M); Expenditures, $73,073; Total giving, $13,000; Grants to individuals, 12 grants totaling $13,000 (high: $1,500, low: $1,000); Loans to individuals, 43 loans totaling $95,840.
Fields of interest: Higher education.
Type of support: Scholarships—to individuals; Student loans—to individuals.
Application information: Applications accepted. Application form required. Interview required.
 Initial approach: Letter, telephone, or e-mail
 Send request by: Mail
 Copies of proposal: 1
 Deadline(s): None
 Applicants should submit the following:
  1) Letter(s) of recommendation
  2) Transcripts
  3) GPA
  4) Financial information
 Additional information: Application should also include a copy of college acceptance letter (first year students only) a signed copy of your most recent tax return, and financial aid award letter. See web site for additional guidelines.
EIN: 310629687

7003
Bluecoats of Louisville
c/o P.N.C. Bank N.A.
P.O. Box 94651
Cleveland, OH 44101-4651

Foundation type: Independent foundation
Purpose: Scholarships and awards to outstanding police and fire department officers in the Louisville, KY area.
Financial data: Year ended 12/31/2012. Assets, $642,254 (M); Expenditures, $33,877; Total giving, $25,551; Grants to individuals, 9 grants totaling $7,500.
Fields of interest: Crime/law enforcement, police agencies.
Type of support: Scholarships—to individuals.
Application information: Applications accepted.
 Initial approach: Letter
 Deadline(s): None
EIN: 616022331

7004
Blancheola Bontrager Medical Scholarship Trust
c/o PNC Bank N.A.
P.O. Box 94651
Cleveland, OH 44101-4651

Foundation type: Independent foundation
Purpose: Scholarships to medical students who are residents of Wayne or Holmes County, OH.
Financial data: Year ended 12/31/2012. Assets, $180,783 (M); Expenditures, $11,973; Total giving, $9,000; Grants to individuals, 3 grants totaling $9,000.
Fields of interest: Medical school/education.
Type of support: Graduate support.
Application information:
 Initial approach: Letter
 Deadline(s): May 1
 Additional information: Application must include three character references.
EIN: 347034110

7005
James D. Boone Trust
c/o KeyBank N.A.
4900 Tiedeman Rd., OH-01-49-0150
Brooklyn, OH 44144-2302
Contact: James D. Boone
Application address: c/o Ashtabula High School, Attn.: Steve Evanson, Selection Committee, 401 W. 44th St., Ashtabula, OH 44004-6807

Foundation type: Independent foundation
Purpose: Scholarships to students living in Ashtabula High School territory or will be graduating from Ashtabula High School and planning on continuing their education at accredited institutions of higher learning on a full time basis.
Financial data: Year ended 12/31/2012. Assets, $139,602 (M); Expenditures, $3,421; Total giving, $1,600.
Fields of interest: Higher education.
Type of support: Support to graduates or students of specific schools.
Application information: Applications accepted. Application form required.
 Deadline(s): May 1
 Applicants should submit the following:
  1) Transcripts
  2) FAF
 Additional information: Application must also include a copy of Student Eligibility Report (SER), applicant must complete course

requirements for the Ohio State Award of Distinction, be enrolled in three honors classes, and must be in the top ten percent of the class. Applications can be obtained from high school. Scholarships are renewable for up to four years.
EIN: 346536046

7006
Willard / Lillian Bosaw Memorial Scholarship Fund
300 High St.
Hamilton, OH 45011-6017 (812) 376-1795

Foundation type: Independent foundation
Purpose: Scholarships to high school graduates of Switzerland County, IN for postsecondary education.
Financial data: Year ended 12/31/2012. Assets, $729,530 (M); Expenditures, $25,022; Total giving, $14,000; Grants to individuals, 14 grants totaling $14,000 (high: $1,000, low: $1,000).
Fields of interest: Higher education.
Type of support: Scholarships—to individuals.
Application information: Applications accepted.
 Initial approach: Letter
 Deadline(s): None
EIN: 351967183

7007
L. & S. Bouchard Scholarship Foundation
c/o KeyBank N.A.
4900 Tiedeman Rd., OH-01-49-0150
Brooklyn, OH 44144-2302
Application address: c/o Guidance Counselor, Oak Hill High School, PO Box 400, Sabattus ME 04280

Foundation type: Independent foundation
Purpose: Scholarship awards to graduating seniors of Oak Hill High School, Litchfield, ME, pursuing a degree in the mechanical or construction field at a vocational or technical institute.
Financial data: Year ended 12/31/2012. Assets, $261,616 (M); Expenditures, $20,316; Total giving, $16,149.
Fields of interest: Vocational education, post-secondary.
Type of support: Support to graduates or students of specific schools.
Application information:
 Initial approach: Letter
 Deadline(s): May 25
 Applicants should submit the following:
  1) Transcripts
  2) SAR
EIN: 527076928

7008
Bowen Scholarship Fund
c/o KeyBank N.A.
4900 Tiedeman Rd., OH-01-49-0150
Brooklyn, OH 44144-2302
Contact: Agnes Marountas
Application address: 127 Public Sq., Cleveland, OH 44114

Foundation type: Independent foundation
Purpose: Interest-free loans to Howard County, IN, high school graduates who have completed undergraduate studies in medicine or nursing at any accredited college or university.
Financial data: Year ended 12/31/2012. Assets, $841,041 (L); Expenditures, $33,475; Total giving, $18,000; Grants to individuals, 2 grants totaling $18,000 (high: $10,000, low: $8,000).

Fields of interest: Medical school/education.
Type of support: Student loans—to individuals;
Graduate support.
Application information: Application form required.
 Copies of proposal: 1
 Deadline(s): May 31
 Applicants should submit the following:
  1) Transcripts
  2) Letter(s) of recommendation
  3) Essay
 Additional information: Application must include
  a paragraph explaining why you want to pursue
  career in medical field. Applicants must repay
  advanced money when financially able.
EIN: 352018090

7009
Bowling Green Community Foundation, Inc.

P.O. Box 1175
Bowling Green, OH   43402-1175   (419)
354-5521
Contact: Sandy Kerr, Exec. Dir.
E-mail: bgcf@bgohcf.org; URL: http://
www.bgohcf.org

Foundation type: Community foundation
Purpose: Scholarships to graduating seniors of
Bowling Green High School, OH for continuing their
education at accredited colleges or universities.
Publications: Application guidelines; Annual report
(including application guidelines); Grants list;
Informational brochure.
Financial data: Year ended 12/31/2011. Assets,
$3,330,331 (M); Expenditures, $120,679; Total
giving, $75,440; Grants to individuals, 19 grants
totaling $25,798.
Fields of interest: Higher education.
Type of support: Support to graduates or students
of specific schools.
Application information: Applications accepted.
Application form required. Application form
available on the grantmaker's web site.
 Additional information: Contact the foundation for
  additional application guidelines.
EIN: 341790526

7010
Bowling Green State University Foundation, Inc.

Mileti Alumni Ctr.
Bowling Green, OH   43403-0054   (419)
372-2551
E-mail: alumni@bgsu.edu; Toll-free tel.: (888)
839-2586; URL: https://www.bgsu.edu/alumni/
about-us/foundation-board.html

Foundation type: Public charity
Purpose: Scholarships to students of Bowling
Green State University, OH.
Financial data: Year ended 06/30/2012. Assets,
$111,372,021 (M); Expenditures, $10,515,826;
Total giving, $6,793,505; Grants to individuals,
totaling $2,221,206.
Fields of interest: Higher education.
Type of support: Support to graduates or students
of specific schools.
Application information: Students should contact
the office of financial aid at the university for further
information.
EIN: 346007199

7011
Dorothy M. Brayton Education Trust

300 High St.
Hamilton, OH   45011-6017

Foundation type: Independent foundation
Purpose: Scholarships to graduating seniors from
Middletown High School, OH, and Bishop Fenwick
High School, OH to pursue their education at a
college, university or other institution of higher
learning.
Financial data: Year ended 01/31/2013. Assets,
$1,052,303 (M); Expenditures, $56,742; Total
giving, $40,000.
Type of support: Support to graduates or students
of specific schools; Undergraduate support.
Application information: Application form required.
Interview required.
 Deadline(s): Mar. 1
 Applicants should submit the following:
  1) Resume
  2) Financial information
  3) SAT
  4) ACT
  5) Transcripts
 Additional information: Application should also
  include a list of school and community
  activities. The scholarship is established
  through a Financial Institution and Middletown
  Community Foundation. Contact your school's
  guidance office for application information.
EIN: 352182651

7012
Brewer & McKay Scholarship Foundation

10 W. 2nd St., 26 Fl.
Dayton, OH   45402
Contact: Eric Waddell
Application Address: C/O Presque Isle High School,
16 Griffin St., Presque Isle, ME

Foundation type: Independent foundation
Purpose: Scholarships to graduating seniors of
Presque Isle High School, ME for continuing
education at institutions of higher learning.
Financial data: Year ended 10/31/2012. Assets,
$360,547 (M); Expenditures, $21,543; Total
giving, $17,000.
Fields of interest: Higher education.
Type of support: Support to graduates or students
of specific schools.
Application information:
 Deadline(s): None
 Additional information: Contact your school
  guidance counselor for application
  information.
EIN: 016135476

7013
Brighten Your Future

30406 Hide Away Hills Rd.
Logan, OH   43138
Contact: Larry Kienzle, Treas.

Foundation type: Independent foundation
Purpose: Scholarships to graduates of the
Logan-Hocking School District, OH, who qualify
under the FAF form.
Financial data: Year ended 06/30/2013. Assets,
$1,531,144 (M); Expenditures, $86,753; Total
giving, $50,910; Grants to individuals, 51 grants
totaling $50,910 (high: $1,000, low: $910).
Type of support: Support to graduates or students
of specific schools; Undergraduate support.
Application information: Applications accepted.
 Deadline(s): May 31

 Additional information: Application should
  include FAF.
EIN: 311255015

7014
Mervin Britton Memorial Scholarship Fund

c/o Security National Bank
40 S. Limestone
Springfield, OH   45502-1222   (937) 325-7671

Foundation type: Independent foundation
Purpose: Scholarships for students from Clark
County, OH, high schools, excluding city high
schools, who are attending or will attend a college
or university for the purpose of receiving formal
training in the field of education.
Financial data: Year ended 12/31/2012. Assets,
$904,312 (M); Expenditures, $44,722; Total
giving, $33,895; Grants to individuals, 23 grants
totaling $33,895 (high: $1,500, low: $1,000).
Fields of interest: Teacher school/education.
Type of support: Support to graduates or students
of specific schools.
Application information: Application form required.
 Deadline(s): Contact Office of Education for
  application deadline
 Applicants should submit the following:
  1) Photograph
  2) Letter(s) of recommendation
  3) Essay
 Additional information: Application should
  include an essay discussing why applicant
  desires to be an educator.
EIN: 316511170

7015
Brown County Foundation

c/o Julie A. McConn-Pirman
P.O. Box 158
Georgetown, OH   45121-0158   (937) 378-6165

Foundation type: Community foundation
Purpose: Awards scholarships to graduating
seniors from Brown County for higher education.
Publications: Informational brochure.
Financial data: Year ended 09/30/2012. Assets,
$288,169 (M); Expenditures, $23,886; Total
giving, $20,066; Grants to individuals, 3 grants
totaling $4,000.
Application information: Scholarships are paid
directly to the recipients' colleges.
EIN: 311589435

7016
Brush Foundation

25350 Rockside Rd., 3rd Fl.
Bedford Heights, OH   44146-3704   (216)
961-8804 x1250
Contact: Judy Wright, Prog. Off.
E-mail: brushfoundation@hotmail.com; URL: http://
fdnweb.org/brush/

Foundation type: Independent foundation
Purpose: Scholarships by nomination only to
students in the Mailman School of Public Health at
Columbia University, NY, for studies in Population
and Reproductive Health and/or Public Policy.
Publications: Application guidelines.
Financial data: Year ended 12/31/2012. Assets,
$6,445,347 (M); Expenditures, $359,057; Total
giving, $290,400.
Type of support: Scholarships—to individuals.
Application information: Applications not
accepted.

Additional information: Unsolicited requests for funds not considered or acknowledged.
EIN: 346000445

7017
Bryan Area Foundation, Inc.
516 E. High St.
P.O. Box 651
Bryan, OH   43506-1316   (419) 633-1156
Contact: Ralph W. Gallagher, Chair.
FAX: (419) 633-9262;
E-mail: foundation@bryanareafoundation.org;
URL: http://www.bryanareafoundation.org

Foundation type: Community foundation
Purpose: Scholarships to residents of the Bryan, OH area for higher education at accredited institutions.
Publications: Application guidelines; Newsletter; Occasional report.
Financial data: Year ended 06/30/2012. Assets, $17,130,361 (M); Expenditures, $626,839; Total giving, $247,028; Grants to individuals, totaling $106,625.
Fields of interest: Higher education.
Type of support: Scholarships—to individuals; Support to graduates or students of specific schools; Undergraduate support.
Application information: Applications accepted. Application form required. Application form available on the grantmaker's web site. Interview required.
  Initial approach: Application
  Send request by: Mail
  Deadline(s): Varies
  Applicants should submit the following:
    1) FAFSA
    2) Essay
    3) Photograph
    4) Financial information
  Additional information: See web site for complete listing of scholarships.
EIN: 237041310

7018
John & Ellen Burnham Educational Trust
c/o KeyBank N.A.
4900 Tiedeman Rd., OH-01-49-0150
Brooklyn, OH   44144-2302
Contact: Florence Slattery
Application address: 2400 Hallowell Rd., Litchfield, ME 04350

Foundation type: Independent foundation
Purpose: Scholarships to individuals, primarily in ME, for higher education.
Financial data: Year ended 12/31/2012. Assets, $133,649 (M); Expenditures, $8,560; Total giving, $6,500; Grants to individuals, 13 grants totaling $6,500 (high: $500, low: $500).
Type of support: Scholarships—to individuals.
Application information: Applications not accepted.
  Additional information: Contributes only to preselected individuals.
EIN: 016131036

7019
Elizabeth B. Bush Memorial Scholarship Trust
c/o KeyBank N.A.
4900 Tiedeman Rd. OH-01-49-0150
Brooklyn, OH   44144-2302

Foundation type: Independent foundation

Purpose: Scholarships to high school graduates who are residents of Lewis, NY. Recipients must seek at least a two-year program of higher study after graduation.
Financial data: Year ended 12/31/2012. Assets, $181,312 (M); Expenditures, $10,682; Total giving, $8,000.
Type of support: Undergraduate support.
Application information: Applications not accepted.
  Additional information: Unsolicited requests for funds not considered or acknowledged.
EIN: 146123826

7020
Butler-Wells Scholarship Fund
c/o Fifth Third Bank
P.O. Box 630858
Cincinnati, OH   45263-0858   (513) 534-5456
Application Address: 38 Fountain SQ. Plz M/D 1090 \CA Cincinnati, OH 45263

Foundation type: Independent foundation
Purpose: Scholarships to students who reside and attend college in IN, OH, IL or PA with preference for residents of Piqua, Cincinnati, or Miami counties, OH.
Financial data: Year ended 12/31/2012. Assets, $751,617 (M); Expenditures, $43,979; Total giving, $36,250.
Type of support: Undergraduate support.
Application information: Applications accepted. Application form required.
  Initial approach: Letter
  Deadline(s): Mar. 15, June 15, Sept. 15 and Dec. 15
  Applicants should submit the following:
    1) Letter(s) of recommendation
    2) Essay
EIN: 316019693

7021
The William M. & A. Cafaro Family Foundation
c/o The Cafaro Co.
2445 Belmont Ave.
P.O. Box 2186
Youngstown, OH   44504-0186
Contact: Ruthanne Brown

Foundation type: Independent foundation
Purpose: Scholarships to qualifying residents of the greater Youngstown, OH area.
Financial data: Year ended 03/31/2013. Assets, $28,588,382 (M); Expenditures, $1,345,469; Total giving, $1,246,605; Grants to individuals, totaling $28,000.
Type of support: Undergraduate support.
Application information: Applications accepted. Application form required.
  Deadline(s): None
  Additional information: Contact foundation for application guidelines.
EIN: 311550874

7022
J. Colin Campbell Scholarship Trust
3040 West Point Rd.
Lancaster, OH   43130-8640   (740) 569-3040
Contact: William J. Sitterley, Tr.
URL: http://www.fairfieldcountyscholarships.com/

Foundation type: Independent foundation

Purpose: Scholarships to graduates of Fairfield County, OH, high schools for attendance at a four-year college or university in OH.
Financial data: Year ended 05/31/2013. Assets, $1,683,839 (M); Expenditures, $72,363; Total giving, $60,000; Grants to individuals, 11 grants totaling $60,000 (high: $6,000, low: $3,000).
Fields of interest: Vocational education, post-secondary; Higher education.
Type of support: Support to graduates or students of specific schools; Technical education support; Undergraduate support.
Application information: Applications accepted. Application form required. Application form available on the grantmaker's web site. Interview required.
  Send request by: Mail
  Deadline(s): Mar. 15
  Applicants should submit the following:
    1) Photograph
    2) Transcripts
    3) GPA
    4) ACT
Program description:
  J. Colin Campbell Scholarship: Scholarships to residents of Fairfield County for a minimum of three years, and have attended a high school in Fairfield County the last three years of their secondary education, including graduation. Students must maintain a good scholastic record, attend accredited state-supported colleges or universities or technical or vocational schools in OH, and must be full-time students with a minimum of 15 hours per term and maintain a 2.0 GPA. Applicants need not be recent high school graduates.
EIN: 316204632

7023
Board of Trustees of Carleton College
P.O. Box 78
Syracuse, OH   45779-0078   (740) 992-2836
Contact: Gordon Fisher, Pres.
Application Address: c/o Gordon Fisher, Duskey St., Syracuse, OH 45779

Foundation type: Independent foundation
Purpose: Scholarships to residents of Syracuse, OH, for attendance at Carleton College, MN.
Financial data: Year ended 12/31/2012. Assets, $55,220 (M); Expenditures, $2,019; Total giving, $1,800; Grants to individuals, 5 grants totaling $1,800 (high: $500, low: $200).
Type of support: Support to graduates or students of specific schools; Undergraduate support.
Application information: Applications accepted. Application form required.
  Deadline(s): Sept. 1
EIN: 311000137

7024
Nellie Martin Carman Scholarship Trust
c/o Key Bank, N.A.
4900 Tiedman Rd., OH-01-49-0150
Brooklyn, OH   44144-2302

Foundation type: Independent foundation
Purpose: Scholarships by nomination only to public high school seniors in King, Snohomish, and Pierce counties, WA, to attend colleges and universities in WA.
Financial data: Year ended 05/31/2013. Assets, $2,497,498 (M); Expenditures, $177,082; Total giving, $127,100; Grants to individuals, 202 grants totaling $126,000 (high: $1,000, low: $500).
Fields of interest: Higher education; Scholarships/financial aid.

Type of support: Scholarships—to individuals; Awards/grants by nomination only; Undergraduate support.
Application information: Interview required.
  Deadline(s): Mar. 1 for new applicants, and Apr. 1 for renewals
  Additional information: Candidates must be nominated by their high schools. Completion of formal nomination required. Nomination forms are available from high school principals and counselors.
Program description:
  Nellie Martin Carman Scholarship: Scholarships of up to $2,000 awarded for one academic year at any university or college in WA. Scholarships are renewable, providing a GPA of at least 3.0 is maintained. First-time applicants must be nominated by their high schools. Renewals must apply directly to the trust. Students majoring in music, sculpture, drawing, interior decorating, or domestic science are ineligible. Candidates must be U.S. citizens.
EIN: 916023774

7025
Helen K. Carney Scholarship Fund
c/o PNC Bank, N.A.
P.O. Box 94651
Cleveland, OH 44101-4651

Foundation type: Independent foundation
Purpose: Scholarships to financially needy graduates of Russell High School, KY, for higher education.
Financial data: Year ended 12/31/2012. Assets, $284,826 (M); Expenditures, $13,937; Total giving, $12,000; Grants to individuals, 12 grants totaling $12,000.
Type of support: Scholarships—to individuals; Support to graduates or students of specific schools.
Application information: Applications accepted. Application form required.
  Deadline(s): Mar. 15
  Additional information: Application should include KY FAF.
EIN: 611163331

7026
Carpenter-Garcia Scholarship Fund
1213 Hillcliff St.
Louisville, OH 44641-2730

Foundation type: Operating foundation
Purpose: Scholarships to graduates of Louisville High School, OH, pursuing a degree in education with the intention of becoming a teacher.
Financial data: Year ended 12/31/2011. Assets, $117,976 (M); Expenditures, $9,801; Total giving, $6,000; Grants to individuals, 4 grants totaling $6,000 (high: $1,500, low: $1,500).
Fields of interest: Higher education.
Type of support: Support to graduates or students of specific schools.
Application information: Applications not accepted.
  Additional information: Contributes only to Louisville High School graduates; unsolicited requests for funds not considered or acknowledged.
EIN: 341702479

7027
The Cassner Foundation
835 S. High St.
Hillsboro, OH 45133-9602

Foundation type: Independent foundation
Purpose: Four-year scholarships to high school seniors in the Highland County school system, OH, for tuition or room and board at a university or college within a 500-mile radius of Highland County.
Financial data: Year ended 03/31/2013. Assets, $4,034,808 (M); Expenditures, $276,722; Total giving, $274,275; Grants to individuals, 26 grants totaling $91,000 (high: $3,500, low: $3,500).
Type of support: Support to graduates or students of specific schools; Undergraduate support.
Application information: Applications not accepted.
  Additional information: Unsolicited requests for funds not considered or acknowledged.
EIN: 386090665

7028
Dr. and Mrs. Theodore J. Castele Foundation
c/o The Catholic Diocese of Cleveland Fdn.
1404 E. 9th St., 8th Fl.
Cleveland, OH 44114-1740   (216) 696-6525

Foundation type: Public charity
Purpose: Scholarships based on academic merit and financial need to residents of the Cleveland, OH area.
Publications: Application guidelines.
Financial data: Year ended 12/31/2011. Assets, $0 (M); Expenditures, $152,547; Total giving, $148,434.
Type of support: Undergraduate support.
Application information: Applications not accepted.
  Additional information: Applicants nominated by their schools. Unsolicited requests for funds not considered or acknowledged.
EIN: 341528050

7029
Catholic Charities Southwestern Ohio
(formerly Catholic Social Services of Southwestern Ohio)
100 E. 8th St.
Cincinnati, OH 45202-2129   (513) 241-7745
Contact: Ted Bergh, C.E.O.
FAX: (513) 241-4333;
E-mail: cgramke@catholiccharitiesswo.org; Toll-free tel.: (888) 256-0379; e-mail for Ted Bergh: tbergh@catholiccharitiesswo.org; URL: http://www.catholiccharitiesswo.org/

Foundation type: Public charity
Purpose: Assistance to individuals and families of southwestern, OH with food, clothing, medical supplies, transportation and other basic needs to improve the quality of their life. Grants to individuals for refugee resettlement and for adoption and foster care assistance.
Publications: Annual report; Informational brochure; Newsletter.
Financial data: Year ended 12/31/2011. Assets, $8,115,902 (M); Expenditures, $13,049,399; Total giving, $402,522; Grants to individuals, 161 grants totaling $209,680.
Fields of interest: Adoption; Foster care; Immigrants/refugees; Economically disadvantaged.
Type of support: Grants for special needs.

Application information: Applications accepted.
  Initial approach: Letter
  Additional information: Some assistance require application. Contact the agency for additional information.
EIN: 310536968

7030
Catholic Mission Aid
17826 Brian Ave.
Cleveland, OH 44119-2933   (216) 481-3155
Contact: Mary Lavrisha, Pers.

Foundation type: Public charity
Purpose: Grants to Catholic missionaries.
Financial data: Year ended 12/31/2012. Assets, $0 (M); Expenditures, $127,405; Total giving, $124,824.
Fields of interest: International relief; Catholic agencies & churches.
Type of support: Grants to individuals.
Application information: Applications accepted.
EIN: 237299558

7031
Hazel M. Chaney Scholarship Trust
c/o KeyBank
4900 Tiedeman, OH-01-49-0150
Brooklyn, OH 44144-2302   (518) 257-8662
Contact: Edward Deluccia
Application address: 66 S. Pearl St., Albany, NY 12207

Foundation type: Independent foundation
Purpose: Scholarships to high school graduates from Wilton, ME, and Franklin County, ME.
Financial data: Year ended 08/31/2013. Assets, $150,290 (M); Expenditures, $13,734; Total giving, $11,000; Grants to individuals, 22 grants totaling $11,000 (high: $600, low: $400).
Type of support: Support to graduates or students of specific schools; Undergraduate support.
Application information: Applications accepted.
  Initial approach: Letter
  Deadline(s): None
EIN: 016007065

7032
Children of Promise International
6844 Loop Rd.
Centerville, OH 45459-2159   (937) 436-5397
FAX: (937) 438-4972; E-mail: info@promise.org; Toll-free tel.: (888) 667-7426; URL: http://www.promise.org

Foundation type: Public charity
Purpose: Specific assistance to needy children around the world with food, clothing, shelter, medical care, higher education opportunities, and other types of support.
Financial data: Year ended 12/31/2011. Assets, $329,605 (M); Expenditures, $1,034,040; Total giving, $961,834.
Fields of interest: Human services; Children, services; Economically disadvantaged.
Type of support: Grants for special needs.
Application information: Applications accepted.
  Additional information: Some assistance require an application. Contact the organization for additional information.
EIN: 431027276

7033
Children's Scholarship Fund of Greater Cincinnati, Inc.
10979 Reed Hartman Hwy.
Blue Ash, OH 45242-2800 (513) 794-9222
FAX: (513) 523-1547; E-mail: csfgclc@one.net;
Toll-free tel.:(888) 332-2408; URL: http://
www.csfcincinnati.org

Foundation type: Public charity
Purpose: Scholarships to low-income students in grades K-8 in the greater Cincinnati, OH area to attend a private, or parochial school of their choice.
Financial data: Year ended 07/31/2011. Assets, $11,246 (M); Expenditures, $158,494; Total giving, $133,176.
Fields of interest: Elementary school/education.
Type of support: Scholarships—to individuals.
Application information: Applications accepted. Application form required.
  Deadline(s): None
  Additional information: All scholarships are need-based and are randomly selected.
EIN: 311682429

7034
Chillicothe-Ross Community Foundation, Inc.
45 E. Main St.
Chillicothe, OH 45601-2504 (740) 774-4438
Contact: Scott Graham, Exec. Dir.
E-mail: scott@crcf.net; URL: http://www.crcf.net/

Foundation type: Community foundation
Purpose: Scholarships to graduating seniors of specific high schools in the South Central, OH, area for higher education.
Financial data: Year ended 12/31/2012. Assets, $1,150,336 (M); Expenditures, $74,534; Total giving, $27,190.
Fields of interest: Vocational education, post-secondary; Higher education.
Type of support: Scholarships—to individuals; Undergraduate support.
Application information: Applications accepted. Application form required. Application form available on the grantmaker's web site.
  Initial approach: Application
  Send request by: Mail or hand deliver
  Deadline(s): Mar. 22
  Applicants should submit the following:
    1) Transcripts
    2) Letter(s) of recommendation
    3) GPA
  Additional information: Students may obtain application from their high school guidance counselors. Each scholarship has its own unique set of eligibility criteria and guideline. See web site for a complete listing.
EIN: 311480939

7035
Christian BusinessCares Foundation
137 S. Main St., Ste. 100
Akron, OH 44308-1416 (330) 762-8825
Application address: P.O. Box 219, Peninsula, OH 44264-0219

Foundation type: Operating foundation
Purpose: Grants to residents of northeast OH for one-time needs which are life-threatening or emergencies such as children and families with medical needs, single moms working to support their children, and the elderly with critical needs.
Financial data: Year ended 10/31/2012. Assets, $57,079 (M); Expenditures, $15,598; Total giving,

$11,792; Grants to individuals, 12 grants totaling $9,545 (high: $3,760, low: $69).
Fields of interest: Human services, emergency aid; Economically disadvantaged.
Type of support: Grants for special needs.
Application information: Applications accepted. Application form required. Interview required.
  Initial approach: Letter or telephone
  Deadline(s): None
EIN: 341377938

7036
Christian Healthcare Ministries, Inc.
127 Hazelwood Ave.
Barberton, OH 44203-1316
E-mail: info@chministries.org; Toll-free tel.: (800) 791-6225; URL: http://www.chministries.org

Foundation type: Public charity
Purpose: Program consists of a nationwide group of Christian individuals and families united to voluntarily share each other's medical bills.
Publications: Newsletter.
Financial data: Year ended 12/31/2011. Assets, $4,122,472 (M); Expenditures, $20,627,578.
Fields of interest: Christian agencies & churches; Mutual aid societies.
Type of support: Grants for special needs.
Application information:
  Initial approach: Letter
  Additional information: Contact the organization for eligibility criteria.
Program description:
  Brother's Keeper: Brother's Keeper is a successful, Bible-centered program enabling CHM participants to meet medical needs that exceed the $125,000 limit per medical incident specified in the CHM Guidelines. Signing up for Brother's Keeper provides an additional $100,000 of medical assistance. With each annual Brother's Keeper renewal, participants receive an additional $100,000 of assistance, up to $1 million. For medical needs exceeding $125,000, Brother's Keeper participants send a quarterly designated gift amount (average amount, $25 per membership unit) to the CHM office, where it is deposited in an audited escrow account.
EIN: 341964742

7037
The Cincinnati Enquirer Foundation
312 Elm St.
Cincinnati, OH 45202-2739

Foundation type: Company-sponsored foundation
Purpose: Scholarships only to children of employees of the Cincinnati Enquirer.
Financial data: Year ended 06/30/2013. Assets, $70,945 (M); Expenditures, $51,262; Total giving, $51,000.
Fields of interest: Scholarships/financial aid.
Type of support: Employee-related scholarships.
Application information: Applications not accepted.
  Additional information: Unsolicted requests for funds not considered or acknowledged.
Company name: Gannett Company, Inc.
EIN: 316037926

7038
Rachel Fiero Clarke Trust
c/o KeyBank N.A.
4900 Tiedeman Rd., OH-01-49-0150
Brooklyn, OH 44144-2302
Application address; c/o Clark Scholarship Fund, Attn.: Chairman, 343 W. Main St., Catskill, NY 12414-1621

Foundation type: Independent foundation
Purpose: Scholarships to graduates of Catskill High School, NY for higher education at accredited colleges or universities.
Financial data: Year ended 06/30/2013. Assets, $1,507,216 (M); Expenditures, $87,241; Total giving, $66,125.
Type of support: Support to graduates or students of specific schools; Undergraduate support.
Application information: Application form required.
  Initial approach: Letter
  Deadline(s): Apr. 15
EIN: 237122166

7039
Clayman Family Foundation Inc.
P.O. Box 200
Canfield, OH 44406

Foundation type: Independent foundation
Purpose: Scholarships primarily to residents of Niles, OH for postsecondary education.
Financial data: Year ended 06/30/2013. Assets, $1,067,173 (M); Expenditures, $63,204; Total giving, $61,115; Grants to individuals, 9 grants totaling $61,115 (high: $10,000, low: $3,333).
Fields of interest: Higher education.
Type of support: Scholarships—to individuals.
Application information: Applications accepted.
  Additional information: Contact the foundation for application guidelines.
EIN: 341685923

7040
Cleveland Alumnae Panhellenic Endowment Fund, Inc.
6735 Ridgecliffe Dr.
Solon, OH 44139

Foundation type: Independent foundation
Purpose: Scholarships to residents of the metropolitan Cleveland, OH, area who are members of the National Panhellenic Conference Women's Sorority.
Financial data: Year ended 05/31/2013. Assets, $249,328 (M); Expenditures, $16,772; Total giving, $16,000; Grants to individuals, 8 grants totaling $16,000 (high: $2,000, low: $2,000).
Fields of interest: Higher education; Students, sororities/fraternities.
Type of support: Graduate support; Undergraduate support.
Application information: Applications accepted. Application form required.
  Send request by: Mail
  Deadline(s): Mar. 1
  Additional information: Application should include two letters of recommendation.
EIN: 341476473

7041
Cleveland Arts Prize

P.O. Box 21126
Cleveland, OH 44121-0126 (440) 523-9889
E-mail: info@clevelandartsprize.org; URL: http://
www.clevelandartsprize.org

Foundation type: Public charity
Purpose: Scholarships to individuals in a graduate
program in dance. Awards and prizes by nomination
only to emerging and mid-career artists who are
residents of Northeast, Ohio.
Financial data: Year ended 12/31/2011. Assets,
$685,924 (M); Expenditures, $160,391; Total
giving, $8,110; Grants to individuals, totaling
$8,110.
Fields of interest: Visual arts; Dance; Arts.
Type of support: Scholarships—to individuals;
Awards/prizes.
Application information: Applications accepted.
Application form required.
  Deadline(s): Varies
  Applicants should submit the following:
    1) Transcripts
    2) Letter(s) of recommendation
    3) Essay
Program descriptions:
  Cleveland Arts Prize Scholarship in Literature: The
  prize is awarded to a high school senior from the
  Cleveland Municipal School District who will attend
  Cleveland State University and demonstrates an
  interest in literature and a need for financial aid.
  Recipients are chosen by Cleveland State
  University.
  Discipline Prizes: Three prizes are awarded in
  literature, visual arts, music and dance, and design:
  Emerging Artist Award of $5,000 to an artist who
  shows remarkable promise and has created a
  significant work or project; Mid-Career Artists Award
  of $5,000 for each discipline for mid-career artists
  who have received national recognition in addition
  to regional and local acclaim; and Lifetime
  Achievement Award to an artist who has worked
  over several decades and whose career and
  achievements have brought great distinction to
  himself and the region.
  John Paul Miller Scholarship in the Visual Arts: The
  tuition scholarship is awarded to a fifth year student
  at the Cleveland Institute of Art.
  Kathryn Karipides Scholarship in Modern Dance:
  Scholarships are awarded to dance students
  nationally who have completed undergraduate work
  with a concentration in dance and have been
  accepted into a graduate program in dance.
  Scholarships of $2,500 are awarded.
  Klaus Roy Scholarship: The scholarship is
  awarded to a student in grades ten through twelve
  at The Cleveland School of the Arts to help them
  purchase an instrument.
  *Martha Joseph Prize for Distinguished Service to
  the Arts:* The prize is awarded annually to an
  individual or an organization that because of
  exceptional commitment, vision, leadership, or
  philanthropy has made a significant contribution to
  the vitality and stature of the arts in Northeast Ohio.
  This contribution may be made through the
  conception and implementation of innovative arts
  events and programs; through the demonstration of
  visionary and/or strategic arts leadership; through
  extraordinary acts of arts patronage or arts
  advocacy; through dedicated and inspiring
  teaching; through the sensitive and effective
  nurturing or artistic talent; or through superb
  performance and/or mastery in an arts discipline.
  Robert P. Bergman Prize: This prize will be
  awarded annually to an exceptional individual who
  has shown passionate leadership and opened his/
  her field more broadly, and whose life and activities
  communicate the joys, excitement, and deep

human relevance of the arts. This prize is open to
national/international candidates. Recipient must
be present for the award event.
EIN: 010627754

7042
Cleveland Browns Foundation

76 Lou Groza Blvd.
Berea, OH 44017-1238 (440) 891-5000
Contact: George W. White, Pres.
FAX: (440) 891-7529; URL: http://
www.clevelandbrowns.com/community/
foundation.html

Foundation type: Public charity
Purpose: Scholarships to high school seniors or
northeast, OH to further their education and pursue
their career dreams.
Publications: Application guidelines; Biennial
report (including application guidelines).
Financial data: Year ended 12/31/2011. Assets,
$908,284 (M); Expenditures, $576,592; Total
giving, $476,103; Grants to individuals, totaling
$100,000.
Fields of interest: Higher education; Youth.
Type of support: Scholarships—to individuals.
Application information: Applications accepted.
Application form required.
  Deadline(s): Nov. 6
  Applicants should submit the following:
    1) Letter(s) of recommendation
    2) Essay
Program description:
  Marion Motley Scholarship: Two scholarships are
  awarded to students for four years to attend
  college. Recipients must demonstrate a
  commitment to and a continued involvement in their
  community. To recognize and honor Marion Motley,
  each applicant will be asked to research his life and
  career and provide insight on how he impacted the
  Cleveland Browns and the NFL.
EIN: 341885593

7043
Cleveland Clinic Foundation Affiliates

9500 Euclid Ave., Ste. JJ19
Cleveland, OH 44195-0001 (216) 636-7389
Contact: Delos M. Cosgrove, Pres. and C.E.O.
URL: http://my.clevelandclinic.org/giving/
how-to-give/corporate.aspx

Foundation type: Public charity
Purpose: Scholarships, fellowships, and research
stipends to individuals working at an affiliate of the
foundation.
Financial data: Year ended 12/31/2012. Assets,
$10,222,859,807 (M); Expenditures,
$6,559,634,961; Total giving, $104,329,822;
Grants to individuals, totaling $90,130,987.
Fields of interest: Health care.
Type of support: Fellowships; Research;
Scholarships—to individuals.
Application information: Contact the foundation for
additional information.
EIN: 912153073

7044
The Cleveland Foundation

1422 Euclid Ave., Ste. 1300
Cleveland, OH 44115-2001 (216) 861-3810
Contact: Ronald B. Richard, C.E.O.
FAX: (216) 861-1729;
E-mail: rrichard@clevefdn.org; TTY: (216)

861-3810; URL: http://
www.clevelandfoundation.org

Foundation type: Community foundation
Purpose: Scholarships to residents of Cuyahoga,
Lake, or Geauga counties to attend an accredited
educational institution.
Publications: Annual report; Informational
brochure; Newsletter; Occasional report.
Financial data: Year ended 12/31/2012. Assets,
$1,883,022,162 (M); Expenditures,
$96,875,460; Total giving, $79,643,582.
Fields of interest: Vocational education; Higher
education.
Type of support: Scholarships—to individuals;
Support to graduates or students of specific
schools; Undergraduate support.
Application information: Applications accepted.
Application form required. Application form
available on the grantmaker's web site.
  Send request by: Mail
  Deadline(s): Varies
  Applicants should submit the following:
    1) Letter(s) of recommendation
    2) GPA
    3) FAFSA
    4) Essay
    5) ACT
  Additional information: See web site for complete
  listing of scholarships. Applicants may apply
  for several, though not all of the scholarships,
  by downloading and completing the
  scholarship form on the web site. See
  individual scholarship descriptions for
  specific instructions.
EIN: 340714588

7045
Cleveland National Air Show Charitable
Foundation

1501 N. Marginal Rd.
Cleveland, OH 44114-3759
URL: http://www.clevelandairshow.com/
foundation/foundation.html

Foundation type: Independent foundation
Purpose: Scholarships to deserving local students
pursuing aviation-related degrees.
Financial data: Year ended 10/31/2011. Assets,
$119,427 (M); Expenditures, $31,285; Total
giving, $25,500.
Fields of interest: Space/aviation.
Type of support: Scholarships—to individuals.
Application information: Applications accepted.
Application form required.
EIN: 341741796

7046
Charles & Hazel Cline Memorial
Scholarship Fund

c/o KeyBank N.A.
4900 Tiedman Rd., OH-01-49-0150
Brooklyn, OH 44144-2302

Foundation type: Independent foundation
Purpose: Scholarships to graduates of high schools
in Linn and Crook counties, OR, for postsecondary
education in OR.
Financial data: Year ended 03/31/2012. Assets,
$1,016,645 (M); Expenditures, $59,291; Total
giving, $45,000.
Fields of interest: Higher education; Scholarships/
financial aid.
Type of support: Support to graduates or students
of specific schools; Undergraduate support.
Application information: Application form required.

Initial approach: Letter
Deadline(s): Spring
Applicants should submit the following:
1) Financial information
2) Transcripts
3) GPA
EIN: 930931552

7047
John L. Cohill Memorial Scholarship Foundation
643 E. Tallmadge Ave.
Akron, OH 44310-2404 (330) 253-9959
Contact: Kenneth Dies, Tr.

Foundation type: Operating foundation
Purpose: Scholarships to graduating seniors on a Northeast Ohio high school wrestling team with a good academic record.
Financial data: Year ended 12/31/2011. Assets, $35,014 (M); Expenditures, $4,000; Total giving, $4,000; Grants to individuals, 5 grants totaling $4,000 (high: $1,000, low: $500).
Application information: Applications accepted.
Initial approach: Letter
Deadline(s): None
EIN: 341584377

7048
Collaborative Network of Lucas County, Inc.
222 N. Clover St.
Fremont, OH 43420-2407 (419) 251-1842

Foundation type: Public charity
Purpose: Emergency assistance to families of Lucas county, Ohio in acquiring the necessary services for children who are at risk for, or have a development disability or delay.
Financial data: Year ended 09/30/2011. Assets, $0 (M); Expenditures, $271,051; Total giving, $131,773; Grants to individuals, totaling $131,773.
Fields of interest: Economically disadvantaged.
Type of support: Emergency funds.
Application information: Contact the organization for assistance.
EIN: 341915282

7049
College Club of Cleveland Foundation
2348 E. Overlook Rd.
Cleveland Heights, OH 44106-2398 (216) 464-8925

Foundation type: Independent foundation
Purpose: Scholarships only to residents of the Cleveland, OH, area.
Financial data: Year ended 12/31/2011. Assets, $426,230 (M); Expenditures, $26,043; Total giving, $19,973; Grants to individuals, 6 grants totaling $19,973 (high: $7,000, low: $500).
Fields of interest: Women.
Type of support: Scholarships—to individuals.
Application information: Applications accepted. Application form required.
Deadline(s): Prior to start of college school year.
EIN: 341569601

7050
College Now Greater Cleveland
(formerly Cleveland Scholarship Programs, Inc., also known as CSP)
500 Public Sq., Ste. 1800
Cleveland, OH 44114-3304 (216) 241-5587
Contact: Alenka M. Winslett, Pres. and C.E.O.
FAX: (216) 241-6184;
E-mail: info@collegenowgc.org; URL: http://www.cspohio.org

Foundation type: Public charity
Purpose: Scholarships to residents of Ashtabula, Cuyahoga, Geauga, Lake, Lorain, Mahoning, Medina, Portage, Stark, Summit, and Trumbull counties, OH.
Publications: Application guidelines; Annual report; Financial statement; Newsletter.
Financial data: Year ended 07/31/2011. Assets, $11,090,420 (M); Expenditures, $5,303,777; Total giving, $2,090,204; Grants to individuals, totaling $2,090,204.
Fields of interest: Higher education; Teacher school/education; Adult/continuing education.
Type of support: Scholarships—to individuals; Graduate support; Precollege support; Undergraduate support.
Application information: Applications accepted. Application form required.
Deadline(s): Apr. 15 for Adult Learners Scholarship
Applicants should submit the following:
1) Transcripts
2) Letter(s) of recommendation
3) Essay
4) Financial information
Additional information: See web site for complete guidelines and application forms.
Program descriptions:
Adult Learner Scholarships: This program provides scholarship opportunities to adult students ages 19 and older who have interrupted their education for one year or more and who are pursuing a non-degree certificate or license in a vocational or technical program, an associate's degree, or a first bachelor's degree. Eligible applicants must: have graduated from high school or have successfully earned their GED; be a resident of Ashtabula, Cuyahoga, Geauga, Lake, Lorain, Mahoning, Medina, Portage, Stark, Summit, or Trumbull counties; and have earned a minimum 2.5 cumulative GPA in either high school or post-secondary education. Scholarships generally range from $500 to $1,000.
CSP Scholarships for High School Seniors: Awards of at least $500 per year to students attending high schools that are currently receiving services from the organization.
EIN: 346580096

7051
Columbia Community Foundation
P.O. Box 567
Columbia Station, OH 44028-0567 (440) 236-8000
FAX: (440) 236-9661;
E-mail: info@columbiacommunityfoundation.org;
URL: http://www.columbiacommunityfoundation.org/

Foundation type: Community foundation
Purpose: Scholarships to graduating seniors of Columbia Township and neighboring communities, for postsecondary education.
Financial data: Year ended 12/31/2012. Assets, $66,108 (M); Expenditures, $18,440; Total giving, $13,925.

Fields of interest: Higher education.
Type of support: Scholarships—to individuals; Undergraduate support.
Application information: Applications accepted. Application form required. Application form available on the grantmaker's web site.
Deadline(s): Apr. 1
Final notification: Applicants notified May 1
Additional information: See web site for a complete listing of scholarships.
EIN: 261095804

7052
Greater Columbus Arts Council, Inc.
100 E. Broad St., Ste. 2250
Columbus, OH 43215-3607 (614) 224-2606
Contact: Milt Baughman, Pres.
FAX: (614) 224-7461; E-mail: info@gcac.org; E-mail for Milt Baughman: mbaughman@gcac.org;
URL: http://www.gcac.org

Foundation type: Public charity
Purpose: Grants to creative artists who are residents of the city of Columbus and/or Franklin county, OH for at least one year prior to date of application.
Publications: Application guidelines; Annual report; Newsletter.
Financial data: Year ended 12/31/2011. Assets, $2,459,407 (M); Expenditures, $5,285,724; Total giving, $3,145,103; Grants to individuals, totaling $90,596.
Fields of interest: Film/video; Visual arts; Theater (playwriting).
Type of support: Grants to individuals.
Application information: Applications accepted.
Send request by: On-line
Deadline(s): Vary
Additional information: Recipients must remain residents of Columbus and/or Franklin county throughout the grant period.
Program description:
Individual Artists Fellowship Program: The program provide unrestricted grants to artists of outstanding talent and ability who currently live in the city of Columbus and/or Franklin county, and have done so for at least one year. Fellowships are awarded in a variety of artistic disciplines. Awards are offered in Visual Arts (2D, 3D, photography, and crafts), Media Arts, Dance/Choreography, Literature and Playwriting each year.
EIN: 310833384

7053
Columbus Blue Jackets Foundation
200 W. Nationwide Blvd.
Columbus, OH 43215-2563 (614) 246-3738
Contact: Jen Bowden, Exec. Dir.
FAX: (614) 246-4625;
E-mail: cbjfoundation@bluejackets.com;
URL: http://www.bluejacketsfoundation.org/

Foundation type: Public charity
Purpose: Scholarships to central Ohio high school seniors who personify the character and leadership of the late John H. McConnell.
Publications: Application guidelines; Annual report; Grants list.
Financial data: Year ended 06/30/2012. Assets, $1,162,011 (M); Expenditures, $402,754; Total giving, $340,991.
Fields of interest: Higher education.
Type of support: Undergraduate support.
Application information:
Deadline(s): Mar. 1
Final notification: Applicants notified in the spring

Additional information: The awards are based on academic performance, to students who demonstrate hard work, perseverance, leadership and community involvement.
EIN: 311688700

7054
Columbus Female Benevolent Society
1234 E. Broad St.
Columbus, OH 43205-1405   (614) 237-6116
Contact: Patricia Offenberg, Treas.
Application address: 33 N. Remington Rd.,
Columbus, OH 43209, tel.: (614) 237-6116

Foundation type: Operating foundation
Purpose: Direct aid on a regular, special, or temporary basis to pensioned widows who are residents of Franklin County, OH. Aid is generally in the form of rent and childcare assistance.
Financial data: Year ended 12/31/2011. Assets, $22,167 (M); Expenditures, $29,084; Total giving, $28,595; Grants to individuals, 34 grants totaling $19,645.
Fields of interest: Housing/shelter, expense aid; Children, services; Economically disadvantaged.
Type of support: Grants for special needs.
Application information: Applications accepted.
Send request by: Mail
Deadline(s): None
EIN: 316042036

7055
Community Action Council of Portage County, Inc.
1036 W. Main St.
P.O. Box 917
Ravenna, OH 44266-0917   (330) 297-1456
FAX: (330) 297-1463; E-mail: info@cacportage.net;
URL: http://cacportage.net

Foundation type: Public charity
Purpose: Assistance to low income residents of Portage county, OH with winter heating, summer cooling, home weatherization, food, shelter and other special needs.
Publications: Application guidelines; Newsletter.
Financial data: Year ended 01/31/2012. Assets, $970,213 (M); Expenditures, $3,776,414; Total giving, $805,106; Grants to individuals, totaling $805,106.
Fields of interest: Human services; Economically disadvantaged.
Type of support: Emergency funds.
Application information: Contact the council for eligibility determination.
EIN: 340967324

7056
Community Action Partnership of the Greater Dayton Area
719 S. Main St.
Dayton, OH 45402-2709   (937) 341-5000
FAX: (937) 341-5002; URL: http://www.cap-dayton.org

Foundation type: Public charity
Purpose: Services to indigent residents of the greater Dayton, OH area, such as transportation services, clothing, food, heating payment assistance, and home weatherization.
Financial data: Year ended 12/31/2011. Assets, $11,309,765 (M); Expenditures, $19,997,924; Total giving, $7,271,333; Grants to individuals, totaling $6,709,602.

Fields of interest: Economically disadvantaged.
Type of support: In-kind gifts; Grants for special needs.
Application information:
Initial approach: Tel.
Additional information: Contact foundation for eligibility criteria.
EIN: 310709198

7057
Community Foundation for Crawford County
(formerly Bucyrus Area Community Foundation)
254 E. Mansfield St.
Bucyrus, OH 44820   (419) 562-3958
E-mail: info@cfcrawford.org; URL: http://cfcrawford.org/

Foundation type: Community foundation
Purpose: Scholarships to students of Crawford county, OH, pursuing a higher education.
Publications: Annual report; Financial statement; Grants list; Informational brochure (including application guidelines); Multi-year report.
Financial data: Year ended 12/31/2012. Assets, $12,582,798 (M); Expenditures, $913,709; Total giving, $523,963; Grants to individuals, 6 grants totaling $5,700.
Fields of interest: Higher education.
Type of support: Scholarships—to individuals; Support to graduates or students of specific schools.
Application information: Applications accepted. Application form required. Application form available on the grantmaker's web site.
Initial approach: Letter, telephone, fax, or e-mail
Send request by: Mail or e-mail
Copies of proposal: 1
Deadline(s): Apr. 10
Final notification: Recipients notified in four weeks
Applicants should submit the following:
1) Transcripts
2) Letter(s) of recommendation
3) GPA
4) Essay
Additional information: Each scholarship for Crawford county students has specific requirements for application. See web site for application guidelines.
EIN: 341465822

7058
The Community Foundation of Lorain County
(formerly The Community Foundation of Greater Lorain County)
9080 Leavitt Rd.
Elyria, OH 44035   (440) 984-7390
Contact: Brian R. Frederick, C.E.O.; For grants: Linda Ong Styer, Sr. Prog. Off.
FAX: (440) 984-7399;
E-mail: info@peoplewhocare.org; Additional e-mail: bfrederick@peoplewhocare.org; Grant inquiry e-mail: lsyter@peoplewhocare.org; URL: http://www.peoplewhocare.org

Foundation type: Community foundation
Purpose: Scholarships to residents of Lorain County, OH for post high school education.
Publications: Application guidelines; Annual report (including application guidelines); Financial statement; Informational brochure (including application guidelines); Newsletter; Program policy statement.

Financial data: Year ended 12/31/2012. Assets, $88,644,009 (M); Expenditures, $4,514,514; Total giving, $4,500,728.
Fields of interest: Print publishing; Medical care, community health systems; Dental care; Nursing care; Health care; Substance abuse, services; Business/industry; Business/industry, trade boards; Engineering.
Type of support: Scholarships—to individuals; Support to graduates or students of specific schools; Graduate support; Technical education support; Undergraduate support.
Application information: Applications accepted. Application form required. Application form available on the grantmaker's web site.
Initial approach: Letter or telephone
Deadline(s): Mar. 1
Final notification: Applicants notified in June
Applicants should submit the following:
1) Transcripts
2) SAT
3) SAR
4) Letter(s) of recommendation
5) GPA
6) Essay
7) ACT
Additional information: Interviews may be required. See web site for a complete listing of scholarships.
EIN: 341322781

7059
Community Foundation of Mount Vernon & Knox County
(formerly The Mount Vernon/Knox County Community Trust)
c/o The First-Knox National Bank
1 S. Main St.
P.O. Box 1270
Mount Vernon, OH 43050-3223   (740) 392-3270
Contact: Samuel Barone, Exec. Dir.
FAX: (740) 399-5296;
E-mail: sbarone@mvkcfoundation.org; URL: http://www.mvkcfoundation.org

Foundation type: Community foundation
Purpose: Scholarships to residents of Knox County, OH, for attendance at accredited colleges or universities as full-time students.
Publications: Application guidelines; Annual report; Informational brochure; Occasional report.
Financial data: Year ended 12/31/2011. Assets, $32,676,632 (M); Expenditures, $1,821,629; Total giving, $1,495,903; Grants to individuals, 251 grants totaling $617,979.
Fields of interest: Higher education.
Type of support: Scholarships—to individuals.
Application information: Applications accepted. Application form required. Application form available on the grantmaker's web site.
Initial approach: Application
Deadline(s): Feb. 18
Applicants should submit the following:
1) SAR
2) FAFSA
3) Photograph
4) Resume
5) Essay
6) Transcripts
7) Letter(s) of recommendation
Additional information: See web site for a complete listing of scholarships and additional guidelines.
EIN: 311768219

7060
The Community Foundation of Shelby County

(formerly The Community Foundation of Sidney and Shelby County)
100 S. Main Ave., Ste. 202
Sidney, OH 45365-2771 (937) 497-7800
Contact: Marian Spicer, Exec. Dir.
FAX: (937) 497-7799;
E-mail: mspicer@commfoun.com; URL: http://www.commfoun.com

Foundation type: Community foundation
Purpose: Scholarships to Shelby County, OH high school seniors. Some scholarships also available for students already in college or the workforce.
Publications: Annual report; Informational brochure; Newsletter.
Financial data: Year ended 12/31/2012. Assets, $18,404,283 (M); Expenditures, $1,102,001; Total giving, $869,479; Grants to individuals, 134 grants totaling $111,590.
Fields of interest: Higher education; Law school/education; Scholarships/financial aid.
Type of support: Scholarships—to individuals; Support to graduates or students of specific schools; Undergraduate support.
Application information: Applications accepted. Application form required. Application form available on the grantmaker's web site.
  Deadline(s): June 2
  Applicants should submit the following:
    1) SAR
    2) FAFSA
    3) Transcripts
  Additional information: Applications are typically available from high school guidance counselors and on the foundation's web site. See web site for additional application guidelines.
Program description:
  Scholarships: Several individuals, families and organizations have established scholarships for the benefit of students in Shelby County, Ohio and the surrounding areas. Each scholarship has its own set of unique eligibility criteria, including graduation from a particular high school. Applications for most of the scholarships are available online.
EIN: 346565194

7061
Community Foundation of Union County, Inc.

(also known as Union County Foundation)
126 N. Main St.
P.O. Box 608
Marysville, OH 43040-0608 (937) 642-9618
Contact: David A. Vollrath, Exec. Dir.
FAX: (937) 642-7376;
E-mail: info@unioncountyfoundation.org;
URL: http://www.unioncountyfoundation.org

Foundation type: Community foundation
Purpose: Scholarships to graduates of Union county high schools pursuing a higher education at postsecondary colleges, universities or technical schools.
Publications: Application guidelines; Annual report; Grants list; Informational brochure.
Financial data: Year ended 12/31/2012. Assets, $6,942,248 (M); Expenditures, $982,821; Total giving, $797,914; Grants to individuals, totaling $110,839.
Fields of interest: Vocational education, post-secondary; Higher education; Scholarships/financial aid.

Type of support: Scholarships—to individuals; Support to graduates or students of specific schools.
Application information: Applications accepted. Application form required.
  Initial approach: Application
  Send request by: Online
  Deadline(s): Apr.
  Additional information: Applicants are selected based on financial need, academic achievement, leadership, character and integrity. See web site for a listing of scholarship programs.
EIN: 310628641

7062
The Community Foundation of West Chester/Liberty

(formerly Key Community Foundation)
5641 Union Centre Dr.
West Chester, OH 45069-4836 (513) 874-5450
Contact: Melissa Benedict, Pres.
FAX: (513) 874-5472;
E-mail: info@wclfoundation.com; Additional e-mail: melissa@wclfoundation.com; URL: http://www.wclfoundation.com

Foundation type: Community foundation
Purpose: Scholarships to students who are residents of West Chester or Liberty township, OH, in pursuit of a higher education.
Publications: Application guidelines; Annual report; Grants list; Informational brochure (including application guidelines); Newsletter.
Financial data: Year ended 12/31/2012. Assets, $9,173,587 (M); Expenditures, $871,776; Total giving, $414,079; Grants to individuals, 77 grants totaling $118,006.
Fields of interest: Higher education; Scholarships/financial aid.
Type of support: Scholarships—to individuals; Support to graduates or students of specific schools; Undergraduate support.
Application information: Applications accepted. Application form required. Application form available on the grantmaker's web site.
  Initial approach: Application
  Copies of proposal: 1
  Deadline(s): Apr. 1
  Applicants should submit the following:
    1) Essay
    2) Transcripts
    3) Letter(s) of recommendation
  Additional information: See web site for a complete listing of scholarship programs.
Program description:
  Scholarship Funds: The foundation has a variety of scholarships available to students looking to pursue higher education. Some of the scholarships have restrictions to students from a specific high school or area of residence. Most scholarships require the applicant to live in West Chester or Liberty Townships. Additional restrictions and requirements are listed with each description, see web site for additional information.
EIN: 311661966

7063
Community Shelter Board

111 Liberty St., Ste. 150
Columbus, OH 43215-5613 (614) 221-9195
FAX: (614) 221-9199; E-mail: info@csb.org;
URL: http://www.csb.org

Foundation type: Public charity

Purpose: Assistance to families and individuals with emergency shelter in central Ohio.
Publications: Application guidelines; Annual report; Newsletter.
Financial data: Year ended 06/30/2012. Assets, $5,807,295 (M); Expenditures, $14,248,332; Total giving, $11,998,718; Grants to individuals, totaling $2,536,740.
Fields of interest: Housing/shelter, temporary shelter; Housing/shelter, homeless.
Type of support: Emergency funds.
Application information: Applications accepted. Application form required.
EIN: 311181284

7064
Community West Foundation

(formerly Fairview Lutheran Foundation)
20545 Center Ridge Rd., Ste. 448
Cleveland, OH 44116-3423 (216) 476-7060
Contact: David T. Dombrowiak, Pres. and C.E.O.
FAX: (216) 476-9730; E-mail: dtd@cwfc.org;
URL: http://www.communitywestfoundation.org/

Foundation type: Public charity
Purpose: Scholarships to high school students of the greater western Cleveland, OH area pursuing a nursing career.
Publications: Application guidelines; Annual report; Informational brochure; Newsletter.
Financial data: Year ended 12/31/2011. Assets, $80,694,147 (M); Expenditures, $4,971,283; Total giving, $3,525,974. Scholarships—to individuals amount not specified.
Fields of interest: Nursing school/education.
Type of support: Scholarships—to individuals.
Application information: Applications accepted.
  Initial approach: Letter, telephone, or fax
  Additional information: Contact the foundation for additional application guidelines.
Program description:
  Nursing Loan Repayment Program at Lutheran Hospital: This program is for new nurses who are willing to commit to a period of employment at Lutheran Hospital by helping them reduce educational debt incurred during nursing education.
EIN: 341456398

7065
Coshocton Foundation

220 S. 4th St.
P.O. Box 55
Coshocton, OH 43812-2019 (740) 622-0010
Contact: Kathy Thompson, Exec. Dir.
FAX: (740) 622-1660;
E-mail: kthompson@coshoctonfoundation.org;
URL: http://www.coshoctonfoundation.org

Foundation type: Community foundation
Purpose: Scholarships to graduates of high schools in Coshocton County, OH.
Publications: Application guidelines; Annual report; Financial statement; Informational brochure (including application guidelines); Newsletter; Occasional report.
Financial data: Year ended 09/30/2012. Assets, $25,437,563 (M); Expenditures, $779,241; Total giving, $539,479; Grants to individuals, totaling $197,524.
Fields of interest: Higher education.
Type of support: Scholarships—to individuals; Undergraduate support.
Application information: Applications accepted. Application form required. Application form available on the grantmaker's web site. Interview required.

Initial approach: Application
Send request by: Mail or in person
Deadline(s): July 29
Additional information: See web site for additional information.
EIN: 316064567

7066
Council for Economic Opportunities in Greater Cleveland
1228 Euclid Ave., Ste. 700
Cleveland, OH 44115-1845 (216) 696-9077
FAX: (216) 696-0770; URL: http://www.ceogc.org
Foundation type: Public charity
Purpose: Financial assistance to Cuyahoga county, OH residents facing foreclosure, eviction, or homelessness and emergency assistance to low income families seeking payments for utility bills.
Publications: Annual report.
Financial data: Year ended 01/31/2012. Assets, $10,858,365 (M); Expenditures, $43,397,405; Total giving, $17,524,892; Grants to individuals, totaling $2,046,659.
Fields of interest: Housing/shelter, home owners; Housing/shelter; Economically disadvantaged.
Type of support: Emergency funds; Grants for special needs.
Application information: Applications accepted.
Additional information: Contact the agency for eligibility determination.
EIN: 340965350

7067
County Corp.
130 W. 2nd St., Ste. 1420
Dayton, OH 45402-1828 (937) 225-6328
Contact: Steve Naas, Pres.
FAX: (937) 225-5089;
E-mail: snaas@countycorp.com; URL: http://www.countycorp.com
Foundation type: Public charity
Purpose: Loans and grants for indigent residents of Montgomery County, OH, and neighboring counties for improved housing.
Financial data: Year ended 09/30/2011. Assets, $21,736,321 (M); Expenditures, $3,613,526; Total giving, $567,387; Grants to individuals, totaling $330,387.
Fields of interest: Housing/shelter; Economically disadvantaged.
Type of support: Loans—to individuals.
Application information: Applications accepted. Application form required. Application form available on the grantmaker's web site.
Initial approach: Letter
Additional information: Contact foundation for eligibility criteria.
Program descriptions:
Access Loan: The program provides funds to make homes more accessible for individuals with documented disabilities. The Access Loan funds are used to remove barriers in the home that inhibit the mobility of the individual. Typically, the program funds exterior ramps, roll-in showers and grab bars, and widening of doorways. The household income must not exceed 80 percent of the area median income based on family size.
Avondale Home Repair Loans: The program provides financial assistance to improve the housing conditions for residents in the Avondale and Woodman 35 neighborhoods in the City of Riverside. These funds are provided as a five-year forgivable loan. As long as the owner occupies the home, no payment is required. Each year 20

percent of the loan is forgiven until, at the end of five years, the balance is forgiven in full.
Housing Trust: The program provides a flexible source of financial resources to address unmet housing needs of low-and moderate-income households in Montgomery County, Ohio.
Individual Development Account Program: The program is a long-term savings plan that earns the family who saves $1,000 another $2,000 in funding from County Corp. The $3,000 is then used for down payment and closing costs on a home the family chooses.
Lifetime Loan: The program provides grants and loans to correct housing conditions that constitute a dire threat to the health and safety of the residents. Up to $3,500 is available for low-income homeowners whose income does not exceed 50 percent of the area median income based on family size. To qualify, the home must be owner occupied. A $25 per month minimum payment is required.
Major Home Improvement Loan: The program provides loans with variable rates and terms, depending on the size of the family and income. The owner must occupy the home and have sufficient income to repay the loan. The maximum major home improvement loan amount is $30,000.
EIN: 310978908

7068
County North Foundation
16806 US 20A, Ste. 14
West Unity, OH 43570 (419) 924-2321
Contact: Lewis Hilkert, Tr.
Foundation type: Independent foundation
Purpose: Scholarships to students for higher education.
Financial data: Year ended 12/31/2012. Assets, $1,021,755 (M); Expenditures, $64,846; Total giving, $55,000; Grants to individuals, 2 grants totaling $5,000 (high: $3,000, low: $2,000).
Type of support: Undergraduate support.
Application information: Applications accepted.
Send request by: Mail
Deadline(s): None
Applicants should submit the following:
1) Class rank
2) Transcripts
Additional information: Application should include high school and graduation date.
EIN: 311596311

7069
The Benny Cowgill Foundation, Inc.
c/o James Cowgill
7414 Myrna Blvd.
Kent, OH 44240-6320 (330) 673-3539
Foundation type: Public charity
Purpose: Financial assistance to children who are eighteen years and younger for cancer treatment to offset the cost of travel, hotel stays and other expenses related to medical care.
Financial data: Year ended 12/31/2011. Assets, $162,085 (M); Expenditures, $6,102; Total giving, $3,500.
Fields of interest: Cancer.
Type of support: Grants for special needs.
Application information: Contact the foundation for eligibility determination.
EIN: 341845596

7070
J. P. Crain Family Scholarship Fund
c/o KeyBank N.A.
P.O. Box 10099
Dayton, OH 45402-0099 (419) 259-8655
Contact: Diane Ohns
Foundation type: Independent foundation
Purpose: Scholarships to financially needy Paulding County, OH high school graduates who are U.S. citizens and are pursuing careers as teachers, doctors of medicine, lawyers, dentists, ministers, engineers, business administrators, farmers, or veterinarians.
Financial data: Year ended 01/31/2013. Assets, $936,509 (M); Expenditures, $54,843; Total giving, $41,500.
Fields of interest: Business school/education; Dental school/education; Law school/education; Medical school/education; Teacher school/education; Engineering school/education; Theological school/education; Veterinary medicine; Agriculture.
Type of support: Support to graduates or students of specific schools; Undergraduate support.
Application information: Applications accepted. Application form required.
Additional information: Application by letter outlining financial need, grades, reasons for request, and a statement of motivation.
EIN: 346985380

7071
The Creech Family Charitable Trust
(formerly The Akey Charitable Trust)
c/o Frederick J. Caspar
10 Courthouse Plz. S.W., Ste. 1100
Dayton, OH 45402-1825
Foundation type: Independent foundation
Purpose: Scholarships to individuals for higher education who presently or in the future anticipate involvement in Christian Ministry.
Financial data: Year ended 12/31/2012. Assets, $732 (M); Expenditures, $1,602; Total giving, $0.
Fields of interest: Higher education.
Type of support: Scholarships—to individuals.
Application information: Applications accepted. Application form required. Interview required.
Deadline(s): Before beginning of any academic semester
Applicants should submit the following:
1) GPA
2) Essay
3) SAT
4) ACT
5) Letter(s) of recommendation
6) Transcripts
EIN: 311574878

7072
Denny Crum Scholarship Foundation
c/o Fifth Third Bank
P.O. Box 630858
Cincinnati, OH 45263-0858 (513) 534-5310
Application address: c/o Fifth Third Bank, Investment Advisors, 401 S. Fourth Ave., Louisville, KY 40202-3426
Foundation type: Public charity
Purpose: Scholarships to high school graduates from the greater Louisville, KY area, under age 23 for postsecondary education at accredited colleges or certificate program.

Financial data: Year ended 12/31/2011. Assets, $432,325 (M); Expenditures, $75,402; Total giving, $69,750.
Fields of interest: Higher education.
Type of support: Scholarships—to individuals.
Application information: Applications accepted. Application form required. Interview required.
  Deadline(s): Mar.
  Final notification: Recipients notified in mid-Apr.
  Applicants should submit the following:
    1) Transcripts
    2) Letter(s) of recommendation
    3) GPA
  Additional information: Scholarships are awarded to those who have demonstrated leadership, community service and academic achievement.
EIN: 611390657

7073
Culture Works
126 N. Main St., Ste. 210
Dayton, OH 45402-1766 (937) 222-2787
Contact: Martine Meredith Collier, Pres. and C.E.O.
E-mail address for scholarships: grants@cultureworks.org
FAX: (937) 222-2786;
E-mail: info@cultureworks.org; E-Mail for Martine Meredith Collier: mcollier@cultureworks.org;
URL: http://www.cultureworks.org

Foundation type: Public charity
Purpose: Scholarships to upper level undergraduate students majoring in the performing arts, visual arts, engineering, and business administration enrolled in a four year college in the Miami Valley, OH.
Publications: Application guidelines.
Financial data: Year ended 06/30/2012. Assets, $3,898,500 (M); Expenditures, $1,134,421; Total giving, $644,018; Grants to individuals, totaling $18,000.
Fields of interest: Visual arts; Performing arts; Business/industry; Engineering.
Type of support: Scholarships—to individuals; Undergraduate support.
Application information: Applications accepted. Application form required. Application form available on the grantmaker's web site.
  Initial approach: Telephone or e-mail
  Send request by: Mail or in person
  Copies of proposal: 6
  Deadline(s): Apr. 30
  Final notification: Recipients announced by June 1
  Applicants should submit the following:
    1) FAFSA
    2) Transcripts
    3) Letter(s) of recommendation
    4) GPA
    5) Financial information
    6) Essay
Program description:
  Leonard Roberts Scholarship: One-year scholarships ranging from $1,000 to $4,000 are available to students entering their junior or senior year of study at a four-year Miami Valley Institution. Applications are accepted from students majoring in business, engineering, art and other majors who demonstrate participation in and patronage of the arts. Applicants must be U.S. citizens.
EIN: 237412338

7074
Charles B. & Margaret E. Cushwa Foundation
c/o KeyBank, N.A.
10 W. 2nd St., 26th Fl.
Dayton, OH 45402
Application Address: c/o Keybank National Association, 101 S. Main st., Elkhart, IN 46516

Foundation type: Independent foundation
Purpose: Scholarships to individuals in OH for higher education.
Financial data: Year ended 12/31/2012. Assets, $1,591,820 (M); Expenditures, $97,376; Total giving, $87,750.
Type of support: Scholarships—to individuals.
Application information: Applications accepted.
  Send request by: Mail
  Deadline(s): None
EIN: 341787513

7075
William & Anna Jean Cushwa Foundation
c/o Key Bank
10th W., 2nd St., 26th Fl.
Dayton, OH 45402

Foundation type: Independent foundation
Purpose: Scholarships to individuals, paid directly to the school.
Financial data: Year ended 12/31/2012. Assets, $1,550,468 (M); Expenditures, $89,037; Total giving, $78,500.
Type of support: Scholarships—to individuals.
Application information: Applications not accepted.
  Additional information: Unsolicited requests for funds not considered or acknowledged.
EIN: 341849990

7076
Cuyahoga Valley National Park Association
1403 W. Hines Hill Rd.
Peninsula, OH 44264-9646 (330) 657-2909
Contact: Deborah Yandala, C.E.O.
FAX: (330) 657-2328; E-mail: info@cvnpa.org;
URL: http://www.cvnpa.org

Foundation type: Public charity
Purpose: Residencies to artists who will integrate their art with the environment in a national park, and share it with park visitors.
Publications: Annual report.
Financial data: Year ended 08/31/2011. Assets, $1,573,679 (M); Expenditures, $2,498,425; Total giving, $207,304; Grants to individuals, totaling $138,046.
Fields of interest: Arts.
Type of support: Residencies.
Application information: Applications accepted. Application form required.
  Initial approach: Letter
  Applicants should submit the following:
    1) Work samples
    2) SASE
    3) Letter(s) of recommendation
    4) Resume
Program description:
  Resident Program: The residential program provides fourth- through eighth-grade classrooms an overnight educational experience that integrates science, nature study, environmental issues, and the arts. Students and their teachers participate in a four-day, three-night interdisciplinary program focusing on the Cuyahoga River. Students learn

natural history and the concepts of watershed, biodiversity, and habitat in the Cuyahoga Valley. In addition, environmental issues and the process of environmental decision-making are explored. The curriculum is designed to meet state standards and teach proficiency skills, especially in science and social studies.
EIN: 341917257

7077
The Danis Foundation, Inc.
3233 Newmark Dr.
Miamisburg, OH 45342-5422
Contact: Karen Applegarth

Foundation type: Company-sponsored foundation
Purpose: Scholarships to children of Danis Industries employees for undergraduate education.
Financial data: Year ended 12/31/2011. Assets, $621,400 (M); Expenditures, $111,834; Total giving, $108,425. Employee-related scholarships amount not specified.
Fields of interest: Higher education.
Type of support: Employee-related scholarships; Undergraduate support.
Application information: Applications not accepted.
  Additional information: Unsolicited requests for funds not considered or acknowledged.
Company name: Danis Building Construction Company
EIN: 316041012

7078
Davey Company Foundation
1500 N. Mantua St.
P.O. Box 5193
Kent, OH 44240-5193 (330) 673-9511
Contact: Marjorie L. Conner, Secy.

Foundation type: Company-sponsored foundation
Purpose: Scholarships to residents of OH for the study of forestry.
Financial data: Year ended 12/31/2012. Assets, $1,004,806 (M); Expenditures, $184,093; Total giving, $177,167.
Fields of interest: Environment, forests.
Type of support: Undergraduate support.
Application information:
  Initial approach: Letter
  Additional information: Contact foundation for eligibility criteria.
EIN: 346555132

7079
The Paul & Carol David Foundation
(formerly The David Family Foundation)
4840 Dressler Rd. N.W., Ste. 200
Canton, OH 44718-2784 (330) 479-0200
Contact: Jeffrey David, Pres.
Scholarship contact: Becky Duplain
FAX: (330) 479-0222;
E-mail: info@davidfoundation.org; URL: http://www.davidfoundation.org

Foundation type: Independent foundation
Purpose: Scholarships to qualified high school students in Stark County, OH.
Financial data: Year ended 12/31/2012. Assets, $58,421,242 (M); Expenditures, $2,369,709; Total giving, $1,618,304; Grants to individuals, totaling $1,169,522.
Type of support: Scholarships—to individuals.

Application information: Applications accepted. Application form required. Application form available on the grantmaker's web site.
  Send request by: Mail
  Deadline(s): Apr. 10
  Applicants should submit the following:
    1) Essay
    2) Transcripts
    3) Letter(s) of recommendation
    4) FAFSA
  Additional information: Application should also include parents' tax returns.
Program description:
  David Scholar Program: The purpose of the David scholarship program is to aid and assist qualified graduating Stark County, Ohio high school students who, due to financial constraints, would find it difficult, if not impossible, to further their education at an accredited college or university. Students must maintain a 2.5 grade point average and take a minimum of twelve credit hours a semester. The foundation focuses on financial need, academic performance, teacher evaluations, character and personal goals, extracurricular and community activities and awards. See foundation web site for complete guidelines and requirements.
EIN: 341319236

7080
The John and Shirley Davies Foundation
(formerly Bishopric Foundation)
7754 Camargo Rd., Ste. 21
Cincinnati, OH 45243-2661 (513) 791-6699

Foundation type: Independent foundation
Purpose: Scholarships to students who graduated from Goshen School District, OH, who are members of One Earth One People (OEOP), Cincinnati, OH, who maintain a 3.0 GPA and a preference for residence in an on-campus dorm.
Financial data: Year ended 12/31/2011. Assets, $641,170 (M); Expenditures, $115,282; Total giving, $68,400.
Fields of interest: Education.
Type of support: Support to graduates or students of specific schools; Undergraduate support.
Application information: Applications accepted.
  Deadline(s): None
  Additional information: Applicant must demonstrate need for financial assistance.
EIN: 311335126

7081
Lewis J. & Nelle A. Davis Foundation
c/o PNC Bank, N.A.
P.O. Box 94651
Cleveland, OH 44101-4651

Foundation type: Independent foundation
Purpose: Scholarships to students who rank in the upper half of the senior class of Galion High School, OH.
Financial data: Year ended 11/30/2012. Assets, $2,469,089 (M); Expenditures, $99,964; Total giving, $77,000; Grants to individuals, 24 grants totaling $77,000.
Type of support: Support to graduates or students of specific schools; Undergraduate support.
Application information: Applications accepted.
  Initial approach: Letter
  Deadline(s): None
EIN: 346942736

7082
The Dayton Foundation
40 N. Main St., Ste. 500
Dayton, OH 45423 (937) 222-0410
Contact: Diane Timmons, V.P., Grants and Progs.
FAX: (937) 222-0636;
E-mail: info@daytonfoundation.org; Additional tel.: (877) 222-0410; Grants inquiry e-mail: dtimmons@daytonfoundation.org@daytonfoundation.org; URL: http://www.daytonfoundation.org

Foundation type: Community foundation
Purpose: Scholarships to students from the greater Dayton, OH, area for postsecondary education.
Publications: Application guidelines; Annual report; Financial statement; Grants list; Informational brochure; Newsletter; Program policy statement.
Financial data: Year ended 06/30/2013. Assets, $416,534,296 (M); Expenditures, $31,669,338; Total giving, $21,906,024.
Fields of interest: Media/communications; Print publishing; Visual arts; Photography; Arts; Vocational education; Higher education; Business school/education; Teacher school/education; Engineering school/education; Crime/law enforcement, police agencies; Government agencies; African Americans/Blacks.
Type of support: Scholarships—to individuals; Support to graduates or students of specific schools; Awards/prizes; Undergraduate support.
Application information: Applications accepted. Application form required. Application form available on the grantmaker's web site.
  Send request by: Online
  Deadline(s): Varies
  Applicants should submit the following:
    1) Transcripts
    2) SAR
    3) Letter(s) of recommendation
    4) GPA
    5) FAFSA
    6) ACT
  Additional information: See web site for a complete listing of scholarships.
Program description:
  Scholarships: The foundation administers over 100 scholarship funds for students residing in the greater Dayton, OH area to attend accredited colleges and universities. Many scholarships are open to all students regardless of high school attended or intended college major or career interest. Some scholarships may list additional selection criteria, such as intended college major or career interest.
EIN: 316027287

7083
Dayton Masonic Foundation
525 Riverview Ave.
Dayton, OH 45405-4702
Contact: Ronald L. Connelly, Pres.

Foundation type: Public charity
Purpose: Scholarships to students from the fourteen-county Dayton, OH, area for higher education.
Financial data: Year ended 07/31/2011. Assets, $826,321 (M); Expenditures, $684,308; Total giving, $587,049; Grants to individuals, totaling $12,500.
Type of support: Undergraduate support.
Application information:
  Initial approach: Letter
  Additional information: Contact foundation for current application deadline/guidelines.
EIN: 311385609

7084
The Edward J. DeBartolo Memorial Scholarship Foundation
c/o Cindy Miller
7620 Market St.
Youngstown, OH 44512-6078 (330) 965-2000
Contact: Shannon Rovnak

Foundation type: Independent foundation
Purpose: Scholarships to individuals who have graduated from a parochial, public or private high school in Columbiana, Mahoning or Trumbull counties, OH.
Financial data: Year ended 12/31/2012. Assets, $1,442,775 (M); Expenditures, $128,844; Total giving, $49,000; Grants to individuals, 7 grants totaling $49,000 (high: $7,000, low: $7,000).
Type of support: Scholarships—to individuals.
Application information: Applications accepted. Application form required.
  Deadline(s): Within 15 days of receiving application.
EIN: 311527910

7085
Colleen DeCrane Family Foundation
17209 Bradgate Ave.
Cleveland, OH 44111-4125 (216) 671-8499
Contact: Sean DeCrane, Pres.
E-mail: rovloc93@aol.com; URL: http://www.colleendecranefoundation.org/

Foundation type: Public charity
Purpose: Grants to seriously ill residents of the Cleveland, OH, metropolitan area for general welfare and medical expenses.
Financial data: Year ended 12/31/2011. Assets, $43,479 (M); Expenditures, $8,511; Total giving, $5,500.
Fields of interest: Economically disadvantaged.
Type of support: Emergency funds; Grants for special needs.
Application information:
  Initial approach: Letter
  Additional information: Contact foundation for current application deadline/guidelines.
EIN: 341912789

7086
Delaware Arts Festival Association, Inc.
P.O. Box 589
Delaware, OH 43015-0589 (740) 363-2695
Application address: Trace Regan, Chair., Scholarship Comm., Delaware Arts Festival Association, Inc., Ohio Wesleyan University, Phillips Hall, Rm. 106C, Delaware, OH 43015, tel.: (740) 368-3648
E-mail: info@delawareartsfestival.org; URL: http://www.delawareartsfestival.org

Foundation type: Public charity
Purpose: Scholarships to Delaware county, OH high school students entering college for the study of visual arts.
Publications: Grants list.
Financial data: Year ended 09/30/2011. Assets, $61,241 (M); Expenditures, $30,724; Total giving, $14,995; Grants to individuals, totaling $14,995.
Fields of interest: Visual arts; Higher education.
Type of support: Scholarships—to individuals.
Application information: Applications accepted. Application form required. Application form available on the grantmaker's web site. Interview required.
  Send request by: Mail
  Deadline(s): Apr. 1

Applicants should submit the following:
1) Transcripts
2) Resume
3) Letter(s) of recommendation
Additional information: Application should also include a personal statement.
EIN: 311053811

7087
Delaware County Foundation
(formerly Community Fdn. of Delaware County)
3954 N. Hampton Dr.
Powell, OH   43065-8430   (614) 764-2332
FAX: (614) 764-2333;
E-mail: foundation@delawarecf.org; URL: http://
www.delawarecf.org

Foundation type: Community foundation
Purpose: Scholarships to graduating seniors in one of the four high schools in Delaware county, OH for attendance at accredited colleges or universities of their choice.
Publications: Application guidelines; Financial statement; Grants list; Informational brochure; Newsletter; Occasional report.
Financial data: Year ended 12/31/2012. Assets, $8,169,147 (M); Expenditures, $934,567; Total giving, $652,740; Grants to individuals, 94 grants totaling $159,300.
Fields of interest: Higher education.
Type of support: Scholarships—to individuals.
Application information: Applications accepted. Application form required.
Initial approach: Letter or telephone
Copies of proposal: 2
Deadline(s): N/A
Applicants should submit the following:
1) Transcripts
2) SAT
3) SAR
4) GPA
5) FAFSA
6) Essay
7) ACT
Additional information: Applications are available from the guidance counselors in the four Delaware county high schools. See web site for a complete listing of scholarship programs.
EIN: 311450786

7088
John T. and Ada Diederich Educational Trust Fund
c/o PNC Bank, N.A.
P.O. Box 94651
Cleveland, OH   44101-4651
Application address: c/o Jenny Templeton, P.O. Box 1919, Ashland, KY 41105-1919, tel.: (859) 281-5276

Foundation type: Independent foundation
Purpose: Scholarships to graduates who have resided for the past three years in one or more of the following Kentucky counties of Boyd, Greenup, Martin, Lawrence, or Carter, and have the desire to pursue a college education.
Financial data: Year ended 12/31/2011. Assets, $4,025,645 (M); Expenditures, $245,425; Total giving, $181,336; Grants to individuals, 60 grants totaling $181,336.
Fields of interest: Higher education.
Type of support: Scholarships—to individuals.
Application information: Application form required.
Deadline(s): May 30
Applicants should submit the following:

1) Letter(s) of recommendation
2) ACT
Additional information: Applications and information available in high school guidance offices.
EIN: 316271680

7089
Dinger Scholarship Fund
(formerly Dinger Scholarship Fund)
P.O. Box 94651
Cleveland, OH   44101-4651
URL: http://www.pnc.com

Foundation type: Independent foundation
Purpose: Scholarships to graduates of Punxsutawney Area High School, PA, who intend to pursue a degree in nursing.
Financial data: Year ended 12/31/2012. Assets, $210,642 (M); Expenditures, $10,710; Total giving, $8,000.
Fields of interest: Nursing school/education.
Type of support: Support to graduates or students of specific schools; Undergraduate support.
Application information: Application form required.
Initial approach: Letter
Deadline(s): Apr. 14
Additional information: Application available from high school guidance office.
EIN: 256291080

7090
Lily E. Drake Scholarship Trust
c/o KeyBank N.A.
4900 Tiedeman Rd.
Brooklyn, OH   44144-2302   (800) 999-9658

Foundation type: Independent foundation
Purpose: Scholarships to single female residents of OR who are registered nurses for further education.
Financial data: Year ended 12/31/2012. Assets, $234,958 (M); Expenditures, $12,981; Total giving, $8,863; Grants to individuals, 5 grants totaling $8,863 (high: $2,633, low: $199).
Fields of interest: Nursing school/education; Women.
Type of support: Postgraduate support.
Application information: Applications accepted.
EIN: 936131516

7091
Evangeline L. Dumesnil Trust
c/o PNC Bank N.A.
P.O. Box 94651
Cleveland, OH   44101-4651

Foundation type: Independent foundation
Purpose: Scholarships to undergraduate and graduate students enrolled in the musical arts program at the University of Michigan and Wayne State University, MI.
Financial data: Year ended 12/31/2012. Assets, $7,837,928 (M); Expenditures, $409,247; Total giving, $350,000.
Fields of interest: Performing arts, education; Higher education.
Type of support: Support to graduates or students of specific schools.
Application information: Applications not accepted.
Additional information: Unsolicited requests for funds not considered or acknowledged.
EIN: 386473007

7092
Frank R. "Bo" Dunlap Foundation, Inc.
4701 Hickory Bend Rd.
Circleville, OH   43113
Scholarship application address: 26541 Immel Rd., Circleville, OH 43113

Foundation type: Independent foundation
Purpose: Scholarships to undergraduates who are residents of Wayne or Union Township, OH, who display financial need and are willing to work to pay part of their college expenses.
Financial data: Year ended 12/31/2012. Assets, $1,101,626 (M); Expenditures, $70,684; Total giving, $51,500; Grants to individuals, 10 grants totaling $47,500 (high: $7,000, low: $4,500).
Type of support: Undergraduate support.
Application information: Applications accepted. Application form required.
Deadline(s): May 15
EIN: 311496488

7093
Caroline F. Dunton Scholarship Fund Trust
c/o KeyBank N.A.
4900 Tiedeman Rd., OH-01-49-0150
Brooklyn, OH   44144-2302

Foundation type: Independent foundation
Purpose: Scholarships to graduates of Belfast High School, ME, for postsecondary education.
Financial data: Year ended 08/31/2013. Assets, $102,492 (M); Expenditures, $6,350; Total giving, $4,500; Grants to individuals, 10 grants totaling $4,500 (high: $1,000, low: $200).
Fields of interest: Vocational education; Higher education.
Type of support: Support to graduates or students of specific schools; Undergraduate support.
Application information: Applications not accepted.
Additional information: Unsolicited requests for funds not considered or acknowledged.
EIN: 016026835

7094
Ruth Dutro Scholarship Fund
P.O. Box 1118 ML CN-OH-W10X
Cincinnati, OH   45201-1118

Foundation type: Independent foundation
Purpose: Scholarships only to students from Nettle Creek school district, IN.
Financial data: Year ended 12/31/2012. Assets, $122,326 (M); Expenditures, $8,894; Total giving, $6,000; Grants to individuals, 2 grants totaling $4,800 (high: $2,400, low: $2,400).
Fields of interest: Higher education.
Type of support: Scholarships—to individuals.
Application information: Unsolicited requests for funds not considered or acknowledged.
EIN: 351997247

7095
Eagles Memorial Foundation, Inc.
1623 Gateway Circle S.
Grove City, OH   43123   (614) 883-2200
Contact: Thomas J. McGriff, Dir.
Additional tel.: (941) 758-4042; Application address for individuals: c/o Richard J. Steinberg, Golden Eagle Fund, P.O. Box 25916, Milwaukee, WI 53225-0916
FAX: (614) 883-2201; E-mail: memorial@foe.com;
URL: http://www.foe.com/charities/
eagles-memorial-foundation.aspx

Foundation type: Public charity
Purpose: Scholarships to the children of deceased Eagle servicemen and women, law officers, or firefighters, and to graduates of Home on the Range for Boys in Sentinel Butte, ND, High Sky Girls Ranch in Midland, TX, and Bob Hope High School in Port Arthur, TX. Medical and dental expense assistance to children of deceased Eagle servicemen and women, law officers, and firefighters..
Publications: Financial statement; Informational brochure.
Financial data: Year ended 05/31/2012. Assets, $9,240,431 (M); Expenditures, $968,664; Total giving, $721,005; Grants to individuals, totaling $98,453.
Fields of interest: Vocational education; Business school/education; Nursing school/education.
Type of support: Support to graduates or students of specific schools; Technical education support; Undergraduate support; Grants for special needs.
Application information: Applications accepted. Application form required.

> *Additional information:* Application should include transcripts. Contact foundation for additional guidelines.

Program description:

Educational Grant: This program provides educational aid to the children of members of the Fraternal Order of Eagles who died from injuries or diseases incurred or aggravated while serving in the armed services, as law enforcement officers, as volunteer firefighters, or as volunteer EMS workers. Grants are available to students under the age of 25 and may be used to attend colleges, universities, or vocational schools. Grants are limited to $6,000 per school year, for a four-year total of $30,000.
EIN: 396126176

7096
Economic Opportunity Planning Association of Greater Toledo, Inc.

c/o E.O.P.A. Administrative Offices
505 Hamilton St.
Toledo, OH   43604-8520   (419) 242-7304
URL: http://eopa.org/

Foundation type: Public charity
Purpose: Emergency and financial assistance for low and moderate income individuals and families of the greater Toledo, OH area with rent, utilities, home energy, mortgage, medical expense and other special needs.
Financial data: Year ended 12/31/2011. Assets, $2,287,325 (M); Expenditures, $17,312,079; Total giving, $1,574,769; Grants to individuals, 11,508 grants totaling $1,574,769.
Fields of interest: Human services; Economically disadvantaged.
Type of support: Emergency funds; Grants for special needs.
Application information:

> *Initial approach:* Telephone
> *Additional information:* All payments are made directly to the vendors on behalf of the clients. Contact the association for eligibility requirements.

EIN: 346562552

7097
Edgerton Area Foundation

P.O. Box 399
Edgerton, OH   43517-0399   (419) 298-2335
Contact: Roger D. Strup, Pres.

Foundation type: Community foundation

Purpose: Scholarships to students in the Edgerton, OH area for higher education.
Publications: Informational brochure.
Financial data: Year ended 06/30/2012. Assets, $2,401,434 (M); Expenditures, $52,946; Total giving, $51,321; Grants to individuals, 22 grants totaling $18,300.
Fields of interest: Higher education; Scholarships/financial aid.
Type of support: Scholarships—to individuals; Undergraduate support.
Application information: Applications accepted.

> *Additional information:* Contact foundation for application guidelines.

EIN: 341593384

7098
Educational Theatre Association

2343 Auburn Ave.
Cincinnati, OH   45219-2815   (513) 421-3900
Contact: Julie Woffington, Exec. Dir.
FAX: (513) 421-7077; E-mail: info@edta.org; E-mail For Julie Woffington:
jwoffington@schooltheatre.org; URL: http://schooltheatre.org/

Foundation type: Public charity
Purpose: Scholarships to high school theatre students to attend the International Thespian Festival; also, grants to assist students and school teachers to cover the registration fee for attending the association's annual conferences.
Publications: Application guidelines; Annual report; Informational brochure.
Financial data: Year ended 07/31/2012. Assets, $6,278,680 (M); Expenditures, $4,193,914; Total giving, $45,234; Grants to individuals, totaling $45,234.
Fields of interest: Theater; Performing arts, education; Higher education; Teacher school/education.
Type of support: Grants to individuals; Scholarships—to individuals; Travel grants.
Application information: Applications accepted. Application form required. Application form available on the grantmaker's web site.

> *Initial approach:* Download application
> *Deadline(s):* Varies
> *Applicants should submit the following:*
> 1) Essay
> 2) Letter(s) of recommendation
> 3) Transcripts

Program descriptions:

Alan D. and Penny Lu Englesman Scholarship: This $500 award will be given to a graduating senior pursuing an education major in theatre, technical theatre, playwriting, or English at college. Annual renewal is possible with this scholarship.

Austin Yeatman Technical Theatre Scholarship: This program provides a one-time award of $1,000, to be used toward tuition and other fees associated with enrollment at a college or university. Eligible applicants must be committed to studying technical theatre in college and to the importance of theatre education.

Bob and Marti Fowler Future Theatre Educator Scholarship: This one-time, $1,500 scholarship is available to members of the International Thespian Society (ITS) who are currently pursuing, or plan to pursue, a theatre education major. Applicants must demonstrate leadership qualities, hard work, the ability to effectively work as a member of a production team, strong character, academic ability, organizational skills, and experience in different aspects of theatre.

Doug Finney Festival Grant: This needs-based grant is given annually to four high-school juniors or

seniors who are members of the International Thespian Society, and who wish to attend the International Thespian Festival (but cannot afford to do so). Grants are intended to cover travel expenses to and from the festival (including round-trip airfare to/from a major airport, shuttle fees, automobile mileage, or bus fare)

Educational Theatre Association Hall of Fame Award: Each year, up to four members of the association are recognized who have dedicated themselves to the cause of theatre education. Recipients will be awarded complimentary dues to the association for a full year, complimentary registration for the association's annual conference, and recognition into the association's Hall of Fame. Eligible applicants must have at least twenty years of service to the association.

Educational Theatre Association Honorary Thespian of the Year: This program recognizes up to three individuals annually who have gone above and beyond the stand duties of an association volunteer, and who have selflessly given their time and ability to help an association-recognized Thespian or Junior Thespian troupe with set construction, chaperoning, fundraising, advocacy, or any other duty to advance their visibility and success. In addition to an award and recognition by the association, the nominator troupe will receive complimentary troupe renewal dues for the following school year. Nominees must be named by an official troupe director.

Educational Theatre Association Michael J. Peitz Scholarship, Recognizing Excellence in Leadership: This $1,000 scholarship is awarded to association-recognized Thespians who successfully demonstrate leadership abilities. Emphasis will be placed on the student's troupe involvement, demonstrated leadership abilities, and demonstrated leadership experiences (both in and out of school). Applicants need not be theatre majors in college.

Educational Theatre Association New Educator's Annual Conference Grant: This program awards up to three grants annually to association members who wish to attend the association's annual conference, including a professional development institute (PDI) course.

Educational Theatre Association Spirit of Thespis: This award annually recognizes up to three schools that have exemplified the adage 'the show must go on' by demonstrating grace under pressure when faced with serious challenges within the previous or current school year. Recipients will be awarded with both association and news recognition, as well as complimentary troupe dues for the following school year. Applicants must be nominated by an official troupe director; eligible schools must be active members of the association in good standing.

Excellence in Theatre Performance Scholarship: This program awards a scholarship annually to a graduating senior who entering a college program to major in the communicative arts (theatre, film, speech, radio and television, broadcasting, music, or dance)

Future Theatre Educator Scholarship: A one-time, $2,500 scholarship is awarded to graduating seniors entering college programs to major in the communicative arts (theatre, film, speech, radio and television, broadcasting, music, or dance)

International Thespian Society (ITS) Leadership Grant: This grant provides registration expenses for one student to attend the International Thespian Festival, with the hopes of enhancing his/her leadership skills.

Jhon Marshall/International Thespian Officers' Outstanding Student Achievement Scholarship: Scholarships of $1,000 each are available to members in good standing of the International

Thespian Society (ITS), who are active members of his/her high school thespian troupe, and who exemplify the ideals of the ITS. Recipients will be selected based on originality of service, contributions of talents, service to the positive image and ideas of educational theatre and the ITS, and benefit of service to productions, programs, schools, community, and/or peers.

Melba Day Henning Scholarship: A $4,000 scholarship, payable for up to four years, is available to a graduating senior working toward a career in theatre education. Recipients are also eligible for a $500 cash stipend, awarded when the recipient secures a teaching position.

Robert L. Johnson/Hector S. Cruz Scholarship: This $500 scholarship, renewable annually for up to four years, is awarded to a graduating senior thespian who demonstrates outstanding professional potential for future success in acting or technical theatre.

Ronald L. Longstreth International Thespian Festival Grant: This grant funds expenses for one international student to attend the International Thespian Festival. Grants cover registration fees, and provide an additional $400 to support transportation to and from the festival (including round trip airfare to/from the festival, shuttle fees to/from airport, automobile mileage, or bus fare). Eligible applicants must be members of a current International Thespian Society (ITS) troupe in a foreign country, or are active participants in a U.S. troupe's activities (if they are exchange students in the U.S.)

Theatre Performance, Technical, or Playwriting Scholarship: A one-time, $2,000 scholarship will be awarded annually to a graduating senior entering a college program to major in theatre performance, technical theatre, or playwriting. Eligible applicants for playwriting scholarships must have been a finalist in the association's Thespian Playworks program during one of the previous four years.
EIN: 310743605

7099
The Elks Morgan Home Company Scholarship Fund of Alliance Ohio
P.O. Box 3515
Alliance, OH 44601-7515   (330) 823-1510
Contact: Terence Taylor, Tr.
Application address: 606 Glamorgan Dr., Alliance, OH 44601-2862

Foundation type: Independent foundation
Purpose: Scholarships to children, step-children, and grandchildren of members of the Alliance Elks Lodge #467 and to other students who demonstrate financial need, leadership and scholastic abilities.
Financial data: Year ended 06/30/2013. Assets, $259,901 (M); Expenditures, $53,808; Total giving, $53,100; Grants to individuals, 17 grants totaling $2,100 (high: $300, low: $100).
Fields of interest: Vocational education, post-secondary; Higher education.
Type of support: Support to graduates or students of specific schools.
Application information: Applications accepted. Application form required.
  Deadline(s): May
  Additional information: Application forms are available at the Lodge.
Program description:
  Elks Scholarship: Scholarships are awarded for postsecondary education including trade school, two-year and four-year accredited degree institutions. The student must be a senior attending one of the seven high schools in the Lodge's

jurisdiction: Alliance, Marlington, West Branch, Sebring, Minerva, St. Thomas Aquinas and Louisville. Scholarships are $1,000 minimum and students must maintain a minimum of 2.5 GPA. Past recipients are eligible to reapply.
EIN: 341639440

7100
Epilepsy Association
2831 Prospect Ave.
Cleveland, OH 44115-2606   (216) 579-1330
FAX: (216) 579-1336;
E-mail: info@epilepsyinfo.org; Toll-free tel.: (800) 653-4300; URL: http://www.epilepsyinfo.org

Foundation type: Public charity
Purpose: Emergency financial assistance to families in Northeast, OH, to help maintain stable living situations.
Publications: Annual report; Newsletter.
Financial data: Year ended 12/31/2011. Assets, $961,411 (M); Expenditures, $643,984; Total giving, $3,173; Grants to individuals, totaling $3,173.
Fields of interest: Epilepsy.
Type of support: Emergency funds.
Application information: Contact agency for additional information on assistance.
EIN: 237198807

7101
Ethnic Voice of America
4606 Bruening Dr.
Parma, OH 44134-4640   (440) 845-0922
Contact: Irene Smirnov, Pres.

Foundation type: Public charity
Purpose: Financial assistance to families residing in OH, for the benefit of children requiring medical treatment.
Financial data: Year ended 10/31/2011. Assets, $447,786 (M); Expenditures, $161,481; Total giving, $75,526.
Type of support: Grants for special needs.
Application information:
  Initial approach: Letter
  Additional information: Contact foundation for program information.
EIN: 341649643

7102
Everhart Scholarship Fund
c/o KeyBank N.A.
4900 Tiedeman Rd., OH-01-49-0150
Brooklyn, OH 44144-2338

Foundation type: Independent foundation
Purpose: Scholarships to Oregon City high school graduates majoring in a social science at OR public schools of higher education.
Financial data: Year ended 12/31/2012. Assets, $666,467 (M); Expenditures, $39,489; Total giving, $30,000.
Fields of interest: Social sciences.
Type of support: Support to graduates or students of specific schools; Undergraduate support.
Application information:
  Initial approach: Letter
  Deadline(s): Apr. 1
  Additional information: Application must reflect financial need, grades, and character.
EIN: 936212186

7103
Paul B. Evers Trust
c/o David L. Pendry
133 E. Market St.
Xenia, OH 45385-3158
Contact: Becky Tittle
Application address: c/o Xenia High School, 303 Kinsey Rd., Xenia, OH 45385-1410

Foundation type: Independent foundation
Purpose: Student loans to graduates of Xenia High School, OH for postsecondary education.
Financial data: Year ended 12/31/2012. Assets, $236,097 (M); Expenditures, $6,415; Total giving, $0.
Fields of interest: Higher education; Scholarships/financial aid.
Type of support: Student loans—to individuals; Support to graduates or students of specific schools; Undergraduate support.
Application information: Applications accepted. Application form required.
  Deadline(s): Mar. 15
  Additional information: Applications are available through high school.
EIN: 316120701

7104
Fairbanks-Horix Foundation
c/o PNC Bank, N.A.
P.O. Box 94651
Cleveland, OH 44101-4651   (412) 768-8538
Contact: John Montoya
Application address: 620 Liberty Ave. 7th Fl., Pittsburgh, PA 15222, tel.: (412) 768-8538

Foundation type: Company-sponsored foundation
Purpose: Scholarships to children of full-time or deceased employees of Horix Manufacturing Company, PA.
Financial data: Year ended 12/31/2012. Assets, $647,578 (M); Expenditures, $35,810; Total giving, $25,500; Grant to an individual, 1 grant totaling $4,000.
Fields of interest: Scholarships/financial aid.
Type of support: Employee-related scholarships.
Application information: Applications not accepted.
  Additional information: Unsolicited requests for funds not considered or acknowledged.
Company name: Horix Manufacturing Company
EIN: 256084211

7105
Fairfield County Foundation
162 E. Main St.
P.O. Box 159
Lancaster, OH 43130-3712   (740) 654-8451
Contact: Amy Eyman, Exec. Dir.; For scholarships: Mindy Farrow, Office Mgr.
Scholarship inquiry e-mail: mfarrow@fairfieldcountyfoundation.org
FAX: (740) 654-3971;
E-mail: aeyman@fairfieldcountyfoundation.org; URL: http://www.fairfieldcountyfoundation.org

Foundation type: Community foundation
Purpose: Scholarships to individuals in the Fairfield County, OH, area for higher education at accredited institutions.
Publications: Application guidelines; Annual report; Financial statement; Grants list; Informational brochure; Informational brochure (including application guidelines); Newsletter.
Financial data: Year ended 12/31/2012. Assets, $32,393,126 (M); Expenditures, $1,888,542;

Total giving, $1,157,813; Grants to individuals, 280 grants totaling $505,342.
Fields of interest: Higher education.
Type of support: Scholarships—to individuals.
Application information: Applications accepted. Application form required. Application form available on the grantmaker's web site.
Initial approach: Application
Send request by: Mail
Copies of proposal: 3
Deadline(s): Mid-Mar. and mid-Oct.
Applicants should submit the following:
1) SAR
2) FAFSA
Additional information: See web site for available scholarships and eligibility criteria for each.
EIN: 341623983

7106
The Fifty Men and Women of Toledo, Inc.
P.O. Box 351135
Toledo, OH   43635
E-mail: the50menandwomen@yahoo.com;
URL: http://www.50menandwomen.com/

Foundation type: Operating foundation
Purpose: College scholarships to promising minority seniors of the Toledo, OH metropolitan area high school.
Financial data: Year ended 12/31/2012. Assets, $987,951 (M); Expenditures, $67,927; Total giving, $51,750; Grants to individuals, 29 grants totaling $37,607 (high: $1,500, low: $222).
Fields of interest: Vocational education, post-secondary; Higher education; Minorities.
Type of support: Scholarships—to individuals.
Application information: Applications accepted. Application form required.
Deadline(s): Apr. 3
Applicants should submit the following:
1) Photograph
2) Class rank
3) Transcripts
4) Letter(s) of recommendation
5) Essay
EIN: 341422066

7107
The Findlay Hancock County Community Foundation
101 W. Sandusky St., Ste. 207
Findlay, OH   45840-3276   (419) 425-1100
Contact: Katherine Kreuchauf, Pres.; Karen Smith, C.F.O.; For scholarships: Shelly Joseph, Scholarship Mgr.
Scholarship tel.: 419-425-1100; Scholarship e-mail: sjoseph@community-foundation.com
FAX: (419) 425-9339;
E-mail: info@community-foundation.com;
URL: http://www.community-foundation.com

Foundation type: Community foundation
Purpose: Scholarships to residents of Hancock County, OH for continuing education at institutions of higher learning.
Publications: Application guidelines; Annual report; Financial statement; Informational brochure; Informational brochure (including application guidelines).
Financial data: Year ended 12/31/2012. Assets, $70,959,790 (M); Expenditures, $3,033,930; Total giving, $1,299,618; Grants to individuals, totaling $3,400.
Fields of interest: Higher education; Scholarships/financial aid.

Type of support: Scholarships—to individuals; Undergraduate support.
Application information: Applications accepted. Application form required. Application form available on the grantmaker's web site.
Send request by: Online
Deadline(s): Apr. 1
Applicants should submit the following:
1) Work samples
2) Transcripts
3) SAT
4) SAR
5) Letter(s) of recommendation
6) GPA
7) FAFSA
8) Essay
9) Curriculum vitae
10) Budget Information
11) ACT
Additional information: See web site for a complete listing of scholarships.
EIN: 341713261

7108
The Fine Arts Association
38660 Mentor Ave.
Willoughby, OH   44094-7715   (440) 951-7500
Contact: Linda Wise, C.E.O.
FAX: (440) 975-4592;
E-mail: faa@fineartsassociation.org; E-Mail for Linda Wise: lwise@fineartsassociation.org;
URL: http://www.fineartsassociation.org

Foundation type: Public charity
Purpose: Grants and scholarships to students of fine arts who are residents of Lake, Geauga or Cuyahoga counties, OH.
Publications: Application guidelines.
Financial data: Year ended 07/31/2011. Assets, $3,652,102 (M); Expenditures, $1,478,552.
Fields of interest: Arts education; Performing arts.
Type of support: Grants to individuals; Scholarships—to individuals.
Application information: Applications accepted. Application form required. Application form available on the grantmaker's web site.
Initial approach: Telephone
Deadline(s): July 22 for Fall session, Dec. 10 for Spring and May 5 for Summer
Additional information: Application must include most recent tax form. Application forms are also available at the Customer Service Center or online.
Program descriptions:
Achievement Scholarships: Students should have been enrolled in classes or lessons at The Fine Arts Association within the past year. Partial scholarships are awarded for each session and must be used in the session for which the scholarship application was made. Students must complete a new scholarship application for each session.
Financial Need Scholarships: Students for financial need scholarships must be residents of Lake county. Scholarships are to be used towards music, art, theatre, and dance for fall, spring, and summer sessions to people whose income meets federal poverty guidelines. Consideration may also be given to students who are experiencing unexpected financial hardship, such as major medical bills or loss of employment.
EIN: 340834212

7109
J. B. Firestone Charitable Trust
106 S. Main St., Ste. 16
Akron, OH   44308

Foundation type: Independent foundation
Purpose: Student loans to students and alumni of Black River High School, OH.
Financial data: Year ended 12/31/2012. Assets, $1,187,892 (M); Expenditures, $95,885; Total giving, $79,275.
Type of support: Student loans—to individuals; Support to graduates or students of specific schools.
Application information: Applications accepted. Application form required.
Additional information: Application must include applicant's and parents' financial information.
EIN: 346577308

7110
Myron Fishel Scholarship Trust
c/o U.S. Bank, N.A.
P.O. Box 4
Cambridge, OH   43725   (740) 432-1334
Contact: Jeffrey C. East, Tr.
Application address: 819 Wheeling Ave., Cambridge, OH 43725-2335

Foundation type: Independent foundation
Purpose: Scholarships to worthy high school seniors of Guernsey county, OH, for undergraduate and graduate study at accredited colleges and universities in OH.
Financial data: Year ended 09/30/2012. Assets, $564,081 (M); Expenditures, $59,956; Total giving, $45,000; Grants to individuals, 30 grants totaling $45,000 (high: $1,500; low: $1,500).
Fields of interest: Higher education; Scholarships/financial aid.
Type of support: Graduate support; Undergraduate support.
Application information: Application form required.
Deadline(s): Apr.
Additional information: In the event there is remaining funds, candidates who are residents of other counties in OH will be considered for the scholarship. Funds are paid directly to the educational institution on behalf of the students. Interviews may be required.
EIN: 237407789

7111
Father James M. Fitzgerald Scholarship Trust
c/o PNC Bank, N.A.
P.O. Box 94651
Cleveland, OH   44101-4651

Foundation type: Independent foundation
Purpose: Scholarships to priesthood students attending Catholic colleges and universities, and to the two highest-ranking students at St. Mark's Catholic School, Peoria, IL, enrolling in any Roman Catholic high school.
Financial data: Year ended 12/31/2012. Assets, $2,602,978 (M); Expenditures, $148,415; Total giving, $120,687.
Fields of interest: Secondary school/education; Theological school/education; Catholic agencies & churches.
Type of support: Scholarships—to individuals; Support to graduates or students of specific schools; Precollege support.

Application information: Applications accepted.
Initial approach: Letter
Deadline(s): None
EIN: 376050189

7112
Foodbank, Inc.
427 Washington St.
Dayton, OH 45402-2500   (937) 461-0265
Contact: Michelle Riley, C.E.O.
FAX: (937) 461-3310;
E-mail: info@thefoodbankdayton.org; URL: http://
www.thefoodbankdayton.org

Foundation type: Public charity
Purpose: Emergency aid to individuals in the form of food clothing and shelter in Montgomery County, OH.
Publications: Newsletter.
Financial data: Year ended 06/30/2012. Assets, $4,009,633 (M); Expenditures, $8,126,511; Total giving, $6,830,889.
Fields of interest: Food services; Homeless.
Type of support: Grants for special needs.
Application information: Applications not accepted.
Additional information: Contact foundation for program information.
EIN: 861082880

7113
S.N. & Ada Ford Fund
c/o KeyBank
4900 Tiedeman Rd, OH-01-49-0150
Brooklyn, OH 44144-2302   (419) 525-7665
Contact: Dana Hammond, Tr.
*Application address:*C/o. KeyBank, N.A., 42 N. Main St., Mansfield, OH 44902, tel.: (419) 525-7665

Foundation type: Independent foundation
Purpose: Scholarships only to qualified residents of Richland County, OH. Relief and medical expense assistance to aged and incurably ill residents of Richland County, OH.
Publications: Annual report.
Financial data: Year ended 12/31/2012. Assets, $11,551,827 (M); Expenditures, $553,730; Total giving, $483,500.
Fields of interest: Vocational education; Aging.
Type of support: Scholarships—to individuals; Grants for special needs.
Application information: Application form required.
Initial approach: Telephone
Deadline(s): None
Program description:
Scholarship Program: The fund provides postsecondary scholarships for study that is preferably designed for the purpose of earning a living.
EIN: 340842282

7114
Donald J. Foss Memorial Employees Trust
604 Madison Ave.
Wooster, OH 44691-4764   (330) 264-4440
Contact: Allan K. Rodd, Tr.

Foundation type: Independent foundation
Purpose: Financial assistance to employees of Wooster Brush Co., Wooster, OH, and their immediate families in time of sickness, death, or other unfortunate circumstances. Officers and directors of the company are ineligible.
Financial data: Year ended 04/30/2013. Assets, $7,159,613 (M); Expenditures, $358,215; Total

giving, $357,766; Grants to individuals, 28 grants totaling $212,766 (high: $8,300, low: $120).
Type of support: Employee-related welfare.
Application information: Applications accepted. Application form required.
Deadline(s): None
Company name: Wooster Brush Company
EIN: 346517801

7115
The Foundation for Appalachian Ohio
36 Public Sq.
P.O. Box 456
Nelsonville, OH 45764-1133   (740) 753-1111
Contact: Cara Dingus Brook, Pres. and C.E.O.
FAX: (740) 753-3333; E-mail: mwanczyk@ffao.org;
Additional e-mail: cbrook@ffao.org; URL: http://
www.appalachianohio.org

Foundation type: Community foundation
Purpose: Scholarships to students across the 32 counties of Appalachian Ohio for higher education.
Publications: Informational brochure.
Financial data: Year ended 12/31/2012. Assets, $12,140,667 (M); Expenditures, $1,296,084; Total giving, $325,421; Grants to individuals, 53 grants totaling $173,186.
Fields of interest: Higher education.
Type of support: Scholarships—to individuals.
Application information: Applications accepted. Application form required.
Initial approach: Telephone
Deadline(s): Mar. 31
Final notification: Applicants notified in May
Additional information: See web site for complete listing of scholarships and application deadlines.
EIN: 311620483

7116
Founders Memorial Fund of the American Sterilizer Company
5960 Heisley Rd.
Mentor, OH 44060-1834   (440) 392-7221
Contact: Hilary Morton

Foundation type: Company-sponsored foundation
Purpose: Scholarships to dependent children of active and retired employees of the American Sterilizer Co. to attend accredited colleges, universities, or technical educational institutions.
Financial data: Year ended 12/31/2012. Assets, $1,815,965 (M); Expenditures, $98,116; Total giving, $87,250; Grants to individuals, 124 grants totaling $87,250 (high: $2,500, low: $350).
Fields of interest: Vocational education.
Type of support: Employee-related scholarships.
Application information: Applications not accepted.
Additional information: Unsolicited requests for funds not considered or acknowledged.
Company name: American Sterilizer Company
EIN: 256062068

7117
Hugh A. Fraser Fund
P.O. Box 1558, Dept. EA4E86
Columbus, OH 43216   (330) 364-7421
Contact: Richard L Stephenson, Chair.
Application Address: New Philadelphia's Lion Club, New Philadelphia, OH 44663

Foundation type: Independent foundation

Purpose: Grants to financially needy children who are residents of Tuskarawas County, OH for speech therapy, medicine, hospital costs, shoes, summer camp and other expenses.
Financial data: Year ended 06/30/2013. Assets, $1,804,575 (M); Expenditures, $98,191; Total giving, $77,995; Grants to individuals, 10 grants totaling $14,225 (high: $2,750, low: $800).
Fields of interest: Children, services; Human services; Children/youth; Economically disadvantaged.
Type of support: Grants for special needs.
Application information: Application form not required.
Initial approach: Letter
Deadline(s): None
EIN: 346622461

7118
Lena Pierce Frederick Trust
c/o KeyBank, N.A.
4900 Tiedeman Rd., OH-01-49-0150
Brooklyn, OH 44144-2302   (207) 930-5376
Application address: c/o Dawson Law Office, Attn.: Elizabeth Dawson, P.O. Box 302, Belfast, ME 04915, tel.: (207) 930-5376

Foundation type: Independent foundation
Purpose: Grants to needy persons of Belfast, ME, for medical and general assistance.
Financial data: Year ended 04/30/2013. Assets, $518,092 (M); Expenditures, $16,343; Total giving, $9,000.
Fields of interest: Health care.
Type of support: Grants for special needs.
Application information: Applications accepted.
Initial approach: Letter
Deadline(s): None
EIN: 016010164

7119
Isabelle Freer Memorial Scholarship Trust
146 E. Center St.
Marion, OH 43302   (740) 387-6000
Contact: John C. Bartram, Tr.

Foundation type: Operating foundation
Purpose: Scholarships to graduates of Marion Harding High School, OH pursuing postsecondary education at institutions of higher learning.
Financial data: Year ended 12/31/2012. Assets, $0 (M); Expenditures, $90,424; Total giving, $88,885; Grants to individuals, 2 grants totaling $4,000.
Fields of interest: Higher education.
Type of support: Support to graduates or students of specific schools; Undergraduate support.
Application information: Applications accepted.
Initial approach: Letter
Deadline(s): None
Additional information: Application should provide details of purpose and use of grant.
EIN: 346866821

7120
The Egbert M. Freese Foundation
126 S. Market St.
Galion, OH 44833-2626   (419) 468-5044

Foundation type: Public charity
Purpose: Scholarships to high school graduates who are residents of Galion, OH.
Financial data: Year ended 12/31/2011. Assets, $8,202,224 (M); Expenditures, $544,137; Total giving, $490,401.

Fields of interest: Higher education.
Type of support: Scholarships—to individuals.
Application information: Contact foundation for current application deadline/guidelines.
EIN: 341901855

7121
Dr. R. A. Gandy, Jr./Mercy Hospital Medical Staff, Inc. Scholarship Fund
c/o Yvonne M. Gandy
2148 Evergreen Rd.
Toledo, OH   43606-2543   (419) 536-8224

Foundation type: Independent foundation
Purpose: Scholarships to students for postgraduate study at the University of Toledo, OH pursuing a degree in a science field.
Financial data: Year ended 12/31/2011. Assets, $82,462 (M); Expenditures, $7,933; Total giving, $7,500; Grant to an individual, 1 grant totaling $7,500.
Fields of interest: Formal/general education.
Type of support: Support to graduates or students of specific schools; Postgraduate support.
Application information: Application form required.
 Deadline(s): July 20
EIN: 311491102

7122
The Lyle B. & Wanda K. Ganyard Scholarship Trust
(formerly The Lyle B. & Wanda K. Ganyard Scholarship Trust)
106 S. Main St., Ste. 16
Akron, OH   44308

Foundation type: Independent foundation
Purpose: Scholarships to graduates of Copley High School and Revere High School, both in OH, who have family residing in one of these schools districts.
Financial data: Year ended 09/30/2013. Assets, $631,214 (M); Expenditures, $46,246; Total giving, $37,303.
Type of support: Support to graduates or students of specific schools; Undergraduate support.
Application information:
 Initial approach: Letter or telephone
 Additional information: Contact high schools for application guidelines.
EIN: 346820819

7123
Jeanne Souers Garcia Scholarship Trust
P.O. Box 1558, Dept. EA4E86
Columbus, OH   43216   (330) 364-0644

Foundation type: Independent foundation
Purpose: Scholarships to graduating students of New Philadelphia High School for postsecondary education at institutions of higher learning.
Financial data: Year ended 06/30/2013. Assets, $147,941 (M); Expenditures, $8,830; Total giving, $6,798; Grants to individuals, 6 grants totaling $6,798 (high: $1,133, low: $1,133).
Fields of interest: Higher education.
Type of support: Support to graduates or students of specific schools.
Application information: Applications accepted. Application form required. Interview required.
 Deadline(s): None
 Applicants should submit the following:
  1) Transcripts
  2) Financial information

Additional information: Application must also include three character reference letters, a biographical statement, including educational background, personal interests, and other pertinent information of yourself. Completed application must be returned to the guidance office.
EIN: 316496564

7124
Gardner Foundation
10 W. 2nd St., 26th Fl.
Dayton, OH   45402-1971
Application address: c/o Eugenie Campbell, 1424 Black Horse Run, Lebanon, OH 45036

Foundation type: Independent foundation
Purpose: Scholarships to graduating seniors of high schools in Edgewood, Franklin, Hamilton County, Madison, and Middletown, OH.
Publications: Application guidelines; Program policy statement.
Financial data: Year ended 05/31/2012. Assets, $3,989,126 (M); Expenditures, $254,663; Total giving, $230,007.
Fields of interest: Scholarships/financial aid.
Type of support: Support to graduates or students of specific schools; Undergraduate support.
Application information: Applications accepted. Application form required.
 Deadline(s): None
 Additional information: Applications available through high school guidance counselors in the specified school districts.
EIN: 316050604

7125
Virginia Gay Fund
c/o PNC Bank, N.A.
P.O. Box 94651
Cleveland, OH   44101-4651

Foundation type: Independent foundation
Purpose: Financial assistance to eligible retired females Ohio school teachers with 20 or more years of public service.
Financial data: Year ended 12/31/2012. Assets, $879,442 (M); Expenditures, $170,635; Total giving, $150,683.
Fields of interest: Education; Aging; Disabilities, people with; Women.
Type of support: Grants for special needs.
Application information: Applications accepted. Application form required. Interview required.
 Deadline(s): None
 Additional information: Application can be obtained from the Secy.-Treas. of the Board of Trustees. Applicant must be at least 55 years of age.
EIN: 314379588

7126
The Norbert Gazin Educational Foundation
c/o KeyBank N.A.
4900 Tiedeman Rd., OH-01-49-0150
Brooklyn, OH   44144-2302
Contact: Julie Burmingham
Application Address: P.O. Box 40, Turin, NY13473

Foundation type: Independent foundation
Purpose: Scholarships to graduates of Lewis County High School, NY pursuing higher education.
Financial data: Year ended 12/31/2012. Assets, $1,985,142 (M); Expenditures, $106,620; Total

giving, $82,086; Grants to individuals, 119 grants totaling $82,086 (high: $1,175, low: $336).
Fields of interest: Higher education.
Type of support: Scholarships—to individuals; Undergraduate support.
Application information:
 Deadline(s): None
 Additional information: Applicant must be a resident of Lewis County, NY for five years, and born in Lewis County.
EIN: 527124691

7127
Muriel Gilbert Memorial Scholarship Fund
c/o KeyBank, N.A.
4900 Tiedeman Rd., OH-01-49-0150
Dayton, OH   45402
Contact: James Hause
Application addresses: 1215 Huron River Rd., Ypsilanti, MI 48197

Foundation type: Independent foundation
Purpose: Scholarships to Eastern Michigan University full-time music majors concentrating on voice with a 3.0 GPA or higher. One-year scholarships also to Milan, MI, area high school seniors who intend to major in music.
Financial data: Year ended 09/30/2013. Assets, $47,783 (M); Expenditures, $26,079; Total giving, $19,908.
Fields of interest: Music; Music (choral); Performing arts, education.
Type of support: Support to graduates or students of specific schools.
Application information: Applications accepted. Application form required.
 Deadline(s): Prior to the end of each academic year
EIN: 386525706

7128
Mary Gonter & Sara O'Brien Scholarship Foundation
P.O. Box 1558, Dept. EA4E86
Columbus, OH   43216   (330) 364-7421
Contact: Larry Markworth
Application address: 232 W.3rd St., Dover, OH 44622-2969, tel.: (330) 364-7421

Foundation type: Independent foundation
Purpose: Scholarships to young OH residents studying to become ordained Protestant Christian ministers.
Financial data: Year ended 06/30/2013. Assets, $332,701 (M); Expenditures, $18,591; Total giving, $14,500.
Fields of interest: Theological school/education; Protestant agencies & churches.
Type of support: Undergraduate support.
Application information: Applications accepted.
 Initial approach: Letter
 Deadline(s): None
EIN: 316317421

7129
Good Samaritan Foundation of Cincinnati, Inc.
619 Oak St., Acctg. 3 W.
Cincinnati, OH   45206-1613   (513) 569-5126

Foundation type: Public charity
Purpose: Scholarships to qualifying employees of the Good Samaritan Hospital of Cincinnati, OH and

its students in the hospital's school of nursing. Support for indigent individuals.
Financial data: Year ended 06/30/2011. Assets, $41,880,969 (M); Expenditures, $3,398,563; Total giving, $1,889,581; Grants to individuals, totaling $71,353.
Fields of interest: Nursing school/education.
Type of support: Employee-related scholarships; Scholarships—to individuals; Grants for special needs.
Application information: Unsolicited requests for funds not considered or acknowledged.
EIN: 311206047

7130
Grace W. Goodridge Charitable Trust
c/o PNC Bank, N.A.
P.O. Box 94651
Cleveland, OH   44101-4651

Foundation type: Independent foundation
Purpose: Scholarships to students from Struthers High School, OH who are in the top 25 percent of the graduating class.
Financial data: Year ended 06/30/2013. Assets, $169,453 (M); Expenditures, $8,300; Total giving, $5,000.
Fields of interest: Higher education.
Type of support: Support to graduates or students of specific schools.
Application information: Application form required.
 Deadline(s): May
 Additional information: Application can be obtained from guidance counselor or principal.
EIN: 346838034

7131
Mark Goodwin Memorial Trust
c/o KeyBank
4900 Tiedeman Rd., OH-01-49-0150
Brooklyn, OH   44144-2302   (518) 257-9661
Contact: Christine Moughton
Application address: 66 S. Pearl St., Albany, NY 12207-1501

Foundation type: Company-sponsored foundation
Purpose: Scholarships to employees and children of employees of Cole Haan Holdings to pursue higher education.
Financial data: Year ended 08/31/2013. Assets, $177,987 (M); Expenditures, $15,240; Total giving, $12,250; Grants to individuals, 23 grants totaling $12,250 (high: $2,000, low: $250).
Fields of interest: Higher education.
Type of support: Employee-related scholarships.
Application information: Applications not accepted.
 Additional information: Unsolicited requests for funds not considered or acknowledged.
EIN: 223226157

7132
The Grace High Washburn Trust
1232 State Rt. 4
Bucyrus, OH   44820-3146   (419) 562-2074
Contact: John R. Clime, Secy.-Treas.

Foundation type: Independent foundation
Purpose: Scholarships to female Protestant residents of Crawford County, OH, to attend Ohio State University and its branch schools. Scholarships are not to exceed four years.
Financial data: Year ended 12/31/2012. Assets, $2,919,694 (M); Expenditures, $155,431; Total

giving, $139,006; Grants to individuals, 53 grants totaling $139,006 (high: $4,714, low: -$1,266).
Fields of interest: Protestant agencies & churches; Adults, women.
Type of support: Support to graduates or students of specific schools; Undergraduate support.
Application information: Applications accepted. Application form required.
 Send request by: Mail
 Deadline(s): May 31
 Applicants should submit the following:
  1) Letter(s) of recommendation
  2) Financial information
EIN: 346521078

7133
The Granville Foundation
P.O. Box 321
Granville, OH   43023-0321   (740) 587-2812
Contact: Doug Plunkett, Exec. Dir.
E-mail: dplunkett@windstream.net; URL: http://www.granvillefoundation.org

Foundation type: Community foundation
Purpose: Scholarships to graduating seniors from the Granville School District, OH for postsecondary education.
Publications: Annual report.
Financial data: Year ended 12/31/2012. Assets, $1,990,835 (M); Expenditures, $94,214; Total giving, $72,046; Grants to individuals, totaling $72,046.
Fields of interest: Higher education.
Type of support: Scholarships—to individuals.
Application information: Applications accepted.
 Additional information: Students should contact their guidance counselor for additional application information.
EIN: 237241045

7134
Greene County Community Foundation
25 Greene St.
Xenia, OH   45385-3101   (937) 562-5550
Contact: Edward Marrinan, Exec. Dir.
FAX: (937) 562-5556;
E-mail: emarrinan@co.greene.oh.us; URL: http://www.greenegiving.org

Foundation type: Community foundation
Purpose: Scholarships to deserving graduating high school seniors of Greene county, OH pursuing higher education.
Publications: Informational brochure.
Financial data: Year ended 12/31/2011. Assets, $8,270,135 (M); Expenditures, $1,353,204; Total giving, $1,186,829; Grants to individuals, totaling $349,828.
Fields of interest: Higher education.
Type of support: Scholarships—to individuals; Support to graduates or students of specific schools.
Application information: Applications accepted.
 Additional information: Contact the foundation for additional application information.
EIN: 311751001

7135
Nora Greenwalt Trust
(formerly Nora Greenwalt Foundation)
P.O. Box 1558, EA4E86
Columbus, OH   43216-1558   (330) 364-1614
Application address: c/o Donald Zimmerman, 140 Fair Ave., P.O. Box 1014, New Philadelphia, OH 44663,

Foundation type: Independent foundation
Purpose: Grants to disabled children in need of financial assistance in the New Philadelphia, OH, area.
Financial data: Year ended 06/30/2013. Assets, $142,818 (M); Expenditures, $7,335; Total giving, $6,606; Grants to individuals, 3 grants totaling $6,606 (high: $4,750, low: $900).
Fields of interest: Children; Disabilities, people with; Economically disadvantaged.
Type of support: Grants for special needs.
Application information:
 Deadline(s): None
EIN: 346521347

7136
Griffith Insurance Education Foundation
623 High St.
Worthington, OH   43085-4146   (614) 880-9870
FAX: (614) 880-9872;
E-mail: info@griffithfoundation.org; URL: http://www.griffithfoundation.org

Foundation type: Public charity
Purpose: Scholarships to OH students who are pursuing insurance, risk management, actuarial science, or insurance-related programs at colleges and universities throughout the U.S.
Publications: Application guidelines.
Financial data: Year ended 12/31/2011. Assets, $2,295,032 (M); Expenditures, $1,415,058; Total giving, $50,585; Grants to individuals, 11 grants totaling $25,585 (high: $15,000, low: $10,585). Subtotal for scholarships: 9 grants totaling $10,585. Subtotal for professorships: 2 grants totaling $15,000.
Fields of interest: Business school/education.
Type of support: Scholarships—to individuals; Graduate support; Undergraduate support.
Application information: Applications accepted. Application form required. Application form available on the grantmaker's web site.
 Send request by: Mail
 Deadline(s): Mar. 10 and Nov. 30
 Additional information: Application should include a current transcript. See web site for additional application guidelines.
Program descriptions:
 Central Ohio Insurance Education Day Scholarships: One $1,500 scholarship, and two $750 scholarships, are available to Ohio-resident business college majors who are attending a college or university anywhere in the U.S., and who commit to take a risk management and insurance (RMI) course, or who are RMI majors. Applicants for the $1,500 scholarship should be planning to enter an insurance-related field upon graduation, and should have a GPA of at least 3.5 or above in their declared major; applicants for the $750 scholarships should be sophomore or junior business college majors who have a GPA of at least 3.5, and who agree to take and complete at least one college insurance and risk management course.
 Central Ohio RIMS Chapter Scholarship: One $2,500 scholarship will be awarded to a U.S. citizen who is a resident of Ohio and who is attending a college or university anywhere in the country.

Applicants must be studying insurance, risk management, or an other insurance-related area, and should be planning to enter an insurance-related field upon graduation; special consideration will be given to central Ohio residents or students.

Francis A. Herzog Scholarship: A $1,000 scholarship will be awarded each year to either a U.S. citizen attending an Ohio college or university, or an Ohio resident attending a college or university anywhere in the U.S., who is a full-time, junior or senior student enrolled in an insurance, risk management, actuarial science, or insurance-related program. Applicants must have a cumulative GPA of at least 2.5, and should be planning to enter an insurance-related field upon graduation; preference will be given to children, stepchildren, or legally-adopted children of Ohio Big I members.

Grand Lake CPCU Chapter Scholarship: This $2,000 scholarship is awarded annually to a U.S. citizen who is a full-time undergraduate resident student attending a college or university anywhere in the U.S., and who is a sophomore or junior enrolled in an insurance program or insurance-related field of study. Applicants must be, or have parents or legal guardians who are, residents of Allen, Auglaize, Mercer, Paulding, Putnam, or Van Wert counties.

Scholarships for Students Attending The Ohio State University: Five scholarships are available to business and actuarial science students who are attending Ohio State University, and who wish to take risk management and insurance courses. Named scholarships available under this program include the Gerald E. Ermlich Memorial Scholarship (providing support to a junior or senior student who is majoring in insurance, and who has a GPA of at least 2.75), the John Conrad Haaf Scholarship Fund (providing support to an undergraduate or graduate insurance major at the university's College of Business, and who has a GPA of at least 2.75), the Fred F. Jaeger Jr. Memorial Insurance Fund (providing scholarship support to further the study of property, casualty, and life insurance), the Norman R. Sleight Endowment Fund (providing scholarship support to undergraduate students), and the Turner and Shepard Fund (providing scholarship support to a full-time graduate or undergraduate student in the university's College of Business)

The Columbus Ohio CPCU Chapter Scholarship: Two scholarships are awarded annually to a student (sophomore or higher) in an insurance program or insurance-related field of study with a GPA of 2.75 or better, and who either resides in the greater central Ohio area or is attending a college or university within Ohio. The Columbus Ohio CPCU Chapter General Scholarship (for $1,000) is available to a student who meets the above criteria; two Columbus Ohio CPCU Chapter Member or Family Member Scholarships (of $1,000 each) are available to students who meet the above criteria, and who are either a Columbus Chapter CPCU member or a relative of a Columbus Chapter CPCU member.

The Motorists Insurance Group Cameron E. Williams Memorial Scholarship: This $2,000 scholarship is awarded each year to a U.S. citizen and full-time student attending a college or university anywhere in the U.S. who is at least a sophomore and enrolled in an insurance, risk management, actuarial science, or insurance-related program. Eligible applicants must have a cumulative GPA of at least 3.0, and should be planning to enter an insurance-related field upon graduation; preference will be given to children,

step-children, and legally-adopted children of The Motorists Insurance Group employees and agents.
EIN: 316052801

7137
Thomas O. Grove Scholarship Fund
4900 Tiedman Rd. OH-01-49-0150
Brooklyn, OH 44144-2302 (800) 999-9658
Contact: Agnes Wolanin
Application address: c/o Agnes Wolanin, 800 Superior St., 4th Fl., Cleveland, OH 44114-2613

Foundation type: Independent foundation
Purpose: Scholarships to students graduating from any high school in Sylvania, OH.
Financial data: Year ended 12/31/2012. Assets, $232,686 (M); Expenditures, $4,100; Total giving, $0.
Type of support: Support to graduates or students of specific schools; Undergraduate support.
Application information:
Deadline(s): None
EIN: 346942668

7138
H.O.P.E. Foundation of Darke County
c/o Rodney Oda
300 W. Main St.
Greenville, OH 45331 (937) 548-4673
Contact: Christy Prakel, Dir.
E-mail: hopefoundation@woh.rr.com; Application address: 201 W Main Rd., Greenville, OH 45331-0438 Tel:(937) 548-4673; URL: http://www.hopedarkecounty.com/

Foundation type: Independent foundation
Purpose: Applicants must be residents of Drake County, OH. The foundation does not generally grant scholarships for first-year studies.
Financial data: Year ended 06/30/2013. Assets, $2,601,923 (M); Expenditures, $186,417; Total giving, $123,081.
Fields of interest: Higher education; Scholarships/financial aid.
Type of support: Scholarships—to individuals; Undergraduate support.
Application information: Applications accepted. Application form required. Interview required.
Deadline(s): June 15
Additional information: Application should include transcripts; Contact foundation for the areas in which they are making grants.
EIN: 311177601

7139
The Hamilton Community Foundation, Inc.
319 N. 3rd St.
Hamilton, OH 45011-1624 (513) 863-1717
Contact: John J. Guidugli, C.E.O.
FAX: (513) 863-2868;
E-mail: info@hamiltonfoundation.org; URL: http://www.hamiltonfoundation.org

Foundation type: Community foundation
Purpose: Scholarships to students of Butler County, OH, pursuing a higher education.
Publications: Application guidelines; Annual report; Informational brochure (including application guidelines); Newsletter.
Financial data: Year ended 12/31/2012. Assets, $76,188,512 (M); Expenditures, $7,776,126; Total giving, $5,522,311; Grants to individuals, 329 grants totaling $515,883.
Fields of interest: Vocational education, post-secondary; Higher education.

Type of support: Scholarships—to individuals; Graduate support; Undergraduate support.
Application information: Applications accepted. Application form required.
Deadline(s): Feb. 7 for Graduating Seniors, June 13 for Students Currently in College and Adult Scholarships
Final notification: Applicants are notified in May for Graduating Seniors
Applicants should submit the following:
1) Essay
2) Transcripts
3) FAFSA
Additional information: See web site for additional application guidelines and eligibility.
EIN: 316038277

7140
Esther Hamilton Fund
(also known as Santa Claus Club Scholarship Fund)
c/o PNC Bank, N.A.
P.O. Box 94651
Cleveland, OH 44101-4651 (330) 742-4309
Contact: George P. Millich
Application address: P. O. Box 450, Youngstown, OH 44503, tel.: (330) 742-4309

Foundation type: Independent foundation
Purpose: Scholarships to financially needy graduating seniors who are in the top 25 percent of their classes at city, county, and parochial high schools in Mahoning County, OH. Recipients must attend Youngstown State University.
Financial data: Year ended 12/31/2011. Assets, $188,696 (M); Expenditures, $9,148; Total giving, $7,800.
Type of support: Support to graduates or students of specific schools; Undergraduate support.
Application information: Applications accepted. Application form required.
Deadline(s): May
Additional information: Applications available from high school principals.
EIN: 346575611

7141
Charles M. and Julia C. Harrington Scholarship Fund
c/o KeyBank
4900 Tiedeman Rd., OH-01-49-0150
Brooklyn, OH 44144-2302
Contact: Alan J. Feazelle
Application address: 1 Clifford Dr., Plattsburgh, NY 12901

Foundation type: Independent foundation
Purpose: Scholarships to graduates of Plattsburg High School, NY, who plan to attend one of several specified colleges.
Financial data: Year ended 12/31/2011. Assets, $90,463 (M); Expenditures, $2,324; Total giving, $1,148.
Type of support: Support to graduates or students of specific schools; Undergraduate support.
Application information:
Send request by: Mail
Deadline(s): Apr. 1
EIN: 146014863

7142
Marjorie Hart Trust
23 E. Broadway St.
P.O. Box 284
Wellston, OH 45692-1225 (740) 384-5440
Contact: Kyle R. Gilliland, Tr.

Foundation type: Independent foundation
Purpose: Scholarships to residents of Wellston, OH.
Financial data: Year ended 12/31/2012. Assets, $380,371 (M); Expenditures, $2,674; Total giving, $2,500; Grants to individuals, 12 grants totaling $2,500 (high: $500; low: $100).
Type of support: Scholarships—to individuals.
Application information: Applications accepted.
  Additional information: Contact foundation for current application deadline/guidelines.
EIN: 311428420

7143
Betty & Randall Hartley Memorial Scholarship Fund
c/o PNC Bank, N.A.
P.O. Box 94651
Cleveland, OH 44101-4651

Foundation type: Independent foundation
Purpose: Scholarships to students attending Ohio State University, Ohio University, University of Pittsburgh or Berea College, who are residents of Guernsey County, OH and are pursuing an education in the teaching profession.
Financial data: Year ended 12/31/2012. Assets, $201,920 (M); Expenditures, $6,722; Total giving, $4,000; Grants to individuals, totaling $4,000.
Fields of interest: Teacher school/education.
Type of support: Support to graduates or students of specific schools; Undergraduate support.
Application information: Applications accepted.
  Send request by: Mail
  Deadline(s): None
  Additional information: Applications should outline financial need.
EIN: 341907881

7144
The Hauss-Helms Foundation, Inc.
P.O. Box 25
Wapakoneta, OH 45895-0025 (419) 738-4911
E-mail: information@hauss-helmsfoundation.org;
URL: http://www.hauss-helmsfoundation.org

Foundation type: Independent foundation
Purpose: Scholarships to financially needy graduating high school students who are residents of Auglaize and Allen counties, OH, and who wish to continue their education at colleges, universities, and technical schools.
Financial data: Year ended 07/31/2012. Assets, $18,480,240 (M); Expenditures, $1,162,627; Total giving, $898,974; Grants to individuals, 167 grants totaling $898,974.
Fields of interest: Vocational education, post-secondary; Higher education.
Type of support: Scholarships—to individuals; Technical education support; Undergraduate support.
Application information: Applications accepted. Application form required. Application form available on the grantmaker's web site.
  Initial approach: Letter
  Send request by: Mail or fax

Copies of proposal: 1
Deadline(s): Apr. 15
Final notification: Applicants notified in two months
Applicants should submit the following:
  1) GPA
  2) FAFSA
  3) Budget Information
  4) Letter(s) of recommendation
  5) Financial information
Program description:
  Educational Grants: Applicants must be of good moral character, rank in the top half of their graduating classes, be unable to fund college on their own, and be recommended for the grant by the principal, guidance counselor, or faculty member in their high school. If already in college, they must be recommended by a faculty advisor at that college. Scholarships are for one year of full-time study, and are renewable providing the student has maintained a GPA of at least 2.0 or its equivalent. In addition, grant recipients will have their grant revoked if they become a member of, or associate with, the Communist Party or any other group advocating the violent overthrow of our government.
EIN: 340975903

7145
Hawkes Scholarship Fund
c/o KeyBank, N.A.
4900 Tiedeman Rd., OH-01-49-01
Brooklyn, OH 44144-2302 (518) 257-9655
Contact: Marilyn Hensel
Application Address: 66 S. Pearl St., Albany, NY, 12207

Foundation type: Independent foundation
Purpose: Scholarships to graduating seniors of Tobique Valley High School in New Brunswick, Canada and Governor Baxter School for the Deaf in Portland, ME. Scholarships also to graduating seniors who are residents of Opportunity Farm for Boys or Sweetser-Children's Home, both in ME, and to members of the Boys and Girls Club of Portland, ME only for the first year of study at a U.S. college, university or technical school.
Financial data: Year ended 07/31/2013. Assets, $1,210,650 (M); Expenditures, $110,856; Total giving, $91,802.
Fields of interest: Vocational education; Boys & girls clubs; Disabilities, people with.
Type of support: Support to graduates or students of specific schools; Undergraduate support.
Application information: Applications not accepted.
  Additional information: Unsolicited requests for funds not considered or accepted.
EIN: 010441158

7146
The Herb Society of America
9019 Kirtland Chardon Rd.
Kirtland, OH 44094-5156 (440) 256-0514
Contact: Katrinka Morgan, Exec. Dir.
FAX: (440) 256-0541;
E-mail: herbs@herbsociety.org; E-Mail for Katrinka Morgan: director@herbsociety.org; URL: http://www.herbsociety.org

Foundation type: Public charity
Purpose: Scholarships to students enrolled in a program for the study of horticulture. Research grants to students, professionals, and individuals engaged in research on the horticultural, scientific, and/or social applications or use of herbs throughout history.

Financial data: Year ended 03/31/2012. Assets, $2,270,845 (M); Expenditures, $390,978; Total giving, $31,447; Grants to individuals, totaling $800.
Fields of interest: Environment, plant conservation; Horticulture/garden clubs; Agriculture.
Type of support: Research; Undergraduate support.
Application information: Applications accepted. Application form required. Application form available on the grantmaker's web site. Interview required.
  Initial approach: Letter
  Copies of proposal: 6
  Deadline(s): Apr. 1 for scholarships
  Applicants should submit the following:
    1) Letter(s) of recommendation
    2) Proposal
    3) Curriculum vitae
  Additional information: See web site for further eligibility criteria.
Program descriptions:
  Grants for Educators: The goal of this grant is the delivery of a project that specifically promotes herbal education, beyond the usual garden activities. Each year, the grant committee anticipates funding one or two grants for a total of $5,000.
  Research Grants: These grants are intended to support small, self-contained research projects that can be carried out in a short period of time. The grant is for a one-year period of work; the maximum amount available is $5,000.
EIN: 341596261

7147
Charles D. "Bud" Hering, Jr. Foundation
84 S. Washington St.
Tiffin, OH 44883-2516 (419) 447-8232
Contact: Fred C. Spurk, Chair.
Application address: P.O. Box 380, Tiffin, OH 44883-0380, tel.: (419) 447-8232

Foundation type: Independent foundation
Purpose: Scholarships to students residing in the Tiffin, OH, area, for higher education.
Financial data: Year ended 12/31/2011. Assets, $333,420 (M); Expenditures, $10,170; Total giving, $8,750; Grants to individuals, 5 grants totaling $8,750 (high: $2,500, low: $1,250).
Type of support: Undergraduate support.
Application information: Applications accepted.
  Initial approach: Letter
  Deadline(s): None
EIN: 341702565

7148
Mildred L. Herzberger Charitable Trust
3040 W. Point Rd.
Lancaster, OH 43130-8640 (740) 569-3040
Contact: William J. Sitterley
URL: https://fairfieldcountyscholarships.com

Foundation type: Independent foundation
Purpose: Scholarships to high school graduates of Fairfield or Hocking county, OH for attendance at accredited OH, colleges or universities.
Financial data: Year ended 05/31/2013. Assets, $458,203 (M); Expenditures, $22,982; Total giving, $18,000; Grants to individuals, 3 grants totaling $18,000 (high: $9,000, low: $9,000).
Fields of interest: Higher education; Scholarships/financial aid.
Type of support: Support to graduates or students of specific schools; Undergraduate support.
Application information: Application form required. Interview required.

Send request by: Mail
Deadline(s): Mar. 15
Applicants should submit the following:
1) Photograph
2) Transcripts
3) GPA
4) ACT
Additional information: Applicant must demonstrate financial need.
EIN: 311435269

7149
Mary E. Higgins Educational Fund
c/o KeyBank N.A.
4900 Tiedeman Rd., OH-01-49-0150
Brooklyn, OH 44144-2302 (207) 657-3323
Application Address: c/o Guidance Dept.
Gray-Gloucester High School, 10 Libby Hill Rd., Gray
ME 04039

Foundation type: Independent foundation
Purpose: Scholarships to residents of Gray, ME, are made payable to the student and the school upon certification of completion of the first semester.
Financial data: Year ended 06/30/2013. Assets, $160,577 (M); Expenditures, $8,500; Total giving, $6,000; Grants to individuals, 6 grants totaling $6,000 (high: $1,000, low: $1,000).
Fields of interest: Vocational education.
Type of support: Support to graduates or students of specific schools; Undergraduate support.
Application information: Applications accepted. Application form required.
EIN: 016067064

7150
Charles F. High Foundation
1232 State Rte. 4 S.
Bucyrus, OH 44820-9589 (419) 562-2074
Contact: John R. Clime, Admin.

Foundation type: Independent foundation
Purpose: Scholarships to male residents of OH to attend Ohio State University.
Financial data: Year ended 12/31/2012. Assets, $6,939,980 (M); Expenditures, $338,416; Total giving, $309,431; Grants to individuals, totaling $309,431.
Fields of interest: Men.
Type of support: Scholarships—to individuals; Support to graduates or students of specific schools.
Application information: Applications accepted.
Initial approach: Letter
Deadline(s): June 1
EIN: 346527860

7151
Holmes County Council for Handicapped Citizens, Inc.
(formerly Holmes County Council for Handicapped Children)
5167 T.R. 629
Millersburg, OH 44654 (330) 674-8045

Foundation type: Public charity
Purpose: Financial assistance and services to members of the organization of Millersburg, OH with transportation, communication devices and adult activities.
Financial data: Year ended 08/31/2012. Assets, $708,430 (M); Expenditures, $141,278; Total giving, $126,309; Grants to individuals, totaling $63,890.

Fields of interest: Human services; Human services, transportation.
Type of support: Grants for special needs.
Application information: Applications not accepted.
Additional information: Funds are disbursed directly to the service providers on behalf of the individuals.
EIN: 341356680

7152
Holmes County Education Foundation
(also known as HCEF)
114 N. Clay St.
Millersburg, OH 44654-1120 (330) 674-7303
Contact: Darla Stitzlein, Exec. Dir.; Anna Patton, Admin. Asst.
FAX: (330) 674-7313; E-mail: info@hcef.net; E-Mail for Darla Stitzlein: hcef@hcef.net; URL: http://www.HCEF.net

Foundation type: Public charity
Purpose: Scholarships to residents of Holmes County, OH, who demonstrate financial need.
Publications: Application guidelines; Annual report; Financial statement; Grants list; Informational brochure; Newsletter.
Financial data: Year ended 12/31/2011. Assets, $8,713,289 (M); Expenditures, $596,782; Total giving, $337,756; Grants to individuals, totaling $315,791.
Type of support: Conferences/seminars; Scholarships—to individuals; Graduate support; Technical education support; Undergraduate support.
Application information: Applications accepted. Application form required. Application form available on the grantmaker's web site.
Send request by: Mail, fax or e-mail
Copies of proposal: 1
Deadline(s): Apr. 24
Final notification: Recipients notified six weeks after deadline
Applicants should submit the following:
1) Pell Grant
2) SAR
3) SAT
4) GPA
5) Financial information
6) ACT
Additional information: Applications available during Jan. to Apr. of each year.
EIN: 341631041

7153
Homeless Families Foundation
33 N. Grubb St.
Columbus, OH 43215-2748 (614) 461-9247
Contact: Adrienne Corbett, Exec. Dir.
FAX: (614) 461-9234;
E-mail: info@homelessfamiliesfoundation.org;
URL: http://www.homelessfamiliesfoundation.org

Foundation type: Public charity
Purpose: Assistance to indigent homeless families and their children with housing, medical and dental care, tutoring and financial counseling in the Columbus, OH area.
Financial data: Year ended 12/31/2012. Assets, $1,890,221 (M); Expenditures, $1,652,370; Total giving, $333,720; Grants to individuals, totaling $333,720.
Fields of interest: Economically disadvantaged.
Type of support: In-kind gifts; Grants for special needs.

Application information: Contact the foundation for eligibility criteria.
EIN: 311179492

7154
The J. Edgar Hoover Foundation
57 E. Washington St.
Chagrin Falls, OH 44022 (216) 623-0900
Contact: John McCaffery, Secy.-Treas.
Application Address: 1111 Superior Ave., Cleveland, OH 44114-2500
FAX: (216) 623-0935;
E-mail: jmccaffrey@mmlitigation.com; URL: http://www.jehooverfoundation.org/

Foundation type: Independent foundation
Purpose: Scholarships to selected college and university students pursuing undergraduate and graduate degrees. Awards to students pursuing a forensic science related career in law enforcement.
Financial data: Year ended 12/31/2012. Assets, $775,690 (M); Expenditures, $99,601; Total giving, $38,000; Grants to individuals, 16 grants totaling $38,000 (high: $25,000, low: $500).
Fields of interest: Law school/education.
Type of support: Scholarships—to individuals; Awards/prizes.
Application information: Applications not accepted.
Additional information: Unsolicited requests for funds not considered or acknowledged.
EIN: 526060988

7155
Blanche and Thomas Hope Memorial Fund
P.O. Box 94651
Cleveland, OH 44101-4651 (859) 281-5276
Contact: June Greenwell
Application address: c/o PNC Bank, N.A., 101 S. 5th St., Louisville, KY 40233, tel.: (859) 281-5276

Foundation type: Independent foundation
Purpose: Scholarships limited to students graduating from high schools in Boyd and Greenup counties, KY, and Lawrence County, OH. Scholarships are based on need, although character, grades, and inclination are important.
Financial data: Year ended 12/31/2011. Assets, $3,129,197 (M); Expenditures, $165,692; Total giving, $139,272; Grants to individuals, totaling $139,272.
Type of support: Support to graduates or students of specific schools.
Application information: Applications accepted. Application form required. Interview required.
Deadline(s): Mar. 1
Applicants should submit the following:
1) Transcripts
2) FAF
EIN: 616067105

7156
Lois U. Horvitz Foundation
(formerly HRH Family Foundation)
1001 Lakeside Ave., Ste. 900
Cleveland, OH 44114-1151 (216) 479-2200

Foundation type: Independent foundation
Purpose: Scholarships to descendants of an employee of The Mainfield Journal, The Lake County News Herald, The Dover-New Philadelphia Times Reporter, The Troy Times Record, The Multi-Channel TV Co., and The Lorain Journal. Scholarships also to high school seniors of Lake, Lorain, Richland,

Tuscarawas counties, OH, or Rensselaer County, NY.
Financial data: Year ended 12/31/2012. Assets, $735,616 (M); Expenditures, $35,389; Total giving, $12,125.
Fields of interest: Higher education; Scholarships/financial aid.
Type of support: Employee-related scholarships; Support to graduates or students of specific schools; Technical education support; Undergraduate support.
Application information: Applications accepted. Application form required.
  Deadline(s): Apr. 1
Program description:
  Scholarship Program: Academic merit is not the most important factor. Awards must be used at an accredited college, university, or nonprofit trade school. Awards are automatically renewable. Payments of the scholarships will be made directly to the schools.
EIN: 341594655

7157
Dr. R. S. Hosler Memorial Educational Fund
P.O. Box 5
Ashville, OH 43103-0005 (740) 983-2557
Contact: Leo J. Hall, Tr.

Foundation type: Independent foundation
Purpose: Scholarships to high school graduates of Teays Valley and Amanda Clearcreek, OH, school systems. The focus is on scholarships for medical school.
Financial data: Year ended 12/31/2012. Assets, $6,279,168 (M); Expenditures, $584,805; Total giving, $465,000; Grants to individuals, 2 grants totaling $45,000 (high: $27,000, low: $18,000).
Fields of interest: Higher education; Medical school/education.
Type of support: Support to graduates or students of specific schools; Undergraduate support.
Application information: Application form required.
  Initial approach: Letter
  Deadline(s): May 1
EIN: 311073939

7158
Hospice of Tuscarawas County, Inc.
716 Commercial Ave., S.W.
New Philadelphia, OH 44663-9367 (330) 343-7605
Contact: Mast Norm, Exec. Dir.
FAX: (330) 343-3542;
E-mail: hospice@myhospice.org; URL: http://www.myhospice.org/

Foundation type: Public charity
Purpose: Specific assistance is provided to individuals with nursing care and counseling for terminally ill patients and their families.
Financial data: Year ended 12/31/2011. Assets, $10,911,009 (M); Expenditures, $6,902,526; Total giving, $2,230,905; Grants to individuals, totaling $2,230,905.
Fields of interest: Terminal illness, people with.
Type of support: Grants for special needs.
Application information: Contact hospice for information on nursing care and other assistance.
EIN: 341522329

7159
The Howley Family Foundation
9725 Lakeshore Blvd.
Bratenahl, OH 44108-1063
E-mail: HowleyScholars@gmail.com

Foundation type: Independent foundation
Purpose: Scholarships and tuition assistance to elementary and high school students in northeast OH.
Financial data: Year ended 12/31/2012. Assets, $17,154,999 (M); Expenditures, $696,390; Total giving, $649,275.
Fields of interest: Elementary/secondary education.
Type of support: Scholarships—to individuals.
Application information: Application form required.
  Initial approach: E-mail
  Deadline(s): See foundation web site for current deadline
  Additional information: Applicant must demonstrate financial need. Application must include two recommendations. See web site for additional application information.
Program description:
  Howley Scholars: The foundation awards scholarships of $1,500- $2,500 renewable for 4 years, for high school tuition in the Cleveland area. Students are recommended by schools and must meet academic and financial criteria.
EIN: 300193364

7160
Ruth M. Hughes Scholarship Trust
P.O. Box 1558 DEPT EA4E86
Columbus, OH 43216-2307 (740) 455-7060

Foundation type: Independent foundation
Purpose: Scholarships to graduates of high schools in Muskingum County, OH, in the top third of their class.
Publications: Annual report.
Financial data: Year ended 12/31/2012. Assets, $5,549,753 (M); Expenditures, $323,717; Total giving, $261,250.
Type of support: Support to graduates or students of specific schools; Undergraduate support.
Application information: Applications accepted. Application form required.
  Deadline(s): May 1
  Applicants should submit the following:
    1) Financial information
    2) Essay
    3) SAT
    4) ACT
    5) Transcripts
  Additional information: Contact foundation for current application guidelines.
EIN: 316442501

7161
J. Brannon Hull Scholarship Fund Inc.
4065 School Dr.
Crooksville, OH 43731 (740) 982-7040

Foundation type: Independent foundation
Purpose: Scholarships to graduates of Crooksville High School, OH, or children of employees of Hull Pottery Company, OH.
Financial data: Year ended 12/31/2012. Assets, $668,322 (M); Expenditures, $45,221; Total giving, $38,678; Grants to individuals, 37 grants totaling $38,678 (high: $1,334, low: $334).
Fields of interest: Higher education.

Type of support: Employee-related scholarships; Support to graduates or students of specific schools.
Application information: Application form required.
  Deadline(s): Mar. 15
  Applicants should submit the following:
    1) Transcripts
    2) SAT
    3) Letter(s) of recommendation
  Additional information: First-time applicants must be under 23 years of age and have a high school GPA of 2.5 or greater.
EIN: 311090015

7162
The Hundred Club of Dayton
500 Kettering Twr.
Dayton, OH 45423-1038 (937) 222-0410
Contact: John E. Voss, Chair.

Foundation type: Public charity
Purpose: Scholarships to spouses of firefighters or police officers killed in the line of duty or to children of full time firefighters or police officers in the Dayton, OH area.
Financial data: Year ended 12/31/2011. Assets, $1,056,608 (M); Expenditures, $60,064; Total giving, $30,500; Grants to individuals, totaling $30,500.
Fields of interest: Crime/law enforcement, police agencies.
Type of support: Scholarships—to individuals.
Application information: Applications accepted. Application form required.
  Deadline(s): Mar.
  Applicants should submit the following:
    1) Transcripts
    2) SAR
    3) SAT
    4) FAFSA
    5) Essay
    6) ACT
  Additional information: Applicant must maintain a 2.5 GPA on a 4.0 scale.
EIN: 237046227

7163
Helen & Joan Hunter Family Trust
P.O. Box 94651
Cleveland, OH 44101-4651

Foundation type: Independent foundation
Purpose: Scholarship awards to individuals who have obtained at least sophomore status in undergraduate school and who are full-time residents of McLean County, IL and are preparing for a career in education.
Financial data: Year ended 12/31/2012. Assets, $193,439 (M); Expenditures, $7,676; Total giving, $3,000; Grants to individuals, totaling $3,000.
Fields of interest: Teacher school/education.
Type of support: Scholarships—to individuals.
Application information: Applications accepted. Application form required.
  Deadline(s): Mar. 1
  Additional information: Contact trust for further application guidelines.
EIN: 376357845

7164
Jane E. Hunter Testamentary Trust
c/o KeyBank N.A. Tax Dept.
4900 Tiedeman Rd., OH-01-49-0150
Brooklyn, OH   44144-2302   (216) 689-5838
Application address: c/o Keycorp Nonprofit Svc.,
127 Public Sq., 16th Fl., Cleveland, OH
44114-1306

Foundation type: Independent foundation
Purpose: Scholarships to young women from Ohio
or South Carolina for higher education.
Financial data: Year ended 12/31/2012. Assets,
$1,981,296 (M); Expenditures, $118,858; Total
giving, $98,850.
Type of support: Undergraduate support.
Application information: Applications accepted.
Application form required.
> *Deadline(s):* May 1
> *Applicants should submit the following:*
>   1) Transcripts
>   2) Letter(s) of recommendation
> *Additional information:* Application should also
>   include first page of prior year tax return, and
>   letter of acceptance. Applicant should have
>   2.5 GPA or better. Unsolicited requests for
>   funds not considered or acknowledged.

EIN: 346699212

7165
The Edward L. Hutton Foundation
255 E. 5th St., Ste. 2600
Cincinnati, OH   45202-4726
Contact: Sandra E. Laney, V.P.
E-mail: sandra.laney@chemed.com

Foundation type: Independent foundation
Purpose: Scholarships to students from I.U.
Bedford N. Lawrence High School, IN; Indiana
University in Bloomington, IN; Bedford North
Lawrence High School, IN; Eastern Greene High
School, IN; Cumberland College, KY; and Montana
University, MT.
Publications: Annual report.
Financial data: Year ended 12/31/2012. Assets,
$12,055,226 (M); Expenditures, $645,850; Total
giving, $611,500.
Type of support: Support to graduates or students
of specific schools; Undergraduate support.
Application information: Applications accepted.
Application form required.
> *Initial approach:* Letter
> *Send request by:* Mail
> *Copies of proposal:* 1
> *Applicants should submit the following:*
>   1) Work samples
>   2) Proposal
>   3) Photograph
>   4) Pell Grant
>   5) Letter(s) of recommendation
>   6) Financial information
>   7) Curriculum vitae

EIN: 311334189

7166
I Know I Can
3798 E. Broad St.
Columbus, OH   43213-1142   (614) 233-9510
Application address: 270 E. State St., Columbus,
OH 43215, tel.: (614) 469-7044, fax: (614)
365-5262
FAX: (614) 233-9512; E-mail: info@iknowican.org;
URL: http://www.iknowican.org

Foundation type: Public charity

Purpose: Scholarships to students of Columbus
City school district, OH for postsecondary
education.
Publications: Application guidelines; Annual report.
Financial data: Year ended 06/30/2011. Assets,
$30,474,114 (M); Expenditures, $2,871,625;
Total giving, $1,433,271.
Fields of interest: Scholarships/financial aid.
Type of support: Support to graduates or students
of specific schools; Undergraduate support.
Application information: Application form required.
Application form available on the grantmaker's web
site.
> *Initial approach:* Letter
> *Deadline(s):* July 1
> *Applicants should submit the following:*
>   1) Financial information
>   2) SAR
> *Additional information:* Applicant must submit a
>   copy of the financial aid award letter from the
>   postsecondary institution the student will
>   attend.

Program description:
> *Last Dollar Grant:* The organization provides up to
> $1,200 annually to cover the gap that exists
> between students' resources and the cost of their
> college education. Applicants must apply within
> three years of high school graduation to be eligible
> to participate in the program. An applicant may
> participate in the program for a total of five years,
> based on the initial year of the program. Applicants
> must have demonstrated unmet need.

EIN: 311229135

7167
A. Gordon & Betty H. Imhoff Scholarship Foundation
311 Oakland Park Ave.
Columbus, OH   43214-4123
E-mail: hammondbl@sbcglobal.net

Foundation type: Independent foundation
Purpose: Scholarship to a senior at Shelby Senior
High School, OH, ranked in the top 40 percent of
their academic class.
Financial data: Year ended 05/31/2013. Assets,
$484,664 (M); Expenditures, $20,644; Total
giving, $12,000; Grants to individuals, 3 grants
totaling $12,000 (high: $4,000, low: $4,000).
Type of support: Support to graduates or students
of specific schools.
Application information: Applications accepted.
> *Initial approach:* Letter
> *Deadline(s):* Mar. 30

EIN: 311353990

7168
Independent Pictures
1392 W. 65th St.
Cleveland, OH   44102-2160   (216) 926-6166
FAX: (216) 651-7317;
E-mail: ohioindiefilmfest@juno.com; URL: http://
www.ohiofilms.com

Foundation type: Public charity
Purpose: Support to emerging media artists from
OH working in the field of independent media.
Publications: Newsletter.
Financial data: Year ended 12/31/2011. Assets,
$1,169 (M); Expenditures, $47,231.
Fields of interest: Film/video; Literature; Arts,
artist's services.
Type of support: Fiscal agent/sponsor.
Application information:
> *Initial approach:* Letter

Additional information: See web site for
> additional guidelines.
Program description:
> *Fiscal Agent Sponsorship Program:* The program
> is available to people seeking funding for film and
> other media projects, and provides a conduit to
> dollars otherwise not available to individual artists,
> writers, directors, producers, and filmmakers.

EIN: 341825319

7169
International Door Association Scholarship Foundation
P.O. Box 117
West Milton, OH   45383-0246   (937) 698-8042
Contact: Peggy Sanders, Scholarship Admin.
Additional tel.: (800) 355-4432
E-mail: psanders@longmgt.com; URL: http://
www.doors.org/Content/NavigationMenu/
MemberServices/ScholarshipProgram/
Overview.htm

Foundation type: Public charity
Purpose: Scholarships to full time employees and
their immediate families or immediate family
members of an employee of an IDA Dealer or
Industry member.
Financial data: Year ended 06/30/2012. Assets,
$413,942 (M); Expenditures, $44,072; Total
giving, $39,000.
Fields of interest: Higher education.
Type of support: Employee-related scholarships.
Application information: Applications accepted.
Application form required.
> *Deadline(s):* July 15

EIN: 760708763

7170
Interthyr Research Foundation
534 4th St.
Marietta, OH   45750   (740) 374-8299
Contact: Dr. William Valente, Pres.

Foundation type: Public charity
Purpose: Research grants to individuals and
laboratory organizations to support endocrine
research.
Financial data: Year ended 12/31/2011. Assets,
$182 (M); Expenditures, $92,589; Total giving,
$85,498.
Type of support: Research.
Application information: See web site for additional
information.

EIN: 521366806

7171
Italian American Cultural Foundation
3659 Green Rd., Ste. 124
Beachwood, OH   44122   (800) 592-5373
URL: http://www.iacfcleveland.org/

Foundation type: Independent foundation
Purpose: Scholarships to graduating seniors in
Cleveland, OH, high schools of Italian descent.
Financial data: Year ended 03/31/2013. Assets,
$23,802 (M); Expenditures, $17,355; Total giving,
$15,150; Grants to individuals, 75 grants totaling
$15,150 (high: $1,000, low: $25).
International interests: Italy.
Type of support: Support to graduates or students
of specific schools.
Application information: Applications accepted.
> *Deadline(s):* Mar. 15

Program description:

Essay Competition: The IACF Essay Competition is open to high school students of Italian descent at participating schools, and all students at participating colleges. Students read a text from the foundation's Literary Collection, which has been donated to each school's library. Students prepare an essay discussing how the test influenced their perspective on Italian American heritage. Essays are judged by a Committee of Academics for content, insight, knowledge, style, grammar and punctuation.
EIN: 341213061

7172
James A. Jackson Trust
(formerly James A. Jackson and Beatrice D. Jackson Scholarship Trust)
c/o KeyBank N.A.
4900 Tideman Rd., OH-01-49-015
Brooklyn, OH 44144-2302
Application address: Superintendent of Oxford County School District, 1570 Main St., No. 11, Oxford, ME 04270-3390

Foundation type: Independent foundation
Purpose: Scholarships to graduating high school seniors who are residents of West Paris, ME, to be used in pursuing Bachelor of Arts degrees. One female and one male resident are selected to receive these scholarships.
Financial data: Year ended 06/30/2013. Assets, $1,625,031 (M); Expenditures, $67,861; Total giving, $43,223; Grants to individuals, totaling $43,223.
Type of support: Undergraduate support.
Application information: Applications accepted.
Initial approach: Letter
Deadline(s): None
EIN: 016128257

7173
The Jamestown Area Foundation, Inc.
133 E. Market St.
Xenia, OH 45385-3110

Foundation type: Independent foundation
Purpose: Scholarships to graduating seniors of Greenview High School and Bellefontaine High School, of Jamestown, Green County, OH.
Financial data: Year ended 12/31/2012. Assets, $10,457,772 (M); Expenditures, $664,766; Total giving, $486,855; Grants to individuals, 26 grants totaling $485,855.
Type of support: Undergraduate support.
Application information:
Initial approach: Letter
Deadline(s): Apr.
Additional information: Applications can be obtained from the foundation or from the guidance office at the Greenview and Bellefontaine high schools.
EIN: 311148328

7174
Jefferson Memorial Foundation
c/o Huntington National Bank
7 Easton Oval
Columbus, OH 43219-6010

Foundation type: Independent foundation
Purpose: Scholarships to high school graduates of Jefferson, OH pursuing higher education.
Financial data: Year ended 12/31/2012. Assets, $243,373 (M); Expenditures, $22,563; Total

giving, $12,700; Grants to individuals, 4 grants totaling $4,000 (high: $1,000, low: $1,000).
Fields of interest: Higher education.
Type of support: Scholarships—to individuals.
Application information: Applications accepted.
Additional information: Students should contact their high school guidance counselors for application or contact the foundation for additional information.
EIN: 346968316

7175
Lela McGuire Jeffery Scholarship Fund Trust
c/o Hyman and Hyman, Ltd.
123 N. Main St.
Paulding, OH 45879-1237
Contact: David A. Hyman
E-mail: dahyman@alltel.net

Foundation type: Operating foundation
Purpose: Scholarships to graduates of Paulding High School, OH.
Financial data: Year ended 12/31/2011. Assets, $308,194 (M); Expenditures, $8,326; Total giving, $6,500; Grants to individuals, 11 grants totaling $6,500 (high: $1,000, low: $300).
Type of support: Support to graduates or students of specific schools.
Application information: Applications accepted. Application form required.
Initial approach: Letter
Deadline(s): Mar. 31
EIN: 166539194

7176
The Robert H. Jentes Scholarship Fund
106 S. Main St., Ste. 16
Akron, OH 44308 (330) 498-1558
Application address: First Merit Bank, N.A., 4481 Munson St. N.W., Canton, OH 44718

Foundation type: Independent foundation
Purpose: Scholarships to students attending Wittenberg College in Springfield, OH, and Malone College in Canton, OH. Scholarships also to children of former employees of Fleming Foods, Co., OH.
Financial data: Year ended 12/31/2012. Assets, $933,087 (M); Expenditures, $54,058; Total giving, $39,000.
Type of support: Support to graduates or students of specific schools; Undergraduate support.
Application information: Applications accepted. Application form required.
Initial approach: Letter
Copies of proposal: 1
Deadline(s): Apr. 1
Applicants should submit the following:
1) Transcripts
2) FAFSA
EIN: 346779406

7177
Jewish Family Service Association of Cleveland
3659 S. Green Rd., Ste. 322
Beachwood, OH 44122-5715 (216) 504-2600
URL: http://www.jfsa-cleveland.org

Foundation type: Public charity
Purpose: Scholarships and interest free loans to Jewish undergraduate and graduate students in the greater Cleveland, OH, area to partially support their

studies. Assistance also to individuals of northeast, OH, with chronic mental disabilities, including mental retardation, severe mental illness, and brain injury.
Publications: Annual report.
Financial data: Year ended 06/30/2011. Assets, $16,289,285 (M); Expenditures, $17,899,023; Total giving, $1,114,065; Grants to individuals, totaling $1,114,065.
Fields of interest: Higher education; Jewish agencies & synagogues; Disabilities, people with; Mentally disabled.
Type of support: Scholarships—to individuals; Student loans—to individuals; Grants for special needs.
Application information: Applications accepted. Application form required.
Initial approach: Telephone
Additional information: Application must include $25 non-refundable fee. See web site for a complete listing of scholarship programs.
Program descriptions:
Eleanor Gerson Award: This is awarded to a needy student who has demonstrated significant academic achievement and community involvement. Awards are also available for graduate students in the field of social work.
Frank Joseph Garron Memorial Scholarship: This is awarded to a full-time graduate or undergraduate student, and can be renewed in competition with others.
Helen and Morris Zupnick Scholarship: This is awarded to an Orthodox Jewish student with defined career goals and high academic credentials.
Howard S. Young Scholarship: This renewable award is given to an academically superior student who is attending Case Western Reserve University; preference will be given to engineering majors.
Irving I. Stone Support Foundation: This is awarded to students attending Yeshiva University or approved seminary/Yeshiva study in Israel.
Jack W. and Shirley Berger Scholarship: This award is given to a scholastically superior high school senior (with a minimum GPA of 3.5) who is seeking a secular education and who agrees to take a course in comparative religion; the award is renewable for additional years if a 3.0 GPA is maintained. This award is non-sectarian in nature.
Jaffe Scholarship: This award is presented to a senior in high school who has demonstrated commitment to volunteerism in the Jewish and general communities.
Morris Abrams Award in International Relations: This non-sectarian award is open to Ph.D. candidates at a graduate school of international affairs, political science, or journalism. Students must be nominated by their department head.
Mrs. Bert Keller Award: This is awarded to a freshman or graduate student pursuing a career in medicine.
Saltzman Scholarship: This is a renewable award given to an undergraduate or graduate student focused on a specific career goal, preferably in the health care field; eligible students must demonstrate significant community service.
Solomon and Jennie Hurvitz Scholarship: This scholarship is given to a scholastically superior, unmarried Jewish student attending a secular college in Ohio.
Sophie and Henry Billys Scholarship: This scholarship is awarded to a full-time student who may not qualify for an academic scholarship but who has overcome a major obstacle in his/her life.
Stanley and Enid Rothenfeld Memorial Scholarship: This is awarded to a non-traditional needy Jewish student who has a minimum GPA of 3.0.

William Wortzman Family Education Fund: This is awarded to a financially-disadvantaged student with a minimum GPA of 3.0; preference will be given to students seeking business or law degrees.
EIN: 340714441

7178
Jewish Federation of Cincinnati
8499 Ridge Rd.
Cincinnati, OH   45236-1300   (513) 985-1500
Contact: Andrew Berger, Pres.
FAX: (513) 985-1503; E-mail: info@jfedcin.org;
URL: http://www.jewishcincinnati.org

Foundation type: Public charity
Purpose: Offers young Jewish people from Cincinnati, OH up to $11,500 for two separate Israel travel opportunities, one for up to $6,500 in high school and another for up to $5,000 post-high school.
Publications: Application guidelines; Financial statement; Grants list.
Financial data: Year ended 12/31/2011. Assets, $88,907,291 (M); Expenditures, $10,592,738; Total giving, $7,533,509; Grants to individuals, totaling $250,313.
Fields of interest: Jewish agencies & synagogues.
Type of support: Travel awards.
Application information: Applications accepted. Application form required. Application form available on the grantmaker's web site.
   Initial approach: Letter or e-mail
   Deadline(s): Applications are accepted year-round, but application must be submitted at least two months before payment is due to the trip provider.
EIN: 310537174

7179
The Johnson Foundation, Inc.
5768 Fairridge Ln.
Hamilton, OH   45011

Foundation type: Independent foundation
Purpose: Grants to financially needy students for the purchase of textbooks.
Financial data: Year ended 12/31/2012. Assets, $3,526 (M); Expenditures, $6,012; Total giving, $0.
Type of support: Grants to individuals; Foreign applicants.
Application information: Applications accepted. Application form required.
   Deadline(s): Aug. 1 preceding senior year
EIN: 943144095

7180
Lillian M. Jones Memorial Foundation
c/o PNC Bank, N.A.
P.O. Box 94651
Cleveland, OH   44101-4651

Foundation type: Independent foundation
Purpose: Scholarships to graduating high school seniors of Ohio County, KY pursuing higher education.
Financial data: Year ended 12/31/2012. Assets, $194,951 (M); Expenditures, $10,394; Total giving, $7,750.
Fields of interest: Higher education.
Type of support: Scholarships—to individuals.
Application information: Applications accepted.
   Additional information: Students should contact their guidance counselor for application

information, or contact the foundation for additional guidelines.
EIN: 616022770

7181
L. Kanhofer Trust
(also known as Lee McKinney Scholarship Trust)
c/o P.N.C. Bank, N.A.
P.O. Box 94651
Cleveland, OH   44101-4651
Application address: c/o Titusville Area High School, Attn.: Guidance Ctr., 302 E. Walnut St., Titusville, PA 16354-1953, tel.: (814) 827-9687

Foundation type: Independent foundation
Purpose: Scholarships to graduates of Titusville Area High School, PA, for undergraduate education at U.S. universities and colleges.
Financial data: Year ended 12/31/2010. Assets, $0 (M); Expenditures, $194,456; Total giving, $189,336.
Type of support: Support to graduates or students of specific schools; Undergraduate support.
Application information: Applications accepted. Application form required.
   Deadline(s): Mar. 1
   Additional information: Contact guidance office for application forms.
EIN: 256227057

7182
Kappa Kappa Gamma Foundation
530 E. Town St.
P.O. Box 38
Columbus, OH   43215-4820   (614) 228-6515
Contact: Beth Burkes, Exec. Dir.
FAX: (614) 228-6303; E-mail: foundation@kkg.org;
Toll-free tel.: (866) KKG-1870; Mailing address:
P.O. Box 38, Columbus, OH 43216-0038;
URL: https://www.kappakappagamma.org/kappa/foundation.aspx?id=264

Foundation type: Public charity
Purpose: Scholarships to qualified Kappas for higher education, and financial assistance to members who are in need.
Publications: Newsletter.
Financial data: Year ended 06/30/2012. Assets, $35,841,940 (M); Expenditures, $2,585,168; Total giving, $1,041,925; Grants to individuals, totaling $668,896.
Fields of interest: Higher education; Students, sororities/fraternities.
Type of support: Undergraduate support.
Application information: Application form required. Application form available on the grantmaker's web site.
   Deadline(s): Feb. 1 for Scholarships
   Applicants should submit the following:
     1) Financial information
     2) Letter(s) of recommendation
     3) Transcripts
     4) Essay
Program descriptions:
   Emergency Assistance Grants: Grants, ranging from $500 to $1,000, are available during the school year to Kappa collegians who face a sudden financial emergency. These grants are confidential. Associate members are not eligible. A recipient must be a full-time student and active in the chapter. A recipient must also remain in school the term following receipt of the grant or refund the award to the foundation.
   Marisol Scholarship: This one time scholarship is awarded to undergraduate members of Kappa Kappa Gamma and provides up to 75 percent of the

costs of the applicant's tuition, fees, books, room and board for one year.
EIN: 316049792

7183
Kati's Hope Foundation for Mesothelioma Research & Support
c/o Kathleen M. Lopresti
27981 N. Woodland Rd.
Cleveland, OH   44124-4518
Application address: P.O. Box 24693, Cleveland, OH 44124-0693

Foundation type: Public charity
Purpose: Financial assistance to individuals who have been diagnosed and are living with mesothelioma. Grants to support medical research to find a cure for mesothelioma.
Financial data: Year ended 12/31/2011. Assets, $70,272 (M); Expenditures, $4,990; Total giving, $3,375; Grants to individuals, 2 grants totaling $3,375. Subtotal for grants to individuals: 2 grants totaling $3,375 (high: $2,000, low: $1,375).
Fields of interest: Cancer research; Lung research.
Type of support: Research; Grants to individuals.
Application information:
   Initial approach: Letter
EIN: 412180901

7184
The Kauffman Family Foundation Inc.
3685 Co. Rd. 25-A
Sidney, OH   45365-9183   (937) 492-1679
Contact: Almeda Jean Wooddell, Pres.

Foundation type: Independent foundation
Purpose: Scholarships to residents of Shelby County, OH.
Financial data: Year ended 12/31/2012. Assets, $308,189 (M); Expenditures, $17,961; Total giving, $16,000.
Type of support: Undergraduate support.
Application information:
   Initial approach: Letter
   Additional information: Contact foundation for eligibility criteria.
EIN: 311621044

7185
Melvin G. & Mary F. Keller Scholarship Fund
c/o PNC Bank, N.A.
P.O. Box 94651
Cleveland, OH   44101-4651   (412) 768-8538
Contact: John Montoya
Application address: 2 PNC Plz., 7th Fl., 620 Liberty Ave., Pittsburgh, PA 15222; URL: http://www.pnc.com

Foundation type: Independent foundation
Purpose: Scholarships to graduates of the Warren County School District, PA, who have resided in Warren County and are pursuing careers in public school teaching.
Financial data: Year ended 12/31/2012. Assets, $1,085,001 (M); Expenditures, $57,204; Total giving, $42,000.
Fields of interest: Teacher school/education.
Type of support: Support to graduates or students of specific schools; Undergraduate support.
Application information: Applications accepted. Application form required.
   Deadline(s): Apr. 30

Additional information: Application forms available upon request.
EIN: 256344325

7186
Edgar E. Kessel Scholarship Fund
(formerly Edgar E. Kessel Trust)
c/o KeyBank, N.A.
4900 Tiedman Rd., OH-01-49-0150
Brooklyn, OH 44144-2302 (216) 689-0416
Contact: Agnes Marountas
Application address: c/o KeyBank N.A., 127 Public Sq., 16th Fl., Cleveland, OH 44114

Foundation type: Independent foundation
Purpose: Scholarships to worthy high school graduates of Euclid public schools, OH for postsecondary education.
Financial data: Year ended 09/30/2013. Assets, $458,086 (M); Expenditures, $28,272; Total giving, $22,000; Grants to individuals, 15 grants totaling $22,000 (high: $2,500, low: $1,000).
Fields of interest: Higher education; Scholarships/financial aid.
Type of support: Scholarships—to individuals; Support to graduates or students of specific schools; Undergraduate support.
Application information: Application form required.
   Send request by: Mail
   Additional information: Preference is given to graduates of public schools in Euclid, OH, though students from other districts may apply.
EIN: 346505938

7187
Ray T. Kest Old Newsboys Goodfellow Memorial Scholarship Fund
2257 Applewood Dr.
Toledo, OH 43615-2907 (419) 536-0873
Contact: Ron Shnider, Chair.
Application address: 3752 Fairwood Dr., Sylvania OH 43560

Foundation type: Operating foundation
Purpose: Scholarships to financially needy students in the Toledo, OH, area.
Financial data: Year ended 05/31/2013. Assets, $145,331 (M); Expenditures, $48,011; Total giving, $39,087; Grants to individuals, 14 grants totaling $39,087 (high: $5,000, low: $96).
Type of support: Scholarships—to individuals.
Application information: Application form required.
   Deadline(s): Oct. 31
EIN: 341668082

7188
KeyBank Community Trust
(formerly Northeastern New York Community Trust)
c/o Keybank, N.A.
4900 Tiedeman, OH-01-49-0150
Brooklyn, OH 44144-2302
*Application address:*c/o Keybank N.A, 66 S Pearl st. Albany, NY 12207

Foundation type: Independent foundation
Purpose: Scholarships to residents of northeastern NY who are children of employees of Albany or state agencies, or KeyCorp and its subsidiaries.
Financial data: Year ended 12/31/2012. Assets, $2,234,274 (M); Expenditures, $117,301; Total giving, $95,000.
Fields of interest: Higher education.
Type of support: Employee-related scholarships.

Application information:
   Initial approach: Letter
   Deadline(s): Nov.
   EIN: 146030063

7189
Kibble Foundation
P.O. Box 1558, Dept. EA4E86
Columbus, OH 43216-1558

Foundation type: Independent foundation
Purpose: Scholarships only to graduates of Meigs County, OH, high schools pursuing four-year degrees or technical degrees on a full-time basis.
Financial data: Year ended 12/31/2012. Assets, $3,425,050 (M); Expenditures, $209,359; Total giving, $168,891.
Fields of interest: Vocational education.
Type of support: Support to graduates or students of specific schools; Technical education support; Undergraduate support.
Application information: Applications not accepted.
   Additional information: Unsolicited requests for funds not considered or acknowledged.
   EIN: 316175971

7190
Kidney Foundation of Ohio, Inc.
2831 Prospect Ave.
Cleveland, OH 44115-2606 (216) 771-2700
Contact: Michael F. Needham, Pres. and C.E.O.
FAX: (216) 771-5114; E-mail: kfolake@kfohio.org; E-mail for Michael F. Needham: mneedham@kfohio.org; URL: http://www.kfohio.org

Foundation type: Public charity
Purpose: Grants to researchers at institutions in the Cleveland, OH area for the study, prevention, and treatment of kidney diseases. Financial assistance to kidney patients in Northeast, OH in need of medication, transportation and other necessary items.
Financial data: Year ended 12/31/2011. Assets, $2,545,713 (M); Expenditures, $703,437; Total giving, $120,249; Grants to individuals, totaling $120,249.
Fields of interest: Kidney diseases; Economically disadvantaged.
Type of support: Research; Grants for special needs.
Application information: Contact the foundation for additional guidelines.
   EIN: 340827748

7191
Kids In Need Foundation
(formerly SHOPA Kids In Need Foundation)
3055 Kettering Blvd., Ste. 119
Dayton, OH 45439-1900 (937) 296-1230
Contact: Dave Smith, Exec. Dir.
E-mail: info@kinf.org; Toll-free tel.: (800) 854-7467; E-mail for Dave Smith: dave.smith@kinf.org; URL: http://www.kinf.org

Foundation type: Public charity
Purpose: Grants to certified K-12 teachers for innovative classroom projects at public, private, charter, or parochial schools within the U.S.
Publications: Application guidelines; Annual report; Grants list; Informational brochure; Newsletter.
Financial data: Year ended 12/31/2011. Assets, $843,767 (M); Expenditures, $48,059,195; Total giving, $210,126; Grants to individuals, totaling $210,126.
Fields of interest: Elementary/secondary education.
Type of support: Project support.
Application information: Applications accepted. Application form required. Application form available on the grantmaker's web site.
   Initial approach: E-mail or fax
   Send request by: Online
   Copies of proposal: 1
   Deadline(s): Sept. 30
   Final notification: Recipients notified by Dec. 1
   Additional information: Pre-school and Home School are not funded.
Program description:
   Kids In Need Teacher Grants: The grants provide K-12 educators with funding to provide innovative learning opportunities for their students. Teacher grant awards range from $100 to $500 each and are used to finance creative classroom projects. Typically, 300 to 600 grants are awarded each year.
   EIN: 311437587

7192
Alice Kindler Scholarship Fund
(formerly Alice Kindler Charitable Fund)
3040 West Point Rd.
Lancaster, OH 43130-8640 (740) 569-3040
Contact: William J. Sitterley, Tr.
URL: http://fairfieldcountyscholarships.com/

Foundation type: Independent foundation
Purpose: Scholarships to graduating seniors of all high schools of Fairfield or Hocking County, OH for postsecondary education at specific colleges or universities in OH.
Financial data: Year ended 05/31/2013. Assets, $1,190,508 (M); Expenditures, $54,562; Total giving, $45,000; Grants to individuals, 8 grants totaling $45,000 (high: $6,000, low: $3,000).
Fields of interest: Higher education; Scholarships/financial aid.
Type of support: Support to graduates or students of specific schools; Technical education support; Undergraduate support.
Application information: Applications accepted. Application form required. Application form available on the grantmaker's web site. Interview required.
   Send request by: Mail
   Deadline(s): Mar. 15
   Applicants should submit the following:
      1) ACT
      2) Class rank
      3) SAT
      4) GPA
      5) Financial information
      6) Transcripts
      7) Photograph
   Additional information: See web site for a listing of four year colleges and universities.
Program description:
   Alice Kindler Scholarship: Scholarships to graduating seniors must be residents of Fairfield or Hocking County for a minimum of three years, and must have attended a high school in Fairfield County the last three years of high school, including graduation. Applicant must demonstrate financial need and agree to attend one of the named four year OH colleges or universities.
   EIN: 311337515

7193
Betty M. Kirkpatrick Scholarship Fund Trust

(also known as Betty Kirkpatrick Scholarship Fund)
300 High St.
Hamilton, OH   45011   (513) 867-4818

Foundation type: Independent foundation
Purpose: Scholarships to graduates of either Switzerland County High School, Vevay, IN or Rising Sun High School, IN, who have completed at least one year at an accredited nursing school.
Financial data: Year ended 12/31/2012. Assets, $118,844 (M); Expenditures, $6,834; Total giving, $4,187; Grant to an individual, 1 grant totaling $4,187.
Fields of interest: Nursing school/education.
Type of support: Support to graduates or students of specific schools.
Application information: Applications accepted. Application form required.
  Initial approach: Letter
  Deadline(s): July 31
  Additional information: Application should include a transcript, a signed letter briefly describing applicant need for the scholarship, plans for the future and career. Also, describe academic and other accomplishments.
EIN: 356548300

7194
Kirtland Athletic Boosters Scholarship Fund Inc.

5000 E. 345th St.
Willoughby, OH   44094-4280   (440) 942-3900
Contact: Keith Martinet, Tr.

Foundation type: Independent foundation
Purpose: Scholarships to graduating seniors of Kirtland High School, OH who are in the athletic program.
Financial data: Year ended 12/31/2011. Assets, $81,168 (M); Expenditures, $11,991; Total giving, $8,000; Grants to individuals, 7 grants totaling $8,000 (high: $2,000, low: $750).
Fields of interest: Higher education; Athletics/sports, school programs.
Type of support: Support to graduates or students of specific schools.
Application information: Applications accepted. Application form required.
  Deadline(s): Jan.
  Additional information: Selection is based on overall scholastic achievement, co-curricular activities and need.
EIN: 340971202

7195
Clara Louise Kiser Memorial Fund

c/o PNC Bank, N.A.
P.O. Box 94651
Cleveland, OH   44101-4651   (814) 677-5085
Application address: c/o Stephen P. Kosak, P.O. Box 374, Oil City, PA 16301, tel.: (814) 677-5085

Foundation type: Independent foundation
Purpose: Scholarships to graduating seniors of Clarion High School, PA.
Financial data: Year ended 12/31/2012. Assets, $661,624 (M); Expenditures, $23,233; Total giving, $15,133.
Type of support: Support to graduates or students of specific schools; Undergraduate support.
Application information: Application form required.
  Deadline(s): Mar. 15

Additional information: Application must include a letter outlining financial need and college CSS profile.
EIN: 256191759

7196
John Anson Kittridge Educational Fund Trust

c/o KeyBank N.A.
4900 Tiedeman Rd., OH-01-49-0150
Brooklyn, OH   44144-2302   (207) 623-5624
Contact: John Mulford
Application address: 286 Water St., Augusta, ME 04330, tel.: (207) 623-562

Foundation type: Independent foundation
Purpose: Grants awarded to artists and scholars for travel to conferences, research, and other artistic or scholarly projects. No scholarships are awarded.
Financial data: Year ended 04/30/2013. Assets, $2,172,636 (M); Expenditures, $112,929; Total giving, $90,175; Grants to individuals, 2 grants totaling $90,175 (high: $10,000, low: $6,000).
Fields of interest: Research; Humanities; Arts, artist's services; Arts.
Type of support: Travel grants.
Application information: Applications accepted.
  Initial approach: Letter
  Deadline(s): None
  Additional information: Application must include purpose, amount requested, period of funding, and supporting letters.
EIN: 016007180

7197
Kiwanis Club of Westshore

(formerly Kiwanis Scholarship Fund)
c/o PNC Bank, N.A.
P.O. Box 94651
Cleveland, OH   44101-4651

Foundation type: Independent foundation
Purpose: Scholarships to young single men graduating from high schools in the City of Lakewood, OH, to study government, civil affairs, foreign languages, public relations, the humanities, or related fields at four-year colleges or universities.
Financial data: Year ended 12/31/2012. Assets, $314,618 (M); Expenditures, $16,300; Total giving, $12,000; Grant to an individual, 1 grant totaling $12,000.
Fields of interest: Humanities; Language (foreign); Political science; Research; Young adults, male.
Type of support: Support to graduates or students of specific schools; Undergraduate support.
Application information: Application form required.
  Deadline(s): Mar.
  Additional information: Completed application forms should be returned to the school's guidance office.
EIN: 346902315

7198
Paul and Alma Klinger Scholarship Trust

c/o PNC Bank N.A.
P.O. Box 94651
Cleveland, OH   44101-4651

Foundation type: Independent foundation
Purpose: Scholarships to students who are members of the Martin Luther Lutheran Church in Youngstown, OH.
Financial data: Year ended 12/31/2012. Assets, $126,098 (M); Expenditures, $5,925; Total giving, $4,000.

Fields of interest: Higher education.
Type of support: Scholarships—to individuals.
Application information: Application form required.
  Initial approach: Letter or telephone
  Additional information: Students must have been members of the Church for the immediate four years preceding the date of submission of the application. The applicant must maintain a GPA of 2.0 on a 4.0 scale.
EIN: 341902577

7199
John S. Knight Memorial Journalism Fund Corp.

4900 Tiedeman Rd., OH-01-49-0150
Brooklyn, OH   44144-2302   (330) 996-3514
Contact: Michael Douglas, Treas.
Application address: c/o Akron Beacon Journal, 44 E. Exchange St., P.O. Box 640, Akron, OH 44309-0640

Foundation type: Independent foundation
Purpose: Scholarship to college students pursuing a degree in journalism, photojournalism, broadcasting or public relations, who either live or attend a college in Summit, Portage, Stark, Medina or Wayne counties, Ohio.
Financial data: Year ended 12/31/2012. Assets, $362,748 (M); Expenditures, $26,436; Total giving, $19,679; Grants to individuals, 10 grants totaling $19,679 (high: $3,000, low: $750).
Fields of interest: Print publishing.
Type of support: Undergraduate support.
Application information:
  Deadline(s): Mar. 2
EIN: 341820183

7200
Leonora H. Knowles Trust B

c/o KeyBank N.A.
4900 Tiedeman Rd., OH-01-49-0150
Brooklyn, OH   44144-2302

Foundation type: Independent foundation
Purpose: Scholarships to financially needy residents of Hancock and Oxford counties, ME, for postsecondary education, including nursing.
Financial data: Year ended 12/31/2012. Assets, $5,796,123 (M); Expenditures, $151,721; Total giving, $76,230.
Fields of interest: Nursing school/education.
Type of support: Undergraduate support.
Application information: Applications not accepted.
  Additional information: Unsolicited requests for funds not considered or acknowledged.
EIN: 222789214

7201
Lake Erie Marine Trades Association Educational Foundation, Inc.

1269 Bassett Rd.
Westlake, OH   44145-1116   (440) 899-5009

Foundation type: Independent foundation
Purpose: Grants to residents of OH for educational purposes in the field of recreational boating.
Financial data: Year ended 04/30/2012. Assets, $16,112 (M); Expenditures, $12,000; Total giving, $12,000; Grants to individuals, 17 grants totaling $12,000 (high: $1,000, low: $250).
Fields of interest: Education; Recreation.
Type of support: Grants to individuals.

Application information: Application form required.
Initial approach: Letter
EIN: 341835791

7202
The Lakeland Foundation
c/o Lakeland Community College
7700 Clocktower Dr.
Kirtland, OH 44094-5198 (440) 525-7094
FAX: (440) 525-7601;
E-mail: lccfoundation@lakelandcc.edu; Toll-free
tel.: (800) 598-8520; E-mail For Bob Cahen:
bcahen@lakelandcc.edu; URL: http://
www.lakelandfoundation.com

Foundation type: Public charity
Purpose: Scholarships to students of Lakeland
Community College, OH pursuing higher education.
Teaching awards for faculty development and
teaching enhancement programs.
Financial data: Year ended 06/30/2012. Assets,
$3,850,069 (M); Expenditures, $741,096; Total
giving, $582,033; Grants to individuals, totaling
$347,650.
Fields of interest: Higher education.
Type of support: Scholarships—to individuals;
Support to graduates or students of specific
schools.
Application information: Applications accepted.
Application form required.
Additional information: Contact the foundation for
additional guidlines.
EIN: 341369714

7203
The LAM Foundation
4015 Executive Park Dr., Ste. 320
Cincinnati, OH 45241-4015 (513) 777-6889
Contact: Leslie Sullivan-Stacey, Pres. and C.E.O.
FAX: (513) 777-4109; E-mail: lam@one.net;
URL: http://www.thelamfoundation.org

Foundation type: Public charity
Purpose: Awards, fellowships and grants to
investigators for research on
lymphangioleiomyomatosis (LAM) to develop better
methods of prevention, diagnosis and treatment of
the disease.
Financial data: Year ended 12/31/2011. Assets,
$1,847,920 (M); Expenditures, $1,043,122; Total
giving, $302,500.
Fields of interest: Medical research; Immunology
research.
Type of support: Research; Postdoctoral support.
Application information: Application form required.
Application form available on the grantmaker's web
site.
Send request by: E-mail
Deadline(s): Sept. 30
Final notification: Applicants will be notified by
Jan. 2
Program descriptions:
Established Investigator Awards: Awards up to
$50,000 to enable faculty-level investigators (M.D.
or Ph.D.) to gather sufficient preliminary data to
apply for more substantial funding from federal
agencies.
Pilot Projects Awards: Awards up to $25,000 to
faculty-level investigators or doctoral-level
investigators (M.D. or Ph.D.) to gather sufficient
preliminary data for more substantial LAM funding.
Post Doctoral Fellowships: Awards up to $50,000
to support postdoctoral-level investigators (M.D. or
Ph.D.) who will be performing LAM research in the

laboratory of an established scientist who is an
expert in areas which are directly pertinent to LAM.
EIN: 311438001

7204
Hypoliet Lapeer Testamentary Trust
c/o PNC Bank, N.A.
P.O. Box 94651
Cleveland, OH 44101 (574) 259-5257
Contact: Carl Loesch
Application address: c/o Marian High School,
Mishawaka, IN 46544, Tel.:(574) 259-5257

Foundation type: Independent foundation
Purpose: Scholarships to Roman Catholic
graduates of Marian High School, Mishawaka, IN,
and St. Joseph High School, South Bend, IN, who
have either Belgian or French ancestry and who plan
to study engineering at Notre Dame University, IN,
or Purdue University, IN.
Financial data: Year ended 12/31/2011. Assets,
$386,675 (M); Expenditures, $21,708; Total
giving, $16,000.
Fields of interest: Engineering school/education;
Catholic agencies & churches.
International interests: Belgium; France.
Type of support: Support to graduates or students
of specific schools; Undergraduate support.
Application information: Application form required.
Initial approach: Letter
Additional information: Forms available from
principal at application address.
EIN: 356508488

7205
William C. & Mildred K. Lehman
Charitable Trust
3040 W. Pt. Rd. S.E.
Lancaster, OH 43130-8640 (740) 569-3040
Contact: William J. Sitterley, Tr.
E-mail: info@sitterleyscholarshiptrusts.com;
URL: http://www.fairfieldcountyscholarships.com

Foundation type: Independent foundation
Purpose: Scholarships to residents of Hocking
County, OH.
Financial data: Year ended 05/31/2013. Assets,
$3,607,597 (M); Expenditures, $171,675; Total
giving, $147,000.
Type of support: Undergraduate support.
Application information: Applications accepted.
Application form required.
Initial approach: Letter
Deadline(s): Mar. 15
Additional information: Contact foundation for
eligibility criteria.
EIN: 311613162

7206
Margaret & Irwin Lesher Foundation
c/o PNC Bank N.A.
P.O. Box 94651
Cleveland, OH 44101-4651 (412) 768-8538
Contact: John Montoya
Application address: 2 PNC Plz., 7th Fl., 620 Liberty
Ave., Pittsburgh, PA 15222

Foundation type: Independent foundation
Purpose: Scholarships to financially needy
graduates of Union Joint High School, PA for
postsecondary education.
Publications: Application guidelines.
Financial data: Year ended 12/31/2012. Assets,
$2,882,425 (M); Expenditures, $98,121; Total
giving, $63,400.

Fields of interest: Vocational education,
post-secondary; Higher education.
Type of support: Support to graduates or students
of specific schools; Undergraduate support.
Application information: Applications accepted.
Application form required.
Initial approach: Letter
Deadline(s): Mar. 15 for first time applicants,
May 20 for renewals
Applicants should submit the following:
1) SAR
2) Class rank
3) Transcripts
4) SAT
Additional information: Application should also
include a signed copy of parents income tax
form.
EIN: 256067843

7207
Marvin Lewis Community Fund
700 W. Pete Rose Way, Ste. 37
Cincinnati, OH 45203-1892 (513) 381-5437
Contact: Barbara Dundee, Exec. Dir.
Scholarship e-mail: scholarship@fuse.net
FAX: (513) 381-5439;
E-mail: bdundee@marvinlewis.org; URL: http://
www.marvinlewis.org

Foundation type: Public charity
Purpose: Scholarships to male and female student
athletes who are residents of greater Cincinnati, OH
for higher education.
Financial data: Year ended 12/31/2011. Assets,
$551,665 (M); Expenditures, $903,785; Total
giving, $159,079; Grants to individuals, totaling
$147,104.
Fields of interest: Athletics/sports, school
programs; Recreation.
Type of support: Scholarships—to individuals.
Application information: Applications accepted.
Application form required.
Send request by: Online
Deadline(s): Apr. 30
Applicants should submit the following:
1) Transcripts
2) SAR
3) Resume
4) Financial information
5) Essay
Additional information: See web site for a listing
of various scholarships and additional
application guidelines.
EIN: 202704690

7208
Jane Lois Ley Trust
P.O. Box 225
Dover, OH 44622-0225

Foundation type: Independent foundation
Purpose: Scholarship to graduates of Dover High
School, Ohio.
Financial data: Year ended 07/31/2013. Assets,
$370,436 (M); Expenditures, $12,066; Total
giving, $11,000; Grants to individuals, 9 grants
totaling $11,000 (high: $3,000, low: $1,000).
Type of support: Scholarships—to individuals;
Support to graduates or students of specific
schools.
Application information: Applications not
accepted.
Additional information: Unsolicited requests for
funds not considered or acknowledged.
EIN: 916540877

7209
Licking County Foundation
30 N. Second St.
P.O. Box 4212
Newark, OH   43058-4212   (740) 349-3863
Contact: Connie Hawk, Dir.
Scholarship inquiry e-mail:
scholarships@thelcfoundation.org
FAX: (740) 322-6260;
E-mail: lcf@thelcfoundation.org; URL: http://
www.thelcfoundation.org

Foundation type: Community foundation
Purpose: Scholarships to graduating high school
seniors and current college students from Licking
County, OH. Grants for public or parochial school
teachers from Newark or Licking County to travel
outside the United State to broaden their
knowledge.
Publications: Application guidelines; Annual report;
Informational brochure; Newsletter.
Financial data: Year ended 12/31/2011. Assets,
$48,755,346 (M); Expenditures, $3,031,979;
Total giving, $2,186,126. Scholarships—to
individuals amount not specified.
Fields of interest: Elementary school/education;
Secondary school/education; Vocational
education; Higher education; Medical school/
education; Nursing school/education; Teacher
school/education; Scholarships/financial aid.
Type of support: Scholarships—to individuals;
Support to graduates or students of specific
schools; Awards/prizes; Graduate support;
Undergraduate support; Travel grants.
Application information: Applications accepted.
Application form required. Application form
available on the grantmaker's web site.
> *Send request by:* On-line
> *Copies of proposal:* 1
> *Deadline(s):* Mar. 5
> *Final notification:* Applicants notified in late June
> *Applicants should submit the following:*
>   1) Transcripts
>   2) FAFSA
>   3) SAR
>   4) Resume
>   5) Essay
> *Additional information:* See web site for
>   application forms, additional application
>   information and complete listing of
>   scholarship funds.
Program descriptions:
Leaders for Learning Grants: The goals for this
program are to: 1) identify and recognize teachers
who exemplify excellence in teaching; 2) provide
opportunities for teachers to participate in
professional growth activities and to support their
classroom activities; and 3) encourage teachers
from the participating districts to join together to
enhance the quality of education in the community.
Each public school district in Licking County may
select one teacher.
Scholarships: The foundation administers
several scholarship funds. Scholarships are
awarded primarily on the basis of financial need and
scholastic achievement. Recipients may attend
undergraduate, graduate, or technical/vocational
schools. Scholarships may be specific as to high
school or college attendance and/or course of
study.
Tibbie Leslie Travel Grants: The Tibbie Leslie
Travel Grant provides stipends of up to $2,000
each for travel outside the continental United
States. The grants will be awarded to teachers and
Newark High School graduating seniors who plan
foreign travel to broaden their experience and
knowledge in their particular field of interest.
EIN: 316018618

7210
James F. Lincoln Arc Welding Foundation
22801 St. Clair Ave.
Cleveland, OH   44117-1199   (216) 481-4300
Application address: P.O. Box 17188, Cleveland, OH
44117-9949; URL: http://www.jflf.org

Foundation type: Operating foundation
Purpose: Awards to high school, undergraduate,
and graduate students, for projects or papers
dealing with arc welding.
Publications: Application guidelines; Informational
brochure (including application guidelines).
Financial data: Year ended 12/31/2012. Assets,
$769,981 (M); Expenditures, $187,740; Total
giving, $83,171.
Fields of interest: Engineering.
Type of support: Awards/prizes; Graduate support;
Precollege support; Undergraduate support.
Application information: Applications accepted.
Application form required. Application form
available on the grantmaker's web site.
> *Send request by:* Mail or online
> *Deadline(s):* June 30 for Divisions I, II and IV
>   awards, Sept. 30 for Division III awards
Program descriptions:
Ag Proficiency Award: The foundation, in
collaboration with the National Future Farmers of
America, awards one $1,000 grant to the individual
who demonstrates outstanding achievement in
agribusiness gained through the establishment of
new business, working for an existing company, or
other hands-on-career experience.
Arc Welding Awards: The foundation makes
awards of cash and welding equipment to students
at various educational levels for projects or papers
relating to design or uses of arc welding. Division I
awards are for high school students age 18 and
under. Division II awards are for career students
ages 19 and over. Division III awards are for Skills
U.S.A. students competing in statewide or national
contests. Division IV awards are for four year
engineering students and their reports on design,
engineering, or fabrication problems relating to any
type of building, bridge, or other generally stationary
structure. Division X awards are for international
career students ages 17 and over. The foundation
is also introducing a new division dedicated to
Associate degree programs or an equivalent that
wish to enter a welding or manufacturing paper.
EIN: 346553433

7211
Douglas W. Lincoln Scholarship
c/o KeyBank N.A.
4900 Tiedeman Rd. OH-01-49-0150
Brooklyn, OH   44144-2302
Appplication Address: c/o Albany High School,
Attn: Principal, 700 Washington Ave., Albany, NY
12203

Foundation type: Independent foundation
Purpose: Scholarships to students of Albany High
School, NY for continuing education at accredited
colleges or universities.
Financial data: Year ended 02/28/2013. Assets,
$86,522 (M); Expenditures, $5,143; Total giving,
$4,000; Grants to individuals, 2 grants totaling
$4,000 (high: $3,000, low: $1,000).
Fields of interest: Higher education.
Type of support: Support to graduates or students
of specific schools.
Application information: Applications accepted.
Application form required.
> *Deadline(s):* May 3
> *Additional information:* Scholarships are awarded
>   to students who demonstrate academic

excellence, character, and financial need.
Applications available from guidance office.
EIN: 146090923

7212
Loeb Foundation
c/o LCNB National Bank
P.O. Box 59
Lebanon, OH   45036-0059   (513) 932-1414
Contact: B.H. Wright, Jr., Tr.
FAX: (513) 932-1492; E-mail: bwright@lcnb.com

Foundation type: Independent foundation
Purpose: Grants and loans to indigent individuals
over the age of 60 to allow them to remain in their
own homes. Limited to Warren County, OH,
residents.
Publications: Annual report.
Financial data: Year ended 09/30/2013. Assets,
$7,368,307 (M); Expenditures, $625,997; Total
giving, $485,580.
Fields of interest: Aging; Economically
disadvantaged.
Type of support: Grants for special needs.
Application information: Applications accepted.
Application form required. Interview required.
> *Initial approach:* Contact Warren County
>   Community Services or send a letter to the
>   Loeb Foundation.
> *Copies of proposal:* 1
> *Deadline(s):* None
> *Final notification:* Applicants are notified within
>   2-3 days
> *Additional information:* Application must include
>   financial information.
EIN: 316225986

7213
The Lorain Foundation
457 Broadway
Lorain, OH   44052

Foundation type: Independent foundation
Purpose: Scholarships to graduates of high schools
in Lorain, OH.
Financial data: Year ended 12/31/2012. Assets,
$1,057,781 (M); Expenditures, $73,636; Total
giving, $52,802; Grants to individuals, 14 grants
totaling $21,000 (high: $1,500, low: $1,500).
Type of support: Support to graduates or students
of specific schools; Undergraduate support.
Application information: Applications accepted.
Application form required.
> *Deadline(s):* Prior to spring break
> *Additional information:* Applications must be
>   submitted to counselor of participating high
>   school.
EIN: 341022034

7214
Alfred J. Loser Memorial Scholarship Fund
457 Broadway
Lorain, OH   44052-1739   (440) 250-7015

Foundation type: Independent foundation
Purpose: Scholarships to financially needy
students who attend high school in Lorain, OH.
Financial data: Year ended 12/31/2011. Assets,
$545,159 (M); Expenditures, $54,856; Total
giving, $26,000; Grants to individuals, 19 grants
totaling $26,000 (high: $3,000, low: $1,000).
Type of support: Undergraduate support.
Application information: Applications accepted.
Application form required.
> *Deadline(s):* Dec. 1

Applicants should submit the following:
1) Photograph
2) Financial information
Additional information: Interviews may be required.
EIN: 346742325

7215
The Louisville Scholarship Foundation
419 E. Main St.
Louisville, OH   44641-1419   (330) 875-5539

Foundation type: Public charity
Purpose: Student loans and scholarships to students of Louisville, OH for postsecondary education.
Financial data: Year ended 12/31/2011. Assets, $1,655,211 (M); Expenditures, $45,407; Total giving, $43,260; Grants to individuals, totaling $43,260.
Fields of interest: Higher education.
Type of support: Scholarships—to individuals; Student loans—to individuals.
Application information: Applications accepted.
Applicants should submit the following:
1) Transcripts
2) SAR
3) Financial information
Additional information: Selection is based on academic and/or financial need. Funds are paid to the educational institution on behalf of the students.
EIN: 237042823

7216
Marguerite Gambill Lyons Scholarship Fund
P.O. Box 94651
Cleveland, OH   44101
Application address: c/o PNC Bank N.A., P.O. Box 1270, Ashland, KY 41105-1270

Foundation type: Independent foundation
Purpose: Scholarships only to students in Boyd, KY, and surrounding counties.
Financial data: Year ended 12/31/2012. Assets, $655,288 (M); Expenditures, $82,954; Total giving, $70,628.
Type of support: Scholarships—to individuals.
Application information: Applications accepted. Application form required.
Additional information: Contact foundation for deadline/guidelines.
EIN: 611121801

7217
Anna M. MacRae Scholarship Trust
c/o PNC Bank, NA
4100 W. 150th St.
Cleveland, OH   44135-1304

Foundation type: Independent foundation
Purpose: Scholarships to graduating students of Cass City High School, Cass City MI or the surrounding area within 20 miles of Cass City, pursuing a nursing career or related medical field.
Financial data: Year ended 12/31/2010. Assets, $190,622 (M); Expenditures, $10,127; Total giving, $7,000; Grants to individuals, 9 grants totaling $7,000 (high: $1,000, low: $500).
Fields of interest: Higher education; Nursing school/education.
Type of support: Support to graduates or students of specific schools.

Application information: Applications accepted. Application form required.
Deadline(s): Apr. 1
Applicants should submit the following:
1) Transcripts
2) SAR
3) FAFSA
4) Letter(s) of recommendation
5) Essay
Additional information: Selection is based on character and intelligence, scholastic record, and the desire and aptitude to pursue his/ her chosen field. Payments are made directly to the educational institution on behalf of the students.
EIN: 386706105

7218
Mary Mansfield Fund for the Aged
c/o Bank Of Cental Kentucky
P.O. Box 630858
Cincinnati, OH   45263-0858   (606) 455-5440
Application address: c/o Fifth Third Bank of Kentucky, 269 W. Main St. Lexington, KY 40507

Foundation type: Independent foundation
Purpose: Grants for medical expenses to indigent residents of Bourbon County, KY.
Financial data: Year ended 12/31/2012. Assets, $393,090 (M); Expenditures, $16,993; Total giving, $10,772; Grants to individuals, 5 grants totaling $1,866 (high: $775, low: $60).
Fields of interest: Aging.
Type of support: Grants for special needs.
Application information: Applications accepted. Application form required.
Initial approach: Letter
Deadline(s): None
EIN: 616021948

7219
Maple Knoll Communities, Inc.
(formerly LifeSphere)
11100 Springfield Pike
Cincinnati, OH   45246-4112   (513) 782-2400
Contact: Shirl Miller, Exec. Asst.
URL: http://www.mkcommunities.org

Foundation type: Public charity
Purpose: Monthly assistance to residents of Cincinnati, OH who are unable to pay full rent.
Financial data: Year ended 06/30/2012. Assets, $135,836,869 (M); Expenditures, $46,213,840; Total giving, $520,849; Grants to individuals, totaling $520,849.
Fields of interest: Human services; Aging; Economically disadvantaged.
Type of support: Grants for special needs.
Application information: Applications accepted.
Additional information: Residents must apply for assistance. Contact the organization for eligibility determination.
EIN: 310544277

7220
Marietta Community Foundation
100 Putnam St.
P.O. Box 77
Marietta, OH   45750-0077   (740) 373-3286
Contact: Carol B. Wharff, Pres. and C.E.O.
FAX: (740) 373-3937;
E-mail: info@mariettacommunityfoundation.org;
Additional e-mail: carol@mcfohio.org; URL: http://www.mariettacommunityfoundation.org

Foundation type: Community foundation
Purpose: Scholarships to graduating high school seniors, or current college students of Washington County, OH, pursuing higher education.
Publications: Application guidelines; Annual report; Grants list; Informational brochure (including application guidelines); Newsletter.
Financial data: Year ended 12/31/2012. Assets, $14,799,613 (M); Expenditures, $864,192; Total giving, $562,776; Grants to individuals, 25 grants totaling $38,940.
Fields of interest: Education.
Type of support: Scholarships—to individuals; Support to graduates or students of specific schools.
Application information: Applications accepted.
Initial approach: Application
Send request by: Online
Copies of proposal: 1
Deadline(s): Apr.
Final notification: Applicants notified in May
Additional information: Recipients are identified and recommended by various school administrators in the area. Contact the foundation for additional guidelines.
EIN: 743054287

7221
Marion Community Foundation, Inc.
(formerly Ohio MedCenter Foundation, Inc.)
504 S. State St.
Marion, OH   43302-5036   (740) 387-9704
Contact: Bradley C. Bebout, C.E.O.
FAX: (740) 375-0665;
E-mail: marionlegacy@frontier.com; URL: http://www.marioncommunityfoundation.org

Foundation type: Community foundation
Purpose: Scholarships to graduating seniors of Marion county, Richwood, and Ridgeway, OH, and Morgan Town, WV for continuing education at accredited colleges or universities.
Publications: Application guidelines; Annual report; Financial statement; Grants list; Informational brochure; Newsletter.
Financial data: Year ended 06/30/2012. Assets, $37,433,438 (M); Expenditures, $1,483,626; Total giving, $914,765. Scholarships—to individuals amount not specified.
Fields of interest: Higher education.
Type of support: Scholarships—to individuals; Support to graduates or students of specific schools.
Application information: Applications accepted. Application form required.
Deadline(s): Mar. 18
Additional information: See web site for requirements and criteria of various scholarships.
EIN: 314446189

7222
Marion Technical College Foundation Inc.
1467 Mount Vernon Ave.
Marion, OH   43302-5628

Foundation type: Independent foundation
Purpose: Financial assistance to students of Marion Technical College, OH for higher education.
Financial data: Year ended 06/30/2012. Assets, $0 (M); Expenditures, $803,962; Total giving, $795,838; Grants to individuals, 61 grants totaling $27,978 (high: $1,500, low: $100).
Fields of interest: College.
Type of support: Grants for special needs.

Application information: Applications accepted. Application form required.

Additional information: Assistance is based on financial need.

EIN: 341475294

7223

Mauger Insurance Fund

P.O. Box 94651

Cleveland, OH 44101-4651 (740) 927-3846
application address: c/o Watskins High School Guidance, 8808 Watskins Rd., Pataskala, OH 43062

Foundation type: Independent foundation

Purpose: Scholarships to high school graduates who have attended Southwest Licking School District, OH, for at least nine years. Scholarships may be used for a university, college, or technical school.

Financial data: Year ended 12/31/2012. Assets, $971,055 (M); Expenditures, $51,000; Total giving, $35,659.

Fields of interest: Vocational education.

Type of support: Support to graduates or students of specific schools; Undergraduate support.

Application information: Application form required.

Deadline(s): May 1

Applicants should submit the following:
1) Letter(s) of recommendation
2) Financial information
3) Transcripts
4) Class rank
5) GPA

Additional information: Application must also include standardized test scores, and handwritten personal statement.

EIN: 316198377

7224

Donald C. and Helene Marienthal McCabe Charitable Foundation

P.O. Box 94651

Cleveland, OH 44101 (507) 931-1682
Application Address: c/o Scholarship Management Services, One Scholarship way Saint Peter, MN, 56082

Foundation type: Independent foundation

Purpose: Undergraduate scholarships primarily to economically disadvantaged and Jewish or Presbyterian residents of Bay, Midland, and Saginaw counties, MI, for tuition at Delta Community College, MI, or Saginaw Valley State University, MI.

Financial data: Year ended 12/31/2012. Assets, $905,455 (M); Expenditures, $55,675; Total giving, $40,994.

Fields of interest: Protestant agencies & churches; Jewish agencies & synagogues.

Type of support: Support to graduates or students of specific schools; Undergraduate support.

Application information: Applications accepted. Application form required.

Deadline(s): Apr. 30

Applicants should submit the following:
1) Letter(s) of recommendation
2) SAR
3) FAFSA

Additional information: Undergraduate scholarships covering tuition up to 32 credits per academic year at Delta Community College, MI, or Saginaw Valley State University, MI, are available to students in Bay, Midland, and Saginaw counties, MI, who demonstrate financial need. First priority is

given to Presbyterian students from Bay County, MI, who live below the federally-defined poverty level, followed by such students who live above the poverty level but still demonstrate financial need. Second priority is given to Presbyterian students from Midland and Saginaw counties, MI, with financial need. Third priority is given to Jewish students from Bay County, MI, followed by such students in Midland and Saginaw counties, MI. Last priority will be given to financially needy Bay County, MI, residents of other religions. All Presbyterian applicants must be recommended by the Board of Trustees of the First Presbyterian Church in Bay City, MI and all Jewish applicants must be recommended by the Bay City Jewish Community Association. Scholarships are renewable.

EIN: 383184550

7225

Edwin L. and Louis B. McCallay Scholarship

300 High St.

Hamilton, OH 45011 (513) 425-7548
Application address: First Financial Bank, 815 S. Breiel Blvd., Middletown, OH 45042

Foundation type: Independent foundation

Purpose: Scholarships to graduates of high schools in the Middletown, OH, city school district, including Fenwick High School, to attend colleges, universities or other institutions of higher learning.

Financial data: Year ended 02/28/2013. Assets, $483,691 (M); Expenditures, $19,171; Total giving, $12,000.

Fields of interest: Higher education; Scholarships/financial aid.

Type of support: Support to graduates or students of specific schools; Technical education support; Undergraduate support.

Application information: Application form required.

Deadline(s): None

Additional information: Applicants should submit financial information; Applications available from high schools in the Middletown, OH, city school district.

EIN: 316111939

7226

J. Bryan and Norma R. McCann Charitable and Educational Trust

14 S. 5th St.

Zanesville, OH 43701-3517 (740) 454-2591
Contact: Jody D. Spencer, Tr.

Foundation type: Independent foundation

Purpose: Scholarships to graduating seniors of Washington County High School, OH for postsecondary education at accredited colleges or universities.

Financial data: Year ended 06/30/2013. Assets, $3,195,726 (M); Expenditures, $176,559; Total giving, $143,427; Grants to individuals, 122 grants totaling $113,201 (high: $12,000, low: $350).

Fields of interest: Higher education.

Type of support: Support to graduates or students of specific schools.

Application information: Applications accepted. Application form required.

Deadline(s): Apr. 25

Applicants should submit the following:
1) SAT
2) Letter(s) of recommendation
3) Financial information

4) ACT

Additional information: Application must also include most recent Federal Income Tax Returns of parents and students.

EIN: 367425931

7227

J. Allen McClain Trust

c/o David L. Pendry
133 E. Market St.
Xenia, OH 45385-3110
Contact: David L. Pendry, Tr.

Foundation type: Independent foundation

Purpose: Loans to graduates of Greene County, OH, high schools for medical school.

Financial data: Year ended 12/31/2011. Assets, $525,753 (M); Expenditures, $8,418; Total giving, $0.

Fields of interest: Medical school/education.

Type of support: Student loans—to individuals; Support to graduates or students of specific schools.

Application information:

Deadline(s): May 31

Additional information: Contact foundation for current application guidelines.

EIN: 316060712

7228

Lucille McComb Memorial Scholarship Fund

105 W. Main St.
Napoleon, OH 43545
Contact: Ryan Wilde
Application address: Napoleon High School, 701 Briartheath, Napoleon, Ohio 43545

Foundation type: Independent foundation

Purpose: Educational grants to economically disadvantaged students from Henry County, OH, to attend colleges, trade, or vocational schools. First consideration is given to Napoleon High School students.

Financial data: Year ended 12/31/2012. Assets, $545,417 (M); Expenditures, $27,387; Total giving, $17,000; Grants to individuals, 7 grants totaling $17,000 (high: $3,000, low: $2,000).

Fields of interest: Vocational education.

Type of support: Support to graduates or students of specific schools; Technical education support; Undergraduate support.

Application information: Applications accepted. Application form required.

Deadline(s): Apr. 1

Additional information: Application must also include a copy of parents' and applicant's federal income tax forms for the previous three years; Interviews may be required.

EIN: 346875773

7229

Ann McConahay Educational Foundation

119 E. State St.
Alliance, OH 44601 (330) 821-2100
Application address: Alliance High School Guidance Counselor, 400 Glamorgan St., Alliance, OH 44601

Foundation type: Independent foundation

Purpose: Scholarships to graduates of Alliance High School, OH for attendance at accredited colleges or universities for tuition and books.

Financial data: Year ended 12/31/2012. Assets, $1,134,501 (M); Expenditures, $76,535; Total giving, $62,750.

Fields of interest: Higher education; Scholarships/financial aid.
Type of support: Support to graduates or students of specific schools; Undergraduate support.
Application information: Application form required.
> *Deadline(s):* June 30
> *Applicants should submit the following:*
> 1) Transcripts
> 2) Letter(s) of recommendation
> *Additional information:* Applicants must demonstrate financial need, maintain at least a 3.0 cumulative GPA and demonstrate good character and integrity. Payments are made directly to the college or university. Recipients may reapply for a total of four years. Applications are available from Alliance High School guidance counselor.

EIN: 341550065

7230
Clark & Laura McCoy Scholarship Trust
P.O. Box 94651
Cleveland, OH 44101-4651

Foundation type: Independent foundation
Purpose: Scholarships to graduates of Wooster High School, OH for continuing their education at institutions of higher education.
Financial data: Year ended 12/31/2011. Assets, $676,021 (M); Expenditures, $27,091; Total giving, $20,440.
Type of support: Support to graduates or students of specific schools.
Application information:
> *Initial approach:* Letter
> *Additional information:* Contact foundation for current application deadline/guidelines.

EIN: 346950704

7231
Joan B. and Frank E. McDonald Charitable Trust Memorial Scholarship Fund for Weir High School
c/o Jane Anderson
401 Market St., Ste. 401
Steubenville, OH 43952
*Application address:*c/o Guidance Depart.Weir Senior High School

Foundation type: Operating foundation
Purpose: Scholarships to financially needy graduates of Weir Senior High School, WV for attendance at a technical school, two or four year college, community college, university, accredited trade, industrial or technical institution.
Financial data: Year ended 09/30/2013. Assets, $708,481 (M); Expenditures, $27,804; Total giving, $23,000; Grants to individuals, 14 grants totaling $23,000 (high: $2,500, low: $1,000).
Fields of interest: Vocational education, post-secondary; Higher education; College (community/junior).
Type of support: Support to graduates or students of specific schools; Technical education support; Undergraduate support.
Application information: Application form required.
> *Deadline(s):* Apr. 1
> *Additional information:* Applications available from the guidance department. Preference is given to individuals who participated as members of a Weir Senior High School sports program.

EIN: 546478360

7232
Joan Bieberson McDonald Charitable Trust Memorial Scholarship Fund for Wheeling Park High School
c/o Jane Anderson
401 Market St., Ste. 401
Steubenville, OH 43952 (304) 243-0400
*Application Address:*c/o Wheeling Park High School Guidance Department, 1976 Parkview Rd. Wheeling, WV 26003

Foundation type: Operating foundation
Purpose: Scholarships to graduates of Wheeling Park High School, Wheeling, WV, to attend a college, university, or accredited trade, industrial, or technical institution.
Financial data: Year ended 09/30/2013. Assets, $1,012,086 (M); Expenditures, $37,898; Total giving, $31,500; Grants to individuals, 12 grants totaling $31,500 (high: $5,000, low: $1,500).
Fields of interest: Vocational education, post-secondary; Higher education.
Type of support: Support to graduates or students of specific schools; Technical education support; Undergraduate support.
Application information: Applications accepted. Application form required.
> *Deadline(s):* Apr. 1
> *Additional information:* Preference is given to individuals who participated on a Wheeling Park High School sports team.

EIN: 546478362

7233
McDonald Memorial Fund Trust
(also known as Angus C. McDonald Memorial Trust)
c/o PNC Bank, N.A.
P.O. Box 94651
Cleveland, OH 44101-4651 (574) 371-5098
Application address: c/o Supt. of the Warsaw Community Schools, 1 Administrative Dr., Warsaw, IN 46580-4846

Foundation type: Independent foundation
Purpose: Student loans for college and professional education to Kosciusko County, IN, residents only.
Publications: Informational brochure.
Financial data: Year ended 12/31/2012. Assets, $2,674,486 (M); Expenditures, $125,090; Total giving, $100,250.
Fields of interest: Higher education; Graduate/professional education.
Type of support: Student loans—to individuals.
Application information: Applications accepted. Application form required. Interview required.
> *Additional information:* Application should include letters of recommendation.

EIN: 356018326

7234
James and Mary McFarlin Charitable Trust
(formerly James and Mary McFarlin Foundation)
c/o Farmers Trust
42 McClurg Rd.
Youngstown, OH 44512

Foundation type: Independent foundation
Purpose: Scholarships to male students of Ohio for continuing education at institutions of higher learning.
Financial data: Year ended 12/31/2012. Assets, $2,480,578 (M); Expenditures, $144,639; Total giving, $100,859.

Fields of interest: Higher education; Young adults, male.
Type of support: Scholarships—to individuals.
Application information: Contact the foundation for additional guidelines.
EIN: 346806350

7235
The Alice & Patrick McGinty Foundation
(formerly McGinty Family Foundation, also known as Alice and Patrick McGinty Foundation)
19541 Roseland Ave.
Euclid, OH 44117 (216) 486-9900
Contact: Jean McGinnis, Secy.
FAX: (216) 464-9531; E-mail: jmcginnis9@aol.com;
URL: http://login.npwebsiteservices.com/mcgintyfamilyfoundation/HomePage.asp

Foundation type: Independent foundation
Purpose: Educational support to outstanding elementary and secondary school teachers in northeastern OH and western MA.
Publications: Application guidelines; Annual report (including application guidelines); Informational brochure (including application guidelines); Newsletter; Occasional report.
Financial data: Year ended 10/31/2012. Assets, $2,660,680 (M); Expenditures, $31,719; Total giving, $15,000.
Fields of interest: Elementary school/education; Secondary school/education; Education.
Type of support: Grants to individuals.
Application information: Application form required.
> *Initial approach:* Letter or telephone
> *Deadline(s):* Aug. 31, Jan. 31 and Apr. 30
> *Final notification:* Applicants notified approximately five weeks after deadline

Program description:
> *Grants to Teachers Program:* The goal of this program is to support the McGinty Family Foundation's fundamental objective of recognizing and encouraging outstanding elementary and secondary educators who develop and implement innovative classroom programs and activities to advance the learning process of their students. Up to $1,000 is awarded to teachers for innovative classroom programs, including materials and/or technological materials to support the program, other educational programs that enhance the curriculum, and attendance at in-service programs or workshops that enhance the curriculum. Applicants must be employed in Cuyahoga or surrounding county schools chartered under the Ohio Department of Education. The foundation does not fund salaries, transportation costs or graduate course tuition.

EIN: 341643124

7236
John McIntire Educational Fund
c/o Huntington National Bank
422 Main St.
P.O. Box 2307
Zanesville, OH 43702-2307 (740) 455-7060
Contact: Kaleen Blosser, Acct. Relationship Assoc.
FAX: (888) 492-6981

Foundation type: Independent foundation
Purpose: Scholarships to residents of Zanesville, OH, who are under 21 years of age. Applicants must have at least a 2.0 or better GPA.
Publications: Annual report.
Financial data: Year ended 06/30/2013. Assets, $12,059,230 (M); Expenditures, $645,851; Total giving, $570,524; Grants to individuals, 162 grants totaling $521,324 (high: $6,008, low: $140).

Type of support: Scholarships—to individuals.
Application information: Application form required.
Deadline(s): May 1
Applicants should submit the following:
1) GPA
2) Transcripts
3) Letter(s) of recommendation
4) Financial information
EIN: 316021239

7237
John McLendon Minority Scholarship Foundation

24651 Detroit Rd.
Westlake, OH 44145-2524   (440) 892-4000
Contact: Joanna McLendon, Admin.
FAX: (440) 892-4007; URL: http://
www.nacda.com/mclendon/scholarship.html

Foundation type: Public charity
Purpose: Postgraduate scholarships to minority students who are planning to pursue a graduate degree in athletics administration.
Financial data: Year ended 12/31/2012. Assets, $1,213,388 (M); Expenditures, $109,943; Total giving, $50,000; Grants to individuals, totaling $50,000.
Fields of interest: Recreation; Minorities; Asians/Pacific Islanders; African Americans/Blacks; Hispanics/Latinos; Native Americans/American Indians.
Type of support: Scholarships—to individuals; Awards/grants by nomination only; Postgraduate support.
Application information:
Send request by: Mail or fax
Deadline(s): Apr.
Applicants should submit the following:
1) Letter(s) of recommendation
2) Essay
Additional information: Application by nomination only.
EIN: 760717270

7238
The Becky Menard Memorial Scholarship Fund

c/o Joe Bick
1600 Scripps Ctr.
312 Walnut St.
Cincinnati, OH 45202-4004
E-mail: prostar@fuse.net

Foundation type: Independent foundation
Purpose: Scholarships to female student athletes graduating from Western Brown High School, OH.
Financial data: Year ended 12/31/2012. Assets, $75,509 (M); Expenditures, $5,113; Total giving, $5,000; Grant to an individual, 1 grant totaling $5,000.
Fields of interest: Higher education.
Type of support: Support to graduates or students of specific schools.
Application information:
Initial approach: Letter
Additional information: Application can be obtained from the principal's office of Western Brown high school, Mt. Orab, OH.
EIN: 311729852

7239
Mentzer Memorial Foundation

(formerly Charles T. Mentzer Memorial Trust)
c/o KeyBank N.A., Trust Div.
4900 Tiedman Rd., OH-01-49-0150
Brooklyn, OH 44144-2302
Application address: c/o KeyBank N.A., Trust Client Svcs., 127 Public Sq., Cleveland, OH 44114-1221

Foundation type: Independent foundation
Purpose: Scholarships to students studying for holy orders.
Financial data: Year ended 12/31/2012. Assets, $453,271 (M); Expenditures, $30,330; Total giving, $24,000.
Fields of interest: Theological school/education.
Type of support: Graduate support; Undergraduate support.
Application information: Contact foundation for current application deadline/guidelines.
EIN: 916273732

7240
The Mercer County Civic Foundation, Inc.

119 W. Fulton St.
P.O. Box 439
Celina, OH 45822-1620   (419) 586-9950
Contact: Glenn H. Hux, Exec. Dir.
E-mail: mccf@bright.net; URL: http://
www.mercercountycivicfdn.org

Foundation type: Community foundation
Purpose: Educational loans and scholarships to students who graduate from Mercer County, OH, high schools.
Publications: Application guidelines; Annual report (including application guidelines); Informational brochure; Newsletter.
Financial data: Year ended 12/31/2012. Assets, $9,313,013 (M); Expenditures, $757,929; Total giving, $654,253. Scholarships—to individuals amount not specified. Student loans—to individuals amount not specified.
Fields of interest: Arts; Vocational education, post-secondary; Higher education; Agriculture.
Type of support: Grants to individuals; Scholarships—to individuals; Student loans—to individuals.
Application information: Applications accepted. Application form required.
Initial approach: Letter
Send request by: Mail
Copies of proposal: 1
Deadline(s): June 1
Applicants should submit the following:
1) Proposal
2) Letter(s) of recommendation
3) Financial information
4) Budget Information
EIN: 346539139

7241
Mercy Regional Foundation

(formerly Community Health Partners Foundation)
3700 Kolbe Rd.
Lorain, OH 44053-1611   (440) 960-4000
Contact: Jane Jonesco JD, Pres.
FAX: (440) 960-3442;
E-mail: Jane.Jonesco@health-partners.org;
URL: http://www.mercyonline.org/
foundation_mercy_regional.aspx

Foundation type: Public charity
Purpose: Scholarships to dependent children of full-time employees of Community Health Partners Regional Health System, and individuals inside and outside the Community Health Partners Regional Health System, also awards for associates of Community Health Partners Regional Health System providing direct care to the poor and underserved.
Publications: Application guidelines.
Financial data: Year ended 12/31/2011. Assets, $21,471,863 (M); Expenditures, $2,192,031; Total giving, $1,741,408; Grants to individuals, totaling $47,997.
Fields of interest: Vocational education, post-secondary; Higher education; Health care, patient services.
Type of support: Scholarships—to individuals; Awards/prizes; Stipends.
Application information: Applications accepted. Application form required.
Deadline(s): Apr. 7
Applicants should submit the following:
1) Transcripts
2) SAT
3) Letter(s) of recommendation
4) ACT
Additional information: Application must also include a personal statement. Application by fax or e-mail not accepted. See web site for additional application information.
Program descriptions:
Denis A. Radefeld, M.D. Humanitarian Award: This award provides a Mercy associate with up to two weeks paid leave as well as a stipend to be used toward qualified expenses to participate in a project providing direct care to the poor and underserved. This award is not restricted to clinical staff, however, applicants must demonstrate they will be involved in providing direct care.
Francis Patterson, M.D. Memorial Scholarship: First preference shall be given to those students interested in pursuing career preparation in the healing arts.
Paul C. Balcom Scholarship: This scholarship is open to all dependent children of full-time employees of the Community Health Partners Regional Health System or a Lorain County, Ohio, affiliate.
Velma Price Memorial Scholarship: This scholarship is open to African American individuals who are enrolled in nursing education at any level, and/or nurses pursuing certification or credentialing in a health care specialty.
EIN: 341504558

7242
Miami County Foundation

(formerly Piqua-Miami County Foundation)
317 N. Wayne St.
P.O. Box 1526
Piqua, OH 45356-1526   (937) 773-9012
Contact: Cheryl Stiefel-Francis, Exec. Dir.
FAX: (937) 773-9012; E-mail: mcf@woh.rr.com;
URL: http://www.miamicountyfoundation.org

Foundation type: Independent foundation
Purpose: Scholarships to students who reside in Newton Township or Miami County, OH for continuing education at colleges or universities.
Publications: Application guidelines; Informational brochure; Newsletter.
Financial data: Year ended 12/31/2012. Assets, $11,721,195 (M); Expenditures, $774,441; Total giving, $440,171.
Fields of interest: Higher education; Formal/general education.
Type of support: Scholarships—to individuals; Support to graduates or students of specific schools; Technical education support; Undergraduate support.

Application information: Applications accepted. Application form required. Application form available on the grantmaker's web site.
   Send request by: Mail or fax
   Copies of proposal: 1
   Deadline(s): Nov. 1 for Dalton Scholarship
   Final notification: Recipients notified in six weeks
   Applicants should submit the following:
      1) SAT
      2) GPA
      3) ACT
   Additional information: Students should call Newton high school for applications. No applications are accepted via e-mail.
Program descriptions:
   Don Favorite Deeter, M.D. Memorial Scholarship: This scholarship program is for Newton High School graduates pursuing a degree in science. For more information contact Newton High School at (937) 676-3081.
   Thelma Ross Dalton Memorial Scholarship: Scholarships up to the amount of $3,000 to Miami County, OH, students for post-high school education at any accredited college, trade/vocational schools, or nursing/health-related facility.
EIN: 311142558

7243
The Howard and Espa Michaud Charitable Trust

(formerly The Michaud Charitable Trust)
c/o KeyBank
10 W. 2nd St., 26th Fl.
Dayton, OH 45402

Foundation type: Independent foundation
Purpose: Scholarships to students attending college in ME.
Financial data: Year ended 10/31/2012. Assets, $1,267,312 (M); Expenditures, $79,814; Total giving, $63,152; Grants to individuals, 29 grants totaling $8,250 (high: $500, low: $250).
Type of support: Undergraduate support.
Application information: Applications accepted.
   Initial approach: Letter
   Deadline(s): None
EIN: 046013647

7244
Ambrose Middleton Trust

c/o KeyBank
4900 Tiedeman Rd., OH-01-49-0150
Brooklyn, OH 44144-2302
Contact: Joann Loper, Pres.
Application address: P.O. Box 237, Malta, OH 43758

Foundation type: Independent foundation
Purpose: Financial assistance to needy individuals of Morgan County, OH with food, clothing, utility, medical expense and other needs.
Financial data: Year ended 08/31/2013. Assets, $330,945 (M); Expenditures, $8,459; Total giving, $7,452; Grants to individuals, 153 grants totaling $7,452 (high: $50, low: $15).
Fields of interest: Human services; Economically disadvantaged.
Type of support: Grants for special needs.
Application information: Applications accepted.
   Deadline(s): None
   Additional information: Morgan county ministries determines needy recipients.
EIN: 346513420

7245
Middletown Community Foundation

300 N. Main St., Ste. 300
Middletown, OH 45042 (513) 424-7369
Contact: T. Duane Gordon, Exec. Dir.
FAX: (513) 424-7555;
E-mail: info@mcfoundation.org; URL: http://www.mcfoundation.org/

Foundation type: Community foundation
Purpose: Scholarships to residents of the Middletown, OH, area for higher education.
Publications: Application guidelines; Annual report; Financial statement; Informational brochure (including application guidelines); Newsletter.
Financial data: Year ended 12/31/2011. Assets, $23,345,511 (M); Expenditures, $2,717,241; Total giving, $1,846,958; Grants to individuals, 350 grants totaling $843,380.
Fields of interest: Higher education.
Type of support: Scholarships—to individuals.
Application information: Applications accepted. Application form required. Application form available on the grantmaker's web site.
   Initial approach: Application
   Send request by: Mail
   Deadline(s): Varies
   Applicants should submit the following:
      1) FAFSA
      2) Letter(s) of recommendation
      3) Resume
   Additional information: See web site for additional guidelines.
EIN: 310898380

7246
Midmark Foundation

P.O. Box 286
Versailles, OH 45380-0286 (937) 526-3662

Foundation type: Company-sponsored foundation
Purpose: Scholarships to high school graduates who are children of a full-time employee of Midmark Corporation.
Financial data: Year ended 12/31/2012. Assets, $976,854 (M); Expenditures, $42,856; Total giving, $23,893. Employee-related scholarships amount not specified.
Fields of interest: Higher education.
Type of support: Employee-related scholarships.
Application information: Applications not accepted.
   Additional information: Unsolicited requests for funds not considered or acknowledged.
Company name: Midmark Corporation
EIN: 237068805

7247
J. William & Lorraine M. Miller Family Foundation

6706 Markwood St.
Worthington, OH 43085

Foundation type: Independent foundation
Purpose: Scholarships to graduates of Saginaw, Bay or Midland County high schools, MI.
Financial data: Year ended 12/31/2012. Assets, $938,027 (M); Expenditures, $50,603; Total giving, $48,000.
Type of support: Support to graduates or students of specific schools; Undergraduate support.
Application information: Application form required.
   Deadline(s): Apr. 10
   Additional information: Applicants should submit transcripts.
EIN: 383009465

7248
Dr. William R. Miller Foundation

1788 Old US Rte. 52
P.O. Box 232
Moscow, OH 45153 (513) 553-3763
Contact: William R. Miller M.D., Tr.

Foundation type: Independent foundation
Purpose: Scholarships to individuals, with preference to residents of Clermont County, OH for study in medical fields.
Financial data: Year ended 12/31/2012. Assets, $7,939 (M); Expenditures, $10,279; Total giving, $8,750.
Fields of interest: Medical school/education.
Type of support: Scholarships—to individuals.
Application information: Applications accepted. Application form required.
   Deadline(s): Rolling
   Additional information: Application should include three references.
EIN: 311657916

7249
The Sydell & Arnold Miller Foundation

(formerly Arnold M. & Sydell L. Miller Foundation)
32333 Aurora Rd., Ste. 300
Solon, OH 44139-2851

Foundation type: Independent foundation
Purpose: Graduate and undergraduate scholarships primarily to fully-dependent children of employees of Matrix Essentials, Inc. and Davida's Salon & Spa, both in OH.
Publications: Financial statement.
Financial data: Year ended 12/31/2012. Assets, $11,093,431 (M); Expenditures, $535,101; Total giving, $525,733.
Fields of interest: Vocational education; Higher education; Graduate/professional education; Scholarships/financial aid.
Type of support: Employee-related scholarships; Graduate support.
Application information: Applications accepted. Application form required.
   Deadline(s): Apr. 15
   Final notification: Recipients notified after May 30
   Applicants should submit the following:
      1) Essay
      2) Transcripts
      3) SAT
      4) ACT
      5) Class rank
      6) Letter(s) of recommendation
      7) Photograph
   Additional information: Application must also include duplicate of application to attending college, personal statement, copy of first page of parents' income tax return or GRE scores for graduate students.
Program description:
   Scholarship Program: Scholarships are awarded on the basis of financial need, academic ability, character, and motivation. Recipients must be full-time students attending accredited colleges, junior colleges, vocational or business schools, graduate, postgraduate, and professional schools. Scholarships are renewable provided recipient has maintained full-time status, worked while attending school, continued to exhibit financial need, and maintained a GPA commensurate with the averages required for other scholarship holders by the school attended.
EIN: 341460324

7250
Jayne L. Miller Scholarship Foundation
P.O. Box 1118, ML CN-OH-W10X
Cincinnati, OH 45201-1118 (765) 965-2295

Foundation type: Independent foundation
Purpose: College scholarships to students of Hagerstown High School, IN for higher education.
Financial data: Year ended 12/31/2011. Assets, $1,457,241 (M); Expenditures, $67,400; Total giving, $49,000.
Fields of interest: Higher education.
Type of support: Scholarships—to individuals; Support to graduates or students of specific schools.
Application information: Applications accepted. Application form required.
>   *Deadline(s):* Mar. 18
>   *Additional information:* Application can be obtained from Hagerstown High School or US Bank.
EIN: 352081769

7251
James Forsythe Milroy Foundation
110 N. Main St.
Bellefontaine, OH 43311-2021 (937) 593-8191
Contact: John R. Hatcher, Tr.
Application address: 1060 Rd. 198, Bellefontaine, OH 43311

Foundation type: Independent foundation
Purpose: Interest-free loans and scholarships to residents of Logan County, OH, studying agriculture or related fields at OH colleges.
Financial data: Year ended 12/31/2012. Assets, $823,545 (M); Expenditures, $38,552; Total giving, $16,500; Grants to individuals, totaling $16,500.
Fields of interest: Agriculture.
Type of support: Scholarships—to individuals; Student loans—to individuals.
Application information: Applications accepted. Application form not required. Interview required.
>   *Deadline(s):* None
EIN: 346516844

7252
Aimee & Frank Mishou Scholarship Fund Trust
c/o KeyBank N.A.
4900 Tiedeman Rd., OH-01-49-0150
Brooklyn, OH 44144-2302

Foundation type: Independent foundation
Purpose: Scholarships to students of Sumner High School or residents of Sullivan, Gouldsboro, or Winter Harbor, ME.
Financial data: Year ended 04/30/2013. Assets, $354,792 (M); Expenditures, $13,488; Total giving, $9,000; Grant to an individual, 1 grant totaling $9,000.
Fields of interest: Education.
Type of support: Support to graduates or students of specific schools; Undergraduate support.
Application information: Applications accepted. Application form required.
>   *Deadline(s):* None
>   *Additional information:* Applications available from high school.
EIN: 016070062

7253
Victor Mohr Memorial Trust
c/o Fifth Third Bank
P.O. Box 630858
Cincinnati, OH 45263-0858 (812) 649-9157
Application address: Principal, South Spencer High School, 1142 N. Orchard Rd., Rockport, IN 47635-9135,

Foundation type: Independent foundation
Purpose: Scholarships to graduates of South Spencer High School, IN, who have a high school average of "C" or better.
Financial data: Year ended 12/31/2012. Assets, $1,038,904 (M); Expenditures, $72,808; Total giving, $51,108.
Fields of interest: Education.
Type of support: Support to graduates or students of specific schools; Undergraduate support.
Application information: Application form required.
>   *Deadline(s):* Apr. 15
>   *Applicants should submit the following:*
>   1) GPA
>   2) Financial information
EIN: 356225418

7254
Dewey H. and Irene G. Moomaw Scholarship Fund
P.O Box 1558, Dept. EA4E86
Columbus, OH 43216 (330) 364-7421

Foundation type: Independent foundation
Purpose: Scholarships to students currently attending or have attended Garaway High School, of Sugarcreek, OH for continuing education at institutions of higher learning.
Financial data: Year ended 09/30/2013. Assets, $516,085 (M); Expenditures, $28,418; Total giving, $22,100.
Fields of interest: Higher education.
Type of support: Support to graduates or students of specific schools.
Application information: Applications accepted.
>   *Deadline(s):* Apr. 30
>   *Additional information:* Contact the fund for additional application guidelines.
EIN: 134211254

7255
Arlene Goist Moore Scholarship Fund
c/o Huntington National Bank
7 Easton Oval
Columbus, OH 43219 (330) 841-0982

Foundation type: Independent foundation
Purpose: Scholarships to Southington High School, OH graduates who are Southington Township residents and have attended Southington Schools for at least four years.
Financial data: Year ended 04/30/2013. Assets, $82,301 (M); Expenditures, $4,388; Total giving, $2,500; Grants to individuals, 5 grants totaling $2,500 (high: $500, low: $500).
Type of support: Support to graduates or students of specific schools; Undergraduate support.
Application information: Application form required.
>   *Initial approach:* Letter
>   *Deadline(s):* Mar. 31
>   *Additional information:* Application must also include academic achievements, nonathletic extracurricular activities, and personal statement on applicant's character and reputation in the community.
EIN: 346863075

7256
Moraine Caddy Scholarship Fund
c/o The Dayton Foundation
500 Kettering Twr.
Dayton, OH 45423-1113 (937) 225-9966
Contact: George G. Malacos, Chair.

Foundation type: Public charity
Purpose: Scholarships to caddies at Moraine Country Club, OH.
Financial data: Year ended 12/31/2011. Assets, $1,047,667 (M); Expenditures, $58,017; Total giving, $69,250; Grants to individuals, totaling $69,250.
Type of support: Undergraduate support.
Application information:
>   *Initial approach:* Letter
>   *Additional information:* Contact foundation for current application guidelines.
EIN: 311773877

7257
Paul Motry Memorial Fund
c/o John Frankel
414 Wayne St.
Sandusky, OH 44871-5001 (419) 627-3100

Foundation type: Independent foundation
Purpose: Financial assistance to physically disabled children who are residents of Erie and Eastern Ottawa counties, OH.
Financial data: Year ended 12/31/2012. Assets, $549,624 (M); Expenditures, $34,194; Total giving, $19,791.
Fields of interest: Physical therapy; Children; Disabilities, people with.
Type of support: Grants for special needs.
Application information: Applications accepted. Application form required.
>   *Deadline(s):* None
>   *Additional information:* Application should include a letter from the doctor, proving need.
EIN: 237420173

7258
Robert L. Munger, Jr. Foundation
1 Cedar Point Dr.
Sandusky, OH 44870-5259
Contact: for Scholarships: R. L. Munger, Secy.
Application addresses: c/o Valley Fair Personnel Dept., 1 Valley Fair Dr., Shakopee, MN 55379-3012, c/o Cedar Point Personnel Dept., 1 Cedar Point Dr., Sandusky, OH 44870-5259

Foundation type: Independent foundation
Purpose: Scholarships to graduating high school seniors who are seasonal and part-time employees of Cedar Point, Sandusky, OH, Valley Fair, Shakopee, MN, or Dorney Park, PA for postsecondary education.
Financial data: Year ended 12/31/2011. Assets, $308,529 (M); Expenditures, $16,471; Total giving, $14,000; Grants to individuals, 7 grants totaling $14,000 (high: $2,000, low: $2,000).
Fields of interest: Education.
Type of support: Employee-related scholarships; Undergraduate support.
Application information: Applications accepted. Application form required. Interview required.
>   *Send request by:* Mail
>   *Deadline(s):* June 30
>   *Applicants should submit the following:*
>   1) Transcripts
>   2) Essay

Additional information: Scholarships are paid directly to the educational institution on behalf of the recipient.
EIN: 341599255

7259
Grant Munro Scholarship Trust
c/o PNC Bank, N.A.
P.O. Box 94651
Cleveland, OH   44101-4651

Foundation type: Independent foundation
Purpose: Scholarships to graduates of a high school in Fairfield County, OH, for degrees in medicine or the ministry.
Financial data: Year ended 05/31/2013. Assets, $6,349,339 (M); Expenditures, $100,989; Total giving, $72,553; Grant to an individual, 1 grant totaling $72,553.
Fields of interest: Medical school/education; Theological school/education.
Type of support: Support to graduates or students of specific schools; Undergraduate support.
Application information: Applications accepted. Application form required.
   Deadline(s): Apr. 15
   Applicants should submit the following:
      1) Letter(s) of recommendation
      2) Transcripts
      3) Financial information
EIN: 316517313

7260
T. R. Murphy Residuary Trust
422 Main St.
Zanesville, OH   43701-3515
Application address: c/o Scott D. Eickelberger, 50 N. 4th St., Zanesville, OH 43701, tel.: (750) 454-2591

Foundation type: Independent foundation
Purpose: Scholarships to graduates of high schools in Muskingum County, OH for postsecondary education.
Financial data: Year ended 06/30/2013. Assets, $3,195,472 (M); Expenditures, $197,903; Total giving, $155,854; Grants to individuals, 362 grants totaling $114,486 (high: $800, low: $200).
Fields of interest: Higher education.
Type of support: Support to graduates or students of specific schools; Undergraduate support.
Application information: Applications accepted. Application form required.
   Deadline(s): May 1
   Applicants should submit the following:
      1) Letter(s) of recommendation
      2) Financial information
      3) SAT
      4) ACT
      5) Transcripts
   Additional information: Application should also include a copy of you/your parents' current Income tax form, and letter of acceptance from college or proof of current attendance.
EIN: 316285970

7261
Murphy Scholarship Trust
c/o PNC Bank N.A.
P.O. Box 94651
Cleveland, OH   44101-4651   (859) 281-5276
Contact: June Greenwall
Application address: c/o PNC Bank, NA, P.O. Box 36010, Louisville, Kentucky 40233-6010

Foundation type: Independent foundation
Purpose: Scholarships to high school seniors in the Louisville, KY area for higher education.
Financial data: Year ended 12/31/2011. Assets, $80,897 (M); Expenditures, $4,678; Total giving, $3,000; Grant to an individual, 1 grant totaling $3,000.
Fields of interest: Higher education.
Type of support: Scholarships—to individuals.
Application information: Applications accepted. Application form required.
   Deadline(s): Mar. 31
   Applicants should submit the following:
      1) Class rank
      2) Transcripts
      3) GPA
      4) Financial information
      5) ACT
   Additional information: Application should also include a copy of parents' most recent W-2 and income tax forms. Application available upon request.
EIN: 616229144

7262
The Albert K. Murray Fine Arts Educational Fund
9665 Young America Rd.
Adamsville, OH   43802

Foundation type: Independent foundation
Purpose: Scholarships for students enrolled in a full time fine arts program at an accredited degree granting college or university at the bachelor's, master's or doctoral level.
Financial data: Year ended 12/31/2012. Assets, $0 (M); Expenditures, $65,692; Total giving, $30,791; Grants to individuals, 23 grants totaling $30,791 (high: $4,339, low: $100).
Fields of interest: Sculpture; Painting; Drawing.
Type of support: Scholarships—to individuals.
Application information: Applications accepted.
   Deadline(s): July 31 for fall , Oct. 31 for winter, Jan. 31 for spring, Apr. 30 for summer
   Additional information: This fine arts scholarship is intended for students who practice or are applying with materials representative of the visual fine arts (illustration, painting/drawing, sculpture).
EIN: 311404573

7263
Muskingum County Community Foundation
534 Putnam Ave.
Zanesville, OH   43701-4933   (740) 453-5192
Contact: David P. Mitzel, Exec. Dir.; For scholarships: Heather Sands, Dir., College Access Progs.
Scholarship Central tel.: (740) 453-5192
FAX: (740) 453-5734; E-mail: giving@mccf.org; URL: http://www.mccf.org

Foundation type: Community foundation
Purpose: Scholarships to residents of Muskingum county, OH pursuing higher education.
Publications: Application guidelines; Annual report; Grants list; Informational brochure; Newsletter.
Financial data: Year ended 12/31/2012. Assets, $22,308,503 (M); Expenditures, $2,401,011; Total giving, $1,621,540.
Fields of interest: Education.
Type of support: Scholarships—to individuals; Graduate support; Undergraduate support.

Application information: Applications accepted. Application form required. Application form available on the grantmaker's web site.
   Deadline(s): Varies
   Applicants should submit the following:
      1) ACT
      2) Essay
      3) Financial information
      4) GPA
      5) Letter(s) of recommendation
      6) Transcripts
   Additional information: See web site for complete listing of scholarships and guidelines.
EIN: 311147022

7264
Myers Church Scholarship
c/o Fifth Third Bank
P.O. Box 630858
Cincinnati, OH   45263-0858   (616) 843-9275
Contact: William Collins
Application address: 6108 Barnhart Rd., Ludington, MI 49431-8625, tel.: (616) 843-9275

Foundation type: Independent foundation
Purpose: Scholarships to graduates of high schools in Mason County, MI or whose parents reside in Mason County.
Financial data: Year ended 12/31/2012. Assets, $166,786 (M); Expenditures, $11,203; Total giving, $6,847; Grants to individuals, totaling $6,847.
Fields of interest: Higher education.
Type of support: Support to graduates or students of specific schools; Undergraduate support.
Application information: Application form required.
   Deadline(s): Apr. 20
   Applicants should submit the following:
      1) Financial information
      2) SAT
      3) GPA
      4) ACT
   Additional information: Application should include two references and a personal statement.
EIN: 383288570

7265
G. Myers Memorial Scholarship Trust
c/o PNC Bank, NA
P.O. Box 94651
Cleveland, OH   44101-4651   800-6288151
Application address: c/o Logansport High School, Attn.: Guidance Dept., 1 Berry Ln., Logansport, IN 46947-3901, tel.: (800) 628-8151

Foundation type: Independent foundation
Purpose: Scholarships to students who have attended Logansport High School, IN, for the last two years of high school, for continuing education at institutions of higher learning.
Financial data: Year ended 12/31/2011. Assets, $196,488 (M); Expenditures, $15,469; Total giving, $12,000; Grants to individuals, 4 grants totaling $12,000 (high: $3,000, low: $3,000).
Fields of interest: Higher education; Scholarships/ financial aid; Volunteer services.
Type of support: Support to graduates or students of specific schools; Undergraduate support.
Application information: Applications accepted. Application form required.
   Deadline(s): Mar. 22
   Applicants should submit the following:
      1) Letter(s) of recommendation
      2) Financial information
      3) Transcripts

Additional information: Application should also include a copy of parents' and student's tax returns and list of school and community activities.
EIN: 356648858

7266
Richard T. Naples Educational Foundation Inc.
2665 N. Main St.
Hubbard, OH 44425-3247 (330) 534-5145
Contact: Richard Naples Sr., Tr.

Foundation type: Independent foundation
Purpose: Scholarships only to residents of Mahoning, Trumbull or Stark counties, OH pursuing higher education.
Financial data: Year ended 06/30/2013. Assets, $69,059 (M); Expenditures, $21,436; Total giving, $20,000; Grants to individuals, 25 grants totaling $20,000 (high: $800, low: $800).
Fields of interest: Higher education.
Type of support: Scholarships—to individuals.
Application information: Applications accepted. Application form required.
  Deadline(s): Mar. 31
  Additional information: Scholarships are for high school students who will be attending college and for students who are already in college. A 2.5 GPA or higher is required. Application can be obtained from the foundation.
EIN: 341851988

7267
National Machinery Foundation Inc.
P.O. Box 747
Tiffin, OH 44883-0747 (419) 443-2306
Contact: Larry F. Baker, Pres.
FAX: (419) 443-2184

Foundation type: Company-sponsored foundation
Purpose: Scholarships to high school seniors and first-year graduates in Seneca county who are children of employees of National Machinery Company, OH. Awards for good citizenship to children in Seneca County, OH. Relief assistance to former employees of National Machinery Company and other needy individuals in Seneca County, OH.
Financial data: Year ended 12/31/2011. Assets, $13,815,873 (M); Expenditures, $773,890; Total giving, $682,147; Grants to individuals, 230 grants totaling $85,590 (high: $1,000, low: $25).
Fields of interest: Higher education; Human services.
Type of support: Employee-related scholarships; Awards/prizes; Employee-related welfare; Graduate support; Undergraduate support; Grants for special needs.
Application information: Applications not accepted.
  Additional information: Unsolicited requests for funds not considered or acknowledged.
Program description:
  National Machinery Citizenship Awards: The foundation annually honors high school students for citizenship, conduct, character, and moral outlook in Seneca, OH. Honorees receive certificates as citizenship award recipients, a pin, and monetary awards ranging from $50 to $300.
EIN: 346520191

7268
New Orphan Asylum Scholarship Foundation
2300 Montana Ave., Ste. 218
Cincinnati, OH 45211-3891 (513) 389-9400
Contact: Tonda Carden
FAX: (513) 389-9401

Foundation type: Independent foundation
Purpose: Scholarships to residents of the greater Cincinnati, OH, area, and to those who attended high school in the greater Cincinnati, OH area.
Financial data: Year ended 12/31/2011. Assets, $2,562,350 (M); Expenditures, $131,277; Total giving, $71,280.
Fields of interest: Vocational education; Higher education.
Type of support: Scholarships—to individuals; Undergraduate support.
Application information: Funds are paid directly to the named institution on behalf of the student. Unsolicited requests for funds not considered or acknowledged.
EIN: 310536683

7269
Horace & Letitia Newton Scholarship Fund
10 W. 2nd St., 26th Fl.
Dayton, OH 45402
Application address: c/o Keybank N.A., Att.: Diane Ohns, P.O. Box 10099, Toledo, OH 43699-0099.

Foundation type: Independent foundation
Purpose: Scholarships primarily to residents of Lucas County, OH, who are graduates or students of Toledo, OH, area schools.
Financial data: Year ended 12/31/2012. Assets, $4,515,009 (M); Expenditures, $284,340; Total giving, $233,039.
Type of support: Scholarships—to individuals; Support to graduates or students of specific schools.
Application information: Applications accepted. Application form required.
  Deadline(s): None
  Additional information: Contact foundation for current application guidelines.
EIN: 346502592

7270
Gilbert & Evelyn Nolley Educational Scholarship Fund
c/o KeyBank N.A.
4900 Tiedeman Rd., OH-01-49-0150
Brooklyn, OH 44144-2302 (216) 689-3759
Contact: Cynthia Clifton
Application address: P.O. Box 89464, Cleveland, OH 44114

Foundation type: Independent foundation
Purpose: Scholarships to students who reside in and attend a high school within the Manchester, OH, school district.
Financial data: Year ended 12/31/2012. Assets, $197,542 (M); Expenditures, $14,235; Total giving, $10,075; Grants to individuals, 13 grants totaling $10,075 (high: $775, low: $775).
Fields of interest: Higher education.
Type of support: Scholarships—to individuals; Support to graduates or students of specific schools.
Application information: Applications accepted.
  Initial approach: Letter
  Copies of proposal: 1
  Deadline(s): None

Applicants should submit the following:
  1) Transcripts
  2) Financial information
  3) Essay
  Additional information: Application should also include letter stating applicant's course of study.
EIN: 346981666

7271
Hartzell Norris Charitable Trust
P.O. Box 630858
Cincinnati, OH 45263-0858
URL: http://www.hartzellindustries.com/careers/community.html

Foundation type: Company-sponsored foundation
Purpose: Scholarships to students, primarily in OH, for higher education.
Financial data: Year ended 10/31/2012. Assets, $4,767,319 (M); Expenditures, $280,175; Total giving, $231,008.
Fields of interest: Higher education.
Type of support: Undergraduate support.
Application information: Applications not accepted.
  Additional information: Unsolicited requests for funds not considered or acknowledged.
EIN: 316024521

7272
The North College Hill Scholarship Foundation
1731 Goodman Ave.
Cincinnati, OH 45239

Foundation type: Independent foundation
Purpose: Scholarships to graduating seniors of North College Hill Schools, OH who are in the top 20 percent of their graduating class.
Financial data: Year ended 12/31/2011. Assets, $324,191 (M); Expenditures, $22,510; Total giving, $21,500; Grants to individuals, 8 grants totaling $21,500 (high: $4,000, low: $1,000).
Fields of interest: Higher education.
Type of support: Scholarships—to individuals.
Application information: Applications accepted. Application form required.
  Deadline(s): May 14
EIN: 200984093

7273
Northwest Ohio Youth Soccer League
135 Chesterfield Ln., Ste. 4
Maumee, OH 43537-2259 (419) 893-2311
Contact: Andrew Olnhausen, Pres.
FAX: (419) 893-2307; E-mail: admin@nwoysl.org; E-mail For Andrew Olnhausen: andrew.oln@gmail.com; URL: http://www.nwoysl.org

Foundation type: Public charity
Purpose: Scholarships to individuals who have participated in NWOYSL as a player or referee.
Financial data: Year ended 12/31/2011. Assets, $310,257 (M); Expenditures, $184,582; Total giving, $10,250; Grants to individuals, totaling $10,250.
Fields of interest: Higher education; Athletics/sports, soccer.
Type of support: Scholarships—to individuals.
Application information: Applications accepted.
  Initial approach: Letter
  Deadline(s): Mar. 1
EIN: 311081583

7274
Northwestern Ohio Community Action Commission
1933 E. Second St.
Defiance, OH 43512-2503 (419) 784-5136
FAX: (419) 782-5648; E-mail: dgerken@nocac.org;
URL: http://www.nocac.org/

Foundation type: Public charity
Purpose: Assistance to low-income individuals and families who are residence of Defiance, Fulton, Henry, Paulding and Williams counties, OH with housing, utility, child development, rent and other special needs.
Publications: Annual report; Newsletter.
Financial data: Year ended 12/31/2011. Assets, $6,315,916 (M); Expenditures, $8,624,388; Total giving, $1,728,962; Grants to individuals, totaling $1,728,962.
Fields of interest: Human services; Economically disadvantaged.
Type of support: Grants for special needs.
Application information: Applications accepted.
Additional information: Some services require application information. Contact the agency for eligibility determination.
EIN: 340971599

7275
Dr. D. R. Nugen Scholarship Fund
c/o KeyBank
4900 Tiedeman Rd., OH-01-49-0150
Brooklyn, OH 44144-2302

Foundation type: Independent foundation
Purpose: Scholarships to graduates of Nooksack Valley High School, OH who attended the school for at least three years.
Financial data: Year ended 12/31/2012. Assets, $38,758 (M); Expenditures, $8,675; Total giving, $6,650.
Fields of interest: Higher education.
Type of support: Support to graduates or students of specific schools.
Application information:
Deadline(s): None
Additional information: Contact school for current application guidelines.
EIN: 916028366

7276
Oberlin Shansi Memorial Association
103 Peters Hall
50 North Prof. Str.
Oberlin, OH 44074-1099 (440) 775-8605
Application e-mail: evelyn.wilkins@oberlin.edu, or hand deliver at Shansi Office, 103 Peters Hall, (Oberlin College campus)
FAX: (440) 775-8116; URL: http://www.oberlin.edu/cgi-bin/cgiwrap/shansi/shansi06.php?section=home

Foundation type: Public charity
Purpose: Fellowships to Oberlin College graduates to study in China, India, Indonesia, and Japan.
Financial data: Year ended 06/30/2011. Assets, $14,147,097 (M); Expenditures, $737,696; Total giving, $97,623; Grants to individuals, 13 grants totaling $20,454.
Fields of interest: Higher education.
International interests: China; India; Indonesia; Japan.
Type of support: Fellowships; Exchange programs.
Application information: Applications accepted. Application form required. Application form

available on the grantmaker's web site. Interview required.
Initial approach: Telephone or fax
Send request by: E-mail or hand deliver
Deadline(s): Oct. for Fellowships
Applicants should submit the following:
1) Transcripts
2) Resume
3) Essay
Additional information: See web site for additional guidelines.
Program descriptions:
Fellowship Program: The program requires candidates to operate independently, respect Shansi's long-term affiliations with their partners in Asia, and be mindful of the partner institution's requirements for the fellows. Candidates must be adaptable and patient, and demonstrate sensitivity to cultures with values that may be very different from their own. Balancing these objectives requires full-time commitment, individual initiative, and determination. The rewards are often rich and life changing. The fellowships are open to all Oberlin students, regardless of academic department, at both the College of Arts and Sciences and the Conservatory of Music.
Visiting Scholars Program: The scholars are faculty or staff chosen competitively from all of the Shansi partner institutions in Asia who spend up to a semester at Oberlin College in support of their scholarly growth. They observe undergraduate teaching, familiarize themselves with the library and its information retrieval system and pursue their areas of research. They are expected to share experiences with their home institution upon their return to Asia.
EIN: 340768350

7277
Ohio Community Pooled Annuity Trust
c/o The Dayton Foundation
500 Kettering Tower
Dayton, OH 45423-1038 (937) 225-9939

Foundation type: Public charity
Purpose: Financial assistance for disabled individuals of Dayton, Ohio.
Financial data: Year ended 06/30/2012. Assets, $3,265,198 (M); Expenditures, $195,529; Total giving, $147,926; Grants to individuals, totaling $137,926.
Fields of interest: Aging; Disabilities, people with.
Type of support: Grants for special needs.
Application information: Applications accepted.
Initial approach: Letter or telephone
Additional information: The organization provides a financial plan for supplemental needs without causing the individuals loss of Medicade and SSI benefits. Contact the trust for eligibillity determination.
EIN: 593788888

7278
Ohio Credit Union Foundation
10 W. Broad St., Ste. 1100
Columbus, OH 43215-3415 (614) 336-2894
Contact: Paul Mercer, Pres.
FAX: (614) 336-2895;
E-mail: oculmail@ohiocul.org; Toll-free tel.: (800) 486-2917; E-mail for Paul Mercer: pmercer@ohiocul.org; URL: http://www.ohiocreditunionfoundation.org/

Foundation type: Public charity
Purpose: Scholarships to high school seniors of various chapters of OH, pursuing postsecondary

education including professional, vocational, and academic studies not limited to colleges and universities.
Publications: Application guidelines; Newsletter.
Financial data: Year ended 12/31/2011. Assets, $819,257 (M); Expenditures, $214,979; Total giving, $213,952; Grants to individuals, totaling $15,000.
Fields of interest: Vocational education, post-secondary; Higher education.
Type of support: Scholarships—to individuals.
Application information: Applications accepted. Application form required. Application form available on the grantmaker's web site. Interview required.
Deadline(s): Feb. 28
Additional information: Each year the foundation awards up to five $3,000 scholarships, and $5,000 by creating a video submission answering a specific question. See web site for additional application guidelines.
EIN: 311582415

7279
Ohio Farm Bureau Foundation
280 N. High St., 6th Fl.
P.O. Box 182383
Columbus, OH 43218-2383 (614) 249-2400
Contact: Dave Rule, Secy.
FAX: (614) 249-2200; E-mail: foundation@ofbf.org;
URL: http://ofbf.org/foundation/

Foundation type: Public charity
Purpose: Scholarships to high school students of OH for attendance at four year accredited colleges or universities, or two year technical schools in pursuit of an agriculture degree.
Publications: Application guidelines; Annual report; Grants list; Informational brochure; Program policy statement.
Financial data: Year ended 12/31/2011. Assets, $697,404 (M); Expenditures, $54,461.
Fields of interest: Vocational education, post-secondary; Higher education; Agriculture.
Type of support: Scholarships—to individuals.
Application information: Applications accepted. Application form required.
Initial approach: Letter, telephone, or conference
Send request by: Mail, fax or e-mail
Copies of proposal: 1
Deadline(s): Mar. 1
Final notification: Apr. 15
Applicants should submit the following:
1) Photograph
2) Transcripts
3) Letter(s) of recommendation
4) Essay
Additional information: All applications must be typed.
Program descriptions:
Cindy Hollingshead Scholarship Fund: This scholarship assists students who plan to pursue careers focusing on agriculture, community service, and association leadership by providing scholarships of at least $1,000. Eligible applicants must be residents of Ohio, and must be members of the Ohio Farm Bureau Federation (OFBF) or must have been active in OFBF youth activities at the county, regional, or state level. Eligible applicants must also have a minimum 2.5 GPA (out of 4.0), and must be enrolled in one of the following courses of study: an accredited high school program, with personal plans to pursue a degree as a full-time student in an accredited two-year technical school or four-year college or university program; a course of study leading to completion in an accredited GED program, with personal plans to pursue a degree as

a full-time student in an accredited two-year technical school or four-year college or university programs; an accredited two-year technical school; an accredited four-year college or university program; or an accredited graduate program.

Darwin Bryan Scholarship Program: This program provides scholarships of at least $1,000 to assist students who have been active in Ohio Farm Bureau Federation (OFBF) youth programs, and/or whose parents are OFBF members, to continue their education. Eligible applicants must also have a minimum 2.5 GPA (out of 4.0), and must be enrolled in one of the following courses of study: an accredited high school program, with personal plans to pursue a degree as a full-time student in an accredited two-year technical school or four-year college or university program; a course of study leading to completion in an accredited GED program, with personal plans to pursue a degree as a full-time student in an accredited two-year technical school or four-year college or university programs; an accredited two-year technical school; an accredited four-year college or university program; or an accredited graduate program.

Foundation Scholar Programs: This program recognizes students for academic effort, community services, and career interests that use agriculture to enhance the partnership between producers and consumers in rural, suburban, and/ or urban settings. Eligible applicants must also have a minimum 2.5 GPA (out of 4.0), and must be enrolled in one of the following courses of study: an accredited high school program, with personal plans to pursue a degree as a full-time student in an accredited two-year technical school or four-year college or university program; a course of study leading to completion in an accredited GED program, with personal plans to pursue a degree as a full-time student in an accredited two-year technical school or four-year college or university programs; an accredited two-year technical school; an accredited four-year college or university program; or an accredited graduate program. Awards of at least $1,000 will be given.

Women's Leadership in Agriculture Scholarship Program: This program provides grants of at least $1,000 to support female education, recreation, and service. Eligible applicants must also have a minimum 2.5 GPA (out of 4.0), and must be enrolled in one of the following courses of study: an accredited high school program, with personal plans to pursue a degree as a full-time student in an accredited two-year technical school or four-year college or university program; a course of study leading to completion in an accredited GED program, with personal plans to pursue a degree as a full-time student in an accredited two-year technical school or four-year college or university programs; an accredited two-year technical school; an accredited four-year college or university program; or an accredited graduate program.
EIN: 311781473

7280
The Ohio Masonic Home
2655 W. National Rd.
Springfield, OH   45504-3617   (967) 525-3067
Contact: Terry W. Posey, Chair.
Toll-free tel.: (877)-679-4869; URL: http://
ohiomasonichome.org/

Foundation type: Public charity
Purpose: Scholarships to relatives of OH Masons.
Publications: Application guidelines; Annual report.
Financial data: Year ended 12/31/2011. Assets, $115,927,887 (M); Expenditures, $11,229,124;

Total giving, $16,834; Grants to individuals, totaling $16,834.
Fields of interest: Fraternal societies.
Type of support: Undergraduate support.
Application information: Applications accepted. Application form required.
  Initial approach: Letter
  Deadline(s): Apr. 1 for scholarships
Program description:
  Scholarship Program: Scholarships are available to provide tuition assistance for eligible students working towards a bachelor's, associate's, or other undergraduate degree program at a qualifying institution. Eligible applicants must have graduated from high school or passed the GED, have at least a 2.3 GPA, be between 16 and 25 years of age, and have a Masonic affiliation by establishing that the applicant's father, step-father, grandfather, or step-grandfather is or was a Mason in good standing of a body recognized by the Grand Lodge of F. & A. M. of Ohio, including, but not limited to, Blue Lodges and Price Hall Lodges. Preference will be given to applicants with financial need due to the father's or step-father's death or disability.
EIN: 310536997

7281
Ohio Newspapers Foundation
1335 Dublin Rd., Ste. 216-B
Columbus, OH   43215-1000   (614) 486-6677
Contact: Dennis Hetzel, Secy. and Exec. Dir.
FAX: (614) 486-4940;
E-mail: fdeaner@ohionews.org; URL: http://
www.ohionews.org/foundation

Foundation type: Public charity
Purpose: Scholarships to graduating seniors enrolled in an Ohio college or university pursuing a career in journalism.
Publications: Application guidelines; Grants list; Informational brochure; Informational brochure (including application guidelines).
Financial data: Year ended 12/31/2011. Assets, $669,730 (M); Expenditures, $431,885; Total giving, $339,980; Grants to individuals, totaling $14,695.
Fields of interest: Journalism school/education.
Type of support: Scholarships—to individuals.
Application information: Applications accepted. Application form required. Application form available on the grantmaker's web site.
  Send request by: Mail
  Deadline(s): Mar. 31
  Final notification: Applicants notified by May 15
  Applicants should submit the following:
    1) Transcripts
    2) Essay
    3) Work samples
    4) Letter(s) of recommendation
Program descriptions:
  Minority Scholarships: Awards $1,500 scholarship to a graduating minority high school senior at an Ohio high school, enrolled as a college freshman at an Ohio college or university. Applicant must be African American, Hispanic, Asian American or American Indian.
  Ohio Newspaper Women's Scholarship: Awards $1,500 to a male or female student who is enrolled as a junior or senior in an Ohio College or university and is majoring in journalism or an equivalent degree program.
  The Harold K. Douthit Regional Scholarship: Awards $1,500 to a high school senior from northern Ohio, enrolled as a sophomore, junior, or senior in a journalism or communications degree program at an Ohio college or university. Applicant must have graduated from a high school from

Cuyahoga, Erie, Geauga, Huron, Lorain, Wood, Sandusky, Ottawa, or Lucas County.
  University Journalism Scholarship: Awards $1,500 each to students who are enrolled as a sophomore, junior or senior at an Ohio college or university and majoring in journalism or an equivalent degree program. Preference will be given to students demonstrating a career commitment to newspaper journalism.
EIN: 310904715

7282
Ohio Osteopathic Foundation
53 W. 3rd Ave.
Columbus, OH   43201-3208   (614) 299-2107
Contact: Jon F. Wills, Exec. Dir.
FAX: (614) 294-0457; E-mail: jwills@ooanet.org;
URL: http://associationdatabase.com/aws/
OOSA/pt/sp/Home_Page

Foundation type: Public charity
Purpose: Scholarships to students for attendance at the Ohio University College of Osteopathic Medicine. Student Loans to provide assistance to Ohio students enrolled in osteopathic colleges.
Financial data: Year ended 04/30/2012. Assets, $1,492,597 (M); Expenditures, $319,282; Total giving, $35,125; Grants to individuals, totaling $20,375.
Fields of interest: Medical school/education.
Type of support: Scholarships—to individuals; Student loans—to individuals; Support to graduates or students of specific schools.
Application information: Applications accepted. Application form required.
  Additional information: Students applying for a scholarship should contact the Office of Student Affairs for additional guidelines. The loan program gives first preference to students from Northwest Ohio, and is based on need.
EIN: 237263316

7283
OHSAA Foundation
4080 Roselea Pl.
Columbus, OH   43214-3069   (614) 267-2502
Contact: Kimberly Combs, Exec. Dir.
FAX: (614) 267-1677; E-mail: kcombs@ohsaa.org;
URL: http://www.ohsaafoundation.org/

Foundation type: Public charity
Purpose: Scholarships to graduating student athletes of OH, for higher education.
Publications: Application guidelines; Newsletter.
Financial data: Year ended 07/31/2011. Assets, $10,884 (M); Expenditures, $84,929; Total giving, $30,000; Grants to individuals, totaling $30,000.
Fields of interest: Higher education; Recreation; Minorities.
Type of support: Scholarships—to individuals.
Application information: Applications accepted. Application form required. Application form available on the grantmaker's web site.
  Send request by: Online
  Applicants should submit the following:
    1) SAT
    2) GPA
    3) ACT
  Additional information: Applicant must have received a minimum of three varsity letter in one OHSAA sanctioned sport or four varsity letters in a combination of any two or more OHSAA sanctioned sports. Each school may submit only one male, one female and one

ethnic minority candidate for scholarship consideration.

Program description:

Scholarships: Awarded with the Ohio High School Athletic Association (OHSAA), the foundation annually provides scholarships to 54 senior student-athletes each year. Recipients are selected based on a points system which rewards students for grade-point averages, ACT and SAT scores, varsity letters earned, individual and team athletic honors. The top two student-athletes from each of the six OHSAA athletic districts receive $2,000 scholarships. In addition, the foundation provides six $1,000 minority scholarships for a student-athlete from each district.

EIN: 311582465

7284
Louis S. Oppenheim Charitable Trust

c/o PNC Bank, N.A.
P.O. Box 94651
Cleveland, OH   44101-4651
URL: http://www.pnc.com

Foundation type: Independent foundation
Purpose: Medical and living expenses to financially needy, blind residents of Peoria County, IL.
Financial data: Year ended 12/31/2012. Assets, $1,218,052 (M); Expenditures, $72,320; Total giving, $54,410; Grants to individuals, 3 grants totaling $13,930 (high: $5,710, low: $3,420).
Fields of interest: Disabilities, people with; Economically disadvantaged.
Type of support: Grants for special needs.
Application information: Applications accepted.
Initial approach: Letter or telephone
Deadline(s): None
Additional information: Applicants must describe financial need.
EIN: 376030392

7285
Louise & Lane Osborn Memorial Trust

P.O. Box 630858
Cincinnati, OH   45263-0858   (812) 456-3215
Application address: c/o Fifth Third Bank, Trust & Investment Mgmt. Div., P.O. Box 719, Evansville, IN 47705-0719, tel.: (812) 456-3215

Foundation type: Independent foundation
Purpose: Scholarships to graduates of Central High School, IN. Scholarships are limited to $2,000 per year, per student.
Financial data: Year ended 07/31/2013. Assets, $1,785,776 (M); Expenditures, $114,602; Total giving, $88,420.
Fields of interest: Higher education.
Type of support: Support to graduates or students of specific schools.
Application information: Application form required.
Deadline(s): Apr. 15
EIN: 356561029

7286
Outdoor Extravaganza

P.O. Box 444
McConnelsville, OH   43756-0444   (740) 297-0690
E-mail: ticketinfo@outdoor-ext.com; URL: http://www.outdoor-ext.com

Foundation type: Public charity
Purpose: Scholarships for residents of Morgan County, OH.

Financial data: Year ended 12/31/2011. Assets, $127,997 (M); Expenditures, $40,606; Total giving, $15,165; Grants to individuals, totaling $5,000.
Type of support: Undergraduate support.
Application information: Applications not accepted.
Additional information: Unsolicited requests for funds not considered.
EIN: 432054551

7287
Hilda M. Padgett Charitable Trust

c/o PNC Bank, NA
P.O. Box 94651
Cleveland, OH   44101-4651
URL: http://www.pnc.com

Foundation type: Independent foundation
Purpose: Scholarships to assist students of Illinois in their educational needs beyond high school.
Financial data: Year ended 12/31/2012. Assets, $1,204,721 (M); Expenditures, $15,003; Total giving, $3,000.
Fields of interest: Higher education.
Type of support: Scholarships—to individuals.
Application information: Applications accepted. Application form required.
Initial approach: Letter
Deadline(s): May 1
Applicants should submit the following:
    1) Transcripts
    2) Financial information
    3) Essay
Additional information: Application should include academic record and anticipated course of study.
EIN: 371338566

7288
C. Paul Palmer Memorial Scholarship Fund

P.O. Box 120
Findlay, OH   45839-0120   (419) 422-4341
Contact: Deb Montooth

Foundation type: Independent foundation
Purpose: Scholarships to children and grandchildren of National Lime and Stone Co. employees.
Financial data: Year ended 12/31/2012. Assets, $191,387 (M); Expenditures, $11,186; Total giving, $8,000.
Type of support: Employee-related scholarships.
Application information: Application form required.
Initial approach: Letter in writing or telephone
Deadline(s): Mar. 15
Company name: National Lime and Stone Company
EIN: 341759012

7289
Parenthesis Family Advocates, Inc.

6500 Taylor Rd., S.W.
Columbus, OH   43068   (614) 751-9112
FAX: (614) 751-9116;
E-mail: parenthe@frontiernet.net; Toll-free tel.: (888) 751-9112

Foundation type: Public charity
Purpose: Assistance to foster parents in and around the Columbus, OH area. Services include respite, mentoring, transportation, community activities, and summer camp.
Financial data: Year ended 06/30/2011. Assets, $645,327 (M); Expenditures, $1,461,412; Total

giving, $663,517; Grants to individuals, totaling $663,517.
Fields of interest: Youth development; Children/youth, services; Foster care.
Type of support: Grants for special needs.
Application information: Contact foundation for further program information.
EIN: 311089582

7290
Parents Advancing Choice in Education

(also known as PACE)
40 S. Perry St., Ste. 120
Dayton, OH   45402-1439   (937) 228-7223
Contact: George E. Loney, Exec. Dir.
FAX: (937) 226-1887;
E-mail: dariastone@pacedayton.org; URL: http://www.pacedayton.org

Foundation type: Independent foundation
Purpose: Scholarships to students from low income families in the Montgomery county, OH area giving parents the choice to send children to a school of their choice.
Publications: Annual report; Informational brochure; Newsletter.
Financial data: Year ended 06/30/2013. Assets, $575,236 (M); Expenditures, $1,372,268; Total giving, $915,567; Grants to individuals, 46 grants totaling $915,567 (high: $267,713, low: $236).
Fields of interest: Education.
Type of support: Scholarships—to individuals.
Application information: Applications not accepted.
Additional information: Unsolicited requests for funds not considered or acknowledged.
Program description:

K-12 Scholarships: Scholarships are available to Ohio students, grades K-12, who wish to attend a private school. A parent or guardian must come to the organization's office and sign up to be on the wait list for a scholarship; from this list, new recipients are chosen. All scholarships are based upon financial need. The organization provides an online annual income eligibility scale, which aids individuals in determining for what amount they might qualify, if selected as a recipient. Parents who receive a scholarship can choose any participating school that their children may attend. New scholarships are added as funds become available.
EIN: 311809977

7291
Park Foundation

c/o The Huntington National Bank
P.O. Box 1558, EA4E
Columbus, OH   43216

Foundation type: Independent foundation
Purpose: Scholarships to high school seniors who reside in Perry County, OH, and attend Southern Local High School their entire senior year.
Financial data: Year ended 06/30/2013. Assets, $534,760 (M); Expenditures, $29,444; Total giving, $21,463.
Type of support: Support to graduates or students of specific schools; Undergraduate support.
Application information: Applications not accepted.
Additional information: Contributes only to preselected individuals.
EIN: 316207775

7292

Partners for a Cure Foundation

c/o Kristin G. Kalnow
2 Grandin Ln.
Cincinnati, OH 45208
URL: http://www.pfacf.org

Foundation type: Independent foundation
Purpose: Financial assistance to cancer patients in the U.S. with day care services, doctors and hospital fees.
Financial data: Year ended 12/31/2012. Assets, $9,921 (M); Expenditures, $14,110; Total giving, $7,500; Grants to individuals, 5 grants totaling $7,500 (high: $1,500, low: $1,500).
Fields of interest: Cancer.
Type of support: Grants for special needs.
Application information: Contact the foundation for eligibility.
EIN: 200800513

7293

PDR Foundation, Inc.

624 Tamarac Trail
Wadsworth, OH 44281 (330) 335-3200
Contact: Patrick L. Ryan, Pres.and Treas.
Application Address: 1 Park Center Dr.,Ste. 301A,Wadsworth,OH,44281

Foundation type: Independent foundation
Purpose: Scholarships to graduates of the Wadsworth and Antwerp school districts in OH.
Financial data: Year ended 12/31/2011. Assets, $2,560,032 (M); Expenditures, $121,822; Total giving, $118,100.
Type of support: Support to graduates or students of specific schools; Undergraduate support.
Application information:
  Initial approach: Letter
  Deadline(s): Mar. 1
EIN: 341881438

7294

Walter G. and Ella M. Peak Scholarship Fund

106 S. Main St., Ste. 16
Akron, OH 44308-1418

Foundation type: Independent foundation
Purpose: Scholarships to graduating students of the Elyria Central School District, OH.
Financial data: Year ended 12/31/2012. Assets, $105,274 (M); Expenditures, $6,166; Total giving, $2,200.
Fields of interest: Higher education.
Type of support: Support to graduates or students of specific schools; Undergraduate support.
Application information: Application form required.
  Deadline(s): Mar. 1
  Additional information: Application can be obtained from and returned to school counselor.
EIN: 341776865

7295

The Pearce Foundation

P.O. Box 1558, Dept. EA4E86
Columbus, OH 43216-1558
Contact: Carol Chamberlain

Foundation type: Independent foundation
Purpose: Scholarships to students in the Ohio area for continuing education at accredited colleges or universities.

Financial data: Year ended 12/31/2012. Assets, $2,199,470 (M); Expenditures, $91,297; Total giving, $64,714.
Fields of interest: Higher education.
Type of support: Scholarships—to individuals.
Application information:
  Initial approach: Letter
  Deadline(s): None
  Additional information: Contact foundation for application guidelines.
EIN: 346572300

7296

Charles Pehna Scholarship Trust

c/o PNC Bank, N.A.
P.O. Box 94651
Cleveland, OH 44101-4651

Foundation type: Independent foundation
Purpose: Scholarships to students, primarily in PA, for higher education.
Financial data: Year ended 12/31/2012. Assets, $300,951 (M); Expenditures, $19,461; Total giving, $15,225.
Type of support: Undergraduate support.
Application information: Applications not accepted.
  Additional information: Unsolicited requests for funds not considered or acknowledged.
EIN: 527155874

7297

Peoples Bancorp Foundation Inc.

138 Putnam St.
P.O. Box 738
Marietta, OH 45750-2923 (740) 376-7128
Contact: Kristi Close, Secy.
Contact for Robert E. Evans Scholarship: Larry E. Holdren

Foundation type: Company-sponsored foundation
Purpose: Scholarships to high school seniors of Ohio, West Virginia and Kentucky, pursuing a four year degree in areas of business or liberal arts. Scholarships also for youth in grades 9 through 12.
Publications: Application guidelines.
Financial data: Year ended 12/31/2012. Assets, $778,016 (M); Expenditures, $242,581; Total giving, $236,400; Grants to individuals, 17 grants totaling $16,150 (high: $1,250, low: $100).
Fields of interest: Visual arts; Humanities; Literature; Business school/education; Education; Science; Social sciences.
Type of support: Scholarships—to individuals; Support to graduates or students of specific schools; Awards/prizes.
Application information: Applications accepted. Application form required. Application form available on the grantmaker's web site.
  Send request by: Mail
  Deadline(s): Mar. 31 for Robert E. Evans Scholarship
  Applicants should submit the following:
    1) SAT
    2) ACT
    3) FAFSA
    4) Essay
    5) Letter(s) of recommendation
Program descriptions:
  Festival of Learning Scholarship: The foundation awards scholarships to students competing for awards by displaying their skills in language arts, business, social science, science/math/health, fine and applied arts, foreign language and family consumer sciences. The scholarships range from $100 to $300. Each participant can compete in up

to two categories and can win up to $600. Scholarships are awarded each year for youth in grades 9 through 12.
  Robert E. Evans Scholarship: The foundation awards scholarships to high school seniors locations in market areas served by Peoples Bank to pursue a four-year degree in business, social sciences, fine art, literature, or the humanities at select universities. Awards will go to students attending Marietta College, Washington State Community College, Ohio Valley University, WVU-Parkersburg, and other college and universities located in market areas served by Peoples Bank. Applicants must have a GPA of 2.8 or higher. Awards are based on demonstration of financial need with preference given to those having a higher need.
EIN: 300222364

7298

Frances E. Perry Fund

c/o KeyBank
4900 Tiedeman Rd., OH-01-49-0150
Brooklyn, OH 44144-2302

Foundation type: Independent foundation
Purpose: Scholarships to individuals for higher education, primarily at New England educational institutions.
Financial data: Year ended 12/31/2012. Assets, $248,427 (M); Expenditures, $16,614; Total giving, $12,000; Grants to individuals, 6 grants totaling $12,000 (high: $2,000, low: $2,000).
Fields of interest: Higher education.
Type of support: Scholarships—to individuals.
Application information: Applications not accepted.
  Additional information: Unsolicited requests for funds not considered or acknowledged.
EIN: 016031448

7299

Perry Scholarship Foundation

(formerly Nathan F. & Edna L. Perry Scholarship)
c/o KeyBank, N.A.
P.O. Box 10099
Toledo, OH 43699-0099 (207) 764-0121

Foundation type: Independent foundation
Purpose: Scholarships to graduates of Presque Isle High School who are residents of Presque Isle, ME.
Financial data: Year ended 05/31/2013. Assets, $480,031 (M); Expenditures, $16,381; Total giving, $9,250; Grants to individuals, 39 grants totaling $9,250 (high: $500, low: $125).
Type of support: Support to graduates or students of specific schools; Undergraduate support.
Application information: Applications not accepted.
  Additional information: Unsolicited requests for funds not considered or acknowledged.
EIN: 510158963

7300

Frank L. and Ruth F. Peters Scholarship B Fund

P.O. Box 1558, Dept. EA4E86
Columbus, OH 43216

Foundation type: Independent foundation
Purpose: Scholarships to graduates of Brookfield High School, OH, pursuing a degree in mathematics at Oberlin College, OH.

Financial data: Year ended 12/31/2012. Assets, $332,477 (M); Expenditures, $19,430; Total giving, $14,500.
Fields of interest: Higher education; Mathematics.
Type of support: Support to graduates or students of specific schools.
Application information: Applications accepted. Application form required.
Additional information: Application must include GPA and two references.
EIN: 237872473

7301
Phi Delta Theta Educational Foundation
2 S. Campus Ave.
Oxford, OH 45056-1801 (513) 523-6966
FAX: (513) 523-9200;
E-mail: foundation@phideltatheta.org

Foundation type: Public charity
Purpose: Undergraduate scholarships and graduate fellowships by nomination only, primarily to members of Phi Delta Theta Fraternity.
Publications: Application guidelines; Newsletter.
Financial data: Year ended 12/31/2011. Assets, $11,329,550 (M); Expenditures, $1,657,105; Total giving, $398,646; Grants to individuals, totaling $206,186.
Type of support: Awards/grants by nomination only.
Application information: Application form required.
Deadline(s): Mar. 15 for Francis D. Lyon Scholarship; May 1 for Graduate Fellowships
EIN: 346539803

7302
Phi Kappa Tau Foundation
5221 Morning Sun Rd.
Oxford, OH 45056-1304 (513) 523-4193
Contact: C. Steven hartman, C.E.O.
FAX: (513) 523-9325;
E-mail: foundation@phikappatau.org; Toll-free tel.: (800) 758-1906; URL: http://phikappatau.org/foundation/foundation-home-page.html

Foundation type: Public charity
Purpose: Scholarships to alumni and undergraduate members of Phi Kappa Tau Fraternity.
Publications: Application guidelines; Annual report.
Financial data: Year ended 06/30/2012. Assets, $10,089,654 (M); Expenditures, $892,935; Total giving, $371,263; Grants to individuals, totaling $24,000.
Fields of interest: Students, sororities/fraternities; Adults, men.
Type of support: Graduate support; Undergraduate support.
Application information: Applications accepted. Application form required. Application form available on the grantmaker's web site.
Initial approach: Letter or telephone
Deadline(s): Apr. 1
Applicants should submit the following:
1) Transcripts
2) Letter(s) of recommendation
3) Financial information
4) GPA
5) Essay
Additional information: Eligible applicants for all scholarships must be initiated members of Phi Kappa Tau who will be entering the next academic year as juniors, seniors, or graduate students, and who have a GPA of 3.0 or higher. Applicants will be evaluated on scholastic achievement, chapter service, and campus and community activities and honors.

Program descriptions:
Heidi Kahle Memorial Scholarships: A $1,000 scholarship will be awarded to a Phi Kappa Tau chapter member from Nebraska Wesleyan, Iowa State University, or the University of Nebraska at Kearney. Candidates must be pre-med or pursuing a degree in an academic field related to medicine and healthcare.
Parents Fund Scholarships: At least two $1,000 scholarships are awarded annually to Phi Kappa Tau members in good standing with their chapters. At least one scholarship will be awarded to an undergraduate student, and at least one to a graduate student.
Paul A. Elfers Omega Scholarships: Six $2,250 scholarships are available to Phi Kappa Tau members in good standing with the fraternity. One scholarship is reserved for an outstanding chapter treasurer.
Phi Kappa Tau Endowed Scholarships: Annual awards of $1,000 each are available to Phi Kappa Tau members in good standing with their chapter. Named scholarships under this program include the J. Oliver Amos Scholarship, Jack L. Anson Scholarship, Rea Andrew Axline Scholarship, Ewing T. Boles Scholarship, E. Thomas Boles Jr. M.D. Scholarship, Thomas C. Cunningham Scholarship, Paul A. Elfers Scholarship, Gregory D. Hollen Scholarship, John Franklin S. McMullan Scholarship, Harold H. Short Scholarship, Ernest H. Volwiler Scholarship, and Joshua Berman Memorial Scholarship.
EIN: 316024975

7303
The Piqua Community Foundation
126 W. High St.
P.O. Box 226
Piqua, OH 45356-2310 (937) 615-9080
Contact: Karen S. Wendeln, Exec. Dir.
FAX: (937) 615-9981;
E-mail: kwendeln@piquacommunityfoundation.org; URL: http://www.piquacommunityfoundation.org

Foundation type: Community foundation
Purpose: Scholarships to high school graduates in Piqua, OH, for higher education.
Publications: Application guidelines; Annual report; Grants list; Informational brochure; Newsletter.
Financial data: Year ended 12/31/2012. Assets, $7,030,230 (M); Expenditures, $823,451; Total giving, $724,026; Grants to individuals, 37 grants totaling $46,500.
Fields of interest: Higher education.
Type of support: Undergraduate support.
Application information: Applications accepted. Application form required. Application form available on the grantmaker's web site.
Initial approach: Letter, telephone or e-mail
Send request by: Mail
Copies of proposal: 1
Deadline(s): Varies
Applicants should submit the following:
1) Transcripts
2) Letter(s) of recommendation
3) GPA
4) ACT
EIN: 311391908

7304
Piqua Education Foundation
719 E. Ash St.
Piqua, OH 45356-2411 (937) 773-4321
E-mail: hillm@piqua.org; URL: http://www.piqua.org/PiquaEducationFoundation.aspx

Foundation type: Public charity
Purpose: Scholarships for high school graduates, and college scholarships for students who are graduates of Piqua High School, OH. Education grants to faculty and staff of Piqua city schools to provide seed money and to support innovative educational undertakings.
Financial data: Year ended 12/31/2011. Assets, $2,861,284 (M); Expenditures, $244,880; Total giving, $212,498; Grants to individuals, totaling $212,498.
Fields of interest: Higher education; College.
Type of support: Grants to individuals; Scholarships—to individuals; Support to graduates or students of specific schools.
Application information: Applications accepted. Application form required. Application form available on the grantmaker's web site.
Send request by: Mail
Deadline(s): Mar. 31 for Scholarships, Aug. 31 for Grants
Additional information: High school students should contact their guidance counselor for application. See web site for additional guidelines.
EIN: 311117501

7305
Alice Plimpton Education Trust
(formerly Alice H. Plimpton Educational Fund)
1422 Euclid Ave., Ste. 1130
Cleveland, OH 44115

Foundation type: Independent foundation
Purpose: Scholarships to students of Norwood High School, MA.
Financial data: Year ended 09/30/2013. Assets, $1,117,000 (M); Expenditures, $63,807; Total giving, $41,000; Grants to individuals, 41 grants totaling $41,000 (high: $1,000, low: $1,000).
Type of support: Scholarships—to individuals; Support to graduates or students of specific schools.
Application information: Applications not accepted.
Additional information: Recipients are selected by the faculty of Norwood High School, MA.
EIN: 046013418

7306
Portage County Sheriff's Association
164 Fairlane Dr.
Ravenna, OH 44266-0786 (330) 296-4774

Foundation type: Independent foundation
Purpose: Grants to residents of Portage County, OH, going through financial hardship.
Financial data: Year ended 12/31/2012. Assets, $146,284 (M); Expenditures, $11,402; Total giving, $8,310; Grants to individuals, 3 grants totaling $1,500 (high: $700, low: $300).
Type of support: Grants for special needs.
Application information: Applications accepted.
Deadline(s): None
EIN: 810616994

7307
Mary E. Powell Trust
112 N. Main St.
Bellefontaine, OH 43311-2021 (937) 593-8510
Contact: D. Fred Burton, Pres.

Foundation type: Independent foundation

Purpose: Financial assistance to elderly ladies who are residents of Logan County, OH to maintain a minimum standard of living.
Financial data: Year ended 12/31/2011. Assets, $47,509 (M); Expenditures, $8,423; Total giving, $5,040; Grants to individuals, 7 grants totaling $5,040 (high: $720, low: $720).
Fields of interest: Aging; Women.
Type of support: Grants for special needs.
Application information:
    Deadline(s): None
EIN: 346532522

7308
Beatrice Prior Memorial Scholarship Trust
146 E. Center St.
Marion, OH   43302-3802

Foundation type: Operating foundation
Purpose: Scholarships by nomination only to graduates of Marion Harding High School, OH.
Financial data: Year ended 12/31/2012. Assets, $0 (M); Expenditures, $306,342; Total giving, $304,028; Grants to individuals, 6 grants totaling $12,000 (high: $2,000, low: $2,000).
Type of support: Support to graduates or students of specific schools; Awards/grants by nomination only; Undergraduate support.
Application information: Applications not accepted.
    Additional information: Scholarships are based on numeric class ranking, no application will be utilized.
EIN: 316637737

7309
PSA No. 3 Agency on Aging, Inc.
200 E. High St., 2nd Fl.
Lima, OH   45801-4424   (419) 222-7723
Contact: Chloe Cole, Ex-Offi.
FAX: (419) 222-8262; Toll-free tel.: (800) 653-7723; URL: http://www.psa3.org

Foundation type: Public charity
Purpose: Grants to elderly residents of Allen, Auglaize, Hancock, Hardin, Mercer, Putnam, and Van Wert counties, OH.
Financial data: Year ended 12/31/2011. Assets, $1,645,905 (M); Expenditures, $14,780,111; Total giving, $11,768,586; Grants to individuals, totaling $11,757,086.
Fields of interest: Aging.
Type of support: Grants for special needs.
Application information: Contact foundation for eligibility requirements.
EIN: 341160526

7310
Psychiatric Research Foundation of Columbus, Inc.
1670 Upham Dr.
Columbus, OH   43210-1250   (614) 293-8204
Contact: Charles Dozer, Chair.

Foundation type: Public charity
Purpose: Research grants and awards to faculty in the department of psychiatry at Ohio State University, OH.
Financial data: Year ended 12/31/2011. Assets, $692,207 (M); Expenditures, $25,869; Total giving, $15,950; Grants to individuals, totaling $5,950.
Fields of interest: Medical school/education; Research.
Type of support: Research; Awards/prizes.

Application information: Contact foundation for complete application deadline/guidelines.
EIN: 237212292

7311
Jack Mary Rains Scholarship Fund
c/o PNC Bank, N.A.
P.O. Box 94651
Cleveland, OH   44101

Foundation type: Independent foundation
Purpose: Scholarships primarily to individuals attending colleges or universities in IN.
Financial data: Year ended 12/31/2011. Assets, $312,726 (M); Expenditures, $19,016; Total giving, $12,000; Grants to individuals, totaling $12,000.
Fields of interest: Higher education.
Type of support: Undergraduate support.
Application information: Applications not accepted.
    Additional information: Unsolicited requests for funds not considered or acknowledged.
EIN: 356337707

7312
Mack Rapp Education Fund Charitable Trust
P.O. Box 94651
Cleveland, OH   44101-4651

Foundation type: Independent foundation
Purpose: Scholarships to individuals studying measurement science and other, related fields.
Financial data: Year ended 12/31/2012. Assets, $200,394 (M); Expenditures, $10,868; Total giving, $8,000.
Fields of interest: Science.
Type of support: Undergraduate support.
Application information: Contact foundation for eligibility requirements.
EIN: 316056686

7313
The Harry Ratner Human Services Fund
25701 Science Park Dr.
Cleveland, OH   44122-7302   (216) 593-2900
Contact: Charles Ratner, Pres.

Foundation type: Public charity
Purpose: Grants to individuals in the Cleveland, OH, area in need of food, clothing, healthcare, shelter, and other basic necessities.
Financial data: Year ended 06/30/2012. Assets, $302,847 (M); Expenditures, $108,369; Total giving, $101,797.
Fields of interest: Economically disadvantaged.
Type of support: Grants for special needs.
Application information: Contact foundation for eligibility requirements.
EIN: 341360076

7314
Ratner, Miller, Shafran Foundation
50 Public Sq.
Cleveland, OH   44113-2295   (216) 416-3475
Contact: Albert Ratner, Secy.

Foundation type: Independent foundation
Purpose: Scholarships to high school graduates in OH, who have maintained good scholastic records to continue their education at the college level.

Financial data: Year ended 11/30/2013. Assets, $38,996 (M); Expenditures, $49,150; Total giving, $39,150; Grants to individuals, 97 grants totaling $39,150 (high: $750, low: -$500).
Fields of interest: Higher education.
Type of support: Scholarships—to individuals.
Application information: Application form required.
    Deadline(s): May 1
    Applicants should submit the following:
    1) Photograph
    2) Transcripts
    3) Letter(s) of recommendation
EIN: 346521216

7315
Reaching Heights, the Cleveland Heights/University Heights Public Schools Foundation
1991 Lee Rd., Ste. 106
Cleveland Heights, OH   44118-2571   (216) 932-5110
E-mail for scholarship: Krista@reachingheights.org
E-mail: patrick@reachingheights.org; URL: http://www.reachingheights.org

Foundation type: Public charity
Purpose: Music scholarship for private music lessons to 5th-9th grade students enrolled in Cleveland Heights-University Heights School District's, OH instrumental music program.
Publications: Application guidelines; Annual report; Financial statement; Grants list; Informational brochure (including application guidelines); Newsletter.
Financial data: Year ended 07/31/2012. Assets, $149,997 (M); Expenditures, $116,442; Total giving, $7,611.
Type of support: Scholarships—to individuals.
Application information: Applications accepted. Application form required.
    Deadline(s): Oct. 29
    Additional information: Award is based on financial need.
EIN: 341604071

7316
George J. Record School Foundation
P.O. Box 581
Conneaut, OH   44030-0581   (216) 599-8283
Contact: Charles N. Lafferty, Pres.

Foundation type: Independent foundation
Purpose: Scholarships to legal residents of Ashtabula County, OH, for tuition and fees at approved private colleges and universities.
Financial data: Year ended 12/31/2012. Assets, $2,441,948 (M); Expenditures, $124,939; Total giving, $67,050; Grants to individuals, totaling $67,050.
Fields of interest: Religion.
Type of support: Undergraduate support.
Application information: Applications accepted. Application form required. Interview required.
    Deadline(s): May 20 for first-year students, June 20 for upper class students
    Applicants should submit the following:
    1) Photograph
    2) Class rank
    3) Letter(s) of recommendation
    4) Transcripts
    5) SAT
    6) GPA
    Additional information: Applicants must attend approved private colleges and complete the

equivalent of six semester hours or nine quarter-hours of religious study.
EIN: 340830818

7317
Religion Newswriters Foundation
P.O. Box 2037
Westerville, OH 43081-2130 (573) 355-5201
Contact: Debra L. Mason, Exec. Dir.

Foundation type: Public charity
Purpose: Scholarships to full-time journalists to cover the costs of taking college religious courses.
Publications: Application guidelines; Annual report.
Financial data: Year ended 06/30/2012. Assets, $332,654 (M); Expenditures, $166,346; Total giving, $49,270; Grants to individuals, totaling $49,270.
Fields of interest: Print publishing; Theological school/education; Religion.
Type of support: Scholarships—to individuals.
Application information: Applications accepted. Application form required. Application form available on the grantmaker's web site.
  Initial approach: Application
  Deadline(s): Apr. 1, July 1, Oct. 1 and Jan. 1for Lilly Scholarships, June 17 for Religion Newswriters Scholarship
  Additional information: See web site for complete application guidelines.
Program descriptions:
  Lilly Scholarships in Religion for Journalists: Journalists will receive scholarships for up to $5,000 each to study religion or spirituality at any accredited college, university, or seminary. Scholarships can cover expenses related to tuition, registration, parking, and books. Online and travel classes also are eligible as long as travel costs are part of the curriculum. Scholarships are available to full-time journalists in the U.S. and Canada.
  Religion Newswriters Association Annual Conference Scholarships: Members of the Religion Newswriters Association can apply for scholarships of up to $1,000 to attend the RNA annual conference. Stipends can be used for registration, hotel, and travel fees. All active RNA members who have not received more than two conference scholarships in the past are eligible. Priority is given to active members who have never received a scholarship.
EIN: 311650883

7318
Remmele Foundation
100 Warren Ave.
Niles, OH 44446

Foundation type: Company-sponsored foundation
Purpose: Scholarships to children of employees (excluding company officers) of Remmele Engineering, Inc., MN. Awards up to $5,000 per year for up to four years for college or university students, and up to $2,000 per year for up to two years for vocational students.
Financial data: Year ended 12/31/2012. Assets, $10,846 (M); Expenditures, $0; Total giving, $0.
Fields of interest: Vocational education.
Type of support: Employee-related scholarships.
Application information: Application form required.
  Deadline(s): Apr. 13
  Final notification: Recipients will be notified by May 15
  Applicants should submit the following:
    1) Essay
    2) Photograph
    3) Transcripts

Additional information: Application must also include results of any aptitude, intelligence, or achievement tests taken and scholastic record form completed by principal or high school counselor.
Company name: Remmele Engineering, Incorporated
EIN: 411356088

7319
Edith Grace Craig Reynolds Estate Foundation
(formerly Edith Grace Reynolds Estate Residuary Trust)
c/o KeyBank N.A.
4900 Tiedeman Rd., OH-01-49-0150
Brooklyn, OH 44144-2302
Contact: Stanley Lepkowski
Application address: 66 S. Pearl St., Albanyn NY 12207

Foundation type: Independent foundation
Purpose: Scholarships to students residing in School District No. 1, Rensselaer County, NY for continuing education at institutions of higher learning.
Financial data: Year ended 03/31/2013. Assets, $1,048,413 (M); Expenditures, $69,507; Total giving, $55,048; Grants to individuals, 76 grants totaling $55,048 (high: $3,600, low: $100).
Fields of interest: Higher education.
Type of support: Scholarships—to individuals.
Application information: Application form required.
  Initial approach: Letter
  Deadline(s): Feb. 15
  Applicants should submit the following:
    1) Transcripts
    2) Financial information
  Additional information: Application must also include a copy of parents' income tax form.
EIN: 237170056

7320
Robert L. Rhoad Testamentary Trust
301 S. Main St., Ste. 3
Findlay, OH 45840-3343
Contact: William E. Clark, Tr.

Foundation type: Independent foundation
Purpose: Scholarships to residents of Hancock County, OH, who are pursuing higher education.
Financial data: Year ended 12/31/2011. Assets, $980,449 (M); Expenditures, $84,111; Total giving, $53,500.
Type of support: Undergraduate support.
Application information: Applications accepted. Application form required.
  Send request by: Mail
  Deadline(s): Apr. 1
  Applicants should submit the following:
    1) Letter(s) of recommendation
    2) Transcripts
EIN: 346959896

7321
Richland County Foundation
(formerly The Richland County Foundation of Mansfield, Ohio)
24 W. 3rd St., Ste. 100
Mansfield, OH 44902-1209 (419) 525-3020
Contact: Bradford Groves, Pres.
FAX: (419) 525-1590;
E-mail: info@rcfoundation.org; Additional e-mail:

bgroves@rcfoundation.org; URL: http://www.richlandcountyfoundation.org/

Foundation type: Community foundation
Purpose: Scholarships for full-time undergraduate study to financially needy residents of Richland County, OH, with at least a 2.5 GPA.
Publications: Application guidelines; Annual report (including application guidelines); Informational brochure; Newsletter.
Financial data: Year ended 12/31/2012. Assets, $105,910,279 (M); Expenditures, $3,133,178; Total giving, $2,470,242; Grants to individuals, 397 grants totaling $346,308.
Fields of interest: Higher education.
Type of support: Undergraduate support.
Application information: Applications accepted. Application form required. Application form available on the grantmaker's web site.
  Initial approach: Letter or telephone
  Send request by: Mail, fax, or e-mail
  Copies of proposal: 1
  Deadline(s): Apr. 1
  Final notification: Recipients notified late June
  Applicants should submit the following:
    1) GPA
    2) FAFSA
EIN: 340872883

7322
Gladys & Evelyn Rickert Memorial Scholarship Fund
c/o PNC Bank, N.A.
P.O. Box 94651
Cleveland, OH 44101-4651 (724) 588-2500

Foundation type: Independent foundation
Purpose: Scholarships to graduating seniors from Greenville Area Senior High School, PA, for higher education.
Financial data: Year ended 12/31/2011. Assets, $250,697 (M); Expenditures, $18,705; Total giving, $15,000; Grants to individuals, 3 grants totaling $15,000 (high: $12,000, low: $1,500).
Fields of interest: Higher education.
Type of support: Support to graduates or students of specific schools; Undergraduate support.
Application information: Applications accepted.
  Initial approach: Letter
  Deadline(s): Jan. 30
  Additional information: Recipients are selected based on financial need, scholastic aptitude and academic performance. Application should include transcripts.
EIN: 237876237

7323
Ruth E. Roach Memorial Scholarship Fund
17608 West River Rd.
Bowling Green, OH 43402 (419) 823-6048
Contact: Sandy Phillips

Foundation type: Independent foundation
Purpose: Scholarships to high school graduates residing in OH, for undergraduate education at U.S. institutions.
Financial data: Year ended 12/31/2011. Assets, $839,365 (M); Expenditures, $45,106; Total giving, $43,550; Grants to individuals, 36 grants totaling $43,550 (high: $2,500, low: $500).
Type of support: Undergraduate support.
Application information: Applications accepted. Application form required.
  Deadline(s): Apr. 1
  Applicants should submit the following:
    1) Transcripts

2) Essay
3) Letter(s) of recommendation
EIN: 341799826

7324
A. F. Robertson Family Memorial Fund
c/o PNC Bank, N.A.
P.O. Box 94651
Cleveland, OH 44101-4651 (216) 222-9815
Contact: Jane Kleinsmith
*Application Address:*1900 E. 9th St. Cleveland, OH
44114

Foundation type: Independent foundation
Purpose: Scholarships to students of Seymour High
School and Brownstown Central High School, both
in IN. Preference is given to residents of
Brownstown and Hamilton Townships.
Financial data: Year ended 12/31/2012. Assets,
$556,612 (M); Expenditures, $23,765; Total
giving, $16,800.
Fields of interest: Higher education.
Type of support: Scholarships—to individuals;
Support to graduates or students of specific
schools.
Application information: Application form required.
Interview required.
Deadline(s): Mar. 1
Applicants should submit the following:
1) SAT
2) Transcripts
3) Letter(s) of recommendation
4) FAFSA
5) FAF
Additional information: Application must also
include an appraisal of qualifications by
principal or counselor. Applications may be
obtained from guidance counselors of
Seymour High School and Brownstown Central
High School, both in IN.
EIN: 356057077

7325
Roddick Fund
(also known as R Johnson)
368 Mentor Ave.
Painesville, OH 44077-2607 (440) 352-0562

Foundation type: Independent foundation
Purpose: Scholarships to residents of the greater
Painesville, OH, community.
Financial data: Year ended 12/31/2011. Assets,
$877,996 (M); Expenditures, $63,935; Total
giving, $49,630.
Fields of interest: Higher education.
Type of support: Scholarships—to individuals.
Application information: Applications accepted.
Application form required.
Initial approach: Letter
Deadline(s): Apr. 1
EIN: 346793439

7326
Bruce & Mary Rogers Student Loan
(formerly Ada M. Rogers Trust, also known as Bruce
& Mary Rogers Memorial Student Loan Fund)
P.O. Box 1558 Dept. EA4E86
Columbus, OH 43216

Foundation type: Independent foundation
Purpose: Student loans to members or children of
members of the Western Reserve Baptist Church,
Trumbull Baptist Association of Churches, Ohio
Baptist Convention, and American Baptist Church

USA. Loans are interest-free if repaid within five
years of graduation.
Financial data: Year ended 08/31/2013. Assets,
$581,499 (M); Expenditures, $8,827; Total giving,
$2,000.
Fields of interest: Christian agencies & churches;
Religion.
Type of support: Student loans—to individuals.
Application information: Applications not
accepted.
Additional information: Application must include
financial information, biographical information
and transcripts. Deadline Feb. 15. Unsolicited
requests for funds not considered or
acknowledged.
EIN: 346631957

7327
Lillian L. Root Scholarship Fund
P.O. Box 630858
Cincinnati, OH 45263-0858

Foundation type: Independent foundation
Purpose: Scholarships primarily to individuals for
attendance at colleges or universities in IN.
Financial data: Year ended 12/31/2012. Assets,
$251,580 (M); Expenditures, $21,502; Total
giving, $16,100.
Fields of interest: Higher education.
Type of support: Scholarships—to individuals.
Application information: Applications not
accepted.
EIN: 351901966

7328
Raymond Rosenberger Award Foundation
P.O. Box 94651
Cleveland, OH 44101-4651

Foundation type: Independent foundation
Purpose: Awards to residents of Fort Wayne, IN who
have performed diligent and faithful service and
have devoted their time to organizations dedicated
to alleviating human suffering.
Financial data: Year ended 06/30/2012. Assets,
$1,475,337 (M); Expenditures, $89,291; Total
giving, $72,000.
Fields of interest: Human services.
Type of support: Awards/grants by nomination only;
Awards/prizes.
Application information: Applications not
accepted.
Additional information: Contributes only to
pre-selected individuals, unsolicited requests
for funds not considered or acknowledged.
EIN: 356627244

7329
Helen L. & Marie F. Rotterman Trust
1900 Kettering Twr.
Dayton, OH 45423-1127
Contact: Jeffrey B. Shulman, Tr.

Foundation type: Independent foundation
Purpose: Scholarships to young Catholic women
primarily from the Dayton, OH, area to attend Trinity
College, Washington, DC.
Financial data: Year ended 07/31/2012. Assets,
$3,430,441 (M); Expenditures, $230,174; Total
giving, $189,000; Grants to individuals, 3 grants
totaling $45,000 (high: $15,000, low: $15,000).
Fields of interest: Catholic agencies & churches;
Women.

Type of support: Scholarships—to individuals;
Support to graduates or students of specific
schools.
Application information:
Initial approach: Letter
Deadline(s): Four to six weeks prior to school year
Additional information: Application must include
a copy of Trinity College application, high
school transcripts, and proof of Catholic
Church affiliation.
EIN: 316236156

7330
Mildred C. Roy Scholarship Fund
211 E. 2nd St.
Port Clinton, OH 43452-1116 (419) 734-4060
Contact: George C. Wilber, Tr.

Foundation type: Operating foundation
Purpose: Scholarships to graduates of Port Clinton
High School, OH.
Financial data: Year ended 12/31/2011. Assets,
$82,591 (M); Expenditures, $5,592; Total giving,
$5,500; Grants to individuals, 4 grants totaling
$5,500 (high: $1,500, low: $1,000).
Type of support: Support to graduates or students
of specific schools; Undergraduate support.
Application information: Applications accepted.
Application form required.
Deadline(s): Feb. 1
Additional information: Applications available
from Port Clinton High School Counselor.
EIN: 341325350

7331
Leroy W. Russell Scholarship Fund
P.O. Box 94651
Cleveland, OH 44101-4651 (216) 257-4701

Foundation type: Independent foundation
Purpose: Scholarships to graduates of Austintown
School District, OH, who will be attending an
accredited college or university.
Financial data: Year ended 06/30/2013. Assets,
$92,647 (M); Expenditures, $5,500; Total giving,
$2,000.
Fields of interest: Higher education.
Type of support: Scholarships—to individuals.
Application information: Applications accepted.
Application form required.
Applicants should submit the following:
1) ACT
2) Class rank
3) GPA
Additional information: Application should
include academic qualifications,
extracurricular activities and work experience.
Contact high school principal's office for more
information.
EIN: 346745005

7332
Mary Rutan Foundation
205 Palmer Ave.
Bellefontaine, OH 43311-2298 (937)
592-4015
E-mail: public.relations@maryrutan.org;
URL: http://www.maryrutan.org/Foundation/
default.aspx

Foundation type: Public charity
Purpose: Scholarships and low-interest loans to
area residents of Logan County, OH, pursuing a
medical career. Benefits to indigent individuals of

Logan county community, with medical, dental, and hospital expenses.
Publications: Application guidelines.
Financial data: Year ended 12/31/2011. Assets, $5,674,042 (M); Expenditures, $313,640; Total giving, $207,201; Grants to individuals, totaling $58,203.
Fields of interest: Medical school/education; Nursing school/education; Health sciences school/education; Human services.
Type of support: Scholarships—to individuals; Student loans—to individuals; Grants for special needs.
Application information: Applications accepted. Application form required. Interview required.
   Deadline(s): Apr. 1 for Scholarships
   Applicants should submit the following:
      1) Letter(s) of recommendation
      2) Transcripts
      3) Photograph
      4) Financial information
   Additional information: Application must also include official letter of acceptance to the chosen medical career field, extracurricular activities, work experience, and academics.
Program description:
   Mary Rutan Foundation Medical Career Scholarship: Applicants must be enrolled in a medical, nursing, or allied health program, and be a resident of Logan County. Scholarships are awarded on the basis of GPA, financial need, association with Mary Rutan Hospital, personality, tuition costs and graduation date.
EIN: 341407262

7333
Salem Community Foundation, Inc.
P.O. Box 553
Salem, OH   44460-2911   (330) 332-4021
Contact: John E. Tonti, Pres.
FAX: (330) 332-4021;
E-mail: Info@salemcommunityfoundation.org;
URL: http://www.salemcommunityfoundation.org

Foundation type: Community foundation
Purpose: Scholarships primarily to residents of Salem, and Columbiana, OH, for undergraduate education.
Publications: Application guidelines; Annual report; Newsletter; Quarterly report.
Financial data: Year ended 12/31/2012. Assets, $16,427,389 (M); Expenditures, $851,898; Total giving, $778,789.
Fields of interest: Higher education; Scholarships/financial aid.
Type of support: Scholarships—to individuals; Undergraduate support.
Application information: Applications accepted. Application form available on the grantmaker's web site.
   Initial approach: Application
   Send request by: Mail
   Deadline(s): June 21
   Applicants should submit the following:
      1) Transcripts
      2) SAT
      3) GPA
      4) Financial information
      5) FAFSA
      6) ACT
   Additional information: Each scholarship has its own set of eligibility criteria. See web site for a complete listing.
EIN: 341001130

7334
Salem Lutheran Foundation
2700 E. Dublin-Granville Rd., Ste. 300
Columbus, OH   43231-4089   (614) 898-7200
Contact: Terrie L. Rice, Secy.

Foundation type: Company-sponsored foundation
Purpose: Scholarships to men studying to become Lutheran ministers in the Wisconsin Evangelical Lutheran Synod.
Financial data: Year ended 12/31/2012. Assets, $73,536 (M); Expenditures, $3,832,646; Total giving, $3,822,583.
Fields of interest: Theological school/education; Protestant agencies & churches; Men.
Type of support: Scholarships—to individuals.
Application information: Applications accepted. Application form required.
   Deadline(s): July 1
   Final notification: Recipients notified after Aug. 1.
   Applicants should submit the following:
      1) Financial information
      2) Essay
      3) Transcripts
      4) Letter(s) of recommendation
   Additional information: Application must also include employment history; Analysis Report required from students of Northwestern University only.
EIN: 316084166

7335
Samaritan Foundation
P.O. Box 97
Haviland, OH   45851-0097   (419) 622-4611
Contact: Todd Stoller, Secy.-Treas.; Craig Stoller, V.P.

Foundation type: Company-sponsored foundation
Purpose: Grants to indigent individuals and scholarships to individuals on the basis of academic qualifications and financial need. Loans to economically disadvantaged individuals, all residing in Paulding County, OH.
Publications: Application guidelines.
Financial data: Year ended 12/31/2011. Assets, $4,652,343 (M); Expenditures, $242,436; Total giving, $240,550.
Type of support: Undergraduate support.
Application information: Applications accepted. Application form required.
   Initial approach: Letter
   Applicants should submit the following:
      1) Photograph
      2) Transcripts
   Additional information: Grants, scholarships and loans will be awarded on an objective and nondiscriminatory basis. Grant, loans and scholarships are based on financial need.
EIN: 341957355

7336
Sandusky/Erie County Community Foundation
135 E. Washington Row
Sandusky, OH   44870-2609   (419) 621-9690
Contact: Anna J. Oertel, Exec. Dir.; For grants: Randall J. Wagner, Dir., Finance
FAX: (419) 621-8420;
E-mail: info@sanduskyfoundation.org; Grant application email: executivedirector@sanduskyfoundation.org; Grant inquiry email: randyw@eriefoundation.org;
URL: http://www.sanduskyfoundation.org

Foundation type: Community foundation

Purpose: Scholarships to residents of Erie County, OH for higher education.
Publications: Application guidelines; Annual report; Financial statement; Grants list; Informational brochure; Newsletter.
Financial data: Year ended 12/31/2012. Assets, $14,934,755 (M); Expenditures, $758,620; Total giving, $415,326; Grants to individuals, 49 grants totaling $65,897.
Fields of interest: Higher education; Scholarships/financial aid.
Type of support: Undergraduate support.
Application information: Applications accepted. Application form required. Application form available on the grantmaker's web site.
   Send request by: Mail
   Copies of proposal: 1
   Deadline(s): Mar. 7
   Final notification: Recipients notified in 60 to 90 days
   Applicants should submit the following:
      1) Transcripts
      2) GPA
      3) FAFSA
      4) ACT
   Additional information: See web site for a complete listing of scholarship funds.
Program description:
   Scholarships: The foundation manages more than 27 named scholarship funds for the benefit of Erie County students for higher education. Each scholarship has its own set of eligibility requirements and application guidelines. Though most recipients are selected based on academic achievement and financial need, some scholarships are to pursue specific areas of study, such as engineering and education. See web site for additional information.
EIN: 341792862

7337
Anastasia Annette Schneider Trust
c/o KeyBank
4900 Tiedeman Rd., OH-01-49-0150
Brooklyn, OH   44144-2302   (866) 238-8650
Contact: Jennifer Ball
Application address: 660 South Pearl St., Albany, ME 12207

Foundation type: Independent foundation
Purpose: Scholarships to graduating students of Cony High School, Gardiner High School and Hall-Dale High School, ME for higher education.
Financial data: Year ended 04/30/2013. Assets, $129,307 (M); Expenditures, $9,800; Total giving, $7,800; Grants to individuals, 9 grants totaling $900 (high: $100, low: $100).
Fields of interest: Higher education.
Type of support: Support to graduates or students of specific schools.
Application information: Application form required.
   Initial approach: Letter
   Deadline(s): None
   Additional information: Letter must state qualification and need.
EIN: 016038182

7338
Scholarship Fund Inc.
9030 Rolling Hill Dr.
Holland, OH   43528-9205

Foundation type: Independent foundation
Purpose: Undergraduate and graduate scholarships to residents of northwest OH, including nonresidents presently living on campus

at the University of Toledo, OH, and Lourdes College, OH, to attend an area college.

Financial data: Year ended 12/31/2012. Assets, $280,763 (M); Expenditures, $20,365; Total giving, $17,424; Grants to individuals, 12 grants totaling $17,424 (high: $1,500, low: $924).

Type of support: Support to graduates or students of specific schools; Graduate support; Undergraduate support.

Application information: Applications not accepted.

Additional information: Unsolicited requests for funds not considered or acknowledged.

EIN: 346533380

7339

The Scioto Foundation

(formerly The Scioto County Area Foundation)
303 Chillicothe St.
P.O. Box 911
Portsmouth, OH 45662 (740) 354-4612
Contact: Kimberly E. Cutlip, Exec. Dir.
FAX: (740) 354-1912;
E-mail: kim.sciotofoundation@verizon.net;
URL: http://www.sciotofoundation.org

Foundation type: Community foundation
Purpose: Scholarships for students in the Scioto County, OH area seeking higher education.
Publications: Application guidelines; Annual report; Financial statement; Grants list; Informational brochure (including application guidelines); Newsletter; Occasional report.
Financial data: Year ended 12/31/2011. Assets, $23,251,000 (M); Expenditures, $1,386,993; Total giving, $942,923. Scholarships—to individuals amount not specified.
Fields of interest: Higher education; Business school/education; Medical school/education; Nursing school/education; Engineering school/ education; Scholarships/financial aid; Environmental education.
Type of support: Scholarships—to individuals.
Application information: Applications accepted. Application form required. Application form available on the grantmaker's web site.
Initial approach: Application
Send request by: Mail or hand deliver
Applicants should submit the following:
1) Transcripts
2) Photograph
3) Letter(s) of recommendation
Additional information: Scholarships are paid directly to the educational institution on behalf of the students. See web site for specific scholarship guidelines.
EIN: 510157026

7340

Scripps Howard Foundation

P.O. Box 5380
312 Walnut St., 28th Fl.
Cincinnati, OH 45201 (513) 977-3035
Contact: Patty Cottingham, V.P., Admin.; Mike Philipps, C.E.O. and Pres.
FAX: (513) 977-3800;
E-mail: mike.philipps@scripps.com; Contact for Roy W. Howard Scripps Howard Competition, National Journalism Awards and Internships: Susan J. Porter, V.P., Progs., tel.: (800) 888-3000, ext. 3030, e-mail: sue.porter@scripps.com. See Web site for information on specific foundation programs.; URL: http://www.scripps.com/ foundation

Foundation type: Company-sponsored foundation

Purpose: Undergraduate scholarships to U.S. citizens pursuing careers in print or broadcast journalism. Awards to professional print/broadcast journalists and college cartoonists and internships to undergradute journalism majors.
Publications: Application guidelines; Annual report.
Financial data: Year ended 12/31/2012. Assets, $65,198,617 (M); Expenditures, $6,300,234; Total giving, $4,618,992; Grants to individuals, 92 grants totaling $368,608 (high: $35,000, low: $500).
Fields of interest: Media/communications; Print publishing.
Type of support: Fellowships; Internship funds; Grants to individuals; Scholarships—to individuals; Awards/prizes.
Application information: See website for application guidelines.
Program descriptions:
Internships: The foundation awards journalism internship grants program for undergraduates offered in cooperation with their partner schools. The schools recommend internship grant recipients and oversee placement in the best workplace, matching aspirations to job-readiness and helping students move to the next level of their budding journalism careers.
Jack R. Howard Fellowships in International Journalism: Two fellowships are awarded to international journalists for a year of study at Columbia University's Graduate School of Journalism.
EIN: 316025114

7341

Sebring - West Branch Area Community Foundation

P.O. Box 176
Sebring, OH 44672 (330) 938-6765
FAX: (330) 938-3408

Foundation type: Community foundation
Purpose: Scholarships to high school seniors in the Sebring, OH area for continuing education at institutions of higher learning.
Financial data: Year ended 06/30/2012. Assets, $2,130,730 (M); Expenditures, $92,803; Total giving, $87,274; Grants to individuals, 40 grants totaling $83,974 (high: $5,000, low: $250).
Fields of interest: Higher education; Scholarships/ financial aid; Education.
Type of support: Scholarships—to individuals; Support to graduates or students of specific schools; Undergraduate support.
Application information: Applications accepted. Application form required.
Additional information: Applications are available at local high school.
EIN: 341665333

7342

Thomas J. Seefred Trust

c/o Bresco Law Firm
23 Lisbon St.
Canfield, OH 44406 (330) 533-9900
Contact: Karen Leetch, Tr.
E-mail: info@seefredtrust.org; URL: http:// www.seefredtrust.org

Foundation type: Independent foundation
Purpose: Scholarships for college students between the ages of 18 and 25 suffering from Juvenile Diabetes and pursuing a bachelor's degree.

Financial data: Year ended 12/31/2012. Assets, $412,261 (M); Expenditures, $21,553; Total giving, $17,000.
Fields of interest: Higher education; Diabetes.
Type of support: Scholarships—to individuals.
Application information: Applications accepted. Application form required.
Deadline(s): Apr. 1
Final notification: Applicants notified July 1
Applicants should submit the following:
1) Transcripts
2) Letter(s) of recommendation
3) Financial information
4) GPA
5) Essay
Additional information: Application should also include current income tax statements for parents and student. Awards are based on academic promise, personal statement, recommendations and financial need.
EIN: 206360111

7343

Sharp Scholarship Fund

P.O. Box 1558, Dept. EA4E86
Columbus, OH 43216-1558 (724) 656-8866
Application address: c/o Dr. C. Joyce Nicksick, Supt., 300 Wood St., New Wilmington, PA 16142-1016, tel.: (724) 656-8866

Foundation type: Independent foundation
Purpose: Scholarships to graduates of the Wilmington School District, PA.
Financial data: Year ended 12/31/2012. Assets, $377,000 (M); Expenditures, $24,201; Total giving, $16,750.
Type of support: Support to graduates or students of specific schools; Undergraduate support.
Application information: Applications accepted.
Additional information: Selection is based on need, aptitude and academic achievement.
EIN: 201757707

7344

The Sharpe Family Foundation

450 E. Town St.
P.O. Box 25
Circleville, OH 43113-0025 (740) 477-1686
Contact: Gary L. Sharpe, Pres.; Connie H. Sharpe, Secy.-Treas.

Foundation type: Operating foundation
Purpose: Scholarships and grants to high school seniors in Pickaway County and contiguous Ohio counties, who have maintained a 2.0 GPA or higher. Applicants also must have been accepted into a college.
Financial data: Year ended 12/31/2012. Assets, $118,309 (M); Expenditures, $350,810; Total giving, $350,000.
Fields of interest: Higher education.
Type of support: Scholarships—to individuals.
Application information: Applications accepted. Application form required.
Initial approach: Letter or application
Deadline(s): None
Additional information: Applications are available at the foundation's main office and through the high school guidance counselors' offices in Pickaway County and in coniguous Ohio counties.
EIN: 201659146

7345
Jasper H. Sheadle Trust
c/o KeyBank N.A.
4900 Tiedeman Rd., OH-01-49-0150
Brooklyn, OH   44144-2338

Foundation type: Independent foundation
Purpose: Annuities to American-born aged couples or aged women (60 and over) of good character residing in Cuyahoga or Mahoning counties, OH.
Financial data: Year ended 12/31/2012. Assets, $2,383,100 (M); Expenditures, $190,203; Total giving, $167,200; Grants to individuals, 28 grants totaling $167,200 (high: $7,500, low: $300).
Fields of interest: Aging; Women.
Type of support: Grants for special needs.
Application information: Applications not accepted.
EIN: 346506457

7346
Leon and Josephine Wade Shepard Scholarship Fund Foundation, Inc.
c/o National City Bank
P.O. Box 94651
Cleveland, OH   44101-4651
Contact: Tara Coffindaffer
Application address: 5 Memorial Dr., Fennville, MI 49408

Foundation type: Independent foundation
Purpose: Scholarships to qualified graduates of Fennville High School, MI, who must attend institutions of higher learning in MI.
Financial data: Year ended 03/31/2012. Assets, $805,560 (M); Expenditures, $40,470; Total giving, $30,500; Grants to individuals, 39 grants totaling $30,500 (high: $1,000, low: $500).
Fields of interest: Higher education.
Type of support: Support to graduates or students of specific schools.
Application information: Applications accepted.
Deadline(s): Mar.
EIN: 386101349

7347
William M. Shinnick Educational Fund
3608 Maple Ave.
Zanesville, OH   43701-3771   (740) 452-2273
Contact: William M. Shinnick, Admin. Asst.

Foundation type: Independent foundation
Purpose: Student loans to worthy students of Muskingum county, OH who otherwise would be unable to secure a college or post-high school education.
Publications: Application guidelines; Informational brochure.
Financial data: Year ended 06/30/2013. Assets, $4,393,437 (M); Expenditures, $365,631; Total giving, $280,000; Grants to individuals, 150 grants totaling $280,000 (high: $2,000, low: $1,000).
Fields of interest: Higher education; Economically disadvantaged.
Type of support: Student loans—to individuals; Undergraduate support.
Application information: Application form required. Interview required.
Initial approach: In person
Deadline(s): June
Applicants should submit the following:
  1) Transcripts
  2) Financial information
Additional information: Applicant must show proof of residence in Muskingum county.
EIN: 314394168

7348
John Q. Shunk Association
P.O. Box 625
Bucyrus, OH   44820-0625   (419) 569-2238
E-mail: pepspatch@marion.net

Foundation type: Independent foundation
Purpose: Scholarships only to graduates of four specified high schools in Crawford County, OH, for attendance at accredited colleges and universities.
Financial data: Year ended 12/31/2012. Assets, $2,039,466 (M); Expenditures, $90,145; Total giving, $60,250.
Fields of interest: Higher education; Scholarships/ financial aid.
Type of support: Support to graduates or students of specific schools; Undergraduate support.
Application information: Applications accepted. Application form required. Interview required.
Initial approach: Letter
Deadline(s): Feb. 15
Applicants should submit the following:
  1) Letter(s) of recommendation
  2) Financial information
Additional information: Application forms may be obtained from guidance offices of the specified high schools.
EIN: 340896477

7349
Sightless Children Club, Inc.
1028 E. 4th St.
Franklin, OH   45005-1834   (937) 671-9171
Contact: Lisa Buckingham, Pres.
E-mail: lisab@sightlesschildren.org; URL: http://www.sightlesschildren.org

Foundation type: Independent foundation
Purpose: Educational equipment, equipment repairs, and seminars for the educational and social development of sightless individuals residing in the Dayton metropolitan, OH, area.
Publications: Informational brochure (including application guidelines); Newsletter.
Financial data: Year ended 10/31/2010. Assets, $2,376,729 (M); Expenditures, $1,926,148; Total giving, $99,456; Grants to individuals, 26 grants totaling $99,456 (high: $7,791, low: -$200).
Fields of interest: Disabilities, people with.
Type of support: Grants for special needs.
Application information: Applications accepted. Application form required.
Initial approach: Letter
Copies of proposal: 3
Deadline(s): May
Applicants should submit the following:
  1) Proposal
  2) Letter(s) of recommendation
Additional information: Application should also include a description of equipment required, estimated cost, and how the equipment will be used.
EIN: 316006092

7350
Esther N. Simmons Charitable Trust
c/o PNC Bank N.A.
P.O. Box 94651
Cleveland, OH   44101-4651

Foundation type: Independent foundation
Purpose: Scholarships to students of Steubenville High School, OH majoring in music.
Financial data: Year ended 05/31/2012. Assets, $2,760,875 (M); Expenditures, $162,507; Total giving, $120,524.

Fields of interest: Music; Higher education.
Type of support: Scholarships—to individuals; Support to graduates or students of specific schools.
Application information:
Deadline(s): None
Additional information: Contact trust for current application guidelines.
EIN: 346743541

7351
Ralph and Mary Simmons Welfare Fund
c/o KeyBank, N.A.
4900 Tiedeman Rd., OH-01-49-0150
Brooklyn, OH   44144-2302
Application address: 286 Water St., Key P., ME 04330

Foundation type: Independent foundation
Purpose: Scholarships to students of Kingfield, ME for higher education.
Financial data: Year ended 08/31/2013. Assets, $568,957 (M); Expenditures, $29,240; Total giving, $27,145; Grants to individuals, totaling $18,500.
Fields of interest: Scholarships/financial aid; Education.
Type of support: Scholarships—to individuals.
Application information: Applications accepted. Application form not required.
Initial approach: Letter
Deadline(s): None
Additional information: Letter must outline need and purpose of grant.
EIN: 016007242

7352
The Slemp Foundation
P.O. Box 1118, ML CN-OH-W10X
Cincinnati, OH   45201-1118
Grant and scholarship application address: c/o Patricia L. Durbin, Tr. Off., U.S. Bank, N.A., Trust Div., P.O. Box 5208, ML CN-OH-W7PT, Cincinnati, OH 45201-5208; tel.: (513) 762-8878; URL: http://www.slempfoundation.org

Foundation type: Independent foundation
Purpose: Undergraduate scholarships limited to individuals residing in Lee and Wise counties, VA, or to individuals who are descendants of residents.
Publications: Application guidelines.
Financial data: Year ended 06/30/2013. Assets, $21,778,722 (M); Expenditures, $1,391,111; Total giving, $1,192,454; Grants to individuals, 130 grants totaling $320,000 (high: $2,500, low: $1,250).
Fields of interest: Higher education; Scholarships/financial aid.
Type of support: Undergraduate support.
Application information: Applications accepted. Application form required. Application form available on the grantmaker's web site.
Initial approach: Letter
Deadline(s): Oct. 15
Final notification: Applicants are notified in December or January
Program description:
Scholarship Program: Approximately 25 new college scholarships are granted each year to qualified individuals. Applications should be made during student's senior year in high school.
EIN: 316025080

7353
Norman W. Smith Charitable Trust
(formerly Norman W. Smith Revolving Loan Trust)
P.O. Box 1558, Dept. EA4E86
Columbus, OH   43216   (304) 348-4582
Contact: Carla Parsons
Application address: Huntington National Bank,
3120 University Ave., Morgantown, WV 26505

Foundation type: Independent foundation
Purpose: Student loans to residents of Berkeley
County, WV, for study at any medical school or any
accredited seminary as a ministerial student.
Financial data: Year ended 12/31/2012. Assets,
$888,348 (M); Expenditures, $57,147; Total
giving, $44,500. Student loans—to individuals
amount not specified.
Fields of interest: Medical school/education;
Theological school/education.
Type of support: Student loans—to individuals.
Application information: Application form not
required.
  Initial approach: Letter
  Additional information: Application must include
    proof of school attendance and evidence of
    residence.
EIN: 556084952

7354
Smith Educational Memorial Fund
(also known as Earl E. & Marie M. Smith
Educational Memorial Fund)
c/o PNC Bank, N.A.
P.O. Box 94651
Cleveland, OH   44101-4651   (260) 461-6218
Contact: Margaret A. Sturm
Application address: c/o PNC Bank, N.A., 110 W.
Berry St., Fort Wayne, IN 46802

Foundation type: Independent foundation
Purpose: Educational loans to residents of
Kosciusko County, IN, only, with preference given to
applicants in the fields of medicine, nursing, and
related clinical pursuits.
Financial data: Year ended 12/31/2012. Assets,
$145,671 (M); Expenditures, $2,542; Total giving,
$0.
Fields of interest: Medical school/education;
Nursing school/education.
Type of support: Student loans—to individuals.
Application information: Applications accepted.
Application form required.
  Deadline(s): None
EIN: 510174338

7355
Arthur Albert Smith Memorial Fund
c/o KeyBank N.A.
10 W. 2nd St., Fl. 26
Dayton, OH   45402

Foundation type: Independent foundation
Purpose: Scholarships to male graduates of
Freeport High School, ME.
Financial data: Year ended 08/31/2012. Assets,
$279,275 (M); Expenditures, $5,910; Total giving,
$0.
Fields of interest: Men.
Type of support: Support to graduates or students
of specific schools; Undergraduate support.
Application information: Applications accepted.
  Initial approach: Letter
  Additional information: Contact fund for current
    application guidelines.
EIN: 016079294

7356
William & Anna Smith Private Foundation
(also known as W. F. & Anna Smith Foundation)
P.O. Box 10099
Toledo, OH   43699-0099

Foundation type: Independent foundation
Purpose: Scholarships to residents primarily of UT
for higher education.
Financial data: Year ended 12/31/2012. Assets,
$63,858 (M); Expenditures, $2,152; Total giving,
$0.
Fields of interest: Higher education.
Type of support: Scholarships—to individuals.
Application information: Applications accepted.
  Initial approach: Letter
  Additional information: Contact the foundation for
    application guidelines.
EIN: 942728399

7357
Charles & Charlotte Bissell Smith
Scholarship Fund
c/o KeyBank
4900 Tiedeman Rd., OH-01-49-0150
Brooklyn, OH   44144-2302   (866) 238-8650
Contact: Marilyn Hensel
Application address: 66 S. Pearl St., Albany, NY
12207; tel.: (866) 238-8650

Foundation type: Independent foundation
Purpose: Scholarships to U.S. citizens who are
graduates of Oneonta High School, NY, with good
scholastic standing and citizenship, who are
involved in two or more extracurricular activities,
and who plan to attend two- and four-year colleges.
Financial data: Year ended 02/28/2013. Assets,
$2,117,652 (M); Expenditures, $104,009; Total
giving, $79,000; Grants to individuals, 79 grants
totaling $79,000 (high: $1,000, low: $1,000).
Fields of interest: Higher education.
Type of support: Support to graduates or students
of specific schools; Undergraduate support.
Application information: Applications accepted.
Application form required.
  Deadline(s): Feb. 15
EIN: 146105261

7358
Helen F. Smucker Memorial Scholarship
Trust
c/o PNC Nank, N.A.
P.O. Box 94651
Cleveland, OH   44101-4651   (330) 682-4661
Application address: c/o Orrville High School,
Attn.: Guidance Dir., 841 N. Ella St., Orrville, OH
44667

Foundation type: Independent foundation
Purpose: Scholarships to graduates of Orrville High
School, OH for continuing education at higher
institutions.
Financial data: Year ended 12/31/2012. Assets,
$285,374 (M); Expenditures, $15,402; Total
giving, $11,065.
Fields of interest: Higher education.
Type of support: Support to graduates or students
of specific schools; Undergraduate support.
Application information: Applications accepted.
  Initial approach: Letter
  Deadline(s): None
EIN: 341296818

7359
W. B. and Mary W. Snow No. 5
Scholarship Fund
106 S. Main St., Ste. 16
Akron, OH   44308-1418   (330) 761-3131
Application address: c/o Office of Career Education,
Attn.:S. Rice 65 Steiner Ave., Rm. 201, Akron, OH
44301,

Foundation type: Independent foundation
Purpose: Scholarships to graduating seniors of
Akron Public School Career Education, OH, pursuing
a skilled trade at a postsecondary institution.
Financial data: Year ended 08/31/2012. Assets,
$181,492 (M); Expenditures, $22,113; Total
giving, $18,000.
Fields of interest: Vocational education,
post-secondary.
Type of support: Scholarships—to individuals;
Technical education support.
Application information: Application form required.
  Initial approach: Letter
  Send request by: Mail
  Deadline(s): Jan.
  Applicants should submit the following:
    1) Transcripts
    2) Letter(s) of recommendation
EIN: 311564522

7360
Social Philosophy and Policy Foundation
P.O. Box 938
Bowling Green, OH   43402-0938   (419)
353-6078
Contact: Fred D. Miller, Jr., Pres.

Foundation type: Public charity
Purpose: Research grants to scholars for study in
the areas of social philosophy and policy.
Financial data: Year ended 12/31/2011. Assets,
$25,064,415 (M); Expenditures, $1,605,239;
Total giving, $432,556; Grants to individuals,
totaling $99,556.
Fields of interest: Philosophy/ethics; Public policy.
Type of support: Research.
Application information: Contact foundation for
current application guidelines.
EIN: 341502497

7361
Southern Perry County Academic
Endowment Fund
P.O. Box 498
Corning, OH   43730-0498   (740) 347-9062
Contact: Rebecca A. Gill, Treas.

Foundation type: Independent foundation
Purpose: Scholarships to graduating seniors of
Miller High School, OH as well as past graduates of
Miller High School for postsecondary education at
an accredited four year college or university.
Financial data: Year ended 12/31/2011. Assets,
$852,949 (M); Expenditures, $12,873; Total
giving, $12,140; Grants to individuals, 23 grants
totaling $12,140 (high: $1,015, low: $300).
Fields of interest: Higher education.
Type of support: Support to graduates or students
of specific schools.
Application information: Application form required.
Interview required.
  Send request by: Mail
  Deadline(s): May 1
  Applicants should submit the following:
    1) Class rank
    2) SAT
    3) GPA

4) ACT
5) Transcripts
6) Financial information
Additional information: Application should also include two letters of reference, letter of acceptance from the college or university applicant will attend as a full time student. Application can be obtained from Miller High School guidance office and the Southern Local School District office.
EIN: 341585950

7362
Spencer Education Foundation
(formerly George and Marie G. Spencer Education Foundation and Trust)
c/o PNC Bank N.A.
P.O. Box 94651
Cleveland, OH 44101-4651
Application address: 619 S. Main St., Tipton, IN 46072, tel.: 317-675-7431

Foundation type: Independent foundation
Purpose: Scholarships to graduates of Tipton High School, IN, and Tri-Central High School, Sharpsville, IN.
Financial data: Year ended 12/31/2011. Assets, $2,715,507 (M); Expenditures, $164,413; Total giving, $135,641.
Fields of interest: Higher education.
Type of support: Support to graduates or students of specific schools; Undergraduate support.
Application information: Application form required.
Deadline(s): Oct. 1
Additional information: Scholarships are renewable.
EIN: 356072759

7363
The Springfield Foundation
333 N. Limestone St., Ste. 201
Springfield, OH 45503 (937) 324-8773
Contact: Ted Vander Roest, Exec. Dir.; For grant application: Joan Elder, Prog. Off.
FAX: (937) 324-1836;
E-mail: info@springfieldfoundation.org; Additional E-mail: joan@springfieldfoundation.org;
URL: http://www.springfieldfoundation.org

Foundation type: Community foundation
Purpose: Scholarships to students of the Clark County, OH area for continuing education at institutions of higher learning.
Publications: Application guidelines; Annual report; Financial statement; Grants list; Informational brochure (including application guidelines); Newsletter; Program policy statement.
Financial data: Year ended 12/31/2012. Assets, $46,413,526 (M); Expenditures, $2,917,480; Total giving, $2,173,863. Scholarships—to individuals amount not specified.
Fields of interest: Higher education; Scholarships/financial aid.
Type of support: Employee-related scholarships; Scholarships—to individuals.
Application information: Applications accepted. Application form required. Application form available on the grantmaker's web site.
Initial approach: Application
Send request by: Online
Deadline(s): Feb. 28
Applicants should submit the following:
1) FAFSA
2) Transcripts
3) SAR
4) Letter(s) of recommendation

Additional information: Each scholarship has different guidelines according to each individual donor's wishes. See web site for a complete program listing.
Program description:
Scholarships: Through the generosity of many families and individuals, the foundation manages more than 50 scholarship funds for the benefit of eligible students. Students benefit from the financial assistance as well as the academic recognition of being a scholarship recipient. Each scholarship fund targets students with different characteristics such as graduation from a particular high school, plans to attend a specific college or selection of a certain field of study such as finance, fine arts, and nursing. See web site for additional information.
EIN: 316030764

7364
Edgar K. Springman Scholarship Fund
(formerly Springman Scholarship Fund)
P.O. Box 630858
Cincinnati, OH 45263-0858 (513) 722-2227

Foundation type: Independent foundation
Purpose: Scholarships to graduates of Goshen High School, OH.
Financial data: Year ended 09/30/2012. Assets, $901,460 (M); Expenditures, $62,792; Total giving, $51,000; Grants to individuals, 17 grants totaling $51,000 (high: $3,000, low: $3,000).
Type of support: Support to graduates or students of specific schools; Undergraduate support.
Application information: Applications not accepted.
EIN: 316455677

7365
St. Marys Community Foundation
146 E. Spring St.
St. Marys, OH 45885 (419) 394-5693
Contact: Michael Makley, Admin. and Treas.
FAX: (419) 394-7694; E-mail: smcf@bright.net;
URL: http://www.thesmcf.org/

Foundation type: Community foundation
Purpose: Scholarships and educational loans to students of the St. Mary's city schools, OH for higher education.
Publications: Annual report; Financial statement; Informational brochure; Occasional report.
Financial data: Year ended 06/30/2013. Assets, $5,535,008 (M); Expenditures, $324,715; Total giving, $277,763; Grants to individuals, 4,772 grants totaling $277,763.
Fields of interest: Higher education.
Type of support: Support to graduates or students of specific schools; Technical education support; Undergraduate support.
Application information:
Initial approach: Letter
Copies of proposal: 1
Deadline(s): Varies
Applicants should submit the following:
1) Financial information
2) Budget Information
Additional information: Applicants must reside in the St. Mary's, OH, area.
EIN: 237372270

7366
Stark Community Foundation
(formerly The Stark County Foundation, Inc.)
400 Market Ave. N., Ste. 200
Canton, OH 44702-2107 (330) 454-3426
Contact: Mark J. Samolczyk, Pres.; For scholarship inquiries: Jackie Gilin, Donor Svcs./Prog. Off.
FAX: (330) 454-5855; E-mail: info@starkcf.org;
Scholarship inquiries: jgilin@starkcf.org;
URL: http://www.starkcf.org/

Foundation type: Community foundation
Purpose: Scholarships and student loans primarily to students who are residents of Stark County, OH.
Publications: Application guidelines; Annual report (including application guidelines); Financial statement; Grants list; Informational brochure; Newsletter; Program policy statement.
Financial data: Year ended 12/31/2012. Assets, $182,082,860 (M); Expenditures, $8,526,030; Total giving, $6,835,359. Scholarships—to individuals amount not specified.
Fields of interest: Elementary school/education; Secondary school/education; Vocational education; Higher education; Graduate/professional education; Nursing school/education.
Type of support: Scholarships—to individuals; Student loans—to individuals; Support to graduates or students of specific schools; Graduate support; Undergraduate support.
Application information: Applications accepted. Application form required. Application form available on the grantmaker's web site.
Deadline(s): Varies
Additional information: See web site for a complete listing of scholarships and application guidelines.
Program description:
Scholarships: The foundation administers over 80 scholarship funds, each varying by deadline date, criteria for selection, eligibility requirements and application information. Scholarships are offered in the following categories: 1) Elementary/High School Scholarships; 2) Undergraduate Scholarships; 3) Vocational, Technical Nursing and Nontraditional Scholarships; 4) Graduate School Scholarships; and 5) Non-Stark County Scholarships. A limited amount of loans are also available. See web site for additional information.
EIN: 340943665

7367
Virginia E. Stauffer Scholarship Fund
c/o KeyBank N.A.
4900 Tiedeman Rd., OH-01-49-0150
Brooklyn, OH 44144-2302
Contact: Nicholas D. Shaw
Application address: 208 N. 24th St., Olean, NY 14760

Foundation type: Independent foundation
Purpose: Scholarships to graduates of high schools within a ten-mile radius of the Exchange Bank of Olean, NY, including Allegany Central School, Hinsdale Central School, Olean High School, Portville Central School, and Walsh (Archbishop) High School.
Financial data: Year ended 08/31/2013. Assets, $422,334 (M); Expenditures, $22,617; Total giving, $16,000; Grants to individuals, 16 grants totaling $16,000 (high: $1,000, low: $1,000).
Type of support: Support to graduates or students of specific schools.
Application information: Applications accepted. Application form required.
EIN: 133143537

7368
Phyllis H. Steigler Trust
c/o KeyBank
4900 Tiedeman Rd., OH-01-49-0150
Brooklyn, OH 44144-2302

Foundation type: Independent foundation
Purpose: Scholarships to residents of ME who are in pursuit of a higher education.
Financial data: Year ended 06/30/2013. Assets, $507,751 (M); Expenditures, $14,629; Total giving, $6,000.
Fields of interest: Education.
Type of support: Scholarships—to individuals.
Application information: Applications accepted.
  Initial approach: Letter
  Additional information: Application must outline financial need and qualifications.
EIN: 016109107

7369
Daniel J. Steiner Scholarship Fund
P.O. Box 1558, Dept. EA4E86
Columbus, OH 43216-1558 (330) 364-0644

Foundation type: Independent foundation
Purpose: Scholarships to students of New Philadelphia High School, OH or Tuscarawas Central Catholic High School, OH for continuing education.
Financial data: Year ended 06/30/2013. Assets, $103,687 (M); Expenditures, $5,779; Total giving, $5,100; Grants to individuals, 4 grants totaling $5,100 (high: $1,275, low: $1,275).
Fields of interest: Education.
Type of support: Support to graduates or students of specific schools.
Application information: Applications accepted. Application form required. Interview required.
  Deadline(s): Apr.
  Additional information: Application must include transcripts, three character references, statement of career objectives/goals, a biographical statement, including educational background, personal interests, financial need and other pertinent information about yourself.
EIN: 316484643

7370
Anna Stinson Trust Agency
c/o KeyBank N.A.
P.O. Box 10099
Toledo, OH 43699-0099
Application address: c/o KeyBank N.A., Attn.: Branch Mgr., 162 High St., Ellsworth, ME 04605, tel.: (207) 669-3051

Foundation type: Independent foundation
Purpose: Scholarships to high school graduates from Surrey or Ellsworth, ME for continuous education at accredited colleges or universities.
Financial data: Year ended 04/30/2012. Assets, $99,312 (M); Expenditures, $7,974; Total giving, $4,000.
Fields of interest: Higher education.
Type of support: Undergraduate support.
Application information: Applications accepted.
  Initial approach: Letter
EIN: 016057075

7371
Student Education Support Association, Inc.
85 Elmwood Pl.
Athens, OH 45701-1902

Foundation type: Independent foundation
Purpose: Scholarships to residents of Athens, OH for higher education.
Financial data: Year ended 12/31/2012. Assets, $25,662 (M); Expenditures, $1,205,023; Total giving, $1,202,774.
Fields of interest: Higher education.
Type of support: Undergraduate support.
Application information: Applications accepted.
  Initial approach: Letter
  Deadline(s): None
  Additional information: Contact foundation for current application guidelines.
EIN: 311387072

7372
Sullivan Scholars Foundation
c/o Cleveland Foundation
1422 Euclid Ave.
Cleveland, OH 44115-2063 (216) 861-3810
URL: http://www.sullivanscholars.org/

Foundation type: Public charity
Purpose: Scholarships to outstanding eighth-grade students in selected Cleveland, OH schools who wish to attend a Catholic or private high school in northeast OH.
Publications: Application guidelines.
Financial data: Year ended 12/31/2011. Assets, $3,605,752 (M); Expenditures, $219,215; Total giving, $180,842; Grants to individuals, 54 grants totaling $180,842.
Fields of interest: Education.
Type of support: Scholarships—to individuals; Support to graduates or students of specific schools.
Application information: Applications accepted. Application form required. Application form available on the grantmaker's web site.
  Send request by: Mail
  Deadline(s): Mar. 1
  Final notification: Applicants notified by mid-May
  Applicants should submit the following:
    1) Transcripts
    2) Letter(s) of recommendation
    3) Essay
  Additional information: Application should also include letter of acceptance from the selected Catholic or private high school, and a copy of the high school's financial aid award notification for the upcoming academic year.
EIN: 421763846

7373
Summerfair Foundation, Inc.
7850 Five Mile Rd.
Cincinnati, OH 45230-2356 (513) 531-0050
Contact: Sharon Strubbe, Exec. Dir.
FAX: (513) 531-0377; *E-mail:* info@summerfair.org; *URL:* http://summerfair.org/

Foundation type: Public charity
Purpose: Grants and scholarships to artists in the Cincinnati, OH, area.
Publications: Application guidelines; Newsletter.
Financial data: Year ended 09/30/2012. Assets, $618,500 (M); Expenditures, $376,047; Total giving, $49,426; Grants to individuals, totaling $13,626.
Fields of interest: Arts, artist's services.

Type of support: Grants to individuals.
Application information: Application form required.
  Deadline(s): Vary
  Final notification: Grants announced mid-Feb.
  Additional information: Grant applications must include slides of artwork and SASE.
Program descriptions:
  Aid to Individual Artists (AIA): This program awards four grants of $3,000 each to artists living within a 40-mile radius of Cincinnati. The artists may use the grants for any purpose as long as it helps advance their artistic vision. Past grants have been used to purchase supplies, rent studio space, or fund exhibits. Eligible applicants must be at least 18 years old.
  Emerging Artists Program: This program annually allows junior and senior art majors from local Cincinnati universities, who represent the next generation of artists to emerge on the local art scene, the opportunity to exhibit their work among their peers. In addition, a $1,000 scholarship will be given to an artist, selected by a jury of professional working artists.
  High School Scholarships: Three scholarships (ranging from $100 to $250) are annually awarded to local high school junior or senior art students, in recognition of outstanding work.
EIN: 237229462

7374
Norma B. Summerville Scholarship Foundation
1655 W. Market St. 525
Akron, OH 44313-2644 (330) 848-4991
Contact: Karen Caley, Secy.
Application address: 2140 13th St., N.W. Akron, OH 44314

Foundation type: Independent foundation
Purpose: Scholarships to female graduates of Kenmore High School, OH with a minimum 3.0 GPA for continuing education at institutions of higher learning.
Financial data: Year ended 12/31/2011. Assets, $461,280 (M); Expenditures, $38,629; Total giving, $37,499; Grants to individuals, totaling $37,499.
Fields of interest: Higher education; Young adults, female.
Type of support: Support to graduates or students of specific schools.
Application information: Applications accepted. Application form required.
  Deadline(s): Apr. 15
  Additional information: Application can be obtained from the principal's office. Application should include an essay.
EIN: 341719340

7375
Taiho Kogyo Tribology Research Foundation
194 Heritage Dr.
Tiffin, OH 44883 (156) 528-2006
Contact: Masato Isobe, Secy.
Additional application address: c/o 2-47 Hosoya-Cho, Toyota City, Aichi Pref. 471-8502 Japan
E-mail: secretariat@ttrf.org; *URL:* http://www.ttrf.org

Foundation type: Independent foundation
Purpose: Grants to individuals for research and development activities in the field of tribology.
Financial data: Year ended 12/31/2012. Assets, $130,289 (M); Expenditures, $186,393; Total

giving, $116,950; Grants to individuals, 6 grants totaling $116,950 (high: $25,000, low: $14,000).
Fields of interest: Research.
Type of support: Research; Grants to individuals.
Application information: Application form required. Application form available on the grantmaker's web site.
>   Deadline(s): Apr. 30 and Oct. 31
>   Applicants should submit the following:
>   1) Curriculum vitae
>   2) Letter(s) of recommendation
EIN: 364399285

7376
Kenneth and Elisabeth Taylor Charitable Trust
3040 W. Point Rd.
Lancaster, OH   43130-8640   (740) 569-3040
Contact: William J Sitterley, Tr.
URL: http://www.fairfieldcountyscholarships.com/

Foundation type: Independent foundation
Purpose: College scholarships to Fairfield County, OH residents for attendance at accredited colleges or universities or accredited technical or vocational schools in Ohio.
Financial data: Year ended 05/31/2013. Assets, $1,283,333 (M); Expenditures, $63,787; Total giving, $54,000; Grants to individuals, 9 grants totaling $54,000 (high: $6,000, low: $5,000).
Fields of interest: Vocational education, post-secondary; Higher education.
Type of support: Scholarships—to individuals.
Application information: Applications accepted. Application form required.
>   Deadline(s): Second Monday in Mar.
>   Applicants should submit the following:
>   1) Class rank
>   2) Transcripts
>   3) GPA
>   4) ACT
>   Additional information: Applicant must demonstrate financial need and ability.
EIN: 316608554

7377
Murtis H. Taylor Human Services System
(formerly Murtis H. Taylor Multi-Service Center)
13422 Kinsman Rd.
Cleveland, OH   44120-4410   (212) 283-4400
Contact: Lovell J. Custard, Pres. and C.E.O.
FAX: (216) 491-9428;
E-mail: Lcustard@murtistaylor.org; URL: http://www.murtistaylor.org

Foundation type: Public charity
Purpose: Emergency assistance to disadvantaged individuals and families of Cuyahoga county, OH, with food, prescriptions, health care, educational programs, transportation and housing assistance.
Financial data: Year ended 12/31/2011. Assets, $5,061,230 (M); Expenditures, $19,830,325; Total giving, $519,593; Grants to individuals, totaling $519,593.
Fields of interest: Human services, emergency aid.
Type of support: Grants for special needs.
Application information: Applications not accepted.
>   Additional information: Contact the organization for eligibility determination. Unsolicited requests for funds not considered or acknowledged.
EIN: 237158458

7378
Oscar and Hildegard Thiele Scholarship Fund
106 S. Main St., Ste. 1600
Akron, OH   44308-1417
Application address: c/o FirstMerit Bank, N.A., P.O. Box 725, Medina, OH 44258

Foundation type: Independent foundation
Purpose: Scholarships to graduating seniors of Buckeye High School, OH, other than the valedictorian or salutatorian, who have at least a "B" average and demonstrate maturity and common sense.
Financial data: Year ended 12/31/2012. Assets, $284,478 (M); Expenditures, $28,547; Total giving, $24,000.
Type of support: Support to graduates or students of specific schools; Undergraduate support.
Application information: Application form required.
>   Deadline(s): Apr. 30
>   Additional information: Application available at Buckeye High School, OH.
EIN: 346854105

7379
Edgel Paul and Garnet E. Thompson Charitable Trust
P.O. Box 630858
Cincinnati, OH   45263-0858   (614) 744-7700
Application address: Fifth Third Bank of Ohio Valley, 21 E. State St., Columbus, OH 43215

Foundation type: Independent foundation
Purpose: Scholarships to individuals residing in Boyd and Lawrence counties, KY, for tuition, books, room, and board.
Financial data: Year ended 02/28/2013. Assets, $394,431 (M); Expenditures, $24,531; Total giving, $18,544.
Fields of interest: Formal/general education; Christian agencies & churches.
Type of support: Undergraduate support.
Application information:
>   Initial approach: Letter
>   Deadline(s): None
EIN: 616206389

7380
Three Arts Scholarship Fund, Inc.
P.O. Box 630858
Cincinnati, OH   45263-0858   (513) 534-5310

Foundation type: Public charity
Purpose: Scholarships primarily to women from OH, PA, and KY to study music, painting, drama, and other arts.
Financial data: Year ended 03/31/2012. Assets, $843,752 (M); Expenditures, $61,905; Total giving, $50,000; Grants to individuals, totaling $50,000.
Fields of interest: Visual arts; Performing arts; Women.
Type of support: Undergraduate support.
Application information:
>   Initial approach: Letter
>   Additional information: Contact foundation for complete eligibility requirements.
EIN: 316024150

7381
The Throckmorton Foundation
39 E. Market St., Ste. 402
Akron, OH   44308-2032   (330) 258-2394
Contact: Mark A. Mosley, Trust Off., Huntington National Bank

Foundation type: Independent foundation
Purpose: Scholarships to individuals of Native American or African-American descent who demonstrate financial need and enroll at Grove City College, PA, or other colleges or universities in eastern OH or western PA.
Financial data: Year ended 06/30/2012. Assets, $5,733,718 (M); Expenditures, $364,607; Total giving, $303,602; Grants to individuals, 33 grants totaling $303,602 (high: $107,000, low: $2,000).
Fields of interest: African Americans/Blacks; Native Americans/American Indians.
Type of support: Support to graduates or students of specific schools; Undergraduate support.
Application information:
>   Initial approach: Letter
EIN: 616288548

7382
Thurber House
77 Jefferson Ave.
Columbus, OH   43215-3840   (614) 464-1032
FAX: (614) 280-3645;
E-mail: thurberhouse@thurberhouse.org; E-Mail For Alison Barret: abarret@thurberhouse.org;
URL: http://www.thurberhouse.org

Foundation type: Public charity
Purpose: Awards and prizes for professionals and aspiring young-adult and humor writers of all ages.
Publications: Application guidelines.
Financial data: Year ended 12/31/2012. Assets, $767,986 (M); Expenditures, $548,808.
Fields of interest: Literature.
Type of support: Awards/prizes; Residencies; Stipends.
Application information:
>   Deadline(s): Apr. 1 for Thurber Prize for American Humorc
Program description:
>   Children's Writers-in-Residence: The organization offers residencies for writers of books for middle-grade children as a seasonal retreat from daily chaos. Residencies offer a quiet living and working environment in a furnished third-floor attic. Residencies include a stipend, opportunities to teach, and time to write.
EIN: 311136182

7383
The Tiffin Charitable Foundation
68 S. Washington St.
Tiffin, OH   44883-2350   (419) 448-1791
E-mail: adm@tiffinfoundation.org; URL: http://www.tiffinfoundation.org

Foundation type: Community foundation
Purpose: Scholarships to graduating high school seniors of Tiffin, OH pursuing higher education at accredited institutions.
Publications: Application guidelines; Annual report; Financial statement; Informational brochure; Newsletter.
Financial data: Year ended 12/31/2012. Assets, $12,637,005 (M); Expenditures, $960,784; Total giving, $877,902; Grants to individuals, totaling $877,902.
Fields of interest: Higher education.
Type of support: Scholarships—to individuals.

Application information: Applications accepted. Application form required.

Deadline(s): Varies

Additional information: Scholarships are paid to the college or university for the benefit of the student. See web site for additional information for scholarship fund criteria.

EIN: 341405286

7384

The Timken Company Charitable and Educational Fund, Inc.

(formerly The Timken Company Educational Fund, Inc.)
1835 Dueber Ave. S.W.
Canton, OH 44706-2728
URL: http://www.timken.com/EN-US/ABOUT/CITIZENSHIP/SCHOLARSHIP/Pages/Scholarship.aspx

Foundation type: Company-sponsored foundation
Purpose: Scholarships to children and dependent stepchildren of employees and retirees of The Timken Company.
Financial data: Year ended 12/31/2012. Assets, $3,591,793 (M); Expenditures, $903,013; Total giving, $828,828; Grants to individuals, 37 grants totaling $818,593.
Type of support: Employee-related scholarships.
Application information: Applications not accepted.

Additional information: Unsolicited requests for funds not considered or acknowledged.

Company name: The Timken Company
EIN: 346520257

7385

Tomlinson's Touching Lives Foundation, Inc.

1360 E. 9th St., Ste. 1100
Cleveland, OH 44114-1717 (216) 920-4800
Contact: LaDanian Tomlinson, Pres.

Foundation type: Public charity
Purpose: Scholarships primarily to indigent residents of the Waco, TX, area.
Financial data: Year ended 12/31/2011. Assets, $141,767 (M); Expenditures, $167,490; Total giving, $31,340; Grants to individuals, totaling $15,000.
Type of support: Scholarships—to individuals.
Application information:

Initial approach: Letter

Additional information: Contact foundation for complete eligibility criteria.

EIN: 201414221

7386

Almeda Leake Toomey Scholarship Fund

P.O. Box 1558, Dept. EA4E86
Columbus, OH 43216-1558 (330) 364-0644
Application address: c/o New Philadelphia High School, 343 Ray Ave. NW, New Philadelphia, OH 44663

Foundation type: Independent foundation
Purpose: Scholarships to graduates of Dover, Central Catholic and New Philadelphia high schools, OH.
Financial data: Year ended 06/30/2013. Assets, $259,266 (M); Expenditures, $15,011; Total giving, $11,315; Grant to an individual, 1 grant totaling $2,515.

Type of support: Support to graduates or students of specific schools; Undergraduate support.
Application information: Applications not accepted.

Additional information: Contributes only to preselected individuals.

EIN: 316630558

7387

The Dennis and Sara Trachsel Foundation

P.O. Box 747
Marion, OH 43301-0747
Application address: c/o Kevin R. Hall, 355 E. Center St., Marion, OH 43302, tel.: (740) 383-6109

Foundation type: Independent foundation
Purpose: Scholarships to graduates of Elgin, Marion Catholic, Marion Harding, Pleasant, Ridgedale, and River Valley counties, and Tri-Rivers Joint Vocational School, OH for attendance at any accredited college, university or technical school.
Financial data: Year ended 12/31/2012. Assets, $5,992,275 (M); Expenditures, $453,050; Total giving, $296,253; Grants to individuals, 28 grants totaling $296,253 (high: $70,000, low: $500).
Fields of interest: Vocational education, post-secondary; Higher education.
Type of support: Support to graduates or students of specific schools; Technical education support; Undergraduate support.
Application information: Applications accepted. Application form required.

Initial approach: Letter

Deadline(s): Apr. 3

Applicants should submit the following:

1) Transcripts
2) Class rank
3) Letter(s) of recommendation
4) GPA
5) Financial information

Additional information: Tri-Rivers students whose home school is located outside of Marion county are also eligible.

EIN: 311472824

7388

The Troy Foundation

216 W. Franklin St.
Troy, OH 45373-2846 (937) 339-8935
Contact: Melissa A. Kleptz, Exec. Dir.; For scholarships: Lisa M. Reynolds, Prog. Off.
FAX: (937) 339-8992;
E-mail: info@thetroyfoundation.org; URL: http://thetroyfoundation.org/

Foundation type: Community foundation
Purpose: Scholarships to local high school seniors of Troy, OH pursuing a postsecondary education.
Publications: Application guidelines; Annual report; Informational brochure; Informational brochure (including application guidelines); Newsletter.
Financial data: Year ended 12/31/2011. Assets, $61,510,606 (M); Expenditures, $3,303,577; Total giving, $2,698,128; Grants to individuals, totaling $231,043.
Fields of interest: Vocational education, post-secondary; Higher education; Business school/education; Nursing school/education.
Type of support: Scholarships—to individuals; Support to graduates or students of specific schools; Undergraduate support.
Application information: Applications accepted. Application form required. Application form available on the grantmaker's web site.

Send request by: Mail

Deadline(s): Mar. 25

Applicants should submit the following:

1) Class rank
2) GPA
3) Essay

Additional information: Contact your high school guidance counselor for application information or see web site for a complete listing of scholarship funds.

Program descriptions:

Apple Grants: This program was established to provide teachers with a monetary source to enhance the educational experience of their students, and is an on-going annual grantmaking program of the foundation. Applications may be for up to $1,000 each and may be received by the foundation at any time throughout the year. Visit foundation web site for application form and guidelines.

Scholarships: The foundation currently holds many scholarship funds that provide scholarships to local high school seniors. Most scholarships are for students pursuing college, vocational or technical training. Some are for students interested in specific subject areas, such as finance, nursing or athletics. Visit foundation web site for more information.

EIN: 316018703

7389

Tuition Assistance Program for Catholic Education

401 Pike St.
Reading, OH 45215-5900 (513) 554-1868

Foundation type: Public charity
Purpose: Tuition assistance for children who are parishioners of Sts. Peter & Paul Roman Catholic Church, Reading OH.
Financial data: Year ended 12/31/2012. Assets, $14,621 (M); Expenditures, $22,750; Total giving, $11,000.
Fields of interest: Education.
Type of support: Support to graduates or students of specific schools.
Application information: Applications not accepted.

Additional information: Contributes only to preselected individuals of the Roman Catholic Church.

EIN: 300295922

7390

The Turco Foundation

1101 Moore Rd.
Avon, OH 44011 (440) 934-1902
Contact: Loreto Turco, Jr., Tr.
Application addresses: c/o Loreto Turco, Jr., 3066 Woodsong Ln., Clearwater, FL 33761; c/o Tracey Lynne McIntosh, 4980 Spring Bluff Dr., Atlanta, GA 30350, tel.: (440) 934-1902,

Foundation type: Independent foundation
Purpose: Scholarships to students accepted for enrollment or currently enrolled at an accredited educational institution with preference to Cleveland residents.
Financial data: Year ended 12/31/2012. Assets, $1,951,400 (M); Expenditures, $106,520; Total giving, $106,285; Grants to individuals, 5 grants totaling $23,000 (high: $6,000, low: $4,000).
Type of support: Undergraduate support.
Application information: Applications accepted. Application form required.

Deadline(s): June 1 and Dec. 1

Applicants should submit the following:
1) Transcripts
2) SAT
3) ACT
4) Letter(s) of recommendation
5) Essay

Additional information: Submit a 500 word essay and include reasons for choosing the professional goals, current experiences, and long range plans after graduation. Recipient must maintain academic record that place them in good standing with institution.
EIN: 341942938

7391
Tuscora Park Health & Wellness Foundation
460 W. Paige Ave.
Barberton, OH 44203-2564 (330) 753-4607
Scholarship application address: c/o Barbara Berlin, Nursing Office, Summa Barberton Hospital, Nursing Scholarship Comm., 155 5th St. N.E., Barberton, OH 44203, tel.: (330) 745-1611, ext. 3352
FAX: (330) 745-3990;
E-mail: tuschealthfdn@yahoo.com; URL: http://www.bcfcharity.org/bcf/tuscorapark_txt.html

Foundation type: Independent foundation
Purpose: Scholarships to residents of Barberton, Kenmore, Manchester, Coventry, Norton, Doylestown, Rittman, Canal Fulton, Green or Clinton, OH, higher education leading to a diploma or degree in professional nursing.
Financial data: Year ended 12/31/2011. Assets, $4,046,948 (M); Expenditures, $243,701; Total giving, $178,709.
Fields of interest: Nursing school/education.
Type of support: Undergraduate support.
Application information: Applications accepted. Application form required. Interview required.
Deadline(s): Mar. 13
Additional information: Application must include transcripts.
EIN: 341193807

7392
Fritts Charles & Margaret TW Scholarship
(formerly Margaret & Charles Fritts Scholarship Trust)
c/o PNC Bank,N.A
P.O. Box 94651
Cleveland, OH 44101-4651 (507) 931-1682
Application Address: c/o Margaret Fritts Scholarship, One Scholarship Way,St. Peter, MN 56082

Foundation type: Independent foundation
Purpose: Scholarships primarily to students attending college or universities in PA and OH.
Financial data: Year ended 12/31/2012. Assets, $827,145 (M); Expenditures, $44,352; Total giving, $33,400.
Type of support: Scholarships—to individuals.
Application information: Applications accepted. Application form required.
Deadline(s): May 5
Additional information: Contact foundation for current application guidelines.
EIN: 206052070

7393
The Twenty First Century Foundation
P.O. Box 543
Norwalk, OH 44857-0543

Foundation type: Independent foundation
Purpose: Grants by nomination only to economically disadvantaged parents of Huron, Erie or Seneca counties in OH for emergencies, disasters and medical expenses.
Financial data: Year ended 06/30/2013. Assets, $13,826,421 (M); Expenditures, $598,056; Total giving, $466,255; Grants to individuals, 5 grants totaling $5,550 (high: $1,500, low: $1,000).
Fields of interest: Health care; Housing/shelter; Safety/disasters.
Type of support: Emergency funds; Grants to individuals; Awards/grants by nomination only; Grants for special needs; Project support.
Application information: Applications not accepted.
Additional information: Unsolicited requests for funds not considered or acknowledged.
EIN: 341852806

7394
Marion C. Tyler Foundation
c/o KeyBank
10 W. 2nd St.,26th Fl.
Dayton, OH 45402

Foundation type: Company-sponsored foundation
Purpose: Pension supplements to retired employees of W.S. Tyler, Inc.
Financial data: Year ended 12/31/2012. Assets, $1,178,745 (M); Expenditures, $55,084; Total giving, $41,999; Grants to individuals, 17 grants totaling $41,999 (high: $4,179, low: $409).
Type of support: Employee-related welfare.
Application information: Application form required.
Additional information: Application should include financial information; Application address: c/o Don Whitehouse, 3200 Bessemer City Rd., Box 8900, Gastonia, NC 28053, tel.: (704) 629-2214. This is an employee-related program all others are ineligible to request funding.
EIN: 346525274

7395
United Labor Agency, Inc.
(also known as United Labor Agency of Ohio)
1020 Bolivar Rd.
Cleveland, OH 44115-1204 (216) 664-2182
FAX: (216) 391-6959

Foundation type: Public charity
Purpose: Grants to economically disadvantaged residents of northeastern OH for medical equipment and other necessities.
Financial data: Year ended 12/31/2012. Assets, $682,919 (M); Expenditures, $4,130,367.
Fields of interest: Economically disadvantaged.
Type of support: Grants for special needs.
Application information:
Initial approach: Letter
Additional information: Contact foundation for complete eligibility requirements.
EIN: 237180005

7396
United Way of Greater Stark County, Inc.
4825 Higbee Ave. N.W., Ste. 101
Canton, OH 44718-2567 (330) 491-0445
FAX: (330) 491-0477; E-mail: info@uwgsc.org;
URL: http://www.uwstark.org/

Foundation type: Public charity

Purpose: Specific assistance to Stark county, OH, residents with food, clothing, shelter, utilities, and medical care.
Publications: Annual report; Financial statement; Informational brochure; Newsletter; Program policy statement.
Financial data: Year ended 03/31/2012. Assets, $10,981,338 (M); Expenditures, $7,116,378; Total giving, $5,183,577; Grants to individuals, totaling $135,623.
Fields of interest: Human services; Economically disadvantaged.
Type of support: In-kind gifts; Grants for special needs.
Application information: Contact the agency for eligibility determination.
EIN: 134254191

7397
United Way of Summit County
90 N. Prospect St.
P.O. Box 1260
Akron, OH 44309-1260 (330) 762-7601
Contact: Bob Kulinski, Pres.
FAX: (330) 762-0317;
E-mail: bkulinski@uwsummit.org; Tel. for Bob Kulinski: (330) 643-5520; URL: http://www.uwsummit.org

Foundation type: Public charity
Purpose: Grants for food, clothing, and shelter to indigents in Summit County, OH.
Publications: Annual report.
Financial data: Year ended 03/31/2012. Assets, $16,796,558 (M); Expenditures, $12,556,353; Total giving, $9,698,364; Grants to individuals, totaling $55,163.
Fields of interest: Human services, emergency aid; Economically disadvantaged.
Type of support: In-kind gifts; Grants for special needs.
Application information: Applications accepted.
Additional information: Contact the agency for eligibility determination.
EIN: 341169257

7398
The University of Toledo Foundation
(formerly Medical University of Ohio Foundation)
2801 W. Bancroft St., MS 319
Toledo, OH 43606-3328 (419) 530-7730
Contact: Brenda Lee, Pres.
FAX: (419) 530-2895;
E-mail: utfoundation@utoledo.edu; Toll-free tel.: (800) 640-0147; e-mail for Brenda Lee: brenda.lee@utoledo.edu; tel. for Brenda Lee : (419) 530-7730; URL: http://www.utoledo.edu/foundation

Foundation type: Public charity
Purpose: Scholarship assistance for students attending the University of Toledo, OH with tuition, books and housing.
Publications: Financial statement.
Financial data: Year ended 06/30/2012. Assets, $217,475,984 (M); Expenditures, $16,916,477; Total giving, $12,766,299; Grants to individuals, totaling $2,569,511.
Fields of interest: Higher education; Medical school/education.
Type of support: Support to graduates or students of specific schools.
Application information: Students should check with the financial aid department for additional information.
EIN: 346555110

7399
Ursuline Foundation
5535 Pfeiffer Rd.
Cincinnati, OH 45242-4813 (513) 791-5791
Contact: Sharon Redmond, Pres.

Foundation type: Public charity
Purpose: Scholarships to students of Ursuline Academy of Cincinnati for higher education.
Financial data: Year ended 06/30/2012. Assets, $7,869,382 (M); Expenditures, $296,694; Total giving, $267,200; Grants to individuals, totaling $92,200.
Fields of interest: Higher education; Young adults, female.
Type of support: Support to graduates or students of specific schools.
Application information: Applications not accepted.
Additional information: Students are selected for the scholarship. Unsolicited requests for funds not considered or acknowledged.
EIN: 311233054

7400
Curt & Margaret Uschmann Memorial Scholarship Fund
c/o KeyBank N.A.
4900 Tiedeman Rd., OH-01-49-0150
Brooklyn, OH 44144-2302
Contact: Karen Gourley
Application address: Lebanon High School Aspire, 1700 S. 5th St., Lebanon, OR 97355

Foundation type: Independent foundation
Purpose: Scholarships to graduates of Lebanon High School, OR, for college or technical schools.
Financial data: Year ended 03/31/2012. Assets, $521,103 (M); Expenditures, $37,422; Total giving, $29,666.
Fields of interest: Vocational education.
Type of support: Support to graduates or students of specific schools; Undergraduate support.
Application information: Applications accepted. Application form required.
Initial approach: Letter
Deadline(s): Apr. 30
EIN: 936146393

7401
Isabel F. Van Horn Scholarship Trust
P.O. Box 3500
Newark, OH 43058-3500
Contact: James D. Young
Application address: 587 Mount Vernon Rd., Newark, OH 43055

Foundation type: Independent foundation
Purpose: Scholarships to men and women entering the seminary in preparation for ministry in the Central Christian Church in Newark, OH.
Financial data: Year ended 12/31/2012. Assets, $896,617 (M); Expenditures, $70,954; Total giving, $61,612.
Fields of interest: Theological school/education; Christian agencies & churches.
Type of support: Graduate support.
Application information: Applications accepted.
Initial approach: Letter
Deadline(s): None
Additional information: Recipients are approved by a majority of the elders of the Church.
EIN: 316464732

7402
Virginia W. Van Hyning Scholarship Fund
P.O. Box 1558, EA4E86
Columbus, OH 43216-1558

Foundation type: Independent foundation
Purpose: Scholarships to graduates of Benjamin Logan High School, Zanesfield, OH.
Financial data: Year ended 12/31/2011. Assets, $205,761 (M); Expenditures, $12,758; Total giving, $10,000.
Type of support: Support to graduates or students of specific schools; Undergraduate support.
Application information: Applications not accepted.
Additional information: Unsolicited requests for funds not considered or acknowledged.
EIN: 316258749

7403
The Van Wert County Foundation
138 E. Main St.
Van Wert, OH 45891-1725 (419) 238-1743
Contact: Larry L. Wendel, Exec. Secy.
FAX: (419) 238-3374; E-mail: vwcf@bright.net

Foundation type: Public charity
Purpose: Scholarships to graduates of high schools in Paulding and Van Wert counties, OH.
Publications: Application guidelines; Informational brochure; Informational brochure (including application guidelines); Newsletter.
Financial data: Year ended 12/31/2011. Assets, $37,583,855 (M); Expenditures, $1,774,297; Total giving, $1,285,995; Grants to individuals, totaling $404,088.
Fields of interest: Arts education; Architecture; Music; Performing arts, education; Literature; Research; Higher education; Medical school/ education; Nursing school/education; Theological school/education; Environment, forests; Horticulture/garden clubs; Veterinary medicine; Agriculture; Nutrition; Home economics; Business/industry; Engineering; Christian agencies & churches; Women; Men.
Type of support: Undergraduate support.
Application information: Applications accepted. Application form required. Interview required.
Initial approach: Letter
Copies of proposal: 1
Deadline(s): June 1
Final notification: Recipients notified in thirty days
Applicants should submit the following:
1) Photograph
2) Financial information
3) Transcripts
4) GPA
5) Curriculum vitae
Program description:
Scholarships: The foundation makes grants to students who reside in Van Wert County and who attend one of the following area high schools: Antwerp High School, Crestview High School, Delphos Jefferson High School, Delphos St. Johns High School, Lincolnview High School, Parkview High School, Paulding High School, Spencerville High School, Van Wert High School, Vantage Vocational School, and Wayne Trace High School. Eligible applicants must maintain a GPA of at least 2.75 during their freshman year of college, and demonstrate a need for financial assistance; to remain eligible for scholarship consideration, students must maintain a GPA of at least 3.0 for their second year in college, and must be enrolled as full-time students.
EIN: 340907558

7404
Fred N. VanBuren Scholarship Fund
107 N. Main St.
P.O. Box 218
Baltimore, OH 43105-1286 (740) 862-4191
Contact: James Keller, Tr.; Stephanie Shook, Tr.; Richard Miller, Tr.

Foundation type: Independent foundation
Purpose: Scholarships to financially needy Liberty Union-Thurston High School students residing in Liberty Township or Liberty Union School District, OH, who are seeking degrees in agriculture or home economics.
Financial data: Year ended 06/30/2013. Assets, $0 (M); Expenditures, $102,489; Total giving, $92,000; Grants to individuals, 92 grants totaling $92,000 (high: $1,000, low: $1,000).
Fields of interest: Scholarships/financial aid; Agriculture; Home economics.
Type of support: Support to graduates or students of specific schools; Undergraduate support.
Application information: Application form required.
Deadline(s): Prior to Apr. 15
Applicants should submit the following:
1) Photograph
2) Transcripts
3) GPA
4) Financial information
Additional information: Applications must also include a completed confidential statement and copies of the last two years tax returns. If under the age of twenty-three a confidential statement of parent's return is required. Applicants must not be users of tobacco, alcoholic beverages, or abusive drugs. Incomplete applications will not be considered.
EIN: 311117779

7405
Helen Vandenbark Scholarship Fund
P.O. Box 1558, Dept EA4E86
Columbus, OH 43216 (740) 455-7060

Foundation type: Independent foundation
Purpose: Scholarships to graduates of Zanesville High School, OH, who are majoring in education.
Financial data: Year ended 12/31/2012. Assets, $104,266 (M); Expenditures, $5,366; Total giving, $3,742.
Fields of interest: Teacher school/education.
Type of support: Support to graduates or students of specific schools; Undergraduate support.
Application information: Application form required.
Initial approach: Letter or telephone
Deadline(s): May 1
Applicants should submit the following:
1) Transcripts
2) Letter(s) of recommendation
3) Financial information
Additional information: Application should also include students' and parents' income tax returns.
EIN: 316226483

7406
Vermillion Family Scholarship Fund, Inc.
1602 Willow Brook Dr.
Warren, OH 44483 (330) 372-6081
Contact: Patricia Diloreto, Secy.

Foundation type: Independent foundation
Purpose: Scholarships to residents of Warren, OH.
Financial data: Year ended 12/31/2011. Assets, $2,507 (M); Expenditures, $14,885; Total giving,

$14,290; Grant to an individual, 1 grant totaling $14,290.
Type of support: Undergraduate support.
Application information: Applications not accepted.
  Additional information: Unsolicited requests for funds not accepted.
EIN: 341906407

7407
W. S. O. S. Community Action Commission, Inc.
109 S. Front St.
P.O. Box 590
Fremont, OH 43420-0590   (419) 334-8911
FAX: (419) 334-8919; Toll Free Tel.: (800)-775-9767; URL: http://www.wsos.org/index.php

Foundation type: Public charity
Purpose: Services to indigent residents of OH, such as small business loans, home weatherization, home repairs, short term housing rental assistance, and utility assistance.
Financial data: Year ended 09/30/2011. Assets, $14,469,815 (M); Expenditures, $28,096,474; Total giving, $7,112,607; Grants to individuals, totaling $4,270,680.
Fields of interest: Economically disadvantaged.
Type of support: In-kind gifts; Grants for special needs.
Application information:
  Initial approach: Letter
  Additional information: Contact foundation for eligibility criteria.
EIN: 340975934

7408
The Wagnalls Memorial Foundation
150 E. Columbus St.
Lithopolis, OH 43136-0217   (614) 837-4765
Contact: Ellen Gruber, Exec. Dir.
E-mail: caspencer@wagnalls.org; URL: http://www.wagnalls.org/

Foundation type: Independent foundation
Purpose: Scholarships for students of Lithopolis and Bloom Township, OH for attending institutions of learning, music and art.
Financial data: Year ended 12/31/2012. Assets, $18,060,730 (M); Expenditures, $697,304; Total giving, $15,500; Grants to individuals, 16 grants totaling $15,500 (high: $2,000, low: $500).
Fields of interest: Higher education; Scholarships/financial aid.
Type of support: Scholarships—to individuals.
Application information: Applications accepted. Application form required. Application form available on the grantmaker's web site. Interview required.
  Initial approach: Letter or telephone
  Send request by: Mail or hand deliver
  Copies of proposal: 1
  Deadline(s): Apr. 15
  Applicants should submit the following:
    1) Photograph
    2) Transcripts
Program description:
  The Mabel Wagnalls Jones Scholarship: Scholarships in the amount of $1,000 are awarded to students with a 2.25 GPA, be within ten years from high school graduation date, and must become a resident of Litopolis or Bloom Township before Sept.1 of the year he/she entered first

grade. Applicants can be currently enrolled in college.
EIN: 314379589

7409
William F. & Gertrude Wahl Scholarship Fund
300 High St.
Hamilton, OH 45011-6037   (812) 376-1795

Foundation type: Independent foundation
Purpose: Scholarships to graduating seniors of Switzerland County High School, IN, who are in the upper quarter of their graduating classes, demonstrate financial need, and are of good standing in the community and school.
Financial data: Year ended 12/31/2012. Assets, $605,599 (M); Expenditures, $21,886; Total giving, $13,900.
Fields of interest: Higher education.
Type of support: Support to graduates or students of specific schools; Undergraduate support.
Application information: Applications accepted.
  Initial approach: Letter
  Deadline(s): None
EIN: 311014220

7410
Carlos E. Wakefield and Beatrice E. Wakefield Scholarship Fund
c/o KeyBank N.A.
4900 Tiedman Rd., OH-01-49-0150
Brooklyn, OH 44144-2302
Contact: Ella Munday
Application address: 53 Main St., Dexter, ME 04930

Foundation type: Independent foundation
Purpose: Scholarships to residents of Dexter or Ripley, ME for postsecondary education.
Financial data: Year ended 08/31/2012. Assets, $753,705 (M); Expenditures, $9,932; Total giving, $0.
Fields of interest: Higher education.
Type of support: Scholarships—to individuals.
Application information: Applications accepted. Application form required.
  Deadline(s): None
  Additional information: Application forms available from the committee.
EIN: 222929235

7411
Anna Marie & Russel Waldron Scholarship Fund
P.O. Box 1558, Dept. EA4E86
Columbus, OH 43216-1558

Foundation type: Independent foundation
Purpose: Scholarships to students of Rutherford B. Hayes High School, who attended Conger Elementary School, OH.
Financial data: Year ended 06/30/2013. Assets, $186,593 (M); Expenditures, $10,491; Total giving, $8,500.
Type of support: Support to graduates or students of specific schools; Undergraduate support.
Application information: Applications not accepted.
  Additional information: Unsolicited requests for funds not considered or acknowledged.
EIN: 311415607

7412
The Wapakoneta Area Community Foundation
P.O. Box 1957
Wapakoneta, OH 45895-1957   (419) 739-9223
Contact: Larry R. Tester, Exec. Dir.
FAX: (419) 739-9220;
E-mail: ltesterwacf@bright.net; URL: http://www.wapakacf.org

Foundation type: Community foundation
Purpose: Scholarships to high school seniors in Wapakoneta, OH, for higher education.
Publications: Annual report; Informational brochure; Newsletter.
Financial data: Year ended 05/31/2013. Assets, $1,667,830 (M); Expenditures, $131,181; Total giving, $97,429; Grants to individuals, 77 grants totaling $97,429.
Fields of interest: Higher education.
Type of support: Scholarships—to individuals.
Application information: Application form required.
  Initial approach: Letter
  Send request by: Mail
  Copies of proposal: 5
  Deadline(s): Apr. 15
EIN: 341615229

7413
Mae Ward Educational Trust
c/o Fifth Third Bank of Ohio Valley
P.O. Box 630858
Cincinnati, OH 45263-0858   (614) 744-7700

Foundation type: Independent foundation
Purpose: Scholarships to students who have attended high schools in Boyd County, KY for at least three years preceding application in pursuit of a college degree.
Financial data: Year ended 12/31/2011. Assets, $532,773 (M); Expenditures, $33,110; Total giving, $25,141.
Type of support: Undergraduate support.
Application information:
  Initial approach: Letter
  Deadline(s): Feb. 15
  Applicants should submit the following:
    1) Class rank
    2) ACT
    3) GPA
    4) Transcripts
  Additional information: Application should also include list of activities.
EIN: 616246093

7414
Warman Scholarship Trust
c/o KeyBank, N.A.
4900 Tiedeman Rd., OH-01-49-0150
Brooklyn, OH 44144-2302   (518) 257-9650
Contact: Joal Savage
Application address: P. O. Box 22042, Albany, NY 12201, tel.: 518-257-9650

Foundation type: Independent foundation
Purpose: College scholarships for graduates of secondary schools in Aroostook and Washington counties, ME.
Financial data: Year ended 03/31/2012. Assets, $529,428 (M); Expenditures, $20,209; Total giving, $13,000; Grants to individuals, 2 grants totaling $13,000 (high: $10,000, low: $3,000).
Type of support: Undergraduate support.
Application information:
  Deadline(s): None
EIN: 046731724

7415
Wayne County Community Foundation
(formerly Greater Wayne County Foundation, Inc.)
517 N. Market St.
Wooster, OH 44691-3405 (330) 262-3877
Contact: Sara L. Patton, Exec. Dir.
FAX: (330) 262-8057; E-mail: wccf@sssnet.com;
Additional e-mail: gwcf@gwcf.net; URL: http://
www.waynecountycommunityfoundation.org

Foundation type: Community foundation
Purpose: Scholarships to individuals residing in the
Wooster, OH, area for undergraduate education at
U.S. colleges and universities.
Publications: Application guidelines; Annual report;
Financial statement; Informational brochure
(including application guidelines).
Financial data: Year ended 06/30/2012. Assets,
$48,947,071 (M); Expenditures, $4,525,111;
Total giving, $4,026,693; Grants to individuals,
totaling $309,279.
Fields of interest: Higher education.
Type of support: Employee-related scholarships;
Scholarships—to individuals; Support to graduates
or students of specific schools; Awards/prizes;
Graduate support; Precollege support;
Undergraduate support.
Application information: Applications accepted.
Application form required. Application form
available on the grantmaker's web site.
  Initial approach: Application
  Send request by: Mail
  Deadline(s): Varies
  Applicants should submit the following:
    1) Transcripts
    2) SAT
    3) Letter(s) of recommendation
    4) GPA
    5) Financial information
    6) Essay
    7) ACT
  Additional information: The foundation
    administers approximately 60 scholarships to
    residents of Akron, Ashland, Dalton,
    Doylestown, Norwayne, Orrville, Rittman,
    Triway, Wayne County, Waynedale, and
    Wooster, OH. See web site for complete
    program information.
EIN: 341281026

7416
Ella Weiss Educational Fund
106 S. Main St., 16th Fl.
Akron, OH 44308 (330) 384-7302
Contact: Toby Blossom
Application address: First Merit Bank

Foundation type: Independent foundation
Purpose: Scholarships to residents of OH under 23
years old for attendance at educational institutions
in OH.
Financial data: Year ended 12/31/2012. Assets,
$618,169 (M); Expenditures, $43,787; Total
giving, $31,500.
Fields of interest: Higher education.
Type of support: Scholarships—to individuals.
Application information: Application form required.
  Initial approach: Letter
  Deadline(s): Mar. 31
  Applicants should submit the following:
    1) Transcripts
    2) Letter(s) of recommendation
EIN: 237133041

7417
Wellness Connection of the Dayton Region
4801 Hempstead Stn. Dr., Ste. B
Kettering, OH 45429-5171 (937) 223-4117
Contact: Jeanine Hufford, Exec. Dir.
FAX: (937) 223-4118;
E-mail: info@wellness-connection.org; Mailing
address: 105 Sugar Camp Cir., Ste. 100, Dayton,
OH 45409-1962; toll-free tel.: (888) 221-4004;
E-mail For Jeanine Hufford:
jhufford@cancersupportwesternohio.org;
URL: http://www.wellness-connection.org

Foundation type: Public charity
Purpose: Medical, dental and hospital expenses to
individuals with heart disease and cancer in the
Miami Valley, OH area.
Publications: Annual report.
Financial data: Year ended 12/31/2011. Assets,
$380,269 (M); Expenditures, $235,910.
Fields of interest: Cancer; Heart & circulatory
diseases.
Type of support: Grants for special needs.
Application information:
  Initial approach: Letter
  Additional information: Contact foundation for
    eligibility.
EIN: 161665552

7418
West Side Ecumenical Ministry
5209 Detroit Ave.
Cleveland, OH 44102-2224 (216) 651-2037
FAX: (216) 651-4145

Foundation type: Public charity
Purpose: Grants to assist individuals and families
of Cleveland, OH for basic necessities, including
food, clothing and other special needs.
Publications: Annual report; Informational
brochure; Newsletter.
Financial data: Year ended 12/31/2011. Assets,
$4,681,758 (M); Expenditures, $7,667,251; Total
giving, $65,218; Grants to individuals, totaling
$65,218.
Fields of interest: Food services; Human services.
Type of support: In-kind gifts; Grants for special
needs.
Application information: Applications not
accepted.
  Additional information: Unsolicited requests for
    funds not considered or acknowledged.
EIN: 237034175

7419
Ward W. and Norabelle Wester Memorial Charitable Foundation
c/o PNC Bank N.A.
P.O. Box 94651
Cleveland, OH 44101-4651

Foundation type: Independent foundation
Purpose: Scholarships to needy individuals who
have received treatment at the Shriners Hospital for
Crippled Children, Cincinnati, OH Burn Institute or
who have received treatment at the Shriners
Hospital for Crippled Children, Erie, PA Unit.
Financial data: Year ended 09/30/2012. Assets,
$1,223,734 (M); Expenditures, $66,777; Total
giving, $54,398.
Fields of interest: Children/youth, services.
Type of support: Scholarships—to individuals.
Application information: Applications accepted.
  Initial approach: Letter
  Deadline(s): None

Additional information: Application must include
social security number and proof of treatment
or benefits from the Shriners Hospitals of
Cincinnati, OH, or Erie, PA.
EIN: 346998992

7420
Western Reserve Area Agency on Aging
925 Euclid Ave., Ste. 600
Cleveland, OH 44115-1405 (216) 621-8010
Toll-free tel.: (800) 626-7277; URL: http://
www.psa10a.org

Foundation type: Public charity
Purpose: Assistance in the form of meals and
homecare services to elderly, low-income residents
of Cuyahoga, Geauga, Lake, Lorain and Medina
counties, OH.
Financial data: Year ended 12/31/2011. Assets,
$15,975,219 (M); Expenditures, $128,315,166.
Fields of interest: Aging.
Type of support: Grants for special needs.
Application information: Applications not
accepted.
  Additional information: Unsolicited requests for
    funds not considered or acknowledged.
EIN: 341620774

7421
Westerville Rotary Foundation
(formerly Westerville Rotary Elderly Housing)
P.O. Box 595
Westerville, OH 43086-0595 (614) 882-3929

Foundation type: Public charity
Purpose: Scholarships to individuals for attendance
at Otterbein College, OH for higher education.
Financial data: Year ended 06/30/2011. Assets,
$244,077 (M); Expenditures, $17,125; Total
giving, $16,250.
Fields of interest: Higher education.
Type of support: Support to graduates or students
of specific schools.
Application information: Contact the foundation for
eligibility requirements.
EIN: 311204959

7422
Wexner Center Foundation
(formerly Wexner Center for the Arts)
c/o Ohio State Univ.
1871 N. High St.
Columbus, OH 43210-1105 (614) 292-0330
Contact: C. Robert Kidder, Pres.
FAX: (614) 292-3369; URL: http://
www.wexarts.org

Foundation type: Public charity
Purpose: Prize by nomination only to a major
contemporary artist. Also, residencies to artists
specializing in the performing arts, media arts (film/
video), and visual arts.
Financial data: Year ended 06/30/2011. Assets,
$6,725,778 (M); Expenditures, $4,661,264; Total
giving, $4,203,648.
Fields of interest: Film/video; Visual arts;
Performing arts; Arts.
Type of support: Awards/grants by nomination only;
Awards/prizes; Residencies.
Application information: Applications accepted.
Program descriptions:
  Artists' Residencies: The foundation provides
  opportunities to artists to interact with the Ohio
  State University community and the public at-large.

Residencies are awarded in the performing arts, media arts (film/video), and visual arts.

Wexner Prize: The program awards a $50,000 prize annually to a major contemporary artist whose work and career must exemplify the institution's goals of embracing exploration and innovation while upholding the highest standards of artistic quality and integrity. Recipients are nominated by the Center's International Arts Advisory Council, whose members are prominent artists and arts professionals from many disciplines.
EIN: 311306419

7423
Wexner Foundation
8000 Walton Pkwy., Ste. 110
New Albany, OH 43054-7074   (614) 939-6060
Fellowship address: The Wexner Israel Fellowship Program, c/o Center for Public Leadership, Harvard Kennedy School, Attn.: Abbey Onn, Coord., Wexner Israel Fellowship Prog. at Harvard University, 79 JFK St., Cambridge, MA 02138, tel.: (617) 496-7113, fax: (617) 495-4988
FAX: (614) 939-6066; E-mail: info@wexner.net; New York address: 599 Lexington Ave., Ste. 27A, New York, NY 10022, tel.: (212) 355-6115; Israel address: 37 Derech Beit Lechem, Jerusalem, Israel 93553, tel.: 02 563-7035, fax: 02 561-2002; MA address: c/o Center for Public Leadership, Harvard Kennedy School, 79 JFK St., Cambridge, MA 02139, tel.: (617) 496-7113; URL: http://www.wexnerfoundation.org

Foundation type: Independent foundation
Purpose: Fellowships for Jewish religious studies in North America. Fellowships to Israeli government officials for study at Harvard University's John F. Kennedy School of Government.
Publications: Informational brochure; Program policy statement.
Financial data: Year ended 12/31/2012. Assets, $4,758,670 (M); Expenditures, $9,450,726; Total giving, $2,182,980.
Fields of interest: Government/public administration; Leadership development; Jewish agencies & synagogues.
Type of support: Fellowships; Support to graduates or students of specific schools; Foreign applicants.
Application information: Application form required.
  Initial approach: Letter
  Copies of proposal: 3
  Deadline(s): See foundation web site for current deadlines
  Applicants should submit the following:
    1) Photograph
    2) Essay
    3) Transcripts
    4) Letter(s) of recommendation
  Additional information: Application must also include GRE scores and acceptance letter from graduate institution applicant is attending; Israeli applicants must also submit scores from a standardized English proficiency test.
Program descriptions:
  Wexner Field Fellowship: In partnership with the Jim Joseph Foundation, three Field Fellows will be accepted as part of incoming classes. Promising Jewish professionals currently working full-time in a Jewish communal organization based in North America, who are seeking professional growth and plan to continue to pursue a career as a professional leader in the North American Jewish community, are eligible. Applicants must: 1) be currently working full-time in a Jewish communal organization based in North America, 2) not have completed graduate studies specifically geared for

the Jewish professional field, 3) be a citizen of the United States, Canada, or Mexico, or have documentation that allows them to work in that country, 4) have at least 3 years of post-baccalaureate full-time work or volunteer experience, 5) be between the ages of 26 and 40 years old, and 6) receive the written support of the executive director and board president of their current organization for full participation in the Fellowship Program. See foundation web site for application information. Contact for questions: Ruthie Warshenbrot, e-mail: rwarshenbrot@wexner.net. Contact for application process: Pam Driftmyer, e-mail: pdriftmyer@wexner.net.
  Wexner Graduate Fellowship/Davidson Scholars: Wexner Graduate Fellowships are awarded to 20 outstanding individuals who seek to prepare themselves through graduate training for careers in the Cantorate, Jewish Education (Davidson Scholars), Jewish Professional Leadership (Davidson Scholars), Jewish Studies, and the Rabbinate. Candidates must be: 1) entering the first or second year of a full-time degree granting graduate program based in North America, that will allow him/her to pursue a career as a professional Jewish leader in North America, 2) a citizen of the United States, Canada, or Mexico, or have documentation that allows him/her to study and to work in that country, and 3) between the ages of 21 and 40 upon entering a graduate program. See foundation web site for specific deadline dates and application information. Contact Linda Smith, Asst. to the Dir. of the Graduate Fellowship/Davidson Scholars Prog., e-mail: lsmith@wexner.net.
EIN: 237320631

7424
G. & M. White Scholarship Fund
c/o KeyBank, N.A.
4900 Tiedman Rd., OH-01-49-0150
Brooklyn, OH 44144-2302

Foundation type: Independent foundation
Purpose: Scholarships to graduating students of Cooperstown High School, NY for higher education at accredited colleges or universities.
Financial data: Year ended 12/31/2012. Assets, $172,313 (M); Expenditures, $11,124; Total giving, $9,000.
Fields of interest: Higher education.
Type of support: Support to graduates or students of specific schools.
Application information: Application form required.
  Deadline(s): None
EIN: 156026002

7425
Elizabeth White Scholarship Trust
c/o KeyBank N.A.
4900 Tiedeman Rd., OH-01-49-0
Brooklyn, OH 44144-2302

Foundation type: Independent foundation
Purpose: Scholarships to graduates of Cooperstown High School, NY, pursuing a major in education.
Financial data: Year ended 12/31/2011. Assets, $122,866 (M); Expenditures, $9,219; Total giving, $7,100.
Fields of interest: Teacher school/education.
Type of support: Support to graduates or students of specific schools; Undergraduate support.
Application information: Applications accepted.

  Initial approach: Letter
  Deadline(s): None
EIN: 146179502

7426
Kay Kelly Wilhelm Memorial Fund
323 S. Marion St.
Cardington, OH 43315-1024   (419) 864-9515

Foundation type: Independent foundation
Purpose: Scholarships to graduating seniors of Cardington Lincoln High School, OH.
Financial data: Year ended 12/31/2011. Assets, $36,016 (M); Expenditures, $6,515; Total giving, $6,000; Grants to individuals, 5 grants totaling $6,000 (high: $2,000, low: $1,000).
Type of support: Support to graduates or students of specific schools; Undergraduate support.
Application information: Applications accepted. Application form required.
  Initial approach: Letter
  Deadline(s): After graduation
  Applicants should submit the following:
    1) Transcripts
    2) Essay
    3) Letter(s) of recommendation
EIN: 237100701

7427
Howell & Lois Williams Memorial Fund
c/o PNC Bank N.A.
P.O. Box 94651
Cleveland, OH 44101-4651   (724) 752-1591
Contact: Donald E. Hollerman
Application address: 501 Crescent Ave., Ellwood City, PA 16117, tel.: 724-752-1591

Foundation type: Independent foundation
Purpose: Scholarships to students of the Ellwood City Area School District, PA, who excel in biology or English.
Financial data: Year ended 04/30/2012. Assets, $323,361 (M); Expenditures, $16,321; Total giving, $11,000.
Fields of interest: Literature; Biology/life sciences.
Type of support: Support to graduates or students of specific schools; Undergraduate support.
Application information: Applications accepted. Application form required.
  Deadline(s): Mar. 1
EIN: 251671119

7428
Jessie A. Williams Trust
(formerly The Frank O. and Clara R. Williams Scholarship Fund)
c/o PNC Bank, N.A.
P.O. Box 94651
Cleveland, OH 44101-4651   (412) 762-4106
Contact: Michael Yoder
Application address: 2 PNC Plz., 7th Fl., 620 Liberty Ave., Pittsburgh, PA 15222 Tel.: (412) 762-4106

Foundation type: Independent foundation
Purpose: Grants and scholarships to graduates of Venango County, PA, high schools.
Publications: Application guidelines.
Financial data: Year ended 12/31/2012. Assets, $6,434,030 (M); Expenditures, $305,348; Total giving, $247,638; Grant to an individual, 1 grant totaling $247,638.
Fields of interest: Scholarships/financial aid.
Type of support: Support to graduates or students of specific schools; Undergraduate support.

Application information: Applications accepted. Application form required. Interview required.
  Initial approach: Letter to request application form
  Deadline(s): Apr. 30
  Final notification: 1 to 2 months
  Additional information: Applicants must intend to enroll in a 4-year college or university. Scholarship preference is for Allegheny College. Application must outline financial need and/or CSS profile. Dependents of National City Bank employees are not eligible.
EIN: 256031440

7429
James Worthington Willmott Memorial Trust II
P.O. Box 94651
Cleveland, OH 44101-4651
URL: https://www.pnc.com/

Foundation type: Independent foundation
Purpose: Scholarships to residents of Bourbon County, KY, and adjacent counties.
Financial data: Year ended 09/30/2012. Assets, $2,331,293 (M); Expenditures, $124,617; Total giving, $108,000; Grants to individuals, 100 grants totaling $108,000.
Type of support: Scholarships—to individuals.
Application information: Applications accepted. Application form required.
  Applicants should submit the following:
    1) Financial information
    2) Transcripts
    3) Letter(s) of recommendation
  Additional information: Application must also include a complete biographical record, statement of educational plans, report on aptitude test results, and a statement of residency.
EIN: 616174229

7430
J. B. & Garnet A. Wilson Charitable Trust
P.O. Box 686
Waverly, OH 45690-0686   (740) 947-2727

Foundation type: Independent foundation
Purpose: Scholarships to individuals for postsecondary education at OH colleges and universities.
Financial data: Year ended 12/31/2012. Assets, $2,106,934 (M); Expenditures, $394,091; Total giving, $365,771; Grants to individuals, totaling $365,771.
Fields of interest: Higher education.
Type of support: Scholarships—to individuals.
Application information: Application form required.
  Deadline(s): Prior to beginning the first year of college
EIN: 310983188

7431
Clark W. Wilson Trust
c/o KeyBank N.A.
4900 Tiedeman Rd. OH-01-49-0
Brooklyn, OH 44144-2302
Application address: c/o Canastota High School, 120 Roberts St., Canastota, NY 13032.

Foundation type: Independent foundation
Purpose: Scholarships to male graduates of Canastota High School, NY pursuing a career in the fields of science and chemistry.

Financial data: Year ended 12/31/2012. Assets, $83,507 (M); Expenditures, $4,426; Total giving, $3,400.
Fields of interest: Medical school/education; Science; Men.
Type of support: Support to graduates or students of specific schools; Undergraduate support.
Application information:
  Deadline(s): None
EIN: 237327739

7432
Wimmer Scholarship Fund
(formerly George G., Elma & Ruth M. Wimmer Scholarship Fund)
c/o PNC Bank, N.A.
P.O. Box 609
Cleveland, OH   15230-9738   (219) 356-4100
Contact: William Gordon Sr.
Application address: 533 Warren St., Huntington, IN 46750

Foundation type: Independent foundation
Purpose: Scholarships to students of Fort Wayne High School, IN, Elmhurst High School, IN, and Huntington North High School, IN, to pursue careers in medicine, nursing, or science.
Financial data: Year ended 08/31/2013. Assets, $2,416,806 (M); Expenditures, $113,476; Total giving, $93,100; Grant to an individual, 1 grant totaling $93,100.
Fields of interest: Medical school/education; Nursing school/education; Science.
Type of support: Support to graduates or students of specific schools; Technical education support; Undergraduate support.
Application information: Application form required.
  Deadline(s): Mar. 31
  Applicants should submit the following:
    1) Photograph
    2) Transcripts
    3) SAT
    4) Letter(s) of recommendation
    5) Financial information
  Additional information: Application should also include statement of no more than 300 words of applicant accomplishments, goals and reason for requesting scholarship. Application available from high school guidance offices.
EIN: 311036448

7433
Ralph Winans Memorial Scholarship Fund
P.O Box 1558, Dept. EA4E86
Columbus, OH 43216
Application address: Huntington National Bank

Foundation type: Independent foundation
Purpose: Scholarships to graduating seniors of the Western Reserve School District, OH.
Financial data: Year ended 12/31/2012. Assets, $7,738 (M); Expenditures, $7,635; Total giving, $7,000.
Type of support: Support to graduates or students of specific schools; Undergraduate support.
Application information: Applications accepted.
  Initial approach: Letter
  Deadline(s): None
EIN: 341631397

7434
Earnest & Maxine Wingett Educational Trust
109 E. 2nd St.
Pomeroy, OH 45769-1031
Contact: Cathy Crow, Dir.
Application Address: P.O. Box 289, Pomeroy, OH 45769

Foundation type: Independent foundation
Purpose: Scholarships to residents of Sutton Township and Meigs County, OH, and to lineal descendants of Ernest and Maxine Wingett.
Financial data: Year ended 06/30/2013. Assets, $271,695 (M); Expenditures, $18,271; Total giving, $15,200; Grants to individuals, 10 grants totaling $6,950 (high: $1,650, low: $1,000).
Type of support: Scholarships—to individuals.
Application information: Applications accepted. Application form required.
  Initial approach: Letter or telephone
  Deadline(s): Mar. 15
EIN: 316411166

7435
Dr. L.G. Wisner & Winfred T. Wisner Scholarship Trust Fund
c/o PNC Bank, N.A.
P.O. Box 94651
Cleveland, OH 44101-4651   (815) 426-2162

Foundation type: Independent foundation
Purpose: Scholarships to financially needy graduating seniors and graduates from Herscher High School, IL.
Financial data: Year ended 04/30/2012. Assets, $210,798 (M); Expenditures, $9,215; Total giving, $7,000.
Type of support: Support to graduates or students of specific schools; Undergraduate support.
Application information: Application form required.
  Deadline(s): Apr. 22
  Applicants should submit the following:
    1) Class rank
    2) GPA
    3) ACT
  Additional information: Applicants who are current Herscher High School students must obtain and complete their application forms in the guidance office. Graduates can secure their application materials from the school district office.
EIN: 366872997

7436
Charles E. Wolf Educational Trust
c/o PNC Bank, N.A.
P.O. Box 94651
Cleveland, OH 44101-4651
URL: https://www.pnc.com

Foundation type: Independent foundation
Purpose: Scholarships primarily to individuals attending college or university in IN.
Financial data: Year ended 09/30/2012. Assets, $559,184 (M); Expenditures, $40,930; Total giving, $33,000.
Fields of interest: Higher education.
Type of support: Undergraduate support.
Application information: Applications not accepted.
  Additional information: Unsolicited requests for funds not considered or acknowledged.
EIN: 900097958

7437
Alice Louise Ridenour Wood Scholarship Fund
P.O. Box 94651
Cleveland, OH 44101-4651

Foundation type: Independent foundation
Purpose: Scholarships to graduating seniors at specific OH high schools for undergraduate and technical/vocational school studies.
Financial data: Year ended 12/31/2011. Assets, $1,596,828 (M); Expenditures, $76,251; Total giving, $56,999; Grants to individuals, 32 grants totaling $56,999.
Fields of interest: Vocational education; Vocational education, post-secondary; College (community/junior); College; University.
Type of support: Support to graduates or students of specific schools; Technical education support; Undergraduate support.
Application information: Application form required.
  Initial approach: Letter or telephone
  Deadline(s): Mar. 15
EIN: 316395426

7438
Ward & Mary Wooddell Scholarship
48 N. South St.
Wilmington, OH 45177-0711
Application address: National Bank Trust Co., P.O. Box 711, Wilmington, OH 45177

Foundation type: Independent foundation
Purpose: Scholarships to graduating seniors from Clinton County, OH, high schools.
Financial data: Year ended 09/30/2013. Assets, $232,294 (M); Expenditures, $14,145; Total giving, $10,164; Grants to individuals, 8 grants totaling $10,164 (high: $3,000, low: $500).
Type of support: Support to graduates or students of specific schools; Undergraduate support.
Application information: Application form required.
  Deadline(s): Apr. 1
  Additional information: Application must include financial statement.
EIN: 316368376

7439
Working Girls Association Inc.
c/o Lee Clay
1825 Sandringham
Toledo, OH 43615-3931 (419) 535-6780
Contact: Cowgee Mangrum, Secy.-Treas.
Application address: 1823 Perth St., Toledo OH 43607

Foundation type: Independent foundation
Purpose: Scholarships to students from low-income disadvantaged families from the Toledo, OH area.
Financial data: Year ended 09/30/2012. Assets, $344,749 (M); Expenditures, $15,447; Total giving, $10,000; Grants to individuals, 7 grants totaling $10,000 (high: $2,000, low: $1,200).
Fields of interest: Education; Economically disadvantaged.
Type of support: Scholarships—to individuals.
Application information: Applications accepted. Application form required.
  Additional information: Applicant must demonstrate economic need, and a minimum GPA must be maintained.
EIN: 344479715

7440
Corale B. Workum Trust
P.O. Box 630858
Cincinnati, OH 45263-0858

Foundation type: Independent foundation
Purpose: Scholarships primarily to students at the University of Cincinnati, OH.
Financial data: Year ended 03/31/2013. Assets, $4,405,912 (M); Expenditures, $249,184; Total giving, $209,001.
Fields of interest: Jewish agencies & synagogues.
Type of support: Scholarships—to individuals.
Application information: Applications accepted.
  Additional information: Contact trust for current application deadline/guidelines.
EIN: 316019902

7441
Charles L. Wright Foundation
P.O. Box 94651
Cleveland, OH 44101-4651 (216) 222-3236
Contact: Laura Bozell
Application address: c/o PNC Bank, N.A., 1900 E. 9th St., Cleveland, OH 44114-3404

Foundation type: Independent foundation
Purpose: Scholarships to seniors in the New Brighton School District, PA, for completion of a two-year degree or nursing program.
Financial data: Year ended 12/31/2011. Assets, $82,038 (M); Expenditures, $6,429; Total giving, $4,500.
Fields of interest: Nursing school/education.
Type of support: Support to graduates or students of specific schools; Undergraduate support.
Application information: Applications accepted. Application form required.
  Deadline(s): None
  Additional information: Application includes an essay.
EIN: 256217209

7442
Kenneth Wyman Trust
(formerly Kenneth B. Wyman Scholarship Trust)
c/o KeyBank, N.A.
4900 Tiedeman Rd. OH-01-49-0150
Brooklyn, OH 44144-2302

Foundation type: Independent foundation
Purpose: Scholarships to students who are residents of Northport, ME, for higher education.
Financial data: Year ended 04/30/2013. Assets, $148,497 (M); Expenditures, $4,582; Total giving, $0.
Type of support: Undergraduate support.
Application information: Applications accepted.
  Initial approach: Letter
  Deadline(s): None
  Additional information: Contact foundation for current application guidelines.
EIN: 016075670

7443
Charles F. & Mary M. Yeiser Foundation
7811 Laurel Ave., Ste. B
Cincinnati, OH 45243-2608 (513) 621-1384
Contact: Charles F. Yeiser, Pres. and Tr.

Foundation type: Independent foundation
Purpose: Scholarships to students of the greater Cincinnati, OH area for undergraduate college degrees.

Financial data: Year ended 12/31/2012. Assets, $8,854 (M); Expenditures, $237,635; Total giving, $237,567; Grants to individuals, 52 grants totaling $237,567 (high: $12,500, low: $500).
Fields of interest: Higher education.
Type of support: Scholarships—to individuals.
Application information: Applications accepted. Application form required.
  Deadline(s): None
  Additional information: Application should include transcript.
EIN: 316033638

7444
Yellow Springs Community Foundation
P.O. Box 55
Yellow Springs, OH 45387-0055 (937) 767-2655
Contact: Virgil Hervey, Fdn. Admin.
E-mail: info@yscf.org; URL: http://www.yscf.org

Foundation type: Community foundation
Purpose: Scholarships to students at Yellow Springs High School, OH for higher education at accredited institutions.
Publications: Application guidelines; Annual report; Grants list; Informational brochure.
Financial data: Year ended 12/31/2012. Assets, $8,091,763 (M); Expenditures, $221,947; Total giving, $146,591; Grants to individuals, 5 grants totaling $5,350.
Fields of interest: Higher education.
Type of support: Scholarships—to individuals; Support to graduates or students of specific schools.
Application information: Applications accepted. Application form required. Application form available on the grantmaker's web site.
  Deadline(s): Apr. 15
  Additional information: Contact the guidance counselor at Yellow Springs High School for specific application information. See web site for additional information.
EIN: 237372791

7445
Yoder Brothers Memorial Scholarship Fund
(formerly Joshua Yoder Memorial Scholarship)
7550 Trails End
Chagrin Falls, OH 44023-1426
URL: http://www.yoderbrothersfoundation.org

Foundation type: Independent foundation
Purpose: Scholarships to students who have participated in at least one sport in their senior year at Berkshire, Newbury and Cardinal high schools in Geauga County, OH.
Financial data: Year ended 12/31/2011. Assets, $820,836 (M); Expenditures, $113,718; Total giving, $68,954; Grants to individuals, 30 grants totaling $68,500 (high: $4,000, low: $1,500).
Fields of interest: Higher education; Athletics/sports, school programs.
Type of support: Support to graduates or students of specific schools; Undergraduate support.
Application information: Application form required.
  Applicants should submit the following:
    1) Essay
    2) Letter(s) of recommendation
    3) Transcripts
  Additional information: Application should also include college acceptance letter.
EIN: 341848189

7446

YSI Foundation Inc.
P.O. Box 279
Yellow Springs, OH 45387-0279 (937)
767-7241
E-mail: smiller@ysi.com

Foundation type: Company-sponsored foundation
Purpose: Scholarships to students and children of employees of YSI, Inc. to pursue higher education and scholarships and equipment to graduate students for research projects.
Financial data: Year ended 12/31/2012. Assets, $4,334 (M); Expenditures, $110,639; Total giving, $107,529.
Fields of interest: Higher education; Scholarships/financial aid; Environment.
Type of support: Travel awards; Research; Employee-related scholarships; Scholarships—to individuals.
Application information: Applications accepted.
  Initial approach: Proposal
  Send request by: E-mail
  Copies of proposal: 1
  Deadline(s): Varies for YSI Scholarships, May 1 for Graduate Student Scholarship and Equipment Loan Program
  Final notification: May 15 for Graduate Student Scholarship and Equipment Loan Program

Additional information: Application should include a curriculum vitae.
Program descriptions:
  Graduate Student Scholarship and Equipment Loan Program: The foundation annually awards four scholarships and loans equipment free of charge to graduate students for original research projects created by the student or in response to a YSI Research Proposal. Special emphasis is directed to the study of environmental variables in oceans, estuaries, rivers, lakes, or laboratory settings. Scholarships of up to $10,000 are awarded and each proposal is eligible for a $1,000 travel grant to a national conference to present the results of investigations.
  YSI Scholarships: The foundation awards scholarships to a local high school student and a YSI employee's child to pursue a two or four-year post-high school continuing education program.
Company name: YSI Incorporated
EIN: 311292180

7447

The Herbert C. Ziegler Foundation
4150 Millennium Blvd. S.E.
Massillon, OH 44646 (330) 834-3332
Contact: William C. Ziegler, Tr.
URL: http://www.bziegler@zieglertire.com

Foundation type: Independent foundation
Purpose: Scholarships to OH employees of The Ziegler Tire and Supply Company and The Ziegler Oil Company, and to their children.
Financial data: Year ended 11/30/2012. Assets, $880,477 (M); Expenditures, $49,100; Total giving, $49,100; Grants to individuals, 21 grants totaling $31,500 (high: $1,500, low: $1,500).
Fields of interest: Education.
Type of support: Employee-related scholarships.
Application information: Applications accepted. Application form required.
  Additional information: Application must include four character references. Unsolicited requests for funds not considered or acknowledged.
EIN: 341381823

OKLAHOMA

7448
Aileen Flanary Educational Fund
2510 Sam Noble Pkwy.
Ardmore, OK 73401 (580) 223-5810
Contact: Michael A. Cawley, Tr.

Foundation type: Independent foundation
Purpose: Scholarships to graduates of high or home schools in Carter County, Oklahoma, attending public institutions in Oklahoma, full time with 2.7 GPA.
Financial data: Year ended 06/30/2013. Assets, $710,042 (M); Expenditures, $41,348; Total giving, $27,500; Grants to individuals, 6 grants totaling $27,500 (high: $5,000, low: $2,500).
Fields of interest: Education.
Type of support: Undergraduate support.
Application information: Applications accepted.
  Initial approach: Letter
  Deadline(s): Apr. 15
  Applicants should submit the following:
    1) Financial information
    2) Class rank
    3) Work samples
    4) SAT
    5) ACT
    6) Transcripts
EIN: 264799010

7449
Ally's House, Inc.
P.O. Box 722767
Norman, OK 73070-9100 (405) 733-2559
Contact: Linda Webb, Exec. Dir.
E-mail: info@allyshouse.net; Toll Free Tel. : (877)-730-2559; URL: http://www.allyshouse.net

Foundation type: Public charity
Purpose: Assist families of children from Oklahoma stricken with cancer by providing financial support, programs and events during their hospital stay.
Publications: Informational brochure; Newsletter.
Financial data: Year ended 12/31/2012. Assets, $76,359 (M); Expenditures, $148,584; Total giving, $75,171; Grants to individuals, totaling $75,171.
Fields of interest: Cancer; Children.
Type of support: Grants for special needs.
Application information: Applications accepted. Application form required.
  Additional information: Families may apply if their child is an Oklahoma resident who has been diagnosed with a form of cancer. See web site for additional information.
EIN: 200726554

7450
Areawide Aging Agency, Inc.
4101 Perimeter Ctr. Dr., Ste. 310
Oklahoma City, OK 73112-5911 (405) 942-8500
Contact: Don Hudman, Exec. Dir.
FAX: (405) 942-8535; Additional Tel.: (405)-943-4344; URL: http://www.areawideaging.org

Foundation type: Public charity
Purpose: Services to indigent elderly in Oklahoma, Logan, Cleveland and Canadian counties, OK, such as free meals and transportation services.

Financial data: Year ended 06/30/2012. Assets, $1,886,921 (M); Expenditures, $6,125,820; Total giving, $5,061,439; Grants to individuals, totaling $92,484.
Fields of interest: Aging; Economically disadvantaged.
Type of support: In-kind gifts.
Application information:
  Initial approach: Tel.
  Additional information: Contact foundation for eligibility criteria.
EIN: 730960311

7451
Bailey Family Memorial Trust
P.O. Box 1620
Tulsa, OK 74101-1620

Foundation type: Independent foundation
Purpose: Grants and fellowships to graduate students at Oklahoma State University studying fine arts.
Financial data: Year ended 08/31/2013. Assets, $2,096,973 (M); Expenditures, $95,150; Total giving, $72,280; Grants to individuals, 8 grants totaling $72,280 (high: $12,000, low: $6,900).
Fields of interest: Humanities.
Type of support: Fellowships; Support to graduates or students of specific schools; Undergraduate support.
Application information: Contact foundation for current application deadline/guidelines.
EIN: 736210018

7452
Bartlesville Public School Foundation, Inc.
1100 S. Jennings
Bartlesville, OK 74003-4730 (918) 336-8600
Contact: Lisa Kennedy
URL: http://www.bps-ok.org

Foundation type: Independent foundation
Purpose: Grants to educators in the Bartlesville Public School System, OK for new and innovative curricula and programs that accelerate and enrich the learning environment of all students.
Financial data: Year ended 06/30/2013. Assets, $1,015,867 (M); Expenditures, $63,877; Total giving, $50,300.
Fields of interest: Education.
Type of support: Program development.
Application information: Application form required. Application form available on the grantmaker's web site.
  Deadline(s): Oct. 1 and Feb. 1 for Classroom Grants; Sept. 15, Jan. 15 and Apr. 15 for Professional Growth; 20th of each month for Experts in Residence Grants
  Additional information: See web site for additional guidelines.
EIN: 731256865

7453
Edward & Helen Bartlett Foundation
(formerly Edward E. Bartlett & Helen Turner Bartlett Foundation)
c/o The Trust Company of Oklahoma
P.O. Box 3627
Tulsa, OK 74101-3627 (918) 744-0553

Foundation type: Independent foundation
Purpose: Scholarships to students attending Oklahoma State University, University of Oklahoma,

Oklahoma State University Institute of Technology, and the University of Tulsa, OK.
Financial data: Year ended 12/31/2012. Assets, $27,270,433 (M); Expenditures, $1,466,184; Total giving, $1,284,463; Grants to individuals, totaling $164,000.
Fields of interest: Higher education.
Type of support: Support to graduates or students of specific schools.
Application information: Applications accepted.
  Initial approach: Letter
  Additional information: Application forms are available at the financial aid office of the mentioned schools.
EIN: 736092250

7454
Cordelia Lunceford Beatty Trust
105 N. Main St.
Blackwell, OK 74631-2226

Foundation type: Independent foundation
Purpose: Postsecondary scholarships and preschool tuition to financially needy residents of Blackwell, OK, who are under the age of 19.
Financial data: Year ended 12/31/2011. Assets, $2,400,416 (M); Expenditures, $161,308; Total giving, $104,527.
Fields of interest: Early childhood education.
Type of support: Precollege support; Undergraduate support.
Application information: Applications accepted. Application form required.
  Initial approach: Letter requesting application
  Deadline(s): Prior to start of school year.
  Additional information: Application should include photograph, GPA, and copy of first two pages of parents' most recent tax return.
EIN: 736094952

7455
Glen Carrier Charitable Trust
P.O. Box 1453
Beaver, OK 73932 (580) 625-3171
Contact: Richard Gardner, Jr., Tr.

Foundation type: Independent foundation
Purpose: Renewable scholarships to students residing in Beaver County, OK, for undergraduate or vocational education.
Publications: Annual report.
Financial data: Year ended 12/31/2012. Assets, $2,313,990 (M); Expenditures, $66,891; Total giving, $50,000; Grants to individuals, totaling $50,000.
Fields of interest: Vocational education, post-secondary.
Type of support: Undergraduate support.
Application information: Application form required.
  Deadline(s): Mar. 31
  Applicants should submit the following:
    1) Letter(s) of recommendation
    2) Transcripts
    3) Financial information
EIN: 731531180

7456
Catholic Foundation of Oklahoma, Inc.
7501 N.W. Expwy.
P.O. Box 32180
Oklahoma City, OK 73123 (405) 721-5651
Contact: Tony Tyler, Pres.; for Scholarships: Toby Boothe, Admin. Asst.
Additional e-mail: tboothe@catharchdioceseokc.org
FAX: (405) 721-4114;
E-mail: tcasso@catharchdioceseokc.org;
URL: http://www.cfook.org

Foundation type: Public charity
Purpose: College scholarships to students from throughout the Archdiocese of Oklahoma City, OK for attendance at colleges or universities.
Financial data: Year ended 06/30/2012. Assets, $48,019,315 (M); Expenditures, $608,261; Total giving, $137,190; Grants to individuals, totaling $137,190.
Fields of interest: Higher education; Catholic agencies & churches.
Type of support: Scholarships—to individuals.
Application information: Applications accepted. Application form required.
  Deadline(s): Apr. 17
  Applicants should submit the following:
    1) Photograph
    2) Transcripts
    3) Letter(s) of recommendation
    4) Financial information
  Additional information: Application must also include a copy of you and your parent's federal income tax return. Scholarships awards are based on academic achievement, service to church and community, and financial need.
EIN: 730773715

7457
Chickasaw Foundation
P.O. Box 1726
Ada, OK 74821-1726 (580) 421-9030
Contact: Johnna R. Walker, Exec. Dir.
Hand deliver address: Chickasaw Foundation, 110 W. 12th St., Ada, OK
E-mail: chickasawfoundation@chickasaw.net;
URL: http://www.chickasawfoundation.org

Foundation type: Public charity
Purpose: Scholarships to eligible Chickasaw, OK students for attendance at accredited colleges or universities.
Publications: Newsletter.
Financial data: Year ended 12/31/2012. Assets, $7,705,786; Expenditures, $1,147,649; Total giving, $96,592; Grants to individuals, totaling $96,592.
Fields of interest: Higher education; Native Americans/American Indians.
Type of support: Scholarships—to individuals; Graduate support; Undergraduate support.
Application information: Applications accepted. Application form required. Application form available on the grantmaker's web site.
  Initial approach: Telephone or e-mail
  Send request by: Mail or hand delivered
  Deadline(s): Jan. 11
  Applicants should submit the following:
    1) Photograph
    2) Essay
    3) Transcripts
    4) Letter(s) of recommendation
  Additional information: Awards are paid directly to the educational institution on behalf of the students. See web site for additional guidelines.
EIN: 731069557

7458
Lynn Colbert Charitable Foundation
c/o BancFirst
P.O. Box 1468
Duncan, OK 73534-1468 (580) 251-7027
Application address: MSC Financial Aid Office, One Murray Campus, Tishomingo, OK 73460, tel.: (580) 371-2371, ext. 143

Foundation type: Public charity
Purpose: Scholarships to freshman and sophomore for attendance at Murray State College, OK with tuition, fees, books, and on-campus housing.
Financial data: Year ended 06/30/2012. Assets, $1,920,914 (M); Expenditures, $134,077; Total giving, $101,495.
Fields of interest: Higher education.
Type of support: Support to graduates or students of specific schools.
Application information: Applications accepted. Application form required.
  Deadline(s): Apr. 15
  Applicants should submit the following:
    1) Transcripts
    2) Resume
    3) SAT
    4) GPA
    5) Essay
    6) ACT
  Additional information: Preference is given to students of Stephen county. Students must reapply for scholarship annually.
EIN: 736131373

7459
Communities Foundation of Oklahoma
(formerly Oklahoma Communities Foundation, Inc.)
2932 N.W. 122nd St., Ste. D
Oklahoma City, OK 73120-1955 (405) 488-1450
Contact: Susan R. Graves, Exec. Dir.; For scholarship inquiries: Lauren Garey, Scholarship Coord.
Scholarship inquiry e-mail: lgarey@cfok.org
FAX: (405) 755-0938; E-mail: sgraves@cfok.org; Additional tel.: (877) 689-7726; URL: http://www.cfok.org

Foundation type: Community foundation
Purpose: Scholarships to students of Ok, for continuing education at institutions of higher learning.
Publications: Annual report; Financial statement; Grants list; Informational brochure.
Financial data: Year ended 06/30/2012. Assets, $73,403,647 (M); Expenditures, $9,693,175; Total giving, $8,478,555; Grants to individuals, totaling $1,090,014.
Fields of interest: Higher education.
Type of support: Scholarships—to individuals; Awards/prizes; Technical education support; Undergraduate support.
Application information: Applications accepted.
  Additional information: The criteria for each scholarship includes established qualifications as to field of study, institution, GPA, and/or need. Contact the foundation for additional guidelines.
EIN: 731396320

7460
Compassionate Care Fund
6161 S. Yale
Tulsa, OK 74136-1902 (918) 494-1585
Contact: Mark Olin Kent, Tr.

Foundation type: Independent foundation
Purpose: Immediate financial assistance to Radiation Oncology patients for medicine, food, housing and/or transportation expenses related to radiation treatment.
Financial data: Year ended 12/31/2011. Assets, $224 (M); Expenditures, $1,764; Total giving, $1,163; Grants to individuals, 14 grants totaling $1,163 (high: $100, low: $30).
Fields of interest: Medical care, in-patient care.
Type of support: Grants for special needs.
Application information: Applications accepted. Application form required.
  Initial approach: Application
  Deadline(s): None
  Additional information: All referrals must be directed to the outpatient radiation oncology social worker. Patients referred to the program must currently be receiving treatment at the Natalie Warren Bryant Cancer Center.
EIN: 736292807

7461
Continue Learning and Strive for Success Foundation
13900 N. Portland
Oklahoma City, OK 73134-4042

Foundation type: Company-sponsored foundation
Purpose: Scholarships to high school graduates for attendance at Oklahoma institutes of higher learning.
Publications: Application guidelines.
Financial data: Year ended 12/31/2012. Assets, $9,604 (M); Expenditures, $5,006; Total giving, $5,000; Grants to individuals, 5 grants totaling $5,000 (high: $1,000, low: $1,000).
Fields of interest: Higher education.
Type of support: Undergraduate support.
Application information: Applications accepted. Application form required. Application form available on the grantmaker's web site.
  Initial approach: Application
  Send request by: Mail
  Deadline(s): Apr. 15
  Final notification: Applicants notified in May
  Applicants should submit the following:
    1) Transcripts
    2) Photograph
    3) GPA
    4) Essay
  Additional information: Essays should be no more than 200 words.
Program description:
  CLASS Scholarship Program: The foundation annually awards $1,000 scholarships to high school seniors who are customers or in the household of customers of Dobson Telephone Company or affiliates Intelleq or Dobson Technologies. Applicants must have a GPA of 3.0 and plan to attend an Oklahoma Institute of higher learning.
EIN: 203393143

7462
Covington-Douglas Scholarship Foundation
c/o Central National Bank & Trust Co.
P.O. Box 3448
Enid, OK 73702-3448
Contact: Karen Holland

Foundation type: Independent foundation
Purpose: Scholarships to graduates of Covington-Douglas Schools, OK or individuals who provide benefit to Covington-Douglas Schools.

Financial data: Year ended 12/31/2013. Assets, $663,170 (M); Expenditures, $21,163; Total giving, $13,000; Grants to individuals, 20 grants totaling $13,000 (high: $2,000, low: -$2,000).
Fields of interest: Higher education.
Type of support: Scholarships—to individuals.
Application information: Applications accepted. Application form required.
   Send request by: Mail
   Deadline(s): Apr.
EIN: 237426494

7463
Russell W. Davis Charitable Trust
P.O. Box 1156
Bartlesville, OK 74005-1156 (918) 337-3470
Contact: John M. Colaw
Application address : P.O. Box 2248, Bartlesville, OK 74005-2248 Tel.: (918)337-3470

Foundation type: Independent foundation
Purpose: Scholarships to worthy students of Bartlesville High School, OK in pursuit of a higher education.
Financial data: Year ended 12/31/2011. Assets, $211,211 (M); Expenditures, $12,928; Total giving, $10,000; Grants to individuals, 9 grants totaling $10,000 (high: $2,000, low: $500).
Fields of interest: Higher education.
Type of support: Scholarships—to individuals; Support to graduates or students of specific schools.
Application information: Applications accepted.
   Initial approach: Letter
   Deadline(s): None
   Additional information: Application should include qualifications and academic standing.
EIN: 736355391

7464
Henry & Elizabeth Donaghey Foundation
c/o Bank of Oklahoma, N.A.
P.O. Box 1620
Tulsa, OK 74101-1620 (918) 813-5100
Application Address: c/o Bank of Texas, P.O. Box 1088, Sherman, TX 75091

Foundation type: Independent foundation
Purpose: Scholarships to graduating seniors of Trenton High School, TX, for postsecondary education.
Financial data: Year ended 12/31/2012. Assets, $1,408,067 (M); Expenditures, $80,742; Total giving, $68,375; Grants to individuals, 11 grants totaling $22,375 (high: $5,000, low: $500).
Fields of interest: Higher education; Scholarships/financial aid.
Type of support: Support to graduates or students of specific schools; Undergraduate support.
Application information: Application form required.
   Deadline(s): None
   Additional information: Students should contact their high school guidance counselor for application information.
EIN: 751937116

7465
Helen Muxlow Driskell Scholarship Trust Fund
c/o BancFirst
P.O. Box 26883
Oklahoma City, OK 73126

Foundation type: Independent foundation

Purpose: Scholarships to graduates of Guthrie High School, OK with preference given to those pursuing a career in nursing.
Financial data: Year ended 12/31/2012. Assets, $338,004 (M); Expenditures, $24,025; Total giving, $18,200; Grants to individuals, 5 grants totaling $18,200 (high: $1,000, low: $500).
Fields of interest: Nursing school/education.
Type of support: Scholarships—to individuals.
Application information: Applications accepted. Application form required.
   Applicants should submit the following:
      1) Transcripts
      2) GPA
EIN: 736226426

7466
Clyde R. Evans Scholarship Award Trust
c/o Heritage Trust Co
P.O. Box 21708
Oklahoma, OK 73156-1708

Foundation type: Independent foundation
Purpose: Scholarships to residents of OK for higher education.
Financial data: Year ended 06/30/2013. Assets, $212,235 (M); Expenditures, $12,174; Total giving, $10,000; Grants to individuals, 2 grants totaling $10,000 (high: $5,000, low: $5,000).
Type of support: Scholarships—to individuals.
Application information: Applications not accepted.
   Additional information: Unsolicited requests for funds not considered or acknowledged.
EIN: 736296081

7467
Charles C. Faranna Scholarship Trust
4008 S. Elm Pl., Ste. F
Broken Arrow, OK 74011-2021

Foundation type: Independent foundation
Purpose: Scholarships to residents of OK.
Financial data: Year ended 06/30/2013. Assets, $0 (M); Expenditures, $468,490; Total giving, $173,471; Grants to individuals, 111 grants totaling $173,471 (high: $36,206, low: $802).
Type of support: Undergraduate support.
Application information: Contact trust for current application deadline/guidelines.
EIN: 736251335

7468
Feed the Children, Inc.
P.O. Box 36
Oklahoma City, OK 73101-0036 (405) 942-0228
FAX: (405) 945-4177;
E-mail: ftc@feedthechildren.org; Toll-free tel.: (800) 627-4556; URL: http://www.feedthechildren.org

Foundation type: Public charity
Purpose: Emergency assistance, including food, clothing, housing and medical supplies, to people in need internationally from natural and man-made disasters.
Publications: Annual report; Financial statement; Newsletter.
Financial data: Year ended 06/30/2012. Assets, $128,711,805 (M); Expenditures, $670,608,915; Total giving, $598,994,339; Grants to individuals, totaling $871,423.
Fields of interest: Safety/disasters; Thrift shops.
Type of support: Emergency funds; Grants for special needs.

Application information: Applications not accepted.
   Additional information: Contact the agency for additional information.
EIN: 736108657

7469
Laura Fields Trust
P.O. Box 2394
Lawton, OK 73502-2394 (580) 250-8441
Contact: Sheila Fountain, Mgr.

Foundation type: Independent foundation
Purpose: Scholarships to the top two students in each of the Comanche County, OK, high schools to attend Cameron University, OK. Loans to approximately ten students each year to attend school.
Publications: Annual report.
Financial data: Year ended 06/30/2013. Assets, $2,372,824 (M); Expenditures, $206,634; Total giving, $103,090.
Fields of interest: Vocational education.
Type of support: Support to graduates or students of specific schools; Undergraduate support.
Application information: Applications accepted. Application form required.
   Initial approach: Letter
   Deadline(s): None
   Additional information: Scholarship is paid to the university on behalf of the students. Interest free loans to students while they attend school and meet certain criteria.
EIN: 736095854

7470
Foundation for Visions
2601 N.W. Expwy., Ste. 612
Oklahoma City, OK 73112-7272 (405) 848-4229
Contact: Donna Kay Harrison, Pres. and Dir.; Stanley T. Harrison, Secy.-Treas. and Dir.

Foundation type: Independent foundation
Purpose: Scholarships to graduating students of OK pursuing postsecondary education at institutions of higher learning.
Financial data: Year ended 12/31/2012. Assets, $259,436 (M); Expenditures, $63,589; Total giving, $62,964; Grant to an individual, 1 grant totaling $2,217.
Fields of interest: Higher education.
Type of support: Scholarships—to individuals; Grants for special needs.
Application information: Applications accepted. Interview required.
   Additional information: Selection is based on recommendation by a school counselor, principal, or teacher, or an employer, minister or other adult.
EIN: 731412490

7471
Anna Collins Franklin Foundation
P.O. Box 144
Ardmore, OK 73401 (580) 223-7967
Contact: Bob Harper
Application address: 1914 6th Ave. N.W., Ardmore, OK 73401, tel.: (580) 223-7967

Foundation type: Independent foundation
Purpose: Scholarships to residents of Carter County, OK.
Financial data: Year ended 12/31/2012. Assets, $2,188,968 (M); Expenditures, $146,749; Total

giving, $110,405; Grants to individuals, 22 grants totaling $110,405 (high: $20,000, low: $875).
Type of support: Scholarships—to individuals.
Application information:
Initial approach: Letter
Deadline(s): None
EIN: 731361437

7472
Frontiers of Science Foundation of Oklahoma
P.O. Box 26967
Oklahoma City, OK   73126-0967   (405) 290-5600

Foundation type: Independent foundation
Purpose: Scholarships to graduating OK high school students who are interested in attending a college or university in OK and pursuing a course of study in applied science.
Financial data: Year ended 06/30/2013. Assets, $814,924 (M); Expenditures, $36,551; Total giving, $33,000.
Fields of interest: Science.
Type of support: Undergraduate support.
Application information: Application form required.
Initial approach: Letter or telephone
Deadline(s): Apr. 1
EIN: 730642039

7473
Funk Educational Foundation
P.O. Box 179
Piedmont, OK   73078   (405) 373-3385
Contact: Julie Bridges, Secy.

Foundation type: Independent foundation
Purpose: Scholarships to graduating students of Piedmont High School, OK for postsecondary education at accredited colleges or universities in OK.
Financial data: Year ended 12/31/2012. Assets, $4,409 (M); Expenditures, $33,304; Total giving, $2,000; Grants to individuals, 4 grants totaling $2,000 (high: $500, low: $500).
Fields of interest: Higher education.
Type of support: Support to graduates or students of specific schools.
Application information: Applications accepted.
Initial approach: Letter
Deadline(s): May 1
Applicants should submit the following:
1) GPA
2) ACT
EIN: 731488498

7474
Katherine and Calvin Gatlin Scholarship Fund
c/o The Trust Co. of Oklahoma
P.O. Box 3627
Tulsa, OK   74101-3627

Foundation type: Independent foundation
Purpose: Scholarships to high school seniors in Vinita, OK.
Financial data: Year ended 12/31/2012. Assets, $1,086,306 (M); Expenditures, $65,191; Total giving, $52,500.
Type of support: Undergraduate support.
Application information: Applications not accepted.

Additional information: Unsolicited requests for funds not considered or acknowledged.
EIN: 736266862

7475
Goldie Gibson Scholarship Fund
P.O. Box 1232
Bartlesville, OK   74005   (918) 337-5277
Contact: Susan Dick, Tr.
Application address: 330 S. Johnstone Ave., Bartlesville, OK 74003

Foundation type: Independent foundation
Purpose: Student loans primarily to residents of OK. Loans are renewable.
Financial data: Year ended 02/28/2012. Assets, $396,553 (M); Expenditures, $4,014; Total giving, $0.
Type of support: Student loans—to individuals.
Application information: Applications accepted. Application form required.
Deadline(s): None
Additional information: Contact foundation for application information.
EIN: 736183311

7476
Global Foundation for Peroxisomal Disorders
5147 S. Harvard Ave
Ste. 181
Tulsa, OK   74135-3587   (918) 230-7713
Application e-mail: grants@thegfpd.org
FAX: (918) 516-0227;
E-mail: contactus@thegfpd.org; URL: http://www.thegfpd.org/

Foundation type: Public charity
Purpose: Grants to investigators to fund research to develop a greater understanding of Peroxisomal Biogenesis Disorder-Zellweger Spectrum disorder (PBD-ZSD)
Financial data: Year ended 12/31/2011. Assets, $74,024 (M); Expenditures, $34,353; Total giving, $28,593; Grants to individuals, totaling $28,593.
Fields of interest: Genetic diseases and disorders research.
Type of support: Grants to individuals.
Application information: Applications accepted. Application form required. Application form available on the grantmaker's web site.
Send request by: Mail or e-mail
Deadline(s): June
Additional information: See web site for additional application guidelines.
Program description:
Small Grants Program: This program provides funding to investigators in obtaining preliminary findings, testing "proof of concept," or conducting other research activities designed to prepare and support competitive, full-scale grant applications related to Peroxisomal Biogenesis Disorder-Zellweger Spectrum Disorder (PBD-ZSD).Clinicans and researchers qualified in any aspect of Peroxisomal Biogenesis Disorder-Zellweger Spectrum Disorder are eligible. The period of the award will be up to two years in length, starting in Sept. of the submission year and amounts up to $25,000 annually for direct costs.
EIN: 273646193

7477
Guthrie Scottish Rite Charitable and Educational Foundation
P. O. Box 70
Guthrie, OK   73044-0070   (405) 282-1281
Contact: Michael L. Wiggins, Pres.
FAX: (405) 282-1250; E-mail: gsrite@sbcglobal.net;
URL: http://guthriescottishrite.org/

Foundation type: Public charity
Purpose: Need-based scholarships to graduates of Guthrie High School, OK, with a GPA of at least 3.0. Applicants whose major interest of study lies in the fine arts or athletics will not be considered. Also, grants to OK teachers for training.
Financial data: Year ended 12/31/2011. Assets, $8,066,497 (M); Expenditures, $449,993; Total giving, $29,500; Grants to individuals, totaling $29,500.
Fields of interest: Higher education.
Type of support: Grants to individuals; Support to graduates or students of specific schools; Undergraduate support.
Application information: Applications accepted. Application form required.
Deadline(s): Apr. 1 for scholarships
Applicants should submit the following:
1) Letter(s) of recommendation
2) SAT
3) ACT
4) Transcripts
5) GPA
EIN: 736105910

7478
Happiness is Helping Foundation
3237 N.W. 62nd St.
Oklahoma City, OK   73112

Foundation type: Operating foundation
Purpose: Financial assistance to low-income families residing in the Oklahoma City, OK metropolitan area.
Financial data: Year ended 12/31/2012. Assets, $74,725 (M); Expenditures, $10,157; Total giving, $9,600.
Fields of interest: Human services; Economically disadvantaged.
Type of support: Grants for special needs.
Application information: Applications not accepted.
Additional information: Unsolicited requests for funds not considered or acknowledged.
EIN: 311695374

7479
The Harold D. and Hazel H. Hathcoat Educational Trust
P.O. Box 286
Nowata, OK   74048

Foundation type: Independent foundation
Purpose: Loans to individuals for higher education.
Financial data: Year ended 12/31/2012. Assets, $654,544 (M); Expenditures, $9,071; Total giving, $0.
Type of support: Student loans—to individuals.
Application information: Applications not accepted.
Additional information: Unsolicited requests for funds not considered or acknowledged.
EIN: 736300011

7480
May Thompson Henry Trust
(formerly Thompson Henry Trust)
c/o Central National Bank & Trust
P.O. Box 3448
Enid, OK 73702-3448
Contact: Karen Holland

Foundation type: Independent foundation
Purpose: Scholarships to high school graduates for attendance at OK state-supported colleges, universities, and technical schools.
Financial data: Year ended 12/31/2012. Assets, $396,021 (M); Expenditures, $17,420; Total giving, $11,000; Grants to individuals, 11 grants totaling $11,000 (high: $1,000, low: $1,000).
Type of support: Scholarships—to individuals; Graduate support; Technical education support; Undergraduate support.
Application information: Application form required.
Send request by: Mail
Deadline(s): Apr. 1
Final notification: Recipients will be contacted no later than the end of May
Applicants should submit the following:
1) Letter(s) of recommendation
2) Transcripts
3) GPA
4) Essay
EIN: 731308178

7481
Merle and Richardine Holton Foundation
402 E. Jackson St.
Hugo, OK 74743-4021 (580) 326-6427
Contact: Bob Rabon, Pres.

Foundation type: Independent foundation
Purpose: College scholarships to graduating students of Hugo, OK for continuing their edcuation at institutions of higher learning.
Financial data: Year ended 12/31/2011. Assets, $116,876 (M); Expenditures, $6,054; Total giving, $4,000; Grants to individuals, 3 grants totaling $4,000 (high: $2,000, low: $1,000).
Fields of interest: Higher education.
Type of support: Scholarships—to individuals.
Application information: Applications accepted. Application form required.
Applicants should submit the following:
1) Letter(s) of recommendation
2) GPA
3) Financial information
Additional information: Applicants must also submit letters of reference, a complete biographical record, a report of academic and professional careers, and statement of plans and commitments after scholarship program.
EIN: 731373753

7482
Indwell Foundation
4221 N.W. 144th Terrace
Oklahoma City, OK 73134-1712

Foundation type: Independent foundation
Purpose: Financial assistance to indigent families of the Houston, TX metropolitan area.
Financial data: Year ended 12/31/2011. Assets, $72 (M); Expenditures, $842; Total giving, $0.
Type of support: Grants for special needs.
Application information: Applications not accepted.
Additional information: Unsolicited requests for funds not accepted.
EIN: 760605921

7483
International Christian Missions, Inc.
4100 S.E. Adams Rd., Ste. D-104
Bartlesville, OK 74006-2826

Foundation type: Independent foundation
Purpose: Financial assistance to priests for administrative costs of running missionary programs in Columbia.
Financial data: Year ended 12/31/2012. Assets, $16,817 (M); Expenditures, $4,674; Total giving, $0.
Fields of interest: Christian agencies & churches.
Type of support: Program development.
Application information: Applications not accepted.
Additional information: Unsolicited requests for funds not considered.
EIN: 260416576

7484
Wyatt F. & Mattie M. Jeltz Scholarship Foundation
P.O. Box 36575
Oklahoma City, OK 73136-6575

Foundation type: Independent foundation
Purpose: Scholarships to needy students who have completed one year of studies at an accredited college or university in OK.
Financial data: Year ended 12/31/2013. Assets, $143,761 (M); Expenditures, $22,412; Total giving, $12,300; Grants to individuals, 11 grants totaling $11,300 (high: $1,000, low: $900).
Fields of interest: Minorities.
Type of support: Scholarships—to individuals.
Application information: Applications accepted.
Deadline(s): Aug. 15 and Dec. 20
Additional information: Contact foundation for application guidelines.
EIN: 730994084

7485
Dexter G. Johnson Educational and Benevolent Trust
P.O. Box 1620
Tulsa, OK 74101-1620
Contact: Betty Crews
Application address: P.O. Box 850250, Yukon, OK 73085

Foundation type: Independent foundation
Purpose: Educational loans limited to financially needy residents of OK for study at OK high schools and vocational schools, and Oklahoma State University, Oklahoma City University, and the University of Oklahoma. Preference is given to physically disabled students, and students who, by misfortune or calamity, cannot otherwise complete their education. Medical expenses to physically disabled children and young men and women of OK.
Financial data: Year ended 12/31/2012. Assets, $4,371,532 (M); Expenditures, $221,890; Total giving, $110,669; Grants to individuals, 6 grants totaling $65,669 (high: $20,000, low: $3,472).
Fields of interest: Secondary school/education; Higher education; Health care; Disabilities, people with.
Type of support: Student loans—to individuals; Support to graduates or students of specific schools; Grants for special needs.
Application information: Application form required.
Additional information: Applications must include financial information, family history, physical

condition, age, education goals, and other data necessary to show need.
EIN: 237389204

7486
The Paul and Louise Johnson Foundation
525 S. Main St., Ste. 700
Tulsa, OK 74103-4500

Foundation type: Operating foundation
Purpose: Scholarships and grants for educational endeavors in the field of dentistry.
Financial data: Year ended 08/31/2012. Assets, $72,160 (M); Expenditures, $995; Total giving, $0.
Fields of interest: Dental school/education.
Type of support: Scholarships—to individuals.
Application information: Applications accepted. Application form required.
Initial approach: Letter or telephone
Deadline(s): None
EIN: 731506406

7487
JWF Quanza Foundation, Inc.
5101 N. Classen Blvd., Ste. 411
Oklahoma City, OK 73118-5258 (405) 843-8444
Contact: Jerry Crabb, Pres.

Foundation type: Independent foundation
Purpose: Scholarships to OK residents for attendance at OK universities and grants for hearing aids for underprivileged children in OK.
Financial data: Year ended 12/31/2011. Assets, $2,241,296 (M); Expenditures, $172,270; Total giving, $104,001.
Fields of interest: Ear, nose & throat diseases; Economically disadvantaged.
Type of support: Undergraduate support; Grants for special needs.
Application information: Applications accepted. Application form required.
Deadline(s): None
Additional information: Applications available at OK universities' financial aid offices and OK audiologists' offices.
EIN: 731467915

7488
Kane Memorial High School Trust
(formerly Robert Kane High School Scholarship Memorial Trust)
P.O. Box 1156
Bartlesville, OK 74005-1156 (918) 337-3433
Application address: c/o Arvest Co., N.A., P.O. Box 2248, Bartlesville, OK 74005-2248

Foundation type: Independent foundation
Purpose: Scholarships to graduating seniors of Bartlesville High School, OK for continuing education at colleges or universities.
Financial data: Year ended 12/31/2011. Assets, $163,352 (M); Expenditures, $12,961; Total giving, $12,344; Grants to individuals, 2 grants totaling $12,344 (high: $8,246, low: $4,098).
Fields of interest: Higher education.
Type of support: Support to graduates or students of specific schools.
Application information: Applications accepted.
Deadline(s): None
Additional information: Application must include scholastic and financial need.
EIN: 736091639

7489

Kappa Alpha PSI OKC Alumni Scholarship Foundation

1801 N.E. 10th St.
Oklahoma City, OK 73117-2815 (405) 424-6040
Contact: Kennith Arinwine, Tr.

Foundation type: Independent foundation
Purpose: Scholarships for graduating high school seniors in the greater OK, city area pursuing higher education.
Financial data: Year ended 12/31/2011. Assets, $127,694 (M); Expenditures, $1,026; Total giving, $5,000; Grants to individuals, totaling $5,000.
Fields of interest: Higher education.
Type of support: Scholarships—to individuals.
Application information: Applications accepted. Application form required.
> *Deadline(s):* Apr. 2
> *Applicants should submit the following:*
> 1) Photograph
> 2) Transcripts
> 3) Letter(s) of recommendation
> 4) Essay
> *Additional information:* Applicants must maintain at least a 2.5 GPA on a 4.0 scale.

EIN: 731417748

7490

Velma Klamm & Ruth Fishburn Foundation

18 N. Adair St.
Pryor, OK 74361-2433 (918) 825-0322
Contact: Julia Neftzger
Application Address: P.O. Box 386, Pryor, OK 74362.

Foundation type: Operating foundation
Purpose: College scholarships to high school students from Pryor and Adair, OK.
Financial data: Year ended 12/31/2013. Assets, $2,977,320 (M); Expenditures, $107,224; Total giving, $84,000; Grants to individuals, 15 grants totaling $84,000 (high: $10,000, low: -$8,000).
Type of support: Undergraduate support.
Application information: Application form required.
> *Deadline(s):* Apr. 30
> *Applicants should submit the following:*
> 1) Essay
> 2) Transcripts

EIN: 731575833

7491

Karl & Georgia Martin, Sr., Anna Belle Flynn, Karl & June Martin, Jr. Foundation

6307 Waterford Blvd., Ste. 215
Oklahoma City, OK 73118 (405) 840-8401
Contact: Joe Womack, Tr.

Foundation type: Independent foundation
Purpose: Scholarships to students at OK colleges and universities primarily studying petroleum, aerospace engineering, energy and engineering.
Financial data: Year ended 12/31/2011. Assets, $5,764,189 (M); Expenditures, $417,724; Total giving, $303,000.
Fields of interest: Environmental education.
Type of support: Undergraduate support.
Application information: Applications accepted. Application form required.
> *Initial approach:* Letter
> *Deadline(s):* Apr. 30

EIN: 731504147

7492

Masonic Charity Foundation of Oklahoma

P.O. Box 2406
Edmond, OK 73083-2406 (405) 348-7500
Contact: John Logan, Exec. Dir.
FAX: (405) 348-9031;
E-mail: information@mcfok.org; Street address: 3424 French Park Dr., Edmond, OK 73034; Toll-free tel.: (877) 562-7667; URL: http://www.mcfok.org

Foundation type: Independent foundation
Purpose: Scholarships to graduating high school seniors of Oklahoma who are members of the Youth Orders for attendance at any accredited college, university, trade or vocational school within or outside of OK.
Publications: Application guidelines; Annual report; Informational brochure.
Financial data: Year ended 12/31/2012. Assets, $86,345,075 (M); Expenditures, $4,177,724; Total giving, $3,292,856; Grants to individuals, 154 grants totaling $152,007.
Fields of interest: Vocational education, post-secondary; Higher education.
Type of support: Emergency funds; Scholarships—to individuals; Grants for special needs.
Application information: Applications accepted. Application form required. Application form available on the grantmaker's web site.
> *Initial approach:* Letter
> *Send request by:* Mail
> *Copies of proposal:* 1
> *Deadline(s):* May 1
> *Applicants should submit the following:*
> 1) Transcripts
> 2) Letter(s) of recommendation
> 3) Financial information

Program description:
> *Youth Scholarship Program:* The program provides scholarships for applicants who must be Oklahoma DeMolay, Rainbow or Job's Daughter majority member or member in good standing at the time of application, and must personally represent the teachings and ideals of the Masonic Bodies. A 2.5 GPA on a 4.0 scale must be maintained for subsequent scholarship applications to be considered. Scholarship amount is approximately $2,000 a year.

EIN: 736097262

7493

Virginia McKenzie Charitable Trust

P.O. Box 1497
Pawhuska, OK 74056
Contact: Harvey Payne, Tr.

Foundation type: Independent foundation
Purpose: Scholarships to residents of Pawhuska, OK.
Financial data: Year ended 12/31/2012. Assets, $2,934,329 (M); Expenditures, $148,554; Total giving, $120,000; Grants to individuals, 120 grants totaling $120,000 (high: $1,000, low: $1,000).
Type of support: Undergraduate support.
Application information:
> *Initial approach:* Letter

EIN: 736309465

7494

Messenger of Salvation

P.O. Box 624
Bethany, OK 73008

Foundation type: Operating foundation
Purpose: Grants to individuals in India to support their missionary work.

Financial data: Year ended 12/31/2011. Assets, $366 (M); Expenditures, $45,990; Total giving, $45,940; Grants to individuals, 41 grants totaling $43,690 (high: $16,835, low: $50).
Fields of interest: Religion.
Type of support: Grants to individuals.
Application information: Applications not accepted.
EIN: 731361590

7495

Mary Clarke Miley Foundation, Inc.

2119 Forister Ct.
Norman, OK 73069-5118
Contact: Stephen W. Bonner, Pres. and Dir.

Foundation type: Independent foundation
Purpose: Scholarships to Native American and African-American students attending the University of Oklahoma who have declared a major in the College of Fine Arts or Journalism/Mass Communication program.
Financial data: Year ended 12/31/2013. Assets, $15,683 (M); Expenditures, $150; Total giving, $0.
Fields of interest: Media/communications; Print publishing; African Americans/Blacks; Native Americans/American Indians.
Type of support: Support to graduates or students of specific schools.
Application information: Applications accepted. Application form required.
> *Deadline(s):* Aug. 1
> *Additional information:* Applications available from the Dean of the College of Fine Arts.

EIN: 731575511

7496

The Ethan A. Mills Foundation

P.O. Box 1146
Bristow, OK 74010
Application address: 121 E. 6th Ave., Bristow, OK 74010

Foundation type: Independent foundation
Purpose: Scholarships to students within the city of Bristow, OK.
Financial data: Year ended 12/31/2011. Assets, $1,156,774 (M); Expenditures, $48,777; Total giving, $35,887; Grants to individuals, 19 grants totaling $35,887.
Type of support: Scholarships—to individuals.
Application information: Applications accepted.
> *Initial approach:* Letter
> *Deadline(s):* Apr. 1

EIN: 731593194

7497

The Samuel Roberts Noble Foundation, Inc.

2510 Sam Noble Pkwy.
P.O. Box 2180
Ardmore, OK 73401-2124 (580) 223-5810
Contact: William Buckner, C.E.O. and Pres.
FAX: (580) 224-6212;
E-mail: Admin-Granting@noble.org; URL: http://www.noble.org

Foundation type: Independent foundation
Purpose: Four-year scholarships to children of OK employees of Noble-affiliated companies and the Noble Foundation and scholarships in the fields of agriculture and technology to southern OK students.

Publications: Application guidelines; Annual report; Grants list; Informational brochure; Quarterly report.
Financial data: Year ended 12/31/2012. Assets, $1,172,213,441 (M); Expenditures, $66,439,961; Total giving, $1,006,333; Grants to individuals, 82 grants totaling $313,750 (high: $6,250, low: $1,250).
Type of support: Employee-related scholarships; Scholarships—to individuals.
Application information: Application form required.
  Deadline(s): Feb. 15
  Additional information: Applications for employee-related scholarships available through parents' employers only.
Program descriptions:
  Noble Educational Fund: Provides a maximum of ten $20,000 ($5,000 per year) four-year scholarship awards to children of employees of Noble companies selected, upon application, by an independent scholarship awards committee.
  Sam Noble Scholarship Program: This scholarship was established by the late Sam Noble to provide scholarships in the fields of agriculture and technology to students residing within one of 15 south central and southeastern Oklahoma counties. To request an application and determine eligibility, please visit the foundation web site.
EIN: 730606209

7498
Oklahoma Bar Foundation
P.O. Box 53036
Oklahoma City, OK   73152-3036   (405) 416-7070
Contact: Nancy Norsworthy, Dir., Admin.
E-mail: nancyn@okbar.org; URL: http://okbarfoundation.org/

Foundation type: Public charity
Purpose: Scholarships to deserving second or third-year law students of OK who intend to practice law in Oklahoma.
Publications: Application guidelines; Grants list.
Financial data: Year ended 12/31/2011. Assets, $9,198,999 (M); Expenditures, $874,652; Total giving, $578,939. Scholarships—to individuals amount not specified.
Fields of interest: Law school/education.
Type of support: Scholarships—to individuals.
Application information: Applications accepted.
  Initial approach: Letter
  Send request by: Mail
  Deadline(s): June 1
  Additional information: Payments are made directly to the educational institution on behalf of the students. See web site for additional guidelines.
Program description:
  OBF Fellows Scholarship: The scholarship is for law students who has been documented continuous legal resident of the State of Oklahoma for the past five years, and displays a demonstrated intent to practice law in OK. The applicant must demonstrate need of financial assistance, good academic standing, diligence of purpose, and evidence of ability to succeed as a lawyer. Preference is given to students with parents and/or grandparents who are or who were members in good standing of the Oklahoma Bar Association and that are or who were members of the Oklahoma Bar Foundation Fellows Program. Special consideration is given to students with an interest in the field of public law or a promise to give back to the community and to the profession. The annual scholarship amount of $5,000 each to a law student from each of the three law schools for a

total of $15,000, with one-half payment each semester.
EIN: 730710244

7499
Oklahoma City Disaster Relief Fund, Inc.
P.O. Box 1146
Oklahoma City, OK   73101-1146   (405) 235-5603

Foundation type: Public charity
Purpose: Financial support to individuals and families of victims of the Oklahoma City bombing with educational assistance, housing, food, clothing, medical expenses, mental health services and other special needs.
Financial data: Year ended 06/30/2012. Assets, $9,976,431 (M); Expenditures, $734,217; Total giving, $460,586; Grants to individuals, totaling $460,586.
Fields of interest: Safety/disasters; Human services.
Type of support: Grants for special needs.
Application information: Applications not accepted.
  Additional information: All grants support the mental and physical healing of the victims of the Oklahoma City bombing. Unsolicited requests for funds not considered or acknowledged.
EIN: 731476117

7500
Oklahoma Elks Major Project, Inc.
219 W. 20th St.
Ada, OK   74820-8203   (405) 672-2987

Foundation type: Public charity
Purpose: Scholarships to high school graduates in OK for higher education.
Financial data: Year ended 03/30/2012. Assets, $300,523 (M); Expenditures, $81,088.
Fields of interest: Higher education.
Type of support: Scholarships—to individuals.
Application information: Contact organization for additional application guidelines.
EIN: 237210114

7501
Oklahoma Foundation for Excellence
120 N. Robinson Ave., Ste. 1420-W
Oklahoma City, OK   73102-7402   (405) 236-0006
Contact: Emily Stratton, Exec. Dir.
FAX: (405) 236-8590; E-mail: info@ofe.org.; Email For Emily Stratton : estratton@ofe.org; URL: http://www.ofe.org

Foundation type: Public charity
Purpose: Scholarships to individual students of OK, through an awards program for excellence, as well as providing scholarships to teachers to encourage professional development.
Publications: Application guidelines.
Financial data: Year ended 06/30/2012. Assets, $6,209,414 (M); Expenditures, $872,135; Total giving, $204,396; Grants to individuals, totaling $196,896.
Fields of interest: Higher education; Teacher school/education.
Type of support: Grants to individuals; Scholarships—to individuals; Awards/prizes.
Application information: Applications accepted.
  Additional information: See foundation web site for information on individual programs.

Program descriptions:
  Academic Awards Program: The foundation recognizes and honors academic excellence in Oklahoma's public schools through a prestigious Awards Program. Awards to be given at the Academic Awards Banquet in May include a $1,000 scholarship to each of the 100 Academic All-State scholars selected from Oklahoma's public high school graduating seniors, and a $5,000 cash award and medal for excellence to five public school educators (one each at the elementary, secondary, community college/regional university, and research university levels, as well as an elementary/secondary school administrator)
  Fund for Teachers: This program awards individual grants of $5,000, and team grants (consisting of two or more eligible teachers) of $10,000 each, to pre-K through 12th grade teachers across Oklahoma who intend to pursue summer professional development opportunities. Applicants must have at least three years' teaching experience, be a full-time employee, and spend at least 50 percent of their time in a classroom setting. In addition, applicants must have the intention of returning to their school and/or district following their summer professional development. Applicants will be selected based on each proposal's merit - the potential for teacher growth and rejuvenation, as well as student, classroom, and school impact.
  Teacher Scholarships for Professional Development: The program awards scholarships to applicants currently employed by a public school district in Oklahoma and teaching in an elementary or secondary classroom, and who have at least two years' teaching experience in Oklahoma prior to the conference or meeting for which the scholarship will be used.
EIN: 731260595

7502
Oklahoma Scholarship Fund, Inc.
5619 N. Classen Blvd.
Oklahoma City, OK   73118-4015   (405) 254-5400
Contact: Karen Horton, Exec. Dir.

Foundation type: Independent foundation
Purpose: Scholarships to financially needy OK students attending second through eighth grade in Oklahoma County, OK to attend any school of their choice.
Financial data: Year ended 11/30/2012. Assets, $1,717 (M); Expenditures, $89,902; Total giving, $89,611; Grants to individuals, 80 grants totaling $89,611 (high: $2,000, low: $232).
Fields of interest: Education.
Type of support: Scholarships—to individuals.
Application information: Applications accepted. Application form required.
  Initial approach: Letter or telephone
  Deadline(s): Apr. 10
  Final notification: Applicants notified by mid-May
  Applicants should submit the following:
    1) Financial information
    2) Essay
  Additional information: Students must be residents of Oklahoma county, OK.
EIN: 731484452

7503
Osteopathic Founders Foundation
8801 S. Yale Ave., Ste. 400
Tulsa, OK 74137-1907 (918) 551-7300
FAX: (918) 551-7336; URL: http://
osteopathicfounders.org/

Foundation type: Public charity
Purpose: Scholarships by nomination only to fourth-year osteopathic medical students.
Publications: Annual report; Newsletter.
Financial data: Year ended 12/31/2011. Assets, $15,766,463 (M); Expenditures, $903,362; Total giving, $270,979; Grants to individuals, totaling $100,664.
Fields of interest: Medical school/education.
Type of support: Awards/grants by nomination only; Doctoral support.
Application information: Applications not accepted.
Additional information: Nomination should be submitted by the dean.
Program description:
Medical Education Grants: Awards an annual $10,000 scholarship to an osteopathic medical student in honor of the foundation's Physician of the Year. The award is presented to a fourth year student attending the Honoree's alma mater, or another osteopathic medical college of the honoree's choice. Nominations for the scholarship award are accepted by the foundation from the Dean of the selected college.
EIN: 730583936

7504
OSU Center for Innovation and Economic Development, Inc.
505 S. Main St.
Stillwater, OK 74074-4058 (405) 744-2325
FAX: (405) 744-2329; URL: http://
www.cied.okstate.edu/

Foundation type: Public charity
Purpose: Fellowships to Oklahoma State University undergraduate students, to spend a semester working in the U.S. Congress.
Publications: Application guidelines; Informational brochure.
Financial data: Year ended 06/30/2011. Assets, $10,936,160 (M); Expenditures, $18,496,922.
Fields of interest: University; Political science.
Type of support: Fellowships.
Application information: Applications accepted. Application form required. Application form available on the grantmaker's web site.
Initial approach: Application
Deadline(s): Mar. 15 for Summer program, June 1 for Fall program, and Nov. 1 for Spring program
Applicants should submit the following:
1) Letter(s) of recommendation
2) Essay
3) Transcripts
Program description:
The Don Nickles Fellowship Program: This program provides an opportunity for Oklahoma State University (OSU) undergraduate students to intern in Washington, D.C. for the spring, summer, or fall. Each fellow will be placed in a position of one of the Oklahoma Congressional offices, and will be given the opportunity to participate in the political and legislative process while representing OSU and Oklahoma state on Capitol Hill. Eligible applicants must be enrolled as a full-time student at Oklahoma State University as a sophomore or above, have a clean academic and behavioral record, and demonstrate good financial standing. Fellowships

include grant money for travel and living expenses, as well as academic credit options.
EIN: 237043186

7505
OWMA Scholarship Fund
(formerly OATCD Scholarship Fund)
P.O. Box 722220
Norman, OK 73070 (405) 360-7667
Contact: Sandra F. Ruble, Exec. Dir.
URL: http://www.owmanet.org/

Foundation type: Independent foundation
Purpose: Scholarships to Oklahoma Wholesale Marketers Association (OWMA) employees, employees' family and family members of OWMA members pursuing higher education.
Financial data: Year ended 12/31/2011. Assets, $12,850 (M); Expenditures, $4,000; Total giving, $4,000; Grants to individuals, 8 grants totaling $4,000 (high: $500, low: $500).
Fields of interest: Higher education.
Type of support: Scholarships—to individuals.
Application information: Applications accepted. Application form required.
Deadline(s): May 15
Additional information: Application should include transcript and proof of enrollment.
EIN: 731351421

7506
Brooksie A. Peyton Foundation
P.O. Drawer Z
Bartlesville, OK 74005 (918) 336-8114

Foundation type: Independent foundation
Purpose: Scholarships to graduating students from Washington county, Oklahoma high schools for attendance at Oklahoma public colleges, universities and technical schools.
Financial data: Year ended 12/31/2012. Assets, $1,513,768 (M); Expenditures, $59,788; Total giving, $38,303; Grants to individuals, 4 grants totaling $38,303 (high: $11,576, low: $6,713).
Fields of interest: Vocational education, post-secondary; Higher education.
Type of support: Scholarships—to individuals.
Application information: Application form required. Interview required.
Deadline(s): Apr.
Applicants should submit the following:
1) Transcripts
2) FAFSA
Additional information: Award is based on the determined needs of the student.
EIN: 113785133

7507
Project Single Parent, Inc.
(formerly Single Parent Assistance Fund, Inc.)
c/o Thomas Kivisto
7107 S. Yale, Ste. 293
Tulsa, OK 74136 (918) 430-8187
Contact: Sharon Pens

Foundation type: Independent foundation
Purpose: Financial assistance to single parents in the Tulsa, OK, area who are seeking to improve the quality of life by furthering their postsecondary education.
Financial data: Year ended 12/31/2012. Assets, $639,379 (M); Expenditures, $24,480; Total giving, $10,400; Grants to individuals, 2 grants totaling $10,400 (high: $5,200, low: $5,200).
Fields of interest: Single parents.

Type of support: Grants for special needs.
Application information: Applications accepted. Application form required.
Initial approach: Letter or telephone
Deadline(s): None
Additional information: Application should include transcript and current enrollment schedule, verification of employment, copies of most recent tax return and birth certificates of all children.
EIN: 731531820

7508
Reining Horse Sports Foundation, Inc.
3000 N.W. 10th St.
Oklahoma City, OK 73107-5302 (405) 946-7400
E-mail: rhsf@nrha.com; URL: http://www.rhsf.com/

Foundation type: Public charity
Purpose: Need-based scholarships to eligible students involved in the sport of reining. Financial support for reiners in need. Also, grants for reining research.
Publications: Application guidelines.
Financial data: Year ended 06/30/2012. Assets, $717,960 (M); Expenditures, $155,694; Total giving, $57,323; Grants to individuals, totaling $44,510.
Fields of interest: Athletics/sports, equestrianism.
Type of support: Research; Undergraduate support; Grants for special needs.
Application information:
Initial approach: E-mail
Additional information: Contact foundation for eligibility criteria.
EIN: 731575062

7509
Rose Family Foundation Trust
c/o The Trust Company of Oklahoma
P.O. Box 128
Muskogee, OK 74402-0128 (918) 967-2374

Foundation type: Independent foundation
Purpose: Scholarships to graduating seniors at Stigler High School, OK.
Financial data: Year ended 06/30/2013. Assets, $181,218 (M); Expenditures, $10,285; Total giving, $8,000; Grants to individuals, 4 grants totaling $8,000 (high: $2,000, low: $2,000).
Type of support: Support to graduates or students of specific schools; Undergraduate support.
Application information: Applications accepted. Application form required.
EIN: 731193406

7510
Saint Francis Home Health, Inc.
6161 S. Yale Ave.
Tulsa, OK 74136-3359 (918) 494-2200
Contact: Jake Henry, Pres. and C.E.O.
E-mail: homehealth@saintfrancis.com; URL: http://www.saintfrancis.com/locations/home_health.aspx

Foundation type: Public charity
Purpose: Grants for pharmaceuticals, medical equipment, inpatient hospital stays, lab processing, radiation therapy, nursing home stays, and ambulance transport for hospice patients.
Financial data: Year ended 06/30/2012. Assets, $2,412,503 (M); Expenditures, $13,617,036; Total giving, $1,683,552; Grants to individuals, totaling $1,683,552.

Fields of interest: Hospitals (general); End of life care.
Type of support: Grants to individuals; Grants for special needs.
Application information: Applications not accepted.
EIN: 731234331

7511
The Frank Sides, Jr. and Edna K. Sides Charitable Trust

P.O. Box 337
Sayre, OK 73662-0337 (580) 243-7013
Contact: J. Robert W. Lakey, Tr.

Foundation type: Independent foundation
Purpose: Financial assistance to individuals with child care, medical, housing, and other expenses in the OK area.
Financial data: Year ended 12/31/2011. Assets, $277,349 (M); Expenditures, $19,775; Total giving, $19,050; Grants to individuals, 6 grants totaling $5,000 (high: $2,200, low: $250).
Fields of interest: Human services.
Type of support: Grants for special needs.
Application information:
  Deadline(s): None
EIN: 736270987

7512
K. L. Smith Scholarship Foundation, Inc.

515 S. Plainview Rd.
Ardmore, OK 73401

Foundation type: Independent foundation
Purpose: Scholarships to deserving young men and women who have graduated from Healdton High School, OK for study at accredited institutions of higher learning.
Financial data: Year ended 09/30/2011. Assets, $68,808 (M); Expenditures, $17,538; Total giving, $4,500; Grants to individuals, 7 grants totaling $4,500 (high: $1,000, low: $500).
Fields of interest: Higher education.
Type of support: Support to graduates or students of specific schools.
Application information: Application form required.
  Initial approach: Letter
  Deadline(s): Apr.
  Applicants should submit the following:
    1) Transcripts
    2) Photograph
    3) Class rank
    4) SAT
    5) Financial information
    6) ACT
  Additional information: Application must also include a brief history of the applicant indicating his or her school activities, honors, extracurricular activities, college plans and other scholarships or grants.
EIN: 731528923

7513
Mabel W. Springfield Trust

716 N.E. 66
Sayre, OK 73662
Application Address: c/o Sayre Public School, 600 Hanna Sayre,OK 73662

Foundation type: Operating foundation
Purpose: Scholarships to students who have attended Sayre High School, OK, for three consecutive years and will graduate in the top 80 percent of their class.

Financial data: Year ended 02/29/2012. Assets, $980,452 (M); Expenditures, $25,419; Total giving, $23,977.
Type of support: Support to graduates or students of specific schools; Undergraduate support.
Application information: Application form required.
  Deadline(s): Mar. 1
EIN: 736101794

7514
St. John Medical Center, Inc.

1923 S. Utica Ave.
Tulsa, OK 74104-6520 (918) 744-2180
URL: http://www.sjmc.org

Foundation type: Public charity
Purpose: Scholarships to employees of St. John Medical Center, Tulsa, OK to further their education.
Publications: Newsletter.
Financial data: Year ended 09/30/2011. Assets, $621,116,777 (M); Expenditures, $456,825,352; Total giving, $4,947,917; Grants to individuals, totaling $481,612.
Fields of interest: Health sciences school/education.
Type of support: Scholarships—to individuals.
Application information: Applications accepted.
  Additional information: The employees are required to complete a specified time of employment with St. John Medical Center. If the employees do not complete the specified time of employment, they must pay back the scholarship.
EIN: 730579286

7515
Jess L. and Miriam B. Stevens Foundation

4000 1 Williams Ctr.
Tulsa, OK 74172-0148 (918) 586-5711
Contact: Joseph J. McCain, Jr., Tr.

Foundation type: Independent foundation
Purpose: Scholarships to needy and worthy students residing in northeastern OK and St. Louis, MO, for undergraduate education.
Financial data: Year ended 07/31/2013. Assets, $13,324,131 (M); Expenditures, $1,024,899; Total giving, $846,440; Grants to individuals, 9 grants totaling $45,000 (high: $7,500, low: $2,500).
Fields of interest: Education.
Type of support: Undergraduate support.
Application information: Applications accepted.
  Initial approach: Letter
  Additional information: Students must be U.S. citizens.
EIN: 731557364

7516
Steward-Newkirk Testamentary Trust

P.O. Box 850
Watonga, OK 73772-0316 (580) 623-4373
Contact: Georgia Forthum, Pres.

Foundation type: Independent foundation
Purpose: Scholarships to students of Blaine county, OK for attendance at trade/vocational schools and church revivals.
Financial data: Year ended 09/30/2012. Assets, $170,410 (M); Expenditures, $2,083; Total giving, $1,400.
Fields of interest: Vocational education, post-secondary.
Type of support: Scholarships—to individuals.

Application information: Application form required.
  Deadline(s): None
EIN: 731612447

7517
Stillwater Medical Center Foundation, Inc.

1606 W. 7th Ave.
Stillwater, OK 74074-4222 (405) 742-5387
FAX: (405) 742-5768;
E-mail: smcfoundation@stillwater-medical.org;
Mailing address: P.O. Box 2048, Stillwater, OK 74076-2408; URL: http://www.smc-foundation.org

Foundation type: Public charity
Purpose: Scholarships to employees of Stillwater Medical Center, OK, for enhancement of their professional growth, and a summer program to high school students contemplating a career in health care; also, fellowships at Stillwater Medical Center, OK, for area high school students who are contemplating a career in healthcare.
Publications: Application guidelines; Annual report; Biennial report; Informational brochure; Newsletter.
Financial data: Year ended 12/31/2011. Assets, $3,847,531 (M); Expenditures, $593,117; Total giving, $359,508; Grants to individuals, totaling $30,076.
Fields of interest: Health care.
Type of support: Employee-related scholarships.
Application information: Applications accepted.
  Deadline(s): Apr. 4 for Student Internships; June 22 and Nov. 22 for Employee Scholarships
  Additional information: Contact foundation for complete program guidelines.
Program descriptions:
  Employee Scholarships: Scholarships are available to assist established employees of Stillwater Medical Center interested in career advancement. Scholarships are available for both collegiate and vocational education opportunities. Eligible applicants must have completed a minimum of nine months of employment at Stillwater Medical Center, must not be on probation or have disciplinary action against them within nine months of the application due date, and must be classified as full-time or permanent part-time employees. Named scholarships include the Dorothy Blackwell Scholarship (a $500 award open to all areas of study), Mike Henson Scholarship (a $500 award open to all areas of study), Maxine Kamm Scholarship (a $500 award open to all areas of study), Betty and Bob Kerns Scholarship (a $500 award restricted to LPNs, RNs, or specialized nursing programs), Mary Randall RN Nursing Scholarship (a $500 award restricted to LPNs, RNs, or specialized nursing programs), Jesse F. Richardson M.D. Scholarships (a $500 award restricted to radiology students), Carolyn Williams RN Nursing Scholarship (a $500 award restricted to LPNs, RNs, or specialized nursing programs), Eric and Mary Williams Scholarship (a $500 award open to all areas of study), Gladys Heath Scholarship (a $500 award open to all areas of study), Alberta Henrickson Nursing Scholarship (a $500 award restricted to male students in the field of nursing), Chuck Hopkins Nursing Scholarship (a $500 award restricted to LPNs, RNs, or specialized nursing programs), Pat Riley RN Nursing Scholarship (a $500 award restricted to LPNs, RNs, or specialized nursing programs), Myr-Lou Rollins-Wade Nursing Scholarship (a $500 award restricted to LPNs, RNs, or specialized nursing programs), Santelmann Staff Development Scholarships (a $500 award to clinical staff members), and Mary Lou and Harold Sare Scholarship (a $500 award open to all areas of study)

Student Internships: The foundation annually offers three summer internships for high-school students. This opportunity allows students to spend six weeks observing and learning from healthcare professionals, and are awarded stipends on successful completion of the internship.
EIN: 731173571

7518
Tulsa Advertising Foundation
P.O. Box 4452
Tulsa, OK 74159-0452   (479) 650-9764
Contact: Danni Powell, Secy.
E-mail: danni.powell@gmail.com

Foundation type: Company-sponsored foundation
Purpose: Scholarships to students who have an interest in advertising, and are residents of Tulsa, OK.
Financial data: Year ended 12/31/2012. Assets, $41,829 (M); Expenditures, $2,901; Total giving, $2,000; Grants to individuals, 3 grants totaling $2,000 (high: $1,000, low: $500).
Fields of interest: Business school/education.
Type of support: Undergraduate support.
Application information:
  Initial approach: Letter
  Applicants should submit the following:
    1) Essay
    2) Proposal
    3) Resume
  Additional information: Proposal should include a narrative on the applicant's interest in marketing and advertising.
EIN: 731253534

7519
Tulsa Community Foundation
7030 S. Yale, Ste. 600
Tulsa, OK 74136   (918) 494-8823
Contact: Phil Lakin, Jr., C.E.O.
FAX: (918) 494-9826; E-mail: info@tulsacf.org;
Additional e-mail: plakin@tulsacf.org; URL: http://www.tulsacf.org

Foundation type: Community foundation
Purpose: Scholarships to students of OK, for higher education. Fellowships also available for PreK-12 teachers.
Publications: Annual report; Financial statement; Informational brochure; Occasional report.
Financial data: Year ended 12/31/2012. Assets, $3,729,789,000 (M); Expenditures, $145,095,000; Total giving, $110,512,000.
Fields of interest: Elementary/secondary education; Vocational education; Higher education; Scholarships/financial aid.
Type of support: Fellowships; Scholarships—to individuals; Support to graduates or students of specific schools; Undergraduate support.
Application information: Applications accepted. Application form required.
  Deadline(s): Varies
  Additional information: See web site for complete listing of scholarships and additional application information.
Program descriptions:
  Fund for Teachers: Fund for Teachers enriches the personal and professional growth of teachers by recognizing and supporting them as they identify and pursue opportunities around the globe that will have the greatest impact on their practice, the academic lives of their students and on their school communities. Believing the teacher knows best how they can make a better impact in their classroom, Fund for Teachers awards fellowships for

self-designed professional growth to PreK-12 teachers who recognize the value of inquiry, the power of knowledge, and their ability to make a difference.
  Scholarships: The foundation maintains dozens of scholarship funds, assisting students locally and nationally. Each fund maintains individual requirements for application, ranging from academic performance and financial need to high school attended, major selected and hometown.
EIN: 731554474

7520
Tulsa County Bar Foundation, Inc.
1446 S. Boston Ave.
Tulsa, OK 74119-3612   (918) 584-5243
Contact: Kevin Cousins, Exec. Dir.
FAX: (918) 592-0208;
E-mail: kevinc@tulsabar.com; URL: http://www.tulsabar.com/tulsa-county-bar-foundation

Foundation type: Public charity
Purpose: Scholarships for law students who are residents of Tulsa county, OK who are accepted to an ABA-accredited law school.
Financial data: Year ended 08/31/2012. Assets, $1,278,814 (M); Expenditures, $77,785; Total giving, $29,664.
Fields of interest: Law school/education.
Type of support: Scholarships—to individuals.
Application information: Applications accepted. Application form required. Interview required.
  Send request by: Mail
  Deadline(s): June 15
  Applicants should submit the following:
    1) Financial information
    2) Transcripts
    3) Letter(s) of recommendation
  Additional information: Application should also include copies of federal income tax forms of yourself and your parents. Applicants must show letter of acceptance in an ABA-accredited law school.
Program description:
  Law School Scholarship: The foundation provides scholarships of up to $2,500 per individual per year entering their first year of law school. At the time of submission of the application, applicant must have achieved undergraduate grades in the top 50 percent of the applicant's college undergraduate class and have LSAT scores in the top 50 percent of the LSAT testing pool. Applicant must be a citizen of the U.S. and have a significant connection to Tulsa county. Students who have completed one or more semesters of law school are not eligible.
EIN: 736092173

7521
Tulsa Royalties Company
500 W. Univ. St.
P.O. Box 61207
Shawnee, OK 74804-2504   (405) 585-5130
Contact: Lloyd White, Pres.

Foundation type: Public charity
Purpose: Scholarships to students of Oklahoma Baptist University, OK.
Financial data: Year ended 12/31/2011. Assets, $196 (M); Expenditures, $1,936,915; Total giving, $1,701,000.
Type of support: Support to graduates or students of specific schools.
Application information: Applications not accepted.

Additional information: Unsolicited requests for funds not considered or acknowledged.
EIN: 736101744

7522
University of Oklahoma Foundation, Inc.
100 Timberdell Rd.
Norman, OK 73019-0685   (405) 321-1174
Contact: Trent Wells, Cont.
FAX: (405) 321-1180; E-mail: twells@ou.edu;
Toll-free tel.: (866) 321-1174; URL: http://www.oufoundation.org

Foundation type: Public charity
Purpose: Scholarships to students attending the University of Oklahoma, OK.
Publications: Annual report; Financial statement; Informational brochure; Newsletter.
Financial data: Year ended 06/30/2012. Assets, $1,007,093,948 (M); Expenditures, $106,731,536; Total giving, $92,817,483; Grants to individuals, totaling $19,050,696.
Fields of interest: University; Scholarships/financial aid.
Type of support: Scholarships—to individuals; Support to graduates or students of specific schools.
Application information: Applications not accepted.
  Additional information: Unsolicited requests for funds not considered or acknowledged.
EIN: 736091755

7523
Wes Watkins Area Vocational-Technical Foundation
7892 Hwy. 9
Wetumka, OK 74883-9522   (405) 452-5500

Foundation type: Public charity
Purpose: Awards to students at Wes Watkins Technology Center, OK, serving schools in Okmulgee, Okfuskee, Hughes, and McIntosh counties, OK.
Financial data: Year ended 12/31/2011. Assets, $59,401 (M); Expenditures, $17,806; Total giving, $16,565.
Type of support: Support to graduates or students of specific schools; Awards/prizes.
Application information: Contact foundation for current application deadline/guidelines.
EIN: 731496435

7524
Watson Family Foundation
P.O. Box 7867
Edmond, OK 73083
Contact: H.B. Watson
Application address: 6349 Harden Dr., Oklahoma City, OK 73118

Foundation type: Independent foundation
Purpose: Scholarships to residents of OK for postsecondary education.
Financial data: Year ended 12/31/2011. Assets, $34,023 (M); Expenditures, $39,514; Total giving, $39,000; Grants to individuals, 4 grants totaling $15,000 (high: $6,000, low: $3,000).
Type of support: Undergraduate support.
Application information: Applications accepted. Application form required.
  Initial approach: Letter
  Deadline(s): None
EIN: 731512470

7525
The George Whitefield Society
4104 Ainsley Ct.
Edmond, OK   73034   (405) 562-4332
Contact: David Gallman

Foundation type: Operating foundation
Purpose: Benevolence grants to individuals, primarily in Oklahoma City, OK.
Financial data: Year ended 12/31/2012. Assets, $22,288 (M); Expenditures, $88,152; Total giving, $67,255; Grants to individuals, 37 grants totaling $67,255 (high: $9,000, low: $250).
Type of support: Grants for special needs.
Application information: Applications not accepted.
EIN: 731492931

7526
R. H. Wilkin Charitable Trust
P.O. Box 32134
Oklahoma City, OK   73123   (405) 722-9393
Contact: Paul A. Porter, Tr.
Application address: P.O. Box 23374, Okc, OK 73123,, tel.: (405) 722-9393

Foundation type: Independent foundation

Purpose: Assistance to needy, crippled children of Oklahoma County, OK, for medical and mental care, and treatment.
Financial data: Year ended 12/31/2012. Assets, $476,259 (M); Expenditures, $17,804; Total giving, $11,238; Grants to individuals, 4 grants totaling $11,238 (high: $4,174, low: $866).
Fields of interest: Children/youth, services; Disabilities, people with.
Type of support: Grants for special needs.
Application information:
  Initial approach: Letter
  Deadline(s): None
  Additional information: Application should include financial information and professional recommendation for special care of minor children. Unsolicited applications not considered or acknowledged.
EIN: 736157614

7527
Patti Johnson Wilson Foundation
c/o The Trust Company of Oklahoma
1924 S. Utica Ave., Ste. 500
Tulsa, OK   74104-6540
Application address: c/o The Trust Company of Oklahoma, Att. Paul E. Kallenberger, P.O. Box 3348, Tulsa, OK 74101-3348

Foundation type: Independent foundation
Purpose: Scholarships to students in the fields of music, engineering, and liberal arts, at the University of Oklahoma, Oklahoma City University, Oklahoma State University, University of Kansas, Kansas State University, University of Tulsa, and University of Arkansas Community College.
Publications: Application guidelines.
Financial data: Year ended 08/31/2012. Assets, $10,823,926 (M); Expenditures, $696,125; Total giving, $331,000; Grants to individuals, 43 grants totaling $102,000 (high: $3,000, low: $1,500).
Fields of interest: Music; Performing arts, education; Humanities; Engineering school/education.
Type of support: Undergraduate support.
Application information: Application form required. Interview required.
  Deadline(s): Mar. 1
  Additional information: Application should include recommendations and standardized test scores.
EIN: 736156280

OREGON

7528
Leo Adler Community Trust
(formerly Leo Adler Trust)
c/o U.S. Bank, N.A.
P.O. Box 3168
Portland, OR 97208-3168
Application address: c/o Michael Sullivan, U.S. Bank, N.A., P.O. Box 7928, Boise, ID 83707, tel.: (208) 383-7217

Foundation type: Independent foundation
Purpose: Scholarships to graduates of high schools in Baker County, OR.
Publications: Informational brochure.
Financial data: Year ended 06/30/2013. Assets, $24,022,013 (M); Expenditures, $1,612,810; Total giving, $1,245,441.
Type of support: Support to graduates or students of specific schools; Undergraduate support.
Application information: Applications accepted.
Additional information: Contact foundation for current application deadline/guidelines.
EIN: 936289087

7529
Aging Community Coordinated Enterprises Supportive Services, Inc.
P.O. Box 4666
Medford, OR 97501-0188 (541) 771-4331
Contact: Jackie Schad, Exec. Dir.
URL: http://www.accessinc.org.au/

Foundation type: Public charity
Purpose: Emergency assistance to low-income individuals, senior citizens and families in the Medford, OR area.
Financial data: Year ended 06/30/2012. Assets, $5,787,253 (M); Expenditures, $10,544,372; Total giving, $4,027,731; Grants to individuals, totaling $4,027,731.
Fields of interest: Economically disadvantaged.
Type of support: Emergency funds; In-kind gifts; Grants for special needs.
Application information: Contact the agency for eligibility determination.
EIN: 930665396

7530
Olga V. Alexandria Trust
P.O. Box 3168
Portland, OR 97208 (801) 581-7200
Application address: University of Utah, Financial Aid, University 200 S., Salt Lake City, UT 84112

Foundation type: Independent foundation
Purpose: Scholarships to young women studying business, law, medicine, or theater at the University of Utah.
Financial data: Year ended 05/31/2013. Assets, $665,532 (M); Expenditures, $43,238; Total giving, $31,000.
Fields of interest: Theater; Performing arts, education; Business school/education; Law school/education; Medical school/education; Women.
Type of support: Support to graduates or students of specific schools; Undergraduate support.
Application information: Applications accepted. Application form required.
Deadline(s): Mar. 1

Additional information: Forms available at the University of Utah.
EIN: 942936907

7531
Mabel V. Almquist-SUHS No. 7J Graduate Assistance Fund, Inc.
c/o Kelley & Kelley
110 N. 2nd Ave.
Silverton, OR 97381 (503) 873-8671
Contact: Don Kelley, Dir.

Foundation type: Operating foundation
Purpose: Scholarships to graduates of Silverton Union High School, OR, who are full-time undergraduate students.
Financial data: Year ended 12/31/2012. Assets, $598,658 (M); Expenditures, $34,406; Total giving, $26,750.
Fields of interest: Higher education.
Type of support: Scholarships—to individuals; Support to graduates or students of specific schools.
Application information: Applications accepted. Application form required.
Deadline(s): Mar. 10
Additional information: Application should include a complete college transcript.
EIN: 931310506

7532
American Tinnitus Association
(also known as ATA)
522 S.W. 5th Ave., Ste. 825
Portland, OR 97204-2143 (503) 248-9985
Contact: Cara James, Exec. Dir.
FAX: (503) 248-0024; E-mail: tinnitus@ata.org;
URL: http://www.ata.org

Foundation type: Public charity
Purpose: Research grants to young scientists relating to the prevention, treatment and cure of Tinnitus.
Publications: Annual report; Informational brochure.
Financial data: Year ended 06/30/2012. Assets, $674,641 (M); Expenditures, $1,029,908; Total giving, $155,594.
Type of support: Research.
Application information: Applications accepted. Application form required.
Initial approach: Proposal
Send request by: E-mail
Deadline(s): June 30
Final notification: Applicants notified in Dec.
Additional information: See web site for additional guidelines.
Program descriptions:
Research Grants: The program awards research grants of up to $50,000 per year for up to three years, for a potential maximum of $150,000, to those scientists and doctors worldwide who are seeking tinnitus-related research funding and are affiliated with non-profit institutions.
Student Research Grants: The program awards grants of up to $10,000 to doctoral candidates or medical residents affiliated with a U.S. non-profit institution. Each candidate must have a qualified mentor supporting their research.
EIN: 930749558

7533
The Arc of Multnomah County, Inc.
6929 N.E Halsey
Portland, OR 97213 (503) 223-7279
Contact: Dee Wright, Admin. and Used Goods Mgr.
FAX: (503) 223-1488; URL: http://www.thearcmult.org/

Foundation type: Public charity
Purpose: Assistance with basic living costs, to adults and children who have developmental disabilities and their families in Multnomah and Clackamas counties, OR.
Publications: Annual report; Financial statement; Informational brochure; Newsletter.
Financial data: Year ended 06/30/2012. Assets, $38,706 (M); Expenditures, $720,227.
Type of support: Grants for special needs.
Application information:
Initial approach: Letter
Additional information: Contact foundation for further information.
EIN: 930439765

7534
Virginia A. Archer Scholarship Trust Fund
520 N.W. Torrey View Ln.
Portland, OR 97229-6540 (503) 292-2733
Contact: Sue A. Close, Tr.
Application address: P.O. Box 219158, Portland, OR 97225

Foundation type: Operating foundation
Purpose: Scholarships to graduating seniors of high schools in Multnomah County, OR, to attend OR colleges and universities.
Financial data: Year ended 06/30/2012. Assets, $157,656 (M); Expenditures, $21,579; Total giving, $9,000; Grants to individuals, 3 grants totaling $9,000 (high: $3,000, low: $3,000).
Fields of interest: Higher education.
Type of support: Support to graduates or students of specific schools; Undergraduate support.
Application information: Applications accepted. Application form required.
Initial approach: Letter
Deadline(s): Apr. 15
Additional information: Contact the fund for application forms.
EIN: 936107007

7535
Astoria School Children's Fund
91771 John Day River Rd.
Astoria, OR 97103

Foundation type: Independent foundation
Purpose: Summer school scholarships to students of Astoria School District, OR.
Financial data: Year ended 12/31/2012. Assets, $61,974 (M); Expenditures, $1,782; Total giving, $500.
Type of support: Support to graduates or students of specific schools.
Application information: Applications not accepted.
Additional information: Unsolicited requests for funds not accepted.
EIN: 931277784

7536
Geraldine Bagley Foundation Trust
P.O. Box 22000
Florence, OR 97439-0141

Foundation type: Independent foundation
Purpose: Scholarships to residents of the Eugene-Springfield, OR area.
Financial data: Year ended 12/31/2012. Assets, $392,767 (M); Expenditures, $34,132; Total giving, $27,500; Grants to individuals, 8 grants totaling $27,500 (high: $5,000, low: $2,500).
Type of support: Undergraduate support.
Application information:
Initial approach: Letter
EIN: 936311484

7537
The Banfield Charitable Trust
8000 N.E. Tillamook St.
P.O. Box 13998
Portland, OR 97213-6655 (503) 922-5801
Contact: Dianne McGill, Exec. Dir. and C.E.O.
FAX: (503) 922-6801;
E-mail: info@banfieldcharitabletrust.org; Toll-free tel.: (866) 802-0566; E-Mail for Dianne McGill: dianne.mcgill@banfieldcharitabletrust.org;
URL: http://www.banfieldcharitabletrust.org

Foundation type: Public charity
Purpose: Scholarships for those pursuing a pet-specific vocation.
Publications: Application guidelines.
Financial data: Year ended 01/31/2013. Assets, $4,797,031 (M); Expenditures, $1,990,657; Total giving, $1,351,380; Grants to individuals, totaling $74,246.
Fields of interest: Animal welfare; Veterinary medicine.
Type of support: Undergraduate support.
Application information: Applications accepted. Application form required. Application form available on the grantmaker's web site.
Initial approach: Letter
Deadline(s): June 30
Applicants should submit the following:
1) Essay
2) Financial information
3) Letter(s) of recommendation
4) SAT
5) ACT
6) Transcripts
EIN: 270044673

7538
Anne Benson Scholarship Trust Fund
P.O. Box 3168
Portland, OR 97208-3168 (406) 657-8139

Foundation type: Independent foundation
Purpose: Scholarships to graduates of Judith Gap High School, MT, for higher education, with preference given to students majoring in education.
Financial data: Year ended 04/30/2013. Assets, $291,947 (M); Expenditures, $20,257; Total giving, $12,000.
Fields of interest: Formal/general education; Education.
Type of support: Support to graduates or students of specific schools; Undergraduate support.
Application information: Application form required.
Send request by: Mail
Deadline(s): Mar. 31
Applicants should submit the following:
1) Financial information
2) Letter(s) of recommendation
3) Transcripts
Program description:
Scholarship Program: Recipients must be pursuing a degree in education, however, if no qualified applicants are majoring in education,

those seeking a college education who have graduated from Judith Gap High School may be considered. Scholarships are for payment costs of tuition, books, expenses, room and board. Relatives of trustee or scholarship committee are ineligible for scholarship.
EIN: 816087202

7539
Benton County Foundation
660 N.W. Harrison Blvd.
Corvallis, OR 97330 (541) 753-1603
Contact: Dick Thompson, Exec. Dir.
Scholarship e-mail:
sue@bentoncountyfoundation.org
E-mail: bcf@peak.org; URL: http://bentoncountyfoundation.org

Foundation type: Community foundation
Purpose: Scholarships to students in Benton County, OR for higher education at accredited colleges or universities.
Publications: Application guidelines; Annual report; Grants list; Informational brochure; Newsletter.
Financial data: Year ended 12/31/2011. Assets, $14,168,886 (M); Expenditures, $503,331; Total giving, $364,412; Grants to individuals, totaling $69,464.
Fields of interest: Vocational education, post-secondary; Higher education.
Type of support: Scholarships—to individuals; Undergraduate support.
Application information: Applications accepted. Application form required. Application form available on the grantmaker's web site.
Initial approach: Letter
Send request by: E-mail
Copies of proposal: 1
Deadline(s): Mar. 7
Final notification: Applicants notified in six weeks
Applicants should submit the following:
1) Class rank
2) Financial information
3) Transcripts
4) GPA
Additional information: See web site for additional application guidelines and a complete list of scholarships.
EIN: 936022916

7540
Black United Fund of Oregon
2828 N.E. Alberta St.
Portland, OR 97211-6351 (503) 282-7973
Contact: Adrienne Livingston, Exec. Dir.
FAX: (503) 282-3482; E-mail: bufor@bufor.org;
E-mail for Adrienne Livingston:
alivingston@bufor.org; URL: http://www.bufor.org

Foundation type: Public charity
Purpose: College scholarships to high school graduates of OR, pursuing higher education.
Publications: Application guidelines.
Financial data: Year ended 12/31/2012. Assets, $1,291,499 (M); Expenditures, $319,353; Total giving, $36,777.
Fields of interest: Higher education; Nursing school/education; Health sciences school/education.
Type of support: Scholarships—to individuals.
Application information: Applications accepted. Application form required.
Additional information: Contact the fund for additional guidelines.

Program descriptions:
Dr. Ethel Simon-McWilliams Scholarship: The scholarship is available to 11th grade African American students who are U.S. citizens with a cumulative GPA between 2.5 to 2.85. Any cumulative GPA over 2.85 does not qualify.
Linfield School of Nursing Scholarship: The scholarship supports students interested in pursuing a degree in nursing or health sciences. This scholarship is available to students who are of African/African American descent. Applicants must reside in Oregon or SW Washington and have a minimum of 34 transferable college credit to apply.
EIN: 930843267

7541
Jane Buttrey Memorial Trust
P.O. Box 3168
Portland, OR 97208

Foundation type: Independent foundation
Purpose: Scholarships to graduating high school seniors or undergraduate college students pursuing a course of study in the humanities or social sciences at specific MT and TX colleges and universities.
Financial data: Year ended 06/30/2013. Assets, $1,310,899 (M); Expenditures, $75,098; Total giving, $60,000.
Fields of interest: Humanities; Social sciences.
Type of support: Support to graduates or students of specific schools; Undergraduate support.
Application information: Applications not accepted.
Additional information: Unsolicited requests for funds not considered or acknowledged.
EIN: 816014941

7542
Caldera
224 N.W. 13th Ave.
P. O. Box 304
Portland, OR 97209-2953 (503) 937-3061
Contact: Tricia Snell, Exec. Dir.
FAX: (503) 937-3085; E-mail: caldera@wk.com;
URL: http://www.calderaarts.org

Foundation type: Public charity
Purpose: Residencies to artists and writers to foster creativity and a deeper appreciation for the environment.
Publications: Application guidelines; Annual report; Financial statement; Informational brochure.
Financial data: Year ended 06/30/2012. Assets, $16,358,151 (M); Expenditures, $1,896,482; Total giving, $10,500; Grants to individuals, totaling $10,500.
Fields of interest: Arts.
Type of support: Residencies.
Application information: Applications accepted. Application form required.
Initial approach: Letter or telephone
Copies of proposal: 4
Deadline(s): June 1
Applicants should submit the following:
1) Letter(s) of recommendation
2) Proposal
3) Resume
4) Work samples
Additional information: Professional non-student applicants are welcomed; Applicants must cover all transportation, supplies and food costs. Recipients notified in eight to ten weeks.
EIN: 943235649

7543
W.C. & Pearl Campbell Scholarship Fund for Linfield College Students
P.O. Box 3168
Portland, OR 97208 (503) 275-6588
Application address: U.S. Bank, Foundation Team, Student

Foundation type: Independent foundation
Purpose: Scholarships to undergraduate and graduate students studying full-time at Linfield College, OR.
Financial data: Year ended 06/30/2012. Assets, $154,372 (M); Expenditures, $11,316; Total giving, $7,500.
Fields of interest: College; Scholarships/financial aid.
Type of support: Support to graduates or students of specific schools; Graduate support; Undergraduate support.
Application information: Applications accepted.
Deadline(s): May 1
Additional information: Contact fund for current application guidelines.
EIN: 936021036

7544
Care To Share
P.O. Box 397
Beaverton, OR 97075-0397 (503) 591-9079
FAX: (503) 591-9084;
E-mail: od@caretosharehelp.org; Additional tel.: (503) 292-4094; URL: http://caretosharehelp.org

Foundation type: Public charity
Purpose: Emergency assistance to economically disadvantaged individuals residing in east Washington County, OR. Assistance includes food, as well as rent and utility assistance.
Publications: Informational brochure; Newsletter.
Financial data: Year ended 12/31/2011. Assets, $315,514 (M); Expenditures, $199,757; Total giving, $63,606; Grants to individuals, totaling $63,606.
Fields of interest: Human services; Economically disadvantaged.
Type of support: Emergency funds; Grants for special needs.
Application information: Applications accepted. Interview required.
Initial approach: Telephone
Deadline(s): None
Additional information: Maximum grant amount is $250.
EIN: 930900348

7545
The Celebration Foundation
3234 N.E. 62nd Ave.
Portland, OR 97213-3949 (503) 493-9770
Contact: Alan Toribio, Secy.-Treas.
URL: http://www.celebrationfoundation.net/

Foundation type: Independent foundation
Purpose: Grants to trained experience artists focusing and functioning at the edge or within the professional arena, primarily in OR.
Financial data: Year ended 06/30/2012. Assets, $58,873 (M); Expenditures, $69,360; Total giving, $50,000; Grants to individuals, 10 grants totaling $40,250 (high: $5,000; low: $3,000).
Fields of interest: Performing arts; Arts.
Type of support: Grants to individuals.
Application information: Applications accepted. Application form required.
Deadline(s): None

Additional information: Applicant must supply four copies of application plus original.
EIN: 931312787

7546
Central Oregon Singers, Inc.
(also known as Youth Choir of Central Oregon)
2125 N.E. Daggett Ln.
P.O. Box 383
Bend, OR 97701 (541) 385-0470
Contact: Beth Basham, Artistic Dir.
FAX: (541) 318-6209; E-mail: choiroffice@ycco.org; Mailing address: P.O. Box 383, Bend, OR 97709; URL: http://www.ycco.org

Foundation type: Public charity
Purpose: Scholarships to qualified singers between the ages of five and eighteen for musical expression and education in a joyful environment.
Financial data: Year ended 06/30/2012. Assets, $41,258 (M); Expenditures, $94,591.
Fields of interest: Music.
Type of support: Scholarships—to individuals.
Application information: Applications accepted. Application form required.
Additional information: Scholarships are awarded on the basis of financial need, and application must include financial information.
EIN: 931193267

7547
Chamber Music Northwest, Inc.
522 S.W. 5th Ave., Ste. 920
Portland, OR 97204-2126 (503) 223-3202
Contact: Linda Magee, Exec. Dir.
FAX: (503) 294-1690; E-mail: info@cmnw.org;
E-Mail for Linda Magee: magee@cmnw.org;
URL: http://www.cmnw.org

Foundation type: Public charity
Purpose: Fellowships to classical musicians aged 12 to 22.
Financial data: Year ended 09/30/2011. Assets, $3,852,533 (M); Expenditures, $1,207,116.
Fields of interest: Music; Music ensembles/groups.
Type of support: Fellowships.
Application information: Application form required.
Initial approach: E-mail
Deadline(s): Dec. 31
Additional information: Application must include biography, 15 minute audition cassette/CD and recommendations.
Program descriptions:
Spring Educational Residency: Chamber Music Northwest's annual Spring Educational Residency brings world-class musicians into Portland-area classrooms and other spaces to expose new audiences to chamber music and to help promising young musicians develop their skills.
Young Artist Fellowship: This program recognizes outstanding young classical musicians, and aims to augment their individual growth by providing opportunities for mentoring, master classes, and community outreach in the context of a world-class chamber music performance. The program is open to all classical musicians aged 12 to 22 who are geographically accessible to Portland for all CMNW offerings and events.
EIN: 237355562

7548
Louis G. & Elizabeth L. Clarke Endowment Fund
P.O. Box 3168
Portland, OR 97208-3168 (503) 226-7827
Contact: Walter Peters
Application address: c/o Scottish Rite Temple, Attn.: Walter L. Peters, Exec. Secy., 709 S.W. 15th Ave., Portland, OR 97205-1906, tel.: (503) 226-7827

Foundation type: Independent foundation
Purpose: Financial assistance to economically disadvantaged Masons and their immediate families requiring hospitalization in Multnomah, Clackamas, and Washington counties, OR.
Financial data: Year ended 12/31/2011. Assets, $1,353,153 (M); Expenditures, $68,160; Total giving, $43,712.
Fields of interest: Economically disadvantaged.
Type of support: Grants for special needs.
Application information: Applications accepted.
Initial approach: Letter
Deadline(s): None
EIN: 936020655

7549
The Clemens Foundation
P.O. Box 24
Alsea, OR 97324-0024
Contact: Susie Sapp
E-mail: clemensfound@peak.org

Foundation type: Independent foundation
Purpose: Tuition grants for high school graduates of Alsea, Crane, Eddyville and Philomath, OR to attend college or an accredited vocational school on a full-time basis.
Financial data: Year ended 12/31/2012. Assets, $28,978,910 (M); Expenditures, $2,022,746; Total giving, $1,929,512.
Fields of interest: Vocational education, post-secondary; Higher education; Medical school/education.
Type of support: Support to graduates or students of specific schools; Undergraduate support.
Application information: Applications accepted. Application form required.
Deadline(s): June 30
Applicants should submit the following:
1) Letter(s) of recommendation
2) Transcripts
Program description:
Scholarship: Students whose families have backgrounds in timber, ranching, farming, mining, manufacturing and occupations in direct support of these areas will only be considered. Students must also be from a pioneer family in the above-mentioned school districts (meaning that at least one of the applicant's parents were born in one of the these school districts and graduated from that high school), as well as students must also live with their parents or court appointed guardian in one of these school districts. Preference will be given to students who are enrolling in trade or vocational schools, members of the 4-H, FFA, the Boy Scouts of America and the Forestry Club, and financial need.
EIN: 936023941

7550
Coalition for Dwarf Advocacy
(also known as CoDA)
22115 N.W. Imbrie Dr., Box 317
Hillsboro, OR 97124-6988
E-mail: info@coda-lp.org; URL: http://
www.dwarfadvocates.com/

Foundation type: Public charity
Purpose: Scholarship to disadvantaged families
with dwarf children for postsecondary education.
Fields of interest: Education.
Type of support: Scholarships—to individuals.
Application information: Applications accepted.
Additional information: Contact the organization
for guidelines.
EIN: 205397605

7551
Cockerline Memorial Fund
P.O. Box 3168
Portland, OR 97208-3168 (541) 684-7218

Foundation type: Public charity
Purpose: College scholarships to graduating
students pursuing a baccalaureate degree at
colleges or universities in OR.
Financial data: Year ended 06/30/2013. Assets,
$680,013 (M); Expenditures, $49,899; Total
giving, $38,250; Grants to individuals, totaling
$38,250.
Fields of interest: Higher education.
Type of support: Support to graduates or students
of specific schools; Undergraduate support.
Application information: Applications accepted.
Application form required.
Final notification: Recipients notified in Apr.
Applicants should submit the following:
1) Transcripts
2) GPA
3) FAFSA
Additional information: Applicant must
demonstrate financial need.
Program description:
Scholarship Program: Scholarships are provided
to students attending four year colleges or
universities in the State of Oregon. Applicants must
be residents of Oregon, be enrolled as a full time
student in a traditional undergraduate daytime
program, and have a high school or college
cumulative GPA of at least 2.50 or above. The
scholarship is for one year and students are
encouraged to reapply each year. Preference is
given to students attending Northwest Christian
College.
EIN: 936029653

7552
Collins - McDonald Trust Fund
1618 S.W. 1st Ave., Ste. 500
Portland, OR 97201-5706 (541) 947-2196
Contact: James C. Lynch, Tr.
Application address: 620 N. 1st Lakeview, OR
97630, tel.: (541) 947-2196

Foundation type: Independent foundation
Purpose: Scholarships to residents of Lake County,
OR. Scholarships also to children of Fremont
Sawmill employees, OR.
Financial data: Year ended 12/31/2012. Assets,
$7,570,523 (M); Expenditures, $491,193; Total
giving, $482,398; Grants to individuals, 50 grants
totaling $285,200 (high: $11,700, low: $2,400).
Fields of interest: Higher education; Scholarships/
financial aid.

Type of support: Employee-related scholarships;
Support to graduates or students of specific
schools; Undergraduate support.
Application information: Applications accepted.
Application form required. Interview required.
Final notification: Recipients notified by Aug. 1
Applicants should submit the following:
1) GPA
2) SAT
Additional information: Contact foundation for
current application deadline/guidelines.
EIN: 936021894

7553
Thomas S. Colvin Scholarship Trust
P.O. Box 1784
Medford, OR 97501-0140
Application address: c/o Clatskanie High School,
Attn.: Ruthann Brown, P.O. Box 68, Clatskanie, OR
97016-0068

Foundation type: Independent foundation
Purpose: Scholarships to graduates of Clatskanie
High School, OR, for the pursuit of a vocational
education at a university, college or trade school.
Financial data: Year ended 12/31/2011. Assets,
$492,159 (M); Expenditures, $28,057; Total
giving, $20,800; Grants to individuals, 7 grants
totaling $20,800 (high: $4,000, low: $2,000).
Fields of interest: Vocational education,
post-secondary.
Type of support: Support to graduates or students
of specific schools; Technical education support;
Undergraduate support.
Application information: Applications accepted.
Initial approach: Letter
Deadline(s): Apr. 15
Applicants should submit the following:
1) Class rank
2) SAT
3) GPA
Additional information: Application must show
financial need, school and community
activities, future plans, and honors received.
EIN: 936267268

7554
Community Action Program of East Central Oregon
721 S.E. 3rd St., Ste. D
Pendleton, OR 97801-3060 (541) 276-1926
FAX: (541) 276-7541; Toll-free tel.: (800)
752-1139; URL: http://www.capeco-works.org

Foundation type: Public charity
Purpose: Rent, home energy assistance, food
supplies, utilities, and lodging assistance in
emergency situations to indigent residents of East
Central Oregon.
Financial data: Year ended 06/30/2012. Assets,
$3,567,743 (M); Expenditures, $7,085,773; Total
giving, $3,954,467; Grants to individuals, totaling
$3,905,875.
Fields of interest: Housing/shelter, expense aid;
Housing/shelter; Economically disadvantaged.
Type of support: In-kind gifts; Grants for special
needs.
Application information:
Initial approach: Tel.
Additional information: Applicants will be asked
to provide proof of income and residence.
EIN: 943060985

7555
Community Action Team, Inc.
125 N. 17th St.
St. Helens, OR 97051-2024 (503) 397-3511
FAX: (503) 397-3290; URL: http://
www.cat-team.org

Foundation type: Public charity
Purpose: Emergency assistance to low income
individuals and families of Clatsop, Columbia, and
Tillamook counties, OR with housing, child care,
weatherization, utility and other needed services.
Publications: Annual report; Newsletter.
Financial data: Year ended 06/30/2012. Assets,
$7,582,165 (M); Expenditures, $9,999,877.
Fields of interest: Human services; Economically
disadvantaged.
Type of support: Emergency funds; Grants for
special needs.
Application information: Applications accepted.
Additional information: Contact the agency for
eligibility determination.
EIN: 930554156

7556
Compassion Ministries
P.O. Box 91516
Portland, OR 97291

Foundation type: Operating foundation
Purpose: Financial support to the needy in OR. Also,
grants to pastors, missionaries and other
individuals involved in Christian service.
Financial data: Year ended 12/31/2011. Assets,
$30,357 (M); Expenditures, $232,995; Total
giving, $130.
Fields of interest: Human services; Christian
agencies & churches.
Type of support: Grants to individuals; Grants for
special needs.
Application information: Applications not
accepted.
Additional information: Unsolicited requests for
funds not considered or acknowledged.
EIN: 931224119

7557
John Larmar Cooper Scholarship Loan Fund
(formerly Cooper Student Aid Fund)
P.O. Box 3168
Portland, OR 97208 (800) 452-8807

Foundation type: Independent foundation
Purpose: Scholarships to graduates at accredited
high schools of Hood River County, OR.
Publications: Informational brochure (including
application guidelines).
Financial data: Year ended 06/30/2013. Assets,
$761,106 (M); Expenditures, $53,587; Total
giving, $34,167.
Fields of interest: Vocational education,
post-secondary; Higher education.
Type of support: Technical education support;
Undergraduate support.
Application information: Applications accepted.
Application form required. Interview required.
Deadline(s): Mar. 1
Additional information: Contact the fund for
additional information.
EIN: 936155856

7558
The Corvallis Clinic Foundation, Inc.
444 N.W. Elks Dr.
Corvallis, OR 97330-3744 (541) 754-1374

Foundation type: Company-sponsored foundation
Purpose: Scholarships to students pursuing higher education in health-related fields or in humanities, and emergency grants to Corvallis employees.
Publications: Application guidelines; Newsletter.
Financial data: Year ended 12/31/2010. Assets, $298,758 (M); Expenditures, $134,513; Total giving, $23,732.
Fields of interest: Humanities; Higher education; Health care.
Type of support: Scholarships—to individuals; Employee-related welfare; Undergraduate support.
Application information: Applications accepted. Application form required.
  Deadline(s): May. 28 for James R. Naibert Scholarship
  Applicants should submit the following:
    1) Letter(s) of recommendation
    2) Essay
    3) Transcripts
  Additional information: Applications are available through school counseling or financial aid offices for Riley and Knox Scholarships. Applications are available through the foundation for Naibert scholarship.
Program descriptions:
  Corvalis Clinic Health Occupations Scholarships: The foundation awards scholarships to five area high school students who have decided to pursue a career in a health-related field.
  Employee Emergency Fund: The foundation awards grants to employees of Corvallis Clinic during times of crisis that results in unexpected financial need.
  George W. Knox Memorial Scholarship: The foundation, in partnership with the George W. Knox family, awards $500 scholarships to Corvallis area high school students who express an interest in entering a health-related career field or the humanities.
  James A. Riley Health Occupation Scholarship: The foundation awards scholarships to Oregon State University students in the College of Science and the College of Health and Human Sciences who have decided to pursue a career in a health-related field. The scholarship is named in honor of a former clinic physician and founder of the foundation, Dr. James A. Riley. The program is administered through the respective OSU colleges.
  James R. Naibert Health Occupation Scholarship: The foundation awards a $1,000 scholarship to a college sophomore or above who demonstrates an interest in a health-related profession that involves direct patient care, including physician, nursing, technical profession, or pharmaceutical studies. The scholarship is named in honor of James R. Naibert, a family physician at The Corvallis Clinic's Waverly Drive facility.
Company name: The Corvallis Clinic, P.C.
EIN: 936021898

7559
Cottage Grove Community Foundation
1450 Birch Ave.
P. O. Box 1326
Cottage Grove, OR 97424 (541) 942-0014
Contact: Frank Simpson, Exec. Dir.
FAX: (541) 942-0032;
E-mail: director@cgcfoundation.org; URL: http://www.cgcfoundation.org

Foundation type: Community foundation

Purpose: Scholarships to graduating seniors who attend schools in Cottage Grove, Creswell, Drain, and Yoncalla, OR for postsecondary education at accredited colleges or universities.
Publications: Application guidelines.
Financial data: Year ended 12/31/2012. Assets, $2,624,647 (M); Expenditures, $181,230; Total giving, $92,744.
Fields of interest: Higher education; Scholarships/financial aid.
Type of support: Scholarships—to individuals; Undergraduate support.
Application information: Applications accepted. Application form required. Application form available on the grantmaker's web site.
  Initial approach: Application
  Send request by: E-mail
  Deadline(s): Apr. 10
  Applicants should submit the following:
    1) Financial information
    2) Essay
    3) Transcripts
    4) GPA
  Additional information: See web site for complete listing of scholarships and additional criteria.
EIN: 943138507

7560
Creative Support, Inc.
930 W. 8th St.
Medford, OR 97501-2908 (541) 864-1673

Foundation type: Public charity
Purpose: Assistance to individuals with developmental disabilities for food, shelter, and clothing necessary in order to allow them to live independently or with families in accordance with the Oregon Department of Disability guidelines.
Financial data: Year ended 06/30/2012. Assets, $1,966,690 (M); Expenditures, $4,722,404; Total giving, $3,595,808; Grants to individuals, totaling $3,595,808.
Type of support: Grants for special needs.
Application information: Applications not accepted.
  Additional information: Unsolicited requests for funds not considered or acknowledged.
EIN: 931299878

7561
Raymond Criswell Scholarship Fund
P.O. Box 3168
Portland, OR 97208-3168 (541) 476-2493
Contact: Clare Winkle
Application address: C/O St. Lukes Episcopal, 224 NW D St., Grants Pass, OR 97526 tel: (541) 476-2493

Foundation type: Independent foundation
Purpose: Scholarships to outstanding seniors of Grants Pass High School, OR, to attend Oregon State University for up to four years.
Financial data: Year ended 06/30/2013. Assets, $228,496 (M); Expenditures, $13,758; Total giving, $6,834.
Fields of interest: Higher education; Scholarships/financial aid; Economically disadvantaged.
Type of support: Support to graduates or students of specific schools; Undergraduate support.
Application information: Applicant must demonstrate financial need.
EIN: 936020612

7562
The Culinary Trust
(formerly The International Association of Culinary Professionals Foundation)
P.O. Box 5485
Portland, OR 97228-5485 (214) 741-4072
Contact: Trina Gribbins, Dir., Admin.
E-mail: tgribbins@hqtrs.com; Mailing Address: P. O. Box 5485, Portland, OR, 97208; URL: http://www.theculinarytrust.org

Foundation type: Public charity
Purpose: Awards and scholarships for training at both the primary and continuing education level to students interested in culinary careers. Grants also for research in the culinary arts and sciences.
Publications: Application guidelines; Annual report; Financial statement; Newsletter.
Financial data: Year ended 06/30/2012. Assets, $425,206 (M); Expenditures, $191,174; Total giving, $153,565; Grants to individuals, totaling $134,441.
Fields of interest: Adult/continuing education; Business/industry.
Type of support: Research; Grants to individuals; Scholarships—to individuals; Awards/prizes; Undergraduate support.
Application information:
  Initial approach: Letter
  Deadline(s): Dec. 1 for Culinary Scholarships
  Additional information: Contact foundation for current application guidelines.
Program descriptions:
  Culinary Trust Scholarship Program: The trust provides both cash and tuition-credit scholarships. The program seeks to encourage, enable, and assist aspiring students and career professionals to advance their knowledge of the culinary arts. Recipients are selected based on merit.
  Harry A. Bell Grants for Food Writers: Assists authors of potentially significant culinary works whose projects require travel and research to complete their pre-contract book proposal. Applicants must describe the project, its scope and the funds necessary to bring their project to a completed book proposal stage. The stipend awarded will vary according to the proposal.
  Julia Child Fund Scholarship: This $5,000 cash scholarship award provides funds for a career professional to conduct independent study and research in France as it relates to French food, wine, history, culture, and traditions. The scholarship offsets expenses for travel, research, and accomodations.
EIN: 521333505

7563
Floyd and Elizabeth Culver Memorial College
(also known as Floyd and Elizabeth Culver Memorial College Scholarship Fund)
P.O. Box 3168
Portland, OR 97208-3168 (360) 690-0378
Contact: Wendy Kelley
Application address: 1613 Broadway St., Vancouver, WA 98660-3435, tel.: (360) 690-0378

Foundation type: Independent foundation
Purpose: Scholarships to graduates from one of the public high schools in Tillamook County, OR for continuing education at colleges or universities.
Financial data: Year ended 09/30/2013. Assets, $451,912 (M); Expenditures, $24,452; Total giving, $15,000.
Fields of interest: Higher education.
Type of support: Scholarships—to individuals.

Application information: Applications accepted.
EIN: 916573013

7564
Aline C. Cutler Charitable Trust
705 W. 10th St.
Medford, OR 97501-3001

Foundation type: Independent foundation
Purpose: Funds to cover medical expenses primarily to individuals in OR.
Financial data: Year ended 06/30/2013. Assets, $373,213 (M); Expenditures, $41,025; Total giving, $30,600; Grants to individuals, 10 grants totaling $9,100 (high: $1,500, low: $200).
Fields of interest: Economically disadvantaged.
Type of support: Grants to individuals.
Application information: Applications not accepted.
  Additional information: Unsolicited requests for funds not considered or acknowledged.
EIN: 931314404

7565
Bernard Daly Educational Fund
P.O. Box 351
Lakeview, OR 97630-0123 (541) 947-2196

Foundation type: Independent foundation
Purpose: Scholarships only to students in Lake County, OR, for study at OR state-supported universities, colleges, and technical schools.
Financial data: Year ended 05/31/2013. Assets, $5,719,677 (M); Expenditures, $426,150; Total giving, $377,000; Grants to individuals, 51 grants totaling $377,000 (high: $7,800, low: $2,600).
Fields of interest: Vocational education.
Type of support: Scholarships—to individuals; Technical education support.
Application information: Applications accepted. Application form required.
  Initial approach: Letter
  Deadline(s): May 1
  Additional information: Scholarships are renewable.
EIN: 936025466

7566
Danicas Foundation, Inc.
1600 Country Commons
Lake Oswego, OR 97034 (503) 344-6944
Contact: Daniel E. Casey M.D., Dir.

Foundation type: Independent foundation
Purpose: Scholarships for students of OR, studying in fields related to mental illness.
Financial data: Year ended 12/31/2012. Assets, $248,548 (M); Expenditures, $12,086; Total giving, $0.
Fields of interest: Mental health, disorders; Schizophrenia.
Type of support: Undergraduate support.
Application information: Applications accepted.
  Initial approach: Letter
  Deadline(s): None
  Additional information: Application should state how the grant will be used.
EIN: 930875917

7567
Thomas R. Dargan Minority Scholarship Fund
(formerly KATU Thomas R. Dargan Minority Scholarship Fund)
P.O. Box 2
Portland, OR 97207-0002
URL: http://www.katu.com/about/scholarship

Foundation type: Company-sponsored foundation
Purpose: Scholarships to students of color from OR or WA who are pursuing careers in broadcasting or communications.
Publications: Application guidelines; Informational brochure (including application guidelines).
Financial data: Year ended 03/31/2013. Assets, $194,547 (M); Expenditures, $11,101; Total giving, $11,000; Grants to individuals, 4 grants totaling $11,000.
Fields of interest: Media/communications; Television; Radio; Web-based media; Minorities.
Type of support: Scholarships—to individuals; Undergraduate support.
Application information: Applications accepted. Application form required. Application form available on the grantmaker's web site. Interview required.
  Initial approach: Application
  Send request by: Mail
  Deadline(s): Apr. 30
  Final notification: Recipients notified July 1
  Applicants should submit the following:
    1) Transcripts
    2) GPA
    3) Letter(s) of recommendation
    4) Essay
Program description:
  KATU Thomas R. Dargan Scholarship: The foundation awards $6,000 scholarships to minority sophomore students who are enrolled in a broadcast, communications, or multi-media curriculum at an institution of higher education in Oregon or Washington or are permanent residents of Oregon or Washington attending an out-of-state institution. Applicants must have a GPA of 3.0 and winners are eligible to receive a paid internship in selected departments at Fisher Broadcasting/ KATU.
EIN: 943101223

7568
Walter L.J. Davies Memorial Scholarship
P.O. Box 3168
Portland, OR 97208-3168 (800) 452-8807
Application address: c/o Oregon Student Assistance Commission, 1500 Valley River Dr., Ste. 100, Eugene, OR 97401-2148,

Foundation type: Independent foundation
Purpose: Scholarships to eligible employees of U.S. Bancorp, or dependents of eligible employees who are graduates of Oregon high schools.
Financial data: Year ended 06/30/2013. Assets, $979,427 (M); Expenditures, $64,836; Total giving, $38,360.
Fields of interest: Higher education.
Type of support: Employee-related scholarships; Scholarships—to individuals.
Application information: Applications accepted. Application form required.
  Deadline(s): Apr. 1
  Applicants should submit the following:
    1) Transcripts
    2) GPA
    3) SAT
    4) ACT
EIN: 936163624

7569
Day Management Educational Foundation
P.O. Box 189
Estacada, OR 97023-0189 (503) 630-4202

Foundation type: Company-sponsored foundation
Purpose: Scholarships to employees of Day Management, and the children or relatives of such employees, for higher education.
Financial data: Year ended 06/30/2013. Assets, $811,994 (M); Expenditures, $31,745; Total giving, $24,000; Grants to individuals, 15 grants totaling $24,000 (high: $2,000, low: $667).
Fields of interest: Higher education.
Type of support: Employee-related scholarships.
Application information: Applications not accepted.
  Additional information: Unsolicted requests for funds not considered or acknowledged.
EIN: 931188551

7570
Deneke's Hope Foundation
2002 N.W. 36th St.
Lincoln City, OR 97367
Contact: Meredith Oksenholt, Pres.
URL: http://www.denekeshope.com

Foundation type: Operating foundation
Purpose: Grants to impoverished individuals in Ethiopia for educational, medical and social needs.
Financial data: Year ended 12/31/2011. Assets, $15,185 (M); Expenditures, $56,031; Total giving, $35,828; Grants to individuals, totaling $28,128.
Fields of interest: Human services; Economically disadvantaged.
Type of support: Grants for special needs.
Application information:
  Deadline(s): None
  Additional information: Contact the foundation for additional information.
EIN: 204812855

7571
Jerri Walker Depriest Memorial Endowment Fund
5225 S.W. Menefee Dr.
Portland, OR 97239 (541) 467-2509
Contact: Thomas A. Walker, Secy.
E-mail: tomwalker_50@hotmail.com

Foundation type: Public charity
Purpose: Scholarships to graduating seniors of Dufur High School, OR for postsecondary education.
Financial data: Year ended 12/31/2012. Assets, $405,848 (M); Expenditures, $17,066; Total giving, $15,417.
Fields of interest: Vocational education, post-secondary; Higher education.
Type of support: Scholarships—to individuals; Support to graduates or students of specific schools.
Application information: Application form required. Interview required.
  Deadline(s): May 2
  Applicants should submit the following:
    1) GPA
    2) Essay
  Additional information: Selection is based on academic performance, financial need and a desire to attend college. Application forms available at Dufur High School.
Program description:
  Scholarship Program: Scholarships are awarded to Dufur High school seniors who have a 2.0 GPA

and wish to advance their education or training through college, vocational, or technical school.
EIN: 931237044

7572
Dewuhs-Keckritz Educational Trust

P.O. Box 1034
Joseph, OR 97846
Contact: Robert S. Williams, Dir.

Foundation type: Independent foundation
Purpose: Scholarships of up to $6,000 each to the top male and female students in Union and Wallowa counties, OR.
Financial data: Year ended 12/31/2012. Assets, $684,706 (M); Expenditures, $42,787; Total giving, $31,250; Grants to individuals, 9 grants totaling $31,250 (high: $5,000, low: $1,250).
Type of support: Undergraduate support.
Application information: Applications accepted. Application form required.
  Deadline(s): Apr. 10
EIN: 936092788

7573
John & Alice Dillard Memorial Trust

P.O. Box 100
Nehalem, OR 97131-0100 (503) 368-6737
Contact: Nancy Dillard, Secy.

Foundation type: Independent foundation
Purpose: College scholarships to high school graduates of the greater Nehalem, OR area for postsecondary education.
Financial data: Year ended 12/31/2012. Assets, $0 (M); Expenditures, $4,407; Total giving, $4,000; Grants to individuals, 5 grants totaling $4,000 (high: $1,000, low: $500).
Fields of interest: Higher education.
Type of support: Scholarships—to individuals.
Application information: Applications accepted. Application form required.
  Initial approach: Letter or telephone
  Deadline(s): Apr. 1
EIN: 936319500

7574
Tosoh Quartz Education Foundation

(also known as Weiss Scientific Foundation)
14380 N.W. Science Park Dr.
Portland, OR 97229-5419 (507) 931-1682

Foundation type: Company-sponsored foundation
Purpose: Scholarships to children of Tosoh Quartz Portland employees residing in CA, OR and TX, with at least four years seniority for higher education.
Financial data: Year ended 12/31/2012. Assets, $370,914 (M); Expenditures, $25,666; Total giving, $15,700; Grants to individuals, 2 grants totaling $15,700 (high: $10,000, low: $5,700).
Type of support: Employee-related scholarships.
Application information:
  Initial approach: Letter
  Deadline(s): July 1
  Applicants should submit the following:
    1) Resume
    2) Transcripts
  Additional information: Application must also include description of extra-curricular and community activities. Contributes only through an employee-related program. Inappropriate request for funds not considered or acknowledged.
Company name: TOSOH Quartz, Inc.
EIN: 930879802

7575
Fanconi Anemia Research Fund, Inc.

1801 Willamette St., Ste. 200
Eugene, OR 97401-8054 (541) 687-4658
Contact: Laura Hays, Exec. Dir.
FAX: (541) 687-0548; E-mail: info@fanconi.org; Toll-free tel.: (888)-326-2664; E-Mail for Laura Hays: laura@fanconi.org; URL: http://www.fanconi.org

Foundation type: Public charity
Purpose: Grants to researchers to find the cause and cure of Fanconia Anemia, and to provide support and education to affected families.
Publications: Application guidelines; Informational brochure; Newsletter.
Financial data: Year ended 12/31/2012. Assets, $5,802,617 (M); Expenditures, $3,009,853; Total giving, $1,813,068.
Fields of interest: Obstetrics/gynecology; Hematology research.
Type of support: Research.
Application information: Applications accepted. Application form required.
  Initial approach: E-mail
  Deadline(s): Ongoing
  Additional information: Application must include proposal. Contact the Fund for additional guidelines.
EIN: 930995453

7576
The Kate Fansler Foundation, Inc.

c/o E. Heilbrun
2175 Jefferson Alley
Eugene, OR 97405 (212) 865-6167
Contact: Susan Heath, Pres.
Application address: 845 West End Ave., Ste. 9A, New York, NY 10025, tel.:(212) 865-6167

Foundation type: Independent foundation
Purpose: Assistance to individuals, with special attention to women in need of such assistance, in order to improve their lives through study, work, or support in their creative efforts.
Financial data: Year ended 05/31/2013. Assets, $132,644 (M); Expenditures, $64,912; Total giving, $59,353; Grants to individuals, 23 grants totaling $59,353 (high: $14,000, low: $68).
Fields of interest: Women.
Type of support: Grants for special needs.
Application information: Applications not accepted.
  Additional information: Unsolicited requests for funds not considered or acknowledged.
EIN: 133979080

7577
Fish Emergency Service, Inc.

1335 S.E. Hawthorne Blvd.
Portland, OR 97214-3615 (503) 233-5533
E-mail: info@fishemergencyservice.org; URL: http://www.fishemergencyservice.org

Foundation type: Public charity
Purpose: Temporary assistance to individuals and families in the Portland, OR area with food, clothing, personal care products and other special needs.
Publications: Annual report.
Financial data: Year ended 09/30/2012. Assets, $651,973 (M); Expenditures, $717,585; Total giving, $455,356; Grants to individuals, totaling $455,356.
Fields of interest: Economically disadvantaged.
Type of support: Grants for special needs.

Application information: Contact the agency for assistance.
EIN: 930638179

7578
The Ford Family Foundation

1600 N.W. Stewart Pkwy.
Roseburg, OR 97471-1957 (541) 957-5574
Contact: Anne C. Kubisch, Pres.
Scholarship application address: The Ford Family Foundation Scholarship Office, 440 E. Broadway, Ste., 200, Eugene, OR 97401, tel.: (541) 485-6211, toll free: (877) 864-2872, e-mail: fordscholarships@tfff.org, fax: (541) 485-6223
FAX: (541) 957-5720; E-mail: info@tfff.org; URL: http://www.tfff.org

Foundation type: Independent foundation
Purpose: Scholarships to deserving high school and community college graduates throughout OR and Siskiyou County, CA, to be used toward a four-year, in-state baccalaureate degree. Fellowships to assist visual artists of Oregon to create new work.
Publications: Informational brochure (including application guidelines); Newsletter.
Financial data: Year ended 12/31/2012. Assets, $721,115,314 (M); Expenditures, $38,571,212; Total giving, $26,159,959; Grants to individuals, 1,370 grants totaling $11,189,835 (high: $36,825, low: $162).
Fields of interest: Visual arts; Adult/continuing education.
Type of support: Fellowships; Employee-related scholarships; Scholarships—to individuals; Technical education support; Undergraduate support.
Application information: Applications accepted. Application form required. Application form available on the grantmaker's web site.
  Initial approach: Application for scholarships
  Send request by: Online
  Copies of proposal: 1
  Deadline(s): Mar. 1 for Scholarships
  Applicants should submit the following:
    1) Essay
    2) FAFSA
    3) GPA
    4) Transcripts
  Additional information: See web site for additional guidelines.
Program descriptions:
  Ford Community Fellows: The award is given to rural residents in Oregon and Siskiyou County, California who have demonstrated a commitment to community service and a dedication to the pursuit of rural community vitality. Ford Community Fellows are nominated by Ford Family Foundation staff and partner contractors who deliver the Ford Institute Leadership Program. Each Fellow receives a $12,000 annual unrestricted monetary award and is eligible for up to two renewal awards. Fellows are expected to develop their own plan to explore, learn, and practice the art of community building. The program promotes community building and vitality by some or all of the following activities: 1) Coaching communities toward their own vision, priorities and measures of success (indicators); 2) Promoting systems thinking and collaboration; 3) Modeling a commitment to "life- long learning" ; 3) Leveraging local resources to draw on external sources, including individuals, philanthropy, non-profits, business, and government ; 4) Encouraging development of projects and programs that draw on best theory and practice; 5) Directing communities to full use of their own resources of time, energy, and dollars to move projects and

programs forward (make things happen); 6) Assisting communities in measuring their own success; 7) Convening individuals, groups and communities to strengthen social capital and networks while learning from each other; and 8) Sustaining strong relationships with key stakeholders, adjoining community leaders, and The Ford Institute for Community Building.

Ford Scholarships: The foundation offers a unique group of financial and program resources to college students. 1) The Ford Scholars Program is open to a) graduating high school seniors b) continuing community college students who are pursuing a bachelor's degree and are ready to transfer to a four-year college. This program is offered in both Oregon and Siskiyou County, California; 2) The Ford Opportunity Program is designed for single parents who are heads of household and who are pursuing a bachelor's degree. This program is offered in both Oregon and Siskiyou County, California; 3) The Scholarship Program for Sons and Daughters of Employees of Roseburg Forest Products Co. serves dependents (21 years of age or younger) of employees of Roseburg Forest Products Co. This program is offered in Oregon, Siskiyou County, California, and other regions; 4) The Ford ReStart Program supports non-traditional adult students beginning or returning to full-time post-secondary education. This program is offered in both Oregon and Siskiyou County, California. For additional information see web site.

Hallie Ford Fellowships in the Visual Arts: The foundation awards up to three unrestricted fellowships per calendar year, each in the amount of $25,000 to Oregon mid-career visual artists who have demonstrated a depth of sophisticated practice and potential for significant future accomplishment. Recipients are chosen based on the quality and evolution of their past and current work and their promise of future potential. They are chosen by a panel of arts professionals familiar with the work of Oregon visual artists, the national contemporary art discipline, and who are experienced in fellowship selection processes. Application is open to any Oregon mid-career visual artist meeting specific criteria and actively producing new work in the fields of contemporary fine art and craft. See web site for eligibility requirements and application and selection schedule.
EIN: 936026156

7579
Ralph H. Foss Memorial Trust
P.O. Box 3168
Portland, OR 97208 (406) 657-8139
Contact: Penny Doak
Application address: U.S. Bank, P.O. Box 30678, Billings, MT 30678

Foundation type: Independent foundation
Purpose: Scholarships to high school graduates of Richland and Dawson counties, MT for postsecondary education.
Financial data: Year ended 12/31/2012. Assets, $448,924 (M); Expenditures, $30,853; Total giving, $22,300.
Fields of interest: Higher education; Scholarships/ financial aid.
Type of support: Undergraduate support.
Application information: Application form required.
   Send request by: Mail
   Deadline(s): Apr. 1
   Applicants should submit the following:
      1) Essay
      2) Financial information

3) Class rank
4) GPA
Additional information: Applications are available from the principal or guidance counselor of high schools in Dawson and Richland counties.
EIN: 816048184

7580
Franks Foundation Fund
P.O. Box 3168
Portland, OR 97208 (800) 452-8807

Foundation type: Independent foundation
Purpose: Student loans to high school students from Deschutes, Crook and Jefferson counties, OR. Second priority is given to students from Harney, Lake, Grant and Klamath counties, OR. Applicants must be enrolled in or planning to enroll in an undergraduate or graduate course of study in theology or nursing.
Financial data: Year ended 06/30/2013. Assets, $354,359 (M); Expenditures, $25,485; Total giving, $14,500.
Type of support: Undergraduate support.
Application information: Applications accepted. Application form required. Interview required.
   Deadline(s): June 1 to June 15
   Applicants should submit the following:
      1) FAFSA
      2) Transcripts
      3) Essay
EIN: 930666994

7581
Elvine & Leroy Gienger Foundation
P.O. Box 337
Chiloquin, OR 97624 (541) 783-2462

Foundation type: Operating foundation
Purpose: Scholarships to residents of the Chiloquin, OR, area for attendance at institutions of higher learning.
Financial data: Year ended 11/30/2013. Assets, $675,159 (M); Expenditures, $25,015; Total giving, $19,208; Grants to individuals, 18 grants totaling $19,208 (high: $2,500, low: -$1,498).
Fields of interest: Higher education.
Type of support: Scholarships—to individuals.
Application information: Application form required.
   Deadline(s): 2 weeks before graduation
   Additional information: Scholarships are renewable. Generally, the foundation chooses two or three new recipients per year.
EIN: 930981050

7582
Edwin C. Goodenough Scholarship Trust
(formerly Edwin C. Goodenough Scholarship Fund)
P.O. Box 2305
Salem, OR 97308-2305

Foundation type: Independent foundation
Purpose: Scholarships to residents of Salem, OR, who are graduating seniors from schools located in the area comprising School District No. 24J in Salem, OR.
Financial data: Year ended 06/30/2013. Assets, $94,500 (M); Expenditures, $9,924; Total giving, $5,396; Grants to individuals, 4 grants totaling $5,396 (high: $1,584, low: $1,224).
Type of support: Support to graduates or students of specific schools; Undergraduate support.

Application information: Application form required. Interview required.
   Initial approach: Letter
   Additional information: Contact foundation for current application deadline/guidelines.
EIN: 936119287

7583
Martha K. Hall Educational Trust
c/o U.S. Bank, N.A.
P.O. Box 3168
Portland, OR 97208-3168 (509) 353-7090

Foundation type: Independent foundation
Purpose: Scholarships to graduates of Lincoln County high schools, WA.
Financial data: Year ended 09/30/2013. Assets, $758,979 (M); Expenditures, $62,559; Total giving, $36,000.
Fields of interest: Higher education.
Type of support: Support to graduates or students of specific schools; Undergraduate support.
Application information: Application form required.
   Initial approach: Letter
   Deadline(s): Apr.
   Applicants should submit the following:
      1) Transcripts
      2) Financial information
EIN: 916173039

7584
Halton Foundation
P.O. Box 3377
Portland, OR 97208-3377 (503) 780-0453
Contact: Susan Halton, Mgr.

Foundation type: Company-sponsored foundation
Purpose: Scholarships only to children of current employees of The Halton Company or related companies.
Financial data: Year ended 08/31/2012. Assets, $1,479,578 (M); Expenditures, $41,852; Total giving, $40,956; Grants to individuals, 7 grants totaling $37,956 (high: $7,901, low: $1,816).
Fields of interest: Higher education.
Type of support: Employee-related scholarships; Graduate support; Technical education support; Undergraduate support.
Application information: Applications not accepted.
   Additional information: Unsolicited requests for funds not considered or acknowledged.
Program description:
   Halton Scholars: The foundation awards college scholarships to children of employees of Halton Co. and its related companies. Employees must be employed for a period of six months before a child can apply. All applicants must be under 28 years of age and plan to pursue higher education as a full-time student. Applicants are evaluated on the basis of financial need, academic achievement, and participation in extracurricular activities, which include athletics, a part-time job, volunteer work, etc.
Company name: Halton Co.
EIN: 936036295

7585
Joann Hamilton Memorial Fund
P.O. Box 3168
Portland, OR 97208-3168 (503) 275-5923
Contact: Rebecca P. Bibleheimer

Foundation type: Independent foundation

Purpose: Scholarships to graduates of Newport High School, OR, or any other Lincoln County, OR, high school pursuing postsecondary education.
Financial data: Year ended 06/30/2013. Assets, $1,356,627 (M); Expenditures, $90,634; Total giving, $62,750.
Fields of interest: Theater; Vocational education.
Type of support: Support to graduates or students of specific schools; Undergraduate support.
Application information: Applications accepted. Application form required.
> *Deadline(s):* Mar. 1
> *Applicants should submit the following:*
> 1) Financial information
> 2) SAT
> 3) Essay
> 4) Letter(s) of recommendation
> 5) Transcripts
> *Additional information:* Applicants should demonstrate academic excellence in any field of study including, but not limited to, speech, drama, and vocational skills. Funds are paid directly to the educational institution on behalf of the students.

EIN: 936249490

7586
Geraldine Heiserman Trust f/b/o Cottey College

(formerly Geraldine Cottey College Trust)
P.O. Box 3168
Portland, OR 97208

Foundation type: Independent foundation
Purpose: Scholarships to residents of CO to attend Cottey College in Nevada, MO.
Financial data: Year ended 12/31/2012. Assets, $337,139 (M); Expenditures, $26,814; Total giving, $19,000.
Fields of interest: Higher education.
Type of support: Support to graduates or students of specific schools.
Application information: Applications accepted.
EIN: 846049131

7587
Pauline and Edna Hellstern Foundation

c/o U.S. Bank, N.A.
P.O. Box 3168
Portland, OR 97208-3168
Contact: Linda McMillan
Application address: c/o Buxman Kwitek and Ohlson, P.C. 601 N. Main St., Ste. 200., Pueblo, CO 81003, tel.: (719) 544-5081

Foundation type: Independent foundation
Purpose: Scholarships to graduates of Pueblo County, CO, schools.
Financial data: Year ended 02/28/2013. Assets, $247,639 (M); Expenditures, $14,627; Total giving, $9,000.
Type of support: Support to graduates or students of specific schools; Undergraduate support.
Application information: Applications accepted. Application form required.
> *Deadline(s):* None
> *Additional information:* Applications available from School District No. 60, Pueblo, CO.

EIN: 742536168

7588
Holce Logging Company Scholarship Foundation Inc

P.O. Box 127
Vernonia, OR 97064-0127

Foundation type: Company-sponsored foundation
Purpose: Scholarships to recent graduates (within five years) of Vernonia High School, OR.
Financial data: Year ended 04/30/2013. Assets, $274,114 (M); Expenditures, $11,037; Total giving, $11,001; Grants to individuals, 7 grants totaling $11,001 (high: $2,000, low: $667).
Fields of interest: Higher education.
Type of support: Support to graduates or students of specific schools; Undergraduate support.
Application information: Applications accepted. Application form required.
> *Send request by:* Mail
> *Deadline(s):* Apr. 15
> *Applicants should submit the following:*
> 1) Transcripts
> 2) SAT
> 3) Resume
> 4) Letter(s) of recommendation
> 5) GPA
> 6) Essay
> 7) ACT
> *Additional information:* Contact guidance counselor of Vernonia High School for application form.

EIN: 930845692

7589
Maria C. Jackson-General George A. White

P.O. Box 3168
Portland, OR 97208-3168 (800) 452-8807

Foundation type: Independent foundation
Purpose: Scholarships to individuals who served or whose parents serve or have served in the U.S. Armed Forces while residing in OR at the time of enlistment, and are residents of OR.
Financial data: Year ended 06/30/2013. Assets, $636,442 (M); Expenditures, $42,711; Total giving, $25,834.
Fields of interest: Higher education; Military/ veterans' organizations.
Type of support: Undergraduate support.
Application information: Applications not accepted.
> *Additional information:* Unsolicited requests for funds not considered or acknowledged.

EIN: 936020316

7590
Jenkins Student Aid Fund

(formerly Jenkins Student Loan Fund)
P.O. Box 3168
Portland, OR 97208 (800) 452-8807
Application address: C/o. Oregon Student Assistance Commission,1500 Valley River Dr., Ste. 100, tel.: (800) 452-8807

Foundation type: Independent foundation
Purpose: Scholarships to graduating seniors of Jefferson High School, Portland, OR for postsecondary education.
Publications: Application guidelines; Program policy statement.
Financial data: Year ended 06/30/2012. Assets, $976,728 (M); Expenditures, $47,979; Total giving, $30,000.
Fields of interest: Higher education.
Type of support: Undergraduate support.

Application information: Application form required.
> *Initial approach:* Letter
> *Applicants should submit the following:*
> 1) Letter(s) of recommendation
> 2) Transcripts
> *Additional information:* Payments are made directly to the educational institution for the named individuals.

EIN: 936020672

7591
Journal Publishing Company Employees Welfare Fund, Inc.

P.O. Box 3168
Portland, OR 97208-3168

Foundation type: Independent foundation
Purpose: Welfare assistance to retired employees of Journal Publishing Co.
Financial data: Year ended 06/30/2010. Assets, $0 (M); Expenditures, $5,020; Total giving, $500.
Type of support: Employee-related welfare.
Application information: Applications accepted.
> *Deadline(s):* None
> *Additional information:* Contact foundation for current application guidelines.

Company name: Journal Publishing Company
EIN: 237066006

7592
Joseph S. Ball Klamath Scholarship Intervivos

P.O. Box 3168
Portland, OR 97208-3168 (800) 522-9100
Application Address: US Bank

Foundation type: Independent foundation
Purpose: Scholarships to current high school students who are members of the Klamath Tribe for attendance at colleges or trade schools.
Financial data: Year ended 07/31/2012. Assets, $686,663 (M); Expenditures, $39,861; Total giving, $27,500.
Fields of interest: Higher education; Native Americans/American Indians.
Type of support: Scholarships—to individuals.
Application information: Applications accepted. Application form required.
> *Deadline(s):* Apr. 15
> *Applicants should submit the following:*
> 1) Transcripts
> 2) GPA
> *Additional information:* Application should also include a letter of reference.

EIN: 916566234

7593
Herbert & Bertha Laird Education Foundation

(formerly Herbert Frank and Bertha Maude Laird Oakland Scottish Rite Memorial Educational Foundation)
c/o Dallas Cason
3131 N.W. Buttercup Dr.
Corvallis, OR 97330-3380

Foundation type: Independent foundation
Purpose: Scholarships by nomination only to public high school students in northern and central CA. Preference is given to electrical engineering majors.
Financial data: Year ended 12/31/2012. Assets, $1,513,328 (M); Expenditures, $85,471; Total giving, $77,250; Grants to individuals, 14 grants totaling $77,250 (high: $7,500, low: $1,750).

Type of support: Undergraduate support.
Application information: Interview required.
Deadline(s): Jan.
Additional information: Applicants must be nominated by high school principals. Individual applications not accepted.
EIN: 237047350

7594
Lampstand Foundation
(formerly Agnes Klingensmith Charitable Foundation)
18160 Cottonwood Rd., No. 244
Sunriver, OR 97707
Contact: David Winn, Tr.

Foundation type: Independent foundation
Purpose: Scholarships and internships to individuals in CA and FL.
Financial data: Year ended 12/31/2012. Assets, $1,298,315 (M); Expenditures, $160,184; Total giving, $121,862.
Type of support: Internship funds; Scholarships—to individuals.
Application information: Applications accepted.
Deadline(s): None
Additional information: Contact foundation for eligibility criteria.
EIN: 911503479

7595
Lane Arts Council
1590 Willamette St., Ste. 200
Eugene, OR 97401-4048 (541) 485-2278
Contact: Liora Sponko, Exec. Dir.
FAX: (541) 485-2478;
E-mail: lanearts@lanearts.org; E-mail for Liora Sponko: liora@lanearts.org; URL: http://www.lanearts.org

Foundation type: Public charity
Purpose: Support to artists throughout Lane County, OR through a fiscal sponsorship program.
Publications: Application guidelines; Annual report.
Financial data: Year ended 06/30/2012. Assets, $64,826 (M); Expenditures, $204,366; Total giving, $49,100.
Fields of interest: Arts, artist's services.
Type of support: Project support; Fiscal agent/sponsor.
Application information: Contact council for further information.
Program description:
Fiscal Sponsorship: The council acts as a fiscal agent/sponsor for arts organizations and artists that fit the council's criteria.
EIN: 930681430

7596
Red and Gena Leonard Foundation
P.O. Box 1024
Hermiston, OR 97838-3024 (541) 564-9177
Contact: Tracy Gammell, Exec. Dir.
FAX: (541) 567-5358;
E-mail: rglfoundation@qwestoffice.net; URL: http://www.leonardfoundation.org

Foundation type: Independent foundation
Purpose: Scholarships to residents of Gilliam, Grant, Morrow, Unmatilla, and Wheeler counties, OR.
Financial data: Year ended 06/30/2013. Assets, $5,507,536 (M); Expenditures, $226,196; Total giving, $158,811.
Type of support: Undergraduate support.

Application information: Applications accepted.
Initial approach: Letter
Applicants should submit the following:
1) Transcripts
2) FAFSA
3) SAR
4) Letter(s) of recommendation
EIN: 931232272

7597
Literary Arts, Inc.
925 S.W. Washington St.
Portland, OR 97205-2919 (503) 227-2583
Contact: Andrew Proctor, Exec. Dir.
FAX: (503) 241-4256; E-mail: la@literary-arts.org; E-mail For Andrew Proctor: andrew@literary-arts.org; URL: http://www.literary-arts.org

Foundation type: Public charity
Purpose: Fellowships and awards to writers residing in OR.
Publications: Application guidelines.
Financial data: Year ended 05/31/2013. Assets, $2,058,321 (M); Expenditures, $1,389,978; Total giving, $29,000; Grants to individuals, totaling $29,000.
Fields of interest: Literature.
Type of support: Fellowships; Awards/prizes.
Application information: Applications accepted. Application form required.
Initial approach: Letter, telephone, or e-mail
Send request by: Mail
Deadline(s): June 24 for Literary Fellowships, Aug. 26 for Book Awards
Applicants should submit the following:
1) Work samples
2) SASE
Additional information: Application for Book Awards should include two copies of the book and an entry fee of $40.00.
Program descriptions:
Oregon Book Awards: These awards are presented annually for the finest accomplishments by Oregon writers who work in genres of poetry, fiction, literary nonfiction, drama and young readers literature. All finalists are promoted in libraries and bookstores across the state, and invited to take part in the Oregon Book Awards Author Tour, which brings finalists to public libraries and independent bookstores in towns throughout Oregon.
Oregon Literary Fellowship: The fellowship helps Oregon writers initiate, develop, or complete literary projects in poetry, fiction, literary nonfiction, drama, and young readers' literature. Writers in the early stages of their career are encouraged to apply.
EIN: 930909494

7598
Carl H. Lytle Scholarship Trust
(formerly Carl H. Lytle Scholarship Trust)
P.O. Box 3168
Portland, OR 97208 (303) 871-4020

Foundation type: Independent foundation
Purpose: Scholarships to financially needy residents of CO to attend the University of Denver. Applicants must have graduated in the upper 25 percent of their high school classes and maintain at least a 3.2 GPA.
Financial data: Year ended 08/31/2013. Assets, $297,930 (M); Expenditures, $21,146; Total giving, $14,500.
Type of support: Support to graduates or students of specific schools; Undergraduate support.
Application information: Application form required.
Deadline(s): None

Additional information: Application must also include student information sheet, certification sheet and financial information.
EIN: 846195232

7599
Major Junior Hockey Education Fund of Oregon
P.O. Box 6405
Portland, OR 97228-6405 (503) 645-3935
Contact: William Deeks, Pres.

Foundation type: Operating foundation
Purpose: Scholarships to individuals who have played amateur hockey for at least one season in the Portland, OR, metropolitan region who are high school graduates and who do not have a career in professional hockey.
Financial data: Year ended 04/30/2013. Assets, $167,783 (M); Expenditures, $57,027; Total giving, $55,040.
Fields of interest: Athletics/sports, training; Athletics/sports, winter sports.
Type of support: Scholarships—to individuals.
Application information: Applications accepted. Application form required.
Initial approach: Letter
Deadline(s): July 15 and Dec. 15
Additional information: Application must also include school admission letter, tuition/fee statement, transcripts and class schedule.
EIN: 930869476

7600
Sophia Byers McComas Foundation
P.O. Box 3168
Portland, OR 97208 (503) 275-5929
Contact: William Dolan
Application address: 111 S.W. 5th Ave., Portland, OR 97204

Foundation type: Independent foundation
Purpose: Financial assistance by recommendation only to aged and indigent persons who are residents of OR and who are not on welfare assistance.
Financial data: Year ended 06/30/2013. Assets, $1,737,415 (M); Expenditures, $126,981; Total giving, $88,700.
Fields of interest: Aging; Economically disadvantaged.
Type of support: Grants for special needs.
Application information: Individual applications not accepted; Applicants are recommended to the trustees by various church groups and service agencies.
EIN: 936019602

7601
Verne Catt McDowell Corporation
P.O. Box 1336
Albany, OR 97321-0440 (541) 924-0976
Contact: Nadine Wood, Mgr.
Application address: 2905 44th Ave., S.E., Albany OR 97322

Foundation type: Independent foundation
Purpose: Scholarships for graduate theological studies to ministers ordained or studying to meet the requirements to be ordained as a minister in the Christian Church (Disciples of Christ). Preference is given to OR residents.
Publications: Application guidelines.
Financial data: Year ended 12/31/2011. Assets, $271,158 (M); Expenditures, $15,717; Total

giving, $11,468; Grants to individuals, 4 grants totaling $8,550 (high: $3,450, low: $1,000).
Fields of interest: Theological school/education; Christian agencies & churches.
Type of support: Graduate support.
Application information: Applications accepted. Application form required. Interview required.
　Initial approach: Letter
　Copies of proposal: 1
　Deadline(s): May 1st
　Applicants should submit the following:
　　1) Transcripts
　　2) Letter(s) of recommendation
　　3) GPA
　　4) Financial information
　Additional information: Application should include educational plans and confirmation by regional minister.
Program description:
Verne Catt McDowell Corporation Scholarship: Applicants must have baccalaureate degrees from accredited liberal arts colleges or universities, and be accepted into professional degree programs at graduate institutions of theological education which are accredited by the General Assembly of the Christian Church (Disciples of Christ). Support is given in the form of a monthly stipend.
EIN: 936022991

7602
John W. McKee Educational Trust
P.O. Box 3168
Portland, OR 97208 (406) 765-1630
Application address: c/o O'Toole Law Firm, Attn.: McKee, 209 N. Main St., Plentywood, MT 59254-1843

Foundation type: Independent foundation
Purpose: Scholarships to undergraduate students who are residents of Sheridan, Roosevelt, or Daniels counties, MT.
Financial data: Year ended 12/31/2012. Assets, $1,162,758 (M); Expenditures, $33,194; Total giving, $22,650; Grants to individuals, 36 grants totaling $22,650 (high: $1,350, low: $250).
Type of support: Undergraduate support.
Application information: Applications accepted. Application form required.
　Deadline(s): July 15
　Additional information: Contact foundation for current application guidelines.
EIN: 237058723

7603
McKenzie River Gathering Foundation
(also known as MRG)
2705 E. Burnside, Ste. 210
Portland, OR 97214-1768 (503) 289-1517
Contact: Marjory Hamann, Exec. Dir.
FAX: (503) 232-1731; Toll-free tel.: (800) 489-6743; URL: http://www.mrgfoundation.org

Foundation type: Public charity
Purpose: Awards to an Oregon woman artist who has been marginalized due to race, sexual orientation, or gender identity.
Publications: Application guidelines; Annual report; Grants list; Informational brochure; Newsletter.
Financial data: Year ended 06/30/2011. Assets, $6,859,130 (M); Expenditures, $1,355,729; Total giving, $602,721.
Fields of interest: Film/video; Women.
Type of support: Awards/prizes.
Application information: Applications accepted. Application form required.

Initial approach: Letter or e-mail
Deadline(s): May 18
Additional information: See web site for additional guidelines.
Program description:
Lilla Jewel Fund for Women Artists: This fund promotes the work of women artists, particularly women of color and queer women, through: inspiring grantees to see the potential of adding art as an organizing tool; using art that especially reflects the struggles and vision of marginalized communities, including people of color and queer or low-income people; providing grantees with access to women artists who will help them create artistic tools and teach them how to create tools on their own in the future; and supporting grantees to make grate use of the tools.
EIN: 930691187

7604
Mercy Foundation, Inc.
2700 Stewart Pkwy.
Roseburg, OR 97470-1281 (541) 677-4818
E-mail: info@mercygiving.org; URL: http://www.mercygiving.org

Foundation type: Public charity
Purpose: Financial assistance and in-kind support to individuals and families in need within Douglas County, OR.
Financial data: Year ended 06/30/2011. Assets, $3,879,074 (M); Expenditures, $1,321,787; Total giving, $366,585; Grants to individuals, totaling $65,950.
Fields of interest: Children/youth, services; Family services; Human services, emergency aid.
Type of support: Emergency funds; In-kind gifts.
Application information: Applications accepted.
　Initial approach: Contact foundation for information
EIN: 936088946

7605
Mid-Columbia Health Foundation
401 E. 3rd St.
The Dalles, OR 97058-2563 (541) 296-7523
FAX: (541) 296-2642; E-mail: mchf@mcmc.net; URL: http://www.mcmc.net

Foundation type: Public charity
Purpose: Scholarships to employees of Mid-Columbia Medical Center, OR. Recipients must have been employees of Mid-Columbia Medical Center for at least one year.
Publications: Application guidelines.
Financial data: Year ended 12/31/2011. Assets, $3,075,338 (M); Expenditures, $931,589; Total giving, $467,622; Grants to individuals, totaling $76,835.
Type of support: Employee-related scholarships.
Application information: Application form required.
　Initial approach: Letter
　Deadline(s): Apr. 30
EIN: 930854433

7606
Ruth Mishler Memorial Trust
P.O. Box 37
Sheridan, OR 97378 (503) 843-3888
Contact: Naomi Kelley, Secy.-Treas.

Foundation type: Independent foundation
Purpose: Scholarships to individuals who have been residents of Sheridan and Willamina, OR, for

at least one year, or local graduates who display need.
Financial data: Year ended 12/31/2012. Assets, $425,491 (M); Expenditures, $18,364; Total giving, $16,500; Grants to individuals, 13 grants totaling $16,500 (high: $5,000, low: $500).
Fields of interest: Higher education.
Type of support: Scholarships—to individuals.
Application information: Applications accepted. Application form required.
　Deadline(s): Apr. 30
　Applicants should submit the following:
　　1) Transcripts
　　2) Letter(s) of recommendation
　Additional information: Applicationshould also include tax returns.
EIN: 943234766

7607
John & Mary Mock Perpetual Memorial Scholarship Fund
P.O. Box 2742
Portland, OR 97208-2742

Foundation type: Independent foundation
Purpose: Scholarships to male graduates of Roosevelt High School, Portland, OR.
Financial data: Year ended 12/31/2011. Assets, $845,897 (M); Expenditures, $43,249; Total giving, $32,472.
Fields of interest: Men.
Type of support: Support to graduates or students of specific schools; Undergraduate support.
Application information: Application form required.
　Deadline(s): Apr. 22
　Applicants should submit the following:
　　1) Letter(s) of recommendation
　　2) Transcripts
EIN: 930727584

7608
Molalla Rotary Foundation
P.O. Box 214
Molalla, OR 97038-0214 (503) 829-3181
Contact: Ilene L. Waldorf, Treas.
E-mail: iwal@molalla.net; Application Address: 221 S. Molalla Ave. Molalla, OR 97038

Foundation type: Operating foundation
Purpose: Scholarships to students from Molalla Union High School, OR.
Financial data: Year ended 06/30/2013. Assets, $108,014 (M); Expenditures, $6,590; Total giving, $3,500; Grants to individuals, 4 grants totaling $3,500 (high: $1,000, low: $500).
Fields of interest: Higher education.
Type of support: Support to graduates or students of specific schools.
Application information: Applications accepted. Application form required.
　Deadline(s): May 1
　Additional information: Applications should include a copy of the student's transcript.
EIN: 930846953

7609
Miles Wendell Moore and Geraldine Moore Scholarship Fund
c/o OregonPacific bank
P.O. Box 1784
Medford, OR 97501 (541) 798-5666
Application address: c/o Lost River High School, Moore Family Scholarship Attn.: Tracie Reed, 23330 Hwy. 50, Merrill, OR 97633-9706

Foundation type: Independent foundation
Purpose: Scholarships to graduating seniors from Lost River High School, OR, pursuing higher education.
Financial data: Year ended 05/31/2013. Assets, $385,761 (M); Expenditures, $15,549; Total giving, $10,000.
Fields of interest: Higher education.
Type of support: Support to graduates or students of specific schools.
Application information: Applications accepted. Application form required.
> *Deadline(s):* May
> *Applicants should submit the following:*
> 1) Letter(s) of recommendation
> 2) Financial information
> 3) Transcripts
> 4) Essay
> *Additional information:* Contact the fund for additional application information.
EIN: 931192772

7610
The Morey Family Foundation
1536 S.W. Highland Pkwy.
Portland, OR 97221-2630 (503) 475-6423

Foundation type: Company-sponsored foundation
Purpose: Scholarships to students for attendance or applying to qualified postsecondary educational institutions.
Financial data: Year ended 08/31/2012. Assets, $512,404 (M); Expenditures, $6,272; Total giving, $5,000.
Fields of interest: Higher education.
Type of support: Scholarships—to individuals.
Application information: Applications accepted. Application form required.
> *Deadline(s):* Spring
> *Additional information:* Application should include a personal statement and a resume. Selection is based on academic performance and financial need.
EIN: 202033108

7611
Mount Angel Community Foundation
P.O. Box 881
Mount Angel, OR 97362 (503) 845-6835
Contact: Lori Pavlicek, Pres.
FAX: (503) 845-6190;
E-mail: mtangelcommfnd@gmail.com; URL: http://www.mtangelcommfnd.org

Foundation type: Community foundation
Purpose: Scholarships to selected local students at John F. Kennedy High School, OR, for attendance at colleges or other schools of higher education.
Publications: Financial statement.
Financial data: Year ended 12/31/2011. Assets, $3,964,129 (M); Expenditures, $76,844; Total giving, $37,963; Grants to individuals, totaling $32,500.
Fields of interest: Higher education.
Type of support: Scholarships—to individuals; Support to graduates or students of specific schools; Undergraduate support.
Application information: Applications accepted.
> *Additional information:* Contact high school guidance counselor to request an application packet.
EIN: 931205915

7612
Marilyn Moyer Charitable Trust
805 S.W. Broadway, Ste. 934
Portland, OR 97205-3360 (503) 241-1111
Contact: Thomas Paul Moyer, Tr.

Foundation type: Independent foundation
Purpose: Grants to residents of Clark County, WA or Oregon for medical expenses not covered by insurance or social or governmental agencies, or for general humanitarian assistance.
Financial data: Year ended 07/31/2012. Assets, $1,741,643 (M); Expenditures, $14,494; Total giving, $0.
Fields of interest: Health care.
Type of support: Grants for special needs.
Application information: Applications accepted. Application form required.
> *Additional information:* Applicants must be legal residents for the past 18 months in Clark county, WA and/or Oregon.
EIN: 936238025

7613
Multnomah Athletic Foundation, Inc.
1849 S.W. Salmon St.
Portland, OR 97205-1726 (503) 223-6251
URL: http://www.themac.com/Default.aspx?p=DynamicModule&pageid=282086&ssid=158059&vnf=1

Foundation type: Public charity
Purpose: Scholarships to athletes residing in the Portland, OR, area for undergraduate education.
Financial data: Year ended 12/31/2011. Assets, $1,756,758 (M); Expenditures, $163,663; Total giving, $92,630; Grants to individuals, totaling $92,630.
Fields of interest: Higher education; Recreation.
Type of support: Awards/grants by nomination only; Undergraduate support.
Application information: Contact foundation for additional guidelines.
EIN: 931014651

7614
National Psoriasis Foundation, Inc.
6600 S.W. 92nd Ave., Ste. 300
Portland, OR 97223-7195 (503) 244-7404
Contact: Randy Beranek, Pres. and C.E.O.
FAX: (503) 245-0626;
E-mail: getinfo@psoriasis.org; Toll-free tel.: (800) 723-9166; URL: http://www.psoriasis.org/

Foundation type: Public charity
Purpose: Awards three $50,000 grants to support innovative psoriasis or psoriatic arthritis research projects in clinical research, genetics, or immunology.
Publications: Application guidelines.
Financial data: Year ended 06/30/2012. Assets, $7,453,451 (M); Expenditures, $7,669,219; Total giving, $1,661,989.
Fields of interest: Skin disorders; Skin disorders research.
Type of support: Research.
Application information: Applications accepted. Application form required.
> *Initial approach:* Letter
> *Deadline(s):* Oct. 16 for Seed Grants
> *Final notification:* Feb. 1 for Seed Grants
EIN: 930571472

7615
Neighborimpact
2303 S.W. 1st St.
Redmond, OR 97756-7133 (541) 548-2380
FAX: (541) 548-6013;
E-mail: info@neighborimpact.org; URL: http://www.neighborimpact.org/

Foundation type: Public charity
Purpose: Emergency assistance to low in-come individuals and families in need throughout central OR.
Financial data: Year ended 06/30/2011. Assets, $8,780,409 (M); Expenditures, $14,303,026; Total giving, $6,327,680; Grants to individuals, 8,373 grants totaling $3,535,609.
Fields of interest: Employment; Nutrition; Housing/shelter; Human services; Family services; Economically disadvantaged.
Type of support: Grants to individuals; In-kind gifts.
Application information: Contact the organization for eligibility determination.
EIN: 930884929

7616
Neskowin Coast Foundation
P.O. Box 65
Otis, OR 97368-0065 (541) 994-5485
FAX: (541) 994-8024; E-mail: info@sitkacenter.org; URL: http://www.sitkacenter.org

Foundation type: Public charity
Purpose: Residencies to visual artists, musicians, and naturalists.
Publications: Application guidelines.
Financial data: Year ended 12/31/2011. Assets, $2,756,306 (M); Expenditures, $453,817.
Fields of interest: Visual arts; Music; Environment.
Type of support: Residencies.
Application information: Applications accepted. Application form required. Application form available on the grantmaker's web site.
> *Send request by:* Mail
> *Deadline(s):* Apr. 22 for Artist and Environmental Scientist Program; Apr. 23 for Recorder Program Residencies
> *Final notification:* Applicants notified by May
> *Applicants should submit the following:*
> 1) Work samples
> 2) SASE
> 3) Letter(s) of recommendation
> 4) Resume
Program descriptions:
> *Artist and Environmental Scientist Program:* This program provides a residency opportunity for visual artists, writers, musicians, naturalists, ecologists, and environmental scientists who are emerging, mid-career, or professional. Up to seven residents at a time live and work on the campus for up to three-and-a-half months, free of charge. All residents are expected to perform community outreach during their stay, offer free exhibits and lectures on campus, present to area schools or community groups, and/or conduct scholarly research for local educational institutions.
> *Recorder Program Residencies:* Residencies, lasting from four to six weeks, are available to recorder players. Applicants are required to demonstrate that they have earned (or presently earn) part of their income from recorder performance or composition; individuals on all sides of the professional spectrum are welcome if they fit the above requirement.
EIN: 237087718

7617
North Coast Scholarship Foundation
8805 S.W. Woodside Dr.
Portland, OR 97225-1745

Foundation type: Independent foundation
Purpose: Scholarships to students for higher education who reside in the north coast of OR.
Financial data: Year ended 12/31/2012. Assets, $462,082 (M); Expenditures, $54,943; Total giving, $43,844.
Type of support: Scholarships—to individuals; Undergraduate support.
Application information: Contact foundation for current program information and guidelines.
EIN: 201930677

7618
Northwest Children's Outreach
P.O. Box 1604
Lake Oswego, OR 97035-0562 (503) 828-1472
Contact: Debbie Sherwood, Pres.
E-mail: info@northwestchildrensoutreach.org;
Additional address (Washington office): 6615 E. Mill Plain, Vancouver, WA 98661-7457, tel.: (360) 576-8024, email: vancouver@northwestchildrensoutreach.org;
URL: http://www.northwestchildrensoutreach.org

Foundation type: Public charity
Purpose: Provides clothing, infant care products, diapers, formula and many of the other necessities indigent parents need for their children in the greater Portland metropolitan area, OR.
Financial data: Year ended 12/31/2011. Assets, $508,365 (M); Expenditures, $2,684,935; Total giving, $2,641,978; Grants to individuals, totaling $2,641,978.
Fields of interest: Economically disadvantaged.
Type of support: In-kind gifts.
Application information:
   Initial approach: Letter
   Additional information: Contact the organization for eligibility criteria.
EIN: 931315508

7619
Northwest Health Foundation
(formerly Northwest Health Foundation (Fund 1))
221 N.W. 2nd Ave., Ste. 300
Portland, OR 97209-3961 (503) 220-1955
Contact: Nichole Maher M.P.H., Pres.
FAX: (503) 220-1335; E-mail: nwhf@nwhf.org;
URL: http://www.northwesthealth.org

Foundation type: Public charity
Purpose: Grants to students in OR, or Clark, Cowlitz, Pacific, Skamania and Wahkiakum counties in WA, to engage in research related to health and medicine. Fellowships to advance the research careers of health practitioners who serve communities in OR and southwest WA.
Publications: Application guidelines; Annual report; Grants list; Newsletter.
Financial data: Year ended 12/31/2011. Assets, $50,599,877 (M); Expenditures, $3,421,727; Total giving, $1,704,006.
Fields of interest: Research; Health care.
Type of support: Fellowships; Research.
Application information: Applications accepted. Application form required. Application form available on the grantmaker's web site.
   Initial approach: E-mail
   Deadline(s): Apr. 24 for Fellowships
   Applicants should submit the following:
      1) Transcripts

2) Resume
3) Letter(s) of recommendation
4) Essay
5) Budget Information
6) Curriculum vitae
Additional information: Contact foundation for application guidelines.
EIN: 911854545

7620
Northwest Osteopathic Medical Foundation
1327 S.E. Tacoma St., Ste. 326
Portland, OR 97202 (503) 222-7161
Contact: David Tate, Exec. Dir.
FAX: (503) 222-2841; E-mail: rosch@nwosteo.org;
Toll-free tel.: (888) 696-7836; E-mail for David Tate: tate@nwosteo.org; URL: http://www.nwosteo.org

Foundation type: Public charity
Purpose: Scholarships and grants to students and professionals residing in AK, ID, MT, OR or WA in the area of osteopathic medicine.
Publications: Application guidelines; Grants list; Informational brochure (including application guidelines); Newsletter.
Financial data: Year ended 12/31/2011. Assets, $5,556,137 (M); Expenditures, $387,663; Total giving, $115,100; Grants to individuals, totaling $94,100.
Fields of interest: Medical school/education; Medical specialties.
Type of support: Program development; Research; Grants to individuals; Graduate support; Doctoral support.
Application information:
   Deadline(s): Apr. 15 for Osteopathic Medical Student Scholarship Program
   Applicants should submit the following:
      1) Essay
      2) Letter(s) of recommendation
      3) Transcripts
      4) Resume
Program description:
   Osteopathic Medical Student Scholarship Program: This program helps defray the cost of osteopathic medical school for students committed to practicing medicine in the Northwest (Alaska, Idaho, Montana, Oregon, and Washington). Eligible applicants must be enrolled in an American Osteopathic Association-approved school. The foundation anticipates that scholarship recipients, upon completion of their medical education, will practice in the Pacific Northwest.
EIN: 930882138

7621
Oapa Scholarship Foundation
1804 N.E. 43rd Ave.
Portland, OR 97213

Foundation type: Operating foundation
Purpose: Scholarships to residents of OR who are majoring in accounting at OR schools.
Financial data: Year ended 06/30/2012. Assets, $258,755 (M); Expenditures, $6,778; Total giving, $6,500; Grants to individuals, 5 grants totaling $6,500 (high: $1,500, low: $500).
Fields of interest: Vocational education; Business school/education; Business/industry.
Type of support: Undergraduate support.
Application information: Applications accepted. Application form required.
   Initial approach: Letter
   Deadline(s): Apr. 1

Additional information: Contact foundation for current application guidelines.
EIN: 930765047

7622
Ochoco Charitable Fund
(formerly Ochoco Scholarship Fund)
P.O. Box 668
Prineville, OR 97754-0668 (541) 416-6900

Foundation type: Company-sponsored foundation
Purpose: Scholarships to graduating students of Crook County High School, OR for higher education at colleges or universities.
Financial data: Year ended 12/31/2011. Assets, $404,609 (M); Expenditures, $31,756; Total giving, $30,800; Grants to individuals, 43 grants totaling $30,800 (high: $1,200, low: $100).
Fields of interest: Higher education.
Type of support: Undergraduate support.
Application information: Applications accepted. Application form not required.
   Initial approach: Letter
   Deadline(s): Varies
   Additional information: Application should include GPA, name of college attended and credit hours. Recipients are selected on the basis of academic standing, financial need, character, personality, and social adjustment. Grants are not usually given for the first college semester. Exceptions are made in cases where the applicant has shown marked ability in high school and is financially unable to enter college without a grant.
EIN: 936024017

7623
Oregon Coast Community Action
(formerly Southwestern Oregon Community)
2110 Newmark Ave.
P.O. Box 899
Coos Bay, OR 97420-2957 (541) 435-7080
Contact: Patricia Gouveia, C.E.O.
FAX: (541) 888-7015; URL: http://www.orcca.us

Foundation type: Public charity
Purpose: Assistance to low-income individuals and families of Coos and Curry counties, OR to become more stable and self-reliant. Food, clothes and housing provided to indigent people.
Publications: Annual report.
Financial data: Year ended 06/30/2011. Assets, $5,211,727 (M); Expenditures, $9,734,157; Total giving, $1,745,888; Grants to individuals, totaling $1,745,888.
Fields of interest: Economically disadvantaged.
Type of support: In-kind gifts; Grants for special needs.
Application information: Applications accepted.
   Additional information: Contact the agency for eligibility determination.
EIN: 930547036

7624
The Oregon Community Foundation
(also known as OCF)
1221 S.W. Yamhill, Ste. 100
Portland, OR 97205-2108 (503) 227-6846
Contact: Megan Schumaker, Prog. Off., Community Grants and Funds
FAX: (503) 274-7771;
E-mail: mschumaker@oregoncf.org; URL: http://www.oregoncf.org

Foundation type: Community foundation

Purpose: Scholarships to students attending specific schools in OR, scholarships to residents of OR and WA for postsecondary education and vocational training, and company-related scholarships to OR residents.
Publications: Application guidelines; Annual report; Newsletter.
Financial data: Year ended 12/31/2013. Assets, $1,698,892,336 (M); Expenditures, $78,143,749; Total giving, $66,052,201.
Fields of interest: Vocational education; Higher education; Graduate/professional education; Scholarships/financial aid.
Type of support: Scholarships—to individuals; Support to graduates or students of specific schools; Undergraduate support.
Application information: Applications accepted. Application form required. Application form available on the grantmaker's web site. Interview required.
  Deadline(s): Mar. 1
  Additional information: Application should include FAFSA.
Program description:
  Scholarship Funds: The foundation's scholarships originate from more than 300 separate funds at OCF established by individual donors and families, schools, civic organizations and employers. Students can find scholarships to help them continue their education in almost any setting, public or private, in Oregon or out of state. Awards range from $200 to $10,000. See web site to view the list of scholarships, www.oregonstudentaid.gov.
EIN: 237315673

7625
Oregon Jewish Community Foundation
(also known as OJCF)
610 S.W. Broadway, Ste. 407
Portland, OR 97205-3431 (503) 248-9328
Contact: Julie Diamond, Exec. Dir.
FAX: (503) 248-9323; E-mail: julie@ojcf.org; URL: http://www.ojcf.org

Foundation type: Public charity
Purpose: Scholarship for higher education and campership for Jewish residents of Oregon.
Publications: Annual report; Informational brochure.
Financial data: Year ended 06/30/2012. Assets, $50,429,928 (M); Expenditures, $2,729,088; Total giving, $2,136,195; Grants to individuals, totaling $85,900.
Fields of interest: Higher education; Jewish agencies & synagogues.
Type of support: Scholarships—to individuals.
Application information: Applications accepted. Application form required. Application form available on the grantmaker's web site.
  Send request by: Mail
  Deadline(s): Mar. 1
  Applicants should submit the following:
    1) Essay
    2) Letter(s) of recommendation
    3) Transcripts
    4) Financial information
  Additional information: Application should also include a copy of you/your parents' income tax return. Scholarship funds are mailed directly to the educational institution on behalf of the student.
Program descriptions:
  Albert J. Kailes College Scholarship: This scholarship is for Jewish students in OR to attend a college or university located within the state of OR. The scholarship does not provide scholarships

for graduate school. Applicant must be a Jewish resident of OR and demonstrate financial need. Only partial scholarships are awarded. The typical award is $1,000.
  Arthur P. Krichevsky Memorial Scholarship: The scholarship was established for the purpose of furthering Jewish education. Consideration will be given to applicants of Jewish Day Schools in Portland, OR (grades 1 and above), Board of Rabbis Teen Israel Experience program, for students pursuing post high school Jewish education through qualified programs offered by accredited educational institutions in the U.S. Greater consideration is given to applicants showing the highest level of commitment to Jewish study, community service and/or outreach. This scholarship does not fund Israel experience trips outside the Oregon Board of Rabbis Teen Isreal Experience Program.
  Rebecca and Sada Tarshis Memorial Scholarship: This scholarship provides tuition assistance to Jewish students for higher education, including college, university and/or graduate school, on the basis of financial need with scholarships of up to $5,000 per recipient per year. The typical award is $1,000. The scholarship does not provide funding for overseas trip or overseas study. Applicant must be a Jewish resident of OR and demonstrate financial need.
EIN: 931019725

7626
Oregon Technical Development Foundation
(also known as Oregon Tech Foundation)
3201 Campus Dr.
Klamath Falls, OR 97601-8801 (541) 885-1130
Additional tel.: (541) 885-1280,
e-mail: scholarships@oit.edu
FAX: (541) 885-1148; E-mail: giving@oit.edu

Foundation type: Public charity
Purpose: Scholarships and student loans to new or enrolled students of Oregon Institute of Technology.
Financial data: Year ended 06/30/2012. Assets, $21,147,019 (M); Expenditures, $1,630,761.
Fields of interest: Higher education.
Type of support: Scholarships—to individuals; Student loans—to individuals.
Application information: Applications accepted. Application form required.
  Deadline(s): Feb. 1
EIN: 237056213

7627
Pacific Northwest Kiwanis Foundation
10184 S.W. Laurel Rd.
Beaverton, OR 97005-3211 (503) 698-8151
FAX: (509) 453-7899;
E-mail: gehcqc@boughton.ca; E-Mail for Jewell Bailey: jewellbailey@comcast.net; URL: http://www.pnwkiwanisfoundation.org

Foundation type: Public charity
Purpose: Scholarships to individuals for higher education.
Publications: Annual report.
Financial data: Year ended 09/30/2011. Assets, $683,179 (M); Expenditures, $46,999; Total giving, $29,232.
Type of support: Scholarships—to individuals.
Application information: Applications accepted. Application form required. Application form available on the grantmaker's web site.
  Deadline(s): Before high school graduation

Additional information: See web site for complete application guidelines.
EIN: 930900103

7628
Pacific Office Automation Charitable Foundation
14747 N.W. Greenbrier Pkwy.
Beaverton, OR 97006-5601

Foundation type: Company-sponsored foundation
Purpose: Scholarships to customers of Pacific Office Automation, who reside in Portland, OR.
Financial data: Year ended 12/31/2011. Assets, $0 (M); Expenditures, $22,120; Total giving, $22,110; Grants to individuals, 6 grants totaling $22,110 (high: $5,000, low: $110).
Type of support: Undergraduate support.
Application information: Applications not accepted.
  Additional information: Unsolicited requests for funds not considered or acknowledged.
EIN: 931283813

7629
Marvin O. Palmer Trust
P.O. Box 3168
Portland, OR 97208

Foundation type: Independent foundation
Purpose: Scholarships to deserving graduates of Park High School, MT, for higher education.
Financial data: Year ended 12/31/2012. Assets, $877,124 (M); Expenditures, $11,836; Total giving, $0.
Type of support: Support to graduates or students of specific schools; Undergraduate support.
Application information: Contact trust for current application deadline/guidelines.
EIN: 816079218

7630
Pass It on Foundation
711 Medford Ctr., Ste.126
Medford, OR 97504

Foundation type: Independent foundation
Purpose: Grants to needy residents of OR, primarily to pay for medical expenses.
Financial data: Year ended 10/31/2012. Assets, $124,392 (M); Expenditures, $37,369; Total giving, $33,804.
Fields of interest: Economically disadvantaged.
Type of support: Grants for special needs.
Application information: Applications not accepted.
  Additional information: Unsolicited requests for funds not considered or acknowledged.
EIN: 900130023

7631
Henry S. Pernot Scholarship Fund
P.O. Box 3168
Portland, OR 97208-3168 (503) 275-5923
Contact: Rebecca Bibleheimer

Foundation type: Independent foundation
Purpose: Scholarships by nomination only to medical students who have completed their first two years at the Oregon Health Sciences University.
Financial data: Year ended 06/30/2013. Assets, $330,868 (M); Expenditures, $24,040; Total giving, $16,000.

Fields of interest: Medical school/education.
Type of support: Scholarships—to individuals; Support to graduates or students of specific schools; Awards/grants by nomination only; Graduate support.
Application information: Applications not accepted.
  Additional information: Students are preselected by the Dean of the Oregon Health Sciences University; The trustee bank then makes the final selection and determines the amount of each scholarship.
  EIN: 237385854

7632
Portland Institute for Contemporary Art
415 SW. 10th Ave., Ste. 300
Portland, OR 97205 (503) 242-1419
Contact: Victoria Frey, Exec. Dir.; Erin Boberg Doughton, Dir, Performing Arts Prog.
FAX: (503) 243-1167; E-mail: pica@pica.org; E-mail for Erin Boberg: erin@pica.org; URL: http://www.pica.org

Foundation type: Public charity
Purpose: Six residencies are available each year to provide artists with materials and working space during a development stage in making a new project.
Publications: Newsletter.
Financial data: Year ended 12/31/2011. Assets, $864,986 (M); Expenditures, $1,080,088.
Fields of interest: Visual arts.
Type of support: Residencies.
Application information: Applications accepted. Application form not required.
  Initial approach: Letter
  Send request by: Mail
  Deadline(s): None
  Applicants should submit the following:
    1) Resume
    2) Work samples
    3) SASE
  Additional information: Application should also include biographic materials, work description, and invitations to upcoming shows.
  EIN: 931177971

7633
Portland Rotary Charitable Trust
619 S.W. 11th Ave., Ste. 123
Portland, OR 97205-2604 (503) 228-1542
Contact: Eric Lochner, Pres.
Application address: c/o Philip Levinson, 7200 SE 34th Ave., Portland, OR 97202, e-mail: pjl4825@comcast.net
FAX: (503) 226-7048; E-mail: info@rotarypdx.org; URL: http://www.rotarypdx.org

Foundation type: Public charity
Purpose: Sponsored scholarships for youth exchange program for high school students of Portland, OR to spend up to a year living with families and attending school in a different country.
Publications: Application guidelines; Informational brochure; Newsletter.
Financial data: Year ended 06/30/2012. Assets, $1,965,268 (M); Expenditures, $232,388; Total giving, $177,229; Grants to individuals, totaling $38,696.
Fields of interest: Higher education.
Type of support: Scholarships—to individuals; Exchange programs.
Application information: Applications accepted. Application form required. Application form

available on the grantmaker's web site. Interview required.
  Initial approach: Telephone
  Send request by: Mail or e-mail
  Deadline(s): Apr. for preliminary application, Oct. for final application
  Additional information: Application should include an essay. Applicants do not have to come from a family in which there is a Rotary member. Everyone is welcome to apply. See web site for additional application guidelines.
  EIN: 936031284

7634
Portland Valley Acacia Fund, Inc.
(formerly Scottish Rite Oregon Consistory Almoner Fund, Inc.)
709 S.W. 15th Ave.
Portland, OR 97205 (503) 226-7827
Contact: Ronald Eggers, Secy.-Treas.

Foundation type: Independent foundation
Purpose: Relief assistance with medical, hospital, or emergency sustenance to distressed Masons, their widows and orphans, and other worthy recipients living in the state of OR.
Financial data: Year ended 12/31/2011. Assets, $436,550 (M); Expenditures, $35,997; Total giving, $15,949; Grants to individuals, totaling $3,200.
Fields of interest: Health care; Human services; Economically disadvantaged.
Type of support: Grants for special needs.
Application information: Applications accepted.
  Initial approach: Letter
  Deadline(s): None
  Additional information: Letter must state why funds are needed.
  EIN: 237154746

7635
Professional Engineers of Oregon Educational Foundation
86 S.W. Century Dr., Ste. 353
Bend, OR 97702

Foundation type: Independent foundation
Purpose: Scholarships for students studying engineering at Portland State University, Oregon State University, and the University of Portland, all in OR.
Financial data: Year ended 12/31/2012. Assets, $84,622 (M); Expenditures, $2,612; Total giving, $0.
Fields of interest: Engineering school/education.
Type of support: Support to graduates or students of specific schools; Undergraduate support.
Application information:
  Initial approach: Letter
  Deadline(s): Spring
  EIN: 930666849

7636
Providence Community Health Foundation
1111 Crater Lake Ave.
Medford, OR 97504-5730 (541) 893-6460
Contact: Jodi Barnard, Exec. Dir.
FAX: (541) 772-2861;
E-mail: jodi.barnard@providence.org; URL: http://oregon.providence.org/patients/programs/

Foundation type: Public charity

Purpose: Scholarship and educational assistance to nursing students pursuing their study in the field of nursing.
Financial data: Year ended 12/31/2012. Assets, $7,010,864 (M); Expenditures, $980,504; Total giving, $634,085; Grants to individuals, totaling $9,250.
Fields of interest: Nursing school/education.
Type of support: Scholarships—to individuals.
Application information: Applications accepted.
  Additional information: Scholarships are granted based on need.
  EIN: 930692907

7637
Providence Milwaukie Foundation
10150 S.E. 32nd
Milwaukie, OR 97222-6516 (503) 513-8325
Contact: Lesley Townsend, Exec. Dir.
URL: http://oregon.providence.org/patients/programs/providence-milwaukie-foundation/Pages/default.aspx

Foundation type: Public charity
Purpose: Prenatal education, medical care and social services to low income pregnant women of the Portland, OR metro area. Also offered are childhood immunizations, youth sports physicals, health screenings, fall prevention clinics and mammograms to indigent residents of the Clackamas County area.
Financial data: Year ended 12/31/2011. Assets, $3,036,982 (M); Expenditures, $593,235; Total giving, $403,284.
Fields of interest: Medical care, community health systems; Health care; Health care, patient services.
Type of support: In-kind gifts.
Application information:
  Initial approach: Letter
  Additional information: Contact foundation for eligibility criteria.
  EIN: 943079515

7638
Providence Newberg Health Foundation
1001 Providence Dr.
Newberg, OR 97132-0610 (503) 537-1671
Contact: Sandra Jordan, Fdn. Asst.
FAX: (503) 537-1814;
E-mail: sandra.jordan@providence.org; URL: http://www.providencefoundations.org/foundations/our-foundations/providence-newberg-health-foundation/pages/default.aspx

Foundation type: Public charity
Purpose: Grants to needy individuals in the Newberg, OR, area.
Financial data: Year ended 12/31/2011. Assets, $1,196,855 (M); Expenditures, $578,531; Total giving, $357,739.
Fields of interest: Economically disadvantaged.
Type of support: Grants for special needs.
Application information: Contact foundation for eligibility information.
  EIN: 930889144

7639
Providence Portland Medical Foundation
4805 N.E. Glisan St.
Portland, OR 97213-2967 (503) 215-7387
FAX: (503) 215-0530;
E-mail: kelly.buechler@providence.org; URL: http://

oregon.providence.org/patients/programs/ providence-portland-medical-foundation/Pages/ default.aspx

Foundation type: Public charity
Purpose: Financial assistance to uninsured patients residing in Portland, OR, for payment of medical bills.
Publications: Annual report.
Financial data: Year ended 12/31/2011. Assets, $48,991,478 (M); Expenditures, $6,409,900; Total giving, $5,775,358; Grants to individuals, totaling $3,750.
Type of support: Grants for special needs.
Application information: Applications accepted. Application form required.
    Initial approach: Letter
    Additional information: Contact foundation for eligibility requirements. Applications must include financial information.
EIN: 931231494

7640
Robert L. Ragel Scholarship Fund
c/o Nikki C. Hatton
1211 S.W. 5th Ave., Ste. 1900
Portland, OR 97204-3795

Foundation type: Independent foundation
Purpose: Scholarships to graduates of Tigard High School, OR, for higher education.
Financial data: Year ended 12/31/2011. Assets, $1,371,244 (M); Expenditures, $50,893; Total giving, $45,834; Grants to individuals, 4 grants totaling $45,834 (high: $20,836, low: $4,166).
Type of support: Support to graduates or students of specific schools; Undergraduate support.
Application information: Application form required.
    Deadline(s): Feb. 1
    Additional information: Applications available from Tigard High School guidance counselors.
EIN: 931254085

7641
Regional Arts and Culture Council
411 N.W. Park Ave., Ste. 101
Portland, OR 97209-3356 (503) 823-5111
Contact: Eloise Damrosch, Exec. Dir.; Fellowships: Lorin Schmit Dunlop
FAX: (503) 823-5432; E-mail: info@racc.org; Fellowships contact tel.: (503) 823-5402, TDD: (503) 823-6868, e-mail: hdaltoso@racc.org; E-mail For Eloise Damrosch: edamrosch@racc.org; URL: http://www.racc.org

Foundation type: Public charity
Purpose: Project grants, fellowships, and professional development grants to artists residing in Clackamas, Multnomah, and Washington counties, OR.
Publications: Application guidelines; Annual report; Informational brochure; Newsletter; Occasional report.
Financial data: Year ended 06/30/2012. Assets, $6,076,936 (M); Expenditures, $7,534,970; Total giving, $2,621,268; Grants to individuals, totaling $451,016.
Fields of interest: Management/technical assistance; Administration/regulation; Media/ communications; Literature; Arts.
Type of support: Program development; Fellowships.
Application information: Applications accepted. Application form required. Application form available on the grantmaker's web site.

Initial approach: Telephone or e-mail
Deadline(s): Varies
Applicants should submit the following:
    1) Work samples
    2) Financial information
    3) Resume
    4) Letter(s) of recommendation
    5) Budget Information
    6) Proposal
Program descriptions:
    Arts Education Fast Track Grants: This program provides funds to private and public schools in Multnomah, Clackamas, and Washington counties to help defray the costs of bring high-quality professional artists or arts organizations into the classroom. grants are awarded for up to $1,000 or half of the total costs (whichever is less)
    Individual Artist Fellowships: Fellowships of up to $20,000 are available to recognize regionally-based individual artistic achievement and excellence, and allows individual artists of high merit to sustain and/or enhance their creative process. Awards are given in three categories (performing arts, visual arts, and media arts/ literature)Eligible applicants must: be a professional artist, as recognized by his/her peers, with a minimum of ten years in the discipline for which they are applying; have been a resident of Oregon for a minimum of five years, and currently be a resident of Clackamas, Multnomah, or Washington counties; have been active on a regular basis in the tri-county area through presenting, performing, or offering arts-related opportunities to area citizens; and be a recognized artist within the general discipline category for which fellowships are being offered in the current fiscal year.
    Professional Development Grants: These grants are intended to assist artists and arts administrators (based in Clackamas, Multnomah, and Washington counties) with opportunities that specifically improve their business management development skills, and/or brings the artist or arts organization to another level artistically. Proposals cannot be geared toward the creation of a specific art project, but must clearly demonstrate how the proposal will benefit the organization or individual in the long term.
    Project Grants: The council provides grants of up to $6,000 to organizations and individuals based in Multnomah, Washington, and Clackamas counties. Applicants must propose a specific art presentation, exhibit, or creating of work that is fully-executed within a specific timeline and contains a public component. Funding is available in three categories: artistic focus (project grants that demonstrate high artistic quality, innovation, creativity in programming and artist selection, and demonstrated ability by the artist or organization); community participation (project grants that support cultural and arts programs and services that involve direct community participation); and arts-in-schools (project grants that encourage and enable members of the professional arts community to work in schools and create arts-rich learning environments)
EIN: 931059037

7642
The Renaissance Foundation
(formerly The Levin Family Foundation)
P.O. Box 80516
Portland, OR 97280-1516
Application address: Renaissance Scholarship Applications, Attn: The Renaissance Foundation, 8405 SW Nimbus Ave., Ste. D, Beaverton, OR

97008, tel.: (971) 722-6119,
e-mail: josh.laurie@pcc.edu
URL: http://www.trfwebsite.org

Foundation type: Independent foundation
Purpose: Renewable scholarships to first generation incoming students of Portland, OR, who demonstrate financial need, a passion for their field of study, and who have shown academic achievement.
Publications: Application guidelines.
Financial data: Year ended 12/31/2012. Assets, $12,705,564 (M); Expenditures, $670,570; Total giving, $589,400. Scholarships—to individuals amount not specified.
Fields of interest: College; University.
Type of support: Scholarships—to individuals; Support to graduates or students of specific schools; Undergraduate support.
Application information: Applications accepted. Application form required. Application form available on the grantmaker's web site.
    Send request by: Mail
    Deadline(s): June
    Applicants should submit the following:
        1) Essay
        2) Transcripts
        3) Letter(s) of recommendation
    Additional information: See web site for additional application guidelines. Scholarships are paid directly to the educational institution on behalf of the students.
EIN: 931306116

7643
Ward Rhoden Athletic Scholarship Fund
2850 N.W. Lon Smith Rd.
Prineville, OR 97754-0460
Contact: Russell Rhoden, Dir.

Foundation type: Independent foundation
Purpose: Scholarships to graduates of Crook County High School, OR who have demonstrated interest and ability in athletics by participating in two major sports in high school for four years.
Financial data: Year ended 12/31/2012. Assets, $112,966 (M); Expenditures, $8,146; Total giving, $7,200; Grants to individuals, 10 grants totaling $7,200 (high: $1,500, low: $400).
Fields of interest: Higher education.
Type of support: Scholarships—to individuals; Support to graduates or students of specific schools.
Application information: Applications accepted. Application form required.
    Deadline(s): Apr. 30
    Applicants should submit the following:
        1) Photograph
        2) Transcripts
        3) Financial information
    Additional information: Recipients will not be required to continue athletic participation in college as a requirement for the acceptance or continuation of this scholarship.
EIN: 237067165

7644
Bob Richardson Memorial Trust
P.O. Box 3168
Portland, OR 97208 (503) 336-5104

Foundation type: Independent foundation
Purpose: Scholarships to worthy students of the city of Toledo, OR, and Lincoln County, OR for

continuing education at institutions of higher learning.
Financial data: Year ended 06/30/2013. Assets, $2,681,673 (M); Expenditures, $177,132; Total giving, $119,000.
Type of support: Scholarships—to individuals.
Application information: Contact trust for current application guidelines.
EIN: 943101770

7645
Richmond Educational Foundation
P.O. Box 518
Phoenix, OR 97535-0518 (760) 445-0651
Contact: James L. Richmond, Tr.
Lois Richmondtel.:(760) 445-0651

Foundation type: Operating foundation
Purpose: Scholarships to high school graduates for continuing education at institutions of higher learning.
Financial data: Year ended 12/31/2011. Assets, $254,596 (M); Expenditures, $60,548; Total giving, $12,149.
Fields of interest: Higher education.
Type of support: Scholarships—to individuals.
Application information: Application form required.
Initial approach: Letter
Deadline(s): Apr. 15
Applicants should submit the following:
1) Letter(s) of recommendation
2) Transcripts
Additional information: Recipients must be willing to work part-time and/or take out student loans in their name. Scholarships will not be renewed for recipients who do not work (after their first semester) unless they notify the selection committee in writing, or there are extenuating circumstances prevent their employment.
EIN: 330638221

7646
Carl and Camilla Rietman Charitable Foundation
P.O. Box D
Lakeside, OR 97449-0803
Scholarship application address: c/o Alfred C. Walsh, Jr., 280 N. Collier, Coquille, OR 97423, tel.: (541) 396-2169

Foundation type: Independent foundation
Purpose: College scholarships to graduates and former students of Coquille High School, OR for attendance at any accredited postsecondary institution.
Financial data: Year ended 09/30/2013. Assets, $6,117,195 (M); Expenditures, $351,286; Total giving, $279,200; Grants to individuals, 70 grants totaling $174,500 (high: $2,500, low: $2,500).
Fields of interest: Higher education.
Type of support: Scholarships—to individuals; Support to graduates or students of specific schools.
Application information: Application form required.
Deadline(s): Apr. 15
Additional information: Application must include references. Financial need is a consideration but not the determining factor in selection.
EIN: 931221623

7647
Jessie May Riggs Student Scholarship Fund
(formerly Riggs Student Scholarship Fund)
P.O. Box 3168
Portland, OR 97208-3168 (503) 275-5923

Foundation type: Independent foundation
Purpose: Scholarships to graduating students of Tillamook High School, Tillamook, OR for higher education at accredited colleges, universities, or vocational/trade schools.
Financial data: Year ended 07/31/2013. Assets, $576,653 (M); Expenditures, $42,580; Total giving, $29,792.
Fields of interest: Higher education.
Type of support: Support to graduates or students of specific schools.
Application information: Application form required.
Deadline(s): Apr. 20
Applicants should submit the following:
1) ACT
2) Transcripts
3) SAT
4) Letter(s) of recommendation
5) Essay
Additional information: Applicant must also include a parent or guardian's most recent completed tax form, a letter of reference from a non-family member addressing the applicant's attitude and character.
EIN: 916565775

7648
Wayne Rinne Memorial Trust
P.O. Box 1030
Astoria, OR 97103-1030
Application address: c/o Neil Branson, 1901 N. Holladay Dr., Seaside, OR 97138-7219, tel.: (503) 738-5589

Foundation type: Independent foundation
Purpose: Scholarships to graduates of Seaside High School, Seaside, OR for higher education at accredited colleges or universities.
Financial data: Year ended 12/31/2011. Assets, $132,771 (M); Expenditures, $2,571; Total giving, $2,500.
Fields of interest: Higher education.
Type of support: Support to graduates or students of specific schools.
Application information: Applications accepted.
Deadline(s): May 1
EIN: 936267824

7649
The Dorothy and Robert Ryan Charitable Foundation
111 S.W. Columbia St.
Portland, OR 97201-5806 (503) 225-1612

Foundation type: Independent foundation
Purpose: Scholarships to individuals of Vancouver, WA, for higher education.
Financial data: Year ended 12/31/2011. Assets, $0 (M); Expenditures, $1,250; Total giving, $500.
Type of support: Undergraduate support.
Application information: Applications not accepted.
Additional information: Contributes only to preselected individuals.
EIN: 911837467

7650
The Salem Foundation
c/o Pioneer Trust Bank, N.A.
P.O. Box 2305
Salem, OR 97308-2305 (503) 363-3136
Contact: Carol Herman, Trust Off.
E-mail: salemfoundation@pioneertrustbank.com;
URL: http://www.salemfoundation.org

Foundation type: Community foundation
Purpose: Scholarships to local students for undergraduate support who live in the Salem, OR, area.
Publications: Application guidelines; Financial statement; Grants list; Informational brochure.
Financial data: Year ended 04/30/2013. Assets, $20,827,737 (M); Expenditures, $1,290,418; Total giving, $1,029,467; Grants to individuals, 22 grants totaling $7,752.
Type of support: Undergraduate support.
Application information: Applications not accepted.
EIN: 936018523

7651
Salem Hospital Foundation
890 Oak St. S.E.
Salem, OR 97301-3905 (503) 561-5576
FAX: (503) 561-4836; E-mail for Greta Mauze: greta.mauze@salemhealth.org.org; tel. for Greta Mauze: (503) 561-5576; URL: http://www.salemhealth.org/foundation/

Foundation type: Public charity
Purpose: Scholarships to individuals residing in Marion, Polk or Yamhill counties, OR, for undergraduate education in a field of healthcare study.
Publications: Application guidelines; Annual report.
Financial data: Year ended 09/30/2011. Assets, $7,964,385 (M); Expenditures, $1,918,115; Total giving, $1,526,082; Grants to individuals, totaling $253,010.
Fields of interest: Health sciences school/education.
Type of support: Undergraduate support.
Application information: Application form required. Application form available on the grantmaker's web site.
Deadline(s): Varies
Applicants should submit the following:
1) Transcripts
2) Resume
3) Letter(s) of recommendation
Additional information: Application must also include a one-page narrative.
Program description:
Scholarships: The foundation provides scholarships to students in medically-related fields of study. Applicants must be a resident of Marion, Polk, or Yamhill counties, and must have applied to a college in their field of healthcare study before applying for the scholarship.
EIN: 237002687

7652
Carl & Mabel Schafer Scholarship Fund
P.O. Box 3168
Portland, OR 97208 (360) 690-0387
Application address: U.S. Bank, 1613 Broadway, Vancouver, WA 98660

Foundation type: Independent foundation
Purpose: Scholarships to graduates of Montesano High School, WA.

Financial data: Year ended 05/31/2012. Assets, $0 (M); Expenditures, $10,802; Total giving, $5,477.
Type of support: Support to graduates or students of specific schools; Undergraduate support.
Application information: Applications accepted. Application form required.
  Initial approach: Letter
  Additional information: Contact high school guidance counselor for application.
EIN: 916023084

7653
Dr. Sam and Cheryl Scheinberg Foundation
1900 S.W. River Dr. 1002 N.
Portland, OR 97201

Foundation type: Independent foundation
Purpose: Scholarships to residents of the Portland, OR area.
Financial data: Year ended 12/31/2012. Assets, $305 (M); Expenditures, $2,678; Total giving, $0.
Type of support: Undergraduate support.
Application information: Applications not accepted.
  Additional information: Unsolicited requests for funds not considered or acknowledged.
EIN: 205490757

7654
Schilling Family Scholarship Fund
(also known as Schilling Family Foundation)
P.O. Box 3168
Portland, OR 97208 (406) 533-2500
Application address: c/o Scholarship Selection Comm., Butte High School, 401 S. Wyoming St., Butte, MT 59701

Foundation type: Independent foundation
Purpose: Scholarships to graduates of Butte High School, MT, who have at least a 3.25 GPA and are full-time students.
Financial data: Year ended 03/31/2013. Assets, $395,048 (M); Expenditures, $25,809; Total giving, $12,000.
Type of support: Support to graduates or students of specific schools; Undergraduate support.
Application information: Application form required.
  Deadline(s): Contact foundation for current application deadline
EIN: 816067894

7655
Walter C. and Marie C. Schmidt Foundation
P.O. Box 3168
Portland, OR 97208-3168 (800) 452-8807

Foundation type: Independent foundation
Purpose: Scholarships to Lane county, OR residents enrolled to become a registered nurse and intend to pursue a career in geriatric health care.
Financial data: Year ended 06/30/2013. Assets, $521,808 (M); Expenditures, $39,963; Total giving, $23,000.
Fields of interest: Nursing school/education; Gerontology.
Type of support: Scholarships—to individuals.
Application information: Applications accepted.

Additional information: Application must include an essay and applicant must be enrolled at least half time.
EIN: 936267092

7656
J.P. and Maude V. Schroeder Memorial Trust
P.O. Box 3168
Portland, OR 97208 (509) 353-7089
Application address: U.S. Bank, P.O. Box 3588, Spokane, WA 99220

Foundation type: Independent foundation
Purpose: Scholarships to graduating high school seniors who are residents of Grant County, WA.
Financial data: Year ended 12/31/2012. Assets, $937,737 (M); Expenditures, $51,025; Total giving, $29,615.
Type of support: Scholarships—to individuals.
Application information: Applications accepted. Application form required.
  Deadline(s): May 1
  Applicants should submit the following:
    1) Transcripts
    2) Letter(s) of recommendation
EIN: 916306402

7657
SCIO District 95-C Scholarships, Inc.
38875 N.W. 1st Ave.
Scio, OR 97374 (503) 394-3276
Contact: Joy Berg

Foundation type: Independent foundation
Purpose: Scholarships to graduating seniors of Scio High School for attendance at accredited colleges or universities.
Financial data: Year ended 06/30/2013. Assets, $276,811 (M); Expenditures, $14,450; Total giving, $8,500.
Fields of interest: Higher education.
Type of support: Support to graduates or students of specific schools.
Application information: Applications accepted. Application form required. Interview required.
  Deadline(s): May 15
  Applicants should submit the following:
    1) Class rank
    2) Transcripts
    3) SAT
    4) Letter(s) of recommendation
    5) GPA
    6) ACT
EIN: 931091492

7658
John M. Shank Memorial Scholarship Fund
11632 N.E. Ainsworth Cir.
Portland, OR 97220-9016 (503) 256-3683
Contact: Johanna Glode, Pres.

Foundation type: Independent foundation
Purpose: Scholarships to students for higher education graduating from Portland, OR school districts.
Financial data: Year ended 12/31/2011. Assets, $94,321 (M); Expenditures, $63,012; Total giving, $62,500.
Fields of interest: Higher education.
Type of support: Scholarships—to individuals; Support to graduates or students of specific schools.

Application information: Applications accepted.
  Initial approach: Letter
  Deadline(s): June 15
  Applicants should submit the following:
    1) Transcripts
    2) Resume
    3) Essay
  Additional information: Essay should describe career goals.
EIN: 270095533

7659
Bertha P. Singer Student Nurses Fund
P.O. Box 3168
Portland, OR 97208-3168 (800) 452-8807
Application address: c/o Oregon Student Assistance Commission, 1500 Valley Dr., Ste. 100, Eugene, OR 97401

Foundation type: Independent foundation
Purpose: Scholarships to financially needy graduates of OR high schools and residents of OR who have been accepted at accredited OR graduate or undergraduate nursing programs.
Financial data: Year ended 06/30/2012. Assets, $393,372 (M); Expenditures, $29,638; Total giving, $17,535.
Fields of interest: Nursing school/education.
Type of support: Graduate support; Undergraduate support.
Application information: Applications accepted. Application form required. Interview required.
  Deadline(s): Jan. 1 to Mar. 15
  Applicants should submit the following:
    1) Transcripts
    2) SAT
    3) GPA
    4) FAFSA
  Additional information: Application must also include proof of acceptance to a nursing program. Applications available from high schools, college financial aid offices, and the OR State Scholarship Commission.
EIN: 510181219

7660
Captain Michael King Smith for Evergreen Aviation Center
500 N.E. Capt. Michael King Smith Way
McMinnville, OR 97128-9402 (503) 434-4185
FAX: (503) 434-4188;
E-mail: events@sprucegoose.org; URL: http://www.evergreenmuseum.org/

Foundation type: Public charity
Purpose: Scholarships to residents of McMinnville, OR who want to study aviation.
Publications: Application guidelines.
Financial data: Year ended 12/31/2011. Assets, $13,467,354 (M); Expenditures, $6,486,333.
Fields of interest: Space/aviation.
Type of support: Undergraduate support.
Application information: Applications not accepted.
  Additional information: Unsolicited requests for funds not accepted.
EIN: 931069203

7661
Snow-Cap Community Charities
P.O. Box 160
Fairview, OR   97024-0160   (503) 674-8785
Contact: Judith Alley, Exec. Dir.
FAX: (503) 674-5355; Additional address: 17805
S.E. Stark St., Portland, OR 97223-4823;
URL: http://www.snowcap.org

Foundation type: Public charity
Purpose: Assistance to low-income individuals and
families of the Fairview, OR, area with food, clothing
(for children), utilities, and other needs.
Publications: Newsletter.
Financial data: Year ended 06/30/2012. Assets,
$1,579,922 (M); Expenditures, $3,173,803; Total
giving, $2,592,549; Grants to individuals, totaling
$2,592,549.
Fields of interest: Human services; Children;
Economically disadvantaged.
Type of support: Grants for special needs.
Application information: Applicant should have
proof of address (mail addressed to you within the
last 30 days) for assistance.
EIN: 237121915

7662
Soapstone - A Writing Retreat for Women
622 S.E. 29th Ave.
Portland, OR   97214-3026   (503) 327-1042
Contact: Ruth Gundle, Admin.
E-mail: retreats@soapstone.org; URL: http://
www.soapstone.org

Foundation type: Public charity
Purpose: Residencies to women writers for one to
four weeks in Portland, OR.
Financial data: Year ended 12/31/2012. Assets,
$157,390 (M); Expenditures, $18,659; Total
giving, $210.
Fields of interest: Literature; Women.
Type of support: Residencies.
Application information: Applications accepted.
Application form required. Application form
available on the grantmaker's web site.
   Initial approach: Application
   Deadline(s): Aug. 1
   Final notification: Recipients notified in two
      months
   Additional information: Application should
      include writing sample and a $20
      nonrefundable application fee.
EIN: 931072551

7663
Society of St. Vincent De Paul of Portland, Oregon
5120 S.E. Milwaukie Ave.
Portland, OR   97242-0157   (503) 235-7837
FAX: (503) 233-5581; E-mail: sharon@svdppdx.org;
Mailing address: Portland Council Office, P.O. Box
42157, Portland, OR 97242-0157; URL: http://
www.svdppdx.org

Foundation type: Public charity
Purpose: Specific assistance to individuals and
families in the Portland, OR, area with food,
clothing, shelter, and other emergency and
temporary needs.
Financial data: Year ended 09/30/2011. Assets,
$4,229,607 (M); Expenditures, $8,921,887; Total
giving, $7,645,455; Grants to individuals, totaling
$7,645,455.
Fields of interest: Human services; Economically
disadvantaged.
Type of support: Grants for special needs.

Application information: Contact the society for
needed assistance.
EIN: 930456525

7664
Southern Oregon Lions Sight & Hearing Center, Inc.
228 N. Holly St.
Medford, OR   97501-2620   (541) 779-3653
FAX: (541) 857-0747; URL: http://www.lions.org

Foundation type: Operating foundation
Purpose: Grants to residents of southern OR,
particularly Jackson County, for vision and hearing
medical care, including exams, surgery,
eyeglasses, hearing aids, and travel expenses.
Publications: Application guidelines; Informational
brochure.
Financial data: Year ended 06/30/2012. Assets,
$1,086,638 (M); Expenditures, $188,729; Total
giving, $32,169.
Fields of interest: Optometry/vision screening;
Health care; Disabilities, people with.
Type of support: Grants for special needs.
Application information: Applications accepted.
   Initial approach: Letter
   Deadline(s): None
   Additional information: Application should outline
      sight and hearing impairments.
EIN: 936042046

7665
Southwestern Oregon Community College Foundation
1988 Newmark Ave.
Coos Bay, OR   97420-2911   (541) 888-7210
Contact: Karen Pringle, Exec. Dir.
FAX: (541) 888-7239;
E-mail: foundation@socc.edu; Toll-free tel.: (800)
962-2838, ext. 7210; E-Mail for Karen Pringle:
karen.pringle@socc.edu; Tel. for Karen Pringle:
(541)-888-7211; URL: http://www.socc.edu/
foundation/

Foundation type: Public charity
Purpose: Scholarships to students at Southwestern
Oregon Community College, OR.
Financial data: Year ended 06/30/2012. Assets,
$3,319,403 (M); Expenditures, $848,300; Total
giving, $529,735; Grants to individuals, totaling
$529,735.
Type of support: Support to graduates or students
of specific schools; Undergraduate support.
Application information: Application form required.
Application form available on the grantmaker's web
site.
   Deadline(s): Mar. 1
   Applicants should submit the following:
      1) Transcripts
      2) FAFSA
      3) Essay
   Additional information: Application must also
      include extracurricular activities, both school
      and community.
EIN: 936031563

7666
J.B. Steinbach Scholarship Fund
(formerly Steinbach Foundation)
P.O. Box 3168
Portland, OR   97208-3168   (800) 452-8807
Application Address: c/o Oregon Student Assistance
Commission, 1500 Valley River Dr. Ste 100,
Eugene OR 97401

Foundation type: Independent foundation
Purpose: Scholarships to worthy U.S. students who
are residents of OR for attendance at trade schools,
colleges or universities.
Financial data: Year ended 06/30/2013. Assets,
$1,141,380 (M); Expenditures, $79,994; Total
giving, $49,167.
Fields of interest: Vocational education,
post-secondary; Higher education.
Type of support: Undergraduate support.
Application information: Application form required.
   Deadline(s): Mar. 1
   Additional information: Applicants must have a
      minimum cumulative college 3.50 GPA,
      entering sophomore or higher undergraduate
      study. The scholarship is for undergraduate
      study.
EIN: 936020885

7667
Mertie & Harley Stevens Memorial Fund
P.O. Box 3168
Portland, OR   97208-3168   (800) 452-8807
Application address: c/o Oregon State Scholarship
Commission, 1500 Valley River Dr., Ste. 100,
Eugene, OR 97401, tel.: (800) 452-8807

Foundation type: Independent foundation
Purpose: Scholarships to graduates of accredited
Clackamas County, OR, high schools for study at
Oregon public colleges or certain protestant-run
private colleges. Student loans are also available.
Financial data: Year ended 06/30/2013. Assets,
$1,121,140 (M); Expenditures, $84,472; Total
giving, $52,949.
Fields of interest: Higher education.
Type of support: Scholarships—to individuals;
Student loans—to individuals.
Application information: Application form required.
Interview required.
   Deadline(s): Jan. 1 and Mar. 15 for scholarships,
      June 1 and June 15 for loans
Program description:
   Mertie and Harvey Stevens Memorial Scholarship:
Presented to graduates from accredited high
schools in Clackamas County, OR, for their first and
fourth year of schooling, who enroll as full-time
undergraduate students. Award recipients are also
eligible for loans for their sophomore and junior
years. Eligible schools include public colleges in OR
or the following private colleges: Concordia,
Corban, George Fox, Lewis and Clark, Linfield,
Multnomah, New Hope Christian, Northwest
Christian, Pacific, Warner Pacific, and Willamette.
Required minimum cumulative GPA for high school
seniors is 3.50 and for college students 3.0. For
loans the minimum is 2.75. Loans are awarded at
three percent interest for the sophomore and junior
years of schooling.
EIN: 936053655

7668
Nadie E. Strayer Scholarship Fund
3480 Pl. St.
Baker City, OR   97814   (541) 523-2800
Contact: Howard Britton, Tr.

Foundation type: Independent foundation
Purpose: Scholarships of $1,000 each to
graduates of Baker County, OR, high schools and
former Baker County graduates attending college.
Financial data: Year ended 12/31/2011. Assets,
$42,435 (M); Expenditures, $4,057; Total giving,
$4,000; Grants to individuals, 4 grants totaling
$4,000 (high: $1,000, low: $1,000).

Fields of interest: Higher education; Scholarships/financial aid.
Type of support: Scholarships—to individuals; Support to graduates or students of specific schools.
Application information: Application form required.
  Deadline(s): May 16
  Applicants should submit the following:
    1) Transcripts
    2) SAR
    3) Letter(s) of recommendation
EIN: 931137546

7669
Albert L. & Ivy B. Thomas Educational Fund
P.O. Box 3168
Portland, OR   97208-3168   (503) 838-0480
Application address: c/o Scholarship Office, 1530 Monmouth St., Independence, OR 97351-1006, tel.: (503) 838-0480
Application address: c/o Scholarship Office, 1530 Monmouth St., Independence, OR 97351-1006, tel.: (503) 838-0480

Foundation type: Independent foundation
Purpose: Scholarships to graduates of the Independence-Monmouth School District 13J in OR.
Financial data: Year ended 12/31/2011. Assets, $986,613 (M); Expenditures, $69,826; Total giving, $36,229.
Fields of interest: Higher education.
Type of support: Support to graduates or students of specific schools; Undergraduate support.
Application information: Applications accepted. Application form required.
  Initial approach: Telephone
  Additional information: Contact the scholarship office for additional information.
EIN: 936196091

7670
Dr. H. A. Trippeer Charitable Foundation
15350 SW Sequoia Prkwy, Ste. 300
Portland, OR   97224   (503) 624-6300
Contact: Candace Clardy
E-mail: candyc@pactrust.com; Application Address: 15350 SW Sequoia Parkway, Ste. 300, Portland, OR 97224; URL: http://trippeerfoundation.org/

Foundation type: Independent foundation
Purpose: Scholarships to graduates of high schools in Walla Walla County, WA, who are attending or who have been accepted to attend four-year undergraduate degree programs at accredited colleges or universities.
Publications: Application guidelines.
Financial data: Year ended 12/31/2012. Assets, $1,984,173 (M); Expenditures, $93,644; Total giving, $74,500.
Fields of interest: Higher education.
Type of support: Support to graduates or students of specific schools; Undergraduate support.
Application information: Applications accepted. Application form required. Application form available on the grantmaker's web site. Interview required.
  Deadline(s): Mar. 19
  Applicants should submit the following:
    1) Photograph
    2) Budget Information
    3) SAT
    4) Transcripts
    5) Letter(s) of recommendation
    6) Essay

Additional information: Application should also include PSAT score, and biography. E-mailed applications are not accepted. See web site for specific application guidelines.
EIN: 916371911

7671
Bismarck H. Turner Scholarship Trust
P.O. Box 3168
Portland, OR   97208-3168   (509) 353-7084
Contact: Robert Hawley; Robert Prince
Application address: c/o U.S. Bank, W. 428 Riverside Ave. Spokane, WA, 99201; tel: (509) 353-7084.

Foundation type: Independent foundation
Purpose: Scholarships to graduates of high schools in Spokane or Pend Oreille counties, WA, or Bonner or Kootenai counties, ID.
Financial data: Year ended 03/31/2012. Assets, $440,150 (M); Expenditures, $30,324; Total giving, $18,275.
Fields of interest: Higher education; Scholarships/financial aid.
Type of support: Support to graduates or students of specific schools; Undergraduate support.
Application information: Application form required.
  Initial approach: Letter
  Deadline(s): Apr. 11
  Applicants should submit the following:
    1) Letter(s) of recommendation
    2) FAFSA
    3) SAR
    4) Transcripts
  Additional information: Funds are paid directly to the educational institution on behalf of the student.
EIN: 916254764

7672
Umpqua Community Action Network
280 Kenneth Ford Dr.
Roseburg, OR   97470-2500   (541) 672-3421
Contact: Mike Fieldman, Exec. Dir.
FAX: (541) 672-1983;
E-mail: mike.fieldman@ucancap.org; URL: http://www.ucancap.org

Foundation type: Public charity
Purpose: Grants to low-income residents of Douglas and Josephine counties, OR.
Financial data: Year ended 06/30/2011. Assets, $15,654,451 (M); Expenditures, $16,377,913; Total giving, $4,257,865; Grants to individuals, totaling $4,257,865.
Fields of interest: Economically disadvantaged.
Type of support: Grants for special needs.
Application information: Applications not accepted.
  Additional information: Unsolicited requests for funds not considered or acknowledged.
EIN: 930587136

7673
Vatheuer Family Foundation, Inc.
4302 S.W. Bertha Ave.
Portland, OR   97239-1578

Foundation type: Operating foundation
Purpose: Scholarships to students at Portland State University School of Engineering and Applied Science, OR, who have financial need, at least junior status, and a cumulative GPA of 3.0.

Financial data: Year ended 12/31/2011. Assets, $572,936 (M); Expenditures, $107,017; Total giving, $0.
Type of support: Support to graduates or students of specific schools; Undergraduate support.
Application information: Applications not accepted.
  Additional information: Unsolicited requests for funds not considered or acknowledged.
EIN: 931218806

7674
Vernier Software & Technology LLC Corporate Giving Program
13979 S.W. Millikan Way
Beaverton, OR   97005-2886
URL: http://www.vernier.com/company/philanthropy/

Foundation type: Corporate giving program
Purpose: Grants to K-12 teachers for the innovative use of data-collection technology using a computer, graphing calculator, or other handheld in the science classroom.
Fields of interest: Elementary/secondary education; Teacher school/education; Education; Formal/general education.
Type of support: Awards/prizes.
Application information: Application form required. Application form available on the grantmaker's web site.
  Deadline(s): Nov. 30
Program description:
  Vernier/NSTA Technology Awards: Through the Vernier/NSTA Technology Awards program, Vernier annually awards seven $3,000 grants to K-12 and college science instructors recognized for the innovative use of data-collection technology using a computer, graphing calculator, or other handheld in the science classroom. Each grant consists of $1,000 in cash, $1,000 in Vernier products, and $1,000 toward expenses to attend the National Science Teachers Association (NSTA) national convention. One grant is awarded to an elementary school instructor, two grants are awarded to middle school instructors, three grants are awarded to high school instructors, and one grant is awarded to a college instructor.

7675
Flora Von der Ahe School Trust
P.O. Box 3168
Portland, OR   97208-3168   (503) 452-8807
Application address: Oregon Student Assistance Commission, 1500 Valley River Dr., Ste. 100, Eugene, OR 97401, tel.: (800) 452-8807

Foundation type: Independent foundation
Purpose: Scholarships to high school graduates of Umatilla County, OR, for full-time undergraduate or graduate study at accredited colleges, universities, and technical schools in OR.
Financial data: Year ended 06/30/2012. Assets, $199,291 (M); Expenditures, $16,813; Total giving, $9,000.
Fields of interest: Vocational education, post-secondary; Higher education.
Type of support: Graduate support; Technical education support; Undergraduate support.
Application information: Applications accepted. Application form required. Interview required.
  Additional information: Application forms are available from OR Student Assistance Commission, high school guidance offices, and the College Financial Aid Office in OR.
EIN: 936066821

7676
Ludwig Vongelstein Foundation, Inc.
18410 Deer Oak Ave.
Lake Oswego, OR 97035
Contact: Diana Braunschweig, Exec. Dir.
E-mail: lvf@earthlink.net

Foundation type: Independent foundation
Purpose: Grants to individuals working in the fine arts (excluding photography, film and video) and in the literary arts, including playwriting.
Publications: Application guidelines.
Financial data: Year ended 12/31/2011. Assets, $1,784 (M); Expenditures, $63,442; Total giving, $0.
Fields of interest: Theater (playwriting); Humanities; Literature.
Type of support: Grants to individuals.
Application information:
 Initial approach: Letter
 Send request by: Mail
 Deadline(s): Mid-spring
 Additional information: Contact the foundation for additional application information.
EIN: 136185761

7677
Watt Brothers Scholars Trust
P.O. Box 999
Tillamook, OR 97141-0999
Application address: c/o Phyllis Wustenberg, P.O. Box 3312, Bay City, OR 97107-3312, tel.: (503) 377-2283

Foundation type: Operating foundation
Purpose: Scholarships to seniors graduating from Tillamook County high schools, OR.
Financial data: Year ended 12/31/2011. Assets, $1,405,365 (M); Expenditures, $189,422; Total giving, $176,993; Grants to individuals, 50 grants totaling $172,993 (high: $6,000, low: $1,332).
Type of support: Support to graduates or students of specific schools; Undergraduate support.
Application information: Applications accepted. Application form required.
 Deadline(s): June 1
 Applicants should submit the following:
  1) SAT
  2) Photograph
  3) Transcripts
 Additional information: Application should also include a handwritten letter of no more than 300 words explaining college plans.
EIN: 931224469

7678
Wattenberg Scholarship Fund
c/o Oregon Pacific Bank
P.O. Box 1784
Medford, OR 97501-0140
Contact: Douglas Spanie

Foundation type: Independent foundation
Purpose: Scholarships to students graduating from high school within the Phoenix-Talent School District No.4, Jackson county, OR to assist students in their initial year of college within the state of OR.
Financial data: Year ended 03/31/2013. Assets, $273,649 (M); Expenditures, $19,288; Total giving, $15,000; Grants to individuals, 6 grants totaling $15,000 (high: $2,500, low: $2,500).
Fields of interest: Higher education.
Type of support: Scholarships—to individuals.
Application information: Students are selected by their principals of each school within the School

District. Criteria for selection is academic achievement and need.
EIN: 204781876

7679
James Weir Memorial Fund-Bigelow District
70544 McKinney Rd.
Wasco, OR 97065-0325 (541) 442-5290
Contact: Kim McKinney
Application Address: 70544 McKinney Rd. Wasco, OR 97065

Foundation type: Independent foundation
Purpose: Scholarships and other educational grants to students and residents of the Bigelow District in Sherman County, OR.
Financial data: Year ended 06/30/2012. Assets, $1,044,641 (M); Expenditures, $81,760; Total giving, $54,377; Grants to individuals, 10 grants totaling $54,377 (high: $15,000, low: $656).
Fields of interest: Education.
Type of support: Scholarships—to individuals.
Application information: Applications accepted.
 Initial approach: Letter
 Deadline(s): Contact foundation for application deadline.
 Additional information: Application should include purpose and amount of funds desired.
EIN: 936041768

7680
Merle S. & Emma J. West Scholarship Fund
(also known as West Scholarship Fund)
c/o U.S. Bank, N.A.
P.O. Box 3168
Portland, OR 97208-3168 (541) 883-3857
Scholarship application address: c/o West Scholarship Comm., Attn.: Jamie M. Fabian, 3720 S. 6th St., Klamath Falls, OR 97603, tel.: (503) 883-3857
URL: http://www.merlewestscholarship.com

Foundation type: Independent foundation
Purpose: Scholarships to graduates of high schools in Klamath County, OR, for postsecondary and vocational education.
Financial data: Year ended 12/31/2012. Assets, $3,525,285 (M); Expenditures, $212,154; Total giving, $157,641.
Fields of interest: Vocational education, post-secondary; Higher education.
Type of support: Support to graduates or students of specific schools; Technical education support; Undergraduate support.
Application information: Applications accepted. Application form required. Application form available on the grantmaker's web site. Interview required.
 Initial approach: Letter or telephone
 Deadline(s): Apr. 1
 Applicants should submit the following:
  1) Transcripts
  2) SAR
  3) Letter(s) of recommendation
  4) GPA
  5) Financial information
  6) FAFSA
  7) Budget Information
  8) ACT
 Additional information: Application can be obtained from any high school in Klamath County. Funds are paid directly to the educational institution on behalf of the

students. See web site for additional application information.
EIN: 936160221

7681
Western Lane Community Foundation
(formerly Western Lane County Foundation)
1525 W. 12th St., Ste. 18
P.O. Box 1589
Florence, OR 97439-8482 (541) 997-1274
Contact: Gayle Waiss, Exec. Dir.
FAX: (541) 997-1274; *E-mail:* wlcf@oregonfast.net; *URL:* http://www.wlcfonline.org/

Foundation type: Community foundation
Purpose: Scholarships to graduates of Sinslaw High School, OR, and Mapleton High School, OR for undergraduate education.
Publications: Application guidelines; Annual report; Informational brochure; Newsletter; Program policy statement.
Financial data: Year ended 12/31/2012. Assets, $5,046,814 (M); Expenditures, $282,457; Total giving, $209,504; Grants to individuals, totaling $24,309.
Type of support: Support to graduates or students of specific schools; Undergraduate support.
Application information: Applications accepted. Application form required.
 Additional information: Application should include GPA. Contact foundation or high school guidance office for further application information.
EIN: 237438503

7682
Clara Wheeler Trust
(formerly Milheim Foundation for Cancer Research)
P.O. Box 3168
Portland, OR 97208 (303) 316-5944
Contact: Sarah Woods
Application address: US Bank, Trust Admin., 200 University, Denver, CO 80206

Foundation type: Independent foundation
Purpose: Grants for research on the prevention, treatment, or cure of cancer to residents of the continental U.S.
Publications: Application guidelines.
Financial data: Year ended 12/31/2011. Assets, $1,035,103 (M); Expenditures, $18,488; Total giving, $0.
Fields of interest: Cancer research.
Type of support: Research.
Application information: Applications accepted. Application form required. Application form available on the grantmaker's web site.
 Initial approach: Letter, telephone
 Copies of proposal: 7
 Deadline(s): Mar. 15
 Final notification: Recipients notified in three months
 Applicants should submit the following:
  1) Proposal
  2) Letter(s) of recommendation
  3) Financial information
  4) Curriculum vitae
  5) Budget Information
 Additional information: The grant award period is for one year. No grants are allowed for travel to meetings or for presentation of papers.
EIN: 846018431

7683
The Craig D. Wiesberg & Calvin P. Ranney Children's Foundation
1000 SW Broadway
Portland, OR   97205
Contact: Steven Wiesberg
*Application Address:*c/o Steven Wiesberg, 2911 Delano Dr. Henderson, NV 89074

Foundation type: Independent foundation
Purpose: Grants and special medical equipment to low-income families in OR.
Financial data: Year ended 12/31/2012. Assets, $1,993 (M); Expenditures, $22; Total giving, $0.
Type of support: Grants for special needs.
Application information: Application form required.
  Initial approach: Letter or telephone
  Deadline(s): Contact foundation for current application deadline
  Applicants should submit the following:
    1) Proposal
    2) Letter(s) of recommendation
  Additional information: Applications should be sent by fax; Time for response to an application is 1-3 days.
EIN: 931228840

7684
E.E. Wilson Scholarship Fund Foundation
P.O. Box 3168
Portland, OR   97208   (541) 737-3374
Contact: Frank Ragulsky
Application address: OSU-118 MU E., Corvallis, OR 97331

Foundation type: Independent foundation
Purpose: Scholarships based on character and scholastic ability to financially needy Benton County, OR, residents to attend Oregon State University.
Financial data: Year ended 06/30/2013. Assets, $815,921 (M); Expenditures, $60,163; Total giving, $42,569.
Type of support: Support to graduates or students of specific schools; Undergraduate support.

Application information: Applications accepted.
  Additional information: Contact fund for current application deadline/guidelines.
EIN: 936022322

7685
Woodmansee Scholarship Fund
P.O. Box 2305
Salem, OR   97308-2305   (503) 363-3136

Foundation type: Independent foundation
Purpose: Scholarships to graduating seniors from OR high schools to attend institutions of higher learning in OR.
Financial data: Year ended 05/31/2013. Assets, $8,884 (M); Expenditures, $8,242; Total giving, $5,698; Grants to individuals, 5 grants totaling $5,698 (high: $1,744, low: $596).
Type of support: Undergraduate support.
Application information: Application form required.
  Initial approach: Letter
  Deadline(s): Mar. 15
  Additional information: Application must include SASE.
EIN: 936195941

7686
Woodrow Foundation
P.O. Box 3168
Portland, OR   97208-3168

Foundation type: Independent foundation
Purpose: One annual scholarship to a worthy and deserving student of Whitworth College, Spokane, WA.
Financial data: Year ended 06/30/2012. Assets, $761,867 (M); Expenditures, $94,260; Total giving, $79,214.
Fields of interest: Higher education.
Type of support: Support to graduates or students of specific schools.
Application information: Application form required.
  Deadline(s): Apr.

Applicants should submit the following:
    1) Financial information
    2) Transcripts
    3) Class rank
    4) SAT
    5) GPA
    6) ACT
  Additional information: Application should also include two letters of reference and a copy of your most recent Income tax return. Applicant must demonstrate need.
EIN: 916326014

7687
Yamhill Community Action Partnership
(formerly Community Action Agency of Yamhill County, Inc.)
1317 N.E. Dustin Court
P.O. Box 621
McMinnville, OR   97128-4408   (503) 472-0457
Contact: Kathy George, Chair.
FAX: (503) 472-5555;
E-mail: contact@yamhillcap.org; Toll-free tel.: (800) 945-9992E-Mail for Lee Means : leem@yamhillcap.orgTel. for Lee Means : (503)-883-4172 Ext. 128; URL: http://yamhillcap.org

Foundation type: Public charity
Purpose: Financial assistance for utilities, and transportation expenses to low-income residents of Yamhill County, OR.
Financial data: Year ended 06/30/2012. Assets, $4,552,424 (M); Expenditures, $5,555,160; Total giving, $23,489.
Fields of interest: Economically disadvantaged.
Type of support: Grants for special needs.
Application information:
  Initial approach: Letter
  Additional information: Contact foundation for eligibility criteria.
EIN: 930758732

PENNSYLVANIA

7688
AAA Scholarship Fund of AAA East Penn
(formerly AAA Scholarship Fund of the Lehigh Valley Motor Club)
1020 Hamilton St.
Allentown, PA 18101 (610) 434-5141
Contact: Thomas Ashley
Application address: Scholarship Selection Committee at AAA East Penn., P.O. Box 1910, Allentown, PA 18105-1910

Foundation type: Independent foundation
Purpose: Scholarships to former members of the AAA safety patrol and to graduates of high schools located within the AAA Lehigh Valley, PA, territory.
Financial data: Year ended 12/31/2012. Assets, $224,755 (M); Expenditures, $9,150; Total giving, $9,000; Grants to individuals, 9 grants totaling $9,000 (high: $1,000, low: $1,000).
Fields of interest: Vocational education; Higher education.
Type of support: Scholarships—to individuals.
Application information: Applications accepted. Application form required.
>   *Deadline(s):* Mar. 1
>   *Applicants should submit the following:*
>   1) GPA
>   2) ACT
>   3) Class rank
>   4) Transcripts
>   5) SAT
>   *Additional information:* Application should also include a personal letter of introduction, two letters of reference, and must be returned to the school's counselor or the scholarship committee.

EIN: 232325177

7689
Abernathy Black Community Development & Educational Fund
(formerly ABCDE Fund)
P.O. Box 177
Washington, PA 15301-0177 (724) 377-0084
Application Address: ABCDEF Fund, P.O. Box 177, Washington. PA 15301-0177

Foundation type: Operating foundation
Purpose: Scholarships to African-American students from the Washington, PA, area to attend colleges and technical schools.
Financial data: Year ended 12/31/2012. Assets, $19,712 (M); Expenditures, $10,249; Total giving, $10,100; Grants to individuals, 24 grants totaling $10,100 (high: $850, low: $250).
Fields of interest: Vocational education; African Americans/Blacks.
Type of support: Technical education support; Undergraduate support.
Application information: Applications accepted. Interview required.
>   *Initial approach:* Letter
>   *Deadline(s):* None
>   *Additional information:* Application must include biographical and educational information.

EIN: 237336423

7690
Abington Memorial Hospital
1200 Old York Rd.
Abington, PA 19001-3720 (215) 481-2000
E-mail: publicrelations@amh.org; URL: http://www.amh.org

Foundation type: Public charity
Purpose: Financial assistance with medically-necessary healthcare services available for all individuals of Abington, PA in a non-discriminatory manner.
Publications: Informational brochure.
Financial data: Year ended 06/30/2011. Assets, $711,714,031 (M); Expenditures, $680,830,235; Total giving, $310,395; Grants to individuals, 183 grants totaling $8,140. Subtotal for emergency funds: 183 grants totaling $8,140.
Fields of interest: Health care.
Type of support: Grants for special needs.
Application information: Applications accepted.
>   *Additional information:* Some services require an application. Unmet needs of vulnerable populations, the poor, minorities, and other underserved groups thoughout the community benefit programs are addressed. Contact the organization for eligibility determination.

EIN: 231352152

7691
Samuel L. Abrams Foundation
c/o BNY Mellon, N.A.
P.O. Box 185
Pittsburgh, PA 15230-0185

Foundation type: Independent foundation
Purpose: Awards grants and interest-free loans to graduates of greater Harrisburg, Pennsylvania, high schools and to faculty and administrative staff of the Harrisburg, PA school district.
Publications: Application guidelines.
Financial data: Year ended 12/31/2012. Assets, $2,970,400 (M); Expenditures, $146,702; Total giving, $123,000; Grants to individuals, 32 grants totaling $123,000 (high: $6,000, low: $1,000).
Fields of interest: Vocational education; Graduate/professional education; Business school/education; Nursing school/education.
Type of support: Student loans—to individuals; Support to graduates or students of specific schools; Undergraduate support.
Application information: Applications accepted. Application form required. Interview required.
>   *Deadline(s):* May 30
>   *Applicants should submit the following:*
>   1) Transcripts
>   2) Financial information
>   *Additional information:* Application should also include copies of most recent income tax returns. See web site for a selection of area schools and additional guidelines.

Program descriptions:
>   *Professional Program:* Grants or interest free loans to eligible individuals of the Harrisburg School District. Applicants must demonstrate initiative, a desire to improve themselves, a need for financial assistance and that the course of study to be pursued will improve their professional skill, ability and understanding. Each applicant must sign a statement agreeing to continue on the faculty or staff of the Harrisburg School District for a minimum of two years after completion of the course of study for which the assistance is granted.
>   *Student Program:* Grants or interest free loans are awarded to graduates of selected Harrisburg area schools who want to continue their education at approved institutions of higher learning including,

but not limited to colleges, universities, junior colleges, community college and business, technical and professional schools. Applicants must demonstrate strong initiatives, a desire for self-improvement and financial need.
EIN: 236408237

7692
James K. & Arlene L. Adams Foundation
1011 Mumma Rd., Ste. 201
Lemoyne, PA 17043-1143 (717) 236-9318
Contact: David H. Radcliff, Tr.

Foundation type: Independent foundation
Purpose: Student loans to individuals graduating from high schools in eastern Cumberland County, PA.
Financial data: Year ended 12/31/2011. Assets, $490,933 (M); Expenditures, $71,586; Total giving, $63,000.
Type of support: Student loans—to individuals; Support to graduates or students of specific schools; Undergraduate support.
Application information: Applications accepted. Application form not required.
>   *Initial approach:* Letter
>   *Deadline(s):* Dec. 31
EIN: 251665127

7693
Aid For Friends
12271 Townsend Rd.
Philadelphia, PA 19154-1288 (215) 464-2224
Contact: Steven Schiavone, Exec. Dir.
FAX: (215) 464-2507;
E-mail: info@aidforfriends.org; URL: http://www.aidforfriends.org

Foundation type: Public charity
Purpose: Emergency financial assistance to those in need throughout the five county greater Philadelphia, PA area. Other assistance to the frail elderly with food, and provide shut-ins with free outreach services.
Publications: Annual report; Newsletter.
Financial data: Year ended 07/31/2011. Assets, $2,855,839 (M); Expenditures, $3,389,562.
Fields of interest: Aging; Disabilities, people with; Economically disadvantaged.
Type of support: Grants for special needs.
Application information: Forms must be completed to recommend someone to Aid For Friends for their Homebound Services. See web site for referral forms.
EIN: 232072722

7694
Alcoa Foundation
Alcoa Corporate Ctr.
201 Isabella St.
Pittsburgh, PA 15212-5858
URL: http://www.alcoa.com/global/en/community/foundation.asp

Foundation type: Company-sponsored foundation
Purpose: Scholarships to children of current or retired employees of Alcoa.
Publications: Application guidelines; Corporate giving report; Grants list; Newsletter; Program policy statement.
Financial data: Year ended 12/31/2012. Assets, $460,142,329 (M); Expenditures, $24,816,126; Total giving, $21,517,932.
Fields of interest: Higher education; Scholarships/financial aid.

Type of support: Employee-related scholarships.
Application information: Applications not accepted.

> *Additional information:* Unsolicited requests for funds not considered or acknowledged.

Program description:

Alcoa Sons and Daughters Scholarship Program: The foundation awards $1,500 college scholarships to children of U.S. employees of Alcoa to pursue two or four-year degree. The program is administered by International Scholarship and Tuition Services.

Company name: Alcoa Inc.
EIN: 251128857

7695
Alex's Lemonade Stand Foundation

333 Lancaster Ave., Ste. 414
Wynnewood, PA   19096-1929   (610) 649-3034
FAX: (610) 949-3038;
E-mail: contact@alexslemonade.com; Toll-free tel.:
(866) 333-1213; URL: http://
www.alexslemonade.org

Foundation type: Public charity
Purpose: Research grants to identify the specific challenges faced in bringing new treatments to children with cancer, and to find better ways to care for children undergoing cancer treatment. Assistance to families who face the need to travel for childhood cancer treatment at select medical institutions in the U.S.
Publications: Application guidelines; Grants list; Informational brochure; Newsletter.
Financial data: Year ended 12/31/2011. Assets, $11,897,960 (M); Expenditures, $7,961,332; Total giving, $5,466,218; Grants to individuals, totaling $70,240.
Fields of interest: Cancer research; Pediatrics research; Children/youth.
Type of support: Grants to individuals; Grants for special needs.
Application information: Applications accepted. Application form required.

> *Deadline(s):* Vary
> *Additional information:* See web site for additional guidelines for funding.

Program descriptions:

'A' Award Grants: This three-year, $375,000 grant will be awarded to young scientists who want to jump-start their career in pediatric oncology research. The ideal candidate has an original project that is not currently being funded. Demonstration of outstanding mentorship and a future commitment to pediatric cancer investigation are critical components of a successful application. Funds must be granted to nonprofit institutions or organizations operating in the United States or Canada. Researchers need not be U.S. citizens.

Innovation Grants: These grants are designed to provide critical and significant seed funding for experienced investigators with a novel and promising approach to finding causes and cures for childhood cancers. The award amount is $250,000 over two years.

Young Investigator Grants: These grants are designed to fill the critical need for start up funds for less experienced researchers to pursue promising research ideas. These grants encourage and cultivate the best and brightest researchers of the future and lead to long term commitments to research projects. Awards are $50,000 per year for two years.

EIN: 562496146

7696
Allegheny County Bar Foundation

400 Koppers Blvd.
436 Seventh Ave.
Pittsburgh, PA   15219-1877
Contact: Lorrie Albert, Dir., Fdn.
E-mail for Lorrie Albert: lalbert@acba.org; tel. for
Lorrie Albert: (412) 402-6640; URL: http://
www.acbf.org/

Foundation type: Public charity
Purpose: Scholarships and loans to students attending select schools in Allegheny County, PA.
Publications: Application guidelines.
Financial data: Year ended 06/30/2011. Assets, $4,151,479 (M); Expenditures, $2,247,979; Total giving, $251,248; Grants to individuals, 50 grants totaling $75,746. Subtotal for scholarships—to individuals: 5 grants totaling $17,000. Subtotal for fellowships: 45 grants totaling $58,746.
Fields of interest: Law school/education.
Type of support: Scholarships—to individuals; Student loans—to individuals.
Application information: Applications accepted. Application form required. Application form available on the grantmaker's web site.

> *Initial approach:* Application
> *Deadline(s):* Apr. 16 for Louis Little Attorneys' Memorial Fund, Honorable Carol Los Mansmann Memorial Fund, James I. Smith III Notre Dame Law School Scholarship Fund, and F.C. Grote Fund, June 15 for Daniel B. Dixon Scholarship Fund
> *Additional information:* See web site for additional guidelines.

Program descriptions:

Daniel B. Dixon Scholarship Fund: This program awards an annual scholarship to a student at The University of Pittsburgh School of Law, who has completed his or her first or second year and who has demonstrated an interest in real estate law, academic excellence, and financial need.

F.C. Grote Fund: Scholarships of $5,000 each will be awarded annually to a student at the University of Pittsburgh School of Law and the University of Pennsylvania Law School.

Gerald K. Gibson Memorial Fund: This fund makes annual cash awards to deserving students participating in the Creditors & Debtors Rights course at the University of Pittsburgh and Duquesne University School of Law.

Honorable Carol Los Mansmann Memorial Fund: Each year, the foundation awards a scholarship to one or more women law students attending Duquesne University School of Law who demonstrate a potential for leadership and a commitment to the advancement of women. Scholarships will be awarded based on the financial need of the student.

James I Smith, III Notre Dame Law School Scholarship Fund: This program provides scholarships to law students from Allegheny County who are enrolled at Notre Dame Law School.

Louis Little Attorneys' Memorial Fund: This program provides low-interest loans to lawyers and law-school students.

Lynette Norton Memorial Fund: This fund provides an annual award to a student graduating from Duquesne University School of Law who has demonstrated academic excellence, skills in oral advocacy through moot court programs, and a keen sense of ethics and professionalism.

EIN: 251383622

7697
William M. & Louise O. Allen Scholarship Fund

c/o PNC Bank, NA
P.O. Box 609
Pittsburgh, PA   15230-9738   (216) 222-9815
Contact: Jane Kleinstein
Application address: C/O PNC Bank, N.A., 1900 E. 9th St., 13th Fl., Cleveland, OH 44114 Tel.: (216) 222-9815

Foundation type: Independent foundation
Purpose: Scholarships to high school graduates from Montgomery County, IN, for attendance at IN colleges or universities.
Financial data: Year ended 09/30/2013. Assets, $161,903 (M); Expenditures, $7,314; Total giving, $5,500; Grants to individuals, totaling $5,500.
Fields of interest: Higher education.
Type of support: Undergraduate support.
Application information: Applications accepted. Application form required.

> *Deadline(s):* May 1
> *Additional information:* Application should include a letter outlining financial need and future plans.

EIN: 356033947

7698
Miriam E. Alsobrooks Educational Fund

c/o Wells Fargo Bank, N.A.
101 N. Independence Mall E., MACY 1372-062
Philadelphia, PA   19106-2112
Application Address: c/o Center for Scholarship Administration, 4320-G Wade Hampton Blvd., Taylors, SC 2687; URL: http://
www.csascholars.org

Foundation type: Independent foundation
Purpose: Scholarships to graduates of Marlboro County High School, SC, who will be attending a college or university in SC and are in need of financial assistance. Preference given to an applicant whose father is deceased.
Financial data: Year ended 12/31/2012. Assets, $180,886 (M); Expenditures, $14,638; Total giving, $10,199.
Type of support: Support to graduates or students of specific schools; Undergraduate support.
Application information: Applications accepted. Application form required.

> *Initial approach:* Letter
> *Deadline(s):* Nov. 3

EIN: 576037000

7699
Alternatives Research and Development Foundation

801 Old York Rd., Ste. 316
Jenkintown, PA   19046-1611   (215) 887-8076
Contact: Sue A. Leary, Pres. and Exec. Dir.
FAX: (215) 887-0771; E-mail: info@ardf-online.org;
Additional E-mail: grants@ardf-online.org;
URL: http://www.ardf-online.org

Foundation type: Public charity
Purpose: Research grants to scientists who explore alternatives to the use of laboratory animals for research.
Publications: Application guidelines; Grants list; Informational brochure.
Financial data: Year ended 12/31/2011. Assets, $7,080,739 (M); Expenditures, $287,173; Total giving, $189,106.
Fields of interest: Medical research.
Type of support: Research.

Application information: Applications accepted. Application form required. Application form available on the grantmaker's web site.
  Initial approach: E-mail
  Send request by: Mail
  Deadline(s): May 2
  Final notification: Applicants notified by July 18
  Applicants should submit the following:
    1) Curriculum vitae
    2) Budget Information
    3) Proposal
EIN: 232740843

7700
Alan Ameche Memorial Foundation
P.O. Box 978
Narberth, PA   19072-0978   (610) 664-8477
Contact: Alan Ameche, Pres.

Foundation type: Public charity
Purpose: Grants to motivated, economically disadvantaged youth in fifth through twelfth grade to help them achieve their educational goals at private, vocational and parochial schools. Giving primarily in Delaware Valley, PA.
Publications: Program policy statement.
Financial data: Year ended 12/31/2012. Assets, $62,765 (M); Expenditures, $32,297; Total giving, $22,250.
Fields of interest: Youth development; Economically disadvantaged.
Type of support: Technical education support; Precollege support.
Application information: Application form required.
  Initial approach: Telephone
  Additional information: Contact foundation for current application deadline/guidelines.
EIN: 232550681

7701
American Association for Cancer Research, Inc.
(also known as AACR)
615 Chestnut St., 17th Fl.
Philadelphia, PA   19106-4404   (215) 440-9300
Contact: Margaret Foti Ph.D., C.E.O.
FAX: (215) 440-9313; E-mail: aacr@aacr.org; Toll Free Tel.: (866)-423-3965; E-Mail for Margaret Foti Ph.D.: executive.office@aacr.org; URL: http://www.aacr.org

Foundation type: Public charity
Purpose: Research grants and travel stipends to scientists for cancer research.
Publications: Application guidelines.
Financial data: Year ended 12/31/2011. Assets, $86,282,981 (M); Expenditures, $51,695,564; Total giving, $14,774,198; Grants to individuals, totaling $14,667,898.
Fields of interest: Cancer research.
Type of support: Fellowships; Research; Travel grants.
Application information: Applications accepted. Application form required. Application form available on the grantmaker's web site.
  Initial approach: E-mail
  Copies of proposal: 2
  Deadline(s): Varies
  Additional information: See web site for detailed program information.
Program descriptions:
  Career Development Awards: Awards are open to junior faculty at an academic, medical, or research institution who completed postdoctoral studies or clinical fellowships no more than four years prior to the start of the grant term.

Fellows Grants: These grants support innovative research by a meritorious young investigator by presenting the fellow with research funds to pursue an independent line of investigation within the context of his/her current fellowship placement. The grant assists the fellow in developing preliminary data to support a future project or investigating a new technique that otherwise would not be possible in the absence of this funding. Candidates must be, at the start of the grant term, in their third, fourth, or fifth year of their fellowship status.
  Research Fellowships: Fellowships foster basic, translational, clinical, and epidemiological research by scientists at the beginning of their careers in the cancer field. They are open to postdoctoral fellows and clinical research fellows at an academic facility, teaching hospital, or research institution who will be in the first, second, or third year of their postdoctoral training at the start of the fellowship term. Fellowships support the salary and benefits of the fellow, with partial funds permitted to be designated to direct research expenses.
EIN: 236251648

7702
American Medical Women's Association Foundation
100 N. 20th St., 4th Fl.
Philadelphia, PA   19103-1443   (215) 320-3716
Contact: Lindsay Groff, Exec. Dir.
FAX: (215) 564-2175;
E-mail: foundation@amwa-doc.org; URL: http://www.amwa-doc.org

Foundation type: Public charity
Purpose: Loans, fellowships and grants provided to students for medical education, research and specialized study.
Publications: Newsletter.
Financial data: Year ended 12/31/2012. Assets, $1,614,507 (M); Expenditures, $525,112; Total giving, $53,343; Grants to individuals, totaling $26,488.
Fields of interest: Medical research; Women.
Type of support: Fellowships; Grants to individuals; Student loans—to individuals.
Application information: Contact foundation for further information.
EIN: 136163539

7703
American Mushroom Institute Community Awareness Scholarship Foundation, Inc.
1284 Gap Newport Pike, Ste. 2
Avondale, PA   19311-9503   (610) 268-7483
Contact: Sara G. Manning

Foundation type: Independent foundation
Purpose: Scholarships to PA high school students pursuing higher education who have completed at least 100 hours of community service and have an interest in the mushroom industry.
Financial data: Year ended 05/31/2013. Assets, $86,723 (M); Expenditures, $64,244; Total giving, $41,625; Grants to individuals, 12 grants totaling $12,000 (high: $1,000, low: $1,000).
Fields of interest: Higher education.
Type of support: Undergraduate support.
Application information: Applications accepted.
  Additional information: Application should include a 500-word essay on "the impact of the mushroom industry to the community"
EIN: 232846736

7704
American Philosophical Society
104 S. 5th St.
Philadelphia, PA   19106-3387   (215) 440-3400
Contact: H. Linda Musumeci, Dir., Grants
FAX: (215) 440-3423;
E-mail: lmusumeci@amphilsoc.org; URL: http://www.amphilsoc.org

Foundation type: Public charity
Purpose: Grants and fellowships to individual scholars for research in a variety of fields.
Publications: Application guidelines.
Financial data: Year ended 12/31/2011. Assets, $147,804,979 (M); Expenditures, $9,939,346; Total giving, $1,701,309; Grants to individuals, totaling $764,596.
Fields of interest: Humanities; Language/linguistics; Philosophy/ethics; Medical research; Research; Ethnic studies.
Type of support: Fellowships; Research; Postdoctoral support.
Application information:
  Initial approach: Letter or e-mail
  Additional information: Proposed use of funds must be stated. See web site for complete program information.
Program descriptions:
  Daland Fellowships in Clinical Investigation: For research in internal medicine, neurology, psychiatry, and pediatrics. Research must be patient-oriented. Candidates are expected to have held an M.D. degree for less than eight years. Applicants must expect to perform their research at an institution in the U.S. under the supervision of a scientific advisor. Awards are for $40,000 per year, and are renewable for a second year.
  Franklin Research Grants: These grants support the cost of research that leads to publication, in all areas of knowledge. Proposals may be in all areas of scholarly knowledge except those in which support by government or corporate enterprise is more appropriate. The program does not accept proposals in the area of journalistic or other writing for general readership; the preparation of textbooks or anthologies; or the work of creative and performing artists. Applicants are expected to have a doctorate or to have published work of doctoral character and quality; Ph.D. candidates are not eligible to apply, but the society is particularly interested in supporting the work of young scholars who have recently received their doctorate. Awards are for up to $6,000 for one year.
  Lewis and Clark Fund for Exploration and Field Research: This fund encourages exploratory field studies for the collection of specimens and data and to provide the imaginative stimulus that accompanies direct observation. Applications are invited from disciplines with a large dependence on field studies, such as archaeology, anthropology, biology, ecology, geography, geology, linguistics, and paleontology, but grants will not be restricted to these fields. Grants are only available to doctoral students; the maximum grant awarded will be $5,000. A separate program in astrobiology for graduate students and post-doctoral and junior scientists is also available.
  Library Resident Research Fellowships: $2,500 per month is awarded to support research in the society's collections for a minimum of one month and a maximum of three months. Some preference will be given to persons whose normal place of residence is outside a 75-mile radius of Philadelphia.
  Phillips Fund Grants for Native American Research: Grants are awarded for research in Native American linguistics and ethnohistory in North America. Work in archaeology, ethnography, psycholinguistics, or pedagogy is ineligible.

Applicants may be graduate students who have passed their qualifying examinations for either master's or doctoral degrees; post-doctoral applicants are eligible. The maximum award is $3,500. Grants are ordinarily given for one year and cover travel, tapes, and consultant fees. Grants are not made for projects in archaeology, ethnography, psycholinguistics, or for the preparation of pedagogical materials.
EIN: 231353269

7705
American Society of Regional Anesthesia and Pain Medicine
239 4th Ave., Ste. 1714
Pittsburgh, PA   15222   (847) 934-7107
Application e-mail: lmafrica@kenes.com, asokumar@aol.com
FAX: (847) 825-5658;
E-mail: j.kahlfeldt@asahq.org; E-Mail for Leonard Mafrica: lmafrica@kenes.com; URL: http://www.asra.com

Foundation type: Public charity
Purpose: Grants for the development and the promotion to further scholarly research in the practice of regional anesthesia.
Publications: Annual report.
Financial data: Year ended 12/31/2011. Assets, $4,834,696 (M); Expenditures, $2,309,954; Total giving, $50,000. Grants to individuals amount not specified.
Fields of interest: Medical specialties research.
Type of support: Research.
Application information: Applications accepted.
  Send request by: E-mail
  Deadline(s): Nov. 30 for Carl Koller Grant
  Final notification: Recipients notified in the Spring
  Additional information: Selection is based on scientific or medical merit. See web site for additional guidelines.
Program description:
  Carl Koller Memorial Research Grant: The purpose of the grant is to encourage anesthesiologists and other researchers who are interested in research related to any aspect of local anesthetics and regional anesthesia and their application to surgery, obstetrics and pain control. The society solicits research grant requests from any of its members for amounts of $500 to $75,000. The grant requests can be for research using laboratory animals for clinical research projects with patients. It is the interest of the society that these awards should provide "seed money" for preliminary investigations leading to continued work supported by other sources. Previous awardees are not encouraged to apply. The award is intended for initiating research at the early part of one's career, with the goal of helping the applicant towards sustained independent funding. The awards are not intended, nor should they be used, to supplement ongoing projects.
EIN: 510163222

7706
Angelo Brothers Company Founders Scholarship Foundation
12401 McNulty Rd.
Philadelphia, PA   19154-3297   (215) 671-2000

Foundation type: Independent foundation
Purpose: Scholarships to children of full-time employees of Angelo Brothers Company or an affiliate.

Financial data: Year ended 12/31/2012. Assets, $328,479 (M); Expenditures, $23,281; Total giving, $23,214; Grants to individuals, 9 grants totaling $23,214 (high: $3,750, low: $1,964).
Fields of interest: Scholarships/financial aid.
Type of support: Employee-related scholarships.
Application information: Application form required.
  Deadline(s): May 1
  Applicants should submit the following:
    1) Financial information
    2) Letter(s) of recommendation
    3) Transcripts
Program description:
  Scholarship Program: Children of Angelo Brothers Company employees are eligible to apply provided the combined family income of the applicant and his or her parents does not exceed $40,000 per year. Criteria for selection includes academic achievement, financial need, extracurricular activities and achievements, community involvement, economic self-help (e.g., part-time and summer employment of the applicant), and recommendations. Scholarships are renewable up to four years provided the recipient continues to be a matriculated degree candidate, maintains a 3.0 GPA, and has not been the subject of disciplinary punishment for misconduct, or convicted of a criminal charge other than routine traffic violations.
EIN: 232825756

7707
AO North America, Inc.
1700 Russell Rd.
Paoli, PA   19301-1224   (610) 993-5100
FAX: (610) 695-2420; E-mail: ellisa@aona.org; Course Info.: c/o AO North America Continuing Medical Education, 1690 Russell Rd., Paoli, PA 19301, tel.: (800) 769-1391 or (610) 695-2459; e-mail: registrar@aona.org; URL: http://www.aona.org

Foundation type: Independent foundation
Purpose: Fellowships to fully-trained orthopedic and general surgeons.
Financial data: Year ended 06/30/2012. Assets, $16,831,445 (M); Expenditures, $12,071,331; Total giving, $547,999.
Fields of interest: Surgery; Nerve, muscle & bone research.
International interests: Europe.
Type of support: Fellowships.
Application information: Application form required.
  Initial approach: Letter, telephone, or fax
  Deadline(s): Jan. 15, Apr. 15, July 15, Oct. 15
  Final notification: Within three weeks of applicable review date.
  Applicants should submit the following:
    1) Curriculum vitae
    2) Photograph
    3) Letter(s) of recommendation
  Additional information: Application must also include copy of medical school diploma, copy of AO Basic Course certificate, and list of publications and lectures. Recipients will be chosen based on their knowledge of orthopaedic medicine and research ability. Grants rarely exceed $5,000 for research projects. Maximum funding for visiting professor program: $3,000 per professor from North America, $6,000 per professor from abroad. Incomplete applications will not be considered.
Program descriptions:
  Jack McDaniel Memorial AO Fellowship: The award, given to one North American Resident, will consist of all travel expenses to the site of the fellowship, and the usual current monthly AO

Fellowship stipend for a period of no more than three months ($2,000 per month). At the Annual North American Spring Basic & Advanced AO Course immediately after completion of the fellowship, the fellow will be invited to be a table instructor and travel expenses and lodging will be covered as for other faculty members. Support for family members is not included.
  John Border Memorial European Trauma Fellowship: Offered to a graduating North American trauma fellow who plans a career in academic trauma surgery. The award will consist of round-trip travel expenses to the site of the fellowship in Europe and a monthly stipend for up to three months to support living expenses at the fellowship site. Support for family members is not included. The fellowship will take place at major AO trauma centers in Europe. The recipient of the fellowship will be invited as a junior faculty member at a North American AO ASIF course in the year following his/her fellowship, with travel and lodging expenses paid by the AO Course organization.
  Martin Allgower Trauma Fellowship: The fellowship, to one practicing North American trauma surgeon, will be granted for three to six months, at a European AO trauma center. The award consists of round-trip travel expenses for the fellow to the site of the fellowship, living quarters for the fellow (and spouse), and a monthly stipend of $2,000 to cover meals and incidentals. Also included in the fellowship is an invitation as a faculty member to the annual AO ASIF Davos Course the year following completion of the fellowship, with the travel and lodging paid for by the course organization. During the course, the fellow may be asked to present a report on his/her fellowship experience.
  Standard AO Fellowship: The award, given to one North American Resident, will consist of all travel expenses to the site of the fellowship, and the usual current monthly AO Fellowship stipend for a period of no more than three months ($2,000 per month). At the Annual North American Spring Basic & Advanced AO Course immediately after completion of the fellowship, the fellow will be invited to be a table instructor and travel expenses and lodging will be covered as for other faculty members. Support for family members is not included.
EIN: 232701788

7708
App Foundation
1010 Stonebridge Dr.
Selinsgrove, PA   17870   (570) 743-1126

Foundation type: Independent foundation
Purpose: Scholarships to high school seniors or college students, domiciled in Snyder county, PA changing his/her career track pursuing a career in nursing, occupational therapy and pharmacy.
Financial data: Year ended 12/31/2012. Assets, $524,251 (M); Expenditures, $43,014; Total giving, $35,500; Grants to individuals, 12 grants totaling $30,250 (high: $4,000, low: $1,250).
Fields of interest: Nursing school/education; Health sciences school/education; Pharmacology.
Type of support: Scholarships—to individuals.
Application information: Applications accepted. Application form required. Interview required.
  Deadline(s): Dec. 31
  Applicants should submit the following:
    1) Transcripts
    2) Financial information
  Additional information: Selection is based on academic achievement, demonstrated

concern for others, financial need and informal educational accomplishments.
EIN: 260848791

7709
Arkema Inc. Foundation
(formerly Atofina Chemicals, Inc. Foundation)
900 First Ave.
King of Prussia, PA 19406-1308 (215) 419-7735
Contact: Diane Milici, Admin.
E-mail: diane.milici@arkema.com; URL: http://www.arkema-inc.com/index.cfm?pag=590

Foundation type: Company-sponsored foundation
Purpose: Scholarships to high school seniors who are children of active or deceased employees of Arkema, Inc.
Publications: Application guidelines.
Financial data: Year ended 12/31/2012. Assets, $280,820 (M); Expenditures, $278,312; Total giving, $272,562; Grants to individuals, 66 grants totaling $32,500 (high: $500, low: $300).
Type of support: Employee-related scholarships.
Application information: Applications not accepted.
  Additional information: Unsolicited requests for funds not considered or acknowledged.
Company name: Arkema Inc.
EIN: 236256818

7710
The Armstrong County Community Foundation
220 S. Jefferson St., Ste. B
Kittanning, PA 16201 (724) 548-5897
Contact: Mindy Knappenberger, Exec. Dir.
FAX: (724) 548-4275;
E-mail: accfound@windstream.net; URL: http://www.accfound.org

Foundation type: Community foundation
Purpose: Educational scholarships to residents of Armstrong County, PA, for higher education.
Publications: Grants list.
Financial data: Year ended 12/31/2012. Assets, $6,117,357 (M); Expenditures, $793,374; Total giving, $639,795; Grants to individuals, 307 grants totaling $290,342.
Fields of interest: Higher education; Scholarships/financial aid.
Type of support: Scholarships—to individuals; Undergraduate support.
Application information: Applications accepted. Application form available on the grantmaker's web site.
  Initial approach: Letter
  Send request by: Mail, fax or e-mail
  Copies of proposal: 1
  Deadline(s): Mar. 15
  Applicants should submit the following:
    1) Transcripts
    2) SAT
    3) Letter(s) of recommendation
    4) Essay
  Additional information: See web site for full list of scholarship programs and additional guidelines.
Program description:
  Scholarships: The foundation offers two different categories of scholarships, one for college and adult students and another for PreK and K through 12 students. College scholarships are available to eligible seniors from Armstrong County that are graduating from a Armstrong County School. Educational Improvement Tax Credit (EITC) program

offers scholarships for eligible students to attend approved preschools and private K through 12 schools in both Armstrong and Butler Counties. See web site for additional information.
EIN: 311625798

7711
Armstrong Foundation
2500 Columbia Ave.
Lancaster, PA 17603-4117
URL: http://www.armstrongfoundation.com/

Foundation type: Company-sponsored foundation
Purpose: Grants to economically disadvantaged employees experiencing financial hardship, natural disasters, or catastrophic illness.
Publications: Application guidelines; Program policy statement.
Financial data: Year ended 12/31/2012. Assets, $1,539,160 (M); Expenditures, $1,443,035; Total giving, $1,424,806.
Fields of interest: Disasters, preparedness/services.
Type of support: Employee-related welfare.
Application information: Applications not accepted.
  Additional information: Unsolicited requests for funds not considered or acknowledged.
Company name: Armstrong World Industries, Inc.
EIN: 232387950

7712
Armstrong Health & Education Foundation
1 Nolte Dr.
Kittanning, PA 16201-7111 (724) 543-8850
URL: http://acmh.org/acmh-foundation/

Foundation type: Public charity
Purpose: Financial assistance to low income cancer patients residing in Armstrong County, PA, who have health costs associated with cancer treatment.
Financial data: Year ended 06/30/2012. Assets, $6,517,236 (M); Expenditures, $435,585; Total giving, $131,089; Grants to individuals, totaling $21,577.
Fields of interest: Cancer.
Type of support: Grants for special needs.
Application information:
  Initial approach: Letter
  Additional information: Contact foundation for further application guidelines.
EIN: 251655867

7713
Arnold Foundation
c/o Paciotti
Plz. 315, 1094 Rte. 315
Wilkes Barre, PA 18702-6943 (570) 823-8855

Foundation type: Independent foundation
Purpose: Scholarships to individuals with preference to residents of the Luzerne County, PA area.
Financial data: Year ended 03/31/2013. Assets, $1,045,221 (M); Expenditures, $58,750; Total giving, $46,568; Grants to individuals, 3 grants totaling $15,368 (high: $7,200, low: $2,000).
Type of support: Scholarships—to individuals.
Application information: Applications accepted.
  Deadline(s): None
  Additional information: Application by letter including brief resume of academic qualifications.
EIN: 236417708

7714
Jack Arpajian Armenian Educational Foundation Inc.
P.O. Box 1090
Exton, PA 19341-0107 (410) 531-7753
Contact: Laurel Connelly, Exec. Dir.
Application address: 6030 Daybreak Cir., Ste. A 150/123, Clarksville, MD 21029, tel.: (410) 531-7753

Foundation type: Independent foundation
Purpose: Scholarships to students of Armenian heritage for higher education.
Financial data: Year ended 12/31/2012. Assets, $485,415 (M); Expenditures, $81,227; Total giving, $48,000; Grants to individuals, 9 grants totaling $48,000 (high: $6,000, low: $3,000).
International interests: Armenia.
Type of support: Undergraduate support.
Application information: Application form required.
  Initial approach: Letter
  Deadline(s): Aug. 1 and Dec. 1
EIN: 232761002

7715
Asbestos Workers Local 14 Scholarship Fund
2014 Hornig Rd.
Philadelphia, PA 19116-4202 (215) 289-4303
FAX: (215) 289-8655; E-mail: info@local-14.org; URL: http://www.local-14.org

Foundation type: Public charity
Purpose: Scholarships to members of Asbestos Workers Local 14 who are employed by participating employers, or their children, for undergraduate education.
Financial data: Year ended 06/30/2012. Assets, $3,347 (M); Expenditures, $25,500; Total giving, $25,500.
Fields of interest: Labor unions/organizations.
Type of support: Employee-related scholarships; Undergraduate support.
Application information:
  Deadline(s): Contact organization for current application deadlines/guidelines
  Additional information: Recipients selected according to leadership, academics and financial need.
EIN: 311729117

7716
The Association for Frontotemporal Dementias
Radnor Station Bldg. No. 2, Ste. 320
290 King of Prussia Rd.
Radnor, PA 19087-5107 (267) 514-7221
Fellowship e-mail: fellowship@ftd-picks.org
E-mail: info@ftd-picks.org; URL: http://www.ftd-picks.org

Foundation type: Public charity
Purpose: Fellowship to an outstanding scientist for research on frontotemporal dementia.
Publications: Application guidelines; Annual report; Informational brochure; Newsletter.
Financial data: Year ended 06/30/2012. Assets, $1,190,461 (M); Expenditures, $478,783; Total giving, $23,004; Grants to individuals, totaling $21,014.
Fields of interest: Brain research.
Type of support: Fellowships; Research.
Application information: Applications accepted. Application form required. Application form available on the grantmaker's web site.

Send request by: On-line
Deadline(s): Nov. 16 for Letter of Intent, Jan. 7 for Postdoctoral Fellowships for application
Final notification: Applicants notified Mar. 1
Applicants should submit the following:
1) Letter(s) of recommendation
2) Resume
3) Budget Information
4) Curriculum vitae
5) Proposal
Additional information: Application should also include a personal statement, two-year research plan, and letter of sponsorship.

Program description:
Postdoctoral Fellowships in Frontotemporal Dementia: A two-year fellowship (of $55,000 for each year) will be available to help foster basic, translational, clinical, and/or epidemiological frontotemporal dementia (FTD) research by an outstanding scientist at the beginning of his/her career. An individual with a Ph.D., M.D., or M.D./Ph.D. at an academic facility, teaching hospital, or research institution who will be in the first, second, or third year of his/her postdoctoral training at the start of the fellowship term is eligible to apply. Awards are intended to cover stipend and benefits, with any remaining balance of these funds permitted to be designated to direct research expenses.
EIN: 412073220

7717
Association for Iron and Steel Technology
186 Thorn Hill Rd.
Warrendale, PA   15086-7528   (724) 814-3000
Contact: Ron Ashburn, Exec. Dir. and Secy.
Application information for the Lincoln, Korf, Fairless, and Schwabe scholarships: contact Lori Wharrey, e-mail: lwharrey@aist.org or tel.: (724) 776-6040 ext. 621; Samson Canadian Scholarship: contact Robert Kneale, AIST Northern Member Chapter, P.O. Box 1734, Cambridge, ON NIR7G8, Canada; Don Nelson Scholarship: contact AIST Midwest Member Chapter Scholarships, c/o Michael Heaney, 3210 Watling St., East Chicago, IN 46312
FAX: (724) 814-3001; E-mail: info@aist.org; E-mail For Ron Ashburn: rashburn@aist.org; URL: http://www.aist.org

Foundation type: Public charity
Purpose: Scholarships to students majoring in engineering, metallurgy, or material sciences.
Publications: Application guidelines.
Financial data: Year ended 06/30/2012. Assets, $17,286,744 (M); Expenditures, $7,829,226; Total giving, $229,386.
Fields of interest: Engineering/technology; Engineering.
International interests: Canada.
Type of support: Scholarships—to individuals.
Application information: Applications accepted. Application form required. Application form available on the grantmaker's web site.
Send request by: Mail or e-mail
Deadline(s): Mar. 5
Applicants should submit the following:
1) SAT
2) ACT
3) Transcripts
4) Letter(s) of recommendation
5) Essay
6) Resume
Additional information: See web site for complete program information.
EIN: 200338690

7718
Association of Theological Schools in the U.S. & Canada
10 Summit Park Dr.
Pittsburgh, PA   15275-1103   (412) 788-6505
Contact: Daniel O. Aleshire, Exec. Dir.
FAX: (412) 788-6510; E-mail: ats@ats.edu; Tel. for Daniel O. Aleshire : (412)-788-6505 Ext. 227;
URL: http://www.ats.edu

Foundation type: Public charity
Purpose: Grants for the enhancement of theological studies to full-time faculty of accredited member schools.
Publications: Application guidelines; Grants list; Informational brochure (including application guidelines); Newsletter.
Financial data: Year ended 06/30/2011. Assets, $19,302,168 (M); Expenditures, $4,615,646; Total giving, $860,929.
Fields of interest: Theological school/education.
International interests: Canada.
Type of support: Fellowships; Research; Sabbaticals.
Application information: Applications accepted. Application form required. Application form available on the grantmaker's web site.
Initial approach: E-mail
Deadline(s): Dec. 1 for Luce Grants; Jan. 5 for Lilly Grants
Applicants should submit the following:
1) Proposal
2) Letter(s) of recommendation
3) Budget Information
Additional information: See web site for complete program information.

Program descriptions:
Henry Luce, III Fellows In Theology: Provides up to $75,000 of matching salary replacement and research funds, and affords Fellows the opportunity to devote a twelve-month leave to research and writing. Awards are given to full-time faculty of member schools of the Association. A conference is held each year where the Fellows have the opportunity to present their conclusions and engage in discussion about their findings and the relation of their work to issues of faith and church life.
Lilly Collaborative Research Grants: As many as four grants of up to $16,000 are available to collaborative research projects from full-time faculty researchers at ATS accredited and candidate schools.
Lilly Faculty Fellowship: Provides up to six fellowships of up to $30,000 for salary and benefit replacement and, if needed, funds for direct research expenses to full-time faculty of member schools of the Association. Awards will be made on a competitive basis for research projects that demonstrate special promise of quality, significance for theological education, and applicability to the life of faith communities and contemporary society.
Lilly Research Expenses Grants: Provides up to $5,000 for six grants to support direct expenses for travel necessary to access material archived elsewhere, for research assistance in gathering or processing data, for essential specialized software, or for similar direct expenses related to faculty research projects. Awards are given to full-time faculty of member schools of the Association. These grants are designed to allow flexibility and encourage creativity on the part of recipients.
Lilly Theological Scholars Grants: Provides up to $12,000 for as many as six grants for full-time faculty of member schools of the Association. The Faculty may request Theological Research Grants for three different patterns of work. Applicants can

request or specify how the money can be used for research.
EIN: 562476876

7719
Aysr Foundation
1388 State Rte. 487
Bloomsburg, PA   17815   (570) 784-0111
Contact: John D. Klingerman, Pres.
Application address: Orangeville, PA 17859

Foundation type: Independent foundation
Purpose: Grants to economically disadvantaged individuals in PA.
Financial data: Year ended 12/31/2012. Assets, $163,715 (M); Expenditures, $32,757; Total giving, $32,707.
Type of support: Grants for special needs.
Application information: Applications accepted.
Initial approach: Letter
Deadline(s): None
EIN: 232966353

7720
Franz and Virginia Bader Fund
2000 Hamilton St., Ste. 700
Philadelphia, PA   19130   (202) 288-4608
URL: http://www.baderfund.org

Foundation type: Independent foundation
Purpose: Grants to visual artists who are 40 years or older and live within 150 miles of Washington, DC.
Financial data: Year ended 12/31/2012. Assets, $860,889 (M); Expenditures, $121,722; Total giving, $75,000; Grants to individuals, 5 grants totaling $75,000 (high: $15,000, low: $15,000).
Fields of interest: Visual arts.
Type of support: Grants to individuals.
Application information: Applications accepted. Application form required. Application form available on the grantmaker's web site.
Send request by: Mail (FedEx, UPS, or USPS)
Deadline(s): Sept. 15
Final notification: Applicants notified before the end of the calendar year
Applicants should submit the following:
1) Resume
2) SASE
Additional information: Application should also include images, slides, and digital files. Applications from filmmakers, video artists, and performance artists not accepted. Applicant must show proof of age. Application by fax or e-mail not accepted.
EIN: 522342875

7721
Mary H. Bailey Trust
c/o BNY Mellon, N.A.
P.O. Box 185
Pittsburgh, PA   15230-0185   (302) 421-2204

Foundation type: Public charity
Purpose: Scholarships to students from Indian River School District and Woodbridge School District, DE.
Financial data: Year ended 06/30/2012. Assets, $760,846 (M); Expenditures, $27,905; Total giving, $15,700.
Fields of interest: Higher education.
Type of support: Support to graduates or students of specific schools; Undergraduate support.

Application information: Unsolicited requests for funds not accepted.
EIN: 236793317

7722

Barrand & Bradford Scholarship
c/o PNC Bank, N.A.
P.O. Box 609
Pittsburgh, PA 15230-9738   (800) 882-3456

Foundation type: Independent foundation
Purpose: Scholarships to incoming freshman for full time attendance at Taylor University, IN,.
Financial data: Year ended 07/31/2013. Assets, $482,977 (M); Expenditures, $7,049; Total giving, $0.
Fields of interest: Higher education.
Type of support: Support to graduates or students of specific schools; Undergraduate support.
Application information: Applications accepted. Application form required.
  Deadline(s): June 1
  Applicants should submit the following:
    1) SAT
    2) Transcripts
    3) GPA
    4) Letter(s) of recommendation
    5) Financial information
    6) Essay
EIN: 356615379

7723

Bartko Foundation
P.O. Box 17160
Pittsburgh, PA 15235-0160   (412) 371-1142
Contact: Carl Ellis Perkins, Exec. Dir. and C.E.O.
E-mail: director@bartkofoundation.com;
URL: http://www.bartkofoundation.com

Foundation type: Public charity
Purpose: Provides assistance to single minority women of PA, with children who are striving to achieve self-sufficiency.
Publications: Application guidelines.
Financial data: Year ended 12/31/2011. Assets, $389,366 (M); Expenditures, $211,787; Total giving, $143,940; Grants to individuals, 23 grants totaling $143,940.
Fields of interest: Minorities; Adults, women; Young adults, female; Single parents.
Type of support: Grants to individuals.
Application information: Applications accepted. Application form required.
  Initial approach: Application
  Send request by: Mail
  Deadline(s): Ongoing
  Final notification: Approximately four weeks
  Additional information: Application should include financial information. See web site for additional application guidelines.
EIN: 522388581

7724

G. Basila Scholarship Fund
517 Ct., St.
Scranton, PA 18508   (570) 342-2676
Contact: Joseph A. Karam, Tr.

Foundation type: Operating foundation
Purpose: Scholarships to students with financial need who attend St. Ann's Maronite Church, Scranton, PA, or St. Joseph's Melkite Church, Scranton, PA.
Financial data: Year ended 12/31/2012. Assets, $270,544 (M); Expenditures, $42,466; Total

giving, $34,606; Grants to individuals, 9 grants totaling $34,606 (high: $6,146, low: $2,210).
Type of support: Scholarships—to individuals.
Application information:
  Initial approach: Letter
  Deadline(s): Prior to start of semester
  Additional information: Application should financial need and include copy of financial aid forms.
EIN: 232614309

7725

Graham Sefton & Anna Mae Sweeney Baskin Foundation
131 Cambridge St.
Indiana, PA 15701-2404   (724) 349-7027
Contact: Edward E. Mackey, Tr.

Foundation type: Independent foundation
Purpose: Scholarships to students who are attending or have attended a high school in Indiana County, PA, to pursue a degree in nursing or physical education.
Financial data: Year ended 12/31/2012. Assets, $1,082,457 (M); Expenditures, $57,785; Total giving, $41,500; Grants to individuals, 28 grants totaling $41,500 (high: $2,500, low: $500).
Fields of interest: Medical school/education; Nursing care; Recreation.
Type of support: Support to graduates or students of specific schools; Undergraduate support.
Application information: Applications accepted. Application form required.
  Deadline(s): Mar. 1
EIN: 251777790

7726

The Beaver County Foundation
P.O. Box 569
Beaver, PA 15009-0569   (724) 728-1331
Contact: Charles O'Data, Pres.
E-mail: cnodata@aol.com; URL: http://www.beavercountyfoundation.com

Foundation type: Community foundation
Purpose: Scholarships to graduates of high schools in Beaver County, PA for postsecondary education.
Publications: Informational brochure.
Financial data: Year ended 12/31/2012. Assets, $6,957,038 (M); Expenditures, $543,916; Total giving, $380,472; Grants to individuals, 35 grants totaling $51,500.
Fields of interest: Higher education.
Type of support: Undergraduate support.
Application information: Applications accepted. Application form not required.
  Initial approach: Letter or e-mail
  Send request by: E-mail
  Copies of proposal: 1
  Deadline(s): None
  Applicants should submit the following:
    1) SAT
    2) Resume
    3) Proposal
    4) Letter(s) of recommendation
    5) GPA
    6) Financial information
    7) Essay
    8) ACT
  Additional information: Awards are made directly to the postsecondary institution on behalf of the students. Application process varies by scholarship fund.
EIN: 251660309

7727

George H. Benford Charities
c/o PNC Bank
620 Liberty Ave., 10th Fl.
Pittsburgh, PA 15222-2705   (412) 762-6633
Contact: Benjamin Ciocco Chari

Foundation type: Independent foundation
Purpose: Student loans only to graduates of the Meyersdale Joint High School, PA.
Financial data: Year ended 09/30/2013. Assets, $2,207,991 (M); Expenditures, $79,627; Total giving, $70,901.
Fields of interest: Education.
Type of support: Student loans—to individuals; Support to graduates or students of specific schools; Undergraduate support.
Application information: Applications accepted. Application form required.
  Deadline(s): None
  Applicants should submit the following:
    1) Financial information
    2) Essay
  Additional information: Contact PNC Bank for loan application and additional requirements.
EIN: 256038490

7728

Robert L. Bennett, Sr. Trust f/b/o Towanda High School Scholarships
c/o Citizens & Northern Bank
90 Main St., Ste. 92
Wellsboro, PA 16901-1517

Foundation type: Independent foundation
Purpose: College scholarships for graduating high school students of Towanda High School, PA for continuing education at accredited colleges or universities.
Financial data: Year ended 12/31/2012. Assets, $499,798 (M); Expenditures, $30,575; Total giving, $24,726; Grants to individuals, 3 grants totaling $24,726 (high: $9,890, low: $4,946).
Fields of interest: Higher education.
Type of support: Support to graduates or students of specific schools.
Application information: Applications accepted.
  Additional information: Contact high school for application information.
EIN: 256622430

7729

William L. & Margaret L. Benz Foundation
c/o BNY Mellon, N.A.
P.O. Box 185
Pittsburgh, PA 15230-0185
Contact: Laurie Moritz, Trust Off., BNY Mellon, N.A.

Foundation type: Independent foundation
Purpose: Scholarships to students of Blairsville High School, PA.
Financial data: Year ended 05/31/2013. Assets, $3,461,953 (M); Expenditures, $180,186; Total giving, $161,750; Grants to individuals, 99 grants totaling $109,200 (high: $2,500, low: $300).
Type of support: Scholarships—to individuals; Support to graduates or students of specific schools.
Application information: Application form required.
  Deadline(s): Apr. 30
  Additional information: Contact Blairsville High School to request application.
EIN: 256276186

7730
Berks County Community Foundation
237 Court St.
Reading, PA 19601 (610) 685-2223
Contact: Kevin K. Murphy, Pres.
FAX: (610) 685-2240; E-mail: info@bccf.org;
URL: http://www.bccf.org

Foundation type: Community foundation
Purpose: Scholarships to individuals in Berks County, PA, for higher education.
Publications: Application guidelines; Annual report; Financial statement; Grants list; Newsletter.
Financial data: Year ended 06/30/2012. Assets, $51,964,330 (M); Expenditures, $4,661,722; Total giving, $2,896,485; Grants to individuals, 287 grants totaling $567,020 (high: $24,474); Loans to individuals, 7 loans totaling $31,499.
Fields of interest: Higher education; Scholarships/financial aid; Education.
Type of support: Scholarships—to individuals; Support to graduates or students of specific schools; Awards/prizes; Technical education support; Undergraduate support.
Application information: Applications accepted. Application form required. Application form available on the grantmaker's web site.
Copies of proposal: 1
Deadline(s): Varies
Additional information: See web site for a complete listing of scholarship funds.
Program description:
Scholarship Funds: The foundation administers scholarship and award funds for Berks County students. These funds often carry the name of the donor, school district, or field of education that the scholarship or award serves. Each scholarship has its own unique set of application guidelines and selection criteria, including school district, enrollment level, major, academic merit and financial need. See web site for additional information.
EIN: 232769892

7731
Bernowski Scholarship Trust Fund
c/o PNC Bank, N.A.
P.O. Box 609
Pittsburgh, PA 15230-9738 (412) 768-8538
Contact: John Montoya
Application address: c/o PNC Bank, N.A., 620 Liberty, 2 PNC Plz., 25th Fl.. Pittsburgh, PA 15222, tel.: (412) 768-8538

Foundation type: Independent foundation
Purpose: Scholarships to graduating seniors of Belle Vernon, Charleroi, and Ringgold, PA, high schools who are under 22, to attend local colleges.
Financial data: Year ended 08/31/2013. Assets, $291,468 (M); Expenditures, $18,075; Total giving, $14,600; Grants to individuals, totaling $14,600.
Fields of interest: Higher education.
Type of support: Support to graduates or students of specific schools; Undergraduate support.
Application information: Applications accepted. Application form required.
Deadline(s): None
Applicants should submit the following:
1) Class rank
2) SAT
3) GPA
EIN: 256534799

7732
Charles G. Berwind Foundation, Inc.
1500 Market St., 3000 Centre Sq. W.
Philadelphia, PA 19102-2100
Contact: Eileen P. Moore

Foundation type: Independent foundation
Purpose: Scholarship to students for attendance at accredited institutions of higher learning in the U.S.
Financial data: Year ended 09/30/2012. Assets, $6,813,125 (M); Expenditures, $357,423; Total giving, $281,009; Grants to individuals, 46 grants totaling $275,009 (high: $15,629, low: $438).
Fields of interest: College.
Type of support: Scholarships—to individuals.
Application information: Applications accepted. Application form required.
Deadline(s): Nov. 30
Applicants should submit the following:
1) Transcripts
2) Letter(s) of recommendation
3) FAFSA
4) SAT
5) ACT
Additional information: Contact the foundation for additional guidelines.
EIN: 203039970

7733
Mary L. C. Biddle Foundation
c/o PNC Bank, N.A.
1600 Market St., No. 4th Fl.
Philadelphia, PA 19103-7240 (412) 768-8192

Foundation type: Independent foundation
Purpose: Financial assistance to women in the Philadelphia, PA, area.
Financial data: Year ended 12/31/2011. Assets, $192,331 (M); Expenditures, $35,007; Total giving, $32,000; Grants to individuals, 11 grants totaling $32,000 (high: $3,000, low: $2,000).
Fields of interest: Women; Economically disadvantaged.
Type of support: Grants for special needs.
Application information: Applications accepted.
Initial approach: Letter
Deadline(s): None
EIN: 236205851

7734
Ingeborg A. Biondo Memorial Trust
(formerly Ingeborg A. Biondo Memorial Trust)
221 Board St.
Milford, PA 18337-0231 (570) 296-5525
Contact: Joseph R. Biondo, Tr.
URL: http://www.biondofoundation.org/

Foundation type: Operating foundation
Purpose: Grants to orphaned and/or physically, mentally, and emotionally handicapped individuals in NY and PA. Scholarships to individuals studying special education.
Financial data: Year ended 12/31/2012. Assets, $1,454,364 (M); Expenditures, $426,601; Total giving, $24,279.
Fields of interest: Residential/custodial care; Disabilities, people with.
Type of support: Scholarships—to individuals; Grants for special needs.
Application information: Applications accepted. Application form required.
Deadline(s): None
EIN: 112801015

7735
Philo & Sarah Blaisdell Foundation
410 Seneca Building
Bradford, PA 16701 (814) 362-6340

Foundation type: Independent foundation
Purpose: Grants for medical, educational and other support to economically disadvantaged residents of McKean County, PA.
Financial data: Year ended 12/31/2012. Assets, $4,296,221 (M); Expenditures, $218,380; Total giving, $136,300; Grants to individuals, 5 grants totaling $1,937 (high: $769, low: $200).
Fields of interest: Education; Economically disadvantaged.
Type of support: Emergency funds; Employee-related scholarships; Grants to individuals; Employee-related welfare; Undergraduate support.
Application information: Contact foundation for current application deadline/guidelines.
EIN: 256035748

7736
Arthur F. Blanchard Trust
c/o BNY Mellon, N.A.
P.O. Box 185
Pittsburgh, PA 15230-0185

Foundation type: Independent foundation
Purpose: Scholarships to residents of Boxborough, MA who attended Blanchard Memorial School, MA.
Financial data: Year ended 08/31/2013. Assets, $18,033,061 (M); Expenditures, $1,403,264; Total giving, $1,256,800.
Type of support: Support to graduates or students of specific schools; Undergraduate support.
Application information: Applications accepted.
Initial approach: Letter
Deadline(s): June 15
Additional information: Contact trust for current application guidelines.
EIN: 046093374

7737
Blues Babe Foundation
2233 N. Broad St., 2nd Fl.
Philadelphia, PA 19132-4502 (267) 324-5600
Contact: Aisha Winfield, Exec. Dir.
E-mail: info@bluesbabefoundation.org; URL: http://bluesbabefoundation.org

Foundation type: Public charity
Purpose: Scholarships to disadvantaged students for undergraduate degrees who reside in the distressed areas of Philadelphia, PA; Camden, NJ; and the Delaware Valley.
Financial data: Year ended 12/31/2011. Assets, $75,820 (M); Expenditures, $150,750.
Fields of interest: Economically disadvantaged.
Type of support: Undergraduate support.
Application information: Applications accepted.
Initial approach: E-mail
Deadline(s): Mar. 1
EIN: 550805127

7738
Bonner-Price Student Loan Fund Trust
c/o Wells Fargo Bank N.A.
101N Inde ndence Mall E MACY1372-062
Philadelphia, PA 19106-2112 (432)685-5300

Foundation type: Independent foundation
Purpose: Loans to high school graduates of McMurry University, Abilene, TX.

Financial data: Year ended 12/31/2012. Assets, $1,226,298 (M); Expenditures, $109,265; Total giving, $63,000.
Fields of interest: Higher education.
Type of support: Student loans—to individuals; Support to graduates or students of specific schools.
Application information: Applications accepted. Application form required.
  Send request by: Mail
  Applicants should submit the following:
    1) Transcripts
    2) Financial information
Program description:
  Student Loan Program: Loans to students for one semester is limited to $7,500 per year. The maximum cumulative amount loaned to a student over the course of the student's academic career shall not exceed $30,000. Upon graduation or termination from McMurry University, the recipient repays the principal and interest on the loan on a monthly installment basis.
EIN: 726084752

7739
Boscov-Berk-Tek, Inc., Scholarship Fund
c/o Nexans Inc.
132 White Oak Rd.
New Holland, PA   17557-8303   (717) 354-6200
Contact: Robert Gascon, Tr.

Foundation type: Company-sponsored foundation
Purpose: Scholarships to children and spouses of employees and qualifying former employees of Berk-Tek, Inc., PA.
Financial data: Year ended 12/31/2012. Assets, $270,460 (M); Expenditures, $13,536; Total giving, $12,000; Grants to individuals, 3 grants totaling $12,000 (high: $4,000, low: $4,000).
Type of support: Employee-related scholarships.
Application information: Applications accepted. Application form required.
  Deadline(s): Contact fund for current application deadline
Company name: Berk-Tek, Incorporated
EIN: 237763668

7740
The Dietrich W. Botstiber Foundation
200 E. State St., Ste. 306-A
Media, PA   19063-3434   (610) 566-3375
Contact: Carlie Numi, Deputy Admin.
FAX: (610) 566-3376; E-mail: cnumi@botstiber.org;
URL: http://www.botstiber.org/

Foundation type: Independent foundation
Purpose: Scholarship to students in the U.S. and abroad for study at Lehigh University in PA.
Publications: Financial statement; IRS Form 990 or 990-PF printed copy available upon request.
Financial data: Year ended 08/31/2012. Assets, $29,001,749 (M); Expenditures, $1,625,230; Total giving, $1,221,373; Grants to individuals, 12 grants totaling $891,607 (high: $25,000, low: $1,400).
Fields of interest: Science; Engineering/technology.
Type of support: Scholarships—to individuals; Graduate support; Undergraduate support.
Application information: Applications accepted. Application form required. Application form available on the grantmaker's web site.
  Additional information: Students are selected on the basis of merit and need. See web site for additional guidelines.

Program description:
  Botstiber Scholars Program: This program provides four-year undergraduate scholarships to young men and women from all over the world for study at Lehigh University in PA. In addition to their course of study, Botstiber scholars participate in monthly seminars on issues of science, ethics and leadership. Students must be of good moral character, and they must study science, technology or commerce. The program looks for students who will return to their home countries and apply their American education for the betterment of their people.
EIN: 237807828

7741
John Boyer First City Troop
(formerly John Boyer First Troop Philadelphia City Cavalry Memorial Fund)
c/o BNY Mellon, N.A
P.O. Box 185
Pittsburgh, PA   15230-0185
Application Address: c/o The First City Troop, 23rd and Market St., Philadelphia, PA 19103

Foundation type: Independent foundation
Purpose: Scholarships by nomination only to members of the 1st City Troop, 23rd & Market St., Philadelphia, PA to study abroad for one year.
Financial data: Year ended 06/30/2013. Assets, $1,544,907 (M); Expenditures, $18,187; Total giving, $658; Grant to an individual, 1 grant totaling $658.
Type of support: Awards/grants by nomination only; Travel grants.
Application information: Applications not accepted.
  Additional information: Candidates must be nominated by a member of Cavalry.
EIN: 236227636

7742
Bernard F. Boyle Memorial Scholarship Fund
c/o BNY Mellon, N.A.
P.O. Box 185
Pittsburgh, PA   15230-0185

Foundation type: Independent foundation
Purpose: Scholarships to students majoring in accounting. First priority is given to residents of Nesquehoning, PA. Second priority is given to residents of Wilkes-Barre, PA.
Financial data: Year ended 12/31/2012. Assets, $914,923 (M); Expenditures, $36,050; Total giving, $23,780; Grants to individuals, 5 grants totaling $23,780 (high: $6,850, low: $1,600).
Fields of interest: Business school/education.
Type of support: Scholarships—to individuals.
Application information: Applications not accepted.
  Additional information: Unsolicited requests for funds not considered or acknowledged.
EIN: 236790683

7743
Bread and Roses Community Fund
(formerly The People's Fund)
1315 Walnut St., Ste. 1300
Philadelphia, PA   19107-4720   (215) 731-1107
Contact: Casey Cook, Exec. Dir.
FAX: (215) 731-0453;
E-mail: info@breadrosesfund.org; E-Mail for Patrice

Green: casey@breadrosesfund.org; URL: http://www.breadrosesfund.org/

Foundation type: Public charity
Purpose: Scholarships awarded to gay men attending accredited colleges, graduate or professional schools, who are residents of or are attending schools in Bucks, Chester, Delaware, Montgomery, Philadelphia, and Camden counties, PA.
Publications: Application guidelines; Grants list; Informational brochure; Newsletter.
Financial data: Year ended 06/30/2011. Assets, $1,440,009 (M); Expenditures, $558,167; Total giving, $139,330; Grants to individuals, totaling $21,000.
Fields of interest: Adults, men; LGBTQ.
Type of support: Graduate support; Undergraduate support.
Application information: Applications accepted. Application form required. Application form available on the grantmaker's web site.
  Initial approach: Letter or telephone
  Deadline(s): Jan. 15
EIN: 232047297

7744
J. P. Brenneman & M. H. Brenneman Fund
c/o BNY Mellon, N.A.
P.O. Box 185
Pittsburgh, PA   15230-0185

Foundation type: Independent foundation
Purpose: Scholarships to residents of York County, PA, for higher education at a university, college, or four-year technical school.
Financial data: Year ended 12/31/2012. Assets, $1,401,203 (M); Expenditures, $91,506; Total giving, $86,750.
Fields of interest: Vocational education.
Type of support: Technical education support; Undergraduate support.
Application information: Applications accepted. Application form required.
  Deadline(s): May 1
  Additional information: Contact the fund in Feb.
EIN: 237850463

7745
Brevillier Village Foundation Inc
5416 E. Lake Rd.
Erie, PA   16510   (814) 899-8600
Contact: George W. Hunter II, Pres.
URL: http://www.brevillier.org/

Foundation type: Independent foundation
Purpose: Scholarships to student nurses employed in the medical field in Erie, PA.
Financial data: Year ended 06/30/2012. Assets, $8,520,330 (M); Expenditures, $1,101,180; Total giving, $12,997; Grants to individuals, 4 grants totaling $12,997 (high: $5,045, low: $576).
Fields of interest: Nursing school/education.
Type of support: Undergraduate support.
Application information:
  Initial approach: Letter
  Deadline(s): None
  Additional information: Agreement is to provide employment services in exchange for non-repayment of scholarship.
EIN: 251548657

7746
Bridge Builders Community Foundation
(formerly Venango Area Community Foundation)
206 Seneca St., National Transit Annex, Ste. 10
P.O Box 374
Oil City, PA 16301-1367 (814) 677-8687
Contact: Jeanne Best, Opers. Dir.
FAX: (814) 677-0653;
E-mail: execdirbbcf@gmail.com; URL: http://
www.bridgebuilderscommunityfoundations.org

Foundation type: Community foundation
Purpose: Scholarships to graduates of high schools
in Venango County, PA.
Publications: Application guidelines; Annual report;
Informational brochure.
Financial data: Year ended 08/30/2012. Assets,
$5,051,722 (M); Expenditures, $424,771; Total
giving, $238,926; Grants to individuals, 148 grants
totaling $150,465.
Fields of interest: Higher education.
Type of support: Support to graduates or students
of specific schools; Technical education support;
Undergraduate support.
Application information: Applications accepted.
Application form required. Application form
available on the grantmaker's web site.
> *Initial approach:* Application
> *Send request by:* Mail
> *Deadline(s):* Apr. 1
> *Additional information:* See web site for
> application forms and complete listing of
> scholarship eligibility criteria per fund.
EIN: 251292553

7747
The Broadbent Family Foundation
(formerly The Broadbent Foundation)
15 Chestnut Hill Dr.
Mohnton, PA 19540-9330 (610) 796-7682
Contact: John H. Broadbent, Jr., Tr.

Foundation type: Independent foundation
Purpose: Scholarships to students at Governor
Mifflin High School, Shillington, PA, for higher
education.
Financial data: Year ended 06/30/2013. Assets,
$2,421,077 (M); Expenditures, $167,181; Total
giving, $142,307.
Type of support: Support to graduates or students
of specific schools; Undergraduate support.
Application information: Application form required.
Interview required.
> *Initial approach:* Letter
> *Send request by:* Mail
> *Applicants should submit the following:*
> 1) Letter(s) of recommendation
> 2) Transcripts
> *Additional information:* Application must also
> include verification of enrollment in school in
> good standing. Contact foundation for current
> application deadline/guidelines.
EIN: 232703271

7748
The Brossman Family Charitable Trust for Scholarships
c/o Ephrata National Bank
P.O. Box 457
Ephrata, PA 17522-0457
Application address: c/o ENB Money Mgmt. Group,
47 E. Main St., Ephrata, PA 17522-2713, tel.: (717)
733-6576

Foundation type: Independent foundation

Purpose: Scholarships to graduates of Ephrata
Senior High School, Ephrata, PA, or high school
residents in an area served by D&E
Communications.
Financial data: Year ended 10/31/2012. Assets,
$0 (M); Expenditures, $365,769; Total giving,
$345,000; Grants to individuals, 121 grants
totaling $345,000 (high: $6,000, low: $500).
Type of support: Support to graduates or students
of specific schools; Undergraduate support.
Application information: Application form required.
> *Deadline(s):* June 15
> *Additional information:* Application available from
> selection committee.
EIN: 232860047

7749
T. Wistar Brown Teacher's Fund
(formerly T. Wistar Brown Trust)
c/o PNC Bank
620 Liberty Ave., 10th Fl.
Pittsburgh, PA 15222-2705 (610) 388-7902
Contact: William D. Ravdin, Tr.
Application address: 122 Kendal Dr., Kennett Sq.,
PA 19348-2329, tel.: (610) 388-7902

Foundation type: Independent foundation
Purpose: Grants to financially needy members of
Philadelphia Yearly Meeting who are 21 years of age
or older. Candidates should be preparing to teach
at the elementary or secondary school level, or
taking or planning to take advanced courses to
enrich their teaching talents.
Financial data: Year ended 09/30/2013. Assets,
$2,148,866 (M); Expenditures, $69,594; Total
giving, $47,825; Grants to individuals, 8 grants
totaling $47,825 (high: $20,000, low: $3,035).
Fields of interest: Teacher school/education;
Education.
Type of support: Grants to individuals.
Application information: Application form required.
> *Deadline(s):* Apr. 15 for summer study, July 1 for
> fall or winter study, Dec. 15 for spring study
> *Applicants should submit the following:*
> 1) Letter(s) of recommendation
> 2) Essay
EIN: 236200741

7750
Florence H. Brown Trust
(also known as H. Fletcher Brown Trust)
c/o PNC Bank, N.A., Tax Department
1600 Market St.
Philadelphia, PA 19103-7240 (302) 429-1338
Contact: Donald W. Davis
Application address: c/o PNC Bank, 222 Delaware
Ave., Wilmington, DE 19899-1637, tel.: (302)
429-1338

Foundation type: Independent foundation
Purpose: Scholarships to financially needy DE
residents who are studying chemistry, engineering,
law, medicine or dentistry.
Financial data: Year ended 12/31/2011. Assets,
$267,368 (M); Expenditures, $29,106; Total
giving, $24,000.
Fields of interest: Dental school/education; Law
school/education; Medical school/education;
Chemistry; Engineering.
Type of support: Scholarships—to individuals.
Application information: Application form required.
Interview required.
> *Deadline(s):* Apr.
> *Applicants should submit the following:*
> 1) Letter(s) of recommendation
> 2) Financial information

3) SAT
4) Transcripts
Additional information: Applications should also
include birth certificate, last two tax returns
and a personal statement.
EIN: 516010596

7751
Pearl S. Buck International, Inc.
(formerly The Pearl S. Buck Foundation, Inc.)
520 Dublin Rd.
Perkasie, PA 18944-3005 (215) 249-0100
FAX: (215) 249-9657; E-mail: psbi@pearlsbuck.org;
E-Mail for Janet L. Mintzer:
jmintzer@pearlsbuck.org; URL: http://
pearlsbuck.org/

Foundation type: Public charity
Purpose: Specific assistance to individuals and
families throughout the world in areas of health,
education, adoption, and other services.
Publications: Annual report; Financial statement;
Newsletter.
Financial data: Year ended 06/30/2012. Assets,
$4,176,831 (M); Expenditures, $2,791,719; Total
giving, $302,772.
Fields of interest: Human services; Economically
disadvantaged.
Type of support: Grants for special needs.
Application information: Contact the organization
for additional information.
EIN: 231637212

7752
Bucks County Foundation
60 E. Court St.
P.O. Box 2073
Doylestown, PA 18901 (215) 997-8566
Contact: Linda Goodwin, Exec. Dir.
FAX: (215) 997-8564;
E-mail: lg@buckscountyfoundation.org;
URL: http://www.buckscountyfoundation.org

Foundation type: Community foundation
Purpose: Scholarships to high school graduates of
Bucks County, PA for postsecondary education.
Publications: Application guidelines; Annual report;
Financial statement; Informational brochure.
Financial data: Year ended 12/31/2012. Assets,
$11,313,113 (M); Expenditures, $536,957; Total
giving, $341,526.
Fields of interest: Higher education.
Type of support: Undergraduate support.
Application information: Applications accepted.
Application form required.
> *Additional information:* Students should apply
> through their high school's guidance office.
> See web site for complete program
> information.
EIN: 239031005

7753
Burch-Setton Student Loan Fund
c/o Wells Fargo Bank N.A.
101N Independence Mall E MACY1372-062
Philadelphia, PA 19106-2112 (806) 293-3658
Application address: c/o First United Methodist
Church, Attn.: Board of Stewards, 1001 W. 7th St.,
Plainview, TX 79072-7701, tel.: (806) 293-3658

Foundation type: Independent foundation
Purpose: Student loans to graduates of high
schools in Briscoe, Castro, Floyd, Hale, Lamb, and
Swisher counties, TX.

Financial data: Year ended 12/31/2012. Assets, $1,859,458 (M); Expenditures, $75,603; Total giving, $0.
Fields of interest: Higher education.
Type of support: Student loans—to individuals; Support to graduates or students of specific schools; Undergraduate support.
Application information: Applications accepted. Application form required.
   Deadline(s): June 1
   Applicants should submit the following:
      1) Transcripts
      2) GPA
      3) Financial information
EIN: 756056226

7754
William E. and Margaret N. Bush Memorial Scholarship Fund
P.O. Box 247
Apollo, PA   15613-0247

Foundation type: Independent foundation
Purpose: Scholarships to individuals.
Financial data: Year ended 12/31/2011. Assets, $640,369 (M); Expenditures, $15,888; Total giving, $7,695.
Type of support: Scholarships—to individuals.
Application information: Applications accepted.
EIN: 251814240

7755
M. Verna Butterer Educational Trust
P.O. Box 273
Fountainville, PA   18923   (215) 249-0503
E-mail: information@butterer.org; URL: http://www.butterer.org

Foundation type: Independent foundation
Purpose: Scholarships and interest free loans to individuals or high school seniors of Bucks County, PA, pursuing a post high school education.
Financial data: Year ended 01/31/2013. Assets, $6,321,758 (M); Expenditures, $189,502; Total giving, $127,801; Grants to individuals, 24 grants totaling $127,801 (high: $10,500, low: $1,027).
Fields of interest: Higher education.
Type of support: Scholarships—to individuals; Student loans—to individuals; Support to graduates or students of specific schools.
Application information: Applications accepted. Application form required. Application form available on the grantmaker's web site.
   Send request by: Mail
   Deadline(s): Mar. 15
   Final notification: Recipients notified in May
   Applicants should submit the following:
      1) Transcripts
      2) SAR
      3) Letter(s) of recommendation
      4) Financial information
      5) FAFSA
   Additional information: Application should also include copies of student and parents' income tax forms, and copy of financial aid award packages accepted from any and all sources. Applications available at public high school guidance departments in Bucks County, PA.
EIN: 237751390

7756
Stephen G. Calvert Memorial Merit Scholarship Foundation
5 Tower Bridge, 300 Barr Harbor Dr., Ste. 600
West Conshohocken, PA   19428-2998

Foundation type: Company-sponsored foundation
Purpose: Scholarships to dependents of Keystone Foods LLC employees.
Financial data: Year ended 10/31/2013. Assets, $16,327 (M); Expenditures, $198,100; Total giving, $177,000.
Type of support: Employee-related scholarships.
Application information: Application form required.
   Initial approach: Letter
   Deadline(s): None
   Applicants should submit the following:
      1) ACT
      2) SAT
      3) Transcripts
      4) Letter(s) of recommendation
Company name: Keystone Foods Corporation
EIN: 232816413

7757
The Cardiovascular Medical Research and Education Fund, Inc.
510 Walnut St., Ste. 500
Philadelphia, PA   19106-3601   (215) 413-2414
Contact: Patricia A. Wolf, Exec. Dir.
E-mail: patt.wolfe@ipahresearch.org; URL: http://www.ipahresearch.org/

Foundation type: Independent foundation
Purpose: Grants to support research of the etiology and pathogenesis of idiopathic pulmonary arterial hypertension, in pursuit of its treatment and cure.
Publications: Application guidelines; Annual report.
Financial data: Year ended 12/31/2012. Assets, $15,250,201 (M); Expenditures, $3,756,722; Total giving, $3,612,675.
Fields of interest: Heart & circulatory research.
Type of support: Research.
Application information:
   Initial approach: Proposal
EIN: 050579911

7758
Carmell Scholarship Trust Fund
(formerly J. Russell & Gladys Irene Carmel Trust)
c/o PNC Bank N.A.
P.O. Box 609
Pittsburgh, PA   15230-9738

Foundation type: Independent foundation
Purpose: Scholarships to graduating students of Saginaw, Bay City, Auburn or Midland, MI who intend to pursue a career in the nursing profession.
Financial data: Year ended 09/30/2013. Assets, $615,777 (M); Expenditures, $21,350; Total giving, $12,648.
Fields of interest: Nursing school/education.
Type of support: Scholarships—to individuals.
Application information: Applications accepted. Application form required.
   Deadline(s): Apr. 30
   Additional information: Application forms can be obtained from the guidance office.
EIN: 347196952

7759
Carnegie Hero Fund Commission
436 7th Ave., Ste. 1101
Pittsburgh, PA   15219-1841
Contact: Jeffrey A. Dooley, Investigations Mgr.
FAX: (412) 281-5751;
E-mail: carnegiehero@carnegiehero.org; Toll free tel.: (800) 447-8900; URL: http://www.carnegiehero.org/

Foundation type: Operating foundation
Purpose: Medals and grants awarded by nomination only for acts of heroism voluntarily performed by civilians within the U.S. and Canada in saving or attempting to save the lives of others.
Publications: Annual report; Informational brochure; Newsletter.
Financial data: Year ended 12/31/2012. Assets, $38,278,724 (M); Expenditures, $1,775,175; Total giving, $920,544; Grants to individuals, totaling $920,544.
Fields of interest: Human services.
Type of support: Awards/grants by nomination only; Awards/prizes.
Application information: Applications accepted. Application form required. Application form available on the grantmaker's web site.
   Initial approach: Letter, including date, time, and place of heroic actions, and addresses of hero and witnesses
   Send request by: Mail or online
   Deadline(s): Within two years of the date of the act for which individual is nominated
Program description:
   Carnegie Hero Fund Program: Medals and grants of $5,000 each awarded in recognition of acts of selfless heroism. Monetary assistance is given to persons who have been awarded the Carnegie Medal and who have need for financial aid as a result of a disabling injury incurred. In addition, grants may be given to the dependents of those who have lost their lives in such heroic manner. Recommendations for awards may be made by any individual having knowledge of an outstanding act of bravery. Scholarship aid is available to all medal recipients as well as dependents of disabled and posthumous awardees. There must be conclusive evidence that the person performing a heroic act voluntarily risked his or her life to an extraordinary degree in saving or attempting to save the life of another person, or voluntarily sacrificed himself or herself in a heroic manner for the benefit of others. The act of rescue must be one in which no full measure of responsibility exists between the rescuer and the rescued. The heroic act must have been performed in the U.S., Canada, or the waters thereof. The following types of people are ineligible for an award: those whose regular vocations require them to perform such acts, unless the rescues are clearly beyond the line of duty; members of the armed services, children considered by the commission to be too young to comprehend the risks involved, and members of the same family, except in cases of outstanding heroism where the rescuer loses his or her life or is severely injured.
EIN: 251062730

7760
Catholic Charities of the Diocese of Pittsburgh
212 9th St.
Pittsburgh, PA   15222-3517   (412) 456-6999
Contact: Susan Rauscher, Exec. Dir.
E-mail: info@ccpgh.org; URL: http://ccpgh.org

Foundation type: Public charity

Purpose: Financial assistance to indigent residents of southwestern PA, for utilities and emergency relief.
Financial data: Year ended 06/30/2012. Assets, $9,892,279 (M); Expenditures, $9,399,483; Total giving, $1,094,921; Grants to individuals, totaling $1,094,921.
Type of support: Emergency funds; Grants for special needs.
Application information:
  Initial approach: Telephone or e-mail
  Additional information: Contact foundation for eligibility requirements.
EIN: 251326213

7761
Center for Community Action
195 Drive In Lane
Everett, PA   15537-6915   (814) 623-1444
Contact: Dorothy Ann Foor, Exec. Dir.

Foundation type: Public charity
Purpose: Assistance towards weatherization, housing services, and human and social services to low- and moderate-low-income residents of Bedford, Fulton, and Huntingdon counties, PA.
Financial data: Year ended 06/30/2012. Assets, $2,373,821 (M); Expenditures, $3,823,468; Total giving, $2,247,248; Grants to individuals, totaling $2,247,248.
Fields of interest: Economically disadvantaged.
Type of support: Grants for special needs.
Application information: Applications not accepted.
  Additional information: Unsolicited requests for funds not considered or acknowledged.
EIN: 251701123

7762
The Center for Emerging Visual Artists
(formerly Creative Artists Network, Inc.)
237 S. 18th St., Ste. 3A
The Barclay
Philadelphia, PA   19103-6161   (215) 546-7775
FAX: (215) 546-7802; E-mail: info@cfeva.org;
E-mail for Lori Dillard Rech: lori@cfeva.org;
URL: http://www.cfeva.org

Foundation type: Public charity
Purpose: Support for emerging visual artists residing within a 100 mile radius of Philadelphia, PA.
Publications: Application guidelines.
Financial data: Year ended 06/30/2012. Assets, $593,013 (M); Expenditures, $480,352.
Fields of interest: Visual arts.
Type of support: Program development.
Application information: Application form required. Application form available on the grantmaker's web site.
  Deadline(s): Oct. 1
  Final notification: Accepted artists notified in Dec. or Jan.
  Applicants should submit the following:
    1) Work samples
    2) SASE
    3) Resume
  Additional information: Application must also include artist's statement, complete slide list, signature page, and $15 application fee.
Program description:
  Career Development Program: This program provides fellowships to advance the professional development of a selected group of emerging visual artists, while encouraging their participating in the region's communities. Fellows are selected

anonymously by an esteemed board of artistic advisors each fall. Selection is based on the merit of the artwork submitted and a brief statement. Artists are accepted into the program regardless of age, educational level, economic status, race, religion, or sexual orientation. The fellows receive up to six exhibition opportunities per year (regionally, nationally, and internationally), a two-person show during the second year, career counseling, mentorship, and intimate workshops geared towards the advancement of his/her career.
EIN: 232250532

7763
Central Susquehanna Community Foundation
(formerly Administers of the Berwick Health and Wellness Fund)
725 West Front St.
Berwick, PA   18603   (570) 752-3930
Contact: Eric DeWald, C.E.O.; For grants: Kara Seesholtz, Prog. Off.
FAX: (570) 752-7435;
E-mail: edewald@csgiving.org; Additional e-mail: kseesholtz@csgiving.org; URL: http://www.csgiving.org

Foundation type: Community foundation
Purpose: Scholarships to graduating high school seniors residing in Columbia and lower Luzerne counties, PA, for higher education.
Publications: Application guidelines; Annual report; Financial statement; Grants list; Informational brochure; Newsletter; Occasional report (including application guidelines).
Financial data: Year ended 12/31/2012. Assets, $38,016,293 (M); Expenditures, $3,024,033; Total giving, $2,105,881; Grants to individuals, 29 grants totaling $157,024.
Fields of interest: Health sciences school/education.
Type of support: Scholarships—to individuals.
Application information: Applications accepted. Application form required. Application form available on the grantmaker's web site.
  Send request by: Online
  Deadline(s): Apr. 10
  Applicants should submit the following:
    1) FAFSA
    2) Transcripts
  Additional information: See web site for complete scholarship listing and eligibility criteria.
EIN: 232982141

7764
Chester County Community Foundation
The Lincoln Bldg.
28 W. Market St.
West Chester, PA   19382-3020   (610) 696-8211
Contact: Karen A. Simmons, C.E.O.; For grants: Beth Harper Briglia, V.P., Grants and Donor Svcs.
FAX: (610) 696-8213; E-mail: info@chescocf.org; Additional e-mail: karen@chescocf.org; Grant application e-mail: grants@chescocf.org; URL: http://www.chescocf.org

Foundation type: Community foundation
Purpose: Scholarships to residents of Chester County, PA, for higher education.
Publications: Application guidelines; Annual report; Financial statement; Informational brochure; Newsletter.
Financial data: Year ended 06/30/2013. Assets, $39,530,395 (M); Expenditures, $2,833,778; Total giving, $1,394,494; Grants to individuals, 154 grants totaling $188,761.

Fields of interest: Higher education.
Type of support: Scholarships—to individuals; Support to graduates or students of specific schools; Undergraduate support.
Application information: Applications accepted. Application form required. Application form available on the grantmaker's web site.
  Initial approach: Application
  Copies of proposal: 1
  Deadline(s): Varies
  Additional information: Each scholarship has its own set of eligibility criteria and guidelines; see web sit for complete listing.
Program description:
  Scholarship Funds: The majority of the scholarships awarded by the foundation are specific to a particular high school or field of study as designated by the fund's donor. That is, the donor establishes a fund for a scholarship that is designated to go to a student who is graduating from a specific high school or pursuing a specific field of study. The high schools' guidance counselors are the foundation's principal contacts for these awards. See web site for additional information.
EIN: 232773822

7765
Children's Scholarship Fund Philadelphia
P.O. Box 22463
Philadelphia, PA   19110-2463   (215) 670-8411
FAX: (215) 670-5899;
E-mail: admin@csfphiladelphia.org; URL: http://www.csfphiladelphia.org

Foundation type: Public charity
Purpose: Four year scholarships to K through 8th grade students from low-income Philadelphia families.
Publications: Financial statement.
Financial data: Year ended 12/31/2011. Assets, $9,980,497 (M); Expenditures, $4,262,689; Total giving, $3,564,599.
Fields of interest: Education.
Type of support: Scholarships—to individuals.
Application information: Applications accepted. Application form required.
  Additional information: Scholarships are need-based and awarded by lottery. Contact the fund for additional information.
EIN: 233078729

7766
Chinese Church Planting Partners
2200 Arch St., Ste. 200
Philadelphia, PA   19103-1315   (215) 568-3120
Contact: Charles Erickson, Dir.

Foundation type: Company-sponsored foundation
Purpose: Grants to support foreign missionaries in China.
Financial data: Year ended 05/31/2010. Assets, $8,226 (M); Expenditures, $105,085; Total giving, $100,407; Grants to individuals, 3 grants totaling $100,407 (high: $35,972, low: $30,340).
Fields of interest: Christian agencies & churches.
International interests: China.
Type of support: Grants to individuals.
Application information: Applications accepted.
  Initial approach: Letter
  Additional information: Application should include financial information.
EIN: 201590078

7767
Elmer S. and Frances R. Christ Scholarship Fund
c/o Union Bank & Trust
115 S.Centre St., Ste. 103
Pottsville, PA 17901
Contact: Michele L. Reber

Foundation type: Operating foundation
Purpose: Scholarships restricted to applicants who have lived within the Pottsville area school district or who have graduated from either Nativity BVM High School or Pottsville High School, PA.
Financial data: Year ended 12/31/2012. Assets, $1,231,047 (M); Expenditures, $48,669; Total giving, $39,000; Grants to individuals, 14 grants totaling $39,000 (high: $4,500, low: $1,500).
Fields of interest: Higher education.
Type of support: Scholarships—to individuals; Support to graduates or students of specific schools.
Application information: Application form required.
Deadline(s): Apr.
Additional information: Application must include financial information, three character references and three academic references.
EIN: 232534508

7768
Kil Chung-Hee Fellowship
7818 Oak Lane Rd.
Cheltenham, PA 19012-1015
Contact: Sangduk Kim, Dir.

Foundation type: Independent foundation
Purpose: Research grants to students and alumni of Korea University Medical College. Upon completion of project, recipient must return to Korea University Medical College within three years to teach or do additional research for a period of no less than three years.
Financial data: Year ended 12/31/2011. Assets, $91,835 (M); Expenditures, $13,102; Total giving, $11,000; Grants to individuals, 2 grants totaling $11,000 (high: $10,000, low: $1,000).
Fields of interest: Medical school/education.
Type of support: Research; Support to graduates or students of specific schools; Postgraduate support.
Application information: Applications accepted.
Initial approach: Proposal
Additional information: Applicants should include a brief resume of academic qualifications.
EIN: 232199550

7769
The Clareth Fund: The Philadelphia Association of Zeta Psi Fraternity
c/o Duane Morris, LLP
30 S. 17th St.
Philadelphia, PA 19103-4196
Contact: Frank G. Cooper, Esq.
Application address: McBee Butcher, 903 Fletcher Rd., Wayne, PA 19087

Foundation type: Independent foundation
Purpose: Loans to students attending the University of Pennsylvania Wharton School, Dental School, or Medical School, or who are in the Sigma chapter of Zeta Psi Fraternity.
Financial data: Year ended 12/31/2013. Assets, $5,454,669 (M); Expenditures, $300,114; Total giving, $223,250; Grants to individuals, 39 grants totaling $183,250 (high: $7,000, low: $250).
Fields of interest: Dental school/education; Medical school/education; Students, sororities/fraternities.

Type of support: Support to graduates or students of specific schools.
Application information: Applications not accepted.
Additional information: Unsolicited requests for funds not considered or acknowledged.
EIN: 232092500

7770
Mary Clark League Trust
(also known as Clark-AFF League Memorial Fund)
c/o BNY Mellon, N.A.
P.O. Box 185
Pittsburgh, PA 15230-0185

Foundation type: Independent foundation
Purpose: Scholarships to students attending medical schools in Philadelphia, PA, including the School of Podiatric Medicine.
Financial data: Year ended 06/30/2013. Assets, $469,326 (M); Expenditures, $21,888; Total giving, $13,000.
Fields of interest: Medical school/education; Podiatry.
Type of support: Support to graduates or students of specific schools; Graduate support.
Application information: Applications accepted. Application form required.
Additional information: Application is available through financial aid office of local medical schools.
EIN: 236225542

7771
Class of 1968 Scholarship, Inc.
1630 N. St.
Philadelphia, PA 19130 (215) 235-2070
Contact: Robert S.V. Platten, Pres.

Foundation type: Operating foundation
Purpose: Scholarships to children of members of the Hobart and William Smith Colleges, PA, class of 1968.
Financial data: Year ended 05/31/2013. Assets, $2,810 (M); Expenditures, $9,468; Total giving, $9,400.
Fields of interest: Higher education.
Type of support: Support to graduates or students of specific schools; Undergraduate support.
Application information: Applications accepted. Application form required.
Initial approach: Letter
Send request by: Mail
Deadline(s): May 31
Additional information: Applicant must demonstrate financial need.
EIN: 222573776

7772
The Clay Studio
137-139 N. 2nd St.
Philadelphia, PA 19106-2009 (215) 925-3453
Contact: Residency: Christopher R. Taylor, Pres.
Additional e-mail: jeff@theclaystudio.org, christina@theclaystudio.org, ctaylor@theclaystudio.org
FAX: (215) 925-7774;
E-mail: info@theclaystudio.org; E-mail For Christopher R. Taylor: ctaylor@theclaystudio.org;
URL: http://www.theclaystudio.org/

Foundation type: Public charity
Purpose: Residencies to ceramic artists.
Financial data: Year ended 05/31/2012. Assets, $1,262,805 (M); Expenditures, $1,505,629.

Fields of interest: Ceramic arts.
Type of support: Residencies.
Application information: Applications accepted. Application form required.
Initial approach: Telephone or e-mail
Deadline(s): Mar. 26
Applicants should submit the following:
1) Work samples
2) Resume
Additional information: Application must also include artist statement and ten slides. Interviews may be required.
EIN: 237380408

7773
Gifford A. Cochran Trust
c/o BNY Mellon, N.A.
P.O. Box 185
Pittsburgh, PA 15230-0185 (617) 722-7121

Foundation type: Independent foundation
Purpose: Scholarships to graduates of high schools in Hancock County, ME, with preference to students from Ellsworth High School, ME.
Financial data: Year ended 08/31/2012. Assets, $223,220 (M); Expenditures, $14,391; Total giving, $10,900.
Type of support: Support to graduates or students of specific schools; Undergraduate support.
Application information: Applications accepted.
Initial approach: Telephone
Additional information: Contact trust for current application deadline/guidelines.
EIN: 046078603

7774
Martin D. Cohen Family Foundation
(formerly J & J Charitable Foundation)
2851 Baglyos Cir., Ste. 200
Bethlehem, PA 18020
Contact: Martin D. Cohen, Pres.

Foundation type: Independent foundation
Purpose: Scholarships only to high school seniors in Lehigh Valley PA, for higher education.
Financial data: Year ended 12/31/2012. Assets, $402,133 (M); Expenditures, $121,150; Total giving, $105,019; Grants to individuals, 62 grants totaling $17,600.
Type of support: Scholarships—to individuals.
Application information: Students should provide financial and academic information. Unsolicited requests for funds not accepted.
EIN: 232294358

7775
Blanche E. Colman Trust
c/o BNY Mellon, N.A.
P.O. Box 185
Pittsburgh, PA 15230-0185 (617) 722-3891
Contact: Sandra Brown-McMullen
Application address: 1 Boston Pl., Boston, MA 02108 Tel.: (617) 722-3891

Foundation type: Independent foundation
Purpose: Grants to worthy artist students residing in the New England area.
Financial data: Year ended 08/31/2013. Assets, $502,778 (M); Expenditures, $34,597; Total giving, $24,500; Grants to individuals, 10 grants totaling $24,500 (high: $4,000, low: $1,000).
Fields of interest: Arts, artist's services.
Type of support: Grants to individuals.
Application information: Application form required.
Deadline(s): Mar. 1

Applicants should submit the following:
1) Letter(s) of recommendation
2) Financial information
EIN: 046094293

7776

Christopher Columbus Scholarship Fund

445 Green Valley Rd.
York, PA 17403-9577 (717) 741-0379
Contact: Richard Arcuri, Pres.
Application address: P.O. Box 5142, York, PA 17405
E-mail: petercucchiara@ccsfyorkpa.org;
URL: http://www.ccsfyorkpa.org

Foundation type: Public charity
Purpose: Scholarships to high school graduates who are residents of York county, PA and have been accepted at an accredited four-year institution of higher learning.
Financial data: Year ended 12/31/2011. Assets, $140,308 (M); Expenditures, $10,480; Total giving, $10,000.
Fields of interest: Higher education.
Type of support: Scholarships—to individuals.
Application information: Applications accepted. Application form required. Application form available on the grantmaker's web site.
Deadline(s): Mar. 31
Final notification: Apr. 27
Applicants should submit the following:
1) Transcripts
2) SAT
3) Essay
4) ACT
Additional information: Applicants are selected based solely on academic potential and financial need. Applications are available at the guidance offices of all York county high schools.
EIN: 232496340

7777

The Comcast Foundation

1 Comcast Ctr., 48th Fl.
Philadelphia, PA 19103-2838 (215) 286-1700
Contact: William D. Black, V.P. and Exec. Dir.
E-mail for Leaders and Achievers Scholarships:
comcast@applyists.com; URL: http://
www.comcast.com/corporate/about/
inthecommunity/foundation/
comcastfoundation.html

Foundation type: Company-sponsored foundation
Purpose: Scholarships by nomination only to high school seniors with leadership potential in eligible Comcast communities.
Publications: Application guidelines.
Financial data: Year ended 12/31/2012. Assets, $4,508,591 (M); Expenditures, $16,196,745; Total giving, $16,170,519; Grants to individuals, 1,790 grants totaling $1,942,000 (high: $10,000, low: $1,000).
Fields of interest: Higher education.
Type of support: Scholarships—to individuals.
Application information: Applications accepted. Application form required.
Initial approach: E-mail
Deadline(s): Dec. 7 for Comcast Leaders and Achievers Scholarship Program
Program descriptions:
Comcast Leaders and Achievers Scholarship Program: The foundation awards $1,000 college scholarships to high school seniors who demonstrate strong commitment to community service and displays leadership ability in school

activities or through work experience. Applicants must have a GPA of 2.8 or higher and must be nominated by a school principal or guidance counselor. The program is administered by International Scholarship and Tuition Services.
Gustave G. Amsterdam Leadership Award: The foundation annually awards $5,000 scholarships to two Philadelphia public high school graduates planning to attend a Philadelphia college or university. The recipients are chosen among Philadelphia area finalists in the Comcast Leaders and Achievers Scholarship Program.
Company name: Comcast Corporation
EIN: 510390132

7778

Commission on Economic Opportunity of Luzerne County

165 Amber Ln.
P.O. Box 1127
Wilkes-Barre, PA 18702-1127 (570) 826-0510
FAX: (570) 829-1665; E-mail: ceo@sunlink.net;
Toll-free tel.: (800) 822-0359; URL: http://
www.ceopeoplehelpingpeople.org

Foundation type: Public charity
Purpose: College tuition assistance and summer camp scholarships to academically talented, economically disadvantaged students of the Wilkes-Barre, PA area.
Financial data: Year ended 06/30/2012. Assets, $10,667,101 (M); Expenditures, $19,005,603; Total giving, $5,000,940; Grants to individuals, totaling $4,674,296.
Fields of interest: Education; Economically disadvantaged.
Type of support: Camperships; Undergraduate support.
Application information:
Initial approach: Tel.
Additional information: Contact foundation for eligibility criteria.
EIN: 231653093

7779

The Community Foundation for the Alleghenies

(also known as The Community Foundation of Greater Johnstown)
116 Market St., Ste. 4
Johnstown, PA 15901-1644 (814) 536-7741
Contact: Michael Kane, Pres.
FAX: (814) 536-5859;
E-mail: info@cfalleghenies.org; URL: http://
www.cfalleghenies.org

Foundation type: Community foundation
Purpose: Grants to individuals who are residents of Bedford, Cambria, Indiana and Somerset counties, PA. Scholarships are also provided.
Publications: Annual report; Annual report (including application guidelines); Grants list; Informational brochure; Newsletter.
Financial data: Year ended 06/30/2013. Assets, $54,986,653 (M); Expenditures, $7,932,893; Total giving, $3,767,341.
Type of support: Undergraduate support; Grants for special needs.
Application information: Application form required.
Deadline(s): Last Fri. in Jan and Aug.
Additional information: Unsolicited applications not accepted.
EIN: 251637373

7780

Community Foundation of Fayette County

2 W. Main St., Ste. 101
Uniontown, PA 15401-3450 (724) 437-8600
Contact: Marilyn J. McDaniel, C.E.O.
FAX: (724) 438-3856;
E-mail: cpascoe@cffayettepa.org; URL: http://
cffayettepa.org

Foundation type: Community foundation
Purpose: Scholarships to graduating high school seniors of Fayette County, PA for higher education.
Publications: Application guidelines; Annual report; Grants list; Informational brochure; Newsletter.
Financial data: Year ended 12/31/2011. Assets, $8,218,402 (M); Expenditures, $793,448; Total giving, $417,051. Scholarships—to individuals amount not specified.
Fields of interest: Higher education.
Type of support: Scholarships—to individuals; Support to graduates or students of specific schools.
Application information: Applications accepted. Application form required. Application form available on the grantmaker's web site.
Initial approach: Application
Send request by: Mail
Deadline(s): Mar. 28
Final notification: Applicants notified in May
Applicants should submit the following:
1) Letter(s) of recommendation
2) FAFSA
3) Class rank
4) Essay
5) SAR
6) ACT
7) Transcripts
8) SAT
9) GPA
Additional information: See web site for a complete listing of scholarships and additional guidelines.
Program description:
Higher Education Scholarship Awards: The foundation offers a variety of educational awards ranging from $100 to $1,500. These awards are available to graduating high school seniors and to students already enrolled in a college, university or business school and non-traditional students. Awards cover a wide range of designations and interests. Applicants must be Fayette County residents to apply.
EIN: 251851158

7781

Community Foundation of Greene County, Pennsylvania

108 E. High St.
P.O. Box 768
Waynesburg, PA 15370 (724) 627-2010
Contact: Bettie B. Stammerjohn, Exec. Dir.; An'Etta Neff, Admin. Asst.
FAX: (724) 627-2011; E-mail: cfgcpa@gmail.com;
URL: http://www.cfgcpa.org

Foundation type: Community foundation
Purpose: Scholarships available to students, Pre-K, K-12, and graduating high school seniors who are residents of Greene County, PA.
Publications: Application guidelines; Annual report; Financial statement; Grants list; Informational brochure; Newsletter; Occasional report; Program policy statement.
Financial data: Year ended 12/31/2012. Assets, $3,253,473 (M); Expenditures, $519,964; Total giving, $297,722; Grants to individuals, 132 grants totaling $137,048.

Fields of interest: Education.
Type of support: Scholarships—to individuals; Support to graduates or students of specific schools; Precollege support; Undergraduate support.
Application information: Applications accepted. Application form required. Application form available on the grantmaker's web site.
  Initial approach: Application
  Deadline(s): Varies
  Applicants should submit the following:
    1) SAR
    2) SAT
  Additional information: See web site for eligibility criteria and additional guidelines.
EIN: 251881899

7782
Community Foundation of the Endless Mountains
(formerly Community Foundation of Susquehanna and Wyoming Counties)
270 Lake Ave.
Montrose, PA   18801   (570) 278-3800
FAX: (570) 278-9608;
E-mail: info@community-foundation.org;
URL: http://www.community-foundation.org/

Foundation type: Community foundation
Purpose: Scholarships to residents of PA from PreK to 12th grade, college and adult students.
Publications: Newsletter.
Financial data: Year ended 12/31/2012. Assets, $8,954,170 (M); Expenditures, $1,722,726; Total giving, $1,496,634; Grants to individuals, totaling $1,496,634.
Fields of interest: Elementary/secondary education; Early childhood education; Vocational education, post-secondary; Higher education.
Type of support: Scholarships—to individuals.
Application information: Applications accepted. Application form required. Application form available on the grantmaker's web site.
  Additional information: See web site for additional application guidelines and eligibility.
EIN: 300011355

7783
Community Foundation of Warren County
(formerly The Warren Foundation)
P.O. Box 691
Warren, PA   16365-0691   (814) 726-9553
Contact: Charles E. MacKenzie M.D., Exec. Dir.
FAX: (814) 726-7099; E-mail: cfwc@westpa.net;
Additional e-mail:
info@communityfoundationofwarrencounty.org;
URL: http://www.communityfoundationofwarrencounty.org
Alternate URL: http://www.warrenfoundationpa.org

Foundation type: Community foundation
Purpose: Scholarships only to residents of Warren County, PA, for nursing education, medical education, and general undergraduate education. Employee family scholarships for employees of Blair Corporation, Whirley Corporation.
Publications: Annual report.
Financial data: Year ended 12/31/2011. Assets, $52,865,589 (M); Expenditures, $2,835,717; Total giving, $2,436,362; Grants to individuals, 390 grants totaling $744,605.
Fields of interest: Higher education; Medical school/education; Nursing school/education.

Type of support: Employee-related scholarships; Graduate support; Technical education support; Undergraduate support.
Application information: Applications accepted. Application form required. Application form available on the grantmaker's web site.
  Initial approach: Application
  Send request by: Mail
  Copies of proposal: 1
  Deadline(s): Apr. 22
  Final notification: Recipients notified first week of July
  Applicants should submit the following:
    1) Transcripts
    2) Resume
    3) Letter(s) of recommendation
    4) GPA
    5) Financial information
  Additional information: See web site for a complete listing of scholarships.
EIN: 251380549

7784
Community Foundation of Western Pennsylvania and Eastern Ohio
(formerly Shenango Valley Foundation)
7 W. State St.
Sharon, PA   16146-2713   (724) 981-5882
Contact: Lawrence E. Haynes, Exec. Dir.; For grants: Amy Atkinson, Assoc. Dir.
FAX: (724) 983-9044;
E-mail: info@comm-foundation.com; URL: http://comm-foundation.org/

Foundation type: Community foundation
Purpose: Scholarships, student loans, and other grants to individuals residing in western PA and eastern OH.
Publications: Application guidelines; Annual report; Informational brochure.
Financial data: Year ended 12/31/2012. Assets, $51,748,231 (M); Expenditures, $4,411,730; Total giving, $3,197,726; Grants to individuals, 791 grants totaling $847,543.
Fields of interest: Higher education.
Type of support: Conferences/seminars; Scholarships—to individuals; Student loans—to individuals.
Application information: Applications accepted. Application form required. Application form available on the grantmaker's web site. Interview required.
  Initial approach: Application
  Send request by: On-line
  Deadline(s): Varies
  Applicants should submit the following:
    1) Transcripts
    2) Letter(s) of recommendation
    3) Essay
  Additional information: See web site for a complete list of programs.
EIN: 251407396

7785
Community Nursing Services in Greensburg Inc.
P.O. Box 98
Greensburg, PA   15601-0098   (724) 837-6827

Foundation type: Independent foundation
Purpose: Scholarships to individuals studying in a health care field, who reside in Greensburg, Hempfield, North Huntingdon, Salem, Sewicky or Unity, PA.
Financial data: Year ended 04/30/2013. Assets, $2,097,833 (M); Expenditures, $74,876; Total

giving, $59,000; Grants to individuals, totaling $59,000.
Fields of interest: Health sciences school/education.
Type of support: Graduate support; Undergraduate support.
Application information: Application form required.
  Initial approach: Letter
  Additional information: Application should include documentation of financial need and interest in a field of study aimed at community health care professions.
EIN: 250967471

7786
Community Progress Council, Inc.
226 E. College Ave.
York, PA   17403-2344   (717) 846-4600
Contact: Robin Rohrbaugh, Pres. and C.E.O.
FAX: (717) 854-8658;
E-mail: rrohrbaugh@yorkcpc.org; URL: http://www.yorkcpc.org/

Foundation type: Public charity
Purpose: Emergency assistance to low-to-moderate income individuals and families of York county, PA with heating bills, rental assistance and other needs.
Financial data: Year ended 06/30/2012. Assets, $2,247,487 (M); Expenditures, $12,033,076.
Fields of interest: Economically disadvantaged.
Type of support: Emergency funds.
Application information: Applications accepted.
  Additional information: Eligible applicants should contact the council for assistance.
EIN: 231653135

7787
Communtiy Action Partnership of Cambria County, Inc.
516 Main St.
Johnstown, PA   15901-2025   (814) 536-9031
Contact: Jeffery Vaughn, Exec. Dir.
E-mail: djzimmerman@capcc.us; URL: http://www.capcc.us

Foundation type: Public charity
Purpose: Support to individuals to help fulfill the basic needs of every citizen in Cambria County, PA for food, shelter, clothing and safety; the need to be accepted; the need for self-esteem; and the need to fulfill one's potential through the mobilization and direction of public, private and human resources.
Financial data: Year ended 06/30/2012. Assets, $3,134,926 (M); Expenditures, $10,573,011.
Fields of interest: Employment, training; Utilities; Infants/toddlers; Children; Women.
Type of support: Grants to individuals.
Application information: Contact the partnership for further information relating to application guidelines and deadlines. See web site for additional information.
EIN: 251150439

7788
John F. Connelly Scholarship Fund
1 Crown Way, Tax Dept.
Philadelphia, PA   19154-4599

Foundation type: Independent foundation
Purpose: Scholarships only to children of employees of Crown Cork & Seal Co., Inc. and its affiliates to pursue undergraduate study at

accredited colleges, universities, and technical/ vocational schools in the U.S. and worldwide.
Financial data: Year ended 12/31/2012. Assets, $3,329,984 (M); Expenditures, $160,000; Total giving, $160,000; Grants to individuals, 80 grants totaling $160,000 (high: $2,000, low: $2,000).
Fields of interest: Vocational education.
Type of support: Employee-related scholarships; Technical education support.
Application information: Applications accepted.
Deadline(s): Apr.
Additional information: Contact fund for current application guidelines.
EIN: 232667541

7789
Conner Family Foundation, Inc.
1030 State St.
Erie, PA   16501-1840   (814) 456-9322
Contact: William B. Conner, Pres. and Secy.-Treas.

Foundation type: Independent foundation
Purpose: Scholarships to graduates of McDowell High School, Erie, PA, for higher education.
Financial data: Year ended 06/30/2013. Assets, $242,969 (M); Expenditures, $23,475; Total giving, $22,500.
Type of support: Support to graduates or students of specific schools; Undergraduate support.
Application information:
Initial approach: Letter
Send request by: Mail
Deadline(s): One month prior to graduation.
Additional information: Application must include transcript and evidence of need.
EIN: 251320114

7790
R.J. Conrad Charitable Foundation
P.O. Box 144
Oakmont, PA   15139-0144   (724) 845-2069
Contact: Robert J. Conrad, Pres.
Application address: 207 Cherry Run Rd., Ford City, PA 16226 tel: (724) 845-2069

Foundation type: Independent foundation
Purpose: Scholarships to students in PA for higher education.
Financial data: Year ended 12/31/2011. Assets, $250,990 (M); Expenditures, $35,380; Total giving, $32,500.
Type of support: Undergraduate support.
Application information: Contact foundation for current application deadline/guidelines.
EIN: 237863991

7791
Coordinated Child Care of Nepa, Inc.
46 S. Washington St.
Wilkes Barre, PA   18701-3026   (570) 822-6500

Foundation type: Public charity
Purpose: Subsidized child care services to residents of Luzerne county, PA who meet financial eligibility requirements.
Financial data: Year ended 06/30/2012. Assets, $857,902 (M); Expenditures, $9,284,769.
Fields of interest: Day care; Family services; Economically disadvantaged.
Type of support: Grants for special needs.
Application information: Contact foundation for further program and application information.
EIN: 232431241

7792
William B. Copp & Grayon S. Copp Agriculture Education Trust
90 Main St., No. 92
Wellsboro, PA   16901   (570) 724-8596
Application address: c/o CN Bank Marla Mcilvain

Foundation type: Independent foundation
Purpose: Scholarships to students of Tioga County, PA high schools pursuing careers in fields related to agriculture.
Financial data: Year ended 12/31/2012. Assets, $1,459,191 (M); Expenditures, $88,160; Total giving, $73,480; Grants to individuals, 6 grants totaling $73,480 (high: $13,360, low: $6,680).
Fields of interest: Higher education; Agriculture/ food.
Type of support: Scholarships—to individuals.
Application information: Applications accepted.
Deadline(s): Before the beginning of the first semester for which the scholarship is sought
Additional information: Application must include financial information.
EIN: 546503829

7793
Corson Foundation
P.O. Box 710
Plymouth Meeting, PA   19462-0710
Contact: John E.F. Corson, Tr.

Foundation type: Independent foundation
Purpose: Scholarships to high school graduates primarily from schools located in the Plymouth-Whitemarsh, PA, area for attendance at colleges or universities.
Financial data: Year ended 12/31/2012. Assets, $2,354,295 (M); Expenditures, $197,982; Total giving, $167,842.
Type of support: Undergraduate support.
Application information: Applications accepted.
Initial approach: Letter
Deadline(s): None
Additional information: Application must include proof of acceptance by an accredited college or university, and two recommendations from high school teachers or from the high school principal.
EIN: 236390878

7794
Theresa Corti Trust
c/o Wells Fargo Bank, N.A.
101N Independence Mall E MACY 1372-062
Philadelphia, PA   19106-2112

Foundation type: Independent foundation
Purpose: Scholarships to graduates of Kern County, CA, high schools who are pursuing an agricultural education at a college or university.
Financial data: Year ended 03/31/2013. Assets, $1,141,347 (M); Expenditures, $75,995; Total giving, $54,703.
Fields of interest: Agriculture.
Type of support: Support to graduates or students of specific schools; Undergraduate support.
Application information: Applications accepted. Application form required.
Deadline(s): Feb. 28
Applicants should submit the following:
1) Transcripts
2) Letter(s) of recommendation
Additional information: Application must also include a letter stating goals and plans; Interviews granted upon request; Application

forms may be obtained from either of the two application contacts.
EIN: 956053041

7795
CPCU- Loman Education Foundation
(formerly CPCU-Harry J. Loman Foundation)
720 Providence Rd.
Malvern, PA   19355-3402
Contact: Millicent W. Workman, Chair.
E-mail: loman@cpcusociety.org; Toll Free Ph.: (800)-932-2728; URL: http:// www.cpculoman.cpcusociety.org

Foundation type: Public charity
Purpose: Scholarships and awards to individuals who are enrolled in an insurance or insurance-related field of study.
Financial data: Year ended 12/31/2011. Assets, $994,124 (M); Expenditures, $154,750; Total giving, $81,211; Grants to individuals, totaling $80,086.
Type of support: Awards/prizes; Undergraduate support.
Application information: Applications not accepted.
Additional information: Recipients must be nominated by a CPCU chapter.
Program description:
Scholarship Program: Scholarship recipients must be enrolled full- or part-time in an insurance or insurance-related field of study. Scholarships are usually in amounts of $1,500 each. CPCU- Loman Education Foundation matches scholarship funds given by individual CPCU chapters.
EIN: 232031260

7796
Crawford Heritage Community Foundation
911 Diamond Park
P.O. Box 933
Meadville, PA   16335   (814) 336-5206
Contact: Christian Maher, Exec. Dir.
FAX: (814) 724-1407;
E-mail: crawfordheritage@zoominternet.net;
URL: http://www.crawfordheritage.org

Foundation type: Community foundation
Purpose: Scholarships to residents of Crawford County, PA pursuing a higher education.
Publications: Application guidelines; Annual report; Grants list; Informational brochure; Newsletter.
Financial data: Year ended 12/31/2012. Assets, $12,741,847 (M); Expenditures, $578,532; Total giving, $439,184; Grants to individuals, 120 grants totaling $135,484.
Fields of interest: Higher education; Dental school/ education; Nursing school/education; Theological school/education.
Type of support: Support to graduates or students of specific schools; Undergraduate support.
Application information: Applications accepted. Application form required.
Deadline(s): Varies
Applicants should submit the following:
1) FAFSA
2) Transcripts
3) SAR
Additional information: Contact your local high school guidance counselor for application or download from the foundation's web site. Each scholarship has different eligibility requirements and selection criteria. See web site for a complete list of programs.
EIN: 251813245

7797
G. Kenneth Crawford and Margaret B. Crawford Memorial Scholarship Fund
P.O. Box 520
Johnstown, PA 15907-0520 (412) 655-8610
Contact: Deborah Madden
Application address: c/o Thomas Jefferson High School, P.O. Box 18019-0019, Pleasant Hills, PA 15236-0019, tel.:(412) 655-8610

Foundation type: Independent foundation
Purpose: Scholarships to graduating seniors of Thomas Jefferson High School, in Pleasant Hills, PA.
Financial data: Year ended 12/31/2011. Assets, $275,032 (M); Expenditures, $16,151; Total giving, $14,000; Grants to individuals, 5 grants totaling $14,000 (high: $2,800, low: $2,800).
Fields of interest: Higher education.
Type of support: Support to graduates or students of specific schools; Undergraduate support.
Application information: Applications accepted. Application form required.
   Deadline(s): Mar. 31
EIN: 251738804

7798
Croatian Fraternal Union Scholarship Foundation, Inc.
100 Delaney Dr.
Pittsburgh, PA 15235-5416 (412) 843-0380
Contact: Bernard M. Luketich

Foundation type: Public charity
Purpose: Scholarships to individuals of Croatian descent residing in Pittsburgh, PA. Applicants should be members of the Croation Fraternal Union, for higher education.
Financial data: Year ended 12/31/2012. Assets, $4,095,427 (M); Expenditures, $250,968; Total giving, $191,325.
International interests: Croatia.
Type of support: Undergraduate support.
Application information: Contact foundation for current application deadline/guidelines.
EIN: 256066985

7799
Alton and Mildred Cross Scholarship Fund
8700 Hanlin Cross Rd.
Union City, PA 16438-7566

Foundation type: Independent foundation
Purpose: Scholarships to high school students of Waterford Borough, Waterford Township, Mill Village Borough, or LeBoeuf Township in Waterford, PA.
Financial data: Year ended 12/31/2012. Assets, $1,298,382 (M); Expenditures, $77,721; Total giving, $64,000; Grants to individuals, 63 grants totaling $64,000 (high: $1,750, low: $500).
Fields of interest: Higher education.
Type of support: Scholarships—to individuals.
Application information: Applications accepted. Application form required.
EIN: 251709602

7800
The Crossroads Foundation
2915 Webster Ave.
Pittsburgh, PA 15219-4209 (412) 621-9422
Contact: Florence Rouzier, Exec. Dir.
FAX: (412) 683-0397; E-mail: info@crfdn.org; E-Mail for Florence Rouzier: frouzier@crfdn.org;
URL: http://www.crossroadsfoundation.org

Foundation type: Public charity
Purpose: Scholarships to students from economically distressed Pittsburgh, PA communities so they can continue to attend area Catholic high schools.
Publications: Annual report; Financial statement; Informational brochure; Newsletter.
Financial data: Year ended 06/30/2012. Assets, $5,284,903 (M); Expenditures, $944,304; Total giving, $283,946; Grants to individuals, totaling $283,946.
Fields of interest: Education; Catholic agencies & churches.
Type of support: Scholarships—to individuals; Support to graduates or students of specific schools.
Application information: Applications accepted. Application form required.
   Additional information: Applicant must demonstrate financial need and academic merit. Student must attend and graduate from one of the designated elementary schools. Funds are paid directly to the educational institution on behalf of the students. Contact the foundation for additional guidelines.
EIN: 251513510

7801
CSI Charities, Inc.
3750 State Rd.
Bensalem, PA 19020-5919 (215) 245-9100
Contact: Linda Madway, Pres.-Secy.

Foundation type: Public charity
Purpose: Assistance to individuals and families of PA, with food, clothing and shelter.
Financial data: Year ended 12/31/2011. Assets, $1,306,714 (M); Expenditures, $751,527; Total giving, $739,606; Grants to individuals, totaling $544,606.
Fields of interest: Economically disadvantaged.
Type of support: Emergency funds.
Application information: Applications not accepted.
   Additional information: Contact the agency for eligibility determination.
EIN: 232612002

7802
T. Manning Curtis Athletic Scholarship Fund
c/o PNC Bank, N.A.
1600 Market St., 4th Fl.
Philadelphia, PA 19103-7240 (717) 421-1990
Application address: c/o Stroudsburg Area School District, Attn.: Supt., 123 Linden St., Stroudsburg, PA 18360-1315, tel.: (717) 421-1990

Foundation type: Independent foundation
Purpose: Scholarships to graduates of Stroudsburg High School, PA, who have participated in a school athletic program and demonstrate financial need.
Financial data: Year ended 12/31/2012. Assets, $140,607 (M); Expenditures, $17,071; Total giving, $14,500.
Fields of interest: Athletics/sports, training.

Type of support: Support to graduates or students of specific schools; Undergraduate support.
Application information: Applications accepted. Application form required.
   Additional information: Applications available at high school guidance office.
EIN: 236979929

7803
Effie H. and Edward H. Curtis Trust Fund
c/o Wells Fargo Bank West, N.A.
101 N. Indepence Mall E. MACY 1372-062
Philadelphia, PA 19106-2112

Foundation type: Independent foundation
Purpose: Grants to permanent residents of Larimer County, CO, who are under 18 years of age and in need of emergency medical and dental assistance.
Publications: Occasional report.
Financial data: Year ended 12/31/2012. Assets, $931,069 (M); Expenditures, $56,282; Total giving, $38,298.
Fields of interest: Dental care; Health care; Children/youth, services.
Type of support: Grants for special needs.
Application information: Applications accepted. Application form required.
   Additional information: Application must include itemized bills and estimates on pre-approvals from the attending physician, and a copy of applicant's latest tax return.
EIN: 846019933

7804
Daly N-N & H Daly Scholarship
c/o The Bank of New York Mellon, N.A.
P.O. Box 185
Pittsburgh, PA 15230-9897

Foundation type: Independent foundation
Purpose: Scholarships only to deserving individuals from Butler County, PA, attending Duquesne University.
Financial data: Year ended 12/31/2012. Assets, $131,491 (M); Expenditures, $14,000; Total giving, $13,000.
Fields of interest: Higher education.
Type of support: Scholarships—to individuals.
Application information: Scholarships are paid directly to the educational institution on behalf of the students.
EIN: 256082584

7805
William G. Davis Charitable Trust
c/o PNC Bank
620 Liberty Ave., 10th Fl.
Pittsburgh, PA 15222-2705 (412) 555-1212
Contact: Ray S. Long
Application address: 125 2nd St., Pittsburgh, PA 15225

Foundation type: Independent foundation
Purpose: Undergraduate scholarships to children of Master Members of Doric Lodge No. 630.
Financial data: Year ended 12/31/2012. Assets, $611,714 (M); Expenditures, $35,411; Total giving, $33,941.
Fields of interest: Fraternal societies.
Type of support: Undergraduate support.
Application information: Applications accepted.
   Initial approach: Letter
   Deadline(s): Dec. 1
EIN: 251289600

7806
Grace Davis Education Trust
c/o S & T Wealth Management
800 Philadelphia St.
Indiana, PA   15701-3908

Foundation type: Independent foundation
Purpose: Scholarships to individuals enrolled at a college or university in PA.
Financial data: Year ended 12/31/2012. Assets, $648,339 (M); Expenditures, $33,538; Total giving, $31,000; Grants to individuals, 29 grants totaling $31,000 (high: $2,000, low: $500).
Type of support: Scholarships—to individuals.
Application information: Applications not accepted.
Additional information: Unsolicited requests for funds not considered or acknowledged.
EIN: 256494236

7807
Thomas and Helen E. Davis Memorial Foundation 31W080010
(formerly Helen D. Whitefield Trust)
P.O. Box 3215, Tax Dept.
Lancaster, PA   17604-3215
Contact: Woodstown High School, Attn.: Guidance Dept.
Application address: 140 East Ave., Woodstown, NJ 08098-1392

Foundation type: Independent foundation
Purpose: Scholarships to graduates of Woodstown High School, NJ.
Publications: Application guidelines.
Financial data: Year ended 02/28/2013. Assets, $138,947 (M); Expenditures, $27,103; Total giving, $22,500; Grants to individuals, 5 grants totaling $22,500 (high: $4,500, low: $4,500).
Type of support: Support to graduates or students of specific schools; Undergraduate support.
Application information: Applications accepted. Application form required.
Deadline(s): May 1
EIN: 222764049

7808
Dorothy Davis Scholarship Fund
c/o PNC Bank, N.A.
160 Market St. Tax Dept. No. 4th Flr.
Philadelphia, PA   19103   (732) 842-1597
Application address: c/o Rumson-Fair Haven Regional HS, 74 Ridge Rd., Rumson, NJ 07760

Foundation type: Independent foundation
Purpose: Merit-based scholarships to graduates of Rumson-Fair Haven High School, NJ, who are residents of Rumson, NJ.
Financial data: Year ended 12/31/2012. Assets, $775,300 (M); Expenditures, $36,931; Total giving, $26,000; Grants to individuals, 7 grants totaling $26,000 (high: $4,000, low: $3,000).
Fields of interest: Higher education; Scholarships/financial aid.
Type of support: Awards/grants by nomination only; Undergraduate support.
Application information:
Initial approach: Letter
Deadline(s): May
Additional information: Application should include personal statement and letters of recommendation. Students must be nominated by their high school principal.
Program description:
George Walter Davis Scholarship: Two scholarships are awarded each year, one to a male student and one to a female student. Applicants must have distinguished academic accomplishments over their last three years. In addition, they must have demonstrated significant accomplishment in a non-academic area such as art, music, sports, community services, leadership. Recipients receive a $3,000 scholarship for the first year of study. Scholarships are renewable for up to four years provided the student remains in good standing. Award amounts may be increased after the first year.
EIN: 226631276

7809
Delaware Valley Senior Citizens Scholarship Trust
115 Connard Dr.
Easton, PA   18042-8755   (610) 330-9767
Contact: Louis DiLullo, Tr.

Foundation type: Independent foundation
Purpose: Scholarships to graduates of Delaware Valley Regional High School, Frenchtown, NJ.
Financial data: Year ended 12/31/2012. Assets, $317,705 (M); Expenditures, $32,676; Total giving, $31,713; Grants to individuals, 22 grants totaling $31,713 (high: $3,000, low: $713).
Type of support: Support to graduates or students of specific schools; Undergraduate support.
Application information: Applications accepted.
Initial approach: Letter
Deadline(s): Apr. 30
Additional information: Application should include a financial aid form.
EIN: 226555205

7810
Delta Phi Epsilon Educational Foundation
251 S. Camac St.
Philadelphia, PA   19107-5609   (215) 732-5901
Contact: Harriette Hirsch, Pres.; Nicole L. DeFeo, Exec. Dir.
FAX: (215) 732-5906; E-mail: info@dphie.org;
URL: http://www.dphie.org/foundation.cfm

Foundation type: Public charity
Purpose: Scholarships to members of Delta Phi Epsilon and their children. Also, grants to current and former members of Delta Phi Epsilon in need.
Publications: Application guidelines; Annual report.
Financial data: Year ended 12/31/2011. Assets, $219,933 (M); Expenditures, $18,563.
Fields of interest: Students, sororities/fraternities.
Type of support: Scholarships—to individuals.
Application information: Application form required. Interview required.
Deadline(s): Mar. 15
Applicants should submit the following:
1) Transcripts
2) Letter(s) of recommendation
EIN: 431661725

7811
G. Fred DiBona, Jr. Memorial Foundation
(formerly G. Fred & Sylvia Dibona Family Foundation)
1035 Waverly Rd.
Gladwyne, PA   19035-1445   (610) 850-3290
Contact: Christine DiBona Lobley, Exec. Dir.
Application address: 775 E. Lancaster Ave., Villanova, PA 19085-1517,
e-mail: Christine@fredsfootsteps.org, fax: (610) 525-1376

Foundation type: Public charity

Purpose: Financial assistance to families in financial crisis due to the costs associated with caring for a critically or chronically ill child.
Financial data: Year ended 12/31/2011. Assets, $3,545,126 (M); Expenditures, $533,063; Total giving, $370,085; Grants to individuals, totaling $370,085.
Fields of interest: Human services; Children.
Type of support: Grants for special needs.
Application information: Applications accepted. Application form required.
Additional information: Application must be submitted by a social worker or other medical professional stating medical diagnosis. Contact the foundation for additional guidelines.
EIN: 232867497

7812
Norris E. Dodd Foundation
c/o Wells Fargo Bank N.A.
101 N Independence Mall E Macy 1372-062
Philadelphia, PA   19106-2112

Foundation type: Independent foundation
Purpose: Scholarships to students in OR for higher education.
Financial data: Year ended 12/31/2012. Assets, $222,517 (M); Expenditures, $8,629; Total giving, $4,000.
Type of support: Scholarships—to individuals.
Application information: Applications not accepted.
Additional information: Unsolicited requests for funds not considered or acknowledged.
EIN: 916449509

7813
Dollar Energy Fund, Inc.
P.O. Box 42329
Pittsburgh, PA   15203-0329   (412) 431-2800
Contact: Cindy Datig, C.E.O.
FAX: (412) 431-2084;
E-mail: info@dollarenergy.org; Toll free tel.: (800) 683-7036; URL: http://www.dollarenergy.org

Foundation type: Public charity
Purpose: Assistance to low income individuals and families in LA, MD, OH, PA, TN, TX, VA and WV experiencing difficulties in affording to pay for utilities.
Publications: Annual report.
Financial data: Year ended 09/30/2012. Assets, $13,023,763 (M); Expenditures, $20,553,199; Total giving, $14,210,530; Grants to individuals, totaling $14,210,530.
Fields of interest: Human services; Economically disadvantaged.
Type of support: Grants for special needs.
Application information: Applications accepted.
Additional information: Applicants must submit to the agency all the necessary eligibility information with their application to receive consideration for a grant.
EIN: 251442933

7814
The Donegal Foundation
(formerly Donegal School District Education Foundation)
P.O. Box 495
Mount Joy, PA 17552-0495 (717) 426-3031
Contact: John Coleman
E-mail: jc@wellspan.org; URL: http://www.donegalfoundation.org

Foundation type: Public charity
Purpose: Scholarships to graduating students of Donegal High School, PA pursuing postsecondary school educational studies in health care related fields.
Publications: Application guidelines.
Financial data: Year ended 06/30/2011. Assets, $197,523 (M); Expenditures, $17,193; Total giving, $14,957.
Fields of interest: Higher education; Formal/general education.
Type of support: Support to graduates or students of specific schools.
Application information: Applications accepted. Application form required. Application form available on the grantmaker's web site.
  Deadline(s): May 1
  Applicants should submit the following:
    1) Class rank
    2) SAT
    3) GPA
    4) FAFSA
    5) Essay
EIN: 232679755

7815
John Dotson, M.D. Fund
c/o PNC Bank, N.A.
1600 Market St., 4th Fl.
Philadelphia, PA 19103 (412) 768-7587

Foundation type: Independent foundation
Purpose: Scholarships to financially needy young women from Closter, NJ.
Financial data: Year ended 12/31/2012. Assets, $192,546 (M); Expenditures, $21,506; Total giving, $19,000.
Fields of interest: Women.
Type of support: Scholarships—to individuals.
Application information: Application form required.
  Initial approach: Letter
  Deadline(s): Apr. 30
EIN: 226040599

7816
J. & R. Doverspike Charitable Foundation
c/o S & T Bank
800 Philadelphia St.
Indiana, PA 15701-0220 (814) 365-5448
Application address: c/o Selection Committee, P.O. Box 1034, Punxsutawney, PA 15767-0834
URL: https://www.stbank.com/

Foundation type: Independent foundation
Purpose: Scholarships to graduates of Punxsutawney School District, PA. Also, grants to cover living expenses of needy PA residents.
Financial data: Year ended 12/31/2012. Assets, $1,233,644 (M); Expenditures, $66,063; Total giving, $55,215; Grants to individuals, 26 grants totaling $36,049 (high: $3,500, low: $500).
Type of support: Scholarships—to individuals; Support to graduates or students of specific schools.

Application information:
  Initial approach: Letter
  Deadline(s): Sept. 30
  Additional information: Contact foundation for current application guidelines.
EIN: 256571881

7817
Early Music America, Inc.
801 Vinial St., Ste 300
Pittsburgh, PA 15212-5177 (412) 642-2778
Contact: Ann Felter, Exec. Dir.
FAX: (412) 642-2779; E-mail: info@earlymusic.org;
E-mail For Ann Felter: ann@earlymusic.org;
URL: http://www.earlymusic.org

Foundation type: Public charity
Purpose: Scholarships to students who wish to study early music at an accredited North American university or summer music workshop.
Publications: Application guidelines.
Financial data: Year ended 06/30/2012. Assets, $197,265 (M); Expenditures, $438,144; Total giving, $17,645; Grants to individuals, totaling $17,645.
Fields of interest: Music.
Type of support: Scholarships—to individuals.
Application information: Applications accepted. Application form required. Application form available on the grantmaker's web site.
  Initial approach: Application
  Send request by: Online
  Deadline(s): Apr. 15 for Summer Workshop Scholarships, May 1 for Barbara Thornton Memorial Scholarship
  Applicants should submit the following:
    1) Essay
    2) Resume
    3) Letter(s) of recommendation
  Additional information: Contact the organization for additional guidelines.
Program descriptions:
  Barbara Thornton Memorial Scholarship: A $2,000 award will be given to an outstanding and highly-motivated (and possibly unconventional) young performer of medieval music who seeks to widen his/her experience through more advanced study and/or auditions in Europe.
  Summer Workshop Scholarships: Scholarships of $750 each are available to students attending early music workshops in the U.S. and Canada. Eligible workshops include any North American workshop sponsored or endorsed by a major early music organizations, such as (but not limited to) the American Recorder Society, Amherst Early Music, Aston magna, Country Dance and Song Society, Early Music Vancouver, Historic Brass Society, Historical Harp Society, Lute Society of America, Oberlin Baroque Performance Institute, San Francisco Early Music Society, and Viola da Gamba Society of America. Applications are open to high school, undergraduate, and graduate students who are enrolled full-time in the spring term of application for the scholarship. Applicants may be of any nationality studying in a North American institution, or North American citizens studying abroad. Priority will be given to applicants who have not previously received awards.
EIN: 133318348

7818
Eastern Pennsylvania Water Pollution Control Operators Association, Inc.
(also known as EPWPCOA)
244 Mountain Top Rd.
Reinholds, PA 17569-9077 (610) 670-6072
Contact: Marykay Steinman, Exec. Dir.
FAX: (610) 670-6076; E-mail: epwpcoa@ptd.net;
URL: http://www.epaops.org/

Foundation type: Public charity
Purpose: Scholarships to members of the Association who are in good standing to continue their education in the water pollution control industry. Student scholarships to children of members who are in good standing or were at the time of their death actively pursuing an education in the environmental field.
Publications: Application guidelines; Newsletter.
Financial data: Year ended 12/31/2011. Assets, $272,987 (M); Expenditures, $218,406; Total giving, $18,000; Grants to individuals, totaling $18,000.
Fields of interest: Higher education; Water pollution; Environment.
Type of support: Employee-related scholarships.
Application information: Applications accepted. Application form required. Interview required.
  Deadline(s): Mar. 31
  Additional information: Scholarships are awarded on the basis of past achievements and contributions to the water pollution control industry, as well as the intended use to enhance or improve the industry. Funds are mailed directly to the college or institution of higher learning on behalf of the students.
Program descriptions:
  Member's Scholarships: Scholarships are awarded to members for tuition assistance to pursue any career path that would enhance and improve the water pollution control industry. Repetitive year applications are accepted. There is a lifetime limit of $10,000 per person.
  Members' Children Scholarships: Scholarships are available to members' children pursuing education in the environmental field. Repetitive year applications are accepted and there is a $10,000 lifetime limit per person.
EIN: 236417070

7819
Howard E. Eckhart Trust
(formerly Edward E. Eckhart Trust)
111 W. Newcastle St.
Zelienople, PA 16063 (724) 452-6610
Contact: Tom Oliverio, Chair.

Foundation type: Independent foundation
Purpose: Financial assistance to needy residents of Zelienople, PA, who are victims of cancer or polio.
Financial data: Year ended 12/31/2012. Assets, $91,376 (M); Expenditures, $1,975; Total giving, $589; Grants to individuals, 2 grants totaling $589 (high: $376, low: $213).
Fields of interest: Cancer.
Type of support: Grants for special needs.
Application information: Applications accepted. Application form required. Interview required.
  Additional information: Application should include physician's statement specifying last date seen by him and nature of illness.
EIN: 256125594

7820
John Henry and Clarissa Arnold Eisenhauer Scholarship Fund
(formerly John Henry & Clarissa A. Eisenhauer, et al. Scholarship Fund)
122 St. Francis Dr.
Lebanon, PA 17042
Contact: Jane L. Kaylor, Tr.
Application address: 225 Bainbridge St., Elizabethtown, PA 17022

Foundation type: Operating foundation
Purpose: Scholarships to financially needy high school seniors of Lebanon County, PA, to attend college.
Financial data: Year ended 06/30/2013. Assets, $131,931 (M); Expenditures, $14,424; Total giving, $13,550; Grants to individuals, 20 grants totaling $13,550 (high: $1,100, low: $320).
Type of support: Support to graduates or students of specific schools; Undergraduate support.
Application information: Applications accepted.
Initial approach: Letter
Deadline(s): None
Additional information: Application must also include recommendations from high school principal and counselor.
EIN: 232020120

7821
Elk County Community Foundation
32 S. St.Marys St.
P.O. Box 934
Saint Marys, PA 15857 (814) 834-2125
Contact: Paula Fritz Eddy, Exec. Dir.
FAX: (814) 834-2126;
E-mail: eccf@windstream.net; URL: http://www.elkcountyfoundation.com

Foundation type: Community foundation
Purpose: Scholarships to individuals residing in Elk County, PA, and surrounding counties.
Publications: Application guidelines; Annual report; Grants list; Informational brochure; Informational brochure (including application guidelines); Newsletter.
Financial data: Year ended 12/31/2012. Assets, $6,072,186 (M); Expenditures, $402,895; Total giving, $302,299; Grants to individuals, 106 grants totaling $84,076.
Fields of interest: Nursing school/education.
Type of support: Scholarships—to individuals; Undergraduate support.
Application information: Applications accepted. Application form required.
Initial approach: Application
Send request by: Mail or fax
Copies of proposal: 1
Deadline(s): Mid-Apr.
Final notification: Recipients notified mid-May
Applicants should submit the following:
1) Essay
2) FAFSA
3) GPA
Additional information: See web site for further application and program information.
EIN: 251859637

7822
Karen Rush Elko Foundation
757 S. Warren Ave.
Malvern, PA 19355-3412

Foundation type: Independent foundation
Purpose: Scholarships to seniors graduating from the Haverford Township School District, PA.

Financial data: Year ended 12/31/2012. Assets, $1,800 (M); Expenditures, $0; Total giving, $0.
Fields of interest: Higher education.
Type of support: Support to graduates or students of specific schools.
Application information:
Deadline(s): None
EIN: 364552991

7823
Charles E. Ellis Grant and Scholarship Fund
c/o PNC Bank, N.A.
1600 Market St., Tax Dept., 4th Fl.
Philadelphia, PA 19103-7240
Application address: c/o Philadelphia Futures, 230 S. Broad St., 7th Fl., Philadelphia, PA 19102-4121

Foundation type: Independent foundation
Purpose: Scholarships to functionally orphaned female students who reside in Philadelphia County, PA, for high school-level education. Scholarships not available for college-level education.
Publications: Application guidelines; Informational brochure; Program policy statement.
Financial data: Year ended 06/30/2013. Assets, $39,400,839 (M); Expenditures, $1,859,206; Total giving, $1,442,039.
Fields of interest: Secondary school/education; Women.
Type of support: Precollege support.
Application information: Applications accepted.
Deadline(s): None
Additional information: The scholarship grants are awarded to individually named recipients. However, all funds are paid directly to the educational institution the individual attends. The fund's use of the term "functionally orphaned" includes girls from single-parent families.
EIN: 236725618

7824
Elwyn, Inc.
111 Elwyn Rd.
Elwyn, PA 19063-4622 (610) 891-2000
Contact: Sandra S. Cornelius Ph.D., Pres.
FAX: (610) 891-2458; E-mail: info@elwyn.org;
URL: http://www.elwyn.org

Foundation type: Public charity
Purpose: Scholarships to adults and children with disabilities and disadvantages.
Financial data: Year ended 06/30/2012. Assets, $172,219,219 (M); Expenditures, $209,584,396.
Fields of interest: Children; Adults; Disabilities, people with.
Type of support: Scholarships—to individuals.
Application information: Applicant must demonstrate need.
EIN: 231352117

7825
Charles C. Ely Trust
c/o BNY Mellon, N.A.
P.O. Box 185
Pittsburgh, PA 15230-0185

Foundation type: Independent foundation
Purpose: Scholarship support for students who have encountered financial difficulties while in school and to low-income and minority students for higher education at schools in the Boston, MA area.

Financial data: Year ended 08/31/2013. Assets, $3,586,605 (M); Expenditures, $205,099; Total giving, $178,000.
Fields of interest: Higher education.
Type of support: Undergraduate support.
Application information:
Deadline(s): May 1
EIN: 046091865

7826
Elizabeth R. England Trust
c/o Mellon Financial Corp.
P.O. Box 185
Pittsburgh, PA 15230-0185

Foundation type: Independent foundation
Purpose: Scholarships to female performing arts majors at Philadelphia High School for Girls or West Philadelphia High School in PA.
Financial data: Year ended 06/30/2013. Assets, $18,090,269 (M); Expenditures, $917,821; Total giving, $883,018; Grants to individuals, 6 grants totaling $135,330 (high: $44,881, low: $510).
Fields of interest: Performing arts, education; Women.
Type of support: Support to graduates or students of specific schools; Undergraduate support.
Application information:
Deadline(s): None
Additional information: Contact trust for current application guidelines.
EIN: 236606334

7827
The Samuel Epstein Foundation Trust
248 Seneca St.
Oil City, PA 16301-1371

Foundation type: Independent foundation
Purpose: Scholarships to residents of PA, primarily from the towns of Sheffield and Clarendon.
Financial data: Year ended 12/31/2012. Assets, $4,726,085 (M); Expenditures, $254,663; Total giving, $181,760.
Type of support: Scholarships—to individuals.
Application information: Applications not accepted.
EIN: 256311365

7828
Gene & Marlene Epstein Humanitarian Fund
1238 Wrightstown Rd.
Newtown, PA 18940-9602 (215) 968-2200
Contact: Gene Epstein, Dir.
E-mail: gboyle@gpboyle.com

Foundation type: Operating foundation
Purpose: Financial assistance for troops stationed in war zones and to aid returning veterans in need.
Financial data: Year ended 12/31/2012. Assets, $0 (M); Expenditures, $190,174; Total giving, $189,974; Grants to individuals, 4 grants totaling $14,450 (high: $5,700, low: $1,650).
Fields of interest: Human services.
Type of support: Grants for special needs.
Application information: Applications accepted.
Initial approach: Letter or telephone
Deadline(s): None
Additional information: Assistance is based on need.
EIN: 061813910

7829
EQT Foundation, Inc.
(formerly Equitable Resources Foundation, Inc.)
1 PNC Plaza
249 Fifth Ave., 3rd Fl.
Pittsburgh, PA 15222 (412) 762-3502
Contact: Bruce Bickel, Exec. Dir.
Application address: 625 Liberty Ave., Pittsburgh,
PA 15222, e-mail: aspire@eqt.com
E-mail: bruce.bickel@pncadvisors.com;
URL: http://www.eqt.com/ourcommunities/
eqt-foundation.aspx

Foundation type: Company-sponsored foundation
Purpose: Scholarships and mentoring for
college-bound high school students in Charleston
and Pittsburgh, PA.
Publications: Application guidelines.
Financial data: Year ended 12/31/2012. Assets,
$24,337,308 (M); Expenditures, $3,156,514;
Total giving, $2,888,936. Scholarships—to
individuals amount not specified.
Fields of interest: Higher education; Scholarships/
financial aid; Youth development, adult & child
programs.
Type of support: Scholarships—to individuals.
Application information: Applications accepted.
Application form required.
  Initial approach: Application
  Send request by: Online during the open
    enrollment period
  Deadline(s): Varies
  Additional information: Students interested in the
    ASPIRE program must be willing to commit to
    a mentoring partnership and must participate
    in all ASPIRE events.
Program description:
  *ASPIRE (Area Students Participating in Rewarding
  Education):* Through ASPIRE, college-bound juniors
  and seniors are provided with one-on-one mentoring
  and scholarships. EQT employees volunteer their
  time to help students and assist them with life
  choices, career development, and personal
  direction. The program awards five $2,500
  scholarships which are renewable for up to six
  years. Scholarship recipients are selected based on
  essay and presentation, participation, and mentor
  partnership. The program is limited to Charleston
  and Pittsburgh, PA.
  EIN: 043747289

7830
Leroy Erickson Scholarship Fund
(formerly Erickson Scholarship Fund)
c/o PNC Bank, N.A.
P.O. Box 609
Pittsburgh, PA 15230-9738
Contact: John Montoya
Application address: 620 Liberty Ave., 7th Fl.,
Pittsburgh, PA 15222-2722, tel.: (412) 768-8538

Foundation type: Independent foundation
Purpose: Scholarships to students who have been
residents of the city of Bradford, the borough of
Lewis Run, or the townships of Bradford, Corydon,
Foster, or Lafayette, PA, for at least the past two
school years and who are graduates of Bradford,
PA, area high schools.
Financial data: Year ended 10/31/2013. Assets,
$953,921 (M); Expenditures, $50,015; Total
giving, $39,783.
Type of support: Scholarships—to individuals;
Support to graduates or students of specific
schools.

Application information: Application form required.
Interview required.
  Deadline(s): May 1
  Final notification: Awards will be announced by
    mid-June
  Applicants should submit the following:
    1) Transcripts
    2) Financial information
    3) Essay
    4) Letter(s) of recommendation
  Additional information: Application should also
    include a list of extracurricular activities.
EIN: 256358243

7831
The Erie Community Foundation
459 W. 6th St.
Erie, PA 16507-1215 (814) 454-0843
Contact: Michael L. Batchelor, Pres.
FAX: (814) 456-4965;
E-mail: mbatchelor@eriecommunityfoundation.org;
Grant inquiry tel.: 814-454-0843; URL: http://
www.eriecommunityfoundation.org

Foundation type: Community foundation
Purpose: Scholarships to individuals residing in the
Erie, PA, area for undergraduate education.
Publications: Application guidelines; Annual report;
Financial statement; Grants list; Informational
brochure (including application guidelines);
Newsletter.
Financial data: Year ended 12/31/2012. Assets,
$187,170,327 (M); Expenditures, $10,975,010;
Total giving, $8,514,550. Scholarships—to
individuals amount not specified.
Fields of interest: Higher education.
Type of support: Scholarships—to individuals;
Support to graduates or students of specific
schools; Undergraduate support.
Application information: Applications accepted.
Application form required.
  Initial approach: Application
  Deadline(s): Varies
  Additional information: Contact your high school
    guidance office, or college financial aid office
    for application. See web site for complete
    listing of scholarships.
EIN: 256032032

7832
The ERM Group Foundation, Inc.
350 Eagleview Blvd., Ste. 200
Exton, PA 19341-1180 (610) 524-3630
Contact: Janice Tapler, Exec. Dir.
FAX: (610) 524-3858;
E-mail: janice.taplar@erm.com; URL: http://
www.erm.com/foundation

Foundation type: Public charity
Purpose: Fellowships to graduate students
interested in environmental issues.
Publications: Application guidelines; Annual report;
Grants list; Informational brochure; Newsletter.
Financial data: Year ended 12/31/2012. Assets,
$265,954 (M); Expenditures, $258,024; Total
giving, $226,220.
Fields of interest: Environment.
Type of support: Fellowships.
Application information: Applications accepted.
Application form required. Application form
available on the grantmaker's web site. Interview
required.
  Initial approach: Application
  Send request by: Online or mail
  Deadline(s): Dec. 16 for ERM Foundation
    Sustainability Fellowship

Applicants should submit the following:
  1) Transcripts
  2) Letter(s) of recommendation
  3) Resume
  4) GPA
  5) Proposal
  6) Budget Information
Program description:
  ERM Foundation Sustainability Fellowship: The
  foundation supports entrepreneurial graduate
  students who want to implement their visions for a
  more sustainable world. In addition to a monetary
  stipend of up to $15,000 for the selected fellow,
  the top five fellowship finalists will be given an
  opportunity to interview for a compensated
  internship position in one of ERM's global offices
  (in Annapolis, MD; Houston, TX; London, UK; or
  Sydney, Australia). Eligible applicants must be
  enrolled in a U.S.-based tax-exempt educational
  organization during the current academic year.
  EIN: 232792333

7833
Eye & Ear Foundation, Inc.
203 Lothrop St., Ste. 251, E&E Inst.
Pittsburgh, PA 15213-2548 (412) 864-1300
Contact: Lawton Snyder, Exec. Dir.
FAX: (412) 864-1305; E-mail: info@eyeandear.org;
E-mail for Lawton Snyder: lawtons@eyeandear.org;
URL: http://www.eyeandear.org

Foundation type: Public charity
Purpose: Awards and prizes to individuals who have
made extraordinary contributions within the field of
otolaryngology.
Financial data: Year ended 06/30/2011. Assets,
$28,180,945 (M); Expenditures, $2,320,740;
Total giving, $1,933,431; Grants to individuals,
totaling $5,300.
Fields of interest: Eye diseases; Ear, nose & throat
diseases.
Type of support: Research; Awards/grants by
nomination only; Awards/prizes.
Application information: Application form required.
  Send request by: Mail
  Deadline(s): Jan. 31
  Additional information: Application should
    include an up-to-date curriculum vitae for the
    nomination. Awards are by nomination only.
Program description:
  Albert C. Muse Prize in Otolaryngology: The prize
  alternates annually between Ophthalmology and
  Otolaryngology, and carries a cash award of
  $5,000, and recognizes those who have made
  significant, progressive contributions to science
  and medicine in these specialties.
  EIN: 251439732

7834
F & M Trust Co., Scholarship Program Trust
P.O. Box 6010
Chambersburg, PA 17201-6010 (717)
264-6116

Foundation type: Company-sponsored foundation
Purpose: Scholarships to children of employees of
Farmers & Merchants Trust Co., for tuition or
related costs of the educational program.
Financial data: Year ended 12/31/2012. Assets,
$148,408 (M); Expenditures, $4,540; Total giving,
$2,700.
Fields of interest: Higher education.
Type of support: Employee-related scholarships.
Application information: Applications not
accepted.

Additional information: Unsolicited requests for funds not considered or acknowledged.
Company name: Farmers and Merchants Trust Company of Chambersburg
EIN: 256823291

7835
The Fabric Workshop and Museum
1222 Arch St.
Philadelphia, PA 19107-2028 (215) 568-1111
FAX: (215) 568-8211;
E-mail: info@fabricworkshopandmuseum.org;
URL: http://www.fabricworkshop.org

Foundation type: Public charity
Purpose: Residencies by invitation only to contemporary artists for the creation of new work using experimental materials and techniques.
Financial data: Year ended 09/30/2011. Assets, $1,727,974 (M); Expenditures, $1,483,596.
Fields of interest: Visual arts; Design.
Type of support: Awards/grants by nomination only; Residencies.
Application information: Applications not accepted.
Additional information: Artists must be nominated by the selection committee. Unsolicited requests for funds not considered or acknowledged.
EIN: 232018929

7836
A. T. Fallquist Memorial Scholarship Fund
P.O. Box 520
Johnstown, PA 15907-0520 (412) 678-9215
Application address: The Consortium for Public Education, 410 9th St., McKeesport, PA 15132-4001

Foundation type: Independent foundation
Purpose: Scholarships to graduates of McKeesport Area High School, PA, who have participated as members of the baseball team.
Financial data: Year ended 12/31/2011. Assets, $299,162 (M); Expenditures, $23,478; Total giving, $18,144; Grants to individuals, 10 grants totaling $18,144 (high: $2,016, low: $1,008).
Fields of interest: Higher education; Athletics/sports, baseball.
Type of support: Support to graduates or students of specific schools.
Application information: Applications accepted. Application form required.
Initial approach: Application
Deadline(s): Apr. 30
Additional information: Students should check with their guidance counselors for additional information.
EIN: 251893905

7837
Farber Foundation
1845 Walnut St., Ste. 800
Philadelphia, PA 19103-4711
Contact: Aaron D. Solomon
Application address: 77 Reese Ln., Millvile, PA 17846

Foundation type: Company-sponsored foundation
Purpose: Scholarships to children of employees pursuing a college degree and whose parents must have been employed at CSS Industries or its subsidiaries.
Financial data: Year ended 12/31/2012. Assets, $684,680 (M); Expenditures, $236,204; Total

giving, $232,510; Grants to individuals, 35 grants totaling $162,080 (high: $12,000, low: -$1,000).
Fields of interest: Higher education.
Type of support: Employee-related scholarships; Undergraduate support.
Application information: Applications not accepted.
Additional information: Unsolicited requests for funds not considered or acknowledged.
Program description:
Faber Foundation Scholarship Program: The foundation awards $2,000 college scholarships to high school seniors who are children of employees of CSS Industries or one of its subsidiaries. Scholarships are awarded based on academic performance, SAT/ACT scores, participation in community and extracurricular activities, and financial need. The foundation also awards a $10,000 scholarship to a top-ranking scholarship recipient who exemplifies the academic ability and personality traits of Jacqueline A. Tully, a coordinator of the Faber Foundation Scholarship who died of ovarian cancer.
Company name: CSS Industries, Inc.
EIN: 236254221

7838
Evelyn Elaine Faust Scholarship Funds
115 S. Centre St., No. 103
Pottsville, PA 17901-3000 570-621-2962
Application address: c/o Pottsville Area High School, Attn.: Guidance Office, Pttsville, PA 17901

Foundation type: Independent foundation
Purpose: Scholarships to students of Pottsville Area High School, PA, who will attend a college or university.
Financial data: Year ended 12/31/2012. Assets, $160,811 (M); Expenditures, $7,262; Total giving, $5,000; Grants to individuals, 4 grants totaling $5,000 (high: $2,000, low: $1,000).
Fields of interest: Higher education.
Type of support: Support to graduates or students of specific schools.
Application information: Applications accepted. Application form required.
Deadline(s): Mar. 25
Additional information: Application forms available at the school guidance office.
EIN: 237985990

7839
The Female Association of Philadelphia
c/o Haverford Trust Company
3 Radnor Corp. Ctr.
Radnor, PA 19087-4580 (610) 527-7400

Foundation type: Independent foundation
Purpose: Relief assistance to women over 60 years of age in the Philadelphia, PA, area with income under $12,000 annually.
Financial data: Year ended 09/30/2013. Assets, $3,069,628 (M); Expenditures, $176,011; Total giving, $144,650.
Fields of interest: Aging; Women.
Type of support: Grants for special needs.
Application information: Applications not accepted.
EIN: 236214961

7840
Fenstermacher Foundation
5 Spruce Ter.
Nesquehoning, PA 18240 (570) 640-6113
Contact: R.T. Fenstermacher, Tr.

Foundation type: Independent foundation
Purpose: Awards and prizes for achievement to an individual of Tamaqua, PA.
Financial data: Year ended 10/31/2013. Assets, $108,677 (M); Expenditures, $5,832; Total giving, $5,000; Grant to an individual, 1 grant totaling $5,000.
Type of support: Awards/prizes.
Application information: Unsolicited requests for funds not considered or acknowledged.
EIN: 236278702

7841
First Community Foundation Partnership of Pennsylvania
(formerly Williamsport-Lycoming Foundation)
330 Pine St., Ste. 401
Williamsport, PA 17701-6242 (570) 321-1500
Contact: For grants and scholarships: Betty Gilmour, Dir., Grantmaking
FAX: (570) 321-6434;
E-mail: jenniferw@fcfpartnership.org; URL: http://www.fcfpa.org

Foundation type: Community foundation
Purpose: Scholarships to residents of Central and Northcentral PA for higher education.
Publications: Application guidelines; Annual report; Financial statement; Informational brochure; Program policy statement.
Financial data: Year ended 12/31/2011. Assets, $61,777,189 (M); Expenditures, $3,681,242; Total giving, $2,038,943.
Fields of interest: Higher education; Scholarships/financial aid.
Type of support: Scholarships—to individuals.
Application information: Applications accepted. Application form required.
Initial approach: Application
Deadline(s): Varies
Additional information: See web site for complete listing of scholarships or contact local high school guidance counselor for application guidelines.
EIN: 246013117

7842
Fischer Memorial Burial Park
c/o Anthony Fischer
1075 Victor Ln.
Bryn Mawr, PA 19010

Foundation type: Independent foundation
Purpose: Grants to provide burial services and grave site maintenance to individuals.
Financial data: Year ended 12/31/2012. Assets, $24,075 (M); Expenditures, $1,119; Total giving, $0.
Fields of interest: Cemeteries/burial services.
Type of support: Grants for special needs.
Application information: Applications not accepted.
Additional information: Unsolicited requests for funds not considered or acknowledged.
EIN: 236263254

7843
Karl Fischer Trust
c/o BNY Mellon, N.A.
P.O. Box 185
Pittsburgh, PA   15230-0185

Foundation type: Independent foundation
Purpose: Scholarships primarily to residents of Marblehead, Salem, and Swampscott, MA.
Financial data: Year ended 08/31/2013. Assets, $511,615 (M); Expenditures, $28,154; Total giving, $20,000; Grants to individuals, 10 grants totaling $20,000 (high: $2,500, low: $1,750).
Type of support: Scholarships—to individuals.
Application information: Application form not required.
   Initial approach: Letter
   Deadline(s): Contact trust for application deadline/guidelines.
EIN: 046411644

7844
T. S. Fitch Memorial Scholarship Fund
c/o BNY Mellon, N.A.
P.O. Box 185
Pittsburgh, PA   15230-0185

Foundation type: Independent foundation
Purpose: Scholarships to students for higher education.
Financial data: Year ended 12/31/2012. Assets, $236,840 (M); Expenditures, $16,511; Total giving, $14,124.
Fields of interest: Higher education.
Type of support: Undergraduate support.
Application information: Contact fund for current application deadline/guidelines.
EIN: 256123538

7845
Herrin Edith Fitton Trust
(formerly Edith Fitton Herrin Trust)
c/o BNY Mellon, N.A.
P.O. Box 185
Pittsburgh, PA   15230-0185

Foundation type: Independent foundation
Purpose: Scholarships to medical students entering or attending any accredited medical school in Philadelphia, PA.
Financial data: Year ended 06/30/2013. Assets, $482,877 (M); Expenditures, $28,717; Total giving, $19,500; Grants to individuals, 9 grants totaling $19,500 (high: $3,250, low: $1,083).
Fields of interest: Medical school/education.
Type of support: Graduate support.
Application information: Application form required.
   Deadline(s): Contact financial aid offices for current application deadline
   Additional information: Applications available at medical schools' financial aid offices.
EIN: 236500294

7846
Clark Flegal Educational Trust
c/o CNB Bank
P.O. Box 42
Clearfield, PA   16830   (814) 765-1683

Foundation type: Independent foundation
Purpose: Educational loans to residents of Clearfield, PA.
Financial data: Year ended 10/31/2012. Assets, $430,560 (M); Expenditures, $4,771; Total giving,
$23,000; Grants to individuals, 8 grants totaling $23,000 (high: $4,000, low: $2,000).
Fields of interest: Scholarships/financial aid.
Type of support: Student loans—to individuals.
Application information: Applications accepted throughout the year; Contact trust for current application guidelines.
EIN: 256030462

7847
Louise Fleischer Memorial Fund Inc.
257 Barrett Dr.
Doylestown, PA   18901   (215) 230-7712
Contact: Erik Fleischer

Foundation type: Independent foundation
Purpose: Scholarships to nursing and horticulture students.
Financial data: Year ended 07/31/2013. Assets, $41,460 (M); Expenditures, $64,440; Total giving, $6,000; Grants to individuals, 5 grants totaling $6,000 (high: $1,500, low: $1,000).
Fields of interest: Nursing school/education; Horticulture/garden clubs.
Type of support: Undergraduate support.
Application information: Contact foundation for current application deadline/guidelines.
EIN: 233099647

7848
Foreman Fleisher Trust No. 2
(also known as Foreman Fleisher Trust No. 2)
c/o PNC Bank, N.A.
620 Liberty Ave., 10th Fl.
Pittsburgh, PA   15222-2705   (215) 832-0519

Foundation type: Independent foundation
Purpose: Scholarships to Jewish women who seek professional education, primarily in PA.
Financial data: Year ended 09/30/2013. Assets, $440,854 (M); Expenditures, $23,058; Total giving, $18,150; Grants to individuals, 9 grants totaling $18,150 (high: $3,150, low: $1,000).
Fields of interest: Jewish agencies & synagogues; Women.
Type of support: Scholarships—to individuals.
Application information: Applications accepted.
   Initial approach: Letter
   Deadline(s): None
EIN: 236201637

7849
FMC Corporation Contributions Program
1735 Market St.
Philadelphia, PA   19103   (215) 299-6000
Contact: Judy Smeltzer, Dir., State Govt. Rels.
URL: http://www.fmc.com/corporateresponsibility/CivicInvolvement/tabid/60/Default.aspx

Foundation type: Corporate giving program
Purpose: Scholarships to students residing in the FMC areas of company operations.
Type of support: Undergraduate support.
Application information: Applications not accepted.
   Additional information: Unsolicited requests for funds not considered.

7850
Foundation for a Christian Civilization, Inc.
P.O. Box 341
Hanover, PA   17331-0341   (717) 225-7147
FAX: (717) 225-7382; E-mail: tfp@tfp.org; Toll-free tel.: (866) 661-0272; URL: http://www.tfp.org/

Foundation type: Public charity
Purpose: Scholarships to individuals involved in the foundation's Exchange-Visitor program.
Publications: Informational brochure.
Financial data: Year ended 06/30/2012. Assets, $6,736,136 (M); Expenditures, $8,066,629; Total giving, $389,788; Grants to individuals, totaling $6,890.
Fields of interest: International exchange; Catholic agencies & churches.
Type of support: Exchange programs; Foreign applicants; Undergraduate support.
Application information: Contact foundation for current application deadline/guidelines.
EIN: 237325778

7851
Foundation for California University of Pennsylvania
250 University Ave.
Campus Box 59
California, PA   15419-1341   (724) 938-4329
Contact: Linda H. Serene, Pres.

Foundation type: Public charity
Purpose: Scholarships to students at California University of Pennsylvania pursuing a regular course of study leading toward a degree and maintain good academic standing throughout the degree program.
Financial data: Year ended 12/31/2011. Assets, $26,723,000 (M); Expenditures, $3,052,812; Total giving, $1,809,974; Grants to individuals, totaling $753,971.
Fields of interest: Higher education.
Type of support: Support to graduates or students of specific schools.
Application information: Scholarship awards are based on the recommendation of an appointed university committee.
EIN: 251540183

7852
The Foundation for Enhancing Communities
(formerly The Greater Harrisburg Foundation)
200 N. 3rd St., 8th Fl.
P.O. Box 678
Harrisburg, PA   17108-0678   (717) 236-5040
Contact: Janice R. Black, C.E.O.; For grants: Jennifer Doyle, Dir., Devel. and Community Investment; For scholarships: Allison Moesta, Prog. Off., Educational Enhancement
Scholarship inquiry e-mail: allison@tfec.org
FAX: (717) 231-4463; E-mail: janice@tfec.org; URL: http://www.tfec.org

Foundation type: Community foundation
Purpose: Scholarships to individuals who are residents of Cumberland, Dauphin, Franklin, Lebanon and Perry counties, PA for higher education.
Publications: Application guidelines; Annual report (including application guidelines); Financial statement; Grants list; Informational brochure (including application guidelines); Newsletter; Program policy statement.

Financial data: Year ended 12/31/2012. Assets, $54,117,886 (M); Expenditures, $6,037,174; Total giving, $3,630,213; Grants to individuals, 218 grants totaling $294,538.
Fields of interest: Higher education; Scholarships/financial aid.
Type of support: Scholarships—to individuals; Undergraduate support.
Application information: Applications accepted. Application form required. Application form available on the grantmaker's web site.
   Initial approach: Letter or telephone
   Send request by: Online
   Copies of proposal: 1
   Deadline(s): Varies
   Final notification: Recipients notified in six to seven weeks
   Applicants should submit the following:
    1) Pell Grant
    2) Budget Information
    3) Work samples
    4) SAR
    5) Resume
    6) Transcripts
    7) SAT
    8) Letter(s) of recommendation
    9) GPA
    10) FAFSA
    11) Essay
    12) Financial information
   Additional information: Contact your local high school guidance offices for additional application information or see web site for additional guidelines.
EIN: 010564355

7853
The Foundation of the Pennsylvania Medical Society

777 E. Park Dr.
P.O. Box 8820
Harrisburg, PA 17105-8820 (717) 558-7750
Contact: Heather A. Wilson, Exec. Dir.
FAX: (717) 558-7818;
E-mail: foundation@pamedsoc.org; Toll-free tel: (800) 228-7823, E-mail for Heather A. Wilson: hwilson@pamedsoc.org; URL: http://www.foundationpamedsoc.org

Foundation type: Public charity
Purpose: Financial assistance to impaired physicians. Loans, scholarships and other educational opportunities for medical career students.
Publications: Application guidelines; Annual report; Financial statement; Newsletter.
Financial data: Year ended 12/31/2011. Assets, $10,071,573 (M); Expenditures, $1,820,102; Total giving, $43,600; Grants to individuals, totaling $43,600.
Fields of interest: Medical school/education.
Type of support: Scholarships—to individuals; Student loans—to individuals; Grants for special needs.
Application information: Applications accepted. Application form required. Application form available on the grantmaker's web site.
   Initial approach: Download application form
   Deadline(s): Mar. 15 for Alliance Medical Scholarship; Apr. 15 for Scott A. Gunder; and Sept. 30 for Lycoming County Medical Society, Myrtle Siegfried and Michael Vigilente Scholarship, and Endowment for South Asian students
Program descriptions:
   Alliance Medical Education Scholarship Fund: Awards several $2,500 scholarships to residents of

Pennsylvania. Applicant must be a second-year or third-year medical student, and must be enrolled full-time in a Pennsylvania medical school.
   Endowment for South Asian Students of Indian Descent Scholarship: Awards $2,000 to a South Asian Indian student enrolled full-time in his/her second, third, or fourth year at an accredited Pennsylvania medical school. Applicants must be residents of Pennsylvania.
   Lycoming County Medical Society (LCMS) Scholarship: The program awards two scholarships of $1,800 to two qualified medical students who are residents of Lycoming County. Preference will be given to first-year students, but all students are encouraged to apply.
   Scott A. Gunder, M.D., DCMS Presidential Scholarship: Awards $1,500 to a second-year medical student from Penn State College of Medicine at the Milton S. Hershey Medical Center. Applicants must be residents of Pennsylvania.
   The Myrtle Siegfried, M.D. and Michael Vigilante, M.D., Scholarship: Awards $1,000 to a qualified first-year medical student residing in Berks, Lehigh, or Northampton county. Applicants must be enrolled full-time in an accredited U.S. medical school.
EIN: 231511600

7854
Foundations Community Partnership

(formerly Delaware Valley Mental Health Foundation)
1456 Ferry Rd., Ste. 404
Doylestown, PA 18901-2391 (267) 247-5584
Contact: Ron Bernstein, Exec. Dir.
E-mail: rbernstein@fcpartnership.org; URL: http://www.fcpartnership.org/

Foundation type: Public charity
Purpose: Scholarship to one senior in each Bucks county public high school, PA for higher education.
Financial data: Year ended 06/30/2012. Assets, $19,479,140 (M); Expenditures, $1,124,592; Total giving, $368,000; Grants to individuals, totaling $48,000.
Fields of interest: Higher education; Human services.
Type of support: Scholarships—to individuals.
Application information: Applications accepted. Application form required.
   Deadline(s): Apr. 30
   Final notification: Applicants notified by May 15
   Additional information: Each high school nominates a student and selection is based on academic excellence and commitment to human services in Bucks county for children, youth and families.
EIN: 236299881

7855
Founder's Trust

236 Park Square Ln.
Pittsburgh, PA 15238
Application address: 5853 Bowcroft St., Unit 3, Los Angeles, CA 90016tel.: (310) 841-6195

Foundation type: Independent foundation
Purpose: Scholarships to young men and women of PA, who have successfully completed a rehabilitation program for attendance at accredited colleges or universities, trade or business schools.
Financial data: Year ended 06/30/2012. Assets, $0 (M); Expenditures, $432; Total giving, $0.
Fields of interest: Vocational education, post-secondary; Higher education; Substance

abuse, treatment; Crime/violence prevention, youth.
Type of support: Scholarships—to individuals.
Application information: Applications accepted. Application form required.
   Deadline(s): 60 days prior to start of academic term
   Applicants should submit the following:
    1) Transcripts
    2) Letter(s) of recommendation
    3) Essay
   Additional information: Application must also include a letter of personal reference and a copy of federal income tax form.
EIN: 251427660

7856
James Frederick Fox Foundation

1 Pitcairn Pl., 165 Township Line Rd., Ste. 2100
Jenkintown, PA 19046-3593 (215) 572-0738
Contact: Robert A. Fox, Mgr.

Foundation type: Independent foundation
Purpose: Scholarships to participants in the Abington, PA School District senior summer basketball program with academic credentials. Also, scholarships to scholar athletes fro the fall football program of the Little Quakers (Pop Warner League) in the Philadelphia, PA area who will attend William Penn Charter School.
Financial data: Year ended 12/31/2013. Assets, $863,975 (M); Expenditures, $7,865; Total giving, $4,367; Grants to individuals, 3 grants totaling $3,000 (high: $1,000, low: $1,000).
Fields of interest: Athletics/sports, basketball; Athletics/sports, football.
Type of support: Support to graduates or students of specific schools.
Application information: Applications accepted. Application form required.
   Deadline(s): None
EIN: 237034155

7857
Freedom Forge Corporation Foundation

(formerly American Welding & Manufacturing Company Foundation)
c/o Kish Bank Asset Management
25 Gateway Dr.
Reedsville, PA 17084-9642

Foundation type: Company-sponsored foundation
Purpose: Scholarships to individuals of PA for continuing education at institutions of higher learning.
Financial data: Year ended 12/31/2012. Assets, $997,180 (M); Expenditures, $97,033; Total giving, $88,551.
Fields of interest: Higher education.
Type of support: Scholarships—to individuals.
Application information: Applications accepted.
   Initial approach: Letter
   Deadline(s): None
EIN: 346516721

7858
The French Benevolent Society of Philadelphia

c/o Clairmont Paciello & Co. PC
250 Tanglewood Ln.
King of Prussia, PA 19406 (610) 935-6995

Foundation type: Independent foundation
Purpose: Scholarships for higher education, either in the U.S. or France, to financially needy French

citizens or immigrants and their descendants, now living in the Philadelphia, PA, metropolitan area. Aid to persons of French extraction in need due to misfortune, age, or illness. Preference is given in the following order: persons of French birth, of French-born parents, and persons of French extraction. Limited to residents of the Philadelphia, PA, metropolitan area.
Publications: Informational brochure (including application guidelines).
Financial data: Year ended 10/31/2013. Assets, $1,208,844 (M); Expenditures, $72,749; Total giving, $21,735; Grants to individuals, 4 grants totaling $21,735 (high: $9,577, low: $2,808).
Fields of interest: Aging.
International interests: France.
Type of support: Scholarships—to individuals; Grants for special needs.
Application information: Applications accepted. Application form required.
  Deadline(s): None
  Additional information: Application should include an official transcript of high school and/or college work done in the U.S. or abroad, a financial disclosure form, and curriculum vitae.
EIN: 231401532

7859
Kennedy T. Friend Education Fund
c/o PNC Bank, N.A.
620 Liberty Ave., 10th Fl.
Pittsburgh, PA 15222-2705   (412) 762-2175

Foundation type: Independent foundation
Purpose: Scholarships to the children of lawyers of Allegheny County, PA, to attend Yale University, CT, or University of Paris, Sorbonne, France.
Financial data: Year ended 12/31/2012. Assets, $7,064,992 (M); Expenditures, $381,301; Total giving, $259,098.
Type of support: Support to graduates or students of specific schools; Undergraduate support.
Application information: Applications accepted. Application form required.
  Initial approach: Letter
  Deadline(s): May 1
EIN: 256026198

7860
Dorothy M. Friend Trust
c/o Wells Fargo Bank, N.A., Trust Tax Dept.
101N. Idenpendence Mall E. MACY1372-062
Philadelphia, PA 19106-2112

Foundation type: Independent foundation
Purpose: Scholarships to graduates who attended Oconee County High School for at least two years.
Financial data: Year ended 12/31/2012. Assets, $1,449,646 (M); Expenditures, $99,430; Total giving, $71,000.
Type of support: Scholarships—to individuals; Support to graduates or students of specific schools.
Application information: Applications accepted. Application form required.
  Initial approach: Letter
  Deadline(s): None
  Additional information: See scholarship web site for application guidelines.
EIN: 576139022

7861
Friendship Fund Inc.
c/o BNY Mellon, N.A.
P.O. Box 185
Pittsburgh, PA 15230-0185

Foundation type: Independent foundation
Purpose: Grants for the advancement of the humanities, the sciences, and the welfare of humanity with emphasis on environmental protection, social services, and international affairs.
Financial data: Year ended 06/30/2012. Assets, $3,894,921 (M); Expenditures, $290,503; Total giving, $241,000.
Fields of interest: Humanities; Natural resources; Human services; International affairs.
Type of support: Undergraduate support.
Application information: Unsolicited applications no longer accepted; All funds for scholarship grants are committed in advance by the trustees.
EIN: 136089220

7862
The Frozen Food Industry Memorial Scholarship Foundation
4755 Linglestown Rd., Ste. 300
Harrisburg, PA 17112-8547   (717) 657-8601

Foundation type: Public charity
Purpose: Scholarships to students in the Harrisburg, PA area pursuing a career in the food industry.
Financial data: Year ended 12/31/2011. Assets, $72,012 (M); Expenditures, $26,472; Total giving, $24,500.
Fields of interest: Food services.
Type of support: Scholarships—to individuals.
Application information: Applications accepted.
  Additional information: Applicant must demonstrate financial need.
EIN: 582456285

7863
Fulton Bank Scholarship Foundation
P.O. Box 3215
Lancaster, PA 17604-3216

Foundation type: Company-sponsored foundation
Purpose: Scholarships to financially needy dependents of employees of Fulton Financial Corporation.
Financial data: Year ended 12/31/2012. Assets, $236 (M); Expenditures, $37,500; Total giving, $37,500; Grants to individuals, 25 grants totaling $37,500 (high: $1,500, low: $1,500).
Type of support: Employee-related scholarships.
Application information: Applications accepted. Application form required.
  Additional information: Application should include transcripts.
Company name: Fulton Financial Corporation
EIN: 236769593

7864
The Gardiner-Cook Cello Endowment
1774 Cambridge Dr.
State College, PA 16803-3263
Contact: Kim D. Cook, Pres.

Foundation type: Independent foundation
Purpose: Scholarships to cello players applying to Pennsylvania State University.
Financial data: Year ended 12/31/2012. Assets, $82,965 (M); Expenditures, $4,926; Total giving,

$4,478; Grant to an individual, 1 grant totaling $1,000.
Fields of interest: Music.
Type of support: Support to graduates or students of specific schools.
Application information: Applications accepted. Application form required.
  Deadline(s): None
  Additional information: Applicants must be current and prospective students of Ms. Cook or another teacher as the foundation designates. Applicants must audition before the selection committee.
EIN: 251864927

7865
John B. Gates Memorial Scholarship Fund
P.O. Box 846
Clearfield, PA 16830-0846

Foundation type: Independent foundation
Purpose: Scholarships to graduating seniors at Curwensville Area High School, PA.
Financial data: Year ended 06/30/2013. Assets, $230,926 (M); Expenditures, $26,017; Total giving, $25,000; Grants to individuals, 2 grants totaling $25,000 (high: $12,500, low: $12,500).
Type of support: Support to graduates or students of specific schools; Undergraduate support.
Application information: Applications not accepted.
  Additional information: Unsolicited requests for funds not considered or acknowledged.
EIN: 251721073

7866
GBU Foundation
4254 Clairton Blvd.
Pittsburgh, PA 15227-3394   (412) 884-5100
FAX: (412) 884-9815; E-mail: info@gbu.org;
Toll-free tel.:(800) 755-4428; URL: http://www.gbu.org

Foundation type: Public charity
Purpose: Scholarships to GBU members in undergraduate, graduate, and two-year programs. Student grants to eighth-grade GBU members for costs associated to their transition into high school.
Publications: Informational brochure (including application guidelines).
Financial data: Year ended 12/31/2011. Assets, $1,808,016 (M); Expenditures, $76,824; Total giving, $72,300; Grants to individuals, totaling $72,300.
Fields of interest: Secondary school/education; Higher education.
Type of support: Scholarships—to individuals.
Application information: Applications accepted. Application form required.
  Initial approach: Letter
  Deadline(s): May 31 for high school freshman grants; Feb.1 for scholarships
  Applicants should submit the following:
    1) Transcripts
    2) Letter(s) of recommendation
    3) Essay
  Additional information: Post-high school scholarship application must also include SAT or ACT scores.
EIN: 256076646

7867
Genesis Employee Foundation
101 E. State St.
Kennett Square, PA   19348-3109   (610)
444-6350
FAX: (610) 347-6217;
E-mail: genesis.employee.foundation@genesishcc.
com

Foundation type: Public charity
Purpose: Provides emergency relief to employees of Genesis HealthCare Corporation, its subsidiaries and affiliates and their dependents who have encountered severe financial hardship beyond their control.
Publications: Occasional report.
Financial data: Year ended 12/31/2011. Assets, $342,859 (M); Expenditures, $807,795; Total giving, $784,864; Grants to individuals, totaling $784,864.
Type of support: Emergency funds; Employee-related welfare; Grants for special needs.
Application information: Applications not accepted.
  Additional information: Unsolicited requests for funds not considered or acknowledged.
EIN: 202301122

7868
William & Marian Ghidotti Foundation
c/o Wells Fargo Bank, N.A., Trust Tax Dept.
101 N. Independence Mall E., MACY1372-062
Philadelphia, PA   19106-2112   (800) 352-3705

Foundation type: Independent foundation
Purpose: Scholarships to residents of Nevada County, CA for continuing education at accredited colleges or universities.
Financial data: Year ended 12/31/2012. Assets, $10,711,937 (M); Expenditures, $646,700; Total giving, $578,233; Grants to individuals, totaling $516,729.
Fields of interest: Education.
Type of support: Scholarships—to individuals.
Application information: Applications accepted. Application form required.
  Deadline(s): Feb. for new scholarships, Aug. for renewals
  Applicants should submit the following:
    1) Transcripts
    2) Resume
  Additional information: Application must also include student and family income statement.
EIN: 946181833

7869
Addison H. Gibson Foundation
1 PPG Pl., Ste. 2230
Pittsburgh, PA   15222-5401   (412) 261-1611
Contact: Rebecca Wallace, Exec. Dir.
E-mail contact for loans: ldunbar@gibson-fnd.org
FAX: (412) 261-5733;
E-mail: rwallace@gibson-fnd.org; URL: http://
www.gibson-fnd.org

Foundation type: Independent foundation
Purpose: Student loans to financially needy residents of western Pennsylvania, enrolled as full time students in a baccalaureate, or graduate program. Financial assistance for hospital and medical costs to needy, self-supporting, long-term western Pennsylvania residents who otherwise cannot afford the medical aid which they require.
Financial data: Year ended 12/31/2012. Assets, $29,263,907 (M); Expenditures, $1,458,636;

Total giving, $918,248; Grants to individuals, totaling $918,248.
Fields of interest: Higher education; Human services; Economically disadvantaged.
Type of support: Student loans—to individuals; Graduate support; Undergraduate support; Grants for special needs.
Application information: Applications not accepted.
  Additional information: The foundation is no longer accepting applications. See web site for information.
Program description:
  Gibson Education Loan Program: Scholarships in the amount of $12,000 maximum, is awarded to undergraduate students and a maximum of $18,000 to graduate students. Applicant must be in good academic standing and be able to demonstrate financial need.
EIN: 250965379

7870
H.G. Gillespie Foundation
13201 Cambridge Springs Rd.
Edinboro, PA   16412-2838
Application address: c/o General McLane Fdn., Therese T. Walter Education Center, 11771 Edinboro Rd., Edinboro, PA 16412-1025

Foundation type: Independent foundation
Purpose: Financial assistance to General McLane school district, PA graduates who have attained at least third year standing in postsecondary educational institutions.
Financial data: Year ended 12/31/2012. Assets, $849,971 (M); Expenditures, $16,573; Total giving, $16,409.
Fields of interest: Higher education.
Type of support: Scholarships—to individuals.
Application information: Applications accepted. Application form required.
  Initial approach: Letter or web site
  Deadline(s): Mar. 27
  Applicants should submit the following:
    1) Essay
    2) SASE
    3) GPA
  Additional information: Application should also include two character references.
EIN: 256035948

7871
GlaxoSmithKline Patient Access
Programs Foundation
1 Franklin Plaza, Rm. 2335
Philadelphia, PA   19101   (888) 825-5249
Additional address: Frank Barrett, 200 N. 16th St., Philadelphia, PA 19102; Tel. for Bridges to Access: (866) 728-4368; Tel. for Commitment to Access: (866) 265-6491; URL: http://
www.gskforyou.com/

Foundation type: Operating foundation
Purpose: Financial aid for the purchase of non-oncology prescription medication to economically disadvantaged patients without prescription drug benefits.
Publications: Application guidelines.
Financial data: Year ended 12/31/2012. Assets, $47,877,145 (M); Expenditures, $620,484,885; Total giving, $599,953,667; Grants to individuals, totaling $599,953,667.
Fields of interest: Health care; Economically disadvantaged.
Type of support: Grants for special needs.

Application information: Applications accepted. Application form available on the grantmaker's web site.
  Initial approach: Application
  Send request by: Mail
  Deadline(s): None
  Additional information: Application should include financial information. Mail proof of current income and other requested documents along with the completed and signed application. Contact the foundation for additional eligibility criteria.
Program descriptions:
  Bridges To Access: Through the Bridges to Access program, the foundation provides non-oncology GSK prescription medicines to eligible low-income U.S. patients without prescription drug benefits. URL: http://www.bridgestoaccess.com/ for additional information.
  Commitment to Access: Through the Commitment to Access program, the foundation provides oncology and specialty pharmacy products, at little or no cost, to patients who qualify. URL: http://
www.gskcta.com/ for additional information.
EIN: 200031992

7872
Golden Slipper Club Charities
215 N. Presidential Blvd. 1st fl.
Bala Cynwyd, PA   19004-1781   (610) 660-0510
FAX: (610) 660-0515;
E-mail: info@goldenslipper.org; URL: https://
goldenslipperclub.org/

Foundation type: Public charity
Purpose: College scholarships to outstanding students in the Philadelphia, PA area pursuing higher education. Assistance to needy families.
Financial data: Year ended 09/30/2011. Assets, $796,138 (M); Expenditures, $868,840; Total giving, $428,342; Grants to individuals, totaling $135,842.
Fields of interest: Vocational education, post-secondary; Higher education.
Type of support: Scholarships—to individuals.
Application information: Applications accepted. Application form required.
  Additional information: Selection is based on leadership, character, service tosociety, career goals and financial need.
EIN: 236430340

7873
Golden Tornado Scholastic Foundation,
Inc.
110 Campus Ln.
Butler, PA   16001-2662   (724) 287-8721
Contact: Carmen Bianco, Pres.

Foundation type: Public charity
Purpose: Scholarships to high school students of Butler Area School District, PA for higher education. Grants to the teaching staff to fund creating teaching.
Financial data: Year ended 12/31/2011. Assets, $1,026,607 (M); Expenditures, $91,152; Total giving, $61,695; Grants to individuals, totaling $58,195.
Fields of interest: Education.
Type of support: Grants to individuals; Scholarships—to individuals.
Application information: Unsolicited requests for funds not considered or acknowledged.
EIN: 251653165

7874
William Goldman Foundation
42 S. 15th St., Ste. 1116
Philadelphia, PA 19102 (215) 568-0411
Contact: William Goldman, Chair.

Foundation type: Independent foundation
Purpose: Scholarships to residents of the metropolitan Philadelphia, PA, area for full-time graduate or medical study at the following nine schools: Bryn Mawr College, Drexel University, Hahnemann University, Medical College of Pennsylvania, Philadelphia College of Osteopathic Medicine, Temple University, Thomas Jefferson University, Jefferson Medical College, University of Pennsylvania, and Villanova University.
Publications: Application guidelines.
Financial data: Year ended 12/31/2012. Assets, $3,115,430 (M); Expenditures, $176,249; Total giving, $127,595.
Fields of interest: Higher education.
Type of support: Support to graduates or students of specific schools; Graduate support.
Application information: Application form required. Interview required.
  Initial approach: Letter
  Deadline(s): Mar. 15
EIN: 236266261

7875
Sarah and Tena Goldstein Memorial Scholarship
c/o Jewish Family and Children's Services
5743 Bartlett St.
Pittsburgh, PA 15217-1515 (412) 422-7200

Foundation type: Independent foundation
Purpose: Scholarships to Jewish students who are residents of Titusville, PA.
Financial data: Year ended 12/31/2012. Assets, $2,658,382 (M); Expenditures, $134,095; Total giving, $111,613; Grants to individuals, 15 grants totaling $111,613 (high: $11,000, low: $1,000).
Fields of interest: Higher education; Jewish agencies & synagogues.
Type of support: Scholarships—to individuals.
Application information:
  Deadline(s): None
  Final notification: Recipients notified in two months
  Additional information: Application must include a brief resume of academic qualifications.
EIN: 251229795

7876
Gooding Group Foundation
345 S. Reading Rd.
Ephrata, PA 17522-1832 (717) 733-1247
Contact: John S. Gooding, Pres.

Foundation type: Company-sponsored foundation
Purpose: Scholarships to employees of GSM Industrial Incorporated, and its subsidiaries.
Financial data: Year ended 12/31/2011. Assets, $436,578 (M); Expenditures, $59,993; Total giving, $41,045.
Type of support: Employee-related scholarships.
Application information: Applications not accepted.
  Additional information: Unsolicited requests for funds not considered.
Company name: GSM Industrial, Inc.
EIN: 232516754

7877
Alva O., Adie E. & Mary J. Goslee Student Loan Fund
c/o Wells Fargo Bank, N.A.
101 N. Independence Mall, MACY1372-062
Philadelphia, PA 19106-2112
Application address: c/o Twin Lakes School Corp., Attn.: Joyce Fulford, 565 S. Main St., Monticello, IN 47960-2473

Foundation type: Independent foundation
Purpose: Scholarships and loans to students of Jefferson & Adams High School and Twin Lakes High School, IN.
Financial data: Year ended 12/31/2012. Assets, $882,799 (M); Expenditures, $42,954; Total giving, $26,150; Grants to individuals, 104 grants totaling $26,150 (high: $650, low: $125).
Fields of interest: Vocational education.
Type of support: Support to graduates or students of specific schools.
Application information: Applications accepted. Application form required.
  Deadline(s): Feb. 8
  Applicants should submit the following:
    1) Transcripts
    2) Letter(s) of recommendation
EIN: 356369633

7878
Grand Lodge of Free & Accepted Masons of Pennsylvania
1 N. Broad St.
Philadelphia, PA 19107-2520 (215) 988-1900
Application address: 1244 Bainbridge Rd., Elizabethtown, PA 17022-9423
URL: http://www.pagrandlodge.org

Foundation type: Public charity
Purpose: Scholarships to those who have a relationship to a Pennsylvania Mason or membership in a Pennsylvania Masonic-sponsored youth group.
Financial data: Year ended 12/31/2011. Assets, $48,743,029 (M); Expenditures, $4,725,949; Total giving, $1,505,850; Grants to individuals, totaling $99,994.
Fields of interest: Fraternal societies.
Type of support: Undergraduate support.
Application information:
  Initial approach: Letter
  Deadline(s): Mar. 15
  Applicants should submit the following:
    1) Letter(s) of recommendation
    2) FAFSA
    3) FAF
    4) Financial information
    5) Transcripts
  Additional information: See http://www.pmyf.org/scholar/app/index.html for additional eligibility criteria.
EIN: 236407467

7879
Greater Erie Community Action Committee
18 W. 9th St.
Erie, PA 16501-1343 (814) 459-4581
Contact: Ronald A. Steele, C.E.O.
FAX: (814) 456-0161; Toll Free Tel.: (800)-769-2436; *URL:* http://www.gecac.org/

Foundation type: Public charity
Purpose: A once a year lump sum grant to indigent residents of Erie, PA customers who have an emergency situation and need temporary help in

paying their electric bill. Also available is a home-heating assistance grant program, which provides assistance to low-income individuals to help pay for energy-related expenses. Eligible individuals can receive a maximum $300 per calendar year to pay overdue heat bills, to purchase fuel or to repair heating equipment.
Financial data: Year ended 09/30/2011. Assets, $11,502,557 (M); Expenditures, $31,995,706; Total giving, $3,838,164; Grants to individuals, totaling $1,521,394.
Fields of interest: Housing/shelter, expense aid; Housing/shelter; Economically disadvantaged.
Type of support: Grants for special needs.
Application information:
  Initial approach: Tel.
  Deadline(s): Oct. 1 through Feb. 28
  Additional information: Applicants must supply proof of income and hardship.
EIN: 256068246

7880
The Greater Pottstown Foundation
934 High St.
Pottstown, PA 19464-0696 (610) 323-7700
Contact: Paul A. Prince Esq., Pres.

Foundation type: Independent foundation
Purpose: Scholarships to seniors graduating from The Hill School, Owen J. Roberts High School, Pottsgrove High School, Pottstown High School or St. Pius X High School, PA.
Financial data: Year ended 12/31/2012. Assets, $1,558,581 (M); Expenditures, $101,852; Total giving, $64,308; Grants to individuals, 5 grants totaling $27,318 (high: $10,000, low: $2,318).
Type of support: Scholarships—to individuals; Support to graduates or students of specific schools.
Application information: Application form required.
  Deadline(s): May 1
  Additional information: Application must include essay.
EIN: 232568998

7881
Dwight R. & Julia Guthrie Scholarship Fund
c/o PNC Bank, N.A.
P.O. Box 609
Pittsburgh, PA 15230-9738

Foundation type: Independent foundation
Purpose: Scholarships to students in PA for higher education.
Financial data: Year ended 01/31/2013. Assets, $300,211 (M); Expenditures, $13,201; Total giving, $9,850.
Type of support: Undergraduate support.
Application information: Applications not accepted.
  Additional information: Unsolicited requests for funds not considered or acknowledged.
EIN: 256638149

7882
Louise H. Haeseler Memorial Fund Trust
c/o Wells Fargo Bank, N.A.
101 N. Independence Mall E MACY1372-062
Philadelphia, PA 19106-2112
Application address: c/o Philadelphia High School for Girls, Bread and Olney Sts., Philadelphia, PA 19141

Foundation type: Independent foundation

Purpose: Grants are awarded to past or present employees of Philadelphia School District, PA, who are in need.
Financial data: Year ended 12/31/2012. Assets, $610,855 (M); Expenditures, $71,847; Total giving, $51,000; Grants to individuals, 6 grants totaling $51,000 (high: $9,600, low: $7,800).
Type of support: Grants to individuals.
Application information: Application form required.
  Deadline(s): None
EIN: 236428035

7883
Carl G. Hahn Academic Athletic Scholarship Award
c/o William J. Sifer
892 2nd St. Pike
Richboro, PA   18954-1005   (215) 322-8300

Foundation type: Public charity
Purpose: Athletic scholarship to worthy students of Central Bucks East High School, PA for higher education.
Financial data: Year ended 12/31/2011. Assets, $96,046 (M); Expenditures, $2,374.
Fields of interest: Higher education.
Type of support: Support to graduates or students of specific schools.
Application information: Contact your high school for eligibility.
EIN: 201302887

7884
Hamot Aid Society
201 State St.
Erie, PA   16550-0002   (814) 871-6000
For Fellowship and Residency Program: Pat Rogers, Prog. Admin., tel.: (814) 877-6257,
e-mail: patricia.rogers@hamot.org
E-mail: info@hamot.org; URL: http://www.hamot.org

Foundation type: Public charity
Purpose: Postdoctoral fellowships and residencies to medical practitioners in PA.
Financial data: Year ended 12/31/2011. Assets, $700,638 (M); Expenditures, $796,116; Total giving, $621,588; Grants to individuals, totaling $16,588.
Fields of interest: Medical school/education; Health sciences school/education; Health care.
Type of support: Fellowships.
Application information: Application form required. Application form available on the grantmaker's web site. Interview required.
  Initial approach: Telephone or e-mail
  Deadline(s): Nov. 1 for Orthopaedic Residency, Dec. 1 for Hand Fellowship, Dec. 31 for Emergency Medicine Residency, Neurology Residency, and Osteopathic Internship, Jan. 31 for Pharmacy Residency
  Applicants should submit the following:
    1) Transcripts
    2) Letter(s) of recommendation
    3) Curriculum vitae
  Additional information: Application must also include board scores, and a personal statement. Contact society for further program and application information.
EIN: 256039041

7885
The George T. Handyside Foundation
c/o Tax Department Build
1019 Rte. 519
Eighty Four, PA   15330-2813   (724) 228-8820

Foundation type: Independent foundation
Purpose: Scholarships to sons, daughters, and spouses of individuals who have been active 84 Lumber Company, Nemacolin Woodlands and 84 Components Company employees for at least two years.
Financial data: Year ended 12/31/2012. Assets, $988,999 (M); Expenditures, $108,039; Total giving, $105,000; Grants to individuals, 16 grants totaling $105,000 (high: $10,000, low: $2,500).
Type of support: Employee-related scholarships.
Application information:
  Initial approach: Letter or telephone
  Deadline(s): Mar. 31
  Additional information: Contact a company office for current application deadline/guidelines.
Company name: 84 Lumber Company
EIN: 251667394

7886
Sylvia M. Harley Nursing Scholarship Fund
260 Sunbury St.
Minersville, PA   17954   (570) 544-1709
Application Address: c/o Sovereigh Bank;
Attn: Wealth Mgmt.Dir.

Foundation type: Independent foundation
Purpose: Scholarships to residents of the Pottsville Area School District, PA, pursuing a career in the nursing profession.
Financial data: Year ended 12/31/2011. Assets, $627,698 (M); Expenditures, $9,798; Total giving, $0.
Fields of interest: Nursing school/education.
Type of support: Scholarships—to individuals; Undergraduate support.
Application information: Application form required.
  Deadline(s): May
  Additional information: Scholarship is based on financial need. Interviews may be required.
EIN: 232402538

7887
Harmon Scholarship Fund
(formerly Marie K. Harmon Scholarship Fund)
c/o Wells Fargo Bank, N.A.
101 N. Independence Mall E MACY 1372-062
Philadelphia, PA   19106-2112
Application address: 4320 Wade Hampton Blvd., Suite G, Taylors, SC 29687

Foundation type: Independent foundation
Purpose: Scholarships to residents of the Jefferson, IA area for higher education.
Financial data: Year ended 12/31/2012. Assets, $308,632 (M); Expenditures, $15,401; Total giving, $6,000.
Type of support: Undergraduate support.
Application information: Applications not accepted.
  Additional information: Unsolicited requests for funds not considered or acknowledged.
EIN: 421318359

7888
George M. & Faye Tabor Harris Charitable Foundation
c/o Wells Fargo Bank N.A.
101 N Independence Mall E Macy1372-062
Philadelphia, PA   19106-2112
Application addresses: c/o Wells Fargo Private Client Services, P.O Box95021 Henderson,NV 89009-5021

Foundation type: Independent foundation
Purpose: Scholarships to high school graduates of MT for attendance at accredited colleges or universities.
Financial data: Year ended 01/31/2013. Assets, $975,691 (M); Expenditures, $67,630; Total giving, $50,829; Grants to individuals, 21 grants totaling $50,829 (high: $10,000, low: $500).
Fields of interest: Higher education.
Type of support: Support to graduates or students of specific schools; Undergraduate support.
Application information:
  Deadline(s): May 1 for general scholarships, Mar. 15 for PEO scholarships
  Applicants should submit the following:
    1) Photograph
    2) Transcripts
    3) Letter(s) of recommendation
    4) Financial information
    5) Essay
  Additional information: Contact the foundation for additional application guidelines.
EIN: 816010110

7889
Raymond J. Harris Educational Trust
c/o BNY Mellon, N.A.
P.O. Box 185
Pittsburgh, PA   15230-0185

Foundation type: Independent foundation
Purpose: Scholarships to Christian men for professional education in medicine, law, engineering, dentistry, or agriculture at nine Philadelphia, PA, area colleges.
Financial data: Year ended 09/30/2013. Assets, $1,064,538 (M); Expenditures, $45,346; Total giving, $30,000.
Fields of interest: Dental school/education; Law school/education; Medical school/education; Engineering school/education; Agriculture; Christian agencies & churches; Men.
Type of support: Support to graduates or students of specific schools; Graduate support; Undergraduate support.
Application information: Applications not accepted.
  Additional information: Applications may be obtained form the nine area colleges. Unsolicited requests for funds not considered or acknowledged.
EIN: 236224306

7890
Harris Scholarship Fund
c/o PNC Bank, N.A.
1600 Market St., Tax Dept.
Philadelphia, PA   19103-7240

Foundation type: Independent foundation
Purpose: Scholarships to academically qualified and financially needy graduates of Salem High School, NJ.
Financial data: Year ended 12/31/2012. Assets, $512,223 (M); Expenditures, $30,158; Total

giving, $24,000; Grants to individuals, 22 grants totaling $24,000 (high: $2,500, low: $500).
Type of support: Support to graduates or students of specific schools; Undergraduate support.
Application information: Applications not accepted.
Additional information: Unsolicited requests for funds not considered or acknowledged.
EIN: 226485592

7891
Paul Hyland Harris Trust
c/o National City Bank
248 Seneca St.
Oil City, PA   16301-1371
Contact: Lynette A. Pedensky, V.P., National City Bank
FAX: (814) 678-3647;
E-mail: lynette.pedensky@nationalcity.com

Foundation type: Independent foundation
Purpose: Scholarships to students graduating from Crawford, Venango, and Warren County high schools, PA, who plan to attend Allegheny College, PA, or Harvard University, MA.
Financial data: Year ended 12/31/2012. Assets, $3,016,740 (M); Expenditures, $146,267; Total giving, $109,038; Grants to individuals, totaling $109,038.
Type of support: Support to graduates or students of specific schools; Undergraduate support.
Application information: Applications accepted. Application form required.
Send request by: Mail
Copies of proposal: 1
Deadline(s): Apr. 1
Final notification: Response to an application within two months
Applicants should submit the following:
1) FAFSA
2) Financial information
3) GPA
4) Letter(s) of recommendation
5) Pell Grant
6) SAT
7) Transcripts
Additional information: Applications available at Allegheny or National City Bank.
EIN: 256013264

7892
Frank and Amanda Hartman Educational Foundation
(formerly Russell L. Hartman Trust)
c/o BNY Mellon, N.A.
P.O. Box 185
Pittsburgh, PA   15230-0185

Foundation type: Independent foundation
Purpose: Scholarships to financially needy residents of Boyertown, PA, and its surrounding areas.
Financial data: Year ended 09/30/2013. Assets, $894,877 (M); Expenditures, $47,310; Total giving, $31,600.
Type of support: Scholarships—to individuals.
Application information: Applications accepted. Application form required.
Deadline(s): May 1
Additional information: Application must include information on academic performance and financial need.
EIN: 236810792

7893
The Hassel Foundation
c/o BNY Mellon Center
1735 Market St., Ste. 600
Philadelphia, PA   19103-7513
Contact: Michael H. Krekstein, Tr.

Foundation type: Independent foundation
Purpose: Scholarships to graduating seniors of Reading Senior High School, Exeter Township Senior High School, and Twin Valley High School, in PA.
Financial data: Year ended 12/31/2012. Assets, $6,548,826 (M); Expenditures, $371,157; Total giving, $303,000.
Fields of interest: Higher education.
Type of support: Support to graduates or students of specific schools; Undergraduate support.
Application information: Applications accepted. Application form not required.
Initial approach: Letter
Deadline(s): None
Additional information: Applications are available through high school principal's office.
EIN: 236251862

7894
Della Lucille Hazelton Charitable Trust
c/o Wells Fargo Bank, N.A.
101N Independence Mall E Macy 1372-062
Philadelphia, PA   19106-2112   (800) 730-4933

Foundation type: Independent foundation
Purpose: Financial assistance to Native Americans who are residents of AZ and MT.
Financial data: Year ended 12/31/2012. Assets, $328,622 (M); Expenditures, $19,833; Total giving, $13,625; Grants to individuals, 40 grants totaling $13,625 (high: $350, low: $350).
Fields of interest: Native Americans/American Indians.
Type of support: Grants for special needs.
Application information: Applications not accepted.
Additional information: Two Native American tribes within each state are contacted on a rotating basis to select needy applicants. Unsolicited requests for funds not considered or acknowledged.
EIN: 746366878

7895
Vivian B. Head Testamentary Trust
c/o Wells Fargo Bank Texas, N.A.
101N Independence Mall E Macy 1372-062
Philadelphia, PA   19106-2112

Foundation type: Independent foundation
Purpose: Scholarships to students majoring in the fine arts and electrical engineering at New Mexico State University, NM and New York University, NY.
Financial data: Year ended 06/30/2012. Assets, $533,919 (M); Expenditures, $31,025; Total giving, $20,000.
Fields of interest: Arts education; Arts; Engineering.
Type of support: Support to graduates or students of specific schools; Undergraduate support.
Application information: Applications not accepted.
Additional information: Unsolicited requests for funds not considered or acknowledged.
EIN: 850319081

7896
William H. Heald Scholarship Fund
c/o PNC Bank, N.A.
1600 Market St.
Philadelphia, PA   19103-7240
Contact: Richard Sutton Esq.
Application address: P.O. Box 1347, Willington, De 19899

Foundation type: Independent foundation
Purpose: Scholarships to male residents of New Castle County, DE, to attend the University of Delaware.
Financial data: Year ended 12/31/2013. Assets, $699,779 (M); Expenditures, $62,916; Total giving, $45,000.
Fields of interest: Men.
Type of support: Support to graduates or students of specific schools; Undergraduate support.
Application information: Deadline May 1; Application by letter.
EIN: 516010547

7897
Health & Educational Trust of Berks County Medical Society
P.O. Box 3215
Lancaster, PA   17604-3215   (610) 332-7143

Foundation type: Public charity
Purpose: Awards to staff members of Berks County Medical Society.
Financial data: Year ended 12/31/2011. Assets, $2,206 (M); Expenditures, $26,365; Total giving, $26,242.
Fields of interest: Health care.
Type of support: Awards/prizes.
Application information: Contact the society for additional guidelines.
EIN: 236415570

7898
Hearn Educational Fund Trust
c/o PNC Bank, N.A.
1600 Market St., Tax Dept.
Philadelphia, PA   19103-7240

Foundation type: Independent foundation
Purpose: Scholarships to students who reside in the Milford, DE, school district, for continuing education at institutions of higher learning.
Publications: Application guidelines; Program policy statement.
Financial data: Year ended 12/31/2012. Assets, $1,608,770 (M); Expenditures, $108,490; Total giving, $74,000.
Fields of interest: Higher education.
Type of support: Scholarships—to individuals; Support to graduates or students of specific schools.
Application information: Applications accepted. Application form required.
Initial approach: Letter
Deadline(s): May 24
EIN: 516015401

7899
Heart of Variety Fund
1520 Locust St., 2nd Fl.
Philadelphia, PA   19102-4404   (215) 735-0803
Contact: Kelly Green, Exec. Dir.

Foundation type: Public charity
Purpose: Scholarships to deserving children with disabilities.

Financial data: Year ended 09/30/2011. Assets, $3,367,385 (M); Expenditures, $4,261,799.
Fields of interest: Children; Disabilities, people with.
Type of support: Scholarships—to individuals.
Application information:
Initial approach: Letter
Additional information: Contact fund for application guidelines.
EIN: 236392728

7900
Heinz Family Foundation
625 Liberty Ave., Ste. 3200
Pittsburgh, PA 15222-3120
FAX: (412) 497-5790; URL: http://www.heinzfamily.org/aboutus/philanthropies.html

Foundation type: Independent foundation
Purpose: Awards by nomination only to individuals for their contributions to the arts and humanities, the environment, the human condition, public policy, technology and the economy.
Financial data: Year ended 12/31/2012. Assets, $117,095,904 (M); Expenditures, $3,691,114; Total giving, $2,222,563; Grant to an individual, 1 grant totaling $215,000.
Fields of interest: Humanities; Arts; Environment; Engineering/technology; Economics; Research.
Type of support: Awards/grants by nomination only; Awards/prizes.
Application information: Recipients are nominated by a foundation-appointed, anonymous council of nominators.
Program description:
Heinz Awards: Established in 1992, the program is the primary activity of the Heinz Family Foundation. The Heinz Awards recognize individuals for their contributions in the areas of arts and humanities, the environment, the human condition, public policy, and technology and the economy. Award nominations are submitted by a Council of Nominators, who serve anonymously, and are reviewed by jurors appointed by the foundation. Award recipients are selected by the Board of Directors of the Heinz Awards upon review of the jurors' recommendations. Awards recipients will receive a cash prize of $250,000 for their unrestricted use. See foundation web site for complete program criteria.
EIN: 251689382

7901
A. M. Helbing Trust for Nursing Education
c/o Mauch Chunk Trust Co.
P.O. Box 289
Jim Thorpe, PA 18229-0289

Foundation type: Independent foundation
Purpose: Scholarships to residents of Carbon County, PA, pursuing nursing education.
Financial data: Year ended 12/31/2012. Assets, $271,435 (M); Expenditures, $16,402; Total giving, $11,950.
Fields of interest: Nursing school/education.
Type of support: Graduate support.
Application information: Applications not accepted.
Additional information: Unsolicited requests for funds not considered or acknowledged.
EIN: 237681690

7902
Bruce R. Helwig Reading High School Scholarship Fund
1136 Penn Ave.
Wyomissing, PA 19610-2034 (610) 378-1933
Contact: Terry Weiler Esq., Tr.

Foundation type: Independent foundation
Purpose: Scholarships to students of Reading High School, PA.
Financial data: Year ended 08/31/2013. Assets, $151,057 (M); Expenditures, $375; Total giving, $0.
Type of support: Support to graduates or students of specific schools; Undergraduate support.
Application information: Applications accepted. Application form required.
Additional information: Contact foundation for current application deadline/guidelines.
EIN: 232843839

7903
M. & G. Henderson Scholarship Fund
c/o The Bank of New York Mellon, Tax Dept.
P.O. Box 185
Pittsburgh, PA 15230-0185

Foundation type: Independent foundation
Purpose: Limited scholarships to graduates of Rye High School, NY for continuing education at accredited colleges or universities.
Financial data: Year ended 12/31/2012. Assets, $134,333 (M); Expenditures, $7,084; Total giving, $6,900.
Fields of interest: Higher education.
Type of support: Support to graduates or students of specific schools.
Application information: Applications accepted.
Initial approach: Letter
Deadline(s): None
Additional information: Applicant must demonstrate financial need.
EIN: 136062187

7904
Marie E. Heyburn Trust
c/o Bank of Malvern
2 W. King St.
Malvern, PA 19355-2410 (610) 579-7745

Foundation type: Independent foundation
Purpose: College scholarships to students of Garnet Valley High School, PA, for attendance at institutions of higher learning.
Financial data: Year ended 12/31/2012. Assets, $271,271 (M); Expenditures, $11,684; Total giving, $7,500; Grants to individuals, 3 grants totaling $7,500 (high: $2,500, low: $2,500).
Fields of interest: Higher education.
Type of support: Support to graduates or students of specific schools; Undergraduate support.
Application information: Applications accepted. Application form required.
Additional information: Contact guidance counselor for current application deadline/guidelines.
EIN: 237776386

7905
David Downes Higbee Trust
c/o PNC Bank, N.A.
620 Liberty Ave., 10th Fl.
Pittsburgh, PA 15222

Foundation type: Independent foundation

Purpose: Scholarships to graduates of Audubon High School, NJ.
Financial data: Year ended 12/31/2012. Assets, $336,559 (M); Expenditures, $25,502; Total giving, $20,000.
Type of support: Support to graduates or students of specific schools; Undergraduate support.
Application information: Applications not accepted.
Additional information: Unsolicited requests for funds not considered or acknowledged.
EIN: 226375372

7906
The S. Dale High Family Foundation
(formerly The High Foundation)
P.O. Box 10008
Lancaster, PA 17605-0008
Contact: Robin D. Stauffer, Exec. Dir.
E-mail: rstauffer@high.net

Foundation type: Independent foundation
Purpose: Scholarships to children of employees of the High companies for undergraduate education at universities and colleges in the U.S.
Publications: Application guidelines; Program policy statement.
Financial data: Year ended 08/31/2013. Assets, $9,994,712 (M); Expenditures, $383,791; Total giving, $310,296; Grants to individuals, 7 grants totaling $32,000 (high: $5,000, low: $4,000).
Fields of interest: College; University.
Type of support: Employee-related scholarships.
Application information: Applications accepted. Application form required.
Deadline(s): Nov. 1
Additional information: Applications available from human resources departments.
EIN: 232149972

7907
Harold Newlin Hill Foundation
c/o BNY Mellon, N.A.
P.O. Box 185
Pittsburgh, PA 15230-0185

Foundation type: Independent foundation
Purpose: Scholarships to children of employees of Asten Group, Inc.
Financial data: Year ended 06/30/2013. Assets, $348,964 (M); Expenditures, $19,337; Total giving, $12,800; Grants to individuals, 15 grants totaling $12,800 (high: $1,000, low: $800).
Type of support: Employee-related scholarships.
Application information: Application form not required.
Company name: Asten Group, Incorporated
EIN: 236228294

7908
David and Edith E. Hill Scholarship Fund
c/o PNC Bank, N.A.
1600 Market St., 4th Fl.
Philadelphia, PA 19103-7240

Foundation type: Independent foundation
Purpose: Scholarships to seniors of Hazelton High School, PA or Bishop Hafey Hig School, PA in pursuit of a higher education.
Financial data: Year ended 12/31/2012. Assets, $112,655 (M); Expenditures, $6,130; Total giving, $4,520.
Fields of interest: Higher education.
Type of support: Support to graduates or students of specific schools.

Application information:
Initial approach: Letter
Deadline(s): None
EIN: 236940311

7909
Ruth A. Hill Trust
c/o BNY Mellon, N.A.
P.O. Box 185
Pittsburgh, PA 15230-0185   (814) 874-5209
Contact: Matthew Loeffler
Application address: 100 State St., Erie, PA 16570
Tel.: (814) 874-5209

Foundation type: Independent foundation
Purpose: Scholarships to financially needy
students who reside in Oil City, PA, and to
African-American students who reside in Venango
County, City of Titusville, or areas served by Forest
County Area Vocational School.
Financial data: Year ended 12/31/2012. Assets,
$7,052,457 (M); Expenditures, $339,653; Total
giving, $313,006.
Fields of interest: Minorities.
Type of support: Support to graduates or students
of specific schools; Undergraduate support.
Application information: Applications accepted.
Application form required.
Deadline(s): Mar. 15
EIN: 256031644

7910
Orris C. Hirtzel and Beatrice Dewey Hirtzel Memorial Foundation
(formerly Elec Material Hirtzel Memorial Foundation)
c/o BNY Mellon, N A
P.O. Box 185
Pittsburgh, PA   15230-0185   (412) 234-0023
Contact: Laurie Moritz
Application address: 500 Grant St., Ste. 3825,
Pittsburgh, PA 15258.

Foundation type: Independent foundation
Purpose: Scholarships to students completing
secondary school with close geographical proximity
to the North East, PA, and Erie County, PA.
Financial data: Year ended 12/31/2012. Assets,
$20,626,922 (M); Expenditures, $992,231; Total
giving, $825,400.
Fields of interest: Higher education.
Type of support: Scholarships—to individuals.
Application information: Application form required.
Initial approach: Letter
EIN: 256018933

7911
Holy Spirit Hospital
503 N. 21st St.
Camp Hill, PA   17011-2204   (717) 763-2100
Contact: Romaine Niemeyer, Pres. and C.E.O.
Tel. for scholarships: (717) 972-4100,
e-mail: applicant@hsh.org
E-mail: pmalone@hsh.org; URL: http://
www.hsh.org

Foundation type: Public charity
Purpose: Reimbursement for the cost of tuition and
textbooks for students at Holy Spirit Health System,
enrolled in the clinical portion of their education in
a RN or CRNA program.
Financial data: Year ended 06/30/2012. Assets,
$268,258,437 (M); Expenditures, $330,131,396;
Total giving, $15,692,256; Grants to individuals,
totaling $265,433.
Fields of interest: Nursing school/education.

Type of support: Scholarships—to individuals.
Application information: Applications accepted.
Application form required.
Deadline(s): Mid-Nov. for Student Nurse Extern
Program
Additional information: See web site for
additional guidelines.
Program descriptions:
Scholarship Program: The RN scholarship
program reimburses up to $5,000 per year.
Students are also eligible to receive medical
benefits at the full time employee rate. The CRNA
scholarship program provides up to $50,000 in
reimbursement and is customized on a
case-by-case basis.
Student Nurse Extern Program: This is a 10-week,
full time, temporary, paid position to student nurses
from NLN accredited nursing programs. The
students in this position will anticipate graduating
the following Dec. or May after completing the
summer externship.
EIN: 231512747

7912
Horn Educational Trust
(formerly Lee A. & Mabel H. Horn Educational Trust)
c/o Wells Fargo Bank, N.A.
101N Independence Mall E. MACY 1372-062
Philadelphia, PA   19106-2112

Foundation type: Independent foundation
Purpose: Scholarships to single students who
graduated from Ida Grove High School, IA, in the
upper third of their class.
Financial data: Year ended 12/31/2012. Assets,
$131,534 (M); Expenditures, $9,509; Total giving,
$4,000.
Type of support: Support to graduates or students
of specific schools; Undergraduate support.
Application information: Applications accepted.
Initial approach: Letter
EIN: 426051539

7913
W. Marshall Hughes, Jr. Scholarship Foundation
2201 Ridgewood Rd., Ste. 180
Wyomissing, PA   19610-1190   (610) 372-6414

Foundation type: Independent foundation
Purpose: Scholarships to graduates of Berks
County, PA, secondary schools to study
architecture, literature, music, or theater.
Scholarships are awarded on the basis of merit and
are renewable for up to seven years (five
undergraduate years and two graduate years)
Financial data: Year ended 12/31/2011. Assets,
$3,153,921 (M); Expenditures, $169,096; Total
giving, $138,901.
Fields of interest: Architecture; Theater; Music;
Performing arts, education; Literature.
Type of support: Support to graduates or students
of specific schools; Undergraduate support.
Application information: Application form required.
Interview required.
Initial approach: Letter
Deadline(s): Mar. 1
Applicants should submit the following:
1) Letter(s) of recommendation
2) Transcripts
Additional information: Application must also
include description of extracurricular and
community activities, statement of career
objectives, certificate of acceptance to

institution, and supporting artistic materials,
if applicable; Auditions may be required.
EIN: 236934996

7914
Otto A. Huth Scholarship Fund Charitable
(formerly Otto A. Huth Scholarship Fund)
c/o Wells Fargo Bank, N.A.
101 N. Independence Mall E MACY 1372-062
Philadelphia, PA   19106-2112   (775) 823-487
Application address: 5340 Kietzke Ln., Ste. 200,
Reno, NV 89511

Foundation type: Independent foundation
Purpose: Scholarships to financially needy high
school seniors who are orphans, and who are
primarily residents of NV.
Financial data: Year ended 12/31/2012. Assets,
$1,004,544 (M); Expenditures, $94,834; Total
giving, $68,699; Grants to individuals, 17 grants
totaling $68,699 (high: $8,079, low: $609).
Fields of interest: Children, services; Residential/
custodial care.
Type of support: Scholarships—to individuals.
Application information: Application form required.
Deadline(s): Prior to college semester
Additional information: Application must include
verification of high school senior status,
estimated cost of education, and a list of
other aid for which student has applied.
EIN: 886059683

7915
II-VI Foundation
(formerly II-VI Incorporated Foundation)
1370 Washington Pike, Ste. 404
Bridgeville, PA   15017-2826   (412) 206-0580
Contact: Richard W. Purnell, Exec. Dir.
FAX: (412) 206-0583;
E-mail: info@ii-vifoundation.com; URL: http://
ii-vifoundation.com/index.html

Foundation type: Independent foundation
Purpose: Scholarships only to students in the areas
where II-VI, Inc. maintains a facility, pursuing an
engineering, science, or mathematics-related
degree at a postsecondary educational institution.
Financial data: Year ended 12/31/2012. Assets,
$26,833,332 (M); Expenditures, $3,537,129;
Total giving, $2,989,866; Grants to individuals,
56 grants totaling $501,837 (high: $10,000, low:
$2,247).
Fields of interest: Higher education.
Type of support: Graduate support; Undergraduate
support.
Application information: Applications accepted.
Application form required. Application form
available on the grantmaker's web site. Interview
required.
Initial approach: Letter
Deadline(s): June 10 for intention, July 10 for
documentation
Final notification: Applicants notified the first
week of Aug.
Applicants should submit the following:
1) Transcripts
2) Letter(s) of recommendation
3) Essay
Additional information: See web site for
additional guidelines.
EIN: 208824719

7916
Independence Foundation
200 S. Broad St., Ste. 1101
Philadelphia, PA 19102-3802 (215) 985-4009
Contact: Susan E. Sherman, C.E.O. and Pres.
FAX: (215) 985-3989; URL: http://
independencefoundation.org/about-us/

Foundation type: Independent foundation
Purpose: Visual and performing arts fellowships by nomination only to residents of the Philadelphia, PA, area, including Bucks, Chester, Delaware, Montgomery, and Philadelphia counties. Fellowships to accomplished young lawyers for compensation and employment benefits who are employed in public interest service.
Publications: Application guidelines; Annual report; Grants list; Occasional report.
Financial data: Year ended 12/31/2012. Assets, $65,788,302 (M); Expenditures, $5,344,409; Total giving, $3,529,147; Grants to individuals, 12 grants totaling $88,600 (high: $10,000, low: $6,200).
Fields of interest: Visual arts; Performing arts; Legal services, public interest law.
Type of support: Fellowships; Awards/grants by nomination only.
Application information: Applications accepted. Application form not required.
> *Initial approach:* Letter
> *Send request by:* Mail
> *Additional information:* Contact foundation for current nomination guidelines.

Program descriptions:
Fellowships in the Arts: The Fellowships in the Arts is an opportunity for exceptional artists to take a key step forward in their professional development. This is the primary goal of the program. Artists are encouraged to be creative in discovering the best possible way to expand their artistic horizons. There are no set boundaries for what is possible or what types of projects might be funded. However, a successful project should be well designed and of maximum practical value to the artist. In addition, the project must provide the artist with an opportunity for artistic growth and improvement in his/her primary area of work; such as assisting the artist in acquiring new skills relevant to his/her work; or providing the artist with a unique developmental opportunity. All applicant artists must be nominated by an official nominating organization. Official nominating organizations are comprised of local non-profit arts and cultural organizations which are grantees of the foundation, and who elect to participate in this program. Criteria for nomination include overall artistic merit; future artistic promise; the strength of the proposed project; the likelihood that the project will be completed; and financial need. All applicant artists must be Pennsylvania residents of the five county Philadelphia region (Bucks, Chester, Delaware, Montgomery or Philadelphia counties). All applicant artists must have 3-5 years professional experience in the visual or performing arts. Artists who have received a Fellowship in the Arts within the last five years are ineligible. There are two grant cycles, one in the visual arts (spring) and one in the performing arts (fall). An application is available on the foundation's web site.
Public Interest Law Fellowships: Through the program, the foundation funds the compensation and cost of employment benefits for accomplished young lawyers who have decided to employ their considerable talents in public interest service. In an additional component of each Fellowship grant, the foundation assists the Public Interest Law Fellows in the repayment of their often substantial educational loans. Thus the foundation enables some of the best and brightest law school graduates to come to the Philadelphia area and obtain employment with an organization based in this region that provides free legal services to poor and disadvantaged people. People served include the elderly, the disabled, the homeless, and others deprived of their human or civil rights. Importantly, the foundation requires that the focus of all fellowship work be on the direct representation of disadvantaged clients. Although the foundation recognizes the value of broad based policy development, the foundation is more interested in supporting direct legal services for those who cannot otherwise obtain the professional assistance they need to navigate the complicated judicial and administrative systems that affect their lives on a daily basis.
EIN: 231352110

7917
Independent Catholic Foundation for the Diocese of Altoona-Johnstown
(formerly Foundation for the Roman Catholic Diocese of Altoona-Johnstown)
320 Frankstown Rd.
Altoona, PA 16602-4231 (814) 201-2080
Contact: William M. Hiergeist, Exec. Dir.
E-mail: director@icfdaj.org; URL: http://
www.independentcatholicfoundation.org

Foundation type: Public charity
Purpose: Scholarships to third- and fourth-year college students who are parishioners at a Roman Catholic Church in Blair County, TX (excluding St. Matthew's Church in Tyrone)
Publications: Application guidelines; Annual report; Informational brochure; Newsletter.
Financial data: Year ended 06/30/2012. Assets, $17,997,226 (M); Expenditures, $662,997.
Fields of interest: College; Scholarships/financial aid.
Type of support: Scholarships—to individuals.
Application information: Applications accepted. Application form required. Application form available on the grantmaker's web site.
> *Initial approach:* Application
> *Deadline(s):* June 1 for Welge Scholarships
> *Additional information:* See web site for additional guidelines.

Program description:
Welge Scholarship: This scholarship provides financial assistance to worthy parishioners of Roman Catholic churches in Blair County (excluding St. Matthew's Church in Tyrone). Eligible applicants must be a member of a Roman Catholic parish (excluding St. Matthew) located in Blair County, a college student entering their junior or senior (third or fourth) year as a full-time undergraduate student at an accredited four-year college or university, and demonstrate financial need. Scholarships of up to $500 will be awarded.
EIN: 251625390

7918
Indiana County Community Action Program, Inc.
827 Water St.
Indiana, PA 15701-1755 (724) 465-2657
FAX: (724) 465-5118; E-mail: lvite@iccap.net;
URL: http://www.iccap.net

Foundation type: Public charity
Purpose: Financial assistance to low income individuals and families of the Indiana county, PA area with food, housing assistance, weatherization, transportation and other special needs.

Financial data: Year ended 06/30/2011. Assets, $1,513,171 (M); Expenditures, $4,874,026; Total giving, $1,866,214; Grants to individuals, totaling $1,866,214.
Fields of interest: Economically disadvantaged.
Type of support: Grants for special needs.
Application information: Contact the agency for eligibility determination.
EIN: 256069770

7919
The Institute for Aegean Prehistory
2133 Arch St., Ste. 300
Philadelphia, PA 19103 (215) 496-9914
Contact: Karen B. Vellucci, Dir., Grants
FAX: (215) 496-9925; E-mail: instap@hotmail.com;
Application e-mail: instapplications@gmail.com;
URL: http://www.aegeanprehistory.net

Foundation type: Operating foundation
Purpose: Research grants to study Aegean prehistory with the expectation of research and publication under the direct supervision and control of the Institute.
Financial data: Year ended 06/30/2012. Assets, $11,787,670 (M); Expenditures, $6,864,553; Total giving, $4,336,990.
Fields of interest: History/archaeology.
International interests: Greece.
Type of support: Publication; Research.
Application information: Applications accepted. Application form required. Application form available on the grantmaker's web site.
> *Initial approach:* Letter
> *Deadline(s):* Nov. 1
> *Applicants should submit the following:*
> 1) Resume
> 2) Budget Information
> *Additional information:* Application must also include project descriptions, relevance to Aegean prehistory, and references.

Program descriptions:
Petrography Internship: The Petrography Internship is to be awarded on a competitive basis to an eligible candidate at the INSTAP Study Center for East Crete (SCEC). This internship is intended for students of archaeology, pottery, geology, and related fields. It is not necessary to have completed the Ph.D. to be eligible. The Petrographer of the SCEC will supervise the intern. The scope of the internship will include projects involving the use of the petrographic microscope. The internship will be awarded in the amount of $2,500 plus reasonable round-trip travel expenses. See institute's web site for application forms and further details.
Post-doctoral Fellowship: This year-long fellowship is intended for scholars in the field of the Aegean Bronze Age/Early Iron Age who have received a Ph.D. degree in the past five years. The fellowship will be awarded in the amount of $24,000, plus up to $4,000 additional for travel expenses. The fellowship will be awarded for a specific project and is not renewable. See the institute's web site for application forms and further details.
Research Fellowship: These six-week fellowships are intended for scholars in the field of the Aegean Bronze Age/Early Iron Age who have already received the Ph.D. Applicants must be prepared to show that travel to the Study Center for East Crete Library or its other facilities is necessary for completing a specific project designed to advance scholarship. The fellowships will be an award of up to $2,500 plus reasonable round-trip travel expenses. Each fellowship will be awarded for a specific project and is not renewable. See

institute's web site for application forms and further details.
EIN: 133137391

7920

International Foundation for Sonography Education and Research

(formerly SDMS Educational Foundation)
929 E. Main St., Ste. 175
Mount Joy, PA 17552 (520) 300-2222
FAX: (888) 488-6598; E-mail: feedback@ifser.org; URL: http://www.ifser.org

Foundation type: Public charity
Purpose: Scholarships to financially needy students with scholastic merit who are enrolled in CAAHEP or CMA accredited diagnostic medical sonography programs, and grants to practicing sonographers. The maximum scholarship amount is $500 per calendar year.
Publications: Application guidelines.
Financial data: Year ended 12/31/2011. Assets, $104,839 (M); Expenditures, $70,962.
Fields of interest: Health sciences school/education.
Type of support: Scholarships—to individuals.
Application information: Applications accepted. Application form required. Application form available on the grantmaker's web site.
   Deadline(s): Mar. 31, July 31 and Nov. 31
   Applicants should submit the following:
      1) SAR
      2) ACT
      3) SAT
      4) Financial information
      5) Transcripts
      6) Essay
EIN: 752262610

7921

Mary Ann Irvin Scholarship Foundation

c/o S&T Wealth Management
800 Philadelphia St.
Indiana, PA 15701-3908
URL: https://www.stbank.com/Content/About-Us/Community-Commitment.aspx

Foundation type: Independent foundation
Purpose: Scholarships to financially needy graduates of Punxsutawney Area High School, PA, entering college or trade school.
Financial data: Year ended 12/31/2012. Assets, $515,262 (M); Expenditures, $26,016; Total giving, $24,000; Grants to individuals, 18 grants totaling $24,000 (high: $2,000, low: $1,000).
Fields of interest: Vocational education.
Type of support: Support to graduates or students of specific schools; Graduate support; Technical education support; Undergraduate support.
Application information: Applications not accepted.
   Additional information: Unsolicited requests for funds not considered or acknowledged.
EIN: 256079669

7922

Agnes and Sophie Dallas Irwin Memorial Fund

c/o PNC Bank, N.A.
1600 Market St., 4th Fl.
Philadelphia, PA 19103-7240

Foundation type: Independent foundation

Purpose: Grants to teachers in private schools for girls, to further their travel, study, and research costs, and/or retirement benefits.
Financial data: Year ended 12/31/2012. Assets, $1,046,118 (M); Expenditures, $50,880; Total giving, $41,000; Grants to individuals, 8 grants totaling $41,000 (high: $15,000, low: $600).
Fields of interest: Education.
Type of support: Grants to individuals.
Application information: Applications accepted.
   Initial approach: Letter
   Deadline(s): None
EIN: 236207350

7923

Ivy Cultural and Educational Foundation, Inc.

P.O. Box 29008
Philadelphia, PA 19151-9008 (703) 217-4242
Contact: Mozelle Clinton Butts, Treas.
E-mail: contact@icef-inc.org; URL: http://icef-inc.org/

Foundation type: Public charity
Purpose: Scholarships to young people attending Philadelphia area high schools for higher education.
Financial data: Year ended 12/31/2011. Assets, $136,003 (M); Expenditures, $27,372; Total giving, $5,759; Grants to individuals, totaling $5,759.
Fields of interest: Higher education; Students, sororities/fraternities.
Type of support: Scholarships—to individuals.
Application information: Applications accepted. Application form required.
   Additional information: Contact the foundation for additional application information.
EIN: 232786339

7924

The Ivy Legacy Foundation

(also known as TILF)
6703 Germantown Ave., Ste. 200
Philadelphia, PA 19119-2109 (215) 576-1086
Contact: Shelia Woods-Skipper, Pres.
E-mail: info@ivylegacy.org; URL: http://www.ivylegacy.org/index.html

Foundation type: Public charity
Purpose: Scholarships to exceptional high school seniors and non-traditional students from the greater Philadelphia, PA area, to further their education.
Publications: Application guidelines; Financial statement; Newsletter.
Financial data: Year ended 12/31/2012. Assets, $24,780 (M); Expenditures, $55,479.
Fields of interest: Higher education; Scholarships/financial aid.
Type of support: Scholarships—to individuals.
Application information: Applications accepted. Application form required. Application form available on the grantmaker's web site.
   Send request by: Mail
   Deadline(s): Mar. 30
   Applicants should submit the following:
      1) Transcripts
      2) Essay
   Additional information: Application should also include three letters of reference.
Program description:
   Scholarships: The foundation awards scholarships to exceptional high school seniors and non-traditional students from the greater Philadelphia area, to further their education. Named scholarships under this program include The Ivy

League Foundation Scholarship (nine scholarships of $2,000 each), The Carrie F. Gethers Memorial Scholarship (one scholarship of $1,250), The Susan Cannon Jones Celebration Scholarship (two scholarships of $1,000 each), The Jarvis Moss Shepherd Memorial Scholarship (one scholarship of $1,500), The John and Roberta Hubbard Family Foundation Scholarship (one scholarships of $1,500), The TILF Philly's Teens are Cookin' Culinary Scholarship (one scholarship of $2,000), The Vicky Rose Jones Scholarship (one scholarship of $1,000), and The Yvonne Cooper Watson Memorial Scholarship (one scholarship of $1,000)
EIN: 232831377

7925

Gaylord L. Jackson Scholarship Fund

c/o PNC Bank, N.A.
P.O. Box 609
Pittsburgh, PA 15230-9738 (216) 222-9815
Contact: Jane Kleinsmith
Application address: c/o PNC Bank, N.A., 1900 E. 9th St., Cleveland, OH 44144 tel.: (216) 222-9815

Foundation type: Independent foundation
Purpose: Scholarships to graduates of Churubusco High School, IN, who are in the top five percent of their academic class.
Financial data: Year ended 11/30/2013. Assets, $162,643 (M); Expenditures, $8,165; Total giving, $5,165; Grants to individuals, totaling $5,165.
Type of support: Support to graduates or students of specific schools.
Application information:
   Initial approach: Letter
   Additional information: Contact fund for further eligibility criteria.
EIN: 356564249

7926

Anna T. Jeanes Foundation

c/o Jeanes Hospital
7600 Central Ave.
Philadelphia, PA 19111-2499 (215) 214-4198
Contact: Robert H. Lefever, Chair.
Scholarship e-mail: scholarship@atjf.org
FAX: (215) 728-3311; E-mail: info@atjf.org; URL: http://www.atjf.org

Foundation type: Public charity
Purpose: Nursing scholarships to high school seniors who are residents of Delaware Valley, PA pursuing the profession of nursing at an institution of higher learning.
Publications: Application guidelines.
Financial data: Year ended 06/30/2012. Assets, $2,293,807 (M); Expenditures, $191,539; Total giving, $189,670; Grants to individuals, totaling $87,500.
Fields of interest: Nursing school/education.
Type of support: Scholarships—to individuals.
Application information: Applications accepted. Interview required.
   Send request by: Mail
   Applicants should submit the following:
      1) Transcripts
      2) Essay
   Additional information: Application should also include two letters of reference. Preference will be given to those who live within the community served by the Jeanes' Hospital.
Program description:
   Dorothy Willits Hallowell Nursing Scholarship: Scholarships to high school seniors who wish to pursue the profession of nursing and have been accepted into an institution of higher education that

offers an approved program of study in professional nursing. During the first and second year, award amounts will be $1,250 per semester (not to exceed $5,000 total), and it is expected that the student will complete pre-nursing course prerequisites. During the third and fourth years, award amounts are $5,000 per semester (not to exceed $20,000). The recipient must be enrolled in nursing course work in an NLN or AACN approved BSN, ADN, or diploma program of study toward professional nursing. The scholarship will be automatically renewable if the student maintains a minimum GPA of 2.85 or equivalent and is successfully matriculated into a nursing program. The money can be used for tuition, fees and other expenses related to attending an institution of higher education.

EIN: 232203406

7927
Ethel Jefferson Scholarship Fund
34 S. State St.
Newtown, PA 18940 (215) 968-4872
Application address: c/o First National Bank Trust Newtown

Foundation type: Independent foundation
Purpose: Scholarships primarily to students of Bucks County, PA.
Financial data: Year ended 12/31/2012. Assets, $1,263,411 (M); Expenditures, $62,556; Total giving, $53,000; Grant to an individual, 1 grant totaling $53,000.
Type of support: Scholarships—to individuals.
Application information: Application form required.
  Deadline(s): Apr. 15
  Additional information: Applications should be requested from the bank's trust dept.
EIN: 237749232

7928
Jewish Family Assistance Fund
P.O. Box 8197
Pittsburgh, PA 15217-1515 (412) 414-6050
Contact: Louise Silk, Tr.

Foundation type: Independent foundation
Purpose: Financial assistance to needy Jewish families for living, personal, food, and medical expenses.
Financial data: Year ended 12/31/2012. Assets, $1,420,894 (M); Expenditures, $181,870; Total giving, $155,475.
Fields of interest: Health care; Jewish agencies & synagogues.
Type of support: Grants for special needs.
Application information: Applications accepted.
  Initial approach: Letter
  Deadline(s): None
EIN: 251512726

7929
Jewish Federation of Greater Philadelphia
2100 Arch St.
Philadelphia, PA 19103-1300 (215) 832-0565
E-mail: info@jfgp.org; URL: http://www.jewishphilly.org

Foundation type: Public charity
Purpose: Scholarships to students throughout the greater Philadelphia, PA area to help further their education.
Publications: Application guidelines; Newsletter.
Financial data: Year ended 08/31/2011. Assets, $230,264,554 (M); Expenditures, $33,044,224;

Total giving, $17,201,584; Grants to individuals, 33 grants totaling $218,400.
Fields of interest: Higher education; Scholarships/financial aid; Vocational rehabilitation.
Type of support: Scholarships—to individuals; Loans—to individuals.
Application information: Applications accepted. Application form available on the grantmaker's web site.
  Initial approach: Application
  Deadline(s): May 15
  Final notification: Recipients notified by Sept. 1
Program descriptions:
  Albert Strickler Memorial Fund: This fund provides an interest-free loan of up to $5,000 to medical students (preferably of the Jewish faith) to aid their pursuit of a medical education. Students should demonstrate a significant need of financial aid, and be enrolled in an accredited U.S. medical or osteopathic school. Funds must be repaid within five years after graduation.
  Ida Foreman Fleisher Fund: This fund provides grants, ranging from $2,000 to $8,000, to allow women (preferably of the Jewish faith) to pursue a graduate degree. Eligible applicants must be from, or attend school in, the greater Philadelphia area (including New Jersey and Delaware).
  Margaret R. Rice Music Scholarship Fund: Grants of up to $2,000 are awarded to students of local music schools, to help further their education.
  Samuel F. and Sara G. Feinman Fund: This fund provides interest-free loans, ranging from $2,000 to $5,000, to assist talented men and women in pursuing their legal or medical education. Applicants must demonstrate financial need and be enrolled in an accredited local medical or law school. Preference will be given to students who live in the greater Philadelphia region, and who are of the Jewish faith. Loan repayment must begin within five years after graduation.
EIN: 231500085

7930
Jewish Federation of the Lehigh Valley
702 N. 22nd St.
Allentown, PA 18104-3904 (610) 821-5500
Contact: for Scholarships: Mark L. Goldstein, Exec. Dir.
E-mail address: markg@jflv.org
FAX: (610) 821-8946; E-mail: mailbox@jflv.org; E-Mail For Mark L. Goldstein: markg@jflv.org; URL: http://www.jewishlehighvalley.org

Foundation type: Public charity
Purpose: Need-based scholarships for Jewish resident summer camps. Scholarships to Jewish teens in grades 9 through 12 who reside in the Lehigh Valley, PA area.
Financial data: Year ended 06/30/2012. Assets, $21,915,309 (M); Expenditures, $3,188,401; Total giving, $2,126,991; Grants to individuals, totaling $67,950.
Fields of interest: Higher education; Jewish agencies & synagogues.
Type of support: Camperships; Scholarships—to individuals.
Application information: Applications accepted. Application form required. Application form available on the grantmaker's web site.
  Send request by: Mail
  Deadline(s): Mar. 20
  Additional information: See web site for additional application guidelines.
EIN: 236396949

7931
Gladys L. Johnson Scholarship Trust
c/o Wells Fargo Bank, N.A.
101N. Indepence Mall E. MACY 1372-062
Philadelphia, PA 19106-2112

Foundation type: Independent foundation
Purpose: Scholarships to residents of east-central MN with preference to those of Protestant faith.
Financial data: Year ended 01/31/2013. Assets, $141,682 (M); Expenditures, $9,365; Total giving, $6,200.
Type of support: Scholarships—to individuals.
Application information: Applications accepted. Application form required. Interview required.
  Initial approach: Letter
  Deadline(s): May 1
EIN: 416225081

7932
William J. and Dora J. Kalnoski Memorial Scholarship Fund
1199 Lightstreet Rd.
Bloomsburg, PA 17815
Contact: Sheri Grozier

Foundation type: Independent foundation
Purpose: Scholarships to students of Columbia County and Schuylkill County, PA pursuing a career in art, architecture or related fields.
Financial data: Year ended 12/31/2012. Assets, $911,303 (M); Expenditures, $53,101; Total giving, $42,000; Grants to individuals, 27 grants totaling $42,000 (high: $2,000, low: $750).
Type of support: Undergraduate support.
Application information: Application form required. Interview required.
  Initial approach: Letter
  Deadline(s): Last Friday in Apr.
  Applicants should submit the following:
    1) Transcripts
    2) Essay
    3) Letter(s) of recommendation
    4) Financial information
    5) GPA
  Additional information: Application should also include a copy of you and your parents' most recent federal income tax return.
EIN: 251882103

7933
Jay F. Keefer Scholarship Trust
c/o Suso Trust
1570 Manheim Pike
P.O. Box 3000
Lancaster, PA 17604-3300

Foundation type: Independent foundation
Purpose: Scholarships to graduating seniors for Loyalsock High School in pursuit of a higher education.
Financial data: Year ended 12/31/2012. Assets, $34,756 (M); Expenditures, $5,025; Total giving, $5,000; Grant to an individual, 1 grant totaling $5,000.
Fields of interest: Higher education.
Type of support: Scholarships—to individuals.
Application information: Applications accepted.
  Additional information: Contact your high school guidance office for application information.
EIN: 236760450

7934

Ruth Keith Scholarship Fund

(also known as Keith Scholarship Fund Foundation)
34 S. State St.
Newtown, PA 18940-1953 (215) 968-4872
Application address: c/o First National Bank & Trust
Co. of Newton

Foundation type: Independent foundation
Purpose: Scholarships primarily to students from
Bucks County, PA for continuing education at
accredited colleges or universities.
Financial data: Year ended 12/31/2012. Assets,
$475,726 (M); Expenditures, $27,848; Total
giving, $22,700; Grants to individuals, 15 grants
totaling $22,700 (high: $3,500, low: $200).
Fields of interest: Scholarships/financial aid;
Education.
Type of support: Undergraduate support.
Application information: Application form required.
Deadline(s): Apr. 15
Additional information: Application can be
obtained from the Bank's Trust Dept.,
scholarships are renewable.
EIN: 236503403

7935

**Kidney Foundation of Central
Pennsylvania**

1500 Paxton St., Ste. 101
Harrisburg, PA 17104-2633 (717) 652-8123
Contact: Tina Fornstrom, Admin. Asst.
FAX: (717) 671-9444; E-mail: info@kfcp.org;
Toll-free tel.: (800) 762-6202; E-mail For Tina
Fornstrom: Tina@kfcp.org; URL: http://
www.kfcp.org/

Foundation type: Public charity
Purpose: Research grants to individuals for the
treatment and study of kidney diseases. Financial
assistance to qualified patients receiving dialysis
treatment in the central PA, area. Scholarships for
postsecondary education to individuals with chronic
kidney failure or disease in the central PA area.
Financial data: Year ended 06/30/2012. Assets,
$283,743 (M); Expenditures, $286,950.
Fields of interest: Education; Kidney diseases.
Type of support: Research; Scholarships—to
individuals; Grants for special needs.
Application information: Application form required.
Additional information: Application for financial
assistance must be submitted through the
social worker at the dialysis center. Applicant
must provide a copy of most recent income tax
form and a brief statement describing
financial need. See web site for additional
information.
EIN: 232113424

7936

The Sidney Kimmel Foundation

1900 Market St.
Philadelphia, PA 19103-3527 (215) 665-2079
Contact: Matthew H. Kamens
Application address: Kimmel Scholars, Gary Cohen,
M.D., Cancer Center GBMC, 6569 N. Charles St.,
Ste. 203 Baltimore, MD 21204, tel.: (443)
849-3729, E-mail: gcohen@gbmc.org
FAX: (215) 701-2257;
E-mail: mkamens@cozen.com; URL: http://
www.kimmel.org

Foundation type: Independent foundation
Purpose: Research grants to physicians and young
investigators for the study of cancer and
translational science.

Financial data: Year ended 07/31/2013. Assets,
$1,957,678 (M); Expenditures, $11,647,173;
Total giving, $11,171,695; Grants to individuals,
45 grants totaling $3,000,000.
Fields of interest: Cancer research; Medical
research.
Type of support: Research; Awards/prizes.
Application information: Application form required.
Application form available on the grantmaker's web
site.
Deadline(s): Dec. 7 for Kimmel Scholar and Dec.
31 for letters of reference
Applicants should submit the following:
1) Letter(s) of recommendation
2) Budget Information
Additional information: Application for Kimmel
Scholar must include personal statement,
research description, and appendix.
Applications not accepted for Translational
Science Program.
Program descriptions:
Kimmel Scholarship Program: Each year the
Kimmel Foundation expects to select up to ten
grant recipients who will receive $100,000 per year
for two years. Qualified applicants must hold an
M.D., Ph.D. or equivalent graduate degree and must
perform research in an American nonprofit
institution during the period of Kimmel Foundation
support. The foundation is seeking accomplished
young investigators dedicated to a career in cancer
research. Applications are limited to those who
achieved the equivalent rank of Assistant Professor
on or after July, 2006. Physicians who have both
clinical and research responsibility are eligible if
appointed on or after July, 2005. These awards are
designed for researchers who do not yet have their
own R01 funding. Applicants will be judged on the
basis of quality of prior work, research proposed
and letters of support. Funding of awards will be
subject to execution of binding agreements setting
forth terms and conditions under which
scholarships will be provided.
Kimmel Translational Science Award: The
foundation provides five additional awards
specifically for physicians engaged in translational
science. Eligibility includes those with M.D. or
equivalent degrees, who have achieved the rank of
Assistant Professor on or after July, 2005.
Candidates must not hold R01 funding for the
laboratory component of their cancer research.
Applicants must demonstrate a significant personal
involvement in the laboratory component of the
translational project described. The translational
aspect may involve either animal or human studies.
EIN: 232698492

7937

Clair H. Kinney Scholarship Fund

(formerly Clair H. Kinney Scholarship and Library
Science Reference Fund)
c/o First Columbia Bank & Trust Co.
1199 Lightstreet Rd.
Bloomsburg, PA 17815 (570) 387-4681
Contact: Sheri Grozier
Application address: 1199 Lightstreet Rd.,
Bloomsburg, PA 17815

Foundation type: Independent foundation
Purpose: Scholarships to graduates of public high
schools in Columbia and Montour counties, PA.
Financial data: Year ended 12/31/2012. Assets,
$132,005 (M); Expenditures, $23,492; Total
giving, $21,000; Grants to individuals, 3 grants
totaling $9,000 (high: $3,000, low: $3,000).
Type of support: Support to graduates or students
of specific schools; Undergraduate support.

Application information: Application form required.
Deadline(s): May 1
Applicants should submit the following:
1) Class rank
2) Transcripts
3) SAT
4) Financial information
Additional information: Application must also
include a copy of parents' federal income tax
return and two references.
EIN: 236664657

7938

G. William Klemstine Foundation

c/o PNC Bank
620 Liberty Ave., 10th Fl.
Pittsburgh, PA 15222-2705 (412) 768-6011
Contact: Anne Scully

Foundation type: Independent foundation
Purpose: Scholarships to residents of Cambria and
Somerset counties, PA for attendance at the
University of Pittsburgh at Johnstown.
Financial data: Year ended 09/30/2013. Assets,
$462,010 (M); Expenditures, $50,736; Total
giving, $40,630.
Fields of interest: Higher education.
Type of support: Scholarships—to individuals.
Application information: Applications accepted.
Initial approach: Letter
Deadline(s): None
EIN: 256058872

7939

Eugene R. Kotur Foundation

c/o PNC Bank, N.A.
620 Liberty Ave., 10th Fl.,
Pittsburgh, PA 15222 (215) 627-2445
Application address: 817 N Franklin St.,Philadelphia
PA. 191232004

Foundation type: Independent foundation
Purpose: Scholarships to individuals of Ukrainian
descent for higher education.
Financial data: Year ended 12/31/2012. Assets,
$338,728 (M); Expenditures, $33,336; Total
giving, $25,412; Grants to individuals, 7 grants
totaling $25,412 (high: $7,206, low: $1,000).
International interests: Ukraine.
Type of support: Undergraduate support.
Application information: Applications accepted.
Application form required.
Deadline(s): June 15
EIN: 256394138

7940

George S. Ladd Memorial Fund

c/o Wells Fargo Bank, N.A.
101N. Indenpendence Mall E. MACY1372-062
Philadelphia, PA 19106-2112

Foundation type: Independent foundation
Purpose: Financial assistance to elderly and retired
employees of Pacific Bell, Nevada Bell, and Pacific
Northwest Bell, primarily in CA and NV.
Financial data: Year ended 12/31/2012. Assets,
$604,797 (M); Expenditures, $43,847; Total
giving, $28,955; Grant to an individual, 1 grant
totaling $28,955.
Fields of interest: Health care; Aging.
Type of support: Employee-related welfare.
Application information: Application form required.
Deadline(s): None
Additional information: Application forms
provided upon request.

Company names: Nevada Bell; Pacific Bell; Pacific Northwest Bell
EIN: 376070933

7941
The Lancaster County Community Foundation

(formerly The Lancaster County Foundation)
24 W. King St., Ste. 201
Lancaster, PA 17603 (717) 397-1629
Contact: Samuel J. Bressi, C.E.O.
FAX: (717) 397-6877;
E-mail: info@lancastercountyfoundation.org;
URL: http://www.lancfound.org/

Foundation type: Community foundation
Purpose: Fellowships to nonprofit leaders in Lancaster County, PA for professional and personal development. Scholarships to residents of Lancaster County and high school seniors or graduates of a high school in Lancaster County, who are already enrolled or planning to enroll in a full-time course of undergraduate study at an accredited two- or four-year college, university, or vocational-technical school.
Publications: Application guidelines; Annual report; Grants list; Informational brochure; Newsletter.
Financial data: Year ended 12/31/2012. Assets, $71,604,558 (M); Expenditures, $5,147,466; Total giving, $3,502,168. Scholarships—to individuals amount not specified.
Fields of interest: Vocational education, post-secondary; Higher education; Leadership development.
Type of support: Fellowships; Scholarships—to individuals.
Application information: Applications accepted. Application form required. Application form available on the grantmaker's web site.
> *Send request by:* Online
> *Deadline(s):* Mar. 28 for fellowships
> *Applicants should submit the following:*
> 1) Transcripts
> 2) Financial information
> *Additional information:* See web site for additional guidelines.

Program descriptions:
John Baldwin Fellowship Program: The John Baldwin Fellowship Program offers a unique experience to Lancaster County community benefit leaders interested in leadership and personal growth. This program is designed to benefit an individual community benefit leader, not the organization that he or she represents. A total of five fellows will be selected for the program, which includes facilitated cohort meetings and $5,000 grants to pursue self-designed journeys of personal reflection and growth. See web site for additional information.
Scholarship Program: The foundation's scholarship program assists area youth who plan to continue education in college or vocational school programs. Applicants must have a cumulative GPA of 2.5 or better on a 4.0 scale. See web site for additional information.
EIN: 200874857

7942
Lancaster Foundation For Educational Enrichment

445 N. Reservoir St.
Lancaster, PA 17602-2447 (717) 391-8660
Contact: Laura Sadler Olin, Assoc. Dir.
FAX: (717) 391-8659; URL: http://lancasteredfnd.org

Foundation type: Public charity
Purpose: Scholarships to graduating McCaskey High School, PA seniors pursuing postsecondary education at institutions of higher learning.
Publications: Newsletter.
Financial data: Year ended 06/30/2012. Assets, $552,071 (M); Expenditures, $407,427; Total giving, $268,149; Grants to individuals, totaling $72,356.
Fields of interest: Higher education.
Type of support: Scholarships—to individuals; Support to graduates or students of specific schools.
Application information: Applications accepted. Application form required.
> *Additional information:* See web site for a complete listing of scholarships, as each scholarship has its own eligibility criteria.
EIN: 232583874

7943
Lancaster General Hospital

555 N. Duke St.
Lancaster, PA 17602-2250 (717) 544-5511
URL: http://www.lancastergeneral.org

Foundation type: Public charity
Purpose: Hospital bill financial assistance to indigent patients of Lancaster General Health affiliated hospitals in PA, whose income is less than 200% Federal Poverty Guidelines.
Financial data: Year ended 06/30/2012. Assets, $784,628,278 (M); Expenditures, $797,015,825; Total giving, $3,658,668; Grants to individuals, totaling $19,346.
Fields of interest: Hospitals (general); Health care, patient services; Economically disadvantaged.
Type of support: Grants for special needs.
Application information: Applications accepted. Application form required.
> *Initial approach:* Tel.
> *Applicants should submit the following:*
> 1) Financial information
> *Additional information:* Contact foundation for eligibility criteria.
EIN: 231365353

7944
Lancaster Medical Society Foundation

480 New Holland Ave., Ste. 8202
Lancaster, PA 17602 (717) 393-9588

Foundation type: Independent foundation
Purpose: Scholarships awarded to medical students who are residents of Lancaster county, PA.
Financial data: Year ended 09/30/2013. Assets, $31,883 (M); Expenditures, $10,661; Total giving, $10,000; Grants to individuals, 3 grants totaling $10,000 (high: $5,000; low: $2,500).
Fields of interest: Medical school/education.
Type of support: Scholarships—to individuals.
Application information: Application form required.
> *Deadline(s):* None
> *Additional information:* Application available upon request.
EIN: 232633979

7945
Lancaster Osteopathic Health Foundation

128 E. Grant St., Ste. 104
Lancaster, PA 17602-2854 (717) 397-8722
Contact: Anna Brendle Kennedy, Exec. Dir.
FAX: (717) 397-8723;
E-mail: info@lohfoundation.org; URL: http://www.lancasterosteopathichealthfoundation.org

Foundation type: Public charity
Purpose: Scholarships to Lancaster County, PA students entering nursing education programs, as well as students already enrolled in one of the programs.
Publications: Financial statement; Grants list; Informational brochure; Newsletter.
Financial data: Year ended 12/31/2011. Assets, $380,183 (M); Expenditures, $22,911; Total giving, $13,650; Grants to individuals, totaling $1,250.
Fields of interest: Nursing school/education.
Type of support: Scholarships—to individuals.
Application information: Applications accepted. Application form required. Application form available on the grantmaker's web site. Interview required.
> *Initial approach:* Application
> *Send request by:* Mail
> *Deadline(s):* May 30
> *Final notification:* Recipients notified in July
> *Additional information:* Scholarships are for tuition only. See web site for additional application guidelines.
Program description:
Nursing Scholarships: The foundation provides tuition scholarships to students entering nursing education programs, as well as already-enrolled students. Tuition excludes books, supplies, fees, room and board or living expenses. The scholarships are applicable for local nursing education programs at Lancaster County Career & Technology Center, PA College of Health Sciences, Harrisburg Area Community College-Lancaster Campus, Eastern Mennonite University, Millersville University, or any accredited BSN, master, post master, doctoral nursing programs and certification classes, including but not limited to school nurse, lactation consultant, and others requiring additional education. Applicants must be a permanent resident of Lancaster County at time of application and already admitted to a nursing education program at time of award/application.
EIN: 222792471

7946
Edith A. Langdale Scholarship Fund

c/o PNC Bank, NA
P.O. Box 609
Pittsburgh, PA 15230-9738 (814) 723-5300

Foundation type: Independent foundation
Purpose: Scholarships to graduates of Warren, PA, area high schools for postsecondary education.
Financial data: Year ended 08/31/2013. Assets, $215,426 (M); Expenditures, $12,491; Total giving, $9,165; Grants to individuals, totaling $9,165.
Fields of interest: Higher education.
Type of support: Support to graduates or students of specific schools; Undergraduate support.
Application information: Applications accepted. Application form required.
> *Deadline(s):* June 1
> *Additional information:* Application available at the guidance counselor office.
EIN: 256164317

7947
Larue-Dawson Scholarship Trust
c/o PNC Bank, N.A.
P.O. Box 609
Pittsburgh, PA 15230-9738

Foundation type: Independent foundation
Purpose: Scholarships to IN students for higher education.
Financial data: Year ended 09/30/2013. Assets, $330,803 (M); Expenditures, $19,462; Total giving, $16,000; Grant to an individual, 1 grant totaling $16,000.
Fields of interest: Higher education.
Type of support: Undergraduate support.
Application information: Applications not accepted.
Additional information: Unsolicited requests for funds not considered or acknowledged.
EIN: 356586275

7948
Harry Laudermilch Scholarship Fund
P.O. Box 3215
Lancaster, PA 17604-3216

Foundation type: Independent foundation
Purpose: Scholarships to graduates of Lebanon High School, PA for attendance at an accredited college or university.
Financial data: Year ended 09/30/2013. Assets, $428,569 (M); Expenditures, $27,579; Total giving, $22,365; Grants to individuals, 5 grants totaling $22,365 (high: $5,500, low: $2,625).
Fields of interest: Higher education; Scholarships/financial aid.
Type of support: Support to graduates or students of specific schools; Undergraduate support.
Application information: Applications accepted. Application form required.
Additional information: Applications may be obtained from high school guidance office.
EIN: 231989571

7949
Jules Laurent & Paulette Leroy Laurent
111 S. Main St.
Greensburg, PA 15601 (724) 832-6052

Foundation type: Independent foundation
Purpose: Limited scholarships to graduating seniors from Deer Lakes High School, PA for postsecondary education.
Financial data: Year ended 05/31/2013. Assets, $175,664 (M); Expenditures, $12,597; Total giving, $10,000; Grants to individuals, 10 grants totaling $10,000 (high: $1,000, low: $1,000).
Fields of interest: Higher education.
Type of support: Support to graduates or students of specific schools.
Application information:
Initial approach: Letter
Deadline(s): Apr. 30
Additional information: Contact your guidance office for application information.
EIN: 256233126

7950
Law School Admissions Council, Inc.
(also known as LSAC)
662 Penn St.
Newtown, PA 18940-0000 (215) 968-1001
E-mail: lsacinfo@lsac.org; TDD: (215) 968-1128; contact email for Kent D. Lollis (Diversity Initiative Fund General Grants, Prelaw Undergraduate

Scholars Program, and Native American Student Workshops): klollis@lsac.org; contact email for Yessenia Z. Garcia-Lebron (Minority Regional Outreach Grants): ygarcia@lsac.org; URL: http://www.lsac.org

Foundation type: Public charity
Purpose: Provides assistance to undergraduate students studying pre-law, and researchers in the fields of investigating precursors to legal training, selection into law schools, legal education, and the legal profession.
Financial data: Year ended 06/30/2012. Assets, $200,602,972 (M); Expenditures, $62,660,743; Total giving, $2,048,209; Grants to individuals, totaling $29,700.
Fields of interest: Law school/education; Minorities.
Type of support: Student aid/financial aid; Research; Scholarships—to individuals.
Application information: Applications accepted.
Additional information: See foundation web site for information on specified programs.
Program descriptions:
Prelaw Undergraduate Scholars Program: Grants of up to $100,000 are available to minority undergraduate students who wish to upgrade their skills in preparation for law school.
Research Grant Program: The program funds empirical research on legal training and legal practice broadly viewed. This includes the study of precursors to legal training (including demographic variables), all varieties of legal training itself and the work that lawyers, judges, law teachers, and other legal professionals do after they complete their training ("law jobs"). The program is open to applicants from all countries.
EIN: 132998164

7951
The Leeway Foundation
The Philadelphia Bldg.
1315 Walnut St., Ste. 832
Philadelphia, PA 19109-1025 (215) 545-4078
FAX: (215) 545-4021; E-mail: info@leeway.org;
URL: http://www.leeway.org/

Foundation type: Independent foundation
Purpose: Grants to women and trans artists 18 years of age and over who reside in the Delaware Valley area.
Publications: Application guidelines; Annual report; Grants list.
Financial data: Year ended 12/31/2012. Assets, $16,849,379 (M); Expenditures, $874,986; Total giving, $214,360; Grants to individuals, 74 grants totaling $214,360 (high: $15,000, low: $100).
Fields of interest: Visual arts; Sculpture; Arts; Adults, women.
Type of support: Program development; Grants to individuals; Awards/prizes.
Application information: Applications accepted. Application form required. Application form available on the grantmaker's web site.
Initial approach: Letter, telephone, or e-mail
Send request by: Mail or in person
Copies of proposal: 1
Deadline(s): Mar. 15 and Sept. 15 for Art and Change Grant; May 15 for Transformation Award
Additional information: Applications by e-mail or fax are not accepted. See web site for further application information.
Program descriptions:
Art and Change Grant Program: The Art and Change Grant Program provides project grants of up to $2,500 to women and trans artists residing in the Delaware Valley region who has financial need

and limited or no access to other financial resources, has an art for social change project or opportunity that impacts a larger group, audience or community, and has a project supported by or in collaboration with a Change Partner (a person, organization, or business that is a part of the project in some way)
Leeway Transformation Award: The Leeway Transformation Award is an unrestricted award of $15,000 given annually to women and trans artists residing in the Delaware Valley region who create art for social change and have done so for the past five years or more, demonstrating a long-term commitment to social change work. All awardees will create a free community event to share their work with others.
EIN: 232727140

7952
Lehigh Carbon Community College Foundation
4525 Education Park Dr.
Schnecksville, PA 18078-2598 (610) 799-1711
Contact: Tim J. Herrlinger M.S.I.T., Exec. Dir.
E-mail: therrlinger@lccc.edu; URL: http://www.lccc.edu/foundation

Foundation type: Public charity
Purpose: Scholarships to deserving students from Lehigh, Carbon, and Schuylkill, PA counties for attendance at Lehigh Carbon Community College.
Financial data: Year ended 06/30/2012. Assets, $11,802,414 (M); Expenditures, $756,201; Total giving, $687,467; Grants to individuals, totaling $59,191.
Fields of interest: Higher education.
Type of support: Scholarships—to individuals; Support to graduates or students of specific schools.
Application information: Applications accepted. Application form required.
Deadline(s): May 15
Applicants should submit the following:
1) Transcripts
2) GPA
Additional information: Selection is based on applicants who show academic promise and demonstrate community involvement.
EIN: 237454575

7953
Lehigh Valley Community Foundation
(formerly Bethlehem Area Foundation)
968 Postal Rd., Ste. 100
Allentown, PA 18109-9301 (610) 266-4284
Contact: Bernard J. Story, C.E.O.; For grants: Ron Horvath, Fiscal Mgr.
FAX: (610) 266-4285;
E-mail: lvcf@lvcfoundation.org; Grant inquiry e-mail: ron@lvcfoundation.org; URL: http://www.lehighvalleyfoundation.org/

Foundation type: Community foundation
Purpose: Scholarships to Lehigh Valley graduating high school seniors for higher education at accredited institutions.
Publications: Application guidelines; Annual report; Grants list; Program policy statement.
Financial data: Year ended 06/30/2012. Assets, $33,471,791 (M); Expenditures, $2,457,612; Total giving, $1,808,035; Grants to individuals, totaling $3,210.
Fields of interest: Higher education; Scholarships/financial aid.

Type of support: Scholarships—to individuals; Support to graduates or students of specific schools; Undergraduate support.
Application information: The foundation manages a number of scholarship funds. Students who would like to learn more about these scholarships and how to apply for these scholarships are encouraged to contact their school's guidance or financial aid department. See web site for additional information.
EIN: 231686634

7954
Vernon S. Lehr Scholarship Fund
c/o PNC Bank, N.A.
1600 Market St., Tax Department
Philadelphia, PA 19103-7240

Foundation type: Independent foundation
Purpose: Scholarships to graduates of Bermudian Springs High School, Delone Catholic High School, Hanover High School, and New Oxford High School, all in PA.
Financial data: Year ended 12/31/2012. Assets, $2,196,125 (M); Expenditures, $99,287; Total giving, $75,000; Grants to individuals, 15 grants totaling $75,000 (high: $5,000, low: $5,000).
Type of support: Support to graduates or students of specific schools; Undergraduate support.
Application information: Applications not accepted.
  Additional information: Unsolicited requests for funds not considered or acknowledged.
EIN: 251872650

7955
Nellie E. Leighow Scholarship Fund
c/o The Northumberland National Bank
245 Front St.
Northumberland, PA 17857-1611

Foundation type: Independent foundation
Purpose: Scholarships to graduating seniors from Shikellamy High School, Sunbury, PA in pursuit of a nursing degree.
Financial data: Year ended 12/31/2012. Assets, $105,588 (M); Expenditures, $3,630; Total giving, $2,100; Grants to individuals, 4 grants totaling $2,100 (high: $1,000, low: $367).
Fields of interest: Nursing school/education.
Type of support: Scholarships—to individuals; Support to graduates or students of specific schools.
Application information: Applications accepted. Application form required.
  Initial approach: Telephone
  Additional information: Applications are available through the guidance counselor at the high school.
EIN: 237692684

7956
The Lenfest Foundation, Inc.
100 N. 18th St., Ste. 800
Two Logan Sq.
Philadelphia, PA 19103-2743 (215) 239-9003
Contact: Bruce Melgary, Exec. Dir.
FAX: (610) 828-0390;
E-mail: lenfestfoundation@lenfestfoundation.org;
URL: http://www.lenfestfoundation.org

Foundation type: Independent foundation
Purpose: Scholarships to students graduating from selected high schools in PA.

Publications: Application guidelines; Informational brochure (including application guidelines).
Financial data: Year ended 06/30/2012. Assets, $102,775,897 (M); Expenditures, $9,629,794; Total giving, $7,855,482; Grants to individuals, totaling $1,006,482.
Fields of interest: Education.
Type of support: Support to graduates or students of specific schools; Undergraduate support.
Application information: Application form required.
  Deadline(s): Feb. 15
  Additional information: Application must include essay and a list of extracurricular activities. See web site for complete list of eligible school districts.
Program description:
  Lenfest College Scholarship Program: The program is open to students in their junior year at the following Pennsylvania high schools: 1) Chambersburg Area Senior High School; 2) Fannett Metal High School; 3) Greencastle Antrim High School; 4) James Buchanan High School; 5) Waynesboro Area Senior High School; 6) Bermudian Springs High School; 7) Biglerville High School; 8) New Oxford High School; 9) Fair Field High School; 10) Pequea Valley High School; 11) Octorara High School; and 12) Upper Perkiomen High School; 13) South Western Senior High School; and 14) Spring Groose Area High School. Students must complete an application along with providing a list of achievements, activities, and an essay. After this initial phase, semifinalists will be identified and asked to provide additional information. Finalists will then be selected and asked to participate in interviews. The selection committee will consider a student's ambition to succeed at a challenging college or university, academic achievement and potential, leadership qualities, personal development and maturity, and family financial need. The program provides up to $12,000 a year for four years toward the cost of an accredited U.S. private college and up to $7,500 a year toward the cost of an accredited U.S. public college.
EIN: 233031350

7957
J. W. Levergood Trust f/b/o Connellsville Area School District
c/o PNC Bank, N.A.
620 Liberty Ave., 10th Fl.
Pittsburgh, PA 15222-2705

Foundation type: Independent foundation
Purpose: Scholarship to a graduate of Connellsville Area School District, PA for higher education.
Financial data: Year ended 12/31/2012. Assets, $87,375 (M); Expenditures, $5,482; Total giving, $3,082; Grant to an individual, 1 grant totaling $3,082.
Fields of interest: Higher education.
Type of support: Support to graduates or students of specific schools.
Application information: Applications not accepted.
  Additional information: Unsolicited requests for funds not considered or acknowledged.
EIN: 206966487

7958
Mabelle McLeod Lewis Memorial Fund
c/o Wells Fargo Bank, N.A.
101N Independence Mall E., MACY1372-062
Philadelphia, PA 19106-2112
Application address: P.O. Box 3730, Stanford, CA 94305

Foundation type: Operating foundation
Purpose: Grants to humanities doctoral candidates in their last year of study or writing, who are attending a northern CA institution of higher learning. No grants for publication of dissertation.
Publications: Application guidelines; Program policy statement.
Financial data: Year ended 03/31/2013. Assets, $4,955,806 (M); Expenditures, $283,530; Total giving, $217,185; Grants to individuals, 9 grants totaling $217,185 (high: $35,306, low: $3,404).
Fields of interest: Humanities.
Type of support: Fellowships.
Application information: Application form required.
  Initial approach: Letter
  Send request by: Mail
  Deadline(s): Jan. 15
  Applicants should submit the following:
    1) Financial information
    2) Resume
    3) Letter(s) of recommendation
EIN: 237079585

7959
Lintner Scholarship Trust
c/o PNC Bank
620 Liberty Ave., 10th Fl.
Pittsburgh, PA 15222-2705 (724) 459-5500
Application address: c/o Blairsville/Saltsburg School District, 102 School Ln., Blairsville, PA 15717

Foundation type: Independent foundation
Purpose: Undergraduate scholarships to residents and children of residents of Blairsville, Burrell, or Black Lick, IN, to attend Pennsylvania State University.
Financial data: Year ended 03/31/2013. Assets, $1,960,604 (M); Expenditures, $108,404; Total giving, $87,090.
Type of support: Support to graduates or students of specific schools; Undergraduate support.
Application information: Applications accepted.
  Initial approach: Letter
  Deadline(s): None
  Additional information: Applicants must submit financial information.
EIN: 256406800

7960
Lock Haven University Foundation
Durrwachter Alumni Conference Ctr., 2nd Fl.
Lock Haven, PA 17745 (570) 484-2293
Contact: Keith Barrows, Exec. Dir.
FAX: (570) 484-2774;
E-mail: info@lhufoundation.org; E-Mail for Keith Barrows: keith.barrows@lhufoundation.org;
URL: http://www.lhufoundation.org/

Foundation type: Public charity
Purpose: Scholarships to students of Lock Haven University, PA.
Financial data: Year ended 06/30/2012. Assets, $67,445,274 (M); Expenditures, $2,797,752; Total giving, $836,832; Grants to individuals, totaling $28,738.
Type of support: Support to graduates or students of specific schools.
Application information: Applications accepted. Application form required. Application form available on the grantmaker's web site.
  Initial approach: Letter
  Deadline(s): Feb. 19

Additional information: See http://www.lhup.edu/development/foundation/scholarships.htm.
EIN: 237007734

7961

Terri Lynne Lokoff Child Care Foundation

100 Ross Rd., Ste. 160
King of Prussia, PA   19406-2110   (610) 992-1140
Contact: Allan S. Miller, Exec. Dir.
FAX: (610) 992-1070;
E-mail: tllccf@childcareabc.org; E-mail for Allan S. Miller: allan@tllccf.org; URL: http://www.childcareabc.org

Foundation type: Public charity
Purpose: Project grants and awards to early childhood education teachers in recognition of excellence in providing quality child care.
Publications: Application guidelines; Annual report; Financial statement; Grants list; Informational brochure; Newsletter.
Financial data: Year ended 12/31/2011. Assets, $488,176 (M); Expenditures, $374,927; Total giving, $96,749; Grants to individuals, totaling $26,000.
Fields of interest: Early childhood education; Day care.
Type of support: Awards/prizes.
Application information: Applications accepted. Application form required. Application form available on the grantmaker's web site.
Initial approach: Proposal
Send request by: Mail
Deadline(s): Dec. 6
Applicants should submit the following:
1) Budget Information
2) Essay
Additional information: See web site for additional application information.
EIN: 222804790

7962

Leon Lowengard Scholarship Fund

c/o BNY Mellon, N.A.
P.O. Box 185
Pittsburgh, PA   15230-0185

Foundation type: Independent foundation
Purpose: Undergraduate and graduate scholarships to Jewish graduates of greater Harrisburg, PA, area high schools.
Financial data: Year ended 09/30/2013. Assets, $3,203,165 (M); Expenditures, $147,717; Total giving, $109,350; Grants to individuals, 72 grants totaling $109,350 (high: $2,750, low: $500).
Fields of interest: Jewish agencies & synagogues.
Type of support: Support to graduates or students of specific schools; Graduate support; Undergraduate support.
Application information: Applications accepted. Application form required.
Deadline(s): Apr. 1
Applicants should submit the following:
1) Transcripts
2) Financial information
EIN: 236236909

7963

Lutron Foundation

1506 Pleasant View Rd.
Coopersburg, PA   18036-9652

Foundation type: Independent foundation

Purpose: Scholarships primarily to students of Penn College, PA who are studying electronics and computer engineering technology.
Financial data: Year ended 12/31/2012. Assets, $3,939,708 (M); Expenditures, $757,941; Total giving, $734,595.
Fields of interest: Engineering school/education; Engineering/technology; Engineering.
Type of support: Support to graduates or students of specific schools.
Application information: Applications not accepted.
Additional information: Unsolicited requests for funds not considered or acknowledged.
EIN: 232322928

7964

The Luzerne Foundation

140 Main St., 2nd Fl.
Luzerne, PA   18709   (570) 714-1570
Contact: Charles M. Barber, C.E.O.
FAX: (570) 300-1712; E-mail: diane@luzfdn.org;
Additional tel.: (877) 589-3386; URL: http://www.luzfdn.org/

Foundation type: Community foundation
Purpose: Scholarships to residents of Luzerne County, PA and the surrounding area.
Publications: Application guidelines; Annual report; Financial statement; Grants list; Informational brochure (including application guidelines); Newsletter; Program policy statement.
Financial data: Year ended 12/31/2012. Assets, $23,734,299 (M); Expenditures, $12,185,930; Total giving, $11,303,725.
Type of support: Graduate support; Undergraduate support.
Application information: Applications accepted. Application form required.
Additional information: See web site for complete program information.
EIN: 232765498

7965

William A. Lynch Trust

c/o BNY Mellon, N.A.
P.O. Box 185
Pittsburgh, PA   15230-0185

Foundation type: Independent foundation
Purpose: Scholarships to deserving Catholic graduates of Beverly, MA, area high schools and Catholic schools for continuing education at institutions of higher learning.
Financial data: Year ended 08/31/2013. Assets, $200,466 (M); Expenditures, $15,282; Total giving, $9,000.
Fields of interest: Higher education; Catholic agencies & churches.
Type of support: Support to graduates or students of specific schools; Undergraduate support.
Application information:
Initial approach: Letter
Additional information: Contact the trust for application information.
EIN: 046093002

7966

Margaret S. Mahler Psychiatric Research Foundation

254 Kent Rd.
Wynnewood, PA   19096-1931   (856) 354-9002
E-mail: contact@margaretmahler.org; URL: http://www.margaretmahler.org

Foundation type: Public charity
Purpose: Awards and prizes to researchers or practitioners whose work contributes to the understanding and developement of separation-individuation theory.
Financial data: Year ended 12/31/2011. Assets, $927,832 (M); Expenditures, $117,766; Total giving, $44,800; Grants to individuals, 2 grants totaling $44,800.
Fields of interest: Psychology/behavioral science.
Type of support: Research; Awards/prizes.
Application information:
Initial approach: Letter
Additional information: Contact the foundation for further information about the prize.
EIN: 231996952

7967

The Christina and William Maley Charitable Foundation

1005 Augusta Way
Pittsburgh, PA   15236-2072   (412) 837-2741
Contact: Karen C. Maley, Tr.

Foundation type: Independent foundation
Purpose: Scholarships to students of the Buena Vista, PA community and general vicinity for postsecondary education.
Financial data: Year ended 12/31/2012. Assets, $9,669,999 (M); Expenditures, $56,419; Total giving, $44,817; Grants to individuals, 16 grants totaling $44,817 (high: $7,228, low: $1,000).
Fields of interest: Higher education.
Type of support: Scholarships—to individuals.
Application information: Applications accepted. Application form required. Interview required.
Deadline(s): Mar. 1
Applicants should submit the following:
1) Transcripts
2) SAT
3) Letter(s) of recommendation
4) Essay
Additional information: Selection is based on good academic performance, involvement in extracurricular activities, satisfactory work and citizenship history. Applications available in the guidance office.
EIN: 207421790

7968

William A. March Education Fund

c/o PNC Bank, N.A., Tax Department
1600 Market St., 4th Fl.
Philadelphia, PA   19103-7240
Application address: c/o PNC Wealth Management, 200 W. Lancaster Ave., Wayne, PA 19087

Foundation type: Independent foundation
Purpose: Interest free student loans to individuals in PA for attendance at colleges or universities.
Financial data: Year ended 12/31/2012. Assets, $1,055,587 (M); Expenditures, $12,472; Total giving, $0; Loans to individuals, totaling $62,500.
Fields of interest: Higher education.
Type of support: Student loans—to individuals.
Application information: Applications accepted. Application form required.
Deadline(s): Ongoing
Applicants should submit the following:
1) Financial information
2) Budget Information
EIN: 236295283

7969
W. Marshall & Margaret Hughes Scholarship Foundation
2201 Ridgewood Rd., Ste. 180
Wyomissing, PA   19610-1190   (800) 826-5534

Foundation type: Independent foundation
Purpose: Scholarships to graduates of Berks County, PA, high schools for undergraduate education in architecture, creative literature, music, or theatre.
Financial data: Year ended 12/31/2011. Assets, $508,470 (M); Expenditures, $26,522; Total giving, $17,000.
Fields of interest: Architecture; Theater; Music; Literature.
Type of support: Support to graduates or students of specific schools.
Application information: Applications accepted. Application form required.
  Send request by: Mail
  Deadline(s): Mar. 1
  Applicants should submit the following:
    1) Work samples
    2) Transcripts
    3) Letter(s) of recommendation
    4) Essay
  Additional information: Application should include proof of enrollment.
EIN: 237813648

7970
J. Clyde Martin Scholarship Trust
c/o S&T Bank
P.O. Box 247
Dubois, PA   15801-0247   (814) 375-3832
Contact: for Scholarships: Tammy Devers

Foundation type: Independent foundation
Purpose: Scholarships to graduating students of the Dubois Area High School, PA for attendance at accredited colleges or universities.
Financial data: Year ended 12/31/2011. Assets, $134,017 (M); Expenditures, $8,298; Total giving, $6,280; Grants to individuals, 4 grants totaling $6,280 (high: $1,570; low: $1,570).
Fields of interest: Higher education.
Type of support: Support to graduates or students of specific schools.
Application information: Applications accepted. Application form required.
  Deadline(s): Apr. 30
  Additional information: Applicant must provide proof of enrollment in a qualified college or university.
EIN: 236403927

7971
Martz Scholarship
(formerly Dolly & George Martz Scholarship Fund)
P.O. Box 3215
Lancaster, PA   17604-3216

Foundation type: Independent foundation
Purpose: Scholarships to students from low and middle income families of PA for higher education.
Financial data: Year ended 12/31/2012. Assets, $86,226 (M); Expenditures, $7,563; Total giving, $5,000; Grants to individuals, 5 grants totaling $5,000 (high: $1,000, low: $1,000).
Fields of interest: Higher education.
Type of support: Undergraduate support.
Application information: Applications accepted.
  Deadline(s): Apr. 30

Additional information: Applications available from Fulton Financial Advisors, N.A.
EIN: 236696968

7972
Mattioli Foundation
(formerly Auto Racing Fraternity Foundation of America, Inc.)
P. O. Box 500
Long Pond, PA   18334-0500   (570) 646-2300

Foundation type: Public charity
Purpose: Scholarships to individuals for higher education, primarily in FL, NC, PA, VA.
Financial data: Year ended 03/31/2012. Assets, $4,853,942 (M); Expenditures, $112,350; Total giving, $110,500.
Fields of interest: Higher education.
Type of support: Scholarships—to individuals.
Application information: Applications not accepted.
  Additional information: Scholarship recipients are determined by the institutions.
EIN: 232136313

7973
The Mattress Factory, Ltd.
500 Sampsonia Way
Pittsburgh, PA   15212-4444   (412) 231-3169
Contact: Catena Bahneman, Asst. Dir.
FAX: (412) 322-2231; E-mail: info@mattress.org;
URL: http://www.mattress.org

Foundation type: Public charity
Purpose: Residencies to artists for the creation of new works by providing studio space for site-specific installations.
Publications: Grants list; Informational brochure; Newsletter; Occasional report.
Financial data: Year ended 12/31/2011. Assets, $4,940,242 (M); Expenditures, $1,605,000.
Fields of interest: Visual arts; Arts.
Type of support: Residencies.
Application information: Applications accepted.
  Additional information: Applications in any form, including 35 millimeter slides, VHS video tapes, or CD-Rom that best represent the artists' work, accepted throughout the year.
Program description:
  Residency Program: The program is open to individual installation artists and artist collaborators at all stages of their professional careers. Residencies range from one week to two months.
EIN: 251338941

7974
Charles McCloskey Memorial Scholarship
c/o Austin Area School District
138 Costello Ave.
Austin, PA   16720   (814) 647-8603
Contact: Jerome Sasala, Tr.

Foundation type: Independent foundation
Purpose: Scholarships to graduates of the Austin Area School District, PA.
Financial data: Year ended 06/30/2012. Assets, $103,266 (M); Expenditures, $3,211; Total giving, $940; Grants to individuals, 3 grants totaling $940 (high: $470, low: $235).
Type of support: Support to graduates or students of specific schools; Undergraduate support.
Application information: Application form required.
  Deadline(s): May
  Final notification: Recipients notified by June 5

Additional information: Application forms available from Austin Area School District, PA.
EIN: 256355191

7975
Lalitta Nash McKaig Foundation
c/o PNC Advisors
620 Liberty Ave., 10th Fl.
Pittsburgh, PA   15222-2705
Application address: Gregory H. Getty, Esq., Admin, c/o Geppert, McMullen, Paye & Getty, 21 Prospect Sq., Cumberland, MD, 21502, tel.: (301) 777-1515

Foundation type: Independent foundation
Purpose: Scholarships to residents of Bedford and Somerset counties, PA, Mineral and Hampshire counties, WV, and Allegany and Garrett counties, MD, for undergraduate, graduate, or professional education at any accredited college or university located in the U.S.
Publications: Application guidelines.
Financial data: Year ended 09/30/2013. Assets, $11,639,782 (M); Expenditures, $626,023; Total giving, $488,650; Grants to individuals, totaling $488,650.
Fields of interest: Higher education; Scholarships/financial aid.
Type of support: Graduate support; Undergraduate support.
Application information: Applications accepted. Application form required. Interview required.
  Deadline(s): May 30
  Additional information: Contact foundation for current application guidelines.
Program description:
  Scholarship Program: Scholarship recipients are selected primarily on the basis of their financial need as computed by the College Scholarship Service from information contained on the FAF and Supplement. The foundation will not normally base any selection of a recipient on his or her past academic performance. Persons applying for a renewal grant, however, will also be evaluated on their scholarship performance during all prior periods of college level education. All persons are eligible to apply for renewal grants provided they resubmit their application and FAF and Supplement for the applicable year and continue to meet the residency requirement. A renewal applicant is not automatically guaranteed a renewal grant.
EIN: 256071908

7976
John McKee Trust
(also known as Trust Under Will of John McKee)
c/o John McKee Scholarship Comm.
P.O. Box 144
Merion Station, PA   19066   (484) 323-1348
Contact: Robert J. Stern, Exec. Secy.
FAX: (610) 640-1965;
E-mail: secretary@mckeescholars.org; URL: http://www.mckeescholars.org

Foundation type: Independent foundation
Purpose: Scholarships for college or vocational training to high school seniors or graduates, not over age 19, who are fatherless boys, in need of financial assistance, native to the five counties of Bucks, Chester, Delaware, Montgomery or Philadelphia, PA.
Publications: Application guidelines.
Financial data: Year ended 12/31/2012. Assets, $5,267,093 (M); Expenditures, $302,880; Total giving, $232,875; Grants to individuals, totaling $232,500.

Fields of interest: Vocational education; Young adults, male.
Type of support: Scholarships—to individuals.
Application information: Applications accepted. Application form required. Application form available on the grantmaker's web site.
  Send request by: Mail, fax or e-mail
  Copies of proposal: 1
  Deadline(s): Feb. 1
  Final notification: Applicants notified mid-March
  Applicants should submit the following:
    1) Transcripts
    2) SAT
    3) ACT
  Additional information: See web site or participating high school guidance offices for forms and conditions. Application and Statement of Understanding Form available on the organization's web site. Applicant must be fatherless boy native to Philadelphia, PA, area, who is under 20 years old. All grants are paid to grantee's school, not to the student directly.
EIN: 237675490

7977
William J. McMannis and A. Haskell McMannis Educational Trust Fund
c/o PNC Bank
620 Liberty Ave., 10th Fl.
Pittsburgh, PA 15222-2708
Scholarship address: c/o PNC Wealth Mgmt., Attn.: Ann O'Neil, P.O. Box 8480, Erie, PA 16553, tel.: (814) 871-9362

Foundation type: Independent foundation
Purpose: Scholarships to students who are U.S. citizens, for study at Gannon University, PA; Mercyhurst College, PA; Pennsylvania State University at Erie, The Behrend College; Dickinson College, PA; University of Pittsburgh, PA; Edinboro University, PA; and Florida State University, Fl.
Publications: Informational brochure (including application guidelines).
Financial data: Year ended 08/31/2013. Assets, $7,481,287 (M); Expenditures, $441,317; Total giving, $347,415; Grants to individuals, 165 grants totaling $347,415 (high: $4,500, low: $500).
Type of support: Support to graduates or students of specific schools; Undergraduate support.
Application information: Application form required.
  Initial approach: Contact participating schools
  Deadline(s): None
  Final notification: June 30
  Additional information: Applications not accepted from individuals and must be submitted through qualified schools.
EIN: 256191302

7978
Wendell W. McMillen Foundation
511 School St.
P.O. Box 638
Sheffield, PA 16347 (814) 968-3241
Contact: Paulette Grove
Application address: c/o W. W. McMillen Foundation, 4058 Rte. 6, Sheffield, PA 16347

Foundation type: Independent foundation
Purpose: Student loans to residents of the Sheffield, PA, area.
Financial data: Year ended 03/31/2013. Assets, $629,463 (M); Expenditures, $9,950; Total giving, $9,950.
Fields of interest: Higher education.
Type of support: Student loans—to individuals.

Application information: Applications accepted. Application form required.
  Initial approach: Letter or telephone
  Deadline(s): None
  Final notification: Applicants notified within two months
  Additional information: Contact the foundation for additional guidelines.
EIN: 256060174

7979
John N. McNeil and Stella McNeil Scholarship Trust
c/o Wells Fargo Bank, N.A.
101 N. Independence Mall E. MACY1372-062
Philadelphia, PA 19106-2112 (906) 776-2670
Contact: Rita Edberg
Application address: c/o Kingsford High School, 431 Hamilton Ave., Kingsford, MI 49802, tel.: (906) 776-2670

Foundation type: Independent foundation
Purpose: Scholarships to graduating seniors of Kingsford High School, MI with a desire to continue their education at an accredited college, university or trade school.
Financial data: Year ended 12/31/2012. Assets, $4,695,945 (M); Expenditures, $228,279; Total giving, $175,500; Grants to individuals, 117 grants totaling $175,500 (high: $1,500, low: $1,500).
Fields of interest: Vocational education, post-secondary; Higher education.
Type of support: Scholarships—to individuals.
Application information: Applications accepted. Application form required.
  Deadline(s): Mar.
  Additional information: Application should include two letters of reference. Applicant requires a 2.0 GPA to apply, full time college attendance and maintain a 2.0 GPA in college.
EIN: 386788691

7980
McRoberts Memorial Law Scholarship Fund
P.O. Box 609
Pittsburgh, PA 15230-9738

Foundation type: Independent foundation
Purpose: Scholarships to students who are residents of Peoria County, IL, for at least five years, and pursuing a law degree.
Financial data: Year ended 06/30/2013. Assets, $766,472 (M); Expenditures, $44,575; Total giving, $35,000; Grant to an individual, 1 grant totaling $35,000.
Fields of interest: Law school/education.
Type of support: Scholarships—to individuals.
Application information: Application form required.
  Deadline(s): May 15
  Applicants should submit the following:
    1) Transcripts
    2) Letter(s) of recommendation
    3) Financial information
  Additional information: Application must also include LSAT scores.
EIN: 376043864

7981
Mellinger Scholarship Fund
(formerly Gertrude & Clarence Mellinger Scholarship Fund)
c/o The Ephrata National Bank
47 E. Main St.
P.O. Box 457
Ephrata, PA 17522-0457 (717) 733-6576

Foundation type: Independent foundation
Purpose: Scholarships to financially needy graduating seniors from Ephrata Area High School, PA, enrolled in a four year degree program or a three year nursing degree program at an institution of higher learning.
Financial data: Year ended 12/31/2012. Assets, $931,500 (M); Expenditures, $55,569; Total giving, $46,250; Grants to individuals, 37 grants totaling $46,250 (high: $1,250, low: $1,250).
Fields of interest: Higher education; Nursing school/education.
Type of support: Support to graduates or students of specific schools; Undergraduate support.
Application information: Application form required.
  Deadline(s): Apr. 25
  Applicants should submit the following:
    1) SAT
    2) Class rank
    3) ACT
  Additional information: Application should also include tax return, extracurricular activities and achievements. Applicant must have been a resident of the school district for at least three years prior to graduation.
EIN: 232833247

7982
Mendenhall-Tyson Scholarship Foundation
c/o PNC Advisors
620 Liberty Ave., P2-PTPP-10-2
Pittsburgh, PA 15222-2705 (412) 768-5895
Contact: David T. Videon, Chair.

Foundation type: Public charity
Purpose: Scholarships to graduates of Upper Darby High School, PA, for continuing education at accredited colleges or universities.
Financial data: Year ended 12/31/2011. Assets, $1,517,247 (M); Expenditures, $73,747; Total giving, $63,000.
Type of support: Support to graduates or students of specific schools.
Application information: Applications accepted.
  Additional information: Students are selected on the basis of qualities of manhood/womanhood, moral character and leadership, ability and achievement, local community and financial need.
EIN: 232983986

7983
Frank J. Michaels Scholarship Fund
c/o Wachovia Bank, N.A.
101 N. Independence Mall E. MACY1372-062
Philadelphia, PA 19108-2112 (866) 608-0001

Foundation type: Independent foundation
Purpose: Scholarships to residents of Oxford, PA, or to those within 25 miles of Oxford, if there are insufficient Oxford applicants.
Financial data: Year ended 01/31/2013. Assets, $2,180,543 (M); Expenditures, $139,408; Total giving, $107,000.
Type of support: Scholarships—to individuals.

Application information: Applications accepted. Application form required.
Deadline(s): Apr. 15
EIN: 236680399

7984
Daniel and Josephine Mikovich Community Foundation, Inc.
53 E. State St.
Albion, PA 16401-1110 (814) 756-4138
Contact: Edward J. Kempf, Jr., V.P.

Foundation type: Independent foundation
Purpose: Scholarships and grants to eligible students in the Albion, PA area for postsecondary education.
Financial data: Year ended 12/31/2011. Assets, $1,315,577 (M); Expenditures, $54,316; Total giving, $44,964; Grants to individuals, 18 grants totaling $18,000.
Fields of interest: Higher education.
Type of support: Undergraduate support.
Application information: Applications not accepted.
Additional information: Unsolicited requests for funds not considered or acknowledged.
EIN: 203528829

7985
Colin & Mary Miller Charitable Trust
P.O. Box 520
Johnstown, PA 15907-0520 (814) 533-5340
Contact: Kimberly Hughes

Foundation type: Independent foundation
Purpose: Scholarships to graduate and undergraduate students who demonstrate financial need, dedication to their community, and academic achievement. First preference is to residents of Pittsburgh, PA.
Financial data: Year ended 12/31/2012. Assets, $239,304 (M); Expenditures, $15,101; Total giving, $10,400; Grants to individuals, 4 grants totaling $10,400 (high: $2,600, low: $2,600).
Type of support: Graduate support; Undergraduate support.
Application information: Applications accepted. Application form required.
Deadline(s): May 15
EIN: 256303529

7986
Don Miller Foundation
c/o Wells Fargo Bank Indiana, N.A.
101 N Independence Mall E Macy 1372-062
Philadelphia, PA 19106-2112 (260) 461-6458
Contact: Jennifer King
Application address: c/o Wells Fargo Bank Indiana, N.A., 111E. Wayne St., Fort Wayne, IN 46802,

Foundation type: Independent foundation
Purpose: Scholarships to children of employees of Miller Pipeline or Miller Cable and to students attending Clyde Greensprings High School in Clyde, OH.
Financial data: Year ended 12/31/2012. Assets, $975,794 (M); Expenditures, $77,242; Total giving, $60,450.
Type of support: Employee-related scholarships; Support to graduates or students of specific schools.
Application information: Application form required.
Deadline(s): Apr. 15
Applicants should submit the following:
1) Transcripts
2) Letter(s) of recommendation
3) Essay
Company names: Miller Pipeline; Miller Cable
EIN: 352004527

7987
John R. Miller Nursing Scholarship
260 Sunbury St.
Minersville, PA 17954 (570) 544-1709
Application address: First National Bank of Minersville, 260 Sunbury St., Minersville, PA 17954

Foundation type: Independent foundation
Purpose: Scholarships to graduating seniors of Blue Mountain High School, PA pursuing a nursing degree.
Financial data: Year ended 12/31/2012. Assets, $268,899 (M); Expenditures, $13,538; Total giving, $11,500; Grants to individuals, totaling $11,500.
Fields of interest: Nursing school/education.
Type of support: Scholarships—to individuals; Support to graduates or students of specific schools.
Application information: Applications accepted. Application form required.
Deadline(s): July 31 for application, Aug. 6 for financial aid
Additional information: Application should include transcripts, and student must have a "C" or better average.
EIN: 237985997

7988
Ed & Edith Miller Scholarship Trust
c/o Wells Fargo Bank N.A. Trust tax Dept.
101N Independence Mall E MACY 1372-Philadelphia, PA 19106-2112
Application Address: Counseling Office, Buckley, WA.

Foundation type: Independent foundation
Purpose: Scholarships to graduates of public high schools in Buckley, WA, to pursue higher education in the areas of engineering, forestry, and mathematics.
Financial data: Year ended 01/31/2013. Assets, $291,154 (M); Expenditures, $20,489; Total giving, $15,000.
Fields of interest: Engineering school/education; Environment, forests; Mathematics.
Type of support: Support to graduates or students of specific schools; Undergraduate support.
Application information: Applications accepted.
Initial approach: Letter
Deadline(s): None
Additional information: Applicants should contact their high school counseling office to apply.
EIN: 916340047

7989
Ruth M. Minear Educational Trust
c/o Wells Fargo Bank, N.A.
101 N. Independence Mall E. MACY 1372-062
Philadelphia, PA 19106-2112

Foundation type: Independent foundation
Purpose: Scholarships to graduates of Wabash High School, IN, for study at an accredited postsecondary school in IN.
Financial data: Year ended 02/28/2013. Assets, $1,769,100 (M); Expenditures, $96,547; Total giving, $62,700.

Type of support: Support to graduates or students of specific schools; Undergraduate support.
Application information: Application form required.
Deadline(s): Feb. 14
Additional information: Application must include transcripts, IN financial aid forms, copy of high school diploma, and certification of acceptance at accredited college; Scholarships are renewable.
EIN: 356335021

7990
Ryan Lee Mohn Memorial Foundation
529 Pine St.
Steelton, PA 17113

Foundation type: Independent foundation
Purpose: Scholarships to worthy students from Steelton-Highspire High School, PA seeking a college education at an educational institution of higher learning.
Financial data: Year ended 12/31/2012. Assets, $0 (M); Expenditures, $34,146; Total giving, $29,886; Grants to individuals, 5 grants totaling $10,000 (high: $2,000, low: $2,000).
Fields of interest: Higher education.
Type of support: Scholarships—to individuals.
Application information: Interview required.
Additional information: Applications can be obtained from your guidance counselors. Scholarship awards are based on academic performance, recommendations, extracurricular activities, including sports, ability and aptitude for college work, and financial need.
EIN: 202338586

7991
The Monroeville Christian Judea Foundation
4363 Northern Pike
Monroeville, PA 15146-2807 (412) 373-3900
FAX: (412) 373-5600;
E-mail: gwen@thecedarsofmonroeville.org;
URL: http://www.thecedarsmonroeville.com

Foundation type: Public charity
Purpose: Scholarships to Gateway High School, PA seniors entering the health care or science fields.
Financial data: Year ended 12/31/2011. Assets, $12,592,781 (M); Expenditures, $9,900,774.
Type of support: Support to graduates or students of specific schools.
Application information: Applications not accepted.
Additional information: Unsolicited requests for funds not considered.
EIN: 251475192

7992
Orlene Drobisch Moore Charitable Foundation
P.O. Box 609
Pittsburgh, PA 15230-9738

Foundation type: Independent foundation
Purpose: Scholarships to high school graduates of Williamsville, IL, School District.
Financial data: Year ended 06/30/2013. Assets, $267,540 (M); Expenditures, $13,726; Total giving, $9,900; Grant to an individual, 1 grant totaling $9,900.
Fields of interest: Higher education.

Type of support: Support to graduates or students of specific schools; Undergraduate support.
Application information: Applications accepted. Application form required.
> *Deadline(s):* None
> *Applicants should submit the following:*
> 1) Letter(s) of recommendation
> 2) SAT
> 3) Financial information
> 4) GPA
> 5) ACT
EIN: 371316048

7993
N. Robert Moore Charitable Scholarship Trust
c/o S&T Bank
P.O. Box 247
Du Bois, PA   15801-0247   (814) 375-3832
Contact: Tammy Divers

Foundation type: Independent foundation
Purpose: Scholarships for graduating students of Dubois Area High School, PA, who will be attending an accredited college or university.
Financial data: Year ended 12/31/2012. Assets, $197,967 (M); Expenditures, $11,578; Total giving, $9,150; Grants to individuals, 5 grants totaling $9,150 (high: $1,830, low: $1,830).
Fields of interest: Higher education.
Type of support: Support to graduates or students of specific schools.
Application information: Applications accepted. Application form required.
> *Additional information:* Contact your school's guidance office for application information.
EIN: 251802886

7994
Elsie B. Moore Scholarship Foundation
c/o PNC Bank, N.A.
1600 Market St., Tax Dept.
Philadelphia, PA   19103-7240
Application address: c/o PNC Bank, N.A., 222 Delaware Ave., 16th Fl., Wilmington, DE 19899

Foundation type: Independent foundation
Purpose: Scholarships to residents of Delaware accepted by an accredited school of medicine.
Financial data: Year ended 08/31/2013. Assets, $389,195 (M); Expenditures, $21,342; Total giving, $13,600.
Fields of interest: Medical school/education.
Type of support: Graduate support.
Application information: Application form required. Interview required.
> *Send request by:* Mail
> *Deadline(s):* Apr. 30
> *Applicants should submit the following:*
> 1) Financial information
> 2) Letter(s) of recommendation
> 3) Transcripts
> *Additional information:* Application must also include MCAT scores, copy of letter of acceptance, and letter describing professional aspirations.
EIN: 516154834

7995
Griffith D. Morgan Memorial Fund
c/o PNC Bank, N.A.
620 Liberty Ave., 10th Fl.
Pittsburgh, PA   15222-2705   (724) 756-7510
Contact: Judith Glackin
Application address: Karns City High School, c/o Judith Glackin-Sedwick, Guidance Counselor, 1446 Kittanning Pike, Karns City, PA 16041-1818

Foundation type: Independent foundation
Purpose: Scholarships to high school graduates of the East Brady Area School District, PA pursuing higher education.
Financial data: Year ended 12/31/2011. Assets, $1,414,869 (M); Expenditures, $76,649; Total giving, $63,138; Grants to individuals, 19 grants totaling $63,138.
Fields of interest: Higher education.
Type of support: Support to graduates or students of specific schools; Undergraduate support.
Application information: Application form required.
> *Initial approach:* Letter
> *Deadline(s):* May 1
> *Additional information:* Application can be obtained from the guidance counselor of Karns City High School.
EIN: 256066552

7996
The William and Louise Moyer Scholarship Fund
6735 Cetronia Rd.
Allentown, PA   18106   (610) 266-6457
Contact: Richard Westover, Secy.
Application address: 216 Church St., Catasauqua, PA 18032

Foundation type: Independent foundation
Purpose: Scholarships to students with 24 hours of credited study at the college level, at one of the eligible colleges as specified by the Trust and the Moyer Will.
Financial data: Year ended 06/30/2012. Assets, $60,365 (M); Expenditures, $24,301; Total giving, $23,000; Grants to individuals, totaling $23,000.
Type of support: Undergraduate support.
Application information: Applications accepted. Application form required.
> *Initial approach:* Letter, e-mail or telephone to request application
> *Deadline(s):* June 1
EIN: 237739199

7997
A. Marlyn Moyer, Jr. Scholarship Foundation
409 Hood Blvd.
Fairless Hills, PA   19030-2901   (215) 943-7400
Contact: Susan M. Harkins, Recording Secy.

Foundation type: Independent foundation
Purpose: Scholarships to residents of Bucks County, PA, who have attended Bucks County high schools and have never attended postsecondary schools.
Financial data: Year ended 12/31/2012. Assets, $698,096 (M); Expenditures, $52,574; Total giving, $44,500; Grants to individuals, 13 grants totaling $44,500 (high: $4,000, low: $1,500).
Type of support: Support to graduates or students of specific schools; Undergraduate support.
Application information: Application form required.
> *Deadline(s):* Apr. 30
> *Additional information:* Contact guidance counselors at local area schools or Bucks

County Chamber of Commerce for application forms.
EIN: 232037282

7998
M. Catherine Murphy Memorial Fund
c/o First Columbia Bank & Trust Co.
1199 Lightstreet Rd.
Bloomsburg, PA   17815
Contact: Sheri Grozier
Application address: 11 W. Main St., Bloomsburg, PA 17815

Foundation type: Independent foundation
Purpose: Interest-free student loans to residents of Catawissa, PA, who are graduates of Southern Columbia Area High School and attend Bloomsburg University, PA.
Financial data: Year ended 12/31/2012. Assets, $341,371 (M); Expenditures, $22,499; Total giving, $17,400; Grants to individuals, 3 grants totaling $17,400 (high: $5,800, low: $5,800).
Type of support: Student loans—to individuals; Support to graduates or students of specific schools.
Application information: Applications accepted. Application form required.
> *Additional information:* Application must also include copy of parents' federal income tax return(s).
EIN: 236648433

7999
Mike Mussina Foundation
999 Loyalsock Ave.
Montoursville, PA   17754-2305
E-mail: info@mikemussinafoundation.org;
URL: http://www.mikemussinafoundation.org/foundation_preloader.swf

Foundation type: Independent foundation
Purpose: Scholarship to a graduating senior from each of twelve area high schools of Lycoming county, PA. Scholarships for college bound students from the north, south, east, and west regions of the U.S.
Financial data: Year ended 12/31/2011. Assets, $197,030 (M); Expenditures, $30,641; Total giving, $28,000; Grants to individuals, 27 grants totaling $28,000 (high: $2,000, low: $1,000).
Fields of interest: Higher education.
Type of support: Scholarships—to individuals.
Application information: Scholarships are awarded on the basis of students who are active in their school and/or community, must be a varsity letter winner or have participated in the school band for at least three years.
Program description:
> *Scholarship Program:* Scholarships in the amount of $1,000 are awarded to one graduating senior from each of the twelve high schools in Lycoming county, including both public and private institutions. Each student receives $1,000 a year for up to four years, as long as they remain in good academic standing. The money can be used at a college, university, community college or Bible college.
EIN: 233022314

8000
National Organization for Hearing Research Foundation
(also known as NOHR Foundation)
P.O. Box 421
Narberth, PA   19072-3404   (610) 649-6114
Contact: Geraldine D. Fox, Pres.
Application e-mail: grants@nohrfoundation.org
FAX: (610) 668-1428;
E-mail: info@nohrfoundation.org; URL: http://www.nohrfoundation.org

Foundation type: Public charity
Purpose: Grants for research into the causes, preventions, treatments, and cures of hearing loss and deafness.
Publications: Annual report; Informational brochure; Occasional report.
Financial data: Year ended 12/31/2011. Assets, $293,162 (M); Expenditures, $329,325; Total giving, $185,075. Grants to individuals amount not specified.
Fields of interest: Ear, nose & throat research.
Type of support: Research.
Application information: Applications accepted. Application form required.
  Initial approach: Letter
  Send request by: Mail or online
  Deadline(s): Apr. 12
  Final notification: Recipients notified by June 28
  Additional information: See web site for additional application guidelines.
EIN: 232528578

8001
National Transplant Assistance Fund, Inc.
150 N. Radnor Chester Rd., Ste. F-120
Radnor, PA   19087-5244
Contact: Lynne Coughlin Samson, Exec. Dir.
FAX: (610) 535-6106;
E-mail: NTAF@transplantfund.org; Toll-free tel.: (800) 642-8399; URL: http://www.transplantfund.org

Foundation type: Public charity
Purpose: Financial assistance to eligible families, to pay for the medically-related costs of life-altering organ/tissue transplantation and catastrophic injury.
Publications: Annual report; Financial statement; Newsletter.
Financial data: Year ended 09/30/2011. Assets, $14,509,899 (M); Expenditures, $8,166,040; Total giving, $6,649,524; Grants to individuals, 1,374 grants totaling $6,543,774. Subtotal for emergency funds: 1,381 grants totaling $6,649,524.
Fields of interest: Organ diseases; Surgery.
Type of support: Grants for special needs.
Application information: Applications accepted. Application form required. Application form available on the grantmaker's web site.
  Initial approach: E-mail
  Additional information: See web site for eligibility criteria.
Program description:
  Financial Assistance: Grants to transplant and catastrophic injury patients for medical expenses including, but not limited to, physician fees, hospital charges, home health care expenses, medical insurance, medication costs, transportation expenses, dental costs, funeral costs, and hardship expenses.
EIN: 521322317

8002
Catherine Hayes Nelson Scholarships, Inc.
1265 S. Garner St.
State College, PA   16801-6327
Contact: John F. Hayes, Pres.

Foundation type: Independent foundation
Purpose: Scholarships to graduates of Brockway Area High School, Dubois Area High School, St. Mary's high schools who have been accepted at the Dubois Campus of the Pennsylvania State University, PA.
Financial data: Year ended 12/31/2011. Assets, $37,442 (M); Expenditures, $36,825; Total giving, $36,500; Grant to an individual, 1 grant totaling $10,000.
Fields of interest: Higher education.
Type of support: Support to graduates or students of specific schools; Undergraduate support.
Application information: Applications accepted. Application form not required.
  Initial approach: Letter
  Applicants should submit the following:
    1) Letter(s) of recommendation
    2) FAFSA
  Additional information: Awards are paid to the educational institution on behalf of the student.
EIN: 251867007

8003
Nephcure Foundation
15 Waterloo Ave., Ste. 200
Berwyn, PA   19312-1730
Contact: Irving Smokler Ph.D., Pres.
E-mail: info@nephcure.org; Toll-free tel.: (866) 637-4287; URL: http://www.nephcure.org

Foundation type: Public charity
Purpose: Research grants for finding a cause and cure for Nephrotic Syndrome and Focal Segmental Glomerulosclerosis.
Publications: Application guidelines; Informational brochure.
Financial data: Year ended 12/31/2011. Assets, $1,607,780 (M); Expenditures, $2,864,274; Total giving, $1,658,609.
Fields of interest: Kidney diseases; Kidney research.
Type of support: Research.
Application information:
  Initial approach: E-mail
  Additional information: See web site for additional guidelines.
Program description:
  Scientific Research Grant Program: The foundation supports research seeking the causes of idiopathic nephrotic syndrome and focal segmental glomerulosclerosis (FSGS), leading to improved treatment and a cure. Grants will be awarded to help understand the cause and mechanics of glomerular disease, with particular emphasis on idiopathic nephrotic syndrome and primary FSGS, with consideration given to work on all forms of idiopathic glomerular disease if this work addresses mechanisms common to glomerular disease. Grants will also be awarded to support the exploration of specific translational and therapeutic approaches that will lead to the development of treatments for glomerular disease and proteinuria. Eligible applicants include post-doctoral fellows (defined as applicants that do not hold a faculty appointment, and who are within ten years of their first doctorate-level degree); young investigators (applicants who are independent investigators holding a faculty-level appointment

and are within the first four years of their first academic appointment at the time the grant commences); established investigators (applicants that are established investigators whose publication history suggest that their work is clearly outside the area of glomerular disease, who seek seed funding for projects that clearly represent a new investigative director for that investigator); and other principal investigators who hold an M.D., Ph.D., or equivalent advanced degree.
EIN: 383569922

8004
Mary Margaret Nestor Foundation
Reiff & West Streets
P.O. Box 147
Lykens, PA   17048

Foundation type: Company-sponsored foundation
Purpose: Scholarships to residents of Dauphin County, PA for postsecondary education.
Financial data: Year ended 06/30/2013. Assets, $1,793 (M); Expenditures, $9,310; Total giving, $7,250; Grants to individuals, 15 grants totaling $7,250 (high: $750, low: $250).
Fields of interest: Higher education; Economically disadvantaged.
Type of support: Scholarships—to individuals; Graduate support.
Application information:
  Initial approach: Letter
  Deadline(s): None
  Additional information: Application should contain a cover letter requesting a scholarship as well as a resume detailing both academic and personal achievements.
EIN: 236277570

8005
Newman Family Charitable Foundation
1120 Ginkgo Ln.
Gladwyne, PA   19035-1038

Foundation type: Independent foundation
Purpose: Grants to individuals for neurodegenerative research and scholarships primarily to students attending Drexel University, PA.
Financial data: Year ended 12/31/2012. Assets, $99,670 (M); Expenditures, $3,330; Total giving, $3,300.
Fields of interest: Brain disorders; Neuroscience; Brain research; Spine disorders research; Neuroscience research; Medical research.
Type of support: Research; Support to graduates or students of specific schools.
Application information: Applications accepted.
  Initial approach: Letter
  Deadline(s): None
  Additional information: Contact foundation for current application guidelines.
EIN: 233045779

8006
Nicholas Family Foundation
119 Valley View Dr.
Edinboro, PA   16412

Foundation type: Independent foundation
Purpose: Grants to residents of western PA for expenses pertaining to medical, housing and educational needs.
Financial data: Year ended 12/31/2011. Assets, $0 (M); Expenditures, $2,251; Total giving,

$1,500; Grant to an individual, 1 grant totaling $1,500.
Fields of interest: Health care; Housing/shelter, repairs.
Type of support: Grants for special needs.
Application information: Application form required.
  Deadline(s): None
  Additional information: Application must include current income and financial need.
EIN: 251855273

8007
L. E. Nicklies Scholarship Fund
c/o PNC Bank, N.A.
620 Liberty Ave., 10th Fl.
Pittsburgh, PA   15222-2722   (502) 485-3221
Contact: Carolyn Quire, Dir.
Application address: P.O. Box 34020, Louisville, KY 40232-4020, tel.: (502) 485-3221

Foundation type: Independent foundation
Purpose: Scholarships to high school graduates of Jefferson County, KY, for attendance at an accredited college or university in Jefferson county.
Publications: Application guidelines.
Financial data: Year ended 07/31/2013. Assets, $735,439 (M); Expenditures, $36,219; Total giving, $32,000.
Fields of interest: Law school/education; Medical school/education; Teacher school/education; Engineering school/education; Theological school/education.
Type of support: Support to graduates or students of specific schools; Undergraduate support.
Application information: Applications accepted. Application form required.
  Initial approach: Letter
  Deadline(s): Mar. 16
  Applicants should submit the following:
    1) Transcripts
    2) Financial information
  Additional information: Application should also include a statement listing extracurricular, leadership and community service activities.
EIN: 310902261

8008
John H. Noll Foundation
c/o PNC Bank, N.A.
P.O. Box 609
Pittsburgh, PA   15230-9738
Application address: c/o PNC Bank, N.A., Attn.: Jane Kleinsmith, 1900 E. 19th St., Cleveland, OH 44114, tel.: (216) 222-9815

Foundation type: Independent foundation
Purpose: Scholarships to graduating seniors of the Fort Wayne public and parochial high schools and Homestead High School, IN.
Financial data: Year ended 09/30/2013. Assets, $3,892,279 (M); Expenditures, $189,912; Total giving, $152,698; Grants to individuals, totaling $152,698.
Type of support: Support to graduates or students of specific schools; Undergraduate support.
Application information: Applications accepted. Application form required.
  Deadline(s): Mar. 31
  Additional information: Application forms are available from guidance counselors of participating high schools.
EIN: 237082877

8009
North Central PA Golf Association
(formerly North Central Pennsylvania Golf Association Scholarship Trust)
131 E., Main St.
Lock Haven, PA   17745   (570) 748-6505
Contact: Robert L. Emert II, Treas.

Foundation type: Independent foundation
Purpose: Scholarships to golfers who are high school seniors participating in the junior golf program.
Financial data: Year ended 12/31/2012. Assets, $174,137 (M); Expenditures, $7,311; Total giving, $6,000; Grants to individuals, 8 grants totaling $6,000 (high: $750; low: $750).
Fields of interest: Athletics/sports, academies.
Type of support: Scholarships—to individuals.
Application information: Applications accepted. Application form required.
  Initial approach: Letter
  Deadline(s): Mar.
  Applicants should submit the following:
    1) Essay
    2) Transcripts
    3) Letter(s) of recommendation
  Additional information: Applicant must be accepted for admission at a college or university and demonstrate knowledge of the rules and etiquette of golf.
EIN: 232500516

8010
North East Community Foundation
P. O. Box 327
North East, PA   16428-0327   (814) 725-7107
Contact: Melissa Fisher, Exec. Assi.
E-mail: melissa_fisher@bayvalleyfoods.com;
URL: http://www.necommunityfoundation.org/

Foundation type: Public charity
Purpose: Scholarships to graduating seniors at North East High School, PA for postsecondary education.
Publications: Application guidelines; Annual report.
Financial data: Year ended 12/31/2011. Assets, $3,303,184 (M); Expenditures, $123,089; Total giving, $92,147; Grants to individuals, totaling $1,000.
Fields of interest: Higher education.
Type of support: Scholarships—to individuals; Support to graduates or students of specific schools.
Application information: Applications accepted. Application form required.
  Additional information: Students should contact their high school guidance counselor for application information. Scholarships are made payable to the educational institution on behalf of the students.
Program descriptions:
  Jared Matthew Bifulco Scholarship Fund: Scholarships are available to students of North East High School, to be used toward their college career.
  Richard Gorzynski Scholarship Fund: Scholarships will be awarded to students at North East High School who have demonstrated competitive traits, spirit, athleticism, and leadership.
EIN: 251650208

8011
Northampton County Area Community College Foundation
3835 Green Pond Rd.
Bethlehem, PA   18020-7568   (610) 861-5300
Contact: Susan K. Kubik, Exec. Dir.
E-mail: skubik@northampton.edu; URL: http://northampton.edu/Offices-and-Services/Foundation.htm

Foundation type: Public charity
Purpose: Scholarships to pre-selected students of Northampton Community College, PA.
Publications: Annual report; Newsletter.
Financial data: Year ended 06/30/2012. Assets, $37,927,734 (M); Expenditures, $2,134,257; Total giving, $1,623,871; Grants to individuals, totaling $13,500.
Type of support: Support to graduates or students of specific schools.
Application information: Applications not accepted.
  Additional information: Unsolicited requests for funds not considered.
EIN: 232064496

8012
The Northeast High School Alumni Foundation
1601 Cottman Ave.
Philadelphia, PA   19111-3430   (215) 728-5018
Contact: Linda Carroll

Foundation type: Independent foundation
Purpose: Scholarships and awards to students and alumni of Northeast High School, PA.
Financial data: Year ended 06/30/2013. Assets, $1,541,306 (M); Expenditures, $114,404; Total giving, $114,404.
Type of support: Support to graduates or students of specific schools.
Application information:
  Initial approach: Letter
  Deadline(s): End of school year for current graduating class
  Additional information: Application must also include financial need and scholastic record.
EIN: 236463349

8013
Northwest Bancorp, Inc. Charitable Foundation
Liberty at 2nd Ave.
Warren, PA   16365   (814) 728-7261
Contact: Vicki Stec, Secy.

Foundation type: Company-sponsored foundation
Purpose: Scholarships to Northwest Bancorp, Inc. employees and their children for undergraduate education.
Financial data: Year ended 06/30/2013. Assets, $1,839,457 (M); Expenditures, $111,767; Total giving, $93,328.
Fields of interest: Higher education.
Type of support: Employee-related scholarships.
Application information: Application form required.
  Deadline(s): End of each calendar quarter
Company name: Northwest Bancorp, MHC
EIN: 251819537

8014
O'Brien-Veba Scholarship Trust
c/o PNC Bank, N.A.
P.O. Box 609
Pittsburgh, PA 15230-9738

Foundation type: Independent foundation
Purpose: Scholarships to residents of IA, IL, IN, MI and WI who are of the Cathoilc faith, for higher education.
Financial data: Year ended 09/30/2013. Assets, $3,588,500 (M); Expenditures, $196,373; Total giving, $156,800; Grants to individuals, totaling $156,800.
Fields of interest: Education; Catholic agencies & churches.
Type of support: Undergraduate support.
Application information: Applications accepted. Application form required.
   Initial approach: Letter
   Deadline(s): None
   Additional information: Application should include educational needs.
EIN: 376277500

8015
ONS Foundation
125 Enterprise Dr.
Pittsburgh, PA 15275-1214 (412) 859-6100
Contact: Linda Worrall, Exec. Dir.
FAX: (412) 859-6163;
E-mail: info@onsfoundation.org; E-Mail for Linda Worrall: lworrall@onsfoundation.org; URL: http://www.onsfoundation.org

Foundation type: Public charity
Purpose: Scholarships to students for postsecondary education pursuing oncology nursing. Grants and awards to help foster nursing research by oncology nurses.
Publications: Application guidelines; Annual report.
Financial data: Year ended 12/31/2011. Assets, $13,263,729 (M); Expenditures, $1,519,635; Total giving, $428,300; Grants to individuals, totaling $360,566.
Fields of interest: Nursing school/education; Cancer.
Type of support: Research; Grants to individuals; Scholarships—to individuals.
Application information: Applications accepted. Application form required. Application form available on the grantmaker's web site.
   Send request by: Online
   Deadline(s): Vary
   Additional information: See web site for additional guidelines and programs.
Program descriptions:
   Academic Scholarships: Scholarships are available to registered nurses who are interested in and committed to oncology nursing to continue their education by pursuing a bachelor's, master's, or doctoral degree. Scholarships range from $2,000 to $5,000. All candidates must have a current license to practice as a registered nurse, and must have an interest in and commitment to oncology nursing.
   Bone Marrow Transplant Career Development Awards: Four $2,000 awards and plaques each are awarded to registered nurses working in bone marrow transplantation by providing financial assistance to attend a continuing education program(s) that will further the nurses' professional goals.
   Cancer Public Education Project Grant: The program provides up to $5,000 in funding for public education projects that provide information to enhance the knowledge and awareness of cancer

prevention, detection, and treatment modalities to the public.
   Congress Scholarship: Awards of up to $1,200 are given to professional nurses who have demonstrated innovation in responding to challenges in practice, and who have made a difference for the patient/family, institution, and/or fellow healthcare professionals. The award is to apply toward ONS Congress registration, travel to and from Congress and per diem Congress expenses.
   Multidisciplinary Cancer Education Grant: One annual grant of $3,000 is awarded to provide seed money to support an oncology registered nurse in developing and/or implementing a cancer-related multidisciplinary education or practice project for healthcare professionals.
   Neuro-Oncology Nursing Research Grant: Awarded in conjunction with the American Brain Tumor Association, this two-year, $10,000 grant will be made available for research on symptom management, support systems, or quality-of-life in neuro-oncology patients and their families. Funding preference will be given to projects that involve nurses in the design and conduct of the research activity, and that promote theoretically-based oncology practice.
   Nurse Leader Career Development Award: A grant of $2,000 is awarded to an oncology nurse for meritorious leadership practice so that the nurse may attend a continuing education program that will further his or her leadership development.
   Pat McCue/New Orleans Chapter End-of-Life Care Nursing Career Development Award: One annual award of $2,500 is given to recognize a registered nurse dedicated to caring for patients and their families during the final stages of life.
   Pearl Moore Career Development Awards: The program rewards three professional nurses for meritorious practice by providing grants of $3,000 each to attend a continuing education program that will further the nurses' professional goals.
EIN: 251410081

8016
Paddington Foundation
(formerly Beard Family Foundation)
125 1st Ave.
Pittsburgh, PA 15222-1590 (412) 391-8510
Contact: Philip E. Beard, Tr.

Foundation type: Independent foundation
Purpose: Scholarships to individuals, primarily in PA, for undergraduate education.
Financial data: Year ended 12/31/2012. Assets, $139,213 (M); Expenditures, $9,099; Total giving, $6,000; Grants to individuals, 3 grants totaling $6,000 (high: $2,500, low: $1,500).
Type of support: Undergraduate support.
Application information: Applications accepted.
   Initial approach: Letter
   Deadline(s): None
   Applicants should submit the following:
      1) Transcripts
      2) Letter(s) of recommendation
      3) Financial information
   Additional information: Application must also include biographical record, statement of goals and demonstration of financial need.
EIN: 256742854

8017
Nick & Paris N. Panagos Charitable Trust
432 Coronet Dr.
Blandon, PA 19510 (610) 944-0774
Contact: Mathew Midouhas, Tr.

Foundation type: Independent foundation
Purpose: Scholarships primarily to residents of PA in pursuit of a higher education.
Financial data: Year ended 12/31/2012. Assets, $566,476 (M); Expenditures, $55,130; Total giving, $31,431.
Fields of interest: Higher education.
Type of support: Scholarships—to individuals.
Application information: Applications accepted. Application form not required.
   Initial approach: Letter
   Deadline(s): None
EIN: 237802567

8018
Pan-Icarian Foundation
P.O. Box 79037
Pittsburgh, PA 15216-0037 (412) 563-0547
Application address: Steve Stratakos, Chair., c/o Pan-Icarian Scholarship Comm., 9305 S. 85th Ct., Hickory Hills, IL 60457; E-mail for additional inquires: generalequity@comcast.net
URL: http://www.pan-icarian.com/foundation

Foundation type: Public charity
Purpose: Scholarships to individuals of Icarian descent for undergraduate and graduate study. Grants to individuals for medical care assistance.
Financial data: Year ended 06/30/2012. Assets, $4,219,477 (M); Expenditures, $112,945; Total giving, $76,500; Grants to individuals, totaling $76,500.
International interests: Greece.
Type of support: Graduate support; Undergraduate support; Grants for special needs.
Application information: Applications accepted. Application form required. Application form available on the grantmaker's web site.
   Send request by: Mail
   Deadline(s): June 30 for scholarships
   Additional information: Applicants for needs based scholarship are not eligible for merit based funding. Download scholarship application from web site. For medical care assistance to the needy contact foundation.
Program descriptions:
   Graduate Merit-Based Pan-Icarian Scholarships: This one-year, $2,000 award covers one year of graduate academic expenses to eligible individuals with a GPA of at least 3.0. Applicants must be of Icarian descent through at least one parent, enrolled full-time in an academically-accredited university graduate program (including law school, medical/dental school, and business school), and have membership (or have a parent who is a member) in the Pan-Icarian Brotherhood for one year immediately prior to the application year.
   Undergraduate Merit-Based Pan-Icarian Scholarship: This $1,500 award is available to applicants of Icarian descent (through at least one parent) who have maintained a minimum 3.0 cumulative GPA. Applicants must be enrolled full-time in an academically-accredited college or university and have, or have a parent who has, membership in the Pan-Icarian Brotherhood for at least a year prior to application.
   Undergraduate Need-Based Pan-Icarian Scholarships: This award provides $1,500 to cover school-based expenses for one academic year. Eligible students may receive the scholarship no more than twice provided that they remain enrolled

full-time, maintain a minimum 2.8 cumulative GPA, and comply with scholarship rules. Eligible applicants must be of Icarian descent through at least one parent, enrolled full-time at an academically-accredited college or university, and must have (or have a parent who has) membership of the Pan-Icarian Brotherhood for at least one year prior to the time of application.
EIN: 256085664

8019
Patton Scholarship Fund
(formerly Patton Scholarship Fund)
c/o Wells Fargo Bank, N.A.
101N. Independence Mall E MACY 1372-062
Philadelphia, PA   19106-2112

Foundation type: Independent foundation
Purpose: Scholarships to graduating high school seniors of Lake City High School, MN, who are members of the Honor Society.
Financial data: Year ended 12/31/2012. Assets, $181,468 (M); Expenditures, $11,790; Total giving, $8,000; Grants to individuals, totaling $8,000.
Fields of interest: Higher education.
Type of support: Support to graduates or students of specific schools.
Application information: Applications accepted.
  Initial approach: Letter
  Deadline(s): None
  Additional information: Applicant must possess outstanding characteristics of leadership and integrity.
EIN: 416059300

8020
PENCON Foundation
90 Lawton Ln.
Milton, PA   17847-9756
URL: http://www.pencon.org/foundation.html

Foundation type: Independent foundation
Purpose: Scholarships to seniors in a secondary school that are in good standing with the PA Energy Consortium and have a 2.0 GPA or better.
Financial data: Year ended 12/31/2012. Assets, $108,045 (M); Expenditures, $35,723; Total giving, $29,150; Grants to individuals, 38 grants totaling $29,150 (high: $1,500, low: $100).
Type of support: Scholarships—to individuals.
Application information: Applications accepted. Application form required.
  Deadline(s): Varies
  Applicants should submit the following:
    1) Financial information
    2) Letter(s) of recommendation
    3) Essay
  Additional information: Contact foundation for further information and application requirements.
EIN: 232992441

8021
William Penn Association Scholarship Foundation
709 Brighton Rd.
Pittsburgh, PA   15233-1805   (412) 231-2979
Contact: Barbara A. House, Chair.
E-mail: scholarship@williampennassociation.org;
URL: http://www.williampennassociation.org/members-scholarship.htm

Foundation type: Public charity

Purpose: Scholarships to students who have been accepted by or are attending an accredited college, university, or school of nursing. Applicants must be an individual Life Benefit Member of the William Penn Association for four years.
Publications: Application guidelines.
Financial data: Year ended 12/31/2011. Assets, $783,857 (M); Expenditures, $85,577; Total giving, $78,000; Grants to individuals, totaling $78,000.
Type of support: Undergraduate support.
Application information: Applications accepted. Application form required.
  Initial approach: Letter
  Applicants should submit the following:
    1) Transcripts
    2) SAT
    3) ACT
  Additional information: See web site for additional eligibility criteria.
EIN: 237059647

8022
Penn National Gaming Foundation
825 Berkshire Blvd., Ste. 200
Wyomissing, PA   19610-1247   (610) 378-8325
Contact: Amanda Garber, Exec. Dir.
FAX: (610) 375-7632; URL: http://www.pngaming.com/Community

Foundation type: Company-sponsored foundation
Purpose: Specific assistance to individuals with short-term financial assistance for emergency food, medical attention, shelter and transportation, and other immediate needs from Hurricane Gustav for affected employees of Penn National Gaming, Inc. and their dependents.
Publications: Application guidelines; Program policy statement.
Financial data: Year ended 12/31/2012. Assets, $114,345 (M); Expenditures, $480,761; Total giving, $474,485.
Fields of interest: Disasters, preparedness/services.
Type of support: Emergency funds; Employee-related welfare.
Application information: Applications accepted. Application form required. Application form available on the grantmaker's web site.
  Send request by: Mail, fax, or on-line
Company name: Penn National Gaming, Inc.
EIN: 203477997

8023
Pennsylvania Automotive Recycling Trade Society Scholarship Foundation
(formerly PARTS Scholarship Foundation)
P.O. Box 1307
Mechanicsburg, PA   17055-1307   (717) 236-5040
URL: http://www.parts.org

Foundation type: Independent foundation
Purpose: Scholarships to members, employees, and their families, of Pennsylvania Automotive Recycling Trade Society (PARTS) for undergraduate or technical school education.
Financial data: Year ended 09/30/2013. Assets, $65,251 (M); Expenditures, $11,237; Total giving, $3,500.
Type of support: Employee-related scholarships; Technical education support.
Application information: Applications accepted. Application form required.
  Deadline(s): Apr. 1

Company name: Pennsylvania Automotive Recycling Trade Society (PARTS)
EIN: 232361314

8024
Pennsylvania Bar Foundation
100 S. St.
Harrisburg, PA   17101-1210   (717) 213-2501
Contact: E. Marie Queen, Exec. Dir.
E-mail: info@pabarfoundation.org; Toll-free tel.: (888) 238-3036; URL: http://www.pabarfoundation.org

Foundation type: Public charity
Purpose: Scholarships to minority law students attending anyone of the eight accredited law schools in PA. Awards to an individual and an organization for legal services to the poor or disadvantaged. One-year loans to qualified attorneys for repayment of undergraduate and law school costs.
Publications: Application guidelines.
Financial data: Year ended 12/31/2012. Assets, $1,198,719 (M); Expenditures, $388,866; Total giving, $327,506; Grants to individuals, totaling $301,255.
Fields of interest: Higher education; Law school/education; Minorities.
Type of support: Scholarships—to individuals; Student loans—to individuals; Awards/prizes.
Application information: Applications accepted.
  Deadline(s): Oct. 14 for Loan Program, Dec. 3 for Scholarships, Mar. 30 for Goffman Awards
  Additional information: Application should include a resume, essay, transcript, financial need and a copy of voter registration card or PA driver's license as proof of residency for Scholarship. See web site for additional guidelines.
Program descriptions:
  James W. Stoudt Scholarship Fund: The fund provides four $3,000 scholarships, two of which are specifically designated to support minority law students, to candidates attending any one of the eight law schools presently serving PA. Applicant must have the potential for making a contribution to society and the legal profession either through anticipated legal field or other efforts as discussed in applicant's essay and evidenced by the applicant's recommendations. The scholarships are provided on an annual basis.
  Louis J. Goffman Awards: This program seeks to recognize and honor an individual and an organization whose commitments to pro-bono work have enhanced the delivery of legal services to Pennsylvania's poor or disadvantaged, making a critical difference in the lives of those in need of legal representation.
  Statewide Loan Assistance Program: This program is designed to help attorneys employed at IOLTA-funded legal services organizations better manage their law school debt, and to help IOLTA-funded legal aid organizations recruit and train the best and brightest attorneys for service in the public good. Loan applicants must be licensed to practice law in PA, or be permitted to practice law under Bar Admission Rule 311, have a valid PA Supreme Court identification number, be in good standing and practice law as an employee of an IOLTA-funded organization, and must have an annual salary of no more than $62,000. First-year program participants are eligible for a maximum loan of $3,500, second-year participants are eligible for up to $4,500 in loans, while third-year participants are eligible for a maximum loan of $6,000.
EIN: 232303925

8025
Pennsylvania Community Real Estate Corporation

1315 Walnut St., 3rd Fl.
Philadelphia, PA   19107-3612   (215) 940-3900

Foundation type: Public charity
Purpose: Financial assistance to low income individuals and families of Philadelphia, PA with food, rent, utility bill and other special needs.
Financial data: Year ended 06/30/2011. Assets, $1,637,658 (M); Expenditures, $7,023,819; Total giving, $5,155,122; Grants to individuals, totaling $5,155,122.
Fields of interest: Housing/shelter; Economically disadvantaged.
Type of support: Emergency funds.
Application information: Application form required.
  Additional information: Contact the agency for eligibility determination.
EIN: 251635266

8026
Pennsylvania Cystic Fibrosis, Inc.

c/o Robert C. Derr
P. O. Box 29
Mifflinburg, PA   17844-0029   (570) 374-2568
Contact: Betty Hollenbach, Pres.
FAX: (570) 374-2612; E-mail: bobderr@ptd.net;
Toll-free tel.: (800) 900-2790; URL: http://www.pacfi.org/

Foundation type: Public charity
Purpose: Grants to PA residents for the purchase of air conditioners, nebulizers, medications and other needs related to cystic fibrosis. Scholarships to PA residents with cystic fibrosis. Research grants for projects related to cystic fibrosis.
Publications: Application guidelines.
Financial data: Year ended 12/31/2011. Assets, $28,093 (M); Expenditures, $63,770; Total giving, $57,240.
Fields of interest: Cystic fibrosis; Cystic fibrosis research.
Type of support: Scholarships—to individuals; Awards/prizes.
Application information: Applications accepted. Application form required. Application form available on the grantmaker's web site.
  Initial approach: Letter or e-mail
  Send request by: Mail, fax or e-mail
  Copies of proposal: 1
  Deadline(s): Feb. 1
  Final notification: Applicants notified in 60 days
EIN: 232573569

8027
Pennsylvania Humanities Council

325 Chestnut St., Ste. 715
Philadelphia, PA   19106-2607   (215) 925-1005
Contact: Laurie Zierer, Exec. Dir.
FAX: (215) 925-3054;
E-mail: phc@pahumanities.org; Toll-free tel. (in PA only): (800) 462-0442; URL: http://www.pahumanities.org

Foundation type: Public charity
Purpose: Grants to PA media artists for works in film, video, radio, or slide projects which deal significantly with the humanities, particularly those of interest to PA residents. Also, awards for outstanding arts commentary.
Publications: Application guidelines; Annual report; Informational brochure; Newsletter.

Financial data: Year ended 10/31/2011. Assets, $1,282,118 (M); Expenditures, $1,446,547; Total giving, $216,541.
Fields of interest: Media/communications; Film/video; Radio; Art history; Arts, artist's services.
Type of support: Fellowships.
Application information:
  Initial approach: Letter or telephone
  Deadline(s): July 1 (large grants) and at least 12 weeks before project start date (for quick and small grants) for Humanities Grants
Program descriptions:
  Arts Commentary Awards: These awards support nonfiction work which educates the broad general public about the contemporary arts. They also promote arts commentators' endeavors to reach larger or newer audiences. Recognizing work in all media, the awards open to the full range of Pennsylvanians producing arts commentary - journalists, broadcast and electronic media professionals, documentary filmmakers, artists, scholars, arts educators, and non-profit professionals. The awards are a partnership between the Pennsylvania Humanities Council and Pennsylvania Council on the Arts (PCA) and is part of PCA's Individual Creative Artists Fellowship program. The program provides awards of $5,000 without matching requirements.
  Humanities Grants: The council provides grants for a variety of humanities projects that promote lifelong learning among Pennsylvanians from all walks of life. Grants work to expand access to the humanities by: funding innovative programming that reaches non-traditional audiences; support experiences that foster an enjoyment of learning; and create opportunities for Pennsylvanians to explore and discuss history, arts, literature, philosophy, and more - and particularly how the ideals integral to these fields both shape and are shaped by the human experience. Three types of grants are available: quick grants (of up to $500); small grants (of up to $3,000); and large grants (of up to $20,000 in outright funds and $16,000 in gift and matching funds). Grants are open to all nonprofits, including arts organizations, history groups, and museums and public libraries.
EIN: 232007911

8028
Pennsylvania Industrial Chemical Corporation-Clairton High School Scholarship Fund

c/o PNC Bank, N.A.
P.O. Box 609
Pittsburgh, PA   15230-9738   (412) 233-9200

Foundation type: Independent foundation
Purpose: Scholarships to graduates of Clarion High School, PA, to attend accredited colleges and universities, and business, nursing, technical, and trade schools.
Financial data: Year ended 06/30/2013. Assets, $504,387 (M); Expenditures, $25,301; Total giving, $19,000; Grant to an individual, 1 grant totaling $19,000.
Fields of interest: Vocational education; Higher education; Business school/education; Nursing school/education.
Type of support: Support to graduates or students of specific schools.
Application information:
  Deadline(s): Apr. 1
  Additional information: Contact fund for current application guidelines.
EIN: 256032785

8029
Pennsylvania Realtors Education Foundation

500 N. 12th St.
Lemoyne, PA   17043-1213
Contact: Brenda Florida, Secy.
FAX: (717) 561-8796; E-mail: info@parealtor.org;
Toll-free tel.: (800) 555-3390; URL: http://www.pref.biz

Foundation type: Public charity
Purpose: Scholarships and grants to individuals to further their education at accredited colleges or universities in PA, in the real estate area.
Publications: Application guidelines.
Fields of interest: Vocational education, post-secondary; Business school/education.
Type of support: Research; Scholarships—to individuals; Support to graduates or students of specific schools; Undergraduate support; Project support.
Application information: Applications accepted. Application form required. Application form available on the grantmaker's web site.
  Initial approach: Telephone
  Send request by: E-mail
  Copies of proposal: 1
  Deadline(s): Mar. 15 for PREF Student Grant-in-Aid Program; none for Educational Program Grants, Project Grants, or Mini-Grants
  Final notification: Applicants notified within 30 days for Educational Program Grants, and within 90 days for Mini-Grants and Project Grants
  Applicants should submit the following:
    1) Transcripts
    2) Letter(s) of recommendation
Program descriptions:
  Mini-Grants: Grants of up to $500 are available to individuals, organizations, and associations whose programs and projects intend to support and benefit the Pennsylvania real estate industry.
  PREF Student Grant-in-Aid Program: Two grants of $1,000 each are available annually to individuals who show interest in pursuing a career in the real estate brokerage business. Grants may be used to pursue an associate or bachelor degree in a real estate-related program at a Pennsylvania university or college. Eligible applicants must be enrolled in a two- or four-year real estate-related program at a Pennsylvania university or college, or document their intent to enroll in such a program within one year of the application deadline; preference will be given to licensed realtors in good standing, their children and spouses, and their employees.
  Project Grants: Grants of at least $500 are available to Pennsylvania-based individuals, organizations, and associations whose programs and projects are designed to benefit the Pennsylvania real estate industry.
  Scholarships: Annually presents up to 20 scholarships to deserving realtors to help them continue their education and professional development. Scholarships can be used for tuition to any realtor designation or broker course offered by a realtor association or their school, as well as reimbursement of lodging and travel expenses. Scholarships will be awarded for up to $500.
EIN: 237028389

8030
Pennsylvania State System of Higher Education Foundation, Inc.

(formerly Fund for the Advancement of the State System of Higher Education, Inc.)
2986 N. 2nd St.
Dixon Univ. Ctr.
Harrisburg, PA   17110-1201   (717) 720-4056
Contact: Jennifer S. Scipioni, Pres. and C.E.O.
FAX: (717) 720-7082;
E-mail: aianiero@thePAfoundation.org; E-mail For Jennifer S. Scipioni:
jscipioni@thePAfoundation.org; URL: http://www.thepafoundation.org

Foundation type: Public charity
Purpose: Scholarships to residents of PA for higher education.
Financial data: Year ended 06/30/2012. Assets, $2,191,995 (M); Expenditures, $530,016; Total giving, $325,577; Grants to individuals, totaling $273,967.
Type of support: Undergraduate support.
Application information: Application form required.
  Additional information: See web site for complete program listings.
EIN: 222686249

8031
H. Stanley & Marie Percival Scholarship Fund

c/o Wells Fargo Bank West, N.A.
101N. Independence Mall E MACY 1372-062
Philadelphia, PA   19106-2112   (406) 447-2050
Application address: c/o Principals of Capital & Helena High, Administration office, 55 S. Rodney, Helena,MT 59601

Foundation type: Independent foundation
Purpose: Scholarships to graduating seniors from Capital High School and Helena High School, MT.
Financial data: Year ended 03/31/2013. Assets, $201,257 (M); Expenditures, $14,321; Total giving, $10,500; Grants to individuals, 2 grants totaling $10,500 (high: $7,000, low: $3,500).
Type of support: Support to graduates or students of specific schools; Undergraduate support.
Application information: Applications accepted. Application form required.
  Initial approach: Letter
  Deadline(s): Apr. 1
  Additional information: Application must include statement of background, activities and achievements, goals and need for assistance.
EIN: 816052962

8032
John Perrone Memorial Scholarship Trust

614 Philadelphia St.
Indiana, PA   15701   (724) 842-0571

Foundation type: Independent foundation
Purpose: Scholarships to residents of Leechburg Area School District, PA for higher education.
Financial data: Year ended 12/31/2012. Assets, $156,639 (M); Expenditures, $7,075; Total giving, $4,800; Grants to individuals, 8 grants totaling $4,800 (high: $600, low: $600).
Fields of interest: Higher education.
Type of support: Scholarships—to individuals.
Application information: Applications accepted. Application form required.
  Deadline(s): Apr. 15
EIN: 256282445

8033
The Pew Charitable Trusts

1 Commerce Sq.
2005 Market St., Ste. 2800
Philadelphia, PA   19103-7077   (215) 575-9050
Contact: Rebecca W. Rimel, C.E.O. and Pres.
FAX: (215) 575-4939; E-mail: info@pewtrusts.org;
Additional address: 901 E St. N.W., Washington, DC 20004-2037; tel.: (202) 552-2000, fax: (202) 552-2299; URL: http://www.pewtrusts.org

Foundation type: Public charity
Purpose: Financial support to dance artists and presenters in the five-county region of metropolitan Philadelphia, PA, and to young scientists in the biomedical field.
Publications: Application guidelines; Grants list; Occasional report.
Financial data: Year ended 06/30/2012. Assets, $736,550,594 (M); Expenditures, $339,908,658; Total giving, $162,255,990.
Fields of interest: Dance; Ballet; Choreography; Theater; Biology/life sciences.
Type of support: Fellowships; Project support.
Application information: Applications accepted. Application form required.
  Initial approach: Letter or e-mail
  Additional information: See web site for individual programs and additional guidelines.
Program descriptions:
  Dance Advance: Awards of project-based grants made to individual dance artists/scholars (including individuals undertaking projects in dance scholarship or theater dance practitioners working in dance). Individual choreographers and dance artists may apply for grants up to $20,000. All applicants must reside in Bucks, Chester, Delaware, Montgomery, or Philadelphia County. Individual applicants must have U.S. citizenship or non-citizen employment eligibility.
  Pew Latin American Fellows Program in the Biomedical Sciences: This program provides support for young scientists from Latin America to receive postdoctoral training in the United States. The program gives these individuals an opportunity to further their scientific knowledge, promotes exchange and collaboration between investigators in the U.S. and Latin America, and advances research in Latin America. The fellowship provides a $30,000 salary stipend in each of two years and an additional $35,000 payment when the Fellow confirms plans to return to Latin America within a maximum of four years from the start date of the grant. The $35,000 portion of the award is for the purchase of supplies and equipment to help establish his/her independent laboratory upon the Fellow's return to Latin America. At the time of application, candidates are not required to have a commitment of a position and laboratory space after the fellowship. However, applicants must submit a written statement of their intent to return to Latin America to continue their research career after the fellowship. To apply, potential candidates need to identify and obtain a commitment from the head of a laboratory in the United States for a postdoctoral position. See foundation web site for complete information, or contact Anita Pepper, Ph.D., Prog. Mgr., tel.: (215) 531-8135; e-mail: apepper@pewtrusts.org.
  Pew Scholars Program in the Biomedical Sciences: This program provides funding to young investigators of outstanding promise in science relevant to the advancement of human health. The program makes grants to selected academic institutions to support the independent research of outstanding individuals who are in their first few years of their appointment at the assistant professor level.
EIN: 562307147

8034
Philadelphia Bar Foundation

1101 Market St., 11th Fl.
Philadelphia, PA   19107-2934   (215) 238-6337
Contact: Gene Sirni, Exec. Dir.
FAX: (215) 238-1159;
E-mail: mmingey@philabar.org; URL: http://www.philadelphiabar.org/page/BarFoundation?appNum=1&wosid=Egftxdg6G4E2vSfOIOGa3M

Foundation type: Public charity
Purpose: Awards and fellowships for the promotion of public interest legal service as a career choice for students and young lawyers.
Publications: Application guidelines; Grants list; Informational brochure.
Financial data: Year ended 12/31/2011. Assets, $6,337,769 (M); Expenditures, $1,173,246; Total giving, $703,250.
Fields of interest: Law school/education.
Type of support: Fellowships; Awards/prizes.
Application information: Applications accepted. Application form required.
  Send request by: Mail
  Deadline(s): Sept. for Shuster Fellowship Program and Foundation Award, Mar. 2 for Judge William M. Marutani Fellowship
  Additional information: See web site for additional guidelines.
Program descriptions:
  Judge William M. Marutani Fellowship: Established in conjunction with the Asian American Bar Association of the Delaware Valley, this fellowship is offered to Asian Pacific American first-year law students at Dickinson School of Law, Rutgers-Camden University School of Law, Temple University James E. Beasley School of Law, University of Pennsylvania School of Law, Villanova University School of Law, Drexel University College of Law, and Widener University School of Law. The fellowship will provide a stipend for a first-year Asian Pacific American law student to subsidize a summer internship position with a non-profit public interest organization or with a federal, state, or municipal government entity (including the judiciary) in the greater Philadelphia area. Each finalist will be selected based upon law school transcripts, past and present work and community service experience, prior accomplishments and awards, character, and an essay. Finalists will be interviewed by a fellowship selection committee. The fellowship recipient will receive a stipend not to exceed $5,000.
  Morris M. Shuster Fellowship: Two fellowships will be awarded to eligible public interest attorneys who have five or more years of work experience, and one additional fellowship will be awarded to an eligible public interest attorney with three or more years of work experience. To be eligible, an applicant must be a full-time lawyer at a qualifying organization who has completed the requisite number of years of work experience at one or more nonprofit organizations principally involved in the delivery of legal services to clients (regardless of geography). An applicant is financially eligible upon demonstration that he or she has an annual student loan repayment obligation that equals or exceeds $5,000 or ten percent of his or her annual gross income, whichever is less. Grants will be awarded for up to $5,000.
  Samuel T. Gomez Award: This award is designed to encourage and recognize outstanding and exemplary community service among law students, regardless of ethnicity by active participation in a legal services program, advocacy on an individual and/or class action basis seeking equal access to medical care, housing, employment, and public assistance, consumer issues, utility issues and INS issues, advocacy on behalf of battered spouses

and other victims of violence and advocacy on behalf of the disabled and patient's rights. The award alternates between Pennsylvania Law School and Temple University School of Law.
EIN: 231660797

8035
Philadelphia College Opportunity Resources for Education
1628 JFK Blvd., Ste. 1975
8 Penn Ctr.
Philadelphia, PA   19103   (215) 507-1690
FAX: (215) 507-1689;
E-mail: scholarship@corephilly.org; URL: http://www.corephilly.org

Foundation type: Public charity
Purpose: Scholarships and college prep assistance to high school students who are residents of Philadelphia, PA to attend select PA colleges and universities.
Publications: Application guidelines.
Financial data: Year ended 12/31/2011. Assets, $345,117 (M); Expenditures, $1,277,538.
Fields of interest: Higher education.
Type of support: Support to graduates or students of specific schools.
Application information: Applications accepted. Application form required. Application form available on the grantmaker's web site.
   Deadline(s): June 30
   Additional information: See web site for additional guidelines and participating colleges or universities.
Program description:
   Scholarships: The organization offers scholarships of up to $2,000 to Philadelphia-area high school seniors to help pay first-year college expenses (including living expenses and books). Eligible applicants must: be a graduate of a school district of a Philadelphia-area public, charter, archdiocese, or private high school; provide proof of residency within the city of Philadelphia; and plan to pursue an associate's or bachelor's degree at a participating college or university.
EIN: 230355320

8036
The Philadelphia Education Fund
1709 Benjamin Franklin Pkwy., Ste. 700
Philadelphia, PA   19103-1218   (215) 665-1400
Contact: Darren Spielman, Pres. and C.E.O.; for Scholarships: Vaneeda Days, Scholarship Coord.
E-mail for Vaneeda Days: vdays@philaedfund.org
FAX: (215) 864-2494;
E-mail: info@philaedfund.org; E-mail For Darren Spielman: dspielman@philaedfund.org;
URL: http://www.philaedfund.org/

Foundation type: Public charity
Purpose: Scholarships to underserved youth in public neighborhood high schools in the Philadelphia, PA area.
Publications: Application guidelines.
Financial data: Year ended 06/30/2012. Assets, $8,944,982 (M); Expenditures, $6,192,405; Total giving, $1,071,053; Grants to individuals, totaling $1,071,053.
Fields of interest: Higher education.
Type of support: Scholarships—to individuals; Residencies.
Application information: Application form required. Application form available on the grantmaker's web site.
   Deadline(s): June 1 for Last Dollar Scholarship
   Applicants should submit the following:

1) Transcripts
2) SAR
3) Financial information
Additional information: Application must also include financial aid award letter from the college/university attending, written verification of completed community service hours.
Program descriptions:
   Philadelphia Scholars - Last Dollar Scholarship Program: Awarded in conjunction with the College Access Program, this program promotes college access and success among Philadelphia's public high school students by providing scholarships for undergraduate study. Scholarships, generally ranging between $200 and $4,000, are awarded when a family's expected family contribution and financial aid package total are less than the cost of attendance, resulting in unmet financial need. Eligible applicants must attend an eligible high school (Benjamin Franklin High School, Thomas A. Edison High School, Thomas Fitzsimons High School, Germantown High School, Simon Gratz High School, Kensington Creative and Performing Arts High School, Kensington International Business and Finance High School, Lankenau High School, E. Washington Rhodes High School, Paul Robeson High School, Roxborough High School, William L. Sayre High School, Strawberry Mansion High School, University City High School, Robert Vaux High School, West Philadelphia High School, Kensington Culinary Arts High School, Northeast High School, Olney East High School, Olney West High School, and Parkway West High School).
   Philadelphia Teacher Residency: This program provides a teacher preparation opportunity for science, technology, engineering, and math (STEM) professionals and recent graduates who want to teach math and science in Philadelphia's high-need middle and high schools. For a full school year, program participants will engage in teaching opportunities with experienced teachers in Philadelphia secondary school classrooms, and will also have the opportunity to take coursework at the University of Pennsylvania Graduate School of Education to earn both a master's degree and Pennsylvania teacher certification. In return, residents commit to teaching in Philadelphia public schools for at least three years after the residency of preparation. Residents receive ongoing professional development activities and networking opportunities, as well as eligibility for local, state, and national loans. Eligible applicants must have a bachelor's degree in a STEM subject, a cumulative undergraduate GPA of at least 3.0, and U.S. citizenship or permanent resident status.
EIN: 222567982

8037
The Philadelphia Foundation
1234 Market St., Ste. 1800
Philadelphia, PA   19107-3794   (215) 563-6417
Contact: R. Andrew Swinney, Pres.; For grants: Alyson Miksitz, Prog. Asst., Philanthropic Svcs.
FAX: (215) 563-6882;
E-mail: almiksitz@philafound.org; URL: http://www.philafound.org

Foundation type: Community foundation
Purpose: Scholarships and grants to individuals residing in Philadelphia, PA.
Publications: Application guidelines; Newsletter.
Financial data: Year ended 12/31/2012. Assets, $334,451,741 (M); Expenditures, $30,812,696; Total giving, $24,679,393.
Fields of interest: Higher education; Nursing school/education.

Type of support: Grants to individuals; Scholarships—to individuals.
Application information: Applications accepted. Application form required. Application form available on the grantmaker's web site.
   Initial approach: Application
   Send request by: Mail
   Deadline(s): Varies
   Additional information: The foundation administers several scholarships that support various educational opportunities for applicants of all ages. See web site for complete scholarship listing and application guidelines.
EIN: 231581832

8038
Philadelphia Futures
(formerly White-Williams Scholars)
215 S. Broad St., 7 Fl.
Philadelphia, PA   19107-5318   (215) 790-1666
Contact: Amy T. Holdsman, Exec. Dir.
FAX: (215) 790-1888; E-mail: info@wwscholars.org; URL: http://www.philadelphiafutures.org/

Foundation type: Public charity
Purpose: Grants to economically disadvantaged Philadelphia, PA, public high school students for school-related expenses such as supplies, books, transportation and food.
Publications: Annual report; Newsletter.
Financial data: Year ended 06/30/2011. Assets, $6,615,955 (M); Expenditures, $1,442,924; Total giving, $321,445; Grants to individuals, totaling $321,445.
Fields of interest: Education.
Type of support: Scholarships—to individuals; Precollege support.
Application information: Applications accepted. Application form required. Application form available on the grantmaker's web site.
   Initial approach: Application
   Send request by: Mail or fax
   Copies of proposal: 1
   Deadline(s): None
   Applicants should submit the following:
1) Transcripts
2) GPA
3) Financial information
   Additional information: Application should include a copy of recent grades and proof of family income.
EIN: 231365983

8039
Philadelphia Nonprofit Advertising Agency
5070 Parkside Ave.
Philadelphia, PA   19131-4747

Foundation type: Independent foundation
Purpose: Scholarships to residents of the Philadelphia, PA metropolitan area.
Financial data: Year ended 06/30/2013. Assets, $2,806,768 (M); Expenditures, $99,626; Total giving, $21,025.
Type of support: Undergraduate support.
Application information: Applications not accepted.
   Additional information: Unsolicited requests for funds not considered.
EIN: 232944224

8040
V. E. & Betty Phillips Scholarship Fund
c/o PNC Bank, N.A.
P.O. Box 609
Pittsburgh, PA 15230-9738   (814) 665-8297
Contact: Michael L. Stahlman
Application address: Corey Area High, 534 E.
Pleasant St., Corry, PA 16407; URL: http://
www.pnc.com

Foundation type: Independent foundation
Purpose: Scholarships to graduates of Corry Area
High School, PA.
Financial data: Year ended 04/30/2013. Assets,
$906,069 (M); Expenditures, $47,961; Total
giving, $33,500.
Type of support: Support to graduates or students
of specific schools; Undergraduate support.
Application information: Application form required.
  Deadline(s): Mar. 1
EIN: 237418046

8041
Phoenixville Community Health Foundation
821 Gay St.
Phoenixville, PA 19460-4410   (610) 917-9890
Contact: Louis J. Beccaria, C.E.O. and Pres.
FAX: (610) 917-9861; E-mail: pchf1@pchf1.org;
URL: http://www.pchf1.org/

Foundation type: Independent foundation
Purpose: Undergraduate scholarships to students
from the greater 19 Township/Borough
Phoenixville, PA, area who plan to pursue careers in
health care.
Publications: Application guidelines; Annual report;
Financial statement; Grants list; Informational
brochure (including application guidelines);
Newsletter; Occasional report; Program policy
statement.
Financial data: Year ended 06/30/2013. Assets,
$50,203,434 (M); Expenditures, $2,390,260;
Total giving, $1,669,118; Grants to individuals,
24 grants totaling $45,000 (high: $3,000, low:
$1,000).
Fields of interest: Health sciences school/
education.
Type of support: Undergraduate support.
Application information: Applications accepted.
Application form required. Application form
available on the grantmaker's web site. Interview
required.
  Initial approach: Application
  Send request by: Mail or fax
  Copies of proposal: 1
  Deadline(s): Apr.
  Final notification: Recipients notified in one
  month
  Applicants should submit the following:
    1) Transcripts
    2) GPA
    3) Financial information
    4) Essay
    5) Curriculum vitae
EIN: 232912035

8042
The Physicians Aid Association of the Delaware Valley
(formerly Aid Association of the Phila County
Medical Society)
684 Ridge Rd.
Spring City, PA 19475-3223
Application address: c/o Sharon Stoeckert, MSW,
9417 Stenton Ave., Erdenheim, PA 19038,
tel.: (215) 499-3240

Foundation type: Independent foundation
Purpose: Financial assistance to needy physicians
and their families who practice in the Philadelphia,
PA, and NJ area and hold an M.D. or D.O. degree.
Financial data: Year ended 12/31/2011. Assets,
$7,604,210 (M); Expenditures, $354,265; Total
giving, $285,728; Grants to individuals, 14 grants
totaling $72,728 (high: $24,000, low: $53).
Fields of interest: Health care; Economically
disadvantaged.
Type of support: Grants for special needs.
Application information: Applications accepted.
EIN: 236266619

8043
Elva and Herbert Pickle Memorial Scholarship Fund
c/o Wells Fargo Bank, N.A.
101 N. Independence Mall E. MACY 1372-062
Philadelphia, PA 19106-2112   (707) 743-2101
Contact: Brent Russert
Application address: C/o. Potter Valley High, P. O.
Box 219, Potter Valley,CA 95469, Tel.: (707)
743-2101

Foundation type: Independent foundation
Purpose: Scholarships to graduates of Potter Valley
High School, CA, to attend accredited junior
colleges, universities, or trade schools.
Financial data: Year ended 03/31/2013. Assets,
$445,757 (M); Expenditures, $12,643; Total
giving, $4,000; Grants to individuals, 2 grants
totaling $4,000 (high: $2,000, low: $2,000).
Fields of interest: Vocational education; College;
University.
Type of support: Support to graduates or students
of specific schools.
Application information: Application form required.
  Deadline(s): None
  Applicants should submit the following:
    1) Letter(s) of recommendation
    2) Essay
  Additional information: Contact foundation for
  application guidelines.
EIN: 946616460

8044
Pinnacle Health Foundation
409 S. 2nd St.
P.O. Box 8700
Harrisburg, PA 17105-8700   (717) 231-8245
Contact: Michael A. Young, Pres. and C.E.O.
URL: http://www.pinnaclehealth.org/

Foundation type: Public charity
Purpose: Financial assistance to employees of
Pinnacle Health System, PA pursuing a nursing
education.
Financial data: Year ended 06/30/2012. Assets,
$58,748,444 (M); Expenditures, $1,877,101;
Total giving, $888,168; Grants to individuals,
totaling $65,745.
Fields of interest: Nursing school/education.
Type of support: Employee-related scholarships;
Grants for special needs.

Application information: Applications accepted.
  Additional information: Recipients are selected
  on various criteria, including GPA and program
  study. the Pinnacle Health System
  department of education and development
  select the recipient annually. The program
  was established to recognize the excellence
  of an internal medicine or family practice
  resident. Applicants are nominated by
  members of the nursing staff.
EIN: 222691718

8045
Roy W. Piper Charitable Trust
P.O. Box 460
Tunkhannock, PA 18657-0460   (717) 836-5454
Contact: William A. Petty, Mgr.

Foundation type: Independent foundation
Purpose: Scholarships to individuals who are
members of a family with a combined household
income of less than $75,000, and who have a
cumulative "C" average through the first term of the
student's senior year in high school. Students who
reside in Lackawanna and Luzerne counties in WY
will have preference.
Financial data: Year ended 12/31/2011. Assets,
$14,442,903 (M); Expenditures, $1,122,116;
Total giving, $439,865; Grants to individuals, 46
grants totaling $372,365 (high: $22,000, low:
$1,041).
Fields of interest: Higher education.
Type of support: Scholarships—to individuals.
Application information: Applications accepted.
  Deadline(s): Mar. 15
  Applicants should submit the following:
    1) Financial information
    2) GPA
  Additional information: Application should also
  include a description of intent to matriculate
  at a college or university. Finalists will be
  required to provide signed income tax returns
  for two fiscal years immediately preceding the
  date of application from each applicant and
  applicant's parent or guardian.
EIN: 207487500

8046
Greater Pittsburgh Arts Council
(formerly ProArts, also known as GPAC)
810 Penn Ave., Ste. 200
Pittsburgh, PA 15222-3401   (412) 391-2060
Contact: Mitch Swain, C.E.O.
FAX: (412) 394-4280;
E-mail: info@pittsburghartscouncil.org; E-Mail for
Mitch Swain: mswain@pittsburghartscouncil.org;
URL: http://www.pittsburghartscouncil.org/

Foundation type: Public charity
Purpose: Grants to individual artists and artist
managers in the Pittsburgh, PA, area.
Publications: Application guidelines; Newsletter.
Financial data: Year ended 06/30/2012. Assets,
$1,746,626 (M); Expenditures, $1,368,944; Total
giving, $277,264; Grants to individuals, totaling
$30,000.
Fields of interest: Arts.
Type of support: Grants to individuals.
Application information: Applications accepted.
Application form required. Application form
available on the grantmaker's web site.
  Initial approach: Letter
  Deadline(s): Mar. 15, July 16, Sept. 1, and Dec.
  1 for Artist Opportunity Grants
  Applicants should submit the following:
    1) SASE

2) Work samples
3) Resume
Additional information: See web site for complete application guidelines.

Program descriptions:

Artist Opportunity Grants: Grants, ranging from $250 to $1,500, are available to Pittsburgh-based individual artists to support expenses related to specific, extraordinary opportunities that have the potential to significantly impact their work and professional development. Eligible applicants must: be 18 years of age or older; be a full-time resident of Allegheny, Armstrong, Beaver, Butler, Fayette, Greene, Indiana, Mercer, Lawrence, Somerset, Venango, Washington, or Westmoreland counties for at least one year immediately prior to the application deadline; and have a record of artistic accomplishment that can be document (including evidence of work that has been publicly performed, exhibited, published, critically reviewed, etc.)

PA Partners in the Arts Program: This program provides grants of up to $3,000 for individual artists, associations, and nonprofit organizations to make arts programs available to every Pennsylvania resident, especially those from underserved communities and regions. Eligible programs for funding include performances, exhibits, readings, and other presentations in any genre (including, but not limited to, visual art, dance, theater, and music). Applicants must be based in Allegheny, Beaver, Butler, Fayette, Green, Lawrence, or Washington counties.
EIN: 251737717

8047
Pittsburgh Center for the Arts, Inc.
477 Melwood Ave.
Pittsburgh, PA   15213-1135   (412) 681-5449
Contact: For Conduit/Fiscal Sponsor Program: Amy Solomon, Dir. Artist Services
FAX: (412) 681-5503; URL: http://pittsburgharts.org/

Foundation type: Public charity
Purpose: Funding and support to artists for the production of projects in media-based disciplines.
Publications: Newsletter.
Financial data: Year ended 06/30/2012. Assets, $6,453,178 (M); Expenditures, $4,344,369.
Fields of interest: Media/communications; Film/video; Photography; Arts, artist's services.
Type of support: Fellowships; Fiscal agent/sponsor.
Application information: Applications accepted.
    Deadline(s): 1st business day of Aug. in alternating years for fellowships; for others contact the organization for application guidelines and deadlines

Program descriptions:

Conduit Program/Fiscal Sponsorship: The program provides artist projects in media-based disciplines with the ability to apply for funding and other resources available only to non-profit organizations. The accepted projects will receive the turnover after a five percent deduction by Pittsburgh Filmmakers.

Folk Arts Apprenticeships: The apprenticeships are offered annually and support artists who practice the traditional arts found in communities across the commonwealth. The funds may be used to 1) Compensate a Master's time; 2) Compensate travel for a Master or Apprentice; or 3) Purchase supplies or film/tape for documentation. The apprentice must be a resident of Pennsylvania, and

preference is given to apprenticeships with a Pennsylvanian master.
EIN: 251229210

8048
The Pittsburgh Foundation
5 PPG Pl., Ste. 250
Pittsburgh, PA   15222-5414   (412) 391-5122
Contact: For grant applications: Jeanne Pearlman, V.P., Prog. and Policy; For scholarships: Deborah Turner, Scholarship Coord.
Scholarship application information, tel.: (412) 394-2649, e-mail: turnerD@pghfdn.org
FAX: (412) 391-7259; E-mail: email@pghfdn.org; URL: http://www.pittsburghfoundation.org

Foundation type: Community foundation
Purpose: Scholarships, awards, and assistance to residents of Pittsburgh and Allegheny County, PA.
Publications: Application guidelines; Annual report; Informational brochure (including application guidelines); Newsletter.
Financial data: Year ended 12/31/2012. Assets, $905,146,642 (M); Expenditures, $57,434,904; Total giving, $43,550,025. Grants to individuals amount not specified.
Fields of interest: Education.
Type of support: Internship funds; Research; Scholarships—to individuals; Camperships.
Application information: Applications accepted. Application form required.
    Initial approach: E-mail or telephone
    Deadline(s): Varies
    Additional information: Each scholarship has its own set of unique eligibility requirements. See web site for additional information for scholarships, awards and assistance.

Program descriptions:

Charles E. Kaufman Award: Honors substantial contributions to science for both the betterment and understanding of human life.

Eben Demarest Award: Supporting the work of independent creative artists and archeologists from across the United States. Each year the trust awards one grant in the amount of $13,000 to an artist or archeologist to support creative and intellectual independence.

Pittsburgh Region Artists Program: Provides resources to professional artists for the breadth of the creative process, from concept to completion.

Scholarships: Scholarship funds benefit students throughout the United States. Most frequently, donors establish funds that assist high school seniors seeking postsecondary education. There are, however, funds that focus on college, graduate or technical school students who are pursuing specific areas of interest. Donors may choose the type of assistance they would like to provide, whether to help pay tuition or purchase school-related items such as books and computers. Some funds have been created to assist elementary school children in obtaining music lessons.
EIN: 250965466

8049
Pittsburgh Glass Center, Inc.
5472 Penn Ave.
Pittsburgh, PA   15206   (412) 365-2145
FAX: (412) 365-2140;
E-mail: pgcinfo@pittsburghglasscenter.org; Toll-free tel.: (866) 742-4527; URL: http://www.pittsburghglasscenter.org

Foundation type: Public charity

Purpose: Residencies for artists working both within and without the glass medium, primarily in PA.
Publications: Informational brochure.
Financial data: Year ended 12/31/2011. Assets, $2,347,911 (M); Expenditures, $1,067,460.
Fields of interest: Arts.
Type of support: Residencies.
Application information: Application form required. Application form available on the grantmaker's web site.
    Initial approach: Letter, telephone, or e-mail.
    Deadline(s): Oct. 1
    Additional information: See foundation's web site for application guidelines.
EIN: 251814656

8050
Elsie L. Plank Trust f/b/o C. Plank Scholarship Trust
c/o BNY Mellon, N.A.
P.O. Box 185
Pittsburgh, PA   15230-0185

Foundation type: Independent foundation
Purpose: Scholarships to graduates of Conestoga Valley High School, for higher education at Frank and Marshall College, PA.
Financial data: Year ended 12/31/2011. Assets, $92,915 (M); Expenditures, $6,149; Total giving, $4,550.
Fields of interest: Higher education.
Type of support: Support to graduates or students of specific schools; Undergraduate support.
Application information: Application form required.
    Deadline(s): Aug. 1
EIN: 236241620

8051
PNC Bank Memorial Foundation
(formerly PNC Bank Memorial Foundation)
c/o PNC Bank
620 Liberty Ave., 10th Fl.
Pittsburgh, PA   15222-2705   (412) 762-3502
Contact: R. Bruce Bickel

Foundation type: Company-sponsored foundation
Purpose: Scholarships only to children of current or deceased employees of PNC Bank, N.A.
Financial data: Year ended 12/31/2012. Assets, $250,205 (M); Expenditures, $11,047; Total giving, $7,200.
Type of support: Employee-related scholarships.
Application information: Application form required.
    Deadline(s): Apr. 30
    Additional information: Application address: PNC Charitable Trust Grant Review C, One PNC Plaza, 249 5th Ave., 20th fl., Pittsburgh, PA 15222, tel.: (412) 762-3413; See web site for application submission guidelines and deadlines.
Company name: PNC Bank, N.A.
EIN: 256487950

8052
The Podiatry Foundation of Pittsburgh
1601 Union Ave., Ste. B
Natrona Heights, PA   15065-2133   (724) 226-0544
Contact: Nicki Nigro, C.E.O. and Treas.
FAX: (724) 226-2172;
E-mail: nickinigro@comcast.net; URL: http://www.podiatryplace.org

Foundation type: Independent foundation

Purpose: Scholarships to podiatry students in PA to further their studies.
Financial data: Year ended 06/30/2013. Assets, $1,270,115 (M); Expenditures, $175,754; Total giving, $124,835; Grants to individuals, 6 grants totaling $46,000 (high: $10,000, low: $1,000).
Fields of interest: Education; Podiatry.
Type of support: Scholarships—to individuals.
Application information: Applications accepted. Application form required. Application form available on the grantmaker's web site.
  Initial approach: Letter
  Copies of proposal: 1
  Deadline(s): Nov. 1
  Applicants should submit the following:
    1) Curriculum vitae
    2) Essay
  Additional information: Students must be studying at podiatric medical schools.
EIN: 251024331

8053

Polish American Board of Education of Berks County, PA

159 Texter Mountain Rd.
Wernersville, PA   19565   (610) 693-9792
Contact: Ann Savitski, Treas.

Foundation type: Independent foundation
Purpose: Scholarships only to high school students who have at least 25 percent Polish heritage, and who are residents of Berks County, PA.
Financial data: Year ended 12/31/2011. Assets, $279,907 (M); Expenditures, $34,427; Total giving, $30,250.
Fields of interest: Higher education.
International interests: Poland.
Type of support: Undergraduate support.
Application information: Application form required.
  Initial approach: Letter
  Deadline(s): None
  Additional information: Application available from Berks County high school offices.
EIN: 232061281

8054

Howard & Edna Postles Scholarship Fund

c/o PNC Bank, N.A.
1600 Market St.
Philadelphia, PA   19103-7240

Foundation type: Independent foundation
Purpose: Scholarships to financially needy high school seniors who are in the top ten percent of their class and who live within a 15-mile radius of Milford, DE, for attendance at any postsecondary institution.
Financial data: Year ended 12/31/2013. Assets, $1,055,498 (M); Expenditures, $70,472; Total giving, $47,000; Grants to individuals, 28 grants totaling $47,000 (high: $3,000, low: $500).
Fields of interest: Vocational education.
Type of support: Undergraduate support.
Application information: Application form required.
  Copies of proposal: 6
  Deadline(s): None
  Applicants should submit the following:
    1) Transcripts
    2) Letter(s) of recommendation
  Additional information: Selection is based on academic performance, extracurricular activities, community service, and financial need.
EIN: 516169946

8055

Wilbur E. Postles Scholarship Fund

c/o PNC Bank, N.A.
1600 Market St., Tax Dept.
Philadelphia, PA   19103-7240
Contact: Aruna Pappu
Application address: c/o PNC Bank, N.A., 222 Delaware Ave., 16th Fl., Wilmington, DE 19801-1637

Foundation type: Independent foundation
Purpose: Scholarships to financially needy students who are residents of Delaware for at least four years to attend college, professional or technical school.
Financial data: Year ended 12/31/2012. Assets, $4,889,211 (M); Expenditures, $343,748; Total giving, $262,942.
Fields of interest: Vocational education; Higher education.
Type of support: Scholarships—to individuals.
Application information: Application form required.
  Deadline(s): May
  Applicants should submit the following:
    1) Letter(s) of recommendation
    2) FAFSA
    3) SAT
    4) Transcripts
  Additional information: The applicant must also include a letter from a parent, guardian, or close friend substantiating the need for financial assistance; a letter indicating the reasons for the selected major and plans for the future; and a copy of the applicant's current driver's license.
EIN: 516010602

8056

Pottstown Symphony Orchestra

P.O. Box 675
Pottstown, PA   19464-0675   (610) 327-3614
Contact: Kevin Wood, Exec. Dir.
Application address for the Kathryn E. MacPhail Young Artist Competition: c/o Kathy Williams, 265 Old State Rd., Royersford, PA 19468; Tel.: (610) 948-4950
E-mail: executivedirector@pottstownsymphony.org;
URL: http://www.pottstownsymphony.org

Foundation type: Public charity
Purpose: Prizes to winners of the Kathryn E. MacPhail Young Artist Competition for musicians, and an opportunity to perform in concert with the Pottstown Symphony.
Publications: Application guidelines.
Fields of interest: Orchestras.
Type of support: Awards/prizes.
Application information: Applications accepted. Application form required. Application form available on the grantmaker's web site.
  Initial approach: Letter
  Deadline(s): Jan. 20
  Additional information: Applications must include a cassette/CD recording of the work to be performed at the audition, plus a $50 application fee.
EIN: 237050084

8057

Howard A. Power Scholarship Fund

c/o PNC Bank, N.A.
620 Liberty Ave. 10th Fl.
Pittsburgh, PA   15222

Foundation type: Independent foundation

Purpose: Scholarships to students attending the University of Pittsburgh School of Medicine.
Financial data: Year ended 12/31/2012. Assets, $648,759 (M); Expenditures, $37,901; Total giving, $29,800; Grants to individuals, 5 grants totaling $29,800 (high: $6,000, low: $5,800).
Fields of interest: Medical school/education.
Type of support: Support to graduates or students of specific schools; Graduate support.
Application information: Applications not accepted.
  Additional information: Contributes only to preselected individuals unsolicited requests for funds not considered or acknowledged.
EIN: 256234582

8058

PPG Industries Foundation

1 PPG Pl., Ste. 7E
Pittsburgh, PA   15272-0001
Contact: Sue Sloan, Exec. Dir.
E-mail: foundation@ppg.com; URL: http://www.ppg.com/en/ppgfoundation/Pages/default.aspx

Foundation type: Company-sponsored foundation
Purpose: Scholarships to outstanding students located in areas of major PPG facilities. Scholarships also to outstanding minorities planning to study chemistry or chemical engineering, as well as scholarships to children of employees of PPG. The program is administered by the National Merit Scholarship Corporation.
Publications: Application guidelines; Annual report (including application guidelines); Financial statement.
Financial data: Year ended 12/31/2012. Assets, $9,337,618 (M); Expenditures, $5,255,340; Total giving, $4,963,751.
Fields of interest: Alliance/advocacy; Chemistry; Engineering/technology; Engineering; Minorities.
Type of support: Employee-related scholarships; Undergraduate support.
Application information:
  Initial approach: Letter
Company name: PPG Industries, Inc.
EIN: 256037790

8059

Torrence Prescott Trust

c/o S&T Wealth Mgmt.
800 Philadelphia St.
Indiana, PA   15701-2605

Foundation type: Independent foundation
Purpose: Scholarships to students of PA for attendance at colleges or universities in PA.
Financial data: Year ended 12/31/2012. Assets, $77,672 (M); Expenditures, $4,150; Total giving, $3,318; Grants to individuals, 3 grants totaling $3,318 (high: $1,493, low: $332).
Fields of interest: Higher education.
Type of support: Scholarships—to individuals.
Application information: Unsolicited requests for funds not considered or acknowledged.
EIN: 237204309

8060

The Presser Foundation

385 Lancaster Ave., No. 205
Haverford, PA   19041-1576   (610) 658-9030
Contact: Mariel Frank, Exec. Dir.
E-mail: mfrank@presserfoundation.org;
URL: http://www.presserfoundation.org

Foundation type: Independent foundation
Purpose: Grants for undergraduate and graduate students of music for attendance at accredited institutions in the U.S. Financial relief to worthy teachers of music in distress.
Publications: Application guidelines.
Financial data: Year ended 06/30/2013. Assets, $61,712,301 (M); Expenditures, $2,965,871; Total giving, $2,707,934; Grants to individuals, totaling $1,092,800.
Fields of interest: Music.
Type of support: Undergraduate support; Grants for special needs.
Application information: Applications accepted. Application form required.
> *Deadline(s):* See foundation web site for current deadlines
> *Additional information:* The participating institutions select the students to receive the awards. The foundation does not give awards directly to individuals. See web site for additional information. Faxed or e-mailed applications are not considered.

EIN: 232164013

8061
Pressley Ridge Foundation
5500 Corporate Dr., Ste. 400
Pittsburgh, PA   15237-5848   (412) 872-9400
FAX: (417) 872-9478; URL: http://www.pressleyridge.org

Foundation type: Public charity
Purpose: Scholarships and financial support to troubled and developmentally-challenged children in the Pressley Ridge program.
Financial data: Year ended 06/30/2012. Assets, $39,745,077 (M); Expenditures, $1,391,889; Total giving, $861,214; Grants to individuals, totaling $68,655.
Fields of interest: Foster care.
Type of support: Scholarships—to individuals; Grants for special needs.
Application information: Contact foundation for eligibility requirements.
EIN: 251653944

8062
Frank W. Preston Memorial Scholarship Trust
125 Mountain Laurel Dr.
Butler, PA   16001
Contact: A. Robert Shott, Pres.

Foundation type: Operating foundation
Purpose: Scholarships to residents of Butler County, PA.
Financial data: Year ended 12/31/2011. Assets, $226,173 (M); Expenditures, $15,067; Total giving, $15,000; Grants to individuals, 5 grants totaling $15,000 (high: $3,000, low: $3,000).
Type of support: Undergraduate support.
Application information:
> *Initial approach:* Letter
> *Deadline(s):* Apr. 15

EIN: 251679290

8063
Print & Graphics Scholarship Foundation
200 Deer Run Rd.
Sewickley, PA   15143-2324   (412) 741-6860

Foundation type: Public charity
Purpose: Scholarships to students in accredited graphic arts courses.

Financial data: Year ended 12/31/2011. Assets, $7,061,923 (M); Expenditures, $520,479; Total giving, $404,900; Grants to individuals, totaling $404,900.
Fields of interest: Visual arts.
Type of support: Scholarships—to individuals.
Application information: Applications accepted.
> *Deadline(s):* Apr. 1
> *Applicants should submit the following:*
>   1) Letter(s) of recommendation
>   2) ACT
>   3) SAT
>   4) Transcripts
> *Additional information:* Contact foundation for eligibility requirements.

EIN: 251668339

8064
Private Industry Council of Lehigh Valley, Inc.
1601 Union Blvd.
P.O. Box 20490
Lehigh Valley, PA   18002-0490   (610) 437-5627

Foundation type: Public charity
Purpose: Employment services through skills assessment, job training, and placement to eligible Lehigh Valley, PA residents.
Financial data: Year ended 06/30/2012. Assets, $1,116,120 (M); Expenditures, $6,732,825; Total giving, $287,021; Grants to individuals, totaling $174,736.
Fields of interest: Employment, services; Employment, training; Employment.
Type of support: In-kind gifts.
Application information:
> *Initial approach:* Letter
> *Additional information:* Contact foundation for eligibility criteria.

EIN: 232143985

8065
Project Management Institute Educational Foundation
14 Campus Blvd.
Newtown Square, PA   19073-3299   (610) 356-4600
Contact: Jeannette Barr, Exec. Dir.
FAX: (610) 356-0357; E-mail: pmief@pmi.org; URL: http://www.pmi.org/Pmief/default.asp

Foundation type: Public charity
Purpose: Scholarships and awards to individuals for the development of future project management professionals worldwide through learning opportunities.
Financial data: Year ended 12/31/2011. Assets, $2,583,106 (M); Expenditures, $1,252,354; Total giving, $397,210; Grants to individuals, totaling $134,425.
Type of support: Scholarships—to individuals; Awards/prizes.
Application information: Applications accepted. Application form available on the grantmaker's web site.
> *Deadline(s):* None
> *Additional information:* See web site for additional program details.

Program descriptions:
> *Scholarships:* Scholarships are open to high school seniors and students at bachelors, masters, and doctoral levels who are studying project management and related fields; primary and secondary school teachers and administrators who wish to implement project-based learning in the classroom; and to employees of nonprofits and

non-governmental organizations who wish to improve the effectiveness and efficiency of their operations.
> *The Donald S. Barrie Award:* This award recognizes the paper that best advances the project management body of knowledge in the field of design, procurement and/or construction by providing a useful contribution to the engineering and construction industry. The award of US$500 is announced at PMI Global Congress-North America.
> *The James R. Snyder International Student Paper of the Year:* The program is available to bachelors, masters, and doctoral students. ISPY award recipients receive a US$500 cash prize plus complimentary registration, travel and lodging to attend the PMI Global Congress in their region. Winning papers are published in Project Management Journal, PMI's academic research quarterly.

EIN: 232630701

8066
Psea Scholarship Trust
c/o Bank of New York Mellon, N.A.
P.O. Box 185
Pittsburgh, PA   15230-0185
Application address: Cameron Scholarship Committee, PSEA - 3rd Fl., 10 S. 19th St., Pittsburgh, PA 15203
E-mail: students@psea.org; URL: http://www.psea.org

Foundation type: Independent foundation
Purpose: Scholarships to one or more outstanding students enrolled at an accredited institution of higher learning for teacher preparation program in PA.
Financial data: Year ended 08/31/2012. Assets, $336,368 (M); Expenditures, $45,342; Total giving, $19,500; Grants to individuals, 8 grants totaling $19,500 (high: $3,000, low: $1,000).
Fields of interest: Teacher school/education.
Type of support: Scholarships—to individuals.
Application information: Applications accepted. Application form required.
> *Send request by:* Mail
> *Deadline(s):* Feb. 28
> *Additional information:* Applicant must be a member in good standing of the Pennsylvania State Education Association.

EIN: 232225710

8067
Leta Potter Puckett Memorial Fund
c/o Wells Fargo Bank, N.A.
101 N. Independence Mall E. MACY 1372-062
Philadelphia, PA   19106-2112   (209) 431-3777

Foundation type: Independent foundation
Purpose: Science and pre-med scholarships to graduates of Roosevelt High School in Fresno, CA. Chapman Scholarships for religious education to graduates of high schools in Fresno County, CA.
Financial data: Year ended 03/31/2013. Assets, $853,191 (M); Expenditures, $41,903; Total giving, $30,000.
Fields of interest: Medical school/education; Theological school/education; Science.
Type of support: Support to graduates or students of specific schools; Undergraduate support.
Application information: Applications accepted. Application form required.
> *Initial approach:* Letter
> *Deadline(s):* Jan. 1 for Chapman Scholarships, Spring for science and pre-med scholarships
> *Applicants should submit the following:*

1) Resume
2) Transcripts
3) Financial information
Additional information: Application must also include statement of goals, and name of college.
EIN: 956731500

8068
Joseph P. Pyle Trust
c/o PNC Bank, N.A. Tax Dept.
1600 Market St.
Philadelphia, PA 19103-7240   (302) 429-1338
Foundation type: Independent foundation
Purpose: Scholarships to high school graduates of Wilmington, DE, between the ages of 17 and 21, entering their first year of college.
Financial data: Year ended 08/31/2013. Assets, $812,085 (M); Expenditures, $38,754; Total giving, $37,904.
Fields of interest: Higher education.
Type of support: Scholarships—to individuals; Undergraduate support.
Application information: Applications accepted. Application form required. Interview required.
  Initial approach: Letter
  Send request by: Mail
  Deadline(s): May 1
  Applicants should submit the following:
    1) Letter(s) of recommendation
    2) Transcripts
    3) SAT
    4) Financial information
  Additional information: Application should also include a list of extracurricular activities and honors.
EIN: 516010048

8069
The Quaker Chemical Foundation
1 Quaker Park
901 Hector St.
Conshohocken, PA 19428-2307   (610) 832-4301
FAX: (610) 832-8682; URL: http:// www.quakerchem.com/about_us/ about_foundation.html
Foundation type: Company-sponsored foundation
Purpose: Scholarships only to CA, MI, and PA employees of Quaker Chemical Corporation.
Publications: Application guidelines.
Financial data: Year ended 06/30/2013. Assets, $24,580 (M); Expenditures, $159,479; Total giving, $155,529; Grants to individuals, totaling $26,000.
Type of support: Employee-related scholarships.
Application information: Contact foundation for current application guidelines. Only one scholarship per year is awarded.
Company name: Quaker Chemical Corporation
EIN: 236245803

8070
Robert D. & Margaret W. Quin Foundation
c/o N.P.I.T.C.
12 E. Broad St.
Hazleton, PA 18201-6521   (570) 459-6745
Contact: Attn. Mary Ann Zubris, Secy.-Treas.
Foundation type: Independent foundation
Purpose: Grants to financially needy individuals who are 19 years old or younger, and who have

been residents for at least one year of an area within a ten-mile radius of Hazleton City Hall, PA.
Financial data: Year ended 12/31/2012. Assets, $20,989 (M); Expenditures, $10,990; Total giving, $10,226; Grants to individuals, 30 grants totaling $8,226 (high: $770, low: $60).
Fields of interest: Education, services; Optometry/ vision screening; Children/youth, services; Day care; Economically disadvantaged.
Type of support: Grants for special needs.
Application information: Applications accepted. Application form required.
  Deadline(s): None
EIN: 222439876

8071
Reading Musical Foundation
P.O. Box 14835
Reading, PA 19612-4835   (610) 376-3395
Contact: Keri Shultz, Program Dir.
FAX: (610) 376-3336;
E-mail: kshultz@readingmusicalfoundation.org;
E-mail for Kerri Shultz:
kshultz@readingmusicalfoundation.org;
URL: http://www.readingmusicalfoundation.org
Foundation type: Public charity
Purpose: Scholarships and awards to music students who reside in Berks County and attend Berks County, PA schools (or homeschooled).
Publications: Application guidelines; Newsletter.
Financial data: Year ended 06/30/2012. Assets, $11,024,386 (M); Expenditures, $661,695; Total giving, $425,922; Grants to individuals, totaling $150,637.
Fields of interest: Music; Performing arts, education; Education; Women.
Type of support: Scholarships—to individuals.
Application information: Application form required.
  Additional information: All scholarship candidates must perform an audition before the scholarship committee. See web site for additional guidelines and a listing of additional programs.
Program descriptions:
  American Guild of Organists Fund of RMF: One award of up to $500 is annually awarded to a Berks County or Schuylkill County student in grades 7-11 who has at least intermediate piano proficiency, and less than one year of organ instruction.
  Charlotte B. Wicklein Scholarship: One award is given annually to a female student of voice, piano, organ, or symphonic/band instruments who has been accepted as a music major by an accredited school of post-secondary education, and who attends school or resides in Berks County.
  David L. Kline Family Mountain Folk Scholarship: At least one award of up to $500 (to be used toward private lessons or for an instrument upgrade) is available to acoustic guitar or banjo students who reside in, or attend school in, Berks County, or who studies with a Berks County-based teacher. Eligible applicants can be of any age; preference will be given to beginner and intermediate students.
  Full Circle Society Acoustic Music Study Program: One award of up to $500 (to be used toward private study) is given annually to an outstanding acoustic guitar, fiddle, mandolin, or banjo student. Eligible applicants must be between the ages of 10 and 25, reside in Berks County, and study with a teacher who is based in Berks County.
  Gladys & Carl Jensen Summer Camp Fellowship Program: Up to two awards of up to $500 each will be awarded to instrumentalists and vocalists in grades 7-11 who have not yet experienced attending a summer music program. Eligible

applicants must attend a school in Berks County, and reside in Berks County.
  Jimbo Jam Memorial Fund: Awards of up to $500 are available to students in grades 7-12 who attend Reading School District schools. Recipients are required to commit to at least 15 hours of community service in the field of their choice for consideration of the award; preference will be given to applicants in grades 9-12.
  Kathleen & Karin Reinsel Early Instrument Scholarship: Scholarships of up to $500 (to be used for private music study) are available for students of any age (excluding professional-level) who are studying early instruments (including recorder, harpsichord, harp, mandolin, and other early-period instruments). Students must reside in and attend school in Berks County.
  Peter J. Brye Cello & Harp Fund: One award of up to $500 will be awarded to a cellist and/or harpist in grades 7-11, to attend a music summer camp. Students must attend a Berks County school and reside in Berks County.
  Ray & Carole Neag Middle School Vocal Program: Need-based awards of up to $500 are annually given to outstanding vocalists in grades 7-9 who attend a Berks County school, and who reside in Berks County, to pursue private study.
  Robert R. Kreitz - Mark A. Hornberger Piano Scholarship: At least two awards (one for students in grades 5-6, and one for students in grades 7-8) are available to piano students who attend Berks County schools, and who reside in Berks County.
  Scheidt/Heslop Jazz Fund: One award of up to $500 is available to a jazz instrumentalist or vocalist in grades K-12, who wishes to attend a music summer camp. Eligible applicants must attend a Berks County school and reside in Berks County.
EIN: 231472487

8072
Realize Your Dream Foundation
c/o Bernard E. Stoecklein, Jr.
609 Epsilon Dr.
Pittsburgh, PA 15238-2940   (412) 967-6200
Contact: Kathleen A. Santelli, Scholarship Coord.
Foundation type: Independent foundation
Purpose: Scholarships to high school seniors attending private and public high schools within the city of Pittsburgh, PA, and those geographic boundaries surrounding the Pittsburgh area: as far east as Lower Burrell, west to Sewickley, north to Butler, and south to the Allegheny and Ohio rivers.
Financial data: Year ended 12/31/2011. Assets, $133,160 (M); Expenditures, $31,275; Total giving, $27,301.
Fields of interest: Higher education.
Type of support: Scholarships—to individuals.
Application information: Application form required.
  Initial approach: Telephone
  Deadline(s): Feb. 28
  Applicants should submit the following:
    1) Essay
    2) Letter(s) of recommendation
    3) GPA
    4) SAT
    5) Transcripts
  Additional information: Contact foundation for current application guidelines; Application must also include total custodial family income, and specific outline of community service projects.
EIN: 232884514

8073
Sophia K. Reeves Foundation Trust
c/o BNY Mellon, N.A.
P.O. Box 185
Pittsburgh, PA 15230-0185
Contact: Annamaria C. Lyles
Application address: c/o BNY Mellon, N.A. , P.O. Box 7236, Philadelphia, PA 19101-0001

Foundation type: Independent foundation
Purpose: Scholarships to children of employees of Philadelphia Gas Works, to residents of Laurel Springs, NJ, and to Protestant residents of the part of Camden County that is contingent to Laurel Springs.
Financial data: Year ended 06/30/2013. Assets, $1,313,801 (M); Expenditures, $111,776; Total giving, $94,251; Grants to individuals, 14 grants totaling $94,251 (high: $10,964, low: $3,501).
Fields of interest: Protestant agencies & churches.
Type of support: Employee-related scholarships.
Application information: Applications accepted. Application form required.
  Deadline(s): Mar. 10
Company name: Philadelphia Gas Works
EIN: 236226072

8074
Henry K. & Evelyn Reitnauer Scholarship Fund
2201 Ridgewood Rd., Ste. 180
Wyomissing, PA 19610-1190 (610) 369-7408
Application address: c/o Boyertown Area School District, Attn: Guidance Dept., 911 Montgomery Ave., Boyertown, PA 19512-9699, tel.: (610) 369-7408

Foundation type: Operating foundation
Purpose: Scholarships to financially needy graduates of Boyertown Area Senior High School, PA, pursuing a teaching degree in special education or another degree that relates to special education.
Financial data: Year ended 12/31/2011. Assets, $1,336,266 (M); Expenditures, $86,061; Total giving, $72,158.
Fields of interest: Education, special; Teacher school/education.
Type of support: Scholarships—to individuals; Support to graduates or students of specific schools.
Application information: Application form required.
  Initial approach: Letter
  Deadline(s): Apr.
  Additional information: Application should be submitted in writing to the scholarship committee.
Program description:
  Scholarship Program: Scholarships are in amounts of up to 80 percent of the recipient's total school costs, with a limit of $5,000 per year. Scholarships are awarded for the entire length of the recipient's period of study. Recipients are chosen by a committee made up of the Superintendent of Schools, the High School Principal, the Director of Pupil Services, and the Senior High School Guidance Department Chairperson.
EIN: 232214468

8075
T. L. Rhoads Foundation
(formerly Leidy-Rhoads Foundation Trust)
c/o BNY Mellon, N.A.
P.O. Box 185
Pittsburgh, PA 15230-0185
Contact: Jean Butt
Application address: 911 Montgomery Ave., Boyertown, PA 19512

Foundation type: Independent foundation
Purpose: Scholarships to residents of Boyertown, PA, primarily for higher education at colleges, universities, and trade schools.
Financial data: Year ended 12/31/2012. Assets, $1,419,966 (M); Expenditures, $80,113; Total giving, $63,000.
Fields of interest: Vocational education.
Type of support: Technical education support; Undergraduate support.
Application information: Applications accepted. Application form required.
  Deadline(s): Early spring
EIN: 236227398

8076
The Rhythm & Blues Foundation, Inc.
100 S. Broad St., Ste. 620
Philadelphia, PA 19110-1017 (215) 772-1514
Contact: Patricia Wilson Aden, Exec. Dir.
FAX: (215) 568-1026;
E-mail: paden@rhythmblues.org; URL: http://www.rhythmblues.org

Foundation type: Public charity
Purpose: Awards by nomination only to pioneers in the rhythm and blues industry. Also, emergency assistance to rhythm and blues artists.
Publications: Application guidelines; Annual report; Financial statement; Informational brochure; Newsletter.
Fields of interest: Music.
Type of support: Awards/grants by nomination only; Awards/prizes; Grants for special needs.
Application information: Applications accepted. Application form required. Application form available on the grantmaker's web site.
  Initial approach: Telephone or e-mail
  Send request by: Mail or fax
  Deadline(s): None
  Additional information: Contact foundation for current application guidelines.
Program descriptions:
  Doc Pomus Financial Assistance Grant Program: The program provides emergency financial assistance to rhythm and blues artists for medications, wheelchairs, dental work, eyeglasses, hearing aids, musical instruments, and funeral expenses.
  Gwendolyn B. Gordy Fuqua Fund: The fund provides emergency financial assistance to former Motown artists of the 1960's and 1970's. Financial assistance may include reimbursements, payments for uninsured medical care and expenses, emergency assistance, burial assistance, and other forms of charitable financial assistance as determined by the foundation.
  Pioneer Awards Program: The program recognizes legendary artists whose lifelong contributions have been instrumental in the development of rhythm and blues music. Awards recipients are nominated by foundation trustees, advisory board and artist steering committee, and past Pioneer Award honorees.
EIN: 521594184

8077
The Riddle HealthCare Foundation
1068 W. Baltimore Pike
Media, PA 19063-5104 (484) 227-3651
Contact: Steven R. Derby, V.P. for Devel.
E-mail: derbys@mlhs.org; URL: http://www.mainlinehealth.org/oth/Page.asp?PageID=OTH001641

Foundation type: Public charity
Purpose: Scholarships only to employees of Riddle Memorial Hospital, PA pursuing a career in the healthcare field.
Financial data: Year ended 06/30/2012. Assets, $26,680,915 (M); Expenditures, $1,681,990; Total giving, $948,473. Employee-related scholarships amount not specified.
Fields of interest: Health sciences school/education.
Type of support: Employee-related scholarships.
Application information: Applications not accepted.
  Additional information: Unsolicited requests for funds not considered or acknowledged.
EIN: 043601189

8078
Rochester Alumni Scholarship Charitable Trust
c/o Jo Shane
1232 Rte. 68
New Brighton, PA 15066-4106
Contact: Thomas R. Goettman, Jr., Pres.
Application address: 626 Farm Ln., Rochester , PA, 15074

Foundation type: Operating foundation
Purpose: Scholarships to students, graduates and faculty/staff at Rochester Area Senior High School, PA.
Financial data: Year ended 12/31/2012. Assets, $96,144 (M); Expenditures, $5,358; Total giving, $5,000; Grants to individuals, 7 grants totaling $5,000 (high: $1,000, low: $500).
Fields of interest: Higher education.
Type of support: Support to graduates or students of specific schools.
Application information: Applications accepted. Application form required.
  Deadline(s): May 8
EIN: 256644260

8079
William G. Rohrer, Jr. Educational Foundation
c/o PNC Bank, N.A.
1600 Market St., Tax Department
Philadelphia, PA 19103-7240 (856) 638-4862
Contact: Ronald L. Caputo, V.P.
Application address: Rte. 38 At Eastgate Dr., Moorestown, NJ 08057

Foundation type: Independent foundation
Purpose: Scholarships to financially needy residents of the Haddon Township, NJ, area.
Financial data: Year ended 12/31/2012. Assets, $882,174 (M); Expenditures, $63,703; Total giving, $48,000; Grants to individuals, 20 grants totaling $48,000 (high: $3,000, low: $2,000).
Type of support: Scholarships—to individuals.
Application information: Applications accepted. Application form required.
  Initial approach: Letter
  Deadline(s): Mar. 31
  Applicants should submit the following:
   1) Financial information

2) Essay
EIN: 226070758

8080

Ronald McDonald House Charities of the Philadelphia Region, Inc.
1525 Valley Center Parkway No. 300
Bethlehem, PA 18017-4500   (856) 582-6843

Foundation type: Public charity
Purpose: Scholarships to college-bound high school students of Hispanic descent from the Philadelphia, PA, area.
Financial data: Year ended 12/31/2011. Assets, $2,418,192 (M); Expenditures, $1,433,752; Total giving, $802,707; Grants to individuals, totaling $42,000.
Fields of interest: Hispanics/Latinos.
Type of support: Undergraduate support.
Application information:
  Applicants should submit the following:
    1) Transcripts
    2) Financial information
  Additional information: Application should also include a list of extracurricular activities.
EIN: 232705170

8081

Art Rooney Scholarship Fund
1 Oxford Ctr., 20th Fl.
Pittsburgh, PA 15219-1410   (412) 562-8800
Contact: Arthur J. Rooney II, Pres. and Treas.

Foundation type: Public charity
Purpose: Scholarships to graduates of Oliver High School, Perry High School, or North Catholic High School, in Pittsburgh, PA for continuing education at a four year college or university.
Financial data: Year ended 12/31/2012. Assets, $82,808 (M); Expenditures, $34,383; Total giving, $33,000.
Fields of interest: Higher education.
Type of support: Support to graduates or students of specific schools.
Application information: Applications accepted.
  Initial approach: Letter
  Deadline(s): June 1
  Additional information: Application must include two letters of recommendation from school staff or administrators. Applicant must have attended the high school for at least three of his or her four years in high school and must have financial need.
EIN: 251605932

8082

Max C. Rosenfeld Trust
c/o BNY Mellon, N.A.
P.O. Box 185
Pittsburgh, PA 15230-0185
Contact: Ruth S. Wolf, Dir.; Max C. Rosenfield

Foundation type: Independent foundation
Purpose: Scholarships or loans to financially needy young Jewish women living in Boston, MA, and its suburbs for continuing their education.
Financial data: Year ended 08/31/2013. Assets, $1,043,354 (M); Expenditures, $71,310; Total giving, $40,500.
Fields of interest: Jewish agencies & synagogues; Women.
Type of support: Scholarships—to individuals.
Application information: Application form required.

Initial approach: Letter
Deadline(s): May 15
EIN: 046044784

8083

The Ross Loan Fund
c/o M&T Investment Group
1 West High St.
Carlisle, PA 17013-2951   (717) 240-4562
Application Address: C/O The Jane R.Ross Trust, 1415 Ritner Hwy. Carlisle, PA. 17013

Foundation type: Independent foundation
Purpose: Low-interest student loans to graduates of Chambersburg Area Senior High School, PA. Graduates from other high schools in Franklin County, PA, will be considered as funds permit.
Financial data: Year ended 12/31/2012. Assets, $4,186,874 (M); Expenditures, $99,665; Total giving, $0.
Fields of interest: Higher education.
Type of support: Student loans—to individuals; Support to graduates or students of specific schools; Undergraduate support.
Application information: Application form required.
  Deadline(s): May 31
  Applicants should submit the following:
    1) Transcripts
    2) Financial information
EIN: 236262609

8084

Gertrude Marion Ruskin Trust
c/o Wells Fargo Bank N.A.
101N Indefendence Mall E MACY 1372-062
Philadelphia, PA 19106-2112   (336) 747-8165
Contact: Michael Boyles
Application address: C/o Wells Fargo Bank, 1 W. 4th St., Winston-Salem, NC 27105

Foundation type: Independent foundation
Purpose: Scholarships to residents of Madison, Buncombe, and Haywood counties, NC, and Cherokee Indian reservations in NC who are of Baptist, Methodist or Presbyterian faith and are of Cherokee Indian descent or Anglo-Saxon descent with ancestors who resided in one of the original thirteen colonies at the time of the Revolutionary War. Preference will be give to students who lost one or both parents.
Financial data: Year ended 01/31/2013. Assets, $437,963 (M); Expenditures, $21,739; Total giving, $17,500.
Fields of interest: Native Americans/American Indians.
Type of support: Scholarships—to individuals.
Application information: Application form required.
  Initial approach: Letter or telephone
  Deadline(s): June 1
EIN: 586187363

8085

The James B. and Eileen Ryan Family Foundation, Inc.
357 Brusselles St.
St.Marys, PA 15827

Foundation type: Independent foundation
Purpose: Scholarships to graduating high school seniors of PA, pursuing higher education.
Financial data: Year ended 12/31/2012. Assets, $19,614 (M); Expenditures, $143,035; Total giving, $139,147; Grants to individuals, 2 grants totaling $2,000 (high: $1,000, low: $1,000).
Fields of interest: Higher education.

Type of support: Scholarships—to individuals.
Application information: Applications accepted.
  Additional information: Selection is based on financial need. Recipients must maintain and provide documentation that the funds were used for qualified tuition expenses, and must also maintain an acceptable GPA.
EIN: 251839459

8086

Charles E. Saak Trust
c/o Wells Fargo Bank, N.A.
101N. Independence Mall E. MACY 1372-062
Philadelphia, PA 19106-2112
Application address: c/o Wells Fargo Bank N.A., P.O. Box 20160, Long Beach, CA 90802

Foundation type: Independent foundation
Purpose: Scholarships to underprivileged students under 21 years of age residing in the Porterville/Poplar area, CA. Dental and emergency medical assistance to children under 21 years of age from low-income families residing in the Porterville/Poplar area, CA.
Publications: Application guidelines.
Financial data: Year ended 01/31/2013. Assets, $1,645,906 (M); Expenditures, $97,984; Total giving, $73,121.
Fields of interest: Higher education; Dental care; Health care; Economically disadvantaged.
Type of support: Scholarships—to individuals; Undergraduate support; Grants for special needs.
Application information: Applications accepted. Application form required.
  Send request by: Mail
  Deadline(s): Mar. 31 for scholarship
  Additional information: Scholarship application should include transcripts, and financial information. Health Care Assistance application should include financial information.
EIN: 946076213

8087

The Clarence Schock Foundation
(formerly The SICO Foundation)
15 Mount Joy St.
P.O. Box 127
Mount Joy, PA 17552-1417
Contact: Dr. Joseph A. Caputo
E-mail: info@sicofoundation.org; URL: http://www.clarenceschockfoundation.org

Foundation type: Independent foundation
Purpose: Scholarships to students attending certain Pennsylvania institutions and residing in specific counties for higher education.
Publications: Annual report; Financial statement; Informational brochure; Newsletter; Program policy statement.
Financial data: Year ended 12/31/2012. Assets, $15,249,812 (M); Expenditures, $1,036,418; Total giving, $587,020.
Fields of interest: Higher education.
Type of support: Scholarships—to individuals; Support to graduates or students of specific schools.
Application information:
  Deadline(s): Oct. 1
  Additional information: All application materials are available from the universities. See web site for additional application guidelines.
Program description:
  Scholarship Program: Scholarships are awarded in the amount of $6,000, payable at $1,200 for freshman year, $1,600 for sophomore year,

$1,800 for junior year, and $2,000 for senior year. Students applying for scholarship must apply to one of the five participating universities on a full-time basis, and must be a legal resident of the following PA counties: Adams, Berks, Chester, Cumberland, Dauphin, Delaware, Lancaster, Lebanon, and York and be a graduate of a secondary school in one of the same counties. The participating universities are: Cheyney University, Kutztown University, Millersville University, Shippensburg University, and West Chester University. The recipient must remain full-time at the university of initial enrollment.
EIN: 236298332

8088
Scholarship Foundation of Erie Scottish Rite

P.O. Box 1364
Erie, PA   16512-1364
Contact: Erie Scottish Rite
URL: http://www.eriescottshrite.org

Foundation type: Independent foundation
Purpose: Scholarships to financially needy high school graduates who are residents of Erie or Crawford counties, PA pursuing undergraduate or graduate degrees form accredited colleges and universities.
Financial data: Year ended 07/31/2012. Assets, $1,103,414 (M); Expenditures, $71,816; Total giving, $61,750; Grants to individuals, 52 grants totaling $61,750 (high: $2,000, low: $750).
Fields of interest: Higher education.
Type of support: Graduate support; Undergraduate support.
Application information: Applications accepted. Application form required.
Initial approach: Letter
Deadline(s): Mar. 12
Final notification: Applicants notified in May
Applicants should submit the following:
1) Essay
2) GPA
3) Transcripts
4) SAT
5) Financial information
EIN: 251710223

8089
The Scholarship Foundation of the Union League of Philadelphia

140 S. Broad St.
Philadelphia, PA   19102-3083   (215) 587-6455
FAX: (215) 851-8789;
E-mail: foundations@unionleague.org; URL: http://www.unionleague.org/scholarship-foundation.php

Foundation type: Public charity
Purpose: Scholarships to high school seniors who are recipients of the Union League Good Citizenship Awards for post high school education at colleges, universities, and trade schools.
Publications: Application guidelines; Informational brochure.
Financial data: Year ended 06/30/2011. Assets, $3,215,332 (M); Expenditures, $244,190; Total giving, $159,680; Grants to individuals, totaling $107,680.
Fields of interest: Vocational education, post-secondary; Higher education.
Type of support: Scholarships—to individuals; Undergraduate support.
Application information: Application form required. Interview required.
Initial approach: Letter or telephone.

Additional information: Applicants are evaluated on character, scholastic ability, personality, leadership potential, financial need, service to society and loyalty to American traditions and principles.
EIN: 236427434

8090
Schuylkill Area Community Foundation

(formerly Ashland Trusts)
216 S. Centre St.
Pottsville, PA   17901-3501   (570) 624-7223
Contact: Eileen Kuperavage, Exec. Dir.
FAX: (570) 624-7256;
E-mail: ekuperavage@verizon.net; URL: http://www.sacfoundation.com

Foundation type: Community foundation
Purpose: Scholarships to undergraduate students in the Pottsville, PA, area.
Financial data: Year ended 12/31/2012. Assets, $13,292,779 (M); Expenditures, $573,421; Total giving, $351,660; Grants to individuals, 104 grants totaling $221,628.
Fields of interest: Education.
Type of support: Scholarships—to individuals.
Application information: Applications accepted. Application form required. Application form available on the grantmaker's web site.
Additional information: See web site for complete program listing.
EIN: 236422789

8091
Schuylkill Community Action

(formerly EOC of Schuylkill)
206 N. 2nd St.
Pottsville, PA   17901-2502   (570) 622-1995
Contact: Theodore R. Dreisbach, Exec. Dir.
URL: http://www.schuylkillcommunityaction.com/

Foundation type: Public charity
Purpose: Financial assistance to individuals of Shuylkill County, PA, for food, housing and other necessities.
Financial data: Year ended 06/30/2012. Assets, $2,507,312 (M); Expenditures, $3,744,164; Total giving, $1,208,778; Grants to individuals, totaling $1,208,778.
Fields of interest: Housing/shelter, services; Economically disadvantaged.
Type of support: Emergency funds; Grants for special needs.
Application information: Eligible applicants must be PA residents. Contact organization for information on assistance.
EIN: 231670456

8092
Schuylkill County Bar Association Scholarship Fund

401 N. 2nd St.
Pottsville, PA   17901
Contact: Margaret A. Ulmer Esq., Mgr.

Foundation type: Operating foundation
Purpose: Scholarships to individuals who are residents of Schuylkill county, PA for three consecutive years, and either must be enrolled in an accredited law school or have taken a law aptitude test and applied for admission at an accredited school.
Financial data: Year ended 12/31/2011. Assets, $182,816 (M); Expenditures, $8,625; Total giving,

$8,000; Grants to individuals, 17 grants totaling $8,000 (high: $850, low: $250).
Fields of interest: Law school/education.
Type of support: Scholarships—to individuals.
Application information: Applications accepted. Application form required.
Deadline(s): July 15
Additional information: Scholarships are for one academic year, applicants must reapply for succeeding years. Interviews may be required.
EIN: 232747769

8093
John Schwab Foundation

2591 Park Ctr. Blvd.
State College, PA   16801   (814) 486-2166
Application address: 421 Broad St., Emporium, PA 15834

Foundation type: Independent foundation
Purpose: Scholarships to financially needy residents of Cameron County, PA, who maintain a specified minimum GPA.
Financial data: Year ended 12/31/2012. Assets, $429,550 (M); Expenditures, $27,242; Total giving, $20,000; Grants to individuals, 17 grants totaling $20,000 (high: $2,000, low: $500).
Type of support: Scholarships—to individuals.
Application information: Application form required.
Deadline(s): June 10
Applicants should submit the following:
1) GPA
2) Transcripts
3) Financial information
EIN: 256029493

8094
The Scranton Area Foundation, Inc.

615 Jefferson Ave., Ste. 102
Scranton, PA   18510   (570) 347-6203
Contact: Laura J. Ducceschi, C.E.O.; For grants: Cathy Fitzpatrick, Donor Svcs. and Comms. Assoc.
FAX: (570) 347-7587; E-mail: safinfo@safdn.org; Grant inquiry e-mail: cathyf@sadfn.org; URL: http://www.safdn.org

Foundation type: Community foundation
Purpose: Scholarships to students in the greater Scranton/Lackawanna Region, PA for continuing education at institutions of higher learning.
Publications: Application guidelines; Annual report; Annual report (including application guidelines); Grants list; Informational brochure; Informational brochure (including application guidelines); Newsletter; Occasional report.
Financial data: Year ended 12/31/2011. Assets, $25,450,403 (M); Expenditures, $1,666,132; Total giving, $1,003,256; Grants to individuals, 73 grants totaling $359,520.
Fields of interest: Higher education; Scholarships/financial aid.
Type of support: Scholarships—to individuals; Support to graduates or students of specific schools; Undergraduate support.
Application information: Applications accepted. Application form required.
Deadline(s): Varies
Additional information: Contact local High School Guidance Counselor for application instructions. Each scholarships has its own unique set of eligibility criteria. See web site for complete listing of scholarship funds.
EIN: 232890364

8095
Scribe Video Center, Inc.
4212 Chestnut St., 3rd Fl.
Philadelphia, PA 19104 (215) 222-4201
FAX: (215) 222-4205; E-mail: inquiry@scribe.org;
URL: http://www.scribe.org

Foundation type: Public charity
Purpose: Support for a limited number of projects by independent film and video artists in the Philadelphia, PA area.
Financial data: Year ended 12/31/2011. Assets, $141,256 (M); Expenditures, $416,467.
Fields of interest: Film/video; Arts, artist's services.
Type of support: Fiscal agent/sponsor.
Application information: Applications accepted.
  Initial approach: Letter
  Copies of proposal: 1
  Deadline(s): None
  Additional information: Contact the Scribe Video Center for more details on how to apply.
Program description:
  Fiscal Sponsorship: The center provides fiscal sponsorship services for a limited number of projects by independent film and video artists in the Philadelphia area. Projects must be non-commercial.
EIN: 232358942

8096
Helen B. Shartzer Scholarship Fund
c/o PNC Bank, N.A.
1600 Market St., 4th Fl.
Philadelphia, PA 19103-7240 (610) 630-5000
Application address: Scholarship Committee of Norristown, 401 N. Whitehall Rd., Norristown, PA 19403

Foundation type: Independent foundation
Purpose: Undergraduate scholarships to worthy residents of Norristown, PA.
Financial data: Year ended 12/31/2012. Assets, $59,603 (M); Expenditures, $6,657; Total giving, $5,000; Grants to individuals, 5 grants totaling $5,000 (high: $2,000, low: $1,000).
Type of support: Undergraduate support.
Application information: Applications accepted.
  Additional information: Contact foundation for current application deadline/guidelines.
EIN: 236398364

8097
The Fred S. Shaulis Foundation Inc.
P.O. Box 121
Friedens, PA 15541 (814) 445-9534
Contact: Randell L. Urban, V.P., Treas. and Dir.

Foundation type: Independent foundation
Purpose: Student loans for college or other post high school education in the Somerset County PA, area.
Financial data: Year ended 02/28/2013. Assets, $757,644 (M); Expenditures, $60,663; Total giving, $0.
Fields of interest: Vocational education, post-secondary; Higher education.
Type of support: Student loans—to individuals.
Application information: Application form required. Interview required.
  Deadline(s): Jan. 5 for spring semester and Aug. 5 for fall semester
  Additional information: Loan application can be obtained from the foundation.
EIN: 521382605

8098
Clyde L. and Mary C. Shaull Education Foundation
c/o PNC Bank, N.A.
620 Liberty Ave.,No. 10th Fl.
Pittsburgh, PA 15222 (717) 730-2275
Contact: Debra A. Smith
*Application address:*c/o PNC Bank N.A, P.O. Box 308, Camp Hill, PA 17001

Foundation type: Independent foundation
Purpose: Scholarships to graduates of Mechanicsburg High School, PA, who are enrolled in postsecondary schools.
Financial data: Year ended 12/31/2012. Assets, $561,583 (M); Expenditures, $35,418; Total giving, $25,764.
Type of support: Scholarships—to individuals; Support to graduates or students of specific schools.
Application information: Applications accepted. Application form required.
  Initial approach: Letter
  Deadline(s): June 1
  Additional information: Application must include financial statement; Application forms available from Mechanicsburg High School guidance counselors.
EIN: 237101845

8099
Howard J. & Ruth H. Sheen Scholarship Fund
c/o PNC Bank, N.A.
620 Liberty Ave. 10th Fl.
Pittsburgh, PA 15222-2705 (814) 665-8297
Application address: c/o Corry Area High School, Attn.: Principal, 534 E. Pleasant St., Corry, PA 16407-2246

Foundation type: Independent foundation
Purpose: Scholarships to graduates of Corry Area High School, PA, who wish to enter medical related fields.
Financial data: Year ended 12/31/2012. Assets, $151,892 (M); Expenditures, $7,902; Total giving, $6,500; Grants to individuals, 5 grants totaling $6,500 (high: $1,300, low: $1,300).
Fields of interest: Medical school/education.
Type of support: Support to graduates or students of specific schools; Undergraduate support.
Application information: Application form required.
  Deadline(s): May 15
EIN: 256257707

8100
John L. & Helen B. Shoemaker Education Trust
c/o PNC Bank, N.A.
1600 Market St., Tax Dept.
Philadelphia, PA 19103-7240

Foundation type: Independent foundation
Purpose: Scholarships to individuals for higher education.
Financial data: Year ended 12/31/2012. Assets, $691,479 (M); Expenditures, $31,835; Total giving, $24,000; Grants to individuals, 4 grants totaling $24,000 (high: $7,000, low: $3,000).
Fields of interest: Higher education.
Type of support: Scholarships—to individuals.
Application information: Unsolicited requests for funds are not accepted.
EIN: 256876449

8101
Ray S. Shoemaker Trust for Shoemaker Scholarship Fund
c/o BNY Mellon, NA
P.O. Box 185
Pittsburgh, PA 15230-0185
Scholarship application address: c/o Office of Financial Aid Svcs., Harrisburg Area Community College, One HACC Dr., Cooper 209, Harrisburg, PA 17110

Foundation type: Independent foundation
Purpose: Undergraduate and graduate scholarships to graduates of high schools in the greater Harrisburg, PA, area.
Financial data: Year ended 09/30/2012. Assets, $5,230,349 (M); Expenditures, $259,474; Total giving, $179,700; Grants to individuals, 254 grants totaling $179,700 (high: $1,900, low: $500).
Type of support: Support to graduates or students of specific schools; Graduate support; Undergraduate support.
Application information: Application form required.
  Deadline(s): Apr. 1
  Applicants should submit the following:
    1) Transcripts
    2) Financial information
EIN: 236237250

8102
The Robbins Shuman Scholarship Fund Trust
c/o Tax Dept.
P.O. Box 3215
Lancaster, PA 17604-3215

Foundation type: Independent foundation
Purpose: Scholarships to residents of Columbia County, PA, for three of the last four years of high school who are attending college full-time and maintaining a GPA of 3.0.
Financial data: Year ended 04/30/2012. Assets, $3,068,488 (M); Expenditures, $185,880; Total giving, $160,996; Grants to individuals, 51 grants totaling $160,996 (high: $4,000, low: $1,500).
Fields of interest: Higher education.
Type of support: Scholarships—to individuals.
Application information: Applications accepted. Application form required.
  Deadline(s): None
  Additional information: Application should include an essay.
EIN: 256857939

8103
Agnes Cecelia J. Siebenthal Scholarship Charitable Fund
c/o PNC Bank, N.A.
P.O. Box 609
Pittsburgh, PA 15230-9738
Application address: 811 S. Griswold St., Peoria, IL 61605, tel.: (309) 672-6600

Foundation type: Independent foundation
Purpose: Scholarships to Peoria, IL, area students who have graduated from Manual High School, IL, to pursue teaching careers.
Financial data: Year ended 09/30/2013. Assets, $752,083 (M); Expenditures, $39,338; Total giving, $33,750.
Fields of interest: Teacher school/education.
Type of support: Support to graduates or students of specific schools; Undergraduate support.
Application information: Applications accepted.

Initial approach: Letter
Deadline(s): Varies
EIN: 376193766

8104
The William G. and M. Virginia Simpson Foundation
52 S. Petrie Rd.
Coraopolis, PA 15108

Foundation type: Independent foundation
Purpose: Scholarships to students attending Lehigh University, University of Pittsburgh, or University of Pennsylvania, all in PA, who are either from, or presently living in, western PA or parts of OH, WV, and MD. Applicants must have had experience working in business or finance, or demonstrated significant interest in working in these areas.
Financial data: Year ended 06/30/2013. Assets, $1,404,197 (M); Expenditures, $127,833; Total giving, $81,000; Grants to individuals, 9 grants totaling $40,000 (high: $6,250, low: $2,000).
Fields of interest: Business school/education; Economics.
Type of support: Support to graduates or students of specific schools; Undergraduate support.
Application information: Applications not accepted.
  Additional information: Recipients are nominated by participating universities.
EIN: 251488701

8105
Dr. James W. Sinden Scholarship Fund
2201 Ridgewood Rd., Ste. 180
Wyomissing, PA 19610-1190 (610) 268-7483
Application address: Dr. James W. Siden Scholarship Committee, American Mushroom Institute, 1284 Gap Newport Pike, Ste. 2, Avondale, PA 19311-9503

Foundation type: Independent foundation
Purpose: Scholarships to students pursuing degrees beyond the baccalaureate level at an accredited college or university within the U.S.
Financial data: Year ended 12/31/2011. Assets, $0 (M); Expenditures, $23,008; Total giving, $22,746.
Fields of interest: Higher education.
Type of support: Scholarships—to individuals; Graduate support; Undergraduate support.
Application information: Applications accepted. Application form required.
  Deadline(s): June
  Applicants should submit the following:
    1) Transcripts
    2) Letter(s) of recommendation
    3) Financial information
EIN: 232170419

8106
Singer Family C & E Foundation
(formerly C & E Foundation)
c/o Judith A. Harris
1611 Pond Rd.
Allentown, PA 18104-2258

Foundation type: Independent foundation
Purpose: Scholarships to graduating students of one Carbon County, PA and two Warren County, NJ high schools.
Financial data: Year ended 12/31/2011. Assets, $5,124,484 (M); Expenditures, $264,300; Total giving, $217,500.

Type of support: Undergraduate support.
Application information: Applications accepted.
  Initial approach: Letter
  Deadline(s): None
EIN: 232929096

8107
Frank Foster Skillman Scholarship
c/o PNC Bank
620 Liberty Ave., 10th Fl.
Pittsburgh, PA 15222-2705 (512) 345-6701

Foundation type: Independent foundation
Purpose: Scholarships to full-time students who are residents of Cincinnati, OH enrolled at accredited institutions.
Financial data: Year ended 09/30/2012. Assets, $495,578 (M); Expenditures, $28,584; Total giving, $20,000.
Fields of interest: Higher education.
Type of support: Scholarships—to individuals.
Application information: Applications accepted. Application form required.
  Deadline(s): Apr. 30
EIN: 316018084

8108
Josiah Sleeper & Lottie S. Hill Fund
c/o PNC Bank, N.A.
620 Liberty Ave., 10th Fl.
Pittsburgh, PA 15222-2705 (412) 762-3792

Foundation type: Public charity
Purpose: Grants to women and children, primarily in PA, to cover rehabilitative and convalescent expenses.
Financial data: Year ended 03/31/2012. Assets, $771,140 (M); Expenditures, $40,800; Total giving, $30,022.
Fields of interest: Medical care, rehabilitation; Nursing home/convalescent facility; Children/youth, services; Women.
Type of support: Grants for special needs.
Application information: Applications not accepted.
  Additional information: Unsolicited requests for funds not considered or acknowledged.
EIN: 232120878

8109
Slippery Rock University Foundation, Inc.
(formerly Slippery Rock Foundation, Inc.)
P.O. Box 233
100 Old Main
Slippery Rock, PA 16057-1313 (724) 738-2047
Contact: Edward R. Bucha, Exec. Dir.
FAX: (724) 738-2520; URL: http://www.sru.edu/advancement/Pages/SRUFoundation.aspx

Foundation type: Public charity
Purpose: Scholarships to students for attendance at Slippery Rock University, PA.
Financial data: Year ended 06/30/2012. Assets, $152,290,095 (M); Expenditures, $20,048,246; Total giving, $2,327,956; Grants to individuals, totaling $2,009,499.
Fields of interest: Higher education.
Type of support: Support to graduates or students of specific schools.
Application information: Applications accepted.
  Initial approach: Letter
EIN: 237093388

8110
Marguerite Carl Smith Foundation
c/o Woodlands Bank
2450 E. 3rd St.
Williamsport, PA 17701

Foundation type: Independent foundation
Purpose: Scholarships to Jersey Shore Area High School, PA seniors and graduates who are in the top third of their class or have a current college GPA of 3.0 or better on a 4.0 scale.
Financial data: Year ended 05/31/2013. Assets, $2,652,610 (M); Expenditures, $158,315; Total giving, $139,000.
Fields of interest: Medical school/education; Nursing school/education; Teacher school/education.
Type of support: Support to graduates or students of specific schools; Undergraduate support.
Application information: Applications accepted. Application form required.
  Initial approach: Letter or telephone
  Deadline(s): Mar. 25
  Applicants should submit the following:
    1) Class rank
    2) Transcripts
    3) SAT
  Additional information: Application should also include three letters of reference, two of which should come from high school or college teachers. Consideration is given first to applicants pursuing studies in teaching, nursing or other medical fields.
EIN: 232564406

8111
Smith Memorial Scholarship Fund
(formerly Patrick M. and Janet T. Smith Scholarship Fund)
5760 Michael Dr.
Bensalem, PA 19020-2455
URL: http://www.smithmemorialscholarshipfund.com/

Foundation type: Independent foundation
Purpose: Scholarships to students attending Archbishop Ryan High School, PA.
Financial data: Year ended 06/30/2012. Assets, $104,375 (M); Expenditures, $27,401; Total giving, $10,050; Grants to individuals, 8 grants totaling $10,000 (high: $1,250, low: $1,250).
Type of support: Support to graduates or students of specific schools; Precollege support.
Application information: Applications not accepted.
  Additional information: Unsolicited requests for funds not considered or acknowledged.
EIN: 232791619

8112
Graycie Campbell Smith Veterinary Trust
701 N. Hermitage Rd.
Hermitage, PA 16148-3234

Foundation type: Independent foundation
Purpose: Scholarships to residents of Dearborn, MI, attending a veterinary school.
Financial data: Year ended 12/31/2011. Assets, $506,406 (M); Expenditures, $44,031; Total giving, $30,000; Grants to individuals, 3 grants totaling $30,000 (high: $10,000, low: $10,000).
Fields of interest: Formal/general education.
Type of support: Undergraduate support.
Application information: Applications not accepted.

Additional information: Unsolicited requests for funds not considered or acknowledged.
EIN: 206387055

8113
The Smithfield Township College Assistance Fund

(formerly Jessie B. Kautz Trust)
c/o BNY Mellon, N.A.
P.O. Box 185
Pittsburgh, PA 15230-0185

Foundation type: Independent foundation
Purpose: Scholarships to graduates of the Smithfield Township Public School, PA and the East Stroudsburg Area High School, PA to attend a non-sectarian college or university pursuing careers in Agriculture, Mining, Chemistry, Business Administration, Geology, Journalism, Pre-medicine, Architecture, Mathematics, Metallurgy, Electronics, Biology, Engineering, Atomic Science, Economics, Physics and Political Science.
Financial data: Year ended 12/31/2012. Assets, $162,267 (M); Expenditures, $9,134; Total giving, $6,000; Grants to individuals, 3 grants totaling $6,000 (high: $2,000, low: $2,000).
Fields of interest: Business school/education; Medical school/education; Engineering school/education; Journalism school/education; Agriculture; Science; Physical/earth sciences; Chemistry; Mathematics; Physics; Biology/life sciences; Economics; Political science.
Type of support: Support to graduates or students of specific schools; Undergraduate support.
Application information: Applications accepted.
  Initial approach: Letter
  Deadline(s): None
  Additional information: Applicants must be residents of Smithfield Township.
EIN: 236720230

8114
Frank L. and Laura L. Smock Foundation

c/o Wells Fargo Bank, N.A.
101 N. Independence Mall E MACY 1372-062
Philadelphia, PA 19106-2112

Foundation type: Independent foundation
Purpose: Medical and nursing care assistance to ailing, needy, crippled, blind, or elderly residents of IN who are members of Presbyterian churches and who have less than $3,000 in assets.
Financial data: Year ended 12/31/2012. Assets, $15,458,775 (M); Expenditures, $800,112; Total giving, $684,724.
Fields of interest: Christian agencies & churches; Protestant agencies & churches; Aging; Disabilities, people with; Blind/visually impaired; Deaf/hearing impaired; Economically disadvantaged.
Type of support: Grants for special needs.
Application information: Applications not accepted.
  Additional information: Giving only to preselected individuals.
EIN: 356011335

8115
Burt Snyder Educational Foundation

c/o Wells Fargo Bank Northwest, N.A.
101 N Independence Mall E Macy 1372-062
Philadelphia, PA 19106-2112 (541) 947-2196
Contact: Jim Lynch
Application address: c/o 620 N. 1st St., Lake View, OR 97630-1506

Foundation type: Independent foundation
Purpose: Scholarships to graduates of public high schools in Lake County, OR.
Financial data: Year ended 06/30/2012. Assets, $426,414 (M); Expenditures, $31,667; Total giving, $24,000; Grants to individuals, 4 grants totaling $24,000 (high: $7,200, low: $7,200).
Fields of interest: Education.
Type of support: Support to graduates or students of specific schools; Undergraduate support.
Application information: Applications accepted.
  Deadline(s): None
  Additional information: Contact foundation for additional application guidelines.
EIN: 936033286

8116
Elmer A. & Anna Belle C. Snyder Scholarship Fund

P.O. Box 1022, 1 Glade Park E.
Kittanning, PA 16201-1901 (724) 548-8101
Contact: Oliver Schaub, Tr.

Foundation type: Independent foundation
Purpose: Scholarships to students of Armstrong county, PA school districts for continuing their education.
Financial data: Year ended 12/31/2011. Assets, $616,566 (M); Expenditures, $35,073; Total giving, $32,000; Grants to individuals, 8 grants totaling $32,000 (high: $4,000, low: $4,000).
Fields of interest: Education.
Type of support: Scholarships—to individuals.
Application information: Applications accepted. Application form required.
  Deadline(s): Apr. 15
EIN: 256373182

8117
Franklin C. Snyder/Longue Vue Club Employee Scholarship Foundation

c/o Ken Pizzica
400 Longue Vue Dr.
Verona, PA 15147-1716 (412) 793-2232
Contact: Kenneth R. Pizzica, V.P., Treas. and Dir.

Foundation type: Independent foundation
Purpose: Scholarships to employees of Longue Vue Club.
Financial data: Year ended 12/31/2012. Assets, $107,427 (M); Expenditures, $35,999; Total giving, $31,500; Grants to individuals, 28 grants totaling $31,500 (high: $1,500, low: $500).
Type of support: Employee-related scholarships.
Application information: Applications accepted. Application form required.
  Initial approach: Letter
  Deadline(s): None
Company name: Longue Vue Club
EIN: 251715070

8118
Harry L. & Ruby T. Soames Educational Foundation

c/o Wells Fargo Bank , N.A.
101 N. Independence Mall E. MACY1372-062
Philadelphia, PA 19106-2112

Foundation type: Independent foundation
Purpose: Scholarships to graduates of Kent School District high schools, WA, who meet entrance requirements for the University of Washington even if this is not the institution they will be attending.
Financial data: Year ended 09/30/2012. Assets, $639,172 (M); Expenditures, $36,890; Total giving, $26,220.
Type of support: Support to graduates or students of specific schools; Undergraduate support.
Application information: Applications accepted.
  Initial approach: Letter
  Deadline(s): June 1
  Additional information: Application must outline grades and reasons for wanting a higher education.
EIN: 916281207

8119
Society for Analytical Chemists of Pittsburgh

300 Penn Ctr. Blvd., Ste. 332
Pittsburgh, PA 15235-5503 (412) 825-3220 ext. 204
Contact: Valerie Daugherty, Admin. Asst.
FAX: (412) 825-3224; E-mail: sacpinfo@pittcon.org; E-mail for Valerie Daughtery: daugherty@pittcon.org; URL: http://www.sacp.org/

Foundation type: Independent foundation
Purpose: Awards to individuals by nomination only for outstanding achievements in the field of analytical chemistry and/or applied spectroscopy in the PA, area. Scholarships to high school seniors and summer internships to college juniors and seniors who are chemistry majors and plan to pursue graduate education in analytical chemistry. Grants to PA science teachers and undergraduate science researchers.
Publications: Informational brochure.
Financial data: Year ended 06/30/2012. Assets, $179,167 (M); Expenditures, $527,035; Total giving, $391,859.
Fields of interest: Education; Science; Chemistry.
Type of support: Program development; Research; Awards/grants by nomination only; Awards/prizes; Undergraduate support.
Application information:
  Deadline(s): Apr. 30
Program descriptions:
  Analytical Chemistry Professor Starter Grant: The society awards one grant of $20,000 per year to an assistant professor in the field of analytical chemistry. The purpose of this grant is to encourage high-quality, innovative research by a new analytical chemistry professor and to promote the training and development of graduate students in this field.
  Elementary/Middle School Science Equipment Grant: The society invites every teacher who teaches science in selected counties of OH, PA, and WV to apply for an SACP Elementary/Middle School Equipment Grant. Applicant need not be designated as an official science teacher. The grant is for a maximum of $500, and at least 60 proposals will be funded.
  High School Science Essay Contest: The society invites every teacher who teaches science in selected counties of OH, PA, and WV to apply for an SACP Elementary/Middle School Equipment Grant. Applicant need not be designated as an official

science teacher. The grant is for a maximum of $500, and at least 60 proposals will be funded.

Keene Dimick Award: $5,000 cash award presented annually for noteworthy accomplishments in the area of gas and supercritical fluid chromatography (GC,SFC). Awards are presented at a symposium arranged by the awardee during the Pittsburgh Conference.

Middle School Science Essay Contest: Prizes of varying cash amounts given to middle school students for winning essays on science topics.

Pittsburgh Analytical Chemistry Award: $2,000 award given in recognition of outstanding research in the field of analytical chemistry.

Undergraduate Analytical Research Program (UARP) Grant: The society has established a $10,000 annual grant to promote high-quality, innovative undergraduate research in the field of analytical chemistry and to promote training and development of undergraduate students in the field of analytical chemistry. Chemistry faculty at U.S. colleges and universities not having a graduate program in the chemical sciences are eligible to apply.

Waters Instrumentation Symposia: Honoraria are paid to participants in this symposium, which recognizes pioneers in the development of scientific instrumentation.
EIN: 256072976

8120
Elizabeth H. Soeder Scholarship Trust
c/o Well Fargo Bank, N.A.
101 N. Independence Mall E. MACY1372-062
Philadelphia, PA   19106-2112   (866) 601-0001

Foundation type: Independent foundation
Purpose: Scholarships to deserving graduating seniors of Cape May County, NJ enrolled at an accredited two or four year public or private, college, university, technical college or vocational school.
Financial data: Year ended 04/30/2013. Assets, $520,889 (M); Expenditures, $34,532; Total giving, $21,400.
Type of support: Support to graduates or students of specific schools; Undergraduate support.
Application information: Applications accepted. Application form required.
   Initial approach: Letter, telephone or e-mail
   Deadline(s): Feb. 16
   Applicants should submit the following:
      1) GPA
      2) Letter(s) of recommendation
   Additional information: Application must also include a list of academic honors, leadership positions, and community service, signed copy of parent's federal tax form and W-2 forms. Applicant must have an unweighted cumulative GPA of 3.0 at the end of the fall term of their senior year in high school, and demonstrate financial need. The scholarship is administered by The Center for Scholarship Administrationn, Inc. Applications may be obtained from CSA at 4320 Wade Hampton, Blvd., Ste. G, Taylors, SC 29687, tel.: (866) 608-0001, e-mail: ljenkinscsa&bellsouth.net.
EIN: 226082438

8121
Somerville Foundation
(formerly Grahame and Thelma Somerville Scholarship Foundation)
c/o PNC Bank
P.O. Box 609
Pittsburgh, PA   15230-9738   (216) 222-9831
Contact: Jane Kleinsmith
Application address: 1900 E. 9th St., Cleveland, OH 44114

Foundation type: Independent foundation
Purpose: Scholarships to nontraditional-aged students of the Fort Wayne, IN, area, who seek an undergraduate degree or vocational training.
Financial data: Year ended 10/31/2013. Assets, $2,838,222 (M); Expenditures, $143,805; Total giving, $115,751; Grant to an individual, 1 grant totaling $115,751.
Fields of interest: Vocational education.
Type of support: Undergraduate support.
Application information: Application form required.
   Deadline(s): July 15
EIN: 356547210

8122
Madeleine H. Soren Trust
c/o BNY Mellon, N.A.
P.O. Box 185
Pittsburgh, PA   15230-0185

Foundation type: Independent foundation
Purpose: Scholarships to financially needy female graduates of MA high schools for studies in music and music education.
Financial data: Year ended 08/31/2012. Assets, $339,712 (M); Expenditures, $22,045; Total giving, $15,000; Grants to individuals, 10 grants totaling $15,000 (high: $2,000, low: $1,000).
Fields of interest: Music; Performing arts, education; Women.
Type of support: Undergraduate support.
Application information: Applications accepted.
   Initial approach: Telepone
   Deadline(s): May 1
   Additional information: Contact the trust for additional information.
EIN: 046092280

8123
South Butler County School District Foundation
328 Knoch Rd.
Saxonburg, PA   16056-9322
Application address: c/o Knoch Senior High School, Attn.: Counseling Center, 345 Knoch Rd., Saxonburg, PA 16056

Foundation type: Independent foundation
Purpose: Scholarships to students of the South Butler County School District, PA.
Financial data: Year ended 06/30/2011. Assets, $2,228,790 (M); Expenditures, $70,186; Total giving, $62,477; Grants to individuals, 23 grants totaling $44,666 (high: $5,000, low: $400).
Type of support: Support to graduates or students of specific schools; Undergraduate support.
Application information: Applications accepted.
   Deadline(s): Mar. 15
EIN: 251735818

8124
South Central Community Action Program, Inc.
153 N. Stratton St.
Gettysburg, PA   17325-1822   (717) 334-7634
Additional address (Chambersburg office): 533 S. Main St., Chambersburg, PA 17201-3505, tel.: (717) 263-5060; URL: http://www.sccap.org/

Foundation type: Public charity
Purpose: A food pantry provides monthly allotments of food, home weatherization, and emergency energy assistance to qualifying indigent families in the Gettysburg area of PA.
Financial data: Year ended 06/30/2011. Assets, $4,324,908 (M); Expenditures, $13,246,076; Total giving, $5,745,251; Grants to individuals, 79,315 grants totaling $5,511,591. Subtotal for grants to individuals: 79,315 grants totaling $5,511,591. Subtotal for in-kind gifts: grants totaling $233,660.
Fields of interest: Economically disadvantaged.
Type of support: In-kind gifts; Grants for special needs.
Application information:
   Initial approach: Letter
   Additional information: Contact foundation for eligibility criteria.
EIN: 232020123

8125
Southern Alleghenies Planning and Development Commission
3 Sheraton Dr.
Altoona, PA   16601-9343   (814) 949-6513
FAX: (814) 949-6505; E-mail: silvetti@sapdc.org;
URL: http://www.sapdc.org

Foundation type: Public charity
Purpose: Support to individuals in Bedford, Blair, Cambria, Fulton, Huntingdon, and Somerset counties, PA who are working to obtain and maintain employment.
Publications: Financial statement.
Financial data: Year ended 06/30/2011. Assets, $19,363,192 (M); Expenditures, $10,662,570; Total giving, $7,042,675; Grants to individuals, 404 grants totaling $1,865,208. Subtotal for stipends: 404 grants totaling $1,865,208.
Fields of interest: Community/economic development.
Type of support: Grants to individuals.
Application information: Contact the organization for additional information.
EIN: 251190505

8126
Isabel Spackman Foundation
c/o PNC Bank, N.A.
1600 Market St.,Tax Dept.
Philadelphia, PA   19103-7240
Contact: Kara Chickson

Foundation type: Independent foundation
Purpose: Financial assistance to primarily needy Episcopalians, in the Philadelphia, PA area.
Financial data: Year ended 12/31/2012. Assets, $969,578 (M); Expenditures, $41,651; Total giving, $23,700; Grants to individuals, 5 grants totaling $23,200 (high: $8,400, low: $1,000).
Fields of interest: Protestant agencies & churches; Economically disadvantaged.
Type of support: Grants for special needs.
Application information: Applications accepted.

Initial approach: Letter
Deadline(s): None
EIN: 237226511

8127

St. Margaret Foundation

100 Medical Arts Bldg., Ste. 100
815 Freeport Rd.
Pittsburgh, PA 15215-3301 (412) 784-4205
Contact: Mary Lee Gannon, Pres.
FAX: (412) 784-4062; E-Mail for Mary Lee Gannon :
gannonm@upmc.eduTel. for Mary Lee Gannon :
(412)-784-4277; URL: http://
www.stmargaretfoundation.org/

Foundation type: Public charity
Purpose: Financial assistance for medical services
and other necessities to residents of the Pittsburg,
PA, area.
Financial data: Year ended 06/30/2011. Assets,
$19,982,011 (M); Expenditures, $1,156,461;
Total giving, $561,139; Grants to individuals,
totaling $8,960.
Fields of interest: Economically disadvantaged.
Type of support: Grants for special needs.
Application information:
Initial approach: Letter
Additional information: Contact foundation for
complete eligibility requirements.
EIN: 251520340

8128

Henry P. and Mary B. Stager Memorial Nursing Scholarship

c/o Tax Dept.
P.O. Box 3215
Lancaster, PA 17604-3215
Application address: Lancaster Health Alliance
School, Financial Aid Admin., 145 E. Lemon St.,
Lancaster, PA 17602

Foundation type: Independent foundation
Purpose: Scholarships to students at the Lancaster
Health Alliance School of Nursing.
Financial data: Year ended 10/31/2012. Assets,
$1,478,285 (M); Expenditures, $93,708; Total
giving, $77,000; Grants to individuals, 114 grants
totaling $77,000 (high: $2,500, low: $125).
Fields of interest: Nursing school/education.
Type of support: Support to graduates or students
of specific schools; Undergraduate support.
Application information: Applications accepted.
Application form required.
Deadline(s): May 1
EIN: 232821372

8129

Matt Stager Memorial Scholarship Fund

c/o Fernley & Fernley, Inc.
100 N. 20th St., 4th Fl.
Philadelphia, PA 19103-1404

Foundation type: Public charity
Purpose: Scholarships to children of Water and
Sewer Distributors Association member company
employees.
Financial data: Year ended 12/31/2011. Assets,
$97,052 (M); Expenditures, $24,621; Total giving,
$17,000.
Type of support: Employee-related scholarships.
Application information: Applications accepted.
Initial approach: Letter
Additional information: Contact foundation for
current application deadline/guidelines.
EIN: 311480297

8130

James Hale Steinman Foundation

8 W. King St.
P.O. Box 128
Lancaster, PA 17608-0128 (717) 291-8676
Contact: Christine Mellinger
E-mail: cmellinger@lnpnews.com

Foundation type: Independent foundation
Purpose: Scholarships to newspaper carriers and
children of employees of Steinman Enterprises,
primarily in Lancaster, PA.
Financial data: Year ended 12/31/2012. Assets,
$32,806,614 (M); Expenditures, $2,079,162;
Total giving, $1,915,621.
Type of support: Employee-related scholarships.
Application information: Application form required.
Deadline(s): Feb. 28
Company name: Steinman Enterprises
EIN: 236266377

8131

John Frederick Steinman Foundation

P.O. Box 128
Lancaster, PA 17608-0128
E-mail: cmellinger@lnpnews.com; Additional
address: c/o M. Steven Weaver, Secy., Fellow, 8 W.
King St., P.O. Box 1328, Lancaster, PA
17603-3824, tel.: (717) 291-8676

Foundation type: Independent foundation
Purpose: Fellowships primarily to residents of
Lancaster, PA, for graduate study in the mental
health field.
Publications: Informational brochure.
Financial data: Year ended 12/31/2012. Assets,
$31,251,661 (M); Expenditures, $1,512,884;
Total giving, $1,359,250.
Fields of interest: Research.
Type of support: Fellowships; Graduate support.
Application information: Application form required.
Deadline(s): Feb. 1
EIN: 236266378

8132

Helen Wolcott Stockwell Trust

c/o BNY Mellon, N.A.
P.O. Box 185
Pittsburgh, PA 15230-0185

Foundation type: Independent foundation
Purpose: Financial assistance to economically
disadvantaged individuals of Stoneham, MA for
medical expenses and other needs.
Financial data: Year ended 08/31/2012. Assets,
$1,016,240 (M); Expenditures, $57,506; Total
giving, $42,503; Grants to individuals, 26 grants
totaling $17,153 (high: $4,690, low: $22).
Fields of interest: Health care; Economically
disadvantaged.
Type of support: Grants for special needs.
Application information: Applications accepted.
Application form required.
Initial approach: Letter, telephone, or in person
Additional information: Payments are made
directly to the medical insitutions and
physicians on behalf of the applicant. Contact
the trust for eligibility requirement.
EIN: 046092050

8133

Stoneleigh Foundation

(formerly A. Stoneleigh Research and Education
Center Serving Children and Youth)
123 S. Broad St., Ste. 1130
Philadelphia, PA 19109-1019 (215) 735-7080
Contact: Cathy M. Weiss, Exec. Dir.
FAX: (215) 735-7089;
E-mail: info@stoneleighfoundation.org;
URL: http://www.stoneleighfoundation.org

Foundation type: Operating foundation
Purpose: Fellowships for research and leadership
development in the areas of child welfare and
juvenile justice.
Publications: Application guidelines.
Financial data: Year ended 06/30/2012. Assets,
$12,478,280 (M); Expenditures, $1,612,904;
Total giving, $905,391; Grant to an individual, 1
grant totaling $75,076.
Fields of interest: Education; Children, services.
Type of support: Fellowships.
Application information: Applications accepted.
Application form required. Application form
available on the grantmaker's web site.
Additional information: See web site for complete
fellowship guidelines and forms.
Program descriptions:
Junior Fellowship Program: This fellowship
cultivates a new generation of leaders in the fields
of child welfare and juvenile justice, and allied fields
such as education and behavioral. It provides an
opportunity for exceptional recent graduates
interested in social policy and public service to work
for one year at an organization in the public or
non-profit sectors in Philadelphia and Harrisburg,
PA. The fellowship is designed to provide dynamic,
hands-on experience for the Junior Fellow resulting
in a tangible work product that advances the career
of the young professional. See foundation web site
for complete guidelines.
Stoneleigh Fellowships: These fellowships are
designed to support creative, accomplished
researchers, practitioners, and policymakers who
have demonstrated leadership in child welfare,
education, juvenile justice, or related fields.
Candidates might be mid- to senior-level
practitioners in youth- or family-serving
organizations or systems. They might also be
seasoned policymakers, analysts, or researchers
working in non-profit, governmental, or academic
institutions. See foundation web site for complete
guidelines.
EIN: 371526458

8134

The Stork Charitable Trust

5727 Twin Silo Rd.
Doylestown, PA 18901-9507 (508) 864-6213
Contact: Erica Zoino Curran, Tr.
Application address: 146 Cockle Cove Rd., S.
Chatham, MA 02659

Foundation type: Independent foundation
Purpose: Scholarships to graduating seniors of
Brockton High School, MA, who have been accepted
to four-year colleges and universities.
Financial data: Year ended 09/30/2012. Assets,
$571,174 (M); Expenditures, $34,945; Total
giving, $35,000; Grants to individuals, 7 grants
totaling $35,000 (high: $5,000, low: $5,000).
Fields of interest: Higher education; Scholarships/
financial aid; Economically disadvantaged.
Type of support: Support to graduates or students
of specific schools; Undergraduate support.

Application information: Applications accepted. Application form required.

>Deadline(s): Mar. 15
>
>Applicants should submit the following:
>1) Transcripts
>2) FAF
>3) Financial information
>
>Additional information: Application should also include a personal statement. Applications available at the school's guidance office. Applicant must demonstrate financial need.

EIN: 236951762

8135
Evelyn E. Stricklin Scholarship

c/o PNC Bank, N.A.
1600 Market St.,
Philadelphia, PA   19103-7240   (302) 429-1115
Contact: Aruna Pappu
Application address: 222 Delaware Ave., 18th Fl., Wilmington, DE 19801

Foundation type: Independent foundation
Purpose: Scholarships to financially needy students who are residents of DE, graduating from a Delaware high school for attendance at the University of Delaware, DE.
Financial data: Year ended 09/30/2012. Assets, $1,598,150 (M); Expenditures, $75,845; Total giving, $56,000; Grants to individuals, totaling $56,000.
Fields of interest: Higher education.
Type of support: Support to graduates or students of specific schools.
Application information: Applications accepted. Application form required.

>Initial approach: Letter
>Deadline(s): Apr. 19
>Applicants should submit the following:
>1) Letter(s) of recommendation
>2) Transcripts
>3) SAT
>
>Additional information: Applicant must demonstrate financial need.

EIN: 016173503

8136
The Clair E. Stuck and Flora E. Stuck Foundation, Inc.

7958 U.S. Hwy. 522 S.
McVeytown, PA   17051-7457   (717) 248-8245
Contact: Gloria A. Shank, Pres.

Foundation type: Independent foundation
Purpose: Scholarships to high school graduates of Mifflin or Juniata counties, PA, for attendance at an institution of higher learning.
Financial data: Year ended 12/31/2011. Assets, $33,623 (M); Expenditures, $28,777; Total giving, $27,972; Grants to individuals, 28 grants totaling $27,972 (high: $999, low: $999).
Fields of interest: Higher education.
Type of support: Scholarships—to individuals.
Application information: Applications accepted. Interview required.

>Deadline(s): Prior to end of school year
>Applicants should submit the following:
>1) Transcripts
>2) Essay
>
>Additional information: Applicant must maintain at least a "C" average through out high school. Funds will be paid directly to the educational institution on behalf of the student. Contact your school's guidance counselor for application information.

EIN: 251709803

8137
Gerald Sutliff Trust f/b/o Hofstra University

c/o BNY Mellon, N.A.
P.O. Box 185
Pittsburgh, PA   15230-0185
Contact: Alfred E. Urban, Jr.
Application address: Post 256, P.O. Box 6, Garden City, NY, 11530-0008

Foundation type: Independent foundation
Purpose: Scholarships to graduates of Garden City High School, NY, who will attend Hofstra University.
Financial data: Year ended 09/30/2013. Assets, $239,242 (M); Expenditures, $11,052; Total giving, $10,000.
Type of support: Support to graduates or students of specific schools; Undergraduate support.
Application information: Applications accepted. Application form required.

>Deadline(s): None

EIN: 133543303

8138
Charles S. Swope Memorial Scholarship Trust

P.O. Box 3105
West Chester, PA   19381-3105
Application address: WCU Foundation, Attn: Swope Scholarship Committee, P.O. Box 541, West Chester, PA 19381, for hand-delivery: WCU Foundation, 202 Carter Dr., West Chester, PA 19382, e-mail: (to be scanned) swopescholarship@gmail.com

Foundation type: Independent foundation
Purpose: Scholarships to full time undergraduate students who have completed at least 45 credit hours at West Chester University, PA, and to graduate students enrolled in a full time program with a minimum 9 credits and must have received their B.A. from West Chester University.
Financial data: Year ended 12/31/2011. Assets, $821,551 (M); Expenditures, $43,323; Total giving, $33,500; Grants to individuals, 13 grants totaling $33,500 (high: $3,500, low: $2,500).
Fields of interest: Higher education.
Type of support: Support to graduates or students of specific schools; Undergraduate support.
Application information: Application form required.

>Send request by: Mail, e-mail or hand deliver
>Deadline(s): Apr. 30
>Final notification: Recipients notified in May
>Applicants should submit the following:
>1) Resume
>2) Curriculum vitae
>3) Letter(s) of recommendation
>
>Additional information: Students must be U.S. citizens and have permanent residence. Scholarships are awarded on the basis of academic achievement, leadership, service, character, industry, and financial need.

EIN: 236390730

8139
Taylor Community Foundation

300 Johnson Ave.
P.O. Box 227
Ridley Park, PA   19078-1834   (610) 461-6571
Contact: Patrick F. O'Brien, Chair.
FAX: (610) 521-6057;
E-mail: info@taylorcommfdn.org; E-mail for Kurt J. Slenn: kslenn@taylorcommfdn.org; URL: http://www.taylorcommfdn.org

Foundation type: Public charity

Purpose: Scholarships to individuals for undergraduate education who will major in an allied health profession and live in the foundation's service area of PA.
Publications: Application guidelines; Annual report; Grants list; Informational brochure (including application guidelines).
Financial data: Year ended 06/30/2012. Assets, $10,247,329 (M); Expenditures, $3,846,627; Total giving, $140,280; Grants to individuals, totaling $1,000.
Fields of interest: Health sciences school/education.
Type of support: Undergraduate support.
Application information: Applications accepted. Application form required. Application form available on the grantmaker's web site. Interview required.

>Initial approach: Application
>Deadline(s): Nov. 30
>Final notification: Recipients notified in Feb.
>Applicants should submit the following:
>1) ACT
>2) Transcripts
>3) SAT
>4) Letter(s) of recommendation
>5) Essay
>
>Additional information: See web site for additional guidelines and TCF Service Area.

Program description:

>Scholarships: Scholarships, generally of $2,500 per year, will be awarded to selected individuals who are interested in pursuing an undergraduate degree in allied health professions which will result in the student, upon graduation, performing work that will enhance the quality of life for people in the foundation's primary service area. Scholarships will be for one to four years and would cover part of the student's total costs. Amounts may vary from one individual to another. Eligible applicants must live in the foundation's service area.

EIN: 232354770

8140
Teamsters Local 830 Scholarship Fund

12298 Townsend Rd.
Philadelphia, PA   19154-1203   (215) 969-1012
Contact: Samuel J. Kenish, Admin.
FAX: (215) 969-3205

Foundation type: Public charity
Purpose: Scholarships to dependent children of Teamsters Local 830 Scholarship Fund in DE, NJ, and PA who are in their senior year of high school. Application forms are mailed out to all employers who participate in the fund.
Publications: Annual report; Financial statement.
Financial data: Year ended 12/31/2011. Assets, $420,155 (M); Expenditures, $163,267; Total giving, $144,000.
Fields of interest: Labor unions/organizations.
Type of support: Undergraduate support.
Application information: Application form required.

>Deadline(s): Feb. 1
>Additional information: Application must include college entrance examination board scores, general scholastic achievements, and transcripts.

EIN: 232003122

8141
John Templeton Foundation

300 Conshohocken State Rd., Ste. 500
West Conshohocken, PA   19428-3801   (610)
941-2828
Contact: Grant Admin.
FAX: (610) 825-1730; E-mail: info@templeton.org;
URL: http://www.templeton.org/

Foundation type: Independent foundation
Purpose: Research grants to scholars of psychology
who hold a Ph.D. degree, and awards by nomination
only to individuals who show extraordinary
originality in advancing humankind's understanding
of God.
Publications: Annual report; Financial statement;
Informational brochure; Newsletter.
Financial data: Year ended 12/31/2012. Assets,
$2,555,855,497 (M); Expenditures,
$135,931,727; Total giving, $105,248,596.
Fields of interest: Film/video; Television;
Psychology/behavioral science; Religion.
Type of support: Research; Grants to individuals;
Awards/grants by nomination only; Awards/prizes.
Application information: Applications accepted.
  Initial approach: Letter
  Deadline(s): July 1 for Templeton Prize
Program description:
  Templeton Prize: The prize honors a living person
  who has made an exceptional contribution to
  affirming life's spiritual dimension, whether through
  insight, discovery, or practical works. It celebrates
  no particular faith tradition or notion of God, but
  rather the quest for progress in humanity's efforts
  to comprehend the many and diverse
  manifestations of the Divine. Men and women of
  any creed, profession, or national origin may be
  nominated. The qualities sought in a nominee
  include creativity and innovation, rigor and impact.
  The judges seek a substantial record of
  achievement that highlights or exemplifies one of
  the various ways in which human beings express
  their yearning for spiritual progress. Consideration
  is given to a nominee's work as a whole, not just
  during the year prior to selection. Nominations are
  especially encouraged in the fields of: 1) Research
  in the human sciences, life sciences, and physical
  sciences; 2) Scholarship in philosophy, theology,
  and other areas of the humanities; 3) Practice,
  including religious leadership, the creation of
  organizations that edify and inspire, and the
  development of new schools of thought; and 4)
  Commentary and journalism on matters of religion,
  virtue, character formation, and the flourishing of
  the human spirit. The prize is a monetary award in
  the amount of 1,000,000 sterling. For additional
  information contact: Judith Marchand, Dir., The
  Templeton Prize Office.
EIN: 621322826

8142
Teva Cares Foundation

(also known as Cephalon Cares Foundation)
1090 Horsham Rd.
P.O. Box 1090
North Wales, PA   19454-1505   (877) 237-4881
Application address: 6900 College Blvd., Ste. 1000,
Overland Park, KS 66211, tel.: (877) 237-4881;
URL: http://www.cephalon.com/
cephaloncares-foundation.html

Foundation type: Operating foundation
Purpose: Financial assistance to provide Cephalon
medication to economically disadvantaged
individuals lacking prescription drug coverage.
Publications: Application guidelines.

Financial data: Year ended 12/31/2012. Assets,
$9,777,194 (M); Expenditures, $47,891,175;
Total giving, $47,191,722; Grants to individuals,
totaling $47,191,722.
Fields of interest: Health care; Economically
disadvantaged.
Type of support: Grants for special needs.
Application information: Applications accepted.
Application form required. Application form
available on the grantmaker's web site.
  Initial approach: Application
  Send request by: Mail or fax
  Deadline(s): None
  Additional information: Application must be
    signed by a physician and should also include
    proof of income. Application for Fentora,
    Nuvigil, Treanda, Gabitril, Tev-Tropin, and
    Trisenox is available.
EIN: 263977456

8143
The Thoburn Foundation for Education

682 Sugar Run Rd.
New Florence, PA   15944-2326   (724) 235-2030
Contact: Terry Thobum Huston, Pres.

Foundation type: Independent foundation
Purpose: Scholarships to graduates of the Ligonier
Valley School District, PA area for attendance at
colleges, universities, technical and vocational
schools.
Financial data: Year ended 05/31/2013. Assets,
$442,292 (M); Expenditures, $30,739; Total
giving, $22,200; Grants to individuals, 14 grants
totaling $15,000 (high: $2,000; low: $1,000).
Fields of interest: Higher education.
Type of support: Scholarships—to individuals;
Support to graduates or students of specific
schools.
Application information: Applications accepted.
Application form required.
  Deadline(s): Mar. 31
  Applicants should submit the following:
    1) Essay
    2) Financial information
  Additional information: Application should also
    include three letters of reference.
EIN: 251494744

8144
John J. Thomas Foundation

c/o PNC Bank
620 Liberty Ave., 10th Fl.
Pittsburgh, PA   15222-2705   (412) 762-2864

Foundation type: Independent foundation
Purpose: Scholarships to men from PA studying for
the priesthood of the Roman Catholic Church and
to women from PA studying nursing.
Financial data: Year ended 09/30/2012. Assets,
$547,837 (M); Expenditures, $31,563; Total
giving, $24,000.
Fields of interest: Nursing school/education;
Theological school/education; Catholic agencies &
churches; Young adults, female; Young adults,
male.
Type of support: Scholarships—to individuals;
Support to graduates or students of specific
schools.
Application information: Applications accepted.
  Initial approach: Letter
  Deadline(s): None
EIN: 251381212

8145
Jack W. Thompson Foundation

c/o Wells Fargo Bank N.A.
101 N Independence Mall E Macy 1372-062
Philadelphia, PA   19106-2112
Application address: P.O. Box 597, Helena, MT
59624-0597

Foundation type: Independent foundation
Purpose: Scholarships to students from Dawson
County, MT for attendance at accredited colleges or
universities.
Financial data: Year ended 10/31/2012. Assets,
$287,333 (M); Expenditures, $34,617; Total
giving, $30,500; Grants to individuals, 30 grants
totaling $30,500 (high: $1,500, low: $1,000).
Fields of interest: Higher education; Scholarships/
financial aid.
Type of support: Undergraduate support.
Application information: Applications accepted.
Application form required.
  Deadline(s): Apr. 1
  Applicants should submit the following:
    1) Transcripts
    2) FAF
  Additional information: Application should also
    include three references. Applicant must
    demonstrate financial need.
EIN: 816010360

8146
Three Rivers Center for Independent
Living

(formerly Center for Independent Living of
Southwestern Pennsylvania, also known as TRCIL)
900 Rebecca Ave.
Pittsburgh, PA   15221-2938
Contact: Cindy Williams
FAX: (412) 371-9430; E-mail: sholbrook@trcil.org;
Toll-free tel.: (800) 633-4588; TTY: (412)
371-6230; E-Mail for Cindy Williams :
cwilliams@trcil.org; URL: http://www.trcil.org

Foundation type: Public charity
Purpose: Services to residents of PA with
disabilities, which include housing assistance,
assistive technology and equipment, transitioning
from nursing home environments into the
community, personal assistance services, and
community service programs for persons with
physical disabilities.
Publications: Newsletter.
Financial data: Year ended 09/30/2011. Assets,
$7,016,295 (M); Expenditures, $24,111,377;
Total giving, $14,843,230; Grants to individuals,
totaling $14,843,230.
Fields of interest: Housing/shelter, services;
Self-advocacy services, disability; Supported living;
Personal assistance services (PAS); Physically
disabled.
Type of support: Grants for special needs.
Application information:
  Initial approach: Letter
  Additional information: Contact organization for
    eligibility criteria.
EIN: 251549226

8147
TLC Foundation

P.O. Box 1564
Greensburg, PA   15601-6564

Foundation type: Independent foundation
Purpose: Scholarships to residents of Greensburg,
PA.

Financial data: Year ended 07/31/2011. Assets, $34,393 (M); Expenditures, $3,200; Total giving, $3,200.
Type of support: Undergraduate support.
Application information:
Initial approach: Letter
Additional information: Contact foundation for eligibility criteria.
EIN: 251548649

8148
Alfred L. Toth Foundation

680 Wetherby Ln.
Devon, PA 19333-1855

Foundation type: Independent foundation
Purpose: Scholarships to disadvantaged students from Transylvania and from minority communities in neighboring countries for tuition and lodging, pursuing a law degree.
Financial data: Year ended 12/31/2010. Assets, $1 (M); Expenditures, $47,321; Total giving, $47,070; Grants to individuals, totaling $47,070.
Fields of interest: Law school/education.
Type of support: Scholarships—to individuals.
Application information: Applications accepted.
EIN: 233000033

8149
Livingston Trout and Mellinger Medical Research Fund

P.O. Box 3215, Tax Dept.
Lancaster, PA 17604-3215
Application address: c/o Fulton Financial Advisors, Attn: Vince Lattanzio, P.O. Box 7989, Lancaster, PA 17602

Foundation type: Independent foundation
Purpose: Grants to doctors in eastern PA for medical research.
Financial data: Year ended 02/28/2013. Assets, $584,296 (M); Expenditures, $45,001; Total giving, $37,184.
Fields of interest: Medical research.
Type of support: Research.
Application information: Applications accepted.
Initial approach: Letter
Deadline(s): None
Additional information: Letter should state purpose of medical research.
EIN: 237660671

8150
Paul A. Troutman Foundation

1570 Manheim Pike
Lancaster, PA 17604-3300
Contact: Christine A. Zanis
Application address: c/o Susquehanna Trust and Investment Co., 48 Orchard Dr., Shamokin Dam, PA 17876

Foundation type: Independent foundation
Purpose: Scholarships to graduating seniors of Millersburgh School District, Millersburgh, PA.
Financial data: Year ended 11/30/2012. Assets, $782,405 (M); Expenditures, $50,402; Total giving, $36,900; Grants to individuals, 8 grants totaling $16,000 (high: $2,000, low: $2,000).
Type of support: Support to graduates or students of specific schools; Undergraduate support.
Application information: Applications accepted.
Deadline(s): None
Additional information: Contact foundation for current application guidelines.
EIN: 232086508

8151
Allene S. Trushel Scholarship Trust

c/o Citizens & Northern Bank
90-92 Main St.
Wellsboro, PA 16901-1517   (814) 274-9150
Application address: c/o Oswayo Valley School District, attn.: Guidance Counselor, P.O. Box 610, Shinglehouse, PA 16478-0610

Foundation type: Independent foundation
Purpose: Scholarships to graduates of Oswayo Valley School District, PA, schools who have completed their entire senior year while residing within the district.
Publications: Application guidelines.
Financial data: Year ended 12/31/2012. Assets, $597,620 (M); Expenditures, $33,429; Total giving, $28,365; Grants to individuals, 5 grants totaling $28,365 (high: $7,790, low: $3,000).
Fields of interest: Medical school/education; Nursing school/education; Veterinary medicine.
Type of support: Support to graduates or students of specific schools; Undergraduate support.
Application information: Applications accepted. Application form required.
Deadline(s): Apr. 15
Additional information: Application should include transcripts and proof of enrollment and specific program. Applications available from the guidance counselor at Oswayo Valley Junior-Senior High School, PA.
Program description:
Trushel Scholarship Program: Scholarships to applicants attending medical school, veterinary school, or nursing school. Secondary consideration will be given to applicants entering their junior year of a pre-medical or pre-veterinary undergraduate program or those attending a one-year LPN program. Scholarships are renewable, but applications must be submitted each year for consideration.
EIN: 251419907

8152
Two Rivers Health and Wellness Foundation

(also known as Two Rivers Hospital Corporation)
1101 Northhampton St., Ste. 101
Easton, PA 18042-4152   (610) 253-7400
Contact: Paul Brunswick, Pres.; Janet A. Mease, Asst. Secy.
FAX: (610) 253-8991;
E-mail: foundation.mail@trhwf.org; Application tel. for Northampton Dental Initiative: (866) 903-9104;
URL: http://www.trhwf.org

Foundation type: Public charity
Purpose: Free dental care to Northampton County, PA underserved residents meeting financial guidelines.
Publications: Application guidelines; Grants list; Newsletter.
Financial data: Year ended 06/30/2011. Assets, $3,372,698 (M); Expenditures, $991,712; Total giving, $452,401; Grants to individuals, totaling $1,000.
Fields of interest: Economically disadvantaged.
Type of support: In-kind gifts; Grants for special needs.
Application information: Applications accepted.
Initial approach: Telephone
Program description:
Northampton Dental Initiative: The foundation provides free dental care to Northampton County residents meeting financial guidelines. The program operates at a selected clinic once a week,

in conjunction with a network of participating dentists.
EIN: 232440924

8153
John Tyndale Scholarship Fund

(also known as John Tyndale Testamentary Trust)
c/o BNY Mellon, N.A.
P.O. Box 185
Pittsburgh, PA 15230-0185

Foundation type: Independent foundation
Purpose: Scholarships to Tyndale family members or graduates of Central High School, PA for higher education.
Financial data: Year ended 09/30/2012. Assets, $232,013 (M); Expenditures, $20,457; Total giving, $16,000.
Fields of interest: Higher education.
Type of support: Scholarships—to individuals; Support to graduates or students of specific schools.
Application information: Applications accepted.
Deadline(s): None
Additional information: Contact fund for current application guidelines.
EIN: 236223859

8154
Union City Community Foundation

P.O. Box 512
Union City, PA 16438-0512   (814) 438-7622
Contact: Kaylynn Ostergard, Admin. Assi.
Application address for Larue Otttaway Scholarship: 459 West 6th St., Erie, PA 16507, Attn: Jane Randall
E-mail: kaylynn@ronjoneshardwood.com;
URL: http://www.unioncitycf.org

Foundation type: Public charity
Purpose: Scholarships to graduating seniors of Union City High School, PA, pursuing a career in health care.
Publications: Application guidelines.
Financial data: Year ended 12/31/2011. Assets, $2,945,162 (M); Expenditures, $159,276; Total giving, $118,140; Grants to individuals, totaling $11,290.
Fields of interest: Higher education; Health sciences school/education.
Type of support: Scholarships—to individuals.
Application information: Applications accepted. Application form required. Application form available on the grantmaker's web site.
Initial approach: Application
Deadline(s): Apr. 15
Additional information: Contact Union City High School guidance counselor for additional application guidelines.
Program description:
Larue Ottaway Scholarship: Scholarships are available to graduates of Union City High School who wish to pursue a career in a health care-related field, and who are currently full-time students studying for a bachelor's degree, associate degree, or equivalent diploma/certificate program in an area of study for health care. Application for this scholarship should include a transcript, and two letters of recommendations from your teachers.
EIN: 251672243

8155
United Way of Greater Philadelphia and Southern New Jersey
(formerly United Way of Southeastern Pennsylvania)
1709 Benjamin Franklin Pkwy.
Philadelphia, PA 19103-1211 (215) 665-2500
Contact: Jill M. Michal, Pres. and C.E.O.
E-mail: contact@uwgpsnj.org; URL: http://
www.unitedforimpact.org/

Foundation type: Public charity
Purpose: Scholarship support to individuals throughout the greater Philadelphia, PA area and southern NJ.
Publications: Financial statement; Newsletter.
Financial data: Year ended 06/30/2012. Assets, $85,308,165 (M); Expenditures, $56,019,343; Total giving, $39,671,019; Grants to individuals, 102 grants totaling $300,660.
Fields of interest: Higher education.
Type of support: Scholarships—to individuals.
Application information: Applications accepted.
  Additional information: Contact the organization for additional information.
EIN: 231556045

8156
Joseph T. Urban and Margaret L. Urban Scholarship Fund
35 S. Main St.
Mahanoy City, PA 17948-2647

Foundation type: Independent foundation
Purpose: Scholarships to graduates of Mahanoy Area School District, PA.
Financial data: Year ended 12/31/2012. Assets, $98,238 (M); Expenditures, $6,850; Total giving, $6,000; Grants to individuals, 3 grants totaling $6,000 (high: $2,000, low: $2,000).
Type of support: Support to graduates or students of specific schools; Undergraduate support.
Application information: Applications not accepted.
  Additional information: Unsolicited requests for funds not considered or acknowledged.
EIN: 237658598

8157
USWA Flint/Glass Industry Conference Lawrence Bankowski Scholarship Award
(formerly The AIL/AFGWU Lawrence Bankowski Scholarship Fund)
5 Gateway Ctr.
Pittsburgh, PA 15222 (419) 343-9412
Contact: Timothy Tuttle, Chair.

Foundation type: Independent foundation
Purpose: Scholarships to children of current members of USWA for higher education.
Financial data: Year ended 12/31/2011. Assets, $103,246 (M); Expenditures, $7,665; Total giving, $5,000; Grants to individuals, 5 grants totaling $5,000 (high: $1,000, low: $1,000).
Fields of interest: Higher education.
Type of support: Scholarships—to individuals.
Application information: Applications accepted.
  Initial approach: Letter
  Deadline(s): Aug. 1
  Additional information: Application should include a 500-word essay on a selected topic.
EIN: 341804857

8158
Valley Will Fund
c/o Wells Fargo Bank, N.A.
101N. Indenpendence Mall E. MACY1372-062
Philadelphia, PA 19106-2112

Foundation type: Independent foundation
Purpose: Scholarships to graduating seniors of accredited MN high schools for full time study at an accredited college or vocational technical school in MN or elsewhere.
Financial data: Year ended 12/31/2012. Assets, $1,449,699 (M); Expenditures, $75,593; Total giving, $42,187.
Fields of interest: Higher education.
Type of support: Undergraduate support.
Application information: Applications accepted.
  Initial approach: Letter
  Additional information: Students are recommended by a representative of his or her high school. The program is administered by Citizens Scholarship Foundation of America.
EIN: 416319887

8159
E. Van Horne Educational Fund
c/o BNY Mellon, N.A.
P.O. Box 185
Pittsburgh, PA 15230-0185 (412) 234-0023

Foundation type: Independent foundation
Purpose: Scholarships to financially needy graduating seniors at Crawford County, PA, high schools, primarily to attend colleges and universities in PA.
Financial data: Year ended 12/31/2012. Assets, $1,284,561 (M); Expenditures, $53,500; Total giving, $39,000.
Fields of interest: Higher education.
Type of support: Scholarships—to individuals.
Application information: Application form required.
  Additional information: Contact the fund for additional guidelines.
EIN: 256220814

8160
J. A., Jr. & W. F. Van Wynen Trust A
(also known as The John A. & Winnifred F. Van Wynen Scholarship Fund)
c/o PNC Bank, N.A.
1600 Market St.
Philadelphia, PA 19103-7240

Foundation type: Independent foundation
Purpose: Scholarships to graduates of the Immaculate Conception High School, Montclair, NJ, and Glen Ridge High School, Glen Ridge, NJ, to attend accredited colleges or trade schools.
Financial data: Year ended 12/31/2012. Assets, $1,010,291 (M); Expenditures, $58,423; Total giving, $44,456.
Fields of interest: Vocational education, post-secondary; Higher education.
Type of support: Support to graduates or students of specific schools; Technical education support; Undergraduate support.
Application information: Applications not accepted.
  Additional information: Unsolicited requests for funds not considered or acknowledged.
EIN: 226502704

8161
The Vang Memorial Foundation
P.O. Box 1430
Camp Hill, PA 17001 (717) 730-2092
Contact: Mary Ann Hosko, Treas.

Foundation type: Independent foundation
Purpose: Grants to economically disadvantaged past, present and future employees, and their dependents, of George Vang, Inc. and related companies.
Financial data: Year ended 12/31/2011. Assets, $1,096,478 (M); Expenditures, $110,939; Total giving, $89,317; Grants to individuals, 11 grants totaling $89,317 (high: $20,400, low: $2,400).
Fields of interest: Economically disadvantaged.
Type of support: Employee-related welfare.
Application information: Applications not accepted.
  Additional information: Application by letter, including copies of previous year's federal and state income tax returns, type of grant requested, and basis of need. Unsolicited requests for funds not considered or acknowledged.
Company name: Vang (George), Incorporated
EIN: 256034491

8162
Otto Ruth Varner-Seneca Valley High School Scholarship Fund
c/o BNY Mellon N.A.
P.O. Box 185
Pittsburgh, PA 15230-0185
Contact: Susan Cencia

Foundation type: Independent foundation
Purpose: Scholarships to residents of Butler, PA, who attend Seneca Valley High School.
Financial data: Year ended 05/31/2013. Assets, $1,146,857 (M); Expenditures, $60,171; Total giving, $53,500; Grants to individuals, 36 grants totaling $53,500 (high: $2,000, low: $1,000).
Fields of interest: Scholarships/financial aid.
Type of support: Scholarships—to individuals; Support to graduates or students of specific schools.
Application information: Application form required.
  Additional information: Contact high school guidance counselor for current application deadline.
EIN: 256292867

8163
George J. & Margaret I. Vasset Memorial Foundation
(formerly George J. & Margaret I. Vasset Memorial Fund)
c/o Wells Fargo Bank, N.A.
101 N. Independence Mail E MACY 1372-062
Philadelphia, PA 19106-2112

Foundation type: Independent foundation
Purpose: Scholarships to members of First Presbyterian Church, Bradenton, FL, for religious education.
Financial data: Year ended 03/31/2012. Assets, $179,864 (M); Expenditures, $10,095; Total giving, $4,600.
Fields of interest: Theological school/education.
Type of support: Scholarships—to individuals.
Application information: Applications accepted.
  Deadline(s): None
EIN: 237320718

8164
Elizabeth Boone Vastine & Katherine Vastine
(formerly Elizabeth Boone Vastine & Katherine Vastine Bernheimer Memorial Fund)
P.O. Box 3215, Tax Dept.
Lancaster, PA 17604-3215
Application address: c/o Danville Senior High School, Attn.: Guidance Counselor, Northumberland Rd., Danville, PA 17821-1507, tel.: (570) 275-4113

Foundation type: Independent foundation
Purpose: Scholarships to graduating seniors of Danville Senior High School, PA, for postsecondary education.
Financial data: Year ended 12/31/2012. Assets, $188,183 (M); Expenditures, $7,480; Total giving, $4,000; Grants to individuals, 2 grants totaling $4,000 (high: $2,000, low: $2,000).
Fields of interest: Higher education; Scholarships/financial aid.
Type of support: Support to graduates or students of specific schools; Undergraduate support.
Application information: Application form required.
  Deadline(s): May 1
  Applicants should submit the following:
    1) Class rank
    2) FAFSA
  Additional information: Contact your school's guidance office for additional application information.
EIN: 232120313

8165
Anna M. Vincent Trust
c/o BNY Mellon, N.A.
P.O. Box 185
Pittsburgh, PA 15230-0185

Foundation type: Independent foundation
Purpose: Scholarships to long-term residents of the five-county Philadelphia, PA area, for graduate or undergraduate study at recognized colleges, universities, and other institutions of higher learning.
Financial data: Year ended 06/30/2012. Assets, $5,967,009 (M); Expenditures, $378,556; Total giving, $270,000; Grants to individuals, 72 grants totaling $270,000 (high: $5,000, low: $2,000).
Fields of interest: Education.
Type of support: Graduate support; Undergraduate support.
Application information: Applications accepted. Application form required.
  Initial approach: Letter
  Deadline(s): Mar. 1
  Additional information: Application forms available at local high schools. Scholarships are paid directly to the educational institution on behalf of the students.
EIN: 236422666

8166
Viropharma Charitable Foundation
730 Stockton Dr.
Exton, PA 19341-1171 (877) 945-1000
FAX: (888) 281-8211;
E-mail: inquiries@cinryzesolutions.com; Additional tel.: (800) 517-2457, fax: (800) 483-6714;
URL: http://www.cinryze.com/hae-patient-assistance.aspx

Foundation type: Company-sponsored foundation

Purpose: Grants of pharmaceutical product CINRYZE to needy individuals with no insurance coverage.
Publications: Application guidelines.
Financial data: Year ended 12/31/2012. Assets, $122,597 (M); Expenditures, $14,774,016; Total giving, $14,774,016; Grants to individuals, 91 grants totaling $14,774,016.
Fields of interest: Health care; Economically disadvantaged.
Type of support: Grants for special needs.
Application information: Applications accepted. Application form required. Application form available on the grantmaker's web site.
  Initial approach: Telephone
  Send request by: On-line or fax
  Deadline(s): None
  Additional information: Patients must work with a Patient Care Coordinator from the Patient Service Center.
EIN: 453132103

8167
Visiting Nurse Association Foundation of Lebanon County
P.O. Box 1203
Lebanon, PA 17042-1203
Contact: Gary Watts, Pres.

Foundation type: Operating foundation
Purpose: Grants to indigent individuals in Lebanon County, PA for expenses related to health care.
Financial data: Year ended 06/30/2013. Assets, $913,362 (M); Expenditures, $53,798; Total giving, $40,815.
Fields of interest: Health care; Economically disadvantaged.
Type of support: Grants for special needs.
Application information: Applications accepted. Application form not required.
  Initial approach: Letter
  Deadline(s): None
EIN: 231365981

8168
The Theodore Vodgis Charitable Trust
c/o PNC Bank, N.A.
1600 Market St., Tax Dept.
Philadelphia, PA 19103-7420

Foundation type: Independent foundation
Purpose: Scholarships to graduates of Frederick High School, MD, for higher education. Scholarships for students attending Athens College in Athens, Greece.
Financial data: Year ended 12/31/2012. Assets, $1,265,021 (M); Expenditures, $59,867; Total giving, $44,926.
Type of support: Support to graduates or students of specific schools; Undergraduate support.
Application information:
  Deadline(s): May
  Applicants should submit the following:
    1) FAFSA
    2) Essay
  Additional information: Contact high school for application information.
EIN: 526101497

8169
Vogeley Memorial Trust
c/o BNY Mellon, N.A.
P.O. Box 185
Pittsburgh, PA 15230-9897

Foundation type: Independent foundation
Purpose: Scholarships to graduates of Butler area Senior High School, PA. for attendance at accredited colleges or universities.
Financial data: Year ended 09/30/2012. Assets, $3,277,453 (M); Expenditures, $194,690; Total giving, $169,110; Grants to individuals, 35 grants totaling $169,110 (high: $19,340, low: $116).
Fields of interest: Higher education.
Type of support: Support to graduates or students of specific schools; Undergraduate support.
Application information: Application form required.
  Additional information: Contact Scholarship committee for additional information.
EIN: 256235851

8170
Dr. Ludwig Von Sallmann Memorial Fund
(formerly Dr. Ludwig Von Sallmann Memorial Fund Trust)
c/o PNC Bank, N.A.
1600 Market St., Tax Dept., No. 4th Fl.
Philadelphia, PA 19103-7240 (212) 305-5688
Application address: Dept. of Ophtalmology-Columbia University, College of Physicians and Surgeons, Attn.: Peter Gouras, M.D., 630 W. 168th St., New York, NY 10032-3702, tel.: (212) 305-5688

Foundation type: Independent foundation
Purpose: Prizes by nomination only awarded biennially to individuals for outstanding research in vision and ophthalmology.
Financial data: Year ended 12/31/2012. Assets, $761,174 (M); Expenditures, $50,265; Total giving, $35,000.
Fields of interest: Eye research.
Type of support: Research; Awards/grants by nomination only.
Application information: Application form required.
  Deadline(s): Mar. 1
  Additional information: Application must include description of nominee's achievements, curriculum vitae, and biography.
EIN: 521224404

8171
Voorhies Scholarship Trust Fund
c/o Wells Fargo Bank, N.A.
101N Indepndence Mall E MACY1372-065
Philadelphia, PA 19106-2112 (810) 252-3024

Foundation type: Operating foundation
Purpose: Scholarships to high school seniors for attendance at accredited colleges or universities in MI, pursuing a degree in engineering.
Financial data: Year ended 12/31/2012. Assets, $565,387 (M); Expenditures, $36,616; Total giving, $25,000.
Fields of interest: Higher education.
Type of support: Scholarships—to individuals.
Application information: Applications accepted.
  Additional information: Contact the fund for application guidelines.
EIN: 656160628

8172
Verneda A. and Leo J. Wachter, Sr. Foundation
(also known as David E. Moses)
412 Union St.
Hollidaysburg, PA 16648-1518

Foundation type: Operating foundation

Purpose: Scholarships to deserving and/or needy students who attend Blair County, PA high schools, for higher education.
Publications: Application guidelines.
Financial data: Year ended 12/31/2011. Assets, $0 (M); Expenditures, $30,711; Total giving, $30,595.
Fields of interest: Higher education.
Type of support: Scholarships—to individuals.
Application information: Applications accepted. Application form required.
   Copies of proposal: 6
   Deadline(s): Mar. 15
   Applicants should submit the following:
      1) Transcripts
      2) Essay
   Additional information: Contact the foundation for application information.
EIN: 251531899

8173
Martin and Awilda Walter Charitable Trust
c/o PNC Bank, N.A.
P.O. Box 609
Pittsburgh, PA   15230-9738

Foundation type: Independent foundation
Purpose: Scholarship to qualified students of IN, pursuing a major in agriculture.
Financial data: Year ended 03/31/2013. Assets, $503,456 (M); Expenditures, $21,562; Total giving, $15,636.
Fields of interest: Higher education; Agriculture.
Type of support: Scholarships—to individuals.
Application information: Applications accepted.
   Additional information: Contact the organization for additional guidelines.
EIN: 352059558

8174
Rew & Edna Walz Scholarship Trust
c/o Wells Fargo Bank, N.A.
101N Independence Mall E MACY 1362-062
Philadelphia, PA   19106-2112
Application address: c/o First Presbyterian Church, Attn.: Scholarship Comm., 710 Kansas City St., Rapid City, SD 57701-2713

Foundation type: Independent foundation
Purpose: Scholarships to students pursuing church-related vocations such as pastor, church music director, Christian education director, missionary, or other church-related positions.
Financial data: Year ended 12/31/2012. Assets, $172,029 (M); Expenditures, $8,095; Total giving, $4,803.
Fields of interest: Theological school/education; Christian agencies & churches; Protestant agencies & churches; Religion.
Type of support: Scholarships—to individuals.
Application information: Applications accepted. Application form required.
   Deadline(s): Apr. 15
   Applicants should submit the following:
      1) Transcripts
      2) Letter(s) of recommendation
      3) Financial information
   Additional information: Applicants must have been active in the First Presbyterian Church or a Presbyterian Church in the SD Presbytery.
EIN: 466093427

8175
The Warren Family Foundation
108 Hunt Club Dr.
Collegeville, PA   19426-3969

Foundation type: Independent foundation
Purpose: Grants for medical and dental expenses primarily to FL residents.
Financial data: Year ended 08/31/2012. Assets, $230,146 (M); Expenditures, $168,075; Total giving, $168,075. Grants to individuals amount not specified.
Fields of interest: Health care.
Type of support: Grants for special needs.
Application information: Applications accepted.
   Initial approach: Letter
   Additional information: Contact foundation for current application deadline/guidelines.
EIN: 562403637

8176
Washington County Community Foundation, Inc.
331 S. Main St.
Washington, PA   15301   (724) 222-6330
Contact: Betsie Trew, C.E.O.
FAX: (724) 222-7960; E-mail: info@wccf.net; Additional e-mail: brtrew@wccf.net; URL: http://www.wccf.net

Foundation type: Community foundation
Purpose: Scholarships to high school graduates of Washington County, PA, pursuing a postsecondary education.
Publications: Application guidelines; Annual report; Financial statement; Informational brochure; Newsletter.
Financial data: Year ended 12/31/2012. Assets, $14,796,203 (M); Expenditures, $878,387; Total giving, $600,971.
Fields of interest: Vocational education, post-secondary; Higher education.
Type of support: Scholarships—to individuals.
Application information: Applications accepted. Application form required. Application form available on the grantmaker's web site.
   Initial approach: Application
   Send request by: Mail
   Deadline(s): Apr. 1
   Applicants should submit the following:
      1) Transcripts
      2) Letter(s) of recommendation
      3) Essay
   Additional information: See web site for eligibility guidelines and a listing of scholarship programs.
EIN: 251726013

8177
Waverly Community House, Inc.
1115 N. Abington Rd.
P.O. Box 142
Waverly, PA   18471-9800   (570) 586-8191
Contact: Maria Wilson, Exec. Dir.
FAX: (570) 586-0185;
E-mail: info@waverlycomm.com; URL: http://www.waverlycomm.com

Foundation type: Public charity
Purpose: Scholarships awarded to residents of the Abingtons or Pocono northeast region of PA who show aptitude and promise in the fine arts.
Publications: Newsletter.
Financial data: Year ended 12/31/2012. Assets, $2,707,267 (M); Expenditures, $562,676; Total

giving, $15,000; Grants to individuals, totaling $15,000.
Fields of interest: Arts education.
Type of support: Scholarships—to individuals.
Application information: Applications accepted. Application form required.
   Initial approach: Letter, telephone or email
   Send request by: Mail
   Deadline(s): Dec. 15
   Final notification: Applicants notified in two months
   Applicants should submit the following:
      1) Work samples
      2) Letter(s) of recommendation
   Additional information: Application should also include a $15 application fee.
EIN: 240798358

8178
Wayne County Community Foundation
214 9th St., 2nd Fl.
Honesdale, PA   18431-1911   (570) 251-9993
Contact: Paul J. Edwards, Exec. Dir.
FAX: (570) 251-9904; E-mail: wccf@ptd.net;
URL: http://www.waynefoundation.org

Foundation type: Community foundation
Purpose: Scholarships to deserving Wayne county, PA graduating seniors for postsecondary education at accredited colleges, universities or vocational schools.
Publications: Application guidelines.
Financial data: Year ended 06/30/2012. Assets, $2,088,785 (M); Expenditures, $278,003; Total giving, $203,890.
Fields of interest: Vocational education, post-secondary; Higher education.
Type of support: Scholarships—to individuals.
Application information: Applications accepted. Application form required. Application form available on the grantmaker's web site.
   Send request by: Mail
   Deadline(s): Apr. 1
   Additional information: Application should include transcripts. Selection criteria is based on academic achievement and financial need.
EIN: 232656896

8179
Benjamin N. Webber Charitable Private Foundation
(also known as Benjamin N. Webber Scholarship Fund)
c/o Wells Fargo Bank, N.A.
101N Independence Mall E MACY1372-062
Philadelphia, PA   19106-2112
Application address: c/o Webber Educational Grants Comm., Arizona Home Economics, 7030 E. Bonnie Brae Dr., Tucson, AZ 85710-3609

Foundation type: Independent foundation
Purpose: Scholarships in home economics and nutrition to Mexican-American bilingual females from mining towns in AZ. Recipients must attend undergraduate programs in AZ colleges and maintain at least a 2.0 GPA. Preference is given to nutrition majors.
Publications: Informational brochure (including application guidelines).
Financial data: Year ended 09/30/2012. Assets, $1,363,701 (M); Expenditures, $54,447; Total giving, $30,532; Grants to individuals, 8 grants totaling $30,532 (high: $9,760, low: $750).
Fields of interest: Nutrition; Home economics; Women.
International interests: Mexico.

Type of support: Undergraduate support.
Application information: Applications accepted. Application form required.
  Deadline(s): None
  Applicants should submit the following:
  1) Transcripts
  2) Letter(s) of recommendation
  3) Financial information
  Additional information: Application must also include educational and professional goals.
EIN: 866136517

8180
Josephine M. Webber Scholarship Fund
c/o Wells Fargo Bank, N.A.
101 N. Independence Mall E
Philadelphia, PA   19106-2112
Application address: c/o Webber Educational Grants Comm., Arizona Home Economics, 7030 E. Bonnie Brae Dr., Tucson, AZ 85710-3609

Foundation type: Independent foundation
Purpose: Scholarships to bilingual, Mexican-American women from mining towns in AZ, majoring in home economics and/or nutrition.
Financial data: Year ended 09/30/2012. Assets, $389,554 (M); Expenditures, $17,528; Total giving, $8,409; Grants to individuals, 6 grants totaling $8,409 (high: $2,152, low: $566).
Fields of interest: Nutrition; Home economics; Hispanics/Latinos; Women.
International interests: Mexico.
Type of support: Scholarships—to individuals.
Application information: Application form required.
  Deadline(s): None
  Additional information: Application should include letters of recommendation. Preference is given to those majoring in nutrition.
EIN: 866136516

8181
Jacques Weber Foundation, Inc.
2548 Old Berwick Rd.
P.O. Box 420
Bloomsburg, PA   17815-0420

Foundation type: Independent foundation
Purpose: Scholarships to residents of Bloomsburg, PA, and Monroe, NC, who are children of employees of Bloomsburg Mills Inc.
Financial data: Year ended 09/30/2012. Assets, $2,974,743 (M); Expenditures, $130,964; Total giving, $95,500; Grants to individuals, 11 grants totaling $50,000 (high: $5,000, low: $2,500).
Type of support: Employee-related scholarships.
Application information: Applications not accepted.
  Additional information: Contributes only to preselected individuals through an employee related program. Inappropriate requests for funds not considered or acknowledged.
Company name: Bloomsburg Mills Incorporated
EIN: 136101161

8182
William Webermeier Scholarship Trust
c/o Wells Fargo Bank, N.A.
101 N. Indenpendence Mall E. MACY1372-062
Philadelphia, PA   19106-2112   (888) 730-4933

Foundation type: Independent foundation
Purpose: Scholarships only to graduates of Milford High School, NE.

Financial data: Year ended 09/30/2012. Assets, $470,831 (M); Expenditures, $24,756; Total giving, $17,625; Grants to individuals, 47 grants totaling $17,625 (high: $375, low: $375).
Type of support: Support to graduates or students of specific schools; Undergraduate support.
Application information: Applications not accepted.
  Additional information: Unsolicited requests for funds not considered or acknowledged.
EIN: 476062610

8183
The Edwin Gardner Weed Ruge
(formerly Isabel R. Ruge Trust, also known as Edwin Gardner Weed Ruge Education Fund)
c/o Wells Fargo Bank, N.A.
101 N. Independence Mall E., MACY 1372-062
Philadelphia, PA   19106-2112
Application address: Center for Scholarship Admin., Inc., 4320 Wade Hampton Blvd., Ste. G, Taylors, SC 29687

Foundation type: Independent foundation
Purpose: Scholarships to dependent children of employees of consolidated Systems, Inc., for higher education.
Financial data: Year ended 12/31/2012. Assets, $346,756 (M); Expenditures, $25,236; Total giving, $17,500.
Fields of interest: Higher education.
Type of support: Undergraduate support.
Application information: Applications accepted.
  Initial approach: Letter
  Deadline(s): Feb. 15
  Additional information: Applicants must be under the age of 25 at the time of application. Selection is based on academic achievement and financial need.
EIN: 596527097

8184
Charles & Dorothy Wein Charitable Fund
P.O. Box 609
Pittsburg, PA   15230-9738

Foundation type: Independent foundation
Purpose: Scholarships for higher education to residents of Clarion County, PA.
Financial data: Year ended 06/30/2013. Assets, $783,064 (M); Expenditures, $44,574; Total giving, $32,300; Grants to individuals, totaling $32,300.
Type of support: Scholarships—to individuals.
Application information: Applications accepted. Application form required.
  Initial approach: Letter
EIN: 256225347

8185
Sara & Warren Welch Foundation
P.O. Box 125
Newville, PA   17241-0125   (717) 263-3910

Foundation type: Independent foundation
Purpose: Student loans to graduates of Big Spring School District, PA for continuing education at accredited colleges or universities.
Financial data: Year ended 04/30/2013. Assets, $438,444 (M); Expenditures, $10,000; Total giving, $0.
Fields of interest: Higher education.
Type of support: Student loans—to individuals; Support to graduates or students of specific schools.

Application information: Applications accepted. Application form required.
  Initial approach: Letter
  Send request by: Mail
  Deadline(s): July 1
EIN: 232130843

8186
Wesley Spectrum Services Foundation
(formerly Spectrum Family Network Foundation)
221 Penn Ave.
Pittsburgh, PA   15221-2101   (412) 342-2300
Contact: Douglas W. Muetzel, C.E.O.
FAX: (412) 831-8868;
E-mail: wssinfo@wesleyspectrum.org; URL: http://wesleyspectrum.org

Foundation type: Public charity
Purpose: Scholarships to students of PA, currently attending Wesley's Academy School for continuing education at institutions of higher learning.
Publications: Newsletter.
Financial data: Year ended 06/30/2012. Assets, $7,926,660 (M); Expenditures, $1,174,238; Total giving, $207,503; Grants to individuals, totaling $6,503.
Fields of interest: Higher education.
Type of support: Scholarships—to individuals; Support to graduates or students of specific schools.
Application information: Applications accepted. Application form required.
  Additional information: Application should include proof of attendance at an institution of higher learning. Funds are paid directly to the educational instituion on behalf of the students.
EIN: 251686715

8187
W. F. & Blanche E. West Educational Fund
c/o Wells Fargo Bank N.A.
101 N Independence Mall E Macy1372-06
Philadelphia, PA   19106-2112

Foundation type: Independent foundation
Purpose: Scholarships to graduates of W.F. West High School, Chehalis, WA, who have lived in Lewis County, WA, for at least two years. Some recipients receive more than one grant.
Financial data: Year ended 12/31/2012. Assets, $2,491,654 (M); Expenditures, $125,172; Total giving, $83,125.
Fields of interest: Education.
Type of support: Support to graduates or students of specific schools.
Application information: Applications accepted. Application form required.
  Deadline(s): July 1 for new applicants
  Additional information: Applications accepted throughout the year for renewals; Application forms available at school.
EIN: 916101769

8188
The H. O. West Foundation
(also known as The Herman O. West Foundation)
530 Heilman O. West Dr.
Exton, PA   19341   (610) 594-2945
Contact: Richard D. Luzzi, Tr.; Maureen B. Goebel, Admin.
E-mail: maureen.goebel@westpharma.com;
URL: http://www.westpharma.com/en/about/Pages/CharitableGiving.aspx

Foundation type: Company-sponsored foundation
Purpose: Scholarships only for dependent children of employees of West Pharmaceutical Services, Inc.
Publications: Application guidelines.
Financial data: Year ended 12/31/2012. Assets, $3,447,277 (M); Expenditures, $788,480; Total giving, $787,663; Grants to individuals, 49 grants totaling $62,023.
Fields of interest: Higher education.
Type of support: Employee-related scholarships.
Application information: Applications not accepted.
 Additional information: Unsolicited requests for funds not considered or acknowledged.
Program description:
 H.O. West Foundation Scholarship Program: The foundation annually awards up to seven college scholarships to children and dependents of employees of West Pharmaceutical Services and its subsidiaries. Winners are selected on the basis of character, maturity, leadership, extra-curricular activities, motivation, interest and desire, patriotism, predicted success in college, and academic achievement. Each scholarship is renewable for 4 years with a maximum of $10,000.
Company name: West Pharmaceutical Services, Inc.
EIN: 383674460

8189
Western Assoc of Ladies IAS
(formerly Western Association of Ladies for the Relief and Employment of the Poor)
5 Radnor Corp. Ctr.
100 Matsonford Rd., Ste. 450
Radnor, PA 19355 (610) 431-4679
Contact: Marlane G. Bohon, Exec. Dir.
Application address: 240 Chatham Way, West Chester, PA 19380; URL: http://westernassociation.org/

Foundation type: Independent foundation
Purpose: Relief to the poor and aged of Philadelphia County, PA. Candidates must be referred by a social service agency and not be covered by government programs or other funding sources.
Financial data: Year ended 12/31/2012. Assets, $2,210,505 (M); Expenditures, $234,094; Total giving, $177,000.
Fields of interest: Aging; Economically disadvantaged.
Type of support: Grants for special needs.
Application information: Applications accepted.
 Deadline(s): None
 Additional information: Application must be submitted in writing through a social worker from an approved organization.
EIN: 231353393

8190
Marian J. Wettrick Charitable Foundation
c/o Citizens & Northern Bank
90-92 Main St.
Wellsboro, PA 16901 (570) 724-8596

Foundation type: Independent foundation
Purpose: Scholarships to female graduates of a PA college who have been accepted to a medical school in PA, with an inclination to practice medicine at Charles Cole Memorial Hospital, Coudersport, PA.
Financial data: Year ended 12/31/2011. Assets, $1,562,536 (M); Expenditures, $84,388; Total giving, $76,000; Grants to individuals, 9 grants totaling $76,000 (high: $12,000; low: $8,000).

Fields of interest: Medical school/education; Women.
Type of support: Graduate support.
Application information: Applications accepted. Application form required. Interview required.
 Deadline(s): May 15
 Additional information: Application should include Medical School Transcript.
EIN: 256545149

8191
Dr. Richard D. Williams Foundation
(formerly Richard D. Williams, Slatington Scholarship Fund and Trust)
300 Edgemont Ave.
Palmerton, PA 18071 (610) 826-6164
Contact: Gerald D. Geiger, Tr.

Foundation type: Independent foundation
Purpose: Scholarships to graduates of the Northern Lehigh School District, PA; and to students at East Strousberg University, PA; Lycoming College, PA; Hood College, MD; University of the Sciences in Philadelphia, PA; Lehigh Carbon Community College, PA; and Cedar Crest College, PA.
Financial data: Year ended 12/31/2012. Assets, $1,311,814 (M); Expenditures, $70,527; Total giving, $69,000.
Type of support: Support to graduates or students of specific schools; Undergraduate support.
Application information: Applications accepted. Application form required.
 Initial approach: Letter
 Deadline(s): May
 Applicants should submit the following:
  1) Budget Information
  2) Transcripts
EIN: 526490235

8192
Charles K. Williams II Trust
c/o BNY Mellon, N.A.
P.O. Box 185
Pittsburgh, PA 15230-0185 (215) 553-3344

Foundation type: Independent foundation
Purpose: Postgraduate fellowships for archaeology research and study.
Financial data: Year ended 11/30/2013. Assets, $134,021 (M); Expenditures, $450,261; Total giving, $450,168; Grants to individuals, 7 grants totaling $285,168 (high: $45,000; low: $4,000).
Fields of interest: History/archaeology.
Type of support: Fellowships; Research; Postgraduate support.
Application information: Applications accepted.
 Initial approach: Proposal
 Deadline(s): None
EIN: 236758319

8193
Charles C. Williams Scholarship Foundation
(formerly Charles Williams Trust)
1500 JFK Blvd.Ste.1400
Philadelphia, PA 19102 (215) 569-3535
Contact: Harry J.J. Bellwoar III, Tr.

Foundation type: Independent foundation
Purpose: Scholarships to graduates of high schools in Philadelphia or Delaware County, PA.
Financial data: Year ended 09/30/2011. Assets, $30,290 (M); Expenditures, $3,650; Total giving, $3,650; Grants to individuals, 7 grants totaling $3,650 (high: $750; low: $400).

Fields of interest: Higher education.
Type of support: Scholarships—to individuals.
Application information: Application form required.
 Initial approach: Letter
 Deadline(s): June 1
 Applicants should submit the following:
  1) Transcripts
  2) Photograph
  3) Letter(s) of recommendation
  4) Financial information
 Additional information: Application should also include copies of parents' recent income tax return.
EIN: 232417678

8194
John G. Williams Scholarship Foundation
3804 Lisburn Rd.
Mechanicsburg, PA 17055 (717) 763-1333
Contact: Connie Williams Jack, Exec. Dir.

Foundation type: Independent foundation
Purpose: Low-interest loans to qualified college students of PA for tuition pursuing higher education.
Financial data: Year ended 03/31/2013. Assets, $649,964 (M); Expenditures, $28,015; Total giving, $0.
Fields of interest: Higher education.
Type of support: Student loans—to individuals; Graduate support; Undergraduate support.
Application information: Applications accepted. Application form required. Application form available on the grantmaker's web site.
 Initial approach: Letter
 Send request by: Mail
 Deadline(s): June 15
 Final notification: Recipients notified mid-Aug.
 Applicants should submit the following:
  1) Essay
  2) Letter(s) of recommendation
  3) Transcripts
  4) Financial information
  5) FAFSA
 Additional information: Application should also include evidence of acceptance/attendance by college or graduate school. Applicant must demonstrate financial need. See web site for additional guidelines.
EIN: 232329462

8195
Williamson Family Educational Trust
349 Union St.
Millersburg, PA 17061-1611 (717) 692-2133

Foundation type: Independent foundation
Purpose: Scholarships to graduating seniors from Millersburg High School, PA.
Financial data: Year ended 12/31/2012. Assets, $918,056 (M); Expenditures, $42,273; Total giving, $33,850; Grants to individuals, 29 grants totaling $33,850 (high: $1,650; low: $1,150).
Type of support: Support to graduates or students of specific schools; Undergraduate support.
Application information: Applications accepted.
 Initial approach: Letter
 Deadline(s): May 1
EIN: 207007479

8196
The Geraldine Diehl Wilson Charitable Foundation of Delanco, New Jersey
c/o S Fuhrman Holin
512 S Bethlehem Pike
Fort Washington, PA   19034-3216
Contact: Susan Fuhrman-Holin, V.P.

Foundation type: Independent foundation
Purpose: Scholarships and financial assistance to worthy high school students going to college and to worthy college students wanting to stay matriculated. Students must be from the South Jersey georgaphic region.
Financial data: Year ended 12/31/2011. Assets, $1,197,989 (M); Expenditures, $75,031; Total giving, $58,592; Grants to individuals, 7 grants totaling $58,592 (high: $15,000, low: $2,000).
Fields of interest: Higher education.
Type of support: Undergraduate support.
Application information:
  Initial approach: Letter
  Applicants should submit the following:
    1) Financial information
    2) Letter(s) of recommendation
    3) Transcripts
  Additional information: Interviews may be required.
EIN: 232829467

8197
George W. Wilson Scholarship Trust
c/o Wells Fargo Bank, N.A.
101N Indepndence Mall E MACY1372-062
Philadelphia, PA   19106-2112
Application address: Superintendents of North South Tool, Toole County High Schools, Shelby, MT 59474, Tel: (406) 727-0888

Foundation type: Independent foundation
Purpose: Scholarships for higher education to graduates of North or South Toole County High Schools, Shelby, MT.
Financial data: Year ended 12/31/2012. Assets, $138,292 (M); Expenditures, $11,006; Total giving, $9,000.
Fields of interest: Higher education.
Type of support: Support to graduates or students of specific schools.
Application information: Applications accepted.
  Deadline(s): May 15
  Additional information: Application should include proof of enrollment and should be submitted to the superintendents of either schools.
EIN: 816024846

8198
Samuel & Emma Winters Foundation
c/o PNC Bank, N.A.
620 Liberty Ave., 10th Fl.
Pittsburgh, PA   15222-2705   (412) 762-7941

Foundation type: Independent foundation
Purpose: Research grants for doctors in the Pittsburgh, PA area in the fields of medicine, dentistry, public health, areas of scientific studies, experimental work or research.
Financial data: Year ended 12/31/2011. Assets, $1,244,137 (M); Expenditures, $59,160; Total giving, $58,100.
Type of support: Research.
Application information: Applications accepted.
  Initial approach: Letter
  Deadline(s): None

Additional information: Letter must describe experimental work and research. Grants are evaluated in Jan. and Feb. of each year.
EIN: 256024170

8199
Buzzy Wittmer Scholarship Fund
P.O. Box 3215
Lancaster, PA   17604-3215
Contact: Atlee Kepler
Application address: 101 Oak Hill Ave., Hagerstown, MD 21742

Foundation type: Independent foundation
Purpose: Scholarships to high school seniors of Washington county, MD for continuing education at accredited colleges or universities.
Financial data: Year ended 12/31/2012. Assets, $185,857 (M); Expenditures, $12,050; Total giving, $9,000; Grants to individuals, 9 grants totaling $9,000 (high: $1,000, low: $1,000).
Fields of interest: Higher education.
Type of support: Scholarships—to individuals.
Application information: Applications accepted. Application form required.
  Deadline(s): Apr. 15
  Additional information: Applications are available from the school's guidance counselors.
EIN: 521084293

8200
Wolf Foundation for Education Trust
c/o Ephrata National Bank
47 E. Main St.
P.O. Box 457
Ephrata, PA   17522-0457   (717) 733-6576

Foundation type: Independent foundation
Purpose: Scholarships to students who graduated from high schools in Ephrata Township and Ephrata Borough, PA. Scholarships are renewable for up to four years of study.
Financial data: Year ended 12/31/2012. Assets, $403,834 (M); Expenditures, $22,360; Total giving, $17,000; Grants to individuals, 34 grants totaling $17,000.
Type of support: Support to graduates or students of specific schools; Undergraduate support.
Application information: Applications accepted. Application form required.
  Applicants should submit the following:
    1) Class rank
    2) SAT
    3) ACT
    4) Financial information
EIN: 236750958

8201
Benjamin & Fredora K. Wolf Memorial Foundation
c/o Thomas Ginsberg
621 Pemberton St.
Philadelphia, PA   19147-2116
Contact: Thomas Ginsberg, Treas.

Foundation type: Independent foundation
Purpose: Scholarships based on merit to residents of the Philadelphia, PA, area.
Financial data: Year ended 05/31/2012. Assets, $2,891,759 (M); Expenditures, $159,066; Total giving, $127,400; Grants to individuals, 242 grants totaling $127,400 (high: $600, low: $300).
Type of support: Scholarships—to individuals.
Application information: Applications accepted.

Initial approach: Letter
Deadline(s): None
Additional information: Contact foundation for current application guidelines.
EIN: 236207344

8202
Walter J. Wolf Trust
c/o PNC Bank, N.A.
1600 Market St., 4th Fl.
Philadelphia, PA   19103   (610) 326-5105

Foundation type: Independent foundation
Purpose: Scholarships to graduates of Pottsgrove High School, PA for continuing education at institutions of higher learning.
Financial data: Year ended 12/31/2012. Assets, $286,910 (M); Expenditures, $15,134; Total giving, $11,600.
Fields of interest: Higher education.
Type of support: Support to graduates or students of specific schools; Undergraduate support.
Application information: Applications accepted.
  Deadline(s): None
  Additional information: Recipients are chosen by Pottsgrove High School, PA.
EIN: 236429959

8203
Women's Center and Shelter of Greater Pittsburgh
P. O. Box 9024
Pittsburgh, PA   15224-0024   (412) 232-7479
Contact: Shirl Regan, Pres. and C.E.O.
FAX: (412) 687-3315;
E-mail: info@wcspittsburgh.org; Tel. for Shirl Regan : (412) 687-8017 ext. 327; Toll free tel. : (877) 338-8255; URL: http://www.wcspittsburgh.org

Foundation type: Public charity
Purpose: Provides financial support to women and their children.
Financial data: Year ended 06/30/2012. Assets, $10,976,861 (M); Expenditures, $4,334,994; Total giving, $103,027; Grants to individuals, 700 grants totaling $103,027.
Application information: Applications not accepted.
EIN: 251264376

8204
Wood Turning Center, Inc.
141 N. 3rd St.
Philadelphia, PA   19106-1002   (215) 923-8000
Contact: Albert LeCoff, Exec. Dir.
FAX: (215) 923-4403;
E-mail: info@woodturningcenter.org; URL: http://www.woodturningcenter.org

Foundation type: Public charity
Purpose: Residencies to artists, scholars, furniture makers, educators and photojournalists interested in lathe-turned art.
Publications: Application guidelines; Annual report; Informational brochure; Newsletter (including application guidelines).
Financial data: Year ended 12/31/2011. Assets, $830,537 (M); Expenditures, $766,264.
Fields of interest: Arts.
Type of support: Residencies.
Application information: Applications accepted. Application form required.

Copies of proposal: 1
Deadline(s): Oct. 1
Applicants should submit the following:
   1) Resume
   2) Proposal
Additional information: Application must also
   include a $25 application fee, and slides of
   recent work.
Program description:
International Turning Exchange Residency: The
program is designed for artists to focus on
advanced technical training innovations,
aesthetics, and techniques and for scholars to
better understand the turning field and its
practitioners. The program is an 8-week residency,
and is available for four lathe artists, one scholar,
one furniture maker/educator, and one
photojournalist selected from the international
community. Residents will receive $400 per week,
roundtrip transportation to the residency location
and housing.
EIN: 222806780

8205
Woods Services Workers Compensation
   ## Trust
P.O. Box 36
Langhorne, PA   19047-0036   (215) 750-4000

Foundation type: Public charity
Purpose: Worker's compensation benefits to
employees of Wood's Services, Inc., PA.
Financial data: Year ended 02/28/2012. Assets,
$2,797,907 (M); Expenditures, $2,282,932.
Fields of interest: Association.
Type of support: Employee-related welfare.
Application information: Applications not
accepted.
   Additional information: Unsolicited requests for
      funds not considered or acknowledged.
EIN: 232407907

8206
Workable Alternatives
(formerly Workable Alternatives Foundation)
2364 Rte. 66
Delmont, PA   15626-1454

Foundation type: Independent foundation
Purpose: Research grants to individuals.
Financial data: Year ended 12/31/2012. Assets,
$1,298,709 (M); Expenditures, $45,219; Total
giving, $45,000; Grants to individuals, 3 grants
totaling $10,000 (high: $5,000, low: $1,000).
Type of support: Research.
Application information: Applications not
accepted.
   Additional information: Unsolicited requests for
      funds not considered or acknowledged.
EIN: 251670751

8207
Workplace Technology Foundation
c/o Michael G. Fiore
316 W. Valley Forge Rd.
King of Prussia, PA   19406-1432   (610)
992-1011

Foundation type: Independent foundation
Purpose: Grants to needy and disabled residents of
PA.
Financial data: Year ended 12/31/2012. Assets,
$164,284 (M); Expenditures, $922,312; Total
giving, $33,908; Grants to individuals, 62 grants
totaling $30,647 (high: $3,882, low: $5).

Fields of interest: Disabilities, people with;
Economically disadvantaged.
Type of support: Grants for special needs.
Application information: Applications accepted.
Application form not required.
   Initial approach: Letter
EIN: 233100879

8208
Salome C. Worthington Scholarship Fund
c/o PNC Bank
620 Liberty Ave., 10th Fl.
Pittsburgh, PA   15222-2722   (502) 776-7608

Foundation type: Independent foundation
Purpose: Scholarships to African American
students who are residents of Kentucky, pursuing a
higher education.
Financial data: Year ended 07/31/2013. Assets,
$148,836 (M); Expenditures, $6,144; Total giving,
$5,500; Grants to individuals, 5 grants totaling
$5,500 (high: $1,500, low: $1,000).
Fields of interest: Higher education; African
Americans/Blacks.
Type of support: Scholarships—to individuals.
Application information: Applications accepted.
   Initial approach: Letter
   Deadline(s): Apr. 1
   Applicants should submit the following:
      1) Financial information
      2) Transcripts
      3) Letter(s) of recommendation
   Additional information: Application should also
      include community involvement and other
      scholarships.
EIN: 616020533

8209
R. R. Wright Educational Fund
c/o BNY Mellon, N.A.
P.O. Box 185
Pittsburgh, PA   15230-0185

Foundation type: Independent foundation
Purpose: Scholarships to graduates of Mercer High
School, PA for continuing education at institutions
of higher learning.
Financial data: Year ended 04/30/2012. Assets,
$278,482 (M); Expenditures, $19,704; Total
giving, $15,250.
Fields of interest: Higher education.
Type of support: Support to graduates or students
of specific schools; Undergraduate support.
Application information: Applications accepted.
Application form required.
   Deadline(s): None
   Additional information: Contact your school
      guidance office for application information.
EIN: 236785914

8210
YMCA of the Brandywine Valley
1 E. Chestnut St.
West Chester, PA   19380-2661   (610) 643-9622
Contact: Denise L. Day, Pres. and C.E.O.
URL: http://www.ymcabwv.org

Foundation type: Public charity
Purpose: Financial assistance to individuals and
families of Chester county, PA to participate in the
YMCA programs and services.
Publications: Annual report.
Financial data: Year ended 12/31/2011. Assets,
$50,224,733 (M); Expenditures, $30,865,458;

Total giving, $2,952,634; Grants to individuals,
totaling $2,952,634.
Fields of interest: Human services; YM/YWCAs &
YM/YWHAs.
Type of support: Grants for special needs.
Application information: Assistance is based on
family size, gross income and available funding.
See web site for additional guidelines.
EIN: 231365994

8211
Yopst Educational Loan Fund Trust
c/o Wells Fargo Bank, N.A.
101N Independence Mall E MACY1372-062
Philadelphia, PA   19106-2112
Contact: J. Stensland
Application address: 112 W. Jefferson Blvd. South
Bend, IN 46601

Foundation type: Independent foundation
Purpose: Educational support to residents of
Wabash County or its five bordering counties for
higher education.
Financial data: Year ended 08/31/2012. Assets,
$1,899,622 (M); Expenditures, $90,348; Total
giving, $53,550.
Fields of interest: Higher education.
Type of support: Support to graduates or students
of specific schools; Undergraduate support.
Application information: Applications accepted.
Application form required.
   Initial approach: Letter
   Deadline(s): None
   Applicants should submit the following:
      1) Transcripts
      2) GPA
   Additional information: Application should also
      include proof of residence, potential for
      educational pursuits, and good character
      references.
EIN: 351971478

8212
York Catholic High School Student Aid
   ## and Endowment Fund
601 E. Springettsbury Ave.
York, PA   17403-2896   (717) 846-8871
Contact: Joseph McFadden, Chair.

Foundation type: Public charity
Purpose: Scholarship assistance for student tuition
aid at York Catholic High School, PA pursuing
postsecondary education.
Financial data: Year ended 12/31/2012. Assets,
$1,054,003 (M); Expenditures, $175,286; Total
giving, $166,158; Grants to individuals, totaling
$166,158.
Fields of interest: Higher education.
Type of support: Scholarships—to individuals;
Support to graduates or students of specific
schools.
Application information: Applications accepted.
Application form required.
   Applicants should submit the following:
      1) Transcripts
      2) Letter(s) of recommendation
   Additional information: Students should contact
      their guidance counselors for additional
      application guidelines.
EIN: 232047570

8213
York County Community Foundation
(formerly York Foundation)
14 W. Market St.
York, PA   17401-1203   (717) 848-3733
Contact: For grants: Jane Conover, V.P., Community Investment; For grants: Sandy Aulbach, Grants Admin.
FAX: (717) 854-7231; E-mail: info@yccf.org; Grant inquiry e-mails: jconover@yccf.org and saulbach@yccf.org; URL: http://www.yccf.org

Foundation type: Community foundation
Purpose: Scholarships to students from York County, PA pursuing higher education. The foundation also administers scholarships for students from K through 12 attending Logos Academy, Susquehanna Waldorf School and York Country Day School.
Publications: Application guidelines; Annual report; Informational brochure; Newsletter.
Financial data: Year ended 12/31/2011. Assets, $66,392,294 (M); Expenditures, $3,643,851; Total giving, $2,547,748; Grants to individuals, 150 grants totaling $214,784.
Fields of interest: Elementary/secondary education; Higher education; Dental school/education; Nursing school/education; Teacher school/education; Engineering school/education.
Type of support: Scholarships—to individuals; Support to graduates or students of specific schools; Precollege support; Undergraduate support.
Application information: Applications accepted. Application form required.
  Deadline(s): Varies
  Additional information: See web site for complete listing of scholarships and application information.
Program descriptions:
  Opportunities Scholarship Program: In an effort to serve a broader spectrum of the community the foundation expanded its scholarship program to include York County students in kindergarten through 12th grade. Through the Opportunities Scholarship Program the foundation serves as the scholarship organization for three local schools that educate York County Students: Logos Academy, Susquehanna Waldorf School and York Country Day School. The schools submit recommendations for student scholarships from these contributions, based on the students financial need; visit foundation web site for more information.
  Scholarships: Some donors have established funds through the foundation that are related to a specific field of study or to benefit a specific institution for scholarship or educational support; visit web site for more information.
EIN: 236299868

8214
Ralph W. Young Family Foundation
1050 Meridian Dr.
Presto, PA   15142-1029

Foundation type: Independent foundation
Purpose: Scholarships primarily to individuals for attendance at PA colleges and universities, as well as for nursing education.
Financial data: Year ended 12/31/2011. Assets, $7,937,318 (M); Expenditures, $319,885; Total giving, $232,022.
Fields of interest: Nursing school/education.
Type of support: Undergraduate support.
Application information: Applications not accepted.

Additional information: Unsolicited requests for funds not considered or acknowledged.
EIN: 306009141

8215
Young Women's Christian Association of Greater Pittsburgh
(also known as YWCA Greater Pittsburgh)
305 Wood St.
Pittsburgh, PA   15222-1914   (412) 391-5100
Contact: Valerie Wheatley, C.F.O.
FAX: (412) 391-5109; E-mail: ywca@ywcapgh.org; URL: http://www.ywcapgh.org

Foundation type: Public charity
Purpose: Housing and emergency assistance to indigents living in Allegheny County, PA. Financial assistance also to low-income women with breast cancer who live in Allegheny County, PA.
Publications: Annual report; Informational brochure.
Financial data: Year ended 06/30/2011. Assets, $50,873,736 (M); Expenditures, $88,297,254; Total giving, $75,489,661; Grants to individuals, totaling $75,489,661.
Fields of interest: Mental health, transitional care; Cancer; Breast cancer; Housing/shelter; Family services; Supported living; Women, centers/services; Homeless, human services; Minorities; Women; Homeless.
Type of support: Grants for special needs.
Application information: Applications not accepted.
Program descriptions:
  Bridge Housing Program: Bridge Housing provides transitional housing and support services to homeless women and their children. Families may stay for a maximum of two years. Support services include case management, life skills education, referrals and assistance with permanent housing placement, referrals to community based health and welfare agencies, assistance and support with vocational and educational goals, an on-site children's learning center and a food pantry. In addition, Bridge Housing offers follow up services to families moving into permanent housing who request ongoing support and assistance. The goal of all services is to help families permanently break the cycles of homelessness and poverty, and achieve lasting self-sufficiency.
  Debora Brueckman Baranik Breast Cancer Fund: This fund was established to support breast education outreach and to provide vouchers for breast cancer survivors who cannot otherwise afford to purchase new wigs, turbans, prostheses, and bras.
  Liz Prine Fund: The Fund provides one-time grants of up to $500 to women to meet needs that pose significant barriers to women's ongoing journey to self-sufficiency.
  W.I.S.H. (Women In Supported Housing) Program: WISH is a permanent, supportive housing program for dually diagnosed women (women who struggle with both drug & alcohol addiction and mental illness), and their children. The program provides housing in leased, scattered site apartments and houses, and intensive support services. The focus is on assisting women with building and maintaining healthy support systems, managing their drug and alcohol and mental health recovery programs, and living independently. The goal is to assist families, particularly those who face the greatest barriers to independence, to achieve and sustain lasting self-sufficiency.
EIN: 250965639

8216
Carl C. Yount Charitable Trust
c/o PNC Bank, N.A.
620 Liberty Ave.10th Fl.
Pittsburgh, PA   15222-2705   (412) 441-8200
Application Address: Chatham College, Woodland Rd., Pittsburg, PA 15232

Foundation type: Independent foundation
Purpose: Scholarship to outstanding students attending an accredited institution majoring in theatrics or music, or be an undergrad pursuing premedical course or in the school of medicine or performing research in orthopedic surgery and allied fields.
Financial data: Year ended 12/31/2011. Assets, $204,524 (M); Expenditures, $12,886; Total giving, $10,000.
Fields of interest: Theater; Music; Medical school/education; Orthopedics research.
Type of support: Research; Scholarships—to individuals; Undergraduate support.
Application information: Applications accepted.
  Initial approach: Letter
  Deadline(s): None
  Additional information: Application should include recommendation letter from a faculty member at Chatham College or University of Pittsburgh. Student must demonstrate financial need.
EIN: 256085369

8217
Harry T. Yule Educational Trust
c/o Wells Fargo Bank Nebraska, N.A.
101 N. Independence Mall E. MACY1372-062
Philadelphia, PA   19106-2112

Foundation type: Independent foundation
Purpose: Scholarships to graduates of Galva-Holstein High School, IA for postsecondary education.
Financial data: Year ended 12/31/2012. Assets, $145,633 (M); Expenditures, $8,552; Total giving, $5,000.
Fields of interest: Higher education.
Type of support: Support to graduates or students of specific schools.
Application information: Applications not accepted.
  Additional information: Unsolicited requests for funds not considered or acknowledged.
EIN: 421293244

8218
Daniel Zaccheus Foundation
c/o PNC Bank, N.A.
620 Liberty Ave., No 10th Fl.
Pittsburgh, PA   15222

Foundation type: Independent foundation
Purpose: Scholarships to graduate students studying astronomy and astrophysics in PA.
Financial data: Year ended 12/31/2012. Assets, $562,231 (M); Expenditures, $31,080; Total giving, $24,000.
Fields of interest: Astronomy; Space/aviation; Physics.
Type of support: Graduate support.
Application information: Applications accepted.
  Initial approach: Letter
  Deadline(s): None
  Additional information: Application should include letter of recommendation from

university department head outlining background and experience of applicant.
EIN: 256065413

8219
Mabel Zimmerman and Adelia Klinger Scholarship Fund
(formerly The Mabel and Adelia Zimmerman Foundation)
P.O. Box 3215
Lancaster, PA   17604-3215
Application address: c/o Fulton Financial Advisors, N.A., P.O. Box 25091, Lehigh Valley, PA 10882-5091

Foundation type: Independent foundation
Purpose: Undergraduate and graduate scholarships to Pine Grove Area High School seniors and graduates who were born in the Pine Grove Area High School District, PA.
Financial data: Year ended 07/31/2012. Assets, $1,104,450 (M); Expenditures, $51,509; Total giving, $39,300; Grants to individuals, 16 grants totaling $39,300 (high: $2,500, low: $2,400).
Fields of interest: Higher education.
Type of support: Support to graduates or students of specific schools; Graduate support; Undergraduate support.

Application information: Application form required.
Deadline(s): Apr. 30
Additional information: Applicant must demonstrate financial need.
EIN: 236887468

8220
R. Zoll FBO Charities
c/o Wells Fargo Bank N.A.
101 N Independence Mall E MACY 1372-062
Philadelphia, PA   19106-2112   (610) 436-2868
Application address: c/o West Chester University 202 Filano Hall, 628 S. High St., West Chester, PA 19383,

Foundation type: Independent foundation
Purpose: Scholarships to students for attendance at West Chester State College, PA for higher education.
Financial data: Year ended 12/31/2012. Assets, $138,442 (M); Expenditures, $6,934; Total giving, $4,500.
Fields of interest: Higher education.
Type of support: Scholarships—to individuals.
Application information: Applications accepted. Application form required.
Deadline(s): Apr. 1
EIN: 236799445

8221
Hattie Zurfluh Scholarship Fund
c/o Wells Fargo Bank N. A.
101 N Independence Mall E MACY 1372-062
Philadelphia, PA   19106-2112   (254) 714-6160
Application address: c/o Wells Fargo Bank, N.A., P.O. Box 2626, Waco, TX 76702-2626

Foundation type: Independent foundation
Purpose: Scholarships to graduating seniors of Waco High School, TX for postsecondary education.
Financial data: Year ended 12/31/2012. Assets, $432,959 (M); Expenditures, $24,951; Total giving, $18,800.
Fields of interest: Higher education.
Type of support: Support to graduates or students of specific schools; Undergraduate support.
Application information: Applications accepted. Application form required.
Deadline(s): Mar.
Applicants should submit the following:
1) Class rank
2) SAT
3) GPA
4) ACT
EIN: 746370513

PUERTO RICO

8222
Harvey Foundation
1st Federal Bldg. Ste. 507
San Juan, PR   00909-1715   (787) 725-1814
Contact: Charles M. Hitt, Pres.

Foundation type: Independent foundation
Purpose: Scholarships to residents of PR for higher education.
Publications: Annual report.
Financial data: Year ended 12/31/2011. Assets, $1,909,548 (M); Expenditures, $97,817; Total giving, $86,600; Grants to individuals, 13 grants totaling $41,000 (high: $6,000, low: $1,000).
Type of support: Scholarships—to individuals.
Application information:
   Initial approach: Letter
   Deadline(s): Jan. 31
EIN: 660271454

8223
Puerto Rico Community Foundation, Inc.
1719 Ponce de Leon Ave.
San Juan, PR   00909-1905   (787) 721-1037
Contact: Juan J. Reyes, Admin.
FAX: (787) 982-1673; E-mail: fcpr@fcpr.og; Mailing address: PO Box 70362, San Juan, PR 00936-8362; URL: http://www.fcpr.org

Foundation type: Community foundation
Purpose: Scholarships to economically disadvantaged residents of Puerto Rico for undergraduate and graduate study in different disciplines.
Publications: Application guidelines; Annual report; Biennial report; Financial statement; Informational brochure (including application guidelines); Newsletter; Occasional report; Program policy statement.
Financial data: Year ended 12/31/2012. Assets, $26,002,495 (M); Expenditures, $3,020,007; Total giving, $1,367,365; Grants to individuals, totaling $288,226.
Fields of interest: Higher education.
Type of support: Scholarships—to individuals; Support to graduates or students of specific schools; Awards/prizes; Undergraduate support.
Application information: Application form available on the grantmaker's web site.
   Send request by: Mail
   Copies of proposal: 5
   Deadline(s): Varies
   Final notification: Applicants notified in two months
   Applicants should submit the following:
      1) Transcripts
      2) Pell Grant
      3) Letter(s) of recommendation
      4) GPA
      5) Financial information
      6) FAFSA
      7) Essay
EIN: 660413230

8224
Unanue Lopez Family Foundation
P.O. Box 60-1467
Bayamon, PR   00960-6067   (787) 740-4900
Contact: Diana L. Lopez Unanue, Tr.

Foundation type: Operating foundation
Purpose: Scholarships to residents of PR for higher education.
Financial data: Year ended 12/31/2011. Assets, $666,982 (M); Expenditures, $65,738; Total giving, $56,383; Grants to individuals, 2 grants totaling $18,733 (high: $9,436, low: $9,297).
Fields of interest: Education.
Type of support: Scholarships—to individuals.
Application information: Contact foundation for application guidelines.
EIN: 660572018

RHODE ISLAND

8225
Additon Scholarship Fund
10 Tripps Ln.
Riverside, RI 02915-7995 (603) 634-7749
Contact: Bill Sirak
Application address: C/O RBS Citizens, N.A., 875 Elm St., Manchester, NH 03105,

Foundation type: Independent foundation
Purpose: Scholarships limited to former employees, or issue of same of Numerica Financial Corp., Manchester, NH, or Citizens Bank New Hampshire, Manchester, NH.
Financial data: Year ended 09/30/2013. Assets, $449,525 (M); Expenditures, $26,843; Total giving, $19,800.
Type of support: Employee-related scholarships.
Application information: Application form required.
  Deadline(s): May 15
  Additional information: Application attainable from the trustee.
Company names: Numerica Financial Corp.; Citizens Bank New Hampshire
EIN: 237435466

8226
Alliance of Artists' Communities
255 S. Main St.
Providence, RI 02903-2910 (401) 351-4320
Contact: Caitlin Strokosch, Exec. Dir.
FAX: (401) 351-4507;
E-mail: info@artistcommunities.org; URL: http://www.artistcommunities.org

Foundation type: Public charity
Purpose: Residency opportunities to underserved and underrepresented artists throughout the U.S.
Publications: Application guidelines.
Financial data: Year ended 12/31/2012. Assets, $487,568 (M); Expenditures, $730,731; Total giving, $73,920; Grants to individuals, totaling $24,000.
Fields of interest: Arts, artist's services.
Type of support: Residencies.
Application information: Applications accepted.
  Initial approach: Application
  Deadline(s): June 7 for Midwestern Voices and Visions Residency Program, none for all others
  Additional information: See web site for list of materials to include with application.
Program descriptions:
  Emergency Funds for Individual Artists: Awarded in partnership with The Joan Mitchell Foundation, this program supports painters and sculptors who have already been accepted to and scheduled to participate in a residency, but who would not otherwise be able to participate due to a sudden change in circumstances, by awarding emergency grants of up to $1,000. Eligible applicants must be painters or sculptors who are legal U.S. residents, who have been accepted and scheduled to participate in a residency program that is an organizational member of the alliance, and who have experienced a recent, unforeseen emergency or triggering event that would otherwise prohibit his/her participation in the planned residency.
  Midwestern Voices and Visions Residency Program: Administered in conjunction with The Joyce Foundation, this program seeks to identify strong voices that represent today's most promising and provocative talent, and reflect the

rich diversity of the Midwest. This program is intended to celebrate, support, and promote the work of highly-talented, yet under-recognized, artists of color, and broaden awareness of and support for the opportunities available at Midwestern residency programs for artists of diverse backgrounds. Eligible artists include those of color who are working in any visual, literary, and/or performance-based media, who display artistic excellence, who are committed to an artistic career, and who are underserved, underrecognized, or underrepresented in the mainstream (including artists who have not had extensive solo exhibitions at galleries or museums, or who have not received any major grants or fellowships for individual artists). Applicants must be permanent residents of IL, IA, MI, MN, MO, NE, OH, or WI, and must not be a degree-seeking student. In addition to a month-long residency opportunity, recipients are given a $4,000 award, to be used at their discretion (e.g., for materials or travel to and from the residency, to offset loss of income during residency)
  Residencies for Artists Affected by a Natural Disaster: On an as-needed basis, the alliance will provide residency opportunities to artists affected by natural disasters. In the event of a natural disaster, the alliance contacts its network of residency programs to identify immediate and short-term availability of residencies. The alliance will then work with affected artists (either through an open call or through a partner organization in the affected area) to take advantage of those residency opportunities.
EIN: 582138525

8227
Warren Alpert Foundation
27 Warren Way
P.O. Box 72743
Providence, RI 02907-2424 (401) 781-9900
URL: http://www.warrenalpert.org/foundation

Foundation type: Independent foundation
Purpose: Medical research grants by nomination only in the form of annual prizes to medical doctors in the U.S. and abroad.
Publications: Grants list.
Financial data: Year ended 12/31/2012. Assets, $198,551,435 (M); Expenditures, $17,633,182; Total giving, $17,406,000; Grants to individuals, 5 grants totaling $256,000 (high: $150,000, low: $6,000).
Fields of interest: Association; Institute.
Type of support: Research; Awards/grants by nomination only; Foreign applicants; Awards/prizes.
Application information: Applications not accepted.
  Additional information: Recipients are chosen in consultation with a panel of medical experts and the faculties of Harvard Medical School and Albert Einstein School of Medicine.
Program description:
  Warren Alpert Foundation Prize: Each year the foundation receives between 30 and 50 award nominations for the prize, which was first awarded in 1987. The goal is to recognize contributions to humanity and breakthroughs in the understanding and curing of major diseases. Prize recipients are selected by the Foundation's Scientific Advisory Committee. Winners are presented with a $200,000 award at the foundation's annual ceremony. For more information contact: Casie Madden, Harvard Medical School, 25 Shattuck St., Rm. 101 Boston, MA 02115, tel.: (617) 432-3638,

e-mail: casie_madden@hms.harvard.edu See foundation web site for online nomination form.
EIN: 050426623

8228
J. Wilfred Anctil Foundation
10 Tripps Ln.
Riverside, RI 02915-7995 (603) 897-1152
Contact: Wayne Nelson
Application address: P.O. Box 96, Nashua NH, 03061-0096

Foundation type: Independent foundation
Purpose: Scholarships for higher education to needy residents of the greater Nashua, NH, area.
Financial data: Year ended 12/31/2012. Assets, $1,157,060 (M); Expenditures, $68,786; Total giving, $52,150; Grants to individuals, 73 grants totaling $52,150 (high: $2,550, low: $250).
Type of support: Scholarships—to individuals.
Application information: Applications accepted.
  Initial approach: Letter
  Deadline(s): May 1
  Applicants should submit the following:
    1) Financial information
    2) Transcripts
EIN: 026007760

8229
Marie B. Andrews Trust
P.O. Box 1802
Providence, RI 02901-1802 (603) 332-0757
Contact: Robert A. Pederson
Application address: C/o. Spaulding High School, Wakefield St., Rochester, NH 03867, tel.: (603) 332-0757

Foundation type: Independent foundation
Purpose: Scholarships for higher education to graduates of Spaulding High School, Rochester, NH, with preference given to applicants receiving their education within the commercial department of the school.
Financial data: Year ended 02/28/2013. Assets, $1,552,683 (M); Expenditures, $69,618; Total giving, $52,832.
Fields of interest: Business school/education.
Type of support: Support to graduates or students of specific schools; Undergraduate support.
Application information:
  Initial approach: Letter or telephone
  Additional information: Contact trust for additional application guidelines.
EIN: 026061834

8230
Benjamin A. Armstrong Trust
P.O. Box 1802
Providence, RI 02901-1802

Foundation type: Independent foundation
Purpose: Scholarships to male graduates of New London High School, CT, and female graduates of the Williams School, CT, for higher education.
Financial data: Year ended 12/31/2012. Assets, $713,382 (M); Expenditures, $39,211; Total giving, $25,000.
Fields of interest: Higher education.
Type of support: Support to graduates or students of specific schools; Undergraduate support.
Application information: Applications accepted. Application form required.
  Deadline(s): June 1
  Applicants should submit the following:
    1) SAT

2) Financial information
3) Transcripts
4) Letter(s) of recommendation
Additional information: Applicants must have attended the respective high schools for at least three years.
EIN: 066026283

8231
Maude E. Arnold Memorial Fund
(formerly Maude E. Arnold Trust for Memorial Fund)
P.O. Box 1802
Providence, RI   02901-1802
Application address: c/o First Baptist Church, Attn: Scholarship Committee Chair., P.O. Box 121, 2-4 North St., Plymouth, CT 06782, tel.: (860) 283-6181

Foundation type: Independent foundation
Purpose: Scholarships to girls who have been residents of Waterbury, CT, for the previous five years.
Financial data: Year ended 12/31/2012. Assets, $208,644 (M); Expenditures, $12,562; Total giving, $9,800.
Fields of interest: Girls.
Type of support: Undergraduate support.
Application information: Applications accepted.
Deadline(s): Apr. 30
Applicants should submit the following:
1) Transcripts
2) Financial information
Additional information: Application should also include activities and grades. Applicants must be U.S. citizens.
EIN: 066140957

8232
Grace Atkins Trust
P.O. Box 1802
Providence, RI   02901-1802
Application address: c/o Bank of America, N.A., 777 Main St., CT2-102-22-02, Hartford, CT 06115

Foundation type: Independent foundation
Purpose: Scholarships and educational grants to residents of Bristol, CT, attending four-year colleges.
Financial data: Year ended 12/31/2012. Assets, $1,447,415 (M); Expenditures, $77,203; Total giving, $54,324.
Fields of interest: Higher education.
Type of support: Scholarships—to individuals.
Application information: Applications accepted. Application form required.
Deadline(s): Mar. 15
Additional information: Application forms are available from public libraries or high school guidance departments.
EIN: 066138990

8233
Fannie August Charitable Trust
P.O. Box 1802
Providence, RI   02901-1802
Application address: c/o Bank of America, N.A., Attn.: Carol Gray, Trust Off., 100 Federal St., Boston, MA 02110

Foundation type: Independent foundation
Purpose: Scholarships to needy, worthy students in the metropolitan Boston, MA, area for medical school.

Financial data: Year ended 12/31/2012. Assets, $316,931 (M); Expenditures, $19,238; Total giving, $13,500.
Fields of interest: Medical school/education.
Type of support: Graduate support.
Application information: Applications accepted.
Initial approach: Letter
Deadline(s): None
Additional information: Contact the trust for additional guidelines.
EIN: 046027010

8234
Waldo & Alice Ayer Trust
10 Tripps Ln.
Riverside, RI   02915-7995   (603) 634-7772
Contact: Maureen Blanchard
Application address: 875 Elm St., Manchester NH, 03101

Foundation type: Independent foundation
Purpose: Scholarships to music students primarily in the state of NH, who are studying to become professional musicians or music teachers.
Financial data: Year ended 09/30/2013. Assets, $817,918 (M); Expenditures, $50,166; Total giving, $37,504.
Fields of interest: Music; Performing arts, education; Teacher school/education.
Type of support: Scholarships—to individuals.
Application information: Applications accepted.
Initial approach: Letter
Deadline(s): None
EIN: 026059690

8235
Lucy C. Ayers Foundation, Inc.
(formerly The Lucy C. Ayres Home for Nurses, Inc.)
2000 Chapel View Blvd.
Cranston, RI   02920   (401) 828-3041
Contact: Nancy Whitaker, Pres.
Application address: Ste. 350, Cranston, RI 02920

Foundation type: Independent foundation
Purpose: Scholarships to nursing students, primarily in RI, and financial support to graduates of the Rhode Island Hospital School of Nursing.
Financial data: Year ended 03/31/2013. Assets, $625,057 (M); Expenditures, $33,775; Total giving, $19,500; Grants to individuals, 33 grants totaling $19,500 (high: $750, low: $500).
Fields of interest: Nursing school/education.
Type of support: Scholarships—to individuals.
Application information: Applications accepted. Application form required.
Additional information: Contact foundation for current application deadline/guidelines.
EIN: 050264853

8236
Betsey E. Babcock Trust
(formerly John C. Babcock Fund)
P.O. Box 1802
Providence, RI   02901-1802

Foundation type: Independent foundation
Purpose: Scholarships to residents of the greater Lynn, MA, area, including Swampscott, Nahant, and Saugus, MA.
Financial data: Year ended 12/31/2012. Assets, $225,148 (M); Expenditures, $12,777; Total giving, $8,000.
Type of support: Scholarships—to individuals.

Application information: Applications accepted. Application form required.
Deadline(s): June 15
EIN: 046043639

8237
Bailey Foundation
(formerly Bailey Foundation Dtd. 11/30/53)
P.O. Box 1802
Providence, RI   02901-1802
Contact: Edwin Bailey
Application address: 414 Main St., Amesbury, MA 01913

Foundation type: Independent foundation
Purpose: Scholarships to students or graduates of Amesbury High School, MA, who are U.S. citizens and residents of Amesbury, MA.
Financial data: Year ended 06/30/2013. Assets, $771,874 (M); Expenditures, $33,807; Total giving, $23,000.
Fields of interest: Higher education.
Type of support: Support to graduates or students of specific schools; Undergraduate support.
Application information: Applications accepted. Application form required.
Deadline(s): Apr. 15
Additional information: Application must include references and a list of hobbies and activities.
Program description:
Scholarship Program: The scholarship is awarded to one new individual each year who is a graduate of Amesbury High School or a resident of Amesbury, MA, and is to be used for tuition, books and supplies, and laboratory expenses for a student pursuing a B.S. or B.A. degree. The scholarship is renewable for a four-year period. Selection is based on a combination of financial need and scholastic record.
EIN: 046095808

8238
Lillian M. Baker Trust
P.O. Box 1802
Providence, RI   02901-1802   (603) 647-7650
Contact: Debra Dunn
Application address: Bank of America,1155 Elm St., Manchester, NH 03101

Foundation type: Independent foundation
Purpose: Scholarships for residents of Maine for higher education.
Financial data: Year ended 12/31/2012. Assets, $785,303 (M); Expenditures, $48,084; Total giving, $35,500; Grants to individuals, 11 grants totaling $29,500 (high: $4,000, low: $1,500).
Fields of interest: Higher education.
Type of support: Support to graduates or students of specific schools; Graduate support; Undergraduate support.
Application information: Application form required.
Initial approach: Letter
Deadline(s): Apr. 15
Additional information: Contact the trust for additional guidelines.
EIN: 046010588

8239
Baker-Adams Scholarship Fund
P.O. Box 1802
Providence, RI   02901-1802
Application address: c/o Georgetown School, 51 N. St., Georgetown, MA 01833

Foundation type: Independent foundation

Purpose: Scholarships to residents of Georgetown, MA, for undergraduate education at American universities.
Financial data: Year ended 12/31/2012. Assets, $632,317 (M); Expenditures, $32,811; Total giving, $20,000.
Fields of interest: Higher education.
Type of support: Support to graduates or students of specific schools; Undergraduate support.
Application information: Applications accepted. Application form required.
  Deadline(s): May 10
  Additional information: Application must include financial information.
EIN: 316636824

8240
Margaret & Dom Barillaro Scholarship Trust
P.O. Box 1802
Providence, RI   02901-1802

Foundation type: Independent foundation
Purpose: Scholarships to young men and women who are enrolled in or are graduates of the public high schools of the community of Danvers, MA seeking a higher education at a recognized college or university.
Financial data: Year ended 07/31/2013. Assets, $279,287 (M); Expenditures, $13,441; Total giving, $8,750.
Fields of interest: Higher education.
Type of support: Scholarships—to individuals.
Application information: Applications accepted. Application form required.
  Deadline(s): June 1
  Additional information: Applicant must demonstrate good character and intelligence, scholastic and extra-curricular achievement, potential for achievement and financial need.
EIN: 046956483

8241
Russell T. & Olive V. Bartlett Trust
10 Tripps Ln.
Riverside, RI   02915-7995   (603) 747-2781

Foundation type: Independent foundation
Purpose: Scholarships to residents of Bath and Haverhill, NH, to attend Dartmouth College, NH. Applicants must have been residents for at least five years prior to application.
Financial data: Year ended 09/30/2013. Assets, $778,575 (M); Expenditures, $49,560; Total giving, $35,400.
Type of support: Support to graduates or students of specific schools; Undergraduate support.
Application information: Applications accepted.
  Send request by: In person
  Deadline(s): None
  Additional information: Applications made in person at the guidance office of Woodsville High School.
EIN: 026003957

8242
Stephen P. Bell, Timothy A. Bell and Tricia Flynn Caley Memorial Scholarship
(formerly Stephen P. Bell and Tricia Flynn Caley Memorial Scholarship Fund)
10 Tripps Ln.
Riverside, RI   02915-7995
Application address: Exeter High School,
Attn.: Principal, 315 Epping Rd., Exeter, NH 03833

Foundation type: Independent foundation
Purpose: Scholarships to graduates of Exeter Area High School, NH, who have been active in student affairs.
Financial data: Year ended 12/31/2012. Assets, $215,393 (M); Expenditures, $14,314; Total giving, $10,000; Grants to individuals, 4 grants totaling $10,000 (high: $2,500, low: $2,500).
Type of support: Support to graduates or students of specific schools; Undergraduate support.
Application information: Applications accepted. Application form required.
  Initial approach: Letter
  Deadline(s): Apr. 1
EIN: 020364166

8243
Janice T. Berry Scholarship
(formerly Janice T. Berry Trust)
10 Tripps Ln.
Riverside, RI   02915-7995   (603) 634-7752
Contact: Bill Sirak
Application address: c/o RBS Citizens, 875 Elm St., Manchester, NH 03101

Foundation type: Independent foundation
Purpose: Scholarships to nursing students, with preference given to students in Manchester, NH.
Financial data: Year ended 12/31/2012. Assets, $403,156 (M); Expenditures, $23,456; Total giving, $15,300.
Fields of interest: Nursing school/education.
Type of support: Undergraduate support.
Application information: Applications accepted. Application form required.
  Initial approach: Letter or telephone
  Deadline(s): July 25
  Additional information: Contact trust for current application guidelines.
EIN: 026067436

8244
Evelyn H. Black Trust
(also known as Art B. and Evelyn H. Black Scholarship Fund)
P.O. Box 1802
Providence, RI   02901-1802   (617) 434-4898
Contact: Carol Gray, Tr.
Application Address: c/o Bank of America, 225 Franklin St., Boston, MA 02110

Foundation type: Independent foundation
Purpose: Scholarships to students who are attending or have attended Concord, MA, public schools.
Publications: Application guidelines.
Financial data: Year ended 12/31/2012. Assets, $1,244,162 (M); Expenditures, $71,741; Total giving, $53,000; Grants to individuals, totaling $53,000.
Fields of interest: Arts education; Vocational education.
Type of support: Support to graduates or students of specific schools; Undergraduate support.
Application information: Applications accepted. Application form required.
  Deadline(s): Apr. 20
  Applicants should submit the following:
    1) Essay
    2) GPA
    3) Transcripts
  Additional information: Application should include copy of parents' tax return.
Program description:
  Scholarship Program: The fund was established to provide scholarships to financially needy, worthy,

and able high school students. To qualify, applicants must have maintained a scholastic standing above their class average during the preceding year. Applicants must also wish to pursue studies or develop a talent in areas where no instruction or additional instruction is available free of charge in the Concord public schools. Scholarships are provided for college or university study, and advanced training in any one of the fine arts, practical arts, or vocations.
EIN: 046141425

8245
Henry L. & Nellie E. Blakeslee Trust for Scholarships
P.O. Box 1802
Providence, RI   02901-1802
Application address: c/o Thomaston High School, 185 Branch Rd., Thomaston, CT 06787

Foundation type: Independent foundation
Purpose: Scholarships to graduates of Thomaston High School, CT for postsecondary education at accredited colleges or universities.
Financial data: Year ended 12/31/2012. Assets, $2,031,191 (M); Expenditures, $98,609; Total giving, $71,250.
Fields of interest: Higher education.
Type of support: Scholarships—to individuals.
Application information: Applications accepted. Application form required.
  Deadline(s): Three weeks before end of school year
  Additional information: Application must include general and financial information.
EIN: 066025519

8246
George Gardner & Fanny Whiting Blanchard Scholarship Fund
P.O. Box 1802
Providence, RI   02901-1802

Foundation type: Independent foundation
Purpose: Scholarships to graduates of Wilton High School, NH.
Financial data: Year ended 03/31/2013. Assets, $484,545 (M); Expenditures, $19,330; Total giving, $17,000.
Fields of interest: Education.
Type of support: Scholarships—to individuals; Support to graduates or students of specific schools.
Application information: Applications accepted. Application form required.
  Deadline(s): None
  Additional information: Application should include transcripts.
EIN: 026004699

8247
Paul O. & Mary Boghossian Foundation
(formerly Paul O. & Mary Boghossian Memorial Trust)
P.O. Box 1802
Providence, RI   02901-1802
Contact: Sharon Driscoll
Application address: 100 Federal St., Boston, MA 02110

Foundation type: Independent foundation
Purpose: Scholarship to residents of Kent County or Pawtucket, Rhode Island for higher education.

Financial data: Year ended 04/30/2013. Assets, $1,974,175 (M); Expenditures, $94,605; Total giving, $61,000.
Fields of interest: Boys & girls clubs; YM/YWCAs & YM/YWHAs; Christian agencies & churches.
International interests: Armenia.
Type of support: Scholarships—to individuals.
Application information: Applications accepted. Application form required.
Copies of proposal: 1
Deadline(s): May 1
Program description:
Scholarship Program: Scholarships are awarded to residents of Kent County, RI, members and former members of the Kent County branch of the YMCA or the Pawtucket Boys Club, members or descendants of members of Park Place Congregation Church in Pawtucket, and individuals who are Armenian by national origin or descent.
EIN: 056051815

8248
Helen C.S. Botsford Trust
P.O. Box 1802
Providence, RI   02901-1802   (413) 458-9582
Contact: Donna D. Rioux
Application address: c/o MT Grey Regional HS, 1781 Cold Spring Rd., Williamstown, MA 01267. Tel.: (413) 458-9582

Foundation type: Independent foundation
Purpose: Scholarships to graduating students of Mount Greylock Regional School District and are residents of Williamstown, MA for higher education.
Financial data: Year ended 03/31/2013. Assets, $195,714 (M); Expenditures, $10,302; Total giving, $6,400.
Fields of interest: Higher education.
Type of support: Scholarships—to individuals.
Application information: Applications accepted. Application form required.
Deadline(s): May 15
Additional information: Applications can be obtained from the guidance office.
EIN: 046130605

8249
Virginia A. Bowmaker Scholarship Trust
(formerly V. A. Bowmaker Scholarship Trust)
P.O. Box 1802
Providence, RI   02901-1802   (585) 546-9303
Application address: Bank of America, NA, c/o Judith Lee, 1 East Ave., Rochester, NY 14638

Foundation type: Independent foundation
Purpose: Scholarships to graduates of Utica, NY, public and parochial schools.
Financial data: Year ended 12/31/2012. Assets, $1,526,135 (M); Expenditures, $93,586; Total giving, $69,000; Grants to individuals, 42 grants totaling $69,000 (high: $2,500, low: $1,000).
Type of support: Support to graduates or students of specific schools; Undergraduate support.
Application information: Applications accepted. Application form required.
Deadline(s): None
EIN: 161381376

8250
The Joan H. Brack Charitable Foundation
c/o RBS Citizens N.A.
10 Tripps Ln.
Riverside, RI   02915-7995
Application address: c/o Kenneth B. Brack, 6 Soule St., Plympton, MA 02367

Foundation type: Independent foundation
Purpose: Scholarship to a senior member of the Varsity Boy's soccer team and one to a senior member of the Varsity Girl's soccer team at Silverlake Regional High School.
Financial data: Year ended 12/31/2012. Assets, $1,464,586 (M); Expenditures, $222,064; Total giving, $183,245.
Fields of interest: Higher education.
Type of support: Support to graduates or students of specific schools.
Application information: Applications accepted. Application form required.
Deadline(s): Apr. 4
Additional information: Application must include a completed personal statement and official transcript. Each recipient will be eligible for second, third and fourth years of college if the recipient maintains a 3.0 GPA or higher during the preceding academic year and maintains his or her status as a full-time student at a qualified school during the preceding academic year.
EIN: 316632672

8251
B. K. Brennan Scholarship Fund, Inc.
P.O. Box 6418
Providence, RI   02940-6418   (401) 737-1457
Contact: Ralph Knox, Secy.

Foundation type: Independent foundation
Purpose: Scholarships to qualified students and craftsmen attending accepted and accredited Graphic Arts schools, colleges or universities of advanced education.
Financial data: Year ended 12/31/2010. Assets, $132,221 (M); Expenditures, $4,865; Total giving, $4,375; Grants to individuals, 4 grants totaling $4,375 (high: $1,775, low: $600).
Fields of interest: Arts education.
Type of support: Scholarships—to individuals.
Application information: Applications accepted. Application form required.
Deadline(s): Nov. 15
Additional information: Application should include transcripts, and letter from school to show enrollment.
EIN: 050519622

8252
Mary E. Brock Trust
10 Tripps Ln.
Riverside, RI   02915-7995

Foundation type: Independent foundation
Purpose: Scholarships to individuals, primarily in N.H.
Financial data: Year ended 12/31/2012. Assets, $533,352 (M); Expenditures, $29,621; Total giving, $21,735.
Type of support: Undergraduate support.
Application information: Applications not accepted.
Additional information: Unsolicited requests for funds not considered or acknowledged.
EIN: 026030934

8253
The John Nicholas Brown Center for the Study of American Civilization
Box 1880
Brown Univ.
Providence, RI   02912-1880   (401) 863-1177
Contact: Steven Lubar, Exec. Dir.
FAX: (401) 863-7777;
E-mail: publichumanities@brown.edu; URL: http://www.brown.edu/jnbc

Foundation type: Public charity
Purpose: Fellowships for staff at Southern New England cultural institutions.
Publications: Application guidelines.
Financial data: Year ended 06/30/2011. Assets, $18,556,393 (M); Expenditures, $975,005.
Fields of interest: Humanities; Literature.
Type of support: Fellowships; Stipends.
Application information: Applications accepted. Application form required.
Initial approach: Letter
Send request by: Mail
Copies of proposal: 1
Deadline(s): Rolling
Applicants should submit the following:
1) Proposal
2) Letter(s) of recommendation
3) Curriculum vitae
Program descriptions:
JNBC Public Humanist-in-Residence: One or two senior practitioners to spend a short period (typically one week) in residence working with students, faculty, and community members. With the assistance of JNBC staff, each resident will design formal and informal opportunities to present their work and their ideas, including within class settings, and to consult on students' and community projects. Residents are accepted by invitation only; applications are not accepted.
JNBC Public Humanities Fellows: These fellowships are intended to encourage writing on issues of the public humanities. Available for periods of up to three months, and open to academics, staff at cultural organizations, and independent scholars, this program will provide a place to work, access to Brown University libraries, participation in a community of interested faculty, students, and public humanists, and a stipend of $2,000 per month. Fellows are expected to make a presentation on their work to the JNBC Public Humanities Colloquium, and to write, for publication on the JNBC web site, a short essay on the subject of their fellowship.
EIN: 222506553

8254
John P. Burke Memorial Fund
1 Button Hole Dr., Ste. 2
Providence, RI   02909-5750   (401) 272-1350
Contact: Maury C. Davitt, Exec. Dir.
FAX: (401) 331-3627;
E-mail: burkefund@rigalinks.org; URL: http://www.burkefund.org

Foundation type: Public charity
Purpose: Scholarships to individuals who have worked at a member club of the Rhode Island Golf Association.
Financial data: Year ended 03/31/2012. Assets, $978,008 (M); Expenditures, $180,518; Total giving, $109,175; Grants to individuals, totaling $109,175.
Fields of interest: Higher education.
Type of support: Scholarships—to individuals.
Application information: Applications accepted. Application form required. Application form

available on the grantmaker's web site. Interview required.
  Initial approach: Letter
  Deadline(s): Apr. 15
  Applicants should submit the following:
    1) Letter(s) of recommendation
    2) SAR
    3) FAFSA
    4) Transcripts
  Additional information: Mail.
EIN: 056008795

8255
Alice L. Carlisle Trust for Children of Goshen Trust
P.O. Box 1802
Providence, RI   02901-1802
Application Address: c/o Bank of America, N.A.

Foundation type: Independent foundation
Purpose: Grants to cover medical expenses for children living in Goshen, CT.
Financial data: Year ended 12/31/2012. Assets, $1,448,345 (M); Expenditures, $79,057; Total giving, $65,252.
Fields of interest: Health care; Children, services.
Type of support: Grants for special needs.
Application information: Applications accepted. Application form required.
  Initial approach: Letter
  Deadline(s): None
  Additional information: Application must include financial information, copy of most recent income tax form and copy of last two weekly earnings statements.
EIN: 066115749

8256
Esther Chandler Trust
P.O. Box 1802
Providence, RI   02901-1802

Foundation type: Independent foundation
Purpose: Scholarships to students who are residents of Kingston, MA, for higher education.
Financial data: Year ended 10/31/2013. Assets, $301,630 (M); Expenditures, $13,885; Total giving, $8,000.
Type of support: Undergraduate support.
Application information:
  Initial approach: Letter
  Deadline(s): Apr. 11
EIN: 046589692

8257
Van and Joanna Christy Scholarship Fund
10 Tripps Ln.
Riverside, RI   02915-7995   (603) 634-7752
Contact: Bill Sirak
Application address: 875 Elm St., Manchester, NH 03101-2104, tel.: (603) 634-7752

Foundation type: Independent foundation
Purpose: Scholarships only to students of Greek descent in the Manchester, NH, area, for higher education.
Financial data: Year ended 08/31/2013. Assets, $1,360,122 (M); Expenditures, $82,418; Total giving, $60,500; Grants to individuals, 25 grants totaling $60,500 (high: $5,000, low: $500).
International interests: Greece.
Type of support: Scholarships—to individuals.

Application information: Applications accepted. Application form required.
  Deadline(s): May 31
EIN: 020484968

8258
Bradford & Dorothy Church Memorial Fund
P.O. Box 1802
Providence, RI   02901-1802

Foundation type: Independent foundation
Purpose: Scholarships to students of Martha's Vineyard Regional High School, MA.
Financial data: Year ended 12/31/2012. Assets, $4,307,918 (M); Expenditures, $187,806; Total giving, $140,744.
Type of support: Support to graduates or students of specific schools; Undergraduate support.
Application information: Applications not accepted.
  Additional information: Unsolicited requests for funds not considered or acknowledged.
EIN: 046135552

8259
Vincent A. Cianci, Jr. Scholarship Fund
P.O. Box 6184
Providence, RI   02940-6184   (401) 944-1067
Contact: Charles R. Mansolillo, Pres.
Application address: 1 Chestnut St., Providence, RI 02903-4155, tel.: (401) 861-1303

Foundation type: Public charity
Purpose: Scholarships to high school seniors from Providence, Rhode Island.
Financial data: Year ended 06/30/2012. Assets, $440,784 (M); Expenditures, $26,803; Total giving, $12,000; Grants to individuals, totaling $12,000.
Type of support: Undergraduate support.
Application information: Application form not required.
  Deadline(s): None
EIN: 050461354

8260
Elwin L. Cilley Trust
10 Tripps Ln.
Riverside, RI   02915-7995   (603) 634-7752
Contact: Carolann Harrington
Application address: c/o RBS Citizens, N.A., 825 Elm St., Manchester, NH 03101

Foundation type: Independent foundation
Purpose: Scholarships to individuals who have resided in Nottingham, NH, for the past five years.
Financial data: Year ended 06/30/2013. Assets, $419,790 (M); Expenditures, $50,857; Total giving, $36,900.
Fields of interest: Higher education.
Type of support: Undergraduate support.
Application information:
  Initial approach: Letter
  Deadline(s): Mar. 31
  Additional information: Application should include an essay. Contact trust for further application guidelines.
EIN: 026044555

8261
Bish & Frannie Cismoski Foundation
P.O. Box 1802
Providence, RI   02901-1802

Foundation type: Independent foundation
Purpose: Grants to priests and pastors.
Financial data: Year ended 12/31/2012. Assets, $68,388 (M); Expenditures, $95,307; Total giving, $93,000.
Fields of interest: Christian agencies & churches.
Type of support: Grants to individuals.
Application information: Contact foundation for current application deadline/guidelines.
EIN: 364434359

8262
Clark Medical Memorial Fund
(formerly Welsford Starr and Mildred M. Clark Medical Memorial Fund)
P.O. Box 1802
Providence, RI   02901-1802

Foundation type: Independent foundation
Purpose: Scholarships to fourth-year medical students who have been CT residents for at least five years.
Financial data: Year ended 12/31/2012. Assets, $3,000,232 (M); Expenditures, $147,269; Total giving, $97,000.
Fields of interest: Medical school/education.
Type of support: Undergraduate support.
Application information: Applications accepted. Application form required. Interview required.
  Deadline(s): Jan. 1
  Applicants should submit the following:
    1) Financial information
    2) Transcripts
    3) Letter(s) of recommendation
  Additional information: Application should also include test results of Part I of the National Boards and statement of medical school expenses.
EIN: 066326364

8263
Club Frontenac, Inc.
1143 Main St.
P.O. Box 137
West Warwick, RI   02893-0137   (401) 821-9846
Contact: David Simas, Pres.

Foundation type: Public charity
Purpose: Scholarships to members of Club Frontenac and their families in RI.
Financial data: Year ended 12/31/2012. Assets, $357,505 (M); Expenditures, $144,171.
Type of support: Scholarships—to individuals.
Application information: Applications accepted.
  Additional information: Contact foundation for complete eligibility information.
EIN: 050248863

8264
Frank & Ellen Cobb Memorial Scholars
P.O. Box 1802
Providence, RI   02901-1802
Application address: c/o Hingham High School, Attn.: Guidance Dept., 17 Union St., Hingham, MA 02043-2922

Foundation type: Independent foundation
Purpose: Scholarships to graduates of Hingham High School, MA, for attendance at a two or four year college.

Financial data: Year ended 08/31/2013. Assets, $1,803,060 (M); Expenditures, $106,392; Total giving, $82,000.
Type of support: Support to graduates or students of specific schools; Undergraduate support.
Application information: Applications accepted. Application form required.
 Deadline(s): Mar. 15
 Additional information: Application can be obtained from the guidance department.
EIN: 036088605

8265
Marion Isabell Coe Fund
P.O. Box 1802
Providence, RI 02901-1802
Contact: Kate Kerchaert, V.P.
Application address: 777 Main St., Hartford, CT 06115
E-mail: kate.kerchaert@ustrust.com; URL: http://www.bankofamerica.com/grantmaking

Foundation type: Independent foundation
Purpose: Relief assistance to worthy adult residents of Goshen, Litchfield, Morris, and Warren, CT, for general living and medical expenses.
Financial data: Year ended 12/31/2012. Assets, $669,315 (M); Expenditures, $39,489; Total giving, $29,000.
Fields of interest: Housing/shelter; Human services; Economically disadvantaged.
Type of support: Grants for special needs.
Application information: Applications accepted.
 Initial approach: Letter
 Deadline(s): None
EIN: 066040150

8266
William H. Coe Medical & Surgical Fund for Education
c/o Bank of America, N.A.
P.O. Box 1802
Providence, RI 02901-1802
Application Address: c/o Auburn Board of Education, Thornton Ave., Auburb, NY 13021

Foundation type: Independent foundation
Purpose: Scholarships to financially needy residents of Cayuga County, NY, who are graduates of high schools within the Auburn School District in NY, primarily those pursuing study in the areas of medicine and/or surgery.
Financial data: Year ended 12/31/2012. Assets, $323,861 (M); Expenditures, $25,451; Total giving, $21,000; Grants to individuals, 8 grants totaling $21,000 (high: $4,500, low: $1,000).
Fields of interest: Medical school/education.
Type of support: Support to graduates or students of specific schools; Undergraduate support.
Application information: Applications accepted. Application form required.
 Deadline(s): Mar. 15
 Additional information: Scholarships are awarded on the basis of need, scholastic standing, character and satisfactory completion of at least one semester of work in a college or university approved by the University of the State of New York.
EIN: 156018065

8267
Helen R. Coe Trust
P.O. Box 1802
Providence, RI 02901-1802
Loan application address: Coe Governing Committee, P.O. Box 185, Center Lovell, ME 04016

Foundation type: Independent foundation
Purpose: Student loans to residents of Lovell, ME.
Financial data: Year ended 03/31/2013. Assets, $2,267,741 (M); Expenditures, $114,400; Total giving, $85,900.
Type of support: Student loans—to individuals.
Application information: Applications accepted.
 Deadline(s): July
 Applicants should submit the following:
  1) Letter(s) of recommendation
  2) Financial information
 Additional information: Application must also include letter showing proof of residency in Lovell, ME, a statement of prior academic performance, and achievement test scores accepted throughout the applicant's senior year of high school.
EIN: 010351827

8268
Rueben J. and Dorothy S. Cohen Scholarship Fund
c/o Bank of America, N.A.
P.O. Box 1802
Providence, RI 02901-1802 (585) 546-9303
Contact: Judith Lee
Application address: East Ave., BC Rochester, NY 14638

Foundation type: Independent foundation
Purpose: Scholarships to financially needy Jewish students admitted to fully accredited medical schools located in Philadelphia, PA.
Financial data: Year ended 12/31/2012. Assets, $476,227 (M); Expenditures, $21,807; Total giving, $17,200.
Fields of interest: Medical school/education; Jewish agencies & synagogues.
Type of support: Support to graduates or students of specific schools; Graduate support.
Application information: Application form required.
 Additional information: Contact foundation for current application deadline/guidelines.
EIN: 226618260

8269
Arthur E. Coia Scholarship & Education Fund
410 S. Main St.
Providence, RI 02903-2956

Foundation type: Public charity
Purpose: Undergraduate scholarships to students who are dependents of members of the Laborers International Union of North America for attendance at Providence College, RI.
Financial data: Year ended 12/31/2012. Assets, $85,861 (M); Expenditures, $81,138; Total giving, $76,000.
Fields of interest: Higher education.
Type of support: Support to graduates or students of specific schools; Undergraduate support.
Application information: Applications accepted. Application form required.
 Deadline(s): Varies
 Additional information: Scholarship selection is based on academic achievements, financial need and potential.
EIN: 050477128

8270
Mary D. Coles Foundation
c/o Bank of America N.A.
P.O. Box 1802
Providence, RI 02901-1802
Contact: Judith Lee

Foundation type: Independent foundation
Purpose: Scholarships to graduates of Martha's Vineyard Regional High School who intend to pursue the study of art, music, architecture, painting, sculpture, theater or other fine arts at the higher education level.
Financial data: Year ended 12/31/2012. Assets, $934,856 (M); Expenditures, $68,469; Total giving, $57,000.
Fields of interest: Arts education; Visual arts; Architecture; Photography; Sculpture; Theater.
Type of support: Support to graduates or students of specific schools.
Application information: Applications not accepted.
 Additional information: Unsolicited requests for funds not considered or acknowledged.
EIN: 527054900

8271
The College Crusade of Rhode Island
134 Thurbers Ave., Ste. 111
Providence, RI 02905-4754 (401) 854-5500
Contact: Todd D. Flaherty Ed.D., Pres. and C.E.O.
FAX: (401) 854-5511;
E-mail: info@thecollegecrusade.org; E-mail for Todd D. Flaherty: tflaherty@thecollegecrusade.org;
URL: http://www.childrenscrusade.org

Foundation type: Public charity
Purpose: Scholarships to students in RI who complete the College Crusade program, demonstrate need, and graduate high school.
Financial data: Year ended 06/30/2012. Assets, $7,448,469 (M); Expenditures, $3,920,765; Total giving, $628,268; Grants to individuals, totaling $628,268.
Type of support: Undergraduate support.
Application information: Applications not accepted.
 Additional information: Unsolicited requests for funds not considered or acknowledged.
EIN: 223031765

8272
Comstock Memorial Scholarship Trust
(formerly James A. Comstock Memorial Scholarship Trust)
c/o Bank of America, N.A.
P.O. Box 1802
Providence, RI 02901-1802 (585) 546-9303
Contact: Judith Lee
Application address: 1 East Ave., NY7-144-04-04, Rochester, NY 14638-2220, tel.: (585) 546-9303

Foundation type: Independent foundation
Purpose: Scholarships to children of employees of Acme Electric/Tracewell Corp.
Financial data: Year ended 05/31/2013. Assets, $2,288,203 (M); Expenditures, $144,141; Total giving, $116,210.
Type of support: Employee-related scholarships.
Application information: Applications accepted. Application form required.
 Deadline(s): Jan. 31
 Applicants should submit the following:
  1) Transcripts
  2) ACT
  3) SAT

4) Letter(s) of recommendation
5) Essay
Additional information: Application must also include proof of tuition.
Company name: Acme Electric Corporation
EIN: 222327403

8273
Almon B. Cook Trust
P.O. Box 1802
Providence, RI   02901-1802

Foundation type: Independent foundation
Purpose: Scholarships to residents of Gloucester or Rockport, MA based on financial need and academic ability.
Financial data: Year ended 10/31/2013. Assets, $135,633 (M); Expenditures, $7,346; Total giving, $5,100.
Fields of interest: Higher education.
Type of support: Scholarships—to individuals.
Application information: Applications accepted. Application form required.
   Initial approach: Application
   Deadline(s): Apr. 20
   Additional information: Application must include parents' tax return and the name of the college or university the applicant plans to attend.
EIN: 046038998

8274
Mary P. Costa Scholarship
(formerly John D. Costa Scholarship Fund Trust)
P.O. Box 1802
Providence, RI   02901-1802
Contact: Carol Gray, Tr.
Application Address: 100 Federal St. Boston, MA 02109

Foundation type: Independent foundation
Purpose: Scholarships by nomination only to the highest ranking graduate of Plymouth-Carver High School, MA.
Financial data: Year ended 07/31/2013. Assets, $220,245 (M); Expenditures, $12,358; Total giving, $8,000.
Type of support: Support to graduates or students of specific schools; Awards/grants by nomination only; Undergraduate support.
Application information: Recipients selected by Plymouth-Carver High School staff.
EIN: 046144750

8275
The Cranston Foundation
c/o The Cranston Fdn. Trustees
1381 Cranston St.
Cranston, RI   02920-6739   (401) 943-4800

Foundation type: Company-sponsored foundation
Purpose: Scholarships for two years only to children of employees, excluding directors and officers, of the Cranston Print Works Company, its divisions, and subsidiaries.
Financial data: Year ended 06/30/2010. Assets, $2,777 (M); Expenditures, $112,371; Total giving, $112,371; Grants to individuals, 5 grants totaling $2,476 (high: $810, low: $207).
Type of support: Employee-related scholarships.
Application information: Applications not accepted.
   Additional information: Unsolicited requests for funds not considered or acknowledged.

Company name: Cranston Print Works Company
EIN: 056015348

8276
Cranston High Schools Athletic Scholarship Fund
c/o John S. Adams
5 Peach Tree Ln.
Coventry, RI   02816-6625   (401) 461-5056
Contact: ark Edward L. Rondeau, Secy.
Application address: 1052 Park Ave., Cranston, RI 02919 Tel.: (401) 461-5056

Foundation type: Independent foundation
Purpose: Scholarships to graduating senior athlete scholars from the two Cranston, RI public high schools pursuing postsecondary education at an accredited institution.
Financial data: Year ended 12/31/2012. Assets, $84,676 (M); Expenditures, $3,695; Total giving, $3,200; Grants to individuals, 7 grants totaling $3,200 (high: $800, low: $200).
Fields of interest: Higher education; Athletics/ sports, training; Athletics/sports, school programs.
Type of support: Support to graduates or students of specific schools; Undergraduate support.
Application information: Applications accepted. Application form required.
   Deadline(s): Apr.
   Applicants should submit the following:
      1) Transcripts
      2) Letter(s) of recommendation
      3) FAFSA
      4) SAR
   Additional information: Application forms are available form the guidance office. Students must demonstrate academic achievement, community service and participation in meaningful school activities.
EIN: 222982274

8277
Robert B. Cranston/Theophilus Pitman Fund
c/o Vernon Harvey
55 Memorial Blvd.
Newport, RI   02840   (401) 847-4260
Contact: John Grant, Dir.
Application address: 18 Market Sq., Newport, RI 02840

Foundation type: Independent foundation
Purpose: Assistance to the aged and economically disadvantaged people of Newport, RI with food, clothing, housing, utilities, travel and medical expense.
Financial data: Year ended 12/31/2012. Assets, $2,419,658 (M); Expenditures, $110,049; Total giving, $90,869; Grant to an individual, 1 grant totaling $90,869.
Fields of interest: Aging; Economically disadvantaged.
Type of support: Grants for special needs.
Application information: Applications accepted. Application form not required.
   Deadline(s): None
   Additional information: Personal appearance or reference from local welfare agencies required to show need.
EIN: 056008897

8278
R. Elaine Croston Scholarship Fund
P.O. Box 1802
Providence, RI   02901-1802   (508) 374-5712
Contact: Karen K. Baker, Principal
Application address: c/o Haverhill High School, Attn.: Karen K. Baker, Principal, 137 Monument St., Haverhill, MA 01832-2697

Foundation type: Independent foundation
Purpose: Scholarships to graduates of Haverhill High School, MA for higher education.
Financial data: Year ended 12/31/2012. Assets, $502,414 (M); Expenditures, $25,552; Total giving, $16,000; Grants to individuals, 6 grants totaling $16,000 (high: $6,000, low: $2,000).
Type of support: Support to graduates or students of specific schools; Undergraduate support.
Application information: Applications accepted.
   Additional information: Contact the principal for application guidelines.
EIN: 046079522

8279
Mary G. Croston TUW #3020001228
10 Tripps Ln.
Riverside, RI   02915-7995   (508) 327-8537
Contact: Fr. Frederick B. McGowan
Application address: c/o St. James Parish, 6 Cottage St., Haver Hill, MA 01830-4920

Foundation type: Independent foundation
Purpose: Scholarships to high school graduates who are members of Saint James Parish in Haverhill, MA.
Financial data: Year ended 08/31/2013. Assets, $246,194 (M); Expenditures, $13,418; Total giving, $9,203.
Fields of interest: Higher education; Christian agencies & churches.
Type of support: Scholarships—to individuals.
Application information: Applications accepted. Application form required.
   Initial approach: Letter
   Deadline(s): Spring
   Additional information: Applications are available from St. James.
EIN: 026027098

8280
Frank J. Cummings Trust
P.O. Box 1802
Providence, RI   02901-1802
Application address: c/o St. Francis of Assisi Church, Attn.: Priest In Charge

Foundation type: Independent foundation
Purpose: Assistance to men residing in Torrington, CT who wish to enter the priesthood.
Financial data: Year ended 12/31/2012. Assets, $182,176 (M); Expenditures, $9,864; Total giving, $5,996.
Fields of interest: Religion.
Type of support: Scholarships—to individuals.
Application information: Applications accepted. Application form required.
   Initial approach: Letter
   Deadline(s): None
EIN: 066134859

8281
Cuno Foundation
P.O. Box 1802
Providence, RI   02901-1802

Foundation type: Independent foundation
Purpose: Scholarships to eligible high school seniors of Meriden, CT and its vicinity who are entering a four year college program. One scholarship is also awarded to a resident of Meriden, CT.
Financial data: Year ended 12/31/2012. Assets, $9,902,889 (M); Expenditures, $513,064; Total giving, $399,562.
Fields of interest: Higher education.
Type of support: Scholarships—to individuals.
Application information: Application form required.
  Initial approach: Letter
  Deadline(s): Mar.
  Applicants should submit the following:
    1) Transcripts
    2) SAT
    3) Letter(s) of recommendation
  Additional information: Two letters of recommendation from teachers are required, one of which may be from a guidance counselor.
EIN: 066033040

8282
CVS Caremark Charitable Trust, Inc.
(formerly CVS/pharmacy Charitable Trust, Inc.)
1 CVS Dr.
Woonsocket, RI 02895-6146 (401) 770-2898
Contact: Joanne Dwyer, Dir., Corporate Comms. & Community Relas.
E-mail: Joanne.Dwyer@cvscaremark.com; General Community Rels. Inquiries: CommunityMailbox@cvscaremark.com;
URL: http://www.cvscaremark.com/community/our-impact/charitable-trust

Foundation type: Company-sponsored foundation
Purpose: Scholarships to children of full-time employees of CVS Corporation and its subsidiaries.
Publications: Grants list; Program policy statement.
Financial data: Year ended 12/31/2012. Assets, $45,651,274 (M); Expenditures, $5,830,000; Total giving, $5,665,193.
Fields of interest: Higher education.
Type of support: Employee-related scholarships.
Application information: Applications not accepted.
  Additional information: Unsolicited requests for funds not considered or acknowledged.
Company name: CVS Caremark Corporation
EIN: 223206973

8283
George W. Davenport Charitable Trust
P.O. Box 1802
Providence, RI 02901-1802
Contact: Thea Katsounakis, Tr., Bank of America, N.A.
Application address: 1 Monarch Pl., Springfield, MA 01144

Foundation type: Independent foundation
Purpose: Financial assistance to single women or couples aged 55 or older who have resided in Bernardston, Leyden, or Greenfield, MA for at least five years.
Financial data: Year ended 12/31/2012. Assets, $531,353 (M); Expenditures, $28,906; Total giving, $18,669.
Fields of interest: Aging; Women; Economically disadvantaged.
Type of support: Grants for special needs.

Application information: Applications accepted. Application form required.
  Deadline(s): None
  Additional information: Application should include detailed financial information. No funds may be used for funeral expenses.
EIN: 046312563

8284
Elmer Hobson DeLoura Trust for Scholarships
(formerly The DeLoura Family Trust)
P.O. Box 1802
Providence, RI 02901-1802
Contact: Susanna Posteo-Castillo
Application address: c/o Scholarship America, Inc., P.O. Box 297, St. Peter, MN 56802
FAX: (617) 434-7567

Foundation type: Independent foundation
Purpose: Scholarships to students of schools in Martha's Vineyard, MA.
Financial data: Year ended 01/31/2013. Assets, $4,445,651 (M); Expenditures, $263,957; Total giving, $156,000.
Fields of interest: Education.
Type of support: Scholarships—to individuals.
Application information: Applications accepted. Application form required.
  Deadline(s): Mar. 15
  Additional information: Applications are available at the guidance office of Martha's Vineyard schools. The program is administered by Scholarship America.
EIN: 046460749

8285
George A. Dix Trust
P.O. Box 1802
Providence, RI 02901-1802
Contact: Michael T. Rivard
Applicatin address: Fitchburg State College, Fitchburg, MA

Foundation type: Independent foundation
Purpose: Scholarships to needy men and women of Tremont, ME for higher education.
Financial data: Year ended 12/31/2012. Assets, $471,150 (M); Expenditures, $26,541; Total giving, $17,581.
Fields of interest: Education; Economically disadvantaged.
Type of support: Scholarships—to individuals.
Application information: Applications accepted.
  Initial approach: Letter
  Deadline(s): None
  Additional information: Applicant must demonstrate need for financial assistance.
EIN: 046023246

8286
Dorot Foundation
401 Elmgrove Ave.
Providence, RI 02906-3451 (401) 351-8866
Contact: Michael Hill, Exec. V.P.
Fellowship e-mail: dfi@dorot.org
FAX: (401) 351-4975; *E-mail:* dorotinfo@dorot.org;
URL: http://www.dorot.org

Foundation type: Independent foundation
Purpose: Fellowships for North American Jews between the ages of 22 to 29.
Publications: Financial statement; Grants list.

Financial data: Year ended 03/31/2013. Assets, $46,511,324 (M); Expenditures, $3,519,963; Total giving, $2,214,621; Grants to individuals, 10 grants totaling $566,930 (high: $57,240, low: $56,140).
Fields of interest: Higher education; Adult/continuing education; International exchange, students; International development; Jewish agencies & synagogues.
International interests: Canada; Israel.
Type of support: Fellowships; Travel grants.
Application information: Applications accepted. Application form required. Application form available on the grantmaker's web site. Interview required.
  Send request by: Online
  Applicants should submit the following:
    1) Photograph
    2) Transcripts
    3) Proposal
    4) Letter(s) of recommendation
    5) Budget Information
    6) Essay
Program description:
  Dorot Fellowship in Israel (DFI): The Fellowship is designed to assemble and empower a network of young Jewish lay leaders to enliven the American Jewish landscape. Between 10 and 15 Dorot Fellows are chosen each year to live in Israel, where they sharpen the characteristics and skills, acquire the experience, and broaden the networks required for Jewish leadership in the 21st Century. The Fellowship encompasses both individual and communal learning experiences and each fellow devises a Personal Learning Program, comprised of formal and experiential learning, and of various volunteer activities. The Fellowship award includes up to $6,000 toward the cost of one's Personal Learning Program, and an $20,000 Living Stipend. See web site for information and application forms.
EIN: 136116927

8287
Duxbury Yacht Club Charitable Foundation
P.O. Box 1802
Providence, RI 02901-1802
Contact: Nancy Masgul, Comm. Chair.
Application address: Duxbury Yacht Club, P.O. BOX 2804, Duxbuty MA 02331

Foundation type: Independent foundation
Purpose: Scholarships to Duxbury, MA, high school graduates.
Financial data: Year ended 12/31/2012. Assets, $323,217 (M); Expenditures, $11,987; Total giving, $10,000.
Type of support: Support to graduates or students of specific schools; Undergraduate support.
Application information: Applications accepted.
  Initial approach: Letter requesting financial aid
  Deadline(s): May 1
EIN: 046115247

8288
Eaton & Reed Scholarship Fund Trust
P.O. Box 1802
Providence, RI 02901-1802

Foundation type: Independent foundation
Purpose: Scholarships to seniors and graduates of Manchester High School, CT.
Financial data: Year ended 09/30/2013. Assets, $647,487 (M); Expenditures, $39,272; Total giving, $27,000.

Type of support: Support to graduates or students of specific schools; Undergraduate support.
Application information: Application form required.
  Deadline(s): Contact Manchester High School guidance office for current application deadline
  Additional information: Application must include page one of parents' 1040 form and the financial aid award package from institution applicant plans to attend or the Needs Analysis Form.
EIN: 237146710

8289
Henry E. Ellsworth Scholarship Fund
P.O. Box 1802
Providence, RI 02901-1802
Application address: c/o Simsbury High School, Attn.: Scholarship Comm., 34 Farms Village Rd., Simsbury, CT 06070-2344

Foundation type: Independent foundation
Purpose: Scholarships to students in the senior class of Simsbury High School, CT.
Financial data: Year ended 12/31/2011. Assets, $84,232 (M); Expenditures, $10,639; Total giving, $9,400.
Type of support: Support to graduates or students of specific schools; Undergraduate support.
Application information: Applications accepted. Application form required.
EIN: 066032904

8290
Herbert Fales Educational Trust
P.O. Box 1802
Providence, RI 02901-1802

Foundation type: Independent foundation
Purpose: Scholarships to individuals who reside within ten miles of Framingham, MA, and have a GPA of at least 2.5.
Financial data: Year ended 12/31/2012. Assets, $838,280 (M); Expenditures, $48,714; Total giving, $33,426.
Fields of interest: Higher education.
Type of support: Scholarships—to individuals.
Application information: Application form required.
  Deadline(s): June 30
EIN: 046044998

8291
Eleanor E. Farrington Trust
P.O. Box 1802
Providence, RI 02901-1802
Application address: c/o Alenia Miles, Guidance Dir., Kennett High School, 176 Main St., Conway, NH 03818-6164

Foundation type: Independent foundation
Purpose: Scholarships to high school seniors from the North Conway, NH school district, who have demonstrated financial need.
Financial data: Year ended 12/31/2012. Assets, $2,595,368 (M); Expenditures, $126,897; Total giving, $100,000.
Fields of interest: Higher education.
Type of support: Support to graduates or students of specific schools; Undergraduate support.
Application information: Application form required.
  Deadline(s): May 29
  Additional information: Application should include a copy of financial aid award letter and copy of first page of SAR.
EIN: 046433574

8292
Eliza H. Faunce Trust
(formerly The Sewall Allen Faunce Fund)
P.O. Box 1802
Providence, RI 02901-1802
Contact: Carol Gray
Application address: c/o Bank of America, N.A.,100 Federal St., Boston, MA 02100-1802

Foundation type: Independent foundation
Purpose: Scholarships to residents of Kingston, MA.
Financial data: Year ended 10/31/2013. Assets, $93,555 (M); Expenditures, $4,229; Total giving, $3,000.
Type of support: Scholarships—to individuals.
Application information: Applications accepted. Application form required.
  Deadline(s): Apr. 11
EIN: 046038603

8293
Fred Forsyth Educational Fund
(formerly Fred Forsyth Educational Trust Fund)
P.O. Box 1802
Providence, RI 02901-1802

Foundation type: Independent foundation
Purpose: Scholarships to graduates of Bucksport High School, ME, attending college.
Financial data: Year ended 07/31/2013. Assets, $854,522 (M); Expenditures, $32,395; Total giving, $18,428; Grants to individuals, 10 grants totaling $18,428 (high: $2,000, low: $428).
Fields of interest: Higher education.
Type of support: Support to graduates or students of specific schools; Undergraduate support.
Application information:
  Initial approach: Letter
  Deadline(s): None
  Additional information: Applications should include financial, scholastic, and employment records.
EIN: 016059631

8294
Louis B. Fox & Julian Karger Scholarship Fund
(formerly Louis B. Fox & Julian Karger Trust)
P.O. Box 1802
Providence, RI 02901-1802
Application address: c/o Revere High School, Attn.: Scholarship Comm., 101 School St., Revere, MA 02151-3099

Foundation type: Independent foundation
Purpose: Scholarships to graduating seniors of Revere High School, MA, for attendance at institutions of higher education.
Financial data: Year ended 12/31/2012. Assets, $101,094 (M); Expenditures, $5,328; Total giving, $3,000; Grants to individuals, totaling $3,000.
Fields of interest: Higher education.
Type of support: Support to graduates or students of specific schools; Undergraduate support.
Application information: Applications accepted.
  Additional information: Students should contact their high school guidance office for additional application information.
EIN: 046334789

8295
Robert Frost Teaching Chairs Trust
P.O. Box 1802
Providence, RI 02901-1802

Foundation type: Independent foundation
Purpose: Awards by nomination only to teachers who have taught in a public high school in the town of Amherst, MA, for at least three years.
Financial data: Year ended 06/30/2013. Assets, $121,657 (M); Expenditures, $6,433; Total giving, $4,824; Grants to individuals, 2 grants totaling $4,824 (high: $2,412, low: $2,412).
Fields of interest: Education.
Type of support: Awards/grants by nomination only; Awards/prizes.
Application information: Applications not accepted.
  Additional information: Unsolicited requests for funds not considered or acknowledged.
EIN: 046027359

8296
Fundacao Beneficente Faialense Inc.
P.O. Box 14291
East Providence, RI 02914-0291 (401) 438-9029
URL: http://www.fundacaofaialense.org/

Foundation type: Independent foundation
Purpose: Scholarships primarily to students residing in Portugal, in the Azores, and in the U.S.
Financial data: Year ended 06/30/2013. Assets, $216,275 (M); Expenditures, $31,841; Total giving, $15,000; Grants to individuals, 10 grants totaling $15,000 (high: $1,500, low: $1,500).
Fields of interest: International exchange, students.
International interests: Portugal.
Type of support: Technical education support; Undergraduate support.
Application information: Applications accepted. Application form required. Application form available on the grantmaker's web site.
  Initial approach: Letter
  Send request by: Mail
  Deadline(s): Feb. 28
  Applicants should submit the following:
    1) Photograph
    2) Essay
    3) Transcripts
    4) Financial information
    5) Letter(s) of recommendation
EIN: 042722163

8297
John T. Galligan Scholarship
P.O. Box 1802
Providence, RI 02901-1802

Foundation type: Independent foundation
Purpose: Scholarships to worthy graduates from Wareham High School or Regional High School, MA for continuing their education at institutions of higher learning.
Financial data: Year ended 12/31/2012. Assets, $211,313 (M); Expenditures, $11,929; Total giving, $8,000; Grants to individuals, 8 grants totaling $8,000 (high: $1,000, low: $1,000).
Fields of interest: Higher education.
Type of support: Support to graduates or students of specific schools.
Application information: Applications accepted. Application form required.
  Deadline(s): May

Additional information: Application must include transcripts. Students are selected based on academic performance, financial need and plans for college.
EIN: 046473132

8298
Mildred E. Gates Trust
P.O. Box 1802
Providence, RI 02901-1802
Contact: Walter Dubzinski
Application address: c/o Gardner High School, Gardner, MA 02108

Foundation type: Independent foundation
Purpose: Scholarships to graduating seniors of Gardner High School, MA for higher education.
Financial data: Year ended 12/31/2011. Assets, $774,345 (M); Expenditures, $52,005; Total giving, $36,000; Grants to individuals, 22 grants totaling $36,000 (high: $1,800, low: $1,800).
Fields of interest: Higher education.
Type of support: Scholarships—to individuals.
Application information: Applications accepted. Application form required.
  Initial approach: Letter
  Deadline(s): Mar. 15
  Additional information: Applicants must live within a 20 mile radius of Gardner City Hall.
EIN: 046643614

8299
Emily Gill Trust
P.O. Box 1802
Providence, RI 02901-1802
Application address: Chicopee H.S. & Chicopee Comp. H.S.

Foundation type: Independent foundation
Purpose: Scholarships to graduates of Chicopee High School and Chicopee Comprehensive High School, MA for postsecondary education.
Financial data: Year ended 12/31/2012. Assets, $306,083 (M); Expenditures, $15,963; Total giving, $12,000.
Fields of interest: Higher education.
Type of support: Support to graduates or students of specific schools; Undergraduate support.
Application information: Applications accepted.
  Initial approach: Letter
  Deadline(s): None
EIN: 046021060

8300
George L. Gooding Trust
P.O. Box 1802
Providence, RI 02901-1802
Application address: c/o Plymouth North High School, Attn.: Guidance Dept., 41 Obery St., Plymouth, MA 02360

Foundation type: Independent foundation
Purpose: Scholarships to graduating seniors of Plymouth High School, Plymouth, MA, for continuing education at institutions of higher learning.
Financial data: Year ended 12/31/2012. Assets, $672,822 (M); Expenditures, $44,784; Total giving, $24,225.
Fields of interest: Higher education.
Type of support: Scholarships—to individuals; Support to graduates or students of specific schools.
Application information: Application form required.
  Deadline(s): Dec. 31

Additional information: Students should contact their high school guidance department.
EIN: 046095797

8301
Gould Scholarship Fund
(formerly Norman J. and Anna B. Gould Scholarship Fund)
P.O. Box 1802
Providence, RI 02901-1802
Contact: M.J. Catoe
Application address: 240 Fall St., Seneca Falls, NY 13148-8745

Foundation type: Company-sponsored foundation
Purpose: Scholarships for Goulds Pumps employees who are residents of Seneca Falls, NY.
Financial data: Year ended 12/31/2012. Assets, $174,341 (M); Expenditures, $11,688; Total giving, $9,300.
Type of support: Employee-related scholarships.
Application information:
  Initial approach: Letter
  Deadline(s): None
Company name: Goulds Pumps, Incorporated
EIN: 166051306

8302
Greater Bridgeport Retired Teachers Fund Inc.
P.O. Box 1802
Providence, RI 02901-1802
Contact: Walter Drozeck, Pres.
Application address : 12 Wilson Ln., Shelton, CT 06484

Foundation type: Independent foundation
Purpose: Grants to retired teachers of the greater Bridgeport, CT, area.
Financial data: Year ended 06/30/2013. Assets, $1,089,101 (M); Expenditures, $57,853; Total giving, $49,441; Grants to individuals, 152 grants totaling $49,441 (high: $750, low: $9).
Fields of interest: Education.
Type of support: Grants for special needs.
Application information: Applications accepted.
  Initial approach: Letter
  Deadline(s): None
  Additional information: Applications should outline reason for financial need and doctor's statement.
EIN: 237258527

8303
Stephanie Weiser Green Scholarship Fund
(formerly Green Scholarship Fund)
P.O. Box 1802
Providence, RI 02901-1802
Application address: c/o Central Regional High School

Foundation type: Independent foundation
Purpose: Scholarships to graduating seniors of Central Regional High School, NJ, pursuing higher education.
Financial data: Year ended 12/31/2012. Assets, $50,079 (M); Expenditures, $10,995; Total giving, $10,000.
Fields of interest: Higher education.
Type of support: Support to graduates or students of specific schools; Undergraduate support.
Application information: Applications accepted. Application form required.
  Deadline(s): None

Additional information: Payments are made directly to the educational institution on behalf of the students.
EIN: 527140821

8304
Vera Grace Greenlaw Trust
P.O. Box 1802
Providence, RI 02901-1802

Foundation type: Independent foundation
Purpose: Scholarships for higher education to residents of Waldo County, ME, and graduates of Waldo County secondary schools.
Financial data: Year ended 04/30/2013. Assets, $592,813 (M); Expenditures, $25,823; Total giving, $16,000.
Type of support: Support to graduates or students of specific schools; Undergraduate support.
Application information: Applications accepted.
  Initial approach: Letter
  Deadline(s): Apr. 30
  Applicants should submit the following:
    1) Letter(s) of recommendation
    2) Transcripts
  Additional information: Application should also include employment history.
EIN: 016080221

8305
Gromack Scholarship Fund
P.O. Box 1802
Providence, RI 02901-1802

Foundation type: Independent foundation
Purpose: Scholarships to students of New Britain High School, CT, who plan on pursuing a Bachelor's degree in the Arts or Sciences, and who have a good academic standing and show financial need.
Financial data: Year ended 04/30/2012. Assets, $422,608 (M); Expenditures, $21,898; Total giving, $12,600.
Type of support: Support to graduates or students of specific schools; Undergraduate support.
Application information: Application form required.
  Deadline(s): Apr. 13
  Applicants should submit the following:
    1) Class rank
    2) Transcripts
  Additional information: Contact foundation for complete program information.
EIN: 061514838

8306
Ernest O. Guertin Trust
P.O. Box 1802
Providence, RI 02901-1802

Foundation type: Independent foundation
Purpose: Scholarships to students of Lebanon High School, NH, for attendance at accredited colleges or universities.
Financial data: Year ended 12/31/2012. Assets, $361,829 (M); Expenditures, $15,369; Total giving, $8,697.
Fields of interest: Higher education.
Type of support: Scholarships—to individuals.
Application information: Applications accepted. Application form required.
  Deadline(s): Apr. 15
  Applicants should submit the following:
    1) FAF
    2) Essay
  Additional information: Application should also include a copy of letter of acceptance, a copy

of financial aid, and financial aid award letter from the college student will attend.
EIN: 026075479

8307
Laura Brooks Harney/P. J. Harney Scholarship Trust
P.O. Box 1802
Providence, RI   02901-1802
Application address: c/o Town of Webb Schools, Attn.: David Clark, Chair., Crosby Blvd., Old Forge, NY 13420
Application address: Town of Webb Schools, Corsby Blvd., Old Forge, NY 13420

Foundation type: Independent foundation
Purpose: Scholarships to students graduating from Town of Webb High School, NY, who will attend school at one of six specific institutions of higher education.
Financial data: Year ended 12/31/2012. Assets, $220,073 (M); Expenditures, $17,756; Total giving, $15,000.
Type of support: Support to graduates or students of specific schools; Undergraduate support.
Application information: Application form required.
  Initial approach: Letter
  Additional information: Contact foundation for current application deadline/guidelines.
EIN: 166283916

8308
B. L. & W. H. Heald Scholarship Trust
P.O. Box 1802
Providence, RI   02901-1802
Application Address: Stafford High School, P.O. Box 87, Stafford CT 06076

Foundation type: Independent foundation
Purpose: Scholarships to graduates from Stafford High School, CT, with an "A" average for postsecondary education.
Financial data: Year ended 09/30/2013. Assets, $346,849 (M); Expenditures, $17,221; Total giving, $13,600.
Fields of interest: Higher education.
Type of support: Support to graduates or students of specific schools; Undergraduate support.
Application information: Students should contact their high school for application guidelines. Applicants must have attended all four years at Stafford High School, live in Stafford and plan to attend an accredited four year college. Scholarship is only for Stafford High School graduates. Unsolicited requests for funds not considered or acknowledged.
EIN: 066087125

8309
Keith Henney Trust
P.O. Box 1802
Providence, RI   02901-1802
Contact: Leona Hurley
Application address: P.O. Box 2, Eaton Center, NH 03832-0002

Foundation type: Independent foundation
Purpose: Scholarships to residents of Eaton, NH, who attended Kennett High School, NH, for at least two years.
Financial data: Year ended 12/31/2011. Assets, $573,392 (M); Expenditures, $34,508; Total giving, $27,038.
Type of support: Support to graduates or students of specific schools; Undergraduate support.

Application information: Applications accepted. Application form required.
  Initial approach: Letter
  Deadline(s): Apr. 10
EIN: 026065480

8310
The George Holopigian Memorial Fund
P.O. Box 1802
Providence, RI   02901-1802
Application addresses: Armenian Students Association of America, P.O. Box 6947, Providence, RI 02904

Foundation type: Independent foundation
Purpose: Scholarships for postsecondary schooling to students of Armenian descent residing in RI.
Financial data: Year ended 06/30/2013. Assets, $464,607 (M); Expenditures, $24,960; Total giving, $18,000; Grants to individuals, 13 grants totaling $18,000 (high: $2,000, low: $1,000).
International interests: Armenia.
Type of support: Undergraduate support.
Application information: Application form required.
  Deadline(s): Contact foundation for current application deadline
  Additional information: Applications are available from the Armenian Students Assn. and Armenian General Benevolent Union.
EIN: 056044531

8311
Edward Wagner and George Hosser Scholarship Fund Trust
c/o Citizens Bank
10 Tripps Ln.
Riverside, RI   02915-7995   (603) 634-7752
Contact: Bill Dirak
Application address: 875 Elm St., Manchester, NH 03101

Foundation type: Independent foundation
Purpose: Undergraduate scholarships to male residents of Manchester, NH.
Financial data: Year ended 06/30/2012. Assets, $5,544,107 (M); Expenditures, $49,282; Total giving, $0.
Fields of interest: Men.
Type of support: Undergraduate support.
Application information: Applications accepted. Application form required.
  Deadline(s): May 31
EIN: 026005491

8312
M. P. Howard Trust
P.O. Box 1802
Providence, RI   02901-1802

Foundation type: Independent foundation
Purpose: Scholarships to graduates of Drury High School, RI, attending a four-year college who are about to enter their junior or senior year.
Financial data: Year ended 12/31/2012. Assets, $203,821 (M); Expenditures, $11,346; Total giving, $7,000.
Type of support: Support to graduates or students of specific schools.
Application information: Application form required.
  Initial approach: Letter
  Deadline(s): May 1
  Additional information: Application must include transcripts.
EIN: 046385719

8313
Grace H. Humphrey Residuary Trust
P.O. Box 1802
Providence, RI   02901-1802

Foundation type: Independent foundation
Purpose: Scholarships to students and graduates of Simsbury High School, CT.
Financial data: Year ended 12/31/2012. Assets, $307,956 (M); Expenditures, $20,024; Total giving, $12,400.
Type of support: Support to graduates or students of specific schools; Undergraduate support.
Application information: Contact foundation for current application deadline/guidelines.
EIN: 066055126

8314
William C. and Mabel D. Hunt Memorial Scholarship
P.O. Box 1802
Providence, RI   02901-1802
Application address: C/o Bank of America, N.A., 1 E. Ave., Rochester, NY 14638

Foundation type: Independent foundation
Purpose: Scholarships to residents of Cape May County, NJ.
Financial data: Year ended 12/31/2012. Assets, $664,868 (M); Expenditures, $27,414; Total giving, $22,000.
Type of support: Scholarships—to individuals.
Application information: Applications accepted. Application form required.
  Deadline(s): May 1
EIN: 222690724

8315
Gerard Jakobi Trust f/b/o Northern Highlands Regional High School
(formerly Northern Highlands Regional High School, Inc.)
P.O. Box 1802
Providence, RI   02901-1802
Application address: 298 Hillside Ave., Allendale, NJ 07401-1447

Foundation type: Independent foundation
Purpose: Scholarships for seniors enrolled at Northern Highlands Regional High School, Allendale, NJ.
Financial data: Year ended 12/31/2012. Assets, $314,904 (M); Expenditures, $18,452; Total giving, $15,000.
Fields of interest: Higher education.
Type of support: Scholarships—to individuals; Support to graduates or students of specific schools.
Application information: Applications accepted. Application form required.
  Deadline(s): Apr. 15
EIN: 226418777

8316
Alfred N. Johnson Memorial Fund Trust
c/o Bank of America
P.O. Box 1802
Providence, RI   02901-1802
Application Address: c/o Gloversville High School, 199 Lincoln St, Gloversville, NY 12708

Foundation type: Independent foundation
Purpose: Scholarships to graduates of Gloversville High School, NY.

Financial data: Year ended 01/31/2013. Assets, $594,521 (M); Expenditures, $50,975; Total giving, $44,375.
Type of support: Support to graduates or students of specific schools; Undergraduate support.
Application information: Application form required.
Deadline(s): May 15
Applicants should submit the following:
1) Letter(s) of recommendation
2) Financial information
Additional information: Application must also include letter of acceptance from college.
EIN: 146099201

8317
Stephanie Kamenski Trust
P.O. Box 1802
Providence, RI 02901-1802
Application address: c/o Principal, Berlin High School, 139 Patterson St., Berlin, CT 06037-3146

Foundation type: Independent foundation
Purpose: Scholarships to graduates of Berlin High School, CT, and New Britain High School, CT for postsecondary education.
Financial data: Year ended 07/31/2013. Assets, $423,481 (M); Expenditures, $28,727; Total giving, $21,600.
Fields of interest: Higher education.
Type of support: Support to graduates or students of specific schools; Undergraduate support.
Application information: Applications accepted.
Initial approach: Letter
Deadline(s): None
Additional information: Application should include transcripts. Also, a copy of parents' 1040 form.
EIN: 066288857

8318
Ralph & Helen Kelley Foundation
P.O. Box 1802
Providence, RI 02901-1802 (888) 866-3275

Foundation type: Independent foundation
Purpose: Scholarship awards to high school students in the Gardner, MA, area.
Financial data: Year ended 12/31/2012. Assets, $11,147,424 (M); Expenditures, $471,178; Total giving, $355,175.
Type of support: Support to graduates or students of specific schools; Undergraduate support.
Application information: Application form required.
Deadline(s): May 1
EIN: 043042476

8319
Margaret J.S. Kennedy Scholarship Trust
P.O. Box 1802
Providence, RI 02901-1802

Foundation type: Independent foundation
Purpose: Scholarships to students at Bucksport High School, ME pursuing higher education.
Financial data: Year ended 04/30/2013. Assets, $337,897 (M); Expenditures, $17,111; Total giving, $11,000.
Fields of interest: Higher education.
Type of support: Support to graduates or students of specific schools; Undergraduate support.
Application information: Application form required.
Deadline(s): Apr. 30
Additional information: Application can be obtained from the guidance counselor and

should include personal data, employment records and references.
EIN: 016027394

8320
Helen U. Kiely Trust
P.O. Box 1802
Providence, RI 02901-1802

Foundation type: Independent foundation
Purpose: Scholarships to residents of Northhampton, Leeds or Florence, MA and graduating seniors of Northampton High School or Catholic High School.
Financial data: Year ended 12/31/2012. Assets, $1,265,217 (M); Expenditures, $70,892; Total giving, $53,680.
Fields of interest: Chemistry; Catholic agencies & churches.
Type of support: Support to graduates or students of specific schools; Awards/prizes; Undergraduate support.
Application information: Application form required.
Initial approach: Letter
Deadline(s): June 30
Applicants should submit the following:
1) Transcripts
2) Financial information
Additional information: Application must also include parents' tax return, transcripts must show final grades and signature of applicant's pastor.
EIN: 046278297

8321
King Scholarship Fund
(also known as Cora E. King Scholarship Fund)
P.O. Box 1802
Providence, RI 02901-1802 (315) 252-3861

Foundation type: Independent foundation
Purpose: Scholarships to residents of Cayuga County, NY, for higher education.
Financial data: Year ended 12/31/2011. Assets, $541,390 (M); Expenditures, $36,130; Total giving, $25,750.
Type of support: Scholarships—to individuals.
Application information: Applications accepted. Application form required.
Deadline(s): May 28
Applicants should submit the following:
1) Transcripts
2) Letter(s) of recommendation
3) Financial information
Additional information: Application must also include autobiography of no more than 300 words, and copy of financial aid form.
EIN: 222589716

8322
The Kingsbury Fund
P.O. Box 1802
Providence, RI 02901-1802

Foundation type: Company-sponsored foundation
Purpose: Scholarships to high school seniors who are children of employees of the Kingsbury Corp. and to company-related undergraduate students, for attendance at technical institutes, colleges, or other accredited schools.
Financial data: Year ended 12/31/2012. Assets, $3,332,026 (M); Expenditures, $168,435; Total giving, $128,784.
Fields of interest: Vocational education; Higher education.

Type of support: Employee-related scholarships.
Application information: Applications not accepted.
Additional information: Unsolicited requests for funds not considered or acknowledged.
Company name: Kingsbury Corporation
EIN: 026004465

8323
James Edward Kinsley Irrevocable Trust
(formerly James Edward Kinsley Educational Foundation)
P.O. Box 1802
Providence, RI 02901-1802
Contact: Carol Gray
Application address: c/o Bank of America, 225 Franklin St., Boston, MA 02110

Foundation type: Independent foundation
Purpose: Scholarships by nomination only to young, unwed mothers who are students of the Acton, MA, public school system.
Financial data: Year ended 05/31/2013. Assets, $317,573 (M); Expenditures, $18,323; Total giving, $13,500; Grants to individuals, 7 grants totaling $13,500 (high: $2,500, low: $1,500).
Fields of interest: Women.
Type of support: Support to graduates or students of specific schools; Awards/grants by nomination only; Undergraduate support.
Application information: Recipients are selected by school committee.
EIN: 046342377

8324
Harry C. Lichman Trust
P.O. Box 1802
Providence, RI 02901-1802

Foundation type: Independent foundation
Purpose: Scholarships to graduating seniors of Keene High School, NH for continuing education at institutions of higher learning.
Financial data: Year ended 12/31/2012. Assets, $675,810 (M); Expenditures, $36,344; Total giving, $25,352.
Fields of interest: Higher education.
Type of support: Support to graduates or students of specific schools.
Application information:
Deadline(s): Prior to graduation
Additional information: Students must write an essay (not over 500 words) on a subject relating to the Life of Abraham Lincoln.
EIN: 597271058

8325
Robert H. Life Trust
P.O. Box 1802
Providence, RI 02901-1802 (413) 584-5898
Application address: c/o Bank of America, N.A., 100 Federal St., Boston, MA 02110-1802

Foundation type: Independent foundation
Purpose: Scholarships to members of the Haydenville Congregational Church from the Second precinct, Boston, MA.
Financial data: Year ended 12/31/2012. Assets, $157,125 (M); Expenditures, $8,109; Total giving, $6,000.
Type of support: Undergraduate support.
Application information:
Initial approach: Letter
Deadline(s): May 1
EIN: 046019151

8326
Edward Little High School Alumni Association Trust
P.O. Box 1802
Providence, RI 02901-1802
Contact: Edward Little
Application address: P.O. Box 1086, Auburn, ME 04211-1086

Foundation type: Independent foundation
Purpose: Scholarships to graduates of Edward Little High School, Auburn, ME, to attend colleges and universities in ME.
Financial data: Year ended 07/31/2013. Assets, $131,458 (M); Expenditures, $4,572; Total giving, $4,000.
Fields of interest: Higher education.
Type of support: Support to graduates or students of specific schools; Undergraduate support.
Application information: Applications accepted. Application form required.
   Deadline(s): None
   Additional information: Application should include personal, academic and financial information.
EIN: 016029596

8327
Dr. Ralph F. & Pearl A. Long Trust
P.O.Box 1802
Providence, RI 02901-1802
Contact: Amy Lynch

Foundation type: Independent foundation
Purpose: Scholarships to financially needy students for higher education. Preference is given to graduates of Terryville High School, CT.
Financial data: Year ended 12/31/2012. Assets, $3,718,808 (M); Expenditures, $206,288; Total giving, $154,000.
Type of support: Support to graduates or students of specific schools; Undergraduate support.
Application information: Applications accepted. Application form required.
   Deadline(s): Mar. 15, and June 15 for renewal
   Applicants should submit the following:
      1) SAT
      2) GPA
      3) Financial information
      4) Letter(s) of recommendation
      5) Transcripts
      6) Essay
   Additional information: Application should include a copy of financial aid package from institution for the next academic year for renewals, and a list of extracurricular activities; Interviews may be required.
EIN: 223010188

8328
Henry C. Lord Scholarship Fund Trust
10 Tripps Ln.
Riverside, RI 02915-7995 (603) 634-7752
Contact: Carolann Harrington
Application address: c/o RBS Citizens, N.A., 875 Elm St., Manchester, NH 03101, tel.: (603) 634-7752

Foundation type: Independent foundation
Purpose: Scholarships to needy residents of Peterborough, NH, and contiguous towns, pursuing an undergraduate program.
Financial data: Year ended 06/30/2013. Assets, $11,275,454 (M); Expenditures, $1,160,794; Total giving, $976,400.
Type of support: Undergraduate support.

Application information: Applications accepted. Application form required.
   Deadline(s): Apr. 30 for first-time applicants, June 15 for reapplicants
EIN: 026051741

8329
D. Maes Trust
P.O. Box 1802
Providence, RI 02901-1802

Foundation type: Independent foundation
Purpose: Scholarships to graduating seniors of Metheun High School, MA.
Financial data: Year ended 12/31/2011. Assets, $120,959 (M); Expenditures, $7,273; Total giving, $5,000.
Type of support: Support to graduates or students of specific schools; Undergraduate support.
Application information: Applications accepted. Application form required.
   Deadline(s): Prior to graduation
EIN: 046660485

8330
Marguerite Magraw Trust
P.O. Box 1802
Providence, RI 02901-1802

Foundation type: Independent foundation
Purpose: Scholarships to financially needy students of Waterbury, CT, and contiguous towns to attend accredited colleges and universities.
Financial data: Year ended 11/30/2013. Assets, $1,353,855 (M); Expenditures, $76,479; Total giving, $54,000; Grants to individuals, 47 grants totaling $54,000 (high: $1,500, low: $1,000).
Type of support: Scholarships—to individuals.
Application information: Applications accepted. Application form required. Interview required.
   Deadline(s): Mar. 31
   Final notification: Recipients notified after June 25.
   Applicants should submit the following:
      1) Transcripts
      2) Financial information
   Additional information: Application available from Scholarship Committee.
EIN: 066113177

8331
The Bruce H. Mahan Scholarship Fund
P.O. Box 1802
Providence, RI 02901-1802

Foundation type: Independent foundation
Purpose: Scholarships to residents of Berlin and New Britain, CT.
Financial data: Year ended 09/30/2013. Assets, $160,229 (M); Expenditures, $9,364; Total giving, $5,500.
Type of support: Undergraduate support.
Application information:
   Initial approach: Letter
   Deadline(s): Jan. 15
EIN: 066256073

8332
Mahana Congregational Church
c/o Marilyn Deal
P.O. Box 1802
Providence, RI 02901-1802

Foundation type: Independent foundation

Purpose: Scholarships to graduating Algona, IA, Community School District students for higher education for attendance at any college or university.
Financial data: Year ended 12/31/2012. Assets, $1,299,153 (M); Expenditures, $70,715; Total giving, $60,000.
Fields of interest: Higher education.
Type of support: Support to graduates or students of specific schools.
Application information: Application form required.
   Initial approach: Letter
   Deadline(s): 3rd week in Apr.
   Additional information: Application available from high school guidance counselors.
EIN: 421391307

8333
Emma F. Makinson Trust
P.O. Box 1802
Providence, RI 02901-1802
Contact: Patricia Lowe
Application address: Office of Supt. of Schools, North Attleboro, MA 02703

Foundation type: Independent foundation
Purpose: Scholarships to high school students from North Attleboro, MA.
Financial data: Year ended 12/31/2012. Assets, $599,135 (M); Expenditures, $21,571; Total giving, $12,000.
Type of support: Support to graduates or students of specific schools; Undergraduate support.
Application information: Applications accepted. Application form required.
   Deadline(s): None
EIN: 046224805

8334
Lloyd R. and Stella Gibboney Manwiller Trust
P.O. Box 1802
Providence, RI 02901-1802
Application address: The Church of Good Shepherd, United Church of Christ, Boyertown, PA 19512

Foundation type: Independent foundation
Purpose: Scholarships to members of any United Church of Christ, primarily in Berks County, PA for seminary education.
Financial data: Year ended 12/31/2012. Assets, $2,382,920 (M); Expenditures, $119,173; Total giving, $95,175.
Fields of interest: Theological school/education; Protestant agencies & churches.
Type of support: Graduate support.
Application information: Applications accepted. Application form required.
   Deadline(s): July 31 or Nov. 30
   Applicants should submit the following:
      1) Transcripts
      2) Letter(s) of recommendation
      3) Financial information
   Additional information: Applicants must plan to serve in the ministry for five years after graduation, or risk full repayment of scholarship funds.
EIN: 236714082

8335
Lorena Marhaver Trust
P.O. Box 1802
Providence, RI 02901-1802
Contact: Judith Lee
Application address: c/o Bank of America, N.A.,
Attn.: Judith Lee, 1 East Ave., Rochester, NY
14638-0002

Foundation type: Independent foundation
Purpose: Grants to residents of the town of Ilion,
NY.
Financial data: Year ended 12/31/2012. Assets,
$144,785 (M); Expenditures, $2,027; Total giving,
$0.
Type of support: Grants to individuals.
Application information: Applications accepted.
  Deadline(s): None
EIN: 166199387

8336
Masonic Grand Lodge Charities of Rhode Island, Inc.
222 Taunton Ave.
East Providence, RI 02914-4556 (401)
435-4650
Contact: Wyman P. Hallstrom, Jr., Secy.

Foundation type: Independent foundation
Purpose: Scholarships to individuals who have
resided in RI for at least five years and to individuals
whose parents or grandparents are RI masons.
Grants to members and widows and children of
members of the Masonic Lodge, who are RI
residents.
Financial data: Year ended 10/31/2011. Assets,
$6,755,227 (M); Expenditures, $531,720; Total
giving, $339,307.
Fields of interest: Fraternal societies; Children;
Women.
Type of support: Scholarships—to individuals;
Grants for special needs.
Application information: Application form required.
  Deadline(s): May 1
  Applicants should submit the following:
  1) Financial information
  2) Transcripts
  Additional information: Application should be
     made through the local masonic lodge.
EIN: 056014340

8337
Margaret & Donald Matheson Scholarship Fund
P.O. Box 1802
Providence, RI 02901-1802

Foundation type: Independent foundation
Purpose: Scholarships to graduating seniors of
Winslow High School, ME, for higher education.
Financial data: Year ended 12/31/2012. Assets,
$604,161 (M); Expenditures, $22,580; Total
giving, $13,000.
Fields of interest: Higher education.
Type of support: Support to graduates or students
of specific schools; Undergraduate support.
Application information: Applications accepted.
  Deadline(s): None
  Additional information: Students who
     demonstrate academic focus and financial
     need will be given highest priority.
EIN: 010504173

8338
Maude -FrancesChildrens Fund
P.O. Box 1802
Providence, RI 02901-1802 (413) 625-9811

Foundation type: Independent foundation
Purpose: Scholarships to graduates of Mulhark
Trail Regional High School, MA, who are also
residents of Shelburne Falls Fire District.
Financial data: Year ended 08/31/2013. Assets,
$573,726 (M); Expenditures, $32,741; Total
giving, $21,000.
Type of support: Support to graduates or students
of specific schools; Undergraduate support.
Application information:
  Initial approach: Letter
  Deadline(s): Apr. 5
  Applicants should submit the following:
  1) Transcripts
  2) Letter(s) of recommendation
  3) Financial information
  Additional information: Application must also
     include list of references.
EIN: 046019146

8339
Imogene M. Maybury Trust
P.O. Box 1802
Providence, RI 02901-1802

Foundation type: Independent foundation
Purpose: Scholarships to graduates of Dexter
Regional High School, Dexter, ME, for study at
colleges, universities, and vocational schools.
Financial data: Year ended 04/30/2013. Assets,
$3,228,694 (M); Expenditures, $142,080; Total
giving, $87,800.
Fields of interest: Vocational education.
Type of support: Support to graduates or students
of specific schools; Undergraduate support.
Application information: Applications accepted.
  Deadline(s): None
  Additional information: Contact guidance
     counselor at high school; Applicants should
     provide all relevant personal data including
     employment information, transcripts, and
     references.
EIN: 016023401

8340
Bernard W. McCormick Scholarship Fund
c/o Bank of America, N.A.
P.O. Box 1802
Providence, RI 02901-1802
Application address: c/o Catholic Central High
School 625 7th Ave., Troy NY 12182

Foundation type: Independent foundation
Purpose: Scholarships to graduates of Catholic
Central High School, Troy, NY, for continuing their
education as full-time students.
Financial data: Year ended 12/31/2012. Assets,
$408,848 (M); Expenditures, $20,999; Total
giving, $16,200.
Fields of interest: Higher education.
Type of support: Support to graduates or students
of specific schools.
Application information: Students are chosen by
the principal of the school.
EIN: 146089372

8341
John B. McLean Scholarship Fund
P.O. Box 1802
Providence, RI 02901-1802 (203) 658-9451

Foundation type: Independent foundation
Purpose: Scholarships to students in the senior
class of the Simsbury High School in pursuit of a
higher education.
Financial data: Year ended 12/31/2012. Assets,
$334,694 (M); Expenditures, $22,564; Total
giving, $16,456.
Fields of interest: Education.
Type of support: Support to graduates or students
of specific schools.
Application information: Applications accepted.
Application form required.
  Deadline(s): Feb. 4
  Additional information: Applications available
     from guidance counselor.
EIN: 066032660

8342
Lucy J. McMurtrie Foundation
(also known as McMurtrie Scholarship Fund)
P.O. Box1802
Providence, RI 02901-1802
Application address: Roxbury High School, Attn.
Guidance Department, 1 Bryant Dr., Succasunna,
NJ 07876

Foundation type: Independent foundation
Purpose: Scholarships to financially needy,
deserving students of Roxbury High School,
Succasunna, NJ.
Financial data: Year ended 12/31/2012. Assets,
$551,713 (M); Expenditures, $29,913; Total
giving, $26,000; Grants to individuals, 24 grants
totaling $26,000 (high: $3,000, low: $1,000).
Type of support: Support to graduates or students
of specific schools; Precollege support.
Application information: Applications accepted.
  Initial approach: Letter
  Deadline(s): May
  Additional information: Application must state
     educational pursuits and financial need.
EIN: 226426610

8343
Bishop Russell J. McVinney Foundation for Religious Vocations
485 Mt. Pleasant Ave.
Providence, RI 02908-3301 (401) 331-1316

Foundation type: Independent foundation
Purpose: Financial assistance to seminarians of
the Roman Catholic Diocese of Providence, RI.
Financial data: Year ended 12/31/2011. Assets,
$979,571 (M); Expenditures, $95,184; Total
giving, $86,317; Grants to individuals, totaling
$86,317.
Fields of interest: Catholic agencies & churches;
Economically disadvantaged.
Type of support: Grants for special needs.
Application information: Applicant must
demonstrate need. Unsolicited requests for funds
not considered or acknowledged.
EIN: 237399394

8344
Meriden Record Journal Foundation
P.O. Box 1802
Providence, RI 02901-1802
Contact: Elliott White
Application address: Mariden Record Journal,
Meriden, CT

Foundation type: Company-sponsored foundation
Purpose: Scholarships to the children of employees
of the Meriden Record Journal, to carriers, and to

residents of the CT circulation area who are studying journalism or journalism-related subjects, such as advertising.
Financial data: Year ended 12/31/2012. Assets, $53,161 (M); Expenditures, $18,450; Total giving, $16,800.
Fields of interest: Media/communications; Print publishing; Business/industry.
Type of support: Employee-related scholarships; Scholarships—to individuals.
Application information: Applications accepted. Application form required.
Company name: Meriden Record Journal
EIN: 066074903

8345
Alice W. Miles HSSF Trust
(formerly Alice W. Miles Trust High School Scholarship)
P.O. Box 1802
Providence, RI   02901-1802

Foundation type: Independent foundation
Purpose: Scholarships to graduating seniors of Worcester Public High School, MA for postsecondary education.
Financial data: Year ended 10/31/2013. Assets, $350,593 (M); Expenditures, $23,233; Total giving, $15,720.
Fields of interest: Higher education.
Type of support: Scholarships—to individuals; Support to graduates or students of specific schools; Undergraduate support.
Application information: Application form required.
  Deadline(s): Feb.
  Additional information: Application should include personal and financial information.
EIN: 046019793

8346
Morey and Helen McCarthy Miller Scholarship Fund
P.O. Box 1802
Providence, RI   02901-1802
Contact: Karen Booth
Application address: Rockland High School, 70 Loveland Hill Rd., Vernon, CT 06066-6836

Foundation type: Independent foundation
Purpose: Scholarships to graduating seniors at Rockville High School, CT, who have been accepted into a college or university.
Financial data: Year ended 02/28/2013. Assets, $3,359,790 (M); Expenditures, $194,311; Total giving, $150,378.
Type of support: Support to graduates or students of specific schools; Undergraduate support.
Application information: Application form required.
  Deadline(s): Apr. 15
  Additional information: Scholarships are awarded based on financial need and academic standing.
EIN: 043222995

8347
F. Roger Miller Trust
P.O. Box 1802
Providence, RI   02901-1802

Foundation type: Independent foundation
Purpose: Scholarships to deserving students who reside in Waldoboro, ME, and attend a college or university in the state of ME.

Financial data: Year ended 12/31/2011. Assets, $703,205 (M); Expenditures, $42,484; Total giving, $31,296.
Fields of interest: College; University.
Type of support: Scholarships—to individuals.
Application information: Application form required.
  Deadline(s): None
EIN: 016048187

8348
Clinton G. Mills Trust
P.O. Box 1802
Providence, RI   02901-1802
Contact: Kerry Sullivan
Application address: 100 Federal St., Boston, MA 02110

Foundation type: Independent foundation
Purpose: Scholarships to graduates of public high schools in Lynn and Swampscott, MA.
Financial data: Year ended 12/31/2012. Assets, $627,123 (M); Expenditures, $34,772; Total giving, $26,219.
Type of support: Support to graduates or students of specific schools; Undergraduate support.
Application information: Contact fund for current application guidelines.
EIN: 046024752

8349
Charles E. Montague Charitable Trust
P.O. Box 1802
Providence, RI   02901-1802
Contact: Carol Gray
Application address: c/o Bank of America, N.A., 100 Federal St., Boston, MA 02110-1802

Foundation type: Independent foundation
Purpose: Assistance to financially needy residents of Wakefield, MA, to help cover hospital bills, including psychotherapy.
Financial data: Year ended 09/30/2012. Assets, $1,390,530 (M); Expenditures, $77,399; Total giving, $55,000.
Fields of interest: Economically disadvantaged.
Type of support: Grants for special needs.
Application information: Applications accepted.
  Deadline(s): None
  Additional information: Applicant must demonstrate financial need.
EIN: 046047134

8350
Darthea Morrow Scholarship Trust
P.O. Box 1802
Providence, RI   02901-1802

Foundation type: Independent foundation
Purpose: Scholarships to graduating seniors of Nauset Regional High School, MA for higher education.
Financial data: Year ended 12/31/2012. Assets, $1,050,209 (M); Expenditures, $64,468; Total giving, $45,000; Grants to individuals, 15 grants totaling $45,000 (high: $3,000, low: $3,000).
Type of support: Support to graduates or students of specific schools; Undergraduate support.
Application information: Applications accepted. Application form required.
  Initial approach: Letter.
  Deadline(s): None
  Additional information: Recipients are chosen during the third week of May.
EIN: 042866532

8351
Harvey H. & Catherine Allis Moses Educational Fund
P.O. Box 1802
Providence, RI   02901-1802
Application address: c/o Ticondegora High School, Guidance Office, Ticondegora, NY 12883

Foundation type: Independent foundation
Purpose: Scholarships to students of Ticonderoga High School, NY, for higher education.
Financial data: Year ended 08/31/2013. Assets, $294,655 (M); Expenditures, $15,806; Total giving, $12,000; Grants to individuals, 8 grants totaling $12,000 (high: $1,500, low: $1,500).
Fields of interest: Higher education.
Type of support: Support to graduates or students of specific schools; Undergraduate support.
Application information: Application form required.
  Deadline(s): Apr. 30
EIN: 046487087

8352
Harold E. Moulton Scholarship Fund
(formerly Helen W. Moulton Scholarship Fund)
c/o Bank of America, N.A.
P.O. Box 1802
Providence, RI   02901-1802
Contact: Judith A. Lee, V.P.
Application address: 1 East Ave., 4th Fl., Rochester, NY 14604

Foundation type: Independent foundation
Purpose: Scholarships to residents of Clarksville, NY, who are attending or have graduated from Bolivar Central School, NY; Richburg Central School, NY; Cuba Rushford School, NY; or Portville Central School, NY. Preference is given to students pursuing dairy or agricultural courses at four-year schools in NY.
Financial data: Year ended 04/30/2013. Assets, $378,051 (M); Expenditures, $18,163; Total giving, $12,500; Grants to individuals, 13 grants totaling $12,500 (high: $1,500, low: $500).
Type of support: Support to graduates or students of specific schools; Undergraduate support.
Application information: Applications accepted. Application form required.
  Initial approach: Letter
  Deadline(s): Apr. 15.
  Applicants should submit the following:
    1) Financial information
    2) Essay
    3) Transcripts
    4) SAT
    5) ACT
EIN: 510197187

8353
William J. Munson Fund
P.O. Box 1802
Providence, RI   02901-1802
Contact: Patrick Sharpe

Foundation type: Independent foundation
Purpose: Scholarships to students of Watertown, CT for undergraduate studies. Medical assistance to qualified residents of Watertown, CT.
Financial data: Year ended 12/31/2012. Assets, $1,611,482 (M); Expenditures, $85,752; Total giving, $59,234; Grants to individuals, 69 grants totaling $59,234 (high: $5,121, low: $20).
Fields of interest: Higher education; Human services.
Type of support: Scholarships—to individuals; Undergraduate support; Grants for special needs.

Application information: Application form required.
Initial approach: Letter
Deadline(s): June 15
Additional information: Application for scholarship available at the high school counseling department. Application for medical assistance available from the Watertwon-Oakville Ecumenical Council of Churches clergy or from any trustee.
EIN: 066024564

8354
Clayton Nash Scholarship Fund
P.O. Box 1802
Providence, RI 02901-1802
Application address: c/o Bank of America, N.A., Attn.: Emme Greene, Trust Off., 100 Federal St., Boston, MA 02110-1802

Foundation type: Independent foundation
Purpose: Scholarships to graduates of Weymouth North and Weymouth South high schools, MA, for higher education.
Financial data: Year ended 05/31/2013. Assets, $245,285 (M); Expenditures, $14,002; Total giving, $10,500.
Type of support: Support to graduates or students of specific schools; Undergraduate support.
Application information: Applications accepted.
Initial approach: Letter
EIN: 222480259

8355
John & Helen Nicholson Scholarship Fund
P.O. Box 1802
Providence, RI 02901-1802
Contact: Carol Gray
Application address: C/o. Bank of America, 100 Federal St., Boston, MA 02110

Foundation type: Independent foundation
Purpose: Scholarships to graduating students of Newburyport High School, MA.
Financial data: Year ended 10/30/2013. Assets, $197,210 (M); Expenditures, $10,853; Total giving, $6,000.
Type of support: Scholarships—to individuals.
Application information: Applications accepted.
EIN: 043545128

8356
Gould Norman & Anna Scholarship fund
(formerly Norman J. and Anna B. Gould Scholarship Fund)
c/o Bank of America, N.A.
P.O. Box 1802
Providence, RI 02901-1802 (315) 258-4811
Contact: Lydia Patti Ruffini
Application address: c/o ITT Corporation, R&CW Auburn, 1 Glouds Dr., Auburn NY, 13021, tel.: (315) 258-4811

Foundation type: Independent foundation
Purpose: Scholarships to children of Goulds Pumps employees and scholarships to children of Seneca Falls, NY residents.
Financial data: Year ended 09/30/2013. Assets, $1,091,883 (M); Expenditures, $71,784; Total giving, $53,234.
Type of support: Employee-related scholarships; Scholarships—to individuals.
Application information: Applications accepted.
Deadline(s): None
Additional information: Contact fund for current application guidelines.

Company name: Goulds Pumps, Incorporated
EIN: 166318641

8357
Frank O'Brion Trust
P.O. Box 1802
Providence, RI 02901-1802

Foundation type: Independent foundation
Purpose: Scholarships to financially needy children of employees of Bank of America, N.A. or any of its subsidiaries located in CT.
Financial data: Year ended 10/31/2012. Assets, $1,235,438 (M); Expenditures, $84,207; Total giving, $59,000.
Fields of interest: Financial services.
Type of support: Employee-related scholarships.
Application information: Application form required.
Deadline(s): Mar. 30
Additional information: Application must include a FAFSA.
EIN: 066154532

8358
Leonard Hubbard Onodaga Nation Scholarship Trust
c/o Bank of America, N.A.
P.O. Box 1802
Providence, RI 02901-1802 (315) 677-7849
Application Address: La Fayette Jr/Sr. High School, Guidance Office, 3122 La Fayette, Lafayette, NY 13084

Foundation type: Independent foundation
Purpose: Scholarships to graduates of Lafayette Senior School, NY who are certified members of Onondaga Nation and enrolled in an accredited college.
Financial data: Year ended 05/31/2013. Assets, $287,330 (M); Expenditures, $11,264; Total giving, $11,500.
Fields of interest: Higher education.
Type of support: Support to graduates or students of specific schools; Undergraduate support.
Application information: Application form required.
Additional information: Students should contact Lafayette Jr./Sr. High School guidance office for application information.
EIN: 226500878

8359
The Orr Foundation
P.O. Box 1802
Providence, RI 02901-1802

Foundation type: Independent foundation
Purpose: Scholarships to high school graduates of Newton North High School, MA, and Newton South High School, MA, for higher education.
Financial data: Year ended 12/31/2011. Assets, $724,180 (M); Expenditures, $51,268; Total giving, $37,000.
Fields of interest: Higher education.
Type of support: Support to graduates or students of specific schools; Undergraduate support.
Application information: Application form required.
Deadline(s): Apr.
Additional information: Application forms available in guidance departments at Newton North and Newton South high schools.
EIN: 046034509

8360
Arline P. Padelford Scholarship Fund
P.O. Box 1802
Providence, RI 02901-1802
Application address: c/o Taunton High School, attn.: Guidance counselor, Taunton, MA

Foundation type: Independent foundation
Purpose: Scholarships to worthy and deserving graduates of Taunton High School, MA.
Financial data: Year ended 12/31/2012. Assets, $335,426 (M); Expenditures, $16,694; Total giving, $12,000.
Fields of interest: Higher education.
Type of support: Support to graduates or students of specific schools; Undergraduate support.
Application information: Application form required.
Additional information: Applications can be obtained from the guidance counselor's office at Taunton high school.
EIN: 046096792

8361
Countess Frances Thorley Palen-Klar Scholarship Fund
P.O. Box 1802
Providence, RI 02901-1802

Foundation type: Independent foundation
Purpose: Scholarships to graduates of Greenwich High School, CT, to attend accredited colleges and universities.
Financial data: Year ended 12/31/2011. Assets, $429,989 (M); Expenditures, $26,314; Total giving, $18,250.
Fields of interest: Higher education.
Type of support: Support to graduates or students of specific schools; Undergraduate support.
Application information: Application form required.
Deadline(s): Mar. 15
EIN: 066033692

8362
Palmer Townsend Trust
P.O. Box 1802
Providence, RI 02901-1802

Foundation type: Independent foundation
Purpose: Scholarships to residents of Montville, CT, who are under the age of 25 and have graduated from Montville High School, CT.
Financial data: Year ended 12/31/2011. Assets, $1,286,837 (M); Expenditures, $95,754; Total giving, $69,585.
Type of support: Scholarships—to individuals; Support to graduates or students of specific schools.
Application information:
Initial approach: Letter
Deadline(s): 1st week of Apr.
Additional information: Contact trust for current application guidelines.
EIN: 066026227

8363
Robert S. Pape Charitable Foundation
P.O. Box 1802
Providence, RI 02901-1802
Contact: James R. Degiacomo Esq., Tr.
Application address: 1 Post Office Sq., Boston, MA 02109

Foundation type: Independent foundation
Purpose: Scholarships to graduates of Cohasset High School, MA, for college or technical school.

Financial data: Year ended 12/31/2012. Assets, $421,634 (M); Expenditures, $25,126; Total giving, $16,998.
Fields of interest: Vocational education; Higher education.
Type of support: Support to graduates or students of specific schools; Technical education support; Undergraduate support.
Application information: Application form required.
Initial approach: Letter or telephone
Deadline(s): May 1
EIN: 046692518

8364
John A. & Irene Papines Scholarship Trust-Ermoupolis

c/o Bank of America, N.A.
P.O. Box 1802
Providence, RI   02901-1802

Foundation type: Independent foundation
Purpose: Scholarships to residents of Ermoupolis, Island of Syra, Greece, who are pursuing a career in medicine.
Financial data: Year ended 12/31/2012. Assets, $241,178 (M); Expenditures, $14,174; Total giving, $11,600.
Fields of interest: Medical school/education.
Type of support: Foreign applicants; Graduate support.
Application information: Application form required.
Additional information: Contact foundation for current application deadline/guidelines.
EIN: 226321386

8365
John A. Pappines Ahepa Tua

(formerly John A. & Irene Papines Scholarship Trust)
c/o Bank of America, N.A.
P.O. Box 1802
Providence, RI   02901-1802
Contact: Judith Lee
Application address: 1 E. Ave., Rochester, NY 14604

Foundation type: Independent foundation
Purpose: Scholarships to residents of Atlantic, Cape May, Cumberland, and Ocean counties, NJ, who are of Greek descent.
Financial data: Year ended 12/31/2012. Assets, $818,374 (M); Expenditures, $46,076; Total giving, $39,996.
Fields of interest: Higher education.
International interests: Greece.
Type of support: Scholarships—to individuals.
Application information: Applications accepted. Application form required.
Deadline(s): May 1
Additional information: Application available from guidance counselor.
EIN: 226321385

8366
Charles Parker Trust for Public Music Fund

P.O. Box 1802
Providence, RI   02901-1802
Contact: Amy Lynch

Foundation type: Independent foundation
Purpose: Scholarship awards to graduating seniors of New Britain High School, CT. The program is administered through Scholarship America.

Financial data: Year ended 03/31/2013. Assets, $235,674 (M); Expenditures, $9,233; Total giving, $6,000.
Type of support: Support to graduates or students of specific schools.
Application information: Applications accepted.
Initial approach: Letter
EIN: 066036450

8367
Katherine L. Peck Trust

P.O. Box 1802
Providence, RI   02901-1802
Application address: c/o First Congregational Church Scholarship Comm., 222 W. Main St., Waterbury, CT 06708, tel.: (203) 757-0331

Foundation type: Independent foundation
Purpose: Scholarships to Protestant girls in the Waterbury, CT, area.
Financial data: Year ended 12/31/2011. Assets, $349,813 (M); Expenditures, $26,348; Total giving, $17,000; Grants to individuals, 17 grants totaling $17,000 (high: $1,000, low: $1,000).
Fields of interest: Education; Protestant agencies & churches; Girls.
Type of support: Scholarships—to individuals.
Application information: Applications accepted.
Initial approach: Letter
Deadline(s): Apr. 15
Applicants should submit the following:
1) Transcripts
2) Financial information
Additional information: Application should also include a list of activities.
EIN: 066024593

8368
Perpetual Benevolent Fund

P.O. Box 1802
Providence, RI   02901-1802
Contact: Augusta Haydock
Application address: 300 Washington St., Newton, Massachusetts 02158

Foundation type: Independent foundation
Purpose: Assistance to financially needy individuals in the greater Boston, MA, area, with preference to residents of Newton and Waltham.
Financial data: Year ended 12/31/2012. Assets, $5,991,511 (M); Expenditures, $321,852; Total giving, $203,880; Grants to individuals, 221 grants totaling $103,480 (high: $1,200).
Fields of interest: Pharmacy/prescriptions; Housing/shelter; Day care; Human services, emergency aid.
Type of support: Grants for special needs.
Application information: Applications accepted. Application form required.
Additional information: Application must include financial information and applicant's social history. Direct applications by individuals not accepted.
EIN: 237011723

8369
Petsas Charitable Trust

P.O. Box 1802
Providence, RI   02901-1802
Application address: c/o Chicopee high School, Attn.: Roland R. Joyal, Principal, 820 Front St., Chicopee, MA 01020

Foundation type: Independent foundation

Purpose: Scholarships to graduating seniors and post graduates of Chicopee High School, and Chicopee Comprehensive High School, Springfield, MA.
Financial data: Year ended 05/31/2013. Assets, $723,758 (M); Expenditures, $39,811; Total giving, $27,333.
Fields of interest: Higher education.
Type of support: Support to graduates or students of specific schools.
Application information: Applications accepted. Application form required.
Deadline(s): May 3
Additional information: Application should include an essay. Awards are based on financial need, character and contributions to the school and community.
EIN: 046421513

8370
Beatrice D. Pierce Trust

P.O. Box 1802
Providence, RI   02901-1802
Contact: Karen Hibbert
Application address: 100 Federal St., Boston, MA 02110

Foundation type: Independent foundation
Purpose: Scholarships to graduates of Lebanon, NH, high schools for higher education at accredited colleges or universities.
Financial data: Year ended 09/30/2013. Assets, $575,605 (M); Expenditures, $37,686; Total giving, $26,000.
Type of support: Support to graduates or students of specific schools; Undergraduate support.
Application information: Applications accepted. Application form required.
Deadline(s): None
Additional information: Contact your school's guidance office for application information.
EIN: 046089261

8371
Evelyn W. Preston Trust

P.O. Box 1802
Providence, RI   02901-1802

Foundation type: Independent foundation
Purpose: Grants to musicians to perform free band and orchestral concerts in Hartford, CT, from June through Sept.
Financial data: Year ended 12/31/2012. Assets, $4,131,709 (M); Expenditures, $221,033; Total giving, $159,124.
Fields of interest: Music; Orchestras; Music ensembles/groups.
Type of support: Grants to individuals.
Application information: Applications accepted. Application form required.
Additional information: Unsolicited requests for funds not considered or acknowledged.
EIN: 060747389

8372
Joseph R. and Florence A. Price Scholarship Fund

P.O. Box 1802
Providence, RI   02901-1802

Foundation type: Independent foundation
Purpose: Scholarships to seniors of Hyde Park High School, MA.

Financial data: Year ended 12/31/2010. Assets, $374,457 (M); Expenditures, $20,112; Total giving, $15,000.
Fields of interest: Higher education.
Type of support: Support to graduates or students of specific schools.
Application information: Applications accepted. Application form required.
 Deadline(s): Apr. 15
 Applicants should submit the following:
   1) Financial information
   2) Letter(s) of recommendation
 Additional information: Applications can be obtained from the school administrator at Hyde Park High School.
EIN: 046031925

8373
Miriam Sutro Price Scholarship Fund Trust
P.O. Box 1802
Providence, RI 02901-1802
Contact: Siobhan Moran
Application address: c/o Bank of America, 200 Glastonbury Blvd. 2nd Fl., Glastonbury City, 06033

Foundation type: Independent foundation
Purpose: Scholarships to residents of towns of New Milford, Bridgewater, Sherman, Roxbury, Kent and Washington CT for higher education.
Financial data: Year ended 06/30/2013. Assets, $181,386 (M); Expenditures, $12,561; Total giving, $7,400.
Fields of interest: Higher education.
Type of support: Scholarships—to individuals.
Application information: Applications accepted. Application form required.
 Deadline(s): May 15
 Additional information: Application forms available at Bank of America.
EIN: 066076246

8374
Nathan D. Prince Trust No. 2
P.O. Box 1802
Providence, RI 02901-1802

Foundation type: Independent foundation
Purpose: Scholarships to graduates of Killingly High School, Danielson, CT who are residents of Killingly, Brooklyn or Plainfield, CT for postsecondary education.
Financial data: Year ended 09/30/2013. Assets, $826,099 (M); Expenditures, $39,440; Total giving, $33,500.
Fields of interest: Higher education.
Type of support: Support to graduates or students of specific schools.
Application information:
 Deadline(s): None
EIN: 066031329

8375
Providence Female Charitable Society
P.O. Box 829
Saunderstown, RI 02874 (401) 294-3183
Contact: Elizabeth Hyman, Treas.

Foundation type: Independent foundation
Purpose: Assistance to economically disadvantaged women who are residents of RI with the purchase of clothing and furniture, income supplement, medical expenses, sending children to summer camp, and payment of rent and utilities.

Financial data: Year ended 03/31/2013. Assets, $586,067 (M); Expenditures, $38,107; Total giving, $28,034.
Fields of interest: Women; Economically disadvantaged.
Type of support: Grants for special needs.
Application information:
 Initial approach: Letter or telephone
 Additional information: Assistance is by referral only.
EIN: 056008631

8376
Pryde Scholarship Fund
P.O. Box 1802
Providence, RI 02901-1802

Foundation type: Independent foundation
Purpose: Scholarships to graduates of Suitland High School, MD and Surrattsville High School, MD pursuing a career in education.
Financial data: Year ended 12/31/2012. Assets, $188,225 (M); Expenditures, $11,952; Total giving, $7,324.
Fields of interest: Teacher school/education.
Type of support: Scholarships—to individuals; Support to graduates or students of specific schools.
Application information: Applications accepted.
 Initial approach: Letter
 Deadline(s): Apr. 1
 Additional information: Contact your high school guidance office for application information.
EIN: 526143655

8377
Franklin H. Putnam Trust
P.O. Box 1802
Providence, RI 02901-1802
Contact: Susana Foster-Castillo
Application address: 100 Federal St., Boston, MA 02110

Foundation type: Independent foundation
Purpose: Scholarships to financially needy young women pursuing an undergraduate education in business or a business-related area of study.
Financial data: Year ended 12/31/2011. Assets, $811,660 (M); Expenditures, $38,927; Total giving, $26,000; Grants to individuals, 8 grants totaling $26,000 (high: $4,000, low: $1,500).
Type of support: Scholarships—to individuals.
Application information: Application form required.
 Deadline(s): June 1
 Final notification: Recipients notified in July
 Applicants should submit the following:
   1) Letter(s) of recommendation
   2) Transcripts
   3) Financial information
EIN: 046009430

8378
Frank B. Randall Trust
P.O. Box 1802
Providence, RI 02901-1802

Foundation type: Independent foundation
Purpose: Scholarships to graduates of Oliver Ames High School, N. Easton, MA for postsecondary education.
Financial data: Year ended 12/31/2011. Assets, $105,150 (M); Expenditures, $5,624; Total giving, $4,000.
Fields of interest: Higher education.

Type of support: Support to graduates or students of specific schools.
Application information: Contact your school guidance office for application information.
EIN: 046063169

8379
Rhode Island Bar Foundation
115 Cedar St.
Providence, RI 02903-1082 (401) 421-5740
Contact: Helen Desmond McDonald, Exec. Dir.
E-mail: info@ribar.com; URL: https://www.ribar.com/Rhode%20Island%20Bar%20Foundation/RhodeIslandBarFoundation.aspx

Foundation type: Public charity
Purpose: Scholarships to RI residents who are entering their first year of law school and will be full-time students.
Publications: Application guidelines.
Financial data: Year ended 06/30/2012. Assets, $2,351,888 (M); Expenditures, $647,906; Total giving, $440,500; Grants to individuals, totaling $40,000.
Fields of interest: Law school/education.
Type of support: Graduate support.
Application information: Applications accepted. Application form required. Application form available on the grantmaker's web site.
 Send request by: Mail
 Deadline(s): Mar. 20
 Applicants should submit the following:
   1) Transcripts
   2) Financial information
   3) SAR
   4) Letter(s) of recommendation
 Additional information: Application must also include a personal statement.
EIN: 056009376

8380
Rhode Island Building Industry Scholarship Fund
29 New York Ave.
Cumberland, RI 02864 (401) 333-3192
Contact: Maureen Myette, Treas.

Foundation type: Independent foundation
Purpose: Scholarships to financially needy RI residents pursuing education related to the building industry.
Financial data: Year ended 12/31/2011. Assets, $86,998 (M); Expenditures, $6,134; Total giving, $5,000; Grants to individuals, 3 grants totaling $5,000 (high: $2,500, low: $1,000).
Type of support: Support to graduates or students of specific schools; Undergraduate support.
Application information: Applications accepted. Interview required.
 Initial approach: Letter
 Send request by: Mail
 Deadline(s): Mar. 1
 Applicants should submit the following:
   1) Resume
   2) Financial information
EIN: 050375250

8381
The Rhode Island Foundation
(also known as The Rhode Island Community
Foundation)
1 Union Station
Providence, RI   02903-1746   (401) 274-4564
FAX: (401) 331-8085;
E-mail: nsteinberg@rifoundation.org; URL: http://
www.rifoundation.org

Foundation type: Community foundation
Purpose: Scholarships and fellowships primarily to
residents of RI.
Publications: Application guidelines; Annual report
(including application guidelines); Financial
statement; Grants list; Informational brochure;
Informational brochure (including application
guidelines); Newsletter; Occasional report; Program
policy statement.
Financial data: Year ended 12/31/2012. Assets,
$678,230,790 (M); Expenditures, $36,048,030;
Total giving, $28,267,948. Scholarships—to
individuals amount not specified. Fellowships
amount not specified.
Fields of interest: Folk arts; Arts education; Film/
video; Design; Music; Performing arts, education;
Vocational education; Higher education; Graduate/
professional education; Scholarships/financial aid;
Students, sororities/fraternities; Nursing care;
Crime/law enforcement, police agencies;
Disasters, fire prevention/control; Volunteer
services; Business/industry; Financial services.
Type of support: Fellowships; Scholarships—to
individuals; Support to graduates or students of
specific schools; Awards/prizes; Graduate support;
Undergraduate support.
Application information: Applications accepted.
Application form required. Application form
available on the grantmaker's web site.
   Send request by: Online
   Copies of proposal: 1
   Deadline(s): Varies
   Additional information: See web site for a
      complete program listing.
Program descriptions:
   Rhode Island Innovation Fellowship: The
foundation will award two applicants up to
$300,000 over three years to develop, test, and
implement innovative ideas that have the potential
to dramatically improve any area of life in Rhode
Island. See web site for additional information.
   Scholarships: The foundation currently manages
nearly 150 scholarship funds. These scholarships
offer assistance to students at a variety of levels,
middle school to post-graduate, for scholars across
Rhode Island, from North Smithfield to Block Island,
and for many different studies, from nursing to
music. See web site for additional information.
EIN: 222604963

8382
Rhode Island Hospital Foundation
167 Point St.
Providence, RI   02903-4771   (401) 444-6500
Contact: Timothy J. Babineau M.D., Pres. and C.E.O.

Foundation type: Public charity
Purpose: The family assistance program funds the
basic living needs of struggling families of patients
at Hasbro Children's Hospital, RI.
Financial data: Year ended 09/30/2011. Assets,
$52,069,813 (M); Expenditures, $11,592,212;
Total giving, $8,933,940; Grants to individuals,
totaling $500.
Fields of interest: Hospitals (general); Children,
services; Family services; Children.
Type of support: Grants for special needs.

Application information:
   Initial approach: Letter
   Additional information: Contact foundation for
      eligibility guidelines.
EIN: 050468736

8383
Robert Rimmele Scholarship Fund
P.O. Box 1802
Providence, RI   02901-1802   (617) 434-4645
Contact: Carol Gray
Application address: 100 Federal St., Boston,MA
02110, tel.: 617-434-4645

Foundation type: Independent foundation
Purpose: Scholarships to graduating high school
students who are residents of Needham, MA.
Financial data: Year ended 12/31/2011. Assets,
$277,967 (M); Expenditures, $15,856; Total
giving, $10,000.
Fields of interest: Higher education.
Type of support: Scholarships—to individuals.
Application information: Application form required.
   Deadline(s): End of Feb.
   Additional information: Application must include
      financial and educational information.
EIN: 046712607

8384
Charlotte M. Robbins Trust
c/o Bank of America, N.A.
P.O. Box 1802
Providence, RI   02901-1802   (617) 897-3209
Contact: Amy Sahler, Tr.
Application address: c/o Bank of America, N.A..,
225 Franklin St., MAO 3, Boston, MA 02110-2804

Foundation type: Independent foundation
Purpose: Financial assistance limited to aged
couples and/or aged women who are residents of
the towns of Ayer, Groton, Harvard, Littleton, or
Shirley, MA or agencies serving the same.
Financial data: Year ended 12/31/2011. Assets,
$393,503 (M); Expenditures, $20,078; Total
giving, $15,000.
Fields of interest: Aging.
Type of support: Grants for special needs.
Application information: Applications accepted.
   Initial approach: Letter
   Deadline(s): None
   Additional information: Application should
      include income and expenses, assets, and
      reason for request.
EIN: 046096044

8385
Fred L. Robbins Trust
P.O. Box 1802
Providence, RI   02901-1802
Contact: Stephen Donovan, Jr.
Application address: c/o Acton-Boxborough
Regional High School, 96 Hayward Rd., Acton, MA
01720-0096

Foundation type: Independent foundation
Purpose: Scholarships to student who are
residents of Acton, MA for postsecondary
education.
Financial data: Year ended 12/31/2012. Assets,
$413,428 (M); Expenditures, $22,797; Total
giving, $17,700.
Fields of interest: Higher education.
Type of support: Scholarships—to individuals.

Application information: Applications accepted.
Application form required.
   Deadline(s): Apr. 1
EIN: 046095991

8386
Blanche A. Robinson Charitable Trust
P.O. Box 1802
Providence, RI   02901-1802   (214) 209-0197
Contact: Melissa W. Mercadante
Application address: 1201 Main St. Dallas, TX
75202-3113

Foundation type: Independent foundation
Purpose: Scholarships to graduating seniors of
Franklin High School, TN for attendance at
accredited colleges or universities.
Financial data: Year ended 12/31/2012. Assets,
$299,839 (M); Expenditures, $16,829; Total
giving, $12,585.
Fields of interest: Higher education.
Type of support: Scholarships—to individuals;
Support to graduates or students of specific
schools.
Application information:
   Deadline(s): None
   Additional information: Contact your guidance
      counselor for application information.
EIN: 626073451

8387
Art & Peg Rolland Scholarship Fund
(formerly Arthur D. & Marvis S. Rolland Scholarship
Fund)
P.O. Box 1802
Providence, RI   02901-1802   (413) 238-5877

Foundation type: Independent foundation
Purpose: Scholarships to individuals who
graduated from secondary school and have been
residents of Worthington, MA, for at least two years.
Financial data: Year ended 12/31/2011. Assets,
$164,301 (M); Expenditures, $9,107; Total giving,
$5,000.
Fields of interest: Higher education.
Type of support: Scholarships—to individuals.
Application information: Applications accepted.
   Deadline(s): June 30
EIN: 046657747

8388
The Paul F. Ronci Memorial Scholarship
Trust
c/o Mary Louise Fonseca
P.O. Box 515
Harmony, RI   02829   (401) 349-4404
URL: http://paulfroncischolarship.org/

Foundation type: Independent foundation
Purpose: Scholarship to a full time student who is
a RI resident and shows academic excellence.
Financial data: Year ended 12/31/2011. Assets,
$517,750 (M); Expenditures, $38,308; Total
giving, $27,700; Grants to individuals, 9 grants
totaling $27,700 (high: $5,000; low: $1,500).
Fields of interest: Higher education.
Type of support: Scholarships—to individuals.
Application information: Applications accepted.
Application form required.
   Deadline(s): Mar. 31
   Applicants should submit the following:
      1) FAFSA
      2) Transcripts
      3) Essay

Additional information: Applicants must demonstrate financial need and must show proof of residence for ten of the last twelve years.
EIN: 586368004

8389
Rostra Engineered Component Sunshine Fund
(formerly Century Brass Sunshine Fund)
P.O. Box 1802
Providence, RI   02901-1802

Foundation type: Company-sponsored foundation
Purpose: Emergency grants and loans and gift baskets for funerals and illnesses to Rostra Engineered Components employees.
Financial data: Year ended 12/31/2012. Assets, $57,149 (M); Expenditures, $7,949; Total giving, $6,500.
Fields of interest: Human services.
Type of support: Employee-related welfare.
Application information: Applications not accepted.
Additional information: Unsolicited requests for funds not considered or acknowledged.
Company name: Rostra Precision Controls, Inc.
EIN: 066219258

8390
Sasso Scholarship Fund Trust
(formerly Sasso Consolidation Fund Trust)
P.O. Box 1802
Providence, RI   02901-1802
Contact: Thomas James

Foundation type: Independent foundation
Purpose: Scholarships to Meriden High School, CT, graduates for attendance at accredited colleges or universities.
Financial data: Year ended 12/31/2012. Assets, $159,643 (M); Expenditures, $11,970; Total giving, $8,500.
Fields of interest: Higher education.
Type of support: Scholarships—to individuals; Support to graduates or students of specific schools.
Application information: Applications accepted.
Initial approach: Letter
Deadline(s): June 1
EIN: 066131106

8391
The Betty Ann Donohue Scavone Scholarship Fund
P.O. Box 1802
Providence, RI   02901-1802

Foundation type: Independent foundation
Purpose: Scholarships to graduates of St. Peter-Marian High School, MA.
Financial data: Year ended 12/31/2011. Assets, $139,425 (M); Expenditures, $10,634; Total giving, $8,500.
Type of support: Support to graduates or students of specific schools.
Application information: Applications not accepted.
Additional information: Unsolicited requests for funds not considered or acknowledged.
EIN: 043071330

8392
Frank H. Scheehl Trust
(also known as Emeline H. Scheehl College Scholarship Fund)
P.O. Box 1802
Providence, RI   02901-1802

Foundation type: Independent foundation
Purpose: Scholarships to seniors of Conard High School, West Hartford, CT.
Financial data: Year ended 06/30/2013. Assets, $211,503 (M); Expenditures, $14,926; Total giving, $9,500; Grants to individuals, 10 grants totaling $9,500 (high: $1,500, low: $500).
Type of support: Support to graduates or students of specific schools; Undergraduate support.
Application information: Applications accepted.
Additional information: Contact school for current application deadline/guidelines.
EIN: 066177823

8393
William J. & Elizabeth M. Schiff Scholarship Fund
P.O. Box 1802
Providence, RI   02901-1802

Foundation type: Independent foundation
Purpose: Scholarships only to graduates of Neptune High School, NJ who intend to pursue a full-time engineering or nursing curriculum.
Financial data: Year ended 12/31/2012. Assets, $951,981 (M); Expenditures, $112,710; Total giving, $99,977.
Fields of interest: Nursing school/education; Engineering school/education.
Type of support: Support to graduates or students of specific schools; Undergraduate support.
Application information: Applications accepted. Application form required.
Deadline(s): May 1
Additional information: Contributes only to preselected individuals, unsolicited requests for funds not considered or acknowledged.
EIN: 226606811

8394
Byron S. Schuyler Child Educational Fund Trust
c/o Bank of America, N.A.
P.O. Box 1802
Providence, RI   02901-1802
Contact: Judith A. Lee, V.P.
Application address: c/o Byron S. Child Educational Trust, 1 East Ave., 4th Fl., NY7-144-04-04 Rochester, NY 14604

Foundation type: Independent foundation
Purpose: Scholarships to graduating seniors of Fulton County, NY for postsecondary education.
Financial data: Year ended 01/31/2013. Assets, $180,542 (M); Expenditures, $11,133; Total giving, $9,000.
Fields of interest: Higher education.
Type of support: Scholarships—to individuals.
Application information: Application form required.
Deadline(s): May 10
Applicants should submit the following:
1) Transcripts
2) Financial information
3) FAFSA
4) Letter(s) of recommendation
5) Class rank
Additional information: Application should also include letter of acceptance from college.
EIN: 146083934

8395
Mary P. Sears Trust
P.O. Box 1802
Providence, RI   02901-1802

Foundation type: Independent foundation
Purpose: Award to a living American poet, selected with reference to his or her genius and need.
Financial data: Year ended 09/30/2013. Assets, $183,311 (M); Expenditures, $11,050; Total giving, $7,000.
Fields of interest: Literature.
Type of support: Awards/grants by nomination only; Awards/prizes.
Application information: Applications not accepted.
Additional information: The award is between $6,000 and $9,000. Application by nomination only.
EIN: 046009466

8396
Winslow F. Sears & Dorothy M. Sears Trust
P.O. Box 1802
Providence, RI   02901-1802

Foundation type: Independent foundation
Purpose: Scholarships to graduating students of Plymouth North High School and Plymouth South High School, MA for postsecondary education.
Financial data: Year ended 04/30/2013. Assets, $817,536 (M); Expenditures, $41,460; Total giving, $29,390.
Fields of interest: Higher education.
Type of support: Support to graduates or students of specific schools.
Application information: Applications accepted. Application form required.
Initial approach: Letter
Deadline(s): Apr. 15
Applicants should submit the following:
1) SAR
2) Financial information
Additional information: Application should also include copies of financial aid awards from all colleges and universities that have accepted you for admission.
EIN: 046702776

8397
John P. Sheehan Scholarship Fund
c/o Bank of America, N.A.
P.O. Box 1802
Providence, RI   02901-1802   (585) 546-9303
Contact: Judith A. Lee
Application address: 1 E. Ave., Rochester, NY 14638, tel.: (585) 546-9303

Foundation type: Independent foundation
Purpose: Scholarships to financially needy graduates of public and parochial high schools in Utica, NY, based on moral fitness, likelihood for success in college, high school academic performance, and financial need.
Financial data: Year ended 12/31/2012. Assets, $366,232 (M); Expenditures, $23,616; Total giving, $18,400; Grants to individuals, 46 grants totaling $18,400 (high: $400, low: $400).
Type of support: Support to graduates or students of specific schools; Undergraduate support.
Application information: Application form required.
Additional information: Contact foundation for current application deadline/guidelines.
EIN: 156014981

8398
Howard E. and Christine Shifler
P.O. Box 1802
Providence, RI   02901-1802
Contact: Judith Lee
Application address: Bank of America, E. Ave., B.C.
1 E. Ave., Rochester, NY 14638

Foundation type: Independent foundation
Purpose: Scholarships to graduates of Southern Regional High School, Manahawkin, NJ, to attend colleges and trade schools.
Financial data: Year ended 12/31/2012. Assets, $260,281 (M); Expenditures, $16,418; Total giving, $14,000.
Fields of interest: Vocational education.
Type of support: Support to graduates or students of specific schools; Technical education support; Undergraduate support.
Application information: Applications accepted. Application form required.
   Deadline(s): Feb. 28
   Additional information: Application must include financial information.
EIN: 226403942

8399
Shriners of Rhode Island Charities Trust
(formerly Palestine Temple Charities Trust)
1 Rhodes Pl.
Cranston, RI   02905-3326   (401) 467-7100
Contact: A. Sheffield Reynolds, Treas.

Foundation type: Independent foundation
Purpose: Medical expense assistance primarily to financially needy individuals living in RI.
Financial data: Year ended 12/31/2012. Assets, $26,797,019 (M); Expenditures, $1,530,267; Total giving, $1,298,818.
Fields of interest: Health care; Economically disadvantaged.
Type of support: Grants for special needs.
Application information: Applications accepted.
   Initial approach: Letter
   Deadline(s): None
   Additional information: Letter should include medical information.
EIN: 223191072

8400
Simionescu Scholarship Foundation
P.O. Box 1802
Providence, RI   02901-1802

Foundation type: Independent foundation
Purpose: Scholarships to financially needy students of Hackensack High School, NJ.
Financial data: Year ended 11/30/2012. Assets, $2,990,823 (M); Expenditures, $150,125; Total giving, $93,424.
Fields of interest: Higher education.
Type of support: Support to graduates or students of specific schools; Undergraduate support.
Application information: Applications accepted. Application form required.
   Deadline(s): May 31
   Additional information: Application forms available at Hackensack High School Guidance Dept.
EIN: 222878206

8401
Peter Sleesman Trust
P.O. Box 1802
Providence, RI   02901-1802

Foundation type: Independent foundation
Purpose: Scholarships to graduating high school seniors at Bridgeton High School, NJ.
Financial data: Year ended 12/31/2011. Assets, $184,300 (M); Expenditures, $12,009; Total giving, $8,750.
Type of support: Support to graduates or students of specific schools; Undergraduate support.
Application information: Applications accepted.
   Initial approach: Letter
   Deadline(s): None
EIN: 216015545

8402
Slowinski Charitable Foundation
(also known as Slowinski Estate Fund Trust)
P.O. Box 1802
Providence, RI   02901-1802

Foundation type: Independent foundation
Purpose: Scholarships to women who have completed their third year of study at Columbia University, NY.
Financial data: Year ended 12/31/2012. Assets, $197,500 (M); Expenditures, $11,063; Total giving, $7,500.
Type of support: Support to graduates or students of specific schools.
Application information: Applications accepted.
   Initial approach: Letter
   Deadline(s): None
EIN: 066314132

8403
Jennie W. Smith Education Fund
(formerly Smith Educational Fund)
P.O. Box 1802
Providence, RI   02901-1802

Foundation type: Independent foundation
Purpose: Scholarships to students of South Hadley, MA for postsecondary education.
Financial data: Year ended 12/31/2012. Assets, $451,868 (M); Expenditures, $24,547; Total giving, $20,475.
Fields of interest: Higher education.
Type of support: Scholarships—to individuals.
Application information: Applications accepted. Application form required.
   Deadline(s): June 10
   Applicants should submit the following:
   1) Class rank
   2) GPA
EIN: 046033742

8404
Pauline Smith Memorial Fund
P.O. Box 1802
Providence, RI   02901-1802
Application address: c/o Mt. Greylock Regional School District, 1781 Cold Spring Rd., Williamstown, MA 01267-2770

Foundation type: Independent foundation
Purpose: Scholarships to graduates of Mount Greylock High School, MA for postsecondary education.
Financial data: Year ended 12/31/2012. Assets, $156,826 (M); Expenditures, $8,700; Total giving,

$5,500; Grants to individuals, 6 grants totaling $5,500 (high: $1,000, low: $500).
Fields of interest: Higher education.
Type of support: Support to graduates or students of specific schools; Undergraduate support.
Application information: Applications accepted. Application form required.
   Initial approach: Letter
   Deadline(s): None
   Additional information: Application should include financial information.
EIN: 046584005

8405
Elmer Smith Scholarship TUW
c/o Bank of America
P.O. Box 1802
Providence, RI   02901-1802
Contact: Judith Lee
Application address: 1 E. , Rochester NY, 14638

Foundation type: Independent foundation
Purpose: Scholarships to students at Cape May County and Holy Spirit high schools, NJ.
Financial data: Year ended 12/31/2012. Assets, $669,749 (M); Expenditures, $38,040; Total giving, $32,500.
Type of support: Support to graduates or students of specific schools; Undergraduate support.
Application information: Applications accepted. Application form required.
   Deadline(s): May 1
   Additional information: Applications available from high schools.
EIN: 226213088

8406
Elizabeth B. Smith Trust
(formerly E. B. and C. G. Smith Scholarship)
P.O. Box 1802
Providence, RI   02901-1802

Foundation type: Independent foundation
Purpose: Scholarships to students from Westfield High School, MA for higher education.
Financial data: Year ended 12/31/2011. Assets, $208,357 (M); Expenditures, $13,315; Total giving, $7,910.
Fields of interest: Higher education.
Type of support: Support to graduates or students of specific schools; Undergraduate support.
Application information: Applications accepted.
   Initial approach: Letter
   Additional information: Contact the trust for additional information.
EIN: 046033567

8407
Ellen V. Smith Trust
(formerly Ellen V. and Robert H. Smith Scholarship Fund)
P.O. Box 1802
Providence, RI   02901-1802
Application address: c/o The Smith Scholarship Selection Comm. P.O. Box 2483 E. Side Sta., Providence RI 02906-0483

Foundation type: Independent foundation
Purpose: Scholarships to residents of South Kingstown, RI, who are between the ages of 15 and 23 years, to attend programs at accredited colleges, universities, and graduate professional schools leading to a bachelor's degree or doctorate. Scholarships are awarded on the basis of need, and are renewable.

Financial data: Year ended 12/31/2012. Assets, $1,621,170 (M); Expenditures, $121,189; Total giving, $102,500.
Type of support: Graduate support; Undergraduate support.
Application information: Application form required.
> *Deadline(s):* Dec. 15 for preliminary application and Feb. 15 for biographical questionnaire and secondary school report or college transcript.
> *Final notification:* Applicants will be notified by Apr. 15
> *Applicants should submit the following:*
> 1) Transcripts
> 2) FAF
> 3) SAT

EIN: 056069745

8408
Elva S. Smith Trust
c/o Citizens Bank
870 Westminster St.
Providence, RI 02903-4024 (412) 624-5230
Application address: c/o University of Pittsburgh, Attn:M. Washington, 509 School of Library and Sciences Building, Pittsburgh, PA 15260

Foundation type: Independent foundation
Purpose: One full scholarship awarded annually for attendance at the School of Library and Information Science at the University of Pittsburgh, PA.
Financial data: Year ended 12/31/2011. Assets, $1,990,258 (M); Expenditures, $131,206; Total giving, $94,877.
Fields of interest: Libraries/library science.
Type of support: Scholarships—to individuals; Support to graduates or students of specific schools.
Application information:
> *Initial approach:* Letter or telephone
> *Additional information:* Contact trust for current application guidelines.

EIN: 026014169

8409
Henry Herbert Smythe Trust
P.O. Box 1802
Providence, RI 02901-1802
Application address: c/o Bank of America, N.A., 100 Federal St., Boston, MA 02110-

Foundation type: Independent foundation
Purpose: Scholarships to students from Falmouth and Adams, MA for continuing education at institutions of higher learning.
Financial data: Year ended 09/30/2012. Assets, $1,838,238 (M); Expenditures, $105,617; Total giving, $81,075.
Fields of interest: Higher education.
Type of support: Scholarships—to individuals.
Application information:
> *Deadline(s):* None

EIN: 046008387

8410
Fred C. Snyder Education Fund
(formerly Fred C. Snyder Fund)
c/o Bank of America N.A.
P.O. Box 1802
Providence, RI 02901-1802 (315) 429-3155
Application address: c/o Dolgeville Central School 38 Slawson St. Ext. Dolgeville, NY 13329

Foundation type: Independent foundation

Purpose: Scholarships to financially needy graduates of Dolgeville Central School, NY.
Financial data: Year ended 12/31/2012. Assets, $611,985 (M); Expenditures, $37,688; Total giving, $27,500.
Type of support: Support to graduates or students of specific schools; Undergraduate support.
Application information: Applications accepted. Application form required.
> *Deadline(s):* July 31

EIN: 156021382

8411
Clifford E. & Melda Snyder Scholarship Fund
(formerly Melda Snyder Scholarship Fund)
c/o Bank of America, N.A.
P.O. Box 1802
Providence, RI 02901-1802
Contact: John Hargreaves
Application Address: Snyder Scholarship Fund, Hunterdon County Board of Agriculture, P.O. Box 2327, Flemington, NJ 08822

Foundation type: Independent foundation
Purpose: Interest-free loans to graduates of Hunterdon County high schools, NJ, pursuing an education in agriculture or a related field.
Financial data: Year ended 12/31/2011. Assets, $729,384 (M); Expenditures, $8,522; Total giving, $0; Loans to individuals, totaling $18,000.
Fields of interest: Vocational education, post-secondary; Formal/general education.
Type of support: Support to graduates or students of specific schools; Undergraduate support.
Application information: Applications accepted. Application form required.
> *Send request by:* Mail
> *Deadline(s):* Apr. 15
> *Applicants should submit the following:*
> 1) Class rank
> 2) SAT
> 3) Financial information
> 4) GPA

Program description:
> *Loan Fund:* The minimum loan amount awarded each year is $2,000 to each individual. Loan recipients must be high school graduates who resided in Hunterdon County, NJ for at least five years immediately prior to graduation. They must be pursuing an education, undergraduate or graduate, in the field of agriculture or fields of related study such as veterinary medicine, agricultural research, food science, farm machinery and general research in agricultural subjects. Applicants must be enrolled in a two or four year college, or a vocational/technical institute, in or outside the U.S.

EIN: 226634349

8412
Inez Sprague Trust
P.O. Box 1802
Providence, RI 02901-1802
Contact: Emma Greene
Application address: c/o Bank of America, N.A., Attn: Emma Greene, 100 Federal St., Boston, MA 02110

Foundation type: Independent foundation
Purpose: Welfare assistance and medical expenses to needy residents of Narragansett, RI.
Financial data: Year ended 06/30/2012. Assets, $781,173 (M); Expenditures, $44,635; Total giving, $28,793; Grants to individuals, 2 grants totaling $1,045 (high: $550, low: $495).

Fields of interest: Health care; Economically disadvantaged.
Type of support: Grants for special needs.
Application information: Applications accepted.
> *Deadline(s):* None
> *Additional information:* Contact trust for current application guidelines.

EIN: 056067971

8413
William F. Starr Fellowship Fund
P.O. Box 1802
Providence, RI 02901-1802

Foundation type: Independent foundation
Purpose: Fellowships to financially needy students attending the University of Connecticut School of Law in Hartford, CT.
Financial data: Year ended 06/30/2013. Assets, $774,478 (M); Expenditures, $42,153; Total giving, $30,910.
Fields of interest: Law school/education; Law/international law.
Type of support: Awards/grants by nomination only.
Application information: Application form not required.
> *Additional information:* Board of trustees chooses award recipients according to merit.

EIN: 066024050

8414
Stauble Scholarship Fund
P.O. Box 1802
Providence, RI 02901-1802

Foundation type: Independent foundation
Purpose: Scholarships to children or stepchildren of employees of Veeder Industries or any of its domestic or foreign subsidiaries or divisions for higher education.
Financial data: Year ended 06/30/2013. Assets, $711,839 (M); Expenditures, $34,791; Total giving, $20,000.
Type of support: Employee-related scholarships.
Application information:
> *Initial approach:* Letter or telephone.
> *Deadline(s):* Jan. 31

EIN: 060993576

8415
Stokes Scholarship Trust
P.O. Box 1802
Providence, RI 02901-1802

Foundation type: Independent foundation
Purpose: Scholarships to residents of Langdon, NH, to attend accredited colleges, universities, vocational schools, or two-year colleges in the U.S. Preference is given to students who attend a school or program for nursing training.
Financial data: Year ended 12/31/2011. Assets, $1,395,737 (M); Expenditures, $74,822; Total giving, $60,000.
Fields of interest: Nursing school/education.
Type of support: Scholarships—to individuals.
Application information: Applications accepted. Application form required. Interview required.
> *Deadline(s):* July 1
> *Applicants should submit the following:*
> 1) Letter(s) of recommendation
> 2) Financial information
> 3) Essay

EIN: 026092657

8416
Streeter Scholarship Fund
(formerly Mallary D. Streeter Scholarship Fund)
c/o Bank Of America, N.A.
P.O. Box 1802
Providence, RI   02901-1802   (315) 946-2200

Foundation type: Independent foundation
Purpose: Scholarships to graduates of the Lyons County Central School District No. 1, NY for postsecondary education.
Financial data: Year ended 12/31/2012. Assets, $309,080 (M); Expenditures, $14,162; Total giving, $9,375; Grants to individuals, totaling $9,375.
Fields of interest: Higher education.
Type of support: Support to graduates or students of specific schools; Undergraduate support.
Application information: Applications accepted. Application form required.
  Initial approach: Letter
  Deadline(s): July 14
  Additional information: Application should include transcript and college verification.
EIN: 166053773

8417
Ruth H. Sutton Trust
P.O. Box 1802
Providence, RI   02901-1802
Contact: Carol Gray
Application address: 225 Franklin St., Boston, MA 02110

Foundation type: Independent foundation
Purpose: Scholarships to selected students of Nantucket High School, MA for undergraduate study.
Financial data: Year ended 09/30/2012. Assets, $269,280 (M); Expenditures, $15,758; Total giving, $10,000; Grant to an individual, 1 grant totaling $4,000.
Fields of interest: Higher education.
Type of support: Support to graduates or students of specific schools; Undergraduate support.
Application information: Applications not accepted.
  Additional information: Contributes only to preselected individuals. Unsolicited requests for funding not considered or acknowledged.
EIN: 046027863

8418
Edward Syder Trust
P.O. Box 1802
Providence, RI   02901-1802   (201) 327-7000
Contact: Edward C. Syder
Application address: 88 West Main St., Ramsey, NJ 07446

Foundation type: Independent foundation
Purpose: Scholarships to students of Ramsey, NJ, who have completed their first year of college, graduate or undergraduate, and demonstrated academic accomplishment, community involvement, and good character.
Financial data: Year ended 12/31/2012. Assets, $571,666 (M); Expenditures, $25,431; Total giving, $20,000; Grants to individuals, totaling $20,000.
Fields of interest: Higher education.
Type of support: Scholarships—to individuals.
Application information: Applications accepted. Application form required.
  Deadline(s): Oct. 15

Additional information: Contact the trust for additional application information.
EIN: 226513992

8419
Betsey W. Taber Trust
(formerly Taber Scholarship Fund)
P.O. Box 1802
Providence, RI   02901-1802

Foundation type: Independent foundation
Purpose: Scholarships to high school graduates of the greater New Bedford, MA, area for postsecondary education.
Financial data: Year ended 09/30/2013. Assets, $545,659 (M); Expenditures, $32,412; Total giving, $21,660.
Fields of interest: Higher education.
Type of support: Scholarships—to individuals.
Application information: Applications accepted. Application form required.
  Deadline(s): None
EIN: 046418554

8420
Eva March Tappan Trust
P.O. Box 1802
Providence, RI   02901-1802

Foundation type: Independent foundation
Purpose: Scholarships to graduates of Worcester County High School, MA, to attend Vassar College.
Financial data: Year ended 10/31/2012. Assets, $826,196 (M); Expenditures, $53,509; Total giving, $35,000. Scholarships—to individuals amount not specified.
Fields of interest: Higher education.
Type of support: Support to graduates or students of specific schools; Undergraduate support.
Application information: Applications accepted.
  Initial approach: Letter
  Deadline(s): Jan. 31
  Applicants should submit the following:
    1) Transcripts
    2) SAT
    3) Letter(s) of recommendation
EIN: 046023587

8421
Willard E. & Ella P. Thompson Educational Fund
P.O. Box 1802
Providence, RI   02901-1802
Application address: c/o Thompson Scholarship Selection Committee, 600 S. Hale, Algona, IA 50511, tel.: (515) 295-7207

Foundation type: Independent foundation
Purpose: Scholarships to graduates of Iowa High School in Algona School District, Algona, IA.
Financial data: Year ended 12/31/2012. Assets, $4,435,844 (M); Expenditures, $249,330; Total giving, $210,829; Grants to individuals, 123 grants totaling $210,829 (high: $3,000, low: $300).
Type of support: Support to graduates or students of specific schools; Undergraduate support.
Application information: Applications not accepted.
  Additional information: Contributes only to preselected individuals.
EIN: 366028029

8422
Thompson Scholarship Fund
c/o William Corcoran
P.O. Box 389
Newport, RI   02840   (401) 847-6235
Application address: Rogers High School, Wickman Rd., Newport, RI 02840

Foundation type: Independent foundation
Purpose: Scholarships to graduating seniors at Rogers High School, Newport, RI, for study at four-year colleges.
Financial data: Year ended 12/31/2012. Assets, $2,198,637 (M); Expenditures, $139,237; Total giving, $104,750; Grants to individuals, 43 grants totaling $104,750 (high: $3,000, low: $1,000).
Type of support: Support to graduates or students of specific schools; Undergraduate support.
Application information: Applications accepted. Application form required.
  Initial approach: Letter or telephone
  Deadline(s): Apr.
  Applicants should submit the following:
    1) Transcripts
    2) Letter(s) of recommendation
    3) Essay
  Additional information: Application must also include copy of most recent tax return.
EIN: 056012968

8423
TMC Foundation
(formerly The Moore Company Foundation)
c/o Alexandra Moore Barber
P.O. Box 538
Westerly, RI   02891-0538

Foundation type: Company-sponsored foundation
Purpose: Scholarships to students for attendance at the University of Rhode Island, RI.
Financial data: Year ended 12/31/2011. Assets, $121,538 (M); Expenditures, $57,181; Total giving, $53,500.
Fields of interest: Higher education.
Type of support: Support to graduates or students of specific schools.
Application information: Applications not accepted.
  Additional information: Checks will be made out directly to the educational institution on behalf of the student. Unsolicited requests for funds not considered or acknowledged.
EIN: 050499128

8424
Todd V. H. and W. R. Foundation
(formerly The Vera H. and William R. Todd Foundation)
P.O. Box 1802
Providence, RI   02901-1802   (860) 952-7405
Contact: Kate Kerchaert
Application address: c/o Bank of America, N.A., 777 Main St., Hartford, CT 06115

Foundation type: Independent foundation
Purpose: Scholarships to residents of Derby or Shelton, CT.
Financial data: Year ended 12/31/2012. Assets, $218,709 (M); Expenditures, $12,359; Total giving, $10,000.
Fields of interest: Education.
Type of support: Scholarships—to individuals.
Application information:
  Initial approach: Letter
  Deadline(s): May 1

Additional information: Scholarships are paid through Scholarship America.
EIN: 066031931

8425
Townsend Aid for the Aged
P.O. Box 1802
Providence, RI   02901-1802
Application address: c/o Townsend Aid for the Aged, Attn: Gina Rymer, 12 Madeline Dr., Newport, RI 02840

Foundation type: Independent foundation
Purpose: Grants to financially needy, elderly residents of Newport, RI, to provide the necessities of life.
Financial data: Year ended 04/30/2012. Assets, $2,937,011 (M); Expenditures, $135,955; Total giving, $115,200; Grants to individuals, totaling $115,200.
Fields of interest: Aging; Economically disadvantaged.
Type of support: Grants for special needs.
Application information: Applications not accepted.
Additional information: Grants are awarded to worthy individuals as directed by an advisory committee, which initiates the application process.
EIN: 056009549

8426
James & Phyllis Tracy Scholarship Foundation
P.O. Box 1802
Providence, RI   02901-1802   (888) 866-3275
Contact: Peter Weston
Application address: 777 Main St., Hartford, CT 06115

Foundation type: Independent foundation
Purpose: Scholarships to students from Waterbury, CT, high schools who have been Waterbury residents for the past five years.
Financial data: Year ended 12/31/2012. Assets, $141,880 (M); Expenditures, $10,690; Total giving, $7,250; Grants to individuals, 3 grants totaling $3,250 (high: $1,250, low: $1,000).
Fields of interest: Vocational education, post-secondary; Higher education; Scholarships/financial aid.
Type of support: Support to graduates or students of specific schools; Precollege support; Undergraduate support.
Application information: Applications accepted. Application form required.
Deadline(s): Apr. 1
Applicants should submit the following:
1) SAT
2) Letter(s) of recommendation
3) GPA
4) FAFSA
5) Transcripts
6) Financial information
EIN: 066025726

8427
Florence J. Tryon Trust
P.O. Box 1802
Providence, RI   02901-1802

Foundation type: Independent foundation
Purpose: Scholarships to male residents of Westfield, MA, between the ages of 16 and 22, who have graduated from St. Mary's High School, MA,

Westfield High School, MA, or Westfield Technical Vocational High, MA.
Financial data: Year ended 10/31/2012. Assets, $382,380 (M); Expenditures, $21,380; Total giving, $14,000.
Fields of interest: Vocational education, post-secondary; Higher education; Men.
Type of support: Support to graduates or students of specific schools; Undergraduate support.
Application information: Applications accepted. Application form required.
Deadline(s): Apr. 30
Applicants should submit the following:
1) Transcripts
2) Letter(s) of recommendation
EIN: 046033568

8428
United States Sailing Foundation
15 Maritime Dr.
P.O. Box 1260
Portsmouth, RI   02871-0907   (401) 683-0800
FAX: (401) 683-0840; *E-mail:* info@ussailing.org;
URL: http://donations.ussailing.org/US_SAILING_Foundation.htm

Foundation type: Public charity
Purpose: Assistance to individuals supporting the United States in international sailing competitions.
Publications: Annual report; Financial statement; Grants list.
Financial data: Year ended 10/31/2011. Assets, $459,436 (M); Expenditures, $58,153; Total giving, $54,485. Grants to individuals amount not specified.
Fields of interest: Athletics/sports, water sports.
Type of support: Grants to individuals.
Application information: Applications accepted.
Initial approach: Letter
Additional information: Contact foundation for eligibility criteria.
EIN: 222667411

8429
Urann Foundation
P.O. Box 1802
Providence, RI   02901-1802   (617) 588-7744
Application address: P.O. Box 1788, Brockton, MA 02403

Foundation type: Independent foundation
Purpose: Giving for scholarships and payment of medical bills to members of Massachusetts families engaged in cranberry production; remainder of giving to a specified university and hospital.
Financial data: Year ended 12/31/2012. Assets, $1,574,745 (M); Expenditures, $1,722,848; Total giving, $1,683,805.
Fields of interest: Higher education; Agriculture.
Type of support: Scholarships—to individuals; Graduate support; Undergraduate support; Grants for special needs.
Application information: Applications accepted.
Initial approach: Letter or telephone
Deadline(s): Apr. 15 for scholarships; None for medical assistance
Additional information: Applications also available at guidance departments of high schools. Applicants for scholarships or medical assistance must show financial need.
EIN: 046115599

8430
The Valley Charitable Trust Fund
P.O. Box 1802
Providence, RI   02901-1802

Foundation type: Independent foundation
Purpose: Scholarships to high school seniors and college students from the Second Congressional District of MA and Hampden County, MA.
Financial data: Year ended 12/31/2012. Assets, $1,343,298 (M); Expenditures, $87,050; Total giving, $65,975; Grants to individuals, 36 grants totaling $51,000 (high: $2,000, low: $500).
Type of support: Undergraduate support.
Application information: Applications accepted. Application form required. Application form available on the grantmaker's web site.
Initial approach: Letter
Send request by: Mail
Deadline(s): Apr. 1
Applicants should submit the following:
1) SAR
2) Transcripts
EIN: 046018361

8431
Harold B. Walker Charitable Trust
P.O. Box 1802
Providence, RI   02901-1802
Contact: Carol M. Brewster
Application address: c/o Ashland High School, Attn.: Carol M. Brewster, 87 W. Union St., Ashland, MA 01721-1408
Application address: c/o Ashland High School, 87 W. Union St., Ashland, MA 01721-1408

Foundation type: Independent foundation
Purpose: Scholarships to graduates of Ashland High School, MA, who are in their third year of college pursuing a degree in science and mathematics.
Financial data: Year ended 12/31/2012. Assets, $501,398 (M); Expenditures, $28,991; Total giving, $19,000.
Fields of interest: College.
Type of support: Support to graduates or students of specific schools.
Application information: Application form required.
Deadline(s): Apr. 30
Additional information: Applicant must demonstrate financial need.
EIN: 046633929

8432
Howard A. Weaver Trust f/b/o Bexley Hall
P.O. Box 1802
Providence, RI   02901-1802

Foundation type: Independent foundation
Purpose: Scholarships for needy students preparing for the ministry within the Episcopal faith.
Financial data: Year ended 12/31/2012. Assets, $2,116,088 (M); Expenditures, $114,953; Total giving, $84,830.
Fields of interest: Theological school/education.
Type of support: Undergraduate support.
Application information: Applications not accepted.
Additional information: Payments are paid directly to the school on behalf of the students. Unsolicited requests for funds not considered or acknowledged.
EIN: 046139771

8433
Hamilton Fish Webster Medical Fund
P.O. Box 1802
Providence, RI 02901-1802

Foundation type: Independent foundation
Purpose: Financial assistance for medical care to needy residents of Aquidnick Island, RI, who are retired or members of the business or professional community.
Financial data: Year ended 12/31/2012. Assets, $1,191,460 (M); Expenditures, $45,208; Total giving, $20,674; Grants to individuals, 5 grants totaling $1,277 (high: $764, low: $30).
Fields of interest: Health care; Business/industry; Economically disadvantaged.
Type of support: Grants for special needs.
Application information: Application form required.
  Deadline(s): None
  Additional information: Applicants may contact any member of the Board of Directors.
EIN: 056007212

8434
Arthur E. Webster Trust
P.O. Box 1802
Providence, RI 02901-1802

Foundation type: Independent foundation
Purpose: Scholarships to graduating seniors of Berlin High School, CT for postsecondary education.
Financial data: Year ended 02/28/2013. Assets, $138,519 (M); Expenditures, $7,109; Total giving, $3,500.
Type of support: Support to graduates or students of specific schools; Undergraduate support.
Application information: Applications accepted.
  Initial approach: Letter
  Deadline(s): Mar.
EIN: 066024231

8435
Fred W. Wells Trust Fund
P.O. Box 1802
Providence, RI 02901-1802

Foundation type: Independent foundation
Purpose: Undergraduate and graduate scholarships for students of Greenfield, Deerfield, Shelburne, Ashfield, Montague, Buckland, Charlemont, Heath, Leyden, Gill, Northfield, Conway, Bernardston, Hawley, Rowe, and Monroe, MA for higher education.
Financial data: Year ended 06/30/2012. Assets, $4,318,472 (M); Expenditures, $217,805; Total giving, $195,202; Grants to individuals, 261 grants totaling $167,517 (high: $1,000, low: $100).
Fields of interest: Higher education.
Type of support: Scholarships—to individuals.
Application information: Selection is based on scholastic ability, financial need, character, leadership skills, integrity, personality and participation in extracurricular activities. Scholarships are renewable for up to four years with a limit of $1,000 per student, per year. Unsolicited requests for funds not considered or acknowledged.
EIN: 046412350

8436
Barbara Thorndike Wiggin Fund
P.O. Box 1802
Providence, RI 02901-1802

Foundation type: Independent foundation

Purpose: Scholarships to financially needy female graduates of high schools in Knox County, ME. Preference is given to graduates of Rockland High School.
Financial data: Year ended 12/31/2012. Assets, $592,290 (M); Expenditures, $27,943; Total giving, $18,000.
Fields of interest: Nursing school/education; Teacher school/education; Women.
Type of support: Support to graduates or students of specific schools; Undergraduate support.
Application information: Applications accepted. Application form required. Interview required.
EIN: 016013826

8437
Rufus & Caroline E. Wiles Scholarship Fund
P.O. Box 1802
Providence, RI 02901-1802
Aoolication Address: c/o Scholarship Fdnd. of Fort Plain, 33 Clinton Ave., Fort Plain., NY 13339 1435

Foundation type: Independent foundation
Purpose: Scholarships to graduating seniors of Fort Plain Central School District, NY for continuing their education at institutions of higher learning.
Financial data: Year ended 12/31/2012. Assets, $103,667 (M); Expenditures, $6,466; Total giving, $5,000.
Fields of interest: Vocational education, post-secondary; Higher education.
Type of support: Scholarships—to individuals.
Application information: Applications accepted.
  Deadline(s): None
EIN: 146014151

8438
George B. Williams Scholarship Foundation Trust
P.O. Box 1802
Providence, RI 02901-1802

Foundation type: Independent foundation
Purpose: Scholarships to graduates of Newington High School, CT.
Financial data: Year ended 04/30/2013. Assets, $327,781 (M); Expenditures, $24,027; Total giving, $17,000.
Type of support: Support to graduates or students of specific schools; Undergraduate support.
Application information: Applications accepted. Application form required.
  Initial approach: Letter
  Additional information: Applications are available at Newington High School guidance office.
EIN: 020682841

8439
Frederick H. Williams Trust f/b/o Williams Scholarship
P.O. Box 1802
Providence, RI 02901-1802
Contact: Lisa Domorod
Application address: 777 Main St., Hartford, CT 06115

Foundation type: Independent foundation
Purpose: Scholarships to residents of Granby, CT for higher education.
Financial data: Year ended 06/30/2012. Assets, $92,794 (M); Expenditures, $6,838; Total giving, $3,300.
Fields of interest: Higher education.

Type of support: Undergraduate support.
Application information: Applications accepted. Application form not required.
  Initial approach: Letter
  Deadline(s): None
  Applicants should submit the following:
    1) Financial information
    2) Transcripts
    3) Resume
    4) Budget Information
EIN: 066023781

8440
Ethel Arnold Wood Scholarship Fund
P.O. Box 1802
Providence, RI 02901-1802
Contact: Douglas R. Medeiros

Foundation type: Independent foundation
Purpose: Scholarships to graduates of Fairhaven High School and Martha's Vineyard Regional High School, MA for attendance at accredited colleges or universities.
Financial data: Year ended 09/30/2012. Assets, $165,097 (M); Expenditures, $15,820; Total giving, $8,500.
Fields of interest: Higher education.
Type of support: Support to graduates or students of specific schools; Undergraduate support.
Application information: Applications accepted. Application form required.
  Initial approach: Letter
  Deadline(s): Sept.
  Applicants should submit the following:
    1) Financial information
    2) Transcripts
EIN: 046332654

8441
Wright Memorial Scholarship
P.O. Box 1802
Providence, RI 02901-1802
Contact: Karen Hibbert
Application address: 100 Federal St., Boston, MA 02110

Foundation type: Independent foundation
Purpose: Scholarships to residents of MA to attend school in New England.
Financial data: Year ended 06/30/2013. Assets, $57,420 (M); Expenditures, $3,793; Total giving, $1,000.
Type of support: Undergraduate support.
Application information: Contact foundation for current application deadline/guidelines.
EIN: 046552717

8442
Helen F. Wylie Foundation
P.O. Box 1802
Providence, RI 02901-1802
Contact: Marilyn L. Hotch, Tr.
Application address: HC 32 Box 41C, Owls Head, ME 04854-9706

Foundation type: Independent foundation
Purpose: Scholarships to students who have been residents of Owls Head, ME, for at least three years prior to the date award is received for postsecondary education at public or private colleges, universities, vocational or professional schools.
Financial data: Year ended 12/31/2012. Assets, $658,005 (M); Expenditures, $33,397; Total giving, $20,600.

Fields of interest: Vocational education, post-secondary; Graduate/professional education.
Type of support: Technical education support; Undergraduate support.
Application information: Applications accepted. Application form required.
 Send request by: Mail
 Deadline(s): Apr. 30
 Applicants should submit the following:
  1) Financial information
  2) SAT
  3) Transcripts
  4) Letter(s) of recommendation
 Additional information: Application should also include a personal statement from the applicant describing career goals and how your educational plans relate to them. Applicant must be 35 years of age or under.
EIN: 010342663

8443
Clement L. Yaeger Trust
(also known as Clement L. Yaeger Scholarship Fund)
P.O. Box 1802
Providence, RI 02901-1802

Foundation type: Independent foundation

Purpose: Scholarships to residents of the New Bedford, MA area who are pursuing studies in library science, music education or design.
Financial data: Year ended 09/30/2012. Assets, $196,163 (M); Expenditures, $10,407; Total giving, $7,000.
Fields of interest: Design; Music; Libraries/library science.
Type of support: Scholarships—to individuals.
Application information: Applications accepted.
 Initial approach: Letter
EIN: 046049740

SOUTH CAROLINA

8444
Airport High School Educational Foundation, Inc.
P. O. Box 2044
West Columbia, SC 29171-2044 (803) 794-3712
Contact: Donny Burkett

Foundation type: Public charity
Purpose: Scholarships to graduating seniors of Airport High School in SC for higher education. Grants to teachers to promote educational programs at Airport High School in SC.
Financial data: Year ended 06/30/2012. Assets, $56,260 (M); Expenditures, $16,294; Total giving, $14,625.
Fields of interest: Higher education.
Type of support: Grants to individuals; Support to graduates or students of specific schools.
Application information: Applications accepted.
 Initial approach: Letter
EIN: 562194610

8445
Alliance for Quality Education
225 S. Pleasantburg Dr., Ste. B1
Greenville, SC 29607-2544 (864) 233-4137
Contact: Grier Mullins, Exec. Dir.
E-mail: grier@afqe.org

Foundation type: Public charity
Purpose: Grants for teachers and administrators in Greenville County School District, SC.
Publications: Application guidelines; Annual report; Grants list; Informational brochure; Newsletter; Occasional report.
Financial data: Year ended 12/31/2011. Assets, $191,525 (M); Expenditures, $313,477; Total giving, $23,541.
Fields of interest: Elementary/secondary education.
Type of support: Grants to individuals.
Application information: Application form required.
 Deadline(s): May 25
Program description:
 Mini-Grant Program: Provides funds (over $900,000 since 1986) through a competitive grant process for teachers and schools to support innovative approaches to improve student learning.
EIN: 570769637

8446
Dick Anderson Chapter 75 United Daughters of the Confederacy Trust
c/o Synovus Trust
P.O. Box 1798
Sumter, SC 29151-1798 (803) 778-8218

Foundation type: Independent foundation
Purpose: Scholarships to students in Sumter and contiguous counties, SC, and to students in SC schools.
Financial data: Year ended 12/31/2011. Assets, $285,912 (M); Expenditures, $13,557; Total giving, $6,000; Grants to individuals, 3 grants totaling $6,000 (high: $2,000, low: $2,000).
Type of support: Scholarships—to individuals.

Application information: Applications accepted. Application form required.
 Deadline(s): Mar.
EIN: 576108972

8447
Anmed Health Foundation
800 N. Fant St.
Anderson, SC 29621-5708 (864) 512-3477
Contact: Michael Cunningham, V.P., Advancement
E-mail: patientadvocate@anmedhealth.org; Toll-free tel.: (800) 994-6610; URL: http://www.anmedhealth.org/body.cfm?id=482

Foundation type: Public charity
Purpose: Financial assistance to patients discharged from the hospital who cannot afford needed medications.
Financial data: Year ended 09/30/2012. Assets, $338,629,199 (M); Expenditures, $421,741; Total giving, $89,928; Grants to individuals, totaling $89,928.
Fields of interest: Economically disadvantaged.
Type of support: Grants for special needs.
Application information: Applications accepted.
 Additional information: Applicant should show proof of income. Application is processed in the order received, and application will be reviewed within 30 days. See web site or contact the foundation for eligibility determination.
EIN: 570817544

8448
The Arts Partnership of Greater Spartanburg
200 E. St. John St.
Spartanburg, SC 29306-5124 (864) 583-2776
FAX: (864) 948-5353;
E-mail: sWong@SpartanArts.org; URL: http://www.spartanarts.org

Foundation type: Public charity
Purpose: Grants to professional artists in Spartanburg, SC, for travel, educational, marketing and other expenses to enhance their careers and promote professional artistic development.
Publications: Application guidelines.
Financial data: Year ended 06/30/2012. Assets, $33,443,850 (M); Expenditures, $2,878,657; Total giving, $575,856; Grants to individuals, totaling $2,000.
Fields of interest: Arts.
Type of support: Fellowships; Residencies; Travel grants.
Application information: Applications accepted. Application form required.
 Initial approach: Telephone
 Deadline(s): Jan. 2, Apr. 1, July 1 and Oct. 1
 Applicants should submit the following:
  1) Work samples
  2) Resume
Program description:
 Professional Artists: Individual artists may apply for $100 to $1,000 in support of travel, registration fees, educational expenses, or other costs directly associated with general cultural programming within the context of career enhancement, professional artistic development, business or management skills development, artist fellowships, or residencies.
EIN: 570986224

8449
Emily & Ellsworth Austin Educational Trust
P.O. Box 428
Camden, SC 29021 (803) 432-7559
Contact: Laura Jones, Tr.
Application address: 2623 Stewart St., Camden, SC 29020

Foundation type: Independent foundation
Purpose: Scholarships to high school residents with 3.0 GPA or better, of Kershaw County, SC, who will attend an accredited post-secondary educational institution.
Financial data: Year ended 12/31/2012. Assets, $1,564,947 (M); Expenditures, $137,430; Total giving, $134,000; Grants to individuals, 34 grants totaling $134,000 (high: $4,000, low: $2,000).
Fields of interest: Higher education.
Type of support: Scholarships—to individuals.
Application information: Application form required.
 Deadline(s): None
 Additional information: Recipient selected from the high school's recommendation list. Scholarships are renewable.
EIN: 306108244

8450
AVX/Kyocera Foundation
1 AVX Blvd.
Fountain Inn, SC 29644-9039

Foundation type: Company-sponsored foundation
Purpose: Undergraduate scholarships to students pursuing a career in Materials Science and Engineering.
Financial data: Year ended 03/31/2013. Assets, $10,243,333 (M); Expenditures, $593,413; Total giving, $503,678.
Fields of interest: Higher education; Engineering/technology.
Type of support: Scholarships—to individuals; Undergraduate support.
Application information: Applications not accepted.
 Additional information: Unsolicited requests for funds not considered or acknowledged.
EIN: 571057142

8451
The Bailey Foundation
c/o TD Bank, N.A.
P.O. Box 494
Clinton, SC 29325-0494 (864) 938-2632
Contact: Robert S. Link, Jr., Admin.
FAX: (864) 938-2669

Foundation type: Operating foundation
Purpose: Scholarships to financially needy graduating seniors of Clinton High School and Laurens High School, SC, for study at accredited four-year colleges and universities. Candidates must rank in the top quarter of their graduating class.
Publications: Annual report; Informational brochure (including application guidelines).
Financial data: Year ended 08/31/2013. Assets, $4,435,587 (M); Expenditures, $310,935; Total giving, $278,510; Grants to individuals, 10 grants totaling $40,000 (high: $5,000, low: $2,500).
Type of support: Support to graduates or students of specific schools; Undergraduate support.
Application information: Application form required.
 Initial approach: Letter
 Deadline(s): Apr. 15

Additional information: Application forms available from high school guidance counselors. Interviews preferred, but not required. Application should include SAT scores.
EIN: 576018387

8452
Boyne Foundation
P.O. Box 1055
Sumter, SC 29151-1055
Contact: Kathryn Boyne Kearney, Pres.
E-mail: Boynefoundation@ftc-i.net; URL: http://boynefoundation.org/index.htm

Foundation type: Independent foundation
Purpose: Scholarships to students enrolled in accredited educational programs that provides training for health care and related services for the elderly.
Financial data: Year ended 08/31/2012. Assets, $1,870,335 (M); Expenditures, $136,331; Total giving, $93,000. Scholarships—to individuals amount not specified.
Fields of interest: Nursing school/education; Health care; Aging.
Type of support: Scholarships—to individuals.
Application information: Applications accepted. Application form required.
Initial approach: Letter or e-mail
Additional information: Application should include recommendations. Grants range from $1,000 to $5,000, and are paid directly to the educational institution on behalf of the students.
EIN: 203861451

8453
James F. Byrnes Foundation
P.O. Box 6781
Columbia, SC 29260-6781 (803) 254-9325
Contact: Kenya White, Exec. Secy.
FAX: (803) 254-9354;
E-mail: info@byrnesscholars.org; URL: http://www.byrnesscholars.org

Foundation type: Operating foundation
Purpose: Undergraduate scholarships to residents of SC who are high school seniors or college freshmen to attend a four-year college or university, and whose parent or parents are deceased.
Publications: Application guidelines; Informational brochure; Newsletter.
Financial data: Year ended 06/30/2011. Assets, $2,403,854 (M); Expenditures, $162,730; Total giving, $83,375.
Fields of interest: Higher education; Economically disadvantaged.
Type of support: Undergraduate support.
Application information: Applications accepted. Application form required. Application form available on the grantmaker's web site. Interview required.
Initial approach: Letter or telephone
Send request by: Mail
Deadline(s): Feb. 15
Final notification: Recipients announced in May
Applicants should submit the following:
1) Letter(s) of recommendation
2) Budget Information
3) Photograph
4) Class rank
5) Transcripts
6) ACT
7) SAT
8) Financial information

Additional information: Application should also include a brief autobiography including a description of educational and career objectives.
Program description:
Byrnes Scholarship: The scholarships are in the amount of approximately $3,250 each year and are renewable for a maximum of four years, contingent upon maintenance of adequate academic standing, personal involvement in the Byrnes Scholarship Program, and continuing need. Applicant must demonstrate financial need, a satisfactory scholastic record, at least a 2.5 GPA, and qualities of character, ability and enterprise that indicate a worthwhile contributor to society.
EIN: 576024756

8454
Dave Cameron Educational Foundation
P.O. Box 181
York, SC 29745-0181 (803) 684-4968

Foundation type: Independent foundation
Purpose: Scholarships to undergraduate students within the York, SC, area pursuing a degree in the agricultural field.
Financial data: Year ended 03/31/2013. Assets, $274,079 (M); Expenditures, $15,603; Total giving, $13,500; Grants to individuals, 9 grants totaling $13,500 (high: $2,000, low: $1,000).
Fields of interest: Agriculture.
Type of support: Undergraduate support.
Application information: Applications accepted. Application form required.
Deadline(s): None
Additional information: Application available upon request.
EIN: 237080657

8455
Carolina Children's Charity, Inc.
1064 Gardner Rd., Ste. 112B
Charleston, SC 29407-4922 (843) 769-7555
Contact: Sonya Beale, Exec. Dir.
FAX: (843) 501-2857;
E-mail: admin@carolinachildren.org; URL: http://www.carolinachildren.org

Foundation type: Public charity
Purpose: Specific assistance to individual patient for patient care, medical services and related activities for birth defects and childhood diseases in the Lowcountry, SC area.
Publications: Application guidelines.
Financial data: Year ended 09/30/2012. Assets, $1,445,256 (M); Expenditures, $459,095; Total giving, $219,190; Grants to individuals, totaling $219,190.
Fields of interest: Genetic diseases and disorders; Children.
Type of support: Grants for special needs.
Application information: Applications accepted. Application form required.
Additional information: Application must include financial information.
Program description:
Grants: The organization provides grants to support patient care, medical services, and related activities to children and families who have been diagnosed with birth defects and/or diseases. Eligible applicants must have a child who has been diagnosed with a birth defect and/or disease, be 18 years of age or younger, and reside in the Lowcountry area of SC (including Berkeley, Charleston, Colleton, and Dorchester counties)
EIN: 570878058

8456
Carolina Community Actions, Inc.
P.O. Box 933
Rock Hill, SC 29731-6993 (803) 329-5195
Contact: Walter Kellogg, Exec. Dir.

Foundation type: Public charity
Purpose: Financial assistance to indigent residents of SC who are enrolled in the Low-Income Home Energy Assistance Program.
Financial data: Year ended 09/30/2011. Assets, $3,560,883 (M); Expenditures, $11,532,069; Total giving, $1,911,650; Grants to individuals, totaling $1,911,650.
Fields of interest: Economically disadvantaged.
Type of support: Grants for special needs.
Application information:
Initial approach: Letter
Additional information: Contact the foundation for further information.
EIN: 570475466

8457
Central Carolina Community Foundation
2711 Middleburg Dr., Ste. 213
Columbia, SC 29204-2486 (803) 254-5601
FAX: (803) 799-6663;
E-mail: info@yourfoundation.org; URL: http://www.yourfoundation.org

Foundation type: Community foundation
Purpose: Scholarships to residents of Calhoun, Clarendon, Fairfield, Kershaw, Lee, Lexington, Newberry, Orangeburg, Richland, Saluda and Sumter counties, SC, for higher education.
Publications: Annual report; Financial statement; Informational brochure; Newsletter.
Financial data: Year ended 06/30/2013. Assets, $96,942,639 (M); Expenditures, $13,580,214; Total giving, $12,814,381. Scholarships—to individuals amount not specified.
Fields of interest: Higher education.
Type of support: Scholarships—to individuals.
Application information:
Initial approach: Application
Send request by: Mail or hand-deliver
Deadline(s): Mar. 17 for most scholarships
Applicants should submit the following:
1) SAR
2) Essay
3) Transcripts
4) Letter(s) of recommendation
Additional information: Each scholarship has its own unique eligibility requirements. See web site for additional information.
Program description:
Scholarships: The foundation manages various scholarship funds benefiting area college students. These scholarships provide educational opportunities for future generations.
EIN: 570793960

8458
Charleston County Human Services Commission, Inc.
1069 King St.
Charleston, SC 29403-3708 (843) 724-6760
Contact: Arnold Collins, Exec. Dir.
FAX: (843) 724-6787;
E-mail: gpringle@cchscom.com; URL: http://www.cchscom.com

Foundation type: Public charity
Purpose: Emergency assistance to low-income Berkeley, Charleston, and Dorchester Counties residents in SC meeting the program guidelines.

Assistance is limited to preventing termination of water and electric services. Help is also available for medication and food.

Financial data: Year ended 12/31/2011. Assets, $4,514,699 (M); Expenditures, $9,292,958; Total giving, $4,489,580; Grants to individuals, totaling $4,489,580.

Fields of interest: Housing/shelter, expense aid; Economically disadvantaged.

Type of support: In-kind gifts; Grants for special needs.

Application information:
  Initial approach: Letter
  Applicants should submit the following:
    1) Financial information
  Additional information: Contact foundation for eligibility criteria.

EIN: 570816782

8459
Charleston Scientific & Cultural Educational Fund

c/o Charlton Desaussure, Jr.
P.O. Box 340
Charleston, SC   29402-0340   (843) 722-3366

Foundation type: Independent foundation

Purpose: Grants to SC natives for scientific, cultural, or educational pursuits in Charleston, SC.

Financial data: Year ended 12/31/2011. Assets, $388,672 (M); Expenditures, $21,342; Total giving, $15,611; Grants to individuals, 8 grants totaling $15,611 (high: $2,400, low: $1,600).

Fields of interest: Education.

Type of support: Grants to individuals.

Application information: Applications accepted. Application form required.
  Deadline(s): Apr. 15
  Additional information: Application should include resume.

EIN: 576019987

8460
Chief's Athlete Scholarship Fund, Inc.

3112 Hermitage Dr.
Little River, SC   29566   (843) 902-3733

Foundation type: Public charity

Purpose: Scholarships to graduating high school seniors of North Myrtle Beach High School, SC for postsecondary education.

Financial data: Year ended 12/31/2011. Assets, $5,933 (M); Expenditures, $13,315; Total giving, $13,000; Grants to individuals, 3 grants totaling $13,000.

Fields of interest: Higher education.

Type of support: Undergraduate support.

Application information: Applications accepted.
  Initial approach: Letter
  Additional information: Funds are paid directly to the educational institution on behalf of the students.

EIN: 571029455

8461
Clemson Community Care, Inc.

105 Anderson Hwy.
Clemson, SC   29631-0271   (864) 653-4460
Contact: Karen Ellers, Exec. Dir.
FAX: (864) 654-5109;
E-mail: ccc@clemsoncommunitycare.org; Mailing address: P.O. Box 271, Clemson, SC 29633; E-mail for Karen Ellers: karenellers@clemsoncommunitycare.org, tel.:

(864)-653-4460 Ext. 107; URL: http://www.clemsoncommunitycare.org

Foundation type: Public charity

Purpose: Financial assistance to economically disadvantaged residents of Clemson County, SC, to help with rent, food, utilities, medical bills and other services.

Publications: Application guidelines.

Financial data: Year ended 12/31/2012. Assets, $506,695 (M); Expenditures, $723,770; Total giving, $572,282; Grants to individuals, totaling $572,282.

Fields of interest: Economically disadvantaged.

Type of support: Grants for special needs.

Application information: Applications accepted.
  Initial approach: Telephone
  Additional information: Some assistance may require an application. Contact the foundation for further guidelines and program information.

EIN: 570868065

8462
Clemson University Research Foundation

391 College Ave., Ste. 401
Clemson, SC   29631   (864) 656-0797
Contact: Casey Porto, Exec. Dir.
FAX: (864) 656-0474; E-mail: cporto@clemson.edu;
URL: http://www.clemson.edu/curf/

Foundation type: Public charity

Purpose: Funding to support the last critical step that will significantly increase the likelihood of commercialization of Clemson intellectual property. Any Clemson faculty member who has had interactions with CURF via the invention disclosure and patenting or copyright process is eligible to submit a proposal for the maturation of their already-disclosed intellectual property.

Financial data: Year ended 06/30/2012. Assets, $16,547,515 (M); Expenditures, $12,975,277; Total giving, $4,838,686.

Fields of interest: Engineering/technology; Engineering.

Type of support: Research.

Application information: Applications accepted. Application form required. Application form available on the grantmaker's web site.
  Initial approach: Proposal
  Deadline(s): June 20
  Applicants should submit the following:
    1) Proposal
  Additional information: For additional information, contact Lisa Perpall, Technology Commercialization Officer: eperpal@clemson.edu.

EIN: 570750000

8463
Clergy Society

(formerly Society for the Relief of the Widows, Orphans, Aged and Disabled Clergy Diocese of South Carolina)
c/o T. Grance Simons
223 Bennett St.
Mount Pleasant, SC   29464-5301   (843) 577-3096
Contact: T.L. Yates
Application address: 205 King St., Charleston, SC 29402, tel.: (843) 577-3096

Foundation type: Operating foundation

Purpose: Grants to clergy and their dependents or survivors, primarily in SC, for medical expenses, living expenses, and children's education.

Financial data: Year ended 12/31/2012. Assets, $1,842,890 (M); Expenditures, $64,385; Total giving, $58,560; Grants to individuals, 5 grants totaling $58,560 (high: $20,960, low: $4,600).

Fields of interest: Christian agencies & churches.

Type of support: Grants for special needs.

Application information: Applications accepted.
  Initial approach: Letter
  Deadline(s): None
  Additional information: Application must outline financial need.

EIN: 576021772

8464
Coastal Community Foundation of South Carolina

(formerly The Community Foundation Serving Coastal South Carolina)
635 Rutledge St., Ste. 201
Charleston, SC   29403   (843) 723-3635
Contact: George C. Stevens, C.E.O.
FAX: (843) 577-3671;
E-mail: info@coastalcommunityfoundation.org;
URL: http://www.coastalcommunityfoundation.org

Foundation type: Community foundation

Purpose: Scholarships primarily to residents of Berkeley, Charleston, Colleton and Dorchester counties, SC.

Publications: Application guidelines; Biennial report; Financial statement; Grants list; Informational brochure (including application guidelines); Newsletter; Occasional report.

Financial data: Year ended 06/30/2011. Assets, $154,468,810 (M); Expenditures, $17,711,955; Total giving, $9,881,331. Scholarships—to individuals amount not specified.

Fields of interest: Arts; Higher education; Scholarships/financial aid; Crime/law enforcement; Athletics/sports, academies; Athletics/sports, racquet sports; Athletics/sports, golf; Business/industry; Catholic agencies & churches; Minorities; African Americans/Blacks; Economically disadvantaged.

Type of support: Scholarships—to individuals; Graduate support; Undergraduate support.

Application information: Applications accepted. Application form required. Application form available on the grantmaker's web site.
  Initial approach: Application
  Send request by: Online
  Deadline(s): Mar. 18
  Applicants should submit the following:
    1) FAFSA
    2) Letter(s) of recommendation
    3) SASE
    4) ACT
    5) Essay
    6) Financial information
    7) GPA
    8) SAT
    9) Transcripts
  Additional information: See web site for a complete listing of scholarships.

Program description:
  Scholarships Funds: Scholarships offered through the foundation have been made possible by the generosity of donors who help students fund their post-secondary education. Scholarship funds within the foundation can be established to benefit students from particular geographic areas or schools, attending certain post-secondary institutions, or entering certain fields of study. Students apply to the program and, if eligible, can be awarded grants from one or more of these different funds. Scholarships are awarded to college-bound students and are based on character

and personality, involvement in extra-curricular and community activities, financial need, academics, aspirations, and ability to overcome obstacles. Awards range generally from $500 to $5,000. See web site for additional information.
EIN: 237390313

8465
Community Foundation of Greenville, Inc.
630 E. Washington St., Ste. A
Greenville, SC 29601 (864) 233-5925
Contact: Robert W. Morris, Pres.; For scholarships: Debbie Cooper, Dir., Donor Svcs.
Scholarship inquiry e-mail: dcooper@cfgreenville.org
FAX: (864) 242-9292;
E-mail: rmorris@cfgreenville.org; URL: http://www.cfgreenville.org

Foundation type: Community foundation
Purpose: Scholarships to graduating seniors of the Greenville, SC area for attendance at accredited colleges or universities.
Publications: Application guidelines; Annual report; Informational brochure; Newsletter; Program policy statement.
Financial data: Year ended 12/31/2012. Assets, $41,548,322 (M); Expenditures, $7,879,235; Total giving, $6,933,642.
Fields of interest: Higher education.
Type of support: Scholarships—to individuals.
Application information: Applications accepted. Application form required. Application form available on the grantmaker's web site.
Send request by: Online
Deadline(s): Varies
Additional information: Eligibility requirements vary per scholarship fund. Scholarship funds are paid directly to the educational institution on behalf of the student. See web site for complete scholarship listing.
EIN: 576019318

8466
Community Foundation of the Lowcountry
(formerly Hilton Head Island Foundation, Inc.)
4 Northridge Dr., Ste. A
P.O. Box 23019
Hilton Head Island, SC 29925-3019 (843) 681-9100
Contact: Denise K. Spencer, C.E.O.
FAX: (843) 681-9101;
E-mail: foundation@cf-lowcountry.org; URL: http://www.cf-lowcountry.org

Foundation type: Community foundation
Purpose: General welfare grants to residents of Beaufort, Colleton, Hampton and Jasper Counties, SC.
Publications: Application guidelines; Annual report; Financial statement; Grants list; Informational brochure; Informational brochure (including application guidelines); Newsletter.
Financial data: Year ended 06/30/2012. Assets, $57,525,194 (M); Expenditures, $5,922,592; Total giving, $4,234,331.
Type of support: Grants for special needs.
Application information: Applications accepted. Application form required.
Initial approach: Letter or telephone
Send request by: Applications should be sent by mail
Deadline(s): None
Final notification: Recipients notified within three months
EIN: 570756987

8467
J. B. Cornelius Foundation
18 Royal Oak Dr.
Greenwood, SC 29649-1313 (864) 229-7604
Contact: John L. Sherrill, Secy.-Treas.

Foundation type: Independent foundation
Purpose: Scholarships to financially needy female students attending a Methodist Church-supported college in NC.
Financial data: Year ended 04/30/2013. Assets, $1,870,500 (M); Expenditures, $124,428; Total giving, $97,000; Grants to individuals, totaling $97,000.
Fields of interest: Women.
Type of support: Support to graduates or students of specific schools.
Application information: Application form required.
Deadline(s): May 1
Additional information: Applications available through colleges.
EIN: 566060705

8468
Cox Foundation
c/o Cox Wood Preserving Co.
P.O. Box 1124
Orangeburg, SC 29116-1124 (803) 837-3782
Contact: Cathy C. Price, Dir.

Foundation type: Company-sponsored foundation
Purpose: Scholarships are granted to family members of full-time SC employees of Cox Industries, Inc., or related companies.
Financial data: Year ended 04/30/2013. Assets, $1,070,692 (M); Expenditures, $73,869; Total giving, $72,779; Grants to individuals, 21 grants totaling $72,779 (high: $4,000, low: $676).
Type of support: Employee-related scholarships.
Application information: Application form required.
Deadline(s): Jan. 31
Company name: Cox Wood Preserving
EIN: 570823753

8469
Cultural Council of Richland and Lexington Counties
930 Richland St.
Columbia, SC 29201-2329 (803) 779-3115
Contact: Norree Boyd-Wicks, Exec. Dir.
FAX: (803) 252-2787; E-mail: info@getcultured.org; E-mail for Norree Boyd-Wicks: norree@smartarts.info; URL: http://www.smartarts.info/

Foundation type: Public charity
Purpose: Grants to individual artists who are residents of Richland or Lexington counties, SC.
Publications: Application guidelines; Financial statement; Informational brochure; Newsletter; Program policy statement.
Financial data: Year ended 06/30/2012. Assets, $275,128 (M); Expenditures, $456,396; Total giving, $202,040.
Fields of interest: Film/video; Visual arts; Theater; Music; Literature; Arts.
Type of support: Seed money; Grants to individuals; Travel grants.
Application information: Application form required. Application form available on the grantmaker's web site.
Initial approach: Telephone or email
Deadline(s): Varies
Applicants should submit the following:
1) Resume
2) Proposal

3) Letter(s) of recommendation
Additional information: Unsolicited applications not accepted.
Program description:
Quarterly Grants for Individual Artists: This program provides grants to support an individual artistic project. Applicants are required to match grant funds with cash.
EIN: 570754328

8470
William B. & Lela P. Earle Scholarship Trust Fund
P.O. Box 40
Walhalla, SC 29691
Contact: John D. Ridley, Tr.
Application address: 140 Hawthorne Ln., Mountain Rest, SC 29664

Foundation type: Operating foundation
Purpose: Scholarships to individuals for attendance at four-year colleges and universities, who are from certain geographical areas in SC, and to those who are handicapped.
Financial data: Year ended 12/31/2012. Assets, $528,738 (M); Expenditures, $17,827; Total giving, $16,475; Grants to individuals, 2 grants totaling $16,475 (high: $12,990, low: $3,485).
Fields of interest: Higher education; Disabilities, people with.
Type of support: Scholarships—to individuals.
Application information: Applications accepted. Application form required.
Deadline(s): Apr. 15
EIN: 586384762

8471
Father-To-Father Project, Inc.
4731 Mixson Ave.
North Charleston, SC 29405-5111 (843) 744-2126

Foundation type: Public charity
Purpose: Financial assistance to indigent young men residing in North Charleston, SC, who have an absentee father.
Financial data: Year ended 09/30/2011. Assets, $38,138 (M); Expenditures, $302,526; Total giving, $7,966; Grants to individuals, totaling $7,966.
Fields of interest: Young adults, male.
Type of support: Grants for special needs.
Application information: Applications not accepted.
Additional information: Unsolicited requests for funds not considered or acknowledged.
EIN: 571121606

8472
The Fund for the Diaconate of the Episcopal Church in the United States
(formerly Retiring Fund for the Women in the Diaconate of the Episcopal Church)
c/o Allerton D. Marshall
33 Old Fort Dr.
Hilton Head Island, SC 29926-2601 (843) 689-6263
Contact: Edwm F. Hallenbeck, Pres.

Foundation type: Public charity
Purpose: Grants to individuals ordained to the ministry of the Episcopal Church who have insufficient funds for their needs in retirement or disability.

Financial data: Year ended 07/31/2012. Assets, $6,217,640 (M); Expenditures, $195,126; Total giving, $128,965; Grants to individuals, totaling $128,965.
Fields of interest: Protestant agencies & churches; Economically disadvantaged.
Type of support: Grants for special needs.
Application information: Contact fund for current application deadline/guidelines.
EIN: 237125960

8473
The Genevieve Mills Gallivan and Henry T. Mills, Jr. Educational Foundation
c/o BB&T Personal Trust, Judy Schoemer
P.O. Box 408
Greenville, SC 29602

Foundation type: Independent foundation
Purpose: Scholarships to members of First Presbyterian Church, Greenville, SC for undergraduate or seminary education.
Financial data: Year ended 12/31/2012. Assets, $669,770 (M); Expenditures, $45,341; Total giving, $35,557.
Fields of interest: Theological school/education.
Type of support: Undergraduate support.
Application information: Applications accepted. Application form required.
EIN: 576167639

8474
Gamecock Club of the University of South Carolina
1300 Rosewood Dr.
Columbia, SC 29208-0001 (803) 777-4276
FAX: (803) 777-1880;
E-mail: gamecockclub@sc.edu; URL: http://uscsports.cstv.com/boosters/scar-boosters.html

Foundation type: Public charity
Purpose: Financial support to student-athletes at the University of South Carolina. This aid is in the form of tuition fees, meal costs, medical costs, injury assistance, and other educational needs.
Publications: Annual report; Informational brochure.
Financial data: Year ended 06/30/2012. Assets, $13,068,575 (M); Expenditures, $13,802,190; Total giving, $8,584,178; Grants to individuals, totaling $8,584,178.
Fields of interest: Education.
Type of support: Undergraduate support.
Application information:
Initial approach: E-mail
Additional information: Contact the foundation for eligibility guidelines.
EIN: 576024939

8475
Gift of Life Trust Fund
22 Centre E.
4200 E. North St.
Greenville, SC 29615-2437 (864) 609-5270
Contact: Tracy Armstrong, C.E.O. and Exec. Dir.
FAX: (864) 609-5387;
E-mail: mblevins@donatelifesc.org; Toll-free tel.: (877) 277-4866; URL: http://www.donatelifesc.org

Foundation type: Public charity
Purpose: Scholarships to residents of SC whose family member was either an organ donor or a transplant recipient. Students can also become eligible if they are seeking a degree in the field of

medicine or social work. Financial assistance to residents of SC who are organ and tissue transplant patients, to help defray the cost of prescriptions and medical supplies.
Publications: Annual report; Newsletter.
Financial data: Year ended 12/31/2011. Assets, $188,404 (M); Expenditures, $190,309.
Fields of interest: Education; Health care, support services; Health care; Organ diseases.
Type of support: Scholarships—to individuals; Grants for special needs.
Application information:
Initial approach: Letter
Additional information: Contact fund for additional information.
EIN: 571052258

8476
Gleamns Human Resources Commission, Inc.
237 N. Hospital St.
P.O. Box 1326
Greenwood, SC 29648-1326 (864) 223-8434
Contact: Sandra Taylor, C.F.O.
FAX: (864) 223-9456;
E-mail: staylor@gleamnshrc.org; URL: http://www.gleamnshrc.org

Foundation type: Public charity
Purpose: Emergency assistance to low income families and individuals of Abbeville, Edgefield, Fairfield, Greenwood, Laurens, Lexington, McCormick, Newberry, Richland, and Saluda counties, SC with education, food, housing, energy and other special needs.
Publications: Newsletter.
Financial data: Year ended 03/31/2012. Assets, $8,912,234 (M); Expenditures, $30,115,598; Total giving, $6,272,151; Grants to individuals, totaling $6,272,151.
Fields of interest: Employment, services; Nutrition; Housing/shelter; Children/youth, services; Family services.
Type of support: Emergency funds; In-kind gifts.
Application information: Application is accepted for some assistance. Contact the organization for eligibility determination.
EIN: 570479691

8477
Greenville Tech Foundation, Inc.
P.O. Box 5616
Greenville, SC 29606-5616 (864) 250-8111
Contact: James C. Morton, Jr., Chair.
FAX: (864) 250-8544;
E-mail: greenvilletech@gvltec.edu; URL: http://www.gvltec.edu/foundation_scholarships/

Foundation type: Public charity
Purpose: Scholarships for students attending Greenville Technical College, SC, pursuing higher education.
Publications: Annual report.
Financial data: Year ended 06/30/2011. Assets, $36,021,074 (M); Expenditures, $4,457,054; Total giving, $170,212; Grants to individuals, totaling $170,212.
Fields of interest: Higher education.
Type of support: Scholarships—to individuals; Support to graduates or students of specific schools.
Application information: Applications accepted. Application form required.
Deadline(s): May 1
Applicants should submit the following:
1) Transcripts

2) Financial information
Additional information: Scholarships are awarded on the basis of need. Contact the financial aid office for additional application information.
EIN: 570565961

8478
Gregg-Graniteville Foundation, Inc.
P.O. Box 418
Graniteville, SC 29829 (803) 663-7552
Contact: Patricia H. Knight, Admin.
FAX: (803) 663-6435

Foundation type: Independent foundation
Purpose: Scholarships only for high school seniors of employees of Avondale Mills Plants in Graniteville, Vaucluse, or Warrenville, SC or Augusta, GA, or residents of Graniteville, Vaucluse, and Warrenville, SC.
Publications: Annual report.
Financial data: Year ended 12/31/2011. Assets, $15,224,200 (M); Expenditures, $830,183; Total giving, $56,500; Grants to individuals, 14 grants totaling $56,500 (high: $6,000; low: $1,500).
Type of support: Employee-related scholarships.
Application information: Applications accepted. Application form required.
Initial approach: Letter or telephone
Send request by: Mail
Copies of proposal: 1
Deadline(s): Four weeks prior to scheduled meeting
Final notification: Recipients notified one week after board meeting
Company name: Avondale Mills, Inc.
EIN: 570314400

8479
Habitat for Humanity of Horry County, Inc.
165 Co-Op Rd.
Myrtle Beach, SC 29588-7375 (843) 650-8815
Contact: Gail Olive, Exec. Dir.; Stephen Carver
FAX: (843) 650-8764;
E-mail: contact@habitatmb.org; Mailing address: P.O. Box 2492, Myrtle Beach, SC 29578-2492; URL: http://www.habitatmb.org

Foundation type: Public charity
Purpose: Assistance to deserving individuals and families of Horry county, SC with the construction of affordable homes.
Publications: Newsletter.
Financial data: Year ended 06/30/2012. Assets, $5,155,227 (M); Expenditures, $1,225,549; Total giving, $511,768; Grants to individuals, totaling $511,768.
Fields of interest: Housing/shelter, rehabilitation; Housing/shelter, home owners.
Type of support: Grants for special needs.
Application information: Applications accepted.
Additional information: Contact the organization for eligibility determination and additional information.
EIN: 570912014

8480
The Reese & Sis Hart Foundation
P.O. Box 860
Pawleys Island, SC 29585 (843) 907-9460
Contact: Craig M. Thomas, Dir.
Application address: 621 Crystal Ln., Murrells Inlet, SC 29576

Foundation type: Operating foundation

Purpose: Scholarships to individuals, primarily in SC, for higher education.
Financial data: Year ended 12/31/2012. Assets, $126,286 (M); Expenditures, $39,163; Total giving, $25,000; Grants to individuals, 3 grants totaling $25,000 (high: $20,000, low: $1,000).
Fields of interest: Higher education; Scholarships/ financial aid.
Type of support: Conferences/seminars; Postdoctoral support; Graduate support; Technical education support; Undergraduate support; Travel grants; Doctoral support.
Application information: Applications accepted. Application form required. Interview required.
  Deadline(s): Contact foundation for current application deadline
  Applicants should submit the following:
    1) Transcripts
    2) Letter(s) of recommendation
EIN: 582435805

8481
Hebrew Orphan Society
(formerly Hebrew Orphan Society of Charleston, SC)
P.O. Box 30011
Charleston, SC   29417-0011   (843) 556-6273
Contact: William Golod, Secy.-Treas.
Application address: 14 Nuffield Rd., Charleston, SC 29407

Foundation type: Independent foundation
Purpose: Scholarships for college bound students and residents, and financial assistance to individuals and families of SC.
Financial data: Year ended 12/31/2011. Assets, $1,430,533 (M); Expenditures, $113,914; Total giving, $95,100.
Fields of interest: Higher education; Economically disadvantaged.
Type of support: Scholarships—to individuals; Grants for special needs.
Application information: Unsolicited application not accepted.
EIN: 576034375

8482
The Ernest Hemingway Foundation, Inc.
(also known as The Hemingway Society)
46 Meredian Rd.
Beaufort, SC   29907-1404   (843) 521-4125
URL: http://hemingwaysociety.org

Foundation type: Public charity
Purpose: Prizes and incentive awards for the best first novel by an American published in the previous year.
Publications: Application guidelines; Newsletter.
Financial data: Year ended 12/31/2011. Assets, $393,832 (M); Expenditures, $34,723; Total giving, $11,000; Grants to individuals, totaling $11,000.
Fields of interest: Literature.
Type of support: Awards/grants by nomination only; Awards/prizes.
Application information: Application form required.
  Deadline(s): Varies
  Final notification: Recipients notified May 1
  Applicants should submit the following:
    1) Budget Information
    2) Proposal
    3) Letter(s) of recommendation
Program descriptions:
  Jim and Nancy Hinkle Travel Grants: This program provides funds to defray travel expenses for graduate students attending the foundation's biennial international conferences. Recipients must

be in good standing of the society, must currently be enrolled in a graduate degree program, and must be planning to present a paper at the conference.
  Pen/Hemingway Award: An $8,000 award is presented annually to a best new work of fiction author.
  Smith-Reynolds Award: Two $1,000 awards are given annually to support research and writing on the work and life of Ernest Hemingway. Awards are given to society members only.
  William P. Corrigan Fellowship for the Study of Hemingway and Cuba: A $1,000 award is available to Hemingway scholars (whether on the undergraduate, graduate, independent, or professorial rank), to support projects of any sort that explore Hemingway's Cuban connections.
EIN: 136195832

8483
Heritage Classic Foundation
71 Lighthouse Rd., Ste. 4200
Hilton Head Island, SC   29928-0244   (843) 671-2448
FAX: (843) 671-6738; Additional tel.: (843) 671-5755; toll-free tel.: (800) 234-1107;
URL: http://www.heritageclassicfoundation.com

Foundation type: Public charity
Purpose: Scholarships to graduating seniors at high schools in Beaufort County, SC.
Financial data: Year ended 12/31/2011. Assets, $3,314,455 (M); Expenditures, $11,299,641; Total giving, $1,263,147.
Type of support: Undergraduate support.
Application information: Applications accepted. Application form required. Application form available on the grantmaker's web site.
  Initial approach: Letter
  Send request by: Online
  Copies of proposal: 1
  Deadline(s): Jan. 12
  Final notification: Applicants notified within two months
  Applicants should submit the following:
    1) Transcripts
    2) SAT
    3) Letter(s) of recommendation
    4) GPA
    5) Financial information
    6) Essay
  Additional information: Application form available through high school counselors.
Program description:
  Scholar Program: Scholarships are available to graduating students from Beaufort County area high schools. Visit http://theheritagescholars.com/ for more information, including application guidelines.
EIN: 570835114

8484
Dick Horne Foundation
P.O. Box 306
Orangeburg, SC   29116-0306

Foundation type: Independent foundation
Purpose: Scholarships to financially needy residents of the trading area served by Horne Motors of Orangeburg and Calhoun counties, SC, for undergraduate education.
Financial data: Year ended 12/31/2011. Assets, $6,110,177 (M); Expenditures, $394,588; Total giving, $330,554.
Fields of interest: Education; Economically disadvantaged.
Type of support: Scholarships—to individuals; Grants for special needs.

Application information: Applications accepted.
  Initial approach: Letter
  Deadline(s): None
  Additional information: Assistance is based on need, character and ability. Application must include financial information and educational background.
EIN: 237015996

8485
IDCA Foundation
305 Asheton Lakes Way
Simpsonville, SC   29681   (202) 841-1538
Contact: Celestino R. Magpayo, Jr., Pres.
URL: http://www.idcafoundation.org/

Foundation type: Company-sponsored foundation
Purpose: Scholarships to residents of Greenville, SC for higher education.
Financial data: Year ended 12/31/2012. Assets, $85,198 (M); Expenditures, $54,931; Total giving, $0.
Type of support: Undergraduate support.
Application information: Applications not accepted.
  Additional information: Unsolicited requests for funds not considered or acknowledged.
EIN: 203128585

8486
Inman-Riverdale Foundation
P.O. Box 207
Inman, SC   29349-0207

Foundation type: Company-sponsored foundation
Purpose: Scholarships only to dependents of Inman Mills employees, SC.
Financial data: Year ended 11/30/2012. Assets, $2,056,109 (M); Expenditures, $652,002; Total giving, $598,779.
Type of support: Employee-related scholarships.
Application information: Applications not accepted.
  Additional information: Unsolicited requests for funds not considered or acknowledged.
Company name: Inman Mills
EIN: 576019736

8487
Kappa Beautillion, Inc.
P.O. Box 7522
Columbia, SC   29202-7522   (803) 606-8752
Contact: Ronald Drayton, C.F.O.
E-mail: info@kappabeautillioninc.org; URL: http:// www.kappasofcolumbiasc.com/ KappaBeautillion.asp

Foundation type: Public charity
Purpose: Scholarships to high school males, juniors and seniors of Midland, SC.
Publications: Annual report; Grants list.
Financial data: Year ended 06/30/2010. Assets, $9,728 (M); Expenditures, $12,453; Total giving, $5,175.
Fields of interest: Higher education; Young adults, male.
Type of support: Undergraduate support.
Application information: Applications accepted. Application form required.
  Additional information: Applicants must attend mandatory workshops.
EIN: 571004533

8488
Deacon Elijah Kelly, Sr. Scholarship
(formerly Deacon Elijah Kelly, Sr. Scholarship Fund)
117 Claude Bundrick Rd.
Blythewood, SC   29016

Foundation type: Operating foundation
Purpose: Scholarships primarily to SC residents for postsecondary education.
Financial data: Year ended 12/31/2012. Assets, $3,349 (M); Expenditures, $6,729; Total giving, $6,000; Grants to individuals, 3 grants totaling $6,000 (high: $2,000, low: $2,000).
Fields of interest: Higher education.
Type of support: Undergraduate support.
Application information: Applications not accepted.
Additional information: Unsolicited requests for funds not considered or acknowledged.
EIN: 570915180

8489
The Kennedy Foundation
(formerly Francis Nathaniel and Katheryn Padgett Kennedy Foundation)
P.O. Box 49
Laurens, SC   29360
Contact: Bev Kennedy
Application address: 301 Hillcrest Dr., Laurens, SC 29360

Foundation type: Independent foundation
Purpose: Student grants only to individuals preparing for full-time Christian service at the college or seminary level. Grants shall be made only to students who are from the South Carolina counties of Abbeville, Anderson, Cherokee, Greenville, Greenwood, Laurens, McCormick, Oconee, Pickens, Spartanburg, Union and York counties. Students from Laurens County shall be given first preference.
Financial data: Year ended 06/30/2013. Assets, $1,203,243 (M); Expenditures, $70,072; Total giving, $47,660; Grants to individuals, 10 grants totaling $31,651 (high: $4,000, low: $2,000).
Fields of interest: Theological school/education.
Type of support: Scholarships—to individuals.
Application information: Application form required.
Initial approach: Letter
Copies of proposal: 1
Deadline(s): June 30
Applicants should submit the following:
   1) Transcripts
   2) Letter(s) of recommendation
   3) Financial information
   4) Budget Information
EIN: 237347655

8490
Kershaw County Vocational Education Foundation, Inc.
P.O. Box 10
Lugoff, SC   29078-0010   (803) 438-4200
Contact: Charles B. Baxley, Chair. and Tr.

Foundation type: Independent foundation
Purpose: Scholarships to residents of Kershaw County, SC, for vocational study.
Financial data: Year ended 12/31/2012. Assets, $821,118 (M); Expenditures, $31,283; Total giving, $21,400; Grants to individuals, 18 grants totaling $18,500 (high: $2,000, low: $500).
Fields of interest: Vocational education.
Type of support: Technical education support.

Application information: Application form required.
Deadline(s): Contact foundation for application deadline.
Additional information: Application must include financial and educational information.
EIN: 570805522

8491
The Lucyle S. Love Foundation
24 Rainflower Dr.
Greenville, SC   29615-6729
Contact: D.R. Mcalister

Foundation type: Independent foundation
Purpose: Scholarships to high school, college, and graduate students to enable them to complete their education in the field of their choice.
Financial data: Year ended 12/31/2012. Assets, $1,952,432 (M); Expenditures, $248,317; Total giving, $195,823.
Fields of interest: Higher education.
Type of support: Scholarships—to individuals; Graduate support; Undergraduate support.
Application information: Application form required.
Initial approach: Letter
Deadline(s): None
Applicants should submit the following:
   1) Letter(s) of recommendation
   2) Transcripts
   3) Essay
   4) Financial information
Additional information: Application must also include employment history and personal references from individuals who are not related to the applicant. Eligible recipients must file their application with the selection commmittee. Children of members of the selection committee are not eligible to apply.
EIN: 570902382

8492
Lowcountry AIDS Services, Inc.
3574 Meeting Street Rd.
North Charleston, SC   29405-1933   (843) 747-2273
FAX: (843) 745-0431;
E-mail: Information@aids-services.com; Toll Free Tel. : (877)-874-0230; URL: http://www.aids-services.com

Foundation type: Public charity
Purpose: Financial assistance and support for eligible people with AIDS or HIV infection in the Charleston, SC area with rent, mortgage, utilities and other special needs.
Financial data: Year ended 12/31/2011. Assets, $1,054,461 (M); Expenditures, $1,175,118; Total giving, $299,029; Grants to individuals, totaling $299,029.
Fields of interest: AIDS, people with; Economically disadvantaged.
Type of support: Grants for special needs.
Application information: Financial assessment required.
EIN: 570905550

8493
Michele Malanga Foundation
10 Game Land Rd.
Bluffton, SC   29910

Foundation type: Independent foundation
Purpose: Scholarships to students attending the University of Basilicata, Italy.

Financial data: Year ended 05/31/2013. Assets, $67,361 (M); Expenditures, $62,526; Total giving, $61,435.
Type of support: Support to graduates or students of specific schools; Foreign applicants.
Application information: Applications accepted.
Additional information: Contact foundation for current application deadline/guidelines.
EIN: 516521243

8494
Miracle Hill Ministries, Inc.
P.O. Box 2546
Greenville, SC   29602-2546   (864) 268-4357
Contact: Reid Lehman, Pres. and C.E.O.
FAX: (864) 268-2283;
E-mail: mhmi@miraclehill.org; Toll-free tel.: (877) 558-4357; URL: http://www.miraclehill.org

Foundation type: Public charity
Purpose: Grants and scholarships to individuals and families of Upstate, SC who have been victimized by poverty, broken homes or other problems.
Publications: Annual report; Financial statement; Informational brochure; Newsletter.
Financial data: Year ended 06/30/2012. Assets, $21,123,552 (M); Expenditures, $11,248,975; Total giving, $412,218; Grants to individuals, totaling $412,218.
Fields of interest: Housing/shelter, temporary shelter; Economically disadvantaged.
Type of support: Scholarships—to individuals; Grants for special needs.
Application information: Applications accepted.
Initial approach: Letter
EIN: 570425826

8495
Alfred Moore Foundation
220 Mockingbird Hill Rd.
Landrum, SC   29356
Contact: C.L. Page, Jr., Chair.

Foundation type: Independent foundation
Purpose: Three four-year scholarships to graduating seniors of Chapman High School, SC, Byrnes High School, SC, and Crescent High School, SC.
Financial data: Year ended 12/31/2012. Assets, $3,001,388 (M); Expenditures, $182,825; Total giving, $150,000.
Fields of interest: Higher education.
Type of support: Support to graduates or students of specific schools; Undergraduate support.
Application information: Application form required.
Initial approach: Letter
Deadline(s): Mar. 31
Additional information: Application forms available from high schools.
EIN: 576018424

8496
Joseph R. Moss Educational & Charitable Trust
P.O. Box 299
York, SC   29745   (803) 684-3559

Foundation type: Independent foundation
Purpose: Scholarships to students of York, SC pursuing higher education.
Financial data: Year ended 08/31/2013. Assets, $1,226,496 (M); Expenditures, $78,622; Total giving, $74,500; Grants to individuals, 34 grants totaling $74,500 (high: $3,500, low: $1,000).
Fields of interest: Higher education.

Type of support: Undergraduate support.
Application information: Applications accepted. Application form required.
  Initial approach: Letter or telephone
  Deadline(s): None
  Additional information: Application forms are available upon request.
EIN: 576162069

8497
Mike Muth Basketball Scholarship Fund
c/o Dale Bell
2 Camelia Cir.
Williamston, SC   29697

Foundation type: Independent foundation
Purpose: College scholarships to students from Palmetto High School, Williamston, SC for attendance at educational institutions of higher learning.
Financial data: Year ended 12/31/2012. Assets, $72,354 (M); Expenditures, $4,600; Total giving, $4,500.
Fields of interest: Higher education.
Type of support: Support to graduates or students of specific schools.
Application information: Applications accepted.
  Initial approach: Letter
  Applicants should submit the following:
    1) Transcripts
    2) Essay
  Additional information: Application should also include letters of references.
EIN: 571019671

8498
NGA of SC Scholarship Foundation
132 Pickens St.
Columbia, SC   29201-4752   (803) 254-8456
E-mail: nginfo@ngasc.org

Foundation type: Public charity
Purpose: Scholarships to dependents of a National Guard member seeking an associate or undergraduate degree. Scholarships are also available to members of the National Guard seeking a graduate degree.
Financial data: Year ended 12/31/2011. Assets, $541,099 (M); Expenditures, $58,991; Total giving, $40,500; Grants to individuals, totaling $40,500.
Fields of interest: Military/veterans.
Type of support: Undergraduate support.
Application information:
  Initial approach: Letter
  Deadline(s): Jan. 31
EIN: 570878323

8499
Ocean View Memorial Foundation, Inc.
P.O. Box 1366
Myrtle Beach, SC   29578-1366   (843) 448-8334

Foundation type: Public charity
Purpose: Scholarships to graduating students who are residents of the Grand Stand community of South Carolina.
Financial data: Year ended 12/31/2012. Assets, $5,472,612 (M); Expenditures, $226,344; Total giving, $174,115; Grants to individuals, totaling $100,000.
Fields of interest: Higher education.
Type of support: Graduate support; Undergraduate support.

Application information: Applications accepted. Application form required.
  Additional information: Application should include GPA.
EIN: 570368086

8500
L. Arthur O'Neill, Jr. Education Fund
P.O. Box 1798
Sumter, SC   29151-2091
Contact: Vivian Brogdon
Application address: P.O. Box 2091, Sumter, SC 29151

Foundation type: Operating foundation
Purpose: Student loans to residents of Sumter County, SC, for full time attendance at SC colleges and universities.
Financial data: Year ended 04/30/2013. Assets, $2,251,952 (M); Expenditures, $61,168; Total giving, $0.
Fields of interest: Higher education.
Type of support: Student loans—to individuals.
Application information: Application form required.
  Deadline(s): Apr. 1 for summer school, May 1 fall term and Nov. 1 for spring term
  Applicants should submit the following:
    1) GPA
    2) Financial information
    3) SAR
    4) Transcripts
  Additional information: Application should also include character reference.
EIN: 237227009

8501
Palmetto Electric Trust
P.O. Box 820
Ridgeland, SC   29936-2644   (843) 726-5551
FAX: (843) 726-5632

Foundation type: Public charity
Purpose: Grants to economically disadvantaged individuals in the tri-county coastal Lowdown area of SC, for food, clothing, shelter, medical and educational costs.
Financial data: Year ended 12/31/2011. Assets, $340,088 (M); Total giving, $325,510; Grants to individuals, totaling $325,510.
Fields of interest: Economically disadvantaged.
Type of support: Scholarships—to individuals; Grants for special needs.
Application information: Application form required.
  Initial approach: Letter
  Additional information: Contact foundation for current application deadline/guidelines.
EIN: 570931978

8502
Rebecca C. Parsons Scholarship Foundation
P.O. Box 1550
Pawleys Island, SC   29585   (843) 237-9125
Contact: Robert D. Harper, Jr., Tr.

Foundation type: Operating foundation
Purpose: Scholarships to qualified high school seniors and graduates of Andrews High School and Waccamaw High School, SC.
Financial data: Year ended 12/31/2011. Assets, $5,033,577 (M); Expenditures, $97,892; Total giving, $58,000.
Fields of interest: Higher education.
Type of support: Scholarships—to individuals.

Application information:
  Initial approach: Essay
  Deadline(s): Apr. 1
EIN: 570990214

8503
Piedmont Care, Inc.
Wachovia Bldg., Intl. Ctr.
101 N. Pine St., Ste. 200
Spartanburg, SC   29302-1604   (864) 582-7773
Contact: Tracey L. Jackson, Exec. Dir.
FAX: (864) 582-8637;
E-mail: tracey@piedmontcare.org; Toll-free tel.: (866) 454-7773; URL: http://www.piedmontcare.org

Foundation type: Public charity
Purpose: Financial assistance to indigent individuals with HIV residing in Spartanburg, Union, and Cherokee counties, SC, for payment of utilities, housing, and medical bills.
Publications: Newsletter.
Financial data: Year ended 03/31/2012. Assets, $228,780 (M); Expenditures, $644,451; Total giving, $157,563; Grants to individuals, totaling $157,563.
Type of support: Grants for special needs.
Application information:
  Initial approach: Letter
  Additional information: Contact foundation for complete eligibility requirements.
EIN: 571036204

8504
Professional Tennis Registry Foundation
(also known as PTR Foundation)
P.O. Box 4739
Hilton Head Island, SC   29938-6754   (843) 785-7244
FAX: (843) 686-2033; E-mail: ptr@ptrtennis.org; Toll-free tel.: (800) 421-6289

Foundation type: Public charity
Purpose: Grants and scholarships to bring tennis to at-risk, needy, or handicapped youth and individuals.
Publications: Application guidelines; Annual report; Informational brochure; Newsletter.
Financial data: Year ended 03/31/2012. Assets, $380,299 (M); Expenditures, $41,154; Total giving, $6,608; Grants to individuals, totaling $6,608.
Fields of interest: Athletics/sports, racquet sports; Disabilities, people with.
Type of support: Grants to individuals; Scholarships—to individuals.
Application information: Applications accepted.
  Additional information: Contact foundation for complete eligibility requirements.
EIN: 942549724

8505
Rural Mission, Inc.
3429 Camp Care Rd.
Johns Island, SC   29455-7131   (843) 768-1720
FAX: (843) 768-7378;
E-mail: info@ruralmission.org; Mailing address: P.O. Box 235, Johns Island, SC 29457-0235; URL: http://www.ruralmission.org

Foundation type: Public charity
Purpose: Economic assistance to low-income families and migrant farm workers on the South Carolina Sea Islands of Johns, Wadmalaw, Yonges, and Edisto.

Financial data: Year ended 12/31/2011. Assets, $338,347 (M); Expenditures, $1,114,756; Total giving, $92,750; Grants to individuals, totaling $92,750. Subtotal for grants for special needs: grants totaling $92,750.
Fields of interest: Human services.
Type of support: Grants for special needs.
Application information: Contact the mission for additional guidelines.
Program descriptions:
  Crisis Assistance and Intervention: This program provides assistance through vouchers to those in dire need of food and emergency assistance with utility bills and rent, when funds are available.
  Hope for the Future: The organization provides assistance to college students in the from of funding for books, clothing, and transportation to and from local colleges and vocational schools.
EIN: 570519864

8506
Sherman College of Straight Chiropractic
P.O. Box 1452
Spartanburg, SC 29304-1452 (864) 578-8770
FAX: (864) 599-4860; Physical address: 2020 Springfield Rd., Spartanburg, SC 29316-7251, toll-free tel.: (800) 849-8771; URL: http://www.sherman.edu/default.asp

Foundation type: Public charity
Purpose: Scholarships to straight chiropractic students based on financial need.
Financial data: Year ended 12/31/2011. Assets, $11,686,867 (M); Expenditures, $5,990,297; Total giving, $303,525; Grants to individuals, totaling $303,525.
Fields of interest: Medical school/education.
Type of support: Scholarships—to individuals.
Application information: Applications accepted.
  Additional information: Contact college for application guidelines.
EIN: 237242844

8507
Jean and Verne Smith Charitable Trust
119 Peachtree Dr.
Greer, SC 29606-6286 (864) 942-1599
Contact: Nancy Lewellyn
tel.: (864) 942-1599

Foundation type: Independent foundation
Purpose: Scholarships to individuals for continuing their education at an institution of higher learning.
Financial data: Year ended 12/31/2011. Assets, $86,955 (M); Expenditures, $36,031; Total giving, $32,148.
Fields of interest: Education.
Type of support: Undergraduate support.
Application information: Applications accepted. Application form required.
  Initial approach: Letter or telephone
  Deadline(s): None
  Additional information: Application must include personal and financial need information, educational background, work experience, extracurricular activities, desire for education and career goals, and basis of worthiness and of scholarship.
EIN: 586404187

8508
Robert L. Smith, Jr. Memorial Education Fund
6171 Crabtree Rd.
Columbia, SC 29206 (252) 753-5138
Contact: Allison Turnage
Application address: c/o Farmville Central High School, P.O. Box 209, Farmville, NC 27828-0209

Foundation type: Independent foundation
Purpose: Scholarships to graduates of Farmville Central High School, NC who have been accepted at one of the state accredited colleges or universities.
Financial data: Year ended 12/31/2011. Assets, $105,236 (M); Expenditures, $4,682; Total giving, $3,500; Grants to individuals, 4 grants totaling $3,500 (high: $1,000, low: $500).
Type of support: Support to graduates or students of specific schools; Undergraduate support.
Application information:
  Initial approach: Letter
  Deadline(s): Apr. 1
EIN: 561709175

8509
Society for the Relief of Families of Deceased & Disabled Indigent Members of the Medical Profession of the State of South Carolina
16 Gibbes St.
Charleston, SC 29401 (843) 722-1554
Contact: Patrick Kelly M.D.

Foundation type: Operating foundation
Purpose: Financial assistance to families of deceased or disabled South Carolina physicians who are in financial need.
Financial data: Year ended 12/31/2012. Assets, $803,456 (M); Expenditures, $60,530; Total giving, $35,500; Grants to individuals, 5 grants totaling $35,500 (high: $11,000, low: $6,000).
Fields of interest: Association; Disabilities, people with; Economically disadvantaged.
Type of support: Grants for special needs.
Application information: Applications not accepted.
  Additional information: The Benevolent Committee evaluates potential recipients throughout the year. There is no requirement that the families live in SC.
EIN: 576021204

8510
Sonoco Products Company Contributions Program
1 N. 2nd St.
Hartsville, SC 29550-3305
URL: http://www.sonoco.com/sustainability/socialresponsibility.aspx

Foundation type: Corporate giving program
Purpose: Scholarships to children of U.S. employees of Sonoco for higher education.
Publications: Corporate giving report.
Fields of interest: College; University.
Type of support: Employee-related scholarships.
Application information: Applications not accepted.
  Additional information: Contributes only to children of U.S. Sonoco employees; unsolicited requests for funds not considered or acknowledged.

Program description:
  Sonoco Scholarship Program: Sonoco annually awards ten $2,000 college scholarships to the children of U.S. employees renewable for an additional three years for a total award of $8,000.
Company name: Sonoco Products Company

8511
South Carolina Junior Golf Foundation
P.O. Box 286
Irmo, SC 29063-0286 (803) 732-9311
Contact: Harrison F. Lathrop, Exec. Dir.
FAX: (803) 732-7406; E-mail: jquick@scgolf.org; E-Mail for Harrison F. Lathrop : happ@scgolf.org; URL: http://scjgf.org/

Foundation type: Public charity
Purpose: Scholarships to junior golfers primarily in SC based on financial need and academic achievement.
Financial data: Year ended 12/31/2012. Assets, $1,196,003 (M); Expenditures, $460,114; Total giving, $227,509; Grants to individuals, totaling $52,509.
Fields of interest: Athletics/sports, golf.
Type of support: Undergraduate support.
Application information: Applications accepted.
  Initial approach: Letter
  Additional information: Application should include letters of recommendation.
EIN: 571021847

8512
South Carolina Nurses Foundation, Inc.
1821 Gadsden St.
Columbia, SC 29201-2344 (803) 252-4781
Contact: Kelly Pabst R.N., M.S.N., V.P.
FAX: (803) 779-3870;
E-mail: leeaw1@windstream.net; E-mail for Marilyn Brady: marilyn.brady@tridenttech.edu; URL: http://www.scnursesfoundation.org

Foundation type: Public charity
Purpose: Scholarships and grants to nursing students of SC, to promote high standards of health care.
Publications: Annual report; Informational brochure; Occasional report.
Financial data: Year ended 12/31/2011. Assets, $478,506 (M); Expenditures, $886,277; Total giving, $834,720; Grants to individuals, totaling $834,720.
Fields of interest: Nursing school/education; Research; Health care.
Type of support: Research; Scholarships—to individuals; Awards/prizes; Undergraduate support.
Application information: Applications accepted. Application form required. Application form available on the grantmaker's web site.
  Deadline(s): Varies
  Additional information: The foundation has currently suspended its Ruth A. Nicholson Award, Healthy Communities Grant, Appalachian District Nurses Association Scholarship, and Evelyn Johnson Entrekin Scholarship. Contact foundation for current status of scholarship programs.
Program descriptions:
  Appalachian District Nurses Association Scholarship: The foundation awards an annual scholarship for an associate-degree, baccalaureate, or higher-degree nursing student who either attend school in one of the four South Carolina Appalachia counties (Anderson, Greenville, Pickens, or Oconee), or is a permanent resident of one of those counties.

Evelyn Johnson Entrekin Scholarship: The foundation provides scholarships to students pursuing a baccalaureate degree in nursing.

Healthy Communities Grant: This grant award will be given to a qualified nurse to assist in his or her continued professional development.

Mary Ellen Hatfield School Nursing Scholarship: Scholarships are awarded to a registered nurse and a licensed practical nurse who are currently practicing nursing in a South Carolina school setting, and who wish to further their education.

Palmetto Gold Undergraduate Scholarships: This scholarship is presented annually to an outstanding student in each of South Carolina's university undergraduate nursing programs.

Renatta S. Loquist Scholarship for Graduate Nursing Education: This scholarship is presented to an outstanding student currently enrolled in a graduate nursing program in a South Carolina school or university.

Ruth A. Nicholson Research Grant: This grant is awarded to a nurse researcher in South Carolina, to support research on a nursing-related topic.

Virginia C. Phillips Scholarships: Scholarships are awarded to undergraduate and graduate students committed to pursuing a career in community/public health nursing.

EIN: 570772080

8513
South Carolina Press Association Foundation

P.O. Box 11429
Columbia, SC   29211-1429   (803) 750-9561

Foundation type: Public charity
Purpose: Scholarships and internships to South Carolina college students pursuing a career in print journalism.
Financial data: Year ended 09/30/2011. Assets, $894,711 (M); Expenditures, $23,757; Total giving, $16,375; Grants to individuals, totaling $16,375.
Fields of interest: Journalism school/education.
Type of support: Internship funds; Scholarships—to individuals.
Application information: Applications accepted. Application form required.
> *Deadline(s):* Jan.
> *Additional information:* Scholarships and internships are awarded to college juniors and seniors. Applicant must attend a SC college. Selection is based on grades, participation in journalistic activities in college and recommendations of faculty members. Financial need may be considered.

EIN: 570735348

8514
The Spartanburg County Foundation

424 E. Kennedy St.
Spartanburg, SC   29302-1916   (864) 582-0138
Contact: Troy M. Hanna, C.E.O.; For grants: Ashley Thomason, Prog. Assoc.
FAX: (864) 573-5378; E-mail: info@spcf.org; Additional e-mail: thanna@spcf.org; Grant inquiry e-mail: athomason@spcf.org; URL: http://www.spcf.org

Foundation type: Community foundation
Purpose: Scholarships to students of Spartanburg County, SC for attendance at Converse College, Wofford College, Spartanburg Community College, Spartanburg Methodist College, USC Upstate and the Spartanburg Day School, SC.

Publications: Application guidelines; Annual report (including application guidelines); Informational brochure; Newsletter.
Financial data: Year ended 12/31/2012. Assets, $109,237,666 (M); Expenditures, $10,850,318; Total giving, $8,696,555. Scholarships—to individuals amount not specified.
Fields of interest: Higher education.
Type of support: Scholarships—to individuals; Support to graduates or students of specific schools.
Application information: Applications accepted. Application form required.
> *Additional information:* Applications available through local high school guidance offices.

EIN: 570351398

8515
The Springs Close Foundation, Inc.

(formerly Springs Foundation, Inc.)
951 Market St., Ste. 205
Fort Mill, SC   29708-6529   (803) 548-2002
Contact: Angela H. McCrae, Pres.
FAX: (803) 548-1797;
E-mail: amccrae@springsfnd.com; Lancaster, SC, office address: 201 W. Gay St., Lancaster, SC 29720, tel.: (803) 286-2197, fax: (803) 416-4626; Chester, SC, office address: 109 Gadsden St., Chester, SC 29706, tel.: (803) 581-7874, fax: (803) 581-2431; URL: http://www.thespringsclosefoundation.org

Foundation type: Independent foundation
Purpose: Student loans to residents of Lancaster County or the townships of Fort Mill and Chester, SC, for undergraduate study, or medical or dental school.
Publications: Application guidelines; Annual report; Annual report (including application guidelines); Grants list.
Financial data: Year ended 12/31/2012. Assets, $41,344,751 (M); Expenditures, $1,568,189; Total giving, $1,115,166.
Type of support: Student loans—to individuals; Graduate support; Undergraduate support.
Application information: Applications accepted. Application form required. Application form available on the grantmaker's web site. Interview required.
> *Initial approach:* Letter or telephone
> *Send request by:* Mail
> *Copies of proposal:* 1
> *Deadline(s):* May 1 and Dec. 1
> *Final notification:* Applicants notified one month after deadline
> *Applicants should submit the following:*
> 1) Essay
> 2) ACT
> 3) GPA
> 4) Letter(s) of recommendation
> 5) SAT
> 6) Transcripts

Program description:
Leroy Springs Student Loan Program: Provides interest-free loans of up to $3,000 per year toward undergraduate education and $4,000 a year toward medical and dental schools. Participants must live in, or parents must work in, Lancaster County, Chester, or Fort Mill, SC, and students must attend four-year colleges or universities in SC. Interest-free loans of up to $1,000 are available to students attending York Technical College; same restrictions apply. An additional book allowance of $500 is available to those who qualify.

EIN: 570426344

8516
Strive, Inc.

P.O. Box 23371
Hilton Head Island, SC   29925-3371

Foundation type: Operating foundation
Purpose: Scholarships to individuals who participated in STRIVE during their high school years, in Hilton Head, SC.
Publications: Newsletter.
Financial data: Year ended 06/30/2012. Assets, $90,447 (M); Expenditures, $4,179; Total giving, $3,950; Grants to individuals, 2 grants totaling $3,950 (high: $3,600, low: $350).
Type of support: Technical education support; Undergraduate support.
Application information:
> *Initial approach:* Letter
> *Additional information:* Contact foundation for application guidelines.

EIN: 570935388

8517
George E. Tucker Educational and Charitable Trust

P.O. Box 181
York, SC   29745-0181   (803) 684-4968

Foundation type: Independent foundation
Purpose: Scholarships to graduating high school seniors from the York, SC area pursuing higher education.
Financial data: Year ended 11/30/2012. Assets, $540,335 (M); Expenditures, $27,975; Total giving, $25,550; Grants to individuals, 21 grants totaling $25,550 (high: $1,600, low: $750).
Fields of interest: Higher education.
Type of support: Scholarships—to individuals; Undergraduate support.
Application information: Applications accepted. Application form required.
> *Deadline(s):* None
> *Applicants should submit the following:*
> 1) Financial information
> 2) Transcripts
> *Additional information:* Application should also include recent tax returns.

EIN: 576103971

8518
United Way of Greenville County, Inc.

105 Edinburgh Ct.
Greenville, SC   29607-2529   (864) 467-3333
Contact: Ted Hendry, Pres.
FAX: (864) 467-3535;
E-mail: info@unitedwaygc.org; URL: http://www.unitedwaygc.org/

Foundation type: Public charity
Purpose: Grants for food, clothing, and shelter to indigents in Greenville County, SC.
Publications: Application guidelines; Annual report.
Financial data: Year ended 12/31/2011. Assets, $25,246,754 (M); Expenditures, $14,372,766; Total giving, $8,856,216; Grants to individuals, totaling $85,771.
Fields of interest: Economically disadvantaged.
Type of support: Grants for special needs.
Application information:
> *Initial approach:* Letter
> *Additional information:* Contact foundation for eligibility criteria.

EIN: 570362066

8519
The West Foundation Inc.
c/o Shelton W. Bosley
P.O. Box 643
Camden, SC 29020-0643 (803) 425-1115
Contact: Tammy C. Hornsby, Exec. Dir.

Foundation type: Independent foundation

Purpose: Scholarships to students attending public and private colleges and universities in the SC, area.

Financial data: Year ended 05/31/2013. Assets, $405,689 (M); Expenditures, $57,764; Total giving, $29,750; Grant to an individual, 1 grant totaling $4,500.

Fields of interest: Higher education.

Type of support: Scholarships—to individuals.

Application information: Applications accepted.
  Initial approach: Letter
  Deadline(s): June 30
  Additional information: Applicant must demonstrate need.

EIN: 237405238

SOUTH DAKOTA

8520
L. A. Amundson Scholarships, Inc.
c/o Barbara J. Hegelund
P.O. Box 1270
Sioux Falls, SD   57101-1270   (605) 335-1508

Foundation type: Independent foundation
Purpose: Scholarships to MN, MT, and ND high school graduates pursuing careers in health care, business, commerce, or technical training who reside in Benson, Byron, Canby, Detroit Lakes, Henning, Lake Benton, Sanborn or Sleepy Eye, MN; Beulah or Robinson, ND; or Fairview, MT.
Financial data: Year ended 12/31/2012. Assets, $6,489,214 (M); Expenditures, $273,211; Total giving, $250,500.
Fields of interest: Business school/education; Health care.
Type of support: Undergraduate support.
Application information: Application form required.
  Deadline(s): Mar. 15
  Additional information: Application should include a letter of acceptance from accredited college or vocational school, official transcript, two letters of recommendation, an essay under 500 words describing applicant's goals, and copy of parents' 1040 form to be considered for financial need. Incomplete applications will not be considered.
EIN: 411692528

8521
Black Hills Area Community Foundation
825 St. Joseph St., 3rd Fl.
P.O. Box 231
Rapid City, SD   57709
Contact: Regina Q. Jahr, Exec. Dir.
E-mail: bhacf@rushmore.com; URL: http://bhacf.org/

Foundation type: Community foundation
Purpose: Scholarships to area students of Black Hills, SD pursuing training or educational opportunities.
Publications: Annual report.
Financial data: Year ended 12/31/2012. Assets, $11,014,247 (M); Expenditures, $910,727; Total giving, $359,776; Grants to individuals, 7 grants totaling $6,500.
Fields of interest: Higher education.
Type of support: Scholarships—to individuals; Undergraduate support.
Application information: Applications accepted. Application form required. Application form available on the grantmaker's web site.
  Initial approach: Application
  Send request by: Mail
  Deadline(s): Spring
  Applicants should submit the following:
    1) Transcripts
    2) Letter(s) of recommendation
    3) Essay
  Additional information: Each available scholarship has its own unique set of eligibility criteria and application guidelines. See web site for a complete listing.
EIN: 363608635

8522
Black Hills Workshop Foundation
3650 Range Rd.
P.O. Box 2104
Rapid City, SD   57709-2104   (605) 343-4550
E-mail: drosby@bhws.com; URL: http://www.bhws.com/

Foundation type: Public charity
Purpose: Assistance to individuals of Rapid City, SD with disabilities for their medical, social and recreational needs. Scholarships for the staff for continuing education and training.
Financial data: Year ended 12/31/2011. Assets, $17,251,385 (M); Expenditures, $523,501; Total giving, $155,236; Grants to individuals, totaling $141,379.
Fields of interest: Education; Disabilities, people with.
Type of support: Scholarships—to individuals; Grants for special needs.
Application information: Applications accepted.
  Additional information: Contact the foundation for eligibility determination.
EIN: 460363653

8523
Brookings Foundation
c/o Kurt Osborne
1028 7th Ave.
Brookings, SD   57006-1312   (605) 274-6012
Contact: Tom Yseth, Pres.

Foundation type: Public charity
Purpose: Assistance to individuals in need in the Brookings, SD area. Postsecondary scholarships for students showing scholastic merit and academic promise.
Financial data: Year ended 03/31/2012. Assets, $1,174,998 (M); Expenditures, $890,596; Total giving, $876,180; Grants to individuals, totaling $182,415.
Fields of interest: Higher education; Human services.
Type of support: Emergency funds; Scholarships—to individuals.
Application information: Contact the foundation for additional guidelines.
EIN: 460342366

8524
Clausen Family Foundation
685 Indian Wells Ct.
Dakota Dunes, SD   57049-5121

Foundation type: Company-sponsored foundation
Purpose: Scholarships to individuals of SD for postsecondary education.
Financial data: Year ended 12/31/2012. Assets, $932,348 (M); Expenditures, $62,631; Total giving, $60,500; Grants to individuals, totaling $10,500.
Fields of interest: Higher education; Education.
Type of support: Scholarships—to individuals.
Application information: Applications accepted.
  Initial approach: Letter
  Send request by: Mail
  Deadline(s): May 15
Program description:
  Clausen Family Scholarship Program: The foundation awards $1,500 scholarships to individuals for postsecondary education. The program is administered by Scholarship America.
EIN: 331158977

8525
William & Ruth Cozard Educational Scholarship Trust
500 E. Norway St.
P.O. Box 1306
Mitchell, SD   57301-1306   (675) 995-7906
Contact: Jean Koehler

Foundation type: Independent foundation
Purpose: Student loans to graduates of Chamberlain High School, SD, for undergraduate study.
Financial data: Year ended 12/31/2012. Assets, $122,189 (M); Expenditures, $31,229; Total giving, $25,000; Grants to individuals, 14 grants totaling $25,000 (high: $2,000, low: $1,500).
Fields of interest: Higher education.
Type of support: Student loans—to individuals; Support to graduates or students of specific schools; Undergraduate support.
Application information: Application form required.
  Initial approach: Letter
  Deadline(s): June 1
  Applicants should submit the following:
    1) Transcripts
    2) Financial information
  Additional information: Application should also include a copy of applicant's, spouse's, or parents' most recent tax return.
EIN: 466039141

8526
Delta Dental Philanthropic Fund
P.O. Box 1157
Pierre, SD   57501-1157   (605) 224-0909
Contact: Scott Jones, Pres.
E-mail: sales@deltadentalsd.com; Toll Free tel. : (800)-627-3961; URL: http://www.deltadentalsd.com/

Foundation type: Public charity
Purpose: Loan repayment for young SD dentists who agree to see a certain percentage of Medicaid patients in their practice and/or work on one of Delta Dental's mobile dental units.
Financial data: Year ended 12/31/2011. Assets, $7,582,114 (M); Expenditures, $2,454,689; Total giving, $569,242; Grants to individuals, totaling $274,839.
Fields of interest: Dental school/education; Dental care.
Type of support: Grants to individuals; Loans—to individuals.
Application information: Applications accepted. Application form required. Application form available on the grantmaker's web site.
  Initial approach: Letter
  Send request by: Mail
  Deadline(s): Apr. 1 and Sept. 1
  Final notification: Applicants notified June 1 and Oct. 1
  Applicants should submit the following:
    1) Essay
    2) Transcripts
    3) Letter(s) of recommendation
  Additional information: Application must also include verification that the employer dentist gives the applicant permission to complete program requirements and documentation of outstanding dental school loans.
EIN: 911776857

8527
Doolittle Memorial Scholarship Trust
1224 3rd St. S.
Aberdeen, SD 57401
Application address: c/o Aberdeen Central High School, 2200 S. Roosevelt St., Aberdeen, SD 57401-8526

Foundation type: Independent foundation
Purpose: Scholarships to graduates of an Aberdeen, SD public school, who attended an Aberdeen public high school for at least two years and enrolled in an accredited four-year college or university.
Financial data: Year ended 12/31/2011. Assets, $88,255 (M); Expenditures, $5,961; Total giving, $3,590; Grants to individuals, 5 grants totaling $3,590 (high: $1,545, low: $250).
Fields of interest: Higher education.
Type of support: Scholarships—to individuals.
Application information: Applications accepted. Application form required.
  Deadline(s): May 15
EIN: 466091497

8528
Blanche Doolittle Private Foundation
c/o First Bank Trust & Financial Svcs.
P.O. Box 1347
Sioux Falls, SD 57101-1347   (605) 978-1129

Foundation type: Independent foundation
Purpose: Scholarships to high school graduates of Sioux Falls, SD, for higher education.
Financial data: Year ended 12/31/2011. Assets, $276,031 (M); Expenditures, $18,576; Total giving, $15,000; Grants to individuals, 6 grants totaling $15,000 (high: $2,500, low: $2,500).
Fields of interest: Higher education.
Type of support: Support to graduates or students of specific schools; Undergraduate support.
Application information: Applications accepted. Application form required.
  Deadline(s): Mar. 15
  Additional information: Contact the foundation for additional application guidelines.
EIN: 466056120

8529
Baron & Emilie Dow Home Inc
P.O. Box 5953
Sioux Falls, SD 57117-5953   (605) 336-1490
Contact: Ralph Jenson
Application address: c/o Ralph Jenson, 1000 N. Lake, Sioux Falls, SD 57104, tel.: (605) 336-1490

Foundation type: Independent foundation
Purpose: General welfare assistance to financially needy residents of Dow Rummel Village, SD.
Financial data: Year ended 12/31/2011. Assets, $1,174,064 (M); Expenditures, $73,444; Total giving, $66,000; Grant to an individual, 1 grant totaling $66,000.
Fields of interest: Economically disadvantaged.
Type of support: Grants to individuals.
Application information: Applications accepted.
  Initial approach: Letter
  Deadline(s): None
EIN: 466018386

8530
First Peoples Fund
P.O. Box 2977
Rapid City, SD 57709-2977   (605) 348-0324
Contact: Lori Pourier, Pres.
FAX: (605) 348-6594;
E-mail: info@firstpeoplesfund.org; URL: http://www.firstpeoplesfund.org

Foundation type: Public charity
Purpose: Grants and fellowships to Native American artists.
Publications: Application guidelines; Newsletter.
Financial data: Year ended 12/31/2011. Assets, $783,161 (M); Expenditures, $761,191; Total giving, $120,127; Grants to individuals, totaling $109,427.
Fields of interest: Visual arts; Performing arts; Literature; Native Americans/American Indians.
Type of support: Program development; Fellowships.
Application information: Applications accepted.
  Send request by: Mail or online
  Deadline(s): Sept. 1 for Cultural Capital, and Artist in Business Leadership
  Additional information: See web site for additional guidelines.
Program descriptions:
  Artists in Business Leadership Program: The program cultivates entrepreneurial artists to a small business level (consistent and reliable income) where business concepts are understood and applied. This is a one-year self-directed program that provides artists with a $5,000 grant, and is supported by individualized professional development training, and working capital funds to strengthen their marketing strategies. Applicants must be in mid-career (five plus years) in their experience in marketing their art at Indian art markets, galleries, and have wholesale experience. Artists must also be members of a Northern Great Plains Tribe located in South Dakota, North Dakota, Montana, Wyoming, Western Dakota of Minnesota, Nebraska, the Eastern Plateau region of Idaho, Oregon, and Washington, a tribe from the Great Lakes Region (Minnesota, Michigan, or Wisconsin), a tribe belonging to the U.S. Eastern Seaboard states, an Alaskan tribe, or Hawaiian Native. Affiliated Canadian First Nations artist applicants are eligible.
  Cultural Capital Program: This program provides up to seven artists per year the opportunity to further their important cultural work in their respective communities with a grant of $5,000. The program is designed to support previous year Community Spirit Award recipients, to engage and reinforce their unique cultural contributions to their communities. The recipients of this fellowship grant are 'master' artists who have ten or more years creating art and who are grounded in the rich cultural heritage of their Tribal Nations.
EIN: 820583682

8531
Dorothy D. Graham Scholarship Fund
c/o First Bank Trust
P.O. Box 1347
Sioux Falls, SD 57101-1347   (605) 575-7400
Contact: Robin Aden, Trust Off.
Application address: c/o Wells Fargo Bank, Trust Dept., Attn.: Nancy Eichacker, 101 N. Phillips Ave., Sioux Falls, SD 57117

Foundation type: Independent foundation
Purpose: Scholarships to high school graduates primarily of SD, for higher education.

Financial data: Year ended 12/31/2011. Assets, $232,276 (M); Expenditures, $15,109; Total giving, $11,486; Grants to individuals, 11 grants totaling $5,750 (high: $750, low: $500).
Fields of interest: Higher education.
Type of support: Scholarships—to individuals.
Application information: Applications accepted. Application form required.
  Initial approach: Letter or telephone
  Deadline(s): None
  Additional information: Application form available upon request.
EIN: 466034811

8532
Walter & Frances Green Charitable Trust
c/o Dan Leikvold
320 S. Main St.
Lead, SD 57754

Foundation type: Independent foundation
Purpose: Scholarships to high school seniors at Lead/Deadwood High School, Lead, SD, for study at colleges or vocational/technical schools.
Financial data: Year ended 12/31/2012. Assets, $1,293,416 (M); Expenditures, $88,021; Total giving, $74,100; Grants to individuals, 25 grants totaling $45,500 (high: $4,000, low: $500).
Fields of interest: Vocational education; Higher education.
Type of support: Support to graduates or students of specific schools; Technical education support; Undergraduate support.
Application information: Applications accepted. Application form required.
  Applicants should submit the following:
    1) Letter(s) of recommendation
    2) Transcripts
    3) Essay
  Additional information: Application must also include a list of extracurricular activities, special awards, and for vocational/technical students, work history.
EIN: 466096446

8533
The Hatterscheidt Foundation Inc.
c/o Dacotah Bank Trust
P.O. Box 1210
Aberdeen, SD 57402-1210
Application address: c/o Tyler DeBoer, 204 S. 1st St., P.O. Box 849, Aberdeen, SD 57402-0849, tel.: (605) 229-8223

Foundation type: Independent foundation
Purpose: Scholarships to high school graduates who are residents of South Dakota, except for scholarships to the two schools in North Dakota.
Financial data: Year ended 12/31/2012. Assets, $4,436,799 (M); Expenditures, $298,153; Total giving, $232,000.
Fields of interest: Higher education.
Type of support: Support to graduates or students of specific schools; Undergraduate support.
Application information: Applications accepted. Application form required.
  Deadline(s): None
  Additional information: Application is available from the foundation, Aberdeen Central and Roncalli High Schools, or the college or university the student plans to attend.
EIN: 466012543

8534
Howard Memorial Fund
404 S. Lincoln St.
P.O. Box 1456
Aberdeen, SD   57402-1456   (605) 225-1000
Contact: Carlyle Richards, Secy.-Treas.

Foundation type: Independent foundation
Purpose: Scholarships to students from Brown County, SD, who attend college in SD, or to students attending Presentation College or Northern State University, SD.
Financial data: Year ended 12/31/2012. Assets, $810,629 (M); Expenditures, $66,936; Total giving, $57,500; Grants to individuals, totaling $42,500.
Fields of interest: Higher education.
Type of support: Scholarships—to individuals; Undergraduate support.
Application information:
  Deadline(s): Apr. 1
  Additional information: Unsolicited requests for funds not considered or acknowledged.
EIN: 466014133

8535
Louie & Frank Kramer Educational Trust
500 E. Norway St.
P.O. Box 1306
Mitchell, SD   57301-1306   (605) 995-7906
Contact: Jean Koehler, Trust Off., First Dakota National Bank

Foundation type: Independent foundation
Purpose: Student loans to residents of Chamberlain, SD.
Financial data: Year ended 12/31/2012. Assets, $42,319 (M); Expenditures, $25,230; Total giving, $21,000; Grants to individuals, 12 grants totaling $21,000 (high: $2,000, low: $1,500).
Type of support: Student loans—to individuals.
Application information: Applications accepted. Application form required.
  Additional information: Application must include transcripts and tax returns.
EIN: 510190074

8536
Don & Marcella McCormick Scholarship Fund
c/o First Bank Trust
P. O. Box 1347
Sioux Falls, SD   57108   (605) 978-1129

Foundation type: Independent foundation
Purpose: Scholarships to high school students of Lake county, SD who have a B average or above for attendance at colleges or universities.
Financial data: Year ended 12/31/2011. Assets, $219,423 (M); Expenditures, $14,477; Total giving, $11,000; Grants to individuals, 29 grants totaling $11,000 (high: $600, low: $300).
Fields of interest: Higher education.
Type of support: Scholarships—to individuals.
Application information: Applications accepted. Application form required.
  Deadline(s): May 15
  Additional information: Applications provided upon request.
EIN: 466105117

8537
Native American Heritage Association
12085 Quaal Rd.
Black Hawk, SD   57718-9862   (605) 341-9110
Contact: David G. Myers, Pres.
FAX: (605) 341-9113; E-mail: info@naha-inc.org;
Additional address (Rapid City address): P.O. Box 512, Rapid City, SD 57709-0512; additional address (Front Royal address): 830-F John Marshall Hwy., Front Royal, VA 22630-3743, tel.: (540) 636-1020, fax: (540) 636-1464; URL: http://www.naha-inc.org

Foundation type: Public charity
Purpose: Financial and non-cash assistance to Native Americans living on and off the tribal reservations in South Dakota and Wyoming with food, clothing, transportation, affordable and temporary housing assistance, and other emergency needs.
Publications: Newsletter.
Financial data: Year ended 08/31/2012. Assets, $20,684,461 (M); Expenditures, $36,236,830; Total giving, $32,303,396; Grants to individuals, totaling $32,303,396.
Fields of interest: Native Americans/American Indians; Economically disadvantaged.
Type of support: In-kind gifts; Grants for special needs.
Application information: Contact the association for eligibility determination.
EIN: 460414390

8538
Sioux Falls Area Community Foundation
200 N. Cherapa Pl.
Sioux Falls, SD   57103   (605) 336-7055
Contact: Candy Hanson, C.E.O.; For grants: Patrick Gale, Prog. Off.
FAX: (605) 336-0038; E-mail: chanson@sfacf.org;
Letter of inquiry e-mail: pgale@sfacf.org;
URL: http://www.sfacf.org

Foundation type: Community foundation
Purpose: Scholarships primarily to students from the Sioux Falls, SD, area, and secondarily to northwest IA, and southeast MN area residents to attend postsecondary schools.
Publications: Application guidelines; Annual report; Financial statement; Grants list; Newsletter.
Financial data: Year ended 06/30/2012. Assets, $86,778,796 (M); Expenditures, $12,087,517; Total giving, $10,917,172; Grants to individuals, 136 grants totaling $226,103.
Fields of interest: Vocational education; Natural resources; Athletics/sports, training; Business/industry; Christian agencies & churches; Protestant agencies & churches; Native Americans/American Indians.
International interests: Norway.
Type of support: Scholarships—to individuals.
Application information: Application form required. Application form available on the grantmaker's web site.
  Initial approach: Contacting college financial aid office or high school counselor's office for scholarships
  Send request by: Mail
  Deadline(s): Varies
  Additional information: Application should include a proposal.
EIN: 311748533

8539
John E. Solem Scholarship Trust
P.O. Box 5186
Sioux Falls, SD   57117-5186   (605) 335-5182
Application addresses: c/o Baltic High School, Attn.: Leonard Bettnemg, 500 3rd St., Baltic, SD 57003, tel.: (605) 529-5466; c/o Dell Rapids High School, Attn.: George Henry, 1216 N. Garfield Ave., Dell Rapids, SD 57002, tel.: (605) 428-5473; c/o Garretson High School, Attn.: Clarence Kooistra, 505 2nd St., Garretson, SD 57030; tel.: (605) 594-3452

Foundation type: Independent foundation
Purpose: Scholarships to high school graduates of Baltic, Dell Rapids, and Garretson, SD, for postsecondary education.
Financial data: Year ended 12/31/2011. Assets, $119,976 (M); Expenditures, $6,121; Total giving, $2,600; Grants to individuals, 7 grants totaling $2,600 (high: $500, low: $100).
Fields of interest: Higher education.
Type of support: Support to graduates or students of specific schools; Undergraduate support.
Application information: Applications accepted. Application form required. Interview required.
  Deadline(s): Apr. 1
  Applicants should submit the following:
    1) Photograph
    2) Transcripts
    3) SAT
    4) ACT
  Additional information: Application should also include two references.
EIN: 466010949

8540
South Dakota Community Foundation
1714 North Lincoln Ave.
P.O. Box 296
Pierre, SD   57501   (605) 224-1025
Contact: Stephanie Judson, Pres.
FAX: (605) 224-5364;
E-mail: stephj16@sdcommunityfoundation.org;
Additional tel.: (800) 888-1842; URL: http://www.sdcommunityfoundation.org

Foundation type: Community foundation
Purpose: Undergraduate scholarships to graduates of SD high schools for higher education.
Publications: Application guidelines; Annual report; Financial statement; Grants list; Informational brochure; Newsletter; Program policy statement.
Financial data: Year ended 12/31/2011. Assets, $128,325,460 (M); Expenditures, $5,217,040; Total giving, $4,230,715; Grants to individuals, totaling $215,163.
Fields of interest: Higher education.
Type of support: Undergraduate support.
Application information: Applications accepted. Application form required.
  Initial approach: Telephone
  Deadline(s): None
EIN: 460398115

8541
South Dakota Humanities Council
1215 Trail Ridge Rd., Ste. A
Brookings, SD   57006-4130   (605) 688-6113
Contact: Sherry DeBoer, Exec. Dir.
FAX: (605) 688-4531;
E-mail: info@sdhumanities.org; E-mail for Sherry DeBoer: sherry.deboer@sdstate.edu, tel. for Sherry de Boer: (605) 688-6114; URL: http://sdhumanities.org

Foundation type: Public charity
Purpose: Grants for scholars researching topics relevant to South Dakota culture and heritage. Grants for teachers to learn about south Dakota's American Indian Culture and history.
Publications: Application guidelines; Annual report; Biennial report (including application guidelines); Grants list; Informational brochure; Newsletter.
Financial data: Year ended 10/31/2012. Assets, $2,020,239 (M); Expenditures, $746,312; Total giving, $236,817.
Fields of interest: Cultural/ethnic awareness; Humanities.
Type of support: Grants to individuals.
Application information: Applications accepted.
Initial approach: Application
Send request by: Online
Deadline(s): Jan. 30 for Research Grants, Sept. 30 for Teachers Grant
Additional information: Mini grant funding is temporarily unavailable at this time. See web site for additional guidelines.
Program description:
Grants: Grants are available in four categories: discussion programs (funding for public presentations such as conferences, lectures, festivals, and symposiums); media programs (incorporating the use of mass media, such as web sites, books, exhibits, documentary films, and radio programs); research programs (awarded to scholars researching relevant to South Dakota culture and heritage, including travel associated with research); and humanities institutes for teachers (providing an intensive one-week institute designed for teachers to learn about South Dakota's American Indian culture and history). Two types of grants will be made available: mini-grants (of $1,000 or less), and major grants (greater than $1,000). Eligible applicants include any South Dakota-based non-profit organization, institution, or community group interested in promoting the humanities.
EIN: 460316222

8542
South Dakota State University Foundation
815 Medary Ave.
P. O. Box 525
Brookings, SD   57007-0499   (605) 697-7475
Contact: Steve Erpenbach, Pres. and C.E.O.
FAX: (605) 697-5641;
E-mail: info@sdsufoundation.org; Toll-free tel.: (888) 747-7378; E-mail For Steve Erpenbach: steve.erpenbach@sdsufoundation.org;
URL: http://www.sdsufoundation.org

Foundation type: Public charity
Purpose: Scholarships to students attending South Dakota State University, SD pursuing higher education.
Financial data: Year ended 12/31/2011. Assets, $144,963,532 (M); Expenditures, $29,468,783; Total giving, $23,399,918. Scholarships—to individuals amount not specified.
Fields of interest: Higher education.
Type of support: Scholarships—to individuals; Support to graduates or students of specific schools.
Application information: Applications not accepted.
Additional information: Scholarships are only for students attending SD State University. Unsolicited requests for funds not considered or acknowledged.
EIN: 460273801

8543
Leland & Lucille Strahl Educational Trust
P.O. Box 1210
Aberdeen, SD   57402-1210   (605) 472-0425
Contact: Leland Strahl
Application address: 26 W. 6th Ave., Apt. 306, Redfield, SD 57469-1165

Foundation type: Operating foundation
Purpose: Undergraduate scholarships to graduates of Redfield and Northwestern school districts, SD.
Financial data: Year ended 06/30/2012. Assets, $475,029 (M); Expenditures, $24,597; Total giving, $19,000; Grants to individuals, 19 grants totaling $19,000 (high: $1,000, low: $1,000).
Type of support: Support to graduates or students of specific schools; Undergraduate support.
Application information: Applications accepted. Application form required.
Initial approach: Letter
EIN: 460412852

8544
Tessier Family Foundation, Inc.
420 S. Pierre St.
P.O. Box 998
Pierre, SD   57501   (605) 224-7392
Contact: Greg Litton
Application address: Bank West

Foundation type: Independent foundation
Purpose: Scholarships to residents of the upper midwest for continuing education at institutions of higher learning.
Financial data: Year ended 12/31/2012. Assets, $1,293,899 (M); Expenditures, $64,181; Total giving, $53,000; Grants to individuals, 9 grants totaling $22,500 (high: $2,500, low: $2,500).
Fields of interest: Higher education.
Type of support: Scholarships—to individuals.
Application information: Applications accepted. Application form required.
Deadline(s): Mar. 1
Additional information: Application should include two letters of recommendation and a brief narrative describing yourself and role in anticipated field of endeavor.
EIN: 203160090

8545
The Glenn E. & Eleanor E. Ullyot Educational Trust
c/o Dacotah Bank
P.O. Box 1210
Aberdeen, SD   57402-1210   (605) 225-5611

Foundation type: Independent foundation
Purpose: Scholarships primarily to Clark residents first, and then to other residents of Clark county, SD.
Financial data: Year ended 12/31/2012. Assets, $144,693 (M); Expenditures, $8,097; Total giving, $6,300; Grants to individuals, 4 grants totaling $6,300 (high: $3,000, low: $300).
Fields of interest: Higher education.
Type of support: Undergraduate support.
Application information: Applications accepted.
Initial approach: Letter
Deadline(s): None
Additional information: Applicant must be a current high school graduate.
EIN: 460355003

8546
Watertown Community Foundation
211 E. Kemp Ave.
P.O. Box 116
Watertown, SD   57201-0116   (605) 882-3731
Contact: Jan DeBerg, Exec. Dir.
FAX: (605) 753-5731;
E-mail: assistant@watertowncommunityfoundation. org; URL: http://
www.watertowncommunityfoundation.org

Foundation type: Community foundation
Purpose: Scholarships to Watertown, SD high school graduates for postsecondary education.
Publications: Annual report (including application guidelines); Informational brochure; Newsletter.
Financial data: Year ended 12/31/2012. Assets, $10,122,925 (M); Expenditures, $683,922; Total giving, $450,946; Grants to individuals, 32 grants totaling $195,452.
Fields of interest: Education.
Type of support: Scholarships—to individuals.
Application information: Recommendations are made to the foundation board by school officials at the students' respective schools.
EIN: 460350319

8547
Westendorf Family Foundation
c/o Neal W. Westendorf
600 Stevens Pt. Dr., Ste. 115
Dakota Dunes, SD   57049

Foundation type: Independent foundation
Purpose: Scholarships to graduates of Onawa School District, IA for higher education.
Financial data: Year ended 10/31/2012. Assets, $590,136 (M); Expenditures, $40,378; Total giving, $31,520; Grants to individuals, 15 grants totaling $30,000 (high: $2,000, low: $2,000).
Fields of interest: Higher education.
Type of support: Scholarships—to individuals.
Application information: Applications not accepted.
Additional information: Unsolicited requests for funds not considered or acknowledged.
EIN: 426373031

8548
Yellow Jacket Foundation, Inc.
c/o Black Hills State Univ.
1200 Univ. Ave., Unit 9506
Spearfish, SD   57799-9673   (605) 642-6385
FAX: (605) 642-6845;
E-mail: stevemeeker@bhsu.edu; URL: http://
www.bhsu.edu/Alumni/
TheYellowJacketFoundation/tabid/143/
Default.aspx

Foundation type: Public charity
Purpose: Scholarships to student athletes at Black Hills State University, SD.
Publications: Annual report; Informational brochure.
Financial data: Year ended 12/31/2011. Assets, $54,139 (M); Expenditures, $578,650; Total giving, $290,000; Grants to individuals, totaling $290,000.
Fields of interest: Higher education; Athletics/ sports, school programs.
Type of support: Scholarships—to individuals; Support to graduates or students of specific schools.
Application information: Unsolicited requests for funds not considered or acknowledged.
EIN: 510151319

TENNESSEE

8549
4-C's Foundation
(also known as 4 C's Foundation)
294 Cleveland St.
Crossville, TN 38555-4854
Contact: Fran Young, Pres.
Application address: 660 Stanley St., Crossville, TN
38555, tel.: (931) 484-6194

Foundation type: Company-sponsored foundation
Purpose: Scholarships to graduates of Cumberland
County High School, or Stone Memorial High School
both in Crossville, TN.
Financial data: Year ended 09/30/2012. Assets,
$11,670 (M); Expenditures, $14,375; Total giving,
$14,225; Grants to individuals, 20 grants totaling
$14,225 (high: $1,000, low: $75).
Fields of interest: Higher education.
Type of support: Support to graduates or students
of specific schools.
Application information: Applications accepted.
Application form required.
 Deadline(s): Apr. 1
 Additional information: A completed 4-C
  scholarship application should be submitted.
EIN: 721586790

8550
The A.I.M. Center, Inc.
472 W. Martin Luther King Blvd.
Chattanooga, TN 37404-3138 (423) 624-4800
Contact: Ginger Storrar, Research Dir.
FAX: (423) 648-9135;
E-mail: ashley@aimcenterinc.org; URL: http://
www.aimcenterinc.org/

Foundation type: Public charity
Purpose: Financial assistance to indigent residents
of the metropolitan Chattanooga, TN, area who
have mental illnesses.
Publications: Annual report; Informational
brochure; Newsletter.
Financial data: Year ended 06/30/2012. Assets,
$7,950,764 (M); Expenditures, $1,798,829.
Fields of interest: Mentally disabled.
Type of support: Grants for special needs.
Application information:
 Initial approach: Letter
 Additional information: Contact the center for
  further information.
EIN: 581718368

8551
Acts Outreach Ministries Inc.
6045 Century Oaks Dr.
Chattanooga, TN 37416 (423) 899-6830
Contact: Anthony Scales, Dir.

Foundation type: Independent foundation
Purpose: Scholarships to individuals of TN, who are
under age 23, for Christian based activity.
Financial data: Year ended 12/31/2011. Assets,
$15,420 (M); Expenditures, $35,656; Total giving,
$35,656.
Fields of interest: Christian agencies & churches.
Type of support: Scholarships—to individuals.
Application information: Applications accepted.
Application form required.
 Deadline(s): 60 days prior to activity

Additional information: Activity brochure or flyer
  must be attached to the application.
EIN: 010751210

8552
Adams Family Foundation
P.O. Box 909
Paris, TN 38242 (731) 642-2940
Contact: David E. Sullivan, Dir.
Application address: 1101 E. Wood St., Paris TN
38242

Foundation type: Independent foundation
Purpose: Financial assistance for indigent
residents of Paris, TN for emergency expenses.
Financial data: Year ended 12/31/2012. Assets,
$225,526 (M); Expenditures, $1,754; Total giving,
$1,000; Grant to an individual, 1 grant totaling
$1,000.
Type of support: Grants for special needs.
Application information: Applications not
accepted.
 Additional information: Unsolicited requests for
  funds not considered.
EIN: 205007846

8553
Aid to Distressed Families of Appalachian Counties, Inc.
(also known as ADFAC)
P.O. Box 5963
Oak Ridge, TN 37831-5963 (865) 425-0256
Contact: Annie Cacheiro, Exec. Dir.
FAX: (865) 481-3822; Mailing address: P.O. Box
5953, Oak Ridge, TN 37831-5953; URL: http://
www.adfac.org

Foundation type: Public charity
Purpose: Emergency financial assistance to
residents of Anderson, County, and the City of Oak
Ridge TN, to help with utility, rent, medicine,
transportation and short-term food. Housing
assistance provided to residents of Anderson,
Campbell, Claiborne, Morgan, Roane and Scott
counties in east, TN, and Whitley County, KY.
Publications: Annual report; Newsletter.
Financial data: Year ended 12/31/2011. Assets,
$2,114,998 (M); Expenditures, $1,520,424; Total
giving, $1,029,396; Grants to individuals, totaling
$1,029,396.
Fields of interest: Human services; Economically
disadvantaged.
Type of support: Grants for special needs.
Application information: Applications not
accepted.
 Additional information: Applicants are screened
  to determine the most appropriate form of aid.
  Assistance is based on basic shelter needs
  and emergency situations.
EIN: 581727751

8554
Alpha Omicron Pi Foundation
(formerly Alpha Omicron Pi Philanthropic
Foundation)
5390 Virginia Wy.
Brentwood, TN 37027-7529 (615) 370-0920
Contact: Barbie Chadwick, Exec. Dir.
FAX: (615) 370-4424;
E-mail: foundation@alphaomicronpi.org; E-Mail for
Barbie Chadwick: bchadwick@alphaomicronpi.org;
URL: http://www.aoiifoundation.org

Foundation type: Public charity

Purpose: Scholarships to collegiate and alumnae
members of Alpha Omicron Pi. Grants to
economically disadvantaged members of Alpha
Omicron Pi to help them through times of financial
crisis. Research grants in the field of arthritis to
further efforts for improving the lives of those with
arthritis.
Publications: Annual report; Biennial report; Grants
list; Informational brochure.
Financial data: Year ended 06/30/2012. Assets,
$5,553,157 (M); Expenditures, $1,043,675; Total
giving, $559,835; Grants to individuals, totaling
$124,594.
Fields of interest: Students, sororities/fraternities;
Arthritis research; Women.
Type of support: Research; Scholarships—to
individuals; Grants for special needs.
Application information: Applications accepted.
Application form required.
 Deadline(s): Mar. 1 for scholarships
 Additional information: Contact foundation for
  current application guidelines.
Program descriptions:
 Diamond Jubilee Scholarships: Scholarships are
 awarded to collegiate and alumnae members who
 exhibit academic excellence as well as dedication
 to serving the community and Alpha Omicron Pi.
 Yearly awards are given in installments based on
 recipient's school semester schedules.
 Education and Training Grants: Educational,
 leadership, and programming grants provide
 opportunities for women in AOII to gain important
 leadership skills, strengthen career achievements,
 enhance personal strengths, and stress the
 importance of today's women serving as positive
 role models for future AOII's.
 Ruby Fund: The fund helps sisters in time of
 extreme financial need when no other resources are
 available for support. All requests and awards
 remain confidential and are handled by the Ruby
 Fund Committee. Senior collegians may be
 considered for fund assistance, although alumnae
 are the main recipients.
EIN: 581343315

8555
Alumni Achievement Awards, Inc.
7201 Shallowford Rd., Ste. 200
Chattanooga, TN 37421-2780 (423) 308-1855
Contact: Melanie Litchfield
E-mail: info@alumniawards.org; URL: http://
alumniawards.org

Foundation type: Operating foundation
Purpose: Awards by nomination only to
accomplished individuals who have attended an
Adventist school and have made global impacts in
their professions and communities. Also, awards by
nomination only to Adventist teachers who have
brought dedication and talent to their classrooms.
Financial data: Year ended 06/30/2013. Assets,
$131,084 (M); Expenditures, $990,551; Total
giving, $545,000; Grants to individuals, 20 grants
totaling $40,000 (high: $2,000, low: $2,000).
Fields of interest: Education.
Type of support: Awards/grants by nomination only;
Awards/prizes.
Application information: Applications accepted.
Application form required. Application form
available on the grantmaker's web site.
 Initial approach: Letter
 Deadline(s): Oct. 31
 Additional information: See web site for
  nomination guidelines and eligibility criteria.
EIN: 592413171

8556

American Association for Cancer Support, Inc.

2210 Country Brook Ln.
Knoxville, TN 37921-2847 (865) 368-2022
Contact: Jula Connatser, Pres.
E-mail: info@americancancersupport.org; Toll-free
tel.: (855) 622-6237; URL: http://
americancancersupport.com/

Foundation type: Public charity
Purpose: Financial assistance to cancer patients in the U.S. to aid with critical need items.
Publications: Annual report; Financial statement.
Financial data: Year ended 12/31/2011. Assets, $24,433 (M); Expenditures, $134,869; Total giving, $80,081; Grants to individuals, totaling $2,662.
Fields of interest: Cancer.
Type of support: Grants for special needs.
Application information: Applications accepted. Application form required. Application form available on the grantmaker's web site.
Send request by: Mail or e-mail
Additional information: Application form must be completed by the patient. The diagnosis verification form must be signed by a medical professional.
Program descriptions:
Cancer Care Card Program: This program is a streamlined method of helping cancer patients financially. The association pre-programs the card with a specific dollar amount, and is then mailed to cancer patients. They can use the card to purchase medicines, pay for co-pay or purchase other needed items anytime they need it.
Cancer Care Package Program: These packages are created to offer quick and sustaining aid. Cancer Care Packages include supplies such as hand sanitizers, toothbrushes, blankets, over the counter medications, nutritional drinks, and body lotion assortments, all of which will help alleviate the individual's and families' struggles during this difficult period.
EIN: 275005215

8557

Appalachian Mountain Project Access

809 S.Roan St.
P.O. Box 973
Johnson City, TN 37601 (423) 232-6700
Contact: Aubrey Everhart, Exec. Dir.
FAX: (423) 232-6707;
E-mail: info@projectaccesseasttn.org; URL: http://
www.projectaccesseasttn.org/

Foundation type: Public charity
Purpose: Emergency assistance to uninsured individuals in need of medical care throughout northeastern TN.
Financial data: Year ended 06/30/2012. Assets, $135,653 (M); Expenditures, $2,811,541; Total giving, $2,659,693; Grants to individuals, totaling $2,659,693.
Fields of interest: Health care; Economically disadvantaged.
Type of support: Grants for special needs.
Application information:
Initial approach: Telephone
Additional information: Applicant must send a referral form to the foundation from the physician or provider.
EIN: 262102040

8558

AutoZone, Inc. Corporate Giving Program

123 S. Front St.
Memphis, TN 38103-3607 (901) 495-6500
E-mail: community.relations@autozone.com;
Application address for matching gifts: AutoZone Matching Gift Prog., P.O. Box 2198, Dept. 8014, Memphis, TN 38101.; URL: http://
www.autozoneinc.com/about_us/
community_relations/index.html

Foundation type: Corporate giving program
Purpose: College scholarships to the children or dependants of AutoZone and ALLDATA associates who have excelled throughout their high school years.
Publications: Application guidelines.
Fields of interest: Higher education.
Type of support: Employee-related scholarships.
Application information: Application form required.
Initial approach: Letter
Additional information: See web site for further program information.
Program description:
AutoZone Scholarships: AutoZone annually awards fifteen $3,000 college scholarships to the children or dependents of AutoZone associates. Eligible recipients must have at least one year of service and have demonstrated academic achievement, leadership, school activity, and community service.

8559

John & Ina Berkshire Educational Operating Foundation

6901 Sherwood Dr.
Knoxville, TN 37919-7468 (865) 583-0502
Contact: Michael K. Hatcher, Pres. and Dir.

Foundation type: Operating foundation
Purpose: Scholarships to seniors graduating from Sevier County, TN, high schools.
Financial data: Year ended 12/31/2011. Assets, $508,504 (M); Expenditures, $36,058; Total giving, $24,000; Grants to individuals, 16 grants totaling $24,000 (high: $1,500, low: $1,500).
Type of support: Support to graduates or students of specific schools; Undergraduate support.
Application information: Applications accepted. Application form required.
Deadline(s): May 30
EIN: 582004367

8560

The Bootstraps Foundation, Inc.

(formerly The Bootstraps Foundation of the Kiwanis Club of Nashville, Inc.)
P. O. Box 159220
Nashville, TN 37215-9220 (615) 577-7644
Contact: Joe White, Chair.
E-mail: info@bootstraps.org; URL: http://
www.bootstraps.org

Foundation type: Public charity
Purpose: Scholarships by nomination only to high school seniors in Davidson, Robertson, Rutherford, Cheatham, Sumner, Wilson and Williamson counties, TN, who have coped with difficulties, problems, or obstacles and are still successful students.
Financial data: Year ended 12/31/2011. Assets, $167,102 (M); Expenditures, $60,232; Total giving, $49,000.
Type of support: Awards/grants by nomination only; Undergraduate support.

Application information: Applicants are chosen by the faculty and principal of each school.
EIN: 621336039

8561

Polly Boyd Scholarship Fund

c/o The Honors Course, Inc.
P.O. Box 23176
Chattanooga, TN 37422-3176
Contact: Joel W. Richardson, Jr., Tr.
Application address: 201 W. Main St., Ste. 205, Chattanooga, TN 37408-1137

Foundation type: Independent foundation
Purpose: Scholarships to employees or caddies of The Honors Course, Inc., in TN.
Financial data: Year ended 12/31/2012. Assets, $605,100 (M); Expenditures, $56,346; Total giving, $56,000; Grants to individuals, 14 grants totaling $56,000 (high: $4,000, low: $4,000).
Fields of interest: Athletics/sports, golf.
Type of support: Employee-related scholarships.
Application information: Application form required. Interview required.
Deadline(s): None
Company name: Honors Course, Incorporated, The
EIN: 626184352

8562

Boys & Girls Clubs of Middle Tennessee, Inc.

1704 Charlotte Pike, Ste. 200
Nashville, TN 37203-2979 (615) 983-6836
Contact: Dan Jernigan, Pres. and C.E.O.
FAX: (615) 833-4381; E-mail: info@bgcmt.org;
URL: http://www.bgcmt.org

Foundation type: Public charity
Purpose: Scholarships to boys and girls ages 6 to 18 of Middle Tennessee to attend post high school, vocational or trade school.
Financial data: Year ended 06/30/2011. Assets, $4,244,104 (M); Expenditures, $1,589,356; Total giving, $4,250; Grants to individuals, totaling $4,250.
Fields of interest: Vocational education; Boys & girls clubs; Youth.
Type of support: Scholarships—to individuals.
Application information: Unsolicited request for funds not considered or acknowledged.
Program description:
Youth of the Year: Scholarships are awarded to outstanding youth throughout mid-Tennessee. One 'youth of the year' will win a $2,500 college scholarship; recipients who are not ready for college will have prize money reserved for them in a trust, which will be available for them when they reach college age.
EIN: 620540402

8563

Cancer Fund of America, Inc.

2901 Breezewood Ln.
Knoxville, TN 37921-1036 (865) 938-5281
FAX: (865) 938-2968; E-mail: info@cfoa.org;
Toll-free tel.: (800) 578-5284; URL: http://
www.cfoa.org

Foundation type: Public charity
Purpose: Financial assistance and other support to indigent cancer patients.
Publications: Application guidelines; Annual report.
Financial data: Year ended 12/31/2011. Assets, $3,745,357 (M); Expenditures, $24,992,585;

Total giving, $16,852,196; Grants to individuals, totaling $2,007,072.
Fields of interest: Cancer.
Type of support: In-kind gifts; Grants for special needs.
Application information: Applications accepted. Application form required. Application form available on the grantmaker's web site.
   Deadline(s): None
Program description:
   Patient Assistance: The fund provides assistance, in the form of needed supplies, to individuals currently in hospice or non-profit health care settings who have cancer. Assistance includes liquid nutrition, diapers, examination gloves, and disposable bed pads.
EIN: 581766061

8564
Robert M. & Lenore W. Carrier Foundation
1100 Ridgeway Loop, Ste. 100
Memphis, TN   38120   (901) 818-7600
Contact: Andrew Carter

Foundation type: Independent foundation
Purpose: Scholarships primarily to MS residents attending the University of Mississippi.
Financial data: Year ended 10/31/2013. Assets, $2,158,585 (M); Expenditures, $116,790; Total giving, $86,615.
Type of support: Support to graduates or students of specific schools; Undergraduate support.
Application information: Application form required.
   Deadline(s): Prior to high school graduation
   Additional information: Application should include transcripts and brief description of academic qualifications.
EIN: 626035575

8565
J. B. Cash Foundation, Inc.
1426 Hilltop Rd.
Shelbyville, TN   37160   (913) 695-5034
Contact: Roy Lawler III, Pres. and Trea.

Foundation type: Independent foundation
Purpose: Scholarships primarily to residents of Homestead, FL.
Financial data: Year ended 12/31/2012. Assets, $4,248,361 (M); Expenditures, $270,100; Total giving, $60,000.
Type of support: Scholarships—to individuals.
Application information:
   Initial approach: Letter
   Additional information: Contact foundation for current application deadline/guidelines.
EIN: 650764220

8566
Catholic Charities of Tennessee, Inc.
30 White Bridge Rd.
Nashville, TN   37205-1401   (615) 352-3087
Contact: William P. Sinclair, Exec. Dir.
FAX: (615) 352-8591;
E-mail: WSinclair@cctenn.org; URL: http://www.cctenn.org

Foundation type: Public charity
Purpose: Giving limited to emergency assistance, including cash, shelter, medical, and non-cash material goods, to individuals in need in TN.
Publications: Annual report; Financial statement.
Financial data: Year ended 06/30/2012. Assets, $2,128,938 (M); Expenditures, $13,822,397;

Total giving, $4,475,705; Grants to individuals, totaling $2,169,738.
Fields of interest: Economically disadvantaged.
Type of support: In-kind gifts; Grants for special needs.
Application information:
   Initial approach: Tel.
   Additional information: For eligibility criteria call 615-760-4436.
EIN: 620679520

8567
Chattanooga Neighborhood Enterprise, Inc.
1301 Market St., Ste. 100
Chattanooga, TN   37402-4455   (423) 756-6201
Contact: Martina Guilfoil, Pres. and C.E.O.
FAX: (423) 756-3851; E-mail: info@cneinc.org;
E-mail For Martina Guilfoil: mguilfoil@cneinc.org;
URL: http://www.cneinc.org

Foundation type: Public charity
Purpose: Loans to low and moderate income families of Chattanooga, TN and its surrounding areas with home purchase to acquire homes of their own.
Financial data: Year ended 06/30/2012. Assets, $9,825,148 (M); Expenditures, $6,609,953; Total giving, $1,427,276; Grants to individuals, totaling $1,427,276.
Fields of interest: Housing/shelter, rehabilitation; Housing/shelter, home owners.
Type of support: Loans—to individuals.
Application information: Applications accepted.
   Additional information: Applicant must reside in the City of Chattanooga and the home must be your primary residence to qualify for the loan. Contact the organization for additional information.
EIN: 621300726

8568
Chattanooga Orthopedic Educational & Research Foundation
975 E. 3rd St.
P.O. Box 260
Chattanooga, TN   37403-2103   (423) 756-6623
Contact: Marshall Jemison M.D., Pres.

Foundation type: Independent foundation
Purpose: Grants to TN orthopaedic physicians for training.
Financial data: Year ended 12/31/2012. Assets, $704,255 (M); Expenditures, $151,363; Total giving, $56,076; Grants to individuals, 21 grants totaling $56,076 (high: $7,787, low: $12).
Fields of interest: Orthopedics.
Type of support: Conferences/seminars; Fellowships; Travel grants.
Application information: Applications accepted. Application form required.
   Initial approach: Letter
   Deadline(s): None
EIN: 237091528

8569
T. Franklin Cheek, Jr. Scholarship Fund
109 Shady Creek Cv.
Ripley, TN   38063   (731) 635-2642
Contact: Joe Bridges
Application address: 254 Jefferson St., Ripley, TN 38063

Foundation type: Independent foundation

Purpose: Scholarships to graduating seniors of Ripley High School, TN, for higher education.
Financial data: Year ended 06/30/2013. Assets, $809,982 (M); Expenditures, $27,476; Total giving, $25,000; Grants to individuals, 25 grants totaling $25,000 (high: $1,000, low: $1,000).
Fields of interest: Higher education.
Type of support: Support to graduates or students of specific schools.
Application information: Application form required.
   Deadline(s): Apr. 1
EIN: 621849605

8570
Elizabeth Chenoweth Foundation, Inc.
P.O. Box 1373
Paris, TN   38242

Foundation type: Independent foundation
Purpose: Scholarships to graduating seniors of Henry County High School, TN, pursuing higher education.
Financial data: Year ended 12/31/2012. Assets, $482,795 (M); Expenditures, $18,388; Total giving, $18,000.
Fields of interest: Education.
Type of support: Support to graduates or students of specific schools; Undergraduate support.
Application information: Applications accepted. Application form required.
   Deadline(s): Apr. 30
   Additional information: Contact the foundation for additional application information.
EIN: 237044756

8571
Chi Omega Foundation
3395 Players Club Pkwy.
Memphis, TN   38125-8863   (901) 748-8600
FAX: (901) 748-8686;
E-mail: chiomega@chiomega.com; URL: http://www.chiomega.com/family/foundation.aspx?item=family/Foundation/A_Overview.xml

Foundation type: Public charity
Purpose: Scholarships to collegiate and alumnae members of Chi Omega fraternity.
Publications: Application guidelines.
Financial data: Year ended 04/30/2012. Assets, $19,816,025 (M); Expenditures, $2,006,360; Total giving, $423,379; Grants to individuals, totaling $317,297.
Fields of interest: Students, sororities/fraternities; Women.
Type of support: Graduate support; Undergraduate support.
Application information: Applications accepted. Application form required. Application form available on the grantmaker's web site.
   Initial approach: Letter
   Send request by: Mail
   Deadline(s): Mar. 6
   Applicants should submit the following:
      1) Transcripts
      2) Photograph
      3) Essay
      4) Letter(s) of recommendation
EIN: 310936294

8572
Children's Cancer Fund of America, Inc.
2317 W. Emory Rd.
Powell, TN 37849-3708 (865) 947-9825
Contact: Rose Perkins, C.E.O.
FAX: (865) 947-9830; E-mail: support@ccfoa.org;
Toll-free tel.: (888) 418-6062; URL: http://
www.ccfoa.org/

Foundation type: Public charity
Purpose: Financial assistance to children afflicted with cancer, as well as their families.
Publications: Application guidelines.
Financial data: Year ended 12/31/2012. Assets, $853,507 (M); Expenditures, $15,513,425; Total giving, $9,054,405; Grants to individuals, totaling $160,861.
Fields of interest: Health care; Children.
Type of support: Grants for special needs.
Application information: Applications accepted. Application form required.
  Initial approach: Telephone
  Deadline(s): None
  Additional information: Applications must be renewed every six months for continued assistance.
EIN: 201226416

8573
Children's Scholarship Fund - Metro Jackson
4027 Hillsboro Pk., Ste. 803
Nashville, TN 37215-2783 (601) 960-7248
Contact: Charles L. LIrby, Chair.

Foundation type: Public charity
Purpose: Provides scholarships of up to $800 per student per year to children in financial need who are attending or will attend private schools. Funds are only available for students entering grades K-12 who are residents of Jackson, MS and the surrounding area.
Financial data: Year ended 08/31/2011. Assets, $15,165 (M); Expenditures, $203,147; Total giving, $165,612.
Fields of interest: Elementary/secondary education; Early childhood education.
Type of support: Scholarships—to individuals.
Application information: Applications accepted. Application form required. Application form available on the grantmaker's web site.
EIN: 640892204

8574
CIC Foundation, Inc.
139 Lake Harbor Dr.
Hendersonville, TN 37075 (615) 386-2296

Foundation type: Company-sponsored foundation
Purpose: Scholarships to students who are residents of Middle Tennessee and South Central Kentucky area pursuing degrees that will prepare them for jobs within the credit industry or closely related financial services industry.
Financial data: Year ended 12/31/2012. Assets, $0 (M); Expenditures, $6,355,437; Total giving, $5,479,421; Grants to individuals, 254 grants totaling $2,211,300 (high: $60,000, low: $1,250).
Fields of interest: Business school/education.
Type of support: Undergraduate support.
Application information: Applications accepted. Application form required.
  Deadline(s): Apr. 1
  Applicants should submit the following:
    1) ACT
    2) Class rank

3) SAT
4) Essay
Additional information: Application should include a copy of a letter of acceptance from an institution of higher education.
EIN: 562348880

8575
Civitan Child Welfare Auxiliary, Inc.
3712 Anderson Ave.
Chattanooga, TN 37412-1809
Contact: J. William Dietzen, Chair.
Application address: 1122 Hilldale Dr., Chattanooga, TN 37411

Foundation type: Independent foundation
Purpose: Assistance for disabled children 16 years old or under who live in the immediate Chattanooga, TN, area.
Financial data: Year ended 12/31/2011. Assets, $1,423,994 (M); Expenditures, $67,135; Total giving, $67,135; Grants to individuals, 16 grants totaling $41,735.
Fields of interest: Children, services; Disabilities, people with.
Type of support: Grants for special needs.
Application information: Applications accepted. Application form not required.
  Initial approach: Letter or telephone
  Copies of proposal: 1
  Deadline(s): None
  Additional information: Application should include information on need and how the grant will be used. For a child, include medical condition, confirmation of condition by a doctor or institution and family's financial status.
EIN: 626036153

8576
E. B. Coburn Scholarship Trust
P.O. Box 370
Dyersburg, TN 38025-0370 (731) 772-1201
Application address: c/o Haywood County High School, 111 College St. Brownsville, TN 38012

Foundation type: Independent foundation
Purpose: Scholarships to high school students at Haywood County High School, TN for higher education.
Financial data: Year ended 12/31/2011. Assets, $137,048 (M); Expenditures, $6,329; Total giving, $4,000.
Type of support: Support to graduates or students of specific schools; Undergraduate support.
Application information: Application form required.
  Initial approach: Letter
  Deadline(s): May 1
EIN: 626199961

8577
The Community Foundation of Greater Chattanooga, Inc.
1270 Market St.
Chattanooga, TN 37402-2713 (423) 265-0586
Contact: Peter T. Cooper, Pres.; For grants: Robin Posey, Prog. Off.; For scholarships: Rebecca Smith, Dir., Scholarships
Scholarship e-mail: rsmith@cfgc.org
FAX: (423) 265-0587; E-mail: info2@cfgc.org;
URL: http://www.cfgc.org

Foundation type: Community foundation
Purpose: Scholarships to residents of the Hamilton County, TN, area for undergraduate study.

Publications: Application guidelines; Annual report; Biennial report (including application guidelines); Grants list; Informational brochure; Informational brochure (including application guidelines).
Financial data: Year ended 12/31/2012. Assets, $104,192,001 (M); Expenditures, $15,312,011; Total giving, $14,098,669; Grants to individuals, 741 grants totaling $1,430,226.
Fields of interest: Higher education; Scholarships/financial aid.
Type of support: Undergraduate support.
Application information: Applications accepted. Application form required. Application form available on the grantmaker's web site. Interview required.
  Initial approach: Application
  Send request by: Mail or hand deliver
  Deadline(s): Varies
  Applicants should submit the following:
    1) SAR
    2) Letter(s) of recommendation
    3) Essay
    4) Transcripts
  Additional information: The foundation manages over 50 different scholarship funds, each with unique eligibility requirements and application guidelines. See web site for a complete listing.
EIN: 626045999

8578
Community Foundation of Greater Memphis
1900 Union Ave.
Memphis, TN 38104-4029 (901) 728-4600
Contact: Robert M. Fockler, Pres.; For grants and scholarships: Vanessa Langston, Grants and Initiatives Assoc.
FAX: (901) 722-0010; E-mail: rfockler@cfgm.org;
Grants and scholarship inquiry tel.: (901) 722-0032, e-mail: vlangston@cfgm.org;
URL: http://www.cfgm.org

Foundation type: Community foundation
Purpose: Scholarships to students residing in the Memphis, TN, area for undergraduate education.
Publications: Application guidelines; Annual report; Newsletter.
Financial data: Year ended 04/30/2013. Assets, $314,940,599 (M); Expenditures, $64,205,129; Total giving, $58,341,057. Scholarships—to individuals amount not specified.
Fields of interest: Music; Vocational education, post-secondary; Higher education; Business school/education.
Type of support: Scholarships—to individuals; Support to graduates or students of specific schools; Undergraduate support.
Application information: Applications accepted. Application form required. Application form available on the grantmaker's web site.
  Initial approach: Application
  Send request by: Mail
  Deadline(s): Apr. 1
  Final notification: Applicants notified June 15
  Applicants should submit the following:
    1) Letter(s) of recommendation
    2) ACT
    3) SAT
    4) SAR
    5) Transcripts
  Additional information: See your high school counselors and financial offices for information on other community-based scholarships. See web site for complete listing of scholarship funds and application.

Program description:

Scholarship Funds: The foundation administers a wide variety of scholarship funds for Memphis-area residents and others attending postsecondary, technical and vocational institutions of higher learning. All applicants must plan to attend an accredited two- or four-year college or university or an accredited vocational or technical institution, enroll as a full-time student (12 credit hours undergraduate), demonstrate academic achievement and demonstrate economic need. Many scholarships have additional eligibility criteria. The foundation publishes updated information each year that describes the criteria and application process for these funds on the web site.
EIN: 581723645

8579
Community Foundation of Middle Tennessee, Inc.

(formerly Nashville Community Foundation, Inc.)
3833 Cleghorn Ave., No. 400
Nashville, TN 37215-2519 (615) 321-4939
Contact: Ellen E. Lehman, Pres.
FAX: (615) 327-2746; E-mail: mail@cfmt.org;
Additional tel.: (888) 540-5200; URL: http://
www.cfmt.org

Foundation type: Community foundation
Purpose: Scholarships to high school seniors of TN for postsecondary education at institution in the U.S.
Publications: Annual report; Informational brochure; Newsletter.
Financial data: Year ended 12/31/2012. Assets, $360,123,135 (M); Expenditures, $78,005,653; Total giving, $72,705,671; Grants to individuals, 407 grants totaling $2,010,613.
Fields of interest: Higher education; Scholarships/ financial aid.
Type of support: Scholarships—to individuals; Support to graduates or students of specific schools; Undergraduate support.
Application information: Applications accepted. Application form required. Application form available on the grantmaker's web site.
  Initial approach: Application
  Send request by: Mail
  Deadline(s): Mar. 15
  Final notification: Recipients notified mid-May
  Applicants should submit the following:
    1) Financial information
    2) Letter(s) of recommendation
    3) Transcripts
  Additional information: Funds are paid directly to the educational institution on behalf of the students. See web site for complete listing of scholarship funds.
Program description:
  Scholarship Program: The foundation's Scholarship Program is made up of more than 60 different scholarship funds established by individuals, firms or organizations wanting to assist individuals in furthering their education. Students apply to the program and, if eligible, can be awarded grants from one or more of these different funds. Scholarship Funds within foundation can be set up to benefit students from particular geographic areas or schools, attending certain postsecondary institutions, or entering certain fields of study, such as fine arts, education, journalism and agriculture. Most scholarships offer varying award amounts, which range from $500 to $2,500. See web site for additional information.
EIN: 621471789

8580
Rosalie Conte Foundation

c/o First Tennessee Bank, N.A.
4385 Poplar Ave.
Memphis, TN 38117

Foundation type: Independent foundation
Purpose: Scholarships for higher education to students who reside within the public school district serving the Great Barrington, MA, area.
Financial data: Year ended 12/31/2012. Assets, $525,135 (M); Expenditures, $28,995; Total giving, $21,500.
Type of support: Undergraduate support.
Application information: Contact foundation for complete application deadline/guidelines.
EIN: 581849183

8581
Cracker Barrel Old Country Store Foundation

305 Hartmann Dr.
Lebanon, TN 37087 (615) 443-5533
Contact: Penny Carroll, Secy.
FAX: (615) 443-9874;
E-mail: pcarroll@crackerbarrel.com; Application address: P.O. Box 787, Lebanon, TN 37088-0787; URL: http://www.crackerbarrel.com/about-us/ employee-scholarship-program/

Foundation type: Company-sponsored foundation
Purpose: Scholarships only to employees of Cracker Barrel Old Country Store and their dependent children for higher education.
Publications: Application guidelines; Informational brochure (including application guidelines); Program policy statement.
Financial data: Year ended 07/31/2012. Assets, $4,404,132 (M); Expenditures, $428,871; Total giving, $414,150; Grants to individuals, 55 grants totaling $82,500 (high: $1,500, low: $1,500).
Fields of interest: Vocational education, post-secondary; Higher education.
Type of support: Employee-related scholarships.
Application information: Applications not accepted.
  Additional information: Unsolicited requests for funds not considered or acknowleged.
Program description:
  Cracker Barrel Foundation Scholarship: The foundation awards 55 $1,500 college scholarships to employees and children of employees of Cracker Barrel Old Country Store. Applicants must enroll in an accredited, not-for-profit college, university, vocational or technical institute as a full time student in the fall of the same calendar year that the scholarship is awarded.
Company name: Cracker Barrel Old Country Store, Inc.
EIN: 621577717

8582
The Dixie Group Foundation, Inc.

(formerly Dixie Yarns Foundation, Inc.)
P.O. Box 25107
Chattanooga, TN 37422-5107 (423) 510-7005
Contact: Starr T. Klein, Secy.-Treas.

Foundation type: Company-sponsored foundation
Purpose: Scholarships to children of employees of The Dixie Group, Inc., Chattanooga, TN. Financial assistance to indigent current or former employees of The Dixie Group, Inc., and its subsidiaries in Chattanooga, TN.
Financial data: Year ended 12/31/2012. Assets, $804,000 (M); Expenditures, $73,348; Total

giving, $67,850; Grants to individuals, 11 grants totaling $22,000 (high: $2,000, low: $2,000).
Fields of interest: Higher education; Human services.
Type of support: Employee-related scholarships; Employee-related welfare.
Application information: Applications not accepted.
  Additional information: Contributes only to preselected individuals. Unsolicited requests for funds not considered or acknowledged.
Company name: Dixie Group, Incorporated, The
EIN: 620645090

8583
Dollar General Employee Assistance Foundation

c/o Denine Torr
100 Mission Ridge
Goodlettsville, TN 37072-2171 (615) 855-5208
Contact: Denie Torr

Foundation type: Operating foundation
Purpose: Aid to distressed Dollar General employees and their families who are experiencing financial hardship due to circumstances beyond their control, such as death or disaster.
Financial data: Year ended 01/31/2013. Assets, $1,265,940 (M); Expenditures, $641,884; Total giving, $621,972; Grants to individuals, 411 grants totaling $621,972 (high: $2,500, low: $89).
Fields of interest: Family services.
Type of support: Emergency funds.
Application information: Applications accepted.
  Additional information: Any police, fire or insurance report filed related to the need must be provided.
EIN: 611492355

8584
The Dollywood Foundation

2700 Dollywood Parks Blvd.
Pigeon Forge, TN 37863-4113 (865) 428-9606
Contact: David C. Dotson, Pres.
FAX: (865) 428-9612;
E-mail: ddotson@dollyfoundation.com; URL: http://www.imaginationlibrary.com/

Foundation type: Public charity
Purpose: Scholarships to graduating high school seniors from Gatlinburg-Pitman High School, Sevier County High School, and Seymour High School, TN, who excel in music, academics, or environmental studies.
Publications: Annual report.
Financial data: Year ended 12/31/2012. Assets, $10,346,582 (M); Expenditures, $1,525,240; Total giving, $314,749; Grants to individuals, totaling $58,125.
Fields of interest: Music; Natural resources.
Type of support: Scholarships—to individuals; Support to graduates or students of specific schools.
Application information: Contact foundation for additional application guidelines.
Program description:
  Dollywood Foundation Scholarships: Nine college scholarships, three per each Sevier County high school (Gatlinburg-Pitman High School, Sevier County High School, and Seymour High School), are awarded annually to graduating seniors in the following areas: music ($1,500), academic achievement ($1,200), and environment ($1,000).

A faculty committee at each high school selects the winners among their students.
EIN: 621348105

8585
Dyersburg-Dyer County Union Mission
213 W. Cedar St.
P.O. Box 179
Dyersburg, TN 38024-5023 (731) 285-0726
FAX: (731) 286-0786;
E-mail: mission@cableone.net; URL: http://dyersburgmission.com

Foundation type: Public charity
Purpose: Financial assistance to needy families for emergency needs and to youth through outreach for camp, recreation club, and youth center who are residents of Dyer County, TN.
Publications: Annual report.
Financial data: Year ended 12/31/2011. Assets, $3,614,514 (M); Expenditures, $6,320,781; Total giving, $5,288,979; Grants to individuals, totaling $5,288,979.
Fields of interest: Youth, services; Human services.
Type of support: Grants for special needs.
Application information: Contact mission for further guidelines.
EIN: 237371023

8586
East Nashville Knights of Columbus Club, Inc.
135 Ellington Pl.
Madison, TN 37115

Foundation type: Independent foundation
Purpose: Scholarships to graduates of John Paul II High School, Hendersonville, Tennessee.
Financial data: Year ended 06/30/2013. Assets, $302,669 (M); Expenditures, $20,596; Total giving, $20,501; Grants to individuals, 6 grants totaling $8,001 (high: $2,000, low: $667).
Type of support: Support to graduates or students of specific schools.
Application information: Applications not accepted.
  Additional information: Unsolicited requests for funds not considered or acknowledged.
EIN: 621431787

8587
East Tennessee Foundation
625 Market St., Ste. 1400
Knoxville, TN 37902-2219 (865) 524-1223
Contact: Michael T. McClamroch, C.E.O. and Pres.; For scholarships: Beth Heller, Scholarship and Prog. Off.
Scholarship inquiry e-mail: bheller@etf.org
FAX: (865) 637-6039; E-mail: etf@etf.org; Toll free tel.: (877) 524-1223; URL: http://www.easttennesseefoundation.org

Foundation type: Community foundation
Purpose: Scholarships to residents of East Tennessee in Anderson, Blount, Campbell, Carter, Claiborne, Cocke, Grainger, Greene, Hamblen, Hancock, Hawkins, Jefferson, Johnson, Knox, Loudon, McMinn, Monroe, Morgan, Roane, Scott, Sevier, Sullivan, Unicoi, Union, and Washington counties for attendance at institutions of higher learning.
Publications: Application guidelines; Annual report; Informational brochure (including application guidelines); Newsletter.

Financial data: Year ended 12/31/2012. Assets, $183,356,380 (M); Expenditures, $11,407,786; Total giving, $8,273,058. Scholarships—to individuals amount not specified.
Fields of interest: Higher education.
Type of support: Scholarships—to individuals; Support to graduates or students of specific schools; Undergraduate support.
Application information: Applications accepted. Application form required. Application form available on the grantmaker's web site.
  Initial approach: Application
  Send request by: Online
  Deadline(s): Mar. 1
  Applicants should submit the following:
    1) Transcripts
    2) Letter(s) of recommendation
  Additional information: Application should include transcripts. See web site or contact your high school guidance counselor for complete listing of scholarships and guidelines See web site or contact your high school guidance counselor for complete listing of scholarships and guidelines.
Program description:
  Scholarships: The foundation administers over 40 scholarship funds for attendance at higher education institutions, ranging from $500 to $40,000 and from one year to four years. Some scholarships are for study of specific subject areas such as science, health care, and business-related degrees. Each scholarship fund has unique eligibility guidelines and deadlines.
EIN: 620807696

8588
East Tennessee Human Resource Agency, Inc.
9111 Cross Park Dr., Ste. D-100
Knoxville, TN 37923-4517 (865) 691-2551
FAX: (865) 531-7216; E-mail: info@ethra.org; TDD: (865) 681-1990; URL: http://www.ethra.org

Foundation type: Public charity
Purpose: Emergency assistance to individuals and families throughout east TN.
Publications: Annual report; Informational brochure.
Financial data: Year ended 06/30/2012. Assets, $15,220,404 (M); Expenditures, $38,022,826; Total giving, $11,485,835; Grants to individuals, totaling $11,485,835.
Fields of interest: Children; Aging; Economically disadvantaged.
Type of support: Emergency funds; In-kind gifts; Grants for special needs.
Application information: Contact the agency for guidelines.
EIN: 621493851

8589
Eastman Chemical Company Contributions Program
P.O. Box 431
Kingsport, TN 37662-0431
Contact: Angie Jobe, Contribs Coord.; George Decroes, Cummunity Rels. Mgr.
FAX: (423) 229-8280;
E-mail: angieb@eastman.com; Pennsylvania application address: c/o Gerald Kuhn, Jefferson Site Mgr., Eastman Chemical Co., P.O. Box 567, West Elizabeth, PA 15088, fax: (412) 384-7311; Texas: c/o Sally Azbell, Eastman Chemical Co., P.O. Box 7444, Longview, TX 75607, fax: (903) 237-5799; URL: http://www.eastman.com/

Company/Sustainability/Social_Responsibility/communities/Pages/Communities.aspx

Foundation type: Corporate giving program
Purpose: Scholarships to employees of Eastman Chemical Company.
Publications: Application guidelines.
Financial data: Year ended 12/31/2012. Total giving, $448,504.
Type of support: Employee-related scholarships.
Application information: Applications not accepted.
  Additional information: Unsolicited requests for funds not considered.
Company name: Eastman Chemical Company

8590
Educational Services of America, Inc.
(also known as ESA)
1321 Murfreesboro Pike, Ste. 702
Nashville, TN 37217-2626 (615) 361-4000
Contact: Mark Claypool, Pres. and C.E.O.
FAX: (615) 577-5695; Toll-free tel.: (888) 979-0004; URL: http://www.esa-education.com

Foundation type: Public charity
Purpose: Scholarships to Florida students with disabilities to attend private schools that best suit their needs.
Financial data: Year ended 12/31/2011. Assets, $1,312,260,913 (M); Expenditures, $56,460,261; Total giving, $831,250; Grants to individuals, totaling $831,250.
Application information: Applications accepted.
  Additional information: See web site for additional guidelines for scholarship.
EIN: 621586836

8591
The Keith W. Fengler Memorial Foundation
453 Essex Park Cir.
Franklin, TN 37069 (615) 472-1977
Contact: Henry J. Fengler, Tr.
URL: http://kwfscholarship.org/

Foundation type: Operating foundation
Purpose: Scholarships to students of Cicero-North Syracuse High School, NY.
Financial data: Year ended 12/31/2012. Assets, $289,542 (M); Expenditures, $16,980; Total giving, $14,638; Grants to individuals, 8 grants totaling $9,682 (high: $1,139, low: $1,139).
Fields of interest: Higher education; Education.
Type of support: Scholarships—to individuals; Support to graduates or students of specific schools.
Application information: Applications accepted. Application form required. Interview required.
  Initial approach: Letter
  Deadline(s): May 1
  Additional information: Contact foundation for further application information.
EIN: 166491840

8592
Fort Sanders Regional Medical Center
1901 Clinch Ave.
Knoxville, TN 37916-2307 (865) 541-1111
URL: http://www.fsregional.com/

Foundation type: Public charity
Purpose: Emergency funds provided to patients of east Tennessee for post-hospitalization transportation and medication needs.

Financial data: Year ended 12/31/2011. Assets, $164,611,848 (M); Expenditures, $295,672,751; Total giving, $149,860; Grants to individuals, totaling $36,544.
Fields of interest: Economically disadvantaged.
Type of support: Emergency funds.
Application information: Patients must demonstrate need.
EIN: 620528340

8593
The Foundation for Geriatric Education
100 E. Vine St.
Murfreesboro, TN 37130-3734 (615) 890-2020
Contact: R. Michael Ussery, Pres.

Foundation type: Public charity
Purpose: Grants to purchase textbooks for those who are studying the field of geriatrics.
Financial data: Year ended 12/31/2011. Assets, $8,263,806 (M); Expenditures, $134,339.
Fields of interest: Geriatrics.
Type of support: Grants to individuals.
Application information:
Initial approach: Letter
Additional information: Contact foundation for further application information.
EIN: 621179417

8594
Goodlark Educational Foundation
404 E. College St., Ste. T
Dickson, TN 37055-1849 (615) 446-9156
Contact: Vanessa Smith

Foundation type: Operating foundation
Purpose: Scholarships for undergraduate studies to financially needy residents of Dickson, Hickman, and Humphreys counties, TN.
Publications: Application guidelines.
Financial data: Year ended 12/31/2012. Assets, $2,699,340 (M); Expenditures, $122,227; Total giving, $91,250; Grant to an individual, 1 grant totaling $91,250.
Fields of interest: Vocational education; Higher education.
Type of support: Undergraduate support.
Application information: Application form required.
Deadline(s): Feb. and Mar.
Applicants should submit the following:
1) Transcripts
2) GPA
Additional information: Application should also include most recent W-2 and income tax forms.
EIN: 581764987

8595
The Mike Grace Memorial Scholarship Fund
c/o Apcom, Inc.
P.O. Box 681149
Franklin, TN 37068-1149 (615) 224-2733

Foundation type: Public charity
Purpose: Scholarships to high school students of TN, who demonstrate a high level of achievement in the area of vocational education.
Financial data: Year ended 06/30/2012. Assets, $399,884 (M); Expenditures, $21,425; Total giving, $20,000.
Fields of interest: Vocational education.
Type of support: Scholarships—to individuals.
Application information: Applications accepted.

Additional information: Contact the fund for additional application guidelines.
EIN: 621175180

8596
Graham Family Foundation Inc.
P.O. Box 789
Linden, TN 37096-0789

Foundation type: Operating foundation
Purpose: Scholarships to graduating needy students of Perry county, TN for attendance at colleges or universities.
Financial data: Year ended 12/31/2012. Assets, $9,737 (M); Expenditures, $47,147; Total giving, $47,000; Grants to individuals, 32 grants totaling $15,800 (high: $500, low: $300).
Fields of interest: Higher education.
Type of support: Scholarships—to individuals.
Application information: Applications accepted.
Additional information: Contact the foundation for application information.
EIN: 201228026

8597
The Hassell Charitable Foundation
129 Main St.
P. O. Box B
Clifton, TN 38425 (931) 676-3371
Contact: Autry Gobbell, Tr.; Martha Gobbell, Tr.

Foundation type: Independent foundation
Purpose: Scholarships to residents within a 125-mile radius of Clifton, TN.
Financial data: Year ended 12/31/2011. Assets, $666,010 (M); Expenditures, $98,516; Total giving, $38,854.
Type of support: Scholarships—to individuals.
Application information: Applications accepted. Application form required.
Initial approach: Letter
Deadline(s): None
EIN: 581485616

8598
E. Maurine Hawkins Memorial Scholarship Fund
P.O. Box 789
Knoxville, TN 37901-0789
Contact: Tom Davenport, Chair.
Application address: c/o Tennessee High School, 112 Edgemont Ave., Bristol, TN 37620

Foundation type: Independent foundation
Purpose: Scholarships to graduates of Tennessee High School, Bristol, TN; and full-time students at University of Tennessee, Knoxville, and Carson Newman College, TN, and Union College, KY.
Financial data: Year ended 12/31/2012. Assets, $267,797 (M); Expenditures, $12,754; Total giving, $10,000; Grants to individuals, 2 grants totaling $10,000 (high: $5,000, low: $5,000).
Type of support: Support to graduates or students of specific schools; Undergraduate support.
Application information: Applications accepted. Application form not required.
Deadline(s): May 1
EIN: 621338535

8599
HCA Hope Fund
P.O. Box 550
Nashville, TN 37202-0550 (877) 857-4673
FAX: (866) 337-4354;
E-mail: hopefund@hcahealthcare.com; URL: http://www.hcahopefund.org

Foundation type: Public charity
Purpose: Grants to HCA employees and their immediate families who were affected by hardship due to an event beyond their control.
Publications: Application guidelines.
Financial data: Year ended 12/31/2011. Assets, $7,932,235 (M); Expenditures, $1,434,025; Total giving, $1,179,578; Grants to individuals, totaling $1,179,578.
Fields of interest: Safety/disasters.
Type of support: Emergency funds; Employee-related welfare; Grants for special needs.
Application information: Applications accepted. Application form required.
Initial approach: Submit application form along with copies of the bills requesting to be paid to your HCA facility's Human Resources department.
Program description:
Emergency Grants: The fund provides grants to HCA employees and their immediate families who were affected by hardship due to an event beyond their control, including disasters, extended illness or injury, and other special situations. Levels of emergency assistance in cases related to a disaster are based on household size and historical levels of emergency assistance provided by disaster relief organizations. Grants in this category will not exceed $2,500. For extended illness/injury and other special circumstances, applicants may receive up to $1,000. Applicants are limited to $5,000 in assistance from the fund over their lifetime.
EIN: 470957872

8600
Heart Support of America, Inc.
2902 Tazewell Pk.
Knoxville, TN 37918-1877 (865) 687-5838
FAX: (865) 687-5840;
E-mail: info@heartsupportofamerica.org; Toll-free tel.: (888) 430-9809; URL: http://www.heartsupportofamerica.org

Foundation type: Public charity
Purpose: Financial assistance to individuals to help pay for cardiac prescription drugs, meals for families of heart patients, and transportation and lodging related to specific cardiac care.
Financial data: Year ended 12/31/2011. Assets, $116,902 (M); Expenditures, $2,826,850; Total giving, $76,372; Grants to individuals, totaling $44,372.
Fields of interest: Heart & circulatory diseases.
Type of support: Grants for special needs.
Application information:
Initial approach: Letter
Additional information: Assistance is based on individual need of the cardiac patient. Contact the organization for additional guidelines.
EIN: 581976599

8601

Ethel Brickey Hicks Charitable Corporation
P.O. Box 1990
Knoxville, TN 37901-1990
Contact: James S. Tipton, Jr., Pres.

Foundation type: Independent foundation
Purpose: Scholarships to medical students who will practice in rural AR.
Financial data: Year ended 12/31/2012. Assets, $793,280 (M); Expenditures, $80,866; Total giving, $57,500; Grants to individuals, 5 grants totaling $57,500 (high: $19,000, low: $9,500).
Fields of interest: Medical school/education.
Type of support: Graduate support.
Application information: Applications accepted. Application form required.
EIN: 710698966

8602

Cathy L. Hodges Memorial Cancer Foundation
9724 Kingston Pike, Ste. 1000
Knoxville, TN 37922-6906 (865) 690-5346
Contact: Bill A. Hodges, Pres.

Foundation type: Independent foundation
Purpose: Grants to economically disadvantaged individuals in eastern Tennessee for medical and other expenses.
Financial data: Year ended 06/30/2013. Assets, $12,076 (M); Expenditures, $58,541; Total giving, $58,269; Grant to an individual, 1 grant totaling $58,269.
Fields of interest: Health care; Economically disadvantaged.
Type of support: Emergency funds; Grants for special needs.
Application information:
 Initial approach: Letter
 Deadline(s): 10th of each month
 Additional information: Letter of no more than two pages describing circumstances.
EIN: 621620282

8603

Hiram W. & Cecil J. Holtsford Scholarship Fund
P.O. Box 692
Lawrenceburg, TN 38464 (931) 762-6620
Contact: Charles Doerflinger, Tr.

Foundation type: Independent foundation
Purpose: Scholarships to residents of Lawrence County, TN, who are single, for attendance at four-year accredited colleges.
Financial data: Year ended 06/30/2012. Assets, $528,268 (M); Expenditures, $8,326; Total giving, $7,500; Grants to individuals, 3 grants totaling $7,500 (high: $3,000, low: $1,500).
Fields of interest: Higher education.
Type of support: Scholarships—to individuals.
Application information: Application form required.
 Deadline(s): Feb. 15
EIN: 626169638

8604

Humanities Tennessee
(formerly Tennessee Humanities Council)
306 Gay St., Ste. 306
Nashville, TN 37201-1189 (615) 770-0006
Contact: Timothy Henderson, Exec. Dir.
FAX: (615) 770-0007;
E-mail: Tim@HumanitiesTennessee.org;
URL: http://www.humanitiestennessee.org

Foundation type: Public charity
Purpose: Awards by nomination to full-time public or private 3rd to 12th grade school teachers in TN who have demonstrated excellence in teaching the humanities.
Publications: Application guidelines; Newsletter.
Financial data: Year ended 12/31/2011. Assets, $275,851 (M); Expenditures, $1,108,776; Total giving, $76,467; Grants to individuals, totaling $10,500.
Fields of interest: Arts education; Music; Humanities; Education.
Type of support: Fellowships; Awards/grants by nomination only; Awards/prizes.
Application information:
 Initial approach: E-mail
 Deadline(s): Dec. 31
 Additional information: Contact foundation for a nomination packet.
Program description:
 Awards of Recognition for Outstanding Teaching of the Humanities: Fellowships of $2,000 each will be awarded to up to six full-time 3rd-12th-grade Tennessee teachers who have demonstrated excellence in teaching the humanities, thus making the humanities an important part of their students' lives. Awards are meant to further the recipients' professional development in the humanities; an addition $1,500 will be awarded to the award recipients' schools to be used for the purchase of humanities instructional materials or for student humanities projects. Eligible nominees include teachers of English, foreign language, history, and social studies; teachers of art, drama, and music are also eligible, provided they employ a solid humanities approach to these subjects. Nominees must also be skillful and dedicated teachers who possess an expansive and in-depth knowledge of the humanities subject they teach, and must have a record of active involvement in community activities and professional organizations (particularly those that promote an understanding of the humanities)
EIN: 620933337

8605

Orion L. & Emma B. Hurlbut Memorial Fund
701 Market St.
Chattanooga, TN 37402-4828
Application address: c/o Kathy Wood, 975 E. 3rd St., Chattanooga, TN 37403-2147; tel.: (423) 778-7503

Foundation type: Independent foundation
Purpose: Financial assistance for medical expenses to economically disadvantaged cancer patients at Erlanger Hospital, outside of Hamilton County, TN.
Financial data: Year ended 04/30/2012. Assets, $19,264,493 (M); Expenditures, $1,216,488; Total giving, $1,040,030.
Fields of interest: Cancer; Economically disadvantaged.
Type of support: Grants for special needs.
Application information: Applications accepted.

 Initial approach: Letter
 Deadline(s): None
 Additional information: Application should include physician's detailed expense vouchers.
EIN: 626034546

8606

International Christian Embassy Jerusalem - USA, Inc.
P.O. Box 332974
Murfreesboro, TN 37133-2974 (615) 895-9830
Contact: Dr. Juergen Buehler, Exec. Dir.
FAX: (615) 895-9829; E-mail: icejusa@icejusa.org;
URL: http://us.icej.org/

Foundation type: Public charity
Purpose: Assistance to eligible individuals and families who wish to immigrate to Israel.
Financial data: Year ended 12/31/2011. Assets, $1,228,072 (M); Expenditures, $1,659,823; Total giving, $407,827; Grants to individuals, totaling $30,000.
Fields of interest: Human services; Immigrants/refugees.
Type of support: Grants to individuals.
Application information: Eligible families must provide proof that permanent residency has been granted, and only eligible expenses such as flight costs are covered. Contact the organization for eligibility determination.
EIN: 621279378

8607

International Paper Company Employee Relief Fund
6400 Poplar Ave.
Memphis, TN 38197-0198 (901) 419-9000
Contact: Kim Wirth, Exec. Dir.
FAX: (901) 419-4092;
E-mail: internationalpaper.comm@ipaper.com;
Toll-free fax: (877)-603-0756; URL: http://www.internationalpaper.com/US/EN/Company/Sustainability/IPGiving.html

Foundation type: Public charity
Purpose: Assistance with basic life necessities to individuals who have encountered financial hardship due to a natural disaster or personal tragedy.
Financial data: Year ended 12/31/2011. Assets, $274,484 (M); Expenditures, $327,118; Total giving, $315,373; Grants to individuals, totaling $96,941.
Fields of interest: Economically disadvantaged.
Type of support: Emergency funds; Grants for special needs.
Application information: Applications not accepted.
 Additional information: Unsolicited requests for funds not considered or acknowledged.
EIN: 621857413

8608

The Daniel Ashley and Irene Houston Jewell Memorial Foundation
c/o George McMillan, Jr.
2221 Fox Run Dr.
Signal Mountain, TN 37377 (404) 624-7636
Contact: D. Ashley Jewell V, Chair. and Tr.
Application address: 115 Old Homestead Dr., Chickamauga, GA 30707, tel.: (404) 624-7636

Foundation type: Independent foundation
Purpose: Scholarships to needy and deserving students who are graduates of Gordon Lee Memorial High School, Chickamauga, Walker County, GA.
Financial data: Year ended 06/30/2013. Assets, $5,225,781 (M); Expenditures, $272,378; Total giving, $230,000; Grants to individuals, 12 grants totaling $48,000 (high: $4,000, low: $4,000).
Fields of interest: Higher education.
Type of support: Scholarships—to individuals; Grants for special needs.
Application information: Applications accepted.
  Initial approach: Letter
  Deadline(s): None
EIN: 586034213

8609
Jewish Family Services, Inc.
6560 Poplar Ave.
Memphis, TN 38138-3656 (901) 767-8511
Contact: Robert Silver, Exec. Dir.
FAX: (901) 763-2348; E-mail: jfsmem@aol.com;
URL: http://www.jfsmemphis.org/contact/

Foundation type: Public charity
Purpose: Scholarships to individuals in the Memphis, TN area. Also, emergency and special assistance to needy individuals and families.
Publications: Financial statement; Newsletter.
Financial data: Year ended 12/31/2011. Assets, $1,656,038 (M); Expenditures, $770,719; Total giving, $65,614; Grants to individuals, totaling $65,614.
Fields of interest: Family services.
Type of support: Grants for special needs.
Application information: Contact foundation for current application deadline/guidelines.
EIN: 620199430

8610
Sandra and Bill Johnson Scholarship Foundation
P.O. Box 169
Shelbyville, TN 37162-0169

Foundation type: Independent foundation
Purpose: Scholarships to students who are members of the Walking Horse Training Association, or are otherwise connected with the walking horse industry to pursue postsecondary education.
Financial data: Year ended 12/31/2010. Assets, $835 (M); Expenditures, $120,415; Total giving, $119,575; Grants to individuals, totaling $119,575.
Fields of interest: Athletics/sports, training; Athletics/sports, equestrianism.
Type of support: Scholarships—to individuals.
Application information: Application form required.
  Deadline(s): Applications are accepted up to the beginning of the current academic year.
  Additional information: Applications can be obtained from the foundation.
EIN: 621622697

8611
JSA Foundation
1310 6th Ave. N.
Nashville, TN 37208 (615) 254-2291
Contact: Margaret L. Behm, Dir.

Foundation type: Independent foundation
Purpose: Scholarships to female residents of TN, 23 years of age or older, who are attending college.

Financial data: Year ended 08/31/2012. Assets, $323,166 (M); Expenditures, $17,410; Total giving, $11,538; Grants to individuals, 2 grants totaling $11,538 (high: $3,000, low: $2,538).
Fields of interest: Women.
Type of support: Scholarships—to individuals.
Application information: Applications accepted. Application form required.
  Deadline(s): One month prior to registration
  Additional information: Application should include transcript.
EIN: 581488121

8612
The Keel Foundation
P.O. Box 1778
Morristown, TN 37816-1778

Foundation type: Independent foundation
Purpose: Scholarships to high school students in pursuit of a higher education.
Financial data: Year ended 12/31/2012. Assets, $1,502,245 (M); Expenditures, $120,301; Total giving, $95,500; Grants to individuals, 9 grants totaling $18,500 (high: $2,500, low: $1,500).
Type of support: Scholarships—to individuals.
Application information: Applications not accepted.
  Additional information: Unsolicited requests for funds not considered or acknowledged.
EIN: 621722004

8613
The Bill and Carol Latimer Charitable Foundation
201 W. Main St., Ste. E
Union City, TN 38261-2132 (731) 885-2888
Contact: William H. Latimer III, Pres.
FAX: (731) 885-3888;
E-mail: bill@latimerfoundation.org; URL: http://www.latimerfoundation.org/

Foundation type: Independent foundation
Purpose: No-interest loans to graduating seniors of Obion, Weakley, and Lake county, TN to secure a college or technical education at accredited schools.
Financial data: Year ended 12/31/2012. Assets, $133,188,510 (M); Expenditures, $11,949,503; Total giving, $11,516,834; Loans to individuals, 8 loans totaling $26,705.
Fields of interest: Higher education.
Type of support: Student loans—to individuals; Support to graduates or students of specific schools; Technical education support; Undergraduate support.
Application information: Applications accepted. Application form required. Application form available on the grantmaker's web site.
  Deadline(s): June 8
  Applicants should submit the following:
    1) FAFSA
    2) Class rank
    3) Financial information
    4) GPA
    5) ACT
    6) Photograph
    7) Letter(s) of recommendation
    8) Essay
  Additional information: Application information and form available on foundation web site.
Program description:
  College Opportunity Fund: Provides interest free loans to students graduating from Obion, Weakly and Lake County, TN, high schools to secure a

college or technical education from an accredited school of their choice.
EIN: 203450991

8614
The Lazarus Foundation, Inc.
340 Martin Luther King Blvd.,Ste. 200
Bristol, TN 37620-2313

Foundation type: Operating foundation
Purpose: Grants by referral only to financially needy individuals, primarily in the Bristol, TN, area.
Financial data: Year ended 12/31/2012. Assets, $387,259 (M); Expenditures, $817,083; Total giving, $677,352.
Type of support: Grants for special needs.
Application information: Applications not accepted.
  Additional information: Individual applications not accepted. Referrals accepted throughout the year.
EIN: 541654943

8615
Le Bonheur Children's Medical Center Foundation
850 Poplar Ave.
Memphis, TN 38105-4585 (901) 287-6308
Contact: Kavanaugh Casey, Exec. Dir.
FAX: (901) 287-5999;
E-mail: kavanaugh.casey@lebonheur.org; Mailing Address : P.O. Box 41817, Memphis, TN 38174-1817; Tel. for Kavanaugh Casey : (901)-287-6332; URL: http://www.lebonheur.org/ways-to-help/about-the-le-bonheur-foundation/

Foundation type: Public charity
Purpose: Residencies and fellowships to pediatricians, pediatric subspecialists, pharmacists, respiratory therapists and orthopaedics at Le Bonheur Hospital, TN.
Financial data: Year ended 12/31/2011. Assets, $24,442,733 (M); Expenditures, $10,086,714; Total giving, $6,895,358; Grants to individuals, totaling $204,345.
Fields of interest: Research; Health care; Pediatrics; Pharmacology; Pediatrics research; Pharmacology research.
Type of support: Fellowships; Residencies.
Application information:
  Initial approach: Tel.
  Additional information: Contact foundation for application guidelines.
EIN: 621872938

8616
The Lead Belly Foundation, Inc.
2441Q Old Fort Pkwy., Ste. 308
Murfreesboro, TN 37128 (615) 403-8091
Contact: Tanya Singh, Exec. Dir.
FAX: (615) 250-8757;
E-mail: leadbellymusic@gmail.com; URL: http://www.leadbelly.org

Foundation type: Operating foundation
Purpose: Music scholarships to individual school-age students who desire to study a musical instrument for the purpose of enriching their lives academically, recreationally, and socially.
Financial data: Year ended 12/31/2012. Assets, $290,967 (M); Expenditures, $145,291; Total giving, $10,375. Scholarships—to individuals amount not specified.
Fields of interest: Arts education; Music.
Type of support: Scholarships—to individuals.

Application information: Applications accepted. Application form required. Application form available on the grantmaker's web site.

Initial approach: Application

Send request by: Mail

Applicants should submit the following:
 1) Essay
 2) Letter(s) of recommendation

Additional information: Letters of recommendations should be sealed, and be from two different sources. Essays are for high scool students only. Copies of certificates, awards or recogntion received, as well as current (past year) grades should also be included.

EIN: 621458267

8617
Arthur K. & Sylvia S. Lee Scholarship Foundation

P.O. Box 681943
Franklin, TN 37068-1943 (615) 771-8300
Contact: James B. Ford, Secy.-Treas.
Application address: 810 Crescent Centre Dr., Ste. 600, Franklin, TN 37067

Foundation type: Company-sponsored foundation
Purpose: Scholarships primarily to children and dependents of employees of United Cities Gas Co.
Financial data: Year ended 12/31/2012. Assets, $1,088,735 (M); Expenditures, $103,188; Total giving, $78,058; Grants to individuals, 111 grants totaling $78,058 (high: $1,400, low: -$3,650).
Fields of interest: Higher education.
Type of support: Employee-related scholarships.
Application information: Application form required.
 Deadline(s): June 1 for applications and June 30 for transcripts.
Company name: Atmos Energy Corporation
EIN: 366069067

8618
Ruthe Edmondson Leyen Memorial Fund

9735 Kingston Pike
Knoxville, TN 37922-3346 (865) 691-2834
Contact: Thomas W. Harper, Secy.

Foundation type: Independent foundation
Purpose: Grants of no more than $1,000 each to various indigent patients for assistance with medical expenses and other living essentials.
Financial data: Year ended 12/31/2012. Assets, $48,862 (M); Expenditures, $8,084; Total giving, $8,062.
Fields of interest: Economically disadvantaged.
Type of support: Grants for special needs.
Application information: Applications accepted.
 Initial approach: Letter
 Deadline(s): 5th of every month
 Additional information: Letter must describe circumstances.
EIN: 311742587

8619
Mercy Health Partners Foundation, Inc.

615 Elsinore Pl.
Knoxville, TN 37917-4505 (513) 639-2800
URL: http://www.mercy.com/foundation_main.asp

Foundation type: Public charity
Purpose: Assistance for patient medical treatment and expenses in the Knoxville, TN area, and for Mercy Health Partners employee scholarships, housing, utilities and other needs.
Publications: Newsletter.

Financial data: Year ended 12/31/2011. Assets, $43,374,879 (M); Expenditures, $5,135,589; Total giving, $4,834,458; Grants to individuals, totaling $170,675.
Fields of interest: Education; Medical care, in-patient care.
Type of support: Scholarships—to individuals; Employee-related welfare.
Application information: Contact the foundation for additional guidelines.
EIN: 621247676

8620
Methodist Healthcare Foundation

1211 Union Ave. Ste. 450
Memphis, TN 38104-6638 (901) 516-0500
Contact: Paula Jacobson, Pres.
E-mail: paula.jacobson@mlh.org; URL: http://methodisthealth.org/

Foundation type: Public charity
Purpose: Scholarships to students in the Methodist Hospital's service area in TN. Also, grants to physicians in the Methodist Healthcare system.
Financial data: Year ended 12/31/2011. Assets, $13,974,850 (M); Expenditures, $6,061,005; Total giving, $3,320,310; Grants to individuals, totaling $1,796,438.
Fields of interest: Health care.
Type of support: Grants to individuals; Undergraduate support.
Application information: Applications accepted. Application form required.
 Initial approach: Letter
 Additional information: Contact foundation for complete eligibility criteria.
EIN: 237320638

8621
Methodist Medical Center

(also known as Methodist Medical Center of Oak Ridge)
990 Oak Ridge Tpke.
Oak Ridge, TN 37831-2529 (865) 835-1000
URL: http://www.mmcoakridge.com/

Foundation type: Public charity
Purpose: Scholarships to graduating high school seniors in the eastern TN, area pursuing a health-related career.
Financial data: Year ended 12/31/2011. Assets, $190,559,810 (M); Expenditures, $187,350,086; Total giving, $92,001; Grants to individuals, totaling $25,242.
Fields of interest: Health sciences school/education; Health care.
Type of support: Scholarships—to individuals.
Application information: Applications accepted. Interview required.
 Initial approach: Letter
 Applicants should submit the following:
  1) Letter(s) of recommendation
  2) SAT
  3) GPA
  4) ACT
 Additional information: Students must be accepted at an accredited college. Selection is based on scholastic record, and recommendations.
Program description:
 Scholarships: Scholarships are provided to assist qualified individuals pursuing professions in the area of health care. Scholarship recipients must be graduating seniors enrolled as full-time students during the award period.
EIN: 620636239

8622
Metropolitan Inter-Faith Association

910 Vance Ave.
Memphis, TN 38126-2911 (901) 527-0208
E-mail: ewhitten@mifa.org; URL: http://www.mifa.org/

Foundation type: Public charity
Purpose: Emergency funds and in-kind gifts to individuals and families in need in Memphis, TN with rent, utilities, food, clothing, and other necessities for families suffering from an unexpected loss of income.
Publications: Annual report; Financial statement; Newsletter.
Financial data: Year ended 06/30/2011. Assets, $8,018,711 (M); Expenditures, $10,975,649; Total giving, $2,585,568; Grants to individuals, totaling $2,585,568.
Fields of interest: Human services; Economically disadvantaged.
Type of support: Emergency funds; Grants for special needs.
Application information: See web site or contact the association for additional information.
EIN: 620803601

8623
Mid-Cumberland Community Action Agency, Inc.

233 Legends Dr., Ste. 103
P.O. Box 310
Lebanon, TN 37087-5306 (615) 742-1113
Contact: Kreda Yokley, Exec. Dir.
FAX: (615) 742-3911; Additional tel.: (615) 453-2243; URL: http://www.mid-cumberlandcaa.com/

Foundation type: Public charity
Purpose: Financial and emergency assistance to low-income individuals and families of middle Tennessee with utility, prescription drug, housing, food and other special needs.
Financial data: Year ended 06/30/2011. Assets, $2,202,236 (M); Expenditures, $18,222,315; Total giving, $7,606,484; Grants to individuals, totaling $7,606,484.
Fields of interest: Human services; Economically disadvantaged.
Type of support: In-kind gifts; Grants for special needs.
Application information: Applications accepted.
 Additional information: Some assistance require application form. Contact the agency for eligibility determination.
EIN: 620859072

8624
Middle Tennessee State University Foundation

c/o Wood-Stegall, MTSU
P.O. Box 109
Murfreesboro, TN 37132-0001 (615) 904-8045
FAX: (615) 898-3345; URL: http://www.mtsu.edu/development/foundation.php

Foundation type: Public charity
Purpose: Scholarships to qualified recipients for higher education.
Financial data: Year ended 06/30/2012. Assets, $66,158,372 (M); Expenditures, $7,623,340; Total giving, $1,251,644; Grants to individuals, totaling $1,251,644.
Fields of interest: Higher education.
Type of support: Scholarships—to individuals.

Application information: Applicant must show financial need, academic merit and major field of study.
EIN: 620695507

8625
Nashville CARES, Inc.
633 Thompson Ln.
Nashville, TN 37204-3616 (615) 259-4866
Contact: LoLita Toney M.A., Pres.
FAX: (615) 259-4849;
E-mail: info@nashvillecares.org; Toll-free tel.: (800) 845-4266; URL: http://www.nashvillecares.org

Foundation type: Public charity
Purpose: Assistance with mortgage, rent and utility bills to HIV/AIDS patients in Middle Tennessee, as well as help with paying for their medicine and medical care.
Publications: Annual report; Newsletter.
Financial data: Year ended 06/30/2012. Assets, $5,168,264 (M); Expenditures, $13,090,685; Total giving, $8,760,142; Grants to individuals, totaling $8,760,142.
Fields of interest: AIDS, people with; Economically disadvantaged.
Type of support: Grants for special needs.
Application information:
Initial approach: Letter
Additional information: Clients experiencing financial concerns must meet with their case manager to discuss the problem. If CARES resources are appropriate to the client's situation, the case manager will assist the client in gathering the needed documentation to seek assistance.
EIN: 621274532

8626
Nashville Predators Foundation
501 Broadway
Nashville, TN 37203-3932 (615) 770-2303
Contact: Sean Henry, Pres.
FAX: (615) 770-2309;
E-mail: ewilhelm@nashvillepredators.com;
URL: http://predators.nhl.com/club/page.htm?id=37108

Foundation type: Public charity
Purpose: Scholarships by nomination only to residents of Nashville and Middle Tennessee area, who have at least a 3.0 GPA.
Publications: Application guidelines; Grants list.
Financial data: Year ended 06/30/2012. Assets, $895,731 (M); Expenditures, $1,042,626; Total giving, $870,195; Grants to individuals, totaling $12,500.
Type of support: Awards/grants by nomination only; Undergraduate support.
Application information: Application form required. Application form available on the grantmaker's web site.
Initial approach: Letter
Applicants should submit the following:
1) Transcripts
2) Letter(s) of recommendation
3) Essay
Additional information: All scholarship candidates must be nominated by a teacher or coach. See web site for additional application requirements.
EIN: 621751832

8627
Nashville Rescue Mission
639 Lafayette St.
Nashville, TN 37203-4226 (615) 255-2475
Contact: Glenn Cranfield, Pres. and C.E.O.
E-mail: rescue@nashvillerescuemission.org;
URL: http://www.nashvillerescuemission.org

Foundation type: Public charity
Purpose: Giving limited to in-kind emergency assistance to needy individuals in the central TN area.
Financial data: Year ended 09/30/2011. Assets, $14,432,070 (M); Expenditures, $11,277,471; Total giving, $2,976,333; Grants to individuals, totaling $1,981,068.
Fields of interest: Human services, emergency aid; Human services.
Type of support: Emergency funds; In-kind gifts.
Application information: Applications not accepted.
EIN: 626018832

8628
National Foundation for Transplants, Inc.
5350 Poplar Ave., Ste. 430
Memphis, TN 38119-3826 (901) 684-1697
Contact: Jackie D. Hancock, Jr., C.E.O.
FAX: (901) 684-1128; E-mail: info@transplants.org;
Toll-free tel.: (800) 489-3863; URL: http://transplants.org

Foundation type: Public charity
Purpose: Financial assistance to organ and tissue transplant candidates and recipients to supplant costs associated with medical expenses and post-transplant care.
Publications: Annual report; Financial statement; Informational brochure; Newsletter.
Financial data: Year ended 06/30/2012. Assets, $5,361,297 (M); Expenditures, $4,290,758; Total giving, $2,613,893; Grants to individuals, totaling $2,613,893.
Fields of interest: Health care; Organ diseases; Surgery.
Type of support: Grants for special needs.
Application information: Eligibility is determined by financial need.
EIN: 581527254

8629
National Storytelling Membership Association
P. O. Box 795
Jonesborough, TN 37659-1368 (423) 913-8201
Contact: Karin Hensley, Dir. of Opers.
FAX: (423) 753-9331; E-mail: nsn@storynet.org;
Toll-free tel.: (800) 525-4514, e-mail:
karin@storynet.org; URL: http://www.storynet.org/

Foundation type: Public charity
Purpose: Grants to support a model storytelling project that can promote change in communities and individuals. Grants also to accomplished and emerging storytellers as well as a membership program.
Publications: Application guidelines.
Financial data: Year ended 12/31/2011. Assets, $383,842 (M); Expenditures, $277,689; Total giving, $38,365; Grants to individuals, totaling $38,365.
Fields of interest: Folk arts; Performing arts; Arts, artist's services.
Type of support: Awards/prizes; Fiscal agent/sponsor.

Application information: Applications accepted. Application form required. Application form available on the grantmaker's web site.
Initial approach: Letter
Deadline(s): Apr. 15 for NSN Member Grants, Apr. 30 for Brimstone Award for Applied Storytelling, Aug. for J.J. Reneaux Mentorship Grant
Final notification: Recipients notified June 15 for NSN Grants, June 5 for Brimstone Award, Oct. for J.J. Reneaux Grant
Additional information: See web site for additional application guidelines.
Program descriptions:
Brimstone Award for Applied Storytelling: Grants of $5,000 will be awarded in support of storytelling projects that are service-oriented, based in a community or local organization, and replicable in other places and situations. Projects should have impact beyond their own communities, organizations, or clients, inspiring excellence in applied storytelling work and communicating to new audiences the humanitarian possibilities of storytelling. Projects may involve various kinds of stories, including traditional tales and myths as well as personal and ad hoc narratives. Although oral storytelling should be central to the project, the work need not be conducted by professional storytellers. Areas of interest include health care, environmental education/activism, community development, law, multicultural awareness, organizational development, leadership, intergenerational initiatives, empowerment of the disabled, substance abuse prevention, and educational curriculum at all levels.
J.J. Reneaux Emerging Artist Grant: This program awards $1,000 to a storyteller of major and unique performing talent who has not yet received wide public recognition. Grants will fund activities that advance storytelling skills, such as workshops, specific courses of study, coaching or work with a director, mentoring by senior tellers, relevant conference attendance, and other forms of training. Recipients should intend to gain at least part of their income for professional storytelling performance, and should not yet have received wide public recognition (such as featuring at a major festival or theater).
J.J. Reneaux Mentorship Artist Grant: This grant awards $1,250 for a gifted younger storyteller (between 18 and 30 years old) to work with a seasoned teller as mentor. Grants will provide $500 to the applicant for expenses related to the plan of work with the mentor (travel, lodging, additional fees, etc.), and $750 to a well-respected, seasoned storyteller who will serve as a mention to the applicant during the grant year by providing individual coaching sessions and/or appropriate workshops. Recipients must intend to gain at least part of their income from professional storytelling performance, have at least one hour of fully developed repertoire, and have yet to receive wide public recognition (such as featuring at a major festival or theater), and should already have several performance credits.
Jack and Carole Ann Huebner Award: This $500 award is given to a National Storytelling Network Member Grant applicant whose proposal involves the telling of traditional folktales and historical stories.
NSN Member Grants: Support is available to National Storytelling Network (NSN) individual, associate, and affiliate members may apply for funding up to $1,000 to develop new projects. Support is available for the development of individual work, collaborative projects, community-based storytelling programs, or for scholarly research. Eligible applicants must be

current NSN individual or affiliate members who have been continuing members before Oct. 31 of the year preceding grant awards. Only one grant is awarded to any one applicant in a single year.

Sponsored Member Program: This program allows independent artists and small storytelling organizations without 501(c)(3) status the opportunity to apply for funds under its nonprofit umbrella and thus makes new sources of funding available to them. Members also receive assistance in preparing proposals for outside funding. The association will charge an administrative fee of eight percent of all grant monies received from successful grant proposals.
EIN: 621760203

8630
Niswonger Foundation, Inc.
c/o Tusculum College
16 Gilland St.
P.O. Box 5112
Greeneville, TN   37743-0001   (423) 798-7836
URL: http://www.niswongerfoundation.org/

Foundation type: Operating foundation
Purpose: Scholarships to individuals for attendance at colleges or universities of their choice.
Publications: Annual report; Informational brochure; Newsletter.
Financial data: Year ended 06/30/2013. Assets, $9,838,518 (M); Expenditures, $4,699,184; Total giving, $93,581; Grants to individuals, 3 grants totaling $6,500 (high: $2,500, low: $2,000).
Fields of interest: Higher education.
Type of support: Scholarships—to individuals.
Application information: Applications accepted. Application form required.
EIN: 621871605

8631
Parkwest Medical Center
9352 Park W. Blvd.
Knoxville, TN   37923-4325   (865) 373-1000
Contact: Rick Lassiter, Pres.
URL: http://www.treatedwell.com/home

Foundation type: Public charity
Purpose: Specific assistance to needy families of West Knox County, Knoxville, TN, with medical, dental and hospital expenses.
Financial data: Year ended 12/31/2011. Assets, $220,502,069 (M); Expenditures, $301,846,742; Total giving, $168,301; Grants to individuals, totaling $113,015.
Fields of interest: Human services.
Type of support: Grants for special needs.
Application information: Applications accepted.
EIN: 581897274

8632
Pearlpoint Cancer Support
(formerly The Minnie Pearl Cancer Foundation)
310 25th Ave. N., Ste. 103
Nashville, TN   37203-6535   (615) 467-1936
Contact: Susan Earl Hosbach, Pres. and C.E.O.
FAX: (615) 467-1940; E-mail: info@pearlpoint.org;
E-mail (for Susan E. Hosbach):
susan@minniepearl.org; toll-free tel.: (877)
467-1936; URL: https://pearlpoint.org/

Foundation type: Public charity
Purpose: Various grants to support cancer patients during their treatment.
Publications: Grants list.

Financial data: Year ended 05/31/2012. Assets, $1,358,644 (M); Expenditures, $1,178,394; Total giving, $30,955; Grants to individuals, totaling $14,824.
Fields of interest: Cancer research.
Type of support: Grants for special needs.
Application information: Applications not accepted.
Additional information: Unsolicited requests for funds not considered.
EIN: 581747771

8633
Precision Rubber Products Foundation, Inc.
6 Hale Ct.
Lebanon, TN   37087-8401

Foundation type: Company-sponsored foundation
Purpose: Scholarships to high school seniors who are children and grandchildren of active employees of Parker Seals at Lebanon and Livingston, TN, for higher education at accredited colleges or universities of their choice.
Financial data: Year ended 06/30/2012. Assets, $1,632,625 (M); Expenditures, $75,119; Total giving, $71,000; Grants to individuals, 5 grants totaling $13,000 (high: $3,000, low: $1,500).
Fields of interest: Higher education.
Type of support: Employee-related scholarships.
Application information: Applications accepted. Application form required.
Deadline(s): Dec.
Additional information: Application should include transcripts, and are available at the Human Resources Office of Parker Seals.
Company name: Wynn's-Precision, Inc.
EIN: 310503347

8634
Rains Foundation
500 N. Main St.
Jamestown, TN   38556-3241   (931) 752-2112
Contact: Steve Rains, Pres.
URL: http://www.rainsfoundation.org/

Foundation type: Company-sponsored foundation
Purpose: Scholarships to graduating high school students in Pickett, Fentress, Cumberland, and Morgan Counties, TN, for higher education.
Financial data: Year ended 05/31/2013. Assets, $12,853 (M); Expenditures, $48,972; Total giving, $26,825; Grants to individuals, 14 grants totaling $24,500 (high: $2,500, low: $1,000).
Fields of interest: Higher education.
Type of support: Scholarships—to individuals.
Application information: Applications accepted. Application form required.
Deadline(s): May 1
Additional information: Application form and essay must be submitted to guidance counselor.
EIN: 201446832

8635
Regal Foundation
7132 Regal Ln.
Knoxville, TN   37918-5803   (865) 925-9435
URL: http://www.regmovies.com/About-Regal/Community-Affairs

Foundation type: Company-sponsored foundation
Purpose: Scholarships to individuals who reside in TN for higher education.

Financial data: Year ended 12/31/2012. Assets, $7,450,049 (M); Expenditures, $3,561,793; Total giving, $3,339,671.
Fields of interest: Higher education.
Type of support: Scholarships—to individuals.
Application information: Applications not accepted.
Additional information: Unsolicited requests for funds not considered or acknowledged.
EIN: 134249812

8636
Richardson Family Henry County Educational Trust
P.O. Box 1090
Paris, TN   38242-1090   (731) 641-9382
Application address: c/o Commercial Bank

Foundation type: Operating foundation
Purpose: Scholarships to residents of Henry County, TN, who graduated from a high school in Henry County while maintaining a four-year GPA of 3.0.
Financial data: Year ended 12/31/2011. Assets, $147,614 (M); Expenditures, $7,036; Total giving, $5,000; Grant to an individual, 1 grant totaling $5,000.
Fields of interest: Higher education.
Type of support: Scholarships—to individuals.
Application information: Applications accepted. Application form required.
Deadline(s): None
Additional information: Application should include a complete biographical background, including academic records, school activities, and awards and honors received.
EIN: 621722603

8637
Mary Elizabeth Roark Scholarship Fund Trust
123 Public Sq.
Gallatin, TN   37066   (615) 452-4611

Foundation type: Independent foundation
Purpose: Scholarships to financially needy graduates of Gallatin High School or Westmoreland High School, TN.
Financial data: Year ended 12/31/2012. Assets, $0 (M); Expenditures, $10,443; Total giving, $9,410; Grants to individuals, 16 grants totaling $9,410 (high: $900, low: $121).
Fields of interest: College.
Type of support: Support to graduates or students of specific schools.
Application information: Applications accepted.
Initial approach: Letter
Deadline(s): None
Applicants should submit the following:
1) Transcripts
2) Resume
Additional information: Application must include personal life history, and work background. Applicant must have scholastic ability.
EIN: 626289349

8638
Betsy Ross Foundation, Inc.
1595 Hwy., 218 Bypass
Paris, TN   38242-6642   (731) 642-6116
Contact: Juliet Williams, Chair.

Foundation type: Independent foundation

Purpose: Financial assistance for indigent individuals and prison inmates in TN. College scholarships to individuals of TN for higher education.
Financial data: Year ended 11/30/2012. Assets, $1,641,244 (M); Expenditures, $32,444; Total giving, $20,350.
Fields of interest: Education; Correctional facilities; Economically disadvantaged.
Type of support: Scholarships—to individuals; Grants for special needs.
Application information: Applications accepted.
  Initial approach: Letter or telephone
  Additional information: Selection is based on financial need.
EIN: 621490795

8639
Ruby Tuesday Team Disaster Response Fund
150 W. Church Ave.
Maryville, TN 37801-4936 (865) 379-5700

Foundation type: Public charity
Purpose: Assistance to Ruby Tuesday employees and their families, who are adversely affected by disaster situations, man-made or natural.
Financial data: Year ended 05/31/2012. Assets, $257,159 (M); Expenditures, $123,510; Total giving, $122,249; Grants to individuals, totaling $122,249.
Fields of interest: Safety/disasters.
Type of support: Emergency funds; Employee-related welfare.
Application information: Applications not accepted.
  Additional information: Unsolicited requests for funds not considered or acknowledged.
EIN: 621868105

8640
Scarlett Family Foundation
4117 Hillsboro Pike, Ste. 103255
Nashville, TN 37215-2728
Contact: Tom Parrish, Exec. Dir.
Scholarship application address: c/o International Scholarship Tuition Services, Inc., 1321 Murfreesboro Rd., Ste. 800, Nashville, TN 37217, tel.: (615) 777-3750, fax: (615) 320-3151, e-mail: info@applyists.com
E-mail: tomparrish@scarlettfoundation.org; URL: http://www.scarlettfoundation.org/

Foundation type: Independent foundation
Purpose: College scholarships to high school seniors, college freshman, sophomores and juniors, who will graduate or have graduated from high school in one of the middle TN counties in pursuit of a business degree. Also eligible are individuals who have obtained a GED in the foundation's designated counties.
Publications: Application guidelines; Grants list.
Financial data: Year ended 06/30/2013. Assets, $53,260,252 (M); Expenditures, $2,221,891; Total giving, $1,712,095; Grants to individuals, 57 grants totaling $397,204 (high: $15,000, low: $2,462).
Fields of interest: Business school/education.
Type of support: Scholarships—to individuals.
Application information: Applications accepted. Application form required. Application form available on the grantmaker's web site.
  Initial approach: Application
  Deadline(s): Sept. 15
  Applicants should submit the following:
    1) Curriculum vitae

2) Essay
3) Financial information
4) GPA
  Additional information: Applicants must demonstrate financial need to be considered for a scholarship. See web site for specific eligibility requirements.
EIN: 201980932

8641
William E. Schmidt Foundation, Inc.
3712 Central Ave., Ste. 500
Nashville, TN 37205
Application address for Schmidt Youth Vocal Competition: c/o Linda McAlister, Coor., 109 Presser Hall, 501 S. Patterson Ave., Miami University, Oxford, OH 45056, tel.: (513) 529-3046; URL: http://www.schmidtfoundation.org/

Foundation type: Independent foundation
Purpose: Awards to talented vocal artists who are currently high school sophomores, juniors, or seniors.
Financial data: Year ended 12/31/2012. Assets, $3,467,374 (M); Expenditures, $312,650; Total giving, $253,650.
Type of support: Scholarships—to individuals.
Application information: Applications accepted. Application form available on the grantmaker's web site.
  Deadline(s): One month prior to competition date
  Additional information: Students are recommended by their vocal teachers or choral directors. Applicants should see their music teacher for application or see web site for additional application information. Unsolicited requests for funds not considered or acknowledged.
EIN: 351884241

8642
The ServiceMaster Foundation
860 Ridgelake Blvd., A3-4019
Memphis, TN 38120-9434 (901) 597-1400
Contact: Jim Fletcher

Foundation type: Company-sponsored foundation
Purpose: Disaster relief grants to ServiceMaster employees affected by natural disasters.
Financial data: Year ended 12/31/2012. Assets, $34,644 (M); Expenditures, $13,500; Total giving, $13,500; Grants to individuals, 12 grants totaling $13,500 (high: $2,500, low: $250).
Type of support: Emergency funds; Employee-related welfare.
Application information: Applications not accepted.
  Additional information: Unsolicited requests for funds not considered.
Company name: The ServiceMaster Company
EIN: 030503230

8643
Shiloh Ministries International, Inc.
5991 Edmondson Pike
Nashville, TN 37211 (615) 832-1978
Contact: Bruce Cambell, Pres.

Foundation type: Operating foundation
Purpose: Grants to ministers of the Gospel of Jesus Christ to support widows, orphans, or single parents.

Financial data: Year ended 12/31/2011. Assets, $39,948 (M); Expenditures, $60,332; Total giving, $58,700.
Fields of interest: Religion; Economically disadvantaged.
Type of support: Grants for special needs.
Application information: Applications not accepted.
EIN: 621768267

8644
Richard Siegel Foundation
P.O. Box 7100
Murfreesboro, TN 37133-1700 (615) 278-7111
Contact: Gina King

Foundation type: Independent foundation
Purpose: Scholarships to residents of Murfreesboro and Rutherford County, TN.
Financial data: Year ended 12/31/2012. Assets, $3,535,797 (M); Expenditures, $185,759; Total giving, $149,864; Grants to individuals, 9 grants totaling $78,614 (high: $1,250, low: $1,250).
Fields of interest: Higher education.
Type of support: Undergraduate support.
Application information:
  Initial approach: Letter
  Additional information: Contact foundation for current application deadline/guidelines.
EIN: 311646336

8645
John W. Simpson, Jr. Foundation Fund
P.O. Box 869
Jasper, TN 37347-0869 (423) 942-3600
Contact: John W. Moore, Treas.

Foundation type: Independent foundation
Purpose: College scholarships to worthy graduates of Marion County High School, Jasper, TN for attendance at colleges or universities.
Financial data: Year ended 12/31/2011. Assets, $114,189 (M); Expenditures, $5,132; Total giving, $4,000; Grants to individuals, 8 grants totaling $4,000 (high: $500, low: $500).
Fields of interest: Higher education.
Type of support: Support to graduates or students of specific schools.
Application information: Applications accepted. Application form required.
  Initial approach: Letter
  Deadline(s): None
  Applicants should submit the following:
    1) Transcripts
    2) Letter(s) of recommendation
  Additional information: Letter must request consideration as a recipient of the scholarship. Applicant must demonstrate need.
EIN: 626052488

8646
Soles4Souls, Inc.
319 Martingale Dr.
Old Hickory, TN 37138-3349 (615) 391-5723
FAX: (615) 391-5730; E-mail: info@giveshoes.org; Toll-free tel.: (866) 521-7463; URL: http://www.soles4souls.org

Foundation type: Public charity
Purpose: Assistance with shoes and clothing to individuals and families suffering from disasters around the globe.
Publications: Annual report.

Financial data: Year ended 06/30/2011. Assets, $16,293,567 (M); Expenditures, $71,861,474; Total giving, $45,428,589; Grants to individuals, 4,890,000 grants totaling $22,538,515.
Fields of interest: Disasters, preparedness/services; Human services, emergency aid.
Type of support: In-kind gifts.
Application information: Applications not accepted.
 Additional information: Unsolicited requests for funds not considered or acknowledged.
EIN: 204023482

8647
Southeast Tennessee Human Resource Agency
312 Resource Rd.
P.O. Box 909
Dunlap, TN 37327-0909 (423) 949-2191
Contact: Bill Harmon, Exec. Dir.
FAX: (423) 949-4023; E-mail: info@sethra.us; E-Mail for Bill Harmon: bharmon@sethra.us; URL: http://www.sethra.us

Foundation type: Public charity
Purpose: Financial and emergency assistance to low income individuals and families, elderly, or handicapped persons of Bledsoe, Bradley, Grundy, Hamilton, Marion, Megis, McMinn, Polk, Rhea, and Sequatchie counties, TN.
Financial data: Year ended 06/30/2011. Assets, $11,399,152 (M); Expenditures, $17,987,890; Total giving, $7,425,236; Grants to individuals, totaling $7,425,236.
Fields of interest: Aging; Disabilities, people with; Economically disadvantaged.
Type of support: Emergency funds; In-kind gifts; Grants for special needs.
Application information: See web site or contact the agency for eligiblilty determination.
EIN: 620926520

8648
Don & Roy Splawn Charitable Foundation
(formerly The Don Splawn Charitable Foundation)
c/o East, Inc.
1163 Gateway Ln.
Nashville, TN 37220-1007
Contact: Jeffrey Gould, Board Member
Scholarship inquiry address:
splawnscholarship@hotmail.com

Foundation type: Independent foundation
Purpose: Scholarships to financially disadvantaged high school seniors of CA, who wish to further their postsecondary education, of an academic or vocational nature.
Financial data: Year ended 12/31/2012. Assets, $3,839,113 (M); Expenditures, $315,894; Total giving, $147,425; Grant to an individual, 1 grant totaling $5,000.
Fields of interest: Vocational education, post-secondary; Higher education.
Type of support: Scholarships—to individuals; Undergraduate support.
Application information: Applications accepted. Application form required.
 Initial approach: Letter
 Deadline(s): Apr.
 Applicants should submit the following:
  1) FAFSA
  2) Essay
  3) Letter(s) of recommendation
  4) Transcripts
  5) Financial information
  6) GPA

Additional information: Selection is based on students who demonstrate significant dedication to their school, family and community.
EIN: 770420822

8649
Mildred T. Stahlman Education Foundation
144 2nd Ave.N. Ste.200
Nashville, TN 37201 (931) 296-2568
Application Address: c/o Humphreys County Scholarship Program, Attn.: Wavery County School Board, 2443 Hig Waverly, TN 37185

Foundation type: Independent foundation
Purpose: Scholarships to students or graduates of high schools in Humphreys County, TN, to attend a fully accredited college or university.
Financial data: Year ended 12/31/2012. Assets, $3,754 (M); Expenditures, $17,299; Total giving, $15,000; Grants to individuals, 6 grants totaling $15,000 (high: $3,000, low: $1,500).
Type of support: Support to graduates or students of specific schools; Undergraduate support.
Application information: Applications accepted. Application form required.
 Deadline(s): Contact foundation for application deadline.
 Applicants should submit the following:
  1) GPA
  2) Transcripts
  3) Financial information
  4) Letter(s) of recommendation
 Additional information: Application must also include personal information.
EIN: 621379222

8650
Stegall Charitable Educational Foundation
107 N. Maple
Murfreesboro, TN 37130 (615) 895-9890
Contact: Whitney Stegall, Jr., Tr.
Application address: P.O. Box 150786, Nashville, TN 37215-0786.
URL: http://foundationcenter.org/grantmaker/stegall/

Foundation type: Independent foundation
Purpose: Scholarships to residents of TN and individuals attending school in TN. First preference goes to individuals who have demonstrated a willingness to serve the public through past community service and second preference goes to individuals who intend to become attorneys.
Financial data: Year ended 12/31/2012. Assets, $895,382 (M); Expenditures, $57,565; Total giving, $35,000; Grants to individuals, 53 grants totaling $35,000 (high: $1,000, low: $500).
Fields of interest: Higher education; Law school/education.
Type of support: Undergraduate support.
Application information: Applications accepted. Application form required. Application form available on the grantmaker's web site.
 Initial approach: Letter
 Send request by: Mail
 Deadline(s): July 1 for fall semester, Dec. 1 for spring semester
 Applicants should submit the following:
  1) FAFSA
  2) Transcripts
  3) Financial information
  4) ACT
  5) GPA

Additional information: Scholarships are in the amount of $500 per semester and is paid directly to the educational institution on behalf of the student.
EIN: 481281001

8651
Joanne W. Stephenson Education Foundation
2719 Wortham Ave.
Nashville, TN 37215

Foundation type: Operating foundation
Purpose: Scholarships to students of Rawa Dolu Secondary School in Katmandu, Nepal.
Financial data: Year ended 11/30/2012. Assets, $147,204 (M); Expenditures, $42,297; Total giving, $39,000.
Type of support: Foreign applicants.
Application information: Applications not accepted.
 Additional information: Unsolicited requests for funds not accepted or acknowledged.
EIN: 256381907

8652
Stuttering Foundation of America, Inc.
(formerly Speech Foundation of America, also known as The Stuttering Foundation)
1805 Moriah Woods Blvd., Ste. 3
Memphis, TN 38117-7121 (800) 992-9392
Contact: Jane Fraser, Pres.
FAX: (901) 761-0484;
E-mail: info@stutteringhelp.org; Mailing address: Stuttering Foundation of America, Inc., c/o Jane Fraser, Pres., P.O. Box 11749, Memphis, TN 38111-0749; URL: http://www.stutteringhelp.org

Foundation type: Operating foundation
Purpose: Grants to professional speech pathologists for training programs designed to improve the treatment of stuttering.
Publications: Annual report; Informational brochure; Newsletter.
Financial data: Year ended 12/31/2012. Assets, $24,966,597 (M); Expenditures, $1,794,623; Total giving, $254,375; Grants to individuals, 35 grants totaling $4,375 (high: $125, low: $125).
Fields of interest: Speech/hearing centers.
Type of support: Program development.
Application information: Applications accepted.
 Initial approach: Letter
 Deadline(s): None
EIN: 626047678

8653
Temple-Inland Foundation
6400 Poplar Ave.
Memphis, TN 38197-0100 (512) 434-3160
FAX: (512) 434-2566; Application address: c/o Karen Lee, 1300 S. Mopac Expwy., Fl. 3N, Austin, TX 78746, tel.: (512) 434-3160.; URL: http://www.templeinland.com/OurMission/CorporateCitizenship/social.asp

Foundation type: Company-sponsored foundation
Purpose: Undergraduate scholarships to children of employees of Temple-Inland, Inc. and its subsidiaries.
Financial data: Year ended 06/30/2012. Assets, $24,995 (M); Expenditures, $1,427,189; Total giving, $1,422,669.
Fields of interest: Higher education.
Type of support: Employee-related scholarships; Undergraduate support.

Application information: Applications not accepted.

Additional information: Unsolicited requests for funds not considered or acknowledged.

Program description:

Temple-Inland Foundation Scholarship Program: The foundation annually awards four-year college scholarships to children of active, retired, or deceased employees of Temple-Inland. The program is designed to recognize students who demonstrate outstanding academic ability, leadership, and other significant qualities.

Company name: Temple-Inland Inc.

EIN: 751977109

8654
The Thomley Foundation Inc.
P.O. Box 1562
Brentwood, TN   37024-1562

Foundation type: Operating foundation

Purpose: Grants to economically disadvantaged individuals in the U.S. and Italy for medical and other assistance.

Financial data: Year ended 12/31/2012. Assets, $264,131 (M); Expenditures, $340,488; Total giving, $146,474.

Fields of interest: Health care; Economically disadvantaged.

International interests: Italy.

Type of support: Foreign applicants; Grants for special needs.

Application information: Applications not accepted.

Additional information: Unsolicited requests for funds not considered or acknowledged.

EIN: 631207742

8655
Tomorrow Scholarship Fund Trust
c/o Allison Barker Watson
P.O. Box 3549
Crossville, TN   38557-3549   (703) 916-0655
Contact: Regina Warner Derzon
Application address: 3320 Grass Hill Ter., Falls Church, VA 22044

Foundation type: Operating foundation

Purpose: Scholarships to graduates of Cumberland County, TN, high schools.

Financial data: Year ended 12/31/2011. Assets, $46,660 (M); Expenditures, $10,000; Total giving, $10,000; Grants to individuals, 10 grants totaling $10,000 (high: $1,000, low: $1,000).

Type of support: Support to graduates or students of specific schools; Undergraduate support.

Application information: Application form required.

Deadline(s): May 1

EIN: 621747882

8656
The Unaka Foundation, Inc.
(formerly Unaka Scholarship Foundation, Inc.)
1500 Industrial Rd.
Greeneville, TN   37745-3541   (423) 639-1171
Contact: Dominick Jackson, Pres.

Foundation type: Company-sponsored foundation

Purpose: Scholarships to children of Unaka Group employees who have worked at least 10 weeks for five seasons with the company, primarily in SC and TN.

Financial data: Year ended 06/30/2012. Assets, $7,685 (M); Expenditures, $74,172; Total giving, $74,150; Grants to individuals, totaling $43,000.

Type of support: Employee-related scholarships.

Application information: Application form required.

Deadline(s): None

Company name: Unaka Group (The)

EIN: 621530053

8657
United Methodist Higher Education Foundation
60 Music Square E., Ste. 350
P.O. Box 340005
Nashville, TN   37203   (615) 649-3990
FAX: (615) 649-3980;
E-mail: umhefscholarships@gbhem.org; Additional tel.: (800) 811-8110; E-Mail for Robert R. Fletcher: bfletcher@umhef.org; URL: http://www.umhef.org

Foundation type: Public charity

Purpose: Scholarships to United Methodist students for attendance at United Methodist related schools for higher education.

Publications: Application guidelines; Annual report; Newsletter.

Financial data: Year ended 12/31/2011. Assets, $43,754,507 (M); Expenditures, $2,410,661; Total giving, $1,305,548; Grants to individuals, totaling $1,290,548.

Fields of interest: Higher education; Theological school/education; Disasters, 9/11/01.

Type of support: Scholarships—to individuals; Support to graduates or students of specific schools.

Application information: Applications accepted. Application form required.

Send request by: Online

Deadline(s): Mar. 1 for United Methodist Dollars for Scholars, and United Methodist Leadership Scholars, Sept. 1 for Foundation Merit Scholars, none for Sept. 11 Memorial Scholarship

Additional information: See web site for additional guidelines.

Program descriptions:

Foundation Merit Scholars Program: The program seeks to foster value-centered education in a Christian context in UM-related educational institutions through scholarship assistance to UM students. Applicants must be full and active members of the United Methodist church for at least one year, have a minimum GPA of 3.0 (or equivalent), demonstrate financial need, enrolled in a full-time degree program at a United Methodist-related institution, citizen or permanent resident of the U.S., and seminary students must be working toward ordination at the master's level. Awards range from $1,000 to $3,000. Recipients are chosen by each United Methodist-related institution.

September 11 Memorial Scholarship Program: The program provides assistance for surviving victims and dependents of victims of the terrorist attacks on September 11. The scholarships are restricted to either: 1) students attending one of the 122 United Methodist-related institutions in the United States, or 2) United Methodist students attending higher education institutions in the United States. Applications will be accepted for candidates who have lost a parent or guardian or have had a parent or guardian disabled as a result of the Sept. 11, 2001 terrorist attacks. Applicants must be U.S. citizens or permanent residents enrolled in a full-time degree program (graduate or undergraduate) and must maintain satisfactory academic progress as defined by the institution he/she is attending.

United Methodist Dollars for Scholars Program: The foundation will provide a $1,000 matching scholarship for churches that raise and provide $1,000 on behalf of student congregational members enrolled or planning to enroll in a United Methodist-related college, university or seminary. These include matching scholarships specifically designated for Hispanic American, Asian American and Native American students who are eligible for HANA funds (funded through the General Board of Higher Education and Ministry). Applicants to the program must be a U.S. citizen or permanent resident enrolled or enrolling as a full-time student in the fall at a UM-related college, university, or seminary and be an active member of the United Methodist Church for at least one year.

United Methodist Leadership Scholars Program: Through the Leadership Scholars program, local churches are encouraged to provide $1,000 scholarships on behalf of students planning to enroll in a participating United Methodist-related college or University located in the Southeastern Jurisdiction. These institutions have agreed to match local church funds for a total award of $2,000. Applications may be submitted only by students who are first time enrolles in a United Methodist-related college or university. Applicants must be active members of the United Methodist Church for at least one year.

EIN: 237077869

8658
United Way of the Mid-South
6775 Lenox Ctr. Ct., Ste. 200
Memphis, TN   38115-4428   (901) 433-4300
FAX: (901) 433-3100; URL: http://www.uwmidsouth.org

Foundation type: Public charity

Purpose: Assistance to individuals and families in need throughout Crittenden, DeSoto, Fayette, Lauderdale, Shelby, Tate, Tipton, and Tunica counties, TN.

Publications: Annual report; Informational brochure; Newsletter.

Financial data: Year ended 12/31/2011. Assets, $28,246,760 (M); Expenditures, $25,532,819; Total giving, $18,801,232; Grants to individuals, 108,694 grants totaling $823,937.

Fields of interest: Employment, job counseling; Human services; United Ways and Federated Giving Programs.

Type of support: Emergency funds; Grants to individuals.

Application information: Applications accepted.

Additional information: Contact the organization for eligibility determination.

EIN: 561010742

8659
Upper East Tennessee Human Development Agency
301 Louis St.
P.O. Box 46
Kingsport, TN   37660-5129   (423) 247-5149
Contact: Lois Smith, Exec. Dir.
FAX: (423) 247-1821; E-mail: lsmith@naxs.com; URL: http://www.uethda.org

Foundation type: Public charity

Purpose: Assistance to low-income individuals and families of Carter, Greene, Hancock, Hawkins, Johnson, Sullivan, Unicoi, and Washington counties, TN, with food, shelter, energy assistance and other special needs.

Financial data: Year ended 06/30/2011. Assets, $3,541,983 (M); Expenditures, $23,898,327;

Total giving, $10,128,505; Grants to individuals, totaling $8,657,772.
Fields of interest: Aging; Disabilities, people with; Economically disadvantaged; Homeless.
Type of support: In-kind gifts; Grants for special needs.
Application information: Applications accepted.
  Additional information: Applicant must demonstrate need of service. See web site for additional guidelines.
EIN: 620902005

8660
Hattie G. Watkins Educational Fund
c/o Regions Bank, Trust Dept.
1100 Ridgeway Loop, Ste. 100
Memphis, TN   38120-4053   (901) 821-8814
Contact: Crystal Mcmahan

Foundation type: Independent foundation
Purpose: Scholarships of up to $750 per semester to individuals for undergraduate education, primarily in TN.
Financial data: Year ended 10/31/2012. Assets, $242,964 (M); Expenditures, $15,808; Total giving, $9,930.
Type of support: Undergraduate support.
Application information: Applications accepted. Application form required.
  Deadline(s): May 31
  Applicants should submit the following:
    1) Transcripts
    2) Resume
    3) Financial information
EIN: 626051024

8661
G. H. Weems Educational Fund
126 E. Main St.
Waverly, TN   37185-2143   (865) 690-4112
Contact: William M. Slayden III, Exec. Dir.
Application address: 122 Debusk Ln., Knoxville, TN 37922, tel.: (865) 690-4112

Foundation type: Independent foundation
Purpose: Scholarships and interest-free honor student loans to residents of Montgomery, Dickson, and Humphreys counties, TN, for study in education-related fields.
Publications: Newsletter.
Financial data: Year ended 12/31/2011. Assets, $683,181 (M); Expenditures, $70,927; Total giving, $39,586; Grants to individuals, totaling $21,250.
Fields of interest: Teacher school/education.
Type of support: Scholarships—to individuals; Student loans—to individuals.
Application information: Applications accepted. Application form required.

Initial approach: Letter
  Deadline(s): Apr. 1
EIN: 626047271

8662
Wellmont Foundation, Inc.
(formerly Holston Valley Health Care Foundation)
1905 American Way
Kingsport, TN   37660-5882   (423) 230-8200
Contact: Todd Norris, Exec. Dir.
URL: http://www.wellmontfoundation.org/

Foundation type: Public charity
Purpose: Financial support to current employees through four emergency funds as well as, a program to assist indigent patients with pharmaceutical, transportation, and other health-related needs.
Financial data: Year ended 06/30/2012. Assets, $32,520,821 (M); Expenditures, $5,523,911; Total giving, $4,492,636; Grants to individuals, totaling $108,730.
Fields of interest: Nursing school/education; Health care.
Type of support: Employee-related scholarships; Scholarships—to individuals; Grants for special needs.
Application information: Applications not accepted.
  Additional information: Contributes only to preselected individuals. Unsolicited requests for funds not considered or acknowledged.
EIN: 581594191

8663
Peary Wilemon National Cotton Ginners Scholarship Foundation
P.O. Box 2995
Cordova, TN   38088-2995   (901) 274-9030
Contact: W. Harrison Ashley, Exec. V.P.
URL: http://www.cotton.org/ncga/scholarship/index.cfm

Foundation type: Independent foundation
Purpose: Scholarships to eligible students pursuing studies related to the cotton ginning industry.
Financial data: Year ended 02/29/2012. Assets, $102,267 (M); Expenditures, $3,062; Total giving, $3,000; Grants to individuals, 3 grants totaling $3,000 (high: $1,000, low: $1,000).
Fields of interest: Higher education; Agriculture.
Type of support: Graduate support; Undergraduate support.
Application information: Applications accepted. Application form required.
  Deadline(s): Mar. 1
  Applicants should submit the following:
    1) Class rank
    2) Transcripts

3) SAT
4) Letter(s) of recommendation
5) GPA
6) ACT
  Additional information: Applicants must be at a minimum university sophomore level for their application to be considered.
EIN: 621595279

8664
Wills Memorial Foundation
(also known as County Executive)
1 N. Washington St.
Brownsville, TN   38012-2554

Foundation type: Independent foundation
Purpose: Scholarships to Haywood High School students in pursuit of an education in the medical field.
Financial data: Year ended 06/30/2013. Assets, $0 (M); Expenditures, $8,895; Total giving, $0.
Fields of interest: Medical school/education.
Type of support: Scholarships—to individuals; Support to graduates or students of specific schools.
Application information: Application form required.
  Deadline(s): Last week in June
  Additional information: Application can be obtained at the county Executive Office.
EIN: 620973997

8665
Woodbury Educational Foundation
26 Maple Dr.
Woodbury, TN   37190
Contact: Richard D. Hunter, Pres.

Foundation type: Independent foundation
Purpose: Scholarships to students of Cannon County, TN, high schools for undergraduate and vocational study.
Financial data: Year ended 05/31/2013. Assets, $662,072 (M); Expenditures, $33,143; Total giving, $30,000; Grants to individuals, 16 grants totaling $30,000 (high: $2,000, low: $1,000).
Fields of interest: Vocational education, post-secondary; Higher education.
Type of support: Support to graduates or students of specific schools; Undergraduate support.
Application information:
  Applicants should submit the following:
    1) ACT
    2) Transcripts
    3) Letter(s) of recommendation
EIN: 620470043

TEXAS

8666
ABG Ministries
511 West Shore Dr.
Richardson, TX 75080

Foundation type: Operating foundation
Purpose: Grants to missionaries of the Gospel who reside in Frisco, TX.
Financial data: Year ended 12/31/2012. Assets, $8,877 (M); Expenditures, $163,646; Total giving, $120,603; Grants to individuals, 2 grants totaling $120,603 (high: $118,003, low: $2,600).
Type of support: Grants to individuals.
Application information: Applications not accepted.
> *Additional information:* Unsolicited requests for funds not accepted.

EIN: 204956474

8667
Advanced Placement Strategies, Inc.
8350 N. Ctr. Expressway, Ste. M-2200
Dallas, TX 75206 (214) 346-1209
FAX: (214) 525-3099;
E-mail: info@apstrategies.org; Toll-free tel.: (888) 949-9702; URL: http://www.apstrategies.org

Foundation type: Public charity
Purpose: Need based and merit scholarships to high school students of Texas for academic preparation and transition to higher education.
Publications: Newsletter.
Financial data: Year ended 12/31/2011. Assets, $14,686,777 (M); Expenditures, $3,795,255; Total giving, $628,434; Grants to individuals, totaling $628,434.
Fields of interest: Higher education.
Type of support: Scholarships—to individuals.
Application information: Applications accepted. Application form required.
> *Additional information:* Applicants are selected based on recommendation of high school administrative personnel.

EIN: 752882595

8668
Affordable Caring Housing, Inc.
2518 Dartmouth St.
College Station, TX 77840-5074
Contact: Jason Bienski, Pres.

Foundation type: Public charity
Purpose: Assistance to low income individuals and families of TX, with affordable housing, assistance with obtaining affordable housing, and care and services for needy and the handicapped.
Financial data: Year ended 09/30/2012. Assets, $8,883,241 (M); Expenditures, $225,234; Total giving, $134,183; Grants to individuals, totaling $134,183.
Fields of interest: Housing/shelter; Physically disabled.
Type of support: Grants for special needs.
Application information: Contact the agency for eligibility determination.
EIN: 743019628

8669
AIDS Arms, Inc.
351 W. Jefferson Blvd., Ste. 300
Dallas, TX 75208-7860 (214) 521-5191
Contact: Raeline Nobles, Exec. Dir.
FAX: (214) 528-5879; TDD: (214) 231-0151;
URL: http://www.aidsarms.org

Foundation type: Public charity
Purpose: Prescription drug payment assistance for individuals with HIV and AIDS who live in or near Dallas, TX.
Publications: Informational brochure.
Financial data: Year ended 12/31/2011. Assets, $3,678,986 (M); Expenditures, $8,192,659; Total giving, $1,595,878; Grants to individuals, totaling $1,595,878.
Fields of interest: Health care, support services; Health care, patient services; AIDS, people with.
Type of support: Grants for special needs.
Application information: Contact foundation for complete program information.
EIN: 752306145

8670
Alamo Colleges Foundation, Inc.
(formerly Alamo Community College District Foundation)
201 W. Sheridan, Ste. C-3
San Antonio, TX 78204-1429
URL: http://legacy.alamo.edu/foundation/index.htm

Foundation type: Public charity
Purpose: Scholarships for needy and deserving students for attendance at Alamo Colleges, TX who would otherwise be unable to pursue a higher education.
Publications: Application guidelines.
Financial data: Year ended 12/31/2011. Assets, $12,767,446 (M); Expenditures, $1,533,328; Total giving, $1,278,025; Grants to individuals, totaling $1,278,025.
Fields of interest: Higher education.
Type of support: Support to graduates or students of specific schools.
Application information: Applications accepted. Application form required.
> *Initial approach:* Application
> *Send request by:* Online
> *Deadline(s):* Sept. 15
> *Applicants should submit the following:*
> 1) FAFSA
> 2) Transcripts
> 3) Essay
> *Additional information:* See web site for additional guidelines.

Program description:
> *Scholarships:* The foundation provides scholarships to students who are enrolled at any of the Alamo Colleges, as either a full- or part-time student. Eligible applicants must be pursuing an associate degree, certificate of completion, or transfer program, and must have and maintain a satisfactory GPA of at least 2.00. Applicant must be a U.S. citizen or eligible non-citizen.

EIN: 742422589

8671
Ralph Buchanan Albaugh Scholarship Trust
c/o Bank of America, N.A.
P.O. Box 831041
Dallas, TX 75283-1041 (254) 753-0181
Contact: Tim Brown, Committee Member
Application address: c/o Methodist Children Home, 1111 Herring Ave., Waco, TX 76708

Foundation type: Independent foundation
Purpose: Scholarships to residents of Methodist Home, Waco, TX, to attend postsecondary educational institutions.
Financial data: Year ended 12/31/2012. Assets, $1,428,502 (M); Expenditures, $78,009; Total giving, $61,720.
Fields of interest: Higher education.
Type of support: Scholarships—to individuals.
Application information: Applications accepted. Application form required.
> *Deadline(s):* None
> *Applicants should submit the following:*
> 1) Transcripts
> 2) Financial information

EIN: 746041694

8672
Alexander Foundation for Orthodontics Research & Education
840 W. Mitchell Dr.
Arlington, TX 76013-2505 (817) 277-3232
Contact: Dr. R. G. Alexander, Pres.
FAX: (817) 277-3826;
E-mail: support@alexanderdiscipline.com

Foundation type: Public charity
Purpose: Scholarships to orthodontics students participating in the Alexander Discipline.
Financial data: Year ended 12/31/2012. Assets, $254,033 (M); Expenditures, $42,334; Total giving, $3,000.
Type of support: Research; Scholarships—to individuals.
Application information: Applications accepted. Application form required.
> *Send request by:* Mail
> *Additional information:* Contact the foundation for additional guidelines.

Program description:
> *Alexander Foundation for Orthodontic Research and Education Grant Program:* The organization provides scholarship opportunities to approved applicants who demonstrate the desire to continue the legacy of the Alexander Discipline.

EIN: 752840046

8673
Alliance for Multicultural Community Services
6440 Hillcroft, Ste. 411
Houston, TX 77081-3104 (713) 776-4700
FAX: (713) 776-4730;
E-mail: info@allianceontheweb.org; URL: http://www.allianceontheweb.org

Foundation type: Public charity
Purpose: Financial assistance and resettlement services to refugees settling in Harris County, TX.
Publications: Annual report; Newsletter.
Financial data: Year ended 09/30/2011. Assets, $3,450,719 (M); Expenditures, $5,316,058; Total giving, $1,070,715; Grants to individuals, totaling $1,070,715.
Fields of interest: Immigrants/refugees.

Type of support: Emergency funds; Grants for special needs.
Application information: Applications accepted.
  Additional information: Contact the agency for eligibility criteria.
EIN: 760171217

8674
Alpha Epsilon Boule
(formerly Alpha Epsilon Boule Education Foundation)
1999 Bryan St., Ste. 3470
Dallas, TX 75201-6823
Contact: Dr. James L. Sweatt, Chair.
Application address: 3735 Blackstone, Dallas, TX

Foundation type: Independent foundation
Purpose: Scholarships to graduating seniors who are African American males of the Dallas Metroplex, TX area.
Financial data: Year ended 12/31/2011. Assets, $26,729 (M); Expenditures, $30,981; Total giving, $13,500; Grants to individuals, 13 grants totaling $13,500 (high: $1,500, low: $1,000).
Fields of interest: Higher education; African Americans/Blacks; Young adults, male.
Type of support: Scholarships—to individuals.
Application information: Applications accepted. Application form required.
  Deadline(s): Mar.
  Applicants should submit the following:
    1) Transcripts
    2) SAT
    3) Letter(s) of recommendation
    4) GPA
    5) Essay
    6) ACT
  Additional information: Faxed applications are not accepted.
EIN: 752541844

8675
Amarillo Area Foundation, Inc.
801 S. Fillmore, Ste. 700
Amarillo, TX 79101-3537 (806) 376-4521
Contact: For grants: Kathie Grant, Grants Coord.
FAX: (806) 373-3656; E-mail: haf@aaf-hf.org;
URL: http://www.amarilloareafoundation.org

Foundation type: Community foundation
Purpose: Scholarships to graduates of high schools in the 26 northernmost counties of the TX Panhandle for higher education.
Publications: Annual report; Informational brochure; Newsletter.
Financial data: Year ended 12/31/2012. Assets, $205,986,892 (M); Expenditures, $9,851,923; Total giving, $6,205,795; Grants to individuals, 783 grants totaling $827,475.
Fields of interest: Higher education; Nursing school/education; Health sciences school/education; Agriculture; Business/industry.
Type of support: Scholarships—to individuals; Support to graduates or students of specific schools; Undergraduate support.
Application information: Applications accepted. Application form required. Application form available on the grantmaker's web site.
  Initial approach: Application
  Send request by: Online
  Deadline(s): Feb. 14
  Applicants should submit the following:
    1) Letter(s) of recommendation
    2) Financial information
    3) SAT
    4) ACT

5) Transcripts
  Additional information: See web site for a complete listing of scholarship funds and online application. Attachments that are not uploaded to the online application must be hand delivered or mailed to the foundation's office by the deadline date or they will not be considered.
Program descriptions:
  Achievement Through Commitment to Education (ACE) Scholarship Program: CE provides access to higher education for students at these schools by providing numerous preparatory activities throughout each student's school career. ACE guarantees payment for tuition, fees, and books for up to 130 semester hours at Amarillo College (AC) or West Texas A&M University (WTAMU). Students receive the greatest benefit if they take 45 hours of core courses first at AC and then continue their education at WTAMU. Students can choose to start at WTAMU, but ACE will pay only as much as the cost of taking 45 hours from AC. ACE is "last money in" meaning all federal and private aid is applied prior to awarding ACE scholarship funds. ACE requires high school students to pledge annually to maintain at least an 80 grade point average, a 95% attendance record and appropriate behavior while attending high school.
  Scholarship Funds: The foundation manages a variety of individual funds awarding scholarships annually for students to attend college. Residents of the 26 northernmost counties of the Texas Panhandle are eligible for scholarships. The foundation offers scholarships in several different fields of study, such as accounting, agriculture, education, governmental services, human sciences, nursing, medical, pharmacology, and general studies. Each scholarship has specific eligibility criteria. See web site for additional information.
EIN: 750978220

8676
Amarillo College Foundation, Inc.
P.O. Box 447
Amarillo, TX 79178-0001 (806) 371-5107
FAX: (806) 371-5370; URL: http://www.actx.edu/foundation/

Foundation type: Public charity
Purpose: Scholarships to students for attendance at Amarillo College, TX for postsecondary education.
Publications: Application guidelines; Annual report; Newsletter.
Financial data: Year ended 08/31/2011. Assets, $28,822,453 (M); Expenditures, $1,158,996; Total giving, $832,648; Grants to individuals, 1,178 grants totaling $818,145.
Fields of interest: Higher education.
Type of support: Scholarships—to individuals; Support to graduates or students of specific schools.
Application information: Applications accepted. Application form required.
  Send request by: Mail or hand deliver
  Deadline(s): Vary
  Applicants should submit the following:
    1) Photograph
    2) Transcripts
    3) GPA
    4) Financial information
  Additional information: See web site for additional application guidelines.
EIN: 756029084

8677
American Academy of Nurse Practitioners Foundation
P.O. Box 12924
Austin, TX 78711-2924 (512) 276-5905
Contact: Kay Todd, Exec. Dir.
FAX: (512) 442-6469;
E-mail: foundation@aanp.org; Administrative address: P.O. Box 10729, Glendale, AZ 85318-0729; URL: http://www.aanp.org/foundation/

Foundation type: Public charity
Purpose: Scholarships, project grants, and research grants to members of the American Academy of Nurse Practitioners.
Publications: Application guidelines.
Financial data: Year ended 12/31/2011. Assets, $1,256,578 (M); Expenditures, $776,244; Total giving, $124,000; Grants to individuals, totaling $124,000.
Fields of interest: Nursing school/education; Allergies research; Asthma research; Alzheimer's disease research; Diabetes research.
Type of support: Research; Scholarships—to individuals.
Application information: Applications accepted. Application form required.
  Initial approach: Telephone, e-mail, or fax
  Send request by: Mail
  Deadline(s): Apr. for 1st funding cycle; Oct. or Nov. for 2nd funding cycle
  Additional information: Application should include application fee.
Program description:
  Student Scholarship: Thirteen scholarships of $3,500, through funding from Johnson and Johnson, is available to students of nursing.
EIN: 742861018

8678
American Heart Association, Inc.
7272 Greenville Ave.
Dallas, TX 75231-4596 (214) 570-5978
Contact: Donna Arnett, Pres.
FAX: (214) 706-1341;
E-mail: Review.personal.info@heart.org;
URL: http://www.heart.org

Foundation type: Public charity
Purpose: Scholarships to students in medical school or in master's or equivalent programs in accredited schools in the U.S. for research training in cardiovascular disease and stroke. Awards to promising and outstanding investigators in the early stages of their careers with interest in basic or clinical research.
Publications: Application guidelines; Annual report; Informational brochure (including application guidelines).
Financial data: Year ended 06/30/2012. Assets, $1,022,717,268 (M); Expenditures, $595,934,019; Total giving, $128,362,259; Grants to individuals, totaling $353,862.
Fields of interest: Medical school/education; Heart & circulatory diseases.
Type of support: Research; Scholarships—to individuals; Awards/prizes.
Application information:
  Send request by: E-mail for Scholarship
  Deadline(s): Mar. 19 for Scholarship
  Additional information: See web site for additional guidelines.
EIN: 135613797

8679
American Lung Association of the Central States, Inc.
(formerly American Lung Association of Missouri, Inc.)
8150 Brookriver Dr., LB-151, S-102
Dallas, TX 75247-4068 (713) 631-5864
E-mail: thalbrook@breathehealthy.org; *URL:* http://www.breathehealthy.org/

Foundation type: Public charity
Purpose: Research grants for the study of lung diseases, MO. Also, scholarships to individuals for asthma camp.
Publications: Annual report.
Financial data: Year ended 06/30/2012. Assets, $11,115,271 (M); Expenditures, $11,630,118.
Fields of interest: Lung research.
Type of support: Research.
Application information: Contact foundation for current application deadline/guidelines.
EIN: 430662525

8680
American Paint Horse Foundation
2800 Meacham Blvd.
Fort Worth, TX 76137-4603
Contact: Rosemary Teate, Treas.
FAX: (817) 834-3152; *E-mail:* rteate@apha.com; Mailing Address: P.O. Box 961023, Ft. Worth, TX 76161-0023, Tel. No. (817) 222-6431, E-mail.: foundation@apha.com; *URL:* http://www.aphfoundation.org

Foundation type: Public charity
Purpose: Scholarships to hard-working young horsemen and horsewomen who are members of the AJPHA or APHA.
Publications: Application guidelines.
Financial data: Year ended 12/31/2011. Assets, $1,467,044 (M); Expenditures, $89,393; Total giving, $44,390; Grants to individuals, totaling $44,390.
Fields of interest: Athletics/sports, training; Athletics/sports, equestrianism.
Type of support: Undergraduate support.
Application information: Applications accepted. Application form required. Application form available on the grantmaker's web site.
Initial approach: Letter
Deadline(s): Mar. 1
Applicants should submit the following:
1) Essay
2) Letter(s) of recommendation
EIN: 752699500

8681
American Porphyria Foundation
4900 Woodway, Ste. 780
Houston, TX 77056-1837 (713) 266-9617
Contact: Desiree H. Lyon, Exec. Dir.
FAX: (713) 840-9552; Toll-free tel.: (866) 273-3635; Mailing address: P.O. Box 22712, Houston, TX 77227-2712; *URL:* http://www.porphyriafoundation.com/

Foundation type: Public charity
Purpose: Grants to researchers in the field of porphyria pathogenesis to improve treatment and ultimately lead to a cure.
Publications: Newsletter.
Financial data: Year ended 12/31/2011. Assets, $230,297 (M); Expenditures, $592,949; Total giving, $141,500; Grants to individuals, totaling $141,500.

Fields of interest: Nerve, muscle & bone research; Diseases (rare) research.
Type of support: Research; Grants to individuals.
Application information: Applications accepted.
Additional information: Contact the foundation for guidelines.
EIN: 364401266

8682
American Quarter Horse Association
1600 Quarter Horse Dr.
Amarillo, TX 79104-3406 (806) 376-4811
URL: http://www.aqha.com

Foundation type: Public charity
Purpose: Financial assistance to members of the association through general, racing, career path and state or regional scholarships.
Publications: Application guidelines; Annual report; Informational brochure; Occasional report.
Financial data: Year ended 09/30/2011. Assets, $56,647,671 (M); Expenditures, $56,717,217; Total giving, $8,165,759; Grants to individuals, totaling $3,873,231.
Fields of interest: Scholarships/financial aid; Athletics/sports, equestrianism.
Type of support: Scholarships—to individuals.
Application information: Applications accepted. Application form required. Application form available on the grantmaker's web site.
Initial approach: Application
Send request by: Mail
Deadline(s): Dec. 1
Additional information: Applicants are selected based on academic achievement, financial need and American Quarter Horse involvement, as well as applicant's outstanding leadership and communication skills.
Program description:
Scholarships: The foundation provides financial assistance to members of the association through a variety of scholarship programs. Four types of scholarships are available through the association: General Scholarships both on the undergraduate and graduate level; Racing Scholarships offering financial support to students seeking a career in the racing industry, including racetrack management, veterinary medicine, or another related field; Career Path Scholarships allowing students to obtain a degree in areas such as animal science, journalism, therapeutic riding, and veterinary medicine; and State and Regional Scholarships for students from Alabama, Arizona, Arkansas, Florida, Indiana, Louisiana, Michigan, Mississippi, Nebraska, New York, Oklahoma, Pennsylvania, Tennessee, and Texas.
EIN: 750725576

8683
American Research Center in Egypt, Inc.
8700 Crownhill Blvd., Ste. 507
San Antonio, TX 78209-1130 (210) 821-7000
Contact: Rachel Mauldin, Asst. Dir. of US Operations
FAX: (210) 821-7007; *E-mail:* info@arce.org; E-Mail for Rachel Mauldin : rmauldin@arce.orgE-Mail for Dina Saad : development@arce.org; *URL:* http://www.arce.org/

Foundation type: Public charity
Purpose: Fellowships to advance graduates and postdoctoral scholars for research in the humanities, social sciences, art and archeology.
Publications: Application guidelines.

Financial data: Year ended 06/30/2012. Assets, $68,253,075 (M); Expenditures, $4,426,025; Total giving, $598,492.
Fields of interest: Humanities; Art history; History/archaeology.
Type of support: Fellowships; Postdoctoral support; Doctoral support.
Application information: Applications accepted. Application form required.
Deadline(s): Dec. 1 for Getty Research Exchange Fellowship, Jan. 15 for all other fellowships
Final notification: Applicants notified in Apr.
Program descriptions:
Antiquities Endowment Fund: The foundation awards one-year grants for highly focused professional projects that serve the conservation, preservation, and documentation needs of Egyptian antiquities that are more than 100 years old.
CAORC Multi-Country Research Fellowship: Ten awards of up to $12,000 each is given to scholars who wish to carry out research on broad questions of multi-country significance in the fields of humanities, social sciences, and related natural sciences.
Fellowships: Ten awards of up to $12,000 each is given to scholars who wish to carry out research on broad questions of multi-country significance in the fields of humanities, social sciences, and related natural sciences.
Research Associate: Individuals enrolled in doctoral programs at North American universities, postdoctoral scholars interested in conducting research in Egypt under an institutional auspice may apply for status as a Research Associate. Research Associates receive all administrative and logistical benefits accorded ARCE Fellows, but do not receive financial support. They may conduct research in Egypt for up to 12 months under the auspices of ARCE.
EIN: 042319500

8684
American Respiratory Care Foundation
9425 N. MacArthur Blvd., Ste. 100
Irving, TX 75063-4706 (972) 243-2272
Contact: Michael T. Amato, Chair.
FAX: (972) 484-2720; *E-mail:* lynch@aarc.org; *URL:* http://www.arcfoundation.org/

Foundation type: Public charity
Purpose: Grants and research opportunities to researchers in the field of respiratory care.
Publications: Application guidelines.
Financial data: Year ended 12/31/2011. Assets, $1,762,829 (M); Expenditures, $331,583; Total giving, $85,119; Grants to individuals, totaling $85,119.
Fields of interest: Lung research.
Type of support: Research; Grants to individuals; Awards/prizes.
Application information: Applications accepted. Application form required. Application form available on the grantmaker's web site.
Initial approach: Application
Deadline(s): Vary
Applicants should submit the following:
1) Essay
2) Letter(s) of recommendation
Additional information: See web site for additional application guidelines.
Program descriptions:
Dr. Charles H. Hudson Award for Cardiopulmonary Public Health: This annual award recognizes efforts to positively influence the public's awareness of cardiopulmonary health and wellness. Recipients are given a plaque, coach airfare, one night lodging,

and registration to the American Association of Respiratory Care Congress.

Forrest M. Bird, M.D., Ph.D., Sc.D. Lifetime Scientific Achievement Award: This award acknowledges outstanding individual scientific contributions in the area of respiratory care of cardiopulmonary disorders. The award consists of a plaque, coach airfare, one night's lodging, and registration to the American Association of Respiratory Care Congress.

H. Frederic Helmholz, Jr., M.D. Educational Research Fund: A $3,000 award is given to support individuals in the respiratory care profession with educational or credentialing research. In addition to the cash award, recipients are awarded a certificate of recognition, airfare, one night lodging and registration for the American Association of Respiratory Care Congress.

Hector Leon Garza, M.D. International Achievement Award: This program recognizes respiratory therapists, physicians, and other health care providers who have had a profound impact on the development of international respiratory care. Recipients are given a crystal sculpture, coach airfare, one night's lodging, and registration to the American Association of Respiratory Care Congress.

Jimmy A. Young Memorial Education Recognition Award: Grants of up to $1,000 are awarded to individuals enrolled in an accredited respiratory care training program, to attend the American Association of Respiratory Care Congress. Eligible applicants must have a GPA of at least 3.0. Preference will be given to nominees of minority origin.

Literary Awards: Awards are given to outstanding articles published in the science journal Respiratory Care. Awards granted under this program are, the Dr. Allen DeVilbiss Literary Award, the IKARIA Literary Award, and Draeger Literary Award. Recipients are given a cash award, certificate of recognition, airfare, one night lodging, and registration to the American Association of Respiratory Care Congress.

Morton B. Duggan, Jr. Memorial Education Recognition Award: This award gives up to $1,000 to individuals enrolled in an accredited respiratory care training program, to attend the American Association of Respiratory Care Congress. Applicants must have a GPA of at least 3.0. Preference will be given to candidates from GA and SC.

NBRC/AMP Gareth B. Gish M.S., RRT Memorial Postgraduate Education Recognition Award: This program, administered in conjunction with the National Board for Respiratory Care and Applied Measurement Professionals Inc., awards up to $1,500 to a respiratory therapist pursuing postgraduate education leading to an advanced degree. Applicants must be a respiratory therapist who has a baccalaureate degree and at least a 3.0 cumulative GPA or better on a 4.0 scale, or the equivalent, and must provide proof of acceptance into an advanced degree program of a fully accredited school. In addition to the cash award, recipients are awarded a certificate of recognition, coach airfare, one night's lodging, and registration to the American Association of Respiratory Care Congress.

NBRC/AMP Robert M. Lawrence, M.D. Education Recognition Award: Awarded in conjunction with the National Board for Respiratory Care and Applied Measurement Professionals Inc., grants of up to $2,500 are available to a third- or fourth-year student enrolled in an accredited respiratory therapy degree that leads to a baccalaureate degree. The award consists of a certificate of recognition, coach airfare, one night's lodging, and

registration for the American Association of Respiratory Care Congress.

Parker B. Francis Respiratory Research Grant: This program makes funds available to provide financial assistance for research programs dealing with respiratory care and related topics. The principal investigator may be a physician or respiratory care practitioner. However, a respiratory care practitioner must be the co-principal investigator if a physician is the principal applicant.

Research Fellowships: The foundation provides a series of fellowships to respiratory clinical researchers. Named awards include the Charles W. Serby COPD Research Fellowship (promoting research and education in the area of chronic obstructive pulmonary disease), the Monaghan/ Trudell Fellowship for Aerosol Technique Development (supporting projects dealing with aerosol delivery issues, including modeling studies, in-vitro studies, and clinical studies), the Philips Respironics Fellowships in Non-Invasive Respiratory Care (fostering projects dealing with non-invasive techniques to provide ventilatory support), the Philips Respironics Fellowship in Mechanical Ventilation (fostering projects dealing with mechanical ventilation, especially outside of the intensive care unit), and the CareFusion Fellowship in Neonatal and Pediatric Therapists (fostering projects in the field of neonatal and pediatric critical care). Each award consists of a plaque, airfare, one night lodging, and registration for the American Association of Respiratory Care Congress.

Thomas L. Petty, M.D. Invacare Award for Excellence in Home Respiratory Care: This award recognizes outstanding individual achievement in home respiratory care. Recipients are given a plaque, coach airfare, one night lodging, and registration to the American Association of Respiratory Care Congress.

William F. Miller, M.D. Postgraduate Education Recognition Award: This program awards up to $1,500 to assist qualified respiratory therapists in the pursuit of postgraduate education leading to an advanced degree. In addition to the cash award, recipients are awarded complimentary registration to the American Association of Respiratory Care Congress. Applicants must have at least a 3.0 cumulative GPA, or better on a 4.0 scale, or the equivalent, and must provide proof of acceptance into an advanced degree program of a fully-accredited school.

William W. Burgin, Jr. M.D. Education Recognition Award: Awards of up to $2,500 are available to a second-year student enrolled in an accredited respiratory therapy program leading to an associate degree. Interested applicants may apply directly, or be nominated by their school or education program. The award consists of a certificate or recognition, one night's lodging, and registration for the American Association of Respiratory Care Congress.
EIN: 237089524

8685
Amigos de las Americas
5618 Star Ln.
Houston, TX 77057-7112 (713) 782-5290
Contact: Sara Nathan, Pres. and C.E.O.
FAX: (713) 782-9267; E-mail: info@amigoslink.org; Toll-free tel.: (800) 213-7796; E-mail For Sara Nathan: snathan@amigoslink.org; URL: http://www.amigoslink.org

Foundation type: Public charity
Purpose: Financial assistance to overseas youth volunteers to help meet expenses.

Publications: Annual report; Informational brochure; Newsletter.
Financial data: Year ended 12/31/2011. Assets, $4,018,519 (M); Expenditures, $3,965,879; Total giving, $47,258; Grants to individuals, totaling $47,258.
Fields of interest: Higher education; Philanthropy/ voluntarism.
Type of support: Grants for special needs.
Application information: Applications accepted.
Send request by: Online
Additional information: Applicant must have successfully completed the field program, be enrolled in a college or university and demonstrate financial need.
EIN: 741547146

8686
Amigos Library Services, Inc.
14400 Midway Rd., Ste. 200
Dallas, TX 75244 (972) 851-8000
Fellowship e-mail: opportunity@amigos.org
FAX: (972) 991-6061; E-mail: amigos@amigos.org; Toll-free tel.: (800) 843-8482; E-mail For Bonnie Juergens: juergens@amigos.org; URL: http://www.amigos.org/

Foundation type: Public charity
Purpose: Fellowships to library and information professionals, (preferably with an ALA accredited master's degree) employed by an Amigos member library.
Publications: Annual report; Newsletter; Occasional report.
Financial data: Year ended 06/30/2012. Assets, $12,340,259 (M); Expenditures, $13,939,088; Total giving, $7,500.
Fields of interest: Libraries/library science.
Type of support: Fellowships.
Application information: Applications accepted. Application form required. Application form available on the grantmaker's web site.
Send request by: Mail or on-line
Deadline(s): Mar. 1
Additional information: See web site for additional guidelines.
EIN: 751627097

8687
Sophie L. Anderson Educational Fund
c/o Bank of America
P.O. Box 831041
Dallas, TX 75283-1041

Foundation type: Independent foundation
Purpose: Scholarships to students attending smaller colleges in WA State.
Financial data: Year ended 03/31/2013. Assets, $208,831 (M); Expenditures, $12,068; Total giving, $7,629.
Fields of interest: History/archaeology; Medical school/education; Nursing school/education; Teacher school/education.
Type of support: Support to graduates or students of specific schools; Undergraduate support.
Application information: Applications accepted.
Additional information: Contact the trust for additional guidelines.
EIN: 916076066

8688
Eugene and Daniela Anderson Scholarship Foundation
309 W. Foster Ave.
Pampa, TX 79065 (806) 669-3397
Contact: Bob Finney, Secy.

Foundation type: Operating foundation
Purpose: Scholarships only to graduates of Pampa High School, TX.
Financial data: Year ended 12/31/2011. Assets, $1,011,138 (M); Expenditures, $55,048; Total giving, $50,000; Grants to individuals, 10 grants totaling $50,000 (high: $7,000, low: $3,000).
Type of support: Support to graduates or students of specific schools; Undergraduate support.
Application information: Applications accepted. Application form required.
　Deadline(s): Dec. 1
　Additional information: Applications available at Pampa High School.
EIN: 752848433

8689
Molly Crouch Anderson Scholarship Foundation
215 Private Rd., Ste 434
Itasca, TX 76055 (817) 917-1868
Contact: Tom Crouch, Pres.

Foundation type: Operating foundation
Purpose: Provides scholarships to students in Itasca, TX and its immediate areas.
Financial data: Year ended 06/30/2013. Assets, $13,869 (M); Expenditures, $9,008; Total giving, $7,750; Grants to individuals, 10 grants totaling $7,750 (high: $1,000, low: $500).
Fields of interest: Higher education.
Type of support: Scholarships—to individuals.
Application information: Applications not accepted.
EIN: 200013938

8690
Arlington Charities, Inc.
811 Secretary Dr.
Arlington, TX 76015-1626 (817) 275-1511

Foundation type: Public charity
Purpose: Relief and assistance in the form of food, clothing and other needs such as gas, car repairs, emergency rental and utility assistance to the poor, elderly and underpriviledged of Arlington, TX.
Financial data: Year ended 12/31/2011. Assets, $258,321 (M); Expenditures, $2,475,776; Total giving, $2,282,120; Grants to individuals, totaling $2,282,120.
Fields of interest: Economically disadvantaged.
Type of support: Grants for special needs.
Application information: Contact the association for eligibility determination.
EIN: 751668092

8691
Associa Cares Inc.
5401 N. Central Expressway, Ste. 300
Dallas, TX 75205-3348 (214) 953-3009
FAX: (214) 239-4538;
E-mail: info@associacares.com; Toll-free tel.: (800) 808-4882; URL: http://www.associacares.com/

Foundation type: Public charity
Purpose: Financial assistance to individuals and families in need, as a result of natural and man-made disasters.

Publications: Annual report; Financial statement; Newsletter.
Financial data: Year ended 12/31/2011. Assets, $1,128,510 (M); Expenditures, $263,556; Total giving, $230,790; Grants to individuals, 197 grants totaling $212,300.
Fields of interest: Human services; Human services, emergency aid.
Type of support: Emergency funds.
Application information:
　Initial approach: Telephone or e-mail
　Additional information: Contact the organization for eligibility determination.
EIN: 205832439

8692
Associated Plumbing-Heating-Cooling Contractors of Texas Charitable and Educational Foundation
145 Trademark Dr.
Buda, TX 78610 (512) 523-8094
Contact: Nancy Jones

Foundation type: Operating foundation
Purpose: Scholarships to graduating high school seniors for attendance at a two year or four year college, or trade school pursuing a career in the plumbing industry.
Financial data: Year ended 12/31/2012. Assets, $146,199 (M); Expenditures, $11,357; Total giving, $9,000; Grants to individuals, 9 grants totaling $9,000 (high: $1,000, low: $1,000).
Fields of interest: Vocational education, post-secondary; Higher education.
Type of support: Scholarships—to individuals.
Application information: Applications accepted. Application form required.
　Deadline(s): Mar. 1
　Additional information: Scholarships are awarded based on academic qualifications, and need.
EIN: 742942085

8693
Nina Heard Astin Charitable Trust
c/o Wells Fargo Bank, N.A., Trust Dept.
P.O. Box 913
Bryan, TX 77805-0913
Scholarship application addresses: c/o Bryan High School Counselors, 3401 E. 29th St., Bryan, TX 77802, tel.: (979) 774-3276; c/o A&M Consolidated High School, 701 West Loop S., Bryan, TX 77840, tel.: (979) 696-0544

Foundation type: Independent foundation
Purpose: Scholarships only to graduates of Bryan High School, TX, and A&M Consolidated High School, TX.
Financial data: Year ended 03/31/2013. Assets, $7,837,833 (M); Expenditures, $338,603; Total giving, $227,750.
Type of support: Support to graduates or students of specific schools; Undergraduate support.
Application information: Applications accepted. Application form required.
　Deadline(s): May 1
EIN: 741721901

8694
Astros in Action Foundation—Fielding the Dreams of Houston
501 Crawford St., Ste. 500
Houston, TX 77002-2113
E-mail for Grand Slam for Youth Baseball Scholarships: scholarships@gsfyb.org
E-mail: foundation@astros.com; Additional address: P.O. Box 288, Houston, TX 77001; Additional tel.: (713) 259-8956; URL: http://houston.astros.mlb.com/NASApp/mlb/hou/community/foundation_mission.jsp

Foundation type: Company-sponsored foundation
Purpose: Scholarships to high school seniors in Houston, TX for postsecondary education.
Publications: Application guidelines.
Financial data: Year ended 12/31/2012. Assets, $2,327,880 (M); Expenditures, $955,531; Total giving, $882,292; Grants to individuals, 25 grants totaling $62,500 (high: $2,500, low: $2,500).
Fields of interest: Higher education; Athletics/sports, baseball.
Type of support: Undergraduate support.
Application information: Applications accepted. Application form required. Application form available on the grantmaker's web site. Interview required.
　Send request by: Mail
　Deadline(s): May 14
　Final notification: Recipients notified June 17
　Applicants should submit the following:
　　1) Letter(s) of recommendation
　Additional information: Applications for Grand Slam for Youth Baseball Scholarships must include proof of acceptance to a post-secondary college or university.
Program description:
　Grand Slam for Youth Baseball Scholarships: The foundation, in partnership with Minute Maid, awards 25 $2,500 college scholarships to Houston area high school seniors who have participated in a youth baseball or softball. The program is designed to assist youth with college expenses.
EIN: 742793078

8695
AT&T Foundation
(formerly SBC Foundation)
208 S. Akard, Ste. 100
Dallas, TX 75202-4206
Additional e-mail: questions@aspirerfp.com; URL: http://www.att.com/gen/landing-pages?pid=7735

Foundation type: Company-sponsored foundation
Purpose: Grants to employees and retirees of AT&T to assist in disaster relief.
Publications: Corporate giving report; Program policy statement.
Financial data: Year ended 12/31/2012. Assets, $9,768,836 (M); Expenditures, $11,312,889; Total giving, $11,012,710; Grants to individuals, 753 grants totaling $153,200 (high: $3,000, low: $100).
Fields of interest: Disasters, preparedness/services.
Type of support: Grants to individuals; Employee-related welfare.
Application information: Applications not accepted.
　Additional information: Unsolicited requests for funds not accepted or acknowledged.
Program description:
　AT&T Foundation Employee Disaster Relief Fund: The foundation provides grants, short-term financial assistance, and long-term financial assistance for

food, clothing, physical and mental health care, housing, transportation, education, and childcare to employees and retirees of AT&T affected by a disaster.
Company name: AT&T Inc.
EIN: 431353948

8696
Austin Community Foundation for the Capital Area, Inc.

(formerly Austin Community Foundation)
4315 Guadalupe St., Ste. 300
Austin, TX   78751   (512) 472-4483
Contact: MariBen Ramsey, V.P.; For scholarships: Amy Allen, Dir., Donor Rels.
Scholarship inquiry e-mail: amyallen@austincommunityfoundation.org
FAX: (512) 472-4486; E-mail: info@austincf.org; Additional e-mail: mbramsey@austincommunityfoundation.org;
URL: http://www.austincommunityfoundation.org

Foundation type: Community foundation
Purpose: Scholarships for all levels of education above high school for residents of the Austin, TX area.
Publications: Application guidelines; Annual report; Informational brochure; Newsletter; Program policy statement.
Financial data: Year ended 12/31/2012. Assets, $140,587,100 (M); Expenditures, $34,251,100; Total giving, $22,509,920.
Fields of interest: Higher education.
Type of support: Scholarships—to individuals; Support to graduates or students of specific schools.
Application information: Applications accepted. Application form required.
> *Deadline(s):* Spring
> *Additional information:* Most applications are available at specific local high schools, though some are available online. Each scholarship has its own unique set of eligibility criteria. See web site for complete listing of scholarships.
EIN: 741934031

8697
Austin Creative Alliance

701 Riverside Dr.
Austin, TX   78704-1269   (512) 247-2531
Contact: Marcy Hoen, Exec. Dir.
E-mail address for scholarship: membership@austincreativealliance.org, subject line: E.L. Scholarship
FAX: (512) 247-2538;
E-mail: info@austincreativealliance.org;
URL: http://www.austincreativealliance.org

Foundation type: Public charity
Purpose: Scholarships to emerging arts leaders of Austin, TX who are current members of the Alliance.
Financial data: Year ended 09/30/2011. Assets, $91,403 (M); Expenditures, $692,274.
Fields of interest: Arts.
Type of support: Scholarships—to individuals; Fiscal agent/sponsor.
Application information: Applications accepted. Application form required.
> *Send request by:* E-mail or hand deliver
> *Deadline(s):* Sept. 14
> *Final notification:* Applicants notified Oct. 31
> *Applicants should submit the following:*
>   1) Essay
>   2) Resume

Program description:
Emerging Arts Leader Scholarship: Scholarships to emerging arts leaders who are at least 23 years of age and have at least two years of employment experience. Applicant must not be a full time student, cannot be a candidate for public office at the time of application and is willing and able to commit the time necessary to complete the program. Applicant must have at least two years experience in Austin's creative community, including both full time, part time paid or volunteer positions.
EIN: 742140348

8698
Austin Film Society

1901 E. 51st St.
Austin, TX   78723-3040   (512) 322-0145
Contact: Rebecca Campbell, Exec. Dir.
FAX: (512) 322-5192; E-mail: afs@austinfilm.org;
URL: http://www.austinfilm.org

Foundation type: Public charity
Purpose: Awards to film and video artists in TX.
Publications: Application guidelines; Grants list; Informational brochure; Newsletter (including application guidelines); Program policy statement.
Financial data: Year ended 08/31/2011. Assets, $2,442,749 (M); Expenditures, $2,191,014; Total giving, $377,012; Grants to individuals, totaling $100,000.
Fields of interest: Film/video; Arts, artist's services.
Type of support: Internship funds; Grants to individuals; Awards/prizes; Fiscal agent/sponsor.
Application information: Applications accepted. Application form required. Application form available on the grantmaker's web site.
> *Initial approach:* Application
> *Copies of proposal:* 4
> *Deadline(s):* June 1
> *Applicants should submit the following:*
>   1) Budget Information
>   2) Proposal
>   3) Letter(s) of recommendation
>   4) Work samples
> *Additional information:* See web site for additional guidelines.
Program descriptions:
Angel Pederast College Scholarship: The scholarship is awarded annually to a high school senior based on artistic potential, strength of character, and dedication to the art of filmmaking or related digital media field.
Fiscal Sponsorship: Through filmmaker membership, the society offers artists eligibility for fiscal sponsorships.
Texas Filmmakers' Production Fund: The fund awards annual grants to emerging film and video artists in the state of Texas. Awards are provided to artists whose work shows promise, skills, and creativity.
Texas Filmmakers' Travel Grant: The grant helps offset travel costs for Texans whose work is invited to prestigious film festivals and events around the world. Eligibility is based on the festival or event that the film has been invited to, not on the film itself, and applicants need not be a member of the Austin Film Society to apply. $500 will be given for a North American festival and $1,000 is given for an international festival. Individual films can receive only one domestic grant and one international grant.
EIN: 742433823

8699
Jeff Austin Trust

P.O. Box 951
Jacksonville, TX   75766-0951   (903) 586-1526
Contact: Ronny E. Lee, Secy.-Treas.

Foundation type: Independent foundation
Purpose: Scholarships to students of the Frankston, TX area pursuing postsecondary education.
Financial data: Year ended 12/31/2012. Assets, $5,177 (M); Expenditures, $57,449; Total giving, $56,905; Grants to individuals, 8 grants totaling $4,500 (high: $1,000, low: $500).
Fields of interest: Higher education.
Type of support: Scholarships—to individuals; Undergraduate support.
Application information: Applications accepted. Application form required.
> *Initial approach:* Letter
> *Additional information:* Application should include schedule of expenses and qualifications. Contact the trust for additional guidelines.
EIN: 756035802

8700
Dr. Samuel & Mildred L. Ayres Student Fund Trust

(formerly Mildred L. Ayres Trust)
c/o Bank of America, N.A.
P.O. Box 831041
Dallas, TX   75283-1041   (401) 278-6043
Contact: Paul Crosby
Application address: 111 Westminster St., Providence, RI 02903

Foundation type: Independent foundation
Purpose: Scholarships to residents of MO attending Midwestern Baptist Seminary, MO, William Jewell College, MO, or the University of Missouri-Columbia to assist with theological and medical training and living expenses. Preference is given to residents of metropolitan Kansas City.
Financial data: Year ended 12/31/2012. Assets, $315,574 (M); Expenditures, $18,697; Total giving, $13,149.
Type of support: Scholarships—to individuals; Student loans—to individuals.
Application information: Applications accepted. Application form required.
> *Initial approach:* Letter
> *Deadline(s):* None
> *Applicants should submit the following:*
>   1) Photograph
>   2) Transcripts
>   3) Financial information
> *Additional information:* Applications available from applicant's high school financial aid office or trust office, and must include, personal statement, and four letters of reference, two personal and two from instructors or advisor.
EIN: 446008191

8701
Baby Lyla's Angel Foundation

6108 LD Lockett Rd.
Colleyville, TX   76034
Contact: Judith M. Thomas, Chair.

Foundation type: Independent foundation
Purpose: Scholarships to individuals for undergraduate education.
Financial data: Year ended 12/31/2011. Assets, $210,733 (M); Expenditures, $35,451; Total

giving, $29,500; Grants to individuals, 7 grants totaling $29,500 (high: $10,000, low: $2,500).
Fields of interest: Higher education.
Type of support: Undergraduate support.
Application information: Applications accepted.
Additional information: Contact foundation for application deadlines/guidelines.
EIN: 203902520

8702
Tom C. Barnsley Foundation
c/o Bank of America, N.A.
P.O. Box 831041
Dallas, TX   75283-1041   (214) 209-1067
Contact: Robert R. Fox

Foundation type: Independent foundation
Purpose: Scholarships to graduates of Crane High School, TX, pursuing a career in agriculture or related field.
Financial data: Year ended 12/31/2012. Assets, $1,201,708 (M); Expenditures, $69,072; Total giving, $45,500; Grants to individuals, 5 grants totaling $45,500 (high: $10,500, low: $7,000).
Fields of interest: Higher education; Agriculture.
Type of support: Scholarships—to individuals; Support to graduates or students of specific schools.
Application information: Applications accepted.
Deadline(s): None
Additional information: Application must include transcript.
EIN: 756248739

8703
Lyle P. Bartholomew Scholarship & Loan Fund f/b/o University of Oregon
c/o Bank of America, N.A.
P.O. Box 831041
Dallas, TX   75283-1041

Foundation type: Independent foundation
Purpose: Scholarships to graduate and undergraduate students of architecture at the University of Oregon.
Financial data: Year ended 04/30/2013. Assets, $543,611 (M); Expenditures, $29,330; Total giving, $21,570.
Fields of interest: Architecture; Higher education.
Type of support: Support to graduates or students of specific schools; Graduate support; Undergraduate support.
Application information: Applications accepted. Application form required.
Deadline(s): May 10
Additional information: Application should include applicant's statement, financial statement and one letter of recommendation from a faculty member.
EIN: 936091423

8704
Harold & Martha Barto Scholarship Trust
c/o Bank of America, N.A.
P.O. Box 831041
Dallas, TX   75283-1041
Contact: Jen Gray
Application address: 400 E. University Way, Ellensburg, WA 98926-7502

Foundation type: Independent foundation
Purpose: Scholarships restricted to full-time students actively pursuing a degree from Central Washington University, WA.

Financial data: Year ended 04/30/2013. Assets, $357,234 (M); Expenditures, $20,136; Total giving, $14,573.
Fields of interest: Higher education.
Type of support: Support to graduates or students of specific schools; Undergraduate support.
Application information: Applications accepted. Application form required.
Deadline(s): Prior to fall semester
Additional information: Funds are paid directly to the educational institution on behalf of the students. Contact the CWU foundation for application.
EIN: 916267640

8705
Bat Conservation International
500 N. Capital of Texas Hwy., Bldg. 1., Ste. 200
Austin, TX   78746-3302   (512) 327-9721
Contact: Jonathan Friedman, Dir., Devel.
FAX: (512) 327-9724; E-mail: info@batcon.org;
URL: http://www.batcon.org

Foundation type: Public charity
Purpose: Scholarships to graduate students and awards to researchers for the study and conservation of the bat.
Publications: Application guidelines; Annual report; Informational brochure; Newsletter.
Financial data: Year ended 05/31/2012. Assets, $3,918,098 (M); Expenditures, $4,020,489; Total giving, $382,846; Grants to individuals, totaling $163,467.
Fields of interest: Animals/wildlife, preservation/protection.
Type of support: Research; Awards/prizes; Graduate support.
Application information: Applications accepted.
Send request by: Online
Deadline(s): Dec. 15 for scholarships
Additional information: Contact foundation for current application guidelines.
Program descriptions:
North American Bat Conservation Fund Grants: This fund provides grants of up to $5,000 to help support projects that most effectively aid bats in the U.S., Canada, and Mexico.
Student Research Scholarship: Scholarships of up to $5,000 are available for graduate students who are performing research dedicated to designated subjects of special concern to bat conservation.
EIN: 742553144

8706
Baumberger Endowment
7201 Broadway, Ste. 300
San Antonio, TX   78209-3774

Foundation type: Independent foundation
Purpose: Scholarships only to graduating seniors of high schools in Bexar County, TX.
Publications: Application guidelines; Program policy statement.
Financial data: Year ended 12/31/2012. Assets, $28,309,826 (M); Expenditures, $1,507,550; Total giving, $1,195,700.
Type of support: Support to graduates or students of specific schools; Undergraduate support.
Application information: Application form required.
Deadline(s): Feb. 15
Applicants should submit the following:
  1) ACT
  2) SAT
  3) Transcripts
  4) Financial information

Additional information: Applications available from high school counselors.
Program description:
Scholarships: The applicant must be a graduating senior of an accredited (TEA) high school within Bexar County, Texas, have resided in Texas for at least 10 years, graduate in the upper one-half of the class, and achieve a minimum total score of 1000 (Critical Reading and Math scorse only) on the Scholastic Achievement Test (SAT) or composite of 22 on the American College Test (ACT). The scholarships are limited to state-supported or non-denominational colleges and universities located in Texas. Baumberger scholars are evaluated on a competitive basis without regard to race, color, ethnic origin, sex, age, or religion and are selected by an impartial committee of professional educators. The scholars are awarded scholarships with the amount of stipend calculated each year based on college costs and student resources and are challenged to pursue quality higher education to the fullest extent culminating in a degree. For additional information, eligible students should contact their high school counselor.
EIN: 237225925

8707
Beaumont Foundation of America
470 Orleans. 1st Fl.
Beaumont, TX   77701-3000   (409) 838-1812
Contact: W. Frank Newton, Pres. and C.E.O.
FAX: (409) 813-1816; Toll-free tel.: (866) 546-2667; URL: http://www.bmtfoundation.com

Foundation type: Public charity
Purpose: Awards laptop computers to the children and spouses of military personnel who gave their lives in the ongoing conflicts in Iraq or Afghanistan.
Publications: Annual report.
Financial data: Year ended 12/31/2011. Assets, $254,605,805 (M); Expenditures, $7,954,566; Total giving, $6,230,091; Grants to individuals, totaling $105,400.
Fields of interest: Military/veterans.
Type of support: In-kind gifts.
Application information:
Initial approach: Tel.
Additional information: To be eligible for the program, a person must be the spouse or child of an active-duty member of the U.S. Armed Forces who died in Iraq or Afghanistan since September 11, 2001. Children must be 18 or younger and must reside in the next of kin's household. Next of kin includes children of the current spouse, former spouse or stepchildren identified as dependents. For additional information contact Hannah Ward at 866-546-2667.
EIN: 760650506

8708
Beefmaster Breeders Universal Brian Murphy Memorial Scholarhip Fund
6800 Park 10 Blvd., Ste. 290 W.
San Antonio, TX   78213-4226   (210) 732-3132
URL: http://www.beefmasters.org

Foundation type: Independent foundation
Purpose: Scholarships to high school graduates under age 21 who are members of the Junior Beefmaster Breeders Association.
Financial data: Year ended 07/31/2013. Assets, $218,022 (M); Expenditures, $11,778; Total giving, $10,800; Grants to individuals, 3 grants totaling $10,800 (high: $3,600, low: $3,600).

Fields of interest: Education.
Type of support: Scholarships—to individuals.
Application information: Applications accepted. Application form required.
  Deadline(s): None
  Additional information: Applicant must have at least a "B" average and sponsored by a "Charter" or "Active" member of Beefmaster Breeders United, a county extension agent or a FFA advisor.
EIN: 746376095

8709
Richard C. and Esther Bellamy Educational Trust
P.O. Box 10109
Liberty, TX 77575 (936) 336-6471
Contact: Glenda Griffin
Application address: c/o First Liberty National Bank, 1900 Sam Houston St., Liberty, TX 77575

Foundation type: Independent foundation
Purpose: Scholarships to financially needy graduates of Liberty County, TX, Independent School Districts, primarily those who rank in the top ten percent of their class.
Financial data: Year ended 12/31/2012. Assets, $975,332 (M); Expenditures, $54,172; Total giving, $12,000; Grants to individuals, 16 grants totaling $12,000 (high: $2,500, low: $2,000).
Fields of interest: Vocational education; Higher education.
Type of support: Support to graduates or students of specific schools; Technical education support; Undergraduate support.
Application information: Applications accepted. Application form required.
  Copies of proposal: 11
  Applicants should submit the following:
    1) SAT
    2) ACT
    3) Transcripts
    4) Photograph
  Additional information: Recipients must attend colleges, universities, or vocational schools in TX. Applications should also include three references, and a handwritten personal statement of about 150 words.
Program description:
  Scholarship Program: Scholarships are awarded on the basis of character, attitude, initiative, stability, leadership, and potential for achievement. Applicants who do not rank in the top ten percent of their graduating classes will be considered if they have a documented extraordinary or outstanding talent. Recipients must attend school full-time at a two-year vocational or technical training program or a four-year college or university in TX. Scholarships are renewable.
EIN: 766002566

8710
Bergman-Davison-Webster Charitable Trust
P.O. Box 1617
Livingston, TX 77351-0029
Application address: c/o Floyd Bush, 306 N. Washington Ave., Livingston, TX 77351-3240; tel.: (936) 327-7181

Foundation type: Independent foundation
Purpose: Scholarships to individuals residing in Livingston and Corrigan, TX, as well as Polk County, TX, for undergraduate education.
Financial data: Year ended 06/30/2012. Assets, $8,778,825 (M); Expenditures, $697,023; Total

giving, $595,063; Grants to individuals, 6 grants totaling $11,000 (high: $2,000, low: $1,000).
Fields of interest: Education.
Type of support: Undergraduate support.
Application information: Applications accepted.
  Initial approach: Letter
  Deadline(s): None
EIN: 760521612

8711
Celia Berwin Memorial Foundation
1880 Country Rd. 3615
Bigfoot, TX 78005-5401 (830) 466-5428
Contact: Janie Mann, Treas.

Foundation type: Independent foundation
Purpose: Scholarships to students in TX for higher education.
Financial data: Year ended 12/31/2012. Assets, $684,255 (M); Expenditures, $37,358; Total giving, $32,000.
Type of support: Undergraduate support.
Application information: Applications accepted.
  Deadline(s): None
  Applicants should submit the following:
    1) Transcripts
    2) Resume
  Additional information: Contact foundation for current application guidelines; Applicant must include professional, educational and character references.
EIN: 746074127

8712
Betts Foundation
c/o Byrleen K. Terry
730 Fonville Dr.
Marlin, TX 76661-2203

Foundation type: Independent foundation
Purpose: Scholarships to graduates of Marlin, TX, area high schools, primarily for undergraduate education at TX institutions.
Financial data: Year ended 12/31/2012. Assets, $32,151 (M); Expenditures, $12,951; Total giving, $11,000; Grants to individuals, 16 grants totaling $11,000 (high: $1,000, low: $250).
Type of support: Undergraduate support.
Application information: Applications accepted. Application form not required.
  Initial approach: Letter
  Deadline(s): None
  Additional information: Contact foundation for further application information.
EIN: 751014070

8713
Jim Black Memorial Scholarship Trust
P.O. Box 2020
Tyler, TX 75710-2020 (903) 535-4276
Application address: Robert E. Lee High School, 411 ESE Loop 323, Tyler, TX 75701

Foundation type: Independent foundation
Purpose: Scholarships to graduating students of Robert E. Lee High School of Tyler, TX pursuing higher education at a four year college.
Financial data: Year ended 12/31/2011. Assets, $45,844 (M); Expenditures, $3,760; Total giving, $2,000; Grants to individuals, 3 grants totaling $2,000 (high: $1,000, low: $500).
Fields of interest: Higher education.
Type of support: Support to graduates or students of specific schools; Undergraduate support.

Application information: Application form required.
  Deadline(s): Feb.
  Additional information: Applicant must maintain a 2.0 GPA on a 4.0 scale. Application should include personal references, financial information, and work experience.
EIN: 756265235

8714
Susan Smith Blackburn Prize, Inc.
3239 Avalon Pl.
Houston, TX 77019-5917 (713) 522-8529
Contact: Leslie Swackhamer, Exec. Dir.
URL: http://www.blackburnprize.org

Foundation type: Public charity
Purpose: Prizes are awarded annually to a woman who deserves recognition for having written a work of outstanding quality for the English-speaking theatre.
Financial data: Year ended 12/31/2011. Assets, $2,143,653 (M); Expenditures, $98,650; Total giving, $29,000; Grants to individuals, totaling $24,000.
Fields of interest: Theater (playwriting); Women.
Type of support: Awards/prizes.
Application information:
  Deadline(s): Sept.
  Additional information: Awards are by nomination only.
Program description:
  Susan Smith Blackburn Prize: Awarded to women playwrights of outstanding quality in English-speaking theatre. The prize awards are: Winner - $20,000, Special Commendation - $5,000, other Finalists - $1,000.
EIN: 741980804

8715
The Mary Bonham Educational Trust
315 Jefferson St.
Sulphur Springs, TX 75482 (903) 885-1044
Contact: Carl D. Bryan, Tr.

Foundation type: Independent foundation
Purpose: Scholarships to undergraduate students from Hopkins County, TX, or another contiguous county who will attend a state-supported college in TX.
Financial data: Year ended 12/31/2012. Assets, $569,055 (M); Expenditures, $19,857; Total giving, $19,411; Grants to individuals, 5 grants totaling $19,411 (high: $7,376, low: $120).
Type of support: Undergraduate support.
Application information: Applications accepted.
  Initial approach: Letter
  Deadline(s): May 1
EIN: 756454600

8716
Borelli Family Scholarship
(formerly Pamela Borelli & Family Scholarship Fund)
c/o USAA Federal Savings Bank
P.O. Box 690827
San Antonio, TX 78269-0827

Foundation type: Independent foundation
Purpose: Scholarships to graduating seniors from Monticello High School, IL and Bement High School, IL. Scholarships for members of the University of Illinois 4-H House Sorority.
Financial data: Year ended 12/31/2012. Assets, $129,182 (M); Expenditures, $5,969; Total giving, $4,194; Grants to individuals, 6 grants totaling $4,194 (high: $1,183, low: $323).

Fields of interest: Higher education.
Type of support: Scholarships—to individuals; Support to graduates or students of specific schools.
Application information: Applications not accepted.
> *Additional information:* Unsolicited requests for funds not considered or acknowledged.

EIN: 376196426

8717
Borton-Ryder Memorial Trust
c/o Bank of America, N.A.
P.O. Box 831041
Dallas, TX   75283-1041   (401) 278-6039
Contact: Maria Botelho
Application address: c/o Bank of America, N.A., 100 Westminster St., Providence, RI 02903 Tel.: (401) 278-6039

Foundation type: Independent foundation
Purpose: Scholarships to students attending the Newman Memorial School of Nursing, Emporia, KS. Payment of medical care for residents of Lyon County, KS.
Financial data: Year ended 06/30/2013. Assets, $322,056 (M); Expenditures, $37,986; Total giving, $32,164; Grants to individuals, 7 grants totaling $32,164 (high: $5,272, low: $532).
Fields of interest: Nursing school/education; Health care.
Type of support: Support to graduates or students of specific schools; Graduate support; Undergraduate support.
Application information: Applications accepted.
> *Initial approach:* Letter
> *Deadline(s):* None

EIN: 486110157

8718
Bour Memorial Scholarship Fund
c/o Bank of America, N.A.
P.O. Box 831041
Dallas, TX   75283-1041   (401) 278-6039
Contact: Maria Botelho
Application address: 111 Westminister St., Providence, RI 02903

Foundation type: Independent foundation
Purpose: Scholarships to financially needy high school graduates residing in Lafayette County, MO, to attend any accredited MO college, junior college, or university.
Financial data: Year ended 12/31/2012. Assets, $594,851 (M); Expenditures, $29,316; Total giving, $19,000.
Type of support: Undergraduate support.
Application information: Applications accepted. Application form required.
> *Deadline(s):* Apr. 1

EIN: 436225461

8719
Bobby Bragan Youth Foundation Scholarship Fund, Inc.
3116 W. 6th St., Ste. 200
Fort Worth, TX   76107-2731   (817) 870-2300
E-mail: bbyf@charterinternet.com

Foundation type: Public charity
Purpose: Scholarships by nomination only to eighth grade students attending public school in Tarrant and Dallas counties, TX.
Financial data: Year ended 12/31/2011. Assets, $1,129,956 (M); Expenditures, $81,680; Total

giving, $81,680; Grants to individuals, totaling $81,680.
Fields of interest: Public education; Elementary/secondary education; Education.
Type of support: Scholarships—to individuals.
Application information:
> *Initial approach:* Letter or telephone
> *Additional information:* Participating public schools nominate 2 students annually. Nomination forms include information on academic and extracurricular achievements. Contact foundation for further application information.

EIN: 752534529

8720
Brazos Community Foundation
108 E. North Ave., Ste. 200
P.O. Box 2622
Bryan, TX   77801   (979) 589-4305
E-mail: president@cfbv.org; URL: http://www.cfbv.org

Foundation type: Community foundation
Purpose: Scholarships to graduating high school seniors of Brazos Valley, TX pursuing higher education.
Financial data: Year ended 12/31/2012. Assets, $2,313,675 (M); Expenditures, $124,619; Total giving, $69,712; Grants to individuals, 12 grants totaling $15,000.
Fields of interest: Higher education.
Type of support: Scholarships—to individuals.
Application information: Applications accepted. Application form required.
> *Deadline(s):* Varies
> *Applicants should submit the following:*
> 1) Transcripts
> 2) Letter(s) of recommendation
> 3) Essay
> *Additional information:* Each scholarship has its own unique eligibility criteria. See web site for a complete listing.

EIN: 320073943

8721
Brisley Scholarship Loan Fund
(formerly Ella Frances Brisley & Noma Brisley Phillips Scholarship Loan Fund)
c/o Bank of America, N.A.
P.O. Box 831041
Dallas, TX   75283-1041   (401) 278-6039
Contact: Maria Botelho
Application address: 111 Westminster St., Providence, RI 02903,tel.: 401-278-6039

Foundation type: Independent foundation
Purpose: Scholarships to financially needy, deserving medical and nursing students attending Methodist colleges. Preference is shown to American-born residents of KS and MO.
Financial data: Year ended 02/28/2013. Assets, $2,747,033 (M); Expenditures, $358,274; Total giving, $310,600.
Fields of interest: Medical school/education; Nursing school/education; Protestant agencies & churches.
Type of support: Awards/grants by nomination only; Graduate support.
Application information: Application form required.
> *Deadline(s):* None
> *Additional information:* Applications available from school.

EIN: 431343600

8722
George K. & Eleanor J. Broady Family Opportunity Foundation
751 Canyon Dr., Ste. 100
Coppell, TX   75019-3857   (972) 484-9637
Contact: George K. Broady, Dir.

Foundation type: Independent foundation
Purpose: Scholarships to high school graduates from the Dallas, TX area for higher education.
Financial data: Year ended 12/31/2012. Assets, $162,283 (M); Expenditures, $240,112; Total giving, $238,267; Grants to individuals, 6 grants totaling $238,267 (high: $72,500, low: $12,500).
Fields of interest: Education.
Type of support: Scholarships—to individuals.
Application information:
> *Deadline(s):* None

EIN: 752739287

8723
Leo J. Brockman Trust
c/o Bank of America, N.A.
P.O. Box 831041
Dallas, TX   75283-1041   (509) 323-6558

Foundation type: Independent foundation
Purpose: Loans to financially needy students of Gonzaga University, WA.
Financial data: Year ended 12/31/2011. Assets, $421,207 (M); Expenditures, $2,148; Total giving, $0.
Fields of interest: Higher education.
Type of support: Student loans—to individuals; Support to graduates or students of specific schools.
Application information: Applications accepted. Application form required.
> *Deadline(s):* None
> *Additional information:* Loan awards are provided for tuition, fees, books, supplies and maintenance but not for transportation.

EIN: 916024372

8724
William A. Brookshire Foundation
c/o Charles Reid
7825 Park Place Blvd.
Houston, TX   77087-4639

Foundation type: Independent foundation
Purpose: Scholarships to full time students attending Lone Star College-CyFair, TX pursuing a career in Drafting, Engineering Technology or Pre-Engineering for tuition, fees, books and other education related expenses.
Financial data: Year ended 06/30/2013. Assets, $22,081,763 (M); Expenditures, $476,091; Total giving, $470,000; Grants to individuals, 33 grants totaling $470,000 (high: $15,000, low: $10,000).
Fields of interest: Higher education.
Type of support: Support to graduates or students of specific schools.
Application information:
> *Deadline(s):* None
> *Additional information:* Applicants must have a 2.5 GPA, working 20 or more hours per week and must be U.S. citizens.

EIN: 760594307

8725
Joe Brown Educational Scholarship Fund
1313 Iroquois
Garland, TX   75043

Foundation type: Independent foundation
Purpose: Scholarships to graduating students in the Garland Independent School District, TX pursuing a degree with a major in education.
Financial data: Year ended 12/31/2012. Assets, $139,461 (M); Expenditures, $4,556; Total giving, $4,000; Grants to individuals, 4 grants totaling $4,000 (high: $1,000, low: $1,000).
Fields of interest: Teacher school/education.
Type of support: Scholarships—to individuals.
Application information: Applications accepted. Application form required.
　　Additional information: Application must include an essay.
EIN: 352167362

8726
The Judge John R. Brown Scholarship Foundation

4615 S. Fwy., Ste. 730
Houston, TX　77019-3312　(713) 899-5188
Scholarship address: c/o K.G. Engerrand, Brown Sims, P.C. 10th Fl., 11777 West Loop S., Houston, TX 77027-9007

Foundation type: Public charity
Purpose: Scholarships to any law student currently enrolled in an accredited law school in the U.S. for excellence in legal writing.
Financial data: Year ended 12/31/2011. Assets, $1,325,787 (M); Expenditures, $2,338.
Fields of interest: Law school/education.
Type of support: Awards/prizes.
Application information:
　　Deadline(s): May 15
　　Final notification: Recipient notified in Aug.
　　Additional information: Applicants must provide four copies of a current legal writing, together with a letter of recommendation by a law school faculty member or legal professional other than the author of the paper.
Program description:
　　Brown Award Excellence in Legal Writing: The award is in the amount of $5,000 to any law student in the U.S. enrolled in an accredited law school seeking a J.D. or LL.B degree. Only one paper may be submitted by any faculty member or legal professional, and only one paper may be submitted on behalf of any student.
EIN: 760397472

8727
Buckner Adoption and Maternity Services, Inc.

600 N. Pearl St., Ste. 2000
Dallas, TX　75201-2896　(214) 758-8000
Contact: Albert L. Reyes, Pres. and C.E.O.
E-mail: adoption@buckner.org; Toll-Free Tel.: (800) 442-4800; URL: http://www.buckner.org/

Foundation type: Public charity
Purpose: Assistance for families and children in hurting and crisis situations in the U.S. and abroad.
Financial data: Year ended 12/31/2011. Assets, $337,460 (M); Expenditures, $564,749; Total giving, $306,703; Grants to individuals, totaling $2,771.
Fields of interest: Adoption.
Type of support: Grants for special needs.
Application information: Applications accepted.
　　Additional information: Assistance is provided through adoption, pre- and post-adoption counseling and humanitarian and social

services support for children. Contact the agency for eligibility determination.
EIN: 752571396

8728
Buckner Children and Family Services, Inc.

600 N. Pearl St., Ste. 2000
Dallas, TX　75201-2896　(214) 758-8023
Contact: Albert I. Reyes, Pres.
E-mail: childrenfamily@buckner.org; URL: http://www.buckner.org

Foundation type: Public charity
Purpose: Rental subsidies and basic needs assistance to individuals and families in need.
Publications: Annual report.
Financial data: Year ended 12/31/2011. Assets, $29,603,457 (M); Expenditures, $36,678,334; Total giving, $11,260,080; Grants to individuals, totaling $6,432,748.
Fields of interest: Housing/shelter, rehabilitation; Human services; Family services; Residential/custodial care, group home.
Type of support: Grants for special needs.
Application information: Applications not accepted.
　　Additional information: Contact foundation for program information.
EIN: 752571395

8729
George Bush Presidential Library Foundation

c/o Texas A & M Univ.
1145 TAMU
College Station, TX　77843-1145　(979) 862-2251
Contact: Frederick D. McClure, C.E.O.
FAX: (979) 862-2253;
E-mail: bushfoundation@georgebushfoundation.org ; URL: http://www.georgebushfoundation.org

Foundation type: Public charity
Purpose: Scholarships to outstanding students to attend undergraduate and graduate schools throughout the U.S.
Publications: Application guidelines.
Financial data: Year ended 12/31/2012. Assets, $59,071,219 (M); Expenditures, $3,293,067; Total giving, $392,123; Grants to individuals, totaling $33,500.
Fields of interest: Higher education.
Type of support: Support to graduates or students of specific schools.
Application information: Applications accepted. Application form required. Application form available on the grantmaker's web site.
　　Initial approach: Application
　　Deadline(s): May 1 for CVN 77 Scholarships
　　Applicants should submit the following:
　　　　1) Transcripts
　　　　2) Letter(s) of recommendation
Program descriptions:
　　CVN 77 Scholarships: Three scholarships of $2,500 each are available for crew members of the U.S.S. George H.W. Bush (CVN 77) and their families. One scholarship is reserved for undergraduate students, while the remaining two are reserved for graduate school study. One to attend the George Bush School of Government and Public Service at Texas A&M University, and one to attend any graduate program in the U.S. Eligible applicants must have a minimum GPA of 3.5, and demonstrate an exemplary record in school and community activities.

　　George Bush Faculty Excellence Awards: Four awards of $2,500 each are annually awarded to faculty members at Texas A&M University. Awards are given in the following categories: teaching (recognizing a faculty member who has made outstanding contributions to the international education of Texas A&M students); research (recognizing a faculty member who has made outstanding contributions to international research); public service (recognizing a faculty member who has made outstanding contributions to the public or non-profit sector in local, statewide, national, or international arenas); and George Bush School faculty.
　　George Bush High School Public Service Scholarship: This program recognizes high-school seniors in the Bryan-College Station, Texas school districts for their community services, with the hopes of inspiring future generations to engage in public service and participate in the building of their communities, states, and the nation as better places in which to work and live for all. Recipients are selected on the basis of academic excellence and community service and receive a $2,000 scholarship. In addition, each recipient's school receives a $2,500 grant, to be used for educational purposes.
EIN: 760345781

8730
H. E. Butt Grocery Company Contributions Program

646 S. Main Ave.
San Antonio, TX　78204-1210　(210) 938-8592
Contact: Dya Campos, Dir., Public Affairs
Excellence in Education Awards: Jill Reynolds, 6929 Airport Blvd., Ste. 176, Austin, TX 78752,
e-mail: reynolds.jill@heb.com
E-mail: campos.dya@heb.com; URL: http://www.heb.com/sectionpage/about-us/community/community-involvement/sd80002

Foundation type: Corporate giving program
Purpose: Awards to K-12 educators for excellence in teaching, primarily in the Dallas, TX area.
Publications: Application guidelines; Grants list.
Fields of interest: Elementary/secondary education.
Type of support: Awards/prizes.
Application information: Applications accepted. Application form required. Application form available on the grantmaker's web site.
　　Send request by: Online
　　Deadline(s): Jan. 6
　　Applicants should submit the following:
　　　　1) Financial information
　　　　2) Essay
　　　　3) Resume
Program description:
　　Excellence in Education Awards: H.E. Butt annually awards grants to K-12 and special area public school educators whose leadership and dedication inspire a love of learning in students of all backgrounds and abilities. The teacher award is divided into three categories: the rising star award, the leadership award, and the lifetime achievement award. Three elementary school and three secondary school teachers and their schools receive $5,000, $10,000, and $25,000, respectively, based on years of service. Thirty regional finalists will also receive $1,000 each plus $1,000 for their schools. Excellence awards also include principal award categories to elementary and secondary school principals and district award categories for large, small, and regional districts. The program is limited to Texas.

8731
C.L.C. Foundation
c/o J.L. Carter
2500 1001 Fannin, Ste. 2831
Houston, TX   77002-6760

Foundation type: Independent foundation
Purpose: Scholarships to residents of Clovis, NM, recommended by advisory trustees associated with Clovis High School.
Financial data: Year ended 12/31/2012. Assets, $266,334 (M); Expenditures, $15,429; Total giving, $15,250.
Fields of interest: Higher education.
Type of support: Support to graduates or students of specific schools.
Application information: Applications accepted.
  Deadline(s): Feb. 15
  Additional information: Application should include resume and statement of financial need.
EIN: 760132112

8732
Cadbury Schweppes Americas Emergency Relief Fund
P.O. Box 259199
Plano, TX   75025-9199   (972) 673-8088

Foundation type: Public charity
Purpose: Grants to current, former, and future employees of CBI Holding and its subsidiaries who suffered hardship as a result of Hurricane Katrina and other disasters.
Financial data: Year ended 12/31/2011. Assets, $72,553 (M); Expenditures, $61,104; Total giving, $60,275.
Fields of interest: Disasters, Hurricane Katrina; Safety/disasters.
Type of support: Grants to individuals; Employee-related welfare.
Application information: Unsolicited requests for funds not accepted.
EIN: 412184477

8733
Camp Mohawk Scholarship Trust
1717 St. James Pl., Ste. 500
Houston, TX   77056   (281) 585-6224

Foundation type: Independent foundation
Purpose: Scholarships to graduating seniors of Alvin Independent School District, TX.
Financial data: Year ended 07/31/2012. Assets, $423,010 (M); Expenditures, $19,994; Total giving, $11,700; Grants to individuals, 3 grants totaling $11,700 (high: $3,900, low: $3,900).
Type of support: Support to graduates or students of specific schools; Undergraduate support.
Application information: Applications accepted. Application form required.
  Deadline(s): Mar. 7
  Applicants should submit the following:
    1) Letter(s) of recommendation
    2) SAT
    3) ACT
    4) Financial information
    5) Transcripts
    6) Essay
EIN: 376387595

8734
Jesse W. Cannon Scholarship Foundation
c/o Bank of America, N.A.
P.O. Box 831041
Dallas, TX   75283-1041

Foundation type: Independent foundation
Purpose: Low-interest educational loans to students attending the University of Arkansas, Fayetteville.
Financial data: Year ended 04/30/2012. Assets, $2,589,674 (M); Expenditures, $197,084; Total giving, $146,969.
Type of support: Student loans—to individuals; Support to graduates or students of specific schools; Undergraduate support.
Application information: Applications accepted. Application form required.
  Initial approach: Letter requesting application
  Deadline(s): None
  Additional information: Applications should be obtained from the financial aid office and include grades and explanation of extenuating circumstances.
EIN: 716099820

8735
Caritas of Austin
611 Neches St.
Austin, TX   78701-3324   (512) 479-4610
FAX: (512) 472-4164;
E-mail: info@caritasofaustin.org; Mailing address: P.O. Box 1947, Austin, TX 78767-1947;
URL: http://www.caritasofaustin.org

Foundation type: Public charity
Purpose: Provides financial assistance and supportive services to residents of Austin, TX who are experiencing a housing crisis or short-term homelessness in order to prevent them from becoming homeless or return them to housing.
Publications: Annual report; Newsletter; IRS Form 990 or 990-PF printed copy available upon request.
Financial data: Year ended 09/30/2011. Assets, $2,970,066 (M); Expenditures, $8,398,838; Total giving, $4,334,824; Grants to individuals, totaling $3,709,116.
Fields of interest: Housing/shelter, expense aid; Housing/shelter; Economically disadvantaged.
Type of support: Grants for special needs.
Application information:
  Initial approach: Tel.
  Applicants should submit the following:
    1) Financial information
  Additional information: Contact foundation for eligibility criteria.
EIN: 741909670

8736
Caritas of Waco
300 S. 15th St.
Waco, TX   76701-1704   (254) 753-4593
Contact: Buddy Edwards, Exec. Dir.
URL: http://www.caritas-waco.org/

Foundation type: Public charity
Purpose: Emergency assistance to individuals and families in the Waco, TX area with food, clothing, utilities, prescription medication and other needs.
Financial data: Year ended 12/31/2011. Assets, $4,709,264 (M); Expenditures, $15,042,174; Total giving, $13,997,910; Grants to individuals, totaling $13,946,070.
Fields of interest: Economically disadvantaged.
Type of support: Emergency funds; In-kind gifts; Grants for special needs.

Application information: Interview required.
  Additional information: Applicants must provide proof of address, identification card and social security cards for all occupants in a household.
EIN: 741711575

8737
Eula Carter & Graham Smith Memorial Scholarship Fund
P.O. Box 985
Mount Vernon, TX   75457-2309   (903) 537-2264
Contact: B.F. Hicks, Tr.

Foundation type: Independent foundation
Purpose: Scholarships to the top five graduates of Mount Vernon High School, TX.
Financial data: Year ended 12/31/2011. Assets, $469,492 (M); Expenditures, $21,412; Total giving, $9,000; Grants to individuals, 6 grants totaling $9,000 (high: $3,500, low: $500).
Type of support: Support to graduates or students of specific schools; Undergraduate support.
Application information: Applications not accepted.
  Additional information: Unsolicited requests for funds not considered or acknowledged.
EIN: 756364952

8738
Amon G. Carter Star-Telegram Employees Fund
306 W. 7th St., Ste. 440
Fort Worth, TX   76102-0480   (817) 332-3535
Contact: Nenetta Carter Tatum, Pres.

Foundation type: Company-sponsored foundation
Purpose: Scholarships to children of employees of the Fort Worth Star-Telegram, KXAS-TV, and WBAP-Radio, all in TX. Pension supplements and medical and hardship assistance to employees of the Fort Worth Star-Telegram, KXAS-TV, and WBAP-Radio, all in TX.
Financial data: Year ended 04/30/2013. Assets, $32,170,263 (M); Expenditures, $1,360,859; Total giving, $1,187,607; Grants to individuals, 200 grants totaling $301,107 (high: $5,000, low: $94).
Type of support: Employee-related scholarships; Employee-related welfare.
Application information: Applications not accepted.
  Additional information: Unsolicted requests for funds not considered or acknowledged.
EIN: 756014850

8739
Catholic Charities Diocese of Fort Worth, Inc.
249 W. Thornhill Dr.
Fort Worth, TX   76105-3012   (817) 534-0814
Contact: Heather Reynolds, Pres.
FAX: (817) 535-8779;
E-mail: infocatholiccharities@ccdofw.org;
URL: http://www.ccdofw.org

Foundation type: Public charity
Purpose: Financial assistance to low income individuals and families in need in the Fort Worth, TX area, with clothing, rent, food, medical, childcare, transportation assistance and other special needs.
Publications: Financial statement; Newsletter.

Financial data: Year ended 12/31/2011. Assets, $20,015,404 (M); Expenditures, $18,963,369; Total giving, $4,026,559; Grants to individuals, totaling $4,026,559.
Fields of interest: Human services, emergency aid; Economically disadvantaged.
Type of support: Grants for special needs.
Application information: Contact the agency for eligibility determination.
EIN: 750808769

8740

Catholic Charities of Dallas, Inc.
9461 LBJ Freeway, Ste. 128
Dallas, TX 75243-4598 (214) 520-6590
Contact: Arne J. Nelson, Pres. and C.E.O.
FAX: (214) 520-6595; URL: http://www.catholiccharitiesdallas.org

Foundation type: Public charity
Purpose: Emergency financial assistance to individuals in need, with focus on the elderly, refugees and immigrants in the Dallas, TX area.
Publications: Annual report.
Financial data: Year ended 06/30/2012. Assets, $13,908,477 (M); Expenditures, $11,572,785; Total giving, $2,267,523; Grants to individuals, totaling $1,584,506.
Fields of interest: Human services; Children/youth; Aging; Immigrants/refugees.
Type of support: Emergency funds; Grants to individuals.
Application information: Contact the organization for information on eligibility and assistance.
EIN: 752745221

8741

Catholic Charities of the Archdiocese of Galveston-Houston
2900 Louisiana St.
Houston, TX 77006-3435 (713) 526-4611
FAX: (713) 526-1546;
E-mail: info@catholiccharities.org; Mailing address: P.O. Box 66508, Houston, TX 77266-6508;
URL: http://www.catholiccharities.org

Foundation type: Public charity
Purpose: Assistance to individuals in need with foster care and adoption, food, family counseling and other special needs throughout the Galveston and Houston metropolitan areas, TX.
Publications: Annual report.
Financial data: Year ended 12/31/2011. Assets, $38,704,642 (M); Expenditures, $29,503,267; Total giving, $10,116,857; Grants to individuals, totaling $10,116,857.
Fields of interest: Human services, emergency aid; Human services; Economically disadvantaged.
Type of support: Emergency funds; In-kind gifts.
Application information: Contact the charity for eligibility requirements.
EIN: 741109733

8742

Frank A. & Gladys F. Chamberlin Scholarship Fund
c/o Bank of America, N.A.
P.O. Box 831041
Dallas, TX 75283-1041 (254) 968-9100
Contact: Dominic Dottavio, Pres.
Application address: c/o Tarleton State Univ., W. Tarleton St., No. T-0001, Stephenville, TX 76402-0001

Foundation type: Independent foundation
Purpose: Seven undergraduate and seven graduate scholarships awarded annually to high school graduates of Erath County, TX, and residents of Erath County, TX, who are attending Tarleton State University, TX.
Financial data: Year ended 07/31/2013. Assets, $820,047 (M); Expenditures, $45,616; Total giving, $34,664; Grants to individuals, 14 grants totaling $34,664 (high: $2,476, low: $2,476).
Type of support: Support to graduates or students of specific schools; Graduate support; Undergraduate support.
Application information: Applications accepted.
  Deadline(s): Apr. 15
  Additional information: Application by FAF available from College Entrance Examination Board.
EIN: 756234715

8743

The Mary Cecile Chambers Charitable Trust
(formerly The Mary Cecile Chambers Scholarship Fund)
c/o Moody National Bank
P.O. Box 1139
Galveston, TX 77553-1139 (409) 765-5561
FAX: (409) 763-8925; E-mail for Luann Bland: LBland@moodytrust.com

Foundation type: Independent foundation
Purpose: Scholarships to financially needy male residents of Chambers, Galveston and Brazoria counties, TX, for full-time study at colleges, universities, and trade schools.
Publications: Application guidelines.
Financial data: Year ended 03/31/2012. Assets, $5,392,349 (M); Expenditures, $358,121; Total giving, $306,200.
Fields of interest: Vocational education; Men; Young adults, male.
Type of support: Scholarships—to individuals; Support to graduates or students of specific schools; Undergraduate support.
Application information: Applications accepted. Application form required.
  Initial approach: Letter or telephone
  Send request by: Mail
  Deadline(s): Apr. 1
  Final notification: Applicants are notified May 31
  Applicants should submit the following:
    1) Class rank
    2) Transcripts
    3) SAT
    4) Letter(s) of recommendation
    5) GPA
    6) Financial information
    7) Essay
    8) ACT
  Additional information: Applications should also include parents' and applicant's financial statements; Application forms available from the trustee or any high school in Chambers, Galveston or Brazoria counties.
EIN: 766071425

8744

Mark A. Chapman Foundation
c/o Lois Krenek
1205 Silliman St.
Sealy, TX 77474-3513

Foundation type: Operating foundation
Purpose: Scholarships to graduating seniors of TX pursuing higher education.

Financial data: Year ended 07/31/2012. Assets, $105,670 (M); Expenditures, $531,179; Total giving, $529,693; Grants to individuals, 80 grants totaling $378,100 (high: $4,125, low: $250).
Fields of interest: Higher education.
Type of support: Scholarships—to individuals.
Application information: Applications accepted. Application form required.
  Additional information: Contact the foundation for additional application guidelines.
EIN: 364460345

8745

Younas & Bushra Chaudhary Foundation
15603 Kuykendahl Rd., No. 200
Houston, TX 77090-3655 (281) 893-9400
Contact: Younas Chaudhary, Dir.

Foundation type: Independent foundation
Purpose: Scholarships to underprivileged individuals residing in the Houston, TX metropolitan area.
Financial data: Year ended 12/31/2011. Assets, $684,903 (M); Expenditures, $95,097; Total giving, $82,801; Grants to individuals, 19 grants totaling $82,801 (high: $37,817, low: $500).
Fields of interest: Economically disadvantaged.
Type of support: Scholarships—to individuals.
Application information: Applications accepted.
  Additional information: Contact foundation for current application guidelines.
EIN: 200479199

8746

Children at Heart Foundation, Inc.
1301 N. Mays St.
Round Rock, TX 78664-2945 (512) 255-3668
FAX: (512) 388-8257;
E-mail: info@childrenatheartministries.org;
URL: http://www.cahfoundation.org

Foundation type: Public charity
Purpose: Scholarships to residents of Texas Baptist Children's Home or Miracle Farm for higher education at an accredited college, university, or vocational school.
Publications: Annual report; Newsletter.
Financial data: Year ended 12/31/2011. Assets, $78,085,660 (M); Expenditures, $8,572,936; Total giving, $7,036,317; Grants to individuals, totaling $168,689.
Fields of interest: Higher education.
Type of support: Scholarships—to individuals.
Application information: Applicants must show written proof of acceptance at accredited institutions, enrolled in at least 12 hours per semester or equivalent, and proof of good standing and passing grades.
EIN: 743007363

8747

Childress Foundation
5773 Woodway, Ste. 191
Houston, TX 77057-1501

Foundation type: Independent foundation
Purpose: Scholarships to graduating seniors from Northbrook Senior High School, TX for continuing education at colleges, universities, or vocational and/or technical education and/or training.
Financial data: Year ended 05/31/2013. Assets, $1,207 (M); Expenditures, $10,815; Total giving, $10,600.
Fields of interest: Vocational education, post-secondary; Higher education.

Type of support: Support to graduates or students of specific schools.

Application information: Applications accepted. Application form required. Interview required.

> *Additional information:* Application should include recommendations from guidance counselors and school principals. Recipients are required to perform 20 hours of community service for any organization of their choice.

Program description:

> *Leadership Award:* This award provides up to $5,000 per year (renewable for up to four years) for college or vocational school expenses. It is available to graduating seniors who have demonstrated leadership qualities and might not otherwise be able to attend undergraduate or vocational and/or technical education and or training institutions.

EIN: 760376247

8748
The Chinati Foundation

1 Cavalry Row
P.O. Box 1135
Marfa, TX   79843-1135   (432) 729-4362
Contact: Rob Weiner, Assoc. Dir.
FAX: (432) 729-4597;
E-mail: information@chinati.org; E-mail for Rob Weiner: rweiner@chinati.org; URL: http://www.chinati.org

Foundation type: Public charity
Purpose: Residencies to artists of diverse ages, backgrounds, and disciplines.
Publications: Newsletter.
Financial data: Year ended 12/31/2011. Assets, $13,489,633 (M); Expenditures, $1,918,285.
Fields of interest: Visual arts.
Type of support: Foreign applicants; Residencies.
Application information:

> *Initial approach:* Letter
> *Deadline(s):* Apr. 1
> *Additional information:* Application must include resume, slides of recent work, and sufficient return postage for materials.

Program descriptions:

> *Artist in Residence:* The foundation provides selected artists with housing, studio space, access to its collection and archives, a stipend of $1,000, and an opportunity to hold an exhibition at the conclusion of the residency. The average residency lasts two to three months.
> *Internships:* The program allows students to engaged directly in all aspects of the museum's daily activities, working closely with staff, resident artists, visiting scholars, architects, and museum professionals. Interns are provided with a stipend of $100 per week.

EIN: 742340423

8749
Christian Community Action

200 S. Mill St.
Lewisville, TX   75057-3944   (972) 219-4357
Contact: Jeffery D. Price, Pres. and C.E.O.
FAX: (972) 219-4330;
E-mail: communications@ccahelps.org;
URL: http://www.ccahelps.org/

Foundation type: Public charity
Purpose: Financial assistance to low income individuals and families of Lewisville, TX to fulfil their immediate and crucial needs during crisis, with food,clothing, shelter, illness, loss of job or the ability to pay their bills.

Publications: Annual report.
Financial data: Year ended 06/30/2012. Assets, $13,954,902 (M); Expenditures, $11,632,613; Total giving, $3,417,503; Grants to individuals, totaling $3,417,503.
Fields of interest: Human services; Economically disadvantaged.
Type of support: In-kind gifts; Grants for special needs.
Application information: Applications accepted. Application form required. Application form available on the grantmaker's web site.

> *Additional information:* Application should include proof of residency, financial need, document income, expenses, and crisis, provide identification for all household members, have a viable action plan, or be willing to form a viable plan, with a CCA caseworker, be cooperative and honest with staff of CCA. Applicant must be 19 years of or older. See web site for eligibility determination.

EIN: 237319371

8750
Christmas in Action - Greater Cleburne, Inc.

(formerly Christmas in April Greater Cleburne, Inc.)
P. O. Box 983
Cleburne, TX   76033-0983   (817) 641-8610
Contact: France Hafford, Pres.
Application address: 212 E. Chambers St., Cleburne, TX 76033

Foundation type: Public charity
Purpose: Financial assistance for home improvement to residents within Johnson county, TX.
Fields of interest: Housing/shelter, services.
Type of support: Grants for special needs.
Application information: Applications accepted. Application form required.

> *Deadline(s):* None
> *Additional information:* Application should include proof of income by copy of previous year income tax return.

EIN: 752874372

8751
Christus Health Gulf Coast Region

919 Hidden Ridge Dr.
Irving, TX   75038   (469) 282-2000
Contact: Ellen M. Jones, Pres. and C.E.O.

Foundation type: Public charity
Purpose: Financial assistance to patients in the Gulf Coast Region who are in need of medication, doctor's visits and other healthcare services.
Financial data: Year ended 06/30/2012. Assets, $314,803,779 (M); Expenditures, $254,100,273; Total giving, $51,533,427; Grants to individuals, totaling $130,882.
Fields of interest: Health care; Economically disadvantaged.
Type of support: In-kind gifts; Grants for special needs.
Application information: Applications accepted.

> *Additional information:* Application form determines your inability to pay for services needed. Contact the organization for eligibility determination.

EIN: 760591592

8752
Alfredo Cisneros Del Moral Foundation, Inc.

735 E. Guenther St.
San Antonio, TX   78210-1235
URL: http://www.sandracisneros.com/foundation.php

Foundation type: Independent foundation
Purpose: Grants to various writers residing in TX, to further their artistic endeavors.
Financial data: Year ended 12/31/2012. Assets, $163,016 (M); Expenditures, $19,275; Total giving, $10,882; Grants to individuals, 3 grants totaling $10,882 (high: $8,882, low: $1,000).
Fields of interest: Literature.
Type of support: Grants to individuals.
Application information: Applications not accepted.

> *Additional information:* Unsolicited requests for funds not considered or acknowledged.

EIN: 742866648

8753
Cleburne Rotary Club Foundation Inc.

P.O. Box 1261
Cleburne, TX   76033-1261
Contact: Kenneth Von Tungeln, Treas.
E-mail: kvontingeln@auldridge.com; Application Address: P.O. Box 1000, Cleburne,TX 76033

Foundation type: Independent foundation
Purpose: Scholarships primarily to residents of Cleburne and Joshua, TX.
Financial data: Year ended 06/30/2013. Assets, $297,468 (M); Expenditures, $48,693; Total giving, $48,650; Grants to individuals, 14 grants totaling $39,250 (high: $6,000, low: $750).
Type of support: Scholarships—to individuals.
Application information: Applications accepted.

> *Additional information:* Contact foundation for current application deadline/guidelines.

EIN: 752886299

8754
Clifford Foundation, Inc.

P.O. Box 1001
Corsicana, TX   75151-1001   (903) 874-4725
Contact: Clifford L. Brown III, Pres.

Foundation type: Independent foundation
Purpose: Scholarships to financially needy graduating seniors of any Navarro county, TX high school who have been accepted to attend a Texas state supported public college, university or technical college.
Financial data: Year ended 06/30/2013. Assets, $3,793,111 (M); Expenditures, $218,632; Total giving, $212,675; Grants to individuals, 35 grants totaling $212,675 (high: $12,962, low: $1,007).
Fields of interest: Vocational education, post-secondary; Higher education.
Type of support: Scholarships—to individuals.
Application information: Applications accepted. Application form required. Interview required.

> *Initial approach:* Telephone
> *Deadline(s):* Mar. 30
> *Applicants should submit the following:*
> 1) Class rank
> 2) GPA
> 3) Transcripts
> 4) SAR
> 5) Financial information
> 6) Essay
> 7) SAT
> 8) ACT

Additional information: Application should also include a copy of students' and parents' previous year's tax return, and college acceptance and financial aid award letters received from the college of your choice.
EIN: 752506394

8755
Coastal Bend Community Foundation
The Six Hundred Bldg.
600 Leopard St., Ste. 1716
Corpus Christi, TX 78473-1111 (361) 882-9745
Contact: Karen W. Selim, C.E.O.; For scholarships: Karen Wesson, Dir., Scholarships
Scholarship inquiry e-mail: kwesson@cbcfoundation.org
FAX: (361) 882-2865;
E-mail: kselim@cbcfoundation.org; URL: http://www.cbcfoundation.org

Foundation type: Community foundation
Purpose: Scholarships to residents of Aransas, Bee, Jim Wells, Kleberg, Nueces, Refugio, and San Patricio counties, TX.
Publications: Application guidelines; Annual report; Grants list; Informational brochure.
Financial data: Year ended 12/31/2011. Assets, $47,066,102 (M); Expenditures, $4,336,939; Total giving, $2,766,890; Grants to individuals, 936 grants totaling $964,968.
Fields of interest: Higher education; Scholarships/financial aid.
Type of support: Scholarships—to individuals; Support to graduates or students of specific schools; Undergraduate support.
Application information: Applications accepted. Application form required. Application form available on the grantmaker's web site.
  Initial approach: Application
  Deadline(s): Mar. 1 for online application, vary for others
  Applicants should submit the following:
    1) Letter(s) of recommendation
    2) Transcripts
    3) SAT
    4) ACT
  Additional information: See web site for additional guidelines for each scholarship.
EIN: 742190039

8756
Coastal Bend Foundation
140 W. Cleveland
Aransas Pass, TX 78336 (361) 758-1608

Foundation type: Independent foundation
Purpose: Scholarships to graduates of the Aransas Pass Independent School District, TX, to attend any secondary education program with a curriculum recognized by the Texas Higher Education Coordinating Board. Awards to outstanding teachers in the Aransas Pass Independent School District, TX.
Financial data: Year ended 12/31/2012. Assets, $1,737,218 (M); Expenditures, $97,093; Total giving, $28,459.
Fields of interest: Higher education.
Type of support: Support to graduates or students of specific schools; Awards/prizes.
Application information:
  Initial approach: Letter
  Additional information: Contact foundation for application guidelines.
EIN: 742129257

8757
College First Foundation
130 E. John Carpenter Freeway
Irving, TX 75062-2708 (972) 999-4560
Contact: Toppy Cantrell, Admin.
FAX: (972) 999-4559

Foundation type: Independent foundation
Purpose: Scholarships for children of active employees, agents, or members of participating companies, organizations and associations.
Financial data: Year ended 12/31/2012. Assets, $560,235 (M); Expenditures, $395,105; Total giving, $325,000; Grants to individuals, 191 grants totaling $325,000 (high: $5,000, low: $1,000).
Fields of interest: Education.
Type of support: Employee-related scholarships.
Application information: Applications accepted.
  Additional information: Recipients should submit formal applications to the scholarship program offered by the organization to which their parent is a member. Unsolicited requests for funds not considered or acknowledged.
EIN: 752638941

8758
Common Grace Ministries Inc.
6010 Hillside Ln.
Garland, TX 75043 (972) 841-9602
Contact: Martin Hironaga, Exec. Dir.
E-mail: toni@commongrace.net

Foundation type: Operating foundation
Purpose: Scholarships to East Dallas, TX students for attendance at Dallas Theological Seminary or an institution of higher education. Grants to individuals or families who reside in East Dallas, TX, with financial or emergency need.
Financial data: Year ended 12/31/2012. Assets, $528,435 (M); Expenditures, $127,825; Total giving, $10,676.
Fields of interest: Theological school/education; Economically disadvantaged.
Type of support: Scholarships—to individuals; Support to graduates or students of specific schools; Grants for special needs.
Application information:
  Deadline(s): Aug. 1 for scholarships, none for assistance
  Additional information: Application form needed for scholarship. Applicant must show proof of financial hardship through a reliable referral for assistance.
EIN: 752727006

8759
Communities Foundation of Texas, Inc.
5500 Caruth Haven Ln.
Dallas, TX 75225-8146 (214) 750-4222
Scholarship enquiry e-mail: scholarships@cftexas.org
FAX: (214) 750-4210;
E-mail: donorservices@cftexas.org; URL: http://www.cftexas.org

Foundation type: Community foundation
Purpose: Scholarships to graduating students from the Dallas, TX area. Some scholarships are available to students from the Dallas-Fort Worth area, as well as Arkansas, Oklahoma and nationwide.
Publications: Application guidelines; Annual report; Financial statement; Newsletter; Program policy statement.

Financial data: Year ended 06/30/2013. Assets, $982,331,000 (M); Expenditures, $103,454,000; Total giving, $82,493,000. Scholarships—to individuals amount not specified.
Fields of interest: Secondary school/education; Higher education.
Type of support: Scholarships—to individuals; Support to graduates or students of specific schools; Undergraduate support.
Application information: Applications accepted. Application form required. Application form available on the grantmaker's web site.
  Initial approach: Application
  Send request by: Online
  Deadline(s): Varies
  Applicants should submit the following:
    1) ACT
    2) SAT
    3) Transcripts
    4) Letter(s) of recommendation
    5) Financial information
    6) Essay
Program description:
  Scholarship Funds: The foundation's trustees award scholarships from over 50 scholarships funds for higher education. Many of these scholarships are awarded exclusively to students graduating from a particular geographical area or high school, attending a specific college or university, or pursuing a particular course of study. See web site for additional information. https://cftexas.academicworks.com.
EIN: 750964565

8760
Community Action Nacogdoches, Inc.
P.O. Box 631938
Nacogdoches, TX 75963-1938 (936) 564-2491
Contact: Karen M. Swenson, Exec. Dir.
FAX: (936) 564-0302

Foundation type: Public charity
Purpose: Emergency assistance to low income individuals and families in the Nacogdoches, TX area with urgent needs for basic needs.
Financial data: Year ended 11/30/2011. Assets, $2,896,251 (M); Expenditures, $21,772,822.
Fields of interest: Economically disadvantaged.
Type of support: Grants for special needs.
Application information: Application form required.
  Initial approach: Telephone
  Additional information: Applicant must attend intake meeting, must show proof of income for all household members, social security number for all household, personal ID, and proof of residency.
EIN: 751226261

8761
Community Council of Greater Dallas
1349 Empire Central, Ste. 400
Dallas, TX 75247-4033 (214) 871-5065
FAX: (214) 871-7442; URL: http://www.ccgd.org

Foundation type: Public charity
Purpose: Emergency assistance to individuals and families in need throughout the greater Dallas, TX metropolitan area with residential repairs and maintenance, medical assistance, food, transportation and other special needs.
Publications: Informational brochure; Occasional report.
Financial data: Year ended 09/30/2011. Assets, $765,353 (M); Expenditures, $9,302,008; Total giving, $1,187,683; Grants to individuals, totaling $1,187,683.

Fields of interest: Children/youth; Aging; Economically disadvantaged.
Type of support: Emergency funds; In-kind gifts; Grants for special needs.
Application information: Contact the council for eligibility determination.
EIN: 750800631

8762
Community Foundation of Abilene
500 Chestnut, Ste. 1634
Abilene, TX   79602-1434
Contact: Katie Alford, C.E.O.
FAX: (325) 676-4206;
E-mail: cfainfo@cfabilene.org; URL: http://www.cfabilene.org

Foundation type: Community foundation
Purpose: Scholarships to area students of Abilene, TX for postsecondary education.
Publications: Application guidelines; Annual report; Informational brochure; Newsletter; Occasional report.
Financial data: Year ended 06/30/2012. Assets, $80,123,372 (M); Expenditures, $6,129,340; Total giving, $5,352,306. Scholarships—to individuals amount not specified.
Fields of interest: Higher education.
Type of support: Scholarships—to individuals.
Application information: Applications accepted. Application form required. Application form available on the grantmaker's web site.
    Send request by: Mail
    Copies of proposal: 1
    Deadline(s): Varies
    Applicants should submit the following:
        1) ACT
        2) Transcripts
        3) SAT
        4) Photograph
        5) Letter(s) of recommendation
        6) GPA
        7) Financial information
        8) Essay
    Additional information: Students should contact their high school counselors for eligibility requirements.
EIN: 752045832

8763
The Community Foundation of Brazoria County, Texas
104 W. Myrtle, Ste. 204
P.O. Box 2392
Angleton, TX   77515   (979) 848-2628
Contact: Barbara Franklin, Exec. Dir.
FAX: (979) 848-0031; E-mail: cfbr@sbcglobal.net;
URL: http://www.cfbr.org

Foundation type: Community foundation
Purpose: Scholarships to deserving students of Brazoria County, TX pursuing higher education.
Publications: Informational brochure; Newsletter.
Financial data: Year ended 06/30/2012. Assets, $1,568,776 (M); Expenditures, $602,925; Total giving, $545,195.
Fields of interest: Higher education.
Type of support: Scholarships—to individuals.
Application information: Applications accepted.
    Deadline(s): Varies
    Additional information: Contact the foundation for additional information.
EIN: 760427068

8764
Community Foundation of North Texas
(formerly The Community Foundation of Metropolitan Tarrant County)
306 W. 7th St., Ste. 850
Fort Worth, TX   76102   (817) 877-0702
Contact: Nancy E. Jones, C.E.O.; For scholarships: Lisa Mund, Scholarship Coord.
For scholarship inquiries: lmund@cfntx.org
FAX: (817) 877-1215;
E-mail: nancyjones@cfntx.org; URL: http://www.cfntx.org

Foundation type: Community foundation
Purpose: Scholarships for students in Hunt, Somervell, and Tarrant counties, TX, as well as various collegiate programs.
Publications: Application guidelines; Annual report; Financial statement; Grants list; Informational brochure; Newsletter; IRS Form 990 or 990-PF printed copy available upon request.
Financial data: Year ended 12/31/2012. Assets, $155,874,668 (M); Expenditures, $12,951,949; Total giving, $11,994,195; Grants to individuals, 213 grants totaling $645,407 (high: $44,000, low: $250).
Fields of interest: Higher education.
Type of support: Scholarships—to individuals.
Application information: Applications accepted. Application form required. Application form available on the grantmaker's web site.
    Deadline(s): Varies
    Additional information: Students should contact their high school counselor for eligibility requirements. Some scholarship application forms and eligibility criteria can be printed from scholarship listings page. See web site for additional information.
EIN: 752267767

8765
Conference U.S.A.
5201 N. O'Connor Blvd., Ste. 300
Irving, TX   75039-3765   (214) 774-1300
URL: http://conferenceusa.cstv.com

Foundation type: Public charity
Purpose: Scholarships by nomination only to student athletes at schools belonging to Conference USA.
Financial data: Year ended 06/30/2012. Assets, $32,331,852 (M); Expenditures, $48,171,582; Total giving, $37,649,452; Grants to individuals, totaling $48,000.
Fields of interest: Athletics/sports, school programs.
Type of support: Support to graduates or students of specific schools; Awards/grants by nomination only; Graduate support; Undergraduate support.
Application information: Student athletes must be nominated by their schools.
EIN: 364021594

8766
Conn Appliances Charitable Foundation Inc.
3295 College St.
Beaumont, TX   77701-4611

Foundation type: Company-sponsored foundation
Purpose: Scholarships to children of employees of Conn Appliances, Inc.
Financial data: Year ended 11/30/2012. Assets, $0 (M); Expenditures, $9,000; Total giving, $9,000.
Type of support: Employee-related scholarships.

Application information: Applications accepted.
    Initial approach: Letter
    Deadline(s): None
Company name: Conn Appliances, Incorporated
EIN: 741884559

8767
James C. & Elizabeth R. Conner Foundation
204 S. Wellington St., Ste. A
Marshall, TX   75670-4056   (903) 938-0331
Contact: Robert L. Duvall, Chair.; R. Michael Hallum, Secy.
FAX: (903) 938-0334

Foundation type: Independent foundation
Purpose: Graduate and doctoral scholarships to deserving students in the fields of business, engineering, medical science, or physical science, who graduated in the top ten percent of their undergraduate class.
Publications: Annual report; Annual report (including application guidelines).
Financial data: Year ended 12/31/2012. Assets, $3,594,290 (M); Expenditures, $226,902; Total giving, $204,687; Grants to individuals, 12 grants totaling $204,687 (high: $37,450, low: $1,689).
Fields of interest: Business school/education; Medical school/education; Engineering school/education; Science; Physical/earth sciences.
Type of support: Graduate support; Doctoral support.
Application information: Applications accepted. Application form required. Interview required.
    Initial approach: Letter or telephone
    Deadline(s): None
    Applicants should submit the following:
        1) Transcripts
        2) Photograph
EIN: 752302882

8768
The Conrad Foundation
2200 Space Park Dr., Ste. 205
Houston, TX   77058   (832) 864-7223
Contact: Jennifer Fotherby, Exec. Dir.
E-mail: info@conradawards.org; URL: http://conradfoundation.org/

Foundation type: Public charity
Purpose: Awards to high school student teams participating in the foundation's Spirit of Innovation Competition.
Financial data: Year ended 12/31/2011. Assets, $303,120 (M); Expenditures, $782,969; Total giving, $80,285; Grants to individuals, totaling $36,035.
Fields of interest: Higher education; Business/industry; Space/aviation; Mathematics; Engineering/technology.
Type of support: Awards/prizes.
Application information:
    Initial approach: Proposal
    Additional information: See web site for additional guidelines.
Program description:
    Spirit of Innovation Challenge: This program invites high school students and their coaches (including teachers and parents) to "get their genius on" during an annual competition. Using science, technology, engineering, and math skills, teams develop innovative products to help solve global sustainability. As part of the program, the challenge matches participants with world-renowned scientists, engineers, and entrepreneurs as mentors to assist with advanced academic and

business principles. Teams compete for awards and recognition, including a chance to attend the foundation's annual Innovation Summit, where they will present their products and vie for seed grants, patent support, and commercial opportunities.
EIN: 262304138

8769
Loring Cook Foundation
900 E. Lakeview Dr.
McAllen, TX 78501-5723 (956) 686-5491
Contact: Kathy Disbro

Foundation type: Independent foundation
Purpose: Scholarships to graduating seniors of McAllen Memorial High School, TX.
Financial data: Year ended 12/31/2012. Assets, $2,412,506 (M); Expenditures, $105,486; Total giving, $81,700.
Type of support: Support to graduates or students of specific schools; Undergraduate support.
Application information: Application form required. Interview required.
> *Deadline(s):* Mar. 1
> *Additional information:* Contact foundation for current application guidelines.

EIN: 746050063

8770
Kelly Gene Cook, Sr. Charitable Foundation, Inc.
230 Kilts Dr.
Houston, TX 77024-6214
Contact: Robert Kneppler, V.P.
E-mail: cookfoundation@sbcglobal.net; Application address: c/o Kathy Pacelli,1675 Lakeland Dr. S., No. 507, Jackson, MS 39216-4841, tel.: (601) 981-1116, e-mail: kathy@kgccf.com

Foundation type: Independent foundation
Purpose: Undergraduate and graduate scholarships to students attending specific schools in MS who are not married, have no children and are not physical education majors.
Financial data: Year ended 12/31/2012. Assets, $21,167,436 (M); Expenditures, $1,380,795; Total giving, $1,050,308.
Fields of interest: Higher education; Scholarships/financial aid.
Type of support: Support to graduates or students of specific schools; Graduate support; Undergraduate support.
Application information: Application form required. Interview required.
> *Deadline(s):* Apr. 15
> *Applicants should submit the following:*
> 1) ACT
> 2) Budget Information
> 3) Essay
> 4) FAFSA
> 5) Financial information
> 6) GPA
> 7) Letter(s) of recommendation
> 8) Pell Grant
> *Additional information:* Financial information should be sent to the financial aid office of the named institutions.

Program description:
> *Scholarship Awards:* To be eligible, students must attend school full-time (15 hours) and maintain a satisfactory GPA. Recipients cannot be physical education majors, married, or have children. Recipients who maintain a 3.0 GPA in their undergraduate studies are eligible to apply for a graduate scholarship.

EIN: 760201807

8771
Frances and Dawson Cooper Educational Trust
c/o Eugene Worthington
P.O. Box 779
Gatesville, TX 76528 (254) 865-2211
Contact: Kenneth Poston

Foundation type: Operating foundation
Purpose: Scholarships to TX residents to cover tuition, fees and books at institutions of higher learning in TX.
Financial data: Year ended 12/31/2012. Assets, $887,559 (M); Expenditures, $16,228; Total giving, $14,678; Grants to individuals, 13 grants totaling $14,678 (high: $2,355, low: $294).
Fields of interest: Higher education.
Type of support: Scholarships—to individuals.
Application information: Applications accepted. Application form required.
> *Deadline(s):* Jan. 1 to May 15
> *Additional information:* Application must include personal tax returns of applicant and parents, personal employment and salary records of applicant and parents, residence verification, proof of enrollment of other family members in college, proof of GPA and hours completed.

EIN: 746494283

8772
Verne Cooper Foundation, Inc.
1400 W. Russell Ave.
Bonham, TX 75418 (903) 583-5574
FAX: (903) 583-9453; URL: http://vernecooper.org/

Foundation type: Independent foundation
Purpose: Scholarships to residents of Fannin County, TX.
Financial data: Year ended 12/31/2011. Assets, $2,410,788 (M); Expenditures, $119,346; Total giving, $110,438; Grants to individuals, 165 grants totaling $108,438 (high: $1,250, low: $350).
Type of support: Scholarships—to individuals.
Application information: Application form required.
> *Deadline(s):* May 1

EIN: 752547151

8773
Corpus Christi Geological Society Scholarship Trust Fund
P.O. Box 1068
Corpus Christi, TX 78403 (361) 884-2443
Contact: Dan Pedrotti, Chair.

Foundation type: Operating foundation
Purpose: Scholarships to students majoring in earth science and attending Texas A&M Corpus Christi, Texas A&M Kingsville, or Del Mar College for higher education.
Financial data: Year ended 12/31/2011. Assets, $129,345 (M); Expenditures, $8,500; Total giving, $8,500; Grants to individuals, 11 grants totaling $8,500 (high: $1,500, low: $500).
Fields of interest: Physical/earth sciences.
Type of support: Support to graduates or students of specific schools.
Application information: Applications accepted. Application form required. Application form available on the grantmaker's web site.
> *Initial approach:* Letter
> *Send request by:* Mail
> *Deadline(s):* Nov. 15 for spring semester, May 1 for fall semesster
> *Applicants should submit the following:*
> 1) Transcripts

> 2) Letter(s) of recommendation
> 3) Essay
> *Additional information:* Scholarship is awarded based on merit and need.

EIN: 742622816

8774
Patricia Joder Cox and Mayor George Foundation
12411 Matisse Ln.
Dallas, TX 75230-1755
Contact: Deborah Cox, Pres.

Foundation type: Independent foundation
Purpose: Scholarships to graduates of Cheyenne High School, Cheyenne, WY.
Financial data: Year ended 12/31/2012. Assets, $15,202 (M); Expenditures, $5,183; Total giving, $5,000; Grant to an individual, 1 grant totaling $5,000.
Fields of interest: Higher education.
Type of support: Scholarships—to individuals.
Application information: Applications accepted. Application form required.
> *Deadline(s):* Feb. 1
> *Applicants should submit the following:*
> 1) SAT
> 2) ACT
> 3) GPA
> *Additional information:* Application available from school guidance counselor and should include a list of extracurricular activities.

EIN: 364532787

8775
Crescent Scholarship Foundation
777 Main St., Ste. 2000
Fort Worth, TX 76102-5366 (817) 321-1000
Contact: Tammy Morgan, Secy.

Foundation type: Company-sponsored foundation
Purpose: Scholarships to children of non-officer employees of Crescent Real Estate Equities, Ltd.
Financial data: Year ended 12/31/2012. Assets, $514,329 (M); Expenditures, $56,072; Total giving, $53,750; Grants to individuals, 16 grants totaling $53,750 (high: $10,000, low: $500).
Type of support: Employee-related scholarships.
Application information:
> *Initial approach:* Letter
> *Deadline(s):* Feb. 28
> *Applicants should submit the following:*
> 1) Resume
> 2) Financial information
> 3) Letter(s) of recommendation
> 4) Photograph
> 5) Essay
> 6) ACT
> 7) Transcripts
> 8) GPA

Company name: Crescent Real Estate Equities Company
EIN: 752993151

8776
CRW Have A Heart Fund, Inc.
4201 Marsh Ln.
Carrollton, TX 75007-1720 (972) 662-5685
Contact: Anne Varano, Pres. and Exec. Dir.

Foundation type: Public charity
Purpose: Financial assistance to employees of Carlson Restaurants Worldwide who are in need of special assistance due to lost of possession,

funeral expenses and medical expenses and other tradegy and disasters.
Financial data: Year ended 12/31/2011. Assets, $1,803,056 (M); Expenditures, $757,147; Total giving, $672,090; Grants to individuals, totaling $672,090.
Fields of interest: Safety/disasters; Human services.
Type of support: Grants for special needs.
Application information: Applications not accepted.
Additional information: Unsolicited requests for funds not considered or acknowledged.
EIN: 161699048

8777
Mark Cuban Foundation
P.O. Box 12388
Dallas, TX 75225-0388
URL: http://www.fallenpatriotfund.org

Foundation type: Independent foundation
Purpose: Grants to the spouses and children of U.S. military personnel who were killed or seriously injured during Operation Iraqi Freedom.
Financial data: Year ended 12/31/2012. Assets, $27,108,439 (M); Expenditures, $120,875; Total giving, $100,400; Grants to individuals, 53 grants totaling $100,400 (high: $2,500, low: $1,000).
Fields of interest: Military/veterans.
Type of support: Grants to individuals.
Application information: Applications accepted. Application form available on the grantmaker's web site.
Deadline(s): None
Additional information: The foundation will proactively contact eligible families. Applications are also available at www.fallenpatriotfund.org.
EIN: 260063142

8778
Culture Shapers
10609 Grant Rd., Bldg. C-D
Houston, TX 77070-6001 (281) 664-1420
Contact: Ernest Fitzpatrick, Pres.
FAX: (281) 664-1417;
E-mail: info@cultureshapers.com; E-mail For Ernie Fitzpatrick: ernie@cultureshapers.com;
URL: http://www.cultureshapers.com

Foundation type: Public charity
Purpose: Awards to visual arts high school students in the greater Houston, TX area.
Publications: Application guidelines.
Financial data: Year ended 12/31/2012. Assets, $33,088 (M); Expenditures, $104,729; Total giving, $55,825; Grants to individuals, totaling $55,825.
Fields of interest: Film/video; Visual arts; Photography; Sculpture; Painting; Drawing.
Type of support: Awards/prizes.
Application information:
Deadline(s): Jan. 20 (electronic media and photography submissions), Mar. 23 (drawing and sculpture submissions), and Oct. 21 (mixed media and painting submissions) for Visual Arts Contest; monthly for Young Voices of Houston
Additional information: Entry fee is $20, with each student receiving a commemorative t-shirt with their entry.
Program descriptions:
Culture Shapers Visual Arts Contest: Through a contest generally held each fall, prizes ranging from $250 to $5,000 are awarded to outstanding artists

attending a high school in Texas in six categories: drawing, electronic media, mixed media, painting, photography, and sculpture. Evaluation criteria include technique, personal expression, organization, and integration. The contest is open to all high school students in Harris, Waller, Liberty, Chambers, Galveston, Brazoria, Fort Bend and Montgomery counties.
Danny Wood "Heart in Art" Award: This award grants a certificate and a check for $1,000 to a high-school student in Brazoria, Chambers, Fort Bend, Harris, Liberty, Montgomery, or Waller counties who exemplifies leadership, social skills, service, positive character, and overcomes adversity. Eligible applicants must be nominated by a teacher and/or peer.
Young Voices of Houston: Awards range from 1st place $500, 2nd place $300, 3rd place $200 and 4 to 12 will receive $25 each. The awards are for a performing arts contest for high school students in the Houston area to encourage and further support efforts to pursue careers in the arts.
EIN: 200568072

8779
Albert B. Cutter Memorial Trust Fund
c/o Bank of America, N.A.
P.O. Box 831041
Dallas, TX 75283-1041
Application Address: c/o Bank of America, 120 Main St., TX1-609-08-05 Dallas, TX 75202-3113

Foundation type: Independent foundation
Purpose: Assistance to the aged, sick and needy people and sick and crippled children who are residents of Riverside, CA.
Financial data: Year ended 12/31/2012. Assets, $955,698 (M); Expenditures, $44,872; Total giving, $23,909; Grants to individuals, 9 grants totaling $12,393 (high: $7,200, low: $125).
Fields of interest: Children; Aging; Disabilities, people with; Economically disadvantaged.
Type of support: Grants for special needs.
Application information: Applications accepted. Application form required. Interview required.
Deadline(s): None
Additional information: Application forms are provided upon request.
EIN: 956112842

8780
Cypress-Fairbanks Educational Foundation
(also known as CFEF)
P.O. Box 1698
Cypress, TX 77410-1698 (281) 807-3591
Contact: Marie Homes, Exec. Dir.
FAX: (832) 634-3434; URL: http://www.thecfef.org

Foundation type: Public charity
Purpose: Scholarships to individuals in the Cypress Fairbanks Independent School District, TX, who are pursuing higher education.
Publications: Application guidelines.
Financial data: Year ended 06/30/2012. Assets, $6,652,502 (M); Expenditures, $497,027; Total giving, $352,525; Grants to individuals, totaling $254,750.
Fields of interest: Higher education.
Type of support: Scholarships—to individuals.
Application information: Applications accepted. Application form available on the grantmaker's web site.
Deadline(s): Feb. 2
Applicants should submit the following:
1) Financial information

2) Transcripts
Additional information: Application should also include a copy of parents' most recent income tax return.
Program descriptions:
Adam Jackson Skinner Memorial Scholarship: A $4,000 scholarship, funded over two years, will be awarded to a male student from Cypress Fairbanks High School with high school drama, choir, team sports, debate, or Boy Scouts of America participation.
Cecil Hall Scholarship: Two scholarships for four years will be available to Cypress-Fairbanks ISD seniors who are planning to attend Texas A&M University. Eligible applicants must have submitted an application and transcript to Texas A&M University.
Cypress Fairbanks Educational Foundation Assistance Scholarships: Scholarships ranging between $2,000 - $10,000 are available to eligible seniors enrolled in the Cypress-Fairbanks ISD. Recipients must forfeit this award if they receive a scholarship/funding of equal or greater value from another source.
Dynegy Scholarship: A $500 award is available to a deserving student of Cypress-Fairbanks ISD.
Edwin C. Schroeder Trust: Multiple scholarships of $1,000 are awarded to students attending a college of the Lone Star College System.
Eric Bassett Memorial Scholarship: One scholarship of $20,000 is awarded over four years to a Cypress-Fairbanks or Cypress-Falls High School student who will attend Texas A & M University.
Kevin Borgfeldt Memorial Scholarship: A $500 scholarship will be awarded to a Cypress Fairbanks High School student who has participated in the band program.
Tenet Healthcare Foundation/Cy-Fair Medical Center Scholarship: Three scholarships of $500 each are available to Cypress-Fairbanks ISD students who plan to pursue studies in the healthcare field.
Watson Family Foundation Scholarship: A $500 award is available to a deserving student of Cypress-Fairbanks ISD.
EIN: 237079589

8781
Clayton Dabney Foundation for Kids With Cancer
6500 Greenville Ave., Ste. 342
Dallas, TX 75206-1828 (214) 361-2600
Contact: John P. Owen, Exec. Dir.
FAX: (214) 217-5199;
E-mail: admin@claytondabney.org; Additional Address: 12335 Kingsride Ste.347, Houston, TX 77024; Additional Tel.: (713)-737-5139; Additional Fax: (713)-973-7751; URL: http://www.claytondabney.org

Foundation type: Public charity
Purpose: Grants to families of children who are terminally ill with cancer to pay for rent and utility bills, and to grant wishes.
Publications: Financial statement; Informational brochure; Newsletter.
Financial data: Year ended 12/31/2012. Assets, $696,638 (M); Expenditures, $805,323; Total giving, $439,722; Grants to individuals, totaling $429,157.
Fields of interest: Cancer; Children.
Type of support: Grants for special needs.
Application information: Applications accepted. Application form required. Application form available on the grantmaker's web site.
Initial approach: Letter or telephone
Send request by: Fax

Copies of proposal: 1
Deadline(s): None
Final notification: Applicants notified in one to
three days
EIN: 752641482

8782
Frank C. Dailey College Scholarship
12041 CR 2210
Grapeland, TX 75844-9705 (936) 687-4661
Contact: Karen Bridges
Application address: 116 W. Myrtle St., Grapeland,
TX, 75844

Foundation type: Operating foundation
Purpose: Scholarships to graduating seniors of
Grapeland Independent School District, TX, for
undergraduate education.
Financial data: Year ended 12/31/2012. Assets,
$254,788 (M); Expenditures, $3,678; Total giving,
$3,000; Grants to individuals, 3 grants totaling
$3,000 (high: $1,500, low: $500).
Type of support: Support to graduates or students
of specific schools.
Application information: Application form required.
Deadline(s): May 15
Additional information: Application must include
transcript.
EIN: 752383547

8783
Dallas Bar Foundation
2101 Ross Ave.
Dallas, TX 75201-2703 (214) 220-7487
Contact: Elizabeth Philipp, Exec. Dir.
FAX: (214) 220-7465;
E-mail: ephilipp@dallasbar.org; URL: http://
www.dallasbarfoundation.org/

Foundation type: Public charity
Purpose: Scholarships to high school graduates of
Dallas, TX pursuing a law degree.
Publications: Application guidelines; Newsletter.
Financial data: Year ended 12/31/2011. Assets,
$10,785,889 (M); Expenditures, $725,251; Total
giving, $210,830; Grants to individuals, totaling
$46,180.
Fields of interest: Law school/education;
Minorities.
Type of support: Scholarships—to individuals.
Application information: Applications accepted.
Application form required.
Send request by: Mail
Deadline(s): Jan. 11 for Justice James Baker
Scholarship, Feb. 15 for Sara T. Hughes
Scholarship
Applicants should submit the following:
1) Transcripts
2) Resume
3) Essay
Additional information: See web site or contact
the foundation for additional application
guidelines.
Program descriptions:
Collins Clerkships: The clerkships are for minority
students in their second year of law school at SMU.
The clerkship is for six weeks and are scheduled
either the first half of second half of the summer.
The clerks are paid $500 a week. The Collins Clerk
placed with the Supreme Court of Texas also
receives a $600 housing allowance.
Sarah T. Hughes Scholarship: This scholarship
enables minority men and women to have the
opportunity to obtain a legal education at Southern
Methodist University Dedman School of Law. The
scholarship covers the full cost of tuition to be

covered for one or more minority students each
year, and is renewed for the second and third years
providing the student remains in good academic
standing.
EIN: 237410031

8784
The Dallas Foundation
Reagan Place at Old Parkland
3963 Maple Ave., Ste. 390
Dallas, TX 75219 (214) 741-9898
Contact: Mary M. Jalonick, Pres.; For grants: Laura
J. Ward, Dir., Community Philanthropy
FAX: (214) 741-9848;
E-mail: info@dallasfoundation.org; URL: http://
www.dallasfoundation.org

Foundation type: Community foundation
Purpose: Scholarships to residents of Dallas, TX for
higher education.
Publications: Application guidelines; Annual report;
Financial statement; Grants list; Newsletter.
Financial data: Year ended 12/31/2012. Assets,
$237,683,349 (M); Expenditures, $34,447,583;
Total giving, $33,204,208. Scholarships—to
individuals amount not specified.
Fields of interest: Higher education; Scholarships/
financial aid.
Type of support: Scholarships—to individuals;
Support to graduates or students of specific
schools; Undergraduate education.
Application information: Applications accepted.
Application form required. Application form
available on the grantmaker's web site.
Send request by: Mail
Deadline(s): Varies
Additional information: See web site for
additional guidelines.
Program description:
Scholarship Funds: The foundation has a number
of scholarship funds to assist area students further
their education at a college/university, vocational
or trade school. Each scholarship has a different
purpose and eligibility criteria, which may include a
proven record of academic achievement,
extracurricular activity, financial need, or particular
area of study such as architecture or journalism.
See web site for additional information.
EIN: 752890371

8785
Dallas Hispanic Bar Association
Scholarship Foundation
2101 Ross Ave.
Dallas, TX 75201-2703 (214) 220-7400
Contact: Catharine M. Maher, Exec. Dir.
FAX: (214) 220-7465;
E-mail: mail@dallashispanicbar.com; E-mail For
Catharine M. Maher: cmaher@dallasbar.org;
URL: http://www.dallasbar.com/content/
dallas-hispanic-law-foundation-amanecer-scholarsh
ip-luncheon

Foundation type: Public charity
Purpose: Scholarships are provided to Texas
residents enrolled in a Texas law school who have
demonstrated high academic performance and
leadership.
Publications: Application guidelines.
Financial data: Year ended 12/31/2011. Assets,
$231,081 (M); Expenditures, $15,650; Total
giving, $15,000.
Fields of interest: Law school/education;
Hispanics/Latinos.
Type of support: Scholarships—to individuals.

Application information: Applications accepted.
Application form required.
Initial approach: E-mail
Additional information: See web site for
additional information.
EIN: 204297699

8786
Dallas Stars Foundation, Inc.
2601 Ave. of the Stars
Frisco, TX 75034-9015 (214) 387-5500
Contact: Jessica Dunn, Exec. Dir.
E-mail address for scholarships:
starscommunity@dallasstars.com
FAX: (214) 387-5610; URL: http://stars.nhl.com/
club/page.htm?id=39286

Foundation type: Public charity
Purpose: Scholarship to deserving graduating high
school seniors of the Dallas/Forth Worth Metroplex,
TX area with demonstrated sportsmanship in
hockey and ice-skating.
Financial data: Year ended 06/30/2012. Assets,
$472,120 (M); Expenditures, $512,318; Total
giving, $221,726; Grants to individuals, totaling
$6,250.
Fields of interest: Higher education; Athletics/
sports, winter sports; Recreation.
Type of support: Scholarships—to individuals;
Support to graduates or students of specific
schools.
Application information: Application form required.
Application form available on the grantmaker's web
site.
Applicants should submit the following:
1) Transcripts
2) SAT
3) Letter(s) of recommendation
4) Essay
5) ACT
Additional information: Application can be
obtained from high school counselor.
Program descriptions:
Bob Gainey Honorary Scholarship: Scholarship in
the amount of $1,250 per year for a maximum of
$5,000 over four years is awarded to a Metroplex
high school senior athlete. Applicant must plan to
attend an accredited two- or four-year U.S. college
or university as a full-time student. The scholarship
is based on academic achievement, community and
extracurricular involvement, and financial need.
Hockey and Figure Skating Scholarships: Dr.
Pepper StarCenter athletes are eligible for hockey
and figure skating scholarships. Applicants must
exhibit strong academic performance, financial
need, involvement in extracurricular and/or
community activities, and exemplary conduct during
practices, games, and competitions.
EIN: 752780401

8787
David Kendall Danciger Charitable
Foundation
18208 Preston Rd., Apt. D9
Dallas, TX 75252 (214) 397-1921
Contact: Cameron Dee Sewell, V.P.
Application address: 2600 Ross Ave., Ste. 2600,
Dallas, TX 75201, tel.: (214) 397-1921

Foundation type: Independent foundation
Purpose: Scholarships to individuals primarily in CO
and TX.
Financial data: Year ended 12/31/2012. Assets,
$568 (M); Expenditures, $2,932; Total giving,
$2,896.
Type of support: Scholarships—to individuals.

Application information: Applications accepted.
Initial approach: Letter
Deadline(s): None
Additional information: Applications should include transcripts.
EIN: 752510985

8788
Mark Deering Foundation
c/o John F. Sheehy, Jr.
510 N. Valley Mills Dr., Ste. 500
Waco, TX 76710-6077 (254) 772-5263
Contact: Mark Deering, Dir.
Application address: 4700 Westchester Dr., Waco, TX 76710-1337

Foundation type: Independent foundation
Purpose: Scholarships to individuals who attend Roman Catholic schools in the greater Waco, TX, area.
Financial data: Year ended 12/31/2011. Assets, $866,781 (M); Expenditures, $63,497; Total giving, $61,375; Grants to individuals, 45 grants totaling $61,375 (high: $3,000, low: $320).
Fields of interest: Catholic agencies & churches.
Type of support: Scholarships—to individuals.
Application information: Applications accepted.
Initial approach: Letter
Deadline(s): None
Final notification: Applicants usually notified within one month
Additional information: Applications should outline financial needs and student qualifications.
EIN: 742726640

8789
The Michael and Susan Dell Foundation
P.O. Box 163867
Austin, TX 78716-3867
FAX: (512) 600-5501; E-mail: info@msdf.org;
URL: http://www.msdf.org/

Foundation type: Independent foundation
Purpose: Scholarships to graduating seniors participating in the foundation's approved college readiness program.
Publications: Grants list.
Financial data: Year ended 12/31/2012. Assets, $803,631,256 (M); Expenditures, $118,834,622; Total giving, $80,821,766.
Fields of interest: Higher education.
Type of support: Scholarships—to individuals.
Application information: Applications accepted. Application form required. Application form available on the grantmaker's web site.
Initial approach: Download application form
Deadline(s): Jan. 15
Applicants should submit the following:
1) FAFSA
2) Pell Grant
Additional information: All applications must be completed online. Application process opens in Nov. and closes the following Jan. Refer to web site for further information concerning guidelines.
Program description:
Dell Scholars Program: The program enables lower-income and underserved students to achieve their greatest potential through higher education. The Dell Scholars Program is offered to high school students participating in an approved AVID program. Each scholar receives $20,000. Candidates are evaluated based on their individual determination to succeed, their stated goals and their demonstrated ability to overcome obstacles

and challenges. Students are not evaluated on academic record or test scores alone, rather on their desire to push themselves in terms of curriculum completed and their ability to communicate their determination to overcome the hardships they have faced. The criteria for application include: 1) Graduation from accredited high school this academic year; 2) Participation in approved college-readiness program; 3) Eligible for a Federal Pell Grant and demonstrated need for financial assistance; 4) 2.4 GPA minimum; 5) Determination in overcoming adversity; and 6) Plan to enter bachelor's degree program at an accredited higher education institution upon graduation. Visit URL: http://www.dellscholars.org for more information.
EIN: 364336415

8790
Delta Delta Delta Foundation
2331 Brookhollow Plz. Dr.
Arlington, TX 76006-7407 (817) 633-8001
Contact: Julie Greene Haskell, Exec. Dir.
FAX: (817) 652-0212;
E-mail: foundation@tridelta.org; Mailing address: P.O. Box 5987, Arlington, TX 76005-5987;
URL: http://www.tridelta.org/foundation

Foundation type: Public charity
Purpose: Scholarships to members of Delta Delta Delta fraternity.
Publications: Application guidelines; Biennial report.
Financial data: Year ended 07/31/2012. Assets, $8,081,094 (M); Expenditures, $905,235; Total giving, $312,108; Grants to individuals, totaling $207,108.
Fields of interest: Students, sororities/fraternities.
Type of support: Undergraduate support.
Application information: Applications accepted. Application form required.
Initial approach: Letter
Deadline(s): Contact foundation for deadline
EIN: 752184529

8791
Denman Family Foundation
4208 Versailles
Dallas, TX 75205

Foundation type: Independent foundation
Purpose: Provides support with medical care and other expenses for individuals in the Dallas, TX area.
Financial data: Year ended 12/31/2012. Assets, $1,370,623 (M); Expenditures, $471,501; Total giving, $460,665; Grants to individuals, 2 grants totaling $4,900 (high: $2,500, low: $2,400).
Fields of interest: Health care.
Type of support: Grants to individuals.
Application information: Applications not accepted.
EIN: 200222678

8792
Daniel B. Deupree Foundation
P.O. Box 345
Bonham, TX 75418-0345 (903) 961-3001
Contact: Lisa Hicks
E-mail: admin@dbdeupree.org; URL: http://dbdeupree.org/

Foundation type: Independent foundation
Purpose: Scholarships to Fannin County, Texas residents and 20 percent to non-Fannin county.

Financial data: Year ended 12/31/2012. Assets, $1,691,842 (M); Expenditures, $71,061; Total giving, $57,370; Grants to individuals, 54 grants totaling $57,370 (high: $1,200, low: $200).
Fields of interest: Education.
Type of support: Scholarships—to individuals.
Application information: Applications accepted. Application form required.
Deadline(s): Mar. 5 for fall semester, Oct. 5 for spring semester
Applicants should submit the following:
1) Transcripts
2) Letter(s) of recommendation
Additional information: Applicant must show need, character, grades and goals. Applications are renewable.
EIN: 759033769

8793
Harry J. Diffenbaugh Trust for Baker University
c/o Bank of America, N.A.
P.O. Box 831041
Dallas, TX 75283-1041

Foundation type: Independent foundation
Purpose: Scholarships to MO residents with financial need attending Baker University, Baldwin, KS.
Financial data: Year ended 12/31/2012. Assets, $204,766 (M); Expenditures, $11,760; Total giving, $8,000.
Type of support: Support to graduates or students of specific schools; Undergraduate support.
Application information: Applications accepted. Application form required.
Initial approach: Letter
Deadline(s): None
EIN: 446008351

8794
H. J. Diffenbaugh Trust for Kansas University
c/o Bank of America, N.A.
P.O. Box 831041
Dallas, TX 75283-1041

Foundation type: Independent foundation
Purpose: Scholarship to financially needy MO residents who wish to attend the University of Kansas.
Financial data: Year ended 12/31/2012. Assets, $242,103 (M); Expenditures, $14,306; Total giving, $9,000.
Type of support: Scholarships—to individuals; Support to graduates or students of specific schools.
Application information: Applications accepted. Application form required.
Initial approach: Letter
Deadline(s): None
Additional information: Application forms available from the University of Kansas or from the Trustee. Applicant must demonstrate financial need.
EIN: 446008349

8795
Harry J. Diffenbaugh-University of Illinois
(formerly H. J. Diffenbaugh Trust for University of Illinois)
c/o Bank of America, N.A.
P.O. Box 831041
Dallas, TX 75283-1041

Foundation type: Independent foundation
Purpose: Scholarships to MO residents attending the University of Illinois at Urbana-Champaign.
Financial data: Year ended 12/31/2012. Assets, $456,130 (M); Expenditures, $22,628; Total giving, $15,000.
Fields of interest: Education.
Type of support: Support to graduates or students of specific schools; Undergraduate support.
Application information: Applications accepted. Application form required.
  Initial approach: Letter or telephone
  Deadline(s): None
  Additional information: Applicant must show financial need. Application available at University of Illinois or from Trustee.
EIN: 446008350

8796
Diverseworks, Inc.

1117 East Freeway
Houston, TX 77002-1108   (713) 223-8346
Contact: Sara Kellner, Exec. Dir.
FAX: (713) 223-4608;
E-mail: info@diverseworks.org; URL: http://www.diverseworks.org

Foundation type: Public charity
Purpose: Residencies to performing and visual artists with preference to residents of Houston, TX.
Publications: Application guidelines.
Financial data: Year ended 08/31/2011. Assets, $147,756 (M); Expenditures, $725,303.
Fields of interest: Visual arts; Performing arts.
Type of support: Residencies.
Application information: Applications accepted.
  Deadline(s): Dec. 17
  Final notification: Applicants notified Jan. 11
  Applicants should submit the following:
    1) Budget Information
    2) Proposal
    3) Work samples
    4) Resume
  Additional information: Application must also include explanation of project, and technical/equipment requirements. See web site for additional guidelines.
EIN: 760035355

8797
Jerry & Lucille Donnelly Scholarship Trust

c/o Bank of America, N.A.
P.O. Box 831041
Dallas, TX 75283-1041   (800) 257-0332
Application address: c/o Bank of America, N.A., P.O. Box 830259, Dallas, TX 75283-0259

Foundation type: Independent foundation
Purpose: Scholarships for students who attended Blackwell, OK public schools for the study of music at an accredited college, university or music school. Also, scholarships to students attending Northern Oklahoma College.
Financial data: Year ended 12/31/2012. Assets, $120,402 (M); Expenditures, $8,264; Total giving, $4,000. Scholarships—to individuals amount not specified.
Fields of interest: Music; Performing arts, education; Higher education.
Type of support: Scholarships—to individuals.
Application information: Applications accepted.
  Deadline(s): None
  Additional information: Application should include a letter of introduction and a resume.
EIN: 731119304

8798
Dreams Scholarship Foundation

P.O. Box 667
Azle, TX 76098   (817) 444-2252
Contact: Trisha McAda, Chair.
Application address: 3103 N. Cardinal Rd., Azle, TX 76020

Foundation type: Operating foundation
Purpose: Scholarships to graduating seniors of Azle and Springtown high schools, TX for attendance at any Texas universities with the exception of University of Texas at Austin.
Financial data: Year ended 02/28/2013. Assets, $241,554 (M); Expenditures, $18,464; Total giving, $18,000; Grants to individuals, 6 grants totaling $18,000 (high: $3,000, low: $3,000).
Fields of interest: Higher education.
Type of support: Support to graduates or students of specific schools.
Application information: Application form required.
  Deadline(s): Mar. 31
  Applicants should submit the following:
    1) Transcripts
    2) FAFSA
EIN: 752738823

8799
Donald Driver Foundation

8951 Ruthby, Exec. Ste. 11/12
P.O. Box 87694
Houston, TX 77061-3140   (832) 831-7273
Contact: Donald J. Driver, C.E.O.
FAX: (713) 644-9402;
E-mail: info@donalddriverfoundation.com;
URL: http://www.donalddriverfoundation.com

Foundation type: Public charity
Purpose: Scholarships to graduating seniors who are residents of MS, TX, and WI for attendance at an accredited college or university.
Publications: Application guidelines.
Financial data: Year ended 12/31/2011. Assets, $488,063 (M); Expenditures, $262,663; Total giving, $160,643; Grants to individuals, totaling $28,092.
Fields of interest: Higher education; Scholarships/financial aid.
Type of support: Scholarships—to individuals.
Application information: Applications accepted. Application form required. Application form available on the grantmaker's web site.
  Send request by: Mail
  Deadline(s): May 30 for Scholarships
  Final notification: Recipients notified July 1
  Applicants should submit the following:
    1) Financial information
    2) Essay
    3) Letter(s) of recommendation
    4) Transcripts
  Additional information: Payments are made directly to the educational institution on behalf of the students.
Program description:
  Donald Driver Foundation Scholarship: Ten scholarships of $1,000 each are available to students living in Mississippi, Texas, or Wisconsin, to be used toward the first semester of an accredited college or university. Eligible applicants must have a G.P.A. of 3.0 or higher (based on a 4.0 scale), have an ACT score of 18 or higher, be accepted to and/or attending an accredited two- or four-year college, university, or technical school, and maintain full-time status. Students must perform and participate in one service project that benefits homelessness, education, or low-income

populations. The service project must be approved by the foundation.
EIN: 760678602

8800
Margaret Dunn Scholarship Trust

c/o Bank of America, N.A.
P.O. Box 831041
Dallas, TX 75283-1041   (509) 573-7021

Foundation type: Independent foundation
Purpose: Scholarships to graduates of Yakima School District 7, WA, for attendance at accredited four year institutions in WA.
Financial data: Year ended 08/31/2013. Assets, $269,136 (M); Expenditures, $15,402; Total giving, $11,000.
Fields of interest: Higher education.
Type of support: Support to graduates or students of specific schools; Undergraduate support.
Application information: Applications accepted. Application form required.
  Deadline(s): Apr. 21
  Applicants should submit the following:
    1) Class rank
    2) GPA
    3) Financial information
  Additional information: Selection is based on financial need, demonstration through scholarship, character and deed achievement and industry in a promise for useful citizenship. See high school counselor for application.
EIN: 916365396

8801
The Naasson K. & Florrie S. Dupre Permanent Educational Scholarship Fund Trust

P.O. Box 1401
Lubbock, TX 79408-1401   (806) 742-2808
Application address: c/o Dean of Agriculture, Texas Tech University, P.O. Box 42131, Lubbock, TX 79409-2131, tel.: (806) 742-2808

Foundation type: Independent foundation
Purpose: Scholarships to juniors, seniors, and graduate students enrolled in the College of Agricultural Sciences at Texas Tech University, who are residents of TX and have maintained at least a "B" average in the semester preceding application.
Financial data: Year ended 12/31/2011. Assets, $134,709 (M); Expenditures, $9,769; Total giving, $7,200; Grants to individuals, 12 grants totaling $7,200 (high: $600, low: $600).
Fields of interest: Natural resources; Agriculture.
Type of support: Support to graduates or students of specific schools; Graduate support; Undergraduate support.
Application information: Applications accepted. Application form required. Interview required.
  Deadline(s): Apr. 1
  Additional information: Scholarships are renewable.
EIN: 756103694

8802
J. Tom Eady Charitable Trust
c/o Community National Bank & Trust
P.O. Box 624
Corsicana, TX 75151-9004
Contact: Les Leskoven, Sr. V.P. and Trust Off.,
Community National Bank & Trust
Tel. and e-mail for L. Leskoven: (903) 654-4528,
e-mail: lleskoven@cbhot.com

Foundation type: Independent foundation
Purpose: Scholarships to Navarro County, TX, high
school students who have been accepted into an
accredited college, university or technical college.
Financial data: Year ended 12/31/2012. Assets,
$9,189,599 (M); Expenditures, $467,025; Total
giving, $429,453; Grants to individuals, 21 grants
totaling $74,903 (high: $7,500, low: $1,250).
Fields of interest: Vocational education,
post-secondary; Higher education.
Type of support: Scholarships—to individuals.
Application information: Applications accepted.
Application form required. Application form
available on the grantmaker's web site.
> *Initial approach:* Letter or telephone requesting
> application form, or download form online
> *Applicants should submit the following:*
> 1) Essay
> 2) SAR
> 3) ACT
> 4) SAT
> 5) Transcripts
> 6) GPA
> *Additional information:* Students should
> demonstrate to the Selection Committee
> good character and academic skills that are
> adequate for continuing their education.
> Emphasis will be placed on acedemic
> performance, standardized test scores,
> financial need, leadership and extracurricular
> activities. Usually, five new scholarships are
> awarded in the current academic year, with a
> value of up to $2,500 per semester.
> Applicants should have an SAT (math and
> reading portions only) minimum total score of
> 1,000, or ACT minimum total score of 21.
> Scholarship Application Form maybe
> downloaded at http://chsgocenter.org/
> EADY_APP.pdf.
EIN: 756604134

8803
East Montgomery County Scholarship Foundation
P.O. Box 1019
New Caney, TX 77357-1019 (281) 354-4419

Foundation type: Public charity
Purpose: Scholarships for graduating seniors or
GED recipients residing within the East Montgomery
County Improvement District boundaries, for
attendance at an accredited college, university, or
technical school.
Financial data: Year ended 09/30/2011. Assets,
$2,306,138 (M); Expenditures, $328,569; Total
giving, $308,476; Grants to individuals, totaling
$308,476.
Fields of interest: Vocational education,
post-secondary; Higher education.
Type of support: Scholarships—to individuals.
Application information: Applications accepted.
Application form required.
> *Additional information:* Application should
> include high school transcript, and proof of
> enrollment. Students should contact their

high school guidance counselor for
assistance.
EIN: 542161804

8804
East Texas Communities Foundation, Inc.
(formerly East Texas Area Foundation)
315 N. Broadway, Ste. 210
Tyler, TX 75702-5757 (903) 533-0208
Contact: Kyle L. Penney, Pres.; For grants: Mary
Lynn Smith, Prog. Off.
FAX: (903) 533-0258; E-mail: etcf@etcf.org; Grant
inquiry e-mail: mlsmith@etcf.org; Additional tel.:
(866) 533-3823; URL: http://www.etcf.org

Foundation type: Community foundation
Purpose: Scholarships to East Texas students for
higher education.
Publications: Annual report; Informational
brochure; Newsletter.
Financial data: Year ended 12/31/2011. Assets,
$47,172,577 (M); Expenditures, $5,212,918;
Total giving, $4,609,602; Grants to individuals,
94 grants totaling $168,996.
Fields of interest: Higher education; Scholarships/
financial aid.
Type of support: Scholarships—to individuals;
Support to graduates or students of specific
schools; Undergraduate support.
Application information: Applications accepted.
> *Deadline(s):* Varies
> *Additional information:* Each scholarship fund
> has its own unique set of eligibility criteria.
> See web site for complete listing of
> scholarships.
EIN: 752309138

8805
Maud and Jack Eddy Foundation
c/o Geron B. Crumley
P.O. Box 443
Lampasas, TX 76550 (512) 556-5722
Contact: Mindi L. Pratus, Tr.

Foundation type: Independent foundation
Purpose: Scholarships to selected graduates of
Lampasas High School, Lampasas, TX.
Financial data: Year ended 12/31/2012. Assets,
$205,050 (M); Expenditures, $13,096; Total
giving, $8,000.
Fields of interest: Higher education.
Type of support: Support to graduates or students
of specific schools.
Application information: Applications accepted.
Application form required.
> *Deadline(s):* May 1
EIN: 746422083

8806
Edinburg Child Care, Inc.
P.O. Box 3487
Edinburg, TX 78540-3487 (956) 383-6789

Foundation type: Public charity
Purpose: Reimbursements to support child
day-care providers in the Edinburg, TX area.
Financial data: Year ended 09/30/2011. Assets,
$408,357 (M); Expenditures, $4,457,442; Total
giving, $3,978,552; Grants to individuals, totaling
$2,416,717.
Fields of interest: Food services; Day care.
Type of support: Grants for special needs.
Application information: Applications accepted.

Additional information: Contact the agency for
eligibility determination.
EIN: 742358732

8807
Education is Freedom Foundation
2711 N. Haskell Ave., Ste. 2070, L.B. 18
Dallas, TX 75204-2906 (214) 432-8551
Contact: Marica Page, C.E.O. and Pres.
Toll-free tel.: (877) 642-6343; URL: http://
www.educationisfreedom.com

Foundation type: Public charity
Purpose: Scholarships to qualifying high school
graduates in a participating school in the Dallas
Independent School District, TX for continuing
education at institutions of higher learning.
Publications: Application guidelines; Annual report.
Financial data: Year ended 12/31/2011. Assets,
$2,407,565 (M); Expenditures, $3,226,890; Total
giving, $91,873; Grants to individuals, totaling
$91,873.
Fields of interest: Higher education.
Type of support: Scholarships—to individuals.
Application information: Contact the foundation for
eligibility determination.
EIN: 043643313

8808
Educational Advancement Foundation
327 Congress Ave., Ste. 500
Austin, TX 78701-3656 (512) 469-1700
E-mail: info@edu-adv-foundation.org; Application
address: c/o Grant Committee: 2303 Rio Grande
St., Austin, TX 78705; URL: http://
www.educationaladvancementfoundation.org

Foundation type: Independent foundation
Purpose: Scholarships primarily to individuals
residing in the Austin, TX, area for undergraduate
education. Scholarships are generally by
nomination only.
Publications: Application guidelines; Informational
brochure.
Financial data: Year ended 12/31/2012. Assets,
$3,616,631 (M); Expenditures, $884,407; Total
giving, $301,307.
Type of support: Awards/grants by nomination only;
Undergraduate support.
Application information: Applications not
accepted.
> *Additional information:* Unsolicited requests for
> funds not considered or acknowledged.
EIN: 237001761

8809
Marguerite R. Edwards Scholarship Trust
1717 St., James Pl., Ste. 500
Houston, TX 77056 (281) 585-6224

Foundation type: Independent foundation
Purpose: Scholarships to graduating seniors of
Alvin High School, TX, who are in the top 15 percent
of their class for attendance at an accredited
college.
Financial data: Year ended 07/31/2012. Assets,
$630,719 (M); Expenditures, $64,913; Total
giving, $16,800; Grants to individuals, 17 grants
totaling $16,800 (high: $2,000, low: $500).
Fields of interest: Higher education; Scholarships/
financial aid.
Type of support: Support to graduates or students
of specific schools; Undergraduate support.
Application information: Applications accepted.
Application form required.

Applicants should submit the following:
1) Letter(s) of recommendation
2) Transcripts
3) Class rank
Additional information: Application should also include personal statement and standardized test scores.
EIN: 746216234

8810
V.M. Ehlers Memorial Fund Inc.
(formerly V. M. Ehlers Memorial Fund, Inc.)
1106 Clayton Ln., Ste. 112 W.
Austin, TX   78723-1066   (512) 459-3124
Contact: Henrietta Atee
E-mail: vm.ehlers@twua.org

Foundation type: Independent foundation
Purpose: Scholarships to active paid members of the Texas Water Utilities Association or their dependent children pursuing a course of study that is related to the water utilities industry.
Financial data: Year ended 06/30/2013. Assets, $499,014 (M); Expenditures, $86,665; Total giving, $84,550; Grants to individuals, 79 grants totaling $84,550 (high: $2,000, low: $200).
Fields of interest: Health sciences school/education; Environmental education.
Type of support: Scholarships—to individuals.
Application information: Application form required.
  Deadline(s): July 1
  Additional information: Application should include transcripts, GED or university grade report which documents current academic status. Students pursuing a graduate degree are not eligible.
EIN: 746062790

8811
El Paso Community Foundation
333 N. Oregon, 2nd Fl.
P.O. Box 272
El Paso, TX   79901   (915) 533-4020
Contact: Richard E. Pearson, Pres.
FAX: (915) 532-0716; *E-mail:* info@epcf.org;
URL: http://www.epcf.org

Foundation type: Community foundation
Purpose: Scholarships to individuals residing in the El Paso, TX, area for undergraduate education.
Publications: Application guidelines; Annual report; Financial statement; Grants list; Informational brochure; Newsletter; Occasional report.
Financial data: Year ended 12/31/2012. Assets, $95,848,181 (M); Expenditures, $7,412,146; Total giving, $3,544,529. Scholarships—to individuals amount not specified.
Fields of interest: Disabilities, people with.
Type of support: Scholarships—to individuals; Undergraduate support.
Application information: Application form required.
  Initial approach: Letter or telephone
  Copies of proposal: 1
  Deadline(s): Jan. 31
  Applicants should submit the following:
    1) Transcripts
    2) Letter(s) of recommendation
    3) Financial information
    4) Essay
  Additional information: See web site for complete listing of programs.
EIN: 741839536

8812
E. O. Elam Scholarship Trust Fund
P.O. Box 111
Hamilton, TX   76531
Application address: P.O. Box 311, Hamilton, TX 76531-0311, tel.: (254) 386-8937

Foundation type: Independent foundation
Purpose: Scholarships to students residing in and attending public school in Hamilton County, TX.
Financial data: Year ended 12/31/2011. Assets, $273,298 (M); Expenditures, $14,085; Total giving, $14,000; Grants to individuals, 5 grants totaling $14,000 (high: $4,000, low: $2,000).
Type of support: Support to graduates or students of specific schools; Undergraduate support.
Application information: Applications not accepted.
  Additional information: Giving only to preselected individuals.
EIN: 746306225

8813
Lee Elizey Family Charitable Trust
c/o Ben Royden Ogletree
112 W. Polk
Livingston, TX   77351   (936) 327-5211
Contact: Ben Royden Ogletree, Jr., Tr.

Foundation type: Independent foundation
Purpose: Scholarships to needy and deserving graduates of the public high school in Livingston, TX who attend state or Protestant college or universities in TX.
Financial data: Year ended 06/30/2012. Assets, $1,686,679 (M); Expenditures, $86,202; Total giving, $78,000; Grants to individuals, 23 grants totaling $57,000 (high: $3,000, low: $1,500).
Fields of interest: Higher education.
Type of support: Undergraduate support.
Application information: Applications accepted. Application form not required.
  Deadline(s): None
EIN: 476246112

8814
Emergency Medicine Foundation
P.O. Box 619911
Dallas, TX   75261-9911
Contact: Robert Heard, Exec. Dir.
E-mail: rheard@emfoundation.org; *Additional address:* 1125 Executive Circle, Irving, TX 75038-2522; *additional tel.:* (800) 798-1822;
URL: http://www.emfoundation.org

Foundation type: Public charity
Purpose: Seed grants to researchers in order to help them develop applications for larger foundation or federal funding in the area of emergency medicine.
Publications: Annual report.
Financial data: Year ended 06/30/2012. Assets, $2,579,656 (M); Expenditures, $858,485; Total giving, $723,166.
Fields of interest: Health care.
Type of support: Research.
Application information: Applications accepted. Application form required.
  Initial approach: Letter
Program descriptions:
  EMF Career Development Grant: A maximum of $50,000 is available to emergency medicine faculty at the instructor or assistant professor level who needs seed money or release time to begin a promising research project that promotes research within the specialty of emergency medicine,

advances emergency medical care, and/or facilitates the academic growth and development of emergency medicine faculty and thereby invest in the future of the specialty of emergency medicine. Eligible applicants must have an M.D., D.O., Ph.D., or equivalent degree; hold the rank of instructor or assistant professor in an accredited U.S. medical school; and have a primary faculty appointment in an approved emergency medicine residency program.
  EMF Health Policy Research Grant: This program awards between $25,000 and $50,000, for up to two years, for research projects in health policy or health services research. Grants are awarded to researchers who have the experience to conduct research on critical health policy issues in emergency medicine. Any proposal relating to health policy or health services topics will be considered, but special consideration will be given to proposals in the following areas of health policy/services research: outcomes measurement tools for emergency care; effects of health insurance on emergency department access and care; cost-effective and patient-centered treatment plans; the role of clinical guidelines or policies on emergency department care; and quality of care. Eligible principal investigators must have a primary faculty appointment in emergency medicine, be recognized as an accomplished investigator in the area of study proposed, and must have proven ability to pursue independent research as evidenced by original research publications in peer-reviewed journals or funding from extramural sources.
  EMF Resident Research Grant: A maximum of $5,000 is available to a junior or senior resident to stimulate research at the graduate level. Grants will be made available to any physician who will be enrolled as a resident in good standing in an Accreditation Council for Graduate Medical Education (ACGME)-approved emergency medicine residency for the proposed funding year. Residents must have a faculty preceptor (M.D., D.O., Ph.D., or equivalent degree) who is capable of ensuring the successful completion of the proposed project; a letter of support from the preceptor is required.
  EMF/ENAF Team Grant: This request for proposals specifically targets research that is designed to investigate the topic of emergency department (ED) overcrowding. Proposals may focus on a number of related areas, including: definitions and outcome measures of ED overcrowding, causes and effects of ED overcrowding, and potential solutions to the problem of ED overcrowding. Applicants must provide evidence of a true collaborative effort between physician and nurse professionals and must delineate the relative roles of the participants in terms of protocol development, data collection, and manuscript preparation. Applications may be enhanced by inclusion of appropriate hospital administrative leaders. Award is for $50,000.
  EMF/FERNE Neurological Emergencies Clinical Research Grant: Co-sponsored by the Foundation for Education and Research in Neurological Emergencies (FERNE), this grant program funds research based towards acute disorders of the neurological system, such as the identification and treatment of diseases and injury to the brain, spinal cord, and nerves. $25,000 will be awarded in this program annually. Only clinical applications will be considered; no basic science applications will be accepted.
  EMF/SAEM Medical Student Research Grant: Co-sponsored by the Society for Academic Emergency Medicine (SAEM), a maximum of $2,400 over three months is available for a medical student to encourage research in and increase exposure to emergency medicine. Applicants may

be either specific medical students or an emergency medicine residency program wishing to sponsor a medical student research project; the specific medical student does not need to be identified at the time of application submission, but preference will be given to an institution naming a student who has already committed to the project.
EIN: 752331221

8815
W. N. and Jane Enger Foundation, Inc.
10672 County Rd. 3909
Athens, TX   75752-3863   (903) 675-6279
Contact: Julie Lively

Foundation type: Independent foundation
Purpose: Scholarships to graduating seniors at Calvin High School, OK, as well as scholarships to students at Oklahoma State University, OK, and Trinity Valley Community College, TX.
Financial data: Year ended 12/31/2012. Assets, $173,316 (M); Expenditures, $96; Total giving, $5,900; Grants to individuals, 5 grants totaling $5,900 (high: $1,650, low: $900).
Fields of interest: Higher education.
Type of support: Support to graduates or students of specific schools.
Application information: Applications accepted. Application form required.
  Initial approach: Application
  Deadline(s): Nov. 1
  Applicants should submit the following:
    1) Transcripts
    2) Letter(s) of recommendation
EIN: 752895683

8816
EOG Scholarship Fund
1111 Bagby, Sky Lobby 2
Houston, TX   77002   (713) 651-6630
Contact: Dorothy Pflughaupt
Application address: P.O. Box 4362, Houston, TX 77210-4362

Foundation type: Operating foundation
Purpose: Scholarships to the unmarried children, adopted children, stepchildren and foster children of employees or retirees of EOG Resources, Inc., or its subsidiary for attendance at an accredited college or university.
Financial data: Year ended 12/31/2012. Assets, $1,141,241 (M); Expenditures, $56,750; Total giving, $56,000; Grants to individuals, 22 grants totaling $56,000 (high: $3,000, low: $500).
Fields of interest: Higher education; Scholarships/financial aid.
Type of support: Employee-related scholarships.
Application information: Application form required.
  Deadline(s): Mar. 31
  Additional information: Application should include high school and college transcripts. Individuals with more than 30 hours of college credit are not required to submit a copy of their official high school transcript. Selection is based on financial need, scholastic achievement, writing skills, demonstrated leadership and community service.
EIN: 760479501

8817
The Fant Foundation
1322 N. Post Oak
Houston, TX   77055-1597

Foundation type: Operating foundation

Purpose: Assistance to financially needy residents of Houston, TX. The foundation helps cover the costs of food, clothing, transportation, guidance, medical expenses, and counseling to impoverished, distressed, and disadvantaged individuals.
Financial data: Year ended 12/31/2012. Assets, $692,687 (M); Expenditures, $756,837; Total giving, $740,613; Grants to individuals, 19 grants totaling $92,143.
Type of support: Grants for special needs.
Application information: Applications accepted. Application form required.
  Initial approach: Letter
EIN: 760443413

8818
E. D. Farmer Relief Fund
c/o Mark Riley
County Judge
Weatherford, TX   76086-4304   (817) 596-5607

Foundation type: Independent foundation
Purpose: Grants to economically disadvantaged individuals residing in Parker County, TX, for medical expenses, supplies, utilities, transportation, and shelter.
Financial data: Year ended 12/31/2010. Assets, $121,914 (M); Expenditures, $923; Total giving, $781.
Fields of interest: Health care; Housing/shelter; Economically disadvantaged.
Type of support: Grants for special needs.
Application information: Applications not accepted.
EIN: 756027759

8819
The Fasken Foundation
P.O. Box 2024
Midland, TX   79702-2024   (432) 683-5401
Contact: Jeff Alsup, Exec. Dir.
FAX: (432) 683-5402;
E-mail: jeff@faskenfoundation.org; URL: http://www.faskenfoundation.org

Foundation type: Independent foundation
Purpose: Scholarships to graduates of Midland County public high schools and Midland Community College for attendance at TX institutions.
Publications: Application guidelines.
Financial data: Year ended 12/31/2012. Assets, $17,332,770 (M); Expenditures, $1,550,314; Total giving, $870,060; Grants to individuals, 39 grants totaling $95,514 (high: $3,300, low: $289).
Fields of interest: Higher education.
Type of support: Support to graduates or students of specific schools; Undergraduate support.
Application information: Applications accepted. Application form required. Application form available on the grantmaker's web site.
  Initial approach: Letter to school
  Applicants should submit the following:
    1) SAT
    2) Resume
    3) Photograph
    4) Pell Grant
    5) Letter(s) of recommendation
    6) GPA
    7) Financial information
    8) Curriculum vitae
    9) Budget Information
EIN: 756023680

8820
The Faulconer Scholarship Programs
611 Chase Dr.
Tyler, TX   75701-9431
Contact: Ron Gleason, V.P. , Secy. and Dir., Scholarship Prog.
E-mail address for Ron Gleason.: rgleason@faulconerscholars.org
E-mail: info@faulconerscholars.org; URL: http://www.faulconerscholars.org

Foundation type: Independent foundation
Purpose: Scholarships to African-American and Hispanic-American students in the Tyler Junior College District of TX, which includes the Independent School Districts in Chapel Hill, Grand Saline, Lindale, Tyler, Van and Winona.
Financial data: Year ended 12/31/2012. Assets, $0 (M); Expenditures, $1,256,848; Total giving, $880,628.
Fields of interest: Higher education; African Americans/Blacks; Hispanics/Latinos.
Type of support: Support to graduates or students of specific schools; Graduate support; Undergraduate support.
Application information: Applications accepted. Application form required. Application form available on the grantmaker's web site.
  Initial approach: Application
  Send request by: Mail
  Deadline(s): Mar. 1
  Applicants should submit the following:
    1) Letter(s) of recommendation
    2) Transcripts
    3) Essay
  Additional information: Applications submitted by e-mail, fax or hand delivered, will not be accepted. Application guidelines and form are available on foundation web site.
Program description:
  Faulconer Graduate Scholarship: A select number of Faulconer Graduate Scholarships are awarded each year. Applicants must be current recipients of the Faulconer Scholarship, have at least a 3.00 cumulative GPA for their last 2 years of undergraduate study and be eligible to be accepted into their chosen graduate program. The awards are based on the mutual agreement of student and program staff regarding the annual costs of tuition, fees and books and will be renewable annually based on full-time work and a minimum GPA of 3.0. The scholarship may be awarded based on the student's application but will not be funded until the applicant is accepted into a graduate program at an accredited Texas college or university. All applications for fall admission must be submitted no later than Apr. 1 of the year applicant plans to begin classes. Applications for spring admission must be submitted no later than Oct. 1 of the prior calendar year. No scholarship will exceed $10,000 per year or be renewable for more than 4 years.
EIN: 010752611

8821
The Arch L. Ferguson Foundation
P.O. Box 1839
Arlington, TX   76004-1839

Foundation type: Independent foundation
Purpose: Grants to financially needy Protestants primarily in Arlington, TX. Aid is also given to ministers and retired ministers.
Financial data: Year ended 12/31/2012. Assets, $7,580,321 (M); Expenditures, $436,457; Total giving, $146,960.
Fields of interest: Christian agencies & churches; Protestant agencies & churches.

Type of support: Grants for special needs.
Application information: Applications not accepted.
> *Additional information:* Unsolicited requests for funds not considered or acknowledged.

EIN: 237103241

8822
First Command Educational Foundation
(formerly USPA & IRA Educational Foundation)
1 FirstComm Plz.
Fort Worth, TX 76109-4999 (817) 569-2940
Contact: Vickie C. Mauldin, C.E.O.
FAX: (817) 569-2970;
E-mail: edufoundation@fcef.com; Toll Free Tel.: 877-872-8289; E-mail for Vicki C. Mauldin: vcmauldin@fcef.com; URL: http://www.firstcommand.org

Foundation type: Public charity
Purpose: Scholarships to individuals for associate, undergraduate and graduate degrees, and to individuals seeking professional certifications and to trade school attendees.
Publications: Annual report; Newsletter.
Financial data: Year ended 12/31/2011. Assets, $1,113,197 (M); Expenditures, $720,777; Total giving, $86,750; Grants to individuals, totaling $86,750.
Fields of interest: Education.
Type of support: Graduate support; Technical education support; Undergraduate support.
Application information: Application form required.
> *Initial approach:* Telephone or e-mail for application details
> *Deadline(s):* None
> *Additional information:* Applications are solicited by various nominating organizations across the U.S.

EIN: 751973894

8823
Fleetwood Memorial Foundation, Inc.
501 S. Fielder Rd.
Arlington, TX 76013-1743
Contact: Tom Cravens, Chair.

Foundation type: Operating foundation
Purpose: Support to certified TX law enforcement officers and fire protection personnel, and their families, who were injured or killed in the line of duty. Some funds are available for retraining if the injury prevents the individual from continuing to work in the police force or the fire department.
Publications: Application guidelines; Informational brochure.
Financial data: Year ended 10/31/2012. Assets, $0 (M); Expenditures, $4,054,317; Total giving, $51,500; Grants to individuals, 21 grants totaling $51,500 (high: $5,000, low: $500).
Fields of interest: Crime/law enforcement; Disasters, fire prevention/control.
Type of support: Employee-related welfare; Grants for special needs.
Application information: Application form required.
> *Deadline(s):* None

EIN: 510163324

8824
The Fluor Foundation
6700 Las Colina Blvd.
Irving, TX 75039-2902 (469) 398-7000
Contact: Terence H. Robinson, Pres.
E-mail: community.relations@fluor.com;
URL: http://www.fluor.com/sustainability/community/Pages/default.aspx

Foundation type: Company-sponsored foundation
Purpose: Scholarships to children of employees of Fluor Corporation to pursue higher education.
Publications: Application guidelines; Financial statement; Informational brochure; IRS Form 990 or 990-PF printed copy available upon request; Program policy statement.
Financial data: Year ended 12/31/2012. Assets, $12,476,435 (M); Expenditures, $4,348,321; Total giving, $4,327,951.
Fields of interest: Higher education; Scholarships/financial aid.
Type of support: Employee-related scholarships.
Application information: Applications not accepted.
> *Additional information:* Unsolicited requests for funds not considered or acknowledged.

Program description:
> *Fluor Scholarship Program:* The foundation annually awards renewable college scholarships of $1,000 to $3,000 to children of employees of Fluor. The program is designed to acknowledge student accomplishments and support their goals to obtain degrees or certificates at universities, colleges, and vocational or technical schools.

Company name: Fluor Corporation
EIN: 510196032

8825
The Forever Foundation for Texas Wildlife
2800 N.E. Loop 410, Ste. 105
San Antonio, TX 78218-1525 (210) 826-2904
Contact: Gary Joiner, C.E.O.
FAX: (210) 826-4933;
E-mail: gjoiner@texas-wildlife.org; URL: http://www.texas-wildlife.org/index.php?option=com_content&view=article&id=99&Itemid=176

Foundation type: Public charity
Purpose: Scholarships to graduating high school seniors and to college students of TX pursuing a career in agriculture and/or natural resource-related majors.
Financial data: Year ended 12/31/2011. Assets, $2,241,255 (M); Expenditures, $1,247,177; Total giving, $1,060,493.
Fields of interest: Natural resources; Animals/wildlife.
Type of support: Scholarships—to individuals.
Application information: Applications accepted. Application form required.
> *Deadline(s):* Mar. 1
> *Applicants should submit the following:*
> 1) Class rank
> 2) Transcripts
> 3) Letter(s) of recommendation
> 4) GPA
> 5) Essay

EIN: 742605516

8826
Formosa Plastics Corporation, Texas—Calhoun High School Scholarship Foundation
525 N. Commerce St.
Port Lavaca, TX 77979-3034 (361) 552-9728

Foundation type: Company-sponsored foundation
Purpose: Scholarships to graduates of Calhoun High School, Port Lavaca, TX, for the first year of postsecondary education.
Financial data: Year ended 12/31/2012. Assets, $1,003,629 (M); Expenditures, $47,607; Total giving, $46,000; Grants to individuals, 23 grants totaling $46,000 (high: $2,000, low: $2,000).
Type of support: Support to graduates or students of specific schools; Undergraduate support.
Application information: Application form required.
> *Initial approach:* Letter
> *Additional information:* Scholarship awards are based strictly on class rank. Applications are available from the office of superintendent.

EIN: 742634043

8827
Fort Worth Hope Center
3625 E. Loop 820 S.
Fort Worth, TX 76119-1822 (817) 451-6288
Contact: Pastor Orlando Reyes, Chair.
FAX: (817) 451-1945; E-mail: info@fwhope.org;
Additional tel.: (817) 451-0093; URL: http://www.fwhope.org/

Foundation type: Public charity
Purpose: Assistance in the form of food supplies and clothing to indigent residents of Fort Worth, TX.
Financial data: Year ended 12/31/2011. Assets, $454,072 (M); Expenditures, $4,887,485; Total giving, $4,480,106; Grants to individuals, totaling $4,480,106.
Fields of interest: Economically disadvantaged.
Type of support: In-kind gifts.
Application information:
> *Initial approach:* Letter
> *Applicants should submit the following:*
> 1) Financial information
> *Additional information:* Contact foundation for eligibility criteria.

EIN: 010801061

8828
Fort Worth Police Officers' Award Foundation
6115 Camp Bowie, Ste. 270
Fort Worth, TX 76116-5500
URL: http://www.fwpoliceawards.org/

Foundation type: Independent foundation
Purpose: Monetary awards and grants to officers of the Fort Worth Police Department, TX, in recognition of their efficiency, skill, and devotion to the citizens of Fort Worth. Grants to Fort Worth police officers for specialized training that would not be available through the city budget.
Financial data: Year ended 12/31/2012. Assets, $695,991 (M); Expenditures, $123,841; Total giving, $35,005.
Fields of interest: Crime/law enforcement, police agencies.
Type of support: Exchange programs; Awards/grants by nomination only; Awards/prizes.
Application information: Applications not accepted.
EIN: 751744211

8829
Fort Worth Stockshow Syndicate
P.O. Box 17005
Fort Worth, TX   76102-0005   (817) 338-0077
Contact: Scott Prince, Chair.
E-mail: fwsss.chairman@gmail.com; Tel. for Larry
Anfin: (817) 401-6633; URL: http://
www.fwsss.com/

Foundation type: Public charity
Purpose: College scholarships to young men and
women of Texas for attendance at a Texas
institution pursuing an agriculture career.
Publications: Application guidelines.
Financial data: Year ended 06/30/2012. Assets,
$1,648,516 (M); Expenditures, $2,629,957; Total
giving, $2,542,225.
Fields of interest: Higher education; Agriculture;
Biology/life sciences.
Type of support: Scholarships—to individuals.
Application information: Applications accepted.
Application form required.
    Additional information: Contact the organization
        for additional guidelines.
Program description:
    Scholarships: Four $10,000 scholarships are
awarded each year to Texas high school students.
The students must attend a Texas institution in
pursuit of a four-year bachelor degree in an
agricultural or life sciences curriculum.
EIN: 751790417

8830
Foundation for Excellence
1628 19th St.
Lubbock, TX   79401-4832   (806) 766-1066

Foundation type: Public charity
Purpose: Financial assistance to students of
Lubbock Independent School District who
participate in an activity that is beyond the scope of
the district's fiscal policy.
Financial data: Year ended 08/31/2011. Assets,
$504,107 (M); Expenditures, $106,694; Total
giving, $103,765; Grants to individuals, totaling
$63,667.
Fields of interest: Education.
Type of support: Scholarships—to individuals;
Support to graduates or students of specific
schools.
Application information: Contact foundation for
application guidelines.
EIN: 752200565

8831
Foundation for the Retarded
3550 W. Dallas St.
Houston, TX   77019-0564   (713) 525-8400
Contact: Eva Aguirre, C.E.O.
E-mail: eaguirre@thecenterhouston.org;
URL: http://www.thecenterhouston.org

Foundation type: Public charity
Purpose: Grants to developmentally disabled
individuals for special needs in Houston, TX.
Publications: Informational brochure; Newsletter.
Financial data: Year ended 06/30/2012. Assets,
$11,283,741 (M); Expenditures, $1,941,515;
Total giving, $1,118,414.
Fields of interest: Developmentally disabled,
centers & services.
Type of support: Grants to individuals; Grants for
special needs.
Application information: Applications not
accepted.

Additional information: Unsolicited requests for
funds not considered or acknowledged.
EIN: 742179425

8832
W. C. Fuller Educational Trust
c/o Bank of America, N.A.
P.O. Box 831041
Dallas, TX   75283-1041   (214) 692-3417
Application address: c/o Southern Methodist Univ.,
Attn: Office of Financial Aid, Box 196, Dallas, TX
75275; c/o Paul Quinn College, Attn: Financial Aid
Director, 3837 Simpson Stuart Rd., Dallas, TX
75241, Tel.: (214) 376-1000

Foundation type: Independent foundation
Purpose: Scholarships to students accepted to or
currently enrolled at Southern Methodist University
or Paul Quinn College, TX.
Financial data: Year ended 10/31/2012. Assets,
$637,279 (M); Expenditures, $35,782; Total
giving, $28,068.
Type of support: Support to graduates or students
of specific schools; Undergraduate support.
Application information: Applications accepted.
Application form required.
    Deadline(s): For SMU: Feb. 1 for freshmen and
        transfer students and Jan. 1 for continuing
        students. For Paul Quinn: Aug. 1
    Additional information: Applicants should apply
        by completing the standard application and
        financial aid forms required by their respective
        schools.
EIN: 756234718

8833
The Fund for Teachers
2000 Post Oak Blvd., Ste. 100
Houston, TX   77056-4497   (713) 296-6127
Contact: Karen K. Webb, Exec. Dir.
FAX: (713) 296-6134;
E-mail: info@fundforteachers.org; Toll Free Tel.:
(800)-681-2667; E-Mail for Karen K. Webb:
karen.kovach-webb@fundforteachers.org; Tel. for
Karen K. Webb: (713)-296-6125; URL: http://
www.fundforteachers.org

Foundation type: Public charity
Purpose: Grants to teachers in designated states
working with students from pre-kindergarten
through 12th grade.
Publications: Application guidelines.
Financial data: Year ended 12/31/2011. Assets,
$21,215,712 (M); Expenditures, $2,273,222;
Total giving, $1,495,809; Grants to individuals,
totaling $1,495,809.
Fields of interest: Education.
Type of support: Grants to individuals.
Application information: Applications accepted.
Application form required.
    Additional information: Grants are awarded to
        teachers based on application quality and
        merit.
Program description:
    Professional Development Grants: The fund
awards fellowships for self-designed professional
growth to teachers who recognize the value of
inquiry, the power of knowledge, and their ability to
make a difference. Fellowship grants are provided
directly to teachers with at least three years of
experience, to support their professional learning
during the summer. Eligible applicants must be
employed by a school district in an eligible
geographic areas, teach in a pre-K through
12th-grade classroom, and spend at least fifty

percent of their time in the classroom or a
classroom-like setting.
EIN: 760679535

8834
Futureus Foundation
P.O. Box 2907
Corpus Christi, TX   78403-2907   (361)
888-7708
Contact: Harold L. Simmons, Jr.
E-mail: donna@mantires.com

Foundation type: Company-sponsored foundation
Purpose: Scholarships and financial relief primarily
to residents of TX and LA.
Financial data: Year ended 10/31/2012. Assets,
$67,761 (M); Expenditures, $9,563; Total giving,
$8,000.
Fields of interest: Human services; Economically
disadvantaged.
Type of support: Undergraduate support; Grants for
special needs.
Application information: Applications accepted.
Application form required.
    Applicants should submit the following:
        1) Letter(s) of recommendation
        2) Transcripts
    Additional information: Contact foundation for
        additional guidelines.
EIN: 270004671

8835
Galena Park ISD Education Foundation, Inc.
14705 Woodforest Blvd.
Houston, TX   77015-0565   (832) 386-1099
Contact: Wayne Oquin, Dir.
E-mail: woquin1@galenaparkisd.com; URL: http://
galenaparkisd.com/departments/foundation/

Foundation type: Public charity
Purpose: Scholarships to students of Galena Park
Independent School District, TX. Career
development scholarships to teachers at Galena
Park Independent School District, TX.
Publications: Application guidelines.
Financial data: Year ended 12/31/2011. Assets,
$366,447 (M); Expenditures, $305,746; Total
giving, $146,431; Grants to individuals, totaling
$146,431.
Type of support: Support to graduates or students
of specific schools.
Application information: Applications accepted.
Application form required. Application form
available on the grantmaker's web site.
    Initial approach: Letter or telephone
    Additional information: Contact foundation for
        current application deadline/guidelines.
EIN: 760563596

8836
Genesis Education Foundation
8910 Walworth Ct.
Houston, TX   77088   (713) 539-6512

Foundation type: Operating foundation
Purpose: Scholarships to graduating high school
seniors to attend colleges in TX.
Financial data: Year ended 12/31/2011. Assets,
$0 (M); Expenditures, $14,647; Total giving,
$13,601; Grants to individuals, 4 grants totaling
$13,601 (high: $5,445, low: $1,747).
Fields of interest: Higher education.
Type of support: Scholarships—to individuals.

Application information: Applications not accepted.

Additional information: Unsolicited requests for funds not considered or acknowledged.

EIN: 760596134

8837
A.P. Giannini Foundation for Employees

c/o Bank of America, N.A.
P.O. Box 831041
Dallas, TX 75283-1041 (877) 444-1012

Foundation type: Company-sponsored foundation
Purpose: Relief assistance to employees and their families of the Bank of America and its subsidiaries for medical bills or other emergencies.
Financial data: Year ended 12/31/2012. Assets, $1,850,970 (M); Expenditures, $91,037; Total giving, $87,500; Grants to individuals, 30 grants totaling $87,500 (high: $10,000, low: $596).
Type of support: Employee-related welfare; Loans —to individuals.
Application information:
Deadline(s): None
Additional information: Application should include reason for grant request, amount requested, and applicant's financial status.
EIN: 946089550

8838
Clorinda Giannini Memorial

c/o Bank of America, N.A.
P.O. Box 831041
Dallas, TX 75283-1041 (877) 444-1012

Foundation type: Company-sponsored foundation
Purpose: Relief assistance to employees, their dependents, and retirees of the Bank of America National Trust and Savings Association who are residents of CA, for illness, accident disability, surgery, medical and nursing care, hospitalization, financial difficulties, loss of income, and other emergencies.
Financial data: Year ended 04/30/2013. Assets, $516,651 (M); Expenditures, $112,528; Total giving, $99,491; Grants to individuals, 36 grants totaling $99,491 (high: $9,947, low: $473).
Fields of interest: Health care.
Type of support: Employee-related welfare.
Application information: Applications not accepted.

Additional information: Unsolicited requests for funds not considered or acknowledged.

Company name: Bank of America National Trust and Savings Association
EIN: 946073513

8839
Giannini-Scatena

(formerly Virginia Scatena Memorial Fund for San Francisco School Teachers)
c/o Bank of America, N.A.
P.O. Box 831041
Dallas, TX 75283-1041 (866) 461-7279

Foundation type: Independent foundation
Purpose: Financial assistance to teachers of the San Francisco Public School District who are needy, sick or disabled.
Financial data: Year ended 12/31/2012. Assets, $166,087 (M); Expenditures, $8,179; Total giving, $7,067.
Fields of interest: Disabilities, people with; Economically disadvantaged.
Type of support: Grants for special needs.

Application information: Applications accepted. Application form required.
Deadline(s): None
EIN: 946073769

8840
The Gill Foundation

1330 Post Oak Blvd., Ste. 2580
Houston, TX 77056-3168

Foundation type: Independent foundation
Purpose: Scholarships to individuals for higher education.
Financial data: Year ended 11/30/2011. Assets, $1,418,324 (M); Expenditures, $142,811; Total giving, $77,000; Grants to individuals, 12 grants totaling $59,000 (high: $20,000, low: $2,000).
Fields of interest: Higher education.
Type of support: Undergraduate support.
Application information: Contact foundation for application guidelines.
EIN: 311506372

8841
Gilman and Gonzalez-Falla Theatre Foundation, Inc.

P.O. Box 18925
Corpus Christi, TX 78480-8925
E-mail: celso@soncel.com; URL: http://www.ggftheater.org/

Foundation type: Independent foundation
Purpose: Awards by nomination only for recognition in American musical theater.
Financial data: Year ended 12/31/2012. Assets, $0 (M); Expenditures, $167,485; Total giving, $27,700.
Fields of interest: Theater.
Type of support: Awards/grants by nomination only; Awards/prizes.
Application information: Application form required.
Deadline(s): None
EIN: 133463382

8842
Gilpatrick Scholarship Trust

P.O. Box 247
Spearman, TX 79081-0247 (806) 659-2584
Contact: Clay Montgomery; David Teal
Application address: 403 E. 11th St., Spearman, TX 79081, tel.:(806) 659-2584

Foundation type: Independent foundation
Purpose: Scholarship awards to students in the top 25 percent of their high school, college, or graduate school class who are residents of Hansford County majoring in the medicine and/or science fields.
Financial data: Year ended 12/31/2012. Assets, $850,693 (M); Expenditures, $17,379; Total giving, $6,468; Grants to individuals, 4 grants totaling $6,468 (high: $2,156, low: $1,078).
Fields of interest: Medical school/education.
Type of support: Scholarships—to individuals.
Application information: Applications accepted. Application form required.
Deadline(s): Varied
Additional information: Contact the trust for further information. Scholarships are renewable.
EIN: 311687792

8843
Richard E. Gnade Charitable Trust

100 W. Houston St.
San Antonio, TX 78205-1414 (210) 220-4959
Contact: Susan T. Palmer

Foundation type: Independent foundation
Purpose: Scholarships to financially needy young men in Bandera County, TX.
Financial data: Year ended 10/31/2013. Assets, $775,525 (M); Expenditures, $46,573; Total giving, $28,422.
Fields of interest: Men.
Type of support: Scholarships—to individuals.
Application information:
Initial approach: Letter
Deadline(s): Contact trust for current application deadline
Additional information: Application should include financial information.
EIN: 746032311

8844
William Jesse Godwin Foundation

P.O. Box 739
Whitesboro, TX 76273-0739 (903) 564-6695

Foundation type: Independent foundation
Purpose: Scholarships to residents of Grayson County, TX.
Financial data: Year ended 12/31/2012. Assets, $0 (M); Expenditures, $27,163; Total giving, $15,300.
Type of support: Scholarships—to individuals.
Application information:
Initial approach: Letter
Deadline(s): None
Additional information: Applications must outline tuition cost, room and board fees, major field of study, and student's future plans.
EIN: 756036128

8845
The Father Bernard C. Goertz Scholarship Trust Fund

136 Tucker Ln.
Red Rock, TX 78662
Contact: Bernard Goertz, Dir.
Application Address: 585 Shiloh Rd.,Bastrop,TX., 78602

Foundation type: Independent foundation
Purpose: Scholarships to qualifying senior graduates of Bastrop Independent School District, TX for continuing education at accredited colleges or universities.
Financial data: Year ended 12/31/2012. Assets, $266,081 (M); Expenditures, $6,571; Total giving, $6,000; Grants to individuals, 6 grants totaling $6,000 (high: $1,000, low: $1,000).
Fields of interest: Higher education.
Type of support: Scholarships—to individuals.
Application information: Applications accepted. Application form required.
Additional information: Applications are available at high school guidance counselors.
EIN: 760577575

8846
Goff Family Foundation

c/o Jennifer Terrell
500 Commerce St., Ste. 700
Fort Worth, TX 76102 (817) 509-3968
Contact: Jill E. Goff, Secy. and Exec. Dir.

Foundation type: Independent foundation
Purpose: Scholarships to individuals in the Fort Worth, TX area for continuing education at institutions of higher learning.
Financial data: Year ended 12/31/2012. Assets, $6,521,720 (M); Expenditures, $323,557; Total giving, $38,428; Grant to an individual, 1 grant totaling $50.
Fields of interest: Higher education.
Type of support: Scholarships—to individuals.
Application information: Applications accepted. Application form required.
  Deadline(s): May 1
  Final notification: Recipients notified May 21
  Applicants should submit the following:
    1) Photograph
    2) Financial information
    3) Letter(s) of recommendation
    4) Essay
    5) Transcripts
    6) SAT
    7) GPA
    8) ACT
  Additional information: Application should also include a personal statement not exceeding 500 words.
EIN: 260562600

8847
Golden Rule Foundation
P.O. Box 3707
Corpus Christi, TX   78463-3707
Contact: Jennifer J. Bowen, Pres.

Foundation type: Independent foundation
Purpose: Scholarships to graduating seniors of Corpus Christi high schools for higher education.
Financial data: Year ended 12/31/2013. Assets, $487,107 (M); Expenditures, $18,863; Total giving, $18,345; Grants to individuals, 31 grants totaling $18,345 (high: $1,000, low: $150).
Fields of interest: Higher education.
Type of support: Scholarships—to individuals.
Application information: Applications accepted.
  Initial approach: Letter
  Additional information: Applicants should include a recommendation from the guidance counselor, and provide receipts for tuition or books to be reimbursed.
EIN: 742701169

8848
The Mary I. Gourley Scholarship Foundation
(formerly M.I.G. Scholarship Foundation)
2630 S. Polaris Dr.
Fort Worth, TX   76137-4803   (817) 834-7533
Contact: Robert C. Albritton, Jr., Pres.
FAX: (817) 834-5093

Foundation type: Public charity
Purpose: Scholarships to high school graduates and/or to mature students who are admitted to a recognized university or seminary in the Fort Worth, TX, area.
Financial data: Year ended 06/30/2012. Assets, $11,376,890 (M); Expenditures, $723,614; Total giving, $394,470.
Fields of interest: Theological school/education; Christian agencies & churches.
Type of support: Support to graduates or students of specific schools.
Application information: Applications accepted. Application form required.
  Applicants should submit the following:
    1) Financial information

    2) Transcripts
  Additional information: Applications must be submitted through the office of the Director of Financial Aid of the college, university, or seminary.
EIN: 752052592

8849
D. D. Hachar Charitable Trust Fund
2200 Post Oak Blvd., 19th Fl.
Houston, TX   77056-4700   (956) 764-2811
FAX: (956) 764-1592; Application address: c/o BBVA Compass Bank, 700 San Bernardo Ave., Laredo, TX 78042, tel.: (956) 727-9311

Foundation type: Independent foundation
Purpose: Scholarships to financially needy residents (of at least 3 years) of Laredo, Webb County, and surrounding counties in TX, who must maintain a GPA of 2.75. Students planning to attend a technical or vocational school will be considered on an individual basis as far as grade point average is concerned.
Publications: Application guidelines; Annual report; Informational brochure; Program policy statement.
Financial data: Year ended 04/30/2013. Assets, $25,257,202 (M); Expenditures, $1,626,472; Total giving, $1,306,818.
Fields of interest: Scholarships/financial aid.
Type of support: Scholarships—to individuals; Undergraduate support.
Application information: Application form required. Interview required.
  Initial approach: Letter or telephone requesting application guidelines
  Deadline(s): Varies
  Applicants should submit the following:
    1) Financial information
    2) Photograph
    3) Transcripts
  Additional information: Incomplete applications will not be accepted. Applicants with gross family incomes over $85,000 and part time students are ineligible. Scholarships are renewable for up to four years providing all existing criteria is met. No scholarships are granted for summer school.
EIN: 742093680

8850
Marie H. Hamilton Scholarship Trust Fund
c/o Bank of America, N.A.
P.O. Box 831041
Dallas, TX   75283-1041   (360) 642-3731
Application address: c/o Ms. Huntley, Ocean Beach School District No. 101, P.O. Box 778, Longbeach, WA 98631, tel.: (360) 642-3731

Foundation type: Independent foundation
Purpose: Scholarships to graduating seniors of Ilwaco High School, WA, for attendance at colleges, universities, junior colleges, trade and technical schools, and business colleges.
Financial data: Year ended 12/31/2012. Assets, $780,733 (M); Expenditures, $44,370; Total giving, $34,091; Grants to individuals, 13 grants totaling $29,424 (high: $5,667, low: $1,000).
Fields of interest: Higher education.
Type of support: Support to graduates or students of specific schools; Technical education support; Undergraduate support.
Application information: Applications accepted. Application form required.
  Deadline(s): Mar.
  Applicants should submit the following:
    1) SAR

    2) SAT
    3) Letter(s) of recommendation
    4) Financial information
    5) FAFSA
    6) ACT
    7) Essay
EIN: 916068558

8851
George and Mary Josephine Hamman Foundation
3336 Richmond, Ste. 310
Houston, TX   77098-3022   (713) 522-9891
Contact: D. Troy Derouen CPA, Exec. Dir.
FAX: (713) 522-9693;
E-mail: HammanFdn@aol.com; URL: http://www.hammanfoundation.org

Foundation type: Independent foundation
Purpose: Undergraduate scholarships to graduating high school seniors residing in the Brazoria, Chambers, Fort Bend, Galveston, Harris, Liberty, Montgomery, or Waller counties, TX. Students must be U.S. citizens.
Publications: Application guidelines; Financial statement; Grants list.
Financial data: Year ended 12/31/2012. Assets, $91,354,903 (M); Expenditures, $5,397,175; Total giving, $4,427,500; Grants to individuals, totaling $924,750.
Fields of interest: Higher education.
Type of support: Scholarships—to individuals.
Application information: Applications accepted. Application form required. Application form available on the grantmaker's web site.
  Initial approach: Application
  Send request by: Mail
  Copies of proposal: 1
  Deadline(s): 3rd Fri. in Feb.
  Final notification: Applicants notified after 60 days
  Applicants should submit the following:
    1) FAFSA
    2) Photograph
    3) Transcripts
    4) SAT
    5) GPA
    6) ACT
    7) Financial information
  Additional information: The award is $16,000, disbursed over 4 years. Applicants must have a minimum SAT score of 1,000 (on the Math and Critical Reading portions combined), and/or ACT score of 21. The recipient may select any major at any four year college or university. Complete application guidelines available on foundation web site.
EIN: 746061447

8852
W. R. Hammond Trust
P.O. Box 41629
Austin, TX   78704-9926

Foundation type: Independent foundation
Purpose: Scholarships to individuals studying medicine, primarily in TX and UT.
Financial data: Year ended 12/31/2011. Assets, $592,224 (M); Expenditures, $39,869; Total giving, $29,000.
Fields of interest: Medical school/education.
Type of support: Graduate support.
Application information: Applications not accepted.

Additional information: Giving only to preselected individuals.
EIN: 756524028

8853

The Haraldson Foundation
25025 I-45 N., Ste. 410
The Woodlands, TX 77380-3034 (281) 362-9909
Contact: Dale A. Dossey, Dir.
FAX: (281) 476-7045;
E-mail: ndossey@haraldsonfoundation.org;
URL: http://www.haraldsonfoundation.org

Foundation type: Operating foundation
Purpose: Scholarships to full-time students attending the University of Texas.
Publications: Application guidelines; Annual report; Grants list; Informational brochure (including application guidelines); Newsletter.
Financial data: Year ended 09/30/2013. Assets, $6,174,859 (M); Expenditures, $469,278; Total giving, $244,400.
Type of support: Support to graduates or students of specific schools; Undergraduate support.
Application information: Applications accepted. Application form required. Interview required.
Initial approach: Letter or e-mail
Applicants should submit the following:
1) Essay
2) Letter(s) of recommendation
Additional information: Application can be obtained from the foundation.
EIN: 760420758

8854

Harding Foundation
P.O Box 130
Raymondville, TX 78580 (956) 689-2706
Contact: Douglas Harding, Pres.

Foundation type: Independent foundation
Purpose: Graduate scholarships to seminary students pursuing master's degrees in theology, leading to ordination in a mainline Protestant church, with special consideration given to those willing to serve in the South Texas Conference.
Financial data: Year ended 12/31/2012. Assets, $972,034 (M); Expenditures, $69,992; Total giving, $12,375; Grants to individuals, 5 grants totaling $9,000 (high: $3,000, low: $1,500).
Fields of interest: Theological school/education; Protestant agencies & churches.
Type of support: Graduate support.
Application information: Applications accepted. Application form required.
Initial approach: Letter
Deadline(s): Jan. 15
Applicants should submit the following:
1) Transcripts
2) Letter(s) of recommendation
Additional information: Application should also include personal statement of no more than 500 words.
EIN: 746025883

8855

Harris County Hospital District Foundation
2525 Holly Hall, Ste. 235
Houston, TX 77054-4124 (713) 566-6409
Contact: Alix CaDavid, Grants Mgr.
FAX: (713) 566-6449;
E-mail: HCHD_Foundation@hchd.tmc.edu;

Additional address: P.O. Box 66769, Houston, TX, 77266-6769; URL: http://www.hchdfoundation.org

Foundation type: Public charity
Purpose: Disaster relief assistance to hospital employees who suffer catastrophic disasters.
Publications: Annual report; Financial statement; Informational brochure; Newsletter.
Financial data: Year ended 02/28/2012. Assets, $38,965,410 (M); Expenditures, $3,737,829; Total giving, $2,628,417.
Fields of interest: Safety/disasters.
Type of support: Grants for special needs.
Application information: Contact the foundation for additional guidelines for relief assistance.
EIN: 760408224

8856

Harris Methodist HEB Auxiliary, Inc.
1600 Hospital Pkwy.
Bedford, TX 76022-6913 (817) 685-4853

Foundation type: Public charity
Purpose: Scholarships to individuals who holds a direct affiliation with Harris Methodist HEB, and plans to attend an institution within TX, pursuing a health care career.
Financial data: Year ended 05/31/2012. Assets, $51,601 (M); Expenditures, $166,610; Total giving, $120,500; Grants to individuals, totaling $10,000.
Fields of interest: Health sciences school/education.
Type of support: Scholarships—to individuals.
Application information: Applications accepted.
Additional information: Selection is based on financial need, academic excellence and a desire to pursue a career in health care.
EIN: 237302201

8857

Havens Foundation, Inc.
25132 Oakhurst Dr., Ste. 220
Spring, TX 77386-1446 (281) 364-3100
Contact: Joe D. Havens, Pres.

Foundation type: Independent foundation
Purpose: Undergraduate scholarships primarily to residents of TX.
Financial data: Year ended 12/31/2011. Assets, $1,387,592 (M); Expenditures, $116,019; Total giving, $105,500; Grant to an individual, 1 grant totaling $2,000.
Fields of interest: Higher education; Religion.
Type of support: Scholarships—to individuals; Undergraduate support.
Application information: Applications accepted. Application form required.
Deadline(s): None
Applicants should submit the following:
1) Transcripts
2) Letter(s) of recommendation
3) GPA
4) Financial information
5) Essay
Additional information: Applicants must include information about their spirituality and church affiliation.
EIN: 760317434

8858

Harry A. Haverlah Foundation
c/o East Texas National Bank
P.O. Box 770
Palestine, TX 75802-0770 (903) 729-6048
Contact: Connie L. Fain, V.P. & Trust Off.

Foundation type: Independent foundation
Purpose: Student loans to graduates of high schools in Anderson County, TX, with at least a "B" average or better for attendance at an accredited college or university in TX.
Financial data: Year ended 12/31/2011. Assets, $349,880 (M); Expenditures, $52,533; Total giving, $40,887; Grants to individuals, 8 grants totaling $40,887 (high: $15,750, low: $91).
Fields of interest: Higher education.
Type of support: Student loans—to individuals; Support to graduates or students of specific schools; Undergraduate support.
Application information: Application form required. Interview required.
Send request by: Mail
Deadline(s): Apr. 25
Applicants should submit the following:
1) SAT
2) ACT
3) Financial information
4) Transcripts
Additional information: Application should also include attendance records, physician's authorization letter, college or university letter, and latest income tax return.
EIN: 751242215

8859

William Z. Hayes Foundation
c/o Bank of America, N.A.
P.O. Box 831041
Dallas, TX 75283-1041 (214) 209-6477
Contact: Jenae Guillory-Boa
Application address: 901 Main St., 19th Fl., Dallas, TX 75202-3714

Foundation type: Independent foundation
Purpose: Scholarships to residents of Dallas County, TX, attending Baylor University, TX, or Southwestern Baptist Theological Seminary, TX.
Financial data: Year ended 01/31/2013. Assets, $627,449 (M); Expenditures, $36,839; Total giving, $25,917.
Fields of interest: Theological school/education; Protestant agencies & churches.
Type of support: Support to graduates or students of specific schools; Undergraduate support.
Application information: Applications accepted. Application form required.
Additional information: Contact foundation for current application deadline/guidelines.
EIN: 756245477

8860

Headliners Foundation of Texas
221 W. 6th St., 20th Fl.
Austin, TX 78701-3400 (512) 479-8080
Contact: Bergan Casey, Exec. Dir.
E-mail: info@headlinersfoundation.org; Mailing Address.: P.O. Box 97, Austin, TX 78767-0097; URL: http://www.headlinersfoundation.org

Foundation type: Public charity
Purpose: Undergraduate scholarships and awards to residents of TX in the field of communications at specified schools in TX.
Publications: Application guidelines.

Financial data: Year ended 07/31/2011. Assets, $2,280,943 (M); Expenditures, $127,183; Total giving, $32,250; Grants to individuals, totaling $32,250.
Fields of interest: Print publishing.
Type of support: Awards/prizes; Undergraduate support.
Application information: Applications accepted. Application form required.
  Initial approach: Letter
  Deadline(s): Feb. 15 for scholarships; Nov. 16 for Charles E. Green Journalism Awards
  Additional information: Application form required for scholarships; Letter for journalism awards.
Program descriptions:
  Charles E. Green Journalism Awards: Each year, the foundation, in cooperation with the Texas Associated Press Managing Editors (TAPME) and the Texas Associated Press Broadcasters (TAPB), sponsors an annual contest to identify the best works in journalism across the state for the previous year. Division winners in each category of the Associated Press contests advance to compete for the Charles E. Green Awards, which represent overall winners in each category. The purpose of these annual awards is to promote professional, balanced journalism; to remind Texans that quality journalism does exist and can be trusted.
  Scholarships: Each year, the foundation awards scholarships to top communication students and college journalists attending universities across Texas.
EIN: 742281076

8861
Healthcare and Nursing Education Foundation
(formerly Visiting Nurse Association of Houston Foundation)
2700 Southwest Freeway, Ste. 209
Houston, TX   77098-4613
FAX: (713) 868-2619; E-mail: info@hnef.org; URL: http://www.hnef.org

Foundation type: Independent foundation
Purpose: Scholarships to individuals with financial need who are pursuing a professional nursing career in the Greater Houston, TX community.
Financial data: Year ended 06/30/2012. Assets, $9,085,729 (M); Expenditures, $372,756; Total giving, $295,794; Grants to individuals, totaling $216,344.
Fields of interest: Nursing school/education.
Type of support: Scholarships—to individuals.
Application information: Applications accepted.
  Deadline(s): None
  Additional information: Scholarships are renewable with acceptable academic performance and continuing financial need.
EIN: 760454511

8862
Steve Heath Memorial ROTC Scholarship Trust
12618 Sandpiper
San Antonio, TX   78233   (210) 655-5317
Contact: Donald Heath, Tr.

Foundation type: Independent foundation
Purpose: Scholarships to individuals who have completed at least one year with the University of Texas at San Antonio AFROTC, Detachment 842.
Financial data: Year ended 12/31/2011. Assets, $49 (M); Expenditures, $1,250; Total giving, $1,250; Grant to an individual, 1 grant totaling $1,250.

Fields of interest: Military/veterans' organizations.
Type of support: Support to graduates or students of specific schools; Undergraduate support.
Application information: Applications accepted. Application form required.
  Send request by: Mail
  Additional information: Application must include transcripts and a 200-300 word handwritten personal history.
EIN: 742591005

8863
Gary & Diane Heavin Community Fund
(formerly The Curves Community Fund, Inc.)
c/o Ronnie Glaesmann
100 Ritchie Rd.
Waco, TX   76712-8544

Foundation type: Company-sponsored foundation
Purpose: Scholarships to current employees of Curves, and their dependents, who plan on studying a subject relating to health.
Financial data: Year ended 12/31/2011. Assets, $17,946,615 (M); Expenditures, $1,981,457; Total giving, $1,768,502.
Type of support: Employee-related scholarships.
Application information:
  Initial approach: Letter
  Additional information: Contact the Corporate Office for further application information.
Company name: Curves International, Inc.
EIN: 743003293

8864
Hefflefinger Scholarship Fund
c/o Bank of America, N.A.
P.O. Box 831041
Dallas, TX   75283-1041
Contact: Michelle Nunley; Lucy Van Scyoc
Application address: Tulare Union High School, Tulare, CA 93274-4353

Foundation type: Independent foundation
Purpose: Scholarships to deserving students attending public schools in the Tulare High School District, CA.
Financial data: Year ended 10/31/2013. Assets, $211,133 (M); Expenditures, $15,714; Total giving, $11,000.
Type of support: Support to graduates or students of specific schools; Undergraduate support.
Application information: Applications accepted. Application form required.
  Initial approach: Letter
  Deadline(s): None
EIN: 953820054

8865
Robert A. and Virginia Heinlein Prize Trust
3106 Beauchamp St., 2nd Fl.
Houston, TX   77019-7206   (713) 861-3600
Contact: Arthur Dula, Dir.
FAX: (713) 861-3620;
E-mail: info@heinleinprize.com; URL: http://www.heinleinprize.com

Foundation type: Independent foundation
Purpose: Awards and grants to individuals who achieve practical accomplishments in the field of commercial space activities.
Financial data: Year ended 12/31/2012. Assets, $12,059,641 (M); Expenditures, $653,484; Total giving, $294,120; Grants to individuals, totaling $25,600.
Fields of interest: Space/aviation.

Type of support: Grants to individuals; Awards/prizes.
Application information:
  Initial approach: Proposal
  Copies of proposal: 1
  Deadline(s): None
  Additional information: Applications are accepted through a world-wide board of advisors. A proposal should be submitted in writing stating how the grant will be used to further the goals and objectives of the foundation.
EIN: 766079186

8866
Hill Country Community Foundation
P.O. Box 848
Burnet, TX   78611   (512) 756-8211
Contact: Pat Williams
E-mail: pwilliams200@austin.rr.com; Additional e-mail: support@thehccf.com; URL: http://www.thehccf.org

Foundation type: Community foundation
Purpose: Scholarships to graduating seniors of Burnet High School for higher education.
Publications: Annual report.
Financial data: Year ended 12/31/2012. Assets, $5,515,008 (M); Expenditures, $341,339; Total giving, $313,987; Grants to individuals, 193 grants totaling $254,532.
Fields of interest: Vocational education, post-secondary; Higher education.
Type of support: Support to graduates or students of specific schools; Undergraduate support.
Application information: Applications accepted. Application form required. Application form available on the grantmaker's web site.
  Send request by: Mail
  Deadline(s): Apr. 1
  Applicants should submit the following:
    1) Class rank
    2) SAT
    3) ACT
  Additional information: Scholarship information is available at your high school guidance office. Funds are paid directly to the educational institution on behalf of the students.
EIN: 742452519

8867
Hill Country Student Help
P.O. Box 1092
Fredericksburg, TX   78624-1092   (830) 997-1013
Contact: Helen V. Birck, Secy.-Treas.

Foundation type: Independent foundation
Purpose: Student loans to graduates of Gillespie County high schools, TX, who have lived and are current residents of Gillespie County for at least two years.
Financial data: Year ended 12/31/2012. Assets, $0 (M); Expenditures, $13,330; Total giving, $0.
Fields of interest: Vocational education, post-secondary; Graduate/professional education; Business school/education.
Type of support: Student loans—to individuals; Graduate support; Undergraduate support.
Application information: Application form required. Interview required.
  Deadline(s): June 30 for fall semester, Nov. 30 for spring semester, Apr. 30 for summer semester
  Applicants should submit the following:
    1) Photograph

2) Transcripts

Additional information: Application should also include a brief letter outlining educational plans and goals, and college acceptance letter or other proof of enrollment.

Program description:

Educational Loans: Loan amount is limited to $1,500 per academic year for the student's first and second years of a college or university education and $2,500 per academic year for the third, fourth, and fifth years up to a total of $10,500 of all loans per student, or $2,500 per year for two years of a trade, business or professional education, up to a grand total of $5,000 per student.

EIN: 741473060

8868

Eric G. Hirsch Memorial Trust

3541 Trail Head Dr.
Kerrville, TX 78028-8515

Foundation type: Independent foundation
Purpose: Scholarships to graduating seniors of Klein Forest High School, Houston, TX.
Financial data: Year ended 07/20/2012. Assets, $0 (M); Expenditures, $73,854; Total giving, $73,835; Grants to individuals, 2 grants totaling $73,835 (high: $36,918, low: $36,917).
Type of support: Support to graduates or students of specific schools; Undergraduate support.
Application information: Application form required.
Deadline(s): Apr.
Additional information: Applications available at high school.
EIN: 760148604

8869

Hispanic American Medical Scholarship Fund

P.O. Box 720374
Houston, TX 77222 (832) 713-3541
Contact: Jose A. Perez M.D, Pres.
Application address: 6550 Fannin St., SM 1001, Houston, TX 77030; URL: http://www.hamah.org/

Foundation type: Independent foundation
Purpose: Scholarships to qualified Hispanic American medical students to further their medical education in the Houston, TX area.
Financial data: Year ended 12/31/2012. Assets, $53,134 (M); Expenditures, $53,349; Total giving, $0.
Fields of interest: Medical school/education; Hispanics/Latinos.
Type of support: Scholarships—to individuals.
Application information: Application form required.
Initial approach: Telephone
EIN: 760341524

8870

Hispanic Association of Colleges and Universities

(also known as HACU)
8415 Datapoint Dr., Ste. 400
San Antonio, TX 78229-3277 (210) 692-3805
Contact: Antonio R. Flores, Pres. and C.E.O.
FAX: (210) 692-0823; E-mail: hacu@hacu.net;
Washington address: Once Dupont Circle N.W., Ste. 430, Washington, D.C. 20036, tel.: (210) 692-3805, fax: (210) 692-0823; Sacramento address: 915 L St., Ste. 1425, Sacramento, CA 95814, tel.(916) 442-0392, (916) 446-4028, e-mail: wro@hacu.net; URL: http://www.hacu.net

Foundation type: Public charity
Purpose: Scholarships to Hispanic students who wish to study engineering and science at a HACU member institution.
Publications: Annual report; Newsletter.
Financial data: Year ended 12/31/2012. Assets, $4,994,486 (M); Expenditures, $11,748,394; Total giving, $99,870; Grants to individuals, 38 grants totaling $99,870.
Fields of interest: Hispanics/Latinos.
Type of support: Undergraduate support.
Application information:
Initial approach: E-mail
Additional information: Application must include letter(s) of recommendation. Contact foundation for further application information.
Program descriptions:
DaimlerChrysler Scholarship Award: This $1,000 scholarship is available to full-time undergraduate students attending an association-affiliated two- or four-year institution. All majors are welcome to apply; eligible students must possess a minimum cumulative GPA of 3.0.
GAP, Inc. Scholarship Award: This $1,000 award is available to a full- or part-time undergraduate or graduate student attending a four-year institution with declared majors in merchandise management, retail management, fashion design, or a related field. Eligible applicants must possess a minimum cumulative GPA of 3.0.
General Motors Engineering Excellence Award: This renewable, $2,000 award is available to full-time undergraduate students at four-year institutions with declared majors in an engineering degree program. Students must provide a minimum cumulative GPA of 3.0. Scholarships are renewable based on the availability of funds and student's continuing eligibility.
HACU-Kellogg Leadership Fellows Program: The program is designed to increase the number of Hispanic senior-level leaders at Hispanic-serving Institutions (HSIs). In an effort to increase this number, the association selects ten Fellows every year and provides them with training aimed at developing the leadership skills needed to be a successful senior-level administrator.
Lockheed Martin Scholarship Award: This $2,800 award is available to full-time undergraduate students at a four-year institution with declared majors in electrical engineering, computer engineering, computer science, or mechanical engineering. Eligible applicants must be interested in Lockheed Martin employment opportunities and possess a minimum cumulative GPA of 3.2.
NASCAR/Wendell Scott Award: These awards are available to undergraduate and graduate students in a two- or four-year institution with a declared major in business, engineering, public relations, mass media, technology, marketing, and sports marketing/management. Undergraduate students must be full-time, able to use the scholarship during their junior or senior year, and possess a minimum cumulative GPA of 3.0 to be eligible for a $1,500 scholarship; graduate students must be attending school at least on a part-time basis and possess a minimum cumulative GPA of 3.0 to be eligible for a $2,000 scholarship.
Office Depot Scholarship: This $1,000 award is available to undergraduate students attending a four-year institution with a minimum cumulative GPA of 3.0 in business, international business, marketing, merchandising, or information technology.
Student Conference Scholarships: Scholarships are available to student representatives of association-affiliated colleges and universities to participate in the association's annual conference. These representatives will be introduced to a national forum that will address critical issues and challenges in higher education and the workplace. Eligible representatives must be currently enrolled in an undergraduate or graduate/professional degree program with a minimum GPA of 3.0. Scholarships cover costs for conference registration, travel and lodging for out-of-state students, conference-related meals, and conference-sponsored entertainment events.
Wachovia Scholarship Award: This $1,000 award is available to full-time undergraduate students attending two- or four-year institutions with a minimum cumulative GPA of 3.0 in finance, accounting, or business administration. Students must be within Wachovia's retail market in Connecticut, New York, New Jersey, Pennsylvania, Delaware, Maryland, District of Columbia, Virginia, North Carolina, South Carolina, Georgia, Florida, Alabama, Tennessee, Mississippi, and Texas.
Wal-Mart Achievers Scholarship: This $1,000 scholarship is for full-time undergraduate students attending a two- to four-year institution with a minimum cumulative GPA of 3.0 in business administration, general management, retail management, or food merchandising. Students must possess an interest in retail and preferably be working while attending school.
EIN: 742466103

8871

Hispanic Women in Leadership

P.O. Box 701065
Houston, TX 77270-1065 (713) 782-7993
FAX: (713) 672-2927; E-mail: info@hwil.org;
URL: http://www.hwil.org

Foundation type: Public charity
Purpose: Scholarships to graduating seniors in the Houston, TX area, based on academic performance, leadership, and economic need.
Publications: Application guidelines.
Fields of interest: Vocational education, post-secondary; Higher education.
Type of support: Scholarships—to individuals.
Application information: Applications accepted. Application form required. Application form available on the grantmaker's web site.
Initial approach: Download application form
Deadline(s): June 8
Applicants should submit the following:
1) Photograph
2) Class rank
3) Transcripts
4) Resume
5) Letter(s) of recommendation
6) Financial information
Additional information: Applicant must be enrolled in a college or university in Texas.
EIN: 760296222

8872

Helen Hodges Educational Charitable Trust

509 W. Wall St.
Midland, TX 79701 (806) 767-7000
Application address: American State Bank-Trust Dept., Attn: Marion, P.O. Box 1401, Lubbock, TX 79408; URL: http://www.ttuhsc.edu/som/fammed/hhect.aspx

Foundation type: Independent foundation
Purpose: College scholarships to students at Texas Tech University or other local universities in the Lubbock, TX area.
Financial data: Year ended 12/31/2011. Assets, $450,925 (M); Expenditures, $26,686; Total

giving, $19,000; Grants to individuals, 15 grants totaling $19,000 (high: $2,000, low: $1,250).
Fields of interest: Higher education.
Type of support: Support to graduates or students of specific schools; Undergraduate support.
Application information: Application form required.
Deadline(s): July 15
Applicants should submit the following:
1) Transcripts
2) Essay
EIN: 510183778

8873
Home Sweet Home Community Redevelopment Company
(also known as HSHCRC Homes, Inc.)
9001 Airport Blvd., Ste. 703
P.O. Box 330217
Houston, TX   77061-3447   (832) 804-6366
Contact: Demetria Reed, Exec. Dir.
FAX: (832) 804-6368;
E-mail: homesweet140@yahoo.com; URL: http://www.homesweethomecommunity.org/

Foundation type: Public charity
Purpose: Housing assistance to low-income individuals in TX, through sales renovation and rental and utility assistance.
Financial data: Year ended 12/31/2011. Assets, $603,539 (M); Expenditures, $528,110; Total giving, $4,445; Grants to individuals, totaling $4,445.
Fields of interest: Housing/shelter, home owners; Housing/shelter, repairs; Economically disadvantaged.
Type of support: Grants for special needs.
Application information: Contact the organization for eligibility requirements.
EIN: 141870063

8874
Frank W. and Gladys G. Hornbrook Scholarship Fund
c/o Broadway National Bank, Trust Dept.
P.O. Box 17001
San Antonio, TX   78217-0001   (210) 820-8875
Application address: c/o Alamo Heights High School, Attn.: Guidance Counselor, 6900 Broadway St., San Antonio, TX 78209-3736, tel.: (210) 820-8875

Foundation type: Independent foundation
Purpose: Scholarships to high school graduates of Alamo Heights High School for postsecondary education at accredited colleges or universities.
Financial data: Year ended 12/31/2012. Assets, $298,785 (M); Expenditures, $20,425; Total giving, $15,000.
Fields of interest: Higher education.
Type of support: Support to graduates or students of specific schools.
Application information: Applications accepted. Application form required.
Initial approach: Letter
Additional information: Application forms available from the guidance office.
EIN: 742881302

8875
Houston Arts Alliance
(formerly Cultural Arts Council of Houston/Harris County)
3201 Allen Pkwy., Ste. 250
Houston, TX   77019-1800   (713) 527-9330
Contact: Jonathon Glus, Pres. and C.E.O.
FAX: (713) 630-5210; E-mail: info@cachh.org;
E-mail for Jonathon Glus: jonathon@haatx.com;
URL: http://www.cachh.org/grants/

Foundation type: Public charity
Purpose: Fellowships and awards to artists of Houston, TX.
Publications: Application guidelines; Annual report; Grants list; Newsletter.
Financial data: Year ended 06/30/2012. Assets, $4,190,385 (M); Expenditures, $7,946,433; Total giving, $3,930,822; Grants to individuals, totaling $188,000.
Fields of interest: Arts, artist's services; Arts.
Type of support: Fellowships; Grants to individuals; Project support.
Application information: Applications accepted. Application form required. Application form available on the grantmaker's web site.
Send request by: Online
Copies of proposal: 1
Deadline(s): Dec. 12
Applicants should submit the following:
1) Work samples
2) Resume
Additional information: Application workshops will be held to assist artists in preparing their materials. See web site for additional guidelines.
Program descriptions:
Grants for Individual Artists: The program seeks to support the development and presentation of new artistic works by local Houston artists to help advance Houston's reputation as a vibrant creative hub and a destination for cultural tourism.
New Works Fellowships: Fellowship of $3,000 supports emerging artists defined as artists who have actively and continually pursued their profession in this discipline for less than three years, and a $7,500 grant to established artists defined as experienced artists who have actively and continually pursued their profession in this discipline for more than three years to produce new works.
EIN: 741946756

8876
Houston Bar Foundation
1001 Fannin St., Ste. 1300
Houston, TX   77002-6732   (713) 759-1133
E-mail: bmcaughan@SMD-IPLaw.com; URL: http://www.hba.org/folder-HBF/HBF.htm

Foundation type: Public charity
Purpose: Limited temporary financial assistance to attorneys in Harris county, TX who are in need. Scholarships to court coordinators for continuing education that is directly related to the administration of justice in Harris county, TX.
Financial data: Year ended 06/30/2012. Assets, $10,172,856 (M); Expenditures, $1,060,631; Total giving, $943,420; Grants to individuals, totaling $19,665.
Type of support: Scholarships—to individuals; Grants for special needs.
Application information: Assistance to lawyers must be approved by the Board.
EIN: 760029594

8877
Houston Center for Contemporary Craft
4848 Main St.
Houston, TX   77002-9718   (713) 529-4848
FAX: (713) 529-1288;
E-mail: nwright@crafthouston.org; E-mail for Julie Farr: jfarr@crafthouston.org; URL: http://www.crafthouston.org

Foundation type: Public charity
Purpose: Residencies to artists working in craft media such as wood, glass, metal, fiber, and clay.
Publications: Application guidelines; Informational brochure; Newsletter.
Financial data: Year ended 06/30/2013. Assets, $959,259 (M); Expenditures, $1,244,321.
Fields of interest: Ceramic arts; Arts.
Type of support: Residencies.
Application information: Applications accepted. Application form required.
Initial approach: Letter
Deadline(s): Mar. 15
Applicants should submit the following:
1) Curriculum vitae
2) Letter(s) of recommendation
Additional information: Application should also include digital images of ten works, created within the last two years, a one page letter of intent and a personal statement.
Program description:
Artist in Residence: This program supports emerging, mid-career and established artists working in craft media, including but not limited to wood, glass, metal, fiber, and clay. Artists selected for the program will receive studio space rent-free and a monthly stipend.
EIN: 760621817

8878
Houston Children's Charity
230 Westcott, Ste. 202
Houston, TX   77007-7023   (713) 524-2878
FAX: (713) 524-3199;
E-mail: hcc@houstonchildrenscharity.org;
URL: http://www.houstonchildrenscharity.org

Foundation type: Public charity
Purpose: Financial assistance to families in emergency crisis situations in the Houston, TX area. Scholarships to enable underprivileged youth in the Houston, TX area to attend college.
Publications: Application guidelines.
Financial data: Year ended 09/30/2011. Assets, $571,456 (M); Expenditures, $3,870,288; Total giving, $2,795,217.
Fields of interest: Higher education; Economically disadvantaged.
Type of support: Scholarships—to individuals; Grants for special needs.
Application information: Contact the Children's Charity for additional information.
EIN: 760135741

8879
Houston Community College System Foundation
3100 Main St., Ste. 12B17
Houston, TX   77002-9312

Foundation type: Public charity
Purpose: Scholarships to qualified and needy students to attend Houston Community College, TX.
Publications: Financial statement.
Financial data: Year ended 08/31/2011. Assets, $8,987,180 (M); Expenditures, $3,002,330; Total

giving, $2,319,927; Grants to individuals, totaling $2,319,927.
Fields of interest: Higher education.
Type of support: Support to graduates or students of specific schools; Undergraduate support.
Application information: Applications accepted. Application form required. Application form available on the grantmaker's web site.
  Initial approach: Letter
  Additional information: Applicant must demonstrate financial need or academic merit.
EIN: 741885205

8880
Greater Houston Community Foundation
5120 Woodway Dr., Ste. 6000
Houston, TX 77056 (713) 333-2200
Contact: Linda Gardner, Dir., Opers.
FAX: (713) 333-2220; E-mail: lgardner@ghcf.org; URL: http://www.ghcf.org

Foundation type: Community foundation
Purpose: Scholarships for higher education to eligible students of the Greater Houston, TX area and elsewhere.
Publications: Annual report; Financial statement; Grants list; Informational brochure; Newsletter; Occasional report; IRS Form 990 or 990-PF printed copy available upon request.
Financial data: Year ended 12/31/2012. Assets, $397,344,831 (M); Expenditures, $76,491,272; Total giving, $72,476,214; Grants to individuals, 200 grants totaling $659,250.
Fields of interest: Higher education.
Type of support: Scholarships—to individuals.
Application information: Applications accepted. Application form required. Application form available on the grantmaker's web site.
  Initial approach: Application
  Send request by: Online
  Deadline(s): Mar. 22
  Additional information: See web site for a complete listing of scholarship funds and guidelines per scholarship type.
EIN: 237160400

8881
Houston Endowment Inc.
600 Travis, Ste. 6400
Houston, TX 77002-3003 (713) 238-8100
Contact: Lydia Hickey, Grant Mgr.
FAX: (713) 238-8101;
E-mail: info@houstonendowment.org; E-mail and tel. for Lydia Hickey:
online@houstonendowment.org; (713) 238-8134; URL: http://www.houstonendowment.org

Foundation type: Independent foundation
Purpose: Scholarships to graduating seniors attending Harris County public schools, TX.
Publications: Application guidelines; Annual report; Financial statement; Grants list; Informational brochure (including application guidelines).
Financial data: Year ended 12/31/2012. Assets, $1,545,616,901 (M); Expenditures, $108,357,045; Total giving, $78,718,050; Grants to individuals, 1,348 grants totaling $4,337,166 (high: $9,400, low: $300).
Fields of interest: Higher education.
Type of support: Scholarships—to individuals.
Application information: Applications not accepted.
  Additional information: Candidates are nominated by their high schools. Unsolicited

requests for funds not considered or acknowledged.
Program description:
  The Jesse H. Jones and Mary Gibbs Jones Scholars Program: Seniors attending most Harris County, TX, public schools may apply and should see their high school college counselor for an application. Candidates are nominated by each participating high school, and a Rotary Club of Houston committee makes the final selection based on scholastic achievement, economic need, community service and leadership. Scholars are eligible to receive up to a total of $16,000 over six academic years. Payments are based on the amount of unmet need and subsidized student loans, limited to $5,000 annually. Some Scholars are likely to receive considerable monetary amounts from scholarships from the university they are attending and from other outside sources. In these cases, total payments on their Jones Scholars award may be substantially less than $16,000.These guidelines apply to all students graduating from high school.
EIN: 746013920

8882
Houston Geological Society Foundation
14811 St. Mary's Ln.
Houston, TX 77079-2922 (713) 463-9476

Foundation type: Independent foundation
Purpose: Scholarships to full time undergraduate students with a geology major at an accredited Texas university.
Financial data: Year ended 06/30/2012. Assets, $294,051 (M); Expenditures, $15,808; Total giving, $15,000; Grants to individuals, 7 grants totaling $15,000 (high: $3,000, low: $2,000).
Fields of interest: Geology.
Type of support: Undergraduate support.
Application information: Applications accepted.
  Initial approach: Letter
  Additional information: Application should include transcripts. Students must be U.S. citizens.
EIN: 760138744

8883
Houston Minority Business Council
3 Riverway Dr., Ste. 555
Houston, TX 77056 (713) 271-7805
FAX: (713) 271-9770; E-mail: info@hmbc.org; Richard A. Huebner E-mail:
richard.huebner@hmsdc.org; URL: http://affiliate.nmsdc.org/hmsdc

Foundation type: Public charity
Purpose: Awards scholarships to individuals to enable them to receive necessary business education and training in the Houston, TX, area.
Publications: Application guidelines; Newsletter.
Financial data: Year ended 12/31/2011. Assets, $416,704 (M); Expenditures, $1,314,536; Total giving, $53,320; Grants to individuals, totaling $53,320.
Fields of interest: Education; Minorities.
Type of support: Scholarships—to individuals.
Application information: Applications accepted. Application form required. Application form available on the grantmaker's web site.
  Initial approach: Letter or telephone
  Copies of proposal: 1
  Deadline(s): May 31
  Additional information: Recipients notified in 90 days. Applications should be sent by fax or mail or delivered to the Council office.

Program description:
  Scholarships: Awards scholarships in an effort to strengthen the management skills of MBEs whose successes could be enhanced by attending educational seminars, to expand public awareness of minority owned businesses and to reward involvement of members in the Houston Minority Business Council.
EIN: 760458224

8884
Houston Osteopathic Hospital Foundation Inc.
1603 N. Main St.
Pearland, TX 77581-2803 (281) 485-3226
Contact: David Armbruster, Pres.
Application Address: 3322 E. Walnut, Ste. 105, Pearland, TX 77581

Foundation type: Independent foundation
Purpose: Scholarships to students at Texas College of Osteopathic Medicine, TX, and licensed physicians enrolled in post-Doctoral courses of study.
Financial data: Year ended 12/31/2012. Assets, $1,070,841 (M); Expenditures, $84,242; Total giving, $40,000.
Fields of interest: Medical school/education; Medical specialties.
Type of support: Support to graduates or students of specific schools; Graduate support; Undergraduate support.
Application information: Application form required.
  Initial approach: Letter
  Additional information: Application must include evidence of enrollment at Texas College of Osteopathic Medicine, as well as biographical, educational, and financial information.
EIN: 742426837

8885
Hubbard Family Foundation
c/o Bank of America, N.A.
P.O. Box 831041
Dallas, TX 75283-1041
Contact: Cindy Keyser, V.P.
E-mail: cindy.s.keyser@ustrust.com; Application address: c/o Bank of America, N.A., P.O. Box 24565 Seattle, WA 98124; URL: http://www.bankofamerica.com/grantmaking

Foundation type: Independent foundation
Purpose: Scholarships to residents of Edmonds and South Snomish counties, WA, for higher education.
Financial data: Year ended 07/31/2013. Assets, $2,322,742 (M); Expenditures, $125,409; Total giving, $91,500.
Type of support: Undergraduate support.
Application information: Applications accepted.
  Additional information: Contact foundation for current application guidelines.
EIN: 916253897

8886
Huddleston Foundation
1221 McKinney Ave., Ste. 3700
Houston, TX 77010 (713) 209-1100
Contact: F.M. Huddleston, Treas.

Foundation type: Independent foundation
Purpose: Scholarships to individuals in the Houston, TX area for attendance at accredited colleges and/or universities within the U.S.

Financial data: Year ended 12/31/2012. Assets, $392,351 (M); Expenditures, $63,913; Total giving, $57,007; Grants to individuals, 14 grants totaling $57,007 (high: $5,000, low: $2,007).
Fields of interest: Higher education.
Type of support: Scholarships—to individuals.
Application information: Applications accepted. Application form required.
> *Applicants should submit the following:*
>   1) Class rank
>   2) SAT
> *Additional information:* Applicant must demonstrate leadership for both school and community, and participated in a minimum of two separate recognized extracurricular activities.
EIN: 760589041

8887
Humanities Texas

(formerly Texas Council for the Humanities)
1410 Rio Grande St.
Austin, TX   78701-1506   (512) 440-1991
Contact: Michael L. Gillette Ph.D., Exec. Dir.
FAX: (512) 440-0115;
E-mail: elupfer@humanitiestexas.org; URL: http://www.humanitiestexas.org/

Foundation type: Public charity
Purpose: Awards by nomination only to humanities teachers.
Publications: Application guidelines; Biennial report; Financial statement; Informational brochure (including application guidelines); Newsletter; Occasional report.
Financial data: Year ended 10/31/2011. Assets, $6,115,776 (M); Expenditures, $2,238,600; Total giving, $329,816; Grants to individuals, totaling $66,000.
Fields of interest: Humanities; Education.
Type of support: Awards/grants by nomination only; Awards/prizes.
Application information: Applications accepted. Application form available on the grantmaker's web site.
> *Initial approach:* Letter or telephone
> *Deadline(s):* Dec. 10 for Outstanding Teaching of the Humanities Award
> *Additional information:* Contact council for current nomination guidelines.
Program descriptions:
> *Humanities Texas Awards:* This program recognizes imaginative leadership in the humanities on a local, regional, or state level by providing two $5,000 awards: one for individual achievement, and one for organizational achievement. Nominees may include (but are by no means limited to) a local library that has started an especially effective reading and lecture series; a group whose work has advanced heritage tourism efforts; or an individual who has developed a significant public program grounded in history, literature, philosophy, archaeology, folklore, or another humanities discipline.
> *Outstanding Teaching of the Humanities Award:* This award recognizes exemplary K-12 humanities teachers. Each year, eleven teachers are selected to receive a $5,000 cash award, as well as an additional $500 award for their respective schools to purchase humanities-based instructional materials. Eligible applicants must be full-time teachers in Texas public and private schools in the areas of English and language arts, foreign languages, history, and social sciences; teachers of art, drama, and music are eligible if they emphasize the history, criticism, and theory of the arts. Named awards under this program include the

James F. Veninga Outstanding Teaching of the Humanities Award, and the Linden Heck Howell Outstanding Teacher of Texas History Award.
EIN: 751493438

8888
Ed and Gladys Hurley Trust Foundation

c/o Bank of America, N.A.
P.O. Box 831041
Dallas, TX   75283-1041   (214) 209-6477
Contact: Jenae Guillory
Application address: c/o Bank of America, 901 Main St. TX1-492-19-05, Dallas, TX 75202-3714

Foundation type: Independent foundation
Purpose: Scholarships to students who reside in the U.S. and wish to study to become ministers, missionaries or religious workers of the Protestant faith, to study at colleges in the state of Texas.
Publications: Informational brochure (including application guidelines).
Financial data: Year ended 08/31/2012. Assets, $1,992,026 (M); Expenditures, $198,893; Total giving, $161,500.
Fields of interest: Theological school/education; Protestant agencies & churches.
Type of support: Graduate support.
Application information: Application form required. Application form available on the grantmaker's web site.
> *Initial approach:* Letter
> *Deadline(s):* Apr. 30.
> *Applicants should submit the following:*
>   1) Letter(s) of recommendation
EIN: 756006961

8889
The Hutton Foundation, Inc.

569 CR 3581
Paradise, TX   76073-3207   (817) 238-6995
Contact: Timothy Hutton, Dir.
Application address: 3980 Boat Club Rd., Ste. 207, Fort Worth, TX 76135 tel: (817) 238-6995

Foundation type: Operating foundation
Purpose: Financial assistance to indigent residents of Fort Worth, TX for medical needs.
Financial data: Year ended 12/31/2012. Assets, $5,336 (M); Expenditures, $73,485; Total giving, $71,250.
Type of support: Grants for special needs.
Application information: Applications not accepted.
> *Additional information:* Unsolicited requests for funds not considered.
EIN: 900122801

8890
IFMA Foundation

1 East Greenway Plz., Ste. 1100
Houston, TX   77046-0104   (713) 623-4362
FAX: (713) 623-6124; URL: http://www.ifmafoundation.org/

Foundation type: Public charity
Purpose: Scholarships to graduate and undergraduate students pursuing degrees in facility management or related fields.
Publications: Application guidelines.
Financial data: Year ended 06/30/2011. Assets, $1,044,232 (M); Expenditures, $538,293; Total giving, $115,381; Grants to individuals, totaling $90,392. Subtotal for stipends: 5 grants totaling $3,465. Subtotal for scholarships—to individuals: 0 grants totaling $111,916.

Fields of interest: Business school/education.
Type of support: Graduate support; Undergraduate support.
Application information: Applications accepted.
> *Deadline(s):* May 31
> *Additional information:* Applicants must attend IFMA's World Workplace Conference and Exhibition as well as educational sessions. See web site for additional guidelines.
Program description:
> *Scholarships:* Scholarships are awarded based on merit and certain applicant restrictions and/or qualification requirements may apply. Applicants are solicited in the spring of each year and funded the following fall. Scholarships provided through the IFMA Foundation are set at a minimum of $1,500 (US) and also include payment for the recipient to attend IFMA's World Workplace event.
EIN: 760313751

8891
May H. Ilgenfritz Testamentary Trust

c/o Bank of America, N.A.
P.O. Box 831041
Dallas, TX   75283-1041   (312) 828-8166
Contact: John Swearingen, Tr.
Application address: P.O. Box 311, Sedalia, MO 65302-0311, tel.: (816) 292-4342

Foundation type: Independent foundation
Purpose: Scholarships to financially needy high school students in the Sedalia, MO, area, who rank in the upper third of their classes.
Financial data: Year ended 12/31/2012. Assets, $4,062,047 (M); Expenditures, $226,531; Total giving, $150,700; Grants to individuals, 69 grants totaling $150,200 (high: $4,050, low: $600).
Fields of interest: Higher education; Scholarships/financial aid; Economically disadvantaged.
Type of support: Undergraduate support.
Application information: Applications accepted.
> *Initial approach:* Letter of no more than three pages
> *Deadline(s):* July and Dec.
> *Additional information:* Application must include two letters of recommendation, one related to character and the other to academic potential.
EIN: 440663403

8892
Imperial Sugar Company Contributions Program

(formerly Imperial Holly Corporation Contributions Program)
8016 Hwy. 90A
P.O. Box 9
Sugar Land, TX   77478-2961
E-mail: DonationRequests@ImperialSugar.com

Foundation type: Corporate giving program
Purpose: Scholarships to high school students residing in Fort Bend County, TX.
Type of support: Undergraduate support.
Application information:
> *Initial approach:* Letter
> *Additional information:* Contact foundation for eligibility requirements.

8893
Joe Ingram Trust

c/o Bank of America, N.A.
P.O. Bank 831041
Dallas, TX   75283-1041   (816) 388-5555

Foundation type: Independent foundation

Purpose: Student loans to residents of Chariton County, MO, who are attending colleges and trade schools. Scholarships to Chariton county high schools seniors. Awards to valedictorians and salutatorians of graduating classes of Chariton County high schools.
Financial data: Year ended 12/31/2012. Assets, $16,011,867 (M); Expenditures, $342,102; Total giving, $910,519; Grants to individuals, 352 grants totaling $783,269 (high: $20,000, low: $105).
Fields of interest: Vocational education, post-secondary; Higher education.
Type of support: Scholarships—to individuals; Student loans—to individuals.
Application information: Application form required.
Initial approach: Letter
Deadline(s): May 1
Applicants should submit the following:
1) Letter(s) of recommendation
2) Transcripts
3) GPA
4) Financial information
Additional information: Application should also include a copy of you and your parents' tax form.
EIN: 446006475

8894
Interdenominational Christian Missions, Inc.
30260 Saratoga Ln.
Fair Oaks Ranch, TX   78015-4232
URL: http://icmweb.org/

Foundation type: Operating foundation
Purpose: Grants to missionaries for ministry work in Costa Rican prisons.
Financial data: Year ended 12/31/2012. Assets, $29,048 (M); Expenditures, $231,213; Total giving, $84,555.
International interests: Costa Rica.
Type of support: Grants to individuals.
Application information: Applications not accepted.
Additional information: Unsolicited requests for funds not considered.
EIN: 742798861

8895
Interfaith Ministries for Greater Houston
3217 Montrose Blvd.
Houston, TX   77006-3929   (713) 533-4900
Contact: Elliot Gershenson, Pres. and C.E.O.
FAX: (713) 800-5110;
E-mail: egershenson@imgh.org; URL: http://www.imgh.org

Foundation type: Public charity
Purpose: Financial assistance, including rental and food assistance, is provided to indigent residents of the greater Houston, TX area.
Financial data: Year ended 06/30/2012. Assets, $6,599,095 (M); Expenditures, $11,375,517; Total giving, $4,474,439; Grants to individuals, totaling $4,474,439.
Fields of interest: Economically disadvantaged.
Type of support: In-kind gifts; Grants for special needs.
Application information:
Initial approach: Letter
Applicants should submit the following:
1) Financial information
Additional information: Contact foundation for eligibility criteria.
EIN: 741488102

8896
Jamaica Foundation of Houston
P.O. Box 710824
Houston, TX   77271-0824   (281) 241-9929
Contact: Arnold Richards, Pres.
FAX: (713) 785-4095;
E-mail: jamaicafoundationhouston@gmail.com;
URL: http://www.jamaicafoundationofhouston.org/

Foundation type: Public charity
Purpose: Scholarships for exceptional college students and high school graduates of Jamaican descent in the Houston, TX metropolitan area.
Publications: Application guidelines; Newsletter.
Financial data: Year ended 12/31/2012. Assets, $128,905 (M); Expenditures, $227,598.
Fields of interest: Higher education.
Type of support: Scholarships—to individuals.
Application information: Applications accepted. Application form required. Application form available on the grantmaker's web site.
Send request by: Mail
Deadline(s): Mar. 31
Applicants should submit the following:
1) Essay
2) Photograph
3) Transcripts
4) Letter(s) of recommendation
Program description:
Scholarships: Scholarships are available to college students and high school graduates in the Houston metropolitan area. Applicants must be enrolled in a four-year or higher accredited program.
EIN: 760641809

8897
The James 127 Foundation
12175 Network Blvd.
San Antonio, TX   78249-3359   (210) 561-5360
Contact: General Welfare: Steven L. Green, Secy.-Treas.

Foundation type: Operating foundation
Purpose: Grants to economically disadvantaged individuals residing in the San Antonio, TX area based on spiritual, emotional, physical, and security needs. Priority is given to single mothers.
Financial data: Year ended 12/31/2011. Assets, $1,426,016 (M); Expenditures, $168,750; Total giving, $90,171; Grants to individuals, 3 grants totaling $14,500 (high: $10,000, low: $2,000).
Fields of interest: Women; Single parents.
Type of support: Grants for special needs.
Application information: Application form required.
Deadline(s): None
EIN: 742959955

8898
Janson Foundation
c/o Bank of America, N.A.
P.O. Box 831041
Dallas, TX   75283-1041   (360) 848-7470
Contact: Ron Wells, Chair.

Foundation type: Independent foundation
Purpose: Scholarships to individuals of Skagit county, WA for undergraduate, post high school studies.
Publications: Application guidelines.
Financial data: Year ended 11/30/2013. Assets, $2,252,542 (M); Expenditures, $125,385; Total giving, $77,416.
Fields of interest: Higher education.
Type of support: Scholarships—to individuals; Undergraduate support.

Application information: Application form required.
Deadline(s): Apr. 15
Applicants should submit the following:
1) Resume
2) Letter(s) of recommendation
3) Essay
4) Financial information
5) Transcripts
Additional information: Applicant must demonstrate financial need, scholastic ability and good moral character. Applications may be obtained from the office of Emmanuel Baptist Church or the Janson Scholarship Committee address.
EIN: 916251624

8899
Jireh Foundation, Inc.
12042 Blanco Rd.
San Antonio, TX   78216-2440   (210) 342-7010
Contact: Edward Ron Acosta, Tr.

Foundation type: Independent foundation
Purpose: Grants for living expenses primarily to individuals in the San Antonio, TX area.
Financial data: Year ended 12/31/2011. Assets, $19,669 (M); Expenditures, $103,826; Total giving, $101,225.
Fields of interest: Economically disadvantaged.
Type of support: Grants for special needs.
Application information: Applications accepted. Application form required.
Deadline(s): None
EIN: 742980977

8900
Johnson Family Foundation
P.O. Box 483
Junction, TX   76849-0483

Foundation type: Independent foundation
Purpose: Scholarships to residents of Kimble, Kerr or Gillespie counties, TX, for higher education.
Financial data: Year ended 12/31/2010. Assets, $143,024 (M); Expenditures, $29,700; Total giving, $28,500.
Type of support: Undergraduate support.
Application information: Application form required.
Deadline(s): Mar. 31
EIN: 752568312

8901
Julie Ann Jones Memorial Theological Scholarship Trust
205 N. Market St.
Brenham, TX   77833-3216
Contact: Sally M. Jones, Tr.

Foundation type: Operating foundation
Purpose: Scholarships to individuals from Washington and surrounding counties in Texas pursuing a degree in the religious field.
Financial data: Year ended 12/31/2012. Assets, $332,346 (M); Expenditures, $5,373; Total giving, $5,250; Grants to individuals, 3 grants totaling $5,250 (high: $3,000, low: $750).
Fields of interest: Higher education; Theological school/education.
Type of support: Scholarships—to individuals.
Application information: Applications accepted.
Final notification: Recipients notified in July and Dec.

Additional information: Applicants should submit a statement showing college, field of study, academic record and statement of need.
EIN: 742219724

8902
Don D. Jordan Scholarship Foundation
(formerly Chairman's Award Foundation)
P.O. Box 4567
Houston, TX 77210-4567 (713) 256-9557
Contact: Dayle Blake
Application address: 1111 Nantucket Dr., Houston, TX, 77057, tel.: (713) 256-9557

Foundation type: Company-sponsored foundation
Purpose: Scholarships to children of employees of Reliant Energy Ventures, Inc. in recognition of volunteer and community service activities.
Financial data: Year ended 12/31/2012. Assets, $1,066,429 (M); Expenditures, $77,349; Total giving, $73,500; Grants to individuals, 21 grants totaling $73,500 (high: $3,500, low: $3,500).
Fields of interest: Volunteer services.
Type of support: Employee-related scholarships.
Application information: Applications accepted. Application form required.
   Deadline(s): Jan. 31
   Additional information: Application must include essay.
Company name: Reliant Energy Ventures, Incorporated
EIN: 760321771

8903
Jerold B. Katz Foundation
P.O. Box 742366
Houston, TX 77274

Foundation type: Independent foundation
Purpose: Scholarships awarded to children of employees of the Katz Controlled Group, and to employees of the State of GA in the State Department of Family and Children's Services. The employees must also be residents of the state of GA.
Financial data: Year ended 11/30/2012. Assets, $1,657,163 (M); Expenditures, $77,875; Total giving, $67,450.
Fields of interest: Higher education.
Type of support: Employee-related scholarships.
Application information: Application form required.
   Deadline(s): None
   Additional information: Scholarship applications must be submitted using the Citizens Scholarship Foundation of America form. The scholarship is administered by the Citizens Scholarship Foundation of America.
EIN: 742164970

8904
Kelly Family Foundation
(formerly Stephen P. and Sandra Lu Kelly Foundation)
9 Stonebrook Ct.
Brownwood, TX 76801 (325) 643-4755
Contact: Sandi Kelly

Foundation type: Independent foundation
Purpose: Scholarships to high school seniors who are residents of Brown County, TX.
Financial data: Year ended 08/31/2012. Assets, $428,699 (M); Expenditures, $30,316; Total giving, $29,720.
Type of support: Undergraduate support.
Application information: Applications accepted.

Initial approach: Letter
Deadline(s): None
Additional information: Application must include a brief resume of academic qualifications.
EIN: 752298202

8905
Kiddies Workshop U.S.A., Inc.
6420 Hillcroft St., Ste. 204
Houston, TX 77081-3103 (713) 988-1929
Contact: Paulette Wiley, Exec. Dir.

Foundation type: Public charity
Purpose: Grants to day care home providers in the Houston, TX area.
Financial data: Year ended 09/30/2011. Assets, $269,743 (M); Expenditures, $2,843,107; Total giving, $2,575,167; Grants to individuals, totaling $2,575,167.
Fields of interest: Day care.
Type of support: Grants to individuals.
Application information: Contact the organization for additional guidelines.
EIN: 760414261

8906
Kimberly-Clark Foundation, Inc.
351 Phelps Dr.
Irving, TX 75038-6507 (972) 281-1200
Application address: P.O. Box 619100, Dallas, TX 75261-9100; URL: http://www.kimberly-clark.com/ourcompany/community/kc_foundation.aspx

Foundation type: Company-sponsored foundation
Purpose: Scholarships to children of U.S. and Canadian employees of Kimberly-Clark.
Publications: Corporate giving report.
Financial data: Year ended 12/31/2012. Assets, $14,395 (M); Expenditures, $4,317,002; Total giving, $4,240,401; Grants to individuals, totaling $1,318,075.
Fields of interest: Higher education.
International interests: Canada.
Type of support: Employee-related scholarships; Undergraduate support.
Application information: Applications not accepted.
   Additional information: Unsolicited requests for funds not considered or acknowledged.
Program description:
   Bright Futures Scholarship Program: Through the Bright Futures Scholarship Program, the foundation awards college scholarships of up to $20,000 to children of U.S. and Canadian employees of Kimberly-Clark.
Company name: Kimberly-Clark Corporation
EIN: 396044304

8907
Howard H. Klein Foundation
1427 Keefer Rd.
Tomball, TX 77375 (281) 370-0300
Contact: Lori Klein, Secy.-Treas.

Foundation type: Independent foundation
Purpose: Scholarships to TX ministers or teachers studying Christianity or TX students attending a Christian university.
Financial data: Year ended 12/31/2010. Assets, $46,955 (M); Expenditures, $7,071; Total giving, $6,950; Grants to individuals, 16 grants totaling $6,950 (high: $1,000, low: $250).
Type of support: Undergraduate support.

Application information:
   Initial approach: Letter
   Additional information: Contact foundation for eligibility criteria.
EIN: 760236778

8908
Louise Knight Scholarship Trust
P.O. Box 925
Madisonville, TX 77864-0924 (936) 348-3543
Contact: Roger Knight, Jr., Tr.

Foundation type: Independent foundation
Purpose: Scholarships to graduates of Madisonville High School, TX, who maintained at least a "C" average, for undergraduate education.
Financial data: Year ended 12/31/2011. Assets, $0 (M); Expenditures, $7,238; Total giving, $7,238; Grants to individuals, 14 grants totaling $7,238 (high: $738, low: $500).
Type of support: Support to graduates or students of specific schools; Undergraduate support.
Application information: Applications accepted. Application form required.
   Deadline(s): Feb. 1
   Applicants should submit the following:
      1) Photograph
      2) Letter(s) of recommendation
      3) Essay
   Additional information: Application must include proof of undergraduate enrollment.
EIN: 746387730

8909
Knights Templar Eye Foundation, Inc.
1033 Long Prairie Rd., Ste. 5
Flower Mound, TX 75022-4230 (214) 888-0220
Contact: Robert W. Bigley, Asst. Secy.
Application online address URL: http://dropbox.yousendit.com/ktef
FAX: (214) 888-0230; E-mail: Manager@KTEF.US; URL: http://www.knightstemplar.org/ktef/

Foundation type: Public charity
Purpose: Research grants to eligible investigators for Pediatric Ophthalmology.
Publications: Application guidelines; Informational brochure.
Financial data: Year ended 06/30/2012. Assets, $91,850,481 (M); Expenditures, $3,639,007; Total giving, $1,557,483; Grants to individuals, totaling $3,583.
Fields of interest: Eye diseases; Pediatrics.
Type of support: Research.
Application information: Applications accepted.
   Initial approach: Proposal
   Send request by: Online
   Deadline(s): Feb. 1 for Competitive Renewal Grants, Feb. 15 for Pediatric Ophthalmology Career-Starter Research Grants
Program descriptions:
   Competitive Renewal Grants: Up to $60,000 per grant to extend the original grant project for one additional year if the data accumulated in the first seven months of the original grant given the previous year are compelling. This grant is only available to awardees of KTEF Career Starter funding in 2012.
   Pediatric Ophthalmology Career-Starter Research Grants: Grants of up to $60,000 are awarded to impact the care of infants and children. Clinical or basic research on conditions that are potentially preventable or correctable such as amblyopia, congenital cataract, congenital glaucoma, retinopathy of prematurity, ocular malformations,

congenital nystagmus, and other hereditary eye diseases such as retinal dystrophies or retinoblastoma. Proposals for support of basic research on the eye and development of the visual system are welcome but must be directly related to pediatric eye diseases. Eligible applicants must live in the U.S. and have received an M.D., Ph.D., or equivalent degree.
EIN: 520686958

8910
Susan G. Komen for the Cure
(formerly The Susan G. Komen Breast Cancer Foundation, Inc.)
5005 Lyndon B. Johnson Fwy., Ste. 250
Dallas, TX   75244-6125   (972) 855-1600
Contact: Judy A. Salerno, Pres. and C.E.O.
FAX: (972) 855-1640; E-mail: grants@komen.org;
Toll-free tel.: (888) 300-5582; URL: http://www.komen.org

Foundation type: Public charity
Purpose: Scholarships to college bound students to assist in their academic pursuits. Awards to honor extraordinary achievement in research and clinical work specifically related to breast cancer survivorship.
Publications: Application guidelines; Annual report; Financial statement; Grants list; Informational brochure; Newsletter.
Financial data: Year ended 03/31/2012. Assets, $313,104,320 (M); Expenditures, $188,358,215; Total giving, $71,697,843.
Fields of interest: Higher education; Breast cancer; Cancer research; Breast cancer research; Population studies.
Type of support: Fellowships; Research; Scholarships—to individuals; Postdoctoral support; Doctoral support.
Application information: Applications accepted. Application form required. Application form available on the grantmaker's web site.
　Initial approach: Letter, telephone, or e-mail
　Deadline(s): Nov. 8 for Scholarships; Mar. 1 for Survivorship Award, Aug. 30 for Research Grants
Program descriptions:
　Brinker Award for Scientific Distinction: This award recognizes outstanding work that has advanced basic research concepts, or affected clinical or social-behavioral applications in the field of breast cancer research, screening, treatment, or prevention. The intent is to recognize scholars for a specific contribution, a consistent pattern of contributions, or leadership in the field that has had a substantial impact on breast cancer. The award is given in two categories. The Basic Science Award is presented to a researcher who has added substantively to the understanding of the basic biology or development of methodologies that further the ability to unravel the genetic and molecular basis of breast cancer. The Clinical Research Award is presented to a clinician who has significantly furthered the identification of new prevention, detection, or treatment approaches for breast cancer and its translation into clinical care. Awards are accompanied by $20,000 to be used to further the recipients' activities in breast cancer research.
　Career Catalyst in Disparities Research (CC-DR): These grants seek to foster independent careers in research exploring the basis for differences in breast cancer outcomes and the translation of this research into clinical and public health practice interventions, particularly among junior scientists from populations affected by breast cancer disparities. Grants will provide up to $450,000 over

three years to support combined programs of research and mentoring that will further research independence for scientists in the early stages of their career. Applicants must hold a doctoral degree or equivalent, must currently hold a faculty appointment, and must not have held any faculty appointment (including non-tenure and tenure-track appointments combined) for a total of more than six years.
　College Scholarship Award: The program assists students who have lost a parent to breast cancer. The program offers college scholarships of up to $10,000 per year, over a four-year period, to young adults (graduating high school to age 25)
　Investigator Initiated Research Grants: This area seeks to stimulate exploration of new ideas and novel approaches that will lead to reductions in breast cancer incidence and/or mortality within the next decade. Special emphasis will be given to studies seeking to understand the basis for differences in breast cancer outcomes and translating research discoveries into clinical and public health practice to eliminate breast cancer disparities. Grants will provide up to $1,000,000 over four years; eligible applicants must have a doctoral degree (e.g., M.D., Ph.D., Dr.PH, D.O., or equivalent)
　Post-Baccalaureate Fellowship in Disparities Research (PBF-DR): These grants seek to attract individuals from populations affected by disparities in breast cancer outcomes into careers seeking to understand and eliminate these disparities; provide the tools and environment in which students very early in their career can begin to define meaningful career paths focused on addressing disparities in breast cancer; and empower these students with the analytic, research, scientific, clinical, and public health skills critical to effectively exploring the basis for differences in breast cancer outcomes and translating research discoveries into clinical and public health practice to eliminate disparities in breast cancer outcomes.
　Postdoctoral Fellowship: The fellowship provides up to $180,000 for direct costs over three years and seeks to attract scientists into careers addressing important research questions about breast cancer, expand the skills and expertise of breast cancer researchers in training, and position trainees for independent careers conducting breast cancer research that will directly affect breast cancer patients.
EIN: 751835298

8911
Vinson & Elkins L.L.P. Scholarship Foundation
1001 Fannin St., Ste. 2500
Houston, TX   77002-6760   (713) 758-2222
Contact: Julie Tran
E-mail: jtran@velaw.com; URL: http://www.vinson-elkins.com/overview/scholarships.aspx?id=476

Foundation type: Company-sponsored foundation
Purpose: Scholarships to financially needy graduating high school seniors at public high schools in the greater Houston, TX, area, who are of African-American or Latino origin, in the top 20 percent of their class and have interest in pursuing a career in law.
Publications: Application guidelines.
Financial data: Year ended 12/31/2012. Assets, $0 (M); Expenditures, $66,249; Total giving, $66,249; Grants to individuals, 16 grants totaling $66,249 (high: $3,749, low: $2,500).
Fields of interest: Law school/education; African Americans/Blacks; Hispanics/Latinos.

Type of support: Undergraduate support.
Application information: Application form required.
　Deadline(s): Apr. 1
　Applicants should submit the following:
　　1) Photograph
　　2) Letter(s) of recommendation
　　3) Transcripts
　　4) Essay
　　5) Class rank
　　6) SAT
　　7) ACT
　Additional information: Applications available only through high school counselors. Scholarships are renewable.
EIN: 760428361

8912
Lake Travis Crisis Ministries
107 R.R. 620 S., Ste. 114
Austin, TX   78734-3900   (512) 266-9810

Foundation type: Public charity
Purpose: Financial and non-cash assistance to low income individuals and families in the Lake Travis, TX area, with food, housing, utilities and other needs.
Financial data: Year ended 12/31/2011. Assets, $60,137 (M); Expenditures, $208,737; Total giving, $180,956; Grants to individuals, totaling $180,956.
Fields of interest: Human services; Economically disadvantaged.
Type of support: In-kind gifts; Grants for special needs.
Application information: Applications accepted. Application form required.
　Additional information: Applicants receiving food or assistance must provide a driver's license or other identification. Cash assistance is paid directly the the vendors.
EIN: 742612401

8913
Lake Travis Education Foundation
P.O. Box 340759
Austin, TX   78734-0013   (512) 533-5968
Contact: Suzanne Stone, Exec. Dir.
FAX: (512) 607-6215;
E-mail: email@laketraviseducationfoundation.org;
URL: http://www.laketraviseducationfoundation.org

Foundation type: Public charity
Purpose: Scholarships to graduating seniors of Lake Travis High School, TX. Grants to educators for creative classroom projects, educational programs, and basic needs that enhance the learning environment for students of Lake Travis Independent School District, TX.
Publications: Application guidelines; Annual report; Grants list.
Financial data: Year ended 05/31/2012. Assets, $648,483 (M); Expenditures, $269,350; Total giving, $222,707; Grants to individuals, totaling $222,707.
Fields of interest: Vocational education, post-secondary; Higher education; Education.
Type of support: Grants to individuals; Scholarships—to individuals; Support to graduates or students of specific schools.
Application information: Applications accepted. Application form available on the grantmaker's web site. Interview required.
　Initial approach: Telephone or e-mail
　Send request by: On-line
　Deadline(s): Feb. for Scholarships

Applicants should submit the following:
1) Letter(s) of recommendation
2) Transcripts
Additional information: See web site for additional guidelines.

Program description:
Scholarships: Scholarships are available to graduating Lake Travis High School seniors. Named scholarships under this program include the Kesley Aydam Memorial Scholarship, Jean Drysdale Memorial Scholarship, Sandi Hanson Memorial Scholarship, Lake Travis Dental Association Scholarship, Grace Massey "Amazing Grace" Scholarship, Rachel Ann Maurer Memorial Scholarship, Carla McDonald Memorial Scholarship, Ella Kate Moore "Moore Love" Scholarship, Ben Perkins Memorial Scholarship, Trevor Searle "Live Life to the Fullest" Scholarship, and Shelley Stillman Memorial Scholarship.
EIN: 742406134

8914
Lanham Foundation
c/o Bank of America, N.A.
P.O. Box 831041
Dallas, TX   75283-1041
Contact: Jay A. Johnson
Application address: P.O. Box 2136, Wenatchee, WA 98807

Foundation type: Independent foundation
Purpose: Awards higher education scholarships to students ages 17-22 who are residents of Chelan County, Washington.
Financial data: Year ended 12/31/2012. Assets, $712,780 (M); Expenditures, $163,232; Total giving, $141,125.
Fields of interest: Vocational education.
Type of support: Technical education support; Undergraduate support.
Application information: Applications accepted. Application form required.
Deadline(s): Apr. 15
Applicants should submit the following:
1) Transcripts
2) Financial information
Additional information: Application must also include a statement on academic performance and progress towards graduation.
EIN: 916020593

8915
Lasco Foundation
P.O Box 292
Liberty Hill, TX   78642
Contact: Marie Burnett, Secy.-Treas.

Foundation type: Independent foundation
Purpose: Scholarships to residents of Leander, TX for continuing education at institutions of higher learning.
Financial data: Year ended 12/31/2012. Assets, $377,296 (M); Expenditures, $29,641; Total giving, $27,900; Grants to individuals, 9 grants totaling $27,900 (high: $5,000, low: $200).
Fields of interest: Higher education.
Type of support: Undergraduate support.
Application information:
Initial approach: Letter
Additional information: Letter should include student's goals, financial resources, and financial needs.
EIN: 742455727

8916
Lawler Foundation
P.O. Box 2888
Humble, TX   77347-2888   (281) 446-0059
Contact: William & Carol Lawler, Mgr.

Foundation type: Independent foundation
Purpose: Scholarships to graduating students attending high school in the Houston, TX, area who will attend a four-year college in TX and graduate within four years.
Financial data: Year ended 11/30/2011. Assets, $190,607 (M); Expenditures, $20,214; Total giving, $17,476; Grants to individuals, 5 grants totaling $11,476 (high: $5,000, low: $976).
Fields of interest: Higher education; Scholarships/financial aid.
Type of support: Awards/grants by nomination only; Undergraduate support.
Application information: Applications not accepted.
Additional information: Students must be nominated by their guidance counselors. Unsolicited requests for funds not considered or acknowledged.
EIN: 760386450

8917
Adam Lee Memorial Scholarship Foundation
4321 Honduras
Corpus Christi, TX   78411

Foundation type: Independent foundation
Purpose: Scholarships to graduating students from the Bayou Vista, TX area for attendance at college or trade school.
Financial data: Year ended 12/31/2012. Assets, $168,324 (M); Expenditures, $7,796; Total giving, $7,750; Grants to individuals, 8 grants totaling $7,750 (high: $1,500, low: $500).
Fields of interest: Vocational education, post-secondary; Higher education.
Type of support: Undergraduate support.
Application information: Applications accepted. Application form required.
Initial approach: Letter
Deadline(s): Mar. 1
Applicants should submit the following:
1) Transcripts
2) Letter(s) of recommendation
EIN: 753174904

8918
Limiar U.S.A., Inc.
P.O.Box 781119
San Antonio, TX   78231-1203   (210) 479-0300
FAX: (210) 479-3835; *E-mail:* limiar@limiar.org; *URL:* http://www.limiar.org

Foundation type: Public charity
Purpose: Grants to provide for medical expenses, education, and financial support to Brazilian orphans.
Financial data: Year ended 12/31/2011. Assets, $1,756 (M); Expenditures, $68,295.
Fields of interest: Adoption.
International interests: Brazil.
Type of support: Grants for special needs.
Application information:
Initial approach: E-mail
Additional information: Contact foundation for further information.
EIN: 341461670

8919
Rufus L. & Helen I. Little Education Trust
(formerly Helen I. Little Education Trust)
P.O. Box 624
Corsicana, TX   75151   (254) 562-5918

Foundation type: Independent foundation
Purpose: Scholarships to members of Christ Episcopal Church, St. Paul's Church, TX, and any Episcopal church, parish or mission in TX.
Financial data: Year ended 12/31/2013. Assets, $1,531,822 (M); Expenditures, $63,432; Total giving, $52,940; Grants to individuals, 4 grants totaling $52,940 (high: $25,800, low: $1,300).
Fields of interest: Protestant agencies & churches.
Type of support: Undergraduate support.
Application information: Application form required.
Deadline(s): Apr. 1.
EIN: 756500051

8920
Live Oak Foundation
c/o Alfred West Ward
290 Cypress Estate Pkwy., W.
Ingram, TX   78025   (361) 492-0567
Contact: Alfred West Ward, Pres.
Application address: P.O. Box 1202, George West, TX 78022

Foundation type: Independent foundation
Purpose: Vocational education scholarships to financially deprived high school students in southern TX.
Financial data: Year ended 12/31/2012. Assets, $151,583 (M); Expenditures, $21,343; Total giving, $15,651.
Fields of interest: Vocational education.
Type of support: Technical education support.
Application information: Applications accepted.
Initial approach: Letter
Deadline(s): None
Additional information: Applicants should submit a resume.
EIN: 742119731

8921
Lockheed Martin Aeronautics Employees Reaching Out Club
(formerly General Dynamics Employees Contribution Club Fort Worth Texas)
P.O. Box 748, MZ 8602
Fort Worth, TX   76101-0748   (817) 935-5847

Foundation type: Public charity
Purpose: General welfare grants to employees of Lockheed Martin and their dependants for emergency aid.
Financial data: Year ended 12/31/2011. Assets, $3,391,155 (M); Expenditures, $3,925,562; Total giving, $3,925,233; Grants to individuals, totaling $371,702.
Type of support: Employee-related welfare.
Application information:
Initial approach: Letter or telephone
Additional information: Contact foundation for further application information.
Company name: Lockheed Martin Corporation
EIN: 756036122

8922
Lockheed Martin Vought Systems Employee Charity Fund
P.O. Box 650003, M/S: PT 42
Dallas, TX 75265-0003 (972) 603-0587
Contact: Hannah Stone, V.P. and Treas.

Foundation type: Company-sponsored foundation
Purpose: Grants to AR and TX employees of Lockheed Martin Missiles and Fire Control in need due to illness, injury, or other catastrophe.
Financial data: Year ended 12/31/2012. Assets, $406,890 (M); Expenditures, $388,576; Total giving, $388,570.
Fields of interest: Health care.
Type of support: Emergency funds; Employee-related welfare.
Application information: Applications not accepted.
  Additional information: Unsolicited requests for funds not considered or acknowledged.
Company name: Lockheed Martin Missiles and Fire Control
EIN: 752528901

8923
L. A. Long Trust
c/o First National Bank in Graham
P.O. Box 540
Graham, TX 76450-0540 (940) 549-2040

Foundation type: Independent foundation
Purpose: Student loans to graduates of Graham Independent School District and graduates of other Young County School District schools, TX.
Financial data: Year ended 07/31/2013. Assets, $643,385 (M); Expenditures, $77,831; Total giving, $58,750; Grant to an individual, 1 grant totaling $58,750.
Type of support: Student loans—to individuals; Support to graduates or students of specific schools.
Application information: Applications accepted.
  Deadline(s): None
  Additional information: Applications by letter.
EIN: 750399970

8924
Linda Lorelle Scholarship Fund, Inc.
2028 Buffalo Ter., Ste. 17
Houston, TX 77019 (713) 942-5805
Contact: Mandi Lovett, Prog. Coor.
FAX: (713) 524-7213;
E-mail: mandi@lindalorelle.org; URL: http://www.lindalorelle.org

Foundation type: Public charity
Purpose: Scholarships to local high school seniors of Houston, TX for postsecondary education.
Financial data: Year ended 06/30/2012. Assets, $836,608 (M); Expenditures, $353,648; Total giving, $148,600; Grants to individuals, totaling $148,600.
Fields of interest: Higher education.
Type of support: Scholarships—to individuals.
Application information: Applications accepted. Application form required.
  Applicants should submit the following:
    1) Transcripts
    2) GPA
    3) Financial information
  Additional information: Application should also include college acceptance letter. Funds are made payable to the educational institution on behalf of the student. Students should

contact their high school counselors for application information.
Program description:
  Scholarships: The fund awards scholarships to local high school seniors who demonstrate at least average ability in their scholastic achievements and show qualities of strong character and determination. Students must be a sophomore or junior currently attending an Independent School District, Private, or Charter school within Harris or Fort Bend counties.
EIN: 760534967

8925
Lowe Syndrome Association
P.O. Box 864346
Plano, TX 75086-4346 (972) 733-1338
Contact: Debbie Jacobs, Pres.
E-mail: info@lowesyndrome.org; URL: http://www.lowesyndrome.org

Foundation type: Public charity
Purpose: Research grants for the study of achieving a better understanding of the metabolic basis of Lowe syndrome; or developing a better understanding of, and/or better treatments for, the major complications of Lowe syndrome. Awards are generally granted between $20,000 and $40,000.
Publications: Application guidelines; Informational brochure.
Financial data: Year ended 12/31/2012. Assets, $355,120 (M); Expenditures, $62,852; Total giving, $50,000; Grants to individuals, 2 grants totaling $50,000 (high: $25,000, low: $25,000).
Fields of interest: Diseases (rare); Diseases (rare) research.
Type of support: Research.
Application information: Applications accepted.
  Additional information: Applications only accepted during the association's call for proposals; requests that fall outside of the RFP process are generally not accepted.
Program description:
  Clinical Research Projects: One-year grants of up to $25,000 will be awarded for projects aimed at promoting a better understanding of the metabolic basis of Lowe syndrome and/or developing a better understanding of and improved treatments for major complications associated with the disease. Researchers of all types are eligible, including but not limited to those affiliated with universities, hospitals, and other nonprofit organizations.
EIN: 311160328

8926
Lubbock Area Foundation, Inc.
2509 80th St.
Lubbock, TX 79423 (806) 762-8061
Contact: Kathleen Stocco, Exec. Dir.; For grants: Tami Swoboda, Dir., Progs. and Comms.
FAX: (806) 762-8551;
E-mail: contact@lubbockareafoundation.org;
Additional E-mail: kathy@lubbockareafoundation.org; Grant inquiry E-mail: tami@lubbockareafoundation.org;
URL: http://www.lubbockareafoundation.org

Foundation type: Community foundation
Purpose: Scholarships for higher education to residents of Lubbock, TX, and the surrounding South Plains counties.
Publications: Application guidelines; Annual report; Financial statement; Grants list; Informational brochure; Newsletter.
Financial data: Year ended 12/31/2011. Assets, $26,026,423 (M); Expenditures, $1,368,251;

Total giving, $820,937; Grants to individuals, 72 grants totaling $124,265.
Fields of interest: Vocational education, post-secondary; Higher education; Graduate/professional education; Nursing school/education; Engineering school/education; Health sciences school/education.
Type of support: Scholarships—to individuals; Support to graduates or students of specific schools; Undergraduate support.
Application information: Applications accepted. Application form required. Application form available on the grantmaker's web site.
  Deadline(s): Varies
  Additional information: See web site for a complete listing of scholarships and additional application information.
Program description:
  Scholarships: The foundation administers various scholarship funds established by donors. Each scholarship has its own unique set of eligibility criteria, including academic achievement, financial need, and areas of study such as nursing, physical sciences, engineering, and law. In all cases, scholarship payments are made directly to the educational institution and can be used for tuition, fees and books only. The application process will vary depending on whether recipients are chosen by the foundation's committee or by an external scholarship committee. See web site for additional information.
EIN: 751709180

8927
The Sam J. Lucas, Jr. Foundation
1929 Allen Pkwy., 9th Fl.
Houston, TX 77019-2506

Foundation type: Operating foundation
Purpose: Scholarships to employees of SCI, their spouses, and their children to further their education.
Financial data: Year ended 12/31/2012. Assets, $10,229 (M); Expenditures, $20,525; Total giving, $15,500; Grants to individuals, 29 grants totaling $15,500 (high: $1,000, low: $250).
Fields of interest: Higher education; Scholarships/financial aid.
Type of support: Employee-related scholarships.
Application information: Applications accepted. Application form required.
  Send request by: Mail
  Deadline(s): Feb. 1
  Final notification: Applicants notified by the end of July
  Applicants should submit the following:
    1) Class rank
    2) Letter(s) of recommendation
    3) Transcripts
    4) SAT
    5) GPA
    6) ACT
    7) Essay
EIN: 760066431

8928
Charles & Nancy Oden Luce Trust
c/o Bank of America, N.A.
P.O. Box 831041
Dallas, TX 75283-1041
Application address: c/o Financial Aid Officer, Umatilla Reservation, 4611 Ti'Mine Way Pendleton, OR 97801

Foundation type: Independent foundation

Purpose: Scholarships to worthy, financially needy members of the federated tribes of the Umatilla Indian Reservation, OR, who wish to obtain a liberal arts, professional, or vocational education.
Financial data: Year ended 12/31/2012. Assets, $267,759 (M); Expenditures, $13,609; Total giving, $9,156.
Fields of interest: Vocational education; Higher education; Native Americans/American Indians.
Type of support: Undergraduate support.
Application information: Applications accepted.
    Deadline(s): None
    Additional information: Contact the Umatilla
        Tribal scholarship committee for additional
        guidelines.
EIN: 916026999

8929
The Luling Foundation
523 S. Mulberry
Luling, TX   78648-2940   (830) 875-2438
URL: http://www.lulingfoundation.org/

Foundation type: Operating foundation
Purpose: Scholarships to graduating high school seniors who are residents of Caldwell, Gonzales, or Guadalupe counties, TX, for studies toward agricultural related and healthcare degrees.
Publications: Application guidelines; Informational brochure; Occasional report.
Financial data: Year ended 12/31/2012. Assets, $4,727,645 (M); Expenditures, $635,953; Total giving, $18,800; Grants to individuals, 15 grants totaling $14,000 (high: $1,000, low: $500).
Fields of interest: Health care; Agriculture.
Type of support: Undergraduate support.
Application information: Applications accepted. Application form required.
    Initial approach: Letter
    Deadline(s): Mar. 31
EIN: 741143102

8930
M. Max Crisp Stewart Scholarship Foundation
1980 Post Oak Blvd., Ste. 800
Houston, TX   77056-3899   (713) 625-8076
Contact: Debbie Wilson, Pres.

Foundation type: Company-sponsored foundation
Purpose: Scholarships to children of employees of Stewart Information Services Corp. and its subsidiaries to attend an accredited state college.
Financial data: Year ended 12/31/2012. Assets, $281 (M); Expenditures, $37,570; Total giving, $37,500; Grants to individuals, 15 grants totaling $27,500 (high: $2,500, low: $2,500).
Fields of interest: College.
Type of support: Employee-related scholarships.
Application information: Applications accepted. Application form required.
    Deadline(s): Jan. 31
Company name: Stewart Information Services Corporation
EIN: 760462905

8931
Minnie L. Maffett Scholarship Trust
c/o Bank of America, N.A.
P.O. Box 831041
Dallas, TX   75283-1041   (214) 768-3490
Contact: Jaynell Dalby, Admin.
Application address: P.O. Box 750181, Dallas, TX 75275-0181

Foundation type: Independent foundation
Purpose: Scholarships to TX students to pursue pre-med or pre-nursing undergraduate degrees. Recipients must attend accredited colleges and universities, state medical college, or an AMA-approved nursing school in TX. Preference is given to residents of Limestone County, TX; Preference that at least one recipient is African American.
Financial data: Year ended 04/30/2013. Assets, $1,473,764 (M); Expenditures, $40,593; Total giving, $20,250; Grants to individuals, 21 grants totaling $20,250 (high: $1,250, low: $750).
Fields of interest: Medical school/education; Nursing school/education; African Americans/ Blacks.
Type of support: Undergraduate support.
Application information: Application form required.
    Deadline(s): Apr. 1
    Additional information: Application should
        include transcripts.
EIN: 756037885

8932
Agnes T. Maguire Trust
P.O. Box 227237
Dallax, TX   75222-7237   (225) 332-3112
Application address: c/o JP Morgan Chase Trust Dept.,P.O Box 912190, Baton Rouge,LA 70821

Foundation type: Independent foundation
Purpose: Student loans to young girls who are residents of LA, pursuing a profession after high school graduation.
Publications: Application guidelines.
Financial data: Year ended 12/31/2012. Assets, $2,582,806 (M); Expenditures, $120,546; Total giving, $65,644.
Fields of interest: Women.
Type of support: Student loans—to individuals; Technical education support; Undergraduate support.
Application information: Applications accepted. Application form required.
    Initial approach: Letter
    Deadline(s): July 1
    Final notification: 6 weeks after deadline
EIN: 726021532

8933
Mallard-Turner Memorial Scholarship Trust
P.O. Box 1908
Uvalde, TX   78802-1908   (830) 278-6231
Contact: Robert K. Baen, Exec. V.P.

Foundation type: Independent foundation
Purpose: Scholarships to one or more qualified and worthy individuals in pursuit of a college education, preferably for attendance at Southwest Texas Junior College, Uvalde, TX, or the Sul Ross State University Rio Grande College, Uvalde, TX.
Financial data: Year ended 12/31/2011. Assets, $871,492 (M); Expenditures, $25,312; Total giving, $21,800; Grants to individuals, 20 grants totaling $21,800 (high: $1,090, low: $1,090).
Fields of interest: Higher education.
Type of support: Support to graduates or students of specific schools.
Application information: Applications accepted. Application form required.
    Deadline(s): Apr. 1
    Additional information: Application forms
        provided by Southwest Texas Junior College.
        Grades will be considered in deciding to

continue aid to a student at the end of each semester.
EIN: 746384709

8934
Ed T. Malloy Foundation
P.O. Box 1755
Orange, TX   77631-1755   (409) 883-3567

Foundation type: Public charity
Purpose: Scholarships to students for higher education in the Orange, TX area.
Financial data: Year ended 09/30/2011. Assets, $6,345,484 (M); Expenditures, $346,136; Total giving, $283,137; Grants to individuals, totaling $3,000.
Fields of interest: Higher education.
Type of support: Scholarships—to individuals.
Application information: Contact foundation for scholarship guidelines.
EIN: 760078695

8935
Teresa Maness Educational Foundation
101 Simonton
Conroe, TX   77301-2840

Foundation type: Independent foundation
Purpose: Scholarships to high school seniors of the Conroe, TX area for postsecondary education.
Financial data: Year ended 12/31/2012. Assets, $1,422,381 (M); Expenditures, $82,540; Total giving, $66,833; Grants to individuals, 30 grants totaling $66,833 (high: $8,000, low: $1,000).
Fields of interest: Higher education.
Type of support: Scholarships—to individuals.
Application information: Contact your school guidance office for application information.
EIN: 416556842

8936
Marti Foundation
1501-D N. Main St.
Cleburne, TX   76033-3876   (817) 558-0079
Contact: Hoylene Harris, Mgr.

Foundation type: Independent foundation
Purpose: Undergraduate scholarships and student loans, and graduate student loans to residents of TX for study at approved institutions. Preference is given to residents of Johnson County.
Financial data: Year ended 12/31/2012. Assets, $14,503,553 (M); Expenditures, $671,961; Total giving, $668,954; Grants to individuals, 278 grants totaling $661,389.
Type of support: Student loans—to individuals; Graduate support; Undergraduate support.
Application information: Applications accepted. Application form required.
    Deadline(s): 60 days prior to the beginning of any
        semester
EIN: 752265837

8937
Mary Kay Foundation
(formerly Mary Kay Ash Charitable Foundation)
P.O. Box 799044
Dallas, TX   75379-9044   (972) 687-6300
Contact: Michael Lunceford, Pres.
E-mail: mkcares@marykayfoundation.org;
Application address: P.O. Box 799044, Dallas, TX 75379-9044; toll-free tel.: (877) 652-2737;
URL: http://www.mkacf.org

Foundation type: Public charity
Purpose: Grants towards translational research in ovarian, uterine, breast, or cervical cancer.
Publications: Application guidelines.
Financial data: Year ended 12/31/2011. Assets, $14,990,850 (M); Expenditures, $4,967,314; Total giving, $4,857,562.
Fields of interest: Cancer research; Medical research; Women.
Type of support: Research.
Application information:
  Initial approach: Letter
  Deadline(s): Feb. 13
Program description:
  Cancer Research Grants: Grants of up to $100,000 each are available towards translational research in ovarian, uterine, breast, or cervical cancer. Grants are for two years. Applications must be submitted by one principal investigator, selected by the institution. Only one grant application will be accepted from each accredited medical school and schools of public health in the United States.
EIN: 752653742

8938

Masonic Home and School of Texas

338 Grapevine Hwy.
Hurst, TX 76054-2409 (817) 503-1500
Contact: Kasha Perkins, Exec. Dir.
FAX: (817) 503-1551; E-mail: info@mhstx.org;
Toll-free tel.: (877) 203-9111; mailing address:
P.O. Box 55189, Hurst, TX 76054-5189; E-mail For Kasha Perkins: kasha@mhstx.org; URL: http://www.mhstx.org

Foundation type: Public charity
Purpose: Scholarships to qualified high school graduates of Masonic Home and School of Texas or Masonic Home Independent School District for continuing education at an accredited college or university.
Publications: Application guidelines.
Financial data: Year ended 06/30/2012. Assets, $83,740,724 (M); Expenditures, $2,840,288; Total giving, $34,644; Grants to individuals, totaling $34,644.
Fields of interest: Higher education.
Type of support: Support to graduates or students of specific schools.
Application information: Application form required.
  Send request by: Mail
  Deadline(s): July 1 for Frank C. Rockabrand Scholarships; none for Masonic Home and School of Texas Scholarships
  Applicants should submit the following:
    1) Letter(s) of recommendation
    2) Transcripts
    3) GPA
Program descriptions:
Frank C. Rockabrand Scholarships: Scholarships are available to students who have attended an organization-related school, to further their educational careers. Applicants must be high-school graduates who reside in western Texas (defined as cities west and along Interstate 35)
Masonic Home and School of Texas Scholarships: Scholarships are available to Texas-based high school graduates who have attended an organization-affiliated school.
EIN: 751528075

8939

M.L. & Jessie Star Mayfield Foundation

27407 E. Fairway Oaks Dr.
Huffman, TX 77336
Contact: Charles F. Presley

Foundation type: Independent foundation
Purpose: Scholarships initially provided as interest bearing loans to residents of TX or LA for attendance at colleges in TX or LA.
Financial data: Year ended 12/31/2013. Assets, $467,971 (M); Expenditures, $21,671; Total giving, $11,739; Grants to individuals, 2 grants totaling $6,309 (high: $3,820, low: $2,489).
Fields of interest: Higher education.
Type of support: Scholarships—to individuals; Student loans—to individuals.
Application information:
  Deadline(s): May 15
  Additional information: Loan will be converted to a grant upon proof of a GPA of 2.5 or better. Applicants must demonstrate financial need by submitting a copy of parents' and personal tax returns for three years.
EIN: 760133546

8940

McCaulay Memorial Masonic Fund

4217 Baybrook Pl.
Midland, TX 79707

Foundation type: Independent foundation
Purpose: Scholarships to former students of the Masonic Home and School of Texas.
Financial data: Year ended 12/31/2012. Assets, $70,982 (M); Expenditures, $62,116; Total giving, $59,500; Grants to individuals, 16 grants totaling $59,500 (high: $7,000, low: $1,000).
Type of support: Scholarships—to individuals.
Application information: Applications not accepted.
EIN: 752443043

8941

Dorsey McCrory Trust for Gonzales County, Texas

919 Congress
Austin, TX 78701 (830) 788-7151

Foundation type: Independent foundation
Purpose: Scholarships to financially needy students from the Gonzales County Commissioner's Precinct No. 2, which includes Waelder, TX, for higher education.
Financial data: Year ended 10/31/2012. Assets, $706,826 (M); Expenditures, $25,995; Total giving, $22,385; Grants to individuals, 16 grants totaling $22,385 (high: $1,947, low: $343).
Type of support: Scholarships—to individuals.
Application information: Applications accepted.
  Initial approach: Letter
  Deadline(s): None
  Additional information: Application must include financial information, evidence of college enrollment, and residency in the Waelder area.
EIN: 746414650

8942

McDaniel Charitable Foundation

P.O. Box 2968
Texas City, TX 77592-2968
FAX: (409) 944-0120;
E-mail: contactus@mcdanielcharitablefoundation.org; URL: http://mcdanielcharitablefoundation.org/

Foundation type: Independent foundation
Purpose: Through the Galveston County Scholarship Program, the foundation provides scholarships based on both need and merit to students who were residents of Galveston County, TX.
Financial data: Year ended 12/31/2012. Assets, $7,550,582 (M); Expenditures, $1,420,875; Total giving, $689,600; Grants to individuals, 38 grants totaling $86,500 (high: $6,000, low: $1,000).
Type of support: Scholarships—to individuals.
Application information: Application form required. Application form available on the grantmaker's web site.
  Initial approach: Application
  Deadline(s): June 1
  Applicants should submit the following:
    1) Financial information
    2) Transcripts
    3) Essay
Program descriptions:
Galveston County Scholarship Program (GCSP): The foundation's Directors established this program to provide scholarships based on both need and merit to students who were residents of Galveston County, TX, at the time of their high school graduation. Scholarship recipients are able to take their award with them to any Texas college. The foundation is currently not accepting new applications for this program. Scholars who currently participate in the program may reapply by completing and submitting a renewal application. See web site for details and renewal application forms.
Lyons Scholarship Program: This program provides funding for four-year need-based scholarships to selected eligible Galveston County students who wish to pursue a degree at Texas A&M University at Galveston. The current program accepts students from all majors. See web site for additional information.
EIN: 760538313

8943

Dan & Dottie McDonald Family Foundation

P.O. Box 33728
Fort Worth, TX 76162-3728 (817) 877-1755

Foundation type: Independent foundation
Purpose: Scholarships up to $6,000 annually for up to four years to members of or involved in the boys and girls club of greater Fort Worth, TX.
Financial data: Year ended 12/31/2012. Assets, $492,653 (M); Expenditures, $22,475; Total giving, $19,276; Grants to individuals, 9 grants totaling $19,276 (high: $4,217, low: $857).
Fields of interest: Higher education.
Type of support: Scholarships—to individuals.
Application information: Applications accepted. Application form required.
  Deadline(s): Feb.
  Applicants should submit the following:
    1) Transcripts
    2) Essay
  Additional information: Applicant must have a GPA of 2.5 out of 4.0 maintained while in

college. Student should be involved in his/her community and possess leadership potential.
EIN: 200610433

8944
McGovern Fund

(formerly McGovern Fund for the Behavioral Sciences)
2211 Norfolk St., Ste. 900
Houston, TX 77098-4062
Contact: Kathrine McGovern, Pres. and V.P.

Foundation type: Independent foundation
Purpose: Scholarships to TX students who have participated in a UIL Academic State Meet during their high school careers.
Financial data: Year ended 11/30/2011. Assets, $227,884 (M); Expenditures, $3,491; Total giving, $0.
Type of support: Undergraduate support.
Application information: Applications accepted. Application form required. Application form available on the grantmaker's web site.
Deadline(s): June 1
Final notification: Applicants notified no later than July 31
Applicants should submit the following:
1) Financial information
2) ACT
3) SAT
4) Transcripts
5) Letter(s) of recommendation
Additional information: See web site for complete list of programs.
EIN: 742086867

8945
The D. Lynd & Terri K. McGowan Foundation

5555 Del Monte Dr., Unit 1007
Houston, TX 77056-4118
Contact: Nora M. McGowan, Pres.

Foundation type: Independent foundation
Purpose: Scholarships to individuals with preference given to those studying finance or education; employees of Investment & Financial Services, Inc. and the children of those employees; and students at the University of Houston, TX or Rice University, TX.
Financial data: Year ended 06/30/2013. Assets, $614,742 (M); Expenditures, $66,803; Total giving, $64,484; Grants to individuals, 5 grants totaling $59,484 (high: $20,226, low: $9,314).
Type of support: Employee-related scholarships; Support to graduates or students of specific schools; Undergraduate support.
Application information: Applications accepted. Application form not required.
Initial approach: Letter
Deadline(s): May 15
Applicants should submit the following:
1) Letter(s) of recommendation
2) Resume
3) Transcripts
Additional information: Application should also include examples of academic work and extracurricular activities.
EIN: 760308875

8946
The MCH Foundation, Inc.

101 E. Park Blvd., Ste. 1039
Plano, TX 75074   (972) 509-0222
Contact: Gary R. Hoskins, Secy.-Treas.

Foundation type: Operating foundation
Purpose: Research grants to individuals for post-graduate study of East Asian textiles, art and artifacts.
Financial data: Year ended 05/31/2013. Assets, $9,770,108 (M); Expenditures, $226,929; Total giving, $19,500; Grant to an individual, 1 grant totaling $6,500.
Fields of interest: Research; Art history; History/archaeology.
International interests: Asia.
Type of support: Research; Postgraduate support.
Application information: Applications accepted.
Deadline(s): None
Additional information: Application must include a resume, academic qualification and intended field of study.
EIN: 752359010

8947
Elmer McKenney Scholarship Trust

P.O. Box 701
Abilene, TX 79604-0701
Contact: Jeri Spiker, Counselor
Address: 2800 N. 6th St., Abilene, TX 79603

Foundation type: Independent foundation
Purpose: Scholarships to graduating seniors from Abilene High School, Cooper High School, and Haskell High School, TX, for attendance at junior or senior colleges or universities.
Financial data: Year ended 07/31/2013. Assets, $247,468 (M); Expenditures, $10,578; Total giving, $4,994.
Fields of interest: Higher education.
Type of support: Support to graduates or students of specific schools; Undergraduate support.
Application information: Application form required.
Deadline(s): Apr. 29
Applicants should submit the following:
1) Transcripts
2) Letter(s) of recommendation
Additional information: Applicant must have a need for financial assistance in order to continue education.
EIN: 756319992

8948
Bruce McMillan, Jr. Foundation Inc.

P.O. Box 9
Overton, TX 75684-0009   (903) 834-3148
Contact: Todd Meadows, Pres.

Foundation type: Independent foundation
Purpose: Scholarships to qualified graduates of eight high schools in the immediate Overton, TX, area.
Publications: Application guidelines.
Financial data: Year ended 06/30/2013. Assets, $19,830,479 (M); Expenditures, $827,820; Total giving, $353,449; Grants to individuals, 15 grants totaling $84,689 (high: $15,000, low: $1,000).
Fields of interest: Higher education; Scholarships/financial aid.
Type of support: Support to graduates or students of specific schools; Undergraduate support.
Application information: Application form required.
Initial approach: Letter
Deadline(s): Apr. 15

Additional information: Interviews required during spring break period of respective high schools.
Program description:
Scholarship Program: The foundation provides scholarship support to qualified high school seniors attending the following high schools within an approximate 15-mile radius of Overton, TX: West Rusk High School, Overton High School, Henderson High School, Leverett Chapel High School, Kilgore High School, Troup High School, Arp High School, and Carlisle High School.
EIN: 750945924

8949
Beth R. Mead Educational Trust

P.O Box 2020
Tyler, TX 75710-2020   (903) 665-2567
Contact: Jesse M. Deware IV, Tr.; Martha Tomlinson, Tr.
Application address: P.O. Box 486, Jefferson, TX 75657

Foundation type: Independent foundation
Purpose: Scholarships to residents of Marion, Harrison, Cass, Morris, Gregg, and Upshur counties, TX for attendance at accredited institutions.
Financial data: Year ended 09/30/2013. Assets, $517,928 (M); Expenditures, $24,091; Total giving, $11,160; Grants to individuals, 11 grants totaling $11,160 (high: $1,750, low: $210).
Fields of interest: Higher education.
Type of support: Scholarships—to individuals.
Application information: Applications accepted. Application form required.
Applicants should submit the following:
1) Letter(s) of recommendation
2) Photograph
3) Transcripts
Additional information: Application must also include a handwritten letter regarding educational field of interest, academic and career goals and an outline of financial need.
EIN: 756310255

8950
The Media Religion and Culture Project

1402 Banks St.
Houston, TX 77006-6018   (713) 524-1628
Contact: Paul Edison-Swift, Treas.

Foundation type: Operating foundation
Purpose: Fellowships focusing primarily on applicants from the Catholic community in Asia-Pacific and Eastern Europe.
Financial data: Year ended 09/30/2012. Assets, $69,362 (M); Expenditures, $21,080; Total giving, $14,774; Grants to individuals, 2 grants totaling $3,294 (high: $2,684, low: $610).
Fields of interest: Education; Christian agencies & churches.
International interests: Asia; Eastern Europe; Europe.
Type of support: Fellowships.
Application information: Contact organization for application deadline and guidelines.
EIN: 201770035

8951
The Mehta Family Foundation
(formerly Bhupat and Jyott Mehta Family Foundation)
20018 Chateau Bend Dr.
Katy, TX   77450-5149
Contact: Bernard Luksich, Exec. Dir.
Application address: c/o Janet Bertolino, U.S. National Bank, 2201 Market St., Galveston, TX 77553, tel.: (409) 770-7165
E-mail: Bernie@MehtaFamilyFoundation.Org

Foundation type: Independent foundation
Purpose: Student loans to TX residents for full-time study at an accredited college or university.
Financial data: Year ended 09/30/2013. Assets, $21,060,532 (M); Expenditures, $953,827; Total giving, $824,671.
Fields of interest: Higher education.
Type of support: Student loans—to individuals; Undergraduate support.
Application information: Application form required.
Initial approach: Letter or telephone
Deadline(s): Jan. 1 to Mar. 31
Additional information: Applicants must be U.S. citizens.
EIN: 760522455

8952
Mensa Education and Research Foundation
1229 Corporate Dr. W.
Arlington, TX   76006-6103   (817) 607-5577
FAX: (817) 649-5232;
E-mail: info@mensafoundation.org; Toll-free tel.: (800) 66-MENSA; URL: http://www.mensafoundation.org

Foundation type: Public charity
Purpose: Scholarships to students enrolled in a degree program in an accredited U.S. institution of higher learning. Scholarships for foreign students enrolled at colleges or universities in the U.S.
Publications: Application guidelines; Annual report.
Financial data: Year ended 03/31/2012. Assets, $2,782,448 (M); Expenditures, $329,527; Total giving, $73,524; Grants to individuals, totaling $73,524.
Fields of interest: Vocational education, post-secondary; Higher education.
Type of support: Scholarships—to individuals; Foreign applicants.
Application information: Applications accepted.
Send request by: Online
Deadline(s): Jan. 15
Additional information: See web site for additional application guidelines.
Program descriptions:
International Scholarship Program: The program is intended to provide scholarships for foreign students enrolled at colleges or universities in the U.S. Eligibility is limited to Mensa members (except American Mensa) or their children age 25 or younger.
U.S. Scholarship Program: The scholarship program bases its awards totally on essays written by the applicants. Consideration is not given to grades, academic program or financial need. Applicants must be a resident of a participating American Mensa Local Group's area and be enrolled in a degree program in an accredited U.S. institution of higher learning during the academic year following the application date. Applicants need not be Mensa members.
EIN: 752857248

8953
The Vandal and Winifred Mercer Texas A & M Educational Foundation
c/o Frost National Bank, Trust Dept.
P.O. Box 8210
Galveston, TX   77553-8210   (409) 770-5665

Foundation type: Operating foundation
Purpose: Educational loans to graduates of TX high schools for attendance at Texas A&M University.
Publications: Informational brochure (including application guidelines).
Financial data: Year ended 12/31/2012. Assets, $1,474,901 (M); Expenditures, $112,295; Total giving, $77,500; Loans to individuals, 31 loans totaling $77,500.
Fields of interest: Higher education.
Type of support: Student loans—to individuals; Support to graduates or students of specific schools; Undergraduate support.
Application information: Application form required.
Initial approach: Letter or telephone
Deadline(s): Mar. 31
Applicants should submit the following:
1) Financial information
2) Essay
Additional information: Application should also include two letters of reference.
EIN: 760472391

8954
Methodist Healthcare Ministries of South Texas, Inc.
4507 Medical Dr.
San Antonio, TX   78229-4401   (210) 692-0234
FAX: (210) 614-7563; E-mail: info@mhm.org;
Toll-free tel.: (800) 959-6673; URL: http://www.mhm.org

Foundation type: Public charity
Purpose: Scholarships to individuals enrolled in an accredited nursing program in San Antonio, TX. Scholarships to graduating high school seniors in TX, who plan to pursue a degree in healthcare.
Publications: Annual report; Informational brochure; Newsletter; Program policy statement.
Financial data: Year ended 12/31/2011. Assets, $666,859,502 (M); Expenditures, $68,594,853; Total giving, $29,056,334; Grants to individuals, totaling $53,825.
Fields of interest: Nursing school/education; Health care.
Type of support: Scholarships—to individuals.
Application information: Applications accepted. Application form required.
EIN: 741287016

8955
Methodist Hospital
6565 Fannin No. GB240
Houston, TX   77030-2707   (713) 790-3311
Contact: Marc L. Boom, Pres. and C.E.O.
URL: http://www.methodisthealth.com/

Foundation type: Public charity
Purpose: Medical fellowships to study at Texas Medical Center campus.
Financial data: Year ended 12/31/2011. Assets, $4,927,064,658 (M); Expenditures, $1,173,242,897; Total giving, $6,482,892; Grants to individuals, totaling $18,600.
Fields of interest: Medical research.
Type of support: Fellowships.
Application information: Applications accepted. Application form required.

Initial approach: Letter
Deadline(s): Varies
Additional information: See web site for eligibility guidelines.
EIN: 741180155

8956
Charles Meyer Foundation
P.O. Box 179
Galveston, TX   77553-0179   (409) 765-5796

Foundation type: Independent foundation
Purpose: Grants to underprivileged Jewish residents of Galveston, TX.
Financial data: Year ended 05/31/2013. Assets, $502,880 (M); Expenditures, $27,814; Total giving, $22,400; Grants to individuals, 4 grants totaling $22,400 (high: $12,600, low: $500).
Fields of interest: Jewish agencies & synagogues; Economically disadvantaged.
Type of support: Grants for special needs.
Application information: Applications accepted.
Deadline(s): None
Additional information: Applications by letter outlining financial need and indicating Jewish faith.
EIN: 746035534

8957
Midland ISD Educational Foundation
P.O. Box 73
Midland, TX   79702-0073   (432) 689-1038
FAX: (432) 689-1087; URL: http://www.midlandisd.net/domain/57

Foundation type: Public charity
Purpose: Scholarships to graduating seniors of Midland, TX high schools pursuing a baccalaureate degree in education.
Financial data: Year ended 12/31/2011. Assets, $492,805 (M); Expenditures, $323,818; Total giving, $260,922; Grants to individuals, totaling $61,900.
Fields of interest: Teacher school/education.
Type of support: Scholarships—to individuals.
Application information: Applications accepted. Application form required.
Send request by: Mail
Deadline(s): Apr. 1
Applicants should submit the following:
1) Transcripts
2) GPA
EIN: 752330628

8958
Millar Scholarship Fund
c/o Bank of America, N.A.
P.O Box 831041
Dallas, TX   75283-1041   (503) 667-3186
Application address: Reynolds High School, Scholarship Coordinator, 1698 S.W. Cherry Park Rd., Troutdale, OR 97060-1481

Foundation type: Independent foundation
Purpose: Scholarships to graduating seniors of Reynolds High School, OR for postsecondary education at colleges or universities in OR.
Financial data: Year ended 06/30/2013. Assets, $355,500 (M); Expenditures, $23,421; Total giving, $17,900.
Fields of interest: Vocational education; Business school/education; Nursing school/education.
Type of support: Support to graduates or students of specific schools; Undergraduate support.

Application information: Applications accepted. Application form required. Interview required.
  Deadline(s): Mar. 30
  Applicants should submit the following:
    1) Transcripts
    2) SAT
    3) Financial information
    4) GPA
  Additional information: Application forms can be obtained from the guidance counselor's office.
EIN: 936054074

8959
The M. W. and Fair Miller Foundation, Inc.
220 W. Sam Rayburn Dr.
Bonham, TX   75418   (903) 583-5715

Foundation type: Independent foundation
Purpose: Scholarships to residents of Bonham, TX, and assistance with health care benefits to needy individuals of Fannin county, TX.
Financial data: Year ended 12/31/2012. Assets, $1,408,239 (M); Expenditures, $20,685; Total giving, $10,159; Grants to individuals, 2 grants totaling $4,200 (high: $2,200, low: $2,000).
Fields of interest: Higher education; Economically disadvantaged.
Type of support: Scholarships—to individuals; Grants for special needs.
Application information:
  Initial approach: Letter
  Deadline(s): None
  Additional information: Letter must address physical handicap of individual needs for assistance.
EIN: 752260316

8960
Arthur M. Miller Fund
c/o Bank of America, N.A.
P.O. Box 831041
Dallas, TX   75283-1041   (800) 257-0332
Application address: 411 N. Akard St., 7th Fl., Dallas, TX 75201-3307

Foundation type: Independent foundation
Purpose: Grants to residents of KS studying or practicing medicine or related fields at accredited institutions.
Financial data: Year ended 12/31/2012. Assets, $396,352 (M); Expenditures, $21,348; Total giving, $16,200; Grants to individuals, 3 grants totaling $16,200 (high: $10,000, low: $1,200).
Fields of interest: Medical school/education.
Type of support: Graduate support.
Application information: Application form required.
  Deadline(s): None
  Applicants should submit the following:
    1) Transcripts
    2) Letter(s) of recommendation
    3) Financial information
  Additional information: Application must also include personal statement; Interviews may be required.
EIN: 481077714

8961
Lila Miller Scholarship Trust
c/o Bank of America, N.A.
P.O. Box 831041
Dallas, TX   75283-1041   (509) 573-7001
Contact: Sharon Surbrook
Application address: 104 N. 4th Ave., Yakima, WA 98902-2636, tel.: (509) 573-7001

Foundation type: Independent foundation
Purpose: Scholarships to students of the three public high schools in Yakima, WA. Applicants must be attending a college, junior college or trade school in the state of WA.
Financial data: Year ended 12/31/2011. Assets, $230,582 (M); Expenditures, $14,651; Total giving, $13,318.
Fields of interest: Higher education.
Type of support: Support to graduates or students of specific schools.
Application information: Applications accepted. Application form required.
  Deadline(s): Apr.
EIN: 916025597

8962
Nettie Millhollon Educational Trust Estate
P.O. Box 643
Stanton, TX   79782-0643
FAX: (432) 756-3956;
E-mail: millhollon@millhollon.com; URL: http://www.millhollon.com

Foundation type: Independent foundation
Purpose: Student loans to financially needy residents of TX, who are under the age of 25.
Financial data: Year ended 06/30/2013. Assets, $5,773,232 (M); Expenditures, $115,436; Total giving, $0.
Type of support: Student loans—to individuals.
Application information: Application form required. Interview required.
  Initial approach: Letter or telephone
  Deadline(s): July 1 for fall semester and Jan. 2 for spring semester
EIN: 756024639

8963
Alfred G. & Elma M. Milotte Scholarship Fund
c/o Bank of America, N.A.
P.O. Box 831041
Dallas, TX   75283-1041   (800) 832-9071
Application address: 1201 Main St., 8th Fl., Dallas, TX 75202
E-mail: info@milotte.org; URL: http://www.milotte.org

Foundation type: Independent foundation
Purpose: Graduate and undergraduate scholarships to college students who are residents of WA for at least five years and have at least a 3.0 GPA and an interest in wilderness areas.
Financial data: Year ended 03/31/2013. Assets, $952,025 (M); Expenditures, $48,492; Total giving, $37,604; Grants to individuals, 7 grants totaling $37,604.
Fields of interest: Arts; Natural resources; Environmental education.
Type of support: Graduate support; Undergraduate support.
Application information: Application form required. Application form available on the grantmaker's web site.
  Send request by: Mail
  Deadline(s): Mar. 31

Applicants should submit the following:
    1) Transcripts
    2) Work samples
  Additional information: Application should also include two letters of reference.
Program description:
  Scholarship Program: A one year scholarship of up to $4,000 to individuals who share their enthusiasm for exploring, chronicling and spreading the magnificence of the wilderness through artistic communication. The scholarship is for post high school education, in a course of study reflecting this devotion.
EIN: 916307731

8964
Minyard Founders Foundation
P.O. Box 679
Gainesville, TX   76241   (940) 668-2220

Foundation type: Independent foundation
Purpose: Scholarships only to full and part-time employees and family for higher education.
Financial data: Year ended 12/31/2011. Assets, $268,260 (M); Expenditures, $18,914; Total giving, $17,250.
Type of support: Employee-related scholarships.
Application information: Contact foundation for current application deadline/guidelines.
EIN: 752368233

8965
Mission Metroplex, Inc.
210 W. South St.
Arlington, TX   76010-7134   (817) 277-6620
Contact: Tillie Burgin, Exec. Dir.
FAX: (817) 277-3388;
E-mail: mission@missionarlington.org; URL: http://www.missionarlington.org

Foundation type: Public charity
Purpose: Assistance to homeless individuals, single parent, and low-income families of the Arlington, TX area with food, clothing, employment, child care, transportation, financial and medical needs.
Publications: Annual report; Financial statement; Informational brochure; Multi-year report; Newsletter.
Financial data: Year ended 12/31/2011. Assets, $15,469,546 (M); Expenditures, $3,066,537; Total giving, $683,505; Grants to individuals, totaling $683,505.
Fields of interest: Economically disadvantaged.
Type of support: Grants for special needs.
Application information: Applications accepted.
  Initial approach: Contact organization by telephone
EIN: 752354962

8966
Montgomery County Community Foundation
1400 Woodloch Forest Dr., Ste. 300-12
The Woodlands, TX   77380   (281) 363-8158
Contact: Shannon L. Kidd, Exec. Dir.
FAX: (281) 363-8191;
E-mail: skidd@mccfoundation.org; URL: http://www.mccfoundation.org

Foundation type: Community foundation
Purpose: Scholarship to assist young adults from Montgomery County, TX in reaching their personal goals and dreams through higher education or technical training.

Publications: Annual report.
Financial data: Year ended 12/31/2012. Assets, $4,332,100 (M); Expenditures, $190,065; Total giving, $113,513; Grants to individuals, 10 grants totaling $7,300.
Fields of interest: Vocational education, post-secondary; Higher education.
Type of support: Scholarships—to individuals.
Application information: Applications accepted. Application form required.
> *Deadline(s):* Varies
> *Additional information:* Students should contact their high school College and Career Counselor or the Financial Aid office of Lone Star College-Montgomery for application information. See web site for a complete listing of scholarships.
EIN: 760082098

8967
The Moody Foundation
2302 Post Office St., Ste. 704
Galveston, TX 77550-1936 (409) 797-1500
Contact: Allan Matthews, Grants Dir.
For scholarships: Samantha Seale, Scholarship Admin., tel.: (409) 797-1511,
e-mail: Samanthas@moodyf.org
FAX: (409) 763-5564; E-mail: info@themoodyf.org;
URL: http://www.moodyf.org

Foundation type: Independent foundation
Purpose: Scholarships to financially needy graduates of high schools in Galveston and Dallas counties, TX, who have a "B+" average. Recipients must attend colleges and universities in TX. Applicants must also be residents of Galveston or Dallas counties, TX.
Publications: Application guidelines; Annual report; Grants list.
Financial data: Year ended 12/31/2012. Assets, $1,241,224,220 (M); Expenditures, $56,639,329; Total giving, $50,007,071; Grants to individuals, totaling $371,325.
Fields of interest: Higher education; Scholarships/financial aid; Volunteer services; Economically disadvantaged.
Type of support: Support to graduates or students of specific schools; Undergraduate support.
Application information: Applications accepted. Application form required.
> *Initial approach:* Letter, telephone, or e-mail
> *Send request by:* Mail
> *Deadline(s):* 6 weeks prior to each board meeting; contact foundation for deadlines
> *Additional information:* Application must include family background, family finances, and scholastic achievement; Applications available only through high school counselors' office.
Program description:
> *Moody Scholars Program:* Applicants must be able to demonstrate high academic ability and some degree of financial need in order to pursue their higher education. To be eligible, the student must be in the top twenty-five percent of their graduating senior class. They also must have a minimum 88 GPA which is determined by the counseling staff. The funds are for undergraduate work only and must be used in the state of Texas. Approximately 75 students are awarded $2,000 per year. The Honor Scholars category of the program is currently only offered in Galveston County. The top ten seniors from each high school are submitted to the foundation by the counseling office. This is a one-time award of $1,000 which

may be directed by the student to their chosen Texas college or university.
EIN: 741403105

8968
Seth & Mabelle Moore Scholarship Trust
P.O. Box 111
Hamilton, TX 76531

Foundation type: Operating foundation
Purpose: Scholarships to graduating seniors of Hamilton High School, TX for postsecondary education.
Financial data: Year ended 12/31/2011. Assets, $197,514 (M); Expenditures, $10,739; Total giving, $10,700; Grants to individuals, 19 grants totaling $10,700 (high: $1,000, low: $400).
Fields of interest: Higher education.
Type of support: Support to graduates or students of specific schools.
Application information: Applications accepted. Application form required.
> *Deadline(s):* May 1
> *Additional information:* Contact the trust for additional application guidelines.
EIN: 742342842

8969
Hardy & Bess Morgan Citzenship Award Fund
P.O. Box 790
Lamesa, TX 79331 (806) 872-5461
Applicatiion address: c/o All Applicants P.O. Box 261 Lamesa, TX 79331

Foundation type: Operating foundation
Purpose: Citizenship awards by nomination only to graduating seniors from high schools in Dawson County, TX.
Financial data: Year ended 12/31/2011. Assets, $0 (M); Expenditures, $7,450; Total giving, $7,125; Grants to individuals, 10 grants totaling $7,125 (high: $1,175, low: $250).
Fields of interest: Higher education.
Type of support: Support to graduates or students of specific schools; Awards/prizes; Undergraduate support.
Application information: Applications accepted.
> *Initial approach:* Letter
> *Deadline(s):* Mar. 1
> *Additional information:* Application must include transcripts, record of nominee's classwork and achievements, and faculty testimonials and vote. Contact high school principals for nomination guidelines.
EIN: 759630846

8970
Morrison Trust
c/o Frost National Bank Trust Dept.
P.O. Box 2950
San Antonio, TX 78299-2950 (210) 220-4438

Foundation type: Independent foundation
Purpose: Grants to support research, scientific study, development of methods of treatment, and the improvement of existing methods of treating and preventing human sickness in the fields of nutrition, blood chemistry, and radionics and electricity, primarily in TX, CA and NM.
Financial data: Year ended 09/30/2012. Assets, $3,540,897 (M); Expenditures, $182,500; Total giving, $164,648; Grants to individuals, 4 grants totaling $164,648 (high: $50,000, low: $28,968).
Fields of interest: Institute; Nutrition.

Type of support: Research.
Application information:
> *Deadline(s):* July 1
> Applicants should submit the following:
> 1) Proposal
> 2) Budget Information
> *Additional information:* Application should also include name of sponsoring institution, individual performing research, summary of research, budget requests, and signature of sponsoring institution representative.
EIN: 746013340

8971
D. W. Morse Family Scholarship Fund
c/o Bank of America, N.A.
P.O. Box 831041
Dallas, TX 75283-1041 (360) 565-1512
Contact: Marielle Eykemans
Application address: 304 E. Park Ave., Port Angeles, WA 98362-6934 tel.: (360) 565-1512

Foundation type: Independent foundation
Purpose: Scholarships to graduates of Port Angeles Senior High School, WA. If funds are available, scholarships may also be given to students residing on the Olympic Peninsula, WA.
Financial data: Year ended 10/31/2013. Assets, $599,649 (M); Expenditures, $38,083; Total giving, $29,450.
Type of support: Support to graduates or students of specific schools; Undergraduate support.
Application information: Application form not required.
> *Deadline(s):* Jan. 6
> *Additional information:* Applicants must prepare a scholarship notebook.
EIN: 916218517

8972
Jerry Don Mouser Foundation
2401 Hwy. 287 N., Ste. 101
Mansfield, TX 76063
Contact: Shirlene D. Miller, Secy.
Application address: P.O. Box 40672, Everman, TX 76140-0672

Foundation type: Operating foundation
Purpose: Scholarships to graduating high school seniors who are dependents of Mouser Electronics Companies employees. Graduating high school students from Grossmont Union High School District in La Mesa, CA, Mansfield Independent School District in Mansfield, TX, and Randolph Township Board of Education in Randolph, NJ may also apply for the scholarship.
Financial data: Year ended 12/31/2011. Assets, $3,359 (M); Expenditures, $12,293; Total giving, $12,071; Grants to individuals, 10 grants totaling $12,071 (high: $2,610, low: $35).
Fields of interest: Higher education.
Type of support: Undergraduate support.
Application information: Application form required.
> *Initial approach:* Letter
> *Deadline(s):* Apr. 20
> *Final notification:* Recipients notified first week in June
> Applicants should submit the following:
> 1) SASE
> 2) Transcripts
> 3) Essay
> 4) SAT
> 5) Letter(s) of recommendation
> 6) ACT
> *Additional information:* Application must also include PSAT/NMSQT, and list of

achievements and honors. Scholarship recipients will receive up to $4,000 for their respective college expenses, must have at least a 3.0 GPA in high school, must be a full time college student with at least twelve hours, or attending a junior college leading to A.A. degree.
EIN: 752548171

8973
John P. Munson Scholarship Fund
c/o Bank of America, N.A.
P.O. Box 831041
Dallas, TX 75283-1041 (509) 963-3109
Application address: Central Washington University, Dir., of Financial Aid, 400 E. University Way, Barge Hall, Ellensburg, WA 98926-7502

Foundation type: Independent foundation
Purpose: Scholarships for needy and deserving students attending Central Washington University, WA.
Financial data: Year ended 12/31/2012. Assets, $268,468 (M); Expenditures, $30,201; Total giving, $25,868; Grants to individuals, totaling $25,868.
Fields of interest: Higher education.
Type of support: Scholarships—to individuals; Support to graduates or students of specific schools.
Application information: Applications accepted. Application form required.
  Send request by: Mail
  Deadline(s): Mar. 1
  Additional information: Application can be obtained from the financial aid office. Unsolicited requests for funds not considered or acknowledged.
EIN: 916025613

8974
Mercedes Murphy Foundation
6550 Fannin St., Ste. 2323
Houston, TX 77030 (713) 795-4300
Contact: Edward C. Murphy, Pres.

Foundation type: Independent foundation
Purpose: Scholarships to qualified students of Houston, TX in pursuit of a college education.
Financial data: Year ended 12/31/2011. Assets, $9,316 (M); Expenditures, $111,270; Total giving, $111,213; Grants to individuals, 7 grants totaling $111,213 (high: $77,427, low: $57).
Fields of interest: Higher education.
Type of support: Scholarships—to individuals.
Application information: Applications accepted.
  Initial approach: Letter
  Deadline(s): None
  Applicants should submit the following:
    1) Transcripts
    2) Resume
  Additional information: Applicant must show academic needs and accomplishments.
EIN: 760150340

8975
The Museum of Fine Arts, Houston
P.O. Box 6826
Houston, TX 77565-6826 (713) 639-7300
FAX: (713) 639-7709; E-mail: core@mfah.org;
URL: http://www.mfah.org

Foundation type: Public charity
Purpose: Residencies to visual artists and art scholars who have completed their undergraduate

or graduate training but have not yet fully developed a professional career.
Publications: Application guidelines; Annual report; Informational brochure; Program policy statement.
Financial data: Year ended 06/30/2012. Assets, $1,118,124,615 (M); Expenditures, $83,082,403; Total giving, $131,727; Grants to individuals, totaling $118,839.
Fields of interest: Visual arts.
Type of support: Fellowships; Postgraduate support; Residencies.
Application information: Applications accepted.
  Initial approach: Letter
  Deadline(s): Apr. 1
  Applicants should submit the following:
    1) SASE
    2) Resume
    3) Letter(s) of recommendation
  Additional information: Application must also include 12 slides.
Program description:
  Core Program: The program awards one- and two-year residencies to highly motivated, exceptional visual artists and art scholars who have completed their undergraduate or graduate training but have not yet fully developed a professional career. Each artist-resident is given approximately 450 square feet of private studio space, 24-hour access to school facilities and equipment, a $11,000 annual stipend, and health insurance. The program runs on an academic calendar, from September through May. Toward the end of each year, the artist residents mount a group show in the school's main gallery, and the critical studies residents prepare essays summarizing aspects of their independent research. These essays, as well as documentation of the resident artists' work, are gathered in a published catalogue.
EIN: 741109655

8976
Music Foundation of San Antonio, Inc.
11918 Vance Jackson Rd.
San Antonio, TX 78230-1444 (210) 696-1973
Contact: Robin Abraham, Pres.

Foundation type: Independent foundation
Purpose: Scholarships to financially needy students of San Antonio, TX for private music instructions.
Financial data: Year ended 12/31/2012. Assets, $1,029,627 (M); Expenditures, $47,581; Total giving, $40,341; Grants to individuals, 40 grants totaling $40,341 (high: $3,645, low: $36).
Fields of interest: Music; Performing arts, education.
Type of support: Scholarships—to individuals.
Application information: Applications accepted. Application form required.
  Deadline(s): None
  Additional information: Contact foundation for additional guidelines.
EIN: 742828454

8977
Mustang Foundation
P.O. Box 78
Cleburne, TX 76033-0078 (817) 556-3255
Contact: Lowell Smith, Jr., Pres. and Tr.

Foundation type: Independent foundation
Purpose: Scholarships to individuals for higher education, and specific assistance to indigent individuals who are residents of TX.

Financial data: Year ended 12/31/2011. Assets, $972,939 (M); Expenditures, $84,041; Total giving, $71,335.
Fields of interest: Higher education; Human services.
Type of support: Undergraduate support; Grants for special needs.
Application information: Applications accepted. Application form required.
  Deadline(s): None
  Additional information: Application forms can be obtained from the foundation.
EIN: 752815383

8978
MVP Foundation
1500 Waters Ridge Dr., Ste. 200
Lewisville, TX 75057 (972) 899-4401
Contact: Paula Pierce, Tr.

Foundation type: Independent foundation
Purpose: Scholarships to individuals of TX, employed in long term care pursuing higher education in nursing, dietary services, physical, occupation or speech therapy, administration or activity certification.
Financial data: Year ended 12/31/2011. Assets, $41,304 (M); Expenditures, $11,878; Total giving, $11,000; Grants to individuals, 4 grants totaling $11,000 (high: $4,000, low: $1,500).
Fields of interest: Nursing school/education; Health sciences school/education.
Type of support: Scholarships—to individuals.
Application information: Applications accepted. Application form required.
  Send request by: Mail
  Deadline(s): Oct. 1 for spring semester, June 1 for fall semester
  Applicants should submit the following:
    1) Essay
    2) Transcripts
    3) Financial information
EIN: 260774983

8979
Nabors Charitable Foundation
515 W. Greens Rd., Ste. 1200
Houston, TX 77067-4536 (281) 874-0035

Foundation type: Independent foundation
Purpose: Financial relief, support and assistance to victims and their family of natural and civil disasters. Educational grants to individuals pursuing higher education.
Financial data: Year ended 12/31/2011. Assets, $431,508 (M); Expenditures, $354,641; Total giving, $353,813; Grants to individuals, 93 grants totaling $353,813 (high: $12,500, low: $620).
Fields of interest: Higher education; Safety/disasters.
Type of support: Grants to individuals; Scholarships—to individuals.
Application information: Applications accepted.
  Additional information: Contact the foundation for additional guidelines for support.
EIN: 030569199

8980
NASA College Scholarship Fund, Inc.
c/o NASA Johnson Space Ctr.
2101 NASA Pkwy.
Houston, TX 77058-3696 (281) 483-3341
Contact: Stephanie Castillo, V.P.

Foundation type: Public charity

Purpose: Undergraduate scholarships to dependents of current and former NASA employees to study engineering and science at U.S. colleges and universities.
Financial data: Year ended 12/31/2012. Assets, $456,708 (M); Expenditures, $34,531; Total giving, $29,500.
Fields of interest: Engineering school/education; Science.
Type of support: Employee-related scholarships.
Application information: Application form required.
Initial approach: Letter or telephone
Deadline(s): Mar. 21
Additional information: Scholarships are a maximum of $2,000 per year, or $8,000 over six years. Application must also include academic records.
EIN: 760039071

8981
Nation Foundation
P.O. Box 180849
Dallas, TX 75218-0849
Contact: James H. Nation, Dir.

Foundation type: Independent foundation
Purpose: Scholarships primarily to TX residents for higher education at accredited colleges or universities.
Financial data: Year ended 12/31/2012. Assets, $4,192,459 (M); Expenditures, $301,692; Total giving, $276,651.
Fields of interest: Higher education.
Type of support: Scholarships—to individuals.
Application information:
Initial approach: Letter
Deadline(s): None
Additional information: Applications must include outline of financial need.
EIN: 752791965

8982
National Association of Latino Arts and Culture
(also known as NALAC)
1208 Buena Vista
San Antonio, TX 78207-4301 (210) 432-3982
FAX: (210) 432-3934; E-mail: info@nalac.org;
URL: http://www.nalac.org

Foundation type: Public charity
Purpose: Grants for U.S.-based Latino working artists in pursuit of social justice through the arts.
Publications: Application guidelines.
Financial data: Year ended 09/30/2012. Assets, $466,913 (M); Expenditures, $831,222; Total giving, $249,598; Grants to individuals, totaling $126,392.
Fields of interest: Arts; Hispanics/Latinos.
Type of support: Grants to individuals.
Application information: Applications accepted.
Send request by: Online
Deadline(s): Jan. 24
Final notification: Recipients notified in Mar.
Applicants should submit the following:
1) Work samples
2) Budget Information
Additional information: See web site for additional guidelines.
Program descriptions:
Fellowship: Fellowship grant of $1,000 to $5,000 supports artists whose work demonstrates excellence and the potential for impacting the Latino arts fields. The fellowship is designed to recognize excellence in an artist's body of work and nurture the creative development of an artist.

Support costs for the creation of new work, travel, study, professional development, living expenses, equipment, hiring of assistants, collaborations, documentation, production expenses and maintenance.
Master Artist Grant: This grant program of $10,000 to $20,000 is created to recognize established Latino artists for their cultural contributions and significance in their communities and also to provide support that enables the Master Artist to serve as a mentor to another artist in their professional and artistic development.
Project Grant: This grant of $1,000 to $10,000 supports project related costs that allow the artist(s) increased time to research and develop ideas or new works. The grant supports creation, development and presentation or work, purchase equipment necessary for artistic production, project research and travel, or professional or career development.
EIN: 742581293

8983
National Athletic Trainers Association Research and Education Foundation, Inc.
2952 Stemmons Freeway, Ste. 200
Dallas, TX 75247-6115 (214) 637-6282
Contact: Rachael Oats, Dir.
FAX: (214) 637-2206; E-mail for Rachael Oats: rachaelo@nata.org; URL: http://www.natafoundation.org

Foundation type: Public charity
Purpose: Scholarships to athletic training students to advance their education. Research grants to investigators to support and advance the athletic training profession.
Publications: Application guidelines.
Financial data: Year ended 12/31/2011. Assets, $2,652,219 (M); Expenditures, $840,513; Total giving, $502,190; Grants to individuals, totaling $421,840.
Fields of interest: Athletics/sports, training.
Type of support: Graduate support; Undergraduate support; Doctoral support.
Application information: Applications accepted.
Send request by: Online
Deadline(s): Feb. 4 for Scholarships, Feb. 15 for Grants
Final notification: Applicants notified by mid-May for Scholarships
Additional information: See web site for additional application guidelines.
Program descriptions:
Doctoral Research Grants: Multiple doctoral grant awards (each for a maximum of $2,500) are available each year. The principal investigator, or an approved co-principal investigator, will be required to present his/her findings at a future foundation annual meeting.
Master's Grants: Multiple master's grant awards (each for a maximum of $1,000) are available each year. The principal investigator, or an approved co-principal investigator, may be requested to present their findings at a future foundation annual meeting, but must do so at their own expense. The purpose of the award is to assist outstanding master's students of athletic training with quality scientific research projects. Proposals in all topic areas will be considered with the highest quality of these being chosen. Osternig Master's Research Grants will not be awarded to individuals to supplement or duplicate projects which are being supported by other funding agencies.
Research Grants: Awards research grants to any healthcare professional, researcher, or educator.

Priority consideration will be given to research proposals that include a foundation-certified athletic trainer as an integral part of the research team. Grant awards for multi-year projects are limited to a maximum of $50,000 in direct costs over no more than three years. The foundation will allow indirect costs up to 15 percent of the total direct costs.
EIN: 752395176

8984
The National Football Foundation and College Hall of Fame, Inc.
433 Las Colinas Blvd. E., Ste. 1130
Irving, TX 75039-6288 (972) 556-1000
Contact: Steven Hatchell, Pres. and C.E.O.
FAX: (972) 556-9032;
E-mail: pharper@footballfoundation.com;
URL: http://www.footballfoundation.com

Foundation type: Public charity
Purpose: Scholarships by nomination only to top local high school student-athletes in the U.S. for attendance at colleges or universities.
Publications: Newsletter.
Financial data: Year ended 12/31/2011. Assets, $717,670 (M); Expenditures, $559,573; Total giving, $345,767.
Fields of interest: Higher education; Athletics/sports, football.
Type of support: Scholarships—to individuals.
Application information: Scholarships are awarded by the chapters based on an individual's academic excellence, athletic ability and leadership qualities. The national office only accepts nominations from the chapters.
EIN: 510226347

8985
National Multiple Sclerosis Society, Lone Star Chapter
8111 N. Stadium Dr., Ste. 100
Houston, TX 77054-1844 (713) 394-2900
Tel. for financial assistance.: (800) 344-4867)
URL: http://txh.nationalmssociety.org

Foundation type: Public charity
Purpose: Scholarships to qualified students who have been diagnosed with MS or who have a parent with MS, for continuing education at institutions of higher learning. Financial assistance to individuals with MS to help them maintain their independence, safety, health and quality of life.
Publications: Newsletter.
Financial data: Year ended 09/30/2011. Assets, $9,243,970 (M); Expenditures, $25,602,617; Total giving, $1,155,669; Grants to individuals, totaling $600,669.
Fields of interest: Higher education; Multiple sclerosis.
Type of support: Scholarships—to individuals; Grants for special needs.
Application information: Applications accepted. Application form required. Application form available on the grantmaker's web site.
Deadline(s): Jan. 15 for Scholarships
Additional information: For scholarships, application should include an essay. Selection is based on financial need, academic achievement, leadership and participation in school or community activities, work experience, outside appraisal, goals and aspirations, and special circumstances. For financial assistance

contact the organization for additional information.
EIN: 741266225

8986
National Relief Charities
(also known as NRC)
500 E. Peyton St.
Sherman, TX   75090-0200   (540) 825-5950
E-mail: info@nrcprograms.org; Toll-free tel.: (800) 416-8102; URL: http://www.nrcprograms.org

Foundation type: Public charity
Purpose: Emergency assistance to Native American individuals and families in need; also, scholarships to deserving Native American students to further their undergraduate and graduate education.
Publications: Application guidelines; Annual report.
Financial data: Year ended 12/31/2011. Assets, $23,678,702 (M); Expenditures, $47,482,819; Total giving, $23,149,965; Grants to individuals, 852,531 grants totaling $23,059,965. Subtotal for scholarships—to individuals: 731 grants totaling $614,223. Subtotal for in-kind gifts: grants totaling $22,445,742.
Fields of interest: Scholarships/financial aid; Education; Human services; Native Americans/American Indians.
Type of support: Emergency funds; Scholarships—to individuals; In-kind gifts.
Application information: Applications accepted. Application form available on the grantmaker's web site.
  Initial approach: Submit application
  Deadline(s): Apr. 4 for scholarships
  Final notification: July
  Applicants should submit the following:
    1) Transcripts
    2) Photograph
    3) Essay
  Additional information: Applications must include proof of tribal enrollment.
EIN: 581888256

8987
The Charles and Dana Nearburg Foundation
P.O. Box 823085
Dallas, TX   75382-3085   (214) 739-1779
Contact: Charles E. Nearburg, Pres.

Foundation type: Operating foundation
Purpose: Scholarships and loans to children of employees of Nearburg Producing Company or other deserving TX community members for enrollment in a private middle or secondary school or an accredited institution of postsecondary education.
Financial data: Year ended 12/31/2012. Assets, $3,927,440 (M); Expenditures, $968,944; Total giving, $948,000; Grants to individuals, 2 grants totaling $4,250 (high: $3,000, low: $1,250).
Fields of interest: Higher education.
Type of support: Employee-related scholarships.
Application information: Applications accepted. Application form required.
  Deadline(s): Aug. 1
  Applicants should submit the following:
    1) Class rank
    2) Transcripts
    3) Letter(s) of recommendation
    4) Financial information
  Additional information: Application should also include the results of a drug test taken within the previous 10 days.
EIN: 752658947

8988
Neighborhood Centers, Inc.
4500 Bissonnet, Ste. 200
Bellaire, TX   77401-3113   (713) 667-9400
Contact: David Chaumette, Chair.
E-mail: nci.info@neighborhood-centers.org;
URL: http://www.neighborhood-centers.org

Foundation type: Public charity
Purpose: Financial assistance to individuals and families in need throughout the Houston, TX metropolitan area, with tuition, employment, elderly and disaster recovery assistance, transportation, and child care.
Publications: Annual report.
Financial data: Year ended 12/31/2011. Assets, $59,118,663 (M); Expenditures, $232,704,079; Total giving, $172,646,213; Grants to individuals, 263,796 grants totaling $171,638,046. Subtotal for grants for special needs: grants totaling $171,639,046.
Fields of interest: Health care; Children/youth; Aging; Economically disadvantaged.
Type of support: Grants for special needs.
Application information: Applications accepted.
  Additional information: Some assistance may require an application. Contact the organization for additional information.
EIN: 237062976

8989
Nichols Foundation, Inc.
9700 Richmond Ave., Ste. 255
Houston, TX   77042-4648   (713) 278-7477
Contact: Rebecca U. Nichols, Pres.

Foundation type: Independent foundation
Purpose: Scholarships to students from Tyler County, TX accepted for enrollment in a junior or four year college who meet the criteria set by the foundation.
Financial data: Year ended 12/31/2011. Assets, $255,706 (M); Expenditures, $10,110; Total giving, $7,500; Grants to individuals, 3 grants totaling $7,500.
Fields of interest: Higher education.
Type of support: Undergraduate support.
Application information: Applications accepted. Application form required.
  Initial approach: Letter
  Deadline(s): Prior to freshman or junior school year
EIN: 760603435

8990
Nielson Scholarship Fund
(formerly Karl A. Nielson and Karen J. Nielson Scholarship Fund)
P.O. Box 247
Spearman, TX   79081   (806) 659-2584
Contact: Clay Montgomery
Application address: 403 E. 11th St. Spearman, TX 79081

Foundation type: Independent foundation
Purpose: Scholarships to graduates of Spearman High School, TX, Gruver High School, TX, and Tekamah-Herman Community Schools, NE, who have been accepted to approved postsecondary educational institutions.
Financial data: Year ended 12/31/2012. Assets, $223,152 (M); Expenditures, $2,762; Total giving, $376; Grants to individuals, 6 grants totaling $376 (high: $82, low: $24).
Fields of interest: Higher education.

Type of support: Support to graduates or students of specific schools; Undergraduate support.
Application information: Application form required.
  Deadline(s): Vary
  Additional information: Contact the fund for additional application guidelines.
EIN: 752065409

8991
Swan C. Norby Scholarship Fund
c/o Bank of America, N.A.
P.O. Box 831041
Dallas, TX   75283-1041   (816) 316-5800

Foundation type: Independent foundation
Purpose: Scholarships to graduating seniors of Grandview High School, MO, to be used at a two-year or four-year college or university.
Financial data: Year ended 12/31/2011. Assets, $311,162 (M); Expenditures, $23,325; Total giving, $17,000; Grants to individuals, 15 grants totaling $17,000 (high: $1,500, low: $1,000).
Type of support: Support to graduates or students of specific schools; Undergraduate support.
Application information: Applications accepted. Application form required.
  Deadline(s): None
  Additional information: Applications available through Grandview High School, MO.
EIN: 431763633

8992
North American Envirothon
P.O. Box 855
League City, TX   77574-0855
FAX: (281) 332-5259

Foundation type: Company-sponsored foundation
Purpose: Scholarships to high school students who place in the top ten at the Canon Envirothon Competition. Awards to highest scoring teams and to teams who demonstrate the most spirit during the Canon Envirothon Competition.
Financial data: Year ended 12/31/2012. Assets, $254,854 (M); Expenditures, $524,557; Total giving, $181,328; Grants to individuals, 47 grants totaling $108,900 (high: $5,000, low: $1,100).
Fields of interest: Natural resources; Environment.
Type of support: Scholarships—to individuals; Awards/prizes.
Application information: Students must contact their state and provincial representatives for local Canon Envirothon Competitions. See web site for additional information.
Program descriptions:
  Canon Scholarships: The foundation awards scholarships of up to $5,000 to students who place in the top 10 at the Canon Envirothon Competition. Scholarships are to be used toward a four year university, two year college, or trade school and students will have up to two years after graduation from high school to use the Canon scholarship money.
  Envirothon Extra Mile Award: The foundation, in partnership with the National Association of Conservation Districts Auxiliary, awards a $100 cash prize and a plaque or trophy to the team demonstrating the most sprit, cooperation, leadership, and friendship during the Canon Envirothon Competition.
  Rookie Team Award: The foundation, in partnership with the National Association of Conservation Districts Auxiliary, awards a $100 cash prize and a plaque or trophy to the highest scoring team representing a state/province that has not previously participated at the Canon

Envirothon Competition. Teams that have participated as a "demonstration team" will also be eligible to compete for the award.
EIN: 300367267

8993
Northwest Assistance Ministries
15555 Kuykendahl Rd.
Houston, TX   77090-3651   (281) 885-4555
Contact: Carlo Little, Pres. and C.E.O.
FAX: (281) 583-5621; E-mail: nam@namonline.org;
URL: http://www.namonline.org

Foundation type: Public charity
Purpose: Social services including food, prescriptions, gasoline vouchers, financial help with rent and utilities, school supplies and clothing, and holiday food and toys to indigent residents of Harris County, TX.
Publications: Annual report.
Financial data: Year ended 09/30/2011. Assets, $4,377,248 (M); Expenditures, $7,855,823; Total giving, $2,873,637; Grants to individuals, totaling $2,873,637.
Fields of interest: Economically disadvantaged.
Type of support: In-kind gifts.
Application information:
   Initial approach: Letter
   Additional information: Contact foundation for
      eligibility criteria.
EIN: 760088702

8994
Davey O'Brien Educational & Charitable Trust
306 W. 7th St., Ste. M-15
Fort Worth, TX   76102-4900   (817) 338-3488
Contact: Danielle Moorman, Exec. Dir.
FAX: (817) 335-7737;
E-mail: info@daveyobrien.org; URL: http://www.daveyobrien.org

Foundation type: Public charity
Purpose: Scholarships to graduating student athletes of Dallas/Fort Worth Metroplex, TX pursuing postsecondary education.
Publications: Application guidelines.
Financial data: Year ended 03/31/2012. Assets, $767,125 (M); Expenditures, $299,670; Total giving, $26,800.
Fields of interest: Higher education; Athletics/sports, school programs; Athletics/sports, football.
Type of support: Scholarships—to individuals; Awards/prizes.
Application information: Applications accepted. Application form required.
   Additional information: See web site for
      additional application information.
Program descriptions:
   Davey O'Brien National Quarterback Award: The award recognizes and honors quarterbacks who excel in both sports and academics, while exhibiting teamwork, sportsmanship and leadership in both academic and athletics. The foundation's selection committee, a nationwide panel of journalists, broadcasters, commentators and former winners, evaluates each candidate on quarterback skills/athletic ability, academics, being a team player, character, leadership, and sportsmanship. The winner will receive a replica bronze of the original Davey O'Brien Trophy and his name is engraved on the base of the original, which is housed in the Davey O'Brien Hall of Fame.
   The Davey O'Brien High School Scholarship Award: Scholarships are provided to outstanding high school senior student-athletes in the Dallas/

Fort Worth, TX area. Recipients are chosen on the basis of scholarship, leadership, character, community service and varsity sports participation. The recipient receives $30,000 scholarship while the four finalists receive a $2,500 scholarship each.
EIN: 751620423

8995
Robert and Willora Oglesby Foundation, Inc.
1409 N. Waterview Dr.
Richardson, TX   75080   (972) 238-4722
Contact: Robert K. Oglesby, Dir.

Foundation type: Independent foundation
Purpose: Scholarships are awarded to private Christian colleges and universities on behalf of financially needy pulpit preacher students.
Financial data: Year ended 12/31/2011. Assets, $575,662 (M); Expenditures, $22,526; Total giving, $20,500; Grants to individuals, 12 grants totaling $18,500 (high: $2,000, low: $500).
Fields of interest: Theological school/education; Christian agencies & churches.
Type of support: Scholarships—to individuals.
Application information: Applications not accepted.
   Additional information: Unsolicited requests for
      funding not considered or acknowledged.
EIN: 752468388

8996
Iona Olson Trust
c/o Ron Olson
7912 Via Verde Dr.
Austin, TX   78739-1981   (512) 329-0550

Foundation type: Independent foundation
Purpose: Scholarships to one outstanding male and one outstanding female student graduating from any high school in Potwin, KS, and who attend Potwin Christian Church and plans to attend an accredited educational institution.
Financial data: Year ended 12/31/2012. Assets, $372,348 (M); Expenditures, $22,066; Total giving, $14,413; Grants to individuals, 2 grants totaling $9,798 (high: $4,899, low: $4,899).
Fields of interest: Higher education; Protestant agencies & churches.
Type of support: Undergraduate support.
Application information: Applications accepted.
   Initial approach: Letter
   Deadline(s): None
EIN: 486328340

8997
The Pat O'Neal Educational Foundation
675 N. Henderson St.
Fort Worth, TX   76107-1479   (817) 625-8246
Contact: Patricia J. O'Neal, Pres.

Foundation type: Independent foundation
Purpose: Scholarships to students graduating from high schools in the Fort Worth, TX area.
Financial data: Year ended 12/31/2011. Assets, $255,251 (M); Expenditures, $205,666; Total giving, $204,268.
Fields of interest: Higher education.
Type of support: Scholarships—to individuals.
Application information: Applications accepted. Application form required.
   Deadline(s): None
   Applicants should submit the following:
      1) SAT

2) ACT
3) Financial information
4) Essay
Additional information: Application should also
   include one or two letters of reference.
EIN: 202055414

8998
OneSight Research Foundation
(formerly Pearle Vision Foundation, Inc.)
2465 Joe Field Rd.
Dallas, TX   75229-3402   (972) 277-6191
Contact: Trina Parasiliti, Secy.
FAX: (972) 277-6422;
E-mail: tparasil@onesight.org; URL: http://www.onesight.org

Foundation type: Operating foundation
Purpose: Scholarships to individual students accepted or enrolled in an optometry school.
Publications: Application guidelines; Grants list.
Financial data: Year ended 12/31/2012. Assets, $1,591,111 (M); Expenditures, $332,772; Total giving, $272,500; Grants to individuals, 20 grants totaling $40,000 (high: $2,000, low: $2,000).
Fields of interest: Optometry/vision screening; Eye diseases.
Type of support: Scholarships—to individuals.
Application information: Applications accepted. Application form required. Application form available on the grantmaker's web site.
   Initial approach: Application
   Send request by: Mail
   Copies of proposal: 1
   Deadline(s): Apr. 15
   Final notification: Applicants notified June 15
   Applicants should submit the following:
      1) GPA
      2) Transcripts
      3) Letter(s) of recommendation
   Additional information: Application should also
      include a list and description of leadership
      responsibilities, a list of accomplishment
      and/or awards received for academic
      excellence, community service, or leadership
      ability, a description of academic and career
      objectives, and a description of the applicants
      vision of diversity and community service.
Program description:
   Dr. Stanley Pearle Scholarship Fund: In 2014, the OneSight Research Foundation will award 10 scholarships in the amount of $5,000 each through the Dr. Stanley Pearle Scholarship Fund. Invitation to apply is extended to second, third and fourth year full-time students starting in the fall, who are pursuing graduate studies leading to a Doctor of Optometry degree. Scholarships will be awarded on a competitive basis, based on scholastic performance, potential, and evidence of a commitment to a career in the optometric profession and to community service.
EIN: 752173714

8999
Operation Homefront, Inc.
8930 Fourwinds Dr., Ste. 340
San Antonio, TX   78239-1971   (210) 659-7756
Contact: Jim Knotts, Pres. and C.E.O.
FAX: (210) 566-7544; Toll-free tel.: (800) 722-6098; URL: http://www.operationhomefront.net

Foundation type: Public charity
Purpose: Emergency and financial assistance to military families of deployed service members with day-to-day issues.

Publications: Annual report; Newsletter; IRS Form 990 or 990-PF printed copy available upon request.
Financial data: Year ended 12/31/2011. Assets, $9,974,830 (M); Expenditures, $24,677,990; Total giving, $19,768,936; Grants to individuals, totaling $19,768,936.
Fields of interest: Military/veterans' organizations.
Type of support: Grants for special needs.
Application information: Applications not accepted.
> *Additional information:* Unsolicited requests for funds not considered or acknowledged.
EIN: 320033325

9000
Jack & Charlotte Owen Educational Scholarship Trust
c/o Capital One Bank, N.A.
P.O. Box 451
Texarkana, TX   75504
Application Address: c/o Individual's School Counselor, Bowie County, TX 75503

Foundation type: Independent foundation
Purpose: Scholarships to high school graduates in Bowie County, TX for postsecondary education.
Financial data: Year ended 12/31/2012. Assets, $1,487,403 (M); Expenditures, $82,210; Total giving, $54,630; Grants to individuals, 40 grants totaling $54,630 (high: $3,000, low: $317).
Fields of interest: Higher education.
Type of support: Scholarships—to individuals.
Application information: Applications accepted. Application form required.
> *Deadline(s):* Apr.
> *Applicants should submit the following:*
> 1) Transcripts
> 2) SAT
> 3) ACT
> *Additional information:* Application should also include a signature letter. Application forms available from high school counselors.
EIN: 756414441

9001
Panasonic Rio Grande Valley Educational Foundation
(formerly Panasonic Tennessee-Japan Cultural Exchange Foundation)
4900 George McVay Dr., Ste. C
McAllen, TX   78503

Foundation type: Company-sponsored foundation
Purpose: Grants to high school students from Knox County, TN, to travel to Japan and high school students from Senri, Japan, to travel to Knoxville, TN, for cultural exchange.
Financial data: Year ended 02/28/2013. Assets, $383,762 (M); Expenditures, $21,567; Total giving, $20,000.
Type of support: Exchange programs; Support to graduates or students of specific schools; Awards/grants by nomination only; Undergraduate support.
Application information: Applications not accepted.
> *Additional information:* Unsolicited requests for funds not considered or acknowledged.
EIN: 621558047

9002
Pardee Cancer Treatment Association of Greater Brazosport
490 This Way, Ste. 220
Lake Jackson, TX   77566

Foundation type: Operating foundation
Purpose: Grants for cancer treatment to individuals who have lived in southern Brazoria County, TX, within one year of being diagnosed with cancer. Grants are for medical expenses and for prescription drugs.
Financial data: Year ended 12/31/2012. Assets, $0 (M); Expenditures, $67,648; Total giving, $49,463.
Fields of interest: Health care; Cancer.
Type of support: Grants for special needs.
Application information: Applications accepted. Application form required.
> *Deadline(s):* None
> *Additional information:* Application includes detailed financial information.
EIN: 510169385

9003
Paris Education Foundation
2255 S. Collegiate
P. O. Box 356
Paris, TX   75461-0356   (903) 737-7400
Contact: Sandra Holt, Exec. Dir.
E-mail: pef@parisjc.edu; URL: http://www.pariseducationfoundation.com/

Foundation type: Public charity
Purpose: Scholarships to graduating seniors of Paris High School who plan to enter a college, university or vocational/technical school.
Financial data: Year ended 06/30/2012. Assets, $1,275,927 (M); Expenditures, $118,108; Total giving, $65,400; Grants to individuals, totaling $65,400.
Fields of interest: Higher education.
Type of support: Scholarships—to individuals; Support to graduates or students of specific schools.
Application information: Applications accepted. Application form required.
> *Additional information:* Scholarships are awarded on the basis of need, academic achievement, school and community involvement and teacher evaluation.
EIN: 752294089

9004
Paris Junior College Memorial Fund Foundation
2400 Clarksville St.
Paris, TX   75460-6258
Contact: George Struve, Chair.

Foundation type: Public charity
Purpose: Scholarships to students for attendance at Paris Junior College, TX pursuing a higher education.
Financial data: Year ended 05/31/2012. Assets, $12,790,342 (M); Expenditures, $373,068; Total giving, $320,859; Grants to individuals, totaling $313,778.
Fields of interest: College (community/junior).
Type of support: Scholarships—to individuals; Support to graduates or students of specific schools.
Application information: Applications accepted.
> *Additional information:* Contact the foundation for additional application guidelines.
EIN: 756035104

9005
Passport to Success Foundation, Inc.
P.O. Box 7411
Waco, TX   76714   (254) 751-7676
Contact: Elizabeth Goins
Application address: 4529 Lakeshore Dr., Waco TX 76710

Foundation type: Independent foundation
Purpose: Scholarships and low interest loans to worthy high school seniors of Waco, TX, for college education or technical training.
Financial data: Year ended 12/31/2012. Assets, $491,644 (M); Expenditures, $74,600; Total giving, $51,395.
Fields of interest: Vocational education, post-secondary; Higher education.
Type of support: Scholarships—to individuals.
Application information: Applications accepted. Application form required.
> *Deadline(s):* June 1
> *Applicants should submit the following:*
> 1) Resume
> 2) FAFSA
EIN: 742499823

9006
Appoline & Simeon Patout Foundation
217 E. Washington
Navasota, TX   77868   (337) 276-4592

Foundation type: Independent foundation
Purpose: Scholarships for high school and college students of LA in pursuit of a college education in a LA college or university.
Financial data: Year ended 07/31/2013. Assets, $283,472 (M); Expenditures, $12,071; Total giving, $12,000; Grants to individuals, 9 grants totaling $12,000 (high: $1,750, low: $750).
Fields of interest: Higher education.
Type of support: Scholarships—to individuals.
Application information: Applications accepted. Application form required.
> *Deadline(s):* 180 days prior to the beginning of the school year
> *Applicants should submit the following:*
> 1) Transcripts
> 2) SAT
> 3) ACT
> 4) Photograph
> 5) Letter(s) of recommendation
> *Additional information:* Application should also include a written statement of financial need and evidence of acceptance for enrollment.
EIN: 581888278

9007
Jack & Katherine Pearce Educational Foundation
c/o Frost National Bank
2201 Market St., Ste. 1010
Galveston, TX   77550-1527
Contact: Janet L. Bertolino, Admin., Frost National Bank

Foundation type: Operating foundation
Purpose: Interest-free student loans to academically worthy young residents of the city of Galveston, TX, who have graduated from Galveston schools. Loans may be used for undergraduate, graduate, postgraduate, or professional education.
Publications: Informational brochure (including application guidelines).
Financial data: Year ended 12/31/2012. Assets, $2,101,541 (M); Expenditures, $211,993; Total

giving, $192,500; Grants to individuals, 39 grants totaling $192,500 (high: $5,000, low: $2,500).
Fields of interest: Higher education.
Type of support: Student loans—to individuals.
Application information: Applications accepted. Application form required.
Initial approach: Letter or telephone
Deadline(s): Mar. 31
Applicants should submit the following:
  1) Photograph
  2) Letter(s) of recommendation
  3) Essay
  4) Budget Information
  5) Transcripts
  6) SAT
  7) ACT
  8) Financial information
Additional information: Application must also include references, and two co-signatures.
EIN: 746035546

9008
Pedernales Electric Cooperative Scholarship Fund
c/o Vicki Hiser
201 South Ave. Apt. F
Johnson City, TX 78636-4827 (830) 868-5112
Contact: Vicki Hiser, Treas.

Foundation type: Company-sponsored foundation
Purpose: Scholarships to graduating high school seniors whose parents or legal guardians are employees of Pedernales Electric Cooperative, TX for attendance at any college, university, junior college, technical school or trade school.
Financial data: Year ended 12/31/2011. Assets, $111,550 (M); Expenditures, $53,005; Total giving, $53,000; Grant to an individual, 1 grant totaling $53,000.
Fields of interest: Vocational education, post-secondary; Higher education; College (community/junior).
Type of support: Employee-related scholarships.
Application information: Applications accepted. Application form required.
Additional information: Selection is based on academic performance, standardized test score, and financial need. Contributes only to pre-selected students through an employee related program, unsolicited requests for funds not considered or acknowledged.
Company name: Pedernales Electric Cooperative, Inc.
EIN: 742897600

9009
Bulah Peery Memorial Scholarship Fund Inc.
P.O. Box 515
Booker, TX 79005-0515 (806) 658-4551
Contact: Pam Sanders, Chair. and Dir.

Foundation type: Independent foundation
Purpose: Scholarships to graduates of Booker High School, TX, who attended the school for at least two years, including senior year.
Financial data: Year ended 07/31/2013. Assets, $477,900 (M); Expenditures, $22,267; Total giving, $20,999; Grants to individuals, 21 grants totaling $20,999 (high: $3,077, low: $375).
Fields of interest: Higher education.
Type of support: Support to graduates or students of specific schools; Undergraduate support.
Application information: Applications accepted.

Additional information: Application must include proof of college enrollment at a U.S. institution.
EIN: 756038523

9010
J. C. Penney Company Fund, Inc.
6501 Legacy Dr., MS 1205
Plano, TX 75024-3612 (972) 431-1431
Contact: Jodi Gibson, Pres. and Exec. Dir.
FAX: (972) 431-1355; URL: http://www.jcpenney.com/jsp/browse/marketing/promotion.jsp?&pageId=pg40037900007

Foundation type: Company-sponsored foundation
Purpose: Emergency assistance grants to employees of J.C. Penney Corporation, displaced by disaster.
Publications: Application guidelines; Corporate giving report.
Financial data: Year ended 02/02/2013. Assets, $10,355,909 (M); Expenditures, $4,847,149; Total giving, $4,846,275.
Type of support: Emergency funds; Employee-related welfare.
Application information: Applications not accepted.
Additional information: Unsolicited requests for funds not considered or acknowledged.
Company name: J. C. Penney Company, Inc.
EIN: 133274961

9011
Penrose Foundation
c/o Patricia Schieffer
777 Main St., Ste. 3250
Fort Worth, TX 76102-5342 (817) 332-1328
Contact: Sharon Schieffer Mayes, Dir.

Foundation type: Independent foundation
Purpose: Scholarships to students of Latino descent who maintain a 3.0 GPA each semester.
Financial data: Year ended 12/31/2011. Assets, $1,213,760 (M); Expenditures, $49,671; Total giving, $21,500; Grants to individuals, 15 grants totaling $21,500 (high: $1,500, low: $1,500).
Fields of interest: Hispanics/Latinos.
Type of support: Scholarships—to individuals.
Application information: Applications accepted.
Initial approach: Letter
Deadline(s): Apr. 1
Applicants should submit the following:
  1) Essay
  2) Transcripts
  3) SAT
  4) Letter(s) of recommendation
  5) ACT
Additional information: Application must also include a copy of parents' last three income tax returns.
EIN: 752456902

9012
Percy Franklin Lucas Memorial Student Loan Fund
(formerly Lottie King Lucas Percy Memorial Trust)
c/o Bank of America, N.A.
P.O. Box 831041
Dallas, TX 75283-1041 (816) 292-4342
Contact: James J. Mueth
Application address: cP.O. Box 219119, Kansas City, MO 64121-9119, tel.: (816) 292-4342

Foundation type: Independent foundation

Purpose: Student loans to financially needy students attending the University of Missouri at Kansas City, MO.
Financial data: Year ended 12/31/2011. Assets, $408,307 (M); Expenditures, $8,789; Total giving, $0.
Fields of interest: Higher education.
Type of support: Student loans—to individuals; Support to graduates or students of specific schools.
Application information: Applications accepted.
Deadline(s): None
Additional information: Loan application forms are available from the University of Missouri at Kansas City (UMKC).
EIN: 446008488

9013
Permian Basin Area Foundation
200 N. Loraine St., Ste. 500
Midland, TX 79701-4711 (432) 617-3213
Contact: Guy McCrary, C.E.O.
FAX: (432) 617-0151; E-mail: gmccrary@pbaf.org;
URL: http://www.pbaf.org

Foundation type: Community foundation
Purpose: Academic scholarships to students pursuing higher education and vocational education from the Permian Basin, TX region.
Publications: Application guidelines; Annual report; Newsletter.
Financial data: Year ended 12/31/2012. Assets, $91,907,173 (M); Expenditures, $9,006,646; Total giving, $7,371,170; Grants to individuals, 266 grants totaling $277,530.
Fields of interest: Music; Vocational education, post-secondary; Higher education; Law school/education; Medical school/education; Nursing school/education; Teacher school/education.
Type of support: Scholarships—to individuals.
Application information: Applications accepted. Application form required. Application form available on the grantmaker's web site.
Initial approach: Telephone or letter
Deadline(s): Mar. 31
Final notification: Applicants notified mid-May
Applicants should submit the following:
  1) Financial information
  2) Transcripts
  3) Letter(s) of recommendation
  4) Essay
Additional information: Applicants must provide proof of acceptance/enrollment to the foundation. Awards are paid directly to the educational institution on behalf of the students. See web site for additional application guidelines.
EIN: 752295008

9014
The Perot Family Foundation
P.O. Box 269014
Plano, TX 75026-9014

Foundation type: Independent foundation
Purpose: Grants to employees and customers of Perot Systems Corp./Deli inc. and its customers who suffered damages as a result of a natural disaster.
Financial data: Year ended 12/31/2012. Assets, $1,640 (M); Expenditures, $0; Total giving, $0.
Fields of interest: Safety/disasters.
Type of support: Emergency funds; Grants to individuals; Employee-related welfare.
Application information: Applications accepted.

Initial approach: Letter
Deadline(s): None
EIN: 752163185

9015
The Pettinger Foundation Inc
305 S. Jupiter Rd., Ste. 100
Allen, TX   75002-3050   (972) 747-9600
Contact: Brandon Pitts, Treas.

Foundation type: Operating foundation
Purpose: Scholarships to high school students in Texas pursuing a career in science and technology.
Financial data: Year ended 08/31/2011. Assets, $0 (M); Expenditures, $11,074; Total giving, $9,000; Grant to an individual, 1 grant totaling $3,000.
Fields of interest: Higher education; Science; Engineering/technology.
Type of support: Scholarships—to individuals.
Application information: Applications accepted.
Initial approach: Letter
Deadline(s): None
Additional information: Applicant must demonstrate financial need.
EIN: 752768241

9016
The Mary L. Peyton Foundation
c/o Stockton Scurry & Smith
4487 N. Mesa St., Ste. 110
El Paso, TX   79902-1149   (915) 533-9698
Contact: Gloria Perry, Exec. Dir.
URL: http://www.marylpeyton.org/program.html

Foundation type: Operating foundation
Purpose: Grants for medical and living expenses and emergency assistance to legal residents of El Paso County, TX. Educational and vocational assistance to qualified needy individuals who are incapacitated or lack sufficient funding.
Financial data: Year ended 05/31/2012. Assets, $3,364,969 (M); Expenditures, $190,141; Total giving, $81,233.
Fields of interest: Vocational education; Higher education; Economically disadvantaged.
Type of support: Grants for special needs.
Application information: Applications accepted. Application form required.
Additional information: Application for economic assistance should be made through social service agencies.
EIN: 741276102

9017
PFLAG/HATCH Youth Scholarship Foundation
c/o OUT for Education
P.O.Box 667010
Houston, TX   77266-7010   (713) 657-0029
E-mail: info@physf.org; *URL:* http://www.physf.org/

Foundation type: Public charity
Purpose: Scholarships for Houston, TX lesbian, gay, bisexual or transgendered students who have demonstrated outstanding achievement while in high school or college.
Publications: Application guidelines.
Financial data: Year ended 12/31/2012. Expenditures, $45,663; Total giving, $40,683.
Fields of interest: LGBTQ.
Type of support: Undergraduate support.
Application information: Applications accepted. Application form required. Application form available on the grantmaker's web site.

Initial approach: Letter
Deadline(s): Mar. 1
EIN: 760596873

9018
Philadelphia Foundation
3757 FM 1781
Rockport, TX   78382-7613
Contact: Susan Yelderman, Secy.

Foundation type: Independent foundation
Purpose: Scholarships to seminary students primarily from TX who are studying to become expository teachers of the Word of God.
Financial data: Year ended 11/30/2012. Assets, $276,010 (M); Expenditures, $15,697; Total giving, $15,000.
Fields of interest: Theological school/education; Christian agencies & churches; Religion.
Type of support: Scholarships—to individuals.
Application information: Applications accepted. Application form required.
Deadline(s): None
Applicants should submit the following:
1) Transcripts
2) Financial information
Additional information: Application should also include biography of Christian life and work.
EIN: 942995658

9019
Phillips-Hernandez Scholarship Foundation
P.O. Box 645
Pampa, TX   79066-0645   (806) 669-3397
Contact: John W. Warner, Secy.-Treas.

Foundation type: Independent foundation
Purpose: Scholarships to graduates of Pampa High School, TX, for higher education, with preference given to minority females.
Financial data: Year ended 12/31/2010. Assets, $80,076 (M); Expenditures, $6,000; Total giving, $6,000; Grants to individuals, 5 grants totaling $6,000 (high: $2,000, low: $1,000).
Fields of interest: Minorities; Women.
Type of support: Support to graduates or students of specific schools; Undergraduate support.
Application information:
Deadline(s): Apr. 1
Additional information: Contact foundation for current application guidelines.
EIN: 752227488

9020
Pioneer Natural Resources Foundation
(formerly Pioneer Natural Resources Scholarship Foundation)
5205 N. O'Connor Blvd., Ste. 200
Irving, TX   75039-3789
Contact: Larry N. Paulsen, V.P. and Treas.
URL: http://www.pxd.com/values/charitable-giving

Foundation type: Company-sponsored foundation
Purpose: Scholarships to any child of a full-time employee who has been employed by Pioneer Natural Resources Company or its affiliates for a minimum of one year, at educational institutions for higher learning. Assistance to employees of Pioneer Natural Resources Company and its affiliates who are victims of a national disaster or civil disaster that is a "qualified disaster"
Financial data: Year ended 12/31/2012. Assets, $53,624 (M); Expenditures, $19,250; Total giving, $19,250.

Fields of interest: Higher education; Safety/disasters.
Type of support: Employee-related scholarships; Grants for special needs.
Application information: Application form required.
Initial approach: Letter or telephone
Deadline(s): June 4 for Scholarships
Additional information: Applications can be obtained from the foundation.
Company name: Pioneer Natural Resources Company
EIN: 752443728

9021
Pipe Line Contractors Association Scholarship Foundation
c/o Pat Tielborg
1700 Pacific Ave.
Dallas, TX   75201-4675
Application address: c/o Scholarship Management Svcs., 1505 Riverview Rd., P.O. Box 297, St. Peter, MN 56082, tel.: (507) 931-1682

Foundation type: Independent foundation
Purpose: Scholarships to children and grandchildren of full-time employees of regular and associate members of the Pipe Line Contractors Assn.
Financial data: Year ended 12/31/2011. Assets, $3,915,285 (M); Expenditures, $355,045; Total giving, $266,250; Grants to individuals, 38 grants totaling $266,250 (high: $7,500, low: -$11,250).
Fields of interest: Higher education; Scholarships/financial aid.
Type of support: Employee-related scholarships.
Application information: Applications accepted. Application form required.
Deadline(s): Jan. 7
EIN: 752744096

9022
Minnie Stevens Piper Foundation
1250 N.E. Loop 410, Ste. 810
San Antonio, TX   78209-1539   (210) 525-8494
Contact: Joyce M. Ellis, Secy. and Exec. Dir.
FAX: (210) 341-6627; *E-mail:* mspf@mspf.org;
URL: http://www.everychanceeverytexan.org/about/scholars/
Additional URL: http://www.everychanceeverytexan.org/about/scholars/

Foundation type: Independent foundation
Purpose: Educational loans and scholarships to TX residents who are full-time college or university students pursuing a graduate or undergraduate degree.
Publications: Application guidelines; Occasional report; Program policy statement.
Financial data: Year ended 12/31/2012. Assets, $22,172,667 (M); Expenditures, $2,002,387; Total giving, $470,800; Grants to individuals, totaling $370,800; Loans to individuals, totaling $149,277.
Fields of interest: Higher education.
Type of support: Scholarships—to individuals; Student loans—to individuals; Awards/prizes; Graduate support; Undergraduate support.
Application information: Applications accepted. Application form required. Application form available on the grantmaker's web site.
Applicants should submit the following:
1) Letter(s) of recommendation
2) Transcripts
Additional information: See web site for additional guidelines.

Program descriptions:

Piper Scholars Program: Four-year scholarships are awarded to academically promising and superior high school seniors, to attend the college or university of their choice in TX. Applicants must be U.S. citizens/permanent residents and TX residents. Students selected must maintain a B average throughout their undergraduate college career to remain in the program. Participation in this program is by invitation only. Nominations are made by principals or counselors for invited high schools in certain counties throughout TX.

Student Loan Program: Loans are made to full-time students who are U.S. citizens/permanent residents and TX residents, attending TX colleges or universities. Maximum of $10,000 may be loaned to one student.

EIN: 741292695

9023
Annie M. & Clarke A. Polk Foundation
P.O. Box 399
Chappell Hill, TX   77426-0399   (979) 251-0887
Contact: Kay Hinton, Secy.

Foundation type: Operating foundation
Purpose: Scholarships to full-time undergraduate students, primarily those residing in Washington County, TX.
Financial data: Year ended 06/30/2013. Assets, $591,135 (M); Expenditures, $41,683; Total giving, $33,250; Grants to individuals, 29 grants totaling $33,250 (high: $1,500, low: $500).
Type of support: Undergraduate support.
Application information: Applications accepted. Application form required. Interview required.
  Initial approach: Letter
  Deadline(s): Apr. 30
  Applicants should submit the following:
    1) Transcripts
    2) Financial information
EIN: 742293811

9024
Poncin Scholarship Fund
c/o Bank of America, N.A.
P.O. Box 831041
Dallas, TX   75283-1041   (206) 358-3079
Contact: Cindy Keyser
Application address: c/o Bank of America, N.A., P.O. Box 24565, Seattle, WA 98124, tel.: (206) 358-3079

Foundation type: Independent foundation
Purpose: Research grants to individuals engaged in medical research in a recognized institution of learning in WA.
Publications: Application guidelines.
Financial data: Year ended 12/31/2012. Assets, $7,010,495 (M); Expenditures, $428,392; Total giving, $342,678; Grants to individuals, 25 grants totaling $342,678 (high: $23,753, low: $9,734).
Fields of interest: Institute.
Type of support: Research.
Application information: Applications accepted.
  Initial approach: Proposal
  Final notification: Recipients notified eight weeks after deadline
  Additional information: Application must include approval from the head of the educational institution's research institute.
EIN: 916069573

9025
Port Arthur Higher Education Foundation, Inc.
1500 Procter St.
Port Arthur, TX   77640-6604   (409) 984-6100
Contact: Donna Schion
E-mail: schiondj@lamarpa.edu; URL: http://www.lamarpa.edu/alumni/foundation.html

Foundation type: Public charity
Purpose: Scholarships to high school seniors for attendance at Lamar State College- Port Arthur, TX based on academic merit and/or financial need.
Financial data: Year ended 12/31/2011. Assets, $3,811,814 (M); Expenditures, $552,109; Total giving, $510,163.
Fields of interest: Higher education.
Type of support: Support to graduates or students of specific schools.
Application information: Applications accepted.
EIN: 237272448

9026
Powdermaker Family Foundation
5901 Cross Timbers Rd.
Flower Mound, TX   75022-3142   (817) 430-9060
Contact: Daniel Byrd, Dir.
Application address: P.O. Box 181684, Dallas TX 75218
E-mail: scholarships@powdermaker.org;
URL: http://powdermaker.org/

Foundation type: Operating foundation
Purpose: Scholarships to graduating students of Dallas County high schools for full time study at an accredited college, university or vocational school.
Financial data: Year ended 12/31/2012. Assets, $221,924 (M); Expenditures, $58,555; Total giving, $55,000; Grants to individuals, 27 grants totaling $55,000 (high: $2,000, low: $2,000).
Fields of interest: Vocational education, post-secondary; Higher education; College (community/junior).
Type of support: Support to graduates or students of specific schools.
Application information: Applications accepted. Application form required. Interview required.
  Deadline(s): Mar. 15
  Applicants should submit the following:
    1) Transcripts
    2) Letter(s) of recommendation
    3) Financial information
EIN: 208366895

9027
Guy & Nyda Prater Scholarship Fund
c/o Bank of America, N.A.
P.O. Box 831041
Dallas, TX   75283-1041

Foundation type: Independent foundation
Purpose: Scholarships to graduates of Dayton High School, Dayton, WA for higher education.
Financial data: Year ended 06/30/2013. Assets, $300,856 (M); Expenditures, $16,786; Total giving, $12,000.
Type of support: Scholarships—to individuals; Support to graduates or students of specific schools.
Application information: Application form required.
  Deadline(s): Apr. 30
  Additional information: Contact fund for application guidelines. Application must include transcript of all grades from grade nine and higher, and completion of the confidential rating sheet (supplied by the selection committee) from two teachers and two adults who are not relatives.
EIN: 916305003

9028
Presbyterian Healthcare Foundation
612 E. Lamar Blvd., Ste. 300
Arlington, TX   76011-4124   (682) 236-5200
Contact: James K. McAuley C.F.R.E., Pres.
E-mail: PHFCommunications@TexasHealth.org;
URL: http://www.presbyhealthfoundation.org

Foundation type: Public charity
Purpose: Hospital bill financial assistance to indigent patients of TX-area hospitals whose income is at or below 200 percent of applicable federal poverty guidelines who lack sufficient funds to pay their bill are eligible for charity care. In addition, patients with significant medical bills and income above 200 percent of applicable federal poverty guidelines may be eligible for charity care.
Publications: Annual report.
Financial data: Year ended 12/31/2011. Assets, $142,562,809 (M); Expenditures, $9,506,862; Total giving, $6,514,199.
Fields of interest: Hospitals (general); Health care; Economically disadvantaged.
Type of support: Grants for special needs.
Application information: Applications accepted. Application form required. Application form available on the grantmaker's web site.
  Initial approach: Letter or tel.
  Applicants should submit the following:
    1) Financial information
  Additional information: For eligibility guidelines, call 682-236-3000 / 800-890-6034, or e-mail customerservice@texashealth.org.
EIN: 752022128

9029
Programs for Human Services, Inc.
3423 Martin St.
Orange, TX   77630-2927   (409) 386-4338
Contact: Tish Foyle-Johnson, Exec. Dir.

Foundation type: Public charity
Purpose: Grants for weatherization assistance and utility bills for needy individuals.
Financial data: Year ended 09/30/2011. Assets, $788,114 (M); Expenditures, $10,115,576; Total giving, $8,767,357; Grants to individuals, totaling $8,767,357.
Fields of interest: Economically disadvantaged.
Type of support: Grants for special needs.
Application information: Applications not accepted.
  Additional information: Unsolicited requests for funds not considered or acknowledged.
EIN: 741939565

9030
Promotional Products Education Foundation
3125 Skyway Cir. N.
Irving, TX   75038-3526   (972) 258-3097
Contact: Sara Besly, Foundation Mgr.
FAX: (972) 594-4097; E-mail: ppef@ppa.org;
URL: http://www.ppa.org/ppef

Foundation type: Public charity
Purpose: College scholarships to students who have a parent working in the promotional products industry or who are working for a company in the industry.

Publications: Application guidelines; Financial statement.
Financial data: Year ended 12/31/2011. Assets, $1,230,830 (M); Expenditures, $154,308; Total giving, $99,000; Grants to individuals, totaling $99,000.
Fields of interest: Higher education; Scholarships/financial aid; Business/industry.
Type of support: Undergraduate support.
Application information: Applications accepted. Application form required. Application form available on the grantmaker's web site.
　Initial approach: Web site or telephone
　Copies of proposal: 1
　Deadline(s): Mar. 15
　Applicants should submit the following:
　　1) Transcripts
　　2) SAT
　　3) Resume
　　4) ACT
　　5) Letter(s) of recommendation
　　6) GPA
　　7) Essay
Program descriptions:
　Chairman's College Scholarship: Awards $2,500 annually for two years (for a total of $5,000) to students entering their junior year of college, actively pursuing a bachelor's degree in an academic field related to promotional products, and express an intent to enter the field related to promotional products as a career. The scholarship is renewable for the senior year, provided the student demonstrates satisfactory progress toward the designated degree and meets the required criteria for scholarship renewal. The scholarship will be awarded on the basis of the student's academic achievement, scholastic and civic leadership, financial need, essay, and letter of recommendation.
　Four-Year College Scholarship for Academic Excellence and Achievement: Awards $1,000 annually for four years to students entering a four-year accredited college or university as a freshman in the fall. The scholarship is renewable for four years of college, provided that the students meet the minimum GPA equipment and current employment in the promotional products industry is maintained by the student or parent. The scholarship will be awarded on the basis of GPA, ACT/SAT test scores, essay, resume, and optional financial need.
　Friends of PPMN Scholarship: This $1,000 scholarship will be awarded to a full-time industry employee for undergraduate or graduate level coursework at an accredited college or university.
　One-Year College Scholarship: Awards $1,000 to students attending a two-year accredited undergraduate college or university who are taking at least six credit hours per semester. Scholarships will be awarded on the basis of GPA, ACT/SAT test scores, essay, resume, and optional financial need.
EIN: 751714221

9031
Rainforest Cafe Friends of the Future Foundation
1510 W. Loop S.
Houston, TX　77027-9505　(713) 386-8094

Foundation type: Public charity
Purpose: Grants for living expenses to survivors of natural disasters in the US.
Financial data: Year ended 12/31/2011. Assets, $798,602 (M); Expenditures, $172,540; Total giving, $158,095.
Type of support: Emergency funds.

Application information: Contact foundation for eligibility information.
EIN: 411909838

9032
The Jerry S. Rawls Scholarship Foundation
6204 17th St.
Lubbock, TX　79416-6133

Foundation type: Independent foundation
Purpose: Scholarships to students who attend Texas Tech University.
Financial data: Year ended 06/30/2012. Assets, $3,506,299 (M); Expenditures, $208,569; Total giving, $167,700; Grants to individuals, 88 grants totaling $167,700 (high: $7,300, low: $700).
Fields of interest: Men.
Type of support: Scholarships—to individuals.
Application information: Applications not accepted.
　Additional information: Unsolicited requests for funds not considered or acknowledged.
EIN: 916530654

9033
Reed Engineering Group Employees Scholarship
2424 Stutz Dr., Ste. 400
Dallas, TX　75235-6500　(214) 350-5600
Contact: Yolanda Hawthrone

Foundation type: Company-sponsored foundation
Purpose: Scholarships to dependents of Reed Engineering Group Employee enrolled or will be entering college or a post-high school vocational institution in pursuit of a degree.
Financial data: Year ended 09/30/2012. Assets, $227,007 (M); Expenditures, $10,501; Total giving, $6,250; Grants to individuals, 3 grants totaling $6,250 (high: $2,500, low: $500).
Fields of interest: Vocational education, post-secondary; Higher education.
Type of support: Employee-related scholarships.
Application information: Applications not accepted.
　Additional information: Unsolicited requests for funds not considered or acknowledged.
Company name: Reed Engineering Group, Inc.
EIN: 752728400

9034
Spence Reese Foundation
c/o Bank of America, N.A.
P.O. Box 831041
Dallas, TX　75283-1041
Application address: c/o Boys & Girls Clubs of Greater San Diego, 115 Woodward Ave., Escondido, CA 92025-2638

Foundation type: Independent foundation
Purpose: Scholarships to four males students who are in their senior year in high school, one each majoring in the fields of medicine, law, engineering, or political science.
Financial data: Year ended 04/30/2013. Assets, $541,854 (M); Expenditures, $67,657; Total giving, $54,000; Grants to individuals, 14 grants totaling $54,000 (high: $6,000, low: $2,000).
Fields of interest: Law school/education; Medical school/education; Engineering; Political science; Men.
Type of support: Scholarships—to individuals.

Application information: Application form required. Application form available on the grantmaker's web site.
　Initial approach: Letter
　Deadline(s): Apr. 15
　Applicants should submit the following:
　　1) SASE
　　2) SAT
　　3) Letter(s) of recommendation
　　4) GPA
　　5) ACT
　Additional information: Applicants are judged on academic ability, financial ability, and potential for good citizenship. Personal interviews may be required.
EIN: 510203269

9035
The Reilly Family Foundation
1017 S. FM Rd. 5
Aledo, TX　76008-4558　(817) 265-2364
Contact: Michael A. Reilly, Chair. and Dir.; Beverly A. Reilly, V.P. and Dir.

Foundation type: Independent foundation
Purpose: Scholarships to students in the Dallas/Fort Worth, TX area in good standing at their current educational institutions.
Financial data: Year ended 12/31/2012. Assets, $1,913,661 (M); Expenditures, $413,672; Total giving, $327,748; Grant to an individual, 1 grant totaling $4,629.
Fields of interest: Education.
Type of support: Undergraduate support.
Application information: Application form required.
　Initial approach: Letter or telephone
　Deadline(s): Vary
　Applicants should submit the following:
　　1) Letter(s) of recommendation
　　2) Transcripts
　　3) Resume
　　4) Financial information
EIN: 752366809

9036
Tom C. & Mary B. Reitch Scholarship Trust
c/o Bank of America, N.A.
P.O. Box 831041
Dallas, TX　75283-1041　(903) 569-3000
Contact: Michelle Dudley
Application address: c/o Mineola High School, 900 W. Patten St., Mineola, TX 75773-1556, tel.: (903) 569-3000

Foundation type: Independent foundation
Purpose: Scholarships to graduates of Mineola High School, Mineola, TX, for tuition to an accredited college or university.
Financial data: Year ended 12/31/2012. Assets, $1,580,495 (M); Expenditures, $90,802; Total giving, $65,000; Grants to individuals, 42 grants totaling $65,000 (high: $3,000, low: $500).
Fields of interest: Higher education.
Type of support: Support to graduates or students of specific schools.
Application information: Applications accepted. Application form required.
　Deadline(s): May 1
　Additional information: Application should include two letters of recommendation.
EIN: 527033946

9037
Reserve Aid, Inc.
2515 McKinney Ave., 11th Fl.
Dallas, TX 75201-1908 (972) 934-4731
Contact: Polly Weidenkopf, Exec. Dir.
FAX: (972) 767-0331;
E-mail: pollyw@reserveaid.org; URL: http://
www.reserveaid.org

Foundation type: Public charity
Purpose: Assistance to U.S. military reserve
personnel in financial need as a result of
deployment.
Publications: Application guidelines; Informational
brochure.
Financial data: Year ended 12/31/2011. Assets,
$1,040,910 (M); Expenditures, $1,202,763; Total
giving, $894,615; Grants to individuals, totaling
$894,615.
Fields of interest: Military/veterans.
Type of support: Grants to individuals; Grants for
special needs.
Application information: Applications accepted.
Application form required.
Send request by: Mail or fax
Additional information: Assistance is for U.S.
military reserve personnel only. Unsolicited
requests for funds not considered or
acknowledged.
Program description:
ReserveAid Grant: Unrestricted, need-based
grants are for military families who have a Reserve
Service member on full-time deployment to a
combat zone or homeland security position, in an
effort to alleviate the emotional and financial
burdens placed on the men and women called to
serve. Eligible applicants include reservists and
National Guard members who is currently deployed
or has returned from deployment within the past 12
months or has been rated 75 percent or greater by
the VA and is not able to work. Applicants must be
referred by a VA representative or service
representative, i.e. Wounded Warrior Advocate or
National Guard Family Assistance coordinator. All
requests require prior approval.
EIN: 412167545

9038
Sid Richardson Memorial Fund
309 Main St.
Fort Worth, TX 76102-4006 (817) 336-0494
Contact: Peggy Laskoski, Coord.
FAX: (817) 332-2176;
E-mail: plaskoski@sidrichardson.org; URL: http://
www.sidrichardson.org

Foundation type: Independent foundation
Purpose: Scholarships to children and
grandchildren of a current or retired employee at
service companies with at least three years of
full-time service.
Financial data: Year ended 12/31/2012. Assets,
$6,855,304 (M); Expenditures, $411,025; Total
giving, $268,750; Grants to individuals, 64 grants
totaling $268,750 (high: $9,000, low: $750).
Fields of interest: Higher education.
Type of support: Employee-related scholarships.
Application information: Applications accepted.
Application form required. Application form
available on the grantmaker's web site.
Initial approach: Letter or fax
Copies of proposal: 1
Deadline(s): Mar. 31
Applicants should submit the following:
1) Transcripts
2) SAT
3) Resume

4) Letter(s) of recommendation
5) GPA
6) Financial information
7) Essay
8) Budget Information
9) ACT
Additional information: Employees service should
be at one of the following companies: Barbnet
Investment Co., BEPCO, L.P., BOPCO, L.P.,
City Club of Ft. Worth, Richardson Aviation,
San Jose Cattle Co., Sid Richardson Carbon
Co., Sid. W. Richardson Foundation and
Sundance Square Management, L.P.
Acceptance is based on academic
achievement and financial need.
EIN: 751220266

9039
Earl N. & Conrad E. Riffe Memorial
Scholarship Trust
(formerly Riffe Memorial Scholarship Trust)
P.O. Box 48
Stratford, TX 79084 (806) 396-5521

Foundation type: Independent foundation
Purpose: Scholarships to graduating high school
students of Stratford, TX.
Financial data: Year ended 12/31/2011. Assets,
$178,167 (M); Expenditures, $8,117; Total giving,
$6,750; Grants to individuals, 5 grants totaling
$6,750 (high: $1,500, low: $750).
Fields of interest: Higher education.
Type of support: Scholarships—to individuals.
Application information: Applications not
accepted.
Initial approach: Letter
Deadline(s): Mar.
EIN: 756325925

9040
Right from the Start Nutrition
4275 Little Rd., Ste. 106
Arlington, TX 76016-5617 (817) 563-7774
Contact: Nguyen Nguyen, Chair.

Foundation type: Public charity
Purpose: Reimbursements to day-care home
providers for nutritional meals served to needy
children from newborn through 15 years old
throughout the Arlington, TX area.
Financial data: Year ended 12/31/2011. Assets,
$543,374 (M); Expenditures, $5,733,161; Total
giving, $5,064,226; Grants to individuals, totaling
$2,603,249.
Fields of interest: Day care.
Type of support: Grants for special needs.
Application information: Contact the agency for
additional information.
EIN: 752771976

9041
Rio Grande Cancer Foundation
10460 Vista Del Sol, Ste. 101
El Paso, TX 79925-7939 (915) 562-7660
FAX: (915) 562-7841; E-mail: rgcf@rgcf.org; E-mail
For Patty Tiscareno: ptiscareno@rgcf.org;
URL: http://www.rgcf.org/

Foundation type: Public charity
Purpose: Financial assistance with free air
transport for cancer patients in El Paso County, TX
who are in need of medical assistance that is
unavailable locally.

Publications: Application guidelines; Grants list;
Informational brochure (including application
guidelines); Newsletter.
Financial data: Year ended 12/31/2012. Assets,
$11,534,130 (M); Expenditures, $837,457; Total
giving, $246,826; Grants to individuals, totaling
$66,976.
Fields of interest: Health care, support services;
Health care, patient services; Cancer.
Type of support: Grants for special needs.
Application information: Applications accepted.
Additional information: Patients apply for
assistance once a referral is obtained from an
El Paso physician. \.
Program description:
Patient Air Transportation Services (PATS): This
program provides free airline transportation
services to cancer patients who are referred outside
the El Paso area for evaluation, treatment, surgical
procedures, or further diagnostic study. Services
are available to any patient whose medical
treatment is unavailable locally and who has a
genuine financial need, as determined by their
referring physician. A round trip airline ticket is
purchased for the patient only.
EIN: 237105159

9042
Velma Lee & John Harvey Robinson
Charitable Foundation
P.O. Box 924
Edna, TX 77957-0924 (361) 782-5737
Contact: John J. Shutt, V.P.

Foundation type: Independent foundation
Purpose: Scholarships are made to Jackson
County, TX, students who will attend a Texas
college, university or trade school, and maintain a
2.75 GPA.
Financial data: Year ended 09/30/2012. Assets,
$24,977,639 (M); Expenditures, $1,385,872;
Total giving, $1,175,000; Grants to individuals,
95 grants totaling $515,230 (high: $5,000, low:
$500).
Type of support: Scholarships—to individuals.
Application information: Applications accepted.
Application form required.
Deadline(s): May 1
Additional information: Scholarship applications
become available to the high school
counselors of the three high schools in
Jackson County, TX, by Apr. 1.
EIN: 742300129

9043
Harry W. and Virginia Robinson Trust
c/o Bank of America, N.A.
P.O. Box 831041
Dallas, TX 75283-1041

Foundation type: Independent foundation
Purpose: Scholarships to students attending
California Institute of Technology Gift and Estate
Planning and Pitzer College for higher education.
Financial data: Year ended 05/31/2012. Assets,
$4,290,950 (M); Expenditures, $242,370; Total
giving, $202,752.
Fields of interest: Higher education.
Type of support: Scholarships—to individuals;
Support to graduates or students of specific
schools.
Application information: Application form not
required.
Additional information: Unsolicited requests for
funds not accepted.
EIN: 956648391

9044
Rolling Plains Management Corporation
P.O. Box 490
Crowell, TX   79227-0490   (940) 684-1571

Foundation type: Public charity
Purpose: Grants to needy individuals in TX for necessities like child care assistance, transportation, and energy assistance.
Financial data: Year ended 11/30/2011. Assets, $4,921,623 (M); Expenditures, $18,240,732; Total giving, $11,175,711; Grants to individuals, totaling $11,175,711.
Fields of interest: Economically disadvantaged.
Type of support: Grants for special needs.
Application information: Contact foundation for eligibility requirements.
EIN: 756047309

9045
The Romsdahl Foundation
295 Circle Dr.
Onalaska, TX   77360-7801   (936) 646-6052
Contact: Virginia M. Romsdahl, Pres.

Foundation type: Independent foundation
Purpose: Scholarships to graduating seniors of Hamlin County High School, South Dakota for continuing education at institutions of higher learning.
Financial data: Year ended 11/30/2012. Assets, $221,118 (M); Expenditures, $13,436; Total giving, $10,000.
Fields of interest: Higher education.
Type of support: Support to graduates or students of specific schools.
Application information: Applications accepted. Application form required.
  Deadline(s): Apr.
  Applicants should submit the following:
    1) Transcripts
    2) Essay
  Additional information: Application should also include two personal references. Scholarship selection is based on extracurricular and community activities, hobbies, work experience and area of study in college.
EIN: 760554765

9046
Rooke Foundation, Inc.
P.O. Box 610
Woodsboro, TX   78393-0610   (361) 543-4533
Contact: Robert E. Rooke, Jr., V.P.
Application address: P.O. Box 7, Woodsboro, TX 78393, tel.: (361) 543-4533

Foundation type: Independent foundation
Purpose: Scholarships to graduates of high schools in Refugio County, TX.
Financial data: Year ended 12/31/2011. Assets, $161,475 (M); Expenditures, $9,263; Total giving, $8,413; Grants to individuals, 10 grants totaling $5,000 (high: $500, low: $500).
Type of support: Support to graduates or students of specific schools; Undergraduate support.
Application information: Applications accepted. Application form required. Interview required.
  Deadline(s): Apr. 1
  Additional information: Applications available from Refugio County high schools.
EIN: 746003460

9047
Rotary Club of Killeen Heights Charitable Corporation
P.O. Box 935
Killeen, TX   76540-0935   (254) 290-0383
Contact: Susan Jones
Application Address: 9782 Arroyo Drive,Belton TX 76513

Foundation type: Independent foundation
Purpose: Scholarships to residents of Bell or Coryell counties TX for attendance at colleges or universities in TX.
Financial data: Year ended 06/30/2011. Assets, $5,547 (M); Expenditures, $10,000; Total giving, $10,000.
Fields of interest: Higher education.
Type of support: Scholarships—to individuals.
Application information: Applications accepted. Application form required.
  Deadline(s): Mar. 1
  Applicants should submit the following:
    1) Transcripts
    2) Letter(s) of recommendation
EIN: 742944842

9048
Nolan Ryan Historical Foundation
P.O. Box 1534
Alvin, TX   77512-1534
Contact: Judy Blunck, Secy.-Treas.
URL: http://www.nolanryanfoundation.org

Foundation type: Public charity
Purpose: Scholarships primarily to residents of Hutto and Alvin, TX.
Financial data: Year ended 01/31/2012. Assets, $1,506,340 (M); Expenditures, $201,732; Total giving, $90,790; Grants to individuals, totaling $57,650.
Type of support: Undergraduate support.
Application information: Contact foundation for eligibility information.
EIN: 760290880

9049
The Ryrie Foundation
3310 Fairmount St., Apt. 5D
Dallas, TX   75201-1232   (972) 383-5700
Contact: Charles C. Ryrie, Tr.

Foundation type: Independent foundation
Purpose: Scholarships to individuals in Texas and throughout the U.S. pursuing a higher education.
Financial data: Year ended 12/31/2011. Assets, $2,430,261 (M); Expenditures, $231,429; Total giving, $219,700.
Fields of interest: Higher education.
Type of support: Scholarships—to individuals.
Application information: Applications accepted. Application form required.
  Deadline(s): None
  Applicants should submit the following:
    1) Photograph
    2) Financial information
  Additional information: Application should also include educational background, goals, current school enrollment status, statement of doctrinal compatibility, and brief autobiography.
EIN: 752001540

9050
S.G.K.&G. Foundation
3629 Greenbrier Dr.
Dallas, TX   75225

Foundation type: Independent foundation
Purpose: Scholarships to students who are residents of Texas for continuing education at institutions of higher learning.
Financial data: Year ended 12/31/2012. Assets, $1,579 (M); Expenditures, $39,677; Total giving, $33,246.
Type of support: Scholarships—to individuals.
Application information: Applications not accepted.
EIN: 205273925

9051
Salesmanship Club of Dallas
106 E. 10th St., Ste. 200
Dallas, TX   75208-6642   (214) 943-9700
FAX: (214) 942-6760;
E-mail: get_involved@scdallas.org; URL: http://www.scdallas.org/

Foundation type: Public charity
Purpose: Grants to needy families, primarily in the Dallas, TX, area. Also, grants by nomination only to junior golfers who excel in junior tournament play, academics, character, and community service.
Financial data: Year ended 10/31/2011. Assets, $12,077,449 (M); Expenditures, $10,155,784; Total giving, $9,177,007; Grants to individuals, totaling $21,482.
Fields of interest: Athletics/sports, golf.
Type of support: Awards/grants by nomination only; Grants for special needs.
Application information: Applications not accepted.
  Additional information: Unsolicited requests for funds not considered or acknowledged.
EIN: 750717135

9052
Salesmanship Club Youth and Family Centers, Inc.
106 E. 10th St.
Dallas, TX   75203-2236   (214) 915-4700
Contact: Michelle Kinder M.Ed., Exec. Dir.
E-mail: info@salesmanshipclub.org; E-Mail for Delane Kinney: mkinder@salesmanshipclub.org; Tel. for Delane Kinney : (214) 915-4776;
URL: http://www.salesmanshipclub.org

Foundation type: Public charity
Purpose: Specific assistance to children and families in the North Oak Cliff area of Dallas, TX, with food, clothing, rent, utilities, school supplies, transportation, and other services. College scholarships to students with help for tuition, books, supplies and housing.
Publications: Annual report.
Financial data: Year ended 10/31/2011. Assets, $10,913,750 (M); Expenditures, $8,762,511; Total giving, $137,250; Grants to individuals, totaling $137,250.
Fields of interest: Higher education; Human services; Children.
Type of support: Scholarships—to individuals; Grants for special needs.
Application information: Scholarship selection is based on merit and need.
EIN: 751855620

9053
San Angelo Area Foundation
221 S. Irving St.
San Angelo, TX 76903-6421 (325) 947-7071
Contact: Matt Lewis, C.E.O.
FAX: (325) 947-7322;
E-mail: infosaaf@saafound.org; Additional e-mail:
mlewis@saafound.org; URL: http://
www.saafound.org

Foundation type: Community foundation
Purpose: Scholarships to residents of Glasscock,
Sterling, Coke, Runnels, Reagan, Irion, Tom Green,
Concho, McCulloch, San Saba, Crockett,
Schleicher, Menard, Mason, Llano, Sutton, and
Kimble counties, TX for higher education.
Publications: Annual report; Grants list;
Informational brochure; Newsletter.
Financial data: Year ended 12/31/2011. Assets,
$58,796,711 (M); Expenditures, $9,380,522;
Total giving, $8,617,547; Grants to individuals,
518 grants totaling $827,697.
Fields of interest: Higher education; Scholarships/
financial aid.
Type of support: Undergraduate support.
Application information: Applications accepted.
Application form required. Application form
available on the grantmaker's web site.
  Initial approach: Application
  Send request by: Online
  Deadline(s): Mar. 1
  Final notification: Recipients notified May 15
  Applicants should submit the following:
    1) Financial information
    2) FAFSA
    3) Letter(s) of recommendation
    4) ACT
    5) SAT
    6) Transcripts
    7) Essay
  Additional information: See web site for a
    complete list of programs and additional
    guidelines.
EIN: 731634145

9054
San Antonio A & M Club Foundation
6205 W. Ave.
San Antonio, TX 78213-2315 (210) 341-1393
Contact: Jim Whiteaker
URL: http://www.aggiepark.com/

Foundation type: Operating foundation
Purpose: Scholarships to Bexar County, TX, high
school students for attendance at Texas A&M
University.
Financial data: Year ended 12/31/2011. Assets,
$1,237,575 (M); Expenditures, $221,353; Total
giving, $52,303.
Fields of interest: Higher education.
Type of support: Support to graduates or students
of specific schools; Undergraduate support.
Application information: Applications accepted.
Application form required.
  Deadline(s): Feb.
EIN: 742247729

9055
San Antonio Area Foundation
303 E. Pearl Pkwy., Ste. 114
San Antonio, TX 78215 (210) 225-2243
Contact: For grant applications: Lydia Saldana,
Prog. Off., Community and Research Grants
FAX: (210) 225-1980; E-mail: info@saafdn.org;
URL: http://www.saafdn.org

Foundation type: Community foundation
Purpose: Scholarships to graduating seniors of
Bexar county, TX attending colleges, universities,
trade, or technical schools.
Publications: Application guidelines; Annual report;
Financial statement; Grants list; Informational
brochure; Newsletter; Quarterly report.
Financial data: Year ended 12/31/2012. Assets,
$227,435,849 (M); Expenditures, $17,612,761;
Total giving, $8,905,911.
Fields of interest: Vocational education,
post-secondary; Higher education.
Type of support: Scholarships—to individuals;
Support to graduates or students of specific
schools; Undergraduate support.
Application information: Applications accepted.
Application form required. Application form
available on the grantmaker's web site.
  Copies of proposal: 1
  Deadline(s): Varies
  Final notification: Applicant notified last week of
    Apr. to first week of May
  Additional information: Applications can be
    obtained from your high school guidance
    counselor. See web site for additional
    application guidelines and a complete list of
    scholarships.
Program description:
  Scholarships: The foundation manages over 80
scholarship funds, each customized to donors'
desires and selection criteria. Established by
generous individuals, families, corporations and
organizations, these scholarship awards are
charitable grants that do not require repayment.
Scholarships may be used for legitimate education
expenses such as tuition, fees, book, and room and
board. Awards range from $500 to $6,000.
EIN: 746065414

9056
San Antonio Dance Umbrella
P.O. Box 830634
San Antonio, TX 78283-0634 (210) 212-6600
E-mail: sadu@sadu.org; Additional address: 106
Auditorium Cir., Ste. 105, San Antonio, TX 78205;
URL: http://www.sadu.org/

Foundation type: Public charity
Purpose: Scholarships to exceptional dancers
between the ages of 13 and 21 in the San Antonio,
TX area who demonstrate ability, artistry, passion
and need to further their dance education.
Financial data: Year ended 09/30/2011. Assets,
$3,185 (M); Expenditures, $45,867.
Fields of interest: Dance; Choreography; Arts,
artist's services.
Type of support: Scholarships—to individuals;
Fiscal agent/sponsor.
Application information: Applications accepted.
Application form required.
  Initial approach: E-mail or telephone
  Applicants should submit the following:
    1) Photograph
    2) Letter(s) of recommendation
  Additional information: Application should also
    include a brief biographical statement
    including all dance study, a videotaped solo
    performance of one to five minutes (format
    should be on VHS or DVD). See web site for
    additional application information.
Program descriptions:
  Fiscal Sponsorship: The organization serves as a
fiscal agent for projects by SADU members to
promote dance in San Antonio and encourage
dancers and choreographers to create new works.
  The Julia L. Cauthorn Scholarship: This
scholarship fund provides aid to young, promising

dancers of the San Antonio area in their pursuit of
a dance education. Scholarships are awarded on
ability, merit, and future potential.
EIN: 742664001

9057
San Antonio Education Fund
131 El Paso St.
San Antonio, TX 78204-3108 (210) 207-4766
Contact: Eyra A. Perez, Exec. Dir.
FAX: (210) 207-4765;
E-mail: Info@saedpartnership.org; URL: http://
www.saedpartnership.org

Foundation type: Public charity
Purpose: Scholarships only to students from
pre-determined public high schools in San Antonio,
TX, who will be attending participating colleges or
universities.
Publications: Informational brochure; Newsletter.
Financial data: Year ended 09/30/2012. Assets,
$2,996,763 (M); Expenditures, $3,619,557; Total
giving, $1,783,124; Grants to individuals, totaling
$1,783,124.
Fields of interest: Higher education.
Type of support: Support to graduates or students
of specific schools; Undergraduate support.
Application information: Applications not
accepted.
  Additional information: Unsolicited requests for
    funds not considered or acknowledged.
EIN: 742547643

9058
San Antonio Livestock Exposition, Inc.
(also known as San Antonio Stock Show and Rodeo)
723 AT&T Center Pkwy.
San Antonio, TX 78219-3609 (210) 225-5851
Contact: Keith Martin, Exec. Dir. and C.E.O.
FAX: (210) 227-7934; E-mail: info@sarodeo.com;
Mailing address: P.O. Box 200230, San Antonio, TX
78220-0230; URL: http://www.sarodeo.com

Foundation type: Public charity
Purpose: Scholarships to 4-H and FFA members
who plan to continue interest in agriculture by
pursuing agricultural studies at a TX college or
university.
Financial data: Year ended 03/31/2012. Assets,
$42,095,858 (M); Expenditures, $28,260,212;
Total giving, $5,124,619.
Fields of interest: Formal/general education;
Agriculture, livestock issues.
Type of support: Undergraduate support.
Application information: Applications accepted.
Application form required. Application form
available on the grantmaker's web site.
  Additional information: Scholarships given
    primarily to participants in San Antonio Stock
    & Rodeo programs.
EIN: 741075466

9059
San Marcos Civic Foundation
2579 Western Trails Blvd., Ste. 110
Austin, TX 78745-1496 (512) 328-6696
Contact: Susan Hinton, Tr.

Foundation type: Independent foundation
Purpose: Grants to train TX professional educators
to design a structured language curriculum for
students who have trouble learning how to read,
write and spell English.

Financial data: Year ended 12/31/2012. Assets, $6,468,951 (M); Expenditures, $451,375; Total giving, $147,608.
Type of support: Program development; Project support.
Application information: Applications accepted.
Deadline(s): None
Additional information: Contact foundation for current application guidelines.
EIN: 746109230

9060
Sand Dollar Foundation
3000 White Settlement Rd.
Fort Worth, TX 76107-1338 (817) 988-6110
Contact: Larry Barker, Dir.
E-mail: lbarker@abahn.com; Additional contact: Stacie Williams, Morgan Stanley, (314) 889-9842, (800) 488-9880, e-mail: Stacie.Williams@mssb.com; URL: http://www.autobahnyouthtour.com/

Foundation type: Company-sponsored foundation
Purpose: Scholarships to winners of Texas Longhorn Breeders Association youth qualifying shows.
Publications: Application guidelines.
Financial data: Year ended 12/31/2012. Assets, $1,090 (M); Expenditures, $630,734; Total giving, $537,811; Grants to individuals, 196 grants totaling $537,811 (high: $17,180, low: $100).
Fields of interest: Athletics/sports, equestrianism.
Type of support: Undergraduate support.
Application information: Applications accepted. Application form available on the grantmaker's web site.
Initial approach: Entry Form
Send request by: Mail
Deadline(s): Varies
Additional information: Applicants are selected through the Texas Longhorn Breeders Association's world show qualifying circuit for youth. Scholarships are publicized as part of each show and the winners of each class in the show are eligible.
Company name: Autobahn Imports, Inc.
EIN: 752957772

9061
Santander Consumer USA Inc. Foundation
(formerly Drive With A Heart Foundation)
8585 N. Stemmons Fwy., Ste. 1100 N.
Dallas, TX 75247-3836 (888) 222-4227
FAX: (214) 237-0533; URL: http://www.santanderconsumerusa.com/about/drive_w_heart.aspx

Foundation type: Company-sponsored foundation
Purpose: Scholarships to K-12 and GED students residing in the Turner Courts housing development in Dallas, Texas.
Financial data: Year ended 12/31/2011. Assets, $243,866 (M); Expenditures, $55,564; Total giving, $55,265.
Type of support: Scholarships—to individuals.
Application information:
Initial approach: Letter
Additional information: Contact foundation for eligibility requirements.
Program description:
Scholarship Program: The foundation awards college scholarships to K-12 and GED students residing in the Turner Courts housing development in Dallas, Texas.
EIN: 201519185

9062
Schull Institute
P.O. Box 131755
Houston, TX 77219-1755
URL: http://www.schullinstitute.com/

Foundation type: Independent foundation
Purpose: Scholarships to individuals for graduate studies in health information sciences in the Houston, TX area.
Financial data: Year ended 12/31/2012. Assets, $41,611 (M); Expenditures, $212,326; Total giving, $196,512; Grants to individuals, 2 grants totaling $182,546 (high: $181,546, low: $1,000).
Fields of interest: Science.
Type of support: Scholarships—to individuals.
Application information: Selection is based on the technical and educational background of the recipients.
EIN: 760637246

9063
Reno O. Schumann Educational Trust
172 W. Coll St.
New Braunfels, TX 78130-5108 (830) 609-7729

Foundation type: Independent foundation
Purpose: Scholarships to members in good standing of First Protestant Church, New Braunfels, TX.
Financial data: Year ended 12/31/2012. Assets, $179,935 (M); Expenditures, $10,151; Total giving, $9,323; Grants to individuals, 10 grants totaling $9,323 (high: $933, low: $932).
Fields of interest: Education; Protestant agencies & churches.
Type of support: Scholarships—to individuals.
Application information: Application form required.
Deadline(s): Apr. 1
Applicants should submit the following:
1) Photograph
2) Resume
3) Letter(s) of recommendation
EIN: 746248871

9064
Schwab-Rosenhouse Memorial Foundation
c/o Wells Fargo Bank, N.A.
P.O. Box 41629, MAC T7061-021
Austin, TX 78704-9926 (609) 243-6549

Foundation type: Independent foundation
Purpose: Scholarships to residents of the four counties in and around Sacramento, CA, to enroll at a postsecondary school located within a 100-mile radius of Sacramento.
Financial data: Year ended 12/31/2012. Assets, $6,342,184 (M); Expenditures, $477,683; Total giving, $325,875; Grants to individuals, 247 grants totaling $325,785 (high: $2,750, low: $500).
Fields of interest: Higher education.
Type of support: Scholarships—to individuals.
Application information: Applications accepted. Application form required.
Send request by: Mail
Deadline(s): Feb. 1
Final notification: Recipients notified in May
Applicants should submit the following:
1) Transcripts
2) Letter(s) of recommendation
EIN: 686136241

9065
The Second Baptist School Foundation, Inc.
6400 Woodway Dr.
Houston, TX 77057-1606 (713) 365-2310
FAX: (713) 365-2355;
E-mail: japplegate@secondbaptistschool.org

Foundation type: Public charity
Purpose: Scholarships to selected students attending Second Baptist School, TX.
Publications: Annual report.
Financial data: Year ended 07/31/2011. Assets, $7,541,514 (M); Expenditures, $945,097; Total giving, $672,047.
Type of support: Support to graduates or students of specific schools.
Application information:
Initial approach: Letter
Additional information: Scholarship is based on financial need.
EIN: 760088961

9066
Second Mile Misson Center
504 FM 1092, Ste. I
Stafford, TX 77477-5419 (281) 261-9199
Contact: Sarah White, Exec. Dir.
FAX: (281) 403-0705; URL: http://www.secondmile.org

Foundation type: Public charity
Purpose: Financial assistance to low-income individuals and families of Fort Bend County, TX, with food, clothing, shelter, utility, medical services, and temporary housing assistance, and rental expense.
Financial data: Year ended 12/31/2011. Assets, $618,959 (M); Expenditures, $4,057,949; Total giving, $3,446,835; Grants to individuals, totaling $3,446,835.
Fields of interest: Economically disadvantaged.
Type of support: Grants for special needs.
Application information: Applications not accepted.
Additional information: Contact the organization for needed assistance.
EIN: 810556112

9067
R. Q. & L. A. Seely Charitable Trust
(formerly Roger Q. & Lovye A. Seely Trust)
P.O. Box 624
Corsicana, TX 75151-9004
Application address: c/o Wortham Independent School District, Attn: C.T. Griffin, P.O. Box 247, Wortham, TX 76693-0247, tel.: (817) 765-3678

Foundation type: Independent foundation
Purpose: Scholarships to high school graduates of the Wortham, TX, area to attend Navarro College. Loans to high school graduates of the Wortham, TX, area to attend colleges and universities in TX.
Financial data: Year ended 02/28/2012. Assets, $505,113 (M); Expenditures, $28,081; Total giving, $23,045.
Fields of interest: Higher education.
Type of support: Support to graduates or students of specific schools; Undergraduate support.
Application information: Applications accepted. Application form required. Interview required.
Deadline(s): May 10.
Applicants should submit the following:
1) Financial information
2) Essay
3) Letter(s) of recommendation

Additional information: Applications available at Wortham High School.
EIN: 756269098

9068
The Abe and Annie Seibel Foundation
c/o Frost National Bank
P.O. Box 179
Galveston, TX   77553-0179   (409) 770-7100
Contact: Janet L. Bertiolino, V.P. and Trust Off., Frost National Bank
FAX: (409) 770-7166

Foundation type: Independent foundation
Purpose: Interest-free undergraduate student loans to TX residents and graduates of TX high schools for full-time attendance at TX colleges and universities.
Publications: Application guidelines; Informational brochure (including application guidelines).
Financial data: Year ended 07/31/2013. Assets, $37,848,774 (M); Expenditures, $5,177,422; Total giving, $4,546,935; Loans to individuals, totaling $4,046,935.
Fields of interest: Higher education.
Type of support: Undergraduate support.
Application information: Application form required.
  Initial approach: Letter or telephone
  Deadline(s): Feb. 28
  Applicants should submit the following:
    1) SAT
    2) Letter(s) of recommendation
    3) GPA
    4) Financial information
    5) Essay
    6) Budget Information
    7) ACT
    8) Transcripts
Program description:
  Seibel Foundation Loan Program: Recipients are selected on the basis of need and GPA and SAT scores. Minimum SAT scores of 1000 (for top 25 percent of the class) or 1100-1200 (for bottom 75 percent of the class) are required. Maximum loan amount is $4,000. Loans must be co-signed. A minimum monthly payment of $35 must be made while in school. Funds are usually made to the student in two disbursements, half of the approved amount for each semester. Upon completion of an undergraduate degree, students will have six years to repay the loan. College students must maintain a 2.75 overall GPA.
EIN: 746035556

9069
Seton Fund of the Daughters of Charity of St. Vincent de Paul, Inc
1201 W. 38th St.
Austin, TX   78705-1006   (512) 324-1990
Application address: 1206 W. 38th St., Ste. 4200, Austin, TX 78705, tel.: (512) 324-3005, e-mail: acook@seton.org
FAX: (512) 324-1989;
E-mail: setonfund@seton.org; URL: http://www.setonfund.org

Foundation type: Public charity
Purpose: Nursing scholarships to Seton employees pursuing a degree in nursing and accepted in an accredited undergraduate or graduating nursing program.
Publications: Newsletter.
Fields of interest: Nursing school/education.
Type of support: Employee-related scholarships.
Application information: Applications accepted. Application form required. Interview required.

Send request by: Mail or e-mail
Deadline(s): May 7
Final notification: Recipients notified early July
Applicants should submit the following:
  1) Transcripts
  2) Letter(s) of recommendation
Additional information: Application should also include proof of acceptance into an accredited school of nursing.
EIN: 742212968

9070
The M. L. Shanor Foundation
P.O. Box 2370
Wichita Falls, TX   76307-2370   (940) 631-9768
Contact: Frank W. Jarratt, Pres.

Foundation type: Independent foundation
Purpose: Grants to residents of Cherokee, Wichita, and Wilbarger counties, TX.
Financial data: Year ended 12/31/2012. Assets, $4,340,830 (M); Expenditures, $198,745; Total giving, $146,350; Grants to individuals, 69 grants totaling $118,350 (high: $3,500, low: $500).
Type of support: Grants to individuals.
Application information: Application form required.
  Deadline(s): Aug. 1
  Applicants should submit the following:
    1) GPA
    2) Financial information
  Additional information: Application must also include two high school references from either two teachers or a teacher and a principal.
EIN: 756012834

9071
Helen Shacklet Shouse Memorial Scholarship Trust
c/o Bank of America, N.A.
P.O. Box 831041
Dallas, TX   75283-1041   (816) 292-4300
Contact: B. Spencer Heddens III
Application address: c/o Bank Of America N.A., P.O. Box 219119, Kansas City, MO 64141-6119, tel.: (816) 292-4300

Foundation type: Independent foundation
Purpose: Scholarships to graduates of Lexington High School, MO for postsecondary education.
Financial data: Year ended 12/31/2012. Assets, $229,231 (M); Expenditures, $13,607; Total giving, $6,300; Grants to individuals, 2 grants totaling $6,000 (high: $3,000, low: $3,000).
Fields of interest: Higher education.
Type of support: Undergraduate support.
Application information: Application form required.
  Deadline(s): Apr. 1
  Additional information: Applicant must demonstrate financial need.
EIN: 431764196

9072
Victoria Livestock Show Foundation
655 E. Lake Dr.
Livingston, TX   77351
Application addresses: c/o Leesa Brown, Chair., Victoria Livestock Show Scholarship Program, 2908 Linda, Victoria, TX 77901, tel.: (361) 218-8516; The County Extension Office, 528 Waco Circle, Victoria, TX 77904, tel.: (361) 575-4581
URL: http://victorialivestockshow.net/Documents/2012_VLS_Scholarship_Appl_and_Info.pdf

Foundation type: Independent foundation

Purpose: Scholarships to graduating seniors who reside in Victoria Court, TX, for higher education at any TX college or university.
Financial data: Year ended 04/30/2011. Assets, $162,133 (M); Expenditures, $16,035; Total giving, $15,500; Grants to individuals, 18 grants totaling $15,500 (high: $1,500, low: $500).
Fields of interest: Higher education; Scholarships/financial aid; Agriculture, livestock issues.
Type of support: Undergraduate support.
Application information: Application form required. Interview required.
  Send request by: Mail
  Deadline(s): Feb. 3
  Final notification: Applicants notified in Mar.
  Applicants should submit the following:
    1) Class rank
    2) Photograph
    3) GPA
    4) Transcripts
  Additional information: Funds are paid directly to the educational institution on behalf of the students.
EIN: 742712669

9073
Silver and Black Give Back
(formerly The San Antonio Spurs Foundation)
1 AT&T Ctr., Pkwy.
San Antonio, TX   78219-3604   (210) 444-5541
Contact: Laura Dixon, Exec. Dir.
FAX: (210) 444-5875; E-mail: sbgb@attcenter.com; URL: http://www.silverandblackgiveback.com

Foundation type: Public charity
Purpose: Scholarships to students in southern TX for higher education.
Financial data: Year ended 06/30/2012. Assets, $2,008,380 (M); Expenditures, $685,668; Total giving, $195,250.
Type of support: Undergraduate support.
Application information: Applications accepted. Application form required.
  Initial approach: Letter
  Deadline(s): Feb.
EIN: 742509544

9074
Rose Silverthorne Foundation
2940 N. O'Connor Rd., Ste. 125
Irving, TX   75062-8802   (972) 252-4200
Contact: William Driscoll, Treas.

Foundation type: Independent foundation
Purpose: Scholarships to individuals in TX for higher education.
Publications: Application guidelines.
Financial data: Year ended 12/31/2012. Assets, $1,940,449 (M); Expenditures, $100,100; Total giving, $79,094; Grants to individuals, 21 grants totaling $79,094 (high: $9,620, low: $310).
Type of support: Undergraduate support.
Application information: Applications accepted. Application form required.
  Initial approach: Letter or telephone
  Copies of proposal: 1
  Deadline(s): Mar.
EIN: 752669407

9075
M. E. Singleton Scholarship Trust
P.O. Box 717
Waxahachie, TX   75168-0717

Foundation type: Independent foundation

Purpose: Scholarships to financially needy students who graduate from high schools in Ellis County, TX.
Financial data: Year ended 07/31/2012. Assets, $3,821,015 (M); Expenditures, $206,755; Total giving, $205,000; Grants to individuals, 134 grants totaling $205,000 (high: $3,000, low: $1,000).
Fields of interest: Higher education; Scholarships/financial aid; Economically disadvantaged.
Type of support: Support to graduates or students of specific schools; Undergraduate support.
Application information: Applications accepted. Application form required.
 Initial approach: Letter requesting application
 Deadline(s): None
EIN: 756037399

9076
Bedford W. Sipes Memorial Student Loan Fund
c/o Wells Fargo Bank, N.A.
P.O. Box 41629
Austin, TX 78704-9926 (361) 886-6600
Application address: c/o Wells Fargo Bank Texas, N.A., Attn.: Lauren Ranly Duke, Trust Off., P.O. Box 900, Corpus Christi, TX, 78403-0900, tel.: (361) 886-6600

Foundation type: Independent foundation
Purpose: Low-interest student loans to students and graduates of Sinton High School, TX, for higher learning at TX institutions.
Financial data: Year ended 02/29/2012. Assets, $201,275 (M); Expenditures, $14,129; Total giving, $3,000; Loan to an individual, 1 loan totaling $3,000.
Fields of interest: Higher education.
Type of support: Student loans—to individuals; Support to graduates or students of specific schools.
Application information: Applications accepted. Application form required.
 Initial approach: Letter outlining financial need
 Deadline(s): None
EIN: 746321954

9077
Clara Lou Vena Siros Foundation
3900 N. 10th St.
McAllen, TX 78501

Foundation type: Independent foundation
Purpose: Scholarships to financially needy students at Laredo Community College, TX, who reside in either Webb County or Laredo, TX.
Financial data: Year ended 12/31/2012. Assets, $998,108 (M); Expenditures, $18,131; Total giving, $0.
Type of support: Support to graduates or students of specific schools; Undergraduate support.
Application information: Application form required.
 Initial approach: Letter or telephone
 Deadline(s): Apr. 27
 Applicants should submit the following:
  1) SAR
  2) Photograph
  3) Letter(s) of recommendation
  4) Transcripts
 Additional information: Application must also include parents' and student's tax returns, and copy of financial aid award letter.
EIN: 742574458

9078
Pat & Emmitt Smith Charities
(formerly Emmitt Smith Charities, Inc.)
c/o Tolleson Wealth Management
5500 Preston Rd.
Dallas, TX 75205-2699 (214) 252-3250
Contact: Emmitt J. Smith III, V.P.
E-mail: info@patandemmittsmithcharities.org;
URL: http://www.smithcharities.wordpress.com/

Foundation type: Independent foundation
Purpose: Scholarships to underserved children of the Dallas, TX area for postsecondary education.
Financial data: Year ended 09/30/2012. Assets, $289,424 (M); Expenditures, $839,512; Total giving, $211,816.
Fields of interest: Higher education.
Type of support: Scholarships—to individuals.
Application information: Applications accepted.
 Initial approach: Letter or telephone
 Additional information: Applicant should explain the purpose for the gift/grant.
EIN: 201895778

9079
Zella M. Smith Scholarship Trust
c/o Bank of America, N.A.
P.O. Box 831041
Dallas, TX 75283-1041

Foundation type: Independent foundation
Purpose: Scholarships to graduating seniors of the Fallbrook Union High School District, CA, for higher education.
Financial data: Year ended 02/28/2013. Assets, $330,469 (M); Expenditures, $15,091; Total giving, $10,300; Grants to individuals, 10 grants totaling $10,300 (high: $2,000, low: $300).
Fields of interest: Higher education.
Type of support: Scholarships—to individuals; Support to graduates or students of specific schools.
Application information: Application form required.
 Initial approach: Letter
 Deadline(s): Apr. 15
 Additional information: Application can be obtained from the guidance counselor office.
EIN: 953653710

9080
Smolin-Melin Scholarship Fund Trust
(formerly Antonia Smolin and Victor Smolin Scholarship Fund Charitable Trust)
c/o Bank of America, N.A.
P.O. Box 831041
Dallas, TX 75283-1041 (415) 771-6400
Contact: Richard Zuckerman, Trust Off., Bank of America, N.A.
Application Address: 1188 Franklin St., Ste. 201, San Francisco, CA 94109

Foundation type: Independent foundation
Purpose: Scholarships to children of members of Local 10 of the International Longshoremen's and Warehousemen's Union.
Financial data: Year ended 12/31/2011. Assets, $461,405 (M); Expenditures, $53,749; Total giving, $45,500; Grants to individuals, 21 grants totaling $45,500 (high: $3,950, low: $1,750).
Fields of interest: Labor unions/organizations.
Type of support: Undergraduate support.
Application information: Applications accepted.
 Initial approach: Letter
EIN: 943070732

9081
Society of Gastrointestinal Radiologists
4550 Post Oak Pl., Ste. 342
Houston, TX 77027-3167 (713) 965-0566
Contact: Dan Johnson M.D., Pres.
FAX: (713) 960-0448; E-mail: info@sgr.org;
URL: http://www.sgr.org

Foundation type: Public charity
Purpose: Grants and awards to individuals for research related to gastrointestinal radiology.
Publications: Application guidelines.
Financial data: Year ended 12/31/2011. Assets, $811,529 (M); Expenditures, $123,757; Total giving, $28,895; Grants to individuals, totaling $28,895.
Fields of interest: Digestive disorders research.
Type of support: Research; Grants to individuals.
Application information:
 Initial approach: Proposal
 Deadline(s): Oct. 1 for Wylie J. Dodds and Howard S. Stern Research Awards
 Additional information: See web site for additional guidelines.
Program descriptions:
 Howard S. Stern Research Grant: This $15,000 grant, sponsored by Bracco Diagnostics Inc., works to facilitate visionary research in medical imaging by making funds available for pilot projects on ideas that are intellectually challenging, but not yet well-enough developed to be suitable for funding by mainstream granting agencies. Eligible applicants must be members of the society.
 Igor Laufer Visiting Professorship Award: This $8,000 award, co-sponsored by Bracco Diagnostics Inc., recognizes and rewards an individual for their contributions to abdominal radiology and the SAR, and to provide Society members with interactions at a local and personal level.
 Richard H. Marshak International Lecturer Award: This $4,000 award is given to a society member, chosen to represent the society at the annual International Education Conference held in a country that cannot support education in the field of Abdominal Radiology.
 Walter B. Canon Medal Award: This award is given annually to a distinguished radiologist who has made an outstanding contribution to the field of gastrointestinal and abdominal radiology.
 Wylie J. Dodds Research Award: This grant is sponsored by Bracco Diagnostics Inc. and GE Medical Systems for SAR members in the amount of $15,000. The research must be relevant to the field of gastrointestinal radiology. At least one author must be a member of the Society of Abdominal Radiology.
EIN: 363032116

9082
Society of St. Vincent De Paul Archdiocese of Galveston-Houston
2403 Holcombe Blvd.
Houston, TX 77021-2023 (713) 741-8234
FAX: (713) 741-3639; URL: http://www.svdphouston.org

Foundation type: Public charity
Purpose: Emergency assistance to individuals and families in the Galveston-Houston, TX area with food, clothing, rent, utilities, transportation, medical and other financial assistance.
Financial data: Year ended 09/30/2011. Assets, $3,512,906 (M); Expenditures, $8,175,593; Total giving, $6,358,508; Grants to individuals, totaling $6,358,508.
Fields of interest: Human services; Economically disadvantaged.

Type of support: In-kind gifts; Grants for special needs.
Application information:
  Initial approach: Telephone
  Additional information: Contact the society for needed assistance.
EIN: 741464210

9083
Some Other Place, Inc.
590 Center St.
Beaumont, TX 77704-0843 (409) 832-7976
Contact: Paula O'Neal, Exec. Dir.
FAX: (409) 832-5921; URL: http://sopbmt.org

Foundation type: Public charity
Purpose: Grants for basic necessities to needy residents of the Beaumont, TX, area.
Financial data: Year ended 12/31/2011. Assets, $2,393,857 (M); Expenditures, $1,833,155; Total giving, $1,243,083; Grants to individuals, totaling $1,243,083.
Fields of interest: Economically disadvantaged.
Type of support: Grants for special needs.
Application information:
  Initial approach: Letter
  Additional information: Contact foundation for complete eligibility requirements.
EIN: 742103171

9084
South Plains Community Action Association, Inc.
411 Austin St.
P.O. Box 610
Levelland, TX 79336-4733 (806) 894-6104
Contact: William D. Powell, Jr., Exec. Dir.
FAX: (806) 894-5349; Toll-free tel.: (800) 780-5028; URL: http://www.spcaa.org

Foundation type: Public charity
Purpose: Assistance to individuals and families of the West Texas area in/near Lubbock, TX, with food, shelter, utility assistance, transportation, health services and child care services.
Financial data: Year ended 02/28/2012. Assets, $15,143,947 (M); Expenditures, $40,726,978; Total giving, $14,064,091; Grants to individuals, totaling $11,637,993.
Fields of interest: Human services; Economically disadvantaged.
Type of support: Grants for special needs.
Application information: Applications accepted.
EIN: 751230219

9085
South Texas Academic Rising Scholars
(also known as STARS)
c/o L&F Distributors, Ltd.
3900 N. McColl Rd.
McAllen, TX 78501-9160 (956) 687-7751
Contact: Laura Escamilla, Exec. Dir.
FAX: (956) 928-0327;
E-mail: helpdesk@StarsScholarship.org; Toll-free tel.: (866) 939-7827; URL: https://www.southtexasstars.org/

Foundation type: Public charity
Purpose: Scholarships to qualified TX students who are attending a college or university.
Publications: Application guidelines.
Financial data: Year ended 07/31/2011. Assets, $1,625,953 (M); Expenditures, $1,002,363; Total

giving, $937,370; Grants to individuals, totaling $937,370.
Fields of interest: Scholarships/financial aid; Education.
Type of support: Scholarships—to individuals.
Application information:
  Initial approach: Application
  Deadline(s): Feb. 29
Program description:
  Scholarships: Scholarships are available to qualified students who attend south Texas schools and who wish to go to an accredited college or university. Eligible applicants must be U.S. citizens or legal permanent residents who have earned at least twelve undergraduate credit hours in a U.S. accredited college our university and have a minimum GPA of 2.7.
EIN: 431977563

9086
South Texas Food Bank
(formerly Laredo-Webb County Food Bank)
1907 Freight St.
Laredo, TX 78041-5675 (956) 726-3120
Contact: Alfonso Casso, Jr., Exec. Dir.
FAX: (956) 725-1309;
E-mail: acasso@southtexasfoodbank.org; Mailing address: P.O. Box 2007, Laredo, TX 78044-2007; URL: http://www.southtexasfoodbank.org

Foundation type: Public charity
Purpose: Food supplies to indigent families of Webb, Zapata, Dimmit, Maverick, Jim Hogg, Val Verde, Kinney and Starr counties, TX.
Financial data: Year ended 12/31/2012. Assets, $4,943,802 (M); Expenditures, $13,453,159; Total giving, $11,816,320; Grants to individuals, totaling $11,816,320.
Fields of interest: Food banks; Food distribution, groceries on wheels; Economically disadvantaged.
Type of support: In-kind gifts.
Application information:
  Initial approach: Letter
EIN: 742574983

9087
Southeast Texas A & M Foundation
P.O. Box 22902
Beaumont, TX 77720-2902 (409) 985-4200
Application address: c/o Joe Peters, 5785 Hooks Ave., Beaumont, TX 77706-6317, tel.: (409) 284-1122

Foundation type: Public charity
Purpose: Scholarships to residents of Jefferson, Hardin or Chambers counties, TX, for attendance at Texas A&M University. Awards to local elementary, middle school and high school teachers.
Financial data: Year ended 12/31/2011. Assets, $66,666 (M); Expenditures, $44,603; Total giving, $23,100.
Fields of interest: Higher education.
Type of support: Support to graduates or students of specific schools; Undergraduate support.
Application information: Application form required.
  Deadline(s): Mar. 21
EIN: 760300907

9088
Southern Union Charitable Foundation
1300 Main St.
Houston, TX 77002

Foundation type: Company-sponsored foundation

Purpose: Scholarships to employees of Southern Union, TX, also provides disaster relief to victims of recent natural disasters.
Financial data: Year ended 12/31/2012. Assets, $0 (M); Expenditures, $3,752; Total giving, $2,000.
Fields of interest: Education; Disasters, preparedness/services.
Type of support: Emergency funds; Employee-related scholarships.
Application information: Applications accepted. Application form required.
  Initial approach: Letter
  Deadline(s): None
  Additional information: Application should include financial information. Applicants should provide statement of damages, and estimates for repair costs. Grants are generally limited to $5,000, but $7,500 for Greensburg, Kansas tornado area.
Company name: Southern Union Company
EIN: 203634627

9089
Southwest Airlines Co. Outreach
c/o Kati Garrett, Charitable Giving
P.O. Box 36611, HDQ-1CV
2702 Love Field Dr.
Dallas, TX 75235-1611 (214) 792-1300
FAX: (214) 792-4200; URL: http://www.southwest.com/donations/

Foundation type: Corporate giving program
Purpose: Flight assistance on Southwest Airlines for individuals who must travel for medical reasons.
Publications: Application guidelines.
Financial data: Year ended 12/31/2011. Total giving, $18,239,850.
Fields of interest: Health care, emergency transport services.
Type of support: Grants for special needs.
Application information: Applications accepted. Application form required. Application form available on the grantmaker's web site.
  Initial approach: Letter, fax, or telephone
  Deadline(s): Applications must be received 30-60 days prior to anticipated travel dates.
  Additional information: Applications must include a physician's statement that confirms the medical reasons for the proposed travel. This statement must be mailed or faxed to the foundation in conjunction with the patient's application.
Company name: Southwest Airlines Co.

9090
Southwest Alternate Media Project, Inc.
(also known as SWAMP)
1519 W. Main St.
Houston, TX 77006-4709 (713) 522-8592
FAX: (713) 522-0953; E-mail: swamp@swamp.org;
E-mail For Mary Lampe: mmlampe@swamp.org;
URL: http://www.swamp.org

Foundation type: Public charity
Purpose: Support through a fiscal sponsorship program and residencies to media artists.
Publications: Application guidelines.
Financial data: Year ended 12/31/2011. Assets, $146,745 (M); Expenditures, $174,087.
Fields of interest: Media/communications; Film/video; Arts, artist's services.
Type of support: Residencies; Fiscal agent/sponsor.
Application information: Applications accepted.

Initial approach: Telephone or letter
Deadline(s): None
Applicants should submit the following:
1) Resume
2) Work samples
3) Budget Information
4) Proposal
Additional information: Application to the Fiscal Sponsorship Program should also include a project timeframe, a list of proposed funding sources, and a $50 non-refundable application fee.

Program description:
Fiscal Sponsorship Program: The organization provides a 501(c)(3) non-profit umbrella for established media artists seeking grants and contributions to develop and produce film and video. Sponsorships will also be considered for installation and performance projects; projects in these areas must reflect a major emphasis on film or video elements, and key personnel must have a film or video background.
EIN: 741925421

9091
Southwest School of Art and Craft
300 Augusta St.
San Antonio, TX 78205-1216 (210) 224-1848
Contact: Paula Owen, Pres.
FAX: (210) 224-9337;
E-mail: information@swschool.org; URL: http://www.swschool.org

Foundation type: Public charity
Purpose: Scholarships to individuals attending Southwest School of Art, TX. Stipends to artists working in various fields in the visual arts.
Publications: Application guidelines.
Financial data: Year ended 07/31/2012. Assets, $23,029,381 (M); Expenditures, $4,359,600; Total giving, $63,824; Grants to individuals, totaling $63,824.
Fields of interest: Arts; Adult/continuing education.
Type of support: Undergraduate support; Residencies.
Application information:
Initial approach: Letter, telephone or e-mail
Deadline(s): Feb. 1 for Guest Artist Program, Ongoing for Artist in Residence Program
Final notification: Applicants notified Mar. 28 for Guest Artist Program
Additional information: Scholarships are based on merit, and individuals must complete an application form and need not be currently enrolled to apply. Applications accepted for residencies should include budget information, letters of recommendation, work samples, proposal, resume and SASE. See web site for additional guidelines.

Program descriptions:
Artist in Residency Program: Artists are encouraged to apply for a residency in one of three departments: Printmaking, Papermaking & Book Arts, Jewelry & Small Metals. Applicants may request a particular block of time during the year and artists may repeat residencies no more than once every five years. Although a stipend is not included with this residency, teaching opportunities may exist based on applicant qualifications. Housing is not provided, however, may be available depending on length and time of residency.
Guest Artist Program: The program is designed to provide opportunities for artists and non-artists to work together and connect through the process of creating a work of art. The program is also an opportunity for artists to develop ideas that challenge assumptions about art by emphasizing

creativity in daily life. Selected projects will emphasize new and/or under-served audiences as well as collaborative and/or interdisciplinary approaches. Collaborations might include social service agencies, schools, health workers, government groups, or any other group or entity. Selected artists will receive a stipend of $1,500, a materials budget, and access to studio facilities, equipment and tools, as well as housing and reimbursement for transportation. The projects should have a specific beginning and ending date. Proposals for the program will be accepted from any artist living in North America.
EIN: 746068932

9092
Southwestern Medical Foundation
3963 Maple Ave., Ste. 100
Dallas, TX 75219 (214) 351-6143
Contact: Kern Wildenthal M.D., Ph.D., Pres. and C.E.O.
FAX: (214) 352-9874; E-mail: info@swmedical.org; URL: http://www.swmedical.org

Foundation type: Public charity
Purpose: Scholarships and student loans to medical students attending the University of Texas Southwestern Medical School, by recommendation of the school. Also, fellowships to individuals at the University of Texas Southwestern Medical Center by recommendation only.
Publications: Annual report.
Financial data: Year ended 12/31/2011. Assets, $778,076,953 (M); Expenditures, $30,120,576; Total giving, $25,332,095; Grants to individuals, totaling $266,500.
Fields of interest: Medical school/education; Medical research.
Type of support: Fellowships; Student loans—to individuals; Support to graduates or students of specific schools; Awards/grants by nomination only; Undergraduate support.
Application information: Applications not accepted.
Additional information: Applicants must be nominated. Unsolicited requests for funds not considered or acknowledged.
EIN: 750945939

9093
SPE Foundation
222 Palisades Creek Dr.
Richardson, TX 75080-2040 (972) 952-9393
Contact: Peter D. Gaffney, Pres.
FAX: (972) 952-9435; URL: http://www.spe.org/spe-app/spe/about/foundation/index.htm

Foundation type: Public charity
Purpose: Scholarships to undergraduates studying petroleum engineering or a related science. Also, graduate fellowships by nomination only to individuals at the Ph.D. level.
Publications: Application guidelines.
Financial data: Year ended 11/30/2012. Assets, $10,553,047 (M); Expenditures, $667,905; Total giving, $483,477; Grants to individuals, totaling $32,000.
Fields of interest: Engineering school/education; Physical/earth sciences; Mathematics; Physics.
Type of support: Undergraduate support.
Application information: Applications accepted. Application form required.
Deadline(s): Mar. 15 for STAR Scholarships and Fellowships; Apr. 30 for Gus Archie Scholarship; Nov. 1 for Nico van Wingen Memorial Graduate Fellowship

Applicants should submit the following:
1) Essay
2) Letter(s) of recommendation
3) Transcripts
Program descriptions:
Gus Archie Scholarship Program: This scholarship program awards $6,000 to an outstanding student who plans to enter a university and pursue an undergraduate degree in petroleum engineering. Applicants must intend to enroll in petroleum engineering in a recognized university program (according to the applicant's country and region) that will lead to an undergraduate degree in petroleum engineering. Scholarships are renewable for up to four years; if awarded a scholarship, applicants must be enrolled in a petroleum engineering class by the beginning of the second year of university, remain in a petroleum engineering degree program, maintain at least two-thirds of a full academic load, and have and maintain a satisfactory average of scores/marks for the current semester and cumulative total to renew scholarship.
Henry DeWitt Smith Fellowship: Fellowships are available to graduate students pursuing a master's or Ph.D. in petroleum engineering or a related field. Eligible applicants must be members of the Society for Petroleum Engineering (SPE), and demonstrate additional sources of income (job, family support, or other fellowships)
Nico Van Wingen Memorial Graduate Fellowship: This fellowship opportunity provides up to two awards, at $5,000 each per year, to outstanding students working and doing research in the field of petroleum engineering. Eligible applicants must be a Society of Petroleum Engineers (SPE) member at an official student chapter, must be at the Ph.D. level, and must intend to pursue a career in academia.
STAR Scholarship and Fellowship: Scholarships (for undergraduates) and fellowships (for graduates) to students pursuing degrees related to the oil and gas industry, for up to a maximum of four years. Eligible applicants must have applied to, or be registered at, a university, or be a current full-time university student, taking or planning to take oil and gas industry-related courses. Applicants must also be members of the Society of Petroleum Engineers (SPE)
EIN: 751575590

9094
Spencer Charitable Foundation
1001 Redbud Trail
Austin, TX 78746-3537 (361) 882-7001

Foundation type: Independent foundation
Purpose: Scholarships primarily to individuals attending Baylor University, TX.
Financial data: Year ended 12/31/2011. Assets, $1,650,997 (M); Expenditures, $90,571; Total giving, $75,000.
Fields of interest: Higher education.
Type of support: Support to graduates or students of specific schools; Undergraduate support.
Application information: Applications not accepted.
Additional information: Unsolicited requests for funds not considered or acknowledged.
EIN: 742900267

9095
St. David's Community Health Care Foundation
811 Barton Springs Rd., Ste. 600
Austin, TX   78704-1164   (512) 879-6600
FAX: (512) 879-6250;
E-mail: info@stdavidsfoundation.org; URL: http://www.sdchf.org

Foundation type: Public charity
Purpose: Grants for medical care for needy residents of central TX.
Publications: Grants list.
Financial data: Year ended 12/31/2011. Assets, $1,414,491 (M); Expenditures, $412,727; Total giving, $402,985.
Type of support: Grants for special needs.
Application information: Contact foundation for complete eligibility guidelines.
EIN: 742206098

9096
St. Joseph Foundation of Bryan, Texas
1530 E. William J. Bryan Pkwy.
Bryan, TX   77803-5005   (979) 774-4087
FAX: (979) 731-8976;
E-mail: gkumzosf@st-joseph.org; Mailing address: P.O. Box 993, Bryan, TX 77805-0993; URL: http://foundation.st-joseph.org

Foundation type: Public charity
Purpose: Scholarships to residents of TX who are studying or working in a healthcare-related field.
Publications: Application guidelines.
Financial data: Year ended 12/31/2011. Assets, $2,972,171 (M); Expenditures, $1,365,387; Total giving, $460,174.
Fields of interest: Health care.
Type of support: Undergraduate support.
Application information: Applications accepted.
Initial approach: Letter or telephone
Deadline(s): Feb. 15
Additional information: Payments are made directly to the educational institution on behalf of the students.
Program descriptions:
Emily Palasota Scholarship in Honor of Mary Ellen "Mel" Rothermel: Scholarship are given to students to pursue medically-related coursework.
Eugene Edge III Scholarship: Scholarship are given to students to pursue medically-related coursework.
Lola M. Cone Healthcare Scholarship: This scholarship provides assistance to graduating high school students in the Brazos Valley who are interested in pursuing a degree in a health-care-related field.
Marshal Verne Ross Foundation Scholarship: This program awards scholarships to students (not restricted to high school) pursuing coursework in a medically-related field, who might not otherwise qualify for a scholarship.
Peter J. Palasota III, M.D. Medical Scholarship: This program assists current and future health caregivers that need financial assistance to expand their educational horizons. Preference will be given to those born in Brazos or Robertson counties.
Sister Gretchen Kunz Healthcare Scholarship: This scholarship annually provides funds to assist current and future caregivers in expanding their educational horizons. Eligible applicants include healthcare professionals in such areas as nursing, laboratory, physical therapy, radiology, pharmacy, medical records, dietary, and other medically-related fields of study.
Sr. Gregory Healthcare Education Fund: This program provides scholarships on an annual basis

to assist current and future caregivers in expanding their education horizons. Scholarships are available to members of St. Joseph Hospital and their dependents.
EIN: 742351158

9097
St. Joseph Hospital Foundation
P.O. Box 1919
Houston, TX   77251-1919   (713) 652-3100
Contact: Les Cave, Pres.
FAX: (713) 652-0760;
E-mail: Les.Cave@CHRISTUSHealth.org; Additional Address : 2615 Fannin at McGowen, Houston, Texas 77002; Tel. for Les Cave : (713)-803-1803; URL: http://www.christusfoundation.org/index.php/en/home/f/c/home/

Foundation type: Public charity
Purpose: Grants for medical research to individuals in the Houston, TX, area.
Financial data: Year ended 06/30/2011. Assets, $59,873,602 (M); Expenditures, $4,311,481; Total giving, $2,761,790; Grants to individuals, totaling $9,135.
Fields of interest: Medical research.
Type of support: Research.
Application information:
Initial approach: Letter
Additional information: Contact foundation for current application deadline/guidelines.
EIN: 746074210

9098
St. Luke's Episcopal Hospital
6720 Bertner Ave.
Houston, TX   77030-2604   (832) 355-1000
URL: http://www.stlukeshouston.com/

Foundation type: Public charity
Purpose: Associate degree scholarships to qualified nursing candidates of St. Luke's Episcopal Hospital, TX. Nursing scholarships for the children of St. Luke's employees. Also, Patient Care Assistant Summer Externships, which is open to local high school students.
Financial data: Year ended 12/31/2011. Assets, $968,830,694 (M); Expenditures, $828,544,359; Total giving, $17,746,619; Grants to individuals, totaling $5,936,586.
Fields of interest: Nursing school/education.
Type of support: Undergraduate support.
Application information: Applications not accepted.
Additional information: Unsolicited requests for funds not considered or acknowledged.
EIN: 741161938

9099
St. Vincent de Paul Rehabilitation Center
314 E. Highland Mall Blvd., Ste. 115
Austin, TX   78752-3729   (512) 453-8833
Contact: Charles Graham, Pres.

Foundation type: Public charity
Purpose: Grants primarily to disabled residents of the Austin, TX metropolitan area.
Financial data: Year ended 12/31/2011. Assets, $1,420,340 (M); Expenditures, $9,215,773.
Fields of interest: Disabilities, people with.
Type of support: Grants for special needs.
Application information: Applications not accepted.

Additional information: Unsolicited requests for funds not considered or acknowledged.
EIN: 742736120

9100
The Stanzel Family Foundation, Inc.
P.O. Box 6
Schulenburg, TX   78956-0006
Application address: c/o Robert R. Stanzel, Pres., 311 Baumgarten St., Schulenberg, TX 78956-2101, tel.: (979) 743-6559

Foundation type: Independent foundation
Purpose: Scholarships to graduating high school seniors who live in the Schulenburg or Weimar Independent school districts or are enrolled in Schulenburg or Weimar high schools, TX. Graduate scholarships may also be available to previous graduates of Schulenburg or Weimar high schools.
Financial data: Year ended 07/31/2011. Assets, $15,594,203 (M); Expenditures, $881,853; Total giving, $284,221; Grants to individuals, 58 grants totaling $225,796 (high: $1,000, low: $225).
Type of support: Support to graduates or students of specific schools; Undergraduate support; Postgraduate support.
Application information: Application form required.
Deadline(s): Mar. 31
EIN: 742579827

9101
Nelda C. and H. J. Lutcher Stark Foundation
P.O. Drawer 909
Orange, TX   77631-0909
Contact: Grant Dept.
Address for physical delivery: 601 W. Green Ave. Orange, TX 77630-5718; URL: http://www.starkfoundation.org/

Foundation type: Operating foundation
Purpose: Scholarships limited to students graduating from Orange County, TX, high schools, who are winners in a reading and declamation contest.
Publications: Annual report.
Financial data: Year ended 12/31/2012. Assets, $564,419,643 (M); Expenditures, $21,014,634; Total giving, $2,901,445; Grants to individuals, 21 grants totaling $49,500 (high: $6,500, low: $1,500).
Fields of interest: Secondary school/education; Research.
Type of support: Fellowships; Scholarships—to individuals; Support to graduates or students of specific schools.
Application information: Application form not required.
Additional information: Contact foundation for current application deadline/guidelines.
Program description:
Miriam Lutcher Stark Contest in Reading and Declamation: In 1976, the Miriam Lutcher Stark Contest in Reading and Declamation became a qualified scholarship program of the Stark Foundation. The contest is now held each spring in each of the five public high schools in Orange County, Texas. The aim of the contest is to encourage student participation and competition to enhance the literary and forensic quality and skills of the students. Upon completion of the contest in the participating school, the First Place winners compete in a countywide final with the determination of the best presentation in

declaiming and the best presentation in interpretative reading.
EIN: 746047440

9102
Student Aid Foundation Enterprises, Inc.
800 Commerce St.
Houston, TX   77002

Foundation type: Independent foundation
Purpose: Scholarships principally to younger students who are residents of Houston, TX, are underprivileged, have learning disabilities or are victims of drug abuse. Students must be nominated by local agencies. College students are eligible only if they are either prior recipients of secondary school assistance or are nominated by a particular college at which the Student Aid Foundation has a program.
Financial data: Year ended 06/30/2013. Assets, $1,298,511 (M); Expenditures, $112,670; Total giving, $54,646.
Fields of interest: Substance abuse, treatment; Learning disorders; Children/youth, services.
Type of support: Awards/grants by nomination only; Foreign applicants.
Application information: Applications not accepted.
  Additional information: Unsolicited requests for funds not considered or acknowledged.
Program description:
  Memorial Hall School Scholarships: Scholarships are given at the secondary school level to disadvantaged children with learning disabilities and/or to dysfunctional foreign students.
EIN: 746060745

9103
Sunnyside Foundation, Inc.
(formerly Sunnyside, Inc.)
8222 Douglas Ave., Ste. 501
Dallas, TX   75225-5936   (214) 692-5686
Contact: Jane McLane, Exec. Dir.
FAX: (214) 692-1968;
E-mail: info@sunnysidetexas.org; Toll free tel.: (888) 293-6918; URL: http://www.sunnysidetexas.org

Foundation type: Independent foundation
Purpose: Scholarships, grants and other assistance to Texas residents who regularly attend a Christian Science Church or Sunday School and are members of a Branch church and/or The First Church of Christ, Scientist in Boston, MA.
Publications: Application guidelines; Informational brochure (including application guidelines); Program policy statement (including application guidelines).
Financial data: Year ended 12/31/2012. Assets, $24,292,144 (M); Expenditures, $1,369,738; Total giving, $1,039,900; Grants to individuals, totaling $1,039,900.
Fields of interest: Education; Camps; Human services; Christian agencies & churches.
Type of support: Scholarships—to individuals; Grants for special needs.
Application information: Applications accepted. Application form required.
  Initial approach: Telephone or fax
  Deadline(s): None
  Additional information: Application for grants and camperships should include Sunday school information and parents' financial information.
EIN: 756037004

9104
Swift Energy Charitable Fund
16825 Northchase Dr., Ste. 400
Houston, TX   77060

Foundation type: Company-sponsored foundation
Purpose: Financial assistance for temporary housing, food, clothing, and other immediate needs for designated disaster zone for hurricanes.
Financial data: Year ended 12/31/2012. Assets, $18,665 (M); Expenditures, $0; Total giving, $22,842; Grants to individuals, 3 grants totaling $8,670 (high: $3,400, low: $2,070).
Fields of interest: Disasters, Hurricane Katrina; Safety/disasters.
Type of support: Grants to individuals; Grants for special needs.
Application information: Applications not accepted.
  Additional information: Unsolicited requests for funds not considered or acknowledged.
EIN: 203402113

9105
Edward F. Swinney Foundation
c/o Bank of America, N.A.
P.O. Box 831041
Dallas, TX   75283-1041   (816) 292-4300
Contact: Spence Heddens, Treas.
Application address: c/o Bank of America, N.A., P.O. Box 219119, Kansas City, MO 64121-9119, tel.: (816) 292-4300

Foundation type: Independent foundation
Purpose: Grants to financially needy employees of Bank of America, N.A.
Financial data: Year ended 12/31/2011. Assets, $853,966 (M); Expenditures, $82,236; Total giving, $68,500; Grants to individuals, 23 grants totaling $9,500 (high: $400, low: $400).
Type of support: Employee-related welfare.
Application information: Applications accepted. Application form required.
  Additional information: Applications are available from the personnel department of Bank of America, N.A., MO.
Company name: Bank of America, N.A.
EIN: 446009677

9106
Edward F. Swinney Student Loan Trust
c/o Bank of America, N.A.
P.O. Box 831041
Dallas, TX   75283-1041   (816) 292-4300
Contact: Spence Heddens
Application address: c/o Bank of America, N.A., P.O. Box 219119, Kansas City, MO 84121-9119, tel.: (816) 292-4300

Foundation type: Independent foundation
Purpose: Low-interest student loans to MO residents with financial need who are attending college or university within the state of MO.
Financial data: Year ended 12/31/2012. Assets, $994,629 (M); Expenditures, $11,667; Total giving, $0.
Fields of interest: Higher education.
Type of support: Student loans—to individuals.
Application information: Applications accepted. Application form required.
  Deadline(s): None
  Additional information: Loan application forms are available upon request from the contact person or from the school's financial aid office.
EIN: 446009266

9107
Sysco Disaster Relief Foundation, Inc.
1390 Enclave Pkwy.
Houston, TX   77077-2025   (281) 584-1471

Foundation type: Independent foundation
Purpose: Disaster relief assistance to current and future employees of SYSCO Corporation and others, to provide relief to victims of disaster.
Financial data: Year ended 07/02/2012. Assets, $11,851 (M); Expenditures, $10,000; Total giving, $10,000; Grants to individuals, 2 grants totaling $10,000 (high: $5,000, low: $5,000).
Fields of interest: Safety/disasters.
Type of support: Employee-related welfare; Grants for special needs.
Application information: Applications accepted.
  Initial approach: Letter
  Deadline(s): None
  Additional information: Letter must include a brief description of reason for funds. How funds are intended to be used and amount needed.
Company name: Sysco Corporation
EIN: 203793783

9108
Targa Resources Employee Relief Organization
1000 Louisiana St., Ste. 4300
Houston, TX   77002-5021

Foundation type: Independent foundation
Purpose: Emergency assistance to relieve the immediate needs of employees suffering from displacement and damage to dwelling from hurricanes.
Financial data: Year ended 12/31/2012. Assets, $0 (M); Expenditures, $142,000; Total giving, $142,000; Grants to individuals, 31 grants totaling $142,000 (high: $10,000, low: $1,500).
Fields of interest: Safety/disasters.
Type of support: Emergency funds.
Application information: Applications not accepted.
  Additional information: Unsolicited requests for funds not considered or acknowledged.
EIN: 710992115

9109
Target Hunger, Inc.
2814 Quitman St.
Houston, TX   77026-6323   (713) 226-4953
FAX: (713) 228-8741;
E-mail: generalinfo@targethunter.org; URL: http://www.targethunger.org

Foundation type: Public charity
Purpose: Grants for food to needy residents of the Houston, TX, area.
Financial data: Year ended 12/31/2011. Assets, $960,063 (M); Expenditures, $3,297,679; Total giving, $2,397,794; Grants to individuals, totaling $2,397,794.
Fields of interest: Economically disadvantaged.
Type of support: Grants for special needs.
Application information: Contact foundation for eligibility requirements.
EIN: 311548849

9110
Hope Pierce Tartt Scholarship Fund
P.O. Box 1964
Marshall, TX   75671-1964
Contact: E.N. Smith, Jr., Chair.

Foundation type: Independent foundation
Purpose: Scholarships for college or university education to United States citizens who have resided in Harrison, Gregg, Marion, Panola, or Upshur Counties, TX, for at least 24 months.
Publications: Application guidelines; Program policy statement.
Financial data: Year ended 05/31/2013. Assets, $16,767,282 (M); Expenditures, $915,250; Total giving, $792,500; Grants to individuals, totaling $792,500.
Fields of interest: Higher education.
Type of support: Scholarships—to individuals.
Application information: Application form required.
  Initial approach: Letter or telephone
  Applicants should submit the following:
    1) FAFSA
    2) GPA
    3) SAT
    4) Financial information
    5) ACT
  Additional information: Scholarship fund is paid directly to the educational institution on behalf of the student. Applicants must have maintained a "C" average in high school and must maintain a 2.0 GPA for continued eligibility. Applicants are judged according to financial need, and must not be a close relative of a member of the Board of Directors, or an officer or employee of Hope Pierce Tart Scholarship Fund. Maximum scholarship per academic year is $5,000. Application forms available through financial aid office of student's chosen school. Application forms can be obtained from the financial aid office of student chosen school.
EIN: 756263272

9111
Robert B. Taylor Educational Trust
P.O. Box 28629
San Antonio, TX   78228-0629

Foundation type: Independent foundation
Purpose: Scholarships to full-time allied health majors at St. Philip's College, TX, who have completed at least 12 hours and possess a 3.0 GPA.
Financial data: Year ended 12/31/2010. Assets, $1,268,238 (M); Expenditures, $18,338; Total giving, $16,000; Grants to individuals, 10 grants totaling $16,000 (high: $1,600, low: $1,600).
Fields of interest: Health sciences school/education.
Type of support: Support to graduates or students of specific schools; Undergraduate support.
Application information:
  Initial approach: Letter or telephone
  Deadline(s): Contact college financial aid for application deadline/guidelines.
EIN: 746364769

9112
Teen Mania Ministries, Inc.
P.O. Box 2000
Lindale, TX   75771-2000   (903) 324-8000
Contact: Ronald Luce, Pres.
URL: http://www.teenmania.com/

Foundation type: Public charity
Purpose: Fellowships to individuals for short-term missionary trips to Latin America, Europe, Africa and Asia.
Financial data: Year ended 08/31/2012. Assets, $7,874,046 (M); Expenditures, $16,219,131; Total giving, $1,850.

Fields of interest: Religion.
Type of support: Fellowships.
Application information: Contact foundation for current application deadline/guidelines.
EIN: 731284606

9113
Blanche G. Terry Educational Trust
c/o Citizens National Bank
400 W. Collin St.
Corsicana, TX   75110-5124

Foundation type: Independent foundation
Purpose: Scholarships to residents of Navarro County, TX.
Financial data: Year ended 05/31/2013. Assets, $751,781 (M); Expenditures, $41,123; Total giving, $29,205; Grants to individuals, 38 grants totaling $29,205 (high: $1,200, low: $300).
Type of support: Scholarships—to individuals.
Application information: Applications accepted. Application form required.
  Deadline(s): Apr. 15
  Final notification: Applicants are notified within two months
EIN: 756173637

9114
Texas Alliance for Minorities In
Engineering
(also known as TAME)
10100 Burnett Rd., Bldg. 16, Rm. 10
Austin, TX   78758-4445   (512) 471-6100
FAX: (512) 471-6797; E-mail: programs@tame.org;
URL: http://www.tame.org/

Foundation type: Public charity
Purpose: Scholarships to TAME students who are residents of TX, pursuing higher education in a science, technology, engineering, or mathematics-related field.
Financial data: Year ended 08/31/2012. Assets, $608,175 (M); Expenditures, $469,020; Total giving, $26,525; Grants to individuals, totaling $26,525.
Fields of interest: Scholarships/financial aid; Education; Science.
Type of support: Scholarships—to individuals.
Application information: See web site for additional information.
EIN: 510192147

9115
Texas Alpha Endowment Fund, Inc.
P.O. Box 28061
Austin, TX   78755-8601

Foundation type: Independent foundation
Purpose: Scholarships primarily to members of the Texas Alpha fraternity.
Financial data: Year ended 06/30/2012. Assets, $1,465,307 (M); Expenditures, $65,683; Total giving, $23,200; Grants to individuals, 26 grants totaling $23,200 (high: $2,200, low: $300).
Type of support: Undergraduate support.
Application information: Applications not accepted.
  Additional information: Unsolicited requests for funds not considered or acknowledged.
EIN: 742560499

9116
Texas and Southwestern Cattle Raisers
Foundation
1600 Gendy St.
Fort Worth, TX   76107-4062   (817) 332-8551
Contact: Patricia W. Riley, Exec. Dir.
FAX: (817) 336-2470;
E-mail: cattleraisersmuseum@gmail.com;
URL: http://www.cattleraisersmuseum.org/

Foundation type: Public charity
Purpose: Scholarships to students pursuing a degree program in animal science, pre-vet, or agribusiness at an accredited Texas or Oklahoma college or university.
Publications: Application guidelines.
Financial data: Year ended 12/31/2011. Assets, $6,692,592 (M); Expenditures, $689,235; Total giving, $299,000; Grants to individuals, 19 grants totaling $49,000.
Fields of interest: Business school/education; Agriculture.
Type of support: Scholarships—to individuals.
Application information: Applications accepted. Application form required. Application form available on the grantmaker's web site.
  Send request by: Mail
  Deadline(s): Jan. 27
  Final notification: Recipients notified by Mar. 16
  Applicants should submit the following:
    1) Photograph
    2) Transcripts
    3) Essay
    4) Letter(s) of recommendation
    5) Financial information
  Additional information: Applicants must be U.S. citizens born in Texas or Oklahoma, sponsored by a member of the TX or Southwestern Cattle Raisers' Association, demonstrate financial need and have a background that includes beef cattle productions. Funds are paid directly to the educational institution on behalf of the students.
Program descriptions:
  Mary and Leonard Stiles Scholarship: A one-year, $5,000 scholarship is available to a graduating high school senior whose family is involved in the ranching or farming industry, and who demonstrates financial need. Applicants must be accepted to an accredited four-year college or university, be a citizen of the U.S., be a member of a family involved in the ranching or farming industry (with special consideration given to applicants who are the first members of their immediate family to attend a college or university), demonstrate financial need, and have a minimum 2.75 GPA.
  Scholarships: The foundation offers scholarships of $2,000 each ($1,000 per semester for two semesters) to students interested in pursuing a degree within the field of agriculture. Applicants must be accepted or enrolled at an accredited university in Texas or Oklahoma and plan to pursue a degree program in agriculture or an agriculture-related field (animals science, pre-vet, agribusiness, range management, or wildlife), be citizens of the U.S., be residents of Texas or Oklahoma, be a member, or be sponsored by a member, of the Texas and Southwestern Cattle Raisers Association, and have a cumulative 2.75 GPA.
EIN: 751762849

9117
The Texas Area Fund Foundation, Inc.
207 W. Spring St.
P.O. Box 283
Palestine, TX 75802-0283   (903) 729-6048
Contact: Connie Fain, Admin.
URL: http://www.txareafundfoundation.org

Foundation type: Community foundation
Purpose: Scholarships to individuals in the Palestine Independent School District, TX.
Financial data: Year ended 12/31/2012. Assets, $1,374,956 (M); Expenditures, $208,736; Total giving, $150,794; Grants to individuals, 15 grants totaling $57,250.
Type of support: Scholarships—to individuals; Support to graduates or students of specific schools.
Application information: Interview required.
> *Additional information:* Contact fund for current application deadline/guidelines.

EIN: 752834546

9118
Texas Bar Foundation
504 Lavaca St., Ste. 1005
Austin, TX 78701-2857   (512) 480-8000
Contact: Andrea Stone, Exec. Dir.
FAX: (512) 480-8005; E-mail: info@txbf.org; E-mail For Morgan Smith: msmith@txbf.org; URL: http://www.txbf.org

Foundation type: Public charity
Purpose: Loans to licensed TX attorneys working full-time to provide legal aid to the poor and continue to work for an approved legal aid organization.
Publications: Application guidelines; Annual report; Grants list; Newsletter.
Financial data: Year ended 05/31/2012. Assets, $19,222,335 (M); Expenditures, $1,476,918; Total giving, $727,439.
Fields of interest: Legal services.
Type of support: Loans—to individuals.
Application information: Applications accepted. Application form required. Application form available on the grantmaker's web site.
> *Initial approach:* Letter
> *Copies of proposal:* 4
> *Deadline(s):* Jan. 15 and Aug. 10
> *Final notification:* Recipients notified in 90 days

EIN: 746074796

9119
Texas Credit Union Foundation
4455 LBJ Freeway, Ste. 1100
Farmers Branch, TX 75244-5998   (800) 953-8283
Contact: Courtney Moran, Exec. Dir.
E-mail: cmoran@tcuf.coop; URL: http://www.tcuf.coop/

Foundation type: Public charity
Purpose: Grants and scholarships to assist credit union staff in achieving professional excellence. Emergency grants to credit union employees to assist with the immediate disaster relief needs.
Financial data: Year ended 12/31/2011. Assets, $1,800,924 (M); Expenditures, $573,574; Total giving, $275,930; Grants to individuals, totaling $129,444.
Fields of interest: Higher education; Safety/disasters.
Type of support: Grants to individuals; Scholarships—to individuals; Grants for special needs.

Application information: Applications accepted. Application form required.
> *Send request by:* Mail
> *Additional information:* See web site for additional guidelines.

Program descriptions:
> *Phase One Disaster Relief Grants:* These grants are provided to credit union employees to assist with immediate disaster relief needs, such as out of pocket costs that may result from being evacuated. These grants are up to $500 per credit union employee, up to 60 days after disaster struck. The intent of these grants is to help stabilize the credit union employee's individual situation so they can return to work.
> *Phase Three Disaster Relief Grants:* These grants are intended to follow-up with those credit union employees who suffered catastrophic loss and are still needing assistance after Phase Two grants have been distributed. Phase Three will begin 180 days after the respective disaster.
> *Phase Two Disaster Relief Grants:* These grants are intended to assist credit union employees with significant needs. Phase two will be implemented following the distribution of Phase One Grants. Amounts of grants will be dependent on the amount of disaster relief funds available, but usually range from $1,000 to $5,000. The Foundation will notify affected credit unions about Phase Two Grant applications, beginning 90 days after disaster has struck. Phase Two Grants could be distributed sooner if insurance claims have been received prior.
> *Professional Development Grants:* This grant allows for designated staff of credit unions to attend professional development training and education workshops offered by or through the Cornerstone Credit Union League. Grants are limited to one entity per calendar year.

EIN: 756039968

9120
Texas Equal Access to Justice Foundation
1601 Rio Grande, Ste. 351
Austin, TX 78701-1149   (512) 320-0099
Contact: Betty Balli Torres, Exec. Dir.
FAX: (512) 469-0112; E-mail: bbtorres@teajf.org; Toll-free tel.: (800) 252-3401; mailing address: P.O. Box 12886, Austin, TX 78711-2886; URL: http://www.txiolta.org

Foundation type: Public charity
Purpose: Student loan repayment assistance to attorneys who choose to pursue careers in legal aid in Texas.
Publications: Application guidelines; Grants list.
Financial data: Year ended 12/31/2011. Assets, $13,575,898 (M); Expenditures, $6,608,989; Total giving, $5,401,920; Grants to individuals, 126 grants totaling $790,935.
Fields of interest: Law school/education.
Type of support: Student loans—to individuals.
Application information: Applications accepted. Application form required. Application form available on the grantmaker's web site.
> *Initial approach:* Email
> *Deadline(s):* Apr. 2
> *Applicants should submit the following:*
>   1) Financial information
>   2) Resume

EIN: 742354575

9121
Texas Industries Foundation
1341 W. Mockingbird Ln., Ste. 700
Dallas, TX 75247   (972) 647-6700

Foundation type: Company-sponsored foundation
Purpose: Scholarships to LA, MS and TX dependents of employees of Texas Industries, Inc. for study at accredited institutions.
Financial data: Year ended 12/31/2012. Assets, $4,049 (M); Expenditures, $25,939; Total giving, $25,000.
Fields of interest: Higher education.
Type of support: Employee-related scholarships.
Application information: Applications not accepted.
> *Additional information:* Unsolicited requests for funds not considered or acknowledged.

EIN: 756043179

9122
Texas Interscholastic League Foundation
(also known as TILF)
1701 Manor Rd.
Austin, TX 78722-2538   (512) 232-4937
Contact: Trudy Richards, Scholarship Coord.
FAX: (512) 232-7311;
E-mail: trichards@uiltexas.org; Mailing address: P.O. Box 8028, Austin, TX 78713-8028; URL: http://www.uiltexas.org/tilf

Foundation type: Public charity
Purpose: Scholarship to residents of TX attending an accredited college or university in Texas.
Publications: Application guidelines.
Financial data: Year ended 05/31/2012. Assets, $10,069,802 (M); Expenditures, $749,562; Total giving, $691,400; Grants to individuals, totaling $691,400.
Fields of interest: Higher education.
Type of support: Scholarships—to individuals.
Application information: Applications accepted. Application form required.
> *Deadline(s):* May 15
> *Final notification:* Recipients notified in June
> *Applicants should submit the following:*
>   1) Class rank
>   2) GPA
>   3) Financial information
> *Additional information:* Selection is based on students who have participated in a UIL Academic State Meet during their high school career. See web site for a listing of additional scholarship programs.

Program descriptions:
> *Abell-Hanger Foundation Nursing Awards:* The foundation awards scholarships of $8,000 each (payable $2,000 each semester of the first two years) to students who plan to major in nursing.
> *Carl B. & Florence E. King Foundation Endowment:* A four-year, $12,000 scholarship is available to selected applicants who have an SAT I/ACT score of 1000/22 or above, completed 15 hours per semester in college, and maintain a minimum 3.0 GPA.
> *CH Foundation Scholarship:* One-year, $3,000 awards are available to students from Cochran, Hockley, Lubbock, or Terry counties; preference will be given to first-generation college students.
> *Clyde V. McKee, Jr. Memorial Scholarship:* A one year, $1,000 scholarship is available to an individual who ranks in the top 25 percent of his/her graduating class and attends a state-supported and fully-accredited four-year college or university. Preference will be given to applicants from Orange, Sabine, Newton and Hardin counties.

Dorothy Sue Whited Memorial Scholarship: A one-year, $1,000 award is available to contestants who have participated in UIL Speech and Debate contests. Recipients must attend the University of Texas at Austin and be enrolled in its business or engineering schools.

H-E-B Pharmacy Scholarship: A one-year, $1,000 scholarship is available to an applicant who declares his/her intent to enter the pharmacy profession, with plans to practice in an area serviced by an H-E-B Pharmacy.

Henry Beckman Memorial Scholarship: A one-year, $1,000 scholarship is available to high school senior who has graduated in the upper 25 percent of his/her graduating class. Recipients must attend the University of Texas at Austin and major in computer sciences, engineering, or natural sciences.

J. O. Webb Memorial Scholarship: A one-year, $1,000 award will be given to an eligible applicant who attends the University of North Texas, Texas Woman's University, Sam Houston State University, West Texas A&M University or Texas State University - San Marcos. Preference will be given to students planning to enter the teaching profession.

Leta Andrews Scholarship: Co-sponsored by Whataburger, Inc. and Southwest Shootout Inc., this one-year, $1,000 award is given to an individual who has competed in girl's high school varsity basketball.

Louise P. and Joe B. Cook Memorial Scholarship Fund: Eight awards of $3,700 each, payable over four years, are available for individuals who have competed in UIL's accounting, calculator applications, computer science, debate, mathematics, number sense, ready writing, science, informative and persuasive speaking, or spelling & vocabulary contests. Students also participating in the UIL State Solo-Ensemble Contest will be given special consideration. Applicants must attend an accredited four-year college or university.

Lynn and Pat Murray Scholarship: This $1,000, one-year award is given to an outstanding UIL State Meet participant. Preference will given to the UIL State One-Act Play Contests. Candidates must attend the University of Texas at Austin and major in theatre teacher training. Recipients must plan to pursue a career in theatre as a theatre arts teacher in public schools or colleges.

Nelda C. & H.J. Lutcher Stark Foundation Scholarship: Fifteen awards of $15,200 each, awarded over four years, are available to eligible applicants who rank in the top 10 percent of their graduating class, have a SAT I/ACT of 1210/27 or above, and attend a state-supported, fully-accredited four-year college or university. Recipients must maintain a minimum 3.0 college GPA. Preference is given to applicants from Orange, Sabine, Newton, and Hardin counties.

Panhandle Chapter of TSCPA Scholarships: Five awards of $2,500 each are available to the top five scorers in the UIL's accounting contest, from the schools within the twenty-five counties that comprise the geographic area of the Panhandle chapter of the Texas Society of Certified Public Accountants. Recipients must enroll full-time as a an accounting major and maintain a minimum 3.0 college GPA.

Red Oak Foundation Scholarship: Three awards of $4,800, payable over four years, are available to contestants in any UIL academic event who declare the intention to teach in the public school system in Texas. Recipients must show a financial need and maintain a 2.75 GPA while taking at least 12 hours each semester at a state-supported four-year university in Texas, or Texas Wesleyan University.

Richard Gibby Memorial Music Scholarship: This one-year, $1,000 award will be made available to eligible applicants who have made a division rating of I or II in a solo performance at the UIL State Solo Contest. Preference will be given to applicants majoring in music who plan on entering the teaching profession.

Steve Barton "Achieving the Dream" Endowed Scholarship: One-year, $3,000 awards are available to applicants who have competed in OAP and will major in theater. Preference is given to multi-skilled applicants in singing, dancing, concert piano, directing, and scenic, costume, and publicity design.

The Meadows Foundation Scholarship: These four-year, $4,000 scholarships will be made available to participants in UIL's ready writing program. Applicants must attend an accredited four-year college or university and maintain a minimum 3.0 college GPA.

The Mike A. Myers Foundation Scholarships: This one-year, $2,000 award will be made to eligible individuals who attend an accredited four-year college or university in the state of Texas. Recipients must maintain a 3.0 college GPA.

The Welch Foundation Scholarship: Twenty awards of $14,000 each, payable over four years, are available for applicants who currently attend any of the Texas colleges or universities approved by The Welch Foundation. Applicants must major in chemistry, biochemistry or chemical engineering, and be willing to engage in chemical research at the graduate level. Recipients must maintain a minimum 3.0 GPA.

UIL Music Directors' Scholarships: Two one-year awards of $1,000 each will be available to individuals who have achieved a division rating of I or II in a solo performance at UIL's state solo contest. Preference will be given to applicants majoring in music.

EIN: 746050081

9123
Texas Knights Templar Educational Foundation

(formerly Templar Educational Foundation)
P.O Box 354
Red Oak, TX   75154   (972) 617-2370
Contact: Jerry Kirby, Treas.

Foundation type: Independent foundation
Purpose: Scholarships to students who need assistance for postsecondary studies, primarily in TX.
Financial data: Year ended 12/31/2012. Assets, $1,193,935 (M); Expenditures, $43,037; Total giving, $24,000; Grants to individuals, 22 grants totaling $24,000 (high: $2,000; low: $1,000).
Type of support: Scholarships—to individuals.
Application information: Applications accepted. Application form required.
  Initial approach: Letter or telephone
  Deadline(s): Contact foundation for application deadline.
  Applicants should submit the following:
    1) Photograph
    2) Transcripts
    3) SAT
    4) Letter(s) of recommendation
    5) GPA
    6) ACT
EIN: 752234779

9124
Texas Medical Association
401 W. 15th St.
Austin, TX   78701-1670   (512) 370-1300
Contact: Louis J. Goodman Ph.D., Exec. Dir.
E-mail: knowledge@texmed.org; Toll-free tel.: (800) 880-1300; URL: http://www.texmed.org/

Foundation type: Public charity
Purpose: Awards to outstanding science teachers and journalists in TX.
Publications: Annual report.
Financial data: Year ended 12/31/2011. Assets, $40,786,029 (M); Expenditures, $22,011,274; Total giving, $463,523; Grants to individuals, totaling $40,185.
Fields of interest: Health care.
Type of support: Awards/prizes.
Application information: Contact foundation for complete application guidelines.
EIN: 741078510

9125
Texas Medical Association Foundation
(formerly Texas Medical Association Education and Research Foundation)
401 W. 15th St.
Austin, TX   78701-1624   (512) 370-1664
Contact: Lisa stark Walsh, Exec. Dir.
FAX: (512) 370-1642;
E-mail: lisa.walsh@texmed.org; URL: http://www.texmed.org/template.aspx?id=245

Foundation type: Public charity
Purpose: Awards by nomination only to outstanding science teachers of TX.
Publications: Application guidelines; Annual report; Grants list; Informational brochure; Newsletter.
Financial data: Year ended 12/31/2011. Assets, $3,807,501 (M); Expenditures, $751,147; Total giving, $300,562. Awards/prizes amount not specified.
Fields of interest: Education; Science.
Type of support: Awards/prizes.
Application information: Applications accepted. Application form available on the grantmaker's web site.
  Deadline(s): Oct. 18 for nomination, Dec. 28 for nominee application
  Applicants should submit the following:
    1) Essay
    2) Letter(s) of recommendation
    3) Curriculum vitae
  Additional information: See web site for additional information.
Program description:
  Ernest and Sarah Butler Awards for Excellence in Science Teaching: Each year, the foundation grants three $5,000 awards to Texas science teachers who exhibit a personal commitment and enthusiasm for teaching any area of science. Eligible applicants must be Texas state-certified, full-time public and/or private school science teachers with a minimum of two years' teaching experience. Both self-nominations and nominations from others are encouraged. In addition to the $5,000 award, the schools of the winning teachers will receive a $2,000 award, three additional science departments will receive $500 each for second-place winners.
EIN: 746073346

9126
Texas Neurofibromatosis Foundation
3030 Olive St.
400 Victory Plaza E.
Dallas, TX 75219-7690 (972) 868-7943
Contact: Cindy Hahn, Exec. Dir.
FAX: (972) 868-7626; E-mail: chahn@texasnf.org;
URL: http://www.texasnf.org

Foundation type: Public charity
Purpose: Scholarships to college students who
have neurofibromatosis for attendance at
institutions of higher learning. Assistance to
families of individuals with neurofibromatosis for
medical visits.
Publications: Newsletter.
Financial data: Year ended 12/31/2011. Assets,
$213,580 (M); Expenditures, $208,109; Total
giving, $32,797; Grants to individuals, totaling
$2,797.
Fields of interest: Higher education; Human
services.
Type of support: Scholarships—to individuals;
Grants for special needs.
Application information: Applications accepted.
Application form required.
Send request by: Mail for scholarship
Deadline(s): July 13 for scholarship
Additional information: Application for
scholarship should include transcripts and a
recent photograph. Only persons with NF1 or
NF2 are eligible for scholarship. Contact
foundation for additional information for
assistance.
EIN: 742138345

9127
Texas Nursery and Landscape Association Education and Research Foundation
7730 S. IH-35
Austin, TX 78745-6621 (512) 280-5182
Contact: Amy Graham, Exec. V.P.
FAX: (512) 280-3012; E-mail: info@txnla.org;
URL: http://www.tnlaonline.org/
EandRFoundation/index.php

Foundation type: Public charity
Purpose: Scholarships to TX residents pursuing
higher education in horticulture at pre-approved TX
institutions.
Publications: Application guidelines.
Financial data: Year ended 06/30/2012. Assets,
$803,657 (M); Expenditures, $68,431; Total
giving, $39,000; Grants to individuals, totaling
$28,000.
Fields of interest: Landscaping.
Type of support: Scholarships—to individuals;
Support to graduates or students of specific
schools.
Application information: Application form required.
Initial approach: Letter or telephone
Deadline(s): June 1
Applicants should submit the following:
1) Photograph
2) Transcripts
3) Letter(s) of recommendation
Additional information: See web site for
additional application guidelines.
Program description:
TNLA Scholarship Program: The foundation
awards scholarships, ranging from $500 to $2,000
(with average awards of $1,000) to horticulture/
landscape students for their continued education.
Eligible applicants must be residents of Texas who
are high school seniors or returning college
students (including seniors and graduates)

majoring in horticulture or a related field at one of
the following schools: Blinn College, Central Texas
College, Houston Community College, Northeast
Texas Community College, Palo Alto College, Prairie
View A&M University, Sam Houston State
University, Stephen F. Austin State University,
Tarleton University, Tarrant County College, Texas
A&M University - College Station, Texas A&M
University - Commerce, Texas A&M University -
Kingsville, Texas State Technical College, Texas
State University, Texas Tech University, Trinity
Valley College, Tyler Junior College, University of
Texas - Arlington, University of Texas - Austin,
Wharton County Jr. College, and Western Texas
College.
EIN: 742637783

9128
Texas Podiatric Medical Foundation
15577 Ranch Rd. 12, Ste. 103
Wimberley, TX 78676-6210
E-mail: staff@txpma.org; Toll-free tel.: (888)
659-4440; toll-free fax: (888) 394-1123;
URL: http://www.txpmf.org

Foundation type: Public charity
Purpose: Scholarships and mission-related travel
grants to podiatry residents, fourth-year podiatric
college students, and fellows.
Financial data: Year ended 12/31/2011. Assets,
$57,854; Expenditures, $75,651; Total giving,
$8,071; Grants to individuals, totaling $8,071.
Fields of interest: Podiatry; Surgery.
Type of support: Scholarships—to individuals;
Postgraduate support.
Application information: Applications accepted.
Additional information: Contact the foundation for
additional application guidelines.
Program description:
Resident Annual Scholarship Grants: The
foundation awards scholarships to podiatry
residents. Named awards under this program
include the Falknor Charitable Outreach Award, the
Mile High Biomechanics Award, the Armstrong Case
Study Award (sponsored by Mile High Orthotics),
and the Fellow Development Award.
EIN: 742952209

9129
Texas Police Chiefs Association Foundation
1312 E. Hway., 290 Rm. C
Elgin, TX 78621 (512) 281-5400
Contact: Chief Barbara Childress, Chair.
FAX: (512) 281-2240; Toll-free tel.: (877)
776-5423; URL: http://www.tpcaf.org/

Foundation type: Public charity
Purpose: Financial assistance to the surviving
spouse, children or parent of a law enforcement
officer of TX, killed in the line of duty.
Financial data: Year ended 09/30/2011. Assets,
$541,598 (M); Expenditures, $257,352; Total
giving, $20,000; Grants to individuals, totaling
$20,000.
Fields of interest: Crime/law enforcement, police
agencies.
Type of support: Emergency funds; Grants for
special needs.
Application information: Applications not
accepted.
Additional information: Unsolicited requests for
funds not considered or acknowledged. The
law enforcement officer does not have to be a
member of any specific law enforcement

agency or does the officer have to be a
member of any law enforcement association.
EIN: 202956522

9130
Texas Rangers Baseball Foundation
P.O. Box 90111
Arlington, TX 76004-3111 (817) 273-5222
URL: http://texas.rangers.mlb.com/tex/
community/foundation.jsp

Foundation type: Public charity
Purpose: Scholarships to students in the
Dallas-Fort Worth, TX, area.
Financial data: Year ended 12/31/2011. Assets,
$1,898,238 (M); Expenditures, $1,865,654; Total
giving, $1,469,742; Grants to individuals, totaling
$900,111.
Fields of interest: Scholarships/financial aid;
Volunteer services.
Type of support: Employee-related scholarships;
Support to graduates or students of specific
schools; Awards/prizes; Precollege support;
Undergraduate support.
Application information:
Initial approach: Telephone
Applicants should submit the following:
1) Transcripts
2) Essay
Additional information: Contact foundation for
application guidelines.
Program descriptions:
Johnny Oates Scholarships: The foundation
awards scholarships to employees and the children
of employees of the Texas Rangers and
Sportservice.
Mark Holtz Scholarships: Four $2,000
scholarships will be awarded to seniors studying
journalism at Texas Christian University and
University of Texas - Austin.
Mentorship Program: This program, sponsored in
conjunction with Chesapeake Energy and
Volunteers of America, helps ten aspiring young
students from Polytechnic High School in Fort Worth
Independent School District, by matching them with
a mentor to guide them throughout the school year.
Mentors and students meet at Rangers Ballpark
each month during the school year for special
sessions, including interviewing and applying for
jobs, financial literacy, the importance of
community service, etiquette, goal-setting, and
healthy living.
Nolan Ryan Scholarships: Two scholarships are
awarded annually to one female and one male
graduating senior from Alvin High School. Awards
are based on academics, school and community
activities, and financial need, and require that the
recipients have participated in a high school sport
for four years.
Richard Greene Scholars: Six scholarships will be
awarded annually to students in the Arlington
Independent School District.
EIN: 752404714

9131
Texas Star Oaks Fund, Inc.
2143 W. Alabama
Houston, TX 77098
Contact: Amy Dillavou
Application Address: 2143 W. Alabama, Houston,
TX 77098

Foundation type: Operating foundation
Purpose: Financial assistance only to needy TX
residents. Grants are given as one-time support or
on a monthly basis for ongoing financial needs.

Financial data: Year ended 03/31/2013. Assets, $96,017 (M); Expenditures, $132,647; Total giving, $123,493; Grants to individuals, 33 grants totaling $123,493 (high: $6,000, low: $402).
Type of support: Grants for special needs.
Application information: Applications accepted. Application form required.
  Initial approach: Letter or telephone
  Deadline(s): None
  Additional information: Application should include letter of recommendation and case history.
EIN: 746047454

9132
Thai Community Center of North Texas
8484 Stults Rd.
Dallas, TX 75243-4021

Foundation type: Independent foundation
Purpose: Financial assistance to Thai residents of northern TX, for help with medical expenses and emergency funds.
Financial data: Year ended 12/31/2011. Assets, $10,544 (M); Expenditures, $39,001; Total giving, $30,173; Grants to individuals, 2 grants totaling $3,946 (high: $2,000, low: $1,946).
Type of support: Grants for special needs.
Application information: Applications not accepted.
  Additional information: Unsolicited requests for funds not considered or acknowledged.
EIN: 752804666

9133
Billie and Gillis Thomas Family Foundation
(formerly The Thomas Foundation)
8333 Douglas Ave., Ste. 1414
Dallas, TX 75225-5821
Contact: Robyn T. Conlon, Pres.

Foundation type: Independent foundation
Purpose: Scholarships to students for continuing education at institutions of higher learning.
Financial data: Year ended 12/31/2012. Assets, $11,496,190 (M); Expenditures, $882,720; Total giving, $823,672; Grants to individuals, 11 grants totaling $155,672 (high: $23,450, low: $2,617).
Fields of interest: Higher education.
Type of support: Scholarships—to individuals.
Application information: Contact the foundation for eligibility determination.
EIN: 752721588

9134
Bessie & Godfrey Thompson Charitable Foundation
c/o Bank of America, N.A.
P.O. Box 831041
Dallas, TX 75283-1041
Contact: Joshua Grant
Application address: P.O. Box 619, Wilbur, WA 99185-0619

Foundation type: Independent foundation
Purpose: Scholarships to individuals in WA.
Financial data: Year ended 06/30/2013. Assets, $1,188,707 (M); Expenditures, $67,235; Total giving, $47,035.
Type of support: Scholarships—to individuals.
Application information: Applications not accepted.
  Additional information: Unsolicited requests for funds not accepted or considered.
EIN: 957078668

9135
A. G. & Phelo Thompson Scholarship Trust
P.O. Box 831
Hamilton, TX 76531

Foundation type: Operating foundation
Purpose: Scholarships to residents of Hamilton, TX.
Financial data: Year ended 12/31/2011. Assets, $184,925 (M); Expenditures, $10,038; Total giving, $10,000; Grants to individuals, 20 grants totaling $10,000 (high: $500, low: $500).
Type of support: Undergraduate support.
Application information: Applications not accepted.
  Additional information: Unsolicited requests for funds not considered or acknowledged.
EIN: 742813801

9136
Ella B. and Lucy Thompson Trust
c/o Bank of America, N.A.
P.O. Box 831041
Dallas, TX 75283-1041

Foundation type: Independent foundation
Purpose: Financial assistance to retired school teachers of the Galveston Public School System, TX.
Financial data: Year ended 12/31/2011. Assets, $514,903 (M); Expenditures, $41,595; Total giving, $33,750; Grants to individuals, 6 grants totaling $33,750 (high: $6,750, low: $5,400).
Fields of interest: Pensions, teacher funds.
Type of support: Employee-related welfare.
Application information: Applications not accepted.
  Additional information: Unsolicited requests for funds not considered or acknowledged.
EIN: 746082981

9137
The Today Foundation
8150 N. Central Expwy., Ste. 1900
Dallas, TX 75206-1833 (214) 572-4487
FAX: (972) 572-1515;
E-mail: info@todayfoundation.org; Mailing address: P.O. Box 225748, Dallas, TX 75222-5748;
URL: http://www.todayfoundation.org

Foundation type: Public charity
Purpose: Scholarships to economically disadvantaged children entering K-8th grade in Dallas county, TX.
Publications: Application guidelines.
Financial data: Year ended 07/31/2012. Assets, $3,227,631 (M); Expenditures, $1,370,928.
Fields of interest: Education.
Type of support: Scholarships—to individuals.
Application information: Applications accepted. Application form required.
  Initial approach: Telephone, letter, e-mail or fax
  Additional information: Scholarships are granted on a first-come, first-served basis.
Program description:
  Children's Education Fund: This program provides Dallas County children with scholarships, in order to allow them to be able to go to the private school of their choice. Applicants must live in Dallas County, be at least five years old, be entering K-8th grade, and demonstrate financial need by meeting the standards of the federal free-lunch program. Scholarships of up to $1,850 per student per year will be awarded. Scholarships are for one year, but are renewable each year up to the eight grade.
EIN: 751864736

9138
George Trimble Special Need Trust Fund
c/o Bank of America, N.A.
P.O. Box 831041
Dallas, TX 75283-1041 (866) 461-7287
Contact: Robert Glew
Application address: c/o Bank of America, N.A., 111 Westminster St., Providence RI 02903 tel.:(866) 461-7287

Foundation type: Independent foundation
Purpose: Scholarships to graduates of El Dorado High School, KS for higher education. Financial assistance to individuals in Butler county, KS with special needs due to a medical condition.
Financial data: Year ended 12/31/2011. Assets, $326,891 (M); Expenditures, $20,589; Total giving, $16,150; Grants to individuals, 13 grants totaling $6,500 (high: $500, low: $500).
Fields of interest: Vocational education; College; Scholarships/financial aid.
Type of support: Support to graduates or students of specific schools; Undergraduate support.
Application information: Applications accepted. Application form required. Interview required.
  Deadline(s): Mar. 1 for scholarship and Dec. 1 for special needs
  Applicants should submit the following:
    1) Letter(s) of recommendation
    2) Essay
    3) Transcripts
  Additional information: Applications may be obtained from the trustee or from the principal's office at El Dorado High School.
EIN: 486319821

9139
TUA Bartholomew Family Foundation
(formerly Bartholomew Family Scholarship & Loan Fund)
c/o Bank of America, N.A.
P.O. Box 831041
Dallas, TX 75283-1041 (503) 363-3660
Application address: c/o First Congregational Church, Attn.: Scholarship Comm., 700 Marion St., N.E., Salem, OR 97301

Foundation type: Independent foundation
Purpose: Scholarships to members of First Congregational Church, Salem, OR, for postsecondary education in OR studying for the ministry.
Financial data: Year ended 11/30/2012. Assets, $458,250 (M); Expenditures, $24,819; Total giving, $20,000.
Fields of interest: Vocational education; Theological school/education; Protestant agencies & churches.
Type of support: Technical education support; Undergraduate support.
Application information: Applications accepted. Application form required.
  Deadline(s): Apr. 30
  Applicants should submit the following:
    1) Financial information
    2) Transcripts
    3) GPA
EIN: 936091422

9140
Lena & Harry Turner Foundation
c/o Bank of America, N.A.
P.O. Box 831041
Dallas, TX 75283-1041
Contact: Marshall Sutton, Tr.
Application address: 110 S.W. 2nd St., Grand
Prairie, TX 75050-5603

Foundation type: Independent foundation
Purpose: Scholarships to residents of Grand
Prairie, TX for higher education.
Financial data: Year ended 12/31/2012. Assets,
$822,464 (M); Expenditures, $67,876; Total
giving, $46,750; Grants to individuals, 11 grants
totaling $19,750 (high: $3,500, low: $750).
Type of support: Scholarships—to individuals.
Application information: Applications accepted.
  Deadline(s): None
EIN: 237416737

9141
UFCW Region 5 Educational Trust
(formerly Meat Cutters Educational Trust)
c/o UFCW, Region 5
1705 W. Northwest Hwy., Ste. 150
Grapevine, TX 76051-8107 (214) 939-9222
Application address: c/o UFCW Scholarship Prog.,
Office of Education, 1701 West N.W. Hwy., Ste.
200, Grapevine, TX 76051

Foundation type: Independent foundation
Purpose: Scholarships to members and children of
members of various UFCW Local Unions.
Publications: Informational brochure (including
application guidelines).
Financial data: Year ended 12/31/2012. Assets,
$105,576 (M); Expenditures, $17,406; Total
giving, $12,000; Grants to individuals, 8 grants
totaling $12,000 (high: $1,500, low: $1,500).
Fields of interest: Higher education.
Type of support: Scholarships—to individuals.
Application information: Applications accepted.
  Deadline(s): Dec. 31
  Applicants should submit the following:
    1) SAT
    2) ACT
  Additional information: Applicants must be high
    school seniors who will graduate the following
    spring, be under 20 years of age as of Mar.
    15 of their graduating year, and plan to enter
    college in the fall.
EIN: 752035368

9142
United Way of Metropolitan Tarrant County
1500 N. Main St., Ste. 200
P.O. Box 4448
Fort Worth, TX 76164-8929 (817) 258-8000
Contact: Tim McKinney, Pres. and C.E.O.
E-mail: tim.mckinney@unitedwaytarrant.org;
Alternate address (Arlington and SE Tarrant
County): 401 W. Sanford St., Ste 2600, Arlington,
TX 76011-7072, tel.: (817) 548-9595, fax: (817)
277-6919; alternate address (NE Tarrant County):
813 Brown Trail, Ste. 7, Bedford, TX 76022-7338,
tel: (817) 282-1160, fax: (817) 282-1275;
URL: http://www.unitedwaytarrant.org

Foundation type: Public charity
Purpose: Grants for basic necessities to needy
residents of Tarran County, TX.
Publications: Financial statement; Newsletter.
Financial data: Year ended 06/30/2012. Assets,
$35,311,244 (M); Expenditures, $32,513,108;

Total giving, $24,527,511; Grants to individuals,
totaling $1,129,269.
Fields of interest: Economically disadvantaged.
Type of support: Grants for special needs.
Application information:
  Initial approach: Letter
  Additional information: Contact foundation for
    complete eligibility requirements.
EIN: 750858360

9143
United Way of South Texas
1200 E. Hackberry Ave., Ste. F
McAllen, TX 78501-5743 (956) 686-6331
FAX: (956) 686-8430; Mailing address: P.O. Box
187, McAllen, TX 78505-0187; URL: http://
www.unitedwayofsotx.org/

Foundation type: Public charity
Purpose: Grants to indigent residents of southern
TX.
Publications: Application guidelines; Annual report;
Informational brochure; Newsletter.
Financial data: Year ended 12/31/2011. Assets,
$5,319,878 (M); Expenditures, $2,465,820; Total
giving, $1,787,227; Grants to individuals, totaling
$203,642.
Fields of interest: Economically disadvantaged.
Type of support: Grants for special needs.
Application information:
  Initial approach: Letter
  Additional information: Contact foundation for
    complete eligibility requirements.
EIN: 742052527

9144
United Way of the Coastal Bend, Inc.
711 N. Carancahua St., Ste. 302
Corpus Christi, TX 78401-0524 (361)
882-2529
FAX: (361) 888-6882; E-mail: unitedway@uwcb.org;
URL: http://www.uwcb.org

Foundation type: Public charity
Purpose: Grants to needy residents of Bee, Jim
Wells, Kelberg, Live Oak, Nueces, and San Patricio
counties, TX.
Publications: Annual report; Newsletter.
Financial data: Year ended 06/30/2012. Assets,
$6,796,644 (M); Expenditures, $4,132,874; Total
giving, $2,995,381.
Fields of interest: Economically disadvantaged.
Type of support: Grants for special needs.
Application information:
  Initial approach: Letter
  Additional information: Contact foundation for
    complete eligibility requirements.
EIN: 741207552

9145
University Medical Center Foundation
1400 Hardaway, Ste. 220
El Paso, TX 79903-3121 (915) 521-7229
Contact: Dennece Knight, Exec. Dir.
FAX: (915) 521-7201;
E-mail: giving@umcelpaso.org; Toll-free tel.: (877)
736-7229; email for Dennece Knight:
dknight@umcelpaso.org; URL: http://
umcfoundationelpaso.org/

Foundation type: Public charity
Purpose: Financial assistance to patients and their
families in the Tucson, AZ area providing rent,
utilities, transportation, food, and other needs that
enable patients to receive the care they need.

Financial data: Year ended 06/30/2011. Assets,
$25,127,742 (M); Expenditures, $6,690,815;
Total giving, $6,423,807; Grants to individuals,
totaling $64,330.
Fields of interest: Human services; Economically
disadvantaged.
Type of support: Grants for special needs.
Application information: Interview required.
  Additional information: Recipients are required to
    complete financial aid referral form to
    determine financial need. Additional
    documentation is required to verify
    information provided in financial aid referral
    form.
EIN: 860572438

9146
Urban Vision Foundation, Inc.
1500 Citywest Blvd., Ste. 450
Houston, TX 77042-2299 (713) 278-5100
Contact: John T. Jones, Pres.

Foundation type: Independent foundation
Purpose: Scholarships primarily to residents of TX
for tuition and textbooks. Grants for needy families
and individuals primarily in Houston, TX.
Financial data: Year ended 12/31/2011. Assets,
$23,435 (M); Expenditures, $17,650; Total giving,
$13,618; Grants to individuals, 4 grants totaling
$13,618 (high: $10,108, low: $250).
Fields of interest: Education; Economically
disadvantaged.
Type of support: Undergraduate support; Grants for
special needs.
Application information: Applications accepted.
Interview required.
  Initial approach: Letter
  Additional information: Contact foundation for
    eligibility requirements.
EIN: 760554508

9147
Valero Scholarship Trust
P.O. Box 696000
San Antonio, TX 78269
Contact: Debbie McNaul

Foundation type: Company-sponsored foundation
Purpose: Scholarships to dependents of employees
of Valero Energy Corp. for higher education.
Financial data: Year ended 12/31/2012. Assets,
$169,409 (M); Expenditures, $229,714; Total
giving, $223,750.
Type of support: Employee-related scholarships.
Application information: Applications not
accepted.
  Additional information: Unsolicited requests for
    funds not considered or acknowledged.
Company name: Valero Energy Corporation
EIN: 746437579

9148
The Vetiver Network
(also known as The Vetiver Network international)
149 E. Rosewood
St. Antonio, TX 78212 (210) 732-7138
Contact: Jim Smyle, Pres. and Dir.
E-mail: info@vetiver.org; URL: http://
www.vetiver.org

Foundation type: Independent foundation
Purpose: Awards to individuals to develop and
disseminate information on the use of Vetiver
System for on farm soil and water conservation,
land rehabilitation, embankment stabilization,

disaster mitigation, water quality enhancement, and pollution control.
Financial data: Year ended 12/31/2012. Assets, $4,186 (M); Expenditures, $3,489; Total giving, $522; Grant to an individual, 1 grant totaling $522.
Fields of interest: Environment, pollution control; Natural resources; Environment, water resources; Environment, land resources.
Type of support: Research; Grants to individuals; Awards/prizes.
Application information: Application form not required.
Initial approach: Letter or telephone
Deadline(s): None
EIN: 541778296

9149
Vietnamese Culture & Science Association
4615 Belle Pk. Dr.
Houston, TX 77072-1819 (281) 933-8118
Scholarship e-mail: Scholarship@vcsa.org
FAX: (281) 933-8187; E-mail: contact@vcsa.org;
URL: http://www.vcsa.org

Foundation type: Public charity
Purpose: Scholarships to Vietnamese-American Students who graduated from local high schools as either Valedictorian or Salutatorian of their current year class.
Publications: Application guidelines; Newsletter.
Financial data: Year ended 12/31/2011. Assets, $160,959 (M); Expenditures, $295,964; Total giving, $89,558; Grants to individuals, totaling $12,959.
Fields of interest: Performing arts; Arts; Higher education.
Type of support: Scholarships—to individuals.
Application information: Applications accepted. Application form required.
Send request by: E-mail
Deadline(s): Apr. 6
Applicants should submit the following:
  1) Essay
  2) Resume
Program description:
VCSA Scholarship Contest: The program will award eight $500 scholarships and certificates to outstanding young community activists who want to attend camp Len Duong and need financial help. Applicants must be active in a Vietnamese community organization or Vietnamese Student Association or some local community organization. Only college students or high school seniors with a cumulative 3.0 GPA or higher on a 4.0 scale may apply.
EIN: 760360557

9150
Dolly Vinsant Memorial Foundation
c/o Border Capital Bank
P.O. Box 5555
McAllen, TX 78502-5555 (956) 399-5763
Contact: Charles Wilson, Chair.
Application Address: c/o Mr. Charles Wilson, 775 North Crockett, San Benito, TX. 78586

Foundation type: Independent foundation
Purpose: Scholarships to graduating students attending high school in Cameron County, TX, to attend a two- or four-year college, university, or vocational-technical school.
Financial data: Year ended 09/30/2012. Assets, $533,888 (M); Expenditures, $85,210; Total giving, $73,000; Grants to individuals, 32 grants totaling $73,000 (high: $5,000, low: $500).

Fields of interest: Vocational education, post-secondary; Medical school/education.
Type of support: Support to graduates or students of specific schools; Technical education support; Undergraduate support.
Application information: Applications accepted. Application form required.
Initial approach: Letter
Deadline(s): None
Applicants should submit the following:
  1) SAT
  2) ACT
  3) GPA
  4) Class rank
  5) Transcripts
  6) Letter(s) of recommendation
  7) Essay
Additional information: Applicant must be in the top 25 percent of their graduating class pursuing a career in the medical related field.
EIN: 741143136

9151
Visible Changes Educational Foundation
1303 Campbell Rd.
Houston, TX 77055-6403

Foundation type: Operating foundation
Purpose: Scholarships only to children of employees of Visible Changes Educational Foundation.
Financial data: Year ended 12/31/2012. Assets, $279,082 (M); Expenditures, $81,200; Total giving, $80,450; Grants to individuals, 50 grants totaling $80,450 (high: $4,000, low: $150).
Type of support: Employee-related scholarships.
Application information: Applications not accepted.
Additional information: Unsolicited requests for funds not considered or acknowledged.
EIN: 760303682

9152
The Von Rosenberg Foundation
1600 Augusta Dr.
Houston, TX 77057

Foundation type: Independent foundation
Purpose: Scholarships to individuals for attendance at accredited colleges or universities in TX.
Financial data: Year ended 10/31/2011. Assets, $93,708 (M); Expenditures, $26,896; Total giving, $26,000; Grants to individuals, 9 grants totaling $26,000 (high: $4,000, low: $2,000).
Fields of interest: Higher education.
Type of support: Scholarships—to individuals.
Application information: Applications not accepted.
Additional information: Unsolicited requests for funds not considered or acknowledged.
EIN: 760520143

9153
Waco Foundation
1105 Wooded Acres, Ste. 701
Waco, TX 76710 (254) 754-3404
Contact: Ashley Allison, Exec. Dir.; Grantmaking: Nicole Wynter, Dir., Grants and Capacity Building
FAX: (254) 753-2887;
E-mail: info@wacofoundation.org; URL: http://www.wacofoundation.org

Foundation type: Community foundation

Purpose: Scholarships to deserving graduating students of McLennan county, TX high schools for attendance at colleges or universities.
Publications: Application guidelines; Annual report; Financial statement; Grants list; Informational brochure; Newsletter.
Financial data: Year ended 03/31/2012. Assets, $62,016,959 (M); Expenditures, $5,134,867; Total giving, $3,816,506; Grants to individuals, 239 grants totaling $345,716.
Fields of interest: Higher education.
Type of support: Scholarships—to individuals.
Application information: Applications accepted. Application form required. Application form available on the grantmaker's web site.
Initial approach: Application
Send request by: On-line
Deadline(s): May 1 for high school students, Dec. 1 for sophomores
Final notification: Recipients notified within 30 days
Applicants should submit the following:
  1) SAR
  2) FAFSA
EIN: 746054628

9154
Kathryn & Otto H. Wagner Charitable Trust
c/o Bank of America, N.A.
P.O. Box 831041
Dallas, TX 75283-1041
Contact: Jodi Gardner, Tr.
Application address: P.O. Box 128, Township, WA 99856-0128

Foundation type: Independent foundation
Purpose: Scholarships to graduating seniors of Okanogan County, WA high schools for higher education.
Financial data: Year ended 12/31/2011. Assets, $769,481 (M); Expenditures, $31,478; Total giving, $14,500; Grants to individuals, 14 grants totaling $14,500 (high: $1,500, low: $1,000).
Fields of interest: Higher education.
Type of support: Scholarships—to individuals.
Application information: Applications accepted. Application form required.
Deadline(s): None
Additional information: Application should include financial information. Applicants are selected by the trustee.
EIN: 916103623

9155
Lillian Waltom Foundation
901 Oak St.
Jourdanton, TX 78026-2847 (830) 769-2001
Contact: W.F. Zuhlke, Jr., Tr.

Foundation type: Independent foundation
Purpose: Scholarships to financially needy students in Atascosa County, TX for study at institutions of higher learning.
Financial data: Year ended 12/31/2011. Assets, $1,673,856 (M); Expenditures, $119,300; Total giving, $83,000.
Fields of interest: Higher education.
Type of support: Scholarships—to individuals.
Application information: Applications accepted. Application form required.
Initial approach: Letter
Additional information: Applicant must demonstrate financial need.
EIN: 742509618

9156
Ward County Council for Handicapped Children, Inc.
819 S. Allen Ave.
Monahans, TX 79756 (432) 943-6335
Contact: Bob Mobley, V.P.

Foundation type: Independent foundation
Purpose: Scholarships for handicapped students of Monahans, Texas to cover tuition and books.
Financial data: Year ended 12/31/2011. Assets, $169,334 (M); Expenditures, $75,965; Total giving, $4,250; Grants to individuals, 14 grants totaling $4,250 (high: $1,000, low: $250).
Type of support: Scholarships—to individuals.
Application information: Applications accepted. Application form required.
   Deadline(s): None
EIN: 751100663

9157
Charles Warnken, Sr. Memorial College Scholarship Fund
P.O. Drawer B
Pleasanton, TX 78064-0060 (830) 569-3808
Contact: Ursula Wauters, Mgr.
Application address: 281 Hwy., Pleasanton, TX 78064

Foundation type: Independent foundation
Purpose: Undergraduate scholarships to graduating seniors at Poth High School, TX.
Financial data: Year ended 06/30/2012. Assets, $118,307 (M); Expenditures, $7,749; Total giving, $6,000; Grants to individuals, 2 grants totaling $6,000 (high: $3,500, low: $2,500).
Type of support: Support to graduates or students of specific schools; Undergraduate support.
Application information: Applications not accepted.
   Additional information: Unsolicited requests for funds not considered or acknowledged.
EIN: 742213880

9158
C. S. Watson Scholarship Foundation
(also known as Clara Stewart Watson Foundation)
c/o Bank of America, N.A.
P.O. Box 831041
Dallas, TX 75283-1041

Foundation type: Independent foundation
Purpose: Scholarships to graduates of high schools in Dallas and Tarrant counties, TX, for undergraduate study at colleges and universities in TX.
Financial data: Year ended 08/31/2012. Assets, $641,646 (M); Expenditures, $38,837; Total giving, $31,000.
Fields of interest: Vocational education, post-secondary; Higher education.
Type of support: Technical education support; Undergraduate support.
Application information: Applications accepted.
   Additional information: Contact the foundation for application guidelines.
EIN: 756064730

9159
Felix H. and Madge B. Watson Scholarship Trust
c/o Wells Fargo Bank, N.A.
P.O. Box 41629
Austin, TX 78704-9926 (940) 766-8300
Contact: Kristin Morris, Trust Off.
Application address: c/o Wells Fargo Bank, N.A., 2301 Kell Blvd., Wichita Falls, TX 76308-1007,

Foundation type: Independent foundation
Purpose: Scholarships to graduating seniors from Clay County, Texas high schools for postsecondary education.
Financial data: Year ended 12/31/2012. Assets, $217,340 (M); Expenditures, $16,076; Total giving, $11,410; Grants to individuals, 5 grants totaling $11,410 (high: $3,000, low: $1,205).
Fields of interest: Higher education.
Type of support: Support to graduates or students of specific schools.
Application information: Applications accepted. Application form required.
   Deadline(s): May 15
   Additional information: Application forms can be obtained from any Clay County, Texas high school.
EIN: 746500001

9160
The Robert A. Welch Foundation
5555 San Felipe, Ste. 1900
Houston, TX 77056-2730
Contact: Norbert Dittrich, Pres.
E-mail: info@welch1.org; URL: http://www.welch1.org

Foundation type: Independent foundation
Purpose: Awards for basic chemistry research at educational institutions in TX. Research grants to support fundamental chemical research at universities, colleges or other educational institutions within the state of TX.
Publications: Application guidelines; Annual report.
Financial data: Year ended 08/31/2012. Assets, $596,206,068 (M); Expenditures, $29,639,999; Total giving, $23,411,861; Grants to individuals, totaling $164,500.
Fields of interest: Chemistry.
Type of support: Research; Awards/prizes.
Application information: Applications accepted. Application form required. Application form available on the grantmaker's web site.
   Send request by: Mail
   Copies of proposal: 1
   Deadline(s): Feb. 1 for Research
   Additional information: See web site for additional application guidelines.
Program descriptions:
   Norman Hackerman Award in Chemical Research: The award was established to recognize the accomplishments of chemical scientist in Texas who are in their early careers and to serve as an encouragement to those who are embarking on careers dedicated to increasing our fundamental understanding of chemistry. The award is intended for the personal benefit of the recipients and carries no requirement for future services as a condition of receiving it. See the foundation's web site for program guidelines.
   Robert A. Welch Award in Chemistry: The purpose of the award is to foster and encourage basic chemical research and to recognize, in a substantial manner, the value of chemical research contributions for the benefit of mankind. Any person can be considered for the award who has made important chemical research contributions which

have had a significant, positive influence on mankind. The award is intended to recognize contributions that have not previously been rewarded in a similar manner. See foundation's web site for guidelines.
EIN: 760343128

9161
Rob and Bessie Welder Wildlife Foundation
P.O. Box 1400
Sinton, TX 78387-1400 (361) 364-2643
Contact: Dr. Selma Glasscock, Asst. Dir.
FAX: (361) 364-2650;
E-mail: welderfoundation@welderwildlife.org;
URL: http://www.welderwildlife.org

Foundation type: Operating foundation
Purpose: Fellowships to M.S. and Ph.D. candidates at accredited U.S. and Canadian colleges and universities to support research and further graduate-level education in wildlife problems and conservation, and to develop scientific methods for increasing wildlife populations.
Publications: Application guidelines; Biennial report; Informational brochure (including application guidelines); Multi-year report; Newsletter.
Financial data: Year ended 12/31/2012. Assets, $26,400,496 (M); Expenditures, $1,123,702; Total giving, $101,198; Grants to individuals, 7 grants totaling $101,198 (high: $23,100, low: $1,495).
Fields of interest: Natural resources; Animals/wildlife, preservation/protection.
Type of support: Fellowships; Internship funds.
Application information: Applications accepted. Application form required. Application form available on the grantmaker's web site.
   Initial approach: Letter
   Copies of proposal: 2
   Deadline(s): Oct. 1
   Final notification: Recipients notified six weeks after deadline
   Applicants should submit the following:
      1) Transcripts
      2) Letter(s) of recommendation
      3) Proposal
      4) Budget Information
      5) GPA
   Additional information: Application should also include GRE scores, timetable and biographical data.
Program description:
   Research Fellowship Program: The Program is designed to promote the education of exceptionally qualified students and provide research information to manage wildlife populations. Fellowships are awarded directly to properly accredited U.S. colleges and universities for bona fide graduate students who are approved candidates for M.S. or Ph.D. degrees after project proposals have been submitted to and approved by the foundation. Complete guidelines available on foundation web site.
EIN: 741381321

9162
West Foundation
15950 N. Dallas Pkwy., Ste. 600
Dallas, TX 75248-6685

Foundation type: Independent foundation
Purpose: Awards by nomination only for excellence in teaching and leadership in public education in the Wichita Falls Independent School District, TX.

Financial data: Year ended 09/30/2013. Assets, $17,714,185 (M); Expenditures, $1,038,851; Total giving, $731,800; Grants to individuals, 20 grants totaling $100,000 (high: $5,000, low: $5,000).
Fields of interest: Education.
Type of support: Support to graduates or students of specific schools; Awards/grants by nomination only; Awards/prizes.
Application information: Applications not accepted.
Additional information: Awards by nomination only. Unsolicited requests for funds not considered or acknowledged.
EIN: 237332105

9163
West Texas Opportunities
603 N. 4th St.
Lamesa, TX 79331-4505 (806) 872-8354
Contact: Jenny Gibson, Exec. Dir.
E-mail: wtxop.info@gowto.org; E-mail For Jenny Gibson: jenny.gibson.wto@gmail.com; URL: http://www.gowto.org

Foundation type: Public charity
Purpose: Grants to low-income residents of western TX.
Financial data: Year ended 06/30/2012. Assets, $4,167,340 (M); Expenditures, $35,950,184; Total giving, $21,169,499; Grants to individuals, totaling $21,169,499.
Fields of interest: Economically disadvantaged.
Type of support: Grants for special needs.
Application information:
Initial approach: Telephone or e-mail
Additional information: Contact foundation for complete eligibility requirements.
EIN: 751226644

9164
Western European Architecture Foundation
306 W. Sunset., Ste. 115
San Antonio, TX 78209-1730 (210) 829-4040
Contact: P.J. Fleming, Pres.
URL: http://www.gabrielprize.org/pages/WEAF.php

Foundation type: Independent foundation
Purpose: Prizes awarded to architects and students of architecture to study the preservation and construction of Western European and French Classical architecture in France.
Financial data: Year ended 12/31/2012. Assets, $2,165,885 (M); Expenditures, $196,950; Total giving, $30,000; Grants to individuals, 2 grants totaling $30,000 (high: $20,000, low: $10,000).
Fields of interest: Architecture.
International interests: Europe; France.
Type of support: Awards/prizes.
Application information: Applications accepted.
Initial approach: Proposal
Deadline(s): Jan. 10
Additional information: Application must detail the amount of money requested and the specific use to which it will be applied. Gabriel Prize application format is available on foundation web site.
Program description:
Gabriel Prize: Each year, the Western European Architecture Foundation awards the Gabriel Prize-a $17,500 grant for the study of classical architecture and landscape in France. Prize winners embark on a three-month itinerary of their own devising. While abroad, Gabriel laureates focus on

some particular aspect of French architecture. The selection process includes three phases, with candidates registering their interest through the submission of pertinent illustrations of personal work and an outline of the studies contemplated. A first jury is empowered to select from such submissions three candidates who are then invited to meet a second jury assembled with the task of naming the final winner and a runner up.
EIN: 742553016

9165
Wichita Falls Area Community Foundation
807 8th St., Ste. 750
Wichita Falls, TX 76301-3334 (940) 766-0829
Contact: Teresa Pontius-Caves, Pres.
FAX: (940) 766-2861; E-mail: wfacf@wfacf.org; Additional e-mail: tpontiuscaves@wfacf.org; URL: http://www.wfacf.org

Foundation type: Community foundation
Purpose: Scholarships to graduating high school seniors, primarily of Wichita Falls, TX.
Publications: Annual report; Informational brochure; Newsletter; Occasional report.
Financial data: Year ended 12/31/2012. Assets, $39,961,797 (M); Expenditures, $5,209,458; Total giving, $4,749,507; Grants to individuals, 163 grants totaling $292,290.
Fields of interest: Higher education.
Type of support: Scholarships—to individuals; Undergraduate support.
Application information: Applications accepted. Application form required. Application form available on the grantmaker's web site.
Deadline(s): Mar. 1
Additional information: Contact your guidance counselor for application information. See web site for a complete scholarship listing and application form.
EIN: 752817894

9166
Edwin E. and Elizabeth Wildner Scholarship Trust
P.O. Box 430
La Grange, TX 78945-0430
Contact: Bill Wagner
Application address: c/o La Grange High School, Attn.: Principal, P.O. Box 100, La Grange, TX 78945-0100, tel.: (979) 968-8378
Application Address: La Grange High School, La Grange TX 78945; tel.: (979) 968-8378

Foundation type: Operating foundation
Purpose: Scholarships to graduates of La Grange High School, TX, pursuing an engineering career.
Financial data: Year ended 12/31/2011. Assets, $196,880 (M); Expenditures, $8,924; Total giving, $8,500; Grants to individuals, 11 grants totaling $8,500 (high: $1,000, low: $500).
Fields of interest: Engineering school/education.
Type of support: Support to graduates or students of specific schools; Undergraduate support.
Application information: Applications accepted. Application form required.
Initial approach: Letter
Deadline(s): None
EIN: 746494527

9167
Bess A. Wilkins Memorial Scholarship Fund
c/o Bank of America, N.A.
P.O. Box 831041
Dallas, TX 75283-1041 (870) 352-3520
Application address: c/o Fordyce Scholarship Assn., P.O. Box 851, Fordyce, AR 71742

Foundation type: Independent foundation
Purpose: College scholarships to graduates of the public high schools in Fordyce county, AR.
Financial data: Year ended 12/31/2012. Assets, $1,117,377 (M); Expenditures, $69,863; Total giving, $46,963; Grants to individuals, 44 grants totaling $46,963 (high: $3,187, low: $13).
Fields of interest: Higher education.
Type of support: Scholarships—to individuals.
Application information: Applications accepted.
Initial approach: Letter
Deadline(s): None
EIN: 716084050

9168
The Roy Williams Safety Net Foundation
8585 N. Stemmons Frwy., Ste. 500
Dallas, TX 75247-3836 (405) 819-5904
FAX: (214) 905-8048;
E-mail: info@roywilliamssafetynet.org

Foundation type: Public charity
Purpose: Grants to single mothers in the Dallas, TX area.
Financial data: Year ended 12/31/2011. Assets, $5,653 (M); Expenditures, $20.
Fields of interest: Single parents.
Type of support: Grants to individuals.
Application information: Applications accepted.
Initial approach: E-mail or letter
Additional information: Contact foundation for eligibility.
EIN: 542110207

9169
Ralph Wilson Plastics Employees Scholarship Fund
600 General Bruce Dr.
Temple, TX 76504-2402 (254) 774-5832
Application address: P.O. Box 625, Temple, TX 76503-0625, tel.: (254) 774-5832

Foundation type: Company-sponsored foundation
Purpose: Scholarships to dependents of TX employees of Wilsonart International, who are full-time students at a college or university.
Financial data: Year ended 06/30/2013. Assets, $1,149,060 (M); Expenditures, $70,653; Total giving, $60,300; Grants to individuals, 34 grants totaling $60,300 (high: $1,800, low: $900).
Type of support: Employee-related scholarships.
Application information: Application form required.
Deadline(s): Apr.
Applicants should submit the following:
1) Transcripts
2) SAT
3) ACT
Additional information: Application should also include copy of letter of acceptance to college or university; Letters of recommendation are optional; Application address for scholarships: c/o Selection Comm., P.O. Box 625, Temple, TX 76503-0625, tel.: (254) 774-5832.
Company name: Wilson (Ralph) Plastics
EIN: 746245026

9170
The Wine and Food Foundation of Texas
(formerly Texas Hill County Wine and Food Foundation)
2121 E. 6th St., Ste. 102
Austin, TX 78702 (512) 327-7555
Contact: Morgan Thomsen, Community Relations Director
FAX: (512) 327-7551;
E-mail: info@winefoodfoundation.org; URL: http://www.winefoodfoundation.org

Foundation type: Public charity
Purpose: Scholarships to residents of TX for higher education in the culinary arts.
Publications: Application guidelines; Informational brochure; Newsletter.
Financial data: Year ended 12/31/2011. Assets, $902,105 (M); Expenditures, $465,643; Total giving, $49,000.
Fields of interest: Vocational education.
Type of support: Conferences/seminars; Research; Grants to individuals; Scholarships—to individuals; Undergraduate support.
Application information: Applications accepted. Application form required. Application form available on the grantmaker's web site.
  Deadline(s): Vary
  Additional information: See web site for additional guidelines.
Program descriptions:
  Pastry Scholarship: Scholarships, ranging from $1,000 to $5,000, are available to outstanding pastry chefs throughout Texas, through a culinary competition. Competitions require applicants to utilize a pre-determined basket of ingredients to create recipes for five pastry categories (including a composed dessert, a traditional Texas dessert, a standard technique dessert, a mignardises plate, and a basic yeast bread). The 2012 Pastry Competition is on hold until 2013.
  Stephan Pyles Scholarship: The scholarship challenges students to create a unique three-course meal utilizing a predetermined 'basket of food' containing many Texas food products. The competition consists of two phases. Phase One is the application phase, whereby menus and application packets are submitted and blindly evaluated. Phase Two consists of the actual cook-off event whereby three finalists will be competing for two days by cooking and serving their menus to a panel of culinary experts. The grand prize is a $15,000 scholarship made payable to the winner's school. The winner also receives a $500 stipend to travel with Chef Pyles to a celebrity chef fundraising event and the opportunity to present a course at the Stephan Pyles Annual Celebrity Chef Dinner & Live Wine Auction. The two remaining finalists will each receive $1,000 scholarships made payable to their respective schools.
EIN: 742846361

9171
David and Eula Wintermann Foundation
P.O. Box 337
Eagle Lake, TX 77434-0337 (979) 234-5551
Contact: Jack Johnson, Pres.

Foundation type: Independent foundation
Purpose: Scholarships to seniors at Rice High School, Eagle Lake, TX, to pursue studies in the medical field.
Financial data: Year ended 09/30/2013. Assets, $14,408,601 (M); Expenditures, $844,049; Total giving, $585,920; Grants to individuals, 4 grants totaling $24,000 (high: $8,000, low: $4,000).

Fields of interest: Medical school/education; Nursing school/education.
Type of support: Support to graduates or students of specific schools; Undergraduate support.
Application information: Applications accepted. Application form required.
  Initial approach: Letter
  Deadline(s): Apr. 1
  Applicants should submit the following:
    1) Transcripts
    2) Financial information
  Additional information: Application should also include field of intended study and a character reference.
EIN: 760082100

9172
Wipe Out Kid's Cancer
1349 Empire Ctr., Ste. 240
Dallas, TX 75247-4123 (214) 987-4662
Contact: Evelyn Costolo, C.E.O.
FAX: (214) 987-4668; E-mail: rmoore@wokc.org; E-mail for Evelyn Costolo: ecostolo@wokc.org; tel. for Evelyn Costolo: (214) 987-4662; fax for Evelyn Costolo: (214) 987-4668; URL: http://www.wokc.org

Foundation type: Public charity
Purpose: Scholarships awards of $2,500 to four survivors of pediatric cancer.
Publications: Application guidelines.
Financial data: Year ended 12/31/2011. Assets, $268,677 (M); Expenditures, $427,171; Total giving, $156,611; Grants to individuals, totaling $27,711.
Fields of interest: Cancer; Pediatrics.
Type of support: Undergraduate support.
Application information: Applications accepted.
  Initial approach: Letter
  Deadline(s): Mar. 15
EIN: 751892051

9173
Erbon & Marie Wise Educational Trust
118 Denny Fox Dr.
Burnet, TX 78611-5001 (337) 527-8308
Contact: Larry Wise, Tr.
Application address: 809 E. Napoleonn St., Sulphur, LA 70663

Foundation type: Independent foundation
Purpose: Scholarships to students of central and southwest LA, majoring in communications or related fields.
Financial data: Year ended 12/31/2012. Assets, $121,382 (M); Expenditures, $8,001; Total giving, $7,500; Grants to individuals, 4 grants totaling $7,500 (high: $2,000, low: $1,500).
Type of support: Undergraduate support.
Application information: Applications accepted. Application form required.
  Deadline(s): Apr. 15
  Applicants should submit the following:
    1) Transcripts
    2) Letter(s) of recommendation
EIN: 726137018

9174
Elroy & Vickie Wisian Ministries, Inc.
4605 14th St.
Lubbock, TX 79416

Foundation type: Independent foundation
Purpose: Scholarships to seminary students of TX, and grants for living expenses.

Financial data: Year ended 05/31/2013. Assets, $0 (M); Expenditures, $119,021; Total giving, $119,021.
Fields of interest: Theological school/education; Christian agencies & churches.
Type of support: Grants to individuals; Undergraduate support.
Application information: Applications not accepted.
  Additional information: Unsolicited requests for funds not considered or acknowledged.
EIN: 200729737

9175
Gus & Ethel Wolters Foundation Trust
c/o Tax Dept.
P.O. Box 2950
San Antonio, TX 78299-2950 (210) 220-4620
Contact: Ryland Howard, V.P.

Foundation type: Independent foundation
Purpose: Scholarships to graduates of Shriner High School or St. Paul's Catholic High School in Shriner, TX, who reside in Lavaca County, TX.
Financial data: Year ended 08/31/2012. Assets, $6,957,304 (M); Expenditures, $338,646; Total giving, $261,438.
Type of support: Support to graduates or students of specific schools; Undergraduate support.
Application information: Applications accepted. Application form required.
  Additional information: Application must include complete biographical data, a report of high school performance, a statement of an academic plan, and a letter of reference; Applications available from the above named schools.
EIN: 742335544

9176
B. M. Woltman Foundation
2525 N. Loop W., Ste. 102
Houston, TX 77008-1024
Application address: c/o Lutheran Church, Missouri Synod, 7900 East Hwy. 290, Austin, TX 78724-2499, tel.: (512) 926-4272

Foundation type: Independent foundation
Purpose: Scholarships to students from TX or students studying in TX, and preparing for the Lutheran ministry or for teaching in Lutheran schools.
Financial data: Year ended 12/31/2012. Assets, $6,002,492 (M); Expenditures, $342,633; Total giving, $278,250; Grants to individuals, 23 grants totaling $59,400 (high: $3,347, low: $1,628).
Fields of interest: Theological school/education.
Type of support: Scholarships—to individuals.
Application information: Applications accepted. Application form required. Interview required.
  Initial approach: Letter
  Deadline(s): Prior to school term
EIN: 741402184

9177
Mildred and Charles Wolverton Scholarship Trust
c/o Bank of America, N.A.
P.O. Box 831041
Dallas, TX 75283-1041
Application address: c/o Bank of America, N.A., Attn.: Janette Pamphile, 1201 Main St., 8th Fl., Dallas TX 75202-3113, tel.: (866) 461-7276

Foundation type: Independent foundation

Purpose: Scholarships to totally blind students who have been residents of CA for at least two years, for study at California Polytechnic College in San Luis Obispo, CA.
Financial data: Year ended 06/30/2012. Assets, $435,373 (M); Expenditures, $28,181; Total giving, $19,682.
Fields of interest: Blind/visually impaired.
Type of support: Scholarships—to individuals; Support to graduates or students of specific schools.
Application information: Applications accepted.
  Initial approach: Letter
  Deadline(s): None
EIN: 956855392

9178
The Women's Fund for Health Education and Research

5353 W. Alabama, Ste. 615
Houston, TX 77056-5940 (713) 623-6543
FAX: (713) 623-6541;
E-mail: katherine@thewomensfund.org;
URL: http://www.thewomensfund.org

Foundation type: Public charity
Purpose: Scholarships to college bound seniors in the greater Houston, TX area for higher learning.
Publications: Application guidelines; Informational brochure; Newsletter.
Financial data: Year ended 12/31/2011. Assets, $106,731 (M); Expenditures, $247,107.
Fields of interest: Higher education.
Type of support: Scholarships—to individuals.
Application information: Applications accepted. Application form required. Application form available on the grantmaker's web site.
  Initial approach: Telephone
  Deadline(s): Apr. 16
  Applicants should submit the following:
    1) Resume
    2) Proposal
    3) Essay
    4) Budget Information
  Additional information: Scholarship winners are chosen by an essay competition.
Program description:
  Scholarships: The fund sponsor an annual scholarship contest to promote good health for women and girls. Two $1,000 scholarships will be awarded to college bound seniors.
EIN: 742013710

9179
Wood Family Charitable Trust

c/o Bank of America, N.A.
P.O. Box 831041
Dallas, TX 75283-1041 (206) 358-3079
E-mail: cindy.s.keyser@ustrust.com; Application address: c/o Bank of America, Attn.: Cindy S. Keyser, 800 5th Ave., Ste. 3300, WA1-501-33-23, Seattle, WA 98104, tel.: (800) 848-7177

Foundation type: Independent foundation
Purpose: Scholarships to graduating seniors of Vale Union High School, OR for postsecondary education at four year undergraduate institutions, community colleges, technical schools and advanced vocational training.
Financial data: Year ended 09/30/2013. Assets, $2,884,699 (M); Expenditures, $129,139; Total giving, $80,167.
Fields of interest: Vocational education, post-secondary; Higher education.
Type of support: Support to graduates or students of specific schools; Undergraduate support.

Application information: Applications accepted. Application form required.
  Deadline(s): Mar. 1
  Applicants should submit the following:
    1) GPA
    2) Financial information
    3) Essay
  Additional information: Applications are to be submitted to the Vale District School Superintendent. Funds are paid directly to the educational institution on behalf of the student.
EIN: 597274218

9180
The Woodhill Foundation

11767 Katy Freeway, Ste. 830
Houston, TX 77079

Foundation type: Independent foundation
Purpose: Grants primarily to individuals residing in TX.
Financial data: Year ended 12/31/2012. Assets, $41,258 (M); Expenditures, $123; Total giving, $0.
Type of support: Grants to individuals.
Application information: Applications not accepted.
  Additional information: Unsolicited requests for funds not considered or acknowledged.
EIN: 760644277

9181
The Woodlands Religious Community, Inc.

4242 Interfaith Way
The Woodlands, TX 77381-2634 (281) 367-1230
FAX: (281) 419-1764; URL: http://www.woodlandsinterfaith.org

Foundation type: Public charity
Purpose: Assistance to families in TX after unexpected events that lead to financial difficulties.
Publications: Newsletter.
Financial data: Year ended 12/31/2011. Assets, $9,298,292 (M); Expenditures, $17,836,564; Total giving, $879,307; Grants to individuals, totaling $879,307.
Type of support: Grants for special needs.
Application information:
  Initial approach: Telephone or e-mail
  Additional information: Contact foundation for eligibility requirements.
EIN: 741804123

9182
Lee J. & Billie B. Woods Memorial Scholarship Fund

P.O. Box 1031
Colorado City, TX 79512-1031 (325) 728-5221
Contact: Dwayne Harris

Foundation type: Independent foundation
Purpose: Scholarships to graduating students of Colorado city, TX for continuing education at accredited colleges or universities.
Financial data: Year ended 12/31/2011. Assets, $102,819 (M); Expenditures, $7,692; Total giving, $6,507; Grants to individuals, 2 grants totaling $6,507 (high: $3,982, low: $2,525).
Fields of interest: Higher education.
Type of support: Scholarships—to individuals.

Application information: Applications accepted. Application form required.
  Deadline(s): Before high school graduation date
  Additional information: Students are selected by school administration.
EIN: 207369859

9183
Bruce & Gladys Wright Charitable Trust

602 N. Wells
P.O. Box 596
Edna, TX 77957 (361) 782-5255
Application address: c/o Edna High School, 1307 W. Gayle St., Edna, TX 77957

Foundation type: Independent foundation
Purpose: Scholarships to graduates of Edna High School, TX, for undergraduate education at a college or university in TX.
Financial data: Year ended 09/30/2013. Assets, $1,121,125 (M); Expenditures, $36,180; Total giving, $36,000; Grants to individuals, 17 grants totaling $34,500 (high: $3,000, low: $500).
Type of support: Support to graduates or students of specific schools; Undergraduate support.
Application information: Applications accepted. Application form required.
  Deadline(s): May 1 and Dec. 1
  Additional information: Applications are available at guidance counselor's office.
EIN: 316647955

9184
W. T. Yett Charitable Foundation

c/o Frost National Bank, Trust Dept.
P.O. Box 2950
San Antonio, TX 78299-2950 210-220-4455
Contact: Linda Namestnik

Foundation type: Independent foundation
Purpose: Scholarships to high school graduates of Blanco County, TX for continuing education at institutions of higher learning.
Financial data: Year ended 12/31/2012. Assets, $783,826 (M); Expenditures, $27,053; Total giving, $20,000.
Fields of interest: Higher education.
Type of support: Undergraduate support.
Application information: Applications accepted.
  Deadline(s): None
  Additional information: Payments are made directly to the educational institution on behalf of the students.
EIN: 742640368

9185
Dustin and Kristen Yoder Memorial Foundation, Inc.

5634 Gebert Rd.
Muldoon, TX 78949
E-mail: yoderken@gmail.com; URL: http://www.yoderfoundation.org

Foundation type: Operating foundation
Purpose: Scholarship to young adults for wilderness experiences through the National Outdoor Leadership School (NOLS), Lander, Wyoming, and for students with an interest in outdoor leadership through the Parks and Recreation Management Program of Northern Arizona University, Flagstaff.
Financial data: Year ended 12/31/2012. Assets, $176,443 (M); Expenditures, $9,676; Total giving, $6,625; Grants to individuals, 7 grants totaling $6,625 (high: $1,250, low: $695).

Fields of interest: Higher education.
Type of support: Scholarships—to individuals.
Application information: Applications accepted.
Application form not required.
> *Initial approach:* Letter
> *Deadline(s):* None
> *Additional information:* See web site for
> additional application guidelines.
EIN: 205214595

9186

The Young Family Foundation

115 W. Putnam Ave.
Ganado, TX   77962   (361) 588-6810
Application addresses: c/o High School Counselo,
510 W. Devers, Ganado, TX 77962, tel: (361)
771-3431; 408 2nd St., Louise TX 77455 tel: (979)
648-2202 ; 1095 Hwy. 35, Elmaton, TX 77440

Foundation type: Independent foundation
Purpose: Scholarships to graduates of Ganado High
School, TX, Louise High School, TX, and Tidehaven
High School, TX for attendance at a TX college or
university.
Financial data: Year ended 09/30/2013. Assets,
$865,128 (M); Expenditures, $51,361; Total
giving, $43,000; Grants to individuals, 16 grants
totaling $30,000 (high: $3,000, low: $1,000).
Fields of interest: Higher education.
Type of support: Support to graduates or students
of specific schools; Undergraduate support.
Application information: Applications accepted.
Application form required.
> *Deadline(s):* Apr. 1
> *Additional information:* Applications available at
> each high school counselor's office.
EIN: 742979295

9187

Young Women's Alliance Foundation

(also known as YWA Foundation)
P.O. Box 684612
Austin, TX   78768-4612   (512) 250-8993
Application e-mail:
scholarships@youngwomensalliance.org
E-mail: foundationpresident@youngwomensalliance
.org; *URL:* http://www.youngwomensalliance.org/
foundation/

Foundation type: Public charity

Purpose: Scholarships to women of Austin, TX who
are in their junior or senior year of college or
graduate school, and to high school seniors coming
out of the Sunrise Leadership Program.
Financial data: Year ended 12/31/2011. Assets,
$81,627 (M); Expenditures, $22,697; Total giving,
$21,000; Grants to individuals, totaling $21,000.
Fields of interest: Vocational education,
post-secondary; Higher education; Women.
Type of support: Scholarships—to individuals.
Application information: Applications accepted.
Application form required. Application form
available on the grantmaker's web site. Interview
required.
> *Send request by:* E-mail
> *Deadline(s):* Mar. 1 for Higher Education
> Scholarship, Mar. 15 for Young Leaders
> Scholarship
> *Applicants should submit the following:*
> 1) Transcripts
> 2) Resume
> 3) Letter(s) of recommendation
> 4) Essay
> *Additional information:* See web site for eligibility
> requirements for each program.
Program descriptions:
> *Austin Sunshine Camps Scholarship:* The
> scholarship is awarded to high school senior
> women in the Austin Sunshine Camps' Sunrise
> Leadership Program.
> *Higher Education Scholarship:* This scholarship is
> available to women attending Central Texas
> universities who have completed 60 hours of
> undergraduate coursework or who are enrolled in
> graduate school. Recipients are chosen based on
> demonstrated financial need, commitment to
> community service, academic achievement and
> leadership potential. Applicant must be a female
> under the age of 40.
> *Young Leaders Scholarship:* The scholarship of
> $2,000 is available to high school seniors who
> demonstrate superior leadership skills and who will
> be attending college or trade school within the
> Austin, TX area. Recipients are chosen based on
> leadership roles, financial need, academic
> achievement, and commitment to community
> service during their high school career.
EIN: 742888276

9188

Zimmer Family Foundation

6380 Rogerdale Rd.
Houston, TX   77072-1646   (800) 777-8580
Contact: Noemi Warren
Application address: 40650 Encyclopedia Cir.,
Fremont, CA 945, tel.: (800) 777-8580

Foundation type: Independent foundation
Purpose: Scholarships to the children of current or
former employees of Men's Wearhouse, Inc. or its
affiliates.
Financial data: Year ended 12/31/2012. Assets,
$1,084,916 (M); Expenditures, $1,165,127; Total
giving, $1,108,946.
Fields of interest: Higher education.
Type of support: Employee-related scholarships.
Application information: Applications accepted.
Application form required.
> *Initial approach:* Letter
> *Send request by:* Mail
> *Deadline(s):* Feb. 11
> *Applicants should submit the following:*
> 1) Letter(s) of recommendation
> 2) ACT
> 3) SAT
> 4) Essay
> 5) Transcripts
> *Additional information:* Application should also
> include a list of athletic, cocurricular,
> extracurricular and community service
> activities.
EIN: 760370782

9189

The Father Joe Znotas Memorial
Scholarship Fund

1201 Plum St.
Lockhart, TX   78644

Foundation type: Operating foundation
Purpose: Scholarships to graduates of high schools
in Austin, TX.
Financial data: Year ended 12/31/2012. Assets,
$1,582 (M); Expenditures, $4,507; Total giving,
$0.
Type of support: Undergraduate support.
Application information: Application form required.
> *Deadline(s):* Apr. 30
EIN: 742157960

UTAH

9190
100% for Kids, Utah Credit Union Education Foundation
1805 S. Redwood Rd., Ste. 200
Salt Lake City, UT   84104-5112   (801) 972-3400
FAX: (801) 975-9301;
E-mail: foundation@ulcu.com; URL: http://www.
100percentforkids.org

Foundation type: Public charity
Purpose: Grants to public school teachers of UT, grades K-12 to cover classroom expenses.
Publications: Application guidelines.
Financial data: Year ended 12/31/2011. Assets, $636,847 (M); Expenditures, $198,278; Total giving, $117,177.
Fields of interest: Education.
Type of support: Grants to individuals.
Application information: Applications accepted. Application form required.
Initial approach: Telephone or e-mail
Send request by: Mail, fax or on-line
Deadline(s): Last day of each month for Mini-Grants, Last day of each quarter beginning June 30 for School Grant and Major Project Grants
Final notification: Teachers notified within 30 days for Mini-Grants, and Aug.15 for School Grants and Major Project Grants
Program descriptions:
Major Project Grants: Grants of $5,000 and up intended for a school-wide project. Examples include a greenhouse, leveled library, and a small computer lab. See web site for details.
Mini Grants: Grants, ranging form $50 to $1,000, are awarded to assist teachers with their out-of-pocket expense during a school year. See web site for details.
School Grants: Grants of $1,000 to $5,000 intended for a multi classroom project, which can be anything from updating the equipment in a school's science lab, to art supplies for an entire grade. See web site for details.
EIN: 421562278

9191
American Indian Services
1902 N. Canyon Rd., Ste. 100
Provo, UT   84604-5894   (801) 375-1777
Contact: Dale Tingey, Exec. Dir.
E-mail for scholarship:
scholarship@americanindianservices.org
E-mail: ais@americanindianservices.org;
URL: http://www.americanindianservices.org/

Foundation type: Public charity
Purpose: College scholarships to students of Native American descent for undergraduate study at accredited colleges, universities, junior college or technical school.
Publications: Application guidelines.
Financial data: Year ended 12/31/2012. Assets, $5,942,399 (M); Expenditures, $2,433,806; Total giving, $2,047,186; Grants to individuals, totaling $2,047,186.
Fields of interest: Vocational education, post-secondary; College (community/junior); University; Native Americans/American Indians.
Type of support: Scholarships—to individuals.

Application information: Applications accepted. Application form required. Application form available on the grantmaker's web site.
Send request by: On-line
Deadline(s): Feb. 15, May 15, Aug. 15, Nov. 15
Applicants should submit the following:
1) Photograph
2) Transcripts
Additional information: Selection criteria is based on academic merit and financial need. See web site for additional guidelines.
Program description:
Scholarships: The scholarship assists applicants who are enrolled in a university, college, junior college or technical school who are one-Quarter Northern Native American Indian Blood.
EIN: 870477049

9192
Loflin Anaya Foundation
285 S. Main St.
Salem, UT   84653

Foundation type: Independent foundation
Purpose: Scholarships to UT students for a postsecondary degree, grants to individuals for medical needs and, loans to assist in the cost of adoption.
Financial data: Year ended 12/31/2011. Assets, $11,388 (M); Expenditures, $36,081; Total giving, $6,725; Grants to individuals, 2 grants totaling $6,725 (high: $4,725, low: $2,000).
Type of support: Scholarships—to individuals; Grants for special needs; Loans—to individuals.
Application information: Applications accepted. Application form required.
Deadline(s): None
EIN: 201607999

9193
Ruth Eleanor Bamberger and John Ernest Bamberger Memorial Foundation
136 S. Main St., Ste. 418
Salt Lake City, UT   84101-1690   (801) 364-2045
Contact: Eleanor Roser, Chair.
E-mail: bambergermemfdn@qwestoffice.net;
URL: http://
www.ruthandjohnbambergermemorialfdn.org

Foundation type: Independent foundation
Purpose: Undergraduate scholarships for UT residents, with preference given to nursing students. Occasional loans awarded for medical education.
Financial data: Year ended 12/31/2012. Assets, $20,566,629 (M); Expenditures, $1,465,329; Total giving, $1,260,112.
Fields of interest: Medical school/education; Nursing school/education.
Type of support: Scholarships—to individuals; Undergraduate support.
Application information: Applications accepted.
Initial approach: Letter
Additional information: Scholarships are paid directly to the educational institution on behalf of the student. Contact foundation for additional application guidelines.
EIN: 876116540

9194
Barrick Mercur Gold Mine Foundation, Inc.
60 Benchview Dr.
Tooele, UT   84074-2409

Foundation type: Independent foundation
Purpose: Scholarships to graduates of Grantsville High School and Tooele High School, both in UT, for higher education.
Financial data: Year ended 12/31/2012. Assets, $148,922 (M); Expenditures, $10,094; Total giving, $7,000.
Type of support: Support to graduates or students of specific schools; Undergraduate support.
Application information: Applications accepted. Application form required.
Initial approach: Letter
Deadline(s): May
Applicants should submit the following:
1) Essay
2) Letter(s) of recommendation
3) Transcripts
EIN: 742546494

9195
The Borax Education Foundation
4700 Daybreak Pkwy.
South Jordan, UT   84095-5120

Foundation type: Company-sponsored foundation
Purpose: Scholarships to dependents of U.S. Borax, Inc. employees.
Financial data: Year ended 12/31/2012. Assets, $0 (M); Expenditures, $6,511; Total giving, $6,511.
Type of support: Employee-related scholarships.
Application information: Applications not accepted.
Additional information: Unsolicited requests for funds not considered or acknowledged.
Company name: U.S. Borax, Incorporated
EIN: 954497752

9196
The Bybee Family Foundation
660 Westfield Rd.
Alpine, UT   84004-1501   (801) 921-6002

Foundation type: Independent foundation
Purpose: Support for education and assistance to individuals and families of Utah, who have sources of income below the national poverty level, and who have exhausted other opportunities for relief.
Financial data: Year ended 12/31/2011. Assets, $2,806 (M); Expenditures, $153,599; Total giving, $149,370; Grants to individuals, 25 grants totaling $147,170 (high: $33,415, low: $200).
Fields of interest: Education; Economically disadvantaged.
Type of support: Scholarships—to individuals; Grants for special needs.
Application information:
Deadline(s): None
Additional information: Letters, personal contacts to foundation officers are considered.
EIN: 202571093

9197
The Cherokee & Walker Foundation
6440 Wasatch Blvd., Ste. 200
Salt Lake City, UT   84121

Foundation type: Independent foundation
Purpose: Grants to residents of UT.
Financial data: Year ended 12/31/2012. Assets, $12,663 (M); Expenditures, $475; Total giving, $0.
Fields of interest: Human services.
Type of support: Grants for special needs.

Application information: Applications accepted.
Deadline(s): None
Additional information: Applications by letter.
EIN: 870635720

9198
Dialysis Research Foundation
5575 S. 500 E.
Ogden, UT 84405-6907 (801) 479-0351
FAX: (801) 476-1766

Foundation type: Independent foundation
Purpose: Educational assistance and textbook stipends to individuals who have undergone dialysis. Research grants to individuals investigating renal disease, including research on dialysis treatment. Preference is given to applicants affiliated with the University of Utah.
Financial data: Year ended 12/31/2012. Assets, $0 (M); Expenditures, $1,002,587; Total giving, $760,890.
Fields of interest: Kidney diseases; Kidney research.
Type of support: Research; Undergraduate support.
Application information: Applications accepted.
Deadline(s): None
Additional information: Contact foundation for current application guidelines.
EIN: 942819009

9199
EnergySolutions Foundation
423 W. 300 S.
Salt Lake City, UT 84101 (801) 649-2286
Contact: Karen Watson
Application address: P.O. Box 510583, Salt Lake City, UT 84151, tel.: (801) 649-2286; URL: http://www.energysolutionsfoundation.org

Foundation type: Independent foundation
Purpose: Scholarships to 10th grade students in selected high schools in GA, ID, IL, NM, OH, SC, TN, UT, WA and Ontario, Canada in areas of study of mathematics, science or engineering.
Financial data: Year ended 12/31/2012. Assets, $1,115,434 (M); Expenditures, $748,875; Total giving, $680,550; Grant to an individual, 1 grant totaling $430,550.
Fields of interest: Higher education; Science; Mathematics; Engineering.
Type of support: Scholarships—to individuals; Support to graduates or students of specific schools.
Application information: Applications accepted. Application form required. Application form available on the grantmaker's web site.
Send request by: Fax or on-line
Deadline(s): Jan 31.
Applicants should submit the following:
1) Letter(s) of recommendation
2) Transcripts
3) Essay
Additional information: Application should also include copy of 10th grade schedule and approved major of study. See web site for additional guidelines.
EIN: 371521992

9200
Andrew Gomez Dream Foundation
c/o Von Curtis Inc.
9756 Sandy Pkwy.
Sandy, UT 84070 (801) 302-8801
E-mail: info@paulmitchelltheschool.com

Foundation type: Public charity
Purpose: Scholarships to high school graduates who are students or a graduate of a beauty school in the U.S.
Financial data: Year ended 12/31/2011. Assets, $1,040,053 (M); Expenditures, $1,595,509; Total giving, $1,477,267; Grants to individuals, totaling $676,549.
Type of support: Scholarships—to individuals.
Application information: Applications accepted. Application form required.
Initial approach: Letter
Deadline(s): 30 days prior to needing scholarship
Applicants should submit the following:
1) Transcripts
2) Letter(s) of recommendation
Additional information: Selection criteria includes applicant must be in good standing with respect to academics and attendance, and should be socially and economically disadvantaged.
EIN: 542125128

9201
Granite Education Foundation, Inc.
2500 S. State St., Ste. D-108
Salt Lake City, UT 84115-3110 (801) 646-4483
Contact: Brent Severe, C.E.O. and Exec. Dir.
FAX: (801) 646-4242;
E-mail: swhipple@graniteschools.org; URL: http://www.graniteeducationfoundation.org

Foundation type: Public charity
Purpose: Scholarships to students from Salt Lake City, UT Granite School District for attendance at accredited secondary or community/technical college.
Publications: Application guidelines; Annual report; Financial statement; Informational brochure; Newsletter.
Financial data: Year ended 06/30/2012. Assets, $2,139,566 (M); Expenditures, $1,145,146; Total giving, $247,225; Grants to individuals, 185 grants totaling $207,225.
Fields of interest: Vocational education, post-secondary; Higher education.
Type of support: Grants to individuals; Support to graduates or students of specific schools.
Application information:
Initial approach: Telephone
Additional information: See web site for additional application information.
Program descriptions:
Excel Outstanding Educator Awards: These awards publicly honor and recognize educators who raise the bar of their profession. Recipients are nominated by school administrators, colleagues, or students through an intensive application process reviewed by a selection committee. Winners will receive a $1,000 check. An additional $500 is awarded to each of the chosen educators' schools for the purpose of expanding school libraries, supplies, and resources.
Mini-Grants for Teachers: This program provides an opportunity for enriching academic experiences for students, as well as recognize and reward outstanding teachers working in the Granite school district, by supporting innovative approaches and creative ideas that are not allocated in school budgets. Mini-grants for one teacher can be up to $500. For multiple teachers, the limit is $750. There is no minimum amount.
Scholarships: The foundation annually awards educational scholarships to students in the Salt Lake City public school district, ranging from $500 to $1,500, in an effort to launch students from high school graduation into an accredited secondary or

community/technical college. Scholarships are intended to be given to those who may not have the opportunity to attend college through traditional means.
EIN: 942951639

9202
The Morgan Groesbeck Foundation
175 S. Main St., Ste. 1310
Salt Lake City, UT 84111 (801) 363-6176

Foundation type: Operating foundation
Purpose: Scholarships to financially needy individuals in the Utah area for continuing their education at institutions of higher learning.
Financial data: Year ended 12/31/2012. Assets, $8,085 (M); Expenditures, $1,526; Total giving, $0.
Fields of interest: Higher education.
Type of support: Scholarships—to individuals.
Application information: Applications accepted. Application form required.
Deadline(s): None
EIN: 870577202

9203
The Marion D. & Maxine C. Hanks Foundation Inc.
P.O. Box 9672
Salt Lake City, UT 84109

Foundation type: Independent foundation
Purpose: General welfare grants and support for medical expenses to needy residents of UT.
Financial data: Year ended 12/31/2012. Assets, $1,282,228 (M); Expenditures, $89,275; Total giving, $65,650; Grants to individuals, 10 grants totaling $16,300 (high: $5,000, low: $300).
Fields of interest: Health care; Economically disadvantaged.
Type of support: Grants for special needs.
Application information:
Initial approach: Letter
Additional information: Contact foundation for current application deadline/guidelines.
EIN: 870503758

9204
The Leon & Arline Harman Foundation
5544 Green St.
Salt Lake City, UT 84123-5798 (801) 313-8000, ext. 8088
Contact: Sherry Prendergast
URL: http://www.scholars.harmans.com/

Foundation type: Independent foundation
Purpose: Scholarships to employees of certain companies in the retail food distribution industry.
Publications: Application guidelines.
Financial data: Year ended 12/31/2012. Assets, $0 (M); Expenditures, $647,996; Total giving, $601,130; Grants to individuals, totaling $601,130.
Fields of interest: Education.
Type of support: Undergraduate support.
Application information: Applications accepted. Application form required. Application form available on the grantmaker's web site.
Initial approach: Scholarship form
Send request by: Mail
Deadline(s): Apr. 30
Applicants should submit the following:
1) Financial information
2) Essay
3) Letter(s) of recommendation

4) Transcripts

Additional information: Applicants must be U.S. citizens or have an alien registration card, and have been working for one of the companies on the foundation's approved list for at least one year by the time school starts. See foundation web site for additional guidelines.
EIN: 201738267

9205
Carlyle and Delta Harmon Scholarship Foundation
(formerly Harmon Women's Scholarship Fund)
2481 W. 1425 S.
Syracuse, UT 84075

Foundation type: Independent foundation
Purpose: Scholarships to single women in UT with dependent children who are enrolled in educational programs to increase their standard of living.
Financial data: Year ended 12/31/2012. Assets, $1,000,547 (M); Expenditures, $95,940; Total giving, $71,210.
Type of support: Undergraduate support.
Application information: Applications not accepted.
Additional information: Unsolicited requests for funds not considered or acknowledged.
EIN: 870508363

9206
Waldo E. Harvey Family Foundation
1785 Fort Douglas Cir.
Salt Lake City, UT 84103-4451 (801) 355-6292
Contact: Clyde E. Harvey, Tr.

Foundation type: Operating foundation
Purpose: Scholarships to residents of Salt Lake City, UT.
Financial data: Year ended 12/31/2013. Assets, $409,696 (M); Expenditures, $1,800; Total giving, $1,800.
Type of support: Undergraduate support.
Application information: Applications accepted.
EIN: 746374603

9207
Helaman Foundation
11 Quietwood Ln.
Sandy, UT 84092-4845
Contact: David J. Lyon, Tr.

Foundation type: Independent foundation
Purpose: Scholarships to residents of AZ, CO, ID and UT, for higher education.
Financial data: Year ended 12/31/2011. Assets, $0 (M); Expenditures, $0; Total giving, $0.
Type of support: Undergraduate support.
Application information: Applications not accepted.
Additional information: Unsolicited requests for funds not considered or acknowledged.
EIN: 311234291

9208
I Care Foundation
496 N. 80 W.
Lindon, UT 84042 (801) 785-1083
Contact: Ilene Olsen, Tr.

Foundation type: Operating foundation
Purpose: Grants to economically disadvantaged individuals and families in the Wasatch Front, UT,

area for food, clothing, educational support, and other necessities.
Financial data: Year ended 12/31/2011. Assets, $24 (M); Expenditures, $6,130; Total giving, $5,430.
Fields of interest: Education; Food services; Economically disadvantaged.
Type of support: Grants for special needs.
Application information: Applications accepted. Application form not required.
Initial approach: Letter or telephone
Deadline(s): None
Additional information: Contact foundation for current application guidelines.
EIN: 870653978

9209
Intermountain Electrical Association Education Fund Scholarship Program
(also known as IEA Educational Scholarship Program)
2125 W. 2300 S.
West Valley City, UT 84119-2017 (801) 484-7900

Foundation type: Public charity
Purpose: Scholarships to individuals for higher education, primarily in UT.
Publications: Application guidelines.
Financial data: Year ended 12/31/2011. Assets, $818,708 (M); Expenditures, $43,257; Total giving, $40,000; Grants to individuals, totaling $40,000.
Type of support: Scholarships—to individuals.
Application information: Applications not accepted.
Additional information: Unsolicited requests for funds not considered or acknowledged.
EIN: 742520009

9210
Intermountain Research and Medical Foundation
(formerly The Deseret Foundation)
5121 S. Cottonwood Dr.
Murray, UT 84157-5701 (801) 507-2408
Contact: Lori T. Piscopo, Exec. Dir.
FAX: (801) 507-5140;
E-mail: lori.piscopo@imail.org

Foundation type: Public charity
Purpose: Research grants for medical research to investigators in the greater Salt Lake City, UT, area.
Publications: Annual report; Informational brochure.
Financial data: Year ended 12/31/2011. Assets, $22,463,551 (M); Expenditures, $2,414,258; Total giving, $1,340,579; Grants to individuals, totaling $353,208.
Fields of interest: Heart & circulatory research; Lung research.
Type of support: Research.
Application information: Applications not accepted.
Additional information: Unsolicited requests for funds not considered or acknowledged.
EIN: 237062016

9211
James IV Association of Surgeons Inc.
30 N. 1900 E. Rm. 3b110
Salt Lake City, UT 84132 (801) 581-7304
Contact: Lisa Marley
E-mail: jamesIVassoc.surg@aol.com

Foundation type: Independent foundation
Purpose: Grants to surgeons for research.
Financial data: Year ended 12/31/2012. Assets, $735,885 (M); Expenditures, $37,065; Total giving, $11,000; Grants to individuals, 2 grants totaling $11,000 (high: $7,500, low: $3,500).
Fields of interest: Surgery.
International interests: Australia; Hong Kong; Mexico.
Type of support: Travel grants.
Application information: Applications not accepted.
Additional information: Unsolicited requests for funds not considered or acknowledged.
EIN: 136138272

9212
Jordan Education Foundation
7387 S. Campus View Dr.
West Jordan, UT 84084-5500 (801) 567-8125
Contact: Steven Hall, Dir.
FAX: (801) 567-8005;
E-mail: steven.hall@jordandistrict.org; URL: http://www.jordaneducationfoundation.org

Foundation type: Public charity
Purpose: Scholarships to Jordan School District, UT, students, for financial need and academic achievement.
Publications: Application guidelines; Annual report; Newsletter.
Financial data: Year ended 06/30/2012. Assets, $730,223 (M); Expenditures, $631,687; Total giving, $631,687; Grants to individuals, totaling $45,535.
Type of support: Support to graduates or students of specific schools; Awards/prizes.
Application information: Applications not accepted.
Additional information: Unsolicited applications not considered or acknowledged.
EIN: 746356280

9213
Robert W. & Barbara J. Keener Foundation
P.O. Box 9360
Salt Lake City, UT 84109-0360

Foundation type: Independent foundation
Purpose: Scholarships to students of Benton High School and Bishop LeBlond High School, UT, planning to attend Kansas University and Missouri Western State College, and to students enrolled in these institutions.
Financial data: Year ended 05/31/2013. Assets, $4,400,656 (M); Expenditures, $200,412; Total giving, $140,590; Grants to individuals, 36 grants totaling $59,090 (high: $2,500, low: $750).
Type of support: Support to graduates or students of specific schools; Undergraduate support.
Application information: Applications not accepted.
Additional information: Unsolicited requests for funds not considered or acknowledged.
EIN: 876232895

9214
The Kolob Foundation
423 Wakara Way, Ste. 212
Salt Lake City, UT 84108-1242 (801) 583-8811

Foundation type: Independent foundation
Purpose: Scholarships to economically disadvantaged individuals in the Salt Lake City, UT, area.

Financial data: Year ended 12/31/2011. Assets, $119,575 (M); Expenditures, $11,745; Total giving, $11,132; Grants to individuals, 5 grants totaling $11,132 (high: $6,131, low: $250).
Fields of interest: Economically disadvantaged.
Type of support: Scholarships—to individuals.
Application information: Applications accepted. Application form required.
  Initial approach: Letter
  Deadline(s): None
EIN: 876231892

9215
Garth B. Last Charitable Foundation
1194 S. 180 West
Hurricane, UT 84737
Contact: Bradley G. Last, Pres.

Foundation type: Independent foundation
Purpose: Financial assistance to economically disadvantaged elderly and/or disabled individuals, primarily in UT, AZ, NV and TX.
Financial data: Year ended 12/31/2011. Assets, $243,038 (M); Expenditures, $56,444; Total giving, $43,391.
Fields of interest: Aging; Economically disadvantaged.
Type of support: Grants for special needs.
Application information: Applications accepted. Application form required.
  Additional information: Contact foundation for current application guidelines.
EIN: 870526622

9216
The Lofthouse Foundation
1596 Cherry Cir.
Farmington, UT 84025-3903   (801) 951-4858
Contact: David L. Stone, Tr.

Foundation type: Independent foundation
Purpose: Scholarships to graduates of Weiser High School, ID for higher education at accredited colleges or universities.
Financial data: Year ended 12/31/2011. Assets, $914,560 (M); Expenditures, $49,748; Total giving, $38,105.
Fields of interest: Higher education.
Type of support: Support to graduates or students of specific schools; Undergraduate support.
Application information: Applications accepted.
  Applicants should submit the following:
    1) Essay
    2) Letter(s) of recommendation
    3) Financial information
    4) GPA
    5) SAT
    6) ACT
  Additional information: Applicants must also submit a statement of background or life experiences, including information regarding leadership and character, awards received, school, community or church service, and participation in school sports, activities and events.
EIN: 752982563

9217
Jessica Elizabeth Luttrell Scholarship Foundation
254 Dammeron Valley Dr. W.
Dammeron Valley, UT 84783-5093   (435) 574-0462

Foundation type: Independent foundation

Purpose: Scholarship to students attending an accredited college, university or school of training on a full-time basis, for cost of tuition, books, supplies, and room and board.
Financial data: Year ended 12/31/2011. Assets, $176,634 (M); Expenditures, $29,749; Total giving, $26,500; Grants to individuals, 8 grants totaling $26,500 (high: $6,000, low: $1,000).
Fields of interest: Vocational education, post-secondary; Higher education.
Type of support: Scholarships—to individuals.
Application information: Applications accepted. Application form required.
  Applicants should submit the following:
    1) Transcripts
    2) Letter(s) of recommendation
    3) Essay
  Additional information: Application must also include student's, parents or guardians current federal tax return and a copy of the acceptance letter indicating student's admission to an accredited institution, or copies of application for admission to each school.
EIN: 141864397

9218
Masonic Foundation of Utah
650 E. S. Temple St.
Salt Lake City, UT 84102-1141   (801) 363-2936
FAX: (801) 363-2938;
E-mail: grandsecretary@utahgrandlodge.org;
URL: http://www.utahgrandlodge.org

Foundation type: Public charity
Purpose: Scholarships to qualified individuals pursuing a four-year degree at colleges or universities primarily in UT.
Financial data: Year ended 12/31/2011. Assets, $5,670,572 (M); Expenditures, $272,135; Total giving, $223,790; Grants to individuals, totaling $84,150.
Fields of interest: Higher education.
Type of support: Undergraduate support.
Application information: Applications accepted. Application form required.
  Initial approach: Telephone and e-mail
  Send request by: Mail
  Copies of proposal: 1
  Applicants should submit the following:
    1) GPA
    2) Transcripts
    3) Letter(s) of recommendation
EIN: 870261722

9219
The McCarthey Dressman Education Foundation
610 E. South Temple St., Ste. 110
Salt Lake City, UT 84102-1208   (801) 578-1260
FAX: (801) 578-1261;
E-mail: info@mccartheydressman.org; URL: http://www.mccartheydressman.org/

Foundation type: Operating foundation
Purpose: Grants to educators and licensed teachers employed by schools and nonprofit organizations for the creation of new curriculum.
Financial data: Year ended 12/31/2011. Assets, $16,791 (M); Expenditures, $260,574; Total giving, $161,309; Grants to individuals, totaling $161,309.
Fields of interest: Child development, education; Teacher school/education; Economically disadvantaged.

Type of support: Grants to individuals; Support to graduates or students of specific schools; Graduate support; Undergraduate support.
Application information: Applications accepted. Application form required. Application form available on the grantmaker's web site. Interview required.
  Deadline(s): May 1
  Applicants should submit the following:
    1) Transcripts
    2) Letter(s) of recommendation
    3) Essay
    4) Budget Information
  Additional information: See web site for additional application information.
Program descriptions:
  Academic Enrichment Grants: Grants awarded to educators to create enrichment programs that serve the intellectual, artistic, and creative abilities of children from low-income households. Grants to individuals in amounts up to $10,000 per year for a maximum of three years, provided the eligibility requirements continue to be met. Applicants must be employed by schools or nonprofit organizations, have direct and regular contact with students in grades Pre-k to 12, work with students from low-income households, and are willing to work in collaboration with the foundation.
  Student Teaching Scholarships/Mentoring: Student teaching scholarships offer support to educators who will be student teaching in their final year of a qualified teacher education program. The foundation offers one-year scholarships in the amount of $6,000 each to college students enrolled in teacher education programs at New Mexico State University; The University of California, Santa Cruz; The University of Texas at Austin; and West Virginia University.
  Teacher Development Grants: Grants are awarded to individuals or small teams of teachers for the formation and implementation of groundbreaking k-12 classroom instruction. Grants are in amounts up to $10,000 per year for a maximum of three years, provided the eligibility requirements continue to be met. Applicants must be licensed k-12 teachers employed in public or private schools, have the background and experience to complete the project successfully and willing to work in collaboration with the foundation.
EIN: 870646265

9220
Larry H. Miller Education Foundation
9350 S. 150 E., Ste. 1000
Sandy, UT 84070-2721

Foundation type: Operating foundation
Purpose: Scholarships to employee's dependents for higher education.
Financial data: Year ended 12/31/2012. Assets, $0 (M); Expenditures, $1,556,883; Total giving, $1,553,552; Grants to individuals, 317 grants totaling $1,553,552 (high: $17,936, low: $184).
Type of support: Scholarships—to individuals.
Application information: Applications not accepted.
  Additional information: Unsolicited requests for funds not considered or acknowledged.
EIN: 870560678

9221
The Park City Foundation
1790 Bonanza Dr., Ste. 250
Park City, UT 84060 (435) 214-7475
Contact: Trisha Worthington, Exec. Dir.
FAX: (435) 214-7489;
E-mail: trisha@theparkcityfoundation.org;
Application address: P.O. Box 681499, Park City,
UT 84068; Grant application e-mail:
katie@theparkcityfoundation.org; URL: http://
www.theparkcityfoundation.org

Foundation type: Community foundation
Purpose: Scholarships to graduating seniors of
Park City, UT for postsecondary education.
Financial data: Year ended 12/31/2011. Assets,
$3,164,645 (M); Expenditures, $798,286; Total
giving, $374,542; Grants to individuals, 6 grants
totaling $53,235.
Fields of interest: Higher education.
Type of support: Scholarships—to individuals.
Application information: Applications accepted.
Application form required.
> *Additional information:* Contact the foundation for
> additional information.
EIN: 300171971

9222
Regence Caring Foundation for Children
(formerly The Caring Foundation, Inc.)
P.O. Box 25185
Salt Lake City, UT 84125 (801) 333-5575
Contact: Kathleen Pitcher, Exec. Dir.
E-mail: Kathleen.PitcherTobey@cambiahealth.com;
Toll-free tel.: (888) 589-5437; additional address:
P.O. Box 2560, Boise, ID 83701-2560, tel.: (208)
395-7741, fax: (208) 333-7873; URL: http://
www.caringfoundationforchildren.org

Foundation type: Public charity
Purpose: Specific assistance to low-income eligible
children residing in UT and ID with free dental care.
Publications: Application guidelines; Annual report.
Financial data: Year ended 12/31/2011. Assets,
$574,751 (M); Expenditures, $810,607; Total
giving, $796,263; Grants to individuals, totaling
$796,263.
Fields of interest: Dental care.
Type of support: Grants for special needs.
Application information: Applications accepted.
Application form required. Application form
available on the grantmaker's web site.
> *Deadline(s):* None
> *Additional information:* Application should
> include copies of two most recent paystubs,
> copy of the first page of last year's tax return
> or a copy of W-2 form.
EIN: 870490448

9223
The Roderick Earl Ross Memorial
Foundation
P.O. Box 2460
Salt Lake City, UT 84110
Contact: Roderick Earl Ross, Tr.

Foundation type: Independent foundation
Purpose: Scholarships by nomination only for
employees and family members of employees of
Equitable Life & Casualty Insurance for attendance
at the University of Utah.
Financial data: Year ended 09/30/2013. Assets,
$30,746 (M); Expenditures, $4,585; Total giving,
$4,000.
Fields of interest: Higher education.
Type of support: Scholarships—to individuals.

Application information: Applications not
accepted.
> *Additional information:* The foundation chooses
> the recipients from among their employees.
> Unsolicited requests for funds not considered
> or acknowledged.
EIN: 237083407

9224
Salt Lake Community College Foundation
4600 S. Redwood Rd.
Salt Lake City, UT 84123-3145
URL: http://www.slcc.edu/development/
give-now.aspx

Foundation type: Public charity
Purpose: Scholarships to students for attendance
at Salt Lake Community College, UT for higher
education.
Financial data: Year ended 06/30/2012. Assets,
$6,941,649 (M); Expenditures, $617,430; Total
giving, $522,065; Grants to individuals, totaling
$522,065.
Fields of interest: Higher education.
Type of support: Support to graduates or students
of specific schools.
Application information: Applications accepted.
Application form required.
> *Deadline(s):* Vary
> *Additional information:* Applicants should contact
> the financial aid office for application
> information. See web site or contact the
> foundation for additional guidelines.
EIN: 942886220

9225
Salt Lake Education Foundation
440 E. 100 South
Salt Lake City, UT 84111-1891 (801) 578-8268
Contact: Michael Williams, Exec. Dir. and C.E.O.
E-mail: cultivating.resources@saltlakeeducationfou
ndation.org; FAX: (801) 578-8440E-Mail for Michael
Williams : michael.williams@slcschools.orgTel. for
Michael Williams : (801)-578-8268; URL: http://
www.sledfoundation.org/

Foundation type: Public charity
Purpose: Research grants to teachers in the Salt
Lake City, UT, area, for the development of
educational curricula.
Publications: Application guidelines; Annual report.
Financial data: Year ended 06/30/2012. Assets,
$2,375,321 (M); Expenditures, $2,475,366; Total
giving, $2,111,605; Grants to individuals, totaling
$99,582.
Fields of interest: Education.
Type of support: Program development; Research.
Application information:
> *Deadline(s):* Varies
> *Additional information:* Application by proposal.
EIN: 742563849

9226
The Skaggs Institute for Research
6190 S. Moffatt Farm Ln.
Salt Lake City, UT 84121-1793 (801) 274-5271

Foundation type: Public charity
Purpose: Scientific research grants to qualified
Skaggs clinical scholars.
Financial data: Year ended 09/30/2011. Assets,
$16,748,890 (M); Expenditures, $3,860,017;
Total giving, $3,717,692.
Fields of interest: Science.
Type of support: Research.

Application information: Contact the institute for
further guidelines.
EIN: 870549234

9227
Sundance Institute
P.O. Box 684429
Park City, UT 84068-4429 (435) 658-3456
Contact: Kenneth Brecher, Exec. Dir.
FAX: (435) 658-3457;
E-mail: institute@sundance.org; Additional
address: 8530 Wilshire Blvd., Beverly Hills, CA
90211-3122; tel.: (310) 360-1981; fax: (310)
360-1969; e-mail: la@sundance.org; URL: http://
www.sundance.org

Foundation type: Public charity
Purpose: Awards and fellowships to film directors,
artists, and writers that involve feature film script
projects.
Publications: Application guidelines.
Financial data: Year ended 08/31/2012. Assets,
$37,587,431 (M); Expenditures, $27,929,227;
Total giving, $1,978,560; Grants to individuals,
totaling $350,135.
Fields of interest: Film/video; Literature; Arts;
Science.
International interests: Europe; Japan.
Type of support: Fellowships; Awards/prizes;
Residencies; Stipends.
Application information: Applications accepted.
Application form required. Application form
available on the grantmaker's web site.
> *Initial approach:* E-mail
> *Deadline(s):* Varies
> *Additional information:* Application should
> include letters of recommendation, script,
> VHS videotape of director's previous work
> (preferably NTSC, with English subtitles if
> possible), bios, and a logline and synopsis.
Program descriptions:
Creative Producing Fellowship and Lab: This
year-long creative and strategic fellowship works to
develop and support the next generation of
American independent producers. Recipients will
also receive a $5,000 living stipend, a $5,000
pre-production grant, year-round mentorship
opportunities from two industry advisors, and
year-round support from institute staff. Candidates
must have produced at least one short or
feature-length narrative or documentary film, but no
more than two narrative features total. Candidates
must also have a completed, legally-optioned,
scripted narrative project in hand with a director
attached to the project, may not be the writer or
director of the submitted project; and must be
based in the U.S., though submitted projects may
be filmed internationally.
Documentary Fund: This program provides grants
to filmmakers worldwide that display artful and
innovative storytelling techniques, global relevance,
contemporary human rights and pressing social
justice issues, and potential for social engagement.
The fund accepts submissions twice a year for
development grants of up to $20,000, production/
post-production grants of up to $50,000, and
audience engagement grants of up to $20,000.
Audience engagement grants are only available to
current Sundance grantees for the support of
strategic audience and community engagement
campaigns. The fund provides grants to about
forty-five to fifty-five projects a year.
Lynn Auerbach Screenwriting Fellowship: This
fellowship opportunity provides concentrated
support to one screenwriter being supported by the
institute's Feature Film Program. Fellows receive a
cash stipend, dedicated yearlong mentorship from

two of the institute's screenwriting advisors, and a produced reading of his/her screenplay.

Maryland Film Fellowship: Awarded in conjunction with the Maryland Film Office, this program awards a fellow of the institute's Directors Lab program with a $10,000 bridge grant as a means to move his or her project forward during the crucial phases of advanced development and preproduction.

Sundance Institute Mahindra Global Filmmaking Award: This grant recognizes and supports emerging independent filmmakers from different regions of the world. Applicants will be selected from fellows supported through the institute's Feature Film Program, screenwriters' lab, and directors' lab. Awards include a cash grant of $10,000 toward a first or second feature film project, attendance at one of the institute's Feature Film Program labs, year-round creative and strategic support from the institute's Feature Film Program staff and creative advisors throughout the life of the project, and attendance at the Sundance Film Festival.

Sundance Institute/Alfred P. Sloan Commissioning Grant: This grant, presented in conjunction with the Alfred P. Sloan Foundation, awards an annual cash stipend of up to $20,000 for a science- or technology-related project that is at an early stage, such as full treatment or early screen draft. Grants also include a small stipend (up to $5,000) for a science advisor to provide support through consultation and feedback, as well as the possibility of inclusion in a screenwriter's lab. Projects must have science or technology as a major theme, or scientists as major characters, science fiction projects, or projects that stray too far from a base scientific reality, will not be considered. Projects must also be narrative features (not documentary in nature), and be English language.

Sundance Institute/Alfred P. Sloan Fellowship: One fellowship is awarded annually to an emerging screenwriter to support the ongoing development of a narrative, feature-length screenplay with science or technology themes. Fellowships include attendance at a screenwriters lab, directors lab, creative producing lab, creative producing summit, or Sundance Film Festival as a fellow; a stipend of up to $5,000 for a science advisor; and creative and strategic support from the institute's Feature Film Program staff.

Time Warner Storytelling Grant: This grant provides up to $5,000 to support artists whose work uniquely positions and advances the concept of storytelling, and allows recipients to focus specifically on the advancement of the narrative and voice in their projects.
EIN: 870361394

9228
Utah Humanities Council
202 W. 300 N.
Salt Lake City, UT   84103-1108   (801) 359-9670
Contact: Cynthia Buckingham, Exec. Dir.
FAX: (801) 531-7869;
E-mail: buckingham@utahhumanities.org; Toll-free tel.: (866) 864-8554; URL: http://www.utahhumanities.org/

Foundation type: Public charity
Purpose: Fellowships by providing financial support for scholars doing research in the humanities.
Publications: Application guidelines; Annual report; Informational brochure; Newsletter.
Financial data: Year ended 10/31/2011. Assets, $1,694,878 (M); Expenditures, $1,035,352; Total giving, $60,470; Grants to individuals, totaling $20,000.

Fields of interest: Humanities.
Type of support: Fellowships; Research.
Application information: Applications accepted. Application form required. Application form available on the grantmaker's web site.
  Initial approach: Letter or telephone
  Copies of proposal: 1
  Deadline(s): Aug. 1 for draft, Sept. 15 for final draft
  Final notification: Recipients are notified approximately two months after deadline
  Applicants should submit the following:
    1) Work samples
    2) Resume
    3) Letter(s) of recommendation
    4) Curriculum vitae
EIN: 870307076

9229
The Utah Motorsports Foundation
764 W. S. Temple
Salt Lake City, UT   84104-1135   (801) 533-9179
Contact: Mike Nish
FAX: (801) 364-8132;
E-mail: mike@utahmotorsportsfoundation.com;
URL: http://www.utahmotorsportsfoundation.com/index.html

Foundation type: Public charity
Purpose: Grants to members of the motorsports community in UT, primarily for medical and funeral expenses.
Financial data: Year ended 04/30/2011. Assets, $421,448 (M); Expenditures, $13,831; Total giving, $10,750; Grants to individuals, totaling $10,750.
Type of support: Grants for special needs.
Application information: Applications accepted.
  Initial approach: Letter
  Deadline(s): None
  Additional information: Contact foundation for complete application guidelines.
EIN: 870628481

9230
Wheelwright Family Charitable Foundation
P.O. Box 662
Oakley, UT   84055-0021   (801) 824-3339
Contact: Steven C. Wheelwright, Tr.
Application address: P.O. Box 21, 1550 Weber Canyon Rd., Oakley, UT 84055,tel.:(801) 824-3339

Foundation type: Independent foundation
Purpose: Scholarships to needy individuals, primarily in UT.
Financial data: Year ended 12/31/2011. Assets, $31 (M); Expenditures, $0; Total giving, $0.
Type of support: Undergraduate support.
Application information: Applications accepted.
  Initial approach: Letter
  Applicants should submit the following:
    1) Budget Information
    2) Transcripts
  Additional information: Application should also include plan for studies and desired degree. Contact foundation for complete eligibility requirements.
EIN: 870672839

9231
The Whiz Kids Foundation
1699 N. 1820 W.
Provo, UT   84604-7201   (801) 636-2517
Contact: David B. Hagen, Dir.

Foundation type: Operating foundation
Purpose: Financial assistance to indigents residing in UT to help pay for medical and living expenses. Scholarships to high school seniors or college students in UT.
Financial data: Year ended 12/31/2010. Assets, $40 (M); Expenditures, $35,606; Total giving, $34,451; Grants to individuals, 13 grants totaling $11,070 (high: $5,520, low: $300).
Fields of interest: Higher education; Economically disadvantaged.
Type of support: Scholarships—to individuals; Grants for special needs.
Application information: Applications accepted.
  Initial approach: Letter
  Applicants should submit the following:
    1) Letter(s) of recommendation
    2) Financial information
  Additional information: Selection is based on academic performance, extracurricular activities, financial need and household income. Applicants from outside UT may also apply.
EIN: 200022998

9232
The H. R. Wing Family Benevolent Agency
1198 N. Spring Creek Pl.
Springville, UT   84663-3039   (801) 489-3684

Foundation type: Independent foundation
Purpose: Financial assistance to indigent residents of UT.
Financial data: Year ended 12/31/2011. Assets, $2,415 (M); Expenditures, $90,650; Total giving, $90,650; Grants to individuals, 4 grants totaling $25,000.
Type of support: Grants for special needs.
Application information: Applications accepted. Application form required.
  Initial approach: Letter
  Deadline(s): None
  Additional information: Contact agency for additional application guidelines.
EIN: 300235381

9233
Marlow & Vella Woodward Foundation, Inc.
1011 W. 400 N.
Logan, UT   84321   (801) 298-4556
Contact: Cliff Lillywhite, Pres.
Application address: 675 N. Main, North Salt Lake, UT 84054

Foundation type: Operating foundation
Purpose: Scholarships and grants to individuals, primarily in UT.
Financial data: Year ended 12/31/2011. Assets, $1,390,108 (M); Expenditures, $32,788; Total giving, $25,664; Grants to individuals, 8 grants totaling $25,664 (high: $5,000, low: $480).
Type of support: Scholarships—to individuals.
Application information: Applications accepted. Application form required.
  Deadline(s): None
  Additional information: Contact foundation for application form.
EIN: 870616969

9234
WTF Foundation
1034 Chartwell Ct.
Salt Lake City, UT   84103-2200
Contact: Sen-Maw Fang, Pres.

Foundation type: Independent foundation
Purpose: Scholarships to students of Chinese heritage who are residents of Salt Lake City, UT.

Financial data: Year ended 12/31/2011. Assets, $1,548,147 (M); Expenditures, $42,793; Total giving, $34,721; Grant to an individual, 1 grant totaling $467.
Fields of interest: Education.
International interests: China.
Type of support: Undergraduate support.

Application information: Applications accepted. Application form required.
  Initial approach: Letter
  Deadline(s): None
  Additional information: Scholarships are paid to the educational institution on behalf of the students.
EIN: 870643999

VERMONT

9235
Arlington Community Public Health Nursing Service, Inc.

P.O. Box 62
Arlington, VT   05250-0062
Contact: Lynn Williams, Pres.

Foundation type: Independent foundation
Purpose: Scholarships to high school graduates of Arlington Memorial High School who are residents of Arlington, Sunderland or Sandgate, VT furthering their education in a health related field.
Financial data: Year ended 12/31/2011. Assets, $386,504 (M); Expenditures, $27,388; Total giving, $4,525; Grants to individuals, 4 grants totaling $4,000 (high: $1,000, low: $1,000).
Fields of interest: Higher education; Health sciences school/education.
Type of support: Scholarships—to individuals; Support to graduates or students of specific schools.
Application information: Applications accepted. Application form required. Interview required.
  Send request by: Mail
  Deadline(s): May 1
  Final notification: Applicants notified by the date of graduation
  Applicants should submit the following:
    1) Transcripts
    2) Letter(s) of recommendation
  Additional information: Scholarships payments are made directly to the educational institution on behalf of the students. Applications can be obtained from Arlington Memorial High School guidance office.
EIN: 030186323

9236
Augustus & Kathleen Barrows Memorial and Trust Fund

271 S. Union St.
Burlington, VT   05401-4513   (802) 863-4531

Foundation type: Independent foundation
Purpose: Scholarships for needy and deserving female students of VT who are under the age of 25.
Financial data: Year ended 12/31/2012. Assets, $91,887 (M); Expenditures, $4,861; Total giving, $3,600; Grant to an individual, 1 grant totaling $3,600.
Fields of interest: Higher education; Adults, women.
Type of support: Scholarships—to individuals.
Application information:
  Initial approach: Letter
  Deadline(s): Prior to entering first semester of college
  Applicants should submit the following:
    1) Transcripts
    2) Letter(s) of recommendation
  Additional information: Applicant must demonstrate need.
EIN: 036010364

9237
The Kelly S. Brush Foundation, Inc.

7 Aspen Dr.
South Burlington, VT   05403-6246   (802) 846-5298
Contact: Betsy Cabrera, Exec. Dir.
FAX: (802) 864-9990;
E-mail: betsycabrera@kellybrushfoundation.org;
URL: http://www.kellybrushfoundation.org

Foundation type: Public charity
Purpose: Grants to economically disadvantaged individuals with paralysis due to a spinal cord injury (SCI) to purchase adaptive sporting equipments such as monoski or a handcycle.
Publications: Application guidelines.
Financial data: Year ended 12/31/2011. Assets, $147,101 (M); Expenditures, $300,556; Total giving, $128,220; Grants to individuals, totaling $78,322.
Fields of interest: Spine disorders.
Type of support: Grants to individuals.
Application information: Applications accepted. Application form required.
  Additional information: Applicant must demonstrate financial need and must be U.S. citizens. See web site for additional guidelines.
EIN: 204560423

9238
The Carving Studio & Sculpture Center

636 Marble St.
P.O. Box 495
West Rutland, VT   05777-0495   (802) 438-2097
Contact: Carol Driscoll, Exec. Dir.
FAX: (802) 438-2020;
E-mail: info@carvingstudio.org; URL: http://www.carvingstudio.org

Foundation type: Public charity
Purpose: Residencies for carvers and sculptors in the U.S., Peru, Kenya and China as they create sculpture and interact with their arts communities.
Publications: Application guidelines.
Financial data: Year ended 12/31/2012. Assets, $566,460 (M); Expenditures, $248,249; Total giving, $10,615; Grants to individuals, totaling $10,615.
Fields of interest: Arts education; Sculpture.
Type of support: Residencies.
Application information: Applications accepted.
  Additional information: See web site for additional information.
Program description:
  Artist Residencies: The foundation works to provide residency opportunities to carvers and sculptors, both at its home studio and around the world. Residencies generally last from one week to one to two months. Specific residency opportunities are also available at Lima, Peru, Kenya, and China's SIAS International University.
EIN: 030325486

9239
Central Vermont Community Action Council, Inc.

20 Gable Pl.
Barre, VT   05641-2267   (802) 479-1053
Contact: Hal Cohen, Exec. Dir.
E-mail: hcohen@cvcac.org; URL: http://www.cvcac.org/

Foundation type: Public charity
Purpose: Emergency and financial assistance to low-income individuals and families of VT.

Financial data: Year ended 09/30/2012. Assets, $7,254,222 (M); Expenditures, $20,646,010; Total giving, $9,892,449; Grants to individuals, totaling $9,892,449.
Fields of interest: Human services; Economically disadvantaged.
Type of support: Emergency funds; Grants for special needs.
Application information: Contact the organization for eligibility determination.
EIN: 030216254

9240
Charitable Foundation of the Bryant Chucking Grinder Company

(formerly Bryant Chucking Grinder Company Charitable Foundation)
53 Cutler Dr.
Springfield, VT   05156   (802) 885-5812
Contact: Richard H. Dexter II, Chair.

Foundation type: Independent foundation
Purpose: Scholarships to students who reside in New England.
Financial data: Year ended 12/31/2012. Assets, $1,097,492 (M); Expenditures, $42,502; Total giving, $11,250.
Type of support: Scholarships—to individuals.
Application information: Applications accepted.
  Initial approach: Letter
  Send request by: Mail
  Deadline(s): None
  Additional information: Contact foundation for current application guidelines.
EIN: 036009332

9241
Ted & Elinor Clifford Scholarship Fund

c/o Northeast Investment Management
190 Mapple St.
White River Junction, VT   05001   (802) 234-9966
Contact: Elinor C. Huntley, Tr.
Application address: R.D. 1, Box 27, Bethel, VT 05032

Foundation type: Independent foundation
Purpose: Scholarships to graduates of Whitcomb Senior High School, Bethel, VT, pursuing undergraduate or graduate degrees.
Financial data: Year ended 12/31/2011. Assets, $333,029 (M); Expenditures, $22,542; Total giving, $20,000; Grants to individuals, 5 grants totaling $20,000 (high: $5,000, low: $3,000).
Fields of interest: Higher education.
Type of support: Support to graduates or students of specific schools; Graduate support; Undergraduate support.
Application information: Applications accepted.
  Deadline(s): May 1
  Applicants should submit the following:
    1) Transcripts
    2) Financial information
  Additional information: Application should also include acceptance letter from academic institution and recommendation of Whitcomb High School committee.
EIN: 036051878

9242
The Copley Fund

P.O. Box 696
Morrisville, VT   05661-0696   (802) 888-2000
Contact: Richard C. Sargent Esq., Tr.

Foundation type: Independent foundation
Purpose: Housing and food assistance for elderly residents of Lamoille County, VT.
Financial data: Year ended 12/31/2012. Assets, $4,010,776 (M); Expenditures, $211,883; Total giving, $195,400; Grants to individuals, 134 grants totaling $120,600.
Fields of interest: Housing/shelter; Aging.
Type of support: Grants for special needs.
Application information:
  Initial approach: Letter
  Deadline(s): Dec. 31
EIN: 036006013

9243
Craft Emergency Relief Fund, Inc.
P.O. Box 838
Montpelier, VT   05601-0838   (802) 229-2306
FAX: (802) 223-6484;
E-mail: info@craftemergency.org; URL: http://www.craftemergency.org

Foundation type: Public charity
Purpose: Grants and loans to eligible craft artists who have suffered career-threatening emergencies.
Publications: Application guidelines; Annual report; Financial statement; Informational brochure; Informational brochure (including application guidelines); Newsletter; Occasional report.
Financial data: Year ended 09/30/2011. Assets, $938,191 (M); Expenditures, $690,092; Total giving, $106,579; Grants to individuals, totaling $106,579.
Fields of interest: Folk arts; Arts, artist's services; Safety/disasters.
Type of support: Emergency funds; Loans—to individuals.
Application information: Applications accepted. Application form required.
  Initial approach: Letter, telephone, fax, or e-mail
  Send request by: Mail
  Copies of proposal: 1
  Deadline(s): None
  Final notification: Recipient notified within two weeks
  Applicants should submit the following:
    1) Work samples
    2) Resume
  Additional information: Application should also include documentation about his/her craft career and the emergency.
Program descriptions:
  Phoenix Loan: This business loan is made available to eligible craft artists to re-establish, improve, or possibly expand his/her work capacity. The program was developed primarily for craft artists who are no longer in the initial stage of emergency recovery. Loans range from $4,000 to $8,000. No interest is charged and loans must be repaid within five years.
  Quick Loans and Emergency Grants: These loans and grants are designed to provide immediate help to eligible craft artists after career-threatening emergencies. The maximum Quick Loan is $4,000 and no interest charged and must be repaid within five years. The maximum Emergency Grant is $2,500. Applicants must be legal U.S. residents.
EIN: 133273980

9244
The Danville School Enrichment Fund, Inc.
c/o DRM
P.O. Box 99
St. Johnsbury, VT   05819-0099

Foundation type: Operating foundation

Purpose: Financial assistance for graduaes of Danville High School pursuing further education.
Financial data: Year ended 12/31/2012. Assets, $177,027 (M); Expenditures, $8,425; Total giving, $6,000; Grants to individuals, 3 grants totaling $6,000 (high: $2,000, low: $2,000).
Fields of interest: Higher education.
Type of support: Scholarships—to individuals; Support to graduates or students of specific schools.
Application information: Applications not accepted.
  Additional information: Unsolicited requests for funds not considered or acknowledged.
EIN: 030368959

9245
Hildegard Durfee Scholarship Fund
44 New England Dr.
Brattleboro, VT   05301-6273   (802) 254-5329
Contact: Charles R. Cummings, Tr.

Foundation type: Independent foundation
Purpose: Undergraduate and graduate scholarships to residents of Windham County, VT.
Financial data: Year ended 12/31/2012. Assets, $607,819 (M); Expenditures, $44,264; Total giving, $32,750; Grants to individuals, 66 grants totaling $32,750 (high: $1,500, low: $250).
Type of support: Graduate support; Undergraduate support.
Application information: Application form required.
  Deadline(s): June 1
  Applicants should submit the following:
    1) Transcripts
    2) FAF
EIN: 226546128

9246
Frank F. England Scholarship Fund
c/o Community Financial Svcs. Group
P.O. Box 120
Newport, VT   05855-0120

Foundation type: Independent foundation
Purpose: Scholarships to graduates of Northfield Elementary and Middle-High School, VT. Recipients must be the first generation of college-bound individuals in their family.
Financial data: Year ended 12/31/2012. Assets, $103,107 (M); Expenditures, $7,220; Total giving, $5,200; Grants to individuals, totaling $5,200.
Fields of interest: Higher education.
Type of support: Support to graduates or students of specific schools; Undergraduate support.
Application information: Applications accepted.
  Send request by: Mail
  Deadline(s): 1st Mon. in June.
  Applicants should submit the following:
    1) Essay
    2) Letter(s) of recommendation
EIN: 036054992

9247
Essex Classical Institute
62 Learned Dr.
Westford, VT   05494   (802) 879-1841
Contact: John Duby, Treas.

Foundation type: Independent foundation
Purpose: Scholarships to graduates of Essex High School who are residents of Essex, VT.
Financial data: Year ended 12/31/2013. Assets, $174,687 (M); Expenditures, $5,594; Total giving,

$5,100; Grants to individuals, 2 grants totaling $4,500 (high: $2,750, low: $1,750).
Type of support: Support to graduates or students of specific schools; Undergraduate support.
Application information: Applications not accepted.
  Additional information: Unsolicited requests for funds not considered or acknowledged.
EIN: 036006448

9248
General Education Fund, Inc.
c/o Merchants Trust Co.
P.O. Box 8490
Burlington, VT   05402-8490
Contact: Dan Stanyon
Application address: General Education Fund (GEF), Inc. Scholarship - NEW, VSAC Scholarship Programs, 10 E. Allen St., P.O. Box 2000, Winooski, VT, 05404-2601
E-mail: jboutin@thecurtisfund.org; URL: http://www.thecurtisfund.org/

Foundation type: Independent foundation
Purpose: Scholarships to deserving high school graduates of VT, for attendance at an accredited postsecondary school approved for federal Title IV funding, pursuing an undergraduate associate's or bachelor's degree.
Publications: Newsletter.
Financial data: Year ended 07/30/2013. Assets, $31,262,653 (M); Expenditures, $1,715,252; Total giving, $1,512,494; Grants to individuals, totaling $1,512,494.
Fields of interest: Higher education.
Type of support: Scholarships—to individuals.
Application information: Applications accepted. Application form required.
  Deadline(s): June 1 for new scholarships, July 1 for renewals
  Additional information: Applicants are nominated by a Vermont Student Assistance Corporation (VSAC) outreach counselor. Applicant must demonstrate financial need.
EIN: 036009912

9249
Green Valley Film & Art Center
300 Maple St.
Burlington, VT   05401
URL: http://www.greenvalleymedia.org/

Foundation type: Independent foundation
Purpose: Grants to non profit filmmakers who are producing educational videos about social issues and various cultures.
Financial data: Year ended 12/31/2012. Assets, $5,207 (M); Expenditures, $18,150; Total giving, $8,500.
Fields of interest: Film/video.
Type of support: Grants to individuals.
Application information: Applications not accepted.
  Additional information: Unsolicited requests for funds not considered.
EIN: 030263918

9250
Sylvia M. Hayes Trust
c/o Community Financial Services Group
P.O. Box 120
Newport, VT 05855-0120
Contact: Reed Korrow
Application address: Northfield High School,
Northfield, VT 05663, tel.: (802) 485-8644

Foundation type: Independent foundation
Purpose: Scholarships to high school graudates of
Northfield High School, VT for continuing education
at two or four year colleges or universities, and
certificate programs.
Financial data: Year ended 12/31/2012. Assets,
$95,531 (M); Expenditures, $7,566; Total giving,
$4,650; Grants to individuals, 3 grants totaling
$4,650 (high: $1,550, low: $1,550).
Fields of interest: Higher education.
Type of support: Support to graduates or students
of specific schools.
Application information: Applications accepted.
Application form required.
  Deadline(s): July 15 for fall semester and Dec. 15
    for spring semester
  Additional information: Application must include
    recommendations. Applicant must
    demonstrate need, and must show character,
    participation in academic,
    extracurricular-church, community or civic
    activities or groups.
EIN: 036055393

9251
Walter Hayes, Sr., Beulah Buffum Hayes & Walter H. Hayes, Jr. Foundation
(also known as The Hayes Foundation)
P.O. Box 424
Wallingford, VT 05773-0424 (802) 446-2877
Nomination address: Mitch Spencer Award, P.O. Box
307, Cuttingsville, VT 05738
E-mail: director@thehayesfoundation.org;
URL: http://www.thehayesfoundation.org/

Foundation type: Independent foundation
Purpose: Educational and financial support for
intellectually gifted children of Rutland county,
Vermont.
Financial data: Year ended 12/31/2012. Assets,
$485,232 (M); Expenditures, $29,995; Total
giving, $19,017; Grants to individuals, 12 grants
totaling $6,317 (high: $1,398, low: $125).
Fields of interest: Music.
Type of support: Grants to individuals.
Application information: Applications accepted.
Application form required. Application form
available on the grantmaker's web site.
  Send request by: Mail or e-mail
  Additional information: Application should
    include a copy of parents' most recent tax
    form.
EIN: 030284264

9252
Marian P. Huffman Educational Foundation
118 S. Main St., Ste. C-1
Stowe, VT 05672 (802) 888-3909
Contact: Donald S. Huffman, Treas.

Foundation type: Independent foundation
Purpose: Scholarships to students of Burlington, VT
who are in good academic standing for attendance
at accredited colleges or universities.
Financial data: Year ended 05/31/2013. Assets,
$46,077 (M); Expenditures, $5,477; Total giving,

$4,590; Grants to individuals, 3 grants totaling
$4,590.
Fields of interest: Higher education.
Type of support: Scholarships—to individuals.
Application information: Applications accepted.
  Initial approach: Letter
  Deadline(s): Apr. 30
  Additional information: Applicant must have a
    minimum of 45 credits earned.
EIN: 571166130

9253
Keal Foundation
c/o Jacobs, Morrisette, Marchand & Assoc.
P.O. Box 385
Burlington, VT 05402 (540) 672-9023
Application address: P.O. Box 647, Orange, VA
22960

Foundation type: Independent foundation
Purpose: Scholarships to graduating high school
seniors in pursuit of a higher education.
Financial data: Year ended 12/31/2011. Assets,
$357,708 (M); Expenditures, $10,000; Total
giving, $10,000; Grants to individuals, 4 grants
totaling $10,000 (high: $2,500, low: $2,500).
Fields of interest: Higher education.
Type of support: Scholarships—to individuals.
Application information: Applications accepted.
Application form required.
  Deadline(s): Mar. 31
  Additional information: Application must include
    a list of high school activities and a brief
    statement of reasons why he/she should
    receive a grant.
EIN: 030280402

9254
Keniston and Dane Educational Fund
553 Mosher Rd.
Sheffield, VT 05866-9705

Foundation type: Operating foundation
Purpose: Scholarships to residents of Wheelock
and Sheffield, VT.
Financial data: Year ended 12/31/2012. Assets,
$1,622,651 (M); Expenditures, $37,182; Total
giving, $23,367; Grants to individuals, 37 grants
totaling $21,249 (high: $797, low: $353).
Type of support: Scholarships—to individuals.
Application information: Applications not
accepted.
  Additional information: Unsolicited requests for
    funds not considered or acknowledged.
EIN: 030341752

9255
Nordic Educational Trust
c/o Vermont Business Roundtable
30 Kimball Ave., Ste. 302
South Burlington, VT 05403 (802) 865-0410
Application address: Lisa Ventriss Nordic
Educational Trust
URL: http://www.vtroundtable.org

Foundation type: Independent foundation
Purpose: Scholarships to residents of Chittenden
and adjacent counties, VT, for study toward degrees
in technical trades and professions at regional
colleges and technical schools.
Financial data: Year ended 12/31/2012. Assets,
$472,539 (M); Expenditures, $27,492; Total
giving, $22,500; Grants to individuals, 5 grants
totaling $22,500 (high: $5,000, low: $2,500).
Fields of interest: Vocational education.

Type of support: Technical education support;
Undergraduate support.
Application information: Applications accepted.
Application form required.
  Deadline(s): Mar. 1
EIN: 222975012

9256
Ohiyesa Corporation
c/o A.M. Peisch & Co., LLP
57 Farmvu Dr.
White River Junction, VT 05001 (802)
649-1282
Contact: Dean J. Seibert, Dir.
Application address: c/o P.O. Box 11, Norwich, VT
05055

Foundation type: Independent foundation
Purpose: Fellowships to undergraduates,
graduates and practitioners with an interest in
serving the needs of the medically underserved
populations.
Financial data: Year ended 12/31/2011. Assets,
$67,164 (M); Expenditures, $42,776; Total giving,
$22,385; Grants to individuals, 31 grants totaling
$22,385 (high: $3,400, low: $125).
Fields of interest: Health care; Economically
disadvantaged.
International interests: Central America.
Type of support: Fellowships; Travel grants.
Application information:
  Initial approach: Letter or proposal
  Deadline(s): None
EIN: 311586691

9257
Ottauquechee Health Center
(also known as Ottauquechee Health Foundation)
32 Pleasant St.
P.O. Box 784
Woodstock, VT 05091-1122 (802) 457-4188
Contact: Milena Zuccotti, Admin. Asst.; Deborah
Heimann, Interim Exec. Dir.
FAX: (802) 457-9072; E-mail: ohfadmin@sover.net;
URL: http://www.ohfvt.org

Foundation type: Public charity
Purpose: Educational grants to individuals residing
in the foundation's service area to assist with
expenses related to training in the health care
professions (including loan forgiveness)
Publications: Application guidelines; Annual report;
Grants list; Newsletter.
Financial data: Year ended 12/31/2011. Assets,
$2,746,367 (M); Expenditures, $295,564; Total
giving, $207,778; Grants to individuals, totaling
$72,434.
Fields of interest: Education; Health care.
Type of support: Grants to individuals.
Application information: Applications accepted.
Application form required.
  Deadline(s): Varies
Program description:
  Educational Grants: Small, one-time educational
    grants are available to assist with expenses related
    to training in health care professionals. Funding is
    available to individuals residing in the health
    center's service area who will be providing health
    care services there.
EIN: 030197766

9258
The Rowland Foundation Inc.
P.O. Box 88
South Londonderry, VT 05155-0088 (802)
824-6400
Contact: Charles Scranton, Exec. Dir.
E-mail: info@therowlandfoundation.org;
URL: http://www.therowlandfoundation.org/

Foundation type: Independent foundation
Purpose: Fellowships to VT high school teachers
seeking professional development and leadership
opportunities to positively affect the culture and
climate at their schools.
Publications: Application guidelines.
Financial data: Year ended 06/30/2013. Assets,
$12,152,100 (M); Expenditures, $723,406; Total
giving, $475,000. Fellowships amount not
specified.
Fields of interest: Elementary/secondary
education.
Type of support: Fellowships; Sabbaticals.
Application information: Applications accepted.
Application form required. Application form
available on the grantmaker's web site. Interview
required.
> *Initial approach:* Letter
> *Deadline(s):* Dec. 31
> *Applicants should submit the following:*
> 1) Letter(s) of recommendation
> 2) Resume
> 3) Proposal
> 4) Budget Information

Program description:
> *Rowland Fellowships:* Each year, up to ten
> Vermont secondary school educators will be chosen
> as Rowland Fellows, whereby their schools will
> receive a $100,000 grant to implement a vision to
> transform an aspect of the school which will
> positively impact its culture and climate. An initial
> grant of $50,000 will cover a sabbatical for each
> fellow (and his/her family, if applicable) to provide
> an opportunity for travel, research, personal
> reflection and renewal, and the development of an
> action plan to be implemented upon the fellow's
> return to his/her school. An additional $50,000
> grant is provided to each school in two installments
> to support initiatives developed by the fellow. The
> first $25,000 is made available upon the fellow's
> return from sabbatical. The balance of the grant is
> made after a visit by the Executive Director to each
> school and the submission of a final report.

EIN: 262698626

9259
Rutland High School Foundation
27 S. Main St.
Rutland, VT 05701-5014
Contact: John H. Bloomer, Jr., Pres.

Foundation type: Independent foundation
Purpose: Scholarships to graduates of Rutland High
School, VT, attending accredited colleges.
Financial data: Year ended 06/30/2011. Assets,
$262,652 (M); Expenditures, $7,017; Total giving,
$7,000; Grants to individuals, 2 grants totaling
$7,000 (high: $3,500, low: $3,500).
Fields of interest: Higher education.
Type of support: Support to graduates or students
of specific schools.
Application information: Applications accepted.
Application form required.
> *Additional information:* Application should
> include a list of extracurricular activities.

EIN: 030334417

9260
Olin Scott Fund, Inc.
P.O. Box 1208
Bennington, VT 05201 (802) 447-1096
Application Address: 407 Main Street,
Bennington,VT 05201

Foundation type: Independent foundation
Purpose: Student loans to young men from
Bennington County, VT, planning to attend VT
colleges and universities.
Financial data: Year ended 06/30/2013. Assets,
$0 (M); Expenditures, $82,230; Total giving,
$7,500.
Fields of interest: Men.
Type of support: Student loans—to individuals;
Undergraduate support.
Application information: Applications accepted.
Application form required. Interview required.
> *Initial approach:* Letter or telephone
> *Deadline(s):* Aug. 1 for fall semester
> *Applicants should submit the following:*
> 1) Letter(s) of recommendation
> 2) Transcripts
> *Additional information:* Application must include
> application fee of $25 for initial loan and for
> each renewal.

EIN: 036005697

9261
Ronald Terrill Memorial Fund, Inc.
P.O. Box 632
Morrisville, VT 05661 (802) 888-2000
Contact: Tim Sargent, Dir.
Application address: P.O. Box 696, Morrisville, VT
0566 tel.: (802) 888-2000

Foundation type: Operating foundation
Purpose: Scholarships to graduating seniors of
Lamoille Union High School, and Peoples Academy
High School, VT, for higher education at two- and
four-year colleges and technical schools.
Financial data: Year ended 12/31/2012. Assets,
$675,168 (M); Expenditures, $28,777; Total
giving, $24,000; Grants to individuals, 11 grants
totaling $24,000 (high: $4,000, low: $500).
Type of support: Support to graduates or students
of specific schools; Technical education support;
Undergraduate support.
Application information: Applications accepted.
> *Initial approach:* Letter
> *Send request by:* Mail
> *Deadline(s):* May 10
> *Applicants should submit the following:*
> 1) Financial information
> 2) Letter(s) of recommendation
> 3) Class rank
> 4) Transcripts
> 5) FAF
> *Additional information:* Application should also
> include educational and vocational goals,
> school or community service, work
> experience, and college entrance scores.

EIN: 030213310

9262
M. Fletcher Tkacyzk & E. Mahaney Memorial Scholarship Trust
c/o Trust Co. of Vermont
P.O. Box 1280
Brattleboro, VT 05302-1280 (802) 257-8922
Application address: c/o Brattleboro Union High
School, 131 Fairground Rd., Brattleboro, VT
05301-6328, tel.: (802) 257-8922

Foundation type: Independent foundation

Purpose: Scholarships to graduating students of
Brattleboro Union High School, VT for attendance at
an accredited college or university earning a BA
degree.
Financial data: Year ended 04/30/2012. Assets,
$434,761 (M); Expenditures, $40,933; Total
giving, $36,000.
Type of support: Support to graduates or students
of specific schools.
Application information:
> *Initial approach:* Letter
> *Deadline(s):* May 30
> *Applicants should submit the following:*
> 1) Transcripts
> 2) Financial information
> *Additional information:* Application should also
> include two references.

EIN: 046981476

9263
Trustees of Chester Academy
P.O. Box 1280
Brattleboro, VT 05302 (802) 875-2146

Foundation type: Independent foundation
Purpose: Scholarships to high school graduates
residing in Chester, VT.
Financial data: Year ended 03/31/2013. Assets,
$583,194 (M); Expenditures, $33,002; Total
giving, $26,100.
Type of support: Undergraduate support.
Application information: Applications not
accepted.
> *Additional information:* Scholarship recipients
> are selected by the Board of Trustees.
> Unsolicited requests for funds not considered
> or acknowledged.

EIN: 036007034

9264
United Way of Lamoille County, Inc.
20 Morrisville Plz., Ste. B
Morrisville, VT 05661-1402 (802) 888-3252
FAX: (802) 888-7298;
E-mail: unitedway@pshift.com; URL: http://
www.uwlamoille.org

Foundation type: Public charity
Purpose: Grants of up to $200 to individuals of
Lamoille county, VT for emergency needs.
Publications: Application guidelines; Annual report;
Financial statement; Informational brochure.
Financial data: Year ended 06/30/2012. Assets,
$356,011 (M); Expenditures, $199,084.
Fields of interest: Economically disadvantaged.
Type of support: Emergency funds.
Application information: Applications not
accepted.
> *Additional information:* Requests for these
> one-time gifts must come at the request of a
> community partner.

EIN: 222774485

9265
VARA Educational Foundation, Inc.
P.O. Box 82
Cavendish, VT 05142 (802) 226-8188
URL: http://www.vara.org/

Foundation type: Company-sponsored foundation
Purpose: Scholarships to residents of VT who are
students of skiing academies or skiing clubs to pay
for tuition and related expenses.
Financial data: Year ended 07/31/2013. Assets,
$188,872 (M); Expenditures, $27,766; Total

giving, $25,400; Grants to individuals, 36 grants totaling $25,400 (high: $2,000, low: $250).
Fields of interest: Athletics/sports, academies.
Type of support: Undergraduate support.
Application information:
  Initial approach: Letter
  Deadline(s): Oct. 15
EIN: 237336991

9266
Vermont Bar Foundation
35-37 Court St.
P.O. Box 1170
Montpelier, VT   05601-1170   (802) 223-1400
Contact: Deborah S. Bailey, Exec. Dir.
FAX: (802) 229-4051;
E-mail: dbailey@vtbarfndn.org; URL: http://www.vtbarfoundation.org/

Foundation type: Public charity
Purpose: Assists VT lawyers working in civil legal services with repayment of their student loans. The purpose of the program is to allow lawyers with high levels of educational loan debt to take and stay in civil legal services jobs in VT.
Financial data: Year ended 12/31/2011. Assets, $963,835 (M); Expenditures, $1,329,228; Total giving, $1,153,372; Grants to individuals, totaling $46,375.
Fields of interest: Law school/education.
Type of support: Student loans—to individuals.
Application information: Applications accepted. Application form required. Application form available on the grantmaker's web site.
  Initial approach: Letter
  Deadline(s): Oct. 29
EIN: 030285318

9267
Vermont Community Foundation
3 Court St.
Middlebury, VT   05753   (802) 388-3355
Contact: For questions about grants: Jen Peterson, V.P., Program and Grants; For questions about accounting and finance: Debra Rooney, V.P., Finance and C.F.O.; For questions about establishing a fund: Peter Espenshade, V.P., Community Philanthropy; For media inquiries or questions about publications: Felipe Rivera, V.P., Communications
FAX: (802) 388-3398; E-mail: info@vermontcf.org; URL: http://www.vermontcf.org

Foundation type: Community foundation
Purpose: Scholarships to students in VT for higher education. Grants to support the development, completion and/or presentation of new work by VT artists.
Publications: Application guidelines; Annual report; Financial statement; Grants list; Newsletter; Occasional report.
Financial data: Year ended 12/31/2012. Assets, $167,245,557 (M); Expenditures, $16,608,412; Total giving, $12,603,915.
Fields of interest: Arts.
Type of support: Grants to individuals; Undergraduate support.
Application information: Applications accepted. Application form required. Application form available on the grantmaker's web site.
  Additional information: Applications for artist grants should be submitted by proposal and also include SASE, resume, financial information, work samples, project description, timeline, and other supporting

materials. See web site for additional information.
Program description:
  Artists Grants: All disciplines and media are eligible. Priority for new works funding will be given to projects which involve artists experimenting and/or proposing to move their work in new directions. Grant amounts range from $300 to $4,000.
EIN: 222712160

9268
Vermont Council on the Arts, Inc.
136 State St., Drawer 33
Montpelier, VT   05633-6001   (802) 828-3291
Contact: Alexander L. Aldrich, Exec. Dir.
FAX: (802) 828-3363;
E-mail: info@vermontartscouncil.org; URL: http://www.vermontartscouncil.org

Foundation type: Public charity
Purpose: Grants to artists in VT with demonstrated artistic merit.
Publications: Application guidelines; Annual report; Informational brochure.
Financial data: Year ended 06/30/2012. Assets, $1,474,442 (M); Expenditures, $1,515,676; Total giving, $540,051; Grants to individuals, totaling $66,611.
Fields of interest: Arts.
Type of support: Awards/prizes; Project support.
Application information: Application form required. Application form available on the grantmaker's web site.
  Initial approach: Telephone or e-mail
  Deadline(s): Varies
  Additional information: See web site for further application information.
Program description:
  Teaching Artist Residency Grants: Grants, ranging from $500 to $1,500, are available to support artist residences in Vermont schools. Eligible activities for this grant include, but are not limited to: school residencies that are a minimum of five days and include a core group who meets with the artist for a minimum of five classes or five hours; residencies that are conducted by a designated teaching artists; and activities in which the teacher is present and participating.
EIN: 030218115

9269
Vermont Student Development Fund, Inc.
P.O. Box 2000
Winooski, VT   05404-2601   (802) 654-3753
Contact: Donald R. Vickers, Pres. and C.E.O.
FAX: (802) 654-3779; E-mail: cromie@vsac.org;
Toll-free tel.: (800) 990-3561, ext. 753;
URL: http://services.vsac.org/wps/wcm/connect/scholarship/donors

Foundation type: Public charity
Purpose: Scholarships and financial assistance to qualified individuals of VT seeking a postsecondary education.
Financial data: Year ended 06/30/2012. Assets, $9,627,079 (M); Expenditures, $5,616,197; Total giving, $5,616,197; Grants to individuals, totaling $5,616,197.
Fields of interest: Higher education.
Type of support: Scholarships—to individuals.
Application information: Applications accepted.
  Send request by: Online
  Additional information: See web site for additional application guidelines.
EIN: 030367034

9270
Vermont Student Opportunity Scholarship Fund, Inc.
P.O. Box 232
Williston, VT   05495-0232   (888) 558-8883
Contact: Ruth Stokes, Exec. Dir.

Foundation type: Public charity
Purpose: Scholarships to residents of VT for K-8 education; Eligibility for scholarships is limited to those students who qualify for participation in the Federal Free and Reduced Lunch program.
Financial data: Year ended 06/30/2010. Assets, $2,704 (M); Expenditures, $23,728; Total giving, $21,754.
Type of support: Precollege support.
Application information: Application form required.
  Additional information: Selection is determined by a lottery drawing. Contact fund for application deadline.
EIN: 030358908

9271
Vermont Studio Center, Inc.
80 Pearl St.
Johnson, VT   05656   (802) 635-2727
Contact: Gary Clark, Pres.
FAX: (802) 635-2730;
E-mail: development@vermontstudiocenter.org;
Mailing address: P.O. Box 613, Johnson, VT 05656-0613; URL: http://www.vermontstudiocenter.org

Foundation type: Public charity
Purpose: Fellowships to painters, printmakers, photographers, sculptors, and writers.
Publications: Application guidelines; Grants list; Informational brochure (including application guidelines).
Financial data: Year ended 12/31/2011. Assets, $7,563,967 (M); Expenditures, $4,074,287; Total giving, $1,467,486; Grants to individuals, totaling $1,467,486.
Fields of interest: Photography; Sculpture; Painting; Literature.
Type of support: Fellowships.
Application information: Application form required.
  Initial approach: Letter or e-mail
  Deadline(s): Feb. 15, Apr. 1, June 15, and Oct. 1
  Applicants should submit the following:
    1) Letter(s) of recommendation
    2) Work samples
    3) Resume
  Additional information: Application should also include $25 application fee, portfolio and first page of income tax return.
Program description:
  Residencies: The organizations offers two- to 12-week studio residencies for 50 artists and writers per month (24 painters/mixed-media artists, 12 sculptors/mixed-media artists, two printmakers, two photographers, and 12 writers). Benefits include: 24-hour access to private studio space appropriate for the medium (for the duration of the residency); simple, private rooms and excellent work; the opportunity to engage in focused, independent work; and opportunities to discuss and share work with fellow residents and a large and diverse creative community. Fellowship costs run from $1,900 (for two weeks) to $3,950; financial assistance is available to those who qualify.
EIN: 222478074

9272
Warner Home for Little Wanderers
4 Forest Hill Dr.
St. Albans, VT 05478-1615
Contact: Donna Roby

Foundation type: Independent foundation
Purpose: Scholarships and financial assistance to needy residents of Franklin County, VT, aged 21 and under, to help defray costs of summer camp; musical instrument rental, purchase, and lessons; art lessons; equipment; and other extracurricular activities.
Financial data: Year ended 04/30/2012. Assets, $1,943,355 (M); Expenditures, $162,339; Total giving, $144,710; Grants to individuals, totaling $144,710.
Fields of interest: Arts education; Performing arts, education; Camps; Children/youth, services.
Type of support: Scholarships—to individuals; Grants for special needs.
Application information: Contact the organization for further information.
EIN: 030179439

9273
The Windham Foundation, Inc.
P.O. Box 70
Grafton, VT 05146-0070 (802) 843-2211
Scholarship e-mail address:
scholarships@windham-foundation.org
FAX: (802) 843-2205;
E-mail: info@windham-foundation.org; URL: http://www.windham-foundation.org

Foundation type: Operating foundation
Purpose: Undergraduate and technical scholarships to Windham County, VT, residents only.
Publications: Application guidelines; Annual report; Informational brochure; Informational brochure (including application guidelines); Newsletter.
Financial data: Year ended 03/31/2012. Assets, $46,600,541 (M); Expenditures, $9,511,790; Total giving, $254,389; Grants to individuals, 18 grants totaling $11,600 (high: $2,500; low: $150).
Fields of interest: Vocational education, post-secondary; Higher education.
Type of support: Scholarships—to individuals; Undergraduate support.
Application information: Applications accepted. Application form required. Application form available on the grantmaker's web site.
  Send request by: Mail
  Copies of proposal: 1
  Deadline(s): Mar. 1
  Applicants should submit the following:
    1) FAFSA
    2) Transcripts
  Additional information: Applicants are required to file with Vermont Student Assistance Corporation (VSAC) and FAFSA to meet foundation deadline.
Program description:
  Windham Foundation Scholarships: Scholarships are limited to Windham County residents studying at the undergraduate level. Awards are paid directly to the institution of study and not to the individual student. The maximum number of scholarships a student may receive is four. While most students enroll in traditional college level institutions, the foundation occasionally provides support for individuals who attend a trade school with a certificate program.
EIN: 136142024

VIRGIN ISLANDS

9274
Community Foundation of the Virgin Islands
(also known as CFVI)
5600 Royal Dane Mall, Ste. 19
Charlotte Amalie, VI 00802-6410 (340) 774-6031
Contact: Dee Baecher-Brown, Pres.
FAX: (340) 774-3852; E-mail: general.info@cfvi.net; Mailing Address: P.O. Box 11790, Charlotte Amalie, VI 00801; Additional e-mail: dbrown@cfvi.net; URL: http://www.cfvi.net/

Foundation type: Community foundation
Purpose: Scholarships to graduating high school students and students enrolled in accredited colleges or universities in St. Croix, St. Thomas, St. John or Water Island, U.S. Virgin Islands.
Publications: Financial statement; Newsletter.
Financial data: Year ended 12/31/2011. Assets, $6,944,548 (M); Expenditures, $2,106,788; Total giving, $1,705,465; Grants to individuals, 482 grants totaling $561,480.
Fields of interest: Higher education.
Type of support: Graduate support; Undergraduate support.
Application information: Applications accepted. Application form required.

Initial approach: Application
Send request by: Mail
Deadline(s): Varies
Additional information: See web site for complete listing of scholarships.
EIN: 660470703

9275
Friends of Virgin Islands National Park
P. O. Box 811
St. John, VI 00831-0811 (340) 779-4940
Contact: Joe Kessler, Pres.
FAX: (340) 693-9973; E-mail: info@friendsvinp.org; Email for scholarships: apenn@friendsvinp.org; URL: http://www.friendsvinp.org

Foundation type: Public charity
Purpose: Scholarships and grants to individuals who wish to conduct research in the Virgin Islands National Park.
Publications: Application guidelines; Informational brochure; Newsletter.
Financial data: Year ended 09/30/2012. Assets, $2,030,240 (M); Expenditures, $942,196; Total giving, $68,499; Grants to individuals, totaling $3,000.
Application information:
Deadline(s): Varies
Program descriptions:
Scholarship Fund: The organization provides scholarship and summer internship opportunities

for two Virgin Islanders to encourage study in fields related to natural resource management.
School Kids in the Park Grants: Grants, ranging from $250 to $500, are available to St. John's-based teachers for creative classroom projects that incorporate the natural and/or cultural resources of the park. Projects must involve an in-class component to the project. Priority will be given to public schools.
EIN: 660463113

9276
Ruby Rutnik Scholarship Fund, Inc.
P.O. Box 348
St. John, VI 00831-0348

Foundation type: Public charity
Purpose: College scholarships to U.S. Virgin Islands female high school graduates.
Financial data: Year ended 12/31/2011. Assets, $194,908 (M); Expenditures, $20,026.
Fields of interest: Higher education; Women.
Type of support: Scholarships—to individuals; Undergraduate support.
Application information:
Deadline(s): May
Final notification: Applicants notified in June
Additional information: Contact the foundation for additional information.
EIN: 660544380

VIRGINIA

9277
A Gift from Ben, Inc.
3526 Governor's Landing Rd.
Williamsburg, VA 23185-1320 (757) 258-9195
URL: http://www.thumpernewman.com/
a_gift_from_ben.htm

Foundation type: Public charity
Purpose: Specific assistance to individuals and families in the Williamsburg, VA area with food and clothing. Cash awards to an outstanding eight grade student diagnosed with a learning disability to further his/her education.
Financial data: Year ended 12/31/2011. Assets, $16,722 (M); Expenditures, $1,333,737; Total giving, $1,980,965.
Fields of interest: Education; Economically disadvantaged.
Type of support: Awards/prizes; Grants for special needs.
Application information: The award depends on the individual need. If the student needs clothing for school or a computer, the award will help fulfill that need.
Program description:
Ben Newman Award: This award consists of a name plaque and a $500 is given annually to an eighth-grade student who has been labeled as learning-disabled, and who has worked the hardest and has given his/her greatest effort.
EIN: 300045747

9278
ACCESS College Foundation
7300 Newport Ave., Ste. 500
Norfolk, VA 23505-3357 (757) 962-6113
Contact: Bonnie B. Sutton, Pres. and C.E.O.
FAX: (757) 962-7314; URL: http://
www.accesscollege.org

Foundation type: Public charity
Purpose: Scholarships to public high school juniors and seniors of Norfolk, Portsmouth, Virginia Beach, Chesapeake, and Suffolk, VA to attend college, university or technical school.
Financial data: Year ended 06/30/2012. Assets, $27,889,235 (M); Expenditures, $2,643,360; Total giving, $553,117; Grants to individuals, 695 grants totaling $553,117.
Fields of interest: Vocational education, post-secondary; Higher education.
Type of support: Support to graduates or students of specific schools.
Application information: Applications accepted.
Additional information: Applicant must demonstrate financial need and have grades of C+ or better.
EIN: 541440734

9279
Advancing Native Missions
P.O. Box 5303
Charlottesville, VA 22905-5303 (540) 456-7111
FAX: (540) 456-7222;
E-mail: requests@adnamis.org; URL: http://
www.adnamis.org

Foundation type: Public charity

Purpose: Assistance to the distribution of medical supplies and books to underserved people around the world.
Publications: Annual report; Financial statement; Newsletter.
Financial data: Year ended 12/31/2011. Assets, $2,640,758 (M); Expenditures, $7,863,929; Total giving, $5,229,074; Grants to individuals, totaling $254,576.
Fields of interest: Human services.
Type of support: In-kind gifts.
Application information: Applications not accepted.
Additional information: Unsolicited requests for funds not considered or acknowledged.
EIN: 752402759

9280
AFP Foundation for Philanthropy
4300 Wilson Blvd., Ste. 300
Arlington, VA 22203-4179 (703) 684-0410
Contact: Paulette V. Maehara, Pres. and C.E.O.
FAX: (703) 684-0540;
E-mail: foundation@afpnet.org; Toll-free tel.: (800) 666-3863; URL: http://www.afpnet.org/
Foundation/

Foundation type: Public charity
Purpose: Grants and scholarships to individuals pursuing research on fundraising and philanthropy related topics Grants and scholarships to individuals pursuing research on fundraising and philanthropy related topics.
Publications: Annual report; Newsletter.
Financial data: Year ended 12/31/2011. Assets, $1,721,949 (M); Expenditures, $969,099; Total giving, $232,955. Scholarships—to individuals amount not specified.
Fields of interest: Fund raising/fund distribution.
Type of support: Grants to individuals; Scholarships—to individuals.
Application information: Applicants must be employed as fundraising professionals and not have attended the international conference in the past.
EIN: 521241128

9281
AHC Community Health Foundation
P.O. Box 1000
Fishersville, VA 22939-1000 (540) 332-4000
Contact: Linda Gail Johnson, Exec. Dir.
FAX: (540) 332-4215;
E-mail: ljohnson@augustamed.com; Toll free tel. : (800)-932-0262; URL: http://
www.augustahealth.com/foundation/
community-needs-assessment

Foundation type: Public charity
Purpose: Scholarships to graduating local high school students of the greater Augusta county, VA area pursuing careers in the health care field of study.
Publications: Application guidelines; Informational brochure.
Financial data: Year ended 12/31/2011. Assets, $10,395,505 (M); Expenditures, $726,752; Total giving, $275,162; Grants to individuals, totaling $15,000.
Fields of interest: Nursing school/education.
Type of support: Scholarships—to individuals; Support to graduates or students of specific schools.
Application information: Contact the foundation for additional application guidelines.

Program descriptions:
Blue Ridge Community College Nursing Student Scholarships: The foundation awards scholarships of $1,000 each to students from the Augusta County area who are enrolled in the nursing program at Blue Ridge Community College.
Dick Graham Scholarship: Scholarships are awarded annually to students who intend to pursue careers in the health care industry.
EIN: 542042365

9282
AHP Foundation
313 Park Ave., Ste. 400
Falls Church, VA 22046-3303 (703) 532-6243
FAX: (703) 532-7170; E-mail: foundation@ahp.org;
URL: http://www.ahp.org/Pages/Home.aspx

Foundation type: Public charity
Purpose: Scholarships to financially needy active AHP members and professional fundraisers for charitable hospitals, who could not attend a conference without scholarship aid.
Publications: Application guidelines; Grants list; Informational brochure; Newsletter.
Financial data: Year ended 06/30/2013. Assets, $1,145,125 (M); Expenditures, $71,846; Total giving, $16,350; Grants to individuals, totaling $16,350.
Fields of interest: Formal/general education; Formal/general education.
Type of support: Conferences/seminars; Postgraduate support.
Application information: Applications accepted. Application form required.
Initial approach: Telephone or e-mail
Deadline(s): Dec. 1
Additional information: Application must include written statement of qualifications, brief history of professional fundraising experience, and any other supporting documentation.
Program description:
AHP Scholarships: Awards $2,000 scholarships to active AHP members to cover registration, lodging, and travel for attendance at either the AHP Institute for Healthcare Philanthropy in Madison, WI or the AHP Annual International Educational Conference. The recipient is responsible for the balance of transportation and per diem expenses.
EIN: 237359389

9283
Air Force Aid Society, Inc.
241 18th St., Ste. 202
Arlington, VA 22202-3405
Contact: John D. Hopper, Jr., C.E.O.
FAX: (703) 607-3022; E-mail: dvosburg@afas.org;
Toll-free tel.: (800) 769-8951; URL: http://
www.afas.org

Foundation type: Public charity
Purpose: Emergency assistance in the form of interest-free loans and grants to full-time active duty and retired personnel, their dependents and survivors of deceased active duty and retired personnel.
Publications: Annual report; Financial statement.
Financial data: Year ended 12/31/2011. Assets, $153,781,514 (M); Expenditures, $13,358,661; Total giving, $8,890,335; Grants to individuals, totaling $7,984,892.
Fields of interest: Higher education; Military/veterans.
Type of support: Emergency funds; Grants to individuals.

Application information: Unsolicited requests for funds not accepted.
EIN: 541797281

9284
Air Force Association
(formerly Aerospace Education Foundation, Inc.)
1501 Lee Hwy.
Arlington, VA 22209-1198 (703) 247-5800
Contact: Craig R. McKinley, Pres.
FAX: (703) 247-5853; E-mail: afastaff@afa.org;
Toll-Free Tel.: (800) 727-3337; E-Mail for Craig R.
McKinley: CMcKinley@AFA.ORG; URL: http://
www.afa.org

Foundation type: Public charity
Purpose: Scholarships to Air Force personnel, their spouses, and AFROTC graduates. Grants to educators for the development of aerospace activities and programs.
Publications: Application guidelines; Annual report.
Financial data: Year ended 12/31/2011. Assets, $22,853,330 (M); Expenditures, $13,646,758; Total giving, $314,608; Grants to individuals, totaling $30,000.
Fields of interest: Science; Space/aviation; Mathematics; Engineering/technology; Military/veterans' organizations.
Type of support: Grants to individuals; Scholarships—to individuals; Awards/prizes; Graduate support; Undergraduate support.
Application information: Applications accepted. Application form required.
  Additional information: See web site for detailed program information.
Program descriptions:
  Air Force Junior ROTC Grants: Provides units and classrooms with up to $250, every other academic year, to support classroom aerospace educational programs, opportunities, activities and interests when no funds are available.
  ANG George W. Bush Award: This award recognizes outstanding civilian employers of traditional Air National Guard members by awarding 12 recipients with $500.
  Awards for Aerospace Education Excellence: These awards are given to motivate and recognize chapter and state participation in association programs, to encourage chapter and state organizations to participate in association programs, and to recognize excellence in the execution of aerospace education programs at the chapter and state level. The program is two-tiered: the first tier is the President's Award and the second tier is the Chairman's Award.
  Captain Jodi Callahan Memorial Scholarship: Provides a $1,000 scholarship to an Air Force active duty full time guard or reserve (officer or enlisted) person who is pursuing a Master's degree in a non-technical field of study.
  Chapter Matching Grants: Promotes aerospace education activities at the association chapter level. The program rewards aggressive chapters with annual grants of up to $1,000 for creating/promoting community educational activities and events in math and sciences.
  Chapter Teacher of the Year Award: Award recognizes teachers of K-12 for science and math who are furthering excellence and making coming to class an adventure. Teachers are awarded $250.
  Civil Air Patrol Aerospace Educator Grant: Classroom teachers who are Aerospace Education or Civil Air Patrol members are eligible to receive one grant every other year. Each school is limited to two grants every other year. Grants cannot exceed $250 per request.

  Civil Air Patrol Unit Grants: Grants of no more than $250 per request for Civil Air Patrol aerospace education programs. Units are eligible to receive one grant every other year.
  Educator Grants: Provides up to $250 per year in support to elementary and secondary classrooms for aerospace education programs, opportunities, and activities when no support is available.
  Full Scholarship to Grantham University: The organization partners with Grantham University to provide one full scholarship, of approximately $36,000, for an active duty dependent, an Air Force Association member, or a dependent of an Air Force Association member. Scholarship includes tuition, required books, and software for winner to complete an online undergraduate or graduate degree through distance learning in the areas of business, science, technology, and related fields.
  Lt. Col. Romeo and Josephine Bass Ferretti Scholarship: This program, made possible through bequest from the estate of Lt. Col. Romeo and Josephine Bass Ferretti, was established for minor dependents of Air Force active duty, reserve, or Air National Guard enlisted airmen pursuing an undergraduate degree in science, technology, engineering, or math.
  Pitsenbarger Award: Provides a one-time grant of $400 to selected top US Air Force-enlisted personnel graduating from the Community College of the Air Force and who plan to pursue a baccalaureate degree.
  Spaatz Award: Awards $1,000 stipend annually to the Air Command and Staff College graduate who writes the best paper on advocacy of Air Force aerospace power.
  Spouse Scholarships: $2,500 scholarships are available to Air Force spouses worldwide to pursue associate/bachelor undergraduate or graduate/post-graduate degrees.
  State Teacher of the Year Award: This award includes a check for $1,000, a certificate, a personalized jacket, and a free Civil Air Patrol Aerospace Education membership for educators selected at the State level who have gone the "extra mile" in increasing student interest in math, science, and technology.
EIN: 526043929

9285
Horatio Alger Association of Distinguished Americans, Inc.
99 Canal Ctr. Plz., Ste. 320
Alexandria, VA 22314-1588 (703) 684-9444
Contact: Terrence J. Giroux, Exec. Dir.
FAX: (703) 548-3822; URL: http://
www.horatioalger.org

Foundation type: Public charity
Purpose: Scholarships to high school seniors who have overcome great obstacles in life.
Publications: Application guidelines; Informational brochure; Occasional report.
Financial data: Year ended 12/31/2011. Assets, $26,214,545 (M); Expenditures, $14,808,234; Total giving, $5,861,158; Grants to individuals, totaling $5,799,158.
Fields of interest: Scholarships/financial aid.
Type of support: Undergraduate support.
Application information: Applications accepted. Application form required. Application form available on the grantmaker's web site.
  Deadline(s): Apr. 15
  Applicants should submit the following:
    1) Financial information
    2) Transcripts
    3) Letter(s) of recommendation

  Additional information: See web site for current application guidelines.
Program descriptions:
  Horatio Alger National Scholarship Program: The $20,000 assists high school students who have faced and overcome great obstacles in their young lives. The program seeks students who have a commitment to use their college degrees in service to others. Applicants must demonstrate financial need.
  State Scholarships: State scholarship programs are available in all U.S. states except Florida, Maryland, and Virginia. See web site for additional details.
EIN: 131669975

9286
All Saints' Scholarship Fund
1968 Woodside Ln.
Virginia Beach, VA 23454 (757) 463-6595

Foundation type: Independent foundation
Purpose: Scholarships to students preparing to enter or continue college for study in accredited degree programs.
Financial data: Year ended 03/31/2013. Assets, $1,117,623 (M); Expenditures, $59,172; Total giving, $51,838; Grants to individuals, 4 grants totaling $51,838 (high: $50,250, low: $150).
Fields of interest: Higher education.
Type of support: Undergraduate support; Postgraduate support.
Application information: Application form required.
  Initial approach: Letter
  Deadline(s): Mid-Feb.
  Additional information: Applications may be obtained from the Virginia Beach public schools web site or the office of All Saints Episcopal Church.
EIN: 541643750

9287
American Academy of Audiology Foundation
11480 Commerce Park Dr., Ste. 220
Reston, VA 20191 (703) 226-1048
Contact: Kathleen Devlin Culver, Dir., Opers. and Devel.
Application address: Audiologist Travel Award Committee, ARO Executive Office, 19 Mantua Rd., Mt. Royal, NJ 08061-1006, tel.: (856) 423-0041, fax: (856) 423-3420, e-mail: headquarters@aro.org
E-mail: aaafoundation@audiology.org; Toll-Free Tel.: (800) 222-2336; E-mail For Kathleen Devlin Culver: kculver@audiology.org; URL: http://
www.audiologyfoundation.org

Foundation type: Public charity
Purpose: Research grants to qualified graduate and post graduate students pursuing a career in audiology and the hearing sciences.
Publications: Application guidelines; Informational brochure.
Financial data: Year ended 06/30/2012. Assets, $750,550 (M); Expenditures, $189,137; Total giving, $93,839; Grants to individuals, totaling $4,900.
Type of support: Research; Postdoctoral support; Graduate support; Travel grants.
Application information: Applications accepted. Application form required.
  Initial approach: Proposal
  Deadline(s): Oct.
  Final notification: Applicants notified in Dec.

Program descriptions:

ARO Travel Awards: Two awards of $500 each to defray travel and lodging costs associated with attendance at the foundation's annual meeting.

James Jerger Awards for Excellence in Student Research: Four students who display their research posters at AudiologyNOW! receive a $500 award for outstanding research from the foundation.

New Investigator Research Award: Awards up to $10,000 to investigators who have recently completed a doctoral degree in audiology and do not have significant sources of research funding.

Student Investigator Research Award: Awards up to $5,000 to graduate students working towards a degree in audiology who wish to complete a research project as a part of their course study.

Student Summer Research Fellowship: Awards a stipend of $2,500 to senior undergraduate students or students currently enrolled in a graduate program in audiology who wish to gain a limited, but significant, exposure to a research environment.
EIN: 621356696

9288
American Academy of Otolaryngic Allergy Foundation

11130 Sunrise Valley Dr., Ste. 100
Reston, VA 20191-5474 (202) 955-5010
Contact: Jami Lucas, C.E.O. and Exec. Dir.
Application address: 11130 Sunrise Valley Dr., Ste. 100, Reston, VA 20191,
e-mail: meetings@aaoaf.org
FAX: (202) 955-5016; E-mail: info@aaoaf.org;
URL: http://www.aaoaf.org

Foundation type: Public charity
Purpose: Research grants to investigators for studies within otolaryngology, focusing on allergy and related inflammatory disease.
Publications: Application guidelines.
Financial data: Year ended 12/31/2011. Assets, $5,219,267 (M); Expenditures, $114,140; Total giving, $54,041; Grants to individuals, totaling $54,041.
Fields of interest: Allergies research.
Type of support: Research; Grants to individuals.
Application information: Applications accepted. Application form required. Application form available on the grantmaker's web site.
  Send request by: Mail, e-mail, or fax
  Deadline(s): June 30 and Dec. 31 for Research Grant, Dec. 31 for ROAD Scholarship Program
  Additional information: See web site for additional guidelines.
Program descriptions:
Research in Otolaryngology & Allergy Development (ROAD) Scholarship Program: The scholarship was developed by the AAOA to partner resident researchers with mentors in order to help develop research in allergy, immunology, inflammatory process, and related respiratory disease. Scholarships of up to $5,000 are available. Grants are considered based on scientific merit and feasibility.
Resident Travel Grants: The travel grant assists residents with costs, the AAOA will offer a stipend award that includes course registration and a monetary award for travel costs. Priority will be given to residents that have not previously been awarded a travel grant.
EIN: 222480270

9289
American Alliance for Health, Physical Education, Recreation, and Dance

1900 Association Dr.
Reston, VA 20191-1598 (703) 476-3400
Contact: E. Paul Roetert, C.E.O.
FAX: (703) 476-9527; Toll-free tel.: (800) 213-7193; URL: http://www.aahperd.org

Foundation type: Public charity
Purpose: Scholarships to undergraduate and graduate students enrolled in health education programs.
Publications: Application guidelines; Informational brochure.
Financial data: Year ended 08/31/2011. Assets, $8,876,596 (M); Expenditures, $13,717,615; Total giving, $3,908,080; Grants to individuals, totaling $12,050.
Fields of interest: Higher education.
Type of support: Graduate support; Undergraduate support.
Application information: Applications accepted. Application form required.
  Additional information: See web site for application guidelines.
EIN: 520886491

9290
American Anthropological Association

2200 Wilson Blvd., Ste. 600
Arlington, VA 22201-3357 (703) 528-1902
Contact: Bill Davis, Exec. Dir.
FAX: (703) 528-3546; URL: http://www.aaanet.org

Foundation type: Public charity
Purpose: Awards and grants to foster, support, and promote the professional interests of anthropologists and the field of anthropology.
Publications: Application guidelines; Annual report; Financial statement.
Financial data: Year ended 12/31/2011. Assets, $11,919,903 (M); Expenditures, $5,023,479; Total giving, $109,039; Grants to individuals, totaling $93,589.
Fields of interest: Anthropology/sociology.
Type of support: Fellowships; Research; Grants to individuals.
Application information: Applications accepted.
  Initial approach: Letter
  Deadline(s): Varies
  Additional information: See web site for complete program information.
Program descriptions:
AAA Leadership Mentoring/Shadow Award Program: This program provides a unique opportunity for young professional anthropologists to learn about the association and leadership opportunities, and to encourage future leadership in the association. Anthropologists who are three to five years beyond the completion of their terminal graduate degree are encouraged to apply. Three to five awardees will be paired with a mentor and be awarded a $500 travel subsidy to attend the association's annual meeting. Eligible applicants must be members of the association.
AAA Minority Dissertation Fellowship Program: Awards a $10,000 writing fellowship to minority doctoral candidates in anthropology. Applicants must be U.S. citizens; a member of an historically underrepresented ethnic minority group, including, but not limited to: African Americans, Alaskan Natives, American Indians or Native Americans, Asian Americans, Latinos/as, Chicanos/as, and Pacific Islanders. Applicants must be enrolled in a full-time academic program leading to a doctoral degree in anthropology at the time of application,

admitted to degree candidacy before the dissertation fellowship is awarded, and be a member of the American Anthropological Association.
AAA/Oxford University Press Award for Excellence in Undergraduate Teaching of Anthropology: This award, given in conjunction with Oxford University Press, recognizes teachers who have contributed to and encouraged the study of anthropology. Awardees will receive a stipend to travel to the association's annual meeting.
Anthropology in Public Policy Award: This biennial award of $500 honors anthropologists whose work has had a significant, positive influence on the course of government decision-making and action.
David M. Schneider Award: The $1,000 award is given in recognition of an original graduate student essay that treats one or more of the topics kinship, cultural theory, and American culture in a fresh and innovative fashion.
Margaret Mead Award: The award is presented to younger scholar for a particular accomplishment, such as a book, film, monograph, or service, which interprets anthropological data and principles in ways that make them meaningful to a broadly concerned public.
Solon T. Kimball Award for Public and Applied Anthropology: This $1,000 award, presented every other year, honors exemplary anthropologists for outstanding recent achievements that have contributed to the development of anthropology as an applied science and have had important impacts on public policy. Nominations can be submitted for individuals or a team (including collaborators outside of anthropology), and is not restricted by nationality, anthropological specialization, or type of employment. The anthropological contribution may be theoretical or methodological; impacts on public policy may be in any area, domestic or international (such as biodiversity, climate change, energy, international relations, medicine, public health, language conservation, education, criminal justice, development, or cultural heritage. Nominations recognizing disciplinary path-breakers who are shaping and strengthening the discipline of anthropology, and which honor those who might otherwise be overlooked, are especially encouraged.
EIN: 530246691

9291
American Association for the Study of Liver Diseases

(also known as AASLD)
1001 N. Fairfax, Ste. 400
Alexandria, VA 22314-2742 (703) 299-9766
Contact: Nellie Sarkissian, C.O.O.
FAX: (703) 299-9622; E-mail: aasld@aasld.org;
E-Mail for Nellie Sarkissian : nsarkissian@aasld.org; URL: http://www.aasld.org

Foundation type: Public charity
Purpose: Fellowships to young investigators, nurse practitioners and physician assistants for training in advanced clinical hepatology.
Publications: Grants list; Newsletter.
Financial data: Year ended 12/31/2011. Assets, $43,670,574 (M); Expenditures, $10,805,001; Total giving, $1,948,250.
Fields of interest: Liver research.
Type of support: Fellowships.
Application information: Applications accepted.
  Additional information: Contact association for further application information.
EIN: 237373091

9292
American Association of Airport Executives Foundation

(also known as AAAE Foundation)
601 Madison St., Ste. 400
Alexandria, VA 22314-1756 (703) 824-0500
Contact: Kelly Johnson, Chair.
FAX: (703) 820-1395; URL: http://www.aaae.org/about_aaae/
aaae_foundationscholarship_program/

Foundation type: Public charity
Purpose: Scholarships to full-time undergraduate or graduate students attending accredited colleges or universities.
Publications: Application guidelines.
Financial data: Year ended 12/31/2011. Assets, $2,138,871 (M); Expenditures, $190,193; Total giving, $168,383; Grants to individuals, totaling $168,383.
Fields of interest: Higher education; Space/aviation; Native Americans/American Indians.
Type of support: Scholarships—to individuals.
Application information: Application form required.
  Deadline(s): Mar. 31
  Additional information: Contact the scholarship or financial aid office at the college you attend for additional scholarship information.
Program descriptions:
  AAAE Foundation Scholarship for Native Americans: Ten $1,000 scholarships are granted each year to a number of students with a junior class standing or higher, who are enrolled in an aviation program and have a GPA of 3.0 or higher. Eligibility is unrelated to membership in AAAE. Only one student from each school is eligible to participate. Criteria for the scholarship are academic records, financial need, participation in school and community activities, work experience, and a personal statement. A recommendation from the school is also required.
  AAAE Foundation Scholarships: Ten $1,000 scholarships are granted each year to a number of students with a junior class standing or higher, who are enrolled in an aviation program and have a GPA of 3.0 or higher. Only one student from each school is eligible to participate. Criteria for the scholarship are academic records, financial need, participation in school and community activities, work experience, and a personal statement. A recommendation from the school is also required.
  Scholarship Program: Students are eligible for scholarships ranging from $900 to $4,000 if they, their spouse, or one of their parents is an active American airport executive.
EIN: 516018128

9293
American Association of School Administrators

(also known as AASA)
1615 Duke St.
Alexandria, VA 22314-3406 (703) 528-0700
Contact: Daniel A. Domenech, Exec. Dir.
Additional e-mail for scholarships:
tributeaward@aasa.org
FAX: (703) 841-1543; E-mail: info@aasa.org;
Additional e-mail: awards@aasa.org; URL: http://www.aasa.org

Foundation type: Public charity
Purpose: Scholarships to high school juniors to attend accredited post high school education or training institute in any career field.
Publications: Application guidelines; Annual report.
Financial data: Year ended 06/30/2012. Assets, $12,998,417 (M); Expenditures, $10,252,393.

Fields of interest: Higher education.
Type of support: Scholarships—to individuals.
Application information: Applications accepted. Application form required. Application form available on the grantmaker's web site.
  Additional information: Contact your guidance office for application materials or see web site for additional guidelines.
Program descriptions:
  American Education Award: This award honors an outstanding American citizen who has distinguished herself or himself through excellence in any profession, and who serves as a role model and teacher to others.
  Distinguished Service Award: These awards are given annually to retired association members who exhibit exemplary leadership throughout their careers and who have enhanced the profession of school administration.
  Dr. Effie H. Jones Humanitarian Award: This award recognize association members who exemplify the professional qualities of advocacy, support, mentorship, and encouragement of diversity in educational leadership.
  Educational Administration Scholarship: These $2,500 scholarships provide incentive, honor, and financial assistance to outstanding graduate students in school administration who intend to make school superintendency a career. A $500 travel allowance is also provided.
  National Superintendent of the Year Program: Co-sponsored with ARAMARK Education, this program seeks to pays tribute to the talent and vision of the men and women who lead the nation's public schools. This program is open to all U.S. public school superintendents and superintendents of American schools abroad who plan to continue in the profession; anyone can nominate a superintendent for this program, including a school board president, parent, community leader, or another superintendent. In addition to other awards, the National Superintendent of the Year presents a $10,000 scholarship to a student in the high school from which he/she graduated.
EIN: 541999773

9294
American College of Toxicology

1821 Michael Faraday Dr., Ste. 300
Reston, VA 20190 (703) 547-0875
Contact: Carol Lemire, Exec. Dir.
FAX: (703) 438-3113; E-mail: acthq@actox.org;
Additional e-mail: clemire@actox.org; URL: http://www.actox.org

Foundation type: Public charity
Purpose: Awards for outstanding toxicology research and travel grants for students.
Publications: Newsletter; Occasional report.
Financial data: Year ended 12/31/2011. Assets, $2,385,172 (M); Expenditures, $823,217; Total giving, $8,000; Grants to individuals, totaling $7,000.
Fields of interest: Medical research.
Type of support: Research; Travel grants.
Application information: Applications accepted. Application form required. Application form available on the grantmaker's web site.
  Initial approach: Application
  Deadline(s): Aug. 1 for ACT Student Travel Awards, Sept. 1 for ACT President's Award for Best Paper Published in the IJT
  Additional information: See web site for additional guidelines.
Program descriptions:
  ACT President's Award for Best Paper Published in the International Journal of Toxicology: Each year,

the International Journal of Toxicology recognizes the authors of the best paper published in the journal with a check for $1,000 and a citation certificate. A paper may be nominated by anyone. Papers that may be considered for this award are those that were published in IJT issues numbers 5 and 6 of the previous year through and including IJT issue number 4 (July to Aug.) of the current year.
  Student Travel Awards: Students are required to attend the annual meeting where students will present their poster at the general posted session in addition to a separate judging session for selection of the Furst Award winner. The Student Travel Award consists of $1,000 cash prize and a certificate. Graduate students may apply for this award.
EIN: 363007817

9295
American Council of the Blind, Inc.

2200 Wilson Blvd., Ste. 650
Arlington, VA 22201-3354 (202) 467-5081
Contact: Ray Campbell, Exec. Dir.
FAX: (703) 465-5085; E-mail: info@acb.org;
Toll-free tel.: (800) 424-8666; additional address (Minneapolis office): 6300 Shingle Creek Pkwy., Ste. 105, Brooklyn Center, MN 55430-2124;
URL: http://www.acb.org

Foundation type: Public charity
Purpose: Undergraduate and graduate scholarships to provide financial assistance to outstanding blind and visually impaired students.
Publications: Application guidelines; Annual report; Financial statement; Informational brochure; Newsletter.
Financial data: Year ended 12/31/2011. Assets, $3,834,727 (M); Expenditures, $1,485,580; Total giving, $31,025; Grants to individuals, totaling $31,025.
Fields of interest: Eye diseases; Disabilities, people with.
Type of support: Graduate support; Undergraduate support.
Application information: Applications accepted. Application form required.
  Initial approach: Letter, telephone, or e-mail
  Deadline(s): Mar.
EIN: 580914436

9296
American Counseling Association Foundation

5999 Stevenson Ave.
Alexandria, VA 22304-3304 (703) 823-9800
URL: http://www.acafoundation.org/

Foundation type: Public charity
Purpose: Grants to support counselors in pursuit of their professional career.
Publications: Application guidelines.
Financial data: Year ended 06/30/2011. Assets, $140,941 (M); Expenditures, $74,606; Total giving, $12,230; Grants to individuals, totaling $12,230.
Type of support: Grants to individuals.
Application information: Applications accepted.
  Initial approach: Telephone
  Additional information: Contact foundation for complete program information.
EIN: 510252372

9297
American Diabetes Association
1701 N. Beauregard St.
Alexandria, VA 22311-1742 (703) 549-1500
Contact: Larry Hausner M.B.A., C.E.O.
FAX: (703) 549-1715;
E-mail: research@diabetes.org; Toll-free tel.: (800) 342-2383; URL: http://www.diabetes.org

Foundation type: Public charity
Purpose: Awards and fellowships for research on diabetes.
Publications: Application guidelines; Annual report; Corporate giving report; Financial statement; Informational brochure; Newsletter; Occasional report; Program policy statement.
Financial data: Year ended 12/31/2011. Assets, $113,516,741 (M); Expenditures, $193,104,772; Total giving, $30,664,039; Grants to individuals, totaling $147,607.
Fields of interest: Eye research; Diabetes research.
Type of support: Professorships; Research; Awards/prizes; Postdoctoral support; Doctoral support.
Application information: Applications accepted. Application form required. Application form available on the grantmaker's web site.
> *Initial approach:* Telephone or e-mail
> *Deadline(s):* Jan. 15 and July 15
> *Additional information:* See web site for complete program information.

Program descriptions:
Development Awards: Awards supporting faculty members' research in diabetes range from $120,000 to $200,000. See web site for further information.
General Research Awards: Multiple awards supporting researchers in diabetes are available to both new and established investigators. Awards range from $50,000 to $200,000. See web site for additional information.
Targeted Awards: Multi-year awards are available to basic and clinical researchers of diabetes. Awards range from $200,000 to $600,000 annually. See web site for additional information.
Training Awards: Awards supporting student research in diabetes at the undergraduate, graduate, and postdoctoral level range from $3,000 to $75,000. Some awards are renewable for up to four years. See web site for additional information.
EIN: 131623888

9298
American Diabetes Association Research Foundation, Inc.
1701 N. Beauregard St.
Alexandria, VA 22311-1742 (703) 549-1500
Contact: Larry Hausner M.B.A., C.E.O.
E-mail: mprice@diabetes.org; Toll-free tel.: (800) 342-2383; URL: http://www.diabetes.org/diabetes-research/ADA-Research-Foundation/researchfoundation.jsp

Foundation type: Public charity
Purpose: Grants and awards for diabetes research, and for the support of investigators in all stages of their careers.
Financial data: Year ended 12/31/2012. Assets, $35,154,688; Expenditures, $36,546,004; Total giving, $35,546,004; Grants to individuals, totaling $132,798.
Fields of interest: Diabetes research.
Type of support: Grants to individuals; Awards/prizes.

Application information: Applications accepted. Application form required.
> *Deadline(s):* July 15 for Core Research and Development Awards, Jan. 15 for Core Training Awards, vary for Targeted Awards
> *Additional information:* See web site for additional application guidelines.

EIN: 541734511

9299
American Floral Endowment
1601 Duke St.
Alexandria, VA 22314-3406 (703) 838-5211
Contact: Debi Aker, Mgr.
FAX: (703) 838-5212; E-mail: afe@endowment.org; URL: http://www.endowment.org

Foundation type: Public charity
Purpose: Scholarships and internships for students studying floriculture and horticulture. Sabbatical leave grants for persons in research, extension, or teaching to leave the home university for professional development. Research grants to benefit the floral industry.
Publications: Application guidelines; Annual report; Informational brochure; Newsletter.
Financial data: Year ended 06/30/2011. Assets, $14,712,634 (M); Expenditures, $593,286; Total giving, $306,702; Grants to individuals, totaling $306,702.
Fields of interest: Horticulture/garden clubs.
Type of support: Professorships; Internship funds; Research; Undergraduate support.
Application information: Applications accepted. Application form required. Application form available on the grantmaker's web site.
> *Send request by:* Online
> *Deadline(s):* Feb. 1 for Paul Ecke Jr., Scholarship, Mar. 1 and Oct. 1 for Mosmiller Intern Scholarship and May 1 for all others
> *Applicants should submit the following:*
> 1) Transcripts
> 2) Letter(s) of recommendation
> *Additional information:* Applicants for sabbaticals must submit request 12 to 24 months previous to time requested.

Program descriptions:
Ball Horticultural Company Scholarship: This scholarship is intended for junior or senior college or university students pursuing a career in commercial floriculture.
Bioworks IPM/Sustainable Practices Scholarship: This scholarship is intended for students pursuing a career in floriculture. Students will be selected on the basis of sound academic performance and a grade point average of 3.0 or better. While not mandatory, it is strongly desired that the student be interested in furthering the use of integrated pest management (IPM) or sustainable practices.
Earl Dedman Memorial Scholarship: This scholarship is awarded to students who are interested in becoming greenhouse growers, are from the northwestern United States, and have sophomore, junior, or senior status.
Ed Markham International Scholarship: The scholarship operates in cooperation with the David Colegrave Foundation in London, England. Each year there will be an exchange of students between the U.S. and Europe, alternating between the two countries. $3,500 scholarships will be made to U.S. students in even numbered years.
Edward Tuinier Memorial Scholarship: This scholarship is awarded to sophomore, junior, or senior undergraduate students enrolled in the floriculture program at Michigan State University.
Fran Johnson Non-Traditional Scholarship: This scholarship goes to students re-entering school

after a minimum five-year absence, who have an interest in bedding and/or floral crops.
Jacob van Namen Marketing Scholarship: This scholarship requires students to have a career interest in agribusiness marketing and distribution of floral products, and be of sophomore, junior, or senior standing.
James Bridenbaugh Memorial Scholarship: This scholarship is for a sophomore, junior, or senior student who is pursuing a career in floral design and marketing of fresh flowers and plants.
James K. Rathmell, Jr. Memorial Scholarship for Horticultural Work/Study Abroad: This scholarship is awarded to junior- or senior-level undergraduates or graduate students who have a specific plan for horticulture work/study outside of the U.S.
John Carew Memorial Scholarship: This scholarship is open to graduate students in horticulture with an interest in greenhouse crops.
John L. Tomasovic, Sr. Scholarship: This scholarship offers consideration for sophomore, junior, or senior undergraduate students with financial need and a grade point average between 3.0 and 3.5.
Lawrence "Bud" Ohlman Memorial Scholarship: This scholarship goes to students with the career goal to become a bedding plant grower for an established business.
Long Island Flower Growers Association (LIFGA) Scholarship: The scholarship is intended for students in the Long Island/New York area studying ornamental horticulture at a community college or a four-year institution.
Mike and Flo Novovesky Scholarship: This scholarship fund aims to help young married students who are working to put themselves through college and have a GPA of 2.5 or higher. Depending on the availability of married applicants, the scholarship may also go to an undergraduate working his or her way through school with financial need and family obligations. Priorities include horticulture and financial need.
Mosmiller Intern Scholarship Program: This program provides retail, wholesale, or allied trade paid internship experiences to floriculture or business students enrolled at two- or four-year schools/universities. Seven awards are available annually, and each includes paid training for 10 to 14 weeks and a $2,000 cash award upon completion.
National Greenhouse Manufacturers Association Scholarships: This program targets students majoring in horticulture and bioengineering or the equivalent, and are at least a junior at an accredited four-year college maintaining a 3.0 GPA.
Paul Ecke, Jr. MS/PhD Floriculture Scholarship: This merit-based scholarship is awarded to an applicant who has completed or is in the process of successfully completing either a BS or MS degree in Horticulture or a related field, such as Agricultural Engineering, Entomology, Agricultural Marketing and Economics, or Plant Pathology, at a U.S. Land-Grant University. The applicant must have the intention of pursuing an MS or PhD degree on a full-time basis in a selected floricultural area and under the direction of a world-renowned floriculture scientist. The recipient, provided s/he makes satisfactory academic progress, will receive a stipend of $8,000 per academic year, for two years in an MS program or three years in a PhD program.
Seed Companies Scholarship: This scholarship requires students to have a career goal within the seed industry, and be junior- or senior-level undergraduates or graduate students.
Vic and Margaret Ball Internship Program: This program provides paid internship experiences to full-time students enrolled in either two- or four-year schools/universities interested in a career in

commercial production (grower). Interns are provided with a scholarship at the end of their internship for the following amounts: $1,500 for a three-month internship, $3,000 for a four-month internship, and $6,000 for a six-month internship.

Vocational (Bettinger, Holden, and Perry) Scholarship: This scholarship requires students to be in a one- or two-year program with the intent to become a grower or greenhouse manager.
EIN: 236268380

9300
American Foundation for Pharmaceutical Education
2107 Wilson Blvd., Ste. 700
Arlington, VA 22201-3042   (703) 875-3095
Contact: Ellen L. Woods, Pres. and Secy.
FAX: (703) 875-3098; E-mail: info@afpenet.org;
URL: http://www.afpenet.org

Foundation type: Public charity
Purpose: Scholarships and fellowships to undergraduate and graduate students, as well as research grants for pharmaceutical studies.
Financial data: Year ended 12/31/2011. Assets, $9,036,676 (M); Expenditures, $859,868; Total giving, $412,462; Grants to individuals, totaling $412,462.
Fields of interest: Health sciences school/education; Pharmacy/prescriptions.
Type of support: Program development; Scholarships—to individuals; Graduate support; Undergraduate support; Doctoral support.
Application information: Applications accepted. Application form required. Application form available on the grantmaker's web site.
   Initial approach: Letter or telephone
   Additional information: See web site for complete program information.
Program descriptions:
   First Year Graduate School Scholarships: Outstanding pharmacy school graduates who are members of Kappa Epsilon, Phi Lambda Sigma and Rho Chi are encouraged to continue their advanced education in graduate school in the pharmaceutical sciences to gain advanced degrees (Ph.D.) of value to the pharmaceutical industry and pharmacy through these scholarships.
   Pharmacy Faculty Development Fellowship in Community Pharmacy Practice: Outstanding pharmacy college faculty members are provided a one-time grant matched by their institution to support a six-month faculty research or faculty development project. This grant program enhances the number and quality of pharmacy faculty committed to research and teaching in the academic pharmacy setting.
   Pharmacy Faculty Development Fellowship in Geriatric Pharmacy: Outstanding pharmacy college faculty members are provided a one-time grant matched by their institution to support a six-month faculty research or faculty development project. This grant program enhances the number and quality of pharmacy faculty committed to research and teaching in the academic pharmacy setting.
   Pre-doctoral Fellowships in Clinical Pharmaceutical Science: Outstanding Pharm.D. graduates who have completed one or more post-doctoral residencies or fellowships can receive up to two years of support to obtain advanced education and training in relevant areas of the biomedical and related basic sciences in order to become competent clinical scientists through this program. A separate fellowships is available to minority candidates.
   Pre-doctoral Graduate Fellowships in the Pharmaceutical Sciences: Outstanding advanced

Ph.D. candidates receive two to three years of support for the Ph.D. degree in the pharmaceutical sciences at a U.S. school or college of pharmacy through this program. Graduates move into professional positions in the pharmaceutical industry and into academic positions to train tomorrow's pharmacists and pharmaceutical scientists. Separate fellowships are available to minority students.
EIN: 530214882

9301
American Friends of Eton College, Inc.
7521 Royal Oak Dr.
McLean, VA 22102-2114
Contact: Henry D. Edelman, Dir.
E-mail: AFEtonC@aol.com

Foundation type: Independent foundation
Purpose: Scholarship award for a U.S. student to attend Eton College, Windsor, England.
Financial data: Year ended 12/31/2012. Assets, $172,006 (M); Expenditures, $488,406; Total giving, $487,841.
Fields of interest: Higher education.
Type of support: Scholarships—to individuals.
Application information:
   Initial approach: E-mail
   Deadline(s): Jan. 31
   Additional information: The foundation accepts use of the U.S. Common Application for Undergraduate College Admissions form, with Eton College addendum. Applicant must be a U.S. student.
EIN: 522273240

9302
American Indian Youth Running Strong, Inc.
(also known as Running Strong for American Indian Youth)
8301 Richmond Hwy.
Alexandria, VA 22309   (703) 317-9881
Contact: Katsi Cook, Exec. Dir.
FAX: (703) 317-9690; E-mail: info@indianyouth.org;
Toll Free Tel. : (888)-491-9859; URL: http://www.indianyouth.org

Foundation type: Public charity
Purpose: Emergency utility assistance and grants for other basic necessities primarily to needy American Indians.
Publications: Application guidelines; Annual report; Financial statement; Informational brochure; Newsletter.
Financial data: Year ended 06/30/2012. Assets, $1,423,021 (M); Expenditures, $3,661,149; Total giving, $2,868,122; Grants to individuals, totaling $90,038.
Fields of interest: Native Americans/American Indians.
Type of support: Emergency funds; Grants for special needs.
Application information: Applications accepted. Application form required.
   Initial approach: Letter or telephone
EIN: 541594578

9303
American Medical Student Association Foundation
45610 Woodland Rd., Ste. 300
Sterling, VA 20166-4220   (703) 620-6600
Contact: Nida Degesys, Pres.
FAX: (703) 620-6445;
E-mail: foundation@amsa.org; Toll-Free Tel.: (800) 767-2266; E-mail For NIda Degesys: pres@amsa.org; URL: http://www.amsafoundation.org

Foundation type: Public charity
Purpose: Fellowship program to introduce medical students to end of life (EOL) care issues.
Financial data: Year ended 04/30/2012. Assets, $1,706,278 (M); Expenditures, $562,359.
Fields of interest: End of life care.
Type of support: Fellowships; Grants to individuals.
Application information: Applications accepted. Application form required.
   Send request by: Mail or e-mail
   Deadline(s): Mar. 22
   Final notification: Recipients notified in Apr.
   Applicants should submit the following:
      1) Letter(s) of recommendation
      2) Resume
      3) Curriculum vitae
      4) Essay
   Additional information: See web site for additional application guidelines.
Program descriptions:
   End of Life Education Fellowship: The fellowship is a six-week summer experience designed to introduce fourteen to sixteen medical students to end-of-life care issues. Students will be part of an interdisciplinary hospice team consisting of doctors, nurses, social workers, chaplains, bereavement counselors, and volunteers. A stipend will be provided to cover most living expenses; there are no funds involved other than paying the student a $375 weekly stipend while they participate in the six-week program (i.e. no flexibility to apply for funds or design own program)
   Widening the Pipeline Mini-Grants: The initiative encourages medical and dental students to go into local middle and high schools to talk to students about health careers and funding is available to assist with program costs. Individual medical or dental students as well as student groups are eligible to apply. Applicants may apply for up to $200 in funding.
EIN: 366116589

9304
American Physical Therapy Association
1111 N. Fairfax St.
Alexandria, VA 22314-1488   (703) 684-2782
Contact: John D. Barnes, C.E.O.
FAX: (703) 684-7343; Toll-free tel.: (800) 999-2782; TDD: (703) 683-6748; URL: http://www.apta.org

Foundation type: Public charity
Purpose: Scholarships in the field of physical therapy to faculty pursuing a post-professional doctoral degree and students who are members of a minority group. Also, grants for research in the field of physical therapy.
Publications: Annual report; Occasional report.
Financial data: Year ended 12/31/2011. Assets, $35,139,405 (M); Expenditures, $36,887,908; Total giving, $1,333,082; Grants to individuals, totaling $42,238.
Fields of interest: Physical therapy; Minorities.
Type of support: Research; Graduate support; Undergraduate support; Doctoral support.

Application information: Applications accepted. Application form required. Application form available on the grantmaker's web site.

> *Copies of proposal:* 7
> *Deadline(s):* Dec. 2
> *Applicants should submit the following:*
> 1) Curriculum vitae
> 2) Essay
> 3) Transcripts

EIN: 131512769

9305
American Psychiatric Publishing, Inc.

(formerly American Psychiatric Association)
1000 Wilson Blvd., Ste. 1825
Arlington, VA   22209-3924   (703) 907-7300
Contact: Paul Burke, Exec. Dir.
FAX: (703) 907-1091; E-mail: appi@psych.org;
Toll-free tel.: (800) 368-5777; URL: http://www.appi.org

Foundation type: Public charity
Purpose: Fellowships and awards to outstanding members of the psychiatric community.
Publications: Newsletter.
Financial data: Year ended 12/31/2011. Assets, $56,448,535 (M); Expenditures, $6,178,469; Total giving, $1,274,609; Grants to individuals, totaling $83,716.
Fields of interest: Psychology/behavioral science; Government/public administration; Minorities.
Type of support: Fellowships; Research; Awards/prizes; Travel grants; Stipends.
Application information: Application form required.
> *Additional information:* Contact foundation for additional application guidelines.

Program description:
> *Awards:* Several awards are offered to individuals, groups, or organizations that have made outstanding efforts or contributions to the field of psychiatry.

EIN: 130433740

9306
American Roentgen Ray Society

44221 Slatestone Ct.
Leesburg, VA   20176-5109   (703) 729-3353
Contact: Susan Brown Cappitelli, Exec. Dir.
FAX: (703) 729-4839; Toll-free tel.: (800) 438-2777; URL: http://www.arrs.org

Foundation type: Public charity
Purpose: Scholarships and awards to deserving individuals in advancing medicine through the science of radiology and its allied sciences.
Publications: Application guidelines; Occasional report.
Financial data: Year ended 12/31/2011. Assets, $16,285,630 (M); Expenditures, $7,777,491; Total giving, $318,200; Grants to individuals, totaling $318,200.
Fields of interest: Science.
Type of support: Scholarships—to individuals; Awards/prizes.
Application information: Applications accepted.
> *Send request by:* E-mail
> *Deadline(s):* Vary
> *Additional information:* See web site or contact the society for eligibility determination.

Program descriptions:
> *ARRS Annual Scholarship Program:* This scholarship is intended to support study in a field selected by the scholar that will enable the scholar to attain his or her professional career goal. A maximum of two scholarships of $140,000 will be funded. Scholars may choose a one-year program

requiring a minimum 80 percent time commitment, or a two-year program requiring a minimum 50 percent time commitment. The funds may be used for salary support, toward the support of the scholar's study or in a way that will contribute to the scholars development and advancement as an academic faculty member. The money may not be spent for the purchase of equipment. Indirect costs may not be paid from this fund.
> *ARRS/Leonard Berlin Scholarship in Medical Professionalism:* These scholarships are intended to support the study and research related to medical ethics, medico-legal principles, patient accountability, sensitivity to patient diversity, and/or topics encompassing medical professionalism. Scholars may choose either a one-year program requiring a minimum 50 percent time commitment to be funded at $100,000, or a two-year program requiring a minimum 25 percent time commitment to be funded at $50,000 each year. Up to $20,000 of the funds may be used in a way that will contribute to the scholar's development and professional advancement, such as tuition and course materials, with the remainder to be used towards salary support. The money may not be spent for the purchase of equipment, or imaging studies. Indirect costs may not be paid from this fund. One scholar will be selected annually.
> *Lee F. Rogers International Fellowship in Radiology Journalism:* The society offers one-month annual fellowships in radiology journalism in the editorial and publications offices of the American Journal of Roentgenology in Birmingham, Alabama. Radiologists practicing abroad are eligible. Successful candidates will each be awarded $12,000, which includes the cost of travel to the editorial and publications offices, living expenses for the month, and an honorarium.
> *Melvin M. Figley Fellowship in Radiology Journalism:* The program offers one-month annual fellowships in radiology journalism in the editorial and publications offices of the American Journal of Roentgenology in Birmingham, Alabama. Radiologists practicing in the U.S. and Canada are eligible for fellowship support every year. Successful candidates will each be awarded $12,000, which includes the cost of travel to the editorial and publications offices, living expenses for the month, and an honorarium.
> *Residents in Radiology Awards:* The awards are available to residents and fellows in radiology and radiological sciences. One of the three awards may be given to a fellow. The President's Award is $2,000, and the Executive Council Awards are $1,000 each.

EIN: 580838728

9307
American Society for Industrial Security Foundation

(also known as ASIS Foundation)
1625 Prince St.
Alexandria, VA   22314-2882   (703) 519-6200
Contact: Robert Rowe, Dir., Devel.
FAX: (703) 519-6299;
E-mail: foundation@asisonline.org; URL: https://www.asisfoundation.org/Pages/default.aspx

Foundation type: Public charity
Purpose: Scholarships to those who are interested in the security profession and who have demonstrated potential to make a contribution to the field of business security. Scholarships by nomination only to those who wish to be a Certified Protection Professional.
Publications: Application guidelines; Informational brochure; Newsletter.

Financial data: Year ended 12/31/2011. Assets, $755,919 (M); Expenditures, $150,516; Total giving, $43,700; Grants to individuals, totaling $43,700.
Fields of interest: Association.
Type of support: Awards/prizes; Graduate support; Undergraduate support.
Application information: Applications accepted. Application form required.
> *Initial approach:* E-mail
> *Deadline(s):* Nov. 30 for Matching Scholarship, Dec. 4 for Student Writing Competition, Dec. 7 for Walsh APC I Award, Jan. 1 for Cross Awards
> *Applicants should submit the following:*
> 1) Letter(s) of recommendation
> 2) Transcripts
> *Additional information:* Application must be signed by ASIS chapter officer and faxed to foundation. See web site for additional information.

Program descriptions:
> *Allan J. Cross Award:* This award, given in conjunction with PPM 2000, Inc., pays the registration fees for thirty society members to attend a certification review course of their choice. Eligible applicants must be society members in good standing who have not previously received the award, and must not be student members or national officers.
> *Matching Scholarships:* Matches one scholarship per chapter per year. Chapters providing scholarships receive one match dollar up to $500 per year. Recipients who are either full- or part-time students are designated at the local chapter level.
> *Roy Bordes Award for Physical Security:* This award pays for a two-day, locally-delivered physical security program for one society chapter each year. Awards cover the costs of instructors, their travel and accommodations, and collateral materials; meeting expenses will be the host chapter's responsibility. Eligible chapters must: have a strong education program, including diverse and plentiful programs on the chapter calendar, and member attendance at society-sponsored programs; support the award by identifying an award champion, capacity to host the program, and a budget for on-site expenses; demonstrate a commitment to its own expansion, including ascending membership numbers and a strategic plan for continued growth; and commit to holding the program within the award year.
> *Student Writing Competition:* Awarded in conjunction with the ASIS Council on Academic Programs in Colleges and Universities, this competition rewards students who conduct research, engage in thoughtful deliberation, and write an academic paper on an issue relevant to the security and assets protection profession. Undergraduate and graduate students compete in separate essay contests; topics are announced on the foundation's web site. Undergraduate winners receive $1,000, while graduate winners receive $1,500; two students will also receive honorable mention awards of $500 each.
> *Timothy J. Walsh APC I Award:* This award pays tuition, transportation, and hotel costs (room fees and taxes for five nights) for a society member to attend an assets protection course (APC). Applicants must be nominated by their chapter, be members in good standing of the society, have not already attended an APC I course, and have at least two years of security experience.

EIN: 520848090

9308
American Society of Clinical Oncology
2318 Mill Rd., Ste. 800
Alexandria, VA 22314-3498 (888) 282-2552
Grants and awards contact: grants@asco.org
FAX: (571) 483-1300;
E-mail: membermail@asco.org; URL: http://
www.asco.org

Foundation type: Public charity
Purpose: Awards and grants to oncologists and cancer researchers.
Financial data: Year ended 12/31/2011. Assets, $162,402,498 (M); Expenditures, $72,368,829; Total giving, $1,923,073.
Fields of interest: Research; Cancer; Cancer research; Medical research.
Type of support: Research; Grants to individuals; Awards/prizes.
Application information: Applications accepted. Application form required. Application form available on the grantmaker's web site.
  Initial approach: Letter, telephone or e-mail
  Deadline(s): Vary
  Applicants should submit the following:
    1) Proposal
    2) Essay
    3) Budget Information
  Additional information: Application must also include IRB approval and list of drugs to be used in research.
Program descriptions:
  David A. Karnofsky Memorial Award and Lecture: This award is presented annually to an individual in the name of David A. Karnofsky, MD in honor of his outstanding contribution to the research, in the diagnosis and or treatment of cancer. The recipient will receive a $25,000 honorarium.
  Distinguished Service Award for Scientific Achievement: Awards a $10,000 honorarium to recognize scientists, practitioners and researchers in all subspecialties of oncology and outstanding, long-term service to ASCO and to clinical oncology. This ward may only be awarded to an individual once.
  Distinguished Service Award for Scientific Leadership: Awards a $10,000 honorarium to a person or person's who have provided extraordinary broad-based leadership in the field of oncology that benefits ASCO members and their patients. This award may only be awarded to an individual once.
  Pediatrics Oncology Lectureship: This lectureship was created to recognize an outstanding pediatric oncologist who has demonstrated outstanding leadership or achievement in the field. The recipient will receive a $5,000 honorarium.
EIN: 136180380

9309
American Society of Consultant Pharmacists Foundation
(formerly American Society of Consultant Pharmacists Research & Education Foundation, also known as The ASCP Foundation)
1321 Duke St.
Alexandria, VA 22314-3507 (703) 739-1300
Contact: Lisa Gables, Exec. Dir.
FAX: (703) 739-1500;
E-mail: info@ascpfoundation.org; Toll-free tel.: (800) 355-2727; URL: http://
www.ascpfoundation.org/

Foundation type: Public charity
Purpose: Traineeships to individuals for pharmacy practice. Grants for pharmacists to establish or expand a fee-for-service component of their senior care pharmacy practice.

Publications: Application guidelines; Annual report; Informational brochure; Newsletter.
Financial data: Year ended 09/30/2011. Assets, $2,081,611 (M); Expenditures, $382,053.
Fields of interest: Pharmacy/prescriptions; Parkinson's disease.
Type of support: Research.
Application information: Applications accepted. Application form required.
  Initial approach: Telephone or e-mail
  Deadline(s): Varies
  Additional information: See web site for complete application information.
Program descriptions:
  Entrepreneur Grants: Seed money grants of up to $3,000 are available to pharmacists seeking to establish or expand a fee-for-service component of their senior care pharmacy practice. Eligible applicants must be active members of ASCP, currently licensed, and actively engaged in senior care pharmacy practice.
  Traineeships: Five-day traineeships are open to pharmacists from all practice settings in the following categories: pain management and Parkinson's disease. The trainees are responsible for all expenses related to travel, meals, and incidental expenses; hotel accommodations will be paid for by the foundation.
EIN: 541358129

9310
American Society of Military Comptrollers
415 N. Alfred St.
Alexandria, VA 22314-2269 (703) 549-0360
FAX: (703) 549-3181;
E-mail: asmchg@asmconline.org; Toll-free tel.: (800) 462-5637; Additional tel. for scholarships: (301) 227-6143; E-mail For Al Runnels: runnels@asmconline.org; URL: http://
www.asmconline.org

Foundation type: Public charity
Purpose: Scholarships to outstanding graduating high school seniors for academic achievement.
Publications: Annual report.
Financial data: Year ended 06/30/2012. Assets, $6,896,683 (M); Expenditures, $3,777,719; Total giving, $47,000; Grants to individuals, totaling $47,000.
Fields of interest: Business school/education; Computer science; Economics; Leadership development.
Type of support: Scholarships—to individuals.
Application information: Application form required. Application form available on the grantmaker's web site.
  Initial approach: Telephone
  Send request by: Mail
  Deadline(s): Mar. 31
  Applicants should submit the following:
    1) SAT
    2) ACT
    3) Financial information
    4) Letter(s) of recommendation
  Additional information: Application should also include copy of college acceptance letter, scholastic achievement, leadership ability, career and academic goals.
Program descriptions:
  Chapter Leadership Awards: The award recognizes individuals for outstanding continuous leadership, accomplishment and support of the society at the chapter level. Nominees must be members or corporate member designees of the society, must have been members for at least three full consecutive years prior to the submission due

date, and must be current members in good standing.
  Corporate Member Award: The award recognizes one corporate member for outstanding contributions made to a local chapter and the national society, in the furtherance of their goals. To be nominated for this award, a corporation must have been a corporate member of the society for at least two consecutive years.
  Individual Achievement Awards: The award recognizes individuals for outstanding accomplishment within one of the functional fields of comptrollership. Any military or civilian person(s), less than four individuals per nomination, currently employed by the Department of Defense or United States Coast Guard may be nominated. A member or non-member of the society may be nominated.
  Member's Essay Award: The award encourages increased authorship within the membership of the society and to provide an additional opportunity for publication in the Armed Forces Comptroller Program. Those entering must be society members in good standing. Winners of the award may have their essays published in the Armed Forces Comptroller magazine. The first-place winner will receive $750, the second-place winner will receive $500, and the third-place winner will receive $250.
  Members' Continuing Education Program: The program provides financial assistance to aid society members in continuing educational endeavors, and to encourage local chapter members' continuing education programs. Up to fifteen grants will be provided annually: ten at $1,000 each, and four awarded at $2,500 each. One winner will be selected as the Dick Vincent Scholarship winner for a $5,000 award.
  National Scholarship Program: The program recognizes outstanding graduating high school seniors for academic achievement, to provide financial assistance to seniors to help them accomplish their future financial management baccalaureate educational goals, and to increase the conduct of local chapter scholarship programs. Eleven scholarships will be awarded to graduating high school seniors: one $3,000 scholarship will be awarded in honor of LTG James F. McCall, former executive director of the society, and five $2,000 scholarships and five $1,000 scholarships will also be awarded.
  Team Achievement Award: The award recognizes a team for outstanding accomplishment within or across any of the functional fields of comptrollership. Any team of military, civilian, or civilian and military persons employed by the Department of Defense or the United States Coast Guard may be nominated.
EIN: 541025128

9311
American Society of Transplant Surgeons
(also known as ASTS)
2461 S. Clark St., Ste. 640
Arlington, VA 22202-3875 (703) 414-7870
Contact: Kim Gifford M.B.A., Exec. Dir.
FAX: (703) 414-7874; E-mail: asts@asts.org; E-mail for Kim Gifford M.B.A.: kim.gifford@asts.org; URL: http://www.asts.org

Foundation type: Public charity
Purpose: Grants and honoraria to society members who wish to perform research in the field of organ and tissue transplantation.
Publications: Application guidelines.
Financial data: Year ended 12/31/2011. Assets, $2,848,379 (M); Expenditures, $4,087,026; Total giving, $94,384.
Fields of interest: Surgery research.

Type of support: Research; Grants to individuals.
Application information: Applications accepted.
Application form required. Application form
available on the grantmaker's web site.

> *Initial approach:* Proposals
> *Send request by:* Online
> *Deadline(s):* Jan. 24
> *Applicants should submit the following:*
> 1) Curriculum vitae
> 2) Budget Information
> *Additional information:* Each award has specific
>   requirements, see web site for guidelines.

Program descriptions:

ASTS Advanced Transplant Provider Award: This
award recognizes the time and effort dedicated to
advancing clinical practice through the translation
of scientific information, the development of
standards, and clinical mentoring of the advanced
transplant provider, with a travel prize to the
society's State-of-the-Art Winter Symposium.
Eligible applicants must be associate members of
the society; awards include expenses (including
registration, two nights' hotel accommodations,
and travel costs of up to $750) to the symposium.

ASTS Presidential Student Mentor Grant: This
program provides $3,500 in stipend and salary
support to medical students working in the field of
organ transplantation by supporting summer
mentorship opportunities under the guidance of a
society member. Eligible applicants must be
medical students with an interest in
transplantation; proposed research projects must
be transplant-related (in either clinical or basic
science) and performed under the direction of a
society member.

ASTS-Astellas Faculty Development Grant:
Awarded in conjunction with Astellas, this grant
program is designed to support a junior faculty
member in the development of transplant research
so that further funding can be obtained. Grants of
up to $50,000 (for up to two years) will support
direct research and educational costs. Eligible
applicants must be members of the society (either
as a regular or candidate member) who are junior
surgical faculty members at a United Network for
Organ Sharing (UNOS)-approved (or Canadian
equivalent) transplant center in the first five years
of faculty appointment, who have completed a
post-residency fellowship or post-doctoral
fellowship at a society-approved fellowship training
program (or foreign equivalent), and who reside in
North America.

ASTS-Fellowship in Transplantation: This program
supports training in the field of solid organ
transplantation with a comprehensive experience in
the clinical aspects of transplant surgery, as well as
involvement in related clinical, translational, and/or
laboratory research. The program provides
$42,500 per year (for up to two years) to support
salary and benefits, as well as direct research
expenses. Eligible applicants must be current
clinical trainees in transplant surgery, or accepted
as a trainee, as a society-approved transplant
fellowship; applicants must also have completed
surgical residency and demonstrated a career
commitment to the area of transplant surgery, and
must reside in North America. Research and clinical
experience must be sponsored by a society
member.

ASTS-Genentech Scientist Scholarship: Awarded
in conjunction with Genentech, this $40,000 award
(per year for up to two years) supports full-time
basic and translational research in the field of
transplantation and transplant immunobiology in
the laboratory of a society member. Eligible
applicants must be either residents in an
Accreditation Council for Graduate Medical
Education (ACGME) program, or have completed an

advanced professional degree (i.e., Ph.D., D.V.M.,
or foreign equivalent) in a discipline germane to
transplantation; applicants must also reside in
North American and have completed at least two
years of clinical training (or one year of post-doctoral
research) in transplantation or transplant
immunobiology. Scholarships are specifically
designed to support research in a laboratory
setting.

ASTS-Pfizer Collaborative Scientist Grant:
Awarded in conjunction with Pfizer, Inc., this
$50,000 award (awarded every year for up to two
years) provides qualified society investigators and
their scientific collaborators with research funding
in the field of solid organ transplantation. Eligible
applicants must: be society members with an
established research effort; have a surgical faculty
appointment at an established United Network of
Organ Sharing (UNOS)-approved transplant center;
and reside in North America. Applicants must apply
in conjunction with a collaborator who has
completed an advanced professional degree (i.e.
M.D., Ph.D., D.V.M., or foreign equivalent),
demonstrate a record of collaborative efforts and
hold a position amenable to proposed scientific
work with the co-applicant, and have a faculty
appointment at an academic institution that has the
ability to support the collaboration.

ASTS-Pfizer Mid-Level Faculty Research Grant:
Awarded in conjunction with Pfizer, Inc., this
$50,000 grant (available for up to two years) is
designed to support on-going research in solid
organ transplantation, so that independent funding
can be obtained, or to fund a new avenue of
research for an established investigator. Eligible
applicants must be society members who: are
mid-level surgical faculty members with an
appointment of full, associate, or assistant
professor at an established United Network for
Organ Sharing (UNOS)-approved transplant center
in years five to ten of post-training; or a director or
associate director of a UNOS-approved transplant
center in years five to ten of post-training. Eligible
applicants must reside in North America; grants are
intended to support only direct research and
educational costs.
EIN: 133048373

9312
American String Teachers, Inc.
4153 Chain Bridge Rd.
Fairfax, VA 22030-4102 (703) 279-2113
Contact: Donna Sizemore Hale, Exec. Dir.
FAX: (703) 279-2114; E-mail: asta@astaweb.com;
E-Mail for Donna Sizemore: donna@astaweb.com;
URL: http://www.astaweb.com

Foundation type: Public charity
Purpose: Grants to music education majors who
play string instruments.
Financial data: Year ended 06/30/2012. Assets,
$2,241,924 (M); Expenditures, $1,907,974.
Fields of interest: Music composition.
Type of support: Scholarships—to individuals.
Application information: Applications accepted.
Application form required.
> *Additional information:* Contact foundation for
>   current application deadline/guidelines.
EIN: 226080964

9313
Americans Helping Americans, Inc.
8301 Richmond Hwy., Ste. 100
Alexandria, VA 22309 (703) 317-9412
Contact: Lynn Thomas, Exec. Dir.
FAX: (703) 317-9690;
E-mail: info@helpingamericans.org; Toll-free tel.:
(888) AHA-5026; URL: http://
www.helpingamericans.org

Foundation type: Public charity
Purpose: Emergency funds to needy individuals
primarily Appalachia, rural communities in West
Virginia, Kentucky, Tennessee, South Carolina and
North Carolina.
Publications: Annual report; Financial statement.
Financial data: Year ended 06/30/2012. Assets,
$88,975 (M); Expenditures, $1,397,127; Total
giving, $1,086,282; Grants to individuals, totaling
$21,000.
Fields of interest: Health care; Food services;
Housing/shelter; Aging; Disabilities, people with;
Economically disadvantaged.
Type of support: Grants for special needs.
Application information: Applications accepted.
Application form required.
> *Initial approach:* Letter or telephone
> *Deadline(s):* July and Dec.
> *Additional information:* Contact foundation for
>   application guidelines.
Program descriptions:

Americans Helping Americans in Appalachia:
Funds are provided for utility assistance, medicine,
medical assistance, homeless prevention, home
repair, enrichment programs, school supplies,
shoes, and holiday gifts for children, and food to the
needy families, disabled, and elderly individuals of
the Appalachian area.

Safe Places Residential Program: The program
provides transitional housing to families who are
determined to safeguard their well being and move
towards self-reliance in homes free from violence.
EIN: 541594577

9314
Arlington Community Foundation
818 N. Quincy St., Ste. 103
Arlington, VA 22203 (703) 243-4785
Contact: Wanda L. Pierce, Exec. Dir.
FAX: (703) 243-4796; E-mail: info@arlcf.org;
URL: http://www.arlcf.org

Foundation type: Community foundation
Purpose: Scholarships to graduating high school
seniors who are residents of Arlington, VA pursuing
a higher education.
Publications: Application guidelines; Annual report;
Financial statement; Grants list; Informational
brochure; Multi-year report; Newsletter; Program
policy statement.
Financial data: Year ended 06/30/2012. Assets,
$9,008,913 (M); Expenditures, $1,192,951; Total
giving, $757,574; Grants to individuals, 142 grants
totaling $326,210.
Fields of interest: Higher education.
Type of support: Scholarships—to individuals.
Application information: Applications accepted.
Application form required. Application form
available on the grantmaker's web site.
> *Initial approach:* Application
> *Send request by:* On-line
> *Deadline(s):* Feb. 10
> *Final notification:* Recipients notified by the
>   middle of Apr.
> *Applicants should submit the following:*
> 1) Transcripts
> 2) SAR

3) SAT
4) Letter(s) of recommendation
5) FAFSA
6) ACT

Additional information: Checks are sent directly to the educational institutions on behalf of the students. See web site for additional application information.

EIN: 541602838

9315
Army Emergency Relief

200 Stovall St.
Alexandria, VA   22332-4005   (703) 428-0000
Additional info.: Kasey L. Phillips, tel.: (703) 428-0035; e-mail: kasey@aerhq.org
FAX: (703) 325-7183; E-mail: aer@aerhq.org;
Toll-free tel.: (866) 878-6378; URL: http://www.aerhq.org

Foundation type: Public charity
Purpose: Emergency assistance and interest-free loans to active and retired army personnel and their dependents in time of need. Scholarships to unmarried dependent children of soldiers, active, retired or deceased, to pursue undergraduate study.
Publications: Application guidelines; Annual report; Informational brochure.
Financial data: Year ended 12/31/2011. Assets, $302,085,345 (M); Expenditures, $24,121,505; Total giving, $16,283,898; Grants to individuals, 121,321 grants totaling $15,252,838. Subtotal for scholarships—to individuals: 3,177 grants totaling $8,095,841. Subtotal for emergency funds: 7,086 grants totaling $6,973,708.
Fields of interest: Higher education; Military/veterans' organizations.
Type of support: Scholarships—to individuals; Undergraduate support; Grants for special needs; Loans—to individuals.
Application information: Applications accepted. Application form required. Application form available on the grantmaker's web site.
  Send request by: Mail or online
  Deadline(s): Apr. 1 for MG James Ursano Scholarship and Stateside Spouse Education Assistance Programs
  Final notification: Recipients notified early June for Ursano Scholarship and Stateside Spouse Education Assistance Program
  Applicants should submit the following:
    1) Transcripts
    2) SAR
    3) GPA

Program descriptions:
  Emergency Assistance: Emergency assistance is available for soldiers on extended active duty and their dependents; members of the Army National Guard and the U.S. Army Reserve on continuous active duty for more than 30 days and their dependents (including soldiers on active duty for training and serving under various sections of title 10 of the United States code); soldiers retired from active duty because of longevity, physical disability, or retirement after reaching age 60, and their dependents; and widow(er)s and orphans of soldiers who died while on active duty or after they retired. Assistance is available for such needs as food, rent, utilities, emergency transportation, vehicle repair, funeral expenses, medical/dental expenses, or personal needs when pay is delayed or stolen.
  MG James Ursano Scholarship Program: The program seeks to help Army families with the costs of post-secondary undergraduate level education, vocational training, and preparation for acceptance

by military service academies for their dependent children. Applicants must be dependent children, stepchildren or legally-adopted children or a ward of Army soldiers on active duty, retired, or deceased while on active duty or after retirement; and children of Reserve or National Guard soldiers mobilized under Title 10 status for the entire academic year. Children of Gray Area Retirees are also eligible for funds. Applicants must be enrolled, accepted, or pending acceptance as full-time dependent students for the entire academic year in post-secondary school for undergraduate study.
  Spouse Education Assistance Program: This program provides scholarships to spouses of active duty U.S. soldiers, assigned and living both within the U.S. and internationally. Eligible applicants must be attending an accredited U.S.-based or international college or university, and must be taking a minimum of six credits (if part-time) or twelve credits (if full-time). Scholarships can only be used toward first undergraduate degrees only. Assistance is not granted for graduate-degree-level courses.
EIN: 530196552

9316
The Army Historical Foundation, Inc

2425 Wilson Blvd.
Arlington, VA   22201-3326   (703) 522-7901
Contact: William W. Hartzog, Pres.
FAX: (703) 522-7929; Toll Free Tel. : (800)-506-2672E-Mail for Creighton Abrams : creighton.abrams@armyhistory.orgTel. for Creighton Abrams : (703)-562-4160; URL: http://www.armyhistory.org

Foundation type: Public charity
Purpose: Annual awards to writers of books and articles that have made a distinctive contribution to U.S. Army history.
Financial data: Year ended 12/31/2012. Assets, $34,841,763 (M); Expenditures, $4,836,243; Total giving, $13,726; Grants to individuals, totaling $5,950.
Fields of interest: Museums (specialized); Literature; Historical activities, war memorials.
Type of support: Awards/prizes.
Application information: Candidates are nominated by their publishers.
Program description:
  Distinguished Writing Awards: Each finalist is judged against four criteria: Significance to U.S. Army History, quality of writing (e.g. clarity, style and analysis), historical accuracy, and presentation (e.g. use of maps, photographs or other materials). The award consists of a distinctive plaque and a nominal cash prize to the author.
EIN: 521367225

9317
Ashoka: Innovators for the Public

1700 N. Moore St., Ste. 2000
Arlington, VA   22209-1939   (703) 527-8300
Contact: William Drayton, Chair. and C.E.O.
FAX: (703) 527-8383; E-mail: info@ashoka.org;
E-mail for individuals working in the U.S.: usprogram@ashoka.org; URL: http://www.ashoka.org

Foundation type: Public charity
Purpose: Fellowships to leading social entrepreneurs who have innovative solutions to social problems and the potential to change patterns across society.
Publications: Application guidelines; Informational brochure; Newsletter.

Financial data: Year ended 08/31/2011. Assets, $85,527,912 (M); Expenditures, $35,555,963; Total giving, $5,736,846; Grants to individuals, 2 grants totaling $105,000. Subtotal for stipends: 69 grants totaling $5,106,846.
Fields of interest: Climate change/global warming; Energy; Equal rights; Recreation; Youth development; Civil/human rights, women; Social entrepreneurship; International studies; Welfare policy/reform; Young adults; Women; Adults, women.
Type of support: Fellowships; Awards/prizes.
Application information:
  Initial approach: Letter or e-mail
  Deadline(s): Varies for all awards
  Additional information: Contact foundation for eligibility requirements.
EIN: 510255908

9318
Asparagus Club

c/o National Grocers Assn.
1005 N. Glebe Rd., Ste. 250
Arlington, VA   22201-5758   (703) 516-0700
Contact: Brian Burnam, Chair.
Scholarship application: c/o Baton Rouge Area Foundation, 402 N. Fourth St, Baton Rouge, LA 70802-5506; Toll-free tel.: (877) 387-6126
FAX: (703) 516-0115;
E-mail: feedback@nationalgrocers.org; URL: http://www.iowagrocers.com/asparagus-club-scholarships-nga.cfm

Foundation type: Public charity
Purpose: Scholarships for full time juniors, seniors or graduate students pursuing a degree in business, food management or another career in the grocery industry.
Publications: Application guidelines.
Financial data: Year ended 05/31/2012. Assets, $55,185 (M); Expenditures, $9,799; Total giving, $9,000.
Fields of interest: Higher education; Business school/education.
Type of support: Scholarships—to individuals.
Application information: Applications accepted. Application form required. Application form available on the grantmaker's web site.
  Send request by: Mail
  Deadline(s): Apr. 30
  Final notification: Applicants notified within two months after receipt of application
  Applicants should submit the following:
    1) GPA
    2) Essay
    3) Letter(s) of recommendation
    4) Transcripts
Program description:
  Scholarships: Scholarship in the amount of $1,500 per semester for a maximum of four consecutive semesters are available for students attending college on a full-time basis. The applicant must demonstrate scholastic achievement by earning a minimum 2.5 GPA and must demonstrate good character. The awards may be used at any accredited, nonprofit college or university in the United States for students who will be entering their senior year.
EIN: 133208336

9319
Associates of the American Foreign Service Worldwide

4001 N. 9th St., Ste. 214
Arlington, VA 22203-1900 (703) 820-5420
Contact: Barbara Reioux, Off. Mgr.
FAX: (703) 820-5421; *E-mail:* office@aafsw.org;
URL: http://www.aafsw.org

Foundation type: Public charity
Purpose: Scholarships and awards for outstanding volunteer activities of U.S. Government employees, spouses, family members over the age of 18, and members of household who work to improve the quality of life at posts abroad.
Financial data: Year ended 06/30/2012. Assets, $324,462 (M); Expenditures, $129,074; Total giving, $30,193.
Fields of interest: Philanthropy/voluntarism.
Type of support: Awards/prizes.
Application information: See web site for additional information.
Program descriptions:
AFSA College Scholarship Program: Scholarships ranging from $1,500 to $3,500 are available to children of Foreign Service employees will attend a four-year undergraduate college. Scholarships are need-based. Academic and merit awards of $1,500 are also available to high school seniors.
Art Contest: Sponsored by the State Department Federal Credit Union, this contest challenges teens to create art in any flat medium based on an annual theme. Nine winners, three in each category, will receive prizes ranging from $100 to $500.
Community Service Award: Two winners will each receive a $1,500 U.S. savings bond to honor youth who have demonstrated outstanding volunteer efforts at home or abroad in community service or in service to their peers.
Dreyfus Fellowship Awards: Scholarships of up to $5,000 are available to incoming students at Yale University, with preference given to students pursuing a master's degree in a field related to foreign affairs.
Environment Contest: The contest challenges Foreign Service youth to create an Earth Day themed event at your school, local community center, or outdoors in a nature setting. Invite one local environmental expert to speak about your chosen environmental issue. Three winners will each receive a cash prize of $500.
Essay Contest: Four winners will receive prizes ranging from $100 to $750 for essays in 1,000 words or less that answer the question about issues to improve in the writers' home country.
KidVid Contest: The contest challenges Foreign Service youth ages 10 to 18 to produce a DVD about life at an overseas post from a kid's perspective. A $1,000 prize will be divided among all winners.
The Avis Bohlen Award: Awards $2,500 in recognition of the accomplishments of a family member of a Foreign Service employee whose relations with the American and foreign communities at post have done the most to advance the interests of the United States.
The J. Kirby Simon Foreign Service Trust: The program supports projects, initiated on a voluntary basis by members of the extended Foreign Service family (American- and locally-engaged employees and family members), that seek, on a modest scale, to improve the health and welfare of people living in their host countries.
The M. Juanita Guess Award: Awards $2,500 to a Community Liaison Officer who has demonstrated outstanding leadership, dedication, initiative or imagination in assisting the families of Americans serving at an overseas post.

The Nelson B. Delavan Award: Awards $2,500 to acknowledge the work of a Foreign Service office management specialist who has made a significant contribution to post or office effectiveness and morale beyond the framework of her/his job responsibilities.
The Secretary of State's Award for Outstanding Volunteerism Abroad: Awards $2,500 in recognition of the outstanding volunteer activities of U.S. government employees and family members over the age of 18 serving overseas. Each year, a winner is chosen from each of State Department's six geographical bureaus.
EIN: 526041153

9320
Association for the Support of Children with Cancer

(also known as ASK)
5211 W. Broad St.
P.O. Box 17184
Richmond, VA 23230 (804) 658-5910
Contact: Amy Godkin, Exec. Dir.
FAX: (804) 658-5952; *E-mail:* agodkin@askweb.org;
URL: http://www.askweb.org

Foundation type: Public charity
Purpose: Medical care for children with cancer and support to give comfort to them and their families.
Publications: Newsletter.
Financial data: Year ended 05/31/2012. Assets, $1,097,566 (M); Expenditures, $554,717; Total giving, $82,040; Grants to individuals, totaling $82,040.
Fields of interest: Cancer; Pediatrics research.
Type of support: Research; Grants for special needs.
Application information: Applications not accepted.
> *Additional information:* Unsolicited requests for funds not considered or acknowledged.
EIN: 510173669

9321
Association of Fundraising Professionals

(formerly National Society of Fund Raising Executives)
4300 Wilson Blvd., Ste. 300
Arlington, VA 22203-4179 (703) 684-0410
FAX: (703) 684-0540; *E-mail:* afp@afpnet.org;
Toll-free tel.: (800) 666-3863; URL: http://www.afpnet.org

Foundation type: Public charity
Purpose: A $3,000 award to the nominated author of a published book or monograph of at least fifty pages that is based on either applied or basic research in fundraising or philanthropy; scholarships also awarded to individuals in the greater New York City area who wish to learn more about philanthropy and fundraising.
Publications: Application guidelines; Annual report.
Financial data: Year ended 12/31/2011. Assets, $5,656,934 (M); Expenditures, $11,667,755; Total giving, $17,293; Grants to individuals, totaling $17,293.
Fields of interest: Literature; Fund raising/fund distribution.
Type of support: Awards/grants by nomination only; Awards/prizes.
Application information:
> *Initial approach:* Letter
> *Deadline(s):* Nov. 1 for Skystone Partners Prize for Research on Fundraising and Philanthropy

Program descriptions:
Greater New York Chapter Scholarships for Fund Raising Day: A limited number of scholarships, generally ranging from $250 to $450, are available to members of the greater New York chapter of the association. Eligible applicants must be currently employed by or volunteer for a 501(c)(3) organization whose budget is under $1 million, and must be either full- or part-time fundraisers who are new to the field, or individuals with extensive volunteer and/or professional experience in the nonprofit sector who seek to expand their knowledge of fundraising.
Skystone Partners Prize for Research on Fundraising and Philanthropy: A $3,000 cash award is available to an author of a published research work on fundraising and philanthropy. Publications must be based on either applied or basic research, and must reflect a standard publisher selection process without regard to the source and sponsorship of the research. Unpublished theses or dissertations, self-published works, directories, op-ed pieces, editorials, or articles will not be considered.
EIN: 132590764

9322
Association of Higher Education Facilities Officers

1643 Prince St.
Alexandria, VA 22314-2818 (703) 684-1446
FAX: (703) 549-2772;
E-mail: webmaster@appa.org; E-mail For E. Lander Medlin: lander@appa.org; Fax: E. Lander Medlin (703) 542-3789; URL: http://www.appa.org

Foundation type: Public charity
Purpose: Scholarships to APPA members for continuing education in facilities management. Also, awards by nomination only to APPA members.
Financial data: Year ended 03/31/2012. Assets, $3,814,229 (M); Expenditures, $4,512,258; Total giving, $106,347; Grants to individuals, totaling $106,347.
Type of support: Scholarships—to individuals; Awards/grants by nomination only; Awards/prizes.
Application information: Applications accepted. Application form required.
> *Additional information:* Contact regional representative for additional guidelines.
Program descriptions:
Award for Excellence in Facilities Management: Given to three individuals each year who have made significant, life-long contributions to the profession of higher education facilities management. Nominee must have been an active member of APPA for a minimum of five years, attended and participated in meetings and other functions at the international level, and demonstrated distinguished service to the association.
Meritorious Service Award: The award is given to no more than three individuals each year who have made significant, life-long contributions to the profession of higher education facilities management. Nominee must have been an active member of APPA for a minimum of five years, attended and participated in meetings and other functions at the international level, and demonstrated distinguished service to the association.
Pacesetter Award: Seven awards are given annually to individuals who have made significant contributions at the regions or chapters and have been active APPA members for a minimum of three years, continued service to the association through the task force, special project, authorship of publication, or presentation at a meeting, and other

voluntary contribution of time, effort, and resources.

President's Award: The award is given to individual APPA members who have demonstrated exceptional achievement in facilities management and who have made outstanding contributions to the association.

Rex Dillow Award: The award is presented to the author or authors of the best article published in Facilities Manager during the previous calendar year. Eligible articles are those written by a full-time employee, from any department, of an APPA member institution of higher education.
EIN: 850211201

9323
Association of Writers and Writing Programs
(also known as AWP)
4400 University Dr., MSN 1E3
Fairfax, VA 22030-4444 (703) 993-4301
Contact: David W. Fenza, Exec. Dir.
FAX: (703) 993-4302;
E-mail: chronicle@awpwriter.org; URL: http://www.awpwriter.org

Foundation type: Public charity
Purpose: Awards to writers and poets. Also, scholarships for emerging writers to attend a writer's conference.
Publications: Application guidelines; Annual report; Informational brochure; Informational brochure (including application guidelines); Newsletter.
Financial data: Year ended 06/30/2012. Assets, $3,091,729 (M); Expenditures, $2,459,941.
Fields of interest: Literature.
Type of support: Conferences/seminars; Scholarships—to individuals; Awards/prizes; Workstudy grants.
Application information: Applications accepted. Application form required.
  Initial approach: E-mail
  Deadline(s): Vary
  Additional information: Application should include entry fee, manuscripts and SASE.
Program descriptions:
  AWP Award Series in the Novel, Poetry, Fiction, and Creative Nonfiction: The series is an annual competition for the publication of excellent new book-length works of poetry, fiction, and creative nonfiction. Winners receive a $2,000 cash honorarium plus publication of their book by University of Pittsburgh Press, University of Massachusetts Press, or University of Georgia Press.
  AWP/ George Garrett Award for Outstanding Community Service in Literature: The award includes a $1,000 honorarium from AWP in addition to travel, accommodations, and registration for attending the AWP Conference.
  Intro Journals Project: A literary competition for the discovery and publication of the best new works by students currently enrolled in the programs of AWP. Winners of this contest receive a $50 cash award and are published in Hayden's Ferry Review, Mid-American Review, Puerto del Sol, Controlled Burn, Quarterly West, Tampa Review, Willow Springs, and Artful Dodge.
  National Program Directors' Prizes for Undergraduate Literary Magazines: This contest awards the best literary magazines produced by undergraduates at AWP member programs - one in content, and one in design - with a $500 cash honorarium.
  WC&C Scholarship Competition: This annual competition provides scholarships for emerging writers who wish to attend a writers' conference,

center, retreat, festival, or residency. Two scholarships of $500 are awarded.
EIN: 050314999

9324
Bedford Community Health Foundation
321 N. Bridge St.
P.O. Box 1104
Bedford, VA 24523-1104 (540) 586-5292
Contact: Donna M. Proctor, Secy. and Exec. Dir.
FAX: (540) 587-5819;
E-mail: info@healthybedford.org; URL: http://www.healthybedford.org

Foundation type: Public charity
Purpose: Scholarships to students or graduates of Bedford City and Bedford County, VA, schools pursuing a health professional career.
Publications: Application guidelines; Annual report; Grants list; Informational brochure; Newsletter.
Financial data: Year ended 12/31/2011. Assets, $3,912,710 (M); Expenditures, $256,442; Total giving, $132,018; Grants to individuals, totaling $38,350.
Fields of interest: Nursing school/education; Health sciences school/education.
Type of support: Scholarships—to individuals; Technical education support.
Application information: Applications accepted. Application form required. Application form available on the grantmaker's web site. Interview required.
  Initial approach: Letter or telephone
  Send request by: Online or hand deliver
  Copies of proposal: 1
  Deadline(s): June 1
Program descriptions:
  Allied Health Scholarship: This program provides up to $1,000 per year for full-time college and post-graduate studies for allied health students that are Bedford City or County residents, enrolled in a Virginia state-approved program of study, maintain a C average in every class, and pursue a certificate or degree. Studies must be in a certificate or degree program.
  David W. and Sandra L.R. Boyes Physician Education Scholarship: The scholarship provides financial assistance for physicians who want to pursue further education that will prepare them for the growing, changing, and unique health needs of seniors. Preference will be given to female physicians, to those specializing in geriatrics, and to those in family practices with a large percentage of senior patients. Specialists of all kinds, including chiropractors and osteopaths, are encouraged to apply. Applicants who currently practice or plan to practice in rural Virginia or southern Appalachian areas are encouraged to apply.
  Janet Boyer Wood Scholarship: Up to $500 per student is available to support continuing education for licensed nurses (including CNAs, LPNs, RNs,) must be employed in Bedford City/County, or must live in Bedford City/County and be employed at the Salem VAMC, studying in a certificate or degree program. Applicant must maintain a "C" or above in each class.
  Maxwell Dudley Davidson Scholarship: Scholarships of $2,000 are available for nursing students willing to work in the Bedford community after graduation. Applicants must be accepted for employment, after graduation, at either Bedford Memorial Hospital or a pre-approved healthcare provider in Bedford City/County. Students must be studying for their ADN, RN or RN/BSN. The scholarship does not pay for the first year of general education classes in a four year degree program. Applicant must be a Bedford City/County resident,

enrolled in a Virginia state approved program of study, maintain a "C" average or above for each class and be a full time student.
EIN: 541088024

9325
The Gloria Wille Bell and Carlos R. Bell Charitable Trust
c/o McGuire Woods, LLP
One James Center
901 E. Cary St.
Richmond, VA 23219-4030
Contact: John O'Grady, Tr.
E-mail for John O'Grady:
jogrady@mcguirewoods.com; URL: http://www.bellscholarship.org

Foundation type: Independent foundation
Purpose: Scholarship awards to first year students attending the University of Michigan, Ann Arbor, entering the College of Engineering or the College of Literature, Science, and the Arts, who are enrolled in an undergraduate degree program in the sciences and who meet specific geographic criteria.
Financial data: Year ended 06/30/2013. Assets, $4,932,289 (M); Expenditures, $355,251; Total giving, $240,000; Grants to individuals, totaling $240,000.
Fields of interest: Engineering school/education; Scholarships/financial aid.
Type of support: Scholarships—to individuals; Support to graduates or students of specific schools.
Application information: Applications not accepted.
  Additional information: Unsolicited requests for funding not considered or acknowledged.
EIN: 546500526

9326
Blair Construction Scholarship Foundation
P.O. Box 612
Gretna, VA 24557-0612 (434) 656-6243
Contact: Fred A. Blair, Pres.

Foundation type: Company-sponsored foundation
Purpose: Scholarships to individuals of the Gretna, VA community in pursuit of a higher education at a two or four year college.
Financial data: Year ended 12/31/2012. Assets, $602 (M); Expenditures, $7,025; Total giving, $7,000; Grants to individuals, 6 grants totaling $7,000 (high: $1,800, low: $600).
Fields of interest: Education.
Type of support: Scholarships—to individuals.
Application information: Applications accepted. Application form required.
  Deadline(s): Feb. 28
EIN: 541915821

9327
Bridgebuilder Scholarship Fund
150 Stonewall Ln.
Quicksburg, VA 22847
Contact: William Logan, Chair.

Foundation type: Operating foundation
Purpose: Scholarships to graduating seniors at Stonewall Jackson High School, Mt. Jackson, VA.
Financial data: Year ended 11/30/2012. Assets, $246,386 (M); Expenditures, $12,391; Total giving, $11,346; Grants to individuals, 7 grants totaling $11,346 (high: $5,000, low: $625).

Fields of interest: Scholarships/financial aid.
Type of support: Support to graduates or students of specific schools; Undergraduate support.
Application information: Applications accepted. Application form required.
> *Deadline(s):* Nov. 1
> *Applicants should submit the following:*
> 1) SAT
> 2) Class rank
> 3) GPA
> 4) Financial information
> *Additional information:* Application should also include work history and a personal statement.

Program description:
> *Scholarship Program:* Scholarships are awarded on the basis of academic ability, leadership and good citizenship, desire for higher education, financial need, and likelihood that applicant will live in the area upon graduation.

EIN: 521262074

9328
Brockbank Education Fund
P.O. Box 752
Crozet, VA 22932

Foundation type: Independent foundation
Purpose: Student loans to undergraduates of Queenstown, Illinge, and Sada, South Africa.
Financial data: Year ended 12/31/2011. Assets, $87,745 (M); Expenditures, $42,174; Total giving, $8,034.
International interests: South Africa.
Type of support: Foreign applicants.
Application information: Applications not accepted.
> *Additional information:* Unsolicited requests for funds not considered or acknowledged.

EIN: 860983317

9329
Ron Brown Scholar Fund
(formerly CAP Charitable Foundation USA)
1160 Pepsi Pl., Ste. 206
Charlottesville, VA 22901-0807 (434) 964-1588
Contact: Michael A. Mallory, Pres. and Exec. Dir.
FAX: (434) 964-1589; E-mail: info@ronbrown.org;
URL: http://www.ronbrown.org

Foundation type: Independent foundation
Purpose: Scholarships to academically talented, highly motivated African American students for undergraduate education.
Publications: Application guidelines; Informational brochure; Newsletter.
Financial data: Year ended 12/31/2012. Assets, $12,211,717 (M); Expenditures, $1,319,616; Total giving, $250,896; Grants to individuals, 49 grants totaling $250,896 (high: $10,000, low: $900).
Fields of interest: Higher education; African Americans/Blacks.
Type of support: Scholarships—to individuals; Undergraduate support.
Application information: Applications accepted. Application form required. Application form available on the grantmaker's web site. Interview required.
> *Send request by:* Mail
> *Deadline(s):* Jan. 9 of senior year in high school
> *Final notification:* Recipients notified Apr. 1
> *Applicants should submit the following:*
> 1) GPA
> 2) Class rank

 3) Essay
 4) Letter(s) of recommendation
 5) ACT
 6) SAT
 7) Transcripts
 8) Financial information
> *Additional information:* Incomplete, e-mailed or faxed applications are not accepted. See web site for complete application guidelines.

Program description:
> *Ron Brown Scholar Program:* The program's mission is to accelerate the progress of African Americans into the mainstream of leadership in business, education, government and a wide spectrum of professions, while instilling a strong dedication to leadership and public service.

EIN: 541832314

9330
The Buchly Charity Fund of Federal Lodge
3819 N. Tazewell St.
Arlington, VA 22207
Contact: Paul D. Dolinsky, Tr.
Application address: 1200 N. Nash St., No. 246, Arlington, VA 22209-1439

Foundation type: Independent foundation
Purpose: Financial assistance to widows and orphans of deceased members of Federal Lodge No. 1 of the Masons, primarily in AZ, DC, MD and VA.
Financial data: Year ended 12/31/2012. Assets, $1,410,121 (M); Expenditures, $35,964; Total giving, $31,475; Grants to individuals, 3 grants totaling $6,475 (high: $2,350, low: $2,050).
Fields of interest: Residential/custodial care; Fraternal societies; Women.
Type of support: Grants for special needs.
Application information:
> *Initial approach:* Letter
> *Additional information:* Unsolicited requests for funds not considered or acknowledged.

Program description:
> *Buchly Charity Fund Program:* Upon the death of a Federal Lodge No. 1 member, a check is issued to assist the widow with her immediate needs. If the widow needs further assistance, she must write to the trustees, who will evaluate her needs and determine whether or not to fund them. The trustees re-evaluate each widow's needs annually.

EIN: 520943739

9331
Burger King Scholars
910 Triangle St.
Blacksburg, VA 24060-7716 (540) 552-7718
Contact: Brittany Shelton
E-mail: burgerkingscholars@scholarshipamerica.org

Foundation type: Company-sponsored foundation
Purpose: Scholarships to graduating high school seniors and Burger King restaurant employees in the U.S., Puerto Rico, and in Canada planning to pursue higher education.
Publications: Application guidelines; Grants list.
Financial data: Year ended 06/30/2013. Assets, $10,130 (M); Expenditures, $75; Total giving, $0.
Fields of interest: Higher education; Education.
Type of support: Employee-related scholarships; Scholarships—to individuals.
Application information: Applications accepted. Application form required. Application form available on the grantmaker's web site.
> *Deadline(s):* Jan. 10
> *Final notification:* Recipients notified in May

> *Additional information:* Applications should include transcripts, a list of work experiences, involvement in school and community activities, and employment information of your application is affiliated with a Burger King employee. The program is administered by Scholarship Management Services.

Company name: Burger King Holdings, Inc.
EIN: 205136286

9332
Camp Foundation
P.O. Box 813
Franklin, VA 23851-0813

Foundation type: Independent foundation
Purpose: Scholarships to graduating high school seniors who are residents of the city of Franklin and the counties of Southampton and Isle of Wight, VA.
Publications: Application guidelines.
Financial data: Year ended 12/31/2012. Assets, $14,924,703 (M); Expenditures, $758,583; Total giving, $692,005.
Fields of interest: Higher education.
Type of support: Undergraduate support.
Application information: Applications accepted. Application form required.
> *Applicants should submit the following:*
> 1) Financial information
> 2) Letter(s) of recommendation
> 3) Photograph
> 4) Transcripts
> *Additional information:* Application should also include a copy of parents 1040 tax form.

EIN: 546052488

9333
Capital One Financial Corporation
Contributions Program
1680 Capital One Dr.
McLean, VA 22102-3491 (703) 720-1000
URL: http://www.capitalone.com/about/? linkid=WWW_1009_Z_A0B2084C0D22A0E8F33F 8CB2G1F85H5AF4I7CC8_GBLFO_F1_01_T_ABT

Foundation type: Corporate giving program
Purpose: Scholarships of $10,000 or $5,000 to graduating high school seniors who demonstrate academic improvement and achievement, community service, extracurricular activities, and financial need.
Publications: Application guidelines.
Fields of interest: Higher education.
Type of support: Undergraduate support.
Application information: Application form required.
> *Additional information:* Contact foundation for further application and program information.

9334
Amory S. Carhart Memorial Fund Trust
c/o Warrenton Hunt
P.O. Box 972
Warrenton, VA 20188-0972 (540) 347-1376
Contact: Kim Nash

Foundation type: Independent foundation
Purpose: Financial assistance to persons who have incurred injury, illness, or disability following activities in a fox hunt, hunter trail, horse show, hound trail, field trial, steeplechase, point to point, hunt race, pony rally, or any similar activity.
Financial data: Year ended 12/31/2012. Assets, $331,245 (M); Expenditures, $28,829; Total giving, $23,992; Grants to individuals, 5 grants totaling $23,992 (high: $7,237, low: $2,000).

Fields of interest: Athletics/sports, training; Athletics/sports, equestrianism.
Type of support: Grants for special needs.
Application information: Applications accepted.
  Send request by: Mail
  Deadline(s): None
  Additional information: Applicants must be residents or visitors within the area registered as the Warrenton Hunt Country, VA, by the Master Fox Hound Association.
EIN: 237418084

9335
Caring Voice Coalition, Inc.

8249 Meadowbridge Rd.
Mechanicsville, VA 23116-2329 (804) 427-6468
Contact: Pamela Harris, Chair. and Pres.
E-mail: cvcinfo@caringvoice.org; Toll-free tel.: (888) 267-1440, toll-free fax: (888) 278-5065; URL: http://www.caringvoice.org

Foundation type: Public charity
Purpose: Financial assistance to patients of alpha-1 antitrypsin deficiency, chronic granulomatous disorder, complex partial seizures, congenital factor XIII deficiency, Huntington's disease, infantile spasms, narcolepsy, or pulmonary hypertension, to pay for medication.
Publications: Application guidelines.
Financial data: Year ended 06/30/2012. Assets, $53,101,166 (M); Expenditures, $52,357,546; Total giving, $46,827,156; Grants to individuals, 12,846 grants totaling $46,826,156. Subtotal for emergency funds: 12,814 grants totaling $46,793,538. Subtotal for travel grants: 32 grants totaling $32,618.
Fields of interest: Health care, insurance; Health care.
Type of support: Emergency funds; Grants to individuals.
Application information: Applications accepted.
  Initial approach: Application
  Send request by: Online
  Deadline(s): None
  Additional information: See web site for additional guidelines.
Program description:
  Financial Assistance Program: The organization provides financial assistance, in the form of monetary grants, to patients of supported diseases (alpha-1 antitrypsin deficiency, chronic granulomatous disorder, complex partial seizures, congenital factor XIII deficiency, Huntington's disease, infantile spasms, narcolepsy, or pulmonary hypertension) to alleviate the burden of medication costs. Grants allow patients to afford copayments for expensive prescription therapies, pay premiums for health insurance coverage, and take care of other self-pay responsibilities related to prescription medications.
EIN: 260058446

9336
Carpenter's Shelter, Inc.

930 N. Henry St.
Alexandria, VA 22314-1621 (703) 548-7500
Contact: Lissette S. Bishins, Exec. Dir.
Scholarship contact: Ashley Speaks, Educ. Prog. Coord.,
e-mail: AshleySpeaks@carpentersshelter.org
FAX: (703) 548-3167;
E-mail: information@carpentersshelter.org; E-mail For Lissette S. Bishins:

LissetteSBishins@carpentersshelter.org;
URL: http://www.carpentersshelter.org

Foundation type: Public charity
Purpose: Scholarships and awards for aftercare clients for school tuition, living stipends, books and computers to pursue their education at higher institutions.
Publications: Newsletter.
Financial data: Year ended 06/30/2012. Assets, $4,656,501 (M); Expenditures, $2,136,022; Total giving, $11,228; Grants to individuals, totaling $11,228.
Fields of interest: Higher education; Economically disadvantaged.
Type of support: Scholarships—to individuals; Grants for special needs.
Application information: Applications accepted.
  Additional information: The scholarship is for any client in good standing in any program.
EIN: 541571849

9337
The Century Foundation

7416 Forest Hill Ave.
Richmond, VA 23225-1528 (804) 330-4400
Contact: William G. Hollowell, Dir.

Foundation type: Company-sponsored foundation
Purpose: Scholarships to residents of VA, for research and training in the construction industry.
Financial data: Year ended 12/31/2011. Assets, $77,109 (M); Expenditures, $4,735; Total giving, $4,000.
Type of support: Undergraduate support.
Application information: Applications accepted. Application form not required.
  Initial approach: Letter
  Copies of proposal: 1
  Additional information: Contact foundation for further application guidelines.
EIN: 541384796

9338
Cherry Blossom Breast Cancer Foundation

P.O. Box 1051
Middleburg, VA 20118-1051 (703) 447-2302
Contact: James P. Atkins, Chair.
E-mail: info@cherryblossombreastcancerfoundation.org; URL: http://www.cherryblossombreastcancerfoundation.org/

Foundation type: Public charity
Purpose: Assistance to local women of Fauquier and Loudoun counties, VA for the treatment of detected breast cancer.
Publications: Newsletter.
Financial data: Year ended 06/30/2012. Assets, $37,074 (M); Expenditures, $158,523; Total giving, $151,000.
Fields of interest: Breast cancer; Women.
Type of support: Grants to individuals; Grants for special needs.
Application information: Contact the foundation for additional information for assistance.
Program description:
  Grants to Individuals: Support to individuals and families facing breast cancer in Loudoun and Fauquier counties, and to educate people on the need for early and regular screenings, for knowing their family medical history, and knowing their own bodies.
EIN: 271416904

9339
Child Nutrition, Inc.

9 N. 3rd St., Ste. 100
Warrenton, VA 20186-3404 (540) 347-3767

Foundation type: Public charity
Purpose: Reimbursements to VA childcare providers, for healthy meals served to children in their care.
Financial data: Year ended 09/30/2011. Assets, $365,089 (M); Expenditures, $3,608,497; Total giving, $3,139,876; Grants to individuals, totaling $3,139,876.
Fields of interest: Food services; Day care.
Type of support: Grants for special needs.
Application information:
  Initial approach: Letter
  Additional information: Contact the organization for eligibility criteria.
EIN: 521312582

9340
Children's AIDS Fund

1329 Shepard Dr., Ste. 7
Sterling, VA 20164-7107 (703) 433-1560

Foundation type: Public charity
Purpose: Provides gifts and support to children with HIV and AIDS.
Financial data: Year ended 12/31/2011. Assets, $1,579,353 (M); Expenditures, $4,462,347; Total giving, $3,626,817.
Fields of interest: AIDS; Children.
Application information: Applications not accepted.
  Additional information: Unsolicited requests for funds not considered or acknowledged.
EIN: 541436973

9341
The Christian Broadcasting Network, Inc.

977 Centerville Tpke.
Virginia Beach, VA 23463-1001 (757) 226-7000
URL: http://www.cbn.com

Foundation type: Public charity
Purpose: Emergency assistance (both cash and in-kind) to individuals in need throughout the world.
Publications: Financial statement.
Financial data: Year ended 03/31/2012. Assets, $190,937,096 (M); Expenditures, $283,961,607; Total giving, $27,565,117; Grants to individuals, 9 grants totaling $49,459.
Fields of interest: Christian agencies & churches; Economically disadvantaged.
Type of support: Emergency funds; Grants to individuals; In-kind gifts.
Application information: Applications accepted.
  Additional information: Some assistance require an application. Contact the organization for additional information.
EIN: 540678752

9342
CIA Officers Memorial Foundation

c/o Arnold & Porter
205 Van Buren St., Ste. 450A
P.O. Box 405
Herndon, VA 20172-0405 (703) 638-5378
E-mail: scholarships@ciamemorialfoundation.org; Additional tel.: (202) 942-5115; additional fax: (202) 942-5999; URL: http://www.ciamemorialfoundation.org/

Foundation type: Public charity
Purpose: Financial assistance to survivors and dependents of CIA officers killed in the line of duty, primarily for postsecondary education for the children of fallen officers.
Financial data: Year ended 12/31/2011. Assets, $7,634,180 (M); Expenditures, $881,737; Total giving, $492,289; Grants to individuals, totaling $492,289.
Fields of interest: Safety/disasters.
Type of support: Grants for special needs.
Application information: Unsolicited requests for funds not accepted.
EIN: 522360463

9343
The Club Foundation
1733 King St.
Alexandria, VA 22314-2720 (703) 739-9500
Contact: Rhonda Schaver, Mgr., Admin. & Schol.
FAX: (703) 739-0124;
E-mail: clubfoundation@clubfoundation.org;
URL: http://www.clubfoundation.org/

Foundation type: Public charity
Purpose: Scholarships to those pursuing a career in private club management.
Publications: Annual report.
Financial data: Year ended 10/31/2011. Assets, $4,296,322 (M); Expenditures, $977,721; Total giving, $345,889; Grants to individuals, totaling $91,269.
Fields of interest: Business school/education.
Type of support: Scholarships—to individuals; Undergraduate support.
Application information: Applications accepted. Application form required.
   Deadline(s): May 1 for Research Grant Program, Sept. 1 for LaRocca Family Executive Scholarship, Nov. 1 and Dec. 1 for Willmoore H. Kendall Scholarship
   Applicants should submit the following:
   1) Resume
   2) Essay
   3) Letter(s) of recommendation
   Additional information: Scholarships by nomination only to assist club managers interested in pursuing the Certified Club Manager (CCM) designation. See web site for additional guidelines.
Program descriptions:
   Faculty Internship Program: The program awards internships to faculty members from established college and university hospitality programs at accredited four-year schools. Candidates must demonstrate strong evidence of their interest in private club management and in the development of a club management curriculum. Preferably, candidates must demonstrate experience teaching course(s) related to club management at the undergraduate or graduate level or be actively involved in teaching in CMAA-sponsored programs, such as The Business Management Institute.
   Faculty Research Grant Program: The program awards two to four grants of up to $2,500 to university faculty members in order for them to have the means to conduct industry-intensive research that may be funded in whole or part.
   Industry Grants: The program awards grants for projects that would be of interest and relevant to club managers and the club industry.
   Jon Perdue Scholarship: The program awards scholarships annually to those individuals actively pursuing a managerial career within the private club industry.
   LaRocca Family Executive Scholarship Application: The scholarship provides financial

support to club managers interested in both furthering their own professional development, as well as helping others achieve their career goals. Scholarships are awarded annually based on the availability of funds and merit of application.
   Willmoore H. Kendall Scholarship Fund: The program provides support to assistant club managers interested in pursuing the Certified Club Manager (CCM) designation. Candidates must be a member of the foundation and an assistant manager actively pursuing the CCM designation, and have at least one BMI course remaining to complete. Candidates must be nominated for the scholarship by their chapter.
EIN: 521642692

9344
The College of William & Mary Foundation
(formerly The Endowment Assocation of the College of William and Mary in Virginia, Inc.)
P.O. Box 8795
Williamsburg, VA 23187-8795 (757) 221-1001
Contact: Lee Foster, Dir., Foundation Oper.
FAX: (757) 221-1313; E-mail: ljfost@wm.edu;
URL: http://www.wm.edu/offices/cwmf/

Foundation type: Public charity
Purpose: Scholarships and fellowships to students of the College of William & Mary, VA.
Publications: Annual report.
Financial data: Year ended 06/30/2012. Assets, $544,308,092 (M); Expenditures, $19,824,482; Total giving, $9,766,480.
Fields of interest: Higher education.
Type of support: Fellowships; Scholarships—to individuals; Support to graduates or students of specific schools.
Application information: Applications not accepted.
   Additional information: Selection of recipients is based on academic achievement, financial need and other similar standards. Students are selected by staff. Unsolicited requests for funds not considered or acknowledged.
EIN: 540734117

9345
Community Foundation for Northern Virginia
2940 Hunter Mill Rd., Ste. 201
Oakton, VA 22124 (703) 879-7640
FAX: (703) 879-7644; E-mail: info@cfnova.org;
URL: http://www.cfnova.org/

Foundation type: Community foundation
Purpose: College scholarships to Northern Virginia students for attendance at full time accredited colleges or universities of their choice.
Publications: Annual report; Financial statement; Grants list; Informational brochure; Informational brochure (including application guidelines); Newsletter; Occasional report.
Financial data: Year ended 06/30/2012. Assets, $33,177,416 (M); Expenditures, $3,525,219; Total giving, $2,003,980; Grants to individuals, 20 grants totaling $194,750.
Fields of interest: Higher education.
Type of support: Scholarships—to individuals; Support to graduates or students of specific schools; Undergraduate support.
Application information: Applications accepted. Application form required. Application form available on the grantmaker's web site.
   Deadline(s): Varies
   Additional information: See web site for additional application guidelines.

Program description:
   Scholarships: The foundation manages six scholarships and administers the funds for approximately twenty other scholarships that support Northern Virginia students pursuing undergraduate degrees. Each scholarship has its own eligibility requirements, including specific areas of study such as elementary education, medicine and computer science. Some scholarships are region-wide, others are specific to one or more high schools. Unless otherwise noted, all scholarships are for full-time attendance at an accredited college or university.
EIN: 510232459

9346
The Community Foundation of the Central Blue Ridge
117 S. Lewis St.
P.O. Box 815
Staunton, VA 24402 (540) 231-2150
Contact: For grants: Susan Lendermon, Dir., Nonprofit Srvs.; For scholarships: Menieka K. Garber, Dir., Opers. and Donor Srvs.
FAX: (540) 242-3387;
E-mail: info@communityfoundationcbr.org;
URL: http://www.communityfoundationcbr.org
Additional URL: http://www.communityfoundationCBR.org

Foundation type: Community foundation
Purpose: Scholarships and awards to improve the quality of life for individuals in Staunton, Waynesboro, Augusta, and Nelson counties, VA.
Publications: Application guidelines; Annual report; Financial statement; Grants list; Informational brochure; Newsletter.
Financial data: Year ended 12/31/2012. Assets, $13,643,841 (M); Expenditures, $725,820; Total giving, $446,951; Grants to individuals, 33 grants totaling $143,175.
Fields of interest: Higher education; Scholarships/financial aid.
Type of support: Scholarships—to individuals; Support to graduates or students of specific schools; Awards/prizes; Technical education support; Undergraduate support.
Application information: Applications accepted. Application form required. Application form available on the grantmaker's web site.
   Initial approach: Application
   Send request by: On-line
   Deadline(s): Mar. 19
   Final notification: Applicants notified in May
   Applicants should submit the following:
   1) Letter(s) of recommendation
   2) Transcripts
   Additional information: Each scholarship has its own specific purpose, selection and eligibility criteria. See web site for a complete listing of scholarships.
EIN: 541647385

9347
Community Foundation of the Dan River Region
(formerly DPC Community Foundation)
541 Loyal St.
Danville, VA 24541 (434) 793-0884
Contact: Debra L. Dodson, Exec. Dir.
FAX: (434) 793-6489; E-mail: info@cfdrr.org;
Additional e-mail: cfdrr@gamewood.net;
URL: http://www.cfdrr.org

Foundation type: Community foundation

Purpose: Scholarships to students living in the region from Martinsville-Henry County, VA to South Boston/Halifax County, VA, including the neighboring NC counties.
Publications: Application guidelines; Annual report; Financial statement; Grants list; Informational brochure; Newsletter.
Financial data: Year ended 06/30/2012. Assets, $23,702,340 (M); Expenditures, $2,168,918; Total giving, $977,625; Grants to individuals, 68 grants totaling $150,552.
Fields of interest: Higher education.
Type of support: Undergraduate support.
Application information: Applications accepted. Application form required. Application form available on the grantmaker's web site.
  Initial approach: Application
  Send request by: Mail
  Deadline(s): Late Feb./Early Mar.
  Final notification: Applicants notified mid-May
  Applicants should submit the following:
    1) Transcripts
    2) Letter(s) of recommendation
    3) Essay
  Additional information: Each scholarship has specific eligibility criteria that were defined by the donor. See web site for complete listing.
EIN: 541823141

9348
Community Foundation of the Rappahannock River Region, Inc.

725 Jackson St., Ste. 114
P.O. Box 208
Fredericksburg, VA 22404-0208 (540) 373-9292
Contact: Teri McNally, Exec. Dir.
FAX: (540) 373-3050; E-mail: info@cfrrr.net;
Additional e-mail: TeriMcNally@cfrrr.org;
URL: http://www.cfrrr.org/

Foundation type: Community foundation
Purpose: Scholarships to students residing in the city of Fredericksburg, and Caroline, Grange, King George, Prince William, Spotsylvania, and Stafford counties, VA.
Publications: Application guidelines; Annual report; Grants list; Informational brochure; Newsletter; Newsletter (including application guidelines); Occasional report; Program policy statement.
Financial data: Year ended 06/30/2012. Assets, $8,755,898 (M); Expenditures, $729,281; Total giving, $493,240; Grants to individuals, 32 grants totaling $60,052 (high: $5,000, low: $500).
Fields of interest: Higher education.
Type of support: Scholarships—to individuals; Undergraduate support.
Application information: Applications accepted. Application form required. Application form available on the grantmaker's web site.
  Initial approach: Application
  Send request by: Mail or hand delivered
  Copies of proposal: 2
  Deadline(s): Early Mar.
  Final notification: Recipients notified in late Apr.
  Applicants should submit the following:
    1) Transcripts
    2) SAT
    3) SAR
    4) Letter(s) of recommendation
    5) GPA
    6) Essay
    7) ACT
  Additional information: Selection is based on academic achievement, need and extracurricular activities.
EIN: 541843987

9349
Community Foundation of Western Virginia

611 S. Jefferson St., Ste. 8
Roanoke, VA 24011 (540) 985-0204
Contact: For grants and scholarships: Michelle Eberly, Prog. Off.
FAX: (540) 982-8175;
E-mail: info@foundationforroanokevalley.org;
Mailing address: P.O. Box 1159, Roanoke, VA 24006; Grant inquiry e-mail: programs@foundationforroanokevalley.org;
URL: http://www.foundationforroanokevalley.org

Foundation type: Community foundation
Purpose: Scholarships to graduating high school seniors and/or non-traditional students of Roanoke Valley, VA for attendance at a college or university.
Publications: Annual report; Financial statement; Informational brochure; Newsletter.
Financial data: Year ended 06/30/2012. Assets, $49,375,293 (M); Expenditures, $4,546,828; Total giving, $3,047,196. Scholarships—to individuals amount not specified.
Fields of interest: Vocational education, post-secondary; Higher education.
Type of support: Scholarships—to individuals; Support to graduates or students of specific schools; Undergraduate support.
Application information: Applications accepted. Application form required. Application form available on the grantmaker's web site.
  Initial approach: Application
  Send request by: Mail
  Deadline(s): Mar. 1
  Final notification: Applicants notified between Apr. and June
  Applicants should submit the following:
    1) Financial information
    2) SAR
    3) Resume
    4) Letter(s) of recommendation
    5) Transcripts
  Additional information: Faxed or e-mail applications are not accepted. See web site for application form and a complete listing of scholarships.
Program description:
  Scholarships: The foundation administers a variety of scholarships to reward and assist capable and deserving students based on the criteria established by the fund donors. Any graduating high school senior and/or non-traditional student planning on attending a college or university may apply, however, there are unique eligibility requirements for every scholarship. Many scholarships are based on academic achievements and financial need. Others seek students pursuing a specific area of study such as music. See web site for additional information.
EIN: 541959458

9350
The Community Foundation Serving Richmond & Central Virginia

(formerly Greater Richmond Community Foundation)
7501 Boulders View Dr., Ste. 110
Richmond, VA 23225-4047 (804) 330-7400
Contact: Darcy S. Oman, C.E.O.; For grants: Susan Hallett, V.P., Progs.; For grants: Elaine

Summerfield, V.P., Progs.; For scholarships: Stacey Keeley, Prog. Assoc.
Scholarship e-mail: skeeley@tcfrichmond.org
FAX: (804) 330-5992;
E-mail: info@tcfrichmond.org; URL: http://www.tcfrichmond.org

Foundation type: Community foundation
Purpose: Scholarships to residents of central VA for higher education. Special grant programs for individuals to pursue professional development activities of their own design.
Publications: Application guidelines; Annual report; Biennial report.
Financial data: Year ended 12/31/2012. Assets, $497,636,734 (M); Expenditures, $36,662,325; Total giving, $32,429,867. Scholarships—to individuals amount not specified.
Fields of interest: Higher education; Graduate/professional education; Scholarships/financial aid; Education.
Type of support: Program development; Grants to individuals; Scholarships—to individuals; Support to graduates or students of specific schools; Awards/prizes; Undergraduate support.
Application information: Applications accepted. Application form required. Application form available on the grantmaker's web site. Interview required.
  Initial approach: Application
  Send request by: Mail
  Deadline(s): Mar. 7 for scholarships, varies for others
  Final notification: Applicants notified mid-May
  Applicants should submit the following:
    1) FAFSA
    2) Letter(s) of recommendation
    3) Transcripts
  Additional information: Eligibility requirements and application materials vary for each scholarship. See web site for a complete listing of scholarships.
Program descriptions:
  R.E.B. Awards for Distinguished Educational Leadership: The awards seek to recognize principals who go beyond the day-to-day demands of their position to create an exceptional educational environment. Four principals will be publicly recognized, one in each school district of the metropolitan area (i.e. the counties of Chesterfield, Hanover, Henrico and the City of Richmond). Each award will consist of a $7,500 cash grant to the principal and an additional $7,500 for school projects chosen by the principal. Nominees must be principals who: 1) manage effectively to promote excellence in education; 2) demonstrate leadership and exemplify commitment; 3) inspire their students and are advocates for their school and faculty; 4) encourage team spirit; 5) foster cooperation between the school and the community; 6) maintain dialogue with students, parents, faculty and staff; 7) have been a principal of their school for at least three years.
  R.E.B. Awards for Teaching Excellence: Grants to individual teachers will be awarded to support professional development and enrichment activities and to share educational ideas and experiences with teacher colleagues. Grants support projects of the teachers' own designs, including grants that support advanced degrees and world travel. Nominations for the R.E.B. Awards for Teaching Excellence are invited from parents, students, educators, and the community at-large. Eligibility is limited to full-time classroom teachers employed by the public school divisions of the City of Richmond, Chesterfield, Hanover, and Henrico Counties, as well as the Department of Juvenile Justice - Division of Education in these localities.

The qualities of an outstanding teacher may include, but are not limited to the following: 1) strong knowledge of subject matter; 2) dedication to the teaching profession; 3) inspires students and peers; 4) motivates students to develop skills and form positive habits towards learning and discipline; 5) utilizes creative methods to engage students in the subject matter.

Scholarships: The foundation administers various scholarships for higher education to graduating high school seniors as well as adult learners. Each scholarship has its own unique set of eligibility criteria (i.e. your high school, area of academic interest, etc.) and application guidelines. See web site for additional information.

Stettinius Awards for Nonprofit Leadership: The Stettinius Fund for Nonprofit Leadership will award cash grants of up to $10,000 to nonprofit professionals who have demonstrated strong leadership potential. Applicants must be employed by a recognized 501(c)(3) nonprofit organizations that serves the greater Richmond or Tri-Cities communities. The award may be used to pursue professional development opportunities of the candidate's own design, including executive seminars, advanced degree course work, best practice or applied research, on-site practice, professional exchange programs and travel. See web site for additional information.

EIN: 237009135

9351
Conquer Cancer Foundation
(formerly ASCO Cancer Foundation)
2318 Mill Rd., Ste. 800
Alexandria, VA 22314-3498 (571) 483-1700
Contact: Jane Chittick C.F.R.E., Dir., Principal Gifts
E-mail: info@conquercancerfoundation.org;
URL: http://www.conquercancerfoundation.org/

Foundation type: Public charity
Purpose: Grants for clinical research in the field of oncology.
Publications: Application guidelines.
Financial data: Year ended 12/31/2011. Assets, $36,980,488 (M); Expenditures, $20,771,487; Total giving, $16,237,145; Grants to individuals, totaling $626,669.
Fields of interest: Cancer; Cancer research.
Type of support: Conferences/seminars; Research; Foreign applicants; Awards/prizes.
Application information: Applications accepted. Application form required. Application form available on the grantmaker's web site.
  Deadline(s): Varies
  Additional information: See web site for complete application information.
Program descriptions:
Advanced Clinical Research Award in Colorectal Cancer: This award is designed to fund mid-career investigators who are committed to colorectal clinical cancer research and who wish to conduct original research not currently funded. Eligible applicants must be a physician with an M.D., D.O., or international equivalent who is in their fourth to ninth year of a full-time, primary faculty appointment in a clinical department at an academic medical institution, and who has completed productive post-doctoral/post-fellowship research and demonstrated the ability to undertake independent investigator-initiated clinical research. Grants will be funded for three years, at $150,000 per year.
Advanced Clinical Research Awards in Breast Cancer and Sarcoma: The program is designed to fund investigators who are committed to clinical cancer study and who wish to conduct original research not currently funded. This research must

have a patient-oriented focus, including a clinical research study and/or translational research involving human subjects. Award amount is $450,000 over three years, paid in increments throughout the award term to the awardee's institution. To be eligible, applicants must be a physician (M.D. or D.O.) who is five to ten years post-final subspecialty training, have a full-time faculty appointment in a clinical department at an academic medical center, have completed productive postdoctoral/post-fellowship research and demonstrated the ability to undertake independent investigator-initiated clinical research, be an active member of the American Society of Clinical Oncology, and expect to spend 75 percent of time during the award period dedicated to research.
Career Development Award: This grant provides a three-year award of up to $200,000 to clinical investigators who have received their initial faculty appointment to establish an independent clinical cancer research program. Specific areas of focus include breast cancer, cancer survivorship, geriatric oncology, health disparities, kidney cancer, multiple myeloma, ovarian cancer, pancreatic cancer, sarcoma, and young adult cancer. Proposals must have a direct patient-oriented focus, preferably including a clinical trial involving human subjects.
Clinical Trials Participation Award: Community-cased practices conducting research for at least five years are eligible for the award, which includes complimentary registration to the ASCO Annual Meeting, a travel grant to assist with expenses attending the Annual meeting, and a $500 award to the practice.
Community Oncology Research Grant: Grants of up to $30,000 each are available to help fund community-based practices and support their efforts to enhance clinical trials programs. Each of the foundation's state and regional affiliates are allowed to nominate one or more community-based practices, which: must be community-based, with high-quality audit reports and investigations in good standing; must have at least one member of ASCO involved in the research program; and must meet basic ethical and scientific standards for a quality clinical trials site.
Comparative Effectiveness Research Professorship (CERP) in Breast Cancer: Awarded in conjunction with the Breast Cancer Research Foundation, this program provides up to $500,000 to outstanding researchers who have made and are continuing to make significant contributions that have changed the direction of breast cancer research, and who provide mentorship to junior researchers. Applicants must have an M.D., D.O., Ph.D., or equivalent degree, have the rank of full professor (or equivalent), with a full-time faculty appointment at an academic medical center, and commit to spending at least 75 percent of time during the award period dedicated to research, including leading a team of research and mentoring physician-scientists.
Improving Cancer Care Grant: Awarded in partnership with Susan G. Komen for the Cure, this grant will provide extramural research funding to address important issues regarding access to healthcare, quality of care, and delivery of care, with general applicability to breast cancer. Eligible research teams will focus on implementing and/or evaluating new solutions to existing problems in quality of, access to, and delivery of care (with general applicability to breast cancer), will be led by a single principal investigator, who must be an active member of the foundation with an M.D., D.O., Ph.D., or equivalent degree, will have a multidisciplinary team of investigators (including, but not limited to, clinicians, nurses, pharmacists,

statisticians, epidemiologists, information technologists, and other research experts), and will be allowed to obtain expertise not represented in the core team through consultants and/or sub-contracts. One grant of $1.35 million will be awarded.
International Development and Education Award: Grants are available to provide support for oncologists in developing countries to attend the foundation's annual meeting and spend additional time at a comprehensive cancer center. The grants are designed to provide continuing medical education, assist in career development, and help establish strong relationships with leading ASCO members who serve as scientific mentors to each recipient. Eligible applicants must have 10 years or less of experience in the field of oncology, and no more than one year of formal training in the U.S., Canada, western Europe, Australia, or New Zealand.
Loan Repayment Program: Funded by Susan G. Komen for the Cure, this program provides repayment of qualifying educational debt to oncologists, or to oncology fellows upon completion of training, who commit to practicing oncology in a medically-underserved region of the U.S. Eligible applicants must be U.S. citizens, U.S. national, or permanent residents of the U.S. who have their M.D., D.O., or equivalent medical doctoral degree from an accredited institution. Up to $35,000 per year for up to two years will be provided.
Long-Term International Fellowships (LIFe): These fellowships provide young oncologists in developing nations with the support and resources needed to advance their training and deepen their relationship with a U.S. or Canadian colleague and his or her institution. Through a one- or two-year fellowship, the recipient will earn valuable training and experience with which they can affect change in their home country.
Medical Student Rotation: Funded by Susan G. Komen for the Cure, this program is designed to facilitate the recruitment and retention of individuals from populations underrepresented in medicine to cancer careers and increase access to quality care for underserved communities. An eight- to ten-week clinical or clinical research oncology rotation for U.S. medical students, as well as a $5,000 stipend for the rotation, plus $1,500 for future travel to the ASCO Annual meeting are provided. An additional $2,000 will be provided to support the student's mentor.
Merit Awards: Grants are available to further promote clinical research by young scientists, and to provide fellows with an opportunity to present their research and interact with other clinical cancer investigators at ASCO scientific meetings. A select number of awards are given annually to recognize outstanding abstracts submitted for consideration for presentation at an ASCO scientific meeting. The awards are given to oncology fellows who are first authors on select abstracts.
Oncology Trainee Travel Awards: These awards provide funding for up to 100 trainees to attend the association's annual meeting, in order to support the continuing education and professional development of trainee oncologists by providing them individual travel grants to defray travel expenses. Grants of up to $1,220 are available to cover travel fare, hotel and transportation costs, meals, and registration.
Resident Travel Awards: Awarded in conjunction with Susan G. Komen for the Cure, this program is designed to facilitate the recruitment and retention of individuals from populations underrepresented in medicine to cancer career, and to increase access to quality care for underserved communities. The award provides financial support for residents from

underrepresented populations to attend the society's annual scientific meeting; grants include a $1,500 travel attendance, complementary registration, and access to housing. Eligible applicants must be enrolled in an ACGME-accredited residency required for future training in a cancer-related subspecialty, be a U.S. citizen (or national or permanent resident), and have a record of good academic standing.

Translational Research Fellowship: This professorship awards outstanding translational researchers who have made, and are continuing to make, significant contributions that have changed the direction of cancer research, and who provide mentorship to future translational researchers. This award is intended to support qualified individuals who are dedicated to bringing advances in basic sciences into the clinical arena and to mentoring other translational researchers.

Young Investigator Award: One-year awards of $50,000 each are available to encourage and promote high-quality research in clinical oncology by providing funds to promising investigators during the transition from a fellowship program to a faculty appointment. Priority consideration will be given to proposals that include patient-oriented and, ultimately, clinical research. Specific areas of focus include breast cancer, cancer survivorship, geriatric oncology, health disparities, kidney cancer, multiple myeloma, ovarian cancer, pancreatic cancer, sarcoma, survivorship, and young adult cancer. Preclinical in-vitro and/or animal studies are acceptable as long as the outcome of these studies may ultimately lead to patient-oriented clinical research.
EIN: 311667995

9352
Jack Kent Cooke Foundation
44325 Woodridge Pkwy.
Lansdowne, VA 20176-5297   (703) 723-8000
Contact: Adrianne Lewis, Prog. Coord.
Application address: Jack Kent Cooke Foundation, ACT, P.O. Box 4030, Iowa City, IA 52243
FAX: (703) 723-8030;
E-mail: jkc@jackkentcookefoundation.org;
URL: http://www.jkcf.org/

Foundation type: Independent foundation
Purpose: Scholarships by nomination only to students or recent alumni from community colleges or two-year institutions who plan to transfer to four-year institutions, and to students recipients who plan to enter a full-time graduate or professional degree program. Scholarships also to students entering high school.
Publications: Application guidelines; Financial statement; Grants list; Informational brochure.
Financial data: Year ended 05/31/2012. Assets, $623,027,806 (M); Expenditures, $29,595,948; Total giving, $20,038,020; Grants to individuals, 744 grants totaling $11,626,060 (high: $89,158, low: $31).
Fields of interest: Higher education; College (community/junior); Graduate/professional education; Disasters, 9/11/01; Youth development.
Type of support: Scholarships—to individuals; Awards/grants by nomination only; Graduate support; Precollege support; Undergraduate support.
Application information: Applications accepted. Application form required.
Deadline(s): Varies
Additional information: Contact foundation for complete program information.

Program descriptions:
Continuing Scholar Graduate Award: The award is open only to students who have received an undergraduate scholarship from the foundation.

Dissertation Fellowship: The fellowship is for up to $25,000 for advanced doctoral students who are completing dissertations that inform the foundation's mission: advancing the education of exceptionally promising students who have financial need. To be eligible, candidates must demonstrate superior academic achievement, have successfully defended their dissertation proposals, and be enrolled full-time in a US graduate degree program.

Graduate Arts Award: The award is for up to $50,000 per year for up to three years to college seniors and recent graduates with significant financial need who will pursue a graduate or professional degree in the visual arts, performing arts, or creative writing. To be eligible, candidates must be nominated by the faculty representative at their undergraduate institution.

Undergraduate Transfer Scholarship Program: This program honors excellence by supporting outstanding community college students with financial need as they transfer to and complete their bachelor's degrees at the nation's top four-year colleges and universities. The foundation selects up to 60 students each year and awards each scholar up to $30,000 annually. Each award is intended to cover a significant share of the student's educational expenses - including tuition, living expenses, books and required fees - for the final two to three years necessary to achieve a bachelor's degree. Awards vary by individual, based on the cost of tuition as well as other grants or scholarships he or she may receive. To be eligible for the program, students must be nominated by the Jack Kent Cooke Foundation Faculty Representative at their two-year institution. Students cannot apply directly to the foundation. Each two-year college may nominate up to two students each year to be considered for the scholarship. The foundation does not offer undergraduate scholarships for freshman, only for transfer students. It does not award grants to institutions, but awards scholarships to individuals.

Young Scholars Program: Through this program, the foundation selects approximately 60 high-achieving youth with financial need and provides them throughout high school with individualized educational services that will enable them to develop their talents and abilities. Students apply for the program in 7th grade, enter the program in 8th grade, and continue through high school. The foundation works closely with Scholars and their families to construct a tailored educational program that includes, but is not limited to, support for summer programs, distance learning courses, and music and art instruction. Some Young Scholars attend a private school if none of their public school options adequately serve their academic potential; however, many stay in their public schools. While there is no formal financial cut-off, since the program's inception, over 90 percent of selected Young Scholars have come from families with Adjusted Gross Incomes (AGI) below $60,000. The foundation takes into consideration: high cost of living expenses in some areas, extraordinary medical expenses, number of dependents in college, number of dependents, and high cost of supporting children with learning differences. Recipients of the Young Scholars program are eligible to apply to the foundation for a one-time award of up to $50,000 to support their graduate or professional studies.
EIN: 541896244

9353
William A. Cooke Foundation
P.O. Box 462
Louisa, VA 23093-0462   (540) 967-0881
Contact: Wallace L. Tingler C.P.A., Pres.
FAX: (540) 967-0711;
E-mail: wtingler@wacooke.com; URL: http://wacookefoundation.com/

Foundation type: Independent foundation
Purpose: Scholarships to residents of Louisa and Orange counties VA for higher education at accredited colleges, universities or vocational schools.
Financial data: Year ended 12/31/2012. Assets, $9,141,972 (M); Expenditures, $442,649; Total giving, $143,100; Grants to individuals, 57 grants totaling $135,000 (high: $5,000, low: $500).
Fields of interest: Vocational education, post-secondary; Higher education.
Type of support: Scholarships—to individuals.
Application information: Applications accepted. Application form required.
Deadline(s): Mar. 15
Applicants should submit the following:
1) Letter(s) of recommendation
2) Essay
3) Transcripts
4) GPA
5) SAT
6) FAFSA
7) SAR
Additional information: Return completed application forms to your high school guidance department. Funds are paid directly to the educational institution on behalf of the students.
EIN: 542012726

9354
Cooley, Dearing and Rinker Educational Trust Fund
P.O. Box 600
Christiansburg, VA 24068-0600

Foundation type: Independent foundation
Purpose: Educational loans to residents of Clarke, Culpeper, Fauquier, Frederick, Loudoun, Rappahanock, and Warren counties, VA, for four-year college and university programs in VA.
Financial data: Year ended 08/31/2013. Assets, $571,240 (M); Expenditures, $12,257; Total giving, $0.
Type of support: Student loans—to individuals.
Application information: Applications not accepted.
Additional information: Unsolicited requests for funds not considered or acknowledged.
EIN: 521274701

9355
The Culpeper Foundation, Inc.
P.O. Box 1521
Culpeper, VA 22701-1029   (540) 825-8310
Application Address: CCHS Guidance Dept., 14240 Achievement Dr., Culpeper, VA 22701

Foundation type: Independent foundation
Purpose: Scholarships to high school graduates from Culpeper County High School VA, for higher education at Virginia colleges and universities.
Financial data: Year ended 06/30/2013. Assets, $563,593 (M); Expenditures, $39,392; Total giving, $16,853; Grants to individuals, 2 grants totaling $1,170 (high: $800, low: $370).
Fields of interest: Higher education.

Type of support: Support to graduates or students of specific schools.
Application information: Application form required.
Deadline(s): Six weeks from date of availability
Applicants should submit the following:
1) Letter(s) of recommendation
2) Essay
Additional information: Application should also include list of activities. Application available from your guidance department.
EIN: 546221677

9356
Cushman Foundation for Foraminiferal Research
489 Brooke Rd.
Fredericksburg, VA 22405-1884
URL: http://www.cushmanfoundation.org

Foundation type: Public charity
Purpose: Grants and fellowships for students to promote foraminiferal research.
Financial data: Year ended 09/30/2012. Assets, $1,834,913 (M); Expenditures, $109,923; Total giving, $30,000; Grants to individuals, 4 grants totaling $13,500.
Fields of interest: Medical research.
Type of support: Grants to individuals.
Application information: Applications accepted. Application form required. Application form available on the grantmaker's web site.
Initial approach: Proposal
Deadline(s): Mar.
Additional information: See web site for additional application guidelines.
Program descriptions:
Johanna M. Resig Foraminiferal Research Fellowship: The fellowship recognizes and forward the careers of outstanding doctoral candidates committed to the advancement of foraminiferal research. The amount of the award will be $25,000.
Joseph A. Cushman Award for Excellence in Foraminiferal Research: The award honors researchers who have made outstanding contributions in the field of foraminiferology. The award consists of recognition of the awardee in the pages of the Journal of Foraminiferal Research, and a plaque embossed with the Foundation's seal, the awardee's name and date of the award.
Joseph A. Cushman Award for Student Research: The award supports master's and doctoral student research projects dealing with the systematics, biostratigraphy, paleoecology, and ecology of fossil or living foraminifera. Current students with developed research projects in these areas are encouraged to apply for support. No award will be made for more than $2,000.
Loeblich and Tappan Student Research Award: The award supports undergraduate and graduate student research on any aspect of living or fossil foraminifera or other protists, such as diatoms, coccolithophorids, dinoflagellates, acritarchs, or radiolaria. Current students with developed research projects in these areas are encouraged to apply for support. No award will be made for more than $2,000.
William V. Sliter Research Award: The award supports graduate student research on Mesozoic and Cenozoic foraminifera. Current students with developed research projects in these areas are encouraged to apply for support. No award will be made for more than $2,000.
EIN: 150616972

9357
Danville Community College Educational Foundation, Inc.
1008 S. Main St.
Danville, VA 24541-4004 (434) 797-8495
Contact: Shannon Hair, Exec. Dir.
FAX: (434) 797-8587; E-mail: shair@dcc.vccs.edu; Additional tel.: (434) 797-8437; URL: http://www.dcc.vccs.edu/foundation/foundation.htm

Foundation type: Public charity
Purpose: College scholarships for students to attend Danville Community College, VA, also scholarships for Danville Community College students to attend four year institutions.
Financial data: Year ended 06/30/2012. Assets, $6,620,152 (M); Expenditures, $509,447; Total giving, $195,254; Grants to individuals, totaling $195,254.
Fields of interest: Higher education.
Type of support: Support to graduates or students of specific schools.
Application information: Applications accepted. Application form required. Application form available on the grantmaker's web site.
Deadline(s): Mar. 16
EIN: 541213521

9358
Datatel Scholars Foundation
4375 Fair Lakes Ct.
Fairfax, VA 22033-4234 (703) 968-9000
Contact: Jane H. Roth, Secy. and Dir.

Foundation type: Company-sponsored foundation
Purpose: Scholarships to undergraduate and graduate students attending a Datatel client college or university.
Financial data: Year ended 12/31/2012. Assets, $133,162 (M); Expenditures, $503; Total giving, $0.
Fields of interest: Higher education.
Type of support: Scholarships—to individuals; Graduate support; Undergraduate support.
Application information: Applications not accepted.
Additional information: The scholarship program is currently on hiatus. The foundation will distribute information when grantmaking resumes.
Program descriptions:
Angelfire Scholarship: The foundation awards $1,700 scholarships to outstanding graduate and undergraduate students currently attending an eligible Datatel client institution who served the U.S. military or is a child or spouse of a veteran.
Datatel Scholars Foundation Scholarship: The foundation awards scholarships of up to $2,400 to undergraduate and graduate students currently attending an eligible Datatel client institution. Applicants must have a GPA of 3.50 or higher and should apply to their educational institutions. Each participating school may nominate two of their most outstanding students for scholarship consideration.
Russ Griffith Memorial Scholarship: The foundation awards $2,000 scholarships to outstanding graduates and undergraduate students currently attending an eligible Datatel client institution who have returned to school after an absence of five years or longer.
EIN: 541604129

9359
Lorimer & Betty Gael Davidson Foundation
c/o Philip J. Sweeney
3815 N. Dickerson St.
Arlington, VA 22207-2968 (507) 931-1682
Application address: Distinguished Scholars Awards, Scholarship America, 1 Scholarship Way, Saint Peter, MN 56082

Foundation type: Independent foundation
Purpose: Scholarships to eligible dependents of employees of GEICO and its affiliates.
Financial data: Year ended 12/31/2012. Assets, $1,180,766 (M); Expenditures, $62,047; Total giving, $47,000; Grants to individuals, 18 grants totaling $47,000 (high: $6,000, low: $2,000).
Type of support: Employee-related scholarships.
Application information: Applications accepted. Application form required.
Initial approach: Letter
Deadline(s): Mar. 31
Additional information: The program is administered by Scholarship America.
Company name: GEICO
EIN: 237230075

9360
Descendants of the Signers of the Declaration of Independence
8507 Henrico Ave.
Richmond, VA 23229 (804) 754-7319
E-mail: president.dsdi@yahoo.com; URL: http://www.dsdi1776.com

Foundation type: Public charity
Purpose: Scholarships to members of Descendents of the Signers of the Declaration of Independence.
Financial data: Year ended 04/30/2012. Assets, $904,794 (M); Expenditures, $63,198; Total giving, $9,000; Grants to individuals, totaling $9,000.
Fields of interest: Historic preservation/historical societies.
Type of support: Undergraduate support.
Application information: Application should include an essay. Contact foundation for current application deadline/guidelines.
EIN: 236397427

9361
Diema's Dream Foundation
9103 Dellwood Dr.
Vienna, VA 22180-6120 (703) 319-9164
Contact: Debra Cockrell, C.F.O. and Exec. Dir.
FAX: (703) 319-0011;
E-mail: debra@diemasdream.com; URL: http://www.diemasdream.com

Foundation type: Public charity
Purpose: Grants to mentally and/or physically disabled children in Eastern Europe and Russia for educational, medical, and other types of support.
Publications: Financial statement; Informational brochure; Newsletter; Program policy statement.
Financial data: Year ended 12/31/2011. Assets, $390,562 (M); Expenditures, $601,749; Total giving, $446,119.
Fields of interest: Children, services; Disabilities, people with.
Type of support: Grants for special needs.
Application information: Applications not accepted.
Additional information: Unsolicited applications not considered or acknowledged.
EIN: 364254630

9362
Dolphin Scholarship Foundation
4966 Euclid Rd. Ste. 109
Virginia Beach, VA   23462-6637   (757)
671-3200
Contact: Andrew Clark, Exec. Dir.
Additional e-mail: scholars@dolphinscholarship.org
FAX: (757) 671-3330;
E-mail: info@dolphinscholarship.org; E-mail for
Amy-Beth Johnson: rklein@dolphinscholarship.org;
URL: http://www.dolphinscholarship.org

Foundation type: Public charity
Purpose: Scholarships to high school or college
children or stepchildren of members or former
members of the U.S. Navy Submarine Service for
attendance at four year colleges or universities and
intend to work toward a BS or BA degree.
Publications: Application guidelines; Informational
brochure; Newsletter.
Financial data: Year ended 06/30/2012. Assets,
$3,841,868 (M); Expenditures, $563,555; Total
giving, $387,437; Grants to individuals, totaling
$387,437.
Fields of interest: Higher education; Military/
veterans' organizations.
Type of support: Scholarships—to individuals.
Application information: Applications accepted.
Application form required. Application form
available on the grantmaker's web site.
> *Deadline(s):* Mar. 15
> *Final notification:* Applicants will be notified in
> Apr.
> *Additional information:* Scholarships are awarded
> on the basis of academic proficiency, financial
> need and commitment and excellence to
> school and community activities.
EIN: 546038828

9363
The Marie A. Dornhecker Foundation
308 Cedar Lakes Dr., 2nd Fl.
Chesapeake, VA   23322-8343   (757) 547-9191
Contact: Robert R. Kinser, Dir.
URL: http://www.dornheckerfoundation.org

Foundation type: Operating foundation
Purpose: Scholarships to students who reside in
the Hampton Roads, VA, area for undergraduate or
graduate study of French language and culture.
Financial data: Year ended 12/31/2012. Assets,
$1,077,032 (M); Expenditures, $51,643; Total
giving, $44,100; Grants to individuals, 23 grants
totaling $43,000 (high: $3,000, low: $500).
Fields of interest: Language (foreign).
International interests: France.
Type of support: Undergraduate support.
Application information: Applications accepted.
Application form required. Application form
available on the grantmaker's web site.
> *Deadline(s):* July 17
> *Applicants should submit the following:*
> 1) Transcripts
> 2) Essay
EIN: 541945504

9364
Major Robertson Doughty III Memorial
Foundation, Inc.
P.O. Box 128
Onley, VA   23418
Contact: Dennis R. Custis, Dir.
Application address: 6 Lake St., Onancock, VA
23417

Foundation type: Independent foundation

Purpose: Scholarships to graduating high school
seniors of Accomack County, VA.
Financial data: Year ended 12/31/2012. Assets,
$143,559 (M); Expenditures, $4,500; Total giving,
$4,400; Grants to individuals, 2 grants totaling
$4,400 (high: $2,200, low: $2,200).
Fields of interest: Higher education.
Type of support: Scholarships—to individuals.
Application information: Applications accepted.
Application form required.
> *Initial approach:* Application
> *Deadline(s):* May 1
> *Additional information:* Applicants must display
> financial need and a "C" average or better
> throughout high school.
EIN: 541280523

9365
Jean B. Duerr Memorial Fund Irrevocable
Trust 001943
P.O. Box 90002
Blacksburg, VA   24062-9002

Foundation type: Independent foundation
Purpose: Scholarships to female residents of VA.
Financial data: Year ended 12/31/2012. Assets,
$165,733 (M); Expenditures, $9,691; Total giving,
$7,400; Grants to individuals, 4 grants totaling
$7,400 (high: $2,000, low: $1,400).
Fields of interest: Higher education; Women.
Type of support: Scholarships—to individuals.
Application information: Applications accepted.
Application form required.
> *Deadline(s):* Mar. 1
EIN: 546317343

9366
Terrell H. Dunnavant Scholarship Fund,
Inc.
30 Willis Mountain Plant Ln.
Dillwyn, VA   23936
Contact: Lakshmi A. Bertram, Dir.

Foundation type: Company-sponsored foundation
Purpose: Scholarships to graduating seniors of
Buckingham County High School, VA, or Prince
Edward County High School, VA.
Financial data: Year ended 12/31/2012. Assets,
$2,727 (M); Expenditures, $8,046; Total giving,
$8,000; Grants to individuals, 4 grants totaling
$8,000 (high: $2,000, low: $2,000).
Fields of interest: Higher education.
Type of support: Support to graduates or students
of specific schools.
Application information: Applications accepted.
Application form required.
> *Deadline(s):* Apr. 15
> *Applicants should submit the following:*
> 1) Letter(s) of recommendation
> 2) Essay
EIN: 611417298

9367
Eastern Virginia AIDS Network
9229 Granby St.
Norfolk, VA   23503-4441   (757) 583-1317
FAX: (757) 583-2749; Additional addresses
(Newport News office): 813 Forrest Dr., Newport
News, VA 23606-4513, tel.: (757) 591-2012, fax:
(757) 591-2015; (Williamsburg office): 479
McLaws Cir., Ste. 2, Williamsburg, VA 23185-5798,
tel.: (757) 220-4606, fax: (757) 253-0001;
URL: http://www.theaidsfund.org/

Foundation type: Public charity
Purpose: Financial assistance to individuals living
with HIV/AIDS in VA with medical expenses, health
care, dental care, food, rent, utilities,
transportation, and household items to make their
lives healthier and happier.
Publications: Annual report.
Financial data: Year ended 06/30/2012. Assets,
$415,488 (M); Expenditures, $2,203,346; Total
giving, $790,920; Grants to individuals, totaling
$392,009.
Fields of interest: Human services; AIDS, people
with.
Type of support: Grants for special needs.
Application information: Contact the network for
assistance.
EIN: 541266663

9368
Eastern Virginia Medical School
Foundation
P.O. Box 5
Norfolk, VA   23501-0005   (757) 446-6070
FAX: (757) 446-7451;
E-mail: info@evmsfoundation.org; URL: http://
www.evms.edu/

Foundation type: Public charity
Purpose: Scholarships for students attending
Eastern Virginia Medical School, Norfolk, VA
pursuing a degree in health related fields.
Financial data: Year ended 06/30/2012. Assets,
$68,032,774 (M); Expenditures, $6,180,961;
Total giving, $5,935,050; Grants to individuals,
totaling $454,428.
Fields of interest: Health sciences school/
education.
Type of support: Support to graduates or students
of specific schools.
Application information: Applications not
accepted.
> *Additional information:* Unsolicited requests for
> funds not considered or acknowledged.
> Scholarships are only for EVMS students.
EIN: 237053028

9369
EastWest Foundation
(formerly The Fenchuk Foundation)
14700 Village Square Pl.
Midlothian, VA   23112-2253

Foundation type: Independent foundation
Purpose: Grants to VA residents primarily for food
and medical expenses.
Financial data: Year ended 09/30/2012. Assets,
$94,135 (M); Expenditures, $17,615; Total giving,
$16,650.
Fields of interest: Human services; Economically
disadvantaged.
Type of support: Grants for special needs.
Application information: Applications not
accepted.
> *Additional information:* Unsolicited requests for
> funds not considered or acknowledged.
EIN: 541391171

9370
Echo, Inc.
7205 Old Keene Mill Rd.
Springfield, VA   22150-3527   (703) 569-9160
FAX: (703) 455-2763; E-mail: echoadmin@cox.net;
URL: http://www.echo-inc.org

Foundation type: Public charity

Purpose: Emergency assistance to families and individuals who are residents of the Burke/Springfield, Fairfax county, VA area experiencing temporary difficulties with food, clothing, household items and financial support.
Publications: Annual report; Financial statement.
Financial data: Year ended 06/30/2012. Assets, $204,038 (M); Expenditures, $1,304,724; Total giving, $1,214,012; Grants to individuals, totaling $993,536.
Fields of interest: Economically disadvantaged.
Type of support: Emergency funds; Grants for special needs.
Application information: Contact the organization for assistance.
EIN: 540852799

9371
EduCap, Inc.
21680 Ridgetop Cir.
Sterling, VA 20166-6590 (703) 674-4718
Contact: Catherine Reynolds, Chair. and C.E.O.
Toll-free tel.: (800) 865-3276; URL: http://www.loantolearn.com

Foundation type: Public charity
Purpose: Educational loans to students who are accepted for enrollment full time or part time in an accredited college, university or private secondary school.
Publications: Application guidelines.
Financial data: Year ended 09/30/2011. Assets, $233,020,365 (M); Expenditures, $19,670,269; Total giving, $3,315,679.
Fields of interest: Higher education.
Type of support: Student loans—to individuals.
Application information: Maximum loan amounts are based on school costs income and debt to income ratio.
Program description:
Loan to Learn Education Loan Program: This program provides unsecured higher education loans based on borrower income and credit, reflecting a store of wisdom and experience accumulated over nearly two decades of education lending. Student loans cover all education-related expenses of up to $50,000 per year.
EIN: 521509402

9372
Education Consumers Foundation
c/o East Tennessee Foundation
1655 N. Fort Myer Dr., Ste. 700
Arlington, VA 22209-3199 (703) 248-2611
Contact: J.E. Stone, Pres.
FAX: (703) 525-8841;
E-mail: ecf@education-consumers.org; E-mail For J.E. Stone: professor@education-consumers.org; URL: http://www.education-consumers.org

Foundation type: Public charity
Purpose: Cash awards honoring TN public school principals for achieving proven records of school performance.
Publications: Occasional report.
Financial data: Year ended 12/31/2012. Assets, $1,239,021 (M); Expenditures, $347,414; Total giving, $36,000; Grants to individuals, totaling $24,000.
Fields of interest: Elementary/secondary education.
Type of support: Awards/prizes.
Application information: Recipients are selected based on their school's most recent three-year average achievement gains in math and reading/language arts. Only principals with five or more years of service are considered.
Program description:
Achievement Awards: The foundation identified principals of the first, second, and third highest performing elementary and middle schools in Tennessee's East, Middle, and West Grand divisions. The awards are $3,000, $2,000 and $1,000.
EIN: 203859268

9373
The English Foundation
(formerly The English Foundation-Trust)
c/o English's Inc.
1522 Main St.
Altavista, VA 24517-1132 (434) 369-4771
Contact: E.R. English, Jr., Tr.

Foundation type: Independent foundation
Purpose: Scholarships to students of Altavista High School, in the Campbell county VA area.
Financial data: Year ended 12/31/2012. Assets, $2,141,434 (M); Expenditures, $207,687; Total giving, $168,350.
Type of support: Support to graduates or students of specific schools; Undergraduate support.
Application information: Application form required.
Deadline(s): None
Additional information: Application forms may be requested from the manager.
EIN: 546036409

9374
The W. C. English Scholarship Foundation
P.O. Box P7000
Lynchburg, VA 24505

Foundation type: Independent foundation
Purpose: Scholarships to students of Lynchburg, VA, attending two or four-year accredited institutions with a preference for four-year programs.
Financial data: Year ended 12/31/2013. Assets, $452,631 (M); Expenditures, $36,219; Total giving, $36,000; Grants to individuals, 33 grants totaling $36,000 (high: $2,250, low: $250).
Type of support: Scholarships—to individuals.
Application information: Application form required.
Initial approach: Letter
Deadline(s): Apr. 1
EIN: 541658362

9375
Epilepsy Therapy Project
P.O. Box 742
10 N. Pendleton St.
Middleburg, VA 20118-0742 (540) 687-8077
Contact: Warren B. Lammert, Chair.
E-mail address for award:
sharktank@epilepsytherapyproject.org
FAX: (540) 687-8066;
E-mail: info@epilepsytherapyproject.org; URL: http://www.epilepsy.com

Foundation type: Public charity
Purpose: Research grants to accelerate new therapies for people with epilepsy and seizures.
Publications: Application guidelines; Annual report.
Financial data: Year ended 12/31/2011. Assets, $500,118 (M); Expenditures, $2,174,839; Total giving, $411,872.
Fields of interest: Disabilities, people with.
Type of support: Grants to individuals; Awards/prizes.

Application information:
Initial approach: Proposal
Send request by: Online
Deadline(s): Jan. 15 for Letter or Intent
Additional information: See web site for additional guidelines.
Program description:
Shark Tank Competition: This award is intended to spur inventors and entrepreneurs to submit proposals for product concepts, therapeutics or technologies with the promise of improving treatment and/or quality-of-life for people living with epilepsy. The top finalists will present their product concepts or therapeutic candidates at the Antiepileptic Drug and Device Trials (AEDD) XII Conference. The winning entry will be selected by live voting at the conference by an expert panel of judges and audience members representing industry, patient advocacy, investment, research and medical communities. The project deemed most innovative will be announced at the conclusion of the conference, and the winner will receive a $100,000 grant to accelerate the idea towards improving the quality of life of people with epilepsy.
EIN: 208640700

9376
Fary Memorial Scholarship Fund
300 Duke St.
P.O. Box 485
Tappahannock, VA 22560-0485 (804) 443-6773
Contact: William L. Lewis, Tr.
FAX: (804) 443-9303; URL: http://www.faryscholarship.org

Foundation type: Independent foundation
Purpose: Scholarships to residents of certain rural counties in VA.
Financial data: Year ended 12/31/2012. Assets, $2,909,959 (M); Expenditures, $196,738; Total giving, $134,578; Grants to individuals, 144 grants totaling $122,578.
Type of support: Scholarships—to individuals.
Application information: Applications accepted. Application form required. Application form available on the grantmaker's web site.
Deadline(s): Dec. 14
Final notification: Applicants notified by late Apr.
Applicants should submit the following:
1) Financial information
2) Letter(s) of recommendation
3) Transcripts
4) SAT
Additional information: See web site for list of eligible counties and additional information.
EIN: 541827276

9377
Focused Ultrasound Surgery Foundation
1230 Cedars Ct., Ste. F
Charlottesville, VA 22902-5306 (434) 220-4993
Contact: Neal Kassell, Chair.
FAX: (434) 220-4978;
E-mail: info@fusfoundation.org; E-Mail for Neal Kassell: nkassell@fusfoundation.org; URL: http://www.fusfoundation.org

Foundation type: Public charity
Purpose: Research and fellowship support for researchers working in the field of MR-guided focused ultrasound.
Publications: Application guidelines.

Financial data: Year ended 12/31/2011. Assets, $8,039,493 (M); Expenditures, $5,670,311; Total giving, $1,611,976; Grants to individuals, totaling $1,407,452.

Fields of interest: Diagnostic imaging; Diagnostic imaging research.

Type of support: Fellowships; Research; Grants to individuals.

Application information: Applications accepted. Application form required. Application form available on the grantmaker's web site.

   Send request by: On-line

   Deadline(s): None

Program descriptions:

   Fellowship Program: This program offers year-long fellowships that provide qualified physicians with combined clinical and research opportunities in the field of magnetic resonance (MR)-guided focused ultrasound. Primarily, this program works to: train clinician and clinician-investigators in MR-guided focused ultrasound treatment and clinical research; accelerate the worldwide adoption of MR-guided focused ultrasound through physician education; facilitate the establishment of MR-guided focused ultrasound surgery centers by increasing the number of clinicians trained in the use of this technology; and establish the standards for training, competencies, certification, and credentialing in MR-guided focused ultrasound. Applicants will receive up to $100,000 of support for a twelve-month period; fellows may be either part-time or full-time, with the amount of funding awarded to part-time fellows dependent on the percentage of effort that the applicant intends to commit to the fellowship. All fellowships must include a clinical training component (i.e., award recipients are expected to be trained in the clinical application of MR-guided focused ultrasound during the fellowship period)

   Research Awards Program: This program provides funding for preclinical research projects and pilot clinical trials related to the application or use of magnetic resonance (MR)-guided focused ultrasound that have high potential for rapidly leading to the development of clinical indications. Goals include: to develop new clinical applications for MR-guided focused ultrasound technology; to increase the awareness of MR-guided focused ultrasound technology and techniques; to facilitate regulatory approval of MR-guided focused ultrasound procedures; and to facilitate reimbursement of focused ultrasound procedures. Awards of approximately $100,000 per recipient will be given, with larger projects and longer funding periods considered for exceptional proposals; grants are generally not intended to fund basic science or discovery-stage research projects, nor for funding projects aimed at developing new technologies.

EIN: 205744808

9378
The Food Allergy & Anaphylaxis Network, Inc.

7925 Jones Branch Dr., Ste. 1100
McLean, VA 22102 (703) 691-3179
Contact: John L. Lehr, C.E.O.
Application address: 515 Madison Ave., Ste. 1912, New York, NY 10022-5403, e-mail:mjmarchisotto@foodallergy.org
FAX: (703) 691-2713; E-mail: faan@foodallergy.org; Toll-free tel.: (800) 929-4040; URL: https://www.foodallergy.org

Foundation type: Public charity

Purpose: Research grants to established investigators who are engaged in food allergy research.

Publications: Application guidelines; Annual report; Newsletter.

Financial data: Year ended 12/31/2011. Assets, $4,147,275 (M); Expenditures, $4,384,544; Total giving, $312,392; Grants to individuals, totaling $52,392.

Fields of interest: Allergies research.

Type of support: Research; Grants to individuals.

Application information: Applications accepted.

   Initial approach: Proposal

   Send request by: On-line or mail

   Deadline(s): Ongoing

   Additional information: See web site for additional guidelines.

EIN: 541605958

9379
Foodbank of Southeastern Virginia

800 Tidewater Dr.
Norfolk, VA 23504-3326 (757) 627-6599
FAX: (757) 627-8588; Mailing address: P.O. Box 1940, Norfolk, VA 23501-1940; toll-free tel.: (877) 486-4379; URL: http://www.foodbankonline.org

Foundation type: Public charity

Purpose: Emergency food assistance to individuals and families in need throughout southeastern VA.

Publications: Newsletter.

Financial data: Year ended 06/30/2012. Assets, $11,367,821 (M); Expenditures, $26,273,824; Total giving, $21,811,318.

Fields of interest: Food services; Food banks.

Type of support: Emergency funds; In-kind gifts.

Application information: Applications not accepted.

   Additional information: Contact the organization for assistance.

EIN: 521219783

9380
The Foundation for Physical Therapy, Inc.

(formerly The Foundation for Physical Therapy Research)
1111 N. Fairfax St.
Alexandria, VA 22314-1484 (703) 684-2782
Contact: Barbara Malm, Exec. Dir.
FAX: (703) 706-8587;
E-mail: info@foundation4pt.org; Toll-free tel.: (800) 875-1378; URL: http://www.foundation4pt.org

Foundation type: Public charity

Purpose: Research grants and doctoral support to students at regionally accredited post professional doctoral programs in physical therapy.

Publications: Application guidelines; Annual report; Financial statement; Grants list; Informational brochure; Multi-year report.

Financial data: Year ended 12/31/2011. Assets, $6,559,772 (M); Expenditures, $1,027,941; Total giving, $285,500; Grants to individuals, totaling $285,500.

Fields of interest: Physical therapy.

Type of support: Fellowships; Research; Scholarships—to individuals; Postgraduate support; Doctoral support.

Application information: Applications accepted. Application form required. Application form available on the grantmaker's web site.

   Initial approach: Letter or e-mail.

   Send request by: Online

   Deadline(s): Jan. 18 for PODS I & II Scholarships

   Final notification: Recipients notified June 1 for scholarships, Dec. for research grants

Applicants should submit the following:

   1) Transcripts

   2) Resume

   3) Proposal

   4) Letter(s) of recommendation

   5) Curriculum vitae

   6) Budget Information

   Additional information: See web site for additional guidelines.

Program descriptions:

   Florence P. Kendall Doctoral Scholarships: A one year scholarship of $5,000 will be awarded to doctoral candidates to meet any type of tuition expense or academic fees reasonably and logically associated with the doctoral program. Priority will be given to applicants who: show promise of completion of full-time or part-time degree requirements in a timely fashion; demonstrate potential for a career as an academic researcher and educator in an accredited physical therapy education program; and are working on research directly related to the mission and goals of the American Physical Therapy Association.

   Geriatric Research Grant: Up to $40,000 funds emerging investigators examining methods to facilitate the translation of research into current physical therapy practice with again adults.

   Magistro Family Foundation Research Grant: The program awards a grant of up to $40,000 to fund research in evaluating the effectiveness of interventions most commonly delivered by physical therapists as determined by current practice patterns. Preferred consideration will be given to applications that examine not only the therapeutic effectiveness of interventions, but their cost effectiveness.

   New Investigator Fellowship Training Initiative (NIFTI) and Health Services Research (NIFTI-HSR) Grants: The program is designed to fund doctorally-prepared physical therapists and physical therapist assistants as developing researchers and to improve their competitiveness in securing external funding for their future research. The foundation seeks to fund the most highly-qualified physical therapists intent upon pursuing a career in research of physical therapy and related health care issues. This is a two-year award; the first year provides $35,000 with an additional $5,000 stipend to defray project expenses, while $38,000 will be awarded for the second year.

   Pediatric Research Grant: The program awards a grant of up to $40,000 to fund research in evaluating one or more of the elements in the physical therapy patient/client management for children with developmental disabilities. The project may focus on examination, diagnosis, prognosis, or intervention (including optimal characteristics of intervention, e.g., intensity or model of service delivery). Priority will be placed on proposals that examine the effectiveness of physical therapy intervention.

   Promotion of Doctoral Studies (PODS) I: The program awards up to $7,500 per year in support of the coursework phase of post-professional doctoral studies prior to candidacy (as defined by the applicant's institution)

   Promotion of Doctoral Studies (PODS) II: The program awards up to $15,000 in support of the post-candidacy phase of post-professional doctoral studies.

   Research Grants: Up to two grants of up to $40,000 each will be made available for research in evaluating the effectiveness of physical therapist interventions. Intervention studies must involve interventions provided by physical therapists, or selected components of the interventions should

be provided by physical therapist assistants under the direction and supervision of physical therapists.
EIN: 136161225

9381
Foundation for Technology and Engineering Educators

1914 Association Dr., Ste. 201
Reston, VA 20191-1538   (703) 860-2100
Contact: Steven A. Barbato, Exec. Dir.
FAX: (703) 860-0353;
E-mail: itea@iteaconnect.org; E-mail For Steven A. Barbato: sbarbato@iteea.org; URL: http://www.iteaconnect.org

Foundation type: Public charity
Purpose: Awards, grants and scholarships for individuals to support the advancement of technology education.
Publications: Application guidelines; Occasional report.
Financial data: Year ended 06/30/2012. Assets, $1,217,820 (M); Expenditures, $55,959; Total giving, $5,000; Grants to individuals, totaling $5,000.
Fields of interest: Engineering/technology.
Type of support: Grants to individuals; Scholarships—to individuals; Awards/prizes.
Application information: Applications accepted. Application form available on the grantmaker's web site.
> *Initial approach:* Application
> *Copies of proposal:* 4
> *Deadline(s):* Dec. 1
> *Applicants should submit the following:*
> 1) Letter(s) of recommendation
> 2) Transcripts
> 3) Resume
> 4) Curriculum vitae
Program descriptions:
Claussen/FTEE Memorial Scholarship for ITEEA TECA Student Professional Development: A $300 grant will be made available to Technology Education Collegiate Association (TECA) members to offset the expenses of attending the association's annual conference. Applicant must be an undergraduate junior or senior TECA member preparing to become a technology and/or engineering education teacher in Grades K-12.
Litherland/FTE Scholarship: The $1,000 scholarship is available to an undergraduate student majoring in technology or engineering education teacher preparation. The award is based upon interest in teaching, academic ability, need and faculty recommendations. Applicant must be a member of the International Technology Education Association, must not be a senior by application deadline, and must be a current, full-time (as defined by the respective institution) undergraduate majoring in technology or engineering education teacher preparation.
Maley/FTE Technology Teacher Scholarship: The program awards a $1,000 scholarship to support teachers in their preparation to increase the positive outcomes of technology and engineering education. Criteria include: evidence of teaching success; plans for action research; recommendations; plans for professional development; and the applicant's need. Applicant must be a member of the International Technology Education Association, and must be a technology and engineering teacher at any grade level who is beginning or continuing graduate study.
Pitsco/Hearlihy/FTE Grant: This $2,000 grant is for a technology teacher at any grade level (K-12). Its purpose is to recognize and encourage the integration of a quality technology and engineering

education program within the school curriculum. Criteria include: evidence of an effective quality technology and engineering education program; documented success in the integration of technology and engineering education with other academic subjects; and plans for professional development via the anticipated grant. Applicant must be a member of the International Technology Education Association, and must be a teacher (elementary or secondary) who is successfully integrating technology education within the school curriculum.
Undergraduate Scholarship: This $1,000 scholarship is for an undergraduate student majoring in technology and engineering education teacher preparation. The award is based upon interest in teaching, academic ability and faculty recommendations. Applicant must be member of the International Technology Education Association, must not be a senior by application deadline, and must be a current, full-time undergraduate majoring in technology and engineering education teacher preparation.
EIN: 521426174

9382
Foundation of the Pierre Fauchard Academy

11654 Plaza American Dr., Ste. 901
Reston, VA 20190   (703) 217-1480
Contact: Jennifer Teale, Exec. Dir.
E-mail: information@foundationpfa.org; Email for completed applications: jteale@foundationpfa.org; URL: http://www.foundationpfa.org

Foundation type: Independent foundation
Purpose: Scholarships to dental school students to promote the study and research of dentistry.
Financial data: Year ended 12/31/2012. Assets, $6,530,970 (M); Expenditures, $403,802; Total giving, $203,800; Grants to individuals, 54 grants totaling $81,000 (high: $1,000, low: $1,000).
Fields of interest: Dental school/education.
Type of support: Scholarships—to individuals; Postdoctoral support; Postgraduate support.
Application information: Applications accepted. Application form required.
EIN: 770120371

9383
Foundation of the Wall & Ceiling Industry

(formerly Association of the Wall & Ceiling Industry-Foundation Office)
513 W. Broad St., Ste. 210
Falls Church, VA 22046-3108   (703) 538-1600
Contact: Steven A. Etkin, Exec. V.P. and C.E.O.
FAX: (703) 534-8307; E-mail: info@awci.org; URL: http://www.awci.org/thefoundation.shtml

Foundation type: Public charity
Purpose: Scholarships to members and dependents of the Association of the Wall and Ceiling Industries and to non-member students who are pursuing a post-high school education in engineering, construction or design. Also, grants to AWCI member company employees and their families who experience a financial hardship caused by unforeseen circumstances.
Publications: Application guidelines; Program policy statement.
Financial data: Year ended 06/30/2012. Assets, $1,423,477 (M); Expenditures, $117,668; Total giving, $13,325; Grants to individuals, totaling $13,325.

Fields of interest: Architecture; Vocational education; Engineering school/education; Business/industry.
Type of support: Graduate support; Technical education support; Undergraduate support.
Application information: Application form required. Interview required.
> *Initial approach:* Telephone or e-mail
> *Deadline(s):* Aug. 1
> *Applicants should submit the following:*
> 1) Letter(s) of recommendation
> 2) GPA
> 3) Essay
Program descriptions:
AWCI Cares Financial Assistance: Grants, ranging from $500 to $8,000, are available to member of the Association of the Wall and Ceiling Industry and their families in financial hardship, from events like an unexpected death or health care costs. Applications should be submitted to the program only after all other available options for financial assistance have been exploited.
FWCI Scholarships: Awards one $10,000 scholarship to undergraduate students in the field of construction management, engineering or architecture, and who maintain at least a 3.0 GPA for the last two full-time semesters of study. Applicants must be related to an employee of the Association of the Wall and Ceiling Industry.
EIN: 521244895

9384
The William and Eva Fox Foundation

P.O. Box 1408
McLean, VA 22101-1408
URL: http://www.tcg.org/fox/index.htm

Foundation type: Independent foundation
Purpose: Fellowships to actors based on their artistic achievements, commitment to the stage, and the strength of the fellowship proposal.
Publications: Grants list.
Financial data: Year ended 06/30/2012. Assets, $5,084,127 (M); Expenditures, $264,620; Total giving, $255,000.
Fields of interest: Theater; Performing arts, education.
Type of support: Fellowships.
Application information: Applications accepted.
> *Initial approach:* E-mail
> *Deadline(s):* Feb. 13
EIN: 133497192

9385
Freedom Alliance

22570 Markey Ct., Ste. 240
Dulles, VA 20166-6919   (703) 444-7940
FAX: (703) 444-9893;
E-mail: info@freedomalliange.org; Toll-free tel.: (800) 475-6620; URL: http://www.freedomalliance.org

Foundation type: Public charity
Purpose: Scholarships to dependents of an active duty service member who died or was permanently disabled in the line of duty, or who is currently certified as POW or MIA. Also, grants to members of the Armed Forces who have been wounded in combat and are recuperating at military hospitals throughout the United States, are currently serving on the frontlines and to grieving military families.
Publications: Application guidelines; Informational brochure (including application guidelines).
Financial data: Year ended 12/31/2011. Assets, $26,167,207 (M); Expenditures, $6,850,149;

Total giving, $1,918,226; Grants to individuals, 501 grants totaling $1,288,348.
Fields of interest: Military/veterans' organizations.
Type of support: Undergraduate support.
Application information: Applications accepted. Application form required. Application form available on the grantmaker's web site.
Initial approach: Letter, telephone or online
Send request by: Mail or online
Deadline(s): July 17 for scholarships; none for grants
Applicants should submit the following:
1) Photograph
2) Letter(s) of recommendation
3) Transcripts
4) Essay
5) Financial information
Additional information: Applications must also include certificate of service/dependency.
Program description:
Scholarships: One-year scholarships are awarded annually to high school seniors, high school graduates, or registered undergraduate students of accredited colleges or to post-high school vocational/technical institutions. Applicants must maintain a GPA of at least 2.0 on a 4.0 scale; applicants must also be dependent children of an active-duty service member who was killed or permanently disabled in the line of duty, or who is currently classified as a POW or MIA.
EIN: 541411430

9386
Friedreich's Ataxia Research Alliance
P.O. Box 1537
Springfield, VA 22151-0537 (540) 895-7188
Contact: Ron Bartek, Pres.
FAX: (703) 425-0643; E-mail: fara@curefa.org; Additional Address: 533 W. Uwchlan Ave.; Downingtown, PA 19335; Additional E-Mail: info@cureFA.org; Additonal Tel.: (484)-879-6160; Fax: (484)-872-1402; URL: http://www.curefa.org

Foundation type: Public charity
Purpose: Grants to individuals for research leading to treatments and a cure for Friedreich's ataxia, and to slow, stop, and reverse the damage caused by this disorder.
Publications: Application guidelines; Informational brochure; Newsletter.
Financial data: Year ended 12/31/2011. Assets, $2,783,758 (M); Expenditures, $3,044,244; Total giving, $2,484,153.
Fields of interest: Nerve, muscle & bone diseases; Neuroscience; Nerve, muscle & bone research; Neuroscience research.
Type of support: Research; Grants to individuals.
Application information: Applications accepted. Application form required.
Initial approach: Download application form
Deadline(s): May 1 for Kyle Bryant Translational Research Awards; Rolling basis for Research and Workshop Grants
Additional information: See web site for further information.
Program descriptions:
Kyle Bryant Translational Research Award: In conjunction with the National Ataxia Foundation, up to $100,000 is available for proposals for pre-clinical/translational research focused on Freidreich's ataxia (FA) with aims targeting one or more of the following: identification of biomarkers for FA that will facilitate drug screening or elucidate disease variability, severity, and/or progression; development of animal models that permit further evaluation of candidate therapeutics; development of tools and technologies that can be directly used

for therapy development; or pre-clinical development and testing of potential targets, biologics, and devices in cells and animals.
Research Grants: These grants are designed to support research, and are offered in three tiers. Smaller, short-range seed grants (usually $25,000 to $60,000 per year for one or two years) are intended to attract new research investigators and assist existing investigators by supporting the early phases of their research, including funds for equipment and post-doctoral fellowships. These seed grants are designed to permit investigators to collect preliminary data and test initial hypotheses. In some cases, significant findings might result, or additional investigators might be attracted to the field; in other cases, the preliminary research will better prepare the investigators to submit successful applications for second-tier grants (usually $60,000 to $100,000 per year for one or two years), to be used to translate more mature research directly into projects of clinical interest or into successful applications for third-tier support from outside organizations.
EIN: 522122720

9387
Goolsby-Gardner Educational Fund
P.O. Box 486
Marion, VA 24354-0486 (276) 783-2705
Contact: J.S. Staley, Jr., Tr.

Foundation type: Independent foundation
Purpose: Scholarships and student loans to financially needy high school graduates in Smyth County, VA.
Financial data: Year ended 12/31/2012. Assets, $1,410,889 (M); Expenditures, $42,218; Total giving, $26,000; Grants to individuals, 41 grants totaling $26,000 (high: $1,000, low: $250).
Fields of interest: Scholarships/financial aid.
Type of support: Undergraduate support.
Application information: Applications accepted. Application form required.
Initial approach: Letter or telephone
Deadline(s): June 30
Applicants should submit the following:
1) FAFSA
2) Letter(s) of recommendation
3) Essay
4) Transcripts
Additional information: Application must also include a list of participation in school and community activities, and leadership positions held.
EIN: 546067955

9388
Greater Williamsburg Community Trust
(also known as Williamsburg Community Foundation)
424 Scotland St.
Williamsburg, VA 23185 (757) 259-1660
Contact: Nancy Cote Sullivan, Exec. Dir.
FAX: (757) 259-1227;
E-mail: office@williamsburgcommunityfoundation.org; Mailing Address: P.O. Box 2821, Williamsburg, VA 23187; Additional e-mail: ncsullivan@williamsburgcommunityfoundation.org; URL: http://www.williamsburgcommunityfoundation.org/

Foundation type: Community foundation
Purpose: Scholarships for graduating students from Jamestown, Lafayette, and Warhill High Schools of Williamsburg, VA for postsecondary education.
Publications: Annual report; Newsletter.

Financial data: Year ended 01/31/2013. Assets, $4,746,769 (M); Expenditures, $600,308; Total giving, $431,175; Grants to individuals, 95 grants totaling $132,097.
Fields of interest: Higher education.
Type of support: Scholarships—to individuals; Support to graduates or students of specific schools; Undergraduate support.
Application information: Applications accepted. Application form required. Application form available on the grantmaker's web site.
Initial approach: Application
Send request by: On-line
Deadline(s): Mar. 23
Applicants should submit the following:
1) Transcripts
2) Letter(s) of recommendation
3) Essay
Additional information: Student need not show financial need in order to be eligible for a scholarship. See web site for application guidelines.
EIN: 541927558

9389
Grobel Scholarship Trust
122 E. Pembroke Ave.
Hampton, VA 23669

Foundation type: Independent foundation
Purpose: Scholarships to high schools graduates in Valley County, MT who are established in postsecondary studies leading to a degree or certification in nursing or a nursing related occupation.
Financial data: Year ended 12/31/2012. Assets, $100,949 (M); Expenditures, $4,000; Total giving, $4,000; Grants to individuals, 2 grants totaling $4,000 (high: $2,000, low: $2,000).
Fields of interest: Nursing school/education.
Type of support: Scholarships—to individuals.
Application information: Applications accepted. Application form required.
Deadline(s): June
Applicants should submit the following:
1) Transcripts
2) Letter(s) of recommendation
3) Essay
Additional information: Applicants must demonstrate scholastic ability, character and integrity, participate in extracurricular and community activities, professional and/or personal accomplishments.
EIN: 810514792

9390
Augusta Schultz Grubbs Charitable Trust
c/o James D. Snyder
P.O. Box 635
Clifton Forge, VA 24422-0635 (540) 863-1700

Foundation type: Independent foundation
Purpose: Scholarships to Alleghany High School seniors, VA, who have a GPA in the top ten percent of their graduating class.
Financial data: Year ended 05/31/2013. Assets, $1,297,833 (M); Expenditures, $62,962; Total giving, $46,829; Grants to individuals, 17 grants totaling $46,829 (high: $12,000, low: $2,829).
Type of support: Support to graduates or students of specific schools; Undergraduate support.
Application information: Applications accepted.
Send request by: Mail
Deadline(s): Deadline Mar. 1.
Additional information: Application should include letter explaining plans for college

education or career in 200 words or less, grade reports and other academic progress, and transcript.
EIN: 541902317

9391

Hampton Roads Community Foundation

(formerly The Norfolk Foundation)
101 W. Main St., Ste. 4500
Norfolk, VA 23510-1644 (757) 622-7951
FAX: (757) 622-1751; URL: http://www.hamptonroadscf.org/

Foundation type: Community foundation
Purpose: Undergraduate, graduate and medical scholarships to residents of the South Hampton Roads, VA area.
Publications: Annual report; Financial statement; Newsletter.
Financial data: Year ended 12/31/2012. Assets, $265,749,751 (M); Expenditures, $16,663,602; Total giving, $14,720,687; Grants to individuals, 349 grants totaling $974,695.
Fields of interest: Higher education; Medical school/education; Theological school/education.
Type of support: Scholarships—to individuals; Graduate support; Undergraduate support.
Application information: Applications accepted. Application form required. Application form available on the grantmaker's web site.
 Initial approach: Application
 Deadline(s): Mar. 1 for most scholarships
 Final notification: Applicants notified in Apr. for undergraduate scholarships
 Additional information: See web site for complete listing of scholarships.
Program description:
 Scholarships: The foundation administers more than 65 permanent scholarship funds. Each has unique criteria set by the donors. Scholarships are awarded through a competitive process. Many of them are for undergraduate study. Graduate and medical school scholarships are also available. Scholarships are awarded based on criteria established by the donors, and most of them, applicant must demonstrate financial need. See web site for additional information.
EIN: 542035996

9392

John Harry & Edith Carter Lewis Carmine Charitable Trust

P.O. Box 1419
Kilmarnock, VA 22482 (804) 435-4247
Contact: Kim Miller

Foundation type: Independent foundation
Purpose: Educational loans to students from Mathews and Gloucester counties, VA, to attend any accredited university, college, or trade school.
Financial data: Year ended 12/31/2012. Assets, $704,002 (M); Expenditures, $42,171; Total giving, $28,060; Grants to individuals, 3 grants totaling $28,060 (high: $13,017, low: $5,199).
Fields of interest: Higher education.
Type of support: Student loans—to individuals.
Application information: Applications accepted.
 Deadline(s): None
 Additional information: Loan application can be obtained from respective high schools in Mathews and Gloucester counties.
EIN: 546262132

9393

The Clyde W. and Mary O. Henley Trust

4025 Indian Trail
Suffolk, VA 23434-7338 (757) 925-3763
Contact: Christopher B. Robinson, Tr.
Application address: 709 W. Washington St., Suffolk, VA 23434-6102

Foundation type: Independent foundation
Purpose: Scholarships to individuals from Suffolk, VA for higher education.
Financial data: Year ended 12/31/2010. Assets, $0 (M); Expenditures, $30,882; Total giving, $21,495; Grant to an individual, 1 grant totaling $2,000.
Type of support: Scholarships—to individuals.
Application information: Applications accepted. Application form required.
 Deadline(s): June 1
 Additional information: Proprietary application form available by request from the trust. Grants must be used to pay for the educational expenses of the applicant. Proof of educational expenditures must be provided to the trust. Applicant must submit a signed copy of their or their parent's most recent federal tax return and the standard FAFSA financial aid form. Applications without these forms will be denied.
EIN: 311651681

9394

Henrico Education Foundation

3820 Nine Mile Rd.
P.O. Box 23120
Richmond, VA 23223-0420 (804) 652-3869
Contact: Susan F. Stanley, Exec. Dir.
FAX: (804) 652-3425;
E-mail: sfstanle@henrico.k12.va.us; URL: http://www.henricofoundation.org/

Foundation type: Public charity
Purpose: Scholarships to graduates of Henrico County public schools, VA. Grants to any teacher, guidance counselor, or school-level administrator employed by the Henrico County School Board for the creation of programs that address objectives or specific curriculum needs at their local school.
Publications: Application guidelines.
Financial data: Year ended 06/30/2012. Assets, $644,524 (M); Expenditures, $301,381; Total giving, $117,097; Grants to individuals, totaling $63,368.
Fields of interest: Education.
Type of support: Support to graduates or students of specific schools.
Application information: Application form required.
 Initial approach: E-mail or letter
 Copies of proposal: 5
 Deadline(s): July 14 for Grants
 Applicants should submit the following:
  1) Budget Information
  2) Proposal
 Additional information: Copies of proposals for grants and application form required. Contact foundation for further application information.
EIN: 541893274

9395

Highlands Community Services Board

(also known as Highlands Community Services Center for Behavioral Health)
610 Campus Dr., Ste. 210
Abingdon, VA 24210-2589 (276) 525-1550
E-mail: tteaster@highlandscsb.org; URL: http://www.highlandscsb.org

Foundation type: Public charity
Purpose: Emergency assistance to individuals with mental, intellectual, and substance-abuse disabilities in Bristol and Washington counties, VA.
Financial data: Year ended 06/30/2012. Assets, $18,783,032 (M); Expenditures, $19,056,899; Total giving, $2,208,066; Grants to individuals, totaling $2,208,066.
Fields of interest: Mental health/crisis services.
Type of support: Grants for special needs.
Application information: Applications accepted.
 Initial approach: Telephone
 Additional information: Contact the agency for additional information.
EIN: 540979632

9396

Hispanic Heritage Foundation

(formerly Hispanic Heritage Awards)
1444 Duke St.
Alexandria, VA 22314-3403 (202) 861-9797
Contact: Jose Antonio Tijerino, Pres. and C.E.O.; For scholarships: Clarissa Sandoval
FAX: (202) 861-9799;
E-mail: info@hispanicheritage.org; URL: http://www.hispanicheritage.org

Foundation type: Public charity
Purpose: Scholarships to graduating high school seniors of Hispanic descent, based on academic achievement and community service.
Publications: Application guidelines; Informational brochure (including application guidelines); Newsletter (including application guidelines).
Financial data: Year ended 12/31/2012. Assets, $160,138 (M); Expenditures, $1,602,865.
Fields of interest: Hispanics/Latinos.
Type of support: Undergraduate support.
Application information: Applications accepted. Application form required. Application form available on the grantmaker's web site.
 Initial approach: E-mail
 Send request by: Mail
 Copies of proposal: 4
 Deadline(s): Contact foundation for current application deadline
 Applicants should submit the following:
  1) Transcripts
  2) Letter(s) of recommendation
  3) GPA
  4) Essay
 Additional information: See Web site for further program information.
EIN: 521818255

9397

Homestretch, Inc.

303 S. Maple Ave., Ste. 400
Falls Church, VA 22046-4418 (703) 237-2035
Contact: Christopher Fay, Exec. Dir.
Tel. for housing assistance: (703) 222-0880
FAX: (703) 237-4540;
E-mail: info@homestretch-inc.org; TTY: (703) 237-2268; URL: http://www.homestretch-inc.org

Foundation type: Public charity
Purpose: Housing assistance to needy individuals and families of northern, VA, with rent, utilities, furnishings and other needs.
Financial data: Year ended 06/30/2012. Assets, $8,293,038 (M); Expenditures, $2,732,577; Total giving, $779,079; Grants to individuals, totaling $779,079.
Fields of interest: Housing/shelter; Economically disadvantaged.
Type of support: Grants for special needs.

Application information: The agency serves families with children, which is the primary eligibility qualification. Housing is provided for two years or more until the family is self-sufficient. Referrals must be made by a referring agency.
EIN: 541894391

9398
Hooker Educational Foundation
P.O Box 4708
Martinsville, VA 24112-2040 (276) 632-2133
Contact: Debbie T. Lawless, Dir.

Foundation type: Company-sponsored foundation
Purpose: Scholarships to children and spouses of full-time employees of Hooker Furniture Corp.
Financial data: Year ended 12/31/2011. Assets, $2,042,471 (M); Expenditures, $78,354; Total giving, $49,250.
Type of support: Employee-related scholarships.
Application information: Application form required.
Deadline(s): Apr. 1
Applicants should submit the following:
1) Transcripts
2) Letter(s) of recommendation
Additional information: Applications should also include college board scores; Application address: c/o Dir., Personnel, Hooker Furniture Corp., P.O. Box 4708, Martinsville VA 24115.
Company name: Hooker Furniture Corporation
EIN: 541583948

9399
Housing and Community Services of Northern Virginia, Inc.
7426 Alban Station Blvd., Ste. B208
Springfield, VA 22150-2323 (703) 372-5440
Contact: Ivan Linero, Exec. Dir.
FAX: (703) 372-5445; E-mail: info@hcsnv.org;
E-mail For Ivan Linero: ilinero@hcsnv.org;
URL: http://www.hcsnv.org

Foundation type: Public charity
Purpose: Short and long term financial assistance to families and individuals in need with affordable housing and promote self-sufficiency in Fairfax county, VA.
Financial data: Year ended 06/30/2011. Assets, $35,312 (M); Expenditures, $297,180; Total giving, $37,477; Grants to individuals, totaling $37,477.
Fields of interest: Housing/shelter, homeless.
Type of support: Grants for special needs.
Application information: Applicant must demonstrate need. See web site for additional information.
EIN: 541711347

9400
Housing Opportunities Made Equal of Virginia
626 E. Broad St., Ste. 400
Richmond, VA 23219-2300 (804) 354-0641
Contact: Heather Mullins Crislip, Pres. and C.E.O.
FAX: (804) 354-0690;
E-mail: help@phonehome.org; E-mail For Heather Mullins Crislip: hcrislip@homeofva.org;
URL: http://www.phonehome.org

Foundation type: Public charity
Purpose: Assistance with down payment and closing cost to low and moderate income first time homebuyers of Richmond, Chesterfield, and Henrico, counties and the Commonwealth of VA.
Financial data: Year ended 06/30/2012. Assets, $1,198,460 (M); Expenditures, $3,166,715; Total giving, $764,328; Grants to individuals, totaling $764,328.
Fields of interest: Housing/shelter; Economically disadvantaged.
Type of support: Grants for special needs.
Application information: Assistance is granted in the form of a secured loan which is forgivable over five years, if the recipient occupies the property throughout the five year forgiveness period. Contact the agency for eligibility determination.
EIN: 237303018

9401
Hughes Memorial Home
P.O. Box 5371
Danville, VA 24540-5371 (434) 724-5757
Contact: Edward O. Blount
Application address: 508 Oxford Pl., Danville, VA 24541

Foundation type: Independent foundation
Purpose: College scholarships to qualified students who cannot afford a college education. Grants to benefit the needy and at-risk children.
Financial data: Year ended 06/30/2012. Assets, $8,897,885 (M); Expenditures, $335,590; Total giving, $418,570.
Fields of interest: Higher education; Economically disadvantaged.
Type of support: Scholarships—to individuals; Grants for special needs.
Application information:
Initial approach: Letter
EIN: 540519574

9402
IDSA Education and Research Foundation
1300 Wilson Blvd.
Arlington, VA 22209-2323 (703) 299-0200
FAX: (703) 299-0204; URL: http://www.idsociety.org/Foundation/

Foundation type: Public charity
Purpose: Awards, fellowships and scholarships to young investigators for research in infectious diseases.
Publications: Application guidelines.
Financial data: Year ended 12/31/2011. Assets, $758,014 (M); Expenditures, $1,448,651; Total giving, $624,187; Grants to individuals, totaling $564,187.
Fields of interest: Medical research.
Type of support: Fellowships; Scholarships—to individuals; Awards/prizes.
Application information: Applications accepted. Application form required.
Deadline(s): Mar.
Additional information: See web site for additional guidelines.
Program descriptions:
ASP/IDSA Young Investigator Award in Geriatrics: This award provides funding for young investigators who develop and implement a basic, clinical, or health services research project focused on a geriatric aspect of infectious diseases. Applicants must have applied for the GEMSSTAR award and received a fundable score as defined by the National Institutes of Health. Award amounts are one two-year award of $150,000 ($100,000 research grant and $50,000 career development award)

Astellas Young Investigator Awards: These awards provide funding to young investigators who have demonstrated outstanding research in any area of current interest in the field of infectious diseases. Two one-year awards of $50,000 will be awarded.
HIVMA Minority Clinical Fellowships: This fellowship works to enable underrepresented minority post-residency physicians to gain HIV clinical experience in an HIV clinical setting, and to increase the number of minority physicians with the expertise and the commitment to provide clinical care to HIV-positive patients from minority communities. Two fellowships will be awarded (one each) to an African-American and Latino applicant (who has an M.D. or D.O.) with a demonstrated interest in HIV medicine, who will have completed their residencies prior to the start of the fellowship, or are in the first five years of medical practice. Fellows will receive up to $60,000, plus fringe benefits, for one year, as well as a one-year membership to the HIV Medicine Association; mentors from sponsoring institutions will receive $10,000.
Medical Scholars Program: This program offers scholarships of up to $2,000 each to medical students with mentorship by an Infectious Disease Society of America (IDSA) member or fellow, in order to attract the best and brightest to the field by giving medical students a first-hand look at the challenges and opportunities of working in infectious diseases. Eligible students can be in any year of their studies at an accredited U.S. medical school scholarship activity must focus on pediatric or adult infectious diseases and may involve either clinical or research activities in one of the following facets of infectious disease, epidemiology, microbiology, diagnosis, treatment, and prevention.
Merle A. Sande/Pfizer Fellowship Award in International Infectious Diseases: This award is intended to encourage young physicians interested in international medicine. The award will be given for important clinical research in infectious diseases and/or HIV/AIDS conducted in a resource-limited setting. The successful applicant will be expected to spend a significant amount of time during the year in country. The award amount is $60,000 for one year. The applicant's research must be conducted in a resource-limited country as defined by the World Bank (low- income and low-middle-income countries), must indicate how much time during the year will be spent in the resource-limited country, and must be from the resource-limited country.
Pfizer Young Investigator Award in Vaccine Development: This annual award provides funding for outstanding research in vaccine development, either through clinical or laboratory investigation. The candidate must have a demonstrated commitment to vaccinology as a career, and must be conducting research or working in a recognized and accredited U.S. institution of higher learning or in a government agency. The award amount is $60,000 over two years ($30,000 per year).
EIN: 311765388

9403
IHFR Foundation
8136 Old Keene Mill Rd., A-312
Springfield, VA 22152-1843 (703) 569-8600
URL: http://www.inhopefreedomrings.org

Foundation type: Operating foundation
Purpose: Scholarships to high school seniors in Fairfax County, VA pursuing higher education.
Publications: Application guidelines.

Financial data: Year ended 12/31/2012. Assets, $17,132 (M); Expenditures, $24,566; Total giving, $20,000; Grants to individuals, 2 grants totaling $20,000 (high: $10,000, low: $10,000).
Fields of interest: Higher education; Scholarships/financial aid.
Type of support: Undergraduate support.
Application information: Applications accepted. Application form required. Application form available on the grantmaker's web site.
> Initial approach: Application
> Send request by: Online
> Deadline(s): Mid Nov.
> Applicants should submit the following:
> 1) Transcripts
> 2) Resume
> 3) Letter(s) of recommendation
> 4) Financial information
> 5) Essay
> Additional information: Applications are also available at a Fairfax County High School career center.

Program description:
In Hope Freedom Rings Foundation Scholarship: The foundation awards $10,000 scholarships to high school seniors who plan to pursue higher education at a two or four-year college or university. Recipients are selected based on academic excellence, financial need, extracurricular activities, and community service. This program is limited to high schools in Fairfax County, Virginia.
EIN: 203849277

9404
Institute for Humane Studies
c/o George Mason University
3301 N. Fairfax Dr., Ste. 440
Arlington, VA 22201-4432 (703) 993-4880
Contact: Marty Zupan, Pres.
FAX: (703) 993-4890; E-mail: ins@gmu.edu;
Toll-free tel.: (800) 697-8799; URL: http://www.theihs.org/

Foundation type: Public charity
Purpose: Scholarships and grants for undergraduates and graduate students pursuing higher education.
Financial data: Year ended 08/31/2011. Assets, $5,062,561 (M); Expenditures, $8,632,911; Total giving, $746,139; Grants to individuals, 278 grants totaling $645,392. Subtotal for fellowships: 298 grants totaling $716,392.
Fields of interest: Media/communications; Film/video; Theater (playwriting); Humanities; Literature; Journalism school/education.
Type of support: Internship funds; Graduate support; Undergraduate support; Postgraduate support; Travel grants.
Application information: Applications accepted. Application form required.
> Deadline(s): Varies
> Additional information: See web site for additional application guidelines.

Program descriptions:
Charles G. Koch Summer Fellow Program: Awards a $1,500 stipend, plus housing assistance and a limited number of travel scholarships, to Fellows to spend the summer completing their own writing projects. Recipients interact with a community of scholars.
Hayek Fund for Scholars: Awards up to $750 to graduate students and untenured faculty members for career-enhancing activities such as travel, research, or participation in career development or enhancing seminars.
Humane Studies Fellowships: Fellowships award amounts from $2,000 to $15,000 to

undergraduates, graduate students, law students, and professional students who are embarking on liberty-advancing careers in ideas.
Journalism Internships: Internships are available to journalism students at Freedom Communications Newspaper and include a $3,200 stipend, travel, and seminar and career workshops.
Summer Graduate Research Fellowships: Awards up to $5,000 in stipend and travel expenses to a graduate student interested in advancing his/her own research agenda by completing their own writing projects, and participating in two interdisciplinary academic conferences.
EIN: 941623852

9405
International Association of Fire Chiefs, Inc.
4025 Fair Ridge Dr., Ste. 300
Fairfax, VA 22033-2868 (703) 273-0911
FAX: (703) 273-9363; URL: http://www.iafc.org

Foundation type: Public charity
Purpose: Scholarships and awards for fire and emergency personnel to further their educational goals.
Publications: Application guidelines.
Financial data: Year ended 12/31/2011. Assets, $7,384,592 (M); Expenditures, $13,565,043.
Fields of interest: Disasters, fire prevention/control.
Type of support: Scholarships—to individuals.
Application information: Applications accepted. Application form required.
> Deadline(s): June 1 for Scholarships
> Additional information: See web site for additional guidelines.

Program descriptions:
Alan Brunacini Fire Service Executive Safety Award: This award is presented annually to the chief executive officer of a fire department (of any size or composition) which has demonstrated a unique commitment to fire service health and safety.
Benjamin Franklin Fire Service Award for Valor: This award recognizes the spirit of service, courage, and heroism that is a tradition among the world's fire and emergency services, by honoring a firefighter for his or her expert training, professional service, and dedication to the duty displayed in saving a human life. Eligible applicants include all active firefighters, career or volunteer, who have saved a human life either on or off duty.
Excellence in Fire and Life Safety Award: This award honors those who have dedicated themselves to saving lives and property through the development of codes, fire-prevention practices, and leadership techniques. Nominees for this award should be individuals whose service, professional abilities, and leadership have been exemplary in promoting the development of codes, and who serve as examples to all fire-prevention and fire-protection professionals. Eligible applicants must be nominated by an association member.
Garry Briese IAFC Safety Performance Award: Co-sponsored by Salamander Technologies, this award is presented annually to an association Safety, Health, and Survival (SHS) Section member in recognition of personal commitment and achievement in the area of health and safety.
James O. Page Award: This award is presented annually to an individual who has played a key role in creating and/or promoting non-clinical innovation and achievements in fire-service EMS management and leadership that has had a positive impact nationally.

John M. Eversole Lifetime Achievement Award: This award recognizes a living individual who has had an exceptionally distinguished career in the field of hazardous-materials emergency response. The award is presented annually to an individual who has distinguished him- or herself through his or her career by leadership and outstanding contributions to further and enhance the hazardous-materials emergency response profession.
Level A Award: This award honors individuals and organizations that have made significant contributions to the hazardous-materials emergency-response profession, and who have provided an exception al level of leadership, service, and commitment to the mission and goals of the profession.
Safety Officer of the Year: Award in conjunction with Elsevier Public Safety and the Fire Department Safety Officers Association, this award is presented annually to a safety officer in a fire department (of any size or composition) who has made a significant contribution to their organization and/or the fire service as a whole in the area of health and safety. Eligible awardees must perform the health and safety officer and/or incident safety officer function in the fire department.
EIN: 131846552

9406
International Council of Airshows Foundation, Inc.
750 Miller Dr., S.E., Ste. F-3
Leesburg, VA 20175-8993 (703) 779-8510
Contact: Caroline Trinkwalder, Chair.
E-mail: info@icasfoundation.org; E-Mail for Caroline Trinkwalder: tntphoto@comcast.net; URL: http://icasfoundation.org

Foundation type: Public charity
Purpose: Scholarships to aspiring pilots, air performers and flight instructors.
Publications: Application guidelines; Financial statement; Program policy statement.
Financial data: Year ended 06/30/2012. Assets, $145,836 (M); Expenditures, $211,050.
Fields of interest: Scholarships/financial aid; Space/aviation; Women.
Type of support: Grants to individuals; Scholarships—to individuals.
Application information: Applications accepted. Application form required. Application form available on the grantmaker's web site.
> Copies of proposal: 1
> Deadline(s): Sept. 1
> Additional information: Application should include a short biography and an essay.

Program descriptions:
Charlie Hillard Memorial Scholarship: This scholarship awards $1,000 each to two U.S. citizens 16 years or older, to support instruction in tailwheel aircraft operations or acrobatic flight.
Family Fund: Provides financial aid to individuals in the air show profession and their families who have suffered a catastrophic event.
French Connection Memorial Scholarship: Awards $1,000 each to a male and female certified flight instructor (CFI) towards pursuing aerobatic flight training.
Jan Jones Memorial Scholarship: Awards $1,000 to a female holding a private pilot certificate, to be used for aerobatic flight training.
Leo Loudenslager Memorial Scholarship: Awards of $2,000 are given in rotation to an enlisted member of the US Navy Blue Angels, the US Air Force Thunderbirds, and the Canadian Forces Snowbirds, to be used for flight training.

Red Barons Memorial Scholarship: This scholarship provides $1,000 to a U.S. citizen who is 16 years or older who is pursuing instruction in tailwheel aircraft operations or aerobatic flight.

Sean DeRosier Memorial Scholarship: Scholarships are available toward aerobatic flight training or schooling towards obtaining an A & P license. Eligible applicants must have a private pilot's license, be between the ages of 18 and 31, and must be a resident of the western U.S. (California, Oregon, Washington, Nevada, or Idaho)
EIN: 382885409

9407
Interstitial Cystitis Association
(formerly Interstitial Cystitis Association of America)
1760 Old Meadow Rd., Ste. 500
McLean, VA 22102 (703) 442-2070
FAX: (703) 506-3266; E-mail: icamail@ichelp.org;
URL: http://www.ichelp.org

Foundation type: Public charity
Purpose: Grants to researchers to support the efforts of finding the cause, cure, treatment and prevention of interstitial cystitis (IC)
Publications: Application guidelines; Annual report; Financial statement.
Financial data: Year ended 09/30/2011. Assets, $1,136,666 (M); Expenditures, $1,104,169; Total giving, $50,832; Grants to individuals, totaling $50,832.
Fields of interest: Medical research.
Type of support: Research.
Application information: Applications accepted.
Initial approach: Proposal
Applicants should submit the following:
1) Curriculum vitae
2) Budget Information
Additional information: See web site for additional guidelines.
Program description:
Research Program: The program funds research in the following areas: etiology of interstitial cystitis, epidemiology of the disease, neurophysiology, serum or urine markers, potential IC treatment modalities, pregnancy and IC, and pain management. Suitable applicants will be specialists with a particular interest in IC in the areas of urology, urogynecology, or pain management. Research projects are normally funded for one year for up to $10,000, and must be completed in one year.
EIN: 133292137

9408
Jefferson Scholars Foundation
112 Clarke Ct.
P.O. Box 400891
Charlottesville, VA 22904-4891 (434) 243-9029
Contact: Jimmy Wright, Pres.
FAX: (434) 243-9081; E-mail: jeffsch@virginia.edu;
E-Mail for Jimmy Wright : jhw2k@virginia.edu;
URL: http://jeffersonscholars.org

Foundation type: Public charity
Purpose: Scholarships to undergraduate students of VA for attendance at the University of Virginia with tuition, fees, books, supplies, room and board, and personal expenses. Fellowships based on academic merit to candidates holding a Ph.D., M.B.A., and J.D. who show outstanding achievement and the highest promise as scholars, teachers, public servants, and business leaders in the U.S. and beyond.

Publications: Application guidelines; Annual report; Financial statement; Grants list; Informational brochure.
Financial data: Year ended 06/30/2012. Assets, $270,275,470 (M); Expenditures, $13,708,043; Total giving, $7,468,045; Grants to individuals, totaling $6,833,727.
Fields of interest: Higher education.
Type of support: Fellowships; Support to graduates or students of specific schools; Graduate support; Undergraduate support.
Application information: See web site for additional guidelines.
EIN: 311755873

9409
Johns Cancer Foundation
1401 Johnston-Willis Dr.
Richmond, VA 23235-4730 (804) 330-2330
Contact: Lawrence M. Lewkow, Pres.
E-mail for patients applying for assistance: grants@thejohnscancerfoundation.com
E-mail: info@johnscancerfoundation.org;
URL: http://www.johnscancerfoundation.org/

Foundation type: Public charity
Purpose: Financial assistance to needy cancer patients in the Richmond, VA area by assisting with everyday living expenses and home health care equipment rental. Oncology nursing scholarship to a student enrolled in the John Tyler Community College.
Financial data: Year ended 12/31/2011. Assets, $212,542 (M); Expenditures, $74,854; Total giving, $59,305; Grants to individuals, totaling $59,305.
Fields of interest: Nursing school/education; Cancer.
Type of support: Scholarships—to individuals; Grants for special needs.
Application information: Applications accepted. Application form required. Application form available on the grantmaker's web site.
Send request by: Mail
Deadline(s): 2nd Monday of the month for patients
Additional information: Applicants are nominated by area Social Workers and Healthcare Providers. Checks are mailed directly to the providers. A maximum of $500 may be requested by the applicant.
EIN: 540788977

9410
Rudi Johnson Foundation, Inc.
3706 Colonnade Dr.
Colonial Heights, VA 23834-5624 (954) 752-2758
FAX: (804) 524-5323;
E-mail: foundation@rudij32.com

Foundation type: Public charity
Purpose: Scholarships to graduating high school seniors in the Virginia area for continuing education at accredited colleges or universities. Assistance to families or individuals in VA who are in crisis due to unforeseen circumstances, or hardship.
Financial data: Year ended 12/31/2011. Assets, $1,773 (M); Expenditures, $155,805.
Fields of interest: Higher education; Economically disadvantaged.
Type of support: Scholarships—to individuals; Grants for special needs.
Application information:
Initial approach: Telephone

Additional information: Scholarship selection is based on need or merit. Contact the foundation for further details.
EIN: 202623664

9411
Judges Athletic Association
P. O. Box 2213
Winchester, VA 22604-1413
Contact: Robert Lawler, Pres.

Foundation type: Public charity
Purpose: Scholarships to Handley High School, VA students who are in an athletic program.
Financial data: Year ended 07/31/2012. Assets, $345,333 (M); Expenditures, $95,269; Total giving, $85,540.
Type of support: Support to graduates or students of specific schools.
Application information: Application form required.
Initial approach: Letter
Deadline(s): Contact foundation for application guidelines
EIN: 546060341

9412
John F. Kane Scholarship Fund, Inc.
12140 Eddystone Ct.
Woodbridge, VA 22192-2213 (703) 494-4779
Contact: Barbara Tivnan

Foundation type: Independent foundation
Purpose: Scholarships to residents of Woodbridge, VA.
Financial data: Year ended 12/31/2012. Assets, $121,372 (M); Expenditures, $12,138; Total giving, $10,500; Grants to individuals, 9 grants totaling $10,500 (high: $3,000, low: $500).
Type of support: Undergraduate support.
Application information: Applications accepted.
Deadline(s): June 1
Applicants should submit the following:
1) Letter(s) of recommendation
2) Essay
3) Transcripts
Additional information: Application should also include list of honors, extracurricular activities and community service. Contact foundation for current application guidelines.
EIN: 541811279

9413
Charles B. Keesee Educational Fund, Inc.
P.O. Box 431
Martinsville, VA 24114-0431 (276) 632-2229
Contact: Mrs. Vernie W. Lewis, Secy.-Treas.
E-mail: cbkeesee@earthlink.net; URL: http://www.cbkeesee.com

Foundation type: Independent foundation
Purpose: Scholarships to students enrolled in a Masters degree program, or to students enrolled in the Doctor of Ministry program at one of the seminaries or divinity schools, and plan to enter the full time Baptist ministry or religious work in the Baptist denomination.
Financial data: Year ended 01/31/2013. Assets, $68,042,090 (M); Expenditures, $3,194,353; Total giving, $2,367,129; Grants to individuals, totaling $1,817,129.
Fields of interest: Theological school/education.
Type of support: Scholarships—to individuals; Support to graduates or students of specific schools.

Application information: Applications accepted. Application form required. Application form available on the grantmaker's web site.

Initial approach: Application
Send request by: Mail
Deadline(s): Apr. 1 for the fall and spring semesters and Oct. 1 for second semester only for the Masters Degree Program. May 1 for fall and spring semesters and Nov. 1 for second semester only for Doctor of Ministry Grant
Additional information: Applications are not accepted via fax or e-mail. See web site for listed schools and additional application guidelines.

Program description:

Ministerial Student Grant Program: Grants to ministerial students who must be United States citizens and a resident of VA, NC or SC for a minimum of twelve months prior to entering any educational institution, where the trustees reserve the right to determine residency. Applicant must be a member of a Baptist church, be preparing to enter the Baptist ministry or religious work in the Baptist denomination, determined by the Board of Trustees. See web site for additional requirements.
EIN: 540490435

9414
Edward R. Kengla Foundation, Inc.
c/o Alexandria American Legion Post 24
P.O. Box 402
Alexandria, VA   22313-0402   (703) 549-9515

Foundation type: Public charity
Purpose: Scholarships to selected students of the Alexandria, VA, post office area for college education.
Financial data: Year ended 12/31/2011. Assets, $811,816 (M); Expenditures, $25,709; Total giving, $22,500; Grants to individuals, totaling $11,500.
Fields of interest: Higher education.
Type of support: Undergraduate support.
Application information: Application form required.
Additional information: Application submitted to local schools.
EIN: 541826229

9415
Kennard Educational Fund, Inc.
c/o Stellarone Wealth Management
P.O. Box 1268
Staunton, VA   24402-1268

Foundation type: Operating foundation
Purpose: Educational loans to residents of the cities of Staunton or Waynesboro, or the county of Augusta, VA.
Financial data: Year ended 09/30/2013. Assets, $1,023,280 (M); Expenditures, $17,418; Total giving, $0.
Type of support: Student loans—to individuals.
Application information: Applications accepted. Application form required.
Initial approach: Letter
Deadline(s): July 1 preceding the academic year
Applicants should submit the following:
1) Financial information
2) Transcripts
Additional information: Application must state purpose and employment history. Forms available at the trust department.
EIN: 541157065

9416
Lawrence R. Klein Fund
c/o Ronald E. Kutscher
21045 Cardinal Pond Terr., Apt. 419
Ashburn, VA   20147-6127

Foundation type: Public charity
Purpose: Awards and prizes to authors of the best written articles in the Bureau of Labor Statistic's Monthly Labor Review.
Financial data: Year ended 12/31/2011. Assets, $2,390 (M); Expenditures, $500; Total giving, $500; Grants to individuals, 5 grants totaling $500.
Fields of interest: Journalism; Literature.
Type of support: Awards/prizes.
Application information: Articles must exhibit originality of ideas or method of analysis, adhere to principles of scientific inquiry, and well written.
EIN: 237017113

9417
Korean American Scholarship Foundation
1952 Gallows Rd., Ste. 310
Vienna, VA   22182-3823   (703) 748-5935
E-mail: feedback@kasf.org; *URL:* http://www.kasf.org

Foundation type: Public charity
Purpose: Scholarships to needy Korean-American students in the U.S. enrolled in a full time undergraduate or graduate program.
Publications: Application guidelines.
Financial data: Year ended 12/31/2012. Assets, $3,796,697 (M); Expenditures, $607,209; Total giving, $426,934; Grants to individuals, totaling $426,934.
Fields of interest: Higher education.
Type of support: Scholarships—to individuals.
Application information: Applications accepted. Application form required.
Deadline(s): Vary
Applicants should submit the following:
1) Financial information
2) Transcripts
3) Letter(s) of recommendation
4) Essay
Additional information: Applicants are selected on the basis of financial need, academic achievement, school activities and community services. Each applicant must submit an application to the respective KASF region, in which each region is designated by the state where school is located. See web site for school locations.
EIN: 237151484

9418
Lee-Jackson Educational Foundation
(formerly The Lee-Jackson Foundation)
P.O. Box 8121
Charlottesville, VA   22906-8121
Contact: Stephanie P. Leech, Secy.
E-mail: leejacksonfoundation@yahoo.com;
URL: http://www.lee-jackson.org

Foundation type: Independent foundation
Purpose: Undergraduate scholarships to juniors and seniors in Virginia public or private high schools or home schools, based on quality of submitted essay.
Financial data: Year ended 03/31/2013. Assets, $0 (M); Expenditures, $260,054; Total giving, $185,000; Grants to individuals, 16 grants totaling $30,000 (high: $10,000, low: $1,000).

Fields of interest: Historical activities, war memorials; Higher education; Scholarships/financial aid.
Type of support: Undergraduate support.
Application information: Applications accepted. Application form required.
Deadline(s): Feb. 15
Additional information: See web site for application guidelines and application form.
EIN: 540581000

9419
Lend-A-Hand, Inc.
c/o Gannett Co.
7950 Jones Branch Dr.
McLean, VA   22107-3302   (703) 854-6000

Foundation type: Public charity
Purpose: Emergency assistance to individuals and/or families who have depleted their resources and do not qualify for assistance from other charities or programs.
Financial data: Year ended 12/31/2011. Assets, $1,448,165 (M); Expenditures, $1,434,811; Total giving, $633,601; Grants to individuals, totaling $176,892.
Fields of interest: Economically disadvantaged.
Type of support: Emergency funds.
Application information: Assistance can be in the form of a one-time cash assistance paid directly to the recipient or by providing food, shelter or medical assistance or any other form needed to assist the individual or families. Contact the agency for eligibility determination.
EIN: 311375444

9420
Lewis-Gale Foundation
1902 Braeburn Dr.
Salem, VA   24153-7304   (540) 444-2925
FAX: (540) 444-2927;
E-mail: jhagadorn@healthfocusswva.org; *Mailing address:* P.O. Box 4692, Roanoke, VA 24015-0692; *URL:* http://www.lewisgalefdn.org

Foundation type: Public charity
Purpose: Scholarships to residents of the southeastern U.S. who have been accepted into a pre-medical program at an accredited college or university.
Publications: Application guidelines.
Financial data: Year ended 12/31/2011. Assets, $835,133 (M); Expenditures, $313,513; Total giving, $165,600.
Fields of interest: Medical school/education.
Type of support: Undergraduate support.
Application information: Applications accepted. Application form required.
Initial approach: Letter or telephone
Deadline(s): May 15 and Dec. 1
EIN: 546051298

9421
The Lincoln-Lane Foundation
c/o Edith Grandy
207 Granby St., Ste. 302
Norfolk, VA   23510-1825   (757) 622-2557
FAX: (757) 623-2698;
E-mail: contact@lincolnlanefoundation.org;
URL: http://www.lincolnlanefoundation.org

Foundation type: Independent foundation
Purpose: Scholarships to college students who are residents of the Tidewater, VA, area.

Publications: Application guidelines; Program policy statement.
Financial data: Year ended 07/31/2013. Assets, $7,152,364 (M); Expenditures, $588,447; Total giving, $377,000; Grants to individuals, 147 grants totaling $377,000 (high: $4,000, low: $250).
Fields of interest: Higher education; Scholarships/financial aid.
Type of support: Scholarships—to individuals; Graduate support; Undergraduate support.
Application information: Applications accepted. Application form required.
   Initial approach: Letter
   Send request by: Mail
   Copies of proposal: 1
   Deadline(s): Nov. 15
   Final notification: Applicants notified in the beginning of Apr.
   Applicants should submit the following:
   1) Financial information
   2) GPA
   3) Letter(s) of recommendation
   4) Photograph
   5) SAT
   6) SAR
   7) Transcripts
Program description:
   Scholarship Program: About 60 new scholarships are awarded annually to college students for full-time study at accredited postsecondary schools, colleges, and universities in the U.S. Applicants are selected on the basis of academic achievement, financial need, community service, and extracurricular activities. Recipients are required to submit periodic progress reports or transcripts to the foundation.
EIN: 540601700

9422
The Linhart Foundation
c/o J. Theodore Linhart
12050 W. Broad St.
Richmond, VA   23233-1001

Foundation type: Company-sponsored foundation
Purpose: Scholarships to students of Henrico County, VA, who are seeking admission to enable them to attend college or university.
Financial data: Year ended 12/31/2012. Assets, $1,022,622 (M); Expenditures, $118,321; Total giving, $100,490.
Type of support: Scholarships—to individuals; Support to graduates or students of specific schools.
Application information: Application form required.
   Initial approach: Letter
   Additional information: Senior students are recommended by the senior guidance counselor of each school.
EIN: 540846082

9423
The Jesse and Rose Loeb Foundation, Inc.
P.O. Box 803
Warrenton, VA   20188-0803   (540) 428-1960
Contact: Thomas H. Kirk, Exec. Dir.
E-mail: kirk@loebfoundation.org; URL: http://www.loebfoundation.org

Foundation type: Independent foundation
Purpose: Scholarships to graduates of Liberty High School in Fauquier County, VA, who are pursuing higher education in VA.
Publications: Application guidelines.
Financial data: Year ended 09/30/2013. Assets, $9,756,847 (M); Expenditures, $518,866; Total

giving, $402,500; Grants to individuals, 11 grants totaling $55,000 (high: $5,000, low: $5,000).
Type of support: Support to graduates or students of specific schools.
Application information: Applications accepted.
   Initial approach: Letter
   Deadline(s): Mid-Apr.
EIN: 541604839

9424
Love Thy Neighbor Community Development & Opportunity Corporation
(formerly Troy Vincent Foundation)
P.O. Box 2670
Purcellville, VA   20134-4670   (609) 989-0290
Application address: The Troy D. Vincent Scholarship Fund, c/o Love Thy Neighbor, P.O. 2670, Purcellville, VA 20132
FAX: (609) 989-5937;
E-mail: contactus@ltncdc.org; URL: http://www.ltncdc.org

Foundation type: Public charity
Purpose: College scholarships to graduating seniors of Pennsbury High School, PA and Trenton Central High School, NJ for postsecondary education.
Financial data: Year ended 05/31/2012. Assets, $44,550 (M); Expenditures, $88,510.
Fields of interest: Higher education.
Type of support: Support to graduates or students of specific schools.
Application information:
   Deadline(s): May 25
   Applicants should submit the following:
   1) Financial information
   2) Essay
   3) Transcripts
   4) Letter(s) of recommendation
   Additional information: Selection is based on leadership, character, scholastic ability, community service, extracurricular activities and financial need. Funds are paid to the educational institution on behalf of the student.
EIN: 113658341

9425
Clare Boothe Luce Policy Institute
112 Elden St., Ste. P
Herndon, VA   20170-4832   (703) 318-0730
Contact: Scholarships: Lil Tuttle, Education Dir.
FAX: (703) 318-8867; E-mail: info@cblpi.org;
Toll-free tel.: (888) 891-4288; URL: http://www.cblpi.org

Foundation type: Public charity
Purpose: Scholarships to individuals for Virginia K through 12 students.
Publications: Application guidelines.
Financial data: Year ended 12/31/2011. Assets, $1,255,470 (M); Expenditures, $1,345,914.
Fields of interest: Higher education.
Type of support: Scholarships—to individuals.
Application information: Applications accepted. Application form required. Application form available on the grantmaker's web site. Interview required.
   Initial approach: Telephone
   Deadline(s): None
Program description:
   CHOICES Scholarship Program: This program is designed to assist Virginia parents in providing their elementary and secondary school-age children a

safe and effective education in the school of their choice by providing $1,000 scholarships to provide financial aid to those who wish to attend, or are currently attending, a K-12 private school or tuition-charging, out-of-district public school. Eligible applicants must be residents of the state of Virginia and of compulsory K-12 age. This program is suspended indefinitely.
EIN: 541672138

9426
Greater Lynchburg Community Trust
101 Paulette Circle, Ste. B
Lynchburg, VA   24504   (434) 845-6500
Contact: Stuart C. Fauber, C.E.O.
FAX: (434) 845-6530; E-mail: challglct@verizon.net; Additional e-mail: sfauberglct@verizon.net; URL: http://www.lynchburgtrust.org

Foundation type: Community foundation
Purpose: Scholarships to deserving students of VA, with financial assistance for attending the college of their choice.
Publications: Application guidelines; Annual report; Informational brochure; Newsletter; Program policy statement.
Financial data: Year ended 06/30/2012. Assets, $29,622,750 (M); Expenditures, $1,626,217; Total giving, $1,331,286; Grants to individuals, 40 grants totaling $30,114.
Fields of interest: Higher education.
Type of support: Scholarships—to individuals; Support to graduates or students of specific schools.
Application information: Applications accepted. Application form required.
   Deadline(s): Varies
   Additional information: Contact local high school guidance department for information on specific scholarships that may apply to you. See web site for complete scholarship listing.
EIN: 546112680

9427
The James Maloney Foundation
1009 Lightfoot Rd.
Williamsburg, VA   23188-9020   (757) 229-2393

Foundation type: Company-sponsored foundation
Purpose: College scholarships to high school graduates for attendance at accredited colleges or universities in the Williamsburg, VA area.
Financial data: Year ended 12/31/2012. Assets, $830,347 (M); Expenditures, $45,539; Total giving, $38,500; Grants to individuals, 7 grants totaling $17,500 (high: $2,500, low: $2,500).
Fields of interest: Higher education.
Type of support: Scholarships—to individuals.
Application information: Applications accepted.
   Initial approach: Letter
   Deadline(s): None
EIN: 203957354

9428
MAPGA Scholarship Foundation, Inc.
1 PGA Dr.
Stafford, VA   22554   (540) 720-7420
Contact: Richard Johns, Exec. Dir.
FAX: (540) 720-7076; URL: http://www.mapga.com/foundationinfo/page_4/

Foundation type: Public charity
Purpose: The foundation provides scholarships to the MAPGA junior golfers pursuing higher education.

Financial data: Year ended 12/31/2012. Assets, $340,237 (M); Expenditures, $58,330; Total giving, $48,905; Grants to individuals, totaling $48,905.
Fields of interest: Higher education; Athletics/sports, golf.
Type of support: Scholarships—to individuals.
Application information: Applications accepted. Application form required. Application form available on the grantmaker's web site.
> *Applicants should submit the following:*
> 1) Transcripts
> 2) Essay
> *Additional information:* Selection is based upon on-course etiquette, academic performance, extracurricular activities, financial need and off course behavior. See web site for additional application guidelines.
EIN: 030418343

9429
Maria's Hope
5730 General Washington Dr.
Alexandria, VA 22312
URL: http://cupscoffeehouse.com/

Foundation type: Operating foundation
Purpose: Financial assistance to individuals of northern Virginia who have experienced a life tragedy, by providing temporary housing and assisting them in building a home or business.
Financial data: Year ended 01/31/2013. Assets, $6,384 (M); Expenditures, $39,974; Total giving, $0.
Fields of interest: Safety/disasters.
Type of support: Emergency funds; Grants for special needs.
Application information:
> *Initial approach:* Letter
> *Deadline(s):* None
> *Additional information:* Applicant must show supporting documents demonstrating need.
EIN: 203910716

9430
Marine Corps Scholarship Foundation, Inc.
909 N. Washington St., Ste. 400
Alexandria, VA 22314 (703) 549-0060
FAX: (703) 549-9474; E-mail: info@mcsf.org;
Toll-free tel.: (866)-496-5462; URL: http://www.mcsf.org

Foundation type: Public charity
Purpose: Scholarships to sons and daughters of active duty or reserve U.S. Marine, veteran U.S. Marine, active duty or reserve U.S. Navy Corpsman, or veteran U.S. Navy Corpsman, for attendance at accredited undergraduate college or vocational/techinal institution.
Publications: Application guidelines; Annual report; Informational brochure; Newsletter.
Financial data: Year ended 12/31/2011. Assets, $47,049,780 (M); Expenditures, $8,948,861; Total giving, $4,344,900; Grants to individuals, totaling $4,344,900.
Fields of interest: Vocational education, post-secondary; Higher education; Military/veterans' organizations.
Type of support: Scholarships—to individuals.
Application information: Applications accepted.
> *Send request by:* Online
> *Deadline(s):* Mar. 1
> *Final notification:* Applicants notified in May

Additional information: Scholarships funds are only for military family. Unsolicited requests for funds not considered or acknowledged.
Program description:
> *Heroes Tribute Scholarship Program for Children of the Wounded:* Scholarship support is provided to eligible children of wounded Marines and Navy Corpsmen attached to Marine units, from all conflicts and wars insuring that these children have the opportunity to attend college or vocational/technical institutions.
EIN: 221905062

9431
MATHCOUNTS Foundation
1420 King St.
Alexandria, VA 22314-2794 (703) 299-9006
Contact: Lou DiGioia, Exec. Dir.; Clay Battin, Dir., Devel.
FAX: (703) 299-5009;
E-mail: info@mathcounts.org; URL: http://mathcounts.org

Foundation type: Public charity
Purpose: Awards to sixth, seventh, or eight graders, "Mathletes," for promoting excellence in math skills among students.
Publications: Annual report; Financial statement; Informational brochure; Newsletter.
Financial data: Year ended 07/31/2011. Assets, $2,279,198 (M); Expenditures, $2,695,897; Total giving, $46,000; Grants to individuals, totaling $46,000.
Fields of interest: Secondary school/education; Mathematics.
Type of support: Awards/prizes; Precollege support.
Application information: Applications not accepted.
Program description:
> *Awards Program:* Awards to the top eight finishers in the national Mathcounts competition held each May in Washington, D.C. The amount of the awards may vary each year. Mathcounts competitors, "Mathletes," are sixth, seventh, and eighth graders.
EIN: 541295407

9432
J. T. - Minnie Maude Charitable Trust
223 Riverview Dr., Ste. G
Danville, VA 24541-3435 (434) 797-3330
Contact: Fred K. Webb, Jr., Exec. Dir.
FAX: (434) 797-3343; URL: http://www.jtmm.org

Foundation type: Independent foundation
Purpose: Scholarship to graduating high school students, individuals who have graduated from high schools, and those who possess a GED diploma from schools in the Danville/Pittsylvania, VA, area, and surrounding counties in NC.
Financial data: Year ended 12/31/2011. Assets, $47,505,145 (M); Expenditures, $2,809,744; Total giving, $1,899,834; Grants to individuals, 504 grants totaling $940,599 (high: $6,500; low: -$500).
Fields of interest: Higher education.
Type of support: Scholarships—to individuals.
Application information: Applications accepted. Application form required. Application form available on the grantmaker's web site. Interview required.
> *Initial approach:* Letter or telephone
> *Deadline(s):* Apr. 2 for traditional students; Feb. 1, June 1, Oct. 1 for non-traditional students

Additional information: See web site for detailed program description and criteria for selection.
EIN: 260771142

9433
MedEvac Foundation International
(formerly The Foundation for Air-Medical Research and Education)
909 N. Washington St., Ste. 410
Alexandria, VA 22314-3143 (703) 836-8732
Contact: Rick Sherlock, Pres. and C.E.O.
Application contact: Kristin Discher, kdischer@aams.org
FAX: (703) 836-8920;
E-mail: jchittick@medevacfoundation.org;
URL: http://www.medevacfoundation.org

Foundation type: Public charity
Purpose: Scholarships to children who have lost a parent in an air medical or critical care ground transport accident. Financial assistance to families of air and ground medical crew members and their patients immediately following a fatal or serious accident to cover unanticipated expenses.
Publications: Application guidelines.
Financial data: Year ended 02/28/2012. Assets, $1,148,805 (M); Expenditures, $578,086; Total giving, $26,028; Grants to individuals, totaling $14,278.
Fields of interest: Higher education; Human services.
Type of support: Scholarships—to individuals; Grants for special needs.
Application information: Applications accepted. Application form required.
> *Send request by:* Mail
> *Deadline(s):* June 30 for Scholarships
> *Applicants should submit the following:*
> 1) Essay
> 2) Transcripts
> 3) Letter(s) of recommendation
> *Additional information:* Selection for scholarship is based on academic achievement, financial need and community service. The award will be paid directly to the educational institution on behalf of the student. See web site for additional application guidelines for scholarships and family grant.
Program description:
> *Children's Scholarship Fund:* This program provides a $2,500 scholarship to a deserving student enrolled or accepted into an accredited college, university, or vocational-technical school who has lost a parent in an air medical accident. Applicant must be a legal U.S. resident.
EIN: 542007236

9434
Melton Foundation
2086 Hunters Crest Way
Vienna, VA 22181-2840 (703) 391-7247
Contact: Winthrop Carty, Exec. Dir.
E-mail: contactus@meltonfoundation.org; E-mail for Winthrop Carty: wcarty@meltonfoundation.org;
URL: http://www.meltonfoundation.org

Foundation type: Public charity
Purpose: Fellowships to address today's global challenges. Fellows participate in inter-cultural training, leadership development, and global education through symposia, travel, online activities, project grants, and social service.
Financial data: Year ended 12/31/2012. Assets, $14,812,749 (M); Expenditures, $813,014; Total giving, $203,789; Grants to individuals, totaling $8,530.

Fields of interest: University.
Type of support: Fellowships.
Application information:
Initial approach: Letter
Additional information: Fellows are selected through a highly competitive process from among the most qualified students at the five participating universities.
Program description:
Fellowships: Fellows are selected as talented undergraduates and undergo training and activities designed to forge the relationships and shared skills that become the basis of a global network for positive change in the world. Fellows enter the program as juniors or seniors in college.
EIN: 541565779

9435
The Mesothelioma Applied Research Foundation, Inc.
(formerly MARF, also known as Meso Foundation)
1317 King St.
Alexandria, VA 22314 (877) 363-6376
Contact: Erin Maas, Operations Mgr.
Research grant application address: P.O. Box 91840, Santa Barbara, CA 93190-1840
FAX: (703) 299-0399; E-mail: info@curemeso.org;
URL: http://www.curemeso.org/

Foundation type: Public charity
Purpose: Research grants to physicians and scientists for the study of mesothelioma and its cure.
Publications: Application guidelines; Annual report; Financial statement; Newsletter.
Financial data: Year ended 12/31/2011. Assets, $2,329,956 (M); Expenditures, $1,989,154; Total giving, $700,000.
Fields of interest: Cancer research; Skin disorders research.
Type of support: Research.
Application information: Applications accepted. Application form required. Application form available on the grantmaker's web site.
Initial approach: Letter or e-mail
Send request by: Mail and e-mail
Copies of proposal: 6
Deadline(s): July 29
Applicants should submit the following:
1) Resume
2) Letter(s) of recommendation
3) Proposal
4) Budget Information
Additional information: See web site for additional program information.
EIN: 752816066

9436
The Military Officers Association of America Scholarship Fund
(formerly The Retired Officers Association Scholarship Fund)
201 N. Washington St.
Alexandria, VA 22314-2539 (703) 549-2311
Contact: Laurie Wavering, Admin.
E-mail: edassist@moaa.org; Toll-free tel.: (800) 234-6622; URL: http://www.moaa.org/scholarshipfund/

Foundation type: Public charity
Purpose: Interest-free student loans and a limited number of scholarships to full-time undergraduates who are dependent children of active, retired, or deceased military officers or enlisted personnel or members of the Retired Officers Association.

Publications: Application guidelines; Financial statement; Informational brochure.
Financial data: Year ended 12/31/2011. Assets, $64,805,847 (M); Expenditures, $988,617; Total giving, $850,000; Grants to individuals, totaling $850,000.
Fields of interest: Vocational education, post-secondary; Higher education; Military/veterans' organizations.
Type of support: Scholarships—to individuals; Student loans—to individuals; Undergraduate support.
Application information: Applications accepted.
Initial approach: Letter or telephone
Send request by: On-line
Deadline(s): Mar. 1
Final notification: Recipients notified in May
Applicants should submit the following:
1) Financial information
2) Transcripts
3) ACT
4) SAT
5) Resume
Program descriptions:
American Patriot Scholarship: This scholarship program is intended to help the children of uniformed services personnel (both officers and enlisted members) who died while in active service as a member of the Regular, Guard, or Reserve forces. Eligible applicants must be a child of a member of the Uniformed Services who died while in active service, and must be under 24 years of age. Scholarships are for up to five years for undergraduate education at an accredited two or four year college of university of their choice.
General John Paul Ratay Educational Fund Grants: Grants of up to $5,000 are reserved for children of surviving spouses of retired officers. A student cannot receive both a MOAA loan and a Ratay grant. Students applying for a loan who also meet the criteria of a Ratay grant automatically is considered.
Interest-Free Loan Program: The fund provides interest-free loans to children of military families who plan to attend an accredited college or university as a full-time student. Loans of up to $5,500 per year (for up to five years) are available to students who have not yet earned an undergraduate degree. Eligible applicants must be 24 years of age and younger, and must be children of former, active, or retired officers, or active or retired enlisted military personnel. Applicants must also have a cumulative GPA of 3.0 or higher (on a 4.0 scale).
EIN: 541659039

9437
Rives C. Minor and Asalie M. Preston Educational Fund, Inc.
P.O. Box 274
Charlottesville, VA 22902-0274 (434) 963-9961
Contact: Brian P. Menard, Exec. Secy. and Dir.
URL: http://minorpreston.org/

Foundation type: Independent foundation
Purpose: Scholarships to residents of the city of Charlottesville, VA, Albemarle County, VA, and all contiguous counties, who are members of a racial minority group or are otherwise culturally disadvantaged enrolled in an educational institution.
Financial data: Year ended 02/28/2013. Assets, $807,211 (M); Expenditures, $132,703; Total giving, $53,892; Grants to individuals, 62 grants totaling $53,892 (high: $1,500, low: $500).
Fields of interest: Education.

Type of support: Scholarships—to individuals.
Application information: Application form required.
Deadline(s): Mar. 15
Additional information: Forms available from high schools.
EIN: 521279007

9438
Missionary Emergency Fund
1403 Pemberton Rd., Ste. 102
Richmond, VA 23238-4474 (804) 740-7350
Additional address: 327 W. Mary St., Bristol, VA 24201-4483

Foundation type: Public charity
Purpose: Scholarships to students who are the sons and daughters of active or retired clergy, missionaries, or others engaged in full time Christian service work, or to students who are preparing to enter full time Christian service as a minister, missionary or teacher at a Christian institution.
Publications: Application guidelines.
Financial data: Year ended 12/31/2011. Assets, $24,879,389 (M); Expenditures, $750,274; Total giving, $573,575; Grants to individuals, totaling $112,275.
Fields of interest: Theological school/education; Formal/general education; Christian agencies & churches.
Type of support: Scholarships—to individuals.
Application information: Applications accepted.
Deadline(s): Apr. 1
Additional information: Contact the organization for additional guidelines.
EIN: 546037002

9439
Cleo Lawson Mitchell Scholarship
P.O. Box 687
Tazewell, VA 24651-0687 (276) 326-1235
Contact: Charlotte Viers, Chair.
Application address: 1 Glen Carlock Dr., Bluefield, VA 24605, tel.: (276) 326-1235

Foundation type: Independent foundation
Purpose: Scholarships to needy and deserving graduates of Graham High School, VA, who are in the top 25 percent of their graduating class.
Financial data: Year ended 06/30/2013. Assets, $201,093 (M); Expenditures, $13,870; Total giving, $11,000.
Fields of interest: Higher education.
Type of support: Support to graduates or students of specific schools; Undergraduate support.
Application information: Applications accepted.
Initial approach: Letter
Deadline(s): Third week of Apr.
Applicants should submit the following:
1) Financial information
2) Essay
Additional information: Application should include course of study the applicant plans to pursue and college selected.
EIN: 237179494

9440
A. D. & A. L. Morgan Memorial Scholarship Fund
c/o George R. Webb
5231 Studeley Ave.
Norfolk, VA 23508-1744 (757) 683-3683

Foundation type: Independent foundation

Purpose: Scholarships for residents of Tidewater south of Hampton Roads, VA, to attend Old Dominion University in Norfolk, VA. Fellowship grants to teachers at Old Dominion University are also granted.

Financial data: Year ended 12/31/2012. Assets, $621,367 (M); Expenditures, $19,661; Total giving, $10,000; Grants to individuals, 5 grants totaling $10,000 (high: $2,000, low: $2,000).

Fields of interest: Education.

Type of support: Professorships; Scholarships—to individuals; Support to graduates or students of specific schools.

Application information: Application form required.

Deadline(s): May

Additional information: Application must also include school records, personal history, and financial status.

EIN: 540309320

9441
Morrow-Stevens Foundation

P.O. Box 3026
Oakton, VA 22124-3026 (703) 319-1527
Contact: Geraldine M. Graham, Dir.

Foundation type: Independent foundation

Purpose: College scholarships to students of Virginia for attendance at four-year accredited VA colleges and universities.

Financial data: Year ended 12/31/2011. Assets, $174,371 (M); Expenditures, $35,727; Total giving, $31,012; Grants to individuals, 3 grants totaling $31,012 (high: $16,684, low: $400).

Fields of interest: Higher education.

Type of support: Undergraduate support.

Application information: Applications accepted. Application form required.

Deadline(s): May 15

Applicants should submit the following:
1) FAF
2) Letter(s) of recommendation
3) Transcripts
4) SAT
5) Essay
6) FAFSA
7) ACT

Additional information: Application must also include proof of VA residency.

EIN: 541949631

9442
Mustard Seed Foundation, Inc.

7115 Leesburg Pike, Ste. 304
Falls Church, VA 22043-2301 (703) 524-5620
Contact: Brian Bakke, Regional Dir., North America
FAX: (703) 533-7340; E-mail: info@msfdn.org;
URL: http://www.msfdn.org

Foundation type: Independent foundation

Purpose: Scholarships and fellowships to Christian graduate students at the country's top universities.

Publications: Application guidelines; Annual report.

Financial data: Year ended 12/31/2012. Assets, $4,063,854 (M); Expenditures, $3,247,838; Total giving, $2,366,694.

Fields of interest: Graduate/professional education; Public policy.

Type of support: Fellowships; Graduate support; Doctoral support.

Application information: Applications accepted. Application form required. Application form available on the grantmaker's web site.

Send request by: E-mail

Deadline(s): Aug. 1- Nov. 1 for the Harvey Fellows

Applicants should submit the following:

1) Curriculum vitae
2) Essay
3) GPA
4) Letter(s) of recommendation
5) Photograph
6) Resume
7) SAT
8) Transcripts
9) Work samples

Additional information: Applications online are available only for the Harvey Fellows. Applications must also include GRE or LSAT scores. See foundation web site for further information.

Program description:

Harvey Fellows: The fellows program provides financial support to Christian graduate students at top tier universities. Harvey Fellows scholarship information and applications may be obtained by visiting URL: http://www.harveyfellows.org or by contacting the foundation office.

EIN: 570748914

9443
Nansemond Charitable Foundation, Inc.

453 W. Washington St.
Suffolk, VA 23434-5344
Contact: Jay A. Dorschel, Chair.

Foundation type: Company-sponsored foundation

Purpose: Scholarships to high school graduates of Nansemond High School, Lakeland High School and Nansemond Academy, VA.

Financial data: Year ended 08/31/2012. Assets, $144,486 (M); Expenditures, $8,778; Total giving, $6,410; Grants to individuals, 3 grants totaling $1,500 (high: $500, low: $500).

Fields of interest: Higher education.

Type of support: Scholarships—to individuals; Support to graduates or students of specific schools.

Application information: Applications accepted. Application form required.

Deadline(s): May 15

Additional information: Application must include letter outlining financial need.

EIN: 541291449

9444
National Association of Biology Teachers, Inc.

(also known as NABT)
1313 Dolley Madison Blvd., Ste. 402
McLean, VA 22101-3926 (703) 790-1745
Contact: Jaclyn Reeves-Pepin, Exec. Dir.
FAX: (703) 790-2672; E-mail: office@nabt.org;
Toll-free tel.: (800) 501-6228; E-Mail For Jaclyn Reeves-Pepin: jreevespepin@nabt.org; URL: http://www.nabt.org

Foundation type: Public charity

Purpose: Scholarship and classroom support for teachers of biology and related subjects.

Publications: Application guidelines; Financial statement.

Financial data: Year ended 06/30/2012. Assets, $119,809 (M); Expenditures, $727,663.

Fields of interest: Scholarships/financial aid; Biology/life sciences.

Type of support: Grants to individuals; Scholarships—to individuals.

Application information: Applications accepted. Application form required. Application form available on the grantmaker's web site.

Deadline(s): Apr. 9 for Biology Educator Leader Scholarships; varies for all others

Applicants should submit the following:
1) Letter(s) of recommendation
2) Essay
3) Curriculum vitae

Program descriptions:

Biology Education Leadership Scholarship: This program works to encourage and support teachers who want to further their education in the life sciences or life sciences education. Recipients are required to be practicing educators who are also enrolled, or who anticipate enrolling, in a graduate program at the master's or doctorate level. Eligible applicants must be association members who have five years or fewer of teaching experience.

Ecology/Environmental Science Teaching Award: This award, sponsored by Vernier Software & Technology, will be given to a secondary school teacher who has successfully developed and demonstrated an innovative approach in the teaching of ecology and/or environmental science, and who has carried his/her commitment to the environment into the community. The award includes a $1,000 stipend, to be used towards travel to the association's annual Professional Development Conference, and $500 of equipment from Vernier.

Evolution Education Award: This $1,000 award, co-sponsored by the American Institute of Biological Sciences and the Biological Sciences Curriculum Study, recognizes innovative classroom teaching and community education efforts to promote the accurate understanding of biological evolution.

Excellence in Encouraging Equity Award: This award, co-sponsored by Ward's Natural Science, recognizes efforts by biology educators to encourage, promote, and strive for equity in the educational community. The award includes an honorarium and a one-year membership to the association.

Four-Year College Biology Teaching Award: This award, sponsored by Benjamin Cummings and the association's Four-Year College Section, honors a four-year college faculty member who demonstrates creativity and innovation in his/her teaching. Such innovation may include, but is not limited to, curriculum design, teaching strategies, and laboratory utilization, and it must have been implemented in the classroom and demonstrated to be effective. The award is open to association members only, and the winner receives $1,000.

Kim Foglia AP Biology Service Award: This award recognizes an AP Biology teacher who displays a willingness to share materials, serves as a mentor to both students and professional colleagues, creates an innovative and student-centered classroom environment, and exemplifies a personal philosophy that encourages professional growth as an AP Biology teacher and member of the community. Recipients are given a $1,000 honorarium, a recognition plaque, and a one-year complimentary association membership.

Kim Foglia AP Biology Travel Fellowship: This award encourages and supports novice AP Biology teachers, and helps them to further their professional development in the biology and life sciences fields, by allowing them to attend the association's annual Professional Development Conference. Fellowships will cover the costs associated with conference registration, travel to and from the conference location, and accommodations for the duration of the conference; in addition, each fellow will receive a one-year complimentary membership to NABT. Applicants must have at most five years of AP Biology teaching experience.

NABT Biotechnology Teaching Award: The award (sponsored by Bio-Rad Laboratories) recognizes a secondary school teacher or undergraduate college biology instructor who has demonstrated outstanding and creative teaching of biotechnology in the classroom. The award may be given for either a short-term series of activities or a long integration of biotechnology into the curriculum. The lessons must include active laboratory work and encompass major principles as well as processes of biotechnology. Topics may include any aspect of basic DNA or protein biotechnology or immunology or applied biotechnology in areas such as medical, forensic, plant and environmental biotechnology. Criteria for selection include creativity, scientific accuracy and currency, quality of laboratory practice and safety, ease of replication, benefit to students and potential significance beyond the classroom. The award, presented annually at NABT's Professional Development Conference, includes a plaque, a one-year complimentary NABT membership and a $500 honorarium.

Outstanding New Biology Teacher Achievement Award: This award recognizes outstanding teaching (grades 7-12) by a "new" biology/life science instructor within his/her first three years of teaching (when nominated) who has developed an original and outstanding program or technique and made a contribution to the profession at the start of his/her career. A recognition plaque is presented to the award winner at the NABT Professional Development Conference, and he/she also receives $500 and a complimentary one-year NABT membership.

Ron Mardigan Biotechnology Teaching Award: Co-sponsored by Bio-Rad Laboratories, this award recognizes a secondary school teacher or undergraduate college biology instructor who has demonstrated outstanding and creative teaching of biotechnology in the classroom. The award may be given for either a short-term series of activities, or a long integration of biotechnology into the curriculum; lesson must include active laboratory work and encompass major principles as well as processes of biotechnology. Topics may include any aspect of basic DNA or protein biotechnology or immunology, or immunology or applied biotechnology in such areas as medical, forensic, plant, and environmental biotechnology. Criteria for selection include creativity, scientific accuracy and currency, the quality of laboratory practice and safety, ease of replication, the benefit to students, and potential significance beyond the classroom. Awards include a recognition plaque, a one-year membership to the association, and $1,500 in travel support and materials/supplies.

Two-Year College Biology Teaching Award: Sponsored by NABT's Two-Year College Section and McGraw-Hill, this award recognizes a two-year college biology educator who employs new and creative techniques in his/her classroom teaching. The primary criterion for the award is skill in teaching, although serious consideration will be given to scholarship, usually demonstrated through publications or innovative techniques relating to teaching strategies, curriculum design, or laboratory utilization. Nominees must be current members of NABT, and the award includes $1,000.
EIN: 810290369

9445
National Association of Child Care Resource & Referral Agencies

(also known as NACCRRA)
1515 N. Courthouse Rd., 11th Fl.
Arlington, VA 22201-4445 (703) 341-4100
Contact: Linda Smith, Exec. Dir.
Additional tel.: (800) 424-2246,
e-mail: msp@naccrra.org
FAX: (703) 341-4101; E-mail: info@naccrra.org;
URL: http://www.naccrra.org

Foundation type: Public charity
Purpose: Fee assistance for child care to eligible Military, Americorps, and Vista members to offset the cost of child care in their communities.
Publications: Application guidelines; Informational brochure.
Financial data: Year ended 09/30/2011. Assets, $18,854,578 (M); Expenditures, $62,386,728; Total giving, $35,649,575; Grants to individuals, totaling $35,649,575.
Fields of interest: Day care.
Type of support: Grants to individuals.
Application information: Applications accepted. Application form required.
  Send request by: Online
  Additional information: Eligibility may vary by military branch. See web site for additional guidelines.
EIN: 943060756

9446
National Association of Secondary School Principals

(also known as NASSP)
1904 Association Dr.
Reston, VA 20191-1537 (703) 860-0200
Contact: Gerald N. Tirozzi, Exec. Dir.; Awards and scholarships: Rosa Aronson
FAX: (703) 476-5432;
E-mail: aronsonr@principals.org; URL: http://www.principals.org

Foundation type: Public charity
Purpose: Scholarships and awards to principals, assistant principals, schools, students, and advisers in the U.S. for their leadership and making positive, siginificant differences in the schools and communities.
Publications: Application guidelines; Annual report; Newsletter.
Financial data: Year ended 06/30/2011. Assets, $17,752,075 (M); Expenditures, $19,686,247; Total giving, $688,000; Grants to individuals, totaling $604,000.
Fields of interest: Education.
Type of support: Awards/grants by nomination only; Awards/prizes; Precollege support; Undergraduate support.
Application information:
  Send request by: Online
  Deadline(s): Varies
  Additional information: See web site for additional guidelines.
Program descriptions:
  Dissertation Competitions: Each year, the association hosts dissertation competitions that works to recognize outstanding leadership research at the middle and high school levels. Competitions are open to doctoral students who have completed and successfully defended their dissertation in the year immediately preceding the award application. Each winner will receive a complimentary one-year membership, a cash award of $1,000 (member) or $500 (non-member), a commemorative plaque, and

a press release to the winner's local community newspaper.

MetLife/NAASP National Principal of the Year Program: This program recognizes and honors outstanding middle-level and high school principals who have succeeded in providing high-quality learning opportunities for students, and who have demonstrated exemplary contributions to the profession. Each year, one middle-level and one high school principal are selected from each state to participate for the national award; one winner in each category will receive a $5,000 grant, while four finalists in each category will receive a $1,500 grant.

NASSP/Herff Jones Principal's Leadership Award: Awarded in conjunction with Herff Jones, Inc., this program affords high-school principals the opportunity to recognize a student leader in his/her schools. Scholarships, ranging from $1,500 to $12,000, will be awarded to 100 outstanding seniors from the U.S. (including its territories). Nominees should be in the top twenty percent of their class and demonstrate outstanding leadership abilities.

NASSP/Virco National Assistant Principal of the Year Program: This program honors secondary school assistant principals in their dedication and success in school leadership, especially through leadership, curriculum, and personalization. Winners receive a $5,000 grant.

Prudential Spirit of Community Awards: Offered in collaboration with Prudential Financial, this award honors middle and high school students for outstanding service to others at the local, state, and national level .The program's goals are to applaud young people who already are making a positive difference in their towns and neighborhoods, and to inspire others to think about how they might contribute to their communities. Any legal resident of the U.S. in grades 5 to 12 who has engaged in volunteer activity within the past year is eligible to apply. See web site for additional information.
EIN: 526006937

9447
National Automobile Dealers Charitable Foundation

8400 Westpark Dr.
McLean, VA 22102-5116 (703) 821-7000
E-mail: nadainfo@nada.org; Toll-free tel.: (800) 248-6232; URL: http://www.nada.org/Advocacy+Outreach/CharitableFoundation/

Foundation type: Public charity
Purpose: Provides grants to members and their families by providing emergency relief to dealership employees victimized by natural disasters.
Financial data: Year ended 12/31/2011. Assets, $8,053,252 (M); Expenditures, $1,097,318; Total giving, $767,231.
Fields of interest: Safety/disasters.
Type of support: Emergency funds.
Application information: Applications accepted. Application form available on the grantmaker's web site.
  Initial approach: Application
  Copies of proposal: 1
  Additional information: Emergency Relief Fund application available on foundation web site.
Program description:
  Emergency Relief Fund: The NADCF Emergency Relief Fund offers emergency assistance to dealership employees who have been affected by unforeseen emergencies and natural disasters, such as hurricanes, tornadoes, fires, etc. Established in 1992, over $4.1 million has been

distributed to more than 6,500 dealership employees in need.
EIN: 541008060

9448
National Board for Professional Teaching Standards, Inc.
1525 Wilson Blvd., Ste. 500
Arlington, VA 22209-2451 (888) 780-7805
Contact: Ronald Thorpe, Pres. and C.E.O.
URL: http://www.nbpts.org/

Foundation type: Public charity
Purpose: Scholarships to teachers pursuing the National Board Certification.
Financial data: Year ended 12/31/2011. Assets, $56,308,443 (M); Expenditures, $40,375,950; Total giving, $549,515; Grants to individuals, totaling $549,515.
Fields of interest: Teacher school/education.
Type of support: Scholarships—to individuals.
Application information: Applications accepted. Application form required. Application form available on the grantmaker's web site.
Additional information: Applicants must hold a bachelor's degree, completed three full years of teaching or school counseling, and possess a valid state teaching or school counseling. Scholarship averages about $750 for candidates from various state jurisdictions in order to assest them in pursuing certification.
EIN: 521512323

9449
National Business Education Association
1914 Association Dr.
Reston, VA 20191-1538 (703) 860-8300
FAX: (703) 620-4483; E-mail: nbea@nbea.org;
URL: http://www.nbea.org

Foundation type: Public charity
Purpose: Scholarships to teachers pursuing continuing education or graduate study in business education.
Financial data: Year ended 06/30/2012. Assets, $2,257,672 (M); Expenditures, $1,218,739; Total giving, $4,600; Grants to individuals, totaling $4,600.
Fields of interest: Business school/education.
Type of support: Scholarships—to individuals; Graduate support.
Application information: Applications accepted. Application form required.
Send request by: Mail
Deadline(s): Dec. 1
Applicants should submit the following:
1) Resume
2) Letter(s) of recommendation
Program description:
Scholarships: Two $1,000 scholarships will recognize and support educators who give evidence of leadership and scholarship potential in the field of business education. Applicants must be currently teaching and plan to continue to teach in the field of business education and be a current professional member of NBEA at the time of application.
EIN: 520886073

9450
National Community Pharmacists Association Foundation
(formerly National Association of Retail Druggists)
100 Daingerfield Rd.
Alexandria, VA 22314-2885 (703) 683-8200
Contact: Sharlea Leatherwood P.D., Pres.
FAX: (703) 683-3619;
E-mail: info@ncpafoundation.org; Toll-free tel.: (800) 544-7447; URL: http://www.ncpafoundation.org/

Foundation type: Public charity
Purpose: Scholarships to pharmacy students and research grants to pharmacists.
Publications: Application guidelines; Annual report; Informational brochure.
Financial data: Year ended 06/30/2012. Assets, $3,821,740 (M); Expenditures, $546,950; Total giving, $54,000; Grants to individuals, totaling $54,000.
Fields of interest: Pharmacy/prescriptions.
Type of support: Conferences/seminars; Awards/prizes.
Application information: Applications accepted. Application form required.
Deadline(s): Varies
Program descriptions:
Independent Pharmacist of the Year: Recipients receive a $1,000 cash award, a commemorative plaque, and a $1,000 scholarship.
Presidential Scholarships: Student members of NCPA with a demonstrated interest in independent pharmacy/ownership are eligible to apply.
EIN: 366072250

9451
National Consortium for Graduate Degrees for Minorities in Engineering and Science, Inc.
1430 Duke St.
Alexandria, VA 22314-3403 (703) 562-3646
Contact: Michele Lezama, Exec. Dir.
FAX: (202) 207-3518;
E-mail: info@gemfellowship.org; E-mail For Michele Lezama: mlezama@gemfellowship.org;
URL: http://gemfellowship.org

Foundation type: Public charity
Purpose: Fellowships to minority students with a masters and doctoral degrees in science and engineering.
Publications: Annual report; Financial statement; Newsletter.
Financial data: Year ended 06/30/2012. Assets, $5,706,273 (M); Expenditures, $2,418,910; Total giving, $1,271,869; Grants to individuals, totaling $1,271,869.
Fields of interest: Engineering school/education; Education; Science; Minorities; African Americans/Blacks; Hispanics/Latinos; Native Americans/American Indians.
Type of support: Fellowships; Graduate support; Doctoral support.
Application information: Applications accepted.
Send request by: Online
Deadline(s): Nov.
Additional information: See web site for additional guidelines.
Program descriptions:
M.S. Engineering Fellowship Program: This program works to promote the benefits of a masters degree within industry. Fellows are provided practical engineering summer work experiences through an employer sponsor and a portable academic year fellowship of tuition, fees, and a stipend which may be used at any participating

consortium member university where the fellow is admitted. Fellows receive a $4,000 living stipend per full time semester up to four semesters (or three quarters), up to two paid summer internships with a GEM Employer Member, and full tuition and fees provided by a GEM University member.
Ph.D. Engineering Fellowship Program: This program offers doctoral fellowships to underrepresented minority students who have either completed, are currently enrolled in a master's in engineering program or received admittance into a PhD program directly from a bachelor's degree program. Fellowships may be used at any participating GEM Member University where the GEM Fellow is admitted. During the first academic year of being awarded the GEM Fellowship, the GEM Consortium remits a stipend and a cost of instruction grant to the institution where the fellow is enrolled. Thereafter, up to the fifth year of the doctoral program, the total fellowship cost is borne by the university. Fellows are provided a practical summer work experience through the Employer Member for at least one summer.
Ph.D. Science Fellowship Program: This program aims to increase the number of minority students who pursue doctoral degrees in the natural science disciplines such as chemistry, physics, earth sciences, mathematics, biological sciences, and computer science. Applicants to this program are accepted as early as their junior undergraduate year, as well as candidates currently enrolled in a Master's of Engineering program and working professionals. Fellowships offered through this program are portable and may be used at any participating GEM Member University where the GEM fellow is admitted. Fellows receive a $16,000 stipend in the first academic year of the GEM Fellowship, GEM Member University provides a living stipend up to the fifth year of PhD Program, equivalent to other funded doctorate students in the department, a minimum of one paid summer internship with a GEM Employer Member, and full tuition and fees at a GEM University Member.
EIN: 310898802

9452
National Council of Teachers of Mathematics
(also known as NCTM's Mathematics Education Trust (MET))
1906 Association Dr.
Reston, VA 20191-1502 (703) 620-9840
Contact: Bob Doucette, Exec. Dir.
FAX: (703) 476-2970; E-mail: nctm@nctm.org;
Toll-free tel.: (800) 235-7566; URL: http://www.nctm.org

Foundation type: Public charity
Purpose: Grants to K-12th grade mathematics teachers for program development, travel grants to NCTM conferences, and research.
Publications: Application guidelines; Annual report; Grants list; Informational brochure.
Financial data: Year ended 05/31/2012. Assets, $24,898,246 (M); Expenditures, $16,419,639; Total giving, $107,710; Grants to individuals, totaling $95,581.
Fields of interest: Education; Mathematics.
Type of support: Program development; Research; Travel grants.
Application information: Applications accepted. Application form required. Application form available on the grantmaker's web site.
Initial approach: Letter, telephone, or e-mail
Send request by: Mail

Copies of proposal: 5
Deadline(s): Varies
Additional information: Applicant should submit budget information. See web site for complete application guidelines and programs.

Program descriptions:

Classroom-Based Research Grants: This grant provides up to $6,000 towards the support and encouragement of classroom-based research in precollege mathematics education in collaboration with college or university mathematics educators. Research must be a significant collaborative effort involving a college or university mathematics educator (a mathematics education researcher or a teacher of mathematics learning, teaching, or curriculum) and one or more grades PreK-6 classroom teachers. The proposal may include, but is not restricted to curriculum development and implementation, involvement of at-risk or minority students, students' thinking about a particular mathematics concept or set of concepts, connection of mathematics to other disciplines, focused learning and teaching of mathematics with embedded use of technology, or innovative assessment or evaluation strategies. This research should lead to a draft article suitable for submission in the mathematics Teacher Educator, Journal for Research in Mathematics Education or in one of the council school journals.

Connecting Mathematics to Other Subject Areas Grants: This grant provides up to $4,000 to current 9th-12th grade mathematics teachers to create senior high school classroom materials or lessons connecting mathematics to other fields and to the everyday world. Materials may be in the form of books, visual displays, computer programs or displays, slide shows, videotapes, or other appropriate medium. Proposals must address the plan for developing and evaluating materials, the connectivity to other fields or disciplines, and anticipated impact on students' learning.

Emerging Teacher Leaders in Elementary School Mathematics: This grant provides up to $6,000 to an elementary school teacher who has a demonstrated commitment to mathematics teaching and learning, to help increase the breadth and depth of mathematics content knowledge. Grant recipients will be expected to provide ongoing professional development to teachers within the school or district to strengthen their mathematical understandings and instructional practices. Funds may be used for college or university coursework pertaining to mathematics, registration fees for conferences, teacher stipends for participation in in-service courses, and materials for teachers to use in the classroom. Eligible applicants must be full-time elementary school teachers with at least three years of experience, and have mathematics as a regular teaching responsibility.

Engaging Students in Learning Mathematics Grants: Up to $3,000 is available to current mathematics teachers in grades 6-8 who wish to incorporate middle-school classroom materials or lessons that actively engage students in tasks and experiences to deepen and connect their content knowledge. Materials may be in the form of books, visual displays, slide shows, videotapes, or other appropriate medium. Proposals must address the following: one or more of the content standards (number and operations, geometry, measurement, and algebra); plan for developing and evaluating materials; and the anticipated impact on students' learning.

Equity in Mathematics Grants: This grant provides up to $8,000 to persons currently teaching mathematics in grades 6-8, to incorporate middle school classroom materials or lessons that will improve the achievement of student groups that

have previous records of underachievement. Proposals must address the mathematics content as defined in the council's Principles and Standards for School Mathematics, the plan for improving achievement of the targeted students, and the anticipated impact on their achievement.

Improving Students' Understanding of Geometry Grants: This grant provides up to $4,000 each to persons currently teaching at the grades PreK-8 level to develop activities that will enable students to better appreciate and understand some aspect of geometry that is consistent with the Principles and Standards for School Mathematics. Projects should include applications of geometry to such disciplines as art, literature, music, architecture, nature, or some other relevant area and may integrate the use of technology into the teaching of geometry. Proposals must address geometry content, the appropriateness of the application, the link between geometry standards and the project's activities, and the anticipated impact on students' learning.

Mathematics Graduate Course Work Scholarships: This grant allocates up to $2,000 to full-time 6-8 teachers to provide financial support for improving teachers' understanding of mathematics by completing graduate course work in mathematics. Primary emphasis is placed on appropriate mathematics content courses. Proposals must address: rationale for the coursework; anticipated instructional improvements and expected impact on student learning outcomes.
EIN: 526057004

9453
National Court Reporters Foundation

8224 Old Courthouse Rd.
Vienna, VA 22182-3808 (703) 556-6272
Contact: B.J. Shorak, Exec. Dir.
FAX: (703) 556-6291;
E-mail: ncrfoundation@ncra.org; Additional tel./ TTY: (703) 556-6289; Toll-free tel.: (800) 272-6272; E-mail for B.J. Shorak: bjshorak@ncra.org; URL: http://www.ncra.org/ Foundation/?navItemNumber=503

Foundation type: Public charity
Purpose: Scholarships and cash awards to student court reporters.
Publications: Application guidelines.
Financial data: Year ended 09/30/2011. Assets, $343,367 (M); Expenditures, $303,888; Total giving, $6,146; Grants to individuals, 4 grants totaling $6,146.
Fields of interest: Scholarships/financial aid; Courts/judicial administration.
Type of support: Scholarships—to individuals; Awards/grants by nomination only.
Application information:
  Send request by: Mail
  Additional information: Applicant must demonstrate financial need. Application by nomination only. See web site for additional guidelines.
Program descriptions:
  Frank Sarli Memorial Scholarship: This $2,000 scholarship is awarded annually to court reporting students. Eligible applicants must be enrolled in a National Court Reporters Association (NCRA)-certified court reporting program, be a member of NCRA, and have a minimum 3.5 GPA.
  New Professional Reporter Grant: Grants of $2,000 each are available to a new employee in his/her first year out of school to help reduce out-of-pocket start-up expenses. Eligible applicants must be enrolled in a National Court Reporters

Association (NCRA)-certified court reporting program, be a member of NCRA, and have a minimum 3.5 GPA.
  Student Intern Scholarship: Two awards of $1,000 each will be made available to students who have completed, or who are in the process of completing, the required internship portion of their court reporting program.
EIN: 541153729

9454
National Guard Youth Foundation

1001 N. Fairfax St., Ste. 205
Alexandria, VA 22314-1595 (703) 684-5437
FAX: (571) 970-3851; E-mail: info@ngyf.org;
URL: http://www.ngyf.org

Foundation type: Public charity
Purpose: Scholarships to assist graduates of the National Guard ChalleNGe who plan to continue their education in college, vocational school programs, or career training.
Financial data: Year ended 12/31/2011. Assets, $4,566,656 (M); Expenditures, $2,001,300; Total giving, $532,000; Grants to individuals, totaling $72,000.
Fields of interest: Vocational education, post-secondary; Higher education.
Type of support: Scholarships—to individuals.
Application information: Applications accepted. Application form required. Application form available on the grantmaker's web site.
  Send request by: Mail
  Deadline(s): Apr. 19
  Final notification: Applicants notified by the end of May
  Additional information: See web site for additional application guidelines.
Program description:
  National Guard Youth ChalleNGe Program (ChalleNGe): Scholarships in the amount of $3,000 for Cadets if they are planning to attend a two-year or vocational program, and $5,000 scholarship if they are planning to attend a four-year program. Applicants must be a current Cadet, graduate in the Post-Residential phase, or individuals who are no more than six months out of the Post-Residential phase of the ChalleNGe Program. Cadets must have a clear understanding of their educational goals and can prove they are attainable, and interested in promoting and supporting the National Guard Youth ChalleNGe Program and the Foundation upon reaching their goals.
EIN: 541940978

9455
National Military Family Association

2500 N. Van Dorn St., Ste. 102
Alexandria, VA 22302-1601 (703) 931-6632
Contact: Joyce Wessel-Raezer, Exce. Dir.
FAX: (703) 931-4600; E-mail: families@nmfa.org;
URL: http://www.militaryfamily.org/

Foundation type: Public charity
Purpose: Scholarships to spouses of Uniformed Services members as well as to spouses of wounded and fallen Uniformed Services members.
Publications: Application guidelines.
Financial data: Year ended 12/31/2011. Assets, $7,755,158 (M); Expenditures, $5,391,585; Total giving, $379,188; Grants to individuals, totaling $379,188.
Fields of interest: Vocational education, post-secondary; Higher education.
Type of support: Scholarships—to individuals; Graduate support.

Application information: Applications accepted. Application form required.

Additional information: Selection is based on completion of some survey questions.

Program description:

Joanne Holbrook Patton Military Spouse Scholarship: Scholarships are awarded to spouses of Uniformed Services members (active duty, National Guard and Reserve, retirees, and survivors) to obtain professional certification or to attend postsecondary or graduate school. Scholarships range in amount from $500 to $1,000, and the number awarded each year varies depending on funding. Scholarship funds may be used for tuition, fees, and school room and board.
EIN: 520899384

9456
National Science and Technology Education Partnership

(also known as NSTEP)
P.O. Box 9644
McLean, VA 22102-0644   (703) 907-7400
Contact: Peter F. McCloskey, C.E.O.
FAX: (703) 907-7727;
E-mail: pmccloskey@nstep-online.org; Additional tel.: (703) 907-7407; Additional e-mail: jcox@nstep-online.org

Foundation type: Public charity
Purpose: Awards to middle and high school students who participate in the TechXplore competition.
Financial data: Year ended 12/31/2011. Assets, $262,170 (M); Expenditures, $477,530; Total giving, $245; Grants to individuals, totaling $245.
Fields of interest: Science.
Type of support: Research; Awards/prizes.
Application information: See web site for information on the competition.
EIN: 521064486

9457
National Science Teachers Association

1840 Wilson Blvd.
Arlington, VA 22201-3000   (703) 243-7100
Contact: David L. Evans, Exec. Dir.
FAX: (703) 243-7177;
E-mail: membership@nsta.org; URL: http://www.nsta.org/

Foundation type: Public charity
Purpose: Awards to teachers for exemplary teaching in science education. Fellowships to promote quality science teaching. Awards to young winners of science fairs.
Publications: Application guidelines.
Financial data: Year ended 05/31/2012. Assets, $34,157,699 (M); Expenditures, $25,257,171; Total giving, $3,162,372; Grants to individuals, totaling $2,919,608.
Fields of interest: Elementary/secondary education; Science.
Type of support: Fellowships; Awards/prizes.
Application information: Applications accepted. Application form available on the grantmaker's web site.

Initial approach: Application
Send request by: On-line
Deadline(s): Varies
Additional information: See web site for additional application guidelines.

Program descriptions:

"Angela" Award: This award honors a female student in grades 5 to 8, who is involved in or has a strong connection to science, and who is enrolled in a full-time public, private, or home school in the U.S. or Canada.

DCAT "Making a Difference" Award: This award recognizes and honors excellence in a science program developed by middle- or high-school-level science teachers in grades 6 to 12. Entries must show innovative and effective teaching strategies, combined with a science program that has influenced students to explore and investigate science and its application to global programs. Awardees receive a $2,500 grant, to be used to enhance or expand the winning science program; the winning school's lead science teacher and principal will also be awarded coach airfare and two nights' hotel accommodation to attend the association's annual national conference.

Delta Education/Frey-Neo/CPO Science Education Awards for Excellence in Inquiry-Based Science Teaching: These awards recognize and honor three full-time pre-kindergarden-12th grade teachers of science who successfully use inquiry-based science to enhance teaching and learning in the classroom. Awardees receive $1,500 toward expenses to attend the association's national conference, and $1,500 to each awardee.

Distinguished Informal Science Education Award: This award honors an association member who has made extraordinary contributions to the advancement of science education in an informal or nontraditional school setting, such as a science-technology center, museum, or community science center. Awardees receive a formal citation, three nights' hotel accommodation, and $500 toward expenses to attend the association's national conference.

Distinguished Service to Science Education Awards: This award honors association members who, through active leadership and scholarly endeavor over a significant period of time, have made extraordinary contributions to the advancement of education in the sciences and science teaching. Awardees receive a formal citation, three nights' hotel accommodation, and up to $500 towards expenses to attend the association's national conference.

Distinguished Teaching Awards: This award honors association members that have made extraordinary contributions to the field of science teaching. Awardees receive a formal citation, three nights' hotel accommodation, and $500 toward expenses to attend the association's national conference.

Faraday Science Communicator Award: This award recognizes both individuals and organizations that have inspired and elevated the public's interest in and appreciation of science. Eligible individuals must not be classroom teachers, but must work in, or have developed a compatible setting for, science communication (i.e., museum, nature center, zoo, state park, aquarium, radio, television, internet, or other science-rich institutions or media); individuals may also be connected to a science setting through his or her involvement with civic organizations and child-education facilities, such as pre-kindergarten child-development centers, 4-H clubs, Girl and Boy Scouts, and Girls and Boys Clubs of America. Eligible organizations must have facilitated and provided exemplary opportunities for science communication to the public, and works to instill the public an appreciation for science through communication efforts at the local, state, and national levels. Awardees will receive an all-expenses-paid trip (of up to $2,500) to attend the association's national conference.

Maitland P. Simmons Memorial Award for New Teachers: This award provides selected up to 25 K-12 teachers in their first five years of teaching with funds to attend the association's National Conference on Science Education. Eligible applicants must be within their first five years (full-time) of their teaching career, and must be a member of the organization in good standing. Awardees receive up to $1,000, to be used to attend the organization's national conference.

NSTA Legacy Award: This award provides grants of up to $500 each to family members of recently-deceased association members who have demonstrated significant lifelong service to the association and contributions to science education.

Robert H. Carleton Award: This award recognizes an individual (from kindergarten to college-level) who has made outstanding contributions to, and provided leadership in, science education at the national level, and especially to the association. Awardees receive $5,000 and an all-expenses-paid trip to the association's national conference.

Ron Mardigian Memorial Biotechnology Explorer Award: This award recognizes and rewards an outstanding high school teacher who has made biotechnology learning accessible to the classroom. Awardees will consist of awards of $750 each towards expenses to attend the association's national conference, a $250 cash award, and $500 in Bio-Rad products.

STEM Educator Award: Awarded in conjunction with PASCO Scientific, this award recognizes excellence and innovation in the field of STEM (science, technology, engineering, and mathematics) education at the elementary, middle school, and high school levels. Eligible applicants must have a minimum of three years' teaching experience in the STEM fields, who have implemented (and continue to implement) innovative inquiry-based, technology-infused programs. One elementary, two middle-level, and two high-school-level recipients will receive a $1,500 award to cover travel expenses to attend the association's national conference, a $1,000 monetary gift, and a $2,000 certificate for PASCO scientific products.

Sylvia Shugrue Award for Elementary School Teachers: This award honors one elementary school teacher who has established (or is establishing) an interdisciplinary, inquiry-based lesson plan. Awardees will receive a $1,000 cash prize, and up to $500 to attend the association's national conference.

Toyota TAPESTRY Grants for Science Teachers: This program provides grants of up to $10,000 to science teachers throughout the U.S. to implement innovative, community-based science projects in environmental science, physical science, and integrating literacy and science.

Vernier Technology Awards: These awards recognize and reward the innovative use of data collection technology using a computer, graphing calculator, or other handheld in the science classroom. Seven awards will be presented annually: one at the elementary level (grades K-5), two awards at the middle level (grades 6-8), three awards at the high-school level (grades 9-12), and one award at the college level. Each award includes $1,000 in cash, $3,000 in Vernier products, and up to $1,500 toward expenses to attend the 2013 NSTA National Conference in San Antonio, Texas. Applicants may be self-nominated or nominated by a colleague.

Wendell G. Mohling Outstanding Aerospace Educator Award: This award recognizes excellence in the field of aerospace education. Eligible applicants include both K-12 teachers of science in formal education settings (e.g., elementary, middle, and high school), and informal education settings (e.g., museums, government, and science centers);

applicants must have a minimum of three years' teaching experience. Awards range from $2,000 to $3,000, to be used to attend the association's national conference.

Zula International-NSTA Early Science Educator Award: This award honors and recognizes two full-time preK-2 teachers who successfully use innovative inquiry-based science to enhance science teaching and learning in their classroom. Awardees will receive $1,000 to attend the association's national conference, and a $400 cash prize.

EIN: 526055229

9458
National Society of Professional Engineers Educational Foundation

(formerly National Society of Professional Engineers)
1420 King St.
Alexandria, VA 22314-2794 (703) 684-2800
Contact: Lawrence A. Jacobson, Exec. Dir.
FAX: (703) 836-4875; E-mail: memserv@nspe.org;
Toll-free tel..: (888)-285-NSPE; URL: http://www.nspe.org

Foundation type: Public charity
Purpose: Scholarships and fellowships in the field of engineering, and awards by nomination only to engineers who have made significant contributions to the field.
Publications: Application guidelines; Informational brochure (including application guidelines).
Financial data: Year ended 06/30/2012. Assets, $1,060,423 (M); Expenditures, $50,210; Total giving, $30,500; Grants to individuals, totaling $30,000.
Fields of interest: Business school/education; Engineering school/education; Engineering/technology; Public affairs; Women.
Type of support: Fellowships; Scholarships—to individuals; Awards/grants by nomination only; Awards/prizes; Graduate support; Undergraduate support.
Application information: Application form required. Application form available on the grantmaker's web site.
> *Deadline(s):* Varies
> *Applicants should submit the following:*
> 1) ACT
> 2) Essay
> 3) GPA
> 4) Letter(s) of recommendation
> 5) SAT
> 6) Transcripts
> *Additional information:* Letter of acceptance must be included in scholarship application.

Program descriptions:
Engineering Education Excellence Award: This national award recognizes one faculty member who has demonstrated an ability to link engineering education with professional practice. The recipients must be licensed and have a tenure-track faculty appointment in an Accreditation Board for Engineering and Technology-Engineering Accreditation Committee (ABET-EAC)-accredited engineering program. This award recognizes mid-career individuals who are 45 years or younger in age at the deadline for submission of the award. The recipients of the award will be recognized at the society's annual meeting and will receive a cash prize of $5,000.

Federal Engineer of the Year Award: This honor is to be awarded to an engineer employed by a federal agency that employs at least 50 engineers worldwide. Candidates are nominated by their employing federal agency, and are judged according

to engineering achievements, education, continuing education, professional/technical society activities and membership, awards or honors, and civic and humanitarian activities.

NSPE Award: This award is presented to an engineer who has made outstanding contributions to the engineering profession, the public welfare, and/or humankind. All engineers of recognized standing are eligible for nomination, provided that they are citizens of the U.S. and are preferably licensed professional engineers. Officers and directors of NSPE are ineligible. Nominations may be made by any member in good standing, but must be approved by the candidate's state society. A state society is not limited to the approval of a single candidate.

NSPE Distinguished Service Award: This award was established to recognize NSPE's members for their exceptional technical contributions to the engineering profession, their contributions to their communities, and to NSPE. Persons holding the membership grade of Member, Life, or Privileged Member in good standing are eligible for selection. Candidates must be recommended by a state society, with endorsement from two other state societies. In addition to completing the nomination, the following biographical information on each candidate should be provided: 500-word personal statement suitable for use as a press release; education; professional achievements; professional and technical society activity; and humanitarian and civic contributions. Each nomination must be made by a NSPE-affiliated state society and endorsed by two other state societies.

PEGASUS Award: This award recognizes the engineer who has made the most outstanding contribution to the advancement and practice of engineering. The honoree must be a registered professional engineer employed by a state, regional, county, special district, or municipal government.

QBS Awards Program: This award recognizes public agencies that make exemplary use of the qualifications-based selection (QBS) process at the state and local levels to hire design professionals.

Scholarships: Scholarships to high school, undergraduate, and graduate students pursuing engineering studies and activities. The NSPE offers over ten scholarships and fellowships that range from $2,000 to $5,000.

Young Engineer of the Year Award: This award recognizes young NSPE members who have made outstanding contributions to the engineering profession and their communities during the early years of their careers. Any licensed professional engineer or engineer-in-training (P.E. or E.I.T.) NSPE member in good standing who is 35 years of age or younger as of Jan. 1 is eligible for nomination. Nominations are to be submitted by an NSPE-affiliated state society or must contain an endorsement from the state society. Only one submission per state will be accepted. The committee makes the selection of the recipient based on the following criteria: 1) educational and collegiate achievements; 2) professional and technical society activities; 3) civic and humanitarian activities; 4) continuing competence; and 5) engineering achievements.

EIN: 526056276

9459
National Wildlife Federation

P.O. Box 1583
Merrifield, VA 22116-1583
Contact: Larry J. Schweiger, Pres. and C.E.O.
URL: http://www.nwf.org

Foundation type: Public charity
Purpose: Fellowships to students for ecological projects on college and university campuses.
Publications: Application guidelines; Annual report.
Financial data: Year ended 08/31/2011. Assets, $64,808,553 (M); Expenditures, $96,260,084; Total giving, $5,830,036; Grants to individuals, totaling $9,300.
Fields of interest: Natural resources; Environment.
Type of support: Fellowships.
Application information: Application form required.
> *Initial approach:* Proposal
> *Deadline(s):* Mar. 31
> *Additional information:* See web site for additional application guidelines.

Program descriptions:
Campus Ecology Fellowship: This program allows college and university students the opportunity to confront global warming on their campuses, and helps to educate and engage the campus community on global warming impacts and solutions. Monetary fellowship grants are awarded to undergraduate and graduate students working with other members of the faculty, staff, or administration on projects designed to help reverse global warming on campus and beyond. In addition to a modest grant, Fellows also receive project support, leadership development, recognition of their accomplishments and other perks.

Emerging Leaders Fellowships: These fellowships are offered to post graduate, young professionals ages 21 to 35, interested in career development and leadership opportunities within the conservation movement. The program is an extension of NWF's successful Campus Ecology Fellows Program. Throughout the fellowship term, selected applicants will be provided with leadership opportunities through the organization and its state affiliates, seed funding for their entrepreneurial efforts, additional leadership and skills trainings, and a diverse support network of peers and mentors.

EIN: 530204616

9460
The NATSO Foundation

1737 King St., Ste. 200
Alexandria, VA 22314-2727 (703) 549-2100
FAX: (703) 684-9667;
E-mail: foundation@natsofoundation.org; Toll-free tel.: (888) 275-6287; URL: http://www.natsofoundation.org

Foundation type: Public charity
Purpose: Scholarships to truck stop industry employees or their dependents who plan to enroll on a full-time basis in postsecondary studies at an accredited school.
Publications: Application guidelines; Informational brochure (including application guidelines); Newsletter.
Financial data: Year ended 12/31/2011. Assets, $2,188,496 (M); Expenditures, $267,918; Total giving, $25,000; Grants to individuals, totaling $25,000.
Fields of interest: Transportation.
Type of support: Employee-related scholarships.
Application information: Applications accepted. Application form required. Application form available on the grantmaker's web site.
> *Deadline(s):* May 1
> *Applicants should submit the following:*
> 1) Transcripts
> 2) Financial information
> 3) Letter(s) of recommendation
> 4) Essay

Program description:

Bill Moon Scholarship: Eight $2,500 scholarships are awarded to truckstop industry employees or their dependents in memory of truckstop industry founding father Bill Moon. Students who plan on enrolling on a full-time basis in postsecondary studies at an accredited school are eligible.

EIN: 541519317

9461
Navy Marine Coast Guard Residence Foundation, Inc.

6251 Old Dominion Dr.
McLean, VA 22101 (703) 538-2970
FAX: (703) 538-2151;
E-mail: development@vinsonhall.org; URL: http://www.nmcgrf.org/

Foundation type: Public charity
Purpose: Financial assistance to former Navy Marine Coast Guard officers currently living in Vinson Hall Retirement Community residences, VA.
Financial data: Year ended 12/31/2011. Assets, $0 (M); Expenditures, $837,924; Total giving, $626,830; Grants to individuals, totaling $123,883.
Fields of interest: Residential/custodial care; Military/veterans' organizations; Aging.
Type of support: Grants for special needs.
Application information: Applications not accepted.

Additional information: Contributes only to the Navy Marine Coast Guard officers; unsolicited requests for funds not considered or acknowledged.

EIN: 526040483

9462
Navy-Marine Corps Relief Society

875 N. Randolph St., Ste. 225
Arlington, VA 22203-0000 (703) 696-4904
Contact: Charles S. Abbot, Pres. and C.E.O.
E-mail: education@hq.nmcrs.org; URL: http://www.nmcrs.org

Foundation type: Public charity
Purpose: Interest free loans and grants to active duty and retired Navy and Marine Corps members, dependents and survivors.
Publications: Application guidelines.
Financial data: Year ended 12/31/2011. Assets, $120,443,471 (M); Expenditures, $24,831,652; Total giving, $4,095,159; Grants to individuals, totaling $4,066,910.
Fields of interest: Higher education; Military/veterans' organizations.
Type of support: Scholarships—to individuals; Loans—to individuals.
Application information: Applications accepted. Application form required.

Send request by: Mail
Deadline(s): May 1 for Vice Admiral E.P. Traverse Loan Program, RADM Courtney G. and Margaret H. Clegg Scholarship and NMCRS Gold Star Scholarship Program, June 1 for Admiral Boorda Loan Program
Applicants should submit the following:
1) Transcripts
2) SAR
3) Essay
Additional information: Selection is based on financial need. Unsolicited requests for funds not considered or acknowledged. Funds are only for Military personnel and their family.

Program descriptions:

Admiral Mike Boorda Loan Program: No-interest loans range from $500 to $3,000 per academic year, to students enrolled in one of the following commissioning programs: Marine Enlisted Commissioning Education Program (MECEP), or Medical Enlisted Commissioning Program (MECP). Applicant must be enrolled as a full time student during the entire academic year and maintain a 2.0 or better GPA on a 4.0 scale.

Joseph A. McAlinden Divers Scholarship Program: This scholarship is offered to active duty Navy or Marine Corps qualified divers, children (under the age 23) of active duty or retired Navy or Marine Corps qualified divers or spouses of active duty or retired Navy or Marine Corps divers. Scholarships range from $500 to $3,000 per academic year for tuition, books, fees, room and board or certifications. Funds are sent directly to the school and are payable to the school and student.

NMCRS Gold Star Scholarship Programs: This program is offered to children (under age 23) of a Sailor or Marine who died while serving on active duty or after retirement, or unmarried Navy and Marine Corps spouses of a service member who died while serving on active duty. Scholarships range from $500 to $2,500 per academic year. Funds are sent directly to the school and payable to the school and student, and it is used for tuition, books, fees, room and board.

RADM Courtney G. Clegg & Mrs. Margaret H. Clegg Scholarship: The scholarship program is for children (under age 23) of active duty Sailors and Marines (including reservists serving on active duty over 90 days), children (under age 23) of retired Sailors and Marines, and spouses of active duty and retired Sailors and Marines (residing within the U.S.). Awards range form $500 to $2,000 per academic year. Funds are for tuition, books, fees, room and board.

Society of Sponsors of the United States Navy Centennial Scholarship Program: This program is for combat wounded Sailors or Marines that served in Iraq or Afghanistan and are pursuing a degree leading to license and certification as a teacher. Applicant must be enrolled as a full time student in an accredited college or university. Scholarship amount is $3,000 per academic year.

Spouse Tuition Aid Loan Program: The loan is for active duty Navy or Marine Corps spouses who are stationed with the service member outside the 50 United States. Applicant must be a part time or full time undergraduate or graduate student enrolled at an accredited college or university. No interest loans are up to $3,000 per 12 month period. Loans may be used for tuition, books and fees.

Vice Admiral E.P. Travers Loan Program: The program provides children under age 23 of active duty Sailors and Marines (including reservists serving on active duty over 90 days), children under age 23 of retired Sailors and Marines, and active duty Navy and Marine Corps spouses (residing within the U.S.) No interest loans range from $500 up to $3,000 per academic year. Funds are sent directly to the school and payable to the school and the student.

EIN: 530204618

9463
Newhouse Scholarship Trust Fund

c/o Stellarone Wealth Management
P.O. Box 1717
Culpeper, VA 22701-6717 (540) 825-8310
Contact: Lisa Walker
Application address: Culpeper County High School, Culpeper, VA 22701

Foundation type: Independent foundation
Purpose: Scholarships primarily to individuals from the Culpeper, VA, area for attendance at colleges and universities in the U.S.
Financial data: Year ended 12/31/2012. Assets, $200,716 (M); Expenditures, $13,204; Total giving, $9,320; Grants to individuals, 4 grants totaling $9,320 (high: $2,330, low: $2,330).
Fields of interest: College; University.
Type of support: Scholarships—to individuals.
Application information: Applications accepted. Application form required. Interview required.

Applicants should submit the following:
1) Transcripts
2) Financial information
Additional information: Contact foundation for current application guidelines.

EIN: 546260176

9464
Newspaper Association of America Foundation

(also known as NAA Foundation)
4401 Wilson Blvd., Ste. 900
Arlington, VA 22203-4195 (571) 366-1000
Contact: Margaret Vassilikos, Sr. V.P. and Treas.
FAX: (571) 366-1195;
E-mail: naafoundation@naa.org; URL: http://www.americanpressinstitute.org/

Foundation type: Public charity
Purpose: Fellowship opportunity for middle and high school newspaper staff to advance their training.
Publications: Application guidelines; Annual report; Newsletter.
Financial data: Year ended 12/31/2011. Assets, $21,458,052 (M); Expenditures, $932,103; Total giving, $96,014; Grants to individuals, totaling $74,014.
Fields of interest: Print publishing.
Type of support: Fellowships; Awards/grants by nomination only.
Application information: Application form required. Application form available on the grantmaker's web site.

Initial approach: Application
Program descriptions:

Minority Fellowship: This program is designed to widen opportunities for 12 minority professionals to enter or advance in newspaper management through providing funding for events and seminars. Newspaper executives and journalism educators are asked to nominate candidates who demonstrate managerial potential. Fellowships cover registration fees and, where applicable, travel, meals, and hotel expenses.

News Challenge: Each spring, the foundation offers a cutting-edge training session for college students interested in digital media career. Students work in teams to develop real-world prototypes for the newspaper industry, and have the opportunity to interact with digital news executives, advertising and marketing directors, community news advocates, educators, and others during a fast-paced week. The program is open to juniors, seniors, or graduate students at accredited colleges and universities; the foundation provides funding for travel, housing, and meals for participating students. Applicants are especially encouraged from the advertising, marketing, business, finance, computer science, computer graphics, and journalism and communications fields of study, though all applicants will be considered.

Teen Fellowship Program: The foundation provides school newspaper editors with the opportunity to nominate their youth staffers for a

fellowship to attend the Newspaper Association of America's Young Reader Conference.
EIN: 136161165

9465
Newton Marasco Foundation
3434 Washington Blvd., 2nd Fl.
Arlington, VA 22201 (703) 284-6059
Contact: Amy Marasco Newton, Pres.
FAX: (540) 668-7711;
E-mail: jan@newtonmarascofoundation.org;
URL: http://www.newtonmarascofoundation.org

Foundation type: Public charity
Purpose: Awards and scholarships to encourage consideration of, and responsibility for, the environment.
Publications: Application guidelines.
Financial data: Year ended 12/31/2011. Assets, $105,055 (M); Expenditures, $293,166; Total giving, $8,575; Grants to individuals, totaling $8,350.
Fields of interest: Environment.
Type of support: Awards/prizes; Undergraduate support.
Application information: Applications accepted. Application form required. Application form available on the grantmaker's web site.
Initial approach: E-mail
Deadline(s): Apr. 2 for Rachel Carson Scholar Program; Dec. 8 for Green Earth Book Award nominations
Program descriptions:
Environmental Stewardship Scholarships: The foundation offers scholarships to graduating high school seniors who are passionate about the environment and want to engage in activities that will help to protect and improve their natural surroundings. Scholarships are a cash award of $500 and can be used for the purchase of books and materials, payment of school fees, and other institutional costs associated with higher education.
Green Earth Book Award: This award focuses on books that best raise awareness of the beauty of the natural world and the responsibility that people have to protect it. The award is intended to teach the ethos of environmental stewardship and to make children more aware of the fragile nature of their local ecosystems and the role each of us can play in nurturing, protecting and defending it. The Children's Fiction award is comprised of a monetary award of $1,250 to the author and $1,250 to the illustrator (or $2,500 if the author and illustrator is the same person). The Young Adult Fiction award is comprised of a $2,500 monetary award to the author. The Nonfiction award is comprised of $2,500 to the author. In addition, a $500 donation will be provided to the environmental organization chosen by each winner and approved by the foundation.
GreenFocus Awards: This award is an environmental still photography contest for high school students who use the art of photography to raise community awareness and foster the environmental education of the nation's youth. This annual contest has two separate components each year: one focusing on sustainable land use for the annual Brownfields Conference, and the other focusing on broader environmental themes for annual foundation-sponsored Earth Day events.
Rachel Carson Scholar Program: This scholarship program is open to Maryland high school juniors and seniors who are concerned about the environment and want to engage in activities and continue studies that will help to protect and improve their natural surroundings. The program

provides $1,000 to the first-place recipient, $750 to the second-place recipient, and $500 to the third-place recipient.
EIN: 201670424

9466
Northern Piedmont Community Foundation
P.O. Box 182
Warrenton, VA 20188 (540) 349-0631
Contact: M. Cole Johnson, Exec. Dir.
FAX: (540) 349-0633; E-mail: info@npcf.org;
URL: http://www.npcf.org

Foundation type: Community foundation
Purpose: Scholarships to graduating seniors attending various high schools in Fauquier, Culpeper, Madison, and Rappahannock counties in the Piedmont region of VA, for higher education.
Publications: Application guidelines; Annual report; Informational brochure; Newsletter.
Financial data: Year ended 06/30/2013. Assets, $6,104,597 (M); Expenditures, $492,450; Total giving, $312,644; Grants to individuals, 23 grants totaling $27,850.
Fields of interest: Higher education; Education.
Type of support: Scholarships—to individuals; Awards/prizes; Undergraduate support.
Application information: Applications accepted. Application form required. Application form available on the grantmaker's web site.
Initial approach: Application
Send request by: Online
Deadline(s): Apr. 19
Additional information: Eligibility criteria varies per scholarship. See web site for a complete listing.
EIN: 311742955

9467
Northern Virginia Delta Education & Community Service Foundation
P.O. Box 2265
Arlington, VA 22202-0310 (703) 715-6140
E-mail: info@dstnovac.org; URL: http://www.nvdecs.org/

Foundation type: Public charity
Purpose: Scholarships to Northern Virginia students pursuing postsecondary education at institutions of higher learning.
Financial data: Year ended 06/30/2012. Assets, $278,666 (M); Expenditures, $103,144; Total giving, $38,170; Grants to individuals, 5 grants totaling $22,500.
Fields of interest: Higher education.
Type of support: Scholarships—to individuals.
Application information: Applications accepted. Application form required.
Applicants should submit the following:
1) Essay
2) Letter(s) of recommendation
3) Transcripts
4) GPA
Additional information: Contact the foundation for additional guidelines.
EIN: 541651048

9468
Northern Virginia Family Service
10455 White Granite Dr., Ste. 100
Oakton, VA 22124-2764 (571) 748-2500
Contact: Mary B. Agee, Exec. Dir.
E-mail: info@nvfs.org; URL: http://www.nvfs.org/

Foundation type: Public charity
Purpose: Emergency support and in-kind gifts to low-income individuals and families throughout northern VA.
Financial data: Year ended 06/30/2012. Assets, $14,039,080 (M); Expenditures, $26,526,588; Total giving, $7,166,764; Grants to individuals, totaling $6,305,531.
Fields of interest: Housing/shelter; Human services; Economically disadvantaged.
Type of support: Emergency funds; In-kind gifts.
Application information: Applicants must submit detailed invoices on a monthly basis to the agency.
EIN: 540791977

9469
The NRA Foundation, Inc.
11250 Waples Mill Rd.
Fairfax, VA 22030-7400 (703) 267-1130
Contact: Wayne Sheets, Exec. Dir.
Application information: Fax: (703) 267-3743, url: http:// www.friendsofnra.org/yes
FAX: (703) 267-3985; E-mail: nraf@nrahq.org;
Toll-free tel.: (800) 423-6894; URL: http://www.nrafoundation.org

Foundation type: Public charity
Purpose: Scholarships to qualified high school sophomores and juniors to participate in the foundation's Youth Education Summit (Y.E.S.)
Publications: Application guidelines; Annual report; Financial statement; Informational brochure (including application guidelines); Newsletter; Occasional report.
Financial data: Year ended 12/31/2011. Assets, $81,140,578 (M); Expenditures, $26,751,339; Total giving, $20,578,246; Grants to individuals, totaling $11,750.
Fields of interest: Higher education.
Type of support: Scholarships—to individuals.
Application information: Applications accepted. Application form required.
Initial approach: E-mail
Send request by: Mail or fax
Deadline(s): Feb. 1
Applicants should submit the following:
1) Transcripts
2) Letter(s) of recommendation
3) Essay
Additional information: Application should also include a personal statement.
EIN: 521710886

9470
The George and Carol Olmsted Foundation
80 E. Jefferson St., Ste. 300B
Falls Church, VA 22046-3566
FAX: (703) 536-5020;
E-mail: scholars@olmstedfoundation.org; Toll-free tel.: (877) 656-7833; URL: http://www.olmstedfoundation.org

Foundation type: Independent foundation
Purpose: Foreign study scholarships by nomination only to career military officers in the Armed Forces.
Publications: Annual report; Informational brochure; IRS Form 990 or 990-PF printed copy available upon request.
Financial data: Year ended 12/31/2012. Assets, $41,309,729 (M); Expenditures, $2,168,169; Total giving, $911,272; Grants to individuals, totaling $514,022.
Fields of interest: Language (foreign); Military/veterans' organizations.
Type of support: Awards/grants by nomination only; Graduate support.

Application information: Applications not accepted.

Additional information: Applications available through Military Services representatives. Unsolicited requests for funds not considered or acknowledged. Funds largely committed.

Program description:

Olmsted Scholar Program: Each year, the Olmsted Scholar Program offers educational grants for two years of graduate study in a foreign language and other educational experiences in a foreign country to competitively selected career line officers from the four branches of the U.S. military. The foundation has the goal of selecting the most highly qualified officers from the Army, Navy, Air Force, and Marine Corps annually, with the number of scholars selected based on the foundation's financial ability to support them and the available pool of qualified candidates. See foundation web site for further information.

EIN: 546049005

9471

Operation Blessing International Relief and Development Corp.

977 Centerville Tpke.
Virginia Beach, VA 23463-1001 (757) 226-3401
Contact: William Horan
FAX: (757) 226-3657; URL: http://www.ob.org

Foundation type: Public charity
Purpose: Assistance to individuals in the U.S. and throughout the world with disaster relief, medical aid, hunger relief, orphan care and clean water.
Publications: Annual report.
Financial data: Year ended 03/31/2012. Assets, $28,545,687 (M); Expenditures, $221,296,053; Total giving, $272,980,225; Grants to individuals, 2,578,155 grants totaling $70,550,817.
Fields of interest: Agriculture/food; Human services; International relief; Children/youth.
Type of support: In-kind gifts; Grants for special needs.
Application information: See web site for additional information.
EIN: 541382657

9472

Operation First Response, Inc.

20037 Dove Hill Rd.
Culpeper, VA 22701-8125
Contact: Peggy Baker, Pres. and C.E.O.
E-mail: info@operationfirstresponse.org; Toll-free tel.: (888) 289-0280Toll-free fax : (888)-505-2795; URL: http://www.operationfirstresponse.org

Foundation type: Public charity
Purpose: Assistance to wounded U.S. service members and their families with personal and financial needs. Examples of services provided included are rent, utilities, vehicle payments, groceries, clothing, and travel expenses to and from major medical facilities.
Financial data: Year ended 12/31/2011. Assets, $227,724 (M); Expenditures, $677,482; Total giving, $534,748; Grants to individuals, totaling $534,748.
Fields of interest: Human services; emergency aid; Military/veterans.
Type of support: In-kind gifts; Grants for special needs.
Application information: Applications accepted. Application form required. Application form available on the grantmaker's web site.
Initial approach: E-mail

Applicants should submit the following:
1) Financial information
EIN: 201622436

9473

Operation Smile, Inc.

3641 Faculty Blvd.
Virginia Beach, VA 23453 (757) 321-7645
Contact: William P. Magee, Jr., C.E.O.
Toll-Free Tel.: (888) 677-6453; URL: http://www.operationsmile.org/

Foundation type: Public charity
Purpose: Free surgeries to treat both indigent children and adults in developing nations who are born with facial deformities, such as cleft lip and cleft palate.
Financial data: Year ended 06/30/2012. Assets, $45,205,335 (M); Expenditures, $51,627,972; Total giving, $7,450,514.
Fields of interest: Health care; Disabilities, people with; Economically disadvantaged.
International interests: Developing Countries.
Type of support: In-kind gifts.
Application information: Applications not accepted.
Additional information: Unsolicited requests not considered or acknowledged.
EIN: 541460147

9474

Orphan Foundation of America

21351 Gentry Dr., Ste. 130
Sterling, VA 20166-8511 (571) 203-0270
Contact: Eileen McCaffrey, Exec. Dir.
FAX: (571) 203-0273; E-mail: help@orphan.org; URL: http://www.orphan.org

Foundation type: Public charity
Purpose: Scholarships and loans to orphans and foster youths pursuing a two- or four-year degree or a certificate in vocational training.
Publications: Application guidelines; Annual report.
Financial data: Year ended 12/31/2011. Assets, $7,613,425 (M); Expenditures, $14,911,882; Total giving, $13,046,731; Grants to individuals, totaling $13,046,731.
Fields of interest: Foster care; Young adults, female.
Type of support: Student loans—to individuals; Technical education support; Undergraduate support.
Application information: Application form required.
Deadline(s): Apr. 1 for scholarships and June 1 for loans
Additional information: See web site for complete guidelines.
Program descriptions:
Burtrez Morrow Educational Loan Program: Provides student loans of up to $5,000 per year for up to two years to young women currently in foster care at the time of their high school graduation. Applicants must be enrolled full-time at a four-year college or university, and entering their junior, or senior year in college. Loans may be used for tuition costs, books, and living expenses.
Casey Family Scholars Program: Provides up to $10,000 to young people under the age of 25 who have spent at least one year in foster care and were not subsequently adopted. Scholarships are awarded for the pursuit of post-secondary education, including vocational/technical training, and are renewable annually based on satisfactory progress and financial need.
Hildegard Lash Merit Scholarship: Provides $5,000 per academic year, paid in two

installments, to college students who have no family supporting their goals and efforts. Students must be currently in foster care at the time of their high school graduation and/or 18th birthday, or entering their sophomore, junior, or senior year as a full-time student at a four-year college or university.
EIN: 521238437

9475

Parkinson Foundation of the National Capital Area, Inc.

7700 Leesburg Pike, Ste. 208
Falls Church, VA 22043-2620 (703) 734-1017
Contact: Jared D. Cohen, Pres. and C.E.O.
FAX: (703) 734-1241;
E-mail: pfnca@parkinsonfoundation.org;
URL: http://www.parkinsonfoundation.org

Foundation type: Public charity
Purpose: Financial assistance for Parkinson's patients with economic hardship. Financial assistance for Caregivers for temporary care for their patients.
Publications: Newsletter.
Financial data: Year ended 06/30/2012. Assets, $401,536 (M); Expenditures, $768,426; Total giving, $7,552; Grants to individuals, totaling $7,552.
Fields of interest: Parkinson's disease.
Type of support: Grants for special needs.
Application information: Applications accepted. Application form required. Application form available on the grantmaker's web site.
Send request by: Mail
Additional information: Patient must demonstrate financial need for medical related services.
Program descriptions:
The Patience Assistance Fund: The grant range is $400 to $800, to Parkinson's patients or the patient's primary Caregiver who demonstrate financial need. The patient must reside in the PFNCA area of service, the Maryland/Virginia/Washington, DC Metropolitan area. Only one grant per person will be provided each 12 month period. There is no limitation to the number of years a person in need may request funding from this program.
The Respite Program for Caregivers: This program provides financial assistance to Caregivers who need to provide temporary care for their Parkinson's patient. The program covers short term care for Parkinson's patients, while the Caregiver is given a small break. There is a maximum contribution grant level of $1,000 per 12 months per applying family and/or individual.
EIN: 542048636

9476

Patient Advocate Foundation

421 Butler Farm Rd.
Hampton, VA 23666-1576
Contact: Alan Richardson, C.D.O.; Nancy Davenport-Ennis, C.E.O.
FAX: (757) 873-8999;
E-mail: help@patientadvocate.org; Toll-free tel.: (800) 532-5274; tel. for Alan Richardson: (757) 952-1372; URL: http://www.patientadvocate.org

Foundation type: Public charity
Purpose: Scholarships to individuals under the age of 25 who are or have been diagnosed with cancer or a critical or life-threatening disease.
Publications: Application guidelines; Annual report; Financial statement; Informational brochure.

Financial data: Year ended 06/30/2012. Assets, $31,786,946 (M); Expenditures, $50,176,681; Total giving, $33,406,623; Grants to individuals, totaling $33,406,323.

Fields of interest: Terminal illness, people with.

Type of support: Scholarships—to individuals.

Application information: Applications accepted. Application form required. Application form available on the grantmaker's web site.

Initial approach: Letter

Send request by: Mail

Copies of proposal: 1

Deadline(s): Apr. 13

Final notification: Applicants notified within two months

Applicants should submit the following:

1) Letter(s) of recommendation

2) GPA

3) Financial information

4) Essay

5) Budget Information

EIN: 541806317

9477

Patient Services, Inc.

P.O. Box 5930

Midlothian, VA   23112-0033   (804) 744-3813

Contact: Dana A. Kuhn Ph.D., Pres.

FAX: (804) 744-5407;

E-mail: uneedpsi@uneedpsi.org; Toll-free tel.: (800) 366-7741; URL: https://www.patientservicesinc.org/

Foundation type: Public charity

Purpose: Health insurance premium assistance, pharmacy co-payment assistance and co-payment waiver assistance for indigent people with specific expensive chronic illnesses.

Publications: Annual report; Newsletter.

Financial data: Year ended 12/31/2012. Assets, $74,975,209 (M); Expenditures, $56,252,372; Total giving, $50,332,148; Grants to individuals, totaling $50,332,148.

Fields of interest: Health care, insurance; Health care, financing; Health care, patient services.

Type of support: Grants for special needs.

Application information: Applications accepted. Application form required.

Initial approach: Telephone or e-mail

Additional information: Contact organization for eligibility criteria.

EIN: 541596178

9478

The Pentagon Federal Credit Union Foundation

2930 Eisenhower Ave.

Alexandria, VA   22314-4557

Contact: Christopher J. Flynn, Pres.

URL: http://www.pentagonfoundation.org

Foundation type: Public charity

Purpose: Assistance for military personnel who were wounded during overseas conflicts. Grants to first time homebuyers for those in service to the U.S. national security.

Financial data: Year ended 12/31/2011. Assets, $1,980,323 (M); Expenditures, $1,411,247; Total giving, $924,268; Grants to individuals, totaling $924,268.

Fields of interest: Military/veterans.

Type of support: Grants to individuals; Grants for special needs.

Application information: Applications not accepted.

Additional information: Unsolicited requests for funds not considered or acknowledged. Assistance is only for military personnel.

Program descriptions:

DreamMakers Grant: This program offers grants for down payments to first-time homebuyers of modest means who valiantly work to protect our country's national security. Military personnel (Active Duty, Reserve, National Guard, or Veteran), Department of Defense and Department of Homeland Security employees may be eligible if they are a first-time home buyer, or have not owned a home for the last three years, or have lost their home through divorce or disaster, and if the gross annual income of all applicants used to qualify for a mortgage is no more than the greater of $55,000 or 80 percent of area median income, adjusted for family size.

Military Heros Fund: This fund provides wounded service members with services for needs that would otherwise be unmet, including child care for families of the wounded recovering at Walter Reed National Military Medical Center, laptop computers for wounded soldiers and their families staying in Fisher Houses at military hospitals, emergency financial support granted to families facing crises due to injuries and natural disasters, and other programs for patients and families.

EIN: 542062271

9479

The James W. Perkins Memorial Trust

c/o Convergence Center IV

301 Bendix Rd., Ste. 500

Virginia Beach, VA   23452-1385   (757) 497-6633

Contact: C. Arthur Robinson II

E-mail: ARobinson@wolriv.com

Foundation type: Independent foundation

Purpose: College scholarships to students of VA, for continuing education at accredited colleges or universities.

Publications: Annual report.

Financial data: Year ended 12/31/2011. Assets, $97,154 (M); Expenditures, $24,226; Total giving, $17,000; Grants to individuals, 5 grants totaling $17,000 (high: $8,000, low: $1,000).

Fields of interest: Higher education.

Type of support: Undergraduate support.

Application information: Application form required.

Initial approach: Letter

Deadline(s): July 1

EIN: 546271058

9480

Petersburg Methodist Home for Girls

P.O. Box 1688

Petersburg, VA   23805-1688   (804) 733-2011

Contact: Jamie S. Morini

Foundation type: Independent foundation

Purpose: College scholarships to students who are residents of Southside, VA for continuing their education at accredited institutions of higher learning.

Financial data: Year ended 12/31/2011. Assets, $2,639,006 (M); Expenditures, $154,083; Total giving, $117,949; Grants to individuals, 41 grants totaling $53,949 (high: $4,000, low: $750).

Type of support: Scholarships—to individuals.

Application information: Application form required.

Deadline(s): July and Feb.

EIN: 540542500

9481

Phoenix Houses of the Mid-Atlantic

(formerly Vanguard Services Unlimited)

521 N. Quincy St.

Arlington, VA   22203-2136

FAX: (703) 841-2316;

E-mail: admissions@phoenixhouse.org;

URL: http://www.phoenixhouse.org/locations/virginia/

Foundation type: Public charity

Purpose: Financial assistance to needy individuals suffering from substance abuse in the Washington, DC, area.

Financial data: Year ended 06/30/2011. Assets, $2,065,086 (M); Expenditures, $8,093,054.

Fields of interest: Substance abusers.

Type of support: Grants for special needs.

Application information:

Initial approach: Letter

Additional information: Contact foundation for complete eligibility requirements.

EIN: 540805530

9482

The Pillay Foundation

P.O. Box 7274

Arlington, VA   22207

Contact: T.P.B. Panicker

Application address: 9H J. M. Crescent, P.G. Anthony Rd., Kochi, 682024, India.

Foundation type: Independent foundation

Purpose: Scholarships to high school students in India for college education.

Financial data: Year ended 12/31/2012. Assets, $188,781 (M); Expenditures, $17,302; Total giving, $12,020; Grants to individuals, 15 grants totaling $12,020 (high: $2,184, low: $100).

Type of support: Foreign applicants; Undergraduate support.

Application information: Applications accepted. Application form required.

Deadline(s): Dec.

Applicants should submit the following:

1) Transcripts

2) Financial information

EIN: 300117203

9483

Plumbing-Heating-Cooling Contractors-National Association Educational Foundation

(also known as PHCC Educational Foundation)

180 S. Washington St

P. O. Box 6808

Falls Church, VA   22046-2900   (703) 237-8100

Contact: Cindy Sheridan C.A.E., C.O.O.

FAX: (703) 237-7442;

E-mail: scholarships@naphcc.org; Toll Free Tel. : (800)-533-7694; E-mail For Cindy Sheridan: sheridan@naphcc.org; URL: http://foundation.phccweb.org/index.cfm?&RDtoken=38908&userID=

Foundation type: Public charity

Purpose: Scholarships to students enrolled in a full time approved certificate or degree program with a major related to the Plumbing-Heating-Cooling (P-H-C) profession.

Publications: Application guidelines.

Financial data: Year ended 12/31/2012. Assets, $9,473,597 (M); Expenditures, $389,761.

Fields of interest: Vocational education, post-secondary; Business school/education; Engineering.

International interests: Canada.
Type of support: Research; Scholarships—to individuals.
Application information: Application form required. Application form available on the grantmaker's web site.
>   *Initial approach:* Telephone or e-mail
>   *Send request by:* Mail or fax
>   *Deadline(s):* May 1
>   *Additional information:* See web site for application guidelines.
Program description:
>   *Scholarship Program:* The foundation awards two $3,000 scholarships to students who are enrolled in either a Plumbing-Heating-Cooling Contractors (PHCC)-approved apprenticeship program or a full-time certificate or degree program at an accredited two-year community college, technical college, or trade school, and three $12,000 scholarships to students who are enrolled in an undergraduate degree program at an accredited four-year college or university.
EIN: 541396371

9484
PMMI Education and Training Foundation
(formerly Packaging Machinery Manufacturers Institute)
11911 Fredom Dr., Ste. 600
Reston, VA   20190-5668   (703) 243-8555
FAX: (703) 243-8556; E-mail: education@pmmi.org

Foundation type: Public charity
Purpose: Scholarships to individuals who work for PMMI member companies for one job-related course per semester, not to exceed $500.
Publications: Application guidelines; Annual report.
Financial data: Year ended 12/31/2011. Assets, $117,114 (M); Expenditures, $123,196; Total giving, $109,511; Grants to individuals, totaling $109,511.
Fields of interest: Higher education; Education.
Type of support: Employee-related scholarships; Scholarships—to individuals.
Application information: Application form required.
>   *Initial approach:* Letter or telephone
>   *Deadline(s):* Dec. 15 for Spring
>   *Additional information:* Application must include recommendations from immediate supervisor and company-designated PMMI executive representative.
Program descriptions:
>   *C. Glenn Davis Scholarships:* Scholarships of $1,000 each are awarded to students enrolled in a packaging machinery mechanic or technician program.
>   *Mark C. Garvey Scholarship:* This scholarship is awarded to students at packaging schools that demonstrate a commitment to excellence in the packaging industry.
>   *Packexpo Travel Scholarships:* Funds are available for students in the packaging and machinery manufacturing industry wishing to travel to association trade shows.
>   *PMMI Member Employee Tuition Reimbursement Program:* This program encourages and supports the efforts of member employees in furthering their education. Individuals employed by a member company can apply for tuition reimbursement of up to $500 to cover the cost of one job-related cost per semester.
EIN: 541820667

9485
Bess R. Poff Scholarship Foundation
P.O. Box 842
Floyd, VA   24091-0842   (540) 745-4111
Contact: Robert Spence, Pres.

Foundation type: Independent foundation
Purpose: Scholarships to graduates of Floyd County High School, Floyd County, VA, for undergraduate education.
Financial data: Year ended 12/31/2012. Assets, $153,638 (M); Expenditures, $1,233; Total giving, $1,000; Grant to an individual, 1 grant totaling $1,000.
Type of support: Support to graduates or students of specific schools.
Application information: Application form required.
>   *Deadline(s):* Apr. 1
>   *Additional information:* Application must include GPA, extracurricular activities, and college choice.
EIN: 541867764

9486
Postal Employees Relief Fund
P.O. Box 7630
Woodbridge, VA   22195-7630   (202) 408-1869
E-mail: perf10268@aol.com; URL: http://www.postalrelief.com

Foundation type: Public charity
Purpose: Relief grants to active or retired postal service employees affected by hurricane, typhoons, earthquakes, floods, tornadoes, wildfires and home fires.
Publications: Application guidelines.
Financial data: Year ended 12/31/2011. Assets, $2,554,516 (M); Expenditures, $671,225; Total giving, $515,000; Grants to individuals, totaling $515,000.
Fields of interest: Safety/disasters.
Type of support: Grants to individuals.
Application information: Applications accepted. Application form required. Application form available on the grantmaker's web site.
>   *Additional information:* Contributes only to postal workers; unsolicited requests for funds not considerer or acknowledged.
Program description:
>   *Financial Assistance:* Grants, ranging from $1,000 to $14,000, are available to active and retired postal employees who incur a significant loss in property damage as a result of a major natural disaster. Covered items eligible for reimbursement include principal dwellings and/or garages, motor vehicles, and content items, such as household appliances, furniture, fixtures, window treatments, clothing, food, medicine, and other day-to-day living items.
EIN: 521666010

9487
Prevent Cancer Foundation
(formerly Cancer Research and Prevention Foundation)
1600 Duke St., Ste.500
Alexandria, VA   22314-3466   (703) 836-4412
Contact: Carolyn R. Aldige, Pres.
FAX: (703) 836-4413;
E-mail: info@preventcancer.org; Toll-free tel.: (800) 277-2732; URL: http://www.preventcancer.org

Foundation type: Public charity
Purpose: Grants for researchers at any academic level who need seed funding to test an innovative hypothesis for the cure of cancer.

Publications: Application guidelines; Annual report; Financial statement; Informational brochure; Newsletter.
Financial data: Year ended 06/30/2012. Assets, $8,978,616 (M); Expenditures, $4,501,393; Total giving, $721,165.
Fields of interest: Cancer research.
Type of support: Research.
Application information:
>   *Initial approach:* Proposal
>   *Deadline(s):* Sept. 14
>   *Additional information:* Contact foundation for further eligibility criteria.
Program descriptions:
>   *Fellowships:* Fellowships are awarded for two years at $40,000 per year for a total of $80,000 to researchers at the postdoctoral level for basic, clinical, translational and population-based research projects; educational programs in cancer prevention; or early detection projects. Fellowship requests should be made by a principal investigator on behalf of the organizational candidate. Researchers need not be U.S. citizens although research must be conducted in the U.S.
>   *Grants:* Grants are awarded for two years at $40,000 per year, for a total of $80,000 for basic, clinical, translational and population-based research projects; educational programs in cancer prevention; or early detection projects. Researchers need not be U.S. citizens although research must be conducted in the U.S.
EIN: 521429544

9488
Public Entity Risk Institute
608 S. King St., No. 200
Leesburg, VA   20175-3924   (303) 651-8720
Contact: Claire L. Reiss, Deputy Exec. Dir.
URL: http://www.riskinstitute.org

Foundation type: Public charity
Purpose: Scholarships to staff and officials of small local governments, schools, and nonprofit organizations for attendance at risk management conferences and training sessions.
Publications: Application guidelines; Grants list; Informational brochure; Newsletter; Program policy statement.
Financial data: Year ended 12/31/2011. Assets, $3,583,556 (M); Expenditures, $1,064,284; Total giving, $59,241; Grants to individuals, totaling $59,241.
Fields of interest: Disasters, preparedness/services; Physical/earth sciences; Engineering; Social sciences.
Type of support: Fellowships; Awards/prizes; Travel grants.
Application information: Application form required.
>   *Deadline(s):* Feb. 1 for PERISHIP Awards
>   *Final notification:* Applicants notified in late May or early June
>   *Applicants should submit the following:*
>   1) Letter(s) of recommendation
>   2) Budget Information
>   3) Proposal
>   4) Curriculum vitae
Program description:
>   *PERISHIP Awards:* Awarded in conjunction with the Natural Hazards Center at the University of Colorado at Boulder, the National Science Foundation, and Swiss Re, this program awards dissertation fellowships in all aspects of natural and human-made hazards, risk, and disasters in all disciplines. Eligible applicants must be ABD (all-but-dissertation) Ph.D. applicants who are affiliated with a U.S. institution, and who are pursuing Ph.D.-level work in hazards, risk, or

disasters in any discipline, including the natural and physical sciences, social and behavioral sciences, engineering, or inter-disciplinary (such as environmental studies)
EIN: 411873459

9489
Radiation Oncology Institute
(formerly ASTRO Education and Development Fund, also known as ASTRO)
8280 Willow Oaks Corp. Dr., Ste. 500
Fairfax, VA 22031-4514 (703) 502-1550
Contact: Laura Thevenot, Exec. Dir.
FAX: (703) 502-7852; E-mail: laurat@astro.org;
Toll-free tel.: (800) 962-7876; URL: http://www.roinstitute.org/

Foundation type: Public charity
Purpose: Fellowships or scholarships, and awards for study of radiology and oncology to U.S. and foreign individuals. One-year fellowships for research in radiation oncology are available to qualified applicants.
Publications: Newsletter.
Financial data: Year ended 12/31/2011. Assets, $9,402,345 (M); Expenditures, $797,420.
Fields of interest: Diagnostic imaging research.
Type of support: Fellowships; Research.
Application information: Applications accepted.
  Initial approach: Letter or telephone
  Additional information: Contact foundation for current application deadline/guidelines.
EIN: 510178702

9490
A. R. Rahman Foundation
3133 Cofer Rd.
Falls Church, VA 22042-4210 (703) 534-6809
Contact: Mohammed Nafia Al-Saigh, Dir.

Foundation type: Operating foundation
Purpose: Grants to needy individuals and families in VA.
Financial data: Year ended 12/31/2012. Assets, $14,259 (M); Expenditures, $39,315; Total giving, $38,658; Grants to individuals, 18 grants totaling $38,658 (high: $6,000, low: $100).
Fields of interest: Economically disadvantaged.
Type of support: Grants for special needs.
Application information:
  Initial approach: Letter
  Deadline(s): None
  Additional information: Application should include endorsements by two prominent citizens.
EIN: 541986384

9491
John Randolph Foundation
112 N. Main St., Ste. B
P.O. Box 1606
Hopewell, VA 23860-2719 (804) 458-2239
Contact: Lisa H. Sharpe, Exec. Dir.
FAX: (804) 458-3754;
E-mail: jrfoundation@covad.net; Email for Lisa H. Sharpe: lsharpe@johnrandolphfoundation.org;
URL: http://johnrandolphfoundation.org

Foundation type: Public charity
Purpose: Scholarships to local students for higher education in professional health fields who reside in Hopewell, Colonial Heights, Petersburg, Emporia, Ft. Lee, Prince George, Dinwiddie, Chesterfield, Charles City, Sussex, Surry, Greensville, Varina, Southeast Henrico, and South of I-64, VA.

Publications: Application guidelines; Informational brochure; Newsletter.
Financial data: Year ended 12/31/2011. Assets, $4,985,885 (M); Expenditures, $662,694; Total giving, $124,995; Grants to individuals, totaling $108,500.
Fields of interest: Health sciences school/education.
Type of support: Scholarships—to individuals; Graduate support; Technical education support; Undergraduate support.
Application information: Applications accepted. Application form required. Application form available on the grantmaker's web site.
  Initial approach: Letter or telephone
  Deadline(s): Apr. 30 for The John Randolph Medical Center Award for Nurse Educators; Feb. 15 for The Drs. Singh and Bhuller Tri-Cities Outstanding Educator of the Year Award and all scholarships
  Additional information: See web site for a listing of additional programs.
Program descriptions:
  Anderson J. Blevins and Thelma L. Hammond Memorial Scholarship Program: Scholarships of $1,000 each are available to students within the foundation's service area who express an interest in attending college as a full- or part-time undergraduate student (at least six hours per semester), and who have a GPA of 3.0 or better.
  Bobby Owen Memorial Scholarship Program: Grants of $2,000 each are available to students who are pursuing careers in fire fighting, law enforcement, or emergency medicine. Eligible applicants must: express an interest in pursuing a course of study or receiving appropriate training as a full- or part-time firefighter, police officer, or emergency medical provider; is currently volunteering or has volunteered as such in the past; or is a dependent of a full- or part-time firefighter, police officer, or emergency medical provider. Applicants must also reside in Prince George County, the Enon District of Chesterfield County, or Varina, and have a GPA of at least 3.0.
  Franklin D. Boyce Annual Health Scholarship Program: Scholarships of $2,500 each are available to students within the foundation's service area who are currently attending, or have an interest in attending, college as a full- or part-time undergraduate or graduate student in a health-related field. Eligible applicants must demonstrate financial need and have a GPA of 3.0 or better.
  Joan Glascock Skaggs Nursing Scholarship Program: Scholarships of up to $2,500 are available to residents of the foundation's service area who are attending, or who express an interest in attending, college as a full- or part-time undergraduate (at least six hours per semester) or graduate student in the nursing field. Eligible applicants must demonstrate financial need and have a GPA of at least 3.0.
  John and Wilber Traylor Scholarship Program: Scholarships of $2,500 each are available to seniors attending Hopewell High School, Prince George High School, Thomas Dale High School, or West End Christian School, who express an interest in attending college as a full- or part-time undergraduate student (at least six hours per semester). Eligible applicants must demonstrate financial need have a GPA of at least 3.0.
  John Randolph Foundation Merit Scholarship Program: Scholarships of $5,000 each are available to high school seniors in Hopewell, Prince George, or the Enon District of Chesterfield County, who express an interest in attending college as a full- or part-time undergraduate student (at least six hours per semester). Applicants must have a

minimum GPA of 3.5, and a minimum SAT score of 1600.
  Plato George Eliades Law Scholarship Program: Scholarships of $1,000 each are available to high-school seniors attending Hopewell High School, Prince George High School, Thomas Dale High School, or Appomattox Regional Governor's School, who express an interest in attending college as a full- or part-time undergraduate student (at least six hours per semester). Eligible applicants must demonstrate financial need and have a GPA of at least 3.0; preference will be given to students pursuing courses of study in the legal and law enforcement fields.
  Prince George High School Memorial Scholarship Program: Scholarships of $1,000 each are available to high-school seniors attending Prince George High School who wish to attend college as a full- or part-time (at least six hours per semester) undergraduate student. Eligible applicants must demonstrate financial need and have a GPA of at least 3.0.
  The Drs. Singh and Bhuller Tri-Cities Outstanding Educator of the Year Award: This award recognizes an outstanding educator from the Tri-Cities area who maintains a standard of excellence in and out of the classroom. The award carries a $2,500 grant.
  The John Randolph Medical Center Award for Nurse Educators: This program recognizes two outstanding nurse educators (one at the high-school level, and one at the college level) who are interested in training others, but who are also challenged by the salary discrepancy between an educational and a clinical setting. Recipients are awarded a $2,500 cash prize, with the hopes of encouraging them to continue training others in their much-needed profession.
EIN: 541649268

9492
Reckitt Benckiser Pharmaceuticals Patient Help Foundation
10710 Midlothian Tpke., Ste. 430
Richmond, VA 23235-4759

Foundation type: Company-sponsored foundation
Purpose: Pharmaceutical assistance used for the treatment of opiate addiction to indigent, uninsured, and low-income individuals.
Financial data: Year ended 12/31/2012. Assets, $0; Expenditures, $24,141,468; Total giving, $22,288,109; Grants to individuals, totaling $22,288,109.
Fields of interest: Health care; Economically disadvantaged.
Type of support: Grants for special needs.
Application information: The program is administered by a third party vendor.
EIN: 800723342

9493
The Research Foundation of CFA Institute
P.O. Box 2083
Charlottesville, VA 22902-2083 (434) 951-5499
Contact: Walter V. Haslett, Jr., Exec. Dir.
FAX: (434) 951-5370; E-mail: rf@cfainstitute.org;
E-Mail for Walter V. Haslett Jr.: bud.haslett@cfainstitute.org; URL: http://www.cfainstitute.org/about/foundation/Pages/index.aspx

Foundation type: Public charity
Purpose: Scholarships to individuals or dependent children, spouses or domestic partners of

individuals who were either permanently disabled in the September 11th terrorist attacks or who are closely related to someone who was killed or permanently disabled in the attacks.
Publications: Application guidelines; Program policy statement.
Financial data: Year ended 08/31/2011. Assets, $10,451,363 (M); Expenditures, $649,726; Total giving, $206,166; Grants to individuals, totaling $194,603.
Fields of interest: Safety/disasters; Disabilities, people with.
Type of support: Undergraduate support.
Application information: Application form required. Application form available on the grantmaker's web site.
  Deadline(s): June 1
Program description:
  September 11 Memorial Scholarship Fund: The fund provides college and university scholarships of up to $25,000 each to individuals who were permanently disabled in the attacks or were the spouses, domestic partners, or dependents of anyone killed or permanently disabled in the attacks and who will pursue university level education in finance, economics, or related fields.
EIN: 546063408

9494
Richmond Jewish Foundation
5403 Monument Ave.
P.O. Box 17128
Richmond, VA   23226-1408   (804) 545-8628
Contact: Robert I. Nomberg, Pres. and C.E.O.
FAX: (804) 282-7507;
E-mail: robert@rjfoundation.org; URL: http://www.rjfoundation.net

Foundation type: Public charity
Purpose: Scholarships to teens in the Richmond/Tidewater, VA metropolitan area, to attend Jewish summer camps and to study in Israel.
Publications: Application guidelines; Annual report.
Financial data: Year ended 06/30/2012. Assets, $28,581,884 (M); Expenditures, $2,185,554; Total giving, $1,646,946.
Fields of interest: Higher education; Jewish agencies & synagogues.
Type of support: Camperships; Scholarships—to individuals.
Application information: Applications accepted. Application form required. Application form available on the grantmaker's web site.
  Send request by: Mail or fax
  Deadline(s): Mar. 1
  Additional information: Application should include a copy of your 1040 income tax form.
Program descriptions:
  Jewish Camp Scholarships: Grants, ranging from $250 to $500, are available to Richmond and Tidewater residents to attend Jewish overnight summer camps.
  Study in Israel Scholarship: Need-based scholarships of up to $1,000 each are available to students interested in studying in Israel.
EIN: 541623966

9495
Robinson, Farmer, Cox Associates Educational Foundation
P.O. Box 6580
Charlottesville, VA   22906-6580   (434) 973-8314
Contact: Robert M. Huff, Pres.
Application address: 530 Westfield Rd., Charlottesville, VA 22901; URL: http://www.rfca.com/index.php?option=com_content&view=article&id=64&Itemid=72

Foundation type: Independent foundation
Purpose: College scholarships to eligible individuals of VA who are pursuing a career in accounting or other majors with a plan to work in public administration.
Financial data: Year ended 12/31/2012. Assets, $292,966 (M); Expenditures, $15,159; Total giving, $9,000.
Fields of interest: Higher education; Business school/education.
Type of support: Scholarships—to individuals.
Application information: Applications accepted. Application form required. Application form available on the grantmaker's web site.
  Initial approach: Letter
  Deadline(s): Nov. 1
  Applicants should submit the following:
    1) Transcripts
    2) Essay
EIN: 542016551

9496
Lucy Pannill Sale Foundation
231 E. Church St., 5th Fl.
Martinsville, VA   24112-2840

Foundation type: Independent foundation
Purpose: Grants and scholarships to residents of VA for the arts, secondary and higher education, and human services.
Financial data: Year ended 05/31/2013. Assets, $537,579 (M); Expenditures, $107,577; Total giving, $98,500.
Fields of interest: Arts; Higher education; Human services.
Type of support: Grants to individuals; Scholarships—to individuals.
Application information:
  Send request by: Mail
  Deadline(s): None
EIN: 541726783

9497
Andrew and Martha Sanford Scholarship Foundation
P.O. Box 1958
Kilmarnock, VA   22482   (804) 435-4137
Contact: Edward Young, Comm.

Foundation type: Independent foundation
Purpose: Scholarships to residents of Westmoreland, Richmond, Lancaster, and Northumberland counties, VA, for attendance at colleges, universities, and trade schools. Scholarships are awarded on the basis of financial need, academic achievement, character, and community and extracurricular activities.
Financial data: Year ended 12/31/2012. Assets, $359,457 (M); Expenditures, $12,173; Total giving, $7,250.
Fields of interest: Vocational education.
Type of support: Technical education support; Undergraduate support.

Application information: Application form required.
  Initial approach: Letter
  Deadline(s): Mar. 15
  Final notification: Recipients notified by May 15
  Applicants should submit the following:
    1) Essay
    2) Transcripts
    3) GPA
    4) Financial information
EIN: 546295578

9498
Sarnoff Cardiovascular Research Foundation, Inc.
731 G-2 Walker Rd.
Great Falls, VA   22066-2834   (703) 759-7600
FAX: (703) 759-7838;
E-mail: dboyd@sarnofffoundation.org; Toll-free tel.: (888) 4-SARNOFF; URL: http://www.sarnofffoundation.org

Foundation type: Public charity
Purpose: Fellowships to medical students enrolled in accredited U.S. medical schools to spend a year conducting intensive work in a biomedical research laboratory, other than the medical school in which they are enrolled, for cardiovascular research.
Publications: Application guidelines; Grants list; Informational brochure; Informational brochure (including application guidelines); Newsletter; Occasional report.
Financial data: Year ended 06/30/2012. Assets, $26,692,000 (M); Expenditures, $1,192,999; Total giving, $503,205; Grants to individuals, totaling $503,205.
Fields of interest: Heart & circulatory research.
Type of support: Fellowships; Research.
Application information: Applications accepted. Application form required. Application form available on the grantmaker's web site.
  Deadline(s): Jan. 12 for Sarnoff Fellowship Program
  Applicants should submit the following:
    1) Letter(s) of recommendation
    2) Curriculum vitae
    3) Transcripts
    4) Essay
  Additional information: Application should also include a personal statement.
Program description:
  Sarnoff Fellowship Program: This program offers medical students enrolled in accredited U.S. medical schools the opportunity to spend a year conducting intense work in a biomedical research facility in the U.S., other than the medical school in which they are enrolled. Fellows receive: a stipend of $28,500; an additional allowance of up to $7,000 for travel to select a preceptor and fellowship laboratory, moving expenses, health insurance, and computer equipment; financial support to attend annual scientific sessions and meetings; and funds for travel to present a paper, based on fellowship research, at two national conferences. Fellows will be accepted from second- and third-year medical students; fourth-year medical students are required to submit an official letter from their medical school granting graduation deferment.
EIN: 521254078

9499
Earle J. Schlarb Scholarship Trust
c/o Jeffrey Lenhart
P.O. Box 1287
Harrisonburg, VA   22803-1287

Foundation type: Independent foundation
Purpose: Scholarships to the top two graduating seniors of each public high school in Shenandoah County, VA, for full-time higher education at a college, university or vocational/technical school.
Financial data: Year ended 12/31/2012. Assets, $623,835 (M); Expenditures, $43,546; Total giving, $24,302; Grants to individuals, 11 grants totaling $24,302 (high: $6,000, low: $434).
Type of support: Support to graduates or students of specific schools; Technical education support; Undergraduate support.
Application information: Applications not accepted.
Additional information: Unsolicited requests for funds not considered or acknowledged.
EIN: 546405104

9500
Scott & Stringfellow Educational Foundation
901 E. Byrd St., Ste. 500
Richmond, VA 23219
FAX: (804) 643-3718

Foundation type: Company-sponsored foundation
Purpose: Scholarships to spouses and dependents of employees of Scott & Stringfellow, Inc. and others in the surrounding areas of company business offices. Also, grants to educators.
Publications: Informational brochure.
Financial data: Year ended 12/31/2012. Assets, $1,124,633 (M); Expenditures, $70,502; Total giving, $58,050; Grants to individuals, 39 grants totaling $56,250 (high: $6,000, low: $500).
Type of support: Employee-related scholarships.
Application information: Applications accepted. Application form required. Application form available on the grantmaker's web site.
Deadline(s): Mar.
Applicants should submit the following:
1) Financial information
2) Transcripts
3) Letter(s) of recommendation
Additional information: Application address: c/o Elizabeth Ronston, 909 E. Main St., Richmond, VA 23219, tel.: (804) 782-7757.
Company name: Scott & Stringfellow, Incorporated
EIN: 541669283

9501
Sentara Healthcare
6015 Poplar Hall Dr.
Norfolk, VA 23502-3819 (757) 455-7020
Contact: Gina L. Pitrone, Exec. Dir.
Toll-free tel.: (800) 736-8272; URL: http://www.sentara.com

Foundation type: Public charity
Purpose: Emergency relief grants to employees of Sentara Healthcare, VA with food, clothing, rent, utilities and other special needs.
Publications: Annual report.
Financial data: Year ended 12/31/2011. Assets, $2,082,820,453 (M); Expenditures, $119,886,255; Total giving, $19,603,445; Grants to individuals, totaling $175,053.
Fields of interest: Housing/shelter, expense aid; Safety/disasters.
Type of support: Grants for special needs.
Application information: Applications accepted. Application form required.
Additional information: Applicants must demonstrate need.

Program description:
H.O.P.E. Fund: This program is funded by donations from employees and managed by a committee of employees to assist coworkers who experience catastrophic financial loss through no fault of their own such as fire, death in the family, flooding, hurricane, tornado, or serious family illness. Applicants must first apply to other emergency assistance programs. Assistance to an individual employee is limited to once per 12-month period and may not exceed $1,000.
EIN: 521271901

9502
Sentara Hospitals
6015 Poplar Hall Dr.
Norfolk, VA 23502-3819 (757) 455-7020
Application address for scholarships: c/o Sentara RN Scholarship Comm., 208 Golden Oak Ct., Ste. 200, Virginia Beach, VA 23452

Foundation type: Public charity
Purpose: Scholarships to current nursing students at Sentara Hospitals, VA accepted at select schools.
Financial data: Year ended 12/31/2011. Assets, $1,082,186,427 (M); Expenditures, $1,694,911,848; Total giving, $57,425,543; Grants to individuals, totaling $118,792.
Fields of interest: College (community/junior); Nursing school/education.
Type of support: Scholarships—to individuals.
Application information: Applications accepted. Application form required.
Applicants should submit the following:
1) Transcripts
2) Letter(s) of recommendation
Additional information: Students essay should not be more than 1,000 words indicating why they have chosen the nursing profession, as well as a description of their career goals. Scholarship selection is based on need and merit.

Program description:
Local Scholarship Program: Scholarships are provided for current nursing students who have successfully completed the prerequisites and have been accepted in to the following schools: Sentara School of Nursing, Hampton University, Thomas Nelson Community College, Tidewater Community College, Norfolk State University, Old Dominion University, and Paul D. Camp Community College. If selected to receive an award the student must sign a work commitment contract with Sentara Healthcare Hospitals. Scholarship funds will be used for the cost of tuition and books. A maximum of $10,000 may be awarded.
EIN: 541547408

9503
N. B. Shingleton Scholarship Fund
P.O. Box 551
Winchester, VA 22604
Contact: Ricky Leonard, Admin.

Foundation type: Independent foundation
Purpose: College scholarships to deserving high school seniors of VA for higher education.
Financial data: Year ended 12/31/2012. Assets, $37,764 (M); Expenditures, $3,696; Total giving, $3,000; Grants to individuals, 6 grants totaling $3,000 (high: $500, low: $500).
Fields of interest: Higher education.
Type of support: Scholarships—to individuals.
Application information: Applications accepted.
Initial approach: Letter

Additional information: Contact fund for current application guidelines.
EIN: 237039441

9504
Devindar Sidhu Foundation Inc.
404 N. Van Buren St.
Falls Church, VA 22046 (410) 329-1115
Contact: Manpreet Sidhu, V.P.

Foundation type: Independent foundation
Purpose: Scholarships to students from MD, VA, DC, and PA who are pursuing electrical, mechanical, computer, or architectural engineering. Preference is given to Sikh students.
Financial data: Year ended 12/31/2012. Assets, $56,641 (M); Expenditures, $6,417; Total giving, $4,328; Grant to an individual, 1 grant totaling $4,328.
Fields of interest: Engineering school/education; Minorities.
Type of support: Undergraduate support.
Application information: Applications accepted. Application form required.
Initial approach: Letter
Deadline(s): Apr. 15
Additional information: Application should include an essay.
EIN: 223850758

9505
Sigma Nu Educational Foundation, Inc.
9 N. Lewis St.
P.O. Box 1869
Lexington, VA 24450-0305 (540) 463-1030
Contact: Bradley L. Hastings, Pres.
FAX: (540) 463-1669;
E-mail: foundation@sigmanu.org; E-Mail for Bradley L. Hastings: brad.hastings@sigmanu.org;
URL: http://www.sigmanu.org/foundation/

Foundation type: Public charity
Purpose: Graduate scholarships, academic awards, and emergency educational aid grants only to Sigma Nu Fraternity members.
Publications: Annual report; Occasional report.
Financial data: Year ended 06/30/2011. Assets, $8,898,208 (M); Expenditures, $1,380,476; Total giving, $100,954; Grants to individuals, totaling $80,865.
Fields of interest: Students, sororities/fraternities.
Type of support: Scholarships—to individuals.
Application information: Contact the foundation for additional guidelines.
EIN: 546035735

9506
SMACNA College of Fellows Foundation
4201 Lafayette Center Dr.
Chantilly, VA 20151 (703) 803-2980
Contact: J. Robert Roach
Application address: P.O. Box 221230, Chantilly, VA 20153-1230
FAX: (703) 803-3732; E-mail: broach@smacna.org; Application Address: P.O. Box 221230 Chantilly, VA 20153; URL: http://www.smacna.org/scholarship/

Foundation type: Independent foundation
Purpose: Scholarships to children of the owners and employees of SMACNA firms, chapters or the national office. Any field of study may be pursued, though preference will be given to those pursuing studies related to the sheet metal industry.

Financial data: Year ended 12/31/2012. Assets, $1,038,843 (M); Expenditures, $94,367; Total giving, $80,000; Grants to individuals, 29 grants totaling $80,000 (high: $3,000, low: $1,000).
Fields of interest: Engineering/technology.
Type of support: Employee-related scholarships.
Application information: Application form required.
Deadline(s): Apr. 30
Company name: SMACNA firms
EIN: 521538775

9507
Gerald F. Smith Scholarship Foundation
P.O. Box 3588
Winchester, VA 22604-2586

Foundation type: Independent foundation
Purpose: Scholarships to individuals for postsecondary education within the U.S.
Financial data: Year ended 12/31/2012. Assets, $8,892 (M); Expenditures, $36,409; Total giving, $32,500; Grants to individuals, 9 grants totaling $32,500 (high: $5,000, low: $2,500).
Type of support: Scholarships—to individuals.
Application information: Contact the foundation for guidelines.
EIN: 541725608

9508
The Smithfield-Luter Foundation, Inc.
200 Commerce St.
Smithfield, VA 23430-1204   (757) 365-3000
Contact: Stewart Leeth, Deputy Dir.
URL: http://www.smithfieldluterfoundation.com/

Foundation type: Company-sponsored foundation
Purpose: Educational scholarships to dependent children or grandchildren of full-time and retired employees of Smithfield and its family of companies, who have been accepted to Fayetteville State University, Iowa State University, Johnson & Wales University, Norfolk State University, Paul D. Camp Community College, Virginia Tech, Virginia Union University or Wake Forest University.
Financial data: Year ended 11/30/2012. Assets, $2,544,357 (M); Expenditures, $2,184,243; Total giving, $2,183,626.
Fields of interest: Higher education.
Type of support: Employee-related scholarships.
Application information: Applications not accepted.
Additional information: Unsolicited requests for funds not considered or acknowledged.
EIN: 542062029

9509
Smith-Melton Foundation
(formerly The Melton Arts Foundation)
2086 Hunters Crest Way
Vienna, VA 22181

Foundation type: Independent foundation
Purpose: Grants and awards to individual artists to improve or enhance literary, artistic, musical, or other skills or talent.
Financial data: Year ended 11/30/2013. Assets, $1,782 (M); Expenditures, $175; Total giving, $0.
Fields of interest: Arts.
Type of support: Grants to individuals.
Application information: Applications accepted.
Initial approach: Letter
Deadline(s): None
Additional information: Applicant must demonstrate financial need and must submit a complete biographical record and

supporting material, including a report on their academic and professional careers, a detailed statement of their training plans, a statement of their plans and commitments after the receipt of the grant, letters of reference and lists of performances, exhibitions, recordings, and/or publications.
EIN: 541648543

9510
Society of Nuclear Medicine
1850 Samuel Morse Dr.
Reston, VA 20190-5316   (703) 708-9000
Contact: Virginia Pappas, C.E.O.
FAX: (703) 708-9015;
E-mail: feedback@snmmi.org; E-Mail for Virginia Pappas: vpappas@snmmi.org; URL: http://www.snm.org

Foundation type: Public charity
Purpose: Scholarships, grants, and awards for students pursuing a career in nuclear medicine.
Financial data: Year ended 09/30/2012. Assets, $10,427,824 (M); Expenditures, $10,218,204; Total giving, $262,050; Grants to individuals, totaling $102,675.
Fields of interest: Health sciences school/education.
Type of support: Grants to individuals; Scholarships—to individuals; Awards/prizes.
Application information: Applications accepted.
Additional information: See web site for additional guidelines.
Program descriptions:
Fellowships: Awards a maximum of $3,000 for at least three months to students enrolled in medical school, pharmacy school or graduate school. Undergraduates who demonstrate outstanding competence in physical and/or biological aspects of radioactive traces will be considered. A $2,000 fellowship for two months will also be considered.
Paul Cole Scholarships: Awards $1,000 to students who are enrolled in or accepted for enrollment in baccalaureate, associate, or certificate programs in nuclear medicine technology.
PDEF Mickey Williams Minority Student Scholarship: Awards $5,000 to an applicant currently accepted or enrolled in a nuclear medicine technology program at the time of application for this scholarship. Award is open to students in associate and baccalaureate level programs only. Individuals with previous certificate or degrees in nuclear medicine sciences are ineligible.
PDEF Professional Development Scholarship: Awards $5,000 to an applicant currently accepted or enrolled in a master's- or doctoral-level program in a field related to advancing their career in nuclear medicine career.
Pilot Research Grants: Awards $10,000 to a top applicant to basic and clinical scientists employed by academically- and research-oriented organizations are invited to apply. Preference is given to individuals who are in the early stages of their careers and who have demonstrated great potential for research careers in the field of nuclear medicine. Up to three other grantees will receive $8,000 each.
EIN: 362496678

9511
Special Libraries Association
(also known as SLA)
331 S. Patrick St.
Alexandria, VA 22314-3501   (703) 647-4900
Contact: Janice R. Lachance, C.E.O.
FAX: (703) 647-4901; E-mail: sla@sla.org; E-Mail For Janice R. Lachance: janice@sla.org;
URL: http://www.sla.org

Foundation type: Public charity
Purpose: Grants and scholarships to individual members of the association who have made outstanding contributions to the fields of library and information science.
Publications: Application guidelines; Annual report; Financial statement; Grants list; Informational brochure; Newsletter.
Financial data: Year ended 12/31/2011. Assets, $8,365,858 (M); Expenditures, $5,432,902.
Fields of interest: Libraries/library science; Libraries (special); Computer science; Minorities.
Type of support: Program development; Publication; Awards/prizes; Postdoctoral support; Graduate support; Doctoral support.
Application information: Applications accepted. Application form required. Application form available on the grantmaker's web site.
Deadline(s): Varies
Program descriptions:
Dialog Member Achievement Award: A $1,000 award will be given to an association member who raises awareness, visibility, and appreciation of the library science profession.
Diversity Leadership Development Program Award: A $1,000 stipend will be awarded to an association member who represents a group typically under-represented in the association. Eligible nominees must have an interest and potential for leadership within the association; recipients must attend the association's annual conference.
Dow Jones Leadership Award: This $2,000 award is presented annually to an association member (or members) in good standing who exemplify leadership as a special librarian through examples of personal and professional competence.
SLA Rising Star Award: Up to five awards are presented annually to recognize a new member who shows exceptional promise of leadership and contribution to the association and the library science profession. Eligible applicants must have from one to five years of professional experience as an information professional, and must have been a member of the association for at most five years. Nominees will be evaluated on their participation in outstanding work and professional activities on behalf of the organization, the development of notable innovations on the job, and active participation within the association. Recipients will be awarded with complimentary registration to the association's annual conference.
EIN: 135404745

9512
Specialized Carriers & Rigging Foundation
5870 trinity Pkwy.
Centreville, VA 20120   (703) 698-0291
Contact: Jackie Roskos, Dir.
URL: http://www.scranet.org/foundatio

Foundation type: Independent foundation
Purpose: Scholarships to children, grandchildren and stepchildren of employees of Specialized Carriers & Rigging Association employees, who are junior and senior high school students pursuing

studies in transportation, cable and rigging, and millwright fields.

Financial data: Year ended 12/31/2012. Assets, $1,688,608 (M); Expenditures, $152,272; Total giving, $30,000; Grants to individuals, 15 grants totaling $30,000 (high: $3,000, low: $500).

Fields of interest: Engineering/technology; Transportation.

Type of support: Employee-related scholarships.

Application information: Applications accepted. Application form required.

   Deadline(s): Jan. 31

Company name: Specialized Carriers & Rigging Assoc.

EIN: 521272278

9513
St. Paul's Church Home
815 E. Grace St.
Richmond, VA 23219-3409 (804) 643-3589

Foundation type: Independent foundation

Purpose: Educational grants to persons between the ages of 17 and 25 who reside in the Richmond, VA, metropolitan area. Grants to needy children to the age of 18 years from the Richmond, VA, metropolitan area for care, maintenance and education, and to destitute, sick individuals of any age in the Richmond, VA, area for care, maintenance, and medical and hospital expenses.

Publications: Application guidelines.

Financial data: Year ended 12/31/2012. Assets, $1,047,063 (M); Expenditures, $57,845; Total giving, $44,990.

Fields of interest: Education; Health care; Children/youth, services; Economically disadvantaged.

Type of support: Undergraduate support; Grants for special needs.

Application information: Applications accepted. Application form required.

   Initial approach: Letter outlining financial need

   Deadline(s): None

   Additional information: Application for educational grant should include two references, financial information, transcripts, and a personal letter outlining educational and academic goals. Applications for special needs should include financial information.

EIN: 546048630

9514
Ralph Stowers Scholarship
c/o National Bank & Trust Co., Trust Dept.
P.O. Box 687
Tazewell, VA 24651-0687 (276) 979-0358

Foundation type: Public charity

Purpose: Scholarships to graduating high school students from Tazewell County, VA.

Financial data: Year ended 12/31/2011. Assets, $2,013,661 (M); Expenditures, $84,496; Total giving, $62,294.

Type of support: Support to graduates or students of specific schools; Undergraduate support.

Application information:

   Deadline(s): None

EIN: 546309437

9515
Strasburg Community Scholarship Trust Fund Inc.
c/o First Bank
112 W. King St.
Strasburg, VA 22657-2220

Foundation type: Independent foundation

Purpose: Scholarships to graduates of Strasburg High School of Strasburg, VA for continuing education at accredited colleges, universities or trade school.

Financial data: Year ended 12/31/2011. Assets, $386,724 (M); Expenditures, $19,730; Total giving, $15,000; Grants to individuals, 10 grants totaling $15,000 (high: $2,500, low: $500).

Fields of interest: Vocational education, post-secondary; Higher education.

Type of support: Support to graduates or students of specific schools; Undergraduate support.

Application information: Applications accepted. Application form required.

   Applicants should submit the following:

     1) Transcripts

     2) Essay

EIN: 541727339

9516
Hattie M. Strong Foundation
6551 Loisdale Ct., Ste. 160
Springfield, VA 22150-1820 (703) 313-6791
FAX: (703) 313-6793;
E-mail: hmsf@hmstrongfoundation.org;
URL: http://www.hmstrongfoundation.org/

Foundation type: Independent foundation

Purpose: Scholarships for college students enrolled in teacher-training programs at selected partnering institutions.

Financial data: Year ended 08/31/2013. Assets, $32,458,699 (M); Expenditures, $1,537,651; Total giving, $975,000; Grants to individuals, 15 grants totaling $150,000 (high: $10,000, low: $10,000).

Fields of interest: Teacher school/education; Scholarships/financial aid.

Type of support: Scholarships—to individuals.

Application information: Applications not accepted.

   Additional information: Unsolicited requests for funds not considered or acknowledged. See web site for participating schools and additional guidelines.

Program description:

   Scholarship Program: This program is aimed at college students enrolled in teacher-training programs. Specifically, the foundation hopes to reduce financial pressure during the student-teaching term, when a student's ability to offset expenses with outside employment is curtailed by the rigor of full-time work in the classroom. Funds for the $5,000 scholarships are distributed via partnership with fifteen institutions, all located near Washington, DC, that have demonstrated leadership in preparing outstanding classroom teachers. Application requirement and student selection will be determined by each institution's scholarship committee in line with the foundation's criteria.

EIN: 530237223

9517
TDC Research Foundation
P.O. Box 1008
Blacksburg, VA 24063

Foundation type: Operating foundation

Purpose: Scientific research grants for the study of chemistry-related areas.

Financial data: Year ended 12/31/2012. Assets, $0 (M); Expenditures, $21,242; Total giving, $14,063.

Fields of interest: Chemistry.

Type of support: Fellowships; Research.

Application information:

   Initial approach: Letter

   Deadline(s): None

EIN: 541574776

9518
Teachers of English to Speakers of Other Languages, Inc.
1925 Ballenger Ave., Ste. 550
Alexandria, VA 22314-4287 (703) 836-0774
FAX: (703) 836-7864; E-mail: info@tesol.org;
Toll-free tel.: (888) 547-3369, E-mail for Deena Boraie: dboraie@aucegypt.edu; URL: http://www.tesol.org

Foundation type: Public charity

Purpose: Awards and grants to English language teaching professionals.

Publications: Application guidelines; Annual report; Informational brochure.

Financial data: Year ended 10/31/2011. Assets, $4,784,781 (M); Expenditures, $4,649,164; Total giving, $43,550; Grants to individuals, totaling $22,050.

Fields of interest: Education.

Type of support: Awards/grants by nomination only; Awards/prizes.

Application information: Application form required.

   Initial approach: Letter or telephone

   Additional information: Application must include letters of recommendation; see web site for additional guidelines for application and nomination.

Program descriptions:

   Global Outreach Fund: This fund supports English language teacher professionals who face personal and/or institutional financial constraints that limit their access to professional development products and services offered by the organization. Eligible applicants include practicing teachers or teacher trainers that reside in a country with a gross national income of less than $15,000 (as determined by the United Nations), or that receive little institutional funding for professional development activities.

   Professional Development Travel Grant for Practicing ESL/EFL Teachers: This program provides grants of $1,500 each to pay the costs of attending organization conferences (including travel, accommodations, and registration fees), in order to support the professional development of ESL/EFL teachers by making it possible for more teachers to attend seminars and conventions. Eligible applicants include practicing ESL/EFL teachers and teacher trainers who need financial support to attend conferences, with preference given to applicants who receive little or no financial support from their institution for professional development, and who have never attended the organization's annual international convention.

   TESOL Award for an Outstanding Paper on NNEST Issues: A $250 award is given to an organization member who has had a proposal accepted for presentation (either a paper or colloquium) on non-native English speakers at the organization's annual convention. Both native and non-native speakers of English may apply for this award.

   TESOL Award for Dedication to Community College ESL Teaching: This $1,000 award honors community college instructors who have demonstrated a commitment to teaching ESL, and will be given to an outstanding community college instructor to facilitate his/her attendance at the organization's annual convention. Eligible applicants will be evaluated on: evidence of dedication to the field of teaching ESL in a community college environment in general, including past and potential future contribution; demonstrated need for professional development; the ability to motivate students; focus on students' learning; and financial need. Applicants must be organizational members with at least three years of ESL community college classroom experience; part-time and adjunct instructors are especially encouraged to apply.

TESOL Award for Distinguished Research: A $1,000 award is available to an organization member who has completed an empirical research project and a subsequent scholarly paper that has been accepted for publication in a scholarly journal. This award is intended to recognize excellence in any area of research on language teaching and learning.

TESOL Award for Teacher as Classroom Action Research: A $1,000 award will be given to recognize excellence in action research on language teaching and learning in an ESL/EFL classroom. Eligible applicants include any instructor who is a member of the organization, who has at least five years of ESL/EFL classroom teaching experience, and who has completed a classroom action research project of significant value to the profession; awards are intended to facilitate attendance and disseminate research findings at the organization's annual convention.

The Albert H. Marckwardt Travel Grants: This $1,000 award honors community college instructors who have demonstrated a commitment to teaching ESL, and will be given to an outstanding community college instructor to facilitate his/her attendance at the organization's annual convention. Eligible applicants will be evaluated on: evidence of dedication to the field of teaching ESL in a community college environment in general, including past and potential future contribution; demonstrated need for professional development; the ability to motivate students; focus on students' learning; and financial need. Applicants must be organizational members with at least three years of ESL community college classroom experience; part-time and adjunct instructors are especially encouraged to apply.

The Mary Finocchiaro Award for Excellence in the Development of Pedagogical Materials: This award recognizes a member (or members) of the organization who has (or have) achieved excellence through the development of practical pedagogical materials not currently under consideration for publication. Materials must be pedagogically innovative and related to some aspect of ESL/EFL teaching, addressing an area such as curriculum, teaching techniques, materials development, testing systems, or computer software. Applications will be available on feasibility, relevance to the classroom, adherence to a rationale or theoretical basis, a clear indication of language level and target population, and style and clarity of expression. Any organization member is eligible to apply; recipients are awarded a $500 grant.

The Ruth Crymes TESOL Fellowship for Graduate Study: The award supports recent or current graduate students in the development of projects with direct application to English as a first- or second-language classroom instruction. Applications are evaluated in terms of the merit of the graduate study project, reasons for pursuing

graduate studies, and financial need. Preference is given to projects with practical classroom applications. The recipient is awarded $1,500 upon selection and acceptance of the award and a convention registration for a subsequent year, when the project is presented.

The TESOL Professional Development Scholarships: The scholarship assists in the professional development of TESOL members by facilitating attendance at the annual convention. Recipients may also choose to attend a pre- or post convention institute (PCI) in addition to the convention. Forty scholarships are awarded for the waiver of convention registration only or convention registration and tuition for one PCI.

The TESOL/TEFL Travel Grant: Grants of up to $2,500 are available to organization members who are currently practicing EFL teachers, teacher trainers, or supervisors with at least five years' experience in a non-English-speaking setting. Grants are intended to offset the costs of travel and basic expenses of attending an organization-sponsored conference; preference will be given to applicants who have previously never attended a conference.

Tina B. Carver Fund: This program provides grants to fund the purchase of student classroom learning materials and/or teacher-related materials (e.g., ancillary materials that can be used in conjunction with textbooks or other instructional materials), to support adult ESL education programs throughout the U.S. Eligible applicants include members of the organization, or members of an organizational affiliate, that submit an application on behalf of a community-based organization, charitable institution, or other U.S.-based nonprofit that provides ESL programming for adults. Priority will be given to organizations that serve the hardest-to-reach students with limited resources.
EIN: 237003530

9519
Thanks USA

1390 Chain Bridge Rd., Ste. 260
McLean, VA 22101-3904
E-mail: shintz@scholarshipamerica.org; *Toll-free tel.:* (888) 849-8720; *URL:* http://www.thanksusa.org

Foundation type: Public charity
Purpose: College, technical, and vocational school scholarships for the children and spouses of those in the United States armed forces.
Publications: Application guidelines.
Financial data: Year ended 12/31/2011. Assets, $2,200,869 (M); Expenditures, $1,697,907; Total giving, $904,600; Grants to individuals, totaling $904,600.
Fields of interest: Military/veterans.
Type of support: Scholarships—to individuals.
Application information: Applications accepted. Application form required.
 Initial approach: Letter
 Deadline(s): May 15
 Additional information: Contact foundation for eligibility criteria. The program is administered by Scholarship America.
Program description:
 Scholarships: Scholarships of $3,000 each are available to dependent children (ages 24 and under) and spouses of active-duty U.S. military service personnel (including those who have served in active duty for at least 180 days since September 11, 2001, including all those who have been killed or wounded in action). Eligible applicants must plan to enroll full-time in an accredited two- or four-year

college, university, vocational school, or technical school, and must have at least a 2.0 cumulative GPA.
EIN: 203973151

9520
Ruby Rowe Thomas Scholarship Trust

P.O. Box 388
Gloucester Point, VA 23062 (804) 642-6111
Contact: Michael T. Soberick, Tr.

Foundation type: Independent foundation
Purpose: Scholarships to graduating seniors of Gloucester High School, VA for postsecondary education.
Financial data: Year ended 12/31/2012. Assets, $12,988 (M); Expenditures, $10,000; Total giving, $8,000; Grants to individuals, 4 grants totaling $8,000 (high: $2,000, low: $2,000).
Fields of interest: Higher education.
Type of support: Support to graduates or students of specific schools.
Application information: Applications accepted. Application form required.
 Deadline(s): May 1
 Applicants should submit the following:
  1) SAR
  2) Letter(s) of recommendation
  3) FAFSA
EIN: 546460652

9521
Mary B. & Perry A. Thompson Educational Trust

P.O. Box 5228
Martinsville, VA 24115 (703) 293-3726
Application Address: c/o 4117 Chain Bridge Rd., Fairfax, VA 22030-4117

Foundation type: Independent foundation
Purpose: Scholarships to legal residents of the city of Fredericksburg, and the counties of Stafford and Spotsylvania, VA for higher education.
Financial data: Year ended 05/31/2013. Assets, $0 (M); Expenditures, $639,490; Total giving, $633,762.
Fields of interest: Higher education.
Type of support: Scholarships—to individuals.
Application information: Applications accepted. Application form required.
 Initial approach: Letter
 Deadline(s): Apr. 15
 Applicants should submit the following:
  1) SAR
  2) Letter(s) of recommendation
  3) SAT
  4) Transcripts
  5) Financial information
 Additional information: Application should also include educational goals and extracurricular activities.
EIN: 546330780

9522
The Tidewater Automobile Association of Virginia - J. Theron "Tim" Timmons Memorial Scholarship Foundation

5366 Virginia Beach Blvd.
Virginia Beach, VA 23462-1828 (757) 233-3825
URL: http://www.aaa.com/

Foundation type: Independent foundation

Purpose: Scholarships to high school graduates whose parents or guardians are members of AAA Tidewater, planning to attend a Virginia school of higher education.
Financial data: Year ended 06/30/2013. Assets, $323,474 (M); Expenditures, $22,975; Total giving, $20,000; Grants to individuals, 4 grants totaling $20,000 (high: $5,000, low: $5,000).
Fields of interest: Higher education.
Type of support: Scholarships—to individuals.
Application information: Applications accepted. Application form required.
 Deadline(s): Apr. 15
 Applicants should submit the following:
  1) Transcripts
  2) SAT
  3) Financial information
  4) Essay
 Additional information: Application should also include parents' income tax return.
EIN: 481288286

9523
Tidewater Builders Association Scholarship Foundation, Inc.
2117 Smith Ave.
Chesapeake, VA 23320-2519 (757) 420-2434
URL: http://www.tbaonline.org/scholarship_foundation.php

Foundation type: Independent foundation
Purpose: Scholarships to high school seniors residing in Chesapeake, Norfolk, Portsmouth, Suffolk, Franklin, Southampton County, Virginia Beach, VA, or the Eastern Shore of VA. Awards to young designers from VA enrolled in drafting and design classes.
Financial data: Year ended 12/31/2012. Assets, $1,053,228 (M); Expenditures, $45,019; Total giving, $9,000.
Fields of interest: Arts education; Visual arts; Design.
Type of support: Scholarships—to individuals; Undergraduate support.
Application information: Application form required.
 Initial approach: Letter or telephone
 Deadline(s): Apr. 7 for Scholarships and Apr. 30 for Young Designers' Scholarship Competition
 Applicants should submit the following:
  1) FAFSA
  2) Resume
  3) SAT
  4) Letter(s) of recommendation
  5) Financial information
  6) Transcripts
 Additional information: Application should also include teacher and counselor evaluations and recommendations, statement of community involvement and a copy of parents' federal income tax return, or W-2 forms, and other income statements.
Program description:
 Young Designers' Scholarship Competition: The scholarship competition is available to students currently enrolled in an approved drafting/design class in any public or private secondary school in Chesapeake, Franklin, Norfolk, Portsmouth, Southampton County, Suffolk, Virginia Beach, or the Eastern Shore of VA. The contest challenges high school designers to create a house to meet a fictional family's needs. First place winner is a $2,000 scholarship. Second place winner is $1,500. Third place winner is $1,000. First honorable mention receives $750 and second honorable mention receives $500. The competition is for CAD designs only, no hand-drawn entries.
EIN: 546057730

9524
Tidewater Jewish Foundation, Inc.
5000 Corporate Woods Dr., Ste. 200
Virginia Beach, VA 23462-4370 (757) 965-6111
Contact: Phillip S. Rovner, Pres. and C.E.O.
FAX: (757) 965-6102; E-mail: tjf-info@ujft.org; E-Mail for Phillip S. Rovner : psrovner@ujft.orgTel. for Phillip S. Rovner : (757)-965-6109; URL: http://www.jewishva.org/tjf-about

Foundation type: Public charity
Purpose: Scholarship to Jewish high school graduates of Hampton Roads, VA for attendance at a nonprofit college or university in the U.S.
Publications: Annual report.
Financial data: Year ended 06/30/2011. Assets, $26,635,210 (M); Expenditures, $3,977,840; Total giving, $2,469,876; Grants to individuals, totaling $22,475.
Fields of interest: Higher education; Jewish agencies & synagogues.
Type of support: Scholarships—to individuals.
Application information: Applications accepted. Application form required. Application form available on the grantmaker's web site.
 Send request by: Mail or hand deliver
 Deadline(s): Mar. 16
 Final notification: Applicants notified in Apr.
 Applicants should submit the following:
  1) Transcripts
  2) Letter(s) of recommendation
  3) Essay
 Additional information: Application should also include a copy of parents' Statement of Family Income and Resources. Scholarship funds are paid directly to the educational institution on behalf of the students. See web site for additional guidelines.
Program description:
 The Stein Family College Scholarship of the TJF: This $10,000 a year scholarship is presented annually for students in the Hampton Roads area (Chesapeake, Norfolk, Portsmouth, Virginia Beach, Suffolk, Isle of Wight County, Hampton, Newport News and the Peninsula) for college tuition. Applicants for the freshman-level scholarship must be high school graduates (or the equivalent) or will graduate from high school at the end of the current school year. Applicants for the sophomore-level scholarship must have completed their freshman year of school at a nonprofit college or university in the U.S. that participates in the Federal Student Aid Program (Title IV)
EIN: 541653165

9525
Jane & Gunby Treakle Charitable and Educational Foundation
P.O. Box 420
Irvington, VA 22480-0420

Foundation type: Independent foundation
Purpose: Scholarships to residents of the Irvington, VA, area.
Financial data: Year ended 11/30/2012. Assets, $838,193 (M); Expenditures, $57,321; Total giving, $20,000; Grants to individuals, 4 grants totaling $20,000 (high: $13,000).
Type of support: Scholarships—to individuals.
Application information: Applications accepted. Application form required.
 Additional information: Contact foundation for current application deadline/guidelines.
EIN: 510215563

9526
The U.S. Civilian Research and Development Foundation
(also known as CRDF Global)
1776 Wilson Blvd., Ste. 300
Arlington, VA 22209-2517 (703) 526-9720
Contact: Carole Russo, Dev. Mgr.
FAX: (703) 526-9721;
E-mail: development@crdf.org; URL: http://www.crdf.org

Foundation type: Public charity
Purpose: Research grants and fellowships to promote scientific and technological collaboration between the U.S. and other countries, primarily the former Soviet Union.
Publications: Application guidelines; Annual report; Informational brochure; Newsletter; Occasional report.
Financial data: Year ended 12/31/2011. Assets, $25,455,564 (M); Expenditures, $25,852,753; Total giving, $12,124,334; Grants to individuals, totaling $693,388.
Fields of interest: Medical research; International exchange; Business/industry; Research; Engineering/technology; Science.
Type of support: Fellowships; Research; Awards/prizes.
Application information: Applications accepted. Application form required. Application form available on the grantmaker's web site.
 Initial approach: Letter
 Deadline(s): Apr. 25 for Biomedical Research Competition; May 4 for George Brown Awards; varies for all others
Program descriptions:
 Biomedical Research Competition: This program supports high-quality and innovative basic or applied research and development by providing up to two years of support to joint research teams of U.S. and international scientists. Eligible general scientific areas include vision research, HIV/AIDS and related infections research, allergies and infectious disease research, and environmental health research. The total maximum grant size is $90,000 for up to two years; at least 80 percent of the funds awarded to each project must be used for the international team's expenses, including institutional support.
 Cooperative Grants Program: Provides up to two years of support to joint U.S. and former Soviet Union (FSU) research teams in all areas of basic and applied research in the natural sciences, mathematics, engineering, and biomedical and behavioral sciences. The average grant is $65,000 and is awarded on a competitive, merit-reviewed basis. Competitions are held every six months and proposals are accepted on a rolling basis.
 George Brown Award for International Scientific Cooperation: A $5,000 award is available to an individual in the policy, business, science, or technology community who is recognized as having contributed substantially to advancing international science and technology cooperation, particularly between the U.S., Eurasia, Middle East, and other regions where the foundation works. Eligible individuals must have made significant advances in international scientific collaboration and positively impacted one or more foundation mission areas (i.e., promoting high-quality research cooperation, infrastructure building, nonproliferation and security, economic development, and education).
 Industry Programs: This program funds pre-commercial research and development (R&D) collaboration between U.S. industry and former Soviet Union (FSU) scientists and engineers. Grants enable FSU scientists and engineers to travel to the United States to learn more about technology

commercialization, fund small projects to assess the commercial potential of technologies for future collaboration, and support market research, business plan development and pre-commercial R&D to prepare selected technologies for the marketplace. Grants range from $3,600 to $125,000.

Junior Scientist Energy Research Fellowship: Fellowships are available to graduate students, postdoctoral students, recent Ph.D. or Kandidat graduates (with degrees completed within the last six years) from Kazakhstan, Russia, Ukraine, and Uzbekistan, for the purposes of traveling to the U.S. for up to three months to work with U.S. specialists on projects that aim to reduce worldwide dependency on non-renewable energy sources. Emphasis will be given to projects that focus on technologies for increased energy efficiency and conservation, and alternative energy development and applications.

Research Grants Program: In cooperation with the Estonia Science Foundation, grants of up to $47,000 are available to joint U.S.-Estonian science and engineering research teams to provide up to two years of support in the areas of information technology and material sciences. Eligible proposals must designate one Estonian Principal Investigator and one U.S. Principal Investigator, each having the following qualifications: each must possess the degree of Ph.D., M.D., or the equivalent research experience; have at least 5 scientific publications in peer-reviewed scientific literature; and work full-time in a civilian research environment. Eligible proposals also must be oriented towards non-military objectives and must be carried out in a civilian research environment.

U.S.-Central Asia Research Travel (CART) Grant Competition: This $45,000 grant allows joint research teams of U.S. and Central Asian scientists and engineers to develop cooperative research projects on environmental issues, including agricultural ecology, alternative energy development and application, atmospheric science, biodiversity, climate change, ecological degradation and recovery, energy conservation, environmental health, hydrology, pollution impact evaluation and management, and soil science. Funds cover travel expenses to the U.S. and Central Asia, equipment materials, and some salaries. Individuals from Kazakhstan, Kyrgyzstan, and Uzbekistan are eligible to submit proposals in collaboration with a U.S. researcher (citizen or permanent resident)
EIN: 541773406

9527
U.S. Committee for Refugees and Immigrants, Inc.
(also known as USCRI)
2231 Crystal Dr., Ste. 350
Arlington, VA 22202-3711 (703) 310-1130
FAX: (703) 769-4241; E-mail: uscri@uscridc.org;
URL: http://www.refugees.org

Foundation type: Public charity
Purpose: Free legal services and direct cash assistance to immigrants and refugees in the United States.
Publications: Annual report; Financial statement.
Financial data: Year ended 09/30/2011. Assets, $12,216,816 (M); Expenditures, $36,979,450; Total giving, $25,318,232.
Fields of interest: Civil/human rights, immigrants; Children's rights; Immigrants/refugees.
Type of support: Grants for special needs.

Application information: Contact organization for further program information.
EIN: 131878704

9528
The United Company Charitable Foundation
(formerly United Coal Company Charitable Foundation)
1005 Glenway Ave.
Bristol, VA 24201-3473 (276) 645-1458
Contact: Martha M. Gayle, Pres.
Scholarship address: Rose Hurley, Mountain Mission School, 1760 Edgewater Dr., Grundy VA 24614, tel.: (276) 791-1514,
e-mail: rhurley@unitedco.net
FAX: (276) 645-1420;
E-mail: mmgayle@unitedco.net

Foundation type: Company-sponsored foundation
Purpose: Scholarships to graduates of Mountain Mission School in Grundy, Virginia to pursue higher education.
Financial data: Year ended 12/31/2011. Assets, $39,394,045 (M); Expenditures, $2,963,482; Total giving, $2,138,236. Scholarships—to individuals amount not specified.
Fields of interest: Higher education.
Type of support: Scholarships—to individuals; Support to graduates or students of specific schools.
Application information: Applications accepted. Application form required.
  Send request by: Mail
  Deadline(s): Jan. 20 for Spring semester and July 1 for Fall semester
  Final notification: Applicants notified in three to four weeks
  Applicants should submit the following:
    1) Transcripts
    2) GPA
    3) SAR
  Additional information: Applications should also include a copy of the applicants college acceptance letter and financial aid award letter.
Program description:
  Scholarship Program: The foundation awards scholarships to graduates of Mountain Mission School in Grundy, Virginia to pursue higher education. The scholarship is designed to cover the cost of tuition, fees, room, board, books, and supplies. Applicants must demonstrate financial need and a GPA of 2.75.
EIN: 541390453

9529
United Daughters of the Confederacy
328 N. Blvd.
Richmond, VA 23220-4009 (804) 355-1636
Contact: Jamesene E. Likins, Pres.
FAX: (804) 353-1396; E-mail: hqudc@rcn.com;
URL: http://www.hqudc.org

Foundation type: Public charity
Purpose: Scholarships to descendents of Confederate soldiers.
Financial data: Year ended 08/31/2012. Assets, $7,104,857 (M); Expenditures, $784,079; Total giving, $49,563; Grants to individuals, totaling $49,563.
Type of support: Graduate support; Undergraduate support.
Application information: Applications accepted. Application form required.
  Initial approach: Letter or e-mail

Copies of proposal: 5
Deadline(s): Mar. 15
Applicants should submit the following:
  1) Financial information
  2) Photograph
  3) Letter(s) of recommendation
  4) Transcripts
Additional information: Application must also include Confederate ancestor's proof of service.
EIN: 540631483

9530
United States Geospatial Intelligence Foundation
2325 Dulles Corner Blvd., Ste. 450
Herndon, VA 20171-4676 (703) 793-0109
Contact: Keith J. Masback, Pres.
Email for the Scholarship Subcommittee:
scholarships@usgif.org
URL: http://www.usgif.org

Foundation type: Public charity
Purpose: Scholarships to students interested in the geospatial sciences.
Financial data: Year ended 06/30/2012. Assets, $6,053,660 (M); Expenditures, $6,438,138; Total giving, $100,500; Grants to individuals, totaling $100,500.
Fields of interest: International affairs, national security.
Type of support: Graduate support; Undergraduate support; Doctoral support.
Application information: Applications accepted. Application form required. Application form available on the grantmaker's web site.
  Initial approach: Email
  Additional information: See http://usgif.org/education/scholarships for additional program criteria.
EIN: 200668409

9531
United Way of South Hampton Roads
2515 Walmer Ave.
P.O. Box 41069
Norfolk, VA 23513-2604 (757) 853-8500
Contact: Mike Hughes, Pres.
FAX: (757) 853-3900;
E-mail: mhughes@unitedwayshr.org; URL: http://www.unitedwayshr.org

Foundation type: Public charity
Purpose: Emergency disaster relief to VA residents suffering from displacement and damage to dwelling from a tornado.
Publications: Annual report; Financial statement; Informational brochure; Newsletter.
Financial data: Year ended 06/30/2012. Assets, $21,289,793 (M); Expenditures, $19,448,103; Total giving, $15,687,503.
Fields of interest: Safety/disasters.
Type of support: Emergency funds.
Application information: Applications not accepted.
EIN: 540506322

9532
United Way-Thomas Jefferson Area
806 E. High St.
Charlottesville, VA 22902-5126 (434) 972-1701
Contact: Cathy Smith Train, Pres.
Contact for child care scholarship eligibility information: Leah Hill at (434) 972-1715
FAX: (434) 972-1719;
E-mail: unitedwaytja@unitedwaytja.org;
URL: http://www.unitedwaytja.org

Foundation type: Public charity
Purpose: Child care scholarships to low income working families in Charlottesville or Albemarle county, VA.
Publications: Application guidelines; Annual report; Informational brochure; Newsletter.
Financial data: Year ended 06/30/2011. Assets, $5,222,787 (M); Expenditures, $2,296,558; Total giving, $1,319,755; Grants to individuals, totaling $365,257.
Fields of interest: Education; Day care.
Type of support: Scholarships—to individuals.
Application information: Applications accepted. Application form required.
  Initial approach: Letter
  Deadline(s): None
Program description:
  Child Care Scholarships: The program helps low-income, working parents maintain their employment and work toward self-sufficiency through partial funding of reliable, safe and educational care for their children.
EIN: 540505882

9533
University of Virginia Medical School Foundation
P.O. Box 800776
Charlottesville, VA 22908-0776 (434) 924-1734
Contact: Barry Collins, Exec. Dir.
FAX: (434) 982-3202;
E-mail: barrycollins@virginia.edu; Toll-free tel.: (866) 315-0947; URL: http://www.healthsystem.virginia.edu/internet/alumni/

Foundation type: Public charity
Purpose: Scholarships to medical students at the University of Virginia, VA.
Publications: Newsletter.
Financial data: Year ended 06/30/2012. Assets, $43,423,399 (M); Expenditures, $3,232,307; Total giving, $2,184,890; Grants to individuals, totaling $984,661.
Fields of interest: Medical school/education.
Type of support: Support to graduates or students of specific schools; Graduate support.
Application information: Applications accepted.
  Initial approach: Letter
  Additional information: See web site for complete list of programs and eligibility criteria.
EIN: 237173411

9534
USAWOA Scholarship Foundation
(also known as United States Army Warrant Officers Associatino Scholarship Foundation)
462 Herndon Pkwy., Ste. 207
Herndon, VA 20170-5235 (703) 742-7727
Contact: Robert D. Scott, Pres. and Exec. Dir.
FAX: (703) 742-7728;
E-mail: usawoasf@cavetel.net; URL: http://www.usawoa.org/scholarship/

Foundation type: Public charity
Purpose: Scholarships to qualified family members of warrant officers serving in or retired from the U.S. Army, the U.S. Army Reserve and the Army National Guard of the various states and territories.
Fields of interest: Military/veterans' organizations.
Type of support: Undergraduate support.
Application information: Applications accepted. Application form required. Application form available on the grantmaker's web site.
  Initial approach: E-mail or telephone
  Deadline(s): Jan. 1 and May 1
  Final notification: 1st week of July
  Additional information: See web site for additional application information.
EIN: 861055533

9535
Utility Wind Integration Group, Inc.
(formerly Utility Wind Interest Group, Inc.)
P.O. Box 2787
Reston, VA 20195-0787 (252) 715-0796
Contact: Charlie Smith, Exec. Dir.
Application address: 620 Mabry Hood Rd., Ste. 300, Knoxville, TN 37932, tel.: (865) 218-4600, ext. 6141, e-mail: sandy@uwig.org
FAX: (865) 218-8998; E-mail: info@uwig.org; URL: http://www.uwig.org/

Foundation type: Public charity
Purpose: Scholarships to students currently enrolled or accepted for enrollment at an accredited trade school or college in the U.S. or Canada pursuing a career related to utility power engineering or operation and maintenance of utility-scale wind equipment.
Financial data: Year ended 12/31/2011. Assets, $985,682 (M); Expenditures, $640,123; Total giving, $14,157; Grants to individuals, totaling $14,157.
Fields of interest: Higher education; Engineering school/education.
Type of support: Scholarships—to individuals.
Application information: Applications accepted. Application form required.
  Send request by: Mail
  Deadline(s): Feb. 17
  Applicants should submit the following:
    1) Transcripts
    2) GPA
    3) Essay
  Additional information: The scholarship covers a single academic year and is not renewable.
Program description:
  UWIG Scholarship: Approximately five scholarships are awarded, with three $2,000 scholarships granted to students enrolled in an undergraduate program at an accredited engineering school who are pursuing a career in power engineering with a focus or major on wind or renewable generation, and up to two $1,000 scholarships granted to students enrolled in an accredited wind technician program.
EIN: 541733337

9536
The Willard A. Van Engel Fellowship Inc.
c/o Virginia Institute of Marine Science
P.O. Box 1346
Gloucester Point, VA 23062-1346

Foundation type: Operating foundation
Purpose: Research fellowships to graduate students at the Virginia Institute of Marine Sciences of the College of William & Mary, VA, who are pursuing an advanced degree in marine science.

Financial data: Year ended 06/30/2013. Assets, $700,510 (M); Expenditures, $23,363; Total giving, $21,152; Grant to an individual, 1 grant totaling $21,152.
Fields of interest: Marine science.
Type of support: Fellowships; Research; Support to graduates or students of specific schools.
Application information: Applications not accepted.
  Additional information: Unsolicited requests for funds not considered or acknowledged.
EIN: 541401233

9537
Vascular Specialists Education Foundation, Inc.
397 Little Neck Rd., Ste. 100
Bldg. 3300 S.
Virginia Beach, VA 23452-5764 (757) 466-6513

Foundation type: Public charity
Purpose: Scholarships to students involved in the care of and research of vascular and end-stage renal disease.
Fields of interest: Kidney diseases.
Type of support: Research; Undergraduate support.
Application information:
  Initial approach: Letter
  Additional information: Contact foundation for complete eligibility requirements.
EIN: 113645252

9538
VAW/VRC Officer's Spouses Association and Memorial Scholarship Fund
P.O. Box 15322
Norfolk, VA 23511-0322 (757) 479-0583
Contact: Kate Cardone, Pres.
E-mail: admin@vaw-vrc-memorialfund.org;
URL: http://www.vaw-vrc-memorialfund.org

Foundation type: Public charity
Purpose: Memorial scholarships to children of members of the VAW/VRC aviation community who died on active duty. Merit scholarships to dependents of U.S. Navy enlisted or officer personnel who have served, or are serving in the VAW/VRC aviation community.
Publications: Application guidelines; Annual report.
Financial data: Year ended 12/31/2011. Assets, $460,860 (M); Expenditures, $69,101; Total giving, $66,488; Grants to individuals, totaling $66,488.
Fields of interest: Vocational education, post-secondary; Higher education; Military/veterans' organizations.
Type of support: Scholarships—to individuals.
Application information: Applications accepted. Application form required.
  Deadline(s): Apr. 28
  Additional information: Tuition is paid directly to the educational institution on behalf of the students. Unsolicited requests for funds not considered or acknowledged.
Program descriptions:
  Memorial Scholarships: These scholarships honor those active duty or reserve service members in the VAW and VRC communities who are lost as a result of a combat aircraft loss or military aviation-related mishap, by helping provide for their children's higher education.
  Merit Scholarships: Scholarships are available each year to spouses or college-age children of current and former members of the VAW/VRC community. Eligible applicants must be graduates

of an accredited high school or equivalent, and must plan to attend an accredited vocational or academic institution to pursue their first undergraduate degree. Scholarships are awarded solely on merit.
EIN: 541673670

9539

Virginia Foundation for the Humanities

(also known as Virginia Foundation for the Humanities and Public Policy)
145 Ednam Dr.
Charlottesville, VA 22903-4629 (434) 924-3296
FAX: (434) 296-4714; E-mail: vfhinfo@virginia.edu;
URL: http://www.virginiafoundation.org
Additional URL: http://www.virginia.edu/VFH

Foundation type: Public charity
Purpose: Fellowships to individuals for research at the Center for the Humanities in Charlottesville, VA.
Publications: Application guidelines; Annual report; Informational brochure (including application guidelines); Newsletter.
Financial data: Year ended 06/30/2012. Assets, $7,695,329 (M); Expenditures, $4,527,346; Total giving, $244,176; Grants to individuals, totaling $73,000.
Fields of interest: Humanities.
Type of support: Seed money; Fellowships; Research.
Application information: Application form required.
Initial approach: Letter or telephone.
Deadline(s): Varies.
Program descriptions:
Discretionary Grant Program: This program allows the foundation to make smaller grants of up to $2,500 at any time during the year. These grants may be used to plan larger projects, or to carry out programs where only a modest amount of funding is required. Potential applicants should consult staff prior to applying.
Fellowships: All fellowship opportunities are open to independent and affiliated scholars, professionals, and others working on projects in the humanities. Applicants need not have advanced degrees, but the foundation generally does not support work toward a degree. Postdoctoral applicants are strongly encouraged to apply for projects other than dissertation revisions. Former foundation fellows must wait three years before applying for another fellowship. Former fellows are welcome to apply for space (without stipend) at any time.
EIN: 541435523

9540

Virginia Foundation of Cooperation, Inc.

P.O. Box 25202
Richmond, VA 23260-5202 (434) 949-1053
Contact: Dixie Watts Dalton
Application address: 109 Campus Dr., Alberta, VA 23821, tel.:(434) 949-1053

Foundation type: Independent foundation
Purpose: Scholarships to students at Virginia Polytechnic Institute and State University. Scholarships for youth to attend the National Institute on Cooperative Education.
Financial data: Year ended 12/31/2011. Assets, $627,965 (M); Expenditures, $9,770; Total giving, $7,065.
Type of support: Scholarships—to individuals; Support to graduates or students of specific schools.
Application information: Applications accepted.

Additional information: Contact foundation for additional application guidelines.
EIN: 510221281

9541

Virginia Scholarship and Youth Development Foundation

468 S. Independence Blvd., Ste. A-100
Virginia Beach, VA 23452-1158 (757) 518-9910
FAX: (757) 410-1470; E-mail: timreid2@cox.net;
URL: http://www.timreid.org

Foundation type: Public charity
Purpose: Scholarships to graduating seniors from Hampton Roads, VA, and the surrounding area who would be unable to afford college without financial aid.
Publications: Grants list.
Financial data: Year ended 04/18/2012. Assets, $1,725 (M); Expenditures, $6,419; Total giving, $1,670.
Type of support: Undergraduate support.
Application information: Applications accepted. Application form required. Application form available on the grantmaker's web site.
Initial approach: Letter
Deadline(s): Apr. 30
Applicants should submit the following:
1) Essay
2) Letter(s) of recommendation
3) Transcripts
4) ACT
5) SAT
6) GPA
Program description:
Scholarships: Scholarships are available to high-school seniors who have graduated from a Virginia-state high school and who plan to enroll in an accredited college or university. Eligible applicants must have an overall GPA of 2.5, and either a minimum score of 900 on the SAT or 19 on the ACT.
EIN: 432029850

9542

Virginia Tech Foundation, Inc.

902 Prices Fork Rd., Ste. 4500
Blacksburg, VA 24061-3260 (540) 231-2861
URL: http://www.vtf.vt.edu

Foundation type: Public charity
Purpose: Scholarships to students of Virginia Polytechnic Institute and State University (Virginia Tech)
Publications: Annual report.
Financial data: Year ended 06/30/2011. Assets, $1,132,039,543 (M); Expenditures, $90,843,928; Total giving, $22,105,224.
Fields of interest: Higher education.
Type of support: Scholarships—to individuals; Support to graduates or students of specific schools.
Application information: Prior to scholarship payments, there must be a VTF Scholarship Award Letter on file with the OSFA. Students should contact the financial aid office for application guidelines.
EIN: 540721690

9543

C. Arthur Ware Testamentary Charitable Trust

P.O. Box 1036
South Boston, VA 24592-6928 (434) 470-1833
Contact: Eilzabeth W. Saunders, Tr.

Foundation type: Independent foundation
Purpose: Scholarships to students of Hailfax County and Essex County, VA pursuing a bachelors degree in business or business related fields of study.
Financial data: Year ended 12/31/2011. Assets, $206,208 (M); Expenditures, $7,367; Total giving, $3,000.
Fields of interest: Business school/education.
Type of support: Scholarships—to individuals.
Application information:
Deadline(s): None
Additional information: Unsolicited requests for funds not considered or acknowledged.
EIN: 546377165

9544

Weaver-Fagan Memorial Fund

2205 Executive Dr.
Hampton, VA 23666 (757) 838-2330
Contact: Allyson Graul
Application address: c/o Alternatives, Inc., Attn.: Allyson Grant, 2021B Cunningham Dr., Hampton, VA 23666-3326
Application address: 2021 Cunninghjam Dr., Hampton, VA 23666 tel: (757) 838-2330

Foundation type: Independent foundation
Purpose: Scholarships to graduating seniors of Bethel, Hampton, Kecoughtan or Phoebus high schools, VA, who have at least a 2.5 GPA, for study at four-year accredited VA colleges and universities.
Financial data: Year ended 12/31/2011. Assets, $1,414,359 (M); Expenditures, $83,059; Total giving, $64,000; Grants to individuals, 25 grants totaling $64,000 (high: $3,000, low: $2,000).
Type of support: Support to graduates or students of specific schools; Undergraduate support.
Application information: Applications accepted. Application form required.
Deadline(s): Mar. 1
Applicants should submit the following:
1) Transcripts
2) Letter(s) of recommendation
3) Essay
Additional information: Application must also include a completed Hampton City Schools Activities Data Sheet.
EIN: 541560569

9545

The Melvin Weinstein Parkinson's Foundation

2324 Harversham Close
Virginia Beach, VA 23454
Contact: Marsha W. Anthony, Dir.; Traci W. Corcoran, Dir.
E-mail: help@mwpf.org; URL: http://www.mwpf.org

Foundation type: Independent foundation
Purpose: Grants to patients with Parkinson's disease to assist with prescription drugs, household expenses, medical expenses, equipment, short term assistance for patients between job loss and the commencement of disability benefits.
Financial data: Year ended 06/30/2012. Assets, $414,838 (M); Expenditures, $120,044; Total giving, $59,614.
Fields of interest: Parkinson's disease.

Type of support: Grants for special needs.
Application information: Applications accepted. Application form required. Application form available on the grantmaker's web site.
  Send request by: Mail
  Deadline(s): None
EIN: 050523378

9546
Western Fairfax Christian Ministries

13981 Metro Tech Dr.
Chantilly, VA 20151-3240 (703) 988-9656
Contact: Melissa Jansen, Exec. Dir.
FAX: (703) 988-9655;
E-mail: mjansen@wfcmva.org; Mailing address: P.O. Box 220802, Chantilly, VA 20153-6802; URL: http://www.wfcmva.org/

Foundation type: Public charity
Purpose: Grants for rent, utilities and other essentials to indigent families in western Fairfax County, VA.
Publications: Annual report; Newsletter.
Financial data: Year ended 06/30/2011. Assets, $335,347 (M); Expenditures, $3,427,614; Total giving, $2,798,764; Grants to individuals, totaling $2,798,764.
Fields of interest: Economically disadvantaged.
Type of support: Grants for special needs.
Application information:
  Initial approach: Letter
  Additional information: Contact foundation for complete eligibility requirements.
EIN: 541606629

9547
Westmoreland County Public School Scholarship Fund

c/o Larry D. Greene, CPA
P.O. Box 639
Montross, VA 22520-0639 (804) 493-8955

Foundation type: Independent foundation
Purpose: Scholarships to college students who are graduates of Westmoreland County Public School System, VA for higher education.
Financial data: Year ended 06/30/2012. Assets, $0 (M); Expenditures, $6,134; Total giving, $6,000; Grants to individuals, 6 grants totaling $6,000 (high: $1,250, low: $500).
Fields of interest: Higher education.
Type of support: Support to graduates or students of specific schools.
Application information: Applications accepted. Application form required.
  Deadline(s): July 31
  Applicants should submit the following:
    1) Transcripts
    2) Letter(s) of recommendation
EIN: 541394300

9548
The Nettie L. and Charles L. Wiley Foundation

P.O. Box 126
Irvington, VA 22480-0126
E-mail: grants@wileyfdn.org; URL: http://www.wileyfdn.org

Foundation type: Independent foundation
Purpose: Scholarships to young students in the northern neck of VA who are interested in teaching. Only college juniors, seniors, or master's degree candidates at Virginia public colleges and universities may apply.
Financial data: Year ended 12/31/2011. Assets, $8,277,390 (M); Expenditures, $414,230; Total giving, $365,300.
Fields of interest: Teacher school/education.
Type of support: Undergraduate support.
Application information: Applications accepted. Application form available on the grantmaker's web site.
  Deadline(s): June 1
  Applicants should submit the following:
    1) Essay
    2) Letter(s) of recommendation
    3) SAT
    4) Transcripts
  Additional information: Specific application guidelines available on foundation web site.
EIN: 521231771

9549
Mary Williamson Educational Loan Fund

P.O. Box 810
New Market, VA 22844-0810 (540) 740-3636
Contact: Allen D. Johnson, Tr.

Foundation type: Independent foundation
Purpose: Loans to deserving college bound students of the New Market, VA, area.
Financial data: Year ended 12/31/2012. Assets, $869,454 (M); Expenditures, $52,557; Total giving, $0.
Fields of interest: Education.
Type of support: Student loans—to individuals.
Application information: Applications accepted. Application form required.
  Additional information: Application should include financial information and three personal references.
EIN: 546043362

9550
Wings Over America Scholarship Foundation

c/o Devel. Assoc. and Scholarship Admin.
4966 Euclid Ave., Ste. 109
Virginia Beach, VA 23462-5834 (757) 671-3200
E-mail: info@wingsoveramerica.us; URL: http://www.wingsoveramerica.us

Foundation type: Public charity
Purpose: Scholarships to dependent children and spouses of all US Navy active duty, retired or deceased.
Publications: Application guidelines; Grants list; Informational brochure.
Financial data: Year ended 09/30/2012. Assets, $357,795 (M); Expenditures, $168,255; Total giving, $103,500; Grants to individuals, totaling $103,500.
Fields of interest: Military/veterans.
Type of support: Undergraduate support.
Application information: Applications accepted. Application form required.
  Initial approach: Prequalification form
  Deadline(s): Mar. 2 for prequalification form; Apr. 1 for application
  Applicants should submit the following:
    1) Transcripts
    2) Letter(s) of recommendation
    3) Essay
EIN: 541846969

9551
Wolf Trap Foundation for the Performing Arts

1645 Trap Rd.
Vienna, VA 22182-2064 (703) 255-1900
Contact: Arvind Manocha, Pres. and C.E.O.; For residencies: Kim Pensinger Witman, Dir.
E-mail: wolftrap@wolftrap.org; URL: http://www.wolftrap.org

Foundation type: Public charity
Purpose: Scholarships and residencies to emerging professional singers and other individuals wishing to work in the arts field.
Publications: Application guidelines; Annual report.
Financial data: Year ended 12/31/2011. Assets, $38,117,149 (M); Expenditures, $26,958,366; Total giving, $23,962; Grants to individuals, 12 grants totaling $23,962. Subtotal for grants to individuals: 12 grants totaling $23,962.
Fields of interest: Opera; Music (choral).
Type of support: Residencies; Stipends.
Application information: Applications accepted. Application form required.
  Initial approach: Letter or e-mail
  Additional information: Applications must include resume, photocopy of passport or birth certificate, $15 application fee, 8x10 black and white photograph, and audio recording.
Program descriptions:
  Internship Program: This program is designed to provide project-based training and experience in the areas of arts administration, education, and technical theater. These internships also provide the opportunity to become an integral member of a team, working with staff and other interns to produce, promote, and administer the full spectrum of the performing arts. Internships are available in the fields of communications and marketing (including marketing, advertising/group sales, graphic design, web communications, creative copywriting for the arts, public relations, photography, and multimedia), opera (including directing, administration, stage management, technical theater, scenic/prop painting, costuming, and videography), education, development (including annual fund, donor relations, and special events), programming and production, human resources, accounting, ticket services, information systems, planning and initiatives, and production and sound. Benefits include: a monetary stipend; college credit (not required); complimentary tickets to many summer performances; field trips to Washington, DC-area metro arts organizations; guest speaker luncheons; performance facility tours; and career development workshops.
  Wolf Trap Grants for High School Performing Arts Teachers: Each year, the foundation awards grants to six outstanding public high school performing arts teachers to honor their exceptional instruction and performance achievements of music, dance, and theater in Washington, DC; Montgomery and Prince George's counties, Maryland; and Loudoun, Arlington, and Fairfax counties, Virginia. These grants support arts education efforts that parallel the foundation's performance and education priorities, including artist residencies, commissions, master classes, and technology in the arts. Grants also give teachers the opportunity to explore and enhance their curriculum through special projects that lead to student performances for the school and community.
EIN: 237011544

9552
Womack Foundation
419 Maple Ln.
Danville, VA   24541-3531
Contact: James A.L. Daniel, Chair.
Application address: P.O. Box 720, Danville, VA
24543-0720,tel.: (434) 792-3911

Foundation type: Independent foundation
Purpose: Student loans and scholarships to
residents of the city of Danville, and Pittsylvania
County, VA and Caswell County, NC.
Financial data: Year ended 03/31/2012. Assets,
$5,139,418 (M); Expenditures, $343,166; Total
giving, $319,410.
Fields of interest: Vocational education; Higher
education; Nursing school/education.
Type of support: Scholarships—to individuals;
Student loans—to individuals.
Application information: Applications accepted.
Application form required. Interview required.
    Deadline(s): None
    Applicants should submit the following:

1) GPA
2) Financial information
3) Essay
EIN: 546053255

9553
Wythe-Bland Community Foundation
180 W. Main St., Ste. 4
P.O. Box 90
Wytheville, VA   24382-0090   (276) 228-8001
Contact: Dr. Gail S. Catron Ph.D., Exec. Dir.
Scholarship address: c/o Wytheville Community
College, 1000 E. Main St., Wytheville, CA 24382
FAX: (276) 228-9001;
E-mail: gcatronwbcf@earthlink.net; URL: http://
www.wbcfoundation.org

Foundation type: Independent foundation
Purpose: Scholarships to qualified Wythe and Bland
county high school graduates (beginning with the
class of 2007) to attend Wytheville Community
College in VA.
Publications: Application guidelines; Annual report;
Financial statement; Grants list; Newsletter.
Financial data: Year ended 09/30/2012. Assets,
$49,739,283 (M); Expenditures, $2,117,134;
Total giving, $1,703,503; Grants to individuals,
totaling $364,087.
Fields of interest: Higher education.
Type of support: Scholarships—to individuals.
Application information: Applications accepted.
Application form required.
    Applicants should submit the following:
    1) Transcripts
    2) FAFSA
    Additional information: By the end of the first
    year, applicants must also complete 40 hours
    of community (volunteer) service with an
    approved agency, and achieve a 2.0 GPA. In
    addition, applicants must also complete 67
    percent of all classes to continue receiving
    the grant for a second year. See web site for
    additional application guidelines.
EIN: 541609065

WASHINGTON

9554
911 Media Arts Center
909 N.E. 43rd St., Ste. 206
Seattle, WA 98105-6020 (206) 682-6552
Contact: Joseph Gray, Pres.
FAX: (206) 464-9009; *E-mail:* info@911media.org

Foundation type: Public charity
Purpose: Residencies and fiscal sponsorship to digital media artists residing in the Seattle, WA area.
Financial data: Year ended 12/31/2011. Assets, $21,600 (M); Expenditures, $127,286; Total giving, $14,100.
Fields of interest: Media/communications; Film/video; Visual arts; Performing arts (multimedia); Arts, artist's services.
Type of support: Residencies; Stipends; Fiscal agent/sponsor.
Application information: Applications accepted. Application form required.
> *Deadline(s):* Mar. 15 for Residencies
> *Additional information:* Application should include resume, work sample and a statement outlining artistic goals for residencies. Contact the arts center for fiscal sponsorship guidelines.

Program descriptions:
Artist Residencies: This program provides a production budget of up to $4,000, production and editing equipment, technical support, and an artist honorarium of $1,000 upon completion of project. Applicants may be emerging or established artists using digital media as an art form (filmmakers, animators, installation artists, performers, etc.)
Fiscal Sponsorship: This program provides support to digital media artists but no monetary support is given.
The Artist Media Scholarship: Practicing artists are eligible for a small stipend to study digital media arts at the 911 Media Arts Center.
EIN: 911271691

9555
AGC of Washington Education Foundation
1200 Westlake Ave. N., Ste. 301
Seattle, WA 98109-3528 (206) 284-4500
Contact: Diane Siderius Kocer, Exec. Dir.
FAX: (206) 284-4595; *E-mail:* dkocer@agcwa.com; *URL:* http://www.constructionfoundation.org

Foundation type: Public charity
Purpose: Scholarships to high school and college students of WA state pursuing a career in the construction industry.
Publications: Application guidelines; Newsletter.
Financial data: Year ended 06/30/2012. Assets, $4,031,700 (M); Expenditures, $750,261; Total giving, $54,491.
Fields of interest: Vocational education, post-secondary; Higher education.
Type of support: Scholarships—to individuals.
Application information: Applications accepted. Application form required. Application form available on the grantmaker's web site. Interview required.
> *Initial approach:* Telephone or e-mail
> *Deadline(s):* Mar. 1
> *Applicants should submit the following:*
>   1) Transcripts
>   2) Letter(s) of recommendation

Additional information: Only students enrolled in WA state construction related programs are considered for the scholarships.
EIN: 911157971

9556
Alaska Pulp Scholarship Foundation
P.O. Box 94122
Seattle, WA 98124-6422 (206) 497-8899
Contact: Franklin Roppel, Pres.
E-mail: info@apc-foundation.com; *URL:* http://www.apc-foundation.com/

Foundation type: Public charity
Purpose: Scholarships to high school seniors in the Sitka and Wrangell, AK school districts to pursue a higher education.
Publications: Application guidelines.
Financial data: Year ended 12/31/2011. Assets, $246,000 (M); Expenditures, $1,525,133; Total giving, $1,506,000; Grants to individuals, totaling $60,000.
Fields of interest: Higher education.
Type of support: Undergraduate support.
Application information: Applications accepted.
> *Initial approach:* Letter
> *Deadline(s):* Mar. 15
> *Applicants should submit the following:*
>   1) Letter(s) of recommendation
>   2) Photograph
>   3) SAT
>   4) Essay
> *Additional information:* Payments are made to the educational institution on behalf of the students.

Program description:
Sasayama Scholarships: Scholarships of up to $2,500 per year (for up to four years) are available to high school seniors attending Sitka- and Wrangell-area school districts who plan to pursue postsecondary education. Selection is based on outstanding academic achievement and/or special talent. Students must remain in good standing and carry a full course load (as prescribed by the postsecondary school) in order to maintain eligibility status for subsequent years.
EIN: 911481897

9557
Alliance for Education
509 Olive Way, Ste. 500
Seattle, WA 98101-2556 (206) 343-0449
Contact: Sara Morris, Pres.-C.E.O.
FAX: (206) 343-0455; *E-mail:* info@alliance4ed.org; *E-mail:* Sara Morris for sara@alliance4ed.org;; *URL:* http://www.alliance4ed.org

Foundation type: Public charity
Purpose: Grants and awards to principals, teachers, and students in the Seattle, WA public schools.
Publications: Annual report.
Financial data: Year ended 12/31/2011. Assets, $12,270,406 (M); Expenditures, $4,701,161; Total giving, $2,818,045; Grants to individuals, totaling $28,750.
Fields of interest: Higher education; Teacher school/education.
Type of support: Scholarships—to individuals; Awards/prizes.
Application information: Applications accepted. Application form required.
> *Deadline(s):* June 15 for Philip B. Swain Scholarship
> *Final notification:* Recipient notified late June or early July

Program descriptions:
The Philip B. Swain Excellence in Teaching Award: $1,000 awards recognize the efforts of secondary school classroom teachers in Seattle Public Schools, particularly those serving large numbers of students eligible for free or reduced-price lunch. Eligible teachers will have taught in grades 6 through 12 for at least three years.
The Philip B. Swain Scholarship: One $1,000 scholarship is awarded to a graduating senior from a Seattle Public high school. Applicants must have a cumulative GPA of 2.5 or better, demonstrate financial need, and anticipate enrollment for fall 2011, and be enrolled at least one-half time at an accredited institution of higher education.
EIN: 911508191

9558
Allied Arts Association
89 Lee Blvd.
Richland, WA 99352-4222 (509) 943-9815
Application address for MFA: Allied Arts MFA Scholarship Competition, c/o Mary Dryburgh, 2211 Harris Ave., Richland, WA 99354-1911
E-mail: publicity@alliedartsrichland.org; *URL:* http://www.alliedartsrichland.org

Foundation type: Public charity
Purpose: Scholarship to a continuing art student at Columbia Basin College, area high school art awards and a regional Master of Fine Arts level scholarship.
Financial data: Year ended 12/31/2011. Assets, $433,740 (M); Expenditures, $155,381.
Fields of interest: Arts education; Visual arts; College.
Type of support: Scholarships—to individuals; Awards/prizes.
Application information: Applications accepted. Application form required. Application form available on the grantmaker's web site.
> *Deadline(s):* Mar. 4 for Master of Fine Arts Scholarship, Apr. 15 for High School Visual Art Award
> *Applicants should submit the following:*
>   1) Resume
>   2) Work samples
>   3) Essay
> *Additional information:* Contact the association for additional information on the awards and scholarships.

Program description:
Scholarships: Each year, Allied Arts provides a high school art award, two college level scholarships, and an Master of Fine Arts level scholarship. Prospectuses for competition for the high school award are sent to Mid-Columbia area school art departments. Columbia Basin College scholarship recipients are chosen by the CBC Foundation, as part of their own broader competition. The MFA competition is open to students in residence at a university in Washington, Oregon and Idaho enrolled in a visual arts MFA program.
EIN: 237359795

9559
Allied Arts Foundation
4111 E. Madison St., Ste. 52
Seattle, WA 98112-3241 (206) 624-0432
Contact: Karen M. Kane, Pres.
FAX: (206) 324-0086;
E-mail: foundation@alliedartsfoundation.org; *URL:* http://www.alliedarts-foundation.org

Foundation type: Public charity

Purpose: Grants to local artists and artist achievement awards to Seattle public high school students. Services for artists are also provided through a fiscal sponsorship program. Giving for grants is limited to the greater Seattle area but the foundation provides fiscal sponsorship beyond that region.

Financial data: Year ended 12/31/2012. Assets, $273,512 (M); Expenditures, $77,544; Total giving, $62,968.

Fields of interest: Performing arts; Music; Arts, artist's services; Arts.

Type of support: Grants to individuals; Support to graduates or students of specific schools; Awards/prizes; Fiscal agent/sponsor.

Application information: Applications accepted. Application form required. Application form available on the grantmaker's web site.

   Initial approach: Letter or e-mail

   Deadline(s): None for Fiscal Sponsorship Program

   Additional information: Application for Fiscal Sponsorship Program should be 1- 1 1/2 pages including contact information, project name, and two or three references. Applications not accepted for Arts Grants Program unless initiated by the foundation. Contact foundation for guidelines regarding high school student art awards.

Program descriptions:

   Arts Grants Program: Grants for artists in the King County area for projects of unique value and significance. The foundation recognition often marks the first entry of an artist into the professional level, and the foundation awards are viewed by peers in the community as a respected endorsement of an emerging talent.

   Fiscal Sponsorship: The foundation provides a nonprofit umbrella for artists in a variety of situations including: those seeking long-term sponsorship, those requiring it only for the duration of a particular project, and those seeking a sponsorship bridge between the time they apply for and receive their own 501(c)(3) status.

   Robert Jackson Block Awards for Excellence in the Arts: Awards are presented annually to three students from each of Seattle's thirteen public high schools for their achievements in literary, visual and performing arts. The awards are in the form of a cash award, certificate and letter to each student.

EIN: 910829974

9560

Alternatives to Hunger

1824 Ellis St.

Bellingham, WA 98225-4619 (360) 676-0392

FAX: (360) 676-0410;

E-mail: info@bellinghamfoodbank.org; URL: http://www.bellinghamfoodbank.org/

Foundation type: Public charity

Purpose: Emergency in-kind assistance of food supplies to individuals and families in need throughout Whatcom County, WA.

Financial data: Year ended 12/31/2011. Assets, $4,256,786 (M); Expenditures, $4,445,257; Total giving, $3,589,140; Grants to individuals, 36,909 grants totaling $3,589,140.

Fields of interest: Food banks; Economically disadvantaged.

Type of support: In-kind gifts.

Application information:

   Initial approach: E-mail

   Additional information: Contact foundation for eligibility criteria.

EIN: 910918619

9561

Arise Charitable Trust

P.O. Box 1014

Freeland, WA 98249-1014 (360) 331-5792

E-mail: info@arisecharitabletrust.org; URL: http://www.arisecharitabletrust.org

Foundation type: Independent foundation

Purpose: Scholarships to students of South Whidbey Island, WA pursuing postsecondary education.

Publications: Informational brochure.

Financial data: Year ended 09/30/2013. Assets, $4,670,278 (M); Expenditures, $245,098; Total giving, $190,462; Grants to individuals, 56 grants totaling $94,842 (high: $3,500, low: $194).

Fields of interest: Vocational education, post-secondary; Higher education; Women.

Type of support: Scholarships—to individuals.

Application information: Applications accepted. Application form required.

   Initial approach: Letter or web site

   Send request by: Mail

   Deadline(s): Apr. 1 and Oct. 1

   Applicants should submit the following:

     1) Transcripts

     2) Letter(s) of recommendation

     3) GPA

     4) Financial information

     5) FAFSA

   Additional information: Application should also include latest income tax return. Awards are paid directly to the educational institution on behalf of the students. See web site for additional guidelines.

EIN: 911350780

9562

ARK Institute of Learning

(formerly ARK Foundation)

c/o Allenmore Medical Ctr.

1916 S. Washington St.

Tacoma, WA 98405-1025 (253) 573-0311

Contact: Pat Himsl, Exec. Dir.

FAX: (253) 573-0211; E-mail: admin@arkinst.org;

Tel. and e-mail for P. Himsl: (253) 759-9682, phimsl@ARKInst.org; URL: http://www.arkinst.org

Foundation type: Public charity

Purpose: Need-based scholarships for students with learning disabilities who could not otherwise afford the cost to attend ARK Institute of Learning.

Financial data: Year ended 12/31/2011. Assets, $1,071,925 (M); Expenditures, $467,502; Total giving, $36,820; Grants to individuals, totaling $36,820.

Fields of interest: Education; Learning disorders.

Type of support: Scholarships—to individuals.

Application information: Applications accepted. Application form required.

   Initial approach: Telephone or e-mail

   Additional information: Scholarship award is based on individual financial need. Recipients are responsible for a portion of the fee and will receive a letter outlining the details. Contact the institute for additional application guidelines.

EIN: 911713751

9563

Arnsberg Scholarship Trust

P.O. Box 386

Republic, WA 99166-8823 (509) 775-2423

Contact: Gary L. Anderson, Tr.

Foundation type: Operating foundation

Purpose: Scholarships to students of Republic High School, WA, for higher education at a WA institution.

Financial data: Year ended 12/31/2011. Assets, $172,753 (M); Expenditures, $6,888; Total giving, $6,800; Grants to individuals, 3 grants totaling $6,800 (high: $5,000, low: $900).

Type of support: Support to graduates or students of specific schools; Undergraduate support.

Application information: Applications accepted.

   Initial approach: Letter

   Deadline(s): First Fri. after spring break

EIN: 916443732

9564

Artist Trust

1835 12th Ave.

Seattle, WA 98122-2437 (206) 467-8734

FAX: (206) 467-9633; E-mail: info@artisttrust.org;

Toll-free tel.: (866) 21TRUST; E-mail for Margit Rankin: margit@artisttrust.org; URL: http://www.artisttrust.org

Foundation type: Public charity

Purpose: Awards and fellowships to professional artists in WA working in all creative disciplines.

Publications: Application guidelines; Annual report; Informational brochure; Newsletter.

Financial data: Year ended 06/30/2012. Assets, $2,880,038 (M); Expenditures, $1,036,315; Total giving, $280,506; Grants to individuals, totaling $280,506.

Fields of interest: Visual arts; Arts; Aging; Women.

Type of support: Fellowships; Grants to individuals; Awards/prizes.

Application information: Applications accepted. Application form required. Application form available on the grantmaker's web site.

   Initial approach: Letter, telephone or e-mail

   Deadline(s): Apr. 15 for Grants for Artists Projects, June 10 for Arts Innovator Awards, Feb. 18 for Fellowships, Dec. 17 for Twining Humber Award, Aug 6 for Conductive Garboil Grant, none for Centrum Residency

   Applicants should submit the following:

     1) Work samples

     2) Resume

     3) Proposal

     4) Budget Information

Program descriptions:

   Arts Innovator Awards: Unrestricted awards of $25,000 given annually to two Washington State generative artists of all disciplines who are originating new work, experimenting with new ideas, taking risks and pushing the boundaries in their respective fields. To be eligible, applicants must be 18 years or older, Washington State residents, and have been working professionally as an artist for a minimum of five years.

   Conductive Garboil Grant: An annual award is available for Seattle artists of all disciplines who have a connection to the Pioneer Square neighborhood and have demonstrated a profound ability to challenge the limits of conductive creative discourse and its effects on our society. This $3,000 grant is administered by Artist Trust and 4Culture with the assistance of the late artist Su Job's personal representative, Lynn Schirmer.

   Fellowships: Fellowships award $7,500 to practicing professional artists of exceptional talent and demonstrated ability. The fellowship is merit-based, not a project-based award. Recipients must present a Meet the Artist Event to a community in Washington State that has little or no access to the artist and their work.

   Grants for Artist Projects (GAP): Grants of up to $1,500 provide support for artist-generated projects, which can include (but are not limited to) the development, completion, or presentation of new work.

Irving and Yvonne Twining Humber Award for Lifetime Artistic Achievement: This unrestricted award of $10,000 is given annually to a Washington state female visual artist, age 60 or over, who has dedicated 25 or more years of her life creating art. The award recognizes creative excellence, professional accomplishment, and dedication to the visual arts.

James W. Ray Venture Project Awards: Two unrestricted awards of $15,000 each are given annually to support artistic excellence and the development of new ideas through individual and collaborative projects. The awards recognize artists of all disciplines living and working in Washington State whose work demonstrates exceptional originality. You must be nominated by an authorized nominator to be eligible for this award. Nominators are selected by Artist Trust. Evaluation of applications and selection of recipients will be performed by selection panels of arts professionals who will adjudicate, conduct site visits or interviews with finalists, and select the recipients of the James W. Ray Venture Project Awards.
EIN: 911353974

9565
Bainbridge Arts & Crafts, Inc.
151 Winslow Way E.
Bainbridge Island, WA 98110-2425 (206) 842-3132
FAX: (206) 780-8149; E-mail: gallery@bacart.org;
URL: http://www.bainbridgeartscrafts.org

Foundation type: Public charity
Purpose: Scholarships to graduates of Bainbridge High School, WA, who intend to pursue full-time art studies.
Publications: Newsletter.
Financial data: Year ended 06/30/2012. Assets, $1,366,804 (M); Expenditures, $422,594; Total giving, $8,535; Grants to individuals, totaling $2,435.
Fields of interest: Arts education.
Type of support: Support to graduates or students of specific schools; Undergraduate support.
Application information: Applications accepted. Application form required.
Initial approach: Letter or e-mail
Additional information: Application must include letters of recommendation.
EIN: 910714664

9566
Bainbridge-Ometepe Sister Islands Association
P. O. Box 4484
Rollingbay, WA 98061-0484 (206) 842-4249
FAX: (206) 842-6907; E-mail: info@bosia.org;
URL: http://www.bosia.org

Foundation type: Public charity
Purpose: Scholarships to students from Ometepe Island, on Lake Nicaragua, to attend college.
Publications: Annual report; Newsletter.
Financial data: Year ended 12/31/2012. Assets, $279,510 (M); Expenditures, $161,891; Total giving, $98,485.
Type of support: Exchange programs; Foreign applicants; Undergraduate support.
Application information: Contact foundation for additional application guidelines.
Program description:
Scholarship Program: Scholarships of $40 to $80 per month are given to Ometepe college

students. Students are selected by three committees of teachers from three different towns on Ometepe. Students must all be from low-income families.
EIN: 911433369

9567
BECU Foundation
(also known as Boeing Employees Credit Union Foundation)
12770 Gateway Dr., Ste. 1011-1
Tukwila, WA 98168-3309 (206) 439-5700
Contact: Deborah Wege, Secy.
URL: http://www.becu.org/who-is/foundation.aspx

Foundation type: Independent foundation
Purpose: Scholarships to BECU members and their families.
Financial data: Year ended 12/31/2011. Assets, $2,056,657 (M); Expenditures, $141,964; Total giving, $100,250; Grants to individuals, 40 grants totaling $100,250 (high: $2,500, low: $2,500).
Type of support: Undergraduate support.
Application information: Applications accepted. Application form required.
Deadline(s): Mar. 31
EIN: 911703337

9568
The Behnke Foundation
(formerly Skinner Foundation)
601 Union St., Ste. 3016
Seattle, WA 98101-3913
FAX: (206) 623-6138;
E-mail: behnkefoundation@aol.com; URL: http://www.behnkefoundation.org/

Foundation type: Company-sponsored foundation
Purpose: Fellowships by nomination only to visual artists residing in the greater Seattle, WA, area.
Publications: Application guidelines; Informational brochure (including application guidelines).
Financial data: Year ended 12/31/2012. Assets, $2,113,984 (M); Expenditures, $164,330; Total giving, $134,800.
Fields of interest: Visual arts; Painting.
Type of support: Fellowships; Awards/grants by nomination only.
Application information: Applications not accepted.
Program description:
Neddy Artist Fellowship: The foundation annually awards two $15,000 fellowships in celebration of Robert E. Behnke's life as an artist. The fellowships are awarded to an artist in painting and one in a rotating discipline. Applicants must be nominated by a group of local artists, collectors, and other members of the arts community. Artists are selected based on their commitment to their art and the community. All nominated artists receive $1,000.
EIN: 916025144

9569
The Bellevue Schools Foundation
12241 Main St., Bldg. 5
P.O. Box 40644
Bellevue, WA 98005 (425) 456-4199
Contact: Roxanne Kroon Shepherd, Exec. Dir.
FAX: (425) 456-4176; E-mail: info@bsfdn.org;
Mailing address: P.O. Box 40644, Bellevue, WA 98015-4644; URL: http://www.bsfdn.org

Foundation type: Public charity

Purpose: Grants to administrators, teachers, staff, students sponsored by certified staff, and parents sponsored by certified staff who work within the Bellevue Schools district, for staff training and enrichment opportunities.
Publications: Application guidelines; Financial statement.
Financial data: Year ended 06/30/2012. Assets, $1,440,618 (M); Expenditures, $1,323,203; Total giving, $848,322; Grants to individuals, totaling $5,070.
Fields of interest: Elementary/secondary education.
Type of support: Grants to individuals.
Application information: Applications accepted. Application form required. Application form available on the grantmaker's web site.
Deadline(s): Sept. 22
Additional information: See web site for additional application.
Program description:
Curriculum Enhancement Grant Program: The purpose of the program is to make funds available to all schools in the Bellevue School District for innovative and creative projects which enhance or expand the curriculum in the classroom and help fulfill the foundation's mission.
EIN: 911080997

9570
Benton-Franklin Community Action Committee, Inc.
710 W. Court St.
Pasco, WA 99301-4178 (509) 545-4042
FAX: (509) 544-9691; URL: http://www.bfcac.org

Foundation type: Public charity
Purpose: Emergency assistance to low-income families and individuals of Franklin and Benton counties, WA with housing, food, utility, transportation, child care and other services, to help them in achieving self sufficiency.
Financial data: Year ended 12/31/2011. Assets, $2,413,132 (M); Expenditures, $6,859,482; Total giving, $4,823,739; Grants to individuals, totaling $4,823,739.
Fields of interest: Human services.
Type of support: Grants for special needs.
Application information: Applicant must meet income eligibility requirements.
EIN: 910792238

9571
Bishop-Fleet Foundation
1420 5th Ave., Ste. 3200
Seattle, WA 98101-2349 (425) 453-8282
Contact: James R. Callaghan, Pres. and Tr.

Foundation type: Independent foundation
Purpose: Scholarships to graduating seniors of WA State for continuing education at accredited colleges or universities.
Financial data: Year ended 12/31/2012. Assets, $2,196,455 (M); Expenditures, $133,850; Total giving, $102,500.
Fields of interest: Higher education.
Type of support: Scholarships—to individuals.
Application information:
Deadline(s): None
EIN: 916031057

9572
Blakemore Foundation

1201 3rd Ave., Ste. 4900
Seattle, WA 98101-3095 (206) 359-8778
Contact: For all inquiries: Cathy Scheibner, Exec. Asst.
FAX: (206) 359-9778;
E-mail: blakemorefoundation@gmail.com;
Additional e-mail: blakemore@perkinscoie.com;
URL: http://www.blakemorefoundation.org

Foundation type: Independent foundation
Purpose: Fellowships to U.S. citizens and permanent U.S. residents studying languages in east and southeast Asia.
Publications: Application guidelines; Annual report; Grants list; Informational brochure.
Financial data: Year ended 12/31/2012. Assets, $8,720,160 (M); Expenditures, $988,047; Total giving, $803,560; Grants to individuals, 31 grants totaling $768,278 (high: $54,036, low: $400).
Fields of interest: Language (foreign).
International interests: Asia.
Type of support: Fellowships.
Application information: Applications accepted. Application form required. Application form available on the grantmaker's web site.
Send request by: Mail
Deadline(s): Dec. 31 for Blakemore Freeman Fellowships and Blakemore Refresher Grants
Final notification: Recipients notified in Mar.
Applicants should submit the following:
1) Curriculum vitae
2) Essay
3) Letter(s) of recommendation
4) Transcripts
Additional information: See web site for additional application guidelines.
Program descriptions:
Blakemore Freeman Fellowships: Blakemore Freeman Fellowships fund an academic year of advanced language study in East or Southeast Asia in approved language programs. An applicant must be an American citizen and permanent resident of the U.S. with a college undergraduate degree and pursuing an academic, professional or business career that involve the regular use of a modern East or Southeast Asian language.
Blakemore Refresher Grants: Blakemore Refresher Grants are intended to provide mid-career professionals an opportunity to refresh their language skills by attending a full-time language program for a summer or semester. Applicants for Refresher Grants must meet all the eligibility requirements for Blakemore Freeman Fellowships, and be a member of one of the following groups: Former Blakemore Freeman Fellows; Professors who are teaching in an Asian field at a university or college in the United States; Professionals working in an Asian field.
EIN: 911505735

9573
Blue Earth Alliance

P.O. Box 4490
Seattle, WA 98194-0490 (206) 725-4913
Contact: Bart J. Cannon, Exec. Dir.
E-mail: submissionsjan12@blueearth.org;
URL: http://www.blueearth.org

Foundation type: Public charity
Purpose: Fiscal sponsorship to individuals with photographic projects whose goal is to educate the public about endangered cultures, threatened environments, or current topics of social concern.
Publications: Application guidelines.

Financial data: Year ended 12/31/2012. Assets, $6,370 (M); Expenditures, $118,763.
Fields of interest: Photography; Design.
Type of support: Grants to individuals; Fiscal agent/sponsor.
Application information: Applications accepted.
Deadline(s): Mar. 21 and Sept. 21
Final notification: Two months after receipt of application
Applicants should submit the following:
1) Work samples
2) Letter(s) of recommendation
3) Resume
4) Budget Information
Additional information: Application must be on a single CD with the following information in doc,.pdf,.xls, or .jpg format as appropriate: Include a brief letter.doc/pdf no more than 3 pages describing the proposed project and your previous work, detailed schedule, a list of who will be approached for funding and 20 images of recent work. Check the web site for further guidelines.
Program description:
Sponsorship for Photographers: Fiscal sponsorships for up to two years are available to photographic projects whose goal is to educate the public about endangered cultures, threatened environments, or current topics of social concern. The alliance is primarily interested in work that is educational and informative in nature, and will consider proposals of any geographic scope, as long as it makes use of the medium of still film. Other benefits include grant-writer services, mentorship, use of office space, and public relations/marketing assistance. The alliance charges a ten-percent fee of all grant monies received.
EIN: 911682270

9574
Blue Mountain Community Foundation

(formerly Blue Mountain Area Foundation)
22 E. Poplar St., Ste. 206
P.O. Box 603
Walla Walla, WA 99362 (509) 529-4371
Contact: Lawson F. Knight, Exec. Dir.
FAX: (509) 529-5284;
E-mail: bmcf@bluemountainfoundation.org;
URL: http://www.bluemountainfoundation.org

Foundation type: Community foundation
Purpose: Scholarships to graduating high school seniors of Walla Walla County, WA for postsecondary education.
Publications: Application guidelines; Annual report; Grants list; Informational brochure; Newsletter.
Financial data: Year ended 06/30/2012. Assets, $30,811,104 (M); Expenditures, $2,170,332; Total giving, $1,661,537; Grants to individuals, totaling $342,091.
Fields of interest: Higher education.
Type of support: Scholarships—to individuals; Graduate support; Undergraduate support.
Application information: Applications accepted. Application form required. Application form available on the grantmaker's web site.
Initial approach: Application
Send request by: Mail or hand deliver
Deadline(s): Mar. 3
Final notification: Recipients notified by June 15
Applicants should submit the following:
1) Essay
2) GPA
3) SAR
4) FAFSA
5) Transcripts

Additional information: Scholarships are paid direcely to the educational institution on behalf of the students. See web site for a complete listing of scholarship eligibility criteria.
EIN: 911250104

9575
Violet R. and Nada V. Bohnett Memorial Foundation

(formerly Violet R. Bohnett Memorial Foundation)
16707 - 188th Pl NE
Woodenville, WA 98072 (425) 495-0901
Contact: James N. Bohnett, Dir.
E-mail: jnbohnett@aol.com; Application Address: 8040 - 161st Ave. N.E PMB 135 Redmond, WA 98052

Foundation type: Independent foundation
Purpose: Scholarships to financially needy individuals, primarily in western WA, CA, AZ, CO, and HI for the study of Christian ministry. Priority is given to students from western WA.
Publications: Informational brochure (including application guidelines); Newsletter.
Financial data: Year ended 12/31/2012. Assets, $2,191,496 (M); Expenditures, $166,555; Total giving, $24,334.
Fields of interest: Theological school/education; Christian agencies & churches.
Type of support: Scholarships—to individuals.
Application information:
Initial approach: Letter
Deadline(s): None
EIN: 956225968

9576
Don L. Bradley Scholarship Trust Fund

301 N. Burlington Blvd.
Burlington, WA 98233-1117 (360) 757-4074
Contact: Jim Clem, Tr.

Foundation type: Independent foundation
Purpose: Scholarships to graduates of Burlington-Edison High School, WA, who have participated in high school sports.
Financial data: Year ended 12/31/2012. Assets, $98,392 (M); Expenditures, $26,660; Total giving, $24,450; Grants to individuals, 38 grants totaling $24,450 (high: $1,250, low: $300).
Fields of interest: Athletics/sports, school programs.
Type of support: Support to graduates or students of specific schools; Undergraduate support.
Application information: Applications accepted. Application form required.
Initial approach: Letter
Deadline(s): Apr. 1
EIN: 916291543

9577
The Bradshaw Trust

304 S. 219th St.
Seattle, WA 98198-4740 (206) 824-2597
Contact: Phillip M. Bradshaw, Tr.; Sherry Bradshaw, Tr.

Foundation type: Operating foundation
Purpose: Scholarships to graduating high school seniors of Guthrie, OK and/or Shelbina, MO who wish to pursue university studies in the field of education.
Financial data: Year ended 12/31/2011. Assets, $85,446 (M); Expenditures, $4,200; Total giving,

$4,000; Grants to individuals, 3 grants totaling $4,000 (high: $2,000, low: $1,000).
Fields of interest: Higher education; Teacher school/education.
Type of support: Scholarships—to individuals.
Application information: Applications accepted. Application form required.
   Deadline(s): 30 days after graduation
   Additional information: Recipient must provide proof of enrollment at an accredited university, and furnish a copy of his/her college transcript to the trust at the end of each semester or quarter of study. Selection is based on the individual's character, motivation, ability and potential are factors considered.
EIN: 943104579

9578
The Bullitt Foundation
1501 E Madison St., Ste. 600
Seattle, WA 98122-4465 (206) 343-0807
Contact: Denis Hayes, Pres.
FAX: (206) 343-0822; E-mail: info@bullitt.org;
URL: http://www.bullitt.org

Foundation type: Independent foundation
Purpose: Fellowships to outstanding, environmentally knowledgeable graduate students who have demonstrated exceptional capacity for leadership as well as scholarship.
Publications: Application guidelines; Grants list.
Financial data: Year ended 12/31/2012. Assets, $105,513,709 (M); Expenditures, $7,622,337; Total giving, $5,345,492; Grants to individuals, 2 grants totaling $100,000.
Fields of interest: Environment, radiation control; Environment, toxics; Climate change/global warming; Minorities.
Type of support: Fellowships; Graduate support.
Application information: Applications accepted. Application form required. Application form available on the grantmaker's web site.
   Deadline(s): Apr. 6
   Applicants should submit the following:
     1) Transcripts
     2) Essay
     3) Resume
     4) Letter(s) of recommendation
Program description:
   Bullitt Environmental Fellowship: The fellowship provides a two-year $50,000 per year award to a graduate student with an outstanding knowledge of the environment and demonstrates an exceptional capacity for leadership as well as scholarship. Applications are encouraged from a broad variety of students with a particular emphasis on students of color and others who have overcome discrimination or other significant hardships.
EIN: 916027795

9579
Burlington Edison Education & Alumni Foundation
927 E. Fairhaven Ave.
P. O. Box 350
Burlington, WA 98233-1918 (360) 422-3659
Contact: Peggy Stowe, Pres.
E-mail: kathiwil@verizon.net

Foundation type: Public charity
Purpose: Scholarships to graduating seniors at Burlington-Edison High School, WA.
Financial data: Year ended 12/31/2011. Assets, $562,768 (M); Expenditures, $41,198; Total

giving, $38,131; Grants to individuals, totaling $38,131.
Type of support: Support to graduates or students of specific schools; Undergraduate support.
Application information: Applications accepted.
EIN: 943199980

9580
Career Path Services-Employment and Training
10 N. Post, Ste. 200
Spokane, WA 99201-0705 (509) 326-7520
Contact: Bill Marchioro, Chair.
FAX: (509) 323-1244; URL: http://careerpathservices.org/

Foundation type: Public charity
Purpose: Assistance to low income individuals with job training and placement in Washington State.
Financial data: Year ended 06/30/2012. Assets, $4,386,126 (M); Expenditures, $12,971,699; Total giving, $5,694,424; Grants to individuals, totaling $5,694,424.
Fields of interest: Employment, job counseling; Employment, training.
Type of support: Grants to individuals.
Application information: See web site for additional information.
Program description:
   Adult Services: The organization provides services to help individuals gain the skills and abilities they need to get and keep 'family-wage' jobs. Available services include skills training (such as on-the-job training, paid work experience, and vocational education), help with resumes and cover letters, workshops on interviewing and job searching, career counseling, guidance, and referrals from employers and to community resources. Eligible applicants must live in Spokane county, be at least 22 years of age, and have low income for the past six months.
EIN: 911032846

9581
Florence Lewis Carkeek Trust
2825 Colby
Everett, WA 98201

Foundation type: Independent foundation
Purpose: Scholarships to graduating seniors of the ten public high schools in Seattle School District No. 1, WA, to attend state-supported institutions.
Financial data: Year ended 03/31/2013. Assets, $3,212,585 (M); Expenditures, $169,191; Total giving, $128,292; Grants to individuals, 277 grants totaling $81,944 (high: $2,500, low: $111).
Type of support: Support to graduates or students of specific schools; Undergraduate support.
Application information:
   Deadline(s): Mar. 15
   Additional information: Applications made through the principals of schools in Seattle School District No. 1. Contact foundation for current application guidelines.
EIN: 916022715

9582
Central Area Motivation Program
722 18th Ave.
Seattle, WA 98122-4704 (206) 812-4940
URL: http://www.campseattle.org

Foundation type: Public charity

Purpose: Emergency assistance to low-income families and individuals in the Seattle, WA, area with food, clothing, shelter, and energy assistance.
Financial data: Year ended 12/31/2011. Assets, $2,073,414 (M); Expenditures, $7,833,168; Total giving, $5,832,395; Grants to individuals, totaling $5,805,222.
Fields of interest: Human services; Economically disadvantaged.
Type of support: Emergency funds; Grants for special needs.
Application information: See web site for additional guidelines or call the organization for assistance.
EIN: 910786727

9583
Centrum Foundation
P.O. Box 1158
Port Townsend, WA 98368-0958 (360) 385-3102
FAX: (360) 385-2470; E-mail: info@centrum.org;
URL: http://www.centrum.org

Foundation type: Public charity
Purpose: Residencies to creative thinkers and artists from all genres.
Publications: Application guidelines; Grants list; Newsletter.
Financial data: Year ended 12/31/2011. Assets, $566,543 (M); Expenditures, $2,217,072.
Fields of interest: Film/video; Photography; Sculpture; Performing arts; Theater (playwriting); Music; Opera; Music composition; Literature; Arts; Science; Social sciences.
Type of support: Residencies.
Application information: Applications accepted. Application form required.
   Initial approach: E-mail
   Deadline(s): Oct. 1
   Applicants should submit the following:
     1) Proposal
     2) Resume
     3) Work samples
   Additional information: Contact foundation for current application guidelines.
Program description:
   Creative Residencies: Provides up to one month residencies to artists where ideas, music, poetry, art, and more can be developed, tried out, and eventually disseminated.
EIN: 237348302

9584
Chelan-Douglas County Community Action Council
620 Lewis St.
Wenatchee, WA 98801-3435 (509) 662-6156
Contact: Robert Soule, Exec. Dir.
FAX: (509) 662-1737; URL: http://www.cdcac.org/

Foundation type: Public charity
Purpose: Assistance towards childcare, food, and low income home energy assistance to indigent residents of the Wenatchee, WA area.
Financial data: Year ended 12/31/2011. Assets, $1,618,964 (M); Expenditures, $4,988,917; Total giving, $2,918,165; Grants to individuals, totaling $2,609,347.
Fields of interest: Economically disadvantaged.
Type of support: Grants for special needs.
Application information: Applications not accepted.
   Additional information: Unsolicited requests for funds not considered or acknowledged.
EIN: 916064514

9585
CHEMCENTRAL Charitable Trust
17425 N.E. Union Hill Rd.
Redmond, WA 98052-3375

Foundation type: Company-sponsored foundation
Purpose: Scholarships to children of employees of CHEMCENTRAL Corporation.
Financial data: Year ended 12/31/2011. Assets, $0 (M); Expenditures, $22,807; Total giving, $22,792.
Type of support: Employee-related scholarships.
Application information: Applications not accepted.
> *Additional information:* Unsolicited requests for funds not considered or acknowledged.
Company name: CHEMCENTRAL Corporation
EIN: 363803848

9586
Judge C. C. Chevelle Foundation
P.O. Box 4742
Rollingbay, WA 98061-0742
Contact: Karen Cammarota-Keefe, Tr.
E-mail: chavelle@chavelle.org

Foundation type: Independent foundation
Purpose: Scholarships to individuals born in the state of WA, for higher education.
Financial data: Year ended 06/30/2012. Assets, $326,938 (M); Expenditures, $46,995; Total giving, $14,500.
Type of support: Undergraduate support.
Application information: Applications accepted. Application form required. Application form available on the grantmaker's web site.
> *Initial approach:* Letter
> *Deadline(s):* Sept.
> *Applicants should submit the following:*
>   1) GPA
>   2) ACT
>   3) SAT
>   4) Resume
> *Additional information:* Application should also include a personal statement of 300 words or less, the addresses and telephone numbers of three references, and birth certificate.
EIN: 911123055

9587
Children's Discovery Foundation
c/o Jim Bredouw
30 Pea Patch Ln.
Eastsound, WA 98245-9728 (360) 376-7177
Contact: Krista Bouchey, Exec. Dir.
Application e-mail address: krista@thefunhouse.org
FAX: (360) 376-7639; URL: http://funhousecommons.org/

Foundation type: Public charity
Purpose: Scholarships to students of Orcas Island High School, WA pursuing higher education.
Financial data: Year ended 12/31/2011. Assets, $966,380 (M); Expenditures, $333,614; Total giving, $5,813; Grants to individuals, totaling $5,813.
Fields of interest: Higher education.
Type of support: Scholarships—to individuals.
Application information: Applications accepted. Application form required. Application form available on the grantmaker's web site.
> *Send request by:* On-line
> *Deadline(s):* May 1
> *Applicants should submit the following:*
>   1) Financial information
>   2) GPA

3) Letter(s) of recommendation
4) Essay
Additional information: Selection is based on academic performance, community service/engagement, years of enrollment in the Orcas Island School District, and participation in HPSSF/Funhouse Commons programs. See web site for additional application guidelines.
EIN: 911806943

9588
Children's Hospital and Regional Medical Center
4800 Sand Point Way, N.E.
Seattle, WA 98105-0371 (206) 987-4846
Contact: Patrick Hagan, Pres. and C.O.O.
Toll-free tel.: (866) 987-2000; URL: http://www.seattlechildrens.org

Foundation type: Public charity
Purpose: Scholarships to employees who are in the process of advancing their careers in the medical field. Assistance also to families in need with various expenses.
Publications: Newsletter.
Financial data: Year ended 09/30/2011. Assets, $1,603,702,328 (M); Expenditures, $784,961,854; Total giving, $4,468,797.
Fields of interest: Medical school/education; Economically disadvantaged.
Type of support: Scholarships—to individuals; Grants for special needs.
Application information:
> *Initial approach:* Telephone
EIN: 910564748

9589
Helen Miller Clancy Scholarship Foundation
P.O. Box 4
Vashon, WA 98070 (206) 463-3608
Application Address: P.O. Box 13476 Burton, WA 98013
E-mail: info@hmcsf.org; URL: http://www.hmcsf.org

Foundation type: Independent foundation
Purpose: Scholarships to graduating high school seniors who are residents of Vashon Island, WA, for higher education.
Financial data: Year ended 12/31/2012. Assets, $395,071 (M); Expenditures, $26,172; Total giving, $23,575; Grants to individuals, 12 grants totaling $23,575 (high: $3,525, low: $400).
Fields of interest: Higher education.
Type of support: Undergraduate support.
Application information: Applications accepted. Application form required. Application form available on the grantmaker's web site. Interview required.
> *Send request by:* Mail
> *Deadline(s):* Apr. 6
> *Final notification:* Recipients notified by May 1
> *Applicants should submit the following:*
>   1) Resume
>   2) Letter(s) of recommendation
>   3) Transcripts
>   4) Essay
EIN: 911658180

9590
Clark Community College District 14 Foundation
1933 Ft. Vancouver Way
Vancouver, WA 98663-3598 (360) 992-2301
Contact: Lisa Gilbert, Pres.
Application address: Clark College, Office of Financial Aid/GHL 101, 1933 Ft. Vancouver Way, Vancouver, WA 98663-3598
FAX: (360) 750-5759;
E-mail: foundation@clark.edu; URL: http://www.clarkcollegefoundation.org

Foundation type: Public charity
Purpose: Scholarships to graduating high school seniors to receive a college education they could not otherwise afford for attendance at Clark College, WA.
Publications: Annual report; Financial statement; Newsletter.
Financial data: Year ended 06/30/2011. Assets, $70,748,179 (M); Expenditures, $4,868,034; Total giving, $501,408; Grants to individuals, totaling $501,408.
Type of support: Support to graduates or students of specific schools.
Application information: Applications accepted. Application form required.
> *Initial approach:* E-mail
> *Deadline(s):* Apr. 10
> *Applicants should submit the following:*
>   1) Transcripts
>   2) Letter(s) of recommendation
> *Additional information:* See web site for additional application guidelines.
EIN: 237315006

9591
Elizabeth Church Clarke Testamentary Trust/Fund Foundation
c/o Davidson Trust Co.
601 W. Riverside, Ste., 1000
Spokane, WA 99201 (503) 226-7827
Application address: Scottish Rite of Freemasonry, 709 S.W. 15th, Portland, OR 97205

Foundation type: Independent foundation
Purpose: Grants to residents of Oregon for medical assistance.
Financial data: Year ended 12/31/2012. Assets, $1,451,874 (M); Expenditures, $80,480; Total giving, $61,194.
Fields of interest: Health care.
Type of support: Grants for special needs.
Application information: Applications accepted.
> *Initial approach:* Letter
> *Deadline(s):* None
> *Additional information:* Payments may be made directly to the individuals or to the physicians and hospitals providing service. Application must detail needs and costs.
EIN: 936024205

9592
Clover Park Foundation
7307 82nd St. Ct. S.W.
Lakewood, WA 98498-3758 (253) 584-4914
Contact: Mark Blanchard, Pres.
E-mail: mark.blanchard@comcast.net; URL: http://cloverparkfoundation.org/

Foundation type: Public charity
Purpose: Grants to Lakewood, WA teachers for classroom assistance to enhance student education.

Financial data: Year ended 08/31/2012. Assets, $77,061 (M); Expenditures, $39,327; Total giving, $21,313.
Fields of interest: Elementary/secondary education.
Type of support: Program development; Project support.
Application information:
Initial approach: Letter
Additional information: Contact foundation for eligibility criteria.
EIN: 911184240

9593
Colf Family Foundation
6816 N.E. Etna Rd.
Woodland, WA   98674-2617

Foundation type: Independent foundation
Purpose: Scholarships to residents of WA for higher education.
Financial data: Year ended 12/31/2012. Assets, $2,310,953 (M); Expenditures, $113,885; Total giving, $100,197.
Type of support: Scholarships—to individuals.
Application information: Applications not accepted.
Additional information: Unsolicited requests for funds not accepted or considered.
EIN: 911815575

9594
College Success Foundation
(formerly Washington Education Foundation)
1605 N.W. Sammamish Rd., Ste. 100
Issaquah, WA   98027-5378   (425) 416-2000
Contact: Tanguy Martin, Exec. Dir.
FAX: (425) 416-2001;
E-mail: info@waedfoundation.org; Toll-free tel. (Issaquah office): (877) 655-4097; additional address (DC office): 1220 12th St., S.E., Ste. 110, Washington, DC 20003-3718, tel.: (202) 207-1800, fax: (202) 207-1801, toll-free tel.: (866) 240-3567; additional address (Tacoma Office): 950 Pacific Ave., Ste. 1250, Tacoma, WA 98402-4423, tel.: (253) 439-5800, fax: (253) 439-5801, toll-free tel.: (877) 655-4097; URL: http://collegesuccessfoundation.org/

Foundation type: Public charity
Purpose: Scholarships to financially needy residents of WA, and to wards of the court or those aging out of foster care.
Financial data: Year ended 12/31/2011. Assets, $44,189,730 (M); Expenditures, $14,240,541; Total giving, $4,574,564; Grants to individuals, totaling $1,144,493.
Fields of interest: College; Foster care; Economically disadvantaged.
Type of support: Undergraduate support.
Application information: Applications accepted. Application form required.
Initial approach: E-mail
Deadline(s): Varies
Applicants should submit the following:
1) GPA
2) Transcripts
3) Essay
Additional information: Contact foundation for further application guidelines.
Program descriptions:
Governor's Scholarship for Foster Youth Program: Awards twenty to thirty scholarships, ranging from $1,000 and $5,000 per year for up to five years for college, to a Washington State high school student

who is a ward of the court or who was before aging out of foster care.
Washington State Achievers Scholarship Program: Awards an average of $20,000 for four years to students in Achievers high schools in Washington state. Students must be in their junior year, plan to obtain a four-year college degree, go to college in Washington state for two years, and have an income that is in the lowest 35 percent of Washington state income levels.
EIN: 912036088

9595
Columbia Basin Foundation
234 1st Ave. N.W. , Ste. B
Ephrata, WA   98823-1603   (509) 754-4596
Contact: Donn Cook, Exec. Dir.
FAX: (509) 754-4194;
E-mail: info@columbiabasinfoundation.org;
Additional e-mail:
dcook@columbiabasinfoundation.org; URL: http://www.columbiabasinfoundation.org

Foundation type: Community foundation
Purpose: Scholarships to individuals in Grant and Adams counties, WA for higher education.
Publications: Application guidelines; Annual report; Informational brochure; Newsletter.
Financial data: Year ended 12/31/2012. Assets, $6,563,234 (M); Expenditures, $641,599; Total giving, $472,361; Grants to individuals, 71 grants totaling $167,850.
Fields of interest: Higher education.
Type of support: Scholarships—to individuals.
Application information: Applications accepted. Application form required. Application form available on the grantmaker's web site.
Initial approach: Application (online PDF)
Send request by: Mail
Copies of proposal: 1
Deadline(s): Feb. 28
Final notification: Recipients notified June 1
Applicants should submit the following:
1) SAR
2) FAFSA
Additional information: Each scholarships has its own unique eligibility criteria. See web site for complete listing of scholarships.
EIN: 911733104

9596
Columbia Endowment Fund
P.O. Box 2166
Battle Ground, WA   98604

Foundation type: Independent foundation
Purpose: Scholarships to needy students attending Columbia Adventist Academy, WA.
Financial data: Year ended 12/31/2011. Assets, $276,587 (M); Expenditures, $15,717; Total giving, $15,000.
Fields of interest: Higher education.
Type of support: Support to graduates or students of specific schools.
Application information: Applications accepted. Application form required.
Deadline(s): Prior to the start of the school term
Additional information: Applications available from school.
EIN: 943090375

9597
Community Action Center
(also known as C.A.C.)
350 S.E. Fairmont Rd.
Pullman, WA   99163-5500   (509) 334-9147
FAX: (509) 334-9105;
E-mail: cac@cacwhitman.com; Toll-free tel.: (800) 482-3991

Foundation type: Public charity
Purpose: Assistance to indigent residents of Whitman County, WA for utilities and food.
Financial data: Year ended 06/30/2012. Assets, $14,942,697 (M); Expenditures, $6,050,367.
Fields of interest: Economically disadvantaged.
Type of support: Grants for special needs.
Application information:
Initial approach: Letter
Additional information: Contact foundation for eligibility criteria.
Program descriptions:
Emergency Food Assistance Program: The program offers help to those who need access to nutritional food. The food bank may be accessed one time in a month for those needing emergency food supplies. Nutritional counseling, information on food purchases and preparation and household budget assistance are also available.
Low Income Home Energy Assistance Program: The program helps pay the winter heating bills or summer cooling bills of low-income and elderly people.
EIN: 943080214

9598
Community Action Council of Lewis Mason and Thurston Counties
420 Golf Club Rd. S.E. Ste. 100
Lacey, WA   98503-1048   (360) 438-1100
Contact: John M. Walsh, C.E.O.
FAX: (360) 491-7729; E-mail: info@caclmt.org; Toll Free Tel.: (800)-952-2125; URL: http://www.caclmt.org/

Foundation type: Public charity
Purpose: Assistance to indigent residents of Lewis, Mason, and Thurston counties, WA, for energy assistance, food, water assistance, and home weatherization.
Financial data: Year ended 09/30/2011. Assets, $11,987,519 (M); Expenditures, $11,557,220; Total giving, $6,203,791; Grants to individuals, totaling $5,319,943.
Fields of interest: Economically disadvantaged.
Type of support: Grants for special needs.
Application information:
Initial approach: Tel.
Applicants should submit the following:
1) Financial information
Additional information: Contact foundation for eligibility criteria.
EIN: 910818368

9599
Community Foundation for Southwest Washington
(formerly Clark County Community Foundation)
1053 Officers Row
Vancouver, WA   98661-3851   (360) 694-2550
Contact: For grant applications: Anne Digenis, Sr. Philanthropic Advisor
FAX: (360) 737-6335; E-mail: director@cfsww.org; URL: http://www.cfsww.org

Foundation type: Community foundation

Purpose: Scholarships to residents of southwest Washington for postsecondary education at a college, university or vocational/technical schools.
Publications: Annual report; Informational brochure; Newsletter.
Financial data: Year ended 12/31/2012. Assets, $62,321,268 (M); Expenditures, $7,026,153; Total giving, $5,936,062. Scholarships—to individuals amount not specified.
Fields of interest: Vocational education, post-secondary; Higher education.
Type of support: Scholarships—to individuals; Support to graduates or students of specific schools; Undergraduate support.
Application information: Applications accepted. Application form required. Application form available on the grantmaker's web site.
  Additional information: See web site for a complete listing of scholarships and applications. Some scholarships listed have applications that may be filled out by the general public.
Program description:
  Scholarship Programs: Each scholarship is unique and supports students with a variety of backgrounds, educational goals and economic status. Individual scholarship awards typically range in size from $1,000 to $5,000. While some scholarship funds award scholarships to graduating high school students, others award scholarships to students currently enrolled in a college or university. Scholarships may be awarded for one year only, while others are awarded for the customary four years of postsecondary education. Each individual scholarship fund is typically designated for students graduating from either a specific high school, are employees or children of employees of specific businesses, or are current college students pursuing a specific career path.
EIN: 911246778

9600
Community Foundation of North Central Washington

(formerly Greater Wenatchee Community Foundation)
9 South Wenatchee Ave.
Wenatchee, WA 98807 (509) 663-7716
Contact: Beth A. Stipe, Exec. Dir.; For grants: Lila Edlund, Prog. and Office Mgr.
Scholarship application e-mail: scholarships@cfncw.org
FAX: (888) 317-8314; E-mail: info@cfncw.org;
URL: http://www.cfncw.org

Foundation type: Community foundation
Purpose: Scholarships to students who are residents of Chelan, Douglas, and Okanogan counties, WA, for higher education.
Publications: Application guidelines; Annual report; Grants list; Informational brochure; Informational brochure (including application guidelines); Newsletter; Occasional report.
Financial data: Year ended 06/30/2012. Assets, $42,422,778 (M); Expenditures, $3,371,939; Total giving, $2,593,807; Grants to individuals, 211 grants totaling $307,458 (high: $14,280).
Fields of interest: Print publishing; Arts; Higher education; Scholarships/financial aid; Education; Christian agencies & churches; Women.
Type of support: Employee-related scholarships; Scholarships—to individuals; Support to graduates or students of specific schools; Undergraduate support.
Application information: Applications accepted. Application form required. Application form available on the grantmaker's web site.

Initial approach: Application
Send request by: E-mail
Deadline(s): Feb. 15
Final notification: Applicants notified in 90 days
Applicants should submit the following:
  1) GPA
  2) FAFSA
  3) Financial information
  4) Letter(s) of recommendation
  5) Transcripts
Additional information: See web site for a complete listing of scholarship funds and application guidelines. No late, incomplete, e-mail or faxed applications are accepted.
Program description:
  Scholarships: The foundation manages over 70 scholarship funds. Scholarship recipients are selected on an objective and competitive basis considering academic and non-academic factors as well as demonstrated financial need. Some awards are made only on the basis of past student performance. Each scholarship has its own award level and selection committee. See web site for additional information.
EIN: 911349486

9601
The Costco Foundation

999 Lake Dr.
Issaquah, WA 98027-8990
Contact: John Matthews, Pres.

Foundation type: Operating foundation
Purpose: Grants to employees of Costco Wholesale Corp. and its subsidiaries for emergency relief.
Financial data: Year ended 09/02/2012. Assets, $5,589 (M); Expenditures, $75,196; Total giving, $75,186; Grants to individuals, 38 grants totaling $75,186 (high: $5,509, low: $500).
Type of support: Employee-related welfare.
Application information: Applications not accepted.
  Additional information: Unsolicited requests for funds not considered or acknowledged.
Company name: Costco Wholesale Corporation
EIN: 911799391

9602
Viola Vestal Coulter Foundation, Inc.

3004 Viewcrest Dr. N.E.
Bremerton, WA 98310-9740
Contact: Mary Lynne Braun, Secy.

Foundation type: Independent foundation
Purpose: Scholarships to students at designated colleges and universities in the western U.S. for graduate and undergraduate degree programs.
Financial data: Year ended 12/31/2011. Assets, $5,633,208 (M); Expenditures, $440,608; Total giving, $310,250.
Fields of interest: Higher education.
Type of support: Scholarships—to individuals.
Application information: Unsolicited applications not accepted.
EIN: 846029641

9603
Helen Davis Scholarship Trust No. 3

(also known as Davis Medical School Scholarships)
P.O. Box 21927, MAC P6540-11K
Seattle, WA 98111 (406) 447-2050
Application address: c/o Wells Fargo Private Client Services, P.O. Box 597, Helena, MT 59624

Foundation type: Independent foundation

Purpose: Scholarships only to residents of MT attending accredited medical schools.
Financial data: Year ended 08/31/2013. Assets, $1,687,305 (M); Expenditures, $97,347; Total giving, $69,000; Grants to individuals, 10 grants totaling $56,000 (high: $7,000, low: $6,000).
Fields of interest: Medical school/education.
Type of support: Graduate support.
Application information: Application form required.
  Deadline(s): July 15
  Applicants should submit the following:
    1) Letter(s) of recommendation
    2) Transcripts
  Additional information: Application must also include federal income tax forms and letter of acceptance from, or proof of enrollment at, an accredited medical school. Applications can be obtained at Wells Fargo Bank, N.A., PCS.
EIN: 816056734

9604
DaVita Children's Foundation

c/o Tax Dept.
1423 Pacific Ave.
Tacoma, WA 98401-2076 (253) 733-4628
FAX: (877) 731-4434;
E-mail: scholarshipfoundations@davita.com

Foundation type: Company-sponsored foundation
Purpose: Scholarships to children and grandchildren of employees of DaVita, Inc., enrolled or preparing to enroll in college.
Financial data: Year ended 12/31/2012. Assets, $200,252 (M); Expenditures, $86,137; Total giving, $86,000; Grants to individuals, 45 grants totaling $86,000 (high: $3,000, low: $1,000).
Type of support: Employee-related scholarships.
Application information: Unsolicited requests for funds not accepted.
Company name: DaVita HealthCare Partners Inc.
EIN: 330932587

9605
Daystar Northwest, Inc.

P.O. Box 46011
Seattle, WA 98146-0011

Foundation type: Operating foundation
Purpose: General welfare support to elderly residents of Daystar Retirement Village, WA.
Financial data: Year ended 12/31/2012. Assets, $79,227 (M); Expenditures, $64,285; Total giving, $60,288; Grants to individuals, 4 grants totaling $60,288 (high: $18,603, low: $11,200).
Fields of interest: Aging.
Type of support: Grants to individuals.
Application information: Applications not accepted.
  Additional information: Unsolicited requests for funds not accepted or considered.
EIN: 910782369

9606
Educational Loan Foundation of Spokane, Inc.

1420 U.S. Bank Bldg.
Spokane, WA 99201 (509) 747-2158
Contact: Joan Bergdorf

Foundation type: Independent foundation
Purpose: Student loans to residents of Spokane, WA.
Financial data: Year ended 05/31/2012. Assets, $69,056 (M); Expenditures, $7,590; Total giving,

$6,000; Grants to individuals, 2 grants totaling $4,000 (high: $2,000, low: $2,000).
Type of support: Student loans—to individuals.
Application information: Applications accepted. Application form required.
> *Deadline(s):* None

EIN: 916031887

9607
Catherine Marie Elvins and Naomi Libby Elvins Scholarship Trust
P.O Box 176
Gig Harbor, WA 98335
Contact: Janelle Braithwait
Application address: 18014 E Montgomery Ave. Greencres, WA 990169306

Foundation type: Independent foundation
Purpose: Scholarships to female medical students from WA who are attending or planning to attend the University of Washington Medical School.
Financial data: Year ended 12/31/2012. Assets, $2,721,062 (M); Expenditures, $141,858; Total giving, $114,990; Grants to individuals, 15 grants totaling $114,990 (high: $10,782, low: $3,592).
Fields of interest: Medical school/education; Women.
Type of support: Support to graduates or students of specific schools.
Application information: Application form required.
> *Deadline(s):* May 1
> *Applicants should submit the following:*
> 1) Transcripts
> 2) Letter(s) of recommendation
> *Additional information:* Application must also include a letter stating importance of obtaining scholarship, future goals, biographical sketch and activities.

EIN: 916470080

9608
The Greater Everett Community Foundation
2823 Rockefeller Ave.
P.O. Box 5549
Everett, WA 98201-3524 (425) 212-4056
Contact: Maddy Metzger-Utt, Pres. and C.E.O.; Karri Matau
FAX: (425) 212-4059;
E-mail: maddy@greatereverettcf.org; Mailing address: P.O. Box 5549, Everett, WA 98206-5549; Additional e-mail: info@greatereverettcf.org; Grant inquiry tel. 425-212-4056; URL: http://www.greatereverettcf.org

Foundation type: Community foundation
Purpose: Scholarships to residents of Everett and Snohomish counties, WA.
Publications: Application guidelines; Annual report.
Financial data: Year ended 12/31/2012. Assets, $10,525,375 (M); Expenditures, $866,736; Total giving, $442,919; Grants to individuals, 16 grants totaling $28,200.
Type of support: Undergraduate support.
Application information: Applications not accepted.
> *Additional information:* Unsolicited requests for funds not considered or acknowledged.

EIN: 943188703

9609
The Evergreen State College Foundation
2700 Evergreen Pkwy. N.W., Ste. L1113
Olympia, WA 98505-0005 (360) 867-6300
Contact: D. Lee Hoemann, Exec. Dir.
Application information and/or application packets should be submitted to The Office of Enrollment Services, The Evergreen State College, Seminar I, Rm. 3165, 2700 Evergreen Pkwy NW, Olympia, WA 98505, tel.: (360) 867-6310,
e-mail: elhardtm@evergreen.edu
URL: http://www.evergreen.edu/give/

Foundation type: Public charity
Purpose: Scholarships and tuition awards to qualified persons for opportunities in education primarily in the Olympia, WA area.
Publications: Annual report.
Financial data: Year ended 06/30/2012. Assets, $9,995,857 (M); Expenditures, $2,017,153; Total giving, $1,387,237; Grants to individuals, totaling $1,387,237.
Fields of interest: College; Scholarships/financial aid.
Type of support: Awards/prizes; Graduate support; Undergraduate support.
Application information: Applications accepted. Application form required.
> *Deadline(s):* Feb. 1 for all Scholarships and Tuition Awards; May 1 for Merit Awards
> *Applicants should submit the following:*
> 1) Transcripts
> 2) Letter(s) of recommendation
> *Additional information:* Scholarships are offered also to new and enrolled students; See web site for further programs and guidelines.

EIN: 910981488

9610
Family Service Spokane
7 S. Howard St., Ste. 321
Spokane, WA 99201-3821 (509) 838-4128
Contact: Jeff Thomas, EXec. Dir.

Foundation type: Public charity
Purpose: Grants for counseling, education, socialization and food services to families in Spokane, WA.
Financial data: Year ended 12/31/2011. Assets, $0 (M); Expenditures, $2,459,960; Total giving, $877,022; Grants to individuals, totaling $877,022.
Fields of interest: Family services; Children.
Type of support: Grants for special needs.
Application information: For providers to be eligible for the grants, they must be a licensed in-home child care facility. Claims submitted for reimbursement, are checked for accuracy before the provider is reimbursed. Contact the agency for eligibility determination.

EIN: 910564952

9611
Joe Fergason Scholarship Fund
P.O. Box 437
South Bend, WA 98586-0437

Foundation type: Operating foundation
Purpose: Scholarships to graduates of South Bend High School, WA for postsecondary education.
Financial data: Year ended 06/30/2013. Assets, $111,332 (M); Expenditures, $5,356; Total giving, $5,000.
Fields of interest: Higher education.
Type of support: Support to graduates or students of specific schools.

Application information: Applications accepted. Application form required.
> *Deadline(s):* Mar. 31
> *Additional information:* Applications should include grades, plans for future education, activities and family information.

EIN: 911322109

9612
First Baptist Church of Everett Foundation
1616 Pacific Ave.
Everett, WA 98201-4026 (425) 259-9167

Foundation type: Public charity
Purpose: Scholarships to graduating high school seniors, college undergraduate, graduate, or ministerial students pursuing higher education.
Fields of interest: Higher education; Theological school/education.
Type of support: Scholarships—to individuals; Graduate support; Undergraduate support.
Application information: Applications accepted.
> *Additional information:* Applicant must be a member of First Baptist Church and be actively involved in church activities, meet a minimum academic standard and participate in school and/or community activities.

EIN: 911313943

9613
Fisher Broadcasting Inc. Minority Scholarship Fund
(formerly KOMO Radio and Television Minority Scholarship Fund)
140 4th Ave. N., Ste. 500
Seattle, WA 98109-4983 (206) 404-7000
FAX: (206) 404-6013; E-mail: jendejan@fsci.com;
URL: http://fsci.com/careers/scholarships-for-minorities/

Foundation type: Company-sponsored foundation
Purpose: Scholarships to minority broadcasting students attending WA, OR, ID, CA or MT schools.
Publications: Application guidelines; Informational brochure; IRS Form 990 or 990-PF printed copy available upon request.
Financial data: Year ended 12/31/2012. Assets, $277,405 (M); Expenditures, $13,631; Total giving, $13,525; Grants to individuals, 6 grants totaling $13,525 (high: $2,500, low: $1,025).
Fields of interest: Media/communications; Television; Radio; Journalism; Minorities.
Type of support: Technical education support; Undergraduate support.
Application information: Applications accepted. Application form required. Application form available on the grantmaker's web site. Interview required.
> *Send request by:* Online
> *Deadline(s):* May 31
> *Final notification:* Recipients notified July 30
> *Applicants should submit the following:*
> 1) Transcripts
> 2) Letter(s) of recommendation
> 3) Essay
> *Additional information:* Applications should also include proof of citizenship.

Program description:
Scholarships for Minorities: The foundation annually awards college scholarships to minority students enrolled in a broadcast oriented curriculum focusing on radio, television, marketing, or broadcast technology. Students must be at the sophomore level or above and have a minimum GPA

of 2.5. Scholarships are awarded based on need, academic achievement, and personal qualities.
EIN: 911500276

9614
Foundation for the Future
16150 N.E. 85th St., Ste. 119
Redmond, WA 98052-3542

Foundation type: Independent foundation
Purpose: Prizes by nomination only to individuals for outstanding achievement in identifying the genetic factors that may have a decisive impact on the survivability of a human population. Also, research grants awarded to scholars for study on the future of humanity.
Financial data: Year ended 12/31/2012. Assets, $7,673,106 (M); Expenditures, $3,693,619; Total giving, $1,385,408; Grant to an individual, 1 grant totaling $7,500.
Fields of interest: Genetic diseases and disorders; Anthropology/sociology.
Type of support: Research; Awards/prizes.
Application information: Application form available on the grantmaker's web site.
  Initial approach: Proposal
  Additional information: Contact foundation for application deadline/guidelines.
EIN: 911732102

9615
Franciscan Foundation Washington
(also known as Francisan Foundation)
1149 Market St.
M.S. 10-02
Tacoma, WA 98402-3515   (253) 428-8411
Contact: Mary McManus, Exec. Asst.
FAX: (253) 428-8466;
E-mail: fhsfoundation@fhshealth.org; Mailing address: P.O. Box 1502, Tacoma, WA 98401-1502; E-mail For Gregory J. Unruh: gregoryunruh@fhshealth.org; URL: http://www.fhshealth.org/Ways_Give.aspx?id=2510&menu_id=322

Foundation type: Public charity
Purpose: Hospital bill assistance to indigent patients of the eight full-service hospitals associated with Franciscan Health System, in Tacoma, WA with family income less than or equal to 130 percent of the Department of Housing and Urban Development very low income guidelines for the area.
Publications: Annual report.
Financial data: Year ended 06/30/2012. Assets, $21,776,319 (M); Expenditures, $5,756,231; Total giving, $4,872,472; Grants to individuals, totaling $58,050.
Fields of interest: Hospitals (general); Health care, patient services; Economically disadvantaged.
Type of support: Grants for special needs.
Application information: Applications accepted. Application form required. Application form available on the grantmaker's web site.
  Initial approach: Tel.
  Deadline(s): None
  Applicants should submit the following:
    1) Financial information
  Additional information: Call 253-396-6700 for eligibility queries.
EIN: 911145592

9616
Fred Hutchinson Cancer Research Center
1100 Fairview Ave. N.
P.O. Box 19024
Seattle, WA 98109-1024   (206) 667-5000
Contact: Larry Corey M.D., Pres.
E-mail: externalrel@fhcrc.org; URL: http://www.fhcrc.org/

Foundation type: Public charity
Purpose: Grants to individuals for cancer research for the prevention and treatment of cancer and related diseases.
Publications: Annual report; Newsletter; Occasional report.
Financial data: Year ended 06/30/2012. Assets, $714,068,907 (M); Expenditures, $436,159,180; Total giving, $79,888,530.
Fields of interest: Cancer research.
Type of support: Grants to individuals.
Application information: Contact the center for additional guidelines.
EIN: 237156071

9617
Frets Educational Trust
20675 Bulson Rd.
Mount Vernon, WA 98274-8032   (360) 445-6007
Contact: Gloria Carbert, Tr.

Foundation type: Independent foundation
Purpose: Scholarships to high school and college students of Skagit County, WA.
Financial data: Year ended 12/31/2012. Assets, $30,632 (M); Expenditures, $9,607; Total giving, $6,700; Grants to individuals, 5 grants totaling $6,700 (high: $2,000; low: $850).
Type of support: Undergraduate support.
Application information: Applications accepted.
  Initial approach: Letter or telephone
  Applicants should submit the following:
    1) Letter(s) of recommendation
    2) Financial information
    3) Transcripts
    4) Resume
EIN: 916341455

9618
Friends of Jose Carreras International Leukemia Foundation
1100 Fairview Ave. N., Ste. D5-100
Seattle, WA 98109-1024
FAX: (206) 667-6124;
E-mail: friendsjc@carrerasfoundation.org;
URL: http://www.carreras-foundation.org/

Foundation type: Independent foundation
Purpose: Fellowships to individual M.D.'s and Ph.D.'s for research into the diagnosis, prevention, and cure of leukemia and related hematologic malignancies.
Financial data: Year ended 06/30/2012. Assets, $130,601 (M); Expenditures, $69,194; Total giving, $19,913.
Fields of interest: Leukemia research.
Type of support: Fellowships; Postdoctoral support.
Application information: Application form required.
  Copies of proposal: 11
  Deadline(s): Nov. 3
  Applicants should submit the following:
    1) Letter(s) of recommendation
    2) Budget Information
    3) Curriculum vitae
  Additional information: See Web site for further application information.

Program description:
  Fellowships: Awards $50,000 for one fellowship, renewable yearly for two additional years upon satisfactory performance. Candidates must hold an M.D. or Ph.D. degree and have completed at least three years postdoctoral training but must be less than ten years post their first doctoral degree when the award begins. There are no restrictions based on nationality, but only one application will be considered from each sponsoring institution.
EIN: 911484924

9619
G.M.L. Foundation Inc.
P.O. Box 916
Port Angeles, WA 98362-0158

Foundation type: Independent foundation
Purpose: Medical expense assistance limited to residents of Clallam County, WA.
Financial data: Year ended 12/31/2012. Assets, $1,138,951 (M); Expenditures, $28,452; Total giving, $21,159; Grants to individuals, 9 grants totaling $21,159 (high: $4,646, low: $205).
Fields of interest: Health care.
Type of support: Grants for special needs.
Application information: Applications not accepted.
  Additional information: Unsolicited requests for funds not accepted or considered.
EIN: 916030844

9620
Gasparovich Memorial Scholarship Award Fund
6701 160th St. S.W.
Edmonds, WA 98026-4535   (206) 252-3892
Application address: c/o Ingraham High School, Attn: Carrie Richard, 1819 N. 135th St., Seattle, WA 98133

Foundation type: Independent foundation
Purpose: Scholarships to high school graduates of Ingraham High School, WA for postsecondary education.
Financial data: Year ended 12/31/2011. Assets, $110,367 (M); Expenditures, $8,845; Total giving, $8,000; Grants to individuals, 4 grants totaling $8,000 (high: $2,000, low: $2,000).
Fields of interest: Higher education.
Type of support: Scholarships—to individuals; Support to graduates or students of specific schools.
Application information: Applications accepted.
  Deadline(s): End of spring
  Additional information: Students are recommended by Ingraham High School athletic department.
EIN: 910986139

9621
Mabelle M. George Educational Trust
43 Kayla Dr.
Montesano, WA 98563-9654   (360) 249-1022
Application address: c/o Brookings-Harbor Scholarship Foundation, Inc., P.O. Box 7673, Brookings, OR 97415-0365

Foundation type: Operating foundation
Purpose: Scholarships to graduates of Brookings-Harbor High School, OR, attending a four-year college or university.
Financial data: Year ended 12/31/2012. Assets, $135,334 (M); Expenditures, $17,237; Total

giving, $15,000; Grants to individuals, 8 grants totaling $15,000 (high: $2,000, low: $1,000).
Type of support: Support to graduates or students of specific schools; Undergraduate support.
Application information: Applications accepted. Application form required.
  Initial approach: Letter
  Deadline(s): None
EIN: 916358636

9622
The Elizabeth George Foundation
P.O. Box 1429
Langley, WA 98260-1429
Contact: Susan Elizabeth George, Dir.
E-mail: georgeassistant@yahoo.com

Foundation type: Independent foundation
Purpose: Grants to unpublished fiction writers and poets.
Publications: Informational brochure.
Financial data: Year ended 10/31/2012. Assets, $804,946 (M); Expenditures, $506,729; Total giving, $500,006; Grants to individuals, 14 grants totaling $197,736 (high: $55,776, low: $2,000).
Fields of interest: Literature.
Type of support: Conferences/seminars; Publication; Fellowships; Scholarships—to individuals; Support to graduates or students of specific schools; Graduate support; Travel grants; Grants for special needs; Project support.
Application information: Applications accepted. Application form not required.
  Initial approach: Letter
  Send request by: Mail
  Copies of proposal: 1
  Deadline(s): July 1 for inquiry; Nov. 1 for application; Nov. 15 for references
  Final notification: Recipients notified in six weeks
  Applicants should submit the following:
    1) Budget Information
    2) Curriculum vitae
    3) Proposal
EIN: 330829947

9623
Gius Foundation
P.O. Box 277
Quincy, WA 98848-0277   (509) 787-3501

Foundation type: Independent foundation
Purpose: Scholarships to students who are graduates of Quincy High School in WA, have a GPA of 2.3 or higher, and plan on attending a two-year community college or technical or trade school to pursue a vocational career.
Financial data: Year ended 12/31/2011. Assets, $5,662,947 (M); Expenditures, $408,234; Total giving, $380,239.
Fields of interest: Vocational education, post-secondary; Higher education.
Type of support: Support to graduates or students of specific schools.
Application information: Applications accepted. Application form required.
  Deadline(s): To be determined by Quincy High School
  Additional information: The scholarship must be used at a program located in the state of WA. Applications available at Quincy High School.
EIN: 911511475

9624
Grays Harbor Community Foundation
707 J St.
P.O. Box 615
Hoquiam, WA 98550-3624   (360) 532-1600
Contact: Jim Daly, Exec. Dir.; For grants: Cassie Lentz, Prog. Off.
FAX: (360) 532-8111; *E-mail:* info@gh-cf.org; Additional e-mail: cassie@gh-cf.org; *URL:* http://www.gh-cf.org

Foundation type: Community foundation
Purpose: Scholarships to graduates of any high school in Grays Harbor County, WA.
Publications: Application guidelines; Annual report; Grants list; Informational brochure; Informational brochure (including application guidelines); Newsletter.
Financial data: Year ended 12/31/2012. Assets, $37,380,788 (M); Expenditures, $1,746,455; Total giving, $1,389,548; Grants to individuals, 237 grants totaling $379,034.
Fields of interest: Higher education; Scholarships/financial aid.
Type of support: Scholarships—to individuals; Undergraduate support.
Application information: Applications accepted. Application form required. Application form available on the grantmaker's web site.
  Initial approach: Application
  Send request by: Mail
  Copies of proposal: 1
  Deadline(s): Mar. 15
  Final notification: Applicants notified by May 30
  Applicants should submit the following:
    1) Transcripts
    2) Resume
    3) Letter(s) of recommendation
    4) GPA
    5) Financial information
    6) Essay
  Additional information: Each scholarships has its own unique set of eligibility criteria. See web site for a complete listing of scholarships.
EIN: 911607005

9625
Fred and Margaret Grimm Foundation
2801 Alaskan Way, Ste. 107
Seattle, WA 98121-1135

Foundation type: Independent foundation
Purpose: Scholarships to individuals for undergraduate education.
Financial data: Year ended 12/31/2012. Assets, $64,279 (M); Expenditures, $58,432; Total giving, $56,387; Grants to individuals, 12 grants totaling $14,667 (high: $2,000, low: $333).
Fields of interest: Higher education.
Type of support: Undergraduate support.
Application information: Applications not accepted.
  Additional information: Unsolicited requests for funds not considered or acknowledged.
EIN: 204005427

9626
Group Health Community Foundation
(formerly The Group Health Foundation)
320 Westlake Ave. N., Ste. 100
Seattle, WA 98109-5233   (206) 448-7330
Contact: Laura Rehrmann, Pres. and C.E.O.
FAX: (206) 877-0646;
E-mail: foundation.ghc@ghc.org; Toll Free Tel.: (866)-389-5532; E-Mail for Laura Rehrmann: rehrmann.l@ghc.org; Tel. for Laura Rehrmann:

(206)-448-7304; *URL:* http://www.ghc.org/foundation/

Foundation type: Public charity
Purpose: Financial assistance to employees of Group Health Cooperative and Group Health Permanente residing in ID, OR, and WA.
Publications: Application guidelines; Annual report; Grants list; Informational brochure; Newsletter; Program policy statement.
Financial data: Year ended 12/31/2011. Assets, $19,374,263 (M); Expenditures, $2,216,292; Total giving, $2,021,478; Grants to individuals, totaling $41,749.
Type of support: Employee-related scholarships; Employee-related welfare; Grants for special needs.
Application information: Applications accepted. Application form required.
  Deadline(s): Contact the foundation for current application deadline
  Additional information: Applications available from personnel office or foundation.
EIN: 911246278

9627
Freeman and Emma Grow Memorial Scholarship Fund
304 Fish Hatchery Rd.
Goldendale, WA 98620   (509) 773-5846
Application Address: c/o Goldendale high School, 525 Simcoe Dr. Goldendale, WA 98620

Foundation type: Independent foundation
Purpose: Scholarships only to graduating seniors of Goldendale High School, WA, to attend institutions of higher learning in WA.
Financial data: Year ended 12/31/2012. Assets, $75,480 (M); Expenditures, $4,240; Total giving, $4,000; Grants to individuals, 4 grants totaling $4,000 (high: $1,000, low: $1,000).
Type of support: Support to graduates or students of specific schools; Undergraduate support.
Application information: Applications accepted. Application form required.
  Deadline(s): None
  Additional information: Scholarships are not renewable.
EIN: 237123616

9628
Joyce Hall Memorial Music Scholarship
14300 N.E. 20th Ave., D-102-204
Vancouver, WA 98686

Foundation type: Company-sponsored foundation
Purpose: Scholarships only to students attending Newport High School, Newport, OR for attendance at an accredited college or university.
Financial data: Year ended 12/31/2012. Assets, $173,835 (M); Expenditures, $13,670; Total giving, $10,000; Grants to individuals, 6 grants totaling $10,000 (high: $2,000, low: $1,000).
Fields of interest: Higher education.
Type of support: Support to graduates or students of specific schools; Undergraduate support.
Application information: Applications not accepted.
  Additional information: Unsolicited requests for funds not considered or acknowledged.
EIN: 931305073

9629
Albert Haller Foundation
P.O. Box 2739
Sequim, WA 98382-2739

Foundation type: Independent foundation
Purpose: Scholarships to students of Clallam County, WA.
Publications: Informational brochure (including application guidelines).
Financial data: Year ended 12/31/2012. Assets, $10,087,409 (M); Expenditures, $537,911; Total giving, $489,958; Grants to individuals, 20 grants totaling $78,000 (high: $4,000, low: $2,000).
Type of support: Scholarships—to individuals.
Application information: Applications not accepted.
> *Additional information:* Applications made through office of the superintendent of applicant's school district. Unsolicited applications not accepted.
EIN: 911556810

9630
Hamilton Agricultural Youth Foundation
P.O. Box 1098
Okanogan, WA   98840-1098   (509) 422-3030
Contact: Greg Hamilton, Pres.

Foundation type: Independent foundation
Purpose: Scholarships to residents of the HFEC trade area in WA who are pursuing higher education in the agricultural field.
Financial data: Year ended 12/31/2012. Assets, $65,534 (M); Expenditures, $20,418; Total giving, $19,143; Grants to individuals, 11 grants totaling $9,600 (high: $1,600, low: $800).
Fields of interest: Agriculture/food.
Type of support: Undergraduate support.
Application information: Applications accepted.
> *Deadline(s):* Apr. 1
> Applicants should submit the following:
> 1) Transcripts
> 2) Letter(s) of recommendation
EIN: 911586443

9631
Doug Hanna Memorial Scholarship Foundation
1340 E. Island Lake Dr.
Shelton, WA   98584-9107   (360) 426-4471
Contact: Via Holman
Application address: Shelton Springs Rd., Shelton, WA 98584, tel.: (360) 426-4471

Foundation type: Independent foundation
Purpose: Scholarships to Shelton High School, WA graduates pursuing a degree in education.
Financial data: Year ended 06/30/2013. Assets, $13,978 (M); Expenditures, $12,362; Total giving, $12,000; Grants to individuals, 5 grants totaling $12,000 (high: $2,500, low: $2,000).
Fields of interest: Higher education.
Type of support: Support to graduates or students of specific schools.
Application information: Applications accepted. Application form required.
> *Deadline(s):* May 1
> Applicants should submit the following:
> 1) SAT
> 2) GPA
> *Additional information:* Application must also include references and applicant must show involvement in school and community activities.
EIN: 911384689

9632
Carl M. Hansen Foundation, Inc.
422 W. Riverside, Ste. 1420
Spokane, WA   99201-0305

Foundation type: Independent foundation
Purpose: Scholarships to residents of the Pacific Northwest for the study of engineering.
Financial data: Year ended 12/31/2012. Assets, $3,024,709 (M); Expenditures, $264,605; Total giving, $229,400.
Fields of interest: Engineering school/education.
Type of support: Scholarships—to individuals.
Application information: Applications not accepted.
> *Additional information:* Unsolicited requests for funds not accepted or considered.
EIN: 916063191

9633
Heily Foundation
c/o Continental Mills, Inc., Attn.: John Haily
P.O. Box 88176
Seattle, WA   98138-2176   (206) 872-8400
Contact: John Heily, Tr.

Foundation type: Independent foundation
Purpose: Scholarships and interest-free or low-interest student loans to WA residents for attendance at postsecondary educational institutions.
Publications: Application guidelines.
Financial data: Year ended 12/31/2012. Assets, $211 (M); Expenditures, $44,290; Total giving, $42,779; Grants to individuals, 3 grants totaling $32,779 (high: $27,057, low: $918).
Fields of interest: Higher education.
Type of support: Scholarships—to individuals; Student loans—to individuals.
Application information:
> *Initial approach:* Letter
> *Deadline(s):* None
> *Additional information:* Application should include biography, including description of educational ambitions, financial need, academic performance and future plans. Financial information should also be included.
EIN: 943041322

9634
Herriges Family Memorial Scholarship Foundation
1817 E. Pinecrest Rd.
Spokane, WA   99203

Foundation type: Independent foundation
Purpose: Scholarships to graduating seniors of Whitefish High School, MT and renewals in subsequent college years.
Financial data: Year ended 12/31/2011. Assets, $0 (M); Expenditures, $4,000; Total giving, $4,000; Grants to individuals, 4 grants totaling $4,000 (high: $1,000, low: $1,000).
Fields of interest: Higher education.
Type of support: Support to graduates or students of specific schools.
Application information: Applications accepted. Application form required.
> *Initial approach:* Letter
> *Deadline(s):* Apr. 1
> *Additional information:* Application must include letter of support. Applicant must demonstrate need. Application forms are available from the foundation.
EIN: 363624208

9635
His Helping Hand Foundation
P.O. Box 1119
Goldendale, WA   98620   (541) 345-0655
Contact: Corinne Fuller, Pres.

Foundation type: Operating foundation
Purpose: Provides partial financial assistance to supplement funds of parents residing in OR and WA who want to enroll their children in Christian schools.
Financial data: Year ended 06/30/2012. Assets, $202,303 (M); Expenditures, $32,296; Total giving, $29,560.
Fields of interest: Elementary/secondary education.
Type of support: Grants to individuals.
Application information: Applications not accepted.
> *Additional information:* Unsolicited requests for funds not considered or acknowledged.
EIN: 911791444

9636
Audrey Holliday Scholarship Fund
c/o Heritage Bank Trust Services
700 Washington St., no. 708
Vancouver, WA   98660
Application address: C/o.Gresham Union High School, Gresham, OR 97080

Foundation type: Independent foundation
Purpose: Scholarships to students at Gresham High School, OR, intending to major in sciences, social studies or liberal arts.
Financial data: Year ended 12/31/2012. Assets, $490,886 (M); Expenditures, $29,167; Total giving, $12,199.
Fields of interest: Humanities; Social sciences.
Type of support: Support to graduates or students of specific schools; Undergraduate support.
Application information: Applications accepted.
> *Deadline(s):* None
> *Additional information:* Students must meet academic requirements to qualify for scholarship. Contact your school guidance office for application guidelines.
EIN: 916340777

9637
Hood Canal Masonic Community Scholarship Foundation
P. O. Box 1424
Belfair, WA   98528   (360) 275-4306
Contact: Cheri A. Pruitt, Vice-Chair.
Application Address: 750 N.E. Old Belfair Hwy., Belfair, WA 98526, tel.: (360) 275-4306

Foundation type: Independent foundation
Purpose: Scholarships to residents of Kitsap and Olympia Counties, WA, attending accredited college and universities in WA.
Financial data: Year ended 03/31/2013. Assets, $106,694 (M); Expenditures, $6,176; Total giving, $5,750; Grants to individuals, 9 grants totaling $5,750 (high: $1,250, low: $500).
Type of support: Undergraduate support.
Application information: Applications accepted. Application form required.
> *Deadline(s):* Mar. 31
> Applicants should submit the following:
> 1) Essay
> 2) Letter(s) of recommendation
> 3) Transcripts

Additional information: Application should also include a 100-word personal statement.
EIN: 371453351

9638
Hopelink
10675 Willows Rd. N.E., Ste. 275
Willows Creek Corporate Ctr.
Redmond, WA 98052-2530 (425) 869-6000
Contact: Lauren Thomas, C.E.O.
E-mail: hopelink@hope-link.org; Mailing Address:
P.O. Box 3577, Redmond, WA, 98073-3577; E-mail
For Lauren Thomas: lthomas@hope-link.org;
URL: http://www.hope-link.org

Foundation type: Public charity
Purpose: Emergency financial assistance to low income individuals and families in the Redmond, WA area. In-kind direct contributions of food, shelter, clothing, transportation and energy to indigent families.
Financial data: Year ended 06/30/2012. Assets, $29,636,300 (M); Expenditures, $58,258,089; Total giving, $7,541,583; Grants to individuals, totaling $7,511,898.
Fields of interest: Economically disadvantaged.
Type of support: Emergency funds; In-kind gifts; Grants for special needs.
Application information: Contact the center for financial assistance.
EIN: 910982116

9639
Richard Hugo House
1634 11th Ave.
Seattle, WA 98122-2419 (206) 322-7030
FAX: (206) 320-8767;
E-mail: welcome@hugohouse.org; URL: http://www.hugohouse.org

Foundation type: Public charity
Purpose: Residencies to outstanding youth and adult writers in the Seattle, WA area.
Publications: Application guidelines.
Financial data: Year ended 12/31/2011. Assets, $241,684 (M); Expenditures, $723,835.
Fields of interest: Literature.
Type of support: Residencies.
Application information:
Initial approach: Letter
Deadline(s): June 4 for Writer-in-Residence Program
Applicants should submit the following:
1) Work samples
2) Curriculum vitae
EIN: 911718383

9640
Eileen M. Hunter Scholarship Fund
c/o Wells Fargo Bank, N.A., Trust Tax
P.O. Box 21927, MAc P6540-11K
Seattle, WA 98111-3927 (307) 733-2704
Contact: Matt Rodesky
Application address: P. O. Box 568, Jackson, WY 83001, tel.; (3070 733-2704

Foundation type: Independent foundation
Purpose: Scholarships to high school graduates of the Teton County School District No. 1, WY.
Financial data: Year ended 12/31/2011. Assets, $481,525 (M); Expenditures, $22,893; Total giving, $17,236.
Type of support: Support to graduates or students of specific schools; Undergraduate support.

Application information: Contact fund for current application deadline/guidelines.
EIN: 836034396

9641
The Jain Foundation, Inc.
9725 3rd Ave. N.E., Ste. 204
Seattle, WA 98115 (425) 882-1492
Contact: Sarah Shira, Prog. Mgr.
E-mail: sshira@jain-foundation.org; URL: http://www.jain-foundation.org

Foundation type: Independent foundation
Purpose: Scientific Forum Award to those involved in LGMD2B/Miyoshi research.
Publications: Application guidelines.
Financial data: Year ended 12/31/2012. Assets, $21,674,038 (M); Expenditures, $2,544,440; Total giving, $1,250,579.
Type of support: Research.
Application information:
Initial approach: Letter
Additional information: Contact foundation for eligibility requirements.
EIN: 200284800

9642
Brett Akio Jensen Memorial Scholarship Fund
3611 102nd Pl. S.E.
Everett, WA 98208

Foundation type: Independent foundation
Purpose: Scholarships to residents of Everett, WA.
Financial data: Year ended 12/31/2012. Assets, $73,954 (M); Expenditures, $10,614; Total giving, $7,000; Grants to individuals, 2 grants totaling $7,000 (high: $3,500, low: $3,500).
Type of support: Undergraduate support.
Application information: Applications not accepted.
Additional information: Unsolicited requests for funds not considered or acknowledged.
EIN: 743074876

9643
Jewish Federation of Greater Seattle
2031 3rd Ave.
Seattle, WA 98121-2412 (206) 443-5400
Contact: for Scholarships: Nancy B. Greer, Interim Pres. and C.E.O.
Additional info. for scholarship.: (206) 774-2221, e-mail: KimG@JewishInSeattle.org
FAX: (206) 443-0303;
E-mail: info@jewishinseattle.org; E-Mail for Nancy B. Greer: NancyBG@JewishInSeattle.org;
URL: http://www.jewishinseattle.org

Foundation type: Public charity
Purpose: Camp scholarship to young Jewish children in the greater Seattle, WA area with camp tuition.
Financial data: Year ended 06/30/2011. Assets, $46,543,228 (M); Expenditures, $7,759,973; Total giving, $3,972,610; Grants to individuals, totaling $212,359.
Type of support: Camperships.
Application information: Application form available on the grantmaker's web site.
Initial approach: Telephone, or e-mail
Deadline(s): Feb. 10
Final notification: Recipients notified Mar. 29

Additional information: Camp scholarships are need-based. See web site or contact the federation for additional guidelines.
EIN: 910575950

9644
The Ji Ji Foundation
2730 Westlake Ave. N.
Seattle, WA 98109-1916 (206) 328-2393
Contact: Anne McEnany
E-mail: anne@jiji.org; URL: http://www.jiji.org

Foundation type: Independent foundation
Purpose: Research grants to individuals for studies of human impact on the environment of the Pacific Coast. Also, small grants and research available for projects related to Baja California, Mexico.
Publications: Application guidelines; Grants list.
Financial data: Year ended 09/30/2012. Assets, $2,853,487 (M); Expenditures, $643,612; Total giving, $601,420; Grants to individuals, 4 grants totaling $79,822 (high: $67,522, low: $2,000).
Fields of interest: Research; Water pollution; Natural resources; Environment.
Type of support: Seed money; Research; Travel grants.
Application information: Applications accepted.
Initial approach: Letter
Send request by: E-mail
Copies of proposal: 1
Final notification: Response given in six to eight weeks
Applicants should submit the following:
1) Proposal
2) Curriculum vitae
3) Budget Information
Additional information: See web site for complete application deadline/guidelines.
EIN: 911664723

9645
The Jordan Fund
P.O. Box 606
Medina, WA 98039 (425) 829-1121
Contact: Huai-Jin Chong, Secy.
URL: http://www.jordanfund.org

Foundation type: Independent foundation
Purpose: Grants to support special needs children and their families.
Financial data: Year ended 12/31/2012. Assets, $4,462,671 (M); Expenditures, $248,104; Total giving, $137,310; Grants to individuals, 10 grants totaling $9,066 (high: $2,000, low: $110).
Fields of interest: Developmentally disabled, centers & services.
Type of support: Grants to individuals.
Application information: Applications accepted.
Initial approach: E-mail
Additional information: Contact foundation for current application guidelines.
EIN: 611437127

9646
JTM Foundation
14031 237th Pl. N.E.
Woodinville, WA 98077 (425) 844-8257
Contact: Thomas Miller, Pres.
E-mail: info@jtmfoundation.org; URL: http://www.jtmfoundation.org

Foundation type: Independent foundation
Purpose: Scholarships to international students for study at a christian college or university within the

U.S. with tuition, room and board, textbooks and course materials.
Financial data: Year ended 12/31/2012. Assets, $215,917 (M); Expenditures, $28,745; Total giving, $25,000; Grants to individuals, 4 grants totaling $25,000 (high: $8,000, low: $1,000).
Fields of interest: Higher education; Theological school/education.
Type of support: Scholarships—to individuals; Foreign applicants.
Application information: Applications accepted. Application form required. Application form available on the grantmaker's web site.
  Deadline(s): Before Spring
  Applicants should submit the following:
    1) Class rank
    2) Transcripts
    3) Letter(s) of recommendation
    4) GPA
  Additional information: Preference is given to U.S. members of the Council for Christian Colleges and Universities (CCCU). See web site for a list of preferred colleges/ universities.
EIN: 203456484

9647
Kawabe Memorial Fund
(also known as Harry S. Kawabe Trust)
c/o Bank of America, Philanthropic Mgmt.
P.O. Box 3977, WA1-501-33-23
Seattle, WA 98124-2477
Contact: Nancy Atkinson, V.P.
E-mail: nancy.l.atkinson@baml.com; Toll-free tel.: 1-800-848-7177; URL: http://fdnweb.org/kawabe

Foundation type: Independent foundation
Purpose: Scholarships to selected graduating seniors of Seward High School, AK.
Publications: Application guidelines.
Financial data: Year ended 12/31/2012. Assets, $3,970,274 (M); Expenditures, $211,628; Total giving, $158,100; Grants to individuals, 9 grants totaling $21,000 (high: $3,400, low: $1,750).
Fields of interest: Higher education; Scholarships/ financial aid; Athletics/sports, academies; Volunteer services; Leadership development.
Type of support: Scholarships—to individuals.
Application information: Applications accepted.
  Initial approach: Proposal
  Copies of proposal: 1
  Deadline(s): Second Fridays of Jan. (Spring cycle), April (Summer cycle) and Aug. (Fall cycle)
  Applicants should submit the following:
    1) Financial information
    2) Budget Information
EIN: 916116549

9648
Kedge Foundation
31620 23rd Ave. S., No. 218
Federal Way, WA 98003

Foundation type: Company-sponsored foundation
Purpose: Scholarships to residents of Snohomish, WA, who have a GPA of 3.0 or higher, and plan on pursuing a teaching-related career.
Financial data: Year ended 12/31/2012. Assets, $69 (M); Expenditures, $33,609; Total giving, $33,550.
Type of support: Undergraduate support.
Application information: Applications not accepted.

Additional information: Unsolicited requests for funds not considered or acknowledged.
EIN: 916506503

9649
Christopher R. Kelly Family Foundation
c/o Christopher R. Kelly
P.O. Box 99342
Seattle, WA 98139 (206) 674-1776
Application address: c/o Ewing C. Kelly Scholarship Fund, P.O. Box 19208, Seattle, WA 98109-1208, tel.: (206) 674-1776

Foundation type: Independent foundation
Purpose: Scholarships to students of the Seattle-Tacoma-Everett, WA, area for continuing education at accredited institutions of higher learning.
Financial data: Year ended 12/31/2011. Assets, $1,515,441 (M); Expenditures, $64,438; Total giving, $56,700.
Fields of interest: Higher education.
Type of support: Undergraduate support.
Application information: Applications accepted. Application form required.
  Initial approach: Letter
  Send request by: Mail
  Deadline(s): Mar. 10
  Final notification: Applicants are notified by Apr. 30
  Applicants should submit the following:
    1) Transcripts
    2) SAT
    3) Letter(s) of recommendation
    4) Financial information
  Additional information: Application should also include a personal statement. Applications can be obtained through the high school counselor. Funds are paid directly to the educational institution on behalf of the student.
EIN: 911876347

9650
Kelly Foundation of Washington
(formerly KCPQ-TV/Kelly Foundation of Washington)
1311 Colchester Dr., S.W.
Port Orchard, WA 98366 (206) 706-8486
Contact: Ewing C. Kelly
Application address: P. O. Box 19208, Seattle, WA 98109-1208, tel.: 206-706-8486

Foundation type: Independent foundation
Purpose: Scholarship to high school seniors from the Cascade Region of Washington.
Financial data: Year ended 12/31/2011. Assets, $3,160,447 (M); Expenditures, $173,873; Total giving, $129,000; Grants to individuals, 32 grants totaling $80,000 (high: $25,000, low: $2,500).
Fields of interest: Higher education; Scholarships/ financial aid.
Type of support: Undergraduate support.
Application information: Application form required.
  Send request by: Mail
  Deadline(s): Mar. 10
  Final notification: Recipients notified Apr. 30
  Applicants should submit the following:
    1) Letter(s) of recommendation
    2) ACT
    3) SAT
    4) Transcripts
    5) Financial information
  Additional information: Applications available through high school counselors.

Program description:
  Ewing C. Kelly Scholarship: Scholarships in the amount of $2,500 are awarded to students who demonstrate good citizenship while striving to attain their academic goals. Applicants are judged on academic merit, extra-curricular achievements- both scholastically and in their community- and financial need.
EIN: 911620836

9651
The Forest C. & Ruth V. Kelsey Foundation
P.O. Box 404
Montesano, WA 98563-0404
Contact: Charles Caldwell, Pres.
E-mail: kelsey@reachone.com

Foundation type: Independent foundation
Purpose: Scholarships to residents of Grays Harbor County, WA for postsecondary education.
Publications: Application guidelines.
Financial data: Year ended 12/31/2012. Assets, $10,881,423 (M); Expenditures, $678,599; Total giving, $532,774; Grants to individuals, 163 grants totaling $438,200 (high: $12,500, low: $900).
Type of support: Scholarships—to individuals.
Application information: Applications accepted. Application form required.
  Applicants should submit the following:
    1) Essay
    2) Budget Information
    3) Letter(s) of recommendation
    4) Transcripts
EIN: 912013369

9652
Kent Community Foundation
524 W. Meeker St., Ste. 1
Kent, WA 98032 (253) 854-1770
Scholarship application address: P.O. Box 128, Kent, WA 98035, e-mail: scholarships@kentcf.com
E-mail: info@kentcf.com; URL: http:// www.kentcf.org/

Foundation type: Community foundation
Purpose: Scholarships for students seeking higher education in the Greater Kent, WA area.
Publications: Application guidelines.
Financial data: Year ended 12/31/2012. Assets, $370,613 (M); Expenditures, $23,598; Total giving, $18,955; Grants to individuals, totaling $17,700.
Fields of interest: Higher education; Scholarships/ financial aid; Athletics/sports, school programs.
Type of support: Scholarships—to individuals.
Application information: Applications accepted. Application form required. Application form available on the grantmaker's web site.
  Initial approach: Application
  Send request by: Mail, on-line
  Deadline(s): Apr. 1 for foundation scholarships, May 27 for Armstrong Tennis Scholarship
  Applicants should submit the following:
    1) Transcripts
    2) Letter(s) of recommendation
    3) Financial information
  Additional information: See web site for application forms available through the foundation.
EIN: 911349506

9653
Almarie King Education Fund
1894 Vista Rama Dr., E.
Port Orchard, WA 98366 (360) 874-5600
Application address: c/o South Kitsap High School,
Attn.: Guidance Office, 425 Mitchell Ave., Port
Orchard, WA 98366-4114, tel.: (360) 874-5600

Foundation type: Independent foundation
Purpose: Scholarships to college bound graduating
seniors of South Kitsap High School, WA pursing a
career in education.
Financial data: Year ended 08/31/2012. Assets,
$129,657 (M); Expenditures, $135; Total giving,
$0.
Fields of interest: Higher education; Teacher
school/education.
Type of support: Support to graduates or students
of specific schools.
Application information: Applications accepted.
Application form required.
  Deadline(s): Mar. 31
  Additional information: Application available at
    high school.
EIN: 200117585

9654
Kitsap Community Foundation
9657 Levin Rd. NW, Ste. L08
P.O. Box 3670
Silverdale, WA 98383 (360) 698-3622
Contact: Kol Medina, Exec. Dir.
FAX: (360) 698-6043;
E-mail: kcf@kitsapfoundation.org; URL: http://
www.kitsapfoundation.org

Foundation type: Community foundation
Purpose: Scholarships to graduating students of
Kitsap County, WA, pursuing higher education.
Publications: Annual report; Biennial report;
Financial statement; Grants list; Informational
brochure; Newsletter.
Financial data: Year ended 09/30/2012. Assets,
$2,915,984 (M); Expenditures, $229,449; Total
giving, $110,825. Scholarships—to individuals
amount not specified.
Fields of interest: Higher education.
Type of support: Support to graduates or students
of specific schools; Undergraduate support.
Application information: Applications accepted.
Application form required. Application form
available on the grantmaker's web site.
  Initial approach: Application
  Send request by: Online
  Deadline(s): Mar. 15
  Final notification: Late May
  Additional information: Funds are paid directly to
    the educational institution on behalf of the
    students. See web site for available
    scholarships.
EIN: 943205217

9655
KLQ Education Foundation
P.O. Box 731087
Puyallup, WA 98373-0049 (253) 539-0516
URL: http://www.klqfoundation.org

Foundation type: Public charity
Purpose: Scholarships to WA students who wish to
pursue a bachelor's degree, associate degree, or
vocational training.
Publications: Application guidelines.
Financial data: Year ended 12/31/2011. Assets,
$214,897 (M); Expenditures, $40,583; Total

giving, $38,120; Grants to individuals, totaling
$28,000.
Fields of interest: Vocational education,
post-secondary; Higher education.
Type of support: Scholarships—to individuals.
Application information: Applications accepted.
Application form required. Application form
available on the grantmaker's web site.
  Initial approach: Application
  Send request by: Mail
  Deadline(s): Apr. 30
  Applicants should submit the following:
    1) Essay
    2) Financial information
    3) Letter(s) of recommendation
    4) Transcripts
    5) SAT
  Additional information: Application should also
    include a copy of parents W-2 form. Funds are
    paid directly to the educational institution on
    behalf of the students.
Program description:
  Scholarships: Scholarships of at least $1,000
each are awarded annually to students who are
interested in earning a bachelor's degree or
associate degree, or who wish to pursue vocational
training. Eligible applicants must be Washington
State residents who are in good standing, must
maintain at least a 2.8 GPA for academic
scholarships, and 2.0 GPA for vocational/technical
scholarships. Application is open to all Quality
Rentals employees' dependents as well as local
high school students and college students.
EIN: 200677836

9656
The KT Family Foundation
1423 Pacific Ave.
Tacoma, WA 98402-4203 (815) 675-2405
Contact: Kay Kargul
E-mail: scholarshipfoundations@davita.com;
Application addreess: 1991 Industrial Dr., DeLand,
FL 32724

Foundation type: Independent foundation
Purpose: Scholarships to children and
grandchildren of DaVita, Inc., employees for higher
education.
Financial data: Year ended 12/31/2012. Assets,
$221,340 (M); Expenditures, $63,322; Total
giving, $63,092; Grants to individuals, 32 grants
totaling $63,092 (high: $3,055, low: $472).
Fields of interest: Education.
Type of support: Undergraduate support.
Application information: Application form required.
  Send request by: Mail, or e-mail
  Deadline(s): Dec. 1
  Applicants should submit the following:
    1) Transcripts
    2) SAT
    3) Letter(s) of recommendation
    4) GPA
    5) ACT
    6) Essay
  Additional information: Applicants must
    demonstrate outstanding leadership,
    community service or academic performance.
EIN: 912151390

9657
Laurendeau Foundation for Cancer Care
P.O. Box 157
Bellingham, WA 98227-0157 (360) 650-1304
Contact: Kay Faulker

Foundation type: Operating foundation

Purpose: Grants to individuals residing in
Bellingham, WA, for outpatient cancer care.
Financial data: Year ended 09/30/2010. Assets,
$20,157 (M); Expenditures, $32,577; Total giving,
$22,123; Grants to individuals, 7 grants totaling
$22,123 (high: $5,468, low: $2,258).
Fields of interest: Medical care, outpatient care;
Cancer.
Type of support: Grants for special needs.
Application information: Applications accepted.
Application form required.
  Deadline(s): Monthly
EIN: 911121989

9658
Paul Lauzier Scholarship Foundation
117 Basin St. N.W.
P.O. Box 1230
Ephrata, WA 98823-1623 (509) 754-3209
Hand delivered address: 117 Basin St. N.W.,
Ephrata, WA
E-mail: ck.lauzier@nwi.net; URL: http://
www.lauzier.org/scholarship-foundation

Foundation type: Independent foundation
Purpose: Scholarships to graduates of Grant
County, WA, high schools who attend a college or
vocational school full time within the State of
Washington. Scholarships to students pursuing
graduate degrees.
Publications: Application guidelines.
Financial data: Year ended 12/31/2012. Assets,
$3,058 (M); Expenditures, $442,216; Total giving,
$438,200; Grants to individuals, 195 grants
totaling $438,200 (high: $5,000, low: $1,000).
Fields of interest: Vocational education,
post-secondary; Higher education.
Type of support: Support to graduates or students
of specific schools; Graduate support;
Undergraduate support.
Application information: Applications accepted.
Application form required. Application form
available on the grantmaker's web site.
  Send request by: Mail or hand deliver
  Deadline(s): Mar. 7
  Applicants should submit the following:
    1) Letter(s) of recommendation
    2) Essay
    3) Transcripts
  Additional information: Applicants must reside in
    Grant county for a minimum of two years prior
    to high school graduation. See web site for
    additional application guidelines.
EIN: 911701545

9659
Margaretta Leavitt Trust
c/o Wells Fargo Bank, N. A.
P.O. Box 21927
Seattle, WA 98111-3927

Foundation type: Independent foundation
Purpose: Scholarships to high school graduates
from the Basin-Greybull area of Big Horn County, WY
for attendance at colleges or universities.
Financial data: Year ended 12/31/2012. Assets,
$136,158 (M); Expenditures, $9,460; Total giving,
$6,000.
Fields of interest: Higher education.
Type of support: Scholarships—to individuals.
Application information: Applications accepted.
EIN: 816091115

9660
Legal Foundation of Washington
1325 Fourth Ave., Ste. 1335
Seattle, WA 98101-2509 (206) 624-2536
Contact: Caitlin Davis Carlson, Exec. Dir.; Dee
Thierry, Office Mgr.
FAX: (206) 382-3396;
E-mail: caitlindc@legalfoundation.org; URL: http://
www.legalfoundation.org

Foundation type: Public charity
Purpose: Summer internships to second-year law
students and above and recent graduates from law
schools across the country for internships with
Washington state nonprofits that provide civil legal
services to the poor.
Publications: Application guidelines; Annual report.
Financial data: Year ended 12/31/2011. Assets,
$8,725,706 (M); Expenditures, $6,350,411; Total
giving, $5,422,846.
Fields of interest: Law school/education; Legal
services, public interest law.
Type of support: Internship funds.
Application information: Applications accepted.
Application form not required. Interview required.
Initial approach: Letter
Copies of proposal: 1
Deadline(s): 2nd Fri. in Oct.
Final notification: Recipients notified 1st Fri. in
Nov. of each year
Applicants should submit the following:
1) Transcripts
2) Resume
3) GPA
4) Essay
Additional information: Unofficial transcript
reflecting current law school enrollment, and
resume with letter required; See web site for
guidelines.
Program description:
Goldmark Internships: The foundation provides
summer internships with specific host programs to
second-year law students. Internships are
advertised with more than 50 schools nationwide.
Three to five finalists are invited for interview.
EIN: 911263533

9661
Lifelong AIDS Alliance
(formerly Northwest AIDS Foundation-Chicken Soup
Brigade)
1002 E. Seneca St.
Seattle, WA 98122-4214 (206) 328-8979
Contact: Randall H. Russell, C.E.O.
FAX: (206) 957-1736; TDD: (206) 323-2685;
URL: http://www.lifelongaidsalliance.org

Foundation type: Public charity
Purpose: Emergency assistance for people living
with HIV/AIDS in King County, WA.
Publications: Annual report.
Financial data: Year ended 06/30/2012. Assets,
$3,054,857 (M); Expenditures, $27,416,336;
Total giving, $21,717,664; Grants to individuals,
totaling $21,707,027.
Fields of interest: AIDS.
Type of support: Grants for special needs.
Application information: Applications accepted.
Initial approach: Letter or telephone
Deadline(s): Fall
Additional information: Contact King Co. Case
Manager for current application guidelines.
EIN: 911215715

9662
William and Esther Littlejohn Foundation
550 W. Hendrickson Rd.
Sequim, WA 98382-3013 (360) 681-4882
Contact: Bill Littlejohn, Dir.

Foundation type: Operating foundation
Purpose: Scholarships to students in the
geographical area of the Sequi School Disctrict,
Callam County, WA. Also, scholarships to students
attending Walla Walla College, WA, and Auburn
Adventist Academy, WA.
Financial data: Year ended 12/31/2012. Assets,
$1,019,304 (M); Expenditures, $74,695; Total
giving, $53,750.
Type of support: Support to graduates or students
of specific schools.
Application information: Applications accepted.
Deadline(s): Sept. 1
EIN: 912135270

9663
The Lochland Foundation
P.O. Box 327
Medina, WA 98039 (425) 548-3482
Contact: Katherine Binder, Secy.-Treas.
Application address: 90 Cascade Key, Bellevue, WA
98006, Tel.: (425) 548-3482

Foundation type: Company-sponsored foundation
Purpose: Scholarships to high school students in
the Seattle, Washington area with demonstrated
financial need.
Financial data: Year ended 12/31/2012. Assets,
$9,457,603 (M); Expenditures, $219,880; Total
giving, $210,500.
Fields of interest: Higher education.
Type of support: Scholarships—to individuals.
Application information: Applications accepted.
Application form required.
Initial approach: Application
Send request by: Mail
Applicants should submit the following:
1) Transcripts
2) Letter(s) of recommendation
3) Financial information
4) Essay
Additional information: Contact foundation for
application information.
EIN: 510420961

9664
Lower Columbia Community Action
Council, Inc.
(also known as Lower Columbia Community Action
Partnership)
1526 Commerce Ave.
P.O. Box 2129
Longview, WA 98632-8232 (360) 425-3430
Contact: Mary Gillespie, Pres.
FAX: (360) 425-6657; E-mail: lisam@lccac.org;
Toll-free tel.: (800) 383-2101; URL: http://
www.lccac.org

Foundation type: Public charity
Purpose: Assistance for low and moderate income
households with energy and rental assistance,
housing rehabilitation, weatherization and other
special needs in the lower Columbia County, WA
area.
Publications: Annual report.
Financial data: Year ended 12/31/2011. Assets,
$6,438,031 (M); Expenditures, $9,115,723; Total
giving, $1,832,949; Grants to individuals, totaling
$1,832,949.

Fields of interest: Employment; Human services;
Community/economic development; Economically
disadvantaged.
Type of support: Grants for special needs.
Application information:
Initial approach: Telephone
Additional information: Contact the agency for
eligibility determination.
EIN: 910814141

9665
Maynard A. Lundberg Education
1590 Bay St.
Port Orchard, WA 98366-5104 (360) 874-5600

Foundation type: Independent foundation
Purpose: Scholarships to college bound graduating
seniors of South Kitsap High School, WA for higher
education.
Financial data: Year ended 06/30/2013. Assets,
$123,434 (M); Expenditures, $8,200; Total giving,
$7,000; Grants to individuals, 7 grants totaling
$7,000 (high: $1,000, low: $1,000).
Fields of interest: Higher education.
Type of support: Scholarships—to individuals.
Application information: Applications accepted.
Application form required.
Deadline(s): May 1
Additional information: Application can be
obtained from high school.
EIN: 911231450

9666
Lynden Memorial Scholarship Fund
P.O. Box 3757
Seattle, WA 98124-3757 (507) 931-1682

Foundation type: Operating foundation
Purpose: Scholarships to dependents of full-time
employees of Lynden, Inc. and its subsidiaries.
Financial data: Year ended 12/31/2012. Assets,
$34,815 (M); Expenditures, $10,495; Total giving,
$9,000; Grants to individuals, 6 grants totaling
$9,000 (high: $1,500, low: $1,500).
Type of support: Employee-related scholarships.
Application information: Applications not
accepted.
Additional information: Unsolicited requests for
funds not considered.
EIN: 911684708

9667
The Market Foundation
85 Pike St., Rm. 500
Seattle, WA 98101-2096 (206) 682-7453
Contact: Lillian Hochstein, Exec. Dir.
FAX: (206) 682-7447;
E-mail: mktfoundation@pikeplacemarket.org;
E-Mail for Lillian Hochstein:
lillian.hochstein@pikeplacemarket.org; Tel. for
Lillian Hochstein: (206)-774-5246; URL: http://
www.pikeplacemarketfoundation.org

Foundation type: Public charity
Purpose: Services for Seattle's low-income
residents, including medical clinics, senior citizen
services, childcare, and food bank.
Publications: Annual report; Newsletter.
Financial data: Year ended 03/31/2012. Assets,
$3,745,287 (M); Expenditures, $1,005,618; Total
giving, $771,810.
Fields of interest: Aging; Minorities; Economically
disadvantaged; Homeless.
Type of support: In-kind gifts.

Application information:
Initial approach: Letter
Additional information: Contact foundation for eligibility criteria.
EIN: 911197625

9668
The Edgar and Holli Martinez Foundation

P.O. Box 50740
Bellevue, WA 98015
E-mail: info@themartinezfoundation.org;
URL: http://themartinezfoundation.com/

Foundation type: Independent foundation
Purpose: Ten undergraduate scholarships of $20,000 each, awarded annually for Latino students in Washington State pursuing careers in education. Scholarships and support programs for graduate students of color to achieve a Master in Teaching degree from the University of Washington, Washington State University, and Seattle University. Students must maintain at least a 2.7 G.P.A.
Financial data: Year ended 12/31/2012. Assets, $1,242 (M); Expenditures, $35,453; Total giving, $35,000.
Fields of interest: Teacher school/education; Minorities; Hispanics/Latinos.
Type of support: Scholarships—to individuals; Support to graduates or students of specific schools.
Application information: See web site for complete scholarship information.
EIN: 261232520

9669
Edmund F. Maxwell Foundation

c/o David G. Johansen
P.O. Box 55548
Seattle, WA 98155-0548
E-mail: admin@maxwell.org; URL: http://www.maxwell.org

Foundation type: Independent foundation
Purpose: Scholarships to residents of western WA requiring financial aid and who are entering or attending accredited, private institutions of higher learning in the western WA state area.
Financial data: Year ended 12/31/2012. Assets, $8,035,674 (M); Expenditures, $400,108; Total giving, $256,671; Grants to individuals, 57 grants totaling $256,271 (high: $5,000, low: $1,981).
Fields of interest: Higher education; Scholarships/financial aid.
Type of support: Scholarships—to individuals; Undergraduate support.
Application information: Applications accepted. Application form required. Application form available on the grantmaker's web site.
Initial approach: Letter, e-mail or web site
Send request by: Mail
Deadline(s): Apr. 30
Final notification: Recipients notified about two months after receipt of application
Applicants should submit the following:
1) GPA
2) Essay
3) Transcripts
4) SAT
5) Financial information
6) ACT
Additional information: Application must also include employment history, and a personal statement.
EIN: 916181008

9670
Frank McCleary Medical Scholarship Fund

(formerly Frank McCleary Medical Scholarship Fund of the Mary Ball Chapter for the Daughters of the American Revolution)
P.O. Box 226
Kapowsin, WA 98344 (253) 318-5679
Contact: Lynne Stallcop

Foundation type: Independent foundation
Purpose: Scholarships to worthy students primarily in the Seattle, WA, area who are U.S. citizens and are enrolled in approved medical schools, colleges, or universities.
Financial data: Year ended 12/31/2012. Assets, $78,474 (M); Expenditures, $22,827; Total giving, $22,400.
Fields of interest: Medical school/education.
Type of support: Graduate support; Undergraduate support.
Application information: Applications accepted. Application form required.
Additional information: Contact foundation for current application deadline/guidelines.
EIN: 510158972

9671
McCoy Scholarship Fund

481 Watkins Way
Yakima, WA 98908-8848 (509) 966-2872

Foundation type: Public charity
Purpose: Scholarships to Highland High School, WA, graduates for higher education.
Financial data: Year ended 12/31/2011. Assets, $425,065 (M); Expenditures, $29,118; Total giving, $15,000.
Fields of interest: Higher education.
Type of support: Scholarships—to individuals.
Application information: Applications accepted.
Initial approach: Contact fund
Program description:
Scholarship Program: The fund provides scholarships between $1,000 and $3,000 for graduating students of Highland High School.
EIN: 916389327

9672
B. Corry and Donna J. McFarland Foundation

P.O. Box 1496
Tacoma, WA 98401-1496 (253) 572-3033

Foundation type: Independent foundation
Purpose: Scholarships to students of the Tacoma, WA area for continuing education at institutions of higher learning.
Financial data: Year ended 12/31/2011. Assets, $14,500 (M); Expenditures, $47,350; Total giving, $42,200.
Fields of interest: Higher education.
Type of support: Scholarships—to individuals.
Application information: Application form required.
Deadline(s): None
Additional information: Application can be obtained from the foundation. Application should include transcripts.
EIN: 916571187

9673
The Robert B. McMillen Foundation

P.O. Box 176
Cle Elum, WA 98922-0176 (425) 313-5711
E-mail: Cassandra@mcmillenfoundation.org;
URL: http://www.mcmillenfoundation.org

Foundation type: Independent foundation
Purpose: Scholarships to students for attendance at accredited institutions of higher learning within the states of Washington and Alaska majoring in the area of visual arts.
Financial data: Year ended 12/31/2012. Assets, $9,413,676 (M); Expenditures, $744,500; Total giving, $497,522; Grants to individuals, 2 grants totaling $57,404 (high: $37,337, low: $20,067).
Fields of interest: Visual arts.
Type of support: Scholarships—to individuals.
Application information: Applications accepted. Application form required. Application form available on the grantmaker's web site. Interview required.
Applicants should submit the following:
1) Transcripts
2) GPA
3) Financial information
4) Essay
Additional information: Applicants must demonstrate outstanding performance in the area of visual art. See web site for additional application guidelines.
EIN: 200011616

9674
Memorial Scholarship of Henry Groth Elsinor Groth and Wayne Elder

c/o Columbia Bank Trust Services
P.O. Box 2156
Tacoma, WA 98401-2156 (360) 473-1000
Application address: c/o Bremerton School District, Attn.: Groth Memorial Scholarship Committee, 134 Marion Ave. N, Bremerton, WA 98312-3542, tel.: (360) 473-1000

Foundation type: Independent foundation
Purpose: Scholarships to graduating seniors from a high school within the geographic boundaries of the Bremerton Washington School District #100-C for attendance at an academic institution of higher learning within the state of WA offering a two or four year academic degree.
Financial data: Year ended 12/31/2011. Assets, $1,592,945 (M); Expenditures, $99,274; Total giving, $80,167.
Fields of interest: Higher education.
Type of support: Scholarships—to individuals.
Application information: Applications accepted. Application form required.
Additional information: Programs focused exclusively on vocational, trade or graduate courses of study are excluded.
EIN: 207271091

9675
Metropolitan Development Council

721 S. Fawcett Ave., Ste. 201
Tacoma, WA 98402-5502 (253) 383-3921
Contact: P. Mark Pereboom, Pres. and C.E.O.
FAX: (253) 593-2400; *TDD:* (253) 591-0147;
URL: http://www.mdc-tacoma.org

Foundation type: Public charity
Purpose: Assistance to low-income residents of Tacoma, WA, with emergency home repairs for the elderly and disabled, energy conservation, health care, and housing assistance.

Financial data: Year ended 12/31/2011. Assets, $16,048,122 (M); Expenditures, $16,605,213; Total giving, $6,580,936; Grants to individuals, totaling $6,580,936.
Fields of interest: Housing/shelter, repairs; Aging; Disabilities, people with.
Type of support: Grants for special needs.
Application information: Contact council for eligibility criteria.
EIN: 910780533

9676
Milton-Freewater Area Foundation
c/o Baker Boyer Trust
P.O. Box 1796
Walla Walla, WA 99362   (509) 525-2000

Foundation type: Independent foundation
Purpose: Scholarships to residents of Milton-Freewater, OR.
Financial data: Year ended 12/31/2012. Assets, $2,619,440 (M); Expenditures, $92,684; Total giving, $72,988.
Type of support: Scholarships—to individuals.
Application information: Applications accepted.
  Additional information: Contact foundation for application guidelines.
EIN: 936025936

9677
Mortar Board Alumni-Tolo Foundation
P.O. Box 53162
Bellevue, WA 98015-3162   (206) 000-0000
E-mail: toloscholars@gmail.com; URL: http://mortarboardtolo.org/

Foundation type: Independent foundation
Purpose: Scholarships to undergraduate and graduate students at the University of Washington and its branch campuses.
Financial data: Year ended 05/31/2013. Assets, $769,413 (M); Expenditures, $38,866; Total giving, $35,000; Grants to individuals, 15 grants totaling $35,000 (high: $2,500, low: $1,000).
Fields of interest: Higher education.
Type of support: Graduate support; Undergraduate support.
Application information: Applications accepted. Application form required. Interview required.
  Send request by: Mail
  Copies of proposal: 3
  Deadline(s): May 4
  Applicants should submit the following:
    1) Transcripts
    2) Letter(s) of recommendation
    3) Essay
  Additional information: Application must also include extracurricular activities.
EIN: 916054386

9678
Museum of Glass
1801 E. Dock St.
Tacoma, WA 98402-3217   (253) 284-4750
Contact: Susan Warner, Exec. Dir.
FAX: (253) 396-1769;
E-mail: info@museumofglass.org; E-Mail for Susan Warner: swarner@museumofglass.org;
URL: http://www.museumofglass.org

Foundation type: Public charity
Purpose: Residencies by invitation to artists.
Publications: Annual report; Newsletter.
Financial data: Year ended 06/30/2012. Assets, $24,510,062 (M); Expenditures, $4,961,698.

Fields of interest: Visual arts.
Type of support: Internship funds; Residencies.
Application information: Applications accepted. Application form required. Application form available on the grantmaker's web site.
  Initial approach: Web site
  Send request by: Mail or e-mail
  Copies of proposal: 1
  Deadline(s): None
Program description:
  Visiting Artist Residency: This program invites internationally-known artists and emerging artists from around the world to work with the museum's resident Hot Shop Team to explore, invent, and create with glass. Offering a diverse mixture of culture, style, focus, and expertise, each artist creates a sense of excitement and wonder for visitors who are given the rare opportunity to witness art being made. Currently, the Visiting Artist residency program is by invitation only.
EIN: 911669422

9679
National Intercollegiate Rodeo Foundation
2033 Walla Walla Ave.
Walla Walla, WA 99362   (509) 529-4402

Foundation type: Independent foundation
Purpose: Scholarships to individuals attending a National Intercollegiate Rodeo Association member college who maintain at least a 3.0 GPA, and meet state financial assistance qualifications.
Financial data: Year ended 06/30/2013. Assets, $1,013,550 (M); Expenditures, $143,427; Total giving, $69,250; Grants to individuals, 4 grants totaling $2,250 (high: $750, low: $500).
Fields of interest: Athletics/sports, equestrianism.
Type of support: Undergraduate support.
Application information: Application form required.
  Initial approach: Letter
  Deadline(s): May 1
  Additional information: Application can be obtained from the foundation.
EIN: 911659631

9680
Native Arts and Cultures Foundation
11109 N.E. 14th St.
Vancouver, WA 98684   (360) 314-2421
Contact: Tara Lulani Arquette, Pres. and C.E.O.; Marshall McKay, Chair.
FAX: (360) 718-2553;
E-mail: info@nativeartsandcultures.org;
URL: http://nativeartsandcultures.org/

Foundation type: Public charity
Purpose: Fellowships to individual Native artists for creation of new work and career development.
Financial data: Year ended 12/31/2011. Assets, $11,309,923 (M); Expenditures, $1,791,713; Total giving, $530,287; Grants to individuals, totaling $86,450.
Fields of interest: Folk arts; Film/video; Visual arts; Ceramic arts; Dance; Music; Literature; Native Americans/American Indians.
Type of support: Fellowships.
Application information: Applications accepted. Application form required. Application form available on the grantmaker's web site.
  Initial approach: Application
  Deadline(s): June 21
  Final notification: Recipients notified in Nov.
Program description:
  Artist Fellowships: These fellowships, which are designed to support Native artists working in dance,

filmmaking, literature, music, traditional arts, and visual arts, are open to American Indian, Alaska Native, and Native Hawaiian artists. Grants of $20,000 will be awarded in recognition of the creativity and expression of exceptional Native artists who have had significant impact in their respective disciplines. To be eligible, artists must be members of federally and state-recognized tribes, Alaska Native, or Native Hawaiian communities.
EIN: 261595870

9681
Roy and Leona Nelson Foundation
P.O. Box 965
Spokane, WA 99210-0965

Foundation type: Independent foundation
Purpose: College scholarships to high school graduates from eastern Washington or northern Idaho high schools for full time study at North Idaho College.
Financial data: Year ended 12/31/2013. Assets, $2,589,190 (M); Expenditures, $133,682; Total giving, $118,000; Grants to individuals, 48 grants totaling $91,000 (high: $2,000, low: $1,000).
Fields of interest: Higher education.
Type of support: Support to graduates or students of specific schools.
Application information: Application form required.
  Deadline(s): Mar. 16
  Applicants should submit the following:
    1) Transcripts
    2) Letter(s) of recommendation
    3) Financial information
    4) FAFSA
  Additional information: Applicant must submit a one page letter describing background, interests, and academic and career goals.
EIN: 710899453

9682
Nikkei Alumni Association
(formerly University Students Club, Inc.)
4021 - 49th Ave. S.
Seattle, WA 98118   (206) 932-8051
Application address: c/o Scholarship Committee, 2703 36th Ave., S.W., Seattle, WA 98126

Foundation type: Independent foundation
Purpose: Scholarships to students of Japanese ancestry planning to attend the University of Washington, Seattle, WA on a full-time basis.
Financial data: Year ended 06/30/2012. Assets, $320,862 (M); Expenditures, $15,366; Total giving, $13,500; Grants to individuals, 6 grants totaling $13,500 (high: $3,000, low: $2,000).
Fields of interest: Higher education; Asians/Pacific Islanders.
Type of support: Support to graduates or students of specific schools.
Application information: Application form required.
  Deadline(s): Apr. 15
  Applicants should submit the following:
    1) GPA
    2) Financial information
  Additional information: Application available from the University of Washington.
EIN: 916035190

9683
North Helpline

12736 33rd Ave. N.E.
Seattle, WA 98125-4504   (206) 367-3477
Contact: Rita Anderson, Exec. Dir.
E-mail: ed@northhelpline.org; URL: http://
www.northhelpline.org

Foundation type: Public charity
Purpose: Provides assistance to indigent residents of North Seattle, WA in the form of services such as money for evictions and utility shutoffs, emergency food, hygiene items, baby cupboard distribution, medical care, referrals to other agencies and organizations and counseling as needed.
Publications: Newsletter.
Financial data: Year ended 12/31/2011. Assets, $1,884,509 (M); Expenditures, $2,254,147; Total giving, $1,943,158; Grants to individuals, totaling $1,943,158.
Fields of interest: Economically disadvantaged.
Type of support: In-kind gifts.
Application information:
  Initial approach: Letter
  Additional information: Contact foundation for eligibility criteria.
EIN: 911475182

9684
Northwest Danish Foundation

(also known as Northwest Danish Association)
1833 N. 105th St., Ste. 101
Seattle, WA 98133-8973   (206) 523-3263
FAX: (206) 729-6997;
E-mail: seattle@nwdanish.org; Toll-free tel. (Seattle office): (800) 564-7736; additional address (Portland office): 4330 N.E. 37th Ave., Portland, OR 97211-8208; URL: http://
www.northwestdanishfoundation.org

Foundation type: Public charity
Purpose: Scholarships only to WA and OR residents, who are either of Danish descent or married to someone of Danish descent, and have shown exceptional involvement in the Danish community. Consideration is also given to those who are not of Danish descent, but only if they have been exceptionally involved in the Danish community.
Publications: Application guidelines; Annual report; Newsletter.
Financial data: Year ended 06/30/2012. Assets, $1,640,783 (M); Expenditures, $136,290; Total giving, $8,500; Grants to individuals, totaling $8,500.
Fields of interest: Language (foreign); Arts; Vocational education.
International interests: Denmark.
Type of support: Scholarships—to individuals.
Application information: Applications accepted. Application form required.
  Initial approach: Letter, telephone, or e-mail
  Deadline(s): Mar. 31
  Final notification: Applicants notified early May
  Applicants should submit the following:
    1) Transcripts
    2) Essay
  Additional information: Application should also include information on Danish background, a character reference, educational reference, and Danish community reference.
Program descriptions:
  scan/design Foundation by Inger and Jens Bruun Scholarship: An annual scholarship of $5,000 each will be available to a student for study in Denmark. Eligible applicants must be 18 years of age or older who wishes to study (in an academic, vocational, or cultural/artistic setting) in Denmark, and who is either a current resident of Oregon or Washington, or who is a student currently registered in a school, university, or other recognized institution of learning in Oregon or Washington.
  The Kaj Christiansen Scholarship for Vocational Training: Each year, the foundation awards a $500 scholarship in support of vocational training. Eligible applicants must: be current members of the association or, upon the receipt of the award, be willing to join at the student level; demonstrate a connection to Denmark through life experiences, travel, study abroad, field of study, or heritage; reside in Oregon or Washington, or be enrolled in an accredited school in Oregon or Washington; and be seeking a academic degree, vocational degree, or re-training for employment possibilities, or be in training for a legitimate artistic career.
EIN: 910565541

9685
Northwest Film Forum

1515 12th Ave.
Seattle, WA 98122-3907   (206) 329-2629
Contact: Lyall Bush, Exec. Dir.
FAX: (206) 329-1193;
E-mail: adams@nwfilmforum.org; E-mail for Lyall Bush: lyall@nwfilmforum.org; URL: http://
www.nwfilmforum.org

Foundation type: Public charity
Purpose: Support to artists who are WA residents through a fiscal sponsorship program.
Publications: Application guidelines.
Financial data: Year ended 09/30/2012. Assets, $303,151 (M); Expenditures, $740,249; Total giving, $11,068; Grants to individuals, totaling $11,068.
Fields of interest: Film/video; Arts, artist's services.
Type of support: Fiscal agent/sponsor.
Application information: Applications accepted.
  Copies of proposal: 1
  Applicants should submit the following:
    1) Proposal
    2) Work samples
  Additional information: See web site for further information.
Program description:
  Fiscal Sponsorship: Through this program, members in good standing may have their projects sponsored. Projects are selected by the board of directors based on artistic merit, organization, and artist need.
EIN: 911702331

9686
Northwest Harvest E.M M.

P.O. Box 12272
Seattle, WA 98102-0272   (206) 625-0755
Contact: Shelley Rotondo, C.E.O.
FAX: (206) 682-3114;
E-mail: info@northwestharvest.org; Additional address (Yakima office): P.O. Box 297, Yakima, WA 98907-0297; Toll Free Tel.: (800)-722-6924; URL: http://www.northwestharvest.org

Foundation type: Public charity
Purpose: Emergency assistance to low-income individuals and families in need of northwest, WA.
Publications: Annual report.
Financial data: Year ended 06/30/2012. Assets, $22,089,165 (M); Expenditures, $40,067,167; Total giving, $32,494,824; Grants to individuals, totaling $1,907,500.
Fields of interest: Economically disadvantaged.

Type of support: Emergency funds; In-kind gifts.
Application information: Contact the agency for assistance.
EIN: 910826037

9687
Northwest Lions Foundation for Sight & Hearing

(formerly Lions Sight and Hearing Foundation of Washington & Northern Idaho)
221 Yale Ave. N., Ste. 450
Seattle, WA 98109-5490   (206) 682-8500
Contact: Monty Montoya, Pres. and C.E.O.
FAX: (206) 838-4627;
E-mail: info@nlfoundation.org; Toll-free tel.: (800) 847-5786; URL: http://www.nlfoundation.org

Foundation type: Public charity
Purpose: Grants to blind and deaf individuals in WA and northern ID, for medical expenses including surgical costs, purchase of hearing aids, and guide-dog training fees. Applicants must be sponsored by a local Lions Club or Lions organization.
Publications: Application guidelines; Informational brochure (including application guidelines); Newsletter.
Financial data: Year ended 12/31/2011. Assets, $10,235,153 (M); Expenditures, $14,938,745; Total giving, $551,716; Grants to individuals, totaling $73,416.
Fields of interest: Health care; Disabilities, people with; Blind/visually impaired; Deaf/hearing impaired.
Type of support: Grants for special needs.
Application information: Application form required.
  Initial approach: Letter
  Deadline(s): Contact foundation for current application deadline
EIN: 237051021

9688
Omega of Sigma Pi Foundation

12909 N.E., 22nd St.
Vancouver, WA 98684   (360) 896-7279
Contact: Don Fitzgerald, Pres.
Application address: 8800 N.E. 58th St., Vancouver, WA 98684 Tel.: (360) 896-7279

Foundation type: Operating foundation
Purpose: Student loans primarily to individuals beyond their sophomore year at a four year university with preference to those attending Oregon State University. Scholarships and/or grants may be provided when funds allow.
Financial data: Year ended 12/31/2013. Assets, $51,886 (M); Expenditures, $81; Total giving, $0.
Fields of interest: Higher education.
Type of support: Student loans—to individuals.
Application information: Applications accepted. Application form required.
  Initial approach: Letter
  Deadline(s): None
EIN: 237191514

9689
Opportunity Council

1111 Cornwall Ave., Ste. C
Bellingham, WA 98225-5039   (360) 734-5121
FAX: (360) 649-5121; Toll-free tel. (Whatcom County): (800) 649-5121; toll-free tel. (San Juan County): (800) 649-2440; additional address (Island County): 1791 N.E. 1st Ave., P.O. Box 922, Oak Harbor, WA 98277-4301, tel. (360) 679-6577,

toll-free tel.: (800) 317-5427, fax: (360) 679-2440;
URL: http://www.oppco.org

Foundation type: Public charity
Purpose: Services to indigent residents of
northwest WA in the form of food, energy
assistance, weatherization, home repairs,
emergency housing, and child care.
Financial data: Year ended 12/31/2011. Assets,
$11,630,105 (M); Expenditures, $23,286,244;
Total giving, $6,817,411; Grants to individuals,
totaling $6,179,954.
Fields of interest: Economically disadvantaged.
Type of support: In-kind gifts.
Application information:
  Initial approach: Telephone
  Additional information: Contact foundation for
    eligibility criteria.
EIN: 910787820

9690
Osteopathic Foundation of Central Washington
(formerly Osteopathic Foundation of Yakima)
P.O. Box 553
Yakima, WA 98907
URL: http://ofcw.org

Foundation type: Independent foundation
Purpose: Scholarships to residents of the Pacific
Northwest who have lived, worked or attended
institutions of higher education in the Pacific
Northwest and enrolled in an American Osteopathic
Association approved school.
Financial data: Year ended 12/31/2012. Assets,
$100,975 (M); Expenditures, $1,148,452; Total
giving, $1,105,750; Grants to individuals, totaling
$80,000.
Fields of interest: Medical school/education.
Type of support: Scholarships—to individuals.
Application information: Applications accepted.
Application form available on the grantmaker's web
site.
  Deadline(s): June 15
  Final notification: Recipients notified in July
  Applicants should submit the following:
    1) Transcripts
    2) Letter(s) of recommendation
  Additional information: See web site for
    additional application information.
EIN: 911640626

9691
Overlake Hospital Auxiliaries
1035 116th Ave. N.E.
Bellevue, WA 98004-4604   (425) 688-5000
Contact: David Aubrey, Exec. Dir.

Foundation type: Public charity
Purpose: Financial assistance for patients in need
at Overlake Medical Center with medical expense,
and assistance for employees of Overlake Hospital
Medical Center due to hardship.
Financial data: Year ended 06/30/2011. Assets,
$831,109 (M); Expenditures, $981,022; Total
giving, $785,424; Grants to individuals, totaling
$7,667.
Fields of interest: Human services; Economically
disadvantaged.
Type of support: Grants for special needs.
Application information: Applications not
accepted.
  Additional information: Unsolicited requests for
    funds not considered or acknowledged.
EIN: 237297831

9692
Pace 8-591 Fallen Workers Memorial Scholarship
47 Alder Ln.
Mount Vernon, WA 98273   (360) 424-3361
URL: http://www.usw12-591.org/

Foundation type: Independent foundation
Purpose: Scholarships to students attending high
schools in Island, Skagit, Snohomish and Whatcom
counties, WA, and to children of Pace Union
members.
Financial data: Year ended 06/30/2013. Assets,
$1,101,308 (M); Expenditures, $57,322; Total
giving, $41,900; Grants to individuals, 51 grants
totaling $41,900 (high: $4,500, low: -$7,500).
Fields of interest: Higher education.
Type of support: Support to graduates or students
of specific schools; Undergraduate support.
Application information: Application form required.
  Deadline(s): Mar. 1
  Applicants should submit the following:
    1) GPA
    2) Essay
EIN: 911986402

9693
Pacific Northwest Ballet Association
301 Mercer St.
Seattle, WA 98109-4600   (206) 441-2424
Contact: D. David Brown, Exec. Dir.
Application tel.: (206) 441-2435
FAX: (206) 441-2420; *E-mail:* marketing@pnb.org;
URL: http://www.pnb.org

Foundation type: Public charity
Purpose: Scholarships to dance students for
furthering their dance education.
Publications: Annual report; Financial statement.
Financial data: Year ended 06/30/2012. Assets,
$8,171,752 (M); Expenditures, $20,901,696;
Total giving, $97,133; Grants to individuals,
totaling $97,133.
Fields of interest: Dance.
Type of support: Scholarships—to individuals.
Application information: Application form required.
  Additional information: Scholarship forms are
    available from the school and must be
    submitted with a $24 application fee.
Program description:
  Scholarship Program: The association provides a
limited number of full and partial scholarship for
students attending ballet school. Scholarships are
awarded on the basis of financial need, class
performance, and potential for a professional
career, and are granted for up to one academic
year.
EIN: 910897129

9694
Jessie Pepper Padelford Scholarship Fund-Sigma Kappa Alumnae
19312 64th Pl. N.E.
Kenmore, WA 98028
Contact: Pamela A. Martin, Treas.

Foundation type: Independent foundation
Purpose: Scholarships to qualified students at the
University of Washington, WA pursuing higher
education.
Financial data: Year ended 07/31/2013. Assets,
$256,614 (M); Expenditures, $16,183; Total
giving, $15,550; Grants to individuals, 15 grants
totaling $15,550 (high: $7,000, low: $50).
Fields of interest: Higher education.

Type of support: Support to graduates or students
of specific schools.
Application information: Applications accepted.
  Deadline(s): None
  Additional information: Awards are based on
    academic performance.
EIN: 911067412

9695
PAH Foundation
500 108th Ave. N.E., Ste. 1750
Bellevue, WA 98004-5576
Contact: Peter A. Horvitz, Pres.

Foundation type: Independent foundation
Purpose: Scholarships to high school seniors who
reside in Lake, Lorain, Richland, Tuscarawas, OH or
Rensselaer, NY counties.
Financial data: Year ended 12/31/2012. Assets,
$305,363 (M); Expenditures, $601,133; Total
giving, $578,292.
Fields of interest: Higher education.
Type of support: Scholarships—to individuals.
Application information: Applications accepted.
Application form required.
  Deadline(s): Apr. 1
  Additional information: Selection is based on
    student with average or above average and
    demonstrate financial need.
EIN: 911866138

9696
R. Merle Palmer Minority Scholarship Foundation
P.O. Box 7119
Tacoma, WA 98417-0119   (253) 572-9008
Contact: Sally Jo Bose, Exec.Dir.
E-mail: info@palmerscholars.org; *URL:* http://
www.palmerscholars.org

Foundation type: Public charity
Purpose: Scholarships to low income minority
graduating high school students who are residents
of Pierce county, WA for postsecondary education
at the college of their choice.
Publications: Newsletter.
Financial data: Year ended 06/30/2012. Assets,
$226,704 (M); Expenditures, $312,411; Total
giving, $170,282; Grants to individuals, totaling
$170,282.
Fields of interest: Higher education; Minorities.
Type of support: Scholarships—to individuals;
Grants for special needs.
Application information: Applications accepted.
Application form required. Application form
available on the grantmaker's web site. Interview
required.
  Deadline(s): Dec. 15
  Final notification: Recipients notified by the end
    of Feb.
  Applicants should submit the following:
    1) Transcripts
    2) Letter(s) of recommendation
    3) GPA
    4) FAFSA
    5) Essay
  Additional information: Applicant must
    demonstrate financial need.
EIN: 911742581

9697
PEMCO Foundation, Inc.
325 Eastlake Ave. E.
Seattle, WA 98109-5407
Contact: Stan W. McNaughton, Pres. and Treas.

Foundation type: Company-sponsored foundation
Purpose: Scholarships to individuals residing in WA for undergraduate education.
Financial data: Year ended 06/30/2013. Assets, $2,127,892 (M); Expenditures, $636,613; Total giving, $634,670.
Type of support: Undergraduate support.
Application information: Applications accepted. Application form required.
  Deadline(s): None
  Final notification: Applicants notified within two months
  Applicants should submit the following:
    1) Transcripts
    2) Letter(s) of recommendation
  Additional information: Application should also include a letter from principal stating academic qualifications.
EIN: 916072723

9698
Paul Pigott Scholarship Foundation
P.O. Box 1518
Bellevue, WA 98009-1518   (425) 468-7890
Contact: Jack Levier

Foundation type: Independent foundation
Purpose: Scholarships only to dependents of employees of PACCAR, Inc. and its subsidiaries, for the first college year or grades 9-12 at non-tax supported secondary schools.
Financial data: Year ended 12/31/2012. Assets, $823,750 (M); Expenditures, $259,854; Total giving, $260,000; Grants to individuals, 26 grants totaling $260,000 (high: $10,000, low: $10,000).
Type of support: Employee-related scholarships; Precollege support; Undergraduate support.
Application information: Applications accepted. Application form required.
  Deadline(s): Nov. 1
  Applicants should submit the following:
    1) SAT
    2) Transcripts
  Additional information: Application must also include school report. Scholarships are not renewable.
Company name: PACCAR, Incorporated
EIN: 916030639

9699
Pioneer Memorial Scholarship Fund
P.O. Box 21927, MAC P6540-11K
Seattle, WA 98111-3927
Application address: c/o Harlowton High School, Attn.: Supt., 304 Division St., P.O. Box 288, Harlowton, MT 59036-0288, tel.: (406) 632-4324

Foundation type: Independent foundation
Purpose: Scholarships to graduates of Harlowton High School, MT for attendance at institutions of higher learning.
Financial data: Year ended 05/31/2010. Assets, $0 (M); Expenditures, $54,771; Total giving, $49,447.
Fields of interest: Higher education.
Type of support: Support to graduates or students of specific schools.

Application information: Applications accepted. Application form required.
  Deadline(s): First Monday in May
EIN: 816010285

9700
Plum Creek Foundation
999 3rd Ave., Ste. 4300
Seattle, WA 98104-4096   (206) 467-3664
Contact: Holly Nicholes
FAX: (206) 467-3795;
E-mail: foundation@plumcreek.com; Contact for Montana Great Classroom Awards: Renee Erickson, tel.: (406) 892-6227, e-mail: renee.erickson@plumcreek.com; Contact for organizations in FL: Rose Fagler, Community Rels. Mgr., tel.: 352-333-3733, e-mail: rose.fagler@plumcreek.com; URL: http://www.plumcreek.com/CommunityInvolvement/tabid/69/Default.aspx

Foundation type: Company-sponsored foundation
Purpose: Grants to public K-12 teachers to improve classrooms and enrich the educational experiences for students in western Montana.
Publications: Application guidelines; Annual report; Grants list; Program policy statement.
Financial data: Year ended 12/31/2012. Assets, $67,819 (M); Expenditures, $1,883,696; Total giving, $1,883,541.
Fields of interest: Elementary/secondary education; Education.
Type of support: Grants to individuals.
Application information: Applications accepted. Application form required. Application form available on the grantmaker's web site.
  Initial approach: Application
  Send request by: Mail
  Deadline(s): June 1 and Dec. 1
  Final notification: Applicants notified in Feb. and Aug.
  Applicants should submit the following:
    1) Budget Information
    2) Proposal
  Additional information: Proposals should not exceed five pages. Teachers may submit only one application per school year. There is no limit to the number of applications that may be submitted by a school or school district. School principals or district administrators must approve the application before any request will be considered. Faxed or e-mailed applications are not accepted.
Program description:
  Montana Great Classroom Awards Program: The foundation awards grants to public K-12 teachers to enhance the learning environment in the classroom and enrich educational experiences of students. The program is designed to promote teacher innovation, learning opportunities beyond the core curriculum, and opportunities to get youth excited about learning. The program is limited to Flathead, Granite, Lake, Lewis & Clark, Lincoln, Mineral, Missoula, Powell, Ravalli, and Sanders counties, MT. Grants range from $2,000 to $5,000.
EIN: 911621028

9701
Potlatch Fund
801 2nd Ave., Ste. 304
Seattle, WA 98104-1512   (206) 624-6076
Application e-mail: grants@potlatchfund.org
FAX: (206) 264-7629;
E-mail: info@potlatchfund.org; URL: http://www.potlatchfund.org

Foundation type: Public charity
Purpose: Grants to Native Americans who reside in Washington, Oregon, Idaho or Montana for projects in traditional or contemporary Native arts and cultures in the Northwest.
Publications: Application guidelines; Annual report; Financial statement; Grants list; Informational brochure; Newsletter.
Financial data: Year ended 12/31/2012. Assets, $716,853 (M); Expenditures, $612,715; Total giving, $190,581; Grants to individuals, totaling $21,326.
Fields of interest: Cultural/ethnic awareness; Native Americans/American Indians.
Type of support: Grants to individuals.
Application information: Applications accepted. Application form required.
  Send request by: Mail, fax, or e-mail
  Deadline(s): July 13
  Applicants should submit the following:
    1) Resume
    2) Letter(s) of recommendation
    3) Budget Information
  Additional information: Application should also include proof of Tribal enrollment or Tribal affiliation, and appropriate documentation of your work.
EIN: 731712905

9702
The Pride Foundation
2014 E. Madison St., Ste. 300
Seattle, WA 98122   (206) 323-3318
Contact: Kris Hermanns, Exec. Dir.
FAX: (206) 323-1017;
E-mail: prideweb@pridefoundation.org; Toll-free tel.: (800) 735-7287; Additional address: P.O. Box 2194, Spokane, WA 99210-2194, tel.: (509) 327-8377, fax: (509) 327-8403, toll-free tel. (WA): (888) 575-7717; URL: http://www.pridefoundation.org

Foundation type: Public charity
Purpose: Scholarships to current and future lesbian, gay, bisexual, transgender and straight-ally leaders and role models from AK, ID, MT, OR, and WA.
Publications: Application guidelines; Financial statement; Grants list; Newsletter.
Financial data: Year ended 03/31/2013. Assets, $48,497,503 (M); Expenditures, $4,505,099; Total giving, $1,161,832; Grants to individuals, totaling $404,843.
Fields of interest: Vocational education, post-secondary; Higher education; LGBTQ.
Type of support: Scholarships—to individuals.
Application information: Applications accepted. Application form required. Application form available on the grantmaker's web site.
  Deadline(s): Jan. 31
  Applicants should submit the following:
    1) Transcripts
    2) Letter(s) of recommendation
  Additional information: Application must be completed online. See web site for complete program listing and additional information.
EIN: 911325007

9703
Providence General Foundation
916 Pacific Ave.
Everett, WA 98201-4147   (425) 258-7500
Contact: Jubie Harvey, Chair. and Pres.
FAX: (425) 258-7507;
E-mail: provgenfoundation@providence.org; Mailing

address: P.O. Box 1067, Everett, WA 98206-1067; URL: http://www.providence.org/everett/foundation/default.htm

Foundation type: Public charity

Purpose: Financial assistance to patients who experience hardship as a result of their cancer diagnosis with payment for food, rent, utilities, prescriptions, therapy and other critical expenses. Assistance to Providence Regional Medical Center Everett employees with financial or medical emergency.

Financial data: Year ended 12/31/2011. Assets, $23,618,153 (M); Expenditures, $4,059,876; Total giving, $2,383,047; Grants to individuals, totaling $90,455.

Fields of interest: Human services; Economically disadvantaged.

Type of support: Grants for special needs.

Application information: Contact the foundation for further guidelines.

EIN: 911041617

9704
Providence Health System - Washington

1801 Lind Ave. S.W., No. 9016
Renton, WA 98057-9016   (425) 525-3985

Foundation type: Public charity

Purpose: Grants for needy individuals in WA.

Financial data: Year ended 12/31/2011. Assets, $5,566,177,800 (M); Expenditures, $3,512,493,322; Total giving, $17,040,598; Grants to individuals, totaling $308,532.

Fields of interest: Economically disadvantaged.

Type of support: Grants for special needs.

Application information: Contact foundation for eligibility information.

EIN: 510216586

9705
Renton Community Foundation

1101 Bronson Way N.
P.O. Box 820
Renton, WA 98057   (425) 282-5199
Contact: Lynn Bohart, Exec. Dir.
FAX: (425) 282-5889;
E-mail: lbohart@rentonfoundation.org; URL: http://www.rentonfoundation.org

Foundation type: Community foundation

Purpose: Scholarships for graduating high school seniors from Renton high schools, WA pursuing higher education at an accredited two or four year college or vocational, technical or trade school.

Publications: Annual report; Grants list; Newsletter.

Financial data: Year ended 12/31/2012. Assets, $6,608,122 (M); Expenditures, $556,136; Total giving, $420,371.

Fields of interest: Vocational education, post-secondary; Higher education; Scholarships/financial aid.

Type of support: Scholarships—to individuals.

Application information: Applications accepted. Application form required.
  Send request by: Mail
  Copies of proposal: 2
  Deadline(s): Apr. 19
  Applicants should submit the following:
    1) Transcripts
    2) Letter(s) of recommendation
    3) Essay

Additional information: Applicant must demonstrate financial need. See web site for additional application guidelines.

EIN: 237069988

9706
Robert W. Richardson Musical Education Scholarship Fund

c/o Baker Boyer National Bank
1149 N. Edison St., Ste. A
Kennewick, WA 99336-1677   (509) 783-6800
Contact: Asha Breintenfeidt

Foundation type: Independent foundation

Purpose: Music scholarships to graduating seniors in the Richland, Pasco, Kennewick, Finley, Burbank, or Kiona-Benton school districts, WA, and to students of Columbia Basin College, Pasco, WA.

Financial data: Year ended 10/31/2011. Assets, $317,035 (M); Expenditures, $22,539; Total giving, $15,828; Grants to individuals, 7 grants totaling $15,828 (high: $3,000, low: $500).

Fields of interest: Music; Performing arts, education.

Type of support: Support to graduates or students of specific schools; Undergraduate support.

Application information: Applications accepted. Application form required. Interview required.
  Send request by: Mail
  Deadline(s): Jan.
  Applicants should submit the following:
    1) Letter(s) of recommendation
    2) Transcripts
  Additional information: Application should also include supplementary background material, and an eight-minute audition cassette tape. Auditions required.

Program description:
  Robert W. Richardson Musical Education Scholarship: These three awards cover the costs of tuition and books, the Robert W. Richardson Award of $5,000, the Leone J. Richardson Award of $3,000, and the Virginia Richardson Stanton Award of $2,000. Applicants need not be music majors. They must, however, have a GPA of at least 2.0 and demonstrate talent and potential in either instrumental or vocal music. Career orientation, academic excellence, and social, civic, and personal responsibility will also be considered. Solo works are preferred, but if a group performance is used, applicant's part must be identified and other performers credited. Selected students will be requested to attend an interview. Those who are successful in the interview stage will then be requested to perform at the Robert W. Richardson Annual Recital in March.

EIN: 916326487

9707
Frank Rider Trust

c/o Hollis Jamison
7451 Garfield-Farmington Rd.
Garfield, WA 99130-8723   (509) 635-1435

Foundation type: Independent foundation

Purpose: Financial assistance only to indigent Freemasons in Whitman, Lincoln, Adams, Franklin, or Grant counties, WA, for medical and other personal needs.

Financial data: Year ended 12/31/2012. Assets, $0 (M); Expenditures, $219,779; Total giving, $77,100; Grants to individuals, 11 grants totaling $77,100 (high: $15,000, low: $2,700).

Fields of interest: Health care; Economically disadvantaged.

Type of support: Grants for special needs.

Application information: Application form required.
  Initial approach: Letter
  Deadline(s): None
  Additional information: Grants are renewable.

EIN: 910641308

9708
Ritzville Warehouse Foundation

201 E. 1st Ave.
Ritzville, WA 99169-0171   (509) 659-0130

Foundation type: Company-sponsored foundation

Purpose: Scholarships to high school seniors living in areas of company operations of Ritzville Warehouse Co., located in WA.

Financial data: Year ended 09/30/2012. Assets, $47,751 (M); Expenditures, $5,000; Total giving, $5,000; Grants to individuals, 1,000 grants totaling $5,000 (high: $1,000, low: $1,000).

Fields of interest: Higher education.

Type of support: Undergraduate support.

Application information: Applications accepted.
  Initial approach: Letter
  Deadline(s): May
  Additional information: Application should include financial background, letter addressing needs and a copy of transcript submitted to the scholarship committee.

EIN: 753027595

9709
Rotalia Foundation

9133 View Ave. N.W.
Seattle, WA 98117-2654   (206) 275-0140
Contact: Mart Kask, Chair.
Application Address: 8 Lindley Rd.Mercer Island, WA 98040

Foundation type: Independent foundation

Purpose: Scholarships and research grants to individuals in the U.S. and abroad who read, speak, and understand Estonian.

Financial data: Year ended 12/31/2012. Assets, $2,512,731 (M); Expenditures, $162,294; Total giving, $141,774; Grants to individuals, 51 grants totaling $138,681 (high: $3,773, low: $2,673).

Fields of interest: Language (foreign); International exchange, students.

International interests: Eastern Europe; Estonia.

Type of support: Research; Exchange programs; Foreign applicants; Graduate support; Undergraduate support; Postgraduate support.

Application information: Application form required.
  Deadline(s): Contact foundation for deadline
  Applicants should submit the following:
    1) Essay
    2) Letter(s) of recommendation
    3) Financial information
  Additional information: Applications must be submitted in Estonian.

EIN: 911409344

9710
Rachel Royston Permanent Scholarship Foundation of Alpha Sigma State of the Delta Kappa Gamma Society International

1501 4th Ave., Ste. 2880
Seattle, WA 98101-1631   (360) 638-1088
Contact: Annamarie Lavieri
Application address: P.O. Box 643, Kelso, WA 98346. Tel.: (360) 638-1088; URL: http://www.deltakappagamma.org/WA/rachel.html

Foundation type: Operating foundation
Purpose: Scholarships for graduate study to female educators who are residents of WA.
Financial data: Year ended 06/30/2013. Assets, $1,146,070 (M); Expenditures, $56,158; Total giving, $23,500; Grants to individuals, 15 grants totaling $23,500 (high: $2,500, low: $1,000).
Fields of interest: Teacher school/education; Education; Women.
Type of support: Graduate support.
Application information: Applications accepted. Application form required. Interview required.
> *Deadline(s):* Dec. 1
> *Additional information:* Application must include letter of acceptance to special project or degree program, three recommendations, progress statement from advisor for doctoral students, budget, and personal statement.
Program description:
> *Scholarship Program:* Recipients may work toward a master's or doctorate degree, or work in a field of special interest. Awards may only be made for one year or a portion thereof, however additional applications may be requested and submitted in later years. Applicants are judged on the basis of their project, its significance to the field of education, and evidence of the candidate's ability to pursue it. Applicants must be residents of WA, must be doing graduate work in an approved institution of higher learning which has been accredited by a regional and/or national accrediting association, and must show promise in a particular field. Recipients are required to submit copies of any written materials produced during the period of the scholarship to the foundation's resource center. Applicants will be notified of the board's decision to be selected for interviews by Mar. of the following year. Finalists will be notified within two weeks of the required interview.
EIN: 916060790

9711
Rural American Scholarship Fund
P.O. Box 2674
Oak Harbor, WA   98277-6674
Contact: Dave Thomas, Secy.-Treas.

Foundation type: Operating foundation
Purpose: Scholarships for higher education to students residing in rural areas of ID, OR, and WA.
Financial data: Year ended 12/31/2013. Assets, $5,407 (M); Expenditures, $39,340; Total giving, $37,500.
Fields of interest: Higher education; Scholarships/financial aid; Rural development; Economically disadvantaged.
Type of support: Scholarships—to individuals; Graduate support; Undergraduate support.
Application information: Applications accepted. Application form required. Application form available on the grantmaker's web site.
> *Deadline(s):* Mar. 1
> *Applicants should submit the following:*
> 1) Photograph
> 2) Transcripts
> 3) SAR
> 4) GPA
> 5) FAFSA
> *Additional information:* Applicants should contact their financial aid office for application.
Program description:
> *Scholarships:* Scholarships range from $1,500 to $5,000 to applicants who have missed the opportunity for college attendance upon completion of high school, be underemployed or hold an unfulfilling job, reside in or come from a rural community, and be at least 23 years of age by Sept.

1. Applicants must also be legal residents of the state in which they will be attending college and have a 2.8 GPA. Master's candidates are eligible to apply.
EIN: 850386189

9712
Rural Resources Community Action
956 S. Main St.
Colville, WA   99114-2505   (509) 684-8421
FAX: (509) 684-4740;
E-mail: info@ruralresources.org; URL: http://www.ruralresources.org

Foundation type: Public charity
Purpose: Financial assistance to low income individuals, families, people with disabilities, and the aged of Northeastern WA, with housing, utilities, transportation, those who suffer abuse and other special needs.
Financial data: Year ended 02/28/2012. Assets, $10,302,936 (M); Expenditures, $14,054,660; Total giving, $4,061,208; Grants to individuals, totaling $4,061,208.
Fields of interest: Aging; Disabilities, people with; Economically disadvantaged.
Type of support: Emergency funds; Grants for special needs.
Application information: Applications accepted.
> *Initial approach:* Telephone
> *Additional information:* Some programs require application forms. Contact the agency for eligibility determination. Assistance payments are made directly to qualified vendors on behalf of the recipients.
EIN: 910793447

9713
The Russell Family Foundation
P.O. Box 2567
Gig Harbor, WA   98335-4567   (253) 858-5050
Contact: Linsey Sauer, Grants Mgr.
FAX: (253) 851-0460; E-mail: info@trff.org; Toll Free tel.: (888) 252-4331; URL: http://trff.org

Foundation type: Independent foundation
Purpose: Fellowships to support grassroot leaders in Pierce county, WA for the improvement of the quality of life in the community.
Publications: Application guidelines; Financial statement; Newsletter.
Financial data: Year ended 12/31/2012. Assets, $135,271,084 (M); Expenditures, $5,575,808; Total giving, $4,958,868; Grants to individuals, 10 grants totaling $97,200.
Fields of interest: Community development, neighborhood development; Leadership development.
Type of support: Fellowships.
Application information: Applications accepted. Application form required. Application form available on the grantmaker's web site.
> *Initial approach:* Letter
> *Send request by:* Mail
> *Copies of proposal:* 1
> *Deadline(s):* Varies
> *Additional information:* Application should include letter of recommendation, and applicants must complete a Jane's Fellowship program application form.
Program description:
> *Jane's Fellowship Program:* In 2004 the foundation launched Jane's Fellowship Program to support grassroots leaders in Tacoma and Pierce County. Each class of fellows participates in a two-year leadership experience before becoming

part of the alumni network. The fellowship focuses on expanding each leader's personal strengths and skills, and offers financial, logistical and educational support for participation. For more information or to have materials mailed to you, call Susan Dobkins: (253) 857-1689 or email: janesfund@trff.org. See web site for brochure and application.
EIN: 911663336

9714
San Juan Island Community Foundation
P.O. Box 1352
Friday Harbor, WA   98250-1352   (360) 378-1001
Scholarship e-mail: scholarships@sjicf.org
E-mail: info@sjicf.org; Additional e-mail: grants@sjicf.org; URL: http://www.sjicf.org

Foundation type: Community foundation
Purpose: Awards scholarships to eligible San Juan Island high school graduates for higher education and career training opportunities for all ages.
Publications: Application guidelines; Annual report; Grants list; Informational brochure; Informational brochure (including application guidelines); Newsletter.
Financial data: Year ended 12/31/2011. Assets, $7,458,254 (M); Expenditures, $2,413,044; Total giving, $2,203,132; Grants to individuals, 29 grants totaling $141,377.
Fields of interest: Higher education; Education.
Type of support: Scholarships—to individuals.
Application information: Applications accepted. Application form required. Application form available on the grantmaker's web site.
> *Initial approach:* Application
> *Send request by:* Mail or hand-deliver
> *Deadline(s):* Varies; none for General Scholarships
> *Additional information:* See web site for additional information.
EIN: 911648730

9715
Margaret Lobdell Schack Memorial Scholarship Fund
2825 Colby
Everett, WA   98201
Contact: Kim Cacae

Foundation type: Independent foundation
Purpose: Scholarships to graduates and graduating seniors of Garfield High School, Seattle, WA.
Financial data: Year ended 03/31/2013. Assets, $148,468 (M); Expenditures, $6,017; Total giving, $3,500.
Type of support: Support to graduates or students of specific schools; Undergraduate support.
Application information: Applications accepted.
> *Send request by:* Mail
> *Deadline(s):* None
> *Additional information:* Contact foundation for current application guidelines.
EIN: 916240991

9716
Herman Oscar Schumacher School Fund
(formerly Herman Oscar Schumacher Scholarship Fund for Men)
717 W. Sprague
Spokane, WA   99201

Foundation type: Independent foundation

Purpose: Scholarships to male Christian residents of Spokane County, WA, who have completed one year of study at an accredited college. Preference is given to orphans and the financially needy. Applicants must be loyal to the principles of democracy and support the Constitution of the U.S.
Financial data: Year ended 06/30/2013. Assets, $445,340 (M); Expenditures, $30,946; Total giving, $22,500; Grants to individuals, 49 grants totaling $22,500 (high: $1,500, low: $500).
Type of support: Undergraduate support.
Application information: Applications accepted. Application form required.
> *Deadline(s):* Oct. 1
> *Additional information:* Application should also include college transcripts and proof of enrollment.
EIN: 916237367

9717
Greater Seattle Business Association Scholarship Fund

(also known as GSBA)
400 E. Pine St., Ste. 322
Seattle, WA 98122-2300 (206) 363-9188
Contact: Louise Chernin, Pres. and C.E.O. and Exec. Dir.
FAX: (206) 568-3123; E-mail: office@thegsba.org;
E-Mail for Louise Chernin: Louise@thegsba.org;
URL: http://www.thegsba.org

Foundation type: Public charity
Purpose: Undergraduate scholarships of up to $5,000 to residents of WA who demonstrate community leadership potential and who foster the understanding and diversity of the sexual minority community.
Publications: Application guidelines; Annual report; Informational brochure; Newsletter.
Financial data: Year ended 12/31/2012. Assets, $1,984,976 (M); Expenditures, $448,281; Total giving, $182,000; Grants to individuals, totaling $182,000.
Fields of interest: LGBTQ.
Type of support: Scholarships—to individuals.
Application information: Applications accepted. Application form required. Application form available on the grantmaker's web site. Interview required.
> *Deadline(s):* Jan. 23
> *Applicants should submit the following:*
> 1) Transcripts
> 2) Letter(s) of recommendation
EIN: 943138514

9718
Seattle Central Community College Foundation

1701 Broadway, Ste. Be-4180
Seattle, WA 98122-0000 (206) 934-5491
Contact: Adam Nance, Exec. Dir.
FAX: (206) 934-4390;
E-mail: scccfoundation@seattlecolleges.edu;
E-mail For Adam Nance:
adam.nance@seattlecolleges.edu; URL: http://www.seattlecentral.edu/foundation/

Foundation type: Public charity
Purpose: Scholarships to students attending Seattle Central College.
Financial data: Year ended 06/30/2012. Assets, $8,059,277 (M); Expenditures, $4,763,937; Total giving, $4,641,185; Grants to individuals, totaling $427,251.
Fields of interest: Education.

Type of support: Support to graduates or students of specific schools.
Application information: Applications accepted. Application form required. Application form available on the grantmaker's web site.
> *Initial approach:* E-mail or tel.
> *Deadline(s):* May 1
> *Additional information:* Email scccscholarships@seattlecolleges.edu with any questions. Help is also available at the Career Services Center: (206) 934-4383.
EIN: 911037870

9719
The Seattle Foundation

1200 5th Ave., Ste. 1300
Seattle, WA 98101-3151 (206) 622-2294
Contact: Ceil Erickson, Dir., Community Progs.
FAX: (206) 622-7673;
E-mail: info@seattlefoundation.org; URL: http://www.seattlefoundation.org

Foundation type: Community foundation
Purpose: Scholarships to qualified residents of Seattle, IL for higher education.
Publications: Annual report; Financial statement; Grants list; Informational brochure; Newsletter; Program policy statement.
Financial data: Year ended 12/31/2012. Assets, $690,275,245 (M); Expenditures, $79,222,798; Total giving, $67,353,039.
Fields of interest: Vocational education, post-secondary; Higher education; Graduate/professional education; Scholarships/financial aid.
Type of support: Scholarships—to individuals; Support to graduates or students of specific schools; Undergraduate support.
Application information: Applications accepted. Application form required. Application form available on the grantmaker's web site.
> *Deadline(s):* Mar. 1
> *Final notification:* Applicants notified mid-Apr.
> *Applicants should submit the following:*
> 1) Transcripts
> 2) Letter(s) of recommendation
> 3) Financial information
> *Additional information:* Funds are paid directly to the educational institution on behalf of the students. See web site for complete listing of scholarships.
Program description:
> *Scholarship Funds:* The foundation holds more than 40 scholarship funds for students from a wide variety of backgrounds. Scholarship opportunities are available for high school seniors, undergraduate and graduate students attending community colleges, four-year colleges and universities, vocational/technical schools and graduate/professional schools. Awards range in size from $500 to $20,000, several are renewable. Each scholarship has its own unique set of eligibility criteria and application guidelines. See web site for additional information, www.theWashBoard.org.
EIN: 916013536

9720
Seattle Parks Foundation

105 S. Main St., Ste. 235
Seattle, WA 98104-3476 (206) 332-9900
FAX: (206) 299-3383;
E-mail: info@seattleparksfoundation.org; E-Mail for Thatcher Bailey:
Thatcher@seattleparksfoundation.org; Tel. for Thatcher Bailey : (206)-332-9900 Ext. 11;
URL: http://www.seattleparksfoundation.org

Foundation type: Public charity
Purpose: Fiscal sponsorship to individuals who meet the foundation's mission to improve and expand Seattle's parks and green spaces.
Publications: Annual report; Newsletter.
Financial data: Year ended 06/30/2012. Assets, $3,185,731 (M); Expenditures, $942,003.
Fields of interest: Parks/playgrounds.
Type of support: Fiscal agent/sponsor.
Application information: Applications accepted.
EIN: 911998597

9721
Second Harvest Food Bank of the Inland Northwest

1234 E. Front Ave.
Spokane, WA 99202-2148 (509) 534-6678
Contact: Jason L. Clark, Pres. and C.E.O.
FAX: (509) 534-8252; E-mail: jclark@2-harvest.org.;
Mailing Address: P.O. Box 3068; Pasco, WA 99302;
URL: http://www.2-harvest.org

Foundation type: Public charity
Purpose: Emergency assistance to individuals and families in need throughout northern IA and eastern WA.
Financial data: Year ended 06/30/2012. Assets, $8,908,568 (M); Expenditures, $35,791,971; Total giving, $31,472,683; Grants to individuals, 100,016 grants totaling $3,131,597.
Fields of interest: Food services; Nutrition; Economically disadvantaged.
Type of support: Emergency funds; In-kind gifts.
Application information: Applications not accepted.
> *Additional information:* See web site for information for assistance.
EIN: 237173826

9722
Sequim Masonic Lodge Foundation

P.O. Box 1500
Sequim, WA 98382
Contact: Robert Rodgers, Secy.
Application address: 242 Forest Haven Dr., Sequim, WA 98382

Foundation type: Independent foundation
Purpose: Scholarships to graduates of the Sequim, WA, school district who are members of recognized youth organizations.
Financial data: Year ended 06/30/2013. Assets, $496,975 (M); Expenditures, $55,106; Total giving, $54,000; Grants to individuals, 54 grants totaling $54,000 (high: $1,000, low: $1,000).
Fields of interest: Higher education.
Type of support: Scholarships—to individuals.
Application information: Applications accepted.
> *Initial approach:* Letter
> *Deadline(s):* Mar. 31
> *Additional information:* Application must include resume outlining participation in youth organizations.
EIN: 910987628

9723
Grace and Harold Sewell Memorial Fund

P.O. Box 685
Issaquah, WA 98027-0025 (425) 392-5520
Contact: Martha Oien, Pres.
URL: http://www.sewellfund.org

Foundation type: Operating foundation

Purpose: Stipends to health sciences librarians and information specialists to attend the national professional meetings of their clients and to increase their identification with medical and health care professionals. Also, funding is provided for sabbatical leaves for librarians.
Financial data: Year ended 12/31/2012. Assets, $1,669,386 (M); Expenditures, $111,805; Total giving, $88,000.
Fields of interest: Libraries/library science.
Type of support: Stipends; Sabbaticals.
Application information: Applications accepted. Application form required.
  Deadline(s): Varies
  Additional information: Application forms available from Dr. Sewell. A 250 word essay is required.
EIN: 200614721

9724
Mary S. Sigourney Award Trust
c/o Barbara C. Sherland
600 University St., Ste. 3600
Seattle, WA 98101-4109 (206) 386-7691
Contact: Barbara Sherland
E-mail: info@sigourney.org; URL: http://sigourneyaward.org/

Foundation type: Independent foundation
Purpose: Awards to individuals nominated by a reputable psychoanalytic society who have published or contributed in a significant way within the last ten years to clinical psychoanalysis or psychoanalytical research, including their application to the field of medicine or related sciences such as psychiatry and psychotherapy.
Publications: Annual report.
Financial data: Year ended 12/31/2012. Assets, $5,046,843 (M); Expenditures, $205,719; Total giving, $100,000; Grants to individuals, 4 grants totaling $100,000 (high: $25,000, low: $25,000).
Fields of interest: Mental health, treatment; Psychology/behavioral science.
Type of support: Research; Awards/grants by nomination only; Awards/prizes.
Application information: Applications not accepted.
  Additional information: Individual applications not accepted; Awards by nomination only.
EIN: 776054596

9725
Skagit Valley Herald Christmas Fund
221 1st Ave. W.
Seattle, WA 98119-4285 (206) 284-7689
Contact: Leighton P. Wood, Pres.

Foundation type: Public charity
Purpose: Grants for basic necessities and for gifts during Christmas to needy residents of Skagit County, WA.
Financial data: Year ended 03/31/2012. Assets, $228,338 (M); Expenditures, $112,244.
Fields of interest: Economically disadvantaged.
Type of support: Grants for special needs.
Application information: Contact foundation for complete eligibility requirements.
EIN: 911304740

9726
SkillSource, Inc.
233 N. Chelan Ave.
Wenatchee, WA 98807-2360 (509) 663-3091
Contact: Dave Petersen, Exec. Dir.
FAX: (509) 663-5649; Toll Free Tel.:
(800)-833-6388; URL: http://www.skillsource.org

Foundation type: Public charity
Purpose: Scholarships to individuals enrolled with Skillsource in WA, for vocational training at community or technical colleges.
Financial data: Year ended 06/30/2012. Assets, $4,913,920 (M); Expenditures, $3,727,863.
Fields of interest: Employment, training.
Type of support: Technical education support.
Application information: Applications accepted. Interview required.
  Initial approach: Telephone or letter
EIN: 911247291

9727
Sarina Slaid Memorial Scholarship Fund
4614 N.E. 45th Pl.
Vancouver, WA 98661-2873 (360) 514-3106
Contact: Donna Maple
Application address: C/o.S.W. Wash Med Ctr. Foundation, P. O. Box 1600, Vancouver, WA 98668, tel.: (360) 514-3106

Foundation type: Independent foundation
Purpose: Scholarships to Mountain View High School, WA, students and to junior volunteers at Southwest Washington Medical Center.
Financial data: Year ended 12/31/2011. Assets, $107,461 (M); Expenditures, $7,199; Total giving, $6,200; Grants to individuals, 2 grants totaling $6,200 (high: $3,100, low: $3,100).
Type of support: Support to graduates or students of specific schools; Undergraduate support.
Application information: Applications not accepted.
  Additional information: Unsolicited requests for funds not considered or acknowledged.
EIN: 943186332

9728
Snohomish County Council of the Society of St. Vincent de Paul
P.O. Box 2269
Everett, WA 98203-0269 (425) 513-6052
Contact: James P. Kehoe, Exec.Dir.
FAX: (425) 513-6051; E-mail: SVDPsno@juno.com; URL: http://snohomishsaintvincent.org

Foundation type: Public charity
Purpose: Financial assistance in the form of shelter, transportation, clothing, food, utilities, and other basic necessities to indigent residents of Snohomish County, WA.
Financial data: Year ended 09/30/2011. Assets, $5,714,018 (M); Expenditures, $2,721,068.
Type of support: Grants for special needs.
Application information:
  Initial approach: Letter
  Additional information: Contact foundation for further information.
EIN: 911022003

9729
Society of St. Vincent de Paul Council of Seattle/King County
(formerly Society of St. Vincent de Paul Council of the Seattle Area)
5950 4th Ave. S.
Seattle, WA 98108-3208 (206) 767-9975
Contact: Ned Delmore, Exec. Dir.
FAX: (206) 767-6439;
E-mail: giving@svdpseattle.org; Additional tel.: (206) 767-6449; URL: http://www.svdpseattle.org

Foundation type: Public charity
Purpose: Emergency and financial assistance to individuals and families in need in the Seattle and King County, WA area with food, clothing, prevention of evictions, hunger, utility shut off and other special needs.
Financial data: Year ended 09/30/2011. Assets, $16,905,027 (M); Expenditures, $11,469,524; Total giving, $3,088,136; Grants to individuals, totaling $3,088,136.
Fields of interest: Human services, emergency aid; Economically disadvantaged.
Type of support: Emergency funds; Grants for special needs.
Application information: Contact the organization for eligibility determination.
EIN: 910583891

9730
Spokane Kiwanis Charities
12426 E. Emory Ln.
Spokane Valley, WA 99206 (509) 358-6176

Foundation type: Public charity
Purpose: College scholarships to qualified disadvantaged youth attempting to further his or her education at the community colleges of Spokane, WA.
Financial data: Year ended 09/30/2011. Assets, $526,074 (M); Expenditures, $17,490; Total giving, $16,158.
Fields of interest: Higher education.
Type of support: Scholarships—to individuals.
Application information: Applications not accepted.
EIN: 910952050

9731
Spokane Neighborhood Action Programs
(also known as SNAP)
2116 E. 1st Ave.
Spokane, WA 99202-3146
FAX: (509) 534-5874; URL: http://www.snapwa.org

Foundation type: Public charity
Purpose: Assistance to homeless and low-income individuals and families of Spokane, WA with energy assistance, utilities, housing, weatherization, and other special needs.
Publications: Annual report; Financial statement.
Financial data: Year ended 12/31/2011. Assets, $14,338,955 (M); Expenditures, $21,478,344; Total giving, $11,925,423; Grants to individuals, totaling $11,925,423.
Fields of interest: Housing/shelter, rehabilitation; Housing/shelter, homeless; Housing/shelter, repairs; Housing/shelter; Economically disadvantaged.
Type of support: Emergency funds; Grants for special needs.
Application information: Applications accepted.

Additional information: Contact the agency for eligibility determination.
EIN: 911311127

9732
St. Luke's Foundation of Bellingham
800 E. Chestnut, Ste. 1B
Bellingham, WA 98225-5641   (360) 671-3349
Contact: Sue Sharpe, Exec. Dir.
FAX: (360) 715-6496;
E-mail: stlukes@stlukesfoundation.org; Mailing address: P.O. Box 5641, Bellingham WA 98225-5641; e-mail for Sue Sharpe: suesharpe@stlukesfoundation.org; tel. for Sue Sharpe: (360) 671-3349 or (360) 739-3027; URL: http://www.stlukesfoundation.org
Foundation type: Public charity
Purpose: Scholarships to students following a program leading to registered nurse and/or continuing in a nursing program toward advanced degrees. Applicants must be residents of Whatcom County, WA.
Publications: Application guidelines; Annual report (including application guidelines); Informational brochure.
Financial data: Year ended 12/31/2011. Assets, $11,477,000 (M); Expenditures, $779,728; Total giving, $522,668; Grants to individuals, totaling $22,500.
Fields of interest: Nursing school/education.
Type of support: Undergraduate support.
Application information:
  Initial approach: Letter
  Deadline(s): May 15 for Nursing Scholarship
EIN: 911192943

9733
Jack Straw Foundation
4261 Roosevelt Way N.E.
Seattle, WA 98105-6999   (206) 634-0919
Contact: Joan Rabinowitz, Exec. Dir.
FAX: (206) 634-0925; E-mail: jsp@jackstraw.org; E-mail for Joan Rabinowitz: joan@jackstraw.org; URL: http://www.jackstraw.org
Foundation type: Public charity
Purpose: Residencies to writers and artists working with sound.
Publications: Newsletter.
Financial data: Year ended 06/30/2012. Assets, $989,960 (M); Expenditures, $422,070.
Fields of interest: Music; Literature; Arts.
Type of support: Residencies.
Application information: Applications accepted.
  Copies of proposal: 7
  Deadline(s): Varies
  Applicants should submit the following:
    1) SASE
    2) Work samples
    3) Resume
  Additional information: Application must also include project form.
Program descriptions:
  Jack Straw Artist Support Program: This program provides up to eight artists in every genre and style (including writers, choreographers, multidisciplinary artists, theatre sound designers, radio producers, film makers, visual artists, and musicians and composers) twenty hours of studio recording and production time with a foundation engineer.
  Jack Straw Writers Program: This program works to introduce local writers to the medium of recorded audio, encourage the creation of new literary work, and present the writer and their work in live readings, in a published anthology, on the web, and

on broadcast radio. Each year, an invited curator selects 12 writers from a large pool of applicants; participating writers receive training in vocal presentation, performance, and microphone technique to prepare them for studio recordings and live recording at public readings. Recorded readings and interviews are then used to produce features on the foundation's web site, for radio broadcast, and for internet podcasts.
EIN: 910776606

9734
The Greater Tacoma Community Foundation
950 Pacific Ave., Ste. 1100
P.O. Box 1995
Tacoma, WA 98402-4423   (253) 383-5622
Contact: For grants and scholarships: Sherrana Kildun, Dir., Community Progs.
FAX: (253) 272-8099; E-mail: info@gtcf.org; URL: http://www.gtcf.org
Foundation type: Community foundation
Purpose: Scholarships to students residing in the greater Tacoma, WA area for attendance at a vocational school or a two or four year accredited university.
Publications: Application guidelines; Annual report; Financial statement; Informational brochure; Informational brochure (including application guidelines); Newsletter.
Financial data: Year ended 06/30/2012. Assets, $79,793,561 (M); Expenditures, $6,312,848; Total giving, $2,704,965. Scholarships—to individuals amount not specified.
Fields of interest: Higher education.
Type of support: Grants to individuals; Scholarships—to individuals.
Application information: Applications accepted. Application form required.
  Initial approach: Telephone or e-mail
  Deadline(s): Varies
  Additional information: Application should include financial information. See web site for additional guidelines.
EIN: 911007459

9735
Three Rivers Community Foundation
1333 Columbia Park Trail, Ste. 310
Richland, WA 99352   (509) 735-5559
Contact: Carrie Green, Secy. and Exec. Dir.
E-mail: carrie@3rcf.org; URL: http://www.3rcf.org
Foundation type: Community foundation
Purpose: Scholarships to residents of Benton or Franklin counties, WA for higher education.
Publications: Grants list.
Financial data: Year ended 12/31/2011. Assets, $1,736,176 (M); Expenditures, $555,646; Total giving, $373,502; Grants to individuals, 12 grants totaling $52,429.
Fields of interest: Higher education.
Type of support: Scholarships—to individuals.
Application information: Applications accepted.
  Additional information: Contact the foundation for additional guidelines.
EIN: 912049302

9736
Treehouse
2100 24th Ave. S., Ste. 220
Seattle, WA 98144-4637   (206) 767-7000
FAX: (206) 767-7773;
E-mail: info@treehouseforkids.org; URL: http://www.treehouse4kids.org
Foundation type: Public charity
Purpose: Grants to foster children for developmental opportunities and educational support.
Publications: Annual report; Newsletter.
Financial data: Year ended 09/30/2011. Assets, $6,373,368 (M); Expenditures, $6,646,592; Total giving, $642,202; Grants to individuals, totaling $642,202.
Fields of interest: Children/youth, services; Foster care.
Type of support: Undergraduate support; Grants for special needs.
Application information: Contact fund for current application deadline/guidelines.
EIN: 911425676

9737
The Tudor Foundation
411 University St., Ste. 1200
Seattle, WA 98101-2519
Contact: Roger Rieger

Foundation type: Operating foundation
Purpose: Scholarships to post high school students for tuition, books, and related expenses.
Financial data: Year ended 12/31/2012. Assets, $1,153,010 (M); Expenditures, $238,632; Total giving, $234,396; Grants to individuals, totaling $177,304.
Fields of interest: Higher education.
Type of support: Undergraduate support.
Application information: Applications not accepted.
  Additional information: Contributes only to preselected individuals.
EIN: 911708176

9738
T.J. Tufts Charitable Foundation
P.O. Box 422
Wilbur, WA 99185-0422   (509) 647-5310
Contact: Charles Wyborney, Tr.

Foundation type: Independent foundation
Purpose: Scholarships to students of Wilbur public schools, WA, who have a minimum 3.0 GPA.
Financial data: Year ended 12/31/2012. Assets, $702,000 (M); Expenditures, $44,384; Total giving, $33,822.
Fields of interest: Higher education.
Type of support: Support to graduates or students of specific schools; Undergraduate support.
Application information: Application form required.
  Deadline(s): Apr. 1
  Additional information: Contact your respective school guidance office for application information.
EIN: 911489095

9739
Ulmschneider Educational Foundation
P.O. Box Q
Greenbank, WA 98253-0191   (360) 678-8049
Contact: M.J. Ellis, Secy.

Foundation type: Independent foundation

Purpose: Scholarships and grants for needy youth to cover living expenses, primarily in NE and WA.
Financial data: Year ended 12/31/2012. Assets, $241,237 (M); Expenditures, $33,579; Total giving, $30,233.
Type of support: Undergraduate support; Grants for special needs.
Application information: Applications accepted. Application form not required.
  Deadline(s): None
EIN: 911886617

9740
Vancouver Methodist Foundation
401 E. 33rd St.
Vancouver, WA 98663-2203 (360) 546-5591
Contact: Ray Johnson, Pres.

Foundation type: Independent foundation
Purpose: Scholarships and study grants primarily to residents of WA.
Financial data: Year ended 12/31/2011. Assets, $1,048,868 (M); Expenditures, $87,741; Total giving, $78,381; Grants to individuals, 25 grants totaling $45,559 (high: $18,000, low: $95).
Fields of interest: Theological school/education.
Type of support: Scholarships—to individuals.
Application information: Applications accepted. Application form required.
  Deadline(s): Apr. 1 for Clark County, none for others
  Applicants should submit the following:
    1) Letter(s) of recommendation
    2) Transcripts
    3) Financial information
  Additional information: Application forms can be obtained from the foundation.
EIN: 910850194

9741
The Martha VanHoff Educational Trust
2129 Crestview Ave.
Richland, WA 99354-1811 (509) 375-1450
Contact: Carl VanHoff, Pres.

Foundation type: Independent foundation
Purpose: Scholarships to individuals from Richland, WA, attending a community college, college, university, or other career-related training program.
Financial data: Year ended 09/30/2012. Assets, $35,976 (M); Expenditures, $16,357; Total giving, $16,000; Grant to an individual, 1 grant totaling $16,000.
Fields of interest: Higher education.
Type of support: Technical education support; Undergraduate support.
Application information: Applications accepted. Application form required.
  Initial approach: Letter
  Deadline(s): Apr. 1
  Final notification: Applicants notified by May 1
  Applicants should submit the following:
    1) Financial information
    2) Essay
    3) Letter(s) of recommendation
    4) Transcripts
  Additional information: Application should also include a copy of acceptance letter, and three letters of reference.
EIN: 912090886

9742
Vista Hermosa
1111 Fishhook Park Rd.
Prescott, WA 99348-9618 (509) 749-2217
Contact: Suzanne Broetje, Exec. Dir.
Scholarship contact: Theresa Morton, Prog. Mgr., tel.: (509) 460-0350
FAX: (509) 749-2354;
E-mail: SuzanneB@firstfruits.com; URL: http://www.firstfruits.com/vista-hermosa-foundation.html

Foundation type: Independent foundation
Purpose: Financial support and encouragement to low-income and first-generation college students who might otherwise not be able to continue their education and pursue their dreams for the future.
Financial data: Year ended 12/31/2012. Assets, $30,099,082 (M); Expenditures, $3,648,640; Total giving, $1,682,905; Grants to individuals, 28 grants totaling $70,010.
Fields of interest: Vocational education, post-secondary; Higher education.
Type of support: Scholarships—to individuals.
Application information: Applications accepted. Application form required. Interview required.
  Initial approach: Telephone
  Send request by: Mail
  Copies of proposal: 1
  Deadline(s): June and Nov.
  Applicants should submit the following:
    1) Transcripts
    2) SAT
    3) Letter(s) of recommendation
    4) GPA
    5) Financial information
    6) Budget Information
    7) Essay
  Additional information: Parent and student must attend Mandatory Orientation Meeting and must sign Acceptance of Scholarship. See web site for additional guidelines.
EIN: 911491438

9743
W & G Scholarship Trust
P.O. Box 277
Port Townsend, WA 98368-0277

Foundation type: Independent foundation
Purpose: Scholarships to residents of Port Townsend, WA, for higher education.
Financial data: Year ended 12/31/2011. Assets, $16,345 (M); Expenditures, $30,000; Total giving, $30,000.
Type of support: Undergraduate support.
Application information: Applications not accepted.
  Additional information: Unsolicited requests for funds not accepted or considered.
EIN: 911941288

9744
Thomas C. Wales Foundation
(formerly Thomas C. Wales Memorial Foundation)
1 Union Sq. Bldg., Ste. 1601
600 University St.
Seattle, WA 98101-1176 (206) 233-2801
FAX: (206) 233-2809;
E-mail: info2009@walesfoundation.org; Mailing address: P.O. Box 2448, Seattle, WA 98111-2448; URL: http://www.walesfoundation.org

Foundation type: Public charity
Purpose: Fellowship support to individuals interested in working with nonprofit organizations

that address critical community issues in the Puget Sound, WA area.
Publications: Application guidelines.
Financial data: Year ended 12/31/2010. Assets, $14,477 (M); Expenditures, $52,569. Fellowships amount not specified.
Fields of interest: Government/public administration; Public affairs, citizen participation; Public affairs.
Type of support: Fellowships.
Application information: Interview required.
Program description:
  TCW Fellowship: The foundation recruits and evaluates organizations that provide valuable learning and leadership opportunities and match them with flexible and motivated interns, known as Fellows, screened for their commitment and ability. Fellows commit to serve their full term in good faith. Organizations commit to maximizing each Fellow's learning opportunities by offering him or her one or more projects to develop and the supervision and mentorship of a senior staff member. Fellows serve between 150 and 200 hours between January and June and may receive academic credit for their efforts. The foundation serves as an independent resource for Fellows and organizations during the fellowship, providing orientations, a series of workshops, and a forum for Fellows to share their experiences.
EIN: 912160664

9745
Walkling Memorial Trust
(formerly Ben & Myrtle Walkling Memorial Trust)
P.O. Box 1588
Port Angeles, WA 98362-0193 (360) 582-3801
Contact: Karen Yakovich

Foundation type: Independent foundation
Purpose: Medical related scholarships to residents of Clallam County schools, WA and to students of Port Angeles High School and other Clallam county high schools.
Financial data: Year ended 12/31/2011. Assets, $2,276,607 (M); Expenditures, $92,296; Total giving, $62,885.
Fields of interest: Vocational education, post-secondary; Medical school/education; Health sciences school/education; Scholarships/financial aid.
Type of support: Support to graduates or students of specific schools; Undergraduate support.
Application information: Applications accepted.
  Deadline(s): Vary
EIN: 943166048

9746
Washington Apple Education Foundation
2900 Euclid Ave.
Wenatchee, WA 98801-8102 (509) 663-7713
Contact: Jennifer Witherbee, Exec. Dir.
FAX: (509) 663-7469; E-mail: waef@waef.org; E-Mail for Jennifer Witherbee: jennifer.witherbee@waef.org; URL: http://www.waef.org

Foundation type: Public charity
Purpose: Scholarships to students who are residents of WA for higher education.
Publications: Application guidelines; Annual report; Financial statement; Grants list; Newsletter.
Financial data: Year ended 12/31/2011. Assets, $4,482,571 (M); Expenditures, $951,001; Total giving, $707,396; Grants to individuals, totaling $508,731.

Fields of interest: Scholarships/financial aid; Agriculture, farmlands; Food services, commodity distribution.
Type of support: Undergraduate support.
Application information: Applications accepted. Application form required. Application form available on the grantmaker's web site.
  Initial approach: Letter
  Deadline(s): Apr. 1
EIN: 911638890

9747
Washington Dental Service Foundation
(also known as WDS Foundation)
9706 4th Ave. N.E.
Seattle, WA 98115-2157 (206) 528-2337
Contact: Laura Smith, Pres. and C.E.O.
Application address: P.O. Box 75983, Seattle, WA 98175-0983, toll free tel.: (800) 572-7835, ext. 5494
FAX: (206) 985-4876;
E-mail: foundation@deltadentalwa.com;
URL: http://www.deltadentalwa.com/Guest/Public/AboutUs/WDS%20Foundation.aspx

Foundation type: Public charity
Purpose: Scholarships to underrepresented minority students from Washington state who are interested in careers as dental hygenists, dental assistants or laboratory technicians.
Publications: Application guidelines; Grants list; Newsletter.
Financial data: Year ended 12/31/2011. Assets, $242,762 (M); Expenditures, $32,187; Total giving, $32,187; Grants to individuals, totaling $1,570.
Fields of interest: Dental school/education; Asians/Pacific Islanders; African Americans/Blacks; Hispanics/Latinos; Native Americans/American Indians.
Type of support: Scholarships—to individuals.
Application information: Applications accepted. Application form required.
  Send request by: Mail
  Deadline(s): July
  Final notification: Recipients notified in Sept.
  Applicants should submit the following:
    1) Financial information
    2) Letter(s) of recommendation
    3) Essay
    4) SAR
    5) FAFSA
Program description:
  Dental Team Scholarships: The foundation offers scholarships for underrepresented minority students who are interested in careers as dental hygienists, dental assistants, and laboratory technicians. Applicants must be Washington state residents and be part of an underrepresented minority group.
EIN: 911281990

9748
The George Washington Foundation
403 E. E St.
Yakima, WA 98901-2400 (506) 965-0706
Contact: James R. Sharples, Secy.
Application address: 2581 Mapleway Rd., Yakima, WA 98908-9673, tel.: (509) 965-0706

Foundation type: Independent foundation
Purpose: Scholarships to graduating local high school seniors in eastern WA for undergraduate study primarily at Yakima Valley College. Scholarships are available, however, for study at institutions nationwide.

Financial data: Year ended 06/30/2012. Assets, $1,225,793 (M); Expenditures, $93,104; Total giving, $81,197.
Type of support: Undergraduate support.
Application information: Applications accepted. Application form required.
  Deadline(s): Apr. 1
  Applicants should submit the following:
    1) Photograph
    2) Transcripts
    3) Financial information
    4) Essay
    5) Letter(s) of recommendation
  Additional information: Applications available from local public high school principals or counselors; Applications must also include student's personal and family data sheet and high school principal's data sheet.
EIN: 916024141

9749
Washington Foundation for Long Term Care
303 Cleveland Ave. S.E.
Tumwater, WA 98501-3340 (360) 652-3304

Foundation type: Independent foundation
Purpose: Scholarships to students of Washington State for postsecondary education pursuing health care related studies.
Financial data: Year ended 05/31/2012. Assets, $10,660 (M); Expenditures, $12,000; Total giving, $12,000; Grants to individuals, 6 grants totaling $12,000 (high: $2,500, low: $1,000).
Fields of interest: Health care.
Type of support: Scholarships—to individuals.
Application information: Applications accepted. Application form required.
  Deadline(s): Vary
  Additional information: Students must be nominated. Application should include letter of acceptance into a long term care related program of study and three letters of recommendation. Application form can be obtained from the foundation office.
EIN: 911725655

9750
Washington Women in Need
c/o The Bradford Ctr.
700 108th Ave. NE, Ste. 207
Bellevue, WA 98004-5102 (425) 451-8838
Contact: Michelle Nitz
FAX: (425) 451-8845; E-mail: programs@wwin.org;
Toll free tel.: (888) 440-9946; URL: http://www.wwin.org

Foundation type: Public charity
Purpose: Educational assistance to low-income women, including payments for tuition and books at accredited universities and technical colleges in Washington state and who reside there. Grants to low-income women who reside in WA, for health care and emergency services.
Publications: Application guidelines; Annual report; IRS Form 990 or 990-PF printed copy available upon request.
Financial data: Year ended 06/30/2012. Assets, $3,619,041 (M); Expenditures, $1,073,115; Total giving, $567,638; Grants to individuals, totaling $567,638.
Fields of interest: Education; Health care; Women.
Type of support: Scholarships—to individuals; Grants for special needs.
Application information: Applications accepted. Application form required.

Additional information: See web site for additional application guidelines.
EIN: 911559848

9751
George T. Welch Testamentary Trust
c/o Baker Boyer National Bank
P.O. Box 1796
Walla Walla, WA 99362-0353
Contact: Peter J. Allen, Trust Off., Baker Boyer National Bank

Foundation type: Independent foundation
Purpose: Scholarships for three undergraduate years to unmarried, financially needy students who are residents of Walla Walla County, WA, and are enrolled in four-year colleges. Medical and welfare assistance to financially needy residents of Walla Walla County, WA.
Publications: Application guidelines; Program policy statement.
Financial data: Year ended 09/30/2013. Assets, $3,803,441 (M); Expenditures, $204,300; Total giving, $163,908; Grants to individuals, 61 grants totaling $106,835 (high: $12,900, low: $114).
Fields of interest: Health care; Economically disadvantaged.
Type of support: Undergraduate support; Grants for special needs.
Application information: Applications accepted. Application form required. Application form available on the grantmaker's web site. Interview required.
  Initial approach: Letter
  Send request by: Mail
  Copies of proposal: 1
  Deadline(s): Apr. 15, May, 15, Aug. 15 and Nov. 15 for medical request and May 1 for academic request
  Final notification: Recipients notified in approximately 60 days
  Additional information: Forms for scholarship applicants available by Jan. 1.
EIN: 916024318

9752
Carrie Welch Trust
P.O. Box 82593
Kenmore, WA 98028-0593 (425) 478-6300
Contact: George Gose, Tr.

Foundation type: Independent foundation
Purpose: Financial assistance to financially needy and/or worthy aged persons residing in WA.
Financial data: Year ended 10/31/2012. Assets, $736,708 (M); Expenditures, $251,660; Total giving, $143,727; Grant to an individual, 1 grant totaling $242.
Fields of interest: Aging.
Type of support: Grants for special needs.
Application information:
  Deadline(s): None
  Additional information: Funds are fully committed.
EIN: 916030361

9753
Wenatchee Valley College Foundation, Inc.
1300 5th St.
Wenatchee, WA 98801-1741 (509) 682-6410
FAX: (509) 682-6401; E-mail: slockhart@wvc.edu;
E-Mail for Stacey Lockhart: (509)-682-6415;

URL: http://www.wvc.edu/directory/departments/wvcfoundation/home.asp

Foundation type: Public charity
Purpose: Scholarships for students attending Wenatchee Valley College, WA.
Financial data: Year ended 06/30/2011. Assets, $12,813,539 (M); Expenditures, $1,463,282; Total giving, $789,124; Grants to individuals, 142 grants totaling $212,029.
Fields of interest: Higher education.
Type of support: Support to graduates or students of specific schools.
Application information: Applications accepted. Application form required. Application form available on the grantmaker's web site.
  Deadline(s): Feb. 1
  Applicants should submit the following:
    1) GPA
    2) Transcripts
    3) Essay
  Additional information: Application should also include one letter of reference. Applications are available from the financial aid office and local high school counselors.
EIN: 237319272

9754
Harold E. & Esther L. Wills Foundation
10 Tala Shore Dr.
Port Ludlow, WA 98365

Foundation type: Operating foundation
Purpose: Provides financial assistance to low income individuals in the Port Ludlow, WA area with medical expense, utilities, rent and other special needs.
Financial data: Year ended 12/31/2011. Assets, $244,709 (M); Expenditures, $9,229; Total giving, $8,751; Grants to individuals, 17 grants totaling $7,251 (high: $1,000, low: $142).
Fields of interest: Economically disadvantaged.
Type of support: Grants for special needs.
Application information: Applications not accepted.
EIN: 911875068

9755
Windermere Foundation
5424 Sand Point Way N.E.
Seattle, WA 98105-2941 (206) 527-3801
URL: http://www.windermere.com/index.cfm?fuseaction=content.libraryHTMl&contentID=39823

Foundation type: Public charity
Purpose: Assistance to homeless and low-income families across the northwest with food, clothing, shelter and other services. Scholarships are also awarded based on need.
Publications: Annual report.
Financial data: Year ended 12/31/2011. Assets, $1,421,277 (M); Expenditures, $1,302,510; Total giving, $1,207,742.
Fields of interest: Housing/shelter, homeless.
Type of support: Grants for special needs.
Application information: Contact Windermere office in your neighborhood for information.
EIN: 911440894

9756
Ray Wittman Scholarship Fund
2320 Vista Ln.
Anacortes, WA 98221 (360) 293-3308
Contact: Glenn Watts, Pres.

Foundation type: Independent foundation
Purpose: Scholarships to individuals seeking a religious vocation in the Catholic church.
Financial data: Year ended 12/31/2012. Assets, $195,378 (M); Expenditures, $8,620; Total giving, $8,000; Grants to individuals, 8 grants totaling $8,000 (high: $1,000, low: $1,000).
Fields of interest: Theological school/education; Catholic agencies & churches.
Type of support: Scholarships—to individuals.
Application information: Applications accepted. Application form required.
  Deadline(s): None
  Additional information: Application must include recommendations. Applications can be obtained through the local Knights of Columbus Council.
EIN: 912093449

9757
Women Helping Women Fund
1325 W. 1st Ave., Ste. 318
Spokane, WA 99201-4136 (509) 328-8285
FAX: (509) 328-8291; E-mail: whwfund@qwest.net; URL: http://www.whwfspokane.org

Foundation type: Public charity
Purpose: Scholarships to young mothers in the greater Spokane, WA area to help them continue their higher education.
Financial data: Year ended 06/30/2012. Assets, $1,441,426 (M); Expenditures, $334,206; Total giving, $271,500; Grants to individuals, totaling $6,000.
Fields of interest: Higher education; Women.
Type of support: Scholarships—to individuals.
Application information: Applications accepted. Application form required.
  Additional information: See web site for additional application guidelines.
Program description:
  Vivian Winston Scholarship: The scholarship was established to assist young mothers in completing their college educations, allowing them to improve their lives, the lives of their children, and their community.
EIN: 911561874

9758
World Vision, Inc.
P.O. Box 9716
Federal Way, WA 98063-9716
E-mail: info@worldvision.org; Toll-free tel.: (888) 511-6443; URL: http://www.worldvision.org

Foundation type: Public charity
Purpose: Emergency assistance to individuals around the world in need with goods and services and help them get back on their feet and on the road to self-reliance, also grants to outstanding youth.
Publications: Annual report; Newsletter.
Financial data: Year ended 09/30/2012. Assets, $249,213,398 (M); Expenditures, $1,061,958,787; Total giving, $808,263,440; Grants to individuals, totaling $80,625.
Fields of interest: Public health; Human services; Christian agencies & churches; Children/youth; Economically disadvantaged.
Type of support: Emergency funds; Grants to individuals; Grants for special needs.
Application information: See web site for additional information.
EIN: 951922279

9759
Richard & Lois Worthington Foundation
15203 Gibralter Rd.
Anacortes, WA 98221-8615 (360) 293-9647
Contact: Barbara Matheson, Pres.

Foundation type: Independent foundation
Purpose: Scholarships to Bothell High School, WA students for postsecondary education.
Financial data: Year ended 09/30/2012. Assets, $5,567,286 (M); Expenditures, $295,120; Total giving, $243,500; Grants to individuals, 7 grants totaling $29,000 (high: $9,000, low: $2,500).
Fields of interest: Higher education.
Type of support: Support to graduates or students of specific schools.
Application information: Applications accepted.
  Deadline(s): Vary
  Additional information: Application available upon request.
EIN: 911909665

9760
Yakima Valley Farm Workers Clinic
518 W. 1st Ave.
P.O. Box 190
Toppenish, WA 98948-1564 (509) 865-5898
FAX: (509) 865-4337; URL: http://www.yvfwc.com

Foundation type: Public charity
Purpose: Assistance to low-income families with medical and dental care, behavioral health care and counseling, pharmacy services, treatment for substance abuse, education, and other services in several Pacific Northwest communities in Washington and Oregon.
Financial data: Year ended 03/31/2012. Assets, $173,007,141 (M); Expenditures, $124,438,579; Total giving, $4,308,251; Grants to individuals, totaling $2,349,764.
Fields of interest: Health care; Human services.
Type of support: Grants for special needs.
Application information: Contact the clinic for eligibility requirements.
EIN: 911019392

9761
Yelm Community Services
P.O. Box 5320
Yelm, WA 98597-5320 (360) 458-7000
Contact: Cindy Cecil, Exec. Dir.

Foundation type: Public charity
Purpose: Financial assistance to indigent residents of Yelm, WA, to help pay for living expenses.
Financial data: Year ended 06/30/2012. Assets, $4,067,042 (M); Expenditures, $2,244,507.
Type of support: Grants for special needs.
Application information:
  Initial approach: Letter
  Additional information: Contact foundation for further information.
EIN: 237226534

9762
Young Womens Christian Association of Seattle-King County-Snohomish City
1118 5th Ave.
Seattle, WA 98101-3001 (206) 490-4380
Contact: Sue Sherbrooke, C.E.O.
E-mail: engage@ywcaworks.org; E-mail For Sue Sherbrooke: ssherb@ywcaworks.org; URL: https://www.ywcaworks.org/netcommunity/

Foundation type: Public charity

Purpose: Assistance to women, children and families in need throughout King county, WA with food, clothing, shelter, child care and other special needs.

Publications: Occasional report.

Financial data: Year ended 12/31/2011. Assets, $149,791,170 (M); Expenditures, $34,809,447; Total giving, $6,826,276; Grants to individuals, totaling $4,880,970.

Fields of interest: Human services, emergency aid; Economically disadvantaged.

Type of support: In-kind gifts; Grants for special needs.

Application information: Contact the organization for eligibility determination.

EIN: 910482890

WEST VIRGINIA

9763
Sally Adams Scholarship Fund
1 Bank Pz.
Wheeling, WV 26003 (304) 234-9400
Contact: Steven Kellas

Foundation type: Independent foundation
Purpose: Scholarships to legal residents of Ohio County, WV, who are financially needy, aged 17 to 25, and graduates of public high schools in Wheeling, WV.
Financial data: Year ended 12/31/2012. Assets, $270,663 (M); Expenditures, $14,565; Total giving, $11,300.
Fields of interest: Education.
Type of support: Support to graduates or students of specific schools; Undergraduate support.
Application information: Applications accepted. Application form required.
Deadline(s): Spring
EIN: 556085702

9764
Arthur's Enterprises, Inc. Scholarship Foundation
P.O. Box 5654
Huntington, WV 25703-0654
Contact: Joan Weisberg, Secy. and Dir.
Application address: P.O. Box 5346, Huntington, WV 25703

Foundation type: Company-sponsored foundation
Purpose: Scholarships to children of employees of Arthur's Enterprises, Inc. and its subsidiaries.
Financial data: Year ended 06/30/2012. Assets, $1,891 (M); Expenditures, $26,602; Total giving, $26,500; Grants to individuals, 27 grants totaling $26,500 (high: $1,000, low: $500).
Fields of interest: Scholarships/financial aid.
Type of support: Employee-related scholarships.
Application information: Applications not accepted.
Additional information: Unsolicited requests for funds not considered or acknowledged.
Company name: Arthur's Enterprises, Inc.
EIN: 550709058

9765
Aurora Project, Inc.
25208 George Washington Hwy.
Aurora, WV 26705-8036 (304) 735-3620
E-mail: info@auroraproject.org; URL: http://www.auroraproject.org

Foundation type: Public charity
Purpose: Residencies to artists specializing in visual arts, film, video, music, and writing, to stay in WV.
Publications: Application guidelines.
Financial data: Year ended 12/31/2011. Assets, $740,088 (M); Expenditures, $126,044.
Fields of interest: Film/video; Visual arts; Architecture; Art conservation; Music; Literature.
Type of support: Residencies.
Application information: Applications accepted.
Initial approach: Letter or e-mail
Additional information: Contact foundation for additional guidelines.

Program description:
Artist Residencies: The organization offers three- to six-week residencies for up to nine artists and scholars per session. Artists can be in any stage of their career (but not be students), and work in the following disciplines: visual arts (photography and media arts, drawing, installation, painting, sculpture, textiles, and fiber arts and mixed media); writing (fiction and literary non-fiction, playwriting, poetry, translation and screenwriting); performing arts (music composition and recording, performance art, and storytelling); design (architecture, industrial design, landscape architecture, urban/rural planning, and scholarly research design); writing (historic preservation, art history and criticism, ecology, and environmental studies); new genres; and interdisciplinary and environmental arts. Accommodations include three meals per day, access to a wood fire kiln, a printmaking studio, a commercial glass blowing company, and community arts opportunities.
EIN: 550783568

9766
Beckley Area Foundation, Inc.
129 Main St., Ste. 203
Beckley, WV 25801-4615 (304) 253-3806
Contact: Susan S. Landis, Exec. Dir.; For scholarships: Sharon Lilly, Prog. Dir. and Off. Mgr.
FAX: (304) 253-7304; E-mail: info@bafwv.org; URL: http://www.bafwv.org/

Foundation type: Community foundation
Purpose: Scholarships to residents of WV who are full-time students with a 2.5 GPA or higher. Mini-grants of $500 to Raleigh County, WV, classroom teachers Pre-K through 12 for supplementary classroom programs.
Publications: Application guidelines; Annual report; Financial statement; Grants list; Informational brochure; Informational brochure (including application guidelines); Newsletter; Occasional report; Program policy statement (including application guidelines).
Financial data: Year ended 03/31/2013. Assets, $31,560,282 (M); Expenditures, $974,282; Total giving, $672,843; Grants to individuals, totaling $4,456.
Fields of interest: Education.
Type of support: Program development; Scholarships—to individuals; Awards/prizes; Graduate support; Technical education support; Undergraduate support.
Application information: Applications accepted. Application form required.
Send request by: Mail
Copies of proposal: 1
Deadline(s): Apr. 1
Final notification: Applicants are informed within three months
Applicants should submit the following:
1) ACT
2) FAFSA
3) Financial information
4) Letter(s) of recommendation
5) SAT
6) Transcripts
Additional information: See web site for a list of eligible schools and additional information. The foundation manages various scholarship funds with specific eligibility criteria.
EIN: 311125328

9767
Big Green Scholarship Foundation, Inc.
P.O. Box 1360
Huntington, WV 25715-1360 (304) 696-4661
FAX: (304) 696-6665;
E-mail: biggreen@marshall.edu; URL: http://herdzone.cstv.com/big-green/

Foundation type: Public charity
Purpose: Scholarships to male and female student athletes of Marshall University, WV for continuing education.
Financial data: Year ended 06/30/2012. Assets, $13,718,083 (M); Expenditures, $3,622,703; Total giving, $1,515,688; Grants to individuals, totaling $670,839.
Fields of interest: Higher education.
Type of support: Support to graduates or students of specific schools.
Application information: Unsolicited requests for funds not considered or acknowledged.
EIN: 550631935

9768
Ethel N. Bowen Foundation
c/o First Century Bank, N.A.
500 Federal St.
Bluefield, WV 24701-3010 (304) 325-8181

Foundation type: Independent foundation
Purpose: Scholarships to students from the coal mining areas of southern WV and southwestern VA.
Financial data: Year ended 12/31/2012. Assets, $8,971,874 (M); Expenditures, $406,944; Total giving, $346,070; Grants to individuals, 411 grants totaling $294,595 (high: $2,000, low: $158).
Type of support: Scholarships—to individuals.
Application information: Applications accepted. Interview required.
Initial approach: Letter
Deadline(s): Prior to beginning of academic year
Applicants should submit the following:
1) Resume
2) Transcripts
Additional information: Applications by letter should also include a biographical outline.
EIN: 237010740

9769
The Warren and Betty Burnside Foundation, Inc.
300 W. Pike St.
Clarksburg, WV 26301-2710 (304) 623-3668
Contact: James C. West, Jr.
E-mail: burnsidefoundation@frontier.com;
URL: http://www.burnsidefoundation.org

Foundation type: Independent foundation
Purpose: Scholarships restricted to residents of Harrison County, WV, who have attended a Harrison County high school for four years for attendance at colleges, universities, and technical schools.
Financial data: Year ended 01/31/2013. Assets, $6,668,370 (M); Expenditures, $318,728; Total giving, $213,000; Grants to individuals, totaling $213,000.
Fields of interest: Vocational education.
Type of support: Support to graduates or students of specific schools; Undergraduate support.
Application information: Application form required.
Deadline(s): Mar. 15
Applicants should submit the following:
1) Transcripts
2) SAT
3) Photograph
4) Letter(s) of recommendation

5) Financial information
6) FAF
7) ACT
Additional information: Application should also include a personal statement of 200 words or less.
EIN: 550709158

9770
Camden-Clark Foundation, Inc.
800 Garfield Ave.
Parkersburg, WV 26101-5340 (304) 424-2200
Contact: Kim Couch, Secy. and Exec. Dir.
Application address: P.O. Box 1834, Parkersburg, WV 26102
FAX: (304) 424-2821; E-mail: kcouch@ccmh.org; URL: http://www.ccmh.org/CommunityConnection/CamdenClarkFoundation.aspx

Foundation type: Public charity
Purpose: Nursing scholarships to students who have been accepted to a nursing program accredited by the National League of Nursing.
Publications: Application guidelines.
Financial data: Year ended 06/30/2012. Assets, $1,610,650 (M); Expenditures, $507,265; Total giving, $307,611; Grants to individuals, totaling $13,000.
Fields of interest: Nursing school/education.
Type of support: Scholarships—to individuals.
Application information: Applications accepted. Application form required. Application form available on the grantmaker's web site.
  Initial approach: Telephone or e-mail
  Send request by: Mail
  Deadline(s): Apr.
  Applicants should submit the following:
    1) Transcripts
    2) Letter(s) of recommendation
    3) Essay
Program description:
  Nursing Scholarships: The foundation awards two $1,500 to nursing students and two $1,500 scholarships to employees of Camden Clark employees who wish to continue their education. Eligible applicants must live in the area served by Camden Clark medical center, which includes eleven counties in WV and OH, have written documentation of acceptance to a nursing program accredited by the National League of Nursing, have successfully completed one year of nursing, and be currently enrolled as a second-year nursing student. The scholarship must be used within the next academic year.
EIN: 550667789

9771
The Valerie Canady Charitable Foundation Trust
c/o Leonard J. George
512 Princeton Ave.
Morgantown, WV 26505-2120 (304) 292-5171
Contact: William J. Canady
Application address: 127 Jackson Ave., Morgantown, WV 26505-6567

Foundation type: Independent foundation
Purpose: Scholarships to high school students in WV, and to those furthering their academic studies in the areas of business and foreign languages.
Financial data: Year ended 12/31/2012. Assets, $61,686 (M); Expenditures, $21,627; Total giving, $20,000; Grants to individuals, 10 grants totaling $20,000 (high: $2,000, low: $2,000).

Fields of interest: Language (foreign); Business school/education.
Type of support: Scholarships—to individuals.
Application information: Applications accepted.
  Deadline(s): May
EIN: 550692616

9772
Carter Family Foundation
P.O. Box 393
Charleston, WV 25322-0393 (304) 256-7301
Contact: Maria L. Miller

Foundation type: Operating foundation
Purpose: Grants to specific WV colleges and universities for scholarships. Priority is shown to WV students, with an emphasis on Raleigh county, WV students.
Financial data: Year ended 06/30/2012. Assets, $13,706,352 (M); Expenditures, $321,653; Total giving, $248,348.
Fields of interest: Education.
Type of support: Support to graduates or students of specific schools.
Application information: Applications accepted.
  Additional information: Applications through financial aid offices at specific schools.
EIN: 550606479

9773
Dante Castrodale Scholarship Foundation
P.O. Box 950
Bluefield, WV 24701-0950 (304) 325-2751

Foundation type: Independent foundation
Purpose: Scholarships to residents of McDowell County, WV.
Financial data: Year ended 12/31/2011. Assets, $506,558 (M); Expenditures, $26,813; Total giving, $23,955; Grants to individuals, 9 grants totaling $23,955 (high: $3,000, low: $2,455).
Type of support: Scholarships—to individuals.
Application information: Applications accepted. Application form required.
  Deadline(s): Jan. to May
  Final notification: Recipients notified in June
  Applicants should submit the following:
    1) Class rank
    2) GPA
  Additional information: Application should also include a personal statement.
EIN: 626198751

9774
The Roy Chambers Foundation
1358 National Rd.
Wheeling, WV 26003-5742
Contact: Linda M. Bordas, Tr.

Foundation type: Independent foundation
Purpose: Grants to needy children of Ohio County, WV, for general welfare, including eye care, clothing, school supplies, and sports camp.
Financial data: Year ended 12/31/2011. Assets, $1,033,919 (M); Expenditures, $44,827; Total giving, $40,612; Grants to individuals, 295 grants totaling $36,112 (high: $2,746, low: $87).
Fields of interest: Optometry/vision screening; Athletics/sports, training; Children/youth, services; Economically disadvantaged.
Type of support: Grants for special needs.
Application information: Applications accepted. Application form required.
  Deadline(s): None
EIN: 556113902

9775
City Hospital Foundation, Inc.
(formerly Gateway Foundation, Inc.)
2000 Foundation Way, Ste. 2310
Martinsburg, WV 25401 (304) 264-1358
FAX: (304) 264-1292

Foundation type: Public charity
Purpose: Scholarships to residents of Berkeley, Jefferson and Morgan counties, WV.
Publications: Financial statement; Informational brochure.
Financial data: Year ended 12/31/2011. Assets, $23,622,052 (M); Expenditures, $1,029,380; Total giving, $193,991.
Type of support: Scholarships—to individuals; Undergraduate support.
Application information: Applications not accepted.
  Additional information: Deadline is Mar. 31. Contact foundation for further application guidelines. Unsolicited applications not accepted or considered.
EIN: 311118075

9776
Community Foundation for the Ohio Valley, Inc.
(also known as CFOV)
1310 Market St.
Wheeling, WV 26003-0085 (304) 242-3144
Contact: Susie Nelson, Exec. Dir.
FAX: (304) 234-4753; E-mail: info@cfov.org; Mailing address: P.O. 670, Wheeling, WV 26003-0085; Additional e-mail: director@cfov.org; URL: http://www.cfov.org

Foundation type: Community foundation
Purpose: Scholarships to qualified students in Belmont and Jefferson counties, OH; and Ohio, Marshall, Tyler, Wetzel, and Brooke counties, WV.
Publications: Application guidelines; Annual report; Annual report (including application guidelines); Grants list; Informational brochure; Newsletter; Program policy statement.
Financial data: Year ended 06/30/2012. Assets, $26,123,744 (M); Expenditures, $1,366,250; Total giving, $1,057,073.
Fields of interest: Higher education.
Type of support: Scholarships—to individuals.
Application information: Applications accepted. Application form required. Application form available on the grantmaker's web site.
  Send request by: Mail
  Deadline(s): Mar. 7
  Applicants should submit the following:
    1) Transcripts
    2) SAT
    3) Letter(s) of recommendation
    4) GPA
    5) Financial information
    6) FAFSA
    7) Essay
    8) Curriculum vitae
    9) Budget Information
    10) ACT
  Additional information: See web site for a complete listing of scholarship programs and criteria.
EIN: 310908698

9777
Community Foundation of the Virginias, Inc.
(formerly Bluefield Area Foundation, Inc.)
128 North St.
P.O. Box 4127
Bluefield, WV   24701-4060   (304) 324-0222
Contact: James H. Shott, Exec. Dir.
FAX: (304) 324-7716; E-mail: admin@cfvinc.org;
Additional e-mail: execdir@cfvinc.org; URL: http://
www.cfvinc.org

Foundation type: Community foundation
Purpose: Scholarships to area high school and college students seeking to further their education. Some scholarships cover Mercer and McDowell Counties, WV and Tazewell, Bland and Buchanan Counties, VA.
Publications: Application guidelines; Annual report; Financial statement; Grants list; Informational brochure (including application guidelines); Newsletter.
Financial data: Year ended 12/31/2012. Assets, $4,319,435 (M); Expenditures, $476,349; Total giving, $360,190; Grants to individuals, totaling $51,220.
Fields of interest: Higher education; Scholarships/financial aid.
Type of support: Scholarships—to individuals; Undergraduate support.
Application information: Applications accepted. Application form required. Application form available on the grantmaker's web site.
    Initial approach: Application
    Send request by: Online
    Deadline(s): Last business day of Mar.
    Final notification: Recipients notified one month after deadline
    Applicants should submit the following:
        1) Transcripts
        2) SAT
        3) Resume
        4) Letter(s) of recommendation
        5) GPA
        6) Essay
        7) ACT
    Additional information: See web site or contact your high school guidance counselors for additional information.
EIN: 550724623

9778
Raymond B. Craig Scholarship Fund
c/o Robert P. Fitzsimmons
1609 Warwood Ave.
Wheeling, WV   26003

Foundation type: Independent foundation
Purpose: Scholarships to students of West Liberty State College, WV.
Financial data: Year ended 12/31/2012. Assets, $142,750 (M); Expenditures, $3,255; Total giving, $3,000; Grants to individuals, 3 grants totaling $3,000 (high: $1,000, low: $1,000).
Fields of interest: Higher education.
Type of support: Scholarships—to individuals; Support to graduates or students of specific schools.
Application information: Applications accepted. Application form required.
    Deadline(s): None
EIN: 550752656

9779
George M. Cruise Charitable Foundation
P.O. Box 950
Bluefield, WV   24701-0950   (304) 325-7151
Contact: George Cruise

Foundation type: Independent foundation
Purpose: Scholarships to area residents of southern WV, or southwestern, VA, to attend U.S. colleges.
Financial data: Year ended 12/31/2012. Assets, $2,995,466 (M); Expenditures, $169,359; Total giving, $141,500.
Type of support: Scholarships—to individuals.
Application information: Applications accepted. Application form required.
    Deadline(s): May
    Applicants should submit the following:
        1) Class rank
        2) Transcripts
        3) SAT
        4) Letter(s) of recommendation
        5) GPA
        6) ACT
EIN: 626214545

9780
Eastern West Virginia Community Foundation
229 E. Martin St., Ste. 4
Martinsburg, WV   25401-4307   (304) 264-0353
Contact: Michael Whalton, Exec. Dir.
FAX: (888) 507-8375; E-mail: info@ewvcf.org;
URL: http://www.ewvcf.org

Foundation type: Community foundation
Purpose: Scholarships to residents of Jefferson, Hampshire, Berkeley and Morgan counties, WV for postsecondary education.
Publications: Application guidelines; Annual report; Financial statement; Grants list; Informational brochure; Newsletter.
Financial data: Year ended 12/31/2012. Assets, $16,684,886 (M); Expenditures, $1,198,615; Total giving, $897,359; Grants to individuals, 46 grants totaling $56,920.
Fields of interest: Higher education; Law school/education.
Type of support: Scholarships—to individuals; Support to graduates or students of specific schools; Undergraduate support.
Application information: Applications accepted. Application form required. Application form available on the grantmaker's web site.
    Initial approach: Application
    Send request by: Online or submit hard copy
    Deadline(s): Mar. 1
    Final notification: Applicants notified by June 1
    Applicants should submit the following:
        1) Financial information
        2) Essay
        3) Transcripts
        4) FAFSA
        5) Letter(s) of recommendation
    Additional information: See web site for complete listing of scholarships. The universal scholarship application is also available on the foundation's web site, or at area school guidance departments.
Program description:
    Scholarship Funds: The foundation administers many different scholarship funds for the benefit of Eastern Panhandle county residents pursuing education in a postsecondary setting. Each scholarship fund has its own selection criteria to evaluate and determine scholarship awards. Some scholarships are for graduates of specific high

schools, while others are require an intent to earn a degree in a specific area of study such as business, agriculture or education. All students must have applied to one or more accredited post-secondary institutions or must be currently enrolled in a college or university at the time of application. See web site for additional information.
EIN: 550742377

9781
The Emerich Scholarship Charitable Trust
P.O. Box 4868
Charleston, WV   25364-4168
Application address: c/o Braxton County High School, Attn.: Principal, 200 Jerry Burton Dr., Sutton, WV 26601-9768

Foundation type: Independent foundation
Purpose: Scholarships to students from Braxton County High School, WV attending a college or university in WV.
Financial data: Year ended 12/31/2012. Assets, $347,468 (M); Expenditures, $18,093; Total giving, $13,500.
Fields of interest: Higher education.
Type of support: Scholarships—to individuals.
Application information: Applications accepted. Application form required.
    Deadline(s): Mar. 1
EIN: 311746382

9782
Fairmont State Foundation, Inc.
1300 Locust Ave.
Fairmont, WV   26554-1436   (304) 367-4213
Contact: K. Jean Ahwesh, Exec. Dir.
FAX: (304) 367-4584;
E-mail: FinancialAid@fairmontstate.edu; Toll Free Tel. : (800)-641-5678 Ext. 2; URL: http://
www.fairmontstate.edu/finaid/funding/
foundation-scholarships

Foundation type: Public charity
Purpose: Scholarships to low-income men and women of West Virginia pursuing a degree at Fairmont State University and Pierpont Community & Technical College.
Publications: Occasional report.
Financial data: Year ended 06/30/2012. Assets, $16,897,103 (M); Expenditures, $1,801,187; Total giving, $1,443,863; Grants to individuals, totaling $992,171.
Fields of interest: Higher education.
Type of support: Support to graduates or students of specific schools.
Application information: Contact the foundation for eligibility determination.
EIN: 556023559

9783
Family Medicine Foundation of West Virginia
650 Main St.
Barboursville, WV   25504-1439   (304) 733-6485
Contact: Robert D. Hess, Pres.
FAX: (304) 733-6486;
E-mail: fam.med.foundation@citynet.net;
URL: http://www.fmfwv.org/

Foundation type: Public charity
Purpose: Scholarships to needy medical students who plan on practicing family medicine in WV.
Publications: Application guidelines; Annual report.

Financial data: Year ended 12/31/2011. Assets, $2,128,476 (M); Expenditures, $317,906; Total giving, $29,534; Grants to individuals, totaling $29,534.
Fields of interest: Medical school/education.
Type of support: Doctoral support.
Application information:
Initial approach: Letter
Additional information: Contact foundation for eligibility criteria.
EIN: 311053219

9784
The Elizabeth S. Faris, Katherine K. Steinbicker, & Paul F. Steinbicker Scholarship Fund
c/o Thomas & Ann Thomas
5 Emerson Rd.
Wheeling, WV 26003-6631

Foundation type: Independent foundation
Purpose: Scholarships to residents of Ohio County, WV.
Financial data: Year ended 12/31/2011. Assets, $460,140 (M); Expenditures, $30,210; Total giving, $25,000; Grants to individuals, 5 grants totaling $25,000 (high: $5,000, low: $5,000).
Type of support: Scholarships—to individuals.
Application information: Applications accepted. Application form required.
Deadline(s): Jan. 31
EIN: 542085195

9785
Charles H. Feoppel Educational Loan Trust
P.O. Box 633
Charleston, WV 25322-0633 (304) 348-4582
Contact: Carla D. Parsons, Tr.
FAX: (304) 348-4552

Foundation type: Independent foundation
Purpose: Student loans to financially needy single boys and girls who are residents of Harrison County, WV, to pursue higher education at WV college or trade school.
Publications: Informational brochure (including application guidelines).
Financial data: Year ended 12/31/2012. Assets, $3,940,025 (M); Expenditures, $43,504; Total giving, $0; Loans to individuals, totaling $87,500.
Fields of interest: Vocational education, post-secondary; Higher education.
Type of support: Student loans—to individuals.
Application information: Application form required.
Deadline(s): May 31
Additional information: Financial need is the prime determinant in granting loans. Loans are given for one year and recipients must reapply each year.
EIN: 556107185

9786
Charles L. and Anna N. Gault Scholarship Fund
c/o United Bank, Inc.
514 Market St.
Parkersburg, WV 26101-5144 (304) 424-8800

Foundation type: Independent foundation
Purpose: Scholarships by nomination only to financially needy senior students attending high schools in Wood and Wirt counties, WV, who are members of the Methodist church.

Financial data: Year ended 12/31/2012. Assets, $760,187 (M); Expenditures, $48,658; Total giving, $39,250; Grants to individuals, 54 grants totaling $39,250 (high: $1,000, low: $250).
Fields of interest: Higher education; Protestant agencies & churches.
Type of support: Support to graduates or students of specific schools; Awards/grants by nomination only; Undergraduate support.
Application information:
Deadline(s): Three months prior to graduation date
Additional information: Contact foundation for current application guidelines.
EIN: 556096793

9787
The Philip A. Haddad Scholarship Fund
1033 Quarrier St., Ste. 511
Charleston, WV 25301-2317 (304) 345-2320
Contact: Edward "Philip" A. Haddad, Tr.
Application address: P.O. Box 4154, Charleston, WV 25364-4154, tel.: (304) 345-2320

Foundation type: Independent foundation
Purpose: Scholarships to individuals who are members of the St. George Orthodox church in Charleston, WV.
Financial data: Year ended 12/31/2010. Assets, $80,974 (M); Expenditures, $4,997; Total giving, $3,700; Grants to individuals, 5 grants totaling $3,700 (high: $800, low: $500).
Fields of interest: Higher education.
Type of support: Scholarships—to individuals.
Application information: Applications accepted. Application form required.
Deadline(s): Oct. 31
Additional information: Contact fund for application guidelines.
EIN: 550668433

9788
James H. Harless Foundation, Inc.
P. O. Box 1210
Gilbert, WV 25621-1210 (304) 664-3227
Contact: James H. Harless, Pres.

Foundation type: Public charity
Purpose: Student loans to residents of the Gilbert, WV, area. Loans to distressed families in the Gilbert, WV, area.
Financial data: Year ended 12/31/2011. Assets, $359,232 (M); Expenditures, $114,468; Total giving, $107,310.
Fields of interest: Family services.
Type of support: Student loans—to individuals; Grants for special needs.
Application information: Application form required.
Deadline(s): None
EIN: 237093387

9789
Adolph & Edith Harries & Eleanor Tippens Scholarship Trust
(also known as Tippens Charitable Trust)
415 Market St.
Parkersburg, WV 26101-5338 (304) 485-8010

Foundation type: Independent foundation
Purpose: Scholarships to financially needy high school students of Wood County, WV, for study at a college, university, or trade school in WV.
Financial data: Year ended 12/31/2011. Assets, $1,919,447 (M); Expenditures, $152,433; Total

giving, $135,084; Grants to individuals, 25 grants totaling $135,084 (high: $19,208, low: $393).
Fields of interest: Vocational education; Higher education.
Type of support: Support to graduates or students of specific schools.
Application information: Applications accepted.
Initial approach: Letter
Deadline(s): Apr. 1
Additional information: The principal and guidance counselor of each high school in Wood County, WV nominates two students.
EIN: 556118733

9790
Hinton Area Foundation
P.O. Box 217
Hinton, WV 25951-0217 (304) 466-5332
Contact: Jerry Beasley, Exec. Dir.
Scholarship application address: Hinton Area Foundation Scholarship Committee, P.O. Box 127, Hinton, WV
25951,e-mail: Scholarships@HintonAreaFoundatio n.com
E-mail: info@hintonareafoundation.com;
URL: http://www.hintonareafoundation.com

Foundation type: Community foundation
Purpose: Scholarships to graduates of Summers County, WV, public schools, for higher education.
Publications: Annual report; Grants list.
Financial data: Year ended 12/31/2012. Assets, $2,897,677 (M); Expenditures, $168,786; Total giving, $129,551; Grants to individuals, 61 grants totaling $101,624.
Fields of interest: Higher education; Medical school/education; Scholarships/financial aid.
Type of support: Scholarships—to individuals; Support to graduates or students of specific schools; Undergraduate support.
Application information: Applications accepted. Application form required. Application form available on the grantmaker's web site.
Initial approach: Application
Send request by: Mail or e-mail
Deadline(s): May 1
Applicants should submit the following:
1) Transcripts
2) Letter(s) of recommendation
3) SAT
4) ACT
5) GPA
6) Class rank
7) SAR
Additional information: See web site for a complete listing of scholarship programs.
EIN: 550716276

9791
P.G. and Ruby Hollandsworth Memorial Trust
349 Buckhannon Ave.
Clarksburg, WV 26301-3134 (304) 624-0022
Contact: Terring M. Weaver, Tr.

Foundation type: Independent foundation
Purpose: Scholarships to graduating seniors of North Central West Virginia with preference given to graduating seniors in Harrison and Nicholas counties, WV with an overall preference given to students with physical impairments as defined by the Americans with Disabilities Act.
Financial data: Year ended 12/31/2012. Assets, $4,592,506 (M); Expenditures, $207,530; Total giving, $182,500; Grants to individuals, 49 grants totaling $72,500 (high: $3,000, low: $500).

Fields of interest: Higher education; Disabilities, people with.
Type of support: Scholarships—to individuals.
Application information: Applications accepted. Application form required.
> *Send request by:* Mail
> *Deadline(s):* May 31
> *Applicants should submit the following:*
> 1) Transcripts
> 2) Letter(s) of recommendation
> 3) Financial information
> *Additional information:* Selection is based on financial need and academic performance.
EIN: 266577320

9792
I.O.O.F. Grand Lodge Educational Fund
c/o Paul L. Hevner
1465 Tremont Ave.
Morgantown, WV 26505-5335
Contact: Carl C. Williams, Secy.
Application address: 371 Thorn Stop Cir., Clarksburg, WV 26301

Foundation type: Independent foundation
Purpose: Scholarships to members of The Independent Order of Odd Fellows of WV and their children.
Financial data: Year ended 12/31/2013. Assets, $458,787 (M); Expenditures, $56,186; Total giving, $54,000.
Type of support: Scholarships—to individuals.
Application information: Applications accepted. Application form required.
> *Deadline(s):* None
> *Additional information:* Application must include transcripts, personal statement, and a letter from the Lodge of I.O.O.F., under seal of Lodge, stating that applicant is eligible.
EIN: 237003391

9793
Jefferson County Tuberculosis Association, Inc.
114 W. 6th Ave.
Ranson, WV 25438 (304) 724-6979
Contact: Kathryn Williams, Treas.

Foundation type: Independent foundation
Purpose: Grants to residents of Jefferson County, WV, related to cardio-pulmonary diseases.
Financial data: Year ended 12/31/2011. Assets, $145,522 (M); Expenditures, $37,522; Total giving, $35,009; Grants to individuals, 6 grants totaling $13,809 (high: $8,295, low: $289).
Fields of interest: Health sciences school/education; Heart & circulatory diseases; Heart & circulatory research.
Type of support: Scholarships—to individuals; Grants for special needs.
Application information: Applications accepted. Application form not required.
> *Initial approach:* Letter or telephone
> *Deadline(s):* None
EIN: 550713040

9794
The Greater Kanawha Valley Foundation
1600 Huntington Sq.
900 Lee St. E.
Charleston, WV 25301-1741 (304) 346-3620
Contact: Rebecca Ceperley, C.E.O.; For grants: Stephanie Hyre, Prog. Off.; For scholarships: Susan Hoover, Scholarship Prog. Off.
Scholarship e-mail: shoover@tgkvf.org
FAX: (304) 346-3640; *E-mail:* tgkvf@tgkvf.org;
URL: http://www.tgkvf.org

Foundation type: Community foundation
Purpose: Scholarships to residents of WV for undergraduate, graduate, vocational, and technical education.
Publications: Application guidelines; Annual report (including application guidelines); Financial statement; Grants list; Informational brochure; Occasional report.
Financial data: Year ended 12/31/2012. Assets, $192,410,440 (M); Expenditures, $7,700,708; Total giving, $6,439,102; Grants to individuals, totaling $473,100.
Fields of interest: Vocational education; Higher education; Graduate/professional education; Scholarships/financial aid.
Type of support: Scholarships—to individuals; Support to graduates or students of specific schools; Graduate support; Technical education support; Undergraduate support.
Application information: Applications accepted. Application form required. Application form available on the grantmaker's web site.
> *Send request by:* Online
> *Deadline(s):* Jan 15
> *Final notification:* Applicants notified May 15
> *Applicants should submit the following:*
> 1) ACT
> 2) Transcripts
> 3) Letter(s) of recommendation
> 4) Financial information
> *Additional information:* See web site for complete listing of scholarship funds.
Program description:
> *Scholarship Funds:* The foundation administers over 90 scholarships established by individuals, firms and organizations wanting to assist West Virginia residents in obtaining a college education. Applicants apply to the program and, if eligible, may be awarded a scholarship. General criteria that applies to most scholarships are as follows: 1) must be a resident of West Virginia with the exception of The Kid's Chance Scholarship; 2) must be a full time student (minimum of 12 Credit Hours); 3) must demonstrate academic achievement (at least a 2.5 GPA); 4) minimum score of 20 on the ACT; and 5) must demonstrate good moral character. Each scholarship has additional specific eligibility criteria. See web site for additional information.
EIN: 556024430

9795
Gay R. Larsen Charitable Education Trust
1 Bank Plz.
Wheeling, WV 26003 (304) 234-9463
Contact: Gay R. Larsen
Aoolication Address: P.O. Box 107, Wheeling, WV. 26003

Foundation type: Independent foundation
Purpose: Scholarships to high school graduates residing in the northern Panhandle counties of WV and OH.
Financial data: Year ended 12/31/2012. Assets, $1,620,326 (M); Expenditures, $106,872; Total

giving, $88,000; Grants to individuals, 41 grants totaling $88,000 (high: $2,500, low: $2,000).
Fields of interest: Vocational education, post-secondary; Higher education; Scholarships/financial aid.
Type of support: Undergraduate support.
Application information: Applications accepted. Application form required.
> *Initial approach:* Telephone
> *Send request by:* Mail
> *Deadline(s):* Feb. 10 for new applicants, June 15 for renewals.
> *Applicants should submit the following:*
> 1) Class rank
> 2) GPA
> 3) Essay
> 4) SAT
> 5) ACT
> *Additional information:* Application should also include extracurricular activities and community service.
EIN: 556128918

9796
George A. Laughlin Trust
1 Bank Plz.
Wheeling, WV 26003-3543 (304) 234-9400
Contact: Lea Ridenhour
E-mail: ridenhour@wesbanco.com

Foundation type: Independent foundation
Purpose: Interest-free home loans to Ohio County, WV, families with one or more dependent children, to purchase homes.
Financial data: Year ended 12/31/2012. Assets, $15,210,366 (M); Expenditures, $795,140; Total giving, $668,078.
Fields of interest: Housing/shelter.
Type of support: Grants for special needs.
Application information: Applications accepted. Application form required. Interview required.
> *Initial approach:* Telephone
> *Send request by:* Mail
> *Deadline(s):* May 31
EIN: 556016889

9797
The Logan County Charitable and Educational Foundation, Inc.
325 Stratton St.
Logan, WV 25601-1367 (304) 855-4574
E-mail: lccandefoundation@verizon.net;
URL: http://logancountycharitableandeducationalfoundation.org/

Foundation type: Public charity
Purpose: Scholarships to local high school students and residents of Logan County, WV.
Publications: Application guidelines; Annual report; Informational brochure.
Financial data: Year ended 12/31/2011. Assets, $2,175,975 (M); Expenditures, $73,138; Total giving, $62,807; Grants to individuals, totaling $62,807.
Type of support: Scholarships—to individuals; Undergraduate support.
Application information: Applications accepted. Application form required.
> *Initial approach:* Letter
> *Copies of proposal:* 1
> *Deadline(s):* Open
> *Applicants should submit the following:*
> 1) Letter(s) of recommendation
> 2) GPA
> 3) Financial information

4) Essay
5) Budget Information
6) ACT
EIN: 311498923

9798
Merwin C. Ludwig Educational Trust
P.O. Box 119
Wardensville, WV 26851-0552 (304) 874-3531
Contact: Patti Combs, Pres.

Foundation type: Independent foundation
Purpose: Scholarships to high school graduates from Hardy and Hampshire counties, WV, for undergraduate education.
Financial data: Year ended 06/30/2013. Assets, $0 (M); Expenditures, $5,051; Total giving, $4,500; Grants to individuals, 5 grants totaling $4,500 (high: $900, low: $900).
Type of support: Undergraduate support.
Application information: Applications accepted.
Send request by: Mail
Deadline(s): None
EIN: 550699102

9799
Ernestine Matthews Trust
P.O. Box 456
Capon Bridge, WV 26711 (301) 330-7630
Application address: P.O. Box 3797, Arlington, VA 22203

Foundation type: Independent foundation
Purpose: Undergraduate scholarships to residents of DC, MD, PA, VA, and WV, who rank in the upper third of their high school classes.
Financial data: Year ended 12/31/2011. Assets, $924,218 (M); Expenditures, $72,062; Total giving, $67,000.
Fields of interest: Higher education.
Type of support: Undergraduate support.
Application information: Application form required.
Send request by: Mail
Deadline(s): Mar. 15
Applicants should submit the following:
1) Class rank
2) Letter(s) of recommendation
3) Financial information
4) Transcripts
Additional information: Application should also include a personal statement. Applicant must demonstrate financial need.
EIN: 526059006

9800
Jay T. McCamic Scholarship Trust
1 Bank Plz.
Wheeling, WV 26003-2905 (304) 234-9000
Contact: P. Kimberly McCluskey, Trust Off., WesBanco Bank, Inc.
E-mail: mccluskey@wesbanco.com

Foundation type: Independent foundation
Purpose: Awards scholarships to dependents of employees of Wheeling National Bank.
Financial data: Year ended 12/31/2012. Assets, $133,721 (M); Expenditures, $7,287; Total giving, $5,787.
Type of support: Employee-related scholarships.
Application information: Application form required.
Initial approach: Letter
EIN: 237155794

9801
Robert W. McCormick Scholarship Fund
c/o Bank of Charles Town
P.O. Drawer 40
Charles Town, WV 25414-0040 (304) 728-2435

Foundation type: Independent foundation
Purpose: Scholarships to students graduating from Jefferson County, WV, high schools with at least a "B" average. Recipients must attend WV public colleges or universities full-time.
Financial data: Year ended 04/30/2013. Assets, $4,363,924 (M); Expenditures, $225,066; Total giving, $169,005; Grants to individuals, 14 grants totaling $130,765 (high: $21,617, low: $1,100).
Fields of interest: Higher education; Scholarships/financial aid.
Type of support: Support to graduates or students of specific schools; Undergraduate support.
Application information: Applications accepted. Application form required.
Deadline(s): Feb. 20
Applicants should submit the following:
1) Transcripts
2) Letter(s) of recommendation
3) FAFSA
4) Essay
EIN: 550734149

9802
The Berkeley Minor and Susan F. Minor Foundation
300 Summers St., Ste. 620
Charleston, WV 25301 (304) 342-1141
Application address: c/o John L. Ray, 109 Capitol St., Ste. 700, Charleston, WV 25301-2609, tel.: (304) 342-1141

Foundation type: Independent foundation
Purpose: Scholarships to residents of WV attending West Virginia University, University of Charleston, University of Virginia, and the Protestant Episcopal Theological Seminary of Virginia.
Financial data: Year ended 12/31/2012. Assets, $2,478,410 (M); Expenditures, $168,976; Total giving, $146,500.
Fields of interest: Theological school/education.
Type of support: Support to graduates or students of specific schools; Undergraduate support.
Application information: Applications accepted.
Initial approach: Letter
Deadline(s): Aug. 1.
Additional information: Application must include names and addresses of parents and siblings, grades and courses in school and college, results of aptitude tests, and recommendations of teachers or others; Only students attending West Virginia University should apply directly to the foundation; Other applicants must be admitted to and recommended for financial aid by the University of Charleston, the University of Virginia, or the Protestant Episcopal Theological Seminary of Virginia.
EIN: 556014946

9803
Morgan-Robertson Memorial Scholarship Fund
(formerly Harvey Morgan Scholarship Fund)
c/o First Community Bank, N.A.
P.O. Box 950
Bluefield, WV 24701-0950

Foundation type: Independent foundation

Purpose: Scholarship to a sophomore student with the highest GPA at the West Virginia University School of Nursing.
Financial data: Year ended 07/31/2013. Assets, $131,116 (M); Expenditures, $11,438; Total giving, $6,273; Grant to an individual, 1 grant totaling $6,273.
Fields of interest: Nursing school/education.
Type of support: Scholarships—to individuals.
Application information: Applications not accepted.
Additional information: Unsolicited requests for funds not considered or acknowledged. Support only for a student attending WV University School of Nursing.
EIN: 556092124

9804
The Mountaintop Foundation
564 W. Main St.
P.O. Box 237
Bruceton Mills, WV 26525 (304) 777-4243

Foundation type: Independent foundation
Purpose: Scholarships to students residing in PA and WV for undergraduate education.
Financial data: Year ended 12/31/2012. Assets, $372,910 (M); Expenditures, $21,696; Total giving, $21,000; Grants to individuals, 14 grants totaling $21,000 (high: $1,500, low: $1,500).
Type of support: Undergraduate support.
Application information: Application form required.
Initial approach: Letter or telephone
Deadline(s): Jan. 31
EIN: 421481840

9805
Nicholas County Community Foundation
P.O. Box 561
Summersville, WV 26651 (304) 872-0202
Contact: Stacy Raffo, Exec. Dir.
E-mail: nccfwv@gmail.com; URL: http://www.nccfwv.com

Foundation type: Community foundation
Purpose: Scholarships for students seeking higher education in Nicholas County, WV.
Publications: Application guidelines.
Financial data: Year ended 12/31/2012. Assets, $2,186,253 (M); Expenditures, $186,616; Total giving, $97,152; Grants to individuals, totaling $3,500.
Fields of interest: Higher education; Scholarships/financial aid.
Type of support: Scholarships—to individuals.
Application information: Applications accepted. Application form required. Application form available on the grantmaker's web site.
Initial approach: Application
Send request by: Mail
Deadline(s): First Friday in Apr.
Applicants should submit the following:
1) Photograph
2) SAR
3) Transcripts
4) Letter(s) of recommendation
Additional information: Students can also check with their guidance counselor for additional application information. See web site for additional application guidelines.
EIN: 205799430

9806
Paden City Foundation, Inc.

P.O. Box 233
Paden City, WV 26159-0233 (304) 337-2205
Contact: Rodney McWilliams, Pres.; Tamara Bowers, Treas.

Foundation type: Independent foundation
Purpose: Scholarships to graduates of Paden City High School, WV for postsecondary education.
Financial data: Year ended 12/31/2011. Assets, $407,630 (M); Expenditures, $17,677; Total giving, $11,973; Grants to individuals, 14 grants totaling $10,525 (high: $1,050, low: $250).
Fields of interest: Higher education.
Type of support: Support to graduates or students of specific schools.
Application information: Applications not accepted.
Additional information: Contributes only to Paden City High School students; unsolicited requests for funds not considered or acknowledged.
EIN: 550678816

9807
The John and Lucia Pais Family Educational Foundation, Inc.

1629 College Ave.
Bluefield, WV 24701 (304) 327-8636
Contact: Elizabeth Pruett, Dir.

Foundation type: Independent foundation
Purpose: Scholarships to graduating students attending McDowell County, WV, public high schools.
Publications: Application guidelines.
Financial data: Year ended 06/30/2013. Assets, $62,194 (M); Expenditures, $11,076; Total giving, $6,000; Grants to individuals, 2 grants totaling $6,000 (high: $4,000, low: $2,000).
Type of support: Scholarships—to individuals; Support to graduates or students of specific schools; Graduate support; Undergraduate support.
Application information: Applications accepted. Application form required. Interview required.
Initial approach: Application
Deadline(s): Apr. 15
Applicants should submit the following:
　1) Transcripts
　2) Letter(s) of recommendation
　3) GPA
　4) Financial information
　5) FAFSA
　6) Essay
　7) Budget Information
　8) ACT
Additional information: Applications available at school.
EIN: 311561732

9808
Parkersburg Area Community Foundation

(also known as Our Community's Foundation)
1620 Park Ave.
P.O. Box 1762
Parkersburg, WV 26102-1762 (304) 428-4438
Contact: Judy Sjostedt, Exec. Dir.; Marian Clowes, Prog. and Devel. Off.
FAX: (304) 428-1200; E-mail: info@pacfwv.com; Additional tel.: (866) 428-4438; Additional e-mail: marian.clowes@pacfwv.com; URL: http://www.pacfwv.com

Foundation type: Community foundation

Purpose: Scholarships to residents of the Mid-Ohio Valley, WV area for continuing education at institutions of higher learning.
Publications: Application guidelines; Annual report; Informational brochure; Newsletter.
Financial data: Year ended 06/30/2011. Assets, $28,536,938 (M); Expenditures, $2,245,062; Total giving, $1,798,270; Grants to individuals, totaling $293,055.
Fields of interest: Vocational education, post-secondary; Higher education; Scholarships/financial aid.
Type of support: Scholarships—to individuals; Support to graduates or students of specific schools; Undergraduate support.
Application information: Applications accepted. Application form required. Application form available on the grantmaker's web site.
Send request by: Online
Copies of proposal: 1
Deadline(s): Varies
Applicants should submit the following:
　1) ACT
　2) Essay
　3) FAFSA
　4) Financial information
　5) GPA
　6) SAT
　7) Transcripts
Additional information: All grants to individuals are prize awards or scholarships to individuals, as directed by specific scholarship endowment agreements. See web site for scholarship award descriptions and specific deadline dates.
Program description:
Scholarships: The foundation manages more than 170 scholarship funds that honor family or friends, celebrate retirements, memorialize loved ones, or ensure that donor values are passed from one generation to the next. Each fund has different eligibility requirements. Many awards are restricted to students graduating from certain high schools, others to students pursuing particular fields of study or attending specific institutions. Most existing scholarships are limited to students who are graduating high school seniors. Only a few are available for students whose undergraduate degree program is already underway or who are "non-traditional" students or in graduate level education. See web site for additional information.
EIN: 556027764

9809
Jonathan Powell Hope Foundation, Inc.

(also known as Jonathan's Hope)
P. O. Box 5527
Princeton, WV 24740-5527 (304) 425-5553
Contact: Melissa Powell, Pres.
URL: http://www.jonathanshope.org/

Foundation type: Public charity
Purpose: Grants to families with children diagnosed with cancer before their 18th birthday who have financial needs related to the diagnosis.
Financial data: Year ended 06/30/2012. Assets, $124,256 (M); Expenditures, $89,112; Total giving, $82,092.
Fields of interest: Cancer; Children.
Type of support: Grants for special needs.
Application information: Applications accepted. Application form required. Application form available on the grantmaker's web site.
Send request by: Mail or fax

Additional information: Application must include a letter of support from a hospital professional.
EIN: 320042188

9810
Herschel C. Price Educational Foundation

P.O. Box 412
Huntington, WV 25708-0412
Contact: Jonna Hughes, Tr.

Foundation type: Independent foundation
Purpose: Scholarships to students residing in WV and/or attending WV colleges and universities.
Financial data: Year ended 04/30/2012. Assets, $4,291,855 (M); Expenditures, $240,504; Total giving, $190,500; Grants to individuals, 79 grants totaling $184,000 (high: $6,000, low: $250).
Fields of interest: Higher education.
Type of support: Scholarships—to individuals.
Application information: Applications accepted. Application form required. Interview required.
Initial approach: Letter
Deadline(s): Apr. 1 for fall and Oct. 1 for spring
Additional information: Letter should indicate where applicant is currently living and college attending.
EIN: 556076719

9811
Albert M. Price Trust

P.O. Box 393
Charleston, WV 25322
Contact: Cathy Houser
Application address: c/o Jackson-Newcomb Scholarship Program, P.O. Box 1508 Parkersburg, WV 26101

Foundation type: Independent foundation
Purpose: Scholarships primarily to Boone County, WV, residents for higher education.
Financial data: Year ended 12/31/2012. Assets, $989,464 (M); Expenditures, $54,816; Total giving, $43,500; Grants to individuals, 58 grants totaling $43,500 (high: $1,125, low: $375).
Fields of interest: Higher education; Scholarships/financial aid.
Type of support: Scholarships—to individuals.
Application information: Applications accepted. Application form required.
Initial approach: Letter
Deadline(s): Mar. 1
Applicants should submit the following:
　1) Letter(s) of recommendation
　2) SAT
　3) GPA
　4) ACT
Additional information: Priority will be given first to Boone county WV residents and then to other WV residents.
EIN: 556081789

9812
Princeton High School Class of 1926 Scholarship Fund

P.O. Box 950
Bluefield, WV 24701 (304) 325-7151
Contact: Jeff Dissibio

Foundation type: Independent foundation
Purpose: Scholarships to students of Princeton Senior High School, WV.
Financial data: Year ended 12/31/2012. Assets, $81,899 (M); Expenditures, $3,061; Total giving,

$2,500; Grants to individuals, 2 grants totaling $2,500 (high: $1,500, low: $1,000).
Type of support: Support to graduates or students of specific schools; Undergraduate support.
Application information: Application form required.
Deadline(s): None
Additional information: Awards restricted to $6,000 over four years per recipient. Recipients are chosen by Princeton Senior High School staff and the foundation's trustees.
EIN: 310889436

9813
Raleigh County Community Action Association, Inc.
111 Willow Ln.
Beckley, WV 25801-1777 (304) 252-6396
Contact: Bobbi Thomas-Bailey, Exec. Dir.
E-mail: bobbi@rccaa.org; URL: http://www.rccaa.org

Foundation type: Public charity
Purpose: Financial assistance to homeless persons residing in Raleigh County, WV to pay for medical, dental, hospital expenses and other special needs.
Financial data: Year ended 12/31/2011. Assets, $2,399,780 (M); Expenditures, $5,089,421; Total giving, $137,941; Grants to individuals, totaling $137,941.
Type of support: Grants for special needs.
Application information:
Initial approach: Letter
Additional information: Contact the association for further guidelines.
EIN: 550480001

9814
Serra Foundation, Inc.
2525 Pennsylvania Ave.
Weirton, WV 26062 (304) 723-4300

Foundation type: Public charity
Purpose: Scholarships to high school seniors and college students in the Weirton, WV area pursuing higher education. Financial assistance to the elderly for rental costs in WV.
Financial data: Year ended 12/31/2011. Assets, $2,005,617 (M); Expenditures, $53,997; Total giving, $46,720; Grants to individuals, totaling $8,500.
Fields of interest: Higher education; Aging; Economically disadvantaged.
Type of support: Scholarships—to individuals; Grants for special needs.
Application information: Applications accepted. Application form required.
Additional information: Contact the foundation for additional guidelines for scholarships and assistance.
EIN: 550696463

9815
Tom C. Smith Charitable Trust
P.O. Box 1216
Huntington, WV 25714 (304) 523-3424
Contact: George Sinkewitz, Tr.

Foundation type: Independent foundation
Purpose: Emergency aid and assistance to financially needy residents of Chesapeake, OH, and Huntington, WV.

Financial data: Year ended 03/31/2013. Assets, $204,346 (M); Expenditures, $71,945; Total giving, $21,755.
Fields of interest: Economically disadvantaged.
Type of support: Grants for special needs.
Application information: Applications accepted.
Initial approach: Letter or telephone
Deadline(s): None
EIN: 550570334

9816
Genevieve Starcher Educational Foundation
c/o United Bank
P.O. Box 393
Charleston, WV 25322 (304) 372-2246
Contact: Kathryn Goodwin, Pres.
Application address: P.O. Box 266, Ripley, WV 25271, tel.: (304) 372-2246

Foundation type: Independent foundation
Purpose: Scholarships to Jackson County, WV, residents to attend colleges and trade schools. Preference is given to graduates of Ripley High School, WV, and less privileged students.
Financial data: Year ended 12/31/2012. Assets, $461,409 (M); Expenditures, $29,506; Total giving, $22,000; Grants to individuals, 23 grants totaling $22,000 (high: $1,000, low: $500).
Fields of interest: Vocational education.
Type of support: Scholarships—to individuals.
Application information: Applications accepted. Application form required.
Deadline(s): May 31
EIN: 510159560

9817
Carl Dee Stickley Educational Fund
c/o The Bank of Romney
P.O. Box 26757
Romney, WV 26757-0876 (304) 822-3541
Contact: Lawrence Foley, Tr.
Application address: c/o 95 E. Main St., Romney, WV 26757

Foundation type: Independent foundation
Purpose: Scholarships to financially disadvantaged graduates of secondary schools in Hampshire County, WV. Recipients must attend a college in WV except for students of the West Virginia School for the Blind and the West Virginia School for the Deaf, who may study out-of-state.
Financial data: Year ended 03/31/2012. Assets, $152,440 (M); Expenditures, $9,381; Total giving, $7,941; Grants to individuals, 7 grants totaling $7,941 (high: $1,664, low: $285).
Fields of interest: Disabilities, people with.
Type of support: Support to graduates or students of specific schools; Undergraduate support.
Application information: Applications accepted. Application form required.
Deadline(s): None
Additional information: Application must include financial information.
EIN: 550682624

9818
George E. Stifel Endowment Fund
c/o Wesbanco Bank
1 Bank Plz.
Wheeling, WV 26003-3543 (304) 234-9400

Foundation type: Public charity
Purpose: Awards and prizes to students in grades five through twelve of Ohio County, WV, achieving

academic excellence. Scholarships to deserving students from public high schools within Ohio County, WV.
Financial data: Year ended 12/31/2011. Assets, $3,433,247 (M); Expenditures, $92,998; Total giving, $77,110; Grants to individuals, totaling $77,110.
Fields of interest: Higher education.
Type of support: Support to graduates or students of specific schools; Awards/prizes; Precollege support.
Application information: Contact the fund for additional guidelines.
EIN: 556018247

9819
O. J. Stout Scholarship Fund
c/o United National Bank
P.O. Box 1508
Parkersburg, WV 26102-1508
Contact: Catherine L. Houser, V.P.

Foundation type: Independent foundation
Purpose: Scholarships and student loans to financially needy, male high school graduates in Wood County, WV, and adjacent WV counties for higher education. Preference is given to students studying to become ministers at West Virginia Wesleyan College.
Financial data: Year ended 12/31/2012. Assets, $7,830,420 (M); Expenditures, $356,607; Total giving, $217,000; Grants to individuals, 121 grants totaling $217,000 (high: $800, low: $100).
Fields of interest: Protestant agencies & churches; Men.
Type of support: Support to graduates or students of specific schools; Graduate support; Undergraduate support.
Application information: Application form required.
Deadline(s): Mar. 31
Applicants should submit the following:
1) Letter(s) of recommendation
2) FAF
3) Transcripts
Additional information: Application must also include first page of parents' 1040. Each recipient is given a scholarship and a student loan. The loan is equivalent to 20 percent of the scholarship amount. Recipients must maintain at least a 2.0 GPA in order to be eligible for additional scholarships and loans.
EIN: 556029015

9820
Hill Stump Disaster Charitable Trust
c/o First Community Bank
P.O. Box 950
Bluefield, WV 24701-0950 (304) 325-7151

Foundation type: Independent foundation
Purpose: Emergency aid to residents of Upshur County, WV, who have suffered loss due to a disaster such as fire, flood, storm, sickness, or death.
Financial data: Year ended 12/31/2012. Assets, $685,355 (M); Expenditures, $23,899; Total giving, $22,260; Grants to individuals, 12 grants totaling $22,260 (high: $1,855, low: $1,855).
Fields of interest: Disasters, floods; Disasters, fire prevention/control; Safety/disasters.
Type of support: Emergency funds.
Application information: Applications accepted. Application form required.
Deadline(s): None

Additional information: Application should include financial information.
EIN: 556104851

9821

The Sun Lumber Company Education Foundation

P.O. Box 590
Weston, WV   26452-0590   (304) 269-1000
Contact: Frank L. Brewster, Tr.

Foundation type: Company-sponsored foundation
Purpose: Scholarships to children of employees of Sun Lumber Company, graduates from certain counties in WV attending Glenville State College and enrolled in forestry, and WV high school graduates enrolled in forestry education.
Financial data: Year ended 12/31/2012. Assets, $32,140 (M); Expenditures, $4,715; Total giving, $4,000.
Fields of interest: Environment, forests.
Type of support: Employee-related scholarships; Support to graduates or students of specific schools; Undergraduate support.
Application information:
  Initial approach: Letter
  Deadline(s): None
  Additional information: Application should include a resume. Contact foundation for further application guidelines.
Company name: Sun Lumber Company, Inc.
EIN: 550780820

9822

Tech Foundation, Inc.

West Virginia Institute of Tech.
405 Fayette Pike Box 21
Montgomery, WV   25136-0000   (304) 442-1003

Foundation type: Public charity
Purpose: Scholarships and awards to students for attendance at West Virginia University Institute of Technology.
Financial data: Year ended 06/30/2011. Assets, $5,124,830 (M); Expenditures, $445,903; Total giving, $46,136; Grants to individuals, 23 grants totaling $46,136.
Fields of interest: Higher education.
Type of support: Support to graduates or students of specific schools.
Application information: Selection is based on academic achievement, financial need and other similar standards.
EIN: 550481587

9823

Timms Family Foundation

c/o Annabel P. Timms
41 Cedar Ln.
Bridgeport, WV   26330-9304   (304) 842-4958
Contact: Leonard J. Timms, Jr., Tr.

Foundation type: Independent foundation
Purpose: Scholarships to residents of Harrison, Marion, Doddridge, or Taylor counties, WV majoring in dance, musical theatre, drama or vocal performance.
Financial data: Year ended 12/31/2012. Assets, $89,178 (M); Expenditures, $4,053; Total giving, $2,800; Grants to individuals, 3 grants totaling $2,800 (high: $1,000, low: $800).
Fields of interest: Dance; Theater (musical); Music (choral); Performing arts, education.
Type of support: Scholarships—to individuals.

Application information: Applications accepted. Application form required.
  Deadline(s): Feb. 15
  Additional information: The scholarship is for one year only, but may be renewed.
EIN: 912052424

9824

Tucker Community Foundation

501 Chestnut St.
P.O. Box 491
Parsons, WV   26287   (304) 478-2930
Contact: Robert A. Burns, Exec. Dir.
FAX: (304) 478-9966; *E-mail:* tcf1@frontiernet.net;
URL: http://www.tuckerfoundation.net

Foundation type: Community foundation
Purpose: Scholarships to residents of Barbour, Grant, Mineral, Pocahontas, Preston, Randolph, and Tucker counties, WV and Garrett county, MD.
Publications: Annual report; Grants list; Newsletter.
Financial data: Year ended 12/31/2011. Assets, $18,556,022 (M); Expenditures, $881,758; Total giving, $646,423; Grants to individuals, 54 grants totaling $36,350.
Fields of interest: Education.
Type of support: Undergraduate support.
Application information: Applications accepted. Application form required. Application form available on the grantmaker's web site.
  Initial approach: Letter or e-mail
  Send request by: Mail
  Deadline(s): Apr. 4
  Applicants should submit the following:
    1) Essay
    2) Photograph
    3) ACT
    4) SAT
    5) Transcripts
  Additional information: See web site for additional application guidelines.
EIN: 550687098

9825

United Way of the River Cities, Inc.

820 Madison Ave.
Huntington, WV   25704-2551   (304) 523-8929
Contact: Laura P. Gilliam, Exec. Dir.
FAX: (304) 523-9811;
E-mail: laura.gilliam@unitedwayrivercities.org;
URL: http://www.unitedwayrivercities.org

Foundation type: Public charity
Purpose: Assistance to low to moderate income individuals and families of West Virginia, to help them become more self-sufficient.
Publications: Annual report; Financial statement; Grants list; Informational brochure; Newsletter.
Financial data: Year ended 12/31/2011. Assets, $3,802,345 (M); Expenditures, $1,452,969; Total giving, $643,179.
Fields of interest: Human services.
Type of support: Grants for special needs.
Application information: Contact the agency for eligibility criteria.
EIN: 550384704

9826

The Vecellio Family Foundation, Inc.

(formerly The Enrico Vecellio Family Foundation, Inc.)
P.O. Box 2438
Beckley, WV   25802-2438

Foundation type: Independent foundation
Purpose: Scholarships to graduating seniors from the high schools in Raleigh County, WV; graduating seniors of Woodrow Wilson High School, WV; graduating seniors of any WV high school who have been a member of the Youth Conservation Program for one year; graduating seniors who are children of employees of Vecellio Group, Inc. and Subsidiaries; and graduating seniors from McDowell County, WV.
Financial data: Year ended 12/31/2012. Assets, $6,592,912 (M); Expenditures, $353,782; Total giving, $304,500; Grants to individuals, 42 grants totaling $105,000 (high: $8,750, low: $1,250).
Fields of interest: Higher education.
Type of support: Employee-related scholarships; Support to graduates or students of specific schools; Undergraduate support.
Application information: Applications accepted. Application form required.
  Initial approach: Letter
  Additional information: The foundation awards only restricted scholarships. Unsolicited requests for funds not considered or acknowledged.
EIN: 550538242

9827

West Virginia Humanities Council, Inc.

1310 Kanawha Blvd. E.
Charleston, WV   25301-2703   (304) 346-8500
Contact: Kenneth Sullivan, Exec. Dir.
FAX: (304) 346-8504;
E-mail: wvhuman@wvhumanities.org; *E-Mail for Kenneth Sullivan:* sullivan@wvhumanities.org;
URL: http://www.wvhumanities.org

Foundation type: Public charity
Purpose: Fellowships to humanities scholars for research support, and project grants to professors in WV.
Publications: Application guidelines; Annual report; Informational brochure; Newsletter.
Financial data: Year ended 10/31/2011. Assets, $1,749,114 (M); Expenditures, $1,335,474; Total giving, $301,705.
Fields of interest: Humanities; Education.
Type of support: Program development; Conferences/seminars; Fellowships; Research; Travel grants.
Application information: Applications accepted. Application form required. Application form available on the grantmaker's web site.
  Initial approach: Letter, telephone or e-mail
  Copies of proposal: 12
  Final notification: Recipients notified in six weeks
  Applicants should submit the following:
    1) Resume
    2) Proposal
    3) Essay
    4) Curriculum vitae
Program descriptions:
  Fellowships Program: Fellowships of $2,500 are awarded on an annual basis to humanities scholars to provide support for individual research within a humanities discipline. The program provides opportunities for advanced study that will enhance scholars' capacities as teachers or interpreters of the humanities.
  Teacher Institutes Grants: Awards a maximum of $25,000 to college and university professors to develop and implement summer seminars or humanities topics suited to the teaching needs of elementary or secondary teachers.
  Travel Assistance Grants: Grants of up to $500 are available towards travel expenses to various

conferences and seminars. Applications must be submitted two months prior to conference date.
EIN: 550553594

9828
Jack Whittaker Foundation, Inc.
2888 Ritter Dr.
Shady Springs, WV   25918   (304) 877-2336
Contact: Andrew J. Whittaker, Pres.
URL: http://www.jackwhittakerfoundation.com

Foundation type: Independent foundation
Purpose: Scholarships to individuals for tuition at institutions of higher education.
Financial data: Year ended 12/31/2011. Assets, $650,983 (M); Expenditures, $49,370; Total giving, $24,814; Grants to individuals, 9 grants totaling $17,250 (high: $4,800, low: $500).
Fields of interest: Scholarships/financial aid.
Type of support: Scholarships—to individuals.
Application information: Applications accepted.
  Deadline(s): None
  Additional information: Applicant should submit a brief description of reason for need.
EIN: 753094074

9829
W. A. Jr. and Phyllis P. Wolfe Foundation, Inc.
500 Federal St.
Bluefield, WV   24701-3010   (304) 325-8181
Contact: John Beckett, Dir.
Application tel.:(304) 325-8181

Foundation type: Independent foundation
Purpose: Scholarships to students residing in the counties of Mercer, McDowell, Monroe, and Wyoming in West Virginia looking to further their educational endeavors.
Financial data: Year ended 12/31/2012. Assets, $3,082,121 (M); Expenditures, $174,486; Total giving, $149,500.

Fields of interest: Higher education.
Type of support: Scholarships—to individuals.
Application information: Applications accepted.
  Initial approach: Letter
  Deadline(s): Apr.
  Additional information: Selection is based on scholastic achievement, college test scores, financial need and teacher recommendations. Application can be obtained from the guidance office.
EIN: 550684389

9830
Workforce Investment Board - Region I, Inc.
200 New River Town Ctr., Ste. 200
Beckley, WV   25801-3709   (304) 253-3611
Contact: Angela M. Henson, Exec. Dir.
E-mail: ahenson@r1workforcewv.org; URL: http://www.region1workforcewestvirginia.org/workforce-investment-board-2/

Foundation type: Public charity
Purpose: Tuition assistance and support, small business development grants, and workforce development grants to eligible individuals throughout WV.
Financial data: Year ended 06/30/2012. Assets, $567,871 (M); Expenditures, $3,134,968; Total giving, $577,033; Grants to individuals, totaling $577,033.
Fields of interest: Employment; Community/economic development.
Type of support: Grants to individuals.
Application information: Applications accepted.
  Additional information: Contact the Board for additional guidelines.
EIN: 550780985

9831
Your Community Foundation, Inc.
(formerly Greater Morgantown Community Trust, Inc.)
111 High St.
P. O. Box 409
Morgantown, WV   26505   (304) 296-3433
Contact: Beth Fuller, Pres.
E-mail: beth@ycfwv.org; URL: http://www.ycfwv.org/

Foundation type: Community foundation
Purpose: Scholarships to graduates of high schools in the North Central, WV area.
Publications: Annual report; Informational brochure.
Financial data: Year ended 12/31/2012. Assets, $9,023,414 (M); Expenditures, $899,105; Total giving, $664,673; Grants to individuals, 58 grants totaling $81,194 (high: $4,684, low: $500).
Fields of interest: Higher education; Scholarships/financial aid; Economically disadvantaged.
Type of support: Scholarships—to individuals; Support to graduates or students of specific schools; Undergraduate support.
Application information: Applications accepted. Application form required. Application form available on the grantmaker's web site.
  Initial approach: E-mail
  Deadline(s): Vary
  Applicants should submit the following:
    1) Transcripts
    2) SAT
    3) Letter(s) of recommendation
    4) GPA
    5) Financial information
    6) Essay
    7) ACT
  Additional information: See web site for complete program information.
EIN: 275249383

WISCONSIN

9832
Earnest F. & Edna P. Aber Scholarship Fund

441 Milwaukee Ave.
Burlington, WI 53105
Contact: Scott Carson, Mgr.
*Application address:*257 Kendall St., Burlington, WI 53105-1809

Foundation type: Independent foundation
Purpose: Scholarships to high school graduates West of I-94, Racine county, WI for attendance at a college or university that is affiliated with, or governed by a Christian organization.
Financial data: Year ended 12/31/2012. Assets, $92,862 (M); Expenditures, $6,526; Total giving, $4,000.
Fields of interest: Higher education.
Type of support: Scholarships—to individuals.
Application information: Applications accepted. Application form required.
Deadline(s): May 1
Applicants should submit the following:
1) Photograph
2) Transcripts
3) SAT
4) Letter(s) of recommendation
5) Financial information
6) ACT
EIN: 911817886

9833
AgSource DHI Foundation, Inc.

P.O. Box 930230
Verona, WI 53593-0230 (608) 845-1900
Application address: 135 Enterprise Dr., Verona, WI 53593-9122

Foundation type: Independent foundation
Purpose: Scholarships primarily to graduating seniors of Wood county, WI pursuing a career in an agriculture-related field of study.
Financial data: Year ended 12/31/2012. Assets, $467,852 (M); Expenditures, $38,417; Total giving, $33,126; Grants to individuals, 25 grants totaling $14,650 (high: $1,500, low: $100).
Fields of interest: Agriculture.
Type of support: Scholarships—to individuals.
Application information: Applications accepted. Application form required.
Deadline(s): Varies
Additional information: Applications available in the school counselor's office.
EIN: 391909207

9834
The American Academy of Allergy, Asthma, and Immunology

555 E. Wells St., Ste. 1100
Milwaukee, WI 53202-3823 (414) 272-6071
E-mail: info@aaaai.org; URL: http://www.aaaai.org

Foundation type: Public charity
Purpose: Grants approximately $1 million annually in awards for allergy / immunology research projects.
Financial data: Year ended 12/31/2011. Assets, $22,052,437 (M); Expenditures, $10,245,784; Total giving, $1,703,268; Grants to individuals, totaling $655,747.
Fields of interest: Allergies; Asthma; Immunology; Allergies research; Asthma research; Immunology research.
Type of support: Research.
Application information:
Initial approach: Letter
Program descriptions:
Faculty Award: Annual awards to AAAAI members for allergy / immunology research projects.
FIT Award: Annual awards to AAAAI members for allergy / immunology research projects.
EIN: 396061326

9835
American Society for Laser Medicine and Surgery, Inc.

2100 Stewart Ave., Ste. 240
Wausau, WI 54401-1709 (715) 845-9283
Contact: Dianne Dalsky, Exec. Dir.
FAX: (715) 848-2493;
E-mail: information@aslms.org; URL: http://www.aslms.org

Foundation type: Public charity
Purpose: Research grants for projects designed to foster the development of lasers and other related technologies in medical and surgical applications.
Publications: Application guidelines.
Financial data: Year ended 12/31/2011. Assets, $3,338,810 (M); Expenditures, $2,402,916; Total giving, $207,289; Grants to individuals, totaling $207,289.
Fields of interest: Surgery research.
Type of support: Research.
Application information: Applications accepted.
Send request by: E-mail
Deadline(s): Jan. 12
Applicants should submit the following:
1) Budget Information
2) Proposal
3) Letter(s) of recommendation
4) Curriculum vitae
Additional information: See web site for complete application guidelines.
EIN: 391397899

9836
AnnMarie Foundation, Inc.

1245 N. Airport Rd.
Phillips, WI 54555 (715) 381-3213
Contact: Lori Feiten
E-mail for Lori Feiten:
lori.feiten@phillipsplastics.com; URL: http://annmariefoundation.org/

Foundation type: Company-sponsored foundation
Purpose: Scholarships to graduates of Phillips High School, WI for continuing education at accredited colleges or universities, or vocational/technical institutions.
Publications: Application guidelines; Program policy statement.
Financial data: Year ended 04/30/2013. Assets, $6,858,560 (M); Expenditures, $307,412; Total giving, $284,922.
Type of support: Support to graduates or students of specific schools.
Application information: Applications not accepted.
Additional information: Unsolicited requests for funds not accepted or considered.
EIN: 237301323

9837
The Anu Family Services Advantage

(formerly PATH Wisconsin, Inc.)
516 2nd St., No. 209
Hudson, WI 54016-1591 (715) 386-1547
Contact: Amelia Franck Meyer, C.E.O.
FAX: (715) 386-2541; E-mail: redwards@anufs.org; URL: http://www.anufs.org/index.asp

Foundation type: Public charity
Purpose: Foster care services for children and youth, adoption and other services for families in Colorado, Minnesota, North Dakota, and Wisconsin.
Financial data: Year ended 06/30/2011. Assets, $862,030 (M); Expenditures, $5,693,256; Total giving, $2,582,216; Grants to individuals, totaling $2,582,216.
Fields of interest: Government agencies; Adoption; Foster care.
Type of support: Grants for special needs.
Application information: Applications not accepted.
EIN: 320023143

9838
Ariens Foundation, Ltd.

655 W. Ryan St.
Brillion, WI 54110-1072
Contact: Leone M. Pahl, V.P.

Foundation type: Company-sponsored foundation
Purpose: Scholarships to residents of Brillion, WI, and the surrounding area.
Financial data: Year ended 06/30/2013. Assets, $402,498 (M); Expenditures, $201,691; Total giving, $201,235; Grants to individuals, totaling $9,750.
Type of support: Scholarships—to individuals.
Application information: Applications accepted.
Deadline(s): None
Additional information: Applicant should submit a brief resume of qualifications.
EIN: 396102058

9839
George W. Askren Memorial Scholarship

(formerly Caroline L. Askren Trust)
c/o JPMorgan Chase Bank, N.A.
P.O. Box 3038
Milwaukee, WI 53201 (317) 684-3115
Application address: c/o Warren Central High School, Attn.: Principal, 9500 E. 16th St., Indianapolis, IN 46229-2008, tel.: (317) 898-6133

Foundation type: Independent foundation
Purpose: Scholarships to graduates of Warren Township Schools, Indianapolis, IN, who are in the upper half of their class.
Financial data: Year ended 10/31/2011. Assets, $311,168 (M); Expenditures, $19,638; Total giving, $13,200; Grants to individuals, 11 grants totaling $13,200 (high: $1,200, low: $1,200).
Type of support: Support to graduates or students of specific schools; Undergraduate support.
Application information: Applications accepted. Application form required.
Deadline(s): Early spring
EIN: 356231596

9840
Hazel Aslakson Scholarship Trust
P.O. Box 12800
Green Bay, WI 54307-2800
Application address: First Lutheran Church, 521 N.
8th St., Manitowoc, WI 54220

Foundation type: Independent foundation
Purpose: Scholarships to members of First
Lutheran Church, Manitowoc, WI, and attend the
Evangelical Lutheran Church at an American
college, university, or seminary.
Financial data: Year ended 12/31/2012. Assets,
$85,200 (M); Expenditures, $2,508; Total giving,
$750; Grants to individuals, 2 grants totaling $750
(high: $600, low: $150).
Fields of interest: Theological school/education.
Type of support: Graduate support; Undergraduate
support.
Application information: Applications accepted.
Application form not required.
  Deadline(s): Contact foundation for current
    application guidelines
  Additional information: Applicant must include
    good character references and have good
    grades.
EIN: 396638318

9841
Associated Banc-Corp Founders Scholarship Fund
P.O. Box 12800
Green Bay, WI 54307-2800 (800) 878-3282
E-mail: Colleaguecare@associatedbank.com

Foundation type: Company-sponsored foundation
Purpose: Scholarships to children of employees of
Associated Banc-Corp and its affiliates.
Financial data: Year ended 12/31/2012. Assets,
$228,188 (M); Expenditures, $47,014; Total
giving, $43,000.
Fields of interest: Higher education; Scholarships/
financial aid.
Type of support: Employee-related scholarships.
Application information: Applications not
accepted.
  Additional information: Unsolicited requests for
    funds not considered or acknowledged.
Company name: Associated Banc-Corp
EIN: 391482448

9842
Ted & Grace Bachhuber Foundation, Inc.
14 Tower Dr.
P.O. Box 228
Mayville, WI 53050-1746
Contact: JoAnn Bachhuber, Pres. and Treas.

Foundation type: Independent foundation
Purpose: Administered by the Mayville Public
School System, the foundation provides
scholarships to graduates of Mayville Public School
System, WI, who plan to pursue an engineering,
business, or technology degree.
Financial data: Year ended 12/31/2012. Assets,
$36,371,855 (M); Expenditures, $1,863,730;
Total giving, $1,677,558.
Fields of interest: Engineering school/education.
Type of support: Support to graduates or students
of specific schools.
Application information: Applications not
accepted.
  Additional information: Unsolicited requests for
    funds not considered.
EIN: 391415821

9843
Carl & Isabel Backlin Trust
c/o BMO Harris Bank, N.A.
P.O. Box 2980
Milwaukee, WI 53201-2977 (414) 287-8845
Application address: c/o BMO Harris Bank, 111 E.
Kilbourn Ave., Milwaukee, WI 53202

Foundation type: Independent foundation
Purpose: Scholarships to students who are
residents of Burlington, WI for attendance at
colleges or universities for tuition and books.
Financial data: Year ended 07/31/2013. Assets,
$153,473 (M); Expenditures, $9,638; Total giving,
$6,589; Grants to individuals, 10 grants totaling
$6,589 (high: $1,089, low: $250).
Fields of interest: Higher education.
Type of support: Scholarships—to individuals.
Application information: Applications accepted.
  Initial approach: Letter
  Applicants should submit the following:
    1) Letter(s) of recommendation
    2) Financial information
EIN: 396717250

9844
Badger Mining Corporate Associate Scholarship Trust
(formerly BMC Associate Scholarship Trust)
P.O. Box 270
Markesan, WI 53946-0270 (920) 398-2358

Foundation type: Company-sponsored foundation
Purpose: College scholarships to employees and
the children and spouses of employees of Badger
Mining.
Financial data: Year ended 12/31/2012. Assets,
$22,224 (M); Expenditures, $20,115; Total giving,
$19,500; Grants to individuals, 13 grants totaling
$19,500 (high: $1,500, low: $1,500).
Type of support: Employee-related scholarships;
Undergraduate support.
Application information: Applications not
accepted.
  Additional information: Contributes only through
    employee-related scholarships.
Company name: Badger Mining Corporation
EIN: 396642667

9845
Badger Mining Scholarship Trust
P.O. Box 270
Markesan, WI 53946-0270 (920) 398-2358

Foundation type: Company-sponsored foundation
Purpose: Scholarships to high school graduates
from Taylor, Berlin, or Markesan, WI, for degrees in
mining engineering, engineering curriculum, or
environmental science.
Financial data: Year ended 12/31/2012. Assets,
$11,549 (M); Expenditures, $28,496; Total giving,
$28,000; Grants to individuals, 12 grants totaling
$28,000 (high: $4,000, low: $1,000).
Fields of interest: Engineering school/education;
Natural resources; Environment; Business/
industry.
Type of support: Undergraduate support.
Application information: Applications accepted.
Application form required.
  Additional information: Application forms
    available from the high schools. Student must
    be full-time and maintain a 2.0 GPA.
EIN: 396433973

9846
Anna Beal Trust
c/o U.S. Bank, N.A.
P.O. Box 2043
Milwaukee, WI 53201-9668 (319) 235-3255

Foundation type: Independent foundation
Purpose: Scholarships to financially needy
residents of IA, studying in agriculture and
biology-related fields, who attend colleges and
universities previously selected by the trustee.
Financial data: Year ended 12/31/2012. Assets,
$592,253 (M); Expenditures, $37,530; Total
giving, $28,196; Grants to individuals, 7 grants
totaling $28,196 (high: $4,028, low: $4,028).
Fields of interest: Agriculture; Biology/life
sciences.
Type of support: Scholarships—to individuals.
Application information: Applications accepted.
  Initial approach: Letter
  Deadline(s): None
  Additional information: Contact foundation for
    current application guidelines.
EIN: 426193621

9847
F. K. Bemis Family Foundation
300 Mill St.
Sheboygan Falls, WI 53085-1807 (920)
467-4621
Contact: Karen Hoefler, Secy.

Foundation type: Company-sponsored foundation
Purpose: Scholarships to residents of Sheboygan
Falls, WI.
Financial data: Year ended 12/31/2012. Assets,
$705,519 (M); Expenditures, $375,824; Total
giving, $375,822.
Type of support: Undergraduate support.
Application information: Applications not
accepted.
  Additional information: Unsolicited requests for
    funds not considered.
EIN: 396067930

9848
Lester R. Birbeck Charitable Trust
c/o BMO HArris Bank
P.O. Box 2980
Milwaukee, WI 53201 (816) 236-1874
Application address: c/o M&I Bank, 4305 Frederick
Blvd., St. Joseph, MO 64506

Foundation type: Independent foundation
Purpose: Scholarships to high school students from
King City or Stanberry, MO, schools for higher
education.
Financial data: Year ended 12/31/2012. Assets,
$2,068,348 (M); Expenditures, $111,594; Total
giving, $93,406.
Type of support: Support to graduates or students
of specific schools; Undergraduate support.
Application information: Applications accepted.
Application form required.
  Deadline(s): Apr. 1
  Applicants should submit the following:
    1) Photograph
    2) Transcripts
EIN: 431725748

9849
Black River Falls Area Foundation
8 Main St.
P.O. Box 99
Black River Falls, WI 54615-1751 (715) 284-3113
Contact: GIlbert L. Homstad, Chair.
URL: http://www.brfareafoundation.org

Foundation type: Community foundation
Purpose: Scholarships to individuals in Jackson County, WI, primarily in Black River Falls, for higher education.
Publications: Application guidelines; Annual report; Informational brochure.
Financial data: Year ended 12/31/2012. Assets, $4,017,730 (M); Expenditures, $180,118; Total giving, $145,502; Grants to individuals, 36 grants totaling $52,500.
Type of support: Undergraduate support.
Application information: Application form required.
 Initial approach: Letter
 Deadline(s): May 15
EIN: 391563654

9850
Karl W. Boer Solar Energy Medal of Merit Award Trust
c/o Ralf R. Boer
777 E. Wisconsin Ave., Ste. 3800
Milwaukee, WI 53202-5367 (414) 297-5609
Contact: for Awards: George C. Hadjipanayis, Exec. Dir.
Nomination address: Institute of Energy Conservation, University of Delaware, Newark, DE 19716, tel.: (302) 831-6200, fax: (302) 831-6226,
URL: http://www.udel.edu/iec/boer_award.html

Foundation type: Public charity
Purpose: A biannual award to an individual who has made significant pioneering contributions to the promotion of solar energy.
Financial data: Year ended 12/31/2011. Assets, $526,266 (M); Expenditures, $52,857; Total giving, $50,000; Grants to individuals, totaling $50,000.
Fields of interest: Energy.
Type of support: Awards/prizes.
Application information: See web site for nomination form. Applicant must include a curriculum vitae and five references.
EIN: 396596448

9851
Briggs & Stratton Corporation Foundation, Inc.
12301 W. Wirth St.
Wauwatosa, WI 53222 (414) 259-5333
Contact: Robert F. Heath, Secy. and Treas.; Jodi A. Chaudoir
Application address for grants to public charities: c/o Robert F. Heath, P.O. Box 702, Milwaukee, WI 53201

Foundation type: Company-sponsored foundation
Purpose: Scholarships to children of employees of the Briggs & Stratton Corporation, who have been employed full-time by the company for at least two years as of the Sept. 1 preceding the deadline.
Financial data: Year ended 11/30/2012. Assets, $13,929,790 (M); Expenditures, $764,860; Total giving, $759,500.
Type of support: Employee-related scholarships.
Application information: Unsolicited requests for funds not considered or acknowledged.

Company name: Briggs & Stratton Corporation
EIN: 396040377

9852
Brillion Foundation Inc.
200 Park Ave.
P.O. Box 127
Brillion, WI 54110 (920) 756-2121
Contact: Julie Malliett, Secy.

Foundation type: Company-sponsored foundation
Purpose: Scholarships to residents of Brillion, WI.
Financial data: Year ended 06/30/2013. Assets, $142,834 (M); Expenditures, $8,779; Total giving, $8,500; Grants to individuals, 4 grants totaling $5,000 (high: $1,250, low: $1,250).
Type of support: Undergraduate support.
Application information:
 Initial approach: Letter
 Deadline(s): None
 Additional information: Contact foundation for eligibility requirements.
EIN: 396043916

9853
Marguerite V. Brown Testamentary Trust
(also known as Le Roy C. Brown Memorial Scholarships)
c/o U.S. Bank, N.A.
P.O. Box 2043
Milwaukee, WI 53201-9668 (712) 366-0571

Foundation type: Independent foundation
Purpose: Scholarships for attendance at colleges and trade schools to financially needy graduates of Abraham Lincoln High School, Thomas Jefferson High School, Lewis Central Senior High School, and the high school at the Iowa School for the Deaf, all in Council Bluffs, IA.
Financial data: Year ended 12/31/2012. Assets, $757,720 (M); Expenditures, $45,655; Total giving, $33,230; Grants to individuals, 46 grants totaling $33,230 (high: $2,000, low: $422).
Fields of interest: Vocational education; Disabilities, people with.
Type of support: Support to graduates or students of specific schools; Technical education support; Undergraduate support.
Application information: Applications accepted. Application form required.
 Deadline(s): Second Mon. in Mar.
 Applicants should submit the following:
  1) GPA
  2) Financial information
 Additional information: Application should also include school and community activities and a self-evaluation. Applications should be submitted to individual high schools.
EIN: 426353639

9854
Joseph & Angela Bruneo Foundation
3505 30th Ave.
Kenosha, WI 53144-1650 (262) 652-5050
Contact: Bruno M. Rizzo, Dir.

Foundation type: Independent foundation
Purpose: Scholarships to students from Kenosha County, WI with financial need who are pursuing a two- or four-year degree in a medical field, with an emphasis on nursing.
Financial data: Year ended 12/31/2010. Assets, $0 (M); Expenditures, $9,291; Total giving, $8,000.

Fields of interest: Medical school/education; Nursing school/education.
Type of support: Scholarships—to individuals.
Application information: Applications accepted.
 Deadline(s): May 1
EIN: 391917743

9855
Michael and Beverly Bruno Family Foundation
1780 Executive Dr.
P.O. Box 84
Oconomowoc, WI 53066-0084 (262) 567-4990

Foundation type: Independent foundation
Purpose: College scholarships to employees of Bruno Independent Living Aids, Inc., or to their dependents who are high school graduates seeking a higher education.
Financial data: Year ended 12/31/2011. Assets, $15,977 (M); Expenditures, $5,010; Total giving, $5,000; Grants to individuals, 5 grants totaling $5,000 (high: $1,000, low: $1,000).
Fields of interest: Higher education.
Type of support: Employee-related scholarships.
Application information: Applications accepted. Application form required.
 Deadline(s): May 31
 Applicants should submit the following:
  1) Transcripts
  2) Letter(s) of recommendation
  3) Essay
 Additional information: Official transcripts must be from all schools attended within the previous three years.
EIN: 113656127

9856
Calumet Area Community Health Foundation
451 E. Brooklyn St., Ste. 6
Chilton, WI 53014-1595 (920) 849-8700
FAX: (920) 849-8707; E-mail: cachfinc@yahoo.com;
URL: http://www.cachf.org

Foundation type: Public charity
Purpose: Scholarships to prior year and current high school graduates of the Calumet county, WI area for attendance at a vocational-technical school, junior and/or community college, four year college or university pursuing a career in a health related field.
Publications: Application guidelines.
Financial data: Year ended 09/30/2012. Assets, $7,126,751 (M); Expenditures, $93,724; Total giving, $31,500; Grants to individuals, totaling $16,000.
Fields of interest: Vocational education, post-secondary; Higher education; College (community/junior); Health sciences school/education.
Type of support: Scholarships—to individuals.
Application information: Applications accepted. Application form required. Application form available on the grantmaker's web site.
 Send request by: Mail
 Deadline(s): Mar. 1
 Applicants should submit the following:
  1) Transcripts
  2) Letter(s) of recommendation
 Additional information: Selection is based on health/health related activities, scholastic achievement, character, personality, initiative, seriousness of purpose, financial need, moral character, citizenship and cooperation. See web site for additional application guidelines.

Program description:
Scholarships: Scholarship are awarded to assist graduating and graduated qualified applicants, as defined in CACHF Health Scholarship Rules, in financing their vocational-technical school, junior and/or community college, four year college or university education. Scholarship amounts vary and will be awarded to eligible graduates.
EIN: 391948002

9857
CAP Services, Inc.
5499 Hwy. 10 E., Ste. A
Stevens Point, WI 54482-9133   (715) 343-7500
Contact: Mary Patoka, Pres. and C.E.O.
FAX: (715) 343-7520; E-mail: info@capmail.org; E-mail For Mary Patoka: mpatoka@capmail.org; URL: http://www.capserv.org

Foundation type: Public charity
Purpose: Financial assistance and other special needs to low-income individuals and families of Marquette, Outagamie, Portage, Waupaca, and Waushara counties, WI to aid in self-sufficiency and enhance the quality of life.
Financial data: Year ended 12/31/2011. Assets, $49,336,040 (M); Expenditures, $17,762,130; Total giving, $2,004,842; Grants to individuals, totaling $1,627,868.
Fields of interest: Economically disadvantaged.
Type of support: Grants for special needs.
Application information: Contact the organization for information on assistance.
EIN: 391080897

9858
Michael Carlisle Charitable Trust 2
P.O. Box 509
Eau Claire, WI 54702-0509   (715) 833-3940
Contact: Robert A. Kerbell, Tr.

Foundation type: Independent foundation
Purpose: Scholarships to students of WI, in pursuit of a higher education and grants to needy individuals.
Financial data: Year ended 12/31/2011. Assets, $1,184,427 (M); Expenditures, $309,627; Total giving, $300,000; Grants to individuals, 2 grants totaling $13,500 (high: $11,000, low: $2,500).
Fields of interest: Higher education; Economically disadvantaged.
Type of support: Scholarships—to individuals; Grants for special needs.
Application information: Applications accepted. Application form required. Interview required.
Deadline(s): Apr. 30 for scholarships
Applicants should submit the following:
1) Transcripts
2) Class rank
3) SAT
4) ACT
5) Financial information
Additional information: Applicants requesting assistance and those applying for scholarships must include income tax returns and financial statements.
EIN: 206001882

9859
Francis F. Carnes Education Charitable Trust
316 N. Main St.
Lake Mills, WI 53551   (920) 648-4456
Contact: Cherie L. Miller, Tr.

Foundation type: Independent foundation
Purpose: Scholarships to graduating seniors who have attended four years of high school at one of the five Jefferson County high schools and maintained a minimum GPA of 2.75.
Financial data: Year ended 01/31/2013. Assets, $1,038,436 (M); Expenditures, $37,995; Total giving, $29,500; Grants to individuals, 12 grants totaling $29,500 (high: $4,000, low: $1,000).
Fields of interest: Scholarships/financial aid.
Type of support: Support to graduates or students of specific schools; Undergraduate support.
Application information: Application form required.
Deadline(s): Mar. 31
EIN: 391968680

9860
William J. & Gertrude R. Casper Foundation
c/o U.S. Bank, N.A.
P.O. Box 3194
Milwaukee, WI 53201-3194   (715) 723-6618
Contact: M. Berry
Application address: c/o The Edward Rutledge Charity, Kim King, 404 N. Bridge St., Chippewa Falls, WI 54729, tel.: (715) 723-6618

Foundation type: Independent foundation
Purpose: Scholarships to residents of the Chippewa Falls, WI, area for study at technical schools, colleges, and universities.
Financial data: Year ended 05/31/2013. Assets, $18,482,374 (M); Expenditures, $922,288; Total giving, $758,900; Grants to individuals, 180 grants totaling $204,450 (high: $2,000, low: $400).
Fields of interest: Vocational education.
Type of support: Technical education support; Undergraduate support.
Application information: Applications accepted. Application form required.
Initial approach: Letter
Deadline(s): None
Program description:
Scholarship Program: Selection is based on financial need, past academic achievement, and character.
EIN: 396484669

9861
Catholic Charities of the Archdiocese of Milwaukee, Inc.
3501 South Lake Dr.
Milwaukee, WI 53207-0912   (414) 769-3420
URL: http://www.archmil.org/Giving/CCMke.htm

Foundation type: Public charity
Purpose: Assistance to indigents residing in Milwaukee, WI, with food, clothing, shelter, and other needs.
Financial data: Year ended 12/31/2012. Assets, $1,870,366 (M); Expenditures, $5,122,175.
Fields of interest: Economically disadvantaged.
Type of support: Grants for special needs.
Application information: Contact the organization for additional information for assistance and eligibility.
EIN: 390806321

9862
Chetek Area Scholarship Foundation, Inc.
P. O. Box 244
Chetek, WI 54728-0244   (715) 237-2477
Contact: Tim Knutson, Pres.
E-mail: info@chetekscholarships.com; URL: http://www.chetekscholarships.com/index.htm

Foundation type: Public charity
Purpose: Scholarships to deserving graduating students of Chetek High School, WI with college or technical school tuition.
Financial data: Year ended 12/31/2012. Assets, $384,941 (M); Expenditures, $34,866; Total giving, $32,750.
Fields of interest: Vocational education, post-secondary; Higher education.
Type of support: Support to graduates or students of specific schools; Undergraduate support.
Application information: Applications accepted. Application form required.
Deadline(s): Mar.
Applicants should submit the following:
1) Essay
2) ACT
3) SAT
4) Class rank
EIN: 311493038

9863
Melanie V. Chmielewski Educational Foundation
2448 S. 102nd St., Ste. 170
West Allis, WI 53227-2141   (414) 545-5450
Contact: Alfred A. Drosen, Jr., Tr.

Foundation type: Independent foundation
Purpose: Scholarships to graduating high school students of WI, pursuing a degree in education.
Financial data: Year ended 12/31/2011. Assets, $2,826 (M); Expenditures, $3,778; Total giving, $2,500.
Fields of interest: Teacher school/education.
Type of support: Undergraduate support.
Application information: Applications accepted. Application form required. Interview required.
Initial approach: Letter
Deadline(s): Prior to the start of the semester or quarter the applicant will attend classes
Additional information: Applications available from Student Service.
EIN: 396531505

9864
Paul & Mary Collins Trust No. 2
c/o U.S. Bank, N.A.
P.O. Box 2043
Milwaukee, WI 53201-9668   (712) 472-2581

Foundation type: Independent foundation
Purpose: Scholarships to individuals enrolling in a college or university, with primary consideration to residents of Lyon County, IA. Relatives of Paul & Mary Collins are ineligible.
Financial data: Year ended 05/31/2013. Assets, $855,787 (M); Expenditures, $45,830; Total giving, $32,425; Grants to individuals, 84 grants totaling $32,425 (high: $625, low: $113).
Type of support: Scholarships—to individuals.
Application information: Application form required.
Deadline(s): June 1
Additional information: Application must include financial statement and a statement of plan for educational progress.
EIN: 426120024

9865
Community Coordinated Child Care, Inc.
5 Odana Ct.
Madison, WI   53719-1120   (608) 271-9181
Contact: Jody Bartnick, Exec. Dir.
FAX: (608) 271-5380; E-mail: info@4-c.org; Toll-free
tel.: (800) 750-KIDS; E-Mail for Jody Bartnick:
jody.bartnick@4-c.org; URL: http://www.4-c.org

Foundation type: Public charity
Purpose: Financial assistance to WI child care
providers to encourage them to serve nutritional
meals to children in their care.
Financial data: Year ended 12/31/2011. Assets,
$1,858,607 (M); Expenditures, $4,195,996; Total
giving, $2,335,591; Grants to individuals, totaling
$2,335,591.
Fields of interest: Day care.
Type of support: Grants to individuals.
Application information:
  Initial approach: Letter
  Additional information: Contact foundation for
    eligibility criteria.
EIN: 391165742

9866
Community Foundation of Central Wisconsin, Inc.
(formerly Community Foundation of Portage County,
Inc.)
1501 Clark St.
P.O. Box 968
Stevens Point, WI   54481-0968   (715)
342-4454
Contact: Terry Rothmann, Exec. Dir.
FAX: (715) 342-5560;
E-mail: foundation@cfcwi.org; Additional E-mail:
terryr@cfpcwi.org; URL: http://www.cfcwi.org/

Foundation type: Community foundation
Purpose: Scholarships to Central Wisconsin area
students for continuing education at institutions of
higher learning.
Publications: Application guidelines; Annual report;
Grants list; Informational brochure.
Financial data: Year ended 06/30/2012. Assets,
$12,921,089 (M); Expenditures, $1,020,130;
Total giving, $831,809; Grants to individuals, 154
grants totaling $138,800.
Fields of interest: Higher education; Nursing
school/education; Scholarships/financial aid;
Athletics/sports, school programs.
Type of support: Scholarships—to individuals;
Support to graduates or students of specific
schools; Undergraduate support.
Application information: Applications accepted.
Application form required. Application form
available on the grantmaker's web site.
  Deadline(s): Mar. 1
  Final notification: Applicants notified by mid-May
  Additional information: See web site for a
    complete listing of scholarships and
    guidelines.
Program description:
  Scholarships: Due to the generosity of donors,
the foundation awards over 120 scholarships to
students every year for educational financial
support. Scholarship awards vary in size from $50
to multi-year awards of up to $4000. Each
scholarship may have its own eligibility
requirements and criteria. Many scholarships are
limited to residents of specific counties or
graduates of specific high schools. See web site for
additional information.
EIN: 390827885

9867
Community Foundation of Dunn County
500 Main St., Ste. 322
P.O. Box 498
Menomonie, WI   54751   (715) 232-8019
Contact: Georgina Tegart, Exec. Dir.
FAX: (715) 232-9636;
E-mail: info@cfdunncounty.org; Additional tel.:
(715) 232-8029; Additional e-mail:
lmcintyre@cfdunncounty.org; URL: http://
www.cfdunncounty.org

Foundation type: Community foundation
Purpose: Scholarships to high school students of
Dunn County, WI for higher education. One annual
scholarship available for area youth under the age
of 19 who suffer from Type I Diabetes to attend
camps specifically designed for young people with
Diabetes.
Publications: Annual report; Informational brochure
(including application guidelines); Newsletter; IRS
Form 990 or 990-PF printed copy available upon
request.
Financial data: Year ended 12/31/2012. Assets,
$3,856,459 (M); Expenditures, $437,812; Total
giving, $59,431; Grants to individuals, totaling
$9,319.
Fields of interest: Higher education; Scholarships/
financial aid; Diabetes.
Type of support: Camperships; Scholarships—to
individuals; Undergraduate support.
Application information: Applications accepted.
Application form required.
  Deadline(s): Varies
  Additional information: Interested applicants
    should apply through their high school
    guidance office unless otherwise indicated on
    foundation's web site. See web site for
    complete listing of scholarships and individual
    eligibility requirements.
EIN: 391819945

9868
Community Foundation of North Central Wisconsin, Inc.
(formerly Wausau Area Community Foundation, Inc.)
500 1st St., Ste. 2600
Wausau, WI   54403   (715) 845-9555
Contact: Jean C. Tehan, Exec. Dir.; For grants: Sue
E. Nelson, Prog. Mgr.
FAX: (715) 845-5423; E-mail: info@cfoncw.org;
Additional tel.: (888) 845-9223; Community Arts
application e-mail: sue@cfoncw.org; URL: http://
www.cfoncw.org

Foundation type: Community foundation
Purpose: Scholarships to residents of the greater
Wausau, WI, area for higher education.
Publications: Application guidelines; Annual report;
Informational brochure (including application
guidelines); Newsletter.
Financial data: Year ended 12/31/2012. Assets,
$37,698,968 (M); Expenditures, $2,035,685;
Total giving, $1,639,469; Grants to individuals,
76 grants totaling $122,550.
Fields of interest: Higher education.
Type of support: Scholarships—to individuals;
Support to graduates or students of specific
schools.
Application information: Applications accepted.
Application form required.
  Send request by: On-line
  Deadline(s): Spring
  Additional information: See web site for a
    complete listing of scholarships and
    guidelines.

Program description:
  Scholarships: Scholarship funds provide benefits
to students that affect their lives and the local
community today and for future generations. Each
scholarship has its own unique set of application
guidelines and eligibility criteria, which ranges from
graduating from particular high schools,
concentration in a particular field of study,
involvement in sports, and demonstrating financial
need. See web site for additional information.
EIN: 391577472

9869
Community Foundation of Southern Wisconsin, Inc.
(formerly United Community Foundation, Inc.)
26 S. Jackson St.
Janesville, WI   53548-3838   (608) 758-0883
Contact: Sue S. Conley, Exec. Dir.; For grants:
Lindsey Hulstrom, Grants and Scholarships Mgr.
FAX: (608) 758-8551; E-mail: info@cfsw.org;
Additional tel.: (800) 995-CFSW; Grant inquiry
e-mail: lindsey@cfsw.org; Additional e-mail:
sueconley@cfsw.org; URL: http://www.cfsw.org

Foundation type: Community foundation
Purpose: Scholarships only to residents of Monroe,
WI, and northern Rock, Iowa, Lafayette, Grant,
Green, Sauk, Vernon, and Walworth counties, WI.
Publications: Application guidelines; Annual report;
Financial statement; Informational brochure
(including application guidelines); Newsletter.
Financial data: Year ended 06/30/2013. Assets,
$35,220,164 (M); Expenditures, $3,112,179;
Total giving, $2,137,193; Grants to individuals,
385 grants totaling $532,263.
Fields of interest: Higher education; Scholarships/
financial aid.
Type of support: Scholarships—to individuals;
Support to graduates or students of specific
schools; Technical education support;
Undergraduate support.
Application information: Applications accepted.
Application form required.
  Initial approach: Telephone
  Send request by: Mail
  Copies of proposal: 1
  Deadline(s): Mar. 1
  Applicants should submit the following:
    1) Transcripts
    2) Letter(s) of recommendation
    3) GPA
    4) ACT
  Additional information: See web site for
    additional information. Applications are
    available on the foundation's web site or at
    your local high school guidance office.
EIN: 391711388

9870
Community Health Network Foundation
(also known as CHN Foundation)
225 Memorial Dr.
Berlin, WI   54923-1243   (920) 361-1313
Contact: Lynn Kleman, Exec. Dir.
FAX: (920) 361-5314;
E-mail: talktous@partnershealth.org; URL: http://
www.communityhealthnetwork.org/getpage.php?
name=foundation

Foundation type: Public charity
Purpose: Grants to WI residents of the Community
Health Network service area who are experiencing
financial strains due to serious medical needs, and
to adults experiencing serious medical problems.

Financial data: Year ended 09/30/2011. Assets, $984,327 (M); Expenditures, $135,142; Total giving, $37,947; Grants to individuals, totaling $14,706.
Fields of interest: Health care.
Type of support: Grants for special needs.
Application information: Applications accepted. Application form required. Application form available on the grantmaker's web site.
 Initial approach: Letter
EIN: 731639346

9871
Noel Compass Foundation, Inc.
1145 Clark St.
Stevens Point, WI 54481-2933
Application address: c/o Sam Dinga, 3300 Business Park, Stevens Point, WI 54482, tel.: (715) 345-1041

Foundation type: Operating foundation
Purpose: Scholarships to financially needy students from at-risk environments attending the University of Wisconsin-Stevens Point, who have shown academic or leadership qualities in their high school careers.
Financial data: Year ended 12/31/2012. Assets, $342,232 (M); Expenditures, $196,658; Total giving, $135,560.
Type of support: Undergraduate support.
Application information: Application form required.
 Deadline(s): Jan. 31
EIN: 391837771

9872
William D. Connor Educational Fund
101 W. 29th St.101 Ste.
Marshfield, WI 54449 (715) 384-2778
Contact: Marietta Drach, Mgr.
Application address: 503 S. Cypress Ave., Marshfield, WI 5444

Foundation type: Independent foundation
Purpose: Scholarships to students at Marshfield, Auburndale and Stratford High Schools, WI, for attendance at Carroll College, UW Marshfield or another UW-system school.
Financial data: Year ended 12/31/2012. Assets, $284,450 (M); Expenditures, $16,192; Total giving, $13,778.
Fields of interest: Higher education.
Type of support: Scholarships—to individuals.
Application information:
 Deadline(s): None
EIN: 396062183

9873
Couleecap, Inc.
201 Melby St.
Westby, WI 54667-1013 (608) 634-7363
Contact: for Scholarships: gi Kadie Brueggen, Devel. Coord.
FAX: (608) 634-3134;
E-mail: contactus@couleecap.org; URL: http://www.couleecap.org

Foundation type: Public charity
Purpose: Scholarships to graduating high school seniors who are residents of Crawford, La Crosse, Monroe, or Vernon county, WI pursuing a career in a human services field. Assistance to low-income individuals and families with food, clothing, energy assistance and home buyer assistance.
Publications: Annual report; Newsletter.

Financial data: Year ended 12/31/2011. Assets, $10,009,244 (M); Expenditures, $11,016,548; Total giving, $4,129,291; Grants to individuals, totaling $4,129,291.
Fields of interest: Higher education; Human services.
Type of support: Scholarships—to individuals; Grants for special needs.
Application information: Applications accepted. Application form required.
 Deadline(s): Feb.
 Final notification: Recipients will be notified in Apr.
 Applicants should submit the following:
  1) Class rank
  2) GPA
  3) Essay
EIN: 391077614

9874
Cuan Foundation, Inc.
c/o Jane Quinlisk
521 S 23rd
La Crosse, WI 54601 (608) 785-0005

Foundation type: Operating foundation
Purpose: Scholarships to residents of the greater La Crosse, WI, area.
Financial data: Year ended 12/31/2012. Assets, $327,036 (M); Expenditures, $49,587; Total giving, $22,437; Grants to individuals, 6 grants totaling $22,437 (high: $6,666, low: $500).
Type of support: Scholarships—to individuals.
Application information: Applications accepted.
 Initial approach: Letter
 Deadline(s): None
EIN: 391714380

9875
Joseph and Sharon Darcey Foundation, Inc.
(formerly Joseph Darcey Foundation, Inc.)
314 W. Main St., Ste. 11
Watertown, WI 53094-7630

Foundation type: Independent foundation
Purpose: Awards to individuals for excellence in teaching in Watertown, WI.
Financial data: Year ended 12/31/2012. Assets, $2,110,809 (M); Expenditures, $95,022; Total giving, $80,000.
Fields of interest: Education.
Type of support: Awards/prizes.
Application information: Applications not accepted.
 Additional information: Unsolicited requests for funds not considered or acknowledged.
EIN: 391715481

9876
Davey Scholarship Foundation
c/o JPMorgan Chase Bank, N.A.
P.O. Box 3038
Milwaukee, WI 53201-1308 (217) 525-9737
Contact: Heather Smith
Application address: 1 East Old State Capital Plz., Springfield, IL 62701 tel.: (217) 525-9737

Foundation type: Independent foundation
Purpose: Loans to high school graduates of Sangamon, Morgan, and Christian counties, IL. Applicants must be between 16 and 25 years of age.

Financial data: Year ended 12/31/2011. Assets, $2,564,115 (M); Expenditures, $48,553; Total giving, $0.
Fields of interest: Higher education.
Type of support: Student loans—to individuals.
Application information: Application form required.
 Send request by: Mail
 Deadline(s): June 15
 Applicants should submit the following:
  1) Transcripts
  2) Class rank
  3) GPA
 Additional information: Application available upon request.
EIN: 376057502

9877
James E. DeLong Foundation, Inc.
1101 W. St. Paul Ave.
Waukesha, WI 53188-4961

Foundation type: Company-sponsored foundation
Purpose: Scholarships only to children of employees of the Waukesha division of Dresser, Inc.
Financial data: Year ended 09/30/2012. Assets, $115,472 (M); Expenditures, $11,850; Total giving, $11,750; Grants to individuals, 10 grants totaling $11,750 (high: $2,250, low: $500).
Fields of interest: Higher education.
Type of support: Employee-related scholarships.
Application information: Applications not accepted.
 Additional information: Unsolicited requests for funds not considered or acknowledged.
EIN: 396050331

9878
Door County Community Foundation, Inc.
228 N. 3rd Ave.
Sturgeon Bay, WI 54235 (920) 746-1786
Contact: Bret Bicoy, Pres. and C.E.O.
FAX: (920) 473-2066;
E-mail: bret@doorcountycommunityfoundation.org;
Mailing Address: P.O. Box 802 Sturgeon Bay, WI 54235; URL: http://www.doorcountycommunityfoundation.org

Foundation type: Community foundation
Purpose: Scholarships to residents of Door County, WI for higher education.
Publications: Informational brochure; Newsletter.
Financial data: Year ended 06/30/2012. Assets, $7,273,204 (M); Expenditures, $654,581; Total giving, $475,583; Grants to individuals, totaling $12,500.
Fields of interest: Higher education.
Type of support: Scholarships—to individuals; Undergraduate support.
Application information: Applications accepted. Application form required. Application form available on the grantmaker's web site.
 Initial approach: Application
 Send request by: Mail or hand deliver
 Deadline(s): Mar. 19
 Additional information: The foundation offers many scholarships, several of which are decided upon by school-based committees of teachers and counselors using the criteria established by the donor. There are no applications publicly available for the school based scholarships. However, students are welcome to apply to any of the public scholarships listed on the foundation's web

site so long as they meet the criteria of the individual scholarship.
EIN: 391980685

9879
Mabel E. Dupee Foundation, Inc.
124 W. Oak St.
Sparta, WI   54656-1713   (608) 269-6737
Contact: Jan Leis, Treas.
Foundation type: Independent foundation
Purpose: Scholarships to graduates of Sparta High School, WI, for undergraduate education. Students beyond their 4th year of post-high school education are ineligible.
Financial data: Year ended 12/31/2012. Assets, $324,958 (M); Expenditures, $17,164; Total giving, $16,400; Grants to individuals, 25 grants totaling $16,400 (high: $1,000, low: $400).
Fields of interest: Higher education.
Type of support: Support to graduates or students of specific schools; Undergraduate support.
Application information: Application form required.
  Deadline(s): Mar. 28
  Applicants should submit the following:
    1) Transcripts
    2) Financial information
  Additional information: Applications can be obtained from the Union National Bank and Trust Co., and at Sparta High School guidance office.
EIN: 391383645

9880
EAA Aviation Foundation, Inc.
P.O. Box 3086
Oshkosh, WI   54903-3086   (920) 426-4800
Contact: Rodney Hightower, Pres.
FAX: (920) 426-6865;
E-mail: scholarships@eaa.org; URL: http://www.eaa.org/support/scholarships.asp
Foundation type: Public charity
Purpose: Scholarships to individuals studying the technologies and skills needed in the field of aviation.
Financial data: Year ended 02/28/2012. Assets, $37,811,798 (M); Expenditures, $2,848,023; Total giving, $1,035,026.
Fields of interest: Engineering school/education; Space/aviation.
Type of support: Scholarships—to individuals; Support to graduates or students of specific schools; Technical education support; Undergraduate support.
Application information: Applications accepted. Application form required. Application form available on the grantmaker's web site.
  Send request by: Online
  Deadline(s): Feb. 28
  Applicants should submit the following:
    1) SAT
    2) ACT
    3) Transcripts
    4) Financial information
  Additional information: Application should include two references and a personal statement of 500 words or less.
Program descriptions:
  Cdr. John Paradiso Scholarship for Women in Aviation/Aerospace: Awards of approximately $750 are available to young women who have a sincere interest in pursuing their dreams of flight.
  Clay Lacy Professional Pilot Scholarship: This scholarship provides highly qualified potential flight students with financial need the opportunity to attend a professional pilot program at the University of North Dakota and participate in flight by living on the EAA Air Academy campus. A possible four scholarships are awarded of up to $12,500 each.
  David Alan Quick Scholarship: Awards one $1,000 renewable scholarship to a junior or senior in good standing, enrolled in an accredited college or university pursuing a degree in Aerospace or Aeronautical Engineering.
  EAA Air Academy Summer Camp Scholarships: Scholarships of $500 to $800 are available to applicants attending EAA Air Academy Summer Camps to cover most or all of the cost of the course and instructional materials.
  H.P. "Bud" Milligan Aviation Scholarship: Awards a renewable $1,000 scholarship to students enrolled in an accredited aviation program at a college, technical school, or aviation academy. Financial need is not a requirement.
  Harrison Ford Education Scholarship Challenge: The fund provides financial assistance to young people seeking to take their FAA written pilot's exam after completing EAA's free online ground school training, take their first formal flying lesson, attend EAA Air Academy residential aviation camp, secure support to obtain their sport pilot's license or further their passion and interest in aviation through tuition support, enabling them to pursue postsecondary education at an institution of their choice.
  Heather McRoberts Memorial Scholarship Fund: A $500 scholarship is available to support females up to 21 years of age to attend EAA's Summer Air Academy. It is awarded to an outstanding applicant who participates in EAA's "Women Soar You Soar" program during AirVenture each summer.
  Payzer Scholarship: Awards one $5,000 scholarship to an individual accepted or enrolled in an accredited college, university or postsecondary school with an emphasis on technical information. The scholarship enables the recipient to pursue a professional career in engineering, mathematics or the physical or biological sciences.
  Russell T. MacFarlane Scholarship Program: Awards from $500 to $1,000 to attend EAA Air Academy Summer Camp dependent upon the youth's individual requirements and Air Academy Internships award range from $1,200 to $1,500 to applicants interested in aviation.
EIN: 391033301

9881
Eckburg Foundation Inc.
636 Wisconsin Ave.
P.O. Box 171
Sheboygan, WI   53082-0171   (608) 263-9725
Contact: Katharyn A. May, Pres.
Application address: U.W. Madison, 600 Highland Ave., Madison, WI 53792
Foundation type: Independent foundation
Purpose: Scholarships to students for attendance at the University of Wisconsin, School of Nursing and the University of Wisconsin, School of Agriculture pursuing careers in Nursing and Dairy fields respectively.
Financial data: Year ended 12/31/2012. Assets, $779,062 (M); Expenditures, $43,671; Total giving, $26,427.
Fields of interest: University; Nursing school/education; Agriculture.
Type of support: Support to graduates or students of specific schools.
Application information: Applications accepted.
  Initial approach: Letter
  Deadline(s): None
EIN: 391837809

9882
Edwin & Lucille Eggen Scholarship Fund
c/o U.S. Bank, N.A.
P.O. Box 7900
Madison, WI   53707-7900   (715) 839-1500
Foundation type: Independent foundation
Purpose: Scholarships to needy and worthy graduates of Memorial High School, North High School, and Regis High School in Eau Claire, WI, and Altoona High School in Altoona, WI.
Financial data: Year ended 06/30/2013. Assets, $1,359,000 (M); Expenditures, $72,244; Total giving, $55,835; Grants to individuals, 32 grants totaling $55,835 (high: $2,584, low: $430).
Type of support: Scholarships—to individuals; Support to graduates or students of specific schools.
Application information: Applications accepted.
  Additional information: Applications should be in written form; submitted to the Eggen Selection Committee at the Eau Claire or Altoona high school the applicant is attending.
EIN: 396769479

9883
Jessie Elfers Scholarship Trust No. 2
c/o U.S. Bank, N.A.
P.O. Box 7900
Madison, WI   53707-7900
Foundation type: Independent foundation
Purpose: Scholarships to graduating seniors of Marshalltown High School, Marshalltown, IA.
Financial data: Year ended 01/31/2013. Assets, $215,530 (M); Expenditures, $10,104; Total giving, $6,000; Grants to individuals, 2 grants totaling $6,000 (high: $3,000, low: $3,000).
Type of support: Support to graduates or students of specific schools; Undergraduate support.
Application information: Applications not accepted.
  Additional information: Unsolicited requests for funds not considered or acknowledged.
EIN: 426546523

9884
Entomological Foundation
4510 Regent St.
Madison, WI   53705-4963   (608) 232-1410
Contact: April Gower, Exec. Dir.
FAX: (608) 232-1440;
E-mail: ipmworks@ipminstitute.org; E-mail for Melodie Dziduch: melodie@entfdn.org; URL: http://www.entfdn.org/
Foundation type: Public charity
Purpose: Scholarships, fellowships, research grants and awards to entomology students in the U.S., Canada and Mexico.
Publications: Annual report; Newsletter.
Financial data: Year ended 12/31/2011. Assets, $332,490 (M); Expenditures, $195,008; Total giving, $23,514.
Fields of interest: Environment; Research; Agriculture.
Type of support: Fellowships; Research; Scholarships—to individuals; Support to graduates or students of specific schools; Awards/prizes; Postdoctoral support; Graduate support; Undergraduate support; Travel grants.
Application information: Applications accepted. Application form required. Application form available on the grantmaker's web site.
  Initial approach: E-mail
  Send request by: Online

Copies of proposal: 1
Deadline(s): July 1
Final notification: Recipients notified in two months
Applicants should submit the following:
1) GPA
2) Curriculum vitae
3) Letter(s) of recommendation
4) Transcripts
Additional information: See web site for additional guidelines.

Program descriptions:

Award for Excellence in Integrated Pest Management: The award recognizes and encourages outstanding contributions to applied integrated pest management in North America and U.S. territories. The amount of the award is dependent on the interest earned from the endowment.

BioQuip Undergraduate Scholarships: An annual $2,000 scholarship is sponsored by BioQuip Products, a major supplier of entomology equipment to encourage student interest in entomology.

George G. Gyrisco Graduate Student Award in Applied Entomology: A $650 award to be used for research purposes is given to an outstanding graduate student in the department of Entomology at Cornell University, Ithaca.

Henry and Sylvia Richardson Research Grant: The purpose of this grant is to provide research funds to postdoctoral members of the society who have at least one year of promising work experience, are undertaking research in selected areas, and have demonstrated a high level of scholarship. The amount of the award is dependent on the interest earned from the endowment.

ICINN Student Recognition Award in Insect Physiology, Biochemistry, Toxicology, and Molecular Biology: The award shall be made on the basis of recognizing and encouraging innovative research in the areas of insect physiology, biochemistry, and toxicology in the broad sense. The amount varies depending upon the interest earned from the endowment.

Integrated Pest Management Team Award: The award recognizes the successful efforts of a small collaborative work team, of no more than 10 members, approach to pest control but must include one entomologist from the private sector and one from the public sector.

Jeffery P. LaFage Graduate Student Research Award: The grant encourages research by graduate students in the field of the biology and control of termites or other insect pests of the urban environment. The amount of the award is dependent on the interest earned from the endowment.

Joseph H. Camin Fellowship: The award supports graduate students in attending the Acarology Summer Program at Ohio State University or an equivalent institution where they can obtain training in the systematics of acarines. Fellowship amount varies annually.

Kenneth and Barbara Starks Plant Resistance to Insects Graduate Student Research Award: This grant encourages research by graduate students in the field of plant resistance to insects in entomology or plant breeding/genetics. The grant is made annually and consists of a plaque and a research grant. The amount is dependent on the interest earned from the endowment.

Larry Larson Graduate Student Award for Leadership in Applied Entomology: This award recognizes master's students who have exhibited exceptional interest in the study and application of entomology through outstanding research and leadership skills. It is hoped that through

recognition of leadership attributes, promising entomology graduate students will be encouraged to further their education to meet the future challenges of agriculture and urban pest management. The amount of the award is dependent on the interest earned from the endowment.

Lillian and Alex Feir Graduate Student Travel Award: The purpose of this award is to encourage graduate students working with insects or other arthropods in the broad areas of physiology, biochemistry, and molecular biology to affiliate with the society's Section B and to attend an annual society meeting or an international Congress of Entomology. The amount of the award is dependent on the interest earned from the endowment.

Pioneer Hi-Bred International Graduate Student Fellowship: The fellowship recognizes innovative research and graduate education in the area of entomology with a focus on key insects or complexes of insects that effect corn, soybeans, canola, alfalfa, or other significant commodity crops. Nominees must attend a college/university in the U.S. and must have demonstrated excellence in the study of entomology or a related discipline. The award is for up to four years of study.

Recognition Award in Urban Entomology: The purpose of this award is to recognize and encourage outstanding extension, research, and teaching contributions in urban entomology, defined as the study of the biology and control of arthropods found in the home or surrounding landscape. The amount of the award is dependent on the interest earned from the endowment.

Snodgrass Memorial Research Award: This award recognizes outstanding research by graduate students who have completed investigations in selected areas of entomology. The award recipient must have completed his/her research thesis or dissertation in related fields of entomology. The amount of the award varies each year.

Stan Beck Fellowship: The purpose of this award is to assist needy students at the graduate or undergraduate level of their education in entomology and related disciplines. The need may be based on physical limitations or economic, minority, or environmental conditions. The annual fellowship varies each year.

Thomas Say Award: This award and certificate is given for significant and outstanding work in the fields of systematics, morphology, or evolution of insects and their allies. The amount of the award is dependent on the interest earned from the endowment.

EIN: 521756169

9885

The Environmental Education Foundation, Inc.

P.O. Box 244
Fontana, WI 53125-0244 (262) 745-0465
Contact: Mary King, Pres.
E-mail: info@envedfdn.org; URL: http://www.envedfnd.org/

Foundation type: Public charity

Purpose: Scholarships to graduating high school students from the Geneva Lakes, WI, area who plan to pursue a major in natural sciences at an accredited college or university. Scholarships also to college undergraduate students and awards to college post-graduate students.

Financial data: Year ended 06/30/2012. Assets, $334,773 (M); Expenditures, $32,386; Total giving, $23,978.

Fields of interest: Physical/earth sciences.

Type of support: Scholarships—to individuals; Support to graduates or students of specific schools; Undergraduate support; Postgraduate support.

Application information: Applications accepted. Application form required.
Deadline(s): Feb. 1 for Undergraduate and Post-Graduate scholarships
Additional information: High school students should contact their guidance counselors, science teachers, and high school scholarship committee chairperson.

Program descriptions:

Charlotte Peterson Elementary and Jr. High Camp Scholarships: Six scholarships are awarded annually, based upon an essay contest, to attend a weeklong Nature Adventure Camp at the Central Wisconsin Environmental Station near Stevens Point, Wisconsin. Students from Geneva Lake Area grade schools are invited to submit an essay of 200 words or less on the given topic. Three winners will be chosen from the 9 to 11 age group and three winners chosen from the 11 to 13 age group.

College Post-Graduate Award: Scholarship up to $2,500 is awarded annually to students registered and actively involved in a natural sciences postgraduate degree program at an accredited college or university. Candidate's academic record, professional goals, relevant work experience and past or present Geneva Lake area residency are all considered by the scholarship committee in making their selection.

College Undergraduate Scholarship: Scholarship of up to $1,500 is awarded annually to qualified college juniors or seniors pursuing a degree in natural sciences at an accredited college or university. Each candidate's academic record, professional goals, relevant work experience and Geneva Lake area past or present residency are evaluated when selecting the top candidate.

High School Graduate Award: Four awards of $2,000 to graduating high school seniors who are recommended by their school and chosen by the foundation and must be registered at an accredited college or university. Scholarship awards are based on academic record, professional goals relevant work experiences and residency.

Thomas E. Reynolds Endowment Scholarship: The scholarship awards a local senior graduating from each of the Geneva Area high schools: Badger High School, Big Foot High School, Williams Bay High School and Faith Christian School. The scholarship assists and encourages young people who demonstrate an interest in conservation, ecology, biology, or other environmentally oriented fields of science. This scholarship awards $2,000 annually for four years, to students who maintain the required 3.0 GPA while actively working toward a degree.

Willard L. Gross Natural Resource Career Workshops for H.S. Juniors and Seniors: Candidates who have an interest in pursuing a career in the environmental sciences are recommended by their teachers to compete for four scholarships that are offered to area high school juniors and seniors to attend a weeklong workshop in the north woods at the Central Wisconsin Environmental Station near Stevens Point, Wisconsin.

EIN: 391394480

9886

Exacto Foundation Inc.

P.O. Box 24
Grafton, WI 53024-0024

Foundation type: Operating foundation

Purpose: Scholarships for undergraduate study to residents of Grafton, WI.
Financial data: Year ended 07/31/2013. Assets, $1,608,743 (M); Expenditures, $112,944; Total giving, $109,444; Grants to individuals, 20 grants totaling $16,250.
Fields of interest: Education; Health care.
Type of support: Undergraduate support.
Application information: Applications not accepted.
  Additional information: Unsolicited requests for funds not considered or acknowledged.
EIN: 237076890

9887
Experimental Aircraft Association, Inc.
3000 Poberezny Rd.
Oshkosh, WI 54902-8939   (920) 426-4800
Contact: Pat Heyer
FAX: (920) 426-6761; E-mail: webmaster@eaa.org; Tel. for Pat Heyer: (920) 426-6507; toll-free tel.: (800) 564-6322; URL: http://www.eaa.org

Foundation type: Public charity
Purpose: Scholarships to outstanding youth who are members of EAA accomplish their aviation interests.
Publications: Annual report; Financial statement.
Financial data: Year ended 02/28/2012. Assets, $36,942,983 (M); Expenditures, $32,654,792; Total giving, $152,666; Grants to individuals, 115 grants totaling $146,895.
Fields of interest: Space/aviation.
Type of support: Internship funds; Scholarships—to individuals; Support to graduates or students of specific schools; Technical education support.
Application information: Applications not accepted.
  Additional information: Contributes only to EAA members, unsolicited requests for funds not considered or acknowledged.
EIN: 390917537

9888
Charles E. Fahrney Education Foundation
(also known as Fahrney Education Foundation)
c/o U.S. Bank, N.A.
P.O. Box 2043
Milwaukee, WI 53201-9668
Application address: c/o US Bank, N.A., Trust Dept., 123 E. 3rd St., Ottumwa, IA 52501, tel.: (641) 683-2053

Foundation type: Independent foundation
Purpose: Undergraduate scholarships to residents of Wapello County, IA, to attend colleges and universities in IA.
Publications: Application guidelines.
Financial data: Year ended 02/28/2013. Assets, $4,935,298 (M); Expenditures, $270,416; Total giving, $215,000; Grants to individuals, 87 grants totaling $215,000 (high: $2,500, low: $1,250).
Fields of interest: Higher education.
Type of support: Undergraduate support.
Application information: Applications accepted. Application form required.
  Deadline(s): Feb. 15
  Additional information: Application should include transcripts, along with a signed personal letter.
EIN: 426295370

9889
Feeding America Eastern Wisconsin, Inc.
1700 W. Fond Du Lac Ave.
Milwaukee, WI 53205-1261   (414) 931-7400
Contact: Bonnie J. Bellehumeur, Pres.
FAX: (414) 931-1996; Toll-free tel.: (800) 236-1208; additional address (Omro office): 1436 Progress Ln., Omro, WI 54963-1569, tel.: (920) 685-6626, toll-free tel.: (888) 643-7074, fax: (920) 685-6639; URL: http://www.feedingamericawi.org/

Foundation type: Public charity
Purpose: Emergency food assistance to individuals and families in need throughout eastern WI.
Financial data: Year ended 06/30/2012. Assets, $14,004,240 (M); Expenditures, $46,397,588; Total giving, $41,232,565; Grants to individuals, 329,400 grants totaling $41,232,565.
Fields of interest: Food services; Food banks; Nutrition; Human services.
Type of support: Emergency funds; In-kind gifts.
Application information: Applications not accepted.
  Additional information: Contact the agency for information for food assistance.
EIN: 391384593

9890
Gertrude A. Fenner Educational Trust
P.O. Box 12800
Green Bay, WI 54307-2800
Contact: Carla Haden
Application address: 1433 S. 8th St., Manitowoc, WI 54220

Foundation type: Independent foundation
Purpose: Scholarships to graduates of Lincoln High School, WI, for undergraduate education.
Financial data: Year ended 12/31/2012. Assets, $198,470 (M); Expenditures, $15,806; Total giving, $12,500.
Type of support: Support to graduates or students of specific schools.
Application information: Applications accepted. Application form required.
  Deadline(s): Mar. 17
EIN: 396741325

9891
Robert W. & Caroline A. Fernstrum Scholarship Foundation Trust
c/o Stephenson National Bank & Trust
P.O. Box 137
Marinette, WI 54143-0137   (906) 863-9951
Application address: 1230 13th St., Menominee, MI 49858

Foundation type: Independent foundation
Purpose: Scholarships to graduating seniors of Menominee High School, MI, for higher education.
Financial data: Year ended 12/31/2012. Assets, $542,107 (M); Expenditures, $33,066; Total giving, $25,314.
Type of support: Support to graduates or students of specific schools; Undergraduate support.
Application information: Applications not accepted.
  Additional information: Unsolicited requests for funds not considered or acknowledged.
EIN: 396625465

9892
Alois A. and Nina M. Fix Scholarship Fund
c/o Jay Carmichael
916 Oak St.
Tomah, WI 54660-1949   (608) 374-7354
Tel.: (608) 374-7354

Foundation type: Independent foundation
Purpose: Scholarships to graduates of Tomah Senior High School, WI.
Financial data: Year ended 12/31/2011. Assets, $233,653 (M); Expenditures, $4,596; Total giving, $3,600.
Type of support: Support to graduates or students of specific schools; Undergraduate support.
Application information: Application form required.
  Deadline(s): Feb. 27
EIN: 396257879

9893
Fond du Lac Area Foundation
384 N. Main St., Ste. 4
Fond du Lac, WI 54935-2310   (920) 921-2215
Contact: Sandi Roehrig, Exec. Dir.
FAX: (920) 921-1036;
E-mail: info@fdlareafoundation.com; URL: http://www.fdlareafoundation.com

Foundation type: Community foundation
Purpose: Scholarships to residents of Fond du Lac, WI.
Publications: Application guidelines; Annual report (including application guidelines); Financial statement; Grants list; Informational brochure (including application guidelines); Newsletter.
Financial data: Year ended 12/31/2012. Assets, $25,537,562 (M); Expenditures, $1,571,343; Total giving, $1,130,037.
Fields of interest: Education.
Type of support: Undergraduate support.
Application information: Applications accepted. Application form required.
  Initial approach: Telephone
  Deadline(s): Varies
  Additional information: The foundation administers numerous scholarships ranging from $250 to $4,000; applications are available in the guidance offices of eligible schools.
EIN: 510181570

9894
Fort Atkinson Community Foundation
244 N. Main St.
Fort Atkinson, WI 53538-1829   (920) 563-3210
Contact: For grants: Sue Hartwick, Prog. Admin.
E-mail: facf@fortfoundation.org; URL: http://fortfoundation.org/

Foundation type: Community foundation
Purpose: Scholarships to Fort Atkinson, WI area high school seniors, college undergraduates, graduate students and individuals considering a vocational or technical education.
Publications: Annual report.
Financial data: Year ended 06/30/2012. Assets, $20,004,392 (M); Expenditures, $655,268; Total giving, $527,135; Grants to individuals, totaling $266,717.
Fields of interest: Higher education.
Type of support: Scholarships—to individuals.
Application information: Applications accepted. Application form required. Application form available on the grantmaker's web site.
  Initial approach: Application

Send request by: Online
Deadline(s): Feb. 15
Additional information: See web site for a complete listing of scholarships and specific eligibility criteria.
EIN: 396220899

9895
The Foundation for Children with Cancer, Inc.

(formerly Reach Our Children, Inc.)
11414 W. Park Pl., Ste. 202
Milwaukee, WI 53324 (414) 716-6250
Contact: Lesley Redman, Exec. Dir.
FAX: (314) 843-9362;
E-mail: info@childrenwithcancer.org; Toll Free: (866)-800-8860; URL: http://www.childrenwithcancer.org

Foundation type: Public charity
Purpose: Grants for mortgage, rent, utilities, and transportation expenses to needy families with a child under the age of 18 diagnosed with cancer.
Publications: Annual report; Financial statement.
Financial data: Year ended 07/31/2012. Assets, $20,499 (M); Expenditures, $331,280; Total giving, $23,037; Grants to individuals, totaling $23,037.
Fields of interest: Cancer; Children.
Type of support: Grants for special needs.
Application information: Applications accepted. Application form required.
  Final notification: Assistance may take up to 2-3 weeks to process
  Additional information: Families must be referred by their physician or assigned social worker.
EIN: 431688473

9896
Four Wheel Drive Foundation

79 8th St.
Clintonville, WI 54929-1518 (715) 823-7961
Contact: John L. Rosenheim, Secy.

Foundation type: Company-sponsored foundation
Purpose: Scholarships to graduating seniors of Clintonville, WI in need of financial assistance pursuing higher education or training for any profession or skill.
Financial data: Year ended 09/30/2012. Assets, $218,922 (M); Expenditures, $6,413; Total giving, $0.
Fields of interest: Higher education.
Type of support: Undergraduate support.
Application information: Applications accepted. Application form required.
  Initial approach: Letter
  Deadline(s): May 10
  Additional information: Application should include transcript and references.
EIN: 396059533

9897
John Cowles Frautschy Scholarship Trust Fund

345 E. Grand Ave.
Beloit, WI 53511 (608) 328-7117

Foundation type: Independent foundation
Purpose: Scholarships to male Protestant graduating seniors of Monroe High School, WI.
Financial data: Year ended 05/31/2013. Assets, $296,665 (M); Expenditures, $10,397; Total

giving, $6,400; Grants to individuals, 5 grants totaling $6,400 (high: $2,800, low: $200).
Fields of interest: Vocational education; Higher education; Protestant agencies & churches; Men.
Type of support: Support to graduates or students of specific schools; Undergraduate support.
Application information: Application form required.
  Deadline(s): Early spring
  Additional information: Applications available from guidance counselors at Monroe High School, WI. Guidance Counselors submit application forms to the Scholarship Selection Group. If requested, the counselors will also present additional information about the applicants, including class rank, aptitude test scores, and an appraisal of financial need. Primary emphasis is given to financial need of the applicants and their record of scholastic accomplishment. Emphasis is also placed on attitude and aptitude. Grants are made for college scholarships or for other training and are awarded to adults as well as to high school seniors.
EIN: 930799642

9898
Freedom From Religion Foundation, Inc.

P.O. Box 750
Madison, WI 53701-0750 (608) 256-8900
Contact: David Groethe, Chair.
FAX: (608) 204-0422; E-mail: info@ffrf.org;
URL: http://www.ffrf.org

Foundation type: Public charity
Purpose: Annual essay competition for graduating high school students, currently enrolled college students, or currently enrolled graduate students.
Financial data: Year ended 12/31/2011. Assets, $8,928,763 (M); Expenditures, $1,518,607; Total giving, $37,286; Grants to individuals, totaling $32,286.
Fields of interest: Higher education.
Type of support: Awards/prizes; Graduate support; Undergraduate support.
Application information:
  Send request by: Mail
  Deadline(s): June 1 for Herbert Bushong Award, June 15 for Michael Hakeem Memorial Award and July 15 for Brian Bolton Award
  Additional information: Application should include an essay.
Program descriptions:
  Brian Bolton Essay Contest for Graduate Students/Mature Students: Awards to currently enrolled graduate student of any age, or any currently enrolled undergraduate age 25 or older, attending a North American college or university. Awards range from $2,000 to $200.
  Herbert Bushong High School Senior Essay Competition: Awards range from $2,000 to $200 to high school seniors graduating in North America and planning on attending college in the fall.
  Michael Hakeem Memorial College Essay Competition: Awards to currently enrolled college student under age 25, currently attending a North American college or university. Awards range from $2,000 to $200.
EIN: 391302520

9899
William and Lena Fricke Foundation

127 Canterbury Rd.
Eau Claire, WI 54701-7105 (603) 305-3201
Contact: Raymond C. Fricke, Tr.
Application address: 2434 Remington Dr., Naperville, IL 60540

Foundation type: Independent foundation
Purpose: Grants to individuals for participation in a program of total abstinence form alcohol and tobacco use.
Financial data: Year ended 12/31/2012. Assets, $337,295 (M); Expenditures, $20,418; Total giving, $18,001; Grants to individuals, 19 grants totaling $18,001 (high: $1,000, low: $667).
Fields of interest: Substance abuse, prevention.
Type of support: Grants to individuals.
Application information:
  Initial approach: Letter
  Deadline(s): Dec. 1
  Additional information: Grants are in the amount of $1,000, and limited to individuals between the ages of 10 and 20 years. Contact the foundation for additional information about the program.
EIN: 396677792

9900
Friends of the Royal Society of Chemistry, Inc.

c/o Lynette N. Zigman
777 E. Wisconsin Ave., Rm. 3600
Milwaukee, WI 53202-5306

Foundation type: Independent foundation
Purpose: Awards prizes to individuals studying chemistry in the United Kingdom in recognition of eminence in that field.
Financial data: Year ended 11/30/2012. Assets, $68,904 (M); Expenditures, $2,448; Total giving, $0.
Fields of interest: Chemistry.
Type of support: Awards/prizes.
Application information: Applications not accepted.
EIN: 391639596

9901
Walter and Mabel Fromm Scholarship Trust

P.O. Box 2043
Milwaukee, WI 53201-9668
E-mail: Gil.Lindemann@USbank.com

Foundation type: Independent foundation
Purpose: Scholarships to graduates of Maple Grove (elementary) School in Hamburg, WI, and Merrill Senior Public High School in Merrill, WI.
Financial data: Year ended 02/28/2012. Assets, $3,332,347 (M); Expenditures, $222,577; Total giving, $172,500; Grants to individuals, 27 grants totaling $172,500 (high: $7,000, low: $1,500).
Fields of interest: Vocational education; Nursing school/education.
Type of support: Support to graduates or students of specific schools; Undergraduate support.
Application information: Applications not accepted.
  Additional information: Unsolicited requests for funds not considered or acknowledged.
EIN: 396250027

9902
Fund for Wisconsin Scholars, Inc.
(formerly Fund for Wisconsin Scholarship, Inc.)
P.O. Box 5506
Madison, WI 53705-0506 (608) 238-2400
Contact: Mary Gulbrandsen, Exec. Dir.
FAX: (608) 238-0044;
E-mail: mgulbrandsen@ffws.org; URL: http://www.ffws.org

Foundation type: Independent foundation
Purpose: Need-based grants to recent graduates of Wisconsin public high schools.
Publications: Annual report.
Financial data: Year ended 06/30/2013. Assets, $159,913,107 (M); Expenditures, $9,784,723; Total giving, $7,886,579; Grants to individuals, 50 grants totaling $25,000.
Fields of interest: Higher education.
Type of support: Scholarships—to individuals.
Application information: Applications not accepted.
Additional information: Students do not need to apply for FFWS grants. They will be eligible to become a grant recipient based on criteria established by FFWS, which include being a PELL recipient, recently graduating from a public high school and attending University of Wisconsin (UW) or Wisconsin Technical College System (WTCS) school full-time. The grants will be awarded to eligible students through a random selection process conducted at the Higher Education Aids Board (HEAB). There is no application process.
EIN: 261412296

9903
Funeral Service Foundation, Inc.
(formerly Funeral Service Educational Foundation)
13625 Bishops Dr.
Brookfield, WI 53005-6607
Contact: Kathy Wisnefski, Exec. Dir.
Key Memories Scholarship Application address: c/o Tim Cocke,400 N. Ashley Dr., Ste. 1900, Tampa, FL 33602
FAX: (262) 789-6977;
E-mail: info@funeralservicefoundation.org; Toll-free tel.: (877) 402-5900; E-mail For Kathy Wisnefski: kwisnefski@funeralservicefoundation.org;
URL: http://www.funeralservicefoundation.org

Foundation type: Public charity
Purpose: Scholarships to full-time students enrolled or accepted in a mortuary science school accredited by the American Board of Funeral Service Education.
Publications: Application guidelines; Annual report.
Financial data: Year ended 12/31/2012. Assets, $6,386,148 (M); Expenditures, $494,992; Total giving, $235,634; Grants to individuals, totaling $7,245.
Fields of interest: Science.
Type of support: Scholarships—to individuals.
Application information: Applications accepted. Application form required.
Deadline(s): Mar. 28 for Key Memories Scholarship, May 11 for Joseph E. Hagan Memorial Scholarship
Additional information: See web site for additional application guidelines.
EIN: 391831612

9904
Romaine Gallmeier Seminarian Scholarship Fund
P.O. Box 12800
Green Bay, WI 54307-2800

Foundation type: Independent foundation
Purpose: Scholarships only to theological students of the American Lutheran Synod.
Financial data: Year ended 12/31/2011. Assets, $265,299 (M); Expenditures, $16,201; Total giving, $13,107.
Fields of interest: Theological school/education.
Type of support: Graduate support.
Application information:
Initial approach: Letter
Deadline(s): None
Additional information: Contact foundation for current application guidelines.
EIN: 396550978

9905
Gehl Foundation
1 Gehl Way
West Bend, WI 53095-3415 (262) 334-9461

Foundation type: Company-sponsored foundation
Purpose: College scholarships to children of employees of Gehl Company or its affiliates for higher education.
Financial data: Year ended 12/31/2012. Assets, $608,766 (M); Expenditures, $52,221; Total giving, $47,000; Grants to individuals, 6 grants totaling $47,000 (high: $16,000, low: $5,000).
Fields of interest: Higher education.
Type of support: Scholarships—to individuals.
Application information: Applications not accepted.
Additional information: Unsolicited requests for funds not considered or acknowledged.
Company name: Manitou Americas, Inc
EIN: 391039217

9906
Giddings & Lewis Foundation, Inc.
P.O. Box 590
Fond Du Lac, WI 54936-0590 (920) 906-9400
Contact: Terri L. Groth, V.P.
Application address: 142 Doty St., Fond Du Lac, WI 549350590

Foundation type: Company-sponsored foundation
Purpose: Scholarships to children of Giddings and Lewis employees with excellent academic standing.
Financial data: Year ended 12/31/2010. Assets, $1,650,188 (M); Expenditures, $67,281; Total giving, $55,730; Grants to individuals, 12 grants totaling $16,000 (high: $2,000, low: $1,000).
Type of support: Employee-related scholarships; Undergraduate support.
Application information: Contact foundation for current application deadline/guidelines.
Company name: Giddings and Lewis
EIN: 396061306

9907
Raymond and Marie Goldbach Foundation, Inc.
(formerly Goldbach Charitable Foundation, Inc.)
c/o John L. Skoug
304 East St.
Marathon, WI 54448-9643
FAX: (715) 443-2928

Foundation type: Independent foundation

Purpose: Scholarships to residents of WI for higher education.
Financial data: Year ended 12/31/2012. Assets, $22,873,702 (M); Expenditures, $674,394; Total giving, $552,039; Grants to individuals, 16 grants totaling $15,500 (high: $1,000, low: $500).
Type of support: Undergraduate support.
Application information: Applications not accepted.
Additional information: Unsolicited requests for funds not considered or acknowledged.
EIN: 391877824

9908
Graef, Anhalt, Schloemer Foundation, Inc.
c/o Richard Bub
One Honey Creek Coporate Center 125 S. 84th St. Ste. 401
Milwaukee, WI 53214-1470 (414) 259-1500
Contact: Richard Bub, Pres.

Foundation type: Independent foundation
Purpose: Scholarships to students enrolled in a postsecondary institution seeking a bachelor's or other advanced degree in the field of Engineering.
Financial data: Year ended 12/31/2012. Assets, $259,216 (M); Expenditures, $14,240; Total giving, $10,000.
Fields of interest: Engineering.
Type of support: Support to graduates or students of specific schools.
Application information: Applications accepted. Application form required.
Deadline(s): Oct.
Applicants should submit the following:
1) Transcripts
2) Letter(s) of recommendation
3) Essay
Additional information: Scholarship funds may be used for tuition, books, or room and board expenses.
EIN: 392033285

9909
Grafton Medical Foundation
P.O. Box 104
Grafton, WI 53024-0104 (262) 377-5525

Foundation type: Independent foundation
Purpose: Scholarship awards to graduates of Grafton High School, Wisconsin.
Financial data: Year ended 12/31/2012. Assets, $114,866 (M); Expenditures, $5,952; Total giving, $5,000; Grants to individuals, 6 grants totaling $5,000 (high: $1,000, low: $500).
Fields of interest: Higher education.
Type of support: Scholarships—to individuals; Support to graduates or students of specific schools.
Application information: Applications accepted.
Initial approach: Letter
Deadline(s): Apr. 1
EIN: 237054743

9910
Greater Green Bay Community Foundation, Inc.
310 W. Walnut St., Ste. 350
Green Bay, WI 54303-2734 (920) 432-0800
Contact: David Z. Pamperin, C.E.O.; For grants: Martha Ahrendt, V.P., Progs.
FAX: (920) 432-5577; E-mail: ggbcf@ggbcf.org; Grant inquiry e-mail: martha@ggbcf.org; Grant

inquiry tel.: 920-432-0800; URL: http://www.ggbcf.org

Foundation type: Community foundation
Purpose: Scholarships to graduates of Brown County high schools, WI pursuing postsecondary education.
Publications: Application guidelines; Annual report; Financial statement; Informational brochure; Occasional report.
Financial data: Year ended 06/30/2012. Assets, $66,121,412 (M); Expenditures, $4,580,878; Total giving, $4,035,684.
Fields of interest: Performing arts, education; Vocational education; Nursing school/education; Agriculture; Women.
Type of support: Support to graduates or students of specific schools; Graduate support; Technical education support; Precollege support; Undergraduate support.
Application information: Applications accepted. Application form required.
  Deadline(s): Varies
  Applicants should submit the following:
    1) Transcripts
    2) Letter(s) of recommendation
    3) GPA
    4) Financial information
    5) FAFSA
    6) Essay
    7) Budget Information
    8) ACT
  Additional information: Applications accepted only through schools, contact your high school guidance counselor for additional application information.
EIN: 391699966

9911
Green Bay Packers Foundation
P.O. Box 10628
1265 Lombardi Ave.
Green Bay, WI 54307-0628   (920) 569-7315
Contact: Margaret J. Meyers, Secy.
FAX: (920) 569-7309;
E-mail: meyersm@packers.com; URL: http://www.packers.com/community/packers-foundation.html

Foundation type: Company-sponsored foundation
Purpose: Scholarships to students in four-year colleges, and two-year associate degree or apprenticeship trades programs at Northeast Wisconsin Technical College, WI.
Publications: Application guidelines; Grants list.
Financial data: Year ended 03/31/2013. Assets, $12,689,918 (M); Expenditures, $704,474; Total giving, $626,200.
Fields of interest: Vocational education, post-secondary; Higher education.
Type of support: Support to graduates or students of specific schools.
Application information:
  Initial approach: Letter
  Deadline(s): Nov. 1
Program description:
  Under the Packers Scholarship Program: The foundation, in partnership with Scholarships, Inc. and Northeast Wisconsin Technical College, awards college scholarships to students in two-year associate degree or apprentice trades programs. Scholarships are based on community service, involvement in athletic activities, academic achievement of at least a 3.0 grade point average, financial need, and residency in Brown County.
EIN: 391577137

9912
Frances Grimm Scholarship Trust
P.O. Box 26
Cassville, WI 53806-0026   (608) 725-5116
Contact: Bruce Boyum
Application address: Cassville High School, 715 E. Amelia Ste., Cassville, WI 53806

Foundation type: Independent foundation
Purpose: College scholarships to graduating seniors of Cassville High School, WI for postsecondary education.
Financial data: Year ended 12/31/2012. Assets, $165,836 (M); Expenditures, $2,674; Total giving, $2,674.
Fields of interest: Higher education.
Type of support: Support to graduates or students of specific schools; Undergraduate support.
Application information: Applications accepted. Application form required.
  Initial approach: Letter
  Deadline(s): One month prior to graduation
  Applicants should submit the following:
    1) Essay
    2) Transcripts
    3) Letter(s) of recommendation
  Additional information: Applicants must have a GPA between 2.70 and 3.40 on a 4.0 scale.
EIN: 206038259

9913
Gundersen Lutheran Medical Foundation, Inc.
1836 South Ave.
La Crosse, WI 54601-5429   (608) 775-6600
Contact: Mark V. Connelly M.D.Q, FACS, Chair.
FAX: (608) 775-6601; E-mail: glmf@gundluth.org; URL: http://www.gundluth.org/foundation/

Foundation type: Public charity
Purpose: Support for transportation, lodging, respite services, tutoring, and adaptive equipment and other living expenses for patients of Gundersen Lutheran Health System, IA.
Financial data: Year ended 12/31/2011. Assets, $58,583,706 (M); Expenditures, $22,980,850; Total giving, $4,340,273; Grants to individuals, totaling $316,868.
Fields of interest: Health care, clinics/centers; Health care.
Type of support: Grants for special needs.
Application information: Contact the foundation for additional information.
EIN: 391249705

9914
Benton & Louise Hale Memorial Scholarship Fund
c/o BMO Harris Bank, N.A.
P.O. Box 2980
Milwaukee, WI 53201-2977   (252) 658-5580

Foundation type: Independent foundation
Purpose: Scholarships for higher education to residents of WI.
Financial data: Year ended 12/31/2012. Assets, $394,681 (M); Expenditures, $25,488; Total giving, $18,874; Grants to individuals, 15 grants totaling $18,874 (high: $2,500, low: $250).
Type of support: Support to graduates or students of specific schools; Undergraduate support.
Application information: Application form required.
  Deadline(s): Apr.
EIN: 396257040

9915
Hamp Foundation Inc.
c/o Godfrey & Kahn, S.C.
780 N. Water St.
Milwaukee, WI 53202   (414) 273-3500
URL: https://sites.google.com/site/hampfoundation/113

Foundation type: Independent foundation
Purpose: Scholarships to graduating seniors enrolled in a Milwaukee county high school for attendance at the University of Wisconsin-Madison or the University of Minnesota-Twin Cities for tuition, room and board, fees and books.
Financial data: Year ended 12/31/2013. Assets, $863,888 (M); Expenditures, $124,201; Total giving, $102,523; Grants to individuals, 7 grants totaling $102,523 (high: $24,125, low: $5,302).
Fields of interest: Higher education.
Type of support: Scholarships—to individuals.
Application information: Application form required.
  Deadline(s): Jan.
  Applicants should submit the following:
    1) Class rank
    2) SAT
    3) GPA
    4) Financial information
    5) ACT
  Additional information: Application should be filed electronically. No hard copy of late applications will be accepted.
EIN: 202059847

9916
Hasselhofer-Wolf Scholarship Fund
c/o U.S. Bank, N.A.
P.O. Box 7900
Madison, WI 53707-7900   (920) 459-6942
*Application address:*C/O St. Peter Clever Parish-Hassel Hoffer, 1444 S. 11 St., Sheboygan, WI 53081

Foundation type: Independent foundation
Purpose: Scholarships to graduates or high school seniors of St. Peter Claver School in Sheboygan, WI, to attend college or technical school.
Financial data: Year ended 05/31/2013. Assets, $236,892 (M); Expenditures, $13,300; Total giving, $10,000; Grants to individuals, 2 grants totaling $10,000 (high: $6,500, low: $3,500).
Type of support: Support to graduates or students of specific schools; Undergraduate support.
Application information:
  Initial approach: Letter
  Deadline(s): May 13
  Final notification: Applicants will be notified by June 1
  Additional information: Contact fund for current application guidelines.
EIN: 396514224

9917
Healthnet of Janesville, Inc.
23 W. Milwaukee St.
Janesville, WI 53548-2981   (608) 756-4638
Contact: Jean Randles, Exec. Dir.
FAX: (608) 756-4928;
E-mail: execdir@healthnetofjanesville.org; E-Mail For Jean Randles: executive-director@healthnet-rock.org; URL: http://www.healthnetofjanesville.org

Foundation type: Public charity
Purpose: Assistance to the uninsured and low income individuals of Rock county Milwaukee, WI with prescription.

Financial data: Year ended 06/30/2012. Assets, $403,884 (M); Expenditures, $3,946,631; Total giving, $3,428,721; Grants to individuals, totaling $3,428,721.

Fields of interest: Pharmacy/prescriptions; Health care.

Type of support: In-kind gifts; Grants for special needs.

Application information: Applications accepted.

Additional information: Medication is provided to patients, vision referrals, specialist refferals, laboratory tests, as well as other resources and services.

EIN: 391778804

9918
Heffel Memorial Scholarship Trust
P.O. Box 15
Evansville, WI   53536-0015   (608) 882-4600
Contact: Randy Keister
Application address: c/o Evansville High School, 420 S. 3rd St., Evansville, WI 53536, tel.: (608) 882-4600

Foundation type: Independent foundation

Purpose: Scholarships to current graduating seniors of Evansville High School, WI for continuing their education at accredited institutions of higher learning.

Financial data: Year ended 12/31/2011. Assets, $105,869 (M); Expenditures, $11,762; Total giving, $10,000; Grants to individuals, 4 grants totaling $10,000 (high: $2,500, low: $2,500).

Fields of interest: Higher education.

Type of support: Support to graduates or students of specific schools.

Application information:
Deadline(s): None
EIN: 746451982

9919
Hemophilia Outreach of Wisconsin Foundation Inc.
2060 Bellevue St.
Green Bay, WI   54311-5622   (920) 965-0606
E-mail: info@hemophiliaoutreach.org; URL: http://www.hemophiliaoutreach.org/programs.php

Foundation type: Operating foundation

Purpose: Scholarships to residents of Brown, Calumet, Door, Florence, Fond du lac, Forest, Kewaunee, Langlade, Manitowoc, Marinette, Menominee, Oconto, Oneida, Outagamie, Shawano, Waupaca and Winnebago counties, WI, who have been diagnosed with hemophilia or von Willebrand's disease, or are children or siblings of individuals who have been diagnosed with hemophilia or von Willebrand's disease.

Financial data: Year ended 12/31/2012. Assets, $12,412,122 (M); Expenditures, $1,350,428; Total giving, $93,000.

Fields of interest: Hemophilia.

Type of support: Grants for special needs.

Application information: Applications accepted. Application form required.

Initial approach: Telephone
Deadline(s): May 1
Applicants should submit the following:
1) Photograph
2) Transcripts
3) FAFSA
EIN: 391858104

9920
Chester Henrizi Scholarship Fund
c/o Paul Schmidt
P.O. Box 100
Sussex, WI   53089-0100   (262) 246-8500

Foundation type: Independent foundation

Purpose: Undergraduate scholarships to male graduates of Menomonee Falls High School, WI, who attend any campus or branch of the University of Wisconsin. Scholarships are renewable for up to four years of undergraduate study.

Financial data: Year ended 11/30/2012. Assets, $188,822 (M); Expenditures, $3,414; Total giving, $0.

Fields of interest: Men.

Type of support: Support to graduates or students of specific schools; Undergraduate support.

Application information: Applications accepted. Application form required.

Initial approach: Letter or telephone
Deadline(s): Contact foundation for current application deadline
EIN: 391501364

9921
Frederick J. Hilgen Foundation, Ltd.
P.O. Box 649
Neenah, WI   54957-0649
*Application address:*c/o Cedarburg Public School System, W68 N611 Evergreen Blvd., Cedarburg, WI 53012, tel.: (262) 376-6100

Foundation type: Independent foundation

Purpose: Scholarships to graduating seniors from Cedarburg High School, WI.

Financial data: Year ended 12/31/2011. Assets, $390,202 (M); Expenditures, $20,354; Total giving, $13,500.

Type of support: Support to graduates or students of specific schools; Undergraduate support.

Application information: Applications not accepted.

Additional information: Unsolicited requests for funds not considered or acknowledged.
EIN: 391287084

9922
Al Hodes Charitable Trust
c/o BMO Harris Bank
P.O. Box 2980
Milwaukee, WI   53201-2977

Foundation type: Independent foundation

Purpose: Scholarships to nursing students attending North Central Technical College in Wausau, WI.

Financial data: Year ended 06/30/2013. Assets, $369,360 (M); Expenditures, $18,963; Total giving, $16,500.

Fields of interest: Nursing school/education.

Type of support: Support to graduates or students of specific schools; Technical education support; Undergraduate support.

Application information: Applications not accepted.

Additional information: Unsolicited requests for funds not considered or acknowledged.
EIN: 396480058

9923
Holt Family Scholarship Foundation
c/o BMO Harris Bank, N.A.
P.O. Box 2980
Milwaukee, WI   53201-2977   (414) 287-7181

Foundation type: Independent foundation

Purpose: Scholarships to graduates of Wautoma High School or Wild Rose High School, WI pursuing post high school education.

Financial data: Year ended 07/31/2013. Assets, $1,077,686 (M); Expenditures, $99,862; Total giving, $56,750.

Type of support: Support to graduates or students of specific schools; Undergraduate support.

Application information: Applications accepted.

Deadline(s): None
Additional information: Contact your guidance office for application information.
EIN: 391734323

9924
Merl Hood Memorial Fund Trust
P.O. Box 2043
Milwaukee, WI   53201-9668   (641) 683-2053
Contact: Laura J. See, Tr.
Application addresses: c/o U.S. Bank, N,A. 123 E. 3rd St. Ottumwa, IA, 52501-8003, tel.: (641) 683-2053

Foundation type: Independent foundation

Purpose: Grants to residents of one of the high-rise or Public Housing Developments within Wapello county, IA (Housing under direction of the Wapello County Public Housing Authority)

Financial data: Year ended 06/30/2013. Assets, $83,082 (M); Expenditures, $6,833; Total giving, $4,400.

Fields of interest: Housing/shelter.

Type of support: Grants to individuals.

Application information: Applications accepted. Application form required.

Deadline(s): Apr. 1 and Oct. 1
Additional information: Applications can be obtained from either trustees or housing authority.
EIN: 421180466

9925
Incourage Community Foundation, Inc.
(formerly Community Foundation of Greater South Wood County, Inc.)
478 E. Grand Ave.
Wisconsin Rapids, WI   54494   (715) 423-3863
Contact: Kelly Ryan, C.E.O.; For grants: Dawn Vruwink, V.P., Community Resources
FAX: (715) 423-3019;
E-mail: hello@incouragecf.org; URL: http://www.incouragecf.org

Foundation type: Community foundation

Purpose: Scholarships to South Wood County residents (Nekoosa, Pittsville, Port Edwards, Rome, Rudolph, Vesper, Wisconsin Rapids, and surrounding communities) for higher education. Grants to K-12 teachers for designing new programs/projects or enhancements of existing programs. Financial assistance to families with children with medical issues.

Publications: Application guidelines; Financial statement; Informational brochure; Newsletter.

Financial data: Year ended 12/31/2012. Assets, $28,535,112 (M); Expenditures, $2,925,655; Total giving, $752,203; Grants to individuals, 116 grants totaling $141,018.

Fields of interest: Secondary school/education; Higher education; Health care.

Type of support: Grants to individuals; Scholarships—to individuals; Support to graduates or students of specific schools; Undergraduate support; Grants for special needs.

Application information: Applications accepted. Application form required. Application form available on the grantmaker's web site.

> *Send request by:* Mail
> *Deadline(s):* Varies for scholarships, none for School Plus Grants and Smile From Lacey Grants
> *Final notification:* Applicants notified end of May for Scholarships
> *Additional information:* See web site for a complete listing of scholarships, and application forms.

Program descriptions:

Scholarships: The foundation provides support to high school students seeking assistance for college tuition, high school tuition, and specific high school programs. There are also scholarships for non-traditional students pursuing a college education, and scholarships for college students in their second year and higher. Each scholarship has its own unique eligibility criteria and application guidelines. See web site for additional information.

School Plus Grants: The program is designed to enhance relationships and communication through effective teaching, learning, and special motivational activities. The foundation provides support to teachers with innovative teaching projects in 4K through Grade 12 in public and parochial schools. Grants requests may be submitted for up to $1,000.

Smile From Lacey Fund Grants: Financial assistance to families with children in need as a result of immediate medical issues related to cancer, major diseases, or major accidents that require extended medical care. One-time grants from the fund are limited to a maximum of $500 per family. The child receiving treatment must reside in the greater south Wood county area and one in northern Adams county; Nekoosa, Pittsville, Port Edwards, Rome, Rudolph, Vesper, and Wisconsin Rapids which includes Biron, Grand Rapids, and surrounding townships.

EIN: 391772651

9926
Indianhead Community Action Agency, Inc.

1000 College Ave. W.
P.O. Box 40
Ladysmith, WI 54848-1839 (715) 532-4222
Contact: Brett Gerber, Exec. Dir.
FAX: (715) 532-7808;
E-mail: 9yZ5x1.q2-6s7@indianheadcaa.org;
URL: http://www.indianheadcaa.org

Foundation type: Public charity
Purpose: Assistance to low and moderate income individuals and families of Burnett, Clark, Rusk, Sawyer, Taylor and Washburn counties in Northwestern, WI to attain skills needed to become self-sufficient.
Publications: Annual report.
Financial data: Year ended 12/31/2011. Assets, $17,270,836 (M); Expenditures, $20,170,907; Total giving, $1,432,700; Grants to individuals, totaling $1,432,700.
Fields of interest: Economically disadvantaged.
Type of support: Grants for special needs.
Application information: Contact the agency for additional information.
EIN: 391086966

9927
International Foundation for Functional Gastrointestinal Disorder

700 W. Virgina St. No. 201
Milwaukee, WI 53204-1549 (414) 964-1799
FAX: (414) 964-7176; E-mail: iffgd@iffgd.org;
URL: http://www.iffgd.org/

Foundation type: Public charity
Purpose: Grants and awards to investigators from around the world to support innovative research into idiopathic gastroparesis.
Financial data: Year ended 12/31/2012. Assets, $5,235,344 (M); Expenditures, $1,142,632; Total giving, $19,000. Grants to individuals amount not specified.
Fields of interest: Digestive disorders research.
Type of support: Grants to individuals.
Application information: Applications accepted.

> *Additional information:* Grants are awarded every two years.

Program descriptions:

IFFGD Competitive Research Grants: This program offers funding for research related to functional gastrointestinal and motility disorders, and neurogastroenterology. Grant awards of $40,000 in direct costs each will be made to three (3) investigators for innovative research related to idiopathic gastroparesis.

IFFGD Noncompetitive Research Grants: These discretionary awards support activities or research related to functional gastrointestinal and motility disorders, and neurogastroenterology. Noncompetitive grants are made occasionally and awarded on a case-by-case basis that considers merit, program need, funding availability, and extraordinary circumstances.
EIN: 391710898

9928
Charles D. Jacobus Family Foundation

11815 W. Bradley Rd.
Milwaukee, WI 53224-2532 (414) 577-0252
Contact: Missy MacLeod, Pres.
FAX: (414) 359-1357;
E-mail: foundation@jacobusenergy.com; Mailing address: P.O. Box 13009, Milwaukee, WI 53213-0009; Toll free tel.: (800) 242-4702 ext. 1252; URL: http://www.cdjff.org

Foundation type: Independent foundation
Purpose: Scholarships to children of full time employees of Jacobus Energy, Inc., or Quick Fuel Fleet Services, LLC.
Publications: Application guidelines.
Financial data: Year ended 12/31/2012. Assets, $4,303,809 (M); Expenditures, $500,085; Total giving, $397,748; Grants to individuals, 4 grants totaling $8,000 (high: $3,000, low: $1,000).
Fields of interest: Higher education.
Type of support: Employee-related scholarships.
Application information: Applications not accepted.

> *Additional information:* Unsolicited requests for funds not considered or acknowledged.

EIN: 391559892

9929
Dan Jansen Foundation, Inc.

1832 Alta Vista Ave.
Milwaukee, WI 53213-2322 (301) 656-1551
Contact: Sean Callahan, V.P.
URL: http://www.djfoundation.org

Foundation type: Public charity

Purpose: Scholarships to one male and one female WI, high school student in pursuit of a higher education.
Publications: Application guidelines; Informational brochure; Informational brochure (including application guidelines).
Fields of interest: Higher education; Women; Young adults, male.
Type of support: Scholarships—to individuals.
Application information: Applications accepted. Application form required. Application form available on the grantmaker's web site.

> *Initial approach:* Letter or telephone
> *Deadline(s):* Open
> *Applicants should submit the following:*
> 1) Class rank
> 2) SAT
> 3) Letter(s) of recommendation
> 4) GPA
> 5) Essay
> 6) ACT

Program description:

Dan Jansen Prep Plus Scholarship: The program awards two $1,000 scholarships for continuing education to Wisconsin high school students (one male and one female) who display the Dan Jansen Spirit toward life, education and overcoming adversity.
EIN: 521864788

9930
Jewish Family Services, Inc.

1300 N. Jackson St.
Milwaukee, WI 53202-2602 (414) 390-5800
Contact: Sylvan Leabman, Pres. and C.E.O.
FAX: (414) 390-5808; E-mail: info@jfsmilw.org;
URL: http://www.jfsmilw.org

Foundation type: Public charity
Purpose: Emergency assistance, resettlement living and arrival expenses, and elderly homecare services to those in need in the Milwaukee, WI area.
Publications: Annual report; Newsletter; Occasional report.
Financial data: Year ended 06/30/2012. Assets, $20,751,919 (M); Expenditures, $7,282,622; Total giving, $1,428,746; Grants to individuals, totaling $224,018.
Fields of interest: Family services; Human services; Jewish agencies & synagogues.
Type of support: Emergency funds; Grants for special needs.
Application information:

> *Initial approach:* Letter, telephone, fax, or e-mail
> *Additional information:* Contact the organization for additional information.

EIN: 390806291

9931
Jewish Federation of Madison

6434 Enterprise Ln.
Madison, WI 53719-1117 (608) 278-1808
Contact: Dina Weinbach, Exec. Dir.
FAX: (608) 278-7814;
E-mail: info@jewishmadison.org; E-mail For Dina Weinbach: dina@jewishmadison.org; URL: http://www.jewishmadison.org

Foundation type: Public charity
Purpose: Scholarships to children in the greater Madison, WI area who wish to attend Jewish day and summer camps, and to graduating seniors to continue their Jewish education.
Financial data: Year ended 02/28/2013. Assets, $6,372,032 (M); Expenditures, $2,352,447; Total

giving, $551,129; Grants to individuals, totaling $13,878.

Fields of interest: Higher education; Recreation; Jewish agencies & synagogues.

Type of support: Scholarships—to individuals.

Application information: Applications accepted.

Deadline(s): Nov. 28 for Midrasha Incentive Award

Additional information: Students must submit a proposal to the committee explaining how he/she plans to use the award.

Program description:

Incentive Award Program: Awards of up to $2,000 to graduating students who attended Midrasha continuously since eight grade. Students will now be eligible to receive up to $1,000 to use during the first year after Midrasha, and the other $1,000 to be used during their second year after they graduate from the Midrasha program. Students must have satisfactory evaluations in terms of attendance, participation, and behavior.

EIN: 390867186

9932
Claire and Marjorie Johnson, Inc.

397 24 3/4 Ave.
Cumberland, WI   54829-8839   (715) 822-5124
Application address: c/o Principal, Cumberland High School, 1000 8th Ave., Cumberland, WI 54829, tel.: (715) 822-5124

Foundation type: Independent foundation

Purpose: Scholarships to selected Cumberland High School, WI graduates for attendance at a four year accredited college or university with college tuition, books and housing expenses.

Financial data: Year ended 12/31/2012. Assets, $5,627,683 (M); Expenditures, $315,664; Total giving, $267,037; Grants to individuals, 59 grants totaling $267,037 (high: $60,000, low: $640).

Fields of interest: Higher education.

Type of support: Support to graduates or students of specific schools.

Application information: Applications accepted. Application form required.

Deadline(s): Apr. 30

Additional information: Application must include a short personal statement, educational goals and areas of study. Applicant must be in good standing and maintain a "B" average. Family income must be under $75,000.

EIN: 391874405

9933
Johnson Controls Foundation, Inc.

(formerly Johnson Controls Foundation)
5757 N. Green Bay Ave.
P.O. Box 591
Milwaukee, WI   53201-0591   (414) 524-2296
Contact: Mary J. Dowell, Dir., Global Community Rels.
E-mail: mary.j.dowell@jci.com; *URL:* http://www.johnsoncontrols.com/publish/us/en/about/our_community_focus/johnson_controls_foundation.html

Foundation type: Company-sponsored foundation

Purpose: Scholarships to children and dependents of employees of Johnson Controls, Inc.

Publications: Application guidelines; Program policy statement.

Financial data: Year ended 12/31/2012. Assets, $21,312,041 (M); Expenditures, $8,103,647; Total giving, $8,041,049.

Fields of interest: Higher education.

Type of support: Employee-related scholarships.

Application information: Applications not accepted.

Additional information: Unsolicited requests for funds not considered or acknowledged.

Program description:

Employee Scholarships: The foundation awards college scholarships to children of employees of Johnson Control. The program is designed to reward students who achieve a balance between academic achievement, leadership, and civic involvement.

Company name: Johnson Controls, Inc.

EIN: 203510307

9934
Johnson Controls, Inc. Corporate Giving Program

5757 N. Green Bay Ave.
Glendale, WI   53209-4408   (414) 524-1200
Address for Igniting Creative Energy: National Energy Foundation, 4516 South 700 East, Ste. 100, Murray, UT 84107
URL: http://www.johnsoncontrols.com/publish/us/en/sustainability/for_our_communities.html

Foundation type: Corporate giving program

Purpose: Awards to K-12 students and teachers for innovative ideas in energy, water conservation, and the environment.

Publications: Corporate giving report.

Financial data: Year ended 12/31/2010. Total giving, $3,210,000.

Fields of interest: Environment, water resources; Energy; Environment.

Type of support: Awards/prizes.

Application information: Applications accepted. Application form required. Application form available on the grantmaker's web site.

Send request by: Online and mail

Deadline(s): Mar. 4

Additional information: Igniting Creative Energy projects are limited to 500 words or 3 pages for documentation or written entries, a 3 minute limit for audio or music entries, and a 10 minute limit for media or electronic entries.

Program description:

Igniting Creative Energy Challenge: Johnson Controls, in partnership with the National Energy Foundation, annually invites K-12 students to design and share innovative ways to make a difference in energy, water conservation, and the environment through competition. Five grand prizes are awarded to 4 students and 1 teacher. Prizes include a trip to Washington, DC for 2 and an invitation to participate in the National Energy Forum in June to share their ideas with energy and government leaders. The highest scoring student in each state will be recognized and participating schools are also eligible to receive a $1,000 grant to beautify their school, educate students, or impact their community.

9935
Ervin W. Johnson Scholarship Fund

434 N. Main St.
Darlington, WI   53530-1428

Foundation type: Independent foundation

Purpose: Scholarships to financially needy high school graduates currently residing in Lafayette County, WI, for study at any recognized institution of higher learning.

Financial data: Year ended 12/31/2012. Assets, $1,965,077 (M); Expenditures, $164,153; Total giving, $157,300.

Fields of interest: Higher education.

Type of support: Scholarships—to individuals; Undergraduate support.

Application information: Applications accepted. Application form required.

Deadline(s): May 1

EIN: 391297197

9936
Emmett & Beulah Jones Educational Fund

c/o BMO Harris bank N.N
P.O. Box 2980
Milwaukee, WI   53201   (816) 781-7700
Application addresses: c/o William Jewell College, Attn.: Office of Student Financial Planning, 500 College Hill, Liberty, MO 64068

Foundation type: Independent foundation

Purpose: Scholarships to residents of Point Lookout and Liberty, MO, primarily for those who are pursuing a Christian ministry or service.

Financial data: Year ended 02/28/2013. Assets, $490,635 (M); Expenditures, $9,604; Total giving, $2,718.

Fields of interest: Theological school/education.

Type of support: Scholarships—to individuals.

Application information: Applications accepted. Application form required.

EIN: 436765443

9937
Harold C. Kallies Charitable Trust

c/o Legacy Private Trust Co.
P.O. Box 649
Neenah, WI   54957-0649   (920) 967-5020

Foundation type: Independent foundation

Purpose: Scholarships to residents of Manitowoc County, WI.

Financial data: Year ended 12/31/2011. Assets, $1,655,641 (M); Expenditures, $218,640; Total giving, $197,588; Grants to individuals, 5 grants totaling $6,500 (high: $1,500, low: $1,250).

Type of support: Undergraduate support.

Application information:

Initial approach: Letter

Additional information: Contact foundation for eligibility criteria.

EIN: 396548517

9938
Kelben Foundation, Inc.

100 E. Wisconsin Ave., St., 2200
Milwaukee, WI   53202-3620   (414) 226-4545
Contact: Mary T. Kellner, Pres. and Treas.
Application address.: 5112 W. Highland, Mequon, WI 53092

Foundation type: Independent foundation

Purpose: Scholarships to graduating seniors from the Milwaukee Public School System in WI, who rank in the top 50 percent of their class, intend to pursue a four-year college degree, and demonstrate a need for financial assistance.

Financial data: Year ended 12/31/2012. Assets, $18,626,995 (M); Expenditures, $1,335,840; Total giving, $1,022,250; Grants to individuals, 157 grants totaling $119,750 (high: $2,000, low: -$1,000).

Fields of interest: Higher education.

Type of support: Support to graduates or students of specific schools; Undergraduate support.

Application information: Application form required.

Deadline(s): Apr.

Final notification: Applicant notified by mid-May

Applicants should submit the following:

1) Transcripts
2) SAT
3) Letter(s) of recommendation
4) ACT
Additional information: Application forms are available at your school's guidance office.
EIN: 391494625

9939
Clarence Keller Scholarship Trust
P.O. Box 2043
Milwaukee, WI 53201-9668 (920) 459-6957
Application address: c/o U.S. Bank, N.A., P.O. Box 0663, Sheboygan, WI 53081-0663, tel.: (920) 459-6957

Foundation type: Independent foundation
Purpose: Giving limited to members of the Foundation Park Methodist Church or participants in the Big Brothers/Big Sisters Program, WI.
Financial data: Year ended 07/31/2013. Assets, $477,619 (M); Expenditures, $24,628; Total giving, $18,050; Grants to individuals, 16 grants totaling $18,050 (high: $2,000, low: $300).
Fields of interest: Big Brothers/Big Sisters; Protestant agencies & churches.
Type of support: Scholarships—to individuals.
Application information: Applications not accepted.
Additional information: Unsolicited requests for funds not considered or acknowledged.
EIN: 396500681

9940
William M. Keller Trust
c/o JPMorgan Chase Bank, N.A.
P.O. Box 3038
Milwaukee, WI 53201-3038 (317) 684-3149
Application address: c/o JPMorgan Chase Bank, 1 E. Ohio St., Indianapolis, IN 46277-1916, tel.: (317) 684-3017

Foundation type: Independent foundation
Purpose: Scholarships to high school graduates residing in Bartholomew County, IN, who intend to pursue careers in the medical, nursing, scientific, engineering, or technical fields at an accredited institution.
Publications: Application guidelines.
Financial data: Year ended 12/31/2011. Assets, $3,516,180 (M); Expenditures, $172,041; Total giving, $120,400; Grants to individuals, 64 grants totaling $120,400 (high: $6,500, low: $500).
Fields of interest: Medical school/education; Nursing school/education; Engineering school/education.
Type of support: Undergraduate support.
Application information: Applications accepted. Application form required.
Deadline(s): Mar. 31
Additional information: Application forms available upon request.
EIN: 351035651

9941
Kenosha Community Foundation
600 52nd St., Ste. 110
Kenosha, WI 53140-3423 (262) 654-2412
Contact: Robert B. Schneider, Exec. Dir.
FAX: (262) 654-2615;
E-mail: email@kenoshafoundation.org; Additional e-mail: rschneider@kenoshafoundation.org;
URL: http://www.kenoshafoundation.org

Foundation type: Community foundation

Purpose: Scholarships to area students of the Kenosha County, WI area for attendance at accredited postsecondary institutions.
Publications: Application guidelines; Annual report; Grants list; Informational brochure.
Financial data: Year ended 12/31/2012. Assets, $5,745,652 (M); Expenditures, $544,953; Total giving, $290,028; Grants to individuals, 45 grants totaling $32,505.
Fields of interest: Higher education.
Type of support: Scholarships—to individuals; Support to graduates or students of specific schools.
Application information: Applications accepted. Application form required.
Additional information: Contact the foundation for additional guidelines.
EIN: 396045289

9942
Kenosha Scholarship Foundation, Inc.
5800 7th Ave.
Kenosha, WI 53140 (262) 656-6310
Contact: Fred E. Ricker, Dir.

Foundation type: Independent foundation
Purpose: Scholarships to graduates of high schools in Kenosha, WI, or Gateway Technical Institute, WI.
Publications: Application guidelines.
Financial data: Year ended 12/31/2012. Assets, $117,234 (M); Expenditures, $11,127; Total giving, $10,000; Grants to individuals, 11 grants totaling $10,000 (high: $1,000, low: $750).
Type of support: Scholarships—to individuals; Technical education support.
Application information: Applications accepted. Application form required.
Initial approach: Letter
Deadline(s): May 15
Additional information: Scholarships are renewable for up to four years of full-time study.
EIN: 391501320

9943
The Kern Foundation, Inc.
204 Wisconsin Ave.
Waukesha, WI 53186-4927 (262) 691-9284

Foundation type: Public charity
Purpose: Assistance to indigent residents of Waukesha County, WI towards veterinary medical care for their companion animals. Services are limited to injuries, illnesses, non-elective surgery, dentistry, necessary immunizations, spaying and neutering.
Financial data: Year ended 04/30/2012. Assets, $194,541 (M); Expenditures, $43,905; Total giving, $42,383.
Fields of interest: Animal welfare; Veterinary medicine; Veterinary medicine, hospital; Economically disadvantaged.
Type of support: In-kind gifts.
Application information: Contact local veterinarian for eligibility criteria.
EIN: 391501332

9944
Herb Kohl Educational Foundation
825 N. Jefferson St., Ste. 350
Milwaukee, WI 53202-3731
Scholarship address: c/o Elaine Strom, Education Consultant, Wisconsin Dept. of Public Instruction, P.O. Box 7841, Madison, WI 53707-7841,

tel.: (608) 266-3089,
e-mail: elaine.strom@dpi.wi.gov
URL: http://www.kohleducation.org

Foundation type: Independent foundation
Purpose: Scholarships to WI students to pursue a postsecondary education in a public or nonpublic university, college or vocational/technical college. Fellowships to Pre K-12 WI teachers for their teaching excellence and innovation.
Financial data: Year ended 12/31/2012. Assets, $931,056 (M); Expenditures, $420,208; Total giving, $392,000; Grants to individuals, 308 grants totaling $392,000 (high: $10,000, low: $1,000).
Fields of interest: Elementary/secondary education; Higher education; Teacher school/education.
Type of support: Fellowships; Undergraduate support.
Application information: Application form required. Application form available on the grantmaker's web site.
Deadline(s): Varies
Applicants should submit the following:
1) Essay
2) Letter(s) of recommendation
3) Transcripts
Additional information: The nomination and application process is divided between public school students, religious and independent school students and homeschooled students. Applicants should contact their schools to determine submission dates. See web site for additional guidelines.
Program description:
Kohl Teacher Fellowship Program: Classroom teachers in Pre-K through grade 12 who are residents of WI and plan on continuing to teach for at least one additional year are eligible for nomination. The foundation awards $1,000 fellowship grants to teachers and each Kohl fellowship recipient's school receives a matching $1,000 grant. To be eligible for a fellowship, teachers must be nominated by parents, teachers, students, community members, or school district administrators. Recipients are chosen on the basis of the degree to which: 1) students have benefited from their leadership, 2) professional colleagues, parents, the community, or the profession itself have benefited from their leadership, 3) they have demonstrated and inspired a love of learning, 4) they have provided services above and beyond what was expected, and 5) they have positively contributed to the improvement of education in general. See foundation web site for further information.
EIN: 391661743

9945
Kohler Foundation, Inc.
725 Woodlake Rd., Ste. X
Kohler, WI 53044-1354 (920) 458-1972
Contact: Terri Yoho, Exec. Dir.
FAX: (920) 458-4280;
E-mail: terri.yoho@kohler.com; URL: http://www.kohlerfoundation.org

Foundation type: Independent foundation
Purpose: Scholarships only to Sheboygan County, WI, graduating high school seniors recommended by their schools.
Financial data: Year ended 12/31/2012. Assets, $201,620,916 (M); Expenditures, $8,845,567; Total giving, $6,926,868; Grants to individuals, 98 grants totaling $356,771 (high: $15,000, low: $1,250).
Fields of interest: Humanities; Science; Mathematics.

Type of support: Undergraduate support.
Application information: Application form required.
Initial approach: Letter
Deadline(s): May 1
Additional information: Contact guidance
counselor for additional information.
Program description:
Scholarships: The foundation has long had a
commitment to higher education evidenced by its
far-reaching program that includes over 45 annual
scholarships awarded to students graduating from
twelve Sheboygan county high schools. The
foundation's most significant scholarships are the
Herbert V. Kohler Scholarship of $80,000 awarded
for outstanding leadership and the new Ruth
DeYoung Kohler Scholarship for $80,000 for
artistic merit. The foundation has established
significant scholarship endowments at eleven
independent colleges in Wisconsin and provides
funds to house the Marie Christine Kohler Fellows
at Knapp House at The Graduate School of the
University of Wisconsin-Madison, as well as a
fellowship in art history.
EIN: 390810536

9946
Kohl's Corporation Contributions Program
c/o Community Rels. Dept.
N56 W.17000 Ridgewood Dr.
Menomonee Falls, WI   53051-5660   (262)
703-7000
E-mail: community.relations@kohls.com; E-mail for
youth soccer sponsorships:
usyouthsoccer@kohls.com; Email for Kohl's Cares
Scholarships for Kids:
Kohls@ScholarshipAmerica.org.; E-mail for
Associates in Action volunteer program:
AssociatesinAction@kohls.com; URL: http://
www.kohlscorporation.com/communityrelations/
community01.htm

Foundation type: Corporate giving program
Purpose: Awards by nomination only to children
aged 6-18 who have gone above and beyond in their
community service activities.
Publications: Application guidelines.
Fields of interest: Volunteer services; Youth
development, community service clubs; Children;
Youth.
Type of support: Awards/prizes; Undergraduate
support.
Application information: Applications accepted.
Application form required. Application form
available on the grantmaker's web site.
Initial approach: Letter, telephone or e-mail
Send request by: Web site
Deadline(s): Mar. 15

9947
Korupp & Waelti Scholarship Fund
c/o U.S. Bank, N.A.
P.O. Box 7900
Madison, WI   53707-7900   (608) 523-4285
Contact: Jubie Simonson
Application address: P.O. Box 117, Blanchardville,
WI 53516-0117, tel.: (608) 523-4285

Foundation type: Independent foundation
Purpose: Scholarships to graduates of Pecatonica
area high schools, WI, for higher education.
Financial data: Year ended 12/31/2012. Assets,
$142,145 (M); Expenditures, $9,711; Total giving,
$6,000; Grants to individuals, 8 grants totaling
$6,000 (high: $900, low: $300).
Fields of interest: Higher education.
Type of support: Scholarships—to individuals.

Application information: Applications accepted.
Application form required.
Deadline(s): First week of Apr.
Applicants should submit the following:
1) Letter(s) of recommendation
2) Financial information
EIN: 396291034

9948
La Crosse Community Foundation
300 2nd St. N., Ste. 320
La Crosse, WI   54601-2001   (608) 782-3223
Contact: Sheila Garrity, Exec. Dir.
FAX: (608) 782-3222;
E-mail: lacrosscommfoundation@centurytel.net;
URL: http://www.laxcommfoundation.com

Foundation type: Community foundation
Purpose: Scholarships limited to residents of La
Crosse County, WI, for higher education.
Publications: Annual report (including application
guidelines).
Financial data: Year ended 12/31/2012. Assets,
$54,458,678 (M); Expenditures, $3,583,541;
Total giving, $2,759,157; Grants to individuals,
186 grants totaling $195,645.
Fields of interest: Print publishing; Music;
Performing arts, education; Higher education;
Theological school/education; Environmental
education; Chemistry; Mathematics.
Type of support: Scholarships—to individuals;
Support to graduates or students of specific
schools; Technical education support;
Undergraduate support.
Application information: Applications accepted.
Application form required. Application form
available on the grantmaker's web site.
Initial approach: Telephone
Deadline(s): Feb. 15
Additional information: Applications available
through the high school guidance office.
Scholarship payments are made to the
educational institution on behalf of the
students.
EIN: 396037996

9949
Lakeland High School Scholarship Fund
P.O. Box 1129
Minocqua, WI   54548   (715) 356-1493
Contact: Joanne M. Long, Secy.

Foundation type: Operating foundation
Purpose: Scholarships to graduates of Lakeland
High School, WI.
Publications: Application guidelines.
Financial data: Year ended 12/31/2012. Assets,
$2,178,103 (M); Expenditures, $121,393; Total
giving, $82,250; Grants to individuals, 33 grants
totaling $82,250 (high: $4,500, low: $500).
Type of support: Support to graduates or students
of specific schools; Undergraduate support.
Application information: Applications accepted.
Application form required.
Copies of proposal: 1
Deadline(s): Feb. 21
EIN: 391259200

9950
Lauterbach Scholarship Fund Trust
c/o US Bank N.A.
P.O. Box 7900
Madison, WI   53707-7900   (319)553-2500
Contact: Rich D. Powers
Application address: 1015 Division St., Cedar Falls,
IA 50613-2372,

Foundation type: Independent foundation
Purpose: Scholarships to female graduates of
Cedar Falls High School, IA, for undergraduate
education at an IA four-year institution.
Financial data: Year ended 12/31/2012. Assets,
$249,820 (M); Expenditures, $13,952; Total
giving, $8,750; Grants to individuals, 10 grants
totaling $8,750 (high: $1,500, low: $500).
Fields of interest: Women.
Type of support: Support to graduates or students
of specific schools; Undergraduate support.
Application information: Applications accepted.
Application form required.
Deadline(s): Mar. 31
Applicants should submit the following:
1) Letter(s) of recommendation
2) Financial information
3) GPA
4) Essay
EIN: 426470008

9951
Brian D. Laviolette Scholarship Fund, Inc.
1135 Pleasant Valley Dr.
Oneida, WI   54155-8619   (920) 405-9929
URL: http://www.briansjourney.com/

Foundation type: Independent foundation
Purpose: Scholarships to deserving college bound
students of northeastern WI.
Financial data: Year ended 12/31/2012. Assets,
$644,734 (M); Expenditures, $128,577; Total
giving, $46,706; Grants to individuals, 39 grants
totaling $46,706 (high: $5,000, low: $500).
Fields of interest: Higher education.
Type of support: Undergraduate support.
Application information: Applications accepted.
Application form required.
Deadline(s): Apr.
Additional information: Contact guidance
counselor for complete application
guidelines.
EIN: 391836591

9952
Leitzell Family Foundation
c/o Karen Sue Hiles
4613 Fox Bluff Ln.
Middleton, WI   53562

Foundation type: Independent foundation
Purpose: College scholarships to students in Ohio
for attendance at accredited colleges or
universities.
Financial data: Year ended 12/31/2012. Assets,
$36,965 (M); Expenditures, $19,587; Total giving,
$16,500; Grants to individuals, 7 grants totaling
$16,500 (high: $3,000, low: $1,500).
Fields of interest: Higher education.
Type of support: Scholarships—to individuals.
Application information: Applications not
accepted.
Additional information: Unsolicited requests for
funds not accepted.
EIN: 562288128

9953
Ray C., Maude E. & Genevieve Lyons Scholarship Fund
345 E. State St.
Beloit, WI 53511 (608) 897-2155

Foundation type: Independent foundation
Purpose: Scholarships to seniors from Brodhead High School, WI.
Financial data: Year ended 04/30/2013. Assets, $572,513 (M); Expenditures, $26,416; Total giving, $18,125.
Type of support: Scholarships—to individuals; Support to graduates or students of specific schools.
Application information: Application form required.
   Deadline(s): Early spring as specified by the high school guidance counselors
   Additional information: Applications available at the guidance office of Brodhead High School, WI.
EIN: 391363244

9954
A. F. MacPherson Trust
(also known as Anonymous Fund)
c/o U.S. Bank, N.A.
P.O. Box 7900
Madison, WI 53707-7900 (608) 252-4172
Application address: c/o U.S. Bank, N.A., 1 S. Pinckney St., Madison, WI 53703

Foundation type: Independent foundation
Purpose: Financial assistance to needy Protestants in the U.S. and Canada, with preference shown to residents of WI.
Financial data: Year ended 12/31/2012. Assets, $506,313 (M); Expenditures, $32,990; Total giving, $17,317; Grants to individuals, 26 grants totaling $17,317 (high: $2,000, low: $100).
Fields of interest: Protestant agencies & churches; Economically disadvantaged.
International interests: Canada.
Type of support: Grants for special needs.
Application information: Application form required.
   Initial approach: Letter
   Additional information: Contact the trust for additional guidelines.
EIN: 396038607

9955
Madison Advertising Federation Foundation
6 Odana Ct.
Madison, WI 53719-1121 (608) 230-1000
Contact: Bill Kennedy, Tres.

Foundation type: Independent foundation
Purpose: Scholarships to students of Madison, WI majoring in Marketing, Communication Arts, Visual Communications, Photography, Journalism, Public Relations, or Advertising.
Financial data: Year ended 06/30/2012. Assets, $88,995 (M); Expenditures, $4,710; Total giving, $4,500; Grants to individuals, 6 grants totaling $4,500 (high: $1,000, low: $500).
Fields of interest: Media/communications; Photography; Journalism school/education.
Type of support: Scholarships—to individuals.
Application information: Applications accepted. Application form required.
   Deadline(s): Apr. 1
   Additional information: Applicants must have at least one semester of undergraduate study remaining after application submission and

must include a statement as to why they merit the award.
EIN: 391630870

9956
Madison Rotary Foundation
22 N. Carroll St., Ste. 202
Madison, WI 53703-3377 (608) 255-9164
FAX: (608) 255-9007;
E-mail: rotaryoffice@rotarymadison.org;
URL: http://rotarymadison.org/

Foundation type: Public charity
Purpose: Scholarships to high school students residing in the Madison, WI, area for postsecondary education.
Publications: Application guidelines; Newsletter.
Financial data: Year ended 06/30/2012. Assets, $8,351,921 (M); Expenditures, $617,762; Total giving, $509,993; Grants to individuals, totaling $264,493.
Fields of interest: Higher education; Scholarships/financial aid; Youth development.
Type of support: Awards/prizes; Precollege support; Undergraduate support.
Application information: Contact your high school guidance counselor for additional information on scholarship selection.
Program descriptions:
   Manfred E. Swarsensky Humanitarian Service Award: This award identifies and honors an individual who has, through his/her voluntary efforts, made a particularly outstanding contribution to humanitarian service in the greater Madison community. A $2,500 award will be given to the charity of the recipient's choice.
   Scholarship Program: Each year twenty-one or more area high school students receive four-year scholarships, ranging from $600 to $5,000. Scholarship is based on students academic standing, character and leadership abilities, and financial need. Scholar nominations are selected on the advice of the high schools guidance counselors.
   Youth Awards: The program recognizes 39 Madison-area high school seniors in academic achievement, academic improvement, and community service.
EIN: 930757050

9957
ManpowerGroup Foundation, Inc.
(formerly Manpower Foundation, Inc.)
10 Manpower
Milwaukee, WI 53212-4030
URL: http://www.manpower.us/en/About-Us/Social-Responsibility.htmresponsibility/philanthropy/default.jsp

Foundation type: Company-sponsored foundation
Purpose: Scholarships to children of permanent, full-time employees of Manpower, Inc., its subsidiaries, or affiliated franchise corporations with at least one year of service.
Financial data: Year ended 12/31/2012. Assets, $551,814 (M); Expenditures, $710,124; Total giving, $710,000; Grants to individuals, 3 grants totaling $12,000 (high: $4,000, low: $4,000).
Fields of interest: Scholarships/financial aid; Education.
Type of support: Employee-related scholarships.
Application information: Applications not accepted.
   Additional information: Unsolicited requests for funds not considered or acknowledged.

Company name: ManpowerGroup Inc.
EIN: 396052810

9958
Mari's Foundation
1229 Merritt Ave.
Oshkosh, WI 54901

Foundation type: Operating foundation
Purpose: Grants to individuals for musical and artistic advancement.
Financial data: Year ended 12/31/2012. Assets, $112,096 (M); Expenditures, $1,070; Total giving, $0.
Fields of interest: Music; Arts.
Type of support: Scholarships—to individuals.
Application information: Applications accepted.
   Deadline(s): None
   Additional information: Application must include how the award will improve or enhance musical or artistic skills and dollar amount needed.
EIN: 396647866

9959
The Markos Foundation, Inc.
P.O. Box 5507
Madison, WI 53705-0507
Contact: Stephanie Mott

Foundation type: Independent foundation
Purpose: Scholarships to individuals in IL, IN and WI for attendance at colleges, universities and technical schools.
Financial data: Year ended 06/30/2012. Assets, $2,059,593 (M); Expenditures, $250,642; Total giving, $215,000.
Type of support: Technical education support; Undergraduate support.
Application information: Applications not accepted.
   Additional information: Unsolicited requests for funds not considered or acknowledged.
EIN: 391836400

9960
Marshfield Area Community Foundation
P.O. Box 456
Marshfield, WI 54449-0456 (715) 384-9029
Contact: Amber Kigins-Leifheit, Exec. Dir.
FAX: (715) 384-9229;
E-mail: macf@marshfieldareacommunityfoundation.org; URL: http://marshfieldareacommunityfoundation.org/

Foundation type: Community foundation
Purpose: Scholarships to residents of the Marshfield, WI, Marquette, WI, and Turkey Valley, IA, areas for higher education.
Publications: Application guidelines; Annual report; Financial statement; Grants list; Informational brochure; Informational brochure (including application guidelines); Newsletter.
Financial data: Year ended 06/30/2012. Assets, $4,883,360 (M); Expenditures, $244,318; Total giving, $148,441; Grants to individuals, 75 grants totaling $54,292.
Type of support: Scholarships—to individuals; Support to graduates or students of specific schools; Technical education support; Undergraduate support; Camperships.
Application information: Applications accepted. Application form required.
   Initial approach: Letter, telephone, or e-mail
   Send request by: Mail or fax

Copies of proposal: 1
Deadline(s): Varies
Final notification: Recipients notified Apr. 30
Applicants should submit the following:
  1) GPA
  2) Letter(s) of recommendation
  3) Financial information
  4) Essay
Additional information: Application should also
  include any other information required in the
  agreement.
EIN: 396578767

9961
Marth Foundation Ltd.
16452 N. Lane Dr.
Marathon, WI 54448-9444 (715) 443-2441

Foundation type: Independent foundation
Purpose: Scholarships to residents of WI who plan
on attending a WI college or university.
Financial data: Year ended 05/31/2013. Assets,
$21,739 (M); Expenditures, $8,523; Total giving,
$8,000.
Type of support: Undergraduate support.
Application information:
  Initial approach: Letter
  Deadline(s): None
  Applicants should submit the following:
    1) Financial information
    2) Essay
  Additional information: Contact foundation for
    further application guidelines.
EIN: 391410550

9962
Dr. Wood Martin Nursing Scholarship
c/o BMO Harris Bank, N.A.
P.O. Box 2980
Milwaukee, WI 53201 (816) 324-3128
Application address: c/o Savannah High School,
Attn.: Counselor, 701 State Rt. E., Savannah, MO
64485-9206

Foundation type: Independent foundation
Purpose: Scholarships to graduates of Savannah
High School, MO who intend to pursue health
related careers with a special emphasis on those
students who intend to become nurses.
Financial data: Year ended 12/31/2012. Assets,
$93,799 (M); Expenditures, $4,875; Total giving,
$2,250.
Fields of interest: Nursing school/education.
Type of support: Support to graduates or students
of specific schools.
Application information: Applications accepted.
Application form required.
  Deadline(s): Feb. 1
  Applicants should submit the following:
    1) Class rank
    2) Transcripts
    3) SAT
    4) GPA
    5) ACT
  Additional information: Applicant must have
    attended Savannah High School for three
    years including all of their senior year.
EIN: 431805119

9963
Meehan Family Foundation
(formerly Daniel E. Meehan Foundation, Inc.)
P.O. Box 270407
West Allis, WI 53227-2950
Contact: Daniel E. Meehan, Chair.

Foundation type: Independent foundation
Purpose: Scholarships to employees and children
of employees of Meehan Seaway Service, Ltd. and
its subsidiaries.
Publications: Application guidelines.
Financial data: Year ended 12/31/2012. Assets,
$2,445,678 (M); Expenditures, $606,776; Total
giving, $600,278.
Fields of interest: Education.
Type of support: Employee-related scholarships.
Application information: Applications accepted.
Application form required.
  Initial approach: Letter or intercompany mail
    outlining financial need and academic
    eligibility.
  Deadline(s): May 15.
  Applicants should submit the following:
    1) SAT
    2) Transcripts
    3) Letter(s) of recommendation
Program description:
  Scholarship Program: Employees of the following
companies are eligible: Meehan Seaway Service,
Ltd., Meehan Seaway Service of Milwaukee, Ltd.,
Meehan Overseas Terminal, Ltd., Meehan
Overseas Terminal of Albany, Ship and Cargo
Agency of Morehead City, Meehan Overseas
Terminal of New London, 4400 Packaging, Inc., and
Seaway Cartage, Ltd. Scholarships are awarded on
the basis of scholastic achievement, standardized
test scores, recommendations, and financial need.
Scholarships may be used for full-time study at the
undergraduate or graduate level. Scholarships
cover the cost of annual tuition, up to $4,000 per
year for up to four years. Recipients must maintain
full-time status and at least a 3.0 GPA to be eligible
for renewals. Applicants are notified of the
scholarship committee's decision by mail.
EIN: 391445333

9964
Melissa Fund, Inc.
c/o BMO Harris Bank, N.A.
111 E. Kilbourn Ave.
Milwaukee, WI 53202

Foundation type: Independent foundation
Purpose: Scholarships to residents of WI who have
attended a public school.
Financial data: Year ended 12/31/2012. Assets,
$81,873 (M); Expenditures, $8,812; Total giving,
$7,750; Grants to individuals, 3 grants totaling
$6,250 (high: $2,500, low: $1,250).
Type of support: Undergraduate support.
Application information: Applications not
accepted.
  Additional information: Unsolicited requests for
    funds not considered or acknowledged.
EIN: 542091457

9965
Menasha Corporation Foundation
P.O. Box 367
Neenah, WI 54957-0367 (920) 751-2036
Contact: Kevin Schuh, Treas.

Foundation type: Company-sponsored foundation
Purpose: Scholarships only to children of
employees of Menasha Corporation.

Financial data: Year ended 12/31/2012. Assets,
$1,567,405 (M); Expenditures, $936,447; Total
giving, $925,232.
Fields of interest: Higher education.
Type of support: Employee-related scholarships.
Application information: Applications accepted.
Application form required.
  Deadline(s): None
  Additional information: Contact foundation for
    application guidelines.
Company name: Menasha Corporation
EIN: 396047384

9966
John P. Mentzer Trust
c/o U.S. Bank, N.A.
P.O. Box 7900
Madison, WI 53707-7900 (319) 377-9894
Contact: Tom Kettmann
Application address: 675 S. 25th St., Marion, IA
52302-4903, tel.: (319) 377-9894

Foundation type: Independent foundation
Purpose: Scholarships to financially needy
graduates of Marion and Linn-Mar high schools,
Marion, IA.
Financial data: Year ended 09/30/2013. Assets,
$170,273 (M); Expenditures, $8,713; Total giving,
$5,300; Grants to individuals, 9 grants totaling
$5,300 (high: $1,000, low: $300).
Type of support: Support to graduates or students
of specific schools; Undergraduate support.
Application information: Application form required.
  Deadline(s): None
  Applicants should submit the following:
    1) Letter(s) of recommendation
    2) Essay
    3) Class rank
    4) Transcripts
    5) GPA
EIN: 426054056

9967
Lee W. Metzner Memorial Fund
c/o M.I. Trust
P.O. Box 2980
Milwaukee, WI 53201-2980 (920) 487-7001
Application address: c/o ALG Guidance Dept., 1715
Division St., Algoma, WI 54201

Foundation type: Independent foundation
Purpose: Scholarships to students of Algoma, Cain
and Luxemberg-Casco High Schools, WI.
Financial data: Year ended 12/31/2012. Assets,
$113,861 (M); Expenditures, $8,948; Total giving,
$5,051; Grants to individuals, 11 grants totaling
$5,051 (high: $1,000, low: $336).
Fields of interest: Higher education.
Type of support: Support to graduates or students
of specific schools.
Application information: Applications accepted.
Application form required.
  Additional information: Application can be
    obtained from the respective high schools.
EIN: 396428655

9968
Steven R. Michels Charitable Foundation
c/o Kathleen A. Loppnow
P.O. Box 128
Brownsville, WI 53006 (561) 625-7800
Application address: c/o William T. Dwyer High
School, Attn.: Guidance Office, 13601 N. Military

Trail, Palm Beach Gardens, FL 33418, tel.: (561) 625-7800

Foundation type: Independent foundation
Purpose: Scholarships to graduating seniors of William T. Dwyer High School, FL.
Financial data: Year ended 12/31/2012. Assets, $461,864 (M); Expenditures, $12,440; Total giving, $10,000; Grants to individuals, 2 grants totaling $10,000 (high: $5,000, low: $5,000).
Fields of interest: Higher education.
Type of support: Support to graduates or students of specific schools.
Application information: Applications accepted. Application form required.
　Additional information: Applications available in school guidance office.
EIN: 721528213

9969
Kathryn J. Michelson Science Scholarship Trust

c/o Pat Cirese
11065 Old Hwy. 51
Arbor Vitae, WI　54568-9721　(715) 356-3282
Contact: Patricia Cirese, Tr.

Foundation type: Operating foundation
Purpose: Scholarships for Arbor Vitae-Woodruff, WI students for attendance at the U.S. Space Camp.
Financial data: Year ended 12/31/2012. Assets, $25,527 (M); Expenditures, $5,487; Total giving, $5,000; Grants to individuals, 4 grants totaling $5,000 (high: $1,250; low: $1,250).
Fields of interest: Space/aviation.
Type of support: Scholarships—to individuals.
Application information: Application form required.
　Deadline(s): Apr. 15
EIN: 396729065

9970
Milwaukee Jewish Federation, Inc.

1360 N. Prospect Ave.
Milwaukee, WI　53202-3016　(414) 390-5700
FAX: (414) 390-5782;
E-mail: info@milwaukeejewish.org; URL: http://www.milwaukeejewish.org

Foundation type: Public charity
Purpose: Scholarships to Milwaukee, WI area residents to participate in recognized Jewish summer overnight camping and summer programs in Israel.
Financial data: Year ended 06/30/2011. Assets, $181,667,200 (M); Expenditures, $26,305,979; Total giving, $14,134,831; Grants to individuals, 225 grants totaling $498,598 (high: $474,153, low: $24,445).
Fields of interest: Jewish agencies & synagogues.
Type of support: Camperships; Scholarships—to individuals.
Application information: Applications accepted. Application form required.
　Send request by: Mail
　Deadline(s): Feb. 2
　Additional information: Application should include a signed copy of page one of the applicant's parents' most recent income tax return and W-2 forms. Applicant must demonstrate financial need.
EIN: 390806312

9971
Milwaukee Times Louvenia Johnson Journalism Scholarship Fund

1938 N. Martin Luther King Dr.
Milwaukee, WI　53212-3642　(414) 263-5088

Foundation type: Public charity
Purpose: Scholarships to African-American residents of WI enrolled in an undergraduate journalism program.
Financial data: Year ended 12/31/2011. Assets, $35,290 (M); Expenditures, $15,000; Total giving, $15,000.
Fields of interest: Journalism school/education; African Americans/Blacks.
Type of support: Undergraduate support.
Application information:
　Initial approach: Letter
EIN: 391680458

9972
Cynthia Asplund Mitchell Medical Scholarship Fund Inc.

407 17th Ave.
Bloomer, WI　54724-1717　(715) 568-5361
Contact: Mary B. Asplund, Dir.

Foundation type: Independent foundation
Purpose: Scholarships to graduating seniors from a Chippewa Valley, WI, high school for attendance at a four-year college of their choice for a career in medicine, nursing, physical or occupational therapy, veterinary medicine, physiology related to medicine, dentistry, other science laboratory fields or other related medical fields.
Financial data: Year ended 12/31/2012. Assets, $519,958 (M); Expenditures, $28,282; Total giving, $26,500; Grants to individuals, 13 grants totaling $26,500 (high: $3,000, low: $500).
Fields of interest: Higher education; Dental school/education; Medical school/education; Nursing school/education; Veterinary medicine; Physical therapy.
Type of support: Support to graduates or students of specific schools.
Application information: Applications accepted.
　Deadline(s): Mar. 31
　Applicants should submit the following:
　　1) Transcripts
　　2) Letter(s) of recommendation
　Additional information: Contributes only to a Chippewa Valley, WI high school; unsolicited requests for funds not considered or acknowledged.
EIN: 391570329

9973
MMAC Community Support Foundation, Inc.

756 N. Milwaukee St.
Milwaukee, WI　53202-3719　(414) 287-4100

Foundation type: Public charity
Purpose: College scholarships to eligible high school graduates from the Metropolitan Milwaukee, WI area.
Financial data: Year ended 06/30/2012. Assets, $474,849 (M); Expenditures, $24,074; Total giving, $18,248; Grants to individuals, totaling $18,248.
Fields of interest: Higher education.
Type of support: Scholarships—to individuals.
Application information: Applications accepted. Application form required. Interview required.
　Applicants should submit the following:
　　1) Transcripts

2) Essay
　Additional information: Contact your respective high schools for application guidelines.
EIN: 391740875

9974
Mildred Jayne & H. J. Ham Moore Trust

c/o U.S. Bank, N.A.
P.O. Box 2043
Milwaukee, WI　53201-9668　(641) 683-2045

Foundation type: Independent foundation
Purpose: Scholarships to graduates of Albia High School, IA, or Twin Cedars High School, IA, pursuing postsecondary education.
Financial data: Year ended 02/28/2013. Assets, $539,983 (M); Expenditures, $31,829; Total giving, $23,000; Grants to individuals, 35 grants totaling $23,000 (high: $2,500, low: $200).
Fields of interest: Higher education.
Type of support: Support to graduates or students of specific schools; Undergraduate support.
Application information: Applications accepted. Application form required.
　Initial approach: Letter or telephone
　Deadline(s): Apr. 1
　Additional information: Applications are available from US Bank, N.A., Ottumwa, IA.
EIN: 426512721

9975
Sarah Mullenbach Memorial Foundation, Inc.

2506 Cedar Creek Ln.
Onalaska, WI　54650-9356　(608) 783-0720
Contact: Cecilia Mullenbach, Secy.-Treas.

Foundation type: Operating foundation
Purpose: Scholarships to students in the La Crosse, WI area for higher education.
Financial data: Year ended 12/31/2011. Assets, $172,520 (M); Expenditures, $8,659; Total giving, $7,912.
Fields of interest: Higher education.
Type of support: Scholarships—to individuals.
Application information: Applications accepted. Application form required.
　Deadline(s): None
EIN: 202277368

9976
Munster Scholarship Trust

(formerly Julia Blake Munster & Adele Blake Scholarship Trust)
P.O. Box 649
Neenah, WI　54957-0649　(262) 268-5500

Foundation type: Independent foundation
Purpose: Scholarships to graduating seniors of Port Washington High School, WI for postsecondary education.
Financial data: Year ended 05/31/2013. Assets, $707,564 (M); Expenditures, $47,846; Total giving, $31,500; Grants to individuals, 23 grants totaling $31,500 (high: $2,000, low: $1,000).
Fields of interest: Higher education.
Type of support: Support to graduates or students of specific schools; Undergraduate support.
Application information: Applications accepted. Application form required.
　Additional information: Applications available through the scholarship committee.
EIN: 396178832

9977
National Lung Cancer Partnership
(formerly Women Against Lung Cancer)
1 Point Pl., Ste. 200
Madison, WI 53719-5072 (608) 833-7905
FAX: (608) 833-7906;
E-mail: info@nationallungcancerpartnership.org;
e-mail for Regina Vidaver, Ph.D.:
regina@nationallungcancerpartnership.org;
URL: http://
www.nationallungcancerpartnership.org
Additional URL: http://www.freetobreathe.org

Foundation type: Public charity
Purpose: Research grants to individuals, and travel grants to individuals to attend specific conferences.
Publications: Application guidelines; Annual report; Informational brochure; Newsletter.
Financial data: Year ended 12/31/2011. Assets, $3,962,401 (M); Expenditures, $2,768,641; Total giving, $833,749.
Fields of interest: Lung research.
Type of support: Research; Travel grants.
Application information: Applications accepted. Application form required. Application form available on the grantmaker's web site.
Initial approach: Full application
Send request by: Mail and e-mail
Copies of proposal: 3
Deadline(s): Varies
Final notification: Recipients notified in six weeks
Applicants should submit the following:
1) Budget Information
2) Letter(s) of recommendation
EIN: 450505050

9978
National Niemann-Pick Disease Foundation, Inc.
401 Madison Ave., Ste. B
P.O. Box 49
Fort Atkinson, WI 53538-0049 (920) 563-0930
Contact: Nadine Hill, Exec. Dir.
FAX: (920) 563-0931; E-mail: nnpdf@nnpdf.org;
Toll-free tel.: (877) 287-3672; E-mail For Nadine Hill: nhill@nnpdf.org; URL: http://www.nnpdf.org

Foundation type: Public charity
Purpose: Supports postdoctoral research fellowships into the pathology and potential cure for Niemann-Pick Type C disease.
Publications: Application guidelines.
Financial data: Year ended 12/31/2011. Assets, $745,298 (M); Expenditures, $524,533.
Fields of interest: Diseases (rare) research.
Type of support: Fellowships; Research.
Application information: Applications accepted. Application form required.
Send request by: E-mail
Deadline(s): May 1
Final notification: Applicants notified Aug. 15
Additional information: See web site for additional application guidelines.
Program description:
Peter G. Pentchev Research Fellowships: These fellowships will provide support of $50,000 per year for two years to postdoctoral research fellows examining the biology of Niemann-Pick Type C (NPC) disease. Researchers who hold an M.D., M.D.-Ph.D., and Ph.D. are eligible to apply for funding; preference will be given to research projects developing new therapies for NPC and identifying biomarkers of disease activity for diagnosis and clinical trials.
EIN: 351844264

9979
Victor & Mary D. Nelson Scholarship Fund
c/o BMO Harris Bank, N.A.
P.O. Box 2980
Milwaukee, WI 53201 (715) 384-0271

Foundation type: Independent foundation
Purpose: Scholarships to graduates of Superior High School, WI, for higher education.
Financial data: Year ended 06/30/2013. Assets, $4,802,303 (M); Expenditures, $273,483; Total giving, $209,833.
Type of support: Support to graduates or students of specific schools; Undergraduate support.
Application information:
Deadline(s): Apr. 15
Additional information: Applications available at school counseling office.
EIN: 396184729

9980
New Glarus Masonic Lodge No. 310 Foundation, Inc.
113 8th Ave.
New Glarus, WI 53574 (608) 938-4194
Application address: 334 S Main St.,Monticello,WI 53570,tel.: (608) 938-4198

Foundation type: Independent foundation
Purpose: Scholarships to graduating high school seniors of Belleville High School, Monticello High School and New Glarus High School of WI, pursuing higher education.
Financial data: Year ended 12/31/2011. Assets, $127,003 (M); Expenditures, $6,925; Total giving, $6,300; Grants to individuals, 9 grants totaling $6,300 (high: $700, low: $700).
Fields of interest: Higher education.
Type of support: Scholarships—to individuals; Support to graduates or students of specific schools.
Application information: Applications accepted. Application form required.
Additional information: Students should contact their respective high school guidance counselor for application information.
EIN: 391985798

9981
James R. Nicholl Memorial Foundation
c/o JPMorgan Chase Bank, N.A.
P.O. Box 3038
Milwaukee, WI 53201-3038 (216) 781-2052

Foundation type: Independent foundation
Purpose: Medical and surgical expense assistance to needy children (2 to 21 years of age) living in Lorain County, OH, for at least two years. Scholarships to residents of Lorain County, enrolled in a post-graduate medical program and plan to return to the area to practice.
Financial data: Year ended 12/31/2011. Assets, $1,156,641 (M); Expenditures, $62,325; Total giving, $44,624.
Fields of interest: Higher education; Health care; Children/youth, services.
Type of support: Postgraduate support; Grants for special needs.
Application information: Applications accepted. Application form required.
Initial approach: Letter
Deadline(s): None
Additional information: Application should indicate the medical need.
EIN: 346574742

9982
Nicolet College Foundation
Univ. Transfer Ctr., 2nd Fl.
Rhinelander, WI 54501-0518 (715) 365-4518
Contact: Heather Schallock, Exec. Dir.
E-mail: hschallock@nicoletcollege.edu; Tel. for Heather Schallock: (715) 365-4518; URL: http://nicoletcollege.edu/about/support-nicolet/nicolet-college-foundation/index.html

Foundation type: Public charity
Purpose: Scholarships to graduating high school seniors for attendance at Nicolet College, WI for higher education.
Financial data: Year ended 06/30/2012. Assets, $1,898,979 (M); Expenditures, $282,214; Total giving, $261,092; Grants to individuals, totaling $225,047.
Fields of interest: Higher education.
Type of support: Support to graduates or students of specific schools.
Application information: Applications not accepted.
Additional information: Scholarships are solely for Nicolet College students. Unsolicited requests for funds not considered or acknowledged.
EIN: 237112418

9983
Freda Nishan Scholarship Trust
c/o U.S. Bank, N.A.
P.O. Box 7900
Madison, WI 53707-7900 (608) 524-2401
Application Address: c/o Nishan Scholarship Committee, 501 K St., Reedburg, WI 539591825

Foundation type: Independent foundation
Purpose: Scholarships to graduates of Reedsburg Area High School, Webb High School, WI, or Sauk County Teacher's College, WI, for attendance at an accredited institution of higher learning in WI.
Financial data: Year ended 12/31/2012. Assets, $974,280 (M); Expenditures, $65,380; Total giving, $46,080; Grants to individuals, 47 grants totaling $46,080 (high: $1,500, low: $250).
Fields of interest: Higher education.
Type of support: Support to graduates or students of specific schools; Undergraduate support.
Application information: Applications accepted.
Initial approach: Letter
Deadline(s): Sept.15
EIN: 396038664

9984
O.J. Noer Research Foundation, Inc.
P.O. Box 94
Juneau, WI 53039-0094
Application address: c/o Jim Spindler, 1711 Wilshire Ct., Lakeland, FL 33813-2373, tel.: (863) 619-9822, fax: (863) 619-7441,
e-mail: spindler@gte.net
URL: http://www.ojnoerfoundation.org

Foundation type: Public charity
Purpose: Financial assistance to graduate students to conduct research in turfgrasses and related fields.
Financial data: Year ended 12/31/2010. Assets, $442,012 (M); Expenditures, $43,038; Total giving, $39,578.
Fields of interest: Research; Environment, land resources; Botanical/horticulture/landscape services.
Type of support: Research; Graduate support.

Application information: Applications accepted. Application form required. Application form available on the grantmaker's web site.
  Initial approach: Letter or e-mail
  Copies of proposal: 15
  Deadline(s): 6 weeks prior to board meetings
EIN: 392672850

9985
Lawrence Norbert & Harry Schwabenlander for Hilbert High School Memorial Scholarship Foundation
N5183 Hwy. 57
Chilton, WI   53014   (920) 849-2790
Contact: Joyce Kopf, Pres.

Foundation type: Independent foundation
Purpose: Scholarships to graduates of Hilbert High School, WI, who have a minimum GPA of 3.0.
Financial data: Year ended 12/31/2012. Assets, $210,154 (M); Expenditures, $11,826; Total giving, $10,000; Grants to individuals, 4 grants totaling $10,000 (high: $2,500, low: $2,500).
Type of support: Support to graduates or students of specific schools.
Application information: Application form required.
  Initial approach: Letter
  Deadline(s): Mar. 15
  Additional information: Application must include an essay.
EIN: 392012927

9986
John and Blanche O'Hara Scholarship Trust
c/o BMO Harris Bank, N.A.
P.O. Box 2980
Milwaukee, WI   53201-2977

Foundation type: Independent foundation
Purpose: Scholarships to graduating seniors of Superior High School, WI, who have been accepted to a junior college, college or university.
Financial data: Year ended 12/31/2012. Assets, $574,874 (M); Expenditures, $27,987; Total giving, $20,000.
Type of support: Support to graduates or students of specific schools; Undergraduate support.
Application information: Applications not accepted.
  Additional information: Giving only to preselected individuals.
EIN: 946659540

9987
Oilgear Ferris Foundation
P.O. Box 2980
Milwaukee, WI   53201-2977   (414) 287-8845
Contact: Deirdre Snyder
Application Address: 111 E. Kilbourn Ave., Milwaukee, WI 53202; tel.:(414) 287-8845

Foundation type: Company-sponsored foundation
Purpose: Scholarships to children of active employees of The Oilgear Company.
Financial data: Year ended 12/31/2012. Assets, $844,577 (M); Expenditures, $59,870; Total giving, $48,000.
Type of support: Employee-related scholarships.
Application information: Applications accepted. Application form not required. Interview required.
  Initial approach: Letter
  Deadline(s): Submissions are reviewed quarterly

Additional information: Application address: Gregory Schmidt, 111 E. Kilbourn Ave., Milwaukee, WI 53202, tel.: (414) 287-8481.
Company name: The Oilgear Company
EIN: 396050126

9988
Oshkosh Area Community Foundation
(formerly Oshkosh Foundation)
230 Ohio St., Ste. 100
Oshkosh, WI   54902   (920) 426-3993
Contact: Diane Abraham, C.E.O.; For grants: Amy Putzer, Dir., Progs.
FAX: (920) 426-6997;
E-mail: info@oshkoshareaf.org; Additional e-mail: diane@oshkoshareacf.org; Grant inquiry e-mail: amy@oshkoshareacf.org; URL: http://www.oshkoshareacf.org

Foundation type: Community foundation
Purpose: Scholarships to graduating high school seniors from Winnebago and Green Lake counties, WI pursuing an undergraduate degree.
Publications: Application guidelines; Annual report; Financial statement; Informational brochure; Newsletter.
Financial data: Year ended 06/30/2013. Assets, $87,475,004 (M); Expenditures, $4,707,217; Total giving, $4,057,085.
Fields of interest: Vocational education, post-secondary; Higher education; Graduate/professional education.
Type of support: Scholarships—to individuals; Support to graduates or students of specific schools; Graduate support; Undergraduate support.
Application information: Applications accepted. Application form required. Application form available on the grantmaker's web site.
  Initial approach: Application
  Send request by: Online
  Deadline(s): Varies
  Final notification: Applicants notified in 12 weeks
  Applicants should submit the following:
    1) Transcripts
    2) SAT
    3) Letter(s) of recommendation
    4) GPA
    5) Financial information
    6) Essay
    7) ACT
  Additional information: Scholarships are paid directly to the educational institution on behalf of the students. See Winnebago County Scholarship Center (www.winnebagocountyscholarships.org) for online application and complete listing of scholarships.
Program descriptions:
  Education Grants: Two types of grants are available to support teachers and schools: 1) Celebrate Education Grants, for K-12 teachers (public and parochial) in the Oshkosh Area School District for a project that enriches the educational experience, motivates or inspires students, fills a specific needs, demonstrates a sense of community and is fun for kids; and 2) Rudoy Awards for Teaching Excellence, for teachers from public and parochial middle and high schools to receive a monetary award to be used for either their own professional development or for a specific program or project in their classrooms. See web site for additional information.
  Scholarships: The foundation offers a wide range of scholarships, each with specific eligibility criteria. Most scholarships are open to graduating high school seniors pursuing an undergraduate

degree, though some graduate school scholarships are also available. Scholarships support both two-year technical and four-year college degrees and typically range from $250 to $1,000. Scholarship awards must be applied to tuition and fees, and cannot be used for books, room and board, or other expenses. See web site for additional information.
EIN: 392034571

9989
Oshkosh Area Community Foundation Corporation
230 Ohio St. Ste. 100
Oshkosh, WI   54902-5894   (920) 426-3993
Contact: Eileen Connolly-Keesler, Pres. and C.E.O.
FAX: (920) 426-6997;
E-mail: info@oshkoshareacf.org; E-Mail for Eileen Connolly-Keesler: eileen@oshkoshareacf.org; URL: http://www.oshkoshareacf.org/

Foundation type: Public charity
Purpose: Scholarships to residents of Oshkosh, WI.
Financial data: Year ended 06/30/2012. Assets, $75,983,529 (M); Expenditures, $5,584,098; Total giving, $4,524,150; Grants to individuals, totaling $549,087.
Fields of interest: Education.
Type of support: Undergraduate support.
Application information: Applications accepted. Application form required.
  Initial approach: E-mail
  Deadline(s): Varies
  Additional information: A full listing of scholarships and a link to the online application is available at FoxRiverScholarshipCenter.org.
EIN: 392034571

9990
Pagel Graphics Arts Scholarship Trust Fund
P.O. Box 34
Elm Grove, WI   53122-0034   (414) 785-9090
Contact: Robert Carlson, Tr.

Foundation type: Operating foundation
Purpose: Scholarships to individuals attending school full time in Wisconsin and pursuing higher education in the print communications industry.
Financial data: Year ended 06/30/2013. Assets, $246,818 (M); Expenditures, $17,785; Total giving, $12,000; Grants to individuals, 17 grants totaling $12,000 (high: $1,250, low: $500).
Fields of interest: Print publishing.
Type of support: Scholarships—to individuals.
Application information: Applications accepted. Application form required.
  Deadline(s): Mar. 1
  Final notification: Applicants notified in Apr.
  Additional information: Application should include transcripts. Scholarships are awarded based on academic performance, activities and financial need.
EIN: 391674169

9991
Partners Advancing Values in Education, Inc.
135 W. Wells St., Ste. 850
Milwaukee, WI   53203-1844   (414) 263-2970
FAX: (414) 263-2975; URL: http://www.pave.org

Foundation type: Public charity

Purpose: Scholarship assistance to students from low income families residing in Milwaukee, WI, enrolled in a private or parochial elementary (K-8) or secondary school in the greater Milwaukee area.
Publications: Financial statement.
Financial data: Year ended 06/30/2012. Assets, $13,283,786 (M); Expenditures, $1,405,774; Total giving, $900,645.
Fields of interest: Education; Economically disadvantaged.
Type of support: Scholarships—to individuals; Grants for special needs.
Application information: Newly enrolled students receive grants solely on need and availability of space.
EIN: 391590212

9992
Bradley A. & Birdell A. Peterson Scholarship Trust
905 Sussex Dr.
Eau Claire, WI   54703   (715) 832-6171
Contact: Michael Markin, Tr.

Foundation type: Operating foundation
Purpose: College scholarships to students who are residents of Eau Claire County, WI.
Financial data: Year ended 07/31/2013. Assets, $24,044 (M); Expenditures, $26,680; Total giving, $23,000; Grants to individuals, 13 grants totaling $23,000 (high: $4,500, low: $1,000).
Fields of interest: Higher education.
Type of support: Scholarships—to individuals.
Application information:
  Initial approach: Letter
  Deadline(s): None
EIN: 391486945

9993
Phillips Plastics Corporation Contributions Program
7 Long Lake Dr.
Phillips, WI   54555-1528
URL: http://www.phillipsplastics.com/about-us/scholarship-programs

Foundation type: Corporate giving program
Purpose: Scholarship to dependent children of regular full- or part-time Phillips Plastics employees in their first year of an Associate, Baccalaureate, or Graduate degree program.
Fields of interest: Higher education.
Type of support: Employee-related scholarships; Graduate support; Undergraduate support.
Application information: Applications not accepted.
  Additional information: Unsolicited requests for funds not considered or acknowledged.
Program descriptions:
  Bob Farley, Jr. Scholarship Program: Philips Plastics award one $1,250 scholarship to students who have completed their first year in an accredited Associate, Baccalaureate, or Graduate degree program. The program is limited to children and dependents of employees of Phillips Plastics and is given in honor of Bob Farley, Jr. Applicants must have a GPA of 3.0, participation in academic and/or non-academic extracurricular activities, and have financial need.
  Philips Plastics Corporation Scholarship Program: Phillips Plastics annually awards ten $1,250 college scholarships to students who have completed the first year of an Associate, Baccalaureate, or Graduate degree program. The program is limited to children and dependents of employees of Phillips Plastics. Applicants must

have a GPA of 3.0, participation in academic and/or non-academic extracurricular activities, and have financial need.
Company name: Phillips-Medisize Corp.

9994
Russell Phillips Trust
c/o BMO Harris Bank, N.A.
P.O. Box 2980
Milwaukee, WI   53201-2980   (715) 342-3254
Application address: c/o BMO Harris Bank, N.A., Attn.: Kim Hilgers, 500 3rd St., Wausau, WI 54402

Foundation type: Independent foundation
Purpose: Scholarships to residents of Portage County, WI, who are studying agriculture, forestry, or conservation at a college in WI.
Financial data: Year ended 12/31/2012. Assets, $96,700 (M); Expenditures, $8,767; Total giving, $4,900.
Fields of interest: Natural resources; Environment, forests; Agriculture.
Type of support: Scholarships—to individuals.
Application information: Application form required.
  Initial approach: Letter specifying amount of tuition needed
  Deadline(s): Mar. 1
EIN: 396276572

9995
Suzanne & Richard Pieper Family Foundation
11602 N. Shorecliff Ln.
Mequon, WI   53092-3528   (262) 241-0527
Contact: Suzanne E. Pieper, Pres.
URL: http://www.srpieperfamilyfoundation.com/

Foundation type: Independent foundation
Purpose: Grants to individuals for the reimbursement of expenses related to character education work in WI.
Financial data: Year ended 10/31/2012. Assets, $2,026,849 (M); Expenditures, $85,445; Total giving, $37,107.
Fields of interest: Education.
Type of support: Grants to individuals.
Application information:
  Deadline(s): None
EIN: 391715108

9996
David J. Porhaska Scholarship Foundation
c/o Mid Wisconsin Trust
134 S. 8th St.
Medford, WI   54451
Applciation Address: c/o Selection Committee, 1700 Edgewood Ave. East, lady smith, Wi 54848
URL: http://www.midwisc.com/about-us/non-profit-foundation2.html

Foundation type: Independent foundation
Purpose: Scholarships to deserving graduating seniors from Ladysmith High School, WI.
Financial data: Year ended 12/31/2012. Assets, $298,929 (M); Expenditures, $20,804; Total giving, $17,625; Grants to individuals, 11 grants totaling $17,625 (high: $2,500, low: $875).
Fields of interest: Higher education.
Type of support: Support to graduates or students of specific schools.
Application information:
  Deadline(s): None
  Additional information: Applicant must write and essay on "Why they deserve to pursue a post

high school education and how they can promote growth of the Ladysmith area"
EIN: 710965198

9997
Prader-Willi Syndrome Association of Wisconsin, Inc.
2701 N. Alexander St.
Appleton, WI   54911-2312   (920) 882-6371
Contact: Mary Lynn Larson, Prog. Dir.
E-mail: wisconsin@pwsausa.org; Toll-free tel.: (866) 797-2947; URL: http://www.pwsaofwi.org

Foundation type: Public charity
Purpose: Financial assistance for families of an individual with PWS of WI, to help meet the needs of the individual.
Financial data: Year ended 12/31/2012. Assets, $58,624 (M); Expenditures, $62,677; Total giving, $2,353.
Fields of interest: Genetic diseases and disorders.
Type of support: Scholarships—to individuals; Grants for special needs.
Application information: Applications accepted. Application form required.
  Send request by: Mail
  Additional information: Applicant must demonstrate financial need. Applicant must reside in the state of WI.
EIN: 391732251

9998
William F. Praiss Memorial Scholarship Fund
P.O. Box 12800
Green Bay, WI   54307-2800

Foundation type: Independent foundation
Purpose: Scholarships to graduating students of Neenah High School, WI with a cumulative average of 2.75 on a 4.0 scale seeking higher education.
Financial data: Year ended 05/31/2013. Assets, $172,814 (M); Expenditures, $14,898; Total giving, $12,000; Grants to individuals, 12 grants totaling $12,000 (high: $1,000, low: $1,000).
Fields of interest: Higher education.
Type of support: Support to graduates or students of specific schools.
Application information: Applications accepted. Application form required.
  Deadline(s): Mar. 1
EIN: 396522494

9999
Prohaska Scholarship Foundation
c/o Mid Wisconsin Trust
134 S. 8th St.
Medford, WI   54451   (800) 643-9477
Application address: Selection Committee
URL: http://www.midwisc.com

Foundation type: Independent foundation
Purpose: Scholarships to graduating seniors of Medford Senior High School, WI for postsecondary education.
Financial data: Year ended 12/31/2011. Assets, $205,490 (M); Expenditures, $23,391; Total giving, $22,500; Grants to individuals, 10 grants totaling $22,500 (high: $3,750, low: $1,250).
Fields of interest: Higher education.
Type of support: Scholarships—to individuals; Support to graduates or students of specific schools.

Application information:
Initial approach: Letter
Deadline(s): None
Additional information: Application should include a personal essay stating why applicant desire to pursue a post high school education and how they can promote growth of the Medford area.
EIN: 391712984

10000
Project Home, Inc.
1966 S. Stoughton Rd.
Madison, WI 53716-2260 (608) 246-3737
FAX: (608) 246-3722;
E-mail: outreach@projecthomewi.org; URL: http://www.projecthomewi.org/

Foundation type: Public charity
Purpose: Assistance to low income homeowners and individuals of Dane and Green counties, WI with home repairs and weatherization services.
Publications: Newsletter.
Financial data: Year ended 12/31/2011. Assets, $4,213,612 (M); Expenditures, $10,768,696; Total giving, $5,597,719; Grants to individuals, totaling $5,579,768.
Fields of interest: Housing/shelter, home owners; Housing/shelter, repairs.
Type of support: Grants for special needs.
Application information:
Initial approach: Telephone
Additional information: Contact the organization for eligibility determination.
EIN: 391279307

10001
Racine Community Foundation, Inc.
(formerly Racine County Area Foundation, Inc.)
245 Main St., Garden Level
Racine, WI 53403-1034 (262) 632-8474
Contact: Mary Beth Mikrut, Exec. Dir.
FAX: (262) 632-3739;
E-mail: info@racinecommunityfoundation.org;
URL: http://www.racinecommunityfoundation.org

Foundation type: Community foundation
Purpose: Scholarships to students of Racine County, WI for continuing education at technical colleges or universities throughout Wisconsin and the nation.
Publications: Application guidelines; Annual report; Financial statement; Informational brochure; Newsletter.
Financial data: Year ended 12/31/2012. Assets, $44,646,488 (M); Expenditures, $1,846,117; Total giving, $1,429,610.
Fields of interest: Vocational education, post-secondary; Higher education.
Type of support: Scholarships—to individuals; Support to graduates or students of specific schools.
Application information: Application form required.
Initial approach: Letter or telephone.
Additional information: Contact your high school guidance counselor for application information and deadlines.
EIN: 510188377

10002
Racine Kenosha Community Action Agency, Inc.
2113 N. Wisconsin St.
Racine, WI 53402-4774 (262) 637-8377
Contact: Sharon F. Schulz, C.E.O.
FAX: (262) 637-6419; URL: http://www.rkcaa.org/RKCAA.htm

Foundation type: Public charity
Purpose: Monthly rent subsidy and home weatherization services to indigent residents of Racine, WI.
Financial data: Year ended 12/31/2011. Assets, $2,011,078 (M); Expenditures, $13,231,367; Total giving, $4,078,565; Grants to individuals, totaling $4,078,565.
Fields of interest: Housing/shelter, expense aid; Housing/shelter; Economically disadvantaged.
Type of support: In-kind gifts; Grants for special needs.
Application information:
Initial approach: Tel.
Applicants should submit the following:
1) Financial information
Additional information: Contact foundation for eligibility criteria.
EIN: 391087210

10003
John E. Raether Scholarship Trust
P.O. Box 649
Neenah, WI 54957-0649
Application address: c/o Manitowoc Public School District, Attn.: Tiffany Gates, 2902 Lindberg Dr., Manitowoc, WI 54220, tel.: (920) 683-4790

Foundation type: Independent foundation
Purpose: Scholarships to students from Manitowoc, WI pursuing a college education.
Financial data: Year ended 12/31/2011. Assets, $0 (M); Expenditures, $179,223; Total giving, $175,702; Grants to individuals, 6 grants totaling $9,000 (high: $1,500; low: $1,500).
Type of support: Undergraduate support.
Application information: Applications accepted. Application form required.
Deadline(s): None
EIN: 396627083

10004
Ramiah Family Foundation
2816 N. Interlaken Dr.
Oconomowoc, WI 53066-4909 (262) 821-0231
Contact: Ramu Ramiah, Tr.

Foundation type: Independent foundation
Purpose: College scholarships to students of WI for higher education at accredited colleges or universities.
Financial data: Year ended 12/31/2012. Assets, $326,156 (M); Expenditures, $22,290; Total giving, $22,278.
Fields of interest: Higher education.
Type of support: Undergraduate support.
Application information: Applications accepted. Application form required. Interview required.
Deadline(s): None
Applicants should submit the following:
1) Letter(s) of recommendation
2) GPA
3) Essay
Additional information: Application can be obtained from the foundation.
EIN: 391980086

10005
Richard F. Redfield Trust
c/o Thomas L. Knudsen
4390 City Hwy. P
Rhinelander, WI 54501-8237

Foundation type: Independent foundation
Purpose: Scholarships to graduates of Rhinelander High School, WI, for higher education.
Financial data: Year ended 05/31/2013. Assets, $693,177 (M); Expenditures, $38,089; Total giving, $29,747; Grants to individuals, 2 grants totaling $29,747 (high: $15,290, low: $14,457).
Fields of interest: Higher education.
Type of support: Support to graduates or students of specific schools; Undergraduate support.
Application information: Application form required.
Deadline(s): Mar. 31
Additional information: Applications can be obtained from Rhinelander Area Scholarship Foundation or Rhinelander High School.
EIN: 396694213

10006
Elwyn Remington Foundation, Inc.
c/o Ruder Ware, LLSC
500 1st St., Ste. 8000
Wausau, WI 54402-8050 (715) 627-4707
Contact: Jeanne Lucht
Application Address: 1504 1st Ave., Antigo WI 54409

Foundation type: Independent foundation
Purpose: Scholarships to graduating students attending accredited colleges or universities in, WI.
Financial data: Year ended 12/31/2012. Assets, $5,047,487 (M); Expenditures, $275,118; Total giving, $214,500.
Fields of interest: Higher education.
Type of support: Scholarships—to individuals.
Application information: Applications not accepted.
EIN: 391633403

10007
Rexnord Foundation Inc.
P.O. Box 2191 Attn Tax Dept
Milwaukee, WI 53201-2191

Foundation type: Company-sponsored foundation
Purpose: Scholarships to children and dependents of Rexnord Corporation employees, including employees of subsidiary companies. Applicants must have a minimum ACT score of 20 or SAT score of 1,000.
Publications: Application guidelines.
Financial data: Year ended 10/31/2012. Assets, $3,903,707 (M); Expenditures, $487,571; Total giving, $477,921.
Fields of interest: Higher education.
Type of support: Employee-related scholarships.
Application information: Applications accepted. Application form not required.
Initial approach: Letter
Deadline(s): May
Additional information: Application must include photocopy of test scores. Scholarship application address: c/o Scholarship Admin., Rexnord Industries, Inc., 4701 W. Greenfield Ave., Milwaukee, WI 53214.
Company name: Rexnord, LLC
EIN: 396042029

10008

The Albert and Mary Rhodes Museum and Charitable Foundation Inc.
c/o Steven D. Shambeau
P.O. Box 111
Waupaca, WI   54981-0111

Foundation type: Independent foundation
Purpose: Scholarships to high school students and college students in the Wisconsin area who are pursuing degrees in ministerial related studies.
Financial data: Year ended 12/31/2011. Assets, $5,735,212 (M); Expenditures, $317,010; Total giving, $262,502.
Fields of interest: Theological school/education.
Type of support: Scholarships—to individuals.
Application information: Applications accepted.
EIN: 391982685

10009

Clarence & Olive Richards Scholarship Trust
c/o U.S. Bank, N.A.
P.O. Box 2043
Milwaukee, WI   53201-9668   (319) 653-2143
Application addresses: Washington High School, 313 S. 4th Ave., Washington, IA 52353; Highland High School, Box B - 1715 Vine Ave., Riverside, IA 52327

Foundation type: Independent foundation
Purpose: Scholarships to high school graduates of the Washington, IA School District and high school graduates residing in Oregon Township, Washington County, IA.
Financial data: Year ended 12/31/2012. Assets, $633,898 (M); Expenditures, $26,089; Total giving, $16,875; Grants to individuals, 24 grants totaling $16,875 (high: $1,500, low: $500).
Fields of interest: Higher education.
Type of support: Support to graduates or students of specific schools; Undergraduate support.
Application information: Application form required.
Additional information: Application forms can be obtained from guidance counselor's office at high school.
EIN: 396672759

10010

Bryon Riesch Paralysis Foundation
P.O. Box 1388
Waukesha, WI   53187-1388   (262) 547-2083
Contact: Bryon Riesch, Pres.
E-mail: info@brpf.org; Additional application address: 1228 Cavalier Dr., Waukesha, WI 53186; URL: http://www.brpf.org

Foundation type: Public charity
Purpose: Grants to researchers looking for a cure for paralysis. Scholarships to students with neurological disabilities, or to children of individuals with neurological disabilities.
Publications: Application guidelines; Grants list.
Financial data: Year ended 09/30/2012. Assets, $300,480 (M); Expenditures, $283,485; Total giving, $227,236; Grants to individuals, totaling $41,251.
Fields of interest: Nerve, muscle & bone diseases; Disabilities, people with.
Type of support: Research; Undergraduate support.
Application information:
Send request by: Mail
Deadline(s): Contact foundation for current application deadline
Applicants should submit the following:
   1) Letter(s) of recommendation

   2) Transcripts
   3) Resume
EIN: 392016568

10011

Riverview Health Care Foundation, Inc.
410 Dewey St.
P. O. Box 8080
Wisconsin Rapids, WI   54495-8080   (715) 421-7488
Contact: Andy Metcalf, Pres. and C.E.O.
E-mail: mettho@rhahealthcare.org; URL: http://www.riverview-foundation.org/

Foundation type: Public charity
Purpose: Scholarships to graduating high school seniors in the Wisconsin Rapids, WI area pursuing a career in the medical field. Emergency assistance to patients at Riverview Hospital.
Publications: Application guidelines; Newsletter.
Financial data: Year ended 12/31/2012. Assets, $3,626,197 (M); Expenditures, $125,983; Total giving, $47,535; Grants to individuals, totaling $22,472.
Fields of interest: Higher education; Medical school/education; Health care.
Type of support: Scholarships—to individuals; Grants for special needs.
Application information: Applications accepted. Application form required.
Applicants should submit the following:
   1) Transcripts
   2) Letter(s) of recommendation
Additional information: Scholarship program must be at least two years in length.
EIN: 391509239

10012

The Leslie C. Robins Family Foundation
N. 9618 Winnebago Park Rd.
Fond du Lac, WI   54935
Contact: Richard Wehner, Tr.
URL: http://www.campwinnegator.com/

Foundation type: Independent foundation
Purpose: Scholarships primarily to WI residents in pursuit of a higher education.
Financial data: Year ended 07/31/2012. Assets, $860,241 (M); Expenditures, $240,600; Total giving, $45,000; Grants to individuals, 3 grants totaling $5,000 (high: $2,000, low: $1,000).
Fields of interest: Higher education.
Type of support: Scholarships—to individuals.
Application information: Applications accepted.
Additional information: Application should include an essay.
EIN: 391805982

10013

Rolfs Educational Foundation, Ltd.
c/o U.S. Bank
P.O. Box 2043
Milwaukee, WI   53201-9668   (262) 335-5405
Contact: Ann Pauli
Application address: c/o West Bend High School, Attn.: Ann Pauli, 1305 E. Decorah Rd., West Bend, WI 53095-4313

Foundation type: Independent foundation
Purpose: Scholarships to students who have attended at least their last two years of high school at the West Bend high schools, WI and who are in the upper ten percent of their class. Also, awards to teachers in the West Bend, WI, area.

Financial data: Year ended 12/31/2011. Assets, $1,476,880 (M); Expenditures, $69,992; Total giving, $63,000; Grants to individuals, 19 grants totaling $63,000 (high: $7,000, low: $1,000).
Fields of interest: Higher education.
Type of support: Support to graduates or students of specific schools; Awards/prizes.
Application information: Applications accepted. Application form required.
Deadline(s): Jan. for Scholarships
Additional information: Unsolicited requests for funds not considered or acknowledged.
EIN: 391651525

10014

Rotary Club of Milwaukee Foundation
(formerly Clifford Randall Memorial Trust)
c/o Rotary Clu
P.O. Box 2043
Milwaukee, WI   53201-9116   (414) 287-3832
Contact: Mary McMormick, Secy. and Exec. Dir.
Application address: 750 N. Lincoln Memorial Dr., Ste. 320, Milwaukee, WI 53202

Foundation type: Public charity
Purpose: Scholarships to Milwaukee, WI area students during their senior year of high school pursuing higher education.
Financial data: Year ended 06/30/2012. Assets, $2,737,518 (M); Expenditures, $260,827; Total giving, $218,538; Grants to individuals, totaling $12,750.
Fields of interest: Vocational education, post-secondary; Higher education.
Type of support: Scholarships—to individuals.
Application information: Applications accepted. Application form required. Application form available on the grantmaker's web site. Interview required.
Send request by: Mail
Deadline(s): Mar.
Applicants should submit the following:
   1) Financial information
   2) SAR
   3) Transcripts
   4) Letter(s) of recommendation
   5) Essay
Additional information: Selection is based on financial need, scholastic achievement, character and leadership ability, breath and depth of community service, and resident of Milwaukee. Contact the foundation for additional application guidelines.
EIN: 930756960

10015

W. E. Ruebush Foundation
c/o U.S. Bank, N.A.
P.O. Box 2043
Milwaukee, WI   53201-9668   (319) 235-3282
Application Address: c/o US Bank NA, P.O. Box 88, Waterloo, IA 507040088

Foundation type: Independent foundation
Purpose: Scholarship to students in journalism, athletics, and any other field designated by the board, in certain designated schools Waterloo, IA and St. Petersburg, FL.
Financial data: Year ended 12/31/2011. Assets, $1,135,295 (M); Expenditures, $59,336; Total giving, $42,500; Grants to individuals, 17 grants totaling $42,500 (high: $2,500, low: $2,500).
Fields of interest: Print publishing; Higher education; Athletics/sports, football.
Type of support: Scholarships—to individuals.

Application information: Applications not accepted.
> *Additional information:* Unsolicited requests for funds not considered or acknowledged.

EIN: 426125502

10016
Edward and Hannah M. Rutledge Charities, Inc.

(formerly Edward Rutledge Charity)
P.O. Box 758
Chippewa Falls, WI   54729-0738

Foundation type: Independent foundation
Purpose: Scholarships to high school graduates who are residents of Chippewa County, WI. Emergency loans to worthy needy residents of Chippewa County, WI.
Financial data: Year ended 05/31/2013. Assets, $23,185,304 (M); Expenditures, $1,114,950; Total giving, $871,252; Grants to individuals, 169 grants totaling $200,950 (high: $3,000, low: $400); Loans to individuals, totaling $657.
Fields of interest: Higher education.
Type of support: Scholarships—to individuals; Grants for special needs; Loans—to individuals.
Application information: Applications accepted. Application form required. Interview required.
> *Deadline(s):* June 1 for scholarships
> *Applicants should submit the following:*
>   1) SAR
>   2) Transcripts
>   3) FAFSA
>   4) Financial information

EIN: 390806178

10017
Sand County Foundation, Inc.

c/o David Allen
16 N. Carroll St., Ste 450
Madison, WI   53703-2784   (608) 663-4605
FAX: (608) 663-4617; E-mail: info@sandcounty.net;
URL: http://www.sandcounty.net

Foundation type: Operating foundation
Purpose: Awards to recognize landowners actively committed to land ethics.
Publications: Annual report; Newsletter.
Financial data: Year ended 12/31/2012. Assets, $8,093,988 (M); Expenditures, $2,412,229; Total giving, $311,000.
Fields of interest: Ethics; Environment, land resources.
Type of support: Awards/prizes.
Application information: See web site for additional information.
Program description:
> *Leopold Conservation Award:* Working with prominent state conservation partners, the foundation presents the award, which consists of $10,000 and a Leopold crystal, in settings that showcase the landowners' achievements among their peers. The award is available in the states of CA, CO, NE, SD, TX, UT, WI and WY, and the specifics may vary from state to state.

EIN: 396089450

10018
W. R. and Floy A. Sauey Family Foundation

715 Lynn Ave.
Baraboo, WI   53913-2488   (608) 356-2130
Contact: Alison Martin, Pres.
Application address: c/o Nordic Group, 414 Broadway, Baraboo, WI 53913; URL: http://www.saueyfamily.org/

Foundation type: Company-sponsored foundation
Purpose: Scholarships to the children or legal guardians of associates of the Nordic Group of Companies, Inc., WI, with an emphasis on business and technical degrees.
Publications: Informational brochure.
Financial data: Year ended 12/31/2011. Assets, $1,118,084 (M); Expenditures, $176,009; Total giving, $153,235.
Fields of interest: Higher education.
Type of support: Scholarships—to individuals.
Application information: Applications not accepted.
> *Additional information:* Unsolicited requests for funds not considered or acknowledged.

Company name: Nordic Group of Companies, Ltd.
EIN: 391934775

10019
Greater Sauk County Community Foundation, Inc.

(formerly Baraboo Area Community Foundation, Inc.)
600 W. Chestnut St.
P.O. Box 544
West Baraboo, WI   53913-0544   (608) 355-0884
Contact: Karen F. Sacia, Exec. Dir.
FAX: (608) 356-8422; E-mail: gsccf@centurytel.net;
URL: http://www.greatersaukcountycf.org

Foundation type: Community foundation
Purpose: Scholarships to graduating seniors of River Valley High School, WI for higher education.
Publications: Application guidelines; Annual report; Informational brochure.
Financial data: Year ended 12/31/2012. Assets, $2,969,017 (M); Expenditures, $208,818; Total giving, $0.
Fields of interest: Higher education.
Type of support: Scholarships—to individuals; Support to graduates or students of specific schools.
Application information: Applications not accepted.
> *Additional information:* Unsolicited requests for funds not considered or acknowledged.

EIN: 391919240

10020
SBC Foundation Inc.

(formerly Stoelting Brothers Company Foundation, Inc.)
P.O. Box 127
Kiel, WI   53042-0127

Foundation type: Company-sponsored foundation
Purpose: Scholarships to graduates of Kiel High School of Kiel, WI for continuing education at institutions of higher learning.
Financial data: Year ended 09/30/2013. Assets, $222,017 (M); Expenditures, $11,207; Total giving, $10,700.
Fields of interest: Higher education.
Type of support: Support to graduates or students of specific schools; Undergraduate support.

Application information:
> *Initial approach:* Letter
> *Additional information:* Application forms are available at Kiel High School guidance offices.

EIN: 396123893

10021
Schield Companies Foundation Inc.

(formerly Weather Shield Manufacturing Foundation, Inc.)
P.O. Box 309
Medford, WI   54451-0309

Foundation type: Company-sponsored foundation
Purpose: College scholarships to children of employees of Weather Shield Manufacturing.
Financial data: Year ended 12/31/2011. Assets, $456,033 (M); Expenditures, $21,900; Total giving, $20,000; Grants to individuals, 32 grants totaling $20,000 (high: $1,000, low: $500).
Fields of interest: Higher education.
Type of support: Employee-related scholarships.
Application information: Applications not accepted.
> *Additional information:* Contributes only through employee related scholarships. Unsolicited requests for funds not considered or acknowledged.

Company name: Weather Shield Manufacturing, Inc.
EIN: 391362989

10022
Niederkon Scholarship Trust

(formerly William J. & Myra L. Niederkorn Scholarship Trust)
P.O. Box 649
Neenah, WI   54957-0649   (262) 268-5500

Foundation type: Independent foundation
Purpose: Scholarships to graduating seniors from Port Washington High School, WI.
Financial data: Year ended 05/31/2013. Assets, $399,485 (M); Expenditures, $22,338; Total giving, $16,000; Grants to individuals, 8 grants totaling $16,000 (high: $3,500, low: $1,000).
Type of support: Support to graduates or students of specific schools; Undergraduate support.
Application information: Applications accepted.
> *Additional information:* Contact scholarship committee for current application deadline/guidelines.

EIN: 396297158

10023
Theodore and Catherine Schulte Foundation

c/o Johnson Bank
555 Main St., Ste. 300
Racine, WI   53403   (414) 632-1667
Contact: Robert Sharp
Application address: 610 Main St., Racine, WI 53403-1258, tel.: (414) 632-1667

Foundation type: Independent foundation
Purpose: Funds for retired Catholic priests from Racine, WI.
Financial data: Year ended 09/30/2013. Assets, $788,906 (M); Expenditures, $41,586; Total giving, $30,400; Grants to individuals, 7 grants totaling $30,400 (high: $5,000, low: $400).
Fields of interest: Housing/shelter; Christian agencies & churches; Catholic agencies & churches.
Type of support: Grants for special needs.

Application information: Applications accepted. Application form not required.

> *Deadline(s):* None
> *Additional information:* Contact foundation for current application guidelines.

EIN: 396222864

10024
Faythe Schwarz Trust f/b/o Stockbridge High School

P.O. Box 149
Chilton, WI 53014-0149

Foundation type: Independent foundation
Purpose: Scholarships to individuals residing in the Chilton WI, area.
Financial data: Year ended 12/31/2012. Assets, $301,637 (M); Expenditures, $11,681; Total giving, $7,680; Grants to individuals, 2 grants totaling $3,840 (high: $1,920, low: $1,920).
Type of support: Undergraduate support.
Application information: Applications not accepted.

> *Additional information:* Unsolicited requests for funds not accepted or considered.

EIN: 806026133

10025
Scoliosis Research Society

555 E. Wells St., Ste. 1100
Milwaukee, WI 53202-3823 (414) 289-9107
Contact: Tressa Goulding C.A.E., C.M.P., Exec. Dir.
FAX: (414) 276-3349; E-mail: info@srs.org;
URL: http://www.srs.org

Foundation type: Public charity
Purpose: Research grants for treatment of patients with pediatric spinal deformities.
Publications: Application guidelines; Grants list.
Financial data: Year ended 12/31/2011. Assets, $8,656,116 (M); Expenditures, $3,683,237; Total giving, $405,145; Grants to individuals, totaling $2,500.
Fields of interest: Spine disorders; Pediatrics research.
Type of support: Research.
Application information: Applications accepted. Application form required.

> *Initial approach:* Proposal
> *Send request by:* Mail or online
> *Deadline(s):* Dec. 1 for preliminary application, Mar. 2 for full application
> *Additional information:* Only SRS members may apply for this grant. Application should include a budget. See web site for additional guidelines.

Program description:

> *Alf Nachemson Evidence Based Medicine Research Grant:* The project may be funded to a maximum of $100,000 over a two-year period. The grants should be used for research on clinical outcome studies using high levels of evidence to evaluate the efficacy of new spinal instrumentation systems and innovative surgical techniques for correcting spinal deformity in children and/or adults, the utility of scoliosis screening in reducing the incidence of severe spinal deformity or the number of patients requiring surgical intervention, and the long term efficacy of non-surgical treatments for spinal deformity.

EIN: 237181863

10026
Select Milwaukee, Inc.

2209 N. Dr. Martin Luther King, Jr. Dr.
Milwaukee, WI 53212-3188 (414) 562-5070
Contact: Raymond Schmidt, Exec. Dir.
FAX: (414) 562-5072;
E-mail: info@selectmilwaukee.org; URL: http://www.selectmilwaukee.org

Foundation type: Public charity
Purpose: Financial assistance to individuals of the greater Milwaukee, WI area with down payment, closing costs and home repair.
Financial data: Year ended 12/31/2011. Assets, $1,534,094 (M); Expenditures, $1,692,119; Total giving, $571,687; Grants to individuals, totaling $571,687.
Fields of interest: Housing/shelter, home owners; Housing/shelter, repairs.
Type of support: Grants for special needs.
Application information: Applications accepted.

> *Additional information:* Contact the organization for eligibility determination.

EIN: 391793410

10027
Seymour Community School Scholarship Trust

200 E. Wisconsin St.
P.O Box 67
Seymour, WI 54165-0067 (920) 833-2356
Contact: Richard Lubinski, Tr.

Foundation type: Independent foundation
Purpose: Scholarships to graduating seniors of the Seymour Community High School, WI, who exhibit leadership abilities and will be attending college.
Financial data: Year ended 12/31/2012. Assets, $1,008,286 (M); Expenditures, $40,994; Total giving, $38,488.
Type of support: Support to graduates or students of specific schools; Undergraduate support.
Application information: Applications accepted. Application form not required.

> *Deadline(s):* Contact trust for current application deadline
> *Additional information:* Recipients must complete the first semester of their freshman year to receive the scholarship.

EIN: 391769065

10028
Allen J. Shafer Irrevocable Trust

c/o U.S. Bank, N.A.
P.O. Box 7900
Madison, WI 53707-7900 (608) 663-1633
Application address: c/o Madison West High School Administra, 30 Ash St. Madison,WI 53726

Foundation type: Independent foundation
Purpose: Scholarships to graduates of West High School, Madison, WI. Recipients are selected by West High School committee.
Financial data: Year ended 12/31/2012. Assets, $159,670 (M); Expenditures, $10,218; Total giving, $7,200; Grants to individuals, 10 grants totaling $7,200 (high: $720, low: $720).
Type of support: Support to graduates or students of specific schools; Undergraduate support.
Application information:

> *Deadline(s):* None

EIN: 396140024

10029
Moses and Caroline Shallow Scholarship Foundation

c/o BMO Harris Bank N.A
P.O. Box 2980
Milwaukee, WI 53201-2980 (715) 856-5276
Contact: Fr. Joseph Dorner
Application address: 507 Church St., Wausaukee, WI 54177

Foundation type: Independent foundation
Purpose: Scholarships to Marinette County, WI residents for postsecondary education pursuing careers in education, engineering, medicine, nursing, pharmaceutics, or science.
Financial data: Year ended 12/31/2012. Assets, $1,084,291 (M); Expenditures, $64,979; Total giving, $52,544; Grants to individuals, totaling $52,544.
Fields of interest: Medical school/education; Nursing school/education; Teacher school/education; Engineering school/education; Science.
Type of support: Scholarships—to individuals; Undergraduate support.
Application information: Applications accepted. Application form required.

> *Initial approach:* Letter or telephone
> *Deadline(s):* July 1
> *Additional information:* Applicants should have a minimum 3.3 GPA, a measure of financial need, and show high moral character.

EIN: 391336290

10030
Robert G. Sharp Trust

P.O. Box 66
Athelstane, WI 54104 (715) 856-5114
Contact: Robert G. Sharp

Foundation type: Independent foundation
Purpose: Scholarships to high school graduates of Oconto and Brown counties, WI, for attendance at Marquette University, Lawrence University, St. Norbert College, Beloit College, and any university in the WI system: Eau Claire, Green Bay, La Crosse, Madison, Milwaukee, Oshkosh, Parkside, Platteville, River Falls, Stevens Point, Stout, Superior, and Whitewater.
Publications: Application guidelines.
Financial data: Year ended 08/31/2013. Assets, $531,064 (M); Expenditures, $37,907; Total giving, $12,500.
Fields of interest: Higher education; Scholarships/financial aid.
Type of support: Support to graduates or students of specific schools; Undergraduate support.
Application information: Application form required.

> *Deadline(s):* Apr. 15
> *Additional information:* Application forms and FAF available from high school counselors in Dec. of each year; Applications should be submitted to the high school guidance counselors.

EIN: 396084979

10031
George Sheets Scholarship Trust

c/o U.S. Bank, N.A.
P.O. Box 2043
Milwaukee, WI 53201-9668 (907) 822-5286
*Application address:*c/o Copper River High School, 1976 Aurora Dr.Glennallen,AK 99588

Foundation type: Independent foundation

Purpose: Scholarships to graduates of Belle Plaine High School, IA, or Copper River High School, AK, with a 3.0 GPA or better.
Financial data: Year ended 12/31/2012. Assets, $301,147 (M); Expenditures, $21,496; Total giving, $14,348; Grants to individuals, 2 grants totaling $14,348 (high: $10,761, low: $3,587).
Type of support: Support to graduates or students of specific schools; Undergraduate support.
Application information: Applications accepted. Application form required.
EIN: 426275922

10032
Shopko Foundation, Inc.
P.O. Box 19060
Green Bay, WI 54307-9060 (920) 497-2211
Additional email:
ShopkoFamilyScholarship@Shopko.com
E-mail: ShopkoFoundation@Shopko.com;
URL: http://www.shopko.com/company/community-giving-shopko-foundation

Foundation type: Public charity
Purpose: Scholarships to Shopko Stores, Inc. employees and their dependants for full time undergraduate course of study at an accredited college, university, vocational or technical school.
Publications: Application guidelines.
Financial data: Year ended 12/31/2011. Assets, $1,148,476 (M); Expenditures, $991,450; Total giving, $903,546; Grants to individuals, 20 grants totaling $46,750.
Fields of interest: Vocational education; Higher education.
Type of support: Employee-related scholarships; Scholarships—to individuals.
Application information: Application form required. Application form available on the grantmaker's web site.
Initial approach: Download application online
Deadline(s): Mar. 1
Final notification: Recipients notified May 15
Applicants should submit the following:
1) Transcripts
2) Letter(s) of recommendation
3) GPA
4) Financial information
5) Essay
Additional information: Application must also include a list of activities, awards, and honors. Checks are mailed directly to the educational institution on behalf of the student.
Program description:
Shopko Teammate and Family Scholarship Program: Scholarships of up to $2,500 are available to full- or part-time Shopko employees and their dependent children (under the age of 24), to attend postsecondary accredited programs, including two- or four-year colleges and universities, as well as vocational and technical schools. Scholarships are awarded based on academic record, leadership, participation in school and community activities, work experience, and recommendations. Applicant must be a U.S. citizen and either a Shopko teammate or a dependent child of Shopko teammate.
Company name: Shopko Stores Operating Co., LLC
EIN: 200917227

10033
Siebert Lutheran Foundation, Inc.
300 N. Corporate Dr., Ste. 200
Brookfield, WI 53045-5862 (262) 754-9160
Contact: Ronald D. Jones, Pres.
FAX: (262) 754-9162;
E-mail: contactus@siebertfoundation.org;
URL: http://www.siebertfoundation.org

Foundation type: Independent foundation
Purpose: Grants to seminary students in Wisconsin to defray educational expenses while attending seminary.
Publications: Application guidelines; Annual report.
Financial data: Year ended 12/31/2012. Assets, $87,443,135 (M); Expenditures, $4,672,349; Total giving, $3,654,723.
Fields of interest: Theological school/education.
Type of support: Grants to individuals.
Application information: Applications accepted. Application form required. Application form available on the grantmaker's web site.
Deadline(s): July 1
Final notification: Recipients notified after Sept. 5
Additional information: Applicants should submit the Siebert Lutheran Foundation Financial Aid Application along with a letter from their pastor verifying membership in the Lutheran Congregation. The letter must be on church letterhead and include the dates of membership. Only original copies are accepted. Students serving a vicarship or internship are not eligible.
Program descriptions:
Seminary Tuition Aid: The foundation annually makes grant money available to assist Wisconsin seminary students with their educational expenses at the seminary. Students must be enrolled, full-time in an accredited seminary for the purpose of ordination or leadership in Lutheran pastoral ministry. Students serving a vicarship or internship are not eligible.
Siebert Pastoral Development Program: This program is designed to allow the pastor to create a personal advanced development program, utilizing existing programs and resources available in the marketplace such as, but not limited to, Ministry Advantage, Pastoral Leadership Institute and Leadership Training Network. The pastor is to prepare a plan to include defined desired outcomes for the advanced development program, and how both the pastor and congregation will benefit when the program is completed. The funding may be used for tuition, books, travel expense and a laptop computer, if required by the program. Applications for programs costing less than $2,500 will not be accepted. This program is temporarily suspended. See foundation web site for updates.
EIN: 396050046

10034
Ida M. Sivyer For Trades School
c/o U.S. Bank, N.A.
P.O. Box 7900
Madison, WI 53707-7900 (414) 212-2400
Application address: c/o Bradley Technical High School, 700 S. 4th St., Milwaukee, WI 53204

Foundation type: Independent foundation
Purpose: Scholarships by nomination only to students at Milwaukee Technical High School, WI.
Financial data: Year ended 06/30/2013. Assets, $234,931 (M); Expenditures, $15,065; Total giving, $10,355; Grants to individuals, 5 grants totaling $10,355 (high: $2,071, low: $2,071).

Type of support: Support to graduates or students of specific schools; Awards/grants by nomination only; Undergraduate support.
Application information: Applications not accepted.
Additional information: Unsolicited requests for funds not considered or acknowledged.
EIN: 396035625

10035
Everett Smith Group Foundation, Ltd.
(formerly Maysteel Foundation, Ltd.)
800 N. Marshall St.
Milwaukee, WI 53202-3911 (414) 223-1560
Contact: Becky J. Beth, Treas.

Foundation type: Independent foundation
Purpose: Undergraduate scholarships to children of employees of Maysteel Corporation.
Financial data: Year ended 11/30/2012. Assets, $2,000,994 (M); Expenditures, $227,710; Total giving, $227,650.
Type of support: Employee-related scholarships; Undergraduate support.
Application information: Applications accepted. Application form not required.
Deadline(s): None
Company name: Maysteel Corporation
EIN: 391480641

10036
The Alice Aber Smith Scholarship Fund
441 Milwaukee Ave.
Burlington, WI 53105-0660
Contact: Markus Wegenast, Fdn. Mgr.
Application address: 455 S. Jefferson St., Waterford, WI 53185-4213, tel.: (262) 763-7616

Foundation type: Independent foundation
Purpose: Scholarships to graduates of Racine County, WI, high schools for attendance at colleges and universities that are affiliated with, or governed by a Christian religious organization.
Financial data: Year ended 12/31/2011. Assets, $611,760 (M); Expenditures, $71,158; Total giving, $63,000.
Fields of interest: Christian agencies & churches.
Type of support: Support to graduates or students of specific schools; Undergraduate support.
Application information: Application form required.
Deadline(s): May 1
Applicants should submit the following:
1) Transcripts
2) Letter(s) of recommendation
EIN: 396628593

10037
Society for Obstetric Anesthesia and Perinatology
6737 W. Washington St., Ste. 1300
Milwaukee, WI 53214 (414) 389-8611
Contact: Jane Svinicki, Exec. Dir.
FAX: (414) 276-7704; E-mail: soap@asahq.org;
E-mail For Jane Svinicki: jane@soap.org;
URL: http://www.soap.org

Foundation type: Public charity
Purpose: Grants and awards to obstetric anesthesiologists for use of research.
Publications: Application guidelines; Informational brochure.
Financial data: Year ended 12/31/2011. Assets, $650,855 (M); Expenditures, $684,448; Total giving, $12,998; Grants to individuals, totaling $2,498.

Fields of interest: Reproductive health, OBGYN/Birthing centers; Anesthesiology research.
Type of support: Grants to individuals; Awards/prizes.
Application information: Applications accepted. Application form available on the grantmaker's web site.
Deadline(s): Mar. 22 for SOAP/Kybele International Outreach Grant, Oct. 1 for SOAP/Gertie Marx Education and Research Grant, varies for all others
Additional information: See web site for additional guidelines.
Program descriptions:
Frederick P. Zuspan Award: This $2,000 award is provided to promote collaborative research and scholarships between obstetricians and obstetric anesthesiologists by rewarding the top research paper co-authored by an obstetrician interfacing with an obstetric anesthesiologist. This award is given to one recipient annually who is chosen from a group from potential candidates following presentation of their abstracts at the society annual meeting.
Research in Education Award: A $500 cash award is provided to an outstanding abstract presented to the society. Abstracts may focus on the education of medical students, residents, patients, obstetric care providers, or the community, all health care providers (anesthesiologists, fellows, residents, obstetricians, nurses, etc.) are eligible as long as they are members of the society, or sponsored by a society member.
SOAP Obstetric History Prize: The prize will be awarded for an outstanding project that discusses a historical event (e.g., the development of a piece of equipment used in obstetric anesthesia) of interest to the organization, or a person who was instrumental in the evolution of the subspecialty. The winner of the competition will receive a $250 prize and will be given the opportunity to write an essay on their topic for publication in the SOAP Newsletter.
SOAP/Gertie Marx Education and Research Grant: This program provides up to $50,000 (over two years) to provide initial funding for projects and investigators to support research in obstetric anesthesia or a closely-related area, with the intention that the results of these projects will form the basis of subsequent grant applications to other society, foundation, or federal sources. Fundable projects may include research in basic physiology, clinical practice, or teaching/training methods. Eligible applicants must: be in the early stages of an investigator's career (primarily at the fellow, instructor, or assistant professor level); be a member of the society; and have a research mentor (unless the applicant is at the rank of associate professor or above)
SOAP/Kybele International Outreach Grant: Awarded in conjunction with Kybele, this program provides funding needed to get involved with international outreach projects, in order to identify and train future leaders in international outreach, with the goal of enhancing the practice of obstetric anesthesia in those countries. Grants of up to $5,000 will be provided to cover travel and related expenses for two trips to a country where a Kybele-sponsored program is ongoing. Eligible applicants must be members of the society in good standing, with a commitment to obstetric anesthesia.
EIN: 943079263

10038
Society of St. Vincent de Paul Manitowoc, Inc.
911 Chicago St.
Manitowoc, WI 54220-4027 (920) 662-9452
Contact: Tim Ascher, Treas.
E-mail: vincent4311@sbcglobal.net

Foundation type: Public charity
Purpose: Grants to economically disadvantaged individuals in WI for medical care, rent, utilities, food, lodging and other expenses.
Financial data: Year ended 09/30/2012. Assets, $667,410 (M); Expenditures, $468,491; Total giving, $169,174; Grants to individuals, totaling $164,174.
Fields of interest: Health care; Food services; Housing/shelter; Economically disadvantaged.
Type of support: Grants for special needs.
Application information: Applications accepted.
Additional information: Some support require an application. Contact the organization for eligibility determination.
EIN: 391096113

10039
Sonnentag Foundation
P.O. Box 100
Marathon, WI 54448-0100
Application address: c/o Carolyn Sonnentag, P.O. Box 435, Astatula, FL 34705, tel.: (715) 848-1365

Foundation type: Independent foundation
Purpose: Scholarships to residents of the Marathon, WI area.
Financial data: Year ended 09/30/2012. Assets, $7,492,849 (M); Expenditures, $88,549; Total giving, $87,935; Grants to individuals, 20 grants totaling $87,935 (high: $69,885, low: $500).
Type of support: Undergraduate support.
Application information: Applications accepted. Application form required.
Deadline(s): None
Additional information: Contact foundation for current application guidelines.
EIN: 391597420

10040
Southwest Wisconsin Workforce Development Board, Inc.
1370 N. Water St.
Platteville, WI 53818-1452 (608) 342-4220
Contact: Robert Borremans, Exec. Dir.
FAX: (608) 342-4429;
E-mail: r.borremans@jobcenter.org; URL: http://www.swwdb.org

Foundation type: Public charity
Purpose: Supportive services, including child care, and other forms of financial assistance to job-seekers residing in southwest WI, who wish to participate in and complete job training.
Publications: Newsletter.
Financial data: Year ended 06/30/2011. Assets, $1,463,082 (M); Expenditures, $5,176,888; Total giving, $2,431,025; Grants to individuals, totaling $1,260,656.
Type of support: Grants for special needs.
Application information: Applications not accepted.
Additional information: Unsolicited request for funds not considered or acknowledged.
EIN: 391451363

10041
Hans & Anna Spartvedt Testamentary Trust
c/o M&I Bank
P.O. Box 2977
Milwaukee, WI 53201-2977 (608) 232-2019

Foundation type: Independent foundation
Purpose: Grants for medical expenses to economically disadvantaged individuals who are residents of WI and under the age of 21.
Financial data: Year ended 12/31/2011. Assets, $0 (M); Expenditures, $50,499; Total giving, $47,177.
Fields of interest: Health care; Children/youth, services; Disabilities, people with; Economically disadvantaged.
Type of support: Grants for special needs.
Application information: Applications accepted.
Send request by: Mail
Deadline(s): None
Additional information: Applications should include medical information and family data.
EIN: 396266732

10042
Hugh & Marie Squires Scholarship Foundation Ltd.
3 N. Jackson St.
Elkhorn, WI 53121 (262) 723-3160
Contact: William J. Trewyn, Treas.

Foundation type: Independent foundation
Purpose: Scholarships to graduating seniors of the Elkhorn, WI area for postsecondary education.
Financial data: Year ended 04/30/2013. Assets, $37,133 (M); Expenditures, $4,216; Total giving, $2,000; Grant to an individual, 1 grant totaling $2,000.
Fields of interest: Higher education.
Type of support: Scholarships—to individuals.
Application information: Applications accepted. Application form required.
Additional information: Application forms can be obtained from the foundation.
EIN: 391354516

10043
St. Croix Valley Foundation
516 2nd St., Ste. 214
Hudson, WI 54016 (715) 386-9490
Contact: Jane Hetland Stevenson, Pres.; For grants: Jill A. Shannon, Dir., Community Partnerships
FAX: (715) 386-1250;
E-mail: info@scvfoundation.org; Additional E-mail: jstevenson@scvfoundation.org; Grant inquiry E-mail: jshannon@scvfoundation.org; URL: http://www.scvfoundation.org/

Foundation type: Community foundation
Purpose: Scholarships to individuals in Chisago and Washington counties, MN and Pierce, Polk and St. Croix counties, WI. Also camperships to children with special needs.
Publications: Application guidelines; Annual report; Financial statement; Informational brochure.
Financial data: Year ended 06/30/2012. Assets, $28,405,554 (M); Expenditures, $1,650,721; Total giving, $1,017,405.
Fields of interest: Higher education; Scholarships/financial aid.
Type of support: Employee-related scholarships; Scholarships—to individuals; Support to graduates or students of specific schools; Undergraduate support.

Application information: Applications accepted. Application form required.

Copies of proposal: 8

Deadline(s): Varies

Additional information: See web site for complete listing of scholarships and guidelines.

Program description:

Scholarships: The foundation administers various scholarships established by donors for residents of the St. Croix Valley region for higher education. Each scholarship has its own unique application guidelines and eligibility criteria, including students who are dependents of certain local companies, students who are graduating from specific high schools, and students pursuing specified majors such as business, music and medicine.

EIN: 411817315

10044
St. Elizabeth Hospital Community Foundation

(formerly St. Elizabeth Hospital Foundation)
1506 S. Oneida St.
Appleton, WI 54915-1305 (920) 831-1475
Contact: Tonya Dedering, Exec. Dir.
FAX: (920) 738-2061;
E-mail: sehf@affinityhealth.org; E-Mail for Tonya Dedering: tdederin@affinityhealth.org; Tel. for Tonya Dedering: (920)-738-2859; URL: http://www.affinityhealth.org/page/about-foundations-elizabeth

Foundation type: Public charity
Purpose: Financial assistance to disadvantaged residents of the Appleton, WI, area.
Publications: Application guidelines; Annual report; Financial statement.
Financial data: Year ended 09/30/2011. Assets, $11,017,849 (M); Expenditures, $2,397,251; Total giving, $1,717,545; Grants to individuals, totaling $53,329.
Fields of interest: Public health; Aging, centers/services; Human services; Economically disadvantaged.
Type of support: Grants for special needs.
Application information: Applications accepted. Application form required. Application form available on the grantmaker's web site.

Initial approach: See foundation web site for information

Program description:

Grants: The foundation accepts applications for funds to address the needs of the poor, elderly, disadvantaged and medically underserved in Appleton, WI and all communities north of Neenah, extending west to New London and Clintonville, and east to Kiel and Chilton.

EIN: 391256677

10045
Wilbert & Evelyn St. John Scholarship Trust

3913 W. Prospect Ave., Ste. 201
Appleton, WI 54914-8209 (920) 986-3351
Application address: c/o Shiocton High School, Attn.: Guidance Counselor, N5650 Broad St., Shiocton, WI, 54170-8626, tel.: (920) 986-3351

Foundation type: Independent foundation
Purpose: Scholarships to graduates of Shiocton High School, WI, who will be attending the University of Wisconsin's Madison, WI, campus.
Financial data: Year ended 12/31/2012. Assets, $774,934 (M); Expenditures, $52,480; Total

giving, $44,999; Grants to individuals, 6 grants totaling $44,999 (high: $11,072, low: $4,640).
Type of support: Support to graduates or students of specific schools; Undergraduate support.
Application information: Applications accepted. Application form required.

Initial approach: Letter

Deadline(s): Mar. 1

Additional information: Application can be obtained from high school guidance counselor.

EIN: 207023185

10046
Arnold P. Stamm Scholarship Trust

P.O. Box 2977
Milwaukee, WI 53201-2977 (920) 867-2156
Contact: David L. Werth
Application address: c/o David L. Werth, P.O. Box 515, Weyauwega, WI 54983-0515 Tel: (920) 867-2156

Foundation type: Independent foundation
Purpose: Scholarships to individuals who reside in the Weyauwega-Fremont School District, WI.
Financial data: Year ended 03/31/2012. Assets, $628,435 (M); Expenditures, $40,274; Total giving, $30,400; Grants to individuals, totaling $30,400 (high: $3,400, low: $400).
Type of support: Scholarships—to individuals.
Application information: Applications accepted.

Deadline(s): May 1

EIN: 396582045

10047
The Stateline Community Foundation

(formerly The Greater Beloit Community Foundation)
690 3rd St., Ste. 110
Beloit, WI 53511-6210 (608) 362-4228
Contact: Tara Jean Tinder, Exec. Dir.
FAX: (608) 362-0056; E-mail: statelinecf@aol.com; Additional E-mail: tara@statelinecf.com; URL: http://www.statelinecf.org

Foundation type: Community foundation
Purpose: Scholarships to residents of the greater Beloit, WI, area for higher education.
Publications: Application guidelines; Annual report; Grants list; Informational brochure; Newsletter.
Financial data: Year ended 12/31/2011. Assets, $9,664,187 (M); Expenditures, $674,848; Total giving, $345,929; Grants to individuals, totaling $133,217.
Fields of interest: Higher education.
Type of support: Scholarships—to individuals; Graduate support; Undergraduate support.
Application information: Applications accepted. Application form required. Application form available on the grantmaker's web site.

Initial approach: Application

Send request by: Online

Deadline(s): Feb. 1

Applicants should submit the following:

1) Letter(s) of recommendation
2) Transcripts
3) FAFSA
4) Essay
5) Photograph
6) Resume
7) SAT
8) ACT
9) Class rank

Additional information: Eligibility criteria varies for each scholarship. See web site for complete application guidelines.

EIN: 391585271

10048
George E. Stifel Scholarship Fund

c/o JPMorgan Chase Bank, N.A.
P.O. Box 3038
Milwaukee, WI 53201-3038 (304) 234-4130
Application address: c/o JPMorgan Chase Bank, N.A., Tr. Dept., 1114 Market St., Wheeling, WV 26003-2906, tel.: (304) 234-4130

Foundation type: Independent foundation
Purpose: Scholarships to graduates of Ohio County, WV, high schools.
Financial data: Year ended 04/30/2012. Assets, $1,421,355 (M); Expenditures, $79,298; Total giving, $57,900; Grants to individuals, 28 grants totaling $57,900 (high: $7,500, low: $500).
Type of support: Undergraduate support.
Application information: Applications accepted. Application form required. Interview required.

Deadline(s): Contact fund for application deadlines.

Additional information: In awarding the scholarships, the trustees consider the personality of each applicant, academic achievement, extracurricular activities, deportment, spirit of cooperation with school authorities, and the general promise the applicant shows of becoming a better citizen if given the opportunity of a college education. Scholarships are renewable for up to four years.

EIN: 556018248

10049
Suder-Pick Foundation, Inc.

c/o George A. Dionisopoulos
777 E. Wisconsin Ave.
Milwaukee, WI 53202-5306 (414) 297-5750

Foundation type: Independent foundation
Purpose: Scholarships to graduating seniors of West Bend High School, WI for postsecondary education.
Financial data: Year ended 12/31/2012. Assets, $65,639 (M); Expenditures, $72,410; Total giving, $66,000; Grants to individuals, 20 grants totaling $66,000 (high: $4,000, low: $2,000).
Type of support: Support to graduates or students of specific schools; Undergraduate support.
Application information: Applications accepted. Application form not required.

Initial approach: Letter

EIN: 396048255

10050
Tate Family Foundation, Inc.

(formerly Joseph P. Tate Foundation)
W326N6611 Sylvian Dr.
Hartland, WI 53029-8544

Foundation type: Independent foundation
Purpose: Scholarships to students attending Fort Atkinson High School, WI, who are related to an employee of Superior Services.
Financial data: Year ended 12/31/2012. Assets, $398,280 (M); Expenditures, $16,393; Total giving, $15,000.
Fields of interest: Education.
Type of support: Scholarships—to individuals.
Application information:

Deadline(s): June 1

Additional information: Contact foundation for current application guidelines.

EIN: 391790720

10051
David E. Thomas Trust
704 Main St.
Wausaukee, WI 54177-8950

Foundation type: Independent foundation
Purpose: Scholarships to graduates of Wausaukee, Pembine and Crivitz high schools, WI.
Financial data: Year ended 12/31/2011. Assets, $1,320,441 (M); Expenditures, $63,938; Total giving, $52,000.
Type of support: Support to graduates or students of specific schools; Undergraduate support.
Application information: Applications not accepted.
  Additional information: Unsolicited requests for funds not considered or acknowledged.
EIN: 396156536

10052
Tomah PTA Scholarship Trust
c/o Clifton Gunderson, LLP
P.O. Box 547
Tomah, WI 54660 (608) 374-7004
Application address: c/o Tomah Senior High School, 129 W. Clifton St., Tomah, WI 54660

Foundation type: Independent foundation
Purpose: Scholarships to graduates of Tomah Senior High School, WI seeking assistance for higher education.
Financial data: Year ended 12/31/2012. Assets, $206,846 (M); Expenditures, $13,226; Total giving, $12,250; Grants to individuals, 13 grants totaling $12,250 (high: $1,000, low: $750).
Fields of interest: Higher education.
Type of support: Support to graduates or students of specific schools.
Application information: Applications accepted. Application form required.
  Additional information: Application should include financial need, scholastic history, and participation in school and community activities.
EIN: 396078616

10053
Trek Scholarship Foundation Inc.
801 W. Madison St.
Waterloo, WI 53594-1379 (920) 478-2191
Contact: Mark Joslyn, Dir.
E-mail: mark_joslyn@trekbikes.com

Foundation type: Independent foundation
Purpose: Scholarships to Wisconsin residents for tuition, housing, books, fees and/or transportation expenses at any accredited postsecondary educational program/institution.
Financial data: Year ended 07/31/2012. Assets, $3,731,284 (M); Expenditures, $273,145; Total giving, $232,750.
Fields of interest: Higher education.
Type of support: Scholarships—to individuals.
Application information: Applications accepted. Application form required. Interview required.
  Deadline(s): Vary
  Final notification: Recipients notified in June
  Applicants should submit the following:
    1) Photograph
    2) Transcripts
    3) Resume
    4) Letter(s) of recommendation
    5) Financial information
    6) Essay
EIN: 204143271

10054
Grace F. Tschirgi Trust
(formerly Grace F. Tschirgi Scholarship Fund)
P.O. Box 2043
Milwaukee, WI 53201-9668 (319) 365-9461

Foundation type: Independent foundation
Purpose: Scholarships to residents of Linn County, IA.
Financial data: Year ended 05/31/2013. Assets, $903,326 (M); Expenditures, $52,798; Total giving, $39,738.
Type of support: Scholarships—to individuals.
Application information: Applications accepted. Application form not required.
  Deadline(s): None
EIN: 426054236

10055
University of Wisconsin Medical Foundation, Inc.
7974 UW Health Ct.
Middleton, WI 53562-5531 (608)821-4223
Contact: Jeffrey Grossman M.D., Pres. and C.E.O.
FAX: (608) 821-4103; URL: http://www.uwhealth.org/about-uwhealth/university-of-wisconsin-medical-foundation/11014

Foundation type: Public charity
Purpose: Scholarships to employees children pursuing a career in the healthcare field.
Financial data: Year ended 06/30/2012. Assets, $406,450,936 (M); Expenditures, $640,051,467; Total giving, $49,127,998; Grants to individuals, totaling $24,750.
Fields of interest: Medical school/education; Health care.
Type of support: Scholarships—to individuals.
Application information: Applications not accepted.
  Additional information: Scholarships for employees children only. Unsolicited requests for funds not considered or acknowledged.
EIN: 391824445

10056
University of Wisconsin River Falls Foundation
410 S. 3rd St.
River Falls, WI 54022-5010 (715) 425-3505
Contact: Alicia Rivard, Off. Mgr.
FAX: (715) 425-3506;
E-mail: foundation@uwrf.edu; Toll-free tel.: (877) 258-6647; Email For Alicia Rivard: alicia.rivard@uwrf.edu; URL: http://www.uwrf.edu/UniversityAdvancement/Foundation/

Foundation type: Public charity
Purpose: Scholarships to students of University of Wisconsin-River Falls.
Publications: Annual report.
Financial data: Year ended 06/30/2012. Assets, $17,908,193 (M); Expenditures, $2,870,787; Total giving, $1,515,425; Grants to individuals, totaling $603,485.
Type of support: Support to graduates or students of specific schools.
Application information: Applications not accepted.
  Additional information: Unsolicited requests for funds not considered or acknowledged.
EIN: 396064630

10057
UW - Whitewater Foundation
800 W. Main St.
Whitewater, WI 53190-1790 (262) 472-1105
Contact: Jonathan C. Enslin, Pres.

Foundation type: Public charity
Purpose: Scholarships and awards for students attending the University of Wisconsin-Whitewater, WI.
Financial data: Year ended 06/30/2012. Assets, $21,005,964 (M); Expenditures, $3,170,183; Total giving, $1,178,141; Grants to individuals, totaling $884,692.
Fields of interest: Higher education.
Type of support: Support to graduates or students of specific schools.
Application information: Applications accepted. Application form required. Application form available on the grantmaker's web site.
  Send request by: Online
  Deadline(s): Feb.
EIN: 396081189

10058
Rino & Ruth Della Vedova Scholarship Trust
c/o U.S. Bank, N.A.
P.O. Box 2043
Milwaukee, WI 53201-9668 (641) 683-2045
Application address: c/o US Bank N.A., 123 E. 3rd St., Ottumwa, IA 52501

Foundation type: Independent foundation
Purpose: Scholarships to graduates of Albia Community High School, IA, who are pursuing an engineering degree.
Financial data: Year ended 06/30/2013. Assets, $1,855,396 (M); Expenditures, $119,113; Total giving, $93,131; Grants to individuals, 13 grants totaling $93,131 (high: $10,000, low: $5,000).
Fields of interest: Engineering school/education.
Type of support: Support to graduates or students of specific schools; Undergraduate support.
Application information: Application form required.
  Deadline(s): Apr. 1
  Additional information: Application should include a one-page letter detailing education and career interests and goals, description of other personal interests and extracurricular activities or extraordinary factors which should be considered.
EIN: 421368808

10059
Viroqua Area Foundation
P. O. Box 262
Viroqua, WI 54665-1605 (608) 637-6850
Contact: Thor Thorson, Pres.
FAX: (608) 637-3394;
E-mail: info@viroquaareafoundation.org; Cell: (608) 778-7199; URL: http://www.viroquaareafoundation.org

Foundation type: Community foundation
Purpose: Scholarships to qualifying students of the Viroqua, WI area for continuing education at accredited colleges or universities.
Financial data: Year ended 12/31/2012. Assets, $585,514 (M); Expenditures, $67,373; Total giving, $65,250; Grants to individuals, 18 grants totaling $8,900.
Fields of interest: Higher education.
Type of support: Scholarships—to individuals.
Application information: Applications accepted. Application form required.

Additional information: See web site for scholarships details.
EIN: 391603279

10060
Edward and Frieda Wagner Scholarship Fund
P.O. Box 12800
Green Bay, WI 54307-2800 (715) 478-3339

Foundation type: Independent foundation
Purpose: Scholarships to two high school graduating seniors of Crandon High School, WI for postsecondary education.
Financial data: Year ended 11/30/2012. Assets, $75,748 (M); Expenditures, $5,959; Total giving, $3,794.
Fields of interest: Higher education.
Type of support: Support to graduates or students of specific schools.
Application information: Applications accepted.
Deadline(s): Apr.
EIN: 396698990

10061
The Wahlin Foundation, Inc.
416 S. Academy St.
P.O. Box 328
Stoughton, WI 53589-0328

Foundation type: Independent foundation
Purpose: Scholarships to residents of WI for attendance at WI schools.
Financial data: Year ended 12/31/2012. Assets, $2,892,838 (M); Expenditures, $167,956; Total giving, $103,300.
Type of support: Undergraduate support.
Application information: Applications not accepted.
Additional information: Unsolicited requests for funds not considered or acknowledged.
EIN: 391948530

10062
Walker Scholarship Grant
c/o US Bank N.A
P.O. Box 7900
Madison, WI 53707-7900 (319) 335-2164
Application address: 314 Gilmore Hall, Iowa City, IA 52242-1376

Foundation type: Operating foundation
Purpose: Scholarships to promising students who are residents of IA, for attending seminary or religious training.
Financial data: Year ended 08/31/2012. Assets, $37,298 (M); Expenditures, $44,117; Total giving, $42,500; Grants to individuals, 7 grants totaling $42,500 (high: $7,500, low: $5,000).
Fields of interest: Theological school/education; Religion.
Type of support: Scholarships—to individuals.
Application information: Applications accepted. Application form required.
Deadline(s): Feb. 15
Additional information: Application can be obtained from the University of Iowa, School of Religion.
EIN: 237435737

10063
Ward Scholarship Fund
P.O. Box 12800
Green Bay, WI 54307-2800

Foundation type: Independent foundation
Purpose: Scholarships only to students of St. Mary's Catholic High School, Menasha, WI or Neenah High School, WI.
Financial data: Year ended 03/31/2013. Assets, $313,063 (M); Expenditures, $19,180; Total giving, $14,642.
Fields of interest: Higher education.
Type of support: Scholarships—to individuals; Support to graduates or students of specific schools.
Application information: Application form required.
Initial approach: Letter
Deadline(s): Mar. 30
Additional information: Applications can be obtained from either high school. Unsolicited requests fro funds not considered or acknowledged.
EIN: 396457338

10064
Watertown Area Community Foundation
c/o Thomas Levi
P.O. Box 351
Watertown, WI 53094-0351 (920) 261-8720
Contact: Tom Schultz, Pres.

Foundation type: Community foundation
Purpose: Scholarships to individuals of Watertown, WI, for higher education based on merit and need.
Financial data: Year ended 06/30/2012. Assets, $4,514,019 (M); Expenditures, $213,895; Total giving, $179,833; Grants to individuals, totaling $160,000.
Fields of interest: Higher education; Nursing school/education.
Type of support: Scholarships—to individuals.
Application information: Contact foundation for application guidelines and a listing of scholarship programs.
EIN: 391708484

10065
Waukesha Ozaukee Washington Workforce Development, Inc.
892 Main St. Ste A
Pewaukee, WI 53072-5808
URL: http://www.wowwdb.org

Foundation type: Public charity
Purpose: Grants to residents of Waukesha, Ozaukee and Washington counties, WI, who were laid off from companies that closed or downsized significantly.
Publications: Annual report.
Financial data: Year ended 06/30/2011. Assets, $1,333,230 (M); Expenditures, $5,548,102; Total giving, $1,332,684; Grants to individuals, totaling $105,552.
Fields of interest: Business/industry.
Type of support: Grants to individuals.
Application information:
Initial approach: Telephone or letter
EIN: 391657328

10066
Weather Shield LITE Foundation
1 Weather Shield Plz.
Medford, WI 54451-2206
Contact: Kevin Schield, Pres.
FAX: (715) 748-6508;
E-mail: litefoundation@weathershield.com;
URL: http://www.weathershield.com/WhyWS/OurStory/LITEFoundation.aspx

Foundation type: Public charity
Purpose: General welfare grants to employees of Weather Shield for assistance with medical bills and expenses due to catastrophic events such as fires and tornadoes.
Publications: Application guidelines.
Financial data: Year ended 12/31/2011. Assets, $7,092 (M); Expenditures, $44,750; Total giving, $44,750; Grants to individuals, totaling $8,840.
Type of support: Emergency funds; Employee-related welfare; Grants for special needs.
Application information: Applications accepted. Application form required.
Initial approach: Letter to request application form
Additional information: See web site for further information.
Company name: Weather Shield Manufacturing, Inc.
EIN: 391978784

10067
Edna Weigel Scholarship Fund Trust
P.O. Box 2977
Milwaukee, WI 53201-2977 (414) 262-7500
Application address: c/o Watertown High School, Attn.: Guidance Off., 825 Endeavour Dr., Watertown, WI 53098-1728, tel.: (414) 262-7500

Foundation type: Independent foundation
Purpose: Scholarships to financially needy graduates of Watertown Senior High School, WI, for full-time enrollment in Wisconsin institutions with accredited baccalaureate programs.
Financial data: Year ended 05/31/2012. Assets, $338,618 (M); Expenditures, $35,579; Total giving, $30,000; Grants to individuals, 7 grants totaling $13,500.
Type of support: Support to graduates or students of specific schools; Undergraduate support.
Application information: Application form required.
Deadline(s): None
EIN: 396618926

10068
Loretta A. Wells Nursing Scholarship Trust
c/o JPMorgan Chase Bank, N.A.
P.O. Box 3038
Milwaukee, WI 53201 (920) 735-1382
Application address: 200 W. College Ave., Fl. 3, Appleton, WI 54911, tel.: (920) 735-1382

Foundation type: Independent foundation
Purpose: Scholarships to nursing students who are residents of Brown county, WI enrolled in their junior or senior year of the BSN program or enrolled in the MSN program.
Financial data: Year ended 07/31/2011. Assets, $1,474,622 (M); Expenditures, $47,522; Total giving, $30,000.
Fields of interest: Nursing school/education.
Type of support: Undergraduate support.
Application information: Applications accepted. Application form required. Interview required.
Deadline(s): Apr. 30

Additional information: Application forms are available from the nursing schools in Brown county, WI.

EIN: 396364734

10069
West Central Wisconsin Community Action Agency, Inc.

525 2nd St.
P.O. Box 308
Glenwood City, WI 54013-0308 (715) 265-4271
Contact: Peter Kilde, Exec. Dir.
FAX: (715) 265-7718; E-mail: westcap@wcap.org; Toll Free Tel.: (800)-606-9227; URL: http://westcap.org/

Foundation type: Public charity
Purpose: Services to indigent residents of west central Wisconsin such as home weatherization, energy/rent/utility/mortgage assistance, transportation, and adult education assistance.
Financial data: Year ended 06/30/2011. Assets, $14,567,212 (M); Expenditures, $11,809,907; Total giving, $4,496,028; Grants to individuals, totaling $4,496,028.
Application information:
   Initial approach: E-mail
   Applicants should submit the following:
      1) Financial information
   Additional information: Contact foundation for eligibility criteria.
EIN: 391076125

10070
Alpha A. Wetenkamp Charitable Trust

2448 S. 102nd St., Ste. 170
West Allis, WI 53227-2141 (414) 545-5450
Contact: Alfred A. Drosen, Jr., Tr.

Foundation type: Independent foundation
Purpose: Scholarships to students of Milwaukee, WI pursuing a degree in one of the required fields of education at a college or university in the Milwaukee Metropolitan area.
Financial data: Year ended 12/31/2011. Assets, $165,984 (M); Expenditures, $1,143; Total giving, $0.
Fields of interest: Higher education.
Type of support: Scholarships—to individuals.
Application information: Applications accepted.
   Deadline(s): Before the start of the semester
EIN: 207086634

10071
Margaret Wiegand Trust

c/o JPMorgan Chase Bank, N.A.
P.O. Box 3038
Milwaukee, WI 53201-1308 (214) 965-2908
Contact: Anne McCullough
Application address: c/o JPMorgan Chase Bank, N.A., 2200 Ross Ave., 5th Fl., Dallas, TX 75201-2744, tel.: (214) 965-2908

Foundation type: Independent foundation
Purpose: Grants to legally blind persons in Waukesha County, WI for their educational needs, care, and maintenance.
Financial data: Year ended 08/31/2011. Assets, $144,632 (M); Expenditures, $8,648; Total giving, $5,200.
Fields of interest: Disabilities, people with.
Type of support: Grants for special needs.
Application information:
   Deadline(s): None

Additional information: Applicants referrals must be from Waukesha Rehabilitation Office and service organizations supporting legally blind individuals.
EIN: 396281352

10072
Charles Joseph Wilber Educational Scholarship Trust

c/o M&I Bank
P.O. Box 2977
Milwaukee, WI 53201 (715) 847-4606
Application address: c/o Supt. of Schools, Tomahawk High School, 1048 E. Kings Rd., Tomahawk, WI 54487

Foundation type: Independent foundation
Purpose: Scholarships to graduates of Tomahawk High School, WI pursuing a career in law or medicine.
Financial data: Year ended 08/31/2012. Assets, $0 (M); Expenditures, $107,678; Total giving, $105,162.
Fields of interest: Law school/education; Medical school/education.
Type of support: Support to graduates or students of specific schools; Undergraduate support.
Application information: Applications accepted. Application form required.
   Additional information: Students should contact their high school guidance office for application information.
EIN: 396371278

10073
Windhover Foundation, Inc.

W224 N3322 Duplainville Rd.
Sussex, WI 53072-4137
E-mail: contact@windhoverfoundation.org; URL: https://www.windhoverfoundation.org/

Foundation type: Company-sponsored foundation
Purpose: Scholarships to children of employees of Quad/Graphics for higher education.
Publications: Application guidelines.
Financial data: Year ended 12/31/2012. Assets, $82,336,076 (M); Expenditures, $3,526,150; Total giving, $3,230,885; Grants to individuals, 188 grants totaling $308,000 (high: $2,500, low: $1,000).
Type of support: Employee-related scholarships.
Application information: Applications not accepted.
   Additional information: Unsolicited requests for funds not considered or acknowledged.
Company name: Quad/Graphics, Inc.
EIN: 391482470

10074
Wisconsin Covenant Foundation, Inc.

2401 International Ln.
Madison, WI 53704-3121
Contact: Amy Kerwin
E-mail: wcfi@wisconsincovenantfoundation.org; Toll-free tel.: (877) 396-6249; URL: https://www.wisconsincovenantfoundation.org/

Foundation type: Public charity
Purpose: Financial assistance to low income students of WI for postsecondary education.
Publications: Occasional report.
Financial data: Year ended 06/30/2012. Assets, $40,893,252 (M); Expenditures, $796,871; Total giving, $763,158; Grants to individuals, totaling $763,158.

Fields of interest: Higher education; Scholarships/financial aid.
Type of support: Scholarships—to individuals.
Application information: Applications accepted.
   Initial approach: Telephone
   Deadline(s): May 9
   Additional information: Contact the foundation for additional application guidelines.
Program description:
   Wisconsin Covenant Program: The Foundation's first public-private partnership began with its pledge to provide additional financial aid to support Wisconsin Covenant Scholars from low-income households. The Wisconsin Covenant program was designed by the state to inspire and reward Wisconsin's young people who work hard in high school and prepare for college. Whereas the Wisconsin Covenant program was open to all state eighth-grade students between 2007 and 2011, the Foundation committed to making grants specifically for those Wisconsin Covenant Scholars who have significant financial need, helping to make higher education possible for all. Although the state program is now closed to new students, the Foundation remains committed to supporting the students who have signed the Wisconsin Covenant pledge and are working to become Scholars. To that end, the Foundation has committed annual grants of up to $1,500 to eligible Scholars for up to four years of college, over a five-year period. This amount works together with the state's Wisconsin Covenant Scholars Grant to provide eligible Scholars up to $2,500 per year, for a total of up to $10,000.
EIN: 261550326

10075
Wisconsin Early Childhood Association, Inc.

744 Williamson St., Ste. 200
Madison, WI 53703-4579 (608) 240-9880
Contact: Ruth Schmidt, Exec. Dir.
FAX: (608) 663-1091;
E-mail: weca@wecanaeyc.org; Additional address: 1556 N. Farwell Ave., Milwaukee, WI 53202, tel.: (414) 278-9322, fax: (414) 278-9336; E-mail for Ruth Schmidt: ruschmidt@wisconsinearlychildhood.org; URL: http://www.wecanaeyc.org/

Foundation type: Public charity
Purpose: Scholarships to WI residents planning to study early childhood education or care at a college or university in WI. Also, grants to child care providers, child care center teachers, assistant teachers, center directors, and administrators in WI.
Publications: Application guidelines; Informational brochure.
Financial data: Year ended 09/30/2011. Assets, $5,719,437 (M); Expenditures, $13,241,349; Total giving, $9,403,327; Grants to individuals, totaling $9,403,327.
Fields of interest: Children/youth, services; Day care.
Type of support: Grants to individuals; Undergraduate support.
Application information: Applications accepted. Application form required. Application form available on the grantmaker's web site.
   Initial approach: Letter
   Final notification: Applicants notified in approximately four to six weeks
   Additional information: See web site for complete program information.
EIN: 391345572

10076
Wisconsin Eastern Star Foundation

1361 Mockingbird Dr.
Oconomowoc, WI 53066-2381 (608) 635-8801
Contact: Karen Carpenter, Secy.
Application address: 908 Hillpoint Ct, Poynette WI
53955

Foundation type: Independent foundation
Purpose: Financial assistance to needy individuals,
primarily in WI.
Financial data: Year ended 12/31/2012. Assets,
$287,242 (M); Expenditures, $28,681; Total
giving, $22,071; Grants to individuals, 27 grants
totaling $21,976 (high: $4,800, low: $25).
Type of support: Grants for special needs.
Application information: Applications accepted.
Application form required.
   Deadline(s): None
   Additional information: Applicant must
      demonstrate need.
EIN: 396059144

10077
Wisconsin Indianhead Technical College Foundation

505 Pine Ridge Dr.
Shell Lake, WI 54871-0452 (715) 468-2815
Contact: Craig Fowler, Exec. Dir.
FAX: (715) 468-2819;
E-mail: craig.fowler@witc.edu; TTY: (715)
468-7755; URL: http://www.witc.edu/foundation

Foundation type: Public charity
Purpose: Scholarships to deserving incoming and
continuing students for attendance at Wisconsin
Indianhead Technical College, WI for postsecondary
education.
Publications: Annual report.
Financial data: Year ended 06/30/2011. Assets,
$2,861,405 (M); Expenditures, $588,269; Total
giving, $157,494; Grants to individuals, totaling
$157,494.
Fields of interest: Vocational education,
post-secondary.
Type of support: Support to graduates or students
of specific schools.
Application information: Applications accepted.
Application form required.
   Deadline(s): Nov. 1 and Apr. 1
   Additional information: Students must be
      enrolled in a minimum of six credits per
      semester to be eligible to apply.
Program description:
   Scholarships: Scholarships ranging from $100 to
$1,000 are available to students enrolled in
associate degree and diploma programs at
Wisconsin Indianhead Technical College campuses
in Ashland, New Richmond, Rice Lake, and
Superior. Scholarships are awarded to students
enrolled in a minimum of six credits per semester
who demonstrate good academic progress and who
have the initiative, desire, and potential to succeed.
EIN: 391313438

10078
Wisconsin Institute of Certified Public Accountants Educational Foundation, Inc.

235 N. Executive Dr., Ste. 200
Brookfield, WI 53005-6000 (262) 785-0445
Contact: Robert A. Gruber, Pres.
FAX: (262) 785-0838;
E-mail: comments@wicpa.org; Toll-free tel.: (800)
772-6939; URL: http://www.wicpa.org

Foundation type: Public charity
Purpose: Scholarships to students studying
accounting at WI universities.
Publications: Application guidelines.
Financial data: Year ended 04/30/2012. Assets,
$1,688,302 (M); Expenditures, $162,982; Total
giving, $59,500; Grants to individuals, totaling
$59,500.
Fields of interest: Business school/education.
Type of support: Scholarships—to individuals.
Application information: Applications accepted.
Application form available on the grantmaker's web
site.
   Deadline(s): Contact funds for deadline
Program description:
   Scholarships: The foundation provides
scholarships to recipients residing in Wisconsin
who are attending a Wisconsin college or university
enrolled in an accounting program which qualifies
the applicant to sit for the C.P.A. exam. Eight
$5,000 scholarships will be awarded to students
pursuing a master's degree and up to three $2,500
scholarships will be awarded to students pursuing
an undergraduate degree in Accounting.
EIN: 237109897

10079
Wisconsin Masonic Foundation

36275 Sunset Dr.
Dousman, WI 53118-9349 (262) 965-2200
Contact: Erika L. Miller, Devel. Coord.
FAX: (262) 965-4211;
E-mail: plannedgiving@gmail.com; URL: http://
www.wisc-freemasonry.org/

Foundation type: Public charity
Purpose: Scholarships to college bound high school
graduates of WI who show leadership for
attendance at a two or four year college.
Publications: Annual report; Informational
brochure.
Financial data: Year ended 04/30/2012. Assets,
$22,066,763 (M); Expenditures, $1,271,709;
Total giving, $1,061,221; Grants to individuals,
totaling $179,508.
Fields of interest: Higher education.
Type of support: Undergraduate support.
Application information:
   Deadline(s): Apr. 29
EIN: 396044637

10080
Wisconsin Medical Society Foundation, Inc.

(formerly State Medical Society Foundation)
330 E. Lakeside St.
P.O. Box 1109
Madison, WI 53715-2074 (608) 442-3800
Contact: Eileen Wilson, Exec. Dir.
E-mail: eileen.wilson@wismed.org; URL: https://
www.wisconsinmedicalsociety.org/about-us/
foundation/

Foundation type: Public charity
Purpose: Scholarships and student loans to
medical school students in WI.
Publications: Application guidelines; Financial
statement; Grants list; Informational brochure;
Newsletter.
Financial data: Year ended 12/31/2011. Assets,
$11,370,544 (M); Expenditures, $752,228; Total
giving, $325,415; Grants to individuals, totaling
$105,250.
Fields of interest: Medical school/education;
Research; Public education; Native Americans/
American Indians.

Type of support: Program development;
Fellowships; Research; Scholarships—to
individuals; Student loans—to individuals; Support
to graduates or students of specific schools;
Awards/prizes; Graduate support; Postgraduate
support; Stipends.
Application information: Applications accepted.
Application form required. Application form
available on the grantmaker's web site.
   Initial approach: Application
   Copies of proposal: 7
   Deadline(s): Feb. 1
   Additional information: Applications for
      scholarships and student loans should
      include an essay, FAFSA, financial
      information, GPA, letter of recommendation,
      and transcripts should be sent via mail.
      Recipients notified in 60 days. Applications
      for health care specialists should include an
      essay, proposal and letter of
      recommendation. Contact foundation for
      further application guidelines.
Program descriptions:
   Amy Hunter-Wilson, M.D., Scholarship: This fund
works to assist American Indians who are pursuing
training or advanced education as doctors of
medicine, nurses, or in related health careers.
Eligible applicants must be a U.S. citizen who is an
enrolled member of a federally-recognized American
Indian tribe; and must be enrolled in an accredited
technical school, college, or university in a medical
or health-related program (including medical
doctors, physician assistants, nurses, technicians,
and other health careers). Eligible applicants also
include adults returning to school in a health
care-related field, or those currently working in a
non-professional health-related field who are
pursuing a professional license or degree, as well
as undergraduate students majoring in a
health-related field or pre-med program. Preference
will be given to candidates from Wisconsin who are
attending an educational institution in Wisconsin;
awards are generally at least $1,000 per year.
   Goodman-Goodell Scholarship: Awards from this
fund are limited to second-year medical students
from the Portage, Wisconsin area who express an
interest in specializing in pulmonary medicine or in
general family practice.
   John D. and Virginia Riesch Scholarship: This fund
provides scholarships for students pursuing
careers as physicians or nurses. Eligible medical
doctors applicants must be attending the University
of Wisconsin School of Medicine and Public Health,
while nursing students must be attending the
University of Wisconsin-Madison. Preference will be
given to students who desire to practice in
Wisconsin.
   Robert Jason Gore Scholarship: Scholarships are
available to Wisconsin medical students who
exemplify the qualities of chivalry, honor, and loyalty
to their patients and the communities in which they
live.
   Robert T. Cooney, M.D. Scholarship: A $5,000
scholarship is available to medical students who
show strong interest in practicing in Wisconsin.
   Rukmini and Joyce Vasudevan Scholarship:
Through this fund, scholarships are made available
to Wisconsin-based female students who will be
entering their third or fourth year in medical school
in the fall.
   *Summer Fellowships in Government and
Community Service:* A $3,500 stipend is awarded to
Wisconsin medical school students to work on a
project in partnership with the public health sector
to advance the foundation's mission.
   Victor A. Baylon, M.D., Memorial Scholarship: This
scholarship program assists outstanding studies
from Racine and Milwaukee counties who wish to

pursue training or advanced education as doctors of medicine, medical technologists, or clinical laboratory scientists. Eligible applicants must be U.S. citizens who are enrolled full-time in an accredited clinical laboratory scientist/medical technologist program, or in medical school. Preference will be given to candidates from Wisconsin who are attending an educational institution in Wisconsin.

Wisconsin Medical Society Presidential Scholar Award: This $3,000 award recognizes a fourth-year medical student who has exemplified the attributes, skills, and desire to become a leader in the medical profession in Wisconsin. Eligible applicants must: be U.S. citizens; be full-time students enrolled in a medical school in Wisconsin and entering their fourth year; and demonstrate active involvement with the Wisconsin Medical Society or a Wisconsin county medical society. Preference will be given to candidates from Wisconsin who are attending an educational institution in Wisconsin, as well as to those applicants who show strong interest in practicing in Wisconsin, especially in areas of need.
EIN: 396045649

10081
Wisconsin Public Service Foundation

(formerly WPS Foundation, Inc.)
700 N. Adams St.
P.O. Box 19001
Green Bay, WI 54307-9001
URL: http://www.wisconsinpublicservice.com/company/foundation.aspx

Foundation type: Company-sponsored foundation
Purpose: Grants to educators or teams of educators with projects designed to improve student achievement. Scholarships to children of WPS employees and to children of customers with a primary residence in WPS territory to pursue higher education. Scholarships to women, minorities, and returning adults to pursue higher education.
Publications: Application guidelines; Grants list; Informational brochure.
Financial data: Year ended 12/31/2012. Assets, $21,638,329 (M); Expenditures, $1,117,131; Total giving, $1,096,489.
Fields of interest: Vocational education, post-secondary; College; Business school/education; Engineering school/education; Adult/continuing education; Environment, forests; Agriculture; Minorities; Women.
Type of support: Employee-related scholarships; Support to graduates or students of specific schools; Technical education support; Undergraduate support.
Application information: Applications accepted. Application form required. Application form available on the grantmaker's web site.
  Deadline(s): Varies
  Final notification: Applicants notified six weeks for Innovative Educator Grant
  Applicants should submit the following:
    1) Essay
    2) Transcripts
    3) Letter(s) of recommendation
    4) GPA
Program descriptions:
  Adult Student Technical College Scholarship Program: Non-renewable scholarships of $250 to $500 will be awarded to adults who are entering or returning to school after a number of years in the workforce. Applicants must be accepted into a two-year associate degree program at Fox Valley Technical College, Lakeshore Technical College,

Northcental Technical College, Nicolet Technical College, Mid-Sate Technical College, or Northeast Wisconsin Technical College.
  Agribusiness/Forestry Scholarship: Awards scholarships to children of employees of WPS or children of a customer with a primary residence in WPS territory to attend select universities or technical colleges. The program is designed to help young people develop skills, leadership, and technical knowledge to meet the challenges of forestry, farming, and farm-related activities. Recipients are awarded $500 for a two-year technical college and $1,000 for a four-year college.
  Business and Technology Scholarships: Awards $1,500 renewable college scholarships to women and minorities majoring in the area of business or engineering, including electrical, mechanical, civil, industrial, chemical, computer, or environmental engineering. Applicants must be a full-time junior or senior in college; attend a four-year institution in Illinois, Indiana, Iowa, Michigan, Minnesota, or Wisconsin; and have a GPA of 2.8.
  College Scholarship: College scholarships of up to $1,500 per year for four years to high school seniors who are children of WPS employees or children of a customer with a primary residence in WPS territory. Applicants must be in the upper 10 percent of his or graduation class and plan to attend a college or university listed in the latest edition of the "Higher Education Directory"
  Innovative Educator Grant: Grants of up to $1,000 to middle school, junior high, or high school educators or teams of educators with projects designed to improve student achievement. Special emphasis is directed toward projects in the areas of math, science, or technology. Grants may be used to purchase equipment or curriculum materials, field trips that are a supplemental learning tool to classroom curriculum, robotics programs, community gardens, engineering mentoring programs, workshops for science teachers, props for energy lessons, history of energy workshops, and marketing energy projects.
  Linus M. Stoll Grant: Two grants at $1,000 each will be awarded for the academic year to high school seniors who are children of employees of WPS or children of a customer with a primary residence in WPS territory. The grants will be renewable for the second year, provided the students maintain at least a 3.0 GPA and are in good standing with their technical college. Applicants must demonstrate high academic standards, exemplary community services, and leadership in extracurricular activities while in high school. Applicant must also plan to attend Fox Valley Technical College, Lakeshore Technical College, Northcentral Technical College, Nicolet Technical College, Mid-State Technical College, or Northeast Wisconsin Technical College.
  Minority and/or Female Northeast Wisconsin Technical College Grant: Awards a non-renewable $500 grants to three non-traditional minority/female students who plan to enroll in technical programs at Northeast Wisconsin Technical College. Applicants must be a high school senior or an adult returning to school. The program is limited to children of employees of WPS or children of a customer with a primary residence in WPS territory.
  Paul D. Ziemer Scholarship: Annual awards of $2,000 college scholarships to children of employees of WPS or children of a customer with a primary residence in WPS territory. Applicants must be in the upper 10 percent of his or her graduation class; plan to attend the University of Wisconsin-Madison; and major in business or engineering.
  Tim Howard Memorial Scholarship: One $1,000 non-renewable scholarship to a high school senior

or returning adult student who is a child of a WPS employee or child of a customer with a primary residence in WPS territory. Applicant must plan to attend Northeast Wisconsin Technical College and pursue a degree in Electrical Power Distribution. The scholarship was established in honor of Tim Howard who endured fatal injuries while restoring electricity in the Wausaukee area.
  UW-Marinette Grant for Returning Adults: These awards are $250 per semester for part-time students and $500 per semester for full-time students, to a maximum of $2,000 to returning adult students who demonstrate financial need, show academic promise and are planning to earn a bachelor's degree. Applicants must be 22 years of age or older when returning to college, entering as a freshman or sophomore at the University of Wisconsin - Marinette and reside in a WPS territory.
  Wayne J. Peterson Memorial Scholarship: Annual awards of $2,000 college scholarships to children of employees of WPS or children of a customer with a primary residence in WPS territory. Applicants must have a GPA of 3.0; plan to attend Marquette University or St. Norbert College; and major in engineering or business.
  Wisconsin Technical Grant: Awards a $500 one-year, non-renewable grant to graduating high school seniors who are children of employees of WPS or children of a customer with a primary residence in WPS territory to attend Fox Valley Technical College, Lakeshore Technical College, Northcentral Technical College, Nicolet Technical College, Mid-State Technical College, or Northeast Wisconsin Technical College.
Company name: Wisconsin Public Service Corporation
EIN: 396075016

10082
Wisconsin State Journal Youth Services, Inc.

1901 Fish Hatchery Rd.
Madison, WI 53713-8056   (608) 252-6297
Contact: William Johnston, Pres.
E-mail: uwf@uwfoundation.wisc.edu

Foundation type: Public charity
Purpose: Financial assistance and non-cash assistance for children of south central WI, with toys and books, and needed items such as school supplies, clothes and food.
Financial data: Year ended 12/31/2011. Assets, $462,847 (M); Expenditures, $574,837; Total giving, $525,652; Grants to individuals, totaling $525,652.
Fields of interest: Human services; Children.
Type of support: In-kind gifts; Grants for special needs.
Application information: Applications accepted.
  Additional information: Families receive toy voucher application and if approved is able to bring their vouchers to the toy depot. Contact the organization for additional information.
EIN: 396051817

10083
Wisconsin Troopers Association Scholarship Fund

4230 E. Towne Blvd., No. 322
Madison, WI 53704-3704
URL: http://www.wi-troopers.org

Foundation type: Independent foundation
Purpose: Scholarships primarily to members of the Wisconsin Troopers Association, their relatives and dependents, and to the general public to pursue

higher education at colleges, universities, and technical schools.
Financial data: Year ended 12/31/2011. Assets, $0 (M); Expenditures, $1,854; Total giving, $1,854.
Fields of interest: Vocational education, post-secondary; Higher education.
Type of support: Technical education support; Undergraduate support.
Application information: Application form required.
Initial approach: Letter
Deadline(s): Mar. 11 for dependents, Aug. 31 for current members and spouses, Nov. 15 for scholarships to the general public
EIN: 391606135

10084
Wisconsin Women's Health Foundation
2503 Todd Dr.
Madison, WI 53713-2341 (608) 251-1675
Contact: Nancy Henderson, Admin. Asst.
FAX: (608) 251-4136; E-mail: wwhf@wwhf.org;
Toll-free tel.: (800) 448-5148; e-mail for Nancy Henderson: nhenderson@wwhf.org; URL: http://www.wwhf.org

Foundation type: Public charity
Purpose: Financial assistance to low-income, uninsured or underinsured individuals in southeastern Wisconsin for cost of breast health screenings, testing, and treatment. Scholarships for breast cancer research throughout Wisconsin.
Publications: Application guidelines; Informational brochure; Newsletter.
Financial data: Year ended 12/31/2012. Assets, $3,725,402 (M); Expenditures, $1,875,154; Total giving, $400,455; Grants to individuals, 649 grants totaling $364,145.
Fields of interest: Nursing school/education; Breast cancer research.
Type of support: Scholarships—to individuals; Grants for special needs.
Application information: Applications accepted. Application form required. Application form available on the grantmaker's web site.
Initial approach: Application
Send request by: Mail or e-mail
Deadline(s): May 1 for Dr. Judith Stitt Women Faculty Scholar Grant and Markos Family Breast Cancer Research Grant, Dec. 15 for Faith Community/Parish Nurse Scholarship, none for Kohl's Southeast Wisconsin Breast Health Assistance Fund
Final notification: Recipients notified Feb. 1 for Faith Community/Parish Nurse Scholarship, Oct. 1 for Dr. Judith Stitt Women Faculty Scholar and Markos Family Breast Cancer Grants
Program descriptions:
Dr. Judith Stitt Women Faculty Scholar Grant: The award for the current year is $25,000 per year for two years, works to provide more women with the opportunity to reach leadership positions where they can introduce women-centered concepts into the training of health care professionals, influence health policy to eliminate gender bias, and contribute to scientific knowledge which should underlie health care practices related to women. This award is for any woman junior faculty member in WI in the health profession, life sciences, biomedical sciences, or social sciences. The application should be submitted via e-mail: nmiller@wwhf.org.
Faith Community/Parish Nurse Scholarship Program: Two scholarships up to $750 each to women dedicated to the role of Faith Community/Parish Nurse. This scholarship is an effective way

to reach underserved women. Faith Community/Parish Nurses function as health advocates, health educators and counselors, referral agents, volunteer coordinators, support group developers and integrators of faith and health. Applicants must hold a current license in Wisconsin as a Registered Nurse. Scholarships are intended to be used for costs related to tuition, travel, books, and supplies. Preference will be given to those demonstrating financial need.
Markos Family Breast Cancer Research Grant: This $10,000 grant is available to support new or existing research in women's health through funding new or continuing research initiatives that will result in new finding about diagnosing, treating, or preventing breast cancer. Applicants include any graduate student, faculty member, or academic staff researcher, or those early in their careers in good standing at any University of Wisconsin campus, the Medical College of Wisconsin, or any other educational institution focusing on women's health matters. Candidates may be in any nationally-accredited school or department, including but not limited to Schools of Medicine, Nursing, Pharmacy, Social Work, Letters and Sciences, Business, or Human Ecology. Preference will be given to candidates whose work is directly relevant to Wisconsin women, and to those with a demonstrated ability to conduct quality peer-reviewed research. Application should be sent via e-mail to nmiller@wwhf.org.
EIN: 391900678

10085
Women's Fund for the Fox Valley Region, Inc.
4455 W. Lawrence St.
P.O. Box 563
Appleton, WI 54912-0563 (920) 830-1290
Contact: Becky Boulanger, Exec. Dir.
FAX: (920) 830-1293;
E-mail: info@womensfundfvr.org; URL: http://www.womensfundfvr.org

Foundation type: Public charity
Purpose: Scholarship to female students of WI, pursuing postsecondary education.
Publications: Application guidelines; Annual report; Grants list.
Financial data: Year ended 06/30/2012. Assets, $1,377,854 (M); Expenditures, $314,777; Total giving, $154,925.
Fields of interest: Higher education; Medical school/education; Nursing school/education; Young adults, female.
Type of support: Scholarships—to individuals.
Application information: Applications accepted. Application form required.
Deadline(s): Mar. for Abraham Scholarship, Mar. 15 for Kratzer Scholarship
Additional information: Financial need is not a requirement for scholarships.
Program descriptions:
Ashley Marie Abraham Scholarship: Awards $2,000 to graduating female high school student from Oshkosh North or Oshkosh West high schools who will pursue a degree in nursing or pre-medicine at a college or university in Wisconsin, including technical colleges. Recipients must have a 3.5 minimum cumulative GPA, a strong academic record and be able to demonstrate school involvement and community service.
Helen Spasoff Kratzer Scholarship: This $2,500 scholarship will be awarded to a graduating female high school student from Appleton East, Appleton North, Appleton West, Fox Valley Lutheran, or Xavier high schools with a minimum 3.6 GPA, a strong

academic record, and demonstrated school and community involvement, who is planning to pursue a degree in Education at a University of Wisconsin System school.
EIN: 203096562

10086
Women's Fund of Greater La Crosse
P.O. Box 654
La Crosse, WI 54602-0654 (608) 780-5710
Contact: Melissa Schultz, Admin. Coord.
E-mail: info@womensfundlacrosse.org; Tel. for Melissa Schultz: (608) 386-4136; URL: http://www.womensfundlacrosse.org

Foundation type: Public charity
Purpose: Provides grants to exceptional women and girls in the La Crosse, WI area to further their education.
Publications: Application guidelines; Newsletter.
Financial data: Year ended 12/31/2012. Assets, $926,090 (M); Expenditures, $68,450; Total giving, $36,295.
Fields of interest: Women; Girls.
Type of support: Grants to individuals.
Application information: Applications accepted.
Initial approach: See fund web site for guidelines
Program description:
Roberta Zurn Women in Leadership Award: This $1,000 award is given to a woman in the greater La Crosse community who has consistently worked on behalf of others. $500 will be awarded to further the recipient's education; the other $500 will be given to a non-profit organization of the recipient's choice.
EIN: 272394065

10087
Women's Fund of Greater Milwaukee, Inc.
316 N. Milwaukee St., Ste. 215
Milwaukee, WI 53202-5831 (414) 290-7350
FAX: (414) 290-7344;
E-mail: info@womensfund.com; URL: http://www.womensfundmke.org/

Foundation type: Public charity
Purpose: Scholarships to women over age 35 seeking to complete degree programs at Milwaukee, WI area colleges and universities.
Publications: Annual report; Financial statement; Grants list; Newsletter.
Financial data: Year ended 12/31/2012. Assets, $2,982,452 (M); Expenditures, $424,082; Total giving, $152,000; Grants to individuals, totaling $28,500.
Fields of interest: Higher education; Women.
Type of support: Scholarships—to individuals.
Application information: Scholarship recipients are selected from applications submitted by participating area colleges. See web site for additional guidelines.
EIN: 203514894

10088
WPS Charitable Foundation
(formerly Ray Koenig Charitable Foundation of WPS Inc.)
1717 W. Broadway
Monona, WI 53713-1834 (608) 221-6881
Contact: Thomas R. Nelson, Secy.-Treas.
E-mail: kim.olsen@wpsic.com; Application address: P.O. Box 7786, Madison, WI 53707-7786 tel.: (608) 221-6881

Foundation type: Company-sponsored foundation

Purpose: Scholarships to children of full-time employees of WPS Health Insurance and its subsidiaries.
Financial data: Year ended 12/31/2012. Assets, $1,230,360 (M); Expenditures, $65,449; Total giving, $58,100; Grants to individuals, 41 grants totaling $43,500 (high: $2,000, low: $100).
Fields of interest: Higher education.
Type of support: Employee-related scholarships; Undergraduate support.
Application information: Applications not accepted.
   Additional information: Unsolicited requests for funds not considered or acknowledged.
Company name: Wisconsin Physicians Service Insurance Corporation
EIN: 391568111

10089
Mary Alice Yakich Educational Foundation Inc.
1640 E. Elm Rd.
Oak Creek, WI   53154-6525   (414) 762-6866
Contact: Jan Drzewiecki, Treas.

Foundation type: Independent foundation
Purpose: Scholarships to financially needy individuals to support and promote education in the Milwaukee, WI and Waco, TX areas.
Financial data: Year ended 12/31/2011. Assets, $353,923 (M); Expenditures, $160,381; Total giving, $159,200; Grants to individuals, 40 grants totaling $103,700 (high: $5,500, low: $1,500).
Fields of interest: Education.
Type of support: Scholarships—to individuals; Grants for special needs.
Application information: Applications accepted. Application form required.
   Deadline(s): Apr. 1
   Applicants should submit the following:
      1) Class rank
      2) Transcripts
      3) SAR
      4) Resume
      5) Letter(s) of recommendation
      6) ACT
   Additional information: Application must also include career goals, extracurricular activities, and awards and honors received.
EIN: 391967691

10090
Howard Young Foundation, Inc.
(formerly Howard Young Health Care Foundation, Inc.)
P.O. Box 470
240 Maple St.
Woodruff, WI   54568-0470   (715) 356-8036
Contact: John R. Lund, Vice-Chair. and Dir.
FAX: (715) 356-8691;
E-mail: john.lund@ministryhealth.org; URL: http://
ministryhealth.org/HYMC/
HowardYoungFoundation.nws
Foundation type: Public charity
Purpose: Emergency support, including medical and dental assistance, food, clothing, rent, and other basic needs, to those in need in the Eagle River, WI area.
Publications: Annual report.
Financial data: Year ended 09/30/2011. Assets, $10,115,607 (M); Expenditures, $1,481,900; Total giving, $634,260; Grants to individuals, totaling $13,796.
Fields of interest: Health care; Human services; Economically disadvantaged.
Type of support: Emergency funds; Grants for special needs.
Application information: Contact the foundation for additional information.
EIN: 391521169

10091
Young Women's Christian Association of Greater Milwaukee
1915 N. Martin Luther King Dr.
Milwaukee, WI   53212-3641   (414) 374-1800
Contact: Paula Penebaker, Pres. and CEO
FAX: (414) 374-2680;
E-mail: communication@ywcasew.org; E-Mail For Paula Penebaker:ppenebaker@ywcasew.org;
URL: http://www.ywcamilw.org

Foundation type: Public charity
Purpose: Child care subsidies in the greater Milwaukee, WI, area to participants in the Wisconsin Works Program, families who need child care to get or keep employment, and teen parents in school.
Publications: Annual report.
Financial data: Year ended 12/31/2011. Assets, $8,451,101 (M); Expenditures, $9,487,797.
Type of support: Grants for special needs.
Application information:
   Initial approach: Letter
EIN: 390806258

10092
Stanley Zebro Foundation
c/o MI Trust Co.
P.O. Box 2977
Milwaukee, WI   53201-2980   (715) 845-3121
Contact: Kim Hilgers
Application address: 500 3rd St., Wausau, WI 54402-4885

Foundation type: Independent foundation
Purpose: Scholarships to graduates of Mosinee High School, WI. Financial assistance to residents of Mosinee, WI for emergency medical care, as well as food and shelter for persons suffering from catastrophic illnesses or from the effects of disasters such as fires and storms.

Financial data: Year ended 12/31/2011. Assets, $316,026 (M); Expenditures, $20,118; Total giving, $15,540; Grants to individuals, 15 grants totaling $15,540 (high: $3,640, low: $500).
Fields of interest: Higher education; Economically disadvantaged.
Type of support: Emergency funds; Support to graduates or students of specific schools; Grants for special needs.
Application information:
   Initial approach: Letter
   Additional information: Contact foundation for further information.
EIN: 391540935

10093
John & Dorothy Zweibel Trust
c/o Talmer Bank & Trust
400 Milwaukee Ave.
Burlington, WI   53105-1231   (262) 767-3268

Foundation type: Independent foundation
Purpose: Scholarships to graduates of Burlington High School or Catholic Central High School of Burlington, WI pursuing full time education beyond high school.
Financial data: Year ended 12/31/2011. Assets, $167,850 (M); Expenditures, $12,313; Total giving, $9,800; Grants to individuals, 10 grants totaling $9,800 (high: $1,300, low: $700).
Fields of interest: Higher education.
Type of support: Support to graduates or students of specific schools.
Application information:
   Deadline(s): Aug. 1
   Additional information: Contact trustee for specific guidelines and a complete copy of submission materials.
EIN: 436921282

WYOMING

10094
Anderson Memorial Educational Trust
P.O. Box 519
Dubois, WY 82513-0519
Contact: Peggy Miller, Tr.
Application address: 7372 Hwy. 26, Crowheart, Wy 82512

Foundation type: Independent foundation
Purpose: Scholarships only to graduates of Dubois High School, WY.
Financial data: Year ended 04/30/2013. Assets, $620,671 (M); Expenditures, $11,214; Total giving, $10,750; Grants to individuals, 19 grants totaling $10,750 (high: $1,000, low: $230).
Type of support: Support to graduates or students of specific schools; Undergraduate support.
Application information: Applications accepted.
> *Initial approach:* Letter
> *Deadline(s):* Apr. 1

EIN: 836025176

10095
Dodd and Dorothy L. Bryan Foundation
2 N. Main, Ste. 401
Sheridan, WY 82801 (307) 672-3535
Application address: P.O. Box 6087, Sheridan, WY 82801

Foundation type: Independent foundation
Purpose: Loans to students from Sheridan, Campbell, and Johnson counties, WY, and from Powder River, Rosebud, and Big Horn counties, MT, who have lived in the county for at least two years prior to application.
Financial data: Year ended 12/31/2012. Assets, $6,267,765 (M); Expenditures, $190,726; Total giving, $75,114.
Fields of interest: Vocational education; Higher education.
Type of support: Student loans—to individuals.
Application information: Applications accepted. Application form required. Interview required.
> *Initial approach:* Letter or in person
> *Deadline(s):* None
> *Applicants should submit the following:*
> 1) Transcripts
> 2) Financial information
> *Additional information:* Contact the foundation for loan application and guidelines.

Program description:
> *Student Loan Program:* Loans are made for higher or vocational education for recipients selected on the basis of financial need and academic achievement. Applicants must be under the age of 25 to be eligible for academic loans. There is no age limit for vocational loans. Recipients must have at least a 2.5 GPA and maintain full-time status. Both of the recipient's parents must co-sign the loan note. Recipients must also carry life insurance with a collateral assignment to the foundation in an amount at least equal to the loan. Repayments are approximately $25 per month per $1,000. Loans are automatically renewed provided the recipient maintains eligibility.

EIN: 836006533

10096
Christian Mission Concerns of Tennessee, Inc.
3125 Tucker Ranch Rd.
Wilson, WY 83014-9703
Contact: Paul P. Piper, Pres.
Application telephone: (307) 733-8112

Foundation type: Independent foundation
Purpose: Grants to individuals for nursing home care.
Financial data: Year ended 12/31/2011. Assets, $20,530,420 (M); Expenditures, $1,668,864; Total giving, $1,152,365.
Type of support: Grants for special needs.
Application information: Contact mission for further information.
EIN: 582021971

10097
Alvin T. Clark Memorial Fund
(formerly Alvin T. Clark Family Memorial Fund)
141 S. Main St.
Buffalo, WY 82834-0400 (307) 684-2211
Contact: Wendy Martin
Application address: Wendy Martin, P.O. Box 400, Buffalo, WY 82834

Foundation type: Independent foundation
Purpose: Interest-free student loans to graduates of Buffalo, WY, high schools for postsecondary education in nursing, forestry, or accredited medical school.
Financial data: Year ended 12/31/2011. Assets, $274,931 (M); Expenditures, $2,225; Total giving, $0; Loans to individuals, 17 loans totaling $23,650.
Fields of interest: Medical school/education; Nursing school/education; Environment, forests.
Type of support: Student loans—to individuals; Support to graduates or students of specific schools.
Application information: Applications accepted. Application form required.
> *Deadline(s):* None
> *Additional information:* Application can be obtained from First National Bank.

EIN: 836025848

10098
Cody Medical Foundation
1108 14th St., No. 422
Cody, WY 82414-3423 (307) 250-0454
Contact: Marty Coe, Exec. Dir.
URL: http://codymedicalfoundation.org

Foundation type: Independent foundation
Purpose: Scholarships to financially needy residents of Park County, WY, for study in a medical-related field.
Financial data: Year ended 06/30/2013. Assets, $1,466,747 (M); Expenditures, $133,461; Total giving, $65,571.
Fields of interest: Medical school/education; Nursing school/education.
Type of support: Graduate support; Undergraduate support.
Application information: Applications accepted.
> *Initial approach:* Letter
> *Send request by:* Mail
> *Deadline(s):* Aug. 1
> *Applicants should submit the following:*
> 1) SAT
> 2) GPA
> 3) ACT

Additional information: Applicant or parents must live in the West Park Hospital District and one year of college work be completed before application is made.
EIN: 836006491

10099
Community Foundation of Jackson Hole
255 E. Simpson St.
P.O. Box 574
Jackson, WY 83001-0574 (307) 739-1026
Contact: For grants: Pam Sather, Finance and Opers. Off.; Katharine Conover, Pres.
Application address for scholarships: c/o Julie Stayner, Guidance Counselor, Jackson Hole High School, P.O. Box 568, Jackson, WY, 83001, tel.: (307) 732-3710, e-mail: jstayner@tcsd.org
FAX: (307) 734-2841;
E-mail: info@cfjacksonhole.org; URL: http://www.cfjacksonhole.org

Foundation type: Community foundation
Purpose: Scholarships to graduating seniors of Jackson Hole, WY for postsecondary education.
Publications: Application guidelines; Annual report; Financial statement; Grants list; Informational brochure.
Financial data: Year ended 12/31/2012. Assets, $7,830,995 (M); Expenditures, $14,043,243; Total giving, $13,742,090. Scholarships—to individuals amount not specified.
Fields of interest: Higher education; Scholarships/financial aid.
Type of support: Scholarships—to individuals; Support to graduates or students of specific schools; Undergraduate support.
Application information: Applications accepted. Application form required.
> *Deadline(s):* Feb. 24
> *Applicants should submit the following:*
> 1) Transcripts
> 2) Letter(s) of recommendation
> 3) Financial information
> *Additional information:* See web site for a complete listing of programs and eligibility criteria.

Program description:
> *Scholarships:* The foundation administers various scholarship funds established by donors who choose to give back to the community through scholarships for local youth. Each scholarship has its own specific application requirements and eligibility criteria, which ranges from financial need, demonstration of public service, and high academic performance to graduation from a particular high school and specific areas of study, such as business and performing arts. See web site for additional information.

EIN: 830308856

10100
Construction Careers Foundation
P.O. Box 965
Cheyenne, WY 82003-0965 (307) 632-0573

Foundation type: Public charity
Purpose: Scholarships to individuals for education and training in the construction industry.
Publications: Informational brochure; Occasional report.
Fields of interest: Vocational education.
Type of support: Technical education support; Undergraduate support.
Application information: Applications accepted. Application form not required.

Initial approach: Letter
Copies of proposal: 3
Applicants should submit the following:
1) Transcripts
2) Resume
3) Proposal
4) Letter(s) of recommendation
5) Budget Information
Additional information: Contact foundation for current application deadlines/guidelines.
EIN: 830319926

10101

Frances Blayney Curtis Foundation
P.O. Box 451
Ranchester, WY 82839-0451 (307) 655-2595
Contact: F. Don Steadman, Secy.-Treas.

Foundation type: Independent foundation
Purpose: Loans to residents of the Sheridan, WY, area to attend colleges, universities, trade schools, and vocational schools in the Rocky Mountain area.
Financial data: Year ended 12/31/2012. Assets, $551,630 (M); Expenditures, $966; Total giving, $0.
Fields of interest: Vocational education, post-secondary; Higher education.
Type of support: Student loans—to individuals; Technical education support; Undergraduate support.
Application information: Application form required.
Deadline(s): 2 months prior to need for funds
Applicants should submit the following:
1) Transcripts
2) Photograph
EIN: 830300312

10102

Davis-Roberts Scholarship Fund, Inc.
5513 Lawrence Ln.
Cheyenne, WY 82009-3524 (307) 632-0491
Contact: Gary D. Skillern, Secy.- Treas.

Foundation type: Independent foundation
Purpose: Scholarships to members or former members of the Order of Nathan Hale or Job's Daughters in WY, for full-time study at any college or university.
Financial data: Year ended 12/31/2012. Assets, $120,742 (M); Expenditures, $5,506; Total giving, $5,000; Grants to individuals, 11 grants totaling $5,000 (high: $500, low: $400).
Fields of interest: Higher education; Scholarships/financial aid.
Type of support: Scholarships—to individuals.
Application information: Application form required.
Initial approach: Letter or telephone
Deadline(s): June 15
Applicants should submit the following:
1) Letter(s) of recommendation
2) Photograph
3) Transcripts
EIN: 836011403

10103

Mark Alan Doherty Scholarship Fund
P.O. Box 369
Cheyenne, WY 82003-0369 (307) 635-0361

Foundation type: Public charity
Purpose: Scholarships to individuals who are, or will be, graduates of a high school in Cheyenne, Wyoming.

Financial data: Year ended 12/31/2011. Assets, $162,887 (M); Expenditures, $16,733; Total giving, $16,250.
Fields of interest: Higher education.
Type of support: Scholarships—to individuals; Support to graduates or students of specific schools.
Application information: Applications accepted.
Additional information: Recipients are determined based on the applicants' past academic record, involvement in school and community activities, and available economic resources for funding their college education. Students participating in golf are given additional consideration.
EIN: 830286668

10104

Henry William Gillet Memorial, Inc.
P.O. Box 730
Pine Bluffs, WY 82082-0730 (307) 245-3222
Contact: Ken E. Malm

Foundation type: Independent foundation
Purpose: Student loans to graduates of Laramie County School District No. 2, WY.
Financial data: Year ended 06/30/2012. Assets, $152,244 (M); Expenditures, $9,040; Total giving, $7,000; Grant to an individual, 1 grant totaling $7,000.
Fields of interest: Higher education.
Type of support: Student loans—to individuals; Support to graduates or students of specific schools; Undergraduate support.
Application information: Applications accepted.
Initial approach: Letter
Deadline(s): None
Additional information: Letter should outline financial need and intentions of education.
EIN: 237135637

10105

Giovanini Foundation
P.O. Box 160
Jackson, WY 83001-0160

Foundation type: Independent foundation
Purpose: Scholarships to students graduating from Dubois High School or Jackson High School, WY.
Financial data: Year ended 12/31/2012. Assets, $1,444,298 (M); Expenditures, $92,877; Total giving, $67,000; Grants to individuals, 10 grants totaling $40,000 (high: $4,000, low: $4,000).
Type of support: Support to graduates or students of specific schools; Undergraduate support.
Application information: Applications not accepted.
Additional information: Unsolicited requests for funds not considered or acknowledged.
EIN: 830308568

10106

The Antonio V. Glassber Educational Foundation
P.O. Box 303
Teton Village, WY 83025
URL: http://www.antonioglassbergfoundation.org/

Foundation type: Independent foundation
Purpose: Scholarships to students of Community School, St. Louis, MO, John Burroughs School, St. Louis, MO, Jackson Hole Community School, Jackson, WY, Sacred Heart Cathedral Preparatory School, San Francisco, CA for tuition expenses.

Financial data: Year ended 12/31/2013. Assets, $127,232 (M); Expenditures, $35,000; Total giving, $35,000.
Fields of interest: Education.
Type of support: Scholarships—to individuals.
Application information: Contact your school for application guidelines. Unsolicited requests for funds not accepted.
EIN: 830334234

10107

Tammy Hladky Foundation
P.O. Box 908
Gillette, WY 82717-0908 (307) 682-9494
Contact: Susan L. Hladky, Dir.
Application address: 211 W. 7th, Gillette, WY 82717, tel.: (307) 682-9494

Foundation type: Independent foundation
Purpose: Scholarship awards to graduates of Campbell County High School, WY.
Financial data: Year ended 06/30/2013. Assets, $1,101,138 (M); Expenditures, $10,890; Total giving, $10,500; Grants to individuals, 7 grants totaling $10,500 (high: $3,500, low: $1,000).
Fields of interest: Scholarships/financial aid.
Type of support: Scholarships—to individuals.
Application information: Applications accepted. Application form required.
Deadline(s): Mar. 1
Applicants should submit the following:
1) GPA
2) Letter(s) of recommendation
3) Class rank
4) Essay
5) ACT
Additional information: Applications must be typed. Include all activities participated in both in and out of school in grades 10-12; three reference letters; personal essay; and honors classes taken. Incomplete applications will not be considered for local scholarships. Contact foundation for further guidelines.
EIN: 830319044

10108

Johnson County High School Scholarship Fund
P.O. Box 400
Buffalo, WY 82834-0400 (307) 684-2211
Contact: Raymond A. Holt, Tr.

Foundation type: Independent foundation
Purpose: Scholarships to graduates of Johnson County, WY, secondary schools for bachelor's degrees and other postsecondary education. Scholarships are renewable for up to four years.
Financial data: Year ended 12/31/2011. Assets, $1,238,883 (M); Expenditures, $55,778; Total giving, $52,900; Grants to individuals, 8 grants totaling $52,900 (high: $6,900, low: $4,600).
Type of support: Support to graduates or students of specific schools; Undergraduate support.
Application information: Applications accepted.
Initial approach: Letter
Deadline(s): Apr. 1
Additional information: Application must indicate references, plans for higher education, name of school planning to attend, courses of study, and dates of attendance. Applicants must be recommended by school administration.
EIN: 836003627

10109
Laing-Weil Scholarship Fund Charitable Trust

P.O. Box 370
Buffalo, WY 82834-0370 (307) 684-2798
Contact: Deanne Bjerke, Dir.
Application address: 611 Klondike Dr., Buffalo, WY 82834, tel.: (307) 684-2798

Foundation type: Operating foundation
Purpose: Scholarships to residents of Buffalo, WY, who are enrolled full-time in a program of study leading to a Bachelor's degree.
Financial data: Year ended 12/31/2011. Assets, $996,614 (M); Expenditures, $37,068; Total giving, $36,000; Grants to individuals, 5 grants totaling $36,000 (high: $10,000, low: $3,000).
Type of support: Undergraduate support.
Application information: Applications accepted.
  Initial approach: Letter
  Deadline(s): Feb. 10
  Applicants should submit the following:
    1) Essay
    2) Transcripts
    3) Resume
EIN: 830324104

10110
LaRue Young Foundation

3021 US Hwy.,No.87
Sheridan, WY 82801
Contact: Paddy Bard, Secy.-Treas.

Foundation type: Independent foundation
Purpose: Grants to physically handicapped individuals over the age of two years and under 21 years who are residents of Big Horn, Powder River, or Rosebud counties, MT or Sheridan county, WY and are in need of financial assistance.
Financial data: Year ended 12/31/2011. Assets, $1,139,859 (M); Expenditures, $103,435; Total giving, $74,358.
Fields of interest: Physically disabled; Economically disadvantaged.
Type of support: Grants for special needs.
Application information: Applications accepted.
  Initial approach: Letter
  Deadline(s): None
  Additional information: Applicant must demonstrate need for financial assistance such as medical insurance coverage, governmental funding, or public health service.
EIN: 810515546

10111
Oletha C. Likins & Loren E. Likins Perpetual Memorial Trust Fund

121 E. 20th Ave.
Torrington, WY 82240

Foundation type: Independent foundation
Purpose: Scholarships only to members of Job's Daughters who are graduates of an accredited high school in Goshen County, WY, with preference given to members of Bethel No. 20, International Order of Job's Daughters, Torrington, WY.
Financial data: Year ended 12/31/2012. Assets, $1,110,386 (M); Expenditures, $67,025; Total giving, $66,000.
Fields of interest: Higher education; Scholarships/financial aid.
Type of support: Scholarships—to individuals; Graduate support; Undergraduate support.

Application information: Applications accepted.
Application form required.
  Deadline(s): Mar. 15
  Applicants should submit the following:
    1) Transcripts
    2) Essay
  Additional information: Application should also include two letters of reference.
EIN: 836039257

10112
Loren E. Linkins Oletha C Linkins, Likins-Masonic Memorial Trust

(formerly Likins-Masonic Memorial Trust, also known as Oletha C. Likins & Loren E. Likins Masonic Memorial Trust)
121 E. 20th Ave.
Torrington, WY 82240

Foundation type: Independent foundation
Purpose: Scholarships only to members of Max Burk Chapter, Order of DeMolay, that graduate from a Goshen County high school, WY.
Financial data: Year ended 12/31/2012. Assets, $1,032,544 (M); Expenditures, $51,264; Total giving, $50,000.
Type of support: Scholarships—to individuals.
Application information: Applications not accepted.
EIN: 836041098

10113
The Ray and Kay Littler Trust

P.O. Box 922
Buffalo, WY 82834-0922 (307) 684-9595

Foundation type: Independent foundation
Purpose: Grants to Johnson County, WY, residents for books and supplies for post-secondary education. Giving also for family travel for children with medical needs.
Financial data: Year ended 06/30/2013. Assets, $754,983 (M); Expenditures, $41,789; Total giving, $28,770.
Fields of interest: Economically disadvantaged.
Type of support: Support to graduates or students of specific schools; Undergraduate support; Grants for special needs.
Application information: Applications accepted.
Application form required.
  Initial approach: Letter demonstrating financial need
  Deadline(s): Apr. 1
EIN: 830320342

10114
Hilda and Raymond Milne Foundation

P.O. Box 3004
Gillette, WY 82717-3004 (307) 682-1313
Contact: Thomas E. Lubnau II
Application address: P.O. Box 1028, Gillette, WY 82717-1028

Foundation type: Independent foundation
Purpose: Scholarships to students in the Campbell County, WY, area, for higher education.
Financial data: Year ended 12/31/2012. Assets, $1,416,655 (M); Expenditures, $58,190; Total giving, $43,250; Grants to individuals, 61 grants totaling $43,250 (high: $2,750, low: $250).
Type of support: Undergraduate support.
Application information: Applications accepted.
  Initial approach: Letter
  Deadline(s): None
EIN: 830305556

10115
Adeline L. Neilson Foundation

P.O. Box 1804
Jackson, WY 83001-1804
Contact: Adeline L. Neilson

Foundation type: Operating foundation
Purpose: Scholarships to students primarily in WY, who plan to attend college, university, or trade school.
Financial data: Year ended 11/30/2012. Assets, $568,079 (M); Expenditures, $58,518; Total giving, $43,830; Grants to individuals, 30 grants totaling $43,830 (high: $2,000, low: $330).
Type of support: Scholarships—to individuals.
Application information: Applications accepted.
Application form required.
  Deadline(s): Apr. 24
  Additional information: Applications available in the guidance office of your school.
EIN: 841423057

10116
Viola Pearson Scholarship Trust

c/o American National Bank & Trust Co.
6020 Yellowstone Rd.
Cheyenne, WY 82009

Foundation type: Independent foundation
Purpose: Scholarships to graduates of East High School, Cheyenne, WY.
Financial data: Year ended 12/31/2011. Assets, $140,931 (M); Expenditures, $7,501; Total giving, $4,243; Grants to individuals, 4 grants totaling $4,243.
Type of support: Support to graduates or students of specific schools; Undergraduate support.
Application information: Applications accepted.
  Initial approach: Letter
  Applicants should submit the following:
    1) Letter(s) of recommendation
    2) Transcripts
    3) Financial information
EIN: 836031271

10117
B. F. & Rose H. Perkins Foundation

45 E. Loucks St., Ste. 110
Sheridan, WY 82801-6329 (307) 674-8871
FAX: (307) 674-8803;
E-mail: bfperkin@fiberpipe.net; URL: http://www.perkinsfoundation.org/

Foundation type: Independent foundation
Purpose: Educational loans and grants to graduates of Sheridan County High School, WY. Medical and dental assistance to children who have resided in Sheridan County, WY, for at least one year.
Publications: Application guidelines; Informational brochure.
Financial data: Year ended 12/31/2012. Assets, $9,428,191 (M); Expenditures, $829,199; Total giving, $670,343; Grants to individuals, 67 grants totaling $79,843; Loans to individuals, 50 loans totaling $238,540.
Fields of interest: Higher education; Dental care; Youth; Economically disadvantaged.
Type of support: Student loans—to individuals; Support to graduates or students of specific schools; Grants for special needs.
Application information: Applications accepted.
Application form required.
  Send request by: Mail or hand delivered
  Applicants should submit the following:
    1) Transcripts

2) GPA
3) Financial information
4) Budget Information
Additional information: Application forms can be obtained from the foundation. Application form for medical assistance should include a copy of their most recent federal tax return. See web site for additional guidelines.
Program descriptions:
Loan Program: Interest-free loans of up to $5,000 a year will be loaned to needy and worthy young men and women who have resided in Sheridan County for more than one year and graduated from an accredited high school located in Sheridan County. Applicant must not be more than 20 years of age when making the initial application.
Medical Program: The foundation funds medical, dental care, eye glasses, and hearing aids for children and young adults from ages one to 20. Applicant must have resided in Sheridan County for at least one year and must show financial need.
EIN: 830138740

10118
Walt & Olga Pilch Foundation
41 E. Burkitt St.
Sheridan, WY 82801-6301   (307) 674-7491

Foundation type: Independent foundation
Purpose: Educational loans and scholarships to students attending Colorado State University, the University of Wyoming, Sheridan College, WY, or an approved vocational school.
Financial data: Year ended 06/30/2013. Assets, $290,858 (M); Expenditures, $13,331; Total giving, $10,000; Grant to an individual, 1 grant totaling $10,000 (high: $1,000).
Type of support: Support to graduates or students of specific schools; Undergraduate support.
Application information: Application form required.
Deadline(s): None
Applicants should submit the following:
1) Transcripts
2) Financial information
EIN: 830323151

10119
Sheridan County Memorial Hospital Foundation
1401 W. 5th St.
P.O. Box 391
Sheridan, WY 82801-0391   (307) 673-2418
Contact: Ada Kirven, Exec. Dir.
E-Mail for Ada Kiven : akirven@sheridanhospital.org;
URL: http://www.sheridanhospital.org/foundation/

Foundation type: Public charity
Purpose: Scholarships to qualified nursing students enrolled at Sheridan Community College, WY.
Financial data: Year ended 06/30/2012. Assets, $9,555,641 (M); Expenditures, $3,616,399; Total giving, $3,363,908; Grants to individuals, totaling $7,500.
Fields of interest: Nursing school/education.
Type of support: Scholarships—to individuals.
Application information: Applications accepted. Application form required.
Additional information: Students must agree to work for Sheridan Memorial Hospital for one year for each year of the scholarship duration. Scholarship payments are based on recommendation from the college nursing

staff that the student is progressing satisfactorily.
EIN: 741905155

10120
SouthEast Wyoming Builders Association Scholarship Trust
P.O. Box 2066
Cheyenne, WY 82003   (307) 778-8222

Foundation type: Independent foundation
Purpose: Scholarships to individuals studying courses related to construction management, primarily in WY.
Financial data: Year ended 12/31/2012. Assets, $220,154 (M); Expenditures, $17,357; Total giving, $10,000; Grants to individuals, 13 grants totaling $10,000 (high: $1,000, low: $500).
Type of support: Scholarships—to individuals.
Application information: Applications accepted.
Initial approach: Letter
Deadline(s): None
EIN: 943161079

10121
Muriel E. Spacht Memorial Trust
P.O. Box 1077
Lusk, WY 82225   (307) 334-2177
Contact: Robert E. Pfister, Tr.

Foundation type: Independent foundation
Purpose: Scholarships and grants to individuals of Niobrara county, WY needing financial assistance to attend college or medical assistance.
Financial data: Year ended 08/31/2012. Assets, $604,551 (M); Expenditures, $91,912; Total giving, $75,700; Grants to individuals, 12 grants totaling $26,700 (high: $10,000, low: $500).
Fields of interest: Higher education; Health care; Economically disadvantaged.
Type of support: Grants to individuals; Scholarships—to individuals; Grants for special needs.
Application information: Applications accepted.
Initial approach: Letter
Deadline(s): None
Additional information: Applicant must demonstrate need.
EIN: 830239195

10122
True Foundation
P.O. Box. 2360
Casper, WY 82602-2360

Foundation type: Company-sponsored foundation
Purpose: Scholarships to dependents of current employees of True Oil Company for postsecondary education.
Financial data: Year ended 11/30/2012. Assets, $2,053,956 (M); Expenditures, $437,263; Total giving, $418,964.
Fields of interest: Higher education.
Type of support: Employee-related scholarships.
Application information: Applications not accepted.
Additional information: Contributes only to dependents of employees of True Oil Company; unsolicited requests for funds not considered or acknowledged.
Company name: True Oil LLC
EIN: 836004596

10123
Ucross Foundation
30 Big Red Ln.
Clearmont, WY 82835-9723   (307) 737-2291
Contact: Sharon Dynak, Pres. and Exec. Dir.
FAX: (307) 737-2322; E-mail: info@ucross.org;
URL: http://www.ucrossfoundation.org

Foundation type: Public charity
Purpose: Residencies to visual artists, composers, and writers from all stages of their professional careers.
Publications: Application guidelines; Financial statement; Informational brochure; Newsletter; Occasional report.
Financial data: Year ended 12/31/2011. Assets, $28,379,733 (M); Expenditures, $1,660,997; Total giving, $10,000; Grants to individuals, totaling $10,000.
Fields of interest: Visual arts; Music composition; Literature.
Type of support: Foreign applicants; Residencies; Stipends.
Application information: Application form required.
Initial approach: E-mail
Deadline(s): Oct. 1 (spring sessions) and Mar. 1 (fall session)
Additional information: Application must also include references and work samples.
Program description:
Residency Program: This program provides 85 residencies per year for two to four weeks and work space for individual artists and writers whose work indicates both involvement in individual creative exploration and significant future accomplishments. Applicants must exhibit professional standing in their field; both mature and emerging artists of promise are welcome to apply. National and international artists are encouraged to apply.
EIN: 742188539

10124
Whitney Benefits, Inc.
P.O. Box 5085
Sheridan, WY 82801-1385   (307) 674-7303
Contact: Patrick Henderson, Exec. Dir.
FAX: (307) 674-4335;
E-mail: assistant@whitneybenefits.org; Physical address: 145 N. Connor St., Ste. 1, Sheridan, WY 82801; URL: http://www.whitneybenefits.org

Foundation type: Independent foundation
Purpose: Interest-free student loans to graduates of high schools in Sheridan and Johnson counties, WY, and to GED recipients from a Sheridan/Johnson County High School or Sheridan College, for undergraduate, graduate or vocational study.
Publications: Annual report.
Financial data: Year ended 06/30/2012. Assets, $123,951,575 (M); Expenditures, $2,565,560; Total giving, $1,564,318; Loans to individuals, totaling $2,107,784.
Fields of interest: Vocational education, post-secondary; Higher education.
Type of support: Support to graduates or students of specific schools; Graduate support; Undergraduate support.
Application information: Applications accepted. Application form required. Application form available on the grantmaker's web site. Interview required.
Initial approach: Letter or telephone
Send request by: On-line
Deadline(s): Sept. 1 for new loans, Oct. 1 and Mar. 1 for current loans
Applicants should submit the following:

1) Photograph
2) Transcripts
Additional information: Applicants up to the age of 24 must have a 2.5 cumulative G.P.A. from high school, or a 2.25 cumulative G.P.A. from college. Applicants who are age 25 and older must have a 2.0 cumulative G.P.A. from high school, or a 2.25 cumulative G.P.A. from college.
EIN: 830168511

10125
The Wilbur & Birdie Williams Trust
(formerly Wilbur & Birdie Williams Scholarship Fund)
P.O. Box 400
Buffalo, WY 82834 (307) 684-2201
Contact: Nick Thom, Tr.

Foundation type: Independent foundation
Purpose: Scholarships to high school seniors in Johnson County, WY who have been in FFA or 4-H activities.
Financial data: Year ended 12/31/2011. Assets, $126,234 (M); Expenditures, $3,758; Total giving, $3,000; Grants to individuals, 3 grants totaling $3,000 (high: $1,500, low: $750).
Fields of interest: Agriculture.
Type of support: Undergraduate support.
Application information: Applications accepted.
Initial approach: Letter
Deadline(s): Apr. 1
Additional information: Application should include educational background and planned course of study.
EIN: 830234332

10126
Wyoming Community Foundation
1472 N. 5th St., Ste. 201
Laramie, WY 82072 (307) 721-8300
Contact: For grants: Samin Dadelahi, C.O.O.
FAX: (307) 721-8333; E-mail: wcf@wycf.org;
URL: http://www.wycf.org

Foundation type: Community foundation
Purpose: Scholarships to graduating seniors of specific WY high schools, and to nursing students in their junior or senior year at the University of Wyoming.
Publications: Application guidelines; Annual report; Grants list; Informational brochure (including application guidelines); Newsletter; Program policy statement.
Financial data: Year ended 12/31/2012. Assets, $87,725,830 (M); Expenditures, $5,607,489; Total giving, $2,598,606; Grants to individuals, 112 grants totaling $114,770.
Fields of interest: Higher education; Nursing school/education; Scholarships/financial aid.
Type of support: Scholarships—to individuals; Support to graduates or students of specific schools; Technical education support; Undergraduate support.
Application information: Applications accepted. Application form required. Application form available on the grantmaker's web site.
Initial approach: Letter
Deadline(s): Feb. 1
Additional information: Application should include transcripts. See web site for complete listing of scholarships.
EIN: 830287513

APPENDIX

This appendix lists those grantmakers that appeared in the 22nd edition of *Foundation Grants to Individuals*, but were excluded from this 23rd edition for the reasons stated. Reasons for exclusion include grantmakers that terminated, those whose status has changed, those no longer making grants to individuals, or those for which no recent information could be obtained. **Grantmakers listed here should not be considered possible sources of funding for individuals.**

A-Peeling Charitable Foundation, Inc., KY
The foundation terminated in 2011.

Adopt an Orca Inc., MI
The foundation gave less than $2,000 to individuals in 2011 and 2012.

AFTRA Heller Memorial Foundation, Inc., NY
The foundation terminated in 2010.

Ahl Scholarship Fund, Helen R., PA
(also known as Ahl Trust, P. Vaughn)
The fund terminated in 2010.

Ahl Trust, P. Vaughn
See Ahl Scholarship Fund, Helen R.

Aitaneet Foundation, OH
Current information not available.

Alamance Educational Foundation, NC
The foundation terminated in 2010.

Alander Scholarship Fund, Robert J., NC
The fund terminated in 2012.

Alpha Zeta Delta of Chi Psi Educational Foundation, WI
The foundation terminated in 2010.

American Association of University Women, HI
The foundation did not provide funding in 2011 and 2012.

American Students' Fund, Inc., MD
(also known as ASF)
The foundation did not provide funding in 2011 and 2012.

Anderson Family Scholarship Trust, IA
The trust terminated in 2010.

Anderson Family Scholarship Trust, John, IA
The trust terminated in 2010.

Anthony Foundation, Barbara Cox, The, GA
The foundation terminated in 2012.

Armstrong Toyota and Ford Family Foundation, FL
Current information not available.

Arrow International Inc., Scholarship Fund, NC
Current information not available.

ASF
See American Students' Fund, Inc.

Baker Memorial Trust, Charles Milton, TN
The trust terminated in 2010.

Ballard Foundation, John & Ann, LA
The foundation terminated in 2010.

Barakat Foundation (USA), The, CA
The foundation terminated in 2011.

Barden Foundation II, Inc., Gary
See Barden Foundation, Inc., Don H.

Barden Foundation, Inc., Don H., MI
(formerly Barden Foundation II, Inc., Gary)
The foundation did not provide funding in 2011 and 2012.

Bissell Fund for Hospital Aid, Inc., Dr. William, CT
The fund terminated in 2011.

Bogan Scholarship Foundation, R. Chad, FL
The foundation terminated in 2011.

BPW Foundation
See Business and Professional Women's Foundation, The

Business and Professional Women's Foundation, The, DC
(formerly BPW Foundation)
The foundation no longer provides funding to individuals.

Catawissa Lumber & Specialty Co., Inc. Trust, PA
The trust terminated in 2012.

Chadwell-Townsend Private Foundation, OH
the foundation terminated in 2011.

Coca-Cola Enterprises Charitable Foundation, The, GA
The foundation terminated in 2011.

Comite Olimpico De Puerto Rico, PR
The foundation did not provide funding in 2012.

Community and Family Services Foundation, WA
The foundation did not provide funding in 2011 and 2012.

ConocoPhillips Dependent Scholarship Program Trust, OK
(formerly Educational Fund for Children of Phillips Petroleum Company Employees)
The trust terminated in 2011.

Corke Educational Trust, Hubert & Alice, AR
The trust terminated in 2013.

Creative Recovery Communities, Inc., TN
The foundation did not provide funding in 2011 and 2012.

Cunningham Scholarship Fund, Wimford E. and Mary E. Benton, OK
The fund terminated in 2013.

Demming Educational Foundation, Robert M. & Margaret O., MO
The foundation terminated in 2010.

Detroit Diesel Scholarship Foundation, Inc., MI
The foundation terminated in 2011.

Dial Educational Trust, Albert, SC
The trust terminated in 2009.

Dinsdale Family Foundation Inc., NE
The foundation did not provide funding in 2012.

Dutka Arts Foundation, Inc., Joyce, NY
The foundation terminated in 2012.

Easthampton Home for Aged Women, Inc.
See Wright Charities Corp.

Educational Fund for Children of Phillips Petroleum Company Employees
See ConocoPhillips Dependent Scholarship Program Trust

El Paso Corporate Foundation, CO
(formerly El Paso Energy Foundation)
The foundation terminated in 2012.

El Paso County Salute to Education Inc, TX
The organization terminated in 2011.

El Paso Energy Foundation
See El Paso Corporate Foundation

Elkhorn Valley Community Development Corporation, NE
The foundation did not provide funding in 2011 and 2012.

EMQ FamiliesFirst, Inc.
See FamiliesFirst, Inc.

FamiliesFirst, Inc., CA
EMQ FamiliesFirst, Inc.
The foundation did not provide funding in 2011 and 2012.

Family Services of Western Pennsylvania, PA
The foundation did not provide funding in 2011 and 2012.

Flying Horse Foundation, Inc., NJ
The foundation terminated in 2012.

Foundation for the Mid South, MS
The foundation did not provide funding in 2011 and 2012.

Fund for Educational Excellence, Inc., MD
The foundation no longer provides funding to individuals.

Georgia-Pacific Foundation, Inc., GA
The foundation has discontinued its ____ program.

Governor's Funding, Inc., LA
The fund terminated in 2011.

Herschend Family Foundation, MO
The foundation does not provide funding to individuals.

Hogsett Foundation, Inc, Robert E., CO
The foundation terminated in 2013.

Hospice Care of Nantucket Foundation, MA
The foundation terminated in 2011.

IAFF Disaster Relief Fund, DC
The fund terminated in 2011.

Inwood Office Furniture Foundation, Inc., IN
(formerly Jasper Table Company Foundation, Inc.)
Current information not available.

Jasper Table Company Foundation, Inc.
See Inwood Office Furniture Foundation, Inc.

Jewish Endowment Foundation, LA
The foundation no longer provides funding to individuals.

Joyard Foundation, The, CA
The foundation terminated in 2013.

Liebmann Fund, Dolores Zohrab, The, TX
Current information not available.

Linda Foundation, John and Mary, NJ
The foundation terminated in 2011.

Lissak Foundation, Inc., The, NJ
The foundation did not provide funding in 2011 and 2012.

Lynch Scholarship Foundation, John B., DE
The foundation terminated in 2011.

M.K. Foundation Inc., NJ
The foundation no longer provides funding to individuals.

Mayer Foundation, Inc., Chaim, NY
Current information not available.

Mellinger Medical Research Memorial Fund, Ralph &. Rose, PA
The foundation terminated in 2012.

Merck-Schering Plough Patient Assistance Program, Inc., NJ
The program terminated in 2012.

Millard Foundation, PA
The foundation terminated in 2010.

Missouri Chamber of Commerce Educational Foundation, Inc., MO
The foundation did not provide funding in 2011 and 2012.

Moore Educational Foundation, Inc., Benjamin, NJ
The foundation terminated in 2009.

Musical Research Society Endowment, OK
(formerly Musical Research Society Endowment Fund, Inc.)
The organization terminated in 2012.

Musical Research Society Endowment Fund, Inc.
See Musical Research Society Endowment

Neinken Scholarship Grant & Loan Foundation, Maurice A., NC
The foundation terminated in 2012.

Nelson Foundation, Inc., WI
(formerly NMC Projects, Inc.)
The foundation terminated in 2012.

NMC Projects, Inc.
See Nelson Foundation, Inc.

Northern Indiana Fuel and Light Company Scholarship Fund, OH
The organization terminated in 2012.

Northwoods Living, Inc., IA
Current information not available.

OCCHA, Inc., OH
The foundation did not provide funding in 2010 and 2011.

Oyler Scholarship Foundation, Inc., Ray, IN
The foundation terminated in 2010.

Pacific Scholarship Foundation, CA
The foundation terminated in 2011.

People in Business Care, Inc., MN
Current information not available.

Perry Scholarship Trust, Mildred R., WI
The trust terminated in 2010.

Pitzer Trust, John, IL
The trust terminated in 2011.

Plitt Southern Theatres, Inc. Employees Fund, TX
The fund terminated in 2012.

Potlatch Foundation for Higher Education, WA
The foundation terminated in 2012.

Quad City Osteopathic Foundation, IA
Current information not available.

Quest Diagnostics Incorporated Contributions Program, NJ
Current information not available.

Ranger-Ryan Scholarship Foundation, TX
The foundation terminated in 2012.

Reger Arts Foundation, Inc., NJ
(formerly Reger Foundation for the Arts, Inc.)
Current information not available.

Reger Foundation for the Arts, Inc.
See Reger Arts Foundation, Inc.

Remington Foundation, Inc.
See Student Votech Foundation, Inc.

Rocky Mountain Natural Gas Memorial Scholarship Fund, CO
Current information not available.

Rogers T.P for C. H. Rogers Memorial Fund, PA
The foundation gave less than $2,000 to individuals in 2011 and 2012.

Rusis Scholarship Fund, Armins, NJ
The fund terminated in 2012.

Sallness Memorial Scholarship Fund, Fritchof T. Sallness and Marian M., MI
The fund terminated in 2010.

Salute to Education, Inc., TX
The organization terminated in 2010.

Schuyler Center for Analysis and Advocacy, NY
(formerly State Communities Aid Association)
The foundation no longer provides funding to individuals.

Shapiro Cancer and Heart Fund, Ruth Newman, NJ
(formerly Shapiro Cancer and Heart Memorial Fund, Ruth Newman)
The foundation gave less than $2,000 to individuals in 2011 and 2012.

Shapiro Cancer and Heart Memorial Fund, Ruth Newman
See Shapiro Cancer and Heart Fund, Ruth Newman

Sigmund Foundation, Bill & Vi, MI
Current information not available.

Stark Trust Fund, Jasper, TN
The fund terminated in 2010.

State Communities Aid Association
See Schuyler Center for Analysis and Advocacy

Student Votech Foundation, Inc., AR
(formerly Remington Foundation, Inc.)
The foundation terminated in 2013.

Stupp Bros. Bridge & Iron Company Foundation, MO
The foundation did not provide funding in 2011 and 2012.

Swyer Foundation, Inc., The, NY
(formerly Swyer Foundation, Lewis A., The)
The foundation terminated in 2011.

Swyer Foundation, Lewis A., The
See Swyer Foundation, Inc., The

Trenton Kappa Foundation, Inc., NJ
The foundation did not provide funding in 2011 and 2012.

Vermillion Civic Council, Inc., SD
The foundation did not provide funding in 2012 and 2013.

Volz Foundation Charitable Trust, MO
The foundation gave less than $2,000 to individuals in 2010 and 2011.

Wacker Foundation, TX
The foundation terminated in 2011.

Ward Educational Trust Agency, Wilbur H., MA
The trust terminated in 2012.

Waterman Trust, Richard, RI
The foundation no longer provides funding to individuals.

Wilbur Foundation, Marguerite Eyer
See Wilbur Foundation, The

Wilbur Foundation, The, CA
(formerly Wilbur Foundation, Marguerite Eyer)
The foundation terminated in 2013.

Woods Foundation, Inc., Tiger, CA
The foundation terminated in 2011.

Wright Charities Corp., MA
(formerly Easthampton Home for Aged Women, Inc.)
The organization terminated in 2011.

GEOGRAPHIC INDEX

The sequence numbers in this index refer to grantmakers which restrict their giving to particular states. Boldface type indicates giving on a national, regional, or international basis. Grantmakers that restrict their giving to particular states, counties, or cities are listed in lighter type following the states in which they give.

ALABAMA

Alexander City: Russell 77
Andalusia: Andalusia 10
Anniston: Community 28
Athens: Franklin 39
Atmore: Mayson 60
Birmingham: AAMN 1, Alabama 3, Alsite 6, **American 8**, American 9, Bashinsky 13, Charity 22, Childcare 23, **Civitan 24**, Community 27, Dixon 31, Grisham 42, Harbert 46, Hawkins 49, **International 54**, Miss 63, Parker 69, Portraits, 70, Protective 72, Regional 74, Southeastern 81, Todd 84, Tractor 85, United 86
Brewton: Brewton 19, Downing 32, Finlay 37, Higdon 50, Owens 67, Reed 73
Camden: Wallace 89
Daphne: Community 25, TAV 83
Decatur: Baker 11, Community 26
Fairhope: Yanamura 95
Florence: Riverbend 76
Foley: Vulcan 88, Woerner 93
Fort Payne: Prewett 71
Guntersville: Marshall-Jackson 58
Haleyville: Winston 92
Huntsville: Decatur 30, Omega 66, WEDC 90
Indian Springs: Smith 80
Mobile: Alsobrook 7, Batre 14, Bedsole 15, Boyd 18, Chapman 21, Dunlap 33, Freels 40, Griswold 43, Gulf 44, Harmeson 47, Harrell 48, Holland 51, Infirmary 52, Killgore 55, Lucash 56, Martin 59, Meharg 61, Middleton 62, Moeschle 64, Padolf 68, Will 91, Wollman 94
Montgomery: Alabama 2, Alabama 4, Alabama 5, Baptist 12, Central 20, Electric 35, Evans 36, Montgomery 65, Reynolds 75, Simpson 79, Venable 87
Opelika: East Alabama 34, Internal 53
Pelham: Gibson 41
Phenix City: Southern 82
Rockford: Hanna 45
Sheffield: Sheffield 78
Tallassee: Blount 17
Tuscaloosa: **Blaylock 16**, Community 29, Fowler 38
Tuskegee: Macon-Russell 57

see also 610, 1614, 2137, 2207, 2247, 3133, 3556, 4653, 4884, 6701, 6707, 6805, 6890, 8575, 8765, 9851

ALASKA

Anchorage: Alaska 97, Alaska 98, Alaska 99, Alaska 100, Alaska 101, Alaskan 102, Aleut 103, Arctic 104, Bristol 107, Calista 108, Chenega 109, Chugach 111, CIRI 113, Eyak 116, Koniag 122, Kuskokwim 123, Norton 128, Old Harbor 129, Providence 131, Rasmuson 132, Schwantes 135, Seybert 137, Tanaq 141, TDX 142, UIC 145, West 149
Cordova: Copper 114
Dillingham: Bristol 106, Choggiung 110, Samuelsen 134
Eagle River: Chugiak-Eagle 112
Fairbanks: Doyon 115, Igloo 119, Monroe 125, Tanana 140, University 146, Usibelli 147
Glennallen: **Ahtna 96**
Homer: Homer 117
Juneau: Huna 118, Juneau 120, Sealaska 136, Territorial 143
Kotzebue: Newlin 127
McGrath: MTNT 126
Nome: Bering 105, Kawerak 121, Pioneer 130, Sitnasuak 138
Point Hope: Tigara 144
Seldovia: SNA 139
Unalaska: McCurdy 124
Wasilla: Valley 148
Wrangell: Rooney 133

see also 321, 536, 4732, 7620, 8759, 9556, 9632, 9644, 9647, 9673, 9690, 9702, 9717, 10031

AMERICAN SAMOA

see 9358

ARIZONA

Apache Junction: Renaissance 232
Avondale: Rosztoczy 234
Cave Creek: **Stott 241**
Chandler: Adelante 151, Arizona 163, East 187, Fisher 192, Food 194
Douglas: Miss 219
Flagsaff: McNeil 216
Flagstaff: **Feed 191**, Northern 222
Gilbert: Positive 230
Glendale: Peoria 225
Gold Canyon: Breeding 173
Kingman: Kingman 207
Kykotsmovi: Hopi 201
Marana: Trico 246
Mesa: Arizona 162, Barlocker 171, **Breast 172**, Prayer 231, Turnbow 249
Miami: McWilliams 217
Phoenix: 100 150, Agape 152, Alhambra 153, Arizona 155, Arizona 156, Arizona 157, Arizona 158, Arizona 159, Arizona 160, Assistance 166, AZHHA 167, Banner 169, Banner 170, Brinker 174, **Cancer 175**, Catholic 176, Catholic 177, Deer 183, **Dickey 184**, Diocesan 185, Dougherty 186, Educare 188, Flinn 193, Foundation 195, Freeport-McMoRan 196, Friedman 197, Grace 199, **Help 200**, Ingebritson 202, Interfaith 204, Knapp 208, Los 212, Major 214, Make-A-Wish 215, Mesa 218, **North 221**, Phoenix 226, Phoenix 227, Piper 229, Seed 236, Squires 239, St. Mary's/Westside 240, Thunderbird 244, Torres 245, Turf 248, US Airways 252, Valley 254, Valley 255, Warner 257, Washington 258
Prescott: Arizona 164, Arizona 165, Christian 179, Education 189
Scottsdale: **Alliance 154**, Arizona 161, Kahvush 206, LaForce 209, Schmitz 235, Spencer 238
Sun City West: Chapman 178
Tempe: Friendship 198, Lewis 211, Patterson 224
Tucson: **Baize 168**, Christian 180, Community 181, Community 182, Educational 190, Institute 203, Jewish 205, Lapan 210, Lupus 213, **Muscular 220**, Old 223, Pima 228, **Research 233**, **Southern 237**, Tucson-Pima 247, United 250, University 251, Valley 253, Youth 259
Willcox: Sulphur 243, Valley 256
Yuma: Sturges 242

see also 417, 440, 478, 999, 1272, 1803, 2357, 2785, 2890, 4238, 5623, 5626, 5628, 5817, 6847, 7894, 8179, 8180, 8188, 9145, 9185, 9207, 9215, 9217, 9330, 9575

ARKANSAS

Amity: Olds 300
Arkadelphia: Sturgis 315
Batesville: Arkansas 263
Bearden: Bearden 270
Benton: Finkbeiner 279
Bentonville: Helping 283, Shewmaker 308, Wal-Mart 324, Wal-Mart 325
Cabot: Cabot 273
Conway: Community 275
Dardanelle: Arvac 267
Dermott: Veasey 322
Dewitt: Moll 291
DeWitt: Thomas 318
El Dorado: El Dorado 277, Murphy 293, Murphy 294, Murphy 295, **Murphy 296**, SHARE 307, Union 321
Eureka Springs: Communication 274
Fayetteville: **Mashburn 289**, Ohlendorf 299, Pierce 302
Flippin: South 311
Fort Smith: Sparks 313, White 326
Harrison: Ozark 301
Hot Springs: Area 261
Hot Springs Village: Riordan 305
Little Rock: Arkansas 262, Arkansas 264, Arkansas 265, Arkansas 266, Baptist 269, Halstead 281, Keltner 287, Terry 317
Magnolia: Southern 312
McGehee: Wallace 323

Mount Ida: Woodson 328
Mountain Home: Hornlein 284, Kelder 286, Nelson 297, Raef 303
Newport: Northeast 298
North Little Rock: Tenenbaum 316, Williams 327
Osceola: Ayres 268
Paragould: Reed 304
Pine Bluff: Munyon 292, Trinity 319
Rogers: Buck 272, Lehman 288
Russellville: Gillespie 280, McDonald 290, Smith 310
Sherwood: Cornerstone 276
Siloam Springs: Allen, 260
Sparkman: Sturgis 314
Springdale: Endeavor 278, Jones 285, RMHC 306, Single 309, Tyson 320
Van Buren: Boggan 271, Hamm 282

see also 7, 81, 610, 1494, 3651, 4884, 5053, 5099, 7527, 8601, 8734, 8922, 9167

CALIFORNIA

Agoura Hills: Community 510, Rader 892
Alameda: **Hager 643**, Justin 715, Lippert 746, McQuinn 780
Aliso Viejo: American 354, Downey 545
Altadena: Five 577
Alturas: Modoc 801
Anaheim: Anaheim 363, Anaheim 364, Angels 366, California 454, **Floor 580**
Anaheim Hills: Jones 713
Apple Valley: High 662
Aptos: Cabrillo 433, Community 512, Graham 634
Arroyo Grande: Johnson 709
Atherton: Menlo 784
Auburn: Placer 870
Bakersfield: Beaver 407, Calcot 440, Twin 1065
Balboa Island: Werner 1089
Bayside: Humboldt 671, Union 1067
Bell: **Children's 491**
Belmont: California 453
Belvedere: Belvedere 411
Berkeley: AEPOCH 341, Alta 350, Baxter 404, Buddhist 426, **Earth 550**, **Impact 678**, Mathematical 776, **San 927**, St. Francis 1011, Through 1047
Beverly Hills: **Academy 334**, Feminist 573, Johnson 710, **PADI 852**, Physicians 867, Tower 1052, Warner 1086, Wayne 1088, Young 1107
Bonita: Child 483
Buena Park: **Global 623**, Tawa 1038, United 1070
Burbank: Burn 429, California 449, Disney 540
Burlingame: California 460, Chicana 482, China 492, Mills-Peninsula 795
Calabasas: Social 998, **Society 1001**
Calistoga: LEF 741
Camarillo: Interface 687, Swift 1036, Ventura 1081
Camp Pendleton: Injured 682
Capistrano Beach: San Felipe 940
Carlsbad: Chopra 494, **Gemological 609**, La 728, **Life 745**, Lynn 762, **NAMM 813**
Carmichael: Hurliman 675
Century City: Bickerstaff 413
Chester: Almanor 349
Chico: North 831, North 832
Chula Vista: Federal 572, Rohr 917
City of Industry: Cacique 434, **Public 886**
Colton: Trinity 1057
Commerce: RCL 900, Smart 993
Corona del Mar: Stedman 1020
Costa Mesa: Assistance 382, **Gala 608**, James 702, **Modglin 800**, **National 815**, National 816
Covina: California 442
Culver City: **Center 473**, **Ramakrishna 895**
Danville: Rainey 894
Davis: American 360

Del Mar: Foundation 585
Del Rey Oaks: Monterey 804
Diamond Bar: Association 390, **SEMA 973**
Dixon: Couch 524, Madden 765, Morris 806
Downey: Stauffer 1019
Dulzura: **Family 568**
El Cajon: Friends 600
El Monte: El Monte 557
Elk Grove: Elk 560
Emeryville: Emery 563
Encinitas: Coastal 504, Rancho 897
Encino: American 353, **A-T 391**, **Gleitsman 620**
Escondido: Truth 1062
Fairfax: Kiersted 720
Fairfield: Darnell 536
Fallbrook: Collister 506
Ferndale: Lytel 763
Forest Ranch: Butte 432
Fremont: Groeniger 639, Washington 1087
Fresno: Alliance 347, Burks 428, Fansler 569, Fresno 595, Fresno 596, Fresno 597, Swanson 1034
Fullerton: California 451, California 459, **Faith's 567**, St. Jude 1014, Sweet 1035
Garden Grove: **Aesthetic 342**, League 738
Gardena: Granoff 636, **Hispanic 664**, Ramona's 896, Shelby 979
Gilroy: St. Joseph's 1013
Glen Ellen: Foundation 590
Glendale: Community 513, Nestle 825, Raies-Murr 893
Glendora: Ameritec 361
Hayward: **Alalusi 345**, Cal 439
Healdsburg: Healdsburg 650, Johnson 712
Hermosa Beach: Sandpipers 953
Hesperia: Oro 847
Hillsborough: GET 613
Hollister: Community 511, Storkan/Hanes 1027
Hollywood: **International 690**
Huntington Beach: Give 618, Golden 627, Huntington 673, Penjoyan 859
Indio: Carreon 465
Inverness: Pacific 850
Irvine: **Beckman 408**, Busch 431, Change 477, Croul 529, Good 629, Philharmonic 866, Project 883, **Rand 898**, **Santa 959**, Warne 1085
Irwindale: Irwindale 697
Jackson: Amador 352
La Canada Flintridge: La Canada 727
La Habra: Missionary 796, Nauheim/Straus 823
La Jolla: Athena 392, Price 878, Price 879, Wilcox 1095
La Mesa: Child 484, Curley 531
La Verne: Jedinstvo 703, Mang 768
Lafayette: Dales 534, Lafayette 730, Turn 1064
Laguna Beach: Science 968
Laguna Niguel: **Chung 499**
Lakeport: Lucky 760
Lakewood: Lakewood 732
Lancaster: Lancaster 735, **Society 1000**
Linden: Machado 764
Livermore: **Hertz 658**, Pedrozzi 858, Taylor 1039
Lodi: Vaccarezza-Murdaca 1075
Long Beach: **Arthritis 376**, Employees 564, Long Beach 754, Redding 904, Vanguard 1077, Whitten 1092
Los Altos: Los Altos 755
Los Angeles: Advertising 339, American 356, **American 358**, Arthritis 375, **Association 389**, BBCN 406, **Bel-Air 410**, California 443, California 445, **Cantor 463**, Celebrity 470, Center 472, Chesley 480, **Children 485**, Chinese 493, Clark 502, Cohen 505, **Colonnades 507**, **Concern 523**, Cops 523, Cure 530, Discovery 539, Dr. 546, Ebell 553, **Elim 559**, Film 575, Flint 579, Found 583, **Foundation 589**, Foundation 591, **French 594**, Fulfillment 604, Fundacion 605, **Getty 614**, Glover 624, **Grass 637**, Hartman 648, Heart 653, Held 655, Inner-City

684, International 689, Jefferies 704, Jewish 708, Korean 723, Korean 724, Kurka 726, Lagrant 731, **Lambda 733**, Laurance 737, Leavey 740, Liberty 744, Loeb 753, Los 757, Los 758, Lynch 761, McComb 778, **Mexican 788**, Military 791, Mills 794, Mitchell 797, National 820, National 821, New 826, Optimist 842, Outpost 848, Performing 861, Pfaffinger 864, Plotkin 871, **Point 875**, QueensCare 891, Recruiting 902, **Screen 969**, Sedler 972, Serra 976, Silverlake 989, **Smiley 994**, Society 999, South 1004, Southern 1005, St. Shenouda 1015, Stern 1024, **Union 1068**, United 1071, **United 1072**, Variety 1078, **Variety 1079**, **Women 1098**
Los Gatos: Urbanek 1074
Los Osos: **Easter 552**
Malibu: Creative 526
Mammoth Lakes: Mammoth 767
Manhattan Beach: Armstrong 371, Nickelson 827, **Pancreatic 854**
Marina del Rey: Association 388
Menlo Park: **Draper 547**, Iranian 696, **Kaiser 716**, Livermore 750, Myotonic 812
Merced: Yosemite 1106
Mill Valley: **Sarcoma 960**
Milpitas: Emergency 562, Housing 669
Mission Viejo: **Association 387**, SCI 967
Modesto: FRAMAX 592, Modesto 798, Modesto 799, Sierra 983, Stanislaus 1017
Montebello: Heart 652
Monterey: Community 516, Monterey 803, Myers 811
Montrose: Schmidt 964
Moraga: **Cystinosis 533**
Mountain View: **Burwen 430**, Cystic 532, Guzik 642, **Marconi 769**, Silicon 986
Napa: Community 518, North 829
Newport Beach: Beckstrand 409, Carlston 464, Chung 498, Hewitt 659, Hoag 665, Hoag 666, Merage 785, Orange 843, Simon 990, Small 992, Strauss 1028
Newport Coast: Kerber 719
North Hills: Penny 860
North Hollywood: **Academy 335**, Deaf 537, Fernando 574, **International 691**
Novato: Gaines 607, Ladies 729, Marin 772
Oakland: American 359, California 450, **Cavalier 469**, **Common 509**, Compass 519, Foster 582, Kaiser 717, Kaiser 718, Level 743, Media 781, Memorial 783, **National 817**, **NMA 828**, Northern 834, Oakland 836, Oaklandish, 837, Open 841, Philanthropic 865, Public 887, Rose 919, Scaife 961, Sulprizio 1031, **Toigo 1049**
Oceanside: Tri 1054
Ojai: Ojai 839
Ontario: Johnson 711
Orange: Assistance 383, Low 759, St 1010
Oxnard: **From 603**
Pacheco: Westphal 1091
Palo Alto: **Association 386**, **Borg 418**, Cherith 479, Dudley-Vehmeyer-Brown 548, Golden 625, Gunn 640, **HP 670**, Pursuit 888, Zider 1109
Palos Verdes Peninsula: Palos Verdes 853
Pasadena: **Armenian 370**, **Avery 395**, California 458, Center 471, National 822, Pasadena 855, Ronald 918, Rosemary 920, Side 981, Sun-Pacific 1033
Pebble Beach: Pebble 857
Placerville: El Dorado 556
Playa Vista: Los 756
Pleasanton: American 355, **International 692**, Morgan 805, Northern 833, Shaklee 977, **World 1102**
Point Reyes Station: Pirkle 869
Pomona: Cal 438, Pomona 876, San Gabriel/Pomona 949
Porterville: Bartlett 400
Portola Valley: Gifford 616, Poole 877
Quincy: Plumas 873
Ramona: Bradley 421

Rancho Cordova: Horn 668, Mercy 786

Rancho Cucamonga: Marino 773

Rancho Santa Fe: Smith 996

Redding: Central 474, Far 570, **McConnell 779**, Richards 910, Roberts 915, Rowan 923, Shasta 978, Sierra 982

Redwood City: Hinckley 663, Legal 742, Sequoia 975

Richmond: West 1090

Rio Vista: Hamilton 646

Riverside: Assistance 384, California 446, Community 514, Locke 751, Riverside 913, Riverside 914

Roseville: Raphael 899

Sacramento: ACEC 337, Alta 351, Cahp 435, California 447, California 448, California 456, GenCorp 610, Girl 617, Health 651, Make-A-Wish 766, Marguerite 770, Quality 890, Sacramento 925, Sacramento 926, **United 1069**

Salinas: Matsui 777

San Bernardino: Children's 488, Foundation 584, Harbison 647, Inland 683

San Carlos: Fischer 576

San Diego: Boyer 420, Brooks 423, **Challenged 476**, Chaparral 478, Conquistador 522, Doe 542, **INCOSE 679**, **Invisible 694**, Jack 699, Klicka 722, **Lambda 734**, Media 782, **Mexico 789**, **Nepal 824**, OZ 849, Pack 851, Promises 884, **QUALCOMM 889**, Rest 908, S.L. 924, San Diego 928, San Diego 929, San Diego 930, San Diego 931, San Diego 932, San Diego 933, San Diego 934, San 935, San Diego 936, San Diego 937, San Diego 938, San Diego 939, Seau 970, **Sempra 974**, Space 1007, Stensrud 1021, Therrien 1045

San Francisco: 826 331, Academic 333, AIDS 344, Allgemeiner 346, **Alliance 348**, **American 357**, Anderson 365, Art 373, **Asia 378**, Asian 379, Aspiration 381, Avery 396, Bartholomew 399, Basic 401, Baskin 402, Bay 405, Black 414, Cal 437, California 441, California 444, California 455, Catholic 467, Children's 487, **Children's 490**, Chronicle 496, **Civic 501**, **Columbia 508**, Community 517, CounterPULSE 525, Dancers' 535, Exploratorium 565, Fleishhacker 578, **Foundation 588**, Frameline 593, Gerbode 612, Giannini 615, Glaucoma 619, Golden 626, **Goldman 628**, Good 631, Herbst 656, Hiebler 660, **Higgins 661**, Horizons 667, Hydrocephalus 676, Independent 680, **Independent 681**, Intersection 693, Italian 698, Jewish 706, Jewish 707, Kimbo 721, Kornberg 725, **Leakey 739**, Liu 749, Martin 774, Masonic 775, Miedema 790, National 819, Olympic 840, **Ploughshares 872**, Pritchett 882, **Red 903**, REDF 905, **Rex 909**, San Francisco 941, **San Francisco 943**, San Francisco 944, San Francisco 945, San Francisco 946, San Francisco 947, San Francisco 948, Schwab 966, Signer 985, Silver 988, Southern 1006, Teachers 1040, Tenderloin 1042, That 1043, Theatre 1044, **Thiel 1046**, **Tides 1048**, Tracy 1053, **Trust 1060**, **Trustees 1061**, **Tuckerman 1063**, University 1073, Visual 1082, Wickham 1094, Williams 1096, Women's 1099, World 1101, Wu 1104

San Jose: **Adobe 338**, Arts 377, Avant! 394, Catalyst 466, Catholic 468, El Puente 558, Good 630, Hallgrimson 645, San 950, Second 971, Silicon 987, **Tech 1041**, Wright 1103

San Luis Obispo: Access 336, San Luis 951, **Shinoda 980**

San Marcos: Griffin 638, Smylie 997

San Marino: Christian 495, Huntington 674, Ward 1084

San Martin: Ioan 695

San Mateo: **Archeo/ 368**, Piedemonte 868, San Mateo 952, Society 1002

San Pedro: Angels 367, Croatian 527

San Rafael: 10,000 329, Art 374, Chrysopolae 497, Ciatti 500, **National 814**, San Francisco 942, **Studenica 1029**

San Ramon: **Croatian 528**

Santa Ana: Breast 422, California 457, Orangewood 845, Sukut 1030, Winnett 1097

Santa Barbara: Bialis 412, Doing 543, **Glenn 621**, Jefferson 705, **Nuclear 835**, Performing 862, **Rivendell 912**, Santa 954, Santa Barbara 955, Scholarship 965, Siff 984, Tri-Counties 1055, **Vogelzang 1083**

Santa Clara: Builder's 427, **Foundation 587**, **Intel 686**

Santa Clarita: Spirit 1008

Santa Cruz: Battered 403, Eastcliff 551, James 700, **Organic 846**

Santa Maria: Santa 957

Santa Monica: 18th 330, Durfee 549, **GRAMMY 635**, Lasso 736, Methodist 787, Milken 792, Mills 793, Musicares 809, Pasarow 856, **Prostate 885**, Veneklasen 1080

Santa Rosa: **Aid 343**, California 452, Community 515, Santa 958

Saratoga: Glennon 622, **Montalvo 802**, Schmidek 963

Sausalito: Arques 372, **Foundation 586**, Headlands 649

Scotts Valley: Santa 956

Seal Beach: Stephens 1022

Sebastopol: True 1059

Sherman Oaks: Childrens 486, Pergo 863

Simi Valley: Reagan 901

Sonoma: Buckley 425, Woodward 1100

Sonora: Ardron 369, Sonora 1003

South El Monte: **Ekstrom 555**

South Gate: Boand 416

South Laguna: Blackburn 415

South Pasadena: **Institute 685**

South San Francisco: Aspiranet 380, **Genentech 611**

St. Helena: **Grace 633**, St. 1012

Stanford: **Stanford 1016**

Stockton: Baker 397, Bank 398, Central 475, Florsheim 581, Friedberger 598, Schiffman 962, **Sponsors 1009**, Stanley 1017, Stockton 1025, Stone 1026, Touhey 1051, Valley 1076, Zeiter 1108

Sun Valley: PMC 874

Sunnyvale: Lockheed 752, SKB 991, Sunnyvale 1032

Sylmar: **Children's 489**

Temecula: Dorland 544

The Sea Ranch: Rosenberg 921

Thousand Oaks: **Amgen 362**, Oakley 838

Toluca Lake: **Rogers 916**

Torrance: Fairmount 566, Gorecki 632, International 688, Little 747, Torrance 1050

Truckee: **Smith 995**, Truckee 1058

Tulare: Cain 436

Tustin: **Little 748**, Orange 844, Trinity 1056

Twentynine Palms: Joshua 714

Ukiah: Chessall 481, Cloud 503, Redwood 906, Redwood 907, Ukiah 1066

Upland: Brown 424, Price 880

Vacaville: Stephenson 1023

Vallejo: Advocates 340

Van Nuys: Bodine 417, North 830

Venice: Conner 521

Victorville: Desert 538, Tatum 1037

Visalia: Price 881

Vista: **Cancer 462**

Walnut Creek: Bossola 419, **Ellison 561**, Farber 571, Friends 599, Haight 644, Heffernan 654, James 701, Muir 808, **National 818**, Rossmoor 922

West Covina: Futuro 606

West Hollywood: Friends 601

Westminster: Heritage 657, Mutual 810

Whittier: Assistance 385, Hunter 672, Rio 911, Whittier 1093

Willits: Guslander 641

Winters: Mariani 771

Woodland: **Immunobiology 677**, Yolo 1105

Woodland Hills: **Autism 393**, California 461, Eglitis 554, Motion 807

Woodside: **Djerassi 541**, Fries 602

Yuba City: Aaron 332

---

see also 200, 210, 1227, 1290, 1385, 1462, 1528, 2021, 2046, 3440, 3738, 3832, 3905, 4087, 4134, 4414, 4526, 4573, 4578, 4731, 5283, 5287, 5289, 5723, 5817, 6036, 6052, 6450, 6531, 6578, 6579, 6585, 6586, 6631, 6648, 6688, 6728, 6742, 6791, 6847, 6874, 7574, 7578, 7593, 7594, 7645, 7794, 7868, 7940, 7958, 8043, 8067, 8069, 8086, 8648, 8779, 8838, 8839, 8864, 8970, 8972, 9021, 9043, 9064, 9079, 9177, 9188, 9204, 9413, 9575, 9613, 9644, 9906, 10017, 10106

COLORADO

Akron: Colorado 1167

Alamosa: Outcalt 1254

Allenspark: Burton 1137

Arvada: Colorado 1155, Eagle 1186, Kaiser 1224, Taddonio 1294

Aspen: Aspen 1123, Boogie's 1131, **Music 1246**, Staley 1290

Aurora: APS 1120, Colfax 1152, Colorado 1153, **Colorado 1165**, Rocky 1273

Avon: Eagle 1187, Vail 1302

Beulah: Hanson 1209

Boulder: American 1117, Boulder 1132, Harvey 1210, I Have 1218, Reach 1265, Young 1311

Breckenridge: Breckenridge 1134, Summit 1293

Broomfield: Broomfield 1135

Carbondale: Carbondale 1140

Castle Rock: Brown 1136, Douglas 1184, Lillis 1232

Centennial: Colorado 1157, Ethridge 1192, Marchello 1237, SEAKR 1279

Colorado Springs: Balke 1127, Care 1141, Christian 1146, Colorado Springs 1166, Community 1173, Curtis 1176, Heathcock 1212, Hughes 1216, Lasater 1229, **National 1248**, Pikes 1257, Pikes 1258, Sachs 1277, Seay 1280, Sharpe 1282, **U.S. 1297**, **United 1298**, **United 1299**, **WaterStone 1305**

Conifer: Morgan 1242

Crawford: Cocker 1151

Delta: Delta 1178, Renfrow 1267, Veirs 1303

Denver: AEG 1113, **AfricAid 1114**, Alexander 1115, **American 1116**, Aorn 1119, Arthritis 1122, Assistance 1124, Bonfils 1130, Boys 1133, Children's 1144, Clark 1149, Colorado 1154, Colorado 1156, Colorado 1159, Colorado 1163, Colorado 1164, **Daniels 1177**, Denver 1179, Denver 1180, Denver 1181, Denver 1182, Denver 1183, East 1188, Food 1196, Foundation 1198, **Foundation 1199**, Gathering 1203, Girl 1204, Goodwill 1205, Helmar 1213, Holt 1214, Jewish 1222, **Johns 1223**, Lupus 1234, Lutheran 1235, Minority 1240, **Morris 1243**, Newland 1249, Nine 1250, Operation 1253, Project 1261, Public 1262, Puddy 1263, Rocky 1270, Rocky 1271, Ronald 1274, Scottish 1278, Stupfel 1292, VSA 1304

Durango: Barr 1128, Community 1172, Durango 1185, Fort 1197, Merry 1238

Edwards: Flatirons 1195

Englewood: Catholic 1142, Cibrowski 1147, Kuzell 1227

Erie: National 1247

Estes Park: Crossroads 1175, MacGregor 1236, YMCA 1310

Evergreen: Evergreen 1193, Mountain 1244

Fort Collins: **Christian 1145**, Colorado 1162, Colorado 1169, Community 1171, Conkling 1174, Griffin 1206, Pathways 1256, Poudre 1260, United 1300

Fort Morgan: Williams 1308

Glendale: Hunter 1217

Glenwood Springs: Advocate 1112, Colorado 1161, Light 1231

Grand Junction: Colorado 1160, Housing 1215, Population 1259, Saccomanno 1276, St. Mary's 1289, Western 1306

Greeley: North 1251, University 1301, Zac's 1313
Greenwood Village: Adventure 1111
Gunnison: Community 1170, Gunnison 1207
Highlands Ranch: CAEYC 1138
Julesburg: Campbell 1139
Kittredge: **Someone 1286**
Lafayette: Sister 1283
Lakewood: ACVIM 1110, **Clan 1148**, Colorado 1168, **Federal 1194**, Jeffco 1220, Jefferson 1221, Keren 1226, Red 1266, Rocky 1272, Stride 1291
Lamar: Rutherford 1275
Littleton: Colorado 1158, Kennedy 1225, Mulford 1245, Servant 1281, Society 1285, **Sonlight 1287**
Longmont: Clark 1150, Layton 1230, Outreach 1255
Louisville: EDUCAUSE 1189, Impact 1219, **Rock 1269**
Loveland: **H.E.L.P. 1208**, Molloy 1241
Manitou Springs: Norwood 1252
Montrose: Elizondo 1191, Langston 1228
Monument: Mikkelson 1239
Pagosa Springs: Archuleta 1121
Parker: El 1190
Penrose: **Galaway 1201**
Pueblo: Assistance 1125, Garone-Nicksich 1202, Hasan 1211, Pueblo 1264, Robinson 1268, Skrifvars 1284, White 1307
Snowmass Village: Anderson 1118
Springfield: Tolbert 1296
Steamboat Springs: Yampa 1309
Sterling: Logan 1233
Superior: **Children 1143**
Telluride: Telluride 1295
Trinidad: Bianco 1129
USAF Academy: **Association 1126**
Walsenburg: Spanish 1288
Westminster: Front 1200
Yuma: Yuma 1312

see also 362, 630, 660, 675, 1083, 1494, 1957, 2552, 2632, 2785, 3902, 4238, 4834, 5099, 5258, 5285, 6653, 6765, 6826, 6841, 7584, 7586, 7587, 7598, 7803, 8787, 9207, 9575, 9837, 10017, 10118

CONNECTICUT

Avon: Cornelia 1370
Bloomfield: **Fidelco 1388**, Operation 1438, Rogow 1451
Branford: Branford 1338, Munger 1427, Zane 1492
Bridgeport: Action 1314, Barden 1329, Borck 1337, Bridgeport 1339, Brown 1341, Eastman 1382, Hurlbutt 1404, International 1407, Scott 1457, Sheridan 1460, Westport-Weston 1484, Workplace 1489
Bristol: Barnes 1330, Main 1419
Brookfield: Macricostas 1417
Burlington: Bristol 1340
Canton: Cawasa 1348
Cheshire: Alexion 1317
Danbury: Albero 1316, **National 1429**
Danielson: Spirol 1462
Darien: Darien 1373, Person-to-Person 1442, **Scudder 1458**, Tierney 1472
East Canaan: Canaan 1345
Easton: Staples 1466
Enfield: Colburn-Keenan 1360
Fairfield: Building 1342
Farmington: **Bonfire 1336**, Graham 1396
Gales Ferry: United 1476
Glastonbury: Charitable 1353, Compass 1364, Macristy 1418, Prasad 1445, Sullivan 1469
Greenwich: Byram 1344, **Cholnoky 1356**, Eagle 1380, Folsom 1390, Gilbert 1395, **Walkabout 1479**
Hartford: American 1321, Capital 1346, Community 1363, Connecticut 1365, Connecticut 1367, Ebony 1383, Fox 1391, Fuller 1393, Hammers 1397, Hartford 1398, Hartford 1399, Hartford 1400, Henries 1402, Hurley 1405, Real 1447, Rubinow 1453, Squier 1463, Urban 1477, Widows 1485, **XL 1491**
Jewett City: Thames 1470
Lakeville: Ash 1325, Bauer 1332, Bauer 1333
Litchfield: CJR 1357
Lyme: Adams 1315
Manchester: Manchester 1420, SBM 1456
Meriden: Clark 1358, Hunter's 1403
Middlebury: Traurig 1475
Middletown: Liberty 1414
Milford: Devon 1376, Milford 1423, Milford 1424
Mystic: **Avatar 1327**
New Britain: American 1322, CCSU 1349, Tomasso 1473
New Canaan: New Canaan 1430, Nolan 1433
New Haven: **Belgian 1334**, Childs 1354, Connecticut 1368, Dolan 1378, Elmseed 1384, Fusco 1394, Jewish 1409, Knights 1411, **Knights 1412**, New Haven 1431, Phelps 1443, Promising 1446, Woman's 1488
New London: Atwood 1326, Bulkeley 1343, Chapman 1351, Community 1361
New Milford: Litchfield 1415, Paul 1440
North Haven: Anthony 1324, North 1434
Norwalk: Center 1350, Chariott 1352, Fairfield 1387, **Multiple 1426**, Norwalk 1435, Norwalk 1436, Wilkerson 1486, Xerox 1490
Norwich: Wells 1483
Old Lyme: MacCurdy 1416
Orange: Orange 1439
Ridgefield: Boehringer 1335, Igstaedter 1406, Ridgefield 1448
Rockville: Fromson 1392
Roxbury: Roxbury 1452
Shartford: Dunning 1379
South Windsor: Rockville 1450
Southington: Miss 1425
Stamford: **Alliance 1318**, **AmeriCares 1323**, Bartlett 1331, Conway 1369, **Criag 1371**, CTE 1372, Deering 1374, First 1389, Miceli-Wings 1422, Peirce 1441, **Pitney 1444**, Senior 1459, Stamford 1464, Stamford 1465, Starks 1467
Stonington: **Coast 1359**, Riot 1449
Suffield: Thomas 1471
Torrington: Community 1362
Trumbull: DiMauro 1377
Wallingford: Eastern 1381
Washington: Steep 1468
Waterbury: Connecticut 1366, Meriden 1421, New 1432, Traalum 1474
Watertown: Watertown 1480
West Hartford: **American 1320**, Balso 1328, Carlson 1347, Endocrine 1385, Jewish 1408, **Kim 1410**, Larrabee 1413, Saybrook 1455, **Society 1461**
Westport: **China 1355**, Equus 1386, Hartley 1401, My 1428, **Save 1454**
Wethersfield: O'Meara 1437
Wilton: Ambler 1319, Deloitte 1375, **Weir 1481**
Windsor: Voya 1478, Windsor 1487
Woodbury: Weller 1482

see also 67, 741, 1858, 2445, 2455, 2513, 2527, 2550, 2577, 2859, 2926, 3986, 3994, 4000, 4029, 4033, 4034, 4064, 4142, 4195, 4268, 4465, 4730, 4960, 5381, 5556, 5579, 5964, 6071, 6171, 6397, 6486, 6514, 6566, 6672, 6771, 7104, 7859, 8230, 8231, 8232, 8245, 8255, 8262, 8265, 8280, 8281, 8288, 8289, 8302, 8305, 8308, 8313, 8317, 8327, 8330, 8331, 8341, 8344, 8346, 8353, 8357, 8361, 8362, 8366, 8367, 8371, 8373, 8374, 8390, 8392, 8413, 8424, 8426, 8434, 8438, 8439, 9240

DELAWARE

Camden: Simpson 1523
Dover: Horsemen's 1513
Lewes: Farpath 1507
Milford: Masten 1516
Newark: Delaware 1502, Gromet 1511, **International 1514**, Quarter 1521, Robinson 1522, University 1526
Rehoboth Beach: Delaware 1504
Wilmington: AstraZeneca 1493, CenturyLink-Clarke 1494, Chaney 1495, Children 1496, Common 1497, CTW 1498, Delaware 1499, Delaware 1500, Delaware 1501, Delaware 1503, **Eleutherian 1505**, Etnier 1506, Frank 1508, Fresh 1509, Gordy 1510, Hirsch 1512, JBL 1515, National 1517, Orange 1518, Ortega 1519, Presto 1520, Splawn 1524, Thomson 1525, Vocational 1527, Westly 1528

see also 3799, 3876, 4884, 5548, 5556, 6890, 7700, 7721, 7737, 7896, 7898, 7929, 7994, 8054, 8055, 8061, 8068, 8135, 8140

DISTRICT OF COLUMBIA

Washington: **AARP 1529**, Abramson 1530, **Accordia 1531**, Afterschool 1532, **Aga 1533**, Air 1534, **Airline 1535**, Albert 1536, **Amazon 1537**, **American 1538**, **American 1539**, American 1540, **American 1541**, **American 1542**, **American 1543**, **American 1544**, **American 1545**, **American 1546**, **American 1547**, **American 1548**, **American 1549**, **American 1550**, **American 1551**, **American 1552**, **American 1553**, **American 1554**, **American 1555**, **American 1556**, **American 1557**, American 1558, **American 1559**, **American 1560**, **American 1561**, **American 1562**, **American 1563**, **American 1564**, **American 1565**, American 1566, **American 1567**, American 1568, American 1569, American 1570, **American 1571**, **American 1572**, **Amyotrophic 1573**, Anacostia 1574, **Animal 1575**, Arab 1576, **Arc 1577**, Arch 1578, **Armed 1579**, Asian 1580, Asian 1581, Asian 1582, **Aspen 1583**, Association 1584, **Association 1585**, **Association 1586**, Association 1587, **Atlas 1588**, **Atlas 1589**, Ayuda 1590, Bell 1591, Best 1592, Black 1593, Block 1594, B'nai 1595, Bogan 1596, **Broadcast 1597**, Capital 1598, Center 1599, Children's 1600, Christ 1601, CIC 1602, **Citizens 1603**, Communications 1604, Community 1605, Community 1606, **Congressional 1607**, Corcoran 1608, Cornerstone 1609, **Council 1610**, **Council 1611**, **Council 1612**, Cox 1613, **Development 1614**, Dingwall 1615, District 1616, District 1617, District 1618, Dutko 1619, Ellington 1620, **Environmental 1621**, **Equal 1622**, Equipment 1623, **Esperantic 1624**, **Families 1625**, **FINRA 1626**, Food 1627, Fordham 1628, **Foundation 1629**, Franciscan 1630, **Freedom 1631**, **Freedom 1632**, **Friendly 1633**, **Fund 1634**, **Fund 1635**, **Gateway 1636**, Gay 1637, **German 1638**, Gerontological 1639, **Glaser 1640**, Global 1641, Hemophilia 1642, **Heritage 1643**, **Hispanic 1644**, Hitachi 1645, Hoffa 1646, Horticultural 1647, **Hurston 1648**, Independent 1649, **Institute 1650**, **Institute 1651**, International 1652, **International 1653**, **International 1654**, **International 1655**, International 1656, **International 1657**, International 1658, **International 1659**, **International 1660**, **Jack 1661**, Jerusalem 1662, Jews 1663, Junior 1664, **Kennedy 1665**, **Kennedy 1666**, **Kennedy 1667**, **Landscape 1668**, Latino 1669, **Legal 1670**, **Lupus 1671**, Marijuana 1672, **Marijuana 1673**, **Marshall 1674**, Masonic 1675, **Melanoma 1676**, **Melanoma 1677**, Mentors 1678, Minbanc 1679, **Monk 1680**, **National 1681**, National 1682, National 1683, **National 1684**, **National 1685**, National 1686, **National 1687**, **National 1688**, **National 1689**, **National 1690**, **National 1691**, **National 1692**, **National 1693**, **National 1694**,

National 1695, National 1696, National 1697, National 1698, **National 1699**, **NEA 1700**, Nonprofit 1701, **Ocean 1702**, Olender 1703, O'Neil 1704, **Optical 1705**, Paralyzed 1706, **Parents, 1707**, **Parkinson's 1708**, **Patient 1709**, Patterson 1710, Patton 1711, **PEN/Faulkner 1712**, People 1713, **Pharmaceutical 1714**, Phi 1715, **Phillips 1716**, Professional 1717, **Radio 1718**, Rainy 1719, Rales 1720, **Recycling 1721**, Red 1722, Resources 1723, **Robinson, 1724**, Ronald 1725, Schimel 1726, **Sheet 1727**, Sigma 1728, **Smithsonian 1729**, **Society 1730**, **Society 1731**, **Sons 1732**, **Spina 1733**, St. John's 1734, **Teamster 1735**, **Travel 1736**, Turner 1737, **U.S. 1738**, **UFCW 1739**, ULI 1740, **Union 1741**, **Union 1742**, **United 1743**, United 1744, **VSA 1745**, Washington 1746, Washington 1747, Washington 1748, Washington 1749, Washington 1750, **Wilderness 1751**, **Wilson 1752**, **Women 1753**, Women's 1754, **World 1755**, Young 1756, **Youth 1757**, **YWCA 1758**

see also 610, 1180, 1385, 1965, 3758, 3810, 3832, 3851, 3853, 3876, 3890, 3907, 3927, 3944, 4884, 5817, 6531, 7082, 7329, 7720, 8061, 9330, 9475, 9481, 9504, 9516, 9799

FLORIDA

Amelia Island: Amos 1776
Apopka: Diocesan 1862
Atlantic Beach: Clint 1832
Belle Glade: Hill 1913
Boca Raton: American 1774, BRRH 1813, **Office 2002**, **Scholarship 2052**, Snow 2066, Sunburst 2079
Bonita Springs: Art 1782
Bradenton: Aurora 1788, Beall 1793, Beall 1794, Beall 1795, Boyer 1804, Manatee 1960, Riechmann 2037, State 2073
Brandon: Florida 1882
Cape Coral: Cape Coral 1815, **Joshua 1932**
Clearwater: Abilities 1763, Amin 1775, Community 1849, Grossman 1897, Gulf 1899, Hein 1909, Momeni 1981, Ott 2009, Petteys 2017, Pinellas 2018
Clermont: Community 1845
Clewiston: Nall 1992
Cocoa Beach: Wolfe 2106
Coconut Creek: **Ataxia 1786**
Cooper City: Renal 2035
Coral Gables: Alpha-1 1767, American 1773
Coral Springs: Morris 1983
Davie: Common 1836, Gwynn 1900
Daytona Beach: Brown 1812, Embassy 1869, LPGA 1955
DeBary: Reed 2032
Delray Beach: Benjamin 1796, Life 1950, Roberts 2039
Dunedin: Pagliara 2010
Englewood: Englewood 1870, Hermitage 1912, Smith 2065
Eustis: Lake 1943
Fellsmere: Operation 2006
Fernandina Beach: Caples 1816
Flagler Beach: Smith 2064
Fort Lauderdale: Arcadian 1779, Broward 1810, Broward 1811, Community 1841, Fort 1889, Fort 1890, **Gamma 1894**, **Multiple 1989**, Senior 2059, Thrush 2087
Fort Myers: Child 1823, Delta 1859, Hellenic 1910, Hillmyer-Tremont 1914, Lloyd 1953, Music 1991, Southwest 2067
Fort Myers Beach: Fort 1891, Ft. 1892
Fort Pierce: Indian 1927, King 1939, United 2095
Ft. Lauderdale: Biegelsen 1798
Gainesville: **Harvest 1906**, North 1998, Operafestival 2005, Santa 2049, University 2096

Hialeah: Starks 2072
Highland City: United 2094
Holiday: **Kids 1938**
Hollywood: Hollywood 1919, Planning 2021
Jacksonville: American 1771, Baptist 1792, Bradish 1805, Callaway 1814, Catholic 1819, Clark 1831, Cohen 1833, Columbus 1835, Community 1838, Corbett 1851, David 1856, duPont 1865, Episcopal 1871, Fuller 1893, Harrelson 1903, Harris 1904, Harrison 1905, Hoeting 1917, Krausman 1942, Lauffer 1947, LeGore 1948, Long 1954, Marco 1962, Mayo 1966, McCurry 1970, Mead 1973, Meador 1974, Meninak 1977, Murray 1990, Northeast 2000, Patterson 2015, Perry 2016, PSS/Gulf 2027, Rayonier 2031, Ruegamer 2042, Ryals 2045, **Samstag 2048**, Space 2068, Spicer 2070, Step 2075, Tracy 2089, Tweed 2091, Washington 2099, Wertzberger 2101
Jacksonville Beach: Jay 1930
Juno Beach: **Prime 2025**
Jupiter: Livingston 1952
Key West: AIDS 1764, Community 1847, Flordia Keys 1883
Kissimmee: Bronson 1808
Lake City: Rogers 2040
Lake Worth: Palm 2011, Palm Beach 2012, Smigiel 2063
Lakeland: Morrison 1984, Watson 2100
Largo: Cousin 1853, Pinellas 2019, Sun 2078
Lauderhill: Scholarship 2051
Lecanto: Citrus 1830
Leesburg: Lake-Sumter 1944
Live Oak: Hurst 1925
Longwood: Christian 1827, Florida 1887
Maitland: Florida 1878, United 2093
Marathon: Schmitt 2050
Marco Island: Art 1783
Melbourne: Brevard 1807, Community 1840, Health 1908, Preeclampsia 2024
Miami: 2 Life 1759, Aqua 1778, AWS 1789, Blac 1800, **Carter 1817**, Cintas 1828, **Cisneros 1829**, **Horizons 1922**, **Julien 1934**, Kelly 1935, Kiwanis 1940, Miami 1978, **Miami 1979**, **National 1996**, **National 1997**, Police 2023, Rayni 2030, Ryder 2046, SWS 2080, Take 2081, Toussant 2088
Miami Beach: Mount 1988
Miami Lakes: Orange 2007
Miami Springs: GMAA 1896
Moore Haven: Glades 1895, Wiggins 2104
Mount Dora: Mount 1986, Mount 1987
Naples: Community 1843, DeVoe 1861, Fabela 1874, Henry 1911, Hma 1916, Immokalee 1926, Leinbach 1949, Maine 1959, Martin 1965, Naples 1993, Naples 1994, Scott 2055, Winged 2105
New Port Richey: Volunteer 2097
New Smyrna Beach: Atlantic 1787
Nokomis: Rhodes 2036
North Miami: Education 1867
North Miami Beach: Moore 1982
Ocala: Colen 1834, Sing 2062
Okeechobee: Okeechobee 2003
Orlando: A Gift 1760, Amateis 1768, American 1769, American 1772, Blankenship 1801, Blount 1802, Bragg 1806, Community 1837, Community 1842, Darden 1855, Deeley 1858, Densch 1860, Dunbar 1864, Florida 1877, Hard 1902, Holt 1920, Hunt 1924, Johnston 1931, Kerouac 1937, Lang 1946, Magic 1958, Martin 1963, McCabe 1967, McCabe 1968, McCune 1969, McKinney 1972, Meiller 1976, National 1995, North 1999, Orlando 2008, Rawls 2029, Rigsby 2038, Rush 2043, Russell 2044, **SeaWorld 2056**, Selinger 2058, **Shepard 2060**, Tangelo 2083, Trolinger 2090, Wagner 2098, Yancey 2109
Oviedo: Hope 1921
Pahokee: Boldin 1803
Palm Beach: Palm 2013, **Whitehall 2103**
Palm Beach Gardens: Northern 2001

Palm Harbor: Stearn 2074, Two 2092
Palmetto Bay: Everglades 1872
Pensacola: Baptist 1791, Fellows 1875, Rehabilitation 2033, Workforce 2108
Ponte Vedra Beach: Players 2022
Port Charlotte: Abernathy 1762
Punta Gorda: Lang 1945
Saint Cloud: Thornton 2086
Sanibel: Change 1822, Reinhold 2034
Sarasota: Community 1844, Community 1848, Miller 1980, Mote 1985, Selby 2057, Sudakoff 2077, Woman's 2107
Sewalls Point: Megaloudis 1975
South Pasadena: Forbes 1888
St. Augustine: **Ashley 1784**
St. Petersburg: Area 1780, Catalina 1818, Catholic 1820, Children's 1824, Edwards 1868, Pinellas 2020, St. Petersburg 2071
Stuart: Allen 1766, Finley 1876, Haven 1907, Martin 1964, Sailfish 2047
Sunrise: Areawide 1781
Tallahassee: **AAST 1761**, Big 1799, Children's 1825, Distilled 1863, Florida 1881, Florida 1884, Florida 1885, Tallahassee 2082
Tampa: All 1765, Bailey 1790, Brooks 1809, Community 1846, Conn 1850, Council 1852, DeBartolo 1857, Florida 1879, Hillsborough 1915, **Holland 1918**, KML 1941, Lutheran 1956, Lynch 1957, Manley 1961, **Patel 2014**, Progress 2026, Sieber 2061, **Special 2069**
Tavares: McGinty 1971
The Villages: Strahan 2076
Titusville: **Astronaut 1785**
Umatilla: Florida 1880
Venice: Bennett 1797, Gulf 1898, Kenney 1936
Vero Beach: Exchange 1873, Judge 1933, Schommer 2053
Wauchula: Olliff 2004
Wellington: Rawlings 2028
West Palm Beach: American 1770, Community 1839, Education 1866, Hand 1901, Jacob 1928, Jacobson 1929, Rubin 2041, School 2054, West Palm Beach 2102
Weston: Taylor 2085
Wewahitchka: Taunton 2084
Windermere: Chamberlain 1821, Lincoln 1951
Winter Park: Anew 1777, Children's 1826, Crealde 1854, Florida 1886, Hungerford 1923

see also 42, 50, 68, 73, 81, 540, 559, 1369, 1451, 1519, 1614, 2400, 2417, 2485, 2487, 2588, 3050, 3816, 3832, 4011, 4238, 4884, 4892, 4899, 5439, 5502, 5916, 5974, 6036, 6450, 6565, 6588, 6628, 6644, 6804, 6915, 7594, 7972, 8163, 8175, 8188, 8565, 8590, 8765, 9656, 9968, 10015

GEORGIA

Acworth: Children 2140
Adel: Dinnerman 2167
Albany: Barnett 2126, Hall 2190, Wetherbee 2262
Alpharetta: **National 2213**
Athens: Adair 2111, Navy 2214, Phillips 2223, Scheffler 2234, University 2254
Atlanta: **100 2110**, Alpha 2112, **American 2113**, **American 2114**, **American 2115**, Arby's 2119, Arthritis 2120, Austin 2121, Ayers 2122, Baker 2123, **Boys 2129**, Burke 2133, Cameron 2135, **Carter 2136**, Cherokee 2138, Chick 2139, Christian 2142, Churches 2143, Club 2144, **Coca 2148**, Community 2150, Council 2155, Cox 2157, CURE 2159, Davies 2160, **DeYoung 2165**, East 2169, Empty 2171, Espy 2172, Families 2176, Fragile 2179, Fulton 2180, Garden 2182, Georgia 2183, Georgia 2184, Georgia 2185, Golden 2189, Healthcare 2195, Hospice 2196, Idaho 2197, **Jewish 2198**, Kajima 2199, Kaplan 2200, Katz

2201, Kids' 2202, Legislative 2205, Make 2207, Medical 2211, **Rosenberg 2229**, Saint 2230, Seven 2236, Southeastern 2237, Southern 2238, Tharpe 2248, **THDF 2249**, Wine 2266, WinShape 2267

Augusta: Duke 2168, **Fadel 2174**, United 2252, Widows 2265

Austell: Parents 2219

Avondale Estates: Dickens 2166

Braselton: **American 2116**, R.A.C.K 2226

Brunswick: **MAP 2208**, Sapelo 2231

Canton: Service 2235

Carrollton: Eternal 2173

Cartersville: Dellinger 2163

Clayton: Stovall 2244

Columbus: Amos-Cheves 2117, Columbus 2149, God's 2188, **Pickett 2224**, Weir 2259

Conyers: Beech 2127

Cordele: Whelchel 2263

Cumming: DeSana 2164

Dalton: United 2251, Whitfield 2264

Decatur: Decatur 2161, DeKalb 2162, Fund 2181

Dewy Rose: Warren 2257

Duluth: Bantly 2125, **NCR 2215**

Eatonton: Peoples 2221

Gainesville: Edmondson 2170, Magnus 2206, Ninth 2216, North 2218

Grayson: Georgia 2187

Greensboro: BankSouth 2124, Reynolds 2228

Hinesville: Tri-County 2250

Jasper: North 2217

Kennesaw: Styles 2246

LaGrange: Callaway 2134

Lagrange: West 2261

Lawrenceville: **Foundation 2178**, Kumar 2203, Marena 2209

Lexington: Brightwell 2131

Macon: Anderson 2118, Bowen 2128, Community 2151, Hamilton 2193, **Pilot 2225**

Madison: Braswell 2130

Marietta: Student 2245, WellStar 2260, Wood 2268

Midway: Coastal 2145

Monroe: Faith 2175, Walker 2256

Moultrie: Community 2153, Southwest 2240

Mount Berry: Hall 2191

Newnan: Coweta 2156

Norcross: Choson 2141, Creative 2158, **Ravi 2227**, Southern 2239, Spears 2241, **TAPPI 2247**, Waffle 2255

Peachtree City: **Phi Mu 2222**

Rabun Gap: Hambidge 2192

Rock Spring: Ladonna 2204

Rome: Fisher 2177

Savannah: Brown 2132, Coastal 2146, Savannah 2232, Savannah 2233, United 2253

Sharpsburg: Cobb 2147

Stockbridge: Georgia 2186

Suwanee: Handweavers 2194

Tallapoosa: Star 2242

Thomasville: Community 2152

Thomson: McDuffie 2210, Watson 2258

Waycross: Concerted 2154, Monroe 2212

West Point: Charter 2137

Woodstock: Stingrays 2243

Zebulon: Park 2220

see also 31, 81, 607, 710, 778, 990, 1385, 1614, 1792, 1814, 1899, 1918, 1924, 1954, 1967, 2031, 2044, 2045, 2046, 2060, 2089, 2109, 2423, 3439, 3556, 3600, 4653, 4731, 4884, 4929, 5723, 6565, 6607, 6718, 6890, 8575, 8608, 8903, 9851

GUAM

see 9358

HAWAII

Aiea: Ishii 2295

Hana: Hana 2287

Hawi: North 2306

Honolulu: Aiea 2269, **Akihito 2270**, Atherton 2271, Bank 2272, Bouslog 2273, **Center 2274**, Ching 2275, Chung 2276, Community 2277, Cottington 2278, Council 2279, Easter 2281, Family 2282, Fukunaga 2283, Gear 2284, Geist 2285, Hawaii 2288, Hawaii 2289, Hawaii 2290, Hawaii 2291, Helping 2292, Hemenway 2293, Imai 2294, Kaiulani 2296, Kaneta 2297, Kokua 2299, Learning 2300, Life 2301, Make-A-Wish 2302, Mink 2304, National 2305, Outrigger 2308, Pacific 2309, Pacific 2310, Palama 2311, Palama 2312, Parents 2313, People 2314, Pope 2315, Rehabilitation 2316, Ross 2317, Sakumoto 2319, Servco 2320, Straub 2321, Takitani 2322, Towle 2323, University 2324, **Watumull 2326**, Zimmerman 2327

Kailua-Kona: Kanuha 2298

Kealakekua: Onizuka 2307

Lihue: Grove 2286

Mililani: Saake 2318

Ocean View: McKee 2303

Wailuku: Diamond 2280

Waimea: Waimea 2325

see also 616, 999, 1511, 4142, 9575

IDAHO

Blackfoot: Stufflebeam 2351

Boise: Boise 2329, Haugse 2332, Home 2333, IDACORP 2334, Idaho 2335, Idaho 2336, Jeker 2337, Lightfoot 2340, Mitchell 2342, Nahas 2343, Perrin 2344, Simplot 2349

Burley: Rotary 2347

Coeur d'Alene: Excel 2331

Hope: Shultz 2348

Idaho Falls: Adams 2328, Rogers 2346

Lewiston: Lewis-Clark 2339

Moscow: Ramsdale 2345

Soda Springs: Chadwick 2330

Twin Falls: Smallwood 2350

Wallace: Kingsbury 2338, Magnuson 2341

see also 197, 1494, 2197, 4142, 5172, 5180, 6596, 6776, 6842, 7179, 7620, 7671, 9207, 9216, 9222, 9613, 9626, 9681, 9687, 9690, 9701, 9702, 9711, 9717

ILLINOIS

Abbott Park: **Abbvie 2354**

Albion: Allhands 2362, Jackson 2655

Arlington Heights: American 2373, **Ewing 2554**, **Foundation 2569**, Magnus 2705, **Plastic 2793**

Aurora: Angelman 2399, Community 2496, Engineering 2547

Barrington: **National 2750**, Oberweiler 2764

Batavia: Hansen 2598, Reach 2809

Beardstown: Reller 2813

Belleville: St. 2868, St. Clair 2869, Suarez 2880

Bensenville: Chicago 2476

Bloomington: Beebe 2418, Brewer 2437, Illinois 2637, Illinois 2641, McLean 2724, United 2906

Bolingbrook: Bolingbrook 2430

Bourbonnais: Olivet 2767

Burr Ridge: Angels 2400, **North 2758**

Bushnell: Bushnell 2451

Canton: Halsey 2597, Jackson 2656

Carbondale: Garwin 2579, Southern 2865

Carlyle: Bender 2419

Carrollton: Costello 2501, District 2517, Pierson 2789

Carterville: Illinois 2634

Centralia: BCMW 2415, Centralia 2467

Champaign: Busey 2450, Wise 2930

Charleston: **Drag 2523**

Chatsworth: Koehler 2674

Chicago: A & B 2352, **Academy 2355**, **ADA 2356**, Adamson 2357, After 2358, AKA 2360, Alberts 2361, American 2367, **American 2368**, American 2369, **American 2370**, **American 2371**, **American 2372**, **American 2374**, **American 2375**, **American 2376**, **American 2377**, **American 2378**, **American 2379**, **American 2380**, **American 2381**, **American 2382**, **American 2385**, **American 2386**, Ann 2401, Aon 2402, APICS 2403, Arbor 2405, ArcelorMittal 2406, Barber 2411, Barnard 2412, Barnes 2413, Barr 2414, Becker 2417, Beneke 2420, Bennett 2422, Berner 2423, Breckinridge 2435, Brege 2436, Brown 2439, Bruton 2444, Bulkley 2445, Bunn 2446, Burton 2449, Business 2452, Cabot 2455, Caestecker 2456, Camp 2458, **Cara 2459**, **Carpe 2460**, Carter 2461, Catholic 2463, Chicago 2472, Chicago 2473, Chicago 2474, Chicago 2475, Children 2477, Children's 2479, Children's 2480, Christ 2481, **Citizens 2482**, CNA 2484, Cochrane 2485, Coleman 2488, Collins 2490, Continental 2498, Corpening 2500, Costilow 2502, Damato 2506, Davis 2508, Davis 2510, de Kay 2513, **Depression 2515**, Dodd 2519, Donnelley 2521, Dreams 2524, Driehaus 2525, Drummond 2526, Dudley 2527, **Dystonia 2529**, Edmunds 2534, Ehrler 2537, **Elks 2540**, Emergency 2542, Ende 2544, English 2548, Erk 2550, Experimental 2555, Fashion 2558, **Feeding 2559**, Ferris 2560, Foundation 2567, Foundation 2568, Francies 2572, Fredenburgh 2575, Gabler 2577, Gaffney 2578, Geyer 2582, Gillenwater 2584, **Gish 2585**, Golden 2586, Gore 2588

chicago: Gorham 2589

Chicago: Graber 2591, **Graham 2592**, Guenther 2595, Hardin 2599, Harper 2600, Hayes 2604, **Health 2606**, **Health 2607**, **Healthy 2608**, Hebrew 2609, **Heed 2610**, Hefti 2611, Herbert 2614, **Hertz 2615**, Higgins 2616, Hirsch 2619, Hirschl 2620, Hohner 2621, **Holocaust 2622**, HOPA 2625, House 2626, Hugg 2628, Hughes 2629, Hyatt 2631, Hynd 2632, Illinois 2633, Illinois 2636, Illinois 2648, Inner 2649, International 2650, Irrevocable 2653, Jewish 2657, Jewish 2658, Journalism 2663, Juvenile 2665, Kander 2666, Kaufman 2669, Kohl 2677, Kooi 2678, Krill 2680, Lakeview 2682, **Lascaris 2685**, Laux 2686, Lawrence 2687, Lewis 2692, Lincoln 2693, Lindsay 2694, Lower 2698, Luley 2700, LUNGevity 2701, **MacArthur 2704**, **Majid 2706**, Make-A-Wish 2707, Martin 2710, Meade 2727, **Medical 2728**, Menn 2731, Miller 2734, Minner 2736, Morrison 2738, Morton 2739, Munson 2740, Murphy 2741, Mutual 2742, **National 2743**, **National 2745**, National 2746, National 2748, **National 2749**, **National 2752**, Neville 2755, Niccum 2756, Nicoll 2757, Oakes 2762, Ott 2773, Ott 2774, Palmer 2777, Peeples 2781, Peterson 2786, Phi 2788, Pingel 2791, **Playboy 2794**, **Poetry 2795**, **Polish 2796**, Presence 2797, Prieto 2799, Pugh 2803, Pullman 2804, Pulmonary 2805, Rainey 2807, **Realtors 2810**, Reiss 2812, **Research 2816**, **Respiratory 2817**, Rinker 2821, Rittenhouse 2822, Robinson 2826, Rockwood 2828, Roesch 2829, Rogers 2830, Roy 2836, Russell 2838, Ryerson 2839, Scherer 2840, Schwarz 2845, Scott 2847, Shinaberry 2852, Short 2853, Shumaker 2854, **Skidmore 2857**, Smith 2859, **Society 2862**, Society 2863, **Special 2866**, Sperling 2867, Stevenson 2873, Stockert 2874, Swiss 2884, **Terra 2889**, Testamentary 2890, Thauer 2891, **Thoracic 2892**, True 2898, **Turnaround 2899**, Uhlich 2900, **Ullery 2901**, Union 2902, Union 2903, Union 2904, Veeder

2908, Villwock 2909, Walters 2916, Walters 2917, Weeks 2920, Wells 2922, Whitney 2926, Willo 2928, WKUS 2931, **Women 2933**, Women's 2934, Wood 2935, **Woodbury 2936**, Woods 2937, Youth 2938

Clifton: REO 2814

Collinsville: St. John's 2870, Tomara 2894

Countryside: Footprints 2566

Crestwood: Bohne 2429

Crystal Lake: AptarGroup 2404, **Engine 2546**, Partners 2779, Steel 2871

Danville: Cunningham 2505

Darien: **American 2388**

Decatur: Arnold 2407, Energy 2545, Evans 2551, Johnson 2659, Richland 2819, Shapiro 2849

Deerfield: American 2387, American 2393, **CF 2469**, Hairy 2596, **International 2652**, Jorndt 2662, Walgreen 2913, **Walgreens 2914**

DeKalb: Northern 2759

Des Plaines: **American 2392, Emergency 2543**, Irwin 2654, Lutheran 2703, Maryville 2711, Smyth 2861

Downers Grove: Sharing 2850

East Moline: Anderson 2395

East St. Louis: East 2530

Edwardsville: Edwardsville 2536

Effingham: Brown 2442, C.E.F.S. 2454, Milburn 2733

Elgin: Community 2492

Elk Grove Village: **American 2366**

Elmwood: Ekstrand 2538

Evanston: Cradle 2503, Dermatology 2516, **Massage 2713, National 2747, Rotary 2835, Sigma 2855**

Fairbury: Karnes 2668, Ross 2832

Fairfield: Davis 2509, Fairfield 2557, Hutchison 2630, Puckett 2802

Fairview Heights: **National 2744**

Flora: Flora 2564

Forrest: Rieger 2820

Frankfort: **Schillings 2841**

Freeport: Zweifel 2943

Galesburg: Brooks 2438

Geneseo: Geneseo 2580

Geneva: Geneva 2581

Germantown: McAllister 2716

Glen Ellyn: O'Malley 2768

Golf: Evans 2552

Granville: Stonier 2875

Greenup: Embarras 2541

Gurnee: **Abbott 2353**

Havana: Lemmer 2688, McFarland 2720, McFarland 2721

Herrin: Harrison 2601, Hill 2617

Highland Park: Friends 2576, Kohl 2676, Old 2766

Hinsdale: Doody 2522

Hoffman Estates: Bechtner 2416

Homewood: Franciscan 2573

Indian Head Park: Burson 2448

Itasca: **National 2751**

Jacksonville: Bound 2432, Ladies 2681

Jerseyville: Catt 2465

Joliet: Catholic 2464

Kankakee: Kankakee 2667, Riverside 2824

Karnak: Shawnee 2851

La Grange: Benjamin 2421

La Grange Park: American 2383

La Salle: Biederstedt 2425, Wagenknecht 2911

Lake Bluff: Piper 2792

Lake Forest: Brunswick 2443, Conway 2499, McMullan 2726, **Ragdale 2806, Scholar 2842**, Schuler 2844

LaSalle: Lang 2683

Lemont: **Lithuanian 2695**

Lewistown: Miller 2735

Lincoln: Bogardus 2428, Larson 2684

Lincolnshire: Children's 2478

Lincolnwood: Grossinger 2594, **Zazove 2939**

Lindenhurst: **Serbian 2848**

Macomb: Wayne 2919, Western 2925

Manteno: HomeStar 2623

Marion: Marion 2708, **TPAA 2895**

Marshall: Marshall 2709

Mattoon: Brown 2440, Burgess 2447, Dole 2520, First 2562, Mason 2712, Oberlin 2763, Smysor 2860, Storey 2876, Stump 2879, Welch 2921

McHenry: McInnes 2722

Melrose Park: **Hasnia 2603**

Metamora: Metamora 2732

Midlothian: Goodgear 2587

Mokena: Ozinga 2775

Moline: Black 2426, Butterworth 2453, Kohen 2675, Moline 2737, Williams 2927

Monmouth: Mellinger 2730, Schweitzer 2846, Titus 2893

Monticello: Betts 2424

Morton: Tazwood 2887

Morton Grove: Gossett 2590

Mount Prospect: McLoraine 2725

Mundelein: Coeli 2486, Medline 2729

Naperville: Edward 2535, Illinois 2639, Koranda 2679, Loaves 2696, Rot 2833, Tree 2896

Nashville: Republic 2815

Normal: Illinois 2646

North Aurora: Fabela 2556

North Riverside: Riverside 2823

Northbrook: Allstate 2363, Blazek 2427, **Chest 2471**, Ohadi 2765

Northfield: College 2489

Oak Brook: **American 2389**, Association 2409, **Foundation 2570**, McDonald's 2719, **Ronald 2831**, Templeton 2888, **Zonta 2942**

Oak Park: Master 2714, Oak Park 2761

Olney: Fildes 2561

Orland Park: Andrew 2396, Andrew 2397

Palatine: Peters 2785, Pilchard 2790

Palos Heights: Paideia 2776, Palos 2778

Paris: BancTrust 2410, Dawson 2512, Dodd 2518, Edgar 2532, Edgar 2533, Henry 2613, McClain 2717, Patterson 2780, Perisho-Nina 2783, Stratton 2877, Wells 2923, Wilson 2929, Zimmerly 2941

Park Ridge: **American 2391, Anesthesia 2398**

Pekin: Everett 2553, Reinheimer 2811, Wolfer 2932

Peoria: Ameren 2364, Central 2466, Community 2494, OSF 2772, Proctor 2801

Peru: Fleurot 2563

Petersburg: Masters 2715, Schroeder 2843

Plainfield: Prest 2798

Princeton: Boyle 2433, Henkel 2612, Zearing 2940

Princeville: Camp 2457

Quincy: Community 2497, Taylor 2886

Rantoul: Long 2697, Smith 2858

River Forest: Daniels 2507, Lutheran 2702

River Grove: Follett 2565

Rock Falls: Tri-County 2897

Rock Island: Rauch 2808, Royal 2837

Rockford: Community 2495, Dawson 2511, Health 2605, Kiwanis 2671, **Nuts, 2760**, Perkins 2784, Rockford 2827, Swedish 2882, Taylor 2885

Rosemont: **American 2384, Cervical 2468, Orthopaedic 2770**

Savoy: **Hill 2618**, Klein 2672

Schaumburg: **American 2365, Foundry 2571**, Levin 2691

Schiller Park: Franklin 2574

Shelbyville: Knecht 2673

Sheldon: Reynolds 2818

Skokie: **Anagnos 2394, International 2651**

Somonauk: Kilts 2670

South Holland: South Holland 2864

Sparta: Boynton-Gillespie 2434, Pflasterer 2787, Rotary 2834

Springfield: Association 2408, Community 2493, Hartke 2602, Hubbard 2627, Illinois 2635, Illinois 2638, Illinois 2640, Illinois 2643, Illinois 2644, Illinois 2645, Illinois 2647, Skelton 2856

St. Charles: Aicardi 2359, Orum 2771

Steeleville: Western 2924

Sterling: CGH 2470, Sterling 2872, Wahl 2912

Stone Park: Joint 2660

Sugar Grove: Waubonsee 2918

Sullivan: Eberhardt 2531

Sycamore: Boulos 2431, Brown 2441, DeKalb 2514, Erickson 2549, Hoover/Hoehn 2624, Jones 2661, Nesbitt 2754, Roberts 2825

Techny: **Gift 2583**

Thayer: Caruso-Sperl 2462

Tinley Park: Claretknoll 2483

Toledo: Neal 2753

Tuscola: Lenore 2689, McDonald 2718

Urbana: Urbana-Champaign 2907

Vandalia: McKee 2723

Vernon Hills: American 2390

Villa Park: Walker 2915

Washington: Sweitzer 2883

Waterloo: Luhr 2699

Waukegan: Community 2491, Just 2664, Prine 2800, United 2905

West Dundee: Coin 2487

West Frankfort: Crosswalk 2504

Westchester: **Organization 2769**

Wheaton: DuPage 2528, Elburn 2539, Peoples 2782, SVI 2881

White Hall: Griswold 2593

Wilmette: **Leukemia 2690**, Strauss 2878

Woodridge: **Vogler 2910**

Wyoming: Illinois 2642

---

see also 43, 56, 365, 701, 710, 1137, 1369, 1385, 1874, 1959, 2986, 3047, 3109, 3173, 3251, 3264, 3278, 3283, 3302, 3318, 4118, 4142, 4331, 4430, 4439, 4445, 4472, 4581, 4595, 4731, 4851, 4936, 4948, 4973, 4989, 5009, 5012, 5021, 5035, 5037, 5043, 5047, 5079, 5082, 5099, 5102, 5103, 5121, 5123, 5236, 5723, 5817, 6654, 6783, 7020, 7111, 7163, 7284, 7287, 7435, 7980, 7992, 8014, 8103, 8716, 8770, 8795, 9876, 9959

INDIANA

Anderson: CIACO 2986, Madison 3106

Angola: Steuben 3193

Attica: Whitehall 3224

Auburn: DeKalb 3015, Peoples 3143

Aurora: PFS 3145

Avon: Hendricks 3057

Batesville: Hillenbrand 3060, Ripley 3164

Bloomfield: Greene 3045

Bloomington: Community 2991, Indiana 3071, **Organization 3132**

Bluffton: Franklin 3037, Wells 3220

Brazil: Raab 3155

Brookville: Brookville 2973, Franklin 3036

Brownsburg: Indianapolis 3072

Cambridge City: Leo 3097

Carmel: Little 3103, Phi 3147, Salin 3170, Tobias 3202, United 3205

Clinton: Vermillion 3211

Columbia City: Whitley 3226

Columbus: Heritage 3059, Keller 3084, Webster 3219

Connersville: Fayette 3028

Corydon: Harrison 3054, McGrain 3111

Covington: Cook 3008, Western 3222

Crawfordsville: Montgomery 3114, Moore 3115

Crown Point: Crown Point 3010, Northwest 3128

Decatur: Adams 2945

East Chicago: Foundations 3033

Elkhart: Elkhart 3024

Evansville: Brown 2976, Catholic 2980, Community 2989, Community 2990, Francisco 3034, Frank 3035, Kiwanis 3088, Koch 3089, Line 3102, Orth 3133, Payton 3141, Public 3152, Randolph 3156, Reeves 3158, Richardt 3160, Stout 3196, Whiteley 3225

Fairland: Coy 3009

Fairmount: Blair 2968, Blair 2969

Ferdinand: Tretter 3203

Fort Wayne: Allen 2947, Cole 2987, Community 2988, Community 2994, Fort 3031, Parkview 3140, United 3207

Fowler: Benton 2966, Henderson 3056

Francesville: Hoch 3061

Frankfort: Laird 3094

Franklin: Gilmore 3044, Johnson 3079, Mann 3108

Goshen: Osteopathic 3135

Gosport: Friends 3039

Greencastle: Putnam 3154

Greensburg: Buerger 2977, Decatur 3013, Harcourt 3052, Humphrey 3066

Greenwood: **Zoltani 3232**

Hammond: Hammond 3048

Hartford City: Blackford 2967

Highland: Peters 3144, Westhaysen 3223

Huntington: Huntington 3067, Huntington 3068

Indianapolis: Alpha 2948, **Alpha 2949**, Alpha 2950, Alpha 2951, **Alpha 2952**, **American 2954**, American 2955, Arsenal 2959, Arts 2960, Association 2962, Bowen 2972, Children's 2982, Children's 2983, Christamore 2984, Christian 2985, Dora 3017, Eskenazi 3027, **Foundation 3032**, **Future 3040**, Gemmill 3042, Independent 3069, Indiana 3070, Indianapolis 3073, Indianapolis 3074, IPALCO 3075, Jewish 3078, **Kappa 3082**, **Lambda 3095**, **Lilly 3099**, **Lilly 3100**, **Lilly 3101**, **National 3121**, **National 3122**, **National 3123**, National 3124, Pacers 3138, **Phi 3146**, RPW 3166, Scholarship 3174, **Sigma 3183**, Simon 3184, Society 3187, Society 3188, Storer 3195, Surina 3197, Thomasson 3198, **Timmy 3200**, **United 3206**, United 3208, **USA 3210**, VSA 3214, Williams 3228, Winchester 3229, Zeta 3230

Jasper: Arvin 2961, Boonshot 2971, Dubois 3019, Dubois 3020, Kimball 3086, King 3087, Loogootee 3105

Knightstown: Reeves 3159

Kokomo: Community 2996

Lafayette: Area 2957, Community 2995, Fitzgerald 3030, Neel 3125

LaGrange: LaGrange 3093

Lawrenceburg: Dearborn 3012

Lebanon: Scering 3171, Thorntown 3199

Liberty: Union 3204

Ligonier: Noble 3127

Logansport: Cass 2979, Logansport 3104, Riddleberger 3163

Lyons: Harris 3053

Madison: Community 2999

Marion: Community 2993

Martinsville: Community 3000

Merrillville: AIDS 2946, Legacy 3096

Michigan City: Hemminger 3055, Levin 3098, Unity 3209

Middlebury: Fenech 3029

Mishawaka: Housing 3064, Saint 3169

Monterey: Frees 3038, Houghton 3063, Keitzer 3083, Russell 3168

Mooresville: Kendrick 3085

Morocco: Scott 3177

Mount Vernon: Schultz 3175

Muncie: Amburn 2953, Ball 2964, Community 3001, Deen 3014, Dunn 3021, Ellison 3025, Epler 3026, Garr 3041, Kuhner 3092, Muncie 3120, Shroyer 3182, Standerford 3191

Munster: Community 3007, Dye 3022, Hammond 3049

Nashville: Brown 2974

New Albany: Community 3003, Horseshoe 3062

New Castle: Henry 3058, Moore 3116, Oberdorfer 3129

New Haven: East 3023

Noblesville: Weaver 3218

North Manchester: Community 3006

North Vernon: Jennings 3077

North Webster: Shoop 3181

Pendleton: South 3189

Peru: Baber 2963, Porter 3149, Sellers 3178

Petersburg: Carroll-Wyatt 2978

Plymouth: Gibson 3043, Marshall 3110

Portland: Portland 3151

Rensselaer: Jasper 3076

Richmond: Belden 2965, Richmond 3161, Richmond 3162, Stiens 3194, Wayne 3217

Ridgeville: Moorman 3117

Rising Sun: Ohio 3131

Rockville: Parke 3139

Rushville: Rush 3167

Salem: Williams 3227

Scottsburg: Scott 3176

Seymour: Abell 2944, Community 2997, Community 2998, Seymour 3179, Shiel 3180

Shelbyville: Blue 2970

South Bend: Charlton 2981, Community 3004, Hannah 3050, Harber 3051, Joshi 3080, Kaminski 3081, Memorial 3113, Moran 3118, Pearson 3142, Plummer 3148, REAL 3157, Slaughter 3185, Smelser 3186, St. Vincent 3190, Stanley 3192, Voland 3213, Zimmer 3231

Spencer: Owen 3136

Syracuse: Mahnken 3107

Tell City: Schergens 3172

Terre Haute: Greenwell 3046, Guiliani 3047, Maris 3109, Nesty 3126, Rose 3165, Schmidt 3173, Wabash 3215, Western 3221

Tipton: Tipton 3201

Valparaiso: Porter 3150, Visiting 3212

Veedersburg: Osborn 3134

Vevay: Community 3005

Vincennes: Pace 3137

Warsaw: Armstrong 2958, Brown 2975, Dead 3011, Kosciusko 3090, Kosciusko 3091

West Lafayette: Delta 3016, Hughes 3065, Morre 3119

Williamsport: McKinney 3112, Warren 3216

Winamac: Pulaski 3153

Winchester: Community 3002

Winona Lake: Dr. 3018

Wolcott: O'Connor 3130

Zionsville: Anna 2956, Community 2992

see also 47, 1017, 1249, 1797, 1961, 2458, 2488, 2510, 2532, 2552, 2616, 2619, 2658, 2698, 2742, 2756, 2762, 2774, 2781, 2821, 2847, 2908, 3555, 3596, 3606, 3618, 4238, 4335, 4406, 4443, 4476, 4502, 4504, 4731, 4851, 5188, 5253, 5261, 5275, 5461, 6577, 6650, 6674, 6732, 6890, 6954, 6956, 6957, 6968, 6985, 7006, 7008, 7020, 7094, 7165, 7193, 7204, 7250, 7253, 7265, 7285, 7311, 7324, 7327, 7328, 7354, 7362, 7409, 7432, 7436, 7697, 7722, 7732, 7925, 7947, 7959, 7989, 8008, 8014, 8114, 8173, 8211, 8641, 9839, 9940, 9959

IOWA

Albert City: Munson 3339

Albia: Bates 3243

Ames: Ames 3236, **Grace 3286**

Anamosa: Vacek 3402

Atlantic: McKenney 3335

Baxter: Diehl 3275

Bettendorf: Community 3264, Life 3326

Bondurant: Garber 3282

Breda: Hermsen 3298

Burlington: Community 3261, Corbin 3267, Great 3287, Raider 3362, Swiler 3394

Carlisle: Schooler 3373

Carroll: Carroll 3253, Community 3265

Cedar Rapids: Affordable 3234, Andersen 3237, Cedar Rapids 3255, Iowa 3309, Johnson 3315, Meier 3336, Schwartz 3376, **Sherwood 3380**, St. Luke's 3387, St. Luke's 3388, United 3399

Cherokee: Brummer 3249, Frisbie 3281, Guest 3292, Mongan 3338, Pritchard 3361

Clarinda: Clarinda 3257

Clio: Leeper 3325

Columbus Junction: Gerling 3284, Shellabarger 3378

Conrad: Smith 3383

Coralville: Iowa 3304

Corydon: Denton 3272, Murphy 3341

Council Bluffs: Jennie 3313

Dakota City: Lindhart 3327

Danville: Bray 3248

Davenport: Community 3260, Genesis 3283, Keppy 3318

Decorah: Carlson 3252

Denison: **Reed 3364**

Des Moines: Camp 3251, Code 3258, Eychaner 3278, Iowa 3307, ISED 3310, **P.E.O. 3349**, **P.E.O. 3350**, **P.E.O. 3351**, **P.E.O. 3352**, Preston 3360, Seidler 3377, United 3400, VDTA 3404, World 3410

DeWitt: Bathalter 3244

Dewitt: Schrader 3374

Durant: Iowa 3306

Eagle Grove: Hill 3299

Eldridge: Rotary 3368

Estherville: Sonstegard 3384

Fairfield: Accelerated 3233, Harper 3295

Fort Dodge: Barr 3242, Credit 3268, Stearns 3389, Trinity 3397

Fort Madison: Andrews 3240, Schlagenbusch 3372

Fremont: U.S. 3398

Graettinger: Upper 3401

Grinnell: Grinnell 3290, Poweshiek 3359, Stewart 3390

Guthrie Center: Taylor 3395

Harlan: Lage 3321, Nishnabotna 3343, West 3407

Hiawatha: Hawkeye 3296

Hudson: Farrell 3279

Ida Grove: Father 3280, Hahn 3294, Parks 3354, Rufer 3369

Indianola: Red 3363

Iowa City: Community 3262, Iowa 3308

Jefferson: Greene 3288, Mahanay 3330

Jewell: King 3319

Johnston: **Pioneer 3358**

Keosauqua: Van Buren 3403

Knoxville: Crozier 3269

Lake View: Hagedorn 3293, Kingfield 3320

Logan: Wood 3409

Manchester: Delaware 3271

Marengo: Bishop 3246

Marshalltown: Hulton 3301, Norris 3344, Pierce 3357

Mason City: Keig 3317, Lee 3324, North 3345

Mitchellville: Carter 3254

Mount Pleasant: Henry 3297

Muscatine: Bishop 3245, Magnus 3329, Marek 3331, Michels 3337

Newton: Jasper 3311

Northwood: Igou 3303, Swensrud 3393

Oelwein: Northeast 3346

Ottumwa: Southern 3385

Panora: Burchfield 3250

Pella: Pella 3355

Pocahontas: Elbert 3277, Sinek 3381

Red Oak: Reifel-Elwood 3365
Reinbeck: Matheson 3332, Palmer 3353
Rippey: Schroeder 3375
Rock Rapids: Murray 3342
Rock Valley: Scanlan 3370, Scanlan 3371
Sergeant Bluff: Winkel 3408
Shenandoah: Anderson 3238, Anderson 3239, Gidley 3285, Hockenberry 3300, Jay 3312, Lake-Matthews 3322
Sioux City: Community 3259, Duggan 3276, Latta 3323, Northwest 3347, Riley 3366, Siouxland 3382, Stubbs 3392
Spencer: Spencer 3386, Vestergaard 3405
Storm Lake: Jepsen 3314, Sherman 3379
Strawberry Point: Munter 3340, Rima 3367
Tipton: Dallas 3270, Petersen 3356
Traer: Traer 3396
Urbandale: Association 3241, Conner 3266, Kansas 3316, Straub 3391
Washington: McKay 3334
Waterloo: Allen 3235, Community 3263, LSB 3328, McElroy 3333, Operation 3348
Waukee: Des Moines 3274
Waverly: Waverly 3406
West Des Moines: Des Moines 3273, Grubb 3291, Hy-Vee 3302, Iowa 3305
Winterset: Black 3247, Chase 3256, Griffith 3289

see also 257, 761, 1186, 1494, 1805, 1949, 1953, 2395, 2604, 2614, 2654, 2808, 2927, 4723, 4779, 4841, 4851, 4859, 4883, 4884, 5099, 5185, 5198, 5201, 5214, 5232, 5259, 6703, 6722, 6745, 6992, 7887, 7912, 7931, 8014, 8217, 8332, 8421, 8538, 8547, 9508, 9721, 9846, 9853, 9883, 9888, 9913, 9924, 9950, 9960, 9966, 9974, 10009, 10015, 10031, 10054, 10058, 10062

KANSAS

Abilene: Brown 3422, Moyer 3491
Ashland: Abell 3411
Atchison: Atchison 3415, Tenholder 3524
Baxter Springs: Mehaffy 3485
Belleville: Boyle 3421
Beloit: Hoy 3458
Chanute: Noah's 3496
Chapman: Hines 3455
Clay Center: Clay 3425
Columbus: Columbus 3428
Concordia: Cloud 3426, Duclos 3434
Council Grove: Stice 3522, Trembly 3529
Dodge City: Community 3429, Murdock 3492, Schmidt 3512, Southwest 3518
Ellsworth: Dolechek 3432
Emporia: Jones 3464
Eureka: Babson's 3416
Fort Scott: Ellis 3439, Key 3473
Fowler: Grasshopper 3448
Fredonia: Patterson 3500
Goodland: Greene 3449
Great Bend: Golden 3447
Gridley: Arnold 3414, French 3445
Hays: Fort 3444, Rush 3509
Hiawatha: Kleppe 3474, Moore 3489, Nelson 3495, Schuneman 3513
Hill City: Vesper 3533, Western 3535
Hoxie: Toothaker 3527
Humboldt: Monarch 3488
Hutchinson: Child 3423, Davis 3431, Hutchinson 3460, Pearce 3501, White 3536
Independence: Independence 3461
Iola: French 3446, Winslow 3541
Junction City: Hoover 3457, Jellison 3462
Kansas City: **Christian 3424**, Terry 3525
Kingman: Spurrier 3520, Woolsey 3542

La Crosse: Baker 3417, Knights 3475
Larned: Fell 3441, Jordaan 3465
Lawrence: Douglas 3433, Kansas 3468, Wildlife 3540
Leawood: **American 3413**
Lewis: Hoar 3456
Logan: Hansen 3451
Manhattan: Journalism 3466, Kansas 3472
Marysville: Pape 3498, Stockard 3523
McLouth: Ehlers 3437, Ehlers 3438
McPherson: McPherson 3483, McPherson 3484
Medicine Lodge: Eggleston 3436
Neodesha: Griffith 3450
Norton: Beal 3419, Davis 3430, Duer 3435, Morgan 3490
Oberlin: Smick 3515
Overland: Trump 3530
Overland Park: Alpha 3412, Fingersh 3442, Jewish 3463, Perdue 3502, Robinson 3508, Spitcaufsky 3519
Paola: Henderson 3454, Preston 3507
Phillipsburg: Nuttycomb 3497, Steffens 3521
Pittsburg: Mitchelson 3486, Throckmorton 3526
Prairie Village: Helping 3453
Pratt: Hartley 3452, McKinnis 3482, Parsons 3499, Porter 3506, South 3517
Salina: Bane 3418, Kansas 3467, Salina 3510
Satanta: Ungles 3531
Shawnee Mission: Pi 3504
Smith Center: Fink 3443, Peterson 3503, Pitts 3505, Sarver 3511
Topeka: Kansas 3469, Kansas 3471, Topeka 3528
Vermillion: Unified 3532
Washington: Mansfield 3481
Wellington: Loofbourrow 3480
Wichita: Beren 3420, Ellis 3440, Hunter 3459, Kansas 3470, Koch 3476, Koch 3477, Laham 3478, Moberley 3487, Naftzger 3493, Nell 3494, Weigand 3534, Wichita 3537, Wichita 3538, Wichita 3539
Winfield: Legacy 3479, Sidwell 3514, Snyder 3516
Yates Center: Coffman 3427

see also 1369, 3050, 3302, 3316, 4935, 4943, 4987, 5023, 5035, 5053, 5075, 5209, 5265, 5607, 7216, 7527, 8717, 8744, 8793, 8794, 8960, 8996, 9088, 9138, 9213

KENTUCKY

Ashland: Kings 3588
Bardstown: Hedrick 3576
Barlow: Jackson 3579
Belfry: McDowell 3595
Berea: Appalachian 3545, Morrill 3599, Morrill 3600
Bowling Green: Rhoads 3619
Burkesville: Norris 3603, Spear 3627
Cold Spring: Disabled 3562, **Disabled 3563**
Covington: Northern 3604
Danville: Murphy 3601
Flemingsburg: Licking 3590
Frankfort: Governors 3574
Gamaliel: Miller 3598
Grayson: Commercial 3557
Hartford: Wells 3636
Hazard: Eastern 3565
Hebron: American 3544
Hopkinsville: PHP 3616
Jackson: Turner 3630
La Grange: Mallory 3594
Lexington: **AAEP 3543**, Blue 3552, Christian 3556, Community 3558, **Energy 3567**, Foundation 3569, God's 3573, Kincaid 3587, **Lexmark 3589**, Mustard 3602, St. 3628, United 3631, **United 3632**, Young 3637
London: Caudill 3554, Pearl 3614, Rose 3621

Louisville: Baker 3547, Bible 3550, Children's 3555, Community 3559, Dream 3564, Farm 3568, Habitat 3575, Kentucky 3582, **Kentucky 3583**, Kentucky 3585, Kentucky 3586, Lincoln 3591, Louisville 3592, Mackin 3593, Metro 3596, Norton 3605, Norton 3606, Operation 3608, Papa 3611, Papa 3612, Quinkert 3618, Rural 3622, School 3623, Scottish 3624, University 3633, University 3634
Madisonville: Trover 3629
Mayfield: Gardner 3571
Milton: Barnett 3548
Monticello: Ogden 3607
Mount Sterling: Boneal 3553
Munfordville: Cox 3561
Owensboro: Horn 3577, Independence 3578, Owensboro 3609, Smith 3625
Owenton: Owenton 3610, Sparks 3626
Paducah: Community 3560, MGM 3597, Paxton 3613
Paintsville: Big 3551
Paris: Batterton 3549
Radcliff: **USA 3635**
Richmond: Kentucky 3584
Shelbyville: KD-FC 3581, Pflughaupt 3615, Process 3617
Somerset: Eastern 3566, Jones 3580
Stanford: River 3620
West Liberty: Gateway 3572
Wilmore: Foundation 3570
Wurtland: Appalachian 3546

see also 81, 362, 2548, 2669, 2755, 2830, 2832, 2920, 3034, 3156, 4884, 6931, 6953, 6954, 7003, 7025, 7072, 7088, 7165, 7180, 7218, 7261, 7379, 7380, 7413, 7429, 8007, 8208, 8553, 8574, 8598, 9313, 9413, 9851

LOUISIANA

Alexandria: Food 3652, Masonic 3667
Arabi: Meraux 3669
Baton Rouge: 100 3638, Academic 3639, Albemarle 3640, Arts 3642, Baton Rouge 3644, Baton Rouge 3645, Louisiana 3662, Olinde 3671, Our 3672
DeRidder: ECD 3650
Gonzales: Ascension 3643
Hammond: Southeastern 3677
Houma: Ledet 3661, St. Vincent 3678
Jennings: Zigler 3684
Keithville: CS 3649
Kenner: Pellerin 3674
Lafayette: Lafayette 3658
Lake Charles: Burton 3648, Lang 3660, **Park 3673**, Tupper 3681
Maurepas: JL Foun 3657
Metairie: Goldring 3654, **Woldenberg 3683**
Minden: Hunter 3656
Morgan City: Brownell 3647
Natchitoches: Louisiana 3666
New Orleans: American 3641, Entergy 3651, Friends 3653, House 3655, Louisiana 3663, Louisiana 3664, Louisiana 3665, National 3670, Pitt's 3675, Putnam 3676, Taylor 3679, Total 3680
Ponchatoula: **Waters 3682**
Ruston: McGinty 3668
Shreveport: Bernstein 3646
Thibodaux: Lafourche 3659

see also 81, 271, 296, 424, 1614, 1902, 2508, 2519, 2739, 2832, 3902, 4497, 4884, 4902, 5099, 5478, 6334, 7813, 8765, 8770, 8834, 8932, 9006, 9104, 9121, 9173, 9296, 9413

MAINE

Auburn: Reid 3729

Augusta: Associated 3687, Augusta 3688, Holocaust 3703, Maine 3709, MELMAC 3718, Russell 3733, Williams 3746

Bangor: Bangor 3689, Gray 3701, Ohmart 3721, Penquis 3725, Spruce 3736

Bar Harbor: Friends 3697

Bath: Corporal 3692, Davenport 3693

Belfast: Gadd 3698, Information 3705, Switzer 3738, Waldo 3744

Brunswick: Maine 3715

Camden: Camden 3691, Montgomery 3719, Thom 3739, Trust 3741

Cape Elizabeth: Portland 3726

Casco: Hancock 3702

Damariscotta: Belknap 3690, Searls 3735

Ellsworth: Down 3694, Goodrich 3700, Lynam 3708, Maine 3712

Falmouth: Maine 3711

Farmington: Franklin 3696

Gardiner: Robinson 3731, Savings 3734

Hallowell: Maine 3710

Houlton: Ricker 3730

Jonesport: Eastern 3695

Newcastle: Watershed 3745

Nobleboro: Kieve 3707

North Anson: Anson 3686

Northeast Harbor: Acadia 3685

Ogunquit: Tramuto 3740

Orono: **Worcester 3748**

Oxford: Oxford 3723

Portland: Hungarian-American 3704, Maine 3713, Maine 3714, Maine 3716, Maine 3717, Opportunity 3722, Paganelli 3724, Powers 3728, Ross 3732, Stich 3737, United 3743, Woman's 3747

Presque Isle: Turner 3742

Rockland: Island 3706, North Haven 3720

Sanford: York 3749

South Portland: Girl 3699

Westbrook: Portland 3727

see also 741, 1358, 1806, 2247, 3940, 3994, 4000, 4075, 4295, 4899, 5353, 5556, 6295, 6974, 6991, 7007, 7012, 7018, 7031, 7093, 7118, 7145, 7149, 7172, 7200, 7243, 7252, 7298, 7299, 7337, 7351, 7355, 7368, 7370, 7410, 7414, 7442, 7773, 8238, 8267, 8285, 8293, 8304, 8319, 8326, 8337, 8339, 8347, 8436, 8442, 9240

MARYLAND

Annapolis: Annapolis 3772, Chesapeake 3799, Ginger 3834, Leadership 3863, Maryland 3872, Maryland 3876

Annapolis Junction: Government 3838

Aquasco: Community 3809

Baltimore: Adams 3750, **Alpha 3755**, **Associated 3777**, Baltimore 3782, Baltimore 3783, Bright 3788, **Casey 3794**, Collegebound 3803, Community 3804, **Evergreen 3824**, Girl 3835, **Global 3836**, Govans 3837, **Humanity 3847**, **International 3849**, Job 3854, Keswick 3857, Kids 3858, Kowalsky 3861, Life 3865, March 3868, **Mid 3884**, Mid-Atlantic 3885, National 3894, **Order 3905**, Passano 3908, Pollak 3914, Sisters 3933, **Sudden 3939**, Truschel 3944

Bel Air: **Pet 3910**

Belcamp: Huether 3845

Berlin: Burbage 3791, Worcester 3953

Bethesda: American 3756, **American 3759**, **American 3765**, American 3766, **American 3767**, Autism 3780, Autism 3781, Cystic 3812, Davies 3813, **ELECTRI 3817**, **Foundation 3829**, Foundation 3830, **Hariri 3839**, **National 3893**, **National 3896**, **National 3897**, Torray 3942

Boonsboro: Sioda 3932

Bowie: Bowie 3786, **Estonian 3823**

Buckeystown: Jorgensen 3855

Camp Springs: Sacco 3923

Capitol Heights: Moore 3889, United 3948

Centreville: **American 3760**, Queen 3918

Charlotte Hall: Charlotte 3798

Chevy Chase: **AICE 3751**, **Endocrine 3818**, GEICO 3832, **Hispanic 3841**, **Hughes 3846**

Clarksburg: Brightfocus 3789

College Park: **American 3757**, **American 3761**, Maryland 3869, Maryland 3873

Columbia: Community 3807, Credit 3810, **Enterprise 3819**, **Foundation 3828**, Talarico 3940, Ulman 3947

Crofton: **Medical 3878**

Crownsville: Raskob 3919

Cumberland: Allegany 3753

Easton: Memorial 3879, Mid-Shore 3887, Neighborhood 3901

Edgewater: Chesapeake 3800

Elkridge: **Phi 3911**

Elkton: Cecil 3796, Steeplechase 3937, Thorn 3941

Ellicott City: Brierley 3787, Brown 3790, Howard 3844, Maryland 3870

Emmitsburg: **National 3895**

Fort Washington: Southern 3936

Frederick: Community 3806, Laughlin 3862, U.S. 3946, United 3949

Freeland: Penn-Mar 3909

Gaithersburg: **HealthWell 3840**, Kattar 3856, Manna 3867, **Osteogenesis 3906**, **Sodexo 3935**

Germantown: **Childhood 3801**, Walton 3950

Glen Burnie: Baltimore 3784, Maryland 3871

Great Mills: Hopkins, 3842

Greenbelt: **Environmental 3820**

Hyattsville: Full 3831, Prince 3915

Ijamsville: Jeremy 3852

Kensington: Crossway 3811, Housing 3843, Moore, 3890, Parent 3907

La Plata: Trustees 3945

Landover: **Epilepsy 3821**, Epilepsy 3822

Lanham: AMVETS 3771, Resource 3921

Largo: Arc 3775

Libertytown: Allemall 3754

Linthicum: **American 3769**, **American 3770**

Lutherville: National 3899, Skaters 3934

Monrovia: Maryland 3874

Mount Rainier: American 3758

Oakland: Moran 3891

Olney: Womens 3952

Owings Mills: Caves 3795, **Central 3797**, Ravens 3920

Oxon Hill: **School 3928**

Phoenix: Malstrom 3866

Port Republic: **Yvorra 3954**

Potomac: Fast 3825

Queenstown: Kirchner 3860

Reisterstown: Roche 3922

Riderwood: **Michels 3883**, Warfield 3951

Rockville: American 3762, **American 3768**, **Aplastic 3774**, **Association 3779**, Beth 3785, **Fisher 3826**, Foulger 3827, Jewish 3853, **King 3859**, McGeehin 3877, Mental 3881, Metropolitan 3882, Montgomery 3888, NASDAQ 3892, National 3898, PNH 3913, Stepping 3938

Salisbury: Community 3808, Salisbury 3924, Salisbury 3925, Shore 3931

Severna Park: **Middle 3886**

Silver Spring: American 3763, **American 3764**, **Anxiety 3773**, Arts 3776, Association 3778, Choice 3802, **Discovery 3815**, Ivy 3851, **National 3900**, Obesity 3904, **Pulmonary 3916**, Pyramid 3917, Sawyer 3927, Seabee 3929

Spencerville: Samet 3926

Stevensville: Maryland 3875

Suitland: Airmen 3752, Ivy 3850

Sykesville: Nexion 3902

Towson: **Carson 3793**, Dellon 3814, Duncan 3816, German 3833, **Immune 3848**, Leister 3864

Tracys Landing: Trueman 3943

Waldorf: Phoenix 3912

Westminster: Carroll 3792, Community 3805, Memorial 3880, Nicolay 3903, Shepherd's 3930

see also 1131, 1495, 1522, 1593, 1594, 1598, 1600, 1614, 1627, 1725, 1728, 1748, 2074, 2595, 4142, 4884, 6192, 6326, 6507, 6531, 6565, 6774, 6890, 7813, 8061, 8104, 8168, 8191, 8199, 8376, 9330, 9465, 9475, 9481, 9504, 9516, 9799, 9824

MASSACHUSETTS

Agawam: Grinspoon 4090

Andover: Andona 3970, Philips 4220, Tenney 4285

Arlington: Sanborn 4256, Terry 4286

Ashburnham: Massachusetts 4166

Ashland: Warren 4311

Avon: Marino 4161, Self-Help 4266

Becket: Jacob's 4129

Beverly: **American 3964**, American 3965, Pope 4227

Boston: AIDS 3961, **American 3966**, American 3967, **American 3969**, Associates 3973, Balfour 3976, **Beebe 3980**, Belmont 3981, Blue 3989, Boston 3991, Boston 3992, Boston 3993, Boston 3995, Bushee 4002, Cabot 4003, **Caring 4010**, Central 4017, Children's 4022, **City 4024**, **Devens 4039**, Du Bois 4044, **Earthwatch 4049**, Eaton 4053, Educational 4054, Edwards 4055, **Elderhostel 4058**, Farmer 4063, Farnam 4064, First 4069, **Fleming 4072**, **Giovanni 4083**, Harvard 4095, Harvard 4096, Hawks 4099, Health 4101, Hill 4105, **Houghton 4115**, Howard 4116, Howes 4118, Howes 4119, Jackson 4128, **Kennedy 4137**, King 4140, **Lalor 4145**, Lend 4146, **Liberty 4148**, **Lowell 4152**, Make-A-Wish 4157, Martin 4162, Massachusetts 4163, Massachusetts 4164, Mitchell 4179, Moakley 4180, Museum 4184, Museum 4185, **National 4190**, New 4194, **New 4196**, Nye 4204, One 4206, Paine 4209, Park 4211, Pierce 4229, Pratt 4229, Progin 4231, Putnam 4232, Red 4240, Rotch 4249, **Roy 4250**, Royal 4251, Salem 4253, SAMFund 4255, Sanders 4257, Swan 4280, **Tanne 4282**, Theta 4287, Travelers 4294, Travelli 4295, University 4305, USO 4307, Weyman 4314, Whiting 4316, **Winter 4319**

Boxford: Benz 3982

Bradford: Costello 4031

Braintree: Campenelli 4005, Costa 4030, Gunning 4092, North 4201, South 4275, Tye 4304

Bridgewater: Bridgewater 3997

Brimfield: Hitchcock 4106

Brockton: Brockton 4001, Mihos 4175, Pilgrim 4224

Brookline: **International 4127**, ROFEH 4246, Smalley 4269

Cambridge: 47 3955, Cambridge 4004, **Farm 4062**, **Genzyme 4080**, **Harvard 4097**, Johnson 4131, Lyceum 4154, President 4230, Real 4239

Canton: Dunkin 4047, **Tourism 4292**

Chestnut Hill: Center 4016, Cohen 4026, Humane 4121

Chilmark: Yard 4327

Concord: Peabody 4213

Danvers: Essex 4059, Fisher 4071, Giving 4084, **Scleroderma 4263**

Dedham: Dedham 4038

Dover: Dover 4043

Duxbury: **Northern 4203**, Trustees 4298

East Boston: First 4070

East Cambridge: East Cambridge 4050

East Longmeadow: East 4051

Easthampton: **Rosenberg 4247**

Essex: Woodman 4320

Fall River: Bristol 3999, Citizens 4023

Fitchburg: North 4200

Foxborough: **Ahern 3959**, Lake View 4144

Framingham: Davis 4036, MetroWest 4173, Take 4281, Trifiro 4297, Young 4328

Gardner: **International 4126**, Stone 4276

Georgetown: Scots 4264, Trustees 4299

Gloucester: Abbott, 3956, Action 3957, Dyer 4048, Needymeds 4191, Perfect 4215

Hanover: Foster 4075, Holmes 4107, Hunt 4122, Ruffini 4252, Taylor 4284, Washburn 4312, West 4313

Haverhill: Community 4028, Haverhill 4098

Hingham: Massachusetts 4168

Holyoke: Holyoke 4109

Hopedale: Hopedale 4112

Hudson: Rice 4242

Hull: **World 4324**

Hyannis: Cape Cod 4008, Heberton 4102, Hopkins 4113, Hutchinson 4124, Jones 4133, Perron 4217, Voght 4308

Ipswich: **New England 4193**

Kingston: South 4273

Lenox: Shultz 4268

Leominster: General 4078

Lexington: Cary 4014, Hayden 4100, Kim 4139, Maloney 4158, Supreme 4279

Lincoln: Carroll 4013

Longmeadow: Carman 4011

Lowell: Lowell 4153, Zampogna 4330

Lunenburg: Chelonian 4020

Lynn: Gerondelis 4082, Molloy 4181

Lynnfield: Hood 4111

Malden: Tri-City 4296

Marblehead: Marblehead 4159, Peach 4214

Marlborough: Crist 4032

Mattapoisett: British 4000

Medford: Jennings 4130

Methuen: College 4027

Middleboro: Pratt 4228

Middlefield: Chester 4021

Nantucket: Coffin's 4025, Donnell 4042, Nantucket 4186, Nantucket 4187, Relief 4241

Natick: Boston 3996, Fassino 4065, Middlesex 4174

Needham: **ALS 3962**, **Jurassic 4134**, McElaney 4171

New Bedford: Association 3974, Howland 4120, New Bedford 4192

Newburyport: **Fraxa 4076**, General 4079, Institution 4125, Kelly 4136, Trustees 4300, Wheelwright 4315

Newton: Segel 4265

Newton Centre: Aid 3960

Newton Highlands: Phillips 4221

North Adams: Massachusetts 4165

North Attleboro: Easter 4052, Miss 4178, North 4199

North Brookfield: Quabaug 4233

North Chatham: Chatham 4019

North Dartmouth: Taylor 4283, University 4306

North Reading: Levin 4147

Northampton: **Global 4085**, Torbet 4291, **Xeric 4326**

Norton: Ouimet 4208

Norwell: Henry 4103, Sullivan 4278

Norwood: Boch 3990, Knights 4141

Oak Bluffs: Permanent 4216

Orange: Orange 4207

Orleans: Faunce 4066, Lowe 4151

Oxford: Philbin 4219

Peabody: North 4202, Scholarship 4261

Pittsfield: Berkshire 3983, Berkshire 3984, Berkshire 3985, Jones 4132, Peabody 4212, Pittsfield 4225, Quirico 4235, South 4272

Plymouth: Plymouth 4226, South 4274

Provincetown: **Fine 4068**

Quincy: Koster 4142, **National 4188**, Quincy 4234, Schaeneman 4260

Raynham: Howard 4117

Raynham Center: Balfour 3977

Reading: Saugus 4259

Revere: Animal 3971

Rockland: Rockland 4245

Salem: Fortin 4074, Mack 4156, Phillips 4222, Samaritan 4254

Sandwich: Pettee 4218, Sandwich 4258, Thorne 4290

Saugus: Austin 3975, Bassett 3978, Blanchard 3988, Brightman 3998, Difelice 4040, Dugan 4045, Essex 4060, Horner 4114, Lynch 4155, Mavrogenis 4169, Nichols 4197, Niconchuk 4198, Richardson 4243, Whittemore 4317, Williams 4318

Sharon: Center 4015

Sheffield: Berkshire 3986

Somerville: **SEVEN 4267**, Thoreau 4289

South Boston: Boston 3994

South Dennis: Elder 4057

South Easton: Goddard 4086

South Yarmouth: Kelley 4135

Southborough: Rotary 4248

Southbridge: American 3968

Springfield: Baystate 3979, Community 4029, D'Amour 4033, D'Amour 4034, Ferdian 4067, Hampden 4093, HAP 4094, Home 4110, New 4195, Smith 4270

Stockbridge: High 4104

Stoughton: Danny 4035, Society 4271

Sudbury: Sudbury 4277

Swampscott: Kernwood 4138

Taunton: Friary 4077

Tewksbury: Holt 4108

Uxbridge: Ocean 4205

Wakefield: **R.O.S.E. 4236**

Walpole: German 4081, McLaughlin 4172

Waltham: **Huntington 4123**, Massachusetts 4167, National 4189, Raytheon 4238, **Transgender 4293**, Turning 4302, **Two 4303**, Von 4309

Watertown: Armenian 3972, **Documentary 4041**, **Milton 4177**

Wellesley: Affordable 3958, Egan 4056, Goldin 4087, Scholarship 4262, **Wurtman 4325**

Wellesley Hills: **Gravity 4089**, Kurzweil 4143

Wellfleet: **Maya 4170**

West Barnstable: Cape 4006

West Springfield: Grinspoon 4091, Millman 4176

Westborough: Beta 3987, Forbes 4073

Westford: Lorden 4150, Riddick 4244

Wilmington: Charles 4018, Golub 4088

Winchendon: Murray 4183

Winchester: Carco 4009, Murphy 4182

Woburn: **Lift 4149**, Trustees 4301

Woods Hole: Deane 4037, Dunham 4046, **Marine 4160**, Thomas 4288, **Woods 4321**

Worcester: **American 3963**, Carroll 4012, Fallon 4061, Pallotta 4210, Ratte 4237, Wagner 4310, Worcester 4322, Worcester 4323, Youth 4329

Yarmouthport: Cape Cod 4007

see also 362, 741, 826, 1333, 1385, 1392, 1395, 1451, 1619, 2323, 3651, 3803, 4386, 4546, 4754, 4960, 5317, 5323, 5343, 5367, 5375, 5556, 5723, 5964, 6032, 6052, 6295, 6327, 6565, 6654, 6829, 7235, 7298, 7305, 7736, 7775, 7825, 7843, 7965, 8082, 8122, 8132, 8134, 8233, 8236, 8237, 8239, 8240, 8244, 8248, 8250, 8256, 8258, 8264, 8270, 8273, 8274, 8275, 8278, 8279, 8283, 8284, 8287, 8290, 8292, 8294, 8295, 8297, 8298, 8299, 8300, 8318, 8320, 8323, 8325, 8329, 8333, 8338, 8345, 8348, 8349, 8350, 8354, 8355, 8359, 8360, 8363, 8368, 8369, 8372, 8377, 8378, 8383, 8384, 8385, 8387, 8391, 8396, 8403, 8404, 8406, 8409, 8417, 8419, 8420, 8427, 8429, 8430, 8431, 8435, 8440, 8441, 8443, 8580, 9240, 9722

MICHIGAN

Adrian: Bixby 4361, Gleaner 4440

Allegan: Allegan 4333, Allegan 4334

Alma: Michigan 4539

Almont: Four 4427

Alpena: Community 4392, Northeast 4559

Ann Arbor: Alliance 4336, Ann Arbor 4338, Ann Arbor 4339, Blaske 4362, **Chang 4378**, **Domino's 4409**, **Earhart 4411**, National 4549, Rislov 4589, **Society 4610**, Winkler 4671

Auburn Hills: Avondale 4341, Come 4389, Easter 4412, Guardian 4452, MEEMIC 4531, Skandalaris 4607

Bad Axe: Huron 4477, Smith 4609

Baraga: Baraga 4344

Battle Creek: Battle Creek 4349, **Kellogg 4496**, **Kellogg 4497**, McCurdy 4529, Michigan 4537, Region 4586, Southwest 4618, Trone 4642, United 4649, Willard 4669, Winship 4672, **Yankama 4676**

Bay City: Bay 4350, Lutheran 4520, Pardee 4572

Bay Harbor: Bay Harbor 4351

Benton Harbor: Southwest 4617, Whirlpool 4666

Benzonia: Johnson 4487

Bingham Farms: Birkenstock 4358, Polakovic 4581

Birmingham: Birmingham 4359, Foundation 4425

Bloomfield Hills: Fallen 4417, **International 4481**, Legion 4515, Thomas 4636

Brighton: Make-A-Wish 4522

Buchanan: Michigan 4538

Byron Center: Buist 4369

Cadillac: Cadillac 4371

Caledonia: Carpenter 4376

Canton: Canton 4372

Caro: Human 4474, Scears 4600, Tuscola 4646

Chelsea: Chelsea 4382

Clarkston: Optimist 4570

Clinton: Clinton 4384

Clinton Township: Italian 4483

Clinton TWP: Nill 4557

Coldwater: Branch 4365, Juhl 4488, Salisbury 4598, Taylor 4633

Dearborn: Oakwood 4567, **Society 4611**

Detroit: Blue 4363, CareLink 4374, Caring 4375, Charity 4379, Chase 4381, Cole 4386, Community 4393, Davenport 4404, Ford 4421, **Ford 4422**, Heat 4459, **Herdegen 4464**, Hospitalers 4470, Hudson 4473, Ilitch 4480, Jackson 4485, Kelly 4498, Kling 4502, Martin 4526, Matrix 4527, Matson 4528, Michigan 4540, Minton 4544, New 4552, Old 4568, Parker 4573, Parks 4574, Phelps 4578, Reuther 4588, Schaap 4601, Society 4612, **Sphinx 4622**, Stokes 4628, Travelers 4640, Tumey 4644, **UAW-Ford 4647**, UAW-GM 4648, **World 4674**, Young 4677

Dexter: Temple 4634

East Jordan: Charlevoix 4380

East Lansing: Junior 4489, Michigan 4534, Michigan 4536

East Tawas: Laidlaw 4509

Escanaba: Community 4399

Evart: Hillier 4466

Farmington Hills: **ACI 4332**, Community 4400, Evereg-Fenesse 4414

Flint: Bees 4354, Bellinger 4355, Brenske 4366, Brenske 4367, Career 4373, Community 4394, Eddy 4413, Flint 4419, Gibbs 4435, Gilles 4436, Hecht 4461, Horgan 4469, Huss 4478, Jeffers 4486, McPherson 4530, Rachor 4583, Reid 4587, Roethke 4591, Trinklein 4641, Whaley 4665, Wilson 4670

Flushing: Welch 4663

Fort Gratiot: I Have 4479

Frankenmuth: Frankenmuth 4428

Franklin: Polan 4582

Fraser: Fraser 4429

Fremont: Fremont 4431, Genesis 4433, **Gerber 4434**, Newaygo 4554

Galesburg: Galesburg-Augusta 4432

Garden City: Stewart 4627

Gaylord: Otsego 4571

Glen Arbor: **Glen Arbor 4441**

Grand Haven: Grand Haven 4444, Wigginton 4668

Grand Rapids: Abbott 4331, Allen 4335, **Ball 4343**, Basilica 4348, Bemis 4356, Ford 4420, Foster 4424, Fredericksen 4430, Gilmore 4437, Glaser 4439, Goodrich 4442, Goss 4443, Grand Rapids 4445, Grand 4446, Gumaer 4453, Habitat 4454, Howe 4472, Humbert 4476, Koch 4504, Morrill 4546, Rudy 4595, Speerstra 4621, Tassell-Wisner-Bottrall 4632, Thresholds 4638, Universal 4653

Greenville: Greenville 4451

Grosse Pointe Park: Ewald 4415, Tamer 4631

Hancock: Keweenaw 4499

Harbor Beach: Krause 4506

Harbor Springs: Harbor 4456, Kiwanis 4501

Hastings: Barry 4347, Pennock 4576

Highland: Baker 4342

Hillsdale: Hillsdale 4467

Holland: Community 4398, Heeringa 4462

Homer: Community 4390

Houghton: Baraga-Houghton 4345

Iron Mountain: Dickinson 4408, Nelson 4551, Trudell 4643

Ironwood: Ironwood 4482

Ithaca: Gratiot 4448, Gratiot 4449

Jackson: Jackson 4484, Michner 4541, Raval 4584, Sigmund 4606

Kalamazoo: Arts 4340, Fabri 4416, **Fetzer 4418**, **Gilmore 4438**, Heyl 4465, Kalamazoo 4492, Kalamazoo 4493, Kalamazoo 4494, **Upjohn 4654**

Kentwood: Paulsen 4575

Lansing: Amy 4337, Delta 4406, Harding 4457, Lansing 4511, Lions 4518, Plumbers 4579, Scholarship 4602, Sparrow 4619, Whiteley 4667

Lapeer: Lapeer 4512

Livonia: Recreational 4585

Lowell: Rotary 4593

Ludington: Birtwistle 4360, Great 4450

Manistee: Tuohy 4645

Marcellus: Hovarter 4471

Marquette: Hammel 4455, Marquette 4523, Marquette 4524

Marshall: Marshall 4525

Mears: HCC 4458

Menominee: M & M 4521

Midland: **Dow 4410**, Midland 4542, United 4651

Milford: Bretzlaff 4368

Monroe: Community 4396, Knabusch 4503, Little 4519, Wells 4664

Morenci: Wirick 4673

Mount Clemens: Mount 4547

Mount Pleasant: Mount Pleasant 4548

Muskegon: Community 4391, Nordman 4558

New Buffalo: Pokagon 4580

Newaygo: Newaygo 4555

Newberry: Tahquamenon 4630

Northport: Leelanau 4514

Northville: Northville 4561, Northville 4562

Novi: Novi 4564, Novi 4565

Okemos: Michigan 4535

Olivet: Vomberg 4659

Ontonagon: Ontonagon 4569

Owosso: Shiawassee 4605

Petoskey: Northern 4560, Petoskey 4577

Pigeon: LaVictoire 4513

Pontiac: Lighthouse 4517, Oakland 4566

Port Huron: Community 4397, United 4652

Redford: Nieman 4556

Remus: Laflin 4508

Rochester: Community 4395, New 4553, Rochester 4590

Rockford: Byrne 4370

Rogers City: United 4650

Romeo: L & L 4507

Roscommon: Roscommon 4592

Roseville: Kiwanis 4500

Royal Oak: Royal 4594

Saginaw: Hebert 4460, Junior 4490, Saginaw 4597, St. Mary's 4625, Watson 4661

Saint Joseph: Berrien 4357, Tiscornia 4639

Saline: Foundation 4426

Sandusky: Coller 4388, Sanilac 4599

Shelby Township: Shelby 4604, Van Hollenbeck 4655

Southfield: Barr 4346, Beaumont 4352, Cunningham 4401, Dancey 4403, National 4550, Sojourner 4613, Southfield 4616, Vetowich 4658

Spring Lake: Sonneveldt 4614

St. Charles: Ruf 4596

St. Clair: Foster 4423

St. Joseph: Lakeland 4510, St. Joseph 4624

Stanton: Central 4377

Sterling Heights: Sterling 4626

Stevensville: Kohn 4505

Sturgis: Sturgis 4629

Tecumseh: Lenawee 4516, Meyers 4532

Temperance: Bedford 4353

Three Rivers: Kadant 4491, Three 4637

Traverse City: **Collectors 4387**, Grand 4447, Northwest 4563, Skrocki 4608

Troy: Children's 4383, Detroit 4407, **Michigan 4533**, Southeastern 4615, Thom 4635

University Center: Delta 4405

Utica: Humane 4475

Van Buren Township: Dana 4402

Warren: Cold 4385

Waterford: Waterford 4660

Wayne: Veteran's 4657

West Bloomfield: Kay 4495

Westland: Spectrum 4620

Willliamston: Schultheiss 4603

Winn: Morey 4545

Wyandotte: Bott 4364, Wayne-Metropolitan 4662, Wyandotte 4675

Wyoming: Home 4468, St. John 4623

Ypsilanti: Hemophilia 4463

Zeeland: Miller 4543, VanKley 4656

---

see also 431, 710, 1095, 2046, 2199, 2247, 2395, 2436, 2552, 2584, 2785, 2886, 3169, 3651, 4142, 4810, 4851, 5643, 5830, 6890, 6975, 6990, 7091, 7127, 7217, 7247, 7264, 7346, 7758, 7931, 7979, 8014, 8069, 8112, 8171, 8188, 9325, 9891, 9906, 10081

MINNESOTA

Ada: Ada 4680

Aitkin: Petraborg 4822

Anoka: Hansen 4753, **Lindbergh 4783**, Thurston 4868

Apple Valley: Minnesota 4807

Bayport: Trinity 4872

Bemidji: Northwest 4817, Region 4836

Blaine: Brooks 4704

Bloomington: Volunteers 4880

Blue Earth: Masonic 4790

Cannon Falls: **Wagner 4883**

Chanhassen: Miracles 4809

Cloquet: Scheidler 4844

Columbia Heights: Columbia 4717

Comfrey: Anderson 4691

Coon Rapids: Minnesota 4805

Crosslake: Crosslake 4724

Detroit Lakes: Mahube 4788

Duluth: Alworth 4685, Arrowhead 4693, Artist 4694, Duluth 4729, Johnson 4773, Minnesota 4804, Moon 4810, Wildey 4891

Eagan: Intertech 4767

Eden Prairie: Birk's 4698

Edina: Chong 4713, Law 4781, Winslow 4893

Ely: Vermilion 4879

Fairmont: Rosen 4841

Fergus Falls: Lake 4777

Foley: Central 4710

Franconia: Franconia 4743

Frazee: Daggett 4725

Fridley: **Grannis-Martin 4751**

Gonvick: Thorbeck 4865

Grand Rapids: Blandin 4700, Grand Rapids 4750, Lemieux 4782, Second 4848

Hastings: Hastings 4755, Hoffman 4761, Welshons 4886

Hector: Sampson 4843

Hermantown: Bowman 4702

Inver Grove Heights: CHS 4715

Lanesboro: Cornucopia 4721

Litchfield: Roberg 4839

Little Falls: Initiative 4764

Mankato: AgStar 4683, Mankato 4789, Minnesota 4806, Siemer 4850, Stillwell 4862

Maple Plain: Pick 4825

Marshall: Southwest 4857, Southwest 4858

Medina: **Polaris 4827**

Mendota Heights: Sun 4863

Minneapolis: Abbott 4679, **American 4686**, Bakken 4697, Bridge 4703, Catholic 4708, Clearway 4716, Community 4718, Crockett 4723, Dolan 4728, Ecotrust 4732, Family 4736, **Francis 4742**, Fredrikson 4745, **Gallagher 4746**, Harvard 4754, Henry 4757, Highpoint 4759, Intermedia 4766, Italian 4768, Jostens 4774, Lakeland 4778, Loft 4784, **Lutheran 4785**, MacPherson 4787, **McKnight 4793**, McKnight 4794, Meyer 4796, Minnesota 4798, Minnesota 4799, Minnesota 4801, Minnesota 4802, Minnesota 4803, National 4811, Northern 4814, Page 4820, Philanthrofund 4824, PLUS 4826, **Pro 4829**, Redmond 4834, Regions 4837, Southern 4855, Target 4864, **Thrivent 4867**, Tiwahe 4869, **UnitedHealthcare 4876**, University 4877, Valspar 4878, Volunteers 4881, VSA 4882, Wallin 4884, Wedum 4885, Woman's 4894

Minnetonka: Baker 4696, Jewish 4772, Providers 4831

Montevideo: Western 4888

Moorhead: Concordia 4719

Moose Lake: Blacklock 4699

Morgan: Gilfillan 4747

Navarre: Wenger 4887

New Ulm: Carson 4707

New York Mills: New York 4812

North Oaks: **Camargo 4706**

Oakdale: ECMC 4730

Perham: Arvig 4695

Plymouth: Bottemiller 4701, **Groot 4752**, Interfaith 4765, Miracle 4808

Red Wing: **Anderson 4690**

Redwood Falls: Farmers 4737, Gilfillan 4748, Redwood 4835

Rochester: Christian 4714, **Foundation 4741**, Franz 4744, Mayo 4791, Mayo 4792, **Restless 4838**, Rochester 4840, Southeastern 4854

Roseville: Petters 4823

Rushford: Semcac 4849

Saint Cloud: Central 4711

Saint Paul: 3-H 4678, Anodyne 4692, Ely-Winton 4733, Forecast 4740, Northern 4816, Soneson 4851, Two 4873, United 4874

Saint Paul Park: South 4853

Shakopee: Rahr 4833, Scott-Carver-Dakota 4846

Shoreview: North 4813

Slayton: Southwest 4856
South Saint Paul: South St. Paul 4852
Springfield: Jenniges 4770
St. Cloud: CentraCare 4709, Child 4712, Ernst 4735, Olson 4818
St. Louis Park: Methodist 4795
St. Paul: Affinity 4682, American 4687, American 4688, American 4689, Bush 4705, Community 4719, Cox 4722, Denfeld 4726, Dietrick-Parks 4727, Ecolab 4731, **Engen 4734**, Gough 4749, HealthEast 4756, Higher 4758, **Hmong 4760**, Hull 4762, IFP 4763, Jaffray 4769, Jerome 4771, Kohl 4775, Koran 4776, Land 4779, Lane 4780, Lutheran 4786, Minnesota 4797, Minnesota 4800, Osborn 4819, **Patterson 4821**, Proshek 4830, Saint Paul 4842, Second 4847, Springboard 4859, St. Paul 4860, Steinke 4861, United 4875, Whiteside 4889, Wilder 4890
St. Peter: **Scholarship 4845**
Staples: Five 4738
Stillwater: Tozer 4870
Wadena: Northern 4815, Tri-County 4871
Waseca: Prairie 4828
Willmar: Adams 4681
Winnebago: Foley 4739
Winona: Alumnae 4684, Pryor 4832, Winona 4892
Zumbrota: Three 4866

see also 238, 1494, 1949, 2226, 2247, 2552, 2768, 2885, 3251, 3302, 3318, 5225, 5622, 5929, 6642, 6708, 6904, 6941, 7023, 7258, 7318, 7931, 8019, 8158, 8520, 8538, 9837, 9913, 10018, 10043

MISSISSIPPI

Amory: Haskell 4910
Biloxi: Bleuer 4898, St. Vincent 4922
Booneville: Franks 4908
Brandon: **Mobile 4916**
Brookhaven: Dunnaway 4905
Columbus: Hazard 4911, Owen 4917, Phillips 4918, Puckett, 4920
Greenwood: Thalheimer 4924
Gulfport: Gulf 4909
Hattiesburg: University 4925
Hernando: Box 4899
Jackson: Community 4902, Feild 4907, Mississippi 4914, Sumners 4923
Lexington: Lexington 4912
Meridian: Care 4901, East 4906
Natchez: AJFC 4895, Biglane 4897
Olive Branch: Skelton 4921
Pascagoula: Bacot/Jolly 4896, **Pine 4919**
Philadelphia: Yates 4926
Ridgeland: C Spire 4900, Mississippi 4915
Tupelo: CREATE 4903
Waveland: McDonald 4913
Yazoo City: Day 4904

see also 21, 81, 294, 2247, 2726, 3556, 3651, 4497, 4884, 5099, 8564, 8573, 8765, 8770, 8799, 9121

MISSOURI

Appleton City: West 5124
Ballwin: Sabada 5081
Bolivar: Bolivar 4940
Bowling Green: North 5065
Bridgeton: **Boys 4941**, **Boys 4942**
Camdenton: Lake 5032
Cape Girardeau: Cape 4951
Chesterfield: Make-A-Wish 5040, Thurman 5114
Chillicothe: Concerned 4965, Hutchinson 5022

Clayton: Evans 4989, Guilander 5009, Kirschner 5030, Leader 5035, Soldwedel 5102, Tilles 5115, Ward 5123
Columbia: **American 4932**, Central 4954, Martin 5044, MFA 5050, Shelter 5099
Dearborn: North 5066
Dexter: Covington 4967
Farmington: Swanson 5110
Fenton: UniGroup 5119
Ferguson: Delta 4973
Forsyth: Gift 4999
Grandview: NASB 5061
Hannibal: Barber 4936, Clayton 4959, Dunlop 4980, Lowrie 5038
Independence: Alpha 4930, Truman 5118
Jefferson City: Hays 5014, Helias 5015, Missouri 5056, Schwartze 5086, Schwartze 5087, Schwartze 5088, Schwartze 5089, Schwartze 5090, Schwartze 5091, Schwartze 5092, Schwartze 5093, Schwartze 5094, Schwartze 5095, Schwartze 5096, St. Marys 5107
Jefferson Cty: MHA 5051
Kansas City: **Agriculture 4928**, **Alpha 4929**, Baptist-Trinity 4935, Butler 4948, Calkins 4949, Community 4964, **Demolay 4974**, Drowns 4979, Ebert 4981, Educational 4983, Employees 4986, Fingersh 4992, Foundation 4994, Goetze 5001, Grant 5003, Green 5005, Hall 5011, Kansas 5023, **Kauffman 5025**, Klapmeyer 5031, Lamb 5033, Mid 5053, Minnesouri 5055, **People 5072**, **PKD 5074**, Poillon 5075, Ronald 5080, **Sertoma, 5098**, Stowers 5109, Tension 5112, United 5120
Keytesville: Finnell 4993
Kirksville: Northeast 5067
Lebanon: Carr 4953
Lee's Summit: Greater 5004, Kansas City 5024
Lexington: Lyons 5039, Mann 5042
Louisiana: Burkhalter 4947
Marshall: Buckner 4945, Missouri 5060, Smith 5101
Maryland Heights: Friedman 4996
Meadville: Doolin 4978
Mexico: Creasey 4971, Ferris 4991, French 4995, Griffin 5007
Moberly: Orscheln 5068
Mount Vernon: Holmes 5018
Nevada: Corbin 4966, Hester 5016, Tompkins 5116
New London: Anderson 4933
Osceola: Fues 4997
Overland: Community 4962
Peculiar: Peculiar 5071
Platte City: Skillman 5100
Portageville: Delta 4972
Princeton: Kauffman 5026
Richland: Missouri 5058
Richmond: Ray 5078
Rock Port: Gibbs 4998
Saint Charles: **Growing 5008**
Saint Joseph: Dodd 4976
Saint Louis: Brey 4943, **Build 4946**, **Chesed 4955**, Cohen 4960, Dental 4975, Gorman 5002, Haddad 5010, Hughes 5019, Kennett 5028, Lange 5034, Lord 5037, Marymount 5046, Miles 5054, Paul 5070, Reynolds 5079, Saint Louis 5082, Schafer 5083, Sprehe 5103, **St. Louis 5105**, St. Louis 5106, Trotter 5117, United 5121
Salem: Young 5126
Salisbury: Huss 5020
Springfield: Bentley 4939, Community 4963, Cox 4968, Coxhealth 4969, Meyer 5049, Missouri 5059, Ozarks 5069
St. Elizabeth: Doerhoff 4977
St. Joseph: Beattie 4937, Campbell 4950, Hirsch 5017, King 5029, Steven 5108
St. Louis: African 4927, American 4931, Arch 4934, Bell 4938, Broida/Sigma-Aldrich 4944, Cardinal 4952, Child 4956, Clay 4958, College 4961, Craft 4970, Edgar 4982, Educational 4984, Emerson

4985, Epilepsy 4987, ESCO 4988, Feraldo 4990, Gilbert 5000, Hamilton 5012, Hayes 5013, Hutchins 5021, Liebling 5036, Mallinckrodt 5041, Marsch 5043, Martino 5045, McElroy 5047, McGlothlan 5048, MICDS 5052, Missouri 5057, **National 5062**, Porter 5076, Queen 5077, Scholarship 5084, Schowengerdt 5085, Scottish 5097, St. Louis 5104, Swope 5111, Urban 5122, **Young 5127**
Town and Country: **Pi 5073**
Trenton: Green 5006, North 5064
Troy: Kelly 5027, Thompson 5113
Webb City: Nichols 5063
Wildwood: Clarkson 4957
Windsor: Windsor 5125

see also 199, 209, 257, 308, 311, 420, 759, 1385, 2046, 2055, 2395, 2502, 2552, 2599, 2807, 2826, 2915, 3251, 3302, 3309, 3439, 3457, 3493, 3816, 4118, 4775, 4884, 5964, 7515, 7586, 8679, 8686, 8700, 8718, 8793, 8794, 8795, 8891, 8893, 8991, 9012, 9071, 9105, 9106, 9213, 9413, 9577, 9848, 9851, 9936, 9962, 10106

MONTANA

Billings: Ashcraft 5129, Bair 5130, Bottrell 5133, District 5142, Montana 5164, Yellowstone 5183
Bozeman: Sacred 5171
Butte: Mike 5162
Chinook: Sweet 5177
Clyde Park: Shields 5173
Cut Bank: Cut Bank 5139
Ennis: Creek 5138
Eureka: Interbel 5160
Geyser: Geyser 5149
Great Falls: Benefis 5132, Gay 5147, Haack 5152, Hawkins 5155, Heisey 5156, Horsman 5158, Nadeau 5166, Senft 5172, Suden 5175
Helena: Bray 5134, Montana 5163, Student 5174, Treacy 5180
Jefferson City: H2 5151
Kalispell: Flathead 5146
Lewistown: Fergus 5145
Malta: Robinson 5168
Missoula: Allegiance 5128, Brondum 5135, Clay 5137, District 5143, Mountain 5165, **National 5167**, **Rocky 5169**, Washington 5182
Plentywood: Hanson 5153
Polson: Clarkson 5136, Harbert 5154, Jarecki 5161, Rolfson 5170, Taber 5178, Unrau 5181
Red Lodge: Beartooth 5131
Roundup: Gebhardt 5148
Sidney: Dayton 5141, Elm 5144, Groskinsky 5150, Svarre 5176
Somers: Daley 5140
Stanford: Hurst 5159
Whitefish: Hinderman 5157
Wibaux: Townley 5179

see also 1237, 1272, 1494, 4172, 4737, 6700, 6719, 6720, 6741, 6824, 6863, 6948, 7165, 7538, 7541, 7579, 7602, 7620, 7629, 7654, 7888, 7894, 8031, 8145, 8197, 8520, 9389, 9603, 9613, 9634, 9690, 9699, 9700, 9701, 9702, 9717, 10095, 10110

NEBRASKA

Alda: Stueven 5264
Alliance: Elliott 5199, Newblom 5247
Atkinson: Weller 5271
Aurora: Hamilton 5212
Benkelman: Hester 5218
Big Springs: Riss 5258
Burwell: Butts 5191

Cambridge: Tri-Valley 5266
Central City: Merrick 5233
Columbus: Federated 5202
Cozad: Cozad 5193, Wilson 5273
Doniphan: Doniphan 5195
Fremont: Fremont 5205
Geneva: Higher 5219
Grand Island: Grand Island 5210
Hastings: Ellis 5200, Hastings 5215, Wilson 5274
Hay Springs: Hay 5217
Holdrege: Phelps 5255
Kearney: Good 5209, Kearney 5223
Lexington: Lexington 5228
Lincoln: BryanLGH 5189, CEDARS 5192, **Dressage 5196**, EducationQuest 5197, Foundation 5204, Girl 5207, Good 5208, Lincoln 5229, Midwest 5235, Nebraska 5237, Nebraska 5238, Nebraska 5239, Nebraska 5241, Nebraska 5243, Nebraska 5245, Nelnet 5246, People's 5254
Loup City: Sherman 5260
Nebraska City: Steinhart 5262
North Platte: Mid-Nebraska 5234
Omaha: Alegent 5184, All 5185, Bemis 5186, Bran 5187, Bryan 5188, **Buffett 5190**, Davis 5194, Edwards 5198, Emerson 5201, Fellman 5203, Genesis 5206, H.H. 5211, Hansen 5213, Hapke 5214, Hawks 5216, Home 5220, Jewish 5221, Kiewit 5224, Killen 5225, Kooper 5226, Leslie 5227, Loessin 5230, Lutheran 5231, McNay 5232, Morrison 5236, Nebraska 5240, Nebraska 5242, Nebraska 5244, OEA 5249, Omaha 5250, Omaha 5251, Patton 5253, Riley 5257, Schmoker 5259, Simon 5261, Strengths 5263, UNMC 5267, Wabash 5268, Walther 5270, Wood 5275, World 5276
Ord: Johnson 5222, Novak 5248
Scottsbluff: Oregon 5252, Regional 5256
Seward: Wake 5269
Superior: Sweet 5265
West Point: West Point 5272
York: York 5277

see also 502, 797, 1494, 3251, 3302, 3330, 3366, 3382, 4722, 4780, 4841, 5053, 5099, 6036, 6687, 6733, 8182, 8188, 8990, 9739, 10017

NEVADA

Boulder City: Korfman 5291
Carson City: Orcutt 5299
Elko: Western 5304
Gardnerville: Snyder 5302
Green Valley: Miracle 5294
Henderson: **A Charitable 5278**, **Marchionne 5293**
Incline Village: Holder 5289
Las Vegas: **Caring 5280**, Catholic 5281, Dawson 5285, Foundation 5288, Laetz 5292, Nevada 5295, Norris 5297, United 5303
Reno: Community 5282, Cummings 5283, Davidson 5284, DiRienzo 5286, Doyle 5287, Kirchner 5290, Nevada 5296, NV 5298, Reno 5300, Renown 5301
Stateline: Berner 5279

see also 174, 208, 711, 999, 4883, 5099, 7914, 7940, 9215, 9217

NEW HAMPSHIRE

Alton Bay: Porter 5362
Barnstead: Lavoie 5337
Berlin: Tri-County 5372
Bethlehem: Somerville 5369
Concord: American 5305, Blandin 5308, Bogni 5309, Butler 5312, Clarke 5313, Cogan 5314, Community 5315, Concord 5316, Davenport 5317, Edmunds 5319, Gifford 5323, Hastings 5327,

James 5331, Manuel 5343, McIninch 5346, Morse 5349, Morton 5350, New Hampshire 5352, New Hampshire 5353, New Hampshire 5355, Ramsaye 5363, Ramsaye 5364, Skrungloo 5368, Vanderhout 5375, White 5377, Wilson 5378
Contoocook: Elliott 5320
Dover: Burtman 5311, Green 5324, Our 5359, Strafford 5371
Exeter: **Lyman 5340**
Gilford: Lakes 5335
Gorham: Randolph 5365
Hooksett: Scots' 5367
Keene: Ladies 5334, Moving 5351
Laconia: Lancaster 5336
Lebanon: Hitchcock 5328
Lincoln: Linwood 5339
Londonderry: Parkland 5360
Manchester: Bruce 5310, Dodge 5318, Fond 5321, Manchester 5342, Moore 5348, New Hampshire 5354, Nye 5357, **U.S. 5373**, Union 5374
Nashua: Griffin 5325, Griffin 5326, Hunt 5330
New London: New London 5356
Newport: Oberkotter 5358
Peterborough: Bean 5307, **MacDowell 5341**
Plymouth: Ayer 5306
Portsmouth: Foundation 5322, Krempels 5332, La Napoule 5333, Letourneau 5338, Plan 5361, Rockingham 5366, Yarnold 5379
Twin Mountain: Stickney 5370
Walpole: Hubbard 5329, Walpole 5376
Wilton: **Money 5347**
Wolfeboro: Martin 5344, Martin 5345

see also 741, 1374, 1455, 3651, 3982, 3994, 4000, 4142, 4264, 4295, 4328, 5556, 6032, 6295, 6327, 7298, 8225, 8228, 8229, 8234, 8241, 8242, 8243, 8252, 8257, 8260, 8291, 8306, 8309, 8311, 8324, 8328, 8370, 8415, 9240

NEW JERSEY

Allwood Station: Kovach 5491
Alpine: **Ostberg 5533**
Annandale: Astle 5390
Atlantic City: Atlanticare 5392, Calvi 5409
Basking Ridge: Grupe 5462, Hannaford, 5465, Lukenda 5499
Bedminster: Bernards 5398, Jackson 5480, Van Doren 5591
Belleville: Belleville 5396
Berlin: Camden 5410
Bloomingdale: Foundation 5450
Branchville: FMI 5447
Brick: Laucius 5495
Bridgeton: Tri-County 5581
Bridgewater: Eastern 5438, **Sanofi 5559**
Burlington: Burlington 5407, Harness 5466
Butler: Payne 5536
Caldwell: Orenstein 5532
Camden: Cooper 5427
Cape May: Kiwanis 5488
Chatham: Chatham 5419
Cherry Hill: BLSJ 5402, Kennedy 5486, Penn 5537, Scholarship 5560
Clark: Bartell 5394, D'Annunzio 5432
Cresskill: **Mahajan 5501**
Denville: WKBJ 5602
East Brunswick: Easter 5437, Hemophilia 5468, New Jersey 5517
East Hanover: **Novartis 5529**
East Rutherford: Giants 5452
Edison: Legal 5497, Middlesex 5507
Egg Harbor Township: Friends 5451, Houton 5474, Previti 5545
Elizabeth: United 5586
Elmer: Miller 5508

Englewood: Anyone 5387
Fairview: **Croatian 5430**
Fanwood: Scotch 5561
Florham Park: Madison 5500
Fords: Woodbridge 5604
Fort Lee: **Southpole 5572**
Gladstone: United 5584
Glassboro: Rowan 5554
Glen Rock: Glen 5453
Hackensack: Arc 5388, **CJ 5425**, Creamer 5429, North 5527, Shoshana 5564, Terplan 5577
Haddonfield: Holman 5471
Hasbrouck Heights: Children's 5423
Haworth: White 5596
Hillsborough: Costume 5428, Gubitosi 5463
Hoboken: **Wiley 5599**
Hohokus: Gruenberg 5461
Iselin: **Siemens 5566**
Jersey City: First 5445, United 5587
Kenilworth: New Jersey 5523
Lakewood: Beth 5400, Dirshu 5434
Lawrenceville: Princeton 5546
Layton: Peters 5539
Lebanon: Van Doren 5590
Linwood: A Place 5380, Hollander 5469, Hollander 5470, Poucher 5544
Little Falls: Townsend 5579
Livingston: Michaels 5506, Silbermann 5567
Long Beach Island: Zahn 5607
Manasquan: Shreve 5565
Maplewood: Bass 5395, **Tang 5575**
Margate City: Avoda 5393
Marlton: NARM 5513, Virtua 5592
Medford: Konstantinos 5490
Mendham: Family 5444
Millburn: Paper 5534
Millville: Pinson 5541, **WheatonArts 5595**
Monmouth Junction: New Jersey 5518
Monroe: Groff 5460
Monroeville: Clayton 5426
Montclair: **Mochary 5509**, Montclair 5510, United 5588
Montvale: KPMG 5492, KPMG 5493
Moorestown: Catholic 5415, Everly 5442, **Knowles 5489**, Moorestown 5511, Parker 5535
Morristown: Honeywell 5472, Rigorous 5551, Wetterberg 5594
Mount Arlington: Child 5420
Mount Laurel: **American 5385**, Chakrabarti 5418, Wound 5605
National Park: Society 5571
Neptune: Child 5422
New Brunswick: **American 5384**, Embrace 5440, **Johnson 5481**, New 5516, New Jersey 5521
New Vernon: Camp 5411
Newark: Buchalter 5406, Butts 5408, Essex 5441, Life 5498, **National 5514**, New Jersey 5519, Newark 5525, Prudential 5547, PSEG 5548, Wight 5598
Newton: Hull 5475
North Brunswick: Segal 5562
Nutley: Wei 5593
Oradell: **DRC 5436**
Palisades Park: **New 5524**
Paramus: Diabetes 5433, United 5585
Park Ridge: Grande 5458, Peterson 5540
Passaic: **American 5383**
Pedricktown: Berkowitz 5397
Pennington: **Glushko 5454**, Kapala 5485, Lasko 5494, McCready 5502, Trial 5580
Perth Amboy: Catholic 5413
Phillipsburg: Northwest 5528
Piscataway: Fortescue 5448, **IEEE 5476**, Ingersoll-Rand 5478
Pittstown: Gonzalez 5456
Pleasantville: Justice 5484

Port Reading: **Foundation 5449**
Princeton: **Center 5416**, **Dow 5435**, Eden 5439, Horowitz 5473, **Infinity 5477**, Islami, 5479, **Johnson 5482**, **LearningAlly 5496**, McLane 5503, **Newcombe 5526**, **Wilson 5600**
Princeton Junction: **Cerebral 5417**
Ramsey: Several 5563
Red Bank: Snyder 5570, Whitfield 5597
Ridgewood: Valley 5589
Ringoes: Skeuse 5568
Ringwood: Boland 5404
Rockaway: Rubenstein 5555
Rumson: Zipf 5608
Saddle River: Saddle 5557, Young 5606
Sea Girt: Adelphic 5381
Short Hills: Grandcolas 5457, **Reeve 5550**
Somers Point: Atlantic 5391
South Plainfield: Ammonius 5386, O'Leary 5531, Robustelli 5552
Springfield: Goldberg 5455, Joint 5483
Summit: Cutter 5431, People 5538, Summit 5573, Summit 5574
Teaneck: **Berrie 5399**, Brookdale 5405, **Puffin 5549**
Tenafly: Union 5583
Toms River: O'Brien's 5530
Totowa: Capezio 5412
Trenton: Bicket 5401, Catholic 5414, Child 5421, New Jersey 5515
Union: Portuguese-American 5543
Vineland: Morello 5512
Voorhees: Akers 5382, Hale 5464, Townsend 5578
Wanaque: Rose 5553
Warren: B'nai 5403, **Chubb 5424**
Washington: Smith 5569
Wayne: **ARCH 5389**, Flynn 5446, Greater 5459, Ryu 5556
West Caldwell: Union 5582
West Collingswood: Excelsior 5443
West Orange: Kessler 5487, Saint 5558
West Trenton: Health 5467, New Jersey 5520
Westfield: Polonsky 5542, Woman's 5603
Whitehouse Station: Merck 5504, **Merck 5505**
Woodbridge: New Jersey 5522
Woodcliff Lake: Tavitian 5576
Wyckoff: **Winn 5601**

see also 406, 591, 1024, 1380, 1467, 1498, 1930, 2146, 2513, 3641, 3872, 4414, 4960, 5363, 5364, 6015, 6016, 6052, 6084, 6109, 6171, 6274, 6336, 6397, 6413, 6471, 6486, 6507, 6531, 6592, 6654, 6693, 6695, 6789, 6868, 6897, 6925, 6963, 7700, 7715, 7737, 7807, 7808, 7809, 7815, 7890, 7905, 7929, 8042, 8073, 8079, 8089, 8106, 8120, 8140, 8155, 8160, 8196, 8303, 8314, 8315, 8342, 8365, 8393, 8398, 8400, 8401, 8405, 8411, 8418, 8972, 9424

NEW MEXICO

Alamogordo: Hamilton 5631
Albuquerque: Albuquerque 5610, **American 5611**, **American 5612**, **Catching 5618**, PRMC-Clovis 5644, SPARX 5653, **SUMMA 5655**
Anthony: Border 5615
Artesia: Berliner 5614, Central 5620, Chase 5621, Penasco 5642, Sacramento 5647
Carlsbad: Carlsbad 5616
Cloudcroft: Otero 5641
Clovis: Clovis 5622, ENMR 5627, ENMR 5628, Farmers' 5629
Deming: Columbus 5623
Espanola: Jemez 5633, Los 5638
Gallup: Community 5625
Grants: Continental 5626
Hobbs: Finis 5630, Leaco 5637, Maddox 5639

Laguna: Laguna 5634
Las Cruces: Community 5624
Las Vegas: Viles 5657
Lovington: Lea 5636
Mountainair: Central 5619
Placitas: **A Room 5609**
Portales: Roosevelt 5645, Roosevelt 5646
Raton: Whited 5658
Santa Fe: B.F. 5613, Helm 5632, **Lannan 5635**, New Mexico 5640, Peninsula 5643, Santa Fe 5648, Santa Fe 5649, **School 5650**, Simon 5651, **Southwestern 5652**, Woodson 5659
Springer: Springer 5654
Taos: Carson 5617, Taos 5656, Wurlitzer 5660

see also 256, 610, 774, 940, 990, 1177, 1272, 1494, 2049, 4497, 4699, 4836, 4847, 6755, 7895, 8731, 8970, 9219

NEW YORK

Albany: **American 5694**, **Civil 5858**, Community 5877, Council 5893, Food 5989, **Foundation 6000**, **World 6533**
Albion: Albion 5678
Amherst: Borchert 5776, **Buffalo 5802**, Lynch 6180, Pressman 6326, Snayberger 6407
Amsterdam: Children's 5848, Wasserman 6503
Armonk: **IBM 6089**
Astoria: Athanasiades 5737, Bon 5773, Queens 6341
Auburn: New York 6272
Austerlitz: **Millay 6216**
Baldwin: Spartan 6419
Batavia: Andrews 5713, Genesee 6020
Bath: Bath 5755
Bay Shore: Breast 5782
Bayside: Agoriani 5673, Tourette 6459
Beacon: Wolf 6525, Wolf 6526
Bellport: Seltzer 6393
Belmont: Allegany 5681
Bethpage: **Lustgarten 6177**
Binghamton: Broome 5799, Foundation 6003, Opportunities 6298
Blue Mountain Lake: **Blue 5770**
Brewster: Brewster 5785
Bridgehampton: Eagleton 5945
Broadalbin: **HASTAGA 6059**
Brockport: McGrath 6205
Bronx: Bronx 5793, Bronx 5794, Bronx 5795, **Wildlife 6520**
Brooklyn: Adams 5666, ArtCouncil 5723, Bonei 5775, Braverman 5781, Brooklyn 5796, Brooklyn 5797, Brooklyn 5798, Brown 5801, Catholic 5825, **Cave 5827**, Community 5882, Dance 5910, Davidson 5916, Elenberg 5956, **Ezer 5971**, FDNY 5978, Foundation 6002, **Franklin 6008**, **Independent 6092**, IRT 6105, Kassenbrock 6130, **Keats 6134**, New 6261, Norwegian 6289, Petra 6314, S.B.H. 6368, Smack 6405, **Social 6409**, Triangle 6462, Tzur 6468, UrbanGlass 6481
Buffalo: Angle 5714, Blosser 5769, Bowman 5778, Buffalo 5803, Community 5875, Early 5947, Farmen 5975, Federman 5980, Fitzpatrick 5985, German 6022, Glazer 6031, Gunglach 6051, Hambay 6055, Herr 6069, Hoffert 6075, Jenkins 6114, Journeys 6124, King 6139, March 6189, McGee 6204, Metzger 6213, **Mikhashoff 6215**, Rau 6345, Reinhardt 6351, Rental 6353, Scalp 6377, Schiffner 6384, Schiffner 6385, **Seneca 6394**, Skaneateles 6400, Squeaky 6423, Statler 6432, Stoner 6439, Tozier 6460, Univera 6480, Witmer 6524
Canandaigua: McConnell 6201, Ontario 6293
Carle Place: **Carnegie 5818**
Cazenovia: Stone 6438
Centereach: Community 5874
Chatham: Giddings 6024

Chestnut Ridge: **Camphill 5811**
Clarence: Cox 5897
Claryville: Carpenter 5819
Clayton: Thousand 6452
Collins: Gernatt 6023
Copiague: Babylon 5746
Corning: **Corning 5886**
Cortland: Cortland 5890
Dix Hills: **Jaffe 6108**
Dunkirk: Northern 6286
East Elmhurst: United 6475
Edmeston: Pathfinder 6307
Elmira: Bloomer 5768, Earl 5946, Parker 6303
Elmsford: Westchester 6514
Far Rockaway: Howard 6078
Flushing: Queens 6340
Forest Hills: Wu 6538
Forestburgh: Goshen 6040
Fort Edward: Washington 6502
Fort Plain: Scholarship 6387
Fresh Meadows: **VonAmelunxen 6496**
Garden City: Biddle 5763, Thompson 6450
Getzville: Foundation 5999
Glen Cove: **Lymphatic 6178**
Glen Head: Human 6081
Glens Falls: Glens Falls 6032, Spain 6417
Glenville: Alexander 5679, Judkins 6125
Goshen: Guarino 6047
Great Neck: Fondation 5987, United 6478
Greenport: Morton 6227, North 6284
Guilderland: New York 6270
Hamilton: **Brackett 5779**, Democracy 5922, Hinman 6070
Harrison: Columbia 5870, Gillroy 6026, Jandon 6110, Rye 6367
Hicksville: NYS 6290
Holley: Webster 6505
Homer: Brockway 5791
Hornell: Buisch 5804, Guenther 6048
Horseheads: Community 5878
Hudson Falls: Sandy 6373
Huntington Station: Klein 6142
Ilion: Brill 5786
Ithaca: Alpha 5683, Community 5873, Epsilon 5962, Saltonstall 6371
Jamestown: Cantor 5815, Chautauqua 5842, Jachym 6107
Jamesville: Muhlenbruck 6230
Jericho: Collins/Chris 5869, Sussman 6442
Johnson City: Community 5876
Katonah: Westchester 6515
Kenmore: Patterson 6308
Lake Placid: Adirondack 5667, Colburn 5864
Larchmont: Gavrin 6018, Kathwari 6131
Latham: Wells 6510
Lincolndale: L.H. 6149
Lindenhurst: Hacker 6053
Little Falls: Burrows 5806
Livingston Manor: Avery 5744
Lockport: Brady 5780, Weeks 6506
Long Island City: AEC 5669, De Karman 5918, Doherty 5929, Gargiulo 6016, SculptureCenter 6391, Socrates 5414, Williams 6521, **Woursell 6537**
Mamaroneck: **Animal 5715**
Mc Connellsville: Harden 6057
Medford: Jay's 6111
Merrick: Ladany 6152, Nolan 6283
Mexico: Grandma 6043
Middletown: Kleeman 6141, Tilt 6456
Mill Neck: Big 5764
Mineola: Chaminade 5840, Dante 5913, Long 6168
Monsey: **Stefansky 6435**
Montebello: Provident 6336
Montgomery: Ashley 5732, Community 5880

Mount Morris: Genesee 6021

New Berlin: Golden 6036

New City: Griffin 6046, **Whitney 6518**

New Lebanon: Authier 5740

New Rochelle: Saagny 6369, **Woodlawn 6530**

New York: **AAAA 5662**, Academy 5663, **ACMP 5664**, **Actors 5665**, Aero 5670, **AFS-USA 5671**, AFTRA 5672, **Agudath 5674**, **AIG 5675**, Ailey 5676, Albee 5677, All 5680, Alliance 5682, Alumni 5684, **Alzheimer's 5685**, **America-Israel 5686**, American 5687, **American 5688**, **American 5689**, American 5690, American 5691, **American 5692**, **American 5693**, American 5695, **American 5696**, **American 5697**, American 5698, **American 5699**, **American 5700**, **American 5701**, **American 5702**, American 5703, American 5705, **American 5706**, **American 5707**, **American 5708**, American 5709, **American 5710**, **American 5711**, **Aperture 5716**, Armenian 5717, Art 5719, Art 5720, Art 5721, Art 5722, **Artis 5724**, Artists 5725, **Arts 5729**, ArtsConnection 5730, ASCAP 5731, **Asia 5733**, **Asian 5734**, Associated 5735, **Astraea 5736**, **Audio 5739**, Authors 5741, **Autism 5742**, **Autism 5743**, **Avon 5745**, Bagby 5749, **Balanchine 5751**, Ballet 5752, Baseball 5754, Bay 5756, Beacon 5757, **Beard 5758**, Bennett 5759, Berntsen 5761, **Bibliographical 5762**, **Blake 5765**, Blake 5766, Blarney 5767, **BMI 5771**, **Bogliasco 5772**, Bone 5774, **Breast 5783**, Breindel 5784, **Bristol 5788**, Broadcasters 5789, **Broadway 5790**, Bronfman 5792, Brown 5800, **Buttonwood 5807**, Camera 5809, Campbell 5810, Cancer 5812, Cancer 5813, Cantor 5814, **Career 5816**, Careers 5817, Carter 5821, Carver 5822, Catholic 5823, Catholic 5824, **CDS 5828**, **CEC 5829**, Center 5830, Center 5831, Center 5832, Center 5833, **Center 5835**, **CFDA 5838**, **Chamber 5839**, chashama 5841, Chest 5845, Children 5846, Children 5847, Children's 5849, Children's 5850, **Children's 5851**, Chinese 5852, Cinereach 5853, Cirio 5855, City 5856, City 5857, Clark 5859, **CNN 5862**, **College 5866**, Collins 5868, **Columbus 5871**, **Commonwealth 5872**, Community 5883, **Conference 5889**, **Correspondents 5889**, Cosby 5891, **Covenant 5895**, **Creative 5898**, Crohn's 5899, Cromwell 5900, **Cuban 5902**, **Cummings 5904**, Cunningham 5905, Dactyl 5908, Daiwa 5909, Dance 5911, **Das 5914**, **Daughters 5915**, De Jur 5917, **Dedalus 5919**, **Delmas 5921**, Dieu 5925, **Direct 5926**, Division 5927, **Do 5928**, Donghia 5930, DonorsChoose.org 5931, Downtown 5933, **Dramatists 5934**, **Dreyfus 5935**, Druckenmiller 5936, **Duke 5938**, **Dungannon 5939**, Dysautonomia 5943, Dystrophic 5944, Eaton 5950, Ebb 5951, **Echoing 5952**, Educational 5954, **Elizabeth 5957**, Elsasser 5958, Ensemble 5959, Episcopal 5960, Episcopal 5961, **ESA 5963**, Eshe 5964, Esiason 5965, **Estonian 5966**, **Explorers 5968**, Exploring 5969, Eyebeam 5970, **Fantasy 5973**, Farber 5974, Fashion 5976, Federation 5979, **Fight 5982**, Figliolia 5983, **Fitch 5984**, **FJC 5986**, **Food 5988**, Forrai 5990, **Foundation 5991**, **Foundation 5992**, **Foundation 5993**, **Foundation 5994**, **Foundation 5995**, Foundation 5996, Foundation 5997, **Foundation 5998**, Foundation 6001, Fountain 6004, **Four 6005**, **Fox 6006**, Fractured 6007, **French 6009**, Friars 6010, Frick 6011, **Friends 6012**, **Friends 6013**, Fund 6014, Gaffney 6015, **General 6019**, Girl 6027, Girls 6028, Glaucoma 6030, **Global 6033**, Glover 6034, **Gottlieb 6041**, Grand 6042, **Graves 6044**, **Grayson-Jockey 6045**, **Guggenheim 6049**, **Guggenheim 6050**, Hadar 6054, **Harvestworks 6058**, **Haven 6060**, Havens 6061, Health 6064, **Hearing 6065**, Hemophilia 6066, Henry 6067, **Hereditary 6068**, Hirth 6071, Hispanic 6072, Historical 6073, Holland 6076, Home 6077, Hudson 6080, Humanas 6082, Humanitas 6083, **Huntington's 6086**, Hutchins 6087, **ID 6090**, **Illuminating 6091**, Independent 6093, Insall 6094, **Institute 6095**, InterExchange 6096, International 6097, **International 6098**, **International 6099**, International 6100, **International 6101**, **International 6102**, **Intrepid 6103**, Inwood 6104, JAM 6109, **Jazz 6112**, Jewish 6115, **Jewish 6117**, Jewish 6119, **Jewish 6120**, **Jockey 6121**, Jonas 6122, Joukowsky 6123, **Juvenile 6127**, Kane 6128, **Kaupp 6132**, **Keren 6135**, **Keren 6136**, Kidney 6137, **King 6138**, Kleban 6140, Klingenstein 6143, **Klingenstein 6144**, **Kosciuszko 6145**, **Koussevitzky 6146**, La 6150, Laboratory 6151, **Lasker 6153**, **LD 6154**, Le Rosey 6155, **League 6156**, Leary 6157, **Legacy 6158**, Lehmann 6159, **Lighthouse 6163**, **Lincoln 6164**, Lissner 6165, Living 6166, London 6167, Looney 6169, L'Oreal 6170, Lortel 6171, Lower 6172, Lower 6173, **Lozynskyj 6174**, **Luce 6175**, Lurcy 6176, **Lymphoma 6179**, MADRE, 6182, Magnum 6183, Maidstone 6184, Malevich 6185, Manhattan 6186, **Mann 6187**, **Marine 6190**, Martin 6192, **Matz 6196**, **Mayday 6197**, Mayer 6198, **McCaddin 6199**, McCall 6200, McCormick 6202, McCrindle 6203, Memorial 6207, Merchant 6209, **MetLife 6210**, **Metropolitan 6211**, Metropolitan 6212, Mitchell 6218, Mitsui 6219, Modest 6220, Moore 6224, Morgan 6225, Morgan 6226, Movement 6228, Moving 6229, Musicians 6231, Musicians 6232, **Musicians 6233**, **Myasthenia 6234**, **Mycenaean 6235**, NAACP 6237, **NARSAD 6238**, **NARSAD: 6239**, National 6240, **National 6242**, **National 6243**, **National 6244**, **National 6246**, National 6247, **National 6248**, **National 6249**, **National 6250**, **National 6251**, **National 6252**, **National 6253**, **National 6254**, **National 6255**, Needham 6257, **Netherland-America 6258**, Netzach 6259, New Alternatives 6260, New Music 6262, New Visions 6263, **New 6264**, **New York 6265**, New York 6266, New York 6267, New York 6268, New York 6269, New York 6271, New York 6273, New York 6274, New York 6275, New York 6276, New York 6277, New 6278, Newhouse 6279, NLN 6280, **Nok 6281**, **Open 6294**, Open 6295, **OPERA 6296**, Opera 6297, **Parapsychology 6301**, Parham 6302, Parodneck 6304, **Pasteur 6306**, Peace 6309, **Pearson 6310**, **PEN 6312**, Performance 6313, **Pfizer 6315**, **Philippe 6316**, **Poetry 6317**, Pollock 6318, **Population 6320**, Prescott 6325, PricewaterhouseCoopers 6328, **Princess 6329**, Professional 6331, **Project 6332**, Project 6334, Project 6335, **Public 6337**, **Public 6338**, Puerto 6339, Radius 6342, **Rainforest 6343**, Randon 6344, Reaching 6346, Realty 6347, REBNY 6348, Reed 6350, Research 6354, Rich 6355, Robinson 6356, **Rockefeller 6359**, Roothbert 6361, Rose 6362, Rottenberg 6363, **Royal 6364**, **Runyon 6365**, **Russian 6366**, Sakhi 6370, **Schalkenbach 6379**, Schepp 6383, Scholarship 6386, Selfhelp 6392, **Shatford 6395**, **Silberman 6396**, Silver 6397, **Skin 6401**, Skowhegan 6402, Sky 6403, **Sloan 6404**, **Smith 6406**, Soanes 6408, Societe 6410, Society 6411, Society 6412, **Soros 6416**, **Sparkplug 6418**, **Spencer 6420**, Sperry 6421, **Sponsors 6422**, St. George's 6425, St. Luke's 6426, Stage 6428, Starlight 6429, **Starr 6430**, Statue 6433, **Stecher 6434**, Steinberg 6436, Stony 6440, Studio 6441, **Teach 6444**, **Teachers 6445**, **Theatre 6448**, THYCA: 6453, **Tibet 6454**, **Tiffany 6455**, Tinker 6457, **Trace 6461**, **Trickle 6463**, **Tsadra 6465**, **Tucker 6466**, Tuttle 6467, UFA 6469, **UJA 6470**, Unique 6471, **United 6472**, United 6473, United 6474, **United 6476**, **V-Day 6487**, Ventures 6488, Viele 6489, **Vietnam 6490**, Vilcek 6491, Visual 6492, Vocational 6494, **Voices 6495**, Wagner 6498, **Wallenberg 6499**, Warren 6501, **Watson 6503**, Weill 6508, Weissberger 6509, **Wenner 6511**, Whiting 6517, **Wiesel 6519**, Windows 6522, **Wine 6523**, Women 6527, **Women's 6528**, Woori 6531, Working 6532, **World 6534**, **Worldstudio 6535**, **Worth 6536**, Yeshiva 6539, Young 6540, **Youth 6541**

Newark Valley: Experimental 5967

Norwich: Baker 5750, Chenango 5843, Costa 5892, Danforth 5912, Dickinson 5924, Ehle 5955, Gillen 6025, Glasgow 6029, Mills 6217, Opportunities 6299, Partridge 6305, Post 6321, Preferred 6324, Schenck 6381, Skahan 6399, Stempfle 6437, Teel 6447, Thompson 6449

Old Westbury: East Williston 5948

Olean: Cattaraugus 5826, Gavin 6017, Hodges 6074, Howe 6079

Oneida: Brink 5787, Calman 5808, Curran 5907, Oneida 6292

Oneonta: Goodell 6039, Haynes 6063, Jenkins 6113, MacKinnon 6181, Potter 6322, Scott 6388

Orchard Park: Hunter's 6085, Krueger 6147

Ossining: Fan 5972

Oyster Bay: Oyster 6300

Pawling: Monahan 6222

Pearl River: Hunter 6084, **St. Elmo 6424**, **Zeta 6542**

Perry: Arts 5728

Pittsford: Mijangos 6214, Reddington 6349

Plainview: National 6245

Plattsburgh: Clinton 5861

Pleasant Valley: Barton 5753

Pleasantville: Professional 6330

Port Washington: Bacon 5748, Lewis 6161, Marino 6191, **North 6285**, Scotts 6389

Poughkeepsie: Bacile 5747, Community 5881, Dutchess 5941

Purchase: **A Child 5661**, Bossak 5777, Central 5836, MasterCard 6195

Purdys: Just 6126

Queensbury: Nolan 6282

Rensselaerville: Huyck 6088

Rochester: Arts 5726, Cure 5906, Father 5977, Jewish 6116, Jewish 6118, Mashomack 6194, Rochester 6357, Rochester 6358, **Visual 6493**, Wegmans 6507

Rock Hill: Project 6333

Rockville Centre: Eastern 5949, Gold 6035, Ivy 6106

Rome: Dyett 5942, Mohawk 6221, Varflex 6485

Rosendale: Women's 6529

Roslyn Heights: Melville 6206

Rye: Dove 5932, Durland 5940

Salem: Burnett 5805

Sanborn: NCCC 6256

Saranac Lake: Saranac 6374

Saratoga Springs: **Corporation 5888**, Duffy 5937, Hawley 6062, Reinhart 6352, Saratoga 6375

Scarsdale: Art 5718, Scarsdale 6378, Schechter 6380

Schenectady: Odasz 6291, Price 6327, Schenectady 6382

South Glens Falls: Solomon 6415

South Salem: America's 5712

Spencerport: Monroe 6223

Spring Valley: Goldstein 6037

Staten Island: **American 5704**, Atlas 5738, Berger 5760, **Chesed 5844**, Cirillo 5854, Council 5894, Dellomo 5920, Staten 6431

Syracuse: Carrier 5820, Central 5837, Crouse 5901, Cultural 5903, **Light 6162**, Martin 6193, Ronald 6360, **United 6477**, Whitcher 6516

Thompson Ridge: Sweitzer 6443

Ticonderoga: Potter 6323

Troy: Arts 5727, Samaritan 6372

Trumansburg: Coleman 5865, Trumansburg 6464

Tuckahoe: Pope 6319

Utica: Cogar 5863, Community 5879, Good 6038, **Sculpture 6390**, Utica 6483, Wadas 6497

Valhalla: Confort 5885, Westchester 6513

Vestal: Stack 6427

Walton: Clark 5860, Eckert 5953, Harby 6056, Memorial 6208, Peck 6311, Walton 6500

Watertown: Northern 6287

Watkins Glen: Northrup 6288

Webster: Cox 5896

West Nyack: Teamsters 6446

West Seneca: **Diamond 5923**
Westport: Gunk 6052
White Plains: College 5867, **Leukemia 6160**, **March 6188**, N Foundation 6236, **National 6241**, **Skadden 6398**, **United States 6479**, **USTA 6482**, Westchester 6512
Whitestone: Society 6413
Willet: Kuhlman 6148
Willsboro: Adirondack 5668
Woodside: Topaz 6458
Woodstock: Center 5834
Wurtsboro: Kaplan 6129, Kautz 6133, Sawyer 6376, Thorwelle 6451
Yonkers: Fermi 5981

see also 406, 521, 540, 710, 794, 984, 1316, 1333, 1369, 1380, 1385, 1428, 1449, 1451, 1467, 1498, 1595, 1779, 1930, 1950, 1965, 2021, 2039, 2062, 2146, 2200, 2201, 2247, 2422, 2513, 2575, 2595, 2620, 2727, 2822, 2859, 2873, 2926, 3050, 3422, 3556, 3651, 3740, 3832, 3872, 3983, 3986, 4011, 4118, 4134, 4142, 4151, 4269, 4282, 4414, 4771, 4812, 4814, 4855, 4960, 5423, 5440, 5452, 5455, 5498, 5542, 5556, 5572, 5579, 5583, 5593, 6847, 6983, 7016, 7019, 7038, 7126, 7141, 7188, 7211, 7319, 7357, 7367, 7424, 7425, 7431, 7734, 7771, 7895, 7903, 8137, 8249, 8266, 8272, 8275, 8301, 8307, 8316, 8321, 8335, 8340, 8351, 8352, 8356, 8358, 8394, 8397, 8402, 8410, 8416, 8420, 8432, 8437, 8591, 9695

NORTH CAROLINA

Apex: **Youth 6933**
Archdale: **United 6908**
Asheboro: Ferree 6656, Tillman 6894
Asheville: Asheville 6561, Asheville 6562, Asheville-Buncombe 6563, Center 6595, Community 6616, Harmon 6694, **Kimmel 6731**, Mission 6775, **Pediatric 6814**, **Rixson 6836**, **Sigma 6860**, Smart 6864, Unruh 6909
Bayboro: Pamlico 6809
Binmore Forest: Taylor 6888
Blowing Rock: Blowing Rock 6575
Boone: **Samaritan's 6849**, Watauga 6914
Boonville: Martin 6757
Brevard: Hughes 6707, Transylvania 6896
Carrboro: Inter-Faith 6714
Carthage: Sandhills 6850
Cary: NC 6785, North 6801, **V Foundation 6910**
Chapel Hill: Child 6599, **Cleft 6604**, Fund 6667, **Institut 6711**, Medical 6769, **Morehead-Cain 6778**, St. Anthony 6873
Charlotte: 100 6543, Area 6555, Arts 6559, Beattie 6570, Carpenter 6592, Children's 6600, Coats 6607, Cotterel 6619, Dilcher 6630, DuVall 6635, Eastern 6641, Evrytanian 6651, Fava 6654, Ferebee 6655, Foundation 6660, Fox 6664, Gift 6671, Gilbert 6672, Giles 6673, Girl 6675, **Graham 6678**, Grimley 6684, Guggenheim 6689, Harris 6695, Hilton 6699, Hoover 6702, Horvat 6704, Huffman 6706, Indian 6710, **Jensen 6717**, Jordan 6725, **Karyae 6726**, Keasbey 6727, Label 6734, Material 6758, McClureTrust 6760, McColl 6761, Mecklenburg 6768, Miller 6774, Myers 6782, Nelson 6789, New 6790, Nucor 6803, Oates 6804, Pappas 6810, Richmond 6832, Ritchie 6835, Robinson 6838, Robinson 6839, Rollison 6840, RSPA 6844, Rumbough 6845, Schug 6854, Shelly 6859, Sirrine 6862, Smith 6867, Stambaugh 6875, Strickland 6882, Thomas 6891, Treen 6897, TW 6903, Watterson 6915, West 6917, Williams 6921, Wolinski 6925, Women's 6926, Yerkes 6930, Zimmerman 6934
Cherokee: Cherokee 6598
Columbus: Forbes 6658
Concord: Little 6744

Conover: Lee 6739
Dallas: Gaston 6669
Dudley: Tri-County 6901
Dunn: Wellons 6916
Durham: American 6549, **American 6550**, Arc 6554, Broad 6582, **Cattell 6594**, **Chordoma 6602**, Durham 6633, Durham 6634, Foundation 6661, Housing 6705, MDC 6767, **Nickel 6792**, North 6795, Southern 6869, **Student 6883**, Triangle 6899
Elizabeth City: Albemarle 6547, Elizabeth 6645, Wiggins 6919
Farmville: Davis 6626
Fayetteville: Better 6573, Bicycle 6574, Cumberland 6624, McAllister 6759, **Military 6773**
Forest City: McNair 6763
Franklin: Macon 6754
Gastonia: Community 6613, First 6657, Gaston 6668
Glade Valley: Religious 6825
Graham: Alamance 6546
Greensboro: Anderson 6552, Armfield 6556, Atlantic 6565, Burlington 6587, Community 6614, Gate 6670, Greensboro 6681, Guilford 6690, Halstead 6692, Latham 6736, North 6793, **Richardson 6831**, Tannenbaum 6885, Triad 6898
Greenville: East 6637, Greenville 6682, Pitt County 6820
Hendersonville: Community 6615, Dietrich 6629, Henderson 6696, **Insurance 6712**, Interfaith 6713, Leever 6740, Western 6918
Hertford: Hunter 6709
Hickory: Beaver 6571, Catawba 6593, Hickory 6698, United 6906
High Point: Fouts 6663, Haggai 6691, Loflin 6747
Hillsborough: **International 6715**, **Music 6781**
Jacksonville: Eastern 6639
Kenansville: Sprunt 6872
Kenly: Edgerton 6643
Kinston: Good 6677
Lenoir: Coffey 6608
Lexington: Team 6889
Little Switzerland: Wildacres 6920
Lumberton: Robeson 6837
Marion: Corpening 6618, Smith 6866
Mocksville: Davie 6625
Monroe: Union 6905
Mooresville: **Earnhardt 6636**, Lowe's 6749
Morehead City: Russell 6846
Morganton: Andrews 6553, Community 6612, Outreach 6807
Murfreesboro: Jordan 6724
New Bern: CarolinaEast 6591, Craven 6621
Newton: Eastern 6640, Isaac 6716
Oriental: Perry 6816, Walker 6913
Pembroke: Lumbee 6750
PineHurst: Clark 6603
Pinehurst: Cole 6611
Raleigh: Accel 6544, **American 6551**, Artspace 6560, Easter 6638, **Environmental 6649**, Foundation 6659, Foundation 6662, Keep 6729, London 6748, NC 6786, NC 6787, NC 6788, North 6794, North Carolina 6796, North Carolina 6797, North 6798, North 6799, North 6800, Pharmacy 6818, Rex 6827, Sloan 6863, Spivey 6871, State 6876, State 6877, Tahquette 6884, **TASCA 6887**, Telamon 6890, Touchstone 6895, Triangle 6900, United 6907, Wake 6911, Wake 6912, With 6924, Woman's 6926
Research Triangle Park: **Bayer 6569**, Brooks 6583, **National 6784**, **S.R.C. 6847**
Rich Square: Choanoke 6601
Rocky Mount: Brewer 6580, Scholarship 6853
Roxboro: Person 6817
Salisbury: **Lion's 6743**, Rowan 6843, Salisbury-Rowan 6848, Smart 6865
Selma: Bridges 6581
Shallotte: Brunswick 6584

Shelby: Cleveland 6606
Smithfield: Johnston 6721
Southern Shores: Outer 6806
Speed: Sheffield 6858
Spindale: Lutz 6753, Stonecutter 6880
Statesville: North Carolina 6802, Steele, 6878
Tarboro: Tarboro 6886
Thomasville: Dixie 6632
Tryon: Polk 6821
Waxhaw: Phoenix 6819
Waynesville: Mountain 6780
Williamston: Barnes 6567
Wilmington: Spire 6870
Wilson: Arps 6558, Atkins 6564, Bass 6568, Crawley 6622, Gray 6680, Grogan 6686, Johns 6718, Leath 6737, Owens 6808, Richardson 6830, Young 6931
Winston Salem: Allen 6548, Arnold 6557, Ballard 6566, Borden 6576, Bowsher 6577, Boye 6578, Brandt 6579, Buck 6585, Burke-Weber 6586, Cady 6589, Chaffer 6596, Chappell 6597, Clements 6605, Coffman 6609, Colburn 6610, Cooke 6617, Cox 6620, Davis 6627, Davis 6628, Dinwiddle 6631, Edmonds 6644, Ella 6646, Ellis 6647, Emerson 6648, Evans 6650, Fairey 6652, Frank 6665, Frasier 6666, Ginder 6674, Gramberg 6679, Grim 6683, Groff 6685, Gross 6687, Grotefend 6688, Harasimik 6693, Hess 6697, Hochmark 6700, Hoffman 6701, Horsey 6703, Hughes 6708, Johnson 6719, Johnson 6720, Jones 6722, Jones 6723, Keena 6728, Kent 6730, Kimmel 6732, Komarek 6733, Lake 6735, Ledward 6738, Lenz 6741, Leverenz 6742, Livingston 6745, Loar 6746, Lundquist 6751, Lundy 6752, Magdalena 6755, Mahalick 6756, McMahan 6762, McNair 6764, McNaught 6765, McRae 6766, Meredith 6770, Midland 6772, Monger 6776, Moore 6777, Morson 6779, Myers 6783, Nichols 6791, Oates 6805, Patch 6811, Patterson 6812, Peckitt 6813, Pennsylvania 6815, Posey 6822, Reich 6823, Reierson 6824, Rennie 6826, Riddick 6833, Risley 6834, Roof 6841, Rouch 6842, Sauvain 6851, Search 6855, Selling 6857, Simpson 6861, Smith 6868, Stagner 6874, Stewart 6879, Stoudenmire 6881, Thomasville 6892, Thomson 6893, Troedson 6902, Two 6904, Wilson 6922
Winston-Salem: AIDS 6545, Bethesda 6572, Butler 6588, Cancer 6590, Crisis 6623, Eddy 6642, Fairfield 6653, Meserve 6771, Reynolds 6828, Richardi 6829, Scholarship 6852, Self 6856, Winston-Salem 6923, Work 6928, Wyly 6929, Young 6932
Yadkinville: Giving 6676

see also 232, 904, 1614, 1763, 1856, 1899, 1903, 2016, 2029, 2247, 2936, 3556, 3600, 4404, 4498, 4544, 4628, 4731, 7713, 7972, 8084, 8181, 8188, 8275, 8467, 8508, 8765, 8770, 9313, 9347, 9413, 9432, 9508, 9516, 9552

NORTH DAKOTA

Bismarck: Brown 6935, Heartland 6942, North Dakota 6946, VFW 6951
Devils Lake: Ernst 6939, Ruger 6947
Fargo: Dakota 6937, Fargo 6940, Forum 6941
Grand Forks: Cronquist 6936, University 6950
Hazelton: Emmons 6938
Langdon: United 6949
Minot: Minot 6945
Sharon: McKenzie 6944
Williston: Martell 6943, Schuetze 6948, Wenstrom 6952

see also 216, 972, 1272, 1494, 4705, 4731, 4737, 4749, 4818, 4851, 4859, 4884, 5133, 5180, 7095, 7931, 8520, 8533, 9837

OHIO

Adamsville: **Murray 7262**

Akron: Akron 6965, Akron 6966, Akron 6967, Christian 7035, Cohill 7047, Firestone 7109, Ganyard 7122, Jentes 7176, Peak 7294, Snow 7359, Summerville 7374, Thiele 7378, Throckmorton 7381, United 7397, Weiss 7416

Albany: Alexander's 6969

Alliance: Elks 7099, McConahay 7229

Ashland: Ashland 6980

Ashtabula: Ashtabula 6981

Ashville: Hosler 7157

Athens: **Student 7371**

Auburn Township: Berlin 6996

Avon: Turco 7390

Baltimore: VanBuren 7404

Barberton: Barberton 6988, **Christian 7036**, Tuscora 7391

Beachwood: Italian 7171, Jewish 7177

Bedford Heights: **Brush 7016**

Bellefontaine: Milroy 7251, Powell 7307, Rutan 7332

Bellevue: Birr 6998

Belpre: Belpre 6994

Berea: Cleveland 7042

Blue Ash: Children's 7033

Bowling Green: Bowling Green 7009, Bowling 7010, Roach 7323, Social 7360

Bratenahl: Howley 7159

Brooklyn: Ames 6973, Atwood 6983, Bean 6991, Beinke 6993, Bentley 6995, Boone 7005, Bouchard 7007, Bowen 7008, Burnham 7018, Bush 7019, Carman 7024, Chaney 7031, Clarke 7038, Cline 7046, Drake 7090, Dunton 7093, Everhart 7102, Ford 7113, Frederick 7118, Gazin 7126, Goodwin 7131, Grove 7137, Harrington 7141, Hawkes 7145, Higgins 7149, Hunter 7164, Jackson 7172, Kessel 7186, KeyBank 7188, Kittridge 7196, Knight 7199, Knowles 7200, Lincoln 7211, Mentzer 7239, Middleton 7244, Mishou 7252, Nolley 7270, Nugen 7275, Perry 7298, Reynolds 7319, Schneider 7337, Sheadle 7345, Simmons 7351, Smith 7357, Stauffer 7367, Steigler 7368, Uschmann 7400, Wakefield 7410, Warman 7414, White 7424, White 7425, Wilson 7431, Wyman 7442

Bryan: Bryan 7017

Bucyrus: Community 7057, Grace 7132, High 7150, Shunk 7348

Cambridge: Agnew 6961, Fishel 7110

Canfield: Clayman 7039, Seefred 7342

Canton: David 7079, Stark 7366, **Timken 7384**, United 7396

Cardington: Wilhelm 7426

Celina: Mercer 7240

Centerville: **Children 7032**

Chagrin Falls: Hoover 7154, Yoder 7445

Chillicothe: Adena 6958, Blosser 7002, Chillicothe 7034

Cincinnati: A Good 6953, Ace 6954, Addison 6957, Alexander 6968, Butler 7020, Catholic 7029, Cincinnati 7037, Crum 7072, Davies 7080, Dutro 7094, **Educational 7098**, Good 7129, Hutton 7165, **Jewish 7178**, LAM 7203, Lewis 7207, Mansfield 7218, Maple 7219, Menard 7238, Miller 7250, Mohr 7253, Myers 7264, New Orphan 7268, Norris 7271, North 7272, Osborn 7285, Partners 7292, Root 7327, Scripps 7340, Slemp 7352, Springman 7364, Summerfair 7373, Thompson 7379, Three 7380, Ursuline 7399, Ward 7413, Workum 7440, Yeiser 7443

Circleville: Dunlap 7092, Sharpe 7344

Cleveland: Anderson 6975, Andrus 6976, Bakes 6985, Barber 6987, Beal 6990, Bluecoats 7003, Bontrager 7004, Carney 7025, Castele 7028, **Catholic 7030**, Cleveland 7041, Cleveland 7043, Cleveland 7044, Cleveland 7045, College 7050, Community 7064, Council 7066, Davis 7081, DeCrane 7085, Diederich 7088, Dinger 7089,

Dumesnil 7091, Epilepsy 7100, Fairbanks-Horix 7104, Fitzgerald 7111, Gay 7125, Goodridge 7130, Hamilton 7140, Hartley 7143, Hope 7155, Horvitz 7156, Hunter 7163, Independent 7168, Jones 7180, Kanhofer 7181, Kati's 7183, Keller 7185, Kidney 7190, Kiser 7195, Kiwanis 7197, Klinger 7198, Lapeer 7204, Lesher 7206, **Lincoln 7210**, Lyons 7216, MacRae 7217, Mauger 7223, McCabe 7224, McCoy 7230, McDonald 7233, Munro 7259, Murphy 7261, Myers 7265, Oppenheim 7284, Padgett 7287, Pehna 7296, Plimpton 7305, Rains 7311, Rapp 7312, Ratner 7313, Ratner, 7314, Rickert 7322, Robertson 7324, Rosenberger 7328, Russell 7331, Shepard 7346, Simmons 7350, Smith 7354, Smucker 7358, Spencer 7362, Sullivan 7372, Taylor 7377, Tomlinson's 7385, TW 7392, United 7395, West Side 7418, Wester 7419, Western 7420, Williams 7427, Williams 7428, Willmott 7429, Wimmer 7432, Wisner 7435, Wolf 7436, Wood 7437, Wright 7441

Cleveland Heights: College 7049, Reaching 7315

Columbia Station: Columbia 7051

Columbus: AGC 6960, American 6971, Bernhard 6997, Columbus 7052, Columbus 7053, Columbus 7054, Community 7063, Fraser 7117, Garcia 7123, Gonter 7128, Greenwalt 7135, Homeless 7153, Hughes 7160, I Know 7166, Imhoff 7167, Jefferson 7174, **Kappa 7182**, Kibble 7189, Moomaw 7254, Moore 7255, Ohio 7278, Ohio 7279, Ohio 7281, Ohio 7282, OHSAA 7283, Parenthesis 7289, Park 7291, Pearce 7295, Peters 7300, Psychiatric 7310, Rogers 7326, Salem 7334, Sharp 7343, Smith 7353, Steiner 7369, Thurber 7382, Toomey 7386, Van Hyning 7402, Vandenbark 7405, Waldron 7411, Wexner 7422, Winans 7433

Conneaut: Allchin 6970, Record 7316

Corning: Southern 7361

Coshocton: Bland 7001, Coshocton 7065

Crooksville: Hull 7161

Dayton: Adams 6956, Brewer 7012, Community 7056, County 7067, Crain 7070, Creech 7071, Culture 7073, Cushwa 7074, Cushwa 7075, Dayton 7082, Dayton 7083, Foodbank 7112, Gardner 7124, Gilbert 7127, Hundred 7162, **Kids 7191**, Michaud 7243, Moraine 7256, Newton 7269, Ohio 7277, Parents 7290, Rotterman 7329, Smith 7355, Tyler 7394

Defiance: Northwestern 7274

Delaware: American 6972, Delaware 7086

Dover: Ley 7208

Dublin: **Arab 6978**

Edgerton: Edgerton 7097

Elyria: Community 7058

Euclid: McGinty 7235

Findlay: Associated 6982, Blanchard 7000, Findlay 7107, Palmer 7288, Rhoad 7320

Franklin: Sightless 7349

Fremont: Collaborative 7048, W. 7407

Galion: Freese 7120

Gallipolis: Annual 6977

Georgetown: Brown 7015

Granville: Granville 7133

Greenville: H.O.P.E. 7138

Grove City: **Eagles 7095**

Hamilton: Bosaw 7006, Brayton 7011, Hamilton 7139, Johnson 7179, Kirkpatrick 7193, McCallay 7225, Wahl 7409

Haviland: Samaritan 7335

Hillsboro: Cassner 7027

Holland: Scholarship 7338

Hubbard: Naples 7266

Kent: Cowgill 7069, Davey 7078

Kettering: Wellness 7417

Kirtland: Herb 7146, Lakeland 7202

Lancaster: Ackers 6955, Campbell 7022, Fairfield 7105, Herzberger 7148, Kindler 7192, Lehman 7205, Taylor 7376

Lebanon: Loeb 7212

Lima: PSA 7309

Lithopolis: Wagnalls 7408

Logan: Brighten 7013

Lorain: Lorain 7213, Loser 7214, Mercy 7241

Louisville: Carpenter-Garcia 7026, Louisville 7215

Mansfield: Richland 7321

Marietta: **Interthyr 7170**, Marietta 7220, Peoples 7297

Marion: Freer 7119, Marion 7221, Marion 7222, Prior 7308, Trachsel 7387

Marysville: Community 7061

Massillon: Ziegler 7447

Maumee: Northwest 7273

McConnelsville: Outdoor 7286

Mentor: Founders 7116

Miamisburg: Danis 7077

Middletown: Middletown 7245

Millersburg: Holmes 7151, Holmes 7152

Moscow: Miller 7248

Mount Vernon: Ariel 6979, Community 7059

Napoleon: McComb 7228

Nelsonville: Foundation 7115

New Albany: Beane 6992, **Wexner 7423**

New Philadelphia: Hospice 7158

Newark: Licking 7209, Van Horn 7401

Niles: Remmele 7318

Norwalk: Twenty 7393

Oberlin: Oberlin 7276

Oxford: **Phi 7301**, Phi Kappa 7302

Painesville: Roddick 7325

Parma: **Ethnic 7101**

Paulding: Jeffery 7175

Peninsula: Cuyahoga 7076

Piqua: Miami 7242, Piqua 7303, Piqua 7304

Pomeroy: Wingett 7434

Port Clinton: Roy 7330

Portsmouth: Scioto 7339

Powell: Delaware 7087

Ravenna: Community 7055, Portage 7306

Reading: Tuition 7389

Reynoldsburg: AJCA 6963

Salem: Salem 7333

Sandusky: Motry 7257, Munger 7258, Sandusky 7336

Sebring: Sebring 7341

Sidney: Barnes 6989, Community 7060, Kauffman 7184

Solon: Cleveland 7040, Miller 7249

Springfield: Britton 7014, Ohio 7280, Springfield 7363

St. Marys: Agape 6959, St. Marys 7365

Steubenville: McDonald 7231, McDonald 7232

Syracuse: Carleton 7023

Tiffin: Hering 7147, National 7267, **Taiho 7375**, Tiffin 7383

Toledo: Anderson 6974, Blade 6999, Economic 7096, Fifty 7106, Gandy 7121, Kest 7187, Perry 7299, Smith 7356, Stinson 7370, University 7398, Working 7439

Troy: Troy 7388

Van Wert: Van Wert 7403

Versailles: Midmark 7246

Wadsworth: PDR 7293

Wapakoneta: Hauss 7144, Wapakoneta 7412

Warren: Vermillion 7406

Waverly: Wilson 7430

Wellington: Aikey 6962

Wellston: Ball 6986, Hart 7142

West Chester: AK Steel 6964, Community 7062

West Milton: International 7169

West Unity: County 7068

Westerville: Religion 7317, Westerville 7421

Westlake: Lake 7201, McLendon 7237

Willoughby: Babcock 6984, Fine 7108, Kirtland 7194

Wilmington: Wooddell 7438

Wooster: Foss 7114, Wayne 7415
Worthington: **Griffith 7136**, Miller 7247
Xenia: Evers 7103, Greene 7134, Jamestown 7173, McClain 7227
Yellow Springs: Yellow Springs 7444, YSI 7446
Youngstown: Cafaro 7021, DeBartolo 7084, McFarlin 7234
Zanesville: McCann 7226, McIntire 7236, Murphy 7260, Muskingum 7263, Shinnick 7347

see also 239, 710, 1462, 1497, 1614, 1756, 1766, 2046, 2201, 2247, 2552, 2572, 2600, 2629, 2680, 2700, 2710, 2798, 2854, 2867, 2909, 2928, 3162, 3544, 3556, 3588, 4406, 4884, 5227, 6389, 6847, 7455, 7784, 7813, 7986, 8061, 8104, 8107, 9695, 9770, 9776, 9795, 9815, 9906, 9952, 9981

OKLAHOMA

Ada: **Chickasaw 7457**, Oklahoma 7500
Ardmore: Aileen 7448, Franklin 7471, Noble 7497, Smith 7512
Bartlesville: Bartlesville 7452, Davis 7463, Gibson 7475, **International 7483**, Kane 7488, Peyton 7506
Beaver: Carrier 7455
Bethany: **Messenger 7494**
Blackwell: Beatty 7454
Bristow: Mills 7496
Broken Arrow: Faranna 7467
Duncan: Colbert 7458
Edmond: Masonic 7492, Watson 7524, Whitefield 7525
Enid: Covington 7462, Henry 7480
Guthrie: Guthrie 7477
Hugo: Holton 7481
Lawton: Fields 7469
Muskogee: Rose 7509
Norman: Ally's 7449, Miley 7495, OWMA 7505, University 7522
Nowata: Hathcoat 7479
Oklahoma: Evans 7466
Oklahoma City: Areawide 7450, Catholic 7456, Communities 7459, Continue 7461, Driskell 7465, **Feed 7468**, **Foundation 7470**, Frontiers 7472, Happiness 7478, Indwell 7482, Jeltz 7484, JWF 7487, Kappa 7489, Martin 7491, Oklahoma 7498, Oklahoma 7499, Oklahoma 7501, Oklahoma 7502, **Reining 7508**, Wilkin 7526
Pawhuska: McKenzie 7493
Piedmont: Funk 7473
Pryor: Klamm 7490
Sayre: Sides 7511, Springfield 7513
Shawnee: Tulsa 7521
Stillwater: OSU 7504, Stillwater 7517
Tulsa: Bailey 7451, Bartlett 7453, Compassionate 7460, Donaghey 7464, Gatlin 7474, Global 7476, Johnson 7485, Johnson 7486, Osteopathic 7503, Project 7507, Saint 7510, St. 7514, Stevens 7515, Tulsa 7518, Tulsa 7519, Tulsa 7520, Wilson 7527
Watonga: Steward-Newkirk 7516
Wetumka: Watkins 7523

see also 1210, 1467, 1614, 2439, 2526, 3439, 3493, 4884, 5053, 5099, 8759, 8765, 8797, 8815, 9116, 9577

OREGON

Albany: McDowell 7601
Alsea: Clemens 7549
Astoria: Astoria 7535, Rinne 7648
Baker City: Strayer 7668
Beaverton: Care 7544, **Pacific 7627**, Pacific 7628, Vernier 7674

Bend: Central 7546, Professional 7635
Chiloquin: Gienger 7581
Coos Bay: Oregon 7623, Southwestern 7665
Corvallis: Benton 7539, Corvallis 7558, Laird 7593
Cottage Grove: Cottage 7559
Estacada: Day 7569
Eugene: **Fanconi 7575**, Fansler 7576, Lane 7595
Fairview: Snow-Cap 7661
Florence: Bagley 7536, Western 7681
Hermiston: Leonard 7596
Hillsboro: Coalition 7550
Joseph: Dewuhs 7572
Klamath Falls: Oregon 7626
Lake Oswego: Danicas 7566, Northwest 7618, **Vongelstein 7676**
Lakeside: Rietman 7646
Lakeview: Daly 7565
Lincoln City: **Deneke's 7570**
McMinnville: Smith 7660, Yamhill 7687
Medford: Aging 7529, Colvin 7553, Creative 7560, Cutler 7564, Moore 7609, Pass 7630, Providence 7636, Southern 7664, Wattenberg 7678
Milwaukie: Providence 7637
Molalla: Molalla 7608
Mount Angel: Mount Angel 7611
Nehalem: Dillard 7573
Newberg: Providence 7638
Otis: Neskowin 7616
Pendleton: Community 7554
Phoenix: Richmond 7645
Portland: Adler 7528, Alexandria 7530, **American 7532**, Arc 7533, Archer 7534, Banfield 7537, Benson 7538, Black 7540, Buttrey 7541, Caldera 7542, Campbell 7543, Celebration 7545, Chamber 7547, Clarke 7548, Cockerline 7551, Collins 7552, Compassion 7556, Cooper 7557, Criswell 7561, **Culinary 7562**, Culver 7563, Dargan 7567, Davies 7568, Depriest 7571, Education 7574, Fish 7577, Foss 7579, Franks 7580, Hall 7583, Halton 7584, Hamilton 7585, Heiserman 7586, Hellstern 7587, Jackson-General 7589, Jenkins 7590, Journal 7591, Klamath 7592, Literary 7597, Lytle 7598, Major 7599, McComas 7600, McKee 7602, McKenzie 7603, Mock 7607, Morey 7610, Moyer 7612, **Multnomah 7613**, **National 7614**, North 7617, Northwest 7619, Northwest 7620, Oapa 7621, Oregon 7624, Oregon 7625, Palmer 7629, Pernot 7631, Portland 7632, Portland 7633, Portland 7634, Providence 7639, Ragel 7640, Regional 7641, Renaissance 7642, Richardson 7644, Riggs 7647, Ryan 7649, Schafer 7652, Scheinberg 7653, Schilling 7654, Schmidt 7655, Schroeder 7656, Shank 7658, Singer 7659, **Soapstone 7662**, Society 7663, Steinbach 7666, Stevens 7667, **Thomas 7669**, Trippeer 7670, Turner 7671, Vatheuer 7673, Von der Ahe 7675, West 7680, Wheeler 7682, Wiesberg 7683, Wilson 7684, Woodrow 7686
Prineville: Ochoco 7622, Rhoden 7643
Redmond: Neighborimpact 7615
Roseburg: Ford 7578, Mercy 7604, Umpqua 7672
Salem: Goodenough 7582, Salem 7650, Salem 7651, Woodmansee 7685
Scio: SCIO 7657
Sheridan: Mishler 7606
Silverton: Almquist 7531
St. Helens: Community 7555
Sunriver: Lampstand 7594
The Dalles: Mid-Columbia 7605
Tillamook: Watt 7677
Vernonia: Holce 7588
Wasco: Weir 7679

see also 630, 850, 940, 1494, 2340, 2344, 2552, 2930, 3743, 4713, 4730, 5593, 6617, 6627, 6723, 6746, 6766, 6811, 6834, 6857, 6902, 7046, 7090, 7102, 7400, 7812, 8115, 8703, 8928, 8958, 9139, 9179, 9574, 9591, 9613,

9621, 9626, 9628, 9632, 9635, 9636, 9676, 9684, 9688, 9690, 9701, 9702, 9711, 9717, 9760

PENNSYLVANIA

Abington: Abington 7690
Albion: Mikovich 7984
Allentown: AAA 7688, **Jewish 7930**, Lehigh Valley 7953, Moyer 7996, Singer 8106
Altoona: Independent 7917, Southern 8125
Apollo: Bush 7754
Austin: McCloskey 7974
Avondale: American 7703
Bala Cynwyd: Golden 7872
Beaver: Beaver 7726
Bensalem: CSI 7801, Smith 8111
Berwick: Central 7763
Berwyn: **Nephcure 8003**
Bethlehem: Cohen 7774, Northampton 8011, Ronald 8080
Blandon: Panagos 8017
Bloomsburg: Aysr 7719, Kalnoski 7932, Kinney 7937, Murphy 7998, Weber 8181
Bradford: Blaisdell 7735
Bridgeville: II-VI 7915
Bryn Mawr: Fischer 7842
Butler: Golden 7873, Preston 8062
California: Foundation 7851
Camp Hill: Holy 7911, **Vang 8161**
Carlisle: Ross 8083
Chambersburg: F & 7834
Cheltenham: Chung-Hee 7768
Clearfield: Flegal 7846, Gates 7865
Collegeville: Warren 8175
Conshohocken: Quaker 8069
Coopersburg: Lutron 7963
Coraopolis: Simpson 8104
Delmont: Workable 8206
Devon: Toth 8148
Doylestown: Bucks 7752, Fleischer 7847, Foundations 7854, Stork 8134
Du Bois: Moore 7993
Dubois: Martin 7970
Easton: Delaware 7809, Two 8152
Edinboro: Gillespie 7870, Nicholas 8006
Eighty Four: **Handyside 7885**
Elwyn: Elwyn 7824
Ephrata: Brossman 7748, Gooding 7876, Mellinger 7981, Wolf 8200
Erie: Brevillier 7745, Conner 7789, Erie 7831, Greater 7879, Hamot 7884, Scholarship 8088
Everett: Center 7761
Exton: Arpajian 7714, **ERM 7832**, **Viropharma 8166**, West 8188
Fairless Hills: Moyer 7997
Fort Washington: Wilson 8196
Fountainville: Butterer 7755
Friedens: Shaulis 8097
Gettysburg: South 8124
Gladwyne: DiBona 7811, Newman 8005
Greensburg: Community 7785, Laurent 7949, TLC 8147
Hanover: **Foundation 7850**
Harrisburg: Foundation 7852, Foundation 7853, Frozen 7862, Kidney 7935, Pennsylvania 8024, Pennsylvania 8030, Pinnacle 8044
Haverford: Presser 8060
Hazleton: Quin 8070
Hermitage: Smith 8112
Hollidaysburg: Wachter 8172
Honesdale: Wayne 8178
Indiana: Baskin 7725, Davis 7806, Doverspike 7816, Indiana 7918, Irvin 7921, Perrone 8032, Prescott 8059

Jenkintown: **Alternatives 7699**, Fox 7856
Jim Thorpe: Helbing 7901
Johnstown: Community 7779, Communtiy 7787, Crawford 7797, Fallquist 7836, Miller 7985
Kennett Square: Genesis 7867
King of Prussia: Arkema 7709, French 7858, **Lokoff 7961**, Workplace 8207
Kittanning: Armstrong 7710, Armstrong 7712, Snyder 8116
Lancaster: Armstrong 7711, Davis 7807, Fulton 7863, Health 7897, High 7906, Keefer 7933, Lancaster 7941, Lancaster 7942, Lancaster 7943, Lancaster 7944, Lancaster 7945, Laudermilch 7948, Martz 7971, Shuman 8102, Stager 8128, Steinman 8130, Steinman 8131, Trout 8149, Troutman 8150, Vastine 8164, Wittmer 8199, Zimmerman 8219
Langhorne: Woods 8205
Lebanon: Eisenhauer 7820, Visiting 8167
Lehigh Valley: Private 8064
Lemoyne: Adams 7692, Pennsylvania 8029
Lock Haven: Lock 7960, North 8009
Long Pond: Mattioli 7972
Luzerne: Luzerne 7964
Lykens: Nestor 8004
Mahanoy City: Urban 8156
Malvern: **CPCU 7795**, Elko 7822, Heyburn 7904
McVeytown: Stuck 8136
Meadville: Crawford 7796
Mechanicsburg: Pennsylvania 8023, Williams 8194
Media: **Botstiber 7740**, Riddle 8077
Merion Station: McKee 7976
Mifflinburg: **Pennsylvania 8026**
Milford: Biondo 7734
Millersburg: Williamson 8195
Milton: PENCON 8020
Minersville: Harley 7886, Miller 7987
Mohnton: Broadbent 7747
Monroeville: Monroeville 7991
Montoursville: Mussina 7999
Montrose: Community 7782
Mount Joy: Donegal 7814, **International 7920**, Schock 8087
Narberth: Ameche 7700, **National 8000**
Natrona Heights: Podiatry 8052
Nesquehoning: Fenstermacher 7840
New Brighton: Rochester 8078
New Florence: Thoburn 8143
New Holland: Boscov 7739
Newtown: Epstein 7828, Jefferson 7927, Keith 7934, **Law 7950**
Newtown Square: Project 8065
Newville: Welch 8185
North East: North 8010
North Wales: Teva 8142
Northumberland: Leighow 7955
Oakmont: Conrad 7790
Oil City: Bridge 7746, Epstein 7827, Harris 7891
Palmerton: Williams 8191
Paoli: **AO 7707**
Perkasie: **Buck 7751**
Philadelphia: Aid 7693, Alsobrooks 7698, **American 7701**, American 7702, **American 7704**, Angelo 7706, Asbestos 7715, Bader 7720, Berwind 7732, Biddle 7733, Blues 7737, Bonner 7738, Bread 7743, Brown 7750, **Cardiovascular 7757**, Center 7762, Children's 7765, **Chinese 7766**, Clareth 7769, Class 7771, Clay 7772, Comcast 7777, **Connelly 7788**, Corti 7794, Curtis 7802, Curtis 7803, Davis 7808, **Delta 7810**, Dodd 7812, Dotson 7815, Ellis 7823, Fabric 7835, Farber 7837, FMC 7849, Friend 7860, Ghidotti 7868, GlaxoSmithKline 7871, Goldman 7874, Goslee 7877, Grand 7878, Haeseler 7882, Harmon 7887, Harris 7888, Harris 7890, Hassel 7893, Hazelton 7894, Head 7895, Heald 7896, Hearn 7898, Heart 7899, Hill 7908, Horn 7912, Huth 7914,

Independence 7916, **Institute 7919**, Irwin 7922, Ivy 7923, Ivy 7924, Jeanes 7926, **Jewish 7929**, Johnson 7931, Kimmel 7936, Ladd 7940, Leeway 7951, Lehr 7954, Lenfest 7956, Lewis 7958, March 7968, McNeil 7979, Michaels 7983, Miller 7986, Miller 7988, Minear 7989, Moore 7994, Northeast 8012, Patton 8019, Pennsylvania 8025, Pennsylvania 8027, Percival 8031, Pew 8033, Philadelphia 8034, Philadelphia 8035, Philadelphia 8036, Philadelphia 8037, Philadelphia 8038, Philadelphia 8039, Pickle 8043, Postles 8054, Postles 8055, Puckett 8067, Pyle 8068, **Rhythm 8076**, Rohrer 8079, Ruskin 8084, Saak 8086, Scholarship 8089, Scribe 8095, Shartzer 8096, Shoemaker 8100, Smock 8114, Snyder 8115, Soames 8118, Soeder 8120, Spackman 8126, Stager 8129, Stoneleigh 8133, Stricklin 8135, Teamsters 8140, Thompson 8145, United 8155, Valley 8158, Van Wynen 8160, Vasset 8163, Vodgis 8168, Von 8170, Voorhies 8171, Walz 8174, Webber 8179, Webber 8180, Webermeier 8182, Weed 8183, West 8187, Williams 8193, Wilson 8197, Wolf 8201, Wolf 8202, Wood 8204, Yopst 8211, Yule 8217, Zoll 8220, Zurfluh 8221
Philedelphia: Burch 7753
Phoenixville: Phoenixville 8041
Pittsburg: Wein 8184
Pittsburgh: Abrams 7691, **Alcoa 7694**, Allegheny 7696, Allen 7697, American 7705, **Association 7718**, Bailey 7721, Barrand 7722, Bartko 7723, Benford 7727, Benz 7729, Bernowski 7731, Blanchard 7736, Boyer 7741, Boyle 7742, Brenneman 7744, Brown 7749, Carmell 7758, **Carnegie 7759**, Catholic 7760, Clark 7770, Cochran 7773, Colman 7775, Croatian 7798, Crossroads 7800, Daly 7804, Davis 7805, Dollar 7813, **Early 7817**, Ely 7825, England 7826, EQT 7829, Erickson 7830, Eye 7833, Fischer 7843, Fitch 7844, Fitton 7845, Fleisher 7848, Founder's 7855, Friend 7859, Friendship 7861, **GBU 7866**, Gibson 7869, Goldstein 7875, Guthrie 7881, Harris 7889, Hartman 7892, **Heinz 7900**, Henderson 7903, Higbee 7905, Hill 7907, Hill 7909, Hirtzel 7910, Jackson 7925, Jewish 7928, Klemstine 7938, Kotur 7946, Langdale 7946, Larue-Dawson 7947, Levergood 7957, Lintner 7959, Lowengard 7962, Lynch 7965, Maley 7967, Mattress 7973, McKaig 7975, McMannis 7977, McRoberts 7980, Mendenhall 7982, Moore 7992, Morgan 7995, Nicklies 8007, Noll 8008, O'Brien-Veba 8014, ONS 8015, Paddington 8016, **Pan 8018**, **Penn 8021**, Pennsylvania 8028, Phillips 8040, Pittsburgh 8046, Pittsburgh 8047, Pittsburgh 8048, Pittsburgh 8049, Plank 8050, PNC 8051, Power 8057, **PPG 8058**, Pressley 8061, Psea 8066, Realize 8072, Reeves 8073, Rhoads 8075, Rooney 8081, Rosenfeld 8082, Shaull 8098, Sheen 8099, Shoemaker 8101, Siebenthal 8103, Skillman 8107, Sleeper 8108, Smithfield 8113, Society 8119, Somerville 8121, Soren 8122, St. Margaret 8127, Stockwell 8132, Sutliff 8137, Thomas 8144, Three 8146, Tyndale 8153, **USWA 8157**, Van Horne 8159, Varner 8162, Vincent 8165, Vogeley 8169, Walter 8173, Wesley 8186, **Williams 8192**, Winters 8198, Women's 8203, Worthington 8208, Wright 8209, Young 8215, Yount 8216, Zaccheus 8218
Plymouth Meeting: Corson 7793
Pottstown: Greater 7880, Pottstown 8056
Pottsville: Christ 7767, Faust 7838, Schuylkill 8090, Schuylkill 8091, Schuylkill 8092
Presto: Young 8214
Radnor: **Association 7716**, Female 7839, **National 8001**, Western 8189
Reading: Berks 7730, Reading 8071
Reedsville: Freedom 7857
Reinholds: Eastern 7818
Richboro: Hahn 7883
Ridley Park: Taylor 8139
Saint Marys: Elk 7821

Saxonburg: South 8123
Schnecksville: Lehigh 7952
Scranton: Basila 7724, Scranton 8094
Selinsgrove: App 7708
Sewickley: Print 8063
Sharon: Community 7784
Sheffield: McMillen 7978
Slippery Rock: Slippery 8109
Spring City: Physicians 8042
St.Marys: Ryan 8085
State College: Gardiner 7864, Nelson 8002, Schwab 8093
Steelton: Mohn 7990
Tunkhannock: Piper 8045
Union City: Cross 7799, Union 8154
Uniontown: Community 7780
Verona: Snyder 8117
Warren: Community 7783, Northwest 8013
Warrendale: **Association 7717**
Washington: Abernathy 7689, Washington 8176
Waverly: Waverly 8177
Waynesburg: Community 7781
Wellsboro: Bennett, 7728, Copp 7792, Trushel 8151, Wettrick 8190
Wernersville: Polish 8053
West Chester: Chester 7764, Swope 8138, YMCA 8210
West Conshohocken: Calvert 7756, **Templeton 8141**
Wilkes Barre: Arnold 7713, Coordinated 7791
Wilkes-Barre: Commission 7778
Williamsport: First 7841, Smith 8110
Wynnewood: **Alex's 7695**, Mahler 7966
Wyomissing: Helwig 7902, Hughes 7913, Marshall 7969, Penn 8022, Reitnauer 8074, Sinden 8105
York: Columbus 7776, Community 7786, York 8212, York 8213
Zelienople: Eckhart 7819

see also 1321, 1369, 1379, 1397, 1506, 1522, 1614, 1704, 1910, 1947, 2792, 3556, 3872, 3932, 4119, 4134, 4179, 4416, 4884, 5382, 5432, 5455, 5504, 5556, 5608, 5714, 5740, 5769, 5778, 5817, 5891, 5936, 5985, 6022, 6031, 6051, 6055, 6069, 6075, 6114, 6139, 6204, 6213, 6225, 6327, 6345, 6360, 6384, 6385, 6407, 6439, 6442, 6460, 6507, 6524, 6531, 6544, 6555, 6570, 6597, 6605, 6630, 6641, 6647, 6664, 6671, 6684, 6685, 6689, 6699, 6704, 6735, 6738, 6756, 6774, 6782, 6810, 6813, 6815, 6832, 6835, 6838, 6851, 6855, 6859, 6891, 6897, 6930, 6934, 7020, 7089, 7104, 7181, 7185, 7195, 7206, 7258, 7296, 7322, 7343, 7380, 7381, 7419, 7427, 7428, 7441, 8268, 8334, 8408, 9424, 9504, 9799, 9804

PUERTO RICO

Bayamon: Unanue 8224
San Juan: Harvey 8222, Puerto Rico 8223

see also 362, 664, 1411, 1519, 1644, 3099, 5547, 5670, 6244, 6315, 9331, 9358

RHODE ISLAND

Coventry: Cranston 8276
Cranston: Ayers 8235, Cranston 8275, Shriners 8399
Cumberland: Rhode Island 8380
East Providence: Fundacao 8296, Masonic 8336
Harmony: Ronci 8388
Newport: Cranston/Theophilus 8277, Thompson 8422
Portsmouth: **United 8428**
Providence: **Alliance 8226**, Alpert 8227, Andrews 8229, Armstrong 8230, Arnold 8231, Atkins 8232, August 8233, Babcock 8236, Bailey 8237, Baker 8238, Baker-Adams 8239, Barillaro 8240, Black

8244, Blakeslee 8245, Blanchard 8246, Boghossian 8247, Botsford 8248, Bowmaker 8249, Brennan 8251, Brown 8253, Burke 8254, Carlisle 8255, Chandler 8256, Church 8258, Cianci 8259, Cismoski 8261, Clark 8262, Cobb 8264, Coe 8265, Coe 8266, Coe 8267, Cohen 8268, Coia 8269, Coles 8270, College 8271, Comstock 8272, Cook 8273, Costa 8274, Croston 8278, Cummings 8280, Cuno 8281, Davenport 8283, DeLoura 8284, Dix 8285, **Dorot 8286,** Duxbury 8287, Eaton 8288, Ellsworth 8289, Fales 8290, Farrington 8291, Faunce 8292, Forsyth 8293, Fox 8294, Frost 8295, Galligan 8297, Gates 8298, Gill 8299, Gooding 8300, Gould 8301, Greater 8302, Green 8303, Greenlaw 8304, Gromack 8305, Guertin 8306, Harney 8307, Heald 8308, Henney 8309, Holopigian 8310, Howard 8312, Humphrey 8313, Hunt 8314, Jakobi 8315, Johnson 8316, Kamenski 8317, Kelley 8318, Kennedy 8319, Kiely 8320, King 8321, Kingsbury 8322, Kinsley 8323, Lichman 8324, Life 8325, Little 8326, Long 8327, Maes 8329, Magraw 8330, Mahan 8331, Mahana 8332, Makinson 8333, Manwiller 8334, Marhaver 8335, Matheson 8337, Maude 8338, Maybury 8339, McCormick 8340, McLean 8341, McMurtrie 8342, McVinney 8343, Meriden 8344, Miles 8345, Miller 8346, Miller 8347, Mills 8348, Montague 8349, Morrow 8350, Moses 8351, Moulton 8352, Munson 8353, Nash 8354, Nicholson 8355, Norman 8356, O'Brion 8357, Onodaga 8358, Orr 8359, Padelford 8360, Palen-Klar 8361, Palmer 8362, Pape 8363, **Papines 8364,** Pappines 8365, Parker 8366, Peck 8367, Perpetual 8368, Petsas 8369, Pierce 8370, Preston 8371, Price 8372, Price 8373, Prince 8374, Pryde 8376, Putnam 8377, Randall 8378, Rhode 8379, Rhode Island 8381, Rhode 8382, Rimmele 8383, Robbins 8384, Robbins 8385, Robinson 8386, Rolland 8387, Rostra 8389, Sasso 8390, Scavone 8391, Scheehl 8392, Schiff 8393, Schuyler 8394, Sears 8395, Sears 8396, Sheehan 8397, Shifler 8398, Simionescu 8400, Sleesman 8401, Slowinski 8402, Smith 8403, Smith 8404, Smith 8405, Smith 8406, Smith 8407, Smith 8408, Smythe 8409, Snyder 8410, Snyder 8411, Sprague 8412, Starr 8413, Stauble 8414, Stokes 8415, Streeter 8416, Sutton 8417, Syder 8418, Taber 8419, Tappan 8420, Thompson 8421, Todd 8424, Townsend 8425, Tracy 8426, Tryon 8427, Urann 8429, Valley 8430, Walker 8431, Weaver 8432, Webster 8433, Webster 8434, Wells 8435, Wiggin 8436, Wiles 8437, Williams 8438, Williams 8439, Wood 8440, Wright 8441, Wylie 8442, Yaeger 8443

Riverside: Additon 8225, Anctil 8228, Ayer 8234, Bartlett 8241, Bell, 8242, Berry 8243, Brack 8250, Brock 8252, Christy 8257, Cilley 8260, Croston 8279, Hosser 8311, Lord 8328

Saunderstown: Providence 8375

West Warwick: Club 8263

Westerly: TMC 8423

Woonsocket: CVS 8282

see also 362, 741, 3050, 3977, 3994, 4000, 4157, 4195, 4238, 5556, 9240, 9508

SOUTH CAROLINA

Anderson: Anmed 8447

Beaufort: **Hemingway 8482**

Bluffton: **Malanga 8493**

Blythewood: Kelly, 8488

Camden: Austin 8449, West 8519

Charleston: Carolina 8455, Charleston 8458, Charleston 8459, Coastal 8464, Hebrew 8481, Society 8509

Clemson: Clemson 8461, Clemson 8462

Clinton: Bailey 8451

Columbia: Byrnes 8453, Central 8457, Cultural 8469, Gamecock 8474, Kappa 8487, NGA 8498, Smith 8508, South 8512, South 8513

Fort Mill: Springs 8515

Fountain Inn: **AVX 8450**

Graniteville: Gregg 8478

Greenville: Alliance 8445, Community 8465, Gallivan 8473, Gift 8475, Greenville 8477, Love 8491, Miracle 8494, United 8518

Greenwood: Cornelius 8467, Gleamns 8476

Greer: Smith 8507

Hartsville: Sonoco 8510

Hilton Head Island: Community 8466, Fund 8472, **Heritage 8483,** Professional 8504, Strive 8516

Inman: Inman 8486

Irmo: South 8511

Johns Island: Rural 8505

Landrum: Moore 8495

Laurens: Kennedy 8489

Little River: Chief's 8460

Lugoff: Kershaw 8490

Mount Pleasant: Clergy 8463

Myrtle Beach: Habitat 8479, Ocean 8499

North Charleston: Father-To-Father 8471, Lowcountry 8492

Orangeburg: Cox 8468, Horne 8484

Pawleys Island: Hart 8480, Parsons 8502

Ridgeland: Palmetto 8501

Rock Hill: Carolina 8456

Simpsonville: IDCA 8485

Spartanburg: Arts 8448, Piedmont 8503, Sherman 8506, Spartanburg 8514

Sumter: Anderson 8446, Boyne 8452, O'Neill 8500

Walhalla: Earle 8470

West Columbia: Airport 8444

Williamston: Muth 8497

York: Cameron 8454, Moss 8496, Tucker 8517

---

see also 81, 1851, 1893, 1899, 2166, 2252, 2258, 3556, 3600, 3855, 4118, 4416, 6565, 6587, 6607, 6636, 6652, 6658, 6660, 6668, 6777, 6821, 6852, 6862, 6881, 6890, 6929, 7164, 7698, 7860, 8656, 9313

SOUTH DAKOTA

Aberdeen: Doolittle 8527, Hatterscheidt 8533, Howard 8534, Strahl 8543, Ullyot 8545

Black Hawk: Native 8537

Brookings: Brookings 8523, South Dakota 8541, South 8542

Dakota Dunes: Clausen 8524, Westendorf 8547

Lead: Green 8532

Mitchell: Cozard 8525, Kramer 8535

Pierre: Delta 8526, South Dakota 8540, Tessier 8544

Rapid City: Black 8521, Black 8522, **First 8530**

Sioux Falls: Amundson 8520, Doolittle 8528, Dow 8529, Graham 8531, McCormick 8536, Sioux Falls 8538, Solem 8539

Spearfish: Yellow 8548

Watertown: Watertown 8546

---

see also 1256, 1494, 3251, 3302, 3382, 4705, 4734, 4737, 4753, 4779, 4841, 4851, 4859, 4883, 4884, 4899, 5230, 5271, 6679, 7931, 8174, 9045, 10017

TENNESSEE

Brentwood: **Alpha 8554,** Thomley 8654

Bristol: Lazarus 8614

Brownsville: Wills 8664

Chattanooga: A.I.M. 8550, Acts 8551, Alumni 8555, Boyd 8561, Chattanooga 8567, Chattanooga 8568, Civitan 8575, Community 8577, Dixie 8582, Hurlbut 8605

Clifton: Hassell 8597

Cordova: Wilemon 8663

Crossville: 4-C's 8549, Tomorrow 8655

Dickson: Goodlark 8594

Dunlap: Southeast 8647

Dyersburg: Coburn 8576, Dyersburg-Dyer 8585

Franklin: Fengler 8591, Grace 8595, Lee 8617

Gallatin: Roark 8637

Goodlettsville: Dollar 8583

Greeneville: Niswonger 8630, Unaka 8656

Hendersonville: CIC 8574

Jamestown: Rains 8634

Jasper: Simpson 8645

Johnson City: Appalachian 8557

Jonesborough: **National 8629**

Kingsport: Eastman 8589, Upper 8659, Wellmont 8662

Knoxville: **American 8556,** Berkshire 8559, **Cancer 8563,** East 8587, East 8588, Fort 8592, Hawkins 8598, **Heart 8600,** Hicks 8601, Hodges 8602, Leyen 8618, Mercy 8619, Parkwest 8631, Regal 8635

Lawrenceburg: Holtsford 8603

Lebanon: Cracker 8581, Mid-Cumberland 8623, Precision 8633

Linden: Graham 8596

Madison: East Nashville 8586

Maryville: Ruby 8639

Memphis: AutoZone 8558, Carrier 8564, Chi Omega 8571, Community 8578, Conte 8580, International 8607, Jewish 8609, Le 8615, Methodist 8620, Metropolitan 8622, **National 8628,** ServiceMaster 8642, Stuttering 8652, Temple 8653, United 8658, Watkins 8660

Morristown: Keel 8612

Murfreesboro: Foundation 8593, **International 8606,** Lead 8616, Middle 8624, Siegel 8644, Stegall 8650

Nashville: Bootstraps 8560, Boys 8562, Catholic 8566, Children's 8573, Community 8579, Educational 8590, HCA 8599, Humanities 8604, JSA 8611, Nashville 8625, Nashville 8626, Nashville 8627, Pearlpoint 8632, **Scarlett 8640,** Schmidt 8641, Shiloh 8643, Splawn 8648, Stahlman 8649, Stephenson 8651, **United 8657**

Oak Ridge: Aid 8553, Methodist 8621

Old Hickory: **Soles4Souls 8646**

Paris: Adams 8552, Chenoweth 8570, Richardson 8636, Ross 8638

Pigeon Forge: Dollywood 8584

Powell: Children's 8572

Ripley: Cheek,Jr. 8569

Shelbyville: Cash 8565, Johnson 8610

Signal Mountain: Jewell 8608

Union City: Latimer 8613

Waverly: Weems 8661

Woodbury: Woodbury 8665

---

see also 18, 40, 48, 51, 59, 81, 94, 610, 1614, 2016, 2832, 3556, 3600, 4884, 4911, 4921, 5099, 6825, 7813, 8386, 8765, 8770, 9001, 9313, 9372

TEXAS

Abilene: Community 8762, McKenney 8947

Aledo: Reilly 9035

Allen: Pettinger 9015

Alvin: Ryan 9048

Amarillo: Amarillo 8675, Amarillo 8676, **American 8682**

Angleton: Community 8763

Aransas Pass: Coastal 8756

Arlington: Alexander 8672, Arlington 8690, **Delta 8790,** Ferguson 8821, Fleetwood 8823, **Mensa 8952,** Mission 8965, Presbyterian 9028, Right 9040, Texas 9130

Athens: Enger 8815

Austin: **American 8677,** Austin 8696, Austin 8697, Austin 8698, **Bat 8705,** Caritas 8735, **Dell 8789,**

Educational 8808, Ehlers 8810, Hammond 8852, Headliners 8860, Humanities 8887, Lake 8912, Lake 8913, McCrory 8941, Olson 8996, San Marcos 9059, Schwab 9064, Seton 9069, Sipes 9076, Spencer 9094, St. David's 9095, St. Vincent 9099, Texas 9114, Texas 9115, Texas 9118, Texas 9120, Texas 9122, Texas 9124, Texas 9125, Texas 9127, Watson 9159, Wine 9170, Young 9187

Azle: Dreams 8798

Beaumont: **Beaumont 8707**, Conn 8766, Some 9083, Southeast 9087

Bedford: Harris 8856

Bellaire: Neighborhood 8988

Bigfoot: Berwin 8711

Bonham: Cooper 8772, Deupree 8792, Miller 8959

Booker: Peery 9009

Brenham: Jones 8901

Brownwood: Kelly 8904

Bryan: Astin 8693, Brazos 8720, St. Joseph 9096

Buda: Associated 8692

Burnet: Hill 8866, Wise 9173

Carrollton: CRW 8776

Chappell Hill: Polk 9023

Cleburne: Christmas 8750, Cleburne 8753, Marti 8936, Mustang 8977

College Station: Affordable 8668, Bush 8729

Colleyville: Baby 8701

Colorado City: Woods 9182

Conroe: Maness 8935

Coppell: Broady 8722

Corpus Christi: Coastal 8755, Corpus Christi 8773, Futureus 8834, Gilman 8841, Golden 8847, Lee 8917, United 9144

Corsicana: Clifford 8754, Eady 8802, Little 8919, Seely 9067, Terry 9113

Crowell: Rolling 9044

Cypress: Cypress 8780

Dallas: Advanced 8667, AIDS 8669, Albaugh 8671, Alpha 8674, **American 8678**, American 8679, Amigos 8686, Anderson 8687, Associa 8691, AT&T 8695, Ayres 8700, Barnsley 8702, Bartholomew 8703, Barto 8704, Borton 8717, Bour 8718, Brisley 8721, Brockman 8723, Buckner 8727, Buckner 8728, Cannon 8734, Catholic 8740, Chamberlin 8742, Communities 8759, Community 8761, Cox 8774, Cuban 8777, Cutter 8779, **Dabney 8781**, Dallas 8783, Dallas 8784, Dallas 8785, Danciger 8787, Denman 8791, Diffenbaugh 8793, Diffenbaugh 8794, Diffenbaugh-University 8795, Donnelly 8797, Dunn 8800, **Education 8807**, **Emergency 8814**, Fuller 8832, Giannini 8837, Giannini 8838, Giannini-Scatena 8839, Hamilton 8850, Hayes 8859, Hefflefinger 8864, Hubbard 8885, Hurley 8888, Ilgenfritz 8891, Ingram 8893, Janson 8898, **Komen 8910**, Lanham 8914, Lockheed 8922, Luce 8928, Maffett 8931, **Mary 8937**, Millar 8958, Miller 8960, Miller 8961, Milotte 8963, Morse 8971, Munson 8973, Nation 8981, National 8983, Nearburg 8987, Norby 8991, **OneSight 8998**, Percy 9012, Pipe 9021, Poncin 9024, Prater 9027, Reed 9033, **Reese 9034**, Reitch 9036, **Reserve 9037**, Robinson 9043, **Ryrie 9049**, S.G.K.&G. 9050, Salesmanship 9051, Salesmanship 9052, Santander 9061, Shouse 9071, Smith 9078, Smith 9079, Smolin 9080, Southwest 9089, Southwestern 9092, Sunnyside 9103, Swinney 9105, Swinney 9106, Texas 9121, Texas 9126, Thai 9132, Thomas 9133, Thompson 9134, Thompson 9136, Today 9137, Trimble 9138, TUA 9139, Turner 9140, Wagner 9154, Watson 9158, West 9162, Wilkins 9167, Williams 9168, Wipe 9172, Wolverton 9177, Wood 9179

Dallax: Maguire 8932

Eagle Lake: Wintermann 9171

Edinburg: Edinburg 8806

Edna: Robinson 9042, Wright 9183

El Paso: El Paso 8811, Peyton 9016, Rio 9041, University 9145

Elgin: Texas 9129

Fair Oaks Ranch: **Interdenominational 8894**

Farmers Branch: Texas 9119

Flower Mound: **Knights 8909**, Powdermaker 9026

Fort Worth: **American 8680**, Bragan 8719, Carter 8738, Catholic 8739, Community 8764, Crescent 8775, **First 8822**, Fort 8827, Fort Worth 8828, Fort Worth 8829, Goff 8846, Gourley 8848, Lockheed 8921, McDonald 8943, O'Brien 8994, O'Neal 8997, Penrose 9011, Richardson 9038, Sand 9060, Texas 9116, United 9142

Fredericksburg: Hill 8867

Frisco: Dallas 8786

Gainesville: Minyard 8964

Galveston: Chambers 8743, Mercer 8953, Meyer 8956, Moody 8967, Pearce 9007, Seibel 9068

Ganado: Young 9186

Garland: Brown 8725, Common 8758

Gatesville: Cooper 8771

Graham: Long 8923

Grapeland: Dailey 8782

Grapevine: UFCW 9141

Hamilton: Elam 8812, Moore 8968, Thompson 9135

Houston: Alliance 8673, American 8681, **Amigos 8685**, Astros 8694, **Blackburn 8714**, Brookshire 8724, Brown 8726, C.L.C. 8731, Camp 8733, Catholic 8741, Chaudhary 8745, Childress 8747, **Conrad 8768**, Cook 8770, Culture 8778, Diverseworks 8796, Driver 8799, Edwards 8809, EOG 8816, Fant 8817, Foundation 8831, Fund 8833, Galena 8835, Genesis 8836, Gill 8840, Hachar 8849, Hamman 8851, Harris 8855, Healthcare 8861, Heinlein 8865, Hispanic 8869, Hispanic 8871, Home 8873, Houston 8875, Houston 8876, **Houston 8877**, Houston 8878, Houston 8879, **Houston 8880**, Houston 8881, Houston 8882, Houston 8883, Huddleston 8886, IFMA 8890, Interfaith 8895, Jamaica 8896, Jordan 8902, Katz 8903, Kiddies 8905, L.L.P. 8911, Lorelle 8924, Lucas 8927, M. 8930, McGovern 8944, McGowan 8945, **Media 8950**, Methodist 8955, Murphy 8974, **Museum 8975**, Nabors 8979, NASA 8980, National 8985, Nichols 8989, Northwest 8993, PFLAG/HATCH 9017, Rainforest 9031, Schull 9062, Second 9065, **Society 9081**, Society 9082, Southern 9088, **Southwest 9090**, St. 9097, St. Luke's 9098, Student 9102, Swift 9104, Sysco 9107, Targa 9108, Target 9109, Texas 9131, Urban 9146, **Vietnamese 9149**, Visible 9151, Von 9152, Welch 9160, Woltman 9176, Women's 9178, Woodhill 9180, Zimmer 9188

Huffman: Mayfield 8939

Humble: Lawler 8916

Hurst: Masonic 8938

Ingram: Live 8920

Irving: **American 8684**, Christus 8751, College 8757, Conference 8765, Fluor 8824, Kimberly 8906, **National 8984**, Pioneer 9020, **Promotional 9030**, Silverthorne 9074

Itasca: Anderson 8689

Jacksonville: Austin 8699

Johnson City: Pedernales 9008

Jourdanton: Waltom 9155

Junction: Johnson 8900

Katy: **Mehta 8951**

Kerrville: Hirsch 8868

Killeen: Rotary 9047

La Grange: Wildner 9166

Lake Jackson: Pardee 9002

Lamesa: Morgan 8969, West 9163

Lampasas: Eddy 8805

Laredo: South 9086

League City: **North 8992**

Levelland: South 9084

Lewisville: Christian 8749, **MVP 8978**

Liberty: Bellamy 8709

Liberty Hill: Lasco 8915

Lindale: Teen 9112

Livingston: Bergman 8710, Ellzey 8813, Show 9072

Lockhart: Znotas 9189

Lubbock: Dupre 8801, Foundation 8830, Lubbock 8926, Rawls 9032, Wisian 9174

Luling: Luling 8929

Madisonville: Knight 8908

Mansfield: Mouser 8972

Marfa: **Chinati 8748**

Marlin: Betts 8712

Marshall: Conner 8767, Tartt 9110

McAllen: Cook 8769, Panasonic 9001, Siros 9077, South 9085, United 9143, Vinsant 9150

Midland: Fasken 8819, Hodges 8872, McCaulay 8940, Midland 8957, Permian 9013

Monahans: Ward 9156

Mount Vernon: Carter 8737

Muldoon: Yoder 9185

Nacogdoches: Community 8760

Navasota: Patout 9006

New Braunfels: Schumann 9063

New Caney: East 8803

Onalaska: Romsdahl 9045

Orange: Malloy 8934, Programs 9029, Stark 9101

Overton: McMillan, 8948

Palestine: Haverlah 8858, Texas 9117

Pampa: Anderson 8688, Phillips 9019

Paradise: Hutton 8889

Paris: Paris 9003, Paris 9004

Pearland: Houston 8884

Plano: Cadbury 8732, Lowe 8925, **MCH 8946**, Penney 9010, Perot 9014

Pleasanton: Warnken 9157

Port Arthur: Port Arthur 9025

Port Lavaca: Formosa 8826

Raymondville: **Harding 8854**

Red Oak: Texas 9123

Red Rock: Goertz 8845

Richardson: **ABG 8666**, Oglesby 8995, **SPE 9093**

Rockport: Philadelphia 9018

Round Rock: Children 8746

San Angelo: San Angelo 9053

San Antonio: Alamo 8670, American 8683, Baumberger 8706, Beefmaster 8708, Borelli 8716, **Butt 8730**, Cisneros 8752, Forever 8825, Gnade 8843, Heath 8862, **Hispanic 8870**, Hornbrook 8874, James 8897, Jireh 8899, **Limiar 8918**, Methodist 8954, Morrison 8970, Music 8976, **National 8982**, **Operation 8999**, Piper 9022, San Antonio 9054, San Antonio 9055, San Antonio 9056, San Antonio 9057, San Antonio 9058, Silver 9073, Southwest 9091, Taylor 9111, Valero 9147, **Western 9164**, Wolters 9175, Yett 9184

Schulenburg: Stanzel 9100

Sealy: Chapman 8744

Sherman: **National 8986**

Sinton: Welder 9161

Spearman: Gilpatrick 8842, Nielson 8990

Spring: Havens 8857

St. Antonio: **Vetiver 9148**

Stafford: Second 9066

Stanton: Millhollon 8962

Stratford: Riffe 9039

Sugar Land: Imperial 8892

Sulphur Springs: Bonham 8715

Temple: Wilson 9169

Texarkana: Owen 9000

Texas City: McDaniel 8942

The Woodlands: Haraldson 8853, Montgomery 8966, Woodlands 9181

Tomball: Klein 8907

Tyler: Black 8713, East 8804, Faulconer 8820, Mead 8949
Uvalde: Mallard 8933
Waco: Caritas 8736, Deering 8788, Heavin 8863, Passport 9005, Waco 9153
Waxahachie: Singleton 9075
Weatherford: Farmer 8818
Whitesboro: Godwin 8844
Wichita Falls: Shanor 9070, Wichita 9165
Wimberley: Texas 9128
Woodsboro: Rooke 9046

see also 64, 305, 710, 1272, 1614, 2046, 2413, 2628, 2694, 2738, 2739, 2740, 2832, 2836, 3651, 3661, 3832, 3902, 4087, 4134, 4238, 4379, 4731, 4883, 4884, 4948, 5053, 5063, 5423, 5580, 5621, 5636, 5723, 7095, 7385, 7464, 7482, 7541, 7574, 7738, 7753, 7813, 7917, 8061, 8221, 9215, 9219, 9413, 10017, 10089

UTAH

Alpine: Bybee 9196
Dammeron Valley: Luttrell 9217
Farmington: Lofthouse 9216
Hurricane: Last 9215
Lindon: I Care 9208
Logan: Woodward 9233
Murray: Intermountain 9210
Oakley: Wheelwright 9230
Ogden: Dialysis 9198
Park City: Park 9221, **Sundance 9227**
Provo: American 9191, Whiz 9231
Salem: Anaya 9192
Salt Lake City: 100% 9190, Bamberger 9193, Cherokee 9197, EnergySolutions 9199, Granite 9201, Groesbeck 9202, Hanks 9203, Harman 9204, Harvey 9206, James 9211, Keener 9213, Kolob 9214, Masonic 9218, McCarthey 9219, Regence 9222, Ross 9223, Salt 9224, Salt 9225, Skaggs 9226, Utah 9228, Utah 9229, WTF 9234
Sandy: Gomez 9200, Helaman 9207, Miller 9220
South Jordan: Borax 9195
Springville: Wing 9232
Syracuse: Harmon 9205
Tooele: Barrick 9194
West Jordan: Jordan 9212
West Valley City: Intermountain 9209

see also 171, 555, 610, 1026, 1177, 1272, 1276, 1494, 3827, 4934, 7356, 7530, 8852, 10017

VERMONT

Arlington: Arlington 9235
Barre: Central 9239
Bennington: Scott 9260
Brattleboro: Durfee 9245, Tkacyzk 9262, Trustees 9263
Burlington: Barrows 9236, General 9248, **Green 9249**, Keal 9253
Cavendish: VARA 9265
Grafton: Windham 9273
Johnson: **Vermont 9271**
Middlebury: Vermont 9267
Montpelier: **Craft 9243**, Vermont 9266, Vermont 9268
Morrisville: Copley 9242, Terrill 9261, United 9264
Newport: England 9246, Hayes 9250
Rutland: Rutland 9259
Sheffield: Keniston 9254
South Burlington: **Brush 9237**, Nordic 9255
South Londonderry: Rowland 9258
Springfield: Charitable 9240
St. Albans: Warner 9272
St. Johnsbury: Danville 9244
Stowe: Huffman 9252
Wallingford: Hayes 9251
West Rutland: **Carving 9238**
Westford: Essex 9247
White River Junction: Clifford 9241, Ohiyesa 9256
Williston: Vermont 9270
Winooski: Vermont 9269
Woodstock: Ottauquechee 9257

see also 741, 1341, 1382, 1455, 1457, 1460, 1462, 3651, 3728, 3983, 3994, 4000, 4091, 4295, 4356, 5309, 5313, 5319, 5327, 5331, 5338, 5349, 5350, 5353, 5358, 5377, 5378, 5556, 6036, 6295, 6327, 7298

VIRGIN ISLANDS

Charlotte Amalie: Community 9274
St. John: Friends 9275, Rutnik 9276

see also 1796, 4884, 6315

VIRGINIA

Abingdon: Highlands 9395
Alexandria: Alger 9285, **American 9291, American 9292, American 9293**, American 9296, **American 9297, American 9298**, American 9299, **American 9302, American 9304, American 9307**, American 9308, **American 9309, American 9310**, Americans 9313, **Army 9315, Association 9322**, Carpenter's 9336, **Club 9343, Conquer 9351, Foundation 9380, Hispanic 9396**, Kengla 9414, **Maria's 9429, Marine 9430, MATHCOUNTS 9431, MedEvac 9433, Mesothelioma 9435, Military 9436, National 9450, National 9451**, National 9454, **National 9455**, National 9458, **NATSO 9460**, Pentagon 9478, Prevent 9487, **Special 9511, Teachers 9518**
Altavista: English 9373
Arlington: AFP 9280, Air 9283, Air 9284, **American 9290, American 9295, American 9300, American 9305**, American 9311, Arlington 9314, **Army 9316, Ashoka: 9317, Asparagus 9318**, Associates 9319, **Association 9321**, Buchly 9330, Davidson 9359, Education 9372, **IDSA 9402, Institute 9404, National 9445**, National 9448, **National 9457**, Navy-Marine 9462, **Newspaper 9464, Newton 9465**, Northern 9467, Phoenix 9481, Pillay 9482, **U.S. 9526, U.S. 9527**
Ashburn: Klein 9416
Bedford: Bedford 9324
Blacksburg: **Burger 9331**, Duerr 9365, TDC 9517, Virginia 9542
Bristol: United 9528
Centreville: Specialized 9512
Chantilly: SMACNA 9506, Western 9546
Charlottesville: **Advancing 9279, Brown 9329, Focused 9377**, Jefferson 9408, Lee-Jackson 9418, Minor 9437, Research 9493, Robinson 9495, United 9532, University 9533, Virginia 9539
Chesapeake: Dornhecker 9363, Tidewater 9523
Christiansburg: Cooley, 9354
Clifton Forge: Grubbs 9390
Colonial Heights: Johnson 9410
Crozet: **Brockbank 9328**
Culpeper: Culpeper 9355, Newhouse 9463, **Operation 9472**
Danville: Community 9347, Danville 9357, Hughes 9401, Maude 9432, Womack 9552
Dillwyn: Dunnavant 9366
Dulles: **Freedom 9385**
Fairfax: **American 9312**, Association 9323, **Datatel 9358, International 9405, NRA 9469, Radiation 9489**
Falls Church: **AHP 9282**, Foundation 9383, Homestretch 9397, **Mustard 9442, Olmsted 9470**, Parkinson 9475, **Plumbing 9483**, Rahman 9490, Sidhu 9504
Fishersville: AHC 9281
Floyd: Poff 9485
Franklin: Camp 9332
Fredericksburg: Community 9348, Cushman 9356
Gloucester Point: Thomas 9520, Van Engel 9536
Great Falls: **Sarnoff 9498**
Gretna: Blair 9326
Hampton: Grobel 9389, Patient 9476, Weaver 9544
Harrisonburg: Schlarb 9499
Herndon: CIA 9342, Luce 9425, **United 9530, USAWOA 9534**
Hopewell: Randolph 9491
Irvington: Treakle 9525, Wiley 9548
Kilmarnock: Harry 9392, Sanford 9497
Lansdowne: **Cooke 9352**
Leesburg: **American 9306**, International 9406, **Public 9488**
Lexington: **Sigma 9505**
Louisa: Cooke 9353
Lynchburg: English 9374, Lynchburg 9426
Marion: Goolsby-Gardner 9387
Martinsville: Hooker 9398, Keesee 9413, Sale 9496, Thompson 9521
McLean: **American 9301**, Capital 9333, **Food 9378, Fox 9384, Interstitial 9407**, Lend-A-Hand 9419, **National 9444, National 9447**, National 9456, Navy 9461, **Thanks 9519**
Mechanicsville: **Caring 9335**
Merrifield: **National 9459**
Middleburg: Cherry 9338, **Epilepsy 9375**
Midlothian: EastWest 9369, Patient 9477
Montross: Westmoreland 9547
New Market: Williamson 9549
Norfolk: ACCESS 9278, Eastern 9367, Eastern 9368, Foodbank 9379, Hampton 9391, Lincoln 9421, Morgan 9440, Sentara 9501, Sentara 9502, United 9531, **VAW/VRC 9538**
Oakton: Community 9345, Morrow 9441, Northern 9468
Onley: Doughty 9364
Petersburg: Petersburg 9480
Purcellville: Love 9424
Quicksburg: Bridgebuilder 9327
Reston: **American 9287, American 9288, American 9289, American 9294, Foundation 9381, Foundation 9382, National 9446**, National 9449, **National 9452, PMMI 9484**, Society 9510, Utility 9535
Richmond: Association 9320, Bell 9325, Century 9337, Community 9350, **Descendants 9360**, Henrico 9394, Housing 9400, Johns 9409, Linhart 9422, Missionary 9438, Reckitt 9492, Richmond 9494, Scott 9500, St. Paul's 9513, **United 9529**, Virginia 9540
Roanoke: Community 9349
Salem: Lewis 9420
Smithfield: Smithfield 9508
South Boston: Ware 9543
Springfield: Echo 9370, **Friedreich's 9386**, Housing 9399, IHFR 9403, Strong 9516
Stafford: MAPGA 9428
Staunton: Community 9346, Kennard 9415
Sterling: American 9303, Children's 9340, **EduCap 9371**, Orphan 9474
Strasburg: Strasburg 9515
Suffolk: Henley 9393, Nansemond 9443
Tappahannock: Fary 9376
Tazewell: Mitchell 9439, Stowers 9514
Vienna: **Diema's 9361**, Korean 9417, **Melton 9434, National 9453**, Smith-Melton 9509, Wolf 9551
Virginia Beach: All 9286, **Christian 9341, Dolphin 9362, Operation 9471**, Operation 9473, Perkins

9479, Tidewater 9522, Tidewater 9524, Vascular 9537, Virginia 9541, Weinstein 9545, **Wings 9550**
Warrenton: Carhart 9334, Child 9339, Loeb 9423, Northern 9466
Williamsburg: A Gift 9277, College 9344, Greater 9388, Maloney 9427
Winchester: Judges 9411, Shingleton 9503, Smith 9507
Woodbridge: Kane 9412, **Postal 9486**
Wytheville: Wythe-Bland 9553

see also 610, 1593, 1594, 1598, 1600, 1614, 1627, 1725, 1748, 1790, 1801, 1802, 1806, 1831, 1833, 1835, 1899, 1904, 1905, 1931, 1951, 1968, 1974, 1976, 2029, 2043, 2045, 2090, 2098, 2534, 2563, 2874, 2886, 3556, 3600, 3832, 3905, 3907, 4238, 4730, 4883, 4884, 5810, 5817, 6507, 6531, 6564, 6565, 6587, 6686, 6697, 6752, 6760, 6840, 6845, 6861, 6890, 7813, 7972, 8061, 8662, 9768, 9770, 9777, 9779, 9799, 9802

WASHINGTON

Anacortes: Wittman 9756, Worthington 9759
Bainbridge Island: Bainbridge 9565
Battle Ground: Columbia 9596
Belfair: Hood 9637
Bellevue: Bellevue 9569, Martinez 9668, Mortar 9677, Overlake 9691, **PAH 9695**, Pigott 9698, Washington 9750
Bellingham: Alternatives 9560, Laurendeau 9657, Opportunity 9689, St. Luke's 9732
Bremerton: Coulter 9602
Burlington: Bradley 9576, Burlington 9579
Cle Elum: McMillen 9673
Colville: Rural 9712
Eastsound: Children's 9587
Edmonds: Gasparovich 9620
Ephrata: Columbia 9595, Lauzier 9658
Everett: Carkeek 9581, Everett 9608, First 9612, Jensen 9642, Providence 9703, Schack 9715, Snohomish 9728
Federal Way: Kedge 9648, **World 9758**
Freeland: Arise 9561
Friday Harbor: San Juan 9714
Garfield: Rider 9707
Gig Harbor: Elvins 9607, Russell 9713
Goldendale: Grow 9627, His 9635
Greenbank: Ulmschneider 9739
Hoquiam: Grays 9624
Issaquah: College 9594, Costco 9601, Sewell 9723
Kapowsin: McCleary 9670
Kenmore: Padelford 9694, Welch 9752
Kennewick: Richardson 9706
Kent: Kent 9652
Lacey: Community 9598
Lakewood: Clover 9592
Langley: George 9622
Longview: Lower 9664
Medina: Jordan 9645, Lochland 9663
Montesano: George 9621, Kelsey 9651
Mount Vernon: Frets 9617, Pace 9692
Oak Harbor: Rural 9711
Okanogan: Hamilton 9630
Olympia: Evergreen 9609
Pasco: Benton-Franklin 9570
Port Angeles: G.M.L. 9619, Walkling 9745
Port Ludlow: Wills 9754
Port Orchard: Kelly 9650, King 9653, Lundberg 9665
Port Townsend: Centrum 9583, W & G 9743
Prescott: **Vista 9742**
Pullman: Community 9597
Puyallup: KLQ 9655
Quincy: Gius 9623

Redmond: CHEMCENTRAL 9585, **Foundation 9614**, Hopelink 9638
Renton: Providence 9704, Renton 9705
Republic: Arnsberg 9563
Richland: Allied 9558, Three 9735, VanHoff 9741
Ritzville: Ritzville 9708
Rollingbay: **Bainbridge 9566**, Chevelle 9586
Seattle: 911 9554, AGC 9555, Alaska 9556, Alliance 9557, Allied 9559, Artist 9564, Behnke 9568, Bishop 9571, Blakemore 9572, Blue 9573, Bradshaw 9577, **Bullitt 9578**, Central 9582, Children's 9588, Davis 9603, Daystar 9605, Fisher 9613, **Fred 9616**, **Friends 9618**, Grimm 9625, Group 9626, Heily 9633, Hugo 9639, Hunter 9640, **Jain 9641**, **Jewish 9643**, **Ji 9644**, Kawabe 9647, Kelly 9649, Leavitt 9659, Legal 9660, Lifelong 9661, Lynden 9666, Market 9667, Maxwell 9669, Nikkei 9682, North 9683, Northwest 9684, Northwest 9685, Northwest 9686, Northwest 9687, Pacific 9693, PEMCO 9697, Pioneer 9699, Plum 9700, Potlatch 9701, Pride 9702, **Rotalia 9709**, Royston 9710, Seattle 9717, Seattle 9718, Seattle 9719, Seattle 9720, Sigourney 9724, Skagit 9725, Society 9729, Straw 9733, Treehouse 9736, Tudor 9737, Wales 9744, Washington 9747, Windermere 9755, Young 9762
Sequim: Haller 9629, Littlejohn 9662, Sequim 9722
Shelton: Hanna 9631
Silverdale: Kitsap 9654
South Bend: Fergason 9611
Spokane: Career 9580, Clarke 9591, Educational 9606, Family 9610, Hansen 9632, Herriges 9634, Nelson 9681, Schumacher 9716, Second 9721, Spokane 9731, Women 9757
Spokane Valley: Spokane 9730
Tacoma: ARK 9562, DaVita 9604, Franciscan 9615, KT Family 9656, McFarland 9672, Memorial 9674, Metropolitan 9675, Museum 9678, Palmer 9696, Tacoma 9734
Toppenish: Yakima 9760
Tukwila: BECU 9567
Tumwater: Washington 9749
Vancouver: Clark 9590, Community 9599, Hall 9628, Holliday 9636, **Native 9680**, Omega 9688, Slaid 9727, Vancouver 9740
Vashon: Clancy 9589
Walla Walla: Blue 9574, Milton 9676, National 9679, Welch 9751
Wenatchee: Chelan-Douglas 9584, Community 9600, SkillSource 9726, Washington 9746, Wenatchee 9753
Wilbur: Tufts 9738
Woodenville: Bohnett 9575
Woodinville: JTM 9646
Woodland: Colf 9593
Yakima: McCoy 9671, Osteopathic 9690, Washington 9748
Yelm: Yelm 9761

see also 111, 362, 365, 610, 695, 850, 1265, 1494, 2031, 2247, 2339, 2552, 5777, 6589, 6609, 6620, 6751, 6772, 6922, 7024, 7189, 7567, 7583, 7584, 7612, 7619, 7620, 7624, 7649, 7652, 7656, 7670, 7671, 7686, 7988, 8118, 8687, 8704, 8723, 8800, 8850, 8885, 8898, 8961, 8963, 8971, 8973, 9024, 9027, 9134, 9154, 9204

WEST VIRGINIA

Aurora: Aurora 9765
Barboursville: Family 9783
Beckley: Beckley 9766, Raleigh 9813, Vecellio 9826, Workforce 9830
Bluefield: Bowen 9768, Castrodale 9773, Community 9777, Cruise 9779, Morgan 9803, Pais 9807, Princeton 9812, Stump 9820, Wolfe 9829
Bridgeport: Timms 9823

Bruceton Mills: Mountaintop 9804
Capon Bridge: Matthews 9799
Charles Town: McCormick 9801
Charleston: Carter 9772, Emerich 9781, Feoppel 9785, Haddad 9787, Kanawha 9794, Minor 9802, Price 9811, Starcher 9816, West Virginia 9827
Clarksburg: Burnside 9769, Hollandsworth 9791
Fairmont: Fairmont 9782
Gilbert: Harless 9788
Hinton: Hinton 9790
Huntington: Arthur's 9764, Big 9767, Price 9810, Smith 9815, United 9825
Logan: Logan 9797
Martinsburg: City 9775, Eastern 9780
Montgomery: Tech 9822
Morgantown: Canady 9771, I.O.O.F. 9792, Your 9831
Paden City: Paden 9806
Parkersburg: Camden-Clark 9770, Gault 9786, Harries 9789, Parkersburg 9808, Stout 9819
Parsons: Tucker 9824
Princeton: Powell 9809
Ranson: Jefferson 9793
Romney: Stickley 9817
Shady Springs: Whittaker 9828
Summersville: Nicholas 9805
Wardensville: Ludwig 9798
Weirton: Serra 9814
Weston: Sun 9821
Wheeling: Adams 9763, Chambers 9774, Community 9776, Craig 9778, Faris, 9784, Larsen 9795, Laughlin 9796, McCamic 9800, Stifel 9818

see also 1725, 2036, 2076, 2420, 2461, 2481, 2500, 2838, 2852, 2874, 2937, 3556, 3588, 3595, 3600, 3932, 4884, 4934, 6557, 6830, 6890, 7231, 7232, 7353, 7813, 8061, 8104, 8765, 9313, 10048

WISCONSIN

Appleton: Prader-Willi 9997, St. Elizabeth 10044, St. John 10045, Women's 10085
Arbor Vitae: Michelson 9969
Athelstane: Sharp 10030
Baraboo: Sauey 10018
Beloit: Frautschy 9897, Lyons 9953, Stateline 10047
Berlin: Community 9870
Black River Falls: Black River 9849
Bloomer: Mitchell 9972
Brillion: Ariens 9838, Brillion 9852
Brookfield: **Funeral 9903**, Siebert 10033, Wisconsin 10078
Brownsville: Michels 9968
Burlington: Aber 9832, Smith 10036, Zweibel 10093
Cassville: Grimm 9912
Chetek: Chetek 9862
Chilton: Calumet 9856, Norbert 9985, Schwarz 10024
Chippewa Falls: Rutledge 10016
Clintonville: Four 9896
Cumberland: Johnson 9932
Darlington: Johnson 9935
Dousman: Wisconsin 10079
Eau Claire: Carlisle 9858, Fricke 9899, Peterson 9992
Elkhorn: Squires 10042
Elm Grove: Pagel 9990
Evansville: Heffel 9918
Fond du Lac: Fond du Lac 9893
Fond Du Lac: Giddings 9906
Fond du Lac: Robins 10012
Fontana: Environmental 9885
Fort Atkinson: Fort 9894, **National 9978**
Glendale: **Johnson 9934**
Glenwood City: West 10069
Grafton: Exacto 9886, Grafton 9909

Green Bay: Aslakson 9840, Associated 9841, Fenner 9890, Gallmeier 9904, Green Bay 9910, Green Bay 9911, Hemophilia 9919, Praiss 9998, Shopko 10032, Wagner 10060, Ward 10063, Wisconsin 10081

Hartland: Tate 10050

Hudson: Anu 9837, St. Croix 10043

Janesville: Community 9869, Healthnet 9917

Juneau: Noer 9984

Kenosha: Bruneo 9854, Kenosha 9941, Kenosha 9942

Kiel: SBC 10020

Kohler: Kohler 9945

La Crosse: Cuan 9874, Gundersen 9913, La Crosse 9948, Women's 10086

Ladysmith: Indianhead 9926

Lake Mills: Carnes 9859

Madison: Community 9865, Eggen 9882, Elfers 9883, **Entomological 9884**, Freedom 9898, Fund 9902, Hasselhofer-Wolf 9916, Jewish 9931, Korupp 9947, Lauterbach 9950, MacPherson 9954, Madison 9955, Madison 9956, Markos 9959, Mentzer 9966, **National 9977**, Nishan 9983, Project 10000, Sand 10017, Shafer 10028, Sivyer 10034, Walker 10062, Wisconsin 10074, Wisconsin 10075, Wisconsin 10080, Wisconsin 10082, Wisconsin 10083, Wisconsin 10084

Manitowoc: Society 10038

Marathon: Goldbach 9907, Marth 9961, Sonnentag 10039

Marinette: Fernstrum 9891

Markesan: Badger 9844, Badger 9845

Marshfield: Connor 9872, Marshfield 9960

Mayville: Bachhuber 9842

Medford: Porhaska 9996, Prohaska 9999, Schield 10021, Weather 10066

Menomonee Falls: Kohl's 9946

Menomonie: Community 9867

Mequon: Pieper 9995

Middleton: Leitzell 9952, University 10055

Milwaukee: American 9834, Askren 9839, Backlin 9843, Beal 9846, Birbeck 9848, Boer 9850, Brown 9853, Casper 9860, Catholic 9861, Collins 9864, Davey 9876, Fahrney 9888, Feeding 9889, Foundation 9895, **Friends 9900**, Fromm 9901, Graef 9908, Hale 9914, Hamp 9915, Hodes 9922, Holt 9923, Hood 9924, International 9927, Jacobus 9928, Jansen 9929, Jewish 9930, Johnson 9933, Jones 9936, Kelben 9938, Keller 9939, Keller 9940, Kohl 9944, ManpowerGroup

9957, Martin 9962, Melissa 9964, Metzner 9967, Milwaukee 9970, Milwaukee 9971, MMAC 9973, Moore 9974, Nelson 9979, Nicholl 9981, O'Hara 9986, Oilgear 9987, Partners 9991, Phillips 9994, Rexnord 10007, Richards 10009, Rolfs 10013, Rotary 10014, Ruebush 10015, Scoliosis 10025, Select 10026, Shallow 10029, Sheets 10031, Smith 10035, **Society 10037**, Spartvedt 10041, Stamm 10046, Stifel 10048, Suder 10049, Tschirgi 10054, Vedova 10058, Weigel 10067, Wells 10068, Wiegand 10071, Wilber 10072, Women's 10087, Young 10091, Zebro 10092

Minocqua: Lakeland 9949

Monona: WPS 10088

Neenah: Hilgen 9921, Kallies 9937, Menasha 9965, Munster 9976, Raether 10003, Scholarship 10022

New Glarus: New Glarus 9980

Oak Creek: Yakich 10089

Oconomowoc: Bruno 9855, Ramiah 10004, Wisconsin 10076

Onalaska: Mullenbach 9975

Oneida: Laviolette 9951

Oshkosh: **EAA 9880**, Experimental 9887, Mari's 9958, Oshkosh 9988, Oshkosh 9989

Pewaukee: Waukesha 10065

Phillips: AnnMarie 9836, Phillips 9993

Platteville: Southwest 10040

Racine: Racine 10001, Racine 10002, Schulte 10023

Rhinelander: Nicolet 9982, Redfield 10005

River Falls: University 10056

Seymour: Seymour 10027

Sheboygan: Eckburg 9881

Sheboygan Falls: Bemis 9847

Shell Lake: Wisconsin 10077

Sparta: Dupee 9879

Stevens Point: CAP 9857, Community 9866, Compass 9871

Stoughton: Wahlin 10061

Sturgeon Bay: Door 9878

Sussex: Henrizi 9920, Windhover 10073

Tomah: Fix 9892, Tomah 10052

Verona: AgSource 9833

Viroqua: Viroqua 10059

Waterloo: Trek 10053

Watertown: Darcey 9875, Watertown 10064

Waukesha: DeLong 9877, Kern 9943, **Riesch 10010**

Waupaca: Rhodes 10008

Wausau: American 9835, Community 9868, Remington 10006

Wausaukee: Thomas 10051

Wauwatosa: Briggs 9851

West Allis: Chmielewski 9863, Meehan 9963, Wetenkamp 10070

West Baraboo: Sauk 10019

West Bend: Gehl 9905

Westby: Couleecap 9873

Whitewater: UW 10057

Wisconsin Rapids: Incourage 9925, Riverview 10011

Woodruff: Young 10090

see also 135, 1020, 1520, 1945, 2034, 2036, 2247, 2361, 2412, 2449, 2456, 2552, 2560, 2578, 2591, 2611, 2653, 2661, 2666, 2677, 2686, 2731, 2757, 2777, 2785, 2803, 2832, 2891, 2909, 2915, 2916, 2917, 2922, 2943, 3179, 3251, 3813, 4302, 4408, 4521, 4683, 4694, 4729, 4731, 4737, 4779, 4810, 4841, 4847, 4851, 4859, 4884, 6665, 7334, 7931, 8014, 8799, 9021

WYOMING

Buffalo: Clark 10097, Johnson 10108, Laing 10109, Littler 10113, Williams 10125

Casper: True 10122

Cheyenne: Construction 10100, Davis 10102, Doherty 10103, Pearson 10116, SouthEast 10120

Clearmont: **Ucross 10123**

Cody: Cody 10098

Dubois: Anderson 10094

Gillette: Hladky 10107, Milne 10114

Jackson: Community 10099, Giovanini 10105, Neilson 10115

Laramie: Wyoming 10126

Lusk: Spacht 10121

Pine Bluffs: Gillet 10104

Ranchester: Curtis 10101

Sheridan: Bryan 10095, LaRue 10110, Perkins 10117, Pilch 10118, Sheridan 10119, Whitney 10124

Teton Village: Glassber 10106

Torrington: Likins 10111, Likins-Masonic 10112

Wilson: Christian 10096

see also 701, 1177, 1196, 1206, 1224, 1272, 1273, 1494, 4934, 5131, 8045, 8537, 8774, 9640, 9659, 10017

INTERNATIONAL GIVING INDEX

List of terms: The names of countries, continents, or regions used in this index are drawn from the complete list below. Terms may appear on the list but not be present in the index.

Index: In the index itself, grantmakers are listed under the countries, continents, or regions in which they have demonstrated giving interests. Within these country or regional groupings, grantmakers are arranged by sequence number. This index indicates support going directly overseas; to learn more about the international interests of grantmakers, see the Subject Index for more information.

Afghanistan
Africa
Albania
Algeria
Andorra
Angola
Anguilla
Antarctica
Antigua & Barbuda
Arctic Region
Argentina
Armenia
Aruba
Asia
Australia
Austria
Azerbaijan
Bahamas
Bahrain
Balkans, The
Bangladesh
Barbados
Belarus
Belgium
Belize
Benin
Bermuda
Bhutan
Bolivia
Bonaire
Bosnia-Herzegovina
Botswana
Brazil
British Virgin Islands
Brunei
Bulgaria
Burkina Faso
Burma (Myanmar)
Burundi
Cambodia
Cameroon
Canada
Cape Verde
Caribbean
Cayman Islands
Central Africa
Central Africa Republic
Central America

Central Asia and the Caucasus
Chad
Chile
China
Colombia
Commonwealth of the Northern
    Mariana Islands
Comoros
Congo
Costa Rica
Croatia
Cuba
Curacao
Cyprus
Czech Republic
Democratic Republic of the Congo
Denmark
Developing countries
Djibouti
Dominica
Dominican Republic
East Africa/Horn of Africa
East Asia
East Jerusalem
East Timor
Eastern & Central Europe
Ecuador
Egypt
El Salvador
England
Equatorial Guinea
Eritrea
Estonia
Ethiopia
Europe
Federated States of Micronesia
Fiji
Finland
France
French Guiana
Gabon
Gambia
Georgia (Republic of)
Germany
Ghana
Gibraltar
Global programs
Greater Antilles

Greece
Greenland
Grenada
Guadeloupe
Guatemala
Guernsey
Guinea
Guinea-Bissau
Guyana
Haiti
Honduras
Hong Kong
Hungary
Iceland
India
Indonesia
Iran
Iraq
Ireland
Isle of Man
Israel
Italy
Ivory Coast
Jamaica
Japan
Jersey
Jordan
Kazakhstan
Kenya
Kiribati
Kosovo
Kuwait
Kyrgyzstan
Laos
Latin America
Latvia
Lebanon
Leeward Islands
Lesotho
Lesser Antilles
Liberia
Libya
Liechtenstein
Lithuania
Luxembourg
Macau
Macedonia
Madagascar

Malawi
Malaysia
Maldives
Mali
Malta
Marshall Islands
Martinique
Mauritania
Mauritius
Mexico
Middle East
Moldova
Monaco
Mongolia
Montenegro
Montserrat
Morocco and the Western Sahara
Mozambique
Namibia
Nauru
Nepal
Netherlands
Netherlands Antilles
New Caledonia
New Zealand
Nicaragua
Niger
Nigeria
North Korea
North Africa
Northern Ireland
Norway
Oceania
Oman
Pakistan
Palau
Panama
Papua New Guinea
Paraguay
Peru
Philippines
Poland
Portugal
Qatar
Romania
Russia
Rwanda
Saint Kitts-Nevis

Saint Lucia
Saint Vincent & the Grenadines
Samoa
Sao Tome and Principe
Saudi Arabia
Scandinavia
Scotland
Senegal
Serbia
Seychelles
Sierra Leone
Singapore
Slovakia
Slovenia
Solomon Islands
Somalia, Somaliland and Puntland

South Africa
South America
South Asia
South Korea
South Sudan
Southeast Asia
Southern Africa
Soviet Union (Former)
Spain
Sri Lanka
Sub-Saharan Africa
Sudan
Suriname
Swaziland
Sweden
Switzerland

Syria
Tahiti
Taiwan
Tajikistan
Tanzania, Zanzibar and Pemba
Thailand
Togo
Tonga
Trinidad & Tobago
Tunisia
Turkey
Turkmenistan
Turks & Caicos Islands
Tuvalu
Uganda
Ukraine

United Arab Emirates
United Kingdom
Uruguay
Uzbekistan
Vanuatu
Vatican City
Venezuela
Vietnam
Wales
West Bank/Gaza
Western Africa
Windward Islands
Yemen
Yugoslavia (Former)
Zambia
Zimbabwe

Africa
California: Leakey 739
District of Columbia: Accordia 1531,
   International 1656
Florida: Joshua 1932
New Jersey: Croatian 5430, Ostberg
   5533
New York: Studio 6441, Wildlife 6520

Albania
New York: American 5692

Algeria
District of Columbia: Arab 1576

Armenia
Michigan: Evereg-Fenesse 4414
New Jersey: Tavitian 5576
Pennsylvania: Arpajian 7714
Rhode Island: Boghossian 8247,
   Holopigian 8310

Asia
New York: Asia 5733, CEC 5829, Luce
   6175, Metropolitan 6211, Wildlife
   6520
Texas: MCH 8946, Media 8950
Washington: Blakemore 9572

Australia
California: 18th 330
Florida: Samstag 2048
Utah: James 9211

Bahamas
Florida: Jacob 1928, Prime 2025

Belgium
Ohio: Lapeer 7204

Belize
California: Foundation 589

Bosnia and Herzegovina
California: Croatian 528
New Jersey: Croatian 5430

Brazil
Missouri: Boys 4942
Nevada: A Charitable 5278
Texas: Limiar 8918

Bulgaria
Massachusetts: American 3966
New York: American 5692

Canada
California: A-T 391
Illinois: American 2389
Michigan: Society 4611
New Hampshire: Fond 5321
New Jersey: New 5524
New York: Alliance 5682, Kosciuszko
   6145, Legacy 6158
North Carolina: Morehead-Cain 6778
Pennsylvania: Association 7717,
   Association 7718
Rhode Island: Dorot 8286
Texas: Kimberly 8906
Virginia: Plumbing 9483
Wisconsin: MacPherson 9954

Central America
California: Foundation 589
Massachusetts: Maya 4170
New Jersey: Croatian 5430
Vermont: Ohiyesa 9256

Chile
California: Avery 395

China
California: Alalusi 345, Avery 395, China
   492, Chinese 493, SKB 991
New York: American 5692, Peace 6309
Ohio: Oberlin 7276
Pennsylvania: Chinese 7766
Utah: WTF 9234

Costa Rica
California: A-T 391
Texas: Interdenominational 8894

Croatia
California: Croatian 527, Croatian 528
New Jersey: Croatian 5430
Pennsylvania: Croatian 7798

Cuba
Florida: Cintas 1828

Czech Republic
New York: American 5692

Denmark
Washington: Northwest 9684

Developing Countries
California: Rivendell 912
District of Columbia: Aga 1533
Massachusetts: International 4127
New York: Wenner 6511
Virginia: Operation 9473

Eastern Europe
California: 18th 330, Getty 614
District of Columbia: German 1638
Massachusetts: International 4127
New Jersey: Tavitian 5576
New York: American 5692, CEC 5829
Texas: Media 8950
Washington: Rotalia 9709

Ecuador
California: Cloud 503

El Salvador
California: Foundation 589

England
California: Gorecki 632
Connecticut: Folsom 1390
North Carolina: Morehead-Cain 6778

Estonia
Florida: Joshua 1932
New York: American 5692
Washington: Rotalia 9709

Europe
California: Getty 614
District of Columbia: German 1638
Illinois: Society 2863
Massachusetts: Beebe 3980
New Jersey: Ostberg 5533
New York: CEC 5829, Legacy 6158
Pennsylvania: AO 7707
Texas: Media 8950, Western 9164
Utah: Sundance 9227

France
District of Columbia: German 1638
Florida: Atlantic 1787
Illinois: Terra 2889
New Hampshire: Fond 5321
New York: French 6009, Lower 6173,
   Lurcy 6176, Metropolitan 6211,
   Pasteur 6306, Philippe 6316,
   Societe 6410
North Carolina: Institut 6711
Ohio: Lapeer 7204
Pennsylvania: French 7858
Texas: Western 9164
Virginia: Dornhecker 9363

Germany
California: Allgemeiner 346
Connecticut: Folsom 1390
District of Columbia: German 1638,
   International 1656
Maryland: German 3833
New York: American 5687, Metropolitan
   6211, Opera 6297

Global Programs
California: 18th 330
District of Columbia: Patterson 1710
Kansas: Davis 3431
Maryland: Aplastic 3774
Mississippi: Dunnaway 4905
New York: Art 5721, Corporation 5888,
   Myasthenia 6234
North Carolina: Environmental 6649

Greece
Massachusetts: Gerondelis 4082
New York: Metropolitan 6211,
  Mycenaean 6235, New York 6268,
  Society 6413
North Carolina: Evrytanian 6651
Pennsylvania: Institute 7919, Pan 8018
Rhode Island: Christy 8257, Pappines
  8365

Guatemala
California: Foundation 589
Massachusetts: Maya 4170
Missouri: Boys 4942

Haiti
Florida: Toussant 2088
New Jersey: Croatian 5430, Ostberg
  5533

Honduras
California: Foundation 589

Hong Kong
Utah: James 9211

Hungary
District of Columbia: German 1638
Florida: Joshua 1932
New Jersey: American 5384, Terplan
  5577
New York: American 5692

India
California: Gala 608
Connecticut: Scudder 1458
Illinois: American 2378
New Jersey: Mahajan 5501
Ohio: Oberlin 7276

Indonesia
New York: HASTAGA 6059
Ohio: Oberlin 7276

Iran
Florida: Momeni 1981
New Jersey: Houton 5474

Ireland
New York: American 5693
North Carolina: Morehead-Cain 6778

Israel
California: American 353, A-T 391,
  Jewish 707
New York: America-Israel 5686,
  American 5693, Chesed 5844, Ezer
  5971, Friends 6012, General 6019,
  Keren 6135, Keren 6136, Legacy
  6158, Matz 6196
Rhode Island: Dorot 8286

Italy
California: A-T 391, Johnson 712
Connecticut: DiMauro 1377

District of Columbia: German 1638,
  National 1693, Sons 1732
Florida: Atlantic 1787, Operafestival
  2005
New York: Dante 5913, Delmas 5921,
  Fermi 5981, Foundation 5998,
  Metropolitan 6211, New York 6268,
  Opera 6297
Ohio: Italian 7171
Tennessee: Thomley 8654

Jamaica
Florida: Horizons 1922

Japan
California: California 453
District of Columbia: International 1656
Florida: Atlantic 1787
Hawaii: Sakumoto 2319
New York: Asian 5734, Peace 6309,
  Social 6409
Ohio: Oberlin 7276
Utah: Sundance 9227

Jordan
California: American 353

Laos
California: McConnell 779

Latin America
New York: Rainforest 6343, Wildlife
  6520

Latvia
Arizona: Kahvush 206
California: Eglitis 554
New York: American 5692

Libya
California: American 353

Lithuania
Illinois: Lithuanian 2695
New York: American 5692

Macedonia
New York: Society 6413

Mexico
California: Carreon 465, Foundation
  589, Hager 643, Johnson 712,
  Ramona's 896
Florida: Atlantic 1787
Illinois: American 2389
Massachusetts: Maya 4170
Minnesota: Gallagher 4746
Missouri: Boys 4942
New York: Wildlife 6520
Pennsylvania: Webber 8179, Webber
  8180
Utah: James 9211

Middle East
District of Columbia: Arab 1576

Morocco
District of Columbia: Arab 1576

Nepal
California: McConnell 779, Nepal 824

Netherlands
California: A-T 391
New York: Netherland-America 6258

New Zealand
New York: Commonwealth 5872

Northern Africa
District of Columbia: Arab 1576

Norway
New York: Norwegian 6289
South Dakota: Sioux Falls 8538

Peru
Missouri: Boys 4942

Poland
California: Gorecki 632
District of Columbia: German 1638
Minnesota: Proshek 4830
New Jersey: Johnson 5482
New York: American 5692, Kosciuszko
  6145
Pennsylvania: Polish 8053

Portugal
District of Columbia: German 1638
Rhode Island: Fundacao 8296

Romania
New Jersey: People 5538
New York: American 5692

Russia
California: Trustees 1061
New York: CEC 5829, Malevich 6185,
  Russian 6366

Scotland
Colorado: Clan 1148
New Hampshire: Scots' 5367

Serbia
Illinois: Serbian 2848

Singapore
New York: National 6251

Slovakia
Minnesota: Proshek 4830
New York: American 5692

South Africa
California: Colonnades 507
Minnesota: Gallagher 4746
Virginia: Brockbank 9328

South America
New York: Russian 6366

South Korea
New Jersey: DRC 5436

Southeastern Asia
California: 18th 330

Spain
District of Columbia: German 1638
Massachusetts: Real 4239

Sub-Saharan Africa
District of Columbia: Accordia 1531

Sweden
Illinois: Hertz 2615
New York: Wallenberg 6499

Switzerland
Illinois: Swiss 2884

Syria
California: American 353

Taiwan
California: 18th 330, SKB 991

Turkey
California: A-T 391
District of Columbia: Institute 1651
Minnesota: Gallagher 4746

Ukraine
Pennsylvania: Kotur 7939

United Kingdom
Massachusetts: British 4000
New York: American 5693, Royal 6364,
  St. George's 6425
North Carolina: Keasbey 6727

Wales
North Carolina: Morehead-Cain 6778

**West Bank/Gaza (Palestinian
Territories)**
California: American 353

Yugoslavia
California: Studenica 1029
Minnesota: Proshek 4830

New York: American 5692

COMPANY NAME INDEX

The numbers following the company names in this index refer to the sequence numbers of entries in the Descriptive Directory section. The specific companies or corporations listed here provide funding directly to employees, former employees, and families of employees.

84 Lumber Company, 7885

A & E Incorporated, 1945
Abbott Laboratories, 2353
Acme Electric Corporation, 8272
AK Steel Holding Corporation, 6964
Albemarle Corporation, 3640
Alcoa Inc., 7694
Aleut Corporation, 103
AMCOL International Corporation, 2416
American Electric Power Company, Inc., 6971
American International Group, Inc., 5675
American National Bank, 3182
American Optical Corporation, 3968
American Sterilizer Company, 7116
American Thread Company, 2242
Amtrak, 6893, 6927
Arch Coal, Inc., 4934
Arkema Inc., 7709
Armstrong World Industries, Inc., 7711
Arnold Industries, Inc., 6790
Arthur's Enterprises, Inc., 9764
Associated Banc-Corp, 9841
Asten Group, Incorporated, 7907
AT&T Inc., 8695
Atlantic Marine, Incorporated, 33
Atmos Energy Corporation, 8617
Autobahn Imports, Inc., 9060
Avondale Mills, Inc., 8478

Badger Mining Corporation, 9844
Bank of America National Trust and Savings Association, 8838
Bank of America, N.A., 9105
Bank of Stockton, 398
BankSouth, 2124
Baptist Hospital, Incorporated, 1791
Barnes Group Inc., 1330
Bay Alarm Company, 1091
Beall's, Inc., 1794, 1795
Beneficial Corporation, 1498
Berk-Tek, Incorporated, 7739
Berkel & Co. Contractors, Inc., 3525
Berkowitz, L.P., J. E., 5397
Biomet, Inc., 3018
Block Communications, Inc., 6999
Bloomsburg Mills Incorporated, 8181
Boeing Company, 4986
BoMarko, 4504
Boston Scientific Corporation, 3996
Branch Banking and Trust Company, 6564
Briggs & Stratton Corporation, 9851
Brown Brothers Harriman & Co., The, 5800
Brunswick Corporation, 2443
Burger King Holdings, Inc., 9331
Burlington Industries, Incorporated, 6587
Butler Manufacturing Company, 4948

Cacique, Inc., 434
Calvi Electric Company, 5409

Carauster Industries, Incorporated, 6673
Carlson Company, Inc., Fred, 3252
Central National Gottesman Division, 5836
Chase Oil Corporation, 5621
CHEMCENTRAL Corporation, 9585
Chenega Corporation, 109
Chicago White Metal Casting Company, Inc., 2476
Chick-fil-A, Inc., 2139
Choice Hotels International, Inc., 3802
Citizens Bank New Hampshire, 8225
CNA Financial Corporation, 2484
Coats American, Inc., 6607
Comcast Corporation, 7777
Conn Appliances, Incorporated, 8766
Conrail, 6893, 6927
Consolidated Container Company LLC, 1369
Consolidated Systems, Inc., 6770
Continental Airlines, Inc., 2498
Corvallis Clinic, P.C., The, 7558
Costco Wholesale Corporation, 9601
Cox Wood Preserving, 8468
Cracker Barrel Old Country Store, Inc., 8581
Cranston Print Works Company, 8275
Creamer Bros., Incorporated, 5429
Crescent Real Estate Equities Company, 8775
CSS Industries, Inc., 7837
Curves International, Inc., 8863
CVS Caremark Corporation, 8282

Daiwa Securities America Inc., 5909
Dana Corporation, 4402
Danis Building Construction Company, 7077
Davidson Pipe Supply Co., Incorporated, 5916
DaVita HealthCare Partners Inc., 9604
Des Moines Golf and Country Club, 3273
Disney Company, Walt, The, 540
Dixie Group, Incorporated, The, 8582
Domino's Pizza, Inc., 4409
Dow Chemical Company, The, 4410

East Cambridge Savings Bank, 4050
Eastman Chemical Company, 8589
Emerson Electric Company, 4985
Entergy Corporation, 3651
Ethan Allen, 6131

Fabri-Kal Corporation, 4416
Farmers and Merchants Trust Company of Chambersburg, 7834
Farmers Union Marketing & Processing Association, 4737
First Merchants Bank, 3182
Flint Association of Plumbing and Mechanical Contractors, Inc., 4602
Fluor Corporation, 8824
Follett Corporation, 2565
Ford Motor Company, 4647
Franklin Electric Company, Inc., 3037
Fulton Financial Corporation, 7863

Gannett Company, Inc., 7037
GEICO, 9359
General Motors Company, 4648
Giddings and Lewis, 9906
Golub Corporation, 6327
Goulds Pumps, Incorporated, 8301, 8356
Grinnell Mutual Reinsurance Company, 3290
Groeniger & Co., 639
GSM Industrial, Inc., 7876
Guardian Industries, 4452
Guardian Life Insurance Company of America, The, 6128

Halton Co., 7584
Hard Rock Cafe International, Inc., 1902
Harden Furniture Company, 6057
Health Management Associates, Inc., 1916
Heffernan Insurance Brokers, 654
Holcim (US), Inc., 4309
Homecrest Industries, Inc., 4701
Honors Course, Incorporated, The, 8561
Hood LLC, HP, 4111
Hooker Furniture Corporation, 9398
Horix Manufacturing Company, 7104
Houghton Mifflin Harcourt Publishing Company, 4115
Howard Miller Clock Company, 4543

IDACORP, Inc., 2334
Imperial Bondware, 1766
Independence Bank, 3578
Inman Mills, 8486
Interlock Industries, Inc., 3593
ITT Corporation, 2590

J. Fletcher Creamer & Son, Incorporated, 5429
J.C. Steele & Sons, Incorporated, 6878
Jack in the Box, Incorporated, 699
John Henry Company, 1911
Johns Manville Corporation, 1223
Johnson Controls, Inc., 9933
Johnston Textiles, Inc., 82
Jostens, Inc., 4774
Journal Publishing Company, 7591
JPMorgan Chase & Co., 1521

Kellogg Company, 4496
Kelly Tractor Company, 1935
Keystone Foods Corporation, 7756
Kimball International, Inc., 3086
Kimberly-Clark Corporation, 8906
Kingsbury Corporation, 8322
Koch Enterprises, Inc., 3089
Koch Industries, Inc., 3477
KPMG LLP, 5492

Lakewood Engineering Equipment Company, Incorporated, 4778
Lee Industries, Inc., 6739
Lexington Furniture Industries, 6632

Lexmark International, Inc., 3589
Lockheed Martin Corporation, 8921
Lockheed Martin Missiles and Fire Control, 8922
Longue Vue Club, 8117

Major League Baseball, 5754
Manitou Americas, Inc, 9905
ManpowerGroup Inc., 9957
Martin Marietta Corporation, 6192
MasterCard Incorporated, 6195
Maysteel Corporation, 10035
Medline Industries, Inc., 2729
Menasha Corporation, 9965
Meriden Record Journal, 8344
Midmark Corporation, 7246
Miller Cable, 7986
Miller Pipeline, 7986
Mitsui & Co. (U.S.A.), Inc., 6219
MN Airlines, LLC, 4863
Murphy Oil Corporation, 296

National Lime and Stone Company, 7288
National Presto Industries, Incorporated, 1520
NCR Corporation, 2215
Needham & Company, LLC, 6257
Nevada Bell, 7940
New Hampshire Retail Grocers Assn. member food
    stores, 5354
New York City Police Department, 2422, 6267
Nexion Health, Inc., 3902
Nikon Inc., 6406
Nordic Group of Companies, Ltd., 10018
Northwest Bancorp, MHC, 8013
Nucor Corporation, 6803
Numerica Financial Corp., 8225

Oilgear Company, The, 9987
Orscheln Group, 5068

PACCAR, Incorporated, 9698
Pacific Bell, 7940
Pacific Northwest Bell, 7940
Papa John's International, Inc., 3611
Pedernales Electric Cooperative, Inc., 9008
Pella Corporation, 3355
Penn Central Corporation, 6893, 6927
Penn Central Transportation Company, 6893
Penn National Gaming, Inc., 8022
Penney Company, Inc., J. C., 9010
Pennsylvania Automotive Recycling Trade Society
    (PARTS), 8023
Pennsylvania Railroad Company, 6893, 6927

Peterson Industries, Inc., 3503
Pharmaceutical Innovations, Inc., 5406
Philadelphia Gas Works, 8073
Philips Electronics North America Corporation, 4220
Phillips-Medisize Corp., 9993
Phototronics, Incorporated, 1417
Pioneer Natural Resources Company, 9020
PNC Bank, N.A., 8051
Polaris Industries, Inc., 4827
PPG Industries, Inc., 8058
Protective Life Corporation, 72

Quad/Graphics, Inc., 10073
Quaker Chemical Corporation, 8069
QUALCOMM Incorporated, 889

Rayonier Inc., 2031
Raytheon Company, 4238
Reagent Chemical and Research, Incorporated, 5568
Reed Elsevier Inc., 4265
Reed Engineering Group, Inc., 9033
Regions Bank, 33
Reliant Energy Ventures, Incorporated, 8902
Remmele Engineering, Incorporated, 7318
Republic of Tea, The, 2815
Rexnord, LLC, 10007
Rock Bottom Restaurants, Inc., 1269
Rockville Financial, Inc., 1450
Roosevelt County Rural Telephone Cooperative, Inc.,
    5646
Rostra Precision Controls, Inc., 8389
Ryerson Inc., 2839

Scott & Stringfellow, Incorporated, 9500
Sempra Energy, 974
Servco Pacific Inc., 2320
ServiceMaster Company, The, 8642
Shadowline Inc., 6616
Shelter Mutual Insurance Company, 5099
Shopko Stores Operating Co., LLC, 10032
Sierra Pacific Industries, 982
Sigma-Aldrich Corporation, 4944
Signs of Safety, 5429
Simplot Company, J.R., 2349
SMACNA firms, 9506
Small Business Service Bureau, Inc., 4012
Sonoco Products Company, 8510
Southern Company, The, 2238
Southern Union Company, 9088
Southern Wine & Spirits of America, Inc., 2080
Southwest Airlines Co., 9089
Specialized Carriers & Rigging Assoc., 9512

Steinman Enterprises, 8130
Stewart Information Services Corporation, 8930
Stop & Shop Supermarket Company LLC, The, 4260
Strauss & Co., Levi, 903
Sun Lumber Company, Inc., 9821
Sysco Corporation, 9107

Temple-Inland Inc., 8653
Tension Envelope Corporation, 5112
Thomasville Furniture Industries, Inc., 6892
Timken Company, The, 7384
TOSOH Quartz, Inc., 7574
True Oil LLC, 10122
Tyson Foods, Inc., 320

U.S. Borax, Incorporated, 9195
U.S. Customs Service, 6496
Unaka Group (The), 8656
United Conveyor Corporation, 2905
United Telephone Mutual Aid Corporation, 6949
Universal Forest Products, Incorporated, 4653
US Airways Group, Inc., 252
Utica Mutual Insurance Company, 6483

Valero Energy Corporation, 9147
Valspar Corporation, The, 4878
Vang (George), Incorporated, 8161
Visteon Corporation, 4647

W & K Management Corporation, 6142
Wal-Mart Stores, Inc., 325
Walgreen Company, 2913
Washington Corporations, The, 5182
Weather Shield Manufacturing, Inc., 10021, 10066
Wegmans Food Markets, Inc., 6507
West Pharmaceutical Services, Inc., 8188
Whirlpool Corporation, 4666
Williams-Sonoma, Inc., 1096
Wilson (Ralph) Plastics, 9169
Wisconsin Physicians Service Insurance Corporation,
    10088
Wisconsin Public Service Corporation, 10081
Wooster Brush Company, 7114
Wynn's-Precision, Inc., 8633

XL America, 1491

Yancey Brothers, Incorporated, 2109
YSI Incorporated, 7446

SPECIFIC SCHOOL INDEX

The numbers following the school names in this index refer to the sequence numbers of entries in the Descriptive Directory section. The index refers to institutions that give educational support only to the graduates of specific high schools or school districts, or students of specific institutions of higher education.

A&M Consolidated High School, TX , 8693
Abilene Christian University, TX , 9110
Abilene High School, KS , 3491
Abilene High School, TX , 8947
Abington High School, MA , 4218
Acalanes High School, CA , 922
Acalanes Union High School District, CA , 730
Acton Public School System, MA , 8323
Ada County high schools, ID , 2332
Ada-Borup High School, MN , 4680
Adair-Casey High School, IA , 3395
Adams High School, MI , 4395
Adel-Minburn-Desoto High School, IA , 5201
Adena High School, OH , 7034
Adirondack High School, NY , 6485
Afton Central High School, NY , 6381, 6447
Airport High School, SC , 8444
Aitkin High School, MN , 4822
Akins High School, TX , 2836
Alamance Community College, NC , 6546
Alameda county high schools, CA , 858
Alameda Unified School District, CA , 746
Alamo Heights High School, TX , 8874
Alaska high schools, AK , 135
Albany High School, NY , 7211
Albany Law School, NY , 5679
Albia Community High School, IA , 10058
Albia High School, IA , 9974
Albion High School, NY , 5678
Albuquerque High School, NM , 5651
Albuquerque high schools, NM , 5610
Alderson-Broaddus College, WV , 9772
Alexander Central High School, NC , 6744
Alexander High School, OH , 6969
Alexander W. Dreyfoos School of the Arts, FL , 2054
Algoma High School, WI , 9967
Algona Community School District, IA , 8332
All Saints Regional School, PA , 7781
Allegany Central School, NY , 7367
Allegany College, PA , 7428
Alleghany High School, VA , 9390
Allegheny College, PA , 7891
Allen County Community College, KS , 3454
Alliance High School, OH , 7229
Almont School District, MI , 4427
Alta Vista High School, CA , 548
Altavista High School, VA , 9373
Altoona High School, WI , 9882
Alvin High School, TX , 8809
Alvin Independent School District, TX , 8733
Amanda Clearcreek School System, OH , 7157
Amarillo College, TX , 8675
American Academy, Rome, Italy, 6268
American Film Institute, CA , 1098
American River College, CA , 926
American School of Classical Studies, Athens, Greece, 6268
Amesbury High School, MA , 8237
Amundsen High School, IL , 2662
Anaheim High School, CA , 990
Anaheim Union High School District, CA , 363
Anchorage West High School, AK , 97

Ancilla College, IN , 3069, 4504
Anderson University, IN , 3069
Andover High School, MA , 3970
Andrew Hill High School, CA , 987
Andrews High School, SC , 8502
Anoka-Hennepin Independent School District No. 11, MN , 4868
Antelope Valley College, CA , 735
Antioch Senior High School, CA , 4578
Antwerp High School, OH , 7403
Antwerp School District, OH , 7293
Appalachian Bible College, WV , 9772
Apple Valley High School, MN , 2226
Appleton High School East, WI , 2686, 2731
Appleton High School West, WI , 2686
Aquinas College, MI , 4445
Aquinas High School, NE , 5269
Aransas Pass Independent School District, TX , 8756
Archbishop Carroll Catholic High School, FL , 2030
Archbishop Ryan High School, PA , 8111
Argos High School, IN , 3142
Argos School Corp., IN , 4504
Arizona State University, AZ , 157, 2890
Arkansas High School, AR , 281
Arkansas State University, Mountain Home, AR , 303
Arkansas Tech University - Ozark, AR , 309
Arkansas Tech University, AR , 310
Arlington High School, NY , 5753
Arlington Memorial High School, VT , 9235
Armada School District, MI , 4427
Armstrong Atlantic State University, GA , 2132
Arp High School, TX , 8948
Arsenal Technical High School, IN , 2959
Art Academy of Ohio- Cincinnati, OH , 6954
Artesia High School, NM , 5621
Arthur Community School District, IL , 2531
Arthur High School, MI , 4591
Asbury Theological Seminary, KY , 3570
Ascension Parish schools, LA , 3643
Asheboro High School, NC , 6894
Asheville High School, NC , 6562
Asheville-Buncombe Community College, NC , 6864
Asheville-Buncombe Technical Community College, NC , 6563
Ashland County high schools, MA , 4248
Ashland County high schools, OH , 6980
Ashland High School, MA , 4311, 8431
Ashtabula High School, OH , 7005
Ashton High School, IL , 2733
Aspen High School, CO , 1195
Astoria High School, IL , 2734
Astoria School District, OR , 7535
Atascadero High School, CA , 6742
Atchinson County public high schools, MO , 4938
Athens College, Greece, 8168
Athens Drive High School, NC , 6926
Atlantic City High School, NJ , 6695
Atlantic City public schools, NJ , 5544
Atlantic County high schools, NJ , 5393
Atlantic County vocational schools, NJ , 5544
Attica School District, IN , 3222
Atwater High School, CA , 1106

Atwood-Hammond High School, IL , 2424
Auburn Adventist Academy, WA , 9662
Auburn School District, NY , 8266
Auburn University, AL , 81, 2247
Audubon High School, NJ , 7905
Augustana College, IL , 2395
Austin Area School District, PA , 7974
Austin High School, TX , 2836
Avon High School, MA , 4161, 4171
Avondale High School, MI , 4341, 4395, 4528

Babylon high schools, NY , 5746
Baca County public high schools, CO , 1214
Baca County School District, CO , 1275
Badger High School, WI , 9885
Bainbridge High School, WA , 9565
Bainville High School, MT , 6948
Baker County high schools, OR , 7528, 7668
Baker University, KS , 8793
Baldwin County high schools, AL , 83
Baldwin High School, MS , 4903
Ball State University, IN , 2964, 3025, 3107
Ballard Memorial High School, KY , 3579
Baltic high schools, SD , 8539
Baptist Health Schools—Little Rock, AR , 269
Baptist Theological Seminary at Richmond, VA , 9413
Barberton High School, OH , 6988
Barnes Academy, GA , 2257
Barnstable High School, MA , 4007
Barrington High School, IL , 2691
Bartlesville High School, OK , 7463, 7488
Baruch College, NY , 6219
Basalt High School, CO , 1231
Batavia High School, NY , 5713
Battle Creek Central High School, MI , 4362
Bauxite public high schools, AR , 319
Baxter Community High School, IA , 3275
Baxter Springs High School, KS , 3485
Bay City Central High School, MI , 4350
Bay City Western High School, MI , 4350
Bay County high schools, MI , 4350
Bay De Noc College, MI , 4643
Bay High School, MS , 4913
Baylor University, TX , 8859, 9094, 9110
Beacon High School, NY , 6526
Beaman-Conrad-Liscomb-Union-Whitten School District, IA , 3383
Bearden High School, AR , 270
Beardstown High School, IL , 2813
Beavercreek High School, OH , 7134
Bedford North Lawrence High School, IN , 7165
Belding High School, MI , 4445
Belen Jesuit School, FL , 2030
Belfast High School, ME , 7093
Belhaven College, MS , 4911
Bellbrook High School, OH , 7134
Belle Plaine High School, IA , 10031
Belle Vernon High School, PA , 7731
Bellefontaine High School, OH , 7173
Belleville High School, NJ , 5396
Belleville High School, WI , 9980
Belleville public high schools, IL , 2812

Bellevue School District, WA , 9569
Bellingham High School, MA , 4245
Bellows Free Academy, VT , 5350
Bellport High School, NY , 6393
Belmont High School, MA , 4009
Belmont High School, NH , 5335
Beloit Jr.-Sr. High School, KS , 3458
Belvidere High School, IL , 2784
Bement High School, IL , 8716
Benedictine College, KS , 3524
Bennet College, NC , 1614, 8467
Bennington County high schools, VT , 5378
Benton Central Junior-Senior High School, IN , 3056
Benton High School, AR , 279
Benton High School, MO , 4979
Benton High School, UT , 9213
Benton public high schools, AR , 319
Bentonville High School, AR , 272, 278
Benzie County high schools, MI , 4487
Berea College, OH , 7143
Berks County high schools, PA , 7969
Berks County Secondary Schools, PA , 7913
Berkshire Community College, MA , 3985
Berlin High School, CT , 8317, 8434
Bermudian Springs High School, PA , 7954
Berry College, GA , 2191, 2267
Bethel College, IN , 3069
Bethel High School, OH , 7388
Bethlehem Area School District, PA , 7953
Bexar County high schools, TX , 9054
Bicol University, School of Nursing, Philippines, 6132
Big Foot High School, WI , 9885
Big Fork High School, MT , 6741
Big Picture High School, CO , 1185
Big Valley High School, CA , 779
Bigelow School District, OR , 7679
Bigfork High School, MN , 4700
Bishop College, TX , 8832
Bishop Fenwick High School, OH , 7011
Bishop Hafey High School, PA , 7908
Bishop Kenny High School, FL , 1816
Bishop LeBlond High School, UT , 9213
Bishop Stang High School, MA , 4283
Black Hills State University, SD , 8548
Black Oak Mine School District, CA , 668
Black River High School, OH , 7109
Blackburn College, IL , 6654
Blackduck High School, MN , 4700
Blackfoot High School, ID , 2351
Blackford High School, IN , 2967
Blair County high schools, PA , 8172
Blairsville High School, PA , 7729
Blanchard Memorial School, MA , 7736
Bland County High School, VA , 9553
Blinn College, TX , 9127
Bloomfield High School, MO , 4967
Bloomsburg University, PA , 7998
Blue Cliff College, AR , 309
Blue Mound High School, IL , 43
Blue Mountain High School, PA , 7987
Blue Ridge Community College, VA , 9281
Bolingbrook High School, IL , 2430
Bolivar Central School, NY , 8352
Bonners Ferry High School, ID , 6776
Booker High School, TX , 9009
Boston College, MA , 6565
Boston English High School, MA , 4297
Boston University, MA , 2323, 4007
Bothell High School, WA , 9759
Botkins High School, OH , 7388
Boulder City High School, NV , 5291
Boulder Valley School District, CO , 1218
Bourbon County high schools, KS , 3446
Bowie High School, TX , 2836
Bowling Green High School, OH , 7009
Bowling Green R-1 School District, MO , 5076
Bowling Green State University, OH , 7010
Boyertown Area Senior High School, PA , 8074
Bradford area high schools, PA , 7830
Bradley University, IL , 2553
Branch County schools, MI , 4633
Branford High School, CT , 1492
Brattleboro Union High School, VT , 4356, 9262
Braxton County High School, WV , 9781

Bremen School Corp., IN , 4504
Bremer County high schools, IA , 3406
Brevard College, NC , 8467
Brewer High School, ME , 3721
Brewster Central School District, NY , 5785
Bridgehampton High School, NY , 5945
Bridgeport High School, NE , 502
Bridgeport High School, WV , 2461, 2500
Bridgeport high schools, CT , 2527
Bridgewater State College, MA , 3997
Brigham Young University, UT , 1026
Brite Divinity School at Texas Christian University, TX , 2832
Broadalbin-Perth High School, NY , 6025
Brockton High School, MA , 4218, 8134
Brockway Area High School, PA , 8002
Brodhead High School, WI , 9953
Brookfield High School, OH , 7300
Brookings-Harbor High School, OR , 9621
Brooklyn Technical High School, NY , 5854
Broome Community College, NY , 6303
Broughton High School, NC , 6926
Broward County High School, FL , 1982
Brown County high schools, KS , 3495
Brown County high schools, WI , 2653
Brownstown Central High School, IN , 7324
Brunswick Senior High School, VA , 6752
Brush High School, OH , 6996
Bryan High School, OH , 7017
Bryan High School, TX , 8693
Bryn Mawr College, PA , 7874
Buchanan High School, James, PA , 6031
Buckeye High School, OH , 7378
Buckingham County Virginia High School, VA , 9366
Buckley public high schools, WA , 7988
Bucknell University, PA , 6664
Bucks County high schools, PA , 7755, 7997
Bucksport High School, ME , 8293, 8319
Buffalo high schools, WY , 10097
Burlington Community High School, IA , 3394
Burlington High School, WI , 10093
Burlington School District, NJ , 5442
Burlington-Edison High School, WA , 9576, 9579
Burnet High School, TX , 8866
Burr Oak High School, MI , 4461
Butler County high schools, KS , 3440
Butler High School, PA , 8169
Butte College, CA , 832
Butte High School, MT , 7654
Byrnes High School, SC , 8495

CA Institute of Technology Gift & Estate Planning, CA , 9043
Cabot High School, AR , 273
Cabrillo College, CA , 402, 433
Cadillac Area public schools, MI , 4371
Cain High School, WI , 9967
Cairo High School, MO , 5068
Caldwell College, NJ , 6654
Caldwell High School, ID , 2343
Calhoun County high schools, WV , 9808
Calhoun County schools, AL , 6701
Calhoun High School, TX , 8826
California Maritime Academy, CA , 3440
California Polytechnic College, CA , 9177
California State Polytechnic University, Pomona, CA , 438
California State Summer School for the Arts, CA , 458
California State University San Bernardino, CA , 584
California State University San Marcos, CA , 897
California State University, CA , 439, 702
California State University, Chico, CA , 832
California State University, Fullerton, CA , 459
California State University, Long Beach, CA , 754
California University of Pennsylvania, PA , 7851
Callistoga High School, CA , 518
Calumet College of St. Joseph, IN , 3069
Calvary Bible College, MO , 4118
Calvary Chapel Christian School, PA , 7781
Calvin College, MI , 4445
Calvin High School, OK , 8815
Camden High School, NC , 6645
Camden High School, NY , 6485

Camden School District, NJ , 5442
Camden-Rockport High School, ME , 3739
Cameron University, OK , 7469
Campbell County High School, WY , 10107
Campbell University Divinity School, NC , 9413
Campbell University, NC , 6812, 6818
Canaan high schools, CT , 1345
Canajoharie High School, NY , 5937, 6352
Canastota High School, NY , 7431
Cannon County high schools, TN , 8665
Canton High School, CT , 1348
Canton High School, IL , 2597, 2656, 2734
Capac School District, MI , 4427
Cape Cod Community College, MA , 4006
Cape Cod Regional High School, MA , 4019
Cape Cod Regional Tech School, MA , 4102
Cape Fear Community College, NC , 6870
Cape Henry Academy, VA , 9286
Cape May County High School, NJ , 8405
Cape May County high schools, NJ , 8120
Capital High School, MT , 8031
Capital High School, NM , 5651
Caprock High School, TX , 8675
Carbon County High School, MT , 5131
Cardinal High School, OH , 7445
Cardinal Mooney High School, FL , 1844
Cardington Lincoln High School, OH , 7426
Career Academy of Hair Design, AR , 309
Carey, OH area high schools, OH , 7082
Carl Sandburg High School, IL , 2396
Carleton College, MN , 7023
Carlisle High School, PA , 5769
Carlisle High School, TX , 8948
Carmichaels High School, PA , 7781
Carroll College, MT , 7541
Carroll Public High School, IA , 3253
Carrollton Community Unit School District No. 1, IL , 2789
Carrollton High School, IL , 2517
Carson-Newman College, TN , 8598
Carter County high schools, KY , 3557
Carterville High School, IL , 2617
Carver high schools, MA , 4107
Case Western Reserve University, OH , 2909
Case Western Reserve University, PA , 7953
Cass City High School, MI , 7217
Cass County high schools, IN , 3163
Cass County public high schools, MO , 5071
Cassville High School, WI , 9912
Caston High School, IN , 2979, 3104
Catasauqua High School, PA , 6813
Catawba College, NC , 6663
Catawba County high schools, NC , 6739
Catawba Valley Community College, NC , 6593
Catholic Central High School, Muskegon, MI , 4444
Catholic Central High School, NY , 8340
Catholic Central High School, WI , 10093
Catholic University of America, DC , 1536
Catskill High School, NY , 7038
Cedar Crest College, PA , 8191
Cedar Falls High School, IA , 9950
Cedar Springs High School, MI , 4445
Cedarburg High School, WI , 9921
Cedarville University, OH , 6954
Centenary College of Louisiana, LA , 2832
Centenary College, LA , 9110
Centennial High School, ID , 2343
Centennial High School, MD , 3787
Centennial High School, NE , 5269
Center Point-Urbana High School, IA , 3237
Centerpoint High School, AR , 300
Centerville-Abington Community Schools, IN , 3217
Central Bucks East High School, PA , 7883
Central Catholic High School, OH , 7386
Central Community College, NE , 5210
Central Community High School, IA , 3374
Central Community School District No. 1, IL , 2549
Central Connecticut State University, CT , 1349
Central Georgia Technical College, GA , 2118
Central High School, IN , 3160, 7285
Central High School, PA , 6689, 8153
Central Lyon High School, IA , 3342
Central Methodist College, MO , 5038
Central Michigan University, MI , 4350, 4545

Central Noble High School, IN , 2774
Central Regional High School, NJ , 8303
Central School District No. 1, NY , 6141
Central State University, OH , 6954
Central Texas College, TX , 9127
Central Valley High School, CA , 474
Central Virginia high schools, VA , 9350
Central Washington University, WA , 8704, 8973
Centralia High School, IL , 5103
Centralia high schools, IL , 2467
Centre College, KY , 2830
Cerro Coso Community College, CA , 767
Chambersburg Area Senior High School, PA , 8083
Chaminade High School, NY , 5840
Champlain Valley Union High School, VT , 1457
Chana High School, CA , 6728
Chapman High School, KS , 3455, 3491
Chapman High School, SC , 8495
Chapman University, CA , 1098
Chareloi High School, PA , 7731
Chariton County high schools, MO , 8893
Charleston Arkansas High Shool, AR , 290
Charlotte County high schools, FL , 1844
Charlotte Valley Central School District, NY , 6063
Chase High School, NC , 6763
Chatham High School, MA , 4019, 4102
Chatham High School, NJ , 5419
Chatham High School, NY , 5761
Chazy Central Rural High School, NY , 6983
Chehalis high schools, WA , 6609
Chelsea High School, VT , 1457
Cherokee Community School District, IA , 3361
Cherokee County high schools, IA , 3249, 3281
Cherokee High School, GA , 2235
Cherryville High School, NC , 1903
Chester High School, PA , 6815
Chetek High School, WI , 9862
Cheyenne High School, WY , 8774
Cheyenne High Schools, WY , 10103
Cheyney University, PA , 8087
Chicago Christian High, IL , 2778
Chicopee Comprehensive High School, MA , 8299,
    8369
Chicopee High School, MA , 8299, 8369
Chief Bug-O-Nay-Ge-Shig School, MN , 4700
Children's Art Center, CA , 941
Chillicothe High School, OH , 7034
Chinook High School, MT , 5177
Chippewa Hills School District, MI , 4508
Chrisman High School, IL , 2929
Christian Life Academy, PA , 7746
Churubusco High School, IN , 7925
Cicero-North Syracuse High School, NY , 8591
Cincinnati Christian University, OH , 6954
Cincinnati State, OH , 6954
Citrus High School, FL , 1830
City College of New York, NY , 1950, 5856, 6277
City University of New York, NY , 5736, 6354
Clallam County high schools, WA , 9745
Clarion High School, PA , 7195, 8028
Clark Atlanta University, GA , 1614
Clark College, WA , 9590
Clark County high schools, OH , 7014
Clark State Community College, OH , 6954
Clark University, MA , 1392
Clatskanie High School, OR , 7553
Clawson High School, MI , 4395
Clay County High School, IN , 3046
Clay County high schools, TX , 9159
Clayton High School, NJ , 5426
Clear Lake High School, CA , 760
Clearwater County high schools, MN , 4865
Clearwater High School, FL , 2009
Clemson University, College of Engineering and
    Science, SC , 6636
Clemson University, SC , 6565, 6929
Clewiston High School, FL , 1992
Clifton Central High School, IL , 2814
Clinton Central High School, IN , 47
Clinton Community College, NY , 5861
Clinton Community Unit No. 15 High School, IL , 2849
Clinton County high schools, OH , 7438
Clinton High School, MI , 431, 4384
Clinton High School, SC , 8451

Clinton Prairie High School, IN , 47
Clinton School District, NY , 6497
Cloudcroft High School, NM , 5647
Cloverdale High School, IN , 3154
Clovis Community College, MN , 5622
Clovis High School, NM , 8731
Coastline Community College, CA , 5287
Coffey County high schools, KS , 3446
Cohasset High School, MA , 8363
Coldwater High School, OH , 7082
Colfax High School, CA , 6728
College of Mount St. Joseph, OH , 6954
College of William & Mary, VA , 9344, 9536
College Park High School, CA , 922
Collier County high schools, FL , 1783
Colorado College, CO , 1149
Colorado Mountain College, CO , 1161
Colorado Mountain College, Vail-Eagle Valley, CO ,
    1302
Colorado School of Mines, CO , 1147, 1149
Colorado Springs School District 11, CO , 1258
Colorado State University, CO , 1149, 10118
Colorado State University-Fort Collins, CO , 1206
Colquitt County High School, GA , 2153
Columbia Adventist Academy, WA , 9596
Columbia Basin College, WA , 9558
Columbia County public high schools, PA , 7937
Columbia Heights High School, MN , 4717
Columbia High School, NJ , 5395
Columbia High School, PA , 6685
Columbia International University, SC , 4118
Columbia Presbyterian Medical Center, NY , 2200
Columbia University Graduate School of Journalism,
    NY , 6202
Columbia University, NY , 5593, 6277, 7016, 8402
Columbus City School District, OH , 7166
Columbus Community School District, IA , 3378
Columbus High School, WI , 9960
Columbus School District, IA , 3284
Columbus State University, GA , 2117
Comanche County high schools, KS , 3487
Comfrey High School, MN , 4691
Community College District No. 503, IL , 2426
Community College of the District of Columbia, DC ,
    1594
Community Colleges of Spokane, WA , 9757
Community School, MO , 10106
Community Unit District 1 High School, IL , 2419, 2716
Conard High School, CT , 8392
Concord Academy, MI , 4577
Concord College, WV , 9772
Concord public schools, MA , 8244
Concordia College, MN , 4720
Conestoga Valley High School, PA , 8050
Conger Elementary School, OH , 7411
Conifer High School, CO , 1244
Connellsville Area School District, PA , 7957
Converse College, SC , 8514
Cony High School, ME , 7337
Cook County High School, MN , 4773
Cook Middle School, NC , 6923
Cooper High School, TX , 8947
Cooperstown High School, NY , 7424, 7425
Copley High School, OH , 7122
Copper River High School, AK , 10031
Coquille High School, OR , 7646
Cornell University, NY , 1333, 5962
Cornerstone Christian School, CT , 1420
Cornerstone College, MI , 4445
Corpus Christi high schools, TX , 8847
Corry Area High School, PA , 8040, 8099
Coshocton High School, OH , 7001
Cosumnes Rvier College, CA , 926
Cottey College, MO , 209, 3309, 7586
Council Grove High School, KS , 3522, 3529
Covington High School, OH , 7388
Covington School District, IN , 3222
Covington-Douglas Schools, OK , 7462
Cranberry Area High School, PA , 7746
Crandon High School, WI , 10060
Crane High School, TX , 8702
Cranston High School East, RI , 8276
Cranston High School West, RI , 8276
Craven Community College, NC , 6621

Crawford County high schools, PA , 7891, 8159
Creekview High School, GA , 2235
Creighton University, NE , 4780
Crescent High School, SC , 8495
Crestview High School, OH , 7403
Cretin-Derham High School, MN , 5929
Crivitz High School, WI , 10051
Crocket High School, TX , 2836
Crook County High School, OR , 7622, 7643
Crooksville High School, OH , 7161
Crosby-Ironton High School, MN , 6708
CrossRoads High School, GA , 2235
Crystal River High School, FL , 1830
CSUCI Oxnard Adult School, CA , 1036
Cuba Rushford School, NY , 8352
Culbertson High School, MT , 6948
Culpeper County High School, VA , 9355
Culver Community School Corporation, IN , 4476
Culver Community School, IN , 3063
Culver-Stocton College, MO , 5038
Cumberland College, KY , 7165
Cumberland County High School, TN , 8549
Cumberland County high schools, PA , 6069
Cumberland County high schools, TN , 8655
Cumberland High School, WI , 9932
Curtis High School, NY , 5738
Curwensville High School, PA , 7865
Cypress Community College, CA , 5287

Dale Bumper College of Agriculture, AR , 264
Dallas County high schools, TX , 9026
Dallas Theological Seminary, TX , 8758
Dane County high schools, WI , 3813
Danville Community College, VA , 9357
Danville Community High School, IN , 1797
Danville High School, VT , 9244
Danville Senior High School, PA , 8164, 8185
Daphne High School, AL , 95
Dartmouth College, NH , 6032, 8241
Dartmouth High School, MA , 4283
Dauphin County High School, NC , 6875
Dauphin County high schools, PA , 6069
Davenport College, MI , 4445
Daviess County School District, KY , 6931
Davis Community College, Jefferson, AL , 37
Dawson County High School, GA , 2246
Dawson County high schools, TX , 8969
Dayton High School, NV , 5299
Dayton High School, WA , 9027
Dayton, OH area high schools, OH , 7082
Daytona State College, FL , 1990
Dean College, MA , 4245
Decatur County high schools, KS , 3515
Decatur District 61 high schools, IL , 2849
Decatur High School, GA , 2161
Decorah High School, IA , 1805
Dedham High School, MA , 4038
Deer Lakes High School, PA , 7949
Deer River High School, MN , 4700
Deer Valley Unified School District, AZ , 183
Deerfield Beach Senior High School, FL , 6588
DeKalb High School, IL , 2431
Dekalb High School, IL , 2514
Del Mar College, TX , 8773
Del Oro High School, CA , 870, 6728
Del Valle Independent School District, TX , 2836
Delavan High School, IL , 2811
Delaware County high schools, IN , 3025, 3195
Delaware County schools, IN , 3021, 3092
Delaware Valley Central High School, NY , 6133, 6451
Delaware Valley High School, PA , 5740
Delaware Valley Regional High School, NJ , 7809
Dell Rapids high schools, SD , 8539
Delone Catholic High School, PA , 7954
Delphos Jefferson High School, OH , 7403
Delphos St. Johns High School, OH , 7403
Delta College, MI , 4350
Delta High School, CO , 1267
Delta-Montrose Area Vocational-Technical Center, CO ,
    1267
Denfeld High School, MN , 4726, 4810
Denison High School, TX , 2740
Dennis-Yarmouth Regional High School, MA , 5323

Denton High School, MT , 5175
Denver high schools, CO , 1192
Denver Metropolitan High Schools, CO , 1179
DePauw University, IN , 2923, 3069
DeRidder High School, LA , 424
Dermott High School, AR , 322
Des Moines County schools, IA , 3362
Des Moines University, Osteopathic Medical Center, IA , 2614
Dexter High School, MO , 4967
Dexter Regional High School, ME , 8339
Diablo Valley College, CA , 922
Dickenson County high schools, VA , 1835
Dickerson High School, Charles O., NY , 6464
Dickinson College, PA , 7977
Dieruff High School, PA , 5740
Dimond High School, AK , 97
Dirigo High School, ME , 3696
Dixon High School, CA , 765, 806
Doddridge County high schools, WV , 9808
Dodge County high schools, WI , 3813
Doherty High School, MA , 4237
Dolgeville Central School, NY , 8410
Donegal High School, PA , 7814
Doniphan High School, MO , 5054
Dorado High School, AR , 321
Douglas County high schools, CO , 1184
Douglas High School, AZ , 2357
Douglas High School, MD , 3868
Douglas High School, NV , 5302
Douglas Southall Freeman high school, VA , 9422
Dover High School, OH , 6997, 7208, 7386
Downey High School, Thomas, CA , 416
Downey Unified School District, CA , 1019
Downs High School, KS , 3443
Downsville School District, NY , 5953
Dr. Phillips High School, FL , 2038
Drake University of Des Moines, IA , 3337
Drexel University, PA , 7874, 8005
Drury High School, RI , 8312
Dryden School District, MI , 4427
Dubois Area High School, PA , 7970, 7993, 8002
Dubois County high schools, IN , 3102
Dubois High School, WY , 10094, 10105
Dufur High School, OR , 7571
Duke Ellington School of the Arts, DC , 1620
Duke University, NC , 6565, 6582, 6737, 6882, 6923, 8467
Dulanely High School, MD , 3866
Duluth high schools, MN , 4851
Dummer High School, MA , 4002
Dunbar High School, MD , 3868
Dundee area high schools, MI , 4664
Dundy County high schools, NE , 5218
Dunedin Comprehensive High School, FL , 1897
Duquesne University, PA , 7804
Durango High School, CO , 1185, 1238
Durham Technical Community College, NC , 6634
Dutchess Community College, NY , 5753
Duxbury Junior and Senior High School, MA , 4298, 8287

Eagle Academy, CO , 1184
Eagle County high schools, CO , 1187
Eanes Independent School District, TX , 2836
Earlham College, IN , 3069, 3217, 6954
East Brady Area School District, PA , 7995
East Butler High School, NE , 5269
East Carolina University, NC , 6637, 6921, 8765
East Catholic High School, CT , 1420
East Central High School, IN , 3012
East Chicago Central High School, IN , 3033
East High School, CO , 1188
East Liverpool High School, OH , 2600
East Rutherford High School, NC , 6763
East Stroudsberg University, PA , 8191
East Stroudsburgh Area High School, PA , 8113
East Tennessee State University, Quillen College of Medicine, TN , 6923
East Texas Baptist University, TX , 9110
Eastern Cumberland County high schools, PA , 7692
Eastern Greene High School, IN , 7165
Eastern Illinois University, IL , 2923

Eastern Kentucky University, KY , 3552
Eastern Michigan University, MI , 7127
Eastern Pulaski Community School, IN , 3063
Eastern Regional High School, NJ , 5464
Eastern Virginia Medical School, VA , 9368
Eastern Washington University, WA , 9757
Eastlake North High School, OH , 6996
Edgar County high schools, IL , 2532
Edgerton High School, OH , 2680
Edgewood high schools, OH , 7124
Edgewood-Colesburg Community School District, IA , 3271
Edinboro University of Pennsylvania, PA , 7977
Edison High School, NJ , 5491
Edison High School, Thomas A., NY , 5946
Edna High School, TX , 9183
Edon High School, OH , 7017
Edwards County High School, IL , 2362
Edwardsville area high schools, IL , 2536
El Dorado High School, CA , 1053
El Dorado High School, KS , 3440, 9138
El Dorado public schools, AR , 277
El Dorado Union High School, CA , 668
Elizabeth City State University, NC , 1614
Elizabethtown College, PA , 8087
Elkton, Pigeon, Bay Port school districts, MI , 4513
Ellsworth High School, ME , 7773
Ellwood City Area School District, PA , 7427
Elmore County high schools, AL , 87
Elmwood Community High School, IL , 2538
Ely High School, MN , 4733
Elyria Central School District, OH , 7294
Emery Unified School District, CA , 563
Emmerich Manual High School, IN , 47
Emporia State University, KS , 3522
Enloe High School, NC , 6926
Enterprise High School, AL , 6707
Ephrata Borough high schools, PA , 8200
Ephrata Senior High School, PA , 7748
Ephrata Township high schools, PA , 8200
Episcopal Theological Seminary of the Southwest, TX , 7541
Escondido High School, CA , 1094
Essex High School, VT , 9247
Essex public high schools, MA , 4060
Essexville-Garber High School, MI , 4350
Estes Park High School, CO , 1236
Eton College, England, 9301
Etowah High School, GA , 2235
Eureka College, IL , 2553
Eustis High School, FL , 1973
Evansville Catholic high schools, IN , 2980
Evansville Deanery, IN , 2980
Evansville High School, WI , 9918
Evart High School, MI , 4466
Evergreen High School, CO , 1244
Exeter Area High School, NH , 8242
Exeter Township Senior High School, PA , 7893

F&M College, PA , 8050
Fairbanks High School, OH , 7061
Fairborn High School, OH , 7134
Fairfield Community High School, IL , 2509, 2802
Fairfield County high schools, OH , 7259
Fairfield University, CT , 1858
Fairhaven High School, MA , 4283, 8440
Fairhope High School, AL , 95
Fairmont State University, WV , 9782
Fairview High School, OH , 7017
Faith Christian School, WI , 9885
Fall Mountain High School, NH , 5358
Fall Mountain Regional High School, NH , 5376
Fallbrook Union High School District, CA , 9079
Fallbrook Union High School, CA , 506
Fannett Metal High School, PA , 6204
Farmington High School, CT , 1396
Farmville Central High School, NC , 8508
Fatima High School, MO , 5087, 5088, 5091, 5092
Fayetteville State University, NC , 9508
Fayetteville-Manlius High School, NY , 5776
Fennville High School, MI , 7346
Ferndale High School, CA , 763
Fillmore County high schools, NE , 5219

Fisk University, TN , 1614
Flathead County high schools, MT , 5155
Flathead High School, MT , 5140, 5158, 5166
Fleetwood Area High School, PA , 7953
Florham Park area high schools, NJ , 5545
Florida A&M University, FL , 1614, 1879
Florida Atlantic University, FL , 1879
Florida Institute of Technology, FL , 1879
Florida International University, FL , 1879
Florida Keys Community College, FL , 1883
Florida State University, FL , 1879, 6565, 7977
Florida University, FL , 1863
Floyd County High School, VA , 9485
Flushing High School, MI , 4663
Foley High School, AL , 88
Folsom Lake College, Placerville Campus, CA , 668
Foran High School, CT , 1376
Forbush High School, NC , 6923
Forest County Area Vocational School, PA , 7909
Forman Community High School, IL , 2418
Forsyth County high schools, GA , 2164
Forsyth County School System, NC , 6923
Forsyth Technical college, NC , 6730
Fort Atkinson High School, WI , 10050
Fort Bragg High School, CA , 6874
Fort Defiance High School, VA , 9346
Fort Hays State University, KS , 3444, 3459
Fort Lauderdale High School, FL , 1890
Fort Lewis College, CO , 1197
Fort Loramie High School, OH , 7388
Fort Madison high schools, IA , 3240
Fort Plain Central School District, NY , 8437
Fort Plain High School, NY , 5937, 6352, 6387
Fort Valley State College, GA , 1614
Fort Valley State University, GA , 2118
Fort Wayne Catholic high schools, IN , 6732
Fort Wayne community schools, IN , 6650
Fort Wayne Elmhurst High School, IN , 7432
Fort Wayne High School, IN , 2994
Fort Wayne parochial high schools, IN , 8008
Fort Wayne public high schools, IN , 8008
Fountain Valley High School, CA , 1022
Foxborough High School, MA , 4052, 4245
Framingham County high schools, MA , 4248
Framingham State College, MA , 4036
Frankenmuth Public Schools, MI , 4641
Frankenmuth School District, MI , 4428
Frankfort Senior High School, IN , 47
Franklin College, IN , 3069
Franklin Community High School, IN , 2781, 3108
Franklin County High School, MA , 4207
Franklin County Vo-Tech, PA , 6439
Franklin High School, IN , 3213
Franklin High School, MA , 4245
Franklin High School, NC , 6879
Franklin High School, PA , 7746
Franklin High School, TN , 8386
Franklin high schools, OH , 7124
Franklin Pierce High School, WA , 6772
Franklin University, AR , 309
Fraser High School, MI , 4429
Frederick High School, MD , 8168
Fredonia High School, KS , 3419, 3500
Fredonia High School, NY , 3740
Freeburg Illinois High School, IL , 56
Freedom High School, NC , 6706
Freeport High School, ME , 7355
Fresno County high schools, CA , 8067
Froid High School, MT , 6948
Front Range Community College, CO , 1200
Frontier High School, IN , 3125
Fruitport High School, MI , 4444
Ft. Madison High School, IA , 3372
Fullerton Community College, CA , 5287
Fulton County high schools, IL , 2919

Gabriel Richard High School, MI , 4364
Gaffney High School, SC , 2166
Galena Park Independent School District, TX , 8835
Galion High School, OH , 7081
Gallatin High School, TN , 8637
Galva-Holstein Community School District, IA , 3392
Galva-Holstein High School, IA , 8217

Galva-Holstein School District, IA , 3314
Galveston County high schools, TX , 8967
Galveston Public School System, TX , 9136
Ganado High School, TX , 9186
Gannon University, PA , 7977
Garaway High School, OH , 7254
Garden City High School, NY , 8137
Garden Spot High School, PA , 6832
Gardiner Area High School, ME , 3731
Gardiner High School, ME , 7337
Gardner High School, MA , 4124, 4330, 8318
Gardner-Webb Divinity School (MCW School of Div.),
    NC , 9413
Garfield High School, CA , 371, 896
Garfield High School, WA , 9715
Garnet Valley High School, PA , 7904
Garretson high schools, SD , 8539
Gaston College, NC , 6669
Gaston County High School, NC , 6657
Gates County High School, NC , 6871
Gateway High School, PA , 7991
Gatlinburg-Pittman High School, TN , 8584
Geauga County high schools, OH , 7445
Genesee Community College, NY , 6020
Geneseo High School, IL , 2580
Geneva High School, IL , 2581
Geneva High School, NY , 6180
Genoa-Kingston High School, IL , 2441, 2624
George Stevens Academy, ME , 3701
George Washington University, DC , 1965
Georgetown High School, MA , 8239
Georgetown University, KY , 6954
Georgia College and State University, GA , 2118
Georgia Insitute of Technology, GA , 2118
Georgia Institute of Technology, GA , 6565
Georgia Southern University, GA , 2118, 2132
Georgia State University, GA , 2118
Gibbon-Fairfax-Winthrop School District, MN , 4707
Gilford High School, NH , 5335
Gillespie County high schools, TX , 8867
Gilmer County high schools, WV , 9808
Gladbrook-Reinbeck Community High School, IA , 3353
Glen Ridge High School, NJ , 8160
Glen Rock High School, NJ , 5453
Glendale Community College, CA , 1084
Glenville State College, WV , 9821
Gloucester High School, MA , 3956, 4048
Gloucester High School, VA , 9520
Gloucester School District, NJ , 5442
Gloversville High School, NY , 5955, 6025, 6437,
    8316
Gold Shores High School, AL , 88
Golden Gate Baptist Theological Seminary, CA , 9413
Golden Sierra High School, CA , 1053
Golden West College, CA , 627
Golden West Community College, CA , 5287
Goldendale High School, WA , 9627
Goldsboro High School, NC , 6576
Gonzaga University, WA , 8723
Gordon College, MA , 4118
Gordon Lee Memorial high school, GA , 8608
Gordon-Conwell Theological Seminary, MA , 4118
Goshen Central School District, NY , 6047
Goshen College, IN , 3069
Goshen County high schools, WY , 10111
Goshen High School, OH , 7364
Goshen School District, OH , 7080
Governor Baxter School for the Deaf, ME , 7145
Governor High School, MA , 4002
Governor Mifflin High School, PA , 7747
Gowanda Central School, NY , 6217
Grace College, IN , 3069
Grafton High School, WI , 9909
Graham County high schools, KS , 3533
Graham High School, VA , 9439
Graham Independent School District, TX , 8923
Grand Haven High School, MI , 4444
Grand Rapids Central High School, MI , 4445
Grand Rapids Community College, MI , 4445
Grand Rapids High School, MN , 4700
Grand Rapids high schools, MN , 4750
Grand Traverse County high schools, MI , 4487
Grand Valley State University, MI , 4445
Grandview High School, MO , 5031, 8991

Granite Hills High School, CA , 400
Grant County high schools, OR , 6766
Grant County high schools, WA , 9658
Grants Pass High School, OR , 7561
Grantsville High School, UT , 9194
Grapeland Independent School District, TX , 8782
Great Path Academy, CT , 1420
Greater Lawrence Regional Vocational Technical High
    School, MA , 3970
Greater Lawrence Technical School, MA , 3970
Greater New Bedford Vocational Technical High School,
    MA , 4283
Green Bay East High School, WI , 2666
Green County Career Center, OH , 7134
Green County high schools, OH , 7227
Green Lake High School, WI , 2456
Greenboro College, NC , 8467
Greencastle High School, IN , 3154
Greene Central School, NY , 6381
Greene High School, NY , 521
Greenleaf High School, ID , 2343
Greensburg Community High School, IN , 2977, 3066
Greensprings High School, Clyde, OH , 7986
Greenview High School, OH , 7173
Greenville Area Senior High School, PA , 7322
Greenville County School District, SC , 8445
Greenville Technical College, SC , 8477
Greenway-Coleraine High School, MN , 4700
Greenwich High School, CT , 8361
Greenwood County high schools, KS , 3416, 3446
Gridley High School, KS , 3414
Griffin High School, GA , 1924
Grinnell College, IA , 1949
Grinnell-Newburg High School, IA , 3390
Grinnell-Newburg School District, Powershiek County,
    IA , 3359
Grove City College, PA , 7381
Gruver High School, TX , 8990
Guernsey County high schools, OH , 6961
Gunn High School, CA , 548, 640
Guthrie Center High School, IA , 3395
Guthrie High School, OK , 7465, 7477

Hackensack High School, NJ , 8400
Haddonfield Memorial High School, NJ , 5471
Hagerstown High School, IN , 7250
Hahnemann University, PA , 7874
Half Hallow Hills High School East, NY , 5869
Hall County high schools, NE , 5264
Hall-Dale High School, ME , 7337
Hamilton County high schools, OH , 7124
Hamilton County public schools, TX , 8812
Hamilton High School, TX , 8968
Hamilton School District, NY , 6070
Hamlin County High School, SD , 9045
Hammondsport Central School District, NY , 2727
Hampton public high schools, VA , 9544
Hampton University, VA , 1614, 9502
Hana High School, HI , 2287
Hancock County high schools, ME , 7773
Handley High School, VA , 9411
Handy Intermediate, T.L., MI , 4350
Hannibal-LaGrange College, MO , 5038
Hanover College, IN , 3005, 3069
Hanover High School, PA , 6782, 7954
Harbor Beach Community School, MI , 4506
Harbor Light Christian, MI , 4577
Harbor Springs High School, MI , 4456, 4577
Harbor Springs School District, MI , 4501
Hardee High School, FL , 2004
Hardin High School, MT , 5147
Hardin-Houston High School, OH , 7388
Harford County high schools, MD , 3845
Harlan Community High School, IA , 3321
Harlowton High School, MT , 6720, 9699
Harmony High School, IA , 3403
Harrisburg area high schools, PA , 7962, 8101
Harrisburg High School, IL , 701
Harrison County high schools, WV , 2937
Hart County High School, GA , 2257
Hartford public high schools, CT , 1391
Hartnell College, CA , 402
Hartwick College, NY , 6039

Harvard University, Division of Medical Sciences, MA ,
    4083
Harvard University, MA , 3988, 4172, 4209, 4230,
    4239, 4754, 6032, 7891
Harwich High School, MA , 4007
Haskell High School, TX , 8947
Hastings College, NE , 6687
Hastings High School, MN , 4886
Hastings High School, NE , 5215
Havana High School, IL , 2688
Haverford Township Senior High School, PA , 7822
Haverhill High School, MA , 4031, 8278
Hawkins County high schools, TN , 48
Hayes High School, Rutherford B., OH , 7411
Haywood County High School, TN , 8576
Haywood High School, TN , 8664
Hazelton High School, PA , 7908
Healdsburg High School, CA , 650, 701
Healdton High School, OK , 7512
Helena High School, MT , 8031
Helene Fuld School of Nursing, NJ , 5592
Helias Catholic High School, MO , 5015
Helias High School, MO , 5093, 5094, 5095
Hemingford High School, NE , 5199
Henderson County High School, KY , 3156
Henderson County High School, NC , 6629
Henderson County public high schools, NC , 6725
Henderson High School, TX , 8948
Henrico County public schools, VA , 9394
Henry County high schools, TN , 8570
Henry County high schools, IL , 2580
Henry High School, Patrick, MN , 4757
Heritage Christian School, IN , 2985
Herkimer County Community College, NY , 5863
Herkimer County High School, NY , 5863
Herrin High School, IL , 2437, 2601, 2865
Herscher High School, IL , 7435
Hiawatha High School, KS , 3513
Hibbing high schools, MN , 4688
Higbee High School, MO , 5068
High Point University, NC , 8467
High School in Union County, NJ , 5582
High Sky Girls Ranch, TX , 7095
Highland County School System, OH , 7027
Highland High School, IA , 10009
Highland High School, WA , 9671
Highland Park High School, IL , 2844
Hilbert High School, WI , 9985
Hill City High School, MN , 4700
Hill High School, Arthur, MI , 4435
Hill High School, The, PA , 7880
Hilltop High School, OH , 7017
Hingham High School, MA , 8264
Hinsdale Central School, NY , 7367
Hobart College, NY , 7771
Hobson High School, MT , 5152
Hocking Technical College, OH , 7189
Hofstra University, NY , 8137
Holland Central High School, NY , 6351
Holland Christian High School, MI , 4444
Holland-Zeeland School District, MI , 4398
Holliston County high schools, MA , 4248
Holy Cross College, IN , 3069
Holy Name School, CT , 1422
Holy Rosary Catholic School, MO , 5027
Holy Spirit High School, NJ , 5451, 8405
Holyoke Community College, MA , 4109
Holyoke High School, MA , 4546
Home on the Range for Boys, ND , 7095
Homedale High School, ID , 2343
Homer High School, AK , 117
Homestead High School, IN , 8008
Homestead High School, WI , 6665
Honeoye Falls-Lima Senior High School, NY , 2822
Hood College, MD , 8191
Hoover High School, CA , 878
Hope (Bob) High School, TX , 7095
Hopedale High School, MA , 4112
Hopkinton County high schools, MA , 4248
Hornell High School, NY , 5804
Hotchkiss High School, CO , 1151
Houghton College, NY , 4118
Houston Community College, TX , 8879, 9127
Howard County high schools, IN , 3148, 6956

Howard Payne University, TX , 9110
Howard University, DC , 1614
Howell Cheney Technical School, CT , 1420
Hudson High School, FL , 1917
Humboldt High School, KS , 3488
Humphreys County high schools, TN , 8649
Hunter College, NY , 5684, 6386
Huntington Beach Union High School District, CA , 5287
Huntington North High School, IN , 3218, 7432
Huntington University, IN , 3069
Huron County high schools, MI , 4609
Hutchinson Community College, KS , 3501
Hutchinson High School, KS , 3431

Ida Grove High School, IA , 7912
Illinois State University, IL , 2646
Illinois University, IL , 2553
Illinois Wesleyan University, IL , 2849
Illion High School, NY , 5786
Ilwaco High School, WA , 8850
Imlay City School District, MI , 4427
Immaculate Conception High School, NJ , 8160
Immanuel Lutheran School, CO , 1212
Immokalee High School, FL , 1926
Independence Community College, KS , 3461
Independence High School, CA , 1053
Independence-Monmouth School District 13J, OR , 7669
Indian Creek High School, IN , 3108
Indian River Community College, FL , 1927
Indian River County public high schools, FL , 1873
Indian River County schools, FL , 1876
Indian River School District, DE , 7721
Indiana County high schools, PA , 7725
Indiana Institute of Technology, IN , 3069
Indiana State University, IN , 3107
Indiana University East, IN , 3217
Indiana University, IN , 2821, 3071, 3107, 3123, 3132, 3140, 3163, 7165
Indiana University, Jacobs School of Music, IN , 3080
Indiana Wesleyan University, IN , 3069
Ingraham High School, WA , 9620
Institute of Forestry - Hetauda Campus, Nepal, 1755
Interlakes Regional High School, NH , 3982
Interstate 35 High School, IA , 3256
Iola High School, KS , 5607
Iona College, NY , 1965
Iona Preparatory School, CT , 1422
Iowa High School, IA , 8421
Iowa Mennonite School, IA , 3331
Iowa State University, IA , 2395, 3278, 3375, 4779, 9508
Iowa Valley Community School District, IA , 3246
Iron Mountain High School, MI , 4455
Ironton Public Schools, MO , 4982
Ironwood Area School District, MI , 4482
Iroquois County high schools, IL , 2818
Irvine Valley Community College, CA , 5287
Island County high schools, WA , 9692
Itasca high schools, MN , 4750
ITT Technical Institute, NM , 5653
Ivy Tech Community College, IN , 3217
Ivy Tech State College, IN , 3045
Ivy Tech, IN , 3163

Jackson County high schools, IN , 2997
Jackson County high schools, WV , 9808
Jackson High School, MI , 4584
Jackson High School, WY , 10105
Jackson Hole Community School, WY , 10106
Jacksonville College, TX , 9110
James E. Rogers College of Law, AZ , 212
James Sprunt Community College, NC , 6872
Jamestown High School, NY , 5815
Jamestown High School, VA , 9388
Jarvis Christian College, TX , 9110
Jay County High School, IN , 3151
Jay High School, ME , 3696
Jeffco public schools, CO , 1221
Jefferson Community College, NY , 6287
Jefferson County high schools, WI , 3813, 9859

Jefferson County North High School, KS , 3437
Jefferson County School District, NY , 6287
Jefferson High School, OR , 7590
Jefferson Medical College, PA , 7874
Jefferson-Morgan High School, PA , 7781
Jersey Shore Area High School, PA , 8110
Jewell County high schools, KS , 5265
Joel Barlow High School, CT , 1482
Joffrey Midwest Workshop, MI , 4419
John A. Logan College, IL , 2865
John Brown University, AR , 309
John Burroughs School, MO , 10106
John Paul II High School, TN , 8586
John Randolph Tucker high school, VA , 9422
John S. Burke Catholic High School, NY , 6443
Johnathan Law High School, CT , 1376
Johnson & Wales University, RI , 9508
Johnson County schools, IN , 3079
Johnson County schools, WY , 10108
Johnson Creek High School, WI , 2361
Johnson High School, NJ , 5394
Johnson High School, TX , 2836
Johnston Community College, NC , 6721
Johnstown High School, NY , 6025
Jonathan Alder High School, OH , 7437
Jones Central High School, NC , 6680
Jordan School District, UT , 9212
Julesburg High School, CO , 1139
Jupiter High School, FL , 1839
Justin-Siaena High School, CA , 518

K.B. Beit Haemek, Israel, 5509
Kalama High School, WA , 6751
Kalamazoo College, MI , 4465
Kalamazoo County high schools, MI , 4493
Kanabec County high schools, MN , 4870
Kaneland High School, IL , 2539
Kaneland School District, IL , 2549
Kansas State University, KS , 3316, 3440, 3472, 3522, 7527
Kansas University, KS , 9213
Kapaa High School, HI , 2286
Kaskaskia College, IL , 5103
Kauai High School, HI , 2286
Kearsage High School, NH , 5358
Keene High School, NH , 8324
Keene public schools, NH , 5334
Kendall College of Art and Design, MI , 4445
Kenmore High School, OH , 7374
Kennedy High School, John F., OR , 7611
Kennesaw State University, GA , 2118
Kennett High School, NH , 8309
Kennett public schools, MO , 2807
Kent County colleges, MI , 4424
Kent School District, WA , 8118
Kent State University, OH , 6962
Kent University, OH , 7366
Kern County high schools, CA , 7794
Ketchikan High School, AK , 97
Kettering University, MI , 4394
Key West High School, FL , 1847
Keystone Central School District, PA , 2792
Keystone High School, PA , 7746
Keystone Junior College, PA , 6597
Keytesville Township School District, MO , 4993
Kiel High School, WI , 10020
Kilgore High School, TX , 8948
Killingly High School, CT , 8374
Kimball Union Academy, NH , 5358
King City high schools, MO , 9848
Kingman City High School, KS , 3520
Kingman High School, KS , 3542
Kings College, TN , 2016
Kingsford High School, MI , 7979
Kingston High School, MA , 4312
Kirby High School, AR , 300
Kirtland High School, OH , 7194
Kishwaukee College, IL , 2431
Klamath County high schools, OR , 7680
Klein Forest High School, TX , 8868
Knightstown High School, IN , 3159, 3167
Knox College, IL , 2553
Knox County High School, TN , 9001

Knox County high schools, ME , 8436
Knoxville High School, IA , 3269
Kolb School, MI , 4350
Koraes School, IL , 2776
Korea University Medical College, South Korea, 7768
Kuna High School, ID , 2343
Kutztown Area High School, PA , 6684
Kutztown University, PA , 8087

La Costa Canyon High School, CA , 728
La Grange High School, TX , 9166
Laboratory Institute Merchandising College, NY , 6151
Laconia High School, NH , 5335
Ladysmith High School, WI , 9996
Lafayette College, PA , 6897
Lafayette High School, VA , 9388
Lafayette Senior High School, NY , 8358
Lafourche Parish School System, LA , 3659
Laguna Beach High School, CA , 415
Lake City High School, MN , 8019
Lake Clifton Senior High School, MD , 2074
Lake County High School, CO , 1293
Lake County high schools, IL , 2664
Lake County public high schools, OR , 8115
Lake Lehman High School, PA , 6855
Lake Region High School, ME , 3702
Lake Region Union High School, VT , 5327
Lake Sumter Community College, FL , 1944
Lake Superior College, MN , 4773
Lake Travis High School, TX , 8913
Lake Worth High School, FL , 1839
Lake Zurich High School, IL , 2764
Lakeland Christian Academy, IN , 3091
Lakeland Community College, OH , 7202
Lakeland High School, VA , 9443
Lakeland High School, WI , 9949
Lakeland School Corporation School District, IN , 3093
Lakeville high schools, MA , 4107
Lamar State College-Port Arthur, TX , 9025
Lamoille Union High School, VT , 9261
Lampasas High School, TX , 8805
Lancaster Health Alliance School of Nursing, PA , 8128
Lancaster High School, OH , 7259
Landrum Public School System, SC , 6658
Langston University, OK , 1614
Laramie County School District #2, WY , 10104
Laredo Community College, TX , 9077
Las Animas County high schools, CO , 1129
Las Lomas High School, CA , 922
LaSalle Catholic School, IL , 2648
LaSalle High School, NY , 6180
LaSalle-Peru High School, IL , 2911
LaSalle-Peru Township High School, IL , 2425
Laurens District 55 high schools, SC , 8451
Laurinburg public high schools, NC , 6764
Laville School Corp., IN , 4504
Lawrence University, WI , 9960
Lawrenceburg High Schools, IN , 3012
Layfayette School District, CA , 730
Lea County high schools, NM , 5630
Lead High School, SD , 8532
Learning Prep School, MA , 4245
Leavenworth High School, KS , 3437
Lebanon County high schools, PA , 7820
Lebanon High School, NH , 5358, 8306
Lebanon High School, OR , 7400
Lebanon High School, PA , 6213, 7948
Lebanon high schools, NH , 8370
Lebanon School District, PA , 6570
Lecanto High School, FL , 1830
Ledford Senior High School, NC , 6923
Lee County public schools, AL , 55
Leelanau County high schools, MI , 4487
Lees-McRae College, NC , 2016
Lehigh Carbon Community College, PA , 7952, 8191
Lehigh University, PA , 6897, 7740, 8104
Lehighton Area High School, PA , 1397
Lehman Catholic High School, OH , 7388
Lemon Bay High School, FL , 1870
Lenawee County High School, MI , 4532
Leonard High School, John I., FL , 1839
LeTourneau University, TX , 9110
Leverett Chapel High School, TX , 8948

Lewis Cass High School, IN , 2979, 3104
Lewis County High School, NY , 7126
Lewis County School District, NY , 6287
Lewis High School, KS , 3456
Lewis S. Mills High School, CT , 1340
Lewisburg High School, PA , 6851
Lewistown High School, IL , 2734
Lewistown School District No. 97, IL , 2735
Lexington High School, NE , 5228
Lexington Theological Seminary, KY , 2832
Liberty High School, CA , 521
Liberty High School, VA , 9423
Liberty Union-Thurston High School, OH , 7404
Lick Wilmerding High School, CA , 985
Ligonier Valley School District, PA , 8143
Lincoln Christian College, IL , 2553
Lincoln County high schools, WA , 7583
Lincoln High School, CA , 878, 896
Lincoln High School, IN , 3097
Lincoln High School, TX , 8967
Lincoln High School, WI , 9890
Lincoln High School, WV , 6830
Lincoln Trail College, IL , 3173
Lincoln University (PA), PA , 1614
Lincoln-Way Central High School, IL , 2778
Lincoln-Way East High School, IL , 2778
Lincolnview High School, OH , 7403
Lindenhurst High School, NY , 6053
Lindsay Elementary School, MI , 4350
Linn High School, MO , 5086, 5096
Linn-Benton Community College, OR , 6811
Linn-Mar High School, IA , 9966
Linton High School, NY , 6291
Linwood Public High School, NH , 5339
Little High School, Edward, ME , 8326
Little Rock Central High School, AR , 317
Little Rock public high schools, AR , 319
Littlefield High School, MI , 4577
Littleton High School, CO , 1245
Livermore Falls High School, ME , 3696
Livermore high schools, CA , 858
Livingston Intermediate School District, TX , 2738
Livingston Manor High School, NY , 5744
Lock Haven University of Pennsylvania, PA , 6664
Lock Haven University, PA , 7960
Lockport School District, NY , 5780
Logan College, John A., IL , 2617
Logan High School, Benjamin, OH , 7402
Logan-Hocking School District, OH , 7013
Logansport High School, IN , 2979, 3104
Logos Academy, PA , 8213
London High School, OH , 7437
Lone Star College-CyFair, TX , 8724
Long Beach City College, CA , 754
Longmont High School, CO , 1150
Longview High School, TX , 64
Loogootee Community School District, IN , 3105
Lorain high schools, OH , 7213
Los Angeles County high schools, CA , 702
Los Angeles Lutheran High School, CA , 964
Lost River High School, OR , 7609
Loudoun County High School, VA , 6861
Loudoun County high schools, VA , 6697
Loudoun Valley High School, VA , 6861
Loudoun Valley high schools, VA , 6697
Louise High School, TX , 9186
Louisiana high schools, MO , 2599
Louisiana State University, LA , 81, 2025, 3646
Louisiana Tech University, LA , 3668
Louisville High School, OH , 7026
Louisville Male Traditional High School, KY , 3592
Lourdes College, OH , 7338
Loveland High School, CO , 1241
Lovington High School, IL , 2424
Lowell High School, CA , 548
Lowell High School, MA , 4244
Lowell High School, MI , 4370, 4445
Lowell Public School District, MI , 4621
Loyalsock High School, PA , 7933
Lubbock Independent School District, TX , 8830
Lucas County high schools, OH , 6993
Ludington Area School District, MI , 4360
Lumen Christi High School, MI , 4541

Luxemberg-Casco High School, WI , 9967
Luxembourg-Casco High School, WI , 2666
Lycoming College, PA , 6664, 8191
Lynn English High School, MA , 4147
Lynn public high schools, MA , 8348
Lyons Central School District No. 1, NY , 8416

MaCalester College, MN , 1949
Macgruder High School, MD , 3877
MacMurray College, IL , 2553
Macomb County high schools, MI , 4655
Macon State College, GA , 2118
Madison Consolidated Schools, IN , 2999
Madison County high schools, MT , 5138
Madison High School, ME , 3696
Madison High School, MO , 5068
Madison High School, NJ , 5500
Madison High School, TX , 8967
Madison high schools, OH , 7124
Madison Plains High School, OH , 7437
Madison School District, NY , 6070
Madisonville High School, TX , 8908
Madonna University, MI , 4385
Mahanoy Area High School, PA , 6756
Mahanoy Area School District, PA , 8156
Mahar Regional High School, Ralph C., MA , 4207
Maharishi University of Management, IA , 761
Mahoning County high schools, OH , 7140
Maine East High School, IL , 2844
Malone College, OH , 7176
Manatee County high schools, FL , 1844
Manatee High School, FL , 2037
Manchester College, IN , 3069
Manchester High School Central, NH , 5318
Manchester High School, CT , 1420, 8288
Manchester High School, NH , 5346
Manchester School District, OH , 7270
Manchester-Essex Regional High School, MA , 4320
Mancos High School, CO , 660
Manual High School, IL , 8103
Mapleton High School, OR , 7681
Mapletown High School, PA , 7781
Marblehead High School, MA , 4214
Marcellus High School, MI , 4471
Marengo Community High School, IL , 2678
Marian Catholic High School, PA , 6756
Marian College, IN , 3228
Marian Educational Outreach, IN , 2980
Marian High School, IN , 7204
Marian University, IN , 3069
Maricopa County high schools, AZ , 211
Marietta College, OH , 7189, 7297
Marion County High School, TN , 8645
Marion County high schools, IN , 2762, 2983
Marion County high schools, TX , 2983
Marion County high schools, MO , 4936
Marion Harding High School, OH , 7119, 7308
Marion High School, IA , 9966
Marist High School, IL , 2522, 2778
Marlboro County High School, SC , 7698
Marquette University, WI , 2832, 9908, 9960
Marriot Hospitality High School, DC , 1559
Marshall County high schools, IA , 3301
Marshall County high schools, IN , 3110
Marshall County public high schools, OK , 2526
Marshall County schools, IN , 3043
Marshall High School, IL , 2709
Marshall University, WV , 8765, 9767
Marshalltown Community High School, IA , 3357
Marshalltown High School, IA , 9883
Marsing High School, ID , 2343
Martha's Vineyard Charter School, MA , 4216
Martha's Vineyard High School, MA , 8284
Martha's Vineyard Regional High School, MA , 4216, 8258, 8270, 8440
Martin County community colleges, FL , 1907
Martin County high schools, FL , 1839, 1907, 1964
Martin University, IN , 3069
Mary Institute and St. Louis Country Day School, MO , 5052
Marysville High School, KS , 3523
Marysville High School, OH , 7061
Marysville Union High School, CA , 332
Mascoma Valley Regional High School, NH , 5358

Mason County high schools, MI , 4485, 7264
Mason County high schools, WV , 9808
Masonic Home and School of Texas, TX , 8938
Masonic Home Independent School District, TX , 8938
Massachusetts College of Liberal Arts, MA , 4165
Massachusetts Institute of Technology, MA , 4209
Masuk High School, CT , 1482
Mattoon High School, IL , 2447
Mattoon Senior High School, IL , 2712
Mayfield Central School, NY , 6025
Maysville Community College, KY , 3552
Mayville Public School System, WI , 9842
McAllen Memorial High School, TX , 8769
McCallie School, The, TN , 4911
McCaskey High School, PA , 7942
McClean County School District, KY , 6931
McCutcheon High School, IN , 3030
McDonough County high schools, IL , 2919
McDonough District high schools, MD , 3945
McDowell County high schools, WV , 9807
McDowell High School, NC , 6866
McDowell High School, PA , 7789
McHenry Community High School, IL , 2800
McIntosh County Academy, GA , 2231
McKeesport Area High School, PA , 7836
McLean County High School, KY , 2548
McMurry University, TX , 7738
McNeese State University, LA , 3681
Mechanicsburg High School, PA , 8098
Medfield High School, MA , 4245
Medford Senior High School, WI , 9999
Medical College of Georgia, GA , 2177
Medical College of Pennsylvania, PA , 7874
Medicine Lake High School, MT , 6948
Meeker High School, CO , 6653
Meigs County high schools, OH , 7189
Melba High School, ID , 2343
Memorial High School,, WI , 9882
Menard County high schools, IL , 2843
Menasha Joint School District, WI , 2611
Mendham High School, NJ , 6015
Mendocino Community College, CA , 481
Menlo School, CA , 1109
Menominee High School, MI , 5643, 9891
Menomonee Falls High School, WI , 9920
Merced High School, CA , 1106
Mercer County high schools, MO , 5026
Mercer High School, PA , 8209
Mercer University, GA , 2045, 2118, 2128
Mercyhurst College, PA , 7977
Meriden High School, CT , 8390
Meridian (Perry) High School, IN , 2510
Meridian High School, ID , 2343
Mesa County high schools, CO , 1191
Methuen High School, MA , 4285, 8329
Metroplex High School, TX , 8786
Mexico High School, MO , 4991, 5005
Miami County high schools, IN , 2963, 3149
Miami County high schools, OH , 7388
Miami East High School, OH , 7388
Miami University, OH , 2247, 6954
Miami-Dade High School, FL , 1982
Mid-Prarie School District, IA , 3331
Mid-Vermont Christian School, VT , 5358
Middle Georgia Technical College, GA , 2118
Middle Tennessee State University, TN , 8611, 8624
Middle-High School, VT , 9246
Middleboro High School, MA , 4312, 4313
Middleboro high schools, MA , 4107
Middleborough High School, MA , 4037, 4046, 4288
Middleton High School, ID , 2343
Middletown High School, OH , 7011
Middletown high schools, OH , 7124
Midland Community College, TX , 8819
Midland County high schools, MI , 7247
Midland County public high schools, TX , 8819
Midway High School, ND , 6936
Midwestern Baptist Theological Seminary, MO , 9413
Milford High School, DE , 1512
Milford High School, MA , 4245
Milford High School, NE , 8182
Milford high schools, CT , 1376
Miller High School, OH , 7361
Millersburg High School, PA , 8195

Millersburgh School District, PA , 8150
Millersville University, PA , 8087
Millikin University, IL , 2553, 2923
Millington High School, MI , 6990
Milton Union High School, OH , 7388
Milwaukee Technical High School, WI , 10034
Minden Public School System, LA , 3656
Mineola High School, TX , 9036
Mineral Point Unified School District, WI , 2591
Minersville Area High School, PA , 6114
Ming de School, China, 6538
Minister High School, OH , 7388
Minneapolis Community and Technical College, MN , 4894
Mira Costa College, CA , 897
Mississippi State University, MS , 81, 2247
Mississippi University for Women, MS , 4911
Missouri School for the Deaf, MO , 5099
Missouri State University, MO , 5059
Missouri Western State College, MO , 5070, 9213
Moberly High School, MO , 5068
Modec High School,, CA , 801
Modesto High School, CA , 1017
Modesto Junior College, CA , 1017
Molalla Union High School, OR , 7608
Molokai High School, HI , 2275
Monache High School, CA , 400
Monmouth County public high schools, NJ , 5597
Mononasen High School, NY , 6291
Monpelier School District, VT , 1460
Monroe County public schools, MI , 4396
Monroe High School, WI , 9897
Montana State University, Billings, MT , 5164, 7541
Montana State University, Bozeman, MT , 7541
Montana State University, MT , 5161, 5182
Montana State University, Northern, MT , 7541
Montana Tech of the University of Montana, MT , 7541
Montana University, MT , 7165
Montclair State University, NJ , 5577
Monterey Peninsula College, CA , 402
Montesano High School, WA , 7652
Montessori School of Rome, GA , 2203
Montevido High School, MN , 4888
Montgomery College, MD , 1594
Monticello High School, IL , 8716
Monticello High School, NY , 5732
Monticello High School, WI , 9980
Montour County public high schools, PA , 7937
Montpelier High School, OH , 7017
Montpelier High School, VT , 5309
Montreat College, NC , 2016
Montrose County High Schools, CO , 1191
Montrose High School, CO , 660, 1228
Montville High School, CT , 8362
Moody Bible Institute, IL , 4118
Moorestown High School, NJ , 5511
Moorpark College, CA , 1036
Morehouse College, GA , 1614
Morenci Public School District, MI , 4673
Morengo Community High School, IL , 2791
Morgan State University, MD , 1614
Morristown High School, TN , 40
Morrisville-Eaton School District, NY , 6070
Morrow County high schools, OR , 6766
Morrow County School District, OR , 6902
Morse High School, ME , 3693
Mosinee High School, WI , 10092
Mother McAuley High School, IL , 2778
Mott Community College, MI , 4394
Moulay Ismail University, Morocco, 6090
Mound Westonka High School, MN , 2768
Mount Desert Island High School, ME , 3700, 3708
Mount Dora area high schools, FL , 1987
Mount Greylock High School, MA , 8404
Mount Hood Community College, OR , 6857
Mount Pleasant High School, NY , 6291
Mount Royal Academy, NH , 5358
Mount San Antonio College, CA , 434
Mount Sinai School of Medicine, NY , 2200
Mount Vernon High School, IL , 5021
Mount Vernon High School, IN , 6957
Mount Vernon High School, OH , 6979
Mount Vernon High School, TX , 8737
Mountain Home Arkansas High School, AR , 284

Mountain Mission School, VA , 9528
Mountain State University, WV , 9772
Mountain Valley High School, ME , 3696
Mountain View High School, ID , 2343
Mountain View High School, WA , 9727
Mountain View Los Altos Union School District, CA , 755
Mt. Abram High School, ME , 3696
Mt. Blue High School, ME , 3696
Mt. Holyoke College, MA , 4124
Mt. Ridge High School, MD , 3891
Mt. Vernon High School, MO , 5018
Mukwonago High School, WI , 2803
Mulhark Trail Regional High School, MA , 8338
Multnomah County high schools, OR , 7534
Murray State College, OK , 7458
Muscatine Community College, IA , 3245, 3337
Muskingum County high schools, OH , 7160, 7260
Mynders Academy, NY , 2575

Nampa Christian High School, ID , 2343
Nampa High School, ID , 2343, 2348
Nansemond Academy, VA , 9443
Nansemond High School, VA , 9443
Nantucket High School, MA , 8417
Napa High School, CA , 518
Napa Valley College, CA , 518
Naperville North High School, IL , 2679
Naples High School, FL , 1861
Napoleon High School, OH , 7228
Nashoba Technical High School, MA , 4150
Nashville High School, IN , 3213
Nashwauk-Keewatin High School, MN , 4700
Natick High School, MA , 4007
Nativity BVM High School, PA , 7767
Naugatuck Valley Community College, CT , 1366
Nauset Regional High School, MA , 4007, 4133, 5343, 5375, 8350
Naval Academy, MD , 2595
Navarro College, TX , 9067
Nebraska Methodist College of Nursing, NE , 5244
Neenah High School, WI , 9998, 10063
Neenah Joint School District, WI , 2611
Neew Glarus High School, WI , 9980
Nelson County High School, VA , 9346
Neodesha High School, KS , 3450
Neptune Township public schools, NJ , 8393
New Bedford High School, MA , 4283
New Brighton School District, PA , 7441
New Britain High School, CT , 8305, 8317, 8366
New Buffalo High School, MI , 4580
New Castle Chrysler High School, IN , 3116, 3129
New Haven public high schools, CT , 1378
New Jersey public high schools, NJ , 5460
New London High School, CT , 8230
New Lothrop High School, MI , 2436
New Mexico State University, NM , 7895, 9219
New Milford High School, CT , 1440
New Orleans Baptist Theological Seminary, LA , 9413
New Oxford High School, PA , 7954
New Philadelphia High School, OH , 7123, 7369, 7386
New Rochelle High School, NY , 6018
New Technology High School, CA , 518
New York City public high schools, NY , 6344
New York Mills School District, NY , 6497
New York State School for the Deaf, NY , 6485
New York University, NY , 6277, 6525, 7895
Newark Senior High School, NY , 1779
Newberry College, SC , 6881
Newburyport High School, MA , 4002
Newburyport High School, MA , 4125
Newburyport High School, MA , 8355
Newington High School, CT , 8438
Newman Memorial School of Nursing, KS , 8717
Newport High School, NH , 5358
Newport High School, OR , 7585, 9628
Newton High School, MS , 2726
Newton High School, OH , 7388
Newton North High School, MA , 4245, 8359
Newton South High School, MA , 8359
Newtown High School, CT , 1482
Niagara County Community College, NY , 6256
Nicolet College, WI , 9982

Niles Senior High School, MI , 4362
Niskayuna High School, NY , 6291
Noble County high schools, IN , 2987
Nooksack Valley High School, OH , 7275
Norfolk Academy, VA , 9286
Norfolk State University, VA , 9502, 9508
Norphlet High School, AR , 321
North Adams high schools, MA , 4217
North Arkansas College, AR , 309
North Attleboro High School, MA , 4199
North Attleboro high schools, MA , 8333
North Brookfield High School, MA , 4233
North Carolina A&T State University, NC , 1614
North Carolina A&T University, NC , 6793
North Carolina School of the Arts, NC , 6730
North Carolina State University, NC , 2247, 6565, 6583
North Carolina Wesleyan College, NC , 4544
North Catholic HIgh School, PA , 8081
North Central Missouri College, MO , 5064
North Central Technical College, WI , 9922
North College Hill Schools, OH , 7272
North Conway School District high schools, NH , 8291
North Crawford High School, WI , 2034
North Dickinson County School, MI , 4551
North East High School, PA , 8010
North Fayette Senior High School, IA , 3317
North Haven High School, CT , 1434
North High School, MN , 4893
North High School, WI , 9882
North Hunterdon High School, NJ , 5590
North Idaho College, ID , 9681
North Judson High School, IN , 3038
North Kansas City High School, MO , 2055
North Myrtle Beach High School, SC , 8460
North Newton High School, IN , 3177
North Platte R-I, MO , 5066
North Plymouth High School, MA , 4252
North Pocono High School, PA , 6605
North Putnam High School, IN , 3154
North Tahoe High School, CA , 1058
North Toole County High School, MT , 8197
North Union High School, OH , 7061
North Vermillion County high schools, IN , 3211
Northampton Community College, PA , 8011
Northampton High School, MA , 4291
Northampton high schools, MA , 8320
Northbrook Senior High School, TX , 8747
Northeast High School, PA , 6859, 8012
Northeast Texas Community College, TX , 9127
Northeast Wisconsin Technical College, WI , 9911
Northeastern High School, IN , 3194
Northeastern Wayne Schools, IN , 3217
Northern Arizona University, AZ , 157, 222, 2890
Northern California public high schools, CA , 961
Northern Highlands Regional High School, NJ , 8315
Northern Illinois University, IL , 2441, 2605, 2759, 3278
Northern Kentucky University, KY , 6954
Northern Lehigh School Disctrict, PA , 8191
Northern Oklahoma College, OK , 8797
Northern Pines High School, WI , 2578
Northern State University, SD , 8534
Northern Virginia Community College, VA , 1594
Northfield Elementary, VT , 9246
Northfield High School, VT , 1457, 9250
Northgate High School, CA , 922
Northome High School, MN , 4700
Northumberland County high schools, PA , 6069
Northview High School, IN , 3126
Northville Central School, NY , 6025
Northville High School, MI , 4561
Northville High School, NY , 6305
Northwest Area High School, PA , 6855
NorthWest Arkansas Community College, AR , 278, 309
Northwest Christian College, OR , 7551
Northwest Technical Institute, AR , 309
Northwestern School District, SD , 8543
Northwestern University, IL , 2788, 2849
Northwood-Kensett High School, IA , 3393
Northwood-Kensett high schools, IA , 3303
Norton Community High School, KS , 3430, 3490
Norwalk Community College, CT , 1435

Norwalk High School, CT , 1352, 2445
Norwell High School, MA , 4103
Norwich High School, NY , 6029
Norwood High School, MA , 7305
Nothern Lehigh High School, PA , 7953
Notre Dame High School, IA , 3394
Notre Dame High School, NJ , 6925
Notre Dame High School, NY , 5713
Notre Dame University, IN , 7204
Nouvel Catholic Central High School, MI , 4366, 4436
Novi Community School District, MI , 4564
Nuckolis County high schools, NE , 5265

O'Fallon Township High School, IL , 4989
Oak Hill High School, ME , 7007
Oak Park Unified School District, CA , 510
Oak Ridge High School, CA , 1053
Oakland City University, IN , 3069
Oakridge High School, OR , 6723
Oberlin College, OH , 7300
Obion County high schools, TN , 8613
Ocean City High School, NJ , 6789
Oconee County High School, SC , 7860
Oconto County high schools, WI , 2653
Odin high schools, IL , 2467
Oelwein Community schools, IA , 3346
Ohio County High School, KY , 3636
Ohio County public high schools, WV , 2420
Ohio State University, OH , 7132, 7143, 7150, 7189,
    7310
Ohio University College of Osteopathic Medicine, OH ,
    7282
Ohio University, OH , 7143, 7189
Ohio Valley University, OH , 7297
Oil City High School, PA , 7746
Okanogan County high schools, WA , 9154
Okeechobee High School, FL , 2003
Oklahoma Baptist University, OK , 7521
Oklahoma City University, OK , 7485, 7527
Oklahoma State Institute of Technology, OK , 7453
Oklahoma State University, OK , 7451, 7453, 7485,
    7491, 7504, 7527, 8815
Olathe High School, CO , 1303
Old Dominion University, VA , 9440, 9502
Olean High School, NY , 7367
Oliver Ames High School, MA , 4175, 8378
Oliver High School, PA , 8081
Olivet Nazerene University, IL , 2767
Olympic Heights High School, FL , 1839
Omaha North High School, NE , 5257
Onaway High School, MI , 2436
Oneonta High School, NY , 6322, 7357
Ontonagon Area High School, MI , 4569
Open Door Christian School, PA , 7781
Orange Coast Community College, CA , 5287
Orange County high schools, CA , 702
Orange County high schools, IN , 3196
Orcas Island High School, WA , 9587
Orchard Park High School, NY , 6147
Ord High School, NE , 5248
Ord public schools, NE , 5222
Oregon City high schools, OR , 7102
Oregon Health Sciences University, OR , 6857, 7631
Oregon Institute of Technology, OR , 7626
Oregon School District No. 24J, OR , 7582
Oregon State University, OR , 5593, 7635, 7684, 9688
Orient-Macksburg High School, IA , 3256
Oriskany High School, NY , 6485
Orrville High School, OH , 7358
Osawatomie High School, KS , 3530
Osceola High School, AR , 299
Osceola public high schools, MO , 4997
Oskaloosa High School, KS , 3437, 3438
Oswayo Valley School District, PA , 8151
Otsego County High School, MI , 4571
Ottawa Hills High School, MI , 4445
Overton High School, TX , 8948
Ovid-Elsie High School, MI , 4435, 4453
Owen County High School, KY , 3626
Owensboro City School District, KY , 6931
Owensville High School, MO , 5083
Oxford School District, MI , 4427
Oxnard College, CA , 1036

PA College of Technology Williamsport, PA , 6664
Paden City High School, WV , 9806
Paint Valley High School, OH , 7034
Palestine Independent School District, TX , 9117
Palm Beach Community College, FL , 1839, 2011
Palm Beach County high schools, FL , 1839
Palm Beach Gardens High School, FL , 1839
Palm Beach Lakes High School, FL , 1839
Palmetto High School, FL , 6644
Palmetto High School, SC , 8497
Palo Alto College, TX , 9127
Palo Alto High School, CA , 548
Palo Duro High School, TX , 8675
Palomar College, CA , 897, 1094
Pamlico County High School, NC , 6913
Pampa High School, TX , 8688, 9019
Panorama Community School District, IA , 3250
Paoli High School, IN , 3141, 3196
Paonia High School, CO , 1151
Paris High School, IL , 2548, 2783
Paris High School, TX , 9003
Paris Junior College, TX , 9004
Park High School, MN , 4853
Park High School, MT , 7629
Park Ridge High School, NJ , 5458
Parkland High School, PA , 7953
Parkside High School, MD , 6326
Parkway High School, OH , 7403
Parma High School, ID , 2342
Pasadena City College, CA , 1084
Patrick County High School, VA , 6686
Paul D. Camp Community College, VA , 9502, 9508
Paulding County High School, OH , 7070
Paulding High School, OH , 7403
Pawnee County high schools, KS , 3465
Pea Ridge High School, AR , 272
Peabody Veterans Memorial High School, MA , 4198
Pekin Community High School, IL , 2932
Pekin High School, IL , 5102
Pelham High School, NY , 1316
Pellston High School, MI , 4577
Pembine High School, WI , 10051
Penn College, PA , 7963
Pennridge High School, PA , 6934
Pennsbury High School, PA , 9424
Pennsylvania State University at Erie, PA , 7977
Pennsylvania State University, PA , 6664, 7864, 7959,
    8002
Pentucket High School, MA , 4002
People's Academy, VT , 5319
Peoples Academy High School, VT , 9261
Peoria Unified School District, AZ , 225
Perdue University, IN , 47
Perkins School of Theology, TX , 9110
Perry County high schools, PA , 6069
Perry High School, PA , 8081
Peru High School, IN , 5275
Petoskey High School, MI , 4577
Pfeiffer College, NC , 8467
Philadelphia College of Osteopathic Medicine, PA ,
    7874
Philadelphia High School for Girls, PA , 7826
Philadelphia medical schools, PA , 8268
Phillips County high schools, MT , 5168
Phillips High School, WI , 9836
Phillipsburg High School, KS , 3521
Phoenix School of Law, AZ , 212
Phoenix Union High School District, AZ , 245
Piedmont High School, OK , 7473
Pierpont Community & Technical College, WV , 9782
Pike Central High School, IN , 2971, 2978
Pike County High School, IL , 2627
Pike County high schools, IL , 4936
Pima Community College, AZ , 190
Pine Bluff public high schools, AR , 319
Pine County high schools, MN , 4870
Pine Grove Area High School, PA , 8219
Pine Tree High School, TX , 64
Pine Valley Central School, NY , 6107
Pine View High School, FL , 1844
Pinedale High School, WY , 701
Pinellas County High School, FL , 68
Pioneer High School, IN , 2979, 3104
Piqua High School, OH , 7304

Pittsfield High School, IL , 2411
Pittsfield High School, MA , 4235
Pitzer College, CA , 9043
Placer High School, CA , 870, 6728
Plattsburg High School, NY , 7141
Pleasants County high schools, WV , 9808
Plentywood High School, MT , 5153, 6948
Plymouth Community Schools, IN , 3192
Plymouth High School, MA , 8300
Plymouth North High School, MA , 8396
Plymouth School Corp., IN , 4504
Plymouth South High School, MA , 8396
Plymouth-Carver High School, MA , 8274
Plymouth/Canton School District, MI , 1095
Pocahontas Area Community School, IA , 3277, 3381
Pocahontas County High School, WV , 2852
Point Loma High School, CA , 624, 878
Polaris High School, GA , 2235
Polk County Public School System, NC , 6658
Polson High School, MT , 5136, 5170, 5181, 6700
Ponderosa High School, CA , 1053
Pope County high schools, AR , 280
Port Angeles High School, WA , 9745
Port Angeles Senior High School, WA , 8971
Port Clinton High School, OH , 7330
Port Huron area high schools, MI , 4479
Port Washington High School, WI , 9976, 10022
PORTA Community Unit School district high schools, IL ,
    2715
Porterville College, CA , 400
Porterville High School, CA , 400
Portland Community College, OR , 6857, 7642
Portland high schools, ME , 3747
Portland high schools, OR , 7658
Portland State University, OR , 6857, 7635, 7642
Portland State University, School of Engineering and
    Applied Science, OR , 7673
Portland Waldorf High School, OH , 6996
Portsmouth High School, NH , 5314
Portville Central School, NY , 7367, 8352
Posey County high schools, IN , 6968
Poth High School, TX , 9157
Pottsgrove High School, PA , 7880, 8202
Pottstown High School, PA , 7880
Pottsville Area High School, PA , 7838
Pottsville High School, PA , 7767
Powell County high schools, MT , 6824
Prairie Central Community Unit District 8 schools, IL ,
    2668
Prairie Grove High School, AR , 302
Prairie Heights Community School Corporation School
    District, IN , 3093
Prairie View A&M University, TX , 1614, 9127
Pratt County Community College, KS , 3506
Pratt County high schools, KS , 3482
Prattsburg Central School District, NY , 6201
Presentation College, SD , 8534
Presque Isle High School, ME , 7012, 7299
Prince Edward County Virginia High School, VA , 9366
Prince George's Community College, MD , 1594
Princeton area secondary schools, NJ , 5503
Princeton Senior High School, WV , 9812
Princeton University, NJ , 6897
Proctor High School, NY , 5907
Prosser High School, WA , 6620
Protestant Episcopal Theological Seminary of Virginia,
    VA , 9802
Providence Catholic High School, IL , 2778
Providence College, RI , 8269
Provincetown High School, MA , 4007
Pueblo County high school, CO , 1209
Pueblo County high schools, CO , 7587
Pullman Free School of Vocational Training, IL , 2804
Punxsutawney Area High School, PA , 7089, 7921
Punxsutawney School District, PA , 7816
Purdue University, IN , 3016, 3107, 3140, 7204
Putnam County Community Unit School District No.
    535, IL , 2875
Putnam County High School, IL , 2433

Quakertown Community High School, PA , 7953
Queens College, NY , 6219, 6340
Quincy High School, WA , 9623

Quincy University, IL , 2553
Quinnipiac University, CT , 1858

Racine Unified School District, WI , 10001
Radcliffe College, MA , 3988
Raleigh high schools, NC , 6779
Rancho Los Alamitos High School, CA , 990
Rancosas Valley high school, NJ , 5552
Randolph County high schools, IN , 3117
Randolph High School, NE , 5257
Randolph Union High School, VT , 1341
Randolphe Southern High School, IN , 3194
Rangeley Lakes Regional School, ME , 3696
Raton High School, NM , 5658
Rawa Dolu Secondary School, Nepal, 8651
Reading High School, PA , 6671, 7902
Reading Senior High School, PA , 6075, 7893
Red Bank Regional High School, NJ , 5460, 5597
Red Rock High School, AZ , 173
Red Rocks Community College, CO , 1266
Red Wing High School, MN , 4796
Redfield School District, SD , 8543
Reed College, OR , 6857
Reedsburg Area High School, WI , 9983
Refugio County high schools, TX , 9046
Regency Beauty Institute, AR , 309
Regional High School, MA , 8297
Regional School District 1, CT , 1332
Regis High School, IL , 2522
Regis High School, WI , 9882
Reinbeck public schools, IA , 3332
Remer High School, MN , 4700
Republic County high schools, KS , 5265
Republic High School, WA , 9563
Revere High School, MA , 8294
Revere High School, OH , 7122
Revere Junior-Senior High School, CO , 1139
Reynolds High School, OR , 8958
Rhinebeck High School, NY , 5753
Rhinelander High School, WI , 2578, 2916, 10005
Rice High School, TX , 9171
Rice University, TX , 8765, 8945
Richburg Central School, NY , 8352
Richland Community College, IL , 2819
Richland County High School, IL , 2561
Richland County high schools, MT , 5144
Richland County School District, ND , 972
Richmond Community Schools, IN , 3217
Richmond High School, IN , 3161
Richmond Senior High School, IN , 1249
Ricker Classical Institute, ME , 3730
Ricker College, ME , 3730
Ricker Junior College, ME , 3730
Ridgefield High School, CT , 1448, 6566
Ridgewood High School, OH , 7001
Rimrock High School, ID , 2343
Ringgold High School, PA , 7731
Rio Hondo College, CA , 385
Ripley High School, TN , 8569
Ripley High School, WV , 9816
Risen Christ Catholic School, MN , 4782
Rising Sun High School, IN , 3131, 6985, 7193
Ritchie County high schools, WV , 9808
Ritenour Senior High School, MO , 2502
River Delta Unified School District, CA , 646
River Valley High School, MI , 4580
River Valley High School, WI , 2412, 10019
Riverheads High School, VA , 9346
Riverside High School, ID , 6776
Riverside-Brookfield High School, IL , 4331, 4430
Riverview High School, OH , 7001
Roane County high schools, WV , 9808
Robert E. Lee High School, TX , 8713
Robert E. Lee High School, VA , 2563, 9346
Roberts High School, Owen J., PA , 7880
Robertsdale High School, AL , 88
Robstown High School, TX , 5580
Rochester Area Senior High School, PA , 8078
Rochester High School, IL , 2551
Rochester High School, MA , 4312
Rochester High School, MI , 4395
Rochester high schools, MN , 4819
Rock Valley College, IL , 2605

Rock Valley Community School, IA , 3371
Rockford High School, IL , 2671
Rockland District High School, ME , 8436
Rockland High School, MA , 4122
Rockport High School, MA , 3956
Rockville High School, CT , 8346
Rocky Mountain College, MT , 7541
Rogers High School, AR , 272, 278
Rogers High School, RI , 8422
Rome Catholic High School, NY , 6485
Rome Free Academy, NY , 6485
Romeo School District, MI , 4427
Roosevelt High School, CA , 896, 8067
Roosevelt High School, OR , 7607
Roosville High Schools, IN , 47
Roscoe Central School District, NY , 5953
Rose-Hulman Institute of Technology, IN , 3069
Roseville High School, CA , 548
Round Lake High School, IL , 2844
Rowan University, NJ , 5554
Roxbury High School, NJ , 8342
Royal College of Music, Benjamin Britten International
    Opera School, England, 3080
Royal Palm Beach High School, FL , 2013
Rumson-Fair Haven High School, NJ , 7808
Rush County high schools, IN , 2488, 2698
Rushville Consolidated High School, IN , 3167
Russell High School, KY , 7025
Rutgers University, School of Law - Newark, NJ , 5521
Ruthland County School District, VT , 5313
Rutland High School, VT , 9259
Rye High School, NY , 6367, 7903

Sacramento City College, CA , 786
Sacramento State University, CA , 926
Sacred heart Cathedral Preparatory School, CA , 10106
Sacred Heart High School, CT , 1858
Saddleback Community College, CA , 968, 5287
Saddleback High School, CA , 990
Saginaw Valley State University, MI , 4350, 4355
Saint Cloud High School, FL , 2086
Salem Central High School, NY , 5805
Salem College, NC , 6730, 6737
Salem High School, MO , 5126
Salem High School, NJ , 6592, 7890
Salem high schools, MA , 4318
Salem State College, MA , 4214
Salinas Valley high schools, CA , 6586
Saline County high schools, AR , 7
Salisbury High School, MO , 5020
Sam Houston State University, TX , 9127
San Diego County high schools, CA , 930
San Diego County schools, CA , 531
San Diego State University, CA , 851, 897
San Francisco State University, CA , 715
San Jose State University, CA , 950
San Lorenzo Valley High School, CA , 4578
San Mateo County high schools, CA , 6585
San Rafael High School, CA , 500
Sandburg High School, Carl, IL , 2778
Sandora high schools, IL , 2467
Sandpoint High School, ID , 5172
Sandra Day O'Connor College of Law, AZ , 212
Sandwich High School, MA , 4007
Sanford High School, ME , 3724
Sanford high schools, ME , 3732
Sangamon County high schools, IL , 2567, 5047
Sanilac County high schools, MI , 4388, 4599
Santa Ana Community College, CA , 5287
Santa Barbara County High School, CA , 955
Santa Cruz High School, CA , 4526, 4573
Santa Fe High School, NM , 5651
Santa Rosa Junior College, CA , 958
Santaluces High School, FL , 1839
Santiago Canyon Community College, CA , 5287
Saranac Lake School District, NY , 6374
Sarasota County high schools, FL , 1844
Saratoga High School, CA , 720
Saratoga Springs high schools, NY , 6062
Sargent College of Rehabilitation, MA , 4007
Satanta High School, KS , 3531
Saugus High School, MA , 4259
Sauk County Teacher's College, WI , 9983

Sauquoit School District, NY , 6497
Savannah High School, MO , 9962
Savannah high schools, MO , 4937
Savannah Technical College, GA , 2132
Sayre High School, OK , 7513
Scarsdale High School, NY , 6378
Schenectady County high schools, NY , 6382
School District No. 60, MO , 4959
School of Podiatric Medicine, PA , 7770
Schulenburg High School, TX , 9100
Scio High School, OR , 7657
Scioto Valley (Ohio) Conference School, OH , 7034
Scobey High School, MT , 5153
Scotch Plains-Fanwood High School, NJ , 5561
Scotland High School, IL , 2929
Seattle Central College, WA , 9718
Seattle high schools, WA , 9559
Seattle Pacific University, WA , 8687
Seattle School District No. 1, WA , 9581
Seattle University, WA , 9668
Second Baptist School, TX , 9065
Sedgwick County high schools, KS , 3494
Sentara School of Nursing, VA , 9502
Sequim School District, WA , 9662
Sequoyah High School, GA , 2235
Serra High School, CA , 522
Seven Rivers Christian School, FL , 1830
Sevier County High School, TN , 8584
Sevier County high schools, TN , 8559
Seward High School, AK , 9647
Seward High School, NE , 5269
Seymour Community School District, WI , 10027
Seymour High School, IN , 3179, 3180, 7324
Seymour High School, TN , 8584
Shasta County high schools, CA , 6688
Sheffield High School, AL , 78
Shelby County High School, KY , 3615
Shelby County high schools, OH , 6989
Shelby Senior High School, OH , 7167
Shelbyville High School, IL , 2673
Shelton High School, CT , 1482
Shelton High School, WA , 9631
Shenandoah Community School District, IA , 3322
Shenandoah County public schools, VA , 9499
Shenandoah High School, IA , 3238, 3285
Shepard High School, Alan B., IL , 2778
Shepaug Valley High School, CT , 2455
Sheridan College, WY , 10118
Sheridan Community College, WY , 10119
Sheridan County high schools, WY , 10117
Sherman County high schools, OR , 6627
Shields Valley High School, MT , 5173
Shiloh C.U.S.D. No. 1, IL , 2518
Shiocton High School, WI , 10045
Shippensburg University, PA , 8087
Shriner High School, TX , 9175
Sikellamny High School, PA , 7955
Sikeston High School, MO , 5049
Siloam Springs High School, AR , 260
Silver Lake Regional High School, MA , 4007
Silverlake Regional High School, MA , 8250
Silverton High School, OR , 6746
Silverton Union High School, OR , 7531
Simla High School, CO , 1229
Simsbury High School, CT , 8289, 8313, 8341
Sinai Academy, NY , 6136
Sinclair Community College, OH , 6954
Sinslaw High School, OR , 7681
Sinton High School, TX , 9076
Sioux Falls high schools, SD , 8528
Skagit County high schools, WA , 9692
Skaneateles Central High School, NY , 6400
Skaneateles High School, NY , 5776
Skowhegan Area High School, ME , 3696
Skyline High School, MO , 759
Skyview High School, ID , 2343, 2348
Slippery Rock University, PA , 8109
Slocomb High School, AL , 6707
Smackover High School, AR , 321
Smith Center High School, KS , 3505
Smith College, William, NY , 7771
Smith County high schools, KS , 5265
Smithfield Township Public School, PA , 8113
Snohomish County high schools, WA , 9692

Somerset County high schools, NJ , 5591
Sonoma Valley High School, CA , 399
Soquel High School, CA , 4573
South Arkansas Community College, AR , 321
South Bay Lutheran High School, CA , 964
South Bend High School, WA , 9611
South Bend high schools, IN , 3185
South Carolina State College, SC , 6852
South Dakota State University, SD , 4779, 8542
South Dearborn High School, IN , 3012
South Hamilton School District, IA , 3319
South Kitsap High School, WA , 9653, 9665
South Lake County high schools, FL , 1845
South Lake High School, CA , 1053
South Park High School, CO , 1293
South Putnam High School, IN , 3154
South Side High School, NY , 6035
South Spencer High School, IN , 7253
South St. Paul Public School District No. 6, MN , 4852
South Tahoe High School, CA , 524
South Toole County High School, MT , 8197
South Valley Academy, NM , 5651
South Vermillion County high schools, IN , 3211
South Western High School, PA , 5778
South Williamsport Area School District, PA , 6555
Southeast Fountain High School, IN , 2908
Southeast Fountain School District, IN , 3134, 3222
Southeast High School, NC , 6926
Southeast Polk High School, IA , 3254
Southeastern Baptist Theological Seminary, NC , 6666, 9413
Southeastern Louisiana University, LA , 3677
Southern Baptist Theological Seminary, KY , 9413
Southern Columbia Area High School, PA , 7998
Southern Connecticut State University, CT , 1858
Southern Illinois University Carbondale, IL , 2865
Southern Illinois University, IL , 2579
Southern Local High School, OH , 7291
Southern Methodist University, TX , 8765, 8832, 9110
Southern Regional High School, NJ , 8398
Southern University, LA , 1614
Southern WV Community and Technical College, WV , 9772
Southington High School, OH , 7255
Southport High School, IN , 2510
Southwest Baptist Theological Seminary, TX , 9110
Southwest Montana high schools, MT , 5162
Southwest Texas Junior College, TX , 8933
Southwestern Baptist Theological Seminary, TX , 8848, 8859, 9413
Southwestern Consolidated Schools, IN , 2999
Southwestern High School, PA , 6782
Southwestern Oregon Community College, OR , 7665
Spanish River High School, FL , 1839
Sparta High School, WI , 9879
Spartanburg Community College, SC , 8514
Spartanburg Methodist College, SC , 8514
Spaulding High School, NH , 8229
Spaulding High School, VT , 5309
Spearfish South Dakota High School, Rapid City Area Schools School District, SD , 8521
Spearman High School, TX , 8990
Spelman College, GA , 1614
Spencer High School, IA , 3386
Spencer High School, WI , 135
Spencerville High School, OH , 7403
Spring Hill College, AL , 14
Spring Lake High School, MI , 4444
Springdale High School, AR , 278
Springfield College, IL , 2553
Springfield School District, MN , 4770
Springs Valley High School, IN , 3087
St. Bernard High School, CT , 1469
St. Charles High School, MI , 4596
St. Clair County high schools, IL , 2869
St. Clair County high schools, MO , 4997
St. Dominic High School, MO , 5027
St. Edward's University, MT , 7541
St. Elizabeth Public School, MO , 4977
St. Francis Borgia Regional High School, MO , 5027
St. Helena High School, CA , 518
St. John Vianney School, MI , 4623
St. John's High School, KS , 3458
St. Johns Public High School, MI , 4670

St. Johnsville High School, NY , 5937, 6352
St. Joseph County schools, IN , 3043
St. Joseph High School, IN , 7204
St. Joseph high schools, MO , 5070
St. Joseph Notre Dame High School, CA , 746
St. Joseph School District, MO , 5036
St. Joseph's College, IN , 3069
St. Laurence High School, IL , 2522
St. Lawrence County School District, NY , 6287
St. Louis County high schools, MO , 5028
St. Louis public high schools, MO , 5111
St. Louis University, MO , 4975
St. Luke's Hospital School of Nursing, PA , 7953
St. Luke's School of Nursing, NY , 6426
St. Mark's Catholic School, IL , 7111
St. Mary's Academy, NY , 6417
St. Mary's Catholic High School, WI , 10063
St. Mary's College, IN , 3069
St. Mary's High School, CO , 1212
St. Mary's High School, MA , 8427
St. Mary's high schools, PA , 8002
St. Mary's Regional Junior-Senior High School, MA , 4181
St. Mary's-Of-The-Woods College, IN , 3069
St. Marys City Schools, OH , 7365
St. Paul's Catholic High School, TX , 9175
St. Paul's Lutheran School, IA , 3315
St. Peter Claver School, WI , 9916
St. Peter-Marian High School, MA , 8391
St. Philip High School, MI , 4362
St. Pius X Grade School, WI , 2034
St. Pius X Grammar School, NY , 5977
St. Pius X High School, PA , 7880
St. Stephen's Episcopal School, TX , 7541
St. Thomas Aquinas High School, FL , 1890
St. Thomas Aquinas High School, NH , 5314
St. Vrain Valley School District, CO , 1230
Stafford High School, CT , 8308
Stagg High School, Amos Alonzo, IL , 2778
Stanberry high schools, MO , 9848
Stanford High School, MT , 5159, 5175
Stanford Law School, CA , 1016
Stanford University, CA , 823
Star City High School, AR , 292
Stark State College of Technology, OH , 7366
State University of New York at Buffalo, NY , 6189
State University of New York, Binghamton, NY , 6303
State University of New York, College at Oneonta, NY , 6113
State University of New York, Cortland, NY , 5890
State University of New York, NY , 2247, 6388
Staunton, Waynesboro, Augusta County High Schools, VA , 9346
Stephen F. Austin State University, TX , 9127
Steubenville High School, OH , 7350
Stevens High School, NH , 5358
Stevens High School, SD , 8521
Stewart County High School, TN , 18
Stigler High School, OK , 7509
Stone Memorial High School, TN , 8549
Stonehill College, MA , 4175
Stonewall Jackson High School, VA , 9327
Stowell School, A.D., MO , 4959
Strasburg High School, VA , 9515
Strathmore High School, CA , 400
Strawberry Point high schools, IA , 3340
Streator Township High School, IL , 2414
Stroudsburg High School, PA , 7802
Struthers High School, OH , 7130
Stuarts Draft High School, VA , 9346
Sturgeon Bay High School, WI , 1020
Suitland High School, MD , 8376
Sul Ross State University Rio Grande College, TX , 8933
Sullivan High School, IN , 3044
Summerfield area high schools, MI , 4664
Summit High School, CO , 1293
Summit High School, NJ , 5431
Sumner County high schools, KS , 3480
Sumner High School, ME , 7252
Superior High School, WI , 9979, 9986
Surrattsville High School, MD , 8376
Susquehanna Waldorf School, PA , 8213
Sussex County high schools, NJ , 5480

Suwannee High School, FL , 1925
Suwannee-Hamilton Area Vocational, Technical, and Adult Cent, FL , 1925
Swampscott High School, MA , 3978
Swampscott public high schools, MA , 8348
Sweet Home High School, OR , 6811
Sweet Springs High School, MO , 5101
Switzerland County High School, IN , 3005, 6985, 7193, 7409
Switzerland County School, IN , 3174
Sycamore High School, IL , 2431, 2825
Sylvania high schools, OH , 7137
Syracuse University, NY , 794

Tamiscal High School, CA , 497
Taquamenon Area School District, MI , 4630
Tarboro High School, NC , 6858
Tarleton State University, TX , 8742
Tarleton University, TX , 9127
Tarrant County College, TX , 8848
Taunton High School, MA , 4077, 8360
Tavares High School, FL , 1971
Taylor High School, IN , 3178
Taylor University, IN , 3069, 7722
Taylorville High School, IL , 43
Taylorville Senior High School, IL , 5037
Tazewell County high schools, VA , 9514
Teays Valley School System, OH , 7157
Tekamah-Herman Community schools, NE , 8990
Tell City High School, IN , 3065
Temple University, PA , 6897, 7874
Tennessee High School, TN , 8598
Tennessee State University, TN , 1614
Tenth School District of Georgetown, CT , 6672
Terrell High School, TX , 5063
Terryville High School, CT , 8327
Teton County School District 1, WY , 9640
Texas A&M Corpus Christi, TX , 8773
Texas A&M Kingsville, TX , 8773
Texas A&M University, Commerce, TX , 9127
Texas A&M University, Kingsville, TX , 9127
Texas A&M University, TX , 8729, 8953, 9054, 9087
Texas Christian University, TX , 8848, 9110
Texas College of Osteopathic Medicine, TX , 8884
Texas Panhandle Area high schools, TX , 8675
Texas State Technical College, TX , 9127
Texas State University, TX , 9127
Texas Tech University, TX , 8801, 8872, 9032, 9127
Texas Wesleyan University, TX , 8848
Texas Women's University, TX , 8848
The Ailey School, NY , 5676
The Juilliard School, NY , 2859, 5808, 6164
The Juilliard School, PA , 7953
The Leland Center, VA , 9413
The Oliverian School, NH , 5358
The Paul Mitchell School, AR , 309
The State College of Florida, Manatee-Sarasota, FL , 2073
The University of Tulsa, OK , 7453
The Wheatley School, NY , 5948
The Williams School, CT , 8230
Thomas Jefferson High School, PA , 7797
Thomas Jefferson University, PA , 7874
Thomas More College, KY , 6954
Thomas Nelson Community College, VA , 9502
Thomaston High School, CT , 8245
Thomasville High School, GA , 778
Thompson Valley High School, CO , 1241
Three Rivers High School, MI , 4491
Ticonderoga High School, NY , 6323, 8351
Tidehaven High School, TX , 9186
Tidewater Community College, VA , 9502
Tillamook County high schools, OR , 7677
Tillamook High School, OR , 7647
Tippecanoe High School, OH , 7388
Tippecanoe Valley High School, IN , 3091
Tipton High School, IN , 3201, 7362
Titusville area high schools, PA , 7181
Tobique Valley High School, Canada, 7145
Toledo area high schools, OH , 7269
Tomah Senior High School, WI , 9892, 10052
Tomahawk High School, WI , 10072
Tomahawk School District, WI , 2677

Toms River High School, NJ , 5530
Tooele High School, UT , 9194
Tottenville High School, NY , 5760
Towanda High School, PA , 7728
Town of Webb High School, NY , 8307
Tr-County Regional Vocational High School, MA , 4245
Travis High School, TX , 2836
Trenton Central High School, NJ , 9424
Trenton High School, TX , 7464
Trenton Public School System, NJ , 5401
Tri-Central High School, IN , 3201, 7362
Tri-State University, IN , 5461
Tri-Valley High School, AK , 147
Trine University, IN , 3069
Trinity College, DC , 7329
Trinity Valley College, TX , 9127
Trinity Valley Community College, TX , 8815
Triton High School, IN , 3091
Triton High School, MA , 4002
Triton Regional High School, MA , 4125
Triton School Corp., IN , 4504
Troup High School, TX , 8948
Troy Christian High School, OH , 7388
Troy High School, ID , 2345
Troy High School, OH , 7388
Truckee High School, CA , 1058
Truman State University, MO , 5001
Trumansburg Central School District, NY , 5865
Trumbull County high Schools, OH , 2700
Trumbull High School, CT , 1482, 2577
Tufts University School of Medicine, MA , 6654
Tufts University, University College of Citizenship, Public Service, MA , 1619
Tulane University, LA , 8765
Tulare District high schools, CA , 8864
Tulare high schools, CA , 436
Tullahoma High School, TN , 51, 94
Tupelo High School, MS , 4903
Tuscarawas Central Catholic High School, OH , 7369
Tuscola County high schools, MI , 4388, 4646
Tuscola High School, IL , 2689
Tuskegee University, AL , 1614
Twin Cedars High School, IA , 9974
Twin Falls County high schools, ID , 2350
Twin Lakes High School, IN , 5253
Twin Valley High School, PA , 7893
Two Harbors High School, MN , 6904
Tygarts Valley High School, WV , 2852
Tyler Junior College, TX , 8820, 9127

Ukiah High School, CA , 481
UNC-Chapel Hill, NC , 6583
UNC-Greensboro, NC , 6583
Unified School District No. 416, KS , 3502
Union 32 School District, VT , 1460
Union City High School, PA , 8154
Union College, KY , 3552, 8598
Union College, NE , 5235
Union County High School, KY , 3034
Union County high schools, AR , 321
Union High School, IN , 3194
Union High School, MI , 4445
Union Joint High School, PA , 7206
Union-Endicott High School, NY , 5787
Unionville-Sebewaing Area High School, MI , 4350
United Township High School, IL , 2395
University City High School, CA , 878
University of Alabama at Birmingham, AL , 8765
University of Alabama, AL , 13, 81
University of Alaska, AK , 97
University of Arizona College of Engineering, AZ , 190
University of Arizona, AZ , 157, 2890
University of Arkansas Community College at Morrilton, AR , 310
University of Arkansas for Medical Sciences, AR , 309
University of Arkansas Fort Smith, AR , 309
University of Arkansas, AR , 81, 289, 309, 317, 7527
University of Arkansas, Fayetteville, AR , 264, 8734
University of Arkansas, Little Rock, AR , 287, 309
University of Basilicata, Italy, 8493
University of Berkeley, CA , 715
University of California, Davis, CA , 832
University of California - Los Angeles, CA , 1098

University of California at San Diego, CA , 897
University of California, Berkeley, CA , 1073
University of California, CA , 453, 702, 926
University of California, Davis, CA , 399
University of Central Florida, FL , 1879, 1958, 1991, 2008, 8765
University of Charleston, WV , 9802
University of Chicago, IL , 2832, 2840, 4445
University of Cincinnati Medical School, OH , 2909
University of Cincinnati, OH , 6954
University of Colorado at Boulder, CO , 1278
University of Colorado Medical School, CO , 6765
University of Colorado, CO , 1149
University of Connecticut, CT , 8413
University of Dayton, OH , 6954
University of Delaware, DE , 1526, 7896, 8135
University of Denver, CO , 1147, 1149, 7598
University of Detroit Mercy, MI , 4350
University of Evansville, IN , 3069, 3158
University of Florida, FL , 81, 1879, 1885, 2025, 2042, 2096, 2487
University of Georgia, GA , 81, 2044, 2089, 2118, 2254, 2266
University of Hawaii, HI , 2293
University of Houston, TX , 8765, 8945
University of Illinois at Urbana-Champaign, IL , 2940, 8795
University of Illinois, College of Medicine, IL , 2605
University of Illinois, IL , 2441, 2520, 2923, 4973, 8716
University of Indianapolis, IN , 3069
University of Iowa, IA , 1186, 3278, 3308, 3375
University of Iowa, School of Religion, IA , 10062
University of Kansas School of Law, KS , 3534
University of Kansas, KS , 3412, 3468, 3504, 3522, 7527, 8794
University of Kentucky, KY , 81, 3552
University of Louisville, KY , 3624, 3633
University of Maine, ME , 2247, 3724
University of Maryland, MD , 6565
University of Massachusetts Amherst, MA , 3987, 4261
University of Memphis, TN , 8765
University of Miami, FL , 1798, 1879, 2417, 6565
University of Michigan Flint, MI , 4394
University of Michigan, MI , 2025, 2199, 2395, 4350, 4445, 4591, 4645, 7091, 9325
University of Minnesota Graduate School, MN , 4894
University of Minnesota Institute of Technology, MN , 2885
University of Minnesota, MN , 2247, 4779, 4787, 4801, 4877
University of Minnesota, Twin Cities, MN , 4830
University of Mississippi, MS , 81, 8564
University of Missouri, Kansas City (UMKC), MO , 9012
University of Missouri, Kansas City, MO , 4975
University of Missouri, School of Agriculture, MO , 5116
University of Missouri-Columbia, MO , 420, 4981, 5085
University of Missouri-Rolla, MO , 420, 5002, 5013
University of Montana, MT , 5182, 7541
University of Nebraska, NE , 502, 4780, 6687
University of Nevada, NV , 5296, 5300
University of New Mexico, NM , 5653
University of North Carolina at Wilmington, NC , 6870
University of North Carolina, Chapel Hill, NC , 6818
University of North Carolina, Greensboro, NC , 6856, 6879
University of North Carolina, Medical School, NC , 6769
University of North Carolina, NC , 6565, 6737
University of North Carolina-Chapel Hill, NC , 6833
University of North Dakota, ND , 6950
University of Northern Colorado, CO , 1206, 1278, 1301
University of Northern Iowa, IA , 3278, 3375
University of Notre Dame Law School, KS , 3534
University of Notre Dame, IN , 1017, 3069
University of Oklahoma, OK , 7453, 7485, 7491, 7495, 7522, 7527
University of Oregon, OR , 8703
University of Paris, Sorbonne, France, 7859
University of Pennsylvania, PA , 6897, 7769, 7874, 8104
University of Pittsburgh, OH , 7143

University of Pittsburgh, PA , 7938, 7977, 8057, 8104
University of Portland, OR , 7635
University of Puget Sound, WA , 8687
University of Rhode Island, RI , 8423
University of Rio Grande, OH , 7189
University of San Diego, CA , 897
University of Singapore, Singapore, 6536
University of South Carolina, SC , 81
University of South Carolina, School of Medicine, SC , 1851
University of South Carolina, Upstate, SC , 8514
University of South Florida, FL , 1879
University of Southern California, CA , 794, 823, 3440
University of Southern Indiana - Evansville, IN , 3107
University of Southern Mississippi, MS , 4925, 8765
University of St. Francis, IN , 3069, 3140
University of Tennessee, TN , 81, 8598
University of Texas at Arlington, TX , 8848
University of Texas at El Paso, TX , 8765
University of Texas at San Antonio, TX , 8862
University of Texas, Arlington, TX , 9127
University of Texas, Austin, TX , 8853, 9127, 9219
University of Texas, Southwestern Medical School, TX , 9092
University of the Ozarks, AR , 278
University of the Sciences in Philadelphia, PA , 8191
University of the West, CA , 688
University of Toledo, OH , 6993, 7121, 7338, 7398
University of Tulsa, OK , 7491, 7527, 8765
University of Utah, UT , 9223
University of Vermont, VT , 5331
University of Virginia, VA , 2045, 2874, 6565, 9408, 9802
University of Washington Medical School, WA , 6922, 9607
University of Washington, WA , 2247, 9668, 9677, 9682, 9694
University of Wisconsin - Marshfield, WI , 9960
University of Wisconsin, Madison, WI , 10045
University of Wisconsin, River Falls, WI , 10056
University of Wisconsin, School of Agriculture, WI , 9881
University of Wisconsin, School of Nursing, WI , 9881
University of Wisconsin, Stevens Point, WI , 9871
University of Wisconsin, WI , 3813, 4779, 9920
University of Wisconsin-Madison Medical School, WI , 2909
University of Wisconsin-Madison, WI , 9908
University of Wisconsin-Milwaukee, WI , 9908
University of Wisconsin-Stevens Point, WI , 2247
University of Wisconsin-Whitewater, WI , 10057
University of Wyoming, WY , 1224, 10118, 10126
University of Wyoming-Laramie, WY , 1206
Upper Darby School District, PA , 7982
Upper Valley Joint Vocational School, OH , 7388
Ursuline Academy of Cincinnati, OH , 7399
US Military Academy, NY , 2595
Utica public and parochial high schools, NY , 8397
Utica public and parochial schools, NY , 8249
Utica public schools, NY , 5907

Vail Mountain School, CO , 1293
Vale Union High School, OR , 9179
Valley High School, WA , 6589
Vallivue High School, ID , 2343
Valparaiso University, IN , 3069
Van Buren Community High School, IA , 3403
Van Buren County high schools, MI , 4493
Van Buren High School, AR , 282
Van Wert High School, OH , 7403
Van-Far School Disctrict No. 1, MO , 5014
Vanderbilt University, TN , 81, 2832
Vanderburgh County high schools, IN , 2976
Vantage Vocational School, OH , 7403
Vassar College, NY , 2926, 8420
Venango County high schools, PA , 7428, 7891
Ventura College, CA , 1036
Vermillion Community College, MN , 4879
Vernon County high schools, MO , 5116
Vernonia High School, OR , 7588
Verona-Vernon-Sherrill High School, NY , 6485
Villanova University, PA , 7874
Vincennes University, IN , 3107

Vineland High School, NJ , 1024
Vintage High School, CA , 518
Virginia Beach high schools, VA , 9286
Virginia Polytechnic Institute & State University, VA ,
9540
Virginia Tech, VA , 6565, 9508
Virginia Union University, VA , 9508
Volunteer State Community College, TN , 59

Wabash College, IN , 3069
Wabash High School, IN , 1961, 2458, 7989
Waccamaw High School, SC , 8502
Waco High School, TX , 8221
Waco Roman Catholic schools, TX , 8788
Wadena High School, MN , 4701
Wadsworth School District, OH , 7293
Waimea High School, HI , 2286
Wake Forest University, Bowman Gray School of
Medicine, NC , 6923
Wake Forest University, NC , 6565, 6730, 6812, 6882,
9508
Wake Technical Community College, NC , 6912
Wakefield High School, NC , 6926
Waldo County high schools, ME , 8304
Walhalla High School, SC , 6929
Walla Walla College, WA , 9662
Walla Walla County high schools, WA , 7670
Walpole High School, MA , 6829
Walsh (Archbishop) High School, NY , 7367
Walsh University, OH , 7366
Waltham High School, MA , 4030, 4245
Walton Central High School, NY , 6056, 6208, 6500
Walton Central School District #1, NY , 5860
Walton Central School District No. 1, NY , 6311
Warde School, Frances Xavier, IL , 2477
Wareham High School, MA , 8297
Warhill High School, VA , 9388
Warren Area High School, PA , 7946
Warren County high schools, PA , 7891
Warren County School District, PA , 7185
Warren G. Harding High School, OH , 2700
Warren Hills Senior High School, NJ , 6868
Warren Township High School, IL , 2844
Warren Township schools, IN , 9839
Warren Wilson College, NC , 2936
Warsaw Community High School, IN , 3091
Warwick Valley Central School District, NY , 6456
Wasco County high schools, OR , 6766
Washburn University School of Law, KS , 3534
Washington Community High School, IL , 2883
Washington Community School District, IA , 3331
Washington County High School, OH , 7226
Washington County high schools, KS , 3481
Washington County high schools, MN , 4870
Washington High School, IA , 3334, 10009
Washington High School, SD , 4753
Washington High School, WI , 3179
Washington State Community College, OH , 7297
Washington State Technical College, WA , 7189
Washington State University, WA , 9668
Washington University School of Architecture, MO ,
4931
Washington University, MO , 2395
Washoe County School District, NV , 5287
Watauga High School, NC , 6914
Waterford public high schools, MI , 4660
Watertown High School, CT , 8353
Watertown High School, WI , 2891
Watertown Senior High School, WI , 10067
Waubonsee Community College, IL , 2549, 2918
Wauconda High School, IL , 4595
Waukegan High School, IL , 2844, 4472
Waukesha County high schools, WI , 2449
Wausau high schools, WI , 2560
Wausaukee High School, WI , 10051
Wautoma High School, WI , 9923
Wawasee High School, IN , 3091
Wayne Community High School, IA , 3341
Wayne Community Junior Senior High School, IA , 3272
Wayne State University, MI , 4342, 7091
Wayne Trace High School, OH , 7403
Waynesboro High School, VA , 9346
Waynesburg Central High School, PA , 7781

Weakly County high schools, TN , 8613
Webb High School, WI , 9983
Webster City High School, IA , 3389
Webster County High School, IA , 2604
Weed High School, NM , 5647
Weehawken High School, NJ , 5364
Weimar High School, TX , 9100
Weir Senior High School, WV , 7231
Weiser High School, ID , 9216
Wellesley College, MA , 1333
Wellington High School, OH , 6976
Wells-Ogunquit High School, ME , 3740
Wellston High School, OH , 6986
Wellsville-Middletown R-1 High School, MO , 4775
Wes Watkins Technology Center, OK , 7523
Wesley's Academy School, PA , 8186
Wesleyan College, GA , 2118, 2128
Wesleyan University, CT , 5381
West Anchorage High School, AK , 149
West Bend high schools, WI , 10049
West Bloomfield High School, MI , 4495
West Chester State College, PA , 8220
West Chester University, PA , 7953, 8087, 8138
West Chicago Community High School District No. 94,
IL , 2421
West Contra Costa Unified School district, CA , 1090
West Delaware County Community School District, IA ,
3271
West Grand High School, CO , 1293
West Greene School District Schools, PA , 7781
West Hempstead School District No. 27, NY , 6283
West High School, W.F., WA , 6609
West High School, WI , 10028
West Jefferson High School, OH , 7437
West Liberty State College, WV , 9778
West Mesa High School, NM , 5651
West Michigan Christian High School, Muskegon, MI ,
4444
West Ottawa High School, MI , 4444
West Philadelphia High School, PA , 7826
West Rusk High School, TX , 8948
West Texas A&M University, TX , 8675
West Virginia University, School of Nursing, WV , 9803
West Virginia University, WV , 2461, 9802
West Virginia Wesleyan College, WV , 9772, 9819
West Washington High School, IN , 3227
Westby High School, MT , 6948
Westchester Community College, NY , 6513
Western Boone High School, IN , 3199
Western Brown High School, OH , 7238
Western High School, MI , 4350
Western Kentucky University, KY , 3607
Western Michigan University, MI , 2247
Western Montana College of the University of Montana,
MT , 7541
Western Reserve School District, OH , 7433
Western Texas College, TX , 9127
Western Wayne Schools, IN , 3217
Westfall High School, OH , 7082
Westfield High School, MA , 8406, 8427
Westfield High School, NJ , 5603
Westfield Technical Vocational High, MA , 8427
Westford Academy, MA , 4150
Westminster High School, MD , 3880
Westmoreland County Community College, PA , 7781
Westmoreland High School, NY , 6485
Westmoreland High School, TN , 8637
Westran High School, MO , 5068
Westview School Corporation School District, IN , 3093
Weyauwega-Fremonth School District, WI , 10046
Weymouth North High School, MA , 8354
Weymouth South High School, MA , 8354
Wharton County Jr. College, TX , 9127
Whatcom County high schools, WA , 9692
Wheaton College, IL , 4118
Wheeler County high schools, OR , 6766
Wheeling Park High School, WV , 7232
Wheeling public schools, WV , 9818
Whitcomb Senior High School, VT , 9241
Whitefish High School, MT , 5157, 9634
Whitesboro School District, NY , 6497
Whitesboro Senior High School, NY , 6399
Whitestown School District, NY , 6497
Whitingham High School, VT , 1382

Whitko High School, IN , 3091
Whitley County high schools, IN , 3226
Whittier College, CA , 385
Whittier Union High School District, CA , 672
Wibaux County High School, MT , 5179
Wichita Falls Independent School District, TX , 9162
Wichita State University, KS , 3539
Wicomico High School, MD , 6326
Wicomico Junior High, MD , 6326
Wilberforce University, OH , 1614
Wilbur public schools, WA , 9738
Wilcox County high schools, AL , 79
Wild Rose High School, WI , 9923
Wiley College, TX , 9110
William Penn Charter School, PA , 7856
William T. Dwyer High School, FL , 9968
Williams Bay High School, WI , 9885
Williamsville School District No. 15, IL , 7992
Willits High School, CA , 641
Willmar School System, MN , 4681
Willoughby South High School, OH , 6996
Wilmington High School, IL , 2736
Wilmington School District, PA , 7343
Wilmington University, OH , 6954
Wilson County public high schools, NC , 6808
Wilson High School, PA , 7953
Wilson Memorial High School, VA , 9346
Winamac Community High School, IN , 3168
Winchester Community High School, IN , 3229
Winchester High School, MA , 4182
Windsor High School, CT , 1487
Windsor High School, IL , 2860
Windsor High School, MO , 5125
Windsor High School, VT , 5358
Winnebago School District, MN , 4739
Winona State University, FL , 4892
Winslow High School, ME , 8337
Winston-Salem College, NC , 6730
Winston-Salem School System, NC , 6923
Winston-Salem State University, NC , 6923
Winterset Community High School, IA , 3289
Winterset High School, IA , 3256
Winthrop University, SC , 6929
Wirt County high schools, WV , 9786
Wisconsin Indianhead Technical College, WI , 10077
Wittenberg College, OH , 7176
Wittenberg University, OH , 6954
WMU Bronson School of Nursing, MI , 4465
Woburn High School, MA , 4301
Wofford College, SC , 8514
Woldoboro High School, ME , 8347
Wood Acres Day School, GA , 2268
Wood County high schools, WV , 9786, 9789, 9808
Wood River High School, ID , 197
Woodbridge High School, NJ , 5431
Woodbridge School District, DE , 7721
Woodbury High School, MN , 4853
Woodrow Wilson High School, DC , 7082
Woodrow Wilson High School, WV , 9826
Woodside High School, CA , 877, 1109
Woodson County high schools, KS , 3427, 3446
Woodstock High School, GA , 2235
Woodstown High School, NJ , 7807
Woodsville High School, NH , 8241
Wooster High School, OH , 7230
Worcester County High School, MA , 8420
Worcester County high schools, MA , 4323
Worcester High School, MA , 4102
Worcester Public High School, MA , 8345
Worcester public high schools, MA , 4269
Wright State University, OH , 6954
WVU-Parkersburg, OH , 7297
Wyandotte Catholic Consolidated School, MI , 4364
Wynne High School, AR , 281
Wyoming County High School, NY , 5728
Wyomissing Area High School, PA , 6385
Wythe County High School, VA , 9553

Xavier University of Louisiana, LA , 1614
Xavier University, OH , 6954
Xenia High School, OH , 7103, 7134

Yadkin County high schools, NC , 6923
Yakima School District 7, WA , 8800
Yakima Valley College, WA , 9748
Yakima Valley Community College, WA , 8961
Yale University, CT , 1443, 4465, 7859
Yellow Springs High School, OH , 7444
Yerba Buena High School, CA , 987
Yeshiva University, NY , 6498

Yeshivah of Flatbush Joel Braverman High School, NY ,
 5781
Ygnacio High School, CA , 922
Yonkers public high shools, NY , 4269
York Catholic High School, PA , 5985, 8212
York College of Pennsylvania, PA , 8213
York Country Day School, PA , 8213
Yorktown High School, IN , 3026

Young County School District, TX , 8923
Youngstown State University, OH , 7140
Yuba City Union High School, CA , 332
Yuba College, CA , 332

Zane Trace High School, OH , 7034
Zanesville High School, OH , 7405

TYPES OF SUPPORT INDEX

The numbers under the types of support in this index refer to the sequence numbers of entries in the Descriptive Directory section of this book. Grantmakers that give nationally, regionally, or internationally are indicated in boldface type following the states in which they are located. Grantmakers that restrict their giving to particular states, counties, or cities are listed in lighter type following the states in which they give. This index is generated to denote the types of support a grantmaker might provide to individuals and does not include the types of support the grantmaker provides to organizations.

Awards/grants by nomination only

Alabama: Mayson 60
Alaska: Alaska 98
Arizona: Community 182, **Research 233**
California: **Alliance 348**, Ameritec 361, Anderson 365, Carlston 464, Fleishhacker 578, Friedberger 598, Gerbode 612, Glaucoma 619, **Gleitsman 620, Glenn 621, Goldman 628**, Herbst 656, Hewitt 659, **Higgins 661**, Kornberg 725, **Lambda 733, Life 745**, Loeb 753, **Marconi 769**, Memorial 783, Merage 785, Modesto 798, Project 883, **Rex 909**, San Diego 929, San Francisco 944, Strauss 1028, **Tech 1041, United 1072**, Ward 1084, **World 1102**
Colorado: Bonfils 1130, EDUCAUSE 1189, **Morris 1243, Rock 1269**, Seay 1280, **WaterStone 1305**, Young 1311
Connecticut: **Avatar 1327, Belgian 1334**
Delaware: Common 1497
District of Columbia: American 1540, **American 1541, American 1544, American 1545, American 1553, American 1559, American 1572**, Community 1605, **German 1638, Independent 1649, International 1660**, National 1682, National 1683, **National 1687, National 1695, National 1699, Optical 1705, Travel 1736**, Washington 1747
Florida: **Astronaut 1785**, Livingston 1952, Rayni 2030, **SeaWorld 2056**, Stearn 2074, Tweed 2091
Georgia: **American 2113**, Arby's 2119, BankSouth 2124, **Foundation 2178**, Healthcare 2195, Seven 2236, **TAPPI 2247**
Hawaii: Rehabilitation 2316
Illinois: **American 2365**, American 2383, Bohne 2429, Ehrler 2537, **Gish 2585**, Golden 2586, Hyatt 2631, **International 2651**, Kohl 2676, **MacArthur 2704**, Oakes 2762, **Playboy 2794, Poetry 2795**, Pullman 2804, **Skidmore 2857**, St. Clair 2869, Testamentary 2890, **TPAA 2895**
Indiana: IPALCO 3075, **Lilly 3099**, Noble 3127, Webster 3219
Iowa: McElroy 3333
Kansas: French 3446
Kentucky: Disabled 3562, Jackson 3579, United 3631
Louisiana: Lafayette 3658
Maine: Augusta 3688
Maryland: **Casey 3794, Global 3836, Hughes 3846**, Laughlin 3862, **National 3896**, Passano 3908
Massachusetts: **Earthwatch 4049, Harvard 4097**, Humane 4121, **Kennedy 4137, Lalor 4145**, Middlesex 4174, Raytheon 4238, Williams 4318

Michigan: Blue 4363, **Gilmore 4438**, Stewart 4627, Vetowich 4658, Wells 4664
Minnesota: Cox 4722, Ecotrust 4732, McKnight 4794, University 4877
Mississippi: McDonald 4913
Missouri: Edgar 4982, Sabada 5081, Tilles 5115
Montana: Heisey 5156, Mountain 5165
Nebraska: **Buffett 5190**, EducationQuest 5197, H.H. 5211
New Hampshire: Wilson 5378
New Jersey: Capezio 5412, **Dow 5435, Glushko 5454, IEEE 5476**, Shoshana 5564, Summit 5573, Wight 5598, **Wiley 5599**
New Mexico: **Lannan 5635**
New York: Academy 5663, **American 5689**, American 5698, ASCAP 5731, Bay 5756, Blake 5766, **BMI 5771**, Bronfman 5792, Buisch 5804, **CNN 5862, College 5866**, Cosby 5891, Cox 5896, **Dreyfus 5935**, Duke 5938, **Dungannon 5939**, Federation 5979, **Foundation 5993, Foundation 5995, Foundation 5998**, Fund 6014, **Graves 6044**, Hadar 6054, Havens 6061, **Hereditary 6068, IBM 6089**, Jenkins 6113, **Lasker 6153**, Le Rosey 6155, **Lighthouse 6163**, L'Oreal 6170, **Luce 6175**, Lurcy 6176, **Lymphoma 6179**, Magnum 6183, **Mann 6187**, McCall 6200, Mills 6217, **National 6243, National 6252, New 6264, PEN 6312**, Petra 6314, **Pollock 6318, Princess 6329**, Scotts 6389, Silver 6397, Skahan 6399, Society 6411, Sperry 6421, Steinberg 6436, **Tiffany 6455, Tucker 6466, Ventures 6488, Watson 6504, Weill 6508**, Weissberger 6509, Whiting 6517, **World 6534**
North Carolina: Buck 6585, DuVall 6635, **International 6715**, Komarek 6733, Martin 6757, **Morehead-Cain 6778**, Reynolds 6828
Ohio: Associated 6982, Carman 7024, McLendon 7237, **Phi 7301**, Prior 7308, Rosenberger 7328, Twenty 7393, Wexner 7422
Oklahoma: Osteopathic 7503
Oregon: **Multnomah 7613**, Pernot 7631
Pennsylvania: Boyer 7741, **Carnegie 7759**, Davis 7808, Eye 7833, Fabric 7835, **Heinz 7900**, Independence 7916, **Rhythm 8076**, Society 8119, **Templeton 8141**, Von 8170
Rhode Island: Alpert 8227, Costa 8274, Frost 8295, Kinsley 8323, Sears 8395, Starr 8413
South Carolina: **Hemingway 8482**
Tennessee: Alumni 8555, Bootstraps 8560, Humanities 8604, Nashville 8626
Texas: Brisley 8721, Conference 8765, Educational 8808, Fort Worth 8828, Gilman 8841, Humanities 8887, Lawler 8916, Panasonic 9001,

Salesmanship 9051, Southwestern 9092, Student 9102, West 9162
Virginia: **Association 9321, Association 9322, Cooke 9352, National 9446, National 9453**, National 9458, **Newspaper 9464, Olmsted 9470, Teachers 9518**
Washington: Behnke 9568, Sigourney 9724
West Virginia: Gault 9786
Wisconsin: Sivyer 10034

Awards/prizes

Alabama: **American 8**
Alaska: Alaska 98, Rasmuson 132, University 146
Arizona: Community 182, Educational 190, Hopi 201, **Research 233**, Sulphur 243
Arkansas: Murphy 293
California: **Academy 335, Aesthetic 342, Alliance 348**, American 356, **American 357**, Ameritec 361, **Amgen 362**, Asian 379, **Association 386**, Association 390, Bay 405, **Beckman 408**, Bialis 412, Boand 416, **Borg 418**, California 442, California 461, Carlston 464, Chesley 480, China 492, Chopra 494, **Civic 501**, Cure 530, **Earth 550, Ellison 561**, Fernando 574, Fleishhacker 578, Found 583, **Foundation 586, Foundation 589, Frameline 593**, Fries 602, Gerbode 612, **Gleitsman 620, Goldman 628**, Guzik 642, Herbst 656, **Higgins 661**, Huntington 674, **Immunobiology 677**, International 689, **International 691**, Intersection 693, Jewish 706, La Canada 727, **Lambda 733**, Loeb 753, Los 758, **Marconi 769**, Martin 774, Mathematical 776, Memorial 783, Milken 792, **National 817**, Nestle 825, **Nuclear 835**, Oaklandish, 837, Ojai 839, Performing 861, Project 883, **Rand 898, Rex 909**, Rosenberg 921, San Diego 929, San Diego 937, **San Francisco 943**, San Francisco 944, San Luis 951, Santa 957, **Tech 1041, Tides 1048**, Wayne 1088, **World 1102**, Young 1107
Colorado: American 1117, Bonfils 1130, Boulder 1132, Burton 1137, Colorado 1169, EDUCAUSE 1189, Young 1311
Connecticut: **Alliance 1318**, Branford 1338, Center 1350, Connecticut 1366, Connecticut 1368, Deloitte 1375, Equus 1386, **Multiple 1426**, New Canaan 1430, Voya 1478, Weller 1482
Delaware: CenturyLink-Clarke 1494, Common 1497, Delaware 1500, **International 1514**, Westly 1528
District of Columbia: **American 1538, American 1539, American 1542, American 1544, American 1545, American 1546, American 1550, American 1552, American 1553, American 1561, American**

1565, American 1570, **American 1572**, Arab 1576, **Association 1585, Atlas 1588**, Block 1594, Community 1605, Cox 1613, **Fund 1634, Fund 1635, German 1638, Glaser 1640, Hitachi 1645**, Hurston 1648, **Independent 1649, International 1660**, Junior 1664, **Kennedy 1665, Monk 1680**, National 1683, **National 1687, National 1691, National 1695, National 1699, Optical 1705, PEN/Faulkner 1712**, Phi 1715, **Society 1731**, ULI 1740, **VSA 1745**, Washington 1746, Washington 1747, Washington 1748, **Youth 1757**

Florida: Community 1844, Hermitage 1912, **Holland 1918**, Lake 1943, Life 1950, Livingston 1952, **National 1997**, Patterson 2015, Planning 2021, Russell 2044, **SeaWorld 2056**, Two 2092

Georgia: **American 2113, American 2114, Foundation 2178**, Golden 2189, Healthcare 2195, **TAPPI 2247**

Hawaii: Rehabilitation 2316

Illinois: Allstate 2363, **American 2365, American 2379, American 2380, American 2382**, American 2383, **American 2386**, American 2390, American 2393, **Anesthesia 2398, Cervical 2468, Chest 2471**, Ehrler 2537, **Elks 2540**, Evans 2552, **Ewing 2554, Feeding 2559, Foundation 2569, Foundation 2570, Gish 2585**, Golden 2586, **Graham 2592, Health 2607**, Hirschl 2620, Hyatt 2631, Illinois 2645, **International 2651, International 2652**, Kohl 2676, **Playboy 2794, Poetry 2795, Ronald 2831, Rotary 2835, Skidmore 2857, Society 2862, Terra 2889**, Union 2904, **Zonta 2942**

Indiana: Allen 2947, Association 2962, Brown 2974, Fort 3031, Hillenbrand 3060, Indianapolis 3072, Indianapolis 3074, IPALCO 3075, Joshi 3080, Keller 3084, **Lilly 3099**, Muncie 3120, **Organization 3132**, Richmond 3162, Society 3187, South 3189

Iowa: Harper 3295, Jasper 3311, McElroy 3333, World 3410

Kansas: Davis 3431, Hansen 3451, Kansas 3472, Koch 3476, Naftzger 3493, Salina 3510, Wildlife 3540

Louisiana: Academic 3639, Arts 3642, Lafayette 3658

Maine: Friends 3697, Maine 3717

Maryland: **American 3757, American 3761**, American 3763, **American 3767, Anxiety 3773**, Arts 3776, Autism 3780, **Carson 3793**, Chesapeake 3799, Cystic 3812, **Discovery 3815, ELECTRI 3817, Endocrine 3818, Foundation 3828, Foundation 3829**, Foundation 3830, Girl 3835, **Global 3836**, Hopkins, 3842, Howard 3844, **International 3849**, Maryland 3870, Maryland 3875, **Medical 3878, National 3896**, Obesity 3904, Passano 3908, Prince 3915, Resource 3921, **School 3928**

Massachusetts: Boston 3991, Chelonian 4020, **Earthwatch 4049, Fine 4068**, Goldin 4087, **Gravity 4089**, Harvard 4096, Humane 4121, **Huntington 4123**, Johnson 4131, **Kennedy 4137**, Lyceum 4154, Museum 4184, **National 4190**, Permanent 4216, President 4230, Putnam 4232

Michigan: Amy 4337, Ann Arbor 4339, Avondale 4341, Blue 4363, Come 4389, Community 4394, Delta 4406, Ford 4420, Fremont 4431, **Gilmore 4438**, Lansing 4511, MEEMIC 4531, **Society 4611, Sphinx 4622**, Winkler 4671

Minnesota: Baker 4696, Central 4710, Ecotrust 4732, Loft 4784, **McKnight 4793**, McKnight 4794, Minnesota 4802, University 4877

Mississippi: Community 4902

Missouri: **American 4932**, Arch 4934, **Build 4946**, Community 4963, Missouri 5056, St. Louis 5106

Montana: Gay 5147, Heisey 5156, Mountain 5165, **National 5167**

Nebraska: **Buffett 5190**, H.H. 5211, Jewish 5221, Strengths 5263

Nevada: Nevada 5295

New Hampshire: New Hampshire 5355

New Jersey: Ammonius 5386, **Berrie 5399**, Capezio 5412, Costume 5428, **Dow 5435**, Foundation 5450, **Glushko 5454, IEEE 5476**, Kessler 5487, Lasko 5494, **LearningAlly 5496**, Life 5498, Newark 5525, Penn 5537, Prudential 5547, **Puffin 5549, Siemens 5566, Wiley 5599**

New Mexico: **A Room 5609, Lannan 5635, School 5650**, Woodson 5659

New York: Academy 5663, Alliance 5682, **American 5688, American 5689**, American 5698, **American 5702, American 5706, American 5710, American 5711, Aperture 5716**, ArtCouncil 5723, ASCAP 5731, **Asia 5733, Asian 5734, Astraea 5736, Autism 5743, Avon 5745**, Bay 5756, **Bibliographical 5762, Blue 5770, BMI 5771**, Bossak 5777, Breast 5783, Brewster 5785, Bronfman 5792, Brown 5801, **Cave 5827**, Center 5831, **CFDA 5838, Chamber 5839, CNN 5862, College 5866**, Community 5878, **Covenant 5895**, Crohn's 5899, Dance 5910, De Jur 5917, **Do 5928, Dungannon 5939**, Ebb 5951, Ensemble 5959, Experimental 5967, **Foundation 5995, Foundation 5998, Fox 6006, Franklin 6008, French 6009**, Fund 6014, Henry 6067, **Hereditary 6068, Illuminating 6091, Jaffe 6108, Jewish 6120, Juvenile 6127, Keats 6134, Lasker 6153, Lighthouse 6163**, London 6167, L'Oreal 6170, **Lymphoma 6179**, Magnum 6183, McCall 6200, McCrindle 6203, Melville 6206, **MetLife 6210, Metropolitan 6211**, Metropolitan 6212, **Mikhashoff 6215, Myasthenia 6234, NARSAD: 6239, National 6241, National 6243, National 6246, National 6251, National 6252, National 6254, New York 6265**, New York 6268, New York 6269, New York 6277, Newhouse 6279, **Pearson 6310, PEN 6312**, Petra 6314, **Poetry 6317, Pollock 6318**, Professional 6331, Queens 6341, **Rockefeller 6359, Schepp 6383**, Scotts 6389, SculptureCenter 6391, **Smith 6406, Social 6409**, Society 6412, **Stecher 6434, Teachers 6445, Theatre 6448, Tiffany 6455, Tucker 6466, United 6476, United States 6479, USTA 6482**, Vilcek 6491, Visual 6492, **Weill 6508**, Weissberger 6509, **Wenner 6511**, Whiting 6517, **Wiesel 6519, Women's 6528, World 6534, Woursell 6537**

North Carolina: Anderson 6552, **Chordoma 6602, Earnhardt 6636, International 6715**, Medical 6769, North 6800, Phoenix 6819, Reynolds 6828, **Sigma 6860**

Ohio: Berlin 6996, Cleveland 7041, Dayton 7082, Hoover 7154, Licking 7209, **Lincoln 7210**, Mercy 7241, National 7267, Peoples 7297, Psychiatric 7310, Rosenberger 7328, Scripps 7340, Thurber 7382, Wayne 7415, Wexner 7422

Oklahoma: Communities 7459, Oklahoma 7501, Watkins 7523

Oregon: **Culinary 7562**, Literary 7597, McKenzie 7603, Vernier 7674

Pennsylvania: Berks 7730, **Carnegie 7759, CPCU 7795**, Eye 7833, Fenstermacher 7840, Health 7897, **Heinz 7900**, Kimmel 7936, Leeway 7951, **Lokoff 7961**, Mahler 7966, Pennsylvania 8024, **Pennsylvania 8026**, Philadelphia 8034, Pottstown 8056, Project 8065, **Rhythm 8076**, Society 8119, **Templeton 8141**

Puerto Rico: Puerto Rico 8223

Rhode Island: Alpert 8227, Frost 8295, Kiely 8320, Rhode Island 8381, Sears 8395

South Carolina: **Hemingway 8482**, South 8512

Tennessee: Alumni 8555, Humanities 8604, **National 8629**

Texas: **American 8678, American 8684**, Austin 8698, **Bat 8705, Blackburn 8714**, Brown 8726, **Butt 8730**, Coastal 8756, **Conrad 8768**, Culture 8778, Fort Worth 8828, Gilman 8841, Headliners 8860, Heinlein 8865, Humanities 8887, Morgan 8969, **North 8992**, O'Brien 8994, Piper 9022, Texas 9124, Texas 9125, Texas 9130, **Vetiver 9148**, Welch 9160, West 9162, **Western 9164**

Utah: Jordan 9212, **Sundance 9227**

Vermont: Vermont 9268

Virginia: A Gift 9277, Air 9284, **American 9297, American 9298, American 9305, American 9306, American 9307**, American 9308, **Army 9316, Ashoka: 9317**, Associates 9319, **Association 9321, Association 9322**, Association 9323, Community 9346, Community 9350, **Conquer 9351**, Education 9372, **Epilepsy 9375, Foundation 9381, IDSA 9402**, Klein 9416, **MATHCOUNTS 9431, National 9446, National 9450**, National 9456, **National 9457**, National 9458, **Newton 9465**, Northern 9466, **Public 9488**, Society 9510, **Special 9511, Teachers 9518, U.S. 9526**

Washington: Alliance 9557, Allied 9558, Allied 9559, Artist 9564, Evergreen 9609, **Foundation 9614**, Sigourney 9724

West Virginia: Beckley 9766, Stifel 9818

Wisconsin: Boer 9850, Darcey 9875, **Entomological 9884**, Freedom 9898, **Friends 9900**, Johnson 9934, Kohl's 9946, Madison 9956, Rolfs 10013, Sand 10017, **Society 10037**, Wisconsin 10080

Camperships

Arizona: Deer 183

California: Coastal 504, Jewish 706, Taylor 1039

Colorado: Adventure 1111

Connecticut: Branford 1338, Person-to-Person 1442

Illinois: Rauch 2808

Indiana: Brown 2974, Community 2994, LaGrange 3093

Iowa: Camp 3251

Kansas: Jewish 3463

Maine: Kieve 3707, Maine 3712, United 3743

Massachusetts: Armenian 3972, Donnell 4042

Michigan: Ann Arbor 4338, Baker 4342, Grand Rapids 4445, Sturgis 4629, Willard 4669

Minnesota: Jewish 4772

Missouri: Kansas 5023

Nebraska: Merrick 5233

New Hampshire: Porter 5362

New York: Adirondack 5668, Federation 5979, Henry 6067, Jonas 6122, Scarsdale 6378

North Carolina: Lumbee 6750

Pennsylvania: Commission 7778, **Jewish 7930**, Pittsburgh 8048

Virginia: Richmond 9494

Washington: **Jewish 9643**

Wisconsin: Community 9867, Marshfield 9960, Milwaukee 9970

Computer technology

Connecticut: Main 1419

Nebraska: Nebraska 5244

New York: LD 6154

Conferences/seminars

Alaska: Alaska 99, Bering 105, CIRI 113

Arizona: Sulphur 243

California: **Arthritis 376, Getty 614**, Johnson 711, Society 999, St. Shenouda 1015

Colorado: Douglas 1184, Rocky 1272

Connecticut: Branford 1338

District of Columbia: **Gay 1637, German 1638**

Illinois: **American 2391, Graham 2592**

Indiana: Community 2994

Maryland: Credit 3810, **School 3928**

Massachusetts: Affordable 3958, Grinspoon 4090

Michigan: United 4649

Missouri: **PKD 5074**

New Mexico: **A Room 5609**, Farmers' 5629

New York: American 5698, **American 5710, Chamber 5839, Echoing 5952**, Manhattan 6186, **New 6264, Wenner 6511**

North Carolina: American 6549
Ohio: Holmes 7152
Pennsylvania: Community 7784
South Carolina: Hart 8480
Tennessee: Chattanooga 8568
Texas: Wine 9170
Virginia: **AHP 9282**, Association 9323, **Conquer 9351, National 9450**
Washington: George 9622
West Virginia: West Virginia 9827

Doctoral support

California: American 359, Arthritis 375, California 441, California 447, Dales 534, **Foundation 589**
Colorado: Aorn 1119, **Morris 1243**
Connecticut: Branford 1338, Deloitte 1375
District of Columbia: **American 1551, American 1565, Council 1612, Institute 1651, U.S. 1738**
Florida: AWS 1789, Florida 1879
Georgia: **American 2113**, Columbus 2149, **Phi Mu 2222**
Hawaii: Mink 2304
Illinois: **American 2371, American 2376, Graham 2592**, Illinois 2638, Illinois 2644, **Medical 2728**, Ott 2773, **Research 2816, Rotary 2835, Zonta 2942**
Indiana: Association 2962, LaGrange 3093, Rush 3167
Kansas: Wildlife 3540
Kentucky: Scottish 3624
Maryland: **Epilepsy 3821, Foundation 3829**, Laughlin 3862
Massachusetts: **Maya 4170**
Michigan: Blue 4363
Minnesota: Philanthrofund 4824
Nevada: Doyle 5287, Nevada 5296
New Jersey: **Johnson 5482**, KPMG 5493, New Jersey 5518, **Tang 5575, Wilson 5600**
New York: **American 5692, American 5693**, American 5695, **American 5711, College 5866, Dedalus 5919, Direct 5926**, Episcopal 5961, **Guggenheim 6049**, Hudson 6080, Huyck 6088, **IBM 6089, Institute 6095, Juvenile 6127, Leukemia 6160**, Memorial 6207, **Myasthenia 6234**, NLN 6280, **Schepp 6383, Social 6409, United 6472, Wenner 6511**, Wine 6523
North Carolina: **American 6550**, Foundation 6661, **Institut 6711, Sigma 6860**
Ohio: **Arab 6978**
Oklahoma: Osteopathic 7503
Oregon: Northwest 7620
South Carolina: Hart 8480
Texas: American 8683, Conner 8767, **Komen 8910**, National 8983
Virginia: **American 9297, American 9300, American 9304, Foundation 9380, Mustard 9442, National 9451, Special 9511, United 9530**
West Virginia: Family 9783

Emergency funds

Alabama: Harbert 46
Alaska: Alaska 100, Kawerak 121
Arizona: Catholic 176, Community 181, **Feed 191**, Jewish 205, Mesa 218, Youth 259
Arkansas: SHARE 307
California: Advertising 339, **Alalusi 345, Armenian 370**, California 447, **Children 485, Children's 489**, Cops 523, El Puente 558, **Family 568**, Fresno 595, **Global 623**, Heart 652, Injured 682, **Intel 686**, Jack 699, Legal 742, Lockheed 752, **Santa 959**, Shaklee 977, **Society 1001**, St. Joseph's 1013, Trinity 1056, Williams 1096
Colorado: Archuleta 1121, Aspen 1123, Care 1141, Evergreen 1193, Jewish 1222, Lupus 1234, Outreach 1255, **Rock 1269**

Connecticut: Branford 1338, Colburn-Keenan 1360, **Pitney 1444**
District of Columbia: **American 1563**, Communications 1604, Community 1606, Rainy 1719, **Teamster 1735, Union 1742**
Florida: 2 Life 1759, Abilities 1763, AIDS 1764, Brown 1812, Change 1822, Darden 1855, Diocesan 1862, Florida 1877, Florida 1880, Florida 1881, **Harvest 1906**, Hma 1916, Hope 1921, **Office 2002**, Pinellas 2020, Ryder 2046, SWS 2080, Volunteer 2097
Georgia: Club 2144, CURE 2159, Faith 2175, Fulton 2180, Southern 2238, Southwest 2240, **THDF 2249**, Tri-County 2250
Hawaii: Family 2282
Idaho: Home 2333
Illinois: **ADA 2356**, BCMW 2415, Catholic 2463, **Elks 2540**, Energy 2545, Lutheran 2702, Prieto 2799, **Realtors 2810**, United 2906
Indiana: Area 2957, Hammond 3048, Warren 3216
Iowa: LSB 3328, Operation 3348, St. Luke's 3388, United 3399
Kansas: Duclos 3434
Kentucky: **Disabled 3563**, God's 3573
Louisiana: Our 3672
Maine: Waldo 3744, York 3749
Maryland: Annapolis 3772, Bowie 3786, Community 3804, Community 3809
Massachusetts: Action 3957, AIDS 3961, Berkshire 3984, British 4000, Community 4028, Giving 4084, Massachusetts 4164, Swan 4280, Travelers 4294
Michigan: Allegan 4334, Baraga-Houghton 4345, **Domino's 4409, Dow 4410**, Hemophilia 4463, Lighthouse 4517, Lions 4518, National 4549, Sparrow 4619
Minnesota: Dolan 4728, Hastings 4755, HealthEast 4756, Interfaith 4765, **Polaris 4827**, Semcac 4849, Springboard 4859, **Thrivent 4867**, Volunteers 4881
Mississippi: AJFC 4895, Box 4899, Lexington 4912
Missouri: Baptist-Trinity 4935, Delta 4972, ESCO 4988
Nebraska: Home 5220, Lutheran 5231, Merrick 5233, Nebraska 5242, UNMC 5267, World 5276
Nevada: **Caring 5280**
New Jersey: Akers 5382, Catholic 5413, Ingersoll-Rand 5478, KPMG 5492, United 5586, United 5588
New York: Aero 5670, AFTRA 5672, **Autism 5743**, Cancer 5812, Cantor 5814, Community 5883, Dystrophic 5944, Episcopal 5960, **Foundation 5995, Gottlieb 6041**, Havens 6061, Hispanic 6072, **International 6101, Jazz 6112**, Kane 6128, Monahan 6222, Morton 6227, Musicians 6231, **Musicians 6233**, New York 6266, New York 6277, New 6278, Project 6334, Rental 6353, **Vietnam 6490**, Williams 6521
North Carolina: Better 6573, Burlington 6587, Hickory 6698, Inter-Faith 6714, **Lion's 6743**, Lumbee 6750, Mission 6775, **Samaritan's 6849**
Ohio: Akron 6967, Collaborative 7048, Community 7055, Community 7063, Council 7066, DeCrane 7085, Economic 7096, Epilepsy 7100, Twenty 7393
Oklahoma: **Feed 7468**, Masonic 7492
Oregon: Aging 7529, Care 7544, Community 7555, Mercy 7604
Pennsylvania: Blaisdell 7735, Catholic 7760, Community 7786, CSI 7801, Genesis 7867, Penn 8022, Pennsylvania 8025, Schuylkill 8091
South Carolina: Gleamns 8476
South Dakota: Brookings 8523
Tennessee: Dollar 8583, East 8588, Fort 8592, HCA 8599, Hodges 8602, International 8607, Metropolitan 8622, Nashville 8627, Ruby 8639, ServiceMaster 8642, Southeast 8647, United 8658
Texas: Alliance 8673, Associa 8691, Caritas 8736, Catholic 8740, Catholic 8741, Community 8761, Lockheed 8922, **National 8986**, Penney 9010,

Perot 9014, Rainforest 9031, Southern 9088, Targa 9108, Texas 9129
Vermont: Central 9239, **Craft 9243**, United 9264
Virginia: Air 9283, **American 9302, Caring 9335, Christian 9341**, Echo 9370, Foodbank 9379, Lend-A-Hand 9419, Maria's 9429, **National 9447**, Northern 9468, United 9531
Washington: Central 9582, Hopelink 9638, Northwest 9686, Rural 9712, Second 9721, Society 9729, Spokane 9731, **World 9758**
West Virginia: Stump 9820
Wisconsin: Feeding 9889, Jewish 9930, Weather 10066, Young 10090, Zebro 10092

Employee-related scholarships

Alabama: Dunlap 33, Protective 72, Southern 82, Tractor 85
Arizona: US Airways 252, Valley 254
Arkansas: **Murphy 296**, Tyson 320, Wal-Mart 325
California: Brooks 423, Cacique 434, Cahp 435, Disney 540, Doe 542, Employees 564, Groeniger 639, Heffernan 654, Jefferies 704, Leavey 740, Little 747, **QUALCOMM 889, Red 903, Sempra 974**, Sierra 982, St 1010, Sun-Pacific 1033, Urbanek 1074, Westphal 1091, Williams 1096
Colorado: **Federal 1194, Johns 1223**, Poudre 1260
Connecticut: Barden 1329, Barnes 1330, Conway 1369, Macricostas 1417, Macristy 1418, **XL 1491**
Delaware: CTW 1498, Ortega 1519, Presto 1520, Quarter 1521
District of Columbia: Community 1605
Florida: Allen 1766, Amos 1776, Baptist 1791, Baptist 1792, Beall 1794, Beall 1795, Cape Coral 1815, Henry 1911, Kelly 1935, Lang 1945, Mount 1988, Naples 1994, Patterson 2015, Rayonier 2031, Sailfish 2047, Yancey 2109
Georgia: Callaway 2134, Chick 2139, Community 2150, East 2169, **NCR 2215**, Star 2242, Weir 2259, WellStar 2260
Hawaii: Rehabilitation 2316, Servco 2320
Idaho: IDACORP 2334, Rogers 2346, Simplot 2349
Illinois: **Abbott 2353**, Andrew 2397, Aon 2402, ArcelorMittal 2406, Bechtner 2416, Bennett 2422, Brunswick 2443, CGH 2470, Chicago 2476, Cochrane 2485, Continental 2498, Conway 2499, Follett 2565, Medline 2729, Old 2766, Republic 2815, Riverside 2824, Ryerson 2839, Taylor 2886, True 2898, United 2905, Wahl 2912
Indiana: Belden 2965, Community 3004, Dora 3017, Dr. 3018, Franklin 3037, Kimball 3086, Koch 3089, Legacy 3096, Memorial 3113, Shroyer 3182
Iowa: Carlson 3252, Des Moines 3273, Grinnell 3290, Hy-Vee 3302, Life 3326, Pella 3355, Trinity 3397, VDTA 3404
Kansas: Koch 3477, Peterson 3503, Spitcaufsky 3519, Terry 3525
Kentucky: Blue 3552, Community 3559, **Lexmark 3589**, Mackin 3593, Papa 3611
Louisiana: Albemarle 3640, Entergy 3651, Goldring 3654, **Woldenberg 3683**
Maryland: Choice 3802, Ginger 3834, Nexion 3902
Massachusetts: American 3968, Boston 3996, Carroll 4012, East Cambridge 4050, Gunning 4092, **Houghton 4115**, Philips 4220, Schaeneman 4260, Segel 4265, Von 4309
Michigan: Ann Arbor 4338, Bay 4350, Community 4398, Dana 4402, Fabri 4416, **Ford 4422**, Grand Rapids 4445, Guardian 4452, Knabusch 4503, Koch 4504, Kohn 4505, L & L 4507, Miller 4543, Scholarship 4602, Southeastern 4615, **UAW-Ford 4647**, UAW-GM 4648, Universal 4653, Whirlpool 4666
Minnesota: Bottemiller 4701, Farmers 4737, Jostens 4774, Koran 4776, Lakeland 4778, **Patterson 4821**, Rahr 4833, Redmond 4834, Sun 4863, Valspar 4878

Missouri: Arch 4934, Broida/Sigma-Aldrich 4944, Butler 4948, Emerson 4985, ESCO 4988, Gilbert 5000, Hall 5011, Minnesouri 5055, Orscheln 5068, Saint Louis 5082, Shelter 5099, St. Marys 5107, Tension 5112, UniGroup 5119

Montana: Beartooth 5131, Montana 5164, Washington 5182

Nebraska: Alegent 5184, Nebraska 5244

New Hampshire: Hunt 5330, New Hampshire 5354

New Jersey: Berkowitz 5397, Buchalter 5406, Calvi 5409, Chakrabarti 5418, **Chubb 5424**, Creamer 5429, Hollander 5469, Skeuse 5568

New Mexico: Chase 5621

New York: **AIG 5675**, **Avon 5745**, Bennett 5759, Brown 5800, Carrier 5820, Central 5836, **Civil 5858**, Confort 5885, Crouse 5901, Daiwa 5909, Davidson 5916, Figliolia 5983, Harden 6057, Hunter 6084, Kathwari 6131, MasterCard 6195, **MetLife 6210**, Mitsui 6219, New York 6266, New York 6267, Price 6327, Realty 6347, Rochester 6357, Silver 6397, **Starr 6430**, Utica 6483, **VonAmelunxen 6496**, Wegmans 6507

North Carolina: Atkins 6564, Coats 6607, Community 6616, Dixie 6632, Foundation 6660, Giles 6673, Meredith 6770, New 6790, Nucor 6803, Steele, 6878, Thomasville 6892, Thomson 6893, Women's 6927

Ohio: AK Steel 6964, American 6971, **Arab 6978**, Blade 6999, Blanchard 7000, Cincinnati 7037, Danis 7077, Fairbanks-Horix 7104, Founders 7116, Good 7129, Goodwin 7131, Horvitz 7156, Hull 7161, International 7169, KeyBank 7188, Midmark 7246, Miller 7249, Munger 7258, National 7267, Palmer 7288, Remmele 7318, Springfield 7363, **Timken 7384**, Wayne 7415, YSI 7446, Ziegler 7447

Oklahoma: Noble 7497, Stillwater 7517

Oregon: Collins 7552, Davies 7568, Day 7569, Education 7574, Ford 7578, Halton 7584, Mid-Columbia 7605

Pennsylvania: **Alcoa 7694**, Angelo 7706, Arkema 7709, Asbestos 7715, Blaisdell 7735, Boscov 7739, Calvert 7756, Community 7783, **Connelly 7788**, Eastern 7818, F & 7834, Farber 7837, Fulton 7863, Gooding 7876, **Handyside 7885**, High 7906, Hill 7907, Miller 7986, Northwest 8013, Pennsylvania 8023, Pinnacle 8044, PNC 8051, **PPG 8058**, Quaker 8069, Reeves 8073, Riddle 8077, Snyder 8117, Stager 8129, Steinman 8130, Weber 8181, West 8188

Rhode Island: Additon 8225, Comstock 8272, Cranston 8275, CVS 8282, Gould 8301, Kingsbury 8322, Meriden 8344, Norman 8356, O'Brion 8357, Stauble 8414

South Carolina: Cox 8468, Gregg 8478, Inman 8486, Sonoco 8510

Tennessee: AutoZone 8558, Boyd 8561, Cracker 8581, Dixie 8582, Eastman 8589, Lee 8617, Precision 8633, Temple 8653, Unaka 8656, Wellmont 8662

Texas: Carter 8738, College 8757, Conn 8766, Crescent 8775, EOG 8816, Fluor 8824, Heavin 8863, Jordan 8902, Katz 8903, Kimberly 8906, Lucas 8927, M. 8930, McGowan 8945, Minyard 8964, NASA 8980, Nearburg 8987, Pedernales 9008, Pioneer 9020, Pipe 9021, Reed 9033, Richardson 9038, Seton 9069, Southern 9088, Texas 9121, Texas 9130, Valero 9147, Visible 9151, Wilson 9169, Zimmer 9188

Utah: Borax 9195

Virginia: **Burger 9331**, Davidson 9359, Hooker 9398, **NATSO 9460**, **PMMI 9484**, Scott 9500, SMACNA 9506, Smithfield 9508, Specialized 9512

Washington: CHEMCENTRAL 9585, Community 9600, DaVita 9604, Group 9626, Lynden 9666, Pigott 9698

West Virginia: Arthur's 9764, McCamic 9800, Sun 9821, Vecellio 9826

Wisconsin: Associated 9841, Badger 9844, Briggs 9851, Bruno 9855, DeLong 9877, Giddings 9906, Jacobus 9928, Johnson 9933, ManpowerGroup 9957, Meehan 9963, Menasha 9965, Oilgear

9987, Phillips 9993, Rexnord 10007, Schield 10021, Shopko 10032, Smith 10035, St. Croix 10043, Windhover 10073, Wisconsin 10081, WPS 10088

Wyoming: True 10122

Employee-related welfare

Alaska: Providence 131

California: Employees 564, Jack 699

Colorado: **Rock 1269**

District of Columbia: Community 1605

Florida: Beall 1795, Brown 1812, Florida 1877, Hma 1916, **Office 2002**, PSS/Gulf 2027, SWS 2080

Georgia: Southern 2238

Illinois: **Abbott 2353**, Aon 2402, CNA 2484, McDonald's 2719, Medline 2729, Walgreen 2913, WKUS 2931

Kentucky: Independence 3578, Papa 3612

Maryland: Memorial 3879

Massachusetts: Dunkin 4047, Park 4211, Raytheon 4238

Michigan: **Domino's 4409**, **Dow 4410**, Ford 4421, Hudson 4473, **Kellogg 4496**

Minnesota: Jaffray 4769, Koran 4776, **Polaris 4827**

Mississippi: Yates 4926

Missouri: Butler 4948, Leader 5035

New York: Baseball 5754, Bennett 5759, Klein 6142, Martin 6192, PricewaterhouseCoopers 6328, Realty 6347, Scarsdale 6378, **VonAmelunxen 6496**

North Carolina: Burlington 6587, Smith 6867

Ohio: Foss 7114, National 7267, Tyler 7394

Oregon: Corvallis 7558, Journal 7591

Pennsylvania: Armstrong 7711, Blaisdell 7735, Genesis 7867, Ladd 7940, Penn 8022, **Vang 8161**, Woods 8205

Rhode Island: Rostra 8389

Tennessee: Dixie 8582, HCA 8599, Mercy 8619, Ruby 8639, ServiceMaster 8642

Texas: AT&T 8695, Cadbury 8732, Carter 8738, Fleetwood 8823, Giannini 8837, Giannini 8838, Lockheed 8921, Lockheed 8922, Penney 9010, Perot 9014, Swinney 9105, Sysco 9107, Thompson 9136

Washington: Costco 9601, Group 9626

Wisconsin: Weather 10066

Exchange programs

California: Community 513, World 1101

Colorado: Yampa 1309

Connecticut: **Belgian 1334**, Branford 1338

District of Columbia: **American 1552, Atlas 1589, German 1638, International 1656, Radio 1718**

Florida: Atlantic 1787

Hawaii: Akihito 2270

Illinois: **Rotary 2835**

Maine: Hungarian-American 3704

Maryland: **Epilepsy 3821**

Michigan: Temple 4634

New Hampshire: La Napoule 5333

New York: American 5687, American 5691, **CDS 5828, Institute 6095**, Lurcy 6176, **Philippe 6316**

North Carolina: Beaver 6571

Ohio: Oberlin 7276

Oregon: Portland 7633

Pennsylvania: **Foundation 7850**

Texas: Fort Worth 8828, Panasonic 9001

Washington: **Bainbridge 9566, Rotalia 9709**

Fellowships

Alabama: Dixon 31

Alaska: Bering 105, CIRI 113, Rasmuson 132, UIC 145

Arizona: **Alliance 154**, Flinn 193, Piper 229

California: **Academy 334**, Arthritis 375, **Arthritis 376**, Arts 377, **Association 389**, California 445, California 446, California 450, Community 512, Creative 526, Cystic 532, **Draper 547**, Durfee 549, Film 575, Fleishhacker 578, **Getty 614**, Giannini 615, Glaucoma 619, **Glenn 621, Grass 637, Hertz 658**, Huntington 674, International 688, Jewish 706, **Kaiser 716**, Kornberg 725, **Leakey 739**, Los 758, Mathematical 776, Merage 785, **National 814, National 818**, National 821, **Pancreatic 854**, Price 878, Price 879, REDF 905, San Diego 939, Southern 1005, **Stanford 1016**, That 1043, **Thiel 1046, Toigo 1049**, Tower 1052, **Trust 1060, United 1072**

Colorado: American 1117, Boulder 1132, Colorado 1153, Colorado 1154, EDUCAUSE 1189, Hasan 1211, **Morris 1243, Music 1246**, National 1247

Connecticut: **American 1320, Belgian 1334**, Branford 1338, Childs 1354, Connecticut 1367, Deloitte 1375, Hartford 1398, **Kim 1410, National 1429**, Tierney 1472

Delaware: **Eleutherian 1505, International 1514**

District of Columbia: Abramson 1530, **Accordia 1531, American 1538, American 1546, American 1547, American 1549, American 1551, American 1552, American 1554, American 1557**, American 1558, **American 1565**, American 1568, **Amyotrophic 1573**, Asian 1581, **Aspen 1583**, Association 1584, Association 1587, **Atlas 1588, Atlas 1589**, Bogan 1596, **Congressional 1607, Council 1610, Council 1611, Council 1612**, Dingwall 1615, Dutko 1619, **Equal 1622, Families 1625**, Fordham 1628, **Friendly 1633, German 1638**, Gerontological 1639, **Heritage 1643, Institute 1650, International 1656, International 1658, International 1660**, Jews 1663, **Kennedy 1666, Kennedy 1667, Lupus 1671, National 1689, National 1695**, Nonprofit 1701, Patterson 1710, Patton 1711, **Pharmaceutical 1714**, Phi 1715, **Phillips 1716, Radio 1718**, Resources 1723, **Smithsonian 1729, Society 1730, U.S. 1738, United 1743**, United 1744, **Wilson 1752**, Women's 1754, **World 1755**

Florida: Alpha-1 1767, American 1772, American 1773, American 1774, AWS 1789, Cintas 1828, Everglades 1872, Florida 1879, Hermitage 1912, Miami 1978

Georgia: **American 2113, American 2115, Carter 2136**, Christian 2142, Columbus 2149, Council 2155, Fund 2181, Hall 2190, **MAP 2208**

Hawaii: **Center 2274, Watumull 2326**

Idaho: Idaho 2336

Illinois: AKA 2360, American 2367, **American 2371, American 2372, American 2378, American 2380, American 2385, American 2392**, American 2393, Ann 2401, Association 2408, Association 2409, Business 2452, Chicago 2472, **Dystonia 2529**, Graham 2592, Health 2607, **Healthy 2608, Heed 2610, Hertz 2615, Holocaust 2622**, International 2650, **Leukemia 2690, MacArthur 2704, Medical 2728**, National 2746, **National 2752, North 2758, Organization 2769**, Ott 2773, **Plastic 2793, Poetry 2795, Sigma 2855, Skidmore 2857**, Society 2863, **Terra 2889, Thoracic 2892, Zonta 2942**

Indiana: Alpha 2948, **Alpha 2949**, Arts 2960, Association 2962, **Lilly 3101, Organization 3132**

Iowa: McElroy 3333

Kansas: Kansas 3472, Wichita 3539

Kentucky: Appalachian 3545, Scottish 3624, University 3634

Louisiana: Academic 3639

Maine: Hungarian-American 3704, Maine 3709, Switzer 3738

Maryland: **American 3761**, American 3762, American 3766, **Associated 3777**, Association 3778, **Casey 3794**, Cystic 3812, **Endocrine 3818, Enterprise 3819, Environmental 3820, Epilepsy 3821, Foundation 3829**, Foundation 3830, Life 3865, **Michels 3883, Middle 3886**, NASDAQ 3892, **National 3897, Osteogenesis 3906**, Prince 3915

Massachusetts: Aid 3960, **American 3963, American 3964,** American 3967, **American 3969,** Blue 3989, Boston 3996, Center 4016, **Earthwatch 4049, Fine 4068,** Fraxa 4076, Harvard 4095, **Harvard 4097,** Health 4101, **International 4127, Kennedy 4137,** Kim 4139, King 4140, **Lalor 4145,** Lyceum 4154, **Marine 4160,** President 4230, Real 4239, **SEVEN 4267,** Smith 4270, **Tanne 4282,** Whiting 4316, **Winter 4319, Woods 4321,** Wurtman 4325

Michigan: **ACI 4332,** Earhart 4411, Heyl 4465, **Kellogg 4497, Society 4610**

Minnesota: **American 4686,** American 4687, Arrowhead 4693, Bakken 4697, Bush 4705, **Camargo 4706,** Ecotrust 4732, IFP 4763, Lake 4777, Loft 4784, Northern 4814, Prairie 4828, Southern 4855

Missouri: **Kauffman 5025, PKD 5074,** Stowers 5109

Montana: Bray 5134, Washington 5182

Nebraska: Foundation 5204

Nevada: Davidson 5284

New Hampshire: Hitchcock 5328, New Hampshire 5353, Plan 5361

New Jersey: Brookdale 5405, **Center 5416, Dow 5435, IEEE 5476, Knowles 5489,** Lasko 5494, Merck 5504, New Jersey 5521, **Newcombe 5526, Reeve 5550, WheatonArts 5595, Wilson 5600**

New Mexico: **American 5611, School 5650, Southwestern 5652, SUMMA 5655**

New York: Academy 5663, American 5687, **American 5688,** American 5690, American 5691, **American 5692, American 5693,** American 5695, **American 5700, American 5701,** American 5703, **American 5704,** American 5705, **American 5710, American 5711,** Armenian 5717, Art 5720, Art 5721, **Autism 5743,** Bibliographical 5762, **BMI 5771,** Bogliasco 5772, Bronx 5793, **Camphill 5811,** Cancer 5813, **CDS 5828,** Center 5833, Center 5834, **Center 5835,** Cinereach 5853, **College 5866, Commonwealth 5872,** Crohn's 5899, **Cummings 5904,** De Karman 5918, **Dedalus 5919, Delmas 5921,** Democracy 5922, Downtown 5933, **Duke 5938,** Dutchess 5941, **Echoing 5952, Elizabeth 5957,** Episcopal 5961, Eyebeam 5970, **Fight 5982, Foundation 5994,** Frick 6011, Golden 6036, Grand 6042, **Guggenheim 6049, Guggenheim 6050,** Hereditary 6068, **Huntington's 6086, IBM 6089,** Insall 6094, **International 6099,** Klingenstein 6143, **Klingenstein 6144,** Kosciuszko 6145, **League 6156, Legacy 6158, Leukemia 6160,** L'Oreal 6170, Lower 6172, **Luce 6175,** Lurcy 6176, **Lymphatic 6178, Lymphoma 6179, Mayday 6197,** Memorial 6207, **Metropolitan 6211,** Moore 6224, **NARSAD 6239, National 6241,** National 6245, **National 6250, National 6251, National 6255,** Netherland-America 6258, New Visions 6263, **New York 6264, New York 6265,** New York 6268, New York 6269, New York 6271, New York 6273, **Open 6294,** Pasteur 6306, **Population 6320, Princess 6329, Public 6337, Rainforest 6343, Royal 6364,** Runyon 6365, **Skadden 6398,** Sloan 6404, **Soanes 6408, Social 6409,** Society 6412, Socrates 6414, **Soros 6416,** Stony 6440, Tourette 6459, **Trace 6461, Tsadra 6465,** UJA 6470, **United 6477,** UrbanGlass 6481, Van Alen 6484, **Watson 6504, Weill 6508, Wenner 6511, Whitney 6518,** Women's 6529, **World 6533, Woursell 6537**

North Carolina: **American 6550,** Broad 6582, **Cattell 6594,** Center 6595, Cherokee 6598, **Institut 6711,** MDC 6767, Mecklenburg 6768, **National 6784,** NC 6785, **Pediatric 6814, S.R.C. 6847, Student 6883**

Ohio: Cleveland 7043, Oberlin 7276, Scripps 7340, **Wexner 7423**

Oklahoma: Bailey 7451, OSU 7504, Tulsa 7519

Oregon: Chamber 7547, Ford 7578, Literary 7597, Northwest 7619, Regional 7641

Pennsylvania: **American 7701,** American 7702, **American 7704, AO 7707, Association 7716,**

Association 7718, **ERM 7832,** Hamot 7884, Independence 7916, Lancaster 7941, Lewis 7958, Pennsylvania 8027, Pew 8033, Philadelphia 8034, Pittsburgh 8047, Steinman 8131, Stoneleigh 8133, **Williams 8192**

Rhode Island: Brown 8253, **Dorot 8286,** Rhode Island 8381

South Carolina: Arts 8448

South Dakota: **First 8530**

Tennessee: Chattanooga 8568, Humanities 8604, Le 8615

Texas: American 8683, Amigos 8686, Houston 8875, **Komen 8910, Media 8950,** Methodist 8955, **Museum 8975,** Southwestern 9092, Stark 9101, Teen 9112, Welder 9161

Utah: **Sundance 9227,** Utah 9228

Vermont: Ohiyesa 9256, Rowland 9258, **Vermont 9271**

Virginia: **American 9290, American 9291,** American 9303, **American 9305, Ashoka: 9317,** College 9344, **Focused 9377, Foundation 9380, Fox 9384, IDSA 9402,** Jefferson 9408, **Melton 9434, Mustard 9442, National 9451, National 9457,** National 9458, **National 9459, Newspaper 9464, Public 9488, Radiation 9489, Sarnoff 9498,** TDC 9517, **U.S. 9526,** Van Engel 9536, Virginia 9539

Washington: Artist 9564, Behnke 9568, Blakemore 9572, **Bullitt 9578, Friends 9618,** George 9622, **Native 9680,** Russell 9713, Wales 9744

West Virginia: West Virginia 9827

Wisconsin: **Entomological 9884,** Kohl 9944, **National 9978,** Wisconsin 10080

Fiscal agent/sponsor

California: AEPOCH 341, Art 373, Arts 377, Aspiration 381, Bay 405, Buddhist 426, Catalyst 466, Celebrity 470, Cloud 503, Community 517, CounterPULSE 525, Creative 526, Dancers' 535, **Earth 550,** Foster 582, Independent 680, International 689, Intersection 693, James 700, Media 781, Media 782, Monterey 803, Oaklandish, 837, Open 841, **Public 886,** Public 887, Rose 919, San Diego 928, **San Francisco 943,** San Francisco 945, San Francisco 948, Side 981, Social 998, Southern 1005, **Trust 1060**

Colorado: Boulder 1132, Colorado 1163

District of Columbia: **Ocean 1702**

Hawaii: North 2306

Illinois: Experimental 2555, Urbana-Champaign 2907

Indiana: LaGrange 3093

Maryland: American 3758, Beth 3785

Massachusetts: Center 4015, **Documentary 4041, Lift 4149**

Minnesota: IFP 4763, Intermedia 4766, Springboard 4859

Nebraska: Nebraska 5241

New York: Art 5718, **Arts 5729,** Brooklyn 5797, Camera 5809, Council 5893, Dance 5910, Dance 5911, Experimental 5967, **FJC 5986,** Foundation 5997, Fractured 6007, **Independent 6092,** Independent 6093, Living 6166, MADRE, 6182, Moving 6229, New York 6277, Performance 6313, Professional 6331, **Public 6338,** Squeaky 6423, Unique 6471, Women 6527, Working 6532

North Carolina: Southern 6869

Ohio: Independent 7168

Oregon: Lane 7595

Pennsylvania: Pittsburgh 8047, Scribe 8095

Tennessee: **National 8629**

Texas: Austin 8697, Austin 8698, San Antonio 9056, **Southwest 9090**

Washington: 911 9554, Allied 9559, Blue 9573, Northwest 9685, Seattle 9720

Foreign applicants

Arizona: Rosztoczy 234

California: Aid 343, Avery 395, **Cantor 463,** Christian 495, **Foundation 587, Foundation 589,** GET 613, Headlands 649, Humboldt 671, **Immunobiology 677,** Leakey 739, Mexico 789, Ramakrishna 895, Studenica 1029, Trustees 1061, Tuckerman 1063

Colorado: **National 1248**

Connecticut: **China 1355, Cholnoky 1356**

District of Columbia: **Accordia 1531, American 1552, American 1557,** Atlas 1588, **Atlas 1589,** Community 1605, **Friendly 1633, German 1638, International 1656, International 1660, Monk 1680, Women 1753**

Florida: Amin 1775, AWS 1789, Cintas 1828, **Horizons 1922,** Jacob 1928, **Prime 2025, Samstag 2048**

Georgia: Coastal 2146, **Pilot 2225**

Hawaii: Towle 2323

Illinois: Anagnos 2394, Hasnia 2603, Lascaris 2685

Iowa: **Grace 3286**

Maryland: **Estonian 3823, Hughes 3846, School 3928**

Massachusetts: **American 3969,** Real 4239

Michigan: **Gilmore 4438**

Minnesota: **Lindbergh 4783**

Missouri: **Alpha 4929, PKD 5074**

New Hampshire: **MacDowell 5341**

New Jersey: **Johnson 5482, Mochary 5509, Ostberg 5533,** Terplan 5577

New York: Agoriani 5673, **American 5692, American 5697, American 5699, American 5711, Brackett 5779,** Children 5847, **Commonwealth 5872, Corporation 5888, Das 5914, Ezer 5971, Friends 6012, International 6098, International 6099,** Jenkins 6113, **Kosciuszko 6145,** L'Oreal 6170, Lurcy 6176, Malevich 6185, **Millay 6216, Open 6294, Pollock 6318,** Scott 6388, **Shatford 6395,** St. George's 6425, UrbanGlass 6481, **Wildlife 6520**

North Carolina: **TASCA 6887**

Ohio: **Arab 6978,** Johnson 7179, **Wexner 7423**

Pennsylvania: **Foundation 7850**

Rhode Island: Alpert 8227, **Papines 8364**

South Carolina: **Malanga 8493**

Tennessee: Stephenson 8651, Thomley 8654

Texas: Chinati 8748, **Mensa 8952,** Student 9102

Virginia: **Brockbank 9328, Conquer 9351,** Pillay 9482

Washington: **Bainbridge 9566,** JTM 9646, **Rotalia 9709**

Wyoming: **Ucross 10123**

Graduate support

Alabama: Alabama 4, **Civitan 24,** Owens 67, Reed 73

Alaska: Bering 105, CIRI 113, Koniag 122, McCurdy 124, Samuelsen 134, SNA 139, Valley 148

Arizona: Arizona 165, AZHHA 167, Major 214, Seed 236

Arkansas: Hornlein 284, Kelder 286, SHARE 307

California: ACEC 337, American 359, American 360, Arques 372, **Association 389,** Association 390, California 453, California 457, **Cancer 462,** China 492, Chung 498, Dales 534, **Foundation 588, Foundation 589, Getty 614,** Golden 626, Guslander 641, **Hertz 658,** Hinckley 663, **Hispanic 664, HP 670, INCOSE 679,** Jewish 708, Joshua 714, Lagrant 731, Lakewood 732, League 738, **Little 748,** Mills 793, Mitchell 797, **Modglin 800,** National 821, North 832, Pasadena 855, Pedrozzi 858, **Rand 898,** RCL 900, San Francisco 944, Scholarship 965, Sedler 972, Smith 996, St. Shenouda 1015, Storkan/Hanes 1027, Ventura 1081, Warner 1086, World 1101

Colorado: AEG 1113, Aorn 1119, **Clan 1148, Galaway 1201,** Mikkelson 1239, National 1247, Sachs 1277, Scottish 1278, Society 1285, Yampa 1309

Connecticut: Ash 1325, **Belgian 1334,** Branford 1338, Community 1361, Community 1362, DiMauro 1377, Folsom 1390, Hartford 1399, New Canaan 1430, Norwalk 1436, **Scudder 1458**

Delaware: Delaware 1500

District of Columbia: **American 1539, American 1559, American 1565,** American 1570, Arab 1576, **Broadcast 1597,** Community 1605, **Congressional 1607, International 1654, Landscape 1668, Monk 1680, National 1685, National 1691, National 1693, Radio 1718, Society 1730, Union 1741, United 1743,** Women's 1754

Florida: American 1770, American 1772, AWS 1789, Brevard 1807, Community 1841, Corbett 1851, Fellows 1875, Harris 1904, Jacob 1928, King 1939, Lauffer 1947, McCabe 1968, McCune 1969, Ruegamer 2042, Sailfish 2047, Wertzberger 2101

Georgia: Callaway 2134, Cobb 2147, Community 2151, **Fadel 2174,** Hall 2191, Kaplan 2200, **Phi Mu 2222, Pilot 2225,** Student 2245

Hawaii: Atherton 2271, **Center 2274,** Kaiulani 2296, Mink 2304, Pope 2315, Ross 2317, Saake 2318

Illinois: **Academy 2355, ADA 2356, American 2368, American 2370, American 2371, American 2376, American 2379, American 2386,** American 2390, **Anagnos 2394,** Aon 2402, APICS 2403, Berner 2423, Bound 2432, Brown 2442, Centralia 2467, Chicago 2476, Christ 2481, Community 2496, DeKalb 2514, **Foundry 2571,** Garwin 2579, Hansen 2598, Knecht 2673, **Lithuanian 2695,** Mellinger 2730, **National 2749, National 2752,** Nesbitt 2754, Ott 2773, Patterson 2780, Peterson 2786, **Polish 2796, Research 2816,** Rinker 2821, Ross 2832, **Rotary 2835,** Scherer 2840, Schwarz 2845, **Sigma 2855,** Smith 2859, Stevenson 2873, Welch 2921, Women's 2934, Zearing 2940

Indiana: Abell 2944, Alpha 2950, **Alpha 2952,** Boonshot 2971, Community 2993, Community 2994, Community 3004, Elkhart 3024, Indiana 3070, Jewish 3078, **Kappa 3082, Lambda 3095, Organization 3132,** Peters 3144, Seymour 3179, Westhaysen 3223, Williams 3228, Zeta 3230

Iowa: Jay 3312, Lee 3324, McElroy 3333, **P.E.O. 3350,** Petersen 3356, **Pioneer 3358,** Pritchard 3361

Kansas: Coffman 3427, Dolechek 3432, Nell 3494, Wildlife 3540

Kentucky: **AAEP 3543,** Batterton 3549, Blue 3552, Community 3559, Morrill 3600, Norris 3603

Louisiana: Bernstein 3646, Lang 3660, Tupper 3681

Maryland: **AICE 3751, Alpha 3755, American 3765, American 3768, Anxiety 3773,** Autism 3781, **Endocrine 3818, Epilepsy 3821,** Fast 3825, **Foundation 3829,** Laughlin 3862, **National 3895**

Massachusetts: Affordable 3958, American 3967, Du Bois 4044, Educational 4054, Edwards 4055, Fortin 4074, **Giovanni 4083, Harvard 4097,** Home 4110, Hopkins 4113, **Huntington 4123,** Kim 4139, Massachusetts 4163, **Maya 4170,** Ocean 4205, Permanent 4216, **Tourism 4292**

Michigan: **ACI 4332,** Baker 4342, Barry 4347, Bay 4350, Birtwistle 4360, Community 4394, **Earhart 4411,** Evereg-Fenesse 4414, Gratiot 4448, Harding 4457, Lapeer 4512, **Michigan 4533,** Mount Pleasant 4548, **Society 4611**

Minnesota: Alworth 4685, Land 4779, Lane 4780, Philanthrofund 4824, PLUS 4826, Stillwell 4862

Mississippi: Feild 4907, Mississippi 4915

Missouri: Baptist-Trinity 4935, **Demolay 4974,** Dental 4975, Drowns 4979, Gorman 5002, Hamilton 5012, Kansas 5023, Schafer 5083, **Sertoma, 5098,** Stowers 5109, Swanson 5110, Truman 5118

Montana: Harbert 5154, Washington 5182

Nebraska: Ellis 5200, Foundation 5204, Grand Island 5210

Nevada: Community 5282, Doyle 5287, Nevada 5296, Western 5304

New Hampshire: Foundation 5322, James 5331, Martin 5345, Plan 5361, Skrungloo 5368, **U.S. 5373**

New Jersey: Atlantic 5391, Essex 5441, Fortescue 5448, **Foundation 5449,** Grupe 5462, **Johnson 5482, Knowles 5489, Mahajan 5501,** Merck 5504, Ryu 5556, Snyder 5570, **Tang 5575,** Wei 5593, Wetterberg 5594, **Wilson 5600**

New Mexico: **American 5611, American 5612,** Berliner 5614, Chase 5621, ENMR 5628, Helm 5632, Laguna 5634

New York: **AAAA 5662,** Alexander 5679, American 5691, **American 5692, American 5696, American 5699,** American 5703, **American 5711,** Angle 5714, Armenian 5717, **Audio 5739,** Buffalo 5803, Cancer 5813, **Career 5816,** Chautauqua 5842, **College 5866,** Collins 5868, Community 5878, Crohn's 5899, **Das 5914, Dedalus 5919, Fight 5982,** Foundation 5999, Foundation 6002, Frick 6011, Grand 6042, **Hearing 6065,** Hudson 6080, **Institute 6095, International 6099, International 6102, Kosciuszko 6145,** La 6150, Lewis 6161, **Lighthouse 6163,** Lurcy 6176, McCormick 6202, **Metropolitan 6211, Myasthenia 6234,** NAACP 6237, National 6247, **Netherland-America 6258,** New York 6270, NLN 6280, Nolan 6282, **Open 6294,** Patterson 6308, Price 6327, **Public 6337,** Puerto 6339, Rochester 6357, Schechter 6380, **Schepp 6395, Shatford 6395,** Snayberger 6407, **Social 6409, Societe 6410,** Society 6412, **Soros 6416, Spencer 6420, St. Elmo 6424,** Tilt 6456, **United 6472,** Warren 6501, Westchester 6514, **Wine 6525,** Wolf 6525, **Women's 6528, Worldstudio 6535, Worth 6536**

North Carolina: Beaver 6571, Boye 6578, Center 6595, Cole 6611, Community 6613, Eddy 6642, **Environmental 6649,** Foundation 6660, Grotefend 6688, Material 6758, McNaught 6765, Myers 6783, Posey 6822, Reich 6823, Rouch 6842, **S.R.C. 6847, Sigma 6860,** Wilson 6922, **Youth 6933**

Ohio: AJCA 6963, **Arab 6978,** Bontrager 7004, Bowen 7008, Cleveland 7040, College 7050, Community 7058, Fishel 7110, **Griffith 7136,** Hamilton 7139, Holmes 7152, Licking 7209, **Lincoln 7210,** Mentzer 7239, Miller 7249, Muskingum 7263, National 7267, Phi Kappa 7302, Scholarship 7338, Stark 7366, Van Horn 7401, Wayne 7415

Oklahoma: **Chickasaw 7457,** Henry 7480

Oregon: Campbell 7543, Halton 7584, McDowell 7601, Northwest 7620, Pernot 7631, Singer 7659, Von der Ahe 7675

Pennsylvania: **Botstiber 7740,** Bread 7743, Clark 7770, Community 7783, Community 7785, Fitton 7845, Gibson 7869, Goldman 7874, Harris 7889, Helbing 7901, II-VI 7915, Irvin 7921, Lowengard 7962, Luzerne 7964, McKaig 7975, Miller 7985, Moore 7994, Nestor 8004, **Pan 8018,** Power 8057, Scholarship 8088, Shoemaker 8101, Sinden 8105, Steinman 8131, Vincent 8165, Wettrick 8190, Williams 8194, Zaccheus 8218, Zimmerman 8219

Rhode Island: August 8233, Baker 8238, Cohen 8268, Manwiller 8334, **Papines 8364,** Rhode 8379, Rhode Island 8381, Smith 8407, Urann 8429

South Carolina: Coastal 8464, Hart 8480, Love 8491, Ocean 8499, Springs 8515

Tennessee: Chi Omega 8571, Hicks 8601, Wilemon 8663

Texas: Bartholomew 8703, **Bat 8705,** Borton 8717, Brisley 8721, Chamberlin 8742, Conference 8765, Conner 8767, Cook 8770, Dupre 8801, Faulconer 8820, **First 8822,** Hammond 8852, **Harding 8854,** Hill 8867, Houston 8884, Hurley 8888, IFMA 8890, Marti 8936, Miller 8960, Milotte 8963, National 8983, Piper 9022

Utah: McCarthey 9219

Vermont: Clifford 9241, Durfee 9245

Virgin Islands: Community 9274

Virginia: Air 9284, **American 9287, American 9289, American 9295, American 9300, American 9304, American 9307, Cooke 9352,** Datatel 9358, Foundation 9383, Hampton 9391, **Institute 9404,** Jefferson 9408, Lincoln 9421, **Mustard 9442,** National 9449, **National 9451, National 9455,** National 9458, **Olmsted 9470,** Randolph 9491, **Special 9511, United 9529, United 9530,** University 9533

Washington: Blue 9574, **Bullitt 9578,** Davis 9603, Evergreen 9609, First 9612, George 9622, Lauzier 9658, McCleary 9670, Mortar 9677, **Rotalia 9709,** Royston 9710, Rural 9711

West Virginia: Beckley 9766, Kanawha 9794, Pais 9807, Stout 9819

Wisconsin: Aslakson 9840, **Entomological 9884,** Freedom 9898, Gallmeier 9904, Green Bay 9910, Noer 9984, Oshkosh 9988, Phillips 9993, Stateline 10047, Wisconsin 10080

Wyoming: Cody 10098, Likins 10111, Whitney 10124

Grants for special needs

Alabama: Alabama 3, Childcare 23, Community 26, Community 29, Decatur 30, Gulf 44, Middleton 62, Montgomery 65, United 86

Alaska: Aleut 103, Kawerak 121, Rooney 133

Arizona: 100 150, Agape 152, Arizona 159, Arizona 160, Assistance 166, **Breast 172, Cancer 175,** Catholic 176, Educational 190, Friendship 198, **Help 200,** Interfaith 204, Make-A-Wish 215, Mesa 218, Old 223, Positive 230, Prayer 231, St. Mary's/Westside 240, Turnbow 249, United 250

Arkansas: Area 261, Arkansas 262, Arvac 267, Community 275, Helping 283, Ozark 301, Riordan 305, RMHC 306, Sparks 313, Wallace 323, Wal-Mart 324

California: Advertising 339, **Aid 343,** AIDS 344, **Alalusi 345,** Allgemeiner 346, Alta 351, American 355, Ardron 369, Assistance 382, Assistance 385, Athena 392, **Autism 393,** Avery 396, Battered 403, Beckstrand 409, Bialis 412, Breast 422, Burks 428, California 451, California 452, Catholic 468, Center 471, Central 475, Child 483, **Children 485,** Childrens 486, Children's 487, Children's 488, **Children's 490,** Christian 495, Chronicle 496, Community 516, El Monte 557, El Puente 558, Emergency 562, **Faith's 567, Family 568,** Far 570, Five 577, **Floor 580,** Florsheim 581, Foundation 591, FRAMAX 592, Fundacion 605, Futuro 606, Girl 617, Give 618, Good 629, Good 630, **Grace 633,** Hoag 666, Housing 669, Huntington 673, Injured 682, Inland 683, Inner-City 684, Interface 687, Ioan 695, Irwindale 697, Italian 698, Jefferson 705, Kaiser 717, Korean 723, Kurka 726, Ladies 729, Laurance 737, Lockheed 752, Los 757, Make-A-Wish 766, Marguerite 770, Marino 773, Masonic 775, Military 791, Modesto 799, Motion 807, Musicares 809, Mutual 810, National 819, New 826, North 829, North 830, Oakley 838, Penny 860, Pfaffinger 864, Physicians 867, Promises 884, **Ramakrishna 895,** Raphael 899, **Red 903,** Redwood 906, Redwood 907, Rest 908, **Rogers 916,** Rohr 917, Rosemary 920, San 935, San Diego 939, San Felipe 940, San Francisco 942, San Gabriel/Pomona 949, Sandpipers 953, **Santa 959, Sarcoma 960,** SCI 967, **Screen 969,** Second 971, Serra 976, Shelby 979, Sierra 983, Small 992, **Society 1001,** Society 1002, South 1004, St 1010, St. 1012, St. Jude 1014, Sunnyvale 1032, Swanson 1034, Sweet 1035, Tatum 1037, Tenderloin 1042, Theatre 1044, Tri-Counties 1055, Trinity 1057, Turn 1064, Twin 1065, Union 1067, United 1070, Valley 1076, Visual 1082, Winnett 1097

Colorado: Advocate 1112, Alexander 1115, Assistance 1125, Balke 1127, Boogie's 1131, Catholic 1142, Colfax 1152, Colorado 1155, Colorado 1159, Colorado 1164, Colorado 1168, Community 1173, Crossroads 1175, Denver 1181, Denver 1182, El 1190, Evergreen 1193, **Federal 1194,** Girl 1204, **H.E.L.P. 1208,** Housing 1215, Hunter 1217, Jeffco 1220, Jewish 1222, Keren 1226, Lillis 1232, Lupus 1234, Lutheran 1235, **National 1248,** Outreach 1255, Pathways 1256, Pikes 1257, **Rock 1269,** Rocky 1273, SEAKR 1279, Servant 1281, Sister 1283, **Someone 1286,** Stride 1291, Telluride 1295, Zac's 1313

Connecticut: Action 1314, Alexion 1317, **AmeriCares 1323**, Boehringer 1335, Branford 1338, Building 1342, Charitable 1353, Colburn-Keenan 1360, Community 1363, CTE 1372, Eastern 1381, **Fidelco 1388**, Hurlbutt 1404, Igstaedter 1406, Larrabee 1413, New 1432, Operation 1438, Orange 1439, Person-to-Person 1442, **Pitney 1444**, Riot 1449, **Save 1454**, Senior 1459, Thames 1470, United 1476, Urban 1477, **Walkabout 1479**, Westport-Weston 1484, Widows 1485, Woman's 1488, Workplace 1489

Delaware: AstraZeneca 1493, Children 1496, Delaware 1502, Delaware 1503, Horsemen's 1513, National 1517

District of Columbia: **Airline 1535**, Anacostia 1574, **Arc 1577**, Ayuda 1590, Christ 1601, Communications 1604, Community 1605, District 1616, Food 1627, **National 1695**, Paralyzed 1706, **Patient 1709**, Professional 1717, Rainy 1719, Red 1722, St. John's 1734, Washington 1749, **Women 1753**, Young 1756

Florida: Abilities 1763, Anew 1777, Area 1780, Aurora 1788, Big 1799, Brown 1812, Catholic 1819, Catholic 1820, Child 1823, Children's 1824, Children's 1826, Christian 1827, Colen 1834, Community 1849, Council 1852, Cousin 1853, Densch 1860, duPont 1865, Edwards 1868, Fabela 1874, Florida 1880, Florida 1881, Fort 1889, Gulf 1899, Harrison 1905, **Harvest 1906**, Jay 1930, **Joshua 1932, Julien 1934, Kids 1938**, King 1939, Lutheran 1956, Miller 1980, **Multiple 1989**, National 1995, North 1998, Pinellas 2020, Police 2023, Rehabilitation 2033, Renal 2035, Rogers 2040, Schmitt 2050, Senior 2059, Sieber 2061, Smigiel 2063, Space 2068, **Special 2069**, Taylor 2085, Trolinger 2090, United 2094, United 2095, Volunteer 2097, Wolfe 2106, Workforce 2108

Georgia: Alpha 2112, **American 2116**, Baker 2123, Burke 2133, Coastal 2146, Concerted 2154, Cox 2157, Creative 2158, CURE 2159, Edmonson 2170, Empty 2171, Fragile 2179, Fulton 2180, God's 2188, Hall 2190, Hospice 2196, Ladonna 2204, Make 2207, Marena 2209, Monroe 2212, Parents 2219, Phillips 2223, **Rosenberg 2229**, Saint 2230, Savannah 2233, Southern 2239, Stovall 2244, **THDF 2249**, United 2251, United 2252, United 2253, West 2261, Whitfield 2264, Widows 2265

Hawaii: Council 2279, Easter 2281, Hana 2287, Hawaii 2289, Helping 2292, Learning 2300, Life 2301, Mink 2304, National 2305, Parents 2313

Idaho: Boise 2329, Home 2333

Illinois: A & B 2352, **Abbvie 2354, ADA 2356**, Aicardi 2359, AKA 2360, Barr 2414, BCMW 2415, Bolingbrook 2430, C.E.F.S. 2454, **Cara 2459**, Catholic 2463, Catholic 2464, Central 2466, Children's 2479, Children's 2480, Coeli 2486, Community 2491, Community 2492, Costello 2501, Crosswalk 2504, Cunningham 2505, Daniels 2507, de Kay 2513, **Drag 2523**, Dreams 2524, Embarras 2541, Emergency 2542, Energy 2545, Fabela 2556, **Gift 2583**, Goodgear 2587, Gore 2588, Gorham 2589, Higgins 2616, Hynd 2632, Illinois 2633, Illinois 2642, Inner 2649, Jewish 2658, Juvenile 2665, Kankakee 2667, Klein 2672, Kohen 2675, Lakeview 2682, Lawrence 2687, Long 2697, Lutheran 2702, Lutheran 2703, **Majid 2706**, Maryville 2711, Morton 2739, Mutual 2742, **National 2744**, Neville 2755, Oak Park 2761, Peoples 2782, Presence 2797, Prieto 2799, Proctor 2801, Reach 2809, Royal 2837, **Serbian 2848**, Sharing 2850, Shawnee 2851, **Special 2866**, St. 2868, Swiss 2884, Tazwood 2887, Tri-County 2897, Uhlich 2900, Union 2902, **Walgreens 2914**, Weeks 2920, Western 2924, Youth 2938

Indiana: AIDS 2946, Anna 2956, Area 2957, Brown 2974, Children's 2982, Christian 2985, CIACO 2986, Community 2988, Community 2989, Community 2992, Coy 3009, Hammond 3048,

Hannah 3050, Housing 3064, Indianapolis 3073, Kosciusko 3090, Levin 3098, **Lilly 3100**, Little 3103, Marshall 3110, McGrain 3111, National 3124, Northwest 3128, Pace 3137, REAL 3157, Rose 3165, St. Vincent 3190, Tobias 3202, United 3207, United 3208, Visiting 3212, Western 3221, Whiteley 3225, Whitley 3226, Zimmer 3231

Iowa: Affordable 3234, Anderson 3239, Barr 3242, Community 3259, Community 3260, Community 3261, Community 3265, Des Moines 3274, Grubb 3291, Hawkeye 3296, Iowa 3307, Iowa 3309, Jennie 3313, Magnus 3329, Operation 3348, Red 3363, **Sherwood 3380**, United 3400, Upper 3401, Waverly 3406, West 3407

Kansas: Cloud 3426, Duclos 3434, Helping 3453, Jones 3464, Kansas 3470, Knights 3475, Sidwell 3514, Southwest 3518, Wichita 3538

Kentucky: American 3544, Appalachian 3546, Bible 3550, Big 3551, Children's 3555, Christian 3556, Community 3558, Eastern 3566, Farm 3568, Foundation 3569, Gardner 3571, Gateway 3572, Kentucky 3585, Kentucky 3586, Kings 3588, Licking 3590, Mallory 3594, Metro 3596, Northern 3604, Operation 3608, PHP 3616, Process 3617, Rose 3621, **USA 3635**

Louisiana: CS 3649, House 3655, JL Foun 3657, Louisiana 3662, National 3670, **Park 3673**, St. Vincent 3678, Total 3680

Maine: Bangor 3689, Belknap 3690, Corporal 3692, Down 3694, Gadd 3698, Girl 3699, Montgomery 3719, Opportunity 3722, Penquis 3725, Portland 3726, Portland 3727, Powers 3728, Spruce 3736, Trust 3741, Waldo 3744, York 3749

Maryland: Allemall 3754, American 3762, Arc 3775, Bowie 3786, Brightfocus 3789, Burbage 3791, Community 3804, Community 3809, Crossway 3811, Full 3831, Govans 3837, **HealthWell 3840**, Housing 3843, **Humanity 3847**, Jeremy 3852, Jewish 3853, Kids 3858, **King 3859**, Kowalsky 3861, Manna 3867, Memorial 3879, Mental 3881, Montgomery 3888, National 3898, Neighborhood 3901, Nexion 3902, **Order 3905**, PNH 3913, Pollak 3914, Salisbury 3924, Shepherd's 3930, Shore 3931, Sisters 3933, Steeplechase 3937, Stepping 3938, United 3948, United 3949, Warfield 3951

Massachusetts: Action 3957, AIDS 3961, Animal 3971, Associates 3973, Association 3974, Balfour 3977, Berkshire 3984, Boston 3993, Boston 3994, Bristol 3999, British 4000, Cape Cod 4008, Central 4017, Citizens 4023, Crist 4032, Danny 4035, **Devens 4039**, Farmer 4063, Farnam 4064, Fisher 4071, Forbes 4073, General 4079, **Genzyme 4080**, German 4081, Giving 4084, HAP 4094, Haverhill 4098, High 4104, Howard 4116, Howes 4119, Howland 4121, Lend 4146, Make-A-Wish 4157, Marblehead 4159, Martin 4162, Needymeds 4191, New 4195, Park 4211, Phillips 4221, Pierce 4223, Pilgrim 4224, Plymouth 4226, Pratt 4229, Quincy 4234, **R.O.S.E. 4236**, Relief 4241, **Roy 4250**, Salem 4253, Samaritan 4254, SAMFund 4255, Sanborn 4256, Sanders 4257, Self-Help 4266, Society 4271, South 4274, South 4275, Swan 4280, Take 4281, Taylor 4284, Terry 4286, Tri-City 4296, Trustees 4299, **Two 4303**, Tye 4304, USO 4307, Worcester 4322, **Xeric 4326**, Youth 4329

Michigan: Baker 4342, Buist 4369, Charity 4379, Children's 4383, Community 4400, Delta 4405, **Domino's 4409**, Easter 4412, Fallen 4417, Ford 4421, Gilmore 4437, Grand 4446, Habitat 4454, Heat 4459, Human 4474, I Have 4479, Italian 4483, Lions 4518, Lutheran 4520, Make-A-Wish 4522, Matrix 4527, National 4549, National 4550, New 4553, Newaygo 4554, Nill 4557, Northeast 4559, Northern 4560, Northville 4562, Northwest 4563, Oakland 4566, Oakwood 4567, Pardee 4572, Pennock 4576, Rochester 4590, Society 4612, Southwest 4617, Southwest 4618, Spectrum 4620, Thresholds 4638, Travelers 4640, Tumey 4644, United 4651, United 4652, Veteran's 4657, Wayne-Metropolitan 4662,

Whaley 4665, Willard 4669, **World 4674, Yankama 4676**

Minnesota: American 4689, Artist 4694, Bridge 4703, Catholic 4708, Community 4718, Community 4719, Gilfillan 4747, Gilfillan 4748, Hastings 4755, Interfaith 4765, Intertech 4767, Law 4781, Lutheran 4786, Mahube 4788, Mayo 4791, Minnesota 4800, Minnesota 4803, Minnesota 4806, Miracle 4808, Miracles 4809, National 4811, Saint Paul 4842, Second 4847, Semcac 4849, Southwest 4857, Three 4866, United 4874, **UnitedHealthcare 4876**, Volunteers 4880, Volunteers 4881, Wilder 4890, Woman's 4894

Mississippi: AJFC 4895, Box 4899, Care 4901, Dunnaway 4905, Lexington 4912, Mississippi 4914, Owen 4917, Phillips 4918, Puckett 4920, Skelton 4921, St. Vincent 4922, Thalheimer 4924

Missouri: Bentley 4939, Cardinal 4952, Central 4954, Clarkson 4957, Community 4964, Concerned 4965, Coxhealth 4969, Employees 4986, Epilepsy 4987, Gift 4999, Green 5006, **Growing 5008**, Hughes 5019, Lamb 5033, Make-A-Wish 5040, Missouri 5056, Missouri 5058, Missouri 5060, **National 5062**, North 5065, Ozarks 5069, **Pi 5073**, Queen 5077, Scottish 5097, Shelter 5099, Trotter 5117, United 5120, United 5121, Urban 5122, West 5124, **Young 5127**

Montana: Brondum 5135, District 5142, District 5143, Montana 5164

Nebraska: Alegent 5184, Nebraska 5240, Nebraska 5242, People's 5254, World 5276

Nevada: Foundation 5288, Miracle 5294, Nevada 5295, United 5303

New Hampshire: Community 5315, Elliott 5320, Griffin 5326, Hunt 5330, Krempels 5332, Lavoie 5337, Manchester 5342, Martin 5344, Moore 5348, Morse 5349, Our 5359, Rockingham 5366, Scots' 5367, Strafford 5371, Tri-County 5372

New Jersey: A Place 5380, Akers 5382, Arc 5388, **ARCH 5389**, Atlanticare 5392, Bass 5395, Burlington 5407, Butts 5408, Catholic 5414, Catholic 5415, Child 5420, Child 5421, Child 5422, Diabetes 5433, Easter 5437, Eastern 5438, Embrace 5440, Family 5444, First 5445, Health 5467, **Johnson 5481, Merck 5505**, New Jersey 5523, North 5527, Northwest 5528, **Novartis 5529**, Orenstein 5532, **Ostberg 5533**, Rose 5553, Saint 5558, **Sanofi 5559**, Several 5563, Society 5571, Summit 5574, Tri-County 5581, United 5585, United 5586, United 5587, United 5588, Virtua 5592, Young 5606

New Mexico: Santa Fe 5649

New York: **Actors 5665**, Adams 5666, Aero 5670, Agorani 5673, **Agudath 5674, American 5697, American 5707**, Artists 5725, Athanasiades 5737, Bagby 5749, Biddle 5763, Bone 5774, Bonei 5775, **Brackett 5779, Bristol 5788**, Broadcasters 5789, **Broadway 5790**, Brockway 5791, Bronx 5795, Cancer 5812, Cantor 5814, **Carnegie 5818**, Carter 5821, Catholic 5823, Catholic 5824, Chest 5845, Chinese 5857, Clark 5859, Community 5874, Community 5883, Corporation 5887, **Correspondents 5889**, Cure 5906, Danforth 5912, Dickinson 5924, Dove 5932, **Dramatists 5934**, Eaton 5950, Episcopal 5960, **Esiason 5965, Estonian 5966, Ezer 5971**, Farber 5974, **General 6019**, Gernatt 6023, **Global 6033**, Goldstein 6037, **Gottlieb 6041**, Griffin 6046, Hambay 6055, **HASTAGA 6059**, Havens 6061, Health 6064, Hispanic 6072, Holland 6076, Hunter's 6085, Hutchins 6087, **International 6101, Intrepid 6103, Jazz 6112**, Jewish 6115, **Jewish 6117**, Jewish 6118, Jewish 6119, **Jockey 6121**, Journeys 6124, Just 6126, **Keren 6135**, Leary 6157, Looney 6169, MacKinnon 6181, Maidstone 6184, **Mann 6187, Matz 6196**, Mayer 6198, Mohawk 6221, Monahan 6222, Morton 6227, Musicians 6232, **Musicians 6233, National 6248**, Netzach 6259, New Alternatives 6260, New Music 6262, New York 6276, North 6284, NYS 6290, Ontario 6293, Opportunities 6298, Parodneck 6304, **Pfizer 6315, Pollock 6318**,

PricewaterhouseCoopers 6328, Project 6335, REBNY 6348, **Russian 6366**, S.B.H. 6368, Saranac 6374, Saratoga 6375, Society 6411, St. George's 6425, Starlight 6429, Sussman 6442, Thompson 6450, Tinker 6457, Tuttle 6467, UFA 6469, United 6475, Variety 6486, **Vietnam 6490**, Vocational 6494, Webster 6505, Windows 6522

North Carolina: AIDS 6545, Albemarle 6547, Arc 6554, Bethesda 6572, Better 6573, Brunswick 6584, Cancer 6590, Cleveland 6606, Community 6613, Corpening 6618, Crisis 6623, Davis 6626, Easter 6638, Eastern 6639, Eastern 6640, Foundation 6660, Giving 6676, Good 6677, Greensboro 6681, Guilford 6690, Hickory 6698, Housing 6705, Hunter 6709, Indian 6710, Interfaith 6713, Inter-Faith 6714, Lake 6735, **Lion's 6743**, Lowe's 6749, Lumbee 6750, Macon 6754, **Music 6781**, NC 6786, Pamlico 6809, Person 6817, Reynolds 6828, **Richardson 6831**, Rowan 6843, Salisbury-Rowan 6848, **Samaritan's 6849**, Sandhills 6850, Tarboro 6886, Telamon 6890, Transylvania 6896, Triad 6898, Triangle 6900, Tri-County 6901, Wellons 6916, Western 6918, With 6924, Work 6928, Young 6932

North Dakota: Heartland 6942, VFW 6951

Ohio: A Good 6953, Agape 6959, Akron 6967, Ames 6973, Associated 6982, Catholic 7029, **Children 7032**, Christian 7035, **Christian 7036**, Columbus 7054, Community 7056, Council 7066, Cowgill 7069, DeCrane 7085, **Eagles 7095**, Economic 7096, **Ethnic 7101**, Foodbank 7112, Ford 7113, Fraser 7117, Frederick 7118, Gay 7125, Good 7129, Greenwalt 7135, Holmes 7151, Homeless 7153, Hospice 7158, Jewish 7177, Kidney 7190, Loeb 7212, Mansfield 7218, Maple 7219, Marion 7222, Middleton 7244, Motry 7257, National 7267, Northwestern 7274, Ohio 7277, Oppenheim 7284, Parenthesis 7289, Partners 7292, Portage 7306, Powell 7307, PSA 7309, Ratner 7313, Rutan 7332, Sheadle 7345, Sightless 7349, Taylor 7377, Twenty 7393, United 7395, United 7396, United 7397, W. 7407, Wellness 7417, West Side 7418, Western 7420

Oklahoma: Ally's 7449, Compassionate 7460, **Feed 7468, Foundation 7470**, Happiness 7478, Indwell 7482, Johnson 7485, JWF 7487, Masonic 7492, Oklahoma 7499, Project 7507, **Reining 7508**, Saint 7510, Sides 7511, Whitefield 7525, Wilkin 7526

Oregon: Aging 7529, Arc 7533, Care 7544, Clarke 7548, Community 7554, Community 7555, Compassion 7556, Creative 7560, **Deneke's 7570**, Fansler 7576, Fish 7577, McComas 7600, Moyer 7612, Oregon 7623, Pass 7630, Portland 7634, Providence 7638, Providence 7641, Snow-Cap 7661, Society 7663, Southern 7664, Umpqua 7672, Wiesberg 7683, Yamhill 7687

Pennsylvania: Abington 7690, Aid 7693, **Alex's 7695**, Armstrong 7712, Aysr 7719, Biddle 7733, Biondo 7734, **Buck 7751**, Catholic 7760, Center 7761, Community 7779, Coordinated 7791, Curtis 7803, DiBona 7811, Dollar 7813, Eckhart 7819, Epstein 7828, Female 7839, Fischer 7842, Foundation 7853, French 7858, Genesis 7867, Gibson 7869, GlaxoSmithKline 7871, Greater 7879, Hazelton 7894, Indiana 7918, Jewish 7928, Kidney 7935, Lancaster 7943, **National 8001**, Nicholas 8006, **Pan 8018**, Physicians 8042, Pinnacle 8044, Presser 8060, Pressley 8061, Quin 8070, **Rhythm 8076**, Saak 8086, Schuylkill 8091, Sleeper 8108, Smock 8114, South 8124, Spackman 8126, St. Margaret 8127, Stockwell 8132, Teva 8142, Three 8146, Two 8152, **Viropharma 8166**, Visiting 8167, Warren 8175, Western 8189, Workplace 8207, YMCA 8210, Young 8215

Rhode Island: Carlisle 8255, Coe 8265, Cranston/ Theophilus 8277, Davenport 8283, Greater 8302, Masonic 8336, McVinney 8343, Montague 8349, Munson 8353, Perpetual 8368, Providence 8375, Rhode 8382, Robbins 8384, Shriners 8399, Sprague 8412, Townsend 8425, Urann 8429, Webster 8433

South Carolina: Anmed 8447, Carolina 8455, Carolina 8456, Charleston 8458, Clemson 8461, Clergy 8463, Community 8466, Father-To-Father 8471, Fund 8472, Gift 8475, Habitat 8479, Hebrew 8481, Horne 8484, Lowcountry 8492, Miracle 8494, Palmetto 8501, Piedmont 8503, Rural 8505, Society 8509, United 8518

South Dakota: Black 8522, Native 8537

Tennessee: A.I.M. 8550, Adams 8552, Aid 8553, **Alpha 8554, American 8556**, Appalachian 8557, **Cancer 8563**, Catholic 8566, Children's 8572, Civitan 8575, Dyersburg-Dyer 8585, East 8588, HCA 8599, **Heart 8600**, Hodges 8602, Hurlbut 8605, International 8607, Jewell 8608, Jewish 8609, Lazarus 8614, Leyen 8618, Metropolitan 8622, Mid-Cumberland 8623, Nashville 8625, **National 8628**, Parkwest 8631, Pearlpoint 8632, Ross 8638, Shiloh 8643, Southeast 8647, Thomley 8654, Upper 8659, Wellmont 8662

Texas: Affordable 8668, AIDS 8669, Alliance 8673, **Amigos 8685**, Arlington 8690, Buckner 8727, Buckner 8728, Caritas 8735, Caritas 8736, Catholic 8739, Christian 8749, Christmas 8750, Christus 8751, Common 8758, Community 8760, Community 8761, CRW 8776, Cutter 8779, **Dabney 8781**, Edinburg 8806, Fant 8817, Farmer 8818, Ferguson 8821, Fleetwood 8823, Foundation 8831, Futureus 8834, Giannini-Scatena 8839, Harris 8855, Home 8873, Houston 8876, Houston 8878, Hutton 8889, Interfaith 8895, James 8897, Jireh 8899, Lake 8912, **Limiar 8918**, Meyer 8956, Miller 8959, Mission 8965, Mustang 8977, National 8985, Neighborhood 8988, **Operation 8999**, Pardee 9002, Peyton 9016, Pioneer 9020, Presbyterian 9028, Programs 9029, **Reserve 9037**, Right 9040, Rio 9041, Rolling 9044, Salesmanship 9051, Salesmanship 9052, Second 9066, Society 9082, Some 9083, South 9084, Southwest 9089, St. David's 9095, St. Vincent 9099, Sunnyside 9103, Swift 9104, Sysco 9107, Target 9109, Texas 9119, Texas 9126, Texas 9129, Texas 9131, Thai 9132, United 9142, United 9143, United 9144, University 9145, Urban 9146, West 9163, Woodlands 9181

Utah: Anaya 9192, Bybee 9196, Cherokee 9197, Hanks 9203, I Care 9208, Last 9215, Regence 9222, Utah 9229, Whiz 9231, Wing 9232

Vermont: Central 9239, Copley 9242, Warner 9272

Virginia: A Gift 9277, **American 9302**, Americans 9313, **Army 9315**, Association 9320, Buchly 9330, Carhart 9334, Carpenter's 9336, Cherry 9338, Child 9339, CIA 9342, **Diema's 9361**, Eastern 9367, EastWest 9369, Echo 9370, Highlands 9395, Homestretch 9399, Housing 9399, Housing 9400, Hughes 9401, Johns 9409, Johnson 9410, Maria's 9429, **MedEvac 9433**, Navy 9461, **Operation 9471, Operation 9472**, Parkinson 9475, Patient 9477, Pentagon 9478, Phoenix 9481, Rahman 9490, Reckitt 9492, Sentara 9501, St. Paul's 9513, **U.S. 9527**, Weinstein 9545, Western 9546

Washington: Benton-Franklin 9570, Central 9582, Chelan-Douglas 9584, Children's 9588, Clarke 9591, Community 9597, Community 9598, Family 9610, Franciscan 9615, G.M.L. 9619, George 9622, Group 9626, Hopelink 9638, Laurendeau 9657, Lifelong 9661, Lower 9664, Metropolitan 9675, Northwest 9687, Overlake 9691, Palmer 9696, Providence 9703, Providence 9704, Rider 9707, Rural 9712, Skagit 9725, Snohomish 9728, Society 9729, Spokane 9731, Treehouse 9736, Ulmschneider 9739, Washington 9750, Welch 9751, Welch 9752, Wills 9754, Windermere 9755, **World 9758**, Yakima 9760, Yelm 9761, Young 9762

West Virginia: Chambers 9774, Harless 9788, Jefferson 9793, Laughlin 9796, Powell 9809, Raleigh 9813, Serra 9814, Smith 9815, United 9825

Wisconsin: Anu 9837, CAP 9857, Carlisle 9858, Catholic 9861, Community 9870, Couleecap

9873, Foundation 9895, Gundersen 9913, Healthnet 9917, Hemophilia 9919, Incourage 9925, Indianhead 9926, Jewish 9930, MacPherson 9954, Nicholl 9981, Partners 9991, Prader-Willi 9997, Project 10000, Racine 10002, Riverview 10011, Rutledge 10016, Schulte 10023, Select 10026, Society 10038, Southwest 10040, Spartvedt 10041, St. Elizabeth 10044, Weather 10066, Wiegand 10071, Wisconsin 10076, Wisconsin 10082, Wisconsin 10084, Yakich 10089, Young 10090, Young 10091, Zebro 10092

Wyoming: Christian 10096, LaRue 10110, Littler 10113, Perkins 10117, Spacht 10121

Grants to individuals

Alabama: **American 8, Blaylock 16**, Franklin 39, Regional 74, Sheffield 78, Southeastern 81, Winston 92, Woerner 93

Alaska: Alaska 100, Alaskan 102, Aleut 103, Bristol 106, CIRI 113, Huna 118

Arizona: **Baize 168**, Food 194, **North 221**, Renaissance 232, Tucson-Pima 247, Turf 248, Valley 255, Washington 258

California: Advocates 340, AEPOCH 341, Alliance 347, American 354, American 356, **Amgen 362**, Archeo/ 368, **Arthritis 376**, Aspiranet 380, **Association 387**, Cal 437, California 447, California 460, Center 472, **Challenged 476**, Cherith 479, Child 484, Children's 487, **Children's 489**, Coastal 504, **Colonnades 507, Columbia 508**, Croatian 527, Dr. 546, Durfee 549, **Earth 550**, Eglitis 554, Foster 582, **Foundation 589**, Foundation 590, **Frameline 593, French 594**, Friends 600, **From 603**, Genentech 611, **Higgins 661, Impact 678, Independent 681, Little 748**, Mang 768, Missionary 796, Musicares 809, **National 814**, National 820, Olympic 840, Open 841, Optimist 842, Pacific 850, **PADI 852**, Pebble 857, Philanthropic 865, Pirkle 869, **Rivendell 912, San 927**, San Diego 928, San Francisco 945, Santa 957, Schwab 966, Silicon 987, **Smith 995**, Southern 1006, St. Francis 1011, Teachers 1040, Theatre 1044, Therrien 1045, **United 1069**, Vanguard 1077, **Variety 1079**, Veneklasen 1080, **Women 1098**, Wu 1104

Colorado: American 1117, Boulder 1132, **Children 1143**, Colorado 1162, **Foundation 1199**, Gathering 1203, Helmar 1213, Lutheran 1235, Operation 1253, Public 1262, Rocky 1270, Rocky 1271, Society 1285, **U.S. 1297, United 1298, United 1299**

Connecticut: Adams 1315, Anthony 1324, Atwood 1326, **Avatar 1327**, Branford 1338, **Criag 1371**, International 1407, My 1428, Orange 1439, Steep 1468, **Walkabout 1479**

Delaware: Farpath 1507

District of Columbia: **American 1547, American 1548, American 1562, American 1565**, American 1566, **Armed 1579, Association 1586**, Bell 1591, Center 1599, Cornerstone 1609, Cox 1613, **Environmental 1621, Equal 1622, FINRA 1626**, Fordham 1628, **Freedom 1632, Fund 1635, Gay 1637, International 1655, Legal 1670, Lupus 1671, Marijuana 1672, National 1684, National 1690, National 1694, NEA 1700, Ocean 1702**, People 1713, Rales 1720, Schimel 1726, **Youth 1757**

Florida: American 1773, Areawide 1781, Beall 1795, Broward 1811, **Cisneros 1829**, Community 1837, Community 1838, Education 1867, Episcopal 1871, Hard 1902, **Julien 1934, National 1997**, Pagliara 2010, Progress 2026, Rawlings 2028, Tangelo 2083, United 2093

Georgia: **American 2116**, Eternal 2173, Families 2176, Golden 2189, Handweavers 2194, Parents 2219

Hawaii: Hawaii 2288, Make-A-Wish 2302, Pacific 2310

Idaho: Excel 2331

Illinois: **Abbvie 2354**, Allstate 2363, **American 2366**, American 2369, **American 2381, American 2384**, American 2387, **American 2389**, Angels 2400, Association 2409, Claretknoll 2483, Cradle 2503, Driehaus 2525, Ende 2544, Foundation 2568, **Graham 2592**, Hairy 2596, **Healthy 2608**, HOPA 2625, Jorndt 2662, LUNGevity 2701, Make-A-Wish 2707, National 2753, **Orthopaedic 2770**, Paideia 2776, Partners 2779, Pulmonary 2805, Rauch 2808, Rockford 2827, Smith 2858, **TPAA 2895, Turnaround 2899**

Indiana: **Alpha 2949**, Alpha 2951, Christian 2985, Community 2991, Community 2998, Community 3001, Decatur 3013, Ohio 3131, Osteopathic 3135, Public 3152, Society 3187, United 3205

Iowa: Bates 3243, **Grace 3286**, Grinnell 3290, Hockenberry 3300, ISED 3310, Keppy 3318, LSB 3328, Operation 3348, United 3399

Kansas: Child 3423, Laham 3478, Noah's 3496, Salina 3510

Kentucky: Dream 3564, Eastern 3565, Mustard 3602, Rural 3622

Louisiana: Academic 3639, Arts 3642, Ascension 3643, Louisiana 3664, Pitt's 3675

Maine: Acadia 3685, Camden 3691, Down 3694, Maine 3712, Trust 3741, United 3743, York 3749

Maryland: **AICE 3751**, Allegany 3753, American 3756, American 3758, **American 3760, American 3769**, Arts 3776, Dellon 3814, Epilepsy 3822, **Foundation 3829**, Foundation 3830, GEICO 3832, Girl 3835, Howard 3844, **Hughes 3846**, Job 3854, Maryland 3875, **Michels 3883**, Obesity 3904, Penn-Mar 3909, **Phi 3911**

Massachusetts: **ALS 3962**, American 3965, Berkshire 3986, Boston 3995, Cabot 4003, Center 4016, Cohen 4026, Danny 4035, Davis 4036, **Documentary 4041**, Dover 4043, Eaton 4053, **Elderhostel 4058**, Grinspoon 4090, Grinspoon 4091, Kim 4139, Knights 4141, Massachusetts 4166, Massachusetts 4167, **New England 4193, New 4196, Northern 4203**, Pierce 4223, President 4230, **Rosenberg 4247**

Michigan: Alliance 4336, Baker 4342, CareLink 4374, **Chang 4378**, Dancey 4403, Foundation 4426, Hudson 4473, Kalamazoo 4492, Lions 4518, McPherson 4530, Northville 4562, Royal 4594, Sparrow 4619, Tamer 4631

Minnesota: American 4687, CentraCare 4709, Child 4712, Ecolab 4731, Family 4736, Five 4738, Forecast 4740, **Groot 4752**, Hastings 4755, Lake 4777, Mayo 4792, Minnesota 4798, Page 4820, Prairie 4828, **Pro 4829**, Providers 4831, Region 4836, Southeastern 4854, Southwest 4856, Southwest 4858, Target 4864, Tiwahe 4869, VSA 4882

Mississippi: C Spire 4900

Missouri: Cape 4951, Child 4956, Delta 4972, Mid 5053, **PKD 5074**, Scholarship 5084, Shelter 5099

Montana: Sacred 5171

Nebraska: Girl 5207, Good 5208, Mid-Nebraska 5234, Nebraska 5237

Nevada: DiRienzo 5286, Norris 5297

New Hampshire: **Money 5347**, Ramsaye 5363

New Jersey: **American 5383, American 5385**, Anyone 5387, **ARCH 5389, Cerebral 5417**, Children's 5423, Costume 5428, **Croatian 5430**, Dirshu 5434, Honeywell 5472, Ingersoll-Rand 5478, KPMG 5492, Montclair 5510, **National 5514**, New Jersey 5515, **Puffin 5549**, Segal 5562, United 5584, United 5587

New Mexico: **A Room 5609**

New York: **ACMP 5664, America-Israel 5686, American 5693**, American 5703, **American 5708**, American 5709, Art 5720, ArtCouncil 5723, **Artis 5724**, Arts 5727, ArtsConnection 5730, **Asian 5734, Autism 5742**, Bagby 5749, Bossak 5777, **Breast 5783**, Breindel 5784, Bronx 5793, **Buttonwood 5807, Camphill 5811**, Cantor 5814, **Career 5816, CEC 5829**, Center 5830, Children 5846, Children's 5850, City 5857, Columbia

5870, Community 5873, Community 5878, Community 5882, **Conference 5884**, Council 5894, **Covenant 5895**, Cox 5897, **Cuban 5902**, Cultural 5903, Dance 5911, DonorsChoose.org 5931, Dysautonomia 5943, Dystrophic 5944, Ebb 5951, Elsasser 5958, **Esiason 5965, Explorers 5968**, Exploring 5969, **Foundation 5995**, Foundation 5996, **Foundation 6000, Four 6005**, Friars 6010, **Friends 6013**, Genesee 6021, Glover 6034, **Grayson-Jockey 6045**, Gunk 6052, **Haven 6060, Hearing 6065**, Hemophilia 6066, Hunter's 6085, **Huntington's 6086, Independent 6092**, InterExchange 6096, Jonas 6122, Kidney 6137, Kleban 6140, **Koussevitzky 6146**, Ladany 6152, Lissner 6165, L'Oreal 6170, Lower 6173, Magnum 6183, Merchant 6209, **Mikhashoff 6215**, Mitchell 6218, Modest 6220, **NARSAD 6238, National 6242, National 6251, National 6254**, New Music 6262, New York 6274, New York 6277, Oyster 6300, **Princess 6329**, Public 6338, Reaching 6346, Reed 6350, Rose 6362, Rottenberg 6363, **Schepp 6383, Silberman 6396, Skadden 6398**, Socrates 6414, St. George's 6425, Stage 6428, Steinberg 6436, Teamsters 6446, THYCA 6453, **Trickle 6463**, Unique 6471, **United States 6479**, Univera 6480, **Wallenberg 6499**, Westchester 6512, **Women's 6528**, Women's 6529

North Carolina: Arts 6559, Asheville 6561, Child 6599, Durham 6633, Gaston 6668, Henderson 6696, **Jensen 6717**, Keep 6729, McAllister 6759, Mission 6775, NC 6787, **Richardson 6831, Rixson 6836**, Robeson 6837, Smart 6865, Telamon 6890, Touchstone 6895, Union 6905, United 6906, Wake 6911, Winston-Salem 6923

Ohio: **Catholic 7030**, Columbus 7052, **Educational 7098**, Fine 7108, Johnson 7179, Kati's 7183, Lake 7201, McGinty 7235, Mercer 7240, Piqua 7304, Scripps 7340, Summerfair 7373, **Taiho 7375**, Twenty 7393

Oklahoma: Global 7476, Guthrie 7477, **Messenger 7494**, Oklahoma 7501, Saint 7510

Oregon: Celebration 7545, Compassion 7556, **Culinary 7562**, Cutler 7564, Neighborimpact 7615, Northwest 7620, **Vongelstein 7676**

Pennsylvania: **Alex's 7695**, American 7702, Bader 7720, Bartko 7723, Blaisdell 7735, Brown 7749, **Chinese 7766**, Colman 7775, Communtiy 7787, Golden 7873, Haeseler 7882, Irwin 7922, Leeway 7951, ONS 8015, Philadelphia 8037, Pittsburgh 8046, Southern 8125, **Templeton 8141**

Rhode Island: Cismoski 8261, Marhaver 8335, Preston 8371, **United 8428**

South Carolina: Airport 8444, Alliance 8445, Charleston 8459, Cultural 8469, Professional 8504

South Dakota: Delta 8526, Dow 8529, South Dakota 8541

Tennessee: Foundation 8593, **International 8606**, Methodist 8620, United 8658

Texas: **ABG 8666**, American 8681, **American 8684**, AT&T 8695, Austin 8698, Cadbury 8732, Catholic 8740, Cisneros 8752, Cuban 8777, Denman 8791, Foundation 8831, Fund 8833, Heinlein 8865, Houston 8875, **Interdenominational 8894**, Kiddies 8905, Lake 8913, Nabors 8979, **National 8982**, Perot 9014, Reserve 9037, Shanor 9070, **Society 9081**, Swift 9104, Texas 9119, **Vetiver 9148**, Williams 9168, Wine 9170, Wisian 9174, Woodhill 9180

Utah: 100% 9190, Granite 9201, McCarthey 9219

Vermont: **Brush 9237, Green 9249**, Hayes 9251, Ottauquechee 9257, Vermont 9267

Virginia: AFP 9280, Air 9283, Air 9284, **American 9288, American 9290**, American 9296, **American 9298**, American 9303, American 9308, American 9311, **Caring 9335**, Cherry 9338, **Christian 9341**, Community 9350, Cushman 9356, **Epilepsy 9375, Focused 9377, Food 9378, Foundation 9381, Friedreich's 9386**, International 9406, **National 9444, National 9445**, Pentagon 9478,

Postal 9486, Sale 9496, Smith-Melton 9509, Society 9510

Washington: Allied 9559, Artist 9564, Bellevue 9569, Blue 9573, Career 9580, Daystar 9605, **Fred 9616**, His 9635, Jordan 9645, Plum 9700, Potlatch 9701, Tacoma 9734, **World 9758**

West Virginia: Workforce 9830

Wisconsin: Community 9865, Fricke 9899, Hood 9924, Incourage 9925, International 9927, Pieper 9995, Siebert 10033, **Society 10037**, Waukesha 10065, Wisconsin 10075, Women's 10086

Wyoming: Spacht 10121

In-kind gifts

Alabama: Community 25, Macon-Russell 57, Marshall-Jackson 58

Arizona: Community 181, **Feed 191**, Pima 228, University 251

Arkansas: RMHC 306

California: **Armenian 370**, Catholic 467, Catholic 468, Childrens 486, **Children's 491**, Nickelson 827, Orange 844, Second 971, Trinity 1057, True 1059, Turn 1064, **Union 1068**, Variety 1079

Colorado: Care 1141, Community 1173, Denver 1181, Food 1196, **H.E.L.P. 1208**, Jewish 1222

Connecticut: **AmeriCares 1323**, New 1432, **Save 1454**

Delaware: AstraZeneca 1493, Children 1496

District of Columbia: **Airline 1535**, Anacostia 1574

Florida: A Gift 1760, Catholic 1819, Children's 1824, Hope 1921, Northeast 2000, Operation 2006, United 2094

Georgia: Hospice 2196, Make 2207, Ninth 2216, North 2217

Illinois: Central 2466, Illinois 2647, Lakeview 2682, Loaves 2696, **Ronald 2831**, Sharing 2850, St. John's 2870, United 2906

Indiana: Area 2957, Community 2988, United 3208

Iowa: Southern 3385

Kansas: Noah's 3496

Kentucky: Christian 3556, Community 3558, **Disabled 3563**, Habitat 3575

Louisiana: Food 3652, **Park 3673**

Maine: Information 3705

Maryland: **Humanity 3847**

Massachusetts: Elder 4057, North 4202, ROFEH 4246, **World 4324**

Michigan: Allegan 4334, Make-A-Wish 4522, Old 4568, Region 4586

Minnesota: Mayo 4791, Scott-Carver-Dakota 4846, Second 4847, Second 4848, Volunteers 4880, Volunteers 4881

Missouri: Community 4962, Northeast 5067, Ronald 5080, United 5121

Nebraska: Lutheran 5231, UNMC 5267

Nevada: Catholic 5281

New Hampshire: Community 5315

New Jersey: Catholic 5413, Legal 5497, Tri-County 5581

New Mexico: Community 5625

New York: Opportunities 6299, Ronald 6360, Washington 6502

North Carolina: Bicycle 6574, Choanoke 6601, Cleveland 6606, Hickory 6698, Mountain 6780, Outreach 6807

Ohio: Community 7056, Homeless 7153, United 7396, United 7397, W. 7407, West Side 7418

Oklahoma: Areawide 7450

Oregon: Aging 7529, Community 7554, Mercy 7604, Neighborimpact 7615, Northwest 7618, Oregon 7623, Providence 7637

Pennsylvania: Private 8064, South 8124, Two 8152

South Carolina: Charleston 8458, Gleamns 8476

South Dakota: Native 8537

Tennessee: **Cancer 8563**, Catholic 8566, East 8588, Mid-Cumberland 8623, Nashville 8627, **Soles4Souls 8646**, Southeast 8647, Upper 8659

Texas: Beaumont 8707, Caritas 8736, Catholic 8741, Christian 8749, Christus 8751, Community 8761, Fort 8827, Interfaith 8895, Lake 8912, **National 8986**, Northwest 8993, Society 9082, South 9086

Virginia: **Advancing 9279, Christian 9341,** Foodbank 9379, Northern 9468, **Operation 9471, Operation 9472,** Operation 9473

Washington: Alternatives 9560, Hopelink 9638, Market 9667, North 9683, Northwest 9686, Opportunity 9689, Second 9721, Young 9762

Wisconsin: Feeding 9889, Healthnet 9917, Kern 9943, Racine 10002, Wisconsin 10082

Internship funds

Alaska: Chenega 109, CIRI 113, Koniag 122

California: **Academy 335, Association 389, Getty 614,** International 689, **International 691, Kaiser 716,** San Diego 928, Schmidek 963

Delaware: **Eleutherian 1505**

District of Columbia: **American 1546,** Arab 1576, Asian 1582, Community 1605, **Congressional 1607, Freedom 1631, Fund 1634,** German 1638, **International 1656, National 1684, Radio 1718**

Florida: Everglades 1872, Mote 1985

Georgia: **Ravi 2227**

Illinois: After 2358

Indiana: **Alpha 2949, Alpha 2952**

Maryland: Foundation 3830, Maryland 3876, Prince 3915

Massachusetts: **Documentary 4041, Kennedy 4137,** Massachusetts 4163

Minnesota: Minnesota 4807

Missouri: Community 4963

New Jersey: Cooper 5427, **Dow 5435,** Lasko 5494, New Jersey 5520, People 5538, **Wilson 5600**

New York: American 5703, **Animal 5715, CDS 5828,** Democracy 5922, Jewish 6118, **Luce 6175, Metropolitan 6211,** Morgan 6226, **National 6241, Pasteur 6306, Public 6337, Spencer 6420,** United 6478, **Women's 6528**

Ohio: Scripps 7340

Oregon: Lampstand 7594

Pennsylvania: Pittsburgh 8048

South Carolina: South 8513

Texas: Austin 8698, Welder 9161

Virginia: American 9299, **Institute 9404**

Washington: Legal 9660, Museum 9678

Wisconsin: Experimental 9887

Loans—to individuals

Alaska: Norton 128

Arizona: Arizona 158, Arizona 160, Mesa 218

Colorado: Colorado 1156

Connecticut: Elmseed 1384

District of Columbia: Cornerstone 1609, **Equal 1622**

Florida: Catholic 1820, Hill 1913

Indiana: Indianapolis 3073

Kentucky: River 3620, Rural 3622

Louisiana: Louisiana 3663

Maine: Maine 3710, York 3749

Michigan: Foundation 4425, Genesis 4433

Minnesota: American 4687, Family 4736, Jewish 4772, **Pro 4829**

Mississippi: East 4906

Montana: Sacred 5171

New York: **A Child 5661,** Authors 5741, Bonei 5775, Community 5874, Jewish 6118

North Carolina: Choanoke 6601, North Carolina 6797, North 6799, Risley 6834

Ohio: County 7067

Pennsylvania: **Jewish 7929**

South Dakota: Delta 8526

Tennessee: Chattanooga 8567

Texas: Giannini 8837, Texas 9118

Utah: Anaya 9192

Vermont: **Craft 9243**

Virginia: **Army 9315,** Navy-Marine 9462

Wisconsin: Rutledge 10016

Postdoctoral support

Arizona: **Muscular 220, Stott 241**

California: American 359, Arthritis 375, **Arthritis 376,** Association 390, **Foundation 589, Getty 614, Grass 637,** Hewitt 659, **Leakey 739,** National 822

Connecticut: **Alliance 1318,** Childs 1354

District of Columbia: **Accordia 1531, American 1542, American 1551, American 1560, American 1565, German 1638, Institute 1651, National 1681**

Florida: Alpha-1 1767, AWS 1789, Biegelsen 1798, **Whitehall 2103**

Georgia: **American 2113,** Hall 2190

Illinois: **American 2371, American 2378,** American 2387, American 2390, Association 2408, **Dystonia 2529, Graham 2592, Hertz 2615, National 2752**

Louisiana: National 3670

Maryland: American 3756, **Anxiety 3773,** Cystic 3812, **Epilepsy 3821, National 3893, National 3897**

Massachusetts: **American 3963, Fraxa 4076, Giovanni 4083,** King 4140, **Lalor 4145,** President 4230, **Winter 4319**

Minnesota: **Foundation 4741**

Missouri: **PKD 5074,** Stowers 5109

New Jersey: Merck 5504, **Reeve 5550**

New York: American 5691, **American 5692, American 5693,** American 5695, **American 5711,** Cancer 5813, Crohn's 5899, **Delmas 5921, Diamond 5923, Duke 5938, Fight 5982, Foundation 5992,** Frick 6011, **Guggenheim 6049, Hereditary 6068,** Human 6081, Huyck 6088, **Institute 6095, International 6102, Juvenile 6127, Myasthenia 6234, NARSAD: 6239, National 6251,** Runyon 6365, **Social 6409,** Tourette 6459, **Wenner 6511**

North Carolina: **Institut 6711**

Ohio: LAM 7203

Pennsylvania: **American 7704**

South Carolina: Hart 8480

Texas: American 8683, **Komen 8910**

Virginia: **American 9287, American 9297, Foundation 9382, Special 9511**

Washington: **Friends 9618**

Wisconsin: **Entomological 9884**

Postgraduate support

Alabama: Dixon 31, Owens 67, Southeastern 81

California: **Asia 378,** California 447, **Foundation 589, Getty 614, INCOSE 679,** Kerber 719, Nauheim/Straus 823, **Tuckerman 1063**

Colorado: Aorn 1119

Connecticut: Cornelia 1370, Fairfield 1387, Orange 1439

District of Columbia: **Aga 1533, American 1551,** American 1558, **Equal 1622**

Florida: **Gamma 1894**

Georgia: Georgia 2187

Hawaii: Atherton 2271

Illinois: American 2367, Berner 2423, Chicago 2472, **Rotary 2835**

Indiana: Community 2994, **Sigma 3183,** South 3189

Iowa: Lee 3324

Maryland: **American 3765, American 3768,** Brown 3790, **Epilepsy 3821,** Thorn 3941

Massachusetts: **Tourism 4292**

Michigan: Grand Rapids 4445

Missouri: American 4931, Friedman 4996, Schafer 5083

Nebraska: Ellis 5200

Nevada: Doyle 5287

New Jersey: **Johnson 5482,** Wetterberg 5594

New Mexico: **American 5611**

New York: **American 5711,** Armenian 5717, **Chesed 5844,** Foundation 6001, **Friends 6012,** Huyck 6088, **Institute 6095, Kosciuszko 6145, Metropolitan 6211, National 6251, Netherland-America 6258, Teach 6444, Tibet 6454, Trace 6461, Women's 6528**

North Carolina: Atlantic 6565, **Environmental 6649,** North Carolina 6797

Ohio: Blanchard 7000, Drake 7090, Gandy 7121, McLendon 7237

Pennsylvania: Chung-Hee 7768, **Williams 8192**

Texas: **MCH 8946, Museum 8975,** Stanzel 9100, Texas 9128

Virginia: **AHP 9282,** All 9286, **Foundation 9380, Foundation 9382, Institute 9404**

Washington: **Rotalia 9709**

Wisconsin: Environmental 9885, Nicholl 9981, Wisconsin 10080

Precollege support

Alabama: Alabama 4

Alaska: Monroe 125

Arizona: Arizona 163, Institute 203

California: Association 390, Baxter 404, **Rand 898,** Sonora 1003, World 1101, Zider 1109

Colorado: Sharpe 1282

Connecticut: Folsom 1390

District of Columbia: **American 1565,** Best 1592, Washington 1747

Illinois: Illinois 2637, McLoraine 2725

Indiana: Elkhart 3024, LaGrange 3093, Marshall 3110, Unity 3209

Iowa: Johnson 3315

Kentucky: Community 3559, School 3623, Sparks 3626

Maryland: **American 3757,** Bright 3788, **School 3928**

Massachusetts: Affordable 3958, Donnell 4042, Home 4110, **Kennedy 4137, Maya 4170**

Michigan: Basilica 4348, Bretzlaff 4368, Evereg-Fenesse 4414, **Herdegen 4464,** Marquette 4524, Novi 4564, St. John 4623, Temple 4634

Missouri: Kansas 5023, Kelly 5027, Reynolds 5079

New Jersey: **Dow 5435,** Peters 5539, Wight 5598

New Mexico: Farmers' 5629

New York: Albion 5678, Center 5831, Elenberg 5956, Harby 6056, Reddington 6349, **Societe 6410**

North Carolina: 100 6543

North Dakota: Schuetze 6948

Ohio: College 7050, Fitzgerald 7111, **Lincoln 7210,** Wayne 7415

Oklahoma: Beatty 7454

Pennsylvania: Ameche 7700, Community 7781, Ellis 7823, Philadelphia 8038, Smith 8111, York 8213

Rhode Island: McMurtrie 8342, Tracy 8426

Texas: Texas 9130

Vermont: Vermont 9270

Virginia: **Cooke 9352, MATHCOUNTS 9431, National 9446**

Washington: Pigott 9698

West Virginia: Stifel 9818

Wisconsin: Green Bay 9910, Madison 9956

Professorships

Alaska: University 146

California: California 447

Florida: Callaway 1814

Illinois: **Terra 2889**

Louisiana: Lang 3660

Virginia: **American 9297,** American 9299, Morgan 9440

Program development

Alaska: Rasmuson 132
Arizona: **Research 233**
California: Cal 437, California 445, Compass 519, Gifford 616, **International 692**, Martin 774, **Ploughshares 872**, Theatre 1044, Truth 1062, World 1101
Colorado: Boulder 1132
Connecticut: Branford 1338, Voya 1478, Xerox 1490
Delaware: CenturyLink-Clarke 1494
District of Columbia: **American 1564, Animal 1575**, Schimel 1726
Florida: Broward 1811
Illinois: **American 2379, CF 2469**, Chicago 2474, Golden 2586, **Graham 2592**, Lincoln 2693, **Massage 2713**
Indiana: Warren 3216
Kentucky: Community 3559, Kentucky 3582, Lincoln 3591
Louisiana: Lafayette 3658
Maryland: **Epilepsy 3821, School 3928**
Massachusetts: **Maya 4170**
Michigan: Arts 4340, Royal 4594, Sojourner 4613, United 4649
Minnesota: **Lindbergh 4783**, Northwest 4817, **UnitedHealthcare 4876**
New Jersey: Giants 5452, **Johnson 5482**, PSEG 5548, **Reeve 5550, Wilson 5600**
New Mexico: **Lannan 5635**
New York: American 5698, ArtsConnection 5730, **Balanchine 5751**, Bossak 5777, Brewster 5785, Broome 5799, **Camphill 5811**, Center 5830, Community 5881, Cromwell 5900, **Do 5928, Echoing 5952**, Gunk 6052, Jenkins 6113, **Juvenile 6127**, Lower 6173, **Lymphoma 6179**, Manhattan 6186, **Mayday 6197**, New 6264, Open 6294, Queens 6341, **Teachers 6445, Theatre 6448, Tsadra 6465, United 6477, Weill 6508, Women's 6528, Woodlawn 6530**
North Carolina: Asheville 6562, Emerson 6648, Pitt County 6820
Ohio: **Arab 6978**
Oklahoma: Bartlesville 7452, **International 7483**
Oregon: Northwest 7620, Regional 7641
Pennsylvania: Center 7762, Leeway 7951, Society 8119
South Dakota: **First 8530**
Tennessee: Stuttering 8652
Texas: San Marcos 9059
Utah: Salt 9225
Virginia: **American 9300**, Community 9350, **National 9452, Special 9511**
Washington: Clover 9592
West Virginia: Beckley 9766, West Virginia 9827
Wisconsin: Wisconsin 10080

Project support

Alaska: Alaska 98
California: Arts 377, Bay 405, Cal 437, Catalyst 466, **Colonnades 507, Columbia 508**, Dancers' 535, **Foundation 589**, International 689, Lafayette 730, Menlo 784, Palos Verdes 853, Public 887, San Diego 934, Theatre 1044, Truth 1062
Colorado: Boulder 1132, Colorado 1163
Connecticut: Branford 1338, Orange 1439, Real 1447, Voya 1478, Xerox 1490
District of Columbia: **Amyotrophic 1573, Melanoma 1677**, Schimel 1726
Florida: Broward 1811, Education 1866
Hawaii: North 2306
Idaho: Idaho 2336
Illinois: **American 2366, CF 2469, Graham 2592, Rotary 2835**
Louisiana: Academic 3639, Lafourche 3659
Michigan: Baker 4342, **Collectors 4387**, United 4649, Waterford 4660

Minnesota: Arrowhead 4693, Forecast 4740, Intermedia 4766, Jerome 4771, Northern 4814, Region 4836, Southern 4855
New Jersey: Giants 5452, PSEG 5548, **Puffin 5549**
New Mexico: **A Room 5609**
New York: **American 5711**, Art 5718, Arts 5726, Bronx 5794, Camera 5809, **Creative 5898**, DonorsChoose.org 5931, International 6100, Lower 6173, Manhattan 6186, Moving 6229, Queens 6341, **Sparkplug 6418, United 6477, Weill 6508**
North Carolina: Arts 6559, North 6800, Touchstone 6895, United 6907
Ohio: **Kids 7191**, Twenty 7393
Oregon: Lane 7595
Pennsylvania: Pennsylvania 8029, Pew 8033
Texas: Houston 8875, San Marcos 9059
Vermont: Vermont 9268
Washington: Clover 9592, George 9622

Publication

California: **Cantor 463**, Huntington 674, **Studenica 1029**
Connecticut: Branford 1338
District of Columbia: **Esperantic 1624, Fund 1635**
Illinois: **American 2389, Graham 2592**
Louisiana: Louisiana 3665
Massachusetts: **Xeric 4326**
Michigan: **Earhart 4411**
Minnesota: Loft 4784, Region 4836
New Mexico: **A Room 5609, Lannan 5635**
New York: Academy 5663, American 5698, Cromwell 5900, Malevich 6185, Radius 6342, **Schalkenbach 6379, Stefansky 6435, Tsadra 6465, Wallenberg 6499, Weill 6508, Wenner 6511**
Pennsylvania: **Institute 7919**
Virginia: **Special 9511**
Washington: George 9622

Research

Alabama: **American 8**, Dixon 31, **International 54**
Alaska: Alaska 99, University 146
Arizona: Banner 170, **Muscular 220, Research 233**, Rosztoczy 234
California: **Aesthetic 342**, American 354, **American 358**, American 359, Ameritec 361, Arthritis 375, **Arthritis 376, Asia 378, A-T 391, Beckman 408, Cantor 463, Concern 520**, Cure 530, Cystic 532, Discovery 539, **Ellison 561**, Farber 571, **Foundation 586, Foundation 589**, Foundation 590, **French 594**, Getty 614, Glaucoma 619, **Glenn 621, GRAMMY 635, Grass 637**, Hewitt 659, **HP 670, Immunobiology 677, INCOSE 679, International 691, International 692**, Joshua 714, **Kaiser 716, Leakey 739, Marconi 769**, Mathematical 776, Milken 792, Myers 811, Myotonic 812, **NAMM 813, National 814, National 818**, National 820, National 822, **Organic 846, PADI 852, Pancreatic 854**, Pasarow 856, **Ploughshares 872, Prostate 885**, San 950, Storkan/Hanes 1027, That 1043, Theatre 1044, Tower 1052, Veneklasen 1080
Colorado: ACVIM 1110, Aorn 1119, Arthritis 1122, Colorado 1162, **Foundation 1199**, Kuzell 1227, Population 1259, Society 1285
Connecticut: **Alliance 1318, American 1320**, Branford 1338, **Cholnoky 1356**, Cornelia 1370, Endocrine 1385, **Multiple 1426, National 1429**, Xerox 1490
Delaware: **International 1514**, University 1526
District of Columbia: **Amazon 1537, American 1541, American 1542, American 1548, American 1551, American 1554, American 1557, American 1560, American 1564, American 1565**, American 1566, American 1568, American 1569, **American 1571, Amyotrophic 1573**, Aspen 1583,

Association 1584, **Association 1585**, B'nai 1595, **Council 1610, Council 1611**, Equipment 1623, **Esperantic 1624, Gateway 1636, German 1638**, Gerontological 1639, **Glaser 1640**, Global 1641, Horticultural 1647, **Institute 1650, Institute 1651, International 1653, International 1656, Jerusalem 1662, Kennedy 1667, Marijuana 1673, Melanoma 1676, Melanoma 1677, National 1681, National 1687, National 1691**, Paralyzed 1706, People 1713, **Pharmaceutical 1714**, Resources 1723, Schimel 1726, **Society 1730**, United 1744
Florida: Alpha-1 1767, American 1771, American 1772, American 1773, American 1774, **Ataxia 1786**, AWS 1789, Biegelsen 1798, Community 1847, Gwynn 1900, Life 1950, **National 1996**, Preeclampsia 2024, Watson 2100, **Whitehall 2103**
Georgia: **American 2113, American 2115**, Arthritis 2120, Bantly 2125, **Carter 2136**, Hall 2190, Southeastern 2237
Hawaii: Hawaii 2290
Illinois: **ADA 2356, American 2365, American 2366**, American 2367, **American 2373, American 2376, American 2377, American 2378, American 2379, American 2380, American 2381, American 2382, American 2385**, American 2387, **American 2388, American 2389**, American 2390, **American 2392**, Angelman 2399, **Cervical 2468, Chest 2471**, Chicago 2473, Children's 2478, **Citizens 2482**, College 2489, **Depression 2515**, Dermatology 2516, **Dystonia 2529, Ewing 2554, Foundation 2569**, Friends 2576, **Graham 2592**, Hairy 2596, **Healthy 2608, Heed 2610**, Hirschl 2620, **Holocaust 2622**, Illinois 2645, **Leukemia 2690**, Lincoln 2693, LUNGevity 2701, **Massage 2713, Medical 2728, National 2744, National 2745**, National 2746, **National 2750, National 2752, North 2758, Plastic 2793**, Pulmonary 2805, **Respiratory 2817, Skidmore 2857, Society 2862, Thoracic 2892**
Indiana: Anna 2956, Dead 3011, Friends 3039, Morre 3119, National 3124, Society 3188
Iowa: Association 3241, Iowa 3308, World 3410
Kansas: **American 3413**, Snyder 3516
Louisiana: ECD 3650, National 3670
Maine: Maine 3711
Maryland: American 3756, **American 3759, American 3761**, American 3762, American 3763, **American 3764**, American 3766, **American 3767, American 3768, American 3770, Anxiety 3773, Aplastic 3774**, Association 3778, Autism 3781, Brightfocus 3789, **Childhood 3801**, Cystic 3812, Dellon 3814, **ELECTRI 3817, Epilepsy 3821, Foundation 3828, Foundation 3829**, Foundation 3830, **Hughes 3846**, Life 3865, Maryland 3874, **Medical 3878, National 3897**, National 3899, Nicolay 3903, **Osteogenesis 3906**, PNH 3913, **Pulmonary 3916, School 3928, Sudden 3939**
Massachusetts: **American 3964**, American 3965, **American 3969, Caring 4010**, Chelonian 4020, **Documentary 4041, Earthwatch 4049, Fraxa 4076, Giovanni 4083**, Harvard 4095, **Harvard 4097, International 4127**, Johnson 4131, **Jurassic 4134, Kennedy 4137**, King 4140, **Lalor 4145, Marine 4160, National 4190, New England 4193**, President 4230, Real 4239, **Scleroderma 4263, SEVEN 4267, Tourism 4292, Woods 4321**
Michigan: **Ball 4343**, Blue 4363, Delta 4406, **Earhart 4411, Fetzer 4418**, Ford 4420, Hemophilia 4463, National 4549, Nill 4557, **Society 4610, Society 4611, Upjohn 4654**
Minnesota: **American 4686**, Bakken 4697, Clearway 4716, Forecast 4740, **Foundation 4741, Lindbergh 4783**, Mayo 4793, **McKnight 4793**, Minnesota 4802, Proshek 4830, **Restless 4838**
Mississippi: **Pine 4919**
Missouri: **Kauffman 5025**, Mallinckrodt 5041, **PKD 5074**, Stowers 5109
Nevada: **A Charitable 5278**, Cummings 5283, **Marchionne 5293**

New Hampshire: Hitchcock 5328

New Jersey: **American 5385**, Ammonius 5386, Anyone 5387, **Cerebral 5417, CJ 5425**, Goldberg 5455, Horowitz 5473, **Infinity 5477, Johnson 5482**, Merck 5504, New 5516, Orenstein 5532, **Reeve 5550**, Silbermann 5567, **Wiley 5599, Winn 5601**

New York: **Alzheimer's 5685**, American 5690, **American 5692, American 5693, American 5694**, American 5695, American 5698, **American 5702**, American 5703, **American 5704, American 5706, American 5710, American 5711, Autism 5743**, Avon 5745, **Bibliographical 5762, Breast 5783**, Cancer 5813, Center 5833, **Children's 5851**, Columbia 5870, **Commonwealth 5872, Corning 5886**, Crohn's 5899, Cromwell 5900, **Delmas 5921, Diamond 5923, Duke 5938**, Dysautonomia 5943, Eshe 5964, **Explorers 5968, Fitch 5984, Food 5988, Foundation 5992, Foundation 5994**, Foundation 5996, **Fox 6006, Friends 6012**, Glaucoma 6030, **Grayson-Jockey 6045, Guggenheim 6049, Hearing 6065**, Hemophilia 6066, Historical 6073, Hudson 6080, Human 6081, **Huntington's 6086**, Huyck 6088, **Juvenile 6127, Keren 6135, Klingenstein 6143, Kosciuszko 6145, Lasker 6153**, Lehmann 6159, **Leukemia 6160, Lighthouse 6163**, L'Oreal 6170, **Lustgarten 6177, Lymphoma 6179**, Malevich 6185, **March 6188, Mayday 6197**, McCall 6200, **MetLife 6210, Metropolitan 6211, Mycenaean 6235, NARSAD: 6239**, National 6245, **National 6248, National 6249, National 6250, National 6251, National 6253**, New York 6271, New York 6273, Open 6295, **Parapsychology 6301, Pasteur 6306, Philippe 6316, Project 6332**, Radius 6342, **Rainforest 6343**, Research 6354, **Runyon 6365, Schalkenbach 6379, Skin 6401, Sloan 6404, Social 6409, Societe 6410**, Stony 6440, THYCA: 6453, Tourette 6459, **Trace 6461, Voices 6495, Weill 6508, Wenner 6511, Whitney 6518, Wildlife 6520, Women's 6528**

North Carolina: **American 6551, Bayer 6569**, Broad 6582, Center 6595, **Cleft 6604**, Eastern 6641, Foundation 6662, **Institut 6711, Nickel 6792, Pediatric 6814, V Foundation 6910**

Ohio: Cleveland 7043, Herb 7146, **Interthyr 7170**, Kati's 7183, Kidney 7190, LAM 7203, Psychiatric 7310, Social 7360, **Taiho 7375**, YSI 7446

Oklahoma: **Reining 7508**

Oregon: **American 7532, Culinary 7562, Fanconi 7575, National 7614**, Northwest 7619, Northwest 7620, Wheeler 7682

Pennsylvania: **Alternatives 7699, American 7701, American 7704**, American 7705, **Association 7716, Association 7718, Cardiovascular 7757**, Chung-Hee 7768, Eye 7833, **Institute 7919**, Kidney 7935, Kimmel 7936, **Law 7950**, Mahler 7966, **National 8000, Nephcure 8003**, Newman 8005, ONS 8015, Pennsylvania 8029, Pittsburgh 8048, Society 8119, **Templeton 8141**, Trout 8149, Von 8170, **Williams 8192**, Winters 8198, Workable 8206, Yount 8216

Rhode Island: Alpert 8227

South Carolina: Clemson 8462, South 8512

Tennessee: **Alpha 8554**

Texas: Alexander 8672, **American 8677, American 8678**, American 8679, American 8681, **American 8684, Bat 8705, Emergency 8814, Knights 8909, Komen 8910**, Lowe 8925, **Mary 8937, MCH 8946**, Morrison 8970, Poncin 9024, **Society 9081**, St. 9097, **Vetiver 9148**, Welch 9160, Wine 9170

Utah: Dialysis 9198, Intermountain 9210, Salt 9225, Skaggs 9226, Utah 9228

Virginia: **American 9287, American 9288, American 9290, American 9294, American 9297**, American 9299, **American 9304, American 9305**, American 9308, **American 9309**, American 9311, Association 9320, **Conquer 9351, Focused 9377, Food 9378, Foundation 9380, Friedreich's 9386, Interstitial 9407, Mesothelioma 9435, National 9452**, National 9456, **Plumbing 9483**, Prevent

9487, **Radiation 9489, Sarnoff 9498**, TDC 9517, **U.S. 9526**, Van Engel 9536, Vascular 9537, Virginia 9539

Washington: **Foundation 9614, Jain 9641, Ji 9644, Rotalia 9709**, Sigourney 9724

West Virginia: West Virginia 9827

Wisconsin: American 9834, American 9835, **Entomological 9884, National 9977, National 9978**, Noer 9984, **Riesch 10010**, Scoliosis 10025, Wisconsin 10080

Residencies

Alaska: Rasmuson 132

Arkansas: Communication 274

California: 18th 330, Angels 367, Bay 405, **Center 473, Common 509**, CounterPULSE 525, Deaf 537, **Djerassi 541**, Dorland 544, Exploratorium 565, Friends 601, **Getty 614**, Headlands 649, Merage 785, **Montalvo 802**, Outpost 848, Riverside 913, **San Francisco 943**

Colorado: Anderson 1118, Carbondale 1140, Public 1262, Sharpe 1282

Connecticut: Center 1350, Steep 1468, **Weir 1481**

Delaware: Delaware 1499

District of Columbia: Arch 1578, **Kennedy 1666**

Florida: Atlantic 1787, Hermitage 1912, Kerouac 1937, Palm Beach 2012

Georgia: Ayers 2122, Hambidge 2192

Illinois: Experimental 2555, **Ragdale 2806, Terra 2889**

Indiana: VSA 3214

Louisiana: Friends 3653

Maine: Eastern 3695, Watershed 3745

Maryland: American 3758, Baltimore 3782, **Evergreen 3824**, Maryland 3872, Metropolitan 3882, **Mid 3884**, Prince 3915, Pyramid 3917

Massachusetts: **American 3963**, Associates 3973, Berkshire 3986, **Fine 4068**, Museum 4185, Nantucket 4187, Yard 4327

Michigan: **Glen Arbor 4441**

Minnesota: American 4687, **Anderson 4690**, Anodyne 4692, Arrowhead 4693, Blacklock 4699, **Camargo 4706**, Cornucopia 4721, Franconia 4743, Highpoint 4759, Intermedia 4766, Minnesota 4799, New York 4812, Northern 4814, Region 4836

Missouri: Craft 4970

Montana: Bray 5134, Clay 5137

Nebraska: Bemis 5186

New Hampshire: La Napoule 5333, **MacDowell 5341**

New Jersey: Peters 5539

New Mexico: Border 5615, Santa Fe 5648, Wurlitzer 5660

New York: Albee 5677, Art 5719, Art 5721, ArtCouncil 5723, ArtsConnection 5730, **Blue 5770, Bogliasco 5772**, Brooklyn 5798, **CEC 5829**, Center 5834, Center 5834, **Chamber 5839**, chashama 5841, **Corning 5886, Corporation 5888, Cuban 5902**, Dactyl 5908, Dance 5911, Dieu 5925, Experimental 5967, Eyebeam 5970, Foundation 5997, **Franklin 6008**, Golden 6036, **Harvestworks 6058**, Henry 6067, Home 6077, **Kosciuszko 6145, Light 6162**, Lower 6172, Lower 6173, **Millay 6216**, Movement 6228, **National 6242**, Performance 6313, **Rockefeller 6359**, Saltonstall 6371, **Sculpture 6390, Skowhegan 6402, Social 6409**, Squeaky 6423, Stone 6438, Studio 6441, **Theatre 6448**, Topaz 6458, Triangle 6462, **Visual 6493**

North Carolina: Artspace 6560, McColl 6761, Wildacres 6920

Ohio: Cuyahoga 7076, Thurber 7382, Wexner 7422

Oregon: Caldera 7542, Neskowin 7616, Portland 7632, **Soapstone 7662**

Pennsylvania: Clay 7772, Fabric 7835, Mattress 7973, Philadelphia 8036, Pittsburgh 8049, Wood 8204

Rhode Island: **Alliance 8226**

South Carolina: Arts 8448

Tennessee: Le 8615

Texas: **Chinati 8748**, Diverseworks 8796, **Houston 8877, Museum 8975, Southwest 9090**, Southwest 9091

Utah: **Sundance 9227**

Vermont: **Carving 9238**

Virginia: Wolf 9551

Washington: 911 9554, Centrum 9583, Hugo 9639, Museum 9678, Straw 9733

West Virginia: Aurora 9765

Wyoming: **Ucross 10123**

Sabbaticals

California: Durfee 549

North Carolina: **Cattell 6594**

Pennsylvania: **Association 7718**

Vermont: Rowland 9258

Washington: Sewell 9723

Scholarships—to individuals

Alabama: AAMN 1, Alabama 2, Alsobrook 7, American 9, Andalusia 10, Baptist 12, Bashinsky 13, Blount 17, Brewton 19, Central 20, Charity 22, Community 27, Community 28, Downing 32, East Alabama 34, Electric 35, Evans 36, Fowler 38, Franklin 39, Gibson 43, Hawkins 49, Infirmary 52, Lucash 56, Martin 59, Meharg 61, Omega 66, Padolf 68, Reynolds 75, Riverbend 76, Russell 77, Simpson 79, Southeastern 81, Will 91

Alaska: **Ahtna 96**, Alaska 97, Alaska 101, Aleut 103, Arctic 104, Bering 105, Bristol 107, Calista 108, Chenega 109, Choggiung 110, Chugiak-Eagle 112, CIRI 113, Copper 114, Doyon 115, Eyak 116, Homer 117, Juneau 120, Kawerak 121, MTNT 126, Seybert 137, Sitnasuak 138, SNA 139, TDX 142, Tigara 144, UIC 145, University 146, Usibelli 147, Valley 148

Arizona: Arizona 155, Arizona 156, Arizona 157, Arizona 158, Arizona 161, Arizona 162, Arizona 164, Assistance 166, Banner 169, Barlocker 171, Catholic 177, Christian 180, Community 182, Deer 183, **Dickey 184**, Diocesan 185, Dougherty 186, East 187, Education 189, Educational 190, Fisher 192, Foundation 195, Freeport-McMoRan 196, Grace 199, Ingebritson 202, Kahvush 206, Kingman 207, Lapan 210, Los 212, Lupus 213, Northern 222, Patterson 224, Phoenix 227, Renaissance 232, Rosztoczy 234, **Southern 237, Stott 241**, Sulphur 243, Thunderbird 244, Torres 245, Valley 253, Warner 257

Arkansas: Arkansas 264, Arkansas 265, Ayres 268, Boggan 271, Cornerstone 276, Jones 285, **Mashburn 289**, Moll 291, Murphy 293, Murphy 295, Nelson 297, Northeast 298, Olds 300, Reed 304, SHARE 307, Thomas 318, Woodson 328

California: 10,000 329, 826 331, **Academy 335**, Access 336, ACEC 337, Alta 350, Amador 352, American 353, American 354, American 356, Anaheim 364, Angels 366, Arques 372, Art 374, Assistance 383, Assistance 384, **Association 387**, Association 388, **Association 389, Avery 395**, Basic 401, Beckstrand 409, **Bel-Air 410**, Belvedere 411, Boand 416, Bodine 417, **Borg 418**, Bradley 421, Burn 429, **Burwen 430**, Butte 432, Calcot 440, California 442, California 443, California 444, California 445, California 447, California 449, California 451, California 454, California 457, California 458, **Cancer 462, Cavalier 469**, Central 474, Change 477, Chaparral 478, Chicana 482, Chrysopolae 497, Chung 498, **Chung 499**, Coastal 504, Cohen 505, Community 510, Community 511, Community 512, Community 514, Community 515, Cops 523, Couch 524, **Croatian 528**, Croul 529, **Cystinosis 533**, Darnell 536, Desert 538, Doing 543, Downey 545, Eastcliff 551, **Easter 552, Ekstrom 555, Elim 559**, Elk 560, Fansler 569, Feminist 573, Fernando 574, Fischer 576, Florsheim 581, Foster

582, Foundation 584, Foundation 585, **Foundation 587, Foundation 588**, Fresno 597, Friends 599, Fulfillment 604, Fundacion 605, Gaines 607, **Gala 608, Gemological 609**, Glennon 622, Golden 625, Golden 627, Good 631, Gorecki 632, **GRAMMY 635, Hager 643**, Haight 644, Hartman 648, Healdsburg 650, Health 651, Heart 653, Held 655, Hiebler 660, High 662, Hoag 665, Horizons 667, Hunter 672, Hurliman 675, Hydrocephalus 676, **INCOSE 679, Institute 685**, International 688, **International 690, Invisible 694**, Iranian 696, Irwindale 697, James 702, Jedinstvo 703, Jewish 706, Jewish 708, Johnson 709, Johnson 711, Jones 713, Kaiser 718, Kerber 719, Kiersted 720, Korean 724, Lagrant 731, **Lambda 734**, Lancaster 735, Lasso 736, **Little 748**, Liu 749, Livermore 750, Locke 751, Long Beach 754, Los 756, Lynch 761, Machado 764, Mammoth 767, Marin 772, Masonic 775, Mathematical 776, Matsui 777, McQuinn 780, Methodist 787, **Mexican 788, Mexico 789**, Miedema 790, Milken 792, Mills-Peninsula 795, Muir 808, National 819, **Nepal 824**, North 831, Northern 833, Northern 834, Orange 843, Orangewood 845, Oro 847, OZ 849, Pack 851, Pasadena 855, Penjoyan 859, Performing 861, Philharmonic 866, PMC 874, Promises 884, QueensCare 891, Rader 892, Rainey 894, Rancho 897, Reagan 901, Recruiting 902, Richards 910, Rio 911, Riverside 914, Roberts 915, **Rogers 916**, S.L. 924, Sacramento 925, Sacramento 926, San Diego 930, San Diego 931, San Diego 934, San Diego 938, San Felipe 940, San Francisco 941, San Francisco 946, San Francisco 947, San Luis 951, Sandpipers 953, Santa 956, Scaife 961, Schiffman 962, Scholarship 965, Seau 970, Sequoia 975, Shasta 978, Shelby 979, Siff 984, Silicon 986, Silver 988, Silverlake 989, Smart 993, **Smiley 994**, Smith 995, Smylie 997, Society 999, Space 1007, **Sponsors 1009**, Stanislaus 1017, Stensrud 1021, Stockton 1025, Stone 1026, **Studenica 1029**, Sulprizio 1031, Tatum 1037, Tawa 1038, Tenderloin 1042, Through 1047, Touhey 1051, Tri 1054, Truckee 1058, **Trustees 1061**, Twin 1065, Vaccarezza-Murdaca 1075, Variety 1078, Ventura 1081, **Vogelzang 1083**, Warner 1086, Werner 1089, West 1090, Whitten 1092, Whittier 1093, Wright 1103, Yolo 1105, Young 1107

Colorado: Adventure 1111, **AfricAid 1114, American 1116**, American 1117, APS 1120, Aspen 1123, Assistance 1124, Assistance 1125, **Association 1126**, Boogie's 1131, Boys 1133, Breckenridge 1134, Broomfield 1135, Brown 1136, Burton 1137, CAEYC 1138, Carbondale 1140, Children's 1144, **Christian 1145**, Clark 1149, Cocker 1151, Colorado 1157, Colorado 1158, Colorado 1160, **Colorado 1165**, Colorado Springs 1166, Colorado 1167, Colorado 1169, Community 1170, Community 1171, Community 1172, Conkling 1174, Curtis 1176, **Daniels 1177**, Delta 1178, Denver 1179, Denver 1183, Durango 1185, Eagle 1186, Eagle 1187, East 1188, Fort 1197, **Galaway 1201**, Garone-Nicksich 1202, Goodwill 1205, Gunnison 1207, Hughes 1216, I Have 1218, Impact 1219, Jefferson 1221, Lillis 1232, Logan 1233, Marchello 1237, Mikkelson 1239, Minority 1240, Morgan 1242, **Morris 1243**, Mountain 1244, Mulford 1245, **Music 1246, National 1248**, Newland 1249, North 1251, Outcalt 1254, Pathways 1256, Pikes 1258, Puddy 1263, Pueblo 1264, Reach 1265, Robinson 1268, Rocky 1272, Ronald 1274, Rutherford 1275, Saccomanno 1276, Scottish 1278, Servant 1281, Skrifvars 1284, Spanish 1288, St. Mary's 1289, Staley 1290, Stupfel 1292, Summit 1293, Taddonio 1294, **United 1298**, United 1300, University 1301, Vail 1302, VSA 1304, Western 1306, White 1307, Williams 1308, Yampa 1309, YMCA 1310

Connecticut: American 1322, Ash 1325, Bartlett 1331, Bauer 1332, Bauer 1333, **Bonfire 1336**, Borck 1337, Branford 1338, Bridgeport 1339, Bristol 1340, Bulkeley 1343, Byram 1344, Capital 1346, Carlson 1347, CJR 1357, Clark 1358, Colburn-Keenan 1360, Community 1361, Community 1362, Compass 1364, Connecticut 1365, Connecticut 1366, Deering 1374, Dolan 1378, Dunning 1379, Eastman 1382, Ebony 1383, Fairfield 1387, First 1389, Fuller 1393, Fusco 1394, Hartford 1399, Hartford 1400, Hunter's 1403, Jewish 1408, Jewish 1409, **Knights 1412**, Liberty 1414, MacCurdy 1416, Macristy 1418, Main 1419, Manchester 1420, Meriden 1421, Milford 1424, Miss 1425, New Canaan 1430, Nolan 1433, Norwalk 1435, Norwalk 1436, O'Meara 1437, Orange 1439, Prasad 1445, Promising 1446, Rockville 1450, Rogow 1451, Saybrook 1455, SBM 1456, **Society 1461**, Stamford 1464, Stamford 1465, Staples 1466, Traalum 1474, Traurig 1475, Watertown 1480, Wells 1483, Westport-Weston 1484

Delaware: Chaney 1495, Delaware 1500, Delaware 1501, Delaware 1504, Fresh 1509, Gromet 1511, Masten 1516, Orange 1518, Robinson 1522, Splawn 1524

District of Columbia: **AARP 1529**, Abramson 1530, Air 1534, Albert 1536, **Amazon 1537, American 1539, American 1543, American 1548, American 1549, American 1550, American 1556, American 1557, American 1561, American 1562, American 1565, American 1567**, Asian 1580, **Aspen 1583**, Bell 1591, Black 1593, Block 1594, Capital 1598, Christ 1601, CIC 1602, Communications 1604, Community 1605, District 1617, District 1618, Ellington 1620, **Foundation 1629, Franciscan 1630**, Hemophilia 1642, **Hispanic 1644, International 1652, International 1657, International 1659**, Latino 1669, **Marshall 1674**, Masonic 1675, Mentors 1678, Minbanc 1679, **National 1685, National 1688, National 1691, National 1696, National 1697**, National 1698, Ocean 1702, Olender 1703, O'Neil 1704, **Parents, 1707, Phillips 1716**, Professional 1717, **Radio 1718**, Red 1722, Sigma 1728, **Spina 1733, Travel 1736, UFCW 1739, Union 1741**, Washington 1750, **Wilderness 1751**

Florida: **AAST 1761**, All 1765, Allen 1766, American 1769, American 1772, Aqua 1778, Art 1782, **Ashley 1784**, Baptist 1792, Beall 1793, Benjamin 1796, Blac 1800, Blankenship 1801, Blount 1802, Boldin 1803, Boyer 1804, Bragg 1806, Bronson 1808, Brooks 1809, Broward 1811, Cape Coral 1815, **Carter 1817**, Catalina 1818, Chamberlain 1821, Children's 1825, Clark 1831, Cohen 1833, Common 1836, Community 1839, Community 1840, Community 1841, Community 1842, Community 1843, Community 1844, Community 1845, Community 1846, Community 1847, Community 1848, Conn 1850, Crealde 1854, Deeley 1858, DeVoe 1861, Dunbar 1864, Embassy 1869, Florida 1878, Florida 1882, Florida 1884, Florida 1885, Florida 1886, Florida 1887, Forbes 1888, Fort 1890, Fort 1891, Ft. 1892, GMAA 1896, Harris 1904, Health 1908, Hellenic 1910, Hillmyer-Tremont 1914, **Holland 1918**, Hollywood 1919, Holt 1920, Hungerford 1923, Indian 1927, Jacobson 1929, Judge 1933, Kelly 1935, Kenney 1936, Kiwanis 1940, KML 1941, Lang 1946, Life 1950, LPGA 1955, Maine 1959, Manatee 1960, Marco 1962, Martin 1964, McCabe 1967, McGinty 1971, McKinney 1972, Meador 1974, Megaloudis 1975, Meiller 1976, Meninak 1977, Miami 1978, **Miami 1979**, Momeni 1981, Moore 1982, Morrison 1984, Mote 1985, Mount 1986, Nall 1992, Naples 1993, Naples 1994, **National 1997**, North 1999, Operafestival 2005, Orange 2007, Orlando 2008, Pagliara 2010, Palm 2013, **Patel 2014**, Petteys 2017, Pinellas 2018, Pinellas 2019, Planning 2021, Police 2023, Rayonier 2031, Reed 2032, Reinhold 2034, Rhodes 2036, Riechmann 2037, Rubin 2041, Rush 2043, **Samstag 2048**, Santa 2049, Scholarship 2051, **Scholarship 2052**, Smith 2064, Smith 2065, Southwest 2067, Space 2068, St. Petersburg 2071, Step 2075, Sudakoff 2077, Sun 2078, Tallahassee 2082, Thrush 2087, Toussant 2088, Wagner 2098, Washington 2099, Watson 2100, Wertzberger 2101, West Palm Beach 2102, Winged 2105, Woman's 2107

Georgia: Alpha 2112, Anderson 2118, Austin 2121, Baker 2123, Braswell 2130, Callaway 2134, Cherokee 2138, Children 2140, Choson 2141, Churches 2143, Coastal 2145, **Coca 2148**, Community 2150, Community 2151, Community 2152, Coweta 2156, Davies 2160, Decatur 2161, Dellinger 2163, **DeYoung 2165**, Dickens 2166, Dinnerman 2167, Edmondson 2170, Fund 2181, Garden 2182, Georgia 2183, Georgia 2184, Georgia 2185, Georgia 2186, Golden 2189, Hamilton 2193, Handweavers 2194, Idaho 2197, **Jewish 2198**, McDuffie 2210, Monroe 2212, **National 2213**, North 2218, Park 2220, Reynolds 2228, Sapelo 2231, Savannah 2232, Service 2235, Spears 2241, Stingrays 2243, **THDF 2249**, Waffle 2255, Warren 2257, WellStar 2260

Hawaii: Aiea 2269, **Akihito 2270, Center 2274**, Chung 2276, Gear 2284, Geist 2285, Grove 2286, Hana 2287, Hawaii 2289, Hawaii 2291, Ishii 2295, Kaneta 2297, Kokua 2299, McKee 2303, Onizuka 2307, Outrigger 2308, Pacific 2309, Pacific 2310, Palama 2312, People 2314, Rehabilitation 2316, Straub 2321, Waimea 2325

Idaho: Adams 2328, Chadwick 2330, Idaho 2335, Lewis-Clark 2339, Lightfoot 2340, Magnuson 2341, Rotary 2347, Stufflebeam 2351

Illinois: AKA 2360, Ameren 2364, **American 2366, American 2368, American 2374, American 2375, American 2376, American 2379, American 2381, American 2382**, American 2383, Arbor 2405, Arnold 2407, BancTrust 2410, BCMW 2415, Beneke 2420, Berner 2423, Bohne 2429, Bolingbrook 2430, Bound 2432, Boynton-Gillespie 2434, Brooks 2438, Brown 2439, Brown 2440, Bruton 2444, Burson 2448, Bushnell 2451, Butterworth 2453, Caestecker 2456, Camp 2457, CGH 2470, Chicago 2472, Collins 2490, Community 2493, Community 2495, Community 2496, Community 2497, Crosswalk 2504, Cunningham 2505, Davis 2509, Dawson 2512, DeKalb 2514, Dodd 2518, East 2530, Edgar 2532, Edgar 2533, Edward 2535, Edwardsville 2536, Ekstrand 2538, **Elks 2540, Emergency 2543, Engine 2546**, Engineering 2547, Erk 2550, Evans 2551, Evans 2552, Fairfield 2557, Fashion 2558, Fildes 2561, Flora 2564, Footprints 2566, Franciscan 2573, Franklin 2574, Gabler 2577, Geneseo 2580, Gore 2588, Grossinger 2594, Hartke 2602, **Hasnia 2603, Health 2606**, Hebrew 2609, Henry 2613, Hill 2617, **Hill 2618**, Hohner 2621, Hubbard 2627, Hughes 2629, Hutchison 2630, Illinois 2633, Illinois 2634, Illinois 2635, Illinois 2636, Illinois 2639, Illinois 2640, Illinois 2643, Illinois 2645, Illinois 2648, Irwin 2654, Jewish 2657, Jewish 2658, Johnson 2659, Joint 2660, Jones 2661, Jorndt 2662, Journalism 2663, Kankakee 2667, Kilts 2670, Koehler 2674, Koranda 2679, Krill 2680, Ladies 2681, Lang 2683, Larson 2684, Levin 2691, Lewis 2692, Luhr 2699, Martin 2710, Maryville 2711, Master 2714, Masters 2715, McDonald 2718, McFarland 2720, McFarland 2721, McInnes 2722, McLean 2724, McLoraine 2725, Meade 2727, **Medical 2728**, Metamora 2732, Milburn 2733, Minner 2736, Moline 2737, Murphy 2741, Mutual 2742, **National 2743, National 2744, National 2751**, Neal 2753, Oak Park 2761, Oberlin 2763, Oberweiler 2764, Ohadi 2765, Ozinga 2775, Perisho-Nina 2783, Pilchard 2790, **Polish 2796**, Riverside 2828, Rockwood 2828, Roesch 2829, Rogers 2830, **Ronald 2831**, Rot 2833, Rotary 2834, **Rotary 2835**, Royal 2837, Russell 2838, **Schillings 2841, Scholar 2842**, Schweitzer 2846, Scott 2847, Shinaberry 2852, Skelton 2856, Smith 2858, Smyth 2861, Southern 2865, Sperling 2867, Stonier 2875, Storey 2876, Suarez 2880, Swedish 2882, Templeton 2888, Titus 2893, **TPAA 2895**, Tree 2896, **Ullery 2901**, Union 2903, Union 2904, Villwock 2909, **Vogler 2910**,

Wayne 2919, Welch 2921, Wells 2922, Western 2924, Western 2925, Williams 2927, Willo 2928, Wise 2930, **Women 2933, Woodbury 2936,** **Zazove 2939,** Zimmerly 2941, **Zonta 2942**

Indiana: Abell 2944, Alpha 2948, **Alpha 2949,** Alpha 2951, Amburn 2953, **American 2954,** American 2955, Arsenal 2959, Association 2962, Benton 2966, Blue 2970, Bowen 2972, Brookville 2973, Brown 2974, Brown 2975, Catholic 2980, Charlton 2981, Children's 2983, Christamore 2984, Community 2990, Community 2991, Community 2993, Community 2994, Community 2995, Community 2996, Community 2998, Community 2999, Community 3000, Community 3001, Community 3002, Community 3003, Community 3004, Community 3005, Community 3006, Community 3007, Coy 3009, Crown Point 3010, Dearborn 3012, Decatur 3013, DeKalb 3015, Delta 3016, Dora 3017, Dubois 3019, East 3023, Elkhart 3024, Eskenazi 3027, Fayette 3028, Fenech 3029, Fitzgerald 3030, Fort 3031, **Foundation 3032,** Foundations 3033, Frank 3035, Franklin 3036, **Future 3040,** Garr 3041, Gemmill 3042, Greene 3045, Hammond 3049, Harcourt 3052, Harrison 3054, Hemminger 3055, Hendricks 3057, Henry 3058, Heritage 3059, Hoch 3061, Horseshoe 3062, Houghton 3063, Hughes 3065, Huntington 3067, Huntington 3068, Independent 3069, Indiana 3070, Indiana 3071, Indianapolis 3072, Indianapolis 3074, Jasper 3076, Jennings 3077, Jewish 3078, Johnson 3079, Joshi 3080, Kaminski 3081, Keitzer 3083, Kendrick 3085, Kiwanis 3088, Kosciusko 3090, Kosciusko 3091, Kuhner 3092, LaGrange 3093, Laird 3094, **Lilly 3099,** Logansport 3104, Madison 3106, Maris 3109, Marshall 3110, McKinney 3112, Moore 3115, Moran 3118, Muncie 3120, **National 3121, National 3122, National 3123,** National 3124, Noble 3127, O'Connor 3130, Ohio 3131, Orth 3133, Owen 3136, Pace 3137, Parke 3139, Parkview 3140, Peoples 3143, Phi 3147, Porter 3150, Public 3152, Putnam 3154, Raab 3155, Richmond 3161, Riddleberger 3163, Ripley 3164, RPW 3166, Rush 3167, Saint 3169, Scering 3171, Scholarship 3174, **Sigma 3183,** Smelser 3186, South 3189, Standerford 3191, Steuben 3193, **Timmy 3200,** Tipton 3201, Tretter 3203, **United 3206,** Unity 3209, **USA 3210,** Vermillion 3211, Visiting 3212, Voland 3213, Wabash 3215, Warren 3216, Wayne 3217, Weaver 3218, Wells 3220, Western 3222, Whitehall 3224, Whitley 3226, Winchester 3229, Zeta 3230, Zimmer 3231, **Zoltani 3232**

Iowa: Accelerated 3233, Allen 3235, Anderson 3238, Anderson 3239, Andrews 3240, Association 3241, Barr 3242, Bishop 3245, Black 3247, Bray 3248, Cedar Rapids 3255, Clarinda 3257, Code 3258, Community 3262, Community 3263, Community 3264, Conner 3266, Corbin 3267, Credit 3268, Garber 3282, Genesis 3283, Gerling 3284, **Grace 3286,** Greene 3288, Griffith 3289, Hahn 3294, Harper 3295, Hermsen 3298, Hockenberry 3300, Igou 3303, Iowa 3305, Iowa 3306, Iowa 3309, Jennie 3313, Keppy 3318, Latta 3323, Leeper 3325, Marek 3331, Meier 3336, Mongan 3338, Munson 3339, Norris 3344, North 3345, Northwest 3347, **P.E.O. 3349, P.E.O. 3350, P.E.O. 3351,** Parks 3354, Petersen 3356, **Pioneer 3358,** Preston 3360, Riley 3366, Rima 3367, Rotary 3368, Schooler 3373, Schwartz 3376, Siouxland 3382, Sonstegard 3384, Stearns 3389, Straub 3391, Trinity 3397, U.S. 3398, Vacek 3402, Van Buren 3403, Vestergaard 3405, Wood 3409

Kansas: Alpha 3412, Atchison 3415, Beren 3420, Boyle 3421, **Christian 3424,** Clay 3425, Columbus 3428, Community 3429, Douglas 3433, Duer 3435, Ellis 3439, Fell 3441, Fingersh 3442, Golden 3447, Grasshopper 3448, Greene 3449, Hoover 3457, Journalism 3466, Kansas 3468, Kansas 3469, Kansas 3472, Laham 3478, Legacy 3479, McKinnis 3482, McPherson 3483, McPherson 3484, Mitchelson 3486, Moore 3489,

Murdock 3492, Nuttycomb 3497, Rush 3509, Salina 3510, South 3517, Stockard 3523, Throckmorton 3526, Topeka 3528, Trembly 3529, Western 3535, Wichita 3537, Wildlife 3540, Winslow 3541

Kentucky: Baker 3547, Barnett 3548, Big 3551, Blue 3552, Caudill 3554, Christian 3556, Community 3560, Cox 3561, Disabled 3562, **Energy 3567,** Governors 3574, Hedrick 3576, Horn 3577, Independence 3578, KD-FC 3581, **Kentucky 3583,** Kentucky 3584, Kings 3588, Metro 3596, Miller 3598, Norton 3605, Owensboro 3609, Paxton 3613, PHP 3616, Quinkert 3618, Rhoads 3619, Turner 3630, **United 3632,** University 3634

Louisiana: 100 3638, American 3641, Baton Rouge 3644, Baton Rouge 3645, Bernstein 3646, Brownell 3647, Goldring 3654, JL Foun 3657, Louisiana 3666, Olinde 3671, Putnam 3676, Taylor 3679, **Waters 3682,** Zigler 3684

Maine: Anson 3686, Associated 3687, Davenport 3693, Hungarian-American 3704, Island 3706, Maine 3711, Maine 3712, Maine 3713, Maine 3716, North Haven 3720, Reid 3729, Stich 3737, Williams 3746, **Worcester 3748**

Maryland: Allemall 3754, **Alpha 3755, American 3757, American 3761,** American 3763, AMVETS 3771, **Aplastic 3774,** Baltimore 3783, Baltimore 3784, **Carson 3793,** Central 3796, **Central 3797,** Charlotte 3798, Chesapeake 3799, Chesapeake 3800, Choice 3802, Collegebound 3803, Community 3805, Community 3806, Community 3807, Community 3808, Credit 3810, **Fisher 3826,** Girl 3835, **Hispanic 3841,** Howard 3844, Ivy 3850, Ivy 3851, Jewish 3853, Jorgensen 3855, Kattar 3856, Leadership 3863, Leister 3864, Maryland 3869, Maryland 3873, Maryland 3874, Maryland 3876, Mid-Atlantic 3885, Mid-Shore 3887, Moore 3889, Moore, 3890, **National 3895, National 3900,** Parent 3907, **Pet 3910, Phi 3911,** Phoenix 3912, **Pulmonary 3916,** Ravens 3920, Roche 3922, Sacco 3923, Salisbury 3925, Samet 3926, Sawyer 3927, **School 3928,** Talarico 3940, Torray 3942, Trueman 3943, Truschel 3944, Ulman 3947, Walton 3950, Womens 3952, **Yvorra 3954**

Massachusetts: 47 3955, Affordable 3958, **Ahern 3959, American 3966,** Andona 3970, Balfour 3976, Belmont 3981, Berkshire 3983, Beta 3987, Boch 3990, Boston 3991, Boston 3992, Brockton 4001, Cambridge 4004, Carman 4011, Charles 4018, Children's 4022, Coffin's 4025, College 4027, Community 4028, Community 4029, Costello 4031, D'Amour 4033, D'Amour 4034, Deane 4037, Difelice 4040, Donnell 4042, Dugan 4045, Dunham 4046, Egan 4056, Essex 4060, Fallon 4061, **Farm 4062,** Fassino 4065, Faunce 4066, Ferdian 4067, First 4069, First 4070, General 4078, General 4079, Goddard 4086, Hawks 4099, Hood 4111, Horner 4114, Howard 4117, Howes 4118, Institution 4125, Jacob's 4129, Jones 4132, Kelley 4135, Lake View 4144, **Liberty 4148,** Lowell 4153, Mack 4156, Massachusetts 4165, McLaughlin 4172, Middlesex 4174, Millman 4176, **Milton 4177,** Moakley 4180, Murray 4183, Nantucket 4186, **National 4188,** National 4189, Nichols 4197, North 4200, North 4201, One 4206, Ouimet 4208, Pallotta 4210, Peabody 4212, Perfect 4215, Permanent 4216, Philbin 4219, Pilgrim 4224, Pittsfield 4225, Pope 4227, President 4230, **R.O.S.E. 4236,** Real 4239, Red 4240, Rice 4242, Richardson 4243, Royal 4251, SAMFund 4255, Sandwich 4258, **SEVEN 4267,** South 4273, Stone 4276, Sullivan 4278, Supreme 4279, Thoreau 4289, Thorne 4290, **Tourism 4292, Transgender 4293,** Travelli 4295, Trustees 4299, Turning 4302, **Two 4303,** Voght 4308, Wagner 4310, Weyman 4314, Wheelwright 4315, **Winter 4319, Woods 4323**

Michigan: Allegan 4333, Allen 4335, Ann Arbor 4338, Avondale 4341, Baker 4342, Baraga 4344, Barry 4347, Battle Creek 4349, Bay Harbor 4351,

Bedford 4353, Bees 4354, Bellinger 4355, Berrien 4357, Birmingham 4359, Bixby 4361, Branch 4365, Buist 4369, Byrne 4370, Canton 4372, Career 4373, Caring 4375, Carpenter 4376, Central 4377, **Chang 4378,** Charlevoix 4380, Chase 4381, Chelsea 4382, Cole 4386, **Collectors 4387,** Come 4389, Community 4390, Community 4391, Community 4392, Community 4393, Community 4394, Community 4395, Community 4396, Community 4397, Community 4398, Cunningham 4401, Delta 4405, Delta 4406, Detroit 4407, Flint 4419, **Ford 4422,** Foster 4423, Four 4427, Frankenmuth 4428, Fremont 4431, **Gerber 4434,** Glaser 4439, Gleaner 4440, Goodrich 4442, Grand Haven 4444, Grand Rapids 4445, Grand 4447, Gratiot 4448, Gratiot 4449, Greenville 4451, Hebert 4460, Hemophilia 4463, Heyl 4465, Hillier 4466, Hillsdale 4467, Home 4468, Horgan 4469, Hospitalers 4470, Howe 4472, Humane 4475, Huron 4477, Juhl 4488, Junior 4489, Junior 4490, Kalamazoo 4492, Kalamazoo 4493, Kalamazoo 4494, Kiwanis 4500, Kling 4502, Kohn 4505, Laidlaw 4509, Lakeland 4510, Lapeer 4512, Leelanau 4514, Legion 4515, Lenawee 4516, M & M 4521, Marquette 4523, Marquette 4524, Marshall 4525, Martin 4526, Meyers 4532, Michigan 4534, Michigan 4537, Michigan 4538, Michigan 4539, Michigan 4540, Midland 4542, Mount 4547, Mount Pleasant 4548, National 4549, Nelson 4551, New 4552, Nieman 4556, Nill 4557, Northville 4561, Novi 4565, Oakwood 4567, Otsego 4571, Parks 4574, Paulsen 4575, Pennock 4576, Phelps 4578, Pokagon 4580, Rachor 4583, Rislov 4589, Rochester 4590, Roscommon 4592, Saginaw 4597, Scears 4600, Schaap 4601, Scholarship 4602, Schultheiss 4603, Shelby 4604, Shiawassee 4605, Sigmund 4606, Skrocki 4608, **Society 4611,** Sonneveldt 4614, Southfield 4616, St. Mary's 4625, Stokes 4628, Sturgis 4629, Tamer 4631, Taylor 4633, Thom 4635, Thomas 4636, Three 4637, United 4650, Watson 4661, Wigginton 4668

Minnesota: 3-H 4678, Abbott 4679, AgStar 4683, Birk's 4698, Bowman 4702, Brooks 4704, Central 4710, Chong 4713, Christian 4714, CHS 4715, Concordia 4720, Crockett 4723, Crosslake 4724, Dietrick-Parks 4727, Duluth 4729, ECMC 4730, **Engen 4734,** Ernst 4735, Five 4738, **Francis 4742,** Franz 4744, Fredrikson 4745, Grand Rapids 4750, **Grannis-Martin 4751,** HealthEast 4756, Higher 4758, **Hmong 4760,** Jewish 4772, Johnson 4773, Kohl 4775, Land 4779, Mankato 4789, Mayo 4792, Methodist 4795, Meyer 4796, Minnesota 4797, Minnesota 4802, Minnesota 4804, Minnesota 4805, National 4811, Northern 4815, Northern 4816, Northwest 4817, Petters 4823, Philanthrofund 4824, PLUS 4826, Proshek 4830, Pryor 4832, Regions 4837, Roberg 4839, Rochester 4840, Rosen 4841, Saint Paul 4842, Sampson 4843, Scheidler 4844, **Scholarship 4845,** South St. Paul 4852, Steinke 4861, Target 4864, Tozer 4870, Tri-County 4871, Two 4873, United 4875, **Wagner 4883,** Wedum 4885, Winona 4892, Woman's 4894

Mississippi: Bacot/Jolly 4896, Bleuer 4898, Care 4901, Community 4902, Franks 4908, Gulf 4909, Haskell 4910, Mississippi 4914, Skelton 4921, Sumners 4923

Missouri: African 4927, **Agriculture 4928,** Alpha 4930, Anderson 4933, Baptist-Trinity 4935, Beattie 4937, Bolivar 4940, **Boys 4942,** Burkhalter 4947, Calkins 4949, **Chesed 4955,** Cohen 4960, Community 4963, Covington 4967, Cox 4968, Coxhealth 4969, Delta 4973, **Demolay 4974,** Dodd 4976, Doolin 4978, Drowns 4979, Ebert 4981, Edgar 4982, Ferris 4991, Fingersh 4992, Foundation 4994, Friedman 4996, Gibbs 4998, Gift 4999, Goetze 5001, Greater 5004, Griffin 5007, Guilander 5009, Haddad 5010, Helias 5015, Hester 5016, Holmes 5018, Hutchinson 5022, Kansas 5023, Kansas City 5024, King 5029, Kirschner 5030, Lake 5032, Lange 5034,

Liebling 5036, Marsch 5043, Martino 5045, MFA 5050, MICDS 5052, Missouri 5057, Missouri 5059, NASB 5061, North 5064, Peculiar 5071, **People 5072**, Saint Louis 5082, Schwartze 5089, Schwartze 5090, Scottish 5097, **Sertoma, 5098**, Shelter 5099, St. Louis 5104, **St. Louis 5105**, St. Louis 5106, St. Marys 5107, Steven 5108, Thurman 5114, Tilles 5115, Truman 5118, Urban 5122, Ward 5123, **Young 5127**

Montana: Allegiance 5128, Beartooth 5131, Bottrell 5133, Bray 5134, Dayton 5141, District 5142, Fergus 5145, Gebhardt 5148, Geyser 5149, H2 5151, Interbel 5160, Mike 5162, **Rocky 5169**, Student 5174, Svarre 5176, Treacy 5180, Washington 5182, Yellowstone 5183

Nebraska: All 5185, BryanLGH 5189, **Buffett 5190**, Butts 5191, CEDARS 5192, Cozad 5193, Davis 5194, Doniphan 5195, **Dressage 5196**, Edwards 5198, Foundation 5204, Grand Island 5210, Hamilton 5212, Hansen 5213, Hastings 5215, Hawks 5216, Hay 5217, Kearney 5223, Kooper 5226, Lexington 5228, Lincoln 5229, Loessin 5230, Merrick 5233, Mid-Nebraska 5234, Morrison 5236, Nebraska 5238, Nebraska 5239, Nebraska 5244, Nebraska 5245, Nelnet 5246, Newblom 5247, Novak 5248, Omaha 5250, Oregon 5252, Phelps 5255, Regional 5256, Riss 5258, Schmoker 5259, Strengths 5263, Stueven 5264, Tri-Valley 5266, Wabash 5268, Walther 5270, West Point 5272

Nevada: Berner 5279, Community 5282, Davidson 5284, Dawson 5285, DiRienzo 5286, Doyle 5287, Kirchner 5290, Korfman 5291, Laetz 5292, Nevada 5295, Norris 5297, NV 5298, Reno 5300, Renown 5301, Western 5304

New Hampshire: American 5305, Ayer 5306, Bean 5307, Blandin 5308, Bruce 5310, Butler 5312, Clarke 5313, Concord 5316, Davenport 5317, Dodge 5318, Fond 5321, Foundation 5322, Hubbard 5329, Lancaster 5336, Lavoie 5337, Letourneau 5338, **Lyman 5340**, Moving 5351, New Hampshire 5353, New London 5356, Nye 5357, Parkland 5360, Plan 5361, Ramsaye 5364, Randolph 5365, Stickney 5370, **U.S. 5373**, Union 5374, Walpole 5376

New Jersey: Bartell 5394, Bass 5395, Bernards 5398, Beth 5400, BLSJ 5402, B'nai 5403, Boland 5404, Camp 5411, **DRC 5436**, Eastern 5438, Eden 5439, Embrace 5440, Flynn 5446, Grandcolas 5457, Greater 5459, Gubitosi 5463, Hemophilia 5468, Hollander 5470, Houton 5474, **IEEE 5476**, Islami, 5479, Justice 5484, Kapala 5485, Kiwanis 5488, Konstantinos 5490, KPMG 5493, Lasko 5494, Lukenda 5499, Middlesex 5507, Morello 5512, NARM 5513, New Jersey 5517, New Jersey 5519, New Jersey 5520, New Jersey 5521, New Jersey 5522, **New 5524, Newcombe 5526**, O'Brien's 5530, O'Leary 5531, Paper 5534, Parker 5535, Penn 5537, Peters 5539, Pinson 5541, Polonsky 5542, Portuguese-American 5543, Princeton 5546, Robustelli 5552, Ryu 5556, Saddle 5557, Scholarship 5560, Shreve 5565, **Siemens 5569**, Smith 5569, Summit 5574, Tavitian 5576, Terplan 5577, Townsend 5579, Union 5582, Union 5583, Virtua 5592, Wei 5593, Woodbridge 5604, Wound 5605, Zipf 5608

New Mexico: Albuquerque 5610, Carlsbad 5616, Carson 5617, **Catching 5618**, Central 5620, Community 5624, ENMR 5627, ENMR 5628, Jemez 5633, Laguna 5634, Los 5638, Maddox 5639, New Mexico 5640, Penasco 5642, PRMC-Clovis 5644, Roosevelt 5645, Santa Fe 5648, Santa Fe 5649, Simon 5651, Taos 5656, Whited 5658

New York: **Actors 5665**, AEC 5669, **AFS-USA 5671**, AFTRA 5672, Ailey 5676, All 5680, Alliance 5682, Alpha 5683, **America-Israel 5686, American 5692**, America's 5712, Andrews 5713, Armenian 5717, Art 5722, Ashley 5732, Athanasiades 5737, Atlas 5738, **Avon 5745**, Bacile 5747, Bacon 5748, Ballet 5752, Barton 5753, Beacon 5757, **Beard 5758**, Berntsen 5761, Blake 5766, Bon 5773,

Breast 5782, Bronx 5795, Brooklyn 5796, **Buffalo 5802**, Burrows 5806, **Buttonwood 5807, Career 5816**, Careers 5817, Carpenter 5819, Carver 5822, Catholic 5825, Cattaraugus 5826, Center 5830, Center 5831, Central 5837, Chautauqua 5842, Chenango 5843, Children's 5848, Cirio 5855, Columbia 5870, **Columbus 5871**, Community 5875, Community 5876, Community 5877, Community 5878, Community 5880, Community 5881, Costa 5892, Cox 5897, Cunningham 5905, Dante 5913, **Direct 5926**, Division 5927, Doherty 5929, Donghia 5930, Durland 5940, Early 5947, Eastern 5949, Eckert 5953, Educational 5954, Elsasser 5958, Episcopal 5960, **ESA 5963, Esiason 5965, Estonian 5966**, Exploring 5969, Fan 5972, **Fantasy 5973**, Fashion 5976, Father 5977, FDNY 5978, Federation 5979, Federman 5980, Figliolia 5983, Fondation 5987, Food 5989, Forrai 5990, Foundation 6001, Foundation 6003, Fountain 6004, Friars 6010, **Friends 6012**, Gavin 6017, Genesee 6020, Gillen 6025, Gillroy 6026, Girl 6027, Glens Falls 6032, Gold 6035, Good 6038, Goodell 6039, Goshen 6040, Haynes 6063, Humanas 6082, Humanitas 6083, **ID 6090, Illuminating 6091**, International 6097, **International 6098, International 6102**, Inwood 6104, Jachym 6107, JAM 6109, Jandon 6110, Jay's 6111, Jewish 6118, **Jewish 6120**, Jonas 6122, Joukowsky 6123, Judkins 6125, Kassenbrock 6130, Kidney 6137, L.H. 6149, La 6150, Le Rosey 6155, **League 6156, Lighthouse 6163**, Long 6168, **Marine 6190**, Marino 6191, Mayer 6198, **McCaddin 6199**, McConnell 6201, McGee 6204, McGrath 6205, Memorial 6207, Mijangos 6214, Monroe 6223, Morgan 6225, Morgan 6226, Morton 6227, Muhlenbruck 6230, N Foundation 6236, National 6240, **National 6244**, National 6247, **National 6252, National 6254**, NCCC 6256, Netzach 6259, New 6261, New Visions 6263, New York 6268, New York 6275, New York 6277, **Nok 6281**, Nolan 6282, Nolan 6283, Northern 6287, **Open 6294**, Opera 6297, **Parapsychology 6301**, Parham 6302, Pathfinder 6307, Peck 6311, Pope 6319, Post 6321, Preferred 6324, Prescott 6325, **Princess 6329**, Professional 6330, Project 6333, Realty 6347, Rochester 6357, Rochester 6358, Roothbert 6361, **Royal 6364**, Saagny 6369, Sakhi 6370, Samaritan 6372, Sandy 6373, Sawyer 6376, Scalp 6377, Schenectady 6382, **Schepp 6383**, Schiffner 6384, Scotts 6389, **Seneca 6394**, Sky 6403, Snayberger 6407, Solomon 6415, Spain 6417, **Spencer 6420**, St. Elmo 6424, Staten 6431, Statler 6432, Statue 6433, **Teach 6444**, Tozier 6460, **Trace 6461, Tsadra 6465**, Tzur 6468, **UJA 6470, United 6472**, United 6474, **United States 6479, USTA 6482, V-Day 6487**, Viele 6489, Visual 6492, Weeks 6506, Wells 6510, Westchester 6514, Whitcher 6516, Witmer 6524, **Women's 6528**, Woori 6531, Wu 6538, Young 6540, **Youth 6541**

North Carolina: Accel 6544, **American 6550**, Arps 6558, Atkins 6564, Barnes 6567, Beattie 6570, Blowing Rock 6575, Brooks 6583, Burke-Weber 6586, CarolinaEast 6591, Chaffer 6596, Children's 6600, **Cleft 6604**, Coffey 6608, Colburn 6610, Community 6612, Community 6613, Community 6614, Community 6615, Community 6616, Craven 6621, Cumberland 6624, Davie 6625, Davis 6628, Dietrich 6629, Dilcher 6630, Dinwiddle 6631, Durham 6634, DuVall 6635, East 6637, Eddy 6642, Edgerton 6643, Elizabeth 6645, Ellis 6647, Evrytanian 6651, Ferebee 6655, Ferree 6656, Foundation 6659, Foundation 6660, Fund 6667, Gate 6670, Gilbert 6672, Ginder 6674, Girl 6675, **Graham 6678**, Greenville 6682, Gross 6687, Haggai 6691, Halstead 6692, Harasimik 6693, Harmon 6694, Henderson 6696, Hilton 6699, Hoover 6702, Horsey 6703, Horvat 6704, Hughes 6708, **Insurance 6712**, Isaac 6716, Johns 6718, Jones 6722, Jordan 6724, **Karyae 6726**, Keasbey 6727, **Kimmel 6731**, Komarek 6733,

Leever 6740, Lenz 6741, Loflin 6747, Lutz 6753, Magdalena 6755, Material 6758, McClureTrust 6760, McMahan 6762, Medical 6769, Meserve 6771, **Military 6773**, Miller 6774, Moore 6777, Myers 6782, North 6794, North 6795, North Carolina 6796, North 6798, North Carolina 6802, Nucor 6805, Oates 6805, Outer 6806, **Pediatric 6814**, Pennsylvania 6815, Phoenix 6819, Polk 6821, Religious 6825, Rex 6827, Robinson 6838, Robinson 6839, Rollison 6840, RSPA 6844, Rumbough 6845, Russell 6846, **S.R.C. 6847**, Schug 6854, Selling 6857, Shelly 6859, Sirrine 6862, Stagner 6874, Stambaugh 6875, State 6876, State 6877, **Student 6883**, Tahquette 6884, **TASCA 6887**, Taylor 6888, Transylvania 6896, Triangle 6899, Troedson 6902, TW 6903, United 6906, **United 6908**, Wake 6912, Walker 6913, Watauga 6914, Williams 6921, Winston-Salem 6923, Woman's 6926

North Dakota: Cronquist 6936, Dakota 6937, Emmons 6938, Ernst 6939, Fargo 6940, Forum 6941, North Dakota 6946, United 6949, Wenstrom 6952

Ohio: Ace 6954, Adams 6956, Adena 6958, AGC 6960, AK Steel 6964, Akron 6965, Akron 6966, Alexander 6968, American 6972, Annual 6977, Ariel 6979, Ashland 6980, Barberton 6988, Bean 6991, Bentley 6995, Bernhard 6997, Birr 6998, Blanchard 7000, Blosser 7002, Bluecoats 7003, Bosaw 7006, **Brush 7016**, Bryan 7017, Burnham 7018, Carman 7024, Carney 7025, Children's 7033, Chillicothe 7034, Clayman 7039, Cleveland 7041, Cleveland 7042, Cleveland 7043, Cleveland 7044, Cleveland 7045, College 7049, College 7050, Columbia 7051, Community 7057, Community 7058, Community 7059, Community 7060, Community 7061, Community 7062, Community 7064, Coshocton 7065, Creech 7071, Crum 7072, Culture 7073, Cushwa 7074, Cushwa 7075, David 7079, Dayton 7082, DeBartolo 7084, Delaware 7086, Delaware 7087, Diederich 7088, Dutro 7094, Edgerton 7097, **Educational 7098**, Fairfield 7105, Fifty 7106, Fine 7108, Fitzgerald 7111, Ford 7113, Foundation 7115, Freese 7120, Gazin 7126, Good 7129, Granville 7133, Greene 7134, **Griffith 7136**, H.O.P.E. 7138, Hamilton 7139, Hart 7142, Hauss 7144, High 7150, Holmes 7152, Hoover 7154, Howley 7159, Hundred 7162, Hunter 7163, Jefferson 7174, Jewish 7177, Jones 7180, Kessel 7186, Kest 7187, Klinger 7198, Lakeland 7202, Lewis 7207, Ley 7208, Licking 7209, Louisville 7215, Lyons 7216, Marietta 7220, Marion 7221, McFarlin 7234, McIntire 7236, McLendon 7237, Mercer 7240, Mercy 7241, Miami 7242, Middletown 7245, Miller 7248, Miller 7250, Milroy 7251, Murphy 7261, **Murray 7262**, Muskingum 7263, Naples 7266, New Orphan 7268, Newton 7269, Nolley 7270, North 7272, Northwest 7273, Ohio 7278, Ohio 7279, Ohio 7281, Ohio 7282, OHSAA 7283, Padgett 7287, Parents 7290, Pearce 7295, Peoples 7297, Perry 7298, Piqua 7304, Plimpton 7305, Ratner 7314, Reaching 7315, Religion 7317, Reynolds 7319, Robertson 7324, Roddick 7325, Root 7327, Rotterman 7329, Russell 7331, Rutan 7332, Salem 7333, Salem 7334, Scioto 7339, Scripps 7340, Sebring 7341, Seefred 7342, Sharpe 7344, Simmons 7350, Simmons 7351, Smith 7356, Snow 7359, Springfield 7363, Stark 7366, Steigler 7368, Sullivan 7372, Taylor 7376, Tiffin 7383, Tomlinson's 7385, Troy 7388, TW 7392, Wagnalls 7408, Wakefield 7410, Wapakoneta 7412, Wayne 7415, Weiss 7416, Wester 7419, Willmott 7429, Wilson 7430, Wingett 7434, Working 7439, Workum 7440, Yeiser 7443, Yellow Springs 7444, YSI 7446

Oklahoma: Catholic 7456, **Chickasaw 7457**, Communities 7459, Covington 7462, Davis 7463, Driskell 7465, Evans 7466, **Foundation 7470**, Franklin 7471, Henry 7480, Holton 7481, Jeltz 7484, Johnson 7486, Kappa 7489, Masonic 7492, Mills 7496, Noble 7497, Oklahoma 7498, Oklahoma 7500, Oklahoma 7501, Oklahoma

7502, OWMA 7505, Peyton 7506, St. 7514, Steward-Newkirk 7516, Tulsa 7519, Tulsa 7520, University 7522

Oregon: Almquist 7531, Benton 7539, Black 7540, Central 7546, Coalition 7550, Corvallis 7558, Cottage 7559, **Culinary 7562**, Culver 7563, Daly 7565, Dargan 7567, Davies 7568, Depriest 7571, Dillard 7573, Ford 7578, Gienger 7581, Klamath 7592, Lampstand 7594, Major 7599, Mishler 7606, Morey 7610, Mount Angel 7611, North 7617, Oregon 7624, Oregon 7625, Oregon 7626, **Pacific 7627**, Pernot 7631, Portland 7633, Providence 7636, Renaissance 7642, Rhoden 7643, Richardson 7644, Richmond 7645, Rietman 7646, Schmidt 7655, Schroeder 7656, Shank 7658, Stevens 7667, Strayer 7668, Wattenberg 7678, Weir 7679

Pennsylvania: AAA 7688, Allegheny 7696, App 7708, Armstrong 7710, Arnold 7713, **Association 7717**, Basila 7724, Benz 7729, Berks 7730, Berwind 7732, Biondo 7734, **Botstiber 7740**, Boyle 7742, Brown 7750, Bush 7754, Butterer 7755, Carmell 7758, Central 7763, Chester 7764, Children's 7765, Christ 7767, Cohen 7774, Columbus 7776, Comcast 7777, Community 7780, Community 7781, Community 7782, Community 7784, Copp 7792, Cross 7799, Crossroads 7800, Daly 7804, Davis 7806, **Delta 7810**, Dodd 7812, Dotson 7815, Doverspike 7816, **Early 7817**, Elk 7821, Elwyn 7824, Epstein 7827, EQT 7829, Erickson 7830, Erie 7831, First 7841, Fischer 7843, Fleisher 7848, Foundation 7852, Foundation 7853, Foundations 7854, Founder's 7855, Freedom 7857, French 7858, Friend 7860, Frozen 7862, **GBU 7866**, Ghidotti 7868, Gillespie 7870, Golden 7872, Golden 7873, Goldstein 7875, Greater 7880, Harley 7886, Hartman 7892, Hearn 7898, Heart 7899, Hirtzel 7910, Holy 7911, Huth 7914, Independent 7917, **International 7920**, Ivy 7923, Ivy 7924, Jeanes 7926, Jefferson 7927, **Jewish 7929, Jewish 7930**, Johnson 7931, Keefer 7933, Kidney 7935, Klemstine 7938, Lancaster 7941, Lancaster 7942, Lancaster 7944, Lancaster 7945, **Law 7950**, Lehigh 7952, Lehigh Valley 7953, Leighow 7955, Maley 7967, Mattioli 7972, McKee 7976, McNeil 7979, McRoberts 7980, Michaels 7983, Miller 7987, Mohn 7990, Mussina 7999, Nestor 8004, North 8009, North 8010, ONS 8015, Panagos 8017, PENCON 8020, Pennsylvania 8024, **Pennsylvania 8026**, Pennsylvania 8029, Perrone 8032, Philadelphia 8036, Philadelphia 8037, Philadelphia 8038, Piper 8045, Pittsburgh 8048, Podiatry 8052, Postles 8055, Prescott 8059, Pressley 8061, Print 8063, Project 8065, Psea 8066, Pyle 8068, Reading 8071, Realize 8072, Reitnauer 8074, Rohrer 8079, Rosenfeld 8082, Ruskin 8084, Ryan 8085, Saak 8086, Schock 8087, Scholarship 8089, Schuylkill 8090, Schuylkill 8092, Schwab 8093, Scranton 8094, Shaull 8098, Shoemaker 8100, Shuman 8102, Sinden 8105, Skillman 8107, Snyder 8116, Stuck 8136, Thoburn 8143, Thomas 8144, Toth 8148, Tyndale 8153, Union 8154, United 8155, **USWA 8157**, Van Horne 8159, Varner 8162, Vasset 8163, Voorhies 8171, Wachter 8172, Walter 8173, Walz 8174, Washington 8176, Waverly 8177, Wayne 8178, Webber 8180, Wein 8184, Wesley 8186, Williams 8193, Wittmer 8199, Wolf 8201, Worthington 8208, York 8212, York 8213, Yount 8216, Zoll 8220

Puerto Rico: Harvey 8222, Puerto Rico 8223, Unanue 8224

Rhode Island: Anctil 8228, Atkins 8232, Ayer 8234, Ayers 8235, Babcock 8236, Barillaro 8240, Blakeslee 8245, Blanchard 8246, Boghossian 8247, Botsford 8248, Brennan 8251, Burke 8254, Christy 8257, Club 8263, Cook 8273, Croston 8279, Cummings 8280, Cuno 8281, DeLoura 8284, Dix 8285, Fales 8290, Faunce 8292, Gates 8298, Gooding 8300, Guertin 8306, Hunt 8314, Jakobi 8315, King 8321, Magraw 8330, Masonic 8336, Meriden 8344, Miles 8345, Miller 8347,

Munson 8353, Nicholson 8355, Norman 8356, Palmer 8362, Pappines 8365, Peck 8367, Price 8373, Pryde 8376, Putnam 8377, Rhode Island 8381, Rimmele 8383, Robbins 8385, Robinson 8386, Rolland 8387, Ronci 8388, Sasso 8390, Schuyler 8394, Smith 8403, Smith 8408, Smythe 8409, Stokes 8415, Syder 8418, Taber 8419, Todd 8424, Urann 8429, Wells 8435, Wiles 8437, Yaeger 8443

South Carolina: Anderson 8446, Austin 8449, **AVX 8450**, Boyne 8452, Central 8457, Coastal 8464, Community 8465, Earle 8470, Gift 8475, Greenville 8477, Hebrew 8481, Horne 8484, Kennedy 8489, Love 8491, Miracle 8494, Palmetto 8501, Parsons 8502, Professional 8504, Sherman 8506, South 8512, South 8513, Spartanburg 8514, Tucker 8517, West 8519

South Dakota: Black 8521, Black 8522, Brookings 8523, Clausen 8524, Doolittle 8527, Graham 8531, Howard 8534, McCormick 8536, Sioux Falls 8538, South 8542, Tessier 8544, Watertown 8546, Westendorf 8547, Yellow 8548

Tennessee: Acts 8551, **Alpha 8554**, Boys 8562, Cash 8565, Children's 8573, Community 8578, Community 8579, Dollywood 8584, East 8587, Fengler 8591, Grace 8595, Graham 8596, Hassell 8597, Holtsford 8603, Jewell 8608, Johnson 8610, JSA 8611, Keel 8612, Lead 8616, Mercy 8619, Methodist 8621, Middle 8624, Niswonger 8630, Rains 8634, Regal 8635, Richardson 8636, Ross 8638, **Scarlett 8640**, Schmidt 8641, Splawn 8648, **United 8657**, Weems 8661, Wellmont 8662, Wills 8664

Texas: Advanced 8667, Albaugh 8671, Alexander 8672, Alpha 8674, Amarillo 8675, Amarillo 8676, **American 8677, American 8678, American 8682**, Anderson 8689, Associated 8692, Austin 8696, Austin 8697, Austin 8699, Ayres 8700, Barnsley 8702, Beefmaster 8708, Borelli 8716, Bragan 8719, Brazos 8720, Broady 8722, Brown 8725, Chambers 8743, Chapman 8744, Chaudhary 8745, Children 8746, Cleburne 8753, Clifford 8754, Coastal 8755, Common 8758, Communities 8759, Community 8762, Community 8763, Community 8764, Cooper 8771, Cooper 8772, Cox 8774, Cypress 8780, Dallas 8783, Dallas 8784, Dallas 8785, Dallas 8786, Danciger 8787, Deering 8788, **Dell 8789**, Deupree 8792, Diffenbaugh 8794, Donnelly 8797, Driver 8799, Eady 8802, East 8803, East 8804, **Education 8807**, Ehlers 8810, El Paso 8811, Forever 8825, Fort Worth 8829, Foundation 8830, Genesis 8836, Gilpatrick 8842, Gnade 8843, Godwin 8844, Goertz 8845, Goff 8846, Golden 8847, Hachar 8849, Hamman 8851, Harris 8856, Havens 8857, Healthcare 8861, Hispanic 8869, Hispanic 8871, Houston 8876, Houston 8878, **Houston 8880**, Houston 8881, Houston 8883, Huddleston 8886, Ingram 8893, Jamaica 8896, Janson 8898, Jones 8901, **Komen 8910**, Lake 8913, Lorelle 8924, Lubbock 8926, Malloy 8934, Maness 8935, Mayfield 8939, McCaulay 8940, McCrory 8941, McDaniel 8942, McDonald 8943, Mead 8949, **Mensa 8952**, Methodist 8954, Midland 8957, Miller 8959, Montgomery 8966, Munson 8973, Murphy 8974, Music 8976, **MVP 8978**, Nabors 8979, Nation 8981, **National 8984**, National 8985, **National 8986, North 8992**, O'Brien 8994, Oglesby 8995, O'Neal 8997, **OneSight 8998**, Owen 9000, Paris 9003, Paris 9004, Passport 9005, Patout 9006, Penrose 9011, Permian 9013, Pettinger 9015, Philadelphia 9018, Piper 9022, Prater 9027, Rawls 9032, **Reese 9034**, Riffe 9039, Robinson 9042, Robinson 9043, Rotary 9047, **Ryrie 9049**, S.G.K.&G. 9050, Salesmanship 9052, San Antonio 9055, San Antonio 9056, Santander 9061, Schull 9062, Schumann 9063, Schwab 9064, Smith 9078, Smith 9079, South 9085, Stark 9101, Sunnyside 9103, Tartt 9110, Terry 9113, Texas 9114, Texas 9116, Texas 9117, Texas 9119, Texas 9122, Texas 9123, Texas 9126, Texas 9127, Texas 9128, Thomas 9133, Thompson 9134, Today

9137, Turner 9140, UFCW 9141, **Vietnamese 9149**, Von 9152, Waco 9153, Wagner 9154, Waltom 9155, Ward 9156, Wichita 9165, Wilkins 9167, Wine 9170, Woltman 9176, Wolverton 9177, Women's 9178, Woods 9182, Yoder 9185, Young 9187

Utah: American 9191, Anaya 9192, Bamberger 9193, Bybee 9196, EnergySolutions 9199, Gomez 9200, Groesbeck 9202, Intermountain 9209, Kolob 9214, Luttrell 9217, Miller 9220, Park 9221, Ross 9223, Whiz 9231, Woodward 9233

Vermont: Arlington 9235, Barrows 9236, Charitable 9240, Danville 9244, General 9248, Huffman 9252, Keal 9253, Keniston 9254, Vermont 9269, Warner 9272, Windham 9273

Virgin Islands: Rutnik 9276

Virginia: AFP 9280, AHC 9281, Air 9284, **American 9292, American 9293, American 9300, American 9301, American 9306, American 9310, American 9312**, Arlington 9314, **Army 9315, Asparagus 9318, Association 9322**, Association 9323, Bedford 9324, Bell 9325, Blair 9326, **Brown 9329, Burger 9331**, Carpenter's 9336, **Club 9343**, College 9344, Community 9345, Community 9346, Community 9348, Community 9349, Community 9350, **Cooke 9352**, Cooke 9353, **Datatel 9358, Dolphin 9362**, Doughty 9364, Duerr 9365, English 9374, Fary 9376, **Foundation 9380, Foundation 9381, Foundation 9382**, Greater 9388, Grobel 9389, Hampton 9391, Henley 9393, Hughes 9401, **IDSA 9402, International 9405**, International 9406, Johns 9409, Johnson 9410, Keesee 9413, Korean 9417, Lincoln 9421, Linhart 9422, Luce 9425, Lynchburg 9426, Maloney 9427, MAPGA 9428, **Marine 9430**, Maude 9432, **MedEvac 9433, Military 9436**, Minor 9437, Missionary 9438, Morgan 9440, Nansemond 9443, **National 9444**, National 9448, National 9449, **National 9453**, National 9454, **National 9455**, National 9458, Navy-Marine 9462, Newhouse 9463, Northern 9466, Northern 9467, **NRA 9469**, Patient 9476, Petersburg 9480, **Plumbing 9483, PMMI 9484**, Randolph 9491, Richmond 9494, Robinson 9495, Sale 9496, Sentara 9502, Shingleton 9503, **Sigma 9505**, Smith 9507, Society 9510, Strong 9516, **Thanks 9519**, Thompson 9521, Tidewater 9522, Tidewater 9523, Tidewater 9524, Treakle 9525, United 9528, United 9532, Utility 9535, **VAW/VRC 9538**, Virginia 9540, Virginia 9542, Ware 9543, Womack 9552, Wythe-Bland 9553

Washington: AGC 9555, Alliance 9557, Allied 9558, Arise 9561, ARK 9562, Bishop 9571, Blue 9574, Bohnett 9575, Bradshaw 9577, Children's 9587, Children's 9588, Colf 9593, Columbia 9595, Community 9599, Community 9600, Coulter 9602, First 9612, Gasparovich 9620, George 9622, Grays 9624, Haller 9629, Hansen 9632, Heily 9633, JTM 9646, Kawabe 9647, Kelsey 9651, Kent 9652, KLQ 9655, Leavitt 9659, Lochland 9663, Lundberg 9665, Martinez 9668, Maxwell 9669, McCoy 9671, McFarland 9672, McMillen 9673, Memorial 9674, Milton 9676, Northwest 9684, Osteopathic 9690, Pacific 9693, **PAH 9695**, Palmer 9696, Pride 9702, Renton 9705, Rural 9711, San Juan 9714, Seattle 9717, Seattle 9719, Sequim 9722, Spokane 9730, Tacoma 9734, Three 9735, Vancouver 9740, **Vista 9742**, Washington 9747, Washington 9749, Washington 9750, Wittman 9756, Women 9757

West Virginia: Beckley 9766, Bowen 9768, Camden-Clark 9770, Canady 9771, Castrodale 9773, City 9775, Community 9776, Community 9777, Craig 9778, Cruise 9779, Eastern 9780, Emerich 9781, Faris 9784, Haddad 9787, Hinton 9790, Hollandsworth 9791, I.O.O.F. 9792, Jefferson 9793, Kanawha 9794, Logan 9797, Morgan 9803, Nicholas 9805, Pais 9807, Parkersburg 9808, Price 9810, Price 9811, Serra 9814, Starcher 9816, Timms 9823, Whittaker 9828, Wolfe 9829, Your 9831

Wisconsin: Aber 9832, AgSource 9833, Ariens 9838, Backlin 9843, Beal 9846, Bruneo 9854, Calumet 9856, Carlisle 9858, Collins 9864, Community 9866, Community 9867, Community 9868, Community 9869, Connor 9872, Couleecap 9873, Cuan 9874, Door 9878, **EAA 9880**, Eggen 9882, **Entomological 9884**, Environmental 9885, Experimental 9887, Fort 9894, Fund 9902, **Funeral 9903**, Gehl 9905, Grafton 9909, Hamp 9915, Incourage 9925, Jansen 9929, Jewish 9931, Johnson 9935, Jones 9936, Keller 9939, Kenosha 9941, Kenosha 9942, Korupp 9947, La Crosse 9948, Leitzell 9952, Lyons 9953, Madison 9955, Mari's 9958, Marshfield 9960, Michelson 9969, Milwaukee 9970, MMAC 9973, Mullenbach 9975, New Glarus 9980, Oshkosh 9988, Pagel 9990, Partners 9991, Peterson 9992, Phillips 9994, Prader-Willi 9997, Prohaska 9999, Racine 10001, Remington 10006, Rhodes 10008, Riverview 10011, Robins 10012, Rotary 10014, Ruebush 10015, Rutledge 10016, Sauey 10018, Sauk 10019, Shallow 10029, Shopko 10032, Squires 10042, St. Croix 10043, Stamm 10046, Stateline 10047, Tate 10050, Trek 10053, Tschirgi 10054, University 10055, Viroqua 10059, Walker 10062, Ward 10063, Watertown 10064, Wetenkamp 10070, Wisconsin 10074, Wisconsin 10078, Wisconsin 10080, Wisconsin 10084, Women's 10085, Women's 10087, Yakich 10089

Wyoming: Community 10099, Davis 10102, Doherty 10103, Glassber 10106, Hladky 10107, Likins 10111, Likins-Masonic 10112, Neilson 10115, Sheridan 10119, SouthEast 10120, Spacht 10121, Wyoming 10126

Seed money

California: Black 414, **Draper 547**, Durfee 549, **Foundation 589, International 691, Ploughshares 872,** Theatre 1044

Connecticut: Branford 1338, Elmseed 1384, Hartley 1401

District of Columbia: **National 1692**

Indiana: Community 2997, Warren 3216

Maine: Maine 3715

Maryland: **Epilepsy 3821, Osteogenesis 3906**

Michigan: **Collectors 4387,** United 4649

Minnesota: Northwest 4817

New Jersey: **Puffin 5549**

New York: **Career 5816, Echoing 5952, New 6264,** Saltonstall 6371, **Trickle 6463**

South Carolina: Cultural 8469

Virginia: Virginia 9539

Washington: **Ji 9644**

Stipends

Alaska: Rasmuson 132

Arizona: Valley 255, Youth 259

Arkansas: Arkansas 266

California: CounterPULSE 525, **Getty 614, Kaiser 716,** LEF 741, Liberty 744, Merage 785, Wu 1104

Connecticut: **Weir 1481**

District of Columbia: Afterschool 1532, **American 1545, Citizens 1603, Congressional 1607**

Florida: Senior 2059

Georgia: **American 2113**

Maine: Maine 3714

Maryland: **American 3761,** Baltimore 3782, **Evergreen 3824, Foundation 3829,** Maryland 3872

Massachusetts: **American 3963,** Baystate 3979, Berkshire 3986, **City 4024,** President 4230, Yard 4327, Youth 4329

Michigan: Beaumont 4352, Oakwood 4567, **Society 4610**

Minnesota: **Camargo 4706,** New York 4812

New Jersey: Honeywell 5472, Newark 5525

New Mexico: Santa Fe 5648

New York: American 5691, **American 5692,** Arts 5726, Associated 5735, **Bibliographical 5762,** Center 5832, chashama 5841, Eyebeam 5970, Federation 5979, **Franklin 6008, Legacy 6158,** MADRE, 6182, Mitchell 6218, **OPERA 6296,** Smack 6405, **Social 6409,** Tzur 6468, **USTA 6482**

North Carolina: **American 6551**

Ohio: Mercy 7241, Thurber 7382

Rhode Island: Brown 8253

Utah: **Sundance 9227**

Virginia: **American 9305,** Wolf 9551

Washington: 911 9554, Sewell 9723

Wisconsin: Wisconsin 10080

Wyoming: **Ucross 10123**

Student aid/financial aid

Georgia: Navy 2214

Missouri: **St. Louis 5105**

Pennsylvania: **Law 7950**

Student loans—to individuals

Alabama: Chapman 21, Dunlap 33

Arizona: Dougherty 186

Arkansas: SHARE 307, Veasey 322

California: Arques 372, Baker 397, Bank 398, Community 513, Health 651, Jewish 707, Methodist 787, Price 880, San Diego 931, Santa 954, Santa Barbara 955, Scholarship 965, SKB 991, Stanley 1018, Warner 1086

Connecticut: Atwood 1326, Orange 1439, Rubinow 1453, Sullivan 1469

Florida: American 1770, AWS 1789, Corbett 1851, Delta 1859, Fellows 1875, Florida 1878, Gulf 1899, KML 1941, Lauffer 1947, Smith 2064

Georgia: Garden 2182, Medical 2211, Student 2245, Walker 2256, Whelchel 2263

Illinois: **American 2375, Anesthesia 2398,** Berner 2423, Bogardus 2428, Catt 2465, Gossett 2590, Griswold 2593, Jewish 2657, Kooi 2678, Lindsay 2694, Marshall 2709, McClain 2717, McKee 2723, Meade 2727, Mellinger 2740, Pingel 2791, Reller 2813, Rogers 2830, Schwarz 2845, Shumaker 2854, Stratton 2877, Woods 2937

Indiana: Alpha 2948, Baber 2963, Henderson 3056, Indiana 3070, Keller 3084, McKinney 3112, Whitley 3226, Williams 3228

Iowa: Burchfield 3250, Community 3264, Gidley 3285, Great 3287, Henry 3297, Hill 3299, King 3319, Lage 3321, Lindhart 3327, Mahanay 3330, Mongan 3338, **P.E.O. 3352,** Pierce 3357, Preston 3360, Pritchard 3361, Scanlan 3370, Scanlan 3371, Van Buren 3403

Kansas: Baker 3417, Fingersh 3442, Kansas 3471, McKinnis 3482, Pape 3498, Porter 3506

Kentucky: Owenton 3610, Trover 3629

Maine: Davenport 3693, Ross 3732, Thom 3739

Maryland: **Central 3797, Hariri 3839,** Jewish 3853, Raskob 3919, Thorn 3941

Massachusetts: Austin 3975, Community 4029, Hopedale 4112, Millman 4176, New 4194, President 4230

Michigan: Brenske 4367, Davenport 4404, Eddy 4413, Jeffers 4486, Kelly 4498, Reid 4587, VanKley 4656

Minnesota: Adams 4681, Petraborg 4822, Redwood 4835, Thurston 4868

Mississippi: Biglane 4897, Day 4904

Missouri: Hamilton 5012, Hutchins 5021, Lowrie 5038, Marymount 5046, Scholarship 5084, Skillman 5100, **St. Louis 5105**

Nebraska: Emerson 5201, Johnson 5222, McNay 5232

New Hampshire: Hitchcock 5328, New Hampshire 5352, New Hampshire 5353

New Jersey: Adelphic 5381, Eastern 5438, Holman 5471, Lasko 5494, McCready 5502

New Mexico: **American 5611**

New York: Bath 5755, Coleman 5865, Hodges 6074, Howe 6079, March 6189, Martin 6193, Northrup 6288, Ontario 6293, Parker 6303, Rau 6345, Schenck 6381

North Carolina: Clark 6603, Cotterel 6619, Ferree 6656, Grim 6683, **Karyae 6726,** NC 6788, Perry 6816, Rennie 6826, Stonecutter 6880, Thomas 6891, Wellons 6916, Winston-Salem 6923

North Dakota: Brown 6935, McKenzie 6944

Ohio: **Arab 6978,** Ashland 6980, Barnes 6989, Blosser 7002, Bowen 7008, Evers 7103, Firestone 7109, Jewish 7177, Louisville 7215, McClain 7227, McDonald 7233, Mercer 7240, Milroy 7251, Ohio 7282, Rogers 7326, Rutan 7332, Shinnick 7347, Smith 7353, Smith 7354, Stark 7366

Oklahoma: Gibson 7475, Hathcoat 7479, Johnson 7485

Oregon: Oregon 7626, Stevens 7667

Pennsylvania: Abrams 7691, Adams 7692, Allegheny 7696, American 7702, Benford 7727, Bonner 7738, Burch 7753, Butterer 7755, Community 7784, Flegal 7846, Foundation 7853, Gibson 7869, March 7968, McMillen 7978, Murphy 7998, Pennsylvania 8024, Ross 8083, Shaulis 8097, Welch 8185, Williams 8194

Rhode Island: Coe 8267

South Carolina: O'Neill 8500, Springs 8515

South Dakota: Cozard 8525, Kramer 8535

Tennessee: Latimer 8613, Weems 8661

Texas: Ayres 8700, Brockman 8723, Cannon 8734, Haverlah 8858, Hill 8867, Ingram 8893, Long 8923, Maguire 8932, Marti 8936, Mayfield 8939, **Mehta 8951,** Mercer 8953, Millhollon 8962, Pearce 9007, Percy 9012, Piper 9022, Sipes 9076, Southwestern 9092, Swinney 9106, Texas 9120

Vermont: Scott 9260, Vermont 9266

Virginia: Cooley, 9354, **EduCap 9371,** Harry 9392, Kennard 9415, **Military 9436,** Orphan 9474, Williamson 9549, Womack 9552

Washington: Educational 9606, Heily 9633, Omega 9688

West Virginia: Feoppel 9785, Harless 9788

Wisconsin: Davey 9876, Wisconsin 10080

Wyoming: Bryan 10095, Clark 10097, Curtis 10101, Gillet 10104, Perkins 10117

Support to graduates or students of specific schools

Alabama: Alsite 6, Alsobrook 7, Batre 14, Boyd 18, Community 27, Finlay 37, Freels 40, Griswold 43, Harmeson 47, Harrell 48, Holland 51, Killgore 55, Lucash 56, Martin 59, Moeschle 64, Owens 67, Padolf 68, Sheffield 78, Simpson 79, TAV 83, Vulcan 88, Wollman 94, Yanamura 95

Alaska: Alaska 97, Homer 117, Schwantes 135, Usibelli 147, West 149

Arizona: Alhambra 153, Arizona 157, Breeding 173, Brinker 174, Community 182, Friedman 197, Ingebritson 202, LaForce 209, Lewis 211, Northern 222, Peoria 225, Phoenix 226

Arkansas: Allen, 260, Baptist 269, Bearden 270, Buck 272, Cabot 273, El Dorado 277, Endeavor 278, Finkbeiner 279, Gillespie 280, Halstead 281, Hamm 282, Hornlein 284, Keltner 287, McDonald 290, Munyon 292, Northeast 298, Ohlendorf 299, Pierce 302, Raef 303, SHARE 307, Smith 310, Southern 312, Terry 317, Trinity 319, Union 321, Veasey 322

California: Aaron 332, Armstrong 371, Asian 379, Assistance 385, Bartholomew 399, Bartlett 400, Baskin 402, Blackburn 415, Boand 416, Boyer 420, Brown 424, Busch 431, Cabrillo 433, Cacique 434, Cain 436, Cal 438, Cal 439, California 445, California 453, California 458, California 459, Central 474, Chessall 481, Chrysopolae 497, Ciatti 500, Clark 502, Coastal 504, Collister 506, Community 510, Community 512, Community 513, Community 518, Conner 521, Conquistador 522,

Curley 531, Dudley-Vehmeyer-Brown 548, Emery 563, Federal 572, Foundation 584, Glover 624, Golden 627, Gunn 640, Guslander 641, Hamilton 646, Harbison 647, Healdsburg 650, **Hertz 658**, Hiebler 660, High 662, Horn 668, Humboldt 671, James 701, James 702, Justin 715, Kiersted 720, Klicka 722, Kornberg 725, La 728, Lancaster 735, Level 743, Lippert 746, Long Beach 754, Los Altos 755, Low 759, Lucky 760, Lynch 761, Lytel 763, Madden 765, Mammoth 767, Marin 772, McComb 778, **McConnell 779**, Mercy 786, Miedema 790, Mills 794, Modoc 801, Morris 806, Pack 851, Placer 870, Poole 877, Pursuit 888, Ramona's 896, Rancho 897, Rio 911, Rossmoor 922, S.L. 924, Sacramento 926, San Diego 934, San Francisco 947, San Luis 951, Santa Barbara 955, Santa 958, Schmidt 964, Scholarship 965, Science 968, Sedler 972, Shasta 978, Siff 984, Signer 985, Silicon 986, Stanislaus 1017, Stauffer 1019, Stedman 1020, Stephens 1022, Stern 1024, Stone 1026, Swift 1036, Tracy 1053, University 1073, Ventura 1081, Ward 1084, Wickham 1094, Wilcox 1095, World 1101, Yosemite 1106, Zider 1109

Colorado: Bianco 1129, Campbell 1139, Cibrowski 1147, Clark 1149, Clark 1150, Cocker 1151, Colorado 1161, Denver 1179, Douglas 1184, Durango 1185, Eagle 1186, Eagle 1187, East 1188, Elizondo 1191, Ethridge 1192, Flatirons 1195, Front 1200, Hanson 1209, Heathcock 1212, Holt 1214, Impact 1219, Jefferson 1221, Kaiser 1224, Langston 1228, Lasater 1229, Layton 1230, Light 1231, MacGregor 1236, Merry 1238, Molloy 1241, Mountain 1244, Mulford 1245, Newland 1249, Norwood 1252, Pikes 1258, Red 1266, Renfrow 1267, Rutherford 1275, Vail 1302, Veirs 1303

Connecticut: Albero 1316, Bauer 1333, Branford 1338, Bristol 1340, Brown 1341, CCSU 1349, Chariott 1352, **Coast 1359**, Community 1361, Connecticut 1366, Devon 1376, Eastman 1382, Fairfield 1387, Fox 1391, Fromson 1392, Fuller 1393, Graham 1396, Hammers 1397, Hartford 1399, **Knights 1412**, Litchfield 1415, Manchester 1420, Miceli-Wings 1422, North 1434, Norwalk 1435, Norwalk 1436, Orange 1439, Paul 1440, Phelps 1443, Ridgefield 1448, Scott 1457, Sheridan 1460, Spirol 1462, Sullivan 1469, Weller 1482, Windsor 1487, Zane 1492

Delaware: Delaware 1500, Gordy 1510, Hirsch 1512

District of Columbia: Albert 1596, Community 1605, **Development 1614**, District 1618, Dutko 1619, Ellington 1620, **Fund 1634, Landscape 1668, Marshall 1674**

Florida: Amateis 1768, Arcadian 1779, Art 1783, Bailey 1790, Beall 1794, Bennett 1797, Bradish 1805, Broward 1810, Caples 1816, Citrus 1830, Columbus 1835, Community 1839, Community 1840, Community 1841, Community 1842, Community 1844, Corbett 1851, Deeley 1858, DeVoe 1861, Distilled 1863, Englewood 1870, Exchange 1873, Finley 1876, Flordia Keys 1883, Florida 1885, Fort 1890, Grossman 1897, Harrelson 1903, Haven 1907, Hoeting 1917, Hunt 1924, Hurst 1925, Immokalee 1926, Indian 1927, Johnston 1931, Lake-Sumter 1944, LeGore 1948, Leinbach 1949, Manley 1961, Martin 1964, Martin 1965, McGinty 1971, Mead 1973, Moore 1982, Mount 1987, Murray 1990, Music 1991, Okeechobee 2003, Olliff 2004, Orange 2007, Orlando 2008, Ott 2009, Palm 2011, Perry 2016, **Prime 2025**, Rayni 2030, Reinhold 2034, Rigsby 2038, Ruegamer 2042, Russell 2044, Ryals 2045, School 2054, Scott 2055, Selinger 2058, Southwest 2067, State 2073, Stearn 2074, Strahan 2076, Sunburst 2079, Thornton 2086, Tracy 2089, University 2096

Georgia: Amos-Cheves 2117, Anderson 2118, Bowen 2128, Brown 2132, Community 2150, Community 2151, Community 2153, Decatur 2161, DeSana 2164, Dickens 2166, Fisher 2177, Hall 2191, Kajima 2199, Kaplan 2200, Kumar 2203, **Phi Mu 2222**, R.A.C.K 2226, Sapelo 2231, Savannah

2232, **TAPPI 2247**, University 2254, Warren 2257, Wetherbee 2262, Wine 2266, WinShape 2267, Wood 2268

Hawaii: Ching 2275, Grove 2286, Hana 2287, Hawaii 2289, Hemenway 2293, Rehabilitation 2316, Towle 2323, University 2324

Idaho: Haugse 2332, IDACORP 2334, Lewis-Clark 2339, Mitchell 2342, Nahas 2343, Ramsdale 2345, Shultz 2348, Smallwood 2350

Illinois: Adamson 2357, Alberts 2361, Allhands 2362, Anderson 2395, Andrew 2396, Barber 2411, Barnard 2412, Barnes 2413, Barr 2414, Becker 2417, Beebe 2418, Bender 2419, Beneke 2420, Benjamin 2421, Betts 2424, Biederstedt 2425, Blazek 2427, Bolingbrook 2430, Boulos 2431, Boyle 2433, Breckinridge 2435, Brege 2436, Brewer 2437, Brown 2441, Bulkley 2445, Burgess 2447, Burton 2449, Cabot 2455, Camp 2458, Carter 2461, Caruso-Sperl 2462, Centralia 2467, Chicago 2475, Children 2477, Coin 2487, Coleman 2488, Community 2496, Community 2497, Corpening 2500, Costilow 2502, Davis 2509, Davis 2510, DeKalb 2514, District 2517, Dodd 2518, Dole 2520, Doody 2522, Drummond 2526, Dudley 2527, Eberhardt 2531, Edwardsville 2536, Ekstrand 2538, Elburn 2539, English 2548, Erickson 2549, Evans 2551, Everett 2553, Ferris 2560, Fildes 2561, Fleurot 2563, Foundation 2567, **Foundry 2571**, Fredenburgh 2575, Gabler 2577, Gaffney 2578, Garwin 2579, Geneseo 2580, Geneva 2581, Graber 2591, Guenther 2595, Halsey 2597, Hardin 2599, Harper 2600, Harrison 2601, Hayes 2604, Health 2605, Hefti 2611, Herbert 2614, Hill 2617, Hoover/Hoehn 2624, Illinois 2646, Illinois 2648, Irrevocable 2653, Jackson 2656, Just 2664, Kander 2666, Karnes 2668, Kiwanis 2671, Knecht 2673, Kohl 2677, Kooi 2678, Koranda 2679, Laux 2686, Lemmer 2688, Lenore 2689, Levin 2691, Lower 2698, Luley 2700, Marion 2708, Marshall 2709, Mason 2712, Masters 2715, McAllister 2716, McMullan 2726, Meade 2727, Menn 2731, Miller 2734, Miller 2735, Moline 2737, Morrison 2738, Munson 2740, Northern 2759, Oak Park 2761, Oakes 2762, Olivet 2767, O'Malley 2768, Ott 2774, Palos 2778, Peeples 2781, Perisho-Nina 2783, Perkins 2784, Pierson 2789, Pilchard 2790, Pingel 2791, Prine 2800, Puckett 2802, Pugh 2803, Rainey 2807, Reinheimer 2811, Reiss 2812, Reller 2813, REO 2814, Reynolds 2818, Richland 2819, Rinker 2821, Rittenhouse 2822, Roberts 2825, Robinson 2826, Ross 2832, Roy 2836, Scherer 2840, Schroeder 2843, Schuler 2844, Shapiro 2849, Shinaberry 2852, Short 2853, Smith 2859, Smysor 2860, Southern 2865, St. Clair 2869, Sterling 2872, Stockert 2874, Sweitzer 2883, Taylor 2885, Testamentary 2890, Thauer 2891, **TPAA 2895**, Veeder 2908, Villwock 2909, Wagenknecht 2911, Walters 2916, Waubonsee 2918, Wells 2923, Whitney 2926, Wilson 2929, Wolfer 2932, **Woodbury 2936**, Woods 2937, Zearing 2940

Indiana: **Alpha 2952**, Arsenal 2959, Baber 2963, Ball 2964, Benton 2966, Blackford 2967, Boonshot 2971, Brookville 2973, Brown 2974, Brown 2976, Buerger 2977, Carroll-Wyatt 2978, Cass 2979, Catholic 2980, Community 2993, Community 2994, Community 2995, Community 2996, Community 2997, Community 2999, Community 3000, Community 3001, Community 3002, Community 3003, Community 3004, Community 3005, Dearborn 3012, Decatur 3013, Dubois 3020, Dunn 3021, Dye 3022, Elkhart 3024, Ellison 3025, Epler 3026, Fayette 3028, Foundations 3033, Francisco 3034, Frees 3038, Gibson 3043, Gilmore 3044, Greene 3045, Greenwell 3046, Harber 3051, Harris 3053, Henderson 3056, Hendricks 3057, Heritage 3059, Houghton 3063, Humphrey 3066, King 3087, Kosciusko 3091, Kuhner 3092, LaGrange 3093, Leo 3097, Line 3102, Logansport 3104, Loogootee 3105, Madison 3106, Mahnken 3107, Mann 3108, Marshall 3110, Montgomery

3114, Moore 3116, Moorman 3117, Neel 3125, Nesty 3126, Oberdorfer 3129, Ohio 3131, **Organization 3132**, Osborn 3134, Payton 3141, Pearson 3142, Plummer 3148, Portland 3151, Putnam 3154, Randolph 3156, Reeves 3158, Reeves 3159, Richardt 3160, Riddleberger 3163, Rush 3167, Russell 3168, Salin 3170, Schmidt 3173, Scholarship 3174, Scott 3177, Sellers 3178, Seymour 3179, Shiel 3180, Shoop 3181, Slaughter 3185, South 3189, Stanley 3192, Steuben 3193, Stiens 3194, Storer 3195, Stout 3196, Thorntown 3199, Tipton 3201, Wayne 3217, Wells 3220, Western 3222, Whitley 3226, Williams 3227, Williams 3228, Winchester 3229

Iowa: Ames 3236, Andersen 3237, Anderson 3238, Andrews 3240, Bathalter 3244, Bishop 3245, Bishop 3246, Brummer 3249, Burchfield 3250, Carroll 3253, Carter 3254, Chase 3256, Community 3263, Crozier 3269, Delaware 3271, Denton 3272, Diehl 3275, Elbert 3277, Eychaner 3278, Frisbie 3281, Gerling 3284, Gidley 3285, Griffith 3289, Hulton 3301, Igou 3303, Iowa 3309, Jay 3312, Jepsen 3314, Johnson 3315, Kansas 3316, Keig 3317, King 3319, Lage 3321, Lake-Matthews 3322, Marek 3331, Matheson 3332, McKay 3334, Michels 3337, Munter 3340, Murphy 3341, Murray 3342, North 3345, Northeast 3346, Palmer 3353, Pierce 3357, Pritchard 3361, Raider 3362, Scanlan 3371, Schlagenbusch 3372, Schrader 3374, Schroeder 3375, Shellabarger 3378, Sherman 3379, Sinek 3381, Siouxland 3382, Spencer 3386, Stearns 3389, Stewart 3390, Stubbs 3392, Swensrud 3393, Swiler 3394, Taylor 3395, Waverly 3406

Kansas: Abell 3411, Arnold 3414, Babson's 3416, Baker 3417, Beal 3419, Coffman 3427, Davis 3430, Davis 3431, Eggleston 3436, Ehlers 3437, Ehlers 3438, Ellis 3440, Fink 3443, Fort 3444, French 3446, Griffith 3450, Henderson 3454, Hines 3455, Hoar 3456, Hoy 3458, Hunter 3459, Independence 3461, Jordaan 3465, Kansas 3468, Kleppe 3474, Loofbourrow 3480, Mansfield 3481, McKinnis 3482, Mehaffy 3485, Moberley 3487, Monarch 3488, Moore 3489, Morgan 3490, Moyer 3491, Nell 3494, Nelson 3495, Pape 3498, Patterson 3500, Pearce 3501, Perdue 3502, Pi 3504, Pitts 3505, Porter 3506, Robinson 3508, Rush 3509, Salina 3510, Schuneman 3513, Smick 3515, South 3517, Spurrier 3520, Steffens 3521, Stice 3522, Stockard 3523, Tenholder 3524, Topeka 3528, Trump 3530, Ungles 3531, Vesper 3533, Weigand 3534, Wichita 3537, Wichita 3539, Woolsey 3542

Kentucky: Blue 3552, Commercial 3557, Foundation 3570, Gardner 3571, Kincaid 3587, Louisville 3592, Pflughaupt 3615, Smith 3625, Sparks 3626, University 3633, Wells 3636

Louisiana: Bernstein 3646, Burton 3648, Hunter 3656, Lang 3660, McGinty 3668, Southeastern 3677, Taylor 3679, Tupper 3681

Maine: Davenport 3693, Franklin 3696, Goodrich 3700, Gray 3701, Hancock 3702, Lynam 3708, Ohmart 3721, Oxford 3723, Paganelli 3724, Ricker 3730, Robinson 3731, Ross 3732, Searls 3735, Thom 3739, Tramuto 3740, Woman's 3747

Maryland: Brierley 3787, Community 3808, Davies 3813, Huether 3845, Malstrom 3866, March 3868, McGeehin 3877, Memorial 3880, Moran 3891, Queen 3918, Ravens 3920, Trustees 3945

Massachusetts: Abbott, 3956, Andona 3970, Bassett 3978, Benz 3982, Berkshire 3985, Beta 3987, Blanchard 3988, Bridgewater 3997, Bushee 4002, Cape 4006, Carco 4009, Chatham 4019, Community 4029, Costa 4030, Costello 4031, Davis 4036, Deane 4037, Dedham 4038, Dunham 4046, Dyer 4048, Easter 4052, First 4069, Friary 4077, Heberton 4102, Henry 4103, Holmes 4107, Holyoke 4109, Hopedale 4112, Howes 4118, Hunt 4122, Hutchinson 4124, Institution 4125, Jones 4133, Levin 4147, Lorden 4150, Marino 4161, McElaney 4171, McLaughlin 4172, Middlesex 4174, Mihos 4175, Molloy 4181, Murphy 4182, Niconchuk 4198, North 4199, Orange 4207, Paine

4209, Peach 4214, Permanent 4216, Perron 4217, Pettee 4218, President 4230, Progin 4231, Quabaug 4233, Quirico 4235, **R.O.S.E. 4236**, Ratte 4237, Red 4240, Riddick 4244, Rockland 4245, Rotary 4248, Ruffini 4252, Saugus 4259, Smalley 4269, Taylor 4283, Tenney 4285, Thomas 4288, Torbet 4291, **Tourism 4292**, Trustees 4298, Trustees 4301, University 4306, Warren 4311, Washburn 4312, West 4313, Williams 4318, Woodman 4320, Worcester 4323, Zampogna 4330

Michigan: Abbott 4331, Barr 4346, Battle Creek 4349, Bellinger 4355, Bemis 4356, Birtwistle 4360, Blaske 4362, Bott 4364, Brenske 4366, Byrne 4370, Cadillac 4371, Clinton 4384, Cold 4385, Coller 4388, Community 4391, Community 4393, Community 4394, Community 4395, Community 4398, Foster 4424, Four 4427, Frankenmuth 4428, Fraser 4429, Fredericksen 4430, Fremont 4431, Galesburg-Augusta 4432, Gibbs 4435, Gilles 4436, Grand Rapids 4445, Greenville 4451, Gumaer 4453, Hammel 4455, Harbor 4456, Hecht 4461, Heyl 4465, Hillier 4466, Howe 4472, Humbert 4476, I Have 4479, Ironwood 4482, Jackson 4484, Jackson 4485, Johnson 4487, Kadant 4491, Kalamazoo 4493, Kay 4495, Kiwanis 4501, Koch 4504, Krause 4506, Laflin 4508, Lapeer 4512, LaVictoire 4513, Martin 4526, Matson 4528, Meyers 4532, Michigan 4536, Michigan 4538, Michner 4541, Midland 4542, Minton 4544, Morey 4545, Morrill 4546, Mount Pleasant 4548, Nordman 4558, Novi 4564, Ontonagon 4569, Otsego 4571, Parker 4573, Petoskey 4577, Phelps 4578, Pokagon 4580, Polakovic 4581, Raval 4584, Roethke 4591, Rudy 4595, Ruf 4596, Salisbury 4598, Sanilac 4599, Shiawassee 4605, Smith 4609, **Society 4611**, Speerstra 4621, St. John 4623, St. Joseph 4624, Tahquamenon 4630, Tiscornia 4639, Trinklein 4641, Trudell 4643, Tuohy 4645, Tuscola 4646, Van Hollenbeck 4655, Waterford 4660, Welch 4663, Wells 4664, Wilson 4670, Winship 4672, Wirick 4673, Wyandotte 4675

Minnesota: Ada 4680, Adams 4681, American 4688, Anderson 4691, Blandin 4700, Bottemiller 4701, Carson 4717, Columbia 4717, Crockett 4723, Crosslake 4724, Denfeld 4726, Duluth 4729, Ely-Winton 4733, Foley 4739, Grand Rapids 4750, Hansen 4753, Harvard 4754, Henry 4757, Hull 4762, Jenniges 4770, Land 4779, Lane 4780, Lemieux 4782, MacPherson 4787, Meyer 4796, Moon 4810, Osborn 4819, Petraborg 4822, Philanthrofund 4824, Roberg 4839, Saint Paul 4842, Soneson 4851, South 4853, Steinke 4861, Thorbeck 4865, Thurston 4868, Tozer 4870, Vermilion 4879, Wallin 4884, Western 4888, Whiteside 4889, Wildey 4891, Winona 4892, Winslow 4893, Woman's 4894

Mississippi: Community 4902, CREATE 4903, Hazard 4911, McDonald 4913, University 4925

Missouri: American 4931, Barber 4936, Bell 4938, Clayton 4959, Community 4963, Covington 4967, Doerhoff 4977, Drowns 4979, Ebert 4981, Edgar 4982, Evans 4989, Ferris 4991, Fingersh 4992, Finnell 4993, Fues 4997, Gorman 5002, Green 5005, Hayes 5013, Hays 5014, Huss 5020, Hutchins 5021, Kansas 5023, Kauffman 5026, Kelly 5027, Kennett 5028, Kirschner 5030, Klapmeyer 5031, Liebling 5036, Lowrie 5038, Martin 5044, McElroy 5047, McGlothlan 5048, Meyer 5049, MICDS 5052, Miles 5054, NASB 5061, Nichols 5063, North 5064, North 5066, Orscheln 5068, Paul 5070, Porter 5076, Saint Louis 5082, Schafer 5083, Schowengerdt 5085, Schwartze 5086, Schwartze 5087, Schwartze 5088, Schwartze 5091, Schwartze 5092, Schwartze 5093, Schwartze 5094, Schwartze 5095, Schwartze 5096, Smith 5101, Soldwedel 5102, Sprehe 5103, Swope 5111, Tompkins 5116, Truman 5118, Windsor 5125, Young 5126

Montana: Bair 5130, Clarkson 5136, Creek 5138, Daley 5140, Elm 5144, Flathead 5146, Gay 5147, Haack 5152, Hanson 5153, Harbert 5154,

Hawkins 5155, Heisey 5156, Hinderman 5157, Horsman 5158, Hurst 5159, Jarecki 5161, Montana 5163, Montana 5164, Nadeau 5166, Robinson 5168, Rolfson 5170, Senft 5172, Shields 5173, Suden 5175, Sweet 5177, Townley 5179, Unrau 5181, Washington 5182

Nebraska: Bryan 5188, Elliott 5199, Emerson 5201, Grand Island 5210, Hapke 5214, Hastings 5215, Hester 5218, Higher 5219, Johnson 5222, Kearney 5223, Lexington 5228, Lincoln 5229, Merrick 5233, Midwest 5235, Nebraska 5244, Novak 5248, Oregon 5252, Patton 5253, Phelps 5255, Riley 5257, Simon 5261, Sweet 5265, Wake 5269, Weller 5271, West Point 5272, Wood 5275

Nevada: Community 5282, Doyle 5287, Korfman 5291, Nevada 5295, Nevada 5296, NV 5298, Orcutt 5299, Snyder 5302

New Hampshire: Bogni 5309, Cogan 5314, Dodge 5318, Edmunds 5319, Gifford 5323, Hastings 5327, James 5331, Lakes 5335, Linwood 5339, Manuel 5343, McIninch 5346, Morton 5350, Oberkotter 5358, Ramsaye 5364, Somerville 5369, Vanderhout 5375, Walpole 5376, Wilson 5378

New Jersey: Adelphic 5381, Avoda 5393, Bartell 5394, Belleville 5396, Bicket 5401, Chatham 5419, Clayton 5426, Cutter 5431, Everly 5442, Friends 5451, Glen 5453, Grande 5458, Groff 5460, Gruenberg 5461, Hale 5464, Holman 5471, Jackson 5480, Kovach 5491, Madison 5500, McLane 5503, Miller 5508, **Mochary 5509**, Moorestown 5511, O'Brien's 5530, Poucher 5544, Previti 5545, Princeton 5546, Rowan 5554, Rubenstein 5555, Scotch 5561, **Southpole 5572**, Terplan 5577, Trial 5580, Van Doren 5590, Van Doren 5591, Wei 5593, Whitfield 5597, Wight 5598, Woman's 5603, Zahn 5607

New Mexico: Albuquerque 5610, B.F. 5613, Carlsbad 5616, Chase 5621, Clovis 5622, Hamilton 5631, New Mexico 5640, Peninsula 5643, Sacramento 5647, Simon 5651, SPARX 5653

New York: Adirondack 5667, Ailey 5676, Albion 5678, Alumni 5684, Andrews 5713, Arts 5728, Associated 5735, **Astraea 5736**, Authier 5740, Avery 5744, Babylon 5746, Barton 5753, Berger 5760, Blarney 5767, Blosser 5769, **BMI 5771**, Borchert 5776, Bowman 5778, Brady 5780, Braverman 5781, Brewster 5785, Brill 5786, Brink 5787, Buisch 5804, Burnett 5805, Calman 5808, Cantor 5815, **Career 5816**, Chaminade 5840, Chautauqua 5842, Cirillo 5854, City 5856, Clark 5860, Clinton 5861, Cogar 5863, Coleman 5865, Collins/Chris 5869, Columbia 5870, Community 5877, Community 5878, Cortland 5890, Curran 5907, Dellomo 5920, Doherty 5929, Duffy 5937, Dyett 5942, Eagleton 5945, Earl 5946, East Williston 5948, Eckert 5953, Ehle 5955, Epsilon 5962, Father 5977, Fitzpatrick 5985, Foundation 6003, Gaffney 6015, Gavrin 6018, Genesee 6020, Giddings 6024, Gillen 6025, Glasgow 6029, Glazer 6031, Glens Falls 6032, Gold 6035, Goodell 6039, Guarino 6047, Guenther 6048, Hacker 6053, Harby 6056, Hawley 6062, Herr 6069, Hinman 6070, Hoffert 6075, **ID 6090**, Jachym 6107, Jenkins 6113, Jenkins 6114, **Kaupp 6132**, Kautz 6133, **Keren 6136, King 6138**, Kleeman 6141, Krueger 6147, Laboratory 6151, **Lincoln 6164, Lozynskyj 6174**, Lynch 6180, March 6189, McConnell 6201, McCormick 6202, Memorial 6208, Metzger 6213, Mijangos 6214, Mills 6217, Mitsui 6219, NCCC 6256, New Visions 6263, New York 6277, Northern 6287, Northrup 6288, Odasz 6291, Parker 6303, Partridge 6305, Peck 6311, Potter 6322, Potter 6323, Project 6333, Queens 6340, Reinhardt 6351, Reinhart 6352, Research 6354, Rochester 6357, Rochester 6358, Rye 6367, Scarsdale 6378, Schenck 6381, Schiffner 6385, Scholarship 6386, Scholarship 6387, Scott 6388, Seltzer 6393, Skahan 6399, Skaneateles 6400, **Social 6409**, Spain 6417, St. Luke's 6426, Stempfle 6437, Stoner 6439, Sweitzer 6443, Teel 6447, Thorwelle 6451, Tilt 6456, Trumansburg

6464, Varflex 6485, Wadas 6497, Wagner 6498, Walton 6500, Westchester 6513, Wolf 6525, Wolf 6526, **Worth 6536**, Wu 6538, Yeshiva 6539

North Carolina: Alamance 6546, Area 6555, Asheville 6562, Asheville-Buncombe 6563, Atlantic 6565, Ballard 6566, Bass 6568, Borden 6576, Brooks 6583, Burke-Weber 6586, Butler 6588, Cady 6589, Catawba 6593, Chappell 6597, Clements 6605, Coffman 6609, Community 6612, Community 6616, Cooke 6617, Cox 6620, Craven 6621, Cumberland 6624, Davie 6625, Davis 6627, Dietrich 6629, Durham 6634, **Earnhardt 6636**, East 6637, Edgerton 6643, Edmonds 6644, Elizabeth 6645, Fairfield 6653, Fava 6654, First 6657, Forbes 6658, Foundation 6660, Fouts 6663, Fox 6664, Frank 6665, Frasier 6666, Gaston 6669, Gift 6671, Gilbert 6672, Gray 6680, Grimley 6684, Groff 6685, Grogan 6686, Gross 6687, Grotefend 6688, Guggenheim 6689, Harris 6695, Henderson 6696, Hess 6697, Hochmark 6700, Hoffman 6701, Huffman 6706, Hughes 6707, Hughes 6708, Johnson 6720, Johnston 6721, Jones 6723, Jordan 6725, Keena 6728, Kent 6730, Kimmel 6732, Leath 6737, Ledward 6738, Lee 6739, Lenz 6741, Leverenz 6742, Little 6744, Livingston 6745, Loar 6746, Lundquist 6751, Lundy 6752, Mahalick 6756, Martin 6757, McNair 6763, McNair 6764, McNaught 6765, McRae 6766, Midland 6772, Monger 6776, **Morehead-Cain 6778**, Morson 6779, Nelson 6789, Nichols 6791, North 6793, Owens 6808, Patch 6811, Patterson 6812, Peckitt 6813, Pennsylvania 6815, Pharmacy 6818, Reierson 6824, Richardi 6829, Richardson 6830, Richmond 6832, Riddick 6833, Ritchie 6835, Scholarship 6852, Search 6855, Self 6856, Selling 6857, Sheffield 6858, Simpson 6861, Smart 6864, Smith 6866, Smith 6868, Spire 6870, Spivey 6871, Sprunt 6872, Stagner 6874, Stambaugh 6875, Stewart 6879, Stoudenmire 6881, Strickland 6882, Tillman 6894, Treen 6897, Triangle 6899, Troedson 6902, Two 6904, Unruh 6909, Wake 6912, Watterson 6915, West 6917, Williams 6921, Wilson 6922, Winston-Salem 6923, Wolinski 6925, Wyly 6929, Young 6931, Zimmerman 6934

North Dakota: Ruger 6947, University 6950

Ohio: Ackers 6955, Adams 6956, Addison 6957, AGC 6960, Agnew 6961, Aikey 6962, Akron 6965, Alexander 6968, Alexander's 6969, Anderson 6975, Andrus 6976, Ariel 6979, Ashland 6980, Ashtabula 6981, Atwood 6983, Babcock 6984, Bakes 6985, Ball 6986, Beal 6990, Beinke 6993, Belpre 6994, Berlin 6996, Bernhard 6997, Bland 7001, Boone 7005, Bouchard 7007, Bowling Green 7009, Bowling 7010, Brayton 7011, Brewer 7012, Brighten 7013, Britton 7014, Bryan 7017, Campbell 7022, Carleton 7023, Carney 7025, Carpenter-Garcia 7026, Cassner 7027, Chaney 7031, Clarke 7038, Cleveland 7044, Cline 7046, Community 7057, Community 7058, Community 7060, Community 7061, Community 7062, Crain 7070, Davies 7080, Davis 7081, Dayton 7082, Dinger 7089, Dumesnil 7091, Dunton 7093, **Eagles 7095**, Elks 7099, Everhart 7102, Evers 7103, Firestone 7109, Fitzgerald 7111, Freer 7119, Gandy 7121, Ganyard 7122, Garcia 7123, Gardner 7124, Gilbert 7127, Goodridge 7130, Grace 7132, Greene 7134, Grove 7137, Hamilton 7140, Harrington 7141, Hartley 7143, Hawkes 7145, Herzberger 7148, Higgins 7149, High 7150, Hope 7155, Horvitz 7156, Hosler 7157, Hughes 7160, Hull 7161, Hutton 7165, I Know 7166, Imhoff 7167, Italian 7171, Jeffery 7175, Jentes 7176, Kanhofer 7181, Keller 7185, Kessel 7186, Kibble 7189, Kindler 7192, Kirkpatrick 7193, Kirtland 7194, Kiser 7195, Kiwanis 7197, Lakeland 7202, Lapeer 7204, Lesher 7206, Ley 7208, Licking 7209, Lincoln 7211, Lorain 7213, MacRae 7217, Marietta 7220, Marion 7221, Mauger 7223, McCabe 7224, McCallay 7225, McCann 7226, McClain 7227, McComb 7228, McConahay 7229, McCoy 7230, McDonald 7231,

McDonald 7232, Menard 7238, Miami 7242, Miller 7247, Miller 7250, Mishou 7252, Mohr 7253, Moomaw 7254, Moore 7255, Munro 7259, Murphy 7260, Myers 7264, Myers 7265, Newton 7269, Nolley 7270, Nugen 7275, Ohio 7282, Osborn 7285, Park 7291, PDR 7293, Peak 7294, Peoples 7297, Perry 7299, Peters 7300, Piqua 7304, Plimpton 7305, Prior 7308, Rickert 7322, Robertson 7324, Rotterman 7329, Roy 7330, Schneider 7337, Scholarship 7338, Sebring 7341, Sharp 7343, Shepard 7346, Shunk 7348, Simmons 7350, Smith 7355, Smith 7357, Smucker 7358, Southern 7361, Spencer 7362, Springman 7364, St. Marys 7365, Stark 7366, Stauffer 7367, Steiner 7369, Sullivan 7372, Summerville 7374, Thiele 7378, Throckmorton 7381, Toomey 7386, Trachsel 7387, Troy 7388, Tuition 7389, University 7398, Ursuline 7399, Uschmann 7400, Van Hyning 7402, VanBuren 7404, Vandenbark 7405, Wahl 7409, Waldron 7411, Wayne 7415, Westerville 7421, **Wexner 7423**, White 7424, White 7425, Wilhelm 7426, Williams 7427, Williams 7428, Wilson 7431, Wimmer 7432, Winans 7433, Wisner 7435, Wood 7437, Wooddell 7438, Wright 7441, Yellow Springs 7444, Yoder 7445

Oklahoma: Bailey 7451, Bartlett 7453, Colbert 7458, Davis 7463, Donaghey 7464, Fields 7469, Funk 7473, Guthrie 7477, Johnson 7485, Kane 7488, Miley 7495, Rose 7509, Smith 7512, Springfield 7513, Tulsa 7519, Tulsa 7521, University 7522, Watkins 7523

Oregon: Adler 7528, Alexandria 7530, Almquist 7531, Archer 7534, Astoria 7535, Benson 7538, Buttrey 7541, Campbell 7543, Clemens 7549, Cockerline 7551, Collins 7552, Colvin 7553, Criswell 7561, Depriest 7571, Goodenough 7582, Hall 7583, Hamilton 7585, Heiserman 7586, Hellstern 7587, Holce 7588, Lytle 7598, Mock 7607, Molalla 7608, Moore 7609, Mount Angel 7611, Oregon 7624, Palmer 7629, Pernot 7631, Professional 7635, Ragel 7640, Renaissance 7642, Rhoden 7643, Rietman 7646, Riggs 7647, Rinne 7648, Schafer 7652, Schilling 7654, SCIO 7657, Shank 7658, Southwestern 7665, Strayer 7668, **Thomas 7669**, Trippeer 7670, Turner 7671, Vatheuer 7673, Watt 7677, West 7680, Western 7681, Wilson 7684, Woodrow 7686

Pennsylvania: Abrams 7691, Adams 7692, Alsobrooks 7698, Bailey 7721, Barrand 7722, Baskin 7725, Benford 7727, Bennett, 7728, Benz 7729, Berks 7730, Bernowski 7731, Blanchard 7736, Bonner 7738, Bridge 7746, Broadbent 7747, Brossman 7748, Burch 7753, Butterer 7755, Chester 7764, Christ 7767, Chung-Hee 7768, Clareth 7769, Clark 7770, Class 7771, Cochran 7773, Community 7780, Community 7781, Conner 7789, Corti 7794, Crawford 7796, Crawford 7797, Crossroads 7800, Curtis 7802, Davis 7807, Delaware 7809, Donegal 7814, Doverspike 7816, Eisenhauer 7820, Elko 7822, England 7826, Erickson 7830, Erie 7831, Fallquist 7836, Faust 7838, Foundation 7851, Fox 7856, Friend 7859, Friend 7860, Gardiner 7864, Gates 7865, Goldman 7874, Goslee 7877, Greater 7880, Hahn 7883, Harris 7888, Harris 7889, Harris 7890, Harris 7891, Hassel 7893, Head 7895, Heald 7896, Hearn 7898, Helwig 7902, Henderson 7903, Heyburn 7904, Higbee 7905, Hill 7908, Hill 7909, Horn 7912, Hughes 7913, Irvin 7921, Jackson 7925, Kinney 7937, Lancaster 7942, Langdale 7946, Laudermilch 7948, Laurent 7949, Lehigh 7952, Lehigh Valley 7953, Lehr 7954, Leighow 7955, Lenfest 7956, Levergood 7957, Lintner 7959, Lock 7960, Lowengard 7962, Lutron 7963, Lynch 7965, Marshall 7969, Martin 7970, McCloskey 7974, McMannis 7977, Mellinger 7981, Mendenhall 7982, Miller 7986, Miller 7987, Miller 7988, Minear 7989, Monroeville 7991, Moore 7992, Moore 7993, Morgan 7995, Moyer 7997, Murphy 7998, Nelson 8002, Newman 8005, Nicklies 8007, Noll 8008, North 8010, Northampton 8011, Northeast 8012, Patton 8019, Pennsylvania 8028,

Pennsylvania 8029, Percival 8031, Philadelphia 8035, Phillips 8040, Pickle 8043, Plank 8050, Power 8057, Puckett 8067, Reitnauer 8074, Rochester 8078, Rooney 8081, Ross 8083, Schock 8087, Scranton 8094, Shaull 8098, Sheen 8099, Shoemaker 8101, Siebenthal 8103, Simpson 8104, Slippery 8109, Smith 8110, Smith 8111, Smithfield 8113, Snyder 8115, Soames 8118, Soeder 8120, South 8123, Stager 8128, Stork 8134, Stricklin 8135, Sutliff 8137, Swope 8138, Thoburn 8143, Thomas 8144, Troutman 8150, Trushel 8151, Tyndale 8153, Urban 8156, Van Wynen 8160, Varner 8162, Vastine 8164, Vodgis 8168, Vogeley 8169, Webermeier 8182, Welch 8185, Wesley 8186, West 8187, Williams 8191, Williamson 8195, Wilson 8197, Wolf 8200, Wolf 8202, Wright 8209, Yopst 8211, York 8212, York 8213, Yule 8217, Zimmerman 8219, Zurfluh 8221

Puerto Rico: Puerto Rico 8223

Rhode Island: Andrews 8229, Armstrong 8230, Bailey 8237, Baker 8238, Baker-Adams 8239, Bartlett 8241, Bell, 8242, Black 8244, Blanchard 8246, Bowmaker 8249, Brack 8250, Church 8258, Cobb 8264, Coe 8266, Cohen 8268, Coia 8269, Coles 8270, Costa 8274, Cranston 8276, Croston 8278, Duxbury 8287, Eaton 8288, Ellsworth 8289, Farrington 8291, Forsyth 8293, Fox 8294, Galligan 8297, Gill 8299, Gooding 8300, Green 8303, Greenlaw 8304, Gromack 8305, Harney 8307, Heald 8308, Henney 8309, Howard 8312, Humphrey 8313, Jakobi 8315, Johnson 8316, Kamenski 8317, Kelley 8318, Kennedy 8319, Kiely 8320, Kinsley 8323, Lichman 8324, Little 8326, Long 8327, Maes 8329, Mahana 8332, Makinson 8333, Matheson 8337, Maude 8338, Maybury 8339, McCormick 8340, McLean 8341, McMurtrie 8342, Miles 8345, Miller 8346, Mills 8348, Morrow 8350, Moses 8351, Moulton 8352, Nash 8354, Onodaga 8358, Orr 8359, Padelford 8360, Palen-Klar 8361, Palmer 8362, Pape 8363, Parker 8366, Petsas 8369, Pierce 8370, Price 8372, Prince 8374, Pryde 8376, Randall 8378, Rhode Island 8380, Rhode Island 8381, Robinson 8386, Sasso 8390, Scavone 8391, Scheehl 8392, Schiff 8393, Sears 8396, Sheehan 8397, Shifler 8398, Simionescu 8400, Sleesman 8401, Slowinski 8402, Smith 8404, Smith 8405, Smith 8406, Smith 8408, Snyder 8410, Snyder 8411, Streeter 8416, Sutton 8417, Tappan 8420, Thompson 8421, Thompson 8422, TMC 8423, Tracy 8426, Tryon 8427, Walker 8431, Webster 8434, Wiggin 8436, Williams 8438, Wood 8440

South Carolina: Airport 8444, Bailey 8451, Cornelius 8467, Greenville 8477, **Malanga 8493**, Moore 8495, Muth 8497, Smith 8508, Spartanburg 8514

South Dakota: Cozard 8525, Doolittle 8528, Green 8532, Hatterscheidt 8533, Solem 8539, South 8542, Strahl 8543, Yellow 8548

Tennessee: 4-C's 8549, Berkshire 8559, Carrier 8564, Cheek,Jr. 8569, Chenoweth 8570, Coburn 8576, Community 8578, Community 8579, Dollywood 8584, East Nashville 8586, East 8587, Fengler 8591, Hawkins 8598, Latimer 8613, Roark 8637, Simpson 8645, Stahlman 8649, Tomorrow 8655, **United 8657**, Wills 8664, Woodbury 8665

Texas: Alamo 8670, Amarillo 8675, Amarillo 8676, Anderson 8687, Anderson 8688, Astin 8693, Austin 8696, Barnsley 8702, Bartholomew 8703, Barto 8704, Baumberger 8706, Bellamy 8709, Black 8713, Borelli 8716, Borton 8717, Brockman 8723, Brookshire 8724, Bush 8729, C.L.C. 8731, Camp 8733, Cannon 8734, Carter 8737, Chamberlin 8742, Chambers 8743, Childress 8747, Coastal 8755, Coastal 8756, Common 8758, Communities 8759, Conference 8765, Cook 8769, Cook 8770, Corpus Christi 8773, Dailey 8782, Dallas 8784, Dallas 8786, Diffenbaugh 8793, Diffenbaugh 8794, Diffenbaugh-University 8795, Dreams 8798, Dunn 8800, Dupre 8801, East 8804, Eddy 8805, Edwards 8809, Elam 8812, Enger 8815, Fasken 8819, Faulconer 8820, Formosa 8826, Foundation 8830, Fuller 8832,

Galena 8835, Gourley 8848, Hamilton 8850, Haraldson 8853, Haverlah 8858, Hayes 8859, Heath 8862, Hefflefinger 8864, Hill 8866, Hirsch 8868, Hodges 8872, Hornbrook 8874, Houston 8879, Houston 8884, Knight 8908, Lake 8913, Long 8923, Lubbock 8926, Mallard 8933, Masonic 8938, McGowan 8945, McKenney 8947, McMillan, 8948, Mercer 8953, Millar 8958, Miller 8961, Moody 8967, Moore 8968, Morgan 8969, Morse 8971, Munson 8973, Nielson 8990, Norby 8991, Panasonic 9001, Paris 9003, Paris 9004, Peery 9009, Percy 9012, Phillips 9019, Port Arthur 9025, Powdermaker 9026, Prater 9027, Reitch 9036, Robinson 9043, Romsdahl 9045, Rooke 9046, San Antonio 9054, San Antonio 9055, San Antonio 9057, Second 9065, Seely 9067, Singleton 9075, Sipes 9076, Siros 9077, Smith 9079, Southeast 9087, Southwestern 9092, Spencer 9094, Stanzel 9100, Stark 9101, Taylor 9111, Texas 9117, Texas 9127, Texas 9130, Trimble 9138, Vinsant 9150, Warnken 9157, Watson 9159, West 9162, Wildner 9166, Wintermann 9171, Wolters 9175, Wolverton 9177, Wood 9179, Wright 9183, Young 9186

Utah: Barrick 9194, EnergySolutions 9199, Granite 9201, Jordan 9212, Keener 9213, Lofthouse 9216, McCarthey 9219, Salt 9224

Vermont: Arlington 9235, Clifford 9241, Danville 9244, England 9246, Essex 9247, Hayes 9250, Rutland 9259, Terrill 9261, Tkacyzk 9262

Virginia: ACCESS 9278, AHC 9281, Bell 9325, Bridgebuilder 9327, College 9344, Community 9345, Community 9346, Community 9349, Community 9350, Culpeper 9355, Danville 9357, Dunnavant 9366, Eastern 9368, English 9373, Greater 9388, Grubbs 9390, Henrico 9394, Jefferson 9408, Judges 9411, Keesee 9413, Linhart 9422, Loeb 9423, Love 9424, Lynchburg 9426, Mitchell 9439, Morgan 9440, Nansemond 9443, Poff 9485, Schlarb 9499, Stowers 9514, Strasburg 9515, Thomas 9520, United 9528, University 9533, Van Engel 9536, Virginia 9540, Virginia 9542, Weaver 9544, Westmoreland 9547

Washington: Allied 9559, Arnsberg 9563, Bainbridge 9565, Bradley 9576, Burlington 9579, Carkeek 9581, Clark 9590, Columbia 9596, Community 9599, Community 9600, Elvins 9607, Fergason 9611, Gasparovich 9620, George 9621, George 9622, Gius 9623, Grow 9627, Hall 9628, Hanna 9631, Herriges 9634, Holliday 9636, Hunter 9640, King 9653, Kitsap 9654, Lauzier 9658, Littlejohn 9662, Martinez 9668, Nelson 9681, Nikkei 9682, Pace 9692, Padelford 9694, Pioneer 9699, Richardson 9706, Schack 9715, Seattle 9718, Slaid 9727, Tufts 9738, Walkling 9745, Wenatchee 9753, Worthington 9759

West Virginia: Adams 9763, Big 9767, Burnside 9769, Carter 9772, Craig 9778, Eastern 9780, Fairmont 9782, Gault 9786, Harries 9789, Hinton 9790, Kanawha 9794, McCormick 9801, Minor 9802, Paden 9806, Pais 9807, Parkersburg 9808, Princeton 9812, Stickley 9817, Stifel 9818, Stout 9819, Sun 9821, Tech 9822, Vecellio 9826, Your 9831

Wisconsin: AnnMarie 9836, Askren 9839, Bachhuber 9842, Birbeck 9848, Brown 9853, Carnes 9859, Chetek 9862, Community 9868, Community 9869, Dupee 9879, **EAA 9880**, Eckburg 9881, Eggen 9882, Elfers 9883, **Entomological 9884**, Environmental 9885, Experimental 9887, Fenner 9890, Fernstrum 9891, Fix 9892, Frautschy 9897, Fromm 9901, Graef 9908, Grafton 9909, Green Bay 9910, Green Bay 9911, Grimm 9912, Hale 9914, Hasselhofer-Wolf 9916, Heffel 9918, Henrizi 9920, Hilgen 9921, Hodes 9922, Holt 9923, Incourage 9925, Johnson 9932, Kelben 9938, Kenosha 9941, La Crosse 9948, Lakeland 9949, Lauterbach 9950, Lyons 9953, Marshfield 9960, Martin 9962, Mentzer 9966, Metzner 9967, Michels 9968, Mitchell 9972, Moore 9974, Munster 9976, Nelson 9979, New Glarus 9980, Nicolet 9982, Nishan 9983, Norbert 9985, O'Hara

9986, Oshkosh 9988, Porhaska 9996, Praiss 9998, Prohaska 9999, Racine 10001, Redfield 10005, Richards 10009, Rolfs 10013, Sauk 10019, SBC 10020, Scholarship 10022, Seymour 10027, Shafer 10028, Sharp 10030, Sheets 10031, Sivyer 10034, Smith 10036, St. Croix 10043, St. John 10045, Suder 10049, Thomas 10051, Tomah 10052, University 10056, UW 10057, Vedova 10058, Wagner 10060, Ward 10063, Weigel 10067, Wilber 10072, Wisconsin 10077, Wisconsin 10080, Wisconsin 10081, Zebro 10092, Zweibel 10093

Wyoming: Anderson 10094, Clark 10097, Community 10099, Doherty 10103, Gillet 10104, Giovanini 10105, Johnson 10108, Littler 10113, Pearson 10116, Perkins 10117, Pilch 10118, Whitney 10124, Wyoming 10126

Technical education support

Alabama: Alabama 4, Wallace 89

Alaska: Aleut 103, Bering 105, Koniag 122, Kuskokwim 123, Newlin 127, Sealaska 136, Territorial 143

Arizona: Alhambra 153, Spencer 238

Arkansas: Cornerstone 276, Hornlein 284, Single 309

California: Bickerstaff 413, Buckley 425, Builder's 427, Community 513, Flint 579, Horizons 667, Jewish 707, Scholarship 965, Ventura 1081, Women's 1099, Yolo 1105

Colorado: Foundation 1198, Yampa 1309

Connecticut: American 1322, Branford 1338, Tomasso 1473, Weller 1482, Xerox 1490

Delaware: Delaware 1500, Thomson 1525, Vocational 1527

District of Columbia: Children's 1600, **International 1654, Union 1741**

Florida: AWS 1789, Community 1839, Hurst 1925, Snow 2066, Take 2081, Taunton 2084, Wiggins 2104

Georgia: Brightwell 2131, DeSana 2164, **Fadel 2174**

Hawaii: Mink 2304

Illinois: Community 2494, District 2517, Donnelley 2521, DuPage 2528, Foundation 2567, Hardin 2599, McAllister 2716, **Nuts, 2760**, Robinson 2826, **Sigma 2855**, Taylor 2885, Walters 2917

Indiana: Armstrong 2958, Community 2990, Community 2997, Community 2999, Community 3001, Dearborn 3012, Kosciusko 3091, LaGrange 3093, Legacy 3096, Noble 3127, Simon 3184, South 3189, Wabash 3215

Iowa: Bishop 3246, Dallas 3270, Father 3280, Guest 3292, Lee 3324, Matheson 3332, Murray 3342, Reifel-Elwood 3365

Kansas: Coffman 3427, Hansen 3451, Jones 3464, Kleppe 3474, Parsons 3499, Perdue 3502, Pitts 3505, Schmidt 3512, Steffens 3521, Toothaker 3527

Kentucky: Community 3559, Jackson 3579

Maryland: Airmen 3752, Autism 3781, **National 3895**

Massachusetts: Affordable 3958, Chester 4021, Home 4110, **Maya 4170**

Michigan: Bay 4350, **Collectors 4387**, Community 4394, Community 4399, Guardian 4452, Petoskey 4577, **Society 4611**, Speerstra 4621

Minnesota: Blandin 4700, Duluth 4729

Missouri: Brey 4943, Clayton 4959, Community 4963, Drowns 4979, Edgar 4982, Lord 5037, Missouri 5059, Reynolds 5079, Schwartze 5088

Montana: Clarkson 5136, Harbert 5154, Suden 5175

Nebraska: Fremont 5205, Weller 5271

Nevada: Doyle 5287, Nevada 5296, Western 5304

New Hampshire: Ladies 5334, New Hampshire 5353, Scots' 5367, Skrungloo 5368, White 5377, Yarnold 5379

New Jersey: Astle 5390, Camden 5410, Poucher 5544

New Mexico: Finis 5630, SPARX 5653, Viles 5657

New York: Babylon 5746, Blosser 5769, **Career 5816**, Colburn 5864, Hawley 6062, Howard 6078,

Rochester 6357, Snayberger 6407, Stony 6440, Witmer 6524

North Carolina: Bass 6568, Beaver 6571, Community 6613, Foundation 6660, Nichols 6791, Rouch 6842

North Dakota: Martell 6943, Schuetze 6948

Ohio: Ackers 6955, Campbell 7022, Community 7058, **Eagles 7095**, Hauss 7144, Holmes 7152, Horvitz 7156, Kibble 7189, Kindler 7192, McCallay 7225, McComb 7228, McDonald 7231, McDonald 7232, Miami 7242, Snow 7359, St. Marys 7365, Trachsel 7387, Wimmer 7432, Wood 7437

Oklahoma: Communities 7459, Henry 7480

Oregon: Colvin 7553, Cooper 7557, Daly 7565, Ford 7578, Halton 7584, Von der Ahe 7675, West 7680

Pennsylvania: Abernathy 7689, Ameche 7700, Berks 7730, Brenneman 7744, Bridge 7746, Community 7783, **Connelly 7788**, Irvin 7921, Pennsylvania 8023, Rhoads 8075, Van Wynen 8160

Rhode Island: Fundacao 8296, Pape 8363, Shifler 8398, Wylie 8442

South Carolina: Hart 8480, Kershaw 8490, Strive 8516

South Dakota: Green 8532

Tennessee: Latimer 8613

Texas: Bellamy 8709, **First 8822**, Hamilton 8850, Lanham 8914, Live 8920, Maguire 8932, TUA 9139, Vinsant 9150, Watson 9158

Vermont: Nordic 9255, Terrill 9261

Virginia: Bedford 9324, Community 9346, Foundation 9383, Orphan 9474, Randolph 9491, Sanford 9497, Schlarb 9499

Washington: Fisher 9613, SkillSource 9726, VanHoff 9741

West Virginia: Beckley 9766, Kanawha 9794

Wisconsin: Brown 9853, Casper 9860, Community 9869, **EAA 9880**, Experimental 9887, Green Bay 9910, Hodes 9922, Kenosha 9942, La Crosse 9948, Markos 9959, Marshfield 9960, Wisconsin 10081, Wisconsin 10083

Wyoming: Construction 10100, Curtis 10101, Wyoming 10126

Travel awards

California: Jewish 706

Colorado: **H.E.L.P. 1208**

District of Columbia: **American 1555, American 1565**, Corcoran 1608

Georgia: **American 2114**

Illinois: **Healthy 2608, International 2652**

Indiana: Association 2962, **Timmy 3200**

Maryland: **Association 3779, Endocrine 3818**

New York: **Soanes 6408, UJA 6470**

Ohio: **Jewish 7178**, YSI 7446

Travel grants

Alabama: **American 8**

Alaska: Aleut 103

Arizona: Sulphur 243

California: **Arthritis 376**, Beaver 407, California 441, **Cantor 463**, China 492, **Foundation 589, Getty 614**, Headlands 649, **Immunobiology 677, International 691**, Johnson 712, **Kaiser 716**, Plotkin 871, Society 999, Theatre 1044, World 1101

Colorado: Society 1285, **WaterStone 1305**

Connecticut: Anthony 1324, **Cholnoky 1356**

District of Columbia: **American 1541, American 1549, American 1552, Association 1585, Association 1586, Congressional 1607, German 1638**, Gerontological 1639, **Institute 1651, International 1656**, National 1686, **Optical 1705, Parkinson's 1708**

Florida: Alpha-1 1767

Georgia: **American 2116**

Illinois: **American 2379, American 2389**, American 2390, **Chest 2471, Ewing 2554, Graham 2592**,

Medical 2728, National 2745, North 2758, Rauch 2808, **Rotary 2835, Skidmore 2857, Terra 2889**

Louisiana: Academic 3639

Maryland: American 3766, **Anxiety 3773, School 3928**

Massachusetts: **American 3963, Beebe 3980, Earthwatch 4049, Global 4085**, Grinspoon 4090, Lyceum 4154, Massachusetts 4166, Massachusetts 4167, **Rosenberg 4247**, Rotch 4249, Whiting 4316

Michigan: Ford 4420

Minnesota: Arrowhead 4693, Bakken 4697, Jerome 4771, Region 4836

Missouri: Alpha 4930

New Hampshire: **Lyman 5340, MacDowell 5341**

New Jersey: Foundation 5450, Honeywell 5472, **IEEE 5476**

New Mexico: **SUMMA 5655**

New York: **American 5692, American 5711, Autism 5742, Commonwealth 5872, Delmas 5921, Foundation 5992**, Foundation 5999, Hudson 6080, **Institute 6095, International 6098, Kosciuszko 6145, Mayday 6197, National 6251, Philippe 6316, Royal 6364, Societe 6410, Theatre 6448, Trace 6461, Watson 6504, Weill 6508**

Ohio: **Educational 7098**, Kittridge 7196, Licking 7209

Pennsylvania: **American 7701**, Boyer 7741

Rhode Island: **Dorot 8286**

South Carolina: Arts 8448, Cultural 8469, Hart 8480

Tennessee: Chattanooga 8568

Utah: James 9211

Vermont: Ohiyesa 9256

Virginia: **American 9287, American 9294, American 9305, Institute 9404, National 9452, Public 9488**

Washington: George 9622, **Ji 9644**

West Virginia: West Virginia 9827

Wisconsin: **Entomological 9884, National 9977**

Undergraduate support

Alabama: Alabama 4, Alabama 5, Baker 11, Bashinsky 13, Batre 14, Bedsole 15, Central 20, **Civitan 24**, Finlay 37, Freels 40, Grisham 42, Griswold 43, Hanna 45, Harmeson 47, Harrell 48, Higdon 50, Holland 51, Internal 53, Killgore 55, Mayson 60, Miss 63, Moeschle 64, Omega 66, Owens 67, Padolf 68, Parker 69, Portraits, 70, Prewett 71, Smith 80, TAV 83, Todd 84, Venable 87, Vulcan 88, Wallace 89, WEDC 90, Wollman 94, Yanamura 95

Alaska: Alaska 97, Arctic 104, Bering 105, Chugach 111, CIRI 113, Doyon 115, Eyak 116, Homer 117, Igloo 119, Koniag 122, Kuskokwim 123, McCurdy 124, Newlin 127, Norton 128, Old Harbor 129, Pioneer 130, Samuelsen 134, Schwantes 135, Sealaska 136, SNA 139, Tanana 140, Tanaq 141, Territorial 143, Valley 148, West 149

Arizona: 100 150, Adelante 151, Alhambra 153, Arizona 157, Arizona 159, Arizona 165, Brinker 174, Chapman 178, Christian 179, Community 182, **Dickey 184**, Educare 188, Flinn 193, Friedman 197, Knapp 208, Lewis 211, Major 214, McNeil 216, McWilliams 217, Miss 219, Phoenix 226, Schmitz 235, Seed 236, Squires 239, Sturges 242, Trico 246, Valley 256

Arkansas: Allen, 260, Arkansas 263, Arkansas 265, Baptist 269, Bearden 270, Cornerstone 276, Finkbeiner 279, Gillespie 280, Hamm 282, Hornlein 284, Kelder 286, Keltner 287, Lehman 288, Murphy 294, Pierce 302, Raef 303, SHARE 307, Shewmaker 308, Single 309, South 311, Sturgis 314, Sturgis 315, Tenenbaum 316, Terry 317, Trinity 319, Union 321, Veasey 322, Wallace 323, Wal-Mart 325, White 326, Williams 327

California: Aaron 332, Academic 333, ACEC 337, **Adobe 338**, Almanor 349, American 360, Anaheim 363, Armstrong 371, Asian 379, Association 390, Avant! 394, Bartholomew 399, Bartlett 400, Baxter 404, BBCN 406, Beaver 407, Bickerstaff 413, Bodine 417, Bossola 419, Boyer 420, Brown 424,

Buckley 425, Builder's 427, Busch 431, Cahp 435, California 445, California 448, California 453, California 455, California 456, California 457, Carreon 465, Chessall 481, China 492, Chinese 493, Chung 498, Ciatti 500, Clark 502, Coastal 504, Collister 506, Community 511, Community 512, Community 513, Community 514, Community 515, Community 518, Conner 521, Curley 531, Dudley-Vehmeyer-Brown 548, Ebell 553, El Dorado 556, Emery 563, Fairmount 566, Federal 572, Flint 579, Fresno 596, Fresno 597, Friedberger 598, **Getty 614**, Gifford 616, Golden 626, Graham 634, Granoff 636, Griffin 638, Gunn 640, Guslander 641, Hallgrimson 645, Hamilton 646, Heritage 657, Hiebler 660, **Hispanic 664**, Horizons 667, Horn 668, **HP 670**, Humboldt 671, **Invisible 694**, James 701, Jewish 707, Jewish 708, Johnson 710, **Kaiser 716**, Kerber 719, Kimbo 721, Klicka 722, Lagrant 731, Lakewood 732, League 738, Lippert 746, Lucky 760, Lynn 762, Mariani 771, **McConnell 779**, Mills 793, Mills 794, Monterey 804, Morgan 805, Morris 806, **National 815**, National 816, **Nepal 824, NMA 828**, North 832, Northern 834, Oakland 836, Olympic 840, Orange 843, Pedrozzi 858, Performing 862, Pergo 863, Piedemonte 868, Plotkin 871, Plumas 873, **Point 875**, Pomona 876, Price 881, Pritchett 882, Pursuit 888, Quality 890, Raies-Murr 893, Ramona's 896, **Rand 898**, Redding 904, Ronald 918, Rossmoor 922, Rowan 923, Sacramento 926, San Diego 932, San Diego 933, San Diego 934, San Diego 936, San Francisco 944, San Luis 951, San Mateo 952, Santa Barbara 955, Scholarship 965, Science 968, **Screen 969**, Sedler 972, **SEMA 973**, Shasta 978, **Shinoda 980**, Signer 985, Silicon 986, Simon 990, Smart 993, Smith 996, **Society 1000, Society 1001**, Sonora 1003, Spirit 1008, Stanislaus 1017, Stephens 1022, Stephenson 1023, Stern 1024, Strauss 1028, Sukut 1030, Torrance 1050, Tracy 1053, Ukiah 1066, United 1071, University 1073, Urbanek 1074, Ventura 1081, Ward 1084, Warne 1085, Warner 1086, Washington 1087, Wilcox 1095, Women's 1099, Woodward 1100, World 1101, Zeiter 1108, Zider 1109

Colorado: AEG 1113, Alexander 1115, Aorn 1119, Barr 1128, Bianco 1129, Campbell 1139, Christian 1146, Cibrowski 1147, **Clan 1148**, Colorado 1168, Community 1171, Denver 1180, Douglas 1184, El 1190, Elizondo 1191, Flatirons 1195, Foundation 1198, Front 1200, **Galaway 1201**, Griffin 1206, Hanson 1209, Harvey 1210, Holt 1214, Kaiser 1224, Kennedy 1225, Langston 1228, Layton 1230, Light 1231, MacGregor 1236, Mikkelson 1239, Molloy 1241, Mulford 1245, National 1247, Nine 1250, Pikes 1258, Project 1261, Sachs 1277, Seay 1280, **Sonlight 1287**, Tolbert 1296, **United 1299**, Vail 1302, Veirs 1303, Western 1306, Yampa 1309, Yuma 1312

Connecticut: Ambler 1319, American 1321, American 1322, Ash 1325, Balso 1328, **Bonfire 1336**, Building 1342, Canaan 1345, Cawasa 1348, Chapman 1351, **Cholnoky 1356, Coast 1359**, Community 1361, Community 1362, Connecticut 1366, Darien 1373, DiMauro 1377, Eagle 1380, Fairfield 1387, Folsom 1390, Fox 1391, Fuller 1393, Gilbert 1395, Graham 1396, Hammers 1397, Hartford 1399, Henries 1402, Hurlbutt 1404, Hurley 1405, Knights 1411, Litchfield 1415, Main 1419, Milford 1423, Munger 1427, Norwalk 1436, Paul 1440, Peirce 1441, Person-to-Person 1442, Ridgefield 1448, Roxbury 1452, SBM 1456, Scott 1457, **Scudder 1458**, Sheridan 1460, Spirol 1462, Squier 1463, Starks 1467, Sullivan 1469, Thomas 1471, Tierney 1472, Tomasso 1473, Watertown 1480, Weller 1482, Wilkerson 1486, Windsor 1487, Woman's 1488, Xerox 1490

Delaware: Chaney 1495, Delaware 1500, Etnier 1506, Frank 1508, Gordy 1510, Hirsch 1512, JBL 1515, Simpson 1523, Thomson 1525

District of Columbia: American 1540, **American 1553, American 1559**, American 1570, Arab 1576, Association 1584, Best 1592, **Broadcast 1597**,

Children's 1600, Communications 1604, Community 1605, **Congressional 1607, Development 1614**, Dingwall 1615, **Foundation 1629, Fund 1634, German 1638, Hoffa 1646**, Horticultural 1647, **International 1654, International 1656, Jack 1661**, Junior 1664, **Landscape 1668, Monk 1680, National 1685, National 1691, National 1693, Phillips 1716, Radio 1718, Recycling 1721, Robinson, 1724**, Ronald 1725, **Sheet 1727, Society 1731, Sons 1732**, Turner 1737, **Union 1741, United 1743**, Washington 1746, Washington 1747, Washington 1749, **YWCA 1758**

Florida: Abernathy 1762, Amateis 1768, American 1770, Amos 1776, Arcadian 1779, Bailey 1790, Baptist 1791, Beall 1794, Bennett 1797, Brevard 1807, BRRH 1813, Citrus 1830, Clint 1832, Columbus 1835, Community 1839, Community 1840, Community 1841, Community 1844, Community 1845, Community 1847, David 1856, DeBartolo 1857, Englewood 1870, Exchange 1873, Fellows 1875, Finley 1876, Fuller 1893, **Gamma 1894**, Glades 1895, GMAA 1896, Grossman 1897, Gulf 1898, Hand 1901, Harrelson 1903, Harris 1904, Haven 1907, Hein 1909, Hillsborough 1915, Hoeting 1917, **Horizons 1922**, Hunt 1924, Hurst 1925, Immokalee 1926, Johnston 1931, King 1939, Krausman 1942, LeGore 1948, Leinbach 1949, Lincoln 1951, Lloyd 1953, Long 1954, Lynch 1957, Magic 1958, Manley 1961, Martin 1963, Mayo 1966, McCabe 1968, McCune 1969, McCurry 1970, Mead 1973, Morris 1983, Mount 1987, Murray 1990, Music 1991, Northern 2001, Ott 2009, Palm 2013, Players 2022, Rawls 2029, Rayni 2030, Rayonier 2031, Roberts 2039, Ruegamer 2042, Sailfish 2047, Schommer 2053, Scott 2055, Selby 2057, Selinger 2058, **Shepard 2060**, Sing 2062, Snow 2066, Southwest 2067, **Special 2069**, Spicer 2070, Starks 2072, Strahan 2076, Sunburst 2079, Take 2081, Taunton 2084, Thornton 2086, Tweed 2091, University 2096, West Palm Beach 2102, Wiggins 2104

Georgia: **100 2110**, Adair 2111, Arby's 2119, Barnett 2126, Beech 2127, Bowen 2128, **Boys 2129**, Brightwell 2131, Callaway 2134, Cameron 2135, Charter 2137, Chick 2139, Cobb 2147, Community 2150, Community 2151, Community 2153, DeKalb 2162, DeSana 2164, Duke 2168, East 2169, Espy 2172, **Fadel 2174**, Hall 2191, Kajima 2199, Kids' 2202, Legislative 2205, Magnus 2206, North 2218, Peoples 2221, **Phi Mu 2222, Pickett 2224, Pilot 2225**, R.A.C.K 2226, **Ravi 2227**, Savannah 2232, Scheffler 2234, Student 2245, Styles 2246, **TAPPI 2247**, Tharpe 2248, Watson 2258, WellStar 2260, Wine 2266, WinShape 2267

Hawaii: Bank 2272, Cottington 2278, Diamond 2280, Fukunaga 2283, Hawaii 2289, Hemenway 2293, Kaiulani 2296, Kanuha 2298, Mink 2304, Palama 2311, Pope 2315, Ross 2317, Saake 2318, Sakumoto 2319, Takitani 2322, Towle 2323, Zimmerman 2327

Idaho: Haugse 2332, IDACORP 2334, Jeker 2337, Kingsbury 2338, Mitchell 2342, Nahas 2343, Perrin 2344, Ramsdale 2345, Shultz 2348, Smallwood 2350

Illinois: **Academy 2355, ADA 2356**, Adamson 2357, Alberts 2361, Ameren 2364, **American 2371**, Anderson 2395, Andrew 2396, Andrew 2397, Aon 2402, APICS 2403, AptarGroup 2404, Barnard 2412, Barnes 2413, Bechtner 2416, Beebe 2418, Bender 2419, Benjamin 2421, Black 2426, Blazek 2427, Boulos 2431, Boyle 2433, Breckinridge 2435, Brege 2436, Brewer 2437, Brown 2441, Bulkley 2445, Bunn 2446, Burgess 2447, Burton 2449, Busey 2450, Cabot 2455, Camp 2458, **Carpe 2460**, Carter 2461, Catt 2465, Centralia 2467, Chicago 2476, Children 2477, Christ 2481, Coin 2487, Coleman 2488, Community 2494, Community 2496, Corpening 2500, Costilow 2502, Damato 2506, Davis 2508, Davis 2510, Dawson 2511, DeKalb 2514, District 2517, Dodd 2519, Dole 2520, Donnelley 2521, Doody 2522,

Drummond 2526, Dudley 2527, DuPage 2528, Eberhardt 2531, Edmunds 2534, Edwardsville 2536, Elburn 2539, **Elks 2540**, Embarras 2541, English 2548, Evans 2552, Everett 2553, Ferris 2560, First 2562, Foundation 2567, **Foundry 2571**, Francies 2572, Fredenburgh 2575, Gaffney 2578, Geyer 2582, Golden 2586, Graber 2591, Halsey 2597, Hansen 2598, Hardin 2599, Harper 2600, Harrison 2601, Hartke 2602, Hayes 2604, Hefti 2611, Henkel 2612, Hirsch 2619, HomeStar 2623, House 2626, Hugg 2628, Hutchison 2630, Illinois 2637, Illinois 2641, Irrevocable 2653, Jackson 2655, Just 2664, Kander 2666, Karnes 2668, Kaufman 2669, Knecht 2673, Kohl 2677, Kooi 2678, **Lascaris 2685**, Laux 2686, Lemmer 2688, **Lithuanian 2695**, Lower 2698, Luley 2700, Magnus 2705, Marion 2708, Marshall 2709, Mason 2712, McAllister 2716, McFarland 2720, McMullan 2726, Mellinger 2730, Miller 2734, Miller 2735, Morrison 2738, Munson 2740, **National 2747, National 2749**, Niccum 2756, Nicoll 2757, **Nuts, 2760**, Oak Park 2761, Oakes 2762, **Organization 2769**, Orum 2771, OSF 2772, Ott 2773, Ott 2774, Palmer 2777, Palos 2778, Patterson 2780, Peeples 2781, Perkins 2784, Peters 2785, Peterson 2786, Pflasterer 2787, Phi 2788, Pierson 2789, Piper 2792, **Polish 2796**, Prest 2798, Puckett 2802, Pugh 2803, Pullman 2804, Rainey 2807, Rauch 2808, Reiss 2812, REO 2814, Reynolds 2818, Rieger 2820, Roberts 2825, Robinson 2826, **Rotary 2835**, Schroeder 2843, Schwarz 2845, Shapiro 2849, Shawnee 2851, Short 2853, **Sigma 2855**, Smith 2859, Smysor 2860, South Holland 2864, **Special 2866**, St. 2868, St. Clair 2869, Steel 2871, Sterling 2872, Strauss 2878, Stump 2879, SVI 2881, Sweitzer 2883, Swiss 2884, Taylor 2885, Taylor 2886, Testamentary 2890, Thauer 2891, Tomara 2894, Tri-County 2897, Union 2904, Veeder 2908, Wagenknecht 2911, Walker 2915, Walters 2916, Waubonsee 2918, Wells 2922, Wells 2923, Whitney 2926, Wood 2935, Zearing 2940, Zweifel 2943

Indiana: Adams 2945, Alpha 2950, **Alpha 2952**, Amburn 2953, Armstrong 2958, Arvin 2961, Baber 2963, Benton 2966, Blair 2968, Blair 2969, Blue 2970, Boonshot 2971, Brown 2976, Buerger 2977, Cass 2979, CIACO 2986, Cole 2987, Community 2990, Community 2992, Community 2993, Community 2994, Community 2995, Community 2996, Community 2997, Community 2999, Community 3000, Community 3001, Community 3003, Community 3004, Community 3005, Cook 3008, Dearborn 3012, Decatur 3013, Deen 3014, DeKalb 3015, Dunn 3021, Elkhart 3024, Ellison 3025, Epler 3026, Fayette 3028, Francisco 3034, Frank 3035, Franklin 3036, Frees 3038, Gemmill 3042, Gibson 3043, Gilmore 3044, Greene 3045, Greenwell 3046, Guiliani 3047, Harber 3051, Harris 3053, Harrison 3054, Hemminger 3055, Henderson 3056, Hendricks 3057, Henry 3058, Heritage 3059, Huntington 3068, Indiana 3070, Jasper 3076, **Kappa 3082**, Keller 3084, Kimball 3086, Koch 3089, Kosciusko 3091, Kuhner 3092, LaGrange 3093, **Lambda 3095**, Legacy 3096, Line 3102, Loogootee 3105, Madison 3106, Marshall 3110, Montgomery 3114, Moorman 3117, Neel 3125, Nesty 3126, Noble 3127, Oberdorfer 3129, Osborn 3134, Pacers 3138, Pearson 3142, PFS 3145, **Phi 3146**, Plummer 3148, Porter 3149, Portland 3151, Pulaski 3153, Putnam 3154, Raab 3155, Randolph 3156, Richardt 3160, Rush 3167, Schergens 3172, Schmidt 3173, Schultz 3175, Scott 3176, Scott 3177, Seymour 3179, Shiel 3180, Shoop 3181, **Sigma 3183**, Simon 3184, Slaughter 3185, Smelser 3186, South 3189, Stanley 3192, Steuben 3193, Stiens 3194, Storer 3195, Stout 3196, Surina 3197, Thomasson 3198, Thorntown 3199, Tipton 3201, Union 3204, Unity 3209, Vermillion 3211, Wabash 3215, Wayne 3217, Webster 3219, Westhaysen 3223,

    FOUNDATION GRANTS TO INDIVIDUALS, 23RD EDITION

Williams 3227, Williams 3228, Winchester 3229, Zeta 3230

Iowa: Bathalter 3244, Bishop 3246, Brummer 3249, Burchfield 3250, Carter 3254, Chase 3256, Clarinda 3257, Community 3263, Crozier 3269, Dallas 3270, Delaware 3271, Denton 3272, Diehl 3275, Duggan 3276, Elbert 3277, Farrell 3279, Father 3280, Genesis 3283, Hagedorn 3293, Hulton 3301, Iowa 3304, Jay 3312, Jepsen 3314, Kansas 3316, Keig 3317, Kingfield 3320, Lage 3321, Lake-Matthews 3322, Lee 3324, Matheson 3332, McKay 3334, McKenney 3335, Michels 3337, Munter 3340, Murphy 3341, Murray 3342, Nishnabotna 3343, **P.E.O. 3352**, Palmer 3353, Petersen 3356, Poweshiek 3359, Pritchard 3361, Raider 3362, **Reed 3364**, Reifel-Elwood 3365, Rufer 3369, Seidler 3377, Shellabarger 3378, Sherman 3379, Sinek 3381, Siouxland 3382, Smith 3383, Spencer 3386, St. Luke's 3387, Stewart 3390, Swensrud 3393, Swiler 3394, Traer 3396, Waverly 3406, Winkel 3408

Kansas: Abell 3411, Arnold 3414, Babson's 3416, Baker 3417, Bane 3418, Coffman 3427, Community 3429, Davis 3431, Eggleston 3436, Ellis 3439, Ellis 3440, French 3445, French 3446, Golden 3447, Griffith 3450, Hansen 3451, Hartley 3452, Henderson 3454, Hines 3455, Hoy 3458, Hunter 3459, Hutchinson 3460, Jellison 3462, Jones 3464, Jordaan 3465, Kansas 3467, Key 3473, Kleppe 3474, Loofbourrow 3480, Mansfield 3481, Moberley 3487, Monarch 3488, Morgan 3490, Moyer 3491, Nell 3494, Nelson 3495, Parsons 3499, Patterson 3500, Pearce 3501, Perdue 3502, Pi 3504, Porter 3506, Preston 3507, Robinson 3508, Salina 3510, Sarver 3511, Schmidt 3512, Smick 3515, Snyder 3516, South 3517, Spitcaufsky 3519, Spurrier 3520, Steffens 3521, Stice 3522, Tenholder 3524, Toothaker 3527, Trump 3530, Ungles 3531, Unified 3532, Vesper 3533, White 3536, Wichita 3539

Kentucky: American 3544, Blue 3552, Boneal 3553, Commercial 3557, Community 3559, Gardner 3571, Jackson 3579, Jones 3580, Kincaid 3587, Louisville 3592, McDowell 3595, MGM 3597, Morrill 3599, Murphy 3601, Norton 3606, Ogden 3607, Papa 3611, Pearl 3614, Smith 3625, Spear 3627, St. 3628, Wells 3636, Young 3637

Louisiana: Baton Rouge 3644, Burton 3648, Hunter 3656, Lang 3660, Ledet 3661, Masonic 3667, Meraux 3669, Pellerin 3674, Tupper 3681

Maine: Goodrich 3700, Gray 3701, Hancock 3702, Holocaust 3703, MELMAC 3718, North Haven 3720, Ohmart 3721, Ricker 3730, Russell 3733, Savings 3734, Searls 3735, Tramuto 3740, Turner 3742, Woman's 3747

Maryland: Adams 3750, Airmen 3752, **American 3757**, American 3763, **American 3765**, AMVETS 3771, Autism 3780, Autism 3781, Baltimore 3783, Bright 3788, Carroll 3792, Caves 3795, Community 3808, Davies 3813, **Discovery 3815**, Duncan 3816, **Endocrine 3818, Estonian 3823**, Fast 3825, Foulger 3827, German 3833, Government 3838, **Hariri 3839**, Huether 3845, **Immune 3848**, Keswick 3857, Maryland 3871, Memorial 3880, Mid-Atlantic 3885, Mid-Shore 3887, Moran 3891, National 3894, **National 3895**, Phoenix 3912, **School 3928**, Seabee 3929, Sioda 3932, Skaters 3934, **Sodexo 3935**, Southern 3936, Thorn 3941, Trustees 3945, U.S. 3946, Worcester 3953

Massachusetts: Abbott, 3956, Affordable 3958, American 3967, Bassett 3978, Berkshire 3986, Blanchard 3988, Brightman 3998, Bushee 4002, Campenelli 4005, Cape Cod 4007, Carroll 4012, Carroll 4013, Cary 4014, Chester 4021, Community 4029, Costa 4030, Dyer 4048, East Cambridge 4050, East 4051, Educational 4054, Edwards 4055, Essex 4059, **Fleming 4072**, Foster 4075, Gerondelis 4082, Golub 4088, Hampden 4093, Hawks 4099, Hayden 4100, Hitchcock 4106, Holmes 4107, Holt 4108, Home 4110, Hopedale 4112, Hopkins 4113, Hunt 4122,

Hutchinson 4124, **International 4126**, Jackson 4128, Jennings 4130, Jones 4133, Kelly 4136, **Kennedy 4137**, Kernwood 4138, Koster 4142, Kurzweil 4143, **Liberty 4148**, Lowe 4151, **Lowell 4152**, Lynch 4155, Maloney 4158, Marino 4161, Massachusetts 4168, Mavrogenis 4169, **Maya 4170**, McElaney 4171, MetroWest 4173, Mihos 4175, Miss 4178, Mitchell 4179, Molloy 4181, Murphy 4182, New Bedford 4192, Niconchuk 4198, North 4199, Nye 4204, Ocean 4205, Orange 4207, Paine 4209, Peabody 4213, Permanent 4216, Perron 4217, Pettee 4218, Phillips 4222, Pittsfield 4225, Pope 4227, Pratt 4228, Quabaug 4233, **R.O.S.E. 4236**, Rotary 4248, Ruffini 4252, Saugus 4259, Schaeneman 4260, Scholarship 4261, Scholarship 4262, Scots 4264, Shultz 4268, Smalley 4269, Smith 4270, South 4272, Sudbury 4277, Sullivan 4278, Taylor 4283, Taylor 4284, Tenney 4285, Theta 4287, **Tourism 4292**, Travelli 4295, Trifiro 4297, Trustees 4298, Trustees 4300, Trustees 4301, University 4305, University 4306, Von 4309, Warren 4311, Whittemore 4317, Williams 4318, Woodman 4320, Worcester 4323, Young 4328, Zampogna 4330

Michigan: Abbott 4331, Allegan 4333, Allen 4335, Ann Arbor 4338, Baker 4342, Barr 4346, Barry 4347, Battle Creek 4349, Bay 4350, Bedford 4353, Bemis 4356, Birkenstock 4358, Birtwistle 4360, Blaske 4362, Bretzlaff 4368, Canton 4372, Cold 4385, Coller 4388, Community 4391, Community 4393, Community 4394, Community 4395, Community 4398, Community 4399, Dickinson 4408, Evereg-Fenesse 4414, Ewald 4415, Foster 4424, Four 4427, Frankenmuth 4428, Fraser 4429, Fremont 4431, Galesburg-Augusta 4432, **Gerber 4434**, Gibbs 4435, Gilles 4436, Goss 4443, Grand Haven 4444, Grand Rapids 4445, Grand 4447, Gratiot 4448, Great 4450, Greenville 4451, Guardian 4452, Hammel 4455, Harding 4457, HCC 4458, Hecht 4461, Heeringa 4462, Humbert 4476, Huron 4477, Huss 4478, Ilitch 4480, **International 4481**, Jackson 4484, Jackson 4485, Johnson 4487, Kadant 4491, Kalamazoo 4492, Kalamazoo 4493, Keweenaw 4499, Kiwanis 4501, Koch 4504, Lansing 4511, Lapeer 4512, LaVictoire 4513, Little 4519, Marquette 4524, Matson 4528, McCurdy 4529, Michigan 4535, Michigan 4538, Michigan 4540, Midland 4542, Minton 4544, Morrill 4546, Mount Pleasant 4548, Newaygo 4555, Nordman 4558, Optimist 4570, Parker 4573, Parks 4574, Pennock 4576, Petoskey 4577, Plumbers 4579, Polakovic 4581, Polan 4582, Raval 4584, Recreational 4585, Reuther 4588, Roscommon 4592, Rotary 4593, Rudy 4595, Ruf 4596, Saginaw 4597, Salisbury 4598, Sanilac 4599, Shiawassee 4605, Skandalaris 4607, Smith 4609, **Society 4611**, Southfield 4616, Speerstra 4621, **Sphinx 4622**, St. Joseph 4624, Sterling 4626, Stewart 4627, Tassell-Wisner-Bottrall 4632, Thomas 4636, Three 4637, Trinklein 4641, Trone 4642, Tuohy 4651, Tuscola 4646, Van Hollenbeck 4655, Vetowich 4658, Vomberg 4659, Welch 4663, Wells 4664, Whiteley 4667, Winship 4672, Wirick 4673, Young 4677

Minnesota: Adams 4681, Affinity 4682, AgStar 4683, Alumnae 4684, Alworth 4685, American 4688, Anderson 4691, Arvig 4695, Blandin 4700, Central 4711, Cox 4722, Daggett 4725, Denfeld 4726, Duluth 4729, Ely-Winton 4733, Foley 4739, **Gallagher 4746**, Gough 4749, Grand Rapids 4750, **Grannis-Martin 4751**, Henry 4757, Hoffman 4761, Hull 4762, Initiative 4764, Italian 4768, Jenniges 4770, **Lutheran 4785**, Mankato 4789, Masonic 4790, Minnesota 4804, Olson 4818, Osborn 4819, Page 4820, Petraborg 4822, Philanthrofund 4824, Pick 4825, Redwood 4835, Rochester 4840, Saint Paul 4842, **Scholarship 4845**, Siemer 4850, Soneson 4851, South 4853, St. Paul 4860, Target 4864, Thorbeck 4865, Thurston 4868, Trinity 4872, United 4874, Wenger

4887, Western 4888, Whiteside 4889, Wildey 4891

Mississippi: Community 4902, CREATE 4903, Day 4904, Feild 4907, Franks 4908, Gulf 4909, Hazard 4911, McDonald 4913, Mississippi 4915, **Mobile 4916**, Sumners 4923

Missouri: **Alpha 4929**, American 4931, Baptist-Trinity 4935, Barber 4936, **Boys 4941, Boys 4942**, Brey 4943, Buckner 4945, Campbell 4950, Carr 4953, Clay 4958, Clayton 4959, College 4961, Community 4963, Corbin 4966, Creasey 4971, **Demolay 4974**, Doerhoff 4977, Drowns 4979, Dunlop 4980, Edgar 4982, Educational 4983, Educational 4984, Feraldo 4990, Finnell 4993, French 4995, Fues 4997, Gorman 5002, Grant 5003, Green 5005, Griffin 5007, Hamilton 5012, Hayes 5013, Hirsch 5017, Kansas 5023, Kauffman 5026, Kennett 5028, Kirschner 5030, Klapmeyer 5031, Lord 5037, Lyons 5039, Mann 5042, Marymount 5046, McElroy 5047, McGlothlan 5048, Meyer 5049, MFA 5050, MHA 5051, Miles 5054, Missouri 5059, Nichols 5063, North 5066, Paul 5070, **Pi 5073**, Poillon 5075, Porter 5076, Ray 5078, Reynolds 5079, Saint Louis 5082, Schafer 5083, Schowengerdt 5085, Schwartze 5086, Schwartze 5087, Schwartze 5088, Schwartze 5091, Schwartze 5092, Schwartze 5094, Schwartze 5095, Schwartze 5096, Scottish 5097, **Sertoma, 5098**, Smith 5101, Soldwedel 5102, Sprehe 5103, Stowers 5109, Swanson 5110, Swope 5111, Thompson 5113, Tilles 5115, Tompkins 5116, Truman 5118, Young 5126

Montana: Ashcraft 5129, Bair 5130, Bottrell 5133, Clarkson 5136, Creek 5138, Cut Bank 5139, Daley 5140, Elm 5144, Flathead 5146, Groskinsky 5150, Haack 5152, Harbert 5154, Hawkins 5155, Hinderman 5157, Horsman 5158, Hurst 5159, Montana 5163, Montana 5164, Robinson 5168, Rolfson 5170, Student 5174, Suden 5175, Sweet 5177, Taber 5178, Townley 5179, Washington 5182

Nebraska: Bran 5187, Bryan 5188, **Buffett 5190**, EducationQuest 5197, Elliott 5199, Emerson 5201, Federated 5202, Fellman 5203, Fremont 5205, Genesis 5206, Good 5209, Grand Island 5210, Hastings 5215, Hay 5217, Hough 5219, Johnson 5222, Kearney 5223, Kiewit 5224, Killen 5225, Leslie 5227, Lexington 5228, Merrick 5233, Nebraska 5243, OEA 5249, Omaha 5251, Oregon 5252, Phelps 5255, Riley 5257, Simon 5261, Steinhart 5262, Sweet 5265, Wake 5269, Weller 5271, Wilson 5273, Wilson 5274, York 5277

Nevada: Community 5282, Doyle 5287, Foundation 5288, Holder 5289, Nevada 5296, Western 5304

New Hampshire: Bogni 5309, Burtman 5311, Cogan 5314, Edmunds 5319, Fond 5321, Foundation 5322, Gifford 5323, Green 5324, Griffin 5325, Hastings 5327, James 5331, Ladies 5334, Lakes 5335, Lancaster 5336, Manuel 5343, Martin 5345, McIninch 5346, Morton 5350, Oberkotter 5358, Plan 5361, Scots' 5367, Skrungloo 5368, Somerville 5369, Vanderhout 5375, White 5377, Wilson 5378, Yarnold 5379

New Jersey: Adelphic 5381, **American 5384**, Astle 5390, Avoda 5393, Bartell 5394, Bicket 5401, Butts 5408, Camden 5410, Chatham 5419, Cooper 5427, Cutter 5431, D'Annunzio 5432, **Dow 5435**, Everly 5442, Excelsior 5443, FMI 5447, **Foundation 5449**, Foundation 5450, Glen 5453, Gonzalez 5456, Groff 5460, Gruenberg 5461, Grupe 5462, Hale 5464, Hannaford 5465, Harness 5466, Hull 5475, Jackson 5480, Joint 5483, Kennedy 5486, Kovach 5491, Laucius 5495, Madison 5500, McLane 5503, Merck 5504, Michaels 5506, Miller 5508, Moorestown 5511, New Jersey 5517, Payne 5536, Peters 5539, Peterson 5540, Poucher 5544, Princeton 5546, Rigorous 5551, Saddle 5557, Saint 5558, Scotch 5561, Snyder 5570, Tavitian 5576, Townsend 5578, Trial 5580, Valley 5589, Van Doren 5590,

Van Doren 5591, White 5596, **Wilson 5600**, WKBJ 5602, Woman's 5603, Zahn 5607

New Mexico: Albuquerque 5610, **American 5612**, B.F. 5613, Berliner 5614, Carlsbad 5616, Central 5619, Columbus 5623, Continental 5626, ENMR 5628, Farmers' 5629, Finis 5630, Hamilton 5631, Laguna 5634, Lea 5636, Leaco 5637, Maddox 5639, Otero 5641, Peninsula 5643, Roosevelt 5646, Sacramento 5647, Santa Fe 5649, SPARX 5653, Springer 5654, Taos 5656, Viles 5657

New York: **AAAA 5662**, Albion 5678, Allegany 5681, Alumni 5684, **American 5696**, Armenian 5717, **Astraea 5736**, Avery 5744, Babylon 5746, Baker 5750, Big 5764, **Blake 5765**, Blake 5766, Blarney 5767, Bloomer 5768, **BMI 5771**, Borchert 5776, Bowman 5778, **Brackett 5779**, Brady 5780, Braverman 5781, Brewster 5785, Brink 5787, Brown 5800, Buffalo 5803, Buisch 5804, Burnett 5805, Campbell 5810, Cantor 5815, **Career 5816**, Carpenter 5819, Carrier 5820, Cattaraugus 5826, Central 5836, Chautauqua 5842, Children's 5848, Children's 5849, Clark 5860, Cogar 5863, Colburn 5864, Coleman 5865, College 5867, Collins 5868, Community 5877, Community 5878, Community 5879, Confort 5885, Cosby 5891, Cox 5896, Curran 5907, **Daughters 5915, Do 5928**, Druckenmiller 5936, Duffy 5937, Dyett 5942, Eagleton 5945, Earl 5946, Elenberg 5953, Farmen 5975, Fermi 5981, **Fight 5982**, Fitzpatrick 5985, Foundation 5991, Foundation 5999, Foundation 6002, Gaffney 6015, Gargiulo 6016, Gavrin 6018, German 6022, Giddings 6024, Gillroy 6026, Glasgow 6029, Glazer 6031, Glens Falls 6032, Goldstein 6037, Grandma 6043, Guarino 6047, Guenther 6048, Gunglach 6051, Hacker 6053, Hawley 6062, Herr 6069, Hinman 6070, Hirth 6071, Hoffert 6075, Howard 6078, Hudson 6080, **Institute 6095**, IRT 6105, Ivy 6106, Jachym 6107, Jenkins 6113, Jewish 6116, Joukowsky 6123, Kaplan 6129, Kathwari 6131, Kautz 6133, **King 6138**, King 6139, Kleeman 6141, **Kosciuszko 6145**, Krueger 6147, Kuhlman 6148, La 6150, Lewis 6161, **Lighthouse 6163, Lincoln 6164**, Lynch 6180, Mashomack 6194, Melville 6206, Memorial 6208, Metzger 6213, Mills 6217, NAACP 6237, **National 6241**, National 6247, Needham 6257, New York 6272, Nolan 6282, **North 6285**, Northern 6286, Northern 6287, Northrup 6288, Norwegian 6289, NYS 6290, Odasz 6291, Oneida 6292, **Open 6294**, Partridge 6305, Patterson 6308, Peace 6309, **Pearson 6310**, Potter 6322, Potter 6323, Pressman 6326, Price 6327, Provident 6336, Randon 6344, Realty 6347, Reddington 6349, Reinhardt 6351, Reinhart 6352, Rich 6355, Robinson 6356, Rochester 6357, Rye 6367, Scarsdale 6378, Schenectady 6382, **Schepp 6383**, Schiffner 6385, Scott 6388, Selfhelp 6392, **Shatford 6395**, Silver 6397, Skaneateles 6400, Snayberger 6407, **Societe 6410**, Society 6413, Spartan 6419, Sperry 6421, **Sponsors 6422, St. Elmo 6424**, St. Luke's 6426, Stack 6427, Stoner 6439, Stony 6440, Sweitzer 6443, Teel 6447, Thompson 6449, Thorwelle 6451, Thousand 6452, Tilt 6456, Trumansburg 6464, UFA 6469, United 6473, Varflex 6485, Wadas 6497, Walton 6500, Warren 6501, Wasserman 6503, **Watson 6504**, Westchester 6515, Windows 6522, Wolf 6526, **Women's 6528, Worldstudio 6535**, Yeshiva 6539, **Youth 6541, Zeta 6542**

North Carolina: 100 6543, Accel 6544, Allen 6548, Andrews 6553, Armfield 6556, Arnold 6557, Atlantic 6565, Ballard 6566, Bass 6568, Beaver 6571, Blowing Rock 6575, Borden 6576, Bowsher 6577, Boye 6578, Brandt 6579, Brewer 6580, Bridges 6581, Buck 6585, Butler 6588, Cady 6589, Carpenter 6592, Chappell 6597, Clements 6605, Coffman 6609, Cole 6611, Community 6613, Community 6616, Cooke 6617, Crawley 6622, Cumberland 6624, Davie 6625, Davis 6627, Eddy 6642, Edmonds 6644, Ella 6646, Evans 6650, Fairey 6652, Fairfield 6653, First 6657, Forbes 6658, Foundation 6660, Fouts

6663, Frank 6665, Frasier 6666, Gift 6671, Gramberg 6679, Greenville 6682, Grimley 6684, Groff 6685, Grogan 6686, Grotefend 6688, Guggenheim 6689, Harris 6695, Hess 6697, Hochmark 6700, Hoffman 6701, Huffman 6706, Hughes 6707, **Insurance 6712**, Johnson 6719, Johnson 6720, Jones 6723, Keena 6728, Kent 6730, **Kimmel 6731**, Kimmel 6732, Label 6734, Latham 6736, Leath 6737, Lee 6739, Leverenz 6742, Little 6744, Livingston 6745, Loar 6746, London 6748, Lundquist 6751, Lundy 6752, Martin 6757, Material 6758, McNair 6764, McRae 6766, Midland 6772, Miller 6774, Moore 6777, **Morehead-Cain 6778**, Morson 6779, Nelson 6789, Nichols 6791, North 6801, North Carolina 6802, Oates 6804, Outer 6806, Owens 6808, Pappas 6810, Patch 6811, Patterson 6812, Pharmacy 6818, Pitt County 6820, Reich 6823, Reierson 6824, Richardi 6829, Ritchie 6835, Roof 6841, Rouch 6842, Sauvain 6851, Scholarship 6853, Shelly 6859, **Sigma 6860**, Sloan 6863, Smith 6866, Spire 6870, Spivey 6871, St. Anthony 6873, Stewart 6879, Stoudenmire 6881, Tannenbaum 6885, Team 6889, Triangle 6899, Two 6904, Unruh 6909, Wiggins 6919, Wilson 6922, Winston-Salem 6923, Wyly 6929, Yerkes 6930, Young 6931, **Youth 6933**, Zimmerman 6934

North Dakota: Brown 6935, Minot 6945, Ruger 6947, Schuetze 6948

Ohio: Ackers 6955, Addison 6957, Agnew 6961, AJCA 6963, AK Steel 6964, Akron 6965, Allchin 6970, Anderson 6974, Anderson 6975, Andrus 6976, Ashtabula 6981, Atwood 6983, Bakes 6985, Barber 6987, Beal 6990, Beane 6992, Beinke 6993, Berlin 6996, Bernhard 6997, Bland 7001, Brayton 7011, Brighten 7013, Bryan 7017, Bush 7019, Butler 7020, Cafaro 7021, Campbell 7022, Carleton 7023, Carman 7024, Cassner 7027, Castele 7028, Chaney 7031, Chillicothe 7034, Clarke 7038, Cleveland 7040, Cleveland 7044, Cline 7046, College 7050, Columbia 7051, Columbus 7053, Community 7058, Community 7060, Community 7062, Coshocton 7065, County 7068, Crain 7070, Culture 7073, Danis 7077, Davey 7078, Davies 7080, Davis 7081, Dayton 7082, Dayton 7083, Dinger 7089, Dunlap 7092, Dunton 7093, **Eagles 7095**, Edgerton 7097, Everhart 7102, Evers 7103, Findlay 7107, Fishel 7110, Freer 7119, Ganyard 7122, Gardner 7124, Gazin 7126, Gonter 7128, Grace 7132, **Griffith 7136**, Grove 7137, H.O.P.E. 7138, Hamilton 7139, Hamilton 7140, Harrington 7141, Hartley 7143, Hauss 7144, Hawkes 7145, Herb 7146, Hering 7147, Herzberger 7148, Higgins 7149, Holmes 7152, Horvitz 7156, Hosler 7157, Hughes 7160, Hunter 7164, Hutton 7165, I Know 7166, Jackson 7172, Jamestown 7173, Jentes 7176, Kanhofer 7181, **Kappa 7182**, Kauffman 7184, Keller 7185, Kessel 7186, Kibble 7189, Kindler 7192, Kiser 7195, Kiwanis 7197, Knight 7199, Knowles 7200, Lapeer 7204, Lehman 7205, Lesher 7206, Licking 7209, **Lincoln 7210**, Lorain 7213, Loser 7214, Mauger 7223, McCabe 7224, McCallay 7225, McComb 7228, McConahay 7229, McDonald 7231, McDonald 7232, Mentzer 7239, Miami 7242, Michaud 7243, Miller 7247, Mishou 7252, Mohr 7253, Moore 7255, Moraine 7256, Munger 7258, Munro 7259, Murphy 7260, Muskingum 7263, Myers 7264, Myers 7265, National 7267, New Orphan 7268, Norris 7271, Ohio 7280, Outdoor 7286, Park 7291, PDR 7293, Peak 7294, Pehna 7296, Perry 7299, Phi Kappa 7302, Piqua 7303, Prior 7308, Rains 7311, Rapp 7312, Record 7316, Rhoad 7320, Richland 7321, Rickert 7322, Roach 7323, Roy 7330, Salem 7333, Samaritan 7335, Sandusky 7336, Scholarship 7338, Sebring 7341, Sharp 7343, Shinnick 7347, Shunk 7348, Slemp 7352, Smith 7355, Smith 7357, Smucker 7358, Spencer 7362, Springman 7364, St. Marys 7365, Stark 7366, Stinson 7370, **Student 7371**, Thiele 7378, Thompson 7379, Three 7380, Throckmorton

7381, Toomey 7386, Trachsel 7387, Troy 7388, Turco 7390, Tuscora 7391, Uschmann 7400, Van Hyning 7402, Van Wert 7403, VanBuren 7404, Vandenbark 7405, Vermillion 7406, Wahl 7409, Waldron 7411, Ward 7413, Warman 7414, Wayne 7415, White 7425, Wilhelm 7426, Williams 7427, Williams 7428, Wilson 7431, Wimmer 7432, Winans 7433, Wisner 7435, Wolf 7436, Wood 7437, Wooddell 7438, Wright 7441, Wyman 7442, Yoder 7445

Oklahoma: Aileen 7448, Bailey 7451, Beatty 7454, Carrier 7455, **Chickasaw 7457**, Communities 7459, Continue 7461, Donaghey 7464, Faranna 7467, Fields 7469, Frontiers 7472, Gatlin 7474, Guthrie 7477, Henry 7480, JWF 7487, Klamm 7490, Martin 7491, McKenzie 7493, **Reining 7508**, Rose 7509, Springfield 7513, Stevens 7515, Tulsa 7518, Tulsa 7519, Watson 7524, Wilson 7527

Oregon: Adler 7528, Alexandria 7530, Archer 7534, Bagley 7536, Banfield 7537, Benson 7538, Benton 7539, Buttrey 7541, Campbell 7543, Clemens 7549, Cockerline 7551, Collins 7552, Colvin 7553, Cooper 7557, Corvallis 7558, Cottage 7559, Criswell 7561, **Culinary 7562**, Danicas 7566, Dargan 7567, Dewuhs 7572, Ford 7578, Foss 7579, Franks 7580, Goodenough 7582, Hall 7583, Halton 7584, Hamilton 7585, Hellstern 7587, Holce 7588, Jackson-General 7589, Jenkins 7590, Laird 7593, Leonard 7596, Lytle 7598, McKee 7602, Mock 7607, Mount Angel 7611, **Multnomah 7613**, North 7617, Oapa 7621, Ochoco 7622, Oregon 7624, Pacific 7628, Palmer 7629, Professional 7635, Ragel 7640, Renaissance 7642, Ryan 7649, Salem 7650, Salem 7651, Schafer 7652, Scheinberg 7653, Schilling 7654, Singer 7659, Smith 7660, Southwestern 7665, Steinbach 7666, **Thomas 7669**, Trippeer 7670, Turner 7671, Vatheuer 7673, Von der Ahe 7675, Watt 7677, West 7680, Western 7681, Wilson 7684, Woodmansee 7685

Pennsylvania: Abernathy 7689, Abrams 7691, Adams 7692, Allen 7697, Alsobrooks 7698, American 7703, Armstrong 7710, Arpajian 7714, Asbestos 7715, Bailey 7721, Barrand 7722, Baskin 7725, Beaver 7726, Benford 7727, Berks 7730, Bernowski 7731, Blaisdell 7735, Blanchard 7736, Blues 7737, **Botstiber 7740**, Bread 7743, Brenneman 7744, Brevillier 7745, Bridge 7746, Broadbent 7747, Brossman 7748, Bucks 7752, Burch 7753, Chester 7764, Class 7771, Cochran 7773, Commission 7778, Community 7779, Community 7781, Community 7783, Community 7785, Conner 7789, Conrad 7790, Corson 7793, Corti 7794, **CPCU 7795**, Crawford 7796, Crawford 7797, Croatian 7798, Curtis 7802, Davis 7805, Davis 7807, Davis 7808, Delaware 7809, Eisenhauer 7820, Elk 7821, Ely 7825, England 7826, Erie 7831, Farber 7837, Fitch 7844, Fleischer 7847, FMC 7849, **Foundation 7850**, Foundation 7852, Friend 7859, Friendship 7861, Gates 7865, Gibson 7869, Grand 7878, Guthrie 7881, Harley 7886, Harmon 7887, Harris 7888, Harris 7889, Harris 7890, Harris 7891, Hassel 7893, Head 7895, Heald 7896, Helwig 7902, Heyburn 7904, Higbee 7905, Hill 7909, Horn 7912, Hughes 7913, II-VI 7915, Irvin 7921, Kalnoski 7932, Keith 7934, Kinney 7937, Kotur 7939, Langdale 7946, Larue-Dawson 7947, Laudermilch 7948, Lehigh Valley 7953, Lehr 7954, Lenfest 7956, Lintner 7959, Lowengard 7962, Luzerne 7964, Lynch 7965, Martz 7971, McCloskey 7974, McKaig 7975, McMannis 7977, Mellinger 7981, Mikovich 7984, Miller 7985, Miller 7988, Minear 7989, Moore 7992, Morgan 7995, Moyer 7996, Moyer 7997, Nelson 8002, Nicklies 8007, Noll 8008, O'Brien-Veba 8014, Paddington 8016, **Pan 8018, Penn 8021**, Pennsylvania 8029, Pennsylvania 8030, Percival 8031, Philadelphia 8039, Phillips 8040, Phoenixville 8041, Plank 8050, Polish 8053, Postles 8054, **PPG 8058**, Presser 8060, Preston 8062, Puckett 8067, Pyle 8068, Rhoads 8075, Ronald 8080, Ross 8083,

Saak 8086, Scholarship 8088, Scholarship 8089, Scranton 8094, Shartzer 8096, Sheen 8099, Shoemaker 8101, Siebenthal 8103, Simpson 8104, Sinden 8105, Singer 8106, Smith 8110, Smith 8112, Smithfield 8113, Snyder 8115, Soames 8118, Society 8119, Soeder 8120, Somerville 8121, Soren 8122, South 8123, Stager 8128, Stork 8134, Sutliff 8137, Swope 8138, Taylor 8139, Teamsters 8140, Thompson 8145, TLC 8147, Troutman 8150, Trushel 8151, Urban 8156, Valley 8158, Van Wynen 8160, Vastine 8164, Vincent 8165, Vodgis 8168, Vogeley 8169, Webber 8179, Webermeier 8182, Weed 8183, Williams 8191, Williams 8194, Williamson 8195, Wilson 8196, Wolf 8200, Wolf 8202, Wright 8209, Yopst 8211, York 8213, Young 8214, Yount 8216, Zimmerman 8219, Zurfluh 8221

Puerto Rico: Puerto Rico 8223

Rhode Island: Andrews 8229, Armstrong 8230, Arnold 8231, Bailey 8237, Baker 8238, Baker-Adams 8239, Bartlett 8241, Bell, 8242, Berry 8243, Black 8244, Bowmaker 8249, Brock 8252, Chandler 8256, Church 8258, Cianci 8259, Cilley 8260, Clark 8262, Cobb 8264, Coe 8266, Coia 8269, College 8271, Costa 8274, Cranston 8276, Croston 8278, Duxbury 8287, Eaton 8288, Ellsworth 8289, Farrington 8291, Forsyth 8293, Fox 8294, Fundacao 8296, Gill 8299, Green 8303, Greenlaw 8304, Gromack 8305, Harney 8307, Heald 8308, Henney 8309, Holopigian 8310, Hosser 8311, Humphrey 8313, Johnson 8316, Kamenski 8317, Kelley 8318, Kennedy 8319, Kiely 8320, Kinsley 8323, Life 8325, Little 8326, Long 8327, Lord 8328, Maes 8329, Mahan 8331, Makinson 8333, Matheson 8337, Maude 8338, Maybury 8339, Miles 8345, Miller 8346, Mills 8348, Morrow 8350, Moses 8351, Moulton 8352, Munson 8353, Nash 8354, Onodaga 8358, Orr 8359, Padelford 8360, Palen-Klar 8361, Pape 8363, Pierce 8370, Rhode Island 8380, Rhode Island 8381, Scheehl 8392, Schiff 8393, Sheehan 8397, Shifler 8398, Simionescu 8400, Sleesman 8401, Smith 8404, Smith 8405, Smith 8406, Smith 8407, Snyder 8410, Snyder 8411, Streeter 8416, Sutton 8417, Tappan 8420, Thompson 8421, Thompson 8422, Tracy 8426, Tryon 8427, Urann 8429, Valley 8430, Weaver 8432, Webster 8434, Wiggin 8436, Williams 8438, Williams 8439, Wood 8440, Wright 8441, Wylie 8442

South Carolina: **AVX 8450**, Bailey 8451, Byrnes 8453, Cameron 8454, Chief's 8460, Coastal 8464, Gallivan 8473, Gamecock 8474, Hart 8480, **Heritage 8483**, IDCA 8485, Kappa 8487, Kelly, 8488, Love 8491, Moore 8495, Moss 8496, NGA 8498, Ocean 8499, Smith 8507, Smith 8508, South 8511, South 8512, Springs 8515, Strive 8516, Tucker 8517

South Dakota: Amundson 8520, Black 8521, Cozard 8525, Doolittle 8528, Green 8532, Hatterscheidt 8533, Howard 8534, Solem 8539, South Dakota 8540, Strahl 8543, Ullyot 8545

Tennessee: Berkshire 8559, Bootstraps 8560, Carrier 8564, Chenoweth 8570, Chi Omega 8571, CIC 8574, Coburn 8576, Community 8577, Community 8578, Community 8579, Conte 8580, East 8587, Goodlark 8594, Hawkins 8598, Latimer 8613, Methodist 8620, Nashville 8626, Siegel 8644, Splawn 8648, Stahlman 8649, Stegall 8650, Temple 8653, Tomorrow 8655, Watkins 8660, Wilemon 8663, Woodbury 8665

Texas: Amarillo 8675, **American 8680**, Anderson 8687, Anderson 8688, Astin 8693, Astros 8694, Austin 8699, Baby 8701, Bartholomew 8703, Barto 8704, Baumberger 8706, Bellamy 8709, Bergman 8710, Berwin 8711, Betts 8712, Black 8713, Bonham 8715, Borton 8717, Bour 8718, Camp 8733, Cannon 8734, Carter 8737,

Chamberlin 8742, Chambers 8743, Coastal 8755, Communities 8759, Conference 8765, Cook 8769, Cook 8770, Dallas 8784, **Delta 8790**, Diffenbaugh 8793, Diffenbaugh-University 8795, Dunn 8800, Dupre 8801, East 8804, Educational 8808, Edwards 8809, El Paso 8811, Elam 8812, Ellzey 8813, Fasken 8819, Faulconer 8820, **First 8822**, Formosa 8826, Fuller 8832, Futureus 8834, Gill 8840, Hachar 8849, Hamilton 8850, Haraldson 8853, Havens 8857, Haverlah 8858, Hayes 8859, Headliners 8860, Heath 8862, Hefflefinger 8864, Hill 8866, Hill 8867, Hirsch 8868, **Hispanic 8870**, Hodges 8872, Houston 8879, Houston 8882, Houston 8884, Hubbard 8885, IFMA 8890, Ilgenfritz 8891, Imperial 8892, Janson 8898, Johnson 8900, Kelly 8904, Kimberly 8906, Klein 8907, Knight 8908, L.L.P. 8911, Lanham 8914, Lasco 8915, Lawler 8916, Lee 8917, Little 8919, Lubbock 8926, Luce 8928, Luling 8929, Maffett 8931, Maguire 8932, Marti 8936, McGovern 8944, McGowan 8945, McKenney 8947, McMillan, 8948, **Mehta 8951**, Mercer 8953, Millar 8958, Milotte 8963, Moody 8967, Morgan 8969, Morse 8971, Mouser 8972, Mustang 8977, National 8983, Nichols 8989, Nielson 8990, Norby 8991, Olson 8996, Panasonic 9001, Peery 9009, PFLAG/HATCH 9017, Phillips 9019, Piper 9022, Polk 9023, **Promotional 9030**, Reilly 9035, Rooke 9046, Ryan 9048, San Angelo 9053, San Antonio 9054, San Antonio 9055, San Antonio 9057, San Antonio 9058, Sand 9060, Seely 9067, Seibel 9068, Shouse 9071, Show 9072, Silver 9073, Silverthorne 9074, Singleton 9075, Siros 9077, Smolin 9080, Southeast 9087, Southwest 9091, Southwestern 9092, **SPE 9093**, Spencer 9094, St. Joseph 9096, St. Luke's 9098, Stanzel 9100, Taylor 9111, Texas 9115, Texas 9130, Thompson 9135, Trimble 9138, TUA 9139, Urban 9146, Vinsant 9150, Warnken 9157, Watson 9158, Wichita 9165, Wildner 9166, Wine 9170, Wintermann 9171, Wipe 9172, Wise 9173, Wisian 9174, Wolters 9175, Wood 9179, Wright 9183, Yett 9184, Young 9186, Znotas 9189

Utah: Bamberger 9193, Barrick 9194, Dialysis 9198, Harman 9204, Harmon 9205, Harvey 9206, Helaman 9207, Keener 9213, Lofthouse 9216, Masonic 9218, McCarthey 9219, Wheelwright 9230, WTF 9234

Vermont: Clifford 9241, Durfee 9245, England 9246, Essex 9247, Nordic 9255, Scott 9260, Terrill 9261, Trustees 9263, VARA 9265, Vermont 9267, Windham 9273

Virgin Islands: Community 9274, Rutnik 9276

Virginia: Air 9284, Alger 9285, All 9286, **American 9289, American 9295**, American 9299, **American 9300, American 9304, American 9307, Army 9315**, Bridgebuilder 9327, **Brown 9329**, Camp 9332, Capital 9333, Century 9337, **Club 9343**, Community 9345, Community 9346, Community 9347, Community 9348, Community 9349, Community 9350, **Cooke 9352, Datatel 9358, Descendants 9360**, Dornhecker 9363, English 9373, Foundation 9383, **Freedom 9385**, Goolsby-Gardner 9387, Greater 9388, Grubbs 9390, Hampton 9391, **Hispanic 9396**, IHFR 9403, **Institute 9404**, Jefferson 9408, Kane 9412, Kengla 9414, Lee-Jackson 9418, Lewis 9420, Lincoln 9421, **Military 9436**, Mitchell 9439, Morrow 9441, **National 9446**, National 9458, **Newton 9465**, Northern 9466, Orphan 9474, Perkins 9479, Pillay 9482, Randolph 9491, Research 9493, Sanford 9497, Schlarb 9499, Sidhu 9504, St. Paul's 9513, Stowers 9514, Strasburg 9515, Tidewater 9523, **United 9529, United 9530, USAWOA 9534**, Vascular 9537, Virginia 9541, Weaver 9544, Wiley 9548, **Wings 9550**

Washington: Alaska 9556, Arnsberg 9563, Bainbridge 9565, **Bainbridge 9566**, BECU 9567, Blue 9574, Bradley 9576, Burlington 9579, Carkeek 9581, Chevelle 9586, Clancy 9589, College 9594, Community 9599, Community 9600, Everett 9608, Evergreen 9609, First 9612, Fisher 9613, Frets 9617, George 9621, Grays 9624, Grimm 9625, Grow 9627, Hall 9628, Hamilton 9630, Holliday 9636, Hood 9637, Hunter 9640, Jensen 9642, Kedge 9648, Kelly 9649, Kelly 9650, Kitsap 9654, KT Family 9656, Lauzier 9658, Maxwell 9669, McCleary 9670, Mortar 9677, National 9679, Pace 9692, PEMCO 9697, Pigott 9698, Richardson 9706, Ritzville 9708, **Rotalia 9709**, Rural 9711, Schack 9715, Schumacher 9716, Seattle 9719, Slaid 9727, St. Luke's 9732, Treehouse 9736, Tudor 9737, Tufts 9738, Ulmschneider 9739, VanHoff 9741, W & G 9743, Walkling 9745, Washington 9746, Washington 9748, Welch 9751

West Virginia: Adams 9763, Beckley 9766, Burnside 9769, City 9775, Community 9777, Eastern 9780, Gault 9786, Hinton 9790, Kanawha 9794, Larsen 9795, Logan 9797, Ludwig 9798, Matthews 9799, McCormick 9801, Minor 9802, Mountaintop 9804, Pais 9807, Parkersburg 9808, Princeton 9812, Stickley 9817, Stout 9819, Sun 9821, Tucker 9824, Vecellio 9826, Your 9831

Wisconsin: Askren 9839, Aslakson 9840, Badger 9844, Badger 9845, Bemis 9847, Birbeck 9848, Black River 9849, Brillion 9852, Brown 9853, Carnes 9859, Casper 9860, Chetek 9862, Chmielewski 9863, Community 9866, Community 9867, Community 9869, Compass 9871, Door 9878, Dupee 9879, **EAA 9880**, Elfers 9883, **Entomological 9884**, Environmental 9885, Exacto 9886, Fahrney 9888, Fernstrum 9891, Fix 9892, Fond du Lac 9893, Four 9896, Frautschy 9897, Freedom 9898, Fromm 9901, Giddings 9906, Goldbach 9907, Green Bay 9910, Grimm 9912, Hale 9914, Hasselhofer-Wolf 9916, Henrizi 9920, Hilgen 9921, Hodes 9922, Holt 9923, Incourage 9925, Johnson 9935, Kallies 9937, Kelben 9938, Keller 9940, Kohl 9944, Kohler 9945, Kohl's 9946, La Crosse 9948, Lakeland 9949, Lauterbach 9950, Laviolette 9951, Madison 9956, Markos 9959, Marshfield 9960, Marth 9961, Melissa 9964, Mentzer 9966, Milwaukee 9971, Moore 9974, Munster 9976, Nelson 9979, Nishan 9983, O'Hara 9986, Oshkosh 9988, Oshkosh 9989, Phillips 9993, Raether 10003, Ramiah 10004, Redfield 10005, Richards 10009, **Riesch 10010**, SBC 10020, Scholarship 10022, Schwarz 10024, Seymour 10027, Shafer 10028, Shallow 10029, Sharp 10030, Sheets 10031, Sivyer 10034, Smith 10035, Smith 10036, Sonnentag 10039, St. Croix 10043, St. John 10045, Stateline 10047, Stifel 10048, Suder 10049, Thomas 10051, Vedova 10058, Wahlin 10061, Weigel 10067, Wells 10068, Wilber 10072, Wisconsin 10075, Wisconsin 10079, Wisconsin 10081, Wisconsin 10083, WPS 10088

Wyoming: Anderson 10094, Cody 10098, Community 10099, Construction 10100, Curtis 10101, Gillet 10104, Giovanini 10105, Johnson 10108, Laing 10109, Likins 10111, Littler 10113, Milne 10114, Pearson 10116, Pilch 10118, Whitney 10124, Williams 10125, Wyoming 10126

Workstudy grants

Connecticut: Branford 1338

Illinois: **National 2749**

New Jersey: Peters 5539

New York: **Institute 6095, National 6241**, Scott 6388, Wegmans 6507

Virginia: Association 9323

SUBJECT INDEX

The numbers under the subject headings in this index refer to the sequence numbers of entries in the Descriptive Directory section of this book. Grantmakers that give nationally, regionally, or internationally are indicated in boldface type following the states in which they are located. Grantmakers that restrict their giving to particular states, counties, or cities are listed in lighter type following the states in which they give. This index is generated to denote the fields of interest a grantmaker might support that are relevant to an individual's needs and does not include the giving interests the grantmaker provides to organizations.

Accessibility/universal design
Adult education—literacy, basic skills & GED
Adult/continuing education
Adults
Adults, men
Adults, women
African Americans/Blacks
Aging
Aging, centers/services
Agriculture
Agriculture, farm bureaus/granges
Agriculture, farmlands
Agriculture, livestock issues
Agriculture, sustainable programs
Agriculture/food
Agriculture/food, formal/general education
Agriculture/food, management/technical
  assistance
Agriculture/food, public education
Agriculture/food, research
AIDS
see also AIDS, people with
AIDS research
AIDS, people with
Alcoholism
Allergies
Allergies research
ALS
ALS research
Alzheimer's disease
Alzheimer's disease research
American studies
Anatomy (animal)
Anatomy (human)
Anesthesiology
Anesthesiology research
Animal population control
Animal welfare
Animals/wildlife
Animals/wildlife, bird preserves
Animals/wildlife, fisheries
Animals/wildlife, formal/general education
Animals/wildlife, preservation/protection
Animals/wildlife, public education
Animals/wildlife, research
Anthropology/sociology
Art history
Arthritis
Arthritis research

Arts
see also dance; film/video; museums; music;
  performing arts; theater; visual arts
Arts education
Arts, administration/regulation
Arts, alliance/advocacy
Arts, artist's services
Arts, cultural/ethnic awareness
Arts, folk arts
Arts, formal/general education
Arts, fund raising/fund distribution
Arts, management/technical assistance
Arts, multipurpose centers/programs
Arts, public education
Arts, research
Arts, services
Arts, volunteer services
Asians/Pacific Islanders
Asthma
Asthma research
Astronomy
Athletics/sports, academies
Athletics/sports, amateur competition
Athletics/sports, amateur leagues
Athletics/sports, baseball
Athletics/sports, basketball
Athletics/sports, equestrianism
Athletics/sports, fishing/hunting
Athletics/sports, football
Athletics/sports, golf
Athletics/sports, Olympics
Athletics/sports, professional leagues
Athletics/sports, racquet sports
Athletics/sports, school programs
Athletics/sports, soccer
Athletics/sports, Special Olympics
Athletics/sports, training
Athletics/sports, water sports
Athletics/sports, winter sports
Autism
Autism research
Big Brothers/Big Sisters
Biology/life sciences
Biomedicine
Biomedicine research
Blind/visually impaired
Botanical/horticulture/landscape services
Botany
Boy scouts
Boys

Boys & girls clubs
Boys clubs
Brain disorders
Brain research
Breast cancer
Breast cancer research
Buddhism
Business school/education
Business/industry
Business/industry, trade boards
Cancer
Cancer research
Cancer, leukemia
Cancer, leukemia research
Catholic agencies & churches
Cemeteries/burial services
Cerebral palsy research
Charter schools
Chemistry
Child development, education
Child development, services
Children
Children's rights
Children, adoption
Children, day care
Children, foster care
Children, services
Children/youth
Children/youth, services
Chiropractic
Christian agencies & churches
Civil liberties, first amendment
Civil rights, race/intergroup relations
see also civil/human rights
Civil/human rights
Civil/human rights, advocacy
Civil/human rights, formal/general education
Civil/human rights, immigrants
Civil/human rights, LGBTQ
Civil/human rights, minorities
Civil/human rights, women
Community development, neighborhood
  associations
Community development, neighborhood
  development
Community development, real estate
Community development, small businesses
Community/economic development
Community/economic development, research

Community/economic development, volunteer
   services
Computer science
Courts/judicial administration
Crime/abuse victims
Crime/law enforcement
Crime/law enforcement, association
Crime/law enforcement, correctional facilities
Crime/law enforcement, formal/general
   education
Crime/law enforcement, government agencies
Crime/law enforcement, police agencies
Crime/law enforcement, reform
Crime/law enforcement, research
Crime/violence prevention
see also domestic violence; gun control
Crime/violence prevention, abuse prevention
see also child abuse; domestic violence
Crime/violence prevention, child abuse
Crime/violence prevention, domestic violence
Crime/violence prevention, sexual abuse
Crime/violence prevention, youth
Cystic fibrosis
Cystic fibrosis research
Deaf/hearing impaired
Dental care
Dental school/education
Developmentally disabled, centers & services
Diabetes
Diabetes research
Diagnostic imaging
Diagnostic imaging research
Digestive diseases
Digestive disorders research
Disabilities, people with
Disasters, 9/11/01
Disasters, domestic resettlement
Disasters, fire prevention/control
Disasters, floods
Disasters, Hurricane Katrina
Disasters, preparedness/services
Disasters, search/rescue
Diseases (rare)
Diseases (rare) research
Down syndrome
Down syndrome research
Ear, nose & throat diseases
Ear, nose & throat research
Economic development
Economically disadvantaged
Economics
Education
Education, administration/regulation
Education, alliance/advocacy
Education, association
Education, continuing education
Education, early childhood education
Education, ESL programs
Education, formal/general education
Education, fund raising/fund distribution
Education, gifted students
Education, management/technical assistance
Education, public education
Education, reading
Education, research
Education, services
Education, single organization support
Education, special
Elementary school/education
Elementary/secondary education
Employment
Employment, association
Employment, government agencies
Employment, job counseling

Employment, labor unions/organizations
Employment, research
Employment, services
Employment, training
Employment, vocational rehabilitation
End of life care
Engineering
Engineering school/education
Engineering/technology
Environment
see also energy; natural resources
Environment, beautification programs
Environment, climate change/global warming
Environment, energy
Environment, ethics
Environment, forests
Environment, formal/general education
Environment, land resources
Environment, legal rights
Environment, natural resources
Environment, plant conservation
Environment, pollution control
Environment, public policy
Environment, radiation control
Environment, recycling
Environment, reform
Environment, research
Environment, toxics
Environment, volunteer services
Environment, waste management
Environment, water pollution
Environment, water resources
Environmental education
Epilepsy
Epilepsy research
Ethnic studies
Eye diseases
Eye research
Family resources and services, disability
Family services
Family services, adolescent parents
Family services, counseling
Family services, domestic violence
Family services, home/homemaker aid
Family services, parent education
Family services, single parents
Financial services
Financial services, credit unions
Food banks
Food distribution, groceries on wheels
Food services
Food services, commodity distribution
Foundations (private grantmaking)
Fraternal societies
Fraternal societies (501(c)(8))
Genetic diseases and disorders
Genetic diseases and disorders research
Geology
Geriatrics
Geriatrics research
Gerontology
Girl scouts
Girls
Government/public administration
Graduate/professional education
Health care
Health care, association
Health care, burn centers
Health care, clinics/centers
Health care, emergency transport services
Health care, EMS
Health care, financing
Health care, formal/general education
Health care, home services

Health care, insurance
Health care, patient services
Health care, public policy
Health care, reform
Health care, research
Health care, support services
Health care, volunteer services
Health organizations, management/technical
   assistance
Health organizations, research
Health organizations, volunteer services
Health sciences school/education
Heart & circulatory diseases
Heart & circulatory research
Hematology
Hematology research
Hemophilia
Hemophilia research
Higher education
Higher education, college
see also higher education
Higher education, college (community/junior)
see also higher education
Higher education, university
see also higher education
Hinduism
Hispanics/Latinos
Historic preservation/historical societies
Historical activities
Historical activities, genealogy
Historical activities, war memorials
History/archaeology
Holistic medicine
Home economics
Homeless
Homeless, human services
see also economically disadvantaged; food services;
   housing/shelter, homeless
Horticulture/garden clubs
Hospitals (general)
Housing/shelter
Housing/shelter, aging
Housing/shelter, development
Housing/shelter, expense aid
Housing/shelter, home owners
Housing/shelter, homeless
Housing/shelter, management/technical
   assistance
Housing/shelter, owner/renter issues
Housing/shelter, rehabilitation
Housing/shelter, repairs
Housing/shelter, services
Housing/shelter, temporary shelter
Human services
Human services, emergency aid
Human services, financial counseling
Human services, gift distribution
Human services, government agencies
Human services, mind/body enrichment
Human services, personal services
Human services, transportation
Human services, travelers' aid
Human services, victim aid
Human services, volunteer services
Humanities
see also history/archaeology; language/linguistics;
   literature; museums
Immigrants/refugees
Immunology
Immunology research
Independent housing for people with disabilities
Independent living, disability
Infants/toddlers
Insurance, providers

International affairs
see also arms control; international peace/security
International affairs, arms control
see also international affairs; international peace/
security
International affairs, foreign policy
International affairs, formal/general education
International affairs, government agencies
International affairs, information services
International affairs, national security
International affairs, public policy
International affairs, research
International conflict resolution
International development
International economic development
International economics/trade policy
International exchange
International exchange, arts
International exchange, students
International human rights
International migration/refugee issues
International peace/security
International relief
International studies
Islam
Jewish agencies & synagogues
Journalism school/education
Kidney diseases
Kidney research
Landscaping
Language (classical)
Language (foreign)
Language/linguistics
Law school/education
Law/international law
Leadership development
see also youth development, services
Learning disorders
Learning disorders research
Legal services
Legal services, public interest law
LGBTQ
Libraries (academic/research)
Libraries (medical)
Libraries (public)
Libraries (school)
Libraries (special)
Libraries/library science
Literature
Liver research
Lung diseases
Lung research
Lupus
Lupus research
Marine science
Mathematics
Media, film/video
Media, journalism
Media, print publishing
Media, radio
Media, television
Media/communications
Medical care, community health systems
Medical care, in-patient care
Medical care, outpatient care
Medical care, rehabilitation
Medical research
Medical research, formal/general education
Medical research, institute
Medical school/education
see also dental school/education; nursing school/
education
Medical specialties
Medical specialties research
Medicine/medical care, public education

Men
Mental health, addictions
Mental health, counseling/support groups
Mental health, depression
Mental health, disorders
Mental health, eating disorders
Mental health, schizophrenia
Mental health, smoking
Mental health, stress
Mental health, transitional care
Mental health, treatment
Mental health/crisis services
Mental health/crisis services, research
Mental health/crisis services, suicide
Mentally disabled
Middle schools/education
Migrant workers
Military/veterans
Military/veterans' organizations
Minorities
see also African Americans/Blacks; Asians/Pacific
Islanders; civil/human rights, minorities;
Hispanics/Latinos; Native Americans/American
Indians
Minorities/immigrants, centers/services
Multiple sclerosis
Multiple sclerosis research
Muscular dystrophy
Muscular dystrophy research
Museums
Museums (art)
Museums (children's)
Museums (history)
Museums (natural history)
Museums (science/technology)
Museums (specialized)
Museums (sports/hobby)
Mutual aid societies
Mutual aid societies, research
Mutual aid societies, volunteer services
Myasthenia gravis
Myasthenia gravis research
Native Americans/American Indians
Neighborhood centers
Nerve, muscle & bone diseases
Nerve, muscle & bone research
Neuroscience
Neuroscience research
Nonprofit management
Nursing care
Nursing home/convalescent facility
Nursing school/education
Nutrition
Obstetrics/gynecology
Obstetrics/gynecology research
Offenders/ex-offenders
Offenders/ex-offenders, rehabilitation
Offenders/ex-offenders, services
Offenders/ex-offenders, transitional care
Optometry/vision screening
Organ diseases
Organ research
Orthopedics
Orthopedics research
Palliative care
Parkinson's disease
Parkinson's disease research
Pathology
Pathology research
Pediatrics
Pediatrics research
Pensions
Pensions, teacher funds
Performing arts
Performing arts (multimedia)

Performing arts centers
Performing arts, ballet
Performing arts, choreography
Performing arts, dance
Performing arts, education
Performing arts, music
Performing arts, music (choral)
Performing arts, music composition
Performing arts, music ensembles/groups
Performing arts, opera
Performing arts, orchestras
Performing arts, theater
Performing arts, theater (musical)
Performing arts, theater (playwriting)
Personal assistance services (PAS)
Pharmacology
Pharmacology research
Pharmacy/prescriptions
Philanthropy/voluntarism
Philanthropy/voluntarism, administration/
regulation
Philanthropy/voluntarism, formal/general
education
Philanthropy/voluntarism, fund raising/fund
distribution
Philanthropy/voluntarism, management/
technical assistance
Philanthropy/voluntarism, volunteer services
Philosophy/ethics
Physical therapy
Physical/earth sciences
Physically disabled
Physics
Podiatry
Political science
Population studies
Poverty studies
Pregnancy centers
Prostate cancer
Prostate cancer research
Protestant agencies & churches
Psychology/behavioral science
Public affairs
Public affairs, administration/regulation
Public affairs, citizen participation
Public affairs, finance
Public affairs, government agencies
Public affairs, political organizations
Public affairs, reform
Public health
Public health school/education
Public health, epidemiology
Public health, obesity
Public health, occupational health
Public health, physical fitness
Public policy, research
Recreation
Recreation, camps
Recreation, community
Recreation, equal rights
Recreation, parks/playgrounds
Recreation, social clubs
Religion
see also Jewish agencies & temples; Protestant
agencies & churches; Catholic agencies &
churches
Religion, formal/general education
Religion, interfaith issues
Religion, public policy
Religion, research
Reproductive health
Reproductive health, fertility
Reproductive health, OBGYN/Birthing centers
Reproductive health, prenatal care

Residential/custodial care
Residential/custodial care, group home
Residential/custodial care, half-way house
Residential/custodial care, hospices
Residential/custodial care, senior continuing
  care
Residential/custodial care, special day care
Rural development
Rural studies
Safety, automotive safety
Safety, education
Safety/disasters
Safety/disasters, ethics
Safety/disasters, government agencies
Safety/disasters, research
Scholarships/financial aid
Science
see also biological sciences; chemistry; computer
  science; engineering/technology; marine science;
  physical/earth sciences
Science, formal/general education
Science, information services
Science, management/technical assistance
Science, public education
Science, public policy
Science, research
Secondary school/education
see also elementary/secondary education
Self-advocacy services, disability
SIDS (Sudden Infant Death Syndrome)
SIDS (Sudden Infant Death Syndrome) research
Single parents
Skin disorders
Skin disorders research
Social entrepreneurship
Social sciences
see also anthropology/sociology; economics; political
  science; psychology/behavioral science

Social sciences, ethics
Social sciences, interdisciplinary studies
Social sciences, public education
Social sciences, public policy
Social sciences, research
Social work school/education
Space/aviation
Speech/hearing centers
Spine disorders
Spine disorders research
Spirituality
Students, sororities/fraternities
Substance abuse, prevention
Substance abuse, services
Substance abuse, treatment
Substance abusers
Supported living
Surgery
Surgery research
Teacher school/education
Telecommunications
Terminal illness, people with
Theological school/education
Theology
Thrift shops
Transportation
Tropical diseases research
United Ways and Federated Giving Programs
Urban studies
Urban/community development
Utilities
Veterinary medicine
Veterinary medicine, hospital
Visual arts
Visual arts, architecture
Visual arts, art conservation
Visual arts, ceramic arts

Visual arts, design
Visual arts, drawing
Visual arts, painting
Visual arts, photography
Visual arts, sculpture
Vocational education
Vocational education, post-secondary
Vocational school, secondary
Voluntarism promotion
Web-based media
Welfare policy/reform
Women
see also civil/human rights, women; reproductive rights
Women's studies
Women, centers/services
YM/YWCAs & YM/YWHAs
Young adults
Young adults, female
Young adults, male
Youth
Youth development
Youth development, adult & child programs
Youth development, agriculture
Youth development, business
Youth development, centers/clubs
Youth development, community service clubs
Youth development, ethics
Youth development, services
Youth development, volunteer services
Youth, pregnancy prevention
Youth, services

Accessibility/universal design

District of Columbia: ULI 1740

Adult education—literacy, basic skills & GED

Delaware: **International 1514**
Florida: Operation 2006
Massachusetts: First 4069
New Jersey: Townsend 5578

Adult/continuing education

Alaska: Kuskokwim 123, Tanana 140
Arkansas: **Murphy 296**
California: **QUALCOMM 889, Sempra 974**
Delaware: Delaware 1500
Idaho: Simplot 2349
Indiana: Community 2998, Public 3152
Iowa: **P.E.O. 3351**
Kentucky: Community 3559
Maine: Maine 3712
New Jersey: Camden 5410
New Mexico: B.F. 5613
New York: **Social 6409**
Ohio: College 7050
Oregon: **Culinary 7562**, Ford 7578
Rhode Island: **Dorot 8286**
Texas: Southwest 9091
Wisconsin: Wisconsin 10081

Adults

California: Alta 351

Colorado: Community 1173
District of Columbia: **Airline 1535, National 1687**
Georgia: Creative 2158
Indiana: Levin 3098
Massachusetts: Knights 4141
Michigan: Community 4390
Minnesota: Catholic 4708, Southwest 4857
New York: **UJA 6470**
North Carolina: Telamon 6890
Pennsylvania: Elwyn 7824

Adults, men

Ohio: Phi Kappa 7302
Pennsylvania: Bread 7743

Adults, women

California: **Aid 343**
Colorado: **Foundation 1199**
Maryland: Choice 3802
Massachusetts: Peabody 4213
Michigan: Sojourner 4613
New Jersey: **Newcombe 5526**
New Mexico: Community 5624
New York: **Avon 5745**
Ohio: Grace 7132
Pennsylvania: Bartko 7723, Leeway 7951
Vermont: Barrows 9236
Virginia: **Ashoka: 9317**

African Americans/Blacks

California: **Adobe 338, Aid 343, Getty 614, HP 670**,
  Lagrant 731, Ronald 918
Colorado: Ronald 1274, Sachs 1277
Connecticut: Connecticut 1366, Promising 1446
District of Columbia: Black 1593, **Development 1614,
  German 1638, Hurston 1648, Jack 1661, United
  1743**
Florida: **Holland 1918**, Magic 1958, Miami 1978,
  Orlando 2008
Georgia: Fund 2181
Hawaii: Towle 2323
Illinois: **Medical 2728, Organization 2769**
Maryland: Adams 3750
Michigan: Come 4389, Community 4394, Grand 4446,
  Kalamazoo 4492, **Sphinx 4622**, Young 4677
Minnesota: Bowman 4702, Higher 4758, Lemieux
  4782, New York 4812
New Jersey: KPMG 5493, Newark 5525
New York: **AAAA 5662**, Camera 5809, **Cave 5827**, Ivy
  6106, **League 6156**, NAACP 6237, **National
  6241, National 6252**, New York 6269, Price 6327,
  Studio 6441, Warren 6501
North Carolina: 100 6543, McAllister 6759
Ohio: AK Steel 6964, Dayton 7082, McLendon 7237,
  Throckmorton 7381
Oklahoma: Miley 7495
Pennsylvania: Abernathy 7689, Worthington 8208
South Carolina: Coastal 8464
Texas: Alpha 8674, Faulconer 8820, L.L.P. 8911,
  Maffett 8931
Virginia: **Brown 9329, National 9451**
Washington: Washington 9747
Wisconsin: Milwaukee 9971

Aging

Alabama: Alabama 3
Arizona: Pima 228
Arkansas: Area 261
California: American 355, **Civic 501**, Italian 698, Marguerite 770, New 826, Oakley 838, San Francisco 942, Second 971
Colorado: Jewish 1222, Lutheran 1235
Connecticut: Larrabee 1413, Senior 1459
District of Columbia: **Families 1625**, Gerontological 1639, **National 1687**
Florida: Area 1780, Areawide 1781, Colen 1834, duPont 1865, Northeast 2000, Senior 2059
Georgia: Concerted 2154, Ladonna 2204, North 2217
Hawaii: Hawaii 2289
Illinois: **Abbott 2353**, C.E.F.S. 2454, Central 2466, Energy 2545, Higgins 2616, Illinois 2642, Morton 2739, **Serbian 2848**, Swiss 2884
Indiana: Area 2957, Northwest 3128
Iowa: Magnus 3329, Waverly 3406
Kansas: Sidwell 3514, Southwest 3518
Maine: Camden 3691, Portland 3726
Maryland: Community 3804, Community 3809, Neighborhood 3901, Warfield 3951
Massachusetts: Association 3974, Bristol 3999, Central 4017, **Devens 4039**, Elder 4057, **Elderhostel 4058**, Farmer 4063, HAP 4094, Howland 4120, Martin 4162, Pierce 4223, Plymouth 4226, Relief 4241, Salem 4253, South 4275, Swan 4280
Michigan: Arts 4340, Blue 4363, Foundation 4425, Gilmore 4437, Italian 4483, Oakland 4566, Region 4586, Rochester 4590
Minnesota: Mahube 4788, Minnesota 4803, Semcac 4849
Missouri: Bentley 4939, Concerned 4965, Missouri 5060, North 5065, Northeast 5067
Nebraska: Home 5220
New Hampshire: Hunt 5330
New Jersey: Brookdale 5405, Northwest 5528, Orenstein 5532, **Ostberg 5533**
New York: Adams 5666, **American 5707**, Bagby 5749, Carter 5821, **Conference 5884**, **Elizabeth 5957**, Federation 5979, Foundation 5996, Holland 6076, Jewish 6115, Jewish 6119, MacKinnon 6181, Parodneck 6304, Saranac 6374, St. George's 6425, Tinker 6457, Tuttle 6467
North Carolina: Indian 6710, Mountain 6780, Telamon 6890
Ohio: Ford 7113, Gay 7125, Loeb 7212, Mansfield 7218, Maple 7219, Ohio 7277, Powell 7307, PSA 7309, Sheadle 7345, Western 7420
Oklahoma: Areawide 7450
Oregon: McComas 7600
Pennsylvania: Aid 7693, Female 7839, French 7858, Ladd 7940, Smock 8114, Western 8189
Rhode Island: Cranston/Theophilus 8277, Davenport 8283, Robbins 8384, Townsend 8425
South Carolina: Boyne 8452
Tennessee: East 8588, Southeast 8647, Upper 8659
Texas: Catholic 8740, Community 8761, Cutter 8779, Neighborhood 8988
Utah: Last 9215
Vermont: Copley 9242
Virginia: Americans 9313, Navy 9461
Washington: Artist 9564, Daystar 9605, Market 9667, Metropolitan 9675, Rural 9712, Welch 9752
West Virginia: Serra 9814

Aging, centers/services

Arizona: Pima 228
Arkansas: Ozark 301
Florida: Area 1780, Areawide 1781
Maine: Camden 3691
Michigan: Region 4586
Wisconsin: St. Elizabeth 10044

Agriculture

Arkansas: Arkansas 265

California: Bodine 417, Calcot 440, California 448, **Foundation 586**, Hamilton 646, **Organic 846**, Smith 996, Stern 1024
Connecticut: Rockville 1450
District of Columbia: **American 1555**, **German 1638**
Florida: Florida 1879, Lauffer 1947
Illinois: First 2562, Geneseo 2580, McClain 2717, McDonald 2718, Schweitzer 2846, Titus 2893
Indiana: Community 2990, **Future 3040**
Iowa: Iowa 3305, Iowa 3306, Marek 3331, **Pioneer 3358**, World 3410
Kentucky: Community 3559
Louisiana: Lang 3660, Louisiana 3666
Michigan: Fremont 4431, Michigan 4534
Minnesota: AgStar 4683, Alworth 4685, Farmers 4737, Land 4779, **Lindbergh 4783**, Northwest 4817, Roberg 4839, Rosen 4841
Missouri: MFA 5050, Tompkins 5116
Nebraska: Nebraska 5238
New York: **Camphill 5811**
North Carolina: Boye 6578, Robinson 6839
Ohio: Crain 7070, Herb 7146, Mercer 7240, Milroy 7251, Ohio 7279, Van Wert 7403, VanBuren 7404
Pennsylvania: Corti 7794, Harris 7889, Smithfield 8113, Walter 8173
Rhode Island: Urann 8429
South Carolina: Cameron 8454
Tennessee: Wilemon 8663
Texas: Amarillo 8675, Barnsley 8702, Dupre 8801, Fort Worth 8829, Luling 8929, Texas 9116
Wisconsin: AgSource 9833, Beal 9846, Eckburg 9881, **Entomological 9884**, Green Bay 9910, Phillips 9994, Wisconsin 10081
Wyoming: Williams 10125

Agriculture, farm bureaus/granges

Iowa: Iowa 3305
Kentucky: Farm 3568
Missouri: Brey 4943

Agriculture, farmlands

Washington: Washington 9746

Agriculture, livestock issues

District of Columbia: Global 1641
New Hampshire: Hubbard 5329
Texas: San Antonio 9058, Show 9072

Agriculture, sustainable programs

California: **Organic 846**

Agriculture/food

Arizona: Community 181
California: **NMA 828**, **Organic 846**
Indiana: **National 3122**
Massachusetts: New 4195
Minnesota: University 4877
Missouri: **Agriculture 4928**
New York: Food 5989, Wegmans 6507
Pennsylvania: Copp 7792
Virginia: **Operation 9471**
Washington: Hamilton 9630

Agriculture/food, formal/general education

Arkansas: Arkansas 264
California: Lytel 763, Woodward 1100
Florida: Blac 1800
Indiana: Decatur 3013, LaGrange 3093
Michigan: Petoskey 4577
Minnesota: 3-H 4678, AgStar 4683, Land 4779
New Jersey: Zahn 5607
Rhode Island: Snyder 8411
Texas: San Antonio 9058

Agriculture/food, management/technical assistance

Minnesota: Farmers 4737

Agriculture/food, public education

Illinois: Wise 2930
Indiana: **Future 3040**
Minnesota: CHS 4715
North Carolina: **Student 6883**

Agriculture/food, research

California: **Organic 846**

AIDS

California: Bickerstaff 413, **Children 485**, **Kaiser 716**
District of Columbia: **Accordia 1531**
Maine: Down 3694
Maryland: Sisters 3933
New Jersey: Several 5563
New York: **New 6264**
Virginia: Children's 9340
Washington: Lifelong 9661

AIDS research

District of Columbia: **Accordia 1531**, **Glaser 1640**
Mississippi: **Pine 4919**
New York: **Foundation 5992**, **New 6264**

AIDS, people with

California: AIDS 344, **Children 485**, Serra 976
Delaware: Delaware 1503
Florida: AIDS 1764, Sieber 2061
Hawaii: Life 2301
Indiana: AIDS 2946
Massachusetts: AIDS 3961
New York: Morton 6227
North Carolina: Triad 6898
South Carolina: Lowcountry 8492
Tennessee: Nashville 8625
Texas: AIDS 8669
Virginia: Eastern 9367

Alcoholism

New York: Carpenter 5819

Allergies

California: **Immunobiology 677**
New York: **Food 5988**
Wisconsin: American 9834

Allergies research

Illinois: **American 2373**, **Foundation 2569**
New York: **Food 5988**
Texas: **American 8677**
Virginia: **American 9288**, **Food 9378**
Wisconsin: American 9834

ALS

North Carolina: Hunter 6709

ALS research

Massachusetts: **ALS 3962**

Alzheimer's disease

California: Oakley 838
New York: **American 5694**
North Carolina: Broad 6582

Alzheimer's disease research

California: **French 594**
Maryland: Brightfocus 3789
Mississippi: **Pine 4919**
New York: **Alzheimer's 5685, MetLife 6210**
North Carolina: Broad 6582
Texas: **American 8677**

American studies

Indiana: **Organization 3132**
Michigan: Ford 4420

Anatomy (animal)

Connecticut: Devon 1376
Massachusetts: **Jurassic 4134**
New York: American 5703

Anatomy (human)

Maryland: American 3756
New York: American 5703

Anesthesiology

Illinois: **American 2391, Anesthesia 2398, Society 2862**

Anesthesiology research

Illinois: **American 2391**
Minnesota: **Foundation 4741**
New York: American 5698
Wisconsin: **Society 10037**

Animal population control

California: Found 583

Animal welfare

California: **United 1069**
Connecticut: Equus 1386
District of Columbia: **Animal 1575,** Global 1641
Massachusetts: Animal 3971, Charles 4018
New Jersey: **Winn 5601**
New York: **Animal 5715, Grayson-Jockey 6045**
North Carolina: **American 6551**
Oregon: Banfield 7537
Wisconsin: Kern 9943

Animals/wildlife

Alaska: University 146
District of Columbia: **Animal 1575**
Illinois: Lincoln 2693
Kansas: Wildlife 3540
Maryland: Allemall 3754, Roche 3922
Michigan: **Ball 4343**
Minnesota: Alworth 4685
Texas: Forever 8825

Animals/wildlife, bird preserves

Alaska: University 146

Animals/wildlife, fisheries

Alaska: Bristol 106

Animals/wildlife, formal/general education

Pennsylvania: Smith 8112

Animals/wildlife, preservation/protection

California: **Foundation 586, Goldman 628**

Colorado: Operation 1253
District of Columbia: **Animal 1575, National 1691**
Florida: **SeaWorld 2056**
Illinois: Lincoln 2693
Massachusetts: **Earthwatch 4049**
Minnesota: **Lindbergh 4783**
Montana: **Rocky 5169**
New Jersey: Hull 5475
New York: **Wildlife 6520**
Texas: **Bat 8705,** Welder 9161

Animals/wildlife, public education

Florida: **SeaWorld 2056**

Animals/wildlife, research

Massachusetts: Chelonian 4020
Michigan: **Ball 4343**
Wisconsin: **Entomological 9884**

Anthropology/sociology

California: **Foundation 589, Leakey 739**
District of Columbia: **German 1638**
Florida: Ruegamer 2042
Illinois: Roberts 2825, Ross 2832
Massachusetts: Du Bois 4044, **Earthwatch 4049**
New Jersey: Horowitz 5473, **Wilson 5600**
New Mexico: **School 5650**
New York: American 5703, **Wenner 6511**
Virginia: **American 9290**
Washington: **Foundation 9614**

Art history

California: **Getty 614**
District of Columbia: American 1558
Illinois: **Terra 2889**
Massachusetts: Jackson 4128
New Jersey: **Foundation 5449**
New York: American 5687, **College 5866, Dedalus 5919,** Delmas 5921, **Metropolitan 6211**
North Carolina: **Institut 6711**
Pennsylvania: Pennsylvania 8027
Texas: American 8683, **MCH 8946**

Arthritis

California: Arthritis 375
Colorado: Arthritis 1122, Kuzell 1227
Georgia: **American 2115**
North Carolina: Emerson 6648

Arthritis research

California: **Arthritis 376**
Colorado: Arthritis 1122
Florida: Biegelsen 1798
Georgia: **American 2115,** Arthritis 2120
Tennessee: **Alpha 8554**

Arts

Alabama: Regional 74
Alaska: Alaska 99
Arizona: Seed 236, Tucson-Pima 247
California: Bay 405, Brown 424, Center 472, **Center 473, Colonnades 507,** Durfee 549, Eglitis 554, **Frameline 593,** Friends 601, **Getty 614, Independent 681,** Inner-City 684, International 689, **International 690,** Martin 774, Open 841, Performing 861, Pirkle 869, Recruiting 902, **Rex 909**
Colorado: Bonfils 1130, Boulder 1132, Gunnison 1207, VSA 1304
Connecticut: Hartford 1398, **Weir 1481**
Delaware: Farpath 1507
District of Columbia: **American 1572,** Community 1605, **PEN/Faulkner 1712,** Phi 1715

Florida: Cintas 1828, Community 1838, Community 1839, Palm Beach 2012, Southwest 2067, United 2093
Illinois: Coin 2487, Erickson 2549, **Gish 2585, MacArthur 2704,** McDonald 2718, Oberlin 2763, O'Malley 2768, Society 2863, Urbana-Champaign 2907
Indiana: Arts 2960, Community 2990, Ellison 3025, Richmond 3161
Kentucky: Kentucky 3582
Louisiana: Arts 3642, Louisiana 3664
Maryland: Allegany 3753, Carroll 3792, Howard 3844, Kattar 3856, **Mid 3884,** Worcester 3953
Massachusetts: **American 3966,** Berkshire 3986, Cabot 4003, **Fine 4068,** Museum 4184, **New 4196, Tanne 4282**
Michigan: Arts 4340, United 4649
Minnesota: **Anderson 4690,** Arrowhead 4693, Blacklock 4699, Forecast 4740, Lake 4777, McKnight 4794, Minnesota 4799, New York 4812, Region 4836, Southeastern 4854, VSA 4882
Missouri: Mid 5053
Nebraska: Ellis 5200
New Hampshire: Nye 5357
New Jersey: Children's 5423, New Jersey 5515, Peters 5539, **Puffin 5549, WheatonArts 5595, Wilson 5600**
New Mexico: **A Room 5609,** Santa Fe 5648, **School 5650, Southwestern 5652,** Whited 5658
New York: American 5687, **American 5689, American 5711, Art 5722, Artis 5724,** Arts 5726, Arts 5727, **Asian 5734,** Broome 5799, Center 5832, **Corning 5886,** Council 5894, **Cuban 5902, Cummings 5904,** Dactyl 5908, Dieu 5925, **Elizabeth 5957,** Ensemble 5959, Experimental 5967, **Fantasy 5973, Foundation 5998,** Fractured 6007, **Friends 6013,** Genesee 6021, **Guggenheim 6050,** Gunk 6052, Lower 6172, Malevich 6185, **MetLife 6210, Metropolitan 6211,** Mitchell 6218, New York 6269, **Rockefeller 6359,** Saltonstall 6371, **Schepp 6383, Social 6409, Tiffany 6455,** Tinker 6457, **Ventures 6488,** Vilcek 6491, Westchester 6512, **Worldstudio 6535**
North Carolina: Cox 6620, Gaston 6668, Martin 6757, Posey 6822, Union 6905, United 6906, United 6907, Wildcares 6920
Ohio: Cleveland 7041, Cuyahoga 7076, Dayton 7082, Kittridge 7196, Mercer 7240, Wexner 7422
Oregon: Caldera 7542, Celebration 7545, Regional 7641
Pennsylvania: Head 7895, **Heinz 7900,** Leeway 7951, Mattress 7973, Pittsburgh 8046, Pittsburgh 8049, Wood 8204
South Carolina: Arts 8448, Coastal 8464, Cultural 8469
Texas: Austin 8697, Houston 8875, **Houston 8877,** Milotte 8963, **National 8982,** Southwest 9091, **Vietnamese 9149**
Utah: **Sundance 9227**
Vermont: Vermont 9267, Vermont 9268
Virginia: Sale 9496, Smith-Melton 9509
Washington: Allied 9559, Artist 9564, Centrum 9583, Community 9600, Northwest 9684, Straw 9733
Wisconsin: Mari's 9958

Arts education

Arizona: Community 182
California: Alliance 347, **Association 389,** California 458, Coastal 504, Philanthropic 865, San Francisco 941, **San Francisco 943,** San Francisco 944
Colorado: Carbondale 1140, **Music 1246,** Sharpe 1282, VSA 1304
Connecticut: Ash 1325, Carlson 1347, Connecticut 1366
District of Columbia: Ellington 1620
Florida: Art 1782, Art 1783, Crealde 1854, Florida 1886, Florida 1887, Mount 1986, School 2054
Georgia: Handweavers 2194
Illinois: Arnold 2407, Bushnell 2451, Erickson 2549, Rockford 2827, **Special 2866,** Union 2904

Indiana: Decatur 3013, Delta 3016, Kosciusko 3091
Kansas: Tenholder 3524
Maine: Maine 3709, Maine 3712
Maryland: Queen 3918
Massachusetts: Massachusetts 4165
Michigan: Grand Rapids 4445, Kalamazoo 4492, United 4650
Minnesota: Central 4710
Missouri: Missouri 5057
New Hampshire: Davenport 5317
New Jersey: Anyone 5387, New Jersey 5519, Peters 5539, Terplan 5577
New York: AFTRA 5672, ArtsConnection 5730, Chautauqua 5842, **Dedalus 5919**, Exploring 5969, Fermi 5981, Kuhlman 6148, **National 6254**, **Sparkplug 6418**, **Worldstudio 6535**
North Carolina: Phoenix 6819, Posey 6822
Ohio: Fine 7108, Van Wert 7403
Pennsylvania: Head 7895, Waverly 8177
Rhode Island: Black 8244, Brennan 8251, Coles 8270, Rhode Island 8381
Tennessee: Humanities 8604, Lead 8616
Vermont: **Carving 9238**, Warner 9272
Virginia: Tidewater 9523
Washington: Allied 9558, Bainbridge 9565

Arts, administration/regulation

Oregon: Regional 7641

Arts, alliance/advocacy

California: **Colonnades 507**
Pennsylvania: **PPG 8058**

Arts, artist's services

California: 18th 330, AEPOCH 341, Art 373, Bay 405, Buddhist 426, California 445, Center 472, Community 515, CounterPULSE 525, Creative 526, Dancers' 535, **Frameline 593**, Friends 601, Independent 680, International 689, Intersection 693, Martin 774, Media 782, Musicares 809, Open 841, San Diego 928, **San Francisco 943**, Side 981, Southern 1005, Sweet 1035, Visual 1082, **Women 1098**
Colorado: Boulder 1132, Sharpe 1282
Florida: Change 1822, Community 1838, Palm Beach 2012
Georgia: Phillips 2223
Illinois: **American 2378**
Maryland: American 3758, Beth 3785, Prince 3915
Massachusetts: Center 4015, **Documentary 4041**
Michigan: Arts 4340
Minnesota: Artist 4694, Forecast 4740, IFP 4763, Intermedia 4766, Southwest 4858, Springboard 4859
Missouri: Mid 5053
New Hampshire: **Money 5347**
New Jersey: **Johnson 5482**, New Jersey 5515, Newark 5525, **Puffin 5549**
New Mexico: Woodson 5659, Wurlitzer 5660
New York: **Actors 5665**, Art 5718, **Artis 5724**, Artists 5725, **Arts 5729**, **Broadway 5790**, Brooklyn 5797, Camera 5809, City 5857, Community 5873, Cultural 5903, Dance 5910, Dance 5911, Episcopal 5960, Experimental 5967, **Explorers 5968**, **Foundation 5995**, Fractured 6007, **Gottlieb 6041**, **Haven 6060**, **Independent 6092**, Ladany 6152, Living 6166, Lower 6173, Magnum 6183, Musicians 6231, Performance 6313, **Pollock 6318**, **Public 6338**, Saltonstall 6371, **Tiffany 6455**, Women 6527, Women's 6529, **Worldstudio 6535**
North Carolina: Durham 6633, Gaston 6668, Southern 6869, Union 6905
Ohio: Independent 7168, Kittridge 7196, Summerfair 7373
Oregon: Lane 7595
Pennsylvania: Colman 7775, Pennsylvania 8027, Pittsburgh 8047, Scribe 8095
Rhode Island: **Alliance 8226**

Tennessee: **National 8629**
Texas: Austin 8698, Houston 8875, San Antonio 9056, **Southwest 9090**
Vermont: **Craft 9243**
Washington: 911 9554, Allied 9559, Northwest 9685

Arts, cultural/ethnic awareness

Alaska: Huna 118
California: Art 374, **Columbia 508**, **Foundation 589**, **International 690**
District of Columbia: **National 1693**
Illinois: Society 2863
Louisiana: Louisiana 3665
Michigan: **Chang 4378**
Minnesota: Intermedia 4766
New Jersey: **Puffin 5549**
New York: **Asian 5734**, Grand 6042, Studio 6441, **Trace 6461**
South Dakota: South Dakota 8541
Washington: Potlatch 9701

Arts, folk arts

Alaska: Rasmuson 132
California: Alliance 347
Florida: Two 2092
Michigan: **Chang 4378**
New Jersey: Peters 5539
New York: Council 5894, Queens 6341, **Tiffany 6455**
North Carolina: Center 6595
Rhode Island: Rhode Island 8381
Tennessee: **National 8629**
Vermont: **Craft 9243**
Washington: **Native 9680**

Arts, formal/general education

Delaware: Delaware 1500
Indiana: Joshi 3080

Arts, fund raising/fund distribution

New York: Moving 6229

Arts, management/technical assistance

District of Columbia: **Kennedy 1666**
Oregon: Regional 7641

Arts, multipurpose centers/programs

Maryland: Pyramid 3917

Arts, public education

Florida: Palm Beach 2012

Arts, research

California: **Getty 614**, **GRAMMY 635**, Veneklasen 1080
New York: McCall 6200
Ohio: Kittridge 7196
Texas: **MCH 8946**

Arts, services

California: Center 472, James 700
New Jersey: New Jersey 5515

Arts, volunteer services

California: Catalyst 466

Asians/Pacific Islanders

California: Asian 379, BBCN 406, California 453, Chinese 493, Lagrant 731, Ronald 918, San Diego 928, SKB 991, Southern 1005
Colorado: Ronald 1274
District of Columbia: Asian 1580, Asian 1582, Community 1605, Dingwall 1615, **United 1743**
Florida: Magic 1958, Orlando 2008
Hawaii: Hawaii 2291, Pacific 2310, Pope 2315
Illinois: **Medical 2728**
New Jersey: Ryu 5556, Wei 5593
New Mexico: **American 5611**
New York: **AAAA 5662**, Children 5847, **National 6244**, Price 6327, Sakhi 6370
Ohio: McLendon 7237
Washington: Nikkei 9682, Washington 9747

Asthma

Wisconsin: American 9834

Asthma research

Illinois: **American 2373**, **Foundation 2569**
Texas: **American 8677**
Wisconsin: American 9834

Astronomy

Arizona: **Research 233**
California: **Hertz 658**
District of Columbia: **National 1693**
Maryland: **American 3761**
New York: American 5703
Pennsylvania: Zaccheus 8218

Athletics/sports, academies

Indiana: Legacy 3096
Pennsylvania: North 8009
South Carolina: Coastal 8464
Vermont: VARA 9265
Washington: Kawabe 9647

Athletics/sports, amateur competition

Hawaii: Outrigger 2308
Indiana: **National 3121**
Maryland: **American 3760**
New York: Oyster 6300
North Carolina: Atlantic 6565, North 6795

Athletics/sports, amateur leagues

California: Olympic 840
District of Columbia: Professional 1717
Michigan: Come 4389, Community 4394, Ilitch 4480

Athletics/sports, baseball

Arizona: Major 214
California: Gifford 616
Kansas: Salina 3510
New York: Baseball 5754, Community 5878
Pennsylvania: Fallquist 7836
Texas: Astros 8694

Athletics/sports, basketball

Colorado: Merry 1238
Florida: Embassy 1869
Indiana: LaGrange 3093
Michigan: Fremont 4431
Pennsylvania: Fox 7856

Athletics/sports, equestrianism

Arizona: Turf 248
Connecticut: Ebony 1383, Equus 1386

Kentucky: **United 3632**
Maryland: **American 3760**, Steeplechase 3937
Nebraska: **Dressage 5196**
New Jersey: United 5584
New York: **Jockey 6121**
Oklahoma: **Reining 7508**
Tennessee: Johnson 8610
Texas: **American 8680**, **American 8682**, Sand 9060
Virginia: Carhart 9334
Washington: National 9679

Athletics/sports, fishing/hunting

Alaska: Territorial 143

Athletics/sports, football

Louisiana: Burton 3648
Missouri: Kansas City 5024
New Jersey: Giants 5452
New York: Cirillo 5854
Pennsylvania: Fox 7856
Texas: **National 8984**, O'Brien 8994
Wisconsin: Ruebush 10015

Athletics/sports, golf

Arizona: **Dickey 184**, Thunderbird 244
Colorado: Merry 1238
Delaware: Delaware 1504
Florida: LPGA 1955
Georgia: **American 2116**, Cherokee 2138, Weir 2259
Hawaii: Ishii 2295
Illinois: Evans 2552, Riverside 2823
Kentucky: Baker 3547
Massachusetts: Belmont 3981, Ouimet 4208
Minnesota: Minnesota 4805
New Jersey: White 5596
New York: Druckenmiller 5936, Long 6168, Westchester 6514
North Carolina: Isaac 6716
South Carolina: Coastal 8464, South 8511
Tennessee: Boyd 8561
Texas: Salesmanship 9051
Virginia: MAPGA 9428

Athletics/sports, Olympics

Colorado: **United 1299**
Indiana: **USA 3210**
New York: Oyster 6300

Athletics/sports, professional leagues

District of Columbia: Professional 1717
Illinois: **Drag 2523**
New Jersey: **National 5514**
North Carolina: Atlantic 6565

Athletics/sports, racquet sports

California: Shasta 978
Georgia: Southern 2239
New York: **United States 6479**, **USTA 6482**
South Carolina: Coastal 8464, Professional 8504

Athletics/sports, school programs

Alaska: Alaska 101
Florida: Lynch 1957
Georgia: R.A.C.K 2226, University 2254
Illinois: Geneva 2581, Koranda 2679
Indiana: Community 3004, Decatur 3013, Hughes 3065, Putnam 3154
Louisiana: Burton 3648
Massachusetts: Philips 4220
Michigan: Fremont 4431
Minnesota: Hansen 4753
Nevada: Snyder 5302
New York: Community 5878, Nolan 6282

Ohio: Kirtland 7194, Lewis 7207, Yoder 7445
Rhode Island: Cranston 8276
South Dakota: Yellow 8548
Texas: Conference 8765, O'Brien 8994
Washington: Bradley 9576, Kent 9652
Wisconsin: Community 9866

Athletics/sports, soccer

Michigan: Community 4394, Vetowich 4658
New Mexico: Albuquerque 5610
New York: Eastern 5949
Ohio: Northwest 7273

Athletics/sports, Special Olympics

California: **Challenged 476**

Athletics/sports, training

Alabama: American 9
California: **Challenged 476**, Community 512, Stephenson 1023
Colorado: Boogie's 1131, **United 1299**
Connecticut: Dolan 1378
Delaware: Delaware 1504
Florida: All 1765, Cape Coral 1815, Community 1839, Winged 2105
Indiana: Ellison 3025, Kosciusko 3091, Legacy 3096, **USA 3210**
Maine: Powers 3728
Maryland: Skaters 3934
Michigan: Ann Arbor 4338
Missouri: Community 4963
Montana: Mountain 5165
New Jersey: Van Doren 5590
New York: Community 5878, **Women's 6528**
Oregon: Major 7599
Pennsylvania: Curtis 7802
Rhode Island: Cranston 8276
South Dakota: Sioux Falls 8538
Tennessee: Johnson 8610
Texas: **American 8680**, National 8983
Virginia: Carhart 9334
West Virginia: Chambers 9774

Athletics/sports, water sports

California: Belvedere 411, Orange 843, **PADI 852**, St. Francis 1011
Florida: **Horizons 1922**
Georgia: Stingrays 2243
Hawaii: Outrigger 2308
Indiana: United 3205
Louisiana: **Waters 3682**
New York: Oyster 6300
Rhode Island: **United 8428**

Athletics/sports, winter sports

Alaska: Alaska 97
California: Mammoth 767
Colorado: Helmar 1213, **U.S. 1297**, **United 1298**
Maine: Powers 3728
Michigan: Community 4394
Minnesota: Baker 4696
New York: Sky 6403
Oregon: Major 7599
Texas: Dallas 8786

Autism

California: **Autism 393**
Maryland: Autism 3780, Autism 3781
Massachusetts: Danny 4035
New Jersey: Eden 5439
New York: **Autism 5743**

Autism research

California: Cure 530
Maryland: Autism 3781
New York: **Autism 5742**, **Autism 5743**

Big Brothers/Big Sisters

Wisconsin: Keller 9939

Biology/life sciences

California: **Beckman 408**, **Glenn 621**, **Grass 637**, **Hertz 658**, Kornberg 725, **Leakey 739**, Storkan/Hanes 1027
Colorado: Colorado 1162
District of Columbia: **National 1691**
Florida: Everglades 1872, Police 2023, Ruegamer 2042
Georgia: Bantly 2125
Illinois: Ehrler 2537, Hirschl 2620
Maryland: **Hughes 3846**, Life 3865, Roche 3922
Massachusetts: **Jurassic 4134**, **Lalor 4145**
Michigan: **Fetzer 4418**, Meyers 4532
Minnesota: Alworth 4685
New Jersey: Merck 5504, Parker 5535
New York: American 5703, Bay 5756, **Explorers 5968**, Huyck 6088, L'Oreal 6170, Open 6295, **Pasteur 6306**, Post 6321, **Sloan 6404**, **Whitney 6518**
Ohio: Williams 7427
Pennsylvania: Pew 8033, Smithfield 8113
Texas: Fort Worth 8829
Virginia: **National 9444**
Wisconsin: Beal 9846

Biomedicine

Kansas: Snyder 3516
Maryland: **National 3897**
Massachusetts: **Marine 4160**
Minnesota: Alworth 4685
Missouri: Stowers 5109
New Jersey: New 5516, Silbermann 5567, **Wiley 5599**
New York: **American 5694**

Biomedicine research

Illinois: Hirschl 2620, **Medical 2728**
Maryland: **Hughes 3846**
Massachusetts: Charles 4018, King 4140
Minnesota: **Lindbergh 4783**
New Jersey: New 5516
New York: Eshe 5964, **Lasker 6153**, **Mayday 6197**, **Pasteur 6306**, Vilcek 6491, **Whitney 6518**

Blind/visually impaired

Connecticut: **Fidelco 1388**
Illinois: Illinois 2647
Massachusetts: **Milton 4177**
Michigan: Lions 4518
New Jersey: **LearningAlly 5496**
New York: **Jewish 6120**, **Lighthouse 6163**
Pennsylvania: Smock 8114
Texas: Wolverton 9177
Washington: Northwest 9687

Botanical/horticulture/landscape services

California: **Shinoda 980**
District of Columbia: Horticultural 1647
Wisconsin: Noer 9984

Botany

Colorado: Colorado 1162, Population 1259
Minnesota: Alworth 4685
Missouri: Swanson 5110
New York: Huyck 6088, Open 6295

Boy scouts

California: Livermore 750
Minnesota: Northern 4816
Nebraska: Bryan 5188
New York: Solomon 6415

Boys

Florida: **Julien 1934**

Boys & girls clubs

California: Schwab 966
Georgia: **Boys 2129**
North Carolina: Lumbee 6750
Ohio: Hawkes 7145
Rhode Island: Boghossian 8247
Tennessee: Boys 8562

Boys clubs

California: Livermore 750
Missouri: Martino 5045

Brain disorders

Georgia: **Pilot 2225**
Illinois: **American 2372**
Massachusetts: Terry 4286
Minnesota: **McKnight 4793**
New York: Tourette 6459
Pennsylvania: Newman 8005

Brain research

Georgia: Southeastern 2237
Illinois: **American 2372**
Maryland: **Childhood 3801**
Massachusetts: **Marine 4160**
Minnesota: Minnesota 4797
New York: **Project 6332**
Pennsylvania: **Association 7716**, Newman 8005

Breast cancer

Arizona: **Breast 172**
California: Breast 422
New York: Babylon 5746, Breast 5782, **Breast 5783**
Pennsylvania: Young 8215
Texas: **Komen 8910**
Virginia: Cherry 9338

Breast cancer research

District of Columbia: National 1686
New York: **Avon 5745**
Texas: **Komen 8910**
Wisconsin: Wisconsin 10084

Buddhism

California: Buddhist 426, International 688
New York: **Tsadra 6465**

Business school/education

Alaska: CIRI 113, Kuskokwim 123
Arizona: Schmitz 235
California: Builder's 427, Kerber 719, Nauheim/Straus 823, Sacramento 926, Shasta 978, **Toigo 1049**
Colorado: Colorado 1158, Reach 1265
Connecticut: Deloitte 1375
Delaware: Chaney 1495
District of Columbia: **American 1539**, Equipment 1623, **German 1638**, **Hispanic 1644**, **Robinson, 1724**
Florida: Community 1839, Florida 1879, Florida 1882, Flordia Keys 1883, Miami 1978
Georgia: Brightwell 2131, Georgia 2183
Hawaii: Fukunaga 2283, Hawaii 2291

Illinois: APICS 2403, Collins 2490, Footprints 2566, Illinois 2643, Oberlin 2763, **Sigma 2855**, **Turnaround 2899**
Indiana: Community 2990, Community 3001, Madison 3106, Putnam 3154, Wabash 3215
Kansas: Salina 3510
Kentucky: Community 3559
Maine: Maine 3713
Maryland: Adams 3750, Mid-Atlantic 3885
Massachusetts: Educational 4054
Michigan: Bay 4350, Community 4394, Grand Rapids 4445, Harding 4457, **Michigan 4533**, Michigan 4540, Petoskey 4577, Whiteley 4667
Minnesota: Crosslake 4724, Petters 4823, PLUS 4826, Scheidler 4844
Mississippi: Community 4902, Mississippi 4915
Missouri: Educational 4984, Lord 5037
Nebraska: Emerson 5201
New Jersey: Chatham 5419, KPMG 5493, Union 5582
New York: **CFDA 5838**, Chautauqua 5842, Community 5878, **Direct 5926**, Foundation 5991, **International 6098**, Laboratory 6151, McGrath 6205, **Spencer 6420**, **Wallenberg 6499**
North Carolina: **American 6550**, Cole 6611, Halstead 6692, Hughes 6707, **Insurance 6712**, Material 6758, NC 6787
Ohio: AJCA 6963, Crain 7070, Dayton 7082, **Eagles 7095**, **Griffith 7136**, Peoples 7297, Scioto 7339, Troy 7388
Oklahoma: Tulsa 7518
Oregon: Alexandria 7530, Oapa 7621
Pennsylvania: Abrams 7691, Boyle 7742, Pennsylvania 8028, Pennsylvania 8029, Simpson 8104, Smithfield 8113
Rhode Island: Andrews 8229
South Dakota: Amundson 8520
Tennessee: CIC 8574, Community 8578, **Scarlett 8640**
Texas: Conner 8767, Hill 8867, IFMA 8890, Millar 8958, Texas 9116
Virginia: **American 9310**, **Asparagus 9318**, **Club 9343**, National 9449, National 9458, **Plumbing 9483**, Robinson 9495, Ware 9543
West Virginia: Canady 9771
Wisconsin: Wisconsin 10078, Wisconsin 10081

Business/industry

California: Builder's 427, California 456, Golden 626, Jewish 707, Loeb 753, Orange 843, Signer 985, Stanislaus 1017
Connecticut: Weller 1482, Woman's 1488
District of Columbia: **American 1559**, **Atlas 1588**, **Hitachi 1645**
Illinois: **American 2381**, APICS 2403, **National 2749**, **Sigma 2855**, Turnaround 2899
Maine: Associated 3687
Maryland: Adams 3750
Massachusetts: Boston 3994, Home 4110, **Two 4303**
Michigan: **ACI 4332**, Genesis 4433
Minnesota: Minnesota 4804, Northwest 4817
Mississippi: Mississippi 4915
Missouri: **Kauffman 5025**
New Hampshire: New Hampshire 5354
New Jersey: **Wilson 5600**
New York: **CDS 5828**, Community 5878, Morgan 6226, Price 6327, Realty 6347, **Wallenberg 6499**, **Wine 6523**
North Carolina: **Kimmel 6731**, NC 6787
Ohio: Community 7058, Culture 7073, Van Wert 7403
Oregon: **Culinary 7562**, Oapa 7621
Rhode Island: Meriden 8344, Rhode Island 8381, Webster 8433
South Carolina: Coastal 8464
South Dakota: Sioux Falls 8538
Texas: Amarillo 8675, **Conrad 8768**, **Promotional 9030**
Virginia: Foundation 9383, **U.S. 9526**
Wisconsin: Badger 9845, Waukesha 10065

Business/industry, trade boards

Ohio: Community 7058

Cancer

Arizona: **Cancer 175**
California: Beckstrand 409, **Cancer 462**, Raphael 899, **Sarcoma 960**, Tower 1052, Vanguard 1077
Colorado: Rocky 1270, Zac's 1313
Connecticut: Connecticut 1365, **Criag 1371**, My 1428
District of Columbia: **Melanoma 1676**
Florida: Jay 1930
Georgia: **American 2113**, Burke 2133, CURE 2159
Hawaii: Hawaii 2288
Illinois: Children's 2480, LUNGevity 2701
Indiana: Kosciusko 3090, Levin 3098, **Lilly 3099**, Morre 3119
Maryland: Jeremy 3852, **National 3896**, Ulman 3947
Massachusetts: SAMFund 4255, Sanborn 4256, Take 4281
Michigan: New 4553, Pardee 4572
Minnesota: Minnesota 4802, Miracles 4809
Missouri: **National 5062**
New Jersey: Embrace 5440, Goldberg 5455, Young 5606
New York: **Avon 5745**, Cancer 5812, Cure 5906, Jay's 6111, **Mann 6187**, **Voices 6495**
North Carolina: Cancer 6590, **Chordoma 6602**
Ohio: Cowgill 7069, Partners 7292, Wellness 7417
Oklahoma: Ally's 7449
Pennsylvania: Armstrong 7712, Eckhart 7819, ONS 8015, Young 8215
Tennessee: **American 8556**, **Cancer 8563**, Hurlbut 8605
Texas: **Dabney 8781**, Pardee 9002, Rio 9041, Wipe 9172
Virginia: American 9308, Association 9320, **Conquer 9351**, Johns 9409
Washington: Laurendeau 9657
West Virginia: Powell 9809
Wisconsin: Foundation 9895

Cancer research

California: **American 358**, **Concern 520**, Farber 571, Foundation 590, **International 691**, **Pancreatic 854**, Tower 1052
Connecticut: **Alliance 1318**, Childs 1354, **Multiple 1426**
District of Columbia: **American 1560**, **Melanoma 1676**
Georgia: **American 2113**
Illinois: **Ewing 2554**, Foundation 2568, HOPA 2625, **Leukemia 2690**, LUNGevity 2701
Indiana: Anna 2956, Morre 3119
Maryland: **Foundation 3829**, **National 3896**
Massachusetts: Aid 3960, **Caring 4010**
Minnesota: Minnesota 4802
New Jersey: Goldberg 5455
New York: **American 5694**, **American 5710**, **Avon 5745**, Cancer 5813, **Leukemia 6160**, L'Oreal 6170, **Lustgarten 6177**, **Lymphoma 6179**, National 6245, **Runyon 6365**, **Skin 6401**, **Voices 6495**
North Carolina: **Chordoma 6602**, **V Foundation 6910**
Ohio: Kati's 7183
Oregon: Wheeler 7682
Pennsylvania: **Alex's 7695**, **American 7701**, Kimmel 7936
Tennessee: Pearlpoint 8632
Texas: **Komen 8910**, **Mary 8937**
Virginia: American 9308, **Conquer 9351**, **Mesothelioma 9435**, Prevent 9487
Washington: **Fred 9616**

Cancer, leukemia

Alaska: Rooney 133
Florida: Jay 1930, **Julien 1934**
Illinois: Children's 2480, Hairy 2596
Louisiana: JL Foun 3657
Michigan: Children's 4383

Cancer, leukemia research

California: Foundation 590
Connecticut: **Alliance 1318**
Illinois: Hairy 2596, **Leukemia 2690**
New York: **American 5694**, Hunter's 6085, **Leukemia 6160**
Washington: **Friends 9618**

Catholic agencies & churches

Alaska: Monroe 125
Arizona: Catholic 177
California: Rader 892
Connecticut: Knights 1411, **Knights 1412**
District of Columbia: Albert 1536
Florida: Council 1852, Forbes 1888, Rayni 2030
Illinois: McLoraine 2725
Indiana: Catholic 2980, Harber 3051
Iowa: Bathalter 3244, Scanlan 3370
Maryland: Truschel 3944
Massachusetts: Dugan 4045, Kelly 4136, Lynch 4155
Michigan: Basilica 4348, Watson 4661
Missouri: Sprehe 5103
New Hampshire: Fond 5321
New York: Bloomer 5768, Catholic 5825, King 6139, **McCaddin 6199**, Reddington 6349
North Carolina: Kimmel 6732
Ohio: **Catholic 7030**, Fitzgerald 7111, Lapeer 7204, Rotterman 7329
Oklahoma: Catholic 7456
Pennsylvania: Crossroads 7800, **Foundation 7850**, Lynch 7965, O'Brien-Veba 8014, Thomas 8144
Rhode Island: Kiely 8320, McVinney 8343
South Carolina: Coastal 8464
Texas: Deering 8788
Washington: Wittman 9756
Wisconsin: Schulte 10023

Cemeteries/burial services

Alaska: Kawerak 121
California: Mutual 810
Pennsylvania: Fischer 7842

Cerebral palsy research

New Jersey: **Cerebral 5417**

Charter schools

Florida: Step 2075
Illinois: Murphy 2741
New York: New Visions 6263

Chemistry

Arizona: **Research 233**
California: **Beckman 408**, **Hertz 658**, Kornberg 725, Science 968
Colorado: Cibrowski 1147
District of Columbia: **American 1548**
Florida: Police 2023, Rayonier 2031
Illinois: Blazek 2427
Indiana: Society 3187
Michigan: Meyers 4532
Missouri: Community 4963
New Jersey: **Siemens 5566**
New York: **Dreyfus 5935**, **Sloan 6404**
North Carolina: **Nickel 6792**
Pennsylvania: Brown 7750, **PPG 8058**, Smithfield 8113, Society 8119
Rhode Island: Kiely 8320
Texas: Welch 9160
Virginia: TDC 9517
Wisconsin: **Friends 9900**, La Crosse 9948

Child development, education

California: **Academy 335**
Florida: Episcopal 1871, Tangelo 2083

North Carolina: Smart 6865, Work 6928
Utah: McCarthey 9219

Child development, services

California: **Rex 909**
Michigan: **Society 4610**
North Carolina: Guilford 6690

Children

California: Alta 351, Celebrity 470, **Children 485**, Inner-City 684, Modesto 799, Raphael 899, Second 971, Taylor 1039, True 1059
Colorado: Colorado 1157, Community 1173, Scottish 1278, Zac's 1313
Connecticut: Connecticut 1367
Delaware: Delaware 1502
District of Columbia: **Airline 1535**, **American 1538**, Children's 1600, Christ 1601
Florida: Children's 1826, Space 2068, Taylor 2085
Georgia: Creative 2158, Fragile 2179, Stovall 2244
Hawaii: Learning 2300, Make-A-Wish 2302
Illinois: Angels 2400, Ann 2401, Dreams 2524, Ende 2544, **Healthy 2608**, **Ronald 2831**
Indiana: Levin 3098, Thomasson 3198
Maryland: Allemall 3754, **Childhood 3801**
Massachusetts: Knights 4141, Make-A-Wish 4157
Michigan: Italian 4483
Minnesota: Catholic 4708, Miracles 4809
Missouri: Make-A-Wish 5040, Missouri 5060, Scottish 5097
Nevada: Miracle 5294
New Jersey: Embrace 5440, Family 5444, Rose 5553
New York: Children 5847, **CNN 5862**, Community 5882, **Keats 6134**, Ronald 6360, **UJA 6470**
North Carolina: Bicycle 6574, Robeson 6837, Telamon 6890
Ohio: Ames 6973, Greenwalt 7135, Motry 7257
Oklahoma: Ally's 7449
Oregon: Snow-Cap 7661
Pennsylvania: Communtiy 7787, DiBona 7811, Elwyn 7824, Heart 7899
Rhode Island: Masonic 8336, Rhode 8382
South Carolina: Carolina 8455
Tennessee: Children's 8572, East 8588
Texas: Cutter 8779, **Dabney 8781**, Salesmanship 9052
Virginia: Children's 9340
Washington: Family 9610
West Virginia: Powell 9809
Wisconsin: Foundation 9895, Kohl's 9946, Wisconsin 10082

Children's rights

Virginia: **U.S. 9527**

Children, adoption

Colorado: Lutheran 1235
Connecticut: **China 1355**
Illinois: **Gift 2583**
Kansas: Kansas 3470
Kentucky: Operation 3608
Michigan: Lutheran 4520
Montana: Sacred 5171
New York: **A Child 5661**, Catholic 5824, **General 6019**, New Alternatives 6260
Ohio: Catholic 7029
Texas: Buckner 8727, **Limiar 8918**
Wisconsin: Anu 9837

Children, day care

Alabama: Gulf 44
Arizona: Valley 255
California: Assistance 382, Center 471, Child 483, Children's 487, Wu 1104
Florida: Child 1823, Community 1837
Hawaii: People 2314

Indiana: Little 3103
Kansas: Child 3423, Noah's 3496
Minnesota: Child 4712, Providers 4831
Mississippi: Skelton 4921
New Jersey: Child 5421, Child 5422
New York: Eaton 5950, Ontario 6293
North Carolina: Child 6599, Guilford 6690
Pennsylvania: Coordinated 7791, **Lokoff 7961**, Quin 8070
Rhode Island: Perpetual 8368
Texas: Edinburg 8806, Kiddies 8905, Right 9040
Virginia: Child 9339, **National 9445**, United 9532
Wisconsin: Community 9865, Wisconsin 10075

Children, foster care

California: Aspiranet 380, Children's 488, Five 577, Futuro 606, Optimist 842, Redwood 906, Rosemary 920, Sierra 983, Trinity 1057, United 1071
Colorado: Lutheran 1235
Georgia: Creative 2158, Families 2176
Hawaii: Geist 2285
Illinois: Children's 2479
Kansas: Kansas 3470
Kentucky: Operation 3608
Maryland: Pollak 3914
Massachusetts: Youth 4329
Michigan: Lutheran 4520
Minnesota: American 4689
Missouri: **Boys 4941**
Nebraska: Nebraska 5240
New York: Catholic 5824, **General 6019**, New Alternatives 6260
Ohio: Catholic 7029, Parenthesis 7289
Pennsylvania: Pressley 8061
Virginia: Orphan 9474
Washington: College 9594, Treehouse 9736
Wisconsin: Anu 9837

Children, services

Arizona: Food 194
Arkansas: RMHC 306
California: Assistance 382, Celebrity 470, Child 484, Children's 487, Children's 488, Fundacion 605, Kurka 726, Mills 793, True 1059, Wu 1104
Florida: Children's 1825, **Kids 1938**, Senior 2059
Hawaii: Hawaii 2288
Kansas: Child 3423
Massachusetts: Quincy 4234
Michigan: Spectrum 4620
Minnesota: Minnesota 4800
Missouri: **Growing 5008**
New Jersey: Child 5420, Child 5422
New York: Cantor 5814, **Foundation 5994**, L.H. 6149
North Carolina: Child 6599, Work 6928
Ohio: **Children 7032**, Columbus 7054, Fraser 7117
Pennsylvania: Huth 7914, Stoneleigh 8133
Rhode Island: Carlisle 8255, Rhode 8382
Tennessee: Civitan 8575
Virginia: **Diema's 9361**

Children/youth

Arizona: Catholic 176, Make-A-Wish 215, Prayer 231
Arkansas: Arkansas 262, RMHC 306
California: **Children's 489**, **Children's 491**, Make-A-Wish 766, Penny 860, Rosemary 920, **World 1102**
Colorado: Rocky 1271, YMCA 1310
Connecticut: **Save 1454**
Florida: Children's 1824, **Kids 1938**
Georgia: Austin 2121, Hall 2190, Make 2207
Illinois: After 2358, Juvenile 2665, Lawrence 2687, Make-A-Wish 2707, **National 2743**, Smyth 2861
Kansas: Jewish 3463
Kentucky: Dream 3564
Maine: York 3749
Maryland: Jeremy 3852, **Middle 3886**
Michigan: McPherson 4530, Old 4568

Minnesota: Providers 4831, **UnitedHealthcare 4876**
Missouri: **Boys 4941**, Ronald 5080
New Hampshire: Morse 5349
New Jersey: Child 5422
New York: Jay's 6111, Just 6126, Ronald 6360
Ohio: Fraser 7117
Pennsylvania: **Alex's 7695**
Texas: Catholic 8740, Community 8761, Neighborhood 8988
Virginia: **Operation 9471**
Washington: **World 9758**

Children/youth, services

Alabama: Meharg 61
California: Allgemeiner 346, Avery 396, Battered 403, **Higgins 661**, Jewish 707, Philanthropic 865, Rest 908, San Felipe 940
Connecticut: Folsom 1390
Florida: Beall 1793, Community 1837, Episcopal 1871, Fabela 1874, Harrison 1905, Take 2081
Hawaii: Parents 2313, People 2314
Illinois: Children's 2480, Claretknoll 2483, Fabela 2556, Gorham 2589, Oak Park 2761, Reach 2809
Indiana: Tobias 3202
Iowa: Black 3247
Kansas: Noah's 3496
Kentucky: Rose 3621
Maine: Portland 3726
Maryland: Montgomery 3888
Massachusetts: Phillips 4221, **Rosenberg 4247**
Michigan: **Herdegen 4464**, Lutheran 4520, Newaygo 4554
Minnesota: Hastings 4755, Miracle 4808, **UnitedHealthcare 4876**
Missouri: **Boys 4941**, Child 4956
Nebraska: Nebraska 5240
New Jersey: Catholic 5413, Several 5563, **Wilson 5600**
New York: Children 5847, Dove 5932, Hambay 6055, Holland 6076, **New 6264**, Ontario 6293, **Russian 6366**, Teamsters 6446
North Carolina: Foundation 6660
Ohio: Parenthesis 7289, Wester 7419
Oklahoma: Wilkin 7526
Oregon: Mercy 7604
Pennsylvania: Curtis 7803, Quin 8070, Sleeper 8108
South Carolina: Gleamns 8476
Texas: Student 9102
Vermont: Warner 9272
Virginia: St. Paul's 9513
Washington: Treehouse 9736
West Virginia: Chambers 9774
Wisconsin: Nicholl 9981, Spartvedt 10041, Wisconsin 10075

Chiropractic

Colorado: **Christian 1145**

Christian agencies & churches

Alabama: Meharg 61, Woerner 93
Arizona: Arizona 164
California: **Armenian 370**, Cherith 479, Christian 495, Foundation 585, Good 629, Johnson 712, Missionary 796, **Modglin 800**, New 826, **Rivendell 912**
Colorado: Adventure 1111, Christian 1146, **National 1248**, Servant 1281, **Sonlight 1287**
Connecticut: Fuller 1393
District of Columbia: **Franciscan 1630**
Florida: Aurora 1788, Morrison 1984, Rawlings 2028
Georgia: Bantly 2125, Eternal 2173, **Ravi 2227**
Hawaii: Atherton 2271
Illinois: **Ullery 2901**, **Women 2933**
Indiana: Thomasson 3198
Iowa: **Grace 3286**
Kansas: McPherson 3483
Maryland: **Middle 3886**
Michigan: Legion 4515
Minnesota: Trinity 4872

Mississippi: Dunnaway 4905
Missouri: Kirschner 5030, McGlothlan 5048
Nebraska: Wood 5275
New Jersey: Butts 5408, **Center 5416**, McCready 5502
New York: Community 5878, Dove 5932, Good 6038, Nolan 6283, United 6473, **Woodlawn 6530**
North Carolina: **Graham 6678**, Horsey 6703, **Rixson 6836**, **Samaritan's 6849**
Ohio: **Christian 7036**, Rogers 7326, Thompson 7379, Van Horn 7401, Van Wert 7403
Oklahoma: **International 7483**
Oregon: Compassion 7556, McDowell 7601
Pennsylvania: **Chinese 7766**, Harris 7889, Smock 8114, Walz 8174
Rhode Island: Boghossian 8247, Cismoski 8261, Croston 8279
South Carolina: Clergy 8463
South Dakota: Sioux Falls 8538
Tennessee: Acts 8551
Texas: Ferguson 8821, Gourley 8848, **Media 8950**, Oglesby 8995, Philadelphia 9018, Sunnyside 9103, Wisian 9174
Virginia: **Christian 9341**, Missionary 9438
Washington: Bohnett 9575, Community 9600, **World 9758**
Wisconsin: Schulte 10023, Smith 10036

Civil liberties, first amendment

Illinois: **Playboy 2794**

Civil rights, race/intergroup relations

California: Allgemeiner 346
Michigan: Bay 4350, Grand Rapids 4445
New York: **New 6264**
North Carolina: Stewart 6879

Civil/human rights

California: **Columbia 508**, **Gleitsman 620**, **Impact 678**, **Tides 1048**
District of Columbia: **Marijuana 1672**
Maine: Holocaust 3703
Massachusetts: Cabot 4003, **Rosenberg 4247**
Michigan: Parks 4574
New York: **Center 5835**, **CNN 5862**, New 6264, **Skadden 6398**

Civil/human rights, advocacy

New York: Petra 6314, **Skadden 6398**

Civil/human rights, formal/general education

New York: Warren 6501

Civil/human rights, immigrants

District of Columbia: Ayuda 1590
Illinois: Hebrew 2609
Virginia: **U.S. 9527**

Civil/human rights, LGBTQ

California: Anderson 365, **Higgins 661**

Civil/human rights, minorities

New Hampshire: **Money 5347**

Civil/human rights, women

District of Columbia: **Women 1753**
Kentucky: Kentucky 3582
Massachusetts: **R.O.S.E. 4236**
Michigan: Sojourner 4613
New Hampshire: **Money 5347**
Virginia: **Ashoka: 9317**

Community development, neighborhood associations

Louisiana: Pitt's 3675

Community development, neighborhood development

California: Nestle 825, **Tides 1048**
District of Columbia: **National 1688**
New York: **Open 6294**
Washington: Russell 9713

Community development, real estate

Connecticut: Devon 1376
New York: Realty 6347

Community development, small businesses

District of Columbia: **Hitachi 1645**

Community/economic development

Alaska: Alaska 99
California: **Children's 489**, **Children's 491**, **Draper 547**, San Diego 929
District of Columbia: Arab 1576, **Independent 1649**, **International 1655**
Illinois: **Massage 2713**
Louisiana: Louisiana 3664
Maryland: **International 3849**
Massachusetts: Cabot 4003, **SEVEN 4267**
Minnesota: Woman's 4894
Missouri: Delta 4972
New York: **Center 5835**, **CNN 5862**, Fund 6014, Health 6064, Manhattan 6186, **New 6264**, **Social 6409**
North Carolina: North 6799
Pennsylvania: Southern 8125
Washington: Lower 9664
West Virginia: Workforce 9830

Community/economic development, research

Massachusetts: **SEVEN 4267**

Community/economic development, volunteer services

California: Milken 792
Colorado: Bonfils 1130
District of Columbia: **Hitachi 1645**
Florida: Spicer 2070
Hawaii: Servco 2320
Illinois: Chicago 2473, **Rotary 2835**
Indiana: Shiel 3180
Missouri: **Build 4946**
New Jersey: Chatham 5419, Prudential 5547
New York: Children's 5849, Community 5878, **Do 5928**
North Carolina: Foundation 6660, London 6748, Martin 6757, Reynolds 6828
Ohio: Myers 7265
Rhode Island: Rhode Island 8381
Texas: Jordan 8902, Moody 8967
Washington: Kawabe 9647

Computer science

California: **Borg 418**, **Hertz 658**, **HP 670**, Stanislaus 1017, **Tides 1048**
Colorado: Colorado 1158, EDUCAUSE 1189, Reach 1265
Connecticut: Devon 1376, Weller 1482
Illinois: Geneseo 2580, Oberlin 2763
Michigan: Michigan 4540, Petoskey 4577
Minnesota: Alworth 4685
Nebraska: Lexington 5228
New Hampshire: **U.S. 5373**
New Jersey: People 5538

New York: **ESA 5963**, **IBM 6089**, Manhattan 6186, Price 6327, **Sloan 6404**, **Social 6409**
North Carolina: Material 6758
Ohio: Birr 6998
Virginia: **American 9310**, **Special 9511**

Courts/judicial administration

Florida: Everglades 1872
Virginia: **National 9453**

Crime/abuse victims

Colorado: Project 1261
New York: **Conference 5884**

Crime/law enforcement

Colorado: Colorado 1168
Florida: Patterson 2015
Georgia: **Foundation 2178**
Kentucky: Appalachian 3545
New Jersey: Gonzalez 5456
New York: New York 6267
South Carolina: Coastal 8464
Texas: Fleetwood 8823

Crime/law enforcement, association

New York: **Marine 6190**
Virginia: **American 9307**

Crime/law enforcement, correctional facilities

California: Doing 543
Tennessee: Ross 8638

Crime/law enforcement, formal/general education

California: Shasta 978
North Carolina: Harmon 6694

Crime/law enforcement, government agencies

Kentucky: Kentucky 3584

Crime/law enforcement, police agencies

California: Huntington 673
Florida: **AAST 1761**, Police 2023
Illinois: Bennett 2422
New Jersey: Camden 5410
New York: New York 6267, New York 6274, NYS 6290
Ohio: Bluecoats 7003, Dayton 7082, Hundred 7162
Rhode Island: Rhode Island 8381
Texas: Fort Worth 8828, Texas 9129

Crime/law enforcement, reform

District of Columbia: **Marijuana 1673**

Crime/law enforcement, research

District of Columbia: **Phillips 1716**

Crime/violence prevention

California: Battered 403, California 461
New York: **Guggenheim 6049**, **Social 6409**

Crime/violence prevention, abuse prevention

Maine: Spruce 3736
New Jersey: A Place 5380

Crime/violence prevention, child abuse

California: Childrens 486, Children's 488, Promises 884
Michigan: Whaley 4665

Crime/violence prevention, domestic violence

California: Battered 403
Colorado: Advocate 1112
Georgia: Tri-County 2250
Maine: Spruce 3736
Massachusetts: **R.O.S.E. 4236**
Minnesota: Dolan 4728
New Jersey: A Place 5380

Crime/violence prevention, sexual abuse

Arizona: Hopi 201
Colorado: Advocate 1112, Archuleta 1121
Michigan: Whaley 4665
New Jersey: A Place 5380

Crime/violence prevention, youth

California: Catalyst 466
New York: Glover 6034
Pennsylvania: Founder's 7855

Cystic fibrosis

California: Cystic 532
New York: **Eslason 5965**
Pennsylvania: **Pennsylvania 8026**

Cystic fibrosis research

California: Cystic 532
Maryland: Cystic 3812
Pennsylvania: **Pennsylvania 8026**

Deaf/hearing impaired

Alabama: Charity 22
California: Deaf 537
Colorado: Conkling 1174
District of Columbia: Bell 1591
Illinois: **American 2377**, Illinois 2647, **Zazove 2939**
Michigan: Lions 4518
Ohio: Ames 6973
Pennsylvania: Smock 8114
Washington: Northwest 9687

Dental care

Arkansas: RMHC 306
California: Assistance 382, Assistance 385, California 447, Jefferson 705, Rest 908
Connecticut: Senior 1459
District of Columbia: **American 1553**
Illinois: **ADA 2356**, **American 2376**, **Healthy 2608**
Indiana: Rose 3165
Kansas: Jones 3464
Maine: Montgomery 3719, Portland 3726
Massachusetts: Permanent 4216
Michigan: Michigan 4535
New York: Saranac 6374
North Carolina: Giving 6676
Ohio: Community 7058
Pennsylvania: Curtis 7803, Saak 8086
South Dakota: Delta 8526
Utah: Regence 9222
Wyoming: Perkins 10117

Dental school/education

California: California 447
Colorado: **Colorado 1165**
Connecticut: Wells 1483
District of Columbia: **American 1553**, **German 1638**

Florida: Delta 1859, King 1939
Georgia: Cobb 2147, Fisher 2177
Illinois: **ADA 2356**, American 2367, **American 2375**, **American 2376**, Illinois 2644, McClain 2717
Indiana: Kendrick 3085, Williams 3228
Kansas: Vesper 3533
Maryland: **Hughes 3846**
Michigan: Cadillac 4371, Delta 4406, Kadant 4491
Missouri: **Demolay 4974**, Dental 4975, Hester 5016
North Carolina: Myers 6783, Reich 6823, Richmond 6832
Ohio: Crain 7070
Oklahoma: Johnson 7486
Pennsylvania: Brown 7750, Clareth 7769, Crawford 7796, Harris 7889, York 8213
South Dakota: Delta 8526
Virginia: **Foundation 9382**
Washington: Washington 9747
Wisconsin: Mitchell 9972

Developmentally disabled, centers & services

California: North 829, San 935
District of Columbia: **Arc 1577**, **Kennedy 1667**
Hawaii: Easter 2281
Maryland: Full 3831
Massachusetts: New 4195
Texas: Foundation 8831
Washington: Jordan 9645

Diabetes

Colorado: Children's 1144
Connecticut: Endocrine 1385
Indiana: **Lilly 3099**
Iowa: Camp 3251
Maine: Gadd 3698
Maryland: American 3766
New Jersey: Diabetes 5433
Ohio: Seefred 7342
Wisconsin: Community 9867

Diabetes research

Colorado: **Children 1143**
Connecticut: Endocrine 1385
Illinois: Friends 2576
New York: **American 5694**, **Juvenile 6127**, **National 6251**
Texas: **American 8677**
Virginia: **American 9297**, **American 9298**

Diagnostic imaging

Virginia: **Focused 9377**

Diagnostic imaging research

Illinois: Association 2409, **Foundation 2570**
New York: **Lymphoma 6179**
Virginia: **Focused 9377**, **Radiation 9489**

Digestive diseases

Maryland: **American 3759**

Digestive disorders research

Illinois: **American 2389**
Maryland: **American 3759**, **Foundation 3829**
New York: Crohn's 5899
Texas: **Society 9081**
Wisconsin: International 9927

Disabilities, people with

Alabama: Community 29
Arizona: Agape 152, Community 182
California: Alta 351, Avery 396, Collister 506, Far 570, Good 630, Inland 683, Los 757, North 830,

Physicians 867, Redwood 907, Rest 908, San
Gabriel/Pomona 949, San Luis 951, South 1004,
Taylor 1039, Through 1047, Tri-Counties 1055,
Valley 1076, **Variety 1079**
Colorado: Breckenridge 1134, Colorado 1157, Conkling
1174, Jewish 1222, VSA 1304
Connecticut: Connecticut 1366
Delaware: Delaware 1502
District of Columbia: Air 1534, **American 1545,**
American 1546, Arc 1577, Cornerstone 1609,
Kennedy 1667, VSA 1745
Florida: Abilities 1763, Aurora 1788, Florida 1881,
Harrison 1905, Northeast 2000
Georgia: Creative 2158, Kids' 2202, **Pilot 2225,**
Scheffler 2234
Hawaii: Easter 2281, Learning 2300
Illinois: Aon 2402, C.E.F.S. 2454, Dreams 2524,
Energy 2545, Gore 2588, Gorham 2589, Hynd
2632, Klein 2672, Morton 2739, **Serbian 2848,**
Special 2866, Weeks 2920
Indiana: Area 2957, Hannah 3050, Northwest 3128
Iowa: Barr 3242, Black 3247
Kansas: Cloud 3426, Southwest 3518
Kentucky: American 3544, **Disabled 3563,** Hedrick
3576, Rose 3621
Maine: Portland 3726
Maryland: **American 3768,** Community 3804, Full
3831, Penn-Mar 3909, Resource 3921
Massachusetts: HAP 4094, Knights 4141, Kurzweil
4143, Phillips 4221, **Roy 4250**
Michigan: Arts 4340, Easter 4412, Gilmore 4437,
Lions 4518, Michigan 4537, Oakland 4566,
Spectrum 4620
Minnesota: Anodyne 4692, Miracle 4808, Semcac
4849, VSA 4882
Mississippi: Care 4901
Missouri: Missouri 5060, North 5065, **Sertoma,**
5098, Trotter 5117
Nebraska: Bemis 5186, Omaha 5251
New Hampshire: Krempels 5332, Moore 5348
New Jersey: Arc 5388, **Cerebral 5417,** Easter 5437,
Essex 5441, Kessler 5487, New Jersey 5522,
Ostberg 5533, Rose 5553, Saddle 5557
New York: Agoriani 5673, **American 5696, American**
5707, Camphill 5811, Catholic 5824, Children
5847, Community 5882, Hambay 6055, **LD 6154,**
Lighthouse 6163, Maidstone 6184, Morton 6227,
Musicians 6232, National 6247, Newhouse 6279,
Ontario 6293, Pathfinder 6307, Project 6335
North Carolina: Bass 6568, Easter 6638, Eddy 6642,
Foundation 6660, Telamon 6890
Ohio: Gay 7125, Greenwalt 7135, Hawkes 7145,
Jewish 7177, Motry 7257, Ohio 7277, Oppenheim
7284, Sightless 7349
Oklahoma: Johnson 7485, Wilkin 7526
Oregon: Southern 7664
Pennsylvania: Aid 7693, Biondo 7734, Elwyn 7824,
Heart 7899, Smock 8114, Workplace 8207
South Carolina: Earle 8470, Professional 8504, Society
8509
South Dakota: Black 8522
Tennessee: Civitan 8575, Southeast 8647, Upper
8659
Texas: Cutter 8779, El Paso 8811, Giannini-Scatena
8839, St. Vincent 9099
Virginia: **American 9295,** Americans 9313, **Diema's**
9361, Epilepsy 9375, Operation 9473, Research
9493
Washington: Metropolitan 9675, Northwest 9687,
Rural 9712
West Virginia: Hollandsworth 9791, Stickley 9817
Wisconsin: Brown 9853, **Riesch 10010,** Spartvedt
10041, Wiegand 10071

Disasters, 9/11/01

California: Twin 1065
Indiana: American 2955
Minnesota: **Scholarship 4845**
New York: Cantor 5814, Leary 6157, Needham 6257,
New York 6274, Windows 6522
Tennessee: **United 8657**

Disasters, domestic resettlement

Florida: 2 Life 1759

Disasters, fire prevention/control

California: Burn 429
District of Columbia: **International 1652, International**
1654
Nebraska: Walther 5270
New Jersey: Camden 5410
New York: Community 5878, Leary 6157, New York
6266, New York 6274, UFA 6469
Rhode Island: Rhode Island 8381
Texas: Fleetwood 8823
Virginia: **International 9405**
West Virginia: Stump 9820

Disasters, floods

California: Musicares 809, Shaklee 977
New York: PricewaterhouseCoopers 6328
West Virginia: Stump 9820

Disasters, Hurricane Katrina

California: **Society 1001**
Florida: PSS/Gulf 2027
Mississippi: C Spire 4900
New Jersey: Ingersoll-Rand 5478
New York: Cantor 5814, Project 6334
Texas: Cadbury 8732, Swift 9104

Disasters, preparedness/services

California: California 460, Musicares 809
Florida: 2 Life 1759
Illinois: Medline 2729
Iowa: United 3399
Massachusetts: Dunkin 4047
North Carolina: Burlington 6587
Pennsylvania: Armstrong 7711, Penn 8022
Tennessee: **Soles4Souls 8646**
Texas: AT&T 8695, Southern 9088
Virginia: **Public 9488**

Disasters, search/rescue

Massachusetts: Humane 4121
New Jersey: Life 5498

Diseases (rare)

California: **Cystinosis 533**
Connecticut: Cornelia 1370
Illinois: Angelman 2399, **National 2744**
Kentucky: Dream 3564
Louisiana: ECD 3650
Massachusetts: **Winter 4319**
Texas: Lowe 8925

Diseases (rare) research

California: National 822
Connecticut: Cornelia 1370, **National 1429**
Illinois: Aicardi 2359, Angelman 2399, **National 2744**
Maryland: PNH 3913
Massachusetts: **Scleroderma 4263**
New York: Dystrophic 5944, **Pasteur 6306**
Texas: American 8681, Lowe 8925
Wisconsin: **National 9978**

Down syndrome

New York: **National 6248**

Down syndrome research

New York: **National 6248**

Ear, nose & throat diseases

District of Columbia: Bell 1591
Oklahoma: JWF 7487
Pennsylvania: Eye 7833

Ear, nose & throat research

Florida: Alpha-1 1767
Maryland: **American 3768, Foundation 3829**
New York: **Hearing 6065**
Pennsylvania: **National 8000**

Economic development

District of Columbia: **Atlas 1588, Citizens 1603**
Illinois: Ameren 2364
Massachusetts: **SEVEN 4267**

Economically disadvantaged

Alabama: Childcare 23, Community 25, Community 26,
Community 29, Macon-Russell 57, United 86,
WEDC 90
Arizona: Arizona 163, Assistance 166, Catholic 176,
Diocesan 185, Educare 188, **Feed 191,** Friendship
198, Interfaith 204, Pima 228, Prayer 231, St.
Mary's/Westside 240, United 250, University 251,
Valley 255
Arkansas: Arkansas 262, Arkansas 266, Arvac 267,
Community 275, Helping 283, Riordan 305, RMHC
306, Sparks 313
California: **Aid 343,** AIDS 344, Anaheim 364, **Armenian**
370, Athena 392, Basic 401, Burks 428, California
447, California 451, California 452, Catholic 467,
Catholic 468, Chessall 481, **Children's 490,**
Chronicle 496, Community 512, Community 516,
CounterPULSE 525, El Monte 557, El Puente 558,
Emergency 562, Employees 564, **Faith's 567,**
Family 568, Five 577, Foundation 591, Fresno
595, Fundacion 605, **Genentech 611,** Good 630,
Grace 633, Hager 643, Heart 652, Hoag 666,
Inner-City 684, Interface 687, Italian 698,
Jefferson 705, Kaiser 721, Klicka 722, Korean
723, Kurka 726, Ladies 729, Legal 742, Masonic
775, Modesto 799, Musicares 809, Oakley 838,
Orange 843, Orange 844, Ronald 918, **San 927,**
San Diego 933, Second 971, Serra 976, Simon
990, **Society 1001,** Society 1002, South 1004, St.
1012, St. Joseph's 1013, St. Jude 1014,
Sunnyvale 1032, Swanson 1034, Sweet 1035,
Tatum 1037, Taylor 1039, Tenderloin 1042, Trinity
1056, Turn 1064, **Union 1068,** Winnett 1097
Colorado: Boogie's 1131, Catholic 1142, Colfax 1152,
Colorado 1159, Community 1173, Denver 1181, El
1190, Evergreen 1193, Food 1196, Goodwill
1205, **H.E.L.P. 1208,** Hunter 1217, Jewish 1222,
Keren 1226, Lillis 1232, Outreach 1255, Pathways
1256, Pikes 1257, Sister 1283, **Someone 1286,**
Stride 1291
Connecticut: Action 1314, **AmeriCares 1323,**
Boehringer 1335, Community 1363, Compass
1364, CTE 1372, Larrabee 1413, New 1432,
Operation 1438, Person-to-Person 1442, **Save**
1454, Thames 1470, Thomas 1471, United 1476,
Urban 1477, **Walkabout 1479,** Westport-Weston
1484
Delaware: AstraZeneca 1493, Children 1496, Delaware
1500, Delaware 1503, Gromet 1511, Horsemen's
1513
District of Columbia: **Airline 1535, American 1562,**
Anacostia 1574, District 1616, **German 1638,**
Legal 1670, Olender 1703, **Teamster 1735,**
Washington 1748, Young 1756
Florida: A Gift 1760, Abilities 1763, Brooks 1809,
Catholic 1819, Catholic 1820, Christian 1827,
Council 1852, Crealde 1854, Darden 1855,
Densch 1860, Diocesan 1862, duPont 1865,

Edwards 1868, Fabela 1874, Fort 1889, Gulf 1899, **Harvest 1906**, Hill 1913, Hope 1921, **Julien 1934**, Northeast 2000, Operation 2006, Pinellas 2020, Rogers 2040, Schmitt 2050, Smigiel 2063, Starks 2072, Take 2081, Taylor 2085, United 2094, United 2095, Wolfe 2106, Workforce 2108

Georgia: Concerted 2154, Edmondson 2170, Empty 2171, Fulton 2180, God's 2188, Ladonna 2204, Marena 2209, Ninth 2216, North 2217, Parents 2219, Saint 2230, Savannah 2233, Scheffler 2234, Stovall 2244, Tri-County 2250, United 2251, United 2252, United 2253, Watson 2258, Whitfield 2264

Hawaii: Council 2279, Hawaii 2289, National 2305

Illinois: A & B 2352, **Abbott 2353**, **Abbvie 2354**, Aicardi 2359, Ameren 2364, Barr 2414, Bunn 2446, C.E.F.S. 2454, **Cara 2459**, Catholic 2463, Central 2466, Coeli 2486, Community 2491, Costello 2501, Crosswalk 2504, Dodd 2519, Embarras 2541, Emergency 2542, Ende 2544, Fabela 2556, Goodgear 2587, Gore 2588, Higgins 2616, Illinois 2633, Illinois 2642, Inner 2649, Kankakee 2667, Kohen 2675, Lakeview 2682, Lawrence 2687, Loaves 2696, Lutheran 2702, Lutheran 2703, **Majid 2706**, Maryville 2711, Mutual 2742, Peoples 2782, Presence 2797, Proctor 2801, **Serbian 2848**, Sharing 2850, Shawnee 2851, **Special 2866**, St. John's 2870, Swiss 2884, Tazwood 2887, Uhlich 2900, Union 2903, **Walgreens 2914**, Weeks 2920, Western 2924, Youth 2938

Indiana: Area 2957, Children's 2982, CIACO 2986, Community 2988, Community 2989, Hammond 3048, Housing 3064, Kosciusko 3090, **Lilly 3100**, McGrain 3111, Northwest 3128, Pace 3137, Rose 3165, United 3207, Western 3221

Iowa: Camp 3251, Community 3259, Community 3260, Community 3261, Community 3265, Des Moines 3274, Hawkeye 3296, Iowa 3307, ISED 3310, Operation 3348, Red 3363, Southern 3385, United 3400, Upper 3401, West 3407

Kansas: Duclos 3434, Helping 3453, Jewish 3463, Knights 3475, Laham 3478, Sidwell 3514, Southwest 3518, Wichita 3538

Kentucky: American 3544, Appalachian 3546, Community 3558, **Disabled 3563**, Eastern 3565, Foundation 3569, Gateway 3572, God's 3573, Kentucky 3585, Lincoln 3591, Metro 3596, PHP 3616, Process 3617, River 3620

Louisiana: CS 3649, Food 3652, JL Foun 3657, Louisiana 3662, Our 3672, St. Vincent 3678, Total 3680

Maine: Bangor 3689, Camden 3691, Corporal 3692, Montgomery 3719, Penquis 3725, Waldo 3744, York 3749

Maryland: American 3762, Bowie 3786, Burbage 3791, Community 3804, Community 3809, Crossway 3811, **HealthWell 3840**, Housing 3843, Kowalsky 3861, Montgomery 3888, Neighborhood 3901, Pollak 3914, Shepherd's 3930, Shore 3931, Stepping 3938, United 3948, United 3949, Warfield 3951

Massachusetts: 47 3955, Action 3957, Bristol 3999, Cape Cod 4008, Crist 4032, **Devens 4039**, Elder 4057, Farmer 4063, German 4081, Giving 4084, HAP 4094, Haverhill 4098, Howes 4119, Make-A-Wish 4157, Marblehead 4159, Martin 4162, New 4195, North 4202, One 4206, Phillips 4222, Pilgrim 4224, Plymouth 4226, Pratt 4229, Quincy 4234, Relief 4241, Salem 4253, Samaritan 4254, Sanders 4257, **SEVEN 4267**, Society 4271, South 4274, Swan 4280, Travelers 4294, Trustees 4299, Turning 4302, **Two 4303**, Worcester 4322, Youth 4329

Michigan: Allegan 4334, Arts 4340, Charity 4379, Davenport 4404, Easter 4412, Gilmore 4437, Grand 4446, Heat 4459, **Herdegen 4464**, I Have 4479, **International 4481**, Italian 4483, **Kellogg 4496**, McPherson 4530, New 4552, Nill 4557, Northern 4560, Oakland 4568, Old 4568, Rochester 4590, Society 4612, Southwest 4617, Southwest 4618, Thresholds 4638, Travelers 4640, Tumey 4644, United 4651, United 4652,

Veteran's 4657, Wayne-Metropolitan 4662, Willard 4669, **World 4674**, **Yankama 4676**

Minnesota: Bowman 4702, Bridge 4703, Catholic 4708, Community 4719, Gilfillan 4748, Higher 4758, Law 4781, Mahube 4788, Minnesota 4803, Minnesota 4806, Scott-Carver-Dakota 4846, Second 4847, Semcac 4849, Southwest 4857, Steinke 4861, **UnitedHealthcare 4876**, Volunteers 4880, Volunteers 4881, Wilder 4890

Mississippi: AJFC 4895, Box 4899, Lexington 4912, Owen 4917, Puckett, 4920, St. Vincent 4922, Thalheimer 4924

Missouri: Baptist-Trinity 4935, Butler 4948, Cardinal 4952, Clarkson 4957, Community 4962, Concerned 4965, Gift 4999, Green 5006, **Growing 5008**, Missouri 5058, North 5065, Ozarks 5069, Ronald 5080, Scottish 5097, United 5121, West 5124, **Young 5127**

Montana: District 5142

Nebraska: Alegent 5184, EducationQuest 5197, Lutheran 5231, People's 5254, UNMC 5267, World 5276

Nevada: Catholic 5281, Foundation 5288, Nevada 5295, United 5303

New Hampshire: Community 5315, Elliott 5320, Lavoie 5337, Martin 5344, Martin 5345, Morse 5349, Scots' 5367, Strafford 5371

New Jersey: **ARCH 5389**, Atlanticare 5392, Bass 5395, Catholic 5413, Catholic 5414, Catholic 5415, Child 5422, **DRC 5436**, Eastern 5438, Family 5444, First 5445, **Johnson 5481**, Legal 5497, **Merck 5505**, Northwest 5528, **Novartis 5529**, **Ostberg 5533**, **Sanofi 5559**, Society 5571, Tri-County 5581, United 5585, United 5586, United 5587, United 5588, WKBJ 5602

New Mexico: Santa Fe 5649

New York: Adams 5666, Agoriani 5673, **Agudath 5674**, **American 5697**, Athanasiades 5737, **Bristol 5788**, Brockway 5791, Bronx 5795, Chest 5845, Children 5847, Children's 5848, Children's 5850, College 5867, Community 5878, Community 5883, Dove 5932, **Global 6033**, Hambay 6055, Havens 6061, Hutchins 6087, IRT 6105, Jenkins 6113, **Jewish 6117**, Jewish 6118, Just 6126, **Keren 6135**, MacKinnon 6181, Mayer 6198, Monahan 6222, Musicians 6232, New York 6269, New York 6276, New 6278, **Open 6294**, Opportunities 6299, Parodneck 6304, **Pfizer 6315**, Project 6334, Realty 6347, REBNY 6348, Rental 6353, Ronald 6360, **Russian 6366**, S.B.H. 6368, Saratoga 6375, **Teach 6444**, Tinker 6457, **Trickle 6463**, Tuttle 6467, Variety 6486, **V-Day 6487**, Vocational 6494, **VonAmelunxen 6496**, Washington 6502, Webster 6505, **Worldstudio 6535**

North Carolina: Better 6573, Choanoke 6601, Corpening 6618, Davis 6626, Eastern 6639, Evans 6650, Foundation 6659, Foundation 6660, Gate 6670, Giving 6676, Indian 6710, Inter-Faith 6714, Magdalena 6755, McAllister 6759, **Music 6781**, NC 6786, Outreach 6807, Rouch 6842, Salisbury-Rowan 6848, Triangle 6900, With 6924

Ohio: Agape 6959, Akron 6967, Catholic 7029, **Children 7032**, Christian 7035, Collaborative 7048, Columbus 7054, Community 7055, Community 7056, Council 7066, County 7067, DeCrane 7085, Economic 7096, Fraser 7117, Greenwalt 7135, Homeless 7153, Kidney 7190, Loeb 7212, Maple 7219, Middleton 7244, Northwestern 7274, Oppenheim 7284, Ratner 7313, Shinnick 7347, United 7395, United 7396, United 7397, W. 7407, Working 7439

Oklahoma: Areawide 7450, Happiness 7478, JWF 7487

Oregon: Aging 7529, Care 7544, Clarke 7548, Community 7554, Community 7555, Criswell 7561, Cutler 7564, **Deneke's 7570**, Fish 7577, McComas 7600, Neighborimpact 7615, Northwest 7618, Oregon 7623, Pass 7630, Portland 7634, Providence 7638, Snow-Cap 7661, Society 7663, Umpqua 7672, Yamhill 7687

Pennsylvania: Aid 7693, Ameche 7700, Biddle 7733, Blaisdell 7735, Blues 7737, **Buck 7751**, Center 7761, Commission 7778, Community 7786, Coordinated 7791, CSI 7801, Dollar 7813, Gibson 7869, GlaxoSmithKline 7871, Greater 7879, Indiana 7918, Lancaster 7943, Nestor 8004, Pennsylvania 8025, Physicians 8042, Quin 8070, Saak 8086, Schuylkill 8091, Smock 8114, South 8124, Spackman 8126, St. Margaret 8127, Stockwell 8132, Stork 8134, Teva 8142, Two 8152, **Vang 8161**, **Viropharma 8166**, Visiting 8167, Western 8189, Workplace 8207

Rhode Island: Coe 8265, Cranston/Theophilus 8277, Davenport 8283, Dix 8285, McVinney 8334, Montague 8349, Providence 8375, Shriners 8399, Sprague 8412, Townsend 8425, Webster 8433

South Carolina: Anmed 8447, Byrnes 8453, Carolina 8456, Charleston 8458, Clemson 8461, Coastal 8464, Fund 8472, Hebrew 8481, Horne 8484, Lowcountry 8492, Miracle 8494, Palmetto 8501, Society 8509, United 8518

South Dakota: Dow 8529, Native 8537

Tennessee: Aid 8553, Appalachian 8557, Catholic 8566, East 8588, Fort 8592, Hodges 8602, Hurlbut 8605, International 8607, Leyen 8618, Metropolitan 8622, Mid-Cumberland 8623, Nashville 8625, Ross 8638, Shiloh 8643, Southeast 8647, Thomley 8654, Upper 8659

Texas: Arlington 8690, Caritas 8735, Caritas 8736, Catholic 8739, Catholic 8741, Chaudhary 8745, Christian 8749, Christus 8751, Common 8758, Community 8760, Community 8761, Cutter 8779, Farmer 8818, Fort 8827, Futureus 8834, Giannini-Scatena 8839, Home 8873, Houston 8878, Ilgenfritz 8891, Interfaith 8895, Jireh 8899, Lake 8912, Meyer 8956, Miller 8959, Mission 8965, Moody 8967, Neighborhood 8988, Northwest 8993, Peyton 9016, Presbyterian 9028, Programs 9029, Rolling 9044, Second 9066, Singleton 9075, Society 9082, Some 9083, South 9084, South 9086, Target 9109, United 9142, United 9143, United 9144, University 9145, Urban 9146, West 9163

Utah: Bybee 9196, Hanks 9203, I Care 9208, Kolob 9214, Last 9215, McCarthey 9219, Whiz 9231

Vermont: Central 9239, Ohiyesa 9256, United 9264

Virginia: A Gift 9277, Americans 9313, Carpenter's 9336, **Christian 9341**, EastWest 9369, Echo 9370, Homestretch 9397, Housing 9400, Hughes 9401, Johnson 9410, Lend-A-Hand 9419, Northern 9468, Operation 9473, Rahman 9490, Reckitt 9492, St. Paul's 9513, Western 9546

Washington: Alternatives 9560, Central 9582, Chelan-Douglas 9584, Children's 9588, College 9594, Community 9597, Community 9598, Franciscan 9615, Hopelink 9638, Lower 9664, Market 9667, North 9683, Northwest 9686, Opportunity 9689, Overlake 9691, Providence 9703, Providence 9704, Rider 9707, Rural 9711, Rural 9712, Second 9721, Skagit 9725, Society 9729, Spokane 9731, Welch 9751, Wills 9754, **World 9758**, Young 9762

West Virginia: Chambers 9774, Serra 9814, Smith 9815, Your 9831

Wisconsin: CAP 9857, Carlisle 9858, Catholic 9861, Indianhead 9926, Kern 9943, MacPherson 9954, Partners 9991, Racine 10002, Society 10038, Spartvedt 10041, St. Elizabeth 10044, Young 10090, Zebro 10092

Wyoming: LaRue 10110, Littler 10113, Perkins 10117, Spacht 10121

Economics

California: **Columbia 508**, Loeb 753

Colorado: Reach 1265

District of Columbia: **Atlas 1588**, Equipment 1623, **FINRA 1626**, **Fund 1634**, **German 1638**

Florida: Everglades 1872

Illinois: **Sigma 2855**

Maryland: Adams 3750, Mid-Atlantic 3885, NASDAQ 3892

Massachusetts: **SEVEN 4267**

Michigan: Bay 4350, Harding 4457
New Jersey: Horowitz 5473
New York: **American 5692, Asia 5733, CDS 5828, Delmas 5921, Schalkenbach 6379, Sloan 6404, Social 6409**
North Carolina: **Institut 6711**
Pennsylvania: **Heinz 7900,** Simpson 8104, Smithfield 8113
Virginia: **American 9310**

Education

Alabama: Sheffield 78
Alaska: CIRI 113, Doyon 115, Monroe 125, Seybert 137, SNA 139, Tanana 140
Arizona: Arizona 161, Arizona 164, Christian 180, Deer 183, East 187, **Research 233,** Seed 236, **Southern 237,** Sulphur 243
Arkansas: Boggan 271, Murphy 293, **Murphy 296,** Thomas 318, Union 321, Wal-Mart 325
California: Basic 401, Boand 416, Carlston 464, **Cavalier 469, Children's 490,** Chopra 494, Cloud 503, Downey 545, **Easter 552,** Emergency 562, Fansler 569, Feminist 573, Florsheim 581, **Grace 633,** Heffernan 654, Herbst 656, Horizons 667, Hydrocephalus 676, **Institute 685,** International 688, Jedinstvo 703, Jewish 706, Johnson 711, Korean 723, La Canada 727, La 728, Lafayette 730, Liu 749, McQuinn 780, Menlo 784, Penjoyan 859, Price 878, Project 883, **QUALCOMM 889,** Richards 910, Scholarship 965, Sedler 972, Shelby 979, Space 1007, Tatum 1037, Tawa 1038, **Thiel 1046,** World 1101, **World 1102**
Colorado: **American 1116,** Assistance 1125, **Clan 1148,** Community 1172, Douglas 1184, El 1190, Garone-Nicksich 1202, Heathcock 1212, Lillis 1232, Pathways 1256, **Someone 1286,** Stupfel 1292, Yampa 1309
Connecticut: Canaan 1345, Hammers 1397, Promising 1446, Rockville 1450, Saybrook 1455, Stamford 1465, Voya 1478, Xerox 1490
Delaware: CenturyLink-Clarke 1494, **International 1514,** Simpson 1523, Vocational 1527
District of Columbia: Afterschool 1532, **American 1554, American 1557, Aspen 1583,** Bell 1591, Christ 1601, CIC 1602, Community 1605, Fordham 1628, **German 1638, International 1657, NEA 1700, Parents, 1707, Sheet 1727,** Washington 1747, Washington 1749
Florida: A Gift 1760, Blankenship 1801, Common 1836, Community 1841, Education 1866, Hollywood 1919, Kelly 1935, Lang 1945, McCabe 1967, **Miami 1979,** Mount 1988, Pagliara 2010, Space 2068
Georgia: Edmondson 2170, Georgia 2185, **Jewish 2198,** Seven 2236, West 2261, Wetherbee 2262
Hawaii: **Center 2274,** Ching 2275, McKee 2303, Palama 2312
Idaho: Excel 2331
Illinois: **Abbott 2353, American 2374, American 2378, American 2386,** Bogardus 2428, Bohne 2429, Bolingbrook 2430, Brewer 2437, Brunswick 2443, Business 2452, Caestecker 2456, Caruso-Sperl 2462, Chicago 2474, Chicago 2476, Crosswalk 2504, Doody 2522, Edmunds 2534, Embarras 2541, English 2548, Erk 2550, Franciscan 2573, Golden 2586, Gore 2588, House 2626, Illinois 2646, Illinois 2648, Kander 2666, Kohl 2676, **Lascaris 2685,** Maryville 2711, **National 2747, National 2749,** Paideia 2776, Peeples 2781, Perkins 2784, **Rotary 2835,** Smith 2858, Smyth 2861, Southern 2865, Swedish 2882, **Turnaround 2899**
Indiana: Coy 3009, Dr. 3018, Foundations 3033, Harber 3051, IPALCO 3075, Kimball 3086, **Lilly 3101, National 3122,** Parkview 3140, Warren 3216, Wells 3220, **Zoltani 3232**
Iowa: Accelerated 3233, Harper 3295, Hockenberry 3300, Iowa 3309, McElroy 3333, Operation 3348, Pella 3355, Schooler 3373, Sonstegard 3384, United 3399
Kansas: Abell 3411, Clay 3425, Davis 3431

Kentucky: Appalachian 3545, Christian 3556, Governors 3574, Independence 3578, Mackin 3593, Papa 3611, PHP 3616
Louisiana: Academic 3639, Ascension 3643, Entergy 3651, Lafayette 3658
Maine: Hungarian-American 3704, Maine 3714, Trust 3741, United 3743
Maryland: **AICE 3751, American 3757, Central 3797,** Credit 3810, Crossway 3811, **Discovery 3815,** Ginger 3834, Maryland 3870, Maryland 3875, Parent 3907, **Sodexo 3935**
Massachusetts: Boston 3992, Cabot 4003, **City 4024,** Community 4028, Dover 4043, **Elderhostel 4058,** Essex 4059, Grinspoon 4090, Grinspoon 4091, **Harvard 4097,** High 4104, Hopedale 4112, **Houghton 4115,** Institution 4125, **National 4188,** North 4200, President 4230, Red 4240, Smith 4270, **Transgender 4293, World 4324**
Michigan: Bott 4364, Career 4373, Caring 4375, Charlevoix 4380, Chelsea 4382, Foster 4423, Foundation 4426, Jackson 4484, L & L 4507, M & M 4521, Marquette 4523, MEEMIC 4531, New 4552, Northville 4562, Polan 4582, Reid 4587, Royal 4594, Scears 4600, **Society 4611,** Stokes 4628
Minnesota: Birk's 4698, Ecolab 4731, **Hmong 4760,** Lemieux 4782, Methodist 4795, Minnesota 4798, Redmond 4834, Sun 4863, Target 4864, Trinity 4872, Two 4873, United 4875, Wedum 4885, Wildey 4891
Mississippi: Bacot/Jolly 4896, Care 4901, Community 4902, Day 4904, Lexington 4912
Missouri: Bolivar 4940, Butler 4948, Cape 4951, Hutchins 5021, MICDS 5052, Shelter 5099, St. Louis 5106, Urban 5122, **Young 5127**
Montana: Heisey 5156
Nebraska: Alegent 5184, Fellman 5203, Hamilton 5212, Hester 5218, Kiewit 5224, Stueven 5264
Nevada: Dawson 5285, Norris 5297
New Hampshire: Concord 5316, Lancaster 5336, Lavoie 5337, **Lyman 5340,** New London 5356
New Jersey: **Dow 5435,** Eastern 5438, Embrace 5440, Montclair 5510, PSEG 5548, Rigorous 5551, Woman's 5603
New Mexico: Berliner 5614
New York: **Agudath 5674,** American 5709, Blarney 5767, **BMI 5771,** Brewster 5785, Burrows 5806, **Buttonwood 5807,** Chautauqua 5842, **Civil 5858,** Community 5881, **Covenant 5895,** De Jur 5917, De Karman 5918, Doherty 5929, Elsasser 5958, Episcopal 5960, Farmen 5975, Food 5989, **Foundation 5994,** Fountain 6004, Gavin 6017, Hodges 6074, **Institute 6095,** Jewish 6116, Jonas 6122, La 6150, **Lighthouse 6163,** MADRE, 6182, Morgan 6225, Morgan 6226, Morton 6227, **New 6264,** New York 6268, Ontario 6293, **Open 6294,** Reaching 6346, Scarsdale 6378, Scott 6388, Snayberger 6407, **Soros 6416,** Statue 6433, **Teach 6444, Teachers 6445, Tibet 6454,** Trumansburg 6464, **United 6472, USTA 6482, V-Day 6487, Watson 6504,** Wegmans 6507
North Carolina: Atkins 6564, Cherokee 6598, Cleveland 6606, Community 6614, Foundation 6659, Henderson 6696, Johns 6718, Leever 6740, Lutz 6753, Martin 6757, Monger 6776, **Morehead-Cain 6778,** NC 6788, Owens 6808, Rennie 6826, **Samaritan's 6849,** Schug 6854, Thomasville 6892, Thomson 6893, Touchstone 6895, Wake 6911, Watauga 6914
Ohio: Addison 6957, Berlin 6996, Davies 7080, Gay 7125, Lake 7201, Marietta 7220, McGinty 7235, Mishou 7252, Mohr 7253, Munger 7258, Muskingum 7263, Parents 7290, Peoples 7297, Sebring 7341, Simmons 7351, Steigler 7368, Steiner 7369, Sullivan 7372, Tuition 7389, Working 7439, Ziegler 7447
Oklahoma: Aileen 7448, Bartlesville 7452, Oklahoma 7502, Stevens 7515
Oregon: Benson 7538, Coalition 7550, Vernier 7674, Weir 7679
Pennsylvania: Benford 7727, Berks 7730, Blaisdell 7735, Brown 7749, Children's 7765, Commission 7778, Community 7781, Crossroads 7800,

Ghidotti 7868, Golden 7873, Irwin 7922, Keith 7934, Kidney 7935, Lenfest 7956, O'Brien-Veba 8014, Philadelphia 8038, Pittsburgh 8048, Podiatry 8052, Reading 8071, Schuylkill 8090, Snyder 8115, Snyder 8116, Society 8119, Stoneleigh 8133, Vincent 8165, West 8187
Puerto Rico: Unanue 8224
Rhode Island: Blanchard 8246, DeLoura 8284, Dix 8285, Frost 8295, Greater 8302, McLean 8341, Peck 8367, Todd 8424
South Carolina: Charleston 8459, Gamecock 8474, Gift 8475, Horne 8484, Smith 8507
South Dakota: Black 8522, Clausen 8524, Watertown 8546
Tennessee: Alumni 8555, Chenoweth 8570, Fengler 8591, Humanities 8604, Mercy 8619, Ross 8638
Texas: Beefmaster 8708, Bergman 8710, Bragan 8719, Broady 8722, College 8757, Deupree 8792, Diffenbaugh-University 8795, **First 8822,** Foundation 8830, Fund 8833, Houston 8883, Humanities 8887, Lake 8913, **Media 8950, National 8986,** Reilly 9035, Schumann 9063, South 9085, Southern 9088, Sunnyside 9103, Texas 9114, Texas 9125, Today 9137, Urban 9146, West 9162
Utah: 100% 9190, Bybee 9196, Harman 9204, I Care 9208, Salt 9225, WTF 9234
Vermont: Ottauquechee 9257
Virginia: A Gift 9277, Blair 9326, **Burger 9331,** Community 9350, Henrico 9394, Minor 9437, Morgan 9440, **National 9446, National 9451, National 9452,** Northern 9466, **PMMI 9484,** St. Paul's 9513, **Teachers 9518,** United 9532, Williamson 9549
Washington: ARK 9562, Community 9600, KT Family 9656, Plum 9700, Royston 9710, San Juan 9714, Seattle 9718, Washington 9750
West Virginia: Adams 9763, Beckley 9766, Carter 9772, Tucker 9824, West Virginia 9827
Wisconsin: Darcey 9875, Exacto 9886, Fond du Lac 9893, ManpowerGroup 9957, Meehan 9963, Oshkosh 9989, Partners 9991, Pieper 9995, Tate 10050, Yakich 10089
Wyoming: Glassber 10106

Education, administration/regulation

Kentucky: Scottish 3624

Education, alliance/advocacy

Illinois: Chicago 2474

Education, association

New York: Catholic 5825

Education, continuing education

Delaware: Fresh 1509
District of Columbia: Hemophilia 1642
New Mexico: Albuquerque 5610

Education, early childhood education

Arkansas: SHARE 307
California: **Academy 335**
Colorado: CAEYC 1138
District of Columbia: Black 1593
Florida: Episcopal 1871
Illinois: Chicago 2474, Illinois 2641
Kansas: Kansas 3467
Minnesota: Child 4712
Missouri: Kansas 5023
New Jersey: Child 5421
North Carolina: Albemarle 6547, Pamlico 6809, Robeson 6837, Smart 6864, Smart 6865
Oklahoma: Beatty 7454
Pennsylvania: Community 7782, **Lokoff 7961**
Tennessee: Children's 8573

Education, ESL programs
Massachusetts: First 4069, New 4195

Education, formal/general education
New York: Community 5878
Oregon: Benson 7538

Education, fund raising/fund distribution
Indiana: **National 3122**
New York: DonorsChoose.org 5931

Education, gifted students
Hawaii: Cottington 2278
Maryland: **Carson 3793**
Nevada: Davidson 5284
New Jersey: **Siemens 5566**

Education, management/technical assistance
Colorado: EDUCAUSE 1189
Indiana: Decatur 3013
Maine: Maine 3712

Education, public education
Colorado: Puddy 1263
District of Columbia: Community 1605
Indiana: Public 3152
Kentucky: Scottish 3624
Nebraska: **Buffett 5190**
New York: Children 5846, **Teachers 6445**
Texas: Bragan 8719

Education, reading
California: Jewish 707
Connecticut: Connecticut 1366
Illinois: Roberts 2825
Kansas: Cloud 3426
Michigan: Come 4389

Education, research
Colorado: EDUCAUSE 1189
Connecticut: Connecticut 1366
Illinois: Golden 2586, **Special 2866**
Nebraska: Strengths 5263
New York: American 5703, Community 5878, Price 6327, Roothbert 6361, **Schalkenbach 6379**
Ohio: Van Wert 7403

Education, services
California: Strauss 1028
Missouri: Kansas 5023
New York: Netzach 6259
Pennsylvania: Quin 8070

Education, single organization support
Massachusetts: Community 4028

Education, special
California: Community 513, Jewish 707
Colorado: Scottish 1278
Connecticut: Connecticut 1366
Illinois: Roberts 2825
Iowa: Corbin 3267
Kansas: Cloud 3426
Massachusetts: Henry 4103
Nebraska: Omaha 5251
New Jersey: Eden 5439, Snyder 5570
New York: Reaching 6346
Pennsylvania: Reitnauer 8074

Elementary school/education
Arizona: Seed 236
California: Basic 401, Chung 498, Coastal 504
Delaware: **International 1514**
District of Columbia: Latino 1669
Florida: Tangelo 2083
Idaho: Idaho 2336
Illinois: Chicago 2474, Golden 2586, Paideia 2776, Williams 2927
Indiana: Amburn 2953, Raab 3155
Kansas: Fingersh 3442
Missouri: Fingersh 4992
New Jersey: PSEG 5548
New York: **Brackett 5779**, Children's 5850, **Columbus 5871**, DonorsChoose.org 5931, McGrath 6205, Trumansburg 6464
North Carolina: Children's 6600
Ohio: Children's 7033, Licking 7209, McGinty 7235, Stark 7366

Elementary/secondary education
Arizona: Arizona 162, Arizona 163, Washington 258
Arkansas: SHARE 307
California: Basic 401, Menlo 784, **NAMM 813**, Palos Verdes 853, Philanthropic 865, San Diego 933, Silicon 987, Ukiah 1066
Colorado: Public 1262
Connecticut: Voya 1478
Delaware: CenturyLink-Clarke 1494, **International 1514**
District of Columbia: **American 1555**, Black 1593
Florida: A Gift 1760, Education 1867, Step 2075
Idaho: Idaho 2336
Illinois: After 2358, Community 2494, Murphy 2741, **Turnaround 2899**
Indiana: Wayne 3217
Maine: Kieve 3707
Maryland: **Discovery 3815**
Michigan: Bretzlaff 4368, Waterford 4660
Minnesota: Target 4864
Missouri: Kansas 5023, **People 5072**
Nebraska: **Buffett 5190**
Nevada: Community 5282
New Jersey: **Siemens 5566**
New York: Dellomo 5920
North Carolina: Pitt County 6820, Touchstone 6895, TW 6903
Ohio: Howley 7159, **Kids 7191**
Oklahoma: Tulsa 7519
Oregon: Vernier 7674
Pennsylvania: Community 7782, York 8213
South Carolina: Alliance 8445
Tennessee: Children's 8573
Texas: Bragan 8719, **Butt 8730**
Vermont: Rowland 9258
Virginia: Education 9372, **National 9457**
Washington: Bellevue 9569, Clover 9592, His 9635, Plum 9700
Wisconsin: Kohl 9944

Employment
Alaska: CIRI 113
Connecticut: Capital 1346
District of Columbia: **American 1556**
Illinois: WKUS 2931
Maine: Information 3705
Maryland: Job 3854
Michigan: Career 4373
Oregon: Neighborimpact 7615
Pennsylvania: Private 8064
Washington: Lower 9664
West Virginia: Workforce 9830

Employment, association
Pennsylvania: Woods 8205

Employment, government agencies
Wisconsin: Anu 9837

Employment, job counseling
Tennessee: United 8658
Washington: Career 9580

Employment, labor unions/organizations
California: California 449, Northern 833, United 1070
District of Columbia: **American 1556**, Communications 1604, Community 1606, **Hoffa 1646**, **UFCW 1739**
Hawaii: Bouslog 2273
Indiana: Community 3004
New Jersey: Joint 5483
Pennsylvania: Asbestos 7715, Teamsters 8140
Texas: Smolin 9080

Employment, research
Michigan: **Upjohn 4654**

Employment, services
Connecticut: Capital 1346
Florida: Operation 2006
Pennsylvania: Private 8064
South Carolina: Gleamns 8476

Employment, training
Alaska: CIRI 113
Connecticut: Capital 1346
New York: Wegmans 6507
Pennsylvania: Communtiy 7787, Private 8064
Washington: Career 9580, SkillSource 9726

Employment, vocational rehabilitation
Pennsylvania: **Jewish 7929**

End of life care
Florida: Big 1799
Oklahoma: Saint 7510
Virginia: American 9303

Engineering
Arizona: Educational 190, Freeport-McMoRan 196, Sulphur 243
Arkansas: Union 321
California: **Adobe 338**, Found 583, **INCOSE 679**, National 821, Signer 985
Colorado: Colorado 1169, Reach 1265, Rocky 1272
Connecticut: Macristy 1418
Delaware: Chaney 1495
District of Columbia: **American 1548**, American 1568, National 1682, **Society 1731**
Florida: Everglades 1872, Florida 1879, Rayonier 2031
Idaho: IDACORP 2334
Illinois: Ameren 2364, **Sigma 2855**
Indiana: Schultz 3175
Kansas: Ellis 3440
Maryland: Jorgensen 3855
Michigan: Community 4396, Michigan 4540, **Society 4611**
Minnesota: Rosen 4841
New Hampshire: Plan 5361
New Jersey: Fortescue 5448, **IEEE 5476**, Snyder 5570, Wei 5593
New York: **Audio 5739**, Community 5878, **IBM 6089**
North Carolina: **Earnhardt 6636**, **S.R.C. 6847**, Taylor 6888
Ohio: Community 7058, Culture 7073, **Lincoln 7210**, Van Wert 7403
Pennsylvania: **Association 7717**, Brown 7750, Head 7895, Lutron 7963, **PPG 8058**

South Carolina: Clemson 8462
Texas: **Reese 9034**
Utah: EnergySolutions 9199
Virginia: **Plumbing 9483**, **Public 9488**
Wisconsin: Graef 9908

Engineering school/education

Alabama: Alsite 6, Vulcan 88
Alaska: Alaska 97, CIRI 113
California: **Foundation 587**, **Hertz 658**, **HP 670**
Colorado: Cibrowski 1147
Connecticut: DiMauro 1377, Fairfield 1387, Spirol 1462
Delaware: Delaware 1500
District of Columbia: Community 1605, **Optical 1705**, **Society 1731**
Florida: Dunbar 1864, Grossman 1897, Lauffer 1947
Georgia: Georgia 2184
Hawaii: Onizuka 2307
Illinois: Blazek 2427, **Foundry 2571**, Meade 2727, **Nuts, 2760**, Steel 2871, Taylor 2885, Walters 2916
Indiana: Community 3001, Community 3004, Dearborn 3012, Decatur 3013, Kuhner 3092, Madison 3106
Kansas: Salina 3510
Louisiana: McGinty 3668
Maryland: Huether 3845, National 3894
Michigan: **ACI 4332**, Cadillac 4371, Community 4394, Kadant 4491, Meyers 4532, Petoskey 4577, **Society 4611**
Minnesota: Alworth 4685, Lakeland 4778, Pick 4825, **Wagner 4883**
Mississippi: Community 4902
Missouri: Gorman 5002, Hayes 5013, Marsch 5043
Nebraska: Lexington 5228
New Jersey: **IEEE 5476**
New Mexico: Albuquerque 5610
New York: AEC 5669, Fitzpatrick 5985, **National 6241**
North Carolina: Nucor 6803
Ohio: AGC 6960, Ariel 6979, Birr 6998, Crain 7070, Dayton 7082, Lapeer 7204, Scioto 7339
Oklahoma: Wilson 7527
Oregon: Professional 7635
Pennsylvania: Harris 7889, Lutron 7963, Miller 7988, Nicklies 8007, Smithfield 8113, York 8213
Rhode Island: Schiff 8393
Texas: Conner 8767, Lubbock 8926, NASA 8980, **SPE 9093**, Wildner 9166
Virginia: Bell 9325, Foundation 9383, **National 9451**, National 9458, Sidhu 9504, Utility 9535
Washington: Hansen 9632
Wisconsin: Bachhuber 9842, Badger 9845, **EAA 9880**, Keller 9940, Shallow 10029, Vedova 10058, Wisconsin 10081

Engineering/technology

California: ACEC 337, **Adobe 338**, **Avery 395**, **Foundation 587**, **HP 670**, **INCOSE 679**, San Diego 937
Colorado: Mikkelson 1239, Rocky 1272
Connecticut: Liberty 1414, Saybrook 1455, Spirol 1462, Weller 1482
District of Columbia: **American 1542**, **Development 1614**, **Hispanic 1644**, National 1682
Florida: **Astronaut 1785**, AWS 1789
Illinois: American 2383, **Hertz 2615**, Peeples 2781, **Zonta 2942**
Indiana: Wabash 3215
Kentucky: Ogden 3607
Maine: Information 3705, Maine 3715
Maryland: **ELECTRI 3817**
Massachusetts: American 3967, Dugan 4045, Wheelwright 4315
Michigan: **Collectors 4387**, **Society 4611**
Minnesota: Alworth 4685, Bakken 4697, **Lindbergh 4783**, Minnesota 4804
New Hampshire: **U.S. 5373**
New Jersey: BLSJ 5402, **Siemens 5566**
New York: Chautauqua 5842, Eyebeam 5970, **IBM 6089**

North Carolina: Foundation 6660, **Kimmel 6731**, Material 6758, Rennie 6826
Pennsylvania: **Association 7717**, **Botstiber 7740**, **Heinz 7900**, Lutron 7963, **PPG 8058**
South Carolina: **AVX 8450**, Clemson 8462
Texas: **Conrad 8768**, Pettinger 9015
Virginia: Air 9284, **Foundation 9381**, National 9458, SMACNA 9506, Specialized 9512, **U.S. 9526**

Environment

Alaska: Alaska 98
California: Cloud 503, **Columbia 508**, **Earth 550**, **Foundation 586**, **Goldman 628**, James 701, Social 998, **Trust 1060**
Colorado: Hasan 1211, Young 1311
District of Columbia: **Amazon 1537**, **Environmental 1621**, **German 1638**, Horticultural 1647, **International 1656**, **National 1690**, **Wilderness 1751**
Florida: Southwest 2067
Illinois: Urbana-Champaign 2907
Kentucky: Eastern 3566, **Energy 3567**
Louisiana: Friends 3653
Maryland: Allemall 3754, Association 3778, **Environmental 3820**
Massachusetts: Berkshire 3986, Cabot 4003, Thoreau 4289
Minnesota: Ecotrust 4732, Minnesota 4804
New Jersey: Honeywell 5472, **Siemens 5566**
New York: **CNN 5862**, **Cummings 5904**, **National 6241**, **Social 6409**, **Worldstudio 6535**
Ohio: YSI 7446
Oregon: Neskowin 7616
Pennsylvania: Eastern 7818, **ERM 7832**, **Heinz 7900**
Texas: **North 8992**
Virginia: **National 9459**, **Newton 9465**
Washington: Ji 9644
Wisconsin: Badger 9845, **Entomological 9884**, **Johnson 9934**

Environment, beautification programs

New York: Scotts 6389

Environment, climate change/global warming

Virginia: **Ashoka: 9317**
Washington: **Bullitt 9578**

Environment, energy

District of Columbia: American 1566, **German 1638**
Kentucky: **Energy 3567**
Minnesota: **Lindbergh 4783**
Virginia: **Ashoka: 9317**
Wisconsin: Boer 9850, **Johnson 9934**

Environment, ethics

Wisconsin: Sand 10017

Environment, forests

Alabama: Alabama 2
Connecticut: Bartlett 1331
Florida: Rayonier 2031
Maryland: Walton 3950
Montana: **National 5167**
New Hampshire: Green 5324
New Jersey: Parker 5535
New York: **Rainforest 6343**
Ohio: Davey 7078, Van Wert 7403
Pennsylvania: Miller 7988
West Virginia: Sun 9821
Wisconsin: Phillips 9994, Wisconsin 10081
Wyoming: Clark 10097

Environment, formal/general education

Maine: Switzer 3738

Environment, land resources

District of Columbia: ULI 1740
Minnesota: Ecotrust 4732
Texas: **Vetiver 9148**
Wisconsin: Noer 9984, Sand 10017

Environment, legal rights

New York: **Open 6294**

Environment, natural resources

California: **Foundation 586**, **Goldman 628**, James 701, Joshua 714
Connecticut: Anthony 1324
District of Columbia: **German 1638**, **National 1691**, Resources 1723, **Wilderness 1751**
Illinois: Illinois 2635
Kentucky: **Energy 3567**
Maine: Switzer 3738
Maryland: Chesapeake 3799, Maryland 3874, Walton 3950
Massachusetts: **Earthwatch 4049**, **New England 4193**, Permanent 4216
Minnesota: **Lindbergh 4783**
New Hampshire: Butler 5312
New Jersey: Chatham 5419, Hull 5475
New York: Bay 5756, **Rainforest 6343**
Pennsylvania: Friendship 7861
South Dakota: Sioux Falls 8538
Tennessee: Dollywood 8584
Texas: Dupre 8801, Forever 8825, Milotte 8963, **North 8992**, **Vetiver 9148**, Welder 9161
Virginia: **National 9459**
Washington: **Ji 9644**
Wisconsin: Badger 9845, Phillips 9994

Environment, plant conservation

District of Columbia: Horticultural 1647
Illinois: Tree 2896
Ohio: Herb 7146

Environment, pollution control

North Carolina: **Nickel 6792**
Texas: **Vetiver 9148**

Environment, public policy

District of Columbia: **Phillips 1716**
Kentucky: **Energy 3567**
New York: **Open 6294**

Environment, radiation control

Washington: **Bullitt 9578**

Environment, recycling

District of Columbia: **Recycling 1721**

Environment, reform

New York: **Open 6294**

Environment, research

District of Columbia: Resources 1723
Maine: Switzer 3738
Massachusetts: **Earthwatch 4049**
Minnesota: Alworth 4685
New York: Hudson 6080, Huyck 6088
North Carolina: **Environmental 6649**
Texas: Stark 9101

Washington: **Ji 9644**
Wisconsin: Noer 9984

Environment, toxics

North Carolina: **Nickel 6792**
Washington: **Bullitt 9578**

Environment, volunteer services

New York: Scotts 6389

Environment, waste management

North Carolina: **Environmental 6649**

Environment, water pollution

California: Monterey 803
District of Columbia: **Ocean 1702**
Kentucky: Eastern 3566
Pennsylvania: Eastern 7818
Washington: **Ji 9644**

Environment, water resources

Arizona: Arizona 165
California: Monterey 803
District of Columbia: **Ocean 1702**
Illinois: **CF 2469**
New Hampshire: American 5305
New York: Hudson 6080
Texas: **Vetiver 9148**
Wisconsin: **Johnson 9934**

Environmental education

Connecticut: Bartlett 1331
Delaware: Chaney 1495
District of Columbia: **National 1691**
Florida: **SeaWorld 2056**
Georgia: Park 2220
Illinois: **CF 2469**, Peters 2785
Kansas: Wildlife 3540
Kentucky: Community 3559
Maryland: Maryland 3874
New Hampshire: Plan 5361
New Jersey: Honeywell 5472, PSEG 5548
North Carolina: Keep 6729
Ohio: Scioto 7339
Oklahoma: Martin 7491
Texas: Ehlers 8810, Milotte 8963
Wisconsin: La Crosse 9948

Epilepsy

Connecticut: **American 1320**
Illinois: Community 2494
Ohio: Epilepsy 7100

Epilepsy research

Connecticut: **American 1320**
Illinois: **Citizens 2482**
Maryland: **Epilepsy 3821**, Epilepsy 3822

Ethnic studies

Pennsylvania: **American 7704**

Eye diseases

California: Discovery 539, Glaucoma 619
Colorado: Rocky 1273
Illinois: **Heed 2610**, Neville 2755
Kentucky: Kentucky 3585
Maryland: **Association 3779**, **Michels 3883**
Massachusetts: Kurzweil 4143, **Milton 4177**

New York: **American 5696**, Glaucoma 6030,
   Lighthouse 6163
Pennsylvania: Eye 7833
Texas: **Knights 8909**, **OneSight 8998**
Virginia: **American 9295**

Eye research

Alabama: **International 54**
California: **American 357**, Glaucoma 619, That 1043
District of Columbia: **Optical 1705**
Florida: American 1772
Georgia: Hall 2190
Illinois: **Heed 2610**, **National 2752**
Maryland: **Association 3779**, Brightfocus 3789,
   Foundation 3828
New York: **Fight 5982**, Glaucoma 6030
Pennsylvania: Von 8170
Virginia: **American 9297**

Family resources and services, disability

New York: New Alternatives 6260
North Carolina: Easter 6638

Family services

Arizona: Turnbow 249
Arkansas: Ozark 301
California: Aspiranet 380, Burks 428, FRAMAX 592,
   Fundacion 605, Injured 682, Interface 687, Marino
   773, Sierra 983
Colorado: Assistance 1125, Colorado 1155
District of Columbia: **Armed 1579**
Florida: Area 1780, Children's 1825, Children's 1826,
   Community 1837
Georgia: Empty 2171
Hawaii: Hawaii 2288, Parents 2313, People 2314
Illinois: Angels 2400
Iowa: Operation 3348
Maine: Information 3705
Maryland: **Casey 3794**, Montgomery 3888
Massachusetts: Pilgrim 4224, **Rosenberg 4247**
Michigan: CareLink 4374, Children's 4383, Lutheran
   4520, Spectrum 4620, Whaley 4665
Minnesota: American 4689, Hastings 4755, Mahube
   4788, **Thrivent 4867**
New Jersey: Catholic 5413, Child 5422
New York: Bonei 5775, Cure 5906, Dove 5932,
   MADRE, 6182
North Carolina: Hickory 6698
Oregon: Mercy 7604, Neighborimpact 7615
Pennsylvania: Coordinated 7791, Young 8215
Rhode Island: Rhode 8382
South Carolina: Gleamns 8476
Tennessee: Dollar 8583, Jewish 8609
Texas: Buckner 8728
Washington: Family 9610
West Virginia: Harless 9788
Wisconsin: Jewish 9930

Family services, adolescent parents

Michigan: Lutheran 4520
Minnesota: **Pro 4829**
New York: Inwood 6104

Family services, counseling

California: Interface 687
Colorado: Lutheran 1235
Michigan: Lutheran 4520

Family services, domestic violence

California: Battered 403, Interface 687
Colorado: Archuleta 1121
Illinois: Prieto 2799
Massachusetts: HAP 4094
New York: Sakhi 6370

Family services, home/homemaker aid

Alabama: Gulf 44

Family services, parent education

California: Interface 687
Maryland: Parent 3907

Family services, single parents

Arkansas: Single 309
Georgia: Ladonna 2204
Oklahoma: Project 7507
Texas: Williams 9168

Financial services

District of Columbia: **FINRA 1626**
Rhode Island: O'Brion 8357, Rhode Island 8381

Financial services, credit unions

Maryland: Credit 3810

Food banks

Alabama: Montgomery 65
Arizona: Community 181, **Feed 191**
Colorado: Care 1141, Food 1196
Illinois: **Feeding 2559**
Louisiana: Food 3652
New Mexico: Community 5625
Texas: South 9086
Virginia: Foodbank 9379
Washington: Alternatives 9560
Wisconsin: Feeding 9889

Food distribution, groceries on wheels

California: El Monte 557
Texas: South 9086

Food services

Arizona: **Feed 191**, Food 194
California: Orange 843
Colorado: Care 1141, **Rock 1269**
District of Columbia: Food 1627
Florida: Densch 1860, Operation 2006, Volunteer
   2097
Illinois: BCMW 2415
Indiana: Pace 3137
Kentucky: Northern 3604
Massachusetts: South 4274
Michigan: Newaygo 4554, **Yankama 4676**
Minnesota: Hastings 4755, Providers 4831, Rosen
   4841, Second 4848
North Carolina: Hickory 6698
North Dakota: Heartland 6942
Ohio: Foodbank 7112, West Side 7418
Pennsylvania: Frozen 7862
Texas: Edinburg 8806
Utah: I Care 9208
Virginia: Americans 9313, Child 9339, Foodbank 9379
Washington: Second 9721
Wisconsin: Feeding 9889, Society 10038

Food services, commodity distribution

Washington: Washington 9746

Foundations (private grantmaking)

New York: **Tsadra 6465**

Fraternal societies

Illinois: **Sigma 2855**
Indiana: **Kappa 3082**, **Lambda 3095**, Scering 3171

Maryland: Samet 3926
Massachusetts: Supreme 4279, Theta 4287
Minnesota: Masonic 4790
Missouri: **Pi 5073**
Montana: Cut Bank 5139
New Jersey: Excelsior 5443, Justice 5484
North Carolina: St. Anthony 6873
Ohio: Ohio 7280
Pennsylvania: Davis 7805, Grand 7878
Rhode Island: Masonic 8336
Virginia: Buchly 9330

Fraternal societies (501(c)(8))

Michigan: Gleaner 4440

Genetic diseases and disorders

California: **Beckman 408, National 818**
District of Columbia: **Spina 1733**
Illinois: **Dystonia 2529**
Maryland: **Foundation 3828**
Minnesota: Alworth 4685
New Hampshire: Hubbard 5329
New York: **March 6188**
South Carolina: Carolina 8455
Washington: **Foundation 9614**
Wisconsin: Prader-Willi 9997

Genetic diseases and disorders research

California: National 822
Connecticut: **Alliance 1318**
Illinois: **International 2651**
Massachusetts: **Fraxa 4076**
New York: **Hereditary 6068, Huntington's 6086,
    March 6188**, New York 6273
North Carolina: **Cleft 6604**
Oklahoma: Global 7476

Geology

Arizona: Freeport-McMoRan 196
Colorado: AEG 1113, Rocky 1272, Society 1285
Florida: Blankenship 1801
Minnesota: Alworth 4685
New York: American 5703
North Carolina: Rennie 6826
Texas: Houston 8882

Geriatrics

District of Columbia: Gerontological 1639
New York: **American 5693**, Foundation 5996
Tennessee: Foundation 8593

Geriatrics research

California: **Ellison 561**
District of Columbia: Gerontological 1639
New York: **American 5693**, American 5698

Gerontology

California: **Glenn 621**
Michigan: **Fetzer 4418**
New York: **American 5693**
Oregon: Schmidt 7655

Girl scouts

California: Girl 617
Colorado: Girl 1204
Maine: Girl 3699
Maryland: Girl 3835
Nebraska: Girl 5207
New York: Girl 6027
North Carolina: Girl 6675

Girls

California: San Francisco 946
Colorado: **AfricAid 1114**, Girl 1204
District of Columbia: Best 1592
Florida: **Julien 1934**
Maryland: Girl 3835
Nebraska: Girl 5207
New Jersey: Camp 5411
New York: **Avon 5745, V-Day 6487**
Rhode Island: Arnold 8231, Peck 8367
Wisconsin: Women's 10086

Government/public administration

Delaware: Common 1497
District of Columbia: **American 1542, Congressional
    1607, German 1638, National 1695**
Illinois: Everett 2553, Francies 2572
Massachusetts: **Kennedy 4137**
Missouri: Community 4963
New Jersey: **Wilson 5600**
New Mexico: Farmers' 5629
Ohio: **Wexner 7423**
Virginia: **American 9305**
Washington: Wales 9744

Graduate/professional education

California: Foundation 584, San Diego 934, **Sempra
    974**
Connecticut: **Belgian 1334**, Community 1361, Fairfield
    1387, Hartford 1399
Delaware: Delaware 1500
Georgia: Callaway 2134
Illinois: **American 2378**, American 2383, Community
    2496, Peterson 2786
Kentucky: Blue 3552
Maine: Maine 3712, Switzer 3738
Maryland: **Alpha 3755**
Michigan: Bretzlaff 4368
Missouri: Hamilton 5012, Kansas 5023, Truman 5118
Nevada: Western 5304
New Mexico: **American 5611**
New York: American 5703, Columbia 5870,
    International 6099, LD 6154, Open 6294, Sperry
    6421
North Carolina: **Insurance 6712**
Ohio: McDonald 7233, Miller 7249, Stark 7366
Oregon: Oregon 7624
Pennsylvania: Abrams 7691
Rhode Island: Rhode Island 8381, Wylie 8442
Texas: Hill 8867, Lubbock 8926
Virginia: Community 9350, **Cooke 9352, Mustard
    9442**
Washington: Seattle 9719
West Virginia: Kanawha 9794
Wisconsin: Oshkosh 9988

Health care

Alabama: East Alabama 34, Middleton 62
Alaska: Kuskokwim 123
Arizona: Seed 236, University 251
Arkansas: Arkansas 262
California: Athena 392, Burks 428, California 441,
    California 450, California 461, Community 516,
    Desert 538, El Monte 557, **Floor 580, Genentech
    611**, Health 651, Hinckley 663, Hoag 665, Hoag
    666, Jefferson 705, Quality 890, QueensCare 891,
    San Francisco 942, **Screen 969**, Shelby 979, St.
    Jude 1014, Stanislaus 1017, Washington 1087,
    Winnett 1097, **World 1102**
Colorado: Balke 1127, Bonfils 1130, **Foundation
    1199**, Rocky 1270, **Someone 1286**, St. Mary's
    1289
Connecticut: Alexion 1317, Colburn-Keenan 1360,
    Larrabee 1413, Senior 1459, Westport-Weston
    1484
District of Columbia: **American 1539, American 1549,
    Families 1625**, Food 1627, **Gay 1637**,
    Gerontological 1639

Florida: Benjamin 1796, Big 1799, Cape Coral 1815,
    Community 1844, Densch 1860, Harrison 1905,
    Mayo 1966, Pagliara 2010, Renal 2035,
    Southwest 2067, Sun 2078, Watson 2100
Georgia: Baker 2123, DeKalb 2162, Edmonson 2170,
    Fragile 2179, God's 2188, Healthcare 2195,
    Hospice 2196, **Phi Mu 2222**, Whitfield 2264
Illinois: Ann 2401, CGH 2470, Daniels 2507, DuPage
    2528, Goodgear 2587, **Health 2607**, Morton
    2739, **Ronald 2831**, Union 2902, **Walgreens 2914**
Indiana: CIACO 2986, Rose 3165, Visiting 3212
Iowa: Anderson 3239, Henry 3297, St. Luke's 3388,
    Van Buren 3403
Kansas: **American 3413**, Duclos 3434, Jones 3464,
    Nell 3494
Kentucky: Children's 3555, Kings 3588, Mallory 3594,
    Norton 3605, Owensboro 3609, Rural 3622
Louisiana: Our 3672
Maine: Belknap 3690, Montgomery 3719, Portland
    3726
Maryland: **American 3769, Aplastic 3774**, Memorial
    3879, National 3898, **National 3900**
Massachusetts: Blue 3989, Boston 3996, Cabot 4003,
    Children's 4022, Crist 4032, Farmer 4063, High
    4104, Koster 4142, Massachusetts 4167,
    Needymeds 4191, ROFEH 4246
Michigan: Blue 4363, Blue 4363, CareLink 4374,
    Laidlaw 4509, Lions 4518, Pardee 4572,
    Southwest 4618
Minnesota: Gilfillan 4747, HealthEast 4756, Intertech
    4767, Mayo 4791, Saint Paul 4842, Tri-County
    4871, **UnitedHealthcare 4876**
Mississippi: Lexington 4912, Owen 4917
Missouri: Buckner 4945, Greater 5004, **National
    5062**, St. Marys 5107
Montana: Brondum 5135
Nebraska: Good 5209, Nebraska 5242, UNMC 5267
Nevada: Foundation 5288, Miracle 5294
New Hampshire: Griffin 5326, Lavoie 5337, Ramsaye
    5363
New Jersey: **American 5385, ARCH 5389**, Atlanticare
    5392, Cooper 5427, Embrace 5440, **Johnson
    5481**, Saint 5558, **Wilson 5600**
New York: Athanasiades 5737, Clark 5859, **CNN
    5862, Commonwealth 5872**, Danforth 5912,
    Dickinson 5924, **Ezer 5971**, Foundation 5996,
    Hambay 6055, Health 6064, **Lasker 6153**,
    Mayday 6197, New 6264, New 6278, North 6284,
    Price 6327, Schechter 6380, Univera 6480
North Carolina: Better 6573, Corpening 6618, Davis
    6626, Foundation 6660, Good 6677, Mission
    6775, NC 6788, Tarboro 6886, **TASCA 6887**
North Dakota: VFW 6951
Ohio: Cleveland 7043, Community 7058, Frederick
    7118, Twenty 7393
Oklahoma: Johnson 7485, Stillwater 7517
Oregon: Corvallis 7558, Moyer 7612, Northwest 7619,
    Portland 7634, Providence 7637, Southern 7664
Pennsylvania: Abington 7690, Curtis 7803,
    GlaxoSmithKline 7871, Hamot 7884, Health 7897,
    Jewish 7928, Ladd 7940, Nicholas 8006,
    Physicians 8042, Saak 8086, Stockwell 8132,
    Teva 8142, **Viropharma 8166**, Visiting 8167,
    Warren 8175
Rhode Island: Carlisle 8255, Shriners 8399, Sprague
    8412, Webster 8433
South Carolina: Boyne 8452, Gift 8475, South 8512
South Dakota: Amundson 8520
Tennessee: Appalachian 8557, Children's 8572,
    Hodges 8602, Le 8615, Methodist 8620,
    Methodist 8621, **National 8628**, Thomley 8654,
    Wellmont 8662
Texas: Borton 8717, Christus 8751, Denman 8791,
    Emergency 8814, Farmer 8818, Giannini 8838,
    Lockheed 8922, Luling 8929, Methodist 8954,
    Neighborhood 8988, Pardee 9002, Presbyterian
    9028, St. Joseph 9096, Texas 9124
Utah: Hanks 9203
Vermont: Ohiyesa 9256, Ottauquechee 9257
Virginia: Americans 9313, **Caring 9335**, Operation
    9473, Reckitt 9492, St. Paul's 9513

Washington: Clarke 9591, G.M.L. 9619, Northwest 9687, Rider 9707, Washington 9749, Washington 9750, Welch 9751, Yakima 9760
Wisconsin: Community 9870, Exacto 9886, Gundersen 9913, Healthnet 9917, Incourage 9925, Nicholl 9981, Riverview 10011, Society 10038, Spartvedt 10041, University 10055, Young 10090
Wyoming: Spacht 10121

Health care, association
Georgia: **MAP 2208**
Massachusetts: **American 3969**, King 4140
New York: Health 6064
North Carolina: Emerson 6648
Rhode Island: Alpert 8227
South Carolina: Society 8509

Health care, burn centers
California: Childrens 486
District of Columbia: **International 1653**

Health care, clinics/centers
Georgia: Columbus 2149
North Carolina: Giving 6676
Wisconsin: Gundersen 9913

Health care, emergency transport services
Massachusetts: Sanborn 4256
Texas: Southwest 9089

Health care, EMS
Connecticut: Hunter's 1403

Health care, financing
California: **Sarcoma 960**
District of Columbia: **Patient 1709**
Kentucky: Mallory 3594
North Carolina: Emerson 6648
Virginia: Patient 9477

Health care, formal/general education
California: Fries 602
Iowa: Greene 3288
Kansas: Snyder 3516
Pennsylvania: Donegal 7814
Virginia: **AHP 9282**

Health care, home services
New York: Saranac 6374

Health care, insurance
Maryland: **HealthWell 3840**
Minnesota: **UnitedHealthcare 4876**
Virginia: **Caring 9335**, Patient 9477

Health care, patient services
California: Kaiser 717, Sierra 983, St. Jude 1014
Colorado: Catholic 1142
Georgia: Burke 2133
Illinois: Presence 2797
Iowa: Iowa 3307
Massachusetts: **Genzyme 4080**, Phillips 4221
Michigan: Northern 4560
Missouri: Cardinal 4952, **National 5062**
Ohio: Mercy 7241
Oregon: Providence 7637
Pennsylvania: Lancaster 7943
Texas: AIDS 8669, Rio 9041
Virginia: Patient 9477

Washington: Franciscan 9615

Health care, public policy
Michigan: Blue 4363
New York: **Commonwealth 5872**

Health care, reform
Colorado: Colorado 1154

Health care, research
District of Columbia: **Accordia 1531**, **Gateway 1636**
Maryland: **American 3764**
Michigan: Blue 4363
Oregon: Northwest 7619
South Carolina: South 8512
Tennessee: Le 8615
Virginia: American 9308
Wisconsin: Wisconsin 10080

Health care, support services
California: **Sarcoma 960**
Kentucky: Kentucky 3585
South Carolina: Gift 8475
Texas: AIDS 8669, Rio 9041

Health care, volunteer services
North Carolina: Giving 6676

Health organizations, management/technical assistance
District of Columbia: **American 1539**

Health organizations, research
District of Columbia: **Accordia 1531**

Health organizations, volunteer services
California: Pomona 876

Health sciences school/education
Alabama: Alabama 5, Andalusia 10, Gibson 41, Infirmary 52, Internal 53
Alaska: CIRI 113, Valley 148
Arkansas: SHARE 307
California: Alta 350, Desert 538, Muir 808, Pomona 876, QueensCare 891, Roberts 915, St 1010
Colorado: Delta 1178, Spanish 1288
Connecticut: Fairfield 1387, Weller 1482
District of Columbia: **American 1551**
Florida: Baptist 1791, Boyer 1804, King 1939
Georgia: Community 2150, **Pickett 2224**, WellStar 2260
Hawaii: Aiea 2269, Zimmerman 2327
Illinois: **Academy 2355**, Illinois 2639, Perkins 2784, **Research 2816**
Indiana: Armstrong 2958, Decatur 3013, Jasper 3076, LaGrange 3093, Logansport 3104, Memorial 3113, Pacers 3138, Saint 3169, Schergens 3172
Iowa: Siouxland 3382, Trinity 3397
Kansas: Douglas 3433, Vesper 3533
Kentucky: KD-FC 3581, Kings 3588, McDowell 3595, Norton 3605, Ogden 3607
Maryland: Association 3778, Baltimore 3784, Laughlin 3862, Womens 3952
Massachusetts: Kelley 4135
Michigan: Bixby 4361, Fremont 4431, Grand Rapids 4445, Hammel 4455, Lakeland 4510, Mount 4547, Oakwood 4567, Pennock 4576, Petoskey 4577
Minnesota: 3-H 4678, Christian 4714, Ely-Winton 4733, **Lindbergh 4783**

Mississippi: **Mobile 4916**
Montana: Beartooth 5131
Nebraska: BryanLGH 5189
New Hampshire: Blandin 5308, Foundation 5322
New Jersey: Kennedy 5486, Princeton 5546
New York: Duffy 5937, Durland 5940, **Seneca 6394**
North Carolina: NC 6785
Ohio: Adena 6958, Rutan 7332
Oklahoma: St. 7514
Oregon: Black 7540, Salem 7651
Pennsylvania: App 7708, Central 7763, Community 7785, Hamot 7884, **International 7920**, Phoenixville 8041, Riddle 8077, Taylor 8139, Union 8154
Tennessee: Methodist 8621
Texas: Amarillo 8675, Ehlers 8810, Harris 8856, Lubbock 8926, **MVP 8978**, Taylor 9111
Vermont: Arlington 9235
Virginia: **American 9300**, Bedford 9324, Eastern 9368, Randolph 9491, Society 9510
Washington: Walkling 9745
West Virginia: Jefferson 9793
Wisconsin: Calumet 9856

Heart & circulatory diseases
California: Shelby 979
Maryland: **Aplastic 3774**, **King 3859**, **Pulmonary 3916**
Ohio: Wellness 7417
Tennessee: **Heart 8600**
Texas: **American 8678**
West Virginia: Jefferson 9793

Heart & circulatory research
District of Columbia: **American 1550**, **Society 1730**
Florida: Biegelsen 1798
Illinois: Children's 2478, **Thoracic 2892**
Maryland: **Pulmonary 3916**
New York: **Duke 5938**
Pennsylvania: **Cardiovascular 7757**
Utah: Intermountain 9210
Virginia: **Sarnoff 9498**
West Virginia: Jefferson 9793

Hematology
District of Columbia: American 1569

Hematology research
District of Columbia: American 1569
Illinois: HOPA 2625
New York: New York 6273
Oregon: **Fanconi 7575**

Hemophilia
California: Orange 843
Connecticut: Colburn-Keenan 1360
District of Columbia: Hemophilia 1642
Michigan: Hemophilia 4463
New Jersey: Hemophilia 5468
New York: Hemophilia 6066, **World 6533**
North Carolina: **Bayer 6569**
Wisconsin: Hemophilia 9919

Hemophilia research
New York: Hemophilia 6066, **National 6250**
North Carolina: **Bayer 6569**

Higher education
Alabama: Alabama 4, Alsobrook 7, Baker 11, Bashinsky 13, Blount 17, Boyd 18, Brewton 19, Central 20, Chapman 21, Charity 22, **Civitan 24**, Community 27, Community 28, Downing 32, East Alabama 34, Electric 35, Grisham 42, Harmeson 47, Harrell 48, Hawkins 49, Higdon 50, Holland 51,

Killgore 55, Martin 59, Mayson 60, Moeschle 64, Owens 67, Padolf 68, Parker 69, Portraits, 70, Reynolds 75, Russell 77, Simpson 79, Smith 80, Southern 82, Tractor 85, Venable 87, Wallace 89, Wollman 94, Yanamura 95

Alaska: **Ahtna 96**, Alaska 97, Alaska 101, Alaskan 102, Arctic 104, Bering 105, Bristol 107, Chenega 109, Chugach 111, Chugiak-Eagle 112, Copper 114, Doyon 115, Eyak 116, Homer 117, Huna 118, Igloo 119, Kawerak 121, Koniag 122, Kuskokwim 123, McCurdy 124, MTNT 126, Schwantes 135, Sitnasuak 138, Tigara 144, UIC 145, University 146

Arizona: 100 150, Adelante 151, Arizona 155, Arizona 156, Arizona 157, Assistance 166, Barlocker 171, Breeding 173, Community 182, **Dickey 184**, Diocesan 185, Dougherty 186, Educational 190, Flinn 193, Freeport-McMoRan 196, Grace 199, Ingebritson 202, Knapp 208, LaForce 209, Lewis 211, McWilliams 217, Northern 222, Patterson 224, Peoria 225, Phoenix 227, Thunderbird 244, Torres 245, US Airways 252, Valley 253, Warner 257

Arkansas: Arkansas 263, Arkansas 264, Arkansas 265, Ayres 268, Buck 272, Cornerstone 276, El Dorado 277, Finkbeiner 279, Halstead 281, Hamm 282, Lehman 288, McDonald 290, Moll 291, Munyon 292, Murphy 294, Murphy 295, **Murphy 296**, Northeast 298, Ohlendorf 299, Olds 300, Pierce 302, Raef 303, Reed 304, South 311, Southern 312, Tyson 320, White 326, Williams 327

California: 10,000 329, 826 331, Access 336, Amador 352, Angels 366, Assistance 383, Assistance 384, Association 390, Baker 397, Bank 398, Bartholomew 399, BBCN 406, Beckstrand 409, Bickerstaff 413, Blackburn 415, Boyer 420, Brooks 423, Buckley 425, **Burwen 430**, Butte 432, Cabrillo 433, Cahp 435, Cal 438, Cal 439, California 443, California 445, California 449, California 451, California 454, California 455, California 456, California 457, California 459, **Cancer 462**, Carreon 465, Change 477, Chicana 482, Chrysopolae 497, Chung 498, **Chung 499**, Ciatti 500, Coastal 504, Community 510, Community 511, Community 512, Community 514, Community 515, Conner 521, Conquistador 522, Cops 523, Couch 524, **Croatian 528**, Curley 531, Darnell 536, Disney 540, Doe 542, Dr. 546, Dudley-Vehmeyer-Brown 548, Eastcliff 551, **Ekstrom 555**, **Elim 559**, Employees 564, Fernando 574, Fischer 576, Flint 579, Foster 582, **Foundation 587**, Fresno 597, Fundacion 605, Gaines 607, **Gemological 609**, Glennon 622, Glover 624, Golden 627, Good 631, Gorecki 632, Graham 634, Granoff 636, Groeniger 639, Harbison 647, Healdsburg 650, Hiebler 660, High 662, **Hispanic 664**, Horn 668, **HP 670**, Hunter 672, Hurliman 675, **INCOSE 679**, **Invisible 694**, Iranian 696, James 701, Jefferies 704, Jewish 707, Jewish 708, Johnson 709, Johnson 710, Jones 713, Kimbo 721, Klicka 722, Korean 724, Lagrant 731, Lancaster 735, Level 743, Lippert 746, **Little 748**, Locke 751, Long Beach 754, Los Altos 755, Los 756, Low 759, Lucky 760, Machado 764, Madden 765, Marin 772, Masonic 775, McComb 778, **McConnell 779**, Methodist 787, Miedema 790, Milken 792, Monterey 804, National 819, **Nepal 824**, North 831, Northern 833, Northern 834, Orange 843, Oro 847, OZ 849, Pack 851, Pasadena 855, Pebble 857, Pedrozzi 858, **Point 875**, Poole 877, Pritchett 882, Promises 884, **QUALCOMM 889**, Rainey 894, Ramona's 896, Rancho 897, Reagan 901, **Red 903**, **Rogers 916**, S.L. 924, Sacramento 925, Sacramento 926, San Diego 930, San Diego 932, San Diego 934, San Diego 938, San Francisco 947, San Luis 951, Santa 956, Schmidt 964, Scholarship 965, **Screen 969**, Seau 970, **SEMA 973**, **Sempra 974**, Silicon 986, Simon 990, SKB 991, **Smiley 994**, Smylie 997, Sonora 1003, Stanislaus 1017, Stanley 1018, Stauffer 1019, Stedman 1020, Stensrud 1021, Stone 1026,

Sukut 1030, Sulprizio 1031, Sun-Pacific 1033, Tenderloin 1042, Through 1047, Truckee 1058, Variety 1078, Ventura 1081, **Vogelzang 1083**, Warner 1086, Werner 1089, West 1090, Whittier 1093, Wickham 1094, Wright 1103, Yolo 1105, Yosemite 1106, Zider 1109

Colorado: **American 1116**, APS 1120, **Association 1126**, Boys 1133, Broomfield 1135, Burton 1137, CAEYC 1138, Campbell 1139, Children's 1144, Clark 1149, Clark 1150, Cocker 1151, Colorado 1160, Colorado Springs 1166, Colorado 1167, Community 1170, Community 1171, Conkling 1174, Curtis 1176, Denver 1179, Denver 1180, Durango 1185, Eagle 1186, Eagle 1187, East 1188, **Federal 1194**, Flatirons 1195, **Galaway 1201**, Griffin 1206, I Have 1218, Impact 1219, Jefferson 1221, Lasater 1229, Light 1231, MacGregor 1236, Marchello 1237, Merry 1238, Minority 1240, Morgan 1242, Mountain 1244, Mulford 1245, Newland 1249, Nine 1250, Norwood 1252, Outcalt 1254, Pikes 1258, Poudre 1260, Puddy 1263, Pueblo 1264, Red 1266, Renfrow 1267, Robinson 1268, Ronald 1274, Saccomanno 1276, Sachs 1277, Seay 1280, Skrivars 1284, **Sonlight 1287**, Staley 1290, Summit 1293, Taddonio 1294, United 1300, Vail 1302, Veirs 1303, Western 1306, White 1307, Williams 1308

Connecticut: Albero 1316, American 1322, Ash 1325, Atwood 1326, Barnes 1330, Borck 1337, Bristol 1340, Brown 1341, Byram 1344, Carlson 1347, Cawasa 1348, Chapman 1351, Chariott 1352, CJR 1357, Clark 1358, Colburn-Keenan 1360, Community 1361, Connecticut 1365, Connecticut 1366, Conway 1369, Darien 1373, Devon 1376, Eastman 1382, Ebony 1383, Fairfield 1387, First 1389, Hartford 1399, Hartford 1400, Hurlbutt 1404, Hurley 1405, Jewish 1408, Knights 1411, **Knights 1412**, Liberty 1414, Litchfield 1415, Macristy 1418, Main 1419, Manchester 1420, Milford 1424, Miss 1425, Munger 1427, New Canaan 1430, Nolan 1433, North 1434, Norwalk 1435, O'Meara 1437, Orange 1439, Paul 1440, Prasad 1445, Rubinow 1453, SBM 1456, Spirol 1462, Sullivan 1469, Westport-Weston 1484, Zane 1492

Delaware: Chaney 1495, Gromet 1511, JBL 1515, Masten 1516, Orange 1518, Robinson 1522

District of Columbia: Abramson 1530, **Aga 1533**, Air 1534, Albert 1536, **American 1547**, **American 1567**, Asian 1580, Block 1594, Capital 1598, Communications 1604, District 1617, District 1618, Dutko 1619, **Foundation 1629**, **International 1659**, **Jack 1661**, **Marshall 1674**, Masonic 1675, Mentors 1678, **National 1691**, **National 1693**, **National 1696**, **National 1697**, National 1698, O'Neil 1704, **Phillips 1716**, Red 1722, Washington 1750

Florida: All 1765, Arcadian 1779, Bennett 1797, Boldin 1803, Boyer 1804, Brooks 1809, Broward 1810, Callaway 1814, Cape Coral 1815, Caples 1816, **Carter 1817**, Citrus 1830, Clint 1832, Community 1839, Community 1840, Community 1842, Community 1843, Community 1844, Community 1845, Community 1846, Community 1848, Deeley 1858, DeVoe 1861, Embassy 1869, Flordia Keys 1883, Florida 1884, Florida 1885, Forbes 1888, Fort 1890, Fort 1891, Ft. 1892, **Gamma 1894**, Glades 1895, Gulf 1898, Gulf 1899, Hand 1901, Harrelson 1903, Harris 1904, Hein 1909, Hellenic 1910, **Holland 1918**, **Horizons 1922**, Indian 1927, Jacobson 1929, Judge 1933, Kenney 1936, Kiwanis 1940, KML 1941, Lang 1946, LeGore 1948, LPGA 1955, Magic 1958, Maine 1959, Manatee 1960, Martin 1963, Martin 1964, Martin 1965, McCabe 1968, McGinty 1971, Mead 1973, Megaloudis 1975, Meiller 1976, Meninak 1977, Miami 1978, Momeni 1981, Moore 1982, Nall 1992, Naples 1993, Naples 1994, Northern 2001, Okeechobee 2003, Olliff 2004, Orange 2007, Orlando 2008, Palm 2013, Patterson 2015, Perry 2016, Petteys 2017, Pinellas 2018, Pinellas 2019, **Prime 2025**, Progress 2026, Rayonier

2031, Reed 2032, Reinhold 2034, Rhodes 2036, Riechmann 2037, Rigsby 2038, Rubin 2041, Ruegamer 2042, Santa 2049, Scholarship 2051, Selby 2057, Selinger 2058, Smith 2065, Spicer 2070, St. Petersburg 2071, Starks 2072, State 2073, Stearn 2074, Tallahassee 2082, Taunton 2084, Thrush 2087, Tweed 2091, Wagner 2098, Washington 2099, Wertzberger 2101, West Palm Beach 2102, Wiggins 2104

Georgia: **100 2110**, Adair 2111, Amos-Cheves 2117, Anderson 2118, Baker 2123, BankSouth 2124, Bowen 2128, Braswell 2130, Brown 2132, Callaway 2134, Cherokee 2138, Chick 2139, Coastal 2145, Cobb 2147, **Coca 2148**, Community 2150, Community 2151, Community 2152, Coweta 2156, Decatur 2161, Dinnerman 2167, Espy 2172, Golden 2189, Hamilton 2193, McDuffie 2210, **National 2213**, Navy 2214, **NCR 2215**, North 2218, Park 2220, Peoples 2221, **Pickett 2224**, Reynolds 2228, Sapelo 2231, Savannah 2232, Scheffler 2234, Service 2235, Spears 2241, Student 2245, **TAPPI 2247**, **THDF 2249**, University 2254, Waffle 2255, Walker 2256, Warren 2257, Weir 2259, Whelchel 2263, Wine 2266, WinShape 2267

Hawaii: **Akihito 2270**, Diamond 2280, Gear 2284, Geist 2285, Grove 2286, Hana 2287, Hawaii 2289, Hemenway 2293, Ishii 2295, Kaiulani 2296, Kaneta 2297, Kokua 2299, Mink 2304, Pacific 2309, Pacific 2310, Ross 2317, Servco 2320, Straub 2321, Takitani 2322, University 2324, Waimea 2325

Idaho: Adams 2328, Chadwick 2330, IDACORP 2334, Idaho 2335, Jeker 2337, Lightfoot 2340, Magnuson 2341, Mitchell 2342, Nahas 2343, Perrin 2344, Rogers 2346, Rotary 2347, Simplot 2349, Smallwood 2350, Stufflebeam 2351

Illinois: AKA 2360, Allhands 2362, American 2383, Andrew 2396, Aon 2402, AptarGroup 2404, Arbor 2405, BancTrust 2410, Barber 2411, Barnard 2412, Barnes 2413, Barr 2414, BCMW 2415, Bender 2419, Betts 2424, Boynton-Gillespie 2434, Brege 2436, Brown 2440, Brunswick 2443, Bunn 2446, Burson 2448, Butterworth 2453, Cabot 2455, **Carpe 2460**, Catt 2465, Cochrane 2485, Community 2493, Community 2495, Community 2496, Community 2497, Conway 2499, Damato 2506, Davis 2509, DeKalb 2514, Dodd 2519, Dole 2520, Donnelley 2521, East 2530, Edgar 2532, Edgar 2533, Edward 2535, Edwardsville 2536, Ekstrand 2538, **Elks 2540**, Engineering 2547, Evans 2551, Fairfield 2557, Fildes 2561, Fleurot 2563, Flora 2564, Footprints 2566, Gabler 2577, Geneseo 2580, Geneva 2581, Golden 2586, Gore 2588, Griswold 2593, Grossinger 2594, Hansen 2598, Harper 2600, Harrison 2601, Hartke 2603, Hasnia 2603, Hayes 2604, **Health 2606**, Hebrew 2609, Henkel 2612, Henry 2613, Herbert 2614, Hill 2617, Hirsch 2619, Hohner 2621, HomeStar 2623, Hoover/ Hoehn 2624, Hubbard 2627, Hugg 2628, Hughes 2629, Illinois 2635, Illinois 2637, Irwin 2654, Jackson 2655, Jackson 2656, Jewish 2657, Jewish 2658, Joint 2660, Jones 2661, Jorndt 2662, Kankakee 2667, Kiwanis 2671, Knecht 2673, Koehler 2674, Kohl 2677, Kooi 2678, Koranda 2679, Krill 2680, Ladies 2681, Lang 2683, Larson 2684, Lemmer 2688, Lenore 2689, Levin 2691, Lewis 2692, Lindsay 2694, Luhr 2699, Magnus 2705, Marshall 2709, McKee 2723, McLean 2724, Medline 2729, Mellinger 2730, Metamora 2732, Milburn 2733, Miller 2734, Minner 2736, Moline 2737, Mutual 2742, Neal 2753, Niccum 2756, Nicoll 2757, Northern 2759, Oak Park 2761, Oberlin 2763, Oberweiler 2764, Ohadi 2765, Old 2766, Olivet 2767, O'Malley 2768, **Organization 2769**, Orum 2771, Ott 2774, Ozinga 2775, Palos 2778, Patterson 2780, Peterson 2786, Pflasterer 2787, Phi 2788, Pierson 2789, Pilchard 2790, Pingel 2791, Piper 2792, **Polish 2796**, Prest 2798, Prine 2800, Puckett 2802, Pullman 2804, Rainey 2807, Reinheimer 2811, Reiss 2812, Reller 2813,

Republic 2815, Reynolds 2818, Richland 2819, Rieger 2820, Rittenhouse 2822, Riverside 2823, Robinson 2826, Rockwood 2828, Rogers 2830, **Ronald 2831**, Rotary 2834, Roy 2836, Royal 2837, Ryerson 2839, Schuler 2844, Schwarz 2845, Schweitzer 2846, Shawnee 2851, Shinaberry 2852, Short 2853, **Sigma 2855**, South Holland 2864, Sperling 2867, St. Clair 2869, Sterling 2872, Strauss 2878, Swiss 2884, True 2898, **Ullery 2901**, Wahl 2912, Wayne 2919, Wells 2922, Western 2924, Western 2925, Whitney 2926, Willo 2928, Wilson 2929, Wolfer 2932, Wood 2935, **Woodbury 2936**, Woods 2937, Zearing 2940

Indiana: Adams 2945, Alpha 2951, **American 2954**, American 2955, Arsenal 2959, Baber 2963, Ball 2964, Belden 2965, Benton 2966, Blackford 2967, Blue 2970, Boonshot 2971, Brookville 2973, Brown 2974, Carroll-Wyatt 2978, Cass 2979, Charlton 2981, Community 2990, Community 2991, Community 2992, Community 2993, Community 2994, Community 2995, Community 2996, Community 2997, Community 2998, Community 2999, Community 3000, Community 3001, Community 3002, Community 3003, Community 3004, Community 3005, Community 3006, Community 3007, Crown Point 3010, Dearborn 3012, Decatur 3013, DeKalb 3015, Delta 3016, Dubois 3019, Dubois 3020, East 3023, Elkhart 3024, Fayette 3028, Fenech 3029, Fitzgerald 3030, Frank 3035, Franklin 3036, Gemmill 3042, Greene 3045, Hammond 3049, Harcourt 3052, Harrison 3054, Hemminger 3055, Henderson 3056, Hendricks 3057, Henry 3058, Heritage 3059, Horseshoe 3062, Hughes 3065, Humphrey 3066, Huntington 3067, Independent 3069, Jasper 3076, Jennings 3077, Jewish 3078, Johnson 3079, Kiwanis 3088, Koch 3089, Kosciusko 3091, Laird 3094, Leo 3097, Logansport 3104, Loogootee 3105, Madison 3106, Mahnken 3107, Mann 3108, Marshall 3110, Montgomery 3114, Moore 3115, Moore 3116, **National 3121**, **National 3123**, National 3124, Neel 3125, Nesty 3126, Noble 3127, Oberdorfer 3129, O'Connor 3130, Ohio 3131, Orth 3133, Osborn 3134, Owen 3136, Pace 3137, Parke 3139, Payton 3141, Pearson 3142, Peoples 3143, Phi 3147, Porter 3150, Portland 3151, Public 3154, Pulaski 3153, Putnam 3156, Reeves 3158, Reeves 3159, Riddleberger 3163, Rush 3167, Russell 3168, Salin 3170, Scering 3171, Scholarship 3174, Scott 3176, Scott 3177, Sellers 3178, Shiel 3180, **Sigma 3183**, Simon 3184, Slaughter 3185, Smelser 3186, South 3189, Standerford 3191, Steuben 3193, Tipton 3201, Tretter 3203, Union 3204, **United 3206**, Unity 3209, Vermillion 3211, Voland 3213, Wabash 3215, Warren 3216, Wayne 3217, Weaver 3218, Wells 3220, Western 3222, Whitehall 3224, Whitley 3226, Zeta 3230, Zimmer 3231

Iowa: Ames 3236, Bray 3248, Carlson 3252, Carroll 3253, Cedar Rapids 3255, Clarinda 3257, Code 3258, Community 3262, Community 3263, Community 3264, Conner 3266, Credit 3268, Dallas 3270, Delaware 3271, Frisbie 3281, Garber 3282, Gerling 3284, Gidley 3285, Great 3287, Griffith 3289, Hahn 3294, Hermsen 3298, Hill 3299, Hy-Vee 3302, Igou 3303, Iowa 3304, Iowa 3305, Iowa 3309, Jay 3312, Kansas 3316, Lage 3321, Leeper 3325, Life 3326, Lindhart 3327, Meier 3336, Michels 3337, Munson 3339, Munter 3340, Murray 3342, Norris 3344, **P.E.O. 3349**, **P.E.O. 3350**, **P.E.O. 3352**, Palmer 3353, Petersen 3356, Pierce 3357, Pritchard 3361, Riley 3366, Rima 3367, Rotary 3368, Scanlan 3371, Schrader 3374, Schroeder 3375, Sherman 3379, Siouxland 3382, Spencer 3386, Stearns 3389, Straub 3391, Stubbs 3392, Taylor 3395, United 3399, Waverly 3406, Winkel 3408

Kansas: Alpha 3412, Atchison 3415, Beal 3419, Coffman 3427, Columbus 3428, Davis 3430, Douglas 3433, Eggleston 3436, Ehlers 3437, Ehlers 3438, Ellis 3439, Fell 3441, Fink 3443, Fort

3444, French 3445, Golden 3447, Hansen 3451, Hartley 3452, Hoy 3458, Hunter 3459, Jellison 3462, Jones 3464, Kansas 3468, Kansas 3471, Koch 3477, Laham 3478, Legacy 3479, Loofbourrow 3480, Mansfield 3481, McPherson 3483, McPherson 3484, Mehaffy 3485, Mitchelson 3486, Monarch 3488, Moore 3489, Morgan 3490, Moyer 3491, Murdock 3492, Nelson 3495, Nuttycomb 3497, Pape 3498, Patterson 3500, Perdue 3502, Peterson 3503, Pitts 3505, Porter 3506, Rush 3509, Salina 3510, Schuneman 3513, South 3517, Stockard 3523, Throckmorton 3526, Toothaker 3527, Topeka 3528, Trembly 3529, Unified 3532, White 3536, Wichita 3537, Woolsey 3542

Kentucky: Baker 3547, Barnett 3548, Big 3551, Blue 3552, Caudill 3554, Commercial 3557, Community 3560, Cox 3561, Disabled 3562, Hedrick 3576, Horn 3577, **Kentucky 3583**, Kentucky 3584, Kincaid 3587, **Lexmark 3589**, Metro 3596, MGM 3597, Miller 3598, Murphy 3601, Papa 3611, Paxton 3613, Pflughaupt 3615, Quinkert 3618, Rhoads 3619, Sparks 3626, University 3633, University 3634, Wells 3636

Louisiana: 100 3638, Albemarle 3640, Baton Rouge 3644, Baton Rouge 3645, Brownell 3647, Entergy 3651, Goldring 3654, McGinty 3668, Meraux 3669, Olinde 3671, Putnam 3676, Southeastern 3677, Taylor 3679, **Woldenberg 3683**

Maine: Anson 3686, Davenport 3693, Franklin 3696, Lynam 3708, Maine 3712, Maine 3713, MELMAC 3718, North Haven 3720, Ohmart 3721, Oxford 3723, Paganelli 3724, Robinson 3731, Ross 3732, Savings 3734, Searls 3735, Stich 3737, Switzer 3738, Thom 3739, Tramuto 3740, Williams 3746

Maryland: Airmen 3752, **Alpha 3755**, AMVETS 3771, Baltimore 3783, Cecil 3796, **Central 3797**, Community 3805, Community 3806, Community 3807, Community 3808, **Fisher 3826**, Government 3838, Ivy 3850, Ivy 3851, Kirchner 3860, March 3868, Maryland 3869, Maryland 3873, Memorial 3880, Mid-Shore 3887, Moore 3890, Moran 3891, Nexion 3902, **Phi 3911**, Raskob 3919, Ravens 3920, Sacco 3923, Samet 3926, **Sodexo 3935**, Talarico 3940, Thorn 3941, Torray 3942, Trueman 3943, U.S. 3946, Ulman 3947, Walton 3950

Massachusetts: **Ahern 3959**, **American 3966**, Andona 3970, Berkshire 3983, Berkshire 3986, Beta 3987, Bridgewater 3997, Cape 4006, Carco 4009, Carman 4011, Cary 4014, Coffin's 4025, College 4027, Community 4029, Costa 4030, Costello 4031, D'Amour 4034, Danny 4035, Dedham 4038, Difelice 4040, Dunham 4046, Dyer 4048, East 4051, Easter 4052, Egan 4056, Ferdian 4067, General 4078, General 4079, Hawks 4099, Heberton 4102, Henry 4103, Hitchcock 4106, Holt 4108, Hood 4111, Howard 4117, Institution 4125, Levin 4147, Lowe 4151, **Lowell 4152**, Lowell 4153, Maloney 4158, Mavrogenis 4169, Middlesex 4174, Mihos 4175, Miss 4178, Moakley 4180, Murphy 4182, Murray 4183, National 4189, Nichols 4197, Niconchuk 4198, North 4199, North 4201, Ocean 4205, One 4206, Ouimet 4208, Pallotta 4210, Peach 4214, Permanent 4216, Philips 4220, Phillips 4222, Pilgrim 4224, Pittsfield 4225, Pope 4227, Pratt 4228, Progin 4231, Quabaug 4233, Quirico 4235, **R.O.S.E. 4236**, Ratte 4237, Rice 4242, Riddick 4244, Royal 4251, Ruffini 4252, Sandwich 4258, Segel 4265, South 4271, Sullivan 4278, Taylor 4283, Taylor 4284, Tenney 4285, Thomas 4288, Thoreau 4289, Thorne 4290, Torbet 4291, **Tourism 4292**, Travelli 4295, Trifiro 4297, Trustees 4299, Trustees 4300, Trustees 4301, Turning 4302, Wagner 4310, Warren 4311, Washburn 4312, West 4313, Whittemore 4317, Worcester 4323, Young 4328, Zampogna 4330

Michigan: Ann Arbor 4338, Avondale 4341, Barry 4347, Battle Creek 4349, Bay Harbor 4351, Bedford 4353, Berrien 4357, Birmingham 4359, Branch 4365, Brenske 4366, Brenske

4367, Buist 4369, Byrne 4370, Cadillac 4371, Canton 4372, Carpenter 4376, Central 4377, Chase 4381, Clinton 4384, Cole 4386, Community 4390, Community 4391, Community 4393, Community 4394, Community 4395, Community 4397, Community 4398, Community 4399, Cunningham 4401, Davenport 4404, Detroit 4407, Eddy 4413, Ewald 4415, Fabri 4416, **Ford 4422**, Four 4427, Frankenmuth 4428, Galesburg-Augusta 4432, **Gerber 4434**, Glaser 4439, Grand Haven 4444, Grand Rapids 4445, Grand 4447, Gratiot 4448, Greenville 4451, Gumaer 4453, Harbor 4456, Hebert 4460, Hecht 4461, Hemophilia 4463, Heyl 4465, Hillier 4466, Hillsdale 4467, Huron 4477, Huss 4478, I Have 4479, Ilitch 4480, Jeffers 4486, Junior 4489, Junior 4490, Kalamazoo 4492, Kalamazoo 4493, Kay 4495, Kiwanis 4500, Knabusch 4503, Kohn 4505, Krause 4506, Lapeer 4512, Leelanau 4514, Lenawee 4516, Marquette 4524, Marshall 4525, Martin 4526, McCurdy 4529, Michigan 4536, Michigan 4538, Michigan 4539, Midland 4542, Minton 4544, Mount Pleasant 4548, National 4549, Nelson 4551, Nieman 4556, Nordman 4558, Northville 4561, Otsego 4571, Parker 4573, Parks 4574, Paulsen 4575, Phelps 4578, Pokagon 4580, Rachor 4583, Raval 4584, Roethke 4591, Roscommon 4592, Ruf 4596, Saginaw 4597, Salisbury 4598, Sanilac 4599, Scholarship 4602, Schultheiss 4603, Shelby 4604, Shiawassee 4605, Sigmund 4606, Skandalaris 4607, Skrocki 4608, Smith 4609, Sonneveldt 4614, Southfield 4616, St. Joseph 4624, St. Mary's 4625, Sterling 4626, Stewart 4627, Sturgis 4629, Tamer 4631, Taylor 4633, Three 4637, Tiscornia 4639, Trudell 4643, Tuohy 4645, Tuscola 4646, Watson 4661, Welch 4663, Wigginton 4668, Wilson 4670, Winship 4672, Wyandotte 4675, Young 4677

Minnesota: Abbott 4679, Ada 4680, Affinity 4682, AgStar 4683, Anderson 4691, Bowman 4702, Central 4711, CHS 4715, Columbia 4717, Concordia 4720, Crockett 4723, Crosslake 4724, Dietrick-Parks 4727, Duluth 4729, ECMC 4730, **Engen 4734**, Farmers 4737, Grand Rapids 4750, HealthEast 4756, Henry 4757, Hull 4762, Jewish 4772, Johnson 4773, Jostens 4774, Kohl 4775, Koran 4776, Mankato 4789, Meyer 4796, Minnesota 4804, Minnesota 4805, Minnesota 4807, Northern 4815, Northern 4816, Olson 4818, Osborn 4819, Page 4820, Philanthrofund 4824, Pryor 4832, Rahr 4833, Rochester 4840, Rosen 4841, Saint Paul 4842, Sampson 4843, Scheidler 4844, **Scholarship 4845**, Siemer 4850, Steinke 4861, Target 4864, Tozer 4870, Valspar 4878, **Wagner 4883**, Wallin 4884, Winona 4892, Woman's 4894

Mississippi: Community 4902, CREATE 4903, Feild 4907, Franks 4908, Gulf 4909, Haskell 4910, Skelton 4921, Sumners 4923, University 4925

Missouri: African 4927, Alpha 4930, Anderson 4933, **Boys 4942**, Burkhalter 4947, Cohen 4960, Covington 4967, Delta 4973, **Demolay 4974**, ESCO 4988, Ferris 4991, Gibbs 4998, Gift 4999, Gilbert 5000, Goetze 5001, Green 5005, Griffin 5007, Guilander 5009, Haddad 5010, Hall 5011, Hamilton 5012, Hays 5014, Helias 5015, Holmes 5018, Hutchins 5021, Hutchinson 5022, Kansas 5023, Kansas City 5024, Kirschner 5030, Lake 5032, Lyons 5039, Mann 5042, McElroy 5047, MFA 5050, Minnesouri 5055, Missouri 5059, North 5064, North 5066, Orscheln 5068, Peculiar 5071, **People 5072**, Poillon 5075, Porter 5076, Reynolds 5079, Saint Louis 5082, Schafer 5083, Scholarship 5084, Schowengerdt 5085, Schwartze 5089, Schwartze 5090, Schwartze 5091, Schwartze 5092, Schwartze 5093, Schwartze 5094, Schwartze 5095, Schwartze 5096, Scottish 5097, Skillman 5100, Smith 5101, Sprehe 5103, St. Louis 5104, **St. Louis 5105**, Steven 5108, Swope 5111, Thompson 5113, Thurman 5114, Tilles 5115, Truman 5118, Urban 5122, Ward 5123, Windsor 5125

Montana: Allegiance 5128, Bair 5130, Creek 5138, Daley 5140, District 5142, Fergus 5145, Flathead 5146, Gay 5147, Gebhardt 5148, Geyser 5149, H2 5151, Hanson 5153, Harbert 5154, Hawkins 5155, Hinderman 5157, Mike 5162, Montana 5163, Robinson 5168, Rolfson 5170, Student 5174, Suden 5175, Svarre 5176, Townley 5179, Unrau 5181, Washington 5182, Yellowstone 5183

Nebraska: All 5185, Bran 5187, **Buffett 5190**, CEDARS 5192, Cozad 5193, Davis 5194, Doniphan 5195, Emerson 5201, Foundation 5204, Fremont 5205, Grand Island 5210, Hansen 5213, Hastings 5215, Hay 5217, Kearney 5223, Kooper 5226, Lexington 5228, Lincoln 5229, Merrick 5233, Mid-Nebraska 5234, Nebraska 5238, Nebraska 5239, Nebraska 5245, Nelnet 5246, Novak 5248, Omaha 5250, Oregon 5252, Patton 5253, Phelps 5255, Riss 5258, Simon 5261, Strengths 5263, Wabash 5268, Wake 5269, West Point 5272, Wood 5275, York 5277

Nevada: Berner 5279, Community 5282, DiRienzo 5286, Doyle 5287, Foundation 5288, Kirchner 5290, Korfman 5291, Nevada 5295, Nevada 5296, NV 5298, Orcutt 5299, Reno 5300, Snyder 5302

New Hampshire: Ayer 5306, Blandin 5308, Bruce 5310, Clarke 5313, Cogan 5314, Dodge 5318, Fond 5321, Gifford 5323, Hunt 5330, Morton 5350, New Hampshire 5353, Nye 5357, Plan 5361, Ramsaye 5364, Randolph 5365, Scots' 5367, Somerville 5369, Stickney 5370, **U.S. 5373**, Walpole 5376, White 5377

New Jersey: Astle 5390, Avoda 5393, Bartell 5394, Bass 5395, Belleville 5396, Berkowitz 5397, Beth 5400, Boland 5404, **Chubb 5424**, Clayton 5426, Cutter 5431, Eden 5439, FMI 5447, Friends 5451, Glen 5453, Grandcolas 5457, Greater 5459, Hale 5464, Harness 5466, Hemophilia 5468, Hollander 5469, Holman 5471, Kapala 5485, Kiwanis 5488, Konstantinos 5490, Lasko 5494, **LearningAlly 5496**, Moorestown 5511, Morello 5512, NARM 5513, New Jersey 5517, New Jersey 5522, O'Brien's 5530, O'Leary 5531, Parker 5535, Payne 5536, Peterson 5540, Pinson 5541, Portuguese-American 5543, Princeton 5546, Robustelli 5552, Rubenstein 5555, Ryu 5556, Saddle 5557, Scholarship 5560, Shreve 5565, **Siemens 5566**, Smith 5569, **Southpole 5572**, Summit 5573, Summit 5574, Terplan 5577, Virtua 5592, Whitfield 5597, Woodbridge 5604

New Mexico: Albuquerque 5610, **American 5612**, Carlsbad 5616, Carson 5617, **Catching 5618**, Central 5620, Chase 5621, Community 5624, Continental 5626, ENMR 5627, ENMR 5628, Farmers' 5629, Finis 5630, Hamilton 5631, Jemez 5633, Laguna 5634, Lea 5636, Los 5638, Maddox 5639, New Mexico 5640, Otero 5641, Penasco 5642, Peninsula 5643, Roosevelt 5645, Roosevelt 5646, Santa Fe 5649, Simon 5651, SPARX 5653, Springer 5654, Taos 5656

New York: Adirondack 5667, AFTRA 5672, **AIG 5675**, All 5680, Allegany 5681, Alpha 5683, America's 5712, Andrews 5713, Armenian 5717, Ashley 5732, Athanasiades 5737, Atlas 5738, Babylon 5746, Bacile 5747, Barton 5753, Bath 5755, Beacon 5757, Berger 5760, Berntsen 5761, Bon 5773, Breast 5782, Bronx 5795, **Buffalo 5802**, Carpenter 5819, Cattaraugus 5826, Central 5837, Children's 5848, Children's 5849, Cirillo 5854, Cirio 5855, City 5856, Clark 5860, Colburn 5864, Coleman 5865, Collins/Chris 5869, Community 5875, Community 5876, Community 5877, Community 5878, Community 5880, Confort 5885, Cortland 5890, Cox 5897, Dante 5913, **Dedalus 5919**, **Direct 5926**, Earl 5946, Early 5947, Eastern 5949, Educational 5954, Ehle 5955, **ESA 5963**, **Esiason 5965**, Fan 5972, Federation 5979, Figliolia 5983, Fondation 5987, Foundation 5999, Foundation 6003, Gaffney 6015, Gavrin 6018, Giddings 6024, Gillen 6025, Gillroy 6026, Glens Falls 6032, Goodell 6039, Goshen 6040, Guenther 6048, Howard 6078, Howe 6079, Humanas 6082, Humanitas 6083, Hunter 6084, **ID 6090**,

Illuminating 6091, **International 6102**, Inwood 6104, IRT 6105, Jachym 6107, Jandon 6110, Jenkins 6113, Jenkins 6114, Jewish 6118, **Jewish 6120**, Judkins 6125, Kaplan 6129, Kassenbrock 6130, Laboratory 6151, Le Rosey 6155, Long 6168, **Lozynskyj 6174**, Marino 6191, Mashomack 6194, MasterCard 6195, Mayer 6198, McGee 6204, Memorial 6208, Monroe 6223, Muhlenbruck 6230, N Foundation 6236, National 6240, **National 6244**, National 6247, New 6261, New Visions 6263, New York 6272, New York 6275, Nolan 6282, Northern 6287, Northrup 6288, Norwegian 6289, NYS 6290, Odasz 6291, **Open 6294**, Parham 6302, Parker 6303, Patterson 6308, **Pearson 6310**, Peck 6311, Pope 6319, Preferred 6324, Prescott 6325, Project 6333, Rau 6345, Realty 6347, Reddington 6349, Reinhardt 6351, Robinson 6356, Rochester 6357, Rochester 6358, Rye 6367, Saagny 6369, Sandy 6373, Sawyer 6376, Scalp 6377, Schenck 6381, Schiffner 6385, Scholarship 6387, Seltzer 6393, Skahan 6399, **Sloan 6404**, Society 6413, Spain 6417, Sperry 6421, **St. Elmo 6424**, Teel 6447, **UJA 6470**, United 6474, Utica 6483, Walton 6500, Wasserman 6503, Weeks 6506, Westchester 6514, Whitcher 6516, Witmer 6524, **Women's 6528**, Woori 6531, Young 6540, **Zeta 6542**

North Carolina: Accel 6544, Arps 6558, Asheville-Buncombe 6563, Atlantic 6565, Barnes 6567, Beattie 6570, Blowing Rock 6575, Brandt 6579, Brooks 6583, Clark 6603, Clements 6605, Coffey 6608, Community 6612, Community 6613, Community 6615, Community 6616, Cooke 6617, Cox 6620, Craven 6621, Cumberland 6624, Davie 6625, Dinwiddle 6631, Durham 6634, **Earnhardt 6636**, Edgerton 6643, First 6657, Foundation 6660, Fox 6664, Fund 6667, Gate 6670, Gilbert 6672, Gray 6680, Greenville 6682, Gross 6687, Haggai 6691, Harasimik 6693, Harmon 6694, Henderson 6696, Hilton 6699, Horsey 6703, Isaac 6716, Johnston 6721, Jones 6723, Jordan 6724, Kent 6730, **Kimmel 6731**, Livingston 6745, Loflin 6747, London 6748, Magdalena 6755, Mahalick 6756, Martin 6757, McClureTrust 6760, McMahan 6762, McNair 6763, Moore 6771, Myers 6782, Nelson 6789, New 6790, Nichols 6791, North Carolina 6796, North 6798, North 6801, North Carolina 6802, Nucor 6803, Oates 6804, Oates 6805, Outer 6806, Patterson 6812, Peckitt 6813, Pennsylvania 6815, Polk 6821, Reierson 6824, Religious 6825, Richardson 6830, Riddick 6833, Ritchie 6835, Robinson 6838, Robinson 6839, Rouch 6842, Russell 6846, Sauvain 6851, Search 6855, Self 6856, Selling 6857, Sheffield 6858, Shelly 6859, Simpson 6861, Sirrine 6862, Smith 6868, Spivey 6871, Sprunt 6872, Stagner 6874, Stambaugh 6875, State 6877, Strickland 6882, Tahquette 6884, Tannenbaum 6885, Thomas 6891, Tillman 6894, Triangle 6899, TW 6903, United 6906, **United 6908**, Unruh 6909, Walker 6913, Watterson 6915, Williams 6921, Winston-Salem 6923, Wolinski 6925, Woman's 6926, Wyly 6929, Yerkes 6930

North Dakota: Brown 6935, Cronquist 6936, Dakota 6937, Emmons 6938, Fargo 6940, North Dakota 6946, Schuetze 6948

Ohio: Ace 6954, Ackers 6955, AJCA 6963, Akron 6965, Akron 6966, Alexander's 6969, Allchin 6970, American 6971, American 6972, Andrus 6976, Annual 6977, Ariel 6979, Ashland 6980, Ashtabula 6981, Babcock 6984, Barberton 6988, Barnes 6989, Bean 6991, Beane 6992, Beinke 6993, Belpre 6994, Bland 7001, Blosser 7002, Boone 7005, Bosaw 7006, Bowling Green 7009, Bowling 7010, Brewer 7012, Bryan 7017, Campbell 7022, Carman 7024, Carpenter-Garcia 7026, Chillicothe 7034, Clayman 7039, Cleveland 7040, Cleveland 7042, Cleveland 7044, Cline 7046, College 7050, Columbia 7051, Columbus 7053, Community 7057, Community 7059, Community 7060, Community 7061, Community 7062, Coshocton 7065, Creech 7071, Crum 7072, Danis 7077, Dayton 7082, Delaware 7086, Delaware 7087,

Diederich 7088, Dumesnil 7091, Dunton 7093, Dutro 7094, Edgerton 7097, **Educational 7098**, Elks 7099, Evers 7103, Fairfield 7105, Fifty 7106, Findlay 7107, Fishel 7110, Foundation 7115, Freer 7119, Freese 7120, Garcia 7123, Gazin 7126, Goodridge 7130, Goodwin 7131, Granville 7133, Greene 7134, H.O.P.E. 7138, Hamilton 7139, Hauss 7144, Herzberger 7148, Horvitz 7156, Hosler 7157, Hull 7161, International 7169, Jefferson 7174, Jewish 7177, Jones 7180, **Kappa 7182**, Kessel 7186, KeyBank 7188, Kindler 7192, Kirtland 7194, Klinger 7198, Lakeland 7202, Lesher 7206, Licking 7209, Lincoln 7211, Louisville 7215, MacRae 7217, Marion 7221, McCallay 7225, McCann 7226, McConahay 7229, McDonald 7231, McDonald 7232, McDonald 7233, McFarlin 7234, Menard 7238, Mercer 7240, Mercy 7241, Miami 7242, Middletown 7245, Midmark 7246, Miller 7249, Miller 7250, Moomaw 7254, Murphy 7260, Murphy 7261, Myers 7264, Myers 7265, Naples 7266, National 7267, New Orphan 7268, Nolley 7270, Norris 7271, North 7272, Northwest 7273, Nugen 7275, Oberlin 7276, Ohio 7278, Ohio 7279, OHSAA 7283, Osborn 7285, Padgett 7287, Peak 7294, Pearce 7295, Perry 7298, Peters 7300, Piqua 7303, Piqua 7304, Rains 7311, Ratner 7314, Reynolds 7319, Richland 7321, Rickert 7322, Robertson 7324, Roddick 7325, Root 7327, Russell 7331, Salem 7333, Sandusky 7336, Schneider 7337, Scioto 7339, Sebring 7341, Seefred 7342, Sharpe 7344, Shepard 7346, Shinnick 7347, Shunk 7348, Simmons 7350, Slemp 7352, Smith 7356, Smith 7357, Smucker 7358, Southern 7361, Spencer 7362, Springfield 7363, St. Marys 7365, Stark 7366, Stinson 7370, **Student 7371**, Summerville 7374, Taylor 7376, Tiffin 7383, Trachsel 7387, Troy 7388, University 7398, Ursuline 7399, Van Wert 7403, Wagnalls 7408, Wahl 7409, Wakefield 7410, Wapakoneta 7412, Wayne 7415, Weiss 7416, Westerville 7421, White 7424, Wilson 7430, Wolf 7436, Yeiser 7443, Yellow Springs 7444, Yoder 7445, YSI 7446

Oklahoma: Bartlett 7453, Catholic 7456, **Chickasaw 7457**, Colbert 7458, Communities 7459, Continue 7461, Covington 7462, Davis 7463, Donaghey 7464, **Foundation 7470**, Funk 7473, Guthrie 7477, Holton 7481, Johnson 7485, Kane 7488, Kappa 7489, Masonic 7492, Oklahoma 7500, Oklahoma 7501, OWMA 7505, Peyton 7506, Smith 7512, Tulsa 7519

Oregon: Almquist 7531, Archer 7534, Benton 7539, Black 7540, Clemens 7549, Cockerline 7551, Collins 7552, Cooper 7557, Corvallis 7558, Cottage 7559, Criswell 7561, Culver 7563, Davies 7568, Day 7569, Depriest 7571, Dillard 7573, Foss 7579, Gienger 7581, Hall 7583, Halton 7584, Heiserman 7586, Holce 7588, Jackson-General 7589, Jenkins 7590, Klamath 7592, Mishler 7606, Molalla 7608, Moore 7609, Morey 7610, Mount Angel 7611, **Multnomah 7613**, Ochoco 7622, Oregon 7624, Oregon 7625, Oregon 7626, Portland 7633, Rhoden 7643, Richmond 7645, Rietman 7646, Riggs 7647, Rinne 7648, SCIO 7657, Shank 7658, Steinbach 7666, Stevens 7667, Strayer 7668, **Thomas 7669**, Trippeer 7670, Turner 7671, Von der Ahe 7675, Wattenberg 7678, West 7680, Woodrow 7686

Pennsylvania: AAA 7688, **Alcoa 7694**, Allen 7697, American 7703, Armstrong 7710, Bailey 7721, Barrand 7722, Beaver 7726, Bennett 7728, Berks 7730, Bernowski 7731, Bonner 7738, Bridge 7746, Bucks 7752, Burch 7753, Butterer 7755, Chester 7764, Christ 7767, Class 7771, Columbus 7776, Comcast 7777, Community 7780, Community 7782, Community 7783, Community 7784, Copp 7792, Crawford 7796, Crawford 7797, Cross 7799, Daly 7804, Davis 7808, Donegal 7814, Eastern 7818, Elko 7822, Ely 7825, EQT 7829, Erie 7831, F & 7834, Fallquist 7836, Farber 7837, Faust 7838, First 7841, Fitch 7844, Foundation 7851, Foundation

7852, Foundations 7854, Founder's 7855, Freedom 7857, **GBU 7866**, Gibson 7869, Gillespie 7870, Golden 7872, Goldman 7874, Goldstein 7875, Hahn 7883, Harris 7888, Hassel 7893, Hearn 7898, Henderson 7903, Heyburn 7904, Hill 7908, Hirtzel 7910, II-VI 7915, Ivy 7923, Ivy 7924, **Jewish 7929, Jewish 7930**, Keefer 7933, Klemstine 7938, Lancaster 7941, Lancaster 7942, Langdale 7946, Larue-Dawson 7947, Laudermilch 7948, Laurent 7949, Lehigh 7952, Lehigh Valley 7953, Levergood 7957, Lynch 7965, Maley 7967, March 7968, Martin 7970, Martz 7971, Mattioli 7972, McKaig 7975, McMillen 7978, McNeil 7979, Mellinger 7981, Mikovich 7984, Mohn 7990, Moore 7992, Moore 7993, Morgan 7995, Mussina 7999, Nelson 8002, Nestor 8004, North 8010, Northwest 8013, Panagos 8017, Patton 8019, Pennsylvania 8024, Pennsylvania 8028, Perrone 8032, Philadelphia 8035, Philadelphia 8036, Philadelphia 8037, Piper 8045, Plank 8050, Polish 8053, Postles 8055, Prescott 8059, Pyle 8068, Realize 8072, Rochester 8078, Rooney 8081, Ross 8083, Ryan 8085, Saak 8086, Schock 8087, Scholarship 8088, Scholarship 8089, Scranton 8094, Shaulis 8097, Shoemaker 8100, Shuman 8102, Sinden 8105, Skillman 8107, Slippery 8109, Stork 8134, Stricklin 8135, Stuck 8136, Swope 8138, Thoburn 8143, Thompson 8145, Tyndale 8153, Union 8154, United 8155, **USWA 8157**, Valley 8158, Van Horne 8159, Van Wynen 8160, Vastine 8164, Vogeley 8169, Voorhies 8171, Wachter 8172, Walter 8173, Washington 8176, Wayne 8178, Weed 8183, Welch 8185, Wesley 8186, West 8188, Williams 8193, Williams 8194, Wilson 8196, Wilson 8197, Wittmer 8199, Wolf 8202, Worthington 8208, Wright 8209, Yopst 8211, York 8212, York 8213, Yule 8217, Zimmerman 8219, Zoll 8220, Zurfluh 8221

Puerto Rico: Puerto Rico 8223

Rhode Island: Armstrong 8230, Atkins 8232, Bailey 8237, Baker 8238, Baker-Adams 8239, Barillaro 8240, Blakeslee 8245, Botsford 8248, Brack 8250, Burke 8254, Cilley 8260, Coia 8269, Cook 8273, Cranston 8276, Croston 8279, Cuno 8281, CVS 8282, **Dorot 8286**, Fales 8290, Farrington 8291, Forsyth 8293, Fox 8294, Galligan 8297, Gates 8298, Gill 8299, Gooding 8300, Green 8303, Guertin 8306, Heald 8308, Jakobi 8315, Kamenski 8317, Kennedy 8319, Kingsbury 8322, Lichman 8324, Little 8326, Mahana 8332, Matheson 8337, McCormick 8340, Miles 8345, Moses 8351, Munson 8353, Onodaga 8358, Orr 8359, Padelford 8360, Palen-Klar 8361, Pape 8363, Pappines 8365, Petsas 8369, Price 8372, Price 8373, Prince 8374, Randall 8378, Rhode Island 8381, Rimmele 8383, Robbins 8385, Robinson 8386, Rolland 8387, Ronci 8388, Sasso 8390, Schuyler 8394, Sears 8396, Simionescu 8400, Smith 8403, Smith 8404, Smith 8406, Smythe 8409, Streeter 8416, Sutton 8417, Syder 8418, Taber 8419, Tappan 8420, TMC 8423, Tracy 8426, Tryon 8427, Urann 8429, Wells 8435, Wiles 8437, Williams 8439, Wood 8440

South Carolina: Airport 8444, Austin 8449, **AVX 8450**, Byrnes 8453, Central 8457, Chief's 8460, Coastal 8464, Community 8465, Earle 8470, Greenville 8477, Hart 8480, Hebrew 8481, Kappa 8487, Kelly, 8488, Love 8491, Moore 8495, Moss 8496, Muth 8497, Ocean 8499, O'Neill 8500, Parsons 8502, Spartanburg 8514, Tucker 8517, West 8519

South Dakota: Black 8521, Brookings 8523, Clausen 8524, Cozard 8525, Doolittle 8527, Doolittle 8528, Graham 8531, Green 8532, Hatterscheidt 8533, Howard 8534, McCormick 8536, Solem 8539, South Dakota 8540, South 8542, Tessier 8544, Ullyot 8545, Westendorf 8547, Yellow 8548

Tennessee: 4-C's 8549, AutoZone 8558, Cheek,Jr. 8569, Community 8577, Community 8578, Community 8579, Cracker 8581, Dixie 8582, East 8587, Fengler 8591, Goodlark 8594, Graham 8596, Holtsford 8603, Jewell 8608, Latimer 8613,

Lee 8617, Middle 8624, Niswonger 8630, Precision 8633, Rains 8634, Regal 8635, Richardson 8636, Siegel 8644, Simpson 8645, Splawn 8648, Stegall 8650, Temple 8653, **United 8657**, Wilemon 8663, Woodbury 8665

Texas: Advanced 8667, Alamo 8670, Albaugh 8671, Alpha 8674, Amarillo 8675, Amarillo 8676, **Amigos 8685**, Anderson 8689, Associated 8692, Astros 8694, Austin 8696, Austin 8699, Baby 8701, Barnsley 8702, Bartholomew 8703, Barto 8704, Bellamy 8709, Black 8713, Borelli 8716, Brazos 8720, Brockman 8723, Brookshire 8724, Bush 8729, C.L.C. 8731, Chapman 8744, Children 8746, Childress 8747, Clifford 8754, Coastal 8755, Coastal 8756, Communities 8759, Community 8762, Community 8763, Community 8764, **Conrad 8768**, Cook 8770, Cooper 8771, Cox 8774, Cypress 8780, Dallas 8784, Dallas 8786, **Dell 8789**, Donnelly 8797, Dreams 8798, Driver 8799, Dunn 8800, Eady 8802, East 8803, East 8804, Eddy 8805, **Education 8807**, Edwards 8809, Ellzey 8813, Enger 8815, EOG 8816, Fasken 8819, Faulconer 8820, Fluor 8824, Fort Worth 8829, Genesis 8836, Gill 8840, Goertz 8845, Goff 8846, Golden 8847, Hamilton 8850, Hamman 8851, Havens 8857, Haverlah 8858, Hill 8866, Hispanic 8871, Hodges 8872, Hornbrook 8874, Houston 8878, Houston 8879, **Houston 8880**, Houston 8881, Huddleston 8886, Ilgenfritz 8891, Ingram 8893, Jamaica 8896, Janson 8898, Jones 8901, Katz 8903, Kimberly 8906, **Komen 8910**, Lake 8913, Lasco 8915, Lawler 8916, Lee 8917, Lorelle 8924, Lubbock 8926, Lucas 8927, Luce 8928, Mallard 8933, Malloy 8934, Maness 8935, Masonic 8938, Mayfield 8939, McDonald 8943, McKenney 8947, McMillan, 8948, Mead 8949, **Mehta 8951**, **Mensa 8952**, Mercer 8953, Miller 8959, Miller 8961, Montgomery 8966, Moody 8967, Moore 8968, Morgan 8969, Mouser 8972, Munson 8973, Murphy 8974, Mustang 8977, Nabors 8979, Nation 8981, **National 8984**, National 8985, Nearburg 8987, Nichols 8989, Nielson 8990, O'Brien 8994, Olson 8996, O'Neal 8997, Owen 9000, Paris 9003, Passport 9005, Patout 9006, Pearce 9007, Pedernales 9008, Peery 9009, Percy 9012, Permian 9013, Pettinger 9015, Peyton 9016, Pioneer 9020, Pipe 9021, Piper 9022, Port Arthur 9025, Powdermaker 9026, **Promotional 9030**, Reed 9033, Reitch 9036, Richardson 9038, Riffe 9039, Robinson 9043, Romsdahl 9045, Rotary 9047, **Ryrie 9049**, Salesmanship 9052, San Angelo 9053, San Antonio 9054, San Antonio 9055, San Antonio 9057, Schwab 9064, Seely 9067, Seibel 9068, Shouse 9071, Show 9072, Singleton 9075, Sipes 9076, Smith 9078, Smith 9079, Southeast 9087, Spencer 9094, Swinney 9106, Tartt 9110, Texas 9119, Texas 9121, Texas 9122, Texas 9126, Thomas 9133, UFCW 9141, **Vietnamese 9149**, Von 9152, Waco 9153, Wagner 9154, Waltom 9155, Watson 9158, Watson 9159, Wichita 9165, Wilkins 9167, Women's 9178, Wood 9179, Woods 9182, Yett 9184, Yoder 9185, Young 9186, Young 9187, Zimmer 9188

Utah: EnergySolutions 9199, Granite 9201, Groesbeck 9202, Lofthouse 9216, Luttrell 9217, Masonic 9218, Park 9221, Ross 9223, Salt 9224, Whiz 9231

Vermont: Arlington 9235, Barrows 9236, Clifford 9241, Danville 9244, England 9246, General 9248, Hayes 9250, Huffman 9252, Keal 9253, Rutland 9259, Vermont 9269, Windham 9273

Virgin Islands: Community 9274, Rutnik 9276

Virginia: ACCESS 9278, Air 9283, All 9286, **American 9289, American 9292, American 9293, American 9301**, Arlington 9314, **Army 9315, Asparagus 9318, Brown 9329, Burger 9331**, Camp 9332, Capital 9333, Carpenter's 9336, College 9344, Community 9345, Community 9346, Community 9347, Community 9348, Community 9349, Community 9350, **Cooke 9352**, Cooke 9353, Culpeper 9355, Danville 9357, **Datatel 9358, Dolphin 9362**, Doughty 9364, Duerr 9365,

Dunnavant 9366, **EduCap 9371**, Greater 9388, Hampton 9391, Harry 9392, Hughes 9401, IHFR 9403, Jefferson 9408, Johnson 9410, Kengla 9414, Korean 9417, Lee-Jackson 9418, Lincoln 9421, Love 9424, Luce 9425, Lynchburg 9426, Maloney 9427, MAPGA 9428, **Marine 9430**, Maude 9432, **MedEvac 9433, Military 9436**, Mitchell 9439, Morrow 9441, Nansemond 9443, National 9454, **National 9455**, Navy-Marine 9462, Northern 9466, Northern 9467, **NRA 9469**, Perkins 9479, **PMMI 9484**, Richmond 9494, Robinson 9495, Sale 9496, Shingleton 9503, Smithfield 9508, Strasburg 9515, Thomas 9520, Thompson 9521, Tidewater 9522, Tidewater 9524, United 9528, Utility 9535, **VAW/VRC 9538**, Virginia 9542, Westmoreland 9547, Womack 9552, Wythe-Bland 9553

Washington: AGC 9555, Alaska 9556, Alliance 9557, Arise 9561, Bishop 9571, Blue 9574, Bradshaw 9577, Children's 9587, Clancy 9589, Columbia 9595, Columbia 9596, Community 9599, Community 9600, Coulter 9602, Fergason 9611, First 9612, Gasparovich 9620, Gius 9623, Grays 9624, Grimm 9625, Hall 9628, Hanna 9631, Heily 9633, Herriges 9634, JTM 9646, Kawabe 9647, Kelly 9649, Kelly 9650, Kent 9652, King 9653, Kitsap 9654, KLQ 9655, Lauzier 9658, Leavitt 9659, Lochland 9663, Lundberg 9665, Maxwell 9669, McCoy 9671, McFarland 9672, Memorial 9674, Mortar 9677, Nelson 9681, Nikkei 9682, Omega 9688, Pace 9692, Padelford 9694, **PAH 9695**, Palmer 9696, Pioneer 9699, Pride 9702, Renton 9705, Ritzville 9708, Rural 9711, San Juan 9714, Seattle 9719, Sequim 9722, Spokane 9730, Tacoma 9734, Three 9735, Tudor 9737, Tufts 9738, VanHoff 9741, **Vista 9742**, Wenatchee 9753, Women 9757, Worthington 9759

West Virginia: Big 9767, Community 9776, Community 9777, Craig 9778, Eastern 9780, Emerich 9781, Fairmont 9782, Feoppel 9785, Gault 9786, Haddad 9787, Harries 9789, Hinton 9790, Hollandsworth 9791, Kanawha 9794, Larsen 9795, Matthews 9799, McCormick 9801, Nicholas 9805, Paden 9806, Parkersburg 9808, Price 9810, Price 9811, Serra 9814, Stifel 9818, Tech 9822, Vecellio 9826, Wolfe 9829, Your 9831

Wisconsin: Aber 9832, Associated 9841, Backlin 9843, Bruno 9855, Calumet 9856, Carlisle 9858, Chetek 9862, Community 9866, Community 9867, Community 9868, Community 9869, Connor 9872, Couleecap 9873, Davey 9876, DeLong 9877, Door 9878, Dupee 9879, Fahrney 9888, Fort 9894, Four 9896, Frautschy 9897, Freedom 9898, Fund 9902, Gehl 9905, Grafton 9909, Green Bay 9911, Grimm 9912, Hamp 9915, Heffel 9918, Incourage 9925, Jacobus 9928, Jansen 9929, Jewish 9931, Johnson 9932, Johnson 9933, Johnson 9935, Kelben 9938, Kenosha 9941, Kohl 9944, Korupp 9947, La Crosse 9948, Laviolette 9951, Leitzell 9952, Madison 9956, Menasha 9965, Metzner 9967, Michels 9968, Mitchell 9972, MMAC 9973, Moore 9974, Mullenbach 9975, Munster 9976, New Glarus 9980, Nicholl 9981, Nicolet 9982, Nishan 9983, Oshkosh 9988, Peterson 9992, Phillips 9993, Porhaska 9996, Praiss 9998, Prohaska 9999, Racine 10001, Ramiah 10004, Redfield 10005, Remington 10006, Rexnord 10007, Richards 10009, Riverview 10011, Robins 10012, Rolfs 10013, Rotary 10014, Ruebush 10015, Rutledge 10016, Sauey 10018, Sauk 10019, SBC 10020, Schield 10021, Sharp 10030, Shopko 10032, Squires 10042, St. Croix 10043, Stateline 10047, Tomah 10052, Trek 10053, UW 10057, Viroqua 10059, Wagner 10060, Ward 10063, Watertown 10064, Wetenkamp 10070, Wisconsin 10074, Wisconsin 10079, Wisconsin 10083, Women's 10085, Women's 10087, WPS 10088, Zebro 10092, Zweibel 10093

Wyoming: Bryan 10095, Community 10099, Curtis 10101, Davis 10102, Doherty 10103, Gillet 10104, Likins 10111, Perkins 10117, Spacht

10121, True 10122, Whitney 10124, Wyoming 10126

Higher education, college

Arizona: Schmitz 235, Trico 246
Arkansas: Endeavor 278, Wal-Mart 325
California: Rio 911
Florida: DeBartolo 1857
Georgia: DeSana 2164, Watson 2258
Idaho: Lewis-Clark 2339
Illinois: Hutchison 2630, Oakes 2762, Walters 2917, Zimmerly 2941, Zweifel 2943
Indiana: Elkhart 3024
Iowa: VDTA 3404
Kansas: Baker 3417, Community 3429, Greene 3449
Kentucky: Disabled 3562
Louisiana: Zigler 3684
Massachusetts: Cambridge 4004, **Liberty 4148**, Whiting 4316
Michigan: Bretzlaff 4368
Minnesota: Concordia 4720, **Gallagher 4746**, Redwood 4835, Whiteside 4889
Missouri: Friedman 4996, NASB 5061
Montana: Treacy 5180
New York: **Columbus 5871**, **LD 6154**, **Youth 6541**
North Carolina: Gaston 6669
Ohio: Marion 7222, Piqua 7304, Wood 7437
Oregon: Campbell 7543, Renaissance 7642
Pennsylvania: Berwind 7732, High 7906, Independent 7917, Pickle 8043
Rhode Island: Miller 8347, Walker 8431
South Carolina: Sonoco 8510
Tennessee: Roark 8637
Texas: M. 8930, Trimble 9138
Virginia: Newhouse 9463
Washington: Allied 9558, College 9594, Evergreen 9609
Wisconsin: Wisconsin 10081

Higher education, college (community/junior)

California: **Cancer 462**, Chessall 481, **Lambda 734**, Mammoth 767, Matsui 777, Orange 843, Pedrozzi 858
Colorado: Assistance 1124, Front 1200
Florida: Lake-Sumter 1944, Palm 2011
Illinois: Community 2494, Fairfield 2557, Hutchison 2630, Illinois 2636, Illinois 2640, Oberlin 2763
Iowa: Iowa 3304
Kansas: Henderson 3454, Independence 3461, Pitts 3505
Kentucky: Disabled 3562
Missouri: Foundation 4994, Friedman 4996, NASB 5061
Nebraska: Weller 5271
Nevada: Western 5304
New Mexico: Clovis 5622
New York: Clinton 5861, Community 5878, Genesee 6020, NCCC 6256
North Carolina: Alamance 6546, Lundy 6752, State 6877, Wake 6912
Ohio: McDonald 7231, Wood 7437
Texas: Paris 9004, Pedernales 9008, Powdermaker 9026
Utah: American 9191
Virginia: **Cooke 9352**, Sentara 9502
Wisconsin: Calumet 9856

Higher education, university

Arizona: **Research 233**, Schmitz 235
Arkansas: Endeavor 278
California: **Lambda 734**
Colorado: University 1301
Florida: Russell 2044
Illinois: Hutchison 2630, Illinois 2640, Zimmerly 2941
Indiana: Indiana 3071
Iowa: VDTA 3404
Kansas: Baker 3417, Community 3429, Kansas 3472
Kentucky: Disabled 3562

Massachusetts: **Farm 4062**, **Liberty 4148**, President 4230, Whiting 4316
Michigan: Bretzlaff 4368
Missouri: Friedman 4996
Nevada: Western 5304
New York: Research 6354
North Carolina: East 6637, Lundy 6752, Strickland 6882
Ohio: Wood 7437
Oklahoma: OSU 7504, University 7522
Oregon: Renaissance 7642
Pennsylvania: High 7906, Pickle 8043
Rhode Island: Miller 8347
South Carolina: Sonoco 8510
Utah: American 9191
Virginia: **Melton 9434**, Newhouse 9463
Wisconsin: Eckburg 9881

Hinduism

California: **Ramakrishna 895**

Hispanics/Latinos

Arizona: Los 212, Torres 245
California: **Adobe 338**, California 447, Carreon 465, Chicana 482, **Getty 614**, **Hispanic 664**, **HP 670**, Lagrant 731, **Mexican 788**, **Mexico 789**, Orange 843, Ramona's 896, Ronald 918
Colorado: Ronald 1274
Delaware: Ortega 1519
District of Columbia: Ayuda 1590, **Congressional 1607**, **Hispanic 1644**, **International 1656**, Latino 1669, **United 1743**
Florida: Kiwanis 1940, Magic 1958, Orlando 2008
Illinois: **Medical 2728**
Maryland: **Hispanic 3841**
Massachusetts: New 4195
Michigan: **Sphinx 4622**
Minnesota: Lemieux 4782
New Jersey: KPMG 5493
New Mexico: Taos 5656
New York: **AAAA 5662**, **Cuban 5902**, Hispanic 6072, La 6150, **National 6241**, New York 6269, Price 6327, Puerto 6339
North Carolina: North 6801
Ohio: McLendon 7237
Pennsylvania: Ronald 8080, Webber 8180
Texas: Dallas 8785, Faulconer 8820, Hispanic 8869, **Hispanic 8870**, L.L.P. 8911, **National 8982**, Penrose 9011
Virginia: **Hispanic 9396**, **National 9451**
Washington: Martinez 9668, Washington 9747

Historic preservation/historical societies

District of Columbia: American 1570, **National 1699**
Florida: Southwest 2067
Illinois: Driehaus 2525, Illinois 2638
Indiana: Community 3004, Kosciusko 3091
Iowa: Bates 3243
Maine: Maine 3712
Massachusetts: **American 3963**
New York: **Fitch 5984**, Frick 6011
Virginia: **Descendants 9360**

Historical activities

California: Cal 437, **Foundation 589**
Delaware: **Eleutherian 1505**
Illinois: Illinois 2645
Indiana: **Organization 3132**
Massachusetts: **American 3963**
New York: New York 6271

Historical activities, genealogy

Connecticut: Folsom 1390

Historical activities, war memorials

Virginia: **Army 9316**, Lee-Jackson 9418

History/archaeology

California: **Archeo/ 368**, **Foundation 589**
Delaware: **Eleutherian 1505**
District of Columbia: **American 1551**, **Phillips 1716**
Illinois: **Holocaust 2622**, Illinois 2645
Indiana: Community 2990, Dead 3011
Massachusetts: **Earthwatch 4049**
Michigan: Bay 4350
New York: American 5703, **Asian 5734**, **Bogliasco 5772**, Center 5833, Cromwell 5900, **Delmas 5921**, Historical 6073, Lehmann 6159, **Mycenaean 6235**, **Wenner 6511**
North Carolina: **Institut 6711**
Pennsylvania: **Institute 7919**, **Williams 8192**
Texas: American 8683, Anderson 8687, **MCH 8946**

Holistic medicine

California: Chopra 494

Home economics

Illinois: Perisho-Nina 2783, Titus 2893
Michigan: Bay 4350
New York: Careers 5817
Ohio: Van Wert 7403, VanBuren 7404
Pennsylvania: Webber 8179, Webber 8180

Homeless

California: Bialis 412, Nickelson 827, **Union 1068**
Colorado: Colorado 1155
Illinois: Emergency 2542
Maryland: Annapolis 3772
Massachusetts: One 4206
Michigan: Wayne-Metropolitan 4662
Minnesota: Mahube 4788
New Jersey: **Ostberg 5533**
New York: Project 6335, REBNY 6348
Ohio: Foodbank 7112
Pennsylvania: Young 8215
Tennessee: Upper 8659
Washington: Market 9667

Homeless, human services

California: Turn 1064
North Carolina: Housing 6705
Pennsylvania: Young 8215

Horticulture/garden clubs

Connecticut: Bartlett 1331
District of Columbia: Horticultural 1647
Florida: American 1773
New Jersey: Parker 5535
New York: Scotts 6389
Ohio: Herb 7146, Van Wert 7403
Pennsylvania: Fleischer 7847
Virginia: American 9299

Hospitals (general)

California: Kaiser 717
Colorado: Catholic 1142
Illinois: Presence 2797
Indiana: Parkview 3140
Iowa: Iowa 3307
Kansas: Jones 3464
Kentucky: Norton 3606
Maine: Belknap 3690
Massachusetts: Baystate 3979, Sanborn 4256
Michigan: Northern 4560
Minnesota: Gilfillan 4748
Missouri: Cardinal 4952
Nebraska: Regional 5256

New York: Crouse 5901
Oklahoma: Saint 7510
Pennsylvania: Lancaster 7943
Rhode Island: Rhode 8382
Texas: Presbyterian 9028
Washington: Franciscan 9615

Housing/shelter

Arizona: Old 223
California: Central 475, El Monte 557, **Floor 580**, Foundation 591, Housing 669, Tenderloin 1042
District of Columbia: Cornerstone 1609
Florida: Abilities 1763, Hill 1913
Georgia: God's 2188
Illinois: Business 2452, Crosswalk 2504, **Realtors 2810**
Indiana: Area 2957, CIACO 2986, Housing 3064, Pace 3137
Iowa: Affordable 3234, Operation 3348
Kentucky: Appalachian 3546, Northern 3604
Maine: Portland 3726, York 3749
Massachusetts: Action 3957, Boston 3993, Boston 3995, HAP 4094, Quincy 4234, ROFEH 4246, South 4274
Michigan: Newaygo 4554
Minnesota: Southwest 4856
Montana: District 5143
New York: Project 6334, Rental 6353
North Carolina: Choanoke 6601, Sandhills 6850, Tarboro 6886
Ohio: Council 7066, County 7067, Twenty 7393
Oregon: Community 7554, Neighborimpact 7615
Pennsylvania: Greater 7879, Pennsylvania 8025, Young 8215
Rhode Island: Coe 8265, Perpetual 8368
South Carolina: Gleamns 8476
Texas: Affordable 8668, Caritas 8735, Farmer 8818
Vermont: Copley 9242
Virginia: Americans 9313, Homestretch 9397, Housing 9400, Northern 9468
Washington: Spokane 9731
West Virginia: Laughlin 9796
Wisconsin: Hood 9924, Racine 10002, Schulte 10023, Society 10038

Housing/shelter, aging

Illinois: Illinois 2642

Housing/shelter, development

Colorado: Housing 1215
Illinois: Driehaus 2525
Iowa: Affordable 3234
Maryland: **Enterprise 3819**
Michigan: Home 4468
New York: REBNY 6348

Housing/shelter, expense aid

Arkansas: Community 275, Ozark 301
California: El Monte 557, Foundation 591, Military 791
Connecticut: Senior 1459
Florida: Catholic 1819
Georgia: Faith 2175
Illinois: Energy 2545
Iowa: Community 3259
Massachusetts: HAP 4094, Massachusetts 4164, Tri-City 4296
Minnesota: Hastings 4755
Mississippi: East 4906
New York: Rental 6353
North Carolina: Choanoke 6601, Corpening 6618
Ohio: Columbus 7054
Oregon: Community 7554
Pennsylvania: Greater 7879
South Carolina: Charleston 8458
Texas: Caritas 8735
Virginia: Sentara 9501
Wisconsin: Racine 10002

Housing/shelter, home owners

Arizona: Old 223
Colorado: Colorado 1156
Connecticut: New Haven 1431
District of Columbia: Rainy 1719
Idaho: Home 2333
Illinois: Partners 2779
Indiana: Indianapolis 3073
Iowa: Affordable 3234
Kentucky: Habitat 3575
Louisiana: Pitt's 3675
Maine: York 3749
Minnesota: Family 4736, Southwest 4856
New York: Community 5874, Parodneck 6304
North Carolina: Lumbee 6750
Ohio: Council 7066
South Carolina: Habitat 8479
Tennessee: Chattanooga 8567
Texas: Home 8873
Wisconsin: Project 10000, Select 10026

Housing/shelter, homeless

California: Emergency 562, Serra 976
Florida: Hope 1921
Idaho: Home 2333
Massachusetts: HAP 4094, New 4195
New York: Mohawk 6221
North Carolina: Housing 6705
Ohio: Community 7063
Virginia: Housing 9399
Washington: Spokane 9731, Windermere 9755

Housing/shelter, management/technical assistance

Massachusetts: Affordable 3958

Housing/shelter, owner/renter issues

North Carolina: Western 6918

Housing/shelter, rehabilitation

California: Tenderloin 1042
Florida: Hill 1913
Illinois: BCMW 2415
Indiana: Indianapolis 3073
Louisiana: Pitt's 3675
New York: Community 5874, L.H. 6149
South Carolina: Habitat 8479
Tennessee: Chattanooga 8567
Texas: Buckner 8728
Washington: Spokane 9731

Housing/shelter, repairs

California: Foundation 591
Colorado: Housing 1215
Florida: Northeast 2000
Illinois: BCMW 2415
Kentucky: Community 3558
Maine: York 3749
Maryland: Salisbury 3924
Massachusetts: Affordable 3958, HAP 4094
Missouri: Green 5006
Pennsylvania: Nicholas 8006
Texas: Home 8873
Washington: Metropolitan 9675, Spokane 9731
Wisconsin: Project 10000, Select 10026

Housing/shelter, services

Arizona: Pima 228
California: Central 475
Illinois: BCMW 2415
Kentucky: Big 3551
Louisiana: Total 3680
Maine: Bangor 3689
North Carolina: Choanoke 6601

Pennsylvania: Schuylkill 8091, Three 8146
Texas: Christmas 8750

Housing/shelter, temporary shelter

California: El Monte 557, Interface 687, Tenderloin 1042
Colorado: Colorado 1155, Gathering 1203
Illinois: BCMW 2415
Ohio: Community 7063
South Carolina: Miracle 8494

Human services

Alabama: Alabama 3, **Blaylock 16**, Franklin 39, Montgomery 65, United 86
Arizona: Catholic 176, Jewish 205, Mesa 218, Positive 230, Valley 255
Arkansas: Area 261, Ozark 301, Wal-Mart 324
California: Advertising 339, Assistance 382, Assistance 385, Catholic 468, **Children's 489**, **Children's 490**, **Children's 491**, Compass 519, Dr. 546, **Earth 550**, Far 570, **Floor 580**, Florsheim 581, **Gleitsman 620**, Good 629, Heart 652, Interface 687, Kurka 726, Laurance 737, Los 757, Marino 773, Modesto 799, Motion 807, Nickelson 827, Orange 844, **Rex 909**, **Rogers 916**, Rohr 917, San Francisco 942, San Luis 951, **Santa 959**, St. 1012, St. Joseph's 1013, Tenderloin 1042, Theatre 1044, Tri-Counties 1055, Trinity 1056, Valley 1076, **World 1102**
Colorado: Aspen 1123, Colorado 1164, Evergreen 1193, Hunter 1217, Jewish 1222, Lupus 1234, Lutheran 1235, Pikes 1257
Connecticut: Action 1314, Boehringer 1335, Eastern 1381, Larrabee 1413, New 1432, Riot 1449, Workplace 1489
Delaware: Children 1496
District of Columbia: **Airline 1535**, **American 1563**, Ayuda 1590, **Freedom 1632**, **Youth 1757**
Florida: 2 Life 1759, Area 1780, Areawide 1781, Change 1822, Community 1837, Florida 1880, Hope 1921, Miller 1980, Southwest 2067, United 2094
Georgia: Coastal 2146, Faith 2175, Families 2176, Make 2207, Parents 2219, Savannah 2233, Southwest 2240, West 2261
Hawaii: Family 2282, Hana 2287, Helping 2292
Idaho: Boise 2329
Illinois: BCMW 2415, Children's 2479, Illinois 2642, Jewish 2658, Lawrence 2687, Lutheran 2703, **MacArthur 2704**, Maryville 2711, Mutual 2742, Neville 2755, Roberts 2825, Sharing 2850, St. John's 2870, United 2906
Indiana: AIDS 2946, Christian 2985, Coy 3009, Northwest 3128, United 3208, Western 3221
Iowa: Community 3261, Hawkeye 3296, Iowa 3309, ISED 3310, Marek 3331, Operation 3348
Kansas: Kansas 3470
Kentucky: Big 3551, Christian 3556, Independence 3578, Licking 3590, Papa 3612, Process 3617
Louisiana: House 3655, **Park 3673**
Maine: Waldo 3744
Maryland: Annapolis 3772, Burbage 3791, **Casey 3794**, Community 3809, Govans 3837, Manna 3867, Memorial 3879, Shepherd's 3930
Massachusetts: Berkshire 3984, Community 4028, General 4079, Giving 4084, High 4104, Howard 4116, New 4195, North 4202, ROFEH 4246, **Rosenberg 4247**, South 4274, Travelers 4294
Michigan: Allegan 4334, CareLink 4374, Easter 4412, Ford 4421, Heat 4459, Hudson 4473, Human 4474, Lighthouse 4517, Matrix 4527, New 4553, Oakland 4566, Society 4612, Southwest 4617, Sparrow 4619, Spectrum 4620, Wayne-Metropolitan 4662, **Yankama 4676**
Minnesota: Dolan 4728, Gilfillan 4748, Koran 4776, Mayo 4792, McKnight 4794, Minnesota 4806, Saint Paul 4842, Second 4847, Semcac 4849, Springboard 4859, Three 4866, **Thrivent 4867**, Volunteers 4881, Woman's 4894

Missouri: Coxhealth 4969, Delta 4972, Epilepsy 4987, Green 5006, Lamb 5033, Make-A-Wish 5040, Missouri 5060, North 5065, Ronald 5080, United 5121, Urban 5122
Montana: Brondum 5135, District 5143
Nebraska: Good 5208, People's 5254
New Hampshire: Moore 5348, Morse 5349, Strafford 5371, Yarnold 5379
New Jersey: Akers 5382, Diabetes 5433, Easter 5437, Eastern 5438, First 5445, **Johnson 5481**, Northwest 5528, Summit 5574, United 5587
New York: Aero 5670, **Camphill 5811**, Carter 5821, Catholic 5823, Community 5878, Community 5883, Eaton 5950, Elsasser 5958, Episcopal 5960, **Estonian 5966**, Federation 5979, **Global 6033**, Hispanic 6072, **International 6099**, **Jazz 6112**, Jewish 6115, **Jewish 6117**, Jewish 6119, Just 6126, MADRE, 6182, Mayer 6198, Modest 6220, **New 6264**, Ronald 6360, **Silberman 6396**, Sussman 6442, Univera 6480
North Carolina: Cleveland 6606, Hickory 6698, NC 6786, **Richardson 6831**, Salisbury-Rowan 6848, Sandhills 6850, Tarboro 6886
North Dakota: Heartland 6942
Ohio: Akron 6967, **Children 7032**, Community 7055, Economic 7096, Fraser 7117, Holmes 7151, Maple 7219, Middleton 7244, National 7267, Northwestern 7274, Rosenberger 7328, Rutan 7332, United 7396, West Side 7418
Oklahoma: Happiness 7478, Oklahoma 7499, Sides 7511
Oregon: Care 7544, Community 7555, Compassion 7556, **Deneke's 7570**, Neighborimpact 7615, Portland 7634, Snow-Cap 7661, Society 7663
Pennsylvania: **Buck 7751**, **Carnegie 7759**, DiBona 7811, Dollar 7813, Epstein 7828, Foundations 7854, Friendship 7861, Gibson 7869, YMCA 8210
Rhode Island: Coe 8265, Munson 8353, Rostra 8389
South Carolina: Rural 8505
South Dakota: Brookings 8523
Tennessee: Aid 8553, Dixie 8582, Dyersburg-Dyer 8585, **International 8606**, Metropolitan 8622, Mid-Cumberland 8623, Nashville 8627, Parkwest 8631, United 8658
Texas: Associa 8691, Buckner 8728, Catholic 8740, Catholic 8741, Christian 8749, CRW 8776, Futureus 8834, Lake 8912, Mustang 8977, **National 8986**, Salesmanship 9052, Society 9082, South 9084, Sunnyside 9103, Texas 9126, University 9145
Utah: Cherokee 9197
Vermont: Central 9239
Virginia: **Advancing 9279**, Eastern 9367, EastWest 9369, **MedEvac 9433**, Northern 9468, **Operation 9471**, Sale 9496
Washington: Benton-Franklin 9570, Central 9582, Lower 9664, Overlake 9691, Providence 9703, **World 9758**, Yakima 9760
West Virginia: United 9825
Wisconsin: Couleecap 9873, Feeding 9889, Jewish 9930, St. Elizabeth 10044, Wisconsin 10082, Young 10090

Human services, emergency aid

Arizona: Interfaith 204
California: Advertising 339, **Armenian 370**, **Children's 491**, El Monte 557, Friends 600, Interface 687, Nickelson 827, Turn 1064
Connecticut: Charitable 1353
District of Columbia: Anacostia 1574
Florida: Diocesan 1862, Rogers 2040, Volunteer 2097
Georgia: Club 2144, Savannah 2233
Hawaii: Helping 2292
Illinois: **ADA 2356**
Indiana: Hammond 3048
Massachusetts: HAP 4094, New 4195
Michigan: Baraga-Houghton 4345
Minnesota: Community 4718, Interfaith 4765
Mississippi: Mississippi 4914, Yates 4926
New York: **Correspondents 5889**
North Carolina: Hickory 6698, Lowe's 6749

Ohio: A Good 6953, Associated 6982, Christian 7035, Taylor 7377, United 7397
Oregon: Mercy 7604
Rhode Island: Perpetual 8368
Tennessee: Nashville 8627, **Soles4Souls 8646**
Texas: Associa 8691, Catholic 8739, Catholic 8741
Virginia: **Operation 9472**
Washington: Society 9729, Young 9762

Human services, financial counseling

California: Schwab 966

Human services, gift distribution

California: El Monte 557

Human services, government agencies

Arizona: 100 150

Human services, mind/body enrichment

Massachusetts: **Rosenberg 4247**

Human services, personal services

New York: Bronfman 5792

Human services, transportation

California: El Monte 557
Massachusetts: **Rosenberg 4247**, Travelers 4294
Minnesota: Interfaith 4765
Ohio: Holmes 7151

Human services, travelers' aid

Massachusetts: **Rosenberg 4247**

Human services, victim aid

Massachusetts: **Rosenberg 4247**
Ohio: A Good 6953

Human services, volunteer services

Texas: Texas 9130

Humanities

Alaska: Alaska 99
California: Arts 377, China 492, **Getty 614**, Huntington 674, Jewish 707, San Francisco 944, Siff 984
Colorado: Bonfils 1130
Connecticut: Connecticut 1366
District of Columbia: **American 1552**, **Council 1611**, **Council 1612**, **National 1681**, Phi 1715
Hawaii: Hawaii 2290
Idaho: Idaho 2336
Illinois: Scherer 2840
Louisiana: Louisiana 3665
Maine: Maine 3714
Maryland: Arts 3776
Massachusetts: **American 3963**
Michigan: **Earhart 4411**
Minnesota: Southwest 4858
New Jersey: **Wilson 5600**
New York: American 5691, **American 5692**, **Guggenheim 6050**, New York 6271, **Open 6294**, **Social 6409**, Vilcek 6491
North Carolina: **National 6784**
Ohio: Kittridge 7196, Kiwanis 7197, Peoples 7297
Oklahoma: Bailey 7451, Wilson 7527
Oregon: Buttrey 7541, Corvallis 7558, **Vongelstein 7676**
Pennsylvania: **American 7704**, Friendship 7861, **Heinz 7900**, Lewis 7958
Rhode Island: Brown 8253

South Dakota: South Dakota 8541
Tennessee: Humanities 8604
Texas: American 8683, Humanities 8887
Utah: Utah 9228
Virginia: **Institute 9404**, Virginia 9539
Washington: Holliday 9636
West Virginia: West Virginia 9827
Wisconsin: Kohler 9945

Immigrants/refugees

California: Feminist 573, Merage 785, **San 927**, **Trustees 1061**, Women's 1099
Connecticut: International 1407
District of Columbia: Arab 1576
Florida: Catholic 1820, Lutheran 1956
Minnesota: Law 4781
Nebraska: Lutheran 5231
New York: **Brackett 5779**, **Foundation 5994**, Journeys 6124, **Social 6409**, **Soros 6416**, Statue 6433, **Tibet 6454**, Vilcek 6491
Ohio: Catholic 7029
Tennessee: **International 8606**
Texas: Alliance 8673, Catholic 8740
Virginia: **U.S. 9527**

Immunology

California: **National 814**
New York: Cancer 5813
Wisconsin: American 9834

Immunology research

California: **Concern 520**, Foundation 590, **Immunobiology 677**
Illinois: American 2390, **Foundation 2569**
Ohio: LAM 7203
Wisconsin: American 9834

Independent housing for people with disabilities

Missouri: Community 4964

Independent living, disability

Michigan: Easter 4412

Infants/toddlers

Maine: York 3749
Pennsylvania: Communtiy 7787

Insurance, providers

Minnesota: **UnitedHealthcare 4876**
New Jersey: Health 5467

International affairs

California: Asia 378, Rex 909
District of Columbia: Atlas 1589, Council 1611, Fund 1634, German 1638, Institute 1650, International 1655, International 1656, U.S. 1738
Hawaii: Pacific 2309
Illinois: Sigma 2855
Massachusetts: SEVEN 4267
New Jersey: **Wilson 5600**
New York: **Social 6409**, World 6534
North Carolina: **Institut 6711**
Pennsylvania: Friendship 7861

International affairs, arms control

California: **Nuclear 835**, Ploughshares 872
New York: New 6264

International affairs, foreign policy

District of Columbia: **German 1638**

International affairs, formal/general education

California: World 1101
New York: Jenkins 6113

International affairs, government agencies

District of Columbia: Cox 1613

International affairs, information services

District of Columbia: **National 1695**

International affairs, national security

Virginia: **United 9530**

International affairs, public policy

District of Columbia: **Fund 1634**

International affairs, research

District of Columbia: **Institute 1650**

International conflict resolution

District of Columbia: **U.S. 1738**

International development

Connecticut: **Save 1454**
Massachusetts: **Lift 4149**
Rhode Island: **Dorot 8286**

International economic development

New York: **Open 6294, Trickle 6463**

International economics/trade policy

Illinois: **Sigma 2855**

International exchange

California: Jewish 707
District of Columbia: **American 1557, Atlas 1589, Institute 1650, International 1656**
Florida: Atlantic 1787
Illinois: **Rotary 2835**
New York: **Open 6294**
Pennsylvania: **Foundation 7850**
Virginia: **U.S. 9526**

International exchange, arts

District of Columbia: **Institute 1650**
New York: **Metropolitan 6211**

International exchange, students

Connecticut: **Belgian 1334**
District of Columbia: **Fund 1634, Jerusalem 1662**
Illinois: **Rotary 2835**
Maine: Hungarian-American 3704
Michigan: Temple 4634
New York: **AFS-USA 5671, American 5699,** American 5703, **Das 5914,** InterExchange 6096, **Kosciuszko 6145,** Lurcy 6176, **Metropolitan 6211, Open 6294,** Scott 6388, **Societe 6410, Wallenberg 6499**
Rhode Island: **Dorot 8286,** Fundacao 8296
Washington: **Rotalia 9709**

International human rights

California: **Gleitsman 620**
Maryland: **Global 3836**
New York: **PEN 6312,** Petra 6314, **Skadden 6398**

International migration/refugee issues

Colorado: Lutheran 1235

International peace/security

California: **Nuclear 835**
District of Columbia: **U.S. 1738**
New York: **New 6264, Social 6409**

International relief

California: **Children's 489**
New Jersey: **Croatian 5430**
New York: **American 5701, Brackett 5779**
Ohio: **Catholic 7030**
Virginia: **Operation 9471**

International studies

California: China 492
District of Columbia: **Institute 1650**
Illinois: **Sigma 2855**
New York: **American 5692, Asia 5733, Asian 5734, Luce 6175**
Virginia: **Ashoka: 9317**

Islam

Georgia: **Fadel 2174**
New York: Radius 6342

Jewish agencies & synagogues

California: Jewish 706, Jewish 707
Connecticut: Jewish 1408
District of Columbia: Jews 1663
Florida: Gulf 1899, **Miami 1979**
Georgia: Coastal 2146, **Jewish 2198, Rosenberg 2229,** Savannah 2233
Illinois: Kohen 2675, Rauch 2808
Indiana: Jewish 3078
Iowa: Des Moines 3274
Kansas: Fingersh 3442, Jewish 3463
Kentucky: Community 3559
Maryland: **Associated 3777,** Jewish 3853
Massachusetts: Grinspoon 4091, ROFEH 4246, **Wurtman 4325**
Minnesota: United 4875
Missouri: **Chesed 4955,** Fingersh 4992
Nebraska: Jewish 5221
New Jersey: **Mochary 5509,** Orenstein 5532
New York: **Agudath 5674, American 5701,** Bonei 5775, **Braverman 5781,** Center 5833, **Chesed 5844, Covenant 5895,** Elenberg 5956, Federman 5980, **Friends 6012,** Jewish 6116, **Jewish 6117,** Jewish 6118, **Keren 6135, Keren 6136,** Lehmann 6159, Martin 6193, Memorial 6207, Netzach 6259, S.B.H. 6368, Selfhelp 6392, **Stefansky 6435,** Teamsters 6446, Tzur 6468, **UJA 6470**
North Carolina: Harris 6695
Ohio: Jewish 7177, **Jewish 7178,** McCabe 7224, **Wexner 7423,** Workum 7440
Oregon: Oregon 7625
Pennsylvania: Fleisher 7848, Goldstein 7875, Jewish 7928, **Jewish 7930,** Lowengard 7962, Rosenfeld 8082
Rhode Island: Cohen 8268, **Dorot 8286**
Texas: Meyer 8956
Virginia: Richmond 9494, Tidewater 9524
Wisconsin: Jewish 9930, Jewish 9931, Milwaukee 9970

Journalism school/education

Alabama: Will 91
California: Community 513, Mammoth 767
Delaware: Delaware 1500
District of Columbia: **Freedom 1631, National 1685, Radio 1718**
Illinois: Joint 2660, Just 2664
Indiana: Indianapolis 3074, LaGrange 3093, Leo 3097
Iowa: Siouxland 3382
Kansas: Journalism 3466
Minnesota: Franz 4744
Mississippi: Community 4902
New Hampshire: Union 5374
New Jersey: New Jersey 5520
New Mexico: Community 5624
New York: AFTRA 5672, Breindel 5784
Ohio: Ohio 7281
Pennsylvania: Smithfield 8113
South Carolina: South 8513
Virginia: **Institute 9404**
Wisconsin: Madison 9955, Milwaukee 9971

Kidney diseases

Alaska: Alaska 100
Arizona: Arizona 159
California: Shelby 979
District of Columbia: **American 1571**
Florida: National 1995, Renal 2035
Hawaii: National 2305
Indiana: National 3124
Louisiana: National 3670
Maryland: American 3762
New York: Kidney 6137, **National 6251**
Ohio: Kidney 7190
Pennsylvania: Kidney 7935, **Nephcure 8003**
Utah: Dialysis 9198
Virginia: Vascular 9537

Kidney research

District of Columbia: **American 1571**
Illinois: National 2746
Indiana: National 3124
Louisiana: National 3670
Maryland: National 3899
Michigan: National 4549
Missouri: **PKD 5074**
New York: **National 6251**
Pennsylvania: **Nephcure 8003**
Utah: Dialysis 9198

Landscaping

District of Columbia: **Landscape 1668**
Illinois: Tree 2896
New Hampshire: Plan 5361
New York: **Bogliasco 5772, Royal 6364**
Texas: Texas 9127

Language (classical)

New York: **Bogliasco 5772,** New York 6268

Language (foreign)

Arkansas: Kelder 286
California: St. Shenouda 1015
District of Columbia: **German 1638, National 1693**
Illinois: **Schillings 2841**
New Jersey: **Wilson 5600**
New York: **American 5692, French 6009, Social 6409, Societe 6410**
North Carolina: **Institut 6711**
Ohio: Kiwanis 7197
Virginia: Dornhecker 9363, **Olmsted 9470**
Washington: Blakemore 9572, Northwest 9684, **Rotalia 9709**
West Virginia: Canady 9771

Language/linguistics

California: Advocates 340, **Foundation 589**
Delaware: **International 1514**
District of Columbia: Dingwall 1615, **Esperantic 1624**
Maryland: **American 3768**, Maryland 3872
New Hampshire: Ramsaye 5364
New York: **Wenner 6511**
North Carolina: **Institut 6711**
Pennsylvania: **American 7704**

Law school/education

Alabama: Alabama 4
Arizona: **Alliance 154**, Arizona 158, Los 212
California: California 444, **Mexican 788**, Mitchell 797, Nauheim/Straus 823, Orange 843, Schiffman 962, Shasta 978, **Stanford 1016**
Connecticut: Devon 1376, Fairfield 1387
Delaware: Delaware 1500
District of Columbia: Asian 1581, **Environmental 1621**, **Equal 1622**, Patton 1711
Florida: Community 1839, Florida 1878, Ryals 2045
Illinois: **American 2368**, American 2369, **American 2370**, **American 2371**, Chicago 2472, Garwin 2579, Illinois 2633, McClain 2717, Ott 2773, Stockert 2874, Walker 2915, Women's 2934
Indiana: **Alpha 2952**, Gemmill 3042, Indiana 3070, Peters 3144
Kansas: Kansas 3469, Salina 3510, Weigand 3534
Kentucky: **Energy 3567**
Louisiana: American 3641, Louisiana 3663
Maine: Maine 3710
Maryland: **Hispanic 3841**
Massachusetts: Dugan 4045, Massachusetts 4163
Michigan: Community 4396, Grand Rapids 4445, Nill 4557, Petoskey 4577
Minnesota: Fredrikson 4745, Lane 4780
Missouri: Missouri 5056
New Hampshire: New Hampshire 5352
New Jersey: Essex 5441, New Jersey 5521, Whitfield 5597
New York: Alexander 5679, Angle 5714, Community 5878, NAACP 6237, Puerto 6339, **Skadden 6398**, Warren 6501, **Worth 6536**
North Carolina: Ledward 6738, Mecklenburg 6768, Myers 6783, North Carolina 6797, Risley 6834
Ohio: Community 7060, Crain 7070, Hoover 7154
Oklahoma: Oklahoma 7498, Tulsa 7520
Oregon: Alexandria 7530
Pennsylvania: Allegheny 7696, Brown 7750, Harris 7889, **Law 7950**, McRoberts 7980, Nicklies 8007, Pennsylvania 8024, Philadelphia 8034, Schuylkill 8092, Toth 8148
Rhode Island: Rhode 8379, Starr 8413
Tennessee: Stegall 8650
Texas: Brown 8726, Dallas 8783, Dallas 8785, L.L.P. 8911, Permian 9013, **Reese 9034**, Texas 9120
Vermont: Vermont 9266
Washington: Legal 9660
West Virginia: Eastern 9780
Wisconsin: Wilber 10072

Law/international law

Georgia: **Foundation 2178**
New York: **CDS 5828**, Cromwell 5900, **Delmas 5921**
Rhode Island: Starr 8413

Leadership development

California: Hinckley 663, Milken 792
Delaware: Common 1497, Westly 1528
District of Columbia: **Atlas 1589**, **Congressional 1607**, **Independent 1649**, Nonprofit 1701, Washington 1747
Florida: Community 1839
Georgia: **100 2110**
Hawaii: Servco 2320
Illinois: Chicago 2473, **MacArthur 2704**
Indiana: **Kappa 3082**
Maryland: Leadership 3863, **Yvorra 3954**

Massachusetts: **Kennedy 4137**, Philips 4220
Michigan: **Kellogg 4497**
Minnesota: Bush 4705
Missouri: **Alpha 4929**
Nebraska: Strengths 5263
New Jersey: Chatham 5419, **Wilson 5600**
New York: **Echoing 5952**, Fund 6014, **International 6099**, **Open 6294**, **Skadden 6398**, **Watson 6504**
North Carolina: London 6748
Ohio: **Wexner 7423**
Pennsylvania: Lancaster 7941
Virginia: **American 9310**
Washington: Kawabe 9647, Russell 9713

Learning disorders

Colorado: Hughes 1216
Connecticut: Adams 1315
Texas: Student 9102
Washington: ARK 9562

Learning disorders research

North Carolina: Eddy 6642

Legal services

California: Legal 742
Colorado: Colorado 1159
District of Columbia: District 1616, **Equal 1622**, **Legal 1670**
Kentucky: Appalachian 3545
New Jersey: Legal 5497
Texas: Texas 9118

Legal services, public interest law

California: **Stanford 1016**
District of Columbia: Abramson 1530
Illinois: Business 2452
New York: **Public 6337**
Pennsylvania: Independence 7916
Washington: Legal 9660

LGBTQ

California: **Frameline 593**, **Higgins 661**, Horizons 667, **Point 875**
Colorado: Alexander 1115
District of Columbia: **American 1562**, **Gay 1637**, **Parents, 1707**
Florida: Aqua 1778, **Gamma 1894**
Illinois: Ohadi 2765
Iowa: Eychaner 3278
Massachusetts: **International 4126**, **Transgender 4293**
Minnesota: Philanthrofund 4824
New Hampshire: **Money 5347**
New York: **Astraea 5736**, North 6284
Pennsylvania: Bread 7743
Texas: PFLAG/HATCH 9017
Washington: Pride 9702, Seattle 9717

Libraries (academic/research)

Massachusetts: **American 3963**

Libraries (medical)

Illinois: **Medical 2728**

Libraries (public)

Illinois: **American 2379**

Libraries (school)

Illinois: **Medical 2728**

Libraries (special)

Virginia: **Special 9511**

Libraries/library science

California: Huntington 674
District of Columbia: **Council 1612**
Illinois: **American 2379**, Bound 2432, Illinois 2638, **Medical 2728**
Iowa: Stewart 3390
Massachusetts: Massachusetts 4166
New York: New York 6270, New York 6271
North Carolina: Cleveland 6606
Rhode Island: Smith 8408, Yaeger 8443
Texas: Amigos 8686
Virginia: **Special 9511**
Washington: Sewell 9723

Literature

Alaska: CIRI 113, Rasmuson 132
Arkansas: Communication 274
California: **Alliance 348**, Angels 367, Cal 437, California 445, **Common 509**, **Djerassi 541**, Dorland 544, Headlands 649, Intersection 693, **Lambda 733**, Martin 774, **Montalvo 802**, **National 817**, **Rand 898**, Riverside 913, Rosenberg 921, Santa Barbara 955, **United 1072**
Colorado: American 1117
Connecticut: Connecticut 1366, Connecticut 1368
Delaware: **International 1514**
District of Columbia: **Association 1585**, **Fund 1635**, **Hurston 1648**, **National 1689**, **National 1695**, **PEN/Faulkner 1712**
Florida: Atlantic 1787, Cintas 1828, Community 1838, Hermitage 1912, Kerouac 1937
Illinois: **Carpe 2460**, **MacArthur 2704**, McDonald 2718, **Poetry 2795**, **Ragdale 2806**, **Skidmore 2857**, Union 2904
Indiana: Ellison 3025
Maine: Eastern 3695, Friends 3697, Holocaust 3703, Maine 3712, Maine 3717
Massachusetts: **American 3963**, Associates 3973, Berkshire 3986, **Fine 4068**, **Kennedy 4137**
Michigan: Amy 4337, **Society 4611**
Minnesota: Anderson 4690, Blacklock 4699, **Camargo 4706**, Central 4710, Cornucopia 4721, Jerome 4771, Loft 4784, Prairie 4828, VSA 4882
Missouri: **American 4932**
New Hampshire: La Napoule 5333, **MacDowell 5341**, **Money 5347**
New Jersey: Anyone 5387, **Puffin 5549**
New Mexico: **A Room 5609**, **Lannan 5635**, Santa Fe 5648
New York: Academy 5663, Albee 5677, Alliance 5682, **American 5692**, **American 5707**, Art 5721, Arts 5727, **Astraea 5736**, Authors 5741, **Bibliographical 5762**, **Blue 5770**, **Bogliasco 5772**, Bronx 5793, Brown 5801, **Carnegie 5818**, **Cave 5827**, **CEC 5829**, **Corporation 5888**, **Cuban 5902**, **Das 5914**, De Jur 5917, **Delmas 5921**, **Dramatists 5934**, **Dungannon 5939**, **Foundation 5995**, **French 6009**, Genesee 6021, **Guggenheim 6050**, Home 6077, **Institute 6095**, **Jaffe 6108**, **Keats 6134**, McCrindle 6203, **Millay 6216**, **National 6243**, New York 6271, **PEN 6312**, **Poetry 6317**, Randon 6344, **Rockefeller 6359**, Saltonstall 6371, **Schepp 6383**, **Trace 6461**, **Visual 6493**, Whiting 6517, **Woursell 6537**
North Carolina: Anderson 6552, Asheville 6561, **Institut 6711**, Wildcares 6920
Ohio: Independent 7168, Peoples 7297, Thurber 7382, Van Wert 7403, Williams 7427
Oregon: Literary 7597, Regional 7641, **Soapstone 7662**, Vongelstein 7676
Pennsylvania: Hughes 7913, Marshall 7969
Rhode Island: Brown 8253, Sears 8395
South Carolina: Cultural 8469, **Hemingway 8482**
South Dakota: **First 8530**
Texas: Cisneros 8752
Utah: **Sundance 9227**

Vermont: **Vermont 9271**
Virginia: **Army 9316, Association 9321**, Association 9323, **Institute 9404**, Klein 9416
Washington: Centrum 9583, George 9622, Hugo 9639, **Native 9680**, Straw 9733
West Virginia: Aurora 9765
Wyoming: **Ucross 10123**

Liver research

Florida: **Alpha-1 1767**
Maryland: **Foundation 3829**
New York: **American 5702**
Virginia: **American 9291**

Lung diseases

Illinois: **American 2380**, LUNGevity 2701, **Respiratory 2817**
New York: Stony 6440
North Carolina: Lake 6735

Lung research

California: American 359
Florida: Alpha-1 1767, American 1771
Illinois: **Chest 2471**, LUNGevity 2701, Pulmonary 2805
New York: Stony 6440
Ohio: Kati's 7183
Texas: American 8679, **American 8684**
Utah: Intermountain 9210
Wisconsin: **National 9977**

Lupus

Arizona: Lupus 213

Lupus research

District of Columbia: **Lupus 1671**
Florida: Biegelsen 1798

Marine science

Alaska: Bristol 106
California: **Beckman 408, Grass 637**, Myers 811, **PADI 852**
Connecticut: Woman's 1488
Florida: Flordia Keys 1883, Mote 1985
Massachusetts: **Earthwatch 4049**, Perfect 4215, **Woods 4321**
Michigan: Recreational 4585
New York: **Schepp 6383**
Virginia: Van Engel 9536

Mathematics

Alaska: CIRI 113
Arizona: Educational 190
California: **Hertz 658**, Mathematical 776, Science 968
Colorado: Mikkelson 1239, Reach 1265
Connecticut: Connecticut 1366
District of Columbia: **Development 1614**, Equipment 1623, **Hispanic 1644, Society 1731**
Florida: Florida 1879
Illinois: Blazek 2427, Kander 2666
Indiana: Wabash 3215
Kansas: White 3536
Maryland: **American 3767**
Massachusetts: American 3967, Putnam 4232
Michigan: Petoskey 4577
Minnesota: Alworth 4685, Redwood 4835, Rosen 4841
Missouri: Community 4963
New Hampshire: Bogni 5309, **U.S. 5373**
New Jersey: Honeywell 5472, **Knowles 5489, Siemens 5566**, Wei 5593
New Mexico: Albuquerque 5610
New York: Fund 6014, **Guggenheim 6050, National 6241, Sloan 6404**
North Carolina: Leverenz 6742, Taylor 6888

Ohio: Peters 7300
Pennsylvania: Miller 7988, Smithfield 8113
Texas: **Conrad 8768, SPE 9093**
Utah: EnergySolutions 9199
Virginia: Air 9284, **MATHCOUNTS 9431, National 9452**
Wisconsin: Kohler 9945, La Crosse 9948

Media, film/video

Alaska: Alaska 98
California: **Academy 334**, American 356, **Association 389**, Bay 405, **Bel-Air 410**, Buddhist 426, Cal 437, **Columbia 508**, Creative 526, **Djerassi 541**, Film 575, **Frameline 593, From 603**, Headlands 649, **Independent 681**, International 689, LEF 741, Media 782, Merage 785, **Montalvo 802**, Motion 807, Ojai 839, Pacific 850, San Diego 928, **San Francisco 943**, San Francisco 944, **Screen 969**, Southern 1005, **Women 1098**
Connecticut: Hartley 1401
District of Columbia: **National 1692**
Georgia: Austin 2121
Hawaii: Pacific 2310
Illinois: **Playboy 2794**
Maine: Maine 3712
Massachusetts: Center 4015, **Documentary 4041**
Michigan: Ann Arbor 4339
Minnesota: **Camargo 4706**, IFP 4763, Intermedia 4766, Jerome 4771
Nebraska: Nebraska 5241
New Hampshire: La Napoule 5333, **MacDowell 5341**, New Hampshire 5355
New Jersey: Newark 5525, **Puffin 5549**
New York: American 5687, Art 5718, **Arts 5729, Asian 5734, Bogliasco 5772**, Camera 5809, Center 5830, chashama 5841, Cinereach 5853, **Corporation 5888, Correspondents 5889**, Council 5894, **Creative 5898**, Dance 5910, Downtown 5933, Experimental 5967, **Harvestworks 6058**, Home 6077, **Independent 6092**, Independent 6093, **King 6138**, Living 6166, Manhattan 6186, **Millay 6216**, Moving 6229, New York 6277, **Open 6294, Princess 6329, Public 6338, Rockefeller 6359**, Smack 6405, Squeaky 6423, **Visual 6493**, Women 6527
North Carolina: Asheville 6561, Southern 6869
Ohio: Columbus 7052, Independent 7168, Wexner 7422
Oregon: McKenzie 7603
Pennsylvania: Pennsylvania 8027, Pittsburgh 8047, Scribe 8095, **Templeton 8141**
Rhode Island: Rhode Island 8381
South Carolina: Cultural 8469
Texas: Austin 8698, Culture 8778, **Southwest 9090**
Utah: **Sundance 9227**
Vermont: **Green 9249**
Virginia: **Institute 9404**
Washington: 911 9554, Centrum 9583, **Native 9680**, Northwest 9685
West Virginia: Aurora 9765

Media, journalism

California: **National 817**, Oakland 836
District of Columbia: **International 1660**
Illinois: Allstate 2363
Virginia: Klein 9416
Washington: Fisher 9613

Media, print publishing

California: **Kaiser 716**, Loeb 753, Recruiting 902, San Francisco 944
Connecticut: Center 1350, Chariott 1352, Connecticut 1366
Delaware: Frank 1508
District of Columbia: **American 1542**, Block 1594, **Council 1610, Friendly 1633, Fund 1634, Fund 1635, German 1638, International 1656**, International 1660, Kennedy 1665, National

1695, Patterson 1710, **Phillips 1716, Radio 1718**, Sigma 1728
Florida: Community 1839, Livingston 1952, Lloyd 1953, St. Petersburg 2071
Georgia: **Carter 2136**
Illinois: Allstate 2363, Journalism 2663, **Playboy 2794**, Urbana-Champaign 2907
Indiana: **Alpha 2952**
Maryland: **American 3761**, Maryland 3873, Maryland 3876
Michigan: Bay 4350, Community 4396, Ford 4420
Missouri: **American 4932**
New Hampshire: Ramsaye 5364
New Jersey: **Dow 5435**, Foundation 5450, Whitfield 5597
New York: **American 5707, Asia 5733**, Bennett 5759, **Blue 5770**, Broadcasters 5789, **CDS 5828, Correspondents 5889**, International 6100, **Jaffe 6108**, Manhattan 6186, McCormick 6202, **Open 6294, PEN 6312, Smith 6406**
North Carolina: American 6549, Anderson 6552
Ohio: Community 7058, Dayton 7082, Knight 7199, Religion 7317, Scripps 7340
Oklahoma: Miley 7495
Rhode Island: Meriden 8344
Texas: Headliners 8860
Virginia: **Newspaper 9464**
Washington: Community 9600
Wisconsin: La Crosse 9948, Pagel 9990, Ruebush 10015

Media, radio

California: Cal 437, **Kaiser 716**, Oakland 836
District of Columbia: **Broadcast 1597**
Illinois: Urbana-Champaign 2907
Massachusetts: **Northern 4203**
New Hampshire: New Hampshire 5355
Oregon: Dargan 7567
Pennsylvania: Pennsylvania 8027
Washington: Fisher 9613

Media, television

California: **Academy 335**, American 356, **Kaiser 716**, Motion 807
District of Columbia: **Broadcast 1597**
Hawaii: Pacific 2310
Illinois: **Playboy 2794**
New Hampshire: New Hampshire 5355
New York: **Correspondents 5889**, Downtown 5933, Independent 6093, Manhattan 6186, New York 6277
Oregon: Dargan 7567
Pennsylvania: **Templeton 8141**
Washington: Fisher 9613

Media/communications

Alaska: Rasmuson 132
California: **Academy 335**, Creative 526, **Djerassi 541**, Good 629, Independent 680, **Kaiser 716**, Media 781, **National 817**, Oakland 836, **San Francisco 943**, San Francisco 944, **United 1072**
Connecticut: Connecticut 1366
Delaware: Common 1497, Delaware 1500
District of Columbia: **Broadcast 1597, Radio 1718**
Florida: Community 1839, Livingston 1952
Georgia: Austin 2121, Cameron 2135
Hawaii: Pacific 2310
Illinois: Illinois 2634, Joint 2660, Just 2664, **Playboy 2794**
Maryland: Arts 3776, Salisbury 3925
Massachusetts: **American 3963, Northern 4203, SEVEN 4267**
Michigan: Michigan 4540
Minnesota: **Camargo 4706**, Franconia 4743, Scheidler 4844
Mississippi: Community 4902
New York: **AAAA 5662**, Arts 5727, Broadcasters 5789, **CDS 5828, Correspondents 5889, Creative**

5898, Genesee 6021, **Harvestworks 6058**, New York 6277, Smack 6405, **Visual 6493**, **World 6534**
North Carolina: McColl 6761, Southern 6869
Ohio: Dayton 7082, Scripps 7340
Oklahoma: Miley 7495
Oregon: Dargan 7567, Regional 7641
Pennsylvania: Pennsylvania 8027, Pittsburgh 8047
Rhode Island: Meriden 8344
Texas: **Southwest 9090**
Virginia: **Institute 9404**
Washington: 911 9554, Fisher 9613
Wisconsin: Madison 9955

Medical care, community health systems
Michigan: **World 4674**
Minnesota: **UnitedHealthcare 4876**
Ohio: Community 7058
Oregon: Providence 7637

Medical care, in-patient care
Florida: Big 1799
New York: MacKinnon 6181
Oklahoma: Compassionate 7460
Tennessee: Mercy 8619

Medical care, outpatient care
New Jersey: Family 5444
New York: MacKinnon 6181
Washington: Laurendeau 9657

Medical care, rehabilitation
California: San Diego 939, SCI 967
Hawaii: Saake 2318
New Jersey: Kessler 5487
New York: MacKinnon 6181
Pennsylvania: Sleeper 8108

Medical research
Arizona: Banner 170
California: Giannini 615, **Grass 637**, **National 814**
Colorado: **Foundation 1199**
Connecticut: Cornelia 1370, **National 1429**, **Walkabout 1479**
District of Columbia: **American 1541**, **American 1549**
Florida: Alpha-1 1767, Preeclampsia 2024
Georgia: **American 2114**, Katz 2201
Illinois: **American 2377**, **American 2382**, **American 2388**, **American 2389**, Angelman 2399, **International 2651**, **National 2744**, **National 2745**
Indiana: Osteopathic 3135
Maine: Maine 3711
Maryland: **American 3770**, Brightfocus 3789, Cystic 3812, **Foundation 3829**, Foundation 3830, **National 3897**
Massachusetts: American 3965, Baystate 3979, Boston 3996, Health 4101, **International 4127**, King 4140, **Marine 4160**
Michigan: Blue 4363
Minnesota: Bakken 4697
Missouri: Mallinckrodt 5041, Stowers 5109
New Hampshire: Hitchcock 5328
New Jersey: Silbermann 5567
New York: American 5698, **Breast 5783**, **Duke 5938**, **Hearing 6065**, **Klingenstein 6144**, **Lasker 6153**, **Lymphatic 6178**, **NARSAD 6238**, **National 6251**, **New York 6265**, New York 6273, **Pasteur 6306**, **Philippe 6316**, THYCA: 6453, Tourette 6459
Ohio: LAM 7203
Pennsylvania: **Alternatives 7699**, American 7702, **American 7704**, Kimmel 7936, Newman 8005, Trout 8149
Texas: **Mary 8937**, Methodist 8955, Southwestern 9092, St. 9097
Virginia: **American 9294**, American 9308, Cushman 9356, **IDSA 9402**, **Interstitial 9407**, **U.S. 9526**

Medical research, formal/general education
New York: **Mayday 6197**

Medical research, institute
California: Ameritec 361, **A-T 391**, **Ellison 561**, Farber 571, Glaucoma 619, **Grass 637**, Hewitt 659, Pasarow 856
Connecticut: Endocrine 1385
District of Columbia: **American 1564**, **International 1653**
Florida: **Ataxia 1786**, Watson 2100
Georgia: Bantly 2125
Illinois: **American 2385**, **Dystonia 2529**, Ehrler 2537
Maryland: **National 3897**, Passano 3908
Massachusetts: **American 3969**, King 4140
Minnesota: **Lindbergh 4783**
New York: Glaucoma 6030, **Whitney 6518**
North Carolina: **International 6715**
Rhode Island: Alpert 8227
Texas: Morrison 8970, Poncin 9024

Medical school/education
Alabama: Andalusia 10, Reed 73
Alaska: Kuskokwim 123
Arkansas: Tenenbaum 316
California: Association 388, Coastal 504, Community 513, Desert 538, **Foundation 587**, Hinckley 663, Lakewood 732, Mills-Peninsula 795, Mitchell 797, North 832, RCL 900, Riverside 914, Roberts 915, San Diego 931, Santa Barbara 955, Schiffman 962, Swift 1036, Torrance 1050
Colorado: Colorado 1153, **Colorado 1165**, Williams 1308
Connecticut: Deering 1374, DiMauro 1377, Dunning 1379, **Scudder 1458**
Delaware: Delaware 1500
District of Columbia: **German 1638**, **National 1696**, **Optical 1705**, **Pharmaceutical 1714**, **Society 1730**
Florida: Amin 1775, Benjamin 1796, Brevard 1807, Corbett 1851, Fellows 1875, Health 1908, Jacob 1928, King 1939, Lauffer 1947, Life 1950, North 1999
Georgia: Community 2150, Georgia 2187, Kaplan 2200, **MAP 2208**, Medical 2211
Hawaii: Zimmerman 2327
Illinois: **American 2382**, **Anagnos 2394**, Brown 2442, Cunningham 2505, Fildes 2561, Garwin 2579, **Hertz 2615**, Marion 2708, McClain 2717, McDonald 2718, McFarland 2721, Nesbitt 2754, Ott 2773, **Research 2816**, Rinker 2821, Ross 2832, Shumaker 2854, Stevenson 2873, Storey 2876, **TPAA 2895**, Villwock 2909, Welch 2921
Indiana: Community 3001, Dunn 3021, Eskenazi 3027, Garr 3041, Kendrick 3085, Kosciusko 3090, Kosciusko 3091, Line 3102, Madison 3106, Pacers 3138, Plummer 3148, **Timmy 3200**, Westhaysen 3223, Williams 3228
Iowa: Barr 3242, Marek 3331, Munson 3339, North 3345, Siouxland 3382, Van Buren 3403
Kansas: Dolechek 3432, Nell 3494, Snyder 3516, Vesper 3533
Kentucky: Batterton 3549, Hedrick 3576, Kings 3588, Morrill 3599, Morrill 3600, Norris 3603, Rural 3622, Trover 3629
Louisiana: Bernstein 3646
Maine: **Worcester 3748**
Maryland: Brown 3790, **Endocrine 3818**, **Hughes 3846**, **National 3900**, Roche 3922
Massachusetts: **American 3969**, Cape Cod 4007, Dugan 4045, Egan 4056, Millman 4176
Michigan: Bay 4350, Beaumont 4352, Blue 4363, Community 4394, Community 4396, Gratiot 4449, Hammel 4455, Kadant 4491, Meyers 4532, Nill 4557, Petoskey 4577, Trone 4642
Minnesota: Alworth 4685, CentraCare 4709, Ely-Winton 4733, Proshek 4830, Stillwell 4862
Missouri: **Demolay 4974**, Greater 5004, Hester 5016, Paul 5070
Nebraska: Tri-Valley 5266

New Hampshire: Foundation 5322, Green 5324, Yarnold 5379
New Jersey: Atlantic 5391, Groff 5460, Grupe 5462, Islami, 5479, **Mahajan 5501**, Middlesex 5507, **Tang 5575**, Valley 5589, Wetterberg 5594
New Mexico: Helm 5632, PRMC-Clovis 5644
New York: Associated 5735, Chautauqua 5842, Chenango 5843, Collins 5868, Crohn's 5899, Duffy 5937, **Duke 5938**, Durland 5940, Glens Falls 6032, March 6189, Mijangos 6214, **Myasthenia 6234**, **National 6251**, **National 6252**, Partridge 6305, **Schepp 6383**, Wagner 6498, Wolf 6525
North Carolina: Komarek 6733, McNaught 6765, Medical 6769, Myers 6783, North 6794, Robinson 6839, Triangle 6899, Wilson 6922
North Dakota: Ruger 6947
Ohio: Adams 6956, Blanchard 7000, Bontrager 7004, Bowen 7008, Crain 7070, Hosler 7157, Licking 7209, McClain 7227, Miller 7248, Munro 7259, Ohio 7282, Psychiatric 7310, Rutan 7332, Scioto 7339, Smith 7353, Smith 7354, University 7398, Van Wert 7403, Wilson 7431, Wimmer 7432
Oklahoma: Osteopathic 7503
Oregon: Alexandria 7530, Clemens 7549, Northwest 7620, Pernot 7631
Pennsylvania: Baskin 7725, Brown 7750, Chung-Hee 7768, Clareth 7769, Clark 7770, Community 7783, Fitton 7845, Foundation 7853, Hamot 7884, Harris 7889, Lancaster 7944, Moore 7994, Nicklies 8007, Power 8057, Puckett 8067, Sheen 8099, Smith 8110, Smithfield 8113, Trushel 8151, Wettrick 8190, Yount 8216
Rhode Island: August 8233, Clark 8262, Coe 8266, Cohen 8268, **Papines 8364**
South Carolina: Sherman 8506
Tennessee: Hicks 8601, Wills 8664
Texas: **American 8678**, Anderson 8687, Brisley 8721, Conner 8767, Gilpatrick 8842, Hammond 8852, Hispanic 8869, Houston 8884, Maffett 8931, Miller 8960, Permian 9013, **Reese 9034**, Southwestern 9092, Vinsant 9150, Wintermann 9171
Utah: Bamberger 9193
Virginia: Hampton 9391, Lewis 9420, University 9533
Washington: Children's 9588, Davis 9603, Elvins 9607, McCleary 9670, Osteopathic 9690, Walkling 9745
West Virginia: Family 9783, Hinton 9790
Wisconsin: Bruneo 9854, Keller 9940, Mitchell 9972, Riverview 10011, Shallow 10029, University 10055, Wilber 10072, Wisconsin 10080, Women's 10085
Wyoming: Clark 10097, Cody 10098

Medical specialties
Illinois: **American 2385**
Oregon: Northwest 7620
Texas: Houston 8884

Medical specialties research
Connecticut: Endocrine 1385
Illinois: **American 2389**
Maryland: **American 3769**, Endocrine 3818, **National 3893**
Minnesota: **Restless 4838**
Nevada: Cummings 5283
New Jersey: Wound 5605
Pennsylvania: American 7705

Medicine/medical care, public education
Wisconsin: Wisconsin 10080

Men
Alabama: AAMN 1, Chapman 21
California: Modesto 799, Scaife 961
Connecticut: Folsom 1390
Florida: Bradish 1805, **Gamma 1894**, Tracy 2089

Illinois: Adamson 2357, Joint 2660
Iowa: Magnus 3329
Kansas: Porter 3506
Kentucky: Louisville 3592
Massachusetts: Cary 4014
Michigan: Bay 4350, Blue 4363
Missouri: **Demolay 4974**, Feraldo 4990, Martino 5045
Nebraska: Bryan 5188
New Hampshire: Cogan 5314
New York: Brink 5787, Dellomo 5920, Scalp 6377
North Carolina: Bowsher 6577, Dietrich 6629
Ohio: High 7150, Salem 7334, Smith 7355, Van Wert 7403, Wilson 7431
Oregon: Mock 7607
Pennsylvania: Harris 7889, Heald 7896
Rhode Island: Hosser 8311, Tryon 8427
Texas: Chambers 8743, Gnade 8843, Rawls 9032, **Reese 9034**
Vermont: Scott 9260
West Virginia: Stout 9819
Wisconsin: Frautschy 9897, Henrizi 9920

Mental health, addictions

Florida: Anew 1777

Mental health, counseling/support groups

Connecticut: Connecticut 1367
Kansas: Cloud 3426
Michigan: Alliance 4336, Community 4400
New Jersey: Young 5606
New York: Cantor 5814
North Carolina: Tarboro 6886

Mental health, depression

Georgia: Phillips 2223
Illinois: **Depression 2515**
Indiana: **Lilly 3099**
New York: **Klingenstein 6144**, NARSAD 6238

Mental health, disorders

Arizona: Agape 152
District of Columbia: **American 1538**
Georgia: Ayers 2122, **Carter 2136**
Illinois: **Depression 2515**
Indiana: **Lilly 3099**
Maryland: **Anxiety 3773**
New York: **Foundation 6000**, Klingenstein 6143, **Klingenstein 6144**, NARSAD 6238
North Carolina: Foundation 6662
Oregon: Danicas 7566

Mental health, eating disorders

Maryland: Obesity 3904
New York: **National 6249**

Mental health, schizophrenia

Indiana: **Lilly 3099**
New York: **NARSAD 6238, NARSAD: 6239**
Oregon: Danicas 7566

Mental health, smoking

District of Columbia: **American 1562**
Minnesota: Clearway 4716

Mental health, stress

Illinois: **International 2652**

Mental health, transitional care

Pennsylvania: Young 8215

Mental health, treatment

California: Hinckley 663
Maryland: American 3763, Laughlin 3862
New York: Collins 5868, **Klingenstein 6144**, Project 6335
Washington: Sigourney 9724

Mental health/crisis services

Alabama: Riverbend 76
California: Rest 908, Sierra 983
Indiana: **Lilly 3099**
Virginia: Highlands 9395

Mental health/crisis services, research

Georgia: **Carter 2136**
New York: **Klingenstein 6144**
Ohio: Psychiatric 7310
Pennsylvania: Steinman 8131

Mental health/crisis services, suicide

New York: American 5695

Mentally disabled

Alabama: Marshall-Jackson 58, Winston 92
California: Inland 683, North 829
Iowa: Corbin 3267
Maryland: Arc 3775, Mental 3881, **Order 3905**
Michigan: CareLink 4374, Community 4400
Missouri: Community 4964
New Jersey: Arc 5388, **Newcombe 5526**, Peterson 5540
New York: Catholic 5824
Ohio: Jewish 7177
Tennessee: A.I.M. 8550

Middle schools/education

California: Chung 498

Migrant workers

Florida: Operation 2006
Massachusetts: New 4195

Military/veterans

Arizona: Arizona 160, Old 223
California: Fischer 576, Nickelson 827
Colorado: **Association 1126**, SEAKR 1279
District of Columbia: **Armed 1579**, Cornerstone 1609
Florida: Florida 1880
Illinois: Community 2494, Guenther 2595
Iowa: Jasper 3311
Kentucky: **Disabled 3563, USA 3635**
Maryland: Airmen 3752, AMVETS 3771
Michigan: Veteran's 4657
Missouri: Poillon 5075
New York: **Intrepid 6103**, United 6478
North Carolina: **Military 6773**, North 6798
Ohio: American 6972
South Carolina: NGA 8498
Texas: **Beaumont 8707**, Cuban 8777, **Reserve 9037**
Virginia: Air 9283, **Operation 9472**, Pentagon 9478, **Thanks 9519, Wings 9550**

Military/veterans' organizations

California: Injured 682
Connecticut: **Coast 1359**, Woman's 1488
District of Columbia: Air 1534, Paralyzed 1706, Red 1722
Florida: American 1769
Indiana: American 2955
Iowa: Anderson 3239
Maine: Portland 3727

Maryland: **Fisher 3826**, GEICO 3832
Massachusetts: Essex 4060, New Bedford 4192, USO 4307
Michigan: Fallen 4417
Missouri: Community 4963
New Jersey: Life 5498
New York: **Daughters 5915**, German 6022
North Dakota: VFW 6951
Oregon: Jackson-General 7589
Texas: Heath 8862, **Operation 8999**
Virginia: Air 9284, **Army 9315, Dolphin 9362, Freedom 9385, Marine 9430, Military 9436**, Navy 9461, Navy-Marine 9462, **Olmsted 9470, USAWOA 9534, VAW/VRC 9538**

Minorities

Alabama: Southeastern 81
Arizona: **Dickey 184**
California: **Adobe 338**, Carreon 465, **Getty 614, HP 670**, Johnson 710, **Kaiser 716**, Level 743, National 821, Ronald 918, San Diego 933, **Tolgo 1049**
Colorado: Minority 1240
Connecticut: Xerox 1490
District of Columbia: **American 1542, American 1543, American 1554, American 1562, Aspen 1583**, Community 1605, **Families 1625, Landscape 1668**, Minbanc 1679, **National 1692, Radio 1718**
Florida: Blac 1800, Hungerford 1923
Georgia: Legislative 2205, Savannah 2233
Illinois: **ADA 2356**, Ameren 2364, **American 2368, American 2370, American 2382, Hill 2618**, Illinois 2634, Kankakee 2667, **Medical 2728**
Indiana: **Organization 3132, Zoltani 3232**
Iowa: Eychaner 3278
Kansas: Atchison 3415
Kentucky: Hedrick 3576, Jackson 3579
Louisiana: Arts 3642
Maryland: **American 3768, National 3897**
Massachusetts: American 3967
Michigan: Arts 4340, Baker 4342, Grand 4446, Kalamazoo 4492, Michigan 4540, **Society 4611, Sphinx 4622**
Minnesota: Fredrikson 4745, Page 4820, Winslow 4893
New Hampshire: **Money 5347**
New Jersey: **Dow 5435**, KPMG 5493, **Newcombe 5526**
New York: **AAAA 5662**, Camera 5809, Cirio 5855, **ESA 5963**, Ivy 6106, Jenkins 6113, Morgan 6226, **National 6241, National 6252, New 6264**, New York 6269, NLN 6280, **Open 6294**, Price 6327, Robinson 6356, Scott 6388, **Social 6409, Sponsors 6422, Worldstudio 6535**
North Carolina: **American 6550**, Gate 6670, **S.R.C. 6847**
Ohio: **Arab 6978**, Fifty 7106, McLendon 7237, OHSAA 7283
Oklahoma: Jeltz 7484
Oregon: Dargan 7567
Pennsylvania: Bartko 7723, Hill 7909, **Law 7950**, Pennsylvania 8024, **PPG 8058**, Young 8215
South Carolina: Coastal 8464
Texas: Dallas 8783, Houston 8883, Phillips 9019
Virginia: **American 9304, American 9305, National 9451**, Sidhu 9504, **Special 9511**
Washington: **Bullitt 9578**, Fisher 9613, Market 9667, Martinez 9668, Palmer 9696
Wisconsin: Wisconsin 10081

Minorities/immigrants, centers/services

New York: **New 6264**

Multiple sclerosis

California: National 819
Delaware: National 1517
Florida: **Multiple 1989**
Illinois: National 2748
Massachusetts: National 4189

Minnesota: National 4811
New York: **National 6253**
Texas: National 8985

Multiple sclerosis research

California: National 820
Michigan: National 4550
New York: **National 6253**

Muscular dystrophy

Arizona: **Muscular 220**
California: Myotonic 812
Florida: Harrison 1905

Muscular dystrophy research

Arizona: **Muscular 220**
California: Myotonic 812

Museums

California: Getty 614
District of Columbia: **American 1545**

Museums (art)

California: Exploratorium 565, **Getty 614**
District of Columbia: Corcoran 1608
New York: **Dedalus 5919, Metropolitan 6211, Soanes 6408**

Museums (children's)

Massachusetts: Museum 4185

Museums (history)

District of Columbia: United 1744
New York: Frick 6011

Museums (natural history)

New York: American 5703

Museums (science/technology)

California: Exploratorium 565, **Tech 1041**
Massachusetts: Museum 4185

Museums (specialized)

District of Columbia: United 1744
Virginia: **Army 9316**

Museums (sports/hobby)

California: St. Shenouda 1015

Mutual aid societies

District of Columbia: **National 1684**
Ohio: **Christian 7036**

Mutual aid societies, research

District of Columbia: **National 1684**

Mutual aid societies, volunteer services

Illinois: Rotary 2835

Myasthenia gravis

New York: **Myasthenia 6234**

Myasthenia gravis research

New York: **Myasthenia 6234**

Native Americans/American Indians

Alaska: Arctic 104, Bering 105, Calista 108, CIRI 113, Copper 114, Eyak 116, Huna 118, Koniag 122, Kuskokwim 123, Newlin 127, Sealaska 136, SNA 139, Tanana 140, Tanaq 141, TDX 142, Tigara 144
California: **Getty 614, HP 670**, Lagrant 731
Colorado: **American 1116**, Pathways 1256
Connecticut: Tierney 1472
District of Columbia: **Freedom 1631, United 1743**
Florida: **Holland 1918**, Magic 1958, Orlando 2008
Hawaii: Pope 2315
Illinois: **Medical 2728**
Maryland: Fast 3825
Massachusetts: Massachusetts 4168, **Maya 4170**
Michigan: Arts 4340, Bay 4350
Minnesota: American 4689, Ecotrust 4732, Gough 4749, Lemieux 4782, Tiwahe 4869, Two 4873
Montana: Washington 5182
New Jersey: KPMG 5493
New Mexico: **American 5611, American 5612, Catching 5618, School 5650, Southwestern 5652**
New York: **AAAA 5662, National 6241**, Price 6327
North Carolina: Cherokee 6598, Ferebee 6655
North Dakota: Ernst 6939
Ohio: McLendon 7237, Throckmorton 7381
Oklahoma: **Chickasaw 7457**, Miley 7495
Oregon: Klamath 7592
Pennsylvania: Hazelton 7894, Ruskin 8084
South Dakota: **First 8530**, Native 8537, Sioux Falls 8538
Texas: Luce 8928, **National 8986**
Utah: American 9191
Virginia: **American 9292, American 9302, National 9451**
Washington: **Native 9680**, Potlatch 9701, Washington 9747
Wisconsin: Wisconsin 10080

Neighborhood centers

Florida: Beall 1793

Nerve, muscle & bone diseases

Arizona: **Muscular 220**
California: Myotonic 812
Connecticut: Endocrine 1385
District of Columbia: **Amyotrophic 1573**
Illinois: **Orthopaedic 2770**
Maryland: **Aplastic 3774**
New York: American 5690, Bone 5774, **Children's 5851**
Virginia: **Friedreich's 9386**
Wisconsin: **Riesch 10010**

Nerve, muscle & bone research

Arizona: **Muscular 220**
California: Myotonic 812
District of Columbia: **Amyotrophic 1573**
Maryland: **Osteogenesis 3906**
New Jersey: New Jersey 5518
New York: **American 5704, Children's 5851**, Dysautonomia 5943
Pennsylvania: **AO 7707**
Texas: American 8681
Virginia: **Friedreich's 9386**

Neuroscience

California: **Grass 637**
District of Columbia: Dingwall 1615
Illinois: **Dystonia 2529, Foundation 2570**
Massachusetts: **Marine 4160**
Minnesota: Alworth 4685, **American 4686**

New York: Collins 5868, Klingenstein 6143, **NARSAD: 6239, Sloan 6404**
Pennsylvania: Newman 8005
Virginia: **Friedreich's 9386**

Neuroscience research

California: **Grass 637**
Maryland: Dellon 3814
Massachusetts: Harvard 4095
Minnesota: **American 4686, McKnight 4793**
New Jersey: **Reeve 5550**
New York: Klingenstein 6143, **NARSAD: 6239**
North Carolina: Broad 6582
Pennsylvania: Newman 8005
Virginia: **Friedreich's 9386**

Nonprofit management

Arizona: Piper 229
California: **Draper 547**
District of Columbia: **Aspen 1583**
North Carolina: Reynolds 6828

Nursing care

California: Bialis 412
Maryland: **American 3764**
Massachusetts: **American 3969**
Ohio: Community 7058
Pennsylvania: Baskin 7725
Rhode Island: Rhode Island 8381

Nursing home/convalescent facility

New York: Clark 5859
Pennsylvania: Sleeper 8108

Nursing school/education

Alabama: AAMN 1, Andalusia 10, Baptist 12, Infirmary 52
Alaska: Alaska 97
Arizona: AZHHA 167, Banner 169, Kingman 207, Valley 254
Arkansas: Baptist 269, Nelson 297, SHARE 307, Smith 310, Union 321
California: Alta 350, American 354, American 359, Fairmount 566, Health 651, Hinckley 663, Hoag 665, Humboldt 671, Kaiser 718, Lakewood 732, Little 747, Mammoth 767, Mercy 786, Mills-Peninsula 795, North 832, QueensCare 891, Sacramento 926, Santa 954, Sequoia 975, Torrance 1050, Tri 1054
Colorado: Aorn 1119, Aspen 1123, Broomfield 1135, **Colorado 1165**, Logan 1233, North 1251
Connecticut: Bridgeport 1339, Connecticut 1366, Fairfield 1387, Norwalk 1436, Weller 1482
Delaware: Delaware 1500
District of Columbia: **American 1543, German 1638, National 1694, National 1696**
Florida: Benjamin 1796, Brevard 1807, BRRH 1813, Embassy 1869, Fellows 1875, Florida 1879, Flordia Keys 1883, Murray 1990, Sailfish 2047, Schommer 2053
Georgia: DeKalb 2162, Georgia 2186, Idaho 2197
Hawaii: Rehabilitation 2316, Zimmerman 2327
Illinois: Camp 2457, CGH 2470, Community 2494, Dawson 2511, Edward 2535, **Emergency 2543**, Hansen 2598, McClain 2717, McFarland 2720, OSF 2772, Peeples 2781, Riverside 2824, Roberts 2825, Welch 2921
Indiana: Abell 2944, **American 2954**, Decatur 3013, Fayette 3028, Garr 3041, Kendrick 3085, Kosciusko 3091, LaGrange 3093, Madison 3106, McKinney 3112, Noble 3127, Plummer 3148, Putnam 3154, Visiting 3212, Wabash 3215, Westhaysen 3223, Williams 3228
Iowa: Allen 3235, Dallas 3270, Genesis 3283, Jennie 3313, Munson 3339, Northwest 3347, Parks

3354, Siouxland 3382, St. Luke's 3387, Van Buren 3403
Kansas: Vesper 3533
Kentucky: Blue 3552, Community 3559, Kings 3588, Morrill 3599, Morrill 3600, Norris 3603, Owensboro 3609, St. 3628
Louisiana: Tupper 3681
Maine: Reid 3729
Maryland: Baltimore 3784, Keswick 3857, Womens 3952
Massachusetts: Children's 4022, Permanent 4216, Philbin 4219
Michigan: Baker 4342, Bay 4350, Bellinger 4355, Community 4394, Dickinson 4408, Gratiot 4449, Guardian 4452, Hammel 4455, Heyl 4465, Kadant 4491, Meyers 4532, Pennock 4576, Petoskey 4577, Sigmund 4606, Three 4637
Minnesota: Alworth 4685, CentraCare 4709, Mayo 4792, Proshek 4830, Regions 4837, United 4874
Missouri: Baptist-Trinity 4935, Cox 4968, Coxhealth 4969, Greater 5004, Hester 5016, Kansas 5023, MHA 5051, St. Marys 5107
Montana: Beartooth 5131
Nebraska: Nebraska 5244, Weller 5271
Nevada: Renown 5301
New Hampshire: Green 5324, Parkland 5360, Yarnold 5379
New Jersey: Groff 5460, Grupe 5462, Hollander 5470, Middlesex 5507, Snyder 5570, Valley 5589, Wound 5605
New York: Chautauqua 5842, Columbia 5870, Community 5878, Durland 5940, Foundation 6001, Foundation 6002, **Myasthenia 6234**, NLN 6280, Post 6321, Samaritan 6372, **Seneca 6394**, St. Luke's 6426, Stoner 6439, Wells 6510
North Carolina: CarolinaEast 6591, Foundation 6660, Gramberg 6679, Mission 6775, Myers 6783, Rex 6827, Richmond 6832, Robinson 6839, Team 6889, Transylvania 6896
Ohio: Adams 6956, Adena 6958, Akron 6966, Blanchard 7000, Community 7064, Dinger 7089, Drake 7090, **Eagles 7095**, Good 7129, Kirkpatrick 7193, Knowles 7200, Licking 7209, MacRae 7217, Rutan 7332, Scioto 7339, Smith 7354, Stark 7366, Troy 7388, Tuscora 7391, Van Wert 7403, Wimmer 7432, Wright 7441
Oklahoma: Driskell 7465
Oregon: Black 7540, Providence 7636, Schmidt 7655, Singer 7659
Pennsylvania: Abrams 7691, App 7708, Brevillier 7745, Carmell 7758, Community 7783, Crawford 7796, Elk 7821, Fleischer 7847, Harley 7886, Helbing 7901, Holy 7911, Jeanes 7926, Lancaster 7945, Leighow 7955, Mellinger 7981, Miller 7987, ONS 8015, Pennsylvania 8028, Philadelphia 8037, Pinnacle 8044, Smith 8110, Stager 8128, Thomas 8144, Trushel 8151, York 8213, Young 8214
Rhode Island: Ayers 8235, Berry 8243, Schiff 8393, Stokes 8415, Wiggin 8436
South Carolina: Boyne 8452, South 8512
Tennessee: Wellmont 8662
Texas: Amarillo 8675, **American 8677**, Anderson 8687, Borton 8717, Brisley 8721, Healthcare 8861, Lubbock 8926, Maffett 8931, Methodist 8954, Millar 8958, **MVP 8978**, Permian 9013, Seton 9069, St. Luke's 9098, Wintermann 9171
Utah: Bamberger 9193
Virginia: AHC 9281, Bedford 9324, Grobel 9389, Johns 9409, Sentara 9502, Womack 9552
Washington: St. Luke's 9732
West Virginia: Camden-Clark 9770, Morgan 9803
Wisconsin: Bruneo 9854, Community 9866, Eckburg 9881, Fromm 9901, Green Bay 9910, Hodes 9922, Keller 9940, Martin 9962, Mitchell 9972, Shallow 10029, Watertown 10064, Wells 10068, Wisconsin 10084, Women's 10085
Wyoming: Clark 10097, Cody 10098, Sheridan 10119, Wyoming 10126

Nutrition

California: Child 484, Rest 908

District of Columbia: **American 1560**, Food 1627
Illinois: **Academy 2355**, **Feeding 2559**, Peeples 2781
Kentucky: God's 3573
Maryland: **School 3928**
Ohio: Van Wert 7403
Oregon: Neighborimpact 7615
Pennsylvania: Webber 8179, Webber 8180
South Carolina: Gleamns 8476
Texas: Morrison 8970
Washington: Second 9721
Wisconsin: Feeding 9889

Obstetrics/gynecology

Maryland: **Medical 3878**
Oregon: **Fanconi 7575**

Obstetrics/gynecology research

Maryland: **Medical 3878**

Offenders/ex-offenders

Michigan: Spectrum 4620

Offenders/ex-offenders, rehabilitation

Hawaii: Community 2277

Offenders/ex-offenders, services

California: Catalyst 466, Doing 543
Massachusetts: **Rosenberg 4247**
Michigan: Easter 4412

Offenders/ex-offenders, transitional care

Hawaii: Community 2277
Michigan: Easter 4412

Optometry/vision screening

California: Rest 908
Florida: American 1772
Georgia: Hall 2190
Illinois: Hynd 2632
Kansas: Jones 3464
Maine: Montgomery 3719, Portland 3726
Oregon: Southern 7664
Pennsylvania: Quin 8070
Texas: **OneSight 8998**
West Virginia: Chambers 9774

Organ diseases

Pennsylvania: **National 8001**
South Carolina: Gift 8475
Tennessee: **National 8628**

Organ research

California: **Pancreatic 854**

Orthopedics

New York: Insall 6094
Tennessee: Chattanooga 8568

Orthopedics research

New York: American 5698
North Carolina: Eastern 6641
Pennsylvania: Yount 8216

Palliative care

Arizona: Valley 254

Parkinson's disease

District of Columbia: **Parkinson's 1708**
Florida: **National 1996**
New York: **Fox 6006**
Virginia: **American 9309**, Parkinson 9475, Weinstein 9545

Parkinson's disease research

District of Columbia: **Parkinson's 1708**
Florida: **National 1996**
New York: **Fox 6006**

Pathology

Illinois: College 2489
Missouri: **Sertoma, 5098**

Pathology research

Illinois: College 2489
New York: **Mayday 6197**

Pediatrics

Connecticut: My 1428
District of Columbia: **Glaser 1640**
Georgia: CURE 2159
Illinois: **American 2366**, American 2387, Ann 2401
Indiana: Society 3188
New York: Cure 5906
Tennessee: Le 8615
Texas: **Knights 8909**, Wipe 9172

Pediatrics research

Alabama: Dixon 31
Illinois: **American 2366**
Maryland: Cystic 3812
Pennsylvania: **Alex's 7695**
Tennessee: Le 8615
Virginia: Association 9320
Wisconsin: Scoliosis 10025

Pensions

Massachusetts: Center 4016

Pensions, teacher funds

Texas: Thompson 9136

Performing arts

Alaska: CIRI 113, Juneau 120, Rasmuson 132
Arizona: Renaissance 232, Tucson-Pima 247
California: Anaheim 363, Arts 377, California 445, **Colonnades 507**, CounterPULSE 525, Deaf 537, **Djerassi 541**, Exploratorium 565, Friends 599, Gerbode 612, Headlands 649, Performing 861, Riverside 913, Silver 988, **United 1072**, Veneklasen 1080
Colorado: Boulder 1132
District of Columbia: **Association 1586**, **Kennedy 1666**
Florida: Atlantic 1787, Community 1838, Florida 1879, **National 1997**, Woman's 2107
Georgia: Ayers 2122
Illinois: **American 2378**, **Carpe 2460**
Indiana: Children's 2983, Ellison 3025, Richmond 3162, VSA 3214
Iowa: **Reed 3364**
Kansas: Koch 3476, Naftzger 3493
Maine: Holocaust 3703
Maryland: American 3758, Arts 3776, Maryland 3872
Massachusetts: **American 3963**, Cohen 4026, Harvard 4096, High 4104
Michigan: Bay 4350

Minnesota: Anodyne 4692, Blacklock 4699, Central 4710, Five 4738, Prairie 4828, Southern 4855, VSA 4882
New Hampshire: La Napoule 5333
New Jersey: Grande 5458, New Jersey 5519, **Puffin 5549**
New York: **Actors 5665, America-Israel 5686, American 5692,** Armenian 5717, Art 5720, **CEC 5829,** chashama 5841, Council 5894, **Creative 5898, Cuban 5902,** Ensemble 5959, **Foundation 5995, Four 6005, Franklin 6008,** Friars 6010, Genesee 6021, Hadar 6054, Home 6077, **Institute 6095,** Living 6166, Merchant 6209, Movement 6228, **Netherland-America 6258,** Performance 6313, **Princess 6329,** Stage 6428, Unique 6471
North Carolina: Arts 6559, Asheville 6561, United 6906
Ohio: Culture 7073, Fine 7108, Three 7380, Wexner 7422
Oregon: Celebration 7545
Pennsylvania: Independence 7916
South Dakota: **First 8530**
Tennessee: **National 8629**
Texas: Diverseworks 8796, **Vietnamese 9149**
Washington: Allied 9559, Centrum 9583

Performing arts (multimedia)

California: Gerbode 612
New York: **Corporation 5888, Creative 5898,** Lower 6173
Washington: 911 9554

Performing arts centers

District of Columbia: **Kennedy 1666**
Michigan: Flint 4419
New York: Home 6077

Performing arts, ballet

Delaware: Delaware 1500
Michigan: Flint 4419
New York: Staten 6431
Pennsylvania: Pew 8033

Performing arts, choreography

Alaska: Rasmuson 132
California: **Djerassi 541,** Gerbode 612
Massachusetts: Yard 4327
New York: **Balanchine 5751, Corporation 5888, Princess 6329**
North Carolina: American 6549
Pennsylvania: Pew 8033
Texas: San Antonio 9056

Performing arts, dance

California: Dancers' 535, Dorland 544, Gerbode 612, Santa 957, Silver 988, Theatre 1044
Indiana: VSA 3214
Kansas: Koch 3476
Maryland: Beth 3785
Massachusetts: Jacob's 4129, Yard 4327
Michigan: Flint 4419
Minnesota: Five 4738, Jerome 4771
New Jersey: Capezio 5412, Paper 5534
New York: Ailey 5676, **Balanchine 5751,** Ballet 5752, **Bogliasco 5772,** Bossak 5777, Brooklyn 5798, **Career 5816,** Cunningham 5905, Dance 5910, Dance 5911, **Foundation 5995,** Foundation 5997, Home 6077, Movement 6228, **Princess 6329,** Queens 6341, Staten 6431, Topaz 6458, Unique 6471
North Carolina: American 6549
Ohio: Cleveland 7041
Pennsylvania: Pew 8033
Texas: San Antonio 9056
Washington: **Native 9680,** Pacific 9693
West Virginia: Timms 9823

Performing arts, education

Alaska: Alaska 97
Arizona: Renaissance 232
Arkansas: **Mashburn 289**
California: Dorland 544, Fresno 596, Memorial 783, Philharmonic 866, Santa Barbara 955
Connecticut: Scott 1457
District of Columbia: Washington 1746
Florida: Community 1839, Music 1991, Operafestival 2005
Illinois: Chicago 2475, Luley 2700, Roesch 2829, Smith 2859, Union 2904
Indiana: Deen 3014, Kosciusko 3091, Porter 3149, Smelser 3186
Iowa: Garber 3282
Massachusetts: Jacob's 4129, South 4272, Weyman 4314
Michigan: Community 4394, Grand Rapids 4445
Minnesota: Central 4710
New Jersey: Paper 5534
New York: ArtsConnection 5730, Bagby 5749, Ballet 5752, **Blake 5765,** Blake 5766, Calman 5808, Chautauqua 5842, **Lincoln 6164,** Moore 6224, Opera 6297, Staten 6431
North Carolina: Allen 6548, Chaffer 6596, Leverenz 6742
Ohio: Dumesnil 7091, **Educational 7098,** Gilbert 7127, Van Wert 7403
Oklahoma: Wilson 7527
Oregon: Alexandria 7530
Pennsylvania: England 7826, Hughes 7913, Reading 8071, Soren 8122
Rhode Island: Ayer 8234, Rhode Island 8381
Texas: Donnelly 8797, Music 8976
Vermont: Warner 9272
Virginia: **Fox 9384**
Washington: Richardson 9706
West Virginia: Timms 9823
Wisconsin: Green Bay 9910, La Crosse 9948

Performing arts, music

Alaska: Alaska 97
Arizona: **North 221**
California: Arques 372, Coastal 504, Dorland 544, Durfee 549, Fresno 596, Gerbode 612, Guzik 642, Hartman 648, Los 758, Memorial 783, **Montalvo 802,** Musicares 809, **NAMM 813,** Performing 862, Philharmonic 866, **Rex 909,** Santa 957, Schmidek 963, Shasta 978, Silverlake 989, **Sponsors 1009, United 1072,** Warne 1085, Wayne 1088, Young 1107
Colorado: **Music 1246,** Vail 1302
Connecticut: Traalum 1474, Weller 1482
District of Columbia: **Kennedy 1666, Monk 1680, VSA 1745,** Washington 1746
Florida: **Ashley 1784,** Manley 1961, Music 1991
Georgia: Barnett 2126
Illinois: Biederstedt 2425, Coin 2487, Luley 2700, Oak Park 2761, Roesch 2829, Smith 2859, Southern 2865, Union 2904
Indiana: Decatur 3013, Fort 3031, Indianapolis 3072, Joshi 3080, Muncie 3120, Richmond 3162, Smelser 3186
Iowa: Garber 3282, Hockenberry 3300, McKay 3334
Kansas: Koch 3476, Naftzger 3493
Maryland: American 3763
Massachusetts: 47 3955, **Beebe 3980,** Boch 3990, Cape Cod 4007, Harvard 4096, High 4104, Nantucket 4186, Nantucket 4187, South 4272, Weyman 4314
Michigan: Ann Arbor 4338, Community 4394, **Gilmore 4438, Glen Arbor 4441,** Rislov 4589
Minnesota: Central 4710, Jerome 4771, Wenger 4887
Missouri: Missouri 5057
New Hampshire: Manchester 5342
New Jersey: Children's 5423, New Jersey 5519, Paper 5534, **Puffin 5549,** Shoshana 5564
New Mexico: Whited 5658
New York: Art 5718, Art 5721, Arts 5727, Bagby 5749, **Blake 5765,** Blake 5766, **BMI 5771, Bogliasco 5772, Chamber 5839,** Chautauqua 5842,

Creative 5898, Cuban 5902, Cunningham 5905, Curran 5907, **Delmas 5921,** Forrai 5990, **Foundation 5995, Harvestworks 6058, Jazz 6112,** Kleban 6140, Kosciuszko 6145, **Koussevitzky 6146, League 6156,** Lissner 6165, **Mikhashoff 6215,** Musicians 6232, **Musicians 6233, National 6243,** New Music 6262, New York 6269, Pressman 6326, Randon 6344, **Rockefeller 6359,** Rose 6362, Schiffner 6384, **Sparkplug 6418, Stecher 6434, Weill 6508**
North Carolina: Asheville 6561, Chaffer 6596, Leverenz 6742, **Music 6781, Sigma 6860,** Wildacres 6920
Ohio: Gilbert 7127, Simmons 7350, Van Wert 7403
Oklahoma: Wilson 7527
Oregon: Central 7546, Chamber 7547, Neskowin 7616
Pennsylvania: **Early 7817,** Gardiner 7864, Hughes 7913, Marshall 7969, Presser 8060, Reading 8071, **Rhythm 8076,** Soren 8122, Yount 8216
Rhode Island: Ayer 8234, Preston 8371, Rhode Island 8381, Yaeger 8443
South Carolina: Cultural 8469
Tennessee: Community 8578, Dollywood 8584, Humanities 8604, Lead 8616
Texas: Donnelly 8797, Music 8976, Permian 9013
Vermont: Hayes 9251
Washington: Allied 9559, Centrum 9583, **Native 9680,** Richardson 9706, Straw 9733
West Virginia: Aurora 9765
Wisconsin: La Crosse 9948, Mari's 9958

Performing arts, music (choral)

Arkansas: **Mashburn 289**
California: San Francisco 946, Silver 988, Society 999, **Society 1001,** Stephens 1022
Colorado: Rocky 1271
Illinois: Biederstedt 2425
Michigan: Marquette 4524
New York: American 5687
Ohio: Gilbert 7127
Virginia: Wolf 9551
West Virginia: Timms 9823

Performing arts, music composition

Alaska: Rasmuson 132
Arkansas: Communication 274
California: **Djerassi 541,** Gerbode 612, Los 758, **Montalvo 802**
District of Columbia: **Kennedy 1666**
Florida: Cintas 1828, Lake 1943
Georgia: Katz 2201
Illinois: Union 2904
Maine: Eastern 3695
Michigan: Rislov 4589
Minnesota: American 4687, **Camargo 4706**
New Hampshire: La Napoule 5333, **MacDowell 5341**
New York: ASCAP 5731, **BMI 5771, Chamber 5839, Corporation 5888,** Dutchess 5941, Home 6077, **Koussevitzky 6146, Mikhashoff 6215, Millay 6216,** New York 6269, **Rockefeller 6359**
Virginia: **American 9312**
Washington: Centrum 9583
Wyoming: **Ucross 10123**

Performing arts, music ensembles/groups

California: San Francisco 945, Society 999
New Jersey: New Jersey 5519
New York: **ACMP 5664, Chamber 5839**
Oregon: Chamber 7547
Rhode Island: Preston 8371

Performing arts, opera

Arizona: Community 182
California: Arques 372
Florida: Operafestival 2005
Indiana: Joshi 3080

New York: American 5687, Lissner 6165, London 6167, Metropolitan 6212, Moore 6224, **OPERA 6296**, Opera 6297, **Tucker 6466**
North Carolina: Jensen 6717
Virginia: Wolf 9551
Washington: Centrum 9583

Performing arts, orchestras

California: Gerbode 612, Los 758, Young 1107
Colorado: Denver 1183, **Music 1246**
Florida: **Ashley 1784**, Florida 1887
Illinois: Chicago 2475
Indiana: Fort 3031, Muncie 3120, Richmond 3162
Michigan: Kalamazoo 4494, **Sphinx 4622**
New York: ASCAP 5731, **League 6156**
Pennsylvania: Pottstown 8056
Rhode Island: Preston 8371

Performing arts, theater

California: Deaf 537, **Montalvo 802**, Santa 957, Theatre 1044
Colorado: American 1117
Delaware: Common 1497, Delaware 1500
Florida: Woman's 2107
Iowa: **Reed 3364**
Kansas: Tenholder 3524
Massachusetts: High 4104
Minnesota: Five 4738, Jerome 4771
New York: American 5687, Art 5718, Arts 5727, **Bogliasco 5772**, Brooklyn 5798, **Creative 5898**, **Delmas 5921**, **Foundation 5995**, Home 6077, **Princess 6329**, Queens 6341, **Theatre 6448**, **United 6477**
Ohio: **Educational 7098**
Oregon: Alexandria 7530, Hamilton 7585
Pennsylvania: Hughes 7913, Marshall 7969, Pew 8033, Yount 8216
Rhode Island: Coles 8270
South Carolina: Cultural 8469
Texas: Gilman 8841
Virginia: **Fox 9384**

Performing arts, theater (musical)

Arkansas: **Mashburn 289**
California: Gerbode 612
Colorado: American 1117
Iowa: **Reed 3364**
Maryland: Salisbury 3925
New York: **American 5689**, **American 5708**, Art 5718, ASCAP 5731, **BMI 5771**, Ebb 5951, **National 6242**, Unique 6471
West Virginia: Timms 9823

Performing arts, theater (playwriting)

California: Chesley 480, Intersection 693, **Montalvo 802**
Colorado: American 1117
District of Columbia: **VSA 1745**
Maryland: Salisbury 3925
New York: Albee 5677, Bronx 5793, Brown 5801, **Dramatists 5934**, Lortel 6171, **National 6243**, **Princess 6329**, **Rockefeller 6359**, Steinberg 6436, **Theatre 6448**, Weissberger 6509
Ohio: Columbus 7052
Oregon: **Vongelstein 7676**
Texas: **Blackburn 8714**
Virginia: **Institute 9404**
Washington: Centrum 9583

Personal assistance services (PAS)

Florida: Area 1780
Pennsylvania: Three 8146

Pharmacology

Alabama: Alabama 5
Pennsylvania: App 7708
Tennessee: Le 8615

Pharmacology research

Tennessee: Le 8615

Pharmacy/prescriptions

California: **Genentech 611**, Lakewood 732, Rest 908
Connecticut: Alexion 1317
Delaware: AstraZeneca 1493
District of Columbia: **American 1564**, **Pharmaceutical 1714**
Illinois: BCMW 2415, Union 2902
Indiana: Kosciusko 3091
Iowa: Association 3241
Kentucky: Northern 3604
Maryland: American 3766, **Foundation 3828**, **HealthWell 3840**
Michigan: Trone 4642
Minnesota: Hastings 4755
New Jersey: **ARCH 5389**, Middlesex 5507, **Sanofi 5559**
New York: **Pfizer 6315**
North Carolina: Burke-Weber 6586, Pharmacy 6818, Transylvania 6896
Rhode Island: Perpetual 8368
Virginia: **American 9300**, **American 9309**, **National 9450**
Wisconsin: Healthnet 9917

Philanthropy/voluntarism

California: **Draper 547**, **San 927**
District of Columbia: **Aspen 1583**, Center 1599, **Independent 1649**
Massachusetts: **Rosenberg 4247**
Texas: **Amigos 8685**
Virginia: Associates 9319

Philanthropy/voluntarism, administration/regulation

Alaska: Rasmuson 132

Philanthropy/voluntarism, formal/general education

Virginia: **AHP 9282**

Philanthropy/voluntarism, fund raising/fund distribution

Virginia: AFP 9280, **Association 9321**

Philanthropy/voluntarism, management/technical assistance

Alaska: Rasmuson 132
District of Columbia: **Aspen 1583**

Philanthropy/voluntarism, volunteer services

California: Durfee 549

Philosophy/ethics

California: **Rand 898**
New York: **American 5692**, Bogliasco 5772, Historical 6073, **Wiesel 6519**
Ohio: Social 7360
Pennsylvania: **American 7704**

Physical therapy

Alabama: Andalusia 10
California: Avery 396
Hawaii: Saake 2318
Illinois: **Massage 2713**
Indiana: Pacers 3138
Kansas: Cloud 3426
Maryland: **American 3765**
Michigan: Bay 4350, Southwest 4618
New York: Schechter 6380
Ohio: Motry 7257
Virginia: **American 9304**, **Foundation 9380**
Wisconsin: Mitchell 9972

Physical/earth sciences

Arizona: **Research 233**
California: **Hertz 658**, National 821
Colorado: Population 1259, Society 1285
District of Columbia: **National 1693**
Florida: Everglades 1872, Sunburst 2079
Idaho: Adams 2328
Massachusetts: American 3967, **Gravity 4089**
Michigan: Meyers 4532
Minnesota: Alworth 4685
New York: American 5703, **Explorers 5968**, Open 6295
North Carolina: **Nickel 6792**
Pennsylvania: Smithfield 8113
Texas: Conner 8767, Corpus Christi 8773, **SPE 9093**
Virginia: **Public 9488**
Wisconsin: Environmental 9885

Physically disabled

California: **Challenged 476**, Stanislaus 1017
Connecticut: **Walkabout 1479**
District of Columbia: Christ 1601
Florida: Northeast 2000, Rehabilitation 2033, Southwest 2067
Illinois: Gore 2588
Indiana: Huntington 3068
New Jersey: **Newcombe 5526**, Peterson 5540
New York: Children 5847, Community 5878, United 6475
Pennsylvania: Three 8146
Texas: Affordable 8668
Wyoming: LaRue 10110

Physics

Arizona: **Research 233**
California: **Hertz 658**, Science 968
Illinois: Blazek 2427, Testamentary 2890
Maryland: **American 3757**, **American 3761**
Minnesota: Alworth 4685
Missouri: Community 4963
New Jersey: Ammonius 5386, **Siemens 5566**
New York: American 5703, **Sloan 6404**
North Carolina: Rennie 6826
Ohio: Birr 6998
Pennsylvania: Smithfield 8113, Zaccheus 8218
Texas: **SPE 9093**

Podiatry

Illinois: **American 2384**
Pennsylvania: Clark 7770, Podiatry 8052
Texas: Texas 9128

Political science

District of Columbia: **Fund 1634**, **German 1638**, **National 1691**
Illinois: Everett 2553, Francies 2572, **Sigma 2855**
Michigan: **Earhart 4411**, Ford 4420
New Jersey: Horowitz 5473
New York: **American 5700**, **CDS 5828**, **Delmas 5921**, **Schalkenbach 6379**, **Social 6409**
Ohio: Kiwanis 7197
Oklahoma: OSU 7504

Pennsylvania: **Smithfield** 8113
Texas: **Reese 9034**

Population studies

District of Columbia: **Association 1585**
Florida: Everglades 1872
Minnesota: **Lindbergh 4783**
New York: **Population 6320**
Texas: **Komen 8910**

Poverty studies

California: **Impact 678**
Massachusetts: **SEVEN 4267**
New York: **World 6534**
North Carolina: Tarboro 6886

Pregnancy centers

Minnesota: **Pro 4829**

Prostate cancer

California: **Prostate 885**

Prostate cancer research

California: **Prostate 885**

Protestant agencies & churches

Alabama: Dixon 31
California: Mang 768
Connecticut: **Society 1461**
Georgia: Baker 2123
Hawaii: Atherton 2271
Illinois: Wells 2922, Wells 2923
Iowa: Preston 3360
Massachusetts: Johnson 4131, Wheelwright 4315
Michigan: Fremont 4431, Kling 4502, Matson 4528,
    VanKley 4656
Minnesota: **Grannis-Martin 4751, Lutheran 4785**
Montana: Hurst 5159
New York: Corporation 5887, Episcopal 5961
North Carolina: Davis 6628, Dilcher 6630, Frasier
    6666, Ginder 6674, Komarek 6733
Ohio: Gonter 7128, Grace 7132, McCabe 7224, Salem
    7334
Pennsylvania: Reeves 8073, Smock 8114, Spackman
    8126, Walz 8174
Rhode Island: Manwiller 8334, Peck 8367
South Carolina: Fund 8472
South Dakota: Sioux Falls 8538
Texas: Brisley 8721, Ferguson 8821, **Harding 8854,**
    Hayes 8859, Hurley 8888, Little 8919, Olson
    8996, Schumann 9063, TUA 9139
West Virginia: Gault 9786, Stout 9819
Wisconsin: Frautschy 9897, Keller 9939, MacPherson
    9954

Psychology/behavioral science

California: **International 692**
District of Columbia: **American 1565, National 1681**
Illinois: O'Malley 2768
Maryland: **American 3768**
Nebraska: Edwards 5198
Nevada: **Marchionne 5293**
New Jersey: Horowitz 5473
New York: **American 5692,** American 5695, American
    5705, Collins 5868, **Guggenheim 6049,**
    Parapsychology 6301, Social 6409
North Carolina: **Cattell 6594**
Pennsylvania: Mahler 7966, **Templeton 8141**
Virginia: **American 9305**
Washington: Sigourney 9724

Public affairs

District of Columbia: **Congressional 1607,**
    International 1656, Marijuana 1672, Patton 1711
Virginia: National 9458
Washington: Wales 9744

Public affairs, administration/regulation

New York: **CDS 5828**

Public affairs, citizen participation

District of Columbia: Asian 1582
New York: Democracy 5922
Washington: Wales 9744

Public affairs, finance

District of Columbia: **FINRA 1626**

Public affairs, government agencies

Ohio: Dayton 7082

Public affairs, political organizations

California: **Rex 909**

Public affairs, reform

District of Columbia: **Marijuana 1673**
New York: Democracy 5922

Public health

California: **Public 886,** Public 887
Colorado: Colorado 1154
District of Columbia: Association 1584, Association
    1587, **Families 1625**
Illinois: DuPage 2528, Marion 2708
Maryland: **Global 3836**
New York: **Lasker 6153, Schepp 6383**
Washington: **World 9758**
Wisconsin: St. Elizabeth 10044

Public health school/education

California: **Foundation 588, Kaiser 716**
District of Columbia: Association 1584
Florida: Benjamin 1796
Georgia: Council 2155
Maryland: Association 3778
Minnesota: Ely-Winton 4733
North Carolina: NC 6785

Public health, epidemiology

Georgia: Council 2155
Maryland: **National 3897**

Public health, obesity

Connecticut: Endocrine 1385

Public health, occupational health

Hawaii: Saake 2318

Public health, physical fitness

Hawaii: Saake 2318

Public policy, research

District of Columbia: **Kennedy 1667,** People 1713,
    Women's 1754
Maryland: **Casey 3794**
Massachusetts: **Kennedy 4137**

New York: **Commonwealth 5872,** New 6264,
    Schalkenbach 6379
Ohio: Kiwanis 7197
Pennsylvania: **Heinz 7900**

Recreation

Alabama: Southeastern 81
Alaska: Alaska 101
California: Community 512, Couch 524, St. Francis
    1011
Florida: Cape Coral 1815, Hillmyer-Tremont 1914,
    Washington 2099, Winged 2105
Hawaii: Outrigger 2308
Illinois: **Drag 2523, Vogler 2910**
Indiana: **National 3121,** RPW 3166
Kentucky: Baker 3547
Maine: Trust 3741
Maryland: Kattar 3856
Massachusetts: Armenian 3972, Lorden 4150
Michigan: Bay 4350, Ilitch 4480, Recreational 4585
New Jersey: Penn 5537
New York: Community 5882
North Carolina: Accel 6544
Ohio: Lake 7201, Lewis 7207, McLendon 7237,
    OHSAA 7283
Oregon: **Multnomah 7613**
Pennsylvania: Baskin 7725
Texas: Dallas 8786
Virginia: **Ashoka 9317**
Wisconsin: Jewish 9931

Recreation, camps

California: Taylor 1039
Colorado: Adventure 1111
Connecticut: Ebony 1383
District of Columbia: Christ 1601
Georgia: Southern 2239
Illinois: Children's 2480, Rauch 2808
Kansas: Jewish 3463
Louisiana: **Waters 3682**
Maine: Kieve 3707, Maine 3712
Minnesota: Brooks 4704
New Hampshire: Porter 5362
New Jersey: Camp 5411
New York: Henry 6067
Texas: Sunnyside 9103
Vermont: Warner 9272

Recreation, community

Illinois: Oak Park 2761

Recreation, equal rights

Virginia: **Ashoka 9317**

Recreation, parks/playgrounds

Michigan: Novi 4565
Washington: Seattle 9720

Recreation, social clubs

Indiana: Legacy 3096

Religion

Alabama: Franklin 39
Arizona: **Baize 168**
California: **Ramakrishna 895,** St. Shenouda 1015
Colorado: **H.E.L.P. 1208, WaterStone 1305**
Connecticut: **Avatar 1327,** Hartley 1401
Florida: Aurora 1788
Georgia: Baker 2123, **Ravi 2227**
Illinois: Peters 2785
Indiana: Brown 2975, Line 3102
Kentucky: Mustard 3602
Massachusetts: Cabot 4003

Michigan: Amy 4337, Legion 4515, Tamer 4631
Mississippi: Dunnaway 4905
Missouri: Kirschner 5030
New Hampshire: **Lyman 5340**
New Jersey: **Wilson 5600**
New York: Netzach 6259, **Wiesel 6519**
North Carolina: **Graham 6678**, Hoover 6702
Ohio: Record 7316, Religion 7317, Rogers 7326
Oklahoma: **Messenger 7494**
Pennsylvania: **Templeton 8141**, Walz 8174
Rhode Island: Cummings 8280
Tennessee: Shiloh 8643
Texas: Havens 8857, Philadelphia 9018, Teen 9112
Wisconsin: Walker 10062

Religion, formal/general education

New York: Catholic 5825, Roothbert 6361
North Carolina: Carpenter 6592, Harasimik 6693
Ohio: Thompson 7379
Virginia: Missionary 9438

Religion, interfaith issues

Minnesota: American 4687

Religion, public policy

Virginia: **Mustard 9442**

Religion, research

California: St. Shenouda 1015
New York: **Friends 6012**

Reproductive health

Alabama: **American 8**
District of Columbia: **American 1551**
New York: MADRE, 6182, **Population 6320**

Reproductive health, fertility

New York: Bonei 5775

Reproductive health, OBGYN/Birthing centers

Wisconsin: **Society 10037**

Reproductive health, prenatal care

District of Columbia: **American 1551**

Residential/custodial care

Arizona: Agape 152
California: Mills 793, Trinity 1057, Turn 1064
Florida: Schmitt 2050
Illinois: Scott 2847
Massachusetts: Austin 3975, Boston 3993
New Mexico: Viles 5657
New York: Catholic 5824, Elenberg 5956, L.H. 6149
Ohio: Bentley 6995
Pennsylvania: Biondo 7734, Huth 7914
Virginia: Buchly 9330, Navy 9461

Residential/custodial care, group home

New York: Inwood 6104, L.H. 6149
Texas: Buckner 8728

Residential/custodial care, half-way house

Michigan: Spectrum 4620

Residential/custodial care, hospices

Alabama: Alabama 3

Residential/custodial care, senior continuing care

Florida: Area 1780
Minnesota: Hastings 4755

Residential/custodial care, special day care

Indiana: Little 3103

Rural development

District of Columbia: **Foundation 1629**
Washington: Rural 9711

Rural studies

Minnesota: AgStar 4683

Safety, automotive safety

Illinois: Allstate 2363

Safety, education

Illinois: **National 2751**
Massachusetts: **National 4190**

Safety/disasters

Alaska: Kawerak 121
Arkansas: Helping 283, Wal-Mart 324
California: **Children's 489**, Give 618, **Global 623**, Jack 699
Connecticut: **AmeriCares 1323**
District of Columbia: **American 1563**, Communications 1604, **Teamster 1735**, **Union 1742**
Florida: Abilities 1763, Brown 1812, Cousin 1853, Hard 1902, Hma 1916, **Office 2002**, PSS/Gulf 2027, Ryder 2046
Georgia: Cox 2157, Southern 2238
Illinois: CNA 2484, McDonald's 2719, **Realtors 2810**, Royal 2837
Iowa: LSB 3328
Kansas: Duclos 3434, Knights 3475
Louisiana: **Park 3673**
Maryland: **Humanity 3847**, Nexion 3902
Massachusetts: Dunkin 4047, Massachusetts 4164, Raytheon 4238
Michigan: Lions 4518
Minnesota: Dolan 4728
Mississippi: Lexington 4912
Nevada: **Caring 5280**
New Jersey: Honeywell 5472, KPMG 5492, North 5527, Virtua 5592
New Mexico: Santa Fe 5648
New York: Aero 5670, New York 6274, PricewaterhouseCoopers 6328
North Carolina: **Lion's 6743**, Lowe's 6749
Ohio: Twenty 7393
Oklahoma: **Feed 7468**, Oklahoma 7499
Tennessee: HCA 8599, Ruby 8639
Texas: Cadbury 8732, CRW 8776, Harris 8855, Nabors 8979, Perot 9014, Pioneer 9020, Swift 9104, Sysco 9107, Targa 9108, Texas 9119
Vermont: **Craft 9243**
Virginia: CIA 9342, Maria's 9429, **National 9447**, **Postal 9486**, Research 9493, Sentara 9501, United 9531
West Virginia: Stump 9820

Safety/disasters, ethics

Massachusetts: Humane 4121

Safety/disasters, government agencies

District of Columbia: Community 1605

Safety/disasters, research

Illinois: **American 2392**

Scholarships/financial aid

Alabama: Bedsole 15, Lucash 56, Mayson 60, Southeastern 81
Arizona: Arizona 157, Arizona 164, Christian 179, Community 182, Freeport-McMoRan 196, **Southern 237**, Sturges 242, Trico 246
Arkansas: Murphy 295, Wal-Mart 325
California: Aaron 332, Almanor 349, Baskin 402, Brown 424, California 456, Chessall 481, Community 510, Community 513, Community 515, **Croatian 528**, **Cystinosis 533**, Disney 540, Eastcliff 551, Ebell 553, Federal 572, Fresno 597, Friedberger 598, Horn 668, Jewish 706, Klicka 722, **McConnell 779**, Orangewood 845, Pritchett 882, San Diego 934, **SEMA 973**, Tracy 1053
Colorado: Aspen 1123, Breckenridge 1134, Campbell 1139, Front 1200, Gunnison 1207, Mulford 1245, Seay 1280, Summit 1293, Vail 1302
Connecticut: **Bonfire 1336**, Cawasa 1348, CJR 1357, Connecticut 1366, Eastman 1382, Fusco 1394, Litchfield 1415, Main 1419, Orange 1439, Promising 1446, Weller 1482
Delaware: Gromet 1511, JBL 1515
District of Columbia: **American 1556**, **Armed 1579**, Community 1605
Florida: Amateis 1768, American 1770, Beall 1794, Cape Coral 1815, **Carter 1817**, Clint 1832, Community 1842, Community 1844, Community 1845, DeVoe 1861, Ft. 1892, Health 1908, Hein 1909, Judge 1933, Kelly 1935, LeGore 1948, **Scholarship 2052**, Selinger 2058, Spicer 2070, Step 2075, Sun 2078, Tweed 2091
Georgia: Arby's 2119, Choson 2141, **Coca 2148**, Sapelo 2231, Scheffler 2234
Hawaii: Servco 2320
Idaho: Simplot 2349, Smallwood 2350
Illinois: Anderson 2395, Andrew 2397, Brunswick 2443, Bunn 2446, Community 2496, Damato 2506, DeKalb 2514, Dodd 2519, **Elks 2540**, Everett 2553, **Foundry 2571**, Hugg 2628, Mellinger 2730, Murphy 2741, Niccum 2756, Oak Park 2761, Pilchard 2790, REO 2814, Short 2853, South Holland 2864, St. Clair 2869, Sterling 2872, Willo 2928, Wood 2935, Zweifel 2943
Indiana: Blue 2970, Community 2995, Community 2996, Community 3000, Community 3002, Community 3004, Community 3005, Dye 3022, Franklin 3037, Hemminger 3055, Hendricks 3057, Heritage 3059, Independent 3069, Indiana 3071, Madison 3106, Montgomery 3114, **National 3121**, Parke 3139, Putnam 3154, Rush 3167, Shiel 3180, Tipton 3201, Vermillion 3211, Warren 3216, Wayne 3217, Wells 3220, Whitley 3226, Winchester 3229
Iowa: Cedar Rapids 3255, Clarinda 3257, Community 3263, Conner 3266, Siouxland 3382
Kansas: Arnold 3414, Douglas 3433, Hansen 3451, Hoy 3458, Kansas 3472, Koch 3477, Loofbourrow 3480, Moore 3489, Stockard 3523, Topeka 3528, Trembly 3529, Wichita 3537
Kentucky: Appalachian 3545, Gardner 3571, Kincaid 3587
Louisiana: Taylor 3679, Zigler 3684
Maine: North Haven 3720, Searls 3735
Maryland: **American 3768**, Baltimore 3783, Community 3808, GEICO 3832, Memorial 3880, Mid-Shore 3887, **Pet 3910**, Thorn 3941
Massachusetts: East 4051, Edwards 4055, **Global 4085**, Hawks 4099, Hitchcock 4106, Hood 4111, Lowe 4151, Mihos 4175, Permanent 4216, Philips 4220, President 4230, Rockland 4245, **Rosenberg 4247**, Von 4309, Worcester 4323
Michigan: Battle Creek 4349, Canton 4372, Come 4389, Community 4391, Community 4393, Community 4395, Community 4398, Cunningham 4401, Dickinson 4408, Eddy 4413, Fremont 4431, **Gerber 4434**, Grand Haven 4444, Grand Rapids 4445, Huron 4477, Kalamazoo 4493, Knabusch

4503, Marquette 4524, McCurdy 4529, Michigan 4538, Midland 4542, Minton 4544, Nordman 4558, Roscommon 4592, Shiawassee 4605, St. Joseph 4624, Tiscornia 4639, Tuscola 4646, Whirlpool 4666, Winship 4672
Minnesota: CentraCare 4709, **Gallagher 4746**, Hull 4762, Jostens 4774, Rochester 4840, Rosen 4841, Saint Paul 4842, Steinke 4861, Two 4873, Whiteside 4889
Missouri: Clay 4958, Dunlop 4980, Edgar 4982, Kelly 5027, Lyons 5039, MFA 5050, Saint Louis 5082, Tilles 5115
Montana: Flathead 5146, Treacy 5180
Nebraska: Davis 5194, Federated 5202, Grand Island 5210, Hawks 5216, Lexington 5228, Phelps 5255, Simon 5261, York 5277
Nevada: Davidson 5284, Nevada 5295
New Hampshire: Lancaster 5336, Moving 5351, Somerville 5369, Wilson 5378
New Jersey: Berkowitz 5397, Harness 5466
New Mexico: Albuquerque 5610, Continental 5626, ENMR 5627, ENMR 5628, Farmers' 5629
New York: **AAAA 5662**, AEC 5669, **AFS-USA 5671**, **Buffalo 5802**, Buisch 5804, **Career 5816**, Cattaraugus 5826, Children's 5848, Children's 5849, Community 5881, Dyett 5942, Jachym 6107, Morgan 6226, New York 6275, Rose 6362, Sperry 6421, **Youth 6541**
North Carolina: **American 6550**, Beaver 6571, Blowing Rock 6575, Community 6613, Cooke 6617, Cumberland 6624, Ferree 6656, Foundation 6660, Livingston 6745, London 6748, Martin 6757, Smith 6868, Strickland 6882, Triangle 6899, Unruh 6909, West 6917, Winston-Salem 6923, Woman's 6926
North Dakota: Brown 6935, United 6949
Ohio: AK Steel 6964, Akron 6965, Anderson 6975, Carman 7024, Cincinnati 7037, Cline 7046, Community 7060, Community 7061, Community 7062, Edgerton 7097, Evers 7103, Fairbanks-Horix 7104, Findlay 7107, Fishel 7110, Gardner 7124, H.O.P.E. 7138, Herzberger 7148, Horvitz 7156, I Know 7166, Kessel 7186, Kindler 7192, Licking 7209, McCallay 7225, McConahay 7229, Miller 7249, Myers 7265, Salem 7333, Sandusky 7336, Scioto 7339, Sebring 7341, Shunk 7348, Simmons 7351, Slemp 7352, Springfield 7363, VanBuren 7404, Wagnalls 7408, Williams 7428, YSI 7446
Oklahoma: Donaghey 7464, Tulsa 7519, University 7522
Oregon: Campbell 7543, Collins 7552, Cottage 7559, Criswell 7561, Foss 7579, Oregon 7624, Strayer 7668, Turner 7671
Pennsylvania: **Alcoa 7694**, Angelo 7706, Armstrong 7710, Berks 7730, Davis 7808, EQT 7829, First 7841, Flegal 7846, Foundation 7852, Independent 7917, Ivy 7924, **Jewish 7929**, Keith 7934, Laudermilch 7948, Lehigh Valley 7953, McKaig 7975, Scranton 8094, Stork 8134, Thompson 8145, Varner 8162, Vastine 8164
Rhode Island: Rhode Island 8381, Tracy 8426
South Carolina: Coastal 8464, Hart 8480
Tennessee: Community 8577, Community 8579
Texas: **American 8682**, Coastal 8755, Cook 8770, Dallas 8784, Driver 8799, East 8804, Edwards 8809, EOG 8816, Fluor 8824, Hachar 8849, Ilgenfritz 8891, Lawler 8916, Lucas 8927, McMillan, 8948, Moody 8967, **National 8986**, Pipe 9021, **Promotional 9030**, San Angelo 9053, Show 9072, Singleton 9075, South 9085, Texas 9114, Texas 9130, Trimble 9138
Virginia: Alger 9285, Bell 9325, Bridgebuilder 9327, Community 9346, Community 9350, Goolsby-Gardner 9387, IHFR 9403, International 9406, Lee-Jackson 9418, Lincoln 9421, **National 9444**, **National 9453**, Strong 9516
Washington: Community 9600, Evergreen 9609, Grays 9624, Kawabe 9647, Kelly 9650, Kent 9652, Maxwell 9669, Renton 9705, Rural 9711, Seattle 9719, Walkling 9745, Washington 9746
West Virginia: Arthur's 9764, Community 9777, Hinton 9790, Kanawha 9794, Larsen 9795, McCormick

9801, Nicholas 9805, Parkersburg 9808, Price 9811, Whittaker 9828, Your 9831
Wisconsin: Associated 9841, Carnes 9859, Community 9866, Community 9867, Community 9869, Madison 9956, ManpowerGroup 9957, Sharp 10030, St. Croix 10043, Wisconsin 10074
Wyoming: Community 10099, Davis 10102, Hladky 10107, Likins 10111, Wyoming 10126

Science

Arizona: Arizona 158, Educational 190, **Research 233**, Seed 236, Sulphur 243
California: American 360, **Amgen 362**, **Association 386**, **Beckman 408**, California 446, Found 583, **Getty 614**, **Hertz 658**, Huntington 674, **Life 745**, **Marconi 769**, Project 883, San Diego 937, Science 968, Shasta 978, Siff 984, **Tech 1041**
Colorado: Bonfils 1130, Bonfils 1130, Colorado 1169, Mikkelson 1239, Reach 1265
Connecticut: Devon 1376, Saybrook 1455, Spirol 1462
Delaware: Common 1497
District of Columbia: **American 1542**, **American 1548**, **Development 1614**, **Hispanic 1644**, National 1683, **National 1695**, **Optical 1705**, **United 1743**, **World 1755**
Florida: American 1774, **Astronaut 1785**, Cape Coral 1815, Grossman 1897, Life 1950, Police 2023, Rayonier 2031, **Whitehall 2103**
Illinois: American 2383, Blazek 2427, Foundation 2567, **Hertz 2615**, International 2650, Kander 2666, Testamentary 2890, **Zonta 2942**
Indiana: Kuhner 3092, Society 3187, Wabash 3215
Kansas: White 3536
Kentucky: Appalachian 3545, Ogden 3607
Maine: Maine 3712
Maryland: American 3756, **American 3767**, Chesapeake 3800, **Discovery 3815**, **Foundation 3829**
Massachusetts: American 3967, Cabot 4003, Dugan 4045, **Giovanni 4083**, **Jurassic 4134**, Kelly 4136, Kim 4139, **Marine 4160**, Wheelwright 4315
Michigan: Baker 4342, Bay 4350, Heyl 4465, Kadant 4491, Meyers 4532, Petoskey 4577
Minnesota: Alworth 4685, Meyer 4796, Pick 4825, Redwood 4835
Missouri: Broida/Sigma-Aldrich 4944, Marsch 5043, Stowers 5109
Nebraska: Ellis 5200, Nebraska 5237
Nevada: Norris 5297
New Hampshire: Bogni 5309, Hubbard 5329, Plan 5361, Ramsaye 5364
New Jersey: Ammonius 5386, **Center 5416**, **Glushko 5454**, Honeywell 5472, **Knowles 5489**, Merck 5504, **Siemens 5566**, **Siemens 5566**, Wei 5593, **Wiley 5599**
New Mexico: Albuquerque 5610, **SUMMA 5655**
New York: American 5703, American 5703, Community 5878, **Delmas 5921**, **Dreyfus 5935**, Fermi 5981, Fund 6014, **Guggenheim 6049**, **IBM 6089**, **Lasker 6153**, **Metropolitan 6211**, **National 6241**, Open 6295, **Sloan 6404**, Society 6412
North Carolina: Horvat 6704, **Institut 6711**, Leverenz 6742, **S.R.C. 6847**, Taylor 6888
Ohio: Peoples 7297, Rapp 7312, Wilson 7431, Wimmer 7432
Oklahoma: Frontiers 7472
Pennsylvania: **Botstiber 7740**, Puckett 8067, Smithfield 8113, Society 8119
Texas: Conner 8767, NASA 8980, Pettinger 9015, Schull 9062, Texas 9114, Texas 9125
Utah: EnergySolutions 9199, Skaggs 9226, **Sundance 9227**
Virginia: Air 9284, **American 9306**, **National 9451**, National 9456, **National 9457**, **U.S. 9526**
Washington: Centrum 9583
Wisconsin: **Funeral 9903**, Kohler 9945, Shallow 10029

Science, formal/general education
California: **Amgen 362**, **Life 745**
District of Columbia: **Society 1731**

Indiana: Decatur 3013
Maryland: **Discovery 3815**, **Hughes 3846**
Ohio: Gandy 7121, Miami 7242
Oregon: Vernier 7674

Science, information services
California: California 446

Science, management/technical assistance
California: California 446

Science, public education
North Carolina: North 6800

Science, public policy
District of Columbia: **National 1691**

Science, research
Arizona: **Research 233**
California: **Beckman 408**, **Hertz 658**, **Leakey 739**, Pasarow 856
Colorado: Society 1285
District of Columbia: **Gateway 1636**
Florida: **Whitehall 2103**
Maine: Maine 3715
Maryland: Life 3865, Passano 3908
Massachusetts: **Lalor 4145**
Minnesota: Bakken 4697, **Lindbergh 4783**
New Jersey: **Johnson 5482**
New York: **Guggenheim 6050**, Human 6081, L'Oreal 6170
North Carolina: **Nickel 6792**
Ohio: **Taiho 7375**
Virginia: **U.S. 9526**

Secondary school/education
Arizona: Youth 259
California: **Association 387**, Chung 498
Colorado: Colorado 1169
Connecticut: Connecticut 1366
District of Columbia: Latino 1669
Florida: Reinhold 2034
Illinois: Murphy 2741, Williams 2927
Indiana: Catholic 2980, Frank 3035
Kansas: Fingersh 3442
Maine: Maine 3712
Massachusetts: Harvard 4096
Michigan: Michner 4541
Missouri: Fingersh 4992, Kelly 5027, **People 5072**
New Jersey: Peters 5539, Wight 5598
New York: **Brackett 5779**, **Columbus 5871**, Community 5878, Confort 5885, **Covenant 5895**, DonorsChoose.org 5931, Father 5977, Figliolia 5983, New 6261, New Visions 6263, Trumansburg 6464
North Carolina: Magdalena 6755
Ohio: Fitzgerald 7111, Licking 7209, McGinty 7235, Stark 7366
Oklahoma: Johnson 7485
Pennsylvania: Ellis 7823, **GBU 7866**
Texas: Communities 8759, Stark 9101
Virginia: **MATHCOUNTS 9431**
Wisconsin: Incourage 9925

Self-advocacy services, disability
Pennsylvania: Three 8146

SIDS (Sudden Infant Death Syndrome)
Maryland: **Sudden 3939**

SIDS (Sudden Infant Death Syndrome) research

Maryland: **Sudden 3939**

Single parents

California: **Aid 343**, Ardron 369, Cacique 434, Downey 545
Pennsylvania: Bartko 7723
Texas: James 8897

Skin disorders

California: **National 814**
District of Columbia: **Melanoma 1676**
Illinois: Dermatology 2516
Oregon: **National 7614**

Skin disorders research

California: **National 814**
District of Columbia: **Melanoma 1676, Melanoma 1677**
Illinois: **American 2365**, Dermatology 2516, **National 2750**
Indiana: Society 3188
Maryland: Nicolay 3903
New York: **American 5706, Skin 6401**
Oregon: **National 7614**
Virginia: **Mesothelioma 9435**

Social entrepreneurship

Delaware: Westly 1528
District of Columbia: **Hitachi 1645**
Virginia: **Ashoka: 9317**

Social sciences

California: China 492, **Getty 614**
Connecticut: Deering 1374
District of Columbia: **Council 1611, National 1681**
Florida: Everglades 1872
Idaho: Adams 2328
Illinois: **American 2371**, Francies 2572, **MacArthur 2704**
Maryland: **Epilepsy 3821**
Massachusetts: Cabot 4003, **SEVEN 4267**
Michigan: Fetzer 4418, Upjohn 4654
New Jersey: **Berrie 5399**, Horowitz 5473, **Wilson 5600**
New York: American 5691, **American 5692**, American 5705, **Guggenheim 6049, Guggenheim 6050, Open 6294, Social 6409**
North Carolina: **Institut 6711**
Ohio: Everhart 7102, Peoples 7297
Oregon: Buttrey 7541
Virginia: **Public 9488**
Washington: Centrum 9583, Holliday 9636

Social sciences, ethics

New Jersey: **Wilson 5600**

Social sciences, interdisciplinary studies

District of Columbia: **Institute 1650**
New York: **Social 6409**

Social sciences, public education

District of Columbia: **American 1552**

Social sciences, public policy

Ohio: Social 7360

Social sciences, research

Michigan: **Earhart 4411**

Pennsylvania: **American 7704**

Social work school/education

Connecticut: **Scudder 1458**
Georgia: Community 2150
Michigan: Community 4394
Minnesota: Christian 4714
Missouri: Kirschner 5030
New York: Community 5878, **Open 6294**

Space/aviation

California: **Hager 643**, Space 1007
Florida: **Astronaut 1785**, GMAA 1896
Illinois: **Organization 2769, Zonta 2942**
Michigan: Meyers 4532, Sigmund 4606
Minnesota: **Lindbergh 4783**
New Jersey: Honeywell 5472
New York: American 5703
Ohio: Cleveland 7045
Oregon: Smith 7660
Pennsylvania: Zaccheus 8218
Texas: **Conrad 8768**, Heinlein 8865
Virginia: Air 9284, **American 9292**, International 9406
Wisconsin: **EAA 9880**, Experimental 9887, Michelson 9969

Speech/hearing centers

Alabama: Andalusia 10
Maryland: **American 3768**
Missouri: **Sertoma, 5098**
Tennessee: Stuttering 8652

Spine disorders

California: SCI 967
Colorado: **Christian 1145**
District of Columbia: **Spina 1733**
Florida: Gwynn 1900
Illinois: **North 2758**
New York: United 6475
Vermont: **Brush 9237**
Wisconsin: Scoliosis 10025

Spine disorders research

California: Ameritec 361
Connecticut: **Walkabout 1479**
District of Columbia: Paralyzed 1706
Illinois: **Cervical 2468, North 2758**
New Jersey: **Reeve 5550**
Pennsylvania: Newman 8005

Spirituality

Maryland: Samet 3926
New York: **Nok 6281**

Students, sororities/fraternities

Florida: Delta 1859
Georgia: Alpha 2112, **Phi Mu 2222**
Illinois: Phi 2788
Indiana: Alpha 2948, **Alpha 2949**, Alpha 2951, **Alpha 2952, Foundation 3032, Phi 3146**, Phi 3147, Zeta 3230
Iowa: Kansas 3316
Maryland: **Alpha 3755**, Ivy 3851, **Phi 3911**
Massachusetts: Beta 3987, Scholarship 4261
Michigan: Bay 4350
Missouri: Alpha 4930, Community 4963, Educational 4983
Nebraska: Nebraska 5245
New York: Alpha 5683, Viele 6489, **Zeta 6542**
North Carolina: **Sigma 6860**
Ohio: Cleveland 7040, **Kappa 7182**, Phi Kappa 7302
Pennsylvania: Clareth 7769, **Delta 7810**, Ivy 7923
Rhode Island: Rhode Island 8381

Tennessee: **Alpha 8554**, Chi Omega 8571
Texas: **Delta 8790**
Virginia: **Sigma 9505**

Substance abuse, prevention

District of Columbia: **American 1562**
Wisconsin: Fricke 9899

Substance abuse, services

Arizona: Old 223
Michigan: Lutheran 4520
New York: Project 6335
Ohio: Community 7058

Substance abuse, treatment

Maryland: American 3763
Missouri: Queen 5077
New York: Carpenter 5819
Pennsylvania: Founder's 7855
Texas: Student 9102

Substance abusers

Virginia: Phoenix 9481

Supported living

Massachusetts: Balfour 3977
Pennsylvania: Three 8146, Young 8215

Surgery

Colorado: Rocky 1273
Illinois: American 2387
Massachusetts: King 4140
New Jersey: **American 5385**
New York: American 5698
Pennsylvania: **AO 7707, National 8001**
Tennessee: **National 8628**
Texas: Texas 9128
Utah: James 9211

Surgery research

California: **Aesthetic 342**
Illinois: Association 2408, **Plastic 2793, Thoracic 2892**
Massachusetts: **American 3964**
New Jersey: **American 5385**
Virginia: American 9311
Wisconsin: American 9835

Teacher school/education

Arizona: Education 189
Arkansas: Union 321
California: California 442, Coastal 504, Community 513, **Life 745**, Menlo 784, Orange 843, Schiffman 962
Colorado: Barr 1128, Ethridge 1192, Layton 1230
Connecticut: Dunning 1379, Scott 1457, **Scudder 1458**, Voya 1478, Weller 1482
Delaware: Delaware 1500
Florida: Community 1839
Georgia: Community 2150, Decatur 2161
Illinois: Breckinridge 2435, Gaffney 2578, Kander 2666, McClain 2717, Ross 2832
Indiana: Amburn 2953, Community 3004, Decatur 3013, Frees 3038, LaGrange 3093, Madison 3106, Public 3152, Williams 3228
Iowa: Dallas 3270, Schlagenbusch 3372, Siouxland 3382
Kansas: Robinson 3508
Kentucky: Hedrick 3576
Maine: Russell 3733
Maryland: Maryland 3871, McGeehin 3877, Sawyer 3927

Michigan: Fremont 4431, Kadant 4491, Kalamazoo 4492, Marquette 4524
Minnesota: Carson 4707, Hansen 4753, Target 4864
Missouri: **Alpha 4929**, Community 4963, Evans 4989, Hester 5016, Kansas 5023
Nebraska: Omaha 5251
New Jersey: Chatham 5419, Grande 5458, Honeywell 5472, Peters 5539, Princeton 5546
New York: Andrews 5713, East Williston 5948, Fund 6014, Schenectady 6382, Stempfle 6437, Trumansburg 6464
North Carolina: Owens 6808, Reich 6823
Ohio: Aikey 6962, Britton 7014, College 7050, Crain 7070, Dayton 7082, **Educational 7098**, Hartley 7143, Hunter 7163, Keller 7185, Licking 7209, Vandenbark 7405, White 7425
Oklahoma: Oklahoma 7501
Oregon: Vernier 7674
Pennsylvania: Brown 7749, Nicklies 8007, Psea 8066, Reitnauer 8074, Siebenthal 8103, Smith 8110, York 8213
Rhode Island: Ayer 8234, Pryde 8376, Wiggin 8436
Tennessee: Weems 8661
Texas: Anderson 8687, Brown 8725, Midland 8957, Permian 9013
Utah: McCarthey 9219
Virginia: National 9448, Strong 9516, Wiley 9548
Washington: Alliance 9557, Bradshaw 9577, King 9653, Martinez 9668, Royston 9710
Wisconsin: Chmielewski 9863, Kohl 9944, Shallow 10029

Telecommunications

District of Columbia: **Foundation 1629**
Illinois: Illinois 2647

Terminal illness, people with

Alabama: Alabama 3
Arizona: Make-A-Wish 215
California: Make-A-Wish 766, Taylor 1039, Theatre 1044
Florida: Children's 1824, **Julien 1934**
Hawaii: Make-A-Wish 2302
Maryland: Sisters 3933
Missouri: Ronald 5080
New York: Ronald 6360
Ohio: Hospice 7158
Virginia: Patient 9476

Theological school/education

Alabama: Dixon 31
Arizona: **Stott 241**
California: Cherith 479, Hinckley 663, Mang 768, Methodist 787, **Modglin 800**, Pasadena 855, Pedrozzi 858
Connecticut: Dunning 1379, **Scudder 1458**, **Society 1461**
District of Columbia: Albert 1536
Florida: Fellows 1875, Forbes 1888
Georgia: Baker 2123, Bantly 2125, Christian 2142, Davies 2160, Fund 2181
Hawaii: Atherton 2271
Illinois: Ross 2832, **Scholar 2842**, **Ullery 2901**, **Women 2933**
Indiana: Abell 2944, Keitzer 3083, Madison 3106, Moran 3118
Iowa: Barr 3242
Kentucky: Bible 3550, Mustard 3602
Massachusetts: Dugan 4045, New 4194
Michigan: Dancey 4403, Fremont 4431, Schaap 4601
Minnesota: Christian 4714, **Grannis-Martin 4751**
Missouri: Hester 5016, Kirschner 5030, McGlothlan 5048
Nebraska: Genesis 5206
New Jersey: **American 5383**, Dirshu 5434, McCready 5502, Snyder 5570
New York: Armenian 5717, Braverman 5781, **Chesed 5844**, **Covenant 5895**, Gillen 6025, **McCaddin 6199**

North Carolina: Davis 6628, Foundation 6661, Frasier 6666, Hoover 6702, Jones 6722, Komarek 6733, Robinson 6839, Scholarship 6853, Stoudenmire 6881, **United 6908**, **Youth 6933**
Ohio: Crain 7070, Fitzgerald 7111, Gonter 7128, Mentzer 7239, Munro 7259, Religion 7317, Salem 7334, Smith 7353, Van Horn 7401, Van Wert 7403
Oregon: McDowell 7601
Pennsylvania: **Association 7718**, Crawford 7796, Nicklies 8007, Puckett 8067, Thomas 8144, Vasset 8163, Walz 8174
Rhode Island: Manwiller 8334, Weaver 8432
South Carolina: Gallivan 8473, Kennedy 8489
Tennessee: **United 8657**
Texas: Common 8758, Gourley 8848, **Harding 8854**, Hayes 8859, Hurley 8888, Jones 8901, Oglesby 8995, Philadelphia 9018, TUA 9139, Wisian 9174, Woltman 9176
Virginia: Hampton 9391, Keesee 9413, Missionary 9438
Washington: Bohnett 9575, First 9612, JTM 9646, Vancouver 9740, Wittman 9756
West Virginia: Minor 9802
Wisconsin: Aslakson 9840, Gallmeier 9904, Jones 9936, La Crosse 9948, Rhodes 10008, Siebert 10033, Walker 10062

Theology

California: St. Shenouda 1015
Georgia: Baker 2123
Indiana: Kuhner 3092

Thrift shops

Oklahoma: **Feed 7468**

Transportation

Delaware: Thomson 1525
Illinois: BCMW 2415
Virginia: **NATSO 9460**, Specialized 9512

Tropical diseases research

Illinois: American 2393

United Ways and Federated Giving Programs

Tennessee: United 8658

Urban studies

Illinois: **Graham 2592**, **Skidmore 2857**
Maryland: **Enterprise 3819**
Minnesota: Higher 4758
New Jersey: Horowitz 5473
New York: **Schalkenbach 6379**

Urban/community development

District of Columbia: ULI 1740
Maryland: **Enterprise 3819**
New York: **Rockefeller 6359**, **Social 6409**

Utilities

Illinois: BCMW 2415
Maine: York 3749
Minnesota: Hastings 4755
Pennsylvania: Communtiy 7787

Veterinary medicine

California: Arques 372
Colorado: ACVIM 1110, **Morris 1243**
Illinois: Berner 2423, Bruton 2444, Ott 2773
Indiana: Schultz 3175, Williams 3228
Kentucky: **AAEP 3543**
Maine: Maine 3716

Maryland: **Pet 3910**
Michigan: Humane 4475
Minnesota: Alworth 4685
Missouri: Ebert 4981, Hester 5016
New Jersey: **Winn 5601**
New York: **North 6285**
North Carolina: **American 6551**
Ohio: Crain 7070, Van Wert 7403
Oregon: Banfield 7537
Pennsylvania: Trushel 8151
Wisconsin: Kern 9943, Mitchell 9972

Veterinary medicine, hospital

Wisconsin: Kern 9943

Visual arts

Alaska: CIRI 113, Rasmuson 132
Arizona: Community 182, Tucson-Pima 247
California: 18th 330, Anaheim 363, Angels 367, Arts 377, Black 414, California 445, Community 512, **Djerassi 541**, Dorland 544, Exploratorium 565, Fleishhacker 578, **Getty 614**, Headlands 649, LEF 741, **Montalvo 802**, Oaklandish, 837, Outpost 848, Performing 861, Pirkle 869, Riverside 913, Santa 957, Side 981, Southern 1006, Veneklasen 1080, Ward 1084
Colorado: Anderson 1118, Boulder 1132, Sharpe 1282
Connecticut: Real 1447, Steep 1468, **Weir 1481**
Delaware: Delaware 1499
District of Columbia: Arch 1578, **VSA 1745**
Florida: Atlantic 1787, Cintas 1828, **Cisneros 1829**, Community 1838, Florida 1879, Lloyd 1953, **National 1997**, Police 2023, **Samstag 2048**, School 2054
Georgia: Hambidge 2192
Illinois: Arnold 2407, Experimental 2555, **Ragdale 2806**, Rockford 2827, Society 2863, **Terra 2889**, Union 2904
Indiana: VSA 3214
Kansas: Koch 3476
Maine: Eastern 3695, Holocaust 3703
Maryland: Arts 3776, **Evergreen 3824**, Maryland 3872, Pyramid 3917, Salisbury 3925
Massachusetts: **American 3963**, Berkshire 3986, Boston 3991, **Fine 4068**, Museum 4184
Michigan: **Glen Arbor 4441**, Kalamazoo 4492, Lansing 4511
Minnesota: Anodyne 4692, Blacklock 4699, **Camargo 4706**, Central 4710, Five 4738, Highpoint 4759, Jerome 4771, Prairie 4828, Southeastern 4854, VSA 4882
Nebraska: Bemis 5186
New Hampshire: La Napoule 5333, **MacDowell 5341**, **Money 5347**, Plan 5361
New Jersey: Peters 5539
New Mexico: **A Room 5609**, **Lannan 5635**, **Southwestern 5652**
New York: Albee 5677, Alliance 5682, **American 5688**, Art 5719, Art 5720, Art 5721, ArtCouncil 5723, Artists 5725, Arts 5727, Arts 5728, **Asian 5734**, **Astraea 5736**, **Bogliasco 5772**, Bronx 5793, Bronx 5794, Center 5834, chashama 5841, **College 5866**, **Corning 5886**, **Corporation 5888**, Council 5894, **Creative 5898**, **Cuban 5902**, **Dedalus 5919**, Dieu 5925, **Elizabeth 5957**, Eyebeam 5970, **Foundation 5995**, Franklin 6008, Genesee 6021, **Gottlieb 6041**, **Graves 6044**, Hadar 6054, **Harvestworks 6058**, Henry 6067, **Institute 6095**, Kuhlman 6148, Lower 6173, **Mann 6187**, McCall 6200, Merchant 6209, **MetLife 6210**, Metropolitan 6211, **Millay 6216**, Mitchell 6218, **Netherland-America 6258**, **Pollock 6318**, Queens 6341, **Rockefeller 6359**, **Skowhegan 6402**, Smack 6405, Stone 6438, **Tiffany 6455**, Topaz 6458, Triangle 6462, Visual 6492, **Visual 6493**
North Carolina: Arts 6559, Artspace 6560, Asheville 6561, Center 6595, United 6906

Ohio: Cleveland 7041, Columbus 7052, Culture 7073, Dayton 7082, Delaware 7086, Peoples 7297, Three 7380, Wexner 7422
Oregon: Ford 7578, Neskowin 7616, Portland 7632
Pennsylvania: Bader 7720, Center 7762, Fabric 7835, Independence 7916, Leeway 7951, Mattress 7973, Print 8063
Rhode Island: Coles 8270
South Carolina: Cultural 8469
South Dakota: **First 8530**
Texas: **Chinati 8748**, Culture 8778, Diverseworks 8796, **Museum 8975**
Virginia: Tidewater 9523
Washington: 911 9554, Allied 9558, Artist 9564, Behnke 9568, McMillen 9673, Museum 9678, **Native 9680**
West Virginia: Aurora 9765
Wyoming: **Ucross 10123**

Visual arts, architecture
California: Friends 601, Humboldt 671, **Montalvo 802, United 1072**
Connecticut: **Kim 1410**
District of Columbia: American 1540, **American 1561, Landscape 1668**
Florida: Cintas 1828
Illinois: **Graham 2592**, Hyatt 2631, **Skidmore 2857**
Maryland: **Enterprise 3819**
Massachusetts: Lyceum 4154, Rotch 4249
Minnesota: Alworth 4685
Missouri: American 4931
New Hampshire: **MacDowell 5341**
New York: **American 5692, Asian 5734, Bogliasco 5772**, Brooklyn 5796, Center 5831, **Delmas 5921, Institute 6095, Royal 6364, Soanes 6408**, Van Alen 6484, Westchester 6515, **Worldstudio 6535**
Ohio: Van Wert 7403
Pennsylvania: Hughes 7913, Marshall 7969
Rhode Island: Coles 8270
Texas: Bartholomew 8703, **Western 9164**
Virginia: Foundation 9383
West Virginia: Aurora 9765

Visual arts, art conservation
California: **Getty 614**
New York: **Metropolitan 6211**
West Virginia: Aurora 9765

Visual arts, ceramic arts
California: **Djerassi 541**
Colorado: Carbondale 1140, National 1247
Maine: Watershed 3745
Maryland: Metropolitan 3882
Massachusetts: Jackson 4128, Nantucket 4187
Michigan: **Glen Arbor 4441**
Minnesota: **Groot 4752**, Northern 4814
Missouri: Craft 4970
Montana: Bray 5134, Clay 5137
New Jersey: Peters 5539
New York: **Tiffany 6455**, UrbanGlass 6481
North Carolina: McColl 6761
Pennsylvania: Clay 7772
Texas: **Houston 8877**
Washington: **Native 9680**

Visual arts, design
California: **Djerassi 541**, Dorland 544, **United 1072**
District of Columbia: American 1570
Florida: Lloyd 1953
Illinois: Fashion 2558, **Graham 2592, Skidmore 2857**
Kansas: Koch 3476
Maryland: Metropolitan 3882
Massachusetts: Jackson 4128
Michigan: Fremont 4431
New Hampshire: La Napoule 5333
New Jersey: Costume 5428

New York: **CFDA 5838**, Donghia 5930, Fashion 5976, **Gottlieb 6041**, Home 6077, **Pollock 6318, Royal 6364, Soanes 6408, Tiffany 6455, Worldstudio 6535**
Pennsylvania: Fabric 7835
Rhode Island: Rhode Island 8381, Yaeger 8443
Virginia: Tidewater 9523
Washington: Blue 9573

Visual arts, drawing
California: **Djerassi 541**
District of Columbia: **National 1695**
Massachusetts: **Xeric 4326**
New Mexico: Border 5615
New York: American 5687
Ohio: **Murray 7262**
Texas: Culture 8778

Visual arts, painting
California: **Djerassi 541**
Illinois: Society 2863, **Terra 2889**
Kansas: Koch 3476
Maine: Acadia 3685
Maryland: Metropolitan 3882
Massachusetts: Jackson 4128, Nantucket 4187
Minnesota: Cornucopia 4721
New Jersey: **Foundation 5449**
New Mexico: Border 5615
New York: Golden 6036, **Gottlieb 6041**, Henry 6067, Lower 6173, Mitchell 6218, **Pollock 6318**, Saltonstall 6371
North Carolina: McColl 6761, Posey 6822
Ohio: **Murray 7262**
Texas: Culture 8778
Vermont: **Vermont 9271**
Washington: Behnke 9568

Visual arts, photography
California: Cal 437, Creative 526, **Djerassi 541**, San Francisco 944
Connecticut: Tierney 1472
District of Columbia: **National 1692**
Illinois: Society 2863
Louisiana: Louisiana 3665
Maryland: Metropolitan 3882
Massachusetts: Jackson 4128, Nantucket 4187
Michigan: **Glen Arbor 4441**
Minnesota: **Camargo 4706**
New Jersey: Foundation 5450, **Puffin 5549**, Segal 5562
New York: **Aperture 5716**, Center 5834, International 6097, **Light 6162**, Lower 6173, Magnum 6183, **Open 6294**, Professional 6331, Saltonstall 6371, **Smith 6406, Visual 6493**
North Carolina: McColl 6761
Ohio: Dayton 7082
Pennsylvania: Pittsburgh 8047
Rhode Island: Coles 8270
Texas: Culture 8778
Vermont: **Vermont 9271**
Washington: Blue 9573, Centrum 9583
Wisconsin: Madison 9955

Visual arts, sculpture
California: **Djerassi 541**
Illinois: Society 2863
Kansas: Koch 3476
Maryland: Baltimore 3782, Metropolitan 3882
Massachusetts: Jackson 4128
Michigan: **Glen Arbor 4441**
Minnesota: Cornucopia 4721, Franconia 4743, **Groot 4752**, New York 4812
New York: Albee 5677, American 5687, **Elizabeth 5957, Gottlieb 6041**, Henry 6067, Lower 6173, Mitchell 6218, **National 6254, Pollock 6318, Sculpture 6390**, SculptureCenter 6391, Socrates 6414, **Tiffany 6455**

North Carolina: McColl 6761, Posey 6822
Ohio: **Murray 7262**
Pennsylvania: Leeway 7951
Rhode Island: Coles 8270
Texas: Culture 8778
Vermont: **Carving 9238, Vermont 9271**
Washington: Centrum 9583

Vocational education
Alaska: Arctic 104, CIRI 113, Doyon 115, Huna 118, Kuskokwim 123
Arizona: Spencer 238
California: Builder's 427, Busch 431, Community 512, Horizons 667, Hunter 672, Jewish 707, Orange 843, Price 880, **QUALCOMM 889**, Sacramento 926, San Diego 934, Santa Barbara 955, **Sempra 974**
Connecticut: Rockville 1450, Tomasso 1473, Weller 1482
Delaware: Gordy 1510, Thomson 1525
District of Columbia: **International 1654**
Florida: Rawls 2029
Georgia: Brightwell 2131, Student 2245
Idaho: IDACORP 2334, Simplot 2349
Illinois: Brunswick 2443, Community 2494, **Engine 2546**, Foundation 2567, Hardin 2599, Lower 2698, Meade 2727, Pullman 2804, **Sigma 2855**
Indiana: Armstrong 2958, Community 2993, Moorman 3117, Portland 3151, Seymour 3179
Iowa: Anderson 3239, Bishop 3246, Guest 3292, Lee 3324, Matheson 3332
Kansas: Baker 3417, Hansen 3451, Jellison 3462, Jones 3464, Kleppe 3474, Moore 3489, Pape 3498, Parsons 3499, Perdue 3502, Robinson 3508, Schmidt 3512
Kentucky: Big 3551, Community 3559
Louisiana: Entergy 3651
Maryland: **Immune 3848**
Massachusetts: Taylor 4283
Michigan: Community 4391, Community 4393, Guardian 4452, Juhl 4488, Midland 4542, Speerstra 4621, Universal 4653
Minnesota: Arvig 4695, Blandin 4700, **Francis 4742**, Minnesota 4804, Redwood 4835, Roberg 4839
Mississippi: Mississippi 4914
Missouri: Brey 4943, Clayton 4959, Community 4963, Lord 5037, Reynolds 5079, Trotter 5117
Montana: Clarkson 5136, Hurst 5159
Nebraska: Oregon 5252
New Hampshire: Ladies 5334, Yarnold 5379
New Jersey: Astle 5390, Camden 5410, Glen 5453
New Mexico: Farmers' 5629, Viles 5657
New York: Community 5878, Fountain 6004, Hawley 6062, Snayberger 6407, Statler 6432, Stony 6440, **Wine 6523**
North Carolina: Bass 6568, **Karyae 6726**, Nucor 6803, Rouch 6842
North Dakota: Martell 6943, North Dakota 6946
Ohio: Cleveland 7044, Dayton 7082, Dunton 7093, **Eagles 7095**, Ford 7113, Founders 7116, Hawkes 7145, Higgins 7149, Kibble 7189, Licking 7209, Mauger 7223, McComb 7228, Miller 7249, New Orphan 7268, Remmele 7318, Stark 7366, Uschmann 7400, Wood 7437
Oklahoma: Fields 7469, Tulsa 7519
Oregon: Daly 7565, Hamilton 7585, Oapa 7621, Oregon 7624
Pennsylvania: AAA 7688, Abernathy 7689, Abrams 7691, Brenneman 7744, **Connelly 7788**, Goslee 7877, Irvin 7921, McKee 7976, Pennsylvania 8028, Pickle 8043, Postles 8054, Postles 8055, Rhoads 8075, Somerville 8121
Rhode Island: Black 8244, Kingsbury 8322, Maybury 8339, Pape 8363, Rhode Island 8381, Shifler 8398
South Carolina: Kershaw 8490
South Dakota: Green 8532, Sioux Falls 8538
Tennessee: Boys 8562, Goodlark 8594, Grace 8595
Texas: Bellamy 8709, Chambers 8743, Lanham 8914, Live 8920, Luce 8928, Millar 8958, Peyton 9016, Trimble 9138, TUA 9139, Wine 9170

Vermont: Nordic 9255
Virginia: Foundation 9383, Sanford 9497, Womack 9552
Washington: Northwest 9684
West Virginia: Burnside 9769, Harries 9789, Kanawha 9794, Starcher 9816
Wisconsin: Brown 9853, Casper 9860, Frautschy 9897, Fromm 9901, Green Bay 9910, Shopko 10032
Wyoming: Bryan 10095, Construction 10100

Vocational education, post-secondary

Alabama: Alabama 4, Boyd 18
Alaska: **Ahtna 96**, Bering 105, Chugach 111, Koniag 122, McCurdy 124, MTNT 126, UIC 145
Arizona: 100 150, Knapp 208, Torres 245
Arkansas: Endeavor 278
California: 10,000 329, 826 331, Buckley 425, California 454, **Cancer 462**, Chrysopolae 497, Community 513, Darnell 536, Foster 582, Healdsburg 650, Humboldt 671, Jewish 708, Kerber 719, **Lambda 734**, **Little 748**, Locke 751, Machado 764, Methodist 787, Pedrozzi 858, **Red 903**, San Francisco 947, Santa 956, Sulprizio 1031, Sun-Pacific 1033, Variety 1078, Ventura 1081, West 1090, Yosemite 1106
Colorado: Assistance 1124, Children's 1144, Colorado Springs 1166, I Have 1218, Renfrow 1267, Ronald 1274
Connecticut: Albero 1316, Ash 1325, Chapman 1351, Connecticut 1365, Manchester 1420
Delaware: Delaware 1500, Vocational 1527
District of Columbia: Capital 1598, **International 1659**
Florida: Bennett 1797, **Carter 1817**, Community 1839, Community 1844, Community 1848, Flordia Keys 1883, Florida 1884, Fort 1890, Ft. 1892, Gulf 1898, Hurst 1925, KML 1941, McGinty 1971, Moore 1982, Naples 1993, Reed 2032, Wiggins 2104
Georgia: Adair 2111, Anderson 2118, Decatur 2161, DeSana 2164, Sapelo 2231
Hawaii: Geist 2285, Mink 2304
Illinois: Aon 2402, Arbor 2405, Barnard 2412, Biederstedt 2425, Brown 2440, Community 2496, East 2530, Footprints 2566, Hartke 2602, Hohner 2621, Illinois 2640, Kooi 2678, **National 2749**, **Nuts, 2760**, Palos 2778, Rainey 2807, Robinson 2826, Royal 2837, True 2898, Walters 2917, Western 2924, Western 2925
Indiana: Benton 2966, Community 2994, Community 2997, Community 2998, Greene 3045, Noble 3127, Owen 3136, Rush 3167, Salin 3170, Zimmer 3231
Iowa: Community 3263, Dallas 3270, Father 3280, Gidley 3285, Iowa 3304, Jay 3312, Lindhart 3327, Murray 3342
Kansas: Coffman 3427, Morgan 3490, Peterson 3503, Pitts 3505, Stockard 3523, Terry 3525, Toothaker 3527, Western 3535
Kentucky: Disabled 3562, Kentucky 3584, Wells 3636
Louisiana: 100 3638
Maine: Oxford 3723, Robinson 3731
Maryland: Airmen 3752, Community 3807, Government 3838, Job 3854, Maryland 3869, Nexion 3902
Massachusetts: Andona 3970, Berkshire 3983, Mack 4156, Middlesex 4174, Murphy 4182, National 4189, Thomas 4288
Michigan: Barry 4347, Community 4399, Fredericksen 4430, Junior 4490, Kalamazoo 4493, Paulsen 4575, Petoskey 4577, Pokagon 4580, Shelby 4604
Minnesota: Crosslake 4724, Duluth 4729, Koran 4776, Moon 4810, Page 4820, **Scholarship 4845**
Mississippi: Community 4902
Missouri: Burkhalter 4947, ESCO 4988, Friedman 4996, Lyons 5039, Minnesouri 5055, NASB 5061, Schwartze 5093, Schwartze 5094, Schwartze 5095, Schwartze 5096
Montana: Bair 5130, Beartooth 5131, District 5142, Fergus 5145, Gebhardt 5148, Hurst 5159, Rolfson 5170, Suden 5175, Yellowstone 5183

Nebraska: All 5185, Emerson 5201, Kearney 5223, Nebraska 5238, Novak 5248, Wabash 5268, Walther 5270, Weller 5271
Nevada: Berner 5279, Doyle 5287, Western 5304
New Hampshire: New Hampshire 5353, Plan 5361, White 5377
New Jersey: BLSJ 5402, Hemophilia 5468, New Jersey 5517, O'Brien's 5530, O'Leary 5531, Peterson 5540, Woodbridge 5604
New Mexico: Finis 5630, Taos 5656
New York: Ashley 5732, Blosser 5769, Guenther 6048, Howard 6078, Jewish 6118, Long 6168, Monroe 6223, Stoner 6439, Westchester 6514
North Carolina: Cox 6620, Kent 6730, Lundy 6752, Nichols 6791, Peckitt 6813, Polk 6821, Search 6855, Sirrine 6862, Tahquette 6884, Watterson 6915
Ohio: American 6972, Bouchard 7007, Campbell 7022, Chillicothe 7034, Community 7061, Elks 7099, Fifty 7106, Hamilton 7139, Hauss 7144, Lesher 7206, McDonald 7231, McDonald 7232, Mercer 7240, Mercy 7241, Ohio 7278, Ohio 7279, Snow 7359, Taylor 7376, Trachsel 7387, Troy 7388, Wood 7437
Oklahoma: Carrier 7455, Masonic 7492, Peyton 7506, Steward-Newkirk 7516
Oregon: Benton 7531, Clemens 7549, Colvin 7553, Cooper 7557, Depriest 7571, Steinbach 7666, Von der Ahe 7675, West 7680
Pennsylvania: Community 7782, Founder's 7855, Golden 7872, Lancaster 7941, McNeil 7979, Pennsylvania 8029, Scholarship 8089, Shaulis 8097, Van Wynen 8160, Washington 8176, Wayne 8178
Rhode Island: Snyder 8411, Tracy 8426, Tryon 8427, Wiles 8437, Wylie 8442
Tennessee: Community 8578, Cracker 8581, Splawn 8648, Woodbury 8665
Texas: Associated 8692, Childress 8747, Clifford 8754, Eady 8802, East 8803, Hill 8866, Hill 8867, Hispanic 8871, Ingram 8893, Lake 8913, Lee 8917, Lubbock 8926, **Mensa 8952**, Montgomery 8966, Passport 9005, Pedernales 9008, Permian 9013, Powdermaker 9026, Reed 9033, San Antonio 9055, Vinsant 9150, Watson 9158, Wood 9179, Young 9187
Utah: American 9191, Granite 9201, Luttrell 9217
Vermont: Windham 9273
Virginia: ACCESS 9278, Community 9349, Cooke 9353, **Marine 9430**, **Military 9436**, National 9454, **National 9455**, **Plumbing 9483**, Strasburg 9515, **VAW/VRC 9538**
Washington: AGC 9555, Arise 9561, Community 9599, Gius 9623, KLQ 9655, Lauzier 9658, Pride 9702, Renton 9705, Seattle 9719, **Vista 9742**, Walkling 9745
West Virginia: Feoppel 9785, Larsen 9795, Parkersburg 9808
Wisconsin: Calumet 9856, Chetek 9862, Green Bay 9911, Oshkosh 9988, Racine 10001, Rotary 10014, Wisconsin 10077, Wisconsin 10081, Wisconsin 10083
Wyoming: Curtis 10101, Whitney 10124

Vocational school, secondary

Massachusetts: Home 4110

Voluntarism promotion

District of Columbia: Junior 1664
Minnesota: Philanthrofund 4824
New Jersey: Chatham 5419
New York: **Do 5928**

Web-based media

Illinois: Allstate 2363
Oregon: Dargan 7567

Welfare policy/reform

Virginia: **Ashoka: 9317**

Women

Alabama: Meharg 61, Miss 63, Owens 67, Southeastern 81, WEDC 90
Arizona: LaForce 209
Arkansas: Keltner 287
California: **Adobe 338**, **Aid 343**, Allgemeiner 346, Ardron 369, Association 388, Baskin 402, Battered 403, **Borg 418**, Breast 422, Chicana 482, Conquistador 522, Marguerite 770, Military 791, Modesto 799, National 821, Rader 892, Santa Barbara 955, Shasta 978, Stanislaus 1017, Wickham 1094, **Women 1098**
Colorado: Advocate 1112, Ethridge 1192, **Foundation 1199**
Connecticut: Connecticut 1366, Larrabee 1413, Miss 1425, Peirce 1441, Widows 1485, Woman's 1488
Delaware: Fresh 1509, Thomson 1525
District of Columbia: **AARP 1529**, **American 1542**, **American 1547**, **American 1551**, Community 1605, **International 1660**, **Women 1753**, Women's 1754, **YWCA 1758**
Florida: Aqua 1778
Georgia: Alpha 2112, **Phi Mu 2222**, Student 2245, Widows 2265
Hawaii: Kaiulani 2296, Mink 2304, Pope 2315
Illinois: Dawson 2511, Ende 2544, **Foundation 2570**, Hansen 2598, Illinois 2642, Joint 2660, Ladies 2681, Mutual 2742, Nesbitt 2754, Royal 2837, Scherer 2840, **Women 2933**, Women's 2934, **Zonta 2942**
Indiana: Kosciusko 3091
Iowa: **P.E.O. 3349**, **P.E.O. 3350**, **P.E.O. 3351**, **P.E.O. 3352**
Kansas: Pi 3504, Schmidt 3512, Tenholder 3524
Kentucky: Community 3559, Morrill 3600, Rhoads 3619, Smith 3625
Maryland: Crossway 3811, Steeplechase 3937, Warfield 3951
Massachusetts: Association 3974, Boston 3993, **Devens 4039**, Farmer 4063, Farnam 4064, Howland 4120, Mack 4156, Miss 4178, Museum 4184, Pierce 4223, Pratt 4229, **R.O.S.E. 4236**, Salem 4253, Swan 4280
Michigan: Ann Arbor 4338, Bemis 4356, Morrill 4546
Minnesota: Blacklock 4699, MacPherson 4787
Mississippi: Hazard 4911
Missouri: **Alpha 4929**, Kauffman 5026, Missouri 5056, Nichols 5063, **Pi 5073**, Queen 5077
Nevada: Nevada 5296
New Hampshire: Dodge 5318, **Money 5347**, Wilson 5378
New Jersey: **ARCH 5389**, **Newcombe 5526**, Several 5563, **Wilson 5600**
New Mexico: **School 5650**, Viles 5657
New York: **AAAA 5662**, **Astraea 5736**, **Avon 5745**, Babylon 5746, **BMI 5771**, Community 5878, **ESA 5963**, Girls 6028, L'Oreal 6170, MADRE, 6182, McCormick 6202, New York 6277, North 6284, Post 6321, Sakhi 6370, Society 6411, Tinker 6457, **V-Day 6487**, **Women's 6528**
North Carolina: **S.R.C. 6847**, Stewart 6879, Woman's 6926
Ohio: College 7049, Drake 7090, Gay 7125, Powell 7307, Rotterman 7329, Sheadle 7345, Three 7380, Van Wert 7403
Oregon: Alexandria 7530, Fansler 7576, McKenzie 7603, **Soapstone 7662**
Pennsylvania: American 7702, Biddle 7733, Communtiy 7787, Dotson 7815, Ellis 7823, England 7826, Female 7839, Fleisher 7848, Reading 8071, Rosenfeld 8082, Sleeper 8108, Soren 8122, Webber 8179, Webber 8180, Wettrick 8190, Young 8215
Rhode Island: Davenport 8283, Kinsley 8323, Masonic 8336, Providence 8375, Wiggin 8436
South Carolina: Cornelius 8467
Tennessee: **Alpha 8554**, Chi Omega 8571, JSA 8611

Texas: **Blackburn 8714**, James 8897, Maguire 8932, **Mary 8937**, Phillips 9019, Young 9187
Virgin Islands: Rutnik 9276
Virginia: **Ashoka: 9317**, Buchly 9330, Cherry 9338, Duerr 9365, International 9406, National 9458
Washington: Arise 9561, Artist 9564, Community 9600, Elvins 9607, Royston 9710, Washington 9750, Women 9757
Wisconsin: Green Bay 9910, Jansen 9929, Lauterbach 9950, Wisconsin 10081, Women's 10086, Women's 10087

Women's studies

New Hampshire: **Money 5347**
New Jersey: **Wilson 5600**

Women, centers/services

California: Interface 687
Colorado: Gathering 1203
Minnesota: **Pro 4829**
Pennsylvania: Young 8215

YM/YWCAs & YM/YWHAs

Colorado: YMCA 1310
District of Columbia: **YWCA 1758**
Illinois: **National 2743**
Pennsylvania: YMCA 8210
Rhode Island: Boghossian 8247

Young adults

California: Catalyst 466, Liberty 744
Colorado: Young 1311
District of Columbia: **American 1538**, **Aspen 1583**
Hawaii: Make-A-Wish 2302
Illinois: Uhlich 2900, Youth 2938
Maryland: Ulman 3947
Michigan: Community 4390
New Jersey: Prudential 5547
New York: **National 6246**, New York 6272, **UJA 6470**
Virginia: **Ashoka: 9317**

Young adults, female

Arizona: **Dickey 184**
California: San Francisco 946
Georgia: **American 2116**
Kansas: Hunter 3459
Massachusetts: Peabody 4213
Michigan: Junior 4490
Missouri: **Pi 5073**
New York: **Asia 5733**, **Avon 5745**, **Daughters 5915**, Professional 6331

Ohio: Summerville 7374, Ursuline 7399
Pennsylvania: Bartko 7723, Thomas 8144
Virginia: Orphan 9474
Wisconsin: Women's 10085

Young adults, male

Arizona: **Dickey 184**
Georgia: **American 2116**
Missouri: **Demolay 4974**, McElroy 5047
Nebraska: Bryan 5188
New York: **Asia 5733**
North Carolina: Bowsher 6577
Ohio: Kiwanis 7197, McFarlin 7234
Pennsylvania: McKee 7976, Thomas 8144
South Carolina: Father-To-Father 8471, Kappa 8487
Texas: Alpha 8674, Chambers 8743
Wisconsin: Jansen 9929

Youth

California: Catalyst 466, Nestle 825, San Diego 928, San Diego 939, Shelby 979, Variety 1078
Colorado: Community 1173, Minority 1240, Young 1311
Connecticut: CJR 1357
District of Columbia: Junior 1664
Florida: Washington 2099
Georgia: Cherokee 2138
Hawaii: Learning 2300
Illinois: **Ronald 2831**, Uhlich 2900
Indiana: Hammond 3049, **Zoltani 3232**
Michigan: Old 4568, Rochester 4590
Minnesota: Southwest 4857
Missouri: North 5065
New York: **National 6246**, Ronald 6360, **United 6476**
North Carolina: Telamon 6890
Ohio: Cleveland 7042
Tennessee: Boys 8562
Wisconsin: Kohl's 9946
Wyoming: Perkins 10117

Youth development

California: Avery 396, **Higgins 661**, **World 1102**
District of Columbia: Washington 1748, **Youth 1757**
Illinois: Chicago 2474
Maryland: **Casey 3794**, **Discovery 3815**, **International 3849**
Massachusetts: **Rosenberg 4247**
Missouri: **Build 4946**
Nebraska: Jewish 5221
New Jersey: Chatham 5419
New York: **Do 5928**, Glover 6034, Wegmans 6507
North Carolina: Cherokee 6598
Ohio: Parenthesis 7289

Pennsylvania: Ameche 7700
Virginia: **Ashoka: 9317**, **Cooke 9352**
Wisconsin: Madison 9956

Youth development, adult & child programs

New York: Scotts 6389
Pennsylvania: EQT 7829

Youth development, agriculture

Maine: Maine 3712

Youth development, business

New York: Wegmans 6507

Youth development, centers/clubs

Missouri: **Build 4946**

Youth development, community service clubs

Missouri: **Build 4946**
Nebraska: Jewish 5221
North Carolina: 100 6543
Wisconsin: Kohl's 9946

Youth development, ethics

District of Columbia: Best 1592

Youth development, services

New York: Children's 5849

Youth development, volunteer services

Wisconsin: Kohl's 9946

Youth, pregnancy prevention

Minnesota: **Pro 4829**

Youth, services

California: Interface 687, Promises 884
Montana: Student 5174
New Jersey: Polonsky 5542, Prudential 5547
New York: Catholic 5824
Tennessee: Dyersburg-Dyer 8585

GRANTMAKER NAME INDEX

This alphabetical index lists all grantmakers with full entries in this volume, as well as those that appeared in the 22nd edition, but no longer qualify and are listed in the Appendix. Numbers following the grantmaker names refer to sequence numbers of entries in the Descriptive Directory section. The letter "A" following a grantmaker name refers to the Appendix.

10,000 Degrees, CA, 329
100 Black Men of America, Greater Charlotte Chapter, Inc., NC, 6543
100 Black Men of America, Inc., GA, 2110
100 Black Men of Greater Charlotte, Inc., NC, see 6543
100 Black Men of Metropolitan Baton Rouge, Ltd., LA, 3638
100 Club of Arizona, The, AZ, 150
100% for Kids, Utah Credit Union Education Foundation, UT, 9190
18th Street Arts Complex, CA, 330

2 Life 18 Foundation, Inc., FL, 1759
2 Strings Connection, Inc., GA, see 2122
2001 Brain Injury Support Fund, Inc., NH, see 5332

3-H Farms Charitable Foundation, MN, 4678

4 C's Foundation, TN, see 8549
4-C's Foundation, TN, 8549
47 Palmer, Inc., MA, 3955

826 Valencia, CA, 331

911 Media Arts Center, WA, 9554
9Health Fair, CO, see 1250

A & A Farone Foundation, DC, see 1536
A & B Family Foundation, IL, 2352
A Charitable Foundation, NV, 5278
A Child Waits Foundation, NY, 5661
A Gift for Teaching, Inc., FL, 1760
A Gift from Ben, Inc., VA, 9277
A Good Day Foundation, OH, 6953
A Place For Us - Atlantic County Womens Center, NJ, 5380
A Room of Her Own Foundation, NM, 5609
A-Peeling Charitable Foundation, Inc., KY, A
A-T Children's Project, FL, see 1786
A-T Medical Research Foundation, CA, 391
A.F.R., Inc., KY, see 3544
A.I.M. Center, Inc., The, TN, 8550
A.M.I.A., CA, see 389
A.P.F., DC, see 1565
A.V.M.F., CO, see 1123
A.W.P.C.A., AZ, see 165
AAA Scholarship Fund of AAA East Penn, PA, 7688
AAA Scholarship Fund of the Lehigh Valley Motor Club, PA, see 7688
AAA, MD, see 3756
AAAA Foundation, Inc., NY, 5662
AAAE Foundation, VA, see 9292
AAAI, CA, see 386
AAAS, DC, see 1542
AACC, DC, see 1541
AACR, PA, see 7701

AAEP Foundation, Inc., KY, 3543
AAFP Foundation, KS, see 3413
AAG, DC, see 1585
AAM, DC, see 1545
AAMN Foundation, AL, 1
Aaron Memorial Trust Scholarship Fund, Mary M., CA, 332
AARP Foundation, DC, 1529
AASA, VA, see 9293
AASLD, VA, see 9291
AAST Scholarship Foundation, FL, 1761
Abbott Foundation, Clara, The, IL, 2353
Abbott Memorial Foundation, Frances H., MI, 4331
Abbott Northwestern Hospital Foundation, MN, 4679
Abbott Patient Assistance Foundation, The, IL, see 2354
Abbott, Jr. Trust, James N., MA, 3956
Abbvie Patient Assistance Foundation, The, IL, 2354
ABCDE Fund, PA, see 7689
Abell Charitable Trust, Joseph and Luella, The, IN, 2944
Abell Education Trust, Jennie G. and Pearl, KS, 3411
Aber Scholarship Fund, Earnest F. & Edna P., WI, 9832
Abernathy Black Community Development & Educational Fund, PA, 7689
Abernathy Port Charlotte Kiwanis Foundation Inc., Inc., FL, 1762
ABG Ministries, TX, 8666
Abilities Rehabilitation Center Foundation, Inc., FL, 1763
Abington Memorial Hospital, PA, 7690
Able Trust, The, FL, see 1881
Abrams Foundation, Samuel L., PA, 7691
Abramson Memorial Foundation, Frederick B., The, DC, 1530
Academic Alliance Foundation for AIDS Care and Prevention in Africa, DC, see 1531
Academic Assistance Fund, CA, 333
Academic Distinction Fund, LA, 3639
Academy Foundation, CA, 334
Academy of American Poets, Inc., NY, 5663
Academy of Nutrition & Dietetics, The, IL, 2355
Academy of Television Arts and Sciences Foundation, CA, 335
Acadia Foundation, ME, 3685
Accel Foundation, NC, 6544
Accelerated Learning Foundation, IA, 3233
ACCESS College Foundation, VA, 9278
Access Foundation, CA, 336
Accordia Global Health Foundation, DC, 1531
Ace Foundation, OH, 6954
ACEC Calfornia Scholarship Foundation, CA, 337
ACGT, CT, see 1318
ACI Foundation, MI, 4332
Ackers Scholarship Trust, Mary Margaret, OH, 6955
ACLS, NY, see 5692
ACMP Foundation, NY, 5664
ACOG, DC, see 1551
ACT Today!, CA, see 393
Action for Bridgeport Community Development, Inc., CT, 1314

Action, Inc., MA, 3957
Actors Fund of America, NY, 5665
Acts Outreach Ministries Inc., TN, 8551
ACVIM Foundation, The, CO, 1110
ADA Foundation, IL, 2356
Ada Scholarship Foundation Inc., MN, 4680
ADA, IL, see 2375
ADAA, MD, see 3773
Adair Scholarship Trust, Wesley G., GA, 2111
Adam's C.A.M.P., CO, see 1157
Adam's Camp, Inc., CO, see 1157
Adams County Community Foundation, IN, 2945
Adams Educational Fund Inc., MN, 4681
Adams Family Foundation, TN, 8552
Adams Foundation, James K. & Arlene L., PA, 7692
Adams Foundation, William L. and Victorine Q., Inc., The, MD, 3750
Adams Memorial Fund, Emma J., Inc., NY, 5666
Adams Rotary Memorial Fund B Trust, Charles & Lovie, OH, see 6956
Adams Rotary Memorial Fund B, OH, 6956
Adams Scholarship Foundation Inc., John & Olive, ID, 2328
Adams Scholarship Fund, Sally, WV, 9763
Adams World Foundation for Dyslexic, CT, 1315
Adamson Scholarship Fund, Dr. E.W., IL, 2357
Addison Trust, Lena A. & Paul F., OH, 6957
Additon Scholarship Fund, RI, 8225
Adelante Foundation Inc., AZ, 151
Adelphic Educational Fund, NJ, 5381
Adena Health Foundation, OH, 6958
ADFAC, TN, see 8553
Adirondack Community Trust, NY, see 5667
Adirondack Foundation, NY, 5667
Adirondack Scholarship Foundation, NY, 5668
Adler Community Trust, Leo, OR, 7528
Adler Trust, Leo, OR, see 7528
Administers of the Berwick Health and Wellness Fund, PA, see 7763
Adobe Systems Incorporated Corporate Giving Program, CA, 338
Adopt an Orca Inc., MI, A
Advanced Placement Strategies, Inc., TX, 8667
Advancing Native Missions, VA, 9279
Adventure Unlimited, CO, 1111
Advertising Industry Emergency Fund, CA, 339
Advocate Safehouse Project, CO, 1112
Advocates for Indigenous California Language Survival, CA, 340
AEC Electrical Scholarship & Educational Fund Corporation, NY, 5669
AEG Foundation, CO, 1113
AEPOCH, CA, 341
Aero Cares, Inc., NY, 5670
Aerospace Education Foundation, Inc., VA, see 9284
AES Educational Foundation, Inc., NY, see 5739
AES, CT, see 1320
Aesthetic Surgery Education and Research Foundation, CA, 342
AFAR, NY, see 5693
AFB, NY, see 5696

Affinity Plus Federal Credit Union Foundation, The, MN, 4682

Affordable Caring Housing, Inc., TX, 8668

Affordable Housing Management Training Foundation, MA, 3958

Affordable Housing Network, Inc., IA, 3234

AFP Foundation for Philanthropy, VA, 9280

AfricAid, Inc., CO, 1114

African American Self-Help Foundation, CA, see 343

African Methodist Episcopal Church Fifth District Economic Development Fund, MO, 4927

AFS-USA, Inc., NY, 5671

After School Matters, Inc., IL, 2358

Afterschool Alliance, DC, 1532

AFTRA Foundation Inc., The, NY, 5672

AFTRA Heller Memorial Foundation, Inc., NY, A

Aga Khan Foundation U.S.A., DC, 1533

Agape Foundation, The, AZ, 152

Agape Minstries, Inc., OH, 6959

AGC of Ohio Education Foundation, OH, 6960

AGC of Washington Education Foundation, WA, 9555

Aging Community Coordinated Enterprises Supportive Services, Inc., OR, 7529

Agnew Foundation, OH, 6961

Agoriani Trust, Athas Zaharis, NY, 5673

Agriculture Future of America, MO, 4928

AgSource DHI Foundation, Inc., WI, 9833

AgStar Fund for Rural America, MN, 4683

Agudath Israel of America, Inc., NY, 5674

AH&LEF, DC, see 1559

AHC Community Health Foundation, VA, 9281

Ahern Scholarship Inc., John J., MA, 3959

Ahl Scholarship Fund, Helen R., PA, A

AHP Foundation, VA, 9282

Ahtna Heritage Foundation, AK, 96

AIA St. Louis Scholarship Fund, MO, see 4931

AIA, DC, see 1561

Aicardi Syndrome Foundation, IL, 2359

AICE, Inc., MD, 3751

AICPA, NC, see 6550

Aid Association of the Phila County Medical Society, PA, see 8042

Aid for Cancer Research, MA, 3960

Aid For Friends, PA, 7693

Aid for Starving Children, CA, 343

Aid to Distressed Families of Appalachian Counties, Inc., TN, 8553

AIDS Action Committee of Massachusetts, Inc., The, MA, 3961

AIDS Arms, Inc., TX, 8669

AIDS Care Service, Inc., NC, 6545

AIDS Emergency Fund, CA, 344

AIDS Help of Monroe County, FL, 1764

AIDS Help, Inc., FL, see 1764

AIDS Task Force of LaPorte & Porter Counties, Inc., IN, 2946

Aiea General Hospital Association Scholarship Fund, HI, 2269

AIG Foundation, Inc., NY, 5675

AIGC Scholars, NM, see 5612

Aikey Foundation, OH, 6962

AIL/AFGWU Lawrence Bankowski Scholarship Fund, The, PA, see 8157

Aileen Flanary Educational Fund, OK, 7448

Ailey Dance Foundation, Alvin, Inc., NY, 5676

Air Force Aid Society, Inc., VA, 9283

Air Force Association, VA, 9284

Air Force Officers Wives Club of Washington DC Welfare Fund, DC, 1534

Airline Ambassadors International, Inc., DC, 1535

Airmen Memorial Foundation, Inc., MD, 3752

Airport High School Educational Foundation, Inc., SC, 8444

Aitaneet Foundation, OH, A

AJCA Educational, Youth Activities & Special Awards Fund, OH, 6963

AJFC Community Action Agency, MS, 4895

AK Steel Foundation, OH, 6964

AKA Educational Advancement Foundation, Inc., IL, 2360

Akers Kicks for Kids, David, Inc., NJ, 5382

Akey Charitable Trust, The, OH, see 7071

Akihito Scholarship Foundation, Crown Prince, HI, 2270

Akron Community Foundation, OH, 6965

Akron General Development Foundation, OH, 6966

Akron Summit Community Action Agency, Inc., OH, 6967

Alabama Forestry Foundation, AL, 2

Alabama Home Health Care, Inc., AL, 3

Alabama Law Foundation, Inc., AL, 4

Alabama Pharmaceutical Association Scholarship Foundation, AL, see 5

Alabama Pharmacy Association Scholarship Foundation, AL, 5

Alalusi Foundation, CA, 345

Alamance Community College Foundation, Inc., NC, 6546

Alamance Educational Foundation, NC, A

Alamo Colleges Foundation, Inc., TX, 8670

Alamo Community College District Foundation, TX, see 8670

Alander Scholarship Fund, Robert J., NC, A

Alaska Community Foundation, The, AK, 97

Alaska Conservation Foundation, AK, 98

Alaska Humanities Forum, AK, 99

Alaska Kidney Foundation, Inc., AK, 100

Alaska Pulp Scholarship Foundation, WA, 9556

Alaska Youth Bowling Foundation, AK, 101

Alaskan International Education Foundation, Inc., AK, 102

Albaugh Scholarship Trust, Ralph Buchanan, TX, 8671

Albee Foundation, Edward, Inc., NY, 5677

Albemarle Foundation, LA, 3640

Albemarle Smart Start Partnership, Inc., NC, 6547

Albero Charitable Trust, Arnold M., The, CT, 1316

Albert E. and Angela T. Farone Foundation, DC, 1536

Alberts Scholarship Trust, Max H., IL, 2361

Albion High School Alumni Foundation, NY, 5678

Albuquerque Community Foundation, NM, 5610

Alcoa Foundation, PA, 7694

Alegent Health-Immanuel Medical Center, NE, 5184

Aleut Foundation, The, AK, 103

Alex's Lemonade Stand Foundation, PA, 7695

Alexander Foundation for Orthodontics Research & Education, TX, 8672

Alexander Foundation, The, CO, 1115

Alexander Memorial Scholarship Fund, John, NY, 5679

Alexander Scholarship Fund, Thomas L., Myrtle R., and Eva, OH, 6968

Alexander's Future Foundation, OH, 6969

Alexandria Trust, Olga V., OR, 7530

Alexion Complement Foundation, CT, 1317

Alger Association of Distinguished Americans, Horatio, Inc., VA, 9285

Alhambra Foundation for the Future, AZ, 153

Aliveness Project of N.W.I., The, IN, see 2946

All Our Kids Inc. Foundation, NE, 5185

All Saints' Scholarship Fund, VA, 9286

All Sports Community Service, Inc., FL, 1765

All Stars Project, Inc., NY, 5680

Allchin Charitable Foundation, Bonnie Schatz, The, OH, 6970

Allegan County Community Foundation, MI, 4333

Allegan County Foundation, MI, see 4333

Allegan County Resource Development Committee, Inc., MI, 4334

Allegany Arts Council, Inc., MD, 3753

Allegany County Area Foundation, Inc., NY, 5681

Allegheny County Bar Foundation, PA, 7696

Allegiance Benefit Foundation, Inc., MT, 5128

Allemall Foundation, Inc., The, MD, 3754

Allen County Education Partnership, Inc., IN, 2947

Allen County Local Education Fund, Inc., IN, see 2947

Allen Foundation, R. E. & Joan S., Inc., FL, 1766

Allen Memorial Hospital Corporation, IA, 3235

Allen Music Scholarship Fund, Iona M., NC, 6548

Allen Scholarship Fund, William M. & Louise O., PA, 7697

Allen Scholarship Trust, MI, 4335

Allen, Sr. Charitable and Scholarship Trust, Charlotte D. and Delbert E., The, AR, 260

Allgemeiner Deutscher Frauen-Hilfsverein, CA, 346

Allhands Education Trust, Jessie V., IL, 2362

Alliance For California Traditional Arts, CA, 347

Alliance for Cancer Gene Therapy, Inc., CT, 1318

Alliance for Education, WA, 9557

Alliance for Gifted Children, MI, 4336

Alliance for Multicultural Community Services, TX, 8673

Alliance for Nonprofit Management, CA, 348

Alliance for Quality Education, SC, 8445

Alliance for Young Artists and Writers, Inc., NY, 5682

Alliance of Artists' Communities, RI, 8226

Allied Arts Association, WA, 9558

Allied Arts Foundation, WA, 9559

Allied Exeter Scholarship Foundation, Inc., CA, see 1033

AlliedSignal Inc. Corporate Giving Program, NJ, see 5472

Allstate Foundation, The, IL, 2363

Ally's House, Inc., OK, 7449

Almanor Scholarship Fund, CA, 349

Almquist-SUHS No. 7J Graduate Assistance Fund, Mabel V., Inc., OR, 7531

Alpert Foundation, Warren, RI, 8227

Alpha Chi Omega Foundation, Inc., IN, 2948

Alpha Delta Kappa Foundation, MO, 4929

Alpha Delta Pi Foundation, Inc., GA, 2112

Alpha Epsilon Boule Education Foundation, TX, see 8674

Alpha Epsilon Boule, TX, 8674

Alpha Epsilon Pi Foundation, Inc., IN, 2949

Alpha Gamma Delta Foundation, Inc., IN, 2950

Alpha Kappa Psi Foundation, Inc., IN, 2951

Alpha Nu Educational Foundation, KS, 3412

Alpha Omicron Pi Foundation, TN, 8554

Alpha Omicron Pi Philanthropic Foundation, TN, see 8554

Alpha Phi Alpha Education Foundation, MD, 3755

Alpha Phi Omega National Service Fraternity, MO, 4930

Alpha Psi of Chi Psi Educational Trust, NY, 5683

Alpha Tau Omega Foundation, Inc., IN, 2952

Alpha Zeta Delta of Chi Psi Educational Foundation, WI, A

Alpha-1 Foundation, FL, 1767

ALS Association, The, DC, see 1573

ALS Therapy Alliance, Inc., MA, 3962

Alsite Scholarships, Inc., AL, 6

Alsobrook Scholarship Trust, W. R., AL, 7

Alsobrooks Educational Fund, Miriam E., PA, 7698

Alta Bates Summit Foundation, CA, 350

Alta Bates Summit Medical Center Foundation, CA, see 350

Alta California Regional Center, Inc., CA, 351

Alternatives Research and Development Foundation, PA, 7699

Alternatives to Hunger, WA, 9560

Alumnae Association of the College of St. Teresa Scholarship Fund, MN, 4684

Alumni Achievement Awards, Inc., TN, 8555

Alumni Association of Hunter College, NY, 5684

Alworth Memorial Fund, Marshall H. and Nellie, MN, 4685

Alzheimer's Drug Discovery Foundation, NY, 5685

AMA Foundation, IL, see 2382

Amador Community Foundation, Inc., CA, 352

Amarillo Area Foundation, Inc., TX, 8675

Amarillo College Foundation, Inc., TX, 8676

Amateis Foundation, Edmond, FL, see 1768

Amateis Irrevocable Trust Foundation, Edmond, FL, 1768

Amazon Conservation Association, DC, 1537

Ambler Trust, Elizabeth Raymond, CT, 1319

Amburn Memorial Scholarship Fund, IN, 2953

Ameche Memorial Foundation, Alan, PA, 7700

Ameren Illinois Corporate Giving Program, IL, 2364

America West Airlines Education Foundation, Inc., AZ, see 252

America's Future Through Academic Progress, Inc., NY, 5712

America's Second Harvest, IL, see 2559

America-Israel Cultural Foundation, Inc., NY, 5686

American Academy & Institute of Arts and Letters, NY, see 5689

American Academy in Berlin, NY, 5687

American Academy in Rome, NY, 5688

American Academy of Allergy, Asthma, and Immunology, The, WI, 9834

American Academy of Arts and Letters, NY, 5689

American Academy of Audiology Foundation, VA, 9287

American Academy of Child & Adolescent Psychiatry, DC, 1538

American Academy of Dermatology, Inc., IL, 2365

American Academy of Family Physicians Foundation, KS, 3413

American Academy of Neurology Foundation, MN, see 4686

American Academy of Nurse Practitioners Foundation, TX, 8677

American Academy of Nursing, DC, 1539

American Academy of Otolaryngic Allergy Foundation, VA, 9288

American Academy of Pediatrics, IL, 2366

American Alliance for Health, Physical Education, Recreation, and Dance, VA, 9289

American Anthropological Association, VA, 9290

American Antiquarian Society, MA, 3963

American Arabic Educational Foundation, CA, 353

American Architectural Foundation, Inc., The, DC, 1540

American Assembly for Men in Nursing Foundation, AL, see 1

American Association for Cancer Research, Inc., PA, 7701

American Association for Cancer Support, Inc., TN, 8556

American Association for Clinical Chemistry, DC, 1541

American Association for the Advancement of Science, DC, 1542

American Association for the Study of Liver Diseases, VA, 9291

American Association of Airport Executives Foundation, VA, 9292

American Association of Anatomists, MD, 3756

American Association of Colleges of Nursing, DC, 1543

American Association of Community Colleges, DC, 1544

American Association of Critical Care Nurses, CA, 354

American Association of Endodontists Foundation, IL, 2367

American Association of Equine Practitioners, KY, see 3543

American Association of Law Libraries, IL, 2368

American Association of Museums, DC, 1545

American Association of People with Disabilities, DC, 1546

American Association of Physics Teachers, MD, 3757

American Association of Plastic Surgeons, MA, 3964

American Association of Retired Persons (AARP) Andrus Foundation, DC, see 1529

American Association of School Administrators, VA, 9293

American Association of State Troopers Scholarship Foundation, Inc., FL, see 1761

American Association of University Women Educational Foundation, DC, 1547

American Association of University Women, HI, A

American Australian Association, Inc., NY, 5690

American Baptist Homes Foundation of the West, Inc., CA, 355

American Bar Association Fund for Justice and Education, IL, 2370

American Bar Association, IL, 2369

American Bar Foundation, IL, 2371

American Berlin Opera Foundation, Inc., The, NY, see 6297

American Brain Foundation, MN, 4686

American Brain Tumor Association, IL, 2372

American Cancer Society, Inc., GA, 2113

American Center Foundation, NY, see 5993

American Charity Council, Inc., FL, see 1853

American Chemical Society, DC, 1548

American College of Allergy, Asthma, and Immunology, IL, 2373

American College of Cardiology Foundation, DC, 1550

American College of Cardiology, DC, 1549

American College of Foot and Ankle Surgeons, IL, 2374

American College of Obstetricians and Gynecologists, DC, 1551

American College of Rheumatology Research and Education Foundation, GA, 2115

American College of Rheumatology, GA, 2114

American College of Toxicology, VA, 9294

American College of Veterinary Internal Medicine Foundation, CO, see 1110

American Colloid Company Foundation, IL, see 2416

American Composers Forum of Washington, DC, Inc., MD, 3758

American Composers Forum, MN, 4687

American Concrete Institute Foundation, MI, see 4332

American Council for Learned Societies, NY, 5691

American Council for the Arts, DC, see 1572

American Council of Learned Societies, NY, 5692

American Council of the Blind, Inc., VA, 9295

American Councils for International Education, DC, 1552

American Counsel Scholarship Foundation, Inc., LA, 3641

American Counseling Association Foundation, VA, 9296

American Dance Festival, Inc., NC, 6549

American Dental Association, IL, 2375

American Dental Education Association, DC, 1553

American Dental Hygienist Association Institute for Oral Health, IL, 2376

American Diabetes Association Research Foundation, Inc., VA, 9298

American Diabetes Association, VA, 9297

American Dietetic Association Foundation, IL, see 2355

American Digestive Health Foundation, MD, see 3829

American Educational Research Association, DC, 1554

American Electric Power System Educational Trust Fund, The, OH, 6971

American Epilepsy Society, CT, 1320

American Ex-Prisoners of War Service Foundation, Inc., NC, see 6773

American Farm Bureau Foundation for Agriculture, DC, 1555

American Federation for Aging Research, Inc., NY, 5693

American Federation for Medical Research, MA, 3965

American Federation of Riders, KY, 3544

American Federation of State, County, and Municipal Employees, DC, 1556

American Fertility Society, The, AL, see 8

American Field Service - USA, Inc., NY, see 5671

American Film Institute, Inc., CA, 356

American Finnish Workers Society Memorial Educational Trust, MN, 4688

American Floral Endowment, VA, 9299

American Foundation for Aging Research, NY, 5694

American Foundation for Bulgaria, Inc., MA, 3966

American Foundation for Pharmaceutical Education, VA, 9300

American Foundation for Suicide Prevention, NY, 5695

American Foundation for the Blind, NY, 5696

American Foundation for Urologic Disease, Inc., MD, see 3770

American Friends of Eton College, Inc., VA, 9301

American Friends of Even Yisroel Charitable Foundation, NJ, 5383

American Friends of Needy Israeli Sephardic Children, The, NY, 5697

American Friends of the Alexander von Humboldt Foundation, DC, 1557

American Gastroenterological Association, MD, 3759

American Geriatrics Society, Inc., NY, 5698

American Glaucoma Society, CA, 357

American Ground Water Trust, NH, 5305

American Head and Neck Society, Inc., The, CA, 358

American Health Assistance Foundation, MD, see 3789

American Hearing Research Foundation, IL, 2377

American Heart Association, Inc., TX, 8678

American Historical Association, DC, 1558

American Horse Trials Foundation, Inc., MD, 3760

American Hotel and Lodging Educational Foundation, DC, 1559

American Hotel and Lodging Foundation, DC, see 1559

American Hungarian Foundation, NJ, 5384

American Indian College Fund, CO, 1116

American Indian Family and Children Services, Inc., MN, 4689

American Indian Family Empowerment Program, MN, see 4869

American Indian Graduate Center Scholars, NM, 5612

American Indian Graduate Center, Inc., NM, 5611

American Indian Services, UT, 9191

American Indian Youth Running Strong, Inc., VA, 9302

American Indonesian Cultural and Educational Foundation, Inc., NY, 5699

American Institute for Cancer Research, DC, 1560

American Institute of Architects St. Louis Scholarship Fund, MO, 4931

American Institute of Architects, The, DC, 1561

American Institute of Certified Public Accountants, NC, 6550

American Institute of Indian Studies, IL, 2378

American Institute of Physics, Inc., MD, 3761

American Jewish Committee, The, NY, 5700

American Jewish Joint Distribution Committee, Inc., The, NY, 5701

American Junior Golf Foundation, Inc., GA, 2116

American Kennel Club Canine Health Foundation, Inc., NC, 6551

American Kidney Fund, Inc., MD, 3762

American Legacy Foundation, DC, 1562

American Legion Charles F. Moran Post No. 475, Scholarship Trust and Baseball Trust, CT, see 1321

American Legion Charles F. Moran Trust, CT, 1321

American Legion Department of Florida, The, FL, 1769

American Legion Department of Ohio Charities, Inc., OH, 6972

American Legion Memorial Scholarship Funds, Inc., FL, 1770

American Legion September 11 Memorial Scholarship Trust Fund, The, IN, 2955

American Legion, The, IN, 2954

American Library Association, IL, 2379

American Liver Foundation, NY, 5702

American Lung Association of California, CA, 359

American Lung Association of Florida, Inc., FL, 1771

American Lung Association of Metropolitan Chicago, IL, see 2817

American Lung Association of Missouri, Inc., TX, see 8679

American Lung Association of the Central States, Inc., TX, 8679

American Lung Association, IL, 2380

American Marketing Association Foundation, IL, 2381

American Massage Therapy Association Foundation, IL, see 2713

American Medical Association Foundation, IL, 2382

American Medical Student Association Foundation, VA, 9303

American Medical Women's Association Foundation, PA, 7702

American Meteorological Society, MA, 3967

American Museum of Natural History, NY, 5703

American Mushroom Institute Community Awareness Scholarship Foundation, Inc., PA, 7703

American Music Therapy Association, MD, 3763

American National Red Cross, DC, 1563

American Nuclear Society, IL, 2383

American Nurses Association Foundation, MD, see 3764

American Nurses Foundation, Inc., MD, 3764

American Occupational Therapy Foundation, MD, 3765

American Optical Foundation, MA, 3968

American Optometric Foundation, FL, 1772

American Orchid Society, Inc., FL, 1773

American Orthopaedic Foot and Ankle Society, IL, 2384

American Orthopaedic Foot Society, IL, see 2384

American Osteopathic Association, IL, 2385

American Osteopathic Foundation, IL, 2386

American Paint Horse Foundation, TX, 8680

American Parkinson's Disease Association, NY, 5704

American Pediatric Surgical Association Foundation, Inc., IL, 2387

American Pharmacists Association Foundation, DC, 1564

American Philosophical Society, PA, 7704

American Physical Therapy Association, VA, 9304

American Physicians Fellowship for Medicine in Israel, MA, 3969

American Porphyria Foundation, TX, 8681

American Psychiatric Association, VA, see 9305

American Psychiatric Publishing, Inc., VA, 9305

American Psychoanalytic Association, NY, 5705

American Psychological Foundation, DC, 1565
American Public Power Association, DC, 1566
American Quarter Horse Association, TX, 8682
American Research Center in Egypt, Inc., TX, 8683
American Respiratory Care Foundation, TX, 8684
American Road & Transportation Builders Association Foundation, DC, 1567
American Roentgen Ray Society, VA, 9306
American Savings Foundation of Connecticut, Inc., CT, see 1322
American Savings Foundation, CT, 1322
American Skin Association, Inc., NY, 5706
American Sleep Medicine Foundation, IL, 2388
American Society for Artificial Internal Organs, FL, 1774
American Society for Engineering Education, DC, 1568
American Society for Enology and Viticulture, CA, 360
American Society for Gastrointestinal Endoscopy Foundation, IL, 2389
American Society for Industrial Security Foundation, VA, 9307
American Society for Laser Medicine and Surgery, Inc., WI, 9835
American Society for Reproductive Immunology, IL, 2390
American Society for Reproductive Medicine, The, AL, 8
American Society for the Defense of Tradition, Family, and Property, The, PA, see 7850
American Society for Theater Research, CO, 1117
American Society of Anesthesiologists, IL, 2391
American Society of Clinical Oncology, VA, 9308
American Society of Consultant Pharmacists Foundation, VA, 9309
American Society of Consultant Pharmacists Research & Education Foundation, VA, see 9309
American Society of Health-System Pharmacists Research and Education Foundation, MD, 3766
American Society of Hematology, Inc., DC, 1569
American Society of Human Genetics, The, MD, 3767
American Society of Interior Designers Foundation, DC, 1570
American Society of Journalists and Authors Charitable Trust, NY, 5707
American Society of Military Comptrollers, VA, 9310
American Society of Nephrology, Inc., DC, 1571
American Society of Newspaper Editors Foundation, MO, 4932
American Society of Regional Anesthesia and Pain Medicine, PA, 7705
American Society of Safety Engineers Foundation, IL, 2392
American Society of Transplant Surgeons, VA, 9311
American Society of Transplantation, NJ, 5385
American Society of Tropical Medicine and Hygiene, IL, 2393
American Speech-Language-Hearing Foundation, MD, 3768
American Sports Medicine Institute, Inc., AL, 9
American String Teachers, Inc., VA, 9312
American Students' Fund, Inc., MD, A
American Symphony Orchestra League, NY, see 6156
American Theatre Wing, Inc., NY, 5708
American Thread Educational Foundation, Inc., NC, see 6607
American Tinnitus Association, OR, 7532
American Turkish Society, Inc., The, NY, 5709
American Urological Association Foundation, MD, 3770
American Urological Association, Inc., MD, 3769
American Welding & Manufacturing Company Foundation, PA, see 7857
American-Israeli Cooperative Enterprise, MD, see 3751
American-Italian Cancer Foundation, NY, 5710
American-Scandinavian Foundation, The, NY, 5711
Americans for the Arts, DC, 1572
Americans Helping Americans, Inc., VA, 9313
AmeriCares Foundation, CT, see 1323
AmeriCares, CT, 1323
Ameritec Foundation, CA, 361
Ames Education Foundation, IA, 3236
Ames Trust, Dorothy, OH, 6973
amfAR & AIDS Research Foundation & American Foundation for AIDS Research, NY, see 5992
Amgen Foundation, Inc., CA, 362

Amigos de las Americas, TX, 8685
Amigos Library Services, Inc., TX, 8686
Amin Foundation Inc., C.M., FL, 1775
Ammonius Foundation, The, NJ, 5386
Amos, Sr. Foundation, W. L., Inc., FL, 1776
Amos-Cheves Foundation, Inc., GA, 2117
Amundson Scholarships, L. A., Inc., SD, 8520
Amusement and Music Operators Educational Foundation, IL, see 2487
AMVETS National Service Foundation, MD, 3771
Amy Foundation, The, MI, 4337
Amyotrophic Lateral Sclerosis Association, The, DC, 1573
Anacostia Community Outreach Center, DC, 1574
Anagnos Educational Foundation, Christina and John, The, IL, 2394
Anaheim Arts Council, CA, 363
Anaheim Community Foundation, CA, 364
Anaya Foundation, Loflin, UT, 9192
Anctil Foundation, J. Wilfred, RI, 8228
Andalusia Health Services Inc., AL, 10
Andersen Family Scholarship Trust, Kenneth N., IA, 3237
Anderson Center for Interdisciplinary Studies, Inc., MN, 4690
Anderson Chapter 75 United Daughters of the Confederacy Trust, Dick, SC, 8446
Anderson Educational Fund, Sophie L., TX, 8687
Anderson Educational Trust, Harold C., MN, 4691
Anderson Family Scholarship Trust, IA, A
Anderson Family Scholarship Trust, John, IA, A
Anderson Foundation, Kay M., IA, 3238
Anderson Foundation, Peyton, Inc., The, GA, 2118
Anderson Foundation, Sherwood, NC, 6552
Anderson Memorial Educational Trust, WY, 10094
Anderson Prize Foundation, CA, 365
Anderson Ranch Arts Center, CO, 1118
Anderson Ranch Arts Foundation, CO, see 1118
Anderson Scholarship Foundation, E. & E., OH, 6974
Anderson Scholarship Foundation, Eugene and Daniela, TX, 8688
Anderson Scholarship Foundation, Molly Crouch, TX, 8689
Anderson Scholarship Trust, Elizabeth M., IL, 2395
Anderson Scholarship Trust, Olson L. Anderson and Catherine Bastow, OH, 6975
Anderson Trust, Etta Mae, MO, 4933
Anderson Veterans Trust, Ralph W., IA, 3239
Andona Society, MA, 3970
Andrew Family Foundation, IL, 2396
Andrew Foundation, Aileen S., IL, 2397
Andrews Charitable Foundation, Carolann K., NY, 5713
Andrews Memorial Foundation, Emily B., The, NC, 6553
Andrews Scholarship Trust, Leah, IA, 3240
Andrews Trust, Marie B., RI, 8229
Andrus Foundation, Alice A., OH, 6976
Anesthesia Foundation, IL, 2398
Anew Foundation, Inc., FL, 1777
Angelman Syndrome Foundation, IL, 2399
Angelo Brothers Company Founders Scholarship Foundation, PA, 7706
Angels Baseball Foundation, CA, 366
Angels for Kids Foundation, Inc., IL, 2400
Angels Gate Cultural Center, Inc., CA, 367
Angle Educational Trust, Faerie L., NY, see 5714
Angle Educational Trust, NY, 5714
Animal Compassion Foundation, DC, see 1641
Animal Umbrella, Inc., MA, 3971
Animal Welfare Institute, DC, 1575
Animal Welfare Trust, NY, 5715
Anmed Health Foundation, SC, 8447
Ann and Robert H. Lurie Children's Hospital of Chicago, IL, 2401
Ann Arbor Area Community Foundation, MI, 4338
Ann Arbor Area Foundation, MI, see 4338
Ann Arbor Film Festival, MI, 4339
Anna Fund, IN, see 2956
Anna Needs Neuroblastoma Answers, IN, 2956
Annapolis Area Ministries, Inc., MD, 3772
AnnMarie Foundation, Inc., WI, 9836
Annual Emancipation Day Celebration, OH, 6977
Anodyne Artist Company, MN, 4692
Anonymous Fund, WI, see 9954

ANS, IL, see 2383
Anson Academy Association, ME, 3686
Anthony Foundation, Barbara Cox, The, GA, A
Anthony Trust Association, The, CT, 1324
Anu Family Services Advantage, The, WI, 9837
Anxiety Disorders Association of America, MD, 3773
Anyone Can Fly Foundation, Inc., NJ, 5387
AO North America, Inc., PA, 7707
Aon Memorial Education Fund, IL, 2402
Aorn Foundation, CO, 1119
AOS, FL, see 1773
Aperture Foundation, NY, 5716
APF, MA, see 3969
APhA Foundation, The, DC, see 1564
APICS Educational & Research Foundation, Inc., IL, 2403
Aplastic Anemia & MDS International Foundation, Inc., MD, 3774
Aplastic Anemia Foundation of America, Inc., MD, see 3774
App Foundation, PA, 7708
APPA, DC, see 1566
Appalachian College Association, KY, 3545
Appalachian Foothills Housing Agency, Inc., KY, 3546
Appalachian Mountain Project Access, TN, 8557
APS Education Foundation, CO, 1120
AptarGroup Charitable Foundation, IL, 2404
Aqua Foundation for Women, FL, 1778
Arab American Institute Foundation, DC, 1576
Arab Student Aid International Corp., OH, 6978
Arbor Falls Foundation, IL, 2405
Arby's Foundation, Inc., GA, 2119
Arc of Bergen and Passaic Counties, Inc., The, NJ, 5388
Arc of Durham County, Inc., The, NC, 6554
Arc of Multnomah County, Inc., The, OR, 7533
Arc of Prince George's County, Inc., The, MD, 3775
Arc of the United States, The, DC, 1577
Arcadian Foundation, The, FL, 1779
ArcelorMittal USA Foundation, Inc., IL, 2406
Arch Coal Foundation, MO, 4934
Arch Development Corporation, DC, 1578
ARCH Foundation, NJ, 5389
Archeo/ Community Foundation, The, CA, 368
Archer Scholarship Trust Fund, Virginia A., OR, 7534
Archuleta County Victims Assistance Program, Inc., CO, 1121
Arctic Education Foundation, AK, 104
Ardron Charitable Foundation, The, CA, 369
Area Agency on Aging of Broward County, FL, see 1781
Area Agency on Aging of Pasco-Pinellas, Inc., FL, 1780
Area Agency on Aging of West Central Arkansas, Inc., AR, 261
Area IV Agency on Aging and Community Action Programs, Inc., IN, 2957
Area Scholastic Awards Trust Fund, NC, 6555
Areawide Aging Agency, Inc., OK, 7450
Areawide Council on Aging of Broward County, Inc., The, FL, 1781
Ariel Foundation, OH, 6979
Ariens Foundation, Ltd., WI, 9838
Arise Charitable Trust, WA, 9561
Arizona Burn Foundation, AZ, 155
Arizona Christian School Tuition Organization, Inc., AZ, see 187
Arizona College Scholarship Foundation, AZ, 156
Arizona Community Foundation, AZ, 157
Arizona Foundation for Legal Services and Education, AZ, 158
Arizona Hospital and Healthcare Association Education Foundation, AZ, see 167
Arizona Kidney Foundation, AZ, 159
Arizona National Guard Emergency Relief Fund, AZ, 160
Arizona Private Education Scholarship Fund, Inc., AZ, 161
Arizona Scholarship Fund, AZ, 162
Arizona School Choice Trust, Inc., AZ, 163
Arizona Tuition Organization, Inc., AZ, 164
Arizona Water and Pollution Control Association, AZ, see 165
Arizona Water Association, AZ, 165
ARK Foundation, WA, see 9562
ARK Institute of Learning, WA, 9562

Arkansas Childrens Hospital, AR, 262
Arkansas Eastman Scholarship Trust, AR, 263
Arkansas Farm Bureau - Romeo E. Short Memorial
　Foundation, AR, 264
Arkansas Farm Bureau Scholarship Foundation, AR,
　265
Arkansas Human Development Corporation, AR, 266
Arkema Inc. Foundation, PA, 7709
Arlington Charities, Inc., TX, 8690
Arlington Community Foundation, VA, 9314
Arlington Community Public Health Nursing Service,
　Inc., VT, 9235
Armed Forces Family Survivors Fund, NY, see 6103
Armed Forces Foundation, DC, 1579
Armenian General Benevolent Union, NY, 5717
Armenian Gospel Mission, CA, 370
Armenian Relief Society, Inc., MA, 3972
Armfield, Sr. Foundation, Edward M., Inc., The, NC,
　6556
Armstrong County Community Foundation, The, PA,
　7710
Armstrong Family Foundation, CA, 371
Armstrong Foundation, Cecil, IN, 2958
Armstrong Foundation, PA, 7711
Armstrong Health & Education Foundation, PA, 7712
Armstrong Toyota and Ford Family Foundation, FL, A
Armstrong Trust, Benjamin A., RI, 8230
Army Emergency Relief, VA, 9315
Army Historical Foundation, Inc, The, VA, 9316
Army Reserve Component Emergency Relief Fund, AZ,
　see 160
Arnold Foundation, PA, 7713
Arnold Industries Scholarship Foundation, NC, see
　6790
Arnold Memorial Fund, Maude E., RI, 8231
Arnold Memorial Scholarship, Heather Lynn, KS, 3414
Arnold Trust for Memorial Fund, Maude E., RI, see 8231
Arnold Trust, George S., NC, 6557
Arnold Trust, William A., IL, 2407
ARNOVA, IN, see 2962
Arnsberg Scholarship Trust, WA, 9563
Arpajian Armenian Educational Foundation Inc., Jack,
　PA, 7714
Arps Memorial Fund Trust, Ernest G., NC, 6558
Arques Charitable Education Trust, CA, 372
Arrow International Inc., Scholarship Fund, NC, A
Arrowhead Regional Arts Council, The, MN, 4693
Arsenal Technical High School Alumni Association, Inc.,
　IN, 2959
Art Bridge Association, Inc., The, NY, 5718
Art in General, Inc., NY, 5719
Art League of Bonita Springs, Inc., FL, 1782
Art League of Marco Island, Inc., FL, 1783
Art Matters, Inc., NY, 5720
Art of the Matter Performance Foundation, CA, 373
Art Omi International Arts Center, NY, 5721
Art Students League of New York, NY, 5722
Art Works Downtown, Inc., CA, 374
Art/Omi, Inc., NY, see 5721
Artadia: The Fund for Art and Dialogue, NY, see 5723
ArtCouncil, Inc., The, NY, 5723
Arthritis Foundation, Inc., CA, 375
Arthritis Foundation, Inc., GA, 2120
Arthritis Foundation, Rocky Mountain Chapter, CO,
　1122
Arthritis National Research Foundation, CA, 376
Arthur's Enterprises, Inc. Scholarship Foundation, WV,
　9764
Artis Contemporary Israeli Art Fund, Inc., NY, 5724
Artis, NY, see 5724
Artist Relief Fund, MN, 4694
Artist Trust, WA, 9564
Artists Fellowship Inc., NY, 5725
Arts & Cultural Council for Greater Rochester, Inc., NY,
　5726
Arts & Industry Council, MI, see 4649
Arts & Science Council, NC, 6559
Arts and Humanities Council of Greater Baton Rouge,
　LA, see 3642
Arts and Humanities Council of Montgomery County,
　MD, 3776
Arts Center of the Capital Region, The, NY, 5727
Arts Council for Wyoming County, NY, 5728

Arts Council of Greater Baton Rouge, Inc., LA, 3642
Arts Council of Greater Kalamazoo, MI, 4340
Arts Council of Indianapolis, Inc., IN, 2960
Arts Council Silicon Valley, CA, 377
Arts Engine, Inc., NY, 5729
Arts Partnership of Greater Spartanburg, The, SC, 8448
ArtsConnection, NY, 5730
Artspace, NC, 6560
Arvac, Inc., AR, 267
Arvig Memorial Scholarship Fund, Royale B. and
　Eleanor M., MN, 4695
Arvig Memorial Scholarship Fund, Royale B., MN, see
　4695
Arvin Family Trust, Frank and Margaret, IN, 2961
Asbestos Workers Local 14 Scholarship Fund, PA,
　7715
ASC, NC, see 6559
ASCAP Foundation, The, NY, 5731
Ascension Fund, Inc., The, LA, 3643
ASCO Cancer Foundation, VA, see 9351
ASCP Foundation, The, VA, see 9309
Ash Charitable Foundation, Mary Kay, TX, see 8937
Ash Scholarship Trust, The, CT, 1325
ASH, DC, see 1569
Ashcraft Foundation Inc., MT, 5129
Asheville Area Arts Council, NC, 6561
Asheville City Schools Foundation, Inc., NC, 6562
Asheville-Buncombe Technical Community College
　Foundation, Inc., NC, 6563
Ashland County Community Foundation, OH, 6980
Ashland Trusts, PA, see 8090
Ashley and Sierra Memorial Scholarship Fund, Inc.,
　The, NY, 5732
Ashley Willwerth Memorial Scholarship Foundation, FL,
　1784
Ashoka: Innovators for the Public, VA, 9317
ASHP Research and Education Foundation, MD, see
　3766
Ashtabula Foundation, Inc., The, OH, 6981
Asia Foundation, The, CA, 378
Asia Society, The, NY, 5733
Asian & Pacific Islander American Scholarship Fund,
　DC, 1580
Asian Cultural Council, NY, 5734
Asian Pacific American Bar Association Educational
　Fund, DC, 1581
Asian Pacific American Institute for Congressional
　Studies, Inc., DC, 1582
Asian Pacific Fund, CA, 379
ASIS Foundation, VA, see 9307
ASK, VA, see 9320
Askren Memorial Scholarship, George W., WI, 9839
Askren Trust, Caroline L., WI, see 9839
Aslakson Scholarship Trust, Hazel, WI, 9840
ASN, DC, see 1571
Asparagus Club, VA, 9318
Aspen Institute, The, DC, 1583
Aspen Music Festival and School, CO, see 1246
Aspen Valley Medical Foundation, Ltd., CO, 1123
ASPH, DC, see 1587
Aspiranet, CA, 380
Aspiration Corporation, CA, 381
Aspirationtech.org, CA, see 381
Assistance League of Denver, CO, 1124
Assistance League of Newport-Mesa California, CA,
　382
Assistance League of Orange California, Inc., CA, 383
Assistance League of Phoenix, Arizona, AZ, 166
Assistance League of Pueblo, Inc., CO, 1125
Assistance League of Riverside, CA, 384
Assistance League of Whittier, CA, 385
Associa Cares, Inc., TX, 8691
Associated Banc-Corp Founders Scholarship Fund, WI,
　9841
Associated Charities of Findlay, Ohio, OH, 6982
Associated General Contractors of Maine Education
　Foundation, ME, 3687
Associated Medical Schools of New York, NY, 5735
Associated Plumbing-Heating-Cooling Contractors of
　Texas Charitable and Educational Foundation, TX,
　8692
Associated: Jewish Community Federation of
　Baltimore, Inc., The, MD, 3777

Associates of the American Foreign Service Worldwide,
　VA, 9319
Associates of the Boston Public Library, MA, 3973
Association for Frontotemporal Dementias, The, PA,
　7716
Association for Iron and Steel Technology, PA, 7717
Association for Prevention Teaching and Research,
　Inc., DC, 1584
Association for Research on Non-Profit Organizations &
　Voluntary Action, IN, 2962
Association for Surgical Education Foundation, IL,
　2408
Association for the Advancement of Artificial
　Intelligence, CA, 386
Association for the Cure of Cancer of the Prostate, CA,
　see 885
Association for the Relief of Aged Women of New
　Bedford, MA, 3974
Association for the Support of Children with Cancer, VA,
　9320
Association Foundation, Iowa Pharmacy, IA, 3241
Association of American Educators Foundation, CA,
　387
Association of American Geographers, DC, 1585
Association of Black Women Physicians, Inc., CA, 388
Association of Fundraising Professionals, VA, 9321
Association of Graduates of the United States Air Force
　Academy, CO, 1126
Association of Higher Education Facilities Officers, VA,
　9322
Association of Moving Image Archivists, CA, 389
Association of Performing Arts Presenters, DC, 1586
Association of Professors & Scholars of Iranian
　Heritage Award Fund, CA, 390
Association of Public Health Laboratories, Inc., MD,
　3778
Association of Schools and Colleges of Optometry, Inc.,
　MD, 3779
Association of Schools of Public Health, Inc., DC, 1587
Association of the Wall & Ceiling Industry-Foundation
　Office, VA, see 9383
Association of Theological Schools in the U.S. &
　Canada, PA, 7718
Association of University Radiologists, IL, 2409
Association of Writers and Writing Programs, VA, 9323
Astin Charitable Trust, Nina Heard, TX, 8693
Astle Memorial Scholarship Foundation, Edward
　Thatcher, The, NJ, 5390
Astoria School Children's Fund, OR, 7535
ASTR, CO, see 1117
Astraea Lesbian Foundation for Justice, Inc., The, NY,
　5736
ASTRAEA, National Lesbian Action Foundation, NY, see
　5736
AstraZeneca Patient Assistance Organization, DE,
　1493
ASTRO Education and Development Fund, VA, see 9489
ASTRO, VA, see 9489
Astronaut Scholarship Foundation, Inc., FL, 1785
Astros in Action Foundation—Fielding the Dreams of
　Houston, TX, 8694
ASTS, VA, see 9311
AT&T Foundation, TX, 8695
ATA, OR, see 7532
Ataxia Telangiectasia Children's Project, FL, 1786
Atchison Community Educational Foundation, KS,
　3415
Atchison Community Foundation, KS, see 3415
Athanasiades Cultural Foundation, Inc., NY, 5737
Athena Charitable Trust, CA, 392
Atherton Family Foundation, HI, 2271
Atkins Educational Trust, Robert G., NC, 6564
Atkins Trust, Grace, RI, 8232
Atlanta Community Foundation, Metropolitan, Inc., GA,
　see 2150
Atlantic Center for the Arts, Inc., FL, 1787
Atlantic Coast Conference, NC, 6565
Atlantic County Medical Society Scholarship Fund, NJ,
　5391
Atlanticare Regional Medical Center, Inc., NJ, 5392
Atlas Economic Research Foundation, DC, 1588
Atlas Foundation, Doctor Theodore A., Inc., The, NY,
　5738

Atlas Service Corps, DC, 1589
Atofina Chemicals, Inc. Foundation, PA, *see* 7709
Atwood Fund, Eugene, CT, 1326
Atwood Trust for Brooks Scholarship Fund, Florence D., OH, 6983
AUA Foundation, MD, *see* 3770
Audio Engineering Society Educational Foundation, Inc., NY, 5739
August Charitable Trust, Fannie, RI, 8233
Augusta Kiwanis Scholarship Foundation, ME, 3688
Aurora Education Foundation, CO, *see* 1120
Aurora Foundation, The, IL, *see* 2496
Aurora Ministries, Inc., FL, 1788
Aurora Project, Inc., WV, 9765
Austin Community Foundation for the Capital Area, Inc., TX, 8696
Austin Community Foundation, TX, *see* 8696
Austin Creative Alliance, TX, 8697
Austin Educational Trust, Emily & Ellsworth, SC, 8449
Austin Film Society, TX, 8698
Austin Foundation, Dallas, Inc., GA, 2121
Austin Trust, Jeff, TX, 8699
Austin Trust, William Harold Francis, MA, 3975
Authier Trust, Jean B., NY, 5740
Authors League Fund, The, NY, 5741
Autism Care & Treatment Today, CA, 393
Autism Science Foundation, NY, 5742
Autism Society of America Foundation, MD, 3781
Autism Society of America, Inc., MD, 3780
Autism Speaks, NY, 5743
Auto Racing Fraternity Foundation of America, Inc., PA, *see* 7972
Autobahn Motorcar Group Youth Scholarship Tour, TX, *see* 9060
AutoZone, Inc. Corporate Giving Program, TN, 8558
Avant! Foundation, The, CA, 394
Avatar Meher Baba Foundation Inc., CT, 1327
Avery Dennison Foundation, CA, 395
Avery International Foundation, CA, *see* 395
Avery Scholarship Foundation, NY, 5744
Avery-Fuller Children's Center, CA, *see* 396
Avery-Fuller-Welch Children's Foundation, CA, 396
Avoda Club of Atlantic County, The, NJ, 5393
Avon Foundation for Women, NY, 5745
Avon Foundation, NY, *see* 5745
Avon Products Foundation, Inc., NY, *see* 5745
Avondale Foundation, MI, 4341
AVX/Kyocera Foundation, SC, 8450
AWP, VA, *see* 9323
AWS Foundation, FL, 1789
Ayer Scholarship Trust, The, NH, 5306
Ayer Trust, Waldo & Alice, RI, 8234
Ayers Foundation for the Artistically Gifted Mentally Ill, Nathaniel Anthony, The, GA, 2122
Ayers Foundation, Lucy C., Inc., RI, 8235
Ayres Home for Nurses, Lucy C., Inc., The, RI, *see* 8235
Ayres Memorial Foundation, Mabel Brickey, Inc., AR, 268
Ayres Student Fund Trust, Dr. Samuel & Mildred L., TX, 8700
Ayres Trust, Mildred L., TX, *see* 8700
Aysr Foundation, PA, 7719
Ayuda, Inc., DC, 1590
AZHHA Education Foundation, AZ, 167
AZTO, AZ, *see* 164

B'nai B'rith, DC, 1595
B'nai Brith Food Industry Lodge Foundation Inc, NJ, 5403
B-G Foundation, The, NC, *see* 6752
B.F. Foundation, NM, 5613
Babcock Fund, John C., RI, *see* 8236
Babcock Trust, Betsey E., RI, 8236
Babcock Trust, Bud H., OH, 6984
Baber Foundation, Weisell, IN, 2963
Babson's Midwest Memorial Foundation, Inc., KS, 3416
Baby Lyla's Angel Foundation, TX, 8701
Babylon Breast Cancer Coalition, Inc., NY, 5746
BAC, NY, *see* 5797
Bachhuber Foundation, Ted & Grace, Inc., WI, 9842
Bacile Scholarship Fund, Victor A., NY, 5747
Backlin Trust, Carl & Isabel, WI, 9843

Bacon Scholarship Fund, Daisy S., NY, 5748
Bacot Foundation, Inc., MS, *see* 4896
Bacot/Jolly McCarty Foundation, Inc., MS, 4896
Bader Fund, Franz and Virginia, PA, 7720
Badger Mining Corporate Associate Scholarship Trust, WI, 9844
Badger Mining Scholarship Trust, WI, 9845
Bagby Foundation for the Musical Arts, Inc., The, NY, 5749
Bagley Foundation Trust, Geraldine, OR, 7536
Bailey Family Foundation, Inc., The, FL, 1790
Bailey Family Memorial Trust, OK, 7451
Bailey Foundation Dtd. 11/30/53, RI, *see* 8237
Bailey Foundation, RI, 8237
Bailey Foundation, The, SC, 8451
Bailey Trust, Mary H., PA, 7721
Bainbridge Arts & Crafts, Inc., WA, 9565
Bainbridge-Ometepe Sister Islands Association, WA, 9566
Bair Memorial Trust, Charles M., MT, 5130
Baize Gospel Preaching Foundation, AZ, 168
Baker Educational Fund, Jessie H., NY, 5750
Baker Foundation, Clark and Ruby, GA, 2123
Baker Foundation, Howard, The, MI, 4342
Baker Foundation, The, AL, 11
Baker Memorial Award Foundation, Hobey, MN, 4696
Baker Memorial Scholarship, Carl & Grace, CA, 397
Baker Memorial Trust, Charles Milton, TN, A
Baker Trust, J. H., KS, 3417
Baker Trust, Lillian M., RI, 8238
Baker-Adams Scholarship Fund, RI, 8239
Baker/Geary Memorial Fund, Inc., KY, 3547
Bakes Scholarship Trust, John E., OH, 6985
Bakken Library of Electricity in Life, MN, *see* 4697
Bakken, The, MN, 4697
Balanchine Foundation, George, Inc., The, NY, 5751
Balfour Foundation, Lloyd G., MA, 3976
Balfour Gold Dusters, MA, 3977
Balke Trust, Rudy, Inc., CO, 1127
Ball State University Foundation, IN, 2964
Ball Trust, Nellie L., OH, 6986
Ball Zoological Society, John, MI, 4343
Ballard Foundation, John & Ann, LA, A
Ballard Memorial Scholarship Fund, Edward L., NC, 6566
Ballet Hispanico of New York, Inc., NY, 5752
Balso Foundation, CT, 1328
Baltimore Clayworks, Inc., MD, 3782
Baltimore Community Foundation, The, MD, 3783
Baltimore Washington Medical Center Foundation, Inc., MD, 3784
Bamberger Memorial Foundation, Ruth Eleanor Bamberger and John Ernest, UT, 9193
Bancorp Hawaii Charitable Foundation, HI, *see* 2272
BancTrust Opportunity Foundation, IL, 2410
Bane Foundation, Earl, KS, 3418
Banfield Charitable Trust, The, OR, 7537
Bangor Fuel Society, ME, 3689
Bank of Hawaii Foundation, HI, 2272
Bank of Stockton Educational Foundation, CA, 398
BankSouth Foundation Ltd., GA, 2124
Banner Health Foundation of Arizona, AZ, 170
Banner Health, AZ, 169
Bantly Charitable Trust, The, GA, 2125
Baptist Health Care Foundation of Montgomery, AL, 12
Baptist Health Care Foundation, Inc., FL, 1791
Baptist Health Foundation, AR, 269
Baptist Health System Foundation, Inc., FL, 1792
Baptist-Trinity Lutheran Legacy Foundation, MO, 4935
Baraboo Area Community Foundation, Inc., WI, *see* 10019
Baraga County Community Foundation, MI, 4344
Baraga-Houghton-Keweenaw Community Action Agency, Inc., MI, 4345
Barakat Foundation (USA), The, CA, A
Barber Family Foundation, IL, 2411
Barber Foundation, C. Glenn, OH, 6987
Barber Scholarship Trust, George and Hazel, MO, 4936
Barbershop Harmony Society, CA, *see* 999
Barberton Community Foundation, OH, 6988
Barden Foundation, Don H., Inc., MI, A
Barden Foundation, Inc., The, CT, 1329
Barillaro Scholarship Trust, Margaret & Dom, RI, 8240

Barlocker Foundation, William A., AZ, 171
Barnard Scholarship Trust, IL, 2412
Barnes Estate Trust, Raeburn E., OH, 6989
Barnes Group Foundation Inc., CT, 1330
Barnes Memorial Trust, Francis M., NC, 6567
Barnes Scholarship Trust, Fay T., IL, 2413
Barnett Foundation, Raymond & Mary D., Inc., KY, 3548
Barnett Jr. Foundation, James M., Inc., GA, 2126
Barnsley Foundation, Tom C., TX, 8702
Barr Foundation, Robert M. Barr and Roberta Armstrong, The, CO, 1128
Barr Foundation, Shelley & Terry, MI, 4346
Barr Trust, Cary C., IL, 2414
Barr Trust, Homer G., IA, 3242
Barrand & Bradford Scholarship, PA, 7722
Barrick Mercur Gold Mine Foundation, Inc., UT, 9194
Barrows Memorial and Trust Fund, Augustus & Kathleen, VT, 9236
Barry Community Foundation, MI, 4347
Bartell Scholarship Foundation Inc., Leslie, NJ, 5394
Bartholomew Family Scholarship & Loan Fund, TX, *see* 9139
Bartholomew Foundation, Frank H., The, CA, 399
Bartholomew Scholarship & Loan Fund f/b/o University of Oregon, Lyle P., TX, 8703
Bartko Foundation, PA, 7723
Bartlesville Public School Foundation, Inc., OK, 7452
Bartlett Foundation, Edward & Helen, OK, 7453
Bartlett Foundation, Edward E. Bartlett & Helen Turner, OK, *see* 7453
Bartlett Tree Foundation, CT, 1331
Bartlett Trust Fund, W. P., CA, 400
Bartlett Trust, Russell T. & Olive V., RI, 8241
Barto Scholarship Trust, Harold & Martha, TX, 8704
Barton Jr. Emerging Artist Fund, James S., NY, 5753
Baseball Assistance Team, NY, 5754
Bashinsky Foundation, Inc., AL, 13
Basic Fund, The, CA, 401
Basila Scholarship Fund, G., PA, 7724
Basilica of St. Adalbert Foundation, MI, 4348
Baskin Foundation, Graham Sefton & Anna Mae Sweeney, PA, 7725
Baskin Foundation, Peggy and Jack, The, CA, 402
Bass Endowment Fund, R. Aumon & Mary Scott, NC, 6568
Bass Memorial Foundation, Inc., NJ, 5395
Bass Memorial Foundation, Ruth, NJ, *see* 5395
Bassett Private Foundation, Lillian M., MA, 3978
Bat Conservation International, TX, 8705
Bates Foundation, Robert T., IA, 3243
Bath Rotary Student Fund, Inc., NY, 5755
Bathalter Scholarship Trust, Oswald and Sophia, IA, 3244
Baton Rouge Area Foundation, LA, 3644
Baton Rouge Jaycee Foundation, LA, *see* 3645
Baton Rouge State Fair Foundation, LA, 3645
Batre Scholarship Trust Fund, Lloyd, AL, 14
Battered Women's Assistance, CA, 403
Batterton Fund Trust, Fred (B. A.), KY, 3549
Battle Creek Community Foundation, MI, 4349
Battle Creek Foundation, Greater, MI, *see* 4349
Bauer Foundation, CT, 1332
Bauer Fund, Frederick R., CT, 1333
Baumberger Endowment, TX, 8706
BAX, NY, *see* 5798
Baxter Family Foundation Inc., K. & F., CA, 404
Bay and Paul Foundations, Inc., The, NY, 5756
Bay Area Community Foundation, MI, 4350
Bay Area Video Coalition, CA, 405
Bay Harbor Foundation, The, MI, 4351
Bayer Hemophilia Awards Program, The, NC, 6569
Baystate Health Foundation, Inc., MA, 3979
BBCN Bank Scholarship Foundation, CA, 406
BCMW Community Services, IL, 2415
Beacon of Learning Foundation, NY, 5757
Beal Scholarship Foundation, Bernard H., OH, 6990
Beal Trust, Anna, WI, 9846
Beal, Jr. Memorial Trust, Jon C., KS, 3419
Beall Family Foundation, Robert & Aldona, The, FL, 1793
Beall Family Foundation, The, FL, *see* 1793
Beall, Sr. Charitable Foundation, R. M., FL, 1794

Beall, Sr. Charitable Operating Foundation, R. M., FL, 1795
Bean Foundation, The, NH, 5307
Bean Scholarship Fund, L. Carl, OH, 6991
Beane Family Foundation, OH, 6992
Beard Family Foundation, PA, see 8016
Beard Foundation, James, Inc., NY, 5758
Bearden Lumber Company Scholarship Foundation, Inc., AR, 270
Beartooth Billings Clinic Foundation, MT, 5131
Beartooth Hospital & Health Center Foundation, MT, see 5131
Beattie Scholarship Fund, John J. and Mildred M., NC, 6570
Beattie Scholarship Trust Fund, Harold W. and Emily K., MO, 4937
Beatty Trust, Cordelia Lunceford, OK, 7454
Beaumont Foundation of America, TX, 8707
Beaumont Hospital, William, MI, 4352
Beaver County Foundation, The, PA, 7726
Beaver Foundation, Dennis and Anne, The, CA, 407
Beaver Scholarship Foundation, Patrick, NC, 6571
Bechtner Education Foundation, Paul, IL, 2416
Becker Scholarship Fund, Davis, IL, 2417
Beckley Area Foundation, Inc., WV, 9766
Beckman Foundation, Arnold and Mabel, CA, 408
Beckstrand Cancer Foundation, Grant, CA, 409
BECU Foundation, WA, 9567
Bedford Community Foundation, MI, 4353
Bedford Community Health Foundation, VA, 9324
Bedford Foundation, MI, see 4353
Bedsole Foundation, J. L., The, AL, 15
Beebe Fund for Musicians, Frank Huntington, MA, 3980
Beebe Scholarship Fund, Charles A., IL, 2418
Beech Foundation, Inc., GA, 2127
Beefmaster Breeders Universal Brian Murphy Memorial Scholarhip Fund, TX, 8708
Bees Scholarship Foundation, John & Nesbeth, MI, 4354
Behnke Foundation, The, WA, 9568
Beinke Scholarship Fund, George C., OH, 6993
Bel-Air Film and Arts Foundation, Inc., CA, 410
Belden Foundation, Joseph C., IN, 2965
Belgian American Educational Foundation, Inc., CT, 1334
Belknap, M.D. Free Bed Fund, Robert W., ME, 3690
Bell and Tricia Flynn Caley Memorial Scholarship Fund, Stephen P., RI, see 8242
Bell Association for the Deaf and Hard of Hearing, Alexander Graham, DC, 1591
Bell Charitable Trust, Gloria Wille Bell and Carlos R., The, VA, 9325
Bell Charitable Trust, Louis E., MO, 4938
Bell, Timothy A. Bell and Tricia Flynn Caley Memorial Scholarship, Stephen P., RI, 8242
Bellamy Educational Trust, Richard C. and Esther, TX, 8709
Belleville Foundation Inc., NJ, 5396
Bellevue Schools Foundation, The, WA, 9569
Bellinger Scholarship Fund, Don & Iva M., MI, 4355
Bellingham Food Bank, WA, see 9560
Belmont Golf Scholarship Fund, Inc., The, MA, 3981
Beloit Community Foundation, Greater, The, WI, see 10047
Belpre Area Community Development Foundation, OH, 6994
Belvedere Cove Foundation, The, CA, 411
Bemis Center for Contemporary Arts, Inc., NE, 5186
Bemis Family Foundation, F. K., WI, 9847
Bemis Scholarship Fund, Samuel L., MI, 4356
Bender Scholarship Trust, Otto, IL, 2419
Beneficial Foundation, Inc., DE, see 1498
Benefis Healthcare Foundation, Inc., MT, 5132
Beneke Scholarship Fund, Phyllis A., IL, 2420
Benford Charities, George H., PA, 7727
Benjamin Foundation, Bennie & Martha, Inc., The, FL, 1796
Benjamin Franklin Bank Charitable Foundation, MA, see 4245
Benjamin Trust Fund, IL, 2421
Bennett Memorial Corporation, James Gordon, The, NY, 5759
Bennett Scholarship Fund, Joe & Mary Helen, FL, 1797

Bennett Scholarship Fund, M. A. & L. J., IL, 2422
Bennett, Sr. Trust f/b/o Towanda High School Scholarships, Robert L., PA, 7728
Benson Scholarship Trust Fund, Anne, OR, 7538
Bentley Charitable Trust, Frank C. and Georgia M., MO, 4939
Bentley Trust, Frank F., OH, 6995
Benton Community Foundation, IN, 2966
Benton County Foundation, OR, 7539
Benton-Franklin Community Action Committee, Inc., WA, 9570
Benz Foundation, William L. & Margaret L., PA, 7729
Benz Trust, Doris L., MA, 3982
Beren Foundation, Lois & Max, KS, 3420
Berger Scholarship Foundation, Herbert, NY, 5760
Bergman-Davison-Webster Charitable Trust, TX, 8710
Bering Straits Foundation, AK, 105
Berkowitz Scholarship Foundation Inc., Edwin J., NJ, 5397
Berks County Community Foundation, PA, 7730
Berkshire Bank Foundation, Inc., MA, 3983
Berkshire Community Action Council, Inc., MA, 3984
Berkshire Community College Foundation, Inc., MA, 3985
Berkshire Educational Operating Foundation, John & Ina, TN, 8559
Berkshire Taconic Community Foundation, MA, 3986
Berlin Family Educational Foundation, OH, 6996
Berliner Foundation Trust, Mary Anne, NM, 5614
Bernards Area Scholarship Assistance, Inc., NJ, 5398
Berner Charitable and Scholarship Foundation, The, IL, 2423
Berner Educational Trust No. 2, NV, 5279
Bernhard-Wentz Scholarship Fund, OH, 6997
Bernowski Scholarship Trust Fund, PA, 7731
Bernstein Scholarship Fund, Nathan, LA, 3646
Bernstine and Henrietta Harris Scholarship Fund, Sadie, The, NC, see 6695
Berntsen Memorial Foundation, Tyler, The, NY, 5761
Berrie Foundation, Russell, The, NJ, 5399
Berrien Community Foundation, Inc., MI, 4357
Berry Fund Charitable Foundation, MA, see 4084
Berry Scholarship, Janice T., RI, 8243
Berry Trust, Janice T., RI, see 8243
Bertelsmann Foundation U.S., Inc., NY, see 6344
Berwin Memorial Foundation, Celia, TX, 8711
Berwind Foundation, Charles G., Inc., PA, 7732
Best Friends Foundation, DC, 1592
Beta Kappa Phi Alpha Gamma Rho Scholarship Foundation, MA, 3987
Beta Kappa Phi Alpha Gamma Rho Scholarship Foundation, The, MA, see 3987
Beth Davis in Good Company, Inc., MD, 3785
Beth Medrash Govoha of Lakewood, Inc., NJ, 5400
Bethesda Center for the Homeless, Inc., NC, 6572
Bethlehem Area Foundation, PA, see 7953
Better Health of Cumberland County, Inc., NC, 6573
Betts Foundation, TX, 8712
Betts Trust No. 113, George V. & Cora, IL, 2424
Bialis Family Foundation, CA, 412
Bianco Foundation, Bernard, CO, 1129
Bible Alliance, Inc., FL, see 1788
Bible Students Aid Foundation, KY, 3550
Bibliographical Society of America, Inc., NY, 5762
Bickerstaff Family Foundation, CA, 413
Bicket Memorial Scholarship Fund Inc., Dr. William J., The, NJ, 5401
Bicycle Man Community Outreach Center, NC, 6574
Bicycleman Community Outreach, NC, see 6574
Biddle Foundation, Mary L. C., PA, 7733
Biddle Paragraph Twelfth Trust, Margaret T., NY, see 5763
Biddle Trust Twelfth, Margaret T., NY, 5763
Biederstedt Scholarship Fund, Evelyn E., IL, 2425
Biegelsen Foundation, Inc., FL, 1798
Big Bend Hospice, Inc., FL, 1799
Big Green Scholarship Foundation, Inc., WV, 9767
Big Guy Foundation, Inc., NY, 5764
Big Sandy Area Community Action Program, Inc., KY, 3551
Biglane Foundation, D.A., MS, 4897
Biomet Foundation, Inc., The, IN, see 3018
Biondo Memorial Trust, Ingeborg A., PA, 7734

Biondo Memorial Trust, Ingeborg A., PA, see 7734
Birbeck Charitable Trust, Lester R., WI, 9848
Birk's HIKE Foundation, Matt, Inc., MN, 4698
Birkenstock Family Foundation, MI, 4358
Birmingham Community Chest, The, AL, see 86
Birmingham Foundation, Greater, The, AL, see 27
Birmingham Student Loan & Scholarship Fund, MI, 4359
Birr Scholarship Foundation, Robert, Inc., The, OH, 6998
Birtwistle Family Foundation, MI, 4360
Birtwistle Foundation, Donald B., MI, see 4360
Bishop Educational Trust, IA, 3245
Bishop Perpetual Scholarship Fund for Iowa Valley Community School District, Rex & Christine, IA, 3246
Bishop-Fleet Foundation, WA, 9571
Bishopric Foundation, OH, see 7080
Bissell Fund for Hospital Aid, Dr. William, Inc., CT, A
Bixby Community Health Foundation, MI, 4361
Blac Hospitality Initiative of Greater Miami, FL, 1800
Black Foundation, Norman, ND, see 6941
Black Hawk College Foundation, IL, 2426
Black Hills Area Community Foundation, SD, 8521
Black Hills Workshop Foundation, SD, 8522
Black Memorial Fund, Abner & Eliza, IA, 3247
Black Memorial Scholarship Trust, Jim, TX, 8713
Black River Falls Area Foundation, WI, 9849
Black Rock Arts Foundation, CA, 414
Black Scholarship Fund, Art B. and Evelyn H., RI, see 8244
Black Student Fund, The, DC, 1593
Black Trust, Evelyn H., RI, 8244
Black United Fund of Oregon, OR, 7540
Blackburn Athletic & Scholarship Foundation, Camron D., CA, 415
Blackburn Prize, Susan Smith, Inc., TX, 8714
Blackford County Community Foundation, Inc., IN, 2967
Blacklock Nature Sanctuary, MN, 4699
Blade Foundation, OH, 6999
Blair Construction Scholarship Foundation, VA, 9326
Blair Scholarship Trust, F. Kelsay, IN, 2968
Blair Scholarship Trust, Lula Mae, IN, 2969
Blaisdell Foundation, Philo & Sarah, PA, 7735
Blake Scholarship Fund, Eubie, NY, see 5765
Blake Scholarship Trust, James Hubert, NY, 5765
Blake Trust, Marion Tyler, NY, 5766
Blakemore Foundation, WA, 9572
Blakeslee Trust for Scholarships, Henry L. & Nellie E., RI, 8245
Blanchard Scholarship Fund, George Gardner & Fanny Whiting, RI, 8246
Blanchard Trust, Arthur F., PA, 7736
Blanchard Trust, Grace T., MA, 3988
Blanchard Valley Health Foundation, OH, 7000
Bland Scholarship Trust, Lenora Ford and W. Jennings, OH, 7001
Blandin Foundation, Charles K., MN, 4700
Blandin Scholarship Trust, Jasper W. & Catherine L., NH, 5308
Blankenship/Justice Scholarship Fund Trust, FL, 1801
Blarney Fund Education Trust, NY, 5767
Blaske-Hill Foundation, MI, 4362
Blaylock Foundation, Inc., AL, 16
Blazek Foundation, Joseph, The, IL, 2427
Blees Educational Foundation, William A., NY, see 5820
Bleuer Scholarship Fund, John M. & Elizabeth Beeman, MS, 4898
Block Foundation, Herb, DC, 1594
Bloomer Charitable Trust, James J., NY, 5768
Bloomington Community Foundation, Inc., IN, see 2991
Blosser Scholarship Trust, Peter J., OH, 7002
Blosser Scholarship Trust, Peter J., OH, see 7002
Blosser Trust, Marlin E., NY, 5769
Blount Educational & Charitable Foundation, Mildred W., The, AL, 17
Blount Educational Foundation, David Strouse, FL, 1802
Blowing Rock Community Foundation, NC, 6575
BLSJ Scholarship Foundation, NJ, 5402
Blue Cross Blue Shield of Massachusetts Foundation, Inc. for Expanding Healthcare Access, MA, 3989

Blue Cross Blue Shield of Michigan Foundation, MI, 4363

Blue Earth Alliance, WA, 9573

Blue Grass Community Foundation, Inc., KY, 3552

Blue Grass Foundation, Inc., KY, see 3552

Blue Mountain Area Foundation, WA, see 9574

Blue Mountain Center, NY, 5770

Blue Mountain Community Foundation, WA, 9574

Blue River Community Foundation, Inc., The, IN, 2970

Blue River Foundation, Inc., The, IN, see 2970

Bluecoats of Louisville, OH, 7003

Bluefield Area Foundation, Inc., WV, see 9777

Blues Babe Foundation, PA, 7737

BMC Associate Scholarship Trust, WI, see 9844

BMI Foundation, Inc., NY, 5771

Boand Family Foundation, CA, 416

Boch Family Foundation, The, MA, 3990

Bodine—Sunkist Memorial Foundation, A. W., CA, 417

Boehringer Ingelheim Cares Foundation, Inc., CT, 1335

Boeing Employees Credit Union Foundation, WA, see 9567

Boer Solar Energy Medal of Merit Award Trust, Karl W., WI, 9850

Bogan Foundation, Beau, The, DC, 1596

Bogan Scholarship Foundation, R. Chad, FL, A

Bogardus Trust, Katherine, IL, 2428

Boggan Scholarship Fund Trust, George S. & Carrie Lee, AR, 271

Boghossian Foundation, Paul O. & Mary, RI, 8247

Boghossian Memorial Trust, Paul O. & Mary, RI, see 8247

Bogliasco Foundation, Inc., The, NY, 5772

Bogni Trust, E. Dante, NH, 5309

Bohne-Pace Memorial Scholarship Fund, Erik, IL, 2429

Bohnett Memorial Foundation, Violet R. and Nada V., WA, 9575

Bohnett Memorial Foundation, Violet R., WA, see 9575

Boise Legacy Constructors Foundation Inc., ID, 2329

Boland, Jr. Memorial Scholarship Fund, Vincent M., NJ, 5404

Boldin Foundation, Anquan, FL, 1803

Bolingbrook Police Benevolent Foundation, IL, 2430

Bolivar Educational Advancement Foundation, MO, 4940

Bon Charitable Trust, Giorgio, The, NY, 5773

Bone Marrow Foundation, Inc., The, NY, 5774

Boneal Charitable Foundation Inc., KY, 3553

Bonei Olam, Inc., NY, 5775

Bonfils-Stanton Foundation, CO, 1130

Bonfire Foundation, The, CT, 1336

Bonham Educational Trust, Mary, The, TX, 8715

Bonner-Price Student Loan Fund Trust, PA, 7738

Bontrager Medical Scholarship Trust, Blancheola, OH, 7004

Boogie's Diner Foundation, CO, 1131

Boone Trust, James D., OH, 7005

Boonshot Memorial Scholarship Trust, James S., IN, 2971

Bootstraps Foundation of the Kiwanis Club of Nashville, Inc., The, TN, see 8560

Bootstraps Foundation, Inc., The, TN, 8560

Borax Education Foundation, The, UT, 9195

Borchert Scholarship Fund, Walter & Cecile, NY, 5776

Borck Family Foundation, Inc., CT, 1337

Borden Foundation, T.A. Frank & Sallie, NC, 6576

Border Art Residency, NM, 5615

Borelli & Family Scholarship Fund, Pamela, TX, see 8716

Borelli Family Scholarship, TX, 8716

Borg Institute for Women and Technology, Anita, CA, 418

Borton-Ryder Memorial Trust, TX, 8717

Bosaw Memorial Scholarship Fund, Willard / Lillian, OH, 7006

Boscov-Berk-Tek, Inc., Scholarship Fund, PA, 7739

Bossak-Heilbron Charitable Foundation, Inc., NY, 5777

Bossola - Colombo Club Scholarship Fund, Lawrence, The, CA, 419

Boston Adult Literacy Fund, MA, see 4069

Boston Art Dealers Association Trust, MA, 3991

Boston Chapter CPCU Trust, MA, 3992

Boston Fatherless & Widows Society, MA, 3993

Boston Leather Trade Benevolent Society, MA, 3994

Boston Local Development Corporation, MA, 3995

Boston Post Office Employees Credit Union Charitable Foundation, MA, see 4070

Boston Scientific Foundation, Inc., MA, 3996

Botsford Trust, Helen C.S., RI, 8248

Botstiber Foundation, Dietrich W., The, PA, 7740

Bott Foundation, Dr. & Mrs. Edmund T., Inc., MI, 4364

Bottemiller Family Foundation, MN, 4701

Bottrell/Dolan Family Foundation, MT, 5133

Bouchard Scholarship Foundation, L. & S., OH, 7007

Boulder County Arts Alliance, CO, 1132

Boulos Foundation, Chris and Katherine, IL, 2431

Bound To Stay Bound Books Foundation, IL, 2432

Bour Memorial Scholarship Fund, TX, 8718

Bouslog Labor Scholarship Fund, Harriet, HI, 2273

Bowen Foundation, Ethel N., WV, 9768

Bowen Foundation, Inc., IN, 2972

Bowen Scholarship Fund, OH, 7008

Bowen Trust, R. A., The, GA, 2128

Bowie Interfaith Pantry and Emergency Aid Fund, MD, 3786

Bowling Green Community Foundation, Inc., OH, 7009

Bowling Green State University Foundation, Inc., OH, 7010

Bowmaker Scholarship Trust, V. A., RI, see 8249

Bowmaker Scholarship Trust, Virginia A., RI, 8249

Bowman Black Catholic Educational Foundation, Sister Thea, MN, 4702

Bowman Scholarship Trust, Robert T. & Beatrice V., NY, 5778

Bowsher Foundation Trust, Nelson P., NC, 6577

Box Project, Inc., The, MS, 4899

Boyd Charitable Foundation Trust, John & Billie, AL, 18

Boyd Memorial Foundation, Thomas H., IL, see 2501

Boyd Scholarship Fund, Polly, TN, 8561

Boye Scholarship Trust, NC, 6578

Boyer First City Troop, John, PA, 7741

Boyer First Troop Philadelphia City Cavalry Memorial Fund, John, PA, see 7741

Boyer M.D. Charitable Foundation, Kevin L., Inc., FL, 1804

Boyer Memorial Scholarship Fund, Marvin, The, CA, see 420

Boyer Scholarship Foundation, Marvin, CA, 420

Boyle Educational Fund of the Margaret Hess Boyle Trust, M C Hess and Margaret Hess, KS, 3421

Boyle Memorial Scholarship Fund, Bernard F., PA, 7742

Boyle Scholarship Fund, Hazel Marie, IL, 2433

Boyle Trust, Margaret Hess, KS, see 3421

Boyne Foundation, SC, 8452

Boynton-Gillespie Memorial Funds, IL, 2434

Boys & Girls Clubs of America, GA, 2129

Boys & Girls Clubs of Middle Tennessee, Inc., TN, 8562

Boys and Girls Clubs of Metro Denver, Inc., CO, 1133

Boys Hope Girls Hope Affiliates, MO, 4941

Boys Hope Girls Hope National, MO, 4942

Brack Charitable Foundation, Joan H., The, RI, 8250

Brackett Foundation, The, NY, 5779

Brackett Refugee Education Fund, The, NY, see 5779

Bradish Memorial Scholarship Fund, FL, 1805

Bradish Trust, Norman C., FL, see 1805

Bradley Foundation, The, CA, 421

Bradley Scholarship Trust Fund, Don L., WA, 9576

Bradshaw Trust, The, WA, 9577

Brady Memorial Scholarship Trust, Lorraine M. And Eugene P., NY, 5780

Bragan Youth Foundation Scholarship Fund, Bobby, Inc., TX, 8719

Bragg Foundation, Herbert E. & Marion K., FL, 1806

Brain and Behavior Research Foundation, NY, see 6239

Bran Inc., NE, 5187

Branch County Community Foundation, MI, 4365

Brandt Scholarship Fund, NC, 6579

Branford Community Foundation, Inc., CT, 1338

Braswell Fund, GA, 2130

Braverman Foundation, Joel, Inc., NY, 5781

Bray Foundation, Archie, MT, 5134

Bray Scholarship, James W. & Carolyn, IA, 3248

Brayton Education Trust, Dorothy M., OH, 7011

Brazos Community Foundation, TX, 8720

BRCH Foundation, Inc., FL, see 1813

Bread and Roses Community Fund, PA, 7743

Breast Cancer Help, Inc., NY, 5782

Breast Cancer Research Foundation, Inc., The, NY, 5783

Breast Cancer Society, Inc., The, AZ, 172

Breast Cancer Survivors, CA, 422

Breckenridge Outdoor Education Center, CO, 1134

Breckinridge Scholarship Fund Trust, Elizabeth, IL, 2435

Breeding Foundation, The, AZ, 173

Brege Memorial Foundation, Jonathan D., IL, 2436

Breindel Memorial Foundation, Eric, Inc., The, NY, 5784

Brennan Scholarship Fund, B. K., Inc., RI, 8251

Brenneman Fund, J. P. Brenneman & M. H., PA, 7744

Brenske Scholarship Fund, C. William, MI, 4366

Brenske Student Loan Fund, Anthony Stephen & Elizabeth E., MI, 4367

Bretzlaff Foundation, Hilda E., Inc., The, MI, 4368

Brevard Heart Foundation, Inc., FL, 1807

Brevillier Village Foundation Inc, PA, 7745

Brewer & McKay Scholarship Foundation, OH, 7012

Brewer Family Foundation, Robert N., IL, 2437

Brewer Foundation Inc., NC, 6580

Brewster Education Foundation, Inc., NY, 5785

Brewton Foundation, Greater, The, AL, 19

Brey Memorial Endowment Fund, Claude Brey and Ina L., MO, 4943

Bridge Builders Community Foundation, PA, 7746

Bridge for Runaway Youth, Inc., The, MN, 4703

Bridgebuilder Scholarship Fund, VA, 9327

Bridgeport Hospital Foundation, Inc., CT, 1339

Bridges Memorial Scholarship, Alton, NC, 6581

Bridgewater State College Foundation, MA, 3997

Brierley Memorial Charitable Foundation, Tim, Inc., MD, 3787

Briggs & Stratton Corporation Foundation, Inc., WI, 9851

Bright Star Foundation, Inc., MD, 3788

Brighten Your Future, OH, 7013

Brightfocus Foundation, MD, 3789

Brightman Scholarship Foundation, Lou and Lucienne, MA, 3998

Brightwell School, A. T., Inc., GA, 2131

Brill Scholarship Foundation, Marion, Inc., NY, 5786

Brillion Foundation Inc., WI, 9852

Bring on the Music, Inc., CA, see 989

Brink Trust Scholarship Fund, E., NY, 5787

Brinker Scholarship Fund, Dorothea, AZ, 174

Brisley & Noma Brisley Phillips Scholarship Loan Fund, Ella Frances, TX, see 8721

Brisley Scholarship Loan Fund, TX, 8721

Bristol Bay Economic Development Corporation, AK, 106

Bristol Bay Native Corp., Education Foundation, AK, 107

Bristol Elder Services, Inc., MA, 3999

Bristol Yale Scholarship Fund Inc., CT, 1340

Bristol-Myers Squibb Patient Assistance Foundation, Inc., The, NY, 5788

British Charitable Society, MA, see 4000

British Society, Inc., MA, 4000

Britton Memorial Scholarship Fund, Mervin, OH, 7014

Broad Biomedical Research Foundation, Ruth K., Inc., The, NC, 6582

Broadbent Family Foundation, The, PA, 7747

Broadbent Foundation, The, PA, see 7747

Broadcast Education Association, DC, 1597

Broadcasters Foundation of America, NY, 5789

Broadcasters Foundation, Inc., NY, see 5789

Broadway Cares/Equity Fights AIDS, NY, 5790

Broady Family Opportunity Foundation, George K. & Eleanor J., TX, 8722

Brock Trust, Mary E., RI, 8252

Brockbank Education Fund, VA, 9328

Brockman Trust, Leo J., TX, 8723

Brockton Rotary Charitable & Educational Fund, Inc., MA, 4001

Brockway Foundation for the Needy of the Village and Township of Homer, New York, NY, 5791

Broderbund Foundation, CA, see 464

Broida/Sigma-Aldrich Scholarship Fund, Dan, Inc., MO, 4944

Brondum Special Assistance Foundation, Marshall and Mary, Inc., MT, 5135

Bronfman Prize Foundation, Charles R., The, NY, 5792
Bronson Scholarship Foundation Inc., R. Carlyle, FL, 1808
Bronx Council on the Arts, NY, 5793
Bronx Museum of the Arts, The, NY, 5794
Bronx Shepherds Restoration Corporation, NY, 5795
Brookdale Foundation, The, NJ, 5405
Brookings Foundation, SD, 8523
Brooklyn Architects Scholarship Foundation, Inc., NY, 5796
Brooklyn Arts Council, The, NY, 5797
Brooklyn Arts Exchange, Inc., NY, 5798
Brooks Charities, Derrick, FL, 1809
Brooks Foundation, Aubrey Lee, NC, 6583
Brooks Foundation, Herb, The, MN, 4704
Brooks Foundation, Sunshine, CA, 423
Brooks Scholarship Foundation, Verl I., IL, 2438
Brookshire Foundation, William A., TX, 8724
Brookville Foundation, IN, 2973
Broome County Arts Council, Inc., NY, 5799
Broomfield Community Foundation, The, CO, 1135
Brossman Family Charitable Trust for Scholarships, The, PA, 7748
Broward Community College Foundation, Inc., FL, 1810
Broward Community Foundation, Inc., FL, 1841
Broward County Grandparents, Inc., FL, see 2059
Broward Education Foundation, FL, 1811
Brown & Brown Disaster Relief Foundation, Inc., FL, 1812
Brown Brothers Harriman & Co. Undergraduate Fund, NY, 5800
Brown Center for the Study of American Civilization, John Nicholas, The, RI, 8253
Brown County Community Foundation, Inc., IN, 2974
Brown County Foundation, OH, 7015
Brown Education Trust, Richard F. Brown & Pearl P., GA, 2132
Brown Educational Scholarship Fund, Joe, TX, 8725
Brown Educational Trust, Selma McKrill, IN, 2975
Brown f/b/o Randolph Uhs, Clayton, CT, 1341
Brown Foundation, Arch and Bruce, The, NY, 5801
Brown Foundation, Ira B., Inc., NJ, see 5423
Brown Foundation, Lucille, CO, 1136
Brown Foundation, Sunny, CA, 424
Brown Memorial Foundation, KS, 3422
Brown Memorial Fund, Fern, IL, 2439
Brown Memorial Scholarship Fund, J. Leonard, IL, 2440
Brown Memorial Scholarships, Le Roy C., WI, see 9853
Brown Scholar Fund, Ron, VA, 9329
Brown Scholarship Foundation, Judge John R., The, TX, 8726
Brown Scholarship Foundation, Lorene, IL, 2441
Brown Scholarship Trust, Marion D., IN, 2976
Brown Teacher's Fund, T. Wistar, PA, 7749
Brown Testamentary Trust, Marguerite V., WI, 9853
Brown Trust No. 363, Raena, IL, 2442
Brown Trust, Florence H., PA, 7750
Brown Trust, Gabriel J., ND, 6935
Brown Trust, H. Fletcher, PA, see 7750
Brown Trust, T. Wistar, PA, see 7749
Brown, Fulton Maryland Scholarship Trust Fund, Vernon W., MD, 3790
Brownell Charitable Fund, Dr. and Mrs. C. R., LA, 3647
BRRH Foundation, Inc., FL, 1813
Bruce Trust, Blanche A., NH, 5310
Brummer-Stiles-Duncan Scholarship Fund, The, IA, 3249
Bruneo Foundation, Joseph & Angela, WI, 9854
Bruno Family Foundation, Michael and Beverly, WI, 9855
Brunswick Family Assistance Agency, NC, 6584
Brunswick Foundation, Inc., The, IL, 2443
Brush Foundation, Kelly S., Inc., The, VT, 9237
Brush Foundation, OH, 7016
Bruton Foundation, Benjamin F. & Ernestine, IL, 2444
Bryan Area Foundation, Inc., OH, 7017
Bryan College Students Fund, Fred A., NE, 5188
Bryan Foundation, Dodd and Dorothy L., WY, 10095
BryanLGH Foundation, NE, 5189
Bryant Chucking Grinder Company Charitable Foundation, VT, see 9240
Buchalter Foundation, Samuel & Esther, Inc., The, NJ, 5406

Buchanan Area Foundation, MI, see 4538
Buchly Charity Fund of Federal Lodge, The, VA, 9330
Buck Educational Foundation, C.A., NC, 6585
Buck Foundation, The, AR, 272
Buck International, Pearl S., Inc., PA, 7751
Buckley Foundation, Helen Ann, CA, 425
Buckner Adoption and Maternity Services, Inc., TX, 8727
Buckner Children and Family Services, Inc., TX, 8728
Buckner Scholarship Trust, Margaret G., MO, 4945
Bucks County Foundation, PA, 7752
Bucyrus Area Community Foundation, OH, see 7057
Buddhist Film Foundation, CA, 426
Buerger Scholarship Fund, Bobby, IN, 2977
Buffalo Media Resources, Inc., NY, see 6423
Buffalo Sabres Alumni Association, NY, 5802
Buffalo Urban League, Inc., NY, 5803
Buffett Foundation, Susan Thompson, The, NE, 5190
Buffett Foundation, The, NE, see 5190
Build-A-Bear Workshop Foundation, Inc., MO, 4946
Builder's Exchange of Santa Clara County Scholarship Fund, CA, 427
Building Hope Foundation, Inc., CT, 1342
Buisch Memorial Scholarship Fund, Elizabeth Roosa, NY, 5804
Buist Foundation, MI, 4369
Bulkeley School, Trustees of the, CT, 1343
Bulkley Foundation Trust, The, IL, see 2445
Bulkley, Jr. Trust, Everett S., IL, 2445
Bullitt Foundation, The, WA, 9578
Buncombe County Partnership for Children, NC, see 6864
Bunn Memorial Fund, Henry, IL, 2446
Burbage Foundation Inc., Jack, MD, 3791
Burch-Setton Student Loan Fund, PA, 7753
Burchfield Trust, Daisy L., IA, 3250
Burden Center for the Aging, Inc., The, NY, see 5821
Burger King Scholars, VA, 9331
Burgess Memorial Scholarship Fund, William, Agnes & Elizabeth, IL, 2447
Burke Foundation, Thomas C., The, GA, 2133
Burke Memorial Fund, John P., RI, 8254
Burke-Weber Memorial Trust, NC, 6586
Burkhalter Educational Fund, The, MO, 4947
Burks Charitable Trust, CA, 428
Burlington County Community Action Program, NJ, 5407
Burlington Edison Education & Alumni Foundation, WA, 9579
Burlington Industries Foundation, NC, 6587
Burlington Medical Center Staff Foundation, IA, see 3287
Burn Foundation, Alisa Ann Ruch, CA, 429
Burnett Foundation, Belle C., NY, 5805
Burnham Educational Trust, John & Ellen, OH, 7018
Burnside Foundation, Warren and Betty, Inc., The, WV, 9769
Burrows Little Falls Foundation, The, NY, 5806
Burson Memorial Scholarship Fund, Dennett L., IL, 2448
Burtman Charity Trust, Abraham, NH, 5311
Burton Charitable Trust, Evelyn Wylie, CO, 1137
Burton Foundation, William T. and Ethel Lewis, The, LA, 3648
Burton Trust, Lila Draper, IL, 2449
Burwen Education Foundation, CA, 430
Busch Family Foundation, CA, 431
Busey-Mills Community Foundation, IL, 2450
Bush Foundation, MN, 4705
Bush Memorial Scholarship Fund, William E. and Margaret N., PA, 7754
Bush Memorial Scholarship Trust, Elizabeth B., OH, 7019
Bush Presidential Library Foundation, George, TX, 8729
Bushee Foundation, Florence Evans, Inc., MA, 4002
Bushnell Arts Foundation, IL, 2451
Business and Professional People for the Public Interest, IL, 2452
Business and Professional Women's Foundation, The, DC, A
Butler Foundation, Alice, NC, 6588
Butler Foundation, The, NH, 5312
Butler Manufacturing Company Foundation, MO, 4948

Butler Memorial Scholarship Foundation, J. D. and Alice, NC, see 6588
Butler-Wells Scholarship Fund, OH, 7020
Butt Grocery Company Contributions Program, H. E., TX, 8730
Butte Creek Foundation, CA, 432
Butterer Educational Trust, M. Verna, PA, 7755
Butterworth Memorial Trust, William, IL, 2453
Buttonwood Foundation, Inc., The, NY, 5807
Buttrey Memorial Trust, Jane, OR, 7541
Butts Memorial Fund, Gertrude, Inc., NJ, 5408
Butts Scholarship Foundation, Art & Clara, NE, 5191
Bybee Family Foundation, The, UT, 9196
Byram Rotary Foundation, CT, 1344
Byram-Cos Cob Rotary Foundation, CT, see 1344
Byrne Family Foundation, MI, 4370
Byrnes Foundation, James F., SC, 8453

C & E Foundation, PA, see 8106
C Spire Wireless Foundation, MS, 4900
C-CAP, NY, see 5817
C.A.C., WA, see 9597
C.E.F., MI, see 4382
C.E.F.S. Economic Opportunity Corporation, IL, 2454
C.L.C. Foundation, TX, 8731
C.M.J. Private Foundation, CA, see 701
C.U.R.E., IL, see 2482
Cabot Scholarship Foundation, Inc., AR, 273
Cabot Scholarship Fund, IL, 2455
Cabot Trust Inc., Ella Lyman, MA, 4003
Cabrillo College Foundation, CA, 433
Cacique Foundation, CA, 434
Cadbury Schweppes Americas Emergency Relief Fund, TX, 8732
Cadillac Area Community Foundation, MI, 4371
Cady Charity Trust, George A., NC, 6589
Caesars Foundation of Floyd County, The, IN, see 3062
Caestecker Foundation, Charles & Marie, IL, 2456
CAEYC, CO, 1138
Cafaro Family Foundation, William M. & A., The, OH, 7021
Cahp Foundation, CA, 435
Cain Family Foundation, The, CA, 436
Cal Humanities, CA, 437
Cal Poly Pomona Foundation, Inc., CA, 438
Cal State East Bay Educational Foundation, CA, 439
Calcot-Seitz Foundation, CA, 440
Caldera, OR, 7542
Calhoun County Arts Council, MI, see 4649
Calhoun County Community Foundation, AL, see 28
California Academy of Family Physicians Foundation, CA, 441
California Association for Bilingual Education, CA, 442
California Association of Realtors Scholarship Foundation, CA, 443
California Bar Foundation, CA, 444
California Bar Foundation, CA, see 444
California Community Foundation, CA, 445
California Council for the Humanities, CA, see 437
California Council on Science and Technology, CA, 446
California Dental Association Foundation, CA, 447
California Dental Association Research Fund, CA, see 447
California Farm Bureau Scholarship Foundation, CA, 448
California Federation of Teachers - AFT 8004, CA, 449
California HealthCare Foundation, CA, 450
California Highway Patrol 11-99 Foundation, The, CA, 451
California Human Development Corporation, CA, 452
California Japanese American Alumni Association, CA, 453
California Job's Daughters Foundation, Inc., CA, 454
California Masonic Foundation, CA, 455
California New Car Dealers Association Scholarship Foundation, CA, see 456
California New Car Dealers Scholarship Foundation, CA, 456
California Scottish Rite Foundation, CA, 457
California Soldiers' Widows Home Association, CA, see 791
California Space Grant Foundation, CA, see 1007

California State Summer School Arts Foundation, CA, 458

California State University, Fullerton, Philanthropic Foundation, CA, 459

California Teachers Association Disaster Relief Fund, CA, 460

California Wellness Foundation, The, CA, 461

Calista Scholarship Fund, AK, 108

Calkins Trust, Ina, MO, 4949

Callaway Foundation, Fuller E., GA, 2134

Callaway Professorial Chairs, Trust for Fuller E., The, FL, 1814

Calman Trust, Henry, NY, 5808

Calumet Area Community Health Foundation, WI, 9856

Calvert Memorial Merit Scholarship Foundation, Stephen G., PA, 7756

Calvi Memorial Foundation, Francis L., NJ, 5409

Camargo Foundation, The, MN, 4706

Cambridge Savings Charitable Foundation Inc., MA, 4004

Camden County Hero Scholarship Fund - 200 Club, Inc., NJ, 5410

Camden Home for Senior Citizens, ME, 3691

Camden Student Trust Fund, ME, see 3741

Camden Trust Fund for Student Loans, ME, see 3741

Camden-Clark Foundation, Inc., WV, 9770

Camellia Foundation, CA, see 789

Camera News, Inc., NY, 5809

Cameron Educational Foundation, Dave, SC, 8454

Cameron Foundation, Ryan, GA, 2135

Camp Arcadia Scholarship Foundation, NJ, 5411

Camp Foundation, VA, 9332

Camp Hertko Hollow, Inc., IA, 3251

Camp Memorial Scholarship Foundation, Joan, IL, 2457

Camp Mohawk Scholarship Trust, TX, 8733

Camp Open Arms, Inc., CA, see 1039

Camp Trust R62440004, Lucille, IL, 2458

Campanelli Charitable Foundation, Alfred, MA, 4005

Campbell Charitable Foundation, Hubert, MO, 4950

Campbell Charitable Trust, Ruth Camp, NY, 5810

Campbell Foundation, Ernest and Lillian E., CO, 1139

Campbell Scholarship Fund for Linfield College Students, W.C. & Pearl, OR, 7543

Campbell Scholarship Trust, J. Colin, OH, 7022

Camphill Foundation, NY, 5811

CAN, CA, see 530

Canaan Exchange Club Charitable Trust, CT, 1345

Canady Charitable Foundation Trust, Valerie, The, WV, 9771

Cancer Aid and Research Fund, AZ, 175

Cancer Care, Inc., NY, 5812

Cancer for College, CA, 462

Cancer Fund of America, Inc., TN, 8563

Cancer Research and Prevention Foundation, VA, see 9487

Cancer Research Fund of the Damon Runyon-Walter Winchell Foundation, NY, see 6365

Cancer Research Institute, Inc., NY, 5813

Cancer Services, Inc., NC, 6590

Cannon Scholarship Foundation, Jesse W., TX, 8734

Canton Community Foundation, MI, 4372

Cantor Art Foundation, B. G., The, CA, see 463

Cantor Fitzgerald Relief Fund, NY, 5814

Cantor Foundation, Iris & B. Gerald, CA, 463

Cantor Foundation, Jasmine L., Inc., NY, 5815

CAP Charitable Foundation USA, VA, see 9329

CAP Services, Inc., WI, 9857

Cape Cod Community College Educational Foundation, Inc., The, MA, 4006

Cape Cod Foundation, The, MA, 4007

Cape Cod Times Needy Fund, Inc., MA, 4008

Cape Coral Community Foundation, FL, 1815

Cape Girardeau Public School Foundation, MO, 4951

Capezio/Ballet Makers Dance Foundation, Inc., NJ, 5412

Capital One Financial Corporation Contributions Program, VA, 9333

Capital Partners for Education, Inc., DC, 1598

Capital Workforce Partners, Inc., CT, 1346

Caples Scholarship Foundation, Katie, Inc., FL, 1816

Cara Program, The, IL, 2459

Carbondale Clay Center, CO, 1140

Carco 31 Charitable Foundation, Robert C., MA, 4009

Cardinal Glennon Childrens Hospital Foundation, MO, 4952

Cardiovascular Medical Research and Education Fund, Inc., The, PA, 7757

Care and Share, Inc., CO, 1141

Care Consistency Foundation, Inc., MS, 4901

Care To Share, OR, 7544

Career Alliance, Inc., MI, 4373

Career Path Services-Employment and Training, WA, 9580

Career Transition For Dancers, NY, 5816

Careers through Culinary Arts Program, Inc., NY, 5817

CareLink Network, Inc., MI, 4374

Carhart Memorial Fund Trust, Amory S., VA, 9334

Caring 4 Kids Foundation, NV, 5280

Caring Athletes Team for Children's and Henry Ford Hospitals, MI, 4375

Caring for Carcinoid Foundation, Inc., MA, 4010

Caring Foundation, Inc., The, UT, see 9222

Caring Voice Coalition, Inc., VA, 9335

Caritas of Austin, TX, 8735

Caritas of Waco, TX, 8736

Carkeek Trust, Florence Lewis, WA, 9581

Carleton College, Board of Trustees of, OH, 7023

Carlisle Charitable Trust 2, Michael, WI, 9858

Carlisle Trust for Children of Goshen Trust, Alice L., RI, 8255

Carlsbad Foundation, Inc., NM, 5616

Carlson Company Foundation, Fred, IA, 3252

Carlson Memorial Scholarship Trust Fund for Performing Arts, Elizabeth, CT, 1347

Carlston Family Foundation, CA, 464

Carman Family Charitable Foundation, The, MA, 4011

Carman Scholarship Trust, Nellie Martin, OH, 7024

Carmel Trust, J. Russell & Gladys Irene, PA, see 7758

Carmell Scholarship Trust Fund, PA, 7758

Carnegie Fund for Authors, NY, 5818

Carnegie Hero Fund Commission, PA, 7759

Carnes Education Charitable Trust, Francis F., WI, 9859

Carney Scholarship Fund, Helen K., OH, 7025

Carolina Children's Charity, Inc., SC, 8455

Carolina Community Actions, Inc., SC, 8456

CarolinaEast Foundation, NC, 6591

Carpe Diem Foundation of Illinois, IL, 2460

Carpenter Foundation, Milton, Inc., NY, 5819

Carpenter Scholarship Trust, Norman & Ardis, MI, 4376

Carpenter Trust, John S., NC, 6592

Carpenter's Shelter, Inc., VA, 9336

Carpenter-Garcia Scholarship Fund, OH, 7026

Carr Foundation Inc., Clinton J., MO, 4953

Carreon, M.D. Foundation, Reynaldo J., CA, 465

Carrier & Bryant Distributors' Educational Foundation, NY, 5820

Carrier Charitable Trust, Glen, OK, 7455

Carrier Foundation, Robert M. & Lenore W., TN, 8564

Carroll Charitable Foundation, MA, 4012

Carroll County Arts Council, MD, 3792

Carroll Foundation Inc., Anne, The, MA, 4013

Carroll High School Memorial Scholarship Fund, IA, 3253

Carroll-Wyatt Testamentary Education Trust, IN, 2978

Carson Electric Education Foundation Inc, Kit, NM, 5617

Carson Scholars Fund, Inc., MD, 3793

Carson Scholarship Fund, Ben & Verna, MN, 4707

Carter & Graham Smith Memorial Scholarship Fund, Eula, TX, 8737

Carter Burden Center for the Aging, Inc., The, NY, 5821

Carter Center, Inc., The, GA, 2136

Carter Family Foundation, WV, 9772

Carter Scholarship Fund, Shawn, FL, 1817

Carter Star-Telegram Employees Fund, Amon G., TX, 8738

Carter Trust Fund For The Southeast Polk School Dist., Marie L. & John L., IA, 3254

Carter Trust Fund, Marie L. & John L., IA, see 3254

Carter Trust, Evelyn C., IL, 2461

Caruso-Sperl Irrevocable Charitable Trust, IL, 2462

Carver Scholarship Fund, Inc., NY, 5822

Carving Studio & Sculpture Center, The, VT, 9238

Cary Educational Fund, Isaac Harris, MA, 4014

Casey Foundation, Annie E., The, MD, 3794

Cash Foundation, J. B., Inc., TN, 8565

Casper Foundation, William J. & Gertrude R., WI, 9860

Cass County Community Foundation, Inc., IN, 2979

Cassner Foundation, The, OH, 7027

Castele Foundation, Dr. and Mrs. Theodore J., OH, 7028

Castrodale Scholarship Foundation, Dante, WV, 9773

Catalina Marketing Charitable Foundation, FL, 1818

Catalyst for Youth, CA, 466

Catawba County Council for the Arts, Inc., NC, see 6906

Catawba Valley Community College Foundation, NC, 6593

Catawissa Lumber & Specialty Co., Inc. Trust, PA, A CATCH, MI, see 4375

Catching the Dream, NM, 5618

Catholic Charities - Diocese of Metuchen, NJ, 5413

Catholic Charities Community Services, Archdiocese of New York, NY, 5823

Catholic Charities Community Services, Inc., AZ, 176

Catholic Charities CYO of the Archdiocese of San Francisco, CA, 467

Catholic Charities Diocese of Fort Worth, Inc., TX, 8739

Catholic Charities of Dallas, Inc., TX, 8740

Catholic Charities of San Jose, CA, 468

Catholic Charities of Santa Clara County, CA, see 468

Catholic Charities of Southern Nevada, NV, 5281

Catholic Charities of St. Paul and Minneapolis, MN, 4708

Catholic Charities of Tennessee, Inc., TN, 8566

Catholic Charities of the Archdiocese of Chicago, IL, 2463

Catholic Charities of the Archdiocese of Galveston-Houston, TX, 8741

Catholic Charities of the Archdiocese of Milwaukee, Inc., WI, 9861

Catholic Charities of the Diocese of Pittsburgh, PA, 7760

Catholic Charities Southwestern Ohio, OH, 7029

Catholic Charities, Diocese of Joliet, IL, 2464

Catholic Charities, Diocese of St. Petersburg, Inc., FL, 1820

Catholic Charities, Diocese of Trenton, NJ, 5414

Catholic Charities, FL, 1819

Catholic Christmas Campaign, Inc., NJ, 5415

Catholic Christmas Crusade, NJ, see 5415

Catholic Education Foundation Diocese of Evansville, IN, 2980

Catholic Foundation of Oklahoma, Inc., OK, 7456

Catholic Guardian Society and Home Bureau, NY, 5824

Catholic Health Initiatives - Colorado, CO, 1142

Catholic Mission Aid, OH, 7030

Catholic Social Services of Southwestern Ohio, OH, see 7029

Catholic Teachers Association of the Diocese of Brooklyn, Inc., NY, 5825

Catholic Tuition Organization of the Diocese of Phoenix, AZ, 177

Catt Educational Fund, Frank and Edith, IL, 2465

Cattaraugus Region Community Foundation, NY, 5826

Cattell Fund, James McKeen, NC, 6594

Cattle Raisers Museum, TX, see 9116

Caudill Optimist Scholarship Fund, Jeff, Inc., KY, 3554

Cavalier Foundation, CA, 469

Cave Canem Foundation, Inc., NY, 5827

Caves Valley Golf Club Foundation, Inc., MD, 3795

Caves Valley Scholars Foundation, Inc., MD, see 3795

Cawasa Grange Memorial Scholarship Fund, Inc., The, CT, 1348

CCH, CA, see 437

CCSNYS, NY, see 5893

CCSU Foundation, Inc., CT, 1349

CDA Foundation, CA, see 447

CDS International, Inc., NY, 5828

CEC ArtsLink, Inc., NY, 5829

Cecil County Bar Foundation, Inc., MD, 3796

Cedar Rapids Community Foundation, Greater, The, IA, 3255

Cedar Rapids Foundation, Greater, The, IA, see 3255

CEDARS Home for Children Foundation, Inc., The, NE, 5192

Cedars of Monroeville, The, PA, see 7991

Celebration Foundation, The, OR, 7545

Celebrity Fund for Children's Charities, CA, 470

Center for Alternative Media and Culture, NY, 5830
Center for Architecture Foundation, NY, 5831
Center for Book Arts, Inc., NY, 5832
Center for Community Action, PA, 7761
Center for Community and Family Services, CA, 471
Center for Contemporary Printmaking, CT, 1350
Center for Craft, Creativity & Design, Inc., NC, 6595
Center for Cultural and Technical Interchange Between East and West, Inc., HI, 2274
Center for Cultural Innovation, CA, 472
Center for Emerging Visual Artists, The, PA, 7762
Center for Independent Documentary, Inc., The, MA, 4015
Center for Independent Living of Southwestern Pennsylvania, PA, see 8146
Center for Jewish History, Inc., The, NY, 5833
Center for Land Use Interpretation, The, CA, 473
Center for Nonprofit Advancement, DC, 1599
Center for Photography of Woodstock, Inc., The, NY, 5834
Center for Retirement Research, MA, 4016
Center for Social Inclusion, NY, 5835
Center of Theological Inquiry, NJ, 5416
CentraCare Health Foundation, MN, 4709
Central Alabama Community Foundation, Inc., AL, 20
Central Area Motivation Program, WA, 9582
Central Boston Elder Services, Inc., MA, 4017
Central Carolina Community Foundation, SC, 8457
Central Illinois Agency on Aging, IL, 2466
Central Minnesota Arts Board, MN, 4710
Central Minnesota Community Foundation, MN, 4711
Central Minnesota Initiative Fund, MN, see 4764
Central Missouri Community Action, MO, 4954
Central Missouri Counties Human Development Corporation, MO, see 4954
Central Montcalm Community Foundation, MI, 4377
Central National-Gottesman Foundation, The, NY, 5836
Central New Mexico Electric Education Foundation, NM, 5619
Central New York Community Foundation, Inc., NY, 5837
Central Oregon Singers, Inc., OR, 7546
Central Scholarship Bureau, Inc., The, MD, 3797
Central Susquehanna Community Foundation, PA, 7763
Central Valley Electric Education Foundation, NM, 5620
Central Valley High School Scholarship Fund, CA, 474
Central Valley Low Income Housing Corporation, CA, 475
Central Vermont Community Action Council, Inc., VT, 9239
Central Wholesale Liquor Foundation, IL, see 2815
Centralia Foundation, IL, 2467
Centrum Foundation, WA, 9583
Century Brass Sunshine Fund, RI, see 8389
Century Foundation, The, VA, 9337
CenturyLink-Clarke M. Williams Foundation, DE, 1494
Cephalon Cares Foundation, PA, see 8142
Cerebral Palsy International Research Foundation, Inc., NJ, 5417
Cervical Spine Research Society, IL, 2468
CF Industries, Inc. Corporate Giving Program, IL, 2469
CFC, MA, see 4023
CFDA Foundation, Inc., NY, 5838
CFEF, TX, see 8780
CFOV, WV, see 9776
CFVI, VI, see 9274
CGH Health Foundation, IL, 2470
Chadwell-Townsend Private Foundation, OH, A
Chadwick Foundation, ID, 2330
Chaffer Scholarship Trust, Joyce A., NC, 6596
Chairman's Award Foundation, TX, see 8902
Chakrabarti Foundation, The, NJ, 5418
Challenged Athletes, Inc., CA, 476
Chalone Wine Foundation, CA, see 1100
Chamber Music America, NY, 5839
Chamber Music Northwest, Inc., OR, 7547
Chamberlain Foundation for Public Enrichment, B. R., FL, 1821
Chamberlin Scholarship Fund, Frank A. & Gladys F., TX, 8742
Chambers Charitable Trust, Mary Cecile, The, TX, 8743
Chambers Foundation, Roy, The, WV, 9774

Chambers Scholarship Fund, Mary Cecile, The, TX, see 8743
Chaminade Development Fund, Inc., NY, 5840
Chandler Trust, Esther, RI, 8256
Chaney Foundation Ltd., DE, 1495
Chaney Foundation, Eugene, Ltd., DE, see 1495
Chaney Scholarship Fund, Hazel M., OH, 7031
Chang Foundation, MI, 4378
Change a Life Foundation, CA, 477
Change, Inc., FL, 1822
Chaparral Foundation, Inc., CA, 478
Chapman Foundation, Mark A., TX, 8744
Chapman Foundation, The, AZ, see 178
Chapman Foundation, William H., CT, 1351
Chapman Fund, The, AZ, 178
Chapman Trust Fund, AL, 21
Chappell Memorial Fund, Corabelle, NC, 6597
Chargers Community Foundation, The, CA, see 929
Chariott Memorial Scholarship Fund, Eugene J., Inc., The, CT, 1352
Charitable Foundation of the Bryant Chucking Grinder Company, VT, 9240
Charitable Society in Hartford, CT, 1353
Charity League, Inc., The, AL, 22
Charity Motors, Inc., MI, 4379
Charles River Foundation, MA, see 4018
Charles River Laboratories Foundation, Inc., MA, 4018
Charleston County Human Services Commission, Inc., SC, 8458
Charleston Scientific & Cultural Educational Fund, SC, 8459
Charlevoix County Community Foundation, MI, 4380
Charlotte Hall School Board of Trustees Inc., MD, 3798
Charlton Educational Trust, Donald L., IN, 2981
Charter Foundation, Inc., The, GA, 2137
Chase Foundation, NM, 5621
Chase Scholarship Fund, Hal S., IA, 3256
Chase Scholarship Fund, Lavere Leonard and Gladys Loraine, MI, 4381
chashama, Inc., NY, 5841
Chatham Citizens Scholarship Trust Fund, The, MA, 4019
Chatham Kiwanis Scholarship Fund, NJ, 5419
Chattanooga Neighborhood Enterprise, Inc., TN, 8567
Chattanooga Orthopedic Educational & Research Foundation, TN, 8568
Chaudhary Foundation, Younas & Bushra, TX, 8745
Chautauqua Region Community Foundation, Inc., NY, 5842
Cheek,Jr. Scholarship Fund, T. Franklin, TN, 8569
Chelan-Douglas County Community Action Council, WA, 9584
Chelonian Research Foundation, MA, 4020
Chelsea Education Foundation, Inc., MI, 4382
CHEMCENTRAL Charitable Trust, WA, 9585
Chenango County Medical Society & The Otsego County Medical Society, NY, 5843
Chenega Future, Inc., AK, 109
Chenoweth Foundation, Elizabeth, Inc., TN, 8570
Cherith Christian Private Foundation, CA, 479
Cherokee & Walker Foundation, The, UT, 9197
Cherokee Caddy Scholarship Foundation, Inc., The, GA, 2138
Cherokee Preservation Foundation, Inc., NC, 6598
Cherry Blossom Breast Cancer Foundation, VA, 9338
Chesapeake Bay Trust, MD, 3799
Chesapeake Research Consortium, Inc., MD, 3800
Chesed Avrhom Hacohn Foundation, NY, 5844
Chesed V'Emet The Avigdor Ben Yosef Family Foundation, MO, 4955
Chesley Foundation, Robert, Inc., The, CA, 480
Chessall Memorial Scholarship Fund, William A., CA, 481
Chest and Foundation of the Fur Industry of the City of New York, Inc., NY, 5845
CHEST Foundation, IL, 2471
Chester County Community Foundation, PA, 7764
Chester High School Alumni Association, MA, 4021
Chetek Area Scholarship Foundation, Inc., WI, 9862
Chevelle Foundation, Judge C. C., WA, 9586
Chi Omega Foundation, TN, 8571
Chicago Bar Foundation, The, IL, 2472
Chicago Community Trust, The, IL, 2473

Chicago Foundation for Education, IL, 2474
Chicago Symphony Orchestra, IL, 2475
Chicago White Metal Charitable Foundation, IL, 2476
Chicana Foundation of Northern CA, CA, 482
Chicana/Latina Foundation, CA, see 482
Chick-fil-A, Inc. Corporate Giving Program, GA, 2139
Chickasaw Foundation, OK, 7457
Chico Community Foundation, CA, see 831
Chico Community Hospital Foundation, CA, see 832
Chief's Athlete Scholarship Fund, Inc., SC, 8460
Child Abuse Prevention Foundation, CA, see 884
Child and Family Resources, Inc., NJ, 5420
Child Care Choices, Inc., MN, 4712
Child Care Connection, Inc., NJ, 5421
Child Care Links Association, KS, 3423
Child Care of Southwest Florida, Inc., FL, 1823
Child Care Resources of Monmouth County, Inc., NJ, 5422
Child Care Services Association, NC, 6599
Child Care Services of Monmouth County, Inc., NJ, see 5422
Child Day Care Association of Saint Louis, MO, 4956
Child Development Associates, Inc., CA, 483
Child Nutrition Foundation, MD, see 3928
Child Nutrition Program of Southern California, Inc., CA, 484
Child Nutrition, Inc., VA, 9339
Childcare Resources, AL, 23
Childhood Brain Tumor Foundation, Inc., The, MD, 3801
Children Affected by AIDS Foundation, CA, 485
Children and Families First Delaware, Inc., DE, 1496
Children at Heart Foundation, Inc., TX, 8746
Children at the Crossroads Foundation, IL, 2477
Children for Children, NY, 5846
Children of China Pediatrics Foundation, NY, 5847
Children of Promise International, OH, 7032
Children of Promise, Inc., GA, 2140
Children with Diabetes Foundation, The, CO, 1143
Children's Aid Association of Amsterdam, NY, NY, 5848
Children's Aid Society, NY, 5849
Children's AIDS Fund, VA, 9340
Children's Bureau, Inc., IN, 2982
Children's Cancer Fund of America, Inc., TN, 8572
Children's Council of San Francisco, CA, 487
Children's Defense Fund, DC, 1600
Children's Diabetes Foundation at Denver, CO, 1144
Children's Discovery Foundation, WA, 9587
Children's Dream Fund, Inc., FL, 1824
Children's Forum, Inc., The, FL, 1825
Children's Foundation for the Arts, Inc., NJ, 5423
Children's Fund, Inc., CA, 488
Children's Health Fund, CA, see 908
Children's Heart Foundation, The, IL, 2478
Children's Home & Aid Society of Illinois, IL, 2479
Children's Home Society of Florida, FL, 1826
Children's Hospital and Regional Medical Center, WA, 9588
Children's Hospital Corporation, MA, 4022
Children's Hospital Foundation, The, KY, 3555
Children's Hunger Fund, CA, 489
Children's Leukemia Foundation of Michigan, MI, 4383
Children's Medifund Corporation, CA, 490
Children's Memorial Hospital, IL, see 2401
Children's Museum of Indianapolis, Inc., The, IN, 2983
Children's Network International, CA, 491
Children's Oncology Services, Inc., IL, 2480
Children's Scholarship Fund - Metro Jackson, TN, 8573
Children's Scholarship Fund Charlotte, NC, 6600
Children's Scholarship Fund of Greater Cincinnati, Inc., OH, 7033
Children's Scholarship Fund Philadelphia, PA, 7765
Children's Scholarship Fund, NY, 5850
Children's Tumor Foundation, NY, 5851
Childrens Burn Foundation, CA, 486
Childress Foundation, TX, 8747
Childs Memorial Fund for Medical Research, Jane Coffin, The, CT, 1354
Chillicothe-Ross Community Foundation, Inc., OH, 7034
China Care Foundation, Inc., CT, 1355
China Times Cultural Foundation, CA, 492

Chinati Foundation, The, TX, 8748

Chinese American Citizens Alliance Foundation, CA, 493

Chinese Church Planting Partners, PA, 7766

Chinese Staff and Workers Association, Inc., NY, 5852

Ching Foundation, Hung Wo & Elizabeth Lau, HI, 2275

Chmielewski Educational Foundation, Melanie V., WI, 9863

CHN Foundation, WI, see 9870

Choanoke Area Development Association, NC, 6601

Choggiung Education Endowment Foundation, AK, 110

Choice Hotels International Foundation, MD, 3802

Cholnoky Foundation, Thomas, Inc., The, CT, 1356

Chong Foundation, Stanley & Marvel, MN, 4713

Chopra Center Foundation, CA, 494

Chordoma Foundation, NC, 6602

Choson Foundation, The, GA, 2141

Christ Child Society, Inc., DC, 1601

Christ Scholarship Fund, Albert A., IL, 2481

Christ Scholarship Fund, Elmer S. and Frances R., PA, 7767

Christamore Aid Society, Inc., IN, see 2984

Christamore House Guild, Inc., IN, 2984

Christian Appalachian Project, Inc., KY, 3556

Christian Broadcasting Network, Inc., The, VA, 9341

Christian BusinessCares Foundation, OH, 7035

Christian Chiropractor's Association, CO, 1145

Christian Community Action, TX, 8749

Christian Community Foundation, CO, see 1305

Christian Fellowship Foundation of the Peace United Church of Christ, MN, 4714

Christian Foundation for Children & Aging, KS, 3424

Christian Foundation of Indiana, Inc., IN, 2985

Christian Healthcare Ministries, Inc., OH, 7036

Christian International Scholarship Foundation, IL, see 2842

Christian Mission Concerns of Tennessee, Inc., WY, 10096

Christian Mission to Gaza, CA, 495

Christian Scholars Foundation, CO, 1146

Christian Scholarship Foundation, AZ, 179

Christian Scholarship Foundation, Inc., GA, 2142

Christian Scholarship Fund of Arizona, AZ, 180

Christian Sharing Center, Inc., The, FL, 1827

Christmas in Action - Greater Cleburne, Inc., TX, 8750

Christmas in April Greater Cleburne, Inc., TX, see 8750

Christus Foundation for Health Care, TX, see 9097

Christus Health Gulf Coast Region, TX, 8751

Christy Scholarship Fund, Van and Joanna, RI, 8257

Chronicle Season of Sharing Fund, CA, 496

Chrysopolae Foundation, CA, 497

CHS Foundation, MN, 4715

Chubb Foundation, The, NJ, 5424

Chugach Heritage Foundation, AK, 111

Chugiak-Eagle River Foundation, AK, 112

Chung Charitable Foundation Inc., The, CA, 498

Chung Kun Ai Foundation, HI, 2276

Chung-Ahm-Jeewon & Jong Lee Scholarship Foundation, Inc., CA, 499

Chung-Hee Fellowship, Kil, PA, 7768

Church Memorial Fund, Bradford & Dorothy, RI, 8258

Churches Homes Foundation, Inc., GA, 2143

CIA Officers Memorial Foundation, VA, 9342

CIACO Inc., IN, 2986

Cianci, Jr. Scholarship Fund, Vincent A., RI, 8259

Ciatti Memorial Foundation, Joseph D., CA, 500

Cibrowski Family Foundation, CO, 1147

CIC Foundation, Inc., TN, 8574

CIC, Inc., DC, 1602

CIF of the San Francisco Foundation, CA, see 517

Cilley Trust, Elwin L., RI, 8260

Cincinnati Enquirer Foundation, The, OH, 7037

Cinereach Ltd., NY, 5853

Cintas Foundation, Inc., FL, 1828

CIRI Foundation, The, AK, 113

Cirillo Scholarship Foundation, Adam, NY, 5854

Cirio Foundation, Inc., NY, 5855

Cismoski Foundation, Bish & Frannie, RI, 8261

Cisneros Del Moral Foundation, Alfredo, Inc., TX, 8752

Cisneros Fontanals Foundation for the Arts, FL, 1829

Citizens Development Corps, Inc., DC, 1603

Citizens for Citizens, Inc., MA, 4023

Citizens Scholarship Foundation, KS, see 3515

Citizens Union Bank Foundation, Ltd., GA, see 2124

Citizens United for Research in Epilepsy, IL, 2482

Citizens' Scholarship Foundation of America, MN, see 4845

Citrus County Circle of Friends, Inc., FL, 1830

City College 21st Century Foundation, Inc., The, NY, 5856

City Hospital Foundation, Inc., WV, 9775

City Parks Foundation, NY, 5857

City Year, Inc., MA, 4024

Civic Ventures, CA, 501

Civil Service Employees Association, Inc., The, NY, 5858

Civitan Child Welfare Auxiliary, Inc., TN, 8575

Civitan International Foundation, AL, see 24

Civitan International, AL, 24

CJ Foundation for SIDS, Inc., The, NJ, 5425

CJR Fund, Inc., CT, 1357

Clan MacBean Foundation, The, CO, 1148

Clancy Scholarship Foundation, Helen Miller, WA, 9589

Clareth Fund: The Philadelphia Association of Zeta Psi Fraternity, The, PA, 7769

Claretknoll Foundation, The, IL, 2483

Clarinda Foundation, The, IA, 3257

Clark Community College District 14 Foundation, WA, 9590

Clark County Community Foundation, WA, see 9599

Clark Educational Fund, Gordon H. & Ruth A., NC, 6603

Clark Family Memorial Fund, Alvin T., WY, see 10097

Clark Foundation, B.M., CT, 1358

Clark Foundation, James T., CO, 1149

Clark Foundation, The, NY, 5859

Clark League Trust, Mary, PA, 7770

Clark Medical Memorial Fund, RI, 8262

Clark Medical Memorial Fund, Welsford Starr and Mildred M., RI, see 8262

Clark Memorial Fund, Alvin T., WY, 10097

Clark Memorial Trust, Royce W., The, NY, 5860

Clark Scholarship Fund, CO, 1150

Clark Scholarship Trust, Donald, CA, 502

Clark Scholarship Trust, FL, 1831

Clark Scholarship Trust, Grace W. Clark, Thomas R. & Elsie T., FL, see 1831

Clark-AFF League Memorial Fund, PA, see 7770

Clarke Endowment Fund, Louis G. & Elizabeth L., OR, 7548

Clarke Testamentary Trust/Fund Foundation, Elizabeth Church, WA, 9591

Clarke Trust, Francis Earl and Edwina Jones, NH, 5313

Clarke Trust, Rachel Fiero, OH, 7038

Clarkson Eyecare Foundation, MO, 4957

Clarkson Scholarship Foundation, George M. & Florence M., MT, 5136

Class of 1968 Scholarship, Inc., PA, 7771

Clausen Family Foundation, SD, 8524

Clay County Educational Endowment Association, Inc., KS, 3425

Clay Scholarship & Research Fund, William L., MO, 4958

Clay Studio of Missoula, The, MT, 5137

Clay Studio, The, PA, 7772

Clayman Family Foundation Inc., OH, 7039

Clayton Kiwanis Scholarship Foundation, NJ, 5426

Clayton Scholarship Trust, Bernard & Anna, MO, 4959

Clearway Minnesota, MN, 4716

Cleburne Rotary Club Foundation Inc., TX, 8753

Cleft Palate Foundation, NC, 6604

Clemens Foundation, The, OR, 7549

Clements Scholarship, H. Lorens, NC, 6605

Clemson Community Care, Inc., SC, 8461

Clemson University Research Foundation, SC, 8462

Clergy Society, SC, 8463

Cleveland Alumnae Panhellenic Endowment Fund, Inc., OH, 7040

Cleveland Arts Prize, OH, 7041

Cleveland Browns Foundation, OH, 7042

Cleveland Clinic Foundation Affiliates, OH, 7043

Cleveland County Partnership for Children, Inc., NC, 6606

Cleveland Foundation, The, OH, 7044

Cleveland National Air Show Charitable Foundation, OH, 7045

Cleveland Scholarship Programs, Inc., OH, see 7050

Clifford Foundation, Inc., TX, 8754

Clifford Scholarship Fund, Ted & Elinor, VT, 9241

Clifton Institute, The, NE, see 5263

Cline Memorial Scholarship Fund, Charles & Hazel, OH, 7046

Clint Foundation, The, FL, 1832

Clinton Community College Foundation, Inc., NY, 5861

Clinton Rotary Scholarship Foundation, MI, 4384

Clopper Memorial Foundation, Paul W., IL, see 2644

Cloud County Children's Trust, KS, 3426

Cloud Forest Institute, CA, 503

Clover Park Foundation, WA, 9592

Clovis Community College Foundation, Inc., NM, 5622

Club Foundation, The, VA, 9343

Club Frontenac, Inc., RI, 8263

Club of Hearts, Inc., GA, 2144

CNA Foundation, IL, 2484

CNA Insurance Companies Foundation, IL, see 2484

CNN Heroes, NY, 5862

COAHSI, NY, see 5894

Coalition for Dwarf Advocacy, OR, 7550

Coast Guard Foundation, Inc., CT, 1359

Coastal Bend Community Foundation, TX, 8755

Coastal Bend Foundation, TX, 8756

Coastal Community Foundation of South Carolina, SC, 8464

Coastal Community Foundation, CA, 504

Coastal EMC Foundation, GA, 2145

Coastal Jewish Foundation, Inc., GA, 2146

Coats North American Educational Foundation, NC, 6607

Cobb Educational Fund, Ty, GA, 2147

Cobb Memorial Scholars, Frank & Ellen, RI, 8264

Coburn Scholarship Trust, E. B., TN, 8576

Coca-Cola Enterprises Charitable Foundation, The, GA, A

Coca-Cola Scholars Foundation, Inc., GA, 2148

Cochran Trust, Gifford A., PA, 7773

Cochrane Educational Trust, William H., IL, 2485

Cocker Kids' Foundation, Inc., CO, 1151

Cockerline Memorial Fund, OR, 7551

CoDA, OR, see 7550

Code Scholarship Fund, IA, 3258

Cody Medical Foundation, WY, 10098

Coe Fund, Marion Isabell, RI, 8265

Coe Medical & Surgical Fund for Education, William H., RI, 8266

Coe Trust, Helen R., RI, 8267

Coeli Foundation Inc., Regina, IL, 2486

Coffey Foundation, Inc., The, NC, 6608

Coffin's Lancasterian School, Admiral Sir Isaac, MA, 4025

Coffman Charitable Education Trust, Otto R., The, KS, 3427

Coffman Scholarship Trust, John F., NC, 6609

Cogan Trust, George T., NH, 5314

Cogar Foundation, Inc., NY, 5863

Cohen Family Foundation, Martin D., PA, 7774

Cohen Foundation Inc., Saul B. and Naomi R., MA, 4026

Cohen Foundation, David J. and Rosetta Adler, The, CA, 505

Cohen Foundation, William & Hannah, MO, 4960

Cohen Scholarship Fund, Rueben J. and Dorothy S., RI, 8268

Cohen Scholarship Fund, Sarah, FL, 1833

Cohill Memorial Scholarship Foundation, John L., OH, 7047

Coia Scholarship & Education Fund, Arthur E., RI, 8269

Coin Op Cares Education & Charitable Foundation, IL, 2487

Colbert Charitable Foundation, Lynn, OK, 7458

Colburn Education Foundation, Deo B., NY, 5864

Colburn Memorial Fund, William Cullen, NC, 6610

Colburn-Keenan Foundation, Inc., CT, 1360

Cold Heading Foundation, The, MI, 4385

Cole Foundation, Olive B., Inc., IN, 2987

Cole Scholarship Trust, Harold M., NC, 6611

Cole Trust, Bradford, MI, 4386

Coleman Scholarship Trust, Lillian R., IL, 2488

Coleman Scholarship Trust, William S. and Lillian R., IL, see 2488

Coleman Student Fund, Inc., NY, 5865

Colen Foundation, Inc., The, FL, 1834
Coles Foundation, Mary D., RI, 8270
Colf Family Foundation, WA, 9593
Colfax Community Network, Inc., CO, 1152
Collaborative Network of Lucas County, Inc., OH, 7048
Collectors Foundation, MI, 4387
College Art Association of America, Inc., NY, see 5866
College Art Association, NY, 5866
College Careers Fund of Westchester, Inc., NY, 5867
College Club of Cleveland Foundation, OH, 7049
College Club of Greater Lawrence, MA, 4027
College Club of St. Louis, MO, 4961
College Crusade of Rhode Island, The, RI, 8271
College First Foundation, TX, 8757
College Now Greater Cleveland, OH, 7050
College of American Pathologists Foundation, IL, 2489
College of William & Mary Foundation, The, VA, 9344
College Success Foundation, WA, 9594
Collegebound Foundation, Inc., MD, 3803
Coller Foundation, MI, 4388
Collins - McDonald Trust Fund, OR, 7552
Collins Foundation, Joseph, NY, 5868
Collins Scholarship Fund, Cardiss, The, IL, 2490
Collins Trust No. 2, Paul & Mary, WI, 9864
Collins/Chris Panatier 9/11 Memorial Foundation, Tom, Inc., NY, 5869
Collister Scholarship Trust, Roberta, CA, 506
Colman Trust, Blanche E., PA, 7775
Colonel's Kids, Inc., KY, see 3583
Colonnades Theatre Lab Inc., CA, 507
Colorado Academy of Family Physicians Foundation, CO, 1153
Colorado Association for the Education of Young Children, CO, see 1138
Colorado Health Foundation, The, CO, 1154
Colorado Homeless Families, Inc., CO, 1155
Colorado Housing Assistance Corporation, CO, 1156
Colorado Institute of Developmental Pediatrics, Inc., CO, 1157
Colorado Insurance and Business Education Foundation, CO, 1158
Colorado Legal Services, CO, 1159
Colorado Masons Benevolent Fund Association, CO, 1160
Colorado Mountain College Foundation, Inc., CO, 1161
Colorado Native Plant Society, CO, 1162
Colorado Nonprofit Development Center, The, CO, 1163
Colorado Professional Fire Fighters Foundation, CO, 1164
Colorado Rural Health Center, CO, 1165
Colorado Springs Camp No. 7226 Modern Woodmen of America Educational Trust, CO, 1166
Colorado State Grange Leadership and Scholarship Foundation, CO, 1167
Colorado State Grange Leadership and Scholarship Foundation, CO, see 1167
Colorado State Patrol Family Foundation, CO, 1168
Colorado State Science Fair, Inc., CO, 1169
Columbia Basin Foundation, WA, 9595
Columbia Community Foundation, OH, 7051
Columbia Endowment Fund, WA, 9596
Columbia Foundation for Public Interest Law, NY, see 6337
Columbia Foundation, CA, 508
Columbia Foundation, The, MD, see 3807
Columbia Heights High School Alumni Scholarship Foundation, MN, 4717
Columbia University-Presbyterian Hospital School of Nursing Alumni Association, NY, 5870
Columbus Arts Council, Greater, Inc., OH, 7052
Columbus Blue Jackets Foundation, OH, 7053
Columbus Citizens Foundation, Inc., NY, 5871
Columbus Community Foundation, KS, 3428
Columbus Electric Scholarship, Inc., NM, 5623
Columbus Female Benevolent Society, OH, 7054
Columbus Phipps Foundation, The, FL, 1835
Columbus Regional Medical Foundation, Inc., GA, 2149
Columbus Scholarship Fund, Christopher, PA, 7776
Colvin Scholarship Trust, Thomas S., OR, 7553
Comcast Foundation, The, PA, 7777
Come Together Foundation, MI, 4389
Comite Olimpico De Puerto Rico, PR, A

Commercial Bank Foundation, KY, 3557
Commission on Economic Opportunity of Luzerne County, PA, 7778
Common Counsel Foundation, CA, 509
Common Grace Ministries Inc., TX, 8758
Common Knowledge Scholarship Foundation, Inc., FL, 1836
Common Wealth Trust, DE, 1497
Commonwealth Fund, The, NY, 5872
Communication Arts Institute, AR, 274
Communications Workers of America Disaster Relief Fund, DC, 1604
Communities Foundation of Oklahoma, OK, 7459
Communities Foundation of Texas, Inc., TX, 8759
Community Action Agency for the Greater Stamford Area, The, CT, see 1372
Community Action Agency of Baldwin, Escambia, Clarke, Monroe, & Conecuh Counties, AL, 25
Community Action Agency of Siouxland, IA, 3259
Community Action Agency of Yamhill County, Inc., OR, see 7687
Community Action Center, WA, 9597
Community Action Council for Lexington-Fayette Bourbon, Harrison, and Nicholas Counties, KY, 3558
Community Action Council of Lewis Mason and Thurston Counties, WA, 9598
Community Action Council of Portage County, Inc., OH, 7055
Community Action Nacogdoches, Inc., TX, 8760
Community Action of Eastern Iowa, IA, 3260
Community Action of Minneapolis, MN, 4718
Community Action of Northeast Indiana, Inc., IN, 2988
Community Action of Southeast Iowa, IA, 3261
Community Action of St. Louis County, Inc., MO, 4962
Community Action Partnership of Lake County, IL, 2491
Community Action Partnership of North Alabama, AL, 26
Community Action Partnership of Ramsey and Washington Counties, MN, 4719
Community Action Partnership of the Greater Dayton Area, OH, 7056
Community Action Program Belknap & Merrimack Counties, Inc., NH, 5315
Community Action Program for Central Arkansas, AR, 275
Community Action Program of East Central Oregon, OR, 7554
Community Action Program of Evansville and Vanderburgh County, Inc., IN, 2989
Community Action Team, Inc., OR, 7555
Community Action, Inc., MA, 4028
Community and Family Services Foundation, WA, A
Community Arts Partnership of Tompkins County, Inc., NY, 5873
Community Assistance Center, HI, 2277
Community Assistance Network, Inc., MD, 3804
Community Contacts, Inc., IL, 2492
Community Coordinated Care for Children, Inc., FL, 1837
Community Coordinated Child Care, Inc., WI, 9865
Community Council of Greater Dallas, TX, 8761
Community Development Corporation of Long Island, Inc., NY, 5874
Community Fdn. of Delaware County, OH, see 7087
Community Food Bank, Inc., AZ, 181
Community Foundation Alliance of Calhoun County, MI, 4390
Community Foundation Alliance, Inc., IN, 2990
Community Foundation for Crawford County, OH, 7057
Community Foundation for Greater Atlanta, The, GA, 2150
Community Foundation for Greater Buffalo, NY, 5875
Community Foundation for Muskegon County, MI, 4391
Community Foundation for Northeast Michigan, MI, 4392
Community Foundation for Northern Virginia, VA, 9345
Community Foundation for Oak Park, CA, 510
Community Foundation for Palm Beach and Martin Counties, Inc., FL, 1839
Community Foundation for San Benito County, CA, 511
Community Foundation for South Central New York, Inc., The, NY, 5876

Community Foundation for Southeast Michigan, MI, 4393
Community Foundation for Southeastern Michigan, MI, see 4393
Community Foundation for Southern Arizona, AZ, 182
Community Foundation for Southwest Washington, WA, 9599
Community Foundation for the Alleghenies, The, PA, 7779
Community Foundation for the Greater Capital Region, Inc., The, NY, 5877
Community Foundation for the Land of Lincoln, IL, 2493
Community Foundation for the National Capital Region, The, DC, 1605
Community Foundation for the Ohio Valley, Inc., WV, 9776
Community Foundation in Jacksonville, The, FL, see 1838
Community Foundation of Abilene, TX, 8762
Community Foundation of Bloomington and Monroe County, Inc., IN, 2991
Community Foundation of Boone County, Inc., IN, 2992
Community Foundation of Brazoria County, Texas, The, TX, 8763
Community Foundation of Brevard County, Inc., FL, see 1840
Community Foundation of Brevard, FL, 1840
Community Foundation of Broward, FL, 1841
Community Foundation of Burke County, NC, 6612
Community Foundation of Cape Cod, The, MA, see 4007
Community Foundation of Carroll County, Inc., MD, 3805
Community Foundation of Central Florida, Inc., FL, 1842
Community Foundation of Central Georgia, Inc., GA, 2151
Community Foundation of Central Illinois, IL, 2494
Community Foundation of Central Wisconsin, Inc., WI, 9866
Community Foundation of Collier County, FL, 1843
Community Foundation of Dunn County, WI, 9867
Community Foundation of Eastern Connecticut, CT, 1361
Community Foundation of Elmira-Corning and the Finger Lakes, Inc., The, NY, 5878
Community Foundation of Fayette County, PA, 7780
Community Foundation of Frederick County, MD, Inc., The, MD, 3806
Community Foundation of Gaston County, Inc., NC, 6613
Community Foundation of Grant County, IN, 2993
Community Foundation of Greater Birmingham, AL, 27
Community Foundation of Greater Chattanooga, Inc., The, TN, 8577
Community Foundation of Greater Flint, MI, 4394
Community Foundation of Greater Fort Wayne, Inc., IN, 2994
Community Foundation of Greater Greensboro, Inc., NC, 6614
Community Foundation of Greater Jackson, MS, 4902
Community Foundation of Greater Johnstown, The, PA, see 7779
Community Foundation of Greater Lafayette, The, IN, 2995
Community Foundation of Greater Lorain County, The, OH, see 7058
Community Foundation of Greater Memphis, TN, 8578
Community Foundation of Greater Rochester, MI, 4395
Community Foundation of Greater South Wood County, Inc., WI, see 9925
Community Foundation of Greater Tampa, Inc., The, FL, see 1846
Community Foundation of Greene County, Pennsylvania, PA, 7781
Community Foundation of Greenville, Inc., SC, 8465
Community Foundation of Gunnison Valley, CO, 1170
Community Foundation of Henderson County, Inc., NC, 6615
Community Foundation of Herkimer & Oneida Counties, Inc., The, NY, 5879
Community Foundation of Howard County, Inc., The, IN, 2996

Community Foundation of Howard County, MD, 3807
Community Foundation of Jackson County Holding, Inc., IN, 2998
Community Foundation of Jackson County, Inc., The, IN, 2997
Community Foundation of Jackson Hole, WY, 10099
Community Foundation of Johnson County, IA, 3262
Community Foundation of Lorain County, The, OH, 7058
Community Foundation of Louisville, Inc., The, KY, 3559
Community Foundation of Madison and Jefferson County, Inc., IN, 2999
Community Foundation of Metropolitan Tarrant County, The, TX, see 8764
Community Foundation of Middle Tennessee, Inc., TN, 8579
Community Foundation of Monroe County, MI, 4396
Community Foundation of Morgan County, Inc., IN, 3000
Community Foundation of Mount Vernon & Knox County, OH, 7059
Community Foundation of Muncie and Delaware County, Inc., The, IN, 3001
Community Foundation of North Central Pennsylvania, PA, see 7821
Community Foundation of North Central Washington, WA, 9600
Community Foundation of North Central Wisconsin, Inc., WI, 9868
Community Foundation of North Texas, TX, 8764
Community Foundation of Northeast Alabama, AL, 28
Community Foundation of Northeast Florida, Inc., The, FL, see 1838
Community Foundation of Northeast Iowa, IA, 3263
Community Foundation of Northern Colorado, CO, 1171
Community Foundation of Northern Illinois, IL, 2495
Community Foundation of Northwest Connecticut, Inc., The, CT, 1362
Community Foundation of Orange and Sullivan, Inc., NY, see 5880
Community Foundation of Orange County, Inc., NY, 5880
Community Foundation of Portage County, Inc., WI, see 9866
Community Foundation of Randolph County, Inc., IN, 3002
Community Foundation of Riverside County, CA, see 514
Community Foundation of Santa Cruz County, The, CA, 512
Community Foundation of Sarasota County, Inc., The, FL, 1844
Community Foundation of Shelby County, The, OH, 7060
Community Foundation of Sidney and Shelby County, The, OH, see 7060
Community Foundation of South Georgia, Inc., GA, 2152
Community Foundation of South Lake County, Inc., FL, 1845
Community Foundation of Southeastern Connecticut, Inc., The, CT, see 1361
Community Foundation of Southern Indiana, IN, 3003
Community Foundation of Southern New Mexico, NM, 5624
Community Foundation of Southern Wisconsin, Inc., WI, 9869
Community Foundation of Southwest Georgia, Inc., GA, see 2152
Community Foundation of Southwest Kansas, KS, 3429
Community Foundation of St. Clair County, MI, 4397
Community Foundation of St. Joseph County, IN, 3004
Community Foundation of Susquehanna and Wyoming Counties, PA, see 7782
Community Foundation of Switzerland County, Inc., IN, 3005
Community Foundation of Tampa Bay, Inc., FL, 1846
Community Foundation of the Central Blue Ridge, The, VA, 9346

Community Foundation of the Chemung County Area and Corning Community Foundation, The, NY, see 5878
Community Foundation of the Dan River Region, VA, 9347
Community Foundation of the Eastern Shore, Inc., MD, 3808
Community Foundation of the Endless Mountains, PA, 7782
Community Foundation of the Florida Keys, Inc., FL, 1847
Community Foundation of the Fox River Valley, IL, 2496
Community Foundation of the Great River Bend, IA, 3264
Community Foundation of the Holland/Zeeland Area, The, MI, 4398
Community Foundation of the Lowcountry, SC, 8466
Community Foundation of the Ozarks, MO, 4963
Community Foundation of the Quincy Area, IL, 2497
Community Foundation of the Rappahannock River Region, Inc., VA, 9348
Community Foundation of the Upper Peninsula, MI, 4399
Community Foundation of the Verdugos, CA, 513
Community Foundation of the Virgin Islands, VI, 9274
Community Foundation of the Virginias, Inc., WV, 9777
Community Foundation of Union County, Inc., OH, 7061
Community Foundation of Wabash County, IN, 3006
Community Foundation of Warren County, PA, 7783
Community Foundation of Waterloo/Cedar Falls and Northeast Iowa, IA, see 3263
Community Foundation of West Chester/Liberty, The, OH, 7062
Community Foundation of West Kentucky, KY, 3560
Community Foundation of Western Massachusetts, MA, 4029
Community Foundation of Western Nevada, NV, 5282
Community Foundation of Western North Carolina, Inc., The, NC, 6616
Community Foundation of Western Pennsylvania and Eastern Ohio, PA, 7784
Community Foundation of Western Virginia, VA, 9349
Community Foundation Serving Coastal South Carolina, The, SC, see 8464
Community Foundation Serving Richmond & Central Virginia, The, VA, 9350
Community Foundation Serving Riverside and San Bernardino Counties, The, CA, 514
Community Foundation Serving Southwest Colorado, CO, 1172
Community Foundation Sonoma County, CA, 515
Community Foundation Trust of Sarasota County, The, FL, 1848
Community Foundation, Inc., MO, see 4963
Community Foundation, Inc., The, FL, 1838
Community Foundations of the Hudson Valley, NY, 5881
Community Health Network Foundation, WI, 9870
Community Health Partners Foundation, OH, see 7241
Community Hospital Auxiliary Scholarship Trust, The, IN, 3007
Community Hospital Foundation, CA, 516
Community Housing Network, MO, 4964
Community Initiative Funds of the San Francisco Foundation, CA, see 517
Community Initiatives, CA, 517
Community Mayors, Inc., NY, 5882
Community Network Services, Inc., MI, 4400
Community Nursing Services in Greensburg Inc., PA, 7785
Community Opportunities, Inc., IA, 3265
Community Pantry, The, NM, 5625
Community Partnership for Child Development, CO, 1173
Community Progress Council, Inc., PA, 7786
Community Projects, Inc., CA, 518
Community Renewal Team, Inc., The, CT, 1363
Community Service Foundation, Inc., FL, 1849
Community Service Programs of West Alabama, Inc., AL, 29
Community Service Society of New York, NY, 5883
Community Services Agency of the Metropolitan Washington Council, DC, 1606

Community Shelter Board, OH, 7063
Community Support Systems, Inc., MD, 3809
Community Welfare Association of Colquitt County, GA, GA, 2153
Community West Foundation, OH, 7064
Communtiy Action Partnership of Cambria County, Inc., PA, 7787
Compass Foundation, Noel, Inc., WI, 9871
Compass Fund, Inc., The, CT, 1364
Compassion Ministries, OR, 7556
Compassionate Care Fund, OK, 7460
CompassPoint Nonprofit Services, CA, 519
Comprehensive Medical Review Course, Inc., NJ, see 5479
Comstock Memorial Scholarship Trust, James A., RI, see 8272
Comstock Memorial Scholarship Trust, RI, 8272
Concern Foundation, CA, 520
Concerned Christians for the Community, Inc., MO, 4965
Concert Competitions & Musical Development, Inc., MI, see 4622
Concerted Services, Inc., GA, 2154
Concord Hospital Associates, NH, 5316
Concordia College Corporation, MN, 4720
Concrete Foundation, Inc., The, NY, see 6350
Concrete Research & Education Foundation, MI, see 4332
Conference on Jewish Material Claims Against Germany, NY, 5884
Conference U.S.A., TX, 8765
Confort Foundation Trust, John, NY, 5885
Congressional Hispanic Caucus Institute, DC, 1607
Conkling Memorial Foundation, Cheryl D., CO, 1174
Conn Appliances Charitable Foundation Inc., TX, 8766
Conn Memorial Foundation, FL, 1850
Connecticut Children's Medical Center Foundation, Inc., CT, 1365
Connecticut Community Foundation, The, CT, 1366
Connecticut Health Foundation, Inc., CT, 1367
Connecticut Young Writers Trust, The, CT, 1368
Connelly Scholarship Fund, John F., PA, 7788
Conner Family Foundation, Inc., PA, 7789
Conner Foundation, Edward & Elizabeth, The, CA, 521
Conner Foundation, James C. & Elizabeth R., TX, 8767
Conner Trust, Alice, IA, 3266
Connor Educational Fund, William D., WI, 9872
ConocoPhillips Dependent Scholarship Program Trust, OK, A
Conquer Cancer Foundation, VA, 9351
Conquistador Trust, The, CA, 522
Conrad Charitable Foundation, R.J., PA, 7790
Conrad Foundation, The, TX, 8768
Conservation Foundation, The, DC, see 1755
Construction Careers Foundation, WY, 10100
Consulting Engineers & Land Surveyors Scholarship Foundation, CA, see 337
Consumer-Farmer Foundation, Inc., The, NY, see 6304
Conte Foundation, Rosalie, TN, 8580
Continental Divide Electric Education Foundation, NM, 5626
Continental Scholarship Fund, IL, 2498
Continue Learning and Strive for Success Foundation, OK, 7461
Conway Farms Golf Club Foundation, IL, 2499
Conway Scholarship Foundation, Carle C., Inc., CT, 1369
Cook Educational Trust, Marvin H. & Gretchen V., IN, 3008
Cook Foundation, Loring, TX, 8769
Cook Inlet Region, Inc. Foundation, The, AK, see 113
Cook Trust, Almon B., RI, 8273
Cook, Sr. Charitable Foundation, Kelly Gene, Inc., TX, 8770
Cooke Educational Fund, Robert W., NC, see 6617
Cooke Educational Trust, Robert W., NC, 6617
Cooke Foundation, Jack Kent, VA, 9352
Cooke Foundation, William A., VA, 9353
Cooley, Dearing and Rinker Educational Trust Fund, VA, 9354
Cooper Educational Trust, Frances and Dawson, TX, 8771
Cooper Foundation, The, NJ, 5427

Cooper Foundation, Verne, Inc., TX, 8772
Cooper Scholarship Loan Fund, John Larmar, OR, 7557
Cooper Student Aid Fund, OR, see 7557
Coopers & Lybrand Foundation, NY, see 6328
Coordinated Child Care of Nepa, Inc., PA, 7791
Copley Fund, The, VT, 9242
Copp Agriculture Education Trust, William B. Copp & Grayon S., PA, 7792
Copper Mountain Foundation, AK, 114
Cops 4 Causes, CA, 523
Corbett Student Loan Program, FL, 1851
Corbett Trust, Laura R & William, FL, see 1851
Corbin Charitable Trust, John Byron, MO, 4966
Corbin Trust, Jessie A., IA, 3267
Corcoran Gallery of Art, DC, 1608
Cordova Native Foundation, AK, see 116
Corke Educational Trust, Hubert & Alice, AR, A
Cornelia de Lange Syndrome Foundation, CT, 1370
Cornelius Foundation, J. B., SC, 8467
Cornerstone Scholarship Charitable Trust, AR, 276
Cornerstone, Inc., DC, 1609
Corning Museum of Glass, The, NY, 5886
Cornucopia Art Center, Inc., MN, 4721
Corpening Trust, Flora, IL, 2500
Corpening, Jr. Memorial Foundation, Maxwell M., NC, 6618
Corporal Works of Mercy Society of St. Mary's Church, ME, 3692
Corporation for Relief of Widows & Children of Clergymen of the Protestant Episcopal Church in NY, NY, 5887
Corporation of Yaddo, The, NY, 5888
Corps of Compassion, NV, see 5280
Corpus Christi Geological Society Scholarship Trust Fund, TX, 8773
Correspondents Fund, The, NY, 5889
Corson Foundation, PA, 7793
Corti Trust, Theresa, PA, 7794
Cortland College Foundation, Inc., NY, 5890
Corvallis Clinic Foundation, Inc., The, OR, 7558
Cosby Foundation, William Henry Cosby, Jr. and Camille Olivia, Inc., NY, 5891
Coshocton Foundation, OH, 7065
Cosmair, Inc. Corporate Giving Program, NY, see 6170
Costa Educational Trust, Jennie & Samuel J., The, MA, 4030
Costa Scholarship Fund Trust, John D., RI, see 8274
Costa Scholarship Fund, Theresa, NY, 5892
Costa Scholarship, Mary P., RI, 8274
Costco Foundation, The, WA, 9601
Costello Scholarship Fund, Bobby, MA, 4031
Costello Trust, Glenn E. & Bessie R., IL, 2501
Costilow Scholarship Trust, O.W., IL, 2502
Costume Society of America, Inc., NJ, 5428
Cottage Grove Community Foundation, OR, 7559
Cotterel Student Loan Trust, R., NC, 6619
Cottey College Trust, Geraldine, OR, see 7586
Cottington Trust for Gifted Children, HI, 2278
Couch Memorial Fund, Randy, CA, 524
Couleecap, Inc., WI, 9873
Coulter Foundation, Viola Vestal, Inc., WA, 9602
Council for Advancement and Support of Education, DC, 1610
Council for Economic Opportunities in Greater Cleveland, OH, 7066
Council for Native Hawaiian Advancement, HI, 2279
Council of American Overseas Research Centers, DC, 1611
Council of American Research Centers, DC, see 1611
Council of Community Services of New York State, Inc., NY, 5893
Council of St. Petersburg Diocese Society of St. Vincent de Paul, Inc., FL, 1852
Council of State and Territorial Epidemiologists, GA, 2155
Council on Library and Information Resources, DC, 1612
Council on the Arts & Humanities for Staten Island, NY, 5894
CounterPULSE, CA, 525
County Corp., OH, 7067
County Executive, TN, see 8664
County North Foundation, OH, 7068

Cousin Foundation Inc., Michael G., The, FL, 1853
Covenant Foundation, The, NY, 5895
Covington Community Foundation, Inc., IN, see 3222
Covington Memorial Scholarship Fund, MO, 4967
Covington-Douglas Scholarship Foundation, OK, 7462
Coweta Community Foundation, Inc., The, GA, 2156
Cowgill Foundation, Benny, Inc., The, OH, 7069
Cox and Mayor George Foundation, Patricia Joder, TX, 8774
Cox Employee Disaster Relief Fund, Inc., GA, 2157
Cox Foundation, James M., MN, 4722
Cox Foundation, SC, 8468
Cox Foundation, Una Chapman, DC, 1613
Cox Foundation, William and Dorothy, NY, 5896
Cox Medical Centers, Lester E., MO, 4968
Cox Memorial Fund, William J., NY, 5897
Cox Memorial Scholarship, Alvah, KY, 3561
Cox Memorial Trust, Hugh W., NC, 6620
Cox Memorial Trust, Hugh W., NC, see 6620
Coxhealth Foundation, MO, 4969
CoxHealth, MO, see 4968
Coy Foundation, Mark W., Inc., The, IN, 3009
Cozad Public Schools Foundation, NE, 5193
Cozard Educational Scholarship Trust, William & Ruth, SD, 8525
CPCU- Loman Education Foundation, PA, 7795
CPCU-Harry J. Loman Foundation, PA, see 7795
Cracker Barrel Old Country Store Foundation, TN, 8581
Cradle Foundation, The, IL, 2503
Craft Alliance, MO, 4970
Craft Emergency Relief Fund, Inc., VT, 9243
Craig Memorial Fund for the Arts, Jennifer, Inc., FL, see 1991
Craig Scholarship Fund, Raymond B., WV, 9778
Crain Family Scholarship Fund, J. P., OH, 7070
Crane-Rogers Foundation, The, DC, see 1650
Cranston Foundation, The, RI, 8275
Cranston High Schools Athletic Scholarship Fund, RI, 8276
Cranston/Theophilus Pitman Fund, Robert B., RI, 8277
Craven Community College Foundation, NC, 6621
Craven Regional Medical Center Foundation, NC, see 6591
Crawford Heritage Community Foundation, PA, 7796
Crawford Memorial Scholarship Fund, G. Kenneth Crawford and Margaret B., PA, 7797
Crawley Memorial Educational Fund, Ethel W., NC, 6622
CRC, MD, see 3800
CRDF Global, VA, see 9526
Crealde School of Art, FL, 1854
Creamer & Son Scholarship Foundation, J. Fletcher, NJ, 5429
Creasey Trust, Roy, MO, 4971
Create Christian Research Education Action Technical Enterprise, Inc., MS, see 4903
CREATE Foundation, MS, 4903
Creative Artists Network, Inc., PA, see 7762
Creative Capital Foundation, NY, 5898
Creative Community Services, GA, 2158
Creative Glass Center of America (CGCA) and Down Jersey Folklife Center, NJ, see 5595
Creative Link for the Arts, NY, see 6200
Creative Recovery Communities, Inc., TN, A
Creative Support, Inc., OR, 7560
Creative Visions Foundation, CA, 526
Credit Bureau of Fort Dodge Trust, IA, 3268
Credit Union Foundation of Maryland and the District of Columbia, Inc., The, MD, 3810
Creech Family Charitable Trust, The, OH, 7071
Creek Preserve Foundation, Jack, Inc., MT, 5138
Crescent Scholarship Foundation, TX, 8775
Criag D. Tifford Foundation, CT, 1371
Crisis Control Ministry, Inc., NC, 6623
Crist Trust, Luther E. Crist and Phyllis C., MA, 4032
Criswell Scholarship Fund, Raymond, OR, 7561
Critzer Trust, Amy, NC, see 6884
Croatian Fraternal Union Scholarship Foundation, Inc., PA, 7798
Croatian National Foundation, CA, 527
Croatian Relief Services, Inc., NJ, 5430
Croatian Scholarship Fund, CA, 528

Crockett Scholarship Trust, Frances Bane Crockett and H. Paul, MN, 4723
Crockett Trust, Frances, MN, see 4723
Crohn's & Colitis Foundation of America, Inc., NY, 5899
Cromwell Foundation for the Research of the Law and Legal History of the Colonial Period of the U.S.A., William Nelson, The, NY, 5900
Cronquist Midway Scholarship Trust, John A. and Yvonne S., ND, 6936
Cross Scholarship Fund, Alton and Mildred, PA, 7799
Crosslake Ideal Scholarship Fund Inc., MN, 4724
Crossroads Foundation, The, PA, 7800
Crossroads Ministry of Estes Park, Inc., CO, 1175
Crosswalk Community Action Agency, Inc., IL, 2504
Crossway Community, Inc., MD, 3811
Croston Scholarship Fund, R. Elaine, RI, 8278
Croston TUW #3020001228, Mary G., RI, 8279
Croul Family Foundation, CA, 529
Crouse Health Foundation, Inc., NY, 5901
Crouse Irving Memorial Foundation, Inc., NY, see 5901
Crown Point Community Foundation, IN, 3010
Crozier Educational Trust, Robert Lloyd and Myrtle Madge, IA, 3269
Cruise Charitable Foundation, George M., WV, 9779
Crum Scholarship Foundation, Denny, OH, 7072
CRW Have A Heart Fund, Inc., TX, 8776
CS Foundation Inc., LA, 3649
CSA, NJ, see 5428
CSB, MD, see 3797
CSI Charities, Inc., PA, 7801
CSP, AL, see 29
CSP, OH, see 7050
CTE, Inc., CT, 1372
CTW Foundation, Inc., DE, 1498
Cuan Foundation, Inc., WI, 9874
Cuban Artists Fund, Inc., NY, 5902
Cuban Foundation, Mark, TX, 8777
Culinary Trust, The, OR, 7562
Culpeper Foundation, Inc., The, VA, 9355
Cultural Arts Council of Houston/Harris County, TX, see 8875
Cultural Council of Richland and Lexington Counties, SC, 8469
Cultural Resources Council of Syracuse & Onondaga County, NY, 5903
Culture Shapers, TX, 8778
Culture Works, OH, 7073
Culver Memorial College Scholarship Fund, Floyd and Elizabeth, OR, see 7563
Culver Memorial College, Floyd and Elizabeth, OR, 7563
Cumberland Community Foundation, Inc., NC, 6624
Cummings Foundation, Nathan, The, NY, 5904
Cummings Foundation, Nicholas & Dorothy, The, NV, 5283
Cummings Trust, Frank J., RI, 8280
Cunningham Dance Foundation, Inc., NY, 5905
Cunningham Foundation, Cameron, IL, 2505
Cunningham Scholarship Foundation, Louis, The, MI, 4401
Cunningham Scholarship Fund, Wimford E. and Mary E. Benton, OK, A
Cuno Foundation, RI, 8281
Curacao Children's Foundation, CA, see 605
Cure Autism Now, CA, 530
CURE Childhood Cancer and Leukemia, Inc., GA, see 2159
Cure Childhood Cancer Association, NY, 5906
CURE Childhood Cancer, Inc., GA, 2159
Curley Foundation, The, CA, 531
Curran Music Scholarship Fund, NY, 5907
Curran Trust f/b/o Curran Music School, Gertrude D., NY, see 5907
Curtis Athletic Scholarship Fund, T. Manning, PA, 7802
Curtis Foundation, Charles Curtis & Patricia Morse, CO, 1176
Curtis Foundation, Frances Blayney, WY, 10101
Curtis Fund, The, VT, see 9248
Curtis Trust Fund, Effie H. and Edward H., PA, 7803
Curves Community Fund, Inc., The, TX, see 8863
Cushman Foundation for Foraminiferal Research, VA, 9356

Cushwa Foundation, Charles B. & Margaret E., OH, 7074

Cushwa Foundation, William & Anna Jean, OH, 7075

Cut Bank Elks Lodge Charitable Corp., MT, 5139

Cutler Charitable Trust, Aline C., OR, 7564

Cutter Memorial Trust Fund, Albert B., TX, 8779

Cutter Trust Fund, William H. & Sadie R., Inc., NJ, 5431

Cuyahoga Valley National Park Association, OH, 7076

CVS Caremark Charitable Trust, Inc., RI, 8282

CVS/pharmacy Charitable Trust, Inc., RI, see 8282

Cypress-Fairbanks Educational Foundation, TX, 8780

Cystic Fibrosis Foundation, MD, 3812

Cystic Fibrosis Research, Inc., CA, 532

Cystinosis Foundation, Inc., CA, 533

D'Amour Fellowship Foundation, Paul H., The, MA, 4033

D'Amour Founders Scholarship for Academic Excellence, Gerald & Paul, The, MA, 4034

D'Annunzio Family Foundation Inc., NJ, 5432

Dabney Foundation for Kids With Cancer, Clayton, TX, 8781

Dactyl Foundation for the Arts & Humanities, Inc., NY, 5908

Dade Community Foundation, FL, see 1978

Dade Public Education Fund, Inc., FL, see 1867

Daggett Scholarship Fund, Inc., MN, 4725

Dailey College Scholarship, Frank C., TX, 8782

DAISY Foundation, CA, see 590

Daiwa Securities America Foundation, NY, 5909

Dakota Foundation, Inc., The, NY, see 6109

Dakota Medical Foundation, ND, 6937

Dales Foundation, George F., CA, 534

Daley Scholarship Foundation, Jim & Doris, MT, 5140

Dallas Bar Foundation, TX, 8783

Dallas Foundation, The, TX, 8784

Dallas Hispanic Bar Association Scholarship Foundation, TX, 8785

Dallas Scholarships, Margaret E., IA, 3270

Dallas Stars Foundation, Inc., TX, 8786

Daly Educational Fund, Bernard, OR, 7565

Daly Scholarship, Daly N-N & H, PA, 7804

Damato Scholarship Trust, Elizabeth B., IL, 2506

Dana Foundation, MI, 4402

Dance Films Association, Inc., NY, 5910

Dance Theater Workshop, Inc., NY, 5911

Dance Theatre Foundation, Inc., NY, see 5676

Dancers' Group, Inc., CA, 535

Dancey Memorial Foundation, Opal, MI, 4403

Danciger Charitable Foundation, David Kendall, TX, 8787

Danforth Memorial Fund, Josiah H., NY, 5912

Danicas Foundation, Inc., OR, 7566

Daniels Fund, CO, 1177

Daniels Hamant Foundation, IL, 2507

Daniels Hamant Patient Assistance Foundation, The, IL, see 2507

Danis Foundation, Inc., The, OH, 7077

Danny Foundation for Autism, The, MA, 4035

Dante Foundation of Nassau County, Inc., NY, 5913

Danville Community College Educational Foundation, Inc., VA, 9357

Danville School Enrichment Fund, Inc., The, VT, 9244

Darcey Foundation, Joseph and Sharon, Inc., WI, 9875

Darcey Foundation, Joseph, Inc., WI, see 9875

Darden Dimes, Inc., FL, 1855

Dargan Minority Scholarship Fund, Thomas R., OR, 7567

Darien Community Association, Inc., CT, 1373

Darnell Scholarship, Agnes Larsen, CA, 536

Das Foundation, Taraknath, NY, 5914

Datatel Scholars Foundation, VA, 9358

Daughters of the Cincinnati, NY, 5915

Davenport Area Foundation, IA, see 3264

Davenport Charitable Trust, George W., RI, 8283

Davenport Educational Fund, Henry & Sidney T., MI, see 4404

Davenport Educational Trust, Henry & Sidney T., MI, 4404

Davenport Foundation, John K. and Thirza F., NH, 5317

Davenport Trust Fund, George P., ME, 3693

Davey Company Foundation, OH, 7078

Davey Scholarship Foundation, WI, 9876

David & Katie B. Bundy Scholarship Trust, Jesse, FL, 1856

David Family Foundation, The, OH, see 7079

David Foundation, Paul & Carol, The, OH, 7079

Davidson Foundation, Lorimer & Betty Gael, VA, 9359

Davidson Institute for Talent Development, NV, 5284

Davidson Krueger Foundation, The, NY, 5916

Davie Community Foundation, Inc., NC, 6625

Davies Educational Foundation of Friendship Class of Peachtree Road Methodist Church, Daisy, GA, see 2160

Davies Educational Foundation, Daisy, GA, 2160

Davies Foundation, John and Shirley, The, OH, 7080

Davies Memorial Scholarship, Walter L.J., OR, 7568

Davies Scholarship Foundation, Joe, MD, 3813

Davis Charitable Trust Fund, R.L., NC, 6626

Davis Charitable Trust, Russell W., OK, 7463

Davis Charitable Trust, William G., PA, 7805

Davis Education Trust, Grace, PA, 7806

Davis Educational Foundation, Charles E., NC, 6627

Davis Foundation Inc., James A. and Juliet L., KS, 3431

Davis Foundation, Esther, KS, 3430

Davis Foundation, Jones S., IL, 2508

Davis Foundation, Lewis J. & Nelle A., OH, 7081

Davis Foundation, William E. & Rose Marie, NE, 5194

Davis Fund for INCAP Alumni, Amelia, MA, 4036

Davis Medical School Scholarships, WA, see 9603

Davis Memorial Foundation 31W080010, Thomas and Helen E., PA, 7807

Davis Memorial Foundation, Fred D., NC, 6628

Davis Memorial Trust, Walter R. Davis & Marie Foley, IL, 2509

Davis Scholarship Fund, Dorothy, PA, 7808

Davis Scholarship Trust No. 3, Helen, WA, 9603

Davis Trust Fund, Margaret L., IL, 2510

Davis-Roberts Scholarship Fund, Inc., WY, 10102

DaVita Children's Foundation, WA, 9604

Dawson Foundation, Alexander, NV, 5285

Dawson Nursing Scholarship Fund, Blanche L., IL, 2511

Dawson Scholarship Trust, James L. & Leona B. & Forrest B. & Muriel R., IL, 2512

Day Management Educational Foundation, OR, 7569

Day Trust, Carl and Virginia, The, MS, 4904

Daystar Northwest, Inc., WA, 9605

Dayton Foundation, MT, 5141

Dayton Foundation, The, OH, 7082

Dayton Masonic Foundation, OH, 7083

DC-CAP, DC, see 1617

DCEF, CO, see 1184

De Jur Trust, Jerome Lowell, NY, 5917

De Karman Scholarship Trust, Josephine, NY, 5918

de Kay Foundation, The, IL, 2513

Dead Sea Scrolls Foundation, IN, 3011

Deaf West Theatre Company, Inc., CA, 537

Deafness Research Foundation, NY, see 6065

DEAN, ME, see 3694

Deane Scholarship Fund, Faye H., MA, 4037

Dearborn Community Foundation, IN, 3012

Dearborn County Community Foundation, IN, see 3012

DeBartolo Family Foundation, FL, 1857

DeBartolo Memorial Scholarship Foundation, Edward J., The, OH, 7084

DebRA of America, NY, see 5944

Decatur County Community Foundation, Inc., IN, 3013

Decatur Education Foundation, Inc., The, GA, 2161

Decatur Policemen & Firemen Death Benefit Fund, AL, 30

DeCrane Family Foundation, Colleen, OH, 7085

Dedalus Foundation, Inc., NY, 5919

Dedham Women's Exchange, Inc., MA, 4038

Deeley Foundation, Thomas and Elsie, The, FL, 1858

Deen Schoeff Scholarship Trust, Dwight & Virginia, IN, 3014

Deer Valley Education Foundation, Inc., AZ, 183

Deering Foundation, Inc., CT, 1374

Deering Foundation, Mark, TX, 8788

DeKalb County Community Foundation (IL), IL, 2514

DeKalb County Community Foundation, Inc., IN, 3015

DeKalb Medical Center Foundation, Inc., GA, 2162

Delaware Arts Festival Association, Inc., OH, 7086

Delaware Center for the Contemporary Arts, Inc., DE, 1499

Delaware Community Foundation, DE, 1500

Delaware Contractors Association Scholarship Trust, DE, 1501

Delaware County Community Foundation, Greater, IA, 3271

Delaware County Foundation, OH, 7087

Delaware Foundation for Retarded Children, Inc., DE, see 1502

Delaware Foundation Reaching Citizens, Inc., DE, 1502

Delaware HIV Consortium, Inc., DE, 1503

Delaware State Golf Association Scholarship Fund, Inc., DE, 1504

Delaware Valley Mental Health Foundation, PA, see 7854

Delaware Valley Senior Citizens Scholarship Trust, PA, 7809

Dell Foundation, Michael and Susan, The, TX, 8789

Dellinger Scholarship Fund, Ray, GA, 2163

Dellomo Scholarship Foundation, Brian A., NY, 5920

Dellon Foundation, MD, 3814

Delmas Foundation, Gladys Krieble, The, NY, 5921

Deloitte & Touche Foundation, CT, see 1375

Deloitte Foundation, CT, 1375

DeLong Foundation, James E., Inc., WI, 9877

DeLoura Family Trust, The, RI, see 8284

DeLoura Trust for Scholarships, Elmer Hobson, RI, 8284

Delta Area Economic Opportunity Corporation, MO, 4972

Delta College Foundation, MI, 4405

Delta County Memorial Hospital Foundation, CO, 1178

Delta Delta Delta Foundation, TX, 8790

Delta Dental Foundation, MI, 4406

Delta Dental Fund, MI, see 4406

Delta Dental Philanthropic Fund, SD, 8526

Delta Phi Benefit Fund, Inc., MO, 4973

Delta Phi Delta, IN, 3016

Delta Phi Educational Fund, Inc., NY, see 6424

Delta Phi Epsilon Educational Foundation, PA, 7810

Delta Sigma Dental Educational Foundation Inc., FL, 1859

Delta Sigma Dental Educational Foundation, Inc., FL, see 1859

Demming Educational Foundation, Robert M. & Margaret O., MO, A

Democracy Matters Institute, Inc., NY, 5922

Demolay Foundation, Inc., MO, 4974

Deneke's Hope Foundation, OR, 7570

Denfeld Foundation, Greater, Inc., MN, 4726

Denman Family Foundation, TX, 8791

Densch Charities, Wayne M., Inc., FL, 1860

Dental Educational Trust, McDavid, MO, 4975

Denton Scholarship Trust, Robert E. & Olive L., IA, 3272

Denver Delta, Inc., CO, 1179

Denver Fire Fighters Burn Foundation, Inc., CO, 1180

Denver Health and Hospitals Foundation, The, CO, 1181

Denver Rescue Mission, CO, 1182

Denver Young Artists Orchestra, CO, 1183

Depression and Bipolar Support Alliance, IL, 2515

Depriest Memorial Endowment Fund, Jerri Walker, OR, 7571

Dept. of the Grand Army of the Republic, George A. Thomas Circle No. 32, CA, see 729

Dermatology Foundation, IL, 2516

Des Moines Golf and Country Club Educational Foundation, IA, 3273

Des Moines Jewish Foundation, IA, 3274

DeSana Educational Fund, Inc., GA, 2164

Descendants of the Signers of the Declaration of Independence, VA, 9360

DeSeranno Educational Foundation, Inc., MI, see 4385

Deseret Foundation, The, UT, see 9210

Desert Valley Charitable Foundation, CA, 538

Detroit Diesel Scholarship Foundation, Inc., MI, A

Detroit Golf Club Caddie Scholarship Foundation, MI, 4407

Deupree Foundation, Daniel B., TX, 8792

Development Fund for Black Students in Science and Technology, DC, 1614

Devens Trust, Sarah A. W., MA, 4039

DeVoe Buick Cadillac Scholarship Trust, Dick, FL, 1861

Devon Rotary Foundation Trust Fund, CT, 1376
Dewuhs-Keckritz Educational Trust, OR, 7572
DeYoung Educational Foundation, Murray, Inc., GA, 2165
DFI, NJ, see 5433
DFRC, DE, see 1502
Diabetes Foundation, Inc., NJ, 5433
Dial Educational Trust, Albert, SC, A
Dialysis Research Foundation, UT, 9198
Diamond Blackfan Anemia Foundation, NY, 5923
Diamond Resort Scholarships, HI, 2280
Dibona Family Foundation, G. Fred & Sylvia, PA, see 7811
DiBona, Jr. Memorial Foundation, G. Fred, PA, 7811
Dickens Family Foundation, The, GA, 2166
Dickey Scholarship Association, Bill, AZ, 184
Dickinson Area Community Foundation, MI, 4408
Dickinson County Area Community Foundation, MI, see 4408
Dickinson Trust, Dorothy, NY, 5924
Diederich Educational Trust Fund, John T. and Ada, OH, 7088
Diehl Trust, Harlan O., IA, 3275
Diema's Dream Foundation, VA, 9361
Dietrich Trust, Emma Fanny, NC, 6629
Dietrick-Parks Foundation, Laurel, MN, 4727
Dieu Donne Papermill, NY, 5925
Dieu Donne, NY, see 5925
Difelice Scholarship Trust, Emilio A. & Mary A., MA, 4040
Diffenbaugh Trust for Baker University, Harry J., TX, 8793
Diffenbaugh Trust for Kansas University, H. J., TX, 8794
Diffenbaugh Trust for University of Illinois, H. J., TX, see 8795
Diffenbaugh-University of Illinois, Harry J., TX, 8795
Dilcher ST LN FD, NC, 6630
Dilcher Student Loan Fund, Harry J. and Mollie S., NC, see 6630
Dillard Memorial Trust, John & Alice, OR, 7573
DiMauro Foundation, Orazio, CT, 1377
Dinger Scholarship Fund, OH, 7089
Dinger Scholarship Fund, OH, see 7089
Dingwall Foundation, William Orr, Inc., DC, 1615
Dinnerman Charitable Trust, Irving & Natalie, GA, 2167
Dinsdale Family Foundation, NE, A
Dinwiddie Scholarship Trust, Nancy, NC, see 6631
Dinwiddie Trust, Howard G. & Nancy C., NC, 6631
Diocesan Council for the Society of St. Vincent de Paul, AZ, 185
Diocesan Council of Orlando - Society of St. Vincent de Paul, FL, 1862
Direct Marketing Educational Foundation, NY, 5926
DiRienzo Foundation, Inc., NV, 5286
Dirshu International, Inc., NJ, 5434
Disabled American Veterans (DAV) Charitable Service Trust, Inc., KY, 3563
Disabled American Veterans, KY, 3562
Discovery Communications, Inc. Corporate Giving Program, MD, 3815
Discovery Eye Foundation, The, CA, 539
Discovery Space Technology Center, CA, see 1007
Disney Company Foundation, Walt, The, CA, 540
Distilled Spirits Wholesalers of Florida Education Foundation, Inc., FL, 1863
District 7 Human Resources Development Council, MT, 5142
District of Columbia Bar Foundation, The, DC, 1616
District of Columbia College Access Program, DC, 1617
District of Columbia College Success Foundation, DC, 1618
District One Foundation for Quality Education, IL, 2517
District XI Human Resource Council, Inc., MT, 5143
Diverseworks, Inc., TX, 8796
Division A Education and Scholarship Fund, NY, 5927
Dix Trust, George A., RI, 8285
Dixie Foundation, Inc., NC, 6632
Dixie Group Foundation, Inc., The, TN, 8582
Dixie Yarns Foundation, Inc., TN, see 8582
Dixon Foundation, The, AL, 31
Djerassi Foundation, The, CA, see 541
Djerassi Resident Artists Program, CA, 541
DMRF, IL, see 2529

Do Something, Inc., NY, 5928
Doctors Hospital of Lakewood Foundation, CA, see 732
Documentary Educational Resources, Inc., MA, 4041
Dodd Educational Trust, W. J. and Amy C., IL, 2518
Dodd Foundation, MO, 4976
Dodd Foundation, Norris E., PA, 7812
Dodd Scholarship Trust, Verna Lilly, IL, 2519
Dodge City Area Foundation, KS, see 3429
Dodge City Business & Professional Women's Club-Elma Schmidt Fund, KS, see 3512
Dodge Scholarship Trust for Girls, NH, 5318
Dodge Scholarship Trust, Adelaide, NH, see 5318
Doe Charitable Trust, Hans and Margaret, CA, 542
Doerhoff Scholarship Trust, Ray & Rosetta, MO, 4977
Doherty Scholarship Fund, James, NY, 5929
Doherty Scholarship Fund, Mark Alan, WY, 10103
Doing His Time, CA, 543
Dolan & Gladys Saulsbury Foundation, Sabina, Inc., CT, 1378
Dolan Media Foundation, MN, 4728
Dole Scholarship Trust, Stephen Dexter and Emily Jane Tipton, IL, 2520
Dolechek Trust, Christine, KS, 3432
Dollar Energy Fund, Inc., PA, 7813
Dollar General Employee Assistance Foundation, TN, 8583
Dollywood Foundation, The, TN, 8584
Dolphin Scholarship Foundation, VA, 9362
Domino's Pizza Partners Foundation, MI, 4409
Don't Stop the Music Foundation, GA, see 2121
Donaghey Foundation, Henry & Elizabeth, OK, 7464
Donegal Foundation, The, PA, 7814
Donegal School District Education Foundation, PA, see 7814
Donghia Foundation, Angelo, Inc., NY, 5930
Doniphan-Trumbull Public School Foundation, NE, 5195
Doniphan/Trumbull Educational Foundation, NE, see 5195
Donnell Trust, Kenneth S., MA, 4042
Donnelley Family Foundation, Mary Barnes, IL, 2521
Donnelly Scholarship Trust, Jerry & Lucille, TX, 8797
DonorsChoose, Inc., NY, see 5931
DonorsChoose.org, NY, 5931
Doody Foundation, Donald J., The, IL, 2522
Doolin Foundation, Clifford, Inc., MO, 4978
Doolittle Memorial Scholarship Trust, SD, 8527
Doolittle Private Foundation, Blanche, SD, 8528
Door County Community Foundation, Inc., WI, 9878
Dora Foundation, James & Shirley, The, IN, 3017
Dorland Mountain Arts Colony, CA, 544
Dornhecker Foundation, Marie A., The, VA, 9363
Dorot Foundation, RI, 8286
Dotson, M.D. Fund, John, PA, 7815
Dougherty Foundation, Inc., AZ, 186
Doughty III Memorial Foundation, Major Robertson, Inc., VA, 9364
Douglas County Community Foundation, KS, 3433
Douglas County Educational Foundation, CO, 1184
Dove Givings Foundation, NY, 5932
Dover and Sherborn Education Fund, Inc., MA, 4043
Doverspike Charitable Foundation, J. & R., PA, 7816
Dow Chemical Company Foundation, The, MI, 4410
Dow Home Inc, Baron & Emilie, SD, 8529
Dow Jones News Fund, Inc., NJ, 5435
Dow Jones Newspaper Fund, Inc., NJ, see 5435
Down East AIDS Network, Inc., ME, 3694
Downey Foundation, James E., The, CA, 545
Downing Educational Trust, Adrian & Marie, AL, 32
Downtown Community Television Center, Inc., NY, 5933
Doyle Foundation, Frank M., Inc., The, NV, 5287
Doyon Foundation, The, AK, 115
DPC Community Foundation, VA, see 9347
Dr. Dane & Mary Louise Miller Foundation, Inc., IN, 3018
Dr. Phil Foundation, The, CA, 546
Drag Racing Association of Women, IL, 2523
Drake Scholarship Trust, Lily E., OH, 7090
Dramatists Guild Fund, Inc., NY, 5934
Draper Richards Foundation, The, CA, see 547
Draper Richards Kaplan Foundation, The, CA, 547
DRAW, IL, see 2523
DRC Sannam Forum, Inc., NJ, 5436

Dream Factory, Inc., The, KY, 3564
Dreams for Kids, Inc., IL, 2524
Dreams Scholarship Foundation, TX, 8798
Dressage Foundation, Inc., The, NE, 5196
Dreyfus Foundation, Camille and Henry, Inc., The, NY, 5935
Driehaus Foundation, Richard H., The, IL, 2525
Driskell Scholarship Trust Fund, Helen Muxlow, OK, 7465
Drive With A Heart Foundation, TX, see 9061
Driver Foundation, Donald, TX, 8799
Drowns Educational Foundation, Bruce V., MO, 4979
Druckenmiller Foundation, NY, 5936
Drummond Foundation, Alfred A. & Tia Juana, IL, 2526
DSGA Junior Golf Scholarship Fund, Inc., DE, see 1504
Du Bois Charitable Trust, Cora, MA, 4044
Dubois County Community Foundation, Inc., IN, 3019
Dubois County High School Scholarship Trust, Inc., IN, 3020
Duclos Foundation, Leva & Frank, KS, 3434
Dudley Fund, Grace Norton, IL, 2527
Dudley-Vehmeyer-Brown Memorial Foundation, CA, 548
Duer Foundation, D. C., KS, 3435
Duerr Memorial Fund Irrevocable Trust 001943, Jean B., VA, 9365
Duffy Foundation, George, NY, 5937
Dugan Foundation, Martin W., MA, 4045
Dugan Trust, Martin W., MA, see 4045
Duggan Scholarship Trust, Cornelius, IA, 3276
Duke Charitable Foundation, Doris, NY, 5938
Duke Scholarship Fund, Margaret S., GA, 2168
Duluth Superior Area Community Foundation, MN, 4729
Dumesnil Trust, Evangeline L., OH, 7091
Dunbar Scholarship Trust A, Howard W., FL, 1864
Duncan Foundation, Harry F., Inc., MD, 3816
Dungannon Foundation, Inc., NY, 5939
Dunham Educational Trust, Arleen and Arthur H., MA, 4046
Dunkin Brands Disaster Relief Fund, Inc., MA, 4047
Dunlap Foundation, Frank R. "Bo", Inc., OH, 7092
Dunlap, Jr. Memorial Trust, David R., AL, 33
Dunlop Scholarship Trust, Mary Frances, MO, 4980
Dunn Memorial Fund Trust, Dr. Ferrell W., IN, 3021
Dunn Scholarship Trust, Margaret, TX, 8800
Dunnavant Scholarship Fund, Terrell H., Inc., VA, 9366
Dunnaway Foundation, Danny M., MS, 4905
Dunning Charitable Trust, W. Gordon, CT, 1379
Dunton Scholarship Fund Trust, Caroline F., OH, 7093
DuPage Medical Society Foundation, IL, 2528
Dupee Foundation, Mabel E., Inc., WI, 9879
duPont Foundation, Alfred I., Inc., FL, 1865
Dupre Permanent Educational Scholarship Fund Trust, Naasson K. & Florrie S., The, TX, 8801
Durango Foundation for Educational Excellence, CO, 1185
Durfee Foundation, The, CA, 549
Durfee Scholarship Fund, Hildegard, VT, 9245
Durham Arts Council, NC, 6633
Durham Technical Community College Foundation, Inc., NC, 6634
Durland Foundation, Agatha, NY, 5940
Dutchess County Arts Council, Inc., NY, 5941
Dutka Arts Foundation, Joyce, Inc., NY, A
Dutko Memorial Foundation, Dan, The, DC, 1619
Dutro Scholarship Fund, Ruth, OH, 7094
DuVall Scholarship Fund, Fred H., NC, 6635
Duxbury Yacht Club Charitable Foundation, RI, 8287
Dye Foundation, James W. & Betty, Inc., IN, 3022
Dyer Trust, J. Franklin, MA, 4048
Dyersburg-Dyer County Union Mission, TN, 8585
Dyett Foundation, Herbert T., Inc., NY, 5942
Dysautonomia Foundation, Inc., NY, 5943
Dystonia Medical Research Foundation, IL, 2529
Dystrophic Epidermolysis Bullosa Research Association of America, Inc., NY, 5944

EAA Aviation Foundation, Inc., WI, 9880
Eady Charitable Trust, J. Tom, TX, 8802
Eagle Foundation Inc., The, CT, 1380
Eagle Foundation, CO, 1186
Eagle River Scholarship Fund, Inc., CO, 1187
Eagles Memorial Foundation, Inc., OH, 7095

Eagleton War Memorial Scholarship Fund, NY, 5945
Earhart Foundation, MI, 4411
Earl & Frances Smith Scholarship, Harrison, NY, 5946
Earle Scholarship Trust Fund, William B. & Lela P., SC, 8470
Early Memorial Scholarship Trust, Caspar S., NY, 5947
Early Music America, Inc., PA, 7817
Earnhardt Foundation, Dale, Inc., The, NC, 6636
Earth Island Institute, Inc., CA, 550
Earthwatch Expeditions, Inc., MA, see 4049
Earthwatch Institute, Inc., MA, 4049
East Alabama Medical Center Foundation, AL, 34
East Allen County Schools Educational Foundation, Inc., IN, 3023
East Angel Friends and Alumni Foundation, CO, 1188
East Cambridge Savings Charitable Foundation, Inc., MA, 4050
East Carolina University Foundation, Inc., NC, 6637
East High Angel Foundation, CO, see 1188
East Lake Community Foundation, Inc., GA, see 2169
East Lake Foundation, Inc., GA, 2169
East Longmeadow Rotary Memorial Scholarship Foundation, Inc., MA, 4051
East Mississippi Development Corporation, MS, 4906
East Montgomery County Scholarship Foundation, TX, 8803
East Nashville Knights of Columbus Club, Inc., TN, 8586
East St. Louis Community Fund, Greater, IL, 2530
East Tennessee Foundation, TN, 8587
East Tennessee Human Resource Agency, Inc., TN, 8588
East Texas Area Foundation, TX, see 8804
East Texas Communities Foundation, Inc., TX, 8804
East Valley Christian School Tuition Organization, Inc., AZ, 187
East Williston Teachers' Association Scholarship Foundation, NY, 5948
East-West Center, HI, see 2274
Eastcliff Foundation, CA, 551
Easter Chapter Order of the Eastern Star Charitable Trust, MA, 4052
Easter Island Foundation, The, CA, 552
Easter Seals Hawaii, HI, 2281
Easter Seals of Michigan, Inc., MI, 4412
Easter Seals of New Jersey, Inc., NJ, 5437
Easter Seals UCP North Carolina and Virginia, Inc., NC, 6638
Easter Seals UCP North Carolina, NC, see 6638
Eastern Carolina Human Services Agency, Inc., NC, 6639
Eastern Catawba Cooperative Christian Ministry, Inc., NC, 6640
Eastern Catawba Cooperative, NC, see 6640
Eastern Choral Society, Inc., The, DC, see 1750
Eastern Frontier Educational Foundation Inc., ME, 3695
Eastern Kentucky Concentrated Employment Program, Inc., KY, 3565
Eastern Kentucky PRIDE, Inc., KY, 3566
Eastern New York Youth Soccer Association Inc., NY, 5949
Eastern Pennsylvania Water Pollution Control Operators Association, Inc., PA, 7818
Eastern Scientific & Education Foundation, NC, 6641
Eastern Star Charity Foundation of Connecticut, Inc., CT, 1381
Eastern Star Charity Foundation of New Jersey, Inc., NJ, 5438
Eastern Virginia AIDS Network, VA, 9367
Eastern Virginia Medical School Foundation, VA, 9368
Eastern West Virginia Community Foundation, WV, 9780
Eastman Chemical Company Contributions Program, TN, 8589
Eastman Memorial Scholarship Fund, Arthur G., CT, 1382
EastWest Foundation, VA, 9369
Eaton & Reed Scholarship Fund Trust, RI, 8288
Eaton Memorial Fund, Georgiana Goddard, MA, 4053
Eaton Society, Annie, Inc., The, NY, 5950
Ebb Foundation, Fred, NY, 5951
Ebell of Los Angeles Scholarship Endowment Fund, CA, 553

Eberhardt Trust, Elsie C., IL, 2531
Ebert Memorial Fund, Hazel C., MO, 4981
Ebony Horsewomen, Inc., The, CT, 1383
ECD Global Alliance, Inc., LA, 3650
Echo, Inc., VA, 9370
Echoing Green Foundation, NY, see 5952
Echoing Green, NY, 5952
Eckburg Foundation Inc., WI, 9881
Eckert Memorial Fund, Dr. Robert, NY, 5953
Eckhart Trust, Edward E., PA, see 7819
Eckhart Trust, Howard E., PA, 7819
Eckmann Foundation, CA, see 585
ECMC Foundation, MN, 4730
ECMC Group Holdings Foundation, MN, see 4730
Ecolab Foundation, MN, 4731
Ecolab Industry Foundation, MN, see 4731
Economic Opportunity Planning Association of Greater Toledo, Inc., OH, 7096
Ecotrust Foundation, MN, 4732
Eddy Family Memorial Fund, C. K., MI, 4413
Eddy Foundation Charitable Trust, NC, see 6642
Eddy Foundation, Maud and Jack, TX, 8805
Eddy Foundation, NC, 6642
Eden Autism Services Foundation, Inc., NJ, 5439
Eden Institute Foundation, NJ, see 5439
Edgar Charitable Foundation, William, MO, 4982
Edgar County Bank & Trust Foundation, IL, 2532
Edgar County Community Foundation, IL, 2533
Edgerton Area Foundation, OH, 7097
Edgerton Murphy Scholarships Trust, NC, 6643
Edinburg Child Care, Inc., TX, 8806
Edmonds Scholarship Trust, George Walter and Violet C., NC, 6644
Edmondson-Telford Foundation, GA, 2170
Edmunds Scholarship Trust, V. Faith, NH, 5319
Edmunds Testamentary Trust, T. Murrell, IL, 2534
EduCap, Inc., VA, 9371
Educare Scholarship Fund, AZ, 188
Education Consumers Foundation, VA, 9372
Education Endowment of Yavapai County, Inc., AZ, 189
Education Foundation of Palm Beach County, The, FL, 1866
Education Foundation, Tosoh Quartz, OR, 7574
Education Fund, Inc., The, FL, 1867
Education is Freedom Foundation, TX, 8807
Educational Advancement Foundation, TX, 8808
Educational Enrichment Foundation, AZ, 190
Educational Foundation for the Fashion Industries, NY, 5954
Educational Foundation of Alpha Gamma Rho, MO, 4983
Educational Foundation of the Massachusetts Society of Certified Public Accountants, MA, 4054
Educational Foundation of the Missouri Society of Certified Public Accountants, Inc., MO, 4984
Educational Loan Foundation of Spokane, Inc., WA, 9606
Educational Services of America, Inc., TN, 8590
Educational Theatre Association, OH, 7098
Educational Trust Fund in Memory of J. Lupton Simpson and Marion Porter Simpson, NC, see 6861
EducationQuest Foundation, NE, 5197
EDUCAUSE, CO, 1189
Edward Foundation, IL, 2535
Edwards Family Foundation, Inc., FL, 1868
Edwards Foundation, William, Inc., FL, see 1868
Edwards Foundation, Winifred, Ruth, Frances & Dorothy, Inc., The, NE, 5198
Edwards Scholarship Fund, MA, 4055
Edwards Scholarship Trust, Marguerite R., TX, 8809
Edwardsville Area Community Foundation, Greater, IL, 2536
EFAF, MO, see 4986
Egan Foundation, Dorothy Harrison, MA, 4056
Eggen Scholarship Fund, Edwin & Lucille, WI, 9882
Eggleston Educational Trust, KS, 3436
Eglitis & Veronika Janelsins Foundation, Anslavs, CA, 554
EHC Lifebuilders, CA, see 562
Ehle Scholarship Foundation, Virgil & Jane Peck, NY, 5955
Ehle Scholarship Trust Fund, Virgil and Jane Peck, NY, see 5955

Ehlers Leavenworth High School Scholarship Charitable Educational Fund Trust, Virginia, KS, 3437
Ehlers Memorial Fund Inc., V.M., TX, 8810
Ehlers Memorial Fund, V. M., Inc., TX, see 8810
Ehlers Oskaloosa High Scholarship Charitable Educational Trust, Marlin & Virginia, KS, 3438
Ehrler Foundation, Dr. Glenn G., IL, 2537
EI Charitable Foundation, CO, 1190
EIA Research and Education Foundation, NC, see 6649
Eisenhauer Scholarship Fund, John Henry and Clarissa Arnold, PA, 7820
Eisenhauer, et al. Scholarship Fund, John Henry & Clarissa A., PA, see 7820
Ekstrand Educational Trust, Marie and Margaret, IL, 2538
Ekstrom Family Foundation, Stanley W., Inc., CA, 555
El Dorado Community Foundation, CA, 556
El Dorado Promise, Inc., AR, 277
El Monte-South El Monte Emergency Resources Association, CA, 557
El Paso Community Foundation, TX, 8811
El Paso Corporate Foundation, CO, A
El Paso County Salute to Education Inc, TX, A
El Puente Charitable Foundation, CA, 558
Elam Scholarship Trust Fund, E. O., TX, 8812
Elbert Trust, Louis J., IA, 3277
Elburn Scholarship Fund, The, IL, 2539
Elder Services of Cape Cod, MA, 4057
Elderhostel, Inc., MA, 4058
Elec Material Hirtzel Memorial Foundation, PA, see 7910
ELECTRI International, MD, 3817
Electric Cooperative Foundation Inc., AL, 35
Electrical Contracting Foundation, Inc., The, MD, see 3817
Elenberg Foundation, Charles and Anna, Inc., NY, 5956
Eleutherian Mills-Hagley Foundation, Inc., DE, 1505
Elfers Scholarship Trust No. 2, Jessie, WI, 9883
Elim Ministry Foundation, CA, 559
Elizabeth City Foundation Committee, NC, 6645
Elizabeth Foundation for the Arts, The, NY, 5957
Elizondo Scholarship Trust, Maria, CO, 1191
Elk County Community Foundation, PA, 7821
Elk Grove Community Foundation, CA, 560
Elkhart County Community Foundation, Inc., IN, 3024
Elkhorn Valley Community Development Corporation, NE, A
Elko Foundation, Karen Rush, PA, 7822
Elks Morgan Home Company Scholarship Fund of Alliance Ohio, The, OH, 7099
Elks National Foundation, IL, 2540
Ella Mount Burr Trust, NC, 6646
Ellington Fund, Inc., The, DC, 1620
Elliott Trust, Mary E., NH, 5320
Elliott-Hemingford Scholarship Foundation, NE, 5199
Ellis Foundation, Danny and Willa, KS, see 3439
Ellis Foundation, The, KS, 3439
Ellis Grant and Scholarship Fund, Charles E., PA, 7823
Ellis Gratuity Fund, Rudolph, NC, 6647
Ellis Scholarship Fund, John G., KS, 3440
Ellis Trust, Jeffrey Wallace, NE, 5200
Ellison Foundation, Lawrence, The, CA, 561
Ellison Medical Foundation, The, CA, see 561
Ellison Scholarship Fund, Harold, IN, 3025
Ellsworth Scholarship Fund, Henry E., RI, 8289
Ellzey Family Charitable Trust, Lee, TX, 8813
Elm Trust, Henry, MT, 5144
Elmseed Enterprise Fund, The, CT, 1384
Elsasser Scholarship Fund, Thomas R., The, NY, 5958
Elvins Scholarship Trust, Catherine Marie Elvins and Naomi Libby, WA, 9607
Elwyn, Inc., PA, 7824
Ely Trust, Charles C., PA, 7825
Ely-Winton Hospital Scholarship Trust, MN, 4733
Embarras River Basin Agency, Inc., IL, 2541
Embassy of Hope Foundation, FL, 1869
EmblemHealth, Inc., NY, see 6064
Embrace Kids Foundation, NJ, 5440
Emergency Fund for the Needy People, IL, see 2542
Emergency Fund, IL, 2542
Emergency Housing Consortium of Santa Clara County, CA, 562
Emergency Medicine Foundation, TX, 8814

Emergency Nurses Association Foundation, IL, 2543
Emerich Scholarship Charitable Trust, The, WV, 9781
Emerson Charitable Trust, MO, 4985
Emerson Foundation, Harland and Genevieve, NE, 5201
Emerson Trust, Anna B. and Thomas H., NC, 6648
Emery Education Foundation, CA, 563
Emmons County Sports Alumni, Inc., ND, 6938
Employees Community Fund of Boeing California, Inc., CA, 564
Employees Emergency Aid Fund of Boeing St. Louis, MO, 4986
Empty Stocking Fund, GA, 2171
ENAF, IL, see 2543
Ende Menzer Walsh & Quinn Retirees' Widows' & Children's Assistance Fund, IL, 2544
Endeavor Foundation, AR, 278
Endocrine Fellows Foundation, CT, 1385
Endocrine Society, MD, 3818
Endowment Assocation of the College of William and Mary in Virginia, Inc., The, VA, see 9344
Endowment of the U.S. Institute of Peace, DC, see 1738
Energy & Mineral Law Foundation, KY, 3567
Energy Assistance Foundation, IL, 2545
EnergySolutions Foundation, UT, 9199
Engen Seminary Student Scholarship Assistance Trust, MN, 4734
Enger Foundation, W. N. and Jane, Inc., TX, 8815
Engine Rebuilders Educational Foundation, The, IL, 2546
Engineering Geology Foundation, CO, see 1113
Engineering Systems Inc., Charitable Foundation, IL, 2547
England Scholarship Fund, Frank F., VT, 9246
England Trust, Elizabeth R., PA, 7826
Englewood Elks Scholarship Trust PC 52-5823900, FL, 1870
English Charitable Trust, Fenton E., IL, 2548
English Foundation, The, VA, 9373
English Foundation-Trust, The, VA, see 9373
English Scholarship Foundation, W. C., The, VA, 9374
ENMR Education Foundation, NM, 5627
ENMR Telephone Education Foundation, NM, see 5627
ENMR-Plateau Corporate Giving Program, NM, 5628
Ensemble Studio Theatre, Inc., The, NY, 5959
Entergy Corporation Contributions Program, LA, 3651
Enterprise Community Partners, Inc., MD, 3819
Enterprise Foundation, The, MD, see 3819
Entertainment Software Association Fdn., NY, see 5963
Entomological Foundation, WI, 9884
Environmental Education Foundation, Inc., The, WI, 9885
Environmental Law Institute, DC, 1621
Environmental Leadership Program, Inc., MD, 3820
Environmental Research and Education Foundation, NC, 6649
EOC of Schuylkill, PA, see 8091
EOG Scholarship Fund, TX, 8816
Epilepsy Association, OH, 7100
Epilepsy Foundation of America, MD, 3821
Epilepsy Foundation of Missouri and Kansas, MO, 4987
Epilepsy Research Foundation, MD, 3822
Epilepsy Therapy Project, VA, 9375
Episcopal Actors Guild of America, Inc., NY, 5960
Episcopal Children's Services, Inc., FL, 1871
Episcopal Church Foundation, NY, 5961
Epler Scholarship Fund, Mabel S., IN, 3026
Epsilon Association Charitable Trust, NY, 5962
Epstein Foundation Trust, Samuel J., PA, 7827
Epstein Humanitarian Fund, Gene & Marlene, PA, 7828
EPWPCOA, PA, see 7818
EQT Foundation, Inc., PA, 7829
Equal Justice Works, DC, 1622
Equipment Leasing and Finance Foundation, DC, 1623
Equitable Resources Foundation, Inc., PA, see 7829
Equus Foundation, Inc., CT, 1386
Erickson Charitable Foundation, Arnold & Mildred, Inc., IL, 2549
Erickson Scholarship Fund, Leroy, PA, 7830
Erickson Scholarship Fund, PA, see 7830

Erie Community Foundation, The, PA, 7831
Erk Charitable Education Trust, Alfred, IL, 2550
ERM Group Foundation, Inc., The, PA, 7832
Ernst Charitable Trust, Helen R., ND, 6939
Ernst Memorial Educational Trust Fund, Catherine, MN, 4735
ESA Foundation, NY, 5963
ESA, TN, see 8590
ESCO Technologies Foundation, MO, 4988
Eshe Fund, The, NY, 5964
Esiason Foundation, Boomer, NY, 5965
Esiason Heroes Foundation, Boomer, NY, see 5965
Eskenazi Health Foundation, Inc., IN, 3027
Esperantic Studies Foundation, Inc., DC, 1624
Espy Foundation, Dacy, Inc., GA, 2172
Essex Classical Institute, VT, 9247
Essex County Bar Foundation, NJ, 5441
Essex County Community Foundation, Inc., MA, 4059
Essex Veterans of World War II, MA, 4060
Estonian Relief Committee, Inc., NY, 5966
Estonian-Revelia Academic Fund, Inc., MD, 3823
Eternal Kingdom Enterprises Inc., GA, 2173
Ethnic Voice of America, OH, 7101
Ethridge Scholarship Foundation, The, CO, 1192
Etnier Charitable Trust, Oliver, DE, 1506
Evans Educational Trust, Zelia Stephans, AL, 36
Evans Memorial Scholarship Fund, Alberta Craig, IL, 2551
Evans Scholars Foundation, IL, 2552
Evans Scholarship Award Trust, Clyde R., OK, 7466
Evans Teacher's Scholarship Trust, LaVerna, MO, 4989
Evans-Moss Fund, NC, 6650
Evereg-Fenesse Educational Society, MI, 4414
Everett Community Foundation, Greater, The, WA, 9608
Everett McKinley Dirksen Endowment Fund, IL, 2553
Everglades Foundation, Inc., The, FL, 1872
Evergreen Christian Outreach, CO, 1193
Evergreen House Foundation, Inc., The, MD, 3824
Evergreen State College Foundation, The, WA, 9609
Everhart Scholarship Fund, OH, 7102
Everly Scholarship Fund Inc., NJ, 5442
Evers Trust, Paul B., OH, 7103
Evrytanian Association of America, NC, see 6651
Evrytanian Association Velouchi, Inc., NC, 6651
Ewald Foundation, H. T., MI, 4415
Ewing Foundation, James, The, IL, 2554
Exacto Foundation Inc., WI, 9886
Excel Foundation, Inc., ID, 2331
Excelsior Scottish Rite Bodies Charity Fund, Inc., NJ, 5443
Exchange Club of Vero Beach Scholarship Foundation Trust, The, FL, 1873
Experimental Aircraft Association, Inc., WI, 9887
Experimental Sound Studio, IL, 2555
Experimental Television Center, Ltd., NY, 5967
Exploratorium, The, CA, 565
Explorers Club, The, NY, 5968
Exploring the Arts, Inc., NY, 5969
Eyak Foundation, The, AK, 116
Eychaner Charitable Foundation, Rich, IA, 3278
Eye & Ear Foundation, Inc., PA, 7833
Eyebeam Atelier, The, NY, 5970
Ezer M'Zion, Inc., NY, 5971

F & M Trust Co., Scholarship Program Trust, PA, 7834
Fabela Family Foundation, The, FL, 1874
Fabela Foundation, Elssy, The, IL, 2556
Fabri-Kal Foundation, MI, 4416
Fabric Workshop and Museum, The, PA, 7835
Fabricators & Manufacturers Association Foundation, IL, see 2760
Fadel Educational Foundation, Inc., The, GA, 2174
Fahrney Education Foundation, Charles E., WI, 9888
Fahrney Education Foundation, WI, see 9888
Fairbanks-Horix Foundation, OH, 7104
Fairey Educational Fund, Kittie M., NC, 6652
Fairfield - Meeker Charitable Trust, Freeman E., NC, 6653
Fairfield Business and Professional Women's Foundation, IL, 2557
Fairfield County Community Foundation, Inc., CT, 1387

Fairfield County Foundation, OH, 7105
Fairmont State Foundation, Inc., WV, 9782
Fairmount Tire Charitable Foundation Inc., CA, 566
Fairview Lutheran Foundation, OH, see 7064
Faith in Serving Humanity, GA, 2175
Faith's Hope Foundation, CA, 567
Fales Educational Trust, Herbert, RI, 8290
Fallen and Wounded Soldier Fund, MI, 4417
Fallon Clinic Foundation, MA, 4061
Fallon Foundation, MA, see 4061
Fallquist Memorial Scholarship Fund, A. T., PA, 7836
Families First, Inc., GA, 2176
Families U.S.A. Foundation, Inc., DC, 1625
FamiliesFirst, Inc., CA, A
Family Care Foundation, Inc., CA, 568
Family Housing Fund, MN, 4736
Family Medicine Foundation of West Virginia, WV, 9783
Family Outreach Foundation, NJ, 5444
Family Programs Hawaii, HI, 2282
Family Service Spokane, WA, 9610
Family Services of Western Pennsylvania, PA, A
FAMSI, CA, see 589
Fan Foundation, Katherine & George, NY, 5972
Fanconi Anemia Research Fund, Inc., OR, 7575
Fansler Foundation, CA, 569
Fansler Foundation, Kate, Inc., The, OR, 7576
Fant Foundation, The, TX, 8817
Fantasy Fountain Fund Inc., NY, 5973
Far Northern Coordinating Council on Developmental Disabilities, CA, 570
Faranna Scholarship Trust, Charles C., OK, 7467
Farber Foundation, Anne & Jason, CA, 571
Farber Foundation, PA, 7837
Farber Memorial Foundation, Charles D., Inc., NY, 5974
Fargo-Moorhead Area Foundation, ND, 6940
Faris, Katherine K. Steinbicker, & Paul F. Steinbicker Scholarship Fund, Elizabeth S., The, WV, 9784
Farm Aid, MA, 4062
Farm Bureau-Arkansas Scholarship Foundation, Inc., AR, see 265
Farm Income Improvement Foundation, Inc., KY, 3568
Farmen Trust for St. Mark's Church, Elizabeth, NY, 5975
Farmer Relief Fund, E. D., TX, 8818
Farmer Trust, Edwin S., MA, 4063
Farmers Union Marketing & Processing Foundation, MN, 4737
Farmers' Electric Education Foundation, NM, 5629
Farnam Trust, Henry, MA, 4064
Farpath Foundation, DE, 1507
Farrell Charitable Trust, Juli Ann, IA, 3279
Farrington Trust, Eleanor E., RI, 8291
Fary Memorial Scholarship Fund, VA, 9376
Fashion Group Foundation of Chicago, Inc., The, IL, 2558
Fashion Group Foundation, Inc., The, NY, 5976
Fasken Foundation, The, TX, 8819
Fassino Foundation, Inc., The, MA, 4065
Fast Scholarship Foundation, Ethel & Emery, Inc., MD, 3825
Father Daily Scholarship Foundation, IA, 3280
Father Murphy Scholarship Fund, NY, 5977
Father-To-Father Project, Inc., SC, 8471
Faulconer Scholarship Programs, The, TX, 8820
Faunce Fund, Sewall Allen, The, RI, see 8292
Faunce Trust, Eliza H., RI, 8292
Faunce Trust, Harriet M., MA, 4066
Faust Scholarship Funds, Evelyn Elaine, PA, 7838
Fava Scholarship Foundation, NC, see 6654
Fava Scholarship Foundation, Philip V. Fava and Nancy Owens D., NC, 6654
Fayette County Foundation, IN, 3028
FCCF, CT, see 1387
FDNY Foundation, NY, 5978
Fed-Mart Foundation, CA, see 572
Federal Employee Education and Assistance Fund, CO, 1194
Federal Employees Scholarship Foundation Inc., CA, 572
Federated Church of Columbus Foundation, Inc., The, NE, 5202
Federation of Protestant Welfare Agencies, Inc., NY, 5979

Federman Scholarship Fund, NY, 5980
FEEA, CO, see 1194
Feed My People Childrens Charities, Inc., AZ, 191
Feed the Children, OK, 7468
Feeding America Eastern Wisconsin, Inc., WI, 9889
Feeding America, IL, 2559
FEF, IL, see 2571
Feild Co-Operative Association Inc., MS, 4907
Fell Foundation, Cliff & Nina, KS, 3441
Fellman Charitable Foundation Trust, Bruce M., NE, 5203
Fellows Memorial Fund, J. Hugh and Earle W., FL, 1875
Female Association of Philadelphia, The, PA, 7839
Feminist Majority Foundation, The, CA, 573
Fenchuk Foundation, The, VA, see 9369
Fenech Foundation, Ron and Lisa, IN, 3029
Fengler Memorial Foundation, Keith W., The, TN, 8591
Fenner Educational Trust, Gertrude A., WI, 9890
Fenstermacher Foundation, PA, 7840
Feoppel Educational Loan Trust, Charles H., WV, 9785
Feraldo Memorial Fund, William Pablo, MO, 4990
Ferdian Education Foundation, Major & Mrs. Frank H., MA, 4067
Ferebee Endowment, Percy B., NC, 6655
Fergason Scholarship Fund, Joe, WA, 9611
Fergus Electric Cooperative, Inc., MT, 5145
Ferguson Foundation, Arch L., The, TX, 8821
Fermi Educational Fund, Enrico, NY, 5981
Fernando Award Foundation, Inc., CA, 574
Fernstrum Scholarship Foundation Trust, Robert W. & Caroline A., WI, 9891
Ferree Educational & Welfare Fund, NC, 6656
Ferris Charitable Trust, Ross D., MO, 4991
Ferris Foundation, Clifford G. & Grace A., IL, 2560
Fetzer Foundation, John E., Inc., MI, see 4418
Fetzer Institute, John E., Inc., MI, 4418
FFB, MD, see 3828
Fidelco Guide Dog Foundation, Inc., CT, 1388
Field, The, NY, see 6313
Fields Trust, Laura, OK, 7469
Fifty Men and Women of Toledo, Inc., The, OH, 7106
Fight for Sight, Inc., NY, 5982
Figliolia Foundation Trust, NY, 5983
Fildes Foundation, Johnsie Fiock, Ltd., The, IL, 2561
Film Forum, NY, see 6229
Film Independent, Inc., CA, 575
Film School Scholarship Grants, CA, see 410
Findlay Hancock County Community Foundation, The, OH, 7107
Fine Arts Association, The, OH, 7108
Fine Arts Work Center in Provincetown, Inc., MA, 4068
Fingersh Charitable Trust Fund, Morris, MO, see 4992
Fingersh Scholarship Fund, Morris, KS, 3442
Fingersh Scholarship Fund, Morris, MO, 4992
Finis Heidel Trust, NM, 5630
Fink Scholarship Trust, Marie G. & Greta M., KS, 3443
Finkbeiner Memorial Fund for Benton High School Graduates, Henry J. and Helen, AR, 279
Finlay Foundation Inc., Curtis, AL, 37
Finley Foundation, Rose McFarland, FL, 1876
Finnell Trust, Dred and Lula, The, MO, 4993
FINRA Investor Education Foundation, DC, 1626
Firestone Charitable Trust, J. B., OH, 7109
First Baptist Church of Everett Foundation, WA, 9612
First Brokers Good Samaritan Fund, NJ, 5445
First Candle, MD, see 3939
First Command Educational Foundation, TX, 8822
First Community Foundation Partnership of Pennsylvania, PA, 7841
First County Bank Foundation, Inc., CT, 1389
First Gaston Foundation, Inc., NC, 6657
First Literacy, Inc., MA, 4069
First Mid-Illinois Bank & Trust, Trust No. 93-111, IL, 2562
First Peoples Fund, SD, 8530
First Priority Credit Union Charitable Foundation, MA, 4070
Fischer Foundation, Friderika, The, NY, see 6491
Fischer Memorial Burial Park, PA, 7842
Fischer Trust, Karl, PA, 7843
Fischer Veterans Assistance Foundation, Dorothy K., CA, 576
Fish Emergency Service, Inc., OR, 7577

FISH, GA, see 2175
Fishel Scholarship Trust, Myron, OH, 7110
Fisher and Fuel Society of Beverly, MA, 4071
Fisher Broadcasting Inc. Minority Scholarship Fund, WA, 9613
Fisher Foundation for Dental Education Foundation, Emile T., Inc., The, GA, 2177
Fisher Foundation, Steven and Lynn, The, AZ, 192
Fisher House Foundation, Inc., MD, 3826
Fitch Charitable Foundation, James Marston, The, NY, 5984
Fitch Memorial Scholarship Fund, T. S., PA, 7844
Fitton Trust, Herrin Edith, PA, 7845
Fitzgerald Foundation, Joseph C. & Louise Skinner, Inc., IN, 3030
Fitzgerald Scholarship Trust, Father James M., OH, 7111
Fitzpatrick Memorial Scholarship Fund, William J., NY, 5985
Five Acres-The Boys & Girls Aid Society of Los Angeles County, CA, 577
Five Wings Arts Council, The, MN, 4738
Fix Scholarship Fund, Alois A. and Nina M., WI, 9892
FJC - A Foundation of Philanthropic Funds, NY, 5986
Flathead Educational Foundation, MT, 5146
Flatirons Foundation, CO, 1195
Fleetwood Memorial Foundation, Inc., TX, 8823
Flegal Educational Trust, Clark, PA, 7846
Fleischer Memorial Fund Inc., Louise, PA, 7847
Fleisher Trust No. 2, Foreman, PA, 7848
Fleisher Trust No. 2, Foreman, PA, see 7848
Fleishhacker Foundation, CA, 578
Fleming Insurance Trust, Albert W., MA, 4072
Fleurot Testamentary Trust, Lillian L., IL, 2563
Flinn Foundation, The, AZ, 193
Flint Cultural Center Corporation, Inc., MI, 4419
Flint Scholarship Endowment Fund, Ebell of Los Angeles/Charles N., The, CA, see 579
Flint Scholarship Endowment Fund, Mr. & Mrs. Charles N., CA, 579
Floor Covering Industry Foundation, CA, 580
Flora School District Academic Foundation, Inc., IL, 2564
Florida Association of Realtors Disaster Relief Fund, FL, 1877
Florida Bar Foundation, The, FL, 1878
Florida Children's Forum, FL, see 1825
Florida Education Fund, Inc., FL, 1879
Florida Elks Charities, Inc., FL, 1880
Florida Endowment Foundation for Vocational Rehabilitation, FL, 1881
Florida FBLA-PBL Foundation, Inc., FL, 1882
Florida Keys Educational Foundation, Inc., FL, 1883
Florida Land Surveyors Scholarship Foundation, Inc., FL, see 1885
Florida Prepaid College Foundation, Inc., FL, 1884
Florida School Choice Fund, Inc., FL, see 2075
Florida Surveying and Mapping Society Scholarship Fund, Inc., FL, 1885
Florida Symphony Youth Orchestra, FL, 1886
Florida Young Artists Orchestra, Inc., FL, 1887
Florsheim Brothers, A California Non-Profit Benefit Corporation, CA, 581
Fluor Foundation, The, TX, 8824
Flying Horse Foundation, Inc., NJ, A
Flynn Scholarship Fund, Margaret and Thomas, NJ, 5446
FMC Corporation Contributions Program, PA, 7849
FMI Scholarship Foundation, Inc., NJ, 5447
Focused Ultrasound Surgery Foundation, VA, 9377
Foley Scholarship Foundation, Harry, MN, 4739
Follett Educational Foundation, IL, 2565
Folsom Foundation, Maud Glover, Inc., CT, 1390
Fond du Lac Area Foundation, WI, 9893
Fond Rev. Edmond Gelinas Inc., NH, 5321
Fondation Sante, NY, 5987
Food Allergy & Anaphylaxis Network, Inc., The, VA, 9378
Food Allergy Initiative, Inc., The, NY, 5988
Food and Friends, Inc., DC, 1627
Food Bank of Central Louisiana, Inc., The, LA, 3652
Food Bank of the Rockies, CO, 1196
Food for Children, Inc., AZ, 194

Food for Thought Endowment Fund, Inc., NY, 5989
Food Industry Scholarship Fund of New Hampshire, NH, see 5354
Foodbank of Southeastern Virginia, VA, 9379
Foodbank, Inc., OH, 7112
Footprints Foundation, The, IL, 2566
Forbes Charitable Foundation, Mary C., FL, 1888
Forbes Foundation, Stuart and Margaret L., Inc., NC, 6658
Forbes Kirkside Foundation Inc., The, MA, 4073
Ford Family Foundation, The, OR, 7578
Ford Foundation, Gerald R., MI, 4420
Ford Fund, S.N. & Ada, OH, 7113
Ford Health System, Henry, MI, 4421
Ford, Jr. Scholarship Program, William C., MI, 4422
Fordham Foundation, Thomas B., DC, 1628
Forecast Public Artworks, MN, 4740
Forever Foundation for Texas Wildlife, The, TX, 8825
Formosa Plastics Corporation, Texas—Calhoun High School Scholarship Foundation, TX, 8826
Forrai Foundation Inc., Olga, NY, 5990
Forsyth Educational Fund, Fred, RI, 8293
Forsyth Educational Trust Fund, Fred, RI, see 8293
Fort Atkinson Community Foundation, WI, 9894
Fort Collins Area Community Foundation, CO, see 1171
Fort Hays State University Endowment Association, KS, see 3444
Fort Hays State University Foundation, KS, 3444
Fort Lauderdale Area Realtors Charitable Foundation Inc., FL, 1889
Fort Lauderdale Rotary 1090 Foundation, Inc., FL, 1890
Fort Lewis College Foundation, Inc., CO, 1197
Fort Myers Beach Chamber of Commerce Foundation, FL, 1891
Fort Pierce Memorial Hospital Scholarship Foundation, Inc., FL, see 1939
Fort Sanders Regional Medical Center, TN, 8592
Fort Wayne Community Foundation, IN, see 2994
Fort Wayne Philharmonic Orchestra, Inc., IN, 3031
Fort Worth Hope Center, TX, 8827
Fort Worth Police Officers' Award Foundation, TX, 8828
Fort Worth Stockshow Syndicate, TX, 8829
Fortescue Fund, Charles Le Geyt, NJ, 5448
Fortin Memorial Foundation, Ernest, Inc., MA, 4074
Forum Communications Foundation, ND, 6941
Foss Memorial Employees Trust, Donald J., OH, 7114
Foss Memorial Trust, Ralph H., OR, 7579
Foster Educational Institute, Marcus A., CA, 582
Foster Family Foundation, MI, 4423
Foster Family Programs of Hawaii, HI, see 2282
Foster Foundation, MI, 4424
Foster Memorial Trust, George B., MA, 4075
Foster Welfare Foundation, MI, see 4424
Foulger Foundation, Sid & Mary, Inc., MD, 3827
Found Advancement Maryland Education, Inc., MD, see 3870
Found Animals Foundation, Inc., CA, 583
Foundation Chapter of Theta Chi Fraternity, Inc., The, IN, 3032
Foundation Fighting Blindness, Inc., MD, 3828
Foundation for a Christian Civilization, Inc., PA, 7850
Foundation for Accounting Education, Inc., NY, 5991
Foundation for Affordable Housing, KY, 3569
Foundation for AIDS Research, Inc., The, NY, 5992
Foundation for Air-Medical Research and Education, The, VA, see 9433
Foundation for Anesthesia Education and Research, MN, 4741
Foundation for Appalachian Ohio, The, OH, 7115
Foundation for Arts Initiatives, NY, 5993
Foundation for Birmingham Senior Residents, MI, 4425
Foundation for Boulder Valley Schools, CO, see 1219
Foundation for Burns and Trauma, Inc., AZ, see 155
Foundation for California State University San Bernardino, CA, 584
Foundation for California University of Pennsylvania, PA, 7851
Foundation for Child Development, NY, 5994
Foundation for Children with Cancer, Inc., The, WI, 9895
Foundation for College Christian Leaders, The, CA, 585
Foundation for Contemporary Arts, NY, 5995

Foundation for Deep Ecology, CA, 586
Foundation for Digestive Health and Nutrition, MD, 3829
Foundation for Educational Advancement, The, CO, see 1210
Foundation for Educational Excellence, CO, 1198
Foundation for Educational Funding, Inc., NE, see 5197
Foundation for Enhancing Communities, The, PA, 7852
Foundation for Excellence, Inc., CA, 587
Foundation for Excellence, TX, 8830
Foundation for Geriatric Education, The, TN, 8593
Foundation for Good Business, NC, 6659
Foundation for Health in Aging, Inc., The, NY, 5996
Foundation for Improvement of Justice Inc., GA, 2178
Foundation for Independent Artists, Inc., NY, 5997
Foundation for Italian Art and Culture, NY, 5998
Foundation for Jewish Philanthropies, Inc., NY, 5999
Foundation for Lincoln Public Schools, The, NE, 5204
Foundation for Manatee Community College, Inc., FL, see 2073
Foundation for Medically Fragile Children, GA, see 2179
Foundation for Montessori Scholarships, AZ, 195
Foundation for Physical Therapy Research, The, VA, see 9380
Foundation for Physical Therapy, Inc., The, VA, 9380
Foundation for Roanoke Valley, VA, see 9349
Foundation for Rural Education & Development, Inc., DC, 1629
Foundation for Saline Area Schools, MI, 4426
Foundation for Seacoast Health, NH, 5322
Foundation for Social Equity, The, NV, 5288
Foundation for Sustainable Development, CA, 588
Foundation for Technology and Engineering Educators, VA, 9381
Foundation for the Advancement of Mesoamerican Studies Inc., CA, 589
Foundation for the Art Renewal Center, Inc., NJ, 5449
Foundation For The Carolinas, NC, 6660
Foundation for the Elimination of Diseases Attacking the Immune System, The, CA, 590
Foundation for the Future, WA, 9614
Foundation for the Jewish Community, The, NY, see 5986
Foundation for the Mid South, MS, A
Foundation for the National Capital Region, The, DC, see 1605
Foundation for the National Institutes of Health, Inc., MD, 3830
Foundation for the Retarded, TX, 8831
Foundation for the Roman Catholic Diocese of Altoona-Johnstown, PA, see 7917
Foundation for Theological Education, A, NC, 6661
Foundation for United Methodists, Inc., KY, 3570
Foundation for Visions, OK, 7470
Foundation for Women's Cancer, IL, 2568
Foundation for Women's Wellness, CO, 1199
Foundation for World Peace, Alexia, Inc., NJ, 5450
Foundation Inc., The, CA, 591
Foundation of Advocacy for Mental Health, Inc., The, NY, 6000
Foundation of Greater Greensboro, Inc., The, NC, see 6614
Foundation of Hope for Research and Treatment of Mental Illness, The, NC, 6662
Foundation of Metropolitan Community College, MO, 4994
Foundation of the Alumnae Association of the Mount Sinai Hospital School of Nursing, Inc., NY, 6001
Foundation of the American College of Allergy, Asthma, and Immunology, IL, 2569
Foundation of the American Society of Neuroradiology, The, IL, 2570
Foundation of The National Student Nurses Association, Inc., NY, 6002
Foundation of the Pennsylvania Medical Society, The, PA, 7853
Foundation of the Pierre Fauchard Academy, VA, 9382
Foundation of the State Bar of California, CA, see 444
Foundation of the State University of New York At Binghamton, Inc., NY, 6003
Foundation of the Wall & Ceiling Industry, VA, 9383
Foundation, Blandin, The, MN, see 4700
Foundation, Jones, Inc., KS, see 3464

Foundation, P&F, IL, 2567
Foundations Community Partnership, PA, 7854
Foundations of East Chicago, Inc., The, IN, 3033
Founder's Trust, PA, 7855
Founders Memorial Fund of the American Sterilizer Company, OH, 7116
Foundry Educational Foundation, The, IL, 2571
Fountain House, Inc., NY, 6004
Four County Community Foundation, MI, 4427
Four County Foundation, MI, see 4427
Four Oaks Foundation, Inc., The, NY, 6005
Four Wheel Drive Foundation, WI, 9896
Fouts Scholarship Fund, Sadie and Hobert, NC, 6663
Fowler Charitable Trust, Blanche N., AL, 38
Fox & Julian Karger Scholarship Fund, Louis B., RI, 8294
Fox & Julian Karger Trust, Louis B., RI, see 8294
Fox Foundation for Parkinson's Research, Michael J., NY, 6006
Fox Foundation, Jacob L. and Lewis, CT, 1391
Fox Foundation, James Frederick, PA, 7856
Fox Foundation, William and Eva, The, VA, 9384
Fox Scholarship Trust, Mary-Ann, NC, 6664
FPWA, NY, see 5979
Fractured Atlas Productions, Inc., NY, 6007
Fragile Kids Foundation, GA, 2179
FRAMAX, Inc., CA, 592
Frameline, CA, 593
France, Donald R., MI, see 4471
Francies Scholarship Fund, IL, 2572
Francis Scholarship Foundation, Joe, MN, 4742
Francisan Foundation, WA, see 9615
Franciscan Community Benefit Services, IL, 2573
Franciscan Foundation for the Holy Land, DC, 1630
Franciscan Foundation Washington, WA, 9615
Francisco Educational Trust, Elenore, IN, 3034
Franconia Sculpture Park, MN, 4743
Frank D. Lanterman Regional Center, CA, see 757
Frank Family Memorial Scholarship, NC, 6665
Frank Scholarship Fund, Jacob, Lillian & Nathan M., IN, 3035
Frank Scholarship Fund, Simon, NC, see 6665
Frank Scholarship Fund, William P., Inc., DE, 1508
Frankenmuth Area Community Foundation, Greater, MI, see 4428
Frankenmuth Community Foundation, MI, 4428
Franklin County Community Foundation, Inc., IN, 3036
Franklin Electric Charitable & Educational Foundation, IN, 3037
Franklin Electric—Edward J. Schaefer and T. W. Kehoe Charitable and Educational Foundation, Inc., The, IN, see 3037
Franklin Foundation, AL, 39
Franklin Foundation, Anna Collins, OK, 7471
Franklin Furnace Archive, Inc., NY, 6008
Franklin Mutual Insurance Scholarship Foundation, Inc., NJ, see 5447
Franklin Park Rotary Club Foundation, IL, 2574
Franklin Savings Bank Community Development Foundation, ME, 3696
Franks Foundation Fund, OR, 7580
Franks Foundation, MS, 4908
Franz Broadcast Journalism Scholarship Trust, Don, MN, 4744
Fraser Area Educational Foundation, MI, 4429
Fraser Fund, Hugh A., OH, 7117
Frasier Charitable Foundation, William G. & Margaret B., NC, 6666
Frautschy Scholarship Trust Fund, John Cowles, WI, 9897
Fraxa Research Foundation, Inc., MA, 4076
Fred Hutchinson Cancer Research Center, WA, 9616
Fredenburgh Scholarship Fund Trust, Harry S., IL, 2575
Frederick Trust, Lena Pierce, OH, 7118
Fredericksen Scholarship Fund, Edwin R., MI, 4430
Fredrikson & Byron Foundation, MN, 4745
Freedom Alliance, VA, 9385
Freedom Forge Corporation Foundation, PA, 7857
Freedom Forum, Inc., The, DC, 1631
Freedom From Religion Foundation, Inc., WI, 9898
Freedom House, Inc., DC, 1632
Freels Scholarship Trust, J. C., AL, 40
Freeport-McMoRan Copper & Gold Foundation, AZ, 196

Freer Memorial Scholarship Trust, Isabelle, OH, 7119
Frees Teaching Scholarship, Irene, IN, 3038
Freese Foundation, Egbert M., The, OH, 7120
Fremont Area Community Foundation, MI, 4431
Fremont Area Community Foundation, NE, 5205
Fremont Area Foundation, The, MI, see 4431
French Alzheimer's Foundation, John Douglas, The, CA, 594
French Benevolent Society of Philadelphia, The, PA, 7858
French Charitable Foundation Inc., Ed, MO, 4995
French Family Educational Foundation, R. E., KS, 3445
French Scholarship Foundation, Blanche E., KS, 3446
French-American Foundation, NY, 6009
Fresh Start Scholarship Foundation, Inc., DE, 1509
Fresno County Economic Opportunities Commission, CA, 595
Fresno Musical Club, CA, 596
Fresno Regional Foundation, CA, 597
Frets Educational Trust, WA, 9617
Friars National Association Foundation, Inc., NY, 6010
Friary Scholarship Trust, Matthew B., MA, 4077
Frick Collection, The, NY, 6011
Fricke Foundation, William and Lena, WI, 9899
Friedberger Educational Fund, CA, 598
Friedman Fund TUW Foundation, AZ, 197
Friedman PDCA Scholarship Fund, A.E. Robert, MO, 4996
Friedman Scholarship Fund, AZ, see 197
Friedreich's Ataxia Research Alliance, VA, 9386
Friend Education Fund, Kennedy T., PA, 7859
Friend Ships Unlimited, LA, see 3673
Friend Trust, Dorothy M., PA, 7860
Friendly Foundation, Alfred, The, DC, 1633
Friends of a Studio in the Woods, LA, 3653
Friends of Acadia, ME, 3697
Friends of Civic Arts Education Fund, CA, 599
Friends of CRAFT, Inc., IN, 3039
Friends of Crest, CA, 600
Friends of Foster Kids, Inc., HI, see 2282
Friends of Hama'ayan Institution Inc., NY, 6012
Friends of Jose Carreras International Leukemia Foundation, WA, 9618
Friends of Marty Wilson, NJ, 5451
Friends of the Mauritshuis, Inc., NY, 6013
Friends of the Royal Society of Chemistry, Inc., WI, 9900
Friends of the Schindler House, CA, 601
Friends of Virgin Islands National Park, VI, 9275
Friends United for Juvenile Diabetes Research, IL, 2576
Friendship Fund Inc., PA, 7861
Friendship Village of Tempe Foundation, Inc., AZ, 198
Fries Foundation, James F. and Sarah T., The, CA, 602
Frisbie Scholarship Fund, Florence, IA, 3281
Fritts Scholarship Trust, Margaret & Charles, OH, see 7392
From the Heart Productions, Inc., CA, 603
Fromm Scholarship Trust, Walter and Mabel, WI, 9901
Fromson Foundation, Howard A., Inc., CT, 1392
Fromson Foundation, Inc., CT, see 1392
Front Range Community College Foundation, CO, 1200
Frontiers of Science Foundation of Oklahoma, OK, 7472
Frost Teaching Chairs Trust, Robert, RI, 8295
Frozen Food Industry Memorial Scholarship Foundation, The, PA, 7862
Ft. Myers Beach Kiwanis Club Foundation, Inc., FL, 1892
Fues Memorial Scholarship Fund, Ruth Perrin, MO, 4997
Fukunaga Scholarship Foundation, HI, 2283
Fulfillment Fund, CA, 604
Full Citizenship of Maryland, Inc., MD, 3831
Fuller Educational Trust, W. C., TX, 8832
Fuller Foundation, C.G., FL, 1893
Fuller Foundation, C.G., FL, 1893
Fuller Trust, Frank R., CT, 1393
Fulton Bank Scholarship Foundation, PA, 7863
Fulton School Employees Charitable Fund, Inc., The, GA, 2180
Fund for American Studies, The, DC, 1634
Fund for Athritis and Infectious Disease Research, CO, see 1227

Fund for Educational Excellence, Inc., MD, A
Fund For Human Possibility, NC, 6667
Fund for Investigative Journalism, DC, 1635
Fund for New York City Public Education, NY, see 6263
Fund for Rural Education & Development, DC, see 1629
Fund for Teachers, The, TX, 8833
Fund for the Advancement of the State System of
   Higher Education, Inc., PA, see 8030
Fund for the City of New York, Inc., NY, 6014
Fund for the Diaconate of the Episcopal Church in the
   United States, The, SC, 8472
Fund for Theological Education, Inc., The, GA, 2181
Fund for Wisconsin Scholars, Inc., WI, 9902
Fund for Wisconsin Scholarship, Inc., WI, see 9902
Fundacao Beneficente Faialense, RI, 8296
Fundacion La Curacao Para Los Ninos, CA, 605
Funeral Service Educational Foundation, WI, see 9903
Funeral Service Foundation, Inc., WI, 9903
Funk Educational Foundation, OK, 7473
Furnas Foundation, Inc., IL, see 2598
Fusco Foundation, Mark R., CT, 1394
Future Farmers of America, IN, 3040
Futureus Foundation, TX, 8834
Futuro Infantil Hispano, CA, 606
FVT Foundation, Inc., AZ, see 198

G.K.C.F.C.A., MO, see 5024
G.M.L. Foundation Inc., WA, 9619
Gabler Scholarship Fund, Arthur, IL, 2577
Gabler Scholarship Trust, Arthur, IL, see 2577
Gadd and F. Frederick Romanow, Jr. Charitable
   Foundation, Alice G., ME, 3698
Gadd Charitable Foundation, Alice G., ME, see 3698
Gaffney Foundation, Joseph N., Inc., NY, 6015
Gaffney Trust, Robert, IL, 2578
Gaines-Jones Education Foundation, The, CA, 607
Gala Foundation, CA, 608
Galaway Foundation, CO, 1201
Galena Park ISD Education Foundation, Inc., TX, 8835
Galesburg-Augusta Community Schools Foundation,
   MI, 4432
Galesburg-Augusta Education Foundation, MI, see
   4432
Gallagher Foundation, The, MN, 4746
Galligan Scholarship, John T., RI, 8297
Gallik Memorial Scholarship Fund, Laura Schriber, NY,
   see 6208
Gallivan and Henry T. Mills, Jr. Educational Foundation,
   Genevieve Mills, The, SC, 8473
Gallmeier Seminarian Scholarship Fund, Romaine, WI,
   9904
Gamecock Club of the University of South Carolina, SC,
   8474
Gamma Mu Foundation, FL, 1894
Gandy, Jr./Mercy Hospital Medical Staff, Inc.
   Scholarship Fund, Dr. R. A., OH, 7121
Ganyard Scholarship Trust, Lyle B. & Wanda K., The,
   OH, 7122
Ganyard Scholarship Trust, Lyle B. & Wanda K., The,
   OH, see 7122
Garber Foundation, Virgil C. Webb, William Garber, and
   Flora Webb, IA, 3282
Garcia Scholarship Trust, Jeanne Souers, OH, 7123
Garden Foundation, Allan C. and Leila J., GA, 2182
Gardiner-Cook Cello Endowment, The, PA, 7864
Gardner Foundation, Annie, KY, 3571
Gardner Foundation, OH, 7124
Gargiulo Local 12 Scholarship Fund, Sal, The, NY, 6016
Garone-Nicksich Foundation, John R., CO, 1202
Garr Scholarship Foundation Trust, Mary K., IN, 3041
Garwin Family Foundation, IL, 2579
Gasparovich Memorial Scholarship Award Fund, WA,
   9620
Gaston Arts Council, The, NC, 6668
Gaston College Foundation, Inc., NC, 6669
Gate City Golf Association Foundation, Inc., NC, 6670
Gates Memorial Scholarship Fund, John B., PA, 7865
Gates Trust, Mildred E., RI, 8298
Gateway Community Action Agency, KY, see 3572
Gateway Community Services Organization, Inc., KY,
   3572
Gateway Foundation, Inc., WV, see 9775
Gateway Global Foundation, DC, 1636

Gathering Place: A Refuge for Rebuilding Lives, The,
   CO, 1203
Gatlin Scholarship Fund, Katherine and Calvin, OK,
   7474
Gault Scholarship Fund, Charles L. and Anna N., WV,
   9786
Gavin Scholarship Trust, NY, 6017
Gavin Scholarship Trust, Ora & Bernard, NY, see 6017
Gavrin Foundation Inc., Arthur J., NY, 6018
Gay and Lesbian Medical Association, DC, 1637
Gay Citizenship Incentive Trust, Melvin, MT, 5147
Gay Fund, Virginia, OH, 7125
Gazin Educational Foundation, Norbert, The, OH, 7126
GBU Foundation, PA, 7866
GCF, IL, see 2568
Gear Up Hawaii Scholarship Trust, HI, 2284
Gebhardt Scholarship Foundation, MT, 5148
Gehl Foundation, WI, 9905
GEICO Philanthropic Foundation, MD, 3832
Geist Foundation, Victoria S. & Bradley L., HI, 2285
Gemmill Foundation, Robert, IN, 3042
Gemological Institute of America, Inc., CA, 609
GenCorp Foundation, Incorporated, CA, 610
Genentech Access To Care Foundation, CA, 611
General Charitable Fund, Inc., MA, 4078
General Charitable Society of Newburyport, MA, 4079
General Dynamics Employees Contribution Club Fort
   Worth Texas, TX, see 8921
General Education Fund, Inc., VT, 9248
General Israel Orphan Home for Girls Jerusalem, Inc.,
   NY, 6019
GenerationOn, NY, see 5846
Genesee Community College Foundation, Inc., The, NY,
   6020
Genesee Valley Council on the Arts, NY, 6021
Genesee/Shiawassee Michigan Works!, MI, see 4373
Geneseo Foundation, IL, 2580
Genesis Education Foundation, TX, 8836
Genesis Employee Foundation, PA, 7867
Genesis Foundation, Inc., NE, 5206
Genesis Health Services Foundation, IA, 3283
Genesis Program Inc., The, MI, 4433
Geneva All-Sports Boosters, Inc., IL, 2581
Genzyme Charitable Foundation, Inc., MA, 4080
George Educational Trust, Mabelle M., WA, 9621
George Foundation, Elizabeth, The, WA, 9622
Georgia Association of Realtors Scholarship
   Foundation, Inc., GA, 2183
Georgia Dental Education Foundation, Inc., GA, see
   2177
Georgia Engineering Foundation, GA, 2184
Georgia Goal Scholarship Program, Inc., GA, 2185
Georgia Health Care Education and Research
   Foundation, Inc., GA, 2186
Georgia Osteopathic Institute, GA, 2187
Georgia-Pacific Foundation, Inc., GA, A
Gerber Companies Foundation and The Gerber Baby
   Food Fund, The, MI, see 4434
Gerber Foundation, The, MI, 4434
Gerbode Foundation, Wallace Alexander, CA, 612
Gerling Scholarship Trust, Roy H. and Joan Huber, The,
   IA, 3284
German Aid Society of Boston Inc., MA, 4081
German Ladies General Benevolent Society, CA, see
   346
German Marshall Fund of the United States, The, DC,
   1638
German Memorial Foundation, Sergeant Philip, NY,
   6022
German Society of Maryland, Inc., The, MD, 3833
Gernatt Family Foundation, Daniel & Flavia, NY, 6023
Gerondelis Foundation Inc., MA, 4082
Gerontological Society of America, DC, 1639
GET Foundation, The, CA, 613
Getty Trust, J. Paul, CA, 614
Geyer Scholarship Fund, John & Dorothy, IL, 2582
Geyser Public School - Strand, MT, 5149
GFF Educational Foundation, Inc., GA, see 2255
GHCAA, MO, see 5006
GHCS, IN, see 3048
Ghidotti Foundation, William & Marian, PA, 7868
Giannini Family Foundation, CA, see 615
Giannini Foundation for Employees, A.P., TX, 8837

Giannini Foundation, A. P., CA, 615
Giannini Memorial, Clorinda, TX, 8838
Giannini-Scatena, TX, 8839
Giants Foundation, Inc., The, NJ, 5452
Gibbs Charitable Trust, Esther A. and Bruce S., MO,
   4998
Gibbs Charitable Trust, Ruby L., MI, 4435
Gibson Foundation, Addison H., PA, 7869
Gibson Foundation, E. L., AL, 41
Gibson Foundation, IN, 3043
Gibson Scholarship Fund, Goldie, OK, 7475
Giddings & Lewis Foundation, Inc., WI, 9906
Giddings Foundation, Alice & Murray, NY, 6024
Gidley Scholarship Fund, Mary Louise, IA, 3285
Gienger Foundation, Elvine & Leroy, OR, 7581
Gifford Foundation, Inc., The, CA, 616
Gifford Fund, Hazel Chase, NH, 5323
Gift of Adoption Fund, IL, 2583
Gift of Hope, Inc., MO, 4999
Gift of Life Trust Fund, SC, 8475
Gift Scholarship Trust, Harold C., NC, 6671
Gilbert Family Foundation, The, CT, 1395
Gilbert Family Foundation, W. A., The, MO, see 5000
Gilbert Foundation, The, MO, 5000
Gilbert Memorial Scholarship Fund, Muriel, OH, 7127
Gilbert Trust - Georgetown School Fund, Edwin, NC,
   6672
Giles Foundation, Edward C., The, NC, see 6673
Giles Foundation, Lucille P. and Edward C., The, NC,
   6673
Gilfillan Memorial, Fanny S., Inc., MN, 4747
Gilfillan Paxton Memorial Foundation, Charles D., MN,
   4748
Gill Foundation, The, TX, 8840
Gill Trust, Emily, RI, 8299
Gillen Scholarship Fund, Conrad H. and Anna Belle, NY,
   6025
Gillen Trust Fund, Conrad H. and Anna Belle, NY, see
   6025
Gillenwater Scholarship Fund R74629008 /
   4400378000, Mary Williams, IL, 2584
Gilles Scholarship Trust, Herbert & Florence, MI, 4436
Gillespie Family Charity Trust, AR, 280
Gillespie Foundation, H.G., PA, 7870
Gillet Memorial, Henry William, Inc., WY, 10104
Gillroy Foundation Inc., James P. & Ruth C., NY, 6026
Gilman and Gonzalez-Falla Theatre Foundation, Inc., TX,
   8841
Gilmore Foundation, The, MI, 4437
Gilmore International Keyboard Festival, Irving S., MI,
   4438
Gilmore Scholarship Trust for Sullivan High School
   Students, Marian Leota, IN, 3044
Gilpatrick Scholarship Trust, TX, 8842
Ginder Memorial Foundation, Clyde O., The, NC, 6674
Ginger Cove Foundation, Inc., MD, 3834
Giovanini Foundation, WY, 10105
Giovanni Armenise-Harvard Foundation for Scientific
   Research, MA, 4083
Girl Scout Council of Greater New York, Inc., NY, 6027
Girl Scouts - Homestead Council, NE, 5207
Girl Scouts Heart of Central California, CA, 617
Girl Scouts Hornets' Nest Council, NC, 6675
Girl Scouts of Central Maryland, Inc., MD, 3835
Girl Scouts of Colorado, CO, 1204
Girl Scouts of Maine, ME, 3699
Girl Scouts of Tierra Del Oro, CA, see 617
Girls Incorporated, NY, 6028
Gish Prize, Dorothy and Lillian, The, IL, 2585
Gius Foundation, WA, 9623
Give A Slice, CA, 618
Giving Children Hope, CA, see 623
Giving Circle, The, MA, 4084
Giving Hand Foundation, Inc., The, NC, 6676
Glades Electric Educational Foundation Inc., FL, 1895
Glaser Pediatric AIDS Foundation, Elizabeth, The, DC,
   1640
Glaser Trust, Sheldon, MI, 4439
Glasgow Foundation, Louis and Florence, NY, 6029
Glassber Educational Foundation, Antonio V., The, WY,
   10106
Glaucoma Foundation, Inc., The, NY, 6030
Glaucoma Research Foundation, CA, 619

GlaxoSmithKline Patient Access Programs Foundation, PA, 7871

Glazer Scholarship Fund, Charles G., NY, 6031

Gleamns Human Resources Commission, Inc., SC, 8476

Gleaner Life Insurance Society Scholarship Foundation, MI, 4440

Gleitsman Foundation, The, CA, 620

Glen Arbor Art Association, MI, 4441

Glen Rock High School Unified Scholarship Council, Inc., NJ, see 5453

Glen Rock Unified Scholarship Council, Inc., NJ, 5453

Glendale Community Foundation, CA, see 513

Glenn Foundation for Medical Research, Inc., CA, 621

Glenn Foundation for Medical Research, Paul F., Inc., CA, see 621

Glennon Foundation, CA, 622

Glens Falls Foundation, The, NY, 6032

Global Animal Partnership, 1641

Global Foundation for Peroxisomal Disorders, OK, 7476

Global Gateway Foundation, DC, see 1636

Global Health Council, MD, 3836

Global Jewish Assistance and Relief Network, NY, 6033

Global Operations and Development, CA, 623

Global Routes, Inc., MA, 4085

Glover Foundation, La'Roi, The, CA, 624

Glover Youth Program, Andrew, NY, 6034

Glushko and Pamela Samuelson Foundation, Robert J., The, NJ, 5454

GMAA -Batchelor Aviation Scholarship Fund Inc., FL, 1896

GMAA Grover Loening Scholarship Fund, FL, see 1896

GMG Foundation, IA, see 3290

Gnade Charitable Trust, Richard E., TX, 8843

God's Gift Foundation, Inc., GA, 2188

God's Pantry Food Bank, Inc., KY, 3573

Goddard Health Services Inc., MA, 4086

Godwin Foundation, William Jesse, TX, 8844

Goertz Scholarship Trust Fund, Father Bernard C., The, TX, 8845

Goetze Educational Foundation Inc., MO, 5001

Goff Family Foundation, TX, 8846

Gold Charitable Trust, Rita & Herbert Z., NY, 6035

Goldbach Charitable Foundation, Inc., WI, see 9907

Goldbach Foundation, Raymond and Marie, Inc., WI, 9907

Goldberg Memorial for Cancer Research, Ruth Estrin, NJ, 5455

Golden Apple Foundation for Excellence in Teaching, IL, 2586

Golden Belt Community Foundation, KS, 3447

Golden Foundation for the Arts, Sam & Adele, NY, 6036

Golden Gate Family Foundation, CA, 625

Golden Gate Restaurant Association Scholarship Foundation, CA, 626

Golden Key International Honour Society, Inc., GA, 2189

Golden Rule Foundation, TX, 8847

Golden Slipper Club Charities, PA, 7872

Golden Tornado Scholastic Foundation, Inc., PA, 7873

Golden West College Foundation, CA, 627

Goldfarb Family Foundation, Andrew and Denise, The, CA, see 863

Goldin Foundation for Excellence in Education, MA, 4087

Goldman Environmental Foundation, CA, 628

Goldman Foundation, William, PA, 7874

Goldring Family Foundation, LA, 3654

Goldstein Family Foundation, NY, 6037

Goldstein Memorial Scholarship, Sarah and Tena, PA, 7875

Golub Educational Trust, Noble Symond Golub and Leila J., MA, 4088

Golub Foundation, NY, see 6327

Gomez Dream Foundation, Andrew, UT, 9200

Gonter & Sara O'Brien Scholarship Foundation, Mary, OH, 7128

Gonzalez Memorial Scholarship Fund, Trooper Scott, NJ, 5456

Good Friend Ministry, CA, 629

Good Neighbor Community Center, Inc., NE, 5208

Good News Foundation of Central New York, Inc., NY, 6038

Good Samaritan Foundation of Cincinnati, Inc., OH, 7129

Good Samaritan Hospital Foundation, NE, 5209

Good Shepherd Foundation Inc., NC, 6677

Good Shepherd Fund, The, CA, 630

Good Tidings Foundation, CA, 631

Goodell Scholarship Endowment Trust, Cora A. Goodell and Menzo W., NY, 6039

Goodenough Scholarship Fund, Edwin C., OR, see 7582

Goodenough Scholarship Trust, Edwin C., OR, 7582

Goodgear Emergency Assistance Foundation, Gary, Inc., IL, 2587

Gooding Group Foundation, PA, 7876

Gooding Trust, George L., RI, 8300

Goodlark Educational Foundation, TN, 8594

Goodrich College Education Fund, David, MI, 4442

Goodrich Scholarship Trust, Arthur George, ME, 3700

Goodrich-Rohr Will-Share Club, CA, see 917

Goodridge Charitable Trust, Grace W., OH, 7130

Goodwill Industries of Denver, CO, 1205

Goodwin Memorial Trust, Mark, OH, 7131

Goolsby-Gardner Educational Fund, VA, 9387

Gordy Family Educational Fund, George E., DE, 1510

Gore Family Memorial Foundation, IL, 2588

Gorecki Scholarship Foundation, Jan, CA, 632

Gorham Memorial Fund, Charles N., IL, 2589

Gorman Foundation, MO, 5002

Goshen Rotary Scholarship Foundation, NY, 6040

Goslee Student Loan Fund, Alva O., Adie E. & Mary J., PA, 7877

Goss Educational Testamentary Trust, Beatrice I., MI, 4443

Gossett Foundation, Earl J., IL, 2590

Gottlieb Foundation, Adolph and Esther, Inc., NY, 6041

Gough Foundation Trust, Helen, MN, 4749

Gould Scholarship Fund, Norman J. and Anna B., RI, see 8301

Gould Scholarship Fund, Norman J. and Anna B., RI, see 8356

Gould Scholarship Fund, RI, 8301

Gourley Scholarship Foundation, Mary I., The, TX, 8848

Govans Ecumenical Development Corporation, MD, 3837

Government Employees Benefit Association Scholarship Foundation, MD, 3838

Governor's Funding, Inc., LA, A

Governors Scholars Program Foundation, Inc., The, KY, 3574

GPAC, PA, see 8046

Graber Scholarship Trust, John, IL, 2591

Grace Family Vineyards Foundation, CA, 633

Grace Foundation, IA, 3286

Grace Foundation, William M. & Ann K., AZ, 199

Grace High Washburn Trust, The, OH, 7132

Grace Memorial Scholarship Fund, Mike, The, TN, 8595

Graef, Anhalt, Schloemer Foundation, Inc., WI, 9908

Grafton Medical Foundation, WI, 9909

Graham & Clemma B. Fancher Scholarship Fund, Florence B., CA, 634

Graham Evangelistic Association, Billy, NC, 6678

Graham Family Foundation Inc., TN, 8596

Graham Foundation for Advanced Studies in the Fine Arts, IL, 2592

Graham Foundation Inc., The, CT, 1396

Graham Scholarship Fund, Dorothy D., SD, 8531

Gramberg-Millner Scholarship Fund, NC, 6679

GRAMMY Foundation, The, CA, 635

Grand Haven Area Community Foundation, Inc., MI, 4444

Grand Island Community Foundation, Inc., NE, 5210

Grand Lodge of Free & Accepted Masons of Pennsylvania, PA, 7878

Grand Marnier Foundation, The, NY, 6042

Grand Rapids Area Community Foundation, MN, 4750

Grand Rapids Community Foundation, MI, 4445

Grand Rapids Foundation, The, MI, see 4445

Grand Rapids Home Builders Association Foundation, Greater, MI, see 4468

Grand Rapids Urban League, MI, 4446

Grand Traverse Regional Community Foundation, MI, 4447

Grandcolas Foundation, Lauren Catuzzi, NJ, 5457

Grande Memorial Foundation, Raven Leigh, Inc., NJ, 5458

Grandma Brown Foundation Inc., NY, 6043

Granite Education Foundation, Inc., UT, 9201

Grannis-Martin Memorial Foundation, MN, 4751

Granoff Foundation, Leon L., CA, 636

Grant Foundation, William T. & Frances D., MO, 5003

Granville Foundation, The, OH, 7133

Grass Foundation, The, CA, 637

Grasshopper Trust, KS, 3448

Gratiot County Community Foundation, MI, 4448

Gratiot Physicians Foundation, MI, 4449

Graves Foundation, Nancy, Inc., NY, 6044

Gravity Research Foundation, MA, 4089

Gray Scholarship Fund, Stella O., NC, 6680

Gray Scholarship Trust, Theodore and Wanda, ME, 3701

Grays Harbor Community Foundation, WA, 9624

Grayson-Jockey Club Research Foundation, NY, 6045

GRCMA Early Childhood Directions, AL, see 44

Great Lakes Castings Corporation Foundation, MI, 4450

Great River Medical Center Staff Foundation, IA, 3287

Greater Berkshire Charitable Foundation, MA, see 3983

Greater Bridgeport Retired Teachers Fund Inc., RI, 8302

Greater Community Educational Foundation, Inc., NJ, 5459

Greater East Texas Community Action Program, TX, see 8760

Greater Erie Community Action Committee, PA, 7879

Greater Lee's Summit Healthcare Foundation, The, MO, 5004

Greater Morgantown Community Trust, Inc., WV, see 9831

Greater Pottstown Foundation, The, PA, 7880

Greater Saint Louis Community Foundation, MO, see 5105

Greater Williamsburg Community Trust, VA, 9388

Green Bay Community Foundation, Greater, Inc., WI, 9910

Green Bay Packers Foundation, WI, 9911

Green Charitable Trust, Walter & Frances, SD, 8532

Green Foundation, Allen P. & Josephine B., MO, 5005

Green Hills Community Action Agency, MO, 5006

Green Scholarship Fund, RI, see 8303

Green Scholarship Fund, Stephanie Weiser, RI, 8303

Green Scholarship Trust, George B., NH, 5324

Green Valley Film & Art Center, VT, 9249

Green Valley Media, VT, see 9249

Greene County Community Foundation, Inc., IN, see 3045

Greene County Community Foundation, OH, 7134

Greene County Foundation, Inc., IN, 3045

Greene County Medical Center Foundation, IA, 3288

Greene Giving, OH, see 7134

Greene Memorial Scholarship Fund, G. E. & E. R., KS, see 3449

Greene Memorial Scholarship Fund, Garnette E. Greene and Ethlyne R., KS, 3449

Greenlaw Trust, Vera Grace, RI, 8304

Greensboro Urban Ministry, Inc., NC, 6681

Greenville Area Community Foundation, MI, 4451

Greenville Area Foundation, MI, see 4451

Greenville Foundation, Greater, Inc., The, NC, 6682

Greenville Tech Foundation, Inc., SC, 8477

Greenwalt Foundation, Nora, OH, see 7135

Greenwalt Trust, Nora, OH, 7135

Greenwell Scholarship Trust, E. E. & Maud, IN, 3046

Gregg-Graniteville Foundation, Inc., SC, 8478

Griffin Educational Fund, Abbie M., NH, 5325

Griffin Family Foundation, Inc., MO, 5007

Griffin Foundation, Inc., The, CO, 1206

Griffin Foundation, Inc., The, NY, 6046

Griffin Hospital Fund, Abbie M., NH, 5326

Griffin Scholarship Foundation, Lloyd Ellis, CA, 638

Griffis Memorial Scholarship in Art and Theatre, The, KS, see 3524

Griffith Family Charitable Foundation, Philip D., The, KS, 3450

Griffith Insurance Education Foundation, OH, 7136

Griffith Scholarship Fund, Paul and Mary, IA, 3289

Grim Educational Fund, Virginia S., NC, 6683
Grimley Scholarship Trust, NC, 6684
Grimm Foundation, Fred and Margaret, WA, 9625
Grimm Scholarship Trust, Frances, WI, 9912
Grinnell Mutual Group Foundation, IA, 3290
Grinspoon Charitable Foundation, Harold, The, MA, 4090
Grinspoon Foundation, Harold, The, MA, 4091
Grisham Scholarship Foundation, Carl H. Grisham and Laura Estella, AL, 42
Griswold Scholarships Fund, Harry E., AL, 43
Griswold Trust, Harry E., AL, see 43
Griswold Trust, Jessie E., IL, 2593
Grobel Scholarship Trust, VA, 9389
Groeniger College Scholarship Fund, Mike & Bev, CA, 639
Groesbeck Foundation, Morgan, The, UT, 9202
Groff Foundation, Frank and Louise, NJ, 5460
Groff Scholarship Trust, Mary S., NC, 6685
Grogan Educational Fund, Beverly W. and Mabel Tudor, The, NC, 6686
Gromack Scholarship Fund, RI, 8305
Gromet Foundation, DE, 1511
Gromet Fund for Disadvantaged Children, Janice & Ben, The, DE, see 1511
Groot Foundation, Candice B., MN, see 4752
Groot Foundation, Virginia A., The, MN, 4752
Groskinsky Foundation, MT, 5150
Gross Memorial Scholarship Fund, Roland, NC, 6687
Grossinger Foundation, Sam & Sarah, IL, 2594
Grossman Scholarship Foundation, Alexander J., FL, 1897
Grotefend Scholarship Fund, George, NC, 6688
Group Health Community Foundation, WA, 9626
Group Health Foundation, The, WA, see 9626
Grove Farm Foundation, HI, 2286
Grove Scholarship Fund, Thomas O., OH, 7137
Grow Memorial Scholarship Fund, Freeman and Emma, WA, 9627
Growing Family Foundation, Inc., MO, 5008
Grubb Charitable Foundation Inc., Stephen R., IA, 3291
Grubbs Charitable Trust, Augusta Schultz, VA, 9390
Gruenberg Foundation, The, NJ, 5461
Grupe Foundation, William F., Inc., NJ, 5462
GSBA, WA, see 9717
Guardian Industries Educational Foundation, MI, 4452
Guardian Life Welfare Trust, The, NY, see 6128
Guarino Family Foundation, Thomas V., NY, 6047
Gubitosi Charitable Fund Inc., Paul, NJ, 5463
Guenther Scholarship Fund, The, NY, 6048
Guenther Trust f/b/o West Point Cadet Fund, Eleanor M., The, IL, 2595
Guertin Trust, Ernest O., RI, 8306
Guest Educational Trust, W. H. Guest & E. M., IA, 3292
Guest Educational Trust, William H. Guest & Edith M., IA, see 3292
Guggenheim Foundation, Harry Frank, The, NY, 6049
Guggenheim Memorial Foundation, John Simon, NY, 6050
Guggenheim Scholarship Fund, Simon, NC, 6689
Guilander Scholarship Trust, Anna M., MO, 5009
Guilford Child Development, Inc., NC, 6690
Guiliani Scholarship Foundation, Albert, IN, 3047
Gulf Coast Community Foundation of Venice, FL, see 1898
Gulf Coast Community Foundation, FL, see 1898
Gulf Coast Community Foundation, Inc., FL, 1898
Gulf Coast Community Foundation, MS, 4909
Gulf Coast Jewish Family and Community Services, Inc., FL, 1899
Gulf Coast Jewish Family Services, Inc., FL, see 1899
Gulf Regional Childcare Management Agency, Inc., AL, 44
Gumaer Scholarship Foundation, Mary L., MI, 4453
Gundersen Lutheran Medical Foundation, Inc., WI, 9913
Gunglach Scholarship Trust, NY, 6051
Gunk Foundation, The, NY, 6052
Gunn Senior High School Foundation, CA, 640
Gunning Scholarship Foundation, Thomas S., Inc., MA, 4092
Gunnison Council for the Arts, CO, 1207

Guslander Masonic Lodge Scholarship Fund, A. B., CA, 641
Guthrie Scholarship Fund, Dwight R. & Julia, PA, 7881
Guthrie Scottish Rite Charitable and Educational Foundation, OK, 7477
Guzik Foundation, The, CA, 642
Gwynn Foundation, Inc., Darrell, FL, 1900
Gygi Foundation, Hans, MA, see 4309
Gynecologic Cancer Foundation, IL, see 2568

H.E.L.P. International, CO, 1208
H.H. Red and Ruth Nelson Foundation, NE, 5211
H.L. Snyder Medical Research Institute, KS, see 3516
H.O.P.E. Foundation of Darke County, OH, 7138
H2 Brensdal Scholarship Fund Trust, The, MT, 5151
Haack Scholarship Trust, Arnold E., MT, 5152
Habig Foundation, The, IN, see 3086
Habitat for Humanity of Horry County, Inc., SC, 8479
Habitat for Humanity of Kent County, Inc., MI, 4454
Habitat for Humanity of Metro Louisville, Inc., KY, 3575
Hachar Charitable Trust Fund, D. D., TX, 8849
Hacker Memorial Scholarship Fund, Starr, NY, 6053
HACU, TX, see 8870
Hadar Foundation, Richard and Mica, The, NY, 6054
Hadar Foundation, The, NY, see 6054
Haddad Scholarship Fund, Philip A., The, WV, 9787
Haddad Welfare Trust Fund, Edna, MO, 5010
Haeseler Memorial Fund Trust, Louise H., PA, 7882
Hagedorn Trust, Mary Catherine, IN, 3293
Hager Hanger Club Foundation, CA, 643
Haggai and Associates Foundation, Tom, NC, 6691
Hagley Museum and Library, DE, see 1505
Hahn Academic Athletic Scholarship Award, Carl G., PA, 7883
Hahn, Jr. Educational Trust, Harry, IA, 3294
Haight Foundation for Foster Children, Lois, CA, 644
Hairy Cell Leukemia Research Foundation, IL, 2596
Hale Memorial Foundation, Jen, Inc., The, NJ, 5464
Hale Memorial Scholarship Fund, Benton & Louise, WI, 9914
Hall Educational Trust, Martha K., OR, 7583
Hall Eye Center, James H., GA, 2190
Hall Eye Center, James H., The, GA, see 2190
Hall Family Foundation, MO, 5011
Hall Memorial Music Scholarship, Joyce, WA, 9628
Hall Trust, John T., GA, 2191
Haller Foundation, Albert, WA, 9629
Hallgrimson Foundation Inc., Steven L., CA, 645
Halsey Educational Trust, James & Lena, IL, 2597
Halstead Charitable Trust, Fred & Florence, AR, 281
Halstead Foundation, Inc., The, MO, 6692
Halstead Scholarship Trust, Fred E., AR, see 281
Halton Foundation, OR, 7584
Hambay Foundation, James T., NY, 6055
Hambidge Center for Creative Arts and Sciences, Inc., GA, 2192
Hamilton Agricultural Youth Foundation, WA, 9630
Hamilton Community Foundation, Inc., NE, 5212
Hamilton Community Foundation, Inc., The, OH, 7139
Hamilton Foundation, John Clifford, CA, 646
Hamilton Foundation, Robert W., NM, 5631
Hamilton Fund, Esther, OH, 7140
Hamilton Holt Kiwanis Scholarship Fund, GA, 2193
Hamilton Memorial Fund, Joann, OR, 7585
Hamilton Scholarship Trust Fund, Marie H., TX, 8850
Hamilton Teachers Scholarship Fund, Helen and June, MO, 5012
Hamm Foundation, Harry O., AR, 282
Hamman Foundation, George and Mary Josephine, TX, 8851
Hammel-Delangis Scholarship Trust, MI, 4455
Hammers Charitable Trust, C. Arthur and Elizabeth, CT, 1397
Hammond Community Services, Greater, Inc., IN, 3048
Hammond Optimist Youth Foundation, IN, 3049
Hammond Trust, W. R., TX, 8852
Hamot Aid Society, PA, 7884
Hamp Foundation Inc., WI, 9915
Hampden Savings Foundation, Inc., MA, 4093
Hampton Pitching in Foundation, Mike, FL, see 1830
Hampton Roads Community Foundation, VA, 9391
Hana Maui Trust, HI, 2287
Hancock Scholarship Fund, Sumner O., ME, 3702

Hand Foundation, Inc., The, FL, 1901
Handweavers Guild of America, Inc., GA, 2194
Handyside Foundation, George T., The, PA, 7885
Hanks Foundation Inc., Marion D. & Maxine C., The, UT, 9203
Hanna Memorial Scholarship Foundation, Doug, WA, 9631
Hanna-Spivey Scholarship Fund, AL, 45
Hannaford, Sr. Foundation Inc., Kevin J., NJ, 5465
Hannah & Friends, IN, 3050
Hansen Charitable Foundation, Albert G. and Bernice F., NE, 5213
Hansen Foundation, Carl M., Inc., WA, 9632
Hansen Foundation, Dane G., KS, 3451
Hansen Scholarship Trust, MN, 4753
Hansen-Furnas Foundation, Inc., IL, 2598
Hanson Charitable Trust, Ruby E., MT, 5153
Hanson Foundation, Maudean & E. L., CO, 1209
HAP, Inc., MA, 4094
Hapke Educational Fund, NE, 5214
Happiness is Helping Foundation, OK, 7478
Haraldson Foundation, The, TX, 8853
Harasimik Trust, Michael, NC, 6693
Harber Educational Trust Foundation, Anna M., IN, 3051
Harbert Employees Reaching Out Foundation, AL, 46
Harbert Scholarship Foundation, Dorris, MT, 5154
Harbison Scholarship Trust, CA, 647
Harbor Springs Educational Foundation, MI, 4456
Harby Scholarship Fund, Ralph Dean & Evelyn Peake, NY, 6056
Harcourt Educational Trust, Russell and Betty B., IN, 3052
Hard Rock Cafe Foundation, Inc., FL, 1902
Harden Foundation, NY, 6057
Hardin Memorial Scholarship Foundation, IL, 2599
Harding Foundation, TX, 8854
Harding Scholarship Fund, George, MI, 4457
Hariri Foundation, MD, 3839
Harless Foundation, James H., Inc., WV, 9788
Harley Nursing Scholarship Fund, Sylvia M., PA, 7886
Harman Foundation, Leon & Arline, The, UT, 9204
Harmeson Trust, Harold L., AL, 47
Harmon Memorial Scholarship Fund, Giles Arthur, Inc., NC, see 6694
Harmon Memorial Scholarship Fund, Giles, NC, 6694
Harmon Scholarship Foundation, Carlyle and Delta, UT, 9205
Harmon Scholarship Fund, Marie K., PA, see 7887
Harmon Scholarship Fund, PA, 7887
Harmon Women's Scholarship Fund, UT, see 9205
Harness Horsemen International Foundation, Inc., NJ, 5466
Harney/P. J. Harney Scholarship Trust, Laura Brooks, RI, 8307
Harper Brush Works Foundation, Inc., IA, 3295
Harper Trust, Carrie M., IL, 2600
Harrell Educational Fund, Clyde W., AL, 48
Harrelson Memorial Scholarship Trust, Dwight H., FL, 1903
Harries & Eleanor Tippens Scholarship Trust, Adolph & Edith, WV, 9789
Harrington Scholarship Fund, Charles M. and Julia C., OH, 7141
Harris & Alice Faye Scholarship Foundation, Phil, Inc., IN, 3053
Harris and Sable Bernstein Fund, Henrietta, NC, 6695
Harris Charitable Foundation, George M. & Faye Tabor, PA, 7888
Harris County Hospital District Foundation, TX, 8855
Harris Educational Fund, Ray M., FL, 1904
Harris Educational Trust, Raymond J., PA, 7889
Harris Methodist HEB Auxiliary, Inc., TX, 8856
Harris Scholarship Fund, PA, 7890
Harris Trust, Paul Hyland, PA, 7891
Harrisburg Foundation, Greater, The, PA, see 7852
Harrison & Conrad Memorial Trust, FL, 1905
Harrison County Community Foundation, Inc., IN, 3054
Harrison Foundation, Fred G., IL, 2601
Harry & Edith Carter Lewis Carmine Charitable Trust, John, VA, 9392
Hart Foundation, Reese & Sis, The, SC, 8480
Hart Trust, Marjorie, OH, 7142

Hartford Arts Council, Greater, Inc., CT, 1398
Hartford Foundation for Public Giving, CT, 1399
Hartford Jaycees Foundation, Greater, Inc., CT, 1400
Hartke Community Foundation, Selma J., The, IL, 2602
Hartley Film Foundation, CT, 1401
Hartley Memorial Scholarship Fund, Betty & Randall, OH, 7143
Hartley Scholarship Trust, Chester and Sylvia, KS, 3452
Hartman Arts and Music Foundation, Dan, CA, 648
Hartman Educational Foundation, Frank and Amanda, PA, 7892
Hartman Foundation for Music, Dan, CA, see 648
Hartman Trust, Russell L., PA, see 7892
Harvard Center for Neurodegeneration and Repair, Inc., MA, 4095
Harvard Club of Minnesota Foundation, MN, 4754
Harvard Musical Association, MA, 4096
Harvard-Yenching Institute, MA, 4097
Harvest of Hope Foundation, Inc., FL, 1906
Harvestworks, Inc., NY, 6058
Harvey Educational Foundation, O. J. & Mary Christine, CO, 1210
Harvey Family Foundation, Waldo E., UT, 9206
Harvey Foundation, PR, 8222
Hasan Family Foundation, CO, 1211
Haskell Scholarship Foundation, Mary Kirkpatrick, Inc., MS, 4910
Hasnia Foundation, IL, 2603
Hassel Foundation, The, PA, 7893
Hasselhofer-Wolf Scholarship Fund, WI, 9916
Hassell Charitable Foundation, The, TN, 8597
HASTAGA Foundation, NY, 6059
Hastings Community Foundation, Inc., NE, 5215
Hastings Family Service, MN, 4755
Hastings Student Aid Fund, Dorothy S., NH, 5327
Hastings Student Aid Fund, NH, see 5327
Hathcoat Educational Trust, Harold D. and Hazel H., The, OK, 7479
Hatterscheidt Foundation Inc., The, SD, 8533
Haugse-Cossey Foundation, ID, 2332
Hauss-Helms Foundation, Inc., The, OH, 7144
Haven Charitable Foundation, Nina, FL, see 1907
Haven Foundation, The, NY, 6060
Haven Scholarships, Nina, Inc., FL, 1907
Havens Foundation, Inc., TX, 8857
Havens Relief Fund Society, The, NY, 6061
Haverhill Female Benevolent Society, MA, 4098
Haverlah Foundation, Harry A., TX, 8858
Hawaii Children's Cancer Foundation, HI, 2288
Hawaii Committee for the Humanities, HI, see 2290
Hawaii Community Foundation, HI, 2289
Hawaii Council for the Humanities, HI, 2290
Hawaii Hotel Industry Foundation, HI, 2291
Hawaiian Foundation, The, HI, see 2289
Hawkes Scholarship Fund, OH, 7145
Hawkeye Area Community Action Program, Inc., IA, 3296
Hawkins Educational Foundation, AL, 49
Hawkins Memorial Scholarship Fund, E. Maurine, TN, 8598
Hawkins Scholarship Foundation, MT, 5155
Hawks Foundation, The, NE, 5216
Hawks Trust, Esther H., MA, 4099
Hawley Foundation for Children, The, NY, 6062
Hay Springs School-Community Foundation, NE, 5217
Hayden Recreation Centre, Josiah Willard, Inc., MA, 4100
Hayes Educational Foundation, Mildred & Milo, IL, see 2604
Hayes Educational Foundation, Milo & Mildred, IL, 2604
Hayes Foundation, The, VT, see 9251
Hayes Foundation, William Z., TX, 8859
Hayes Scholarship Fund, Dale Irwin, MO, 5013
Hayes Trust, Sylvia M., VT, 9250
Hayes, Jr. Foundation, Walter Hayes, Sr., Beulah Buffum Hayes & Walter H., VT, 9251
Haynes Trust, Charles O. and Elsie, NY, 6063
Hays Memorial Scholarship Trust, J. L. & D. A., MO, 5014
Hazard Memorial Foundation, Mary & Annie, MS, 4911
Hazelton Charitable Trust, Della Lucille, PA, 7894

HBA Foundation, MI, see 4468
HCA Hope Fund, TN, 8599
HCC Foundation, MI, 4458
HCEF, OH, see 7152
Head Testamentary Trust, Vivian B., PA, 7895
Headlands Center for the Arts, CA, 649
Headliners Foundation of Texas, TX, 8860
Heald Scholarship Fund, William H., PA, 7896
Heald Scholarship Trust, B. L. & W. H., RI, 8308
Healdsburg Education Foundation, The, CA, see 650
Healdsburg Educational Legacy Partnership Foundation, CA, 650
Health & Educational Trust of Berks County Medical Society, PA, 7897
Health and Welfare Fund Local 456, NJ, 5467
Health Careers Foundation, IL, 2605
Health Education and Relief, IL, 2606
Health First Foundation, Inc., FL, 1908
Health Focus of Southwest Virginia, VA, see 9420
Health Insurance Plan of Greater New York, NY, 6064
Health Professions Education Foundation, CA, 651
Health Research and Educational Trust, IL, 2607
Health Resources in Action, Inc., MA, 4101
Healthcare and Nursing Education Foundation, TX, 8861
Healthcare Georgia Foundation, Inc., GA, 2195
HealthEast Foundation, MN, 4756
Healthnet of Janesville, Inc., WI, 9917
HealthONE Alliance, CO, see 1154
Healthtrac Foundation, CA, see 602
HealthWell Foundation, The, MD, 3840
Healthy Smiles, Healthy Children: The Foundation of the AAPD, IL, 2608
Hearing Health Foundation, NY, 6065
Hearn Educational Fund Trust, PA, 7898
Heart of Compassion Distribution, CA, 652
Heart of Los Angeles Youth, Inc., CA, 653
Heart of Variety Fund, PA, 7899
Heart Support of America, Inc., TN, 8600
Heartland Child Nutrition, Inc., ND, 6942
Heat & Frost Insulators Local 12 Officers Scholarship Fund, NY, see 6016
Heat and Warmth Fund, The, MI, 4459
Heath Memorial ROTC Scholarship Trust, Steve, TX, 8862
Heathcock Accordance, Bettye, CO, 1212
Heavin Community Fund, Gary & Diane, TX, 8863
Hebert Memorial Scholarship Fund, MI, 4460
Heberton Scholarship Trust, K. A., MA, see 4102
Heberton Scholarship Trust, Katharine A., MA, 4102
Hebrew Immigrant Aid Society of Chicago, IL, 2609
Hebrew Orphan Society of Charleston, SC, SC, see 8481
Hebrew Orphan Society, SC, 8481
Hecht Scholarship Fund, Maurice and Virginia, MI, 4461
Hedrick & Janice O. Lantz Charitable Foundation, Jim, The, KY, 3576
Heed Ophthalmic Foundation, The, IL, 2610
Heeringa Foundation, George and Lucile, The, MI, 4462
Heffel Memorial Scholarship Trust, WI, 9918
Heffernan Group Foundation, CA, 654
Hefflefinger Scholarship Fund, TX, 8864
Hefti Trust, Frances Sawyer, IL, 2611
Heily Foundation, WA, 9633
Hein Family Foundation Corporation, FL, 1909
Heinlein Prize Trust, Robert A. and Virginia, TX, 8865
Heinz Family Foundation, PA, 7900
Heiserman Trust f/b/o Cottey College, Geraldine, OR, 7586
Heisey Foundation, The, MT, 5156
Helaman Foundation, UT, 9207
Helbing Trust for Nursing Education, A. M., PA, 7901
Held Foundation, The, CA, 655
Helias Foundation, Inc., MO, 5015
Hellenic Foundation, FL, 1910
Hellstern Foundation, Pauline and Edna, OR, 7587
Helm Scholarship Fund, John Y. & Willie Mae, NM, 5632
Helmar Skating Fund, CO, 1213
Help From Above, AZ, 200
Help the Children, CA, see 491
HelpHopeLive, Inc., PA, see 8001

Helping Hand Foundation, KS, 3453
Helping Hands Hawaii, HI, 2292
Helping Hands of Benton County, AR, 283
Helping Hands Thrift Shop, Inc., AR, see 283
Helwig Reading High School Scholarship Fund, Bruce R., PA, 7902
Hemenway Scholarship Trust, Charles R., HI, 2293
Hemingford Scholarship Foundation, NE, see 5199
Hemingway Foundation, Ernest, Inc., The, SC, 8482
Hemingway Society, The, SC, see 8482
Hemminger Scholarship Foundation, Susan Hay, IN, 3055
Hemophilia Association of New Jersey, NJ, 5468
Hemophilia Association of New York, Inc., NY, 6066
Hemophilia Federation of America, Inc., DC, 1642
Hemophilia Foundation of Michigan, MI, 4463
Hemophilia Outreach of Wisconsin Foundation Inc., WI, 9919
Henderson County Education Foundation, Inc., NC, 6696
Henderson Scholarship Foundation, Herbert & Gertrude, KS, 3454
Henderson Scholarship Fund, Helen L., IN, 3056
Henderson Scholarship Fund, M. & G., PA, 7903
Hendricks County Community Foundation, IN, 3057
Henfield Foundation, The, NY, see 6203
Henkel Scholarship Trust, Father Leo, IL, 2612
Henley Trust, Clyde W. and Mary O., The, VA, 9393
Henney Trust, Keith, RI, 8309
Henrico Education Foundation, VA, 9394
Henries Scholarship Trust, Doris Banks, CT, 1402
Henrizi Scholarship Fund, Chester, WI, 9920
Henry Company—Lou Brand Scholarship Foundation, John, The, FL, 1911
Henry County Community Foundation, Inc., IN, 3058
Henry County Health Center Foundation, IA, 3297
Henry Foundation for Autism, Evan, Inc., MA, 4103
Henry High School Foundation, Patrick, MN, 4757
Henry Scholarship Trust, Iva W. & Roy, IL, 2613
Henry Street Settlement, NY, 6067
Henry Trust, May Thompson, OK, 7480
Henry Trust, Thompson, OK, see 7480
Herb Society of America, The, OH, 7146
Herbert Scholarship Trust, Bernard & Pauline, IL, 2614
Herbst Foundation, Inc., The, CA, 656
Herdegen Trust, Elizabeth A., MI, 4464
Hereditary Disease Foundation, NY, 6068
Hering, Jr. Foundation, Charles D. "Bud", OH, 7147
Heritage Classic Foundation, SC, 8483
Heritage Club - A Christian Molokan Association, CA, 657
Heritage Foundation, The, DC, 1643
Heritage Fund - The Community Foundation of Bartholomew County, IN, 3059
Heritage Fund of Bartholomew County, Inc., IN, see 3059
Heritage Fund of Huntington County, Inc., IN, see 3067
Hermitage Artist Retreat, Inc., The, FL, 1912
Hermsen Memorial Foundation, Chink and Annie, IA, 3298
Hero Foundation, AL, see 46
Herr Foundation, Irvin E., NY, 6069
Herriges Family Memorial Scholarship Foundation, WA, 9634
Herrin Trust, Edith Fitton, PA, see 7845
Herschend Family Foundation, MO, A
Hertz Foundation, Fannie and John, CA, 658
Hertz Foundation, Hellmuth, IL, 2615
Hertz Foundation, The, CA, see 658
Herzberger Charitable Trust, Mildred L., OH, 7148
Hess Educational Fund Trust, George R., NC, 6697
Hess Educational Trust, Hazel Porter Hess and George R., NC, see 6697
Hester - Dundy County Public Schools Foundation, Elmer E., NE, 5218
Hester Student Memorial Trust, Leonard W. & Helen L., MO, 5016
Hewitt Foundation for Medical Research, George E., CA, 659
Heyburn Trust, Marie E., PA, 7904
Heyl Science Scholarship Fund, F. W. & Elsie, MI, 4465
HGA, GA, see 2194

Hickory Cooperative Christian Ministry, Greater, NC, 6698

Hicks Charitable Corporation, Ethel Brickey, TN, 8601

Hiebler Memorial Scholarship Fund Trust, Thomas & Jennie, CA, 660

Higbee Trust, David Downes, PA, 7905

Higdon Charitable Foundation, Laura Calfee, AL, 50

Higgins Educational Fund, Mary E., OH, 7149

Higgins Foundation, Colin, CA, 661

Higgins Trust for Avelena Fund, William, IL, 2616

High Desert Community Foundation, CA, 662

High Family Foundation, S. Dale, The, PA, 7906

High Foundation, Charles F., OH, 7150

High Foundation, The, PA, see 7906

High Meadow Foundation, Inc., MA, 4104

Higher Education Consortium for Urban Affairs, Inc., MN, 4758

Higher Education Trust, NE, 5219

Highlands Community Services Board, VA, 9395

Highlands Community Services Center for Behavioral Health, VA, see 9395

Highpoint Center for Printmaking, MN, 4759

Hilgen Foundation, Frederick J., Ltd., WI, 9921

Hill Charitable Foundation, Paul and Julia Mercer, IL, 2617

Hill Country Community Foundation, TX, 8866

Hill Country Student Help, TX, 8867

Hill Foundation Inc., Howard E., FL, 1913

Hill Foundation, Harold Newlin, PA, 7907

Hill House, Inc., MA, 4105

Hill Scholarship Fund, David and Edith E., PA, 7908

Hill Trust, Elizabeth, IA, 3299

Hill Trust, Ruth A., PA, 7909

Hill-Plath Foundation, IL, 2618

Hillenbrand Memorial Fund, John W., IN, 3060

Hillier Scholarship Fund of Evart, MI, 4466

Hillmyer-Tremont Student Athlete Foundation, Inc., FL, 1914

Hillsborough Educational Partnership Foundation, Inc., FL, 1915

Hillsdale County Community Foundation, MI, 4467

Hilton Head Island Foundation, Inc., SC, see 8466

Hilton Trust, Helen Reber, NC, 6699

Hinckley Fund, William & Alice, CA, 663

Hinderman Scholarship Memorial, E. A., MT, 5157

Hines Honorary Scholarship, Jud W., KS, 3455

Hinman Charitable Foundation, Grove W. and Agnes M., NY, 6070

Hinton Area Foundation, WV, 9790

Hirsch Educational Endowment Fund, Florence, MO, 5017

Hirsch Foundation, Armin & Esther, IL, 2619

Hirsch Foundation, The, DE, see 1512

Hirsch Memorial Trust, Eric G., TX, 8868

Hirsch Scholarship Fund, L., DE, 1512

Hirschl Trust, Irma T., IL, 2620

Hirth Family Foundation, Inc., NY, 6071

Hirtzel Memorial Foundation, Orris C. Hirtzel and Beatrice Dewey, PA, 7910

His Helping Hand Foundation, WA, 9635

His Trust Foundation, Inc., GA, see 2117

Hispanic American Medical Scholarship Fund, TX, 8869

Hispanic Association of Colleges and Universities, TX, 8870

Hispanic College Fund, Inc., DC, 1644

Hispanic Federation, NY, 6072

Hispanic Heritage Awards, VA, see 9396

Hispanic Heritage Foundation, VA, 9396

Hispanic National Bar Foundation, Inc., MD, 3841

Hispanic Scholarship Fund, CA, 664

Hispanic Women in Leadership, TX, 8871

Historical Research Foundation, Inc., NY, 6073

Hitachi Foundation, The, DC, 1645

Hitchcock Foundation, NH, 5328

Hitchcock Free Academy, MA, 4106

Hladky Foundation, Tammy, WY, 10107

Hma Employee Disaster Relief Fund, Inc., FL, 1916

Hmong National Development, Inc., MN, 4760

HNBF, MD, see 3841

Hoag Hospital Foundation, CA, 665

Hoag Memorial Hospital Presbyterian, CA, 666

Hoar Memorial Scholarship Fund, Jimmy V. & Lucile A., KS, 3456

Hoch Memorial Trust, J. Herbert Hoch & Martha, IN, 3061

Hochmark Scholarship Foundation, Bertram & Alta Heartt, NC, 6700

Hochmark Scholarship Trust, B. A., NC, see 6700

Hockenberry Foundation, Charles, IA, 3300

Hodes Charitable Trust, Al, WI, 9922

Hodges Educational Charitable Trust, Helen, TX, 8872

Hodges Educational Fund Trust, J. M., NY, 6074

Hodges Memorial Cancer Foundation, Cathy L., TN, 8602

Hoeting Scholarship Trust, John F., FL, 1917

Hoffa Memorial Scholarship Fund, James R., Inc., DC, 1646

Hoffert Scholarship Trust, Valeria E., NY, 6075

Hoffman & McNamara Foundation, MN, 4761

Hoffman Scholarship Trust, James M., NC, 6701

Hogsett Foundation, Robert E., Inc, CO, A

Hohner Scholarship Fund, Joseph J., IL, 2621

Holce Logging Company Scholarship Foundation Inc, OR, 7588

Holder Family Foundation, The, NV, 5289

Holland & Knight Charitable Foundation, Inc., FL, 1918

Holland Community Foundation, Inc., MI, see 4398

Holland Lodge Foundation Inc., NY, 6076

Holland Scholarship Foundation for Tullahoma School System Grds., C.V. Maybelle & John I, AL, 51

Holland Scholarship Fund, C.V. Holland, Maybelle Holland, & John, AL, see 51

Hollander Scholarship Foundation, Adelaide, Inc., NJ, 5469

Hollander Scholarship Fund for Registered Nurses Inc., Pauline, NJ, 5470

Hollandsworth Memorial Trust, P.G. and Ruby, WV, 9791

Holliday Scholarship Fund, Audrey, WA, 9636

Hollywood Rotary Foundation, Inc., FL, 1919

Holman Foundation, Jeffrey S., The, NJ, 5471

Holmes County Council for Handicapped Children, OH, see 7151

Holmes County Council for Handicapped Citizens, Inc., OH, 7151

Holmes County Education Foundation, OH, 7152

Holmes Scholarship Fund, Bonnie L., MO, 5018

Holmes Trust f/b/o Elizabeth V. Cushman Scholarship Fund, Ruth H., MA, see 4107

Holmes Trust, Ruth H., MA, 4107

Holocaust and Human Rights Center of Maine, ME, 3703

Holocaust Educational Foundation, The, IL, 2622

Holopigian Memorial Fund, George, The, RI, 8310

Holston Valley Health Care Foundation, TN, see 8662

Holt & Bugbee Foundation, Inc., MA, 4108

Holt Corporate Foundation, R. B., CO, see 1214

Holt Family Scholarship Foundation, WI, 9923

Holt Foundation of Central Florida, Lois, FL, 1920

Holt Foundation, R. B., CO, 1214

Holton Foundation, Merle and Richardine, OK, 7481

Holtsford Scholarship Fund, Hiram W. & Cecil J., TN, 8603

Holy Land Trust, MD, see 3886

Holy Spirit Hospital, PA, 7911

Holyoke Community College Foundation, Inc., MA, 4109

Home and Building Association Foundation, MI, 4468

Home Builders Foundation of Western Massachusetts, Inc., MA, 4110

Home Depot Foundation, GA, see 2249

Home for Contemporary Theater and Art, NY, 6077

Home Instead Senior Care Disaster Relief Foundation, NE, 5220

Home Partership Foundation, Inc., The, ID, 2333

Home Sweet Home Community Redevelopment Company, TX, 8873

Homecrest Foundation, MN, see 4701

Homeless Families Foundation, OH, 7153

Homer Foundation, The, AK, 117

Homer Fund, The, GA, see 2249

HomeStar Education Foundation Inc., IL, 2623

Homestretch, Inc., VA, 9397

Honeywell Corporate Giving Program, NJ, 5472

Hood Canal Masonic Community Scholarship Foundation, WA, 9637

Hood Fund, Charles H., MA, 4111

Hood Memorial Fund Trust, Merl, WI, 9924

Hooker Educational Foundation, VA, 9398

Hoover Foundation, J. Edgar, The, OH, 7154

Hoover Scholarship Foundation, O. Robert, IL, see 2624

Hoover Trust Fund, Daniel R., NC, 6702

Hoover-Koken Foundation, Inc., KS, 3457

Hoover/Hoehn Scholarship Foundation, IL, 2624

Hoover/Hohen Scholarship Foundation, IL, see 2624

HOPA Research Foundation, IL, 2625

HOPE Center, The, TX, see 8827

Hope Foundation for the Homeless, FL, 1921

Hope Memorial Fund, Blanche and Thomas, OH, 7155

Hopedale Foundation, The, MA, 4112

Hopelink, WA, 9638

Hopi Foundation Barbara Chester Endowment Fund, AZ, 201

Hopkins Scholarship Fund, Dorothy K., MA, 4113

Hopkins, Jr., Arts Endowment, George Cragg, Inc., MD, 3842

Horgan Charitable Trust, Charles & Alda, MI, 4469

Horizons Foundation Inc., The, FL, 1922

Horizons Foundation, CA, 667

Horn Educational Trust, Lee A. & Mabel H., PA, see 7912

Horn Educational Trust, PA, 7912

Horn Family Foundation Inc., Michael E., KY, 3577

Horn Scholarship Trust, Evelyn, CA, 668

Hornbrook Scholarship Fund, Frank W. and Gladys G., TX, 8874

Horne Foundation, Dick, SC, 8484

Horner Charitable Foundation, Ednah, MA, 4114

Hornlein Scholarship Trust, AR, 284

Horowitz Foundation for Research in Social Policy, Irving Louis, NJ, 5473

Horsemen's Welfare Trust, DE, 1513

Horseshoe Foundation of Floyd County, IN, 3062

Horsey Educational Fund Trinity Episcopal, NC, 6703

Horsman Foundation, MT, 5158

Horticultural Research Institute Endowment Fund, Inc., DC, 1647

Horvat Foundation, Dr. Arthur J. & Helen M., NC, 6704

Horvitz Foundation, Lois U., OH, 7156

Hosler Memorial Educational Fund, Dr. R. S., OH, 7157

Hospice Care of Nantucket Foundation, MA, A

Hospice of the Emerald Coast, Inc., GA, 2196

Hospice of the Valley, AZ, see 254

Hospice of Tuscarawas County, Inc., OH, 7158

Hospitalers Committee of Detroit Commandery No. 1 Knights Templar, MI, A

Hosser Scholarship Fund Trust, Edward Wagner and George, RI, 8311

Houghton Memorial Trust, Everett R. & Frieda G., IN, 3063

Houghton Mifflin Harcourt Publishing Company Contributions Program, MA, 4115

House Educational Trust, Susan Cook, IL, 2626

House of Ruth, Inc., LA, 3655

Housing and Community Services of Northern Virginia, Inc., VA, 9399

Housing Assistance Office, Inc., IN, 3064

Housing for New Hope, NC, 6705

Housing Industry Foundation, CA, 669

Housing Opportunities Community Partners, MD, 3843

Housing Opportunities Made Equal of Virginia, VA, 9400

Housing Resources of Western Colorado, CO, 1215

Houston Arts Alliance, TX, 8875

Houston Bar Foundation, TX, 8876

Houston Center for Contemporary Craft, TX, 8877

Houston Children's Charity, TX, 8878

Houston Community College System Foundation, TX, 8879

Houston Community Foundation, Greater, TX, 8880

Houston Endowment Inc., TX, 8881

Houston Geological Society Foundation, TX, 8882

Houston Minority Business Council, TX, 8883

Houston Osteopathic Hospital Foundation Inc., TX, 8884

Houton Scholarship Foundation, NJ, 5474

Hovarter Scholarship Fund Trust, Leon & Audrey, MI, see 4471

Hovarter Scholarship Fund Trust, MI, 4471

Howard Association, John, HI, see 2277
Howard Benevolent Society, MA, 4116
Howard County Arts Council, MD, 3844
Howard Funds 1993, Trustees of the, MA, 4117
Howard Memorial Fund, NY, 6078
Howard Memorial Fund, SD, 8534
Howard Trust, M. P., RI, 8312
Howe Educational Fund Trust, J.E., NY, 6079
Howe Scholarship Fund, M & H, MI, 4472
Howe Scholarship Trust, M. & H., MI, see 4472
Howe Scholarship Trust, Marjorie W. Howe & Howard
    C., MI, see 4472
Howes Trust f/b/o Sick & Needy Persons, Ernest G.,
    MA, 4119
Howes Trust, Samuel C., MA, 4118
Howland Fund for Aged Women, MA, 4120
Howley Family Foundation, The, OH, 7159
Hoy Family Scholarship Fund, George, KS, 3458
HP Corporate Giving Program, CA, 670
HRH Family Foundation, OH, see 7156
HSHCRC Homes, Inc., TX, see 8873
Hubbard Family Foundation, TX, 8885
Hubbard Farms Charitable Foundation, NH, 5329
Hubbard Scholarship & Charitable Trust, Laurence E.
    Hubbard and Ruth J., IL, 2627
Huddleston Foundation, TX, 8886
Hudson River Foundation for Science & Environmental
    Research, NY, 6080
Hudson-Webber Foundation, MI, 4473
Huether Foundation, Inc., The, MD, see 3845
Huether/McClelland Foundation, Inc., The, MD, 3845
Huffman Educational Foundation, Marian P., VT, 9252
Huffman-Cornwell Foundation, NC, 6706
Hugg Trust, Leola W. and Charles H., IL, 2628
Hughes Business Scholarship, Raymond, NC, see 6707
Hughes Educational Trust, Walter M., IL, 2629
Hughes Foundation, Charles J., CO, 1216
Hughes Foundation, Larry, MO, 5019
Hughes Medical Institute, Howard, MD, 3846
Hughes Memorial Home, VA, 9401
Hughes Owen Memorial Scholarship Fund, IN, see
    3065
Hughes Owen Memorial Scholarship Trust, IN, 3065
Hughes Scholarship Fund, Raymond, NC, 6707
Hughes Scholarship Trust, Cedric L., NC, 6708
Hughes Scholarship Trust, Ruth M., OH, 7160
Hughes, Jr. Scholarship Foundation, W. Marshall, PA,
    7913
Hugo House, Richard, WA, 9639
Hull Educational Foundation, Orson A. & Minnie E., MN,
    4762
Hull Scholarship Fund Inc., J. Brannon, OH, 7161
Hull Scholarship Fund, Herbert J. and Geneva S., Inc.,
    NJ, 5475
Hulton Educational Trust, Phyllis Perry, IA, 3301
Human Development Commission, MI, 4474
Human Growth Foundation, NY, 6081
Humanas, Inc., NY, 6082
Humane Society of Macomb Foundation, Inc., MI, 4475
Humane Society of the Commonwealth of
    Massachusetts, MA, 4121
Humanitas Scholarship Trust, NY, 6083
Humanities Tennessee, TN, 8604
Humanities Texas, TX, 8887
Humanity First U.S.A., MD, 3847
Humbert Scholarship Trust, Paul A., MI, 4476
Humboldt Area Foundation, The, CA, 671
Humphrey Residuary Trust, Grace H., RI, 8313
Humphrey Scholarship Trust, Bernie H. & Mary L., IN,
    3066
Huna Heritage Foundation, AK, 118
Hundred Club of Dayton, The, OH, 7162
Hungarian-American Enterprise Scholarship Fund, ME,
    3704
Hungerford Chapel Trust, Robert, FL, 1923
Hunt Community, Inc., NH, 5330
Hunt Memorial Scholarship, William C. and Mabel D.,
    RI, 8314
Hunt Trust, Agnes B., The, FL, 1924
Hunt Trust, Helena W., MA, 4122
Hunter ALS Foundation, Jim "Catfish", NC, 6709
Hunter Douglas Foundation Inc., NY, 6084
Hunter Family Trust, Helen & Joan, OH, 7163

Hunter Foundation, Dorothy P. and Howard D., CA, 672
Hunter Scholarship Fund, Eileen M., WA, 9640
Hunter Scholarship Fund, Larry & Gladys, Inc., LA, 3656
Hunter Scholarship Trust, Ralph & Lucile, KS, 3459
Hunter Testamentary Trust, Jane E., OH, 7164
Hunter Trust, A. V., Inc., CO, 1217
Hunter's Hope Foundation, Inc., NY, 6085
Hunter's Scholarship Fund in Memory of Bill Lawton &
    Carol Gillooly, CT, 1403
Huntington Beach Police Officers Foundation, CA, 673
Huntington County Community Foundation, Inc., IN,
    3067
Huntington County Help Inc. for Disabled Citizens, IN,
    3068
Huntington Fund, Samuel, Inc., The, MA, 4123
Huntington Library and Art Gallery, Henry E., CA, 674
Huntington's Disease Society of America, Inc., NY,
    6086
Hurlbut Memorial Fund, Orion L. & Emma B., TN, 8605
Hurlbutt Memorial Fund, Horace C., CT, 1404
Hurley Scholarship Foundation, Doc, Inc., CT, 1405
Hurley Trust Foundation, Ed and Gladys, TX, 8888
Hurliman Scholarship Foundation, The, CA, 675
Huron County Community Foundation, MI, 4477
Hurst Scholarship Trust, Lonnie Bob, FL, 1925
Hurst-Sorenson Memorial Fund, MT, 5159
Hurston & Richard Wright Foundation, Zora Neale, DC,
    1648
Huss Charitable Trust, Helen, MO, 5020
Huss Memorial Fund, Theodore Huss, Sr. and Elsie
    Endert, MI, 4478
Hutchins Foundation Fund, Harold J., MO, 5021
Hutchins Foundation, Mary J., Inc., NY, 6087
Hutchinson Community Foundation, KS, 3460
Hutchinson Foundation, C. P. and Dorthea, Inc., MO,
    5022
Hutchinson Scholarship Fund, Marjorie and Doris, MA,
    4124
Hutchison Foundation, IL, 2630
Huth Scholarship Fund Charitable, Otto A., PA, 7914
Huth Scholarship Fund, Otto A., PA, see 7914
Hutton Foundation, Edward L., The, OH, 7165
Hutton Foundation, Inc., The, TX, 8889
Huyck Preserve Inc., Edmund Niles, The, NY, 6088
Hy-Vee Foundation Inc., IA, 3302
Hyatt Foundation, IL, 2631
Hydrocephalus Association, CA, 676
Hynd and Nancy Johnson Trust, James, IL, 2632

I Care Foundation, UT, 9208
I Have a Dream Foundation - Port Huron, MI, 4479
I Have a Dream Foundation of Boulder County, CO,
    1218
I Know I Can, OH, 7166
I.O.O.F. Grand Lodge Educational Fund, WV, 9792
IAFF Burn Foundation, DC, see 1653
IAFF Disaster Relief Fund, DC, A
IAFF, DC, see 1652
IBM International Foundation, NY, 6089
IBM South Africa Projects Fund, NY, see 6089
ICRDA/SDA Scholarship Foundation, NC, see 6844
ID Identifying Discourse, Inc., NY, 6090
IDA, CA, see 689
IDACORP, Inc. Corporate Giving Program, ID, 2334
Idaho Community Foundation, ID, 2335
Idaho Humanities Council, ID, 2336
Idaho Nurses Foundation Inc., GA, 2197
IDCA Foundation, SC, 8485
IDSA Education and Research Foundation, VA, 9402
IEA Educational Scholarship Program, UT, see 9209
IEEE Foundation, Inc., NJ, 5476
IFF, NY, see 6099
IFGE, MA, see 4126
IFMA Foundation, TX, 8890
IFP Minneapolis/St. Paul, MN, see 4763
IFP Minnesota Center for Media Arts, MN, 4763
IFP, NY, see 6092
Igloo No. 4 Foundation, AK, 119
Igou Scholarship Fund, Carrie and Oren, IA, 3303
Igstaedter Foundation, Leonard & Mildred, CT, 1406
IHFR Foundation, VA, 9403
II-VI Foundation, PA, 7915
II-VI Incorporated Foundation, PA, see 7915

Ilgenfritz Testamentary Trust, May H., TX, 8891
Ilitch Charities for Children, Inc., MI, see 4480
Ilitch Charities, Inc., MI, 4480
Illinois Bar Foundation, IL, 2633
Illinois Broadcasters Association Minority Intern
    Program, Inc., IL, 2634
Illinois Conservation Foundation, IL, 2635
Illinois Education Foundation, IL, 2636
Illinois High School Activities Foundation, IL, 2637
Illinois Historic Preservation Agency Trust, IL, 2638
Illinois Hospital Research and Educational Foundation,
    IL, 2639
Illinois Lumber and Material Dealers Association
    Educational Foundation, Inc., IL, 2640
Illinois Network of Child Care Resource and Referral
    Agencies, IL, 2641
Illinois P.E.O. Home Fund, Inc., IL, 2642
Illinois Power Company Contributions Program, IL, see
    2364
Illinois Real Estate Educational Foundation, IL, 2643
Illinois State Dental Society Foundation, IL, 2644
Illinois State Historical Society, The, IL, 2645
Illinois State University Foundation, IL, 2646
Illinois Telecommunications Access Corporation, IL,
    2647
Illinois Valley Educational Foundation Inc., IL, 2648
Illuminating Engineering Society of North America, NY,
    see 6091
Illuminating Engineering Society, NY, 6091
Imai Shin Buddhist Scholarship Charitable Foundation,
    Richard and Eleanor, HI, 2294
Imhoff Scholarship Foundation, A. Gordon & Betty H.,
    OH, 7167
Immokalee Foundation, Inc., FL, 1926
Immune Deficiency Foundation, Inc., MD, 3848
Immunobiology Research Fund, CA, 677
Impac Literary Awards for Young Writers Trust, The,
    CT, see 1368
Impact Fund, The, CA, 678
Impact on Education, CO, 1219
Imperial Holly Corporation Contributions Program, TX,
    see 8892
Imperial Sugar Company Contributions Program, TX,
    8892
INCOSE Foundation, CA, 679
Incourage Community Foundation, Inc., WI, 9925
Independence Community College Foundation, KS,
    3461
Independence Community Foundation, MO, see 5118
Independence Foundation, Inc., KY, 3578
Independence Foundation, PA, 7916
Independent Arts and Media, CA, 680
Independent Catholic Foundation for the Diocese of
    Altoona-Johnstown, PA, 7917
Independent Colleges of Indiana, Inc., IN, 3069
Independent Feature Project, Inc., NY, 6092
Independent Feature Project/West, CA, see 575
Independent Pictures, OH, 7168
Independent Production Fund, Inc., NY, 6093
Independent Sector, DC, 1649
Independent Television Service, CA, 681
Indian River Community College Foundation, FL, see
    1927
Indian River County Foundation for the Elderly, NC,
    6710
Indian River State College Foundation, Inc., FL, 1927
Indiana Bar Foundation, IN, 3070
Indiana County Community Action Program, Inc., PA,
    7918
Indiana University Foundation, IN, 3071
Indianapolis Matinee Musicale, IN, 3072
Indianapolis Neighborhood Housing Partnership, Inc.,
    IN, 3073
Indianapolis Press Club Foundation, Inc., IN, 3074
Indianhead Community Action Agency, Inc., WI, 9926
Indianhead/Viking Council, Boy Scouts of America,
    Inc., MN, see 4816
Indwell Foundation, OK, 7482
Infinity Foundation, Inc., The, NJ, 5477
Infirmary Foundation, Inc., AL, 52
Information Technology Exchange, ME, 3705
ING Life Insurance and Annuity Company Contributions
    Program, CT, see 1478

Ingebritson Family Foundation, The, AZ, 202
Ingersoll-Rand Charitable Foundation, NJ, 5478
Ingram Trust, Joe, TX, 8893
Initiative Foundation, MN, 4764
Injured Marine Semper Fi Fund, CA, 682
Inland Counties Regional Center, Inc., CA, 683
Inman-Riverdale Foundation, SC, 8486
Inner Voice, Inc., The, IL, 2649
Inner-City Arts, CA, 684
Insall Foundation for Orthopaedics Inc., John N., NY, 6094
Institut Francais d'Amerique, NC, 6711
Institut Francais de Washington, NC, see 6711
Institute for Aegean Prehistory, The, PA, 7919
Institute for Better Education, AZ, 203
Institute for Educational Advancement, CA, 685
Institute for Humane Studies, VA, 9404
Institute for Inclusive Work Environments, CA, see 743
Institute of Current World Affairs, Inc., DC, 1650
Institute of International Education, Inc., NY, 6095
Institute of Turkish Studies, DC, 1651
Institution for Savings Charitable Foundation, Inc., MA, 4125
Institution for Savings in Newburyport & Its Vicinity Charitable Foundation, Inc., MA, see 4125
Insurance Scholarship Foundation of America, NC, 6712
Intel Corporation Contributions Program, CA, 686
Inter-American Wildlife Foundation, CA, see 552
Inter-Faith Council for Social Service, Inc., NC, 6714
Interbel Education Foundation, MT, 5160
Interdenominational Christian Missions, Inc., TX, 8894
InterExchange, Inc., NY, 6096
Interface Children Family Services, CA, 687
Interfaith Assistance Ministry, Inc., NC, 6713
Interfaith Cooperative Ministries, AZ, 204
Interfaith Ministries for Greater Houston, TX, 8895
Interfaith of the Woodlands, TX, see 9181
Interfaith Outreach and Community Partners, MN, 4765
Intermedia Arts Minnesota, Inc., MN, 4766
Intermountain Electrical Association Education Fund Scholarship Program, UT, 9209
Intermountain Research and Medical Foundation, UT, 9210
Internal Medicine Associates Scholarship Fund, Inc., AL, 53
International Association of Culinary Professionals Foundation, The, OR, see 7562
International Association of Fire Chiefs, Inc., VA, 9405
International Association of Fire Fighters Burn Foundation, DC, 1653
International Association of Fire Fighters Scholarship Fund, DC, 1654
International Association of Fire Fighters, DC, 1652
International Buddhist Education Foundation, CA, 688
International Burn Foundation of the United States, NC, 6715
International Campaign for Tibet, DC, 1655
International Center for Journalists, Inc., The, DC, 1656
International Center of Photography, NY, 6097
International Christian Embassy Jerusalem - USA, Inc., TN, 8606
International Christian Missions, Inc., OK, 7483
International City/County Management Association, DC, 1657
International Council of Airshows Foundation, Inc., VA, 9406
International Council of Shopping Centers Educational Foundation, Inc., NY, 6098
International Development Fund for Higher Education, MI, 4481
International Documentary Association, CA, 689
International Documentary, CA, see 689
International Door Association Scholarship Foundation, OH, 7169
International Fellowships Fund, NY, 6099
International Foundation for Ethical Research, The, IL, 2650
International Foundation for Functional Gastrointestinal Disorder, WI, 9927
International Foundation for Gender Education, Inc., MA, 4126

International Foundation for Music Research, CA, see 813
International Foundation for Sonography Education and Research, PA, 7920
International Gospel Mission, CA, see 629
International House of Blues Foundation, Inc., CA, 690
International Institute of Connecticut, Inc., CT, 1407
International Leadership Foundation, DC, 1658
International Myeloma Foundation, CA, 691
International Palace of Sports, Inc., IN, see 3181
International Paper Company Employee Relief Fund, TN, 8607
International Print Center New York, NY, 6100
International Reading Association, Inc., DE, 1514
International Rescue Committee, Inc., NY, 6101
International Retinal Research Foundation, Inc., AL, 54
International Sephardic Education Foundation, NY, 6102
International Society for Infectious Diseases, Inc., MA, 4127
International Society for Stem Cell Research, IL, 2651
International Society for Traumatic Stress Studies, The, IL, 2652
International Transactional Analysis Association, CA, 692
International Union of Painters and Allied Trades, DC, 1659
International Women's Media Foundation, DC, 1660
International Youth Foundation, MD, 3849
Intersection for the Arts, CA, 693
Interstitial Cystitis Association of America, VA, see 9407
Interstitial Cystitis Association, VA, 9407
Intertech Foundation, MN, 4767
Interthyr Research Foundation, OH, 7170
Intrepid Fallen Heroes Fund, The, NY, 6103
Invisible Children, Inc., CA, 694
Invitrogen Corporation Contributions Program, CA, see 745
Inwood House, NY, 6104
Inwood Office Furniture Foundation, Inc., IN, A
Ioan Foundation, The, CA, 695
IOCP, MN, see 4765
Iowa City Area Association of Realtors Scholarship Foundation, IA, 3304
Iowa East Central T.R.A.I.N., IA, see 3260
Iowa Farm Bureau Federation, IA, 3305
Iowa Foundation for Agricultural Advancement, IA, 3306
Iowa Health Foundation, IA, 3307
Iowa Measurement Research Foundation, IA, 3308
Iowa P.E.O. Project Fund, Inc., IA, 3309
IPALCO Enterprises, Inc. Corporate Giving Program, IN, 3075
IPF, NY, see 6093
Iranian Scholarship Foundation, CA, 696
Ironwood Area Scholarship Foundation, MI, 4482
Irrevocable Scholarship Trust, Rathke, Edward, IL, 2653
IRT Foundation, NY, 6105
Irvin Scholarship Foundation, Mary Ann, PA, 7921
Irwin Memorial Fund, Agnes and Sophie Dallas, PA, 7922
Irwin Scholarship Foundation, Tiffany, IL, 2654
Irwindale Educational & Scholarship Foundation, CA, see 697
Irwindale Educational Foundation, CA, 697
Isaac Scholarship Foundation, Betty & Ken, Inc., NC, 6716
ISED Ventures, IA, 3310
Ishii Foundation, David S., HI, 2295
ISID, MA, see 4127
Islami, M.D. Foundation Inc., Abdol H., NJ, 5479
Island Institute, ME, 3706
ISSCR, IL, see 2651
Italian American Club Foundation, Inc., MN, 4768
Italian American Cultural Foundation, OH, 7171
Italian American Delegates, Inc., MI, 4483
Italian Welfare Agency, Inc., CA, see 698
Italian-American Community Services Agency, CA, 698
ITT Rayonier Foundation, The, FL, see 2031
ITVS, CA, see 681
Ivy Community Charities of Prince George's County, Inc., The, MD, 3850

Ivy Cultural and Educational Foundation, Inc., PA, 7923
Ivy Foundation of Suffolk-Nassau, NY, 6106
Ivy Legacy Foundation, The, PA, 7924
Ivy Vine Charities, Inc., MD, 3851
IYF, MD, see 3849

J & J Charitable Foundation, PA, see 7774
Jachym Scholarship Fund, Amelia G., NY, 6107
Jack and Jill of America Foundation, DC, 1661
Jack in the Box Foundation, CA, 699
Jackson Community Foundation, MI, 4484
Jackson County Community Foundation, The, MI, see 4484
Jackson Education Trust, Genelle V., IL, 2655
Jackson Foundation, Corwill and Margie, Co., MI, 4485
Jackson Foundation, Greater, MS, see 4902
Jackson Memorial Fund, Bruce & Nellie M., IL, 2656
Jackson Scholarship Foundation, George, NJ, 5480
Jackson Scholarship Fund, Gaylord L., PA, 7925
Jackson Scholarship Trust, James A. Jackson and Beatrice D., OH, see 7172
Jackson Scholarship, Beatrice, KY, 3579
Jackson Trust, George, NJ, see 5480
Jackson Trust, James A., OH, 7172
Jackson Trust, Wilhelmina W., MA, 4128
Jackson-General George A. White, Maria C., OR, 7589
Jacob Foreman U.S. Scholarship Trust, Myron, FL, 1928
Jacob's Pillow Dance Festival, Inc., MA, 4129
Jacobson Charitable Trust, Robert and Deborah, The, FL, 1929
Jacobus Family Foundation, Charles D., WI, 9928
Jaffe Foundation, Rona, The, NY, 6108
Jaffray Employees Trust, Clive T., MN, 4769
Jain Foundation, Inc., The, WA, 9641
Jakobi Trust f/b/o Northern Highlands Regional High School, Gerard, RI, 8315
JAM Anonymous Foundation, Inc., NY, 6109
Jamaica Foundation of Houston, TX, 8896
James 127 Foundation, The, TX, 8897
James Association, William, CA, 700
James Family Foundation, CA, 701
James IV Association of Surgeons Inc., UT, 9211
James Publishing's Kids, CA, 702
James Scholarship Fund, William & Glenna, NH, 5331
Jamestown Area Foundation, Inc., The, OH, 7173
Jandon Foundation, NY, 6110
Jansen Foundation, Dan, Inc., WI, 9929
Janson Foundation, TX, 8898
Janssen Ortho Patient Assistance Foundation, Inc., NJ, see 5481
Jarecki Foundation, MT, 5161
JASA, NY, see 6115
Jasper Community Foundation, IA, 3311
Jasper Foundation, Inc., IN, 3076
Jay Fund Foundation, Tom Coughlin, Inc., FL, 1930
Jay Memorial Trust, George S. & Grace A., IA, 3312
Jay's World Childhood Cancer Foundation, NY, 6111
Jazz Foundation of America, Inc., NY, 6112
JBL Scholarship Trust, DE, 1515
Jeanes Foundation, Anna T., PA, 7926
Jedinstvo Athletic Club, Inc., CA, 703
Jeffco Action Center, Inc., CO, 1220
Jefferies Educational Grant Program, Boyd & Stephen, CA, see 704
Jefferies Family Scholarship, CA, 704
Jeffers Memorial Education Fund, Michael, MI, 4486
Jefferson County Tuberculosis Association, Inc., WV, 9793
Jefferson Endowment Fund, John Percival and Mary C., CA, 705
Jefferson Foundation, The, CO, 1221
Jefferson Memorial Foundation, OH, 7174
Jefferson Scholars Foundation, VA, 9408
Jefferson Scholarship Fund, Ethel, PA, 7927
Jeffery Scholarship Fund Trust, Lela McGuire, OH, 7175
Jeker Family Trust, ID, 2337
Jellison Benevolent Society Inc., KS, 3462
Jeltz Scholarship Foundation, Wyatt F. & Mattie M., OK, 7484
Jemez Mountains Electric Foundation, NM, 5633
Jemez Mountains Electric Foundation, NM, see 5633
Jenkins Fund, Scott, NY, 6113

Jenkins Scholarship Fund, Melvin H. & Thelma N., NY, 6114

Jenkins Student Aid Fund, OR, 7590

Jenkins Student Loan Fund, OR, *see* 7590

Jennie Edmundson Memorial Hospital, IA, 3313

Jenniges Education Trust, Vernon & Leoma, MN, 4770

Jennings County Community Foundation, Inc., IN, 3077

Jennings Foundation, John J.and Nora, Inc., The, MA, 4130

Jensen Foundation, Fritz and Lavinia, NC, 6717

Jensen Memorial Scholarship Fund, Brett Akio, WA, 9642

Jentes Scholarship Fund, Robert H., The, OH, 7176

Jepsen Educational Trust, IA, 3314

Jeremy Foundation, Inc., MD, 3852

Jerome Foundation, MN, 4771

Jerusalem Fund for Education and Community Development, The, DC, 1662

Jerusalem Fund, The, DC, *see* 1662

JESNA, NY, *see* 6117

Jewell Memorial Foundation, Daniel Ashley and Irene Houston, The, TN, 8608

Jewish Association for Services for the Aged, NY, 6115

Jewish Children's Home of Rochester, New York, NY, 6116

Jewish Community Federation of San Francisco, the Peninsula, Marin and Sonoma Counties, CA, 706

Jewish Community Foundation of Greater Hartford, Inc., CT, 1408

Jewish Education Service of North America, Inc., NY, 6117

Jewish Endowment Foundation, LA, A

Jewish Family & Children's Service of Southern Arizona, Inc., AZ, 205

Jewish Family & Childrens Service of Minneapolis, MN, 4772

Jewish Family and Children's Services of San Francisco, the Peninsula, Marin and Sonoma Counties, CA, 707

Jewish Family Assistance Fund, PA, 7928

Jewish Family Service Association of Cleveland, OH, 7177

Jewish Family Service of Colorado, Inc., CO, 1222

Jewish Family Service of Rochester, Inc., NY, 6118

Jewish Family Services, Inc., TN, 8609

Jewish Family Services, Inc., WI, 9930

Jewish Federation of Cincinnati, OH, 7178

Jewish Federation of Greater Atlanta, GA, 2198

Jewish Federation of Greater Indianapolis, Inc., IN, 3078

Jewish Federation of Greater Kansas City, KS, 3463

Jewish Federation of Greater Philadelphia, PA, 7929

Jewish Federation of Greater Seattle, WA, 9643

Jewish Federation of Madison, WI, 9931

Jewish Federation of Metropolitan Chicago, IL, 2657

Jewish Federation of Omaha, Inc., NE, 5221

Jewish Federation of the Lehigh Valley, PA, 7930

Jewish Foundation for the Righteous, Inc., The, NY, 6119

Jewish Guild for the Blind, The, NY, 6120

Jewish Home for Children, CT, 1409

Jewish Social Service Agency, MD, 3853

Jewish Vocational Service - Los Angeles, CA, 708

Jewish Vocational Service and Employment Center, IL, 2658

Jews United for Justice, DC, 1663

JFCS, CA, *see* 707

Ji Ji Foundation, The, WA, 9644

Jireh Foundation, Inc., TX, 8899

JL Foundation, The, LA, 3657

Job Opportunities Task Force, Inc., MD, 3854

Jockey Club Foundation, The, NY, 6121

Johns Cancer Foundation, VA, 9409

Johns Manville Fund, Inc., CO, 1223

Johns Scholarships Foundation, Marvin A. and Lillie M., NC, 6718

Johnson & Johnson Patient Assistance Foundation, Inc., NJ, 5481

Johnson Charitable Scholarship Foundation, Donald K., IA, 3315

Johnson Charitable Trust, Ralph and Marguerita, The, CA, 709

Johnson Controls Foundation, Inc., WI, 9933

Johnson Controls Foundation, WI, *see* 9933

Johnson Controls, Inc. Corporate Giving Program, WI, 9934

Johnson Corporation Scholarship Foundation, MI, *see* 4491

Johnson County Community Foundation, Greater, IN, *see* 3079

Johnson County Community Foundation, Inc., IN, 3079

Johnson County High School Scholarship Fund, WY, 10108

Johnson Educational and Benevolent Trust, Dexter G., OK, 7485

Johnson Educational Trust, Ethan Allen and Caroline H., IL, 2659

Johnson Family Foundation, TX, 8900

Johnson Foundation, Barbara Piasecka, NJ, 5482

Johnson Foundation, Inc., The, OH, 7179

Johnson Foundation, Lloyd K., MN, 4773

Johnson Foundation, Magic, Inc., CA, 710

Johnson Foundation, Paul and Louise, The, OK, 7486

Johnson Foundation, Paul T. & Frances B., MI, 4487

Johnson Foundation, Richard Myles, CA, 711

Johnson Foundation, Rudi, Inc., VA, 9410

Johnson Memorial Fund for Scholarly Research on Christian Science, Marlene F., MA, 4131

Johnson Memorial Fund Trust, Alfred N., RI, 8316

Johnson Missionary Foundation, John and Dorothy, CA, 712

Johnson Scholarship Foundation, John A., NC, 6719

Johnson Scholarship Foundation, Sandra and Bill, TN, 8610

Johnson Scholarship Fund, Ervin W., WI, 9935

Johnson Scholarship Fund, Ray and Nell, NC, 6720

Johnson Scholarship Trust, Gladys L., PA, 7931

Johnson Student Scholarship & Loan Foundation, NE, 5222

Johnson, Claire and Marjorie, Inc., WI, 9932

Johnson, R, OH, *see* 7325

Johnston Community College Foundation, Inc., NC, 6721

Johnston Foundation, F. W., FL, *see* 1931

Johnston Scholarship Fund, F. W., FL, 1931

Joint Civic Committee of Italian Americans, IL, 2660

Joint Council No. 73 Scholarship Fund, NJ, 5483

Jonas Foundation, Louis August, Inc., NY, 6122

Jonathan's Hope, WV, *see* 9809

Jones Charitable Foundation, Thomas B. Jones & Grace Stevenson, IL, 2661

Jones Charitable Trust No. 2, Harvey and Bernice, The, AR, 285

Jones Educational Foundation Inc., The, KY, 3580

Jones Educational Fund, Emmett & Beulah, WI, 9936

Jones Foundation, Deacon, CA, 713

Jones Foundation, Walter S. and Evan C., KS, 3464

Jones Memorial Foundation, Lillian M., OH, 7180

Jones Memorial Theological Scholarship Trust, Julie Ann, TX, 8901

Jones Memorial Trust, Clinton O. & Lura Curtis, MA, 4132

Jones Ministerial Trust, Adora S., NC, 6722

Jones Scholarship Foundation, Claude R. and Sadie B., NC, 6723

Jones Trust, Grace B., MA, 4133

Jones Trust, Grace, MA, *see* 4133

Jordaan Foundation, Inc., KS, 3465

Jordan Charitable Trust, Roderick J. & Gertrude B., NC, 6724

Jordan Education Foundation, UT, 9212

Jordan Fund, The, WA, 9645

Jordan Scholarship Foundation, Don D., TX, 8902

Jordan Scholarship Fund, Bessie Noble and Willie Lou, The, NC, 6725

Jorgensen Foundation Inc., Roy, The, MD, 3855

Jorndt Amundsen High School Learning Foundation, Dan and Pat, Inc., IL, 2662

Joshi Foundation Inc, Georgina, The, IN, 3080

Joshua Foundation, Inc., The, FL, 1932

Joshua Tree National Park Association, CA, 714

Jostens Foundation, Inc., The, MN, 4774

Joukowsky Family Foundation, NY, 6123

Journal Publishing Company Employees Welfare Fund, Inc., OR, 7591

Journalism Education Association, KS, 3466

Journalism Foundation of Metropolitan St. Louis, IL, 2663

Journeys End Refugee Services, Inc., NY, 6124

Joyard Foundation, The, CA, A

JSA Foundation, TN, 8611

JSW Adoption Foundation, Inc., The, IL, *see* 2583

JTM Foundation, WA, 9646

Judge Foundation, Bryan W. & Minnie, FL, 1933

Judges Athletic Association, VA, 9411

Judkins Scholarship Fund, Ernest L. & Florence L., NY, 6125

Juhl Scholarship Fund, George W. & Sadie Marie, MI, 4488

Julien Collot Foundation, The, FL, 1934

Juneau Arts & Humanities Council, AK, 120

Junior League of Lansing, Michigan, MI, 4489

Junior League of Saginaw Valley, MI, 4490

Junior League of Washington, Inc., DC, 1664

Jurassic Foundation Inc., The, MA, 4134

Just Foundation, F. Ward, IL, 2664

Just Imagine Making Miracles Yours, NY, 6126

Just Scholarship Foundation, F. Ward, IL, *see* 2664

Justice Lodge No. 285 F. & A. M., Educational Trust, NJ, 5484

Justin Foundation, Herbert W. and Jeanne A., The, CA, 715

Juvenile Diabetes Research Foundation International, NY, 6127

Juvenile Protective Association, IL, 2665

JWF Quanza Foundation, Inc., OK, 7487

K21 Health Foundation, IN, *see* 3090

Kadant Johnson, Inc. Scholarship Foundation, MI, 4491

Kahvush Trust, Janis & Milly, The, AZ, 206

Kaiser Family Foundation, Henry J., The, CA, 716

Kaiser Foundation Health Plan of Colorado, CA, 717

Kaiser Foundation Hospitals, CA, 718

Kaiser Foundation, Inc., CO, 1224

Kaiulani Home for Girls Trust, HI, 2296

Kajima Foundation, Inc., GA, 2199

Kalamazoo Communities in Schools Foundation, MI, 4492

Kalamazoo Community Foundation, MI, 4493

Kalamazoo Foundation, MI, *see* 4493

Kalamazoo Public Education Foundation, MI, *see* 4492

Kalamazoo Symphony Orchestra, MI, 4494

Kallies Charitable Trust, Harold C., WI, 9937

Kalnoski Memorial Scholarship Fund, William J. and Dora J., PA, 7932

Kamenski Trust, Stephanie, RI, 8317

Kaminski Foundation, IN, *see* 3081

Kaminski Sylvester & Tessie Foundation, IN, 3081

Kanawha Valley Foundation, Greater, The, WV, 9794

Kander Scholarship Fund, Stephen D., IL, *see* 2666

Kander Scholarship Fund, Stephen Douglas, IL, 2666

Kane Guardian Life Welfare Trust, Edward, The, NY, 6128

Kane High School Scholarship Memorial Trust, Robert, OK, *see* 7488

Kane Memorial High School Trust, OK, 7488

Kane Scholarship Fund, John F., Inc., VA, 9412

Kaneta Charitable Foundation, HI, *see* 2297

Kaneta Foundation, HI, 2297

Kanhofer Trust, L., OH, 7181

Kankakee County Community Services, Inc., IL, 2667

Kansas Association of Child Care Resource and Referral Agencies, KS, 3467

Kansas Athletics Inc., KS, 3468

Kansas Bar Association, KS, 3469

Kansas Bar Foundation, KS, *see* 3469

Kansas Children's Service League, KS, 3470

Kansas City Community Foundation and Affiliated Trusts, Greater, The, MO, *see* 5023

Kansas City Community Foundation, Greater, MO, 5023

Kansas City Football Coaches Association, Greater, MO, 5024

Kansas Cultural Trust, KS, *see* 3476

Kansas Masonic Foundation, Inc., KS, 3471

Kansas State Alpha Tau Omega Students' Aid Endowment Fund, IA, 3316

Kansas State University Foundation, KS, 3472

Kanuha and Stella Kaipo Fern Foundation, Betty C., HI, see 2298
Kanuha Foundation, Betty C., The, HI, 2298
Kapala Scholarship Trust, Walter S., The, NJ, 5485
Kaplan Foundation, Lazare and Charlotte, NY, 6129
Kaplan Scholarship Foundation, Seymour L., The, GA, 2200
Kappa Alpha PSI OKC Alumni Scholarship Foundation, OK, 7489
Kappa Alpha Theta Foundation, IN, 3082
Kappa Beautillion, Inc., SC, 8487
Kappa Kappa Gamma Foundation, OH, 7182
Karnes Memorial Fund, The, IL, 2668
Karyae Benevolent Foundation, NC, 6726
Kassenbrock Brothers Memorial Scholarship Fund, Inc., NY, 6130
Kathwari Foundation Inc., Irfan, NY, 6131
Kati's Hope Foundation for Mesothelioma Research & Support, OH, 7183
Kattar Memorial Fund, Kerri Ann, Inc., MD, 3856
KATU Thomas R. Dargan Minority Scholarship Fund, OR, see 7567
Katz Foundation, Abraham J. & Phyllis, GA, 2201
Katz Foundation, Jerold B., TX, 8903
Kauffman Family Foundation Inc., The, OH, 7184
Kauffman Foundation, Ewing Marion, MO, 5025
Kauffman Scholarship Foundation, Gene, Inc., MO, 5026
Kaufman & Coffman Scholarship Fund, IL, 2669
Kaupp Foundation, Hanna, NY, 6132
Kautz Foundation, Charles and Pauline, NY, 6133
Kautz Trust, Jessie B., PA, see 8113
Kawabe Memorial Fund, WA, 9647
Kawabe Trust, Harry S., WA, see 9647
Kawerak, Inc., AK, 121
Kay Scholarship Foundation, Ryan Michael, MI, 4495
KBRK, Inc., NY, see 6158
KCPQ-TV/Kelly Foundation of Washington, WA, see 9650
KD-FC, Inc., KY, 3581
Keal Foundation, VT, 9253
Kearney Area Community Foundation, NE, 5223
Keasbey Memorial Fund, H. G. and A. G., NC, 6727
Keats Foundation, Ezra Jack, Inc., NY, 6134
Kedge Foundation, WA, 9648
Keefer Scholarship Trust, Jay F., PA, 7933
Keel Foundation, The, TN, 8612
Keena Trust, Lorene Lobner, NC, 6728
Keener Foundation, Robert W. & Barbara J., UT, 9213
Keep North Carolina Clean and Beautiful, Inc., NC, 6729
Keeping Kids Warm, PA, see 7801
Keesee Educational Fund, Charles B., Inc., VA, 9413
Keig Scholarship Fund, E. R. Keig and Alice, IA, 3317
Keith Scholarship Fund Foundation, PA, see 7934
Keith Scholarship Fund, Ruth, PA, 7934
Keitzer Memorial Trust C, Charles B. & Lenore M., IN, 3083
Kelben Foundation, Inc., WI, 9938
Kelder Scholarship Trust, Mickey and Ross, AR, 286
Keller Foundation, Lucille L., IN, 3084
Keller Scholarship Fund, Melvin G. & Mary F., OH, 7185
Keller Scholarship Trust, Clarence, WI, 9939
Keller Trust, William M., WI, 9940
Kelley Foundation, Edward Bangs and Elza, Inc., MA, 4135
Kelley Foundation, Ralph & Helen, RI, 8318
Kellogg Company 25-Year Employees Fund, Inc., MI, 4496
Kellogg Foundation, W. K., MI, 4497
Kelly Charitable Trust, C.L., MI, 4498
Kelly Family Charitable Foundation, MO, 5027
Kelly Family Foundation, Christopher R., WA, 9649
Kelly Family Foundation, TX, 8904
Kelly Foundation of Washington, WA, 9650
Kelly Foundation, Inc., FL, 1935
Kelly Foundation, Stephen P. and Sandra Lu, TX, see 8904
Kelly Scholarship Fund, Mary A., MA, 4136
Kelly, Sr. Scholarship Fund, Deacon Elijah, SC, see 8488
Kelly, Sr. Scholarship, Deacon Elijah, SC, 8488
Kelsey Foundation, Forest C. & Ruth V., The, WA, 9651

Keltner Foundation for Women, Phyllis A., AR, 287
Kendrick Foundation, Inc., IN, 3085
Kendrick Memorial Hospital, Inc., IN, see 3085
Kengla Foundation, Edward R., VA, 9414
Keniston and Dane Educational Fund, VT, 9254
Kennard Educational Fund, Inc., VA, 9415
Kennedy Center for Justice and Human Rights, Robert F., The, DC, 1665
Kennedy Center for the Performing Arts, John F., The, DC, 1666
Kennedy Foundation, CO, 1225
Kennedy Foundation, Francis Nathaniel and Katheryn Padgett, SC, see 8489
Kennedy Foundation, The, SC, 8489
Kennedy Health Care Foundation, Inc., NJ, see 5486
Kennedy Health System, Inc., NJ, 5486
Kennedy Library Foundation, John F., Inc., MA, 4137
Kennedy Memorial, Robert F., DC, see 1665
Kennedy Scholarship Trust, Margaret J.S., RI, 8319
Kennedy, Jr. Foundation, Joseph P., The, DC, 1667
Kennestone Regional Foundation, Inc., GA, see 2260
Kenneth Rech, IA, see 3365
Kennett Educational Fund, Arthur, MO, 5028
Kenney Foundation, Ruth, FL, 1936
Kenosha Community Foundation, WI, 9941
Kenosha Scholarship Foundation, Inc., WI, 9942
Kent Community Foundation, WI, 9652
Kent Foundation, Senah C. and C.A., NC, 6730
Kentucky Foundation for Women, Inc., KY, 3582
Kentucky Fried Chicken Foundation, Inc., KY, 3583
Kentucky Law Enforcement Memorial Foundation, KY, 3584
Kentucky Lions Eye Foundation, Inc., KY, 3585
Kentucky Racing Health and Welfare Fund, Inc., KY, 3586
Keppy Charitable Foundation, Wilbert J. & Carol A., IA, 3318
Kerber Memorial Foundation, Ralph A., CA, 719
Keren America, CO, 1226
Keren Keshet - The Rainbow Foundation, NY, 6135
Keren Tifereth Yisroel Foundation, NY, 6136
Kern Foundation, Inc., The, WI, 9943
Kernwood Scholarship Foundation, MA, 4138
Kerouac Project of Orlando, Inc., The, FL, 1937
Kershaw County Vocational Education Foundation, Inc., SC, 8490
Kessel Scholarship Fund, Edgar E., OH, 7186
Kessel Trust, Edgar E., OH, see 7186
Kessler Foundation, NJ, 5487
Kest Old Newsboys Goodfellow Memorial Scholarship Fund, Ray T., OH, 7187
Keswick Foundation, Inc., MD, 3857
Keweenaw Community Foundation, MI, 4499
Key Charitable Trust, KS, 3473
Key Community Foundation, OH, see 7062
KeyBank Community Trust, OH, 7188
Kibble Foundation, OH, 7189
Kiddies Workshop U.S.A., Inc., TX, 8905
Kidney & Urology Foundation of America, Inc., NY, 6137
Kidney Foundation of Central Pennsylvania, PA, 7935
Kidney Foundation of Ohio, Inc., OH, 7190
Kids Campaign, Inc., MD, 3858
Kids In Need Foundation, OH, 7191
Kids Wish Network, Inc., FL, 1938
Kids' Chance of Georgia, Inc., GA, 2202
Kids' Chance, GA, see 2202
Kiely Trust, Helen U., RI, 8320
Kiersted Memorial Scholarship, Robert W., CA, 720
Kieve Affective Education, ME, see 3707
Kieve-Wavus Education, Inc., ME, 3707
Kiewit Foundation, Peter, NE, 5224
Killen Scholarship Trust, NE, 5225
Killgore Scholarship Trust Fund, J. A. & Ophelia, AL, 55
Kilts Foundation, The, IL, 2670
Kilts Foundation: Alverda & Edwards Kilts, The, IL, see 2670
Kim Architectural Fellowship Foundation, Tai Soo, CT, 1410
Kim Foundation for The History of Science and Technology In East Asia, D., Inc., The, MA, 4139
Kimball International—Habig Foundation Inc., The, IN, 3086
Kimberly-Clark Foundation, Inc., TX, 8906

Kimbo Foundation, The, CA, 721
Kimmel & Associates, Inc. Corporate Giving Program, NC, 6731
Kimmel Foundation, Sidney, The, PA, 7936
Kimmel Scholarship Foundation, Eugene E., NC, 6732
Kincaid Foundation, KY, 3587
Kindler Charitable Fund, Alice, OH, see 7192
Kindler Scholarship Fund, Alice, OH, 7192
King Cardiac Foundation, Larry, The, MD, 3859
King Charity Fund Trust, Jane R., IA, 3319
King Education Fund, Almarie, WA, 9653
King Education Trust, Maurice & Evelyn, IN, 3087
King Educational Trust, William Toben, MO, 5029
King Family Foundation, Charles & Lucille, Inc., NY, 6138
King Scholarship Foundation, Basil L., Inc., FL, 1939
King Scholarship Fund, Cora E., RI, see 8321
King Scholarship Fund, RI, 8321
King Trust, Charles A., MA, 4140
King-St. Ferdinand College Scholarship Foundation, George Leech, NY, 6139
Kingfield Memorial Scholarship Trust, Marcella, IA, 3320
Kingman Regional Hospital Foundation, AZ, 207
Kings Daughters Health Foundation, Inc., KY, 3588
Kingsbury Fund, The, RI, 8322
Kingsbury Scholarship Fund, Mr. & Mrs. Henry B., ID, 2338
Kinney Scholarship and Library Science Reference Fund, Clair H., PA, see 7937
Kinney Scholarship Fund, Clair H., PA, 7937
Kinsley Educational Foundation, James Edward, RI, see 8323
Kinsley Irrevocable Trust, James Edward, RI, 8323
Kirchner Educational Scholarship Trust, A. G. and Hattie Odell, NV, 5290
Kirchner Family Foundation, Inc., The, MD, 3860
Kirkpatrick Scholarship Fund Trust, Betty M., OH, 7193
Kirkpatrick Scholarship Fund, Betty, OH, see 7193
Kirkside, Inc., The, MA, see 4073
Kirschner Educational Trust, John E., MO, 5030
Kirtland Athletic Boosters Scholarship Fund Inc., OH, 7194
Kiser Memorial Fund, Clara Louise, OH, 7195
Kitsap Community Foundation, WA, 9654
Kittridge Educational Fund Trust, John Anson, OH, 7196
Kiwanis Charities of Rockford, Inc., IL, 2671
Kiwanis Club Foundation, Inc., IN, 3088
Kiwanis Club of Cape May Foundation, Inc., NJ, 5488
Kiwanis Club of Shorewood Foundation, MI, 4500
Kiwanis Club of Westshore, OH, 7197
Kiwanis Foundation of Harbor Springs, MI, 4501
Kiwanis of Little Havana Foundation, Inc., FL, 1940
Kiwanis Scholarship Fund, OH, see 7197
Klamath Scholarship Intervivos, Joseph S. Ball, OR, 7592
Klamm & Ruth Fishburn Foundation, Velma, OK, 7490
Klapmeyer Grandview High School Foundation, Ray & Mary, MO, 5031
Kleban Foundation, Inc., The, NY, 6140
Kleeman, Jr. Scholarship Fund, A. M., NY, 6141
Klein Foundation, Howard H., TX, 8907
Klein Fund, Lawrence R., VA, 9416
Klein Trust Fund, Arlen Francis, IL, 2672
Klein-Kaufman Family Foundation, The, NY, 6142
Klemstine Foundation, G. William, PA, 7938
Kleppe Scholarship Fund, Cecil H., KS, 3474
Klicka Foundation, Jessie, CA, 722
Kling Scholarship, Verne O. & Dorothy M., MI, 4502
Klingensmith Charitable Foundation, Agnes, OR, see 7594
Klingenstein Fund, Esther A. & Joseph, Inc., The, NY, 6143
Klingenstein Third Generation Foundation, The, NY, 6144
Klinger Scholarship Trust, Paul and Alma, OH, 7198
KLQ Education Foundation, WA, 9655
KML Foundation, Inc., FL, 1941
Knabusch Scholarship Foundation, Edward M. and Henrietta M., MI, 4503
Knapp Foundation Trust, Russell and Edna, AZ, 208
Knapp Foundation, AZ, see 208

Knecht Trust, Beulah, IL, 2673
Knight Memorial Journalism Fund Corp., John S., OH, 7199
Knight Scholarship Trust, Louise, TX, 8908
Knights of Columbus Charities Aid Foundation, KS, 3475
Knights of Columbus Charities USA, Inc., CT, 1412
Knights of Columbus Charities, Inc., CT, 1411
Knights of Columbus Massachusetts State Council Charity Fund, MA, 4141
Knights Templar Eye Foundation, Inc., TX, 8909
Knowles Foundation, Janet H. and C. Harry, Inc., NJ, 5489
Knowles Science Teaching Foundation (KSTF), NJ, see 5489
Knowles Trust B, Leonora H., OH, 7200
Koch Bomarko Founders Scholarship Fund, Robert & Margaret, MI, 4504
Koch Cultural Trust, KS, 3476
Koch Foundation, Fred C. and Mary R., Inc., The, KS, 3477
Koch Foundation, Fred C., The, KS, see 3477
Koch Foundation, Inc., IN, 3089
Koch Sons Foundation, George, Inc., IN, see 3089
Koehler Fund, John G., IL, 2674
Kohen Non-Exempt Charitable Trust, Elsie, IL, 2675
Kohl Education Foundation, Dolores, IL, 2676
Kohl Educational Foundation, Herb, WI, 9944
Kohl Educational Foundation, Victor E. and Hazel V., MN, 4775
Kohl Scholarship Trust, Leila, IL, 2677
Kohl's Corporation Contributions Program, WI, 9946
Kohler Foundation, Inc., WI, 9945
Kohn-Bancroft Family Foundation, The, MI, 4505
Kokua Foundation, The, HI, 2299
Kolob Foundation, The, UT, 9214
Komarek Charitable Trust, NC, 6733
Komen Breast Cancer Foundation, Susan G., Inc., The, TX, see 8910
Komen for the Cure, Susan G., TX, 8910
KOMO Radio and Television Minority Scholarship Fund, WA, see 9613
Koniag Education Foundation, AK, 122
Konstantinos Scholarship Foundation, K. Kiki, NJ, 5490
Kooi Education Fund, Elmer J. Kooi, Beatrice A. Kooi and Robert J., IL, see 2678
Kooi Education Fund, IL, 2678
Kooper Charitable Foundation Trust, Robert H. and Dorothy G., NE, 5226
Koran Trust, Ida C., MN, 4776
Koranda Scholarship Foundation, Rob, IL, 2679
Korean American Scholarship Foundation, VA, 9417
Korean American Volunteer Corps., CA, 723
Korean Heritage Scholarship Foundation, CA, 724
Korfman Scholarship Foundation, Michelle, NV, 5291
Kornberg Family Foundation, CA, 725
Korner Gift Shop, NC, see 6827
Korupp & Waelti Scholarship Fund, WI, 9947
Kosciusko 21st Century Foundation, Inc., IN, 3090
Kosciusko County Community Foundation, Inc., IN, 3091
Kosciuszko Foundation, Inc., NY, 6145
Koster Insurance Scholarship Fund Inc., MA, 4142
Kotur Foundation, Eugene R., PA, 7939
Koussevitzky Music Foundation, Inc., NY, 6146
Kovach Memorial Trust, Judith Kirsch, NJ, 5491
Kowalsky Memorial Ahavas Yisroel Fund, Rabbi Chaim Nachman, Inc., MD, 3861
KPMG Disaster Relief Fund, NJ, 5492
KPMG Foundation, The, NJ, 5493
KPMG Peat Marwick Foundation, The, NJ, see 5493
Kramer Educational Trust, Louie & Frank, SD, 8535
Krause Foundation, Cmdr. and Mrs. Robert, MI, 4506
Krausman Scholarships, August P. & Essie W., FL, see 1942
Krausman Trust, Essie W., FL, 1942
Krempels Brain Injury Foundation, The, NH, 5332
Krill Scholarship Fund, Verlin and Laverne, IL, 2680
Krueger Memorial Foundation, Scott S., Inc., The, NY, 6147
KT Family Foundation, The, WA, 9656
Kuhlman Foundation, Barbara L., Inc., NY, 6148

Kuhner Scholarship Foundation, IN, 3092
Kumar Memorial Scholarship Fund, Swarna, GA, 2203
Kurka Children's Health Fund, Kathryn L., Inc., CA, 726
Kurzweil Foundation, Inc., MA, 4143
Kuskokwim Educational Foundation, AK, 123
Kuzell Foundation, William C., CO, 1227

L & L Educational Foundation, MI, 4507
L'Oreal USA, Inc. Corporate Giving Program, NY, 6170
L.H. Foundation, Inc., NY, 6149
L.L.P. Scholarship Foundation, Vinson & Elkins, TX, 8911
La Canada Flintridge Educational Foundation, CA, 727
La Costa Canyon High School Foundation, Inc., CA, 728
La Crosse Community Foundation, WI, 9948
La Napoule Art Foundation, NH, 5333
La Unidad Latina Foundation, NY, 6150
Label Memorial Scholarship Trust, Frances, NC, 6734
Laboratory Institute of Merchandising Fashion Education Foundation, Inc., NY, 6151
Ladany Foundation Inc., Emory and Ilona E., NY, 6152
Ladd Memorial Fund, George S., PA, 7940
Ladies Charitable Society of Keene, NH, 5334
Ladies Education Society, IL, 2681
Ladies of the Grand Army of the Republic, CA, 729
Ladonna Cares and Shares Inc., GA, 2204
Laetz Fund Inc., Sumi, NV, 5292
Lafayette Arts & Science Foundation, CA, 730
Lafayette Education Foundation, LA, 3658
Laflin Scholarship Fund, William T., Inc., MI, 4508
LaForce Scholarship and Grant Fund, Elizabeth, AZ, 209
Lafourche Education Foundation, Inc, LA, 3659
Lage Loan & Scholarship Trust Fund, H. Carl & William, IA, 3321
LaGrange County Community Foundation, Inc., IN, 3093
Lagrant Foundation, CA, 731
Laguna Education Foundation, Inc., NM, 5634
Laham Family Foundation, KS, 3478
Laidlaw Foundation, Helen, The, MI, 4509
Laing-Weil Scholarship Fund Charitable Trust, WY, 10109
Laird Education Foundation, Herbert & Bertha, OR, 7593
Laird Oakland Scottish Rite Memorial Educational Foundation, Herbert Frank and Bertha Maude, OR, see 7593
Laird Testamentary Trust, Andrew, IN, 3094
Lake Area Civic Association, Inc., MO, 5032
Lake Erie Marine Trades Association Educational Foundation, Inc., OH, 7201
Lake Eustis Institute, Inc., FL, 1943
Lake Foundation, William B., NC, 6735
Lake Region Arts Council, Inc., MN, 4777
Lake Travis Crisis Ministries, TX, 8912
Lake Travis Education Foundation, TX, 8913
Lake View Pavilion Charitable Foundation, MA, 4144
Lake-Matthews Educational Fund, IA, 3322
Lake-Sumter Community College Foundation, Inc., FL, 1944
Lakeland Foundation, The, OH, 7202
Lakeland Group Foundation, Inc., The, MN, 4778
Lakeland Health Foundation, Niles, MI, 4510
Lakeland High School Scholarship Fund, WI, 9949
Lakes Region Scholarship Foundation, NH, 5335
Lakeview Pantry, IL, 2682
Lakewood Medical Center Foundation, CA, 732
Lalor Foundation, Inc., The, MA, 4145
LAM Foundation, The, OH, 7203
Lamb Community Services, Della, MO, 5033
Lamb Neighborhood House, Della C., MO, see 5033
Lambda Chi Alpha Educational Foundation, Inc., IN, 3095
Lambda Literary Foundation, CA, 733
Lambda Theta Nu Sorority, Inc., CA, 734
Lampstand Foundation, OR, 7594
Lancaster County Community Foundation, The, PA, 7941
Lancaster County Foundation, The, PA, see 7941
Lancaster Foundation For Educational Enrichment, PA, 7942
Lancaster General Hospital, PA, 7943

Lancaster Medical Society Foundation, PA, 7944
Lancaster Osteopathic Health Foundation, PA, 7945
Lancaster Trust, Lela M., NH, 5336
Lancaster West Rotary Foundation, CA, 735
Land O'Lakes Foundation, MN, 4779
Landry's Foundation, TX, see 9031
Landscape Architecture Foundation, DC, 1668
Lane Arts Council, OR, 7595
Lane Foundation, Winthrop and Frances, MN, 4780
Lang Benevolent Trust, Ruth E. Patterson, IL, 2683
Lang Family Foundation Inc., FL, 1945
Lang Foundation, Fritz, The, LA, 3660
Lang Foundation, Inc., Kenard, FL, 1946
Langdale Scholarship Fund, Edith A., PA, 7946
Lange Charitable Trust, H. K., MO, 5034
Langston Memorial Scholarship Trust, Bonnie, CO, 1228
Lanham Foundation, TX, 8914
Lannan Foundation, NM, 5635
Lansing Art Gallery, Inc., MI, 4511
Lapan Educational Loan Foundation, Inc., AZ, see 210
Lapan Memorial Sunshine Foundation, Inc., AZ, 210
Lapeer County Community Foundation, MI, 4512
Lapeer County Community Fund, MI, see 4512
Lapeer Testamentary Trust, Hypoliet, OH, 7204
Laredo-Webb County Food Bank, TX, see 9086
Larrabee Fund Association, CT, 1413
Larsen Charitable Education Trust, Gay R., WV, 9795
Larson Scholarship Trust, Lucille Flick, IL, 2684
LaRue Young Foundation, WY, 10110
Larue-Dawson Scholarship Trust, PA, 7947
Lasater Scholarship Foundation, CO, 1229
Lascaris Scholarship Trust, Michael, IL, 2685
Lasco Foundation, TX, 8915
Lasker Foundation, Albert and Mary, Inc., NY, 6153
Lasko Foundation, John C., NJ, 5494
LASO Public/Private Partnership Foundation, CA, see 736
Lasso Foundation, CA, 736
Last Charitable Foundation, Garth B., UT, 9215
Latham Foundation Inc., Walter, NC, 6736
Latimer Charitable Foundation, Bill and Carol, The, TN, 8613
Latino Student Fund, DC, 1669
Latta Charitable Trust, Lucile, IA, 3323
Laucius Educational and Charitable Foundation, Stephanie E., NJ, 5495
Laudermilch Scholarship Fund, Harry, PA, 7948
Lauffer Scholarship Fund, FL, 1947
Lauffer Trust, Charles A., FL, see 1947
Laughlin Foundation, Dr. Henry P. and Marion Page Durkee, Inc., MD, 3862
Laughlin Trust, George A., WV, 9796
Laurance Family Foundation, CA, 737
Laurendeau Foundation for Cancer Care, WA, 9657
Laurent, Jules Laurent & Paulette Leroy, PA, 7949
Lauterbach Scholarship Fund Trust, WI, 9950
Laux Memorial Trust, Madalynne F., IL, 2686
Lauzier Scholarship Foundation, Paul, WA, 9658
LaVictoire Memorial Scholarship, Daisy Harder, MI, 4513
Laviolette Scholarship Fund, Brian D., Inc., WI, 9951
Lavoie Foundation, NH, 5337
Law Review Inc., MN, 4781
Law School Admissions Council, Inc., PA, 7950
Lawler Foundation, TX, 8916
Lawrence Hall Youth Services, IL, 2687
Layton Scholarship Fund, Edna A., CO, 1230
Lazarus Foundation, Inc., The, TN, 8614
LD Resources Foundation, Inc., NY, 6154
Le Bonheur Children's Medical Center Foundation, TN, 8615
Le Rosey Foundation, NY, 6155
Lea County Electric Education Foundation, NM, 5636
Leaco Rural Telephone Education Foundation, NM, 5637
Lead Belly Foundation, Inc., The, TN, 8616
Leader Foundation, MO, 5035
Leadership Maryland, Inc., MD, 3863
League of American Orchestras, NY, 6156
League of United Latin American Citizens California Educational Foundation, CA, 738

Leakey Foundation for Research Related to Human Origins, Behavior and Survival, L. S. B., CA, see 739
Leakey Foundation, L. S. B., The, CA, 739
Learning Disabilities Association of Hawaii, HI, 2300
LearningAlly, NJ, 5496
Leary Firefighters Foundation, NY, 6157
Leath Foundation, Thomas H. and Mary Hadley Conner, NC, 6737
Leavey Foundation, Thomas & Dorothy, CA, 740
Leavitt Trust, Margaretta, WA, 9659
Ledet Foundation, Jerry, The, LA, 3661
Ledward Memorial Foundation, J. Dehaven, NC, see 6738
Ledward Memorial Scholarship, Carol J., NC, 6738
Lee Endowment Foundation, IA, 3324
Lee Industries Educational Foundation, Inc., NC, 6739
Lee Memorial Scholarship Foundation, Adam, TX, 8917
Lee Scholarship Foundation, Arthur K. & Sylvia S., TN, 8617
Lee-Jackson Educational Foundation, VA, 9418
Lee-Jackson Foundation, The, VA, see 9418
Leelanau Township Community Foundation, Inc., MI, 4514
Leeper Scholarship Foundation, The, IA, 3325
Leever Foundation, The, NC, 6740
Leeway Foundation, The, PA, 7951
LEF Foundation, CA, 741
Legacy Foundation, Inc., IN, 3096
Legacy Heritage Fund Limited, NY, 6158
Legacy, A Regional Community Foundation, KS, 3479
Legal Aid Society of Metropolitan Denver, CO, see 1159
Legal Aid Society of San Mateo County, CA, 742
Legal Foundation of Washington, WA, 9660
Legal Services Corporation, DC, 1670
Legal Services of New Jersey, Inc., NJ, 5497
Legion Foundation, The, MI, 4515
Legislative Black Caucus of the Georgia General Assembly, Inc., GA, 2205
LeGore Scholarship Fund, FL, 1948
Lehigh Carbon Community College Foundation, PA, 7952
Lehigh Valley Community Foundation, PA, 7953
Lehman Charitable Foundation, Carmen, Inc., The, AR, 288
Lehman Charitable Trust, William C. & Mildred K., OH, 7205
Lehmann Foundation, Manfred & Anne, NY, 6159
Lehr Scholarship Fund, Vernon S., PA, 7954
Leidy-Rhoads Foundation Trust, PA, see 8075
Leighow Scholarship Fund, Nellie E., PA, 7955
Leinbach Foundation, Edith, Samuel and Elizabeth, Inc., FL, 1949
Leister Foundation Inc, Klein G. & Mary Lee, MD, 3864
Leitzell Family Foundation, WI, 9952
Lemieux Charitable Trust, Geraldine N., MN, 4782
Lemmer-Blazer Scholarship Fund, IL, 2688
Lenawee Community Foundation, MI, 4516
Lend A Hand Society, MA, 4146
Lend-A-Hand, Inc., VA, 9419
Lenfest Foundation, Inc., The, PA, 7956
Lenore Cletcher-Wessale Trust, IL, 2689
Lenz Foundation, Dorsey S. & Eugenie C., NC, 6741
Leo House Scholarship Fund, Raymond, IN, 3097
Leonard Foundation, Red and Gena, OR, 7596
Lesher Foundation, Margaret & Irwin, OH, 7206
Leslie Scholarship Fund, NE, 5227
Letourneau Educational Foundation, Raymond & Lorraine, NH, 5338
Leukemia & Lymphoma Society of America, Inc., The, NY, see 6160
Leukemia & Lymphoma Society, Inc., The, NY, 6160
Leukemia Research Foundation, Inc., IL, 2690
Level Field Fund, ME, see 3728
Level Playing Field Institute, CA, 743
Leverenz Scholarship Trust, Mr. & Mrs. Walter F., NC, see 6742
Leverenz Trust, Walter & Hazel, NC, 6742
Levergood Trust f/b/o Connellsville Area School District, J. W., PA, 7957
Levin Family Foundation, The, OR, see 7642
Levin Foundation, Nicole Lynn, IL, 2691
Levin Trust f/b/o Lynn English, Elizabeth, MA, 4147
Levin Trust, Mosette, IN, 3098

Lewis Community Fund, Marvin, OH, 7207
Lewis Foundation, Harvey R., Inc., NY, 6161
Lewis Foundation, T. W., AZ, 211
Lewis Memorial Fund, Mabelle McLeod, PA, 7958
Lewis Scholarship Fund, Roberta Bachmann, IL, 2692
Lewis-Clark State College Foundation, Inc., ID, 2339
Lewis-Gale Foundation, VA, 9420
Lexington Community Foundation, NE, 5228
Lexington Foundation, The, MS, 4912
Lexmark International Group, Inc. Corporate Giving Program, KY, see 3589
Lexmark International, Inc. Corporate Giving Program, KY, 3589
Ley Trust, Jane Lois, OH, 7208
Leyen Memorial Fund, Ruthe Edmondson, TN, 8618
LFT Pacific Trust Foundation, CA, see 737
Liberty Bank Foundation, Inc., CT, 1414
Liberty Hill Foundation, CA, 744
Liberty Mutual Group Corporate Giving Program, MA, 4148
Lichman Trust, Harry C., RI, 8324
Licking County Foundation, OH, 7209
Licking Valley Community Action Program, KY, 3590
Liebling Foundation for Worthy Students, The, MO, 5036
Liebling Foundation, The, MO, see 5036
Liebmann Fund, Dolores Zohrab, The, TX, A
Life Foundation Inc., Lois Pope, FL, 1950
Life Foundation, HI, 2301
Life Investors Fortunaires Club, IA, 3326
Life Saving Benevolent Association of New York, NJ, 5498
Life Sciences Research Foundation, MD, 3865
Life Technologies Corporation Contributions Program, CA, 745
Life Trust, Robert H., RI, 8325
Lifelong AIDS Alliance, WA, 9661
LifeSphere, OH, see 7219
Lift Up Africa, MA, 4149
Light Ranch at Old Snowmass Charitable Trust, Inc., CO, 1231
Light Work Visual Studies, Inc., NY, 6162
Lightfoot Foundation, E.L. & B.G., The, ID, see 2340
Lightfoot Foundation, The, ID, 2340
Lighthouse Emergency Services, Inc., MI, 4517
Lighthouse International, NY, 6163
Likins Masonic Memorial Trust, Oletha C. Likins & Loren E., WY, see 10112
Likins Perpetual Memorial Trust Fund, Oletha C. Likins & Loren E., WY, 10111
Likins-Masonic Memorial Trust, Loren E. Linkins Oletha C Linkins,, WY, 10112
Likins-Masonic Memorial Trust, WY, see 10112
Lillis Foundation, The, CO, 1232
Lilly and Company Contributions Program, Eli, IN, 3099
Lilly Cares Foundation, Inc., IN, 3100
Lilly Endowment Inc., IN, 3101
LIM Fashion Education Foundation, Inc., NY, see 6151
Limiar U.S.A., Inc., TX, 8918
Lincoln Arc Welding Foundation, James F., OH, 7210
Lincoln Center for the Performing Arts, Inc., NY, 6164
Lincoln Center, Inc., NY, see 6164
Lincoln Community Foundation, Inc., NE, 5229
Lincoln Foundation, FL, 1951
Lincoln Foundation, Inc., NE, see 5229
Lincoln Foundation, KY, 3591
Lincoln Park Zoological Society, IL, 2693
Lincoln Scholarship, Douglas W., OH, 7211
Lincoln-Lane Foundation, The, VA, 9421
Linda Foundation, John and Mary, NJ, A
Lindbergh Foundation, Charles A. and Anne Morrow, The, MN, 4783
Lindbergh Foundation, MN, see 4783
Lindhart Educational Trust, IA, 3327
Lindsay Trust, Franklin, IL, 2694
Line Scholarship Fund Trust II, Alma Verne, IN, 3102
Line Scholarship Fund Trust II, Claude & Verne, IN, see 3102
Linhart Foundation, The, VA, 9422
Lintner Scholarship Trust, PA, 7959
Linwood Educational Trust Fund, Inc., NH, 5339
Lion's Pride Foundation, Inc., The, NC, 6743
Lions of Michigan Service Foundation, Inc., MI, 4518

Lions Sight and Hearing Foundation of Washington & Northern Idaho, WA, see 9687
Lippert Foundation, Robert L., CA, 746
Lissak Foundation, Inc., The, NJ, A
Lissner Foundation, Gerda, Inc., NY, 6165
Litchfield County University Club, CT, 1415
Literary Arts, Inc., OR, 7597
Lithuanian Foundation, IL, 2695
Little Buns, Inc., IN, 3103
Little Company of Mary Community Health Foundation, CA, 747
Little Education Trust, Helen I., TX, see 8919
Little Education Trust, Rufus L. & Helen I., TX, 8919
Little High School Alumni Association Trust, Edward, RI, 8326
Little People of America, Inc., CA, 748
Little Scholarship Loan Fund, Solon E. & Espie Watts, Inc., NC, 6744
Little Scholarship Trust, Earle and Elsie, The, MI, 4519
Littlejohn Foundation, William and Esther, WA, 9662
Littler Trust, Ray and Kay, The, WY, 10113
Liu Foundation, Margaret, The, CA, 749
Live Oak Foundation, TX, 8920
Livermore Trust, Frank, CA, 750
Living Archives, Inc., NY, 6166
Livingston Educational Trust, James S. & Peggy M., NC, 6745
Livingston Foundation, Mollie Parnis, Inc., FL, 1952
Lloyd Family Foundation, FL, 1953
LMCC, NY, see 6173
Loar Scholarship Foundation, P. A. & Marie B., NC, 6746
Loaves and Fishes Community Pantry, IL, 2696
Local 758 S & E Fund, NY, see 5927
Lochland Foundation, The, WA, 9663
Lock Haven University Foundation, PA, 7960
Locke Memorial Foundation, Owen, CA, 751
Lockheed Martin Aeronautics Employees Reaching Out Club, TX, 8921
Lockheed Martin Employees' Foundation, CA, 752
Lockheed Martin Vought Systems Employee Charity Fund, TX, 8922
Lockheed MSC Employees Bucks of the Month Club, CA, see 752
Loeb Foundation, G. and R., Inc., The, CA, 753
Loeb Foundation, Jesse and Rose, Inc., The, VA, 9423
Loeb Foundation, OH, 7212
Loessin Memorial Scholarship Trust, Merle, NE, 5230
Loflin Educational Foundation, Charles B., NC, 6747
Loft Literary Center, The, MN, see 4784
Loft, Inc., The, MN, 4784
Lofthouse Foundation, The, UT, 9216
Logan County Charitable and Educational Foundation, Inc., The, WV, 9797
Logan County Nurses Scholarship Association, CO, 1233
Logansport Memorial Hospital Foundation, IN, 3104
Lokoff Child Care Foundation, Terri Lynne, PA, 7961
London Educational Foundation, George and Frances, NC, 6748
London Foundation for Singers, George, Inc., NY, 6167
Long Beach Rotary Scholarship Foundation, CA, 754
Long Charitable Trust, Lucy B., FL, 1954
Long Foundation, Jackie, IL, 2697
Long Island Caddie Scholarship Fund, Inc., NY, 6168
Long Trust, Dr. Ralph F. & Pearl A., RI, 8327
Long Trust, L. A., TX, 8923
Loofbourrow Educational Trust, KS, 3480
Loogootee Community School Scholarship, IN, 3105
Looney Memorial Fund, Charles, NY, 6169
Lorain Foundation, The, OH, 7213
Lord Educational Fund, MO, 5037
Lord Scholarship Fund Trust, Henry C., RI, 8328
Lorden II Memorial Scholarship Corp., Michael J., MA, 4150
Lorelle Scholarship Fund, Linda, Inc., TX, 8924
Lortel Foundation, Lucille, The, NY, 6171
Los Abogados Hispanic Bar Association, AZ, 212
Los Alamos National Laboratory Foundation, NM, 5638
Los Altos Community Foundation, CA, 755
Los Angeles Clippers Foundation, CA, 756
Los Angeles County Developmental Services Foundation, CA, 757

Los Angeles Philharmonic Association, CA, 758
Loser Memorial Scholarship Fund, Alfred J., OH, 7214
Louisiana Association of Community Action
Partnerships, Inc., The, LA, 3662
Louisiana Bar Foundation, LA, 3663
Louisiana Cultural Economy Foundation, LA, 3664
Louisiana Endowment for the Humanities, LA, 3665
Louisiana Poultry Industries Educational Foundation,
Inc., LA, 3666
Louisville Community Foundation, Inc., KY, see 3559
Louisville Male High School Foundation, Inc., KY, 3592
Louisville Scholarship Foundation, The, OH, 7215
Love Foundation, Lucyle S., The, SC, 8491
Love Thy Neighbor Community Development &
Opportunity Corporation, VA, 9424
Low Foundation, Claude & Ada, Inc., CA, 759
Lowcountry AIDS Services, Inc., SC, 8492
Lowe Memorial Educational Fund, Mary Friese, MA,
4151
Lowe Syndrome Association, TX, 8925
Lowe's Employee Relief Fund, NC, 6749
Lowell 10th Clause Trust, Amy, MA, 4152
Lowell Community Foundation, Greater, MA, 4153
Lowengard Scholarship Fund, Leon, PA, 7962
Lower Columbia Community Action Council, Inc., WA,
9664
Lower Columbia Community Action Partnership, WA,
see 9664
Lower East Side Printshop, Inc., NY, 6172
Lower Manhattan Cultural Council, Inc., NY, 6173
Lower Memorial Scholarship Fund, Ora T. & Dessie H.,
IL, 2698
Lowrie Student Loan Fund, Pearl, MO, 5038
Lozynskyj Foundation, NY, 6174
LPA, CA, see 748
LPGA Foundation, The, FL, 1955
LSAC, PA, see 7950
LSB Foundation, IA, 3328
LSC, DC, see 1670
Lubbock Area Foundation, Inc., TX, 8926
Lucas, Jr. Foundation, Sam J., The, TX, 8927
Lucash Charitable Private Foundation Trust, John R.,
AL, 56
Lucash Scholarship Trust, John R., AL, see 56
Luce Foundation, Henry, Inc., The, NY, 6175
Luce Policy Institute, Clare Boothe, VA, 9425
Luce Trust, Charles & Nancy Oden, TX, 8928
Lucky Scholarship Trust, Oatha & Una, CA, 760
Ludwig Educational Trust, Merwin C., WV, 9798
Luhr Foundation, Alois and Twyla, IL, 2699
Lukenda Educational & Scholarship Foundation Inc.,
Raymond, The, NJ, 5499
Luley Scholarship & Educational Fund, Founces M., IL,
2700
Luling Foundation, The, TX, 8929
Lumbee Nation Tribal Programs, Inc., NC, 6750
Lundberg Education, Maynard A., WA, 9665
Lundquist Scholarship Foundation, Walter E., NC, 6751
Lundy Foundation, Turner and Louise, The, NC, 6752
LUNGevity Foundation, Inc., IL, 2701
Lupus Foundation of America, Inc., DC, 1671
Lupus Foundation of Colorado, Inc., The, CO, 1234
Lupus Inspiration Foundation for Excellence, AZ, 213
Lurcy Charitable and Educational Trust, Georges, NY,
6176
Lustgarten Pancreatic Cancer Foundation, Marc, NY,
6177
Lutheran Child & Family Service of Michigan, Inc., MI,
4520
Lutheran Child and Family Services of Illinois, IL, 2702
Lutheran Community Foundation, MN, 4785
Lutheran Family Services of Colorado, CO, see 1235
Lutheran Family Services of Nebraska, Inc., NE, 5231
Lutheran Services Florida, Inc., FL, 1956
Lutheran Social Service of Colorado, CO, 1235
Lutheran Social Service of Minnesota, MN, 4786
Lutheran Social Services of Illinois, IL, 2703
Lutron Foundation, PA, 7963
Luttrell Scholarship Foundation, Jessica Elizabeth, UT,
9217
Lutz Foundation, Inc., NC, 6753
Luzerne Foundation, The, PA, 7964
Lyceum Fellowship, Inc., The, MA, 4154

Lyman Fund, Inc., NH, 5340
Lymphatic Research Foundation, NY, 6178
Lymphoma Research Foundation, NY, 6179
Lynam Trust, Hattie A. and Fred C., ME, 3708
Lynch Foundation For Consciousness-Based Education
and World Peace, David, CA, 761
Lynch Foundation, John, Inc., The, FL, 1957
Lynch Scholarship Foundation, John B., DE, A
Lynch Scholarship Fund, Cornelius T. & Elizabeth, NY,
6180
Lynch Scholarship Trust, Cornelius T. & Elizabeth, NY,
see 6180
Lynch Trust, William A., MA, 4155
Lynch Trust, William A., PA, 7965
Lynchburg Community Trust, Greater, VA, 9426
Lynden Memorial Scholarship Fund, WA, 9666
Lynn Foundation, Berneice U., CA, 762
Lyons Memorial Foundation, Charles, Inc., MO, 5039
Lyons Scholarship Fund, Marguerite Gambill, OH, 7216
Lyons Scholarship Fund, Ray C., Maude E. &
Genevieve, WI, 9953
Lytel Foundation, Bertha Russ, CA, 763
Lytle Scholarship Trust, Carl H., OR, 7598
Lytle Scholarship Trust, Carl H., OR, see 7598

M & M Area Community Foundation, MI, 4521
M. C. G. Foundation, MI, see 4547
M. Max Crisp Stewart Scholarship Foundation, TX,
8930
M.I.G. Scholarship Foundation, TX, see 8848
M.K. Foundation Inc., NJ, A
MacArthur Foundation, John D. and Catherine T., The,
IL, 2704
MacCurdy Salisbury Educational Foundation, Inc., The,
CT, 1416
MacCurdy Salisbury Foundation, Inc., The, CT, see
1416
MacDowell Colony, Inc., NH, 5341
MacGregor Charitable Trust, Muriel L., CO, 1236
MacGregor Ranch, CO, see 1236
Machado Foundation, Christopher Michael, CA, 764
Mack Industrial School, MA, 4156
Mackin Foundation, Inc., KY, 3593
MacKinnon Fund, Mary W., NY, 6181
Macon County Care Network, NC, 6754
Macon-Russell Community Action Agency, Inc., AL, 57
MacPherson Memorial Scholarship Fund, Carol E., MN,
4787
MacPherson Trust, A. F., WI, 9954
MacRae Scholarship Trust, Anna M., OH, 7217
Macricostas Scholarship Trust, Inc., CT, 1417
Macristy Foundation, William & Ellen E., CT, 1418
Madden Memorial Trust, Angus, CA, 765
Maddox Foundation, J. F., NM, 5639
Made in Dover Foundation, The, NJ, see 5602
Madison Advertising Federation Foundation, WI, 9955
Madison County Community Foundation, IN, 3106
Madison Rotary Foundation, WI, 9956
Madison Scholarship Committee, NJ, 5500
MADRE, Inc., NY, 6182
Maes Trust, D., RI, 8329
Maffett Scholarship Trust, Minnie L., TX, 8931
MAG Foundation, GA, see 2211
Magdalena School District Gear up Scholarship Trust,
NC, 6755
Magic Action Community Fund, Inc., FL, see 1958
Magic Action Team Community Fund, Inc., FL, 1958
Magnum Cultural Foundation, NY, 6183
Magnum Foundation, The, NY, see 6183
Magnus Charitable Trust, IL, 2705
Magnus Foundation, James D. and Diane S., Inc., GA,
2206
Magnus Home, A. J., IA, 3329
Magnuson Foundation, Rick and Amy, Inc., ID, 2341
Magraw Trust, Marguerite, RI, 8330
Maguire Trust, Agnes T., TX, 8932
Mahajan Memorial Trust, Varoon, Inc., NJ, 5501
Mahalick Scholarship Fund, Stanley & Mary, NC, 6756
Mahan Scholarship Fund, Bruce H., The, RI, 8331
Mahana Congregational Church, RI, 8332
Mahanay Educational Trust, Dora, IA, 3330
Mahler Psychiatric Research Foundation, Margaret S.,
PA, 7966

Mahnken Foundation, Elizabeth A., Inc., The, IN, 3107
Mahube Community Council, MN, 4788
Maidstone Foundation, Inc., NY, 6184
Main Street Community Foundation, CT, 1419
Maine Alliance for Arts Education, ME, 3709
Maine Bar Foundation, ME, 3710
Maine Cancer Foundation, ME, 3711
Maine Community Foundation, Inc., The, ME, 3712
Maine Higher Education Assistance Foundation, ME,
3713
Maine Humanities Council, ME, 3714
Maine South Scholarship Fund, Will Dushek, FL, 1959
Maine Technology Institute, ME, 3715
Maine Veterinary Education Foundation, ME, 3716
Maine Writers and Publishers Alliance, ME, 3717
Majid Family Foundation, IL, 2706
Major Junior Hockey Education Fund of Oregon, OR,
7599
Major League Baseball Equipment Managers
Association, AZ, 214
Make A Wish Foundation of Georgia and Alabama, GA,
2207
Make It Right, LA, see 3675
Make-A-Wish Foundation of Arizona, Inc., AZ, 215
Make-A-Wish Foundation of Illinois, Inc., IL, 2707
Make-A-Wish Foundation of Massachusetts, Inc., MA,
4157
Make-A-Wish Foundation of Metro St. Louis, Inc., MO,
5040
Make-A-Wish Foundation of Michigan, MI, 4522
Make-A-Wish Foundation of Sacramento and
Northeastern CA, CA, 766
Make-A-Wish Hawaii, Inc., HI, 2302
Makinson Trust, Emma F., RI, 8333
Malanga Foundation, Michele, SC, 8493
Malevich Society, The, NY, 6185
Maley Charitable Foundation, Christina and William,
The, PA, 7967
Mallard-Turner Memorial Scholarship Trust, TX, 8933
Mallinckrodt, Jr. Foundation, Edward, MO, 5041
Mallory-Taylor Foundation, Inc., KY, 3594
Malloy Foundation, Ed T., TX, 8934
Maloney Foundation, James, The, VA, 9427
Maloney Foundation, William E., MA, 4158
Malstrom Memorial Foundation, Brandon James, Inc.,
MD, 3866
Mammoth Lakes Foundation, CA, 767
Manatee Community Foundation, Inc., FL, 1960
Manchester Community Music School, NH, 5342
Manchester Scholarship Foundation, Inc., CT, 1420
Maness Educational Foundation, Teresa, TX, 8935
Mang Foundation, So, CA, 768
Manhattan Community Access Corporation, NY, see
6186
Manhattan Neighborhood Network, NY, 6186
Mankato Area Foundation, Inc., MN, 4789
Manley Music Scholarship Trust, FL, 1961
Mann Foundation, Rema Hort, Inc., NY, 6187
Mann Scholarship Trust, Roderic and Mildred, The, IN,
3108
Mann, Jr. Memorial Fund, Joe L., MO, 5042
Manna Food Center, Inc., MD, 3867
Manpower Foundation, Inc., WI, see 9957
ManpowerGroup Foundation, Inc., WI, 9957
Mansfield Family Foundation, KS, 3481
Mansfield Fund for the Aged, Mary, OH, 7218
Manuel Trust, Viola G., NH, 5343
Manwiller Trust, Lloyd R. and Stella Gibboney, RI, 8334
MAP International, GA, 2208
MAPGA Scholarship Foundation, Inc., VA, 9428
Maple Knoll Communities, Inc., OH, 7219
Marblehead Female Humane Society, Inc., MA, 4159
March Education Fund, William A., PA, 7968
March of Dimes Birth Defects Foundation, NY, see
6188
March of Dimes Foundation, NY, 6188
March Scholarship Foundation, Thelma, The, MD, 3868
March Scholarship Fund, Clara A., NY, 6189
Marchello Scholarship Foundation, Stephen T., CO,
1237
Marchionne Foundation for Scientific Study of Human
Relations, A., NV, 5293

Marchionne Foundation for Scientific Study, A., NV, *see* 5293

Marco Island Women's Club Foundation, FL, 1962

Marconi Society Inc., CA, 769

Marek Trust Fund, IA, 3331

Marena Foundation, Inc., The, GA, 2209

MARF, VA, *see* 9435

Marguerite Home, a Charitable Trust, The, CA, *see* 770

Marguerite Home, The, CA, 770

Marhaver Trust, Lorena, RI, 8335

Mari's Foundation, WI, 9958

Maria's Hope, WA, 9429

Mariani Nut Company Foundation, Inc., CA, 771

Marietta Community Foundation, OH, 7220

Marijuana Policy Project Foundation, DC, 1673

Marijuana Policy Project, DC, 1672

Marin Community Foundation, CA, 772

Marin Education Fund, CA, *see* 329

Marine Biological Laboratory, MA, 4160

Marine Corps Scholarship Foundation, Inc., VA, 9430

Marine Corps-Law Enforcement Foundation, Inc., NY, 6190

Marino Foundation, John Michael, Inc., NY, 6191

Marino Memorial Foundation, James J., CA, 773

Marino Scholarship Fund, Maria, MA, 4161

Marion Community Foundation, Inc., OH, 7221

Marion Memorial Health Foundation, IL, 2708

Marion Technical College Foundation Inc., OH, 7222

Maris Scholarship Foundation, Irena, IN, 3109

Market Foundation, The, WA, 9667

Markos Foundation, Inc., The, WI, 9959

Marquette Area Public Schools Education Foundation, MI, 4523

Marquette Community Foundation, MI, *see* 4524

Marquette County Community Foundation, MI, 4524

Marsch Charitable Trust, Louis and Temple, MO, 5043

Marshall & Margaret Hughes Scholarship Foundation, W., PA, 7969

Marshall Civic Foundation, MI, *see* 4525

Marshall College Fund, Thurgood, DC, 1674

Marshall Community Foundation, MI, 4525

Marshall County Community Foundation, Inc., IN, 3110

Marshall Educational Trust Fund, The, IL, 2709

Marshall Scholarship Fund, Thurgood, DC, *see* 1674

Marshall-Jackson Mental Retardation Authority, Inc., AL, 58

Marshfield Area Community Foundation, WI, 9960

Martell Memorial Foundation, C.F., ND, 6943

Marth Foundation Ltd., WI, 9961

Marti Foundation, TX, 8936

Martin Charitable Trust, G. Roxy & Elizabeth C., FL, 1963

Martin Charitable Trust, Loy Crump, MO, 5044

Martin County Community Foundation, Inc., FL, 1964

Martin Education Trust, IL, 2710

Martin Family Foundation, Patrick J., The, FL, 1965

Martin Foundation for the Creative Arts, Peter and Madeleine, CA, 774

Martin Foundation, Glenn L., NY, 6192

Martin Fund, Henry B., Inc., MA, 4162

Martin Nursing Scholarship, Dr. Wood, WI, 9962

Martin Scholarship Fund, Dewey & Louise, AL, 59

Martin Scholarship Trust Fund, Albert and Jessie D., NC, 6757

Martin Scholarship Trust, J. Clyde, PA, 7970

Martin Scholarship, Marcus K., MI, 4526

Martin Trust 1, Mary R., NH, 5344

Martin Trust Fund, David M., NY, 6193

Martin Trust No. 2, Mary R., NH, 5345

Martin Trust, Gertrude E., MI, *see* 4526

Martin, Jr. Foundation, Karl & Georgia Martin, Sr., Anna Belle Flynn, Karl & June, OK, 7491

Martinez Foundation, Edgar and Holli, The, WA, 9668

Martinez Foundation, The, WA, *see* 9668

Martino Trust, Joseph W., MO, 5045

Martz Scholarship Fund, Dolly & George, PA, *see* 7971

Martz Scholarship, PA, 7971

Mary Institute Scholarship Fund, MO, *see* 5052

Mary Kay Foundation, TX, 8937

Maryland 4-H Foundation, Inc., MD, 3869

Maryland Association of Elementary School Principals, Inc., MD, 3870

Maryland Congress of Parents and Teachers, Inc., MD, 3871

Maryland Credit Union Foundation, Inc., The, MD, *see* 3810

Maryland Hall for the Creative Arts, Inc., MD, 3872

Maryland Instructional Computers Coordinators Association, MD, *see* 3875

Maryland Media, Inc., MD, 3873

Maryland Ornithological Society, Inc., MD, 3874

Maryland PTA, MD, *see* 3871

Maryland Society for Educational Technology, MD, 3875

Maryland-Delaware-D.C. Press Foundation, Inc., MD, 3876

Marymount Foundation, Mother Joseph Rogan, MO, 5046

Maryville Academy, IL, 2711

Mashburn Scholarship Foundation, AR, 289

Mashomack Foundation, NY, 6194

Mason Scholarship Fund, Daisy, IL, 2712

Mason Scholarship Fund, IL, *see* 2712

Masonic Benevolence, MN, 4790

Masonic Charity Foundation of Oklahoma, OK, 7492

Masonic Educational Foundation Inc., LA, 3667

Masonic Foundation of the District of Columbia, The, DC, 1675

Masonic Foundation of Utah, UT, 9218

Masonic Grand Lodge Charities of Rhode Island, Inc., RI, 8336

Masonic Home and School of Texas, TX, 8938

Masonic Homes of California, CA, 775

Massachusetts Bar Foundation, Inc., MA, 4163

Massachusetts Charitable Fire Society, MA, 4164

Massachusetts College of Liberal Arts Foundation, Inc., MA, 4165

Massachusetts Library Aid Association, MA, 4166

Massachusetts Medical Society, MA, 4167

Massachusetts Society of Mayflower Descendants, MA, 4168

Massage Therapy Foundation, Inc., IL, 2713

Masten Charitable Scholarship Trust, Raymond W. & Edith W., DE, 1516

Master Educational Assistance Foundation, IL, 2714

MasterCard Incorporated Corporate Giving Program, NY, 6195

Masters Trust Fund, Edith L., IL, 2715

Mat-Su Health Foundation, AK, *see* 148

Material Handling Educational Foundation, Inc., NC, 6758

MATHCOUNTS Foundation, VA, 9431

Mathematical Sciences Research Institute, CA, 776

Matheson Scholarship Fund, Margaret & Donald, RI, 8337

Matheson Scholarship Trust Fund, James Matheson & Marian, IA, 3332

Matrix Human Services, MI, 4527

Matson Trust, Lorraine D., MI, 4528

Matsui Foundation, CA, 777

Matthews Trust, Ernestine, WV, 9799

Mattioli Foundation, PA, 7972

Mattress Factory, Ltd., The, PA, 7973

Matz Foundation, Israel, NY, 6196

Maude -FrancesChildrens Fund, RI, 8338

Maude Charitable Trust, J. T. - Minnie, VA, 9432

Mauger Insurance Fund, OH, 7223

Mauldin Scholarship Charitable Trust, AR, *see* 276

Mavrogenis Trust Fund, Dennis and Marion, MA, 4169

Maxwell Foundation, Edmund F., WA, 9669

Maya Educational Foundation, MA, 4170

Maybury Trust, Imogene M., RI, 8339

Mayday Fund, The, NY, 6197

Mayer Foundation, Chaim, Inc., NY, A

Mayer Foundation, The, NY, 6198

Mayfield Foundation, M.L. & Jessie Star, TX, 8939

Mayo Clinic - St. Mary's Hospital, MN, 4792

Mayo Clinic Jacksonville, FL, 1966

Mayo Clinic Rochester, MN, *see* 4791

Mayo Clinic, MN, 4791

Mayson Scholarship Grant Fund, Charles G. & Alice R., The, AL, 60

Maysteel Foundation, Ltd., WI, *see* 10035

MBL, MA, *see* 4160

McAllister Christmas Fund, James, NC, 6759

McAllister Scholarship Fund, Cheryl A., IL, 2716

MCBA, MN, *see* 4799

MCCA, MD, *see* 3888

McCabe Charitable Foundation, Donald C. and Helene Marienthal, OH, 7224

McCabe Testamentary Trust - Georgia, E.R. Warner, FL, 1967

McCabe Testamentary Trust, E.R. Warner, FL, 1968

McCaddin-McQuirk Foundation, Inc., The, NY, 6199

McCall Foundation, Penny, Inc., The, NY, 6200

McCallay Scholarship, Edwin L. and Louis B., OH, 7225

McCamic Scholarship Trust, Jay T., WV, 9800

McCann Charitable and Educational Trust, J. Bryan and Norma R., OH, 7226

McCarthey Dressman Education Foundation, The, UT, 9219

McCaulay Memorial Masonic Fund, TX, 8940

McClain Scholarship Trust, IL, 2717

McClain Trust, J. Allen, OH, 7227

McCleary Medical Scholarship Fund of the Mary Ball Chapter for the Daughters of the American Revolut, Frank, WA, *see* 9670

McCleary Medical Scholarship Fund, Frank, WA, 9670

McCloskey Memorial Scholarship, Charles, PA, 7974

McClureTrust, John S., NC, 6760

McColl Center for Visual Arts, NC, 6761

McComas Foundation, Sophia Byers, OR, 7600

McComb Fund, CA, 778

McComb Memorial Scholarship Fund, Lucille, OH, 7228

McConahay Educational Foundation, Ann, OH, 7229

McConnell Foundation and Scholarship Fund, Lynn E. and Mattie G., The, NY, *see* 6201

McConnell Foundation, The, CA, 779

McConnell Scholarship Foundation, The, NY, 6201

McCormick Memorial Fund, Anne O'Hare, Inc., NY, 6202

McCormick Scholarship Fund, Bernard W., RI, 8340

McCormick Scholarship Fund, Don & Marcella, SD, 8536

McCormick Scholarship Fund, Robert W., WV, 9801

McCourtney Trust, Flora S., IL, *see* 2567

McCoy Scholarship Fund, WA, 9671

McCoy Scholarship Trust, Clark & Laura, OH, 7230

McCready Scholarship Fund, Stephen F., NJ, 5502

McCrindle Foundation, Joseph F., NY, 6203

McCrory Trust for Gonzales County, Texas, Dorsey, TX, 8941

McCune Scholarship Foundation Trust, C.N., FL, 1969

McCurdy Memorial Scholarship Foundation, MI, 4529

McCurdy Scholarship Foundation, Edna P., AK, 124

McCurry Foundation Inc., The, FL, 1970

McDaniel Charitable Foundation, TX, 8942

McDavid Dental Education Trust, G. N. and Edna, MO, *see* 4975

McDonald Charitable Trust Memorial Scholarship Fund for Weir High School, Joan B. and Frank E., OH, 7231

McDonald Charitable Trust Memorial Scholarship Fund for Wheeling Park High School, Joan Bieberson, OH, 7232

McDonald Family Foundation, Dan & Dottie, TX, 8943

McDonald Memorial Fund Trust, OH, 7233

McDonald Memorial Scholarship Fund, Katrina Overall, MS, 4913

McDonald Memorial Trust, Angus C., OH, *see* 7233

McDonald Scholarship Fund, John & Lee Ella, AR, 290

McDonald Trust, Georgine B., IL, 2718

McDonald's Family Charity, Inc., IL, 2719

McDonnell Douglas-West Personnel Community Services Inc., CA, *see* 564

McDougall Charitable Trust, Ruth Camp, NY, *see* 5810

McDowell Corporation, Verne Catt, OR, 7601

McDowell Foundation, Ephraim, KY, 3595

McDuffie Scholarship & Loan Foundation, Inc., GA, 2210

McElaney Trust f/b/o Town of Avon, John, MA, 4171

McElroy Charitable Foundation, William E., MO, 5047

McElroy Trust, R. J., IA, 3333

McFarland Charitable Foundation, IL, 2720

McFarland Foundation, B. Corry and Donna J., WA, 9672

McFarland Medical Trust, IL, 2721

McFarlin Charitable Trust, James and Mary, OH, 7234

McFarlin Foundation, James and Mary, OH, see 7234
McGee Trust, NY, 6204
McGeehin Educational Foundation Inc., The, MD, 3877
McGinty Family Foundation, OH, see 7235
McGinty Foundation, Alice & Patrick, The, OH, 7235
McGinty Foundation, Alice and Patrick, OH, see 7235
McGinty Scholarship Fund Trust, Ellanora, The, FL, 1971
McGinty Trust, Garnie W. & Zoe, LA, 3668
McGlothlan Trust, Arthur B. and Anna F., MO, 5048
McGovern Fund for the Behavioral Sciences, TX, see 8944
McGovern Fund, TX, 8944
McGowan Foundation, D. Lynd & Terri K., The, TX, 8945
McGrain Cedar Glade Foundation for the Needy of Harrison County, Thomas D., IN, 3111
McGrath Charitable Foundation Scholarship Fund, Margaret A., NY, 6205
MCH Foundation, Inc., The, TX, 8946
McIninch Scholarship Fund, The, NH, 5346
McInnes College Scholarship Fund, Eva E., IL, 2722
McIntire Educational Fund, John, OH, 7236
McKaig Foundation, Lalitta Nash, PA, 7975
McKay Trust, Milburn A., IA, 3334
McKee Educational Trust, John W., OR, 7602
McKee Foundation, Ella G., IL, 2723
McKee Foundation, H., Inc., HI, 2303
McKee Trust, John, PA, 7976
McKenney Scholarship Trust, Elmer, TX, 8947
McKenney Trust, Leona Thiele, IA, 3335
McKenzie Charitable Trust, Virginia, OK, 7493
McKenzie County Education Trust, ND, 6944
McKenzie River Gathering Foundation, OR, 7603
McKinney Charitable Trust, Edgar & Nona, FL, 1972
McKinney Foundation, Edgar P. & Nona B., FL, see 1972
McKinney Nursing School Loan Trust, Ralph E., IN, 3112
McKinney Scholarship Trust, Lee, OH, see 7181
McKinnis Educational Trust, Ira and Dena, The, KS, 3482
McKnight Endowment Fund for Neuroscience, The, MN, 4793
McKnight Foundation, The, MN, 4794
McLane Association, Dorothea van Dyke, NJ, 5503
McLaughlin Foundation, The, MA, 4172
McLean Memorial Fund, Herbert, IL, 2724
McLean Scholarship Fund, John B., RI, 8341
McLendon Minority Scholarship Foundation, John, OH, 7237
McLoraine Educational Trust, Reverend John A., IL, 2725
McMahan Trust, Mildred R., NC, 6762
McMannis Educational Trust Fund, William J. McMannis and A. Haskell, PA, 7977
McMillan, Jr. Foundation Inc., Bruce, TX, 8948
McMillen Foundation, Robert B., The, WA, 9673
McMillen Foundation, Wendell W., PA, 7978
McMullan Family Foundation, James and Madeleine, IL, 2726
McMullan Foundation, James and Milton, IL, see 2726
McMurtrie Foundation, Lucy J., RI, 8342
McMurtrie Scholarship Fund, RI, see 8342
McNair Educational Foundation, Robert and Janice, NC, 6763
McNair Memorial Fund Trust, John F., NC, 6764
McNaught Scholarship Fund, Dr. Francis, NC, 6765
McNaught Scholarship Fund, Grace I. McNaught-Dr. Francis, NC, see 6765
McNay Educational Trust, Harry & Winnie, NE, 5232
McNeil Scholarship Fund, Roy and Yvonne, AZ, 216
McNeil Scholarship Trust, John N. McNeil and Stella, PA, 7979
McPherson Church of Christ Scholarship and Charitable Trust, KS, 3483
McPherson County Community Foundation, KS, 3484
McPherson Trust, R. S., MI, 4530
McQuinn Scholarship Foundation, Margaret L., CA, 780
McRae Scholarship Charity, Gertrude L., NC, 6766
McRoberts Memorial Law Scholarship Fund, PA, 7980
McVinney Foundation for Religious Vocations, Bishop Russell J., RI, 8343
McWilliams Trust, Ed and Patricia, Inc., AZ, 217

MDC, Inc., NC, 6767
MDF, CA, see 812
Mead Educational Trust, Beth R., TX, 8949
Mead Scholarship Trust, Edwin Budge, FL, 1973
Meade Memorial Science Fund, IL, 2727
Meador Scholarship Trust, L. & M., FL, 1974
Meat Cutters Educational Trust, TX, see 9141
Mecklenburg Bar Foundation, NC, 6768
MedEvac Foundation International, VA, 9433
Media Alliance, CA, 781
Media Arts Center San Diego, CA, 782
Media Religion and Culture Project, The, TX, 8950
Medical Association of Georgia Foundation, Inc., GA, 2211
Medical Education Foundation in Gynecology & Obstetrics, MD, 3878
Medical Foundation of North Carolina, Inc., The, NC, 6769
Medical Foundation, The, MA, see 4101
Medical Library Association, IL, 2728
Medical University of Ohio Foundation, OH, see 7398
Medline Foundation, The, IL, 2729
MEED, CO, see 1240
Meehan Family Foundation, WI, 9963
Meehan Foundation, Daniel E., Inc., WI, see 9963
MEEMIC Foundation for the Future of Education, MI, 4531
Megaloudis Foundation, Nicole, The, FL, 1975
Mehaffy Foundation, Amy E., Inc., The, KS, 3485
Meharg Scholarship Trust, Lena Y., AL, 61
Mehta Family Foundation, Bhupat and Jyott, TX, see 8951
Mehta Family Foundation, The, TX, 8951
Meier Scholarship Trust, J. Ralph and Gladys, IA, 3336
Meiller Educational Trust, Lucy E., FL, 1976
Melanoma Research Alliance Foundation, DC, 1676
Melanoma Research Foundation, DC, 1677
Melissa Fund, Inc., WI, 9964
Mellinger Educational Foundation, Edward Arthur, Inc., IL, 2730
Mellinger Medical Research Memorial Fund, Ralph &. Rose, PA, A
Mellinger Scholarship Fund, Gertrude & Clarence, PA, see 7981
Mellinger Scholarship Fund, PA, 7981
MELMAC Education Foundation, ME, 3718
Melton Arts Foundation, The, VA, see 9509
Melton Foundation, VA, 9434
Melville House Inc., NY, 6206
Memorial Foundation for Jewish Culture, Inc., NY, 6207
Memorial Foundation, CA, see 915
Memorial Health Foundation, Inc., IN, 3113
Memorial Hospital Foundation, Inc., MD, 3879
Memorial Scholarship Foundation of the Music Teachers Association of California, Alameda County Branch, CA, 783
Memorial Scholarship Foundation of the Rotary Club of Westminster, Maryland in Memory of Colonel Sherman E. Flanagan, Jr., MD, 3880
Memorial Scholarship of Henry Groth Elsinor Groth and Wayne Elder, WA, 9674
Memorial Scholarship, Laura's Galik, NY, 6208
Menard Memorial Scholarship Fund, Becky, The, OH, 7238
Menasha Corporation Foundation, WI, 9965
Mendenhall-Tyson Scholarship Foundation, PA, 7982
Meninak Charity Foundation Trust, FL, 1977
Meninak Foundation of Jacksonville, FL, see 1977
Menlo Park-Atherton Education Foundation, CA, 784
Menn Foundation, Gregory, IL, 2731
Mensa Education and Research Foundation, TX, 8952
Mental Health Association of Montgomery County, MD, Inc., MD, 3881
Mental Health Foundation, The, NY, see 6000
Mentors, Inc., DC, 1678
Mentzer Memorial Foundation, OH, 7239
Mentzer Memorial Trust, Charles T., OH, see 7239
Mentzer Trust, John P., WI, 9966
Merage Foundation for U.S.- Israel Trade, CA, 785
Meraux Charitable Foundation, Arlene & Joseph, Inc., LA, 3669
Mercer County Civic Foundation, Inc., The, OH, 7240

Mercer Texas A & M Educational Foundation, Vandal and Winifred, The, TX, 8953
Merchant and Ivory Foundation, Ltd., NY, 6209
Merck Institute for Science Education, Inc., NJ, 5504
Merck Patient Assistance Program, Inc., NJ, 5505
Merck-Schering Plough Patient Assistance Program, Inc., NJ, A
Mercy Foundation, Inc., OR, 7604
Mercy Health Partners Foundation, Inc., TN, 8619
Mercy Hospital Foundation, CA, 786
Mercy Regional Foundation, OH, 7241
Meredith, Jr. Foundation, Thomas C., NC, 6770
Meriden Foundation, The, CT, 1421
Meriden Record Journal Foundation, RI, 8344
Merrick Foundation, Inc., NE, 5233
Merry Basketball Scholarship Fund, Bryan, CO, 1238
Mesa Angels Foundation, Inc., AZ, 218
Meserve Memorial Fund, Albert & Helen C., NC, 6771
Meso Foundation, VA, see 9435
Mesothelioma Applied Research Foundation, Inc., The, VA, 9435
Messenger of Salvation, OK, 7494
Metamora Community Foundation, IL, 2732
Methodist Foundation of Santa Monica, CA, 787
Methodist Healthcare Foundation, TN, 8620
Methodist Healthcare Ministries of South Texas, Inc., TX, 8954
Methodist Hospital, MN, 4795
Methodist Hospital, TX, 8955
Methodist Medical Center of Oak Ridge, TN, see 8621
Methodist Medical Center, TN, 8621
MetLife Foundation, NY, 6210
Metro United Way, Inc., KY, 3596
Metropolitan Center for the Visual Arts, MD, 3882
Metropolitan Development Council, WA, 9675
Metropolitan Inter-Faith Association, TN, 8622
Metropolitan Museum of Art, The, NY, 6211
Metropolitan Opera Association, Inc., NY, 6212
MetroWest Community Health Care Foundation, Inc., MA, see 4173
MetroWest Health Foundation, MA, 4173
Metzger Scholarship Fund, Stella E., NY, 6213
Metzner Memorial Fund, Lee W., WI, 9967
Mexican American Legal Defense and Educational Fund, CA, 788
Mexico Foundation, CA, 789
Meyer Foundation, Charles, TX, 8956
Meyer Foundation, Roy E. and Merle, MN, 4796
Meyer Scholarship Trust, Paul & Regina, MO, 5049
Meyers Foundation, Allen H. and Nydia, MI, 4532
Meyers Foundation, Allen H., MI, see 4532
MFA Foundation, MO, 5050
MGM Charitable/Scholarship Foundation, KY, 3597
MHA Center for Education, MO, 5051
Miami County Foundation, OH, 7242
Miami Foundation, The, FL, 1978
Miami Jewish Federation, Greater, Inc., FL, 1979
MICDS Scholarship Fund, MO, 5052
Miceli-Wings of Hope Foundation, Justin Samela, The, CT, 1422
Michaels Foundation, Fern, Inc., NJ, 5506
Michaels Scholarship Fund, Frank J., PA, 7983
Michaud Charitable Trust, Howard and Espa, The, OH, 7243
Michaud Charitable Trust, The, OH, see 7243
Michels Charitable Foundation, Steven R., WI, 9968
Michels Family Educational Trust, IA, 3337
Michels Fellowship Foundation, Ronald G., Inc., MD, 3883
Michelson Science Scholarship Trust, Kathryn J., WI, 9969
Michigan Accountancy Foundation, MI, 4533
Michigan Agri-Business Association Educational Trust Fund, MI, 4534
Michigan Agri-Dealers Educational Trust, MI, see 4534
Michigan Dental Foundation, MI, 4535
Michigan Education Association Scholarship Fund, MI, 4536
Michigan Elks Association Charitable Grant Fund, MI, 4537
Michigan Gateway Community Foundation, MI, 4538

Michigan Health Care Education and Research Foundation/MHCERF, MI, *see* 4363

Michigan Masonic Charitable Foundation, MI, 4539

Michigan Masonic Home Charitable Foundation, MI, *see* 4539

Michigan Minority Business Development Council, Inc., MI, 4540

Michner Educational Foundation, Joseph & Lottie, MI, 4541

Mid Atlantic Arts Foundation, MD, 3884

Mid-America Arts Alliance, MO, 5053

Mid-Atlantic Securities Traders Foundation, Inc., The, MD, 3885

Mid-Columbia Health Foundation, OR, 7605

Mid-Cumberland Community Action Agency, Inc., TN, 8623

Mid-Nebraska Community Foundation, Inc., NE, 5234

Mid-Shore Community Foundation, Inc., MD, 3887

Middle East Fellowship, MD, 3886

Middle Tennessee State University Foundation, TN, 8624

Middlesex County Medical Society Foundation, NJ, 5507

Middlesex Savings Charitable Foundation, Inc., MA, 4174

Middleton Fund, Kate Kinloch, AL, 62

Middleton Trust, Ambrose, OH, 7244

Middletown Community Foundation, OH, 7245

Midland Area Community Foundation, MI, 4542

Midland Community Club Scholarship Foundation, NC, 6772

Midland Foundation, MI, *see* 4542

Midland ISD Educational Foundation, TX, 8957

Midmark Foundation, OH, 7246

Midwest Foundaton for Higher Education, NE, 5235

Miedema Trust, Madeline, CA, 790

Mihos Youth Foundation, Christina M., MA, 4175

Mijangos, Jr. Foundation, Dr. Jose Antonio, NY, 6214

Mike Venner Memorial Scholarship Fund, Inc., MT, 5162

Mikhashoff Trust for New Music, Yvar, NY, 6215

Mikkelson Foundation, The, CO, 1239

Mikovich Community Foundation, Daniel and Josephine, Inc., PA, 7984

Milburn Trust, Weaver Milburn, Jr. and Lenore Pauline, IL, 2733

Miles Educational Foundation, MO, 5054

Miles HSSF Trust, Alice W., RI, 8345

Miles Trust High School Scholarship, Alice W., RI, *see* 8345

Miley Foundation, Mary Clarke, Inc., OK, 7495

Milford Chamber of Commerce Trust Fund, CT, 1423

Milford Hospital, Inc., CT, 1424

Milheim Foundation for Cancer Research, OR, *see* 7682

Military Ex-Prisoners of War Foundation, Inc., NC, 6773

Military Officers Association of America Scholarship Fund, The, VA, 9436

Military Women In Need Foundation, CA, 791

Milken Family Foundation, The, CA, 792

Millar Scholarship Fund, TX, 8958

Millard Foundation, PA, A

Millay Colony for the Arts, Inc., The, NY, 6216

Miller Charitable Trust, Colin & Mary, PA, 7985

Miller Education Foundation, Larry H., UT, 9220

Miller Family Charitable Foundation, Inc., FL, 1980

Miller Family Foundation, J. William & Lorraine M., OH, 7247

Miller Foundation, Arnold M. & Sydell L., OH, *see* 7249

Miller Foundation, Don, PA, 7986

Miller Foundation, Dr. William R., OH, 7248

Miller Foundation, Howard, MI, 4543

Miller Foundation, M. W. and Fair, Inc., The, TX, 8959

Miller Foundation, Sydell & Arnold, The, OH, 7249

Miller Fund of the American Society of Journalists and Authors Charitable Trust, Llewellyn, The, NY, *see* 5707

Miller Fund, Arthur M., TX, 8960

Miller Nursing Scholarship, John R., PA, 7987

Miller Scholarship Foundation, Jayne L., OH, 7250

Miller Scholarship Fund, Morey and Helen McCarthy, RI, 8346

Miller Scholarship Fund, Perry W. & Lucy Compton, KY, 3598

Miller Scholarship Trust, Ed & Edith, PA, 7988

Miller Scholarship Trust, IL, 2734

Miller Scholarship Trust, Lila, TX, 8961

Miller Trust Fund for Education, Daniel R., NC, 6774

Miller Trust, F. Roger, RI, 8347

Miller Trust, George W. and Wilma F., IL, 2735

Miller Trust, Sadie H., NJ, 5508

Millhollon Educational Trust Estate, Nettie, TX, 8962

Millman Foundation, Dr. Max & Ida L., MA, 4176

Mills Foundation, Ethan A., The, OK, 7496

Mills Scholarship Foundation, Casper, CA, 793

Mills Scholarship Trust, Thomas and Lois, NY, 6217

Mills Trust B, William R., CA, 794

Mills Trust, Clinton G., RI, 8348

Mills-Peninsula Hospital Foundation, CA, 795

Milne Foundation, Hilda and Raymond, WY, 10114

Milotte Scholarship Fund, Alfred G. & Elma M., TX, 8963

Milroy Foundation, James Forsythe, OH, 7251

Milton Society for the Blind, John, MA, 4177

Milton-Freewater Area Foundation, WA, 9676

Milwaukee Jewish Federation, Inc., WI, 9970

Milwaukee Times Louvenia Johnson Journalism Scholarship Fund, WI, 9971

Minbanc Foundation, Inc., DC, 1679

Minear Educational Trust, Ruth M., PA, 7989

Mink Education Foundation for Low Income Women & Children, Patsy Takemoto, HI, 2304

Minner Family Charitable Foundation, IL, 2736

Minnesota American Legion Auxiliary Brain Science Foundation, MN, *see* 4797

Minnesota American Legion, Auxiliary & The Sons of The American Legion Brain Science Foundation, MN, 4797

Minnesota Business Partnership, MN, 4798

Minnesota Center for Book Arts, MN, 4799

Minnesota Licensed Family Child Care Association, Inc., MN, 4800

Minnesota Medical Foundation, MN, 4801

Minnesota Ovarian Cancer Alliance, MN, 4802

Minnesota P.E.O. Home Fund, MN, 4803

Minnesota Power Foundation, MN, 4804

Minnesota Section PGA Foundation, MN, 4805

Minnesota Valley Action Council, Inc., MN, 4806

Minnesota Zoo Foundation, MN, 4807

Minnesouri Scholarship Foundation, MO, 5055

Minor and Asalie M. Preston Educational Fund, Rives C., Inc., VA, 9437

Minor Foundation, Berkeley Minor and Susan F., The, WV, 9802

Minority Enterprise & Educational Development, CO, 1240

Minority Health Professions Education Foundation, CA, *see* 651

Minot Rotary Scholarship Foundation, ND, 6945

Minton Educational Fund, Helen Lancaster, MI, 4544

Minyard Founders Foundation, TX, 8964

Miracle Flights For Kids, NV, 5294

Miracle Hill Ministries, Inc., SC, 8494

Miracle-Ear Children's Foundation, MN, 4808

Miracles of Mitch Foundation, MN, 4809

Mishler Memorial Trust, Ruth, OR, 7606

Mishou Scholarship Fund Trust, Aimee & Frank, OH, 7252

Miss Alabama Pageant, Inc., The, AL, 63

Miss Arizona Scholarship Foundation, AZ, 219

Miss Connecticut Scholarship Corporation, CT, 1425

Miss Massachusetts Scholarship Foundation, MA, 4178

Mission Healthcare Foundation, Inc., NC, 6775

Mission Metroplex, Inc., TX, 8965

Missionary Emergency Fund, VA, 9438

Missionary Enterprises, CA, 796

Mississippi Bar Foundation, Inc., MS, 4914

Mississippi Society of Certified Public Accountants Foundation, MS, 4915

Missouri Bar Foundation, MO, 5056

Missouri Chamber of Commerce Educational Foundation, Inc., MO, A

Missouri Federation of Music Clubs, MO, 5057

Missouri Ozarks Community Action, Inc., MO, 5058

Missouri State University Foundation, MO, 5059

Missouri Valley Community Action Agency, MO, 5060

Mitchell Foundation, Bruce, ID, 2342

Mitchell Foundation, Everett W. & Marion E., MA, 4179

Mitchell Foundation, Joan, Inc., The, NY, 6218

Mitchell Medical Scholarship Fund Inc., Cynthia Asplund, WI, 9972

Mitchell Scholarship, Cleo Lawson, VA, 9439

Mitchell, Jr. Trust Scholarship Fund, Oscar, MN, *see* 4891

Mitchell-Gantz Educational & Charitable Trust, CA, 797

Mitchelson Foundation, Inc., The, KS, 3486

Mitsui U.S.A. Foundation, The, NY, 6219

Mittal Steel USA Foundation, Inc., IL, *see* 2406

MMAC Community Support Foundation, Inc., WI, 9973

Moakley Charitable Foundation, John Joseph, Inc., MA, 4180

Moberley F H Scholarship Trust, KS, 3487

Mobile Medical Mission Hospital, Inc., MS, 4916

MOCA, MN, *see* 4802

Mochary Family Foundation Corp., Kasser, NJ, 5509

Mock Perpetual Memorial Scholarship Fund, John & Mary, OR, 7607

MoCo Arts, NH, *see* 5351

Modern Poetry Association, The, IL, *see* 2795

Modest Needs Foundation, NY, 6220

Modesto Rotary Club Foundation, CA, 798

Modesto Union Gospel Mission, Inc., CA, 799

Modglin Family Foundation, The, CA, 800

Modoc Scholarship Fund, Inc., CA, 801

Moeschle Scholarship Fund, Cecile, AL, 64

Mohawk Valley Community Action Agency, Inc., NY, 6221

Mohn Memorial Foundation, Ryan Lee, PA, 7990

Mohr Memorial Trust, Victor, OH, 7253

Molalla Rotary Foundation, OR, 7608

Moline Foundation, The, IL, 2737

Moll Scholarship Trust, Vida June, AR, 291

Molloy Scholarship Fund, Mary, CO, 1241

Molloy Scholarship Trust Fund, Michael A., MA, 4181

Momeni Foundation, FL, 1981

Monahan and Alberta W. Laighton Memorial Fund, Margaret B., NY, *see* 6222

Monahan-Laighton Memorial Fund, NY, 6222

Monarch Cement Co. Academic Achievement Award, KS, *see* 3488

Monarch Cement Company Academic Achievement Award, The, KS, 3488

Money for Women Barbara Deming Memorial Fund, Inc., NH, 5347

Mongan Trust, Carroll C., IA, 3338

Monger Scholarship Fund, NC, 6776

Monius Institute, A.M., Inc., NJ, *see* 5386

Monk Institute of Jazz, Thelonious, DC, 1680

Monroe 2 Orleans Educational Foundation, Inc., NY, 6223

Monroe Foundation, Inc., AK, 125

Monroe Welfare Foundation, GA, 2212

Monroeville Christian Judea Foundation, The, PA, 7991

Montague Charitable Trust, Charles E., RI, 8349

Montalvo Arts Center, CA, 802

Montalvo Association, CA, *see* 802

Montana Community Foundation, MT, 5163

Montana State University Billings Foundation, MT, 5164

Montclair Fund for Educational Excellence, Inc., NJ, 5510

Monterey Bay Marine Sanctuary Foundation, CA, 803

Monterey County Association of Realtors, CA, 804

Montgomery Area Community Foundation, Inc., AL, *see* 20

Montgomery Area Food Bank, Inc., AL, 65

Montgomery Child Care Association, Inc., MD, 3888

Montgomery County Community Foundation, IN, 3114

Montgomery County Community Foundation, TX, 8966

Montgomery Foundation, Anita Card, ME, 3719

Moody Foundation, The, TX, 8967

Moomaw Scholarship Fund, Dewey H. and Irene G., OH, 7254

Moon Scholarship Foundation, Jack, MN, 4810

Moore Center Services, Inc., NH, 5348

Moore Charitable Foundation, James B., IN, 3115

Moore Charitable Foundation, Orlene Drobisch, PA, 7992

Moore Charitable Scholarship Trust, N. Robert, PA, 7993

Moore Company Foundation, The, RI, *see* 8423

Moore Educational Foundation, Benjamin, Inc., NJ, A

Moore Foundation, Alfred, SC, 8495

Moore Foundation, Nat, Inc., The, FL, 1982

Moore Fund for American Opera, Douglas, Inc., The, NY, 6224

Moore Scholarship Foundation, Elsie B., PA, 7994

Moore Scholarship Fund Trust, Doris Floyd, NC, 6777

Moore Scholarship Fund, Arlene Goist, OH, 7255

Moore Scholarship Fund, Miles Wendell Moore and Geraldine, OR, 7609

Moore Scholarship Fund, Roy L. & Aleata M., KS, 3489

Moore Scholarship Trust, Billy J. and Christina R., IN, 3116

Moore Scholarship Trust, M. Eddie, MD, 3889

Moore Scholarship Trust, Seth & Mabelle, TX, 8968

Moore Scholarships, J. W. and Doris Floyd, NC, *see* 6777

Moore Trust, Mildred Jayne & H. J. Ham, WI, 9974

Moore, Jr. Charitable Trust, Aaron R., The, MD, 3890

Moorestown Education Foundation, NJ, 5511

Moorman Orphans Home, James, IN, 3117

Moraine Caddy Scholarship Fund, OH, 7256

Moran Religious Education Foundation, Maude M., IN, 3118

Moran Scholarship Trust, Edward & Sarah, MD, 3891

Morehead Foundation, John Motley, The, NC, *see* 6778

Morehead-Cain Foundation, The, NC, 6778

Morello Foundation, The, NJ, 5512

Morey Family Foundation, The, OR, 7610

Morey Foundation, The, MI, 4545

Morgan Citzenship Award Fund, Hardy & Bess, TX, 8969

Morgan Family Foundation, CO, 1242

Morgan Family Foundation, Inc., CA, 805

Morgan Foundation, John E., Inc., NY, 6225

Morgan Irrevocable Trust No. 1, Thomas D., KS, 3490

Morgan Memorial Fund, Griffith D., PA, 7995

Morgan Memorial Scholarship Fund, A. D. & A. L., VA, 9440

Morgan Scholarship Fund, Harvey, WV, *see* 9803

Morgan Stanley Foundation, Inc., NY, 6226

Morgan Stanley Foundation, NY, *see* 6226

Morgan-Robertson Memorial Scholarship Fund, WV, 9803

Morre Research Inc., Harvey H. and Donna M., IN, 3119

Morrill Fund, J. L., KY, 3599

Morrill Fund, Louisa S., KY, 3600

Morrill Scholarship Fund, James K., MI, 4546

Morris Animal Foundation, CO, 1243

Morris Educational Foundation, Muriel M., CA, 806

Morris Family Foundation, Winifred, FL, 1983

Morrison Education Foundation, NE, 5236

Morrison Education Foundation, NE, *see* 5236

Morrison Foundation, Glenn W. & Hazelle Paxson, Inc., FL, 1984

Morrison Foundation, IL, 2738

Morrison Foundation, Ollege and Minnie, IL, *see* 2738

Morrison Trust, TX, 8970

Morrow Scholarship Trust, Darthea, RI, 8350

Morrow-Stevens Foundation, VA, 9441

Morse Family Scholarship Fund, D. W., TX, 8971

Morse Fund, William A., NH, 5349

Morson Memorial Scholarship Fund, Hugh, NC, 6779

Mortar Board Alumni-Tolo Foundation, WA, 9677

Morton Foundation, Alan, NY, 6227

Morton Memorial Fund, Mark, IL, 2739

Morton Memorial Trust, Alice E., NH, 5350

MOS, MD, *see* 3874

Moses Educational Fund, Harvey H. & Catherine Allis, RI, 8351

Moses, David E., PA, *see* 8172

Moss Educational & Charitable Trust, Joseph R., SC, 8496

Mote Marine Laboratory, Inc., FL, 1985

Motion Picture & Television Fund, CA, 807

Motry Memorial Fund, Paul, OH, 7257

Moulton Scholarship Fund, Harold E., RI, 8352

Moulton Scholarship Fund, Helen W., RI, *see* 8352

Mount Angel Community Foundation, OR, 7611

Mount Clemens Regional Health Care Foundation, MI, 4547

Mount Dora Center for the Arts, FL, 1986

Mount Dora Community Trust, FL, 1987

Mount Pleasant Area Community Foundation, MI, 4548

Mount Pleasant Community Foundation, MI, *see* 4548

Mount Sinai Medical Center Foundation, Inc., FL, 1988

Mount Vernon/Knox County Community Trust, The, OH, *see* 7059

Mountain Projects, Inc., NC, 6780

Mountain Protective Association Scholarship Fund, CO, 1244

Mountain West Track & Field Club, Inc., The, MT, 5165

Mountaintop Foundation, The, WV, 9804

Mouser Foundation, Jerry Don, TX, 8972

Movement Research, Inc., NY, 6228

Moving Company Dance Center, NH, 5351

Moving Image, Inc., The, NY, 6229

Moyer Brothers Educational Trust, KS, 3491

Moyer Charitable Trust, Marilyn, OR, 7612

Moyer Scholarship Fund, William and Louise, The, PA, 7996

Moyer, Jr. Scholarship Foundation, A. Marlyn, PA, 7997

MRF, DC, *see* 1677

MRG, OR, *see* 7603

MS Foundation, FL, *see* 1989

MSET, MD, *see* 3875

MSRI, CA, *see* 776

MTI, ME, *see* 3715

MTNT Foundation, Inc., AK, 126

Muhlenbruck Foundation, Kenneth, Inc., NY, 6230

Muir Health, John, CA, 808

Mulford Scholarship Foundation, Louis K., The, CO, 1245

Mullenbach Memorial Foundation, Sarah, Inc., WI, 9975

Multiple Myeloma Research Foundation, Inc., The, CT, 1426

Multiple Sclerosis Foundation, Inc., FL, 1989

Multnomah Athletic Foundation, Inc., OR, 7613

Muncie Civic & College Symphony Association, Inc., IN, 3120

Munger Scholarship Fund, Henry J. & Marie, CT, 1427

Munger, Jr. Foundation, Robert L., OH, 7258

Munoz Foundation, Anthony, OH, *see* 6954

Munro Scholarship Trust, Grant, OH, 7259

Munson Foundation, W. B., IL, 2740

Munson Fund, William J., RI, 8353

Munson Scholarship Fund, John P., TX, 8973

Munson Trust, Elsie H., IA, 3339

Munster & Adele Blake Scholarship Trust, Julia Blake, WI, *see* 9976

Munster Medical Foundation, Inc., IN, *see* 3007

Munster Scholarship Trust, WI, 9976

Munter Charitable Trust, Duane & Evelyn, IA, 3340

Munyon Scholarship Trust, Julian M., AR, 292

Murdock Educational Trust, Irene, KS, 3492

Murphy Education Program, Inc., AR, 293

Murphy Foundation, M. W., AR, 294

Murphy Foundation, Mercedes, TX, 8974

Murphy Foundation, The, AR, 295

Murphy Jr. Trust, Sam, KY, 3601

Murphy Jr., Charitable Trust, Mary E. Murphy and John F., The, MA, 4182

Murphy Memorial Fund, M. Catherine, PA, 7998

Murphy Oil Corporation Contributions Program, AR, 296

Murphy Residuary Trust, T. R., OH, 7260

Murphy Scholarship Fund, Daniel, IL, 2741

Murphy Scholarship Trust, Dennis L. & Hildreth M., IA, 3341

Murphy Scholarship Trust, OH, 7261

Murray Fine Arts Educational Fund, Albert K., The, OH, 7262

Murray Memorial Scholarship Trust Fund, William H., FL, 1990

Murray Scholarship Fund, F. Leo Murray & Irene D., MA, 4183

Murray Trust, IA, 3342

Murray XII Trust, IA, *see* 3342

Muscular Dystrophy Association, Inc., AZ, 220

Museum of Fine Arts, Houston, The, TX, 8975

Museum of Fine Arts, MA, 4184

Museum of Glass, WA, 9678

Museum of Science, MA, 4185

Music Associates of Aspen, Inc., CO, 1246

Music Drives Us, MA, *see* 3990

Music Foundation of San Antonio, Inc., TX, 8976

Music Foundation of Southwest Florida, The, FL, 1991

Music Maker Relief Foundation, Inc., NC, 6781

Musical Research Society Endowment, OK, A

Musicares Foundation, Inc., CA, 809

Musicians Emergency Fund Inc., NY, 6231

Musicians Emergency Relief Fund-Local 802, NY, 6232

Musicians Foundation, Inc., NY, 6233

Muskegon County Community Foundation, Inc., MI, *see* 4391

Muskingum County Community Foundation, OH, 7263

Mussina Foundation, Mike, PA, 7999

Mustang Foundation, TX, 8977

Mustard Seed Foundation, Inc., VA, 9442

Mustard Seed Foundation, The, KY, 3602

Muth Basketball Scholarship Fund, Mike, SC, 8497

Mutual After Life Foundation, The, CA, 810

Mutual Service Foundation, IL, 2742

MVP Foundation, TX, 8978

My Child's Hand Foundation Trust, CT, 1428

Myasthenia Gravis Foundation of America, Inc., NY, 6234

Mycenaean Foundation, NY, 6235

Myers Charitable Trust, NC, *see* 6783

Myers Church Scholarship, OH, 7264

Myers Memorial Scholarship Trust, G., OH, 7265

Myers Oceanographic & Marine Biology Trust, CA, 811

Myers Scholarship Fund, Malcolm W. & Anna G., NC, 6782

Myers Trust, NC, 6783

Myers-Ti-Caro Foundation, Inc., NC, *see* 6657

Myotonic Dystrophy Foundation, CA, 812

N Foundation, Inc., The, NY, 6236

N.C.E.C.A., CO, *see* 1247

NAA Foundation, VA, *see* 9464

NAACP Legal Defense and Education Fund, Inc., NY, 6237

NAAF, CA, *see* 814

NAASO, The Obesity Society, MD, *see* 3904

Nabors Charitable Foundation, TX, 8979

NABT, VA, *see* 9444

NACCRRA, VA, *see* 9445

NACME, NY, *see* 6241

Nadeau & Louise E. Nelson Scholarship Foundation, Stella M. Nelson, MT, 5166

Nadeau & Louise E. Nelson Senft Scholarship Foundation, Stella M. Nelson, MT, *see* 5166

Naftzger Fund for Fine Arts, KS, 3493

Nahas Educational Scholarship Foundation, Robert T., ID, 2343

NAHJ, DC, *see* 1685

NALAC, TX, *see* 8982

Nall Scholarship Fund, Campbell E., Inc., FL, 1992

NAMM Foundation, CA, 813

NAMT, NY, *see* 6242

Nansemond Charitable Foundation, Inc., VA, 9443

Nantucket Community Music Center, MA, 4186

Nantucket Island School of Design and the Arts, Inc., MA, 4187

NAPA Valley Student Enrichment Program, CA, *see* 633

Naples Educational Foundation Inc., Richard T., OH, 7266

Naples Woman's Club, Inc., FL, 1993

Naples Yacht Club Blue Gavel Scholarship Fund, FL, 1994

Nara Bank Scholarship Foundation, The, CA, *see* 406

NARAS Foundation, The, CA, *see* 635

NARM Scholarship Foundation, Inc., NJ, 5513

NARSAD Research Institute, Inc., NY, 6238

NARSAD: The World's Leading Charity Dedicated to Mental Health Research, NY, 6239

NAS, DC, *see* 1683

NASA College Scholarship Fund, Inc., TX, 8980

NASB Foundation, Inc., MO, 5061

NASD Investor Education Foundation, DC, *see* 1626

NASDAQ OMX Group Educational Foundation, Inc., MD, 3892

Nasdaq Stock Marked Educational Foundation, Inc., The, MD, see 3892

Nash Scholarship Fund, Clayton, RI, 8354

Nashville CARES, Inc., TN, 8625

Nashville Community Foundation, Inc., TN, see 8579

Nashville Predators Foundation, TN, 8626

Nashville Rescue Mission, TN, 8627

NASS, IL, see 2758

NASSP, VA, see 9446

Nation Foundation, TX, 8981

National Academy Foundation, NY, 6240

National Academy of Education, The, DC, 1681

National Academy of Engineering Fund, DC, 1682

National Academy of Sciences, DC, 1683

National Academy of Social Insurance, DC, 1684

National Action Council for Minorities in Engineering, Inc., NY, 6241

National Alliance for Musical Theatre, Inc., NY, 6242

National Alliance for Research on Schizophrenia and Depression, NY, see 6239

National Alopecia Areata Foundation, CA, 814

National Arts Club, The, NY, 6243

National Association for Public Interest Law, DC, see 1622

National Association of Asian Professionals, Inc., The, NY, 6244

National Association of Biology Teachers, Inc., VA, 9444

National Association of Child Care Resource & Referral Agencies, VA, 9445

National Association of Hispanic Journalists, DC, 1685

National Association of Insurance Women (International) Education Foundation, NC, see 6712

National Association of Latino Arts and Culture, TX, 8982

National Association of Retail Druggists, VA, see 9450

National Association of Secondary School Principals, VA, 9446

National Athletic Trainers Association Research and Education Foundation, Inc., TX, 8983

National Automobile Dealers Charitable Foundation, VA, 9447

National Blood Foundation Research and Education Trust Fund, MD, 3893

National Board for Professional Teaching Standards, Inc., VA, 9448

National Breast Cancer Coalition Fund, DC, 1686

National Business Education Association, VA, 9449

National Cancer Center, Inc., NY, 6245

National Center for Creative Aging, DC, 1687

National Charity League, Inc., CA, 815

National Charity League-Newport Chapter, CA, 816

National Child Labor Committee, NY, 6246

National Children's Cancer Society, Inc., MO, 5062

National Christian Charitable Foundation, Inc., GA, 2213

National Collegiate Athletic Association, IN, 3121

National Community Pharmacists Association Foundation, VA, 9450

National Consortium for Graduate Degrees for Minorities in Engineering and Science, Inc., VA, 9451

National Council of Jewish Women - New York Section, NY, 6247

National Council of Teachers of Mathematics, VA, 9452

National Council of YMCAs of the USA, IL, 2743

National Council on Crime and Delinquency, CA, 817

National Council on Education for the Ceramic Arts, CO, 1247

National Court Reporters Foundation, VA, 9453

National Credit Union Foundation, Inc., DC, 1688

National Down Syndrome Society, NY, 6248

National Eating Disorders Association, NY, 6249

National Electronic Museum, Inc., MD, 3894

National Endowment for the Arts, DC, 1689

National Environmental Education & Training Foundation, Inc., The, DC, see 1690

National Environmental Education Foundation, DC, 1690

National F.F.A. Organization, IN, see 3040

National Fallen Firefighters Foundation, MD, 3895

National FFA Foundation, Inc., IN, 3122

National Fire Protection Association, MA, 4188

National Fish and Wildlife Foundation, DC, 1691

National Football Foundation and College Hall of Fame, Inc., The, TX, 8984

National Football League Alumni, Inc., NJ, 5514

National Forest Foundation, MT, 5167

National Foundation for Advancement in the Arts, FL, see 1997

National Foundation for Cancer Research, MD, 3896

National Foundation for Ectodermal Dysplasias, IL, 2744

National Foundation for Infectious Diseases, The, MD, 3897

National Foundation for Transplants, Inc., TN, 8628

National Foundation, Inc., CO, 1248

National Fragile X Foundation, The, CA, 818

National G.E.M. Consortium, VA, see 9451

National Gaucher Care Foundation, Inc., MD, 3898

National Geographic Society, DC, 1692

National Guard Youth Foundation, VA, 9454

National Gymnastics Foundation, IN, 3123

National Headache Foundation, IL, 2745

National Hemophilia Foundation, The, NY, 6250

National Humanities Center, NC, 6784

National Institute for the Food Service Industry, IL, see 2749

National Intercollegiate Rodeo Foundation, WA, 9679

National Italian American Foundation, Inc., DC, 1693

National Kidney Foundation of Florida, Inc., FL, 1995

National Kidney Foundation of Hawaii, HI, 2305

National Kidney Foundation of Illinois, Inc., IL, 2746

National Kidney Foundation of Indiana, Inc., IN, 3124

National Kidney Foundation of Louisiana, Inc., LA, 3670

National Kidney Foundation of Maryland, Inc., MD, 3899

National Kidney Foundation of Michigan, Inc., MI, 4549

National Kidney Foundation, Inc., NY, 6251

National League for Nursing, Inc., DC, 1694

National Lung Cancer Partnership, WI, 9977

National Machinery Foundation Inc., OH, 7267

National Medical Association, Inc., MD, 3900

National Medical Fellowships, Inc., NY, 6252

National Merit Scholarship Corporation, IL, 2747

National Military Family Association, VA, 9455

National Multiple Sclerosis Society - Delaware Chapter, DE, 1517

National Multiple Sclerosis Society - Greater Illinois Chapter, IL, 2748

National Multiple Sclerosis Society Michigan Chapter, Inc., MI, 4550

National Multiple Sclerosis Society Northern California Chapter, The, CA, 819

National Multiple Sclerosis Society, Central New England Chapter, MA, 4189

National Multiple Sclerosis Society, Lone Star Chapter, TX, 8985

National Multiple Sclerosis Society, Minnesota Chapter, MN, 4811

National Multiple Sclerosis Society, NY, 6253

National Multiple Sclerosis Society, Southern California Chapter, CA, 820

National Neurofibromatosis Foundation, Inc., NY, see 5851

National Niemann-Pick Disease Foundation, Inc., WI, 9978

National Organization for Hearing Research Foundation, PA, 8000

National Organization for Rare Disorders, Inc., CT, 1429

National Osteopathic Foundation, IL, see 2386

National Parkinson Foundation, Inc., FL, 1996

National Patient Safety Foundation, MA, 4190

National Physical Science Consortium, CA, 821

National Press Foundation, Inc., DC, 1695

National Psoriasis Foundation, Inc., OR, 7614

National Psychiatric Endowment Fund, Inc., MD, see 3862

National Relief Charities, TX, 8986

National Restaurant Association Educational Foundation, IL, 2749

National Rosacea Society, IL, 2750

National Safety Council, IL, 2751

National Science and Technology Education Partnership, VA, 9456

National Science Teachers Association, VA, 9457

National Sculpture Society, Inc., NY, 6254

National Society Daughters of the American Revolution, DC, 1696

National Society of Collegiate Scholars, DC, 1697

National Society of Fund Raising Executives, VA, see 9321

National Society of Professional Engineers Educational Foundation, VA, 9458

National Society of Professional Engineers, VA, see 9458

National Society of the Daughters of the American Revolution, North Carolina, NC, see 6903

National Society to Prevent Blindness, IL, 2752

National Storytelling Membership Association, TN, 8629

National Storytelling Network, TN, see 8629

National Student Achievement Awards, DC, 1698

National Transplant Assistance Fund, Inc., PA, 8001

National Trust for Historic Preservation in the United States, DC, 1699

National Urban Fellows, Inc., NY, 6255

National Urea Cycle Disorders Foundation, CA, 822

National Wildlife Federation, VA, 9459

National YoungArts Foundation, FL, 1997

Native American Heritage Association, SD, 8537

Native Arts and Cultures Foundation, WA, 9680

NATSO Foundation, The, VA, 9460

Nauheim/Straus Charitable Foundation, Inc., CA, 823

Navarro Family Foundation, Inc., CT, see 1364

Navy Marine Coast Guard Residence Foundation, Inc., VA, 9461

Navy Supply Corps Foundation, Inc., GA, 2214

Navy-Marine Corps Relief Society, VA, 9462

NBCCF, DC, see 1686

NC Beautiful, NC, see 6729

NC Foundation for Advanced Health Programs, Inc., NC, 6785

NC Foundation for Public School Children, NC, 6786

NC HEF, NC, see 6787

NC Hospitality Education Foundation, NC, 6787

NC LEAF, NC, see 6797

NC Medical Society Foundation, Inc., NC, 6788

NCAA, IN, see 3121

NCCA, DC, see 1687

NCCC Foundation, Inc., NY, 6256

NCPA Foundation, VA, see 9450

NCR Scholarship Foundation, GA, 2215

NCSTA, NC, see 6800

NCTM's Mathematics Education Trust (MET), VA, see 9452

NDCF, ND, see 6946

NEA Foundation for the Improvement of Education, The, DC, see 1700

NEA Foundation, DC, 1700

Neal Foundation, IL, 2753

Nearburg Foundation, Charles and Dana, The, TX, 8987

Nebraska Academy of Sciences, NE, 5237

Nebraska Cattlemen Research and Education Foundation, NE, 5238

Nebraska Community Foundation, NE, 5239

Nebraska Friends of Foster Children Foundation, NE, 5240

Nebraska Independent Film Projects, NE, 5241

Nebraska Medical Center, The, NE, 5242

Nebraska Medical Foundation, Inc., NE, 5243

Nebraska Methodist Hospital Foundation, NE, 5244

Nebraska Wesleyan University Theta Chi Scholarship Fund Inc., NE, 5245

Needham September 11th Scholarship Fund, NY, 6257

Needymeds, Inc., MA, 4191

Neel Scholarship Fund, Harold M. Neel and Katharine Klepinger, IN, 3125

NEFA, MA, see 4196

Neighborhood Centers, Inc., TX, 8988

Neighborhood Service Center, Inc., MD, 3901

Neighborimpact, OR, 7615

Neilson Foundation, Adeline L., WY, 10115

Neinken Scholarship Grant & Loan Foundation, Maurice A., NC, A

Nell Trust, Lawrence R., KS, 3494

Nelnet Foundation, NE, 5246

Nelson and Morgan Hand II Memorial Scholarship Fund, Cecelia Hand, NC, 6789

Nelson Foundation, Inc., WI, A

Nelson Foundation, Roy and Leona, WA, 9681

Nelson Scholarship Fund, Donald E. and Margaret L., MI, 4551

Nelson Scholarship Fund, Hazel T., KS, 3495

Nelson Scholarship Fund, Victor & Mary D., WI, 9979

Nelson Scholarship Fund, William H. & Helen L., AR, 297

Nelson Scholarships, Catherine Hayes, Inc., PA, 8002

Nepal Educational Fund, Inc., CA, 824

Nephcure Foundation, PA, 8003

Nesbitt Medical Student Foundation, IL, 2754

Neskowin Coast Foundation, OR, 7616

Neslab Charitable Foundation, NH, see 5312

Nestle USA, Inc. Corporate Giving Program, CA, 825

Nestor Foundation, Mary Margaret, PA, 8004

Nesty Charitable Trust, Ted & Anna, IN, 3126

Netherland-America Foundation, Inc., The, NY, 6258

Netzach Foundation, NY, 6259

Neuroradiology Education and Research Foundation, The, IL, see 2570

Nevada Community Foundation, Inc., NV, 5295

Nevada Women's Fund, NV, 5296

Neville Trust, Linda, IL, 2755

New Alternatives for Children, Inc., NY, 6260

New Bedford Port Society, Ladies Branch of the, MA, 4192

New Canaan Community Foundation, Inc., CT, 1430

New Common School Foundation, The, MI, 4552

New Day Foundation for Families, The, MI, 4553

New England Biolabs Foundation, MA, 4193

New England Education Society, MA, 4194

New England Farm Workers Council, Inc., MA, 4195

New England Foundation for the Arts, MA, 4196

New England Society in the City of Brooklyn, NY, 6261

New Glarus Masonic Lodge No. 310 Foundation, Inc., WI, 9980

New Hampshire Bar Foundation, NH, 5352

New Hampshire Charitable Foundation, NH, 5353

New Hampshire Food Industries Education Foundation, NH, 5354

New Hampshire Humanities Council, Inc., NH, 5355

New Haven Community Loan Fund, Greater, Inc., CT, 1431

New Horizons Foundation, CA, 826

New Jersey Council on the Arts, NJ, 5515

New Jersey Health Foundation, Inc., NJ, 5516

New Jersey Motor Truck Association Scholarship Fund, NJ, 5517

New Jersey Osteopathic Education Foundation, NJ, 5518

New Jersey Performing Arts Center, Corp., NJ, 5519

New Jersey Press Foundation, NJ, 5520

New Jersey State Bar Foundation, NJ, 5521

New Jersey State Elks Association Special Children's Committee, Inc., NJ, 5522

New Jersey State Firemen's Association, NJ, 5523

New London Service Organization, Inc., NH, 5356

New Mexico Community Foundation, The, NM, 5640

New Music USA, Inc., NY, 6262

New Opportunities, Inc., CT, 1432

New Orphan Asylum Scholarship Foundation, OH, 7268

New Penn Motor Express Scholarship Foundation, NC, 6790

New Visions for Public Schools, Inc., NY, 6263

New World Foundation, The, NY, 6264

New World Gospel Mission, Inc., NJ, 5524

New York Academy of Medicine, NY, 6265

New York City "Bravest" Scholarship Fund, NY, 6266

New York City Police Foundation, Inc., NY, 6267

New York Classical Club, The, NY, 6268

New York Community Trust, The, NY, 6269

New York Foundation for Architecture, Inc., NY, see 5831

New York Library Association, NY, 6270

New York Live Arts, NY, see 5911

New York Mills Arts Retreat, MN, 4812

New York Public Library Astor, Lenox and Tilden Foundations, The, NY, 6271

New York Public Library, The, NY, see 6271

New York State 4-H Foundation, Inc., NY, 6272

New York Stem Cell Foundation, Inc., NY, 6273

New York Stock Exchange Fallen Heroes Fund, The, NY, 6274

New York Times Company Foundation Inc., The, NY, 6275

New York Times Neediest Cases Fund, Inc., The, NY, 6276

New York Women in Film & Television, Inc., NY, 6277

New York-Presbyterian Fund, Inc., NY, 6278

Newark Museum Association, The, NJ, 5525

Newaygo County Community Services, MI, 4554

Newaygo Public Schools Educational Advancement Foundation, MI, 4555

Newblom Foundation, Darold A., NE, 5247

Newcombe Foundation, Charlotte W., The, NJ, 5526

Newhouse Foundation, Samuel I., Inc., NY, 6279

Newhouse Scholarship Trust Fund, VA, 9463

Newland Trust in Memory of Anna L. Frinfrock, Sadie G., CO, 1249

Newlin, Sr. Memorial Trust, Robert "Aqqaluk", AK, 127

Newman Family Charitable Foundation, PA, 8005

Newnan-Coweta Chamber Foundation, GA, see 2156

Newspaper Association of America Foundation, VA, 9464

Newton Marasco Foundation, VA, 9465

Newton Scholarship Fund, Horace & Letitia, OH, 7269

Newton Television Foundation, The, MA, see 4015

Nexion Health Foundation, MD, 3902

NFID, MD, see 3897

NGA of SC Scholarship Foundation, SC, 8498

NH Bar Foundation, NH, see 5352

Niccum Educational Trust Foundation, IL, 2756

Nicholas County Community Foundation, WV, 9805

Nicholas Family Foundation, PA, 8006

Nicholl Memorial Foundation, James R., WI, 9981

Nichols Foundation, Inc., TX, 8989

Nichols Scholarship Trust, Howard and Mamie, NC, 6791

Nichols Trust, Mary, MA, 4197

Nichols, Jr. Scholarship Foundation, Robert L., MO, 5063

Nicholson Scholarship Fund, John & Helen, RI, 8355

Nickel Producers Environmental Research Association, Inc., NC, 6792

Nickelson Memorial Foundation for Homeless Veterans, Kenny, Inc., The, CA, 827

Nicklies Scholarship Fund, L. E., PA, 8007

Nicolai Memorial Scholarship Fund, David K., AK, see 108

Nicolay Melanoma Foundation, Joanna M., MD, 3903

Nicolet College Foundation, WI, 9982

Nicoll Educational Trust, Robert and Ida, IL, 2757

Niconchuk Scholarship Trust, Anna, MA, 4198

Niederkorn Scholarship Trust, William J. & Myra L., WI, see 10022

Nielson Scholarship Fund, Karl A. Nielson and Karen J., TX, see 8990

Nielson Scholarship Fund, TX, 8990

Nieman Scholarship Fund, Sara L., MI, 4556

NIFP, NE, see 5241

Nikkei Alumni Association, WA, 9682

Nill Foundation, Dr. William F. and Mabel E., Inc., MI, 4557

Nine Health Services, Inc., CO, 1250

Ninth District Opportunity, Inc., GA, 2216

NiPERA, NC, see 6792

Nishan Scholarship Trust, Freda, WI, 9983

Nishnabotna Valley Foundation, IA, 3343

Niswonger Foundation, Inc., TN, 8630

NJPAC, NJ, see 5519

NLN Foundation for Nursing Education, NY, 6280

NMA Scholarship Foundation, CA, 828

NMSC, IL, see 2747

Noah's Ark Christian Day Care Center, Inc., KS, 3496

Noble County Community Foundation, IN, 3127

Noble Foundation, Samuel Roberts, Inc., The, OK, 7497

Noer Research Foundation, O.J., Inc., WI, 9984

NOHR Foundation, PA, see 8000

Nok Charitable Organization, Inc., NY, 6281

NOK Foundation, Inc., NY, see 6281

Nolan Foundation, L. Douglas, Inc., CT, 1433

Nolan Foundation, Robert J., Inc., NY, 6282

Nolan Memorial Fund, St. Thomas Knights/Maureen, NY, 6283

Noll Foundation, John H., PA, 8008

Nolley Educational Scholarship Fund, Gilbert & Evelyn, OH, 7270

Nonprofit Roundtable of Greater Washington, The, DC, 1701

Norbert & Harry Schwabenlander for Hilbert High School Memorial Scholarship Foundation, Lawrence, WI, 9985

Norby Scholarship Fund, Swan C., TX, 8991

Nordic Educational Trust, VT, 9255

Nordman Charitable Trust, Amos, MI, see 4558

Nordman Foundation Charitable Trust, Amos, MI, 4558

Norfolk Foundation, The, VA, see 9391

Norman & Anna Scholarship fund, Gould, RI, 8356

Norris Charitable Trust, Hartzell, OH, 7271

Norris Foundation, Elwood and Stephanie, The, NV, 5297

Norris Memorial Foundation, Nick, IA, 3344

Norris Scholarship, Shelley R. and Alice S., KY, 3603

North American Artist Foundation, AZ, 221

North American Envirothon, TX, 8992

North American Philips Foundation, MA, see 4220

North American Savings Bank Foundation, Inc., MO, see 5061

North American Spine Society, IL, 2758

North Attleboro Scholarship Foundation, MA, 4199

North Bay Developmental Disabilities Services, Inc., CA, 829

North Carolina A&T University Foundation, Inc., NC, 6793

North Carolina Academy of Family Physicians Foundation, NC, 6794

North Carolina Amateur Sports, Inc., NC, 6795

North Carolina Community Foundation, NC, 6796

North Carolina Legal Education Assistance Foundation, NC, 6797

North Carolina National Guard Association Education Foundation, NC, 6798

North Carolina Rural Economic Development Center, Inc., NC, 6799

North Carolina Science Teacher Association, NC, 6800

North Carolina Society of Hispanic Professionals, Inc., NC, 6801

North Carolina State Grange Foundation, Inc., NC, 6802

North Central Florida Health Planning Council, Inc., FL, 1998

North Central Massachusetts Community Foundation, Inc., MA, 4200

North Central Missouri College Foundation, Inc., MO, 5064

North Central PA Golf Association, PA, 8009

North Central Pennsylvania Golf Association Scholarship Trust, PA, see 8009

North Coast Scholarship Foundation, OR, 7617

North College Hill Scholarship Foundation, The, OH, 7272

North Colorado Medical Center Foundation, Inc., CO, 1251

North Dakota Community Foundation, ND, 6946

North East Community Action Corporation, MO, 5065

North East Community Foundation, PA, 8010

North East Roofing Educational Foundation, Inc., MA, 4201

North Fork Women for Women Fund, Inc., NY, 6284

North Georgia Community Action, Inc., GA, 2217

North Georgia Community Foundation, GA, 2218

North Haven Foundation, ME, 3720

North Haven Rotary Foundation, Inc., CT, 1434

North Helpline, WA, 9683

North Iowa Area Community College Foundation, IA, 3345

North Jersey Media Group Foundation, Inc., NJ, 5527

North Kohala Community Resource Center, HI, 2306

North Los Angeles County Regional Center, Inc., CA, 830

North Manchester Community Foundation, IN, see 3006

North Orange Memorial Hospital Trust, FL, 1999

North Platte Foundation, The, MO, 5066

North Shore Animal League America, Inc., NY, 6285
North Shore Community Action Programs, Inc., MA, 4202
North Suburban Community Foundation, MN, 4813
North Valley Community Foundation, CA, 831
North Valley Health Education Foundation, CA, 832
Northampton County Area Community College Foundation, PA, 8011
Northeast Arkansas Higher Education Charitable Foundation, Inc., AR, 298
Northeast Educational Services, Inc., MA, see 4289
Northeast Florida Builders Association Builders Care, Inc., FL, 2000
Northeast High School Alumni Foundation, The, PA, 8012
Northeast Iowa Charitable Foundation, IA, 3346
Northeast Michigan Community Foundation, MI, see 4392
Northeast Michigan Community Service Agency, Inc., MI, 4559
Northeast Missouri Area Agency on Aging, MO, 5067
Northeastern New York Community Trust, OH, see 7188
Northern Arizona University Foundation, Inc., AZ, 222
Northern California DX Foundation, The, MA, 4203
Northern California Laborers Scholarship Foundation, CA, 833
Northern California Scholarship Foundation and the Scaife Scholarship Foundation, The, CA, see 834
Northern California Scholarship Foundation, The, CA, 834
Northern Chautauqua Community Foundation, Inc., NY, 6286
Northern Clay Center, MN, 4814
Northern Coop Foundation, MN, 4815
Northern Highlands Regional High School, Inc., RI, see 8315
Northern Illinois University Foundation, IL, 2759
Northern Indiana Fuel and Light Company Scholarship Fund, OH, A
Northern Kentucky Community Action Commisson, Inc., KY, 3604
Northern Michigan Hospital Foundation, MI, 4560
Northern New York Community Foundation, Inc., NY, 6287
Northern Palm Beach County Youth Foundation Inc., The, FL, 2001
Northern Piedmont Community Foundation, VA, 9466
Northern Star Council, Boy Scouts of America, Inc., MN, 4816
Northern Virginia Delta Education & Community Service Foundation, VA, 9467
Northern Virginia Family Service, VA, 9468
Northrup Educational Foundation Inc., NY, 6288
Northstar Partners Scholarship Fund, MN, see 4884
Northville Community Foundation, MI, 4561
Northville Educational Foundation, MI, 4562
Northwest AIDS Foundation-Chicken Soup Brigade, WA, see 9661
Northwest Assistance Ministries, TX, 8993
Northwest Bancorp, Inc. Charitable Foundation, PA, 8013
Northwest Children's Outreach, OR, 7618
Northwest Danish Association, WA, see 9684
Northwest Danish Foundation, WA, 9684
Northwest Film Forum, WA, 9685
Northwest Harvest E.M M., WA, 9686
Northwest Health Foundation (Fund 1), OR, see 7619
Northwest Health Foundation, OR, 7619
Northwest Indiana Community Action Corporation, IN, 3128
Northwest Iowa Hospital Corporation, IA, 3347
Northwest Lions Foundation for Sight & Hearing, WA, 9687
Northwest Michigan Human Services, Inc., MI, 4563
Northwest Minnesota Foundation (NWMF), MN, 4817
Northwest New Jersey Community Action Program, Inc., NJ, 5528
Northwest Ohio Youth Soccer League, OH, 7273
Northwest Osteopathic Medical Foundation, OR, 7620
Northwestern Ohio Community Action Commission, OH, 7274
Northwoods Living, Inc., IA, A
Norton Healthcare Foundation, Inc., KY, 3606

Norton Healthcare, Inc., KY, 3605
Norton Sound Economic Development Corporation, AK, 128
Norwalk Community College Foundation, CT, 1435
Norwalk Hospital Foundation, Inc., CT, 1436
Norwegian Children's Home Association of New York, Inc., The, NY, 6289
NORWESCAP, NJ, see 5528
Norwood Foundation, The, CO, 1252
Novak Scholarship Foundation, Frank J. & Joe E., NE, 5248
Novartis Patient Assistance Foundation, Inc., NJ, 5529
Novi Educational Foundation, MI, 4564
Novi Parks Foundation, MI, 4565
NPSC, CA, see 821
NRA Foundation, Inc., The, VA, 9469
NRC Foundation, Inc., CT, see 1491
NRC, TX, see 8986
NSDAR, DC, see 1696
NSTEP, VA, see 9456
Nuclear Age Peace Foundation, CA, 835
Nucor Foundation, NC, 6803
NUF, Inc., NY, see 6255
Nugen Scholarship Fund, Dr. D. R., OH, 7275
Nuts, Bolts, and Thingamajigs: The Foundation of the Fabricators and Manufacturers Association, Inc., IL, 2760
Nuttycomb Charitable Trust No. 2, S. T. & Mabel I., KS, see 3497
Nuttycomb Charitable Trust, S. T. & Mabel I., KS, 3497
NV Energy Charitable Foundation, NV, 5298
NV Energy Foundation, NV, see 5298
NYContemporary Glass Center, Inc., NY, see 6481
Nye Charitable Trust, Avis M., NH, 5357
Nye Scholarship Trust, Grace Swift Nye & Alfred Gibbs, MA, 4204
NYS Fraternal Order of Police Empire State Foundation, NY, see 6290
NYS Fraternal Order of Police Foundation, NY, 6290
NYWIFT, NY, see 6277

O'Brien Educational & Charitable Trust, Davey, TX, 8994
O'Brien's Irish Angel Endowment Fund, NJ, 5530
O'Brien-Veba Scholarship Trust, PA, 8014
O'Brion Trust, Frank, RI, 8357
O'Connor Educational Trust, Charles D. & Gertrude H., IN, 3130
O'Hara Scholarship Trust, John and Blanche, WI, 9986
O'Leary Foundation, Simone, NJ, 5531
O'Malley Foundation, The, IL, 2768
O'Meara Foundation, Inc., The, CT, 1437
O'Neal Educational Foundation, Pat, The, TX, 8997
O'Neil Foundation, Claire Williams, DC, 1704
O'Neill, Jr. Education Fund, L. Arthur, SC, 8500
Oak Park/River Forest Community Foundation, IL, 2761
Oakes Foundation, Frank L., IL, 2762
Oakland A's Community Fund, The, CA, see 836
Oakland Athletics Community Fund, The, CA, 836
Oakland Innovators Awards Fund, CA, see 837
Oakland Livingston Human Service Agency, MI, 4566
Oaklandish, LLP Corporate Giving Program, CA, 837
Oakley Foundation, Mary, Inc., The, CA, 838
Oakwood Healthcare, Inc., MI, 4567
Oapa Scholarship Foundation, OR, 7621
OATCD Scholarship Fund, OK, see 7505
Oates Scholarship Fund Trust, L.R., NC, 6804
Oates Scholarship Trust, Forrest C. & Minnie Less, NC, 6805
Oberdorfer Scholarship Trust Fund, Julia S., IN, 3129
Oberkotter Family Foundation, Robert & Joyce, NH, 5358
Oberlin Charitable Trust, IL, 2763
Oberlin Shansi Memorial Association, OH, 7276
Oberweiler Foundation, IL, 2764
Obesity Society, The, MD, 3904
Oblinger Trust f/b/o Stephen Dexter and Emily Jane Tipton Dole Scholarship, Emily, IL, see 2520
OCCHA, Inc., OH, A
Ocean Foundation, The, DC, 1702
Ocean State Power Scholarship Foundation, Ltd., MA, 4205
Ocean View Memorial Foundation, Inc., SC, 8499

OCF, OR, see 7624
Ochoco Charitable Fund, OR, 7622
Ochoco Scholarship Fund, OR, see 7622
Odasz Trust, Jeanette, NY, 6291
OEA Foundation, Inc., NE, 5249
Office Depot Foundation, FL, 2002
Ogden College Foundation, KY, 3607
Oglesby Foundation, Robert and Willora, Inc., TX, 8995
Ohadi Memorial Foundation, Jean Paul, IL, 2765
Ohio Community Pooled Annuity Trust, OH, 7277
Ohio County Community Foundation, Inc., IN, 3131
Ohio Credit Union Foundation, OH, 7278
Ohio Farm Bureau Foundation, OH, 7279
Ohio Masonic Home, The, OH, 7280
Ohio MedCenter Foundation, Inc., OH, see 7221
Ohio Newspapers Foundation, OH, 7281
Ohio Osteopathic Foundation, OH, 7282
Ohiyesa Corporation, VT, 9256
Ohlendorf Scholarship Fund, Harold & Bruce, AR, 299
Ohmart Memorial Fund, David Marshall, ME, 3721
OHSAA Foundation, OH, 7283
Oilgear Ferris Foundation, WI, 9987
Ojai Film Festival, CA, 839
OJCF, OR, see 7625
Okeechobee Educational Foundation, Inc., FL, 2003
Oklahoma Bar Foundation, OK, 7498
Oklahoma City Disaster Relief Fund, Inc., OK, 7499
Oklahoma Communities Foundation, Inc., OK, see 7459
Oklahoma Elks Major Project, Inc., OK, 7500
Oklahoma Foundation for Excellence, OK, 7501
Oklahoma Scholarship Fund, Inc., OK, 7502
Old Elm Scholarship Foundation, IL, 2766
Old Harbor Scholarship Foundation, AK, 129
Old Newsboys Goodfellow Fund of Detroit, MI, 4568
Old Pueblo Community Services, AZ, 223
Olds Foundation, AR, 300
Olean Community Foundation, Greater, NY, see 5826
Olender Foundation, Jack H. & Lovell R., DC, 1703
Olinde, Jr. Family Foundation, Humphrey T., The, LA, 3671
Olivet Nazarene College Foundation, IL, see 2767
Olivet Nazarene University Foundation, IL, 2767
Olliff Foundation, Matred Carlton, FL, 2004
Olmsted Foundation, George and Carol, The, VA, 9470
Olson Trust, C.P. & Irene, MN, 4818
Olson Trust, Iona, TX, 8996
Olympic Club Foundation, The, CA, 840
Omaha Schools Foundation, NE, 5250
Omaha Volunteers for Handicapped Children, NE, 5251
Omega Men of North Alabama, Inc., AL, 66
Omega of Sigma Pi Foundation, WA, 9688
On Top of the World Foundation, Inc., The, FL, see 1834
One Family, Inc., MA, 4206
One Million Degrees, IL, see 2636
Oneida Savings Bank Charitable Foundation, NY, 6292
OneSight Research Foundation, TX, 8998
Onizuka Scholarship Fund-Kona, Ellison S., Inc., HI, 2307
Onodaga Nation Scholarship Trust, Leonard Hubbard, RI, 8358
ONS Foundation, PA, 8015
Ontario Children's Foundation, NY, 6293
Ontario Children's Home, NY, see 6293
Ontonagon Area Scholarship Foundation, The, MI, 4569
Open Circle Foundation, CA, 841
Open Society Institute, NY, 6294
Open Space Institute, NY, 6295
OPERA America, NY, 6296
Opera Foundation, Inc., The, NY, 6297
Operafestival di Roma, Inc., FL, 2005
Operation Blessing International Relief and Development Corp., VA, 9471
Operation First Response, Inc., VA, 9472
Operation Fuel, Inc., CT, 1438
Operation Game Thief, Inc., CO, 1253
Operation Homefront, Inc., TX, 8999
Operation Hope of Brevard, Inc., FL, 2006
Operation Open Arms, Inc., KY, 3608
Operation Smile, Inc., VA, 9473
Operation Threshold, Inc., IA, 3348
Oppenheim Charitable Trust, Louis S., OH, 7284

Opportunities for Broome, Inc., NY, 6298
Opportunities for Chenango, Inc., NY, 6299
Opportunity Alliance, The, ME, 3722
Opportunity Council, WA, 9689
Optical Society of America, DC, 1705
Optimist Boys Home and Ranch, Inc., CA, 842
Optimist Club Foundation, The, MI, 4570
Optimist Youth Homes and Family Services, CA, see 842
Orange Bowl Committee, Inc., FL, 2007
Orange County Community Foundation, CA, 843
Orange County Rescue Mission, Inc., CA, 844
Orange Foundation, CT, 1439
Orange Foundation, Inc., DE, see 1518
Orange Home, Inc., DE, 1518
Orange Scholarship Foundation, MA, 4207
Orangewood Children's Foundation, CA, 845
Orcutt Memorial Foundation, Mary, NV, 5299
Orcutt Memorial Scholarship Foundation, Mary, NV, see 5299
Order of the Alhambra Charity Fund, Inc., MD, 3905
OREF, IL, see 2770
Oregon Coast Community Action, OR, 7623
Oregon Community Foundation, The, OR, 7624
Oregon Jewish Community Foundation, OR, 7625
Oregon Tech Foundation, OR, see 7626
Oregon Technical Development Foundation, OR, 7626
Oregon Trail Community Foundation, Inc., NE, 5252
Orenstein Foundation, Henry and Carolyn Sue, Inc., NJ, 5532
Organic Farming Research Foundation, CA, 846
Organization of American Historians, IN, 3132
Organization of Black Aerospcae Professionals, The, IL, 2769
Organization of Black Airline Pilots, IL, see 2769
Orlando Magic Foundation, Inc., FL, 2008
Orlando Magic Youth Foundation, FL, see 2008
Orlando Magic Youth Fund, FL, see 2008
Oro Grande Foundation, CA, 847
Orphan Foundation of America, VA, 9474
Orr Foundation, The, RI, 8359
Orscheln Industries Foundation Inc., MO, 5068
Ortega Charitable Foundation, DE, 1519
Orth Scholarship Fund, Alfred H., IN, 3133
Orthopaedic Research Education Foundation, IL, 2770
Orum Memorial Foundation, Stig P., Inc., IL, 2771
Osborn Memorial Trust, Louise & Lane, OH, 7285
Osborn Scholarship Trust, Joyce L., MN, 4819
Osborn Scholarship Trust, Lawrence L., IN, 3134
OSF Healthcare System, IL, 2772
Oshkosh Area Community Foundation Corporation, WI, 9989
Oshkosh Area Community Foundation, WI, 9988
Oshkosh Foundation, WI, see 9988
Ostberg Foundation, Inc., The, NJ, 5533
Osteogenesis Imperfecta Foundation, Inc., MD, 3906
Osteopathic Foundation of Central Washington, WA, 9690
Osteopathic Foundation of Yakima, WA, see 9690
Osteopathic Founders Foundation, OK, 7503
Osteopathic Institute of the South, GA, see 2187
Osteopathic Medical Foundation, Inc., IN, 3135
OSU Center for Innovation and Economic Development, Inc., OK, 7504
Otero County Electric Education Foundation, NM, 5641
Otsego County Community Foundation, MI, 4571
Ott Scholarship Foundation, Richard F., FL, 2009
Ott Scholarship Fund, Raymond J., IL, 2773
Ott Scholarship Trust, Harlan, Ruby & Phil E., IL, 2774
Ott Scholarships, Phil E., IL, see 2774
Ottauquechee Health Center, VT, 9257
Ottauquechee Health Foundation, Inc., VT, see 9257
Ottauquechee Health Foundation, VT, see 9257
Ouimet Scholarship Fund, Francis, Inc., The, MA, 4208
Our Community's Foundation, WV, see 9808
Our House for Girls, Inc., NH, 5359
Our Lady of the Lake Regional Medical Center, LA, 3672
Outcalt Foundation, CO, 1254
Outdoor Extravaganza, OH, 7286
Outer Banks Community Foundation, Inc., NC, 6806
Outpost for Contemporary Art, CA, 848
Outreach Center, The, NC, 6807

Outreach United Resource Center, Inc., CO, 1255
Outrigger Duke Kahanamoku Foundation, HI, 2308
Overlake Hospital Auxiliaries, WA, 9691
Owen County Community Foundation, IN, 3136
Owen Educational Scholarship Trust, Jack & Charlotte, TX, 9000
Owen Foundation, Herman and Hazel, The, MS, 4917
Owens Foundation, Elizabeth Anne, AL, 67
Owens Scholarship Trust Co., NC, see 6808
Owens Scholarship Trust, Peewee and Myrtle, NC, 6808
Owensboro Medical Health System, Inc., KY, 3609
Owenton Rotary Student Loan Fund, KY, 3610
OWMA Scholarship Fund, OK, 7505
Oxford Foundation, Inc., IN, see 3198
Oxford Hills Scholarship Foundation, ME, 3723
Oxygen Society, The, IN, see 3187
Oyler Scholarship Foundation, Ray, Inc., IN, A
Oyster Bay Sailing Foundation, The, NY, 6300
OZ Foundation, CA, 849
Ozark Opportunities, Inc., AR, 301
Ozarks Area Community Action Corporation, MO, 5069
Ozinga Memorial Scholarship Foundation, Janet, IL, 2775

P.E.O. Foundation, IA, 3349
P.E.O. International Peace Scholarship Fund, IA, 3350
P.E.O. Program for Continuing Education, IA, 3351
P.E.O. Sisterhood International, California Chapter, IA, 3352
PAAC, HI, see 2309
Pace 8-591 Fallen Workers Memorial Scholarship, WA, 9692
Pace Community Action Agency, Inc., IN, 3137
PACE, OH, see 7290
Pacers Basketball Corporation Foundation, Inc., IN, see 3138
Pacers Foundation, Inc., IN, 3138
Pacific and Asian Affairs Council, HI, 2309
Pacific Islanders in Communications, HI, 2310
Pacific Northwest Ballet Association, WA, 9693
Pacific Northwest Kiwanis Foundation, OR, 7627
Pacific Office Automation Charitable Foundation, OR, 7628
Pacific Pioneer Fund, Inc., CA, 850
Pacific Scholarship Foundation, CA, A
Pack Foundation, CA, 851
Packaging Machinery Manufacturers Institute, VA, see 9484
Paddington Foundation, PA, 8016
Padelford Scholarship Fund, Arline P., RI, 8360
Padelford Scholarship Fund-Sigma Kappa Alumnae, Jessie Pepper, WA, 9694
Paden City Foundation, Inc., WV, 9806
Padgett Charitable Trust, Hilda M., OH, 7287
PADI Foundation, CA, 852
Padolf Foundation, Lou & Lillian, AL, 68
Paducah Area Community Foundation, KY, see 3560
Paganelli Trust, A. Nina, ME, 3724
Page Education Foundation, MN, 4820
Pagel Graphics Arts Scholarship Trust Fund, WI, 9990
Pagliara Charitable Foundation, The, FL, 2010
PAH Foundation, WA, 9695
Paideia Foundation, The, IL, 2776
Paine Scholarship Fund Trust, Charles J., MA, 4209
Pais Family Educational Foundation, John and Lucia, Inc., The, WV, 9807
Palama Scholarship Foundation Inc., HI, 2311
Palama Settlement, HI, 2312
Palen-Klar Scholarship Fund, Countess Frances Thorley, RI, 8361
Palestine Temple Charities Trust, RI, see 8399
Pallotta Foundation, Marc & Ernest, Inc., MA, 4210
Palm Beach Community College Foundation, Inc., FL, 2011
Palm Beach County Community Foundation, FL, see 1839
Palm Beach County Cultural Council, FL, 2012
Palm Beach Rotary Foundation, FL, 2013
Palmer & Ben A. Miller Scholarship Trust, Elise Miller, IA, 3353
Palmer Memorial Scholarship Fund, C. Paul, OH, 7288

Palmer Minority Scholarship Foundation, R. Merle, WA, 9696
Palmer Scholarship Trust, Walter Curtis, The, IL, 2777
Palmer Townsend Trust, RI, 8362
Palmer Trust, Marvin O., OR, 7629
Palmetto Electric Trust, SC, 8501
Palos Bank Foundation, Inc., IL, 2778
Palos Verdes Peninsula Education Foundation, CA, 853
Pamlico Partnership for Children, Inc., NC, 6809
PAN Foundation, DC, see 1709
Pan-Icarian Foundation, PA, 8018
Panagos Charitable Trust, Nick & Paris N., PA, 8017
Panasonic Rio Grande Valley Educational Foundation, TX, 9001
Panasonic Tennessee-Japan Cultural Exchange Foundation, TX, see 9001
Pancreatic Cancer Action Network, Inc., CA, 854
Papa John's International, Inc. Corporate Giving Program, KY, 3611
Papa John's Team Member Emergency Relief Fund, Inc., KY, 3612
Pape Charitable Foundation, Robert S., RI, 8363
Pape Educational Fund Trust, Arthur F., KS, 3498
Paper Mill Playhouse, NJ, 5534
Papines Scholarship Trust, John A. & Irene, RI, see 8365
Papines Scholarship Trust-Ermoupolis, John A. & Irene, RI, 8364
Pappas Trust I, N. J., NC, 6810
Pappines Ahepa Tua, John A., RI, 8365
Paralyzed Veterans of America, DC, 1706
Parapsychology Foundation, Inc., NY, 6301
Pardee Cancer Treatment Association of Greater Brazosport, TX, 9002
Pardee Cancer Treatment Fund of Bay County, MI, 4572
Parent Encouragement Program, MD, 3907
Parenthesis Family Advocates, Inc., OH, 7289
Parents Advancing Choice in Education, OH, 7290
Parents and Children Together, HI, 2313
Parents With A Purpose, Inc., GA, 2219
Parents, Families & Friends of Lesbians and Gays, Inc., DC, 1707
Parham Fund for Scholastic Excellence, Ron, NY, 6302
Paris Education Foundation, TX, 9003
Paris Junior College Memorial Fund Foundation, TX, 9004
Park Charitable Foundation, Clyde, MA, 4211
Park City Foundation, The, UT, 9221
Park Foundation, OH, 7291
Park Memorial Scholarship Fund, Leanna Bray, GA, 2220
Park Trust, Clyde, MA, see 4211
Park West Children's Fund, Inc., LA, 3673
Parke County Community Foundation, Inc., IN, 3139
Parker Charitable Trust, Pauline R., NY, 6303
Parker Family Foundation, AL, 69
Parker Scholarship Foundation, Winston E., NJ, 5535
Parker Scholarship Fund, Winston E., NJ, see 5535
Parker Scholarship Trust, Henry & Louise, MI, 4573
Parker Trust for Public Music Fund, Charles, RI, 8366
Parkersburg Area Community Foundation, WV, 9808
Parkinson Foundation of the National Capital Area, Inc., VA, 9475
Parkinson's Action Network, DC, 1708
Parkland Medical Center Nursing Memorial Scholarship Fund, NH, 5360
Parks Scholarship Foundation, Rosa L., Inc., MI, 4574
Parks Trust for the Education of Nurses, Ruth, IA, 3354
Parkview Foundation, Inc., IN, see 3140
Parkview Hospital Foundation, Inc., IN, 3140
Parkwest Medical Center, TN, 8631
Parodneck Foundation for Self-Help, Housing & Community Development, Inc., The, NY, 6304
Parsons Scholarship Foundation, Rebecca C., SC, 8502
Parsons Scholarship Foundation, W.N., KS, 3499
Partners Advancing Values in Education, Inc., WI, 9991
Partners for a Cure Foundation, OH, 7292
Partners in Charity, Inc., IL, 2779
Partridge Memorial Scholarship Fund, William G. & Rhoda B., NY, 6305
PARTS Scholarship Foundation, PA, see 8023
Pasadena Methodist Foundation, CA, 855

Pasarow Foundation, Robert J. & Claire, CA, 856
Pass It on Foundation, OR, 7630
Passano Foundation, Inc., The, MD, 3908
Passim Folk Music & Cultural Center, MA, see 3955
Passport to Success Foundation, Inc., TX, 9005
Pasteur Foundation, NY, 6306
Patch Scholarship Trust, Grace, NC, 6811
PATCH, HI, see 2314
Patel Family Foundation, Drs. Kiran & Pallavi, Inc., FL, 2014
PATH Wisconsin, Inc., WI, see 9837
Pathfinder Village Foundation, Inc., NY, 6307
Pathways to Spirit, CO, 1256
Patient Access Network Foundation, DC, 1709
Patient Advocate Foundation, VA, 9476
Patient Services, Inc., VA, 9477
Patout Foundation, Appoline & Simeon, TX, 9006
Patterson Charitable Trust, Charles A. & Odette W., FL, 2015
Patterson Dental Foundation, MN, see 4821
Patterson Foundation, Alicia, DC, 1710
Patterson Foundation, Father Joseph, AZ, 224
Patterson Foundation, MN, 4821
Patterson Perpetual Fund, Nicholas, NY, 6308
Patterson Trust, Frances, KS, 3500
Patterson Trust, G. F., IL, 2780
Patterson, Jr. Scholarship Fund, Ola Warren & John W., NC, 6812
Patton Boggs Foundation, DC, 1711
Patton Scholarship Fund, PA, 8019
Patton Scholarship Fund, PA, see 8019
Patton Scholarship Trust, NE, 5253
Paul Foundation, Josephine Bay Paul and C. Michael, Inc., NY, see 5756
Paul Memorial Trust, Thomas M., MO, 5070
Paul Scholarship Fund, Elizabeth and John, CT, 1440
Paulsen Trust, MI, 4575
Pawating Health Foundation, MI, see 4510
Paxton Memorial Scholarship Fund, Jack, Inc., KY, 3613
Payne Scholarship Fund, Charles K., Inc., NJ, 5536
Payton Scholarship Trust, Alene, IN, 3141
PDR Foundation, Inc., OH, 7293
Peabody Foundation Inc., Grace And Bill, MA, 4212
Peabody School for Girls, Henry O., MA, 4213
Peace Foundation Inc., James Bradley, NY, 6309
Peach Scholarship Fund, Donald H. and Helen D., MA, 4214
Peak Scholarship Fund, Walter G. and Ella M., OH, 7294
Pearce Educational Foundation, Jack & Katherine, TX, 9007
Pearce Foundation, The, OH, 7295
Pearce Trust, George & Belle, KS, 3501
Pearl Cancer Foundation, Minnie, The, TN, see 8632
Pearl S. Buck Foundation, Inc., The, PA, see 7751
Pearl Scholarship Fund, Charles G., KY, 3614
Pearle Vision Foundation, Inc., TX, see 8998
Pearlpoint Cancer Support, TN, 8632
Pearson Charitable Foundation, NY, 6310
Pearson Scholarship Trust, IN, 3142
Pearson Scholarship Trust, Viola, WY, 10116
Pebble Beach Company Foundation, CA, 857
Peck Memorial Fund, Dr. Abel E., NY, 6311
Peck Trust, Katherine L., RI, 8367
Peckitt Scholarship Trust, Hattie M., NC, 6813
Peckitt Scholarship Trust, Leonard Carlton, NC, see 6813
Peculiar Charitable Foundation, MO, 5071
Pedernales Electric Cooperative Scholarship Fund, TX, 9008
Pediatric Brain Tumor Foundation of the United States, Inc., NC, 6814
Pedrozzi Scholarship Foundation, Mario, CA, 858
Peeples Trust, Marion A. & Eva S., IL, 2781
Peery Memorial Scholarship Fund Inc., Bulah, TX, 9009
Pehna Scholarship Trust, Charles, OH, 7296
Peirce Scholarship Foundation, Victoria Glenn, CT, 1441
Pella Rolscreen Foundation, IA, 3355
Pellerin Foundation, Willis & Mildred, LA, 3674
PEMCO Foundation, Inc., WA, 9697
PEN American Center, Inc., NY, 6312

PEN/Faulkner Foundation, DC, 1712
Penasco Valley Telephone Education Foundation, NM, 5642
PENCON Foundation, PA, 8020
Peninsula Foundation, The, NM, 5643
Penjoyan Educational Trust, Richard, CA, 859
Penn Association Scholarship Foundation, William, PA, 8021
Penn Jersey Youth Umpires School, Inc., NJ, 5537
Penn National Gaming Foundation, PA, 8022
Penn-Mar Organization, Inc., MD, 3909
Penney Company Fund, J. C., Inc., TX, 9010
Pennock Foundation, MI, 4576
Pennsylvania Automotive Recycling Trade Society Scholarship Foundation, PA, 8023
Pennsylvania Bar Foundation, PA, 8024
Pennsylvania Community Real Estate Corporation, PA, 8025
Pennsylvania Cystic Fibrosis, Inc., PA, 8026
Pennsylvania Humanities Council, PA, 8027
Pennsylvania Industrial Chemical Corporation-Clairton High School Scholarship Fund, PA, 8028
Pennsylvania Industrial Chemical, NC, 6815
Pennsylvania Realtors Education Foundation, PA, 8029
Pennsylvania State System of Higher Education Foundation, Inc., PA, 8030
Penny Lane Centers, CA, 860
Penquis Community Action Program, ME, 3725
Penquis, ME, see 3725
Penrose Foundation, TX, 9011
Pentagon Federal Credit Union Foundation, The, VA, 9478
People Attentive to Children, HI, 2314
People For the American Way Foundation, DC, 1713
People in Business Care, Inc., MN, A
People Technology Foundation, Inc., The, NJ, 5538
People to People International, MO, 5072
People's City Mission, NE, 5254
People's Fund, The, PA, see 7743
People's Regional Opportunity Program, ME, see 3722
Peoples Bancorp Foundation Inc., OH, 7297
Peoples Bank Foundation, Ltd., The, GA, 2221
Peoples Charitable Foundation, Inc., IN, 3143
Peoples Resource Center, IL, 2782
Peoria Area Community Foundation, IL, see 2494
Peoria Educational Enrichment Foundation, Inc., AZ, 225
Percival Scholarship Fund, H. Stanley & Marie, PA, 8031
Percy Franklin Lucas Memorial Student Loan Fund, TX, 9012
Percy Memorial Trust, Lottie King Lucas, TX, see 9012
Perdue Education Fund, Evelyn, KS, see 3502
Perdue Education Trust, Evelyn, KS, 3502
Perfect Storm, Inc., The, MA, 4215
Performance Zone, Inc., The, NY, 6313
Performing Arts Center of Los Angeles County, CA, 861
Performing Arts Scholarship Foundation, CA, 862
Pergo Foundation, The, CA, 863
Perisho-Nina Rall McConkey Scholarship Trust, Mary, IL, 2783
Perkins Foundation, B. F. & Rose H., WY, 10117
Perkins Memorial Trust, James W., The, VA, 9479
Perkins Scholarship Fund, Alden and Dorothy, IL, 2784
Permanent Endowment Fund for Martha's Vineyard, MA, 4216
Permian Basin Area Foundation, TX, 9013
Pernot Scholarship Fund, Henry S., OR, 7631
Perot Family Foundation, The, TX, 9014
Perpetual Benevolent Fund, RI, 8368
Perrin Foundation, Charles Hugh & Wilma Marie, ID, 2344
Perron Memorial Trust f/b/o Graduates of High School Serving the City of North Adams, Charles A., MA, see 4217
Perron Memorial Trust, Charles & Olivina, MA, 4217
Perrone Memorial Scholarship Trust, John, PA, 8032
Perry Fund, Frances E., OH, 7298
Perry Memorial Scholarship Trust, FL, 2016
Perry Memorial Scholarships, Frank H. & Annie Belle Whilhelm, FL, see 2016
Perry Scholarship Foundation, OH, 7299
Perry Scholarship Trust, Mildred R., WI, A

Perry Scholarship, Nathan F. & Edna L., OH, see 7299
Perry-Griffin Foundation, The, NC, 6816
Person County Partnership for Children, NC, 6817
Person-to-Person, Inc., CT, 1442
Pet Care Trust, The, MD, 3910
Peters Foundation, Herman & Katherine, Corp., The, IL, 2785
Peters Scholarship B Fund, Frank L. and Ruth F., OH, 7300
Peters Trust, Glenn D., IN, 3144
Peters Valley Craftsman, Inc., NJ, 5539
Petersburg Methodist Home for Girls, VA, 9480
Petersen Educational Trust, Siegfried, IA, 3356
Peterson Charitable Foundation, Alan & Mildred, IL, 2786
Peterson Foundation, John P., NJ, 5540
Peterson Industries Foundation, KS, 3503
Peterson Scholarship Trust, Bradley A. & Birdell A., WI, 9992
Petoskey-Harbor Springs Area Community Foundation, MI, 4577
Petra Foundation Charitable Trust, NY, 6314
Petraborg Educational Trust Fund, Hans and Thora, MN, 4822
Petsas Charitable Trust, RI, 8369
Pettee-Chace Memorial Scholarship Fund, MA, 4218
Petters Foundation, John T., The, MN, 4823
Petteys Trust, Agnes F., FL, 2017
Pettinger Foundation Inc, The, TX, 9015
Pew Charitable Trusts, The, PA, 8033
Peyton Foundation, Brooksie A., OK, 7506
Peyton Foundation, Mary L., The, TX, 9016
Pfaffinger Foundation, CA, 864
Pfizer Patient Assistance Foundation, Inc., NY, 6315
PFLAG, DC, see 1707
PFLAG/HATCH Youth Scholarship Foundation, TX, 9017
Pflasterer, M.D. Private Foundation, Orlan W., IL, 2787
Pflughaupt Charitable Foundation, Eugene B. and Margery Ames, Inc., KY, see 3615
Pflughaupt Charitable Foundation, KY, 3615
PFS Community Foundation, IN, 3145
PFund Foundation, MN, see 4824
Pharmaceutical Research and Manufacturers of America Foundation, Inc., DC, 1714
Pharmacy Network Foundation, Inc., The, NC, 6818
PHCC Educational Foundation, VA, see 9483
Phelps Association, CT, 1443
Phelps County Community Foundation, Inc., NE, 5255
Phelps Dodge Foundation, AZ, see 196
Phelps Scholarship Trust, Roger S., MI, 4578
Phi Beta Kappa Society, The, DC, 1715
Phi Chapter Educational Foundation of Phi Gamma Delta Fraternity, IL, 2788
Phi Delta Theta Educational Foundation, OH, 7301
Phi Kappa Psi Fraternity, Endowment Fund of, Inc., The, IN, 3146
Phi Kappa Tau Foundation, OH, 7302
Phi Kappa Theta National Foundation, IN, 3147
Phi Mu Foundation, GA, 2222
Phi Sigma Sigma Foundation, Inc., MD, 3911
Philadelphia Bar Foundation, PA, 8034
Philadelphia College Opportunity Resources for Education, PA, 8035
Philadelphia Education Fund, The, PA, 8036
Philadelphia Foundation, The, PA, 8037
Philadelphia Foundation, TX, 9018
Philadelphia Futures, PA, 8038
Philadelphia Nonprofit Advertising Agency, PA, 8039
Philanthrofund Foundation, MN, 4824
Philanthropic Foundation of Cape Coral, Inc., FL, see 1815
Philanthropic Ventures Foundation, CA, 865
Philbin Memorial Fund, Catherine E., The, MA, 4219
Philharmonic Society of Orange County, CA, 866
Philippe Foundation, Inc., NY, 6316
Philips Electronics North American Foundation, MA, 4220
Phillips Foundation, Edwin, MA, 4221
Phillips Foundation, Inc., The, DC, 1716
Phillips Foundation, MS, 4918
Phillips Memorial Charitable Trust, Stephen, MA, 4222
Phillips Memorial Foundation, Nuci, The, GA, 2223

Phillips Plastics Corporation Contributions Program, WI, 9993

Phillips Scholarship Fund, V. E. & Betty, PA, 8040

Phillips Trust, Russell, WI, 9994

Phillips-Hernandez Scholarship Foundation, TX, 9019

Phoenix Challenge Foundation, Inc., NC, 6819

Phoenix Foundation Trust Fund, AZ, 226

Phoenix Houses of the Mid-Atlantic, VA, 9481

Phoenix Scholarship Foundation Inc., MD, 3912

Phoenix Suns Charities, Inc., AZ, 227

Phoenixville Community Health Foundation, PA, 8041

Photronics Scholarship Foundation, Inc., CT, see 1417

PHP, Inc., KY, 3616

PhRMA Foundation, DC, see 1714

Physicians Aid Association of the Delaware Valley, The, PA, 8042

Physicians Aid Association, CA, 867

Pi Beta Phi Educational Foundation, KS, 3504

Pi Beta Phi Foundation, MO, 5073

Pick Foundation, Vernon J., The, MN, 4825

Pickett & Hatcher Educational Fund, Inc., GA, 2224

Pickle Memorial Scholarship Fund, Elva and Herbert, PA, 8043

Piedmonte Charitable Trust, CA, 868

Piedmont Care, Inc., SC, 8503

Pieper Family Foundation, Suzanne & Richard, WI, 9995

Pierce Charitable Foundation, Mills O. Pierce & Mount Vernon, AR, 302

Pierce Trust, Beatrice D., RI, 8370

Pierce Trust, Frank, IA, 3357

Pierce Trust, Katharine C., MA, 4223

Pierson Trust, Julia, IL, 2789

PIF, GA, see 2225

Pigott Scholarship Foundation, Paul, WA, 9698

Pikes Peak Community Action Agency, Inc., CO, 1257

Pikes Peak Community Foundation, CO, 1258

Pilch Foundation, Walt & Olga, WY, 10118

Pilchard Foundation, A. Franklin, IL, 2790

PILF, NY, see 6337

Pilgrim Foundation, MA, 4224

Pillay Foundation, The, VA, 9482

Pilot International Foundation, Inc., GA, 2225

Pima Council on Aging, Inc., AZ, 228

Pine Family Foundation, MS, 4919

Pinellas County Community Foundation, FL, 2018

Pinellas County Education Foundation, Inc., FL, 2019

Pinellas County Urban League, Inc., FL, 2020

Pingel Educational Fund, Edward H. & Cora W., IL, 2791

Pinnacle Health Foundation, PA, 8044

Pinson Scholarship Foundation, Edward, NJ, 5541

Pioneer Fund, Inc., CA, see 850

Pioneer Hi-Bred International, Inc. Foundation, IA, 3358

Pioneer Igloo No. 1, AK, 130

Pioneer Memorial Scholarship Fund, WA, 9699

Pioneer Natural Resources Foundation, TX, 9020

Pioneer Natural Resources Scholarship Foundation, TX, see 9020

Pipe Line Contractors Association Scholarship Foundation, TX, 9021

Piper Charitable Trust, Roy W., PA, 8045

Piper Charitable Trust, Virginia G., The, AZ, 229

Piper Foundation, Inc., The, IL, 2792

Piper Foundation, Minnie Stevens, TX, 9022

Piqua Community Foundation, The, OH, 7303

Piqua Education Foundation, OH, 7304

Piqua-Miami County Foundation, OH, see 7242

Pirkle Jones Foundation, CA, 869

Pistons-Palace Foundation, The, MI, see 4389

Pitney Bowes Relief Fund Charitable Trust, The, CT, 1444

Pitt County Educational Foundation, Inc., NC, 6820

Pitt's Make It Right Foundation, Brad, LA, 3675

Pitts Scholarship Fund, Donald R. Pitts & Zelma C., KS, 3505

Pittsburgh Arts Council, Greater, PA, 8046

Pittsburgh Center for the Arts, Inc., PA, 8047

Pittsburgh Foundation, The, PA, 8048

Pittsburgh Glass Center, Inc., PA, 8049

Pittsfield Rotary Club Foundation Inc., MA, 4225

Pitzer Trust, John, IL, A

PKD Foundation, MO, 5074

Placer Community Foundation, CA, 870

Plan NH - The Foundation for Shaping the Built Environment, NH, 5361

Plank Trust f/b/o C. Plank Scholarship Trust, Elsie L., PA, 8050

Planning & Visual Education (P.A.V.E.), FL, see 2021

Planning & Visual Education Partnership, Inc., FL, 2021

Plastic Surgery Educational Foundation, IL, see 2793

Plastic Surgery Foundation, The, IL, 2793

Playboy Foundation, The, IL, 2794

Players Championship Charities, The, FL, 2022

Plimpton Education Trust, Alice, OH, 7305

Plimpton Educational Fund, Alice H., OH, see 7305

Plitt Southern Theatres, Inc. Employees Fund, TX, A

Plotkin Foundation, Peter & Masha, CA, 871

Ploughshares Fund, CA, 872

Plum Creek Foundation, WA, 9700

Plumas Community Foundation, CA, 873

Plumbers and Pipefitters Local No. 333 Scholarship Plan, MI, 4579

Plumbing-Heating-Cooling Contractors-National Association Educational Foundation, VA, 9483

Plummer Scholarship Fund, IN, 3148

PLUS Foundation, MN, 4826

Plymouth Fragment Society, MA, 4226

PMC Foundation, The, CA, 874

PMMI Education and Training Foundation, VA, 9484

PNC Bank Memorial Foundation, PA, 8051

PNC Bank Memorial Foundation, PA, see 8051

PNH Research & Support Foundation, The, MD, 3913

Podiatry Foundation of Pittsburgh, The, PA, 8052

Poetry Foundation, The, IL, 2795

Poetry Society of America, NY, 6317

Poff Scholarship Foundation, Bess R., VA, 9485

Poillon Memorial Scholarship Trust, John Williams, MO, 5075

Point Foundation, CA, 875

Pokagon Fund, Inc., The, MI, 4580

Polakovic Charitable Trust, John, MI, 4581

Polan Foundation, Jennifer Gordon, MI, 4582

Polaris Foundation, The, MN, 4827

Police Officer Assistance Trust, FL, 2023

Polish American Board of Education of Berks County, PA, PA, 8053

Polish American Congress Charitable Foundation, IL, 2796

Polk County Community Foundation, Inc., The, NC, 6821

Polk Foundation, Annie M. & Clarke A., TX, 9023

Pollak Project, Martin, Inc., The, MD, 3914

Pollock-Krasner Foundation, Inc., The, NY, 6318

Polonsky Brothers Foundation, NJ, 5542

Polycystic Kidney Research Foundation, MO, see 5074

Pomona Valley Community Hospital LTD-Womens Auxiliary, CA, 876

Poncin Scholarship Fund, TX, 9024

Poole Foundation, Leslie, The, CA, 877

Pope Foundation, Generoso, The, NY, 6319

Pope Foundation, The, NY, see 6319

Pope Memorial Scholarship Fund, Ida M., HI, 2315

Pope Scholarship Fund, Thomas H., MA, 4227

Population Biology Foundation, CO, 1259

Population Council, Inc., The, NY, 6320

Porhaska Scholarship Foundation, David J., WI, 9996

Port Arthur Higher Education Foundation, Inc., TX, 9025

Portage County Sheriff's Association, OH, 7306

Porter Art Foundation Trust, OH, 7149

Porter County Community Foundation, Inc., IN, 3150

Porter Educational Fund, Edwin M., MO, 5076

Porter Foundation, John & Anna Newton, NH, 5362

Porter Trust, Laura E., KS, 3506

Portland Female Charitable Society, ME, 3726

Portland Foundation, The, IN, 3151

Portland Institute for Contemporary Art, OR, 7632

Portland Rotary Charitable Trust, OR, 7633

Portland Seamen's Friend Society, ME, 3727

Portland Valley Acacia Fund, Inc., OR, 7634

Portraits, Inc. Scholarship Foundation, AL, 70

Portraits, Inc., Scholarship Foundation, AL, see 70

Portuguese-American Scholarship Foundation, NJ, 5543

Posey Foundation, Leslie T. & Frances U., NC, 6822

Positive Impact, Inc., AZ, 230

Post Trust, Ralph B., NY, 6321

Postal Employees Relief Fund, VA, 9486

Postles Scholarship Fund, Howard & Edna, PA, 8054

Postles Scholarship Fund, Wilbur E., PA, 8055

Potlatch Foundation for Higher Education, WA, A

Potlatch Fund, WA, 9701

Potter Foundation, Philip E., The, NY, 6322

Potter Memorial Foundation, Stephen J., Inc., NY, 6323

Pottstown Symphony Orchestra, PA, 8056

Poucher Memorial Fund, Frank C. Poucher & Lillian S., NJ, 5544

Poudre Valley Health System Foundation, CO, 1260

Poudre Valley Hospital Foundation, CO, see 1260

Powdermaker Family Foundation, TX, 9026

Powell Hope Foundation, Jonathan, Inc., WV, 9809

Powell Trust, Mary E., OH, 7307

Power Scholarship Fund, Howard A., PA, 8057

Powers Foundation, Ross, ME, 3728

Poweshiek Community Foundation, Greater, IA, 3359

PPG Industries Foundation, PA, 8058

Prader-Willi Syndrome Association of Wisconsin, Inc., WI, 9997

Prairie Lakes Regional Arts Council, MN, 4828

Praiss Memorial Scholarship Fund, William F., WI, 9998

Prasad Family Foundation, Inc., The, CT, 1445

Prater Scholarship Fund, Guy & Nyda, TX, 9027

Pratt Free School, Trustees of the, MA, 4228

Pratt Trust Clause No. 31, Fannie B., MA, 4229

Prayer Child Foundation, AZ, 231

Precision Rubber Products Foundation, Inc., TN, 8633

Preeclampsia Foundation, FL, 2024

Preferred Mutual Insurance Company Foundation, NY, 6324

Presbyterian Healthcare Foundation, TX, 9028

Presbyterian Healthcare Services, NM, see 5644

Prescott Christian School Scholarship Foundation, AZ, see 179

Prescott Fund for Children & Youth, Inc., NY, 6325

Prescott Trust, Torrence, PA, 8059

Presence Health Foundation, IL, 2797

President and Fellows of Harvard College, MA, see 4230

President and Fellows of Harvard Corporation, MA, 4230

Presser Foundation, The, PA, 8060

Pressley Ridge Foundation, PA, 8061

Pressman Co. Trust, William, NY, 6326

Prest Educational Trust Fund, Joe, IL, 2798

Presto Foundation, The, DE, 1520

Preston & Belvah McFadden Scholarship Fund, William, KS, 3507

Preston Educational Trust, Elmer O. & Ida, IA, 3360

Preston Memorial Scholarship Trust, Frank W., PA, 8062

Preston Trust, Evelyn W., RI, 8371

Prevent Blindness America, IL, see 2752

Prevent Cancer Foundation, VA, 9487

Previti Family Charitable Foundation, A.A., Inc., NJ, see 5545

Previti Foundation, A. A., NJ, 5545

Prewett, Jr. Educational Foundation, V. I., AL, 71

Price Charities, CA, 878

Price Chopper's Golub Foundation, NY, 6327

Price Educational Foundation, Herschel C., WV, 9810

Price Family Charitable Fund, The, CA, 879

Price Foundation, Inc., CA, 880

Price Foundation, M. B., Inc., CA, 881

Price Foundation, Sol & Helen, The, CA, see 879

Price Scholarship Fund Trust, Miriam Sutro, RI, 8373

Price Scholarship Fund, Joseph R. and Florence A., RI, 8372

Price Trust, Albert M., WV, 9811

PricewaterhouseCoopers Charitable Foundation, Inc., NY, 6328

Pride Foundation, The, WA, 9702

Prieto Community Board, Dr. Jorge, IL, 2799

Prime Time Foundation, Inc., FL, 2025

Prince George's Arts and Humanities Council, MD, see 3915

Prince George's Arts Council, Inc., MD, 3915

Prince Trust No. 2, Nathan D., RI, 8374

Princess Grace Foundation - U.S.A., NY, 6329

Princeton Area Community Foundation, Inc., NJ, 5546

Princeton Area Foundation, Inc., The, NJ, see 5546

Princeton High School Class of 1926 Scholarship Fund, WV, 9812
Prine Scholarship Award Foundation, Ricky, IL, 2800
Print & Graphics Scholarship Foundation, PA, 8063
Prior Memorial Scholarship Trust, Beatrice, OH, 7308
Pritchard Educational Trust, IA, 3361
Pritchett Trust, Scott R., CA, 882
Private Industry Council of Lehigh Valley, Inc., PA, 8064
PRMC-Clovis Hospital Auxiliary, NM, 5644
Pro-Choice Resources, MN, 4829
ProArts, PA, see 8046
Process Machinery Charitable Foundation, Inc., KY, 3617
Proctor Health Care Foundation, IL, 2801
Professional Association of Diving Instructors Foundation, CA, see 852
Professional Athletes Foundation, DC, 1717
Professional Engineers of Oregon Educational Foundation, OR, 7635
Professional Horsemen's Scholarship Fund, NY, 6330
Professional Tennis Registry Foundation, SC, 8504
Professional Women Photographers, Inc., NY, 6331
Progin Scholarship Fund, George K., The, MA, 4231
Programs for Human Services, Inc., TX, 9029
Progress Village Foundation, FL, see 2026
Progress Village Foundation, Inc., FL, 2026
Prohaska Scholarship Foundation, WI, 9999
Project A.L.S., Inc., NY, 6332
Project Dream Foundation, NY, 6333
Project Home Again Foundation, NY, 6334
Project Home, Inc., WI, 10000
Project Management Institute Educational Foundation, PA, 8065
Project PAVE, Inc., CO, 1261
Project Renewal, Inc., NY, 6335
Project Single Parent, Inc., OK, 7507
Project Tomorrow, CA, 883
Promises 2 Kids, CA, 884
Promising Scholars Fund, CT, 1446
Promotional Products Education Foundation, TX, 9030
Proshek Foundation, Charles E., MN, 4830
Prostate Cancer Foundation, CA, 885
Protective Life Foundation, AL, 72
Provenzano Scholarship Fund, Josephine, NJ, see 5483
Providence Alaska Foundation, AK, 131
Providence Community Health Foundation, OR, 7636
Providence Female Charitable Society, RI, 8375
Providence General Foundation, WA, 9703
Providence Health System - Washington, WA, 9704
Providence Little Company of Mary Foundation, CA, see 747
Providence Milwaukie Foundation, OR, 7637
Providence Newberg Health Foundation, OR, 7638
Providence Portland Medical Foundation, OR, 7639
Provident Bank Charitable Foundation, NY, 6336
Providers Choice, Inc., MN, 4831
Prudential Financial, Inc. Corporate Giving Program, NJ, 5547
Pryde Scholarship Fund, RI, 8376
Pryor Foundation, Mark R., MN, 4832
PSA No. 3 Agency on Aging, Inc., OH, 7309
Psea Scholarship Trust, PA, 8066
PSEG Foundation, Inc., NJ, 5548
PSS/Gulf South Employee Relief Fund Inc., FL, 2027
Psychiatric Research Foundation of Columbus, Inc., OH, 7310
PTR Foundation, SC, see 8504
Public Education & Business Coalition, CO, 1262
Public Education Foundation of Evansville, Inc., IN, 3152
Public Entity Risk Institute, VA, 9488
Public Health Foundation Enterprises, Inc., CA, 886
Public Health Institute, CA, 887
Public Interest Law Foundation at Columbia, NY, 6337
Public Media, Inc., NY, 6338
Public Service Electric and Gas Company Foundation, Inc., NJ, see 5548
Puckett Foundation, IL, 2802
Puckett Memorial Fund, Leta Potter, PA, 8067
Puckett, Jr. Family Foundation, Allen B., MS, 4920
Puddy Educational Foundation, CO, 1263
Pueblo Hispanic Education Foundation, CO, 1264

Puerto Rican Bar Association Scholarship Fund, Inc., NY, 6339
Puerto Rico Community Foundation, Inc., PR, 8223
Puffin Foundation, Ltd., NJ, 5549
Pugh Foundation Scholarship Fund, Hazel & Ben, IL, see 2803
Pugh Foundation Scholarship Fund, IL, 2803
Pulaski County Community Foundation, Inc., IN, 3153
Pullman Educational Foundation, George M., IL, 2804
Pulmonary Fibrosis Foundation, IL, 2805
Pulmonary Hypertension Association, MD, 3916
Pursuit of Excellence, CA, 888
Putnam County Community Foundation, The, IN, 3154
Putnam Cultural Endowment, Oscar Lee, LA, 3676
Putnam Prize Fund for the Promotion of Scholarship, William Lowell, MA, 4232
Putnam Trust, Franklin H., RI, 8377
Pyle Trust, Joseph P., PA, 8068
Pyramid Atlantic, Inc., MD, 3917

Quabaug Corporation Charitable Foundation, MA, 4233
Quad City Osteopathic Foundation, IA, A
Quaker Chemical Foundation, The, PA, 8069
QUALCOMM Incorporated Corporate Giving Program, CA, 889
Quality Care Health Foundation, Inc., CA, 890
Quarter Century Club Scholarship Fund, DE, 1521
Queen Anne's County Art Council, Inc., MD, 3918
Queen of Peace Center, MO, 5077
Queens College Foundation, Inc., NY, 6340
Queens Council on the Arts, Inc., NY, 6341
QueensCare, CA, 891
Quest Diagnostics Incorporated Contributions Program, NJ, A
Quin Foundation, Robert D. & Margaret W., PA, 8070
Quincy Area Community Foundation, IL, see 2497
Quincy Community Action Programs, Inc., MA, 4234
Quinkert Memorial Foundation, Shayne, KY, 3618
Quirico Educational Foundation, Francis J., The, MA, 4235
Qwest Foundation, DE, see 1494

R.A.C.K Foundation, GA, 2226
R.B. Ranch, CO, see 1155
R.O.S.E. Fund, Inc., The, MA, 4236
Raab Educational Trust, Herbert and Gwendolyn, IN, 3155
Rabideau Education Scholarship Fund, Omer E., IL, see 2814
Rachor Family Foundation, Ltd., MI, 4583
Rachor Professional School Scholarship Fund, Michael Garry, Ltd., MI, see 4583
Racine Community Foundation, Inc., WI, 10001
Racine County Area Foundation, Inc., WI, see 10001
Racine Kenosha Community Action Agency, Inc., WI, 10002
Rader Education Foundation Inc., Lucille, CA, 892
Radiation Oncology Institute, VA, 9489
Radio and Television News Directors Foundation, DC, 1718
Radio Television Digital News Association, DC, see 1718
Radius Foundation, Inc., The, NY, 6342
Raef Scholarship Fund Trust, Arthur J. & Blanche D., AR, 303
Raether Scholarship Trust, John E., WI, 10003
Ragdale Foundation, The, IL, 2806
Ragel Scholarship Fund, Robert L., OR, 7640
Rahman Foundation, A. R., VA, 9490
Rahr Foundation, MN, 4833
Raider Memorial Trust, Helen, IA, 3362
Raies-Murr Educational Trust, CA, 893
Rainey Memorial Trust, Bish, IL, 2807
Rainey Scholarship Fund Inc., Micki, CA, 894
Rainforest Alliance, Inc., NY, 6343
Rainforest Cafe Friends of the Future Foundation, TX, 9031
Rains Foundation, TN, 8634
Rains Scholarship Fund, Jack Mary, OH, 7311
Rainy Day Foundation, Inc., DC, 1719
RAISE, CA, see 902

Raleigh County Community Action Association, Inc., WV, 9813
Rales Foundation, Norman R. Rales and Ruth, The, DC, 1720
Ramakrishna Foundation, CA, 895
Ramiah Family Foundation, WI, 10004
Ramona's Mexican Food Products Scholarship Foundation, CA, 896
Ramsaye Medical Trust, Helene, NH, 5363
Ramsaye Scholarship Trust, Helene, NH, 5364
Ramsdale Scholarship Fund, Edward, Inc., ID, 2345
Rancho Santa Fe Community Foundation, CA, see 897
Rancho Santa Fe Foundation, CA, 897
Rand Institute/The Center for the Advancement of Objectivism, Ayn, CA, 898
Randall Memorial Trust, Clifford, WI, see 10014
Randall Trust, Frank B., RI, 8378
Randolph Foundation, John, VA, 9491
Randolph Foundation, The, NH, 5365
Randolph Memorial Scholarship Trust, IN, 3156
Randon House Foundation, Inc., NY, 6344
Ranger-Ryan Scholarship Foundation, TX, A
Raphael Memorial for Neuroblastoma, Keaton, Inc., The, CA, 899
Rapp Education Fund Charitable Trust, Mack, OH, 7312
Raskob Foundation, Bill, Inc., The, MD, 3919
Rasmuson Foundation, AK, 132
Ratner Human Services Fund, Harry, The, OH, 7313
Ratner, Miller, Shafran Foundation, OH, 7314
Ratte Charitable Foundation, Michael G., MA, 4237
Rau Trust, Alexander and Cassia, NY, 6345
Rauch Family Foundation II, Inc., IL, 2808
Raval Education Foundation Inc., The, MI, 4584
Ravens All-Community Team Foundation, Inc., MD, 3920
Ravens Foundation for Families, Inc., MD, see 3920
Ravi Zacharias International Ministries, GA, 2227
Rawlings Foundation, Inc., The, FL, 2028
Rawls Educational Trust, Walter C. & Ella, FL, 2029
Rawls Scholarship Foundation, Jerry S., The, TX, 9032
Ray Koenig Charitable Foundation of WPS Inc., WI, see 10088
Ray-Carroll County Grain Growers Scholarship Fund, Inc., MO, see 5078
Ray-Carroll Scholarship Fund, MO, 5078
Rayni Foundation, Inc., The, CA, 2030
Rayonier Foundation, The, FL, 2031
Raytheon Company Contributions Program, MA, 4238
RCL Foundation, CA, 900
Reach for The Moon Foundation, IL, 2809
Reach Our Children, Inc., WI, see 9895
Reach Scholars Foundation, CO, 1265
Reaching Heights, the Cleveland Heights/University Heights Public Schools Foundation, OH, 7315
Reaching Up, Inc., NY, 6346
Reading Musical Foundation, PA, 8071
READY Foundation, Inc., NJ, see 5551
Reagan Presidential Foundation, Ronald, The, CA, 901
Real Art Ways, CT, 1447
Real Colegio Complutense, Inc., MA, 4239
REAL Services, Inc., IN, 3157
Realize Your Dream Foundation, PA, 8072
Realtors Relief Foundation, IL, 2810
Realty Foundation of New York, NY, 6347
REBNY Foundation Inc., The, NY, 6348
Reckitt Benckiser Pharmaceuticals Patient Help Foundation, VA, 9492
Record School Foundation, George J., OH, 7316
Recording for the Blind & Dyslexic, NJ, see 5496
Recreational Boating Industries Educational Foundation, MI, 4585
Recruiting Advancement of Instruction & Scholarship for Education in the Graphic Arts, Inc., CA, 902
Recycling Research Foundation, DC, 1721
Red Circle Foundation, DC, 1722
Red Rock Area Community Action Program, Inc., IA, 3363
Red Rocks Community College Foundation, CO, 1266
Red Sox Foundation, Inc., The, MA, 4240
Red Tab Foundation, The, CA, 903
Redding Family Foundation, CA, 904
Reddington Scholarship Fund & Trust, John A., NY, 6349

Reddy Charitable Foundation, Dr. Prem, CA, *see* 538

REDF, CA, 905

Redfield Trust, Richard F., WI, 10005

Redmond Foundation, Thomas M., MN, 4834

Redwood Area Communities Foundation, Inc., MN, 4835

Redwood Children's Services, Inc., CA, 906

Redwood Coast Developmental Services Corporation, CA, 907

Reed Charitable Trust, Elsie Seller, FL, 2032

Reed Engineering Group Employees Scholarship, TX, 9033

Reed Foundation for the Performing Arts, Donna, The, IA, 3364

Reed Foundation, Judge J. P. & Elizabeth, AR, 304

Reed Foundation, Peter S., Inc., NY, 6350

Reed Medical Scholarship Trust, Joanna F., AL, 73

Reese Foundation, Spence, TX, 9034

Reeve Foundation, Christopher and Dana, NJ, *see* 5550

Reeve Foundation, Christopher, NJ, 5550

Reeves Foundation Trust, Sophia K., PA, 8073

Reeves Foundation, IN, 3158

Reeves Foundation, Inc., IN, 3159

Regal Foundation, TN, 8635

Regence Caring Foundation for Children, UT, 9222

Reger Arts Foundation, Inc., NJ, A

Region 2 Arts Council, MN, 4836

Region 3b Area Agency on Aging, MI, 4586

Regional Arts and Culture Council, OR, 7641

Regional Cultural Alliance of Greater Birmingham, Inc., AL, 74

Regional West Foundation, NE, 5256

Regions Hospital Foundation, MN, 4837

Rehabilitation Foundation of Northwest Florida, Inc., FL, 2033

Rehabilitation Hospital of the Pacific Foundation, HI, 2316

Reich Education Foundation, Edgar and Lois, NC, 6823

Reid Charitable & Student Loan, C. M. & A. A., MI, 4587

Reid Scholarship Fund, W. Scott, The, ME, 3729

Reierson Foundation, Olive Rice, NC, 6824

Reifel-Elwood Educational Foundation, IA, 3365

Reilly Family Foundation, The, TX, 9035

Reinhardt Family Scholarship Trust, The, NY, 6351

Reinhart Memorial Scholarship Foundation, Floyd J., NY, 6352

Reinheimer Trust, Mildred, IL, 2811

Reinhold Scholarship Trust, Grace E., FL, *see* 2034

Reinhold Scholarship Trust, Grace Fleming, FL, 2034

Reining Horse Sports Foundation, Inc., OK, 7508

Reiss Foundation, William M., IL, 2812

Reitch Scholarship Trust, Tom C. & Mary B., TX, 9036

Reitnauer Scholarship Fund, Henry K. & Evelyn, PA, 8074

Relief Association Trust, MA, *see* 4241

Relief Association, Inc., MA, 4241

Religion Newswriters Foundation, OH, 7317

Religious Institutional Finance Corporation of America, NC, 6825

Reller Memorial Scholarship Fund, Elizabeth, IL, 2813

Remington Foundation, Elwyn, Inc., WI, 10006

Remmele Foundation, OH, 7318

Renaissance Foundation, The, OR, 7642

Renaissance Performing Arts Co., AZ, 232

Renal Assistance, Inc., FL, 2035

Renfrow Foundation, L. & A., CO, 1267

Rennie Scholarship Fund, Waldo E., NC, 6826

Reno County Child Care Association, Inc., KS, *see* 3423

Reno Rodeo Foundation, NV, 5300

Renown Health Foundation, NV, 5301

Rental Assistance Corporation of Buffalo, NY, 6353

Renton Community Foundation, WA, 9705

REO Educational Scholarship Fund, IL, 2814

Republic of Tea Foundation, The, IL, 2815

Research & Education Foundation of the American Association for the Surgery of Trauma, IL, 2816

Research Corporation for Science Advancement, AZ, 233

Research Foundation of CFA Institute, The, VA, 9493

Research Foundation of The City University of New York, NY, 6354

Reserve Aid, Inc., TX, 9037

Resource Connections of Prince George's County, Inc., MD, 3921

Resources for the Future, DC, 1723

Respiratory Health Association of Metropolitan Chicago, IL, 2817

Rest Haven Preventorium for Children, Inc., CA, 908

Restless Legs Syndrome Foundation, Inc., MN, 4838

Resurrection Development Foundation, IL, *see* 2797

Retired Officers Association Scholarship Fund, The, VA, *see* 9436

Retiring Fund for the Women in the Diaconate of the Episcopal Church, SC, *see* 8472

Reuther Memorial Fund, MI, *see* 4588

Reuther Memorial Fund, Walter and May, MI, 4588

Rex Foundation, CA, 909

Rex Hospital Guild, Inc., NC, 6827

Rexnord Foundation Inc., WI, 10007

Reynolds Estate Foundation, Edith Grace Craig, OH, 7319

Reynolds Estate Residuary Trust, Edith Grace, OH, *see* 7319

Reynolds Foundation, Catherine B., VA, *see* 9371

Reynolds Foundation, Inc., GA, *see* 2228

Reynolds Foundation, Z. Smith, Inc., NC, 6828

Reynolds Plantation Foundation, Inc., GA, 2228

Reynolds Scholarship Trust, S. M. and Jessie Dell, AL, 75

Reynolds Trust, Harry Bertram, MO, 5079

Reynolds-Barwick Scholarship Fund, IL, 2818

RFF, DC, *see* 1723

Rhoad Testamentary Trust, Robert L., OH, 7320

Rhoads Foundation, T. L., PA, 8075

Rhoads Scholarship Trust, KY, 3619

Rhode Island Bar Foundation, RI, 8379

Rhode Island Building Industry Scholarship Fund, RI, 8380

Rhode Island Community Foundation, The, RI, *see* 8381

Rhode Island Foundation, The, RI, 8381

Rhode Island Hospital Foundation, RI, 8382

Rhoden Athletic Scholarship Fund, Ward, OR, 7643

Rhodes Museum and Charitable Foundation Inc., Albert and Mary, The, WI, 10008

Rhodes Scholarship Fund, Marguerite A., FL, 2036

Rhythm & Blues Foundation, Inc., The, PA, 8076

Rice Aid Fund Inc., William B., MA, 4242

Rich Memorial Foundation, Gordon A., The, NY, 6355

Richardi Scholarship Trust, Richard, NC, 6829

Richards Education Foundation, Barbara Keene, The, CA, 910

Richards Scholarship Trust, Clarence & Olive, WI, 10009

Richardson Family Henry County Educational Trust, TN, 8636

Richardson Foundation, Robert L. and Shirla B., NC, 6830

Richardson Fund Corporation, Mary T. & William A., MA, 4243

Richardson Fund, Mary Lynn, The, NC, 6831

Richardson Memorial Fund, Sid, TX, 9038

Richardson Memorial Trust, Bob, OR, 7644

Richardson Musical Education Scholarship Fund, Robert W., WA, 9706

Richardt Charitable Trust, Charlotte M., IN, 3160

Richey Foundation, Beverly Aronson, The, IN, *see* 3009

Richland Community College Foundation, IL, 2819

Richland County Foundation of Mansfield, Ohio, The, OH, *see* 7321

Richland County Foundation, OH, 7321

Richmond Art Museum, IN, 3161

Richmond Community Foundation, Greater, VA, *see* 9350

Richmond Educational Foundation, OR, 7645

Richmond Jewish Foundation, VA, 9494

Richmond Symphony Orchestra Association, IN, 3162

Richmond Unified Education Fund, CA, *see* 1090

Richmond-Pennock Family Scholarship Fund, NC, 6832

Ricker College Endowment Fund, ME, 3730

Rickert Memorial Scholarship Fund, Gladys & Evelyn, OH, 7322

Riddick Foundation, The, NC, 6833

Riddick Memorial Scholarship Fund, Raymond E., MA, 4244

Riddle HealthCare Foundation, The, PA, 8077

Riddleberger Scholarship Trust, Faye, IN, 3163

Ride For Kids Foundation, Inc., NC, *see* 6814

Rider Trust, Frank, WA, 9707

Ridgefield Scholarship Group, Inc., CT, 1448

Riechmann Foundation, B. Beall & R. Kemp, FL, 2037

Rieger Foundation, Herman, IL, 2820

Riesch Paralysis Foundation, Bryon, WI, 10010

Rietman Charitable Foundation, Carl and Camilla, OR, 7646

RIFCA, NC, *see* 6825

Riffe Memorial Scholarship Trust, Earl N. & Conrad E., TX, 9039

Riffe Memorial Scholarship Trust, TX, *see* 9039

Riggs Student Scholarship Fund, Jessie May, OR, 7647

Riggs Student Scholarship Fund, OR, *see* 7647

Right from the Start Nutrition, TX, 9040

Rigorous Educational Assistance for Deserving Youth Foundation, Inc., NJ, 5551

Rigsby Memorial Fund, John & David, Inc., The, FL, 2038

Riley Family Scholarship Fund, Leo B., IA, 3366

Riley Foundation, Grace O. & Harry D., The, NE, 5257

Rima Memorial Scholarship, Michelle, Inc., IA, 3367

Rimmele Scholarship Fund, Robert, RI, 8383

Rinker Medical Scholarship Fund, Dr. E.B., IL, *see* 2821

Rinker Trust, Lila, IL, 2821

Rinne Memorial Trust, Wayne, OR, 7648

Rio Grande Cancer Foundation, TX, 9041

Rio Hondo College Foundation, CA, 911

Riordan Foundation, Cle & Dennis, AR, 305

Riot Relief Fund, The, CT, 1449

Ripley County Community Foundation, Inc., IN, 3164

Risley Educational Trust, Jean, NC, 6834

Rislov Foundation, Sigurd & Jarmila, MI, 4589

Riss Trust, Lois E., NE, 5258

Ritchie Memorial Fund, Lieutenant Robert Bolenius, NC, 6835

Rittenhouse Charitable Foundation, Lloyd W. & Virginia D., IL, 2822

Rittenhouse Foundation, IL, *see* 2822

Ritzville Warehouse Foundation, WA, 9708

Rivendell Stewards' Trust, CA, 912

River Foundation, Inc., The, KY, 3620

Riverbend Foundation, AL, 76

Riverside Arts Council, CA, 913

Riverside County Physicians Memorial Foundation, CA, 914

Riverside Golf Club Memorial Scholarship Fund For Caddies Foundation, The, IL, 2823

Riverside HealthCare Foundation, IL, 2824

Riverview Health Care Foundation, Inc., WI, 10011

Rixson Foundation, Oscar C., Inc., NC, 6836

RMC Foundation, Inc., IL, *see* 2824

RMCMI, CO, *see* 1272

RMHC of Arkoma, Inc., AR, 306

Roach Memorial Scholarship Fund, Ruth E., OH, 7323

Roark Scholarship Fund Trust, Mary Elizabeth, TN, 8637

Robbins Trust, Charlotte M., RI, 8384

Robbins Trust, Fred L., RI, 8385

Roberg Endowment Trust, Louis A., MN, 4839

Roberts Memorial Foundation, Robert R., CA, 915

Roberts Memorial Scholarship Fund, Diana, FL, 2039

Roberts Scholarship Foundation, Mary K., IL, 2825

Robertson Family Memorial Fund, A. F., OH, 7324

Robeson County Partnership for Children, Inc., NC, 6837

Robins Family Foundation, Leslie C., The, WI, 10012

Robinson Charitable Foundation, Velma Lee & John Harvey, TX, 9042

Robinson Charitable Trust, Blanche A., RI, 8386

Robinson Foundation, Harold and Ruth, The, CO, 1268

Robinson Foundation, Jackie, Inc., NY, 6356

Robinson Fund, Fred L., MT, 5168

Robinson Memorial Scholarship Fund, C. E., DE, *see* 1522

Robinson Memorial Scholarship, Charles E., DE, 1522

Robinson Scholarship Trust, Florence M., KS, 3508

Robinson Trust f/b/o Scholarship Fund, A., NC, 6838

Robinson Trust Foundation, Emmet and Mary, NC, 6839

Robinson Trust, Harry W. and Virginia, TX, 9043

Robinson Trust, Mary H., IL, 2826

Robinson Welfare Trust, John W., ME, 3731

Robinson, Farmer, Cox Associates Educational Foundation, VA, 9495

Robinson, Jr. Memorial Foundation, Angus, DC, 1724

Robustelli Family Foundation, NJ, 5552

Roche Memorial Fund, Ellen Marie, Inc., MD, 3922

Rochester Alumni Scholarship Charitable Trust, PA, 8078

Rochester Area Community Foundation Initiatives, Inc., NY, 6358

Rochester Area Community Foundation, Greater, MI, see 4395

Rochester Area Community Foundation, NY, 6357

Rochester Area Foundation, MN, 4840

Rochester Area Neighborhood House, Inc., MI, 4590

Rock Bottom Foundation, CO, 1269

Rock River Valley Health Foundation, IL, see 2470

Rockefeller Foundation, The, NY, 6359

Rockford Area Arts Council, IL, 2827

Rockford Community Foundation, IL, see 2495

Rockingham County Community Action, Inc., NH, 5366

Rockland Trust Charitable Foundation, MA, 4245

Rockville Bank Community Foundation, Inc., CT, see 1450

Rockville Bank Foundation, Inc., CT, 1450

Rockwood Foundation, The, IL, 2828

Rocky Mountain Cancer Assistance, CO, 1270

Rocky Mountain Cancer Centers Foundation, CO, see 1270

Rocky Mountain Children's Choir, CO, 1271

Rocky Mountain Coal Mining Institute, CO, 1272

Rocky Mountain Elk Foundation, Inc., MT, 5169

Rocky Mountain Lions Eye Bank, CO, 1273

Rocky Mountain Natural Gas Memorial Scholarship Fund, CO, A

Roddick Fund, OH, 7325

Roesch Vocal Scholarship Trust, Polly W., IL, 2829

Roethke Scholarship Fund, Otto & Helen, MI, 4591

ROFEH, Inc., MA, 4246

Rogers Brothers Foundation, ID, 2346

Rogers Educational Trust, Lon & Jessie, IL, 2830

Rogers Foundation, Buck, Inc., FL, 2040

Rogers Institute, Will, CA, see 916

Rogers Memorial Student Loan Fund, Bruce & Mary, OH, see 7326

Rogers Motion Picture Pioneers Foundation, Will, CA, 916

Rogers Student Loan, Bruce & Mary, OH, 7326

Rogers T.P for C. H. Rogers Memorial Fund, PA, A

Rogers Trust, Ada M., OH, see 7326

Rogow Birken Foundation, Inc., The, CT, see 1451

Rogow Greenberg Foundation, Inc., The, CT, 1451

Rohr Employees Will-Share Club, CA, 917

Rohrer, Jr. Educational Foundation, William G., PA, 8079

Rolfs Educational Foundation, Ltd., WI, 10013

Rolfson Scholarship Trust, Mars & Verna, MT, 5170

Rolland Scholarship Fund, Art & Peg, RI, 8387

Rolland Scholarship Fund, Arthur D. & Marvis S., RI, see 8387

Rolling Plains Management Corporation, TX, 9044

Rollison Educational Scholarship Trust, John W., NC, 6840

Romsdahl Foundation, The, TX, 9045

Ronald McDonald Children's Charities, IL, see 2831

Ronald McDonald House Charities of Arkoma, Inc., AR, see 306

Ronald McDonald House Charities of Central New York, Inc., NY, 6360

Ronald McDonald House Charities of Denver, Inc., CO, 1274

Ronald McDonald House Charities of Greater Washington, DC, Inc., DC, 1725

Ronald McDonald House Charities of Kansas City, Inc., MO, 5080

Ronald McDonald House Charities of Southern California, Inc., CA, 918

Ronald McDonald House Charities of the Heart of America, Inc., MO, see 5080

Ronald McDonald House Charities of the Philadelphia Region, Inc., PA, 8080

Ronald McDonald House Charities, IL, 2831

Ronci Memorial Scholarship Trust, Paul F., The, RI, 8388

Roof Memorial Scholarship Fund, Freda T., NC, 6841

Rooke Foundation, Inc., TX, 9046

Rooney Scholarship Fund, Art, PA, 8081

Rooney Wrangell Community Foundation, Peter, AK, 133

Roosevelt County Electric Education Foundation, NM, 5645

Roosevelt County Rural Telephone Education Foundation, NM, 5646

Root Scholarship Fund, Lillian L., OH, 7327

Roothbert Fund Inc., The, NY, 6361

Roscommon County Community Foundation, MI, 4592

Rose Family Foundation Trust, OK, 7509

Rose Foundation for Communities and the Environment, CA, 919

Rose Foundation, Scott, Inc., KY, 3621

Rose Fund for Music, Susan W., Inc., NY, 6362

Rose Fund, Mary Therese, The, NJ, 5553

Rose Ladies Aid Society, IN, 3165

Rosemary Childrens Services, CA, 920

Rosen Family Foundation, Inc., The, MN, 4841

Rosenberg Foundation, Murray & Sydell, Inc., GA, 2229

Rosenberg Foundation, Murray M., GA, see 2229

Rosenberg Fund for Children, Inc., MA, 4247

Rosenberg Fund, Anna Davidson, CA, see 921

Rosenberg Memorial Fund, Dorothy Sargent, CA, 921

Rosenberger Award Foundation, Raymond, OH, 7328

Rosenfeld Trust, Max C., PA, 8082

Ross Foundation, Betsy, Inc., TN, 8638

Ross Foundation, John M., HI, 2317

Ross Loan Fund, The, PA, 8083

Ross Memorial Foundation, Roderick Earl, The, UT, 9223

Ross Scholarship Loan, ME, 3732

Ross Trust, Charles M., IL, 2832

Rossmoor Scholarship Foundation, CA, 922

Rostra Engineered Component Sunshine Fund, RI, 8389

Rosztoczy Foundation, AZ, 234

Rot Foundation, Albert J. and Susan E., IL, 2833

Rotalia Foundation, WA, 9709

Rotary Club Education Fund of Framingham, MA, 4248

Rotary Club of Burley, Idaho Scholarship Trust, ID, 2347

Rotary Club of Killeen Heights Charitable Corporation, TX, 9047

Rotary Club of Lowell Community Foundation, MI, 4593

Rotary Club of Milwaukee Foundation, WI, 10014

Rotary Club of North Scott Educational Foundation, IA, 3368

Rotary Club of Sparta-Henderson Memorial Foundation, Inc., IL, 2834

Rotary Foundation of Rotary International, The, IL, 2835

Rotary Service Foundation of San Mateo, CA, see 952

Rotch Travelling Scholarship, Inc., MA, 4249

Rottenberg Foundation, Herman & Lenore, NY, 6363

Rotterman Trust, Helen L. & Marie F., OH, 7329

Rouch Boys Foundation, A. P. and Louise, NC, see 6842

Rouch Foundation Charitable Trust, NC, 6842

Rowan Family Foundation, CA, 923

Rowan Helping Ministries, NC, 6843

Rowan Partnership for Children, Inc., NC, see 6865

Rowan University Foundation, Inc., NJ, 5554

Rowland Foundation Inc., The, VT, 9258

Roxbury Scholarship Foundation, Inc., CT, 1452

Roy Foundation, Travis, MA, 4250

Roy Scholarship Fund Charitable Trust, IL, see 2836

Roy Scholarship Fund, IL, see 2836

Roy Scholarship Fund, Mildred C., OH, 7330

Roy Scholarship Trust, IL, 2836

Royal Arcanum Scholarship Fund, Inc., MA, 4251

Royal Neighbors of America Foundation, IL, 2837

Royal Oak Foundation for Public Education, MI, 4594

Royal Oak Foundation, NY, 6364

Royston Permanent Scholarship Foundation of Alpha Sigma State of the Delta Kappa Gamma Society International, Rachel, WA, 9710

RPW Foundation, Inc., IN, 3166

RSPA Scholarship Foundation, Inc., NC, 6844

Rubenstein Family Foundation, S., Inc., NJ, 5555

Rubenstein Memorial Scholarship Foundation, David, CA, see 626

Rubin Foundation, J. M., Inc., FL, 2041

Rubinow Scholarship Fund Trust, Mary B. Rubinow and William, CT, 1453

Ruby Tuesday Team Disaster Response Fund, TN, 8639

Rudy Scholarship Fund, MI, 4595

Rudy Scholarship, MI, see 4595

Ruebush Foundation, W. E., WI, 10015

Ruegamer Charitable Trust, W. R. & A. F., FL, 2042

Ruf Scholarship Trust, Clara A., MI, 4596

Rufer Scholarship Trust, Merlin & Ethyl, IA, 3369

Ruffini Charitable Foundation, MA, 4252

Ruge Education Fund, Edwin Gardner Weed, PA, see 8183

Ruge Trust, Isabel R., PA, see 8183

Ruger Trust, Dr. Henry Hobert, ND, 6947

Rumbaugh Fund, James Hickey, NC, see 6845

Rumbough Trust, Constance H., NC, 6845

Running Strong for American Indian Youth, VA, see 9302

Runyon Cancer Research Foundation, Damon, NY, 6365

Runyon Cancer Research Foundation, Damon, NY, see 6365

Rural American Scholarship Fund, WA, 9711

Rural Kentucky Medical Scholarship Fund, KY, 3622

Rural Mission, Inc., SC, 8505

Rural Resources Community Action, WA, 9712

Rush County Community Foundation, Inc., IN, 3167

Rush Educational Trust, David and Mary P., KS, 3509

Rush Testamentary Trust, Lonza L., FL, 2043

Rush Trust, R. Roy, FL, see 2043

Rusis Scholarship Fund, Armins, NJ, A

Ruskin Trust, Gertrude Marion, PA, 8084

Russell Educational and Charitable Foundation, Benjamin and Roberta, Inc., AL, see 77

Russell Family Foundation, The, WA, 9713

Russell Foundation, Benjamin & Roberta, Inc., AL, 77

Russell Foundation, Richard B., FL, 2044

Russell Medical Educational Trust, Edmund J., IN, 3168

Russell Scholarship Fund, Clyde, ME, 3733

Russell Scholarship Fund, Helen B. & Robert H., IL, see 2838

Russell Scholarship Fund, IL, 2838

Russell Scholarship Fund, Leroy W., OH, 7331

Russell Testamentary Trust, Nancy D., NC, 6846

Russian Children's Welfare Society, Inc., NY, 6366

Rutan Foundation, Mary, OH, 7332

Rutherford Foundation, CO, 1275

Rutland High School Foundation, VT, 9259

Rutledge Charities, Edward and Hannah M., Inc., WI, 10016

Rutledge Charity, Edward, WI, see 10016

Rutnik Scholarship Fund, Ruby, VI, 9276

Ryals Scholarship Fund, Thomas E., FL, 2045

Ryan Charitable Foundation, Dorothy and Robert, The, OR, 7649

Ryan Family Foundation, James B. and Eileen, Inc., The, PA, 8085

Ryan Historical Foundation, Nolan, TX, 9048

Ryder System Charitable Foundation, Inc., The, FL, 2046

Rye Rotary Foundation Inc., NY, 6367

Ryerson Foundation, IL, 2839

Ryerson Tull Foundation, IL, see 2839

Ryka Rose Foundation, MA, see 4236

Ryrie Foundation, The, TX, 9049

Ryu Family Foundation, Inc., NJ, 5556

S.B.H. Community Service Network, Inc., NY, 6368

S.G.K.&G. Foundation, TX, 9050

S.L. Scholarship Foundation, CA, 924

S.N.H.S., MD, see 3924

S.R.C. Education Alliance, NC, 6847

Saagny Foundation, Inc., The, NY, 6369

Saak Foundation, Charles E., PA, 8086

Saake Foundation, Dr. Alvin & Monica, HI, 2318

Sabada Memorial Scholarship Foundation, Darrik S., MO, 5081

Sacco Scholarship Fund, Joseph, MD, 3923

Saccomanno Higher Education Foundation, CO, 1276

Sachs Foundation, CO, 1277

Sacramento Association of REALTORS Scholarship Foundation Trust, CA, 925

Sacramento Board of Realtors Scholarship Foundation Trust, CA, see 925

Sacramento Mountain Scholarship Fund, Inc., NM, 5647

Sacramento Region Community Foundation, CA, 926

Sacramento Regional Foundation, CA, see 926

Sacred Portion Children's Outreach, Inc., The, MT, 5171

Saddle River Valley Lions Charities, Inc., NJ, 5557

SAF, NC, see 6883

Saginaw Community Foundation, MI, 4597

Sailfish Point Foundation, Inc., FL, 2047

Saint Barnabas Development Foundation, NJ, 5558

Saint Barnabas Medical Center Foundation, The, NJ, see 5558

Saint Francis Home Health, Inc., OK, 7510

Saint Joseph's Regional Medical Center, Inc., IN, 3169

Saint Louis Community Foundation, Greater, MO, 5082

Saint Paul Foundation, The, MN, 4842

Saint Vincent De Paul Society, Inc., GA, 2230

Sakhi for South Asian Women, NY, 6370

Sakumoto Charitable Trust, Toyo, HI, 2319

Sale Foundation, Lucy Pannill, VA, 9496

Salem Community Foundation, Inc., OH, 7333

Salem Female Charitable Society, MA, 4253

Salem Foundation, The, OR, 7650

Salem Hospital Foundation, OR, 7651

Salem Lutheran Foundation, OH, 7334

Salesmanship Club of Dallas, TX, 9051

Salesmanship Club Youth and Family Centers, Inc., TX, 9052

Salin Foundation, Inc., IN, 3170

Salina Community Foundation, Greater, KS, 3510

Salisbury Memorial Scholarship Fund, Burl E., MI, 4598

Salisbury Neighborhood Housing Service, Inc., MD, 3924

Salisbury Wicomico Arts Council, MD, 3925

Salisbury-Rowan Community Action Agency, Inc., NC, 6848

Salisbury-Rowan Community Service Council, Inc., NC, see 6848

Sallness Memorial Scholarship Fund, Fritchof T. Sallness and Marian M., MI, A

Salt Lake Community College Foundation, UT, 9224

Salt Lake Education Foundation, UT, 9225

Saltonstall Foundation for the Arts, Constance, Inc., NY, 6371

Salute to Education, Inc., TX, A

Samaritan Foundation, OH, 7335

Samaritan Foundation, The, AZ, see 170

Samaritan Hospital School of Nursing Alumni Association Charitable Foundation, NY, 6372

Samaritan Society, MA, 4254

Samaritan's Purse, NC, 6849

Samet Foundation, Jerold J. & Margaret M., MD, 3926

SAMFund, The, MA, 4255

Sampson Family Foundation, MN, 4843

Samstag Fine Arts Trust, Gordon, FL, 2048

Samuelsen Scholarship Trust, Harvey, AK, 134

San Angelo Area Foundation, TX, 9053

San Antonio A & M Club Foundation, TX, 9054

San Antonio Area Foundation, TX, 9055

San Antonio Dance Umbrella, TX, 9056

San Antonio Education Fund, TX, 9057

San Antonio Education Partnership, TX, see 9057

San Antonio Livestock Exposition, Inc., TX, 9058

San Antonio Spurs Foundation, The, TX, see 9073

San Antonio Stock Show and Rodeo, TX, see 9058

San Carlos Foundation, The, CA, 927

San Diego Asian Film Foundation, CA, 928

San Diego Chargers Charities, CA, 929

San Diego Community Foundation, CA, see 934

San Diego County Citizens Scholarship Foundation, CA, 930

San Diego County Medical Society Foundation, CA, 931

San Diego County Salute to Education, CA, 932

San Diego Education Fund, CA, 933

San Diego Foundation, The, CA, 934

San Diego Imperial Counties Developmental Services, Inc., CA, 935

San Diego Martin Luther King Jr. Foundation, CA, 936

San Diego Revitalization Corporation, CA, see 878

San Diego Science & Engineering Fair, Greater, CA, 937

San Diego Scottish Rite Community Foundation, CA, 938

San Diego Sports Medicine Foundation, CA, 939

San Felipe del Rio, Inc., CA, see 940

San Felipe Humanitarian Alliance, CA, 940

San Francisco Children's Art Center, CA, 941

San Francisco Family Foundation, CA, 942

San Francisco Film Society, CA, 943

San Francisco Foundation, The, CA, 944

San Francisco Friends of Chamber Music, CA, 945

San Francisco Girls Chorus, CA, 946

San Francisco School Alliance, CA, 947

San Francisco Study Center, Inc., CA, 948

San Gabriel/Pomona Valleys Developmental Services, Inc., CA, 949

San Jose State University Foundation, CA, 950

San Jose State University Research Foundation, CA, see 950

San Juan Island Community Foundation, WA, 9714

San Luis Obispo County Community Foundation, CA, 951

San Marcos Civic Foundation, TX, 9059

San Mateo Rotary Foundation, CA, 952

Sanborn Foundation for the Treatment and Cure of Cancer, Elizabeth and George L., Inc., MA, 4256

Sand County Foundation, Inc., WI, 10017

Sand Dollar Foundation, TX, 9060

Sanders Fund, Inc., MA, 4257

Sandhills Community Action Program, Inc., NC, 6850

Sandler and Co., Aleck, CA, see 867

Sandpipers Philanthropy Trust Fund, CA, 953

Sandusky/Erie County Community Foundation, OH, 7336

Sandwich Women's Club, The, MA, 4258

Sandy Hill Foundation, The, NY, 6373

Sanford Scholarship Foundation, Andrew and Martha, VA, 9497

Sangamon County Foundation, IL, see 2493

Sanilac County Community Foundation, MI, 4599

Sanofi Foundation for North America, NJ, 5559

Sanofi-aventis Patient Assistance Foundation, NJ, see 5559

Santa Barbara Cottage Hospital Foundation, CA, 954

Santa Barbara Foundation, CA, 955

Santa Claus Club Scholarship Fund, OH, see 7140

Santa Cruz County Community Foundation, Greater, CA, see 512

Santa Cruz County Rotary Endowment, CA, 956

Santa Fe Art Institute, NM, 5648

Santa Fe College Foundation, Inc., FL, 2049

Santa Fe Community Foundation, NM, 5649

Santa Maria Arts Council, Inc., CA, 957

Santa Rosa Junior College Foundation, CA, 958

Santa Verena Charity, Inc., CA, 959

Santander Consumer USA Inc. Foundation, TX, 9061

Sapelo Foundation, Inc., The, GA, 2231

Sapelo Island Research Foundation, Inc., GA, see 2231

Saranac Lake Voluntary Health Association, Inc., NY, 6374

Sarasota County Community Foundation, Inc., The, FL, see 1844

Saratoga County Economic Opportunity Council, NY, 6375

Sarcoma Alliance, The, CA, 960

Sarnoff Cardiovascular Research Foundation, Inc., VA, 9498

Sarver Charitable Trust, KS, 3511

Sasso Consolidation Fund Trust, RI, see 8390

Sasso Scholarship Fund Trust, RI, 8390

Sauey Family Foundation, W. R. and Floy A., WI, 10018

Saugus High School Scholarship Fund, Inc., MA, 4259

Sauk County Community Foundation, Greater, Inc., WI, 10019

Sauvain Scholarship Fund, NC, see 6851

Sauvain Trust, Walter H., NC, 6851

Savannah Community Foundation, The, GA, 2232

Savannah Foundation, The, GA, see 2232

Savannah Jewish Council, Inc., GA, 2233

Savannah Jewish Federation, GA, see 2233

Save The Children Federation, Inc., CT, 1454

Savings Bank of Maine Scholarship Foundation, Gardiner Savings Institution FSB Scholarship Foundation, ME, see 3734

Savings Bank of Maine Scholarship Foundation, ME, 3734

Sawyer Scholarship Foundation, NY, 6376

Sawyer Teacher Scholarship Trust Fund, Lillie Murray, MD, 3927

Saybrook Charitable Trust, CT, 1455

SBC Foundation Inc., WI, 10020

SBC Foundation, TX, see 8695

SBM Charitable Foundation, Inc., CT, 1456

Scaife Scholarship Foundation, CA, 961

Scalp and Blade Scholarship Trust, NY, 6377

Scanlan Foundation, IA, 3370

Scanlan Memorial Scholarship Fund, IA, 3371

Scarlett Family Foundation, TN, 8640

Scarsdale Foundation, NY, 6378

Scatena Memorial Fund for San Francisco School Teachers, Virginia, TX, see 8839

Scavone Scholarship Fund, Betty Ann Donohue, The, RI, 8391

Scears Foundation of Akron Michigan, MI, 4600

Scering Trust, Board of Trustees of, IN, see 3171

Scering Trust, IN, 3171

Schaap Foundation, A. Paul and Carol C., The, MI, 4601

Schack Memorial Scholarship Fund, Margaret Lobdell, WA, 9715

Schaeneman, Jr. Memorial Scholarship Foundation, Lewis G., Inc., MA, 4260

Schafer Scholarship Fund, Carl & Mabel, OR, 7652

Schafer Scholarship Fund, Frank and Elizabeth, MO, 5083

Schalkenbach Foundation, Robert, Inc., NY, 6379

Schechter Foundation, The, NY, 6380

Scheehl College Scholarship Fund, Emeline H., RI, see 8392

Scheehl Trust, Frank H., RI, 8392

Scheffler Family Foundation, GA, 2234

Scheidler Scholarship Foundation, Floy Gilman, Inc., MN, 4844

Scheinberg Foundation, Dr. Sam and Cheryl, OR, 7653

Schenck Estate Trust, Jane, NY, see 6381

Schenck Fund 003490, Jane I, NY, 6381

Schenectady Foundation, The, NY, 6382

Schepp Foundation, Leopold, NY, 6383

Scherer Foundation, Karla, The, IL, 2840

Schergens Foundation, Edgar & Lucile, Inc., IN, 3172

Schield Companies Foundation Inc., WI, 10021

Schiff Scholarship Fund, William J. & Elizabeth M., RI, 8393

Schiffman Memorial Foundation, CA, 962

Schiffner Music Fund, Kathryn, NY, 6384

Schiffner Scholarship Fund, Helen M., NY, 6385

Schilling Family Foundation, OR, see 7654

Schilling Family Scholarship Fund, OR, 7654

Schillings Foundation, Corinne Jeannine, IL, 2841

Schimel Lode, The, DC, 1726

Schlagenbusch Scholarship Trust, Marjorie, IA, 3372

Schlarb Scholarship Trust, Earle J., VA, 9499

Schmidek Charitable Foundation, Damir I. and Virginia A., CA, 963

Schmidt Foundation, Clara, Inc., CA, 964

Schmidt Foundation, Walter C. and Marie C., OR, 7655

Schmidt Foundation, William E., Inc., TN, 8641

Schmidt Scholarship Fund, Elma, KS, 3512

Schmidt Trust, Walter F., IN, 3173

Schmitt Charitable Foundation, C. B., Inc., FL, 2050

Schmitz Foundation Inc., Shirley G., AZ, 235

Schmoker Trust, Cecil Mae, NE, 5259

Schneider Trust, Anastasia Annette, OH, 7337

Schock Foundation, Clarence, The, PA, 8087

Scholar Leaders International, IL, 2842

Scholarship America, MN, 4845

Scholarship and Welfare Fund of the Alumni Association of Hunter College, Inc., NY, 6386

Scholarship Assistance Foundation, FL, 2051

Scholarship Association of Fort Plain Inc., NY, 6387

Scholarship Foundation of Erie Scottish Rite, PA, 8088

Scholarship Foundation of Santa Barbara, CA, 965

Scholarship Foundation of St. Louis, The, MO, 5084

Scholarship Foundation of the Union League of Philadelphia, The, PA, 8089

Scholarship Foundation, Denglade, Inc., IN, 3174

Scholarship Foundation, The, NJ, 5560

Scholarship Fund for Ethiopian Jews, FL, 2052

Scholarship Fund for South Carolina State College, NC, 6852

Scholarship Fund Inc., OH, 7338

Scholarship Fund of Flint Plumbing & Pipefitting Industry, MI, 4602

Scholarship Fund of Kappa Sigma Fraternity Inc., MA, 4261

Scholarship Fund of Tau Beta Beta, Inc., MA, 4262

Scholarship Headquarters, Inc., NC, 6853

Scholarship Trust, Niederkon, WI, 10022

Scholastic Art & Writing Awards, NY, see 5682

Schommer Memorial Scholarship Fund for Nursing, Matthew Alan, The, FL, 2053

School CHOICE Scholarships, Inc., KY, 3623

School for Advanced Research on the Human Experience, NM, 5650

School Nutrition Foundation, MD, 3928

School of American Research, NM, see 5650

School of the Arts Foundation, Inc., FL, 2054

Schooler Scholarship Trust Fund, Karl, IA, 3373

Schowengerdt Family Scholarship Fund, MO, 5085

Schrader Trust, Florence M., IA, 3374

Schroeder Memorial Trust, J.P. and Maude V., OR, 7656

Schroeder Scholarship Trust, William Archie, IL, 2843

Schroeder Trust, Dale D., IA, 3375

Schuetze Foundation, Maude M., ND, 6948

Schug Foundation, NC, 6854

Schuler Family Foundation, IL, 2844

Schull Institute, TX, 9062

Schuller Fund, Inc., CO, see 1223

Schulte Foundation, Theodore and Catherine, WI, 10023

Schultheiss Foundation, Elizabeth, MI, 4603

Schultz Trust, Kate W., IN, 3175

Schumacher Scholarship Fund for Men, Herman Oscar, WA, see 9716

Schumacher School Fund, Herman Oscar, WA, 9716

Schumann Educational Trust, Reno O., TX, 9063

Schuneman Scholarship Trust, Paul A. & Daisy E., KS, 3513

Schuyler Center for Analysis and Advocacy, NY, A

Schuyler Child Educational Fund Trust, Byron S., RI, 8394

Schuylkill Area Community Foundation, PA, 8090

Schuylkill Community Action, PA, 8091

Schuylkill County Bar Association Scholarship Fund, PA, 8092

Schwab Foundation, Charles, CA, 966

Schwab Foundation, John, PA, 8093

Schwab-Rosenhouse Memorial Foundation, TX, 9064

Schwantes Scholarship Fund, Elmer & Ruth, AK, 135

Schwartz Foundation, Ernie P., IA, 3376

Schwartze Linn High School Scholarship Fund Trust I, A.J., MO, 5086

Schwartze Scholarship Fund Trust II, A.J., MO, 5088

Schwartze Scholarship Fund Trust, A. J., MO, 5087

Schwartze Trust - Chamois High School I, A.J., MO, 5089

Schwartze Trust - Chamois High School II, A. J., MO, 5090

Schwartze Trust - Scholarship Fund III, A. J., MO, 5091

Schwartze Trust - Scholarship Fund IV, A. J., MO, 5092

Schwartze Trust Helias High School Scholarship Fund II, A. J., MO, 5094

Schwartze Trust Helias High School Scholarship Fund III, A. J., MO, 5095

Schwartze Trust Helias High School Scholarship Fund, A. J., MO, 5093

Schwartze Trust Linn High School Scholarship Fund Trust II, A.J., MO, 5096

Schwarz Charitable Trust for Education, Evalee C., The, IL, 2845

Schwarz Trust f/b/o Stockbridge High School, Faythe, WI, 10024

Schweitzer Agriculture Education Foundation, Alice Wilson Schweitzer & William J., IL, 2846

SCI Special Fund, CA, 967

Science Scholarship Foundation, CA, 968

Science Service, Inc., DC, see 1731

SCIO District 95-C Scholarships, Inc., OR, 7657

Scioto County Area Foundation, The, OH, see 7339

Scioto Foundation, The, OH, 7339

Scleroderma Foundation, Inc., MA, 4263

Scoliosis Research Society, WI, 10025

Scotch Plains Fanwood Scholarship Foundation, NJ, 5561

Scots Charitable Society of Boston, Massachussetts, Woman's Auxiliary Board of the, MA, 4264

Scots' Charitable Society of Boston, NH, 5367

Scott & Stringfellow Educational Foundation, VA, 9500

Scott County Community Foundation, Inc., IN, 3176

Scott Foundation, Richard L. & F. Annette, FL, 2055

Scott Fund, Olin, Inc., VT, 9260

Scott Memorial Trust, Arthur H., CT, 1457

Scott Trust, Ethel Voris, IL, 2847

Scott Trust, Gordon and Ann, IN, 3177

Scott-Carver-Dakota Cap Agency, Inc., MN, 4846

Scott-Jenkins Fund, NY, 6388

Scottish Rite Foundation in Kentucky, KY, 3624

Scottish Rite Foundation of Colorado, CO, 1278

Scottish Rite Foundation of Missouri, Inc., MO, 5097

Scottish Rite Oregon Consistory Almoner Fund, Inc., OR, see 7634

Scotts Miracle-Gro Foundation, NY, 6389

Scranton Area Foundation, Inc., The, PA, 8094

Screen Actors Guild Foundation, The, CA, 969

Scribe Video Center, Inc., PA, 8095

Scripps Howard Foundation, OH, 7340

SCS Foundation, NY, see 6392

Scudder Association Inc., The, CT, 1458

Sculpture Space, Inc., NY, 6390

SculptureCenter, NY, 6391

SDF, NC, see 6869

SDMS Educational Foundation, PA, see 7920

Seabee Memorial Scholarship Association, MD, 3929

SEAKR Foundation, CO, 1279

Sealaska Heritage Foundation, AK, see 136

Sealaska Heritage Institute, AK, 136

Search Scholarship Fund, Betty I. and Karl B., NC, 6855

Searls Scholarship Fund, William, ME, 3735

Sears Trust, Mary P., RI, 8395

Sears Trust, Winslow F. Sears & Dorothy M., RI, 8396

Seattle Business Association Scholarship Fund, Greater, WA, 9717

Seattle Central Community College Foundation, WA, 9718

Seattle Foundation, The, WA, 9719

Seattle Parks Foundation, WA, 9720

Seau Foundation, Junior, CA, 970

SeaWorld & Busch Gardens Conservation Fund, FL, 2056

Seay Foundation, CO, 1280

Sebring - West Branch Area Community Foundation, OH, 7341

Second Baptist School Foundation, Inc., The, TX, 9065

Second Harvest Food Bank of Santa Clara and San Mateo Counties, CA, 971

Second Harvest Food Bank of the Inland Northwest, WA, 9721

Second Harvest Heartland, MN, 4847

Second Harvest North Central Food Bank, Inc., MN, 4848

Second Mile Misson Center, TX, 9066

SECU Foundation, NC, see 6877

Securities Association of Virginia Foundation, Inc., The, MD, see 3885

Sedler Scholarship Fund, Theodore H., CA, 972

Seed Money for Growth Foundation, Inc., AZ, 236

Seefred Trust, Thomas J., OH, 7342

Seely Charitable Trust, R. Q. & L. A., TX, 9067

Seely Trust, Roger Q. & Lovye A., TX, see 9067

Segal Foundation, George & Helen, NJ, 5562

Segel Memorial Scholarship Fund Inc., Ronald G., MA, 4265

Seibel Foundation, Abe and Annie, The, TX, 9068

Seidler Foundation, The, IA, 3377

Selby Foundation, William G. Selby and Marie, FL, 2057

Select Milwaukee, Inc., WI, 10026

Self Foundation, Sara Smith, Inc., The, NC, 6856

Self-Help, Inc., MA, 4266

Selfhelp Community Services Foundation, Inc., NY, 6392

Selinger Educational Fund, FL, 2058

Selinger Educational Trust Fund, Sydney & Grace, FL, see 2058

Sellers Scholarship Fund, Lloyd & Gene, IN, 3178

Selling Scholarship Loan Fund, Ben, NC, 6857

Seltzer Memorial Scholarship Foundation, Ronald, NY, 6393

SEMA Memorial Scholarship Fund, CA, 973

Semcac, Inc., MN, 4849

Sempra Energy Corporate Giving Program, CA, 974

Seneca Diabetes Foundation, NY, 6394

Senft Scholarship Foundation, Louise E., MT, 5172

Senior Services of Stamford, Inc., CT, 1459

Senior Volunteer Services, Inc., FL, 2059

Sentara Healthcare, VA, 9501

Sentara Hospitals, VA, 9502

Sephardic Bikur Holim & Ma'oz La'ebyon, NY, see 6368

Sequim Masonic Lodge Foundation, WA, 9722

Sequoia Hospital Foundation, CA, 975

Serbian Brothers Help, Inc., IL, 2848

Serra Ancillary Care Corporation, CA, 976

Serra Foundation, Inc., WV, 9814

Serra Project, The, CA, see 976

Sertoma, Inc., MO, 5098

Servant Leadership Foundation, The, CO, 1281

Servco Foundation, HI, 2320

Service League of Cherokee County, GA, 2235

ServiceMaster Foundation, The, TN, 8642

Seton Fund of the Daughters of Charity of St. Vincent de Paul, Inc, TX, 9069

SEVEN Fund, MA, 4267

Seven Oaks Foundation, Inc., GA, 2236

Several Sources Foundation, Inc., NJ, 5563

Sewell Memorial Fund, Grace and Harold, WA, 9723

Seybert Memorial Scholarship Fund, Jennie J., AK, 137

Seymour Community School Scholarship Trust, WI, 10027

Seymour Trust Fund, Greater, IN, 3179

SFAI, NM, see 5648

Shafer Irrevocable Trust, Allen J., WI, 10028

Shaklee Cares, CA, 977

Shallow Scholarship Foundation, Moses and Caroline, WI, 10029

Shank Memorial Scholarship Fund, John M., OR, 7658

Shanor Foundation, M. L., The, TX, 9070

Shapiro Cancer and Heart Fund, Ruth Newman, NJ, A

Shapiro Testamentary Scholarship Trust, Ida, IL, 2849

SHARE Foundation, AR, 307

Sharing Connections, Inc., IL, 2850

Sharp Scholarship Fund, OH, 7343

Sharp Trust, Robert G., WI, 10030

Sharpe Art Foundation, Marie Walsh, The, CO, 1282

Sharpe Family Foundation, The, OH, 7344

Shasta Regional Community Foundation, CA, 978

Shatford Memorial Trust, J. D., NY, 6395

Shaulis Foundation Inc., Fred S., The, PA, 8097

Shaull Education Foundation, Clyde L. and Mary C., PA, 8098

Shawn Carter Foundation, FL, see 1817

Shawnee Development Council, Inc., IL, 2851

Sheadle Trust, Jasper H., OH, 7345

Sheehan Scholarship Fund, John P., RI, 8397

Sheen Scholarship Fund, Howard J. & Ruth H., PA, 8099

Sheet Metal Workers' International Scholarship Foundation, Inc., DC, 1727

Sheets Scholarship Trust, George, WI, 10031

Sheffield Education Foundation, AL, 78

Sheffield Scholarship Fund, Elizabeth Braswell, NC, 6858

Shelby Children's Foundation, Carroll, CA, see 979

Shelby Community Foundation, MI, 4604

Shelby Foundation, Carroll, The, CA, 979

Shellabarger Educational Trust, Charles E., IA, 3378

Shelly Scholarship Fund, Buck and S.Louise, NC, 6859

Shelter Insurance Foundation, MO, 5099

Shenango Valley Foundation, PA, see 7784

Shepard Scholarship Fund Foundation, Leon and Josephine Wade, Inc., OH, 7346

Shepard Trust, Charles E., FL, 2060

Shepherd's Staff, Inc., MD, 3930
Sheridan County Memorial Hospital Foundation, WY, 10119
Sheridan Memorial Scholarship, Harry R., CT, 1460
Sherman College of Straight Chiropractic, SC, 8506
Sherman County Community Foundation, Inc., NE, 5260
Sherman Educational Fund, Mabel E., IA, 3379
Sherwood Trust, Nellie R., IA, 3380
Shewmaker Family Scholarship Trust, AR, 308
Shiawassee Community Foundation, MI, 4605
Shiawassee Foundation, MI, see 4605
Shiel Trust, John F. and Mary E., IN, 3180
Shields Valley Foundation Inc., MT, 5173
Shifler, Howard E. and Christine, RI, 8398
Shiloh Ministries International, Inc., TN, 8643
Shinaberry Public Scholarship Trust, IL, 2852
Shingleton Scholarship Fund, N. B., VA, 9503
Shinnick Educational Fund, William M., OH, 7347
Shinoda Memorial Scholarship Foundation, Joseph, CA, 980
Shire Philanthropic Foundation, CA, see 1046
Shoemaker Education Trust, John L. & Helen B., PA, 8100
Shoemaker Trust for Shoemaker Scholarship Fund, Ray S., PA, 8101
Shoop Sports and Youth Foundation Inc., IN, 3181
SHOPA Kids In Need Foundation, OH, see 7191
Shopko Foundation, Inc., WI, 10032
Shoppers Village/Maureen Nolan Memorial Fund, NY, see 6283
Shore Up!, Inc., MD, 3931
Short Foundation, Romeo E., AR, see 264
Short Scholarship Fund, J. Leo, IL, 2853
Shoshana Foundation Inc., NJ, 5564
Shouse Memorial Scholarship Trust, Helen Shacklet, TX, 9071
Show Foundation, Victoria Livestock, TX, 9072
Shreve Foundation, William A. & Mary A., NJ, 5565
Shriners of Rhode Island Charities Trust, RI, 8399
Shroyer Scholarship Fund, IN, 3182
Shultz Eagle Scout Foundation, Bernard E., ID, 2348
Shultz Trust, Ruth A., MA, 4268
Shumaker Foundation, Paul and Adelyn C., IL, 2854
Shuman Scholarship Fund Trust, Robbins, The, PA, 8102
Shunk Association, John Q., OH, 7348
SICO Foundation, The, PA, see 8087
Side Street Projects, CA, 981
Sides Charitable Trust, Frank Sides, Jr. and Edna K., The, OK, 7511
Sidhu Foundation Inc., Devindar, VA, 9504
Sidwell Charitable Trust, KS, 3514
Siebenthal Scholarship Charitable Fund, Agnes Cecelia J., PA, 8103
Sieber Foundation, Fred B., The, FL, 2061
Siebert Lutheran Foundation, Inc., WI, 10033
Siegel Foundation, Richard, TN, 8644
Siemens Foundation, NJ, 5566
Siemer Foundation Inc., Dennis K. and Vivian D., MN, 4850
Sierra Pacific Foundation, CA, 982
Sierra Vista Child & Family Services, CA, 983
Siff Educational Foundation, Philip and Aida, CA, 984
Siff Educational Foundation, Philip Francis, CA, see 984
Sightless Children Club, Inc., OH, 7349
Sigma Alpha Iota Philanthropies, Inc., NC, 6860
Sigma Chi Foundation, IL, 2855
Sigma Delta Chi Foundation of Washington, DC, DC, 1728
Sigma Gamma Rho National Education Fund, IN, 3183
Sigma Nu Educational Foundation, Inc., VA, 9505
Sigmund Foundation, Bill & Vi, MI, A
Sigmund Foundation, Bill and Vi, MI, 4606
Signer Memorial Trust Fund, John J., CA, 985
Sigourney Award Trust, Mary S., WA, 9724
Silberman Fund, Lois and Samuel, Inc., The, NY, 6396
Silbermann Foundation, Rosanne H., Inc., The, NJ, 5567
Silicon Valley Community Foundation, CA, 986
Silicon Valley Education Foundation, CA, 987
Silver and Black Give Back, TX, 9073
Silver Foundation, Steve, Inc., CA, 988

Silver Shield Foundation, Inc., NY, 6397
Silverlake Conservatory of Music, CA, 989
Silverthorne Foundation, Rose, TX, 9074
Simionescu Scholarship Foundation, RI, 8400
Simmons Charitable Trust, Esther N., OH, 7350
Simmons Welfare Fund, Ralph and Mary, OH, 7351
Simon Charitable Foundation, The, NM, 5651
Simon Educational Irrevocable Trust Foundation, NE, 5261
Simon Family Foundation, Ronald M., CA, see 990
Simon Foundation for Education and Housing, CA, 990
Simon Youth Foundation, Inc., IN, 3184
Simplot Company Contributions Program, J. R., ID, 2349
Simpson Education Trust, NC, see 6861
Simpson Educational Fund Inc., W.B., DE, 1523
Simpson Foundation, The, AL, 79
Simpson Foundation, William G. and M. Virginia, The, PA, 8104
Simpson Scholars Trust, NC, 6861
Simpson, Jr. Foundation Fund, John W., TN, 8645
Sinden Scholarship Fund, Dr. James W., PA, 8105
Sinek Scholarship Trust, Joseph J., IA, 3381
Sing Association, Lin, Inc., FL, 2062
Singer Family C & E Foundation, PA, 8106
Singer Student Nurses Fund, Bertha P., OR, 7659
Single Parent Assistance Fund, Inc., OK, see 7507
Single Parent Scholarship Fund of Northwest Arkansas, Inc., AR, 309
Single Parent Scholarship Fund of Washington County, Inc., AR, 309
Singleton Scholarship Trust, M. E., TX, 9075
Sioda Family Foundation Inc, The, MD, 3932
Sioux Falls Area Community Foundation, SD, 8538
Siouxland Community Foundation, IA, 3382
Siouxland Foundation, IA, see 3382
Sipes Memorial Student Loan Fund, Bedford W., TX, 9076
Siros Foundation, Clara Lou Vena, TX, 9077
Sirrine High School Fund, J. E., NC, 6862
Sister Carmen Community Center, Inc., CO, 1283
Sisters Together and Reaching, Inc., MD, 3933
Sitka Center for Art and Ecology, OR, see 7616
Sitnasuak Foundation, AK, 138
SIU Scholarship Foundation and Trust, MD, see 3923
Sivyer For Trades School, Ida M., WI, 10034
Skadden Fellowship Foundation, Inc., The, NY, 6398
Skadden, Arps, Slate, Meagher & Flom Fellowship Foundation, NY, see 6398
Skaggs Institute for Research, The, UT, 9226
Skagit Valley Herald Christmas Fund, WA, 9725
Skahan Memorial Fund, Joan, NY, 6399
Skandalaris Family Foundation, MI, 4607
Skaneateles Central School Endowment Foundation, NY, 6400
Skaneateles Central School Endowment Foundation, NY, see 6400
Skaters Education & Training Fund, Inc., The, MD, 3934
SKB Foundation, CA, 991
Skelton Charitable Foundation, Homer, MS, 4921
Skelton Scholarship Fund, IL, 2856
Skelton Trust Fund, Ila M., IL, see 2856
Skeuse Scholarship Fund Inc., Thomas J. and Rita T., The, NJ, 5568
Skidmore, Owings & Merrill Foundation, IL, 2857
Skillman Scholarship Fund, Chris A., MO, 5100
Skillman Scholarship, Frank Foster, PA, 8107
SkillSource, Inc., WA, 9726
Skin Cancer Foundation, Inc., The, NY, 6401
Skinner Foundation, WA, 9568
Skowhegan School of Painting & Sculpture, NY, 6402
Skrifvars Scholarship Fund, Warren, CO, 1284
Skrocki Foundation, Chester J. & Angela M., MI, 4608
Skrungloo Farms, Inc., NH, 5368
Sky Rink Winter Games Training Facilities, Inc., NY, 6403
SLA Foundation, CO, see 1158
SLA, VA, see 9511
Slaid Memorial Scholarship Fund, Sarina, WA, 9727
Slater Dance Theater, Deborah, CA, see 373
Slaughter Scholarship Trust, IN, 3185
Sleeper & Lottie S. Hill Fund, Josiah, PA, 8108
Sleesman Trust, Peter, RI, 8401

Slemp Foundation, The, OH, 7352
Slipher Trust, V. M., IL, see 2890
Slippery Rock Foundation, Inc., PA, see 8109
Slippery Rock University Foundation, Inc., PA, 8109
Sloan Foundation, Alfred P., NY, 6404
Sloan, Jr. Foundation, Carole C. and O. Temple, NC, 6863
Slowinski Charitable Foundation, RI, 8402
Slowinski Estate Fund Trust, RI, see 8402
Smack Mellon Studios, Inc., NY, 6405
SMACNA College of Fellows Foundation, VA, 9506
Small Angels Foundation and Endowment, CA, 992
Small Business Service Bureau, Inc. Charitable Foundation, MA, see 4012
Smalley Foundation, Inc., The, MA, 4269
Smallwood Scholarship Foundation, ID, 2350
Smart & Final Scholarship Foundation, CA, 993
Smart Start of Buncombe County, Inc., NC, 6864
Smart Start Rowan, Inc., NC, 6865
SME Education Foundation, MI, see 4611
Smelser Scholarship Fund, Hazel Dell Neff, IN, 3186
SMFG Foundation, Inc., AZ, see 236
Smick Memorial Loan Fund, KS, 3515
Smigiel Foundation to Benefit Children and Families Inc., FL, 2063
Smiley Foundation, Tavis, CA, 994
Smith Charitable Trust, Henry J., IL, 2858
Smith Charitable Trust, Jean and Verne, SC, 8507
Smith Charitable Trust, Norman W., OH, 7353
Smith Charitable Trust, Tom C., WV, 9815
Smith Charitable Trust, William Harold, NC, 6866
Smith Charities, Emmitt, Inc., TX, see 9078
Smith Charities, Pat & Emmitt, TX, 9078
Smith Education Fund, Jennie W., RI, 8403
Smith Educational Foundation, Charles C., NJ, 5569
Smith Educational Fund, RI, see 8403
Smith Educational Memorial Fund, Earl E. & Marie M., OH, see 7354
Smith Educational Memorial Fund, OH, 7354
Smith for Evergreen Aviation Center, Captain Michael King, OR, 7660
Smith Foundation, Jean M. R., MI, 4609
Smith Foundation, Marguerite Carl, PA, 8110
Smith Foundation, McGregor, FL, 2064
Smith Foundation, McGregor, The, FL, see 2064
Smith Foundation, W. F. & Anna, OH, see 7356
Smith Fund, Horace, The, MA, 4270
Smith Group Foundation, Everett, Ltd., WI, 10035
Smith Memorial Foundation, Douglas Franklin, CA, 995
Smith Memorial Foundation, Winthrop H., Inc., NC, 6867
Smith Memorial Fund, Arthur Albert, OH, 7355
Smith Memorial Fund, Pauline, RI, 8404
Smith Memorial Fund, W. Eugene, Inc., NY, 6406
Smith Memorial Scholarship Fund, Mace C. Smith and Dee, MO, 5101
Smith Memorial Scholarship Fund, PA, 8111
Smith Private Foundation, William & Anna, OH, 7356
Smith Revolving Loan Trust, Norman W., OH, see 7353
Smith Scholarship Foundation, Edward Craig, AR, 310
Smith Scholarship Foundation, Gerald F., VA, 9507
Smith Scholarship Foundation, J. Craig and Page T., Inc., AL, 80
Smith Scholarship Foundation, K. L., Inc., OK, 7512
Smith Scholarship Fund, Alice Aber, The, WI, 10036
Smith Scholarship Fund, Charles & Charlotte Bissell, OH, 7357
Smith Scholarship Fund, Ellen V. and Robert H., RI, see 8407
Smith Scholarship Fund, Hugh Bell, KY, 3625
Smith Scholarship Fund, J.A. & Flossie Mae, CA, 996
Smith Scholarship Fund, Kathleen A., NC, 6868
Smith Scholarship Fund, Patrick M. and Janet T., PA, see 8111
Smith Scholarship Trust, Alice F., FL, 2065
Smith Scholarship Trust, Zella M., TX, 9079
Smith Scholarship TUW, Elmer, RI, 8405
Smith Scholarship, E. B. and C. G., RI, see 8406
Smith Trust, Arline J., IL, 2859
Smith Trust, Elizabeth B., RI, 8406
Smith Trust, Ellen V., RI, 8407
Smith Trust, Elva S., RI, 8408
Smith Trust, Freda B. & William H., IA, 3383

Smith Veterinary Trust, Gracie Campbell, PA, 8112
Smith, Jr. Memorial Education Fund, Robert L., SC, 8508
Smith-Melton Foundation, VA, 9509
Smithfield Township College Assistance Fund, The, PA, 8113
Smithfield-Luter Foundation, Inc., The, VA, 9508
Smithsonian Institution, DC, 1729
Smock Foundation, Frank L. and Laura L., PA, 8114
Smolin Scholarship Fund Charitable Trust, Antonia Smolin and Victor, TX, see 9080
Smolin-Melin Scholarship Fund Trust, TX, 9080
Smucker Memorial Scholarship Trust, Helen F., OH, 7358
Smylie Foundation, John & Charlene, CA, 997
Smysor Memorial Fund, Harry L. & John L., IL, 2860
Smyth Standing Tall Charitable Foundation, Rev. John, The, IL, 2861
Smythe Trust, Henry Herbert, RI, 8409
SNA Foundation, AK, 139
SNAP, WA, see 9731
Snayberger Memorial Foundation, Harry E. and Florence W., NY, 6407
Snayberger Memorial Foundation, NY, see 6407
Snohomish County Council of the Society of St. Vincent de Paul, WA, 9728
Snow Foundation, George, Inc., FL, see 2066
Snow No. 5 Scholarship Fund, W. B. and Mary W., OH, 7359
Snow Scholarship Fund, George, Inc., FL, 2066
Snow-Cap Community Charities, OR, 7661
Snyder Education Fund, Fred C., RI, 8410
Snyder Educational Foundation, Burt, PA, 8115
Snyder Foundation, Harold B. and Dorothy A., The, NJ, 5570
Snyder Fund, Fred C., RI, see 8410
Snyder Medical Foundation, H. L., KS, 3516
Snyder Memorial Fund, Nicole, Inc., NV, 5302
Snyder Scholarship Fund, Clifford E. & Melda, RI, 8411
Snyder Scholarship Fund, Elmer A. & Anna Belle C., PA, 8116
Snyder Scholarship Fund, Melda, RI, see 8411
Snyder/Longue Vue Club Employee Scholarship Foundation, Franklin C., PA, 8117
Soames Educational Foundation, Harry L. & Ruby T., PA, 8118
Soanes Museum Foundation, Sir John, Inc., NY, 6408
Soapstone - A Writing Retreat for Women, OR, 7662
Social and Environmental Entrepreneurs, CA, 998
Social Equity Venture Fund, MA, see 4267
Social Philosophy and Policy Foundation, OH, 7360
Social Science Research Council, NY, 6409
Societe des Professeurs Francais en Amerique, NY, 6410
Societe des Professeurs Francais en Amerique, NY, see 6410
Society for Ambulatory Anesthesia, IL, 2862
Society for Analytical Chemists of Pittsburgh, PA, 8119
Society for Arts, Ltd., The, IL, 2863
Society for Cardiovascular Angiography and Interventions, The, DC, 1730
Society for Free Radical Biology and Medicine, IN, 3187
Society for Obstetric Anesthesia and Perinatology, WI, 10037
Society for Organizing Charity of the City of Salem, New Jersey, Inc., The, NJ, 5571
Society for Pediatric Dermatology, IN, 3188
Society for Research in Child Development, Inc., MI, 4610
Society for Science and the Public, Inc., DC, 1731
Society for the Increase of the Ministry, The, CT, 1461
Society for the Preservation & Encouragement of Barbershop Quartet Singing in America, CA, 999
Society for the Relief of Families of Deceased & Disabled Indigent Members of the Medical Profession of the State of South Carolina, SC, 8509
Society for the Relief of the Widows, Orphans, Aged and Disabled Clergy Diocese of South Carolina, SC, see 8463
Society for the Relief of Women & Children, NY, 6411
Society of Cincinnati - Virginia Trust, FL, see 1968
Society of Cincinnati, Georgia Trust, FL, see 1967

Society of Cosmetic Chemists, NY, 6412
Society of Economic Geologists Foundation, Inc., CO, 1285
Society of Experimental Test Pilots Scholarship Foundation, CA, 1000
Society of Gastrointestinal Radiologists, TX, 9081
Society of Kastorians Omonoia, Inc., NY, 6413
Society of Manufacturing Engineers Education Foundation, MI, 4611
Society of Nuclear Medicine, VA, 9510
Society of Singers, Inc., CA, 1001
Society of St. Vincent de Paul - Detroit, MI, 4612
Society of St. Vincent De Paul Archdiocese of Galveston-Houston, TX, 9082
Society of St. Vincent de Paul Council of Seattle/King County, WA, 9729
Society of St. Vincent de Paul Council of the Seattle Area, WA, see 9729
Society of St. Vincent de Paul Manitowoc, Inc., WI, 10038
Society of St. Vincent De Paul of Portland, Oregon, OR, 7663
Society of St. Vincent De Paul, MA, 4271
Society of St. Vincent de Paul, Particular Council of San Mateo, Inc., CA, 1002
Socrates Sculpture Park, NY, 6414
Sodexho Foundation, Inc., MD, see 3935
Sodexo Foundation, Inc., MD, 3935
Soeder Scholarship Trust, Elizabeth H., PA, 8120
Sojourner Foundation, MI, 4613
Soldwedel Foundation, MO, 5102
Solem Scholarship Trust, John E., SD, 8539
Soles4Souls, Inc., TN, 8646
Solomon Freedom Foundation Inc., Gerald B., NY, 6415
Some Other Place, Inc., TX, 9083
SOME, Inc., CA, see 1009
Someone Cares Charitable Trust, CO, 1286
Somerville Foundation, PA, 8121
Somerville Scholarship Foundation, Grahame and Thelma, PA, see 8121
Somerville Trust, Jason C., NH, 5369
Soneson Scholarship Fund Trust, Walter & Anna, MN, 4851
Sonlight Curriculum Foundation, CO, 1287
Sonnentag Foundation, WI, 10039
Sonneveldt Foundation, The, MI, 4614
Sonoco Products Company Contributions Program, SC, 8510
Sonoma County Community Foundation, The, CA, see 515
Sonora Area Foundation, CA, 1003
Sons of Italy Foundation, DC, 1732
Sons of Iwo Jima, Inc., NY, see 6309
Sonstegard Scholarship Foundation, Goodwin, IA, 3384
Soren Trust, Madeleine H., PA, 8122
Soros Fellowships for New Americans, Paul & Daisy, NY, 6416
Soros Foundation, Paul & Daisy, NY, see 6416
South Butler County School District Foundation, PA, 8123
South Carolina Junior Golf Foundation, SC, 8511
South Carolina Nurses Foundation, Inc., SC, 8512
South Carolina Press Association Foundation, SC, 8513
South Central Community Action Program, Inc., PA, 8124
South Central Community Foundation, KS, 3517
South Central Los Angeles Regional Center for Developmentally Disabled Persons, Inc., CA, 1004
South Dakota Community Foundation, SD, 8540
South Dakota Humanities Council, SD, 8541
South Dakota State University Foundation, SD, 8542
South Holland Business Association Foundation, IL, 2864
South Lake County Community Foundation, Inc., FL, see 1845
South Madison Community Foundation, IN, 3189
South Mountain Association, MA, 4272
South Plains Community Action Association, Inc., TX, 9084
South Shore Antique Auto Foundation, Inc., MA, 4273
South Shore Community Action Council, Inc., MA, 4274

South Shore Elder Services, Inc., MA, 4275
South Shore Foundation, AR, 311
South St. Paul Educational Foundation, MN, 4852
South Texas Academic Rising Scholars, TX, 9085
South Texas Food Bank, TX, 9086
South Washington County Scholarship Committee, MN, 4853
Southeast Tennessee Human Resource Agency, TN, 8647
Southeast Texas A & M Foundation, TX, 9087
SouthEast Wyoming Builders Association Scholarship Trust, WY, 10120
Southeastern Brain Tumor Foundation, GA, 2237
Southeastern Conference, AL, 81
Southeastern Louisiana University Development Foundation, LA, 3677
Southeastern Michigan Chapter NECA Educational and Research Foundation, MI, 4615
Southeastern Minnesota Arts Council, Inc., The, MN, 4854
Southern Alleghenies Planning and Development Commission, PA, 8125
Southern Arizona Foundation for Education-Lutheran, AZ, 237
Southern Arkansas University Foundation, Inc., AR, 312
Southern California Asian American Studies Central, Inc., CA, 1005
Southern Company Charitable Foundation, Inc., GA, 2238
Southern Documentary Fund, The, NC, 6869
Southern Exposure, CA, 1006
Southern Illinois University Foundation, IL, 2865
Southern Iowa Economic Development Association, IA, 3385
Southern Oregon Lions Sight & Hearing Center, Inc., OR, 7664
Southern Perry County Academic Endowment Fund, OH, 7361
Southern Phenix Textiles Scholarship Fund Inc., AL, 82
Southern Prince George's County Community Charities, MD, 3936
Southern Tennis Patrons Foundation, GA, 2239
Southern Theater Foundation, MN, 4855
Southern Union Charitable Foundation, TX, 9088
Southfield Community Foundation, MI, 4616
Southpole Foundation Inc., NJ, 5572
Southwest Airlines Co. Outreach, TX, 9089
Southwest Alternate Media Project, Inc., TX, 9090
Southwest Florida Community Foundation, Inc., The, FL, 2067
Southwest Georgia Community Action Council, Inc., GA, 2240
Southwest Kansas Area Agency On Aging, Inc., KS, 3518
Southwest Michigan Community Action Agency, MI, 4617
Southwest Michigan Rehab Foundation, MI, 4618
Southwest Minnesota Housing Partnership, MN, 4856
Southwest Minnesota Private Industry Council, Inc., MN, 4857
Southwest MN Arts and Humanities Council, MN, 4858
Southwest School of Art and Craft, TX, 9091
Southwest Wisconsin Workforce Development Board, Inc., WI, 10040
Southwestern Association for Indian Arts, Inc., NM, 5652
Southwestern Medical Foundation, TX, 9092
Southwestern Oregon Community College Foundation, OR, 7665
Southwestern Oregon Community, OR, see 7623
Space Grant Education and Enterprise Institute, CA, 1007
Space Shuttle Children's Trust Fund, The, FL, 2068
Spacht Memorial Trust, Muriel E., WY, 10121
Spackman Foundation, Isabel, PA, 8126
Spain Scholarship Foundation, E. Leo and Louise F., The, NY, 6417
Spanish Peaks Healthcare Foundation, CO, 1288
Sparkplug Foundation, The, NY, 6418
Sparks Employee Good Neighbor Foundation, AR, 313
Sparks Scholarship Fund, Bessie, KY, 3626
Sparrow Foundation, MI, 4619

Sparrow Hospital Memorials and Endowment Foundation, MI, *see* 4619
Spartan Masonic Educational Foundation, NY, 6419
Spartanburg County Foundation, The, SC, 8514
Spartvedt Testamentary Trust, Hans & Anna, WI, 10041
SPARX/Lorenzo Antonio Foundation, NM, 5653
SPE Foundation, TX, 9093
Spear Scholarship, Hugh and Della, Inc., KY, 3627
Spears Foundation, John and L. A., Inc., The, GA, 2241
SPEBSQSA - Far Western District, CA, *see* 999
Special Libraries Association, VA, 9511
Special Operations Warrior Foundation, FL, 2069
Special People in Need, IL, 2866
Specialized Carriers & Rigging Foundation, VA, 9512
Spectrum Family Network Foundation, PA, *see* 8186
Spectrum Human Services, Inc., MI, 4620
Speech Foundation of America, TN, *see* 8652
Speerstra Scholarship Fund Trust, Peter and Evelyn, MI, 4621
Spencer Charitable Foundation, TX, 9094
Spencer Community School Foundation, IA, 3386
Spencer Education Foundation and Trust, George and Marie G., OH, *see* 7362
Spencer Education Foundation, OH, 7362
Spencer Educational Foundation, Inc., NY, 6420
Spencer Scholarship Foundation, AZ, 238
Sperling Memorial Foundation, Haley, IL, 2867
Sperry Fund, The, NY, 6421
Sphinx Organization, The, MI, 4622
Spicer Scholarship Fund, Kathleen C., FL, 2070
Spina Bifida Association of America, DC, 1733
Spire Foundation, Abigail L., Inc., NC, 6870
Spirit Educational Foundation, CA, 1008
Spirol International Charitable Foundation Inc., CT, 1462
Spitcaufsky Memorial Foundation, Melvin, KS, 3519
Spivey Scholarship Trust, NC, 6871
Splawn Charitable Foundation West, Don and Roy, Inc., DE, 1524
Splawn Charitable Foundation, Don & Roy, TN, 8648
Splawn Charitable Foundation, Don, The, TN, *see* 8648
Splawn Charitable Foundation, Roy L., DE, *see* 1524
Spokane Kiwanis Charities, WA, 9730
Spokane Neighborhood Action Programs, WA, 9731
Sponsors for Educational Opportunity, Inc., NY, 6422
Sponsors of Musical Enrichment, Inc., CA, 1009
Sprague Trust, Inez, RI, 8412
Sprehe Scholarship Trust, Ralph & Bernice, MO, 5103
Springboard for the Arts, MN, 4859
Springer Electric Cooperative Education Foundation, NM, 5654
Springfield Foundation, The, OH, 7363
Springfield Trust, Mabel W., OK, 7513
Springman Scholarship Fund, Edgar K., OH, 7364
Springman Scholarship Fund, OH, *see* 7364
Springs Close Foundation, Inc., The, SC, 8515
Springs Foundation, Inc., SC, *see* 8515
Spruce Run Association, ME, 3736
Sprunt Foundation, James, Inc., NC, 6872
Spurrier Scholarship Fund, Rose, KS, 3520
Squeaky Wheel, NY, 6423
Squier Trust, C. Weaver, CT, 1463
Squires Educational Foundation, William D., Inc., The, AZ, 239
Squires Scholarship Foundation Ltd., Hugh & Marie, WI, 10042
SRCD, MI, *see* 4610
SSES, MA, *see* 4275
SSRC, NY, *see* 6409
SSVEC Foundation, AZ, *see* 243
St Joseph Hospital of Orange, CA, 1010
St. Anthony Educational Foundation, Inc., NC, 6873
St. Clair County Community Action Agency, IL, 2868
St. Clair County Scholarship Trust Fund, IL, 2869
St. Croix Valley Foundation, WI, 10043
St. David's Community Health Care Foundation, TX, 9095
St. Elizabeth Hospital Community Foundation, WI, 10044
St. Elizabeth Hospital Foundation, WI, *see* 10044
St. Elmo Foundation, NY, 6424
St. Francis Yacht Club Foundation, CA, 1011

St. George's Society of New York, NY, 6425
St. Helena Family Center, CA, 1012
St. John Medical Center, Inc., OK, 7514
St. John Scholarship Trust, Wilbert & Evelyn, WI, 10045
St. John Vianney Educational Foundation, MI, *see* 4623
St. John Vianney Foundation, MI, 4623
St. John's Healing Community Board, IL, 2870
St. John's Home and Community Care, IL, *see* 2870
St. John's Mite Association, DC, 1734
St. Joseph Foundation of Bryan, Texas, TX, 9096
St. Joseph Hospital Foundation, Inc., KY, 3628
St. Joseph Hospital Foundation, TX, 9097
St. Joseph Kiwanis Foundation, MI, 4624
St. Joseph's Family Center, CA, 1013
St. Jude Hospital, Inc., CA, 1014
St. Louis Carpenters District Council Scholarship Fund, Inc., MO, 5104
St. Louis Chapters American Institute of Architects Scholarship Fund, MO, *see* 4931
St. Louis Community Foundation, Inc., MO, 5105
St. Louis Community Foundation, MO, *see* 5082
St. Louis Public Schools Foundation, MO, 5106
St. Luke's Episcopal Hospital, TX, 9098
St. Luke's Foundation of Bellingham, WA, 9732
St. Luke's Health Care Foundation, IA, 3387
St. Luke's Methodist Hospital, IA, 3388
St. Luke's Nurses' Benefit Fund, NY, 6426
St. Luke's Regional Medical Center, IA, *see* 3347
St. Margaret Foundation, PA, 8127
St. Mary's Hospital and Medical Center, Inc., CO, 1289
St. Mary's Hospital Foundation, MI, *see* 4625
St. Mary's Hospital of Rochester, MN, *see* 4792
St. Mary's of Michigan Foundation, MI, 4625
St. Mary's/Westside Food Bank Alliance, AZ, 240
St. Marys Community Foundation, OH, 7365
St. Marys Health Center Jefferson City Missouri Foundation, MO, 5107
St. Paul College Club, Inc. - AAUW Scholarship Trust, MN, 4860
St. Paul's Church Home, VA, 9513
St. Petersburg Times Fund, Inc., FL, 2071
St. Petersburg Times Scholarship Fund, FL, *see* 2071
St. Shenouda the Archimandrite Coptic Society, CA, 1015
St. Vincent de Paul Community Pharmacy, Inc., MS, 4922
St. Vincent de Paul Rehabilitation Center, TX, 9099
St. Vincent de Paul Society of St. Joseph County, Inc., IN, 3190
St. Vincent de Paul Store of Houma, LA, 3678
Stack Memorial Scholarship Fund, Dick, NY, 6427
Stage Directors and Choreographers Foundation, NY, 6428
Stager Memorial Nursing Scholarship, Henry P. and Mary B., PA, 8128
Stager Memorial Scholarship Fund, Matt, PA, 8129
Stagner Charitable Trust, Mabel, NC, 6874
Stahlman Education Foundation, Mildred T., TN, 8649
Staley Educational Foundation, Richard Seth, The, CO, 1290
Staley Foundation for Psychological Development, Richard Seth, CO, *see* 1290
Staley Foundation, Richard S., CA, *see* 900
Stambaugh Scholarship Fund, William S. & Arthur, NC, *see* 6875
Stambaugh Scholarship Private Foundation, NC, 6875
Stamford Rotary Trust Fund, CT, 1464
Stamford Woman's Club Inc., CT, 1465
Stamm Scholarship Trust, Arnold P., WI, 10046
Standerford Trust, H. Wayne, IN, 3191
Stanford Public Interest Law Foundation, CA, 1016
Stanislaus Community Foundation, CA, 1017
Stanley Scholarship Trust, Eugene & Florence O., IN, 3192
Stanley Scottish Rite Memorial Fund, Charles E., CA, 1018
Stanzel Family Foundation, Inc., The, TX, 9100
Staples Free School Trust, CT, 1466
Star Foundation Inc., GA, 2242
Starcher Educational Foundation, Genevieve, WV, 9816
Stark Community Foundation, OH, 7366
Stark County Foundation, Inc., The, OH, *see* 7366

Stark Foundation, Nelda C. and H. J. Lutcher, TX, 9101
Stark Trust Fund, Jasper, TN, A
Starks Charitable Foundation, FL, 2072
Starks Foundation, John L., Inc., CT, 1467
Starlight Children's Foundation, NY/NJ/CT, NY, 6429
Starr Fellowship Fund, William F., RI, 8413
Starr Foundation, The, NY, 6430
STARS, TX, *see* 9085
State College of Florida Foundation, Inc., FL, 2073
State Employees Association of North Carolina Scholarship Fund, Inc., NC, 6876
State Employees' Credit Union Foundation, NC, 6877
State Medical Society Foundation, WI, *see* 10080
Stateline Community Foundation, The, WI, 10047
Staten Island Ballet Theater, Inc., NY, 6431
Statler Foundation, The, NY, 6432
Statue Foundation, Inc., The, NY, 6433
Stauble Scholarship Fund, RI, 8414
Stauffer Foundation, Mary R., CA, 1019
Stauffer Scholarship Fund, Virginia E., OH, 7367
Staunton Augusta Waynesboro Community Foundation, VA, *see* 9346
Stearn Foundation, Alexander William, Inc., FL, 2074
Stearns Trust, Teresa Treat, IA, 3389
Stecher and Horowitz Foundation, The, NY, 6434
Stedman Foundation, Ella May, CA, 1020
Steel Founders' Society Foundation, IL, 2871
Steele, Jr. Scholarship Foundation, J. C., Inc., NC, 6878
Steep Rock Arts Association Co., CT, 1468
Steeplechase Fund, The, MD, 3937
Stefansky Charitable Trust, Meir and Ruth, The, NY, 6435
Steffens Scholarship Trust, Fred T. & John H., KS, 3521
Stegall Charitable Educational Foundation, TN, 8650
Steigler Trust, Phyllis H., OH, 7368
Steinbach Foundation, OR, *see* 7666
Steinbach Scholarship Fund, J.B., OR, 7666
Steinberg Charitable Trust, Harold & Mimi, The, NY, 6436
Steiner Scholarship Fund, Daniel J., OH, 7369
Steinhart Foundation, Inc., The, NE, 5262
Steinke Perpetual Scholarship, A. L., MN, 4861
Steinman Foundation, James Hale, PA, 8130
Steinman Foundation, John Frederick, PA, 8131
Stempfle Fund Trust, Evelyn E., NY, *see* 6437
Stempfle Scholarship, Evelyn E., NY, 6437
Stensrud Foundation, The, CA, 1021
Step Up for Students, FL, 2075
Stephens Charitable Foundation, Cecile, CA, 1022
Stephenson Education Foundation, Joanne W., TN, 8651
Stephenson Scholarship Foundation, CA, *see* 1023
Stephenson-Beelard Scholarship Foundation, CA, 1023
Stepping Stones Shelter, Inc., MD, 3938
Sterling Heights Community Foundation, MI, 4626
Sterling-Rock Falls Community Trust, IL, 2872
Stern Family Foundation, The, CA, *see* 1024
Stern Foundation, Marc and Eva, The, CA, 1024
Sternberger Foundation, Sigmund, Inc., NC, *see* 6885
Steuben County Community Foundation, IN, 3193
Steven Scholarship Trust, James & Cecile, MO, 5108
Stevens Foundation, Jess L. and Miriam B., OK, 7515
Stevens Memorial Fund, Mertie & Harley, OR, 7667
Stevenson Foundation Trust, IL, 2873
Steward-Newkirk Testamentary Trust, OK, 7516
Stewart Management Group Charitable Foundation, MI, 4627
Stewart School Trust, Marie Palmer, NC, 6879
Stewart Trust, Helen T. & Mildred, IA, 3390
Stice Trust, Ross W., KS, 3522
Stich Scholarship Fund, Eleanor F., ME, 3737
Stickley Educational Fund, Carl Dee, WV, 9817
Stickney Educational Trust, The, NH, 5370
Stiens Trust, Robert F. Stiens and Glenda M., IN, 3194
Stifel Endowment Fund, George E., WV, 9818
Stifel Scholarship Fund, George E., WI, 10048
Stillwater Medical Center Foundation, Inc., OK, 7517
Stillwell Foundation, Dr. W. C., MN, 4862
Stingrays, Inc., GA, 2243
Stinson Trust Agency, Anna, OH, 7370
Stockard Charitable Trust, KS, 3523

Stockert Foundation, Tom, IL, 2874
Stockton Fire Fighters Gladys Benerd Trust, CA, 1025
Stockwell Trust, Helen Wolcott, PA, 8132
Stoelting Brothers Company Foundation, Inc., WI, see 10020
Stokes Scholarship Trust, Olive A., MI, 4628
Stokes Scholarship Trust, RI, 8415
Stone Family Foundation, Max D., Inc., CA, 1026
Stone Fund, Albert H. & Ruben S., MA, 4276
Stone Quarry Hill Art Park, NY, 6438
Stonecutter Foundation, Inc., NC, 6880
Stoneleigh Foundation, PA, 8133
Stoneleigh Research and Education Center Serving Children and Youth, A., PA, see 8133
Stoner Trust, Katherine M., NY, 6439
Stonier Educational Trust, I. F. Doug Stonier and Ella, IL, 2875
Stony Wold-Herbert Fund, Inc., NY, 6440
Storer Scholarship Foundation, Oliver W., IN, 3195
Storey Scholarship Fund, Irene, IL, 2876
Stork Charitable Trust, The, PA, 8134
Storkan Foundation, Richard C., The, CA, see 1027
Storkan/Hanes McCaslin Research Foundation, CA, 1027
Stott Ministries, John, AZ, 241
Stoudenmire Education Fund, Lottie D., NC, 6881
Stout Foundation, C. B., IN, 3196
Stout Scholarship Fund, O. J., WV, 9819
Stovall Hope Foundation, Inc., GA, 2244
Stowers Institute for Medical Research, MO, 5109
Stowers Medical Institute, MO, see 5109
Stowers Scholarship, Ralph, VA, 9514
Strafford County Community Action Committee, Inc., NH, 5371
Strahan Educational Foundation, David L., Inc., The, FL, 2076
Strahl Educational Trust, Leland & Lucille, SD, 8543
Strasburg Community Scholarship Trust Fund Inc., VA, 9515
Stratton Trust, Gladys, IL, 2877
Straub Family Foundation, IA, 3391
Straub Foundation, IA, see 3391
Straub Trust Estate, Gertrude S., HI, 2321
Strauss Opportunity Trust, Helaine & Edgar, IL, 2878
Strauss Scholarship Foundation, Donald A., CA, 1028
Straw Foundation, Jack, WA, 9733
Strayer Scholarship Fund, Nadie E., OR, 7668
Streams in the Desert Foundation, CA, see 662
Streeter Scholarship Fund, Mallary D., RI, see 8416
Streeter Scholarship Fund, RI, 8416
Strengths Institute, Clifton, NE, 5263
Strickland Memorial Fund, Charles A., NC, 6882
Stricklin Scholarship, Evelyn E., PA, 8135
Stride, CO, 1291
Strive, Inc., SC, 8516
Strong Foundation, Hattie M., VA, 9516
Stubbs Scholarship Trust, R. L. and Ethel, IA, 3392
Stuck Foundation, Clair E. Stuck and Flora E., Inc., The, PA, 8136
Studenica Foundation, CA, 1029
Student Action with Farmworkers, NC, 6883
Student Aid Foundation Enterprises, Inc., TX, 9102
Student Aid Foundation Inc., GA, 2245
Student Assistance Foundation, MT, 5174
Student Education Support Association, Inc., OH, 7371
Student Votech Foundation, Inc., AR, A
Studio Museum in Harlem, The, NY, 6441
Stueven Charitable Foundation, The, NE, 5264
Stufflebeam Educational Foundation, Dwain H. and Joyce L., Inc., ID, 2351
Stump Disaster Charitable Trust, Hill, WV, 9820
Stump Memorial Scholarship Fund, IL, 2879
Stupfel Trust, E. Isabella, CO, 1292
Stupp Bros. Bridge & Iron Company Foundation, MO, A
Sturges Charitable Trust, Stephen H. Sturges & Rose P., The, AZ, 242
Sturgis Area Community Foundation, MI, 4629
Sturgis Foundation, MI, see 4629
Sturgis Foundation, Roy & Christine, AR, 314
Sturgis Foundation, W. P., AR, 315
Stuttering Foundation of America, Inc., TN, 8652
Stuttering Foundation, The, TN, see 8652

Styles Memorial Scholarship Fund Foundation, The, GA, 2246
Suarez Charitable Foundation, Seg and Harty, IL, 2880
Sudakoff Foundation, Roberta Leventhal, Inc., FL, 2077
Sudbury Foundation, MA, 4277
Sudden Infant Death Syndrome Alliance, Inc., MD, 3939
Suden Scholarship Trust Fund, Rudy, MT, 5175
Suder-Pick Foundation, Inc., WI, 10049
Suffridge UFCW Scholarship Fund, James A., DC, see 1739
Sukut Family Foundation, The, CA, 1030
Sullivan Foundation, Ray & Pauline, CT, 1469
Sullivan Memorial Foundation, Bob, MA, 4278
Sullivan Scholars Foundation, OH, 7372
Sulphur Springs Valley Electric Cooperative Foundation, Inc., AZ, 243
Sulprizio Scholarship Fund, Georgia Frasier, The, CA, 1031
SUMMA Foundation, NM, 5655
Summerfair Foundation, Inc., OH, 7373
Summerville Scholarship Foundation, Norma B., OH, 7374
Summit Area Public Foundation, The, NJ, 5573
Summit Foundation, The, CO, 1293
Summit Home for Children Chesebrough Foundation, NJ, 5574
Sumners Foundation, Mr. & Mrs. E. H., MS, 4923
Sun Coast Hospital Foundation, Inc., FL, see 2078
Sun Coast Osteopathic Foundation, Inc., FL, 2078
Sun Country Airlines Foundation, MN, 4863
Sun Lumber Company Education Foundation, The, WV, 9821
Sun-Pacific Scholarship Foundation, Inc., CA, 1033
Sunburst Foundation, Inc., FL, 2079
Sundance Institute, UT, 9227
Sunnyside Foundation, Inc., TX, 9103
Sunnyside, Inc., TX, see 9103
Sunnyvale Community Services, CA, 1032
Support Center for Nonprofit Management, CA, see 519
Supreme Council Education and Charity Fund, MA, 4279
Surina Scholarship Fund, Jeanette Lyons, Inc., IN, 3197
Sussman Trust, Otto, NY, 6442
Sutliff Trust f/b/o Hofstra University, Gerald, PA, 8137
Sutton Trust, Ruth H., RI, 8417
Svarre Foundation, MT, 5176
SVI Scholarship Fund, IL, 2881
SWAIA, NM, see 5652
SWAMP, TX, see 9090
Swan Society in Boston, MA, 4280
Swanson Fund f/b/o Fresno Lodge No. 247, F. & A. M, CA, 1034
Swanson Fund, Annette Monson, CA, see 1034
Swanson Memorial Scholarship Trust, Ernest and Lillian, MO, 5110
Swedish American Hospital, IL, 2882
Sweet Education Foundation, Lloyd D., MT, 5177
Sweet Foundation, Harry B., Inc., NE, 5265
Sweet Relief Musicians Fund, CA, 1035
Sweitzer American Legion Trust, Willard F., IL, 2883
Sweitzer Memorial Fund, Timothy, Inc., NY, 6443
Swensrud Scholarship Fund, Sidney A., IA, 3393
Swift Energy Charitable Fund, TX, 9104
Swift Memorial Health Care Foundation, CA, 1036
Swiler Memorial Scholarship Trust Fund, Wesley and Barbara, IA, 3394
Swinney Foundation, Edward F., TX, 9105
Swinney Student Loan Trust, Edward F., TX, 9106
Swiss Benevolent Society of Chicago, IL, 2884
Switzer Foundation, ME, see 3738
Switzer Foundation, Robert and Patricia, ME, 3738
Swope Memorial Scholarship Trust, Charles S., PA, 8138
Swope Trust, Gerald, MO, 5111
SWS Charitable Foundation, Inc., FL, 2080
Swyer Foundation, Inc., The, NY, A
Syder Trust, Edward, RI, 8418
Sysco Disaster Relief Foundation, Inc., TX, 9107

T.O.T.A., CA, see 1064
T.R.H. Development Foundation, IA, see 3397

Taber Educational Trust, George & Blanche, MT, 5178
Taber Scholarship Fund, RI, see 8419
Taber Scholarship Trust, George and Blanche, MT, see 5178
Taber Trust, Betsey W., RI, 8419
Tacoma Community Foundation, Greater, The, WA, 9734
Taddonio Family Foundation, Salvatore, The, CO, 1294
Tahquamenon Education Foundation, MI, 4630
Tahquette Education Trust, Chief John Alfred, NC, 6884
Taiho Kogyo Tribology Research Foundation, OH, 7375
Take a Swing at Cancer, Inc., MA, 4281
Take Stock in Children, Inc., FL, 2081
Takitani Foundation, Inc., HI, see 2322
Takitani Foundation, Mamoru & Aiko, Inc., HI, 2322
Talarico Scholarship Fund, Louis C., MD, 3940
Tallahassee Quarterback Club Foundation, Inc., FL, 2082
Taller de Salud Compesina, NC, see 6887
Tam Charitable Foundation, Gordon Tam & Elsie K., CA, see 613
TAME, TX, see 9114
Tamer Foundation, MI, 4631
Tanana Chiefs Conference, AK, 140
Tanaq Foundation, AK, 141
Tang Foundation for Education, Jane and Tom, Inc., NJ, 5575
Tangelo Park Pilot Program Inc., FL, 2083
Tanne Foundation, MA, 4282
Tannenbaum-Sternberger Foundation, Inc., NC, 6885
Taos Community Foundation, NM, 5656
Tappan Trust, Eva March, RI, 8420
TAPPI Foundation, Inc., GA, 2247
Tarboro Community Outreach, Inc., NC, 6886
Targa Resources Employee Relief Organization, TX, 9108
Target Corporation Contributions Program, MN, 4864
Target Hunger, Inc., TX, 9109
Tartt Scholarship Fund, Hope Pierce, TX, 9110
TASCA, NC, 6887
Tassell Foundation, Leslie E., The, MI, see 4632
Tassell-Wisner-Bottrall Foundation, MI, 4632
Tate Family Foundation, Inc., WI, 10050
Tate Florida Prepaid College Foundation, Stanley G., FL, see 1884
Tate Foundation, Joseph P., WI, see 10050
Tatum Foundation, The, CA, 1037
Taunton Family Children's Home, FL, 2084
TAV Foundation, AL, 83
Tavitian Foundation, Inc., NJ, 5576
Tawa Charitable Foundation, CA, 1038
Taylor Charitable Trust, Kenneth and Elisabeth, OH, 7376
Taylor Community Foundation, PA, 8139
Taylor Educational Fund, Frank C. Taylor & Helen M., MA, 4283
Taylor Educational Trust, Robert B., TX, 9111
Taylor Family Foundation, The, CA, 1039
Taylor Foundation, Jason, Inc., FL, 2085
Taylor Foundation, Mr. & Mrs. George W., IL, 2885
Taylor Foundation, Patrick F., LA, 3679
Taylor Fund, Nathaniel, Inc., MA, 4284
Taylor Human Services System, Murtis H., OH, 7377
Taylor Multi-Service Center, Murtis H., OH, see 7377
Taylor Perpetual Charitable Trust, Brent, IL, 2886
Taylor Scholarship, C. H. "Buck", IA, 3395
Taylor Trust Scholarship Trust, H., MI, 4633
Taylor Trust, Sally Smith, NC, 6888
Tazewood Community Services, Inc., IL, 2887
TDC Research Foundation, VA, 9517
TDX Foundation, AK, 142
Teach For America, NY, 6444
Teachers Housing Cooperative, CA, 1040
Teachers Network, The, NY, 6445
Teachers of English to Speakers of Other Languages, Inc., VA, 9518
Team Scholarship Fund, Dr. Robert A., NC, 6889
Teamster Disaster Relief Fund, DC, 1735
Teamsters BBYO Scholarship Fund, NY, 6446
Teamsters Local 830 Scholarship Fund, PA, 8140
Tech Foundation, Inc., WV, 9822
Tech Museum of Innovation, The, CA, 1041
Tecumseh Community Fund Foundation, MI, see 4516

Teel Charitable Trust, Fred M., NY, 6447
Teen Mania Ministries, Inc., TX, 9112
Telamon Corporation, NC, 6890
Telluride Foundation, CO, 1295
Templar Educational Foundation, TX, see 9123
Temple-Inland Foundation, TN, 8653
Temple-Krick YFU Scholarship Fund, Inc., MI, 4634
Templeton Foundation, John, PA, 8141
Templeton Trust Foundation, John B., IL, 2888
Tenderloin Neighborhood Development Corporation, CA, 1042
Tenenbaum Educational Trust, AR, 316
Tenholder Trust, Richard J. & Florence J., KS, 3524
Tennessee Humanities Council, TN, see 8604
Tenney Educational Fund, Inc., MA, 4285
Tension Envelope Foundation, MO, 5112
Teresan Scholarship Fund, MN, see 4684
Terplan Family Foundation, Inc., NJ, 5577
Terra Foundation for American Art, IL, 2889
Terrill Memorial Fund, Ronald, Inc., VT, 9261
Territorial Sportsmen Scholarship, AK, 143
Terry Educational Trust, Blanche G., TX, 9113
Terry Memorial Scholarship Trust Fund, Seymour, AR, 317
Terry Scholarship Foundation, C. D., KS, 3525
Terry, Jr. Foundation, Robert F., The, MA, 4286
Tessier Family Foundation, Inc., SD, 8544
Testamentary Trust, V. M. Slipher, IL, 2890
Teva Cares Foundation, PA, 8142
Texas Alliance for Minorities In Engineering, TX, 9114
Texas Alpha Endowment Fund, Inc., TX, 9115
Texas and Southwestern Cattle Raisers Foundation, TX, 9116
Texas Area Fund Foundation, Inc., The, TX, 9117
Texas Bar Foundation, TX, 9118
Texas Council for the Humanities, TX, see 8887
Texas Credit Union Foundation, TX, 9119
Texas Equal Access to Justice Foundation, TX, 9120
Texas Hill County Wine and Food Foundation, TX, see 9170
Texas Industries Foundation, TX, 9121
Texas Interscholastic League Foundation, TX, 9122
Texas Knights Templar Educational Foundation, TX, 9123
Texas Medical Association Education and Research Foundation, TX, see 9125
Texas Medical Association Foundation, TX, 9125
Texas Medical Association, TX, 9124
Texas Neurofibromatosis Foundation, TX, 9126
Texas Nursery and Landscape Association Education and Research Foundation, TX, 9127
Texas Podiatric Medical Foundation, TX, 9128
Texas Police Chiefs Association Foundation, TX, 9129
Texas Rangers Baseball Foundation, TX, 9130
Texas Star Oaks Fund, Inc., TX, 9131
Texas Wildlife Association Foundation, Inc., TX, see 8825
THA Foundation, NC, see 6691
Thai Community Center of North Texas, TX, 9132
Thai Physicians Association of America Foundation, IL, see 2895
Thalheimer Charitable Trust, Louise W., MS, 4924
Thames Valley Council for Community Action, Inc., CT, 1470
Thanks USA, VA, 9519
Tharpe Foundation, Robert H. and Kathryne B., The, GA, see 2248
Tharpe Foundation, The, GA, 2248
That Man May See, Inc., CA, 1043
Thatcher Foundation, The, CO, see 1307
Thauer Scholarship Fund, Muriel, IL, 2891
THAW, MI, see 4459
THDF II, Inc., GA, 2249
Theatre Bay Area, CA, 1044
Theatre Communications Group, NY, 6448
Therrien Foundation, Corinne Rentfrow, The, CA, 1045
Theta Delta Chi Educational Foundation, Inc., MA, 4287
Theta Omega Omega Charities, Inc., MD, see 3851
Thiel Foundation, The, CA, 1046
Thiele Scholarship Fund, Oscar and Hildegard, OH, 7378
Third World Newsreel, NY, see 5809
Thoburn Foundation for Education, The, PA, 8143

Thom Charitable Foundation, Carl and Elinor Glyn, MI, 4635
Thom Memorial Corporation, Douglas A., ME, 3739
Thomas Circle No. 32, Ladies of the Grand Army of the Republic, George H., CA, see 729
Thomas Educational Fund, Albert L. & Ivy B., OR, 7669
Thomas Estate Student Aid Trust, Harvey, NC, 6891
Thomas Family Foundation, Billie and Gillis, TX, 9133
Thomas Foundation, Godfrey, AR, 318
Thomas Foundation, J and K, The, CT, 1471
Thomas Foundation, John J., PA, 8144
Thomas Foundation, The, TX, see 9133
Thomas Scholarship Fund, Albert A. and Ruth W., MA, 4288
Thomas Scholarship Fund, Russ, MI, 4636
Thomas Scholarship Trust, Ruby Rowe, VA, 9520
Thomas Trust, David E., WI, 10051
Thomas Trust, Ruth W., MA, see 4288
Thomasson Foundation, The, IN, 3198
Thomasville Furniture Industries Foundation, NC, 6892
Thomley Foundation Inc., The, TN, 8654
Thompson Charitable Foundation, Bessie & Godfrey, TX, 9134
Thompson Charitable Trust, Edgel Paul and Garnet E., OH, 7379
Thompson Educational Fund, Willard E. & Ella P., RI, 8421
Thompson Educational Trust, Mary B. & Perry A., VA, 9521
Thompson Family Charitable Foundation, Donald E., The, MO, 5113
Thompson Foundation, Jack W., PA, 8145
Thompson Foundation, Otis A., Inc., NY, 6449
Thompson Fund, Wm. B., NY, 6450
Thompson Scholarship Fund, RI, 8422
Thompson Scholarship Trust, A. G. & Phelo, TX, 9135
Thompson Trust, Ella B. and Lucy, TX, 9136
Thomson Foundation, John Edgar, The, DE, 1525
Thomson Scholarships, TD Frank, NC, 6893
Thoracic Surgery Foundation for Research and Education, The, IL, 2892
Thorbeck Foundation, Inc., MN, 4865
Thoreau Foundation, Henry David, Inc., MA, 4289
Thorn, Jr. Foundation, Columbus W., MD, 3941
Thorne Foundation Inc., John M. & Ethel C., MA, 4290
Thornton III Memorial Scholarship Trust, Haywood R., FL, 2086
Thorntown Businessmen's Educational Foundation, Inc., IN, 3199
Thorwelle Foundation, Charles, NY, 6451
Thousand Islands Foundation, Inc., NY, 6452
Three Arts Scholarship Fund, Inc., OH, 7380
Three Rivers Area Community Foundation, MI, 4637
Three Rivers Center for Independent Living, PA, 8146
Three Rivers Community Action, Inc., MN, 4866
Three Rivers Community Foundation, MI, see 4637
Three Rivers Community Foundation, WA, 9735
Thresholds, Inc., MI, 4638
Thrivent Financial For Lutherans, MN, 4867
Throckmorton Foundation, The, OH, 7381
Throckmorton-Riser Foundation, Inc., KS, 3526
Through the Looking Glass, CA, 1047
Thrush Charitable Trust, Robert A., FL, 2087
Thunderbird Junior Golf Foundation, AZ, 244
Thurber House, OH, 7382
Thurman Educational Foundation Inc., Rabbi Samuel, MO, 5114
Thurston Foundation, Harlan R., MN, 4868
THYCA: Thyroid Cancer Survivors' Association, Inc., NY, 6453
Tibet Fund, The, NY, 6454
Tides Foundation, CA, 1048
Tidewater Automobile Association of Virginia - J. Theron "Tim" Timmons Memorial Scholarship Foundation, The, VA, 9522
Tidewater Builders Association Scholarship Foundation, Inc., VA, 9523
Tidewater Jewish Foundation, Inc., VA, 9524
Tierney Family Foundation, Inc., The, CT, 1472
Tiffany Foundation, Louis Comfort, The, NY, 6455
Tiffany Pines Community Outreach Center, NC, see 6574
Tiffin Charitable Foundation, The, OH, 7383

Tigara Educational Foundation Inc., AK, 144
TILF, PA, see 7924
TILF, TX, see 9122
Tilles Fund, The, MO, 5115
Tilles Nonsectarian Charity Fund, Rosalie, MO, see 5115
Tillman Scholarship Trust, John Shaw and Anna Walters, NC, 6894
Tilt Scholarship Trust, Margaret B., NY, 6456
Timken Company Charitable and Educational Fund, Inc., The, OH, 7384
Timken Company Educational Fund, Inc., The, OH, see 7384
Timms Family Foundation, WV, 9823
Timmy Foundation, Inc., IN, see 3200
Timmy Global Health, IN, 3200
Tinker Association for Women, Annie, Inc., The, NY, 6457
Tinker Memorial Fund, Annie Rensselaer, NY, see 6457
Tippens Charitable Trust, WV, see 9789
Tipton County Foundation, Inc., IN, 3201
Tiscornia Foundation, Inc., The, MI, 4639
Titus Trust, Evelyn K., IL, 2893
Tiwahe Foundation, MN, 4869
Tkacyzk & E. Mahaney Memorial Scholarship Trust, M. Fletcher, VT, 9262
TLC Foundation, PA, 8147
TMC Foundation, RI, 8423
TMCF, DC, see 1674
Tobias Foundation, Randall L., Inc., IN, 3202
Today Foundation, The, TX, 9137
Todd Foundation, Vera H. and William R., The, RI, see 8424
Todd Scholarship Fund, Robert H., AL, 84
Todd V. H. and W. R. Foundation, RI, 8424
Toigo Foundation, Robert, CA, 1049
Tolbert Charitable Trust, Emma Belle, The, CO, 1296
Tomah PTA Scholarship Trust, WI, 10052
Tomara Corporation, IL, 2894
Tomasso Family Foundation, Inc., The, CT, see 1473
Tomasso Foundation Inc., William J., The, CT, 1473
Tomlinson's Touching Lives Foundation, OH, 7385
Tomorrow Scholarship Fund Trust, TN, 8655
Tompkins Trust, Martin L. & Mary Ellen Tompkins & John A., MO, 5116
Toomey Scholarship Fund, Almeda Leake, OH, 7386
Toothaker Trust, Willis & Imogene, KS, 3527
Topaz Arts, Inc., NY, 6458
Topeka Community Foundation, KS, 3528
Torbet Scholarship Trust, Ernest & Anna, MA, 4291
Torrance Memorial Medical Center Health Care Foundation, CA, 1050
Torray Family Foundation, Robert E. Torray and Anne P., MD, 3942
Torres Memorial Scholarship Fund, Rosa Carrillo, AZ, 245
Torrington Area Foundation for Public Giving Trust Entity, CT, see 1362
Total Community Action, Inc., LA, 3680
Toth Foundation, Alfred L., PA, 8148
Touchstone Energy Bright Ideas Grant Program, NC, 6895
Touhey Scholarship Fund, Eleanora P., CA, 1051
Tourette Syndrome Association, Inc., NY, 6459
Tourism Cares for Tomorrow, Inc., MA, see 4292
Tourism Cares, Inc., MA, 4292
Toussant/Roger Radloff Foundation, Pierre, FL, 2088
Tower Hematology Oncology Cancer Research Foundation, CA, 1052
Towle Scholarship Trust, Mildred, HI, 2323
Townley Educational Trust, Harry and Minerva, MT, 5179
Townsend Aid for the Aged, RI, 8425
Townsend Foundation, Inc., The, NJ, 5578
Townsend Scholarship Fund, Ethel C., NJ, 5579
Tozer Foundation, Inc., MN, 4870
Tozier Memorial Scholarship Trust, Gladys, NY, 6460
TPAA Foundation, IL, 2895
Traalum Trust, Hertha, CT, 1474
Trace Foundation, NY, 6461
Trachsel Foundation, Dennis and Sara, The, OH, 7387
Tractor and Equipment Company Foundation, The, AL, 85

Tracy Scholarship Foundation, James & Phyllis, RI, 8426

Tracy Scholarship Fund, Perry S. and Stella H., CA, 1053

Tracy, CFSA and 1st Lieutenant William G. Burt, Jr., USAF Fund, Brigadier General Edward Dorr, FL, 2089

Traer Community Foundation, IA, 3396

Tramuto Foundation, Donato J., ME, 3740

Transgender Scholarship and Education Legacy Fund, MA, 4293

Transylvania Community Hospital Foundation, Inc., NC, 6896

Traurig Scholarship Trust, Louis D., CT, 1475

Travel Industry Association of America Foundation, DC, 1736

Travelers Aid Family Services, Inc., MA, 4294

Travelers Aid Society of Metropolitan Detroit, MI, 4640

Travelli Fund, Charles Irwin, The, MA, 4295

TRCIL, PA, see 8146

Treacy Company, MT, 5180

Treacy Foundation, MT, see 5180

Treakle Charitable and Educational Foundation, Jane & Gunby, VA, 9525

TREE Fund, IL, see 2896

Tree Research and Education Endowment Fund, IL, 2896

Treehouse, WA, 9736

Treen Fund, Henrietta S., NC, 6897

Trek Scholarship Foundation Inc., WI, 10053

Trembly Foundation, John E., KS, 3529

Trenton Kappa Foundation, Inc., NJ, A

Tretter Foundation, Edwin C., Inc., IN, 3203

Tri-City Community Action Program, Inc., MA, 4296

Tri-City Hospital Foundation, CA, 1054

Tri-Counties Association for the Developmentally Disabled, Inc., CA, 1055

Tri-County Community Action Agency, Inc., NJ, 5581

Tri-County Community Action Program, Inc., NH, 5372

Tri-County Electric Foundation, NC, 6901

Tri-County Hospital, Inc., MN, 4871

Tri-County Opportunities Council, IL, 2897

Tri-County Protective Agency, Inc., GA, 2250

Tri-Valley Medical Foundation, NE, 5266

Triad Health Project, The, NC, 6898

Trial Lawyers Foundation for Youth Education, NJ, 5580

Triangle Arts Association, NY, 6462

Triangle Community Foundation, NC, 6899

Triangle Family Services, Inc., NC, 6900

Trickle Up Program, Inc., NY, 6463

Trico Foundation, AZ, 246

Trifiro Foundation, Richard J., MA, 4297

Trimble Special Need Trust Fund, George, TX, 9138

Trinity Christian Center of Santa Ana, Inc., CA, 1056

Trinity Foundation, AR, 319

Trinity Health Foundation, IA, 3397

Trinity Lutheran Scholarship Fund, MN, 4872

Trinity Youth Services, CA, 1057

Trinklein Educational Trust, Otto, MI, 4641

Trippeer Charitable Foundation, Dr. H. A., OR, 7670

Troedson Educational Fund, Carl W., NC, 6902

Trolinger Trust, The, FL, 2090

Trone Scholarship Trust, Blanche Barr, MI, 4642

Trotter Charitable Trust, Esther L., MO, 5117

Trout and Mellinger Medical Research Fund, Livingston, PA, 8149

Troutman Foundation, Paul A., PA, 8150

Trover Clinic Foundation, Inc., KY, 3629

Troy Foundation, The, OH, 7388

Truckee Tahoe Community Foundation, CA, 1058

Trudell Scholarship Trust, MI, 4643

True Foundation, WY, 10122

True to Life Children's Services, CA, 1059

True Value Foundation, IL, 2898

Trueman Educational Trust, Florence B., MD, 3943

Truman Heartland Community Foundation, MO, 5118

Trumansburg Charitable Trust, The, NY, 6464

Trump Scholarship Fund, Paul and Ida, KS, 3530

Truschel Charitable Foundation Inc., Theresa F., MD, 3944

Trushel Scholarship Trust, Allene S., PA, 8151

Trust for Conservation Innovation, CA, 1060

Trust for Higher Education of Graduates of Accredited Fillmore County, Nebraska High Schools, NE, see 5219

Trust Fund, Camden Student, ME, 3741

Trust Under Will of John McKee, PA, see 7976

Trustees of Chester Academy, VT, 9263

Trustees of Ivan V. Koulaieff Educational Fund, CA, 1061

Trustees of McDonough Charity School, The, MD, 3945

Trustees of Partridge Academy in Duxbury, MA, 4298

Trustees of the Perley Free School, MA, 4299

Trustees of the Putnam Free School, MA, 4300

Trustees of Warren Academy, MA, 4301

Truth Seeker Foundation, The, CA, 1062

Tryon Trust, Florence J., RI, 8427

Tsadra Foundation, NY, 6465

Tschirgi Scholarship Fund, Grace F., WI, see 10054

Tschirgi Trust, Grace F., WI, 10054

TSELF, MA, see 4293

TUA Bartholomew Family Foundation, TX, 9139

Tucker Community Foundation, WV, 9824

Tucker Educational and Charitable Trust, George E., SC, 8517

Tucker Music Foundation, Richard, The, NY, 6466

Tuckerman Foundation, Elizabeth, CA, 1063

Tucson-Pima Arts Council, Inc., AZ, 247

Tudor Foundation, The, WA, 9737

Tufts Charitable Foundation, T.J., WA, 9738

Tuition Assistance Program for Catholic Education, OH, 7389

Tulsa Advertising Foundation, OK, 7518

Tulsa Community Foundation, OK, 7519

Tulsa County Bar Foundation, Inc., OK, 7520

Tulsa Royalties Company, OK, 7521

Tumey & Grand Lodge, Jeremiah, MI, see 4644

Tumey Fund, Jeremiah, MI, 4644

Tuohy-University of Michigan Student Loan Fund, Berndine MacMullen, MI, 4645

Tupper Foundation, Olive, LA, 3681

Turco Foundation, The, OH, 7390

Turn On To America, CA, 1064

Turnaround Management Association, IL, 2899

Turnbow Foundation, The, AZ, 249

Turner Educational Foundation, Marie R. & Ervine, Inc., KY, 3630

Turner Foundation, Lena & Harry, TX, 9140

Turner Foundation, Mark E. and Emily, ME, 3742

Turner Memorial Trust, Cirtie Mae, DC, 1737

Turner Scholarship Trust, Bismarck H., OR, 7671

Turning Leaf Foundation Inc., MA, 4302

Tuscola County Community Foundation, MI, 4646

Tuscora Park Health & Wellness Foundation, OH, 7391

Tuttle Fund, Isaac H., NY, 6467

TW National Society Dar, Et Al, NC, 6903

TW Scholarship, Fritts Charles & Margaret, OH, 7392

Tweed Scholarship Endowment Trust, Ethel H. and George W., FL, 2091

Twenty First Century Foundation, The, OH, 7393

Twin Towers Orphan Fund, CA, 1065

Two Feathers Endowment, The, MN, 4873

Two Harbors High School Senior Scholarship Fund, NC, 6904

Two Red Roses the Foundation, Inc., FL, 2092

Two Rivers Health and Wellness Foundation, PA, 8152

Two Rivers Hospital Corporation, PA, see 8152

Two Ten Footwear Foundation, Inc., MA, 4303

Tyche Foundation for Archaeology and Community, CA, see 368

Tye Medical Aid Foundation, Ray, MA, 4304

Tyler Foundation, Marion C., OH, 7394

Tyndale Scholarship Fund, John, PA, 8153

Tyndale Testamentary Trust, John, PA, see 8153

Tyo-St. Ferdinand College Scholarship Foundation, Ray, NY, see 6139

Tyson Family Foundation, Inc., AR, 320

Tzur Foundation Inc., Maoz, NY, 6468

U.S. Bobsled & Skeleton Federation, Inc., CO, 1297

U.S. Civilian Research and Development Foundation, The, VA, 9526

U.S. Committee for Refugees and Immigrants, Inc., VA, 9527

U.S. Foundation for the Inspiration & Recognition Science & Technology, NH, 5373

U.S. Institute of Peace, DC, 1738

U.S. Navy Warner Trust, IA, 3398

U.S. Silica Company Education Foundation, The, MD, 3946

UAW-Ford National Programs, MI, 4647

UAW-GM Center for Human Resources, MI, 4648

UCAN, IL, see 2900

Ucross Foundation, WY, 10123

UFA Widow's and Children's Fund, NY, 6469

UFCW 324, CA, see 1070

UFCW Region 5 Educational Trust, TX, 9141

UFCW Suffridge/Jimerson Scholarship Fund, DC, 1739

Uhlich Children's Advantage Network, IL, 2900

UIC Foundation, Inc., AK, 145

UJA - Federation of New York, NY, 6470

Ukiah Educational Foundation, CA, 1066

ULI Foundation, DC, 1740

Ullery Charitable Trust, Jimmie, IL, 2901

Ullyot Educational Trust, Glenn E. & Eleanor E., The, SD, 8545

Ulman Cancer Fund for Young Adults, The, MD, 3947

Ulmschneider Educational Foundation, WA, 9739

Umpqua Community Action Network, OR, 7672

Unaka Foundation, Inc., The, TN, 8656

Unaka Scholarship Foundation, Inc., TN, see 8656

Unanue Lopez Family Foundation, PR, 8224

Ungles Educational Trust, H. T., KS, 3531

Unified School District No. 380 Endowment Association, KS, 3532

UniGroup Incorporated Scholarship, MO, 5119

Union City Community Foundation, PA, 8154

Union County Community Arts Council, Inc., NC, 6905

Union County Community Foundation, Inc., AR, 321

Union County CPA Scholarship Fund, NJ, 5582

Union County Foundation, Inc., IN, 3204

Union County Foundation, OH, see 7061

Union Health Service, Inc., IL, 2902

Union Labor Health Foundation, CA, 1067

Union Labor Hospital Association, CA, see 1067

Union Leader Charitable Fund, Inc., NH, 5374

Union League Boys and Girls Clubs, IL, 2903

Union League Civic & Arts Foundation, IL, 2904

Union Mutual Foundation, NJ, 5583

Union Plus Disaster Relief Fund, DC, see 1742

Union Plus Education Foundation, DC, 1741

Union Privilege Relief Fund Trust, DC, 1742

Union Rescue Mission, CA, 1068

Unique Projects, Inc., NY, 6471

United Animal Nations, CA, 1069

United Arts Council of Calhoun County, MI, 4649

United Arts Council of Catawba County, NC, 6906

United Arts Council of Gaston County, NC, see 6668

United Arts Council of Raleigh and Wake County, Inc., NC, 6907

United Arts of Central Florida, Inc., FL, 2093

United Board for Christian Higher Education in Asia, NY, 6472

United Cerebral Palsy Research and Educational Foundation, Inc., The, NJ, see 5417

United Coal Company Charitable Foundation, VA, see 9528

United Communities Against Poverty, Inc., MD, 3948

United Communities Foundation, MI, 4650

United Community Foundation, Inc., WI, see 9869

United Company Charitable Foundation, The, VA, 9528

United Conveyor Foundation, IL, 2905

United Daughters of the Confederacy, VA, 9529

United Fire Group Foundation, IA, 3399

United Food and Commercial Workers Union Local 324, CA, 1070

United Friends of the Children, CA, 1071

United Help, Inc., NY, see 6392

United Hospital Foundation, MN, 4874

United Jewish Fund and Council of St. Paul, The, MN, see 4875

United Jewish Fund and Council, MN, 4875

United Labor Agency of Ohio, OH, see 7395

United Labor Agency, Inc., OH, 7395

United Methodist City Society, The, NY, 6473

United Methodist Higher Education Foundation, TN, 8657

United Negro College Fund, Inc., DC, 1743

United Neighborhood Houses of New York, Inc., NY, 6474

United Services Community Action Agency, MO, 5120

United Society of Friends Women Trust, NC, 6908

United Spinal Association, Inc., NY, 6475

United States Achievement Academy Scholarship Foundation, Inc., KY, 3631

United States Army Warrant Officers Associatino Scholarship Foundation, VA, see 9534

United States Artists, CA, 1072

United States Diving Foundation, Inc., IN, 3205

United States Equestrian Federation, Inc., KY, 3632

United States Equestrian Team Foundation, Inc., NJ, 5584

United States Figure Skating Association, CO, 1298

United States Fund for UNICEF, NY, 6476

United States Geospatial Intelligence Foundation, VA, 9530

United States Gymnastics Federation, IN, see 3210

United States Holocaust Memorial Museum, The, DC, 1744

United States Institute for Theatre Technology, Inc., NY, 6477

United States Merchant Marine Academy Alumni Foundation, Inc., NY, 6478

United States Olympic Committee, CO, 1299

United States Sailing Foundation, RI, 8428

United States Tennis Association, NY, 6479

United Student Aid Funds, Inc., IN, 3206

United Telephone Educational Foundation Inc., ND, 6949

United Way of Allen County, Inc., IN, 3207

United Way of Bergen County, NJ, 5585

United Way of Central Alabama, Inc., AL, 86

United Way of Central Florida, Inc., FL, 2094

United Way of Central Indiana, IN, 3208

United Way of Central Iowa, IA, 3400

United Way of Frederick County, Inc., MD, 3949

United Way of Greater Philadelphia and Southern New Jersey, PA, 8155

United Way of Greater Portland, ME, see 3743

United Way of Greater St. Louis, Inc., MO, 5121

United Way of Greater Stark County, Inc., OH, 7396

United Way of Greater Union County, Inc., NJ, 5586

United Way of Greenville County, Inc., SC, 8518

United Way of Hudson County, NJ, 5587

United Way of Lamoille County, Inc., VT, 9264

United Way of Larimer County, CO, 1300

United Way of McLean County, IL, 2906

United Way of Metropolitan Tarrant County, TX, 9142

United Way of Midland County, MI, 4651

United Way of North Essex, NJ, 5588

United Way of Northwest Georgia, Inc., GA, 2251

United Way of South Hampton Roads, VA, 9531

United Way of South Texas, TX, 9143

United Way of Southeastern Connecticut, Inc., CT, 1476

United Way of Southeastern Pennsylvania, PA, see 8155

United Way of Southern Nevada, NV, 5303

United Way of St. Clair County, MI, 4652

United Way of St. Lucie County, Inc., FL, 2095

United Way of Summit County, OH, 7397

United Way of the Central Savannah River Area, Inc., GA, 2252

United Way of the Coastal Bend, Inc., TX, 9144

United Way of the Coastal Empire, Inc., GA, 2253

United Way of the Mid-South, TN, 8658

United Way of the River Cities, Inc., WV, 9825

United Way of Tucson and Southern Arizona, Inc., AZ, 250

United Way, Inc., ME, 3743

United Way-Thomas Jefferson Area, VA, 9532

UnitedHealthcare Children's Foundation, MN, 4876

Unity Foundation of La Porte County, Inc., IN, 3209

Univera Community Health, Inc., NY, 6480

Universal Companies, Inc. Education Foundation, MI, see 4653

Universal Forest Products Education Foundation, MI, 4653

University Athletic Association, Inc., FL, 2096

University Club Scholarship Fund, MA, 4305

University Medical Center Corporation, AZ, 251

University Medical Center Foundation, TX, 9145

University of Alaska Foundation, AK, 146

University of Arizona Medical Center Corporation, The, AZ, see 251

University of California Chinese Alumni Foundation, CA, 1073

University of Delaware Research Foundation, DE, 1526

University of Georgia Athletic Association, Inc., GA, 2254

University of Hawai'i Foundation, HI, 2324

University of Kansas Athletic Corp., KS, see 3468

University of Louisville Foundation, Inc., KY, 3633

University of Louisville Research Foundation, Inc., KY, 3634

University of Massachusetts Dartmouth Foundation, Inc., MA, 4306

University of Minnesota Foundation, MN, 4877

University of North Dakota Foundation, ND, 6950

University of Northern Colorado Foundation, Inc., CO, 1301

University of Oklahoma Foundation, Inc., OK, 7522

University of Southern Mississippi Foundation, The, MS, 4925

University of Toledo Foundation, The, OH, 7398

University of Virginia Medical School Foundation, VA, 9533

University of Wisconsin Medical Foundation, Inc., WI, 10055

University of Wisconsin River Falls Foundation, WI, 10056

University Students Club, Inc., WA, see 9682

UNMC Physicians, NE, 5267

Unrau Scholarship Foundation, Peggy L., MT, 5181

Unruh Foundation, Darryl E., Inc., NC, 6909

Upjohn Institute for Employment Research, W.E., MI, see 4654

Upjohn Unemployment Trustee Corp., W. E., MI, 4654

Upper Des Moines Opportunity, Inc., IA, 3401

Upper East Tennessee Human Development Agency, TN, 8659

Upper Peninsula Community Foundation Alliance, MI, see 4399

Urann Foundation, RI, 8429

Urban League of Greater Hartford, Inc, The, CT, 1477

Urban League of Metropolitan St. Louis, Inc., MO, 5122

Urban Scholarship Fund, Joseph T. Urban and Margaret L., PA, 8156

Urban Vision Foundation, Inc., TX, 9146

Urbana-Champaign Independent Media Center, IL, 2907

Urbanek-Levy Education Fund, CA, 1074

UrbanGlass, NY, 6481

Ursuline Foundation, OH, 7399

US Airways Education Foundation, Inc., AZ, 252

USA Cares, Inc., KY, 3635

USA Gymnastics, IN, 3210

USA, CA, see 1072

USAWOA Scholarship Foundation, VA, 9534

Uschmann Memorial Scholarship Fund, Curt & Margaret, OH, 7400

USCRI, VA, see 9527

USEF, KY, see 3632

Usibelli Foundation, The, AK, 147

USO Council of New England, Inc., MA, 4307

USPA & IRA Educational Foundation, TX, see 8822

USTA Serves - Foundation for Academics. Character. Excellence., NY, 6482

USTA Tennis and Education Foundation, NY, see 6482

USWA Flint/Glass Industry Conference Lawrence Bankowski Scholarship Award, PA, 8157

Utah Humanities Council, UT, 9228

Utah Motorsports Foundation, The, UT, 9229

Utica Foundation, Inc., NY, see 5879

Utica National Group Foundation, Inc., NY, 6483

Utility Wind Integration Group, Inc., VA, 9535

Utility Wind Interest Group, Inc., VA, see 9535

UW - Whitewater Foundation, WI, 10057

V Foundation for Cancer Research, The, NC, 6910

V-Day, NY, 6487

V.G.I.F., NY, see 5685

Vaccarezza-Murdaca Family Foundation, The, CA, 1075

Vacek Scholarship Trust, Mabel, IA, 3402

Vail Valley Foundation, Inc., CO, 1302

Valero Scholarship Trust, TX, 9147

Valley Charitable Trust Fund, The, RI, 8430

Valley Foundation, The, AZ, 253

Valley Hospital Association, Inc., AK, 148

Valley Hospital Auxiliary, The, NJ, 5589

Valley Mountain Regional Center, Inc., CA, 1076

Valley of the Sun Hospice Association, AZ, 254

Valley of the Sun United Way, AZ, 255

Valley Telephone Cooperative Foundation, AZ, 256

Valley Will Fund, PA, 8158

Valspar Foundation, The, MN, 4878

Van Alen Institute, NY, 6484

Van Buren Foundation, Inc., The, IA, 3403

Van Doren Memorial Scholarship Fund, Scott, NJ, 5590

Van Doren Scholarship Fund, Peter Ellis, NJ, see 5591

Van Doren Scholarship Trust 008963, NJ, 5591

Van Engel Fellowship Inc., Willard A., The, VA, 9536

Van Hollenbeck Foundation, Homer J., MI, 4655

Van Horn Scholarship Trust, Isabel F., OH, 7401

Van Horne Educational Fund, E., PA, 8159

Van Hyning Scholarship Fund, Virginia W., OH, 7402

Van Wert County Foundation, The, OH, 7403

Van Wynen Scholarship Fund, John A. & Winnifred F., The, PA, see 8160

Van Wynen Trust A, J. A., Jr. & W. F., PA, 8160

VanBuren Scholarship Fund, Fred N., OH, 7404

Vancouver Methodist Foundation, WA, 9740

Vandenbark Scholarship Fund, Helen, OH, 7405

Vanderhout Trust, William, NH, 5375

Vang Memorial Foundation, The, PA, 8161

Vanguard Cancer Foundation, CA, 1077

Vanguard Services Unlimited, VA, see 9481

VanHoff Educational Trust, Martha, The, WA, 9741

VanKley Educational Foundation, Dr. Lavern and Betty, MI, 4656

VARA Educational Foundation, Inc., VT, 9265

Varflex Educational Foundation II, The, NY, 6485

Variety - The Children's Charity of Southern California, Tent 25, CA, 1078

Variety - The Children's Charity of the U.S., CA, 1079

Variety Club Foundation of New York, Inc., NY, 6486

Varner-Seneca Valley High School Scholarship Fund, Otto Ruth, PA, 8162

Vascular Specialists Education Foundation, Inc., VA, 9537

Vasset Memorial Foundation, George J. & Margaret I., PA, 8163

Vasset Memorial Fund, George J. & Margaret I., PA, see 8163

Vastine & Katherine Vastine Bernheimer Memorial Fund, Elizabeth Boone, PA, see 8164

Vastine & Katherine Vastine, Elizabeth Boone, PA, 8164

Vatheuer Family Foundation, Inc., OR, 7673

VAW/VRC Officer's Spouses Association and Memorial Scholarship Fund, VA, 9538

VDTA Bernie Epstein Scholarship Fund, IA, 3404

Veasey Educational Foundation Inc., Ruth, AR, 322

Vecellio Family Foundation, Enrico, Inc., The, WV, see 9826

Vecellio Family Foundation, Inc., The, WV, 9826

Vedova Scholarship Trust, Rino & Ruth Della, WI, 10058

Veeder Scholarship Fund Trust, Peter Simon, IL, 2908

Veirs Scholarship Fund, Eldon E., CO, 1303

Venable Educational Trust, Austin L. and Nell S., AL, 87

Venango Area Community Foundation, PA, see 7746

Veneklasen Research Foundation, Paul S., CA, 1080

Ventura County Community Foundation, CA, 1081

Ventures Foundation, A. E., Inc., NY, 6488

Vermilion Community College Foundation, MN, 4879

Vermillion Civic Council, Inc., SD, A

Vermillion County Community Foundation, IN, 3211

Vermillion Family Scholarship Fund, Inc., OH, 7406

Vermont Arts Council, VT, see 9268

Vermont Bar Foundation, VT, 9266

Vermont Community Foundation, VT, 9267

Vermont Council on the Arts, Inc., VT, 9268

Vermont Student Development Fund, Inc., VT, 9269

Vermont Student Opportunity Scholarship Fund, Inc., VT, 9270

Vermont Studio Center, Inc., VT, 9271
Vernier Software & Technology LLC Corporate Giving Program, OR, 7674
Vesper Educational Trust, Vernon A. & Ada L., KS, 3533
Vestergaard Memorial Scholarship Fund, Adolph and Esther, IA, 3405
Veteran's Haven, Inc., MI, 4657
Vetiver Network international, The, TX, see 9148
Vetiver Network, The, TX, 9148
Vetovich Family Foundation, MI, 4658
VFW Charitable Trust, ND, 6951
Viele Scholarship Trust, Frances S., NY, 6489
Vietnam Relief Effort, NY, 6490
Vietnamese Culture & Science Association, TX, 9149
Vilcek Foundation, Inc., The, NY, 6491
Viles Foundation, NM, 5657
Villwock Medical Educational Scholarship Fund, Otto, IL, 2909
Vincent Foundation, Troy, VA, see 9424
Vincent Trust, Anna M., PA, 8165
Vinsant Memorial Foundation, Dolly, TX, 9150
Virginia Foundation for the Humanities and Public Policy, VA, see 9539
Virginia Foundation for the Humanities, VA, 9539
Virginia Foundation of Cooperation, Inc., VA, 9540
Virginia Scholarship and Youth Development Foundation, VA, 9541
Virginia Tech Foundation, Inc., VA, 9542
Viropharma Charitable Foundation, PA, 8166
Viroqua Area Foundation, WI, 10059
Virtua Health Foundation, Inc., NJ, 5592
VisArts at Rockville, MD, see 3882
Visible Changes Educational Foundation, TX, 9151
Vision Fund, Inc., The, CT, see 1342
Visiting Nurse Association Foundation of Lebanon County, PA, 8167
Visiting Nurse Association Foundation, Inc., IN, 3212
Visiting Nurse Association of Houston Foundation, TX, see 8861
Visiting Nurse Association of Rye, Inc., The, NY, see 5940
Visitor Industry Human Resource Development Council, FL, see 1800
Vista Hermosa, WA, 9742
Visual Aid: Artists for AIDS Relief, CA, 1082
Visual Arts Foundation, Inc., NY, 6492
Visual Communications, CA, see 1005
Visual Studies Workshop, Inc., NY, 6493
Vocational Foundation, Inc., NY, 6494
Vocational Technical Educational Foundation of Delaware, DE, 1527
Vodgis Charitable Trust, Theodore, The, PA, 8168
Vogeley Memorial Trust, PA, 8169
Vogelzang Foundation, Mary Beth and James C., CA, see 1083
Vogelzang Foundation, Mary Beth, CA, 1083
Voght Scholarship Fund, MA, see 4308
Voght Trust, Mary G., MA, 4308
Vogler Scholarship Foundation, Rich, Inc., IL, 2910
Voices Against Brain Cancer Foundation, NY, 6495
Voland Scholarship Trust, James A., IN, 3213
Volunteer Way, Inc., The, FL, 2097
Volunteers Enlisted to Assist People, MN, 4880
Volunteers of America, MN, 4881
Volz Foundation Charitable Trust, MO, A
Vomberg Foundation, The, MI, 4659
Von der Ahe School Trust, Flora, OR, 7675
Von Rosenberg Foundation, The, TX, 9152
Von Sallmann Memorial Fund Trust, Dr. Ludwig, PA, see 8170
Von Sallmann Memorial Fund, Dr. Ludwig, PA, 8170
Von Wyss Foundation, Gygi, MA, 4309
VonAmelunxen Foundation, Roger L., Inc., NY, 6496
Vongelstein Foundation, Ludwig, Inc., OR, 7676
Voorhies Scholarship Trust Fund, PA, 8171
Voya Financial, Inc. Contributions Program, CT, 1478
VSA arts of Colorado, Inc., CO, 1304
VSA arts of Indiana, IN, 3214
VSA arts of Minnesota, MN, see 4882
VSA arts, DC, 1745
VSA Colorado/Access Gallery, CO, see 1304
VSA Minnesota, MN, 4882
Vulcan Scholarships, Inc., AL, 88

W & G Scholarship Trust, WA, 9743
W!se, NY, see 6532
W. S. O. S. Community Action Commission, Inc., OH, 7407
Wabash County Scholarship Trust, NE, 5268
Wabash Valley Community Foundation, Inc., IN, 3215
Wabash Valley Human Services, Inc., IN, see 3137
Wachter, Sr. Foundation, Verneda A. and Leo J., PA, 8172
Wacker Foundation, TX, A
Waco Foundation, TX, 9153
Wadas Foundation, Edwin J., Inc., NY, 6497
Waffle House Foundation, Inc., GA, 2255
Wagenknecht Scholarship Trust, Frank C., IL, 2911
Wagnalls Memorial Foundation, The, OH, 7408
Wagner Charitable Trust, Kathryn & Otto H., TX, 9154
Wagner Estate Heinbach-Wagner Trust, Claire, NY, 6498
Wagner Foundation, Ross, MN, 4883
Wagner Scholarship Fund, Arno & Roberta E., MA, 4310
Wagner Scholarship Fund, Edward and Frieda, WI, 10060
Wagner Trust, Elizabeth C., FL, 2098
Wahl Foundation, Leo J., IL, 2912
Wahl Scholarship Fund, William F. & Gertrude, OH, 7409
Wahlin Foundation, Inc., The, WI, 10061
Waimea Educational & Cultural Association, HI, 2325
Wake Charitable Foundation, NE, 5269
Wake Education Partnership, NC, 6911
Wake Technical Community College Foundation, Inc., NC, 6912
Wake Technical Institute Foundation, Inc., NC, see 6912
Wakefield Scholarship Fund, Carlos E. Wakefield and Beatrice E., OH, 7410
Wal-Mart Associates in Critical Need Fund, AR, 324
Wal-Mart Foundation, AR, see 325
Wal-Mart Foundation, Inc., The, AR, 325
Waldo Community Action Partners, ME, 3744
Waldron Scholarship Fund, Anna Marie & Russel, OH, 7411
Wales Foundation, Thomas C., WA, 9744
Wales Memorial Foundation, Thomas C., WA, see 9744
Walgreen Benefit Fund, IL, 2913
Walgreens Assistance, Inc., IL, 2914
Walkabout Foundation, The, CT, 1479
Walker Charitable Trust, Harold B., RI, 8431
Walker Foundation, Charles M., Inc., GA, 2256
Walker Scholarship Fund, Darleen J. and Robert L., IL, 2915
Walker Scholarship Fund, Richard Wells, Inc., NC, 6913
Walker Scholarship Grant, WI, 10062
Walkling Memorial Trust, Ben & Myrtle, WA, see 9745
Walkling Memorial Trust, WA, 9745
Wallace Educational Trust, Allyrae, AL, 89
Wallace Trust Foundation, AR, 323
Wallenberg Foundation, Marcus, The, NY, 6499
Wallin Education Partners, MN, 4884
Walmart Associates in Critical Need Fund, AR, see 324
Walmart Foundation, The, AR, see 325
Walpole Village District Nursing Association, NH, 5376
Walter Charitable Trust, Martin and Awilda, PA, 8173
Walters Scholarship Fund, IL, 2916
Walters Technical Scholarship Fund, IL, 2917
Walther Scholarship Fund, Charles & Alberta, NE, 5270
Waltom Foundation, Lillian, TX, 9155
Walton Central School District Trust No. 1, NY, 6500
Walton League of America - Rockville Chapter, Izaak, MD, 3950
Walz Scholarship Trust, Rew & Edna, PA, 8174
Wapakoneta Area Community Foundation, The, OH, 7412
Ward County Council for Handicapped Children, Inc., TX, 9156
Ward Educational Scholarship, MO, 5123
Ward Educational Trust Agency, Wilbur H., MA, A
Ward Educational Trust, Mae, OH, 7413
Ward Educational Trust, MO, see 5123
Ward Faith Foundation, Jeanne, CA, see 1084
Ward Foundation, Jeanne, CA, 1084
Ward Scholarship Fund, WI, 10063

Ware Testamentary Charitable Trust, C. Arthur, VA, 9543
Warfield Memorial Fund, Anna Emory, Inc., MD, 3951
Warman Scholarship Trust, OH, 7414
Warne Family Charitable Foundation, CA, 1085
Warner Educational Trust, Mary Ellen, CA, 1086
Warner First Things First Foundation, Kurt, AZ, 257
Warner Home for Little Wanderers, VT, 9272
Warnken, Sr. Memorial College Scholarship Fund, Charles, TX, 9157
Warren Benevolent Fund, Inc., MA, 4311
Warren Charitable Trust, Harold, GA, 2257
Warren County Community Foundation, Inc., IN, 3216
Warren Family Foundation, The, PA, 8175
Warren Foundation, The, PA, see 7783
Warren Legal Training Program, Earl, Inc., NY, 6501
Washburn Scholarship Fund, Ann White, MA, 4312
Washington Apple Education Foundation, WA, 9746
Washington County Community Foundation, Inc., PA, 8176
Washington County Economic Opportunity Council, Inc., NY, 6502
Washington Dental Service Foundation, WA, 9747
Washington Education Foundation, Inc., The, AZ, 258
Washington Education Foundation, WA, 9594
Washington Foundation for Long Term Care, WA, 9749
Washington Foundation, Dennis & Phyllis, Inc., MT, 5182
Washington Foundation, Dennis R., Inc., MT, see 5182
Washington Foundation, George, The, WA, 9748
Washington Group Foundation, ID, see 2329
Washington Kids Foundation, MaliVai, Inc., FL, 2099
Washington Performing Arts Society, DC, 1746
Washington Post Company Educational Foundation, The, DC, 1747
Washington Sports & Entertainment Charities, Inc., DC, 1748
Washington Tennis & Education Foundation, DC, 1749
Washington Township Hospital Service League, Inc., CA, 1087
Washington Women in Need, WA, 9750
Washington Youth Choir, DC, see 1750
Washington Youth Choir, The, DC, 1750
Washoe Medical Foundation, Inc., NV, see 5301
Wasserman Scholarship Fund, David, Inc., NY, 6503
Watauga Education Foundation, Inc., NC, 6914
Waterbury Foundation, The, CT, see 1366
Waterford Foundation for Public Education, MI, 4660
Waterman Trust, Richard, RI, A
Waters Scholarship Fund, Roy A., LA, 3682
Watershed Center for Ceramic Arts, ME, 3745
WaterStone, CO, 1305
Watertown Area Community Foundation, WI, 10064
Watertown Community Foundation, SD, 8546
Watertown Foundation, Inc., CT, 1480
Watertown Foundation, Inc., NY, see 6287
Watkins Area Vocational-Technical Foundation, Wes, OK, 7523
Watkins Educational Fund, Hattie G., TN, 8660
Watson Clinic Foundation, Inc., FL, 2100
Watson Family Foundation, OK, 7524
Watson Foundation, Clara Stewart, TX, see 9158
Watson Foundation, John W. and Rose E., MI, 4661
Watson Foundation, Thomas J., The, NY, 6504
Watson Scholarship Foundation, C. S., TX, 9158
Watson Scholarship Trust, Felix H. and Madge B., TX, 9159
Watson-Brown Foundation, Inc., GA, 2258
Watt Brothers Scholars Trust, OR, 7677
Wattenberg Scholarship Fund, OR, 7678
Watterson Trust, Grace Margaret, NC, 6915
Watumull Estate, J., Inc., HI, see 2326
Watumull Fund, J., HI, 2326
Waubonsee Community College Foundation, IL, 2918
Waukesha Ozaukee Washington Workforce Development, Inc., WI, 10065
Wausau Area Community Foundation, Inc., WI, see 9868
Waverly Community Foundation, IA, 3406
Waverly Community House, Inc., PA, 8177
Wayne County Community Foundation, OH, 7415
Wayne County Community Foundation, PA, 8178
Wayne County Foundation, Greater, Inc., OH, see 7415

Wayne County Foundation, IN, see 3217

Wayne County, Indiana Foundation, Inc., IN, 3217

Wayne Foundation, Lenore & Richard, CA, 1088

Wayne Scholarship Trust, John, IL, 2919

Wayne-Metropolitan Community Action Agency, MI, 4662

Ways & Means Homelessness Prevention, VA, see 9546

WDA, KS, see 3540

WDS Foundation, WA, see 9747

Weather Shield LITE Foundation, WI, 10066

Weather Shield Manufacturing Foundation, Inc., WI, see 10021

Weaver Popcorn Foundation, Inc., IN, 3218

Weaver Trust f/b/o Bexley Hall, Howard A., RI, 8432

Weaver-Fagan Memorial Fund, VA, 9544

Webber Charitable Private Foundation, Benjamin N., PA, 8179

Webber Scholarship Fund, Benjamin N., PA, see 8179

Webber Scholarship Fund, Josephine M., PA, 8180

Weber Foundation, Jacques, Inc., PA, 8181

Webermeier Scholarship Trust, William, PA, 8182

Webster Aid Association, Emma Reed, Inc., NY, 6505

Webster Medical Fund, Hamilton Fish, RI, 8433

Webster Scholarship Fund, Guyneth B., IN, 3219

Webster Trust, Arthur E., RI, 8434

WEDC Foundation, Inc., AL, 90

Wedum Foundation, J.A., MN, 4885

Weed Ruge, Edwin Gardner, The, PA, 8183

Weeks Family Foundation, The, NY, 6506

Weeks Trust, George S., IL, 2920

Weems Educational Fund, G. H., TN, 8661

Wegmans Food Markets, Inc. Corporate Giving Program, NY, 6507

Wei Family Private Foundation, NJ, 5593

Weigand, Jr. Notre Dame Legal Education Trust, J.L., The, KS, 3534

Weigel Scholarship Fund Trust, Edna, WI, 10067

Weill Foundation for Music, Kurt, Inc., NY, 6508

Wein Charitable Fund, Charles & Dorothy, PA, 8184

Weinglass Foundation, Inc., The, CO, see 1131

Weinstein Parkinson's Foundation, Melvin, The, VA, 9545

Weir Farm Trust, Inc., CT, 1481

Weir Memorial Fund-Bigelow District, James, OR, 7679

Weir Scholarship Foundation Trust, Shirley and Billy, GA, 2259

Weiss Educational Fund, Ella, OH, 7416

Weiss Scientific Foundation, OR, see 7574

Weissberger Foundation, Anna L., Ltd., NY, 6509

Weisz Private Foundation, Mordechai, Inc., NY, see 6046

Welch Charitable Foundation, Lorna A., MI, 4663

Welch Foundation, Robert A., The, TX, 9160

Welch Foundation, Sara & Warren, PA, 8185

Welch Memorial Trust, Anna B., IL, 2921

Welch Testamentary Trust, George T., WA, 9751

Welch Trust, Carrie, WA, 9752

Welder Wildlife Foundation, Rob and Bessie, TX, 9161

Wellchild, the Foundation of Health for Life, MA, see 3989

Weller Foundation, Inc., The, CT, 1482

Weller Foundation, Inc., The, NE, 5271

Wellmont Foundation, Inc., TN, 8662

Wellness Connection of the Dayton Region, OH, 7417

Wellons Foundation, Inc., NC, see 6916

Wellons Foundation, John H., Inc., NC, 6916

Wells County Foundation, Inc., The, IN, 3220

Wells Education Fund, Glen, Frieda and John, KY, 3636

Wells Memorial Educational Foundation Inc., Julia O., NY, 6510

Wells Nursing Scholarship Trust, Loretta A., WI, 10068

Wells Scholarship Fund, Lucile, IL, 2922

Wells Trust Fund, Fred W., RI, 8435

Wells Trust Fund, Horace, CT, 1483

Wells Trust Fund, IL, 2923

Wells Trust, Leon, MI, 4664

WellStar Foundation, Inc., GA, 2260

Welshons Family Scholarship Trust, MN, 4886

Wenatchee Community Foundation, Greater, WA, see 9600

Wenatchee Valley College Foundation, Inc., WA, 9753

Wenger Foundation, MN, 4887

Wenner-Gren Foundation for Anthropological Research, Inc., NY, 6511

Wenstrom Foundation, Frank A. & M. Esther, ND, 6952

Werner Educational Opportunity Charitable Trust, Lawrence M. and Susan, CA, 1089

Wertzberger Trust, Frances R., FL, 2101

Wesley Spectrum Services Foundation, PA, 8186

West Central Community Action, IA, 3407

West Central Development Corporation, IA, see 3407

West Central Missouri Community Action Agency, Inc., MO, 5124

West Central Wisconsin Community Action Agency, Inc., WI, 10069

West Contra Costa Public Education Fund, CA, 1090

West Educational Fund, W. F. & Blanche E., PA, 8187

West Foundation Inc., The, SC, 8519

West Foundation, H. O., The, PA, 8188

West Foundation, Herman O., The, PA, see 8188

West Foundation, TX, 9162

West Georgia Health Foundation, Inc., GA, 2261

West High Alumni Association, AK, 149

West Memorial Foundation Trust, Dudley R., NC, 6917

West Palm Beach Rotary Club Charity Fund, Inc., FL, 2102

West Point Community Foundation, NE, 5272

West Scholarship Fund, Marion Huxley, MA, 4313

West Scholarship Fund, Merle S. & Emma J., OR, 7680

West Scholarship Fund, OR, see 7680

West Side Ecumenical Ministry, OH, 7418

West Texas Opportunities, TX, 9163

West Virginia Humanities Council, Inc., WV, 9827

Westchester Arts Council, Inc., NY, 6512

Westchester Community College Foundation, Inc., NY, 6513

Westchester Foundation, IL, see 2930

Westchester Golf Association Caddie Scholarship Fund, Inc., NY, 6514

Westchester Mid Hudson Chapter American Institute of Architects Scholarship Fund, NY, 6515

Westendorf Family Foundation, SD, 8547

Wester Memorial Charitable Foundation, Ward W. and Norabelle, OH, 7419

Westerhold Family Foundation, IL, see 2828

Western Assoc of Ladies IAS, PA, 8189

Western Association of Ladies for the Relief and Employment of the Poor, PA, see 8189

Western Carolina Community Action, Inc., NC, 6918

Western Colorado Community Foundation, Inc., CO, 1306

Western Egyptian Economic Opportunity Council, Inc., IL, 2924

Western European Architecture Foundation, TX, 9164

Western Fairfax Christian Ministries, VA, 9546

Western Illinois Regional Council Community Action Agency, IL, 2925

Western Indiana Community Action Agency, Inc., IN, 3221

Western Indiana Community Foundation, Inc., IN, 3222

Western Industrial Training Foundation, KS, 3535

Western Lane Community Foundation, OR, 7681

Western Lane County Foundation, OR, see 7681

Western Minnesota Masonic Foundation, MN, 4888

Western Reserve Area Agency on Aging, OH, 7420

Western Shoshone Scholarship Foundation, NV, 5304

Westerville Rotary Elderly Housing, OH, see 7421

Westerville Rotary Foundation, OH, 7421

Westhaysen Medical Education Trust, Peter V., IN, 3223

Westly Foundation, Steve and Anita, The, DE, 1528

Westmoreland County Public School Scholarship Fund, VA, 9547

Westphal Family Foundation, The, CA, 1091

Westport-Weston Foundation Trust, CT, 1484

Wetenkamp Charitable Trust, Alpha A., WI, 10070

Wetherbee Foundation, Harold and Sara, GA, 2262

Wetterberg Foundation, Harold, The, NJ, 5594

Wettrick Charitable Foundation, Marian J., PA, 8190

Wexner Center for the Arts, OH, see 7422

Wexner Center Foundation, OH, 7422

Wexner Foundation, OH, 7423

Weyman Trust, Wesley, MA, 4314

Whaley Children's Center, Inc., MI, 4665

Wheaton Village, Inc., NJ, see 5595

WheatonArts and Cultural Center, NJ, 5595

Wheeler Trust, Clara, OR, 7682

Wheelright Family Charitable Foundation, UT, 9230

Wheelwright Scientific School, MA, 4315

Whelchel Student Aid, Dr. & Mrs. A. J., GA, 2263

Whircher Trust, Peter N., NY, 6516

White Beeches Country Club Caddy Scholarship Fund, Inc., NJ, 5596

White Foundation, Grant T., AR, 326

White Foundation, Mahlon Thatcher, The, CO, 1307

White Foundation, Marvin, Inc., KS, 3536

White Lick Heritage Community Foundation, Inc., The, IN, 3057

White Scholarship Fund, G. & M., OH, 7424

White Scholarship Trust, Elizabeth, OH, 7425

White Trust, Eleanor, NH, 5377

White-Williams Scholars, PA, see 8038

Whited Foundation, NM, 5658

Whitefield Society, George, The, OK, 7525

Whitefield Trust, Helen D., PA, see 7807

Whitehall Educational Trust, Lee, IN, 3224

Whitehall Foundation, Inc., FL, 2103

Whiteley Charity Fund Trust, Burt, IN, 3225

Whiteley Foundation, John and Elizabeth, The, MI, 4667

Whiteside Scholarship Fund Trust, MN, 4889

Whiteside Scholarship Fund, Robert B. and Sophia, MN, see 4889

Whitfield Foundation, Howard, NJ, 5597

Whitfield Healthcare Foundation, Inc., GA, 2264

Whiting Foundation, Marion and Jasper, MA, 4316

Whiting Foundation, Mrs. Giles, NY, 6517

Whiting Foundation, NY, see 6517

Whitley County Community Foundation, IN, 3226

Whitney Benefits, Inc., WY, 10124

Whitney Foundation, Helen Hay, The, NY, 6518

Whitney Scholarship Trust, B. Belle, IL, 2926

Whittaker Foundation, Jack, Inc., WV, 9828

Whittemore Trust, Edna May, MA, 4317

Whitten Trust, Kathryn M., CA, 1092

Whittier Host Lions Club Foundation, CA, 1093

Whiz Kids Foundation, The, UT, 9231

WHY, NY, see 6534

Wichita Community Foundation, Greater, KS, see 3537

Wichita Community Foundation, KS, 3537

Wichita Consistory Midian Temple Crippled Children's Fund, KS, 3538

Wichita Falls Area Community Foundation, TX, 9165

Wichita State University Foundation, KS, 3539

Wickam Scholarship Trust, Ivie Frances, CA, 1094

Widding Foundation for Women, Phyllis A., AR, see 287

Widows Home, GA, 2265

Widows Society in Boston, MA, see 4280

Widows Society, CT, 1485

Wiegand Trust, Margaret, WI, 10071

Wiesberg & Calvin P. Ranney Children's Foundation, Craig D., The, OR, 7683

Wiesel Foundation for Humanity, Elie, The, NY, 6519

Wiggin Fund, Barbara Thorndike, RI, 8436

Wiggins Foundation, Lloyd M. & Doris B., NC, 6919

Wiggins Memorial Trust, J.J., FL, 2104

Wigginton Educational Foundation, MI, 4668

Wight Foundation, Inc., The, NJ, 5598

Wilber Educational Scholarship Trust, Charles Joseph, WI, 10072

Wilbur Foundation, The, CA, A

Wilcox Family Foundation, The, CA, 1095

Wildacres Retreat, NC, 6920

Wilder Foundation, Amherst H., MN, 4890

Wilder Foundation, MN, see 4890

Wilderness Society, The, DC, 1751

Wildey Mitchell Scholarship Fund, Oscar and Mary, MN, 4891

Wildlife Conservation Society, NY, 6520

Wildlife Disease Association, Inc., KS, 3540

Wildner Scholarship Trust, Edwin E. and Elizabeth, TX, 9166

Wilemon National Cotton Ginners Scholarship Foundation, Peary, TN, 8663

Wiles Scholarship Fund, Rufus & Caroline E., RI, 8437

Wiley Foundation, Inc., The, NJ, 5599

Wiley Foundation, Nettie L. and Charles L., The, VA, 9548

Wilhelm Memorial Fund, Kay Kelly, OH, 7426

Wilkerson Scholarship Fund LLC, CT, 1486

Wilkin Charitable Trust, R. H., OK, 7526

Wilkins Memorial Scholarship Fund, Bess A., TX, 9167

Will Journalism Scholarship Foundation, John M., AL, 91

Willard Trust, George & Emily Harris, MI, 4669

Williams Charitable Foundation, Don E. & Charlotte J., Inc., IL, 2927

Williams Charitable Trust, Ted and Betty, AR, 327

Williams Charitable Trust, Ted, AR, see 327

Williams Family Foundation, The, CO, 1308

Williams Foundation, Dr. Richard D., PA, 8191

Williams Fund for Barnard School for Girls, A. F., NY, see 6521

Williams Fund for Teachers, A. F., NY, 6521

Williams II Trust, Charles K., PA, 8192

Williams Memorial Fund, Horace, The, ME, 3746

Williams Memorial Fund, Howell & Lois, OH, 7427

Williams Memorial Scholarship Fund, Charles and Ada, Inc., IN, 3227

Williams Safety Net Foundation, Roy, The, TX, 9168

Williams Scholarship Foundation Trust, George B., RI, 8438

Williams Scholarship Foundation, Charles C., PA, 8193

Williams Scholarship Foundation, John G., PA, 8194

Williams Scholarship Fund, Frank O. and Clara R., The, OH, see 7428

Williams Scholarship Fund, Margaret F., NC, 6921

Williams Scholarship Fund, Wilbur & Birdie, WY, see 10125

Williams Scholarship Loan Fund, Inc., IN, 3228

Williams Sonoma Foundation, CA, 1096

Williams Trust f/b/o Williams Scholarship, Frederick H., RI, 8439

Williams Trust, Charles, PA, see 8193

Williams Trust, Jessie A., OH, 7428

Williams Trust, Milton L., MA, 4318

Williams Trust, Wilbur & Birdie, The, WY, 10125

Williams, Slatington Scholarship Fund and Trust, Richard D., PA, see 8191

Williamsburg Community Foundation, VA, see 9388

Williamson Educational Loan Fund, Mary, VA, 9549

Williamson Family Educational Trust, PA, 8195

Williamsport-Lycoming Foundation, PA, see 7841

Willmott Memorial Trust II, James Worthington, OH, 7429

Willo Scholarship Fund, Veronica, IL, 2928

Wills Foundation, Harold E. & Esther L., WA, 9754

Wills Memorial Foundation, TN, 8664

Willwerth Foundation, Ashley, The, FL, see 1784

Wilson Charitable Foundation of Delanco, New Jersey, Geraldine Diehl, The, PA, 8196

Wilson Charitable Trust, J. B. & Garnet A., OH, 7430

Wilson Foundation, John & Mary, NC, 6922

Wilson Foundation, NE, 5273

Wilson Foundation, Patti Johnson, OK, 7527

Wilson Foundation, Warren and Velda, NE, 5274

Wilson International Center for Scholars, Woodrow, DC, 1752

Wilson National Fellowship Foundation, Woodrow, The, NJ, 5600

Wilson Plastics Employees Scholarship Fund, Ralph, TX, 9169

Wilson Scholarship Fund Foundation, E.E., OR, 7684

Wilson Scholarship Fund, Dee, IL, 2929

Wilson Scholarship Fund, Marty, NJ, see 5451

Wilson Scholarship Fund, MI, 4670

Wilson Scholarship Fund, Rodney B., MI, see 4670

Wilson Scholarship Trust, George W., PA, 8197

Wilson Scholarship Trust, John R., NH, 5378

Wilson Trust, Clark W., OH, 7431

Wimmer Scholarship Fund, George G., Elma & Ruth M., OH, see 7432

Wimmer Scholarship Fund, OH, 7432

Winans Memorial Scholarship Fund, Ralph, OH, 7433

Winchester Foundation, The, IN, 3229

Windermere Foundation, WA, 9755

Windham Foundation, Inc., The, VT, 9273

Windhover Foundation, Inc., WI, 10073

Windows of Hope Family Relief Fund, NY, 6522

Windsor High School Alumni Scholarship Fund, CT, 1487

Windsor High School Master Scholarship Endowment Fund, Inc., MO, 5125

Wine & Spirits Wholesalers of Georgia Foundation, Inc., GA, 2266

Wine and Food Foundation of Texas, The, TX, 9170

Wine Spectator California Scholarship Foundation, NY, 6523

Wing Family Benevolent Agency, H. R., The, UT, 9232

Winged Foot Scholarship Foundation, FL, 2105

Wingett Educational Trust, Earnest & Maxine, OH, 7434

Wings Over America Scholarship Foundation, VA, 9550

Winkel Family Foundation, IA, 3408

Winkler Memorial Trust, John J., MI, 4671

Winn Feline Foundation, The, NJ, 5601

Winn Foundation for Cat Research, Robert H., Inc., NJ, see 5601

Winnett Foundation, CA, 1097

Winona State University Foundation, MN, 4892

WinShape Centre, Inc., GA, see 2267

WinShape Foundation, Inc., GA, 2267

Winship Memorial Scholarship Foundation, MI, 4672

Winslow Education Trust, Lloyd E. & Katherine S., The, KS, 3541

Winslow Foundation, MN, 4893

Winston-Marion Counties Association for Retarded Citizens, Inc., AL, 92

Winston-Salem Foundation, The, NC, 6923

Winter Course in Infectious Diseases, Inc., MA, 4319

Wintermann Foundation, David and Eula, TX, 9171

Winters Foundation, Samuel & Emma, PA, 8198

Wipe Out Kid's Cancer, TX, 9172

Wirick Foundation, Evelyn and Ronald, MI, 4673

Wisconsin Covenant Foundation, Inc., WI, 10074

Wisconsin Early Childhood Association, Inc., WI, 10075

Wisconsin Eastern Star Foundation, WI, 10076

Wisconsin Indianhead Technical College Foundation, WI, 10077

Wisconsin Institute of Certified Public Accountants Educational Foundation, Inc., WI, 10078

Wisconsin Masonic Foundation, WI, 10079

Wisconsin Medical Society Foundation, Inc., WI, 10080

Wisconsin Public Service Foundation, WI, 10081

Wisconsin State Journal Youth Services, Inc., WI, 10082

Wisconsin Troopers Association Scholarship Fund, WI, 10083

Wisconsin Women's Health Foundation, WI, 10084

Wise Associates Foundation, Murray, IL, 2930

Wise Educational Trust, Erbon & Marie, TX, 9173

Wishard Memorial Foundation, Inc., IN, see 3027

Wisian Ministries, Elroy & Vickie, Inc., TX, 9174

Wisner Scholarship Trust Fund, Dr. L.G. Wisner & Winfred T., OH, 7435

With Love From Jesus Ministries, Inc., NC, 6924

Witmer Trust, Mabel M., NY, 6524

Wittman Scholarship Fund, Ray, WA, 9756

Wittmer Scholarship Fund, Buzzy, PA, 8199

WKBJ Partnership Foundation, NJ, 5602

WKUS Benefits Trust, IL, 2931

Woerner Foundation for World Missions, Inc., The, AL, 93

Woerner Foundation, The, AL, see 93

Woldenberg Foundation, Dorothy & Malcolm, LA, see 3683

Woldenberg Foundation, The, LA, 3683

Wolf Educational Trust, Charles E., OH, 7436

Wolf Foundation for Education Trust, PA, 8200

Wolf Memorial Foundation, Benjamin & Fredora K., PA, 8201

Wolf Scholarship Fund, Charles F., NY, 6525

Wolf Scholarship Fund, Elizabeth, NY, 6526

Wolf Trap Foundation for the Performing Arts, VA, 9551

Wolf Trust, Walter J., PA, 8202

Wolfe Foundation Inc., Frank M., The, FL, 2106

Wolfe Foundation, W. A. Jr. and Phyllis P., Inc., WV, 9829

Wolfer Scholarship Fund, J. Edgar, IL, 2932

Wolinski Trust f/b/o Notre Dame High School Trust, E., NC, 6925

Wollman, Dorothy Armstrong Wollman and Ella Armstrong Scholarship Fund, O. G., The, AL, 94

Wolters Foundation Trust, Gus & Ethel, TX, 9175

Woltman Foundation, B. M., TX, 9176

Wolverton Scholarship Trust, Mildred and Charles, TX, 9177

Womack Foundation, VA, 9552

Woman's Club of Minneapolis, The, MN, 4894

Woman's Club of Raleigh, Inc., The, NC, 6926

Woman's Club of Westfield, Inc., NJ, 5603

Woman's Exchange, Inc. of Sarasota, FL, 2107

Woman's Literary Union, The, ME, 3747

Woman's Seamen's Friend Society of Connecticut Inc., CT, 1488

Women Against Lung Cancer, WI, see 9977

Women for Women International, DC, 1753

Women Helping Women Fund, WA, 9757

Women in Film Foundation, CA, 1098

Women Make Movies, Inc., NY, 6527

Women of the Evangelical Lutheran Church in America, IL, 2933

Women's Aid of Penn Central School IAS, NC, 6927

Women's Aid Scholarship, NC, see 6927

Women's Bar Foundation, IL, 2934

Women's Center and Shelter of Greater Pittsburgh, PA, 8203

Women's Economic Development Council Foundation, AL, see 90

Women's Foundation of California, CA, 1099

Women's Fund for Health Education and Research, The, TX, 9178

Women's Fund for the Fox Valley Region, Inc., WI, 10085

Women's Fund of Greater La Crosse, WI, 10086

Women's Fund of Greater Milwaukee, Inc., WI, 10087

Women's Research & Education Institute, DC, 1754

Women's Sports Foundation, NY, 6528

Women's Studio Workshop, Inc., NY, 6529

Womens Board of Montgomery General Hospital, MD, 3952

Wood Acres Educational Foundation, Inc., GA, 2268

Wood Charitable Trust, L. S., IL, 2935

Wood Family Charitable Trust, TX, 9179

Wood Foundation, Jim and Marie, The, IA, 3409

Wood Scholarship Fund, Alice Louise Ridenour, OH, 7437

Wood Scholarship Fund, Ethel Arnold, RI, 8440

Wood Trust, Hester C., NE, 5275

Wood Turning Center, Inc., PA, 8204

Woodbridge Rotary Scholarship Foundation, Inc., NJ, 5604

Woodbury Educational Foundation, TN, 8665

Woodbury Foundation, IL, 2936

Wooddell Scholarship, Ward & Mary, OH, 7438

Woodhill Foundation, The, TX, 9180

Woodlands Religious Community, Inc., The, TX, 9181

Woodlawn Foundation, Inc., NY, 6530

Woodman Scholarship Fund Inc., Mr. & Mrs. L. Dexter, MA, 4320

Woodmansee Scholarship Fund, OR, 7685

Woodrow Foundation, OR, 7686

Woods Educational Trust, Woodrow W., IL, 2937

Woods Foundation, Tiger, Inc., CA, A

Woods Hole Oceanographic Institution, MA, 4321

Woods Memorial Scholarship Fund, Lee J. & Billie B., TX, 9182

Woods Services Workers Compensation Trust, PA, 8205

Woodson Foundation, The, NM, 5659

Woodson Sampley Educational Foundation, Robert E and Catherine, Inc., AR, 328

Woodward Foundation, Marlow & Vella, Inc., UT, 9233

Woodward/Graff Wine Foundation, CA, 1100

Woolsey Scholarship Fund, KS, 3542

Woori America Bank Scholarship Foundation Inc., NY, 6531

Worcester Community Action Council, Inc., MA, 4322

Worcester Community Foundation, Greater, Inc., MA, 4323

Worcester County Arts Council, MD, 3953

Worcester Institute for Student Exchange, ME, 3748

Work Family Resource Center, Inc., NC, 6928

Workable Alternatives Foundation, PA, see 8206

Workable Alternatives, PA, 8206
Workforce Escarosa, Inc., FL, 2108
Workforce Investment Board - Region I, Inc., WV, 9830
Working Girls Association Inc., OH, 7439
Working in Support of Education, NY, 6532
Workplace Technology Foundation, PA, 8207
Workplace, Inc., The, CT, 1489
Workum Trust, Corale B., OH, 7440
World Affairs Council of Northern California, CA, 1101
World Computer Exchange, Inc., MA, 4324
World Federation of Hemophilia - USA, NY, 6533
World Food Prize Foundation, IA, 3410
World Hemophilia Alliance, NY, see 6533
World Hunger Year, Inc., NY, 6534
World Medical Relief, Inc., MI, 4674
World of Children, Inc., CA, 1102
World Vision, Inc., WA, 9758
World Wildlife Fund, DC, 1755
World-Herald Goodfellows Charities, Inc., NE, 5276
Worldstudio Foundation, Inc., NY, 6535
Worth Memorial Foundation, Kathryn Aguirre, Inc., The, NY, 6536
Worthington Foundation, Richard & Lois, WA, 9759
Worthington Scholarship Fund, Salome C., PA, 8208
Wound Ostomy Continence Nurses Foundation, NJ, 5605
Woursell Foundation, Abraham, NY, 6537
WPAS, DC, see 1746
WPS Charitable Foundation, WI, 10088
WPS Foundation, Inc., WI, see 10081
WPS Scholarship Foundation, MI, see 4675
Wright Charitable Trust, Bruce & Gladys, TX, 9183
Wright Charities Corp., MA, A
Wright Education Fund, Mabel B., CA, 1103
Wright Educational Fund, R. R., PA, 8209
Wright Foundation, Charles L., OH, 7441
Wright Memorial Scholarship, RI, 8441
Writers Emergency Assistance Fund, NY, see 5707
Writers' Colony at Dairy Hollow, AR, see 274
WTF Foundation, UT, 9234
Wu Yee Children's Services, CA, 1104
Wu Zhong-Yi Scholarship Foundation Inc., NY, 6538
Wurlitzer Foundation of New Mexico, Helene, The, NM, 5660
Wurster Foundation, IN, see 3166
Wurtman Foundation, MA, see 4325
Wurtman Ner David Foundation, Inc., MA, 4325
Wyandotte Public Schools Foundation, MI, see 4675
Wyandotte Public Schools Scholarship Foundation, MI, 4675
Wylie Foundation, Helen F., RI, 8442
Wyly Scholarship Fund, NC, 6929
Wyman Scholarship Trust, Kenneth B., OH, see 7442
Wyman Trust, Kenneth, OH, 7442
Wyoming Community Foundation, WY, 10126
Wythe-Bland Community Foundation, VA, 9553

Xeric Foundation, MA, 4326
Xerox Foundation, CT, 1490
XL America Foundation, Inc., CT, 1491

Yaeger Scholarship Fund, Clement L., RI, see 8443
Yaeger Trust, Clement L., RI, 8443

Yakich Educational Foundation Inc., Mary Alice, WI, 10089
Yakima Valley Farm Workers Clinic, WA, 9760
Yamhill Community Action Partnership, OR, 7687
Yampa Valley Community Foundation, CO, 1309
Yanamura Educational Fund, Marian Gaynor, Inc., AL, 95
Yancey Foundation, Charm & Goodloe, FL, 2109
Yankama Feed the Children Charitable Foundation, MI, 4676
Yard, Inc., The, MA, 4327
Yarnold Scholarship Trust, Alice M. & Samuel, NH, 5379
Yates Emergency Relief Foundation, MS, 4926
Yeiser Foundation, Charles F. & Mary M., OH, 7443
Yellow Jacket Foundation, Inc., SD, 8548
Yellow Springs Community Foundation, OH, 7444
Yellowstone Boys and Girls Ranch Foundation, Inc., MT, 5183
Yelm Community Services, WA, 9761
Yerkes Scholarship Foundation, Martha E., NC, see 6930
Yerkes Scholarship Trust, Martha E., NC, 6930
Yeshiva Endowment Foundation, Inc., NY, 6539
Yett Charitable Foundation, W. T., TX, 9184
YMCA of the Brandywine Valley, PA, 8210
YMCA of the Rockies, CO, 1310
YMF, CA, see 1107
Yoder Brothers Memorial Scholarship Fund, OH, 7445
Yoder Memorial Foundation, Dustin and Kristen, Inc., TX, 9185
Yoder Memorial Scholarship, Joshua, OH, see 7445
Yolo Community Foundation, CA, 1105
Yopst Educational Loan Fund Trust, PA, 8211
York Catholic High School Student Aid and Endowment Fund, PA, 8212
York Community Foundation, NE, 5277
York County Community Action Corporation, ME, 3749
York County Community Foundation, PA, 8213
York Foundation, PA, see 8213
Yosemite Lodge No. 99 Scholarship Fund, CA, 1106
Young Family Foundation, Ralph W., PA, 8214
Young Family Foundation, The, TX, 9186
Young Foundation, Coleman A., MI, 4677
Young Foundation, Howard, Inc., WI, 10090
Young Health Care Foundation, Howard, Inc., WI, see 10090
Young Heroes Project, CO, 1311
Young Memorial Educational Foundation, Judson, MO, 5126
Young Memorial Foundation, Leonard, The, NJ, 5606
Young Memorial Fund, John B. & Brownie, NC, 6931
Young Men's Christian Association of Greater St. Louis, MO, 5127
Young Men's Christian Association of Northwest North Carolina, NC, 6932
Young Musicians Foundation, CA, 1107
Young Scholarship Foundation, Pauline C., Inc., KY, 3637
Young Trust, Alden N., MA, 4328
Young Women's Alliance Foundation, TX, 9187
Young Women's Christian Association of Greater Milwaukee, WI, 10091

Young Women's Christian Association of Greater Pittsburgh, PA, 8215
Young Women's Christian Association of Greater Toledo, DC, 1756
Young Women's Leadership Foundation, Inc., The, NY, see 6540
Young Women's Leadership Network, Inc., NY, 6540
Young Womens Christian Association of Seattle-King County-Snohomish City, WA, 9762
Yount Charitable Trust, Carl C., PA, 8216
Your Community Foundation, IL, see 2536
Your Community Foundation, Inc., WV, 9831
Youth Choir of Central Oregon, OR, see 7546
Youth Foundation, Inc., NY, 6541
Youth Ministry Inc., NC, 6933
Youth On Their Own, AZ, 259
Youth Opportunities Upheld, Inc., MA, 4329
Youth Outreach Services, Inc., IL, 2938
Youth Service America, DC, 1757
YSI Foundation Inc., OH, 7446
Yule Educational Trust, Harry T., PA, 8217
Yuma Community Foundation, CO, 1312
Yvorra Leadership Development, Inc., MD, 3954
YWA Foundation, TX, see 9187
YWCA Greater Pittsburgh, PA, see 8215
YWCA of Greater Toledo, DC, see 1756
YWCA of the USA, DC, 1758

Zac's Legacy Foundation, Inc., CO, 1313
Zaccheus Foundation, Daniel, PA, 8218
Zahn FFA Scholarship Trust at the Iola High School, Edward B., NJ, 5607
Zampogna Scholarship Fund, Angela M., MA, 4330
Zane Foundation, Inc., CT, 1492
Zazove Foundation, Louise Tumarkin, Inc., The, IL, 2939
Zearing Trust, Delyte K. Zearing and Robert I., IL, 2940
Zebro Foundation, Stanley, WI, 10092
Zeiter Charitable Foundation, Henry and Carol, CA, 1108
Zeta Psi Educational Foundation, NY, 6542
Zeta Tau Alpha Foundation, Inc., IN, 3230
Zider Scholarship Fund, Christopher, The, CA, 1109
Ziegler Foundation, Herbert C., The, OH, 7447
Zigler Foundation, Fred B. and Ruth B., LA, 3684
Zimmer Family Foundation, TX, 9188
Zimmer Memorial Fund, C. Thomas, IN, 3231
Zimmerly Educational Trust, I.P. and Lola, IL, 2941
Zimmerman and Adelia Klinger Scholarship Fund, Mabel, PA, 8219
Zimmerman Foundation, Hans and Clara Davis, HI, 2327
Zimmerman Foundation, Mabel and Adelia, The, PA, see 8219
Zimmerman Scholarship Fund, NC, 6934
Zimmerman Scholarship Trust, Martin H., NC, see 6934
Zipf Memorial Scholarship Foundation, Inc., NJ, 5608
Znotas Memorial Scholarship Fund, Father Joe, The, TX, 9189
Zoll FBO Charities, R., PA, 8220
Zoltani Foundation, Geza & Judit, Inc., IN, 3232
Zonta International Foundation, IL, 2942
Zurfluh Scholarship Fund, Hattie, PA, 8221
Zweibel Trust, John & Dorothy, WI, 10093
Zweifel Trust, Harry R. & Gertrude, IL, 2943